PEARS

CYCLOPAEDIA

2006–2007

A BOOK OF REFERENCE AND BACKGROUND
INFORMATION FOR ALL THE FAMILY

EDITED BY

CHRISTOPHER COOK

M.A. CANTAB., D.PHIL. OXON., F.R. HIST. S.

One Hundred and Fifteenth Edition

The Editor desires to express his gratitude to readers for their constructive suggestions and to all those who in one way or another have contributed to this latest edition. Correspondence on editorial and any related matters should be addressed to Dr Christopher Cook, *Pears Cyclopaedia*, Penguin Press (Editorial), 80 Strand, London WC2R 0RL

PENGUIN BOOKS

Published by the Penguin Group
Penguin Books Ltd, 80 Strand, London WC2R ORL
Penguin Group (USA) Inc., 375 Hudson Street, New York, New York 10014, USA
Penguin Group (Canada), 90 Eglinton Avenue East, Suite 700, Toronto, Ontario, Canada M4P 2Y3
(a division of Pearson Penguin Canada Inc.)
Penguin Group (Australia), 250 Camberwell Road, Camberwell, Victoria 3124, Australia
(a division of Pearson Australia Group Pty Ltd)
Penguin Group (NZ), cnr Airborne and Rosedale Roads, Albany, Auckland 1310, New Zealand
(a division of Pearson New Zealand Ltd)

Penguin Books Ltd, Registered Offices: 80 Strand, London WC2R ORL, England

www.penguin.com

First published 1897
115th edition published 2006
Copyright, © Penguin Books Ltd 2006
Visit our website at www.penguin.com

Pears is a trademark of Penguin Books Ltd

Typeset by Rowland Phototypesetting Ltd, Bury St Edmunds, Suffolk
Printed in England by Clays Ltd., St Ives plc

A CIP catalogue record for this book is available from the British Library

ISBN-13: 978-0-140-515-572
ISBN-10: 0-140-515-577

CONTENTS

Sections are arranged alphabetically, or chronologically, or have a detailed Table of Contents. The following summary is intended as a general guide.

THE
HISTORICAL
WORLD

Historical events from the ancient world to the present day. Also included is a wide-ranging selection of common historical terms, a selection of famous places in British history and miscellaneous tables of monarchs and prime ministers. Entries on many of the famous figures in history cited here may be found in Section B, Prominent People. Current political events (including the background to developments around the globe) are discussed in detail in Section C, World Affairs.

PART I. HISTORICAL EVENTS

B.C.

PREHISTORY

70,000,000 Earliest known primate (*Plesiadapis*).

35,000,000 *Aegyptopithecus*, ancestral ape from the Fayum.

20,000,000 *Proconsul*, possible ancestor of hominids in East Africa

3,700,000 First hominids in East Africa – *Australopithecus*.

2,100,000 First hominid stone toolmaker – *Homo habilis*; present in Africa until 1,800,000 years ago.

1,600,000 Earliest *Homo erectus* in East Africa, present there and in Europe and Far East until 200,000 years ago.

500,000 Archaic modern man, *Homo sapiens*, present in Africa until 30,000 years ago.

100,000 Neanderthal Man, present in Europe until 35,000 years ago: Anatomically modern man, *Homo sapiens sapiens* present in Africa, dispersed worldwide.

70,000 Neanderthalers (Europe, Asia, N. Africa). Rhodesian Man (S. Africa). Solo Man (Java). Flake tools.

40,000 First cold phase ends. Neanderthal race becoming extinct. Second cold phase. *Homo sapiens* (modern man). Implements show significant advances: small knife-blades, engraving tools. Paintings and sculpture; magic rites and ceremonies. Cro-Magnons with Aurignacian culture.

18,000 Final culmination of last ice age.

Aurignacian culture dying out to be replaced by Solutrean and then by the Magdalenian cultures. Great flowering of Palaeolithic art.

15,000 First immigrants from Asia to cross Bering Straits?

15,000 Last glaciers in Britain disappeared. Proto-Neolithic in Middle East. Agricultural settlements (*e.g.*, Jericho). Settled way of life leading to such skills as weaving, metallurgy; inventions such as ox-drawn plough, wheeled cart.

5,000 Britain becomes an island (land connection with continent severed by melting ice-sheets).

CIVILISATION IN THE MIDDLE EAST

4300–3100 Formation of urban settlements in S. Mesopotamia during the Uruk Period. Cuneiform writing developed.

3150 First Egyptian Dynasty; capital at Memphis. Hieratic writing already perfected. Early Minoan Age (Crete). Pictorial writing, copper, silver, gold in use. Early Mycenaean civilisation begins.

2900–2334 Early Dynastic Mesopotamia (Sumer & Akkad). Sumerian dominance; Royal Cemetery of Ur.

2870 First settlements at Troy.

2850 Golden Age of China begins (legendary).

2700–2200 Old Kingdom (Pyramid Age) in Egypt.

2400 Aryan migrations.

B.C.

2334–2279 Sargon of Agade; his Akkadian empire collapses soon after the death of his grandson Naram-Sin in 2218.

2205 Hsia Dynasty begins in China (legendary).

2200 Middle Minoan Age: pottery, linear writing in pen and ink

1800–1400 Stonehenge built and rebuilt.

1792–1750 Hammurabi king of Babylon; law code

1766–1122 Shang Dynasty in China.

1720–1550 Hyksos in Egypt. War chariots introduced. Hebrews entered Egypt (Joseph) *c.* 1600.

1552–1069 Egyptian New Kingdom: at zenith under XVIIIth Dynasty. Chronology more certain: Late Minoan Age; Linear B script.

1500 Powerful Mitanni (Aryan) kingdom in Asia Minor. Phoenicia thriving—trade with Egypt and Babylonia. Vedic literature in India.

1450 Zenith of Minoan civilisation.

1400 Ugarit (N. Syria) culture at its zenith. Cretan civilisation ends: Knossos burnt. Temple at Luxor built.

1352–1338 Amenhotep IV (Akhenaten), the "heretic" Pharaoh. Diplomatic archive of Tell el-Amarna.

1350 Zenith of Hittite civilisation.

1275 Israelite oppression (Rameses II); Exodus from Egypt (Moses). Phoenician settlements—Hellas and Spain (Cadiz). Tyre flourishing.

1250 Israelites invade Palestine (Joshua).

1200 Attacks on Egypt by "Peoples of the Sea". Downfall of Hittite kingdom. Siege of Troy (Homeric). Beginning of sea-power of independent Phoenician cities.

1122–256 Chou (Zhou) Dynasty in China.

1115 Magnetic needle reputed in China.

1005–925 Kingdom of David and Solomon: Jerusalem as Sanctuary.

1000 *Rig Veda* (India).

925–722 Israel and Judah divided.

893 Assyrian chronological records begin.

850 Foundation of Carthage (traditional).

781 Chinese record of an eclipse.

776 First Olympiad to be used for chronological purposes.

753 Foundation of Rome (traditional).

750 Greek colonists settling in Southern Italy.

745 Accession of Tiglath-Pileser III; Assyrian Power at its height.

722 Capture of Samaria by Sargon II: Israel deported to Nineveh.

700 Homer's poems probably written before this date. Spread of the iron-using Celtic Hallstatt culture about this time.

625 Neo-Babylonian (Chaldean) Empire (Nineveh destroyed 612).

621 Publication of Athenian laws by Draco.

610 Spartan constitution, made rigid after Messenian Wars: later attributed to Lycurgus.

594 Athenian constitution reformed by Solon.

586 Capture of Jerusalem: Judah deported to Babylon (partial return 538).

B.C.
561 Pisistratus tyrant of Athens.

560 Accession of Croesus—prosperity of Lydia.

538 Babylon taken by Persians: Empire founded by Cyrus, soon covers almost all of civilised Middle East.

509 Roman Republic founded (traditional).

508 Democratic constitution in Athens.

500 Etruscans at height of their power in Northern Italy.

GREAT AGE OF GREECE

499 Revolt of Ionian Greek cities against Persian king Darius.

494 Secession of Plebeians from Rome. Tribunes established.

490 Battle of Marathon: Athenian repulse of Persian attack.

480 Death of Buddha. Battle of Thermopylae: Spartans under Leonidas wiped out by Persians. Battle of Salamis: Persian fleet defeated by Athenians under Themistocles; Persian invasion of Greece halted.

479 Battles of Plataea and Mycale: Greek victories by land and sea respectively destroy Persian invasion force. Death of Confucius.

477 League of Delos founded by Athens for defence against Persia; soon becomes Athenian Empire. (467 Naxos kept in by force.)

461 Pericles comes to power in Athens.

458 Cincinnatus saves Rome (traditional).

456 Death of Aeschylus.

447 Building of Parthenon begun.

431 Death of Phidias. Outbreak of Great Peloponnesian War between Athens and Sparta. Pericles "Funeral Oration" (according to Thucydides).

425 Death of Herodotus.

416 Massacre of Melos by Athenians.

415 Sicilian Expedition: flight of Alcibiades from Athens to Sparta.

413 Loss of entire Athenian expeditionary force at Syracuse.

406 Death of Euripides and Sophocles.

405 Battle of Aegospotami: Athenian navy destroyed by Sparta.

404 Athenian surrender to Sparta: beginning of Spartan hegemony in Greece.

403 Beginning of epoch of Warring States in China.

400 Death of Thucydides, Greek historian (?).

399 Death of Socrates.

390 Occupation of Rome by Gauls under Brennus.

371 Battle of Leuctra: Spartans defeated by Thebans; beginning of Theban hegemony in Greece.

370 Death of Hippocrates of Cos (?).

347 Death of Plato.

PERSIAN CONQUEST OF EGYPT

343 Last native Egyptian Dynasty ends; Persians reconquer Egypt.

338 Battle of Chaeronea: Greek city-states defeated by Philip II of Macedon, who becomes supreme in Greece.

336 Assassination of Philip of Macedon: accession of Alexander.

334 Alexander's invasion of Persian Empire. Battle of Granicus, first victory.

333 Battle of Issus: Alexander defeats Darius of Persia.

332 Alexander's siege and capture of Tyre, occupation of Egypt.

B.C.
331 Battle of Arbela (Gaugamela)—final defeat of Darius.

330 Death of Darius and end of Persian Empire. Alexander heir to civilisations of Middle East.

326 Battle of Hydaspes: Alexander conquers the Punjab.

323 Death of Alexander at Babylon. Beginning of Hellenistic Age in Middle East and Eastern Mediterranean. Ptolemy I founds dynasty in Egypt. Alexandria becomes intellectual centre of Hellenic world.

322 Death of Demosthenes and Aristotle.

321 Maurya dynasty unites N. India.

312 Seleucus I founds dynasty in Asia.

300 Zeno the Stoic, Epicurus and Euclid flourishing.

ROME: CONQUESTS AND DECAY OF REPUBLICAN INSTITUTIONS

290 End of Third Samnite War. Rome dominates Central Italy.

280 Translation of Pentateuch into Greek.

275 Battle of Beneventum: Rome finally defeats Pyrrhus and the Greek cities of Southern Italy. Rome dominates all Italy.

274 Asoka becomes ruler of two-thirds of Indian sub-continent.

264 Beginning of First Punic War (Rome v. Carthage).

260 Battle of Mylae: first great Roman naval victory.

255 Defeat and capture of Regulus by Carthaginians.

250 Incursion of "La Tène" Iron Age people into Britain.

241 End of First Punic War. Sicily becomes first Province of Rome.

221 Kingdom of Ch'in (Qin) completes conquest of all Chinese states under Shih Huang-ti.

218 Outbreak of Second Punic War: Hannibal crosses Alps.

216 Battle of Cannae: Hannibal wipes out great Roman army.

214 Great Wall of China constructed (by linking existing walls).

213 Burning of Chinese classics.

212 Capture of Syracuse by Romans and death of Archimedes.

207 Battle of Metaurus: defeat and death of Hasdrubal. End of Hannibal's hopes of overcoming Rome.

205 Roman provinces organised in Spain.

202 Battle of Zama: Hannibal defeated by Scipio Africanus, 202-A.D. 220 Han Dynasty in China.

201 End of Second Punic War. Rome dominates Western Mediterranean.

196 After defeating Macedon, Rome proclaims independence of Greek city-states. Death of Eratosthenes the geographer (?).

160 Death in battle of Judas Maccabaeus: Jewish revolt against Seleucids continues successfully.

149 Outbreak of Third Punic War.

146 Carthage destroyed. Roman province of Africa formed. Roman provinces of Macedonia and Achaea formed, and most of remainder of Greece reduced to vassal status.

134 First Servile War; Revolt of slaves in Sicily under Eunus. Suppressed 132.

133 Siege and destruction of Numantia by Romans. Tiberius Gracchus Tribune. Attempted land reforms. Murdered 132.

129 Roman province of Asia formed from lands bequeathed by Attalus of Pergamum.

124 Chinese Grand College to train Civil Service officials.

123 Caius Gracchus Tribune. Attempted land reforms. Murdered 121.

110 Chinese expansion to include most of south-east of modern China, under Emperor Wu Ti. Commercial activity in Indian Ocean.

B.C.

106 Jugurtha captured by Marius and Sulla.

104 Second Servile War: revolt of slaves in Sicily under Tryphon and Athenion. Suppressed 101.

102 Chinese expedition to Ferghana and possible knowledge of West.

101 Battle of Vercellae: Marius ends threat of Cimbri to Rome.

91 Social War: revolt of Italian cities against Rome. Suppressed 88. Roman franchise granted to most Italians.

88 Civil Wars of Marius and Sulla begin.

87 Massacre in Rome by Marius.

82 Proscriptions in Rome by Sulla.

75 Belgic invasion of south-eastern Britain.

73 Third Servile War: revolt of slaves in southern Italy under Spartacus the gladiator. Suppressed 71.

63 Conspiracy of Catiline exposed by Cicero.

60 First Triumvirate: Pompey, Caesar, Crassus.

58 Beginning of Caesar's conquest of Gaul.

55 Caesar's first British expedition: second, 54.

53 Battle of Carrhae: destruction of Roman army under Crassus by Persians.

52 Revolt of Vercingetorix against Caesar.

50 Migration to Britain of Commius and his followers.

49 Caesar crosses the Rubicon. Beginning of war against Pompey and the Senate.

48 Battle of Pharsalus: defeat of Pompey by Caesar.

46 Caesar's calendar reforms.

44 Murder of Caesar.

43 Second Triumvirate: Antony, Octavian, Lepidus.

42 Battle of Philippi: defeat and death of Brutus and his associates.

31 Battle of Actium: naval victory of Octavian over Antony and Cleopatra. Octavian unchallenged master of the Roman world.

THE ROMAN EMPIRE

27 Octavian given the title of Augustus by the Senate.

19 Death of Virgil.

8 Death of Horace.

4 Birth of Jesus (date not certain).

A.D.

6 Civil Service Examination system in China.

9 Radical reforms by Wang Mang (short Hsin dynasty 9–23). Annihilation of Roman army under Varus by Teutonic tribesmen under Arminius.

10 Cunobelinus reigning over much of southeast Britain from Colchester.

14 Death of Augustus.

17 Death of Livy.

18 Death of Ovid.

30 Crucifixion of Jesus (date not certain).

43 Roman invasion of Britain under Aulus Plautius.

51 Caractacus taken to Rome as prisoner.

60 Revolt of Boudicca.

63 Great Fire of Rome.

64 Death of St. Paul (date not certain).

65 Death of Seneca.

66 Jews of Palestine rebelled against Roman rule.

68 Death of Nero—end of Julio-Claudian line of Roman Emperors.

70 Jerusalem taken and Jewish revolt suppressed by Titus.

79 Destruction of Pompeii and Herculaneum by eruption of Vesuvius.

A.D.

80 Completion of Colosseum (Flavian Amphitheatre).

83 Battle of Mons Graupius: Agricola crushes Caledonians.

96 Accession of Nerva: first of the "Five Good Emperors."

97 Chinese expedition under Kang Yin (lieutenant of Pan Ch'ao) penetrates to Persian Gulf.

117 Death of Trajan, accession of Hadrian. Roman Empire at its greatest extent.

122 Beginning of Hadrian's Wall (Tyne–Solway) by Aulus Platorius Nepos.

176 Suppression of Bar-Cochba's revolt and Dispersion of Jews.

142 Construction of Antonine Wall (Forth–Clyde) by Quintus Lollius Urbicus.

180 Death of Marcus Aurelius, last of the "Five Good Emperors." Beginning of the "Decline" of the Roman Empire (Gibbon).

193 Praetorian guards murder Emperor Pertinax, sell Empire to highest bidder (Didius Julianus).

196 Clodius Albinus, governor, withdraws forces from Britain to support his attempt to become Emperor. Northern Britain overrun by barbarians.

208 Septimius Severus visits Britain to punish Caledonians (death at York 211).

212 Edict of Caracalla. Roman citizenship conferred on all free inhabitants of Empire.

220 End of Han Dynasty: China divided and frequently invaded for next three centuries.

227 Sassanid Empire in Persia.

230 Emperor Sulin—Japanese history emerging from legendary stage.

251 Goths defeat and kill Emperor Decius.

259 Break-away "Gallic Empire" set up: suppressed 273.

273 Defeat of Zenobia and destruction of Palmyra by Emperor Aurelian.

284 Accession of Diocletian, who reorganises Roman Empire (293) with rigid social laws and heavy taxation.

287 Carausius attempts to found independent "Empire of Britain": suppressed 297.

306 Constantine proclaimed Emperor at York.

313 Edict of Milan. Christianity tolerated in Roman Empire.

320 Gupta dynasty reunites India.

325 Council of Nicaea: first general Council of the Church.

367 Successful attack on Britain by Picts, Scots, Saxons.

369 Restoration of Roman authority in Britain by Theodosius.

378 Battle of Adrianople: Goths defeat and kill Eastern Roman Emperor Valens.

383 Magnus Maximus withdraws forces from Britain to support his attempt to conquer north-western part of Empire.

388 Magnus Maximus defeated and killed in Italy.

395 Death of Emperor Theodosius the Great: the division of the Empire into East and West at his death proves eventually to be the final one.

406 Usurper Constantine III withdraws forces from Britain to support his claims: probable end of Roman military occupation of Britain.

410 Sack of Rome by Alaric the Goth. Emperor Honorius tells Britons to arrange for their own defence.

THE BARBARIAN INVASIONS

415 Visigoths begin conquest of Spain.

419 Visigothic kingdom of Toulouse recognised by Roman government.

429 Vandals begin conquest of North Africa.

432 St. Patrick begins mission in Ireland.

A.D.

446 "Groans of the Britons"—last appeal to Rome (traditional).

451 Châlons: Attila the Hun repelled from Gaul by mixed Roman–Barbarian forces.

452 Attila's raid into Italy: destruction of Aquileia and foundation of Venice by refugees.

455 Rome pillaged by Vandals.

476 Romulus Augustulus, last Western Roman Emperor, deposed by Odovacar: conventionally the end of the Western Roman Empire.

481 Clovis becomes King of the Franks, who eventually conquer Gaul (d. 511).

493 Theodoric founds Ostrogothic Kingdom in Italy (d. 526).

515 Battle of Mount Badon: West Saxon advance halted by Britons, perhaps led by Arthur (?).

BYZANTIUM AND ISLAM

527 Accession of Justinian I (d. 565).

529 Code of Civil Law published by Justinian. Rule of St. Benedict put into practice at Monte Cassino (traditional).

534 Byzantines under Belisarius reconquer North Africa from Vandals.

552 Byzantine reconquest of Italy complete.

563 St. Columba founds mission in Iona.

568 Lombard Kingdom founded in Italy.

570 Birth of Mohammed.

577 Battle of Deorham. West Saxon advance resumed.

581–618 Sui Dynasty in China.

590 Gregory the Great becomes Pope.

597 St. Augustine lands in Kent.

605 Grand Canal of China constructed.

618–907 T'ang Dynasty in China: their administrative system lasts in essentials for 1,300 years.

622 Hejira or flight from Mecca to Medina of Mohammed: beginning of Mohammedan era.

627 Battle of Nineveh: Persians crushed by Byzantines under Heraclius.

632 Death of Mohammed: all Arabia now Muslim. Accession of Abu Bakr, the first Caliph.

634 Battle of Heavenfield: Oswald becomes king of Northumbria, brings in Celtic Christianity.

638 Jerusalem captured by Muslims.

641 Battle of Mehawand: Persia conquered by Muslims.

643 Alexandria taken by Muslims.

645 Downfall of Soga clan in Japan, after establishing Buddhism: beginning of period of imitation of Chinese culture.

650 Slav occupation of Balkans now complete.

663 Synod of Whitby: Roman Christianity triumphs over Celtic Christianity in England.

685 Nectansmere: end of Northumbrian dominance in England.

698 Carthage taken by Muslims.

711 Tarik leads successful Muslim invasion of Spain.

718 Failure of second and greatest Muslim attack on Constantinople. Pelayo founds Christian kingdom of Asturias in Northern Spain.

726 Byzantine Emperor Leo III begins Iconoclast movement: opposed by Pope Gregory II, and an important cause of difference between Roman and Byzantine churches.

THE HOLY ROMAN EMPIRE AND THE TRIUMPH OF CHRISTIANITY IN EUROPE: NORSEMEN AND NORMANS

732 Poitiers: Muslim western advance halted by Charles Martel.

735 Death of Bede.

750 Beginning of Abbasid Caliphate (replacing Omayyads)

A.D.

751 Pepin King of the Franks: founds Carolingian dynasty. Ravenna taken by Lombards: end of Byzantine power in the West.

754 Pepin promises central Italy to Pope: beginning of temporal power of the Papacy.

778 Roncesvalles: defeat and death of Roland.

786 Accession of Haroun-al-Rashid in Baghdad.

793 Sack of Lindisfarne: Viking attacks on Britain begin.

795 Death of Offa: end of Mercian dominance in England.

800 Coronation of Charlemagne as Emperor by Pope Leo III in Rome.

814 Death of Charlemagne: division of empire.

825 Ellandun: Egbert defeats Mercians and Wessex becomes leading kingdom in England.

827 Muslim invasion of Sicily.

840 Muslims capture Bari and occupy much of Southern Italy.

843 Treaty of Verdun: final division of Carolingian Empire, and beginning of France and Germany as separate states.

844 Kenneth MacAlpin becomes king of Picts as well as Scots: the kingdom of Alban.

862 Rurik founds Viking state in Russia: first at Novgorod, later at Kiev.

866 Fujiwara period begins in Japan. Viking "Great Army" in England: Northumbria, East Anglia and Mercia subsequently overwhelmed.

868 Earliest dated printed book in China.

872 Harold Fairhair King of Norway.

874 Iceland settled by Norsemen.

885–6 Viking attack on Paris.

893 Simeon founds first Bulgar Empire in Balkans.

896 Arpad and the Magyars in Hungary.

899 Death of Alfred the Great.

900 Ghana at the height of its power in North West Africa.

907–960 Five Dynasties in China: partition.

910 Abbey of Cluny founded: monastic reforms spread from here.

911 Rolf (or Rollo) becomes ruler of Normandy.

912 Accession of Abderrahman III: the most splendid period of the Omayyad Caliphate of Cordova (d. 961).

928 Brandenburg taken from the Slavs by Henry the Fowler, King of Germany.

929 Death of Wenceslas, Christian King of Bohemia.

937 Battle of Brunanburh: crowning victory of Athelstan. West Saxon kings now masters of England.

955 Battle of Lechfeld: Magyars finally defeated by Otto the Great and settle in Hungary.

960–1279 Sung (Song) Dynasty in China.

965 Harold Bluetooth king of Denmark, accepts Christianity.

966 Mieszko I king of Poland, accepts Christianity.

968 Fatimids begin their rule in Egypt.

982 Discovery of Greenland by Norsemen.

987 Hugh Capet king of France: founder of Capetian dynasty.

988 Vladimir of Kiev accepts Christianity.

991 Battle of Maldon: defeat of Byrhtnoth of Essex by Vikings—renewed Viking raids on England.

993 Olof Skutkonung, king of Sweden, accepts Christianity.

1000 Leif Ericsson discovers North America.

1001 Coronation of St. Stephen of Hungary with crown sent by the Pope.

1002 Massacre of St. Brice's Day: attempt by Ethelred to exterminate Danes in England.

A.D.

1014 Battle of Clontarf: victory of Irish under Brian Boru over Vikings.

1016 Canute becomes king of England; builds short-lived Danish "empire."

1018 Byzantines under Basil 11 complete subjection of Bulgars.

1040 Attempts to implement Truce of God.

1046 Normans under Robert Guiscard in southern Italy.

1054 Beginning of Almoravid (Muslim) conquests in West Africa.

1060 Normans invade Sicily.

1066 Norman conquest of England under William I.

1069 Reforms of Wang An-Shih in China.

THE CRUSADES

1071 Manzikert: Seljuk Turks destroy Byzantine army and overrun Anatolia.

1073 Hildebrand (Gregory VII) becomes Pope. Church discipline and Papal authority enforced.

1075 Seljuk Turks capture Jerusalem.

1076 Kumbi, capital of Ghana, sacked by Almoravids: subsequent break-up of Ghana Empire,

1084 Carthusians founded by St. Bruno at Chartreuse.

1086 Compilation of Domesday Book.

1094 El Cid takes Valencia.

1095 Council of Clermont: Urban II preaches First Crusade.

1098 Cistercians founded by St. Robert at Citeaux.

1099 First Crusade under Godfrey of Bouillon takes Jerusalem.

1100 Death of William Rufus in the New Forest. Baldwin I: Latin Kingdom of Jerusalem founded.

1106 Tinchebrai: Henry I of England acquires Normandy, captures his brother Robert.

1115 Abelard teaching at Paris. St. Bernard founds monastery at Clairvaux.

1119 Order of Knights Templars founded.

1120 Loss of the White Ship and heir to English throne.

1122 Concordat of Worms: Pope and Emperor compromise on the Investiture Controversy, but continue to quarrel over other matters (Guelfs and Ghibellines).

1135 Stephen takes English crown: civil wars with Matilda and anarchy ensue.

1143 Alfonso Henriques proclaimed first king of Portugal.

1144 Muslims take Edessa (Christian stronghold).

1148 Second Crusade fails to capture Damascus.

1150 Carmelites founded about this time by Berthold.

1152 Accession of Emperor Frederick Barbarossa.

1154 Henry of Anjou succeeds Stephen: first of Plantagenet kings of England. Adrian IV (first English pope, Nicholas Breakspear).

1161 Explosives used in warfare in China.

1169 Strongbow invades Ireland: beginning of Anglo-Norman rule. Saladin ruling in Egypt.

1170 Murder of Thomas Becket in Canterbury cathedral.

1171 Spanish knightly Order of Santiago founded.

1176 Battle of Legnano: Frederick Barbarossa defeated by the Lombard League. Italian autonomy established.

1185 Kamakura Period in Japan: epoch of feudalism: until 1333.

1187 Hattin: destruction of Latin kingdom of Jerusalem by Saladin.

1189 Third Crusade launched: leaders—Frede-

A.D.

rick Barbarossa, Philip Augustus of France, Richard Lionheart of England.

1191 Capture of Acre by Crusaders.

1192 End of Third Crusade without regaining Jerusalem. Richard I seized and held to ransom in Austria on return journey.

1198 Innocent III becomes Pope.

1202 Fourth Crusade, diverted by Venetians takes Zara from Byzantines.

1204 Fourth Crusade captures Constantinople, founds Latin Empire. King John of England loses Normandy to France.

1206 Temujin proclaimed Genghiz Khan (Very Mighty King) of all the Mongols: soon controls all of Central Asia.

1208 Albigensian Crusade launched: the first against Christians.

1212 Battle of Las Navas de Tolosa: decisive victory of Spaniards over Moors. The Children's Crusade.

THE CULMINATION OF THE MIDDLE AGES

1215 Fourth Lateran Council: the authority of the mediaeval Church and Papacy at its zenith. Dominicans recognised by the Pope. Magna Carta extorted by barons from John.

1223 Franciscans recognised by the Pope.

1229 Emperor Frederick II, through diplomacy, recognised by Muslims as King of Jerusalem.

1230 Teutonic Knights established in Prussia.

1237 Golden Horde (Mongols) begin subjugation of Russia.

1241 Mongol incursions into Central Europe.

1250 St. Louis of France captured on his Crusade in Egypt. Mamelukes become rulers of Egypt. Mandingo king declares his independence of Ghana and embraces Islam.

1256 Conference of Baltic ports; the first form of the Hanseatic League.

1258 Provisions of Oxford: barons under Simon de Montfort force reforms on Henry III of England. Baghdad destroyed by Mongols.

1264 Battle of Lewes: Montfort's party become rulers of England.

1265 Simon de Montfort's Parliament. Battle of Evesham: defeat and death of de Montfort.

1274 Death of Thomas Aquinas.

1279–1368 Mongol (Yuan) Dynasty in China (Kublai Khan).

1281 Repulse of Mongol attack on Japan.

1282 Sicilian Vespers: rising of Sicilians against French ruler.

1284 Completion of Edward I of England's conquest of Wales.

1290 Expulsion of Jews from England. Death of Maid of Norway: Edward I begins attempts to rule Scotland.

1291 Fall of Acre: end of Crusading in Holy Land. Everlasting League of Uri: beginnings of Swiss Confederation.

1294 Death of Roger Bacon (see **B5**).

1295 "Model Parliament" of Edward I (anticipated in 1275).

1308 Death of Duns Scotus.

THE DECLINE OF THE MIDDLE AGES

1309 Papacy moves to Avignon: beginning of the Babylonish Captivity.

1312 Suppression of Templars by king of France and Pope.

1314 Battle of Bannockburn: victory of Robert Bruce secures Scottish independence.

1320 Declaration of Arbroath.

1321 Death of Dante.

1325 Zenith of Mandingo Empire of Mali (North West Africa) under Mansa Musa; superseded at end of 15th century by Songhai empire.

1327 Deposition of Edward II; subsequently murdered.

A.D.
1336 Ashikaga Period in Japan: great feudal lords semi-independent of authority of Shogun.

1337 Death of Giotto.

1338 Beginning of Hundred Years' War between England and France.

1340 Battle of Sluys: English capture French fleet.

1344 Swabian League: weakness of Imperial authority in Germany obliges towns to form leagues for mutual protection.

1346 Battles of Crecy and Neville's Cross: spectacular English victories over French and Scots.

1347 Calais taken by Edward III of England. Cola di Rienzi attempts to reform government of Rome: killed 1354.

1348 Black Death reaches Europe (England 1349, Scotland 1350).

1351 Statute of Labourers: attempt by English Parliament to freeze wages.

1353 Statute of Praemunire: restraints placed on Papal intervention in England.

1354 Ottoman Turks make first settlement in Europe, at Gallipoli.

1355 Death of Stephen Dushan: collapse of Serbian Empire which he had built.

1356 Battle of Poitiers: capture of King John of France by Black Prince. "Golden Bull" regulates Imperial elections in such a way as to place power in the hands of the German princes: valid until 1806.

1358 The Jacquerie: rising of French peasants.

1360 Peace of Bretigny: Edward III makes great territorial gains in France.

1362 English becomes the official language in Parliament and the Law Courts.

1363 Timur (Tamerlane) begins his career of conquest in Asia.

1368–1644 Ming Dynasty in China.

1370 Bertrand du Guesclin Constable of France: regains much territory from the English. Peace of Stralsund: Hansa in complete control of Baltic Sea.

1377 Pope returns to Rome: End of Babylonish Captivity.

1378 Disputed Papal Election: Beginning of Western Schism.

1380 Battle of Chioggia: decisive victory of Venice over Genoa. Battle of Kulikovo: Dmitri Donskoi of Moscow wins first major Russian victory over Golden Horde.

1381 Peasants' Revolt in England under Wat Tyler.

1384 Death of John Wyclif.

1385 Battle of Aljubarotta: Portugal safeguards independence from Castile.

1386 Battle of Sempach: Swiss safeguard independence from Habsburgs. Jagiello (Vladislav V) unites Lithuania and Poland.

1389 Battle of Kosovo: crushing defeat of Serbs and neighbouring nations by Turks.

1396 Battle of Nicopolis: "the last crusade" annihilated by Turks.

1397 Union of Kalmar: Denmark, Norway and Sweden united under one crown: dissolved 1448.

1398 Timur invades and pillages Northern India.

1399 Richard II deposed by Henry IV: first of the Lancastrian kings of England.

1400 Owen Glendower revolts in Wales. Death of Chaucer.

1401 De Haeretico Comburendo: the burning of heretics made legal in England.

1410 Battle of Tannenberg: Poles and Lithuanians break power of Teutonic Knights.

1415 Battle of Agincourt: great success of Henry V of England in France. Council of Constance ends Western Schism, burns John Hus.

1420 Treaty of Troyes: English claims to French throne recognised. Hussite Wars begin: Bohemian heretics defend themselves successfully.

A.D.
1429 Relief of Orleans by Joan of Arc.

1431 Burning of Joan of Arc.

1433 Rounding of Cape Bojador: first great achievement in exploration ordered by Henry the Navigator.

1434 Cosimo die Medici begins his family's control of Florence.

1435 Congress of Arras: Burgundians withdraw support from England, in favour of France.

1438 Albert II became German king and began Hapsburg rule over Holy Roman Empire, 1438–1806.

1440 Death of Jan van Eyck.

1450 Rebellion of Jack Cade against government of Henry VI of England.

1453 Battle of Castillon: final English defeat and end of Hundred Years' War. Constantinople taken by Ottoman Turks: end of Byzantine or Eastern Roman Empire.

RENAISSANCE, DISCOVERIES, "NEW MONARCHIES"

1454 First dated printing from movable types in Europe: Papal indulgence printed at Mainz.

1455 First battle of St. Albans: beginning of Wars of the Roses.

1458 Mathias Corvinus becomes king of Hungary. George of Podiebrad becomes king of Bohemia.

1461 Battle of Towton: Yorkist victory in a particularly bloody battle. Louis XI becomes king of France.

1467 Charles the Bold becomes Duke of Burgundy.

1469 Marriage of Ferdinand of Aragon with Isabella of Castile: union of the main kingdoms of Spain (1474). Lorenzo the Magnificent becomes ruler of Florence.

1470 Warwick ("The Kingmaker") turns Lancastrian, dethrones Edward IV.

1471 Return of Edward IV: Lancastrians crushed at Barnet and Tewkesbury. Ivan III of Moscow takes Novgorod: Muscovy rising to supremacy in Russia.

1476 Caxton sets up his press at Westminster.

1477 Battle of Nancy: defeat and death of Charles the Bold: end of the greatness of Burgundy.

1479 Pazzi conspiracy against the Medici in Florence.

1481 Inquisition becomes active in Castile (1484 in Aragon).

1485 Battle of Bosworth Field: beginning of Tudor period in England.

1497 Lambert Simnel's rising fails.

1488 Bartholomew Diaz rounds Cape of Good Hope.

1491 Brittany acquired by King of France (by marriage).

1492 Rodrigo Borgia becomes Pope Alexander VI. Granada, last Moorish foothold in Western Europe, conquered by Spain. Christopher Columbus discovers the West Indies.

1493 Sonni Ali brings Songhai Empire to height of its prestige: Timbuktu renowned centre of literary culture.

1494 Italy invaded by French led by Charles VIII: beginning of Italian Wars and "modern" European diplomacy and international relations. Treaty of Tordesillas: Spain and Portugal agree to divide unexplored part of world; subsequently approved by Pope.

1496 Habsburg–Spanish marriages: foundation of later empires.

1497 Perkin Warbeck captured by Henry VII (hanged 1499). John Cabot discovers Newfoundland.

1498 Savonarola burned. Vasco da Gama at Calicut: the sea route to India found.

1499 Amerigo Vespucci charts part of the South American coast.

A.D.
1500 Brazil discovered by Pedro Cabral.
1503 Casa de Contratación established at Seville; beginnings of Spanish colonial government. Fall of Caesar Borgia.
1507 Alfonso de Albuquerque becomes Viceroy of Portuguese Empire in the East.
1513 Accession of Pope Leo X, zenith of Renaissance Papacy. Machiavelli writes *The Prince.* Balboa discovers the Pacific (South Sea). Battle of Flodden: James IV of Scotland defeated and killed by English.
1514 Battle of Chaldiran: Turkish victory begins long series of wars between Turkish and Persian Empires.

REFORMATION, HAPSBURG–VALOIS WARS

1515 Francis I becomes king of France: victory of Marignano ends legend of Swiss invincibility. Thomas Wolsey becomes Lord Chancellor of England and Cardinal.
1516 Algiers taken by Barbarossa; beginning of the Corsairs.
1517 Martin Luther nails up his Ninety-five Theses: beginning of the Reformation. Turks conquer Egypt.
1519 Charles V inherits Habsburg lands and elected emperor. Magellan begins first circumnavigation of the world. Death of Leonardo da Vinci.
1520 Suleiman the Magnificent becomes Sultan; Turkish power at its height. Field of Cloth of Gold; celebrated diplomatic meeting, spectacular but with no results.
1521 Mexico conquered by Hernando Cortes. Belgrade taken by the Turks. Diet of Worms; Luther commits himself irrevocably. Charles V divides his dominions: Austrian and Spanish Habsburgs.
1522 Rhodes taken by the Turks; Knights of St. John move to Malta. Election of Adrian VI, first non-Italian Pope since 1378.
1523 Swedes expel Danish overlords, elect Gustavus Vasa King.
1524 Peasants' War in Germany (suppressed 1525).
1525 Battle of Pavia: defeat and capture of Francis I by Imperialists.
1526 Battle of Mohács: Turkish victory ends Hungarian independence. Foundation of Danubian Habsburg Monarchy (Hungarian and Bohemian crowns united with Austrian patrimony of Habsburgs): Holy Roman Empire prolonged for 300 years. Battle of Panipat: Babar begins Muslim conquest of India, founds Mogul Empire.
1527 Sack of Rome by Imperialists. Italy under control of Charles V.
1529 Siege of Vienna by the Turks. Peace of Cambrai; pause in Habsburg–Valois struggle, end of serious French intervention in Italy. Diet of Speyer: origin of the name Protestant.
1532 Peru conquered by Francisco Pizarro.
1533 Ivan IV (the Terrible) becomes Tsar. Marriage of Henry VIII and Catherine of Aragon declared null.
1534 Act of Supremacy: Henry VIII asserts control over English Church.
1535 Coverdale's English Bible printed. Execution of Thomas More and John Fisher.
1536 Execution of Anne Boleyn. Dissolution of smaller Monasteries by Henry VIII and Thomas Cromwell (remainder dissolved 1539). Pilgrimage of Grace: Northern rising because of religious grievances.
1538 Chibchas of Bogota conquered by Gonzalo de Quesada.
1540 Francisco de Coronado begins explorations in North America. Society of Jesus recognised by Pope.
1541 John Calvin regains authority in Geneva.
1542 First Portuguese reach Japan. New Laws of the Indies: first attempt to legislate for welfare of colonial natives, by Spanish government.
1543 Death of Copernicus.
1545 Opening of Council of Trent: the Counter Reformation.

A.D.
1547 Death of Henry VIII: Somerset Protector in the name of the boy king, Edward VI.
1549 First English Book of Common Prayer. Kett's Rebellion in Norfolk, because of economic grievances.
1550 Deposition of Protector Somerset: Northumberland rules England.
1553 Lady Jane Grey proclaimed Queen by Northumberland on death of Edward VI: Mary I succeeds. Servetus burned by Calvin.
1555 Latimer and Ridley burned by Mary. Religious Peace of Augsburg: policy of *cuius regio, eius religio* accepted in Germany.
1556 Charles V abdicated imperial powers in favour of brother Ferdinand. Cranmer burned. Akbar becomes Mogul Emperor (d. 1605).
1557 Macao becomes permanent Portuguese port in China.
1558 Calais lost by English to French. Elizabeth I becomes Queen of England.
1559 Peace of Cateau-Cambrésis: end of Hapsburg–Valois duel.

RELIGIOUS WARS

1561 Mary, Queen of Scots, returns to Scotland.
1562 First War of Religion in France: wars continue intermittently until 1598.
1563 Thirty-nine Articles define Elizabethan Church settlement.
1564 Birth of Shakespeare; death of Michelangelo.
1565 Malta beats off Ottoman threat.
1567 Deposition of Mary, Queen of Scots. Alva in the Netherlands: severe rule.
1568 Flight of Mary, Queen of Scots, to England: imprisonment. San Juan de Ulua: defeat of Hawkins, and end of his slave-trading voyages. Beginning of Anglo-Spanish maritime feud. Revolt of Moriscos of Granada (suppressed 1570).
1569 Rebellion of Northern Earls (Catholic) in England.
1570 Elizabeth I anathematised by Pope.
1571 Battle of Lepanto: spectacular defeat of Turkish sea-power by Don John of Austria. Bornu (or Kanem) in Central Sudan at its zenith under Idris III.
1572 Dutch "Sea Beggars" take Brill. Massacre of St. Bartholomew in France. Polish Crown elective again, on death of Sigismund II.
1576 Catholic League formed in France, led by Guise family.
1577 Drake begins voyage round world (returns 1580).
1578 Battle of Alcazar-Quivir: death of King Sebastian of Portugal. Parma re-establishes Spanish rule in Southern Netherlands.
1579 Union of Utrecht: seven northern provinces of Netherlands form what becomes Dutch Republic. Death of Grand Vizier Sokolli: decline of Turkish power begins.
1580 Philip II of Spain becomes king of Portugal.
1582 Gregorian Calendar (or New Style) introduced by Pope Gregory XIII.
1584 Assassination of William the Silent.
1585 Hidéyoshi Dictator of Japan: unification of the country. English intervention in Spanish–Dutch War.
1587 Execution of Mary, Queen of Scots. Drake "singes King of Spain's beard." Shah Abbas I (the Great) becomes ruler of Persia (d. 1629).
1588 Spanish Armada defeated.
1589 Death of Catherine de' Medici, Queen-Mother of France.
1592 Moorish conquest of African Songhai Empire.
1593 Henry IV of France becomes Catholic.
1598 Edict of Nantes: French Protestants guaranteed liberty of worship. End of French Wars of Religion.
1600 English East India Company founded. Tokugawa Period begins in Japan (Ieyasu takes title of Shogun, 1603): lasts until 1868.

A.D.
1601 Rebellion and execution of Earl of Essex, Elizabethan Poor Law.

1602 Dutch East India Company founded.

1603 Irish revolts finally suppressed by Mountjoy. Accession of James VI of Scotland as James I of England: Union of English and Scottish Crowns.

1604 Hampton Court Conference: James I disappoints Puritans.

1605 Gunpowder Plot.

1607 Virginia colonised by London company: Jamestown founded.

1608 Quebec founded by Champlain.

1609 Twelve Years' Truce between Spain and United Provinces: Dutch independence in fact secured. Expulsion of Moriscos from Spain.

1610 Assassination of Henry IV of France.

1611 Plantation of Ulster with English and Scottish colonists. Authorised Version of the Bible in England.

1613 Michael Romanov becomes Tsar: the first of the dynasty.

1614 Napier publishes his explanation of logarithms.

1616 Death of Shakespeare and Cervantes. Edict of Inquisition against Galileo's astronomy.

1618 "Defenestration of Prague": Bohemian assertion of independence begins Thirty Years' War

1620 Pilgrim Fathers settle in New England.

1624 "Massacre of Amboina": English driven out of spice islands by Dutch. Richelieu becomes Chief Minister in France.

1628 Murder of Duke of Buckingham. Petition of Right by Commons to Charles I. Fall of La Rochelle. French Protestants lose political power. Harvey publishes his work on the circulation of blood.

1629 Charles I begins Personal Rule.

1630 Gustavus Adolphus of Sweden enters Thirty Years' War, turns tide against Imperialists.

1631 Sack of Magdeburg, one of the worst incidents of the Thirty Years' War.

1632 Battle of Lützen: death of Gustavus Adolphus.

1633 William Laud appointed Archbishop of Canterbury. Thomas Wentworth takes up his post as Lord Deputy of Ireland.

1634 Dismissal and murder of Imperialist general Wallenstein.

1635 John Hampden refuses to pay Ship Money.

1636 Japanese forbidden to go abroad.

1637 Russian pioneers reach shores of Pacific.

1638 Covenant widely signed in Scotland.

1639 First Bishops' War: Charles I comes to terms with Scots.

1640 Second Bishops' War: Charles I defeated by Scots. Long Parliament begins: abolition of Royal prerogatives. Great Elector (Frederick William) becomes ruler of Brandenburg. Revolt of Catalonia (finally suppressed 1659). Revolt of Portugal: Duke of Braganza proclaimed king.

1641 Japanese exclude all foreigners (except for small Dutch trading fleet). Massacre of Protestants in Ireland. Wentworth (Earl of Strafford) executed. Grand Remonstrance of Commons to Charles I.

1642 Charles I attempts to arrest the Five Members. Outbreak of English Civil War: first general engagement, Edgehill. Death of Richelieu.

1643 Mazarin becomes Chief Minister of France. Battle of Rocroi: French victory, end of Spanish reputation for invincibility. English Parliament agrees to Solemn League and Covenant, secures services of Scots army.

1644 Marston Moor: decisive battle of English Civil War. North lost to Charles I. Tippemuir: Montrose begins victorious Royalist

A.D.
campaign in Scotland. 1644–1911 Manchu (Qing) dynasty in China.

1645 Formation of New Model Army. Naseby: main Royalist army crushed. Battle of Philiphaugh: Montrose's army destroyed.

1646 Charles I surrenders to Scots.

1647 Charles I handed over to Parliament. Charles I seized by Army. Charles I flees to Carisbrooke Castle.

1648 Second Civil War: New Model Army defeats Scots and Royalists. "Pride's Purge": Parliament refashioned by Army. Peace of Westphalia ends Thirty Years' War.

ASCENDANCY OF FRANCE

1649 Charles I executed. England governed as Commonwealth. Cromwell in Ireland. New Code of Laws in Russia completes establishment of serfdom.

1651 Battle of Worcester: Cromwell's final victory, now master of all Britain. First English Navigation Act. Hobbes' *Leviathan* published.

1652 Foundation of Cape Colony by Dutch under Van Riebeek. First Anglo-Dutch War begins (ends 1654).

1653 Cromwell dissolves Rump, becomes Protector.

1655 Major-Generals appointed to supervise districts of England. Jamaica seized by English.

1656 Grand Vizier Kiuprili: revival of Turkish government.

1658 Death of Cromwell.

1659 Peace of the Pyrenees: France replaces Spain as greatest power in Western Europe.

1660 Restoration of monarch in Britain: Charles II. Royal Society founded.

1661 Death of Mazarin: Louis XIV now rules in person. "Clarendon Code"; beginning of persecution of Non-conformists in England.

1664 New York taken by English: Second Anglo-Dutch War ensues (ends 1667).

1665 Great Plague of London.

1666 Great Fire of London. Newton's discovery of law of gravitation.

1667 Dutch fleet in the Medway. War of Devolution begins: first of Louis XIV's aggressions.

1668 Portuguese Independence recognised by Spain.

1669 Death of Rembrandt.

1670 Secret Treaty of Dover between Charles II and Louis XIV. Revolt of peasants and Don Cossacks under Stenka Razin (suppressed 1671).

1672 Third Anglo-Dutch War begins (ends 1674). Murder of De Witt brothers: William of Orange becomes leader of Dutch against French invasion.

1673 Test Act deprives English Catholics and Non-conformists of public offices. Death of Molière.

1675 Battle of Fehrbellin: Swedes defeated by Great Elector: rise of Prussian military power. Greenwich Royal Observatory founded.

1678 "Popish Plot" of Titus Oates utilised by Shaftesbury and the Whigs to bring pressure on Charles II.

1679 Bothwell Brig: suppression of Scottish Covenanters. Habeas Corpus Act passed.

1680 Chambers of Reunion: Louis XIV uses legal arguments to complete annexation of Alsace.

1681 Oxford Parliament: Charles II overcomes his opponents, begins to rule without Parliament.

1683 Rye House Plot. Siege of Vienna by the Turks: last major Turkish attack on Europe.

1685 Sedgemoor: Monmouth's rebellion crushed by James II. Revocation of Edict of Nantes: persecution of French Protestants by Louis XIV.

A.D.

1688 Seven Bishops protest against James II's policy of toleration, and are acquitted. William of Orange lands in England: flight of James II. "The Glorious Revolution."

1689 Derry relieved: failure of James II to subdue Irish Protestants. Killiecrankie: death of Dundee and collapse of Highland rising. Bill of Rights defines liberties established by "Glorious Revolution."

1690 Locke's *Two Treatises on Government* published. Beachy Head: French victory over Anglo-Dutch fleet. Boyne: defeat of James II by William III.

1691 Capitulation of Limerick: surrender of Irish supporters of James II on conditions which are not fulfilled.

1692 Massacre of Glencoe: Government's "lesson" to Highlanders. La Hogue: Anglo-Dutch fleet regains command of the sea.

1693 National Debt of England begun.

1694 Bank of England founded.

1695 Press licensing abandoned: freedom of the press in England.

1696 Peter the Great sole Czar.

1697 Peace of Ryswyck between Louis XIV and William III. Peter journeys "incognito" to the West.

1699 Treaty of Karlowitz: great Turkish concessions to Austrians. Death of Racine.

1700 Great Northern War, involving all Baltic powers, begins (ends 1721). Battle of Narva: Russians defeated by Charles XII of Sweden. Death of Charles II of Spain: under French influence Louis XIV's grandson Philip of Anjou named successor.

1701 War of the Spanish Succession begins. Hungarian revolt led by Francis Rakoczi against Austrians. Elector of Brandenburg receives title of King of Prussia. Act of Settlement establishes Protestant Hanoverian Succession in England.

1703 Methuen Treaty between England and Portugal. St. Petersburg founded.

1704 Gibraltar taken by Rooke. Blenheim: Marlborough stops France from winning war.

1706 Ramillies: Marlborough's second great victory. Turin: Eugene defeats French in Italy.

1707 Almanza: Anglo-Austrian forces in Spain defeated by French under Berwick. Act of Union: English and Scottish Parliaments united. Death of Aurungzib, last powerful Mogul.

1708 Oudenarde: Marlborough's third great victory.

1709 Pultava: Charles XII's invasion of Russia smashed by Peter the Great. Malplaquet: Marlborough's fourth great victory—at great cost in lives.

1710 Tory government in England.

1711 Dismissal of Marlborough.

1713 Peace of Utrecht: England makes advantageous peace with Louis XIV. Bourbon king of Spain grants Asiento (monopoly of Spanish American slave trade) to England.

1714 Peace of Rastatt between France and Austria. Death of Queen Anne: accession of George I. Beginning of Hanoverian Dynasty in Britain. Whig oligarchy rules.

1715 Jacobite Rising defeated at Preston and Sheriffmuir. Death of Louis XIV. France under Regent Orleans.

ENLIGHTENED DESPOTS: FIRST BRITISH EMPIRE

1716 Septennial Act: English Parliament prolongs its life from three to seven years. Prince Eugène of Savoy defeated Turks at Petrovaradin (Yugoslavia).

1720 Collapse of Law's system of banking ("Mississippi Bubble") in France. "South Sea Bubble" in England.

A.D.

1721 Robert Walpole becomes first Prime Minister. Peace of Nystad: Sweden no longer a major power at end of Great Northern War. Russian gains.

1723 Death of Christopher Wren.

1727 First Indemnity Act for Non-conformists.

1729 Methodists begin at Oxford.

1730 Resignation from government of Townshend, who becomes agricultural pioneer.

1733 First Family Compact between Bourbon kings of France and Spain. Withdrawal of Walpole's Excise Bill. John Kay invents flying shuttle, first of the great textile inventions. Jethro Tull publishes *The Horse-Hoeing Husbandry*, advocating new agricultural methods.

1738 Lorraine ceded to France.

1739 Nadir Shah with Persian army sacks Delhi, ruins Mogul power. War of Jenkins' Ear begins between Spain and Britain.

1740 Frederick II (the Great) becomes king of Prussia. Maria Theresa succeeds to Austrian dominions. Frederick seizes Silesia, begins War of the Austrian Succession.

1742 Fall of Walpole.

1743 Dettingen: George II, last British king to command his army in the field, defeats French.

1745 Fontenoy: Duke of Cumberland defeated by Marshal Saxe. Jacobite Rebellion under Prince Charles Edward: initial success, victory of Prestonpans, march to Derby.

1746 Culloden: Jacobites destroyed by Cumberland.

1748 Treaty of Aix-la-Chapelle: Frederick retains Silesia, elsewhere status quo.

1750 Death of J. S. Bach.

1751 First volume of the *Encyclopédie* published in France. Clive takes and holds Arcot: checks plans of Dupleix in Southern India. Chinese conquest of Tibet.

1752 Britain adopts New Style calendar.

1753 British Museum begun by government purchase of Sloane's collection.

1755 Lisbon earthquake. Braddock's defeat and death at the hands of French and Indians.

1756 Diplomatic Revolution (alliance of Austria with France) achieved by Kaunitz; Britain and Prussia perforce became allies. Seven Years' War begins. Minorca taken from British by French (Byng executed 1757). Black Hole of Calcutta: suffocation of many British prisoners.

1757 Pitt Secretary of State, main influence in British government. Rossbach: one of Frederick II's numerous victories against heavy odds. Plassey: Clive conquers Bengal.

1759 "Year of Victories" for Britain: Quebec, Minden, Lagos, Quiberon Bay. James Brindley designs Worsley-Manchester Canal: the beginning of this form of transport in Britain. Voltaire publishes *Candide*. Death of Handel.

1760 Wandewash: decisive defeat of French in India, by Coote.

1761 Panipat: Mahrattas heavily defeated by Afghans. Fall of Pitt.

1762 Catherine II (the Great) becomes Czarina. Rousseau's *Social Contract* and *Emile* published.

1763 Peace of Paris: British colonial gains, First British Empire at its height. Peace of Hubertusburg: Frederick II retains his gains. Pontiac's Conspiracy: failure of Red Indian attempt to destroy British power.

1764 John Wilkes expelled from Commons. James Hargreaves invents spinning jenny.

1766 Henry Cavendish proves hydrogen to be an element.

1768 Royal Academy of Arts founded.

1769 Richard Arkwright erects spinning mill (invention of water frame).

1770 Struensee comes to power in Denmark (executed 1772). "Boston Massacre." James Cook discovers New South Wales.

1772 First Partition of Poland between Russia, Prussia and Austria.

A.D.

1773 Society of Jesus suppressed by Pope (restored 1814). Revolt led by Pugachov in Russia (suppressed 1775). "Boston Tea Party."

1774 Warren Hastings appointed first Governor-General of India. Treaty of Kutchuk Kainarji; great Turkish concessions to Russia. Karl Scheele discovers chlorine. Joseph Priestley's discovery of oxygen.

1775 Watt and Boulton in partnership at Soho Engineering Works, Birmingham. Lexington: first action in American War of Independence.

1776 American Declaration of Independence. Adam Smith's *Wealth of Nations* published.

1777 Saratoga: surrender of British army under Burgoyne to Americans.

1779 Beginning of great Franco-Spanish siege of Gibraltar (raised finally, 1783). Samuel Crompton invents spinning mule.

1780 Joseph II assumes sole power in Austria. Armed neutrality of maritime nations to restrain British interference with shipping.

1781 Joseph II introduces religious toleration, abolishes serfdom in Austria. Yorktown: surrender of British under Cornwallis.

1782 Battle of the Saints: Rodney's victory save British West Indies.

1783 Treaty of Versailles: American independence recognised. Pitt the Younger becomes Prime Minister of Britain. First flights in hot air (Montgolfier) and hydrogen (Charles) balloons.

1784 Death of Dr. Samuel Johnson.

1785 Edmund Cartwright invents the power loom.

1787 American Constitution drafted.

1788 Impeachment of Warren Hastings begins (ends 1795). English fleet commanded by Captain Arthur Phillip landed in Australia.

FRENCH REVOLUTION AND NAPOLEON

1789 Washington the first President of USA. French Revolution begins. Storming of the Bastille (July 14).

1790 Civil constitution of the Clergy in France.

1791 Flight of Louis XVI and Marie Antoinette to Varennes.

1792 Battle of Valmy: French Revolution saved from intervention of European kings. Denmark becomes first country to prohibit slave trade. France becomes a Republic.

1793 Louis XVI beheaded. Second partition of Poland.

1794 "Glorious First of June." Fall of Robespierre and end of Jacobin Republic. Negro revolt in Haiti led by Toussaint L'Ouverture.

1795 The Directory established. "Whiff of Grapeshot": Napoleon Bonaparte disperses Paris mob, Oct. 5. Batavian Republic set up by France.

1796 First Italian campaign of Bonaparte: victories of Lodi, Arcola.

1797 Treaty of Campo Formio: Bonaparte compels Austria to make peace. Britain left to fight France alone.

1798 Bonaparte goes to Egypt. Battle of the Nile. Vinegar Hill rebellion in Ireland suppressed.

1799 New coalition against France: Suvorov and Russians victorious in Italy. Bonaparte returns to France. *Coup d'état* of Brumaire, Nov. 9. Consulate set up.

1800 Parliamentary Union of Great Britain and Ireland.

1801 Treaty of Lunéville: Austria makes peace; great French gains in Germany.

1802 Peace of Amiens between Britain and France. *Charlotte Dundas*, first practical steamship, on Clyde.

1803 Insurrection in Ireland under Robert Emmet. Britain again at war with France.

A.D.

1804 Bonaparte becomes Emperor. Spain declares war against Great Britain. Serbian revolt against Turks under Kara George.

1805 Battle of Trafalgar, Nelson's great victory and death, Oct. 21. Battle of Austerlitz, Dec. 2.

1806 Death of Pitt, Jan. 23. Confederation of the Rhine: Napoleon's reorganisation of Germany, July 12. End of Holy Roman Empire, Aug. 6. Prussia overthrown at Jena. Napoleon declares Great Britain in a state of blockade—"Continental System."

1807 Slave trade abolished in British Empire. Treaty of Tilsit: with Alexander of Russia his friend, Napoleon controls all of Europe. Occupation of Portugal by French, to enforce Continental Blockade.

1808 Occupation of Spain by French. Spanish rising: guerilla warfare. Peninsular War begins. Battle of Vimeiro (defeat of French by Wellington), Aug. 21.

1809 Battle of Corunna and death of Sir John Moore, Jan. 16. Attempted risings in Germany against Napoleon: Austria renews war. Treaty of Schönbrunn, Oct. 14.

1810 Self-government established in Argentina: first South American state to become independent of Spain.

1811 Massacre of Mamelukes at Cairo. Luddite riots.

1812 Retreat from Moscow: destruction of Napoleon's Grand Army.

1813 War of Liberation starts in Germany. Defeat of French by Wellington at Vitoria, June 21

1814 Soult defeated by Wellington at Toulouse, April 10. Abdication of Napoleon, April 11; Louis XVIII king of France. Congress of Vienna (concluded June 1815) under guidance of Metternich. Resettlement of Europe, usually by restoration of kings. Germanic Confederation under Austrian supervision. Poland ruled by Czar. Kingdom of Netherlands to include Belgium.

THE OLD ORDER RESTORED

1815 Escape of Napoleon from Elba. Battle of Waterloo, June 18. Corn Law in Britain to safeguard agricultural interests by keeping up prices. Quadruple Alliance (Austria, Russia, Prussia, Britain) to maintain Vienna settlement and hold regular meetings ("Congress System")—frequently confused with Holy Alliance which was simply a declaration of Christian principles. Napoleon sent to St. Helena, Oct. 16.

1818 Bernadotte made king of Sweden (Charles XIV), Feb. 6.

1819 Singapore founded by Stamford Raffles. Beginning of Zollverein (Customs Union) in Germany under Prussian influence. Parliamentary reform meeting at Manchester dispersed by military ("Peterloo"), Aug. 16.

1820 Death of George III, Jan. 29.

1821 Death of Napoleon at St. Helena, May 5

1822 Congress of Verona: congress system breaks down with refusal of Britain (Canning) to intervene against revolutions.

1823 "Monroe Doctrine" announced by USA. President. Dec. 2.

1824 Repeal of Combination Acts in Britain which had forbidden Trades Unions. Charles X king of France.

1825 Independence of all Spanish American mainland now achieved. Nicholas I Czar of Russia. First railway, Stockton to Darlington, opened.

1826 First crossing of Atlantic under steam by Dutch ship *Curaçao*. Menai suspension bridge opened.

1827 Battle of Navarino, Turkish and Egyptian fleet destroyed. Death of Beethoven.

1828 Death of Chaka, great Zulu conqueror.

1829 Greece independent. Catholic Emancipation Act in Britain. Metropolitan Police established.

A.D.
1830 Death of George IV, June 26. Louis Philippe ousts Charles X. Belgium breaks away from Holland. Russian Poland revolts.

1831 First Reform Bill introduced by Lord John Russell. Leopold of Saxe-Coburg becomes king of independent Belgium. British Association founded. Faraday discovers electromagnetic induction.

1832 Reform Bill passed, June 7. Walter Scott, Jeremy Bentham, and Goethe die. Electric telegraph invented by Morse.

1833 Beginning of "Oxford Movement" in English Church. First government grant made to English schools. First British Factory Act.

1834 Poor Law Amendment Act: tightening up of relief in Britain. "Tolpuddle Martyrs" victimised to discourage British working-class movement. Carlist wars begin in Spain.

1835 Municipal Reform Act revises British local government. The word "socialism" first used. "Tamworth Manifesto" of Peel defines aims of Conservative Party.

1836 People's Charter states programme of Chartists. Great Trek of Boers from British South African territory. Texas achieves independence of Mexico.

1837 Queen Victoria succeeds to the throne.

1838 National Gallery (opened in 1824) moved to its Trafalgar Square site.

1839 First Afghan war begins. Chartist riots at Birmingham and Newport. Anti-Corn Law League founded. Aden annexed by Britain.

1840 Penny postage instituted. Queen Victoria marries Prince Albert of Saxe-Coburg-Gotha. "Opium War" with China begins. Union Act gives Canada responsible government. Last convicts landed in New South Wales.

1841 Hong Kong acquired by Britain.

1842 Chartists present second national petition and put themselves at the head of strikes. Great potato famine in Ireland begins.

1846 Repeal of the Corn Laws. Peel resigns.

1847 British Museum opened.

REVOLUTIONS AND NEW NATIONS

1848 Monster meeting of Chartists on Kennington Common, procession abandoned, Apr. 10. General revolutionary movement throughout the Continent. Louis Philippe abdicates: French Republic proclaimed. Swiss Federal Constitution established after defeat of Sonderbund (Catholic succession movement). Rising in Vienna: flight of Metternich, accession of Francis Joseph. Nationalist risings in Bohemia and Hungary. Frankfurt Parliament: attempt to unite Germany on liberal principles. Communist Manifesto produced by Marx and Engels. Gold discovered in California.

1849 Collapse of revolutionary movements. Rome republic besieged by French (June 3), defended by Garibaldi, holds out until July 2. Austrians take Venice, Aug. 22. Repeal of old Navigation Laws. Punjab annexed by Britain.

1850 Cavour becomes Prime Minister of Sardinia. Don Pacifico affair: privileges of British citizenship at their highest defended by Palmerston.

1851 Great Exhibition in Hyde Park. First satisfactory submarine telegraph cable between Dover and Calais laid. Gold in Australia.

1852 Independence of Transvaal recognised by Britain. Napoleon III Emperor of the French.

1853 U.S. Commodore Perry lands in Japan: beginning of Western influence. Russia and Turkey at war.

1854 War declared against Russia by France and Britain. Allied armies land in Crimea, Sept. 14 (Alma, Siege of Sevastopol, Balaklava, Inkerman). Orange Free State set up.

1855 Sardinia joins Britain and France against Russia. Fall of Sevastopol and end of Crimean War. Alexander II Czar of Russia.

A.D.
1856 Peace Treaty signed at Paris. Bessemer invents process for large-scale production of steel. Livingstone completes journey across Africa.

1857 Indian Mutiny. Relief of Lucknow. Canton captured by English and French.

1858 *Great Eastern* launched. Crown assumes government of India. Treaty of Aigun, by which China cedes Amur region to Russia.

1859 Darwin publishes *Origin of Species*. French support for Piedmont in war with Austria (Magenta, Solferino). Piedmont receives Lombardy. Harper's Ferry raid: John Brown hanged, Dec. 2.

1860 Garibaldi and the Thousand Redshirts in Sicily and Naples; most of Italy united to Piedmont. Vladivostok founded; Russia strongly established on N.W. Pacific.

1861 Abraham Lincoln takes office as Pres. of USA. American Civil War commences with 11 states breaking away to form Southern Confederacy. Bull Run (July 21) Confederate success ends Federal hopes of easy victory. Victor Emmanuel proclaimed by first Italian Parliament as king of Italy. Emancipation of Serfs in Russia. Death of Prince Albert, Dec. 14.

1862 Bismarck becomes leading minister in Prussia. Garibaldi attempts to seize Rome but wounded at Aspromonte. Aug. 29. Cotton famine in Lancashire.

1863 Polish rising against Russia (suppressed 1864). French in Mexico. Battle of Gettysburg, July 1–3. Maximilian of Austria made emperor of Mexico.

1864 Cession of Schleswig-Holstein to Prussia and Austria. First Socialist International formed. Taiping rebellion in China ended. Federal army enters Atlanta, Sept. 2: General Sherman captures Savannah ("From Atlanta to the sea"). Dec. 22. Geneva Convention originated.

1865 Death of Cobden, Apr. 2. General Lee surrenders to Grant, Apr. 9. Lincoln assassinated, Apr. 14. Thirteenth Amendment to Constitution: slavery abolished in USA. Death of Palmerston, Oct. 18. Lister introduces antiseptic surgery in Glasgow. Tashkent becomes centre of Russian expansion in Central Asia. Mendel experiments on heredity. William Booth founds Salvation Army.

1866 Austro-Prussian War over Schleswig-Holstein ("Seven Weeks War"). Prussian victory at Sadowa (July 3). Venice secured for Italy, who had, however, been defeated by Austrians at Custozza (June 24) and Lissa (July 20). Treaty of Prague, Aug. 23.

1867 North German Confederation founded. Emperor Maximilian of Mexico shot. Dominion of Canada established. Russia sells Alaska to America for $7 million. Garibaldi makes second attempt to seize Rome, but defeated by Pope with French support at Mentana, Nov. 3. Second Parliamentary Reform Bill passed (Disraeli "dished the Whigs").

1868 Shogunate abolished in Japan: Meiji period of rapid Westernisation under Imperial leadership begins. Ten Years' War (1868–78): struggle for Cuban independence from Spain. Impeachment of President Johnson (USA). Disraeli succeeds Derby as Prime Minister but defeated in general election by Gladstone, Nov.

1869 General Grant, Pres. of USA. Irish Church disestablished. Suez Canal formally opened.

1870 Napoleon III declares war against Prussia. French defeated at Woerth, Gravelotte, and Sedan. Paris besieged. Rome and Papal states annexed to kingdom of Italy. Irish Land Act passed. Forster's Education Act puts elementary education within reach of all children. Papal Infallibility announced.

1871 William I of Prussia proclaimed German emperor at Versailles, Jan. 18. Paris capitulates, Jan. 28. Commune of Paris proclaimed, Mar. 28. Peace signed at Frankfurt-on-Main, May 10. Government troops enter Paris and

A.D.

crush Communards, May 28. Thiers President of the Republic, Aug. 31. Mont Cenis tunnel opened. Trade Unions in Britain legalised.

RIVAL IMPERIAL POWERS

1872 Secret ballot introduced in Britain. Death of Mazzini, Mar. 10.

1873 Death of Livingstone, May 4. Ashanti war.

1874 Disraeli succeeds Gladstone as Prime Minister.

1875 England purchases Khedive's shares in Suez Canal, Nov.

1876 Bulgarian massacres. Serbo-Turkish war. Bell invents the telephone. Custer defeated and killed in last large-scale Red Indian success. Porfirio Diaz in power in Mexico (until 1911). Victoria declared Empress of India.

1877 Transvaal annexed to British Empire. War between Russia and Turkey. Satsuma rebellion in Japan.

1878 Congress of Berlin: general Balkan settlement. Cyprus leased to Britain (annexed 1914). Second war with Afghanistan (ended 1880). Edison and Swan produce first successful incandescent electric light.

1879 Dual control (Britain and France) in Egypt. Zulu War. Gladstone's Midlothian Campaign. Tay Bridge destroyed, Dec. 28.

1880 Beaconsfield ministry succeeded by second Gladstone ministry. Transvaal declared a republic.

1881 British defeat at Majuba: independence of Transvaal recognised. France occupies Tunis. Gambetta becomes Prime Minister of France. Revolt of the Mahdi in the Sudan. Pasteur's famous immunisation experiment to show that inoculated animals can survive anthrax.

1882 Lord Frederick Cavendish, Irish Secretary, assassinated in Phoenix Park, Dublin, May 6. Triple Alliance (Germany, Austria, Italy) first formed. Alexandria bombarded, July 11. Cairo occupied by British troops, Sept. 14.

1883 National Insurance begun in Germany. Death of Wagner.

1884 Wolseley heads expedition to Khartoum to rescue Gordon. French establish complete protectorate in Indo-China. Evelyn Baring takes over administration of Egypt. Russians capture Merv. Berlin Conference defines rights of European Powers in Africa. Third Parliamentary Reform Bill. Parsons invents his turbine. Greenwich meridian internationally recognised as prime meridian. Fabian Society founded.

1885 Khartoum captured; Gordon slain, Jan. 26.

1886 Upper Burma annexed by Britain. Home Rule Bill defeated in Commons. All Indians in USA now in Reservations. Daimler produces his first motor car. Completion of Canadian Pacific Railway. Gold discovered in the Transvaal.

1887 Queen Victoria's Golden Jubilee, June 21.

1888 William II German Emperor. County Councils set up in Britain.

1889 Mayerling: tragic death of Prince Rudolf of Austria, Jan. 30. Flight of General Boulanger, after attempting to become master of France. Second Socialist International set up. Great London dock strike, Aug. 15–Sept. 16.

1890 Parnell ruined by divorce case: Irish politicians split. Sherman Anti-Trust Law: first attempt in USA to break cartels. Opening of Forth Bridge, Mar. 4. Bismarck resigns, Mar. 17. Caprivi succeeds. Heligoland ceded to Germany.

1891 The United States of Brazil formed.

1892 Panama Canal financial scandals in France.

1893 Home Rule Bill passes third reading in Commons, Sept. 1: Lords reject Bill, Sept. 8.

1894 Opening of Manchester Ship Canal, Jan. 1. Gladstone resigns, Mar. 3, Lord Rosebery succeeds. Armenian massacres by Turks: repeated at intervals for next quarter of century.

A.D.

Japan declares war against China. Dreyfus convicted of treason.

1895 Opening of Kiel canal, June 21. Rosebery resigns, June 22; Salisbury Ministry succeeds. Treaty of Shimonoseki: Japan gets Formosa, free hand in Korea. New Cuban revolution breaks out against Spanish. Marconi sends message over a mile by wireless. Röntgen discovers X-rays. Freud publishes his first work on psycho-analysis. Jameson Raid, Dec. 29.

1896 Jameson raiders defeated by Boers, Jan. 1. Adowa: Italian disaster at hands of Abyssinians, the first major defeat of a white colonising power by "natives." Gold discovered in the Klondike.

1897 Cretan revolt leads to Greek-Turkish War. Hawaii annexed by USA. Queen Victoria's Diamond Jubilee, June 22. Great Gold Rush began.

1898 Port Arthur ceded to Russia. Spanish-American War. *Maine*, U.S. warship blown up in Havana harbour. Treaty of Paris, Dec. 10: Cuba freed, Puerto Rico and Guam ceded to USA, Phillippines surrendered for β20 million. Death of Gladstone, May 19. Battle of Omdurman, decisive defeat of Mahdists, Sept. 2. Empress of Austria assassinated, Sept. 10. The Curies discovered Radium.

THE BOER WAR

1899 Boer War begins, Oct. 10.

1900 Boers attack Ladysmith, Jan. 6. Battle of Spion Kop, Buller repulsed with severe losses, Jan. 14. Relief of Kimberley, Feb. 15. Ladysmith relieved, Feb. 28. Mafeking relieved, May 17. Boxer outbreak in China, May. Annexation of Orange Free State, May 26. Roberts occupies Johannesburg, May 31. "Khaki Election." Annexation of the Transvaal, Oct. 25. Australian Commonwealth proclaimed, Dec. 30.

1901 Queen Victoria dies, Jan. 22. Trans-Siberian Railway opened for single-track traffic.

1902 Anglo-Japanese Alliance, Jan. 30. Death of Cecil Rhodes, Mar. 26. Treaty of Vereeniging ends Boer War, May 31.

1903 Congo scandal: celebrated case of misrule and exploitation. Royal family of Serbia assassinated, May 29. First controlled flight in heavier-than air machine Orville and Wilbur Wright at Kitty Hawk, USA, Dec. 17.

1904 Russo-Japanese War begins, Feb. 8. Japanese victory at Yalu River, May 1. British forces under Younghusband reach Lhasa, Aug. 3. Treaty with Tibet signed at Lhasa, Sept. 7.

1905 Port Arthur falls to Japanese, Jan. 3. "Bloody Sunday" massacre at St. Petersburg, Jan. 22. Destruction of Russian fleet under Rozhdestvenski at Tsushima by Admiral Togo (May). Treaty of Portsmouth (USA) ends Russo-Japanese war. Separation of Church and State in France. Norway separates from Sweden.

1906 General strike in Russia. San Francisco destroyed by earthquake and fire, Apr. 18. Simplon tunnel opened for railway traffic, June 1. First Duma (Parliament with limited powers) in Russia. Liberal "landslide" majority in Britain: Labour MPs appear. Movement for Women's Suffrage becomes active in Britain. Algeciras Conference: Franco-German crises resolved in favour of France. Death of Ibsen. Vitamins discovered by F. G. Hopkins.

1907 New Zealand becomes a dominion.

1908 Annexation of Congo by Belgium. Young Turk revolution. Annexation of Bosnia and Herzegovina by Austria: severe rebuff for Russia. Asquith becomes Prime Minister of Britain.

1909 Old Age Pensions in Britain. Peary reaches North Pole. Blériot makes first cross-Channel flight. House of Lords rejects Lloyd George's budget. Union of South Africa formed. Henry Ford concentrates on producing Model T chassis: beginnings of cheap motors.

A.D.

1910 Accession of George V on death of Edward VII, May 6. Liberals win two General Elections. Labour Exchanges established in Britain. Death of Tolstoy and Florence Nightingale.

1911 Parliament Act: power of Lords decisively reduced. British MPs paid for first time. National Insurance in Britain. Great British rail strike. Tripoli taken from Turkey by Italy. Chinese Revolution. Amundsen reaches South Pole, Dec. 14.

1912 China becomes a Republic under Sun Yat Sen. *Titanic* disaster off Cape Race, Apr. 14–15. Great British coal strike. Scott's last expedition. Outbreak of Balkan Wars

1913 Treaty of Bucharest: most of Turkey-in-Europe divided among Balkan states.

FIRST WORLD WAR

1914 Archduke Francis Ferdinand, heir to the Hapsburg thrones, assassinated at Sarajevo, June 28. Austria–Hungary declares war against Serbia, July 28. Germany declares war against Russia, Aug. 1. Germany declares war against France, Aug. 3. German invasion of Belgium: Great Britain declares war against Germany, Aug. 4. Great Britain declares war on Austria–Hungary, Aug. 12. British Expeditionary Force concentrated before Mauberge, Aug. 20. Battle of Mons; Japan declared war on Germany, Aug. 23. Battle of the Marne, Sept. 5–9. Trench warfare began on Aisne salient, Sept. 16. Three British cruisers (*Aboukir*, *Hogue*, and *Cressy*) sunk by one U-boat, Sept. 22. First Battle of Ypres, Oct. 12–Nov. 11. Raiding of German cruiser *Emden* until destroyed, Nov. 9. Battle of Coronel: German cruisers *Scharnhorst* and *Gneisenau* sink British cruisers *Good Hope* and *Monmouth*, Nov. 1. Great Britain declares war against Turkey, Nov. 5. Destruction of German squadron off Falkland Is., Dec. 8. British protectorate over Egypt proclaimed, Dec. 17. First Zeppelin appeared over British coast, Dec. 20.

1915 Turkish army defeated in Caucasus, Jan 5. Great Britain declared blockade of Germany, Mar. 1. Battle of Neuve Chapelle, Mar. 10–13. Naval attack on Dardanelles called off, Mar. 22. First landing of British, Australian, New Zealand troops on Gallipoli Peninsula, Apr. 25. Second Battle of Ypres, Apr. 22–May 25: Germans first used gas. Sinking of *Lusitania*, May 7. Battle of Aubers Ridge, May 9–25. Italy declares war on Austria, May 22. British Coalition Government formed, May 26. Italian army crosses Isonzo, June 2. Zeppelin destroyed by R. A. J. Warneford, June 7. Second landing of Allied troops at Suvla Bay. Italy declares war on Turkey, Aug. 20. Turks defeated at Kut-el-Amara, Sept 28. Serbia conquered by Austria and Bulgaria, Nov. 28. French and British troops occupy Salonika, Dec. 13. British troops withdraw from Anzac and Suvla, Dec. 20.

1916 Evacuation of Gallipoli completed, Jan 8. Opening of Battle of Verdun, Feb. 21. Republican rising in Ireland, Apr. 24. First Daylight Saving Bill passed. Fall of Kut, Apr. 29. Battle of Jutland, May 31. Brusilov's offensive in Galicia begins, June 4. Kitchener drowned when *Hampshire* struck mine, June 5. Battle of the Somme, July 1–Nov. 13: British losses: 420,000. Italians capture Gorizia, Aug. 10. Hindenburg and Ludendorff chiefs of German staff, Aug. 27. Rumania declares war against Austria and Germany. Aug. 27. Tanks first used by British, Sept. 15. Death of Francis Joseph of Austria, Nov. 21. Lloyd George forms War Cabinet, Dec. 6. Joffre replaced by Nivelle, early Dec.

1917 Unrestricted submarine warfare begins, Feb. 1. British troops occupy Baghdad, Mar. 11. Revolution in Russia, Mar. 12. USA declares war on Germany, April 6. Battle of Arras, Apr. 9–14: Vimy Ridge taken by Canadians, Apr. 10. Pétain replaced Nivelle, May 15. Messines Ridge taken by British, June 7. First American contingents arrive in France, June 26. Allenby assumes Palestine

A.D.

command, June 29. Third Battle of Ypres opened, July 31. Russia proclaimed a Republic, Sept. 15. British victory on Passchendaele Ridge, Oct. 4. French victory on the Aisne, Oct. 23. Caporetto: Italians severely defeated by Austrians. Oct. 24. Bolshevik Revolution, Nov. 7 (Oct. 25 O.S.). Passchendaele captured by British, Nov. 6. Balfour declaration recognised Palestine as "a national home" for the Jews, Nov. 8. Hindenburg Lines smashed on 10-mile front, Nov. 20. Fall of Jerusalem, Dec. 9. Russo-German armistice signed, Dec. 15.

1918 Treaty of Brest-Litovsk, Mar. 2. German offensive against British opened on Somme, Mar 21. Battle of Arras, Mar 21 Apr. 4. Second German offensive against British, Apr. 9–25. British naval raid on Zeebrugge and Ostend, Apr. 23. Foch appointed C.-in-C. Allied armies, Apr. 14. Peace signed between Rumania and Central Powers, May 7. *Vindictive* sunk in Ostend harbour, May 9. Last German offensive against French, July 15. British, Canadians, and Australians attack in front of Amiens, Aug. 8. Allenby destroyed last Turkish army at Megiddo, Sept. 19. Bulgarians signed armistice, Sept. 29. General Allied offensive in West began, Sept. 26. Germans accepted Wilson's Fourteen Points, Oct. 23. Great Italian advance, Oct. 24. Turkey surrenders, Oct 30. Austria accepts imposed terms, Nov. 3. Popular government in Poland (Lublin), Nov. 7. Revolutionary movement begins in Germany, Nov. 8. Kaiser abdicates and escapes to Holland, Nov. 9. Armistice signed by Germans, Nov. 11. Proclamation of Kingdom of Serbs, Croats and Slovenes in Belgrade, Dec. 1.

THE INTERWAR YEARS

1919 Peace Conference in Paris, Jan. 18. Einstein's theory of Relativity confirmed experimentally during solar eclipse, March 29. First direct flight across Atlantic by Sir J. Alcock and Sir A. W. Brown, June 15. Interned German fleet scuttled at Scapa Flow, June 19. Treaty of Peace with Germany signed at Versailles, June 28. Treaty of St. Germain: break-up of Austrian Empire, Sept. 10.

1920 Peace Treaty ratified in Paris. First meeting of League of Nations, from which Germany, Austria, Russia, and Turkey are excluded, and at which the USA is not represented. Prohibition in USA Peace Treaty with Turkey signed at Sèvres: Ottoman Empire broken up Aug. 10. Degrees first open to women at Oxford Univ., Oct. 14.

1921 Riots in Egypt, May 23. In complete disregard of the League of Nations, Greece makes war on Turkey. Heligoland fortresses demolished, Oct. 14. Irish Free State set up by Peace Treaty with Britain, Dec. 6.

1922 Four-Power Pacific Treaty ratified by U.S. Senate, Mar. 24. Heavy fighting in Dublin, as Four Courts blown up, July 2. Defeat of Greek armies by the Turks, Aug.–Sept. Mussolini's Fascist "March on Rome," Oct. 28.

1923 French troops despatched to Ruhr, Jan. 11. Treaty of Lausanne, July 24. Earthquake in Japan, Tokyo and Yokohama in ruins, Sept. 1. Rhine Republic proclaimed, Bavaria defies the Reich, Oct. 20. Turkish Republic proclaimed; Kemal Pasha, first President, Oct. 29.

1924 Lenin dies, Jan. 21. First Labour Ministry in Britain under MacDonald, Jan. 22; lasts 9 months. George II of Greece deposed and a Republic declared, Mar. 25. Dawes Plan accepted by London conference; Ruhr evacuation agreed to, Aug. 16.

1925 Hindenburg elected German President, Mar. 26. Treaty of Locarno signed in London, Dec. 1. Summer Time Act made permanent.

1926 Ibn Saud proclaimed king of the Hedjaz in Jeddah, Jan. 11. Evacuation of Cologne by British forces, Jan. 31. General strike in Britain.

1927 Lindbergh flies Atlantic alone, May 21.

1928 Earthquake in Greece, Corinth destroyed. Apr. 23. Capt. Kingsford-Smith flies the

A.D.

Pacific, June 9. General Nobile rescued by aeroplane from Arctic one month after disaster, June 24. Kellogg Pact accepted by Gt. Britain, July 18. German airship with 60 persons crosses Atlantic, Oct. 15. Women in Britain enfranchised on same basis as men.

1929 Second Labour Ministry under MacDonald. Graf Zeppelin makes numerous successful intercontinental flights. Commander Byrd flies over South Pole, Nov. 30. American slump and Wall Street crash.

1930 *R.101* destroyed in France on first flight to India, 48 lives lost, Oct. 5—end of British interest in airships.

1931 Great floods in China. Resignation of Labour Government and formation of Coalition under MacDonald. Invergordon naval mutiny.

1932 Manchuria erected into Japanese puppet state of Manchukuo, Feb. 18. Sydney Harbour Bridge opened, Mar. 19. Ottawa Imperial Conference.

1933 Hitler appointed Chancellor by Hindenburg, Jan. 30, and step by step gains supreme control. German Reichstag set on fire, Feb. 27.

1934 Dollfuss, Austrian Chancellor, murdered by Austrian Nazis, July 25. Death of Hindenburg, Aug. 2. Hitler becomes Dictator. Alexander of Yugoslavia assassinated in Marseilles, Oct. 9.

1935 Saar plebiscite for return to Germany, Jan. 13. Baldwin succeeds MacDonald as Prime Minister, June 7. War begins between Italy and Abyssinia, Oct. 3. Ineffectual economic "sanctions" by League of Nations against Italy, Nov. 18.

1936 Accession of King Edward VIII, Jan. 20. Repudiation of Locarno Treaty by Germany, Mar. 7. Remilitarisation of Rhineland, Mar. 8. Italian troops occupy Addis Ababa, May 5. Civil War breaks out in Spain, July 18. Inauguration of BBC high definition TV, Nov. 2. King Edward VIII abdicates after a reign of 325 days, Dec. 10. The Duke of York succeeds his brother as King George VI, Dec. 12.

1937 Coalition Ministry under Chamberlain, May 28. Japanese begin attempted conquest of China—"China incident," July 7.

1938 Austria annexed by Germany, Mar. 13. British navy mobilised, Sept. 28. Munich Agreement between Chamberlain, Daladier, Hitler, and Mussolini, Sept. 29.

1939

February 27 Great Britain recognises General Franco's Government.

March 16 Bohemia and Moravia annexed by Hitler and proclaimed a German Protectorate. **22** Memel ceded to Germany by Lithuania. **28** Anti-Polish press campaign begun by Germany.

April 1 Spanish War ends **7** Italy seizes Albania. **14** First British talks with Russia. **27** Conscription introduced in Great Britain. **28** Hitler denounces Anglo-German Naval agreement and the Polish Non-Aggression Treaty.

May 12 Great Britain signs defensive agreement with Turkey. **22** Italy and Germany sign pact. **23** France and Turkey sign defensive agreement. **25** Anglo-Polish treaty signed in London.

July 10 Chamberlain re-affirms British pledge to Poland.

August 23 German-Soviet Pact signed by von Ribbentrop. **25** Japan breaks away from the Anti-Comintern Pact. **28** Holland mobilises. **31** British fleet mobilised.

SECOND WORLD WAR

September 1 Poland invaded by German forces. Great Britain and France mobilise. **1–4** Evacuation schemes put in motion in England and Wales: 1,200,000 persons moved. **2** Compulsory military service for all men in Britain aged 20 to 41. **3** War declared (11 a.m.) between Britain and Germany as from 5 p.m. **4** British liner *Athenia* sunk by submarine. RAF raid the Kiel Canal entrance and bomb German warships. **6** First enemy air raid on Britain. **8** Russia mobilises. Russian troops on Polish border. **11** British troops on French soil. **17**

A.D.

Russian troops cross the Polish frontier along its entire length. Russian and German troops meet near Brest Litovsk: loss of *Courageous*. **27** Capitulation of Warsaw. **29** Nazi-Soviet pact signed in Moscow approving partition of Poland: Introduction of petrol rationing in Britain.

October 14 *Royal Oak* sunk in Scapa Flow with a loss of 810 lives.

November 8 Bomb explosion in the Bürgerbräukeller at Munich after Hitler's speech. Germans using magnetic mines. **29** Diplomatic relations between Russia and Finland severed. **30** Finland attacked by Russia.

December 11 Italy leaves the League of Nations. **13** Battle of the River Plate: engagement of German warship *Admiral Graf Spee* by the cruisers *Exeter*, *Ajax*, and *Achilles*. **14** Rejection by Russia of the League of Nations' offer of mediation in the Russo-Finnish war. Russia expelled from the League of Nations. **17** *Admiral Graf Spee* scuttles herself in the entrance of Montevideo harbour.

1940

February 14 Finnish advanced posts captured by Russians. **16** 299 British prisoners taken off the German Naval Auxiliary *Altmark* in Norwegian waters. **26** Finns lose the island fortress of Kolvisto. Finns retreat from Petsamo.

March 12 British ships to be fitted with a protective device against magnetic mines. Finland concludes a peace treaty whereby she cedes to Russia the Karelian Isthmus, the town of Vipuri and a military base on Hango Peninsula.

April 9 Invasion of Denmark and Norway by Germany. **15** British troops arrive in Norway. **19** British soldiers land in the Faroes.

May 2 British troops withdrawn from Norway. **10** Holland, Belgium and Luxembourg invaded by German forces. Parachute troops landed near Rotterdam. British troops cross the Belgian border. British troops land in Iceland. Rotterdam bombed. **11** National Government formed under Churchill. **13** Queen Wilhelmina arrives in London. **14** Rotterdam captured. Holland ceases fighting. Allied troops land near Narvik. **17** Belgian Government moves to Ostend. **24** German forces enter Boulogne. **27** Belgian army capitulates on the order of King Leopold. British forces to be withdrawn from Flanders. Narvik captured by Allied forces. **29** Ostend, Ypres, Lille and other Belgian and French towns lost to the Germans.

June Evacuation of British army from Dunkirk (May 27–June 4): 299 British warships and 420 other vessels under constant attack evacuate 335,490 officers and men. **5** Hitler proclaims a war of total annihilation against his enemies. **8** German armoured forces penetrate French defences in the West near Rouen. **10** Italy declares war on Great Britain and France. **14** Paris captured by German forces. **15** Soviet troops occupy Lithuania, Latvia and Estonia. **22** French delegates accept terms for an Armistice. **25** Hostilities in France cease at 12.35 a.m.

July 1 Channel Islands occupied by Germany. **3** French naval squadron at Oran immobilised. **10** Battle of Britain began.

August 19 British withdraw from Somaliland. **25** British began night bombing of Germany.

September 6 King Carol of Rumania abdicates in favour of his son Michael. **7** London sustains severe damage in the largest aerial attack since war commenced. **15** Battle of Britain ends with British victory: German aeroplanes destroyed, 1,733; RAF losses, 915. **23** Japanese troops enter Indo-China.

October 7 German troops enter Rumania. **28** Greece rejects an Italian ultimatum.

November 1 Greeks repel Italian attacks, **5** HMS *Jervis Bay* lost defending Atlantic convoy from German warship *Admiral Scheer*. **11** Italian fleet at Taranto crippled by Fleet Air Arm. **14** Coventry heavily attacked, the Cathedral destroyed. **22** Albanian town of Koritza captured by the Greeks.

December 2 Bristol heavily bombed. **11** Sidi Barrani captured by British forces: beginning

A.D.

of Wavell's destruction of Italian forces in Cyrenaica. **29** City of London severely burned by incendiary bombs; Guildhall and eight Wren Churches destroyed.

1941

January 5 Bardia captured. **22** Tobruk captured by Australian troops.
February 7 Benghazi captured. **26** Mogadishu, capital of Italian Somaliland, occupied by Imperial troops. German mechanised troops in Libya.
March 4 British raid Lofoten Islands. **11** U.S. Lease and Lend Bill signed by Roosevelt. **27** Keren—main battle in British conquest of Abyssinia and Somaliland **28** Cape Matapan: Italian fleet routed by British. **30** Rommel opens attack in N. Africa.
April 4 Addis Ababa entered by Imperial troops. **6** Greece and Yugoslavia invaded by German troops. **8** Massawa capitulates. **11** Belgrade occupied by German forces. **13** Bardia given up by British. Tobruk holds out. **24** Empire forces withdrawing from Greece. **27** Athens captured by the Germans.
May 2 Evacuation from Greece completed. **10** Rudolf Hess descends by parachute in Scotland. **20** Crete invaded by German air-borne troops. **24** HMS *Hood* sunk. **27** German battleship *Bismarck* sunk; British forces withdrawn from Crete.
June 2 Clothes rationing commences. **4** William II (ex-Kaiser of Germany) dies. **18** Treaty of friendship between Turkey and Germany signed. **22** Germany attacks Russia. **24** Russia loses Brest Litovsk.
July 3 Palmyra (Syria) surrenders to Allied forces. **7** U.S. forces arrive in Iceland. **9** General Dentz, the French High Commissioner in Syria, asks for Armistice terms. **25** Fighting round Smolensk.
August 25 British and Russian troops enter Persia. **27** The Dnepropetrovsk dam blown up by the Russians.
September 18 Crimea cut off from mainland. **19** Kiev entered by Germans.
October 6 German attack on Moscow. **16** Soviet Government leaves Moscow. Odessa occupied by German and Rumanian troops. **19** Taganrog on Sea of Azov captured by Germans. **26** Kharkov captured by the Germans.
November 14 *Ark Royal* sunk. **18** Libyan battle opens: Eighth Army's first offensive. **23** Bardia and Fort Capuzzo captured by British. **24** HMS *Dunedin* torpedoed. **25** HMS *Barham* sunk. **30** Russians re-take Rostov.
December 1 Points rationing scheme in force in Britain. **4** German attack on Moscow halted. **7** Japanese attack on Pearl Harbor. **8** Japanese forces land in Malaya. **9** British forces in Tobruk relieved. **10** HMS *Repulse* and *Prince of Wales* sunk off Malaya by Japanese. Phillippines invaded by Japanese. **25** Hongkong surrenders to Japanese.

1942

January 2 Manila and Cavite taken by Japanese. **23** Japanese forces land in New Guinea and the Solomon Islands.
February 9 Soap rationed. **12** Escape through English Channel of German ships *Scharnhorst*, *Gneisenau*, and *Prinz Eugen*. **15** Singapore surrenders to Japanese. **27** Battle of Java Sea.
March 9 Surrender of Java to Japanese.
April 15 George Cross awarded to the island of Malta.
May 4–8 Battle of Coral Sea. **7** Madagascar invaded by British forces. **7** U.S. forces sink 11 Japanese warships off the Solomon Islands. **30** Over 1,000 bombers raid Cologne. Canterbury bombed.
June 3–7 Midway Island: U.S. naval victory turns tide in Pacific. **20** Tobruk captured by the Germans.
July 16 RAF make first daylight raid on the Ruhr.
August 6 Germans advancing towards the Caucasus. **10** American forces land in the Solomon

A.D.

Islands. **11** Malta convoy action (loss of HMS *Eagle*, *Manchester*, *Cairo*, and one destroyer). **19** Raid on Dieppe. **23–25** Battle of Solomons.
September 6 Germans halted at Stalingrad.
October 23 El Alamein: Allied offensive opens in Egypt.
November 4 Rommel's army in full retreat. **5** Red Army holding firm at Stalingrad. **7** Allied invasion of N. Africa. **27** German forces enter Toulon. French Fleet scuttled.
December 2 First self-sustained, controlled nuclear chain reaction in uranium achieved by group working under Enrico Fermi at Chicago. **24** Admiral Darlan assassinated.

1943

January 6 German armies in the Caucasus and the Don elbow in retreat. **18** Leningrad 16-month siege ended. **23** Tripoli occupied by the Eighth Army. **27** American bombers make their first attack on Germany. **31** Remnants of the German army outside Stalingrad surrender.
February 9 Guadalcanal Island cleared of Japanese troops. **16** Kharkov retaken by the Russians.
March 1–3 Battle of Bismarck Sea. **23** 8th Army penetrates the Mareth Line.
May 7 Tunis and Bizerta captured by Allies. **12** All organised German resistance in Tunisia ceases. **16** Dams in the Ruhr breached by the RAF. **22** Moscow dissolves the Comintern.
June 3 French Committee for National Liberation formed in Algiers.
July 5 Battle of Kursk begins; largest tank battle in history ends in Russian victory; **10** Allied invasion of Sicily. **25** Mussolini overthrown. **28** Fascist Party in Italy dissolved.
August 17 Sicily in Allied hands.
September 3 Italian mainland invaded. **7** Italy surrenders. **9** British and American troops land near Naples. **10** Rome seized by the Germans. **14** Salamaua captured from the Japanese. **23** *Tirpitz* severely damaged (sunk Nov. 12, 1944). **25** Smolensk taken by the Russians.
October 1 Naples taken. **25** Russians capture Dnepropetrovsk and Dneprodzerzhinck.
November 6 Kiev taken by the Russians. **26** Second Battle of Solomons. **28** Churchill, Roosevelt, and Stalin meet in Teheran.
December 2 Men between 18 and 25 to be directed to the mining industry by ballot in Britain. **26** Sinking of German battleship *Scharnhorst*.

1944

January 22 Allied landings at Anzio. **28** Argentina breaks with the Axis Powers.
February 1 American forces land on the Marshall Islands. **2** Russians penetrate Estonia.
March 15 Cassino (Italy) destroyed by US bombers.
May 9 Sevastopol captured by Russians. **18** Capture of Cassino and Abbey by Allies. **19** 50 Allied officers shot after escaping from a German prison camp. **30** Battle for Rome commences.
June 4 Allied forces enter Rome. King of Italy signs decree transferring his powers to Prince Umberto, his son. **6** *D-Day*: invasion of Europe (over 4,000 ships in invasion fleet). **7** Defeat of Japanese thrust at India, outside Imphal. **9** Heavy fighting near Caen. **12** First V-1 falls on England. **18** Cherbourg peninsula cut by the Americans. Russians break through the Mannerheim Line.
July 3 Minsk captured by Russians. **9** Caen captured by Allies. **20** "Bomb plot" on Hitler's life. **21** Guam captured by Americans.
August 1 Uprising in Warsaw. **4** Myitkyina falls to Allied forces. **15** Allied forces land in southern France. Marseilles taken. Rumania surrenders. **25** Paris liberated. Rumania declares war on Germany.
September 3 Allies in Belgium. **4** Antwerp and Brussels taken by Allies. Holland entered. Finland "ceases fire." **6** Bulgaria asks for an armistice. **7** Boulogne entered by Allies. Bulgaria declares war on Germany. **8** First V-2 falls on England. **11** Allied forces fighting on

A.D.
Reich territory. **17** Allied airborne troops landed at Arnhem. **22** 1st Battle of Philippines.
October 3 Warsaw rising crushed by Germany. **14** Allies occupied Athens. **15** Hungary requested armistice. **20** US troops took Aachen. **25** Battle of Leyte Gulf: Japan's sea-power broken.
December 6 Civil war in Athens. **16** German counter-attack in Ardennes.

1945

January 5 Athens fighting ended. **9** US troops landed on Luzon. **13** Red Army occupied Budapest. **17** Red Army occupied Warsaw. **27** Red Army entered Auschwitz. **28** Burma Rd to China reopened.
February 4 Yalta Conference. **14** Dresden bombed. **19** US troops landed on Iwo Jima.
March 6 Allies took Cologne.
April 1 US invaded Okinawa. **11** Red Army entered Vienna. **12** Pres Roosevelt died. **27** Russian–US link-up in Germany. **28** Mussolini killed by Italian partisans. **29** German and Italian armies in Italy surrendered. **30** Suicide of Hitler.
May 2 Russians took Berlin. **3** British took Rangoon. **4** German forces in NW Germany, Holland and Denmark surrendered. **8** World War II ended; VE Day. **28** Air attacks on Japan.
June 26 World Security Charter to establish UN signed in San Francisco.
July 5 Allies recognised Polish government. **26** Labour won General Election: new PM Clement Attlee. **31** Potsdam Conference.
August 6 Atomic bomb destroyed Hiroshima. **9** Nagasaki atom bomb. **14** Unconditional surrender of Japan. **15** VJ Day.
September 5 Allies reoccupied Singapore.

"COLD WAR": AFRO-ASIAN INDEPENDENCE

October 15 Laval executed. **24** Quisling executed.
November 16 UNESCO founded in Paris. **20** Nuremberg trial opened.
December 27 IMF and World Bank established.

1946

February 1 Trygve Lie 1st UN Secretary-General.
March 5 Churchill's "Iron Curtain" speech.
April 18 League of Nations wound up.
May 25 Jordan independent.
June 30 US atom bomb test at Bikini.
July 13 £937m US loan to Britain. **22** King David Hotel, British HQ in Jerusalem, blown up.
August 1 Paris Peace Conference.
October 16 Nuremberg sentences carried out: Goering's suicide. **23** General Assembly of UN opened in New York.

1947

January 1 Coal nationalised. **14** Vincent Auriol 1st Pres of French IVth Republic.
February 20 Lord Mountbatten last Viceroy of India.
June 5 "Marshall Plan" inaugurated.
August 3 UN mediation ended Indonesia fighting. **15** India and Pakistan independent after partition.
October 6 International organisation of Communist Parties Cominform set up. **14** Sound barrier broken.
November 20 Princess Elizabeth married.
December 15 "Big 4" talks on Germany broke down.

1948

January 1 Railways nationalised. **4** Burma independent. **30** Gandhi assassinated.
February 1 Malayan federal constitution came into force. **27** Communists seized power in Czechoslovakia.
March 10 Czech Foreign Minister Jan Masaryk found dead.
April 1 Electricity nationalised. **16** OEEC set up.
May 14 British Mandate in Palestine ended: new State of Israel proclaimed.

A.D.
June 16 State of Emergency declared in Malaya. **28** Cominform expelled Yugoslavia.
July 1 Berlin airlift. **5** NHS inaugurated.
August 1 Economic union of French, US and British zones in Germany.
September 4 Queen Wilhelmina of Netherlands abdicated. **9** N Korea independent, following S Korea. **17** UN mediator in Palestine assassinated.
November 3 Harry Truman elected US Pres. **14** Prince Charles born.
December 10 UN adopted Declaration of Human Rights.

1949

January 22 Chinese Communists took Peking.
April 1 Newfoundland became province of Canada. **4** 12 nations signed N Atlantic Treaty. **18** Republic of Ireland proclaimed.
May 1 Gas nationalised. **12** Berlin blockade lifted. **23** Federal Republic of Germany proclaimed.
August 5 1st meeting of Council of Europe.
September 14 Dr Adenauer 1st Chancellor of FDR. **21** Soviet atom bomb test.
October 1 People's Republic of China proclaimed under Chairman Mao Tse-tung. **12** German Democratic Republic proclaimed in Soviet sector.
December 8 Chinese Nationalist government set up Formosa HQ. **27** Indonesia independent.

1950

January 26 Indian republic proclaimed under Pres Rajendra Prasad.
February 14 USSR–China alliance signed. **23** Labour won General Election.
June 25 N Korea invaded S Korea. **27** US air, naval, and later ground forces supported S Korea.
July 8 Gen MacArthur C in C of UN forces in Korea.
August 1 Chinese membership rejected by UN. **7** US offensive in Korea.
September 6 British troops in action in Korea.
October 19 UN forces took Pyongyang. **21** China invaded Tibet. **26** New Chamber of House of Commons opened.
November 26 Chinese offensive into N Korea.
December 4 Chinese took Pyongyang. **19** Gen Eisenhower appointed head of NATO forces.

1951

January 4 N Korean and Chinese troops captured Seoul. **17** French held back Viet Minh offensive in Tonkin.
March 19 Treaty of Paris signed to create European Coal & Steel Community.
April 11 Gen MacArthur replaced by Lt-Gen Ridgway.
May 2 Persian oil industry nationalised. **3** Festival of Britain opened.
June 7 British diplomats Burgess and Maclean vanished.
July 8 Korean ceasefire talks. **16** King Leopold of Belgians abdicated. **20** King Abdullah of Jordan assassinated.
September 1 Tripartite Security Treaty between US, Australia and New Zealand. **8** Japanese peace treaty.
October 16 Pakistan's PM Ali Khan assassinated. **19** British troops seized Suez Canal Zone. **25** Conservatives won General Election: Churchill PM.
December 24 Libya independent.

1952

February 6 George VI died: Accession of Queen Elizabeth II.
March 21 Kwame Nkrumah Gold Coast's 1st PM.
April 23 Japan regained sovereign and independent status.
May 27 European Defence Community Treaty signed.
June 23 US air attack on N Korea hydro-electric plants.
July 23 Military coup in Egypt: later King Faroukh abdicated. **26** Eva Peron died.

A.D.
August 1 Parliament ratified Bonn Agreement: W Germany again independent. **16** Lynmouth floods. **26** S African protests against racial laws.
September 8 Gen Neguib military Gov-Gen of Egypt.
October 3 Britain's 1st atomic bomb test in Monte Bello Is. **20** State of Emergency in Kenya over Mau Mau atrocities.
November 4 Republican Gen Eisenhower won US Presidental Election. **30** US hydrogen bomb test reported.

1953

February 3 E coast floods.
March 5 Stalin died. **14** Krushchev emerged as USSR leader. **24** Queen Mary died. **25** Polio vaccine announced. **31** New UN Sec-Gen Dag Hammarskjöld.
April 8 Mau Mau leader Jomo Kenyatta jailed.
May 29 Hillary and Tensing climbed Everest.
June 2 Elizabeth II crowned: ceremony televised. **17** E Berlin anti-Soviet riots. **18** Egyptian republic proclaimed.
July 27 Korean armistice signed.
August 14 Soviet hydrogen bomb test.
November 21 Piltdown skull exposed as hoax. **29** French took Dien Bien Phu.
December 23 Former KGB chief Beria executed.

1954

February 3 1st Central African Federation parliament opened.
March 22 London gold market reopened.
April 18 Nasser took power as Egypt's PM. **21** USSR joined UNESCO.
May 4 Roger Bannister's 4-min mile. **8** Dien Bien Phu fell to Viet Minh. **17** Racial segregation banned in US state schools.
June 2 New Irish PM John Costello. **17** New French PM Pierre Mendès-France.
July 5 Food rationing ended. **21** Sino-French pact to end Indo-China war.
August 5 Persian oil dispute settled.
October 19 Anglo-Egyptian Suez Canal Agreement.
November 1 Algerian nationalist riots.
December 2 Senator McCarthy censured by Congress. **18** Cyprus riots for union with Greece.

1955

February 8 Marshall Bulganin Soviet PM and 1st Sec of Communist Party. **23** New French PM Edgar Fauré. **25** 1st meeting of SEATO.
April 5 Sir Winston Churchill resigned: new PM Sir Anthony Eden. **18** Hungarian PM Imre Nagy dismissed. **24** Afro-Asian Conference of 29 non-aligned nations. **29** Vietnam civil war.
May 5 W Germany attained full sovereignty; Western European Union established. **26** Conservatives won General Election.
June 2 Soviet-Yugoslav relations normalised. **15** UK–US nuclear cooperation agreed.
July 18 "Big 4" Geneva conference.
August 20 Riots in Algeria and Morocco.
September 15 EOKA guerrillas outlawed: British troops in Cyprus. **19** Gen Peron ousted. **22** ITV 1st broadcast.
October 6 New Greek PM Constantine Karamanlis. **20** Syria–Egypt mutual defence treaty. **26** S Vietnam declared independent republic.
November 2 New Israeli PM David Ben-Gurion.
December 7 Clement Attlee resigned. **14** New Labour Party leader Hugh Gaitskell.

1956

January 1 Sudan proclaimed independent republic.
February 25 Krushchev denounced Stalin. **29** Alabama race riots.
March 2 King Hussein of Jordan dismissed Lt-Gen Glubb, Commander of Arab Legion. **9** Archbishop Makarios deported to Seychelles. **23** Pakistan Islamic Republic within Commonwealth.
April 18 Krushchev and Bulganin in London.
June 13 British troops left Canal Zone. **23** Nasser elected Pres of Egypt unopposed. **29** Polish anti-Soviet riots.
July 26 Egypt seized Canal Zone.
October 23 Hungarian uprising against Soviet domination. **25** Anti-Soviet Polish unrest. **29**

A.D.
Israel invaded Egypt seizing Sinai peninsula. **31** Anglo-French forces bombed Egyptian targets.
November 1 Premium bonds launched. **4** Soviet tanks crushed Hungarian revolt. **5** Anglo-French troops seized Canal Zone. **6** Pres Eisenhower re-elected. **8** UN Canal Zone ceasefire. **16** Canal blocked. **21** UN troops controlled Canal Zone. **30** Flood of Hungarian refugees.
December 5 140 arrests in S Africa for alleged treason. **7** Anglo-French troops left Port Said.

1957

January 1 Egypt abrogated 1954 Anglo-Egyptian Treaty, Saarland returned to W Germany. **9** Sir Anthony Eden resigned: new PM Harold Macmillan.
February 15 New Soviet Foreign Minister Andrei Gromyko.
March 6 Ghana independent; De Valera won Irish General Election. **25** Treaty of Rome setting up EEC and EAEC (Euratom) signed by Benelux, France, Germany and Italy.
April 8 Suez Canal reopened. **17** Archbishop Makarios in Athens.
May 15 UK's 1st hydrogen bomb test.
June 11 Canada's new Convervative government under John Diefenbaker.
July 8 State of Emergency against IRA proclaimed in Republic of Ireland. **25** Tunisia became republic under Pres Bourguiba.
August 8 Myxomatosis rife. **30** Malaya independent.
September 4 Wolfenden Report published. **15** Chancellor Adenauer re-elected. **23** Asian flu epidemic. **25** National Guard sent in to enforce desegregation in Little Rock, Arkansas.
October 4 Soviet satellite launched. **11** Jodrell Bank radio telescope inaugurated.
November 3 Soviet satellite carrying dog in orbit.
December 19 NATO conference agreed US nuclear bases in Europe.

EUROPEAN INTEGRATION

1958

January 1 Treaty of Rome came into force. **3** British W Indies Federation inaugurated. **28** Turkish Cypriot riots. **31** US satellite launched.
February 1 Syria and Egypt proclaimed United Arab Republic. **6** Munich plane crash: Manchester Utd lost 8 players. **14** Short-lived Jordan–Iraq union. **17** CND founded.
March 2 Dr Vivian Fuchs completed 1st crossing of Antarctica. **8** Yemen entered federation with UAR. **27** Bulganin ousted.
April 1 1st Aldermaston march. **17** Nationalists won S African General Election. **21** Maltese PM Dom Mintoff resigned.
May 13 Algerian French nationalists rebelled. **23** Hovercraft unveiled. **29** Gen de Gaulle returned to power.
June 9 Gatwick airport opened. **20** Greek Cypriots rejected British peace plan.
July 14 King Faisal of Iraq assassinated: republic established. **15** US marines in Lebanon. **17** British troops in Jordan. **24** 1st life peers announced.
August 5 US nuclear submarine passed under N Pole.
September 2 New S African PM Dr Verwoerd. **9** Notting Hill race riots. **28** French referendum approved Vth Republic.
October 4 EOKA campaign renewed. **9** Pope Pius XII died. **28** Angelo Roncalli elected Pope as John XXIII. **31** 1st heart pacemaker implanted.
December 8 Draft agreement at 3-power Geneva test ban talks. **21** De Gaulle 1st Pres of Vth Republic. **27** Soviet cooperation agreed with UAR on Aswan dam project. **31** Thalidomide implicated in birth defects.

1959

January 1 Cuba's Batista regime overthrown by Fidel Castro. **12** USSR *Lunik I* satellite 1st to escape Earth's gravity.
February 2 Indira Gandhi leader of India's Congress Party. **23** Archbishop Makarios returned to

A.D.

Cyprus. **26** State of Emergency in S Rhodesia: black nationalist parties dissolved.
March 4 Anti-British riots in Nyasaland: Hastings Banda arrested. **17** Lhasa uprising against Chinese rule: Dalai Lama fled.
May 6 "Cod war" with Iceland. **15** Jodrell Bank transmitted radio message to USA via moon.
June 17 Eamon de Valera voted Ireland's Pres. **26** St Lawrence Seaway opened.
July 5 3 animals recovered safely after Soviet space flight. **18** Castro assumed Cuba's Presidency.
August 18 BMC launched Mini.
September 14 Soviet *Lunik II* landed on moon. **27** Ceylon's PM Bandaranaike assassinated.
October 8 Conservatives won General Election. **26** *Lunik III* sent back photos of dark side of moon.
November 1 Nationalist riots in Belgian Congo. **2** M1 motorway opened. **20** EFTA agreement signed.
December 1 12 nations signed Antarctic Treaty. **3** Fréjus dam disaster. **14** Archbishop Makarios 1st Pres of Cyprus.

1960

January 1 French "new franc" introduced. **29** French settlers' revolt in Algeria.
February 2 De Gaulle granted emergency powers. **3** Harold Macmillan's "Wind of change" speech in Cape Town. **13** French atomic test in Sahara. **29** Agadir earthquake.
March 21 Sharpeville massacre in S Africa: 67 dead.
April 1 Hastings Banda freed. **9** Murder attempt on Dr Verwoerd. **19** Flood of E German refugees. **27** S Korean Pres Synghman Rhee resigned.
May 1 US U-2 reconnaissance aircraft shot down over USSR. **7** Leonid Brezhnev new Soviet PM. **17** Paris "Big 4" Summit failed; Kariba Dam inaugurated.
June 22 Krushchev attacked Mao and Chinese policies. **30** Belgian Congo became independent republic of Congo under PM Patrice Lumumba.
July 1 Ghana and Somalia became republics. **6** Congolese army mutiny: whites fled Leopoldville. **11** Katanga declared independence from Congo under Moise Tshombe. **21** Mrs Bandaranaike world's 1st woman PM. **31** Emergency in Malaya officially ended.
August 8 Coup in Laos: new PM Prince Souvanna Phouma. **16** Cyprus declared republic.
September 14 Congolese army took power under Col Mobutu.
October 2 Talks to end "Cod war". **12** Disruptive behaviour from Krushchev at UN General Assembly. **20** *Lady Chatterley's Lover* trial.
November 9 Democrat John Kennedy elected US Pres. **21** Fighting between Congolese army and UN troops.
December 2 Lumumba arrested, Archbishop of Canterbury met Pope. **31** National Service ended; Farthing abolished.

1961

January 8 Referendum in France and Algeria backed de Gaulle; Portland spy ring arrests.
February 13 Lumumba dead.
March 21 US military aid to Laos. **26** French army rising in Algiers collapsed after 4 days.
April 12 Yuri Gagarin in 1st manned space flight. **19** Cuban exiles in Bay of Pigs invasion. **20** Angolan revolt.
May 1 1st betting shops opened. **5** Alan Shephard made 1st US manned space flight. **17** S Korean military coup. **31** S Africa independent and left Commonwealth.
June 3 Kennedy-Krushchev Vienna talks. **27** Michael Ramsay enthroned as 100th Archbishop of Canterbury.
August 10 Britain formally applied to join EEC. **13** E Berlin border sealed: later Berlin Wall erected. **14** Kenyatta freed.
September 18 Dag Hammarskjöld killed in Congo plane crash. **30** Syria seceded from UAR.
October 10 Volcanic eruption on Tristan da Cunha: entire population evacuated. **23** 30 megaton Soviet atomic test. **24** Malta independent. **30** Stalin's body moved from Red Sq.
November 7 Adenauer elected Chancellor for 4th term. **28** UN condemned S African apartheid policy.
December 15 Eichmann sentenced to death for

A.D.

crimes against Jewish people. **17** Indian troops invaded Goa and other Portuguese colonies in India.

1962

January 4 More US military aid for S Vietnam. **14** UK smallpox outbreak.
February 8 OAS bomb campaign in France and Algeria.
March 2 Nehru's Congress Party won Indian General Election. **14** Geneva disarmament talks reopened. **15** Liberals won Orpington by-election.
April 8 Algerian peace accord. **13** International agreement on marine pollution. **26** 1st UK satellite *Ariel* launched.
May 10 US troops in Laos. **13** New Indian Pres Dr Radhakrishnan. **25** Coventry cathedral consecrated.
July 1 Commonwealth Immigrants Act came into force. **3** Algeria independent. **10** 1st live tv US–Europe link-up via *Telstar*.
August 22 De Gaulle escaped 4th assassination attempt.
September 3 Trans-Canada highway opened. **27** Yemen proclaimed republic.
October 22 Cuban missile crisis. **28** Soviet missile sites in Cuba to be dismantled. **26** Fighting on China–India border.
November 7 Nelson Mandela jailed for incitement. **20** US Cuban blockade lifted. **21** Ceasefire in China–India border dispute. **26** US Turkish bases to be removed. **29** Anglo-French agreement on Concorde. **30** New UN Sec-Gen U Thant.
December 8 British troops clashed with Brunei rebels opposing Malaysian Federation. **9** Dr Julius Nyrere 1st Pres of Tanganyika. **15** Right-wing victory in S Rhodesian General Election.

1963

January 15 Moise Tshombe finally ended Katanga secession. **18** Hugh Gaitskell died. **22** Franco–German Treaty on political and military cooperation. **29** Britain refused EEC membership; "Kim" Philby disappeared from Beirut.
February Nyasaland self-governing under PM Hastings Banda. **8** Military coup in Iraq: PM Kassim executed. **9** Joshua Nkomo jailed in S Rhodesia. **14** Harold Wilson new Labour leader: 1st successful kidney transplant.
March 8 Military coup in Syria. **27** Beeching Report axed railways. **29** Central African Federation collapsed.
April 6 US–UK Polaris agreement. **8** Liberals won Canadian General Election. **23** New German Chancellor Ludwig Erhart.
May 11 Greville Wynne in Moscow spy trial. **18** Federal troops sent to quell Alabama race riots. **20** Sukarno Life Pres of Indonesia. **25** OAU founded. **27** Kenyatta elected PM in Kenya's 1st General Election.
June 3 John XXIII died. **5** John Profumo, Secretary of State for War, resigned. **6** Martial law in Teheran after Ayatollah Khomeini arrested. **13** Buddhist riots in Saigon. **16** Valentina Tereshkova 1st woman in space. **21** Giovanni Battista Montini elected Pope as Paul VI. **26** Pres Kennedy in W Berlin.
July 22 Stephen Ward on trial in "Profumo affair" aftermath. **26** Skopje earthquake.
August 8 "Great Train Robbery": £2·6m. mailbags stolen. **8** US–UK–USSR test ban treaty. **28** Dr Martin Luther King's "Freedom March" on Washington. **30** Moscow–Washington "hot line" inaugurated.
September 16 Federation of Malaysia created: anti-British riots. **17** Fylingdales early warning missile system operational.
October 1 Nigeria declared republic within Commonwealth. **18** Harold Macmillan resigned: new PM Earl of Home, later Sir Alec Douglas-Home.
November 1 Military coup in S Vietnam. **22** Pres Kennedy assassinated: Vice-Pres Lyndon Johnson sworn in.
December 12 Kenya independent.

1964

January 4 Pope visited Holy Land. **29** Further S Vietnam military coup.
February 11 Turkish–Greek Cypriot fighting.

A.D.
March 19 UN peacekeeping troops in Cyprus.
April 9 Labour won 1st GLC elections. **13** New S Rhodesian PM Ian Smith. **21** BBC-2 on air. **22** Tanganyika and Zanzibar united as Tanzania.
May 27 Nehru died.
June 2 New Indian PM Lal Shastri; PLO founded. **4** Britain's *Blue Streak* rocket launched. **12** Life sentence on Nelson Mandela for treason. **14** Francois Duvallier Haitian Pres-for-Life.
July 2 US Civil Rights Act. **6** Nyasaland independent as Malawi. **10** Congo's new PM Moise Tshombe.
August 2 US destroyer attacked by N Vietnam in Gulf of Tonkin: US air raids in reprisal.
September 2 Indonesian troops landed in Malaysia. **21** Malta independent within Commonwealth.
October 15 Krushchev deposed: new Communist Party leader Leonid Brezhnev, new PM Kosygin; Labour won General Election: new PM Harold Wilson. **16** Chinese atomic test. **24** N Rhodesia independent as Zambia under Pres Kaunda.
November 1 Vietcong guerrillas attacked US S Vietnamese base. **2** King Saud of Saudi Arabia deposed by brother Faisal. **3** Pres Johnson won US Presidential Election. **17** Arms embargo on S Africa. **26** Belgian paratroopers rescued hostages from Congo rebels.
December 12 Kenya proclaimed republic under Pres Kenyatta.

1965

January 12 Indonesia left UN. **24** Churchill died.
February 7 US air raid on N Vietnam. **24** US bombed Vietcong in S Vietnam.
March 7 US marines in S Vietnam. **18** Soviet cosmonaut made 1st spacewalk. **25** Ceylon's new PM Senanayaka. **28** Alabama civil rights protest. **30** US Saigon embassy bombed.
April 30 US marines in Dominica after military coup.
May 7 Rhodesia Front won Rhodesian General Election. **11** E Pakistan cyclone: 16,000 dead.
June 19 Algerian Pres Ben Bella ousted by Col Boumedienne. **29** US offensive against Vietcong.
July 29 Edward Heath new Conservative leader.
August 9 Singapore seceded from Malaysia. **11** Riots in Watts, Los Angeles.
September 8 India invaded Pakistan after Kashmir fighting: Pakistan air raids on New Delhi and later Bombay. **12** 50,000 more US troops in S Vietnam. **30** UK's 1st woman High Court judge.
October 7 Post Office Tower opened. **17** US and UK anti-Vietnam war protests. **22** India and Pakistan accepted UN ceasefire. **29** Rhodesia conciliation talks failed.
November 11 Rhodesian UDI: Britain declared regime illegal: sanctions imposed. **25** Gen Mobutu deposed Congo's Pres Kasavubu.
December 8 Vatican Council II closed. **17** Rhodesian oil embargo. **19** Pres de Gaulle re-elected.

1966

January 11 Indian PM Shastri died: new PM Indira Gandhi. **15** Army coup in Nigeria. **31** US bombing of N Vietnam resumed: UK Rhodesia trade ban.
February 24 Army coup in Ghana while Pres Nkrumah abroad.
March 31 Labour won General Election.
April 19 Australian troops in Vietnam.
June 30 France left NATO; US bombed Hanoi.
July 20 6-month pay and prize freeze. **30** US bombed Vietnam demilitarised zone; England won World Cup. **31** US urban race riots.
Augst 11 Indonesia–Malaysia peace agreement. **13** Chinese cultural revolution began.
September 6 Dr Verwoerd assassinated: new S African PM John Vorster. **30** Bechuanaland became independent republic of Botswana; Ancient statues saved from waters of Aswan Dam.
October 3 Basutoland independent as Lesotho; Nigerian tribal fighting. **21** Aberfan coal tip disaster.
November 1 Vietcong shelled Saigon. **9** Florence floods; new Irish PM Jack Lynch.
December 1 Dr Kiesinger new W German Chancellor. **2** Harold Wilson and Ian Smith in inconclusive talks on HMS *Tiger*. **16** UN mandatory oil

A.D.
sanctions against Rhodesia. **22** Rhodesia left Commonwealth.

1967

January 18 New Liberal leader Jeremy Thorpe. **27** Flash fire killed 3 US astronauts during ground test.
February 22 Gen Suharto in power in Indonesia. **26** Major US offensive against Vietcong.
March 9 Stalin's daughter defected to West. **18** *Torrey Canyon* wrecked off Land's End: major pollution. **24** Army coup in Sierra Leone.
April 1 UK's 1st Ombudsman. **14** Conservatives won GLC elections. **21** Greek colonels seized power.
May 11 Britain applied to join EEC. **30** Biafra seceded from Nigeria.
June 5 6 Day War: Israel seized territory from Egypt, Jordan and Syria. **17** 1st Chinese H-bomb test.
July 1 Moise Tshombe arrested when plane hijacked to Algiers; BBC-2 began colour broadcasts. **7** Nigerian troops invaded Biafra. **15** De Gaulle in Quebec. **27** US urban race riots.
August 9 Biafran troops in Nigeria.
September 1 Majority verdicts allowed in UK criminal courts. **3** Swedish traffic switched to right. **20** *QEII* launched.
October 9 Che Guevara killed; New drink-driving laws. **22** Anti-Vietnam war demonstrations in US, UK and W Europe. **25** Abortion Bill passed. **31** Foot-and-mouth disease epidemic.
November 19 £ devalued. **29** Aden independent republic as S Yemen.
December 3 1st successful human heart transplant. **17** Australian PM Harold Holt drowned.

1968

January 5 Alexander Dubcek new moderate Czechoslovak PM. **9** New Australian PM John Gorton. **23** Intelligence ship *USS Pueblo* seized by N Korea. **31** Vietcong Tet offensive against S Vietnam cities: raid on US Saigon embassy.
February 24 US and S Vietnam troops recaptured Hue.
March 6 Black Rhodesians hanged in defiance of Queen's reprieve. **15** Foreign Secretary George Brown resigned. **17** Grosvenor Sq anti-Vietnam war demonstration.
April 4 Martin Luther King assassinated: riots throughout USA. **6** New Canadian Liberal PM Pierre Trudeau. **12** Student riots throughout Europe after shooting of W German student leader Rudi Dutschke. **21** Enoch Powell's immigration speech.
May 3 Student riots in Paris began. **9** Soviet troops on Czech border. **16** Ronan Point tower block collapsed. **19** French General Strike. **30** De Gaulle dissolved National Assembly and called General Election.
June 5 Robert Kennedy assassinated. **30** De Gaulle won landslide victory in French General Election.
July 1 Last EEC customs barriers removed; 36 nations signed Nuclear Non-Proliferation Treaty. **10** Couve de Murville succeeded Pompidou as French PM. **29** Papal encyclical against artificial contraception.
August 22 Warsaw Pact troops invaded Czechoslovakia.
September 11 Soviet tanks left Prague. **16** UK 2-tier postal system. **26** Theatre censorship abolished. **27** France vetoed UK EEC membership.
October 4 Warsaw Pact troops to remain in Czechoslovakia. **6** Londonderry riots against sectarian discrimination. **9** HMS *Fearless* Rhodesia talks failed.
November 1 US halted bombing of N Vietnam. **5** Republican Richard Nixon won US Presidential Election. **7** Prague anti-Soviet demonstrations.
December 27 3 US astronauts completed 10 orbits of moon.

1969

January 3 N Ireland sectarian violence. **19** Student Jan Palach set himself on fire in Wenceslas Sq in anti-Soviet protest.
February 3 Yasser Arafat PLO leader.
March 2 Soviet–China border clashes. **17** New Israeli PM Golda Meir. **19** British troops in

A.D.

Anguilla. **25** Pres Ayub Khan ousted by army coup under Gen Yahya Khan.

April 17 More troops sent to N Ireland; Dubcek replaced as Czech Communist Party leader by Gustav Husak. **18** Bernadette Devlin, civil rights worker, elected in Mid-Ulster by-election, UK's youngest MP. **23** Nigerian troops took Umuahia. **28** De Gaulle resigned after referendum defeat. **29** N Ireland PM Terence O'Neill resigned.

May 1 New N Ireland PM Maj James Chichester-Clark.

June 8 Spain closed Gibraltar border. **15** New French Pres Georges Pompidou: PM Jacques Chaban-Delmas.

July 1 Prince of Wales invested at Caernarvon. **21** Neil Armstrong and "Buzz" Aldrin 1st men on moon; Sen Edward Kennedy in court over Chappaquiddick drowning. **22** Gen Franco named Prince Juan Carlos as future Spanish King.

August 12 3 days of riots in Londonderry after Apprentice Boys' March. **15** British troops took over N Ireland security.

September 1 King Idris of Libya deposed by army revolutionaries under Muammar Gaddafi: republic proclaimed. **3** Ho Chi Minh died. **10** 7,000 troops in N Ireland. **24** Ton Duc Thang new N Vietnamese Pres. **28** Army erected Belfast "peace line": barricades dismantled: traffic curfew.

October 1 Olaf Palme Swedish PM. **10** N Ireland "B Specials" disbanded. **12** Troops used tear gas in N Ireland. **14** 50p coin issued. **15** "Vietnam moratorium" in USA. **21** New W German Chancellor Willi Brandt.

November 2 Starvation in Biafran refugee camps: Nigeria banned Red Cross aid.

December 18 UK death penalty permanently abolished.

1970

January 1 UK age of majority 18. **12** Biafra capitulated. **16** New Libyan PM Gaddafi; UK Hong Kong flu epidemic.

February 9 Equal Pay Bill passed in Commons. **11** Decentralisation of NHS announced.

March 1 US planes bombed "Ho Chi Minh trail" in E Laos. **2** Rhodesia declared republic. **18** Cambodia's Prince Sihanouk ousted. **19** 1st meeting between E and W German leaders.

April 2 Battle between Israeli and Syrian troops. **8** Israeli air raid on Nile delta village. **16** Clifford Dupont 1st Pres of Rhodesia. **17** *Apollo 13* crew rescued. **30** US troops in Cambodia.

May 4 4 student anti-war protesters shot dead at Kent State University, Ohio.

June 7 Jordan troops attempted to expel Palestinian guerrillas. **19** Conservatives won General Election; new PM Edward Heath. **26** Dubcek expelled from Communist Party. **30** UK, Denmark, Ireland and Norway opened talks on EEC entry.

August 2 1st use of rubber bullets in N Ireland. **30** Malayan PM Tengku Abdul Rahman resigned.

September 4 New Chilean Pres Socialist Salvador Allende. **12** Palestinian terrorists blew up 3 hijacked airliners in Jordan desert: 56 hostages held. **14** Palestinian guerrillas in control of N Jordan and Jordan's 2nd city Irbid. **22** New Malayan PM Abdul Razak. **27** Jordan–PLO truce signed in Cairo: PLO expelled from Jordan. **28** Nasser died. **30** All Western hostages freed in exchange for terrorists held by UK, W Germany and Switzerland.

October 5 New Egyptian Pres Anwar Sadat; Quebec separatists kidnapped British diplomat. **10** Quebec Minister Pierre Laporte kidnapped. **16** Trudeau outlawed FLQ and invoked emergency powers. **18** Laporte found dead. **19** Major oil find in N Sea by BP.

November 9 De Gaulle died. **13** Defence Minister Gen Assad seized power in Syria. **20** E Pakistan tidal wave: 150,000 dead.

December 3 Kidnapped British diplomat freed. **8** Pakistan's 1st free elections: Zulfikar Ali Bhutto victorious in W, Sheikh Mujibur Rahman in E.

December 14 Anti-government riots in Poland's Baltic ports: Communist Party leader Gomulka replaced by Gierek.

1971

January 1 Divorce Reform Act in force. **2** Ibrox Park football disaster. **3** Open University inaugu-

A.D.

rated. **8** British ambassador to Uruguay kidnapped by Tupamaros guerrillas. **15** Aswan High Dam inaugurated. **25** Ugandan Pres Obote ousted by army coup under Idi Amin.

February 4 Rolls-Royce bankrupt; Swiss women given vote in national elections. **9** 1st British soldier killed in N Ireland. **15** UK decimal day. **20** Idi Amin Uganda's self-appointed Pres.

March 23 New N Ireland PM Brian Faulkner. **26** Sheikh Mujibur Rahman declared E Pakistan independent as Bangladesh: civil war erupted: Rahman jailed. **29** Lt Calley found guilty of My Lai massacre.

April 5 Thousands dead in E Pakistan fighting. **10** Split between "official" and "provisional" IRA. **18** UAR, Syria and Libya formed Federation of Arab Republics. **22** Jean Claude Duvallier succeeded as Haitian Pres.

May 3 Erich Honeker Gen Sec of E German Communist Party. **13** Labour took over GLC. **14** 2m E Pakistan refugees in India. **28** Egypt–USSR friendship treaty.

June 6 Cholera epidemic in W Bengal: border with Bangladesh sealed. **15** Education Sec Mrs Thatcher announced end of free school milk. **30** 3 Soviet cosmonauts dead at end of space flight.

July 20 Anglo-Maltese defence talks collapsed.

August 10 Internment without trial in N Ireland: riots and firebomb attacks. **22** Right-wing coup in Bolivia.

September 9 British ambassador freed in Uruguay. **24** 90 Soviet diplomats expelled as spies. **27** Chequers talks on N Ireland between 3 PMs.

October 25 China admitted to UN. **27** Congo changed name to Zaire. **28** Parliament voted to join EEC. **31** IRA bomb at PO Tower.

November 23 India–Pakistan border fighting. **24** Rhodesia agreement signed.

December 3 Pakistan declared war on India. **6** India recognised Bangladesh. **7** Libya nationalised £80m BP assets. **17** Pakistan agreed ceasefire. **20** New Pakistan PM Zulfikar Ali Bhutto. **21** New UN Sec-Gen Kurt Waldheim. **26** US resumed N Vietnam bombing.

1972

January 9 Miners' strike. **12** Sheikh Mujibur Rhaman PM of Bangladesh. **13** Ghana coup led by Col Acheampong. **20** UK unemployment passed 1m. **22** Treaty of Brussels signed to admit UK, Denmark, Ireland and Norway to EEC. **30** "Bloody Sunday": army shot 13 Derry marchers dead; Pakistan left Commonwealth.

February 2 British embassy in Dublin burned down. **16** Widespread prolonged power cuts as miners' crisis deepened: State of Emergency declared. **22** IRA Aldershot bomb: 7 dead. **25** Miners ended strike.

March 4 2 killed, 146 injured by Belfast restaurant bomb. **21** 6 died in Belfast shops bombing. **30** Direct rule imposed in N Ireland; N Vietnamese offensive.

April 10 46 nations signed convention to ban biological warfare. **14** US retaliatory bombing of Hanoi and Haiphong. **18** Bangladesh joined Commonwealth.

May 3 Hue evacuated. **9** Israeli troops freed 92 hostages and killed Black September guerrillas at Lydda airport. **16** Segregationist Gov Wallace of Alabama crippled by gunman. **22** Ceylon became republic of Sri Lanka. **28** Duke of Windsor died. **29** Brezhnev–Nixon talks. **30** Tel Aviv airport massacre by PFLP; Official IRA agreed ceasefire.

June 16 5 burglars caught in Watergate building, Democrat campaign HQ; W German Army Red Faction guerrillas captured. **22** Provisional IRA ceasefire. **23** £ floated.

July 1 Pres Nixon's campaign manager resigned. **14** N Ireland ceasefire failed. **31** "Operation Motorman": army dismantled N Ireland barricades.

August 6 50,000 Ugandan Asians expelled to UK. **11** Last ground troops left Vietnam. **20** S Vietnamese troops retreated.

September 1 New Icelandic fishing limit 50 miles. **5** Black September guerrillas killed Israeli athletes at Munich Olympics, kidnapped others: hostages, 5 guerrillas and policeman killed in airport gun battle. **12** Icelandic gunboat sank 2 British trawlers.

October 5 United Reformed Church formed. **13** Bank rate abolished (new term MLR).

A.D.
November 6 Government froze prices, pay, rent and dividend increases for 90 days. **7** Pres Nixon re-elected. **19** Chancellor Brandt re-elected. **20** Silver Wedding of Queen and Prince Philip.

December 2 Gough Whitlam 1st Australian Labor PM since 1946. **18** US resumed bombing of N Vietnam. **21** Treaty between W and E Germany. **23** Nicaraguan earthquake devastated Managua.

1973
January 1 UK, Ireland and Denmark joined EEC. **27** Vietnam ceasefire signed.

February 1 EEC Common Agricultural Policy came into effect. **5** 1st Loyalists detained without trial in N Ireland. **12** 1st US prisoners released by N Vietnam. **21** Israeli fighters brought down Libyan Boeing 727: 104 dead.

March 1 Fine Gael and Labour coalition won Irish General Election: new PM Liam Cosgrave. **8** 2 bombs in central London. **9** N Ireland referendum: 591,820 in favour of retaining UK links. **11** French General Election: Gaullists and allies won absolute majority.

April 1 VAT introduced in UK.

May 7 Pres Nixon denied all knowledge of Watergate. **10** Elections for 36 new metropolitan district councils. **18** Royal Navy frigates sent to protect British trawlers in disputed 50-mile limit off Iceland. **31** Erskine Childers succeeded Pres de Valera of Eire.

June 1 Greece declared republic. **7** Skylab astronauts freed solar panels saving mission. **21** Mr Brezhnev and Pres Nixon signed arms limitation agreement.

July 31 1st sitting of N Ireland Assembly ended in chaos.

August 2 Summerland fire at Douglas, IOM. **19** George Papadopoulos 1st Pres of Greece.

September 3 Dr Henry Kissinger new US Secretary of State. **7** Len Murray new TUC General Secretary. **11** Allende government overthrown in Chile. **14** King Gustav of Sweden died. **20** Chelsea barracks bombed.

October 6 Arab–Israeli war began. **8** UK's 1st commercial radio station opened. **10** US Vice Pres Spiro Agnew resigned. **12** Gen Peron new Pres of Argentina with his wife as Vice Pres **16** Government embargo on arms sales to Middle East. **17** Arab oil producers cut supplies until Israel withdrew from occupied territories. **22** UN ceasefire agreed by Israel, Egypt and Jordan. **31** 3 Provisional IRA leaders freed from Mountjoy prison by hijacked helicopter.

November 8 UK–Iceland "cod war" ended. **12** Miners began overtime ban and ambulance drivers selective strikes. **14** Wedding of Princess Anne and Capt Mark Phillips. **25** Army coup in Greece.

December 5 50 mph speed limit imposed to conserve fuel. **6** Gerald Ford new US Vice Pres. **12** Rail drivers union ASLEF began overtime ban. **20** Spain's PM Admiral Carrero Blanco assassinated. **31** 3-day week imposed.

1974
January 1 Direct rule in N Ireland ended: new N Ireland Executive took office; Golda Meir won Israeli General Elections. **8** Lord Carrington Energy Secretary at head of new department. **9** Commons debate on energy crisis. **18** Israel and Egypt agreed withdrawal of forces. **22** Loyalists expelled from N Ireland Assembly.

February 10 Miners strike began. **28** UK General Election: no clear majority.

March 4 Edward Heath resigned: new minority Labour government. **9** UK resumed 5-day week. **11** Miners returned to work.

A.D.
April 10 Golda Meir and Cabinet resigned. **14** Fighting on Golan Heights and Mt Hermon. **24** S African General Election: Nationalist party won. **25** Army uprising in Portugal: regime in power since 1926 overthrown.

May 6 Chancellor Brandt resigned on discovery of E German spy in Chancellery. **15** Gen Spinola new Pres of Portugal; Israeli troops stormed village school in Ma'alot where children held hostage by Arab terrorists. **16** Herr Schmidt new W German Chancellor. **19** Giscard d'Estaing won French General Election. **28** N Ireland Executive collapsed. direct rule from Westminster resumed.

June 1 Flixborough chemical works explosion. **3** New Israeli PM Mr Rabin.

July 1 Death of General Peron. **9** Pierre Trudeau won Canadian General Election. **13** Senate Watergate Committee Report. **15** Pres Makarios overthrown in Cyprus coup. **17** Bomb at Tower of London. **18** Statutory incomes policy ended. **20** Turkish invasion of Cyprus. **24** Supreme Court ordered surrender of 64 White House tape recordings. **26** Greek junta collapsed: Mr Karamanlis returned to power. **27** 3 articles of impeachment adopted by Judiciary Committee of House of Representatives against Pres Nixon.

August 2 Pres Nixon resigned. **9** Gerald Ford sworn in as US Pres.

September 8 Emperor Haile Selassie deposed. **30** New Portuguese Pres Gen da Costa Gomes.

October 5 Guildford pub bombings: 2 dead, 70 hurt. **10** Labour won UK General Election: overall majority of 3. **15** Riots at Maze prison.

November 2 Vladivostock Summit between Pres Ford and Mr Brezhnev. **7** Woolwich pub bombings: 2 dead. **17** Mr Karamanlis won 1st Greek General Election since 1967. **21** Birmingham pub bombings: 21 dead, 120 hurt. **29** Anti-Terrorism Act proscribing IRA.

December 3 Defence cuts announced. **7** Archbishop Makarios returned to Cyprus. **18** Wave of bombs in London. **25** Cyclone devastated Darwin.

1975
January 1 Watergate defendants found guilty. **24** Dr Coggan enthroned 101st Archbishop of Canterbury. **25** Shaikh Mujibur Rahman new Pres of single party state in Bangladesh.

February 11 Mrs Thatcher elected leader of Conservative Party. **13** Turkish Cypriots declared separate state.

March 13 Portugal's new Supreme Revolutionary Council took power. **25** King Faisal of Saudi Arabia assassinated. **26** S Vietnamese troops evacuated Hué and Da Nang.

April 17 Phnom Penh government surrendered to Khmer Rouge. **21** Pres Thieu resigned as N Vietnamese troops encircled Saigon. **25** 1st elections in Portugal for 50 years. **30** Vietnam War ended.

June 5 Referendum on membership of European Community: UK in favour by 2:1 majority. **5** Suez Canal reopened. **12** Mrs Gandhi convicted of illegal use of government officials in 1971 campaign.

July 1 S S Ramphal the new Commonwealth Secretary-General. **29** Military coup in Nigeria: new Head of State Brig Murtala Mohammed.

August 7 Hottest-ever August day in London. **15** Pres Rahman of Bangladesh assassinated. **27** Bombings in Caterham and London.

September 9 Prince Sihanouk returned to Cambodia. **24** Government steps to check unemployment.

October 3 Dutch industrialist kidnapped in Limerick. **15** Iceland extended fishing rights to 200

A.D.

miles. 21 UK unemployment over 1m. 26 Battles in Beirut between Christian Phalangists and left-wing Muslims.

November 3 Queen formally inaugurated North Sea oil. 11 Angolan independence; Australian Governor-General dismissed Labor government. 22 Prince Juan Carlos crowned King of Spain.

December 4 Detention without trial ended in N Ireland. 10 "Cod war" began. 11 IRA Balcombe St siege in London. 14 Liberal Country Party won Australian General Election. 18 Education Bill compelling comprehensive education published. 29 Sex Discrimination and Equal Pay Acts came into force.

1976

January 19 Commons Devolution debate.

February 11 MPLA recognised as Angola's legal government by OAU. 13 Nigerian Pres Murtala Mohammed assassinated.

March 5 Ulster Convention dissolved: direct rule continued. 16 Harold Wilson resigned. 24 Senora Peron of Argentina deposed. 25 Basil Hume enthroned as Archbishop of Westminster.

April 5 New PM James Callaghan.

May 10 Jeremy Thorpe resigned Liberal leadership. 28 Soviet–US treaty on underground nuclear explosions.

June 1 "Cod war" ended. 16 Riots in African township Soweto near Johannesburg. 24 Vietnam reunified.

July 2 Government emergency powers to control water shortage. 4 Israeli raid on Entebbe airport to free 100 hostages. 7 David Steel new Liberal leader. 10 Explosion at Hoffman-La Roche plant at Seveso: contamination over 7km radius. 14 Official handing-over to Tanzania and Zambia of Chinese-built Tanzam railway. 21 UK ambassador to Ireland assassinated. 28 Earthquake destroyed Tangshan, China.

August 25 PM Chirac of France resigned.

September 2 European Commission on Human Rights found Britain guilty of torture in N Ireland. 19 Zagreb air collision. 20 Sweden's Social Democratic Party ousted after 20 years. 24 Ian Smith accepted UK and US proposals for Rhodesian majority rule.

October 8 Bishop Muzorewa returned to Rhodesia from exile. 4 British Rail high-speed train entered service. 6 Military coup in Thailand. 25 National Theatre officially opened. 28 Geneva conference on Rhodesia's future.

November 1 Jimmy Carter elected Pres of USA. 15 Formal end of Lebanon's civil war: Syrian peacekeeping troops in Beirut.

December 16 Michael Manley won Jamaican General Election. 17 Vladimir Bukovsky, Soviet dissident, and Senor Corvalán, Chilean Communist veteran, exchanged.

1977

January 1 EEC extended fishing limits to 200 miles. 24 Rhodesia talks collapsed.

February 15 1976 deaths exceeded live births for 1st time. 17 Uganda's archbishop and 2 Cabinet ministers killed in mysterious circumstances.

March 1 James Callaghan's government went into minority. 7 Zulfikar Ali Bhutto won Pakistan election. 22 Mrs Gandhi resigned after election defeat. 23 Lib-Lab pact: no-confidence vote defeated. 24 New Indian PM Moraji Desai and Janata Party government sworn in. 27 Tenerife airport disaster.

April 21 Martial law in Pakistan. 22 Ekofisk Bravo oilfield disaster.

A.D.

May 13 N Ireland 11-day strike collapsed. 17 Menachem Begin's Likud Party won Israel election. 18 International Commission of Jurists reported Ugandan atrocities.

June 1 New UK road speed limits. 7 Silver Jubilee celebrations in London. 11 11-day S Moluccan sieges ended in Holland. 15 1st Spanish elections since 1936, won by PM Suarez's Union of Democratic Centre. 16 Fianna Fail won Irish General Election.

July 5 Pakistan army deposed PM Bhutto. 21 Mrs Bandaranaika's Sri Lanka Freedom Party defeated.

August 10 Panama Canal Agreement concluded. 13 Violence at Lewisham National Front march. 25 Scarman Report on Grunwick dispute.

October 31 Effective revaluation of £.

November 4 Mandatory UN arms embargo on S Africa. 14 Firemen's strike. 15 Son for Princess Anne. 19 Egyptian Pres Sadat and Israeli PM Begin met in Israel; Bay of Bengal cyclone killed 25,000. 30 National Party won S African General Election.

December 10 Malcolm Fraser's Conservative coalition won Australian General Election: Labor leader Gough Whitlam resigned. 21 OPEC froze oil prices.

1978

January 1 Air India plane crash off Bombay. 4 PLO London representative shot dead. 25 Government defeat on Scottish devolution. 29 Rhodesia talks in Malta with Joshua Nkomo and Robert Mugabe.

February 4 Ethiopian Ogaden offensive. 19 Egyptian commandos stormed hijacked plane at Larnaca.

March 3 Internal settlement agreed in Rhodesia between Ian Smith and 3 black Nationalist leaders. 8 New Italian PM Giulio Andreotti. 15 Israeli thrust into S Lebanon. 16 Aldo Moro, 5 times Italy's PM, kidnapped and murdered; Amoco Cadiz aground off Brittany: massive pollution.

April 3 1st regular radio broadcasts from Parliament. 10 Transkei, 1st tribal homeland to gain independence, cut diplomatic links with S Africa. 17. No cases of smallpox anywhere during previous year. 26 Arab terrorist attack on bus on West Bank. 27 Afghanistan's Pres Daoud deposed in pro-Soviet coup.

May 1 1st UK May Day Bank Holiday. 24 Princess Margaret and Lord Snowdon divorced.

June 3 New Bangladeshi Pres Gen Zia ur-Rahman. 12 Provisional IRA leader Seamus Twomey sentenced in Dublin.

July 5 Ghanaian Pres Acheampong resigned. 9 Former Iraqi PM Gen Razzale al-Naif shot in London. 25 World's 1st "test tube" baby born. 31 Lib-Lab pact ended.

August 6 Pope Paul VI died. 13 Beirut PLO HQ bombed. 22 Gunmen held hundreds hostage in Nicaraguan parliament. 26 Cardinal Albino Luciani of Venice elected as Pope John Paul I.

September 8 Martial law in Tehran. 11 Martial law in Nicaragua. 16 Earthquake in Iran killed 11,000. 17 Camp David talks between Pres Sadat and PM Begin concluded framework for Middle East peace treaty. 28 Pope John Paul I died; New S African PM Pieter Botha.

October 10 New Kenyan Pres Daniel arap Moi. 15 Cardinal Karol Wojtyla of Cracow 1st non-Italian Pope for 450 years as John Paul II. 20 4-week siege of Beirut lifted.

November 25 National Party won New Zealand

A.D.
General Election. **26** Clashes in Iran during 24-hour general strike. **27** Japanese PM Fukuda resigned. **30** Publication of *The Times* suspended until 13 Nov 1979.

December 17 OPEC announced oil price rise. **20** Israeli attack on Lebanese terrorist bases.

1979

January 1 New Iranian PM Dr. Bakhtiar. **4** Guadeloupe Summit between UK, US, W Germany and France. **7** Phnom Penh captured by Vietnamese and rebel troops. **15** Road haulage strike. **16** Shah left Iran. **17** UK admitted Vietnamese refugees. **30** Rhodesian whites-only referendum. 6:1 in favour of transfer to majority rule.

February 1 Ayatollah Khomeini returned to Iran from exile in Paris. **5** New Iranian PM Dr Bazargan. **14** "Concordat" between government and TUC. **15** Army take-over in Chad. **28** Final meeting of white Rhodesian House of Assembly.

March 1 Scots voting in favour of devolution failed to reach 40% requirement: Welsh voted overwhelmingly against devolution. **13** Government of Grenada overthrown. **26** Israel–Egypt peace treaty signed. **28** Radiation leak at Three Mile Island nuclear plant, Pennsylvania. **30** Shadow N Ireland Secretary Airey Neave assassinated. **31** Final withdrawal of British navy from Malta.

April 1 Islamic Republic in Iran. **2** 1st visit of Israeli PM to Egypt. **4** Former Pakistani PM Bhutto executed. **11** Kampala captured by Tanzanian troops and Ugandan exiles: new Ugandan leader Prof Yusofo Lule. **23** 1 died, 300 arrested in clashes at Southall National Front march.

May 3 UK General Election: Margaret Thatcher 1st woman PM: Conservative overall majority 43. **16** Government removed legal obligation towards comprehensive education. **22** Joe Clark's Progressive Conservatives formed minority Canadian government. **29** Bishop Muzorewa Zimbabwe Rhodesia's 1st black MP.

June 4 S African Pres Vorster resigned after "Muldergate" scandal. **11** Conservatives won UK European elections. **18** Pres Carter and Pres Brezhnev signed SALT II treaty. **20** Ugandan Pres Lule deposed. **22** Jeremy Thorpe acquitted in Old Bailey conspiracy trial.

July 13 Abortion Law tightened. **17** Pres Somoza fled Nicaragua.

August 18 Heart transplant carried out at Papworth Hospital near Cambridge. **19** Former Cambodian leader Pol Pot convicted in his absence of murder of 3m people. **27** Earl Mountbatten killed by bomb on boat in Sligo.

September 10 London talks on Zimbabwe Rhodesia constitution. **19** 3-party non-Socialist coalition won Swedish elections. **20** Emperor Bokassa of Central Africa Empire ousted. **26** UK compulsory metrication abandoned. **29** 1st-ever Papal visit to Eire.

October 1 Civilian rule restored in Nigeria. **17** El Salvador colonels imposed martial law. **19** ITV strike ended. **23** Foreign exchange controls removed.

November 1 Military coup in Bolivia. **4** Iranian students occupied US embassy in Tehran. **9** US computer fault led to full-scale nuclear alert. **14** Iranian assets in US frozen.

December 7 Dutch Parliament rejected NATO's Cruise missile plan. **11** New Irish PM Charles Haughey. **12** NATO approved stationing of US missiles in Europe. **21** Rhodesian treaty signed. **27** Afghanistan's Pres Amin ousted in Soviet-backed coup.

1980

January 7 Mrs Gandhi's Congress Party won

A.D.
Indian General Election. **22** Dr Andrei Sakharov, winner of 1975 Nobel peace prize, sent into USSR internal exile. **27** Israel–Egypt border reopened.

February 12 Publication of Brandt Report "North South". **18** Pierre Trudeau won Canadian General Election.

March 4 Robert Mugabe's ZANU(PF) party formed government with absolute majority in Zimbabwe Rhodesia. **24** Archbishop Romero shot dead at altar in San Salvador. **25** Robert Runcie enthroned as Archbishop of Canterbury. **27** Oil accommodation rig overturned in North Sea.

April 2 Riots in St Pauls area of Bristol. **3** 13-week steel strike ended. **9** Israeli troops moved into Lebanon. **13** US Olympic Committee voted to boycott Moscow Games. **18** Rhodesia became independent as Zimbabwe. **25** Unsuccessful attempt to free US hostages in Iran. **30** Queen Beatrix of the Netherlands invested.

May 5 SAS stormed besieged Iranian embassy in London. **18** Mount St Helens erupted.

June 22 Liberals won Japanese General Election. **23** Sanjay Gandhi, son of Indian PM, died in plane crash.

July 17 Military coup in Bolivia. **19** Moscow Olympics opened.

August 13 French fishermen blockaded Channel ports.

September 7 Hua Guofeng resigned as Chinese leader: replaced by Zhao Ziyang. **10** Libya and Syria to merge as unitary Arab state. **22** Outbreak of Iran–Iraq War.

October 5 Helmut Schmidt re-elected W German Chancellor. **10** Algerian earthquake: 4,000 dead. **15** James Callaghan resigned as Labour leader. **18** Liberal and Country coalition won Australian General Election. **23** Soviet PM Kosygin resigned. **24** Polish independent trade union Solidarity recognised by Polish authorities. **27** Hunger strike at Maze prison.

November 4 Ronald Reagan elected Pres of USA. **10** New Labour leader Michael Foot. **23** Earthquake in S Italy.

December 8 Dublin Summit between Mrs Thatcher and Charles Haughey; John Lennon shot dead in New York. **15** Dr Milton Obote sworn in as Ugandan Pres. **17** Prof Alan Walters appointed PM's personal economic adviser.

1981

January 1 Greece joined EEC. **20** US hostages left Iran. **21** Sir Norman Stronge and his son, former Stormont MPs, killed by IRA. **25** Roy Jenkins, Shirley Williams, William Rodgers and David Owen launched Council for Social Democracy; Mao's widow Jiang Qing convicted. **27** Joshua Nkomo appointed Minister without Portfolio in attempt to prevent Zimbabwe confrontation.

February 3 Norway's first woman PM Dr Gro Harlem Brundtland. **12** Rupert Murdoch bought *The Times*. **23** Failed military coup in Spain.

March 26 Social Democratic Party born. **30** Pres Reagan shot outside Hilton Hotel in Washington.

April 5 Pres Brezhnev in Czechoslovakia talks on Polish crisis. **11** Brixton riots.

May 9 Bomb exploded at Sullum Voe during Royal inauguration. **10** François Mitterrand won French Presidential Election. **13** Pope shot by Turkish gunman. **22** Peter Sutcliffe convicted of Yorkshire Ripper murders. **30** Bangladeshi Pres Zia ur-Rahman assassinated.

June 8 Israeli planes destroyed Iraqi nuclear reactor. **10** 8 IRA prisoners escaped from Crumlin Rd jail. **13** Blanks fired at Queen during

A.D.
Trooping of Colour. 16 Liberal-SDP alliance announced. 21 Socialists won French General Election. 22 Ayatollah Khomeini dismissed Iran's Pres Bani-Sadr. 30 PM Begin secured continuation of Israeli coalition government; New Irish PM Dr Garret FitzGerald.

July 3 Southall race riots. 4 Toxteth riots. 15 Red Cross to mediate at Maze prison. 29 Wedding of Prince Charles and Lady Diana Spencer.

August 20 MLR suspended. 25 S African troops crossed into Angola. 30 Iran's Pres and PM killed by bomb.

September 1 Army take-over in Central African Republic. 18 France abolished capital punishment.

October 4 Maze hunger strike ended. 6 Pres Sadat assassinated. 10 IRA bomb in Chelsea: 2 dead. 14 New Egyptian Pres Hosni Mubarak. 18 Gen Jaruzelski new leader of Polish Communist Party. 26 Oxford St IRA bomb killed disposal expert.

November 6 Anglo-Irish Intergovernmental Council agreed. 14 Unionist MP Rev Robert Bradford shot dead.

December 8 Arthur Scargill new leader of National Union of Mineworkers. 11 Javier Perez de Cuellar new UN Secretary-General. 13 Martial law in Poland. 14 Israel annexed Golan Heights. 19 Penlee lifeboat lost during rescue attempt.

1982

January 4 EEC rejected USSR and Poland sanctions. 26 UK unemployment reached 3m.

February 5 Laker Airways collapsed. 19 De Lorean car company failed.

March 9 Charles Haughey new Irish PM. 16 Pres Brezhnev froze deployment of Soviet missiles in Europe. 18 Argentinians in S Georgia to dismantle whaling station raised Argentinian flag. 19 3-year ban on England cricketers in unofficial S African tour. 24 Martial law in Bangladesh after coup.

April 2 Argentina invaded Falkland Is. 5 Lord Carrington and 2 Foreign Office ministers resigned: new Foreign Secretary Francis Pym. 25 British troops recaptured S Georgia; Israel handed over Sinai to Egypt.

May 2 Argentine cruiser *General Belgrano* sunk in British attack. 4 British destroyer HMS *Sheffield* hit by Exocet missile. 7 Britain extended total exclusion zone to within 12 miles of Argentine coast. 15 British commando raid on Argentine airstrip at Pebble I. 21 British troops established bridgehead at San Carlos. 28 Paratroops captured Goose Green and Darwin; Papal visit to UK.

June 3 Israeli ambassador shot in London. 4 Israel bombed Beirut's Palestinian quarter. 6 British took Bluff Cove and Fitzroy. 7 Argentine raid on *Sir Tristram* and *Sir Galahad* off Bluff Cove. 14 Falklands ceasefire. 17 Argentinan Pres Gen Galtieri ousted. 21 Prince William of Wales born. 23 Labour National Executive acted against Militant Tendency. 25 New US Secretary of State George Shultz.

July 1 New Argentinian Pres Gen Bignone. 2 Roy Jenkins new SDP leader. 20 IRA bombs in Hyde Park and Regent's Park.

August 4 Israeli tanks invaded W Beirut. 12 Ceasefire in Lebanon. 17 China and US agreed Taiwan policy. 21 PLO guerrillas left Beirut.

September 4 Princess Grace of Monaco died; Lebanese leader Bashire Gemayal killed by bomb. 17 Palestinian refugees killed in W Beirut camps. 19 Swedish Social Democrats won General Election.

October 1 New W German Chancellor Christian Democrat leader Helmut Kohl. 8 Polish govern-

A.D.
ment dissolved Solidarity. 11 Tudor warship *Mary Rose* raised. 21 SDLP and Sinn Fein refused to take seats won in Ulster Assembly election. 28 Socialists elected in Spain. 31 Thames barrier inaugurated.

November 1 Channel 4 TV opened. 10 Soviet leader Leonid Brezhnev died: new leader Yuri Andropov. 24 El Al went into liquidation. 25 Ireland's new government formed by Fine Gael and Labour coalition.

December 6 Bomb at bar in Ballykelly killed 16. 12 30,000 women ringed Greenham Common missile base in protest.

1983

January 25 EEC agreed common fishing policy. 31 New UK seat belt law.

February 9 Derby winner Shergar stolen in Co Kildare.

March 5 Labor Party won Australian General Election. 6 Christian Democrats won W German General Election. 22 New Israeli Pres Chaim Herzog.

April 18 US embassy in W Beirut bombed: many dead. 21 New UK £1 coin. 24 Austrian Chancellor Dr Bruno Kreisky resigned. 26 8 famine relief workers kidnapped in Ethiopia by Tigré People's Liberation Front.

May 1 Demonstrations in 20 Polish cities. 16 1st use of wheel clamps by London police. 17 Israel-Lebanon agreement on troop withdrawal. 18 State of Emergency in Sri Lanka. 23 S African raids on Maputo.

June 9 Conservative majority of 144 in UK General Election. 13 New SDP leader David Owen. 14 All-party Commons defence committee endorsed "Fortress Falklands" policy. 15 New Speaker of Commons Bernard Weatherill. 16 Mr Andropov elected Soviet Pres. 24 Syria expelled PLO leader Yasser Arafat.

July 3 Home of former Ulster MP Gerry Fitt burnt out by IRA. 15 6 killed by bomb at Orly airport. 16 20 killed in helicopter crash near Scilly Is.

August 4 Italy's 1st Socialist PM since 1946 Bettino Craxi. 5 Lebanese mosque explosion: 19 dead. 11 Chad town Faya-Largeau fell to Libyan troops. 14 French troops in NE Chad. 21 Philippine opposition leader shot dead at Manila airport. 31 S Korean airliner disappeared near Japan: USSR later admitted shooting it down.

September 4 Israeli army withdrew from Chouf mountains above Beirut. 15 Israeli PM Begin resigned. 23 Abu Dhabi air crash: 112 dead. 25 38 IRA prisoners escaped from Maze prison: prison officer stabbed to death. 26 *Australia II* won America's Cup.

October 2 New Labour leader Neil Kinnock. 10 New Israeli government led by Yitzhak Shamir. 14 Cecil Parkinson resigned. 19 Grenada's PM Maurice Bishop shot by troops: Gen Hudson Austin in control. 23 Suicide bombers killed 229 US marines and 58 French paratroops in Beirut. 25 Troops from US and 6 Caribbean states invaded Grenada. 30 Radical Party leader Raul Alfonsin won Argentine General Election.

November 3 S African white minority voted to give limited representation to Asians and Coloureds. 12 New leader of Irish Republican movement Gerry Adams. 14 1st Cruise missiles at Greenham Common. 15 Turkish Cypriot UDI under Rauf Denktash. 16 Yasser Arafat retreated to Tripoli. 21 Unionist Party withdrew from N Ireland Assembly in protest at Darkley Gospel Hall killings. 23 USSR quit Geneva disarmament talks. 26 £26m Heathrow bullion robbery. 27 Air crash near Madrid: 181 dead. 28 European space lab launched at Cape Canaveral.

December 6 1st UK heart–lung transplant. 7 Official Unionist Edgar Graham shot dead at

A.D.

Queen's University Belfast. **10** Bomb at Woolwich barracks. **15** NGA industrial action ended. **17** Harrods bomb: 6 dead, many injured. **31** Military coup in Nigeria: new leader Maj-Gen Mohammed Buhari.

1984

January 9 Share prices exceeded 800 on FT index. **20** £1m Christie's diamond robbery. **25** Government ban on union membership at GCHQ.

February 5 Lebanese Cabinet resigned. **8** British peacekeeping troops left Lebanon followed by French, Italians and US. **9** Soviet Pres Andropov died: succeeded by Konstantin Chernenko. **15** Druze and Shi'ite militiamen drove Lebanese army from 8 Beirut. **29** Canadian PM Pierre Trudeau resigned.

March 12 Miners strike against pit closures. **15** £5m Woburn Abbey silver robbery. **20** UK blamed for collapse of EEC Summit. **23** Foreign Office clerk jailed for leaking documents to *The Guardian*.

April 3 Coup in Guinea after death of Pres Sekou Touré. **17** WPC Yvonne Fletcher shot dead outside Libyan embassy: 10-day siege.

May 7 Christian Democrat Napoleon Duarté won Salvadorean Presidential election. **8** USSR and Warsaw Pact countries boycotted Olympics. **13** Angolan rebels freed 16 hostages. **18** IRA killed 4 members of security forces. **23** Lancs underground pumping station explosion: 15 dead.

June 1 Pres Reagan visited Ireland; Mrs Thatcher and PM Botha in Chequers talks. **5** US increased military role in Gulf. **6** Sikh fanatics in Golden Temple of Amritsar surrendered to Indian army: leader died. **14** UK European elections: Conservatives kept majority. **16** New Canadian Liberal Party leader and PM John Turner. **20** Education Secretary announced new GCSE examinations.

July 9 York Minster fire. **12** Robert Maxwell acquired Mirror Group newspapers. **13** Labour Party won New Zealand General Election. **17** French government resigned. **25** Soviet cosmonaut 1st woman to walk in space. **29** Los Angeles Olympics opened.

August 21 S African Coloured elections won by Labour Party: many arrests. **26** Wakefield salmonella outbreak. **31** TUC backed pit strike.

September 3 Riots in Transvaal townships. **4** Conservatives won Canadian General Election: new PM Brian Mulroney. **5** New Israeli government of national unity; TUC rejoined Neddy. **24** US Beirut embassy bombed. **26** Sino-British declaration on Hong Kong's future.

October 12 IRA bomb at Grand Hotel, Brighton. **23** Violence in S African townships. **30** Kidnapped Polish priest Fr Popieluszko found dead; Famine in Ethiopia. **31** Indian PM Mrs Gandhi assassinated by Sikh bodyguard: new PM her son Rajiv.

November 4 New Nicaraguan Pres Daniel Ortega. **6** Pres Reagan re-elected. **19** Mexico City gas explosion: 600 dead.

December 1 Labor Party won Australian General Election. **3** Leak of poison gas from pesticide factory in Bhopal, India: 2,500 dead, thousands blinded; Massive gains in 1st day's trading in British Telecom shares. **18** Local authorities told to cut capital spending by £1bn in 1985. **28** Rajiv Gandhi won Indian General Election

THE END OF THE COLD WAR

1985

January 3 12,000 Ethiopian Jews airlifted to Israel. **15** Civilian Pres for Brazil. **20** Tamil bomb on Sri Lankan train: 36 dead. **23** 1st House of Lords debate televised. **29** Oxford University refused PM honorary degree.

A.D.

February 4 Spain–Gibraltar border reopened. **18** Riots at Crossroads shanty town, S Africa. **19** S African anti-apartheid leaders arrested. **20** PM addressed joint session of US Congress. **25** £ at record low against $. **28** IRA bombed Newry police station.

March 3 Miners' strike ended. **4** New Zealand PM reaffirmed ban on nuclear weapons. **8** Beirut car bomb: 80 dead. **10** Pres Chernenko died: succeeded by Mikhail Gorbachev. **12** Geneva arms control talks. **15** Belgian government agreed to deploy Cruise missiles. **21** 19 blacks shot dead in Uitenhage on Sharpeville anniversary.

April 6 Sudanese Pres Numeiri deposed by army. **11** Tamil bomb killed 24 in Colombo just prior to Mrs Thatcher's arrival.

May 1 US trade ban on Nicaragua; Ethiopia's largest famine relief camp cleared by troops. **10** Pres Reagan froze defence spending. **11** Bradford City FC fire: 55 dead. **15** Sri Lankan Tamil terrorists killed 146. **22** Fighting in Beirut. **24** Tidal wave swamped Bangladesh islands: thousands dead. **29** 38 killed when wall collapsed at Heysel stadium, Brussels, before Liverpool v Juventus match.

June 10 Israel completed withdrawal from Lebanon. **12** Shi'ite gunmen blew up Jordanian aircraft after releasing hijack hostages.

July 2 New USSR Pres Andrei Gromyko: Foreign Minister Eduard Schevardnadze. **7** Robert Mugabe won Zimbabwe General Election. **10** Greenpeace ship *Rainbow Warrior* sunk in Auckland, NZ. **13** Live Aid concert for African famine relief. **19** Dam collapse at Stava, Italy: 260 dead. **21** S African State of Emergency. **27** Ugandan Pres Obote ousted.

August 12 Japanese Boeing 747 crashed near Tokyo: 524 dead. **17** E Beirut car bomb killed 54. **22** Manchester airport disaster: 54 dead. **27** Nigerian government ousted.

September 9 Riots in Handsworth, Birmingham. **11** S African citizenship restored to 8m blacks in tribal homelands. **17** Chancellor Kohl's secretary defected to E Berlin. **28** Brixton riots.

October 1 Israeli air raid on PLO's Tunisian HQ. **6** Policeman killed in riots on Broadwater Farm estate, Tottenham. **7** Italian cruise ship *Achille Lauro* hijacked by PLO. **20** Commonwealth leaders agreed measures against S Africa.

November 2 S African government controls on media riot coverage. **14** W Colombian volcano erupted: 20,000 dead. **15** N Ireland agreement signed by Mrs Thatcher and Dr Garret FitzGerald. **21** Reagan–Gorbachev Summit. **24** Egyptian commandos stormed hijacked Boeing in Malta.

December 1 UK to withdraw from UNESCO. **6** UK to participate in US Strategic Defence Initiative (SDI). **13** Westland helicopters in deal with US and Italian consortium. **27** Terrorist attacks on Israeli check-in desks at Rome and Vienna airports.

1986

January 7 Pres Reagan cut economic links with Libya. **9** Michael Heseltine and later Leon Brittan resigned over Westland affair: George Younger new Defence Secretary. **20** Anglo-French twin tunnel Channel rail link agreed. **24** N Ireland by-elections due to mass resignation of MPs. **26** *Sunday Times* and *News of the World* printed at Wapping despite print union action. **28** *Challenger* shuttle crashed on take-off.

February 7 Jean-Claude Duvalier left Haiti. **16** Mario Suares won Portuguese Presidential Election. **25** Mrs Corazon Aquino took power in Philippines. **28** Swedish PM Olof Palme assassinated.

March 2 Legal independence for Australia. **12** New Swedish PM Ingvar Carlsson. **16** New French PM

A.D.

Jacques Chirac. **24** US navy destroyed missile battery on Gulf of Sidra. **31** GLC and 6 Metropolitan councils abolished.

April 15 US bombed Benghazi and Tripoli in retaliation for Libyan terrorism. **17** 2 UK hostages killed in Lebanon. **26** Major accident at Chernobyl nuclear power plant, USSR: 19 deaths, radioactive cloud over Scandanavia. **30** Police invaded Golden Temple at Amritsar.

May 19 S African commando attacks on Zimbabwe, Zambia and Botswana.

June 6 Chief Constable of W Yorks to replace John Stalker in N Ireland "shoot-to-kill" inquiry. **8** New Austrian Pres Dr Kurt Waldheim. **12** Renewed State of Emergency in S Africa. **20** S Africa legalised 180-day detention without trial; Ban on sheep movement in Cumbria and N Wales due to radiation. **27** EEC Summit called for release of Mandela and recognition of ANC; International Court of Justice ruled US support for Nicaraguan Contras illegal.

July 6 Liberal Democratic Party won Japanese General Election. **22** Commons voted to ban corporal punishment in schools. **23** Prince Andrew named Duke of York on marriage to Sarah Ferguson. **25** Appeal Court banned publications by former MI5 officer Peter Wright.

August 5 Commonwealth sanctions against S Africa. **7** Ulster loyalist mob crossed border into Eire. **18** Mr Gorbachev announced unilateral freeze on nuclear testing. **25** Gas escape from volcanic crater in Cameroon: 1,500 dead.

September 1 Soviet cruise liner sank after collision: 400 dead. **5** Commandos stormed hijacked PanAm jet at Karachi. **10** Kinross goldmine fire in Transvaal: 177 dead.

October 2 US sanctions against S Africa. **7** *The Independent* newspaper launched; New state-funded city technology colleges announced. **12** Reagan–Gorbachev Summit collapsed over Star Wars programme; Queen visited China. **19** Pres Samora Michel of Mozambique killed in S Africa plane crash: new Pres Joaquim Chissano. **20** New Israeli PM Likud leader Yitzhak Shamir. **26** Conservative Party deputy chairman Jeffrey Archer resigned. **27** "Big Bang" day in City: computer failed. **29** Final section of M25 opened.

November 10 EEC (except Greece) backed sanctions against Syria. **19** Pres Reagan admitted arms sales to Iran. **24** Barclays Bank pulled out of S Africa. **25** John Poindexter and Col Oliver North dismissed over sale of arms to Contras.

December 1 DTI investigation into Guinness affair. **23** Dr Andrei Sakharov returned to Moscow.

1987

January 12 Rate Support Grant settlement: cuts of up to 30% imposed on 20 local authorities. **16** General Secretary of Chinese Communist Party Hu Yaobang resigned. **20** Archbishop of Canterbury's special envoy Terry Waite kidnapped in Beirut. **25** Chancellor Kohl's centre-right coalition won German election. **27** Mr Gorbachev offered Soviet people choice of election candidates: criticism of Brezhnev era.

February 10 140 political prisoners released in USSR. **12** Peaceful Moscow human rights demonstration dispersed violently. **22** 4,000 Syrian troops in W Beirut to enforce peace.

March 6 Zeebrugge ferry disaster: 193 dead. **10** Ireland's new PM Charles Haughey.

April 13 9 trains set alight in Soweto. **25** Lord Justice Gibson and Lady Gibson killed by N Ireland car bomb.

May 1 Government abandoned plan to dump nuclear waste. **5** Congressional hearing into Irangate affair. **6** National Party won S African whites-only election: 1m blacks on protest strike.

A.D.

14 Coup led by Lt-Col Sitiveni Rabuka in Fiji. **17** USS *Stark* hit by Iraqi Exocet: 37 dead. **26** US authorised Kuwaiti tankers in Gulf to fly US flag; Sri Lankan government offensive to recapture Jaffna Peninsula. **29** German Matthius Rust landed in Red Sq; S African commandos attacked Maputo targets.

June 1 Lebanese PM Rashid Karami murdered. **11** UK General Election: Conservatives won 3rd term with 101 majority. **12** Princess Anne created Princess Royal. **15** Christian Democrats won Italian General Election.

July 3 Former Gestapo chief Klaus Barbie found guilty of crimes against humanity. **13** Labor Party won Australian General Election. **17** France and Iran cut diplomatic relations. **20** Social Democrats won Portuguese General Election. **29** Indo–Sri Lankan peace accord signed: Colombo riots.

August 6 David Owen resigned as SDP leader after party voted to open merger talks with Liberals. **12** Pres Reagan accepted responsibility for Iran–Contra affair: no knowledge of diversion of funds. **17** Suicide of Rudolf Hess. **19** Hungerford massacre: 16 dead. **27** Pres Aquino crushed 5th coup in 18 months. **29** New SDP leader Robert Maclennan.

September 3 Bangladesh monsoon: 24m homeless. **4** UN Security Council endorsed Iran–Iraq peace plan. **5** Israeli air raid on Palestinian refugee camp: 40 dead. **7** Lebanese kidnappers released W German hostage. **9** Iraqi air raids on Iran. **23** Home Secretary ended sale of arms to Iran.

October 1 Los Angeles earthquake: 7 dead; 5 foreign tankers attacked in Gulf. **6** Fiji declared a republic. **15** Coup in Burkina Faso; US-protected supertanker hit by Iranian Silkworm missile. **16** Hurricane in S England: 19 dead. **17** Indian army crushed Jaffna rebels. **19** "Black Monday": London and NY shares crashed. **22** Iran attacked Kuwait oil loading terminal. **26** Lord Mackay succeeded Lord Havers as Lord Chancellor.

November 1 Deng Xiaoping resigned from Chinese Politburo: replaced by Zhao Ziyang. **5** Former ANC chairman Govan Mbeki released after 23 years. **8** Enniskillen Remembrance Day bomb: 11 dead. **11** Moscow reformist leader Boris Yeltsin dismissed; Arab Summit declared support for Iraq. **18** King's Cross fire: 31 dead. **24** US and USSR agreed to scrap intermediate range nuclear weapons.

December 8 Pres Reagan and Mr Gorbachev signed INF agreement. **16** Roh Tae Woo won allegedly rigged S Korean Presidential Election. **17** Milos Jakes succeeded Czechoslovakian Pres Husak. **20** Manila ferry disaster: 2,000 drowned. **29** Space record of 11 months by Soviet cosmonaut. **31** Robert Mugabe executive Pres of Zimbabwe: Joshua Nkomo 1 of 2 Vice Pres.

1988

January 3 Mrs Thatcher longest-serving 20th century UK PM. **4** Purchases by W German and Japanese banks halted US $ slide. **8** Further Wall St crash. **11** Secret Belfast talks between SDLP and Sinn Fein. **17** Leslie Manigat won Haitian General Election amid protests.

February 2 3 women abseiled into Lords in Clause 28 protest. **5** 2 UN relief workers kidnapped in Lebanon. **7** W Bank and Gaza strip violence. **14** PLO officials killed by bomb in Limassol. **16** Prevention of Terrorism Act made permanent. **17** US Lt-Col William Higgins kidnapped in S Lebanon. **21** New Cyprus Pres George Vassiliou.

March 1 31 dead in riots in Azerbaijan city Sumga'it: Soviet tanks moved in. **3** Liberals and SDP formed Social & Liberal Democrats. **6** 3 IRA members shot dead in Gibraltar after bomb plan uncovered. **10** Prince Charles' friend Hugh Lindsay killed by avalanche: Prince escaped. **14** Gulf War flared; Israel imposed curfew in Gaza and W Bank. **16** Loyalist gunman killed 3 at IRA

A.D.

funeral. **17** US troops in Honduras. **18** State of Emergency in Panama. **19** 2 British soldiers lynched in vicinity of Republican funeral. **25** Government review of justice in N Ireland. **28** S African commandos killed 4 in Botswana.

April 4 3,000 Indian troops moved to Pakistan border. **5** Kuwait Airways 747 hijacked to Mashad, Larnaca, then Algiers. **7** ANC lawyer Albie Sachs injured by car bomb in Mozambique. **10** 80 killed in Islamabad and Rawalpindi arsenal fire. **14** Geneva accord on withdrawal from Afghanistan. **15** PLO military commander Abu Jihad murdered. **17** Iraq recaptured Faw penin sula. **18** John Demjanjuk found guilty on Treblinka charges. **22** Kanak militants rioted in New Caledonia.

May 1 IRA killed 3 British servicemen in Holland. **2** Israeli troops in Lebanon rounded up Palestinian guerrillas. **8** Pres Mitterrand re-elected: new French PM Michel Rocard. **10** Coalition re-elected in Denmark. **17** Commandos stormed Golden Temple. **22** Hungarian Communist Party leader ousted. **27** Syrian troops moved into Shi'ite S Beirut. **29** Moscow Summit: Pres Reagan and Mr Gorbachev signed INF treaty.

June 2 Mine disaster in Borken, W Germany. **10** Millenium of Christianity celebrated in USSR; S Africa extended press curbs. **15** IRA bomb killed 6 soldiers at Lisburn fun-run. **19** Haitian coup: civilian leader fled. **21** Toronto Economic Summit. **23** IRA shot down army helicopter at Crossmaglen; EEC agreed farm price freeze. **26** A320 airbus crash at French air show. **27** 57 dead in Gare de Lyon train crash.

July 1 Communist Party conference approved Gorbachev's democratising proposals. **3** USS *Vincennes* shot down Iranian airbus "by mistake": 200 dead. **5** Former priest held in Brussels over IRA arms procurement. **6** Explosion on North Sea oil rig Piper Alpha: 170 dead. **12** Nagorno-Karabakh's Armenian majority voted to leave Azerbaijan. **19** Soviet team at Greenham Common for missile check. **22** New EEC Commissioner Leon Brittan. **23** 3 killed by IRA landmine intended for Justice Higgins. **25** Ne Win retired as leader of Burma's ruling Socialist Party after 26 years; UN Gulf peace talks. **28** New SLD leader Paddy Ashdown.

August 1 Bomb at N London barracks killed soldier. **6** Train crash at Gare de l'Est: SNCF Chairman resigned. **8** Iran-Iraq ceasefire; Soviet troops withdrew from Kabul. **11** 6,000 North Sea seals died from canine distemper. **12** Burmese leader Sein Lwin resigned after week of violence: 1,000 dead. **17** Pakistan's Pres Zia killed in plane explosion. **21** 24,000 massacred in Burundi. **22** All-day opening in English and Welsh pubs. **25** Heart of Lisbon gutted by fire. **28** Ramstein air disaster. **31** Nelson Mandela suffering from TB.

September 3 Lee Kuan Yew won Singapore's General Election. **6** Kurdish leader's appeal to UN to intervene against genocide. **7** 2 stranded cosmonauts landed successfully. **12** W German hostage freed in Beirut. **14** Papal Mass pilgrims held hostage in Maseru: S African troops stormed bus. **17** Seoul Olympics opened. **18** Further coup in Burma. **19** Polish PM resigned. **20** New Pres of UN General Assembly Argentina's Dante Caputo. **22** Lebanon's Pres Gemayal appointed Christian PM. **31** Mr Gorbachev new Soviet Pres.

October 2 Estonian Popular Front founded. **6** State of Emergency in Algiers. **9** Serb protests in Yugoslavia. **10** Czechoslovakian PM resigned. **19** Ban on broadcast interviews with pro-violence groups in N Ireland. **20** Criminals' right to silence abolished in N Ireland. **28** Police crushed Prague rally.

November 8 George Bush won US Presidential Election. **10** Hungary legalised political opposition parties. **14** Agreement to end Sudan civil war. **21** Brian Mulroney won Canadian General Election. **22** State of Emergency in Azerbaijan. **23** "Sharpeville 6" reprieved. **24** Police clashed with students in Westminster student loans

A.D.

protest. **27** US banned PLO leader. **30** New Pakistani PM Benazir Bhutto.

December 4 Edwina Currie, junior Health Minister, in "salmonella in eggs" row. **7** Yasser Arafat voiced Palestinian recognition of Israel's existence; Disastrous Armenian earthquake: Pres Gorbachev abandoned US trip. **12** Clapham rail crash. **21** PanAm jumbo jet crashed on Lockerbie: 281 killed: caused by terrorist bomb. **22** Namibian independence accord signed by S Africa, Cuba and Angola. **29** Rajiv Gandhi on 1st working visit to Pakistan by Indian PM for 28 years.

1989

January 4 US jets shot down 2 Libyan MiGs. **7** Emperor Hirohito of Japan died. **8** Boeing 737 crashed on M1 embankment near Kegworth, Leics. **18** 1st steps towards legalisation of Solidarity. **20** Nagorno-Karabakh under Moscow's direct control. **31** White Paper proposed market-orientated NHS.

February 3 Alfredo Stroessner ousted in Paraguay after 35 years: replaced by Gen Rodriguez; Michael Manley won Jamaican General Election. **14** Ayatollah Khomeini ordered execution for blasphemy of Salman Rushdie, author of *The Satanic Verses*. **21** Leading Czech playwright Vaclav Havel jailed; 2 of Winnie Mandela's bodyguards charged with murder of young activist.

March 2 EC agreed to ban CFCs by 2000. **7** China imposed martial law in Lhasa. **24** *Exxon Valdez* aground off Alaska: 12m gallons oil spilt. **26** Soviet General Election: many senior officials defeated: Moscow victory for Boris Yeltsin.

April 14 Georgia's Communist leader, Pres and PM resigned. **15** 95 Liverpool supporters crushed to death in Hillsborough disaster; Death of Hu Yaobang sparked Beijing student riots.

May 13 Briton Jackie Mann kidnapped in Beirut. **14** Peronist Carlos Menem won Argentine General Election.

June 2 Tiananmen Sq massacre. **3** Ayatollah Khomeini died. **4** Solidarity won Polish elections. **15** Labour won UK European elections.

July 5 Pres Botha met Nelson Mandela. **19** Gen Jaruzelski executive Pres of Poland. **21** Burmese opposition leader Aung San Suu Kyi under house arrest. **24** Cabinet re-shuffle: Geoffrey Howe deputy PM and Leader of Commons, John Major Foreign Secretary.

August 1 1st Cruise missiles left Greenham Common. **14** Pres Botha resigned: acting S African Pres F W de Klerk. **23** Independence demonstration in Baltic states. **24** 1st non-communist Polish PM for 45 years.

September 6 Pres de Klerk's National Party won S African General Election. **11** Hungary opened border allowing E German refugees to escape. **13** Huge peaceful anti-apartheid protest in Cape Town. **18** Hungary announced transition to democracy. **19** Vietnamese army left Cambodia.

October 1 Thousands of E German refugees escaped through Warsaw and Prague embassies. **2** E Germany closed borders after demonstrations for reform. **4** Soviet workers given right to strike. **13** ANC's Walter Sisulu released after 25 years. **16** CITES banned ivory trade to save African elephant. **17** San Francisco earthquake. **18** E German leader Erich Honecker resigned: succeeded by Egon Krenz. **19** "Guildford 4" released. **26** Chancellor of Exchequer Nigel Lawson resigned: new Chancellor John Major, Douglas Hurd Foreign Secretary.

November 8 E German cabinet and politburo resigned. **9** E Germany opened borders to West: demolition of Berlin Wall began. **10** Bulgarian Communist leader Zhivkov ousted. **12** SWAPO won Namibian General Election. **17** Violent anti-government demonstration in Prague. **23** S African troops withdrew from Namibia after 74 years.

A.D.
24 Communist leader Milos Jakes and Czechoslovak politburo resigned. **28** Soviet parliament restored Azerbaijan's powers over Nagorno-Karabakh. **29** Indian PM Rajiv Gandhi resigned.

December 1 Czechoslovakia began demolition of Iron Curtain along Austrian border; E German Communist Party voted away monopoly of power. **3** Malta Summit: Pres Bush and Pres Gorbachev declared end of Cold War. **6** Egon Krenz resigned. **7** Lithuanian parliament abolished guarantee of Communist supremacy. **10** Czechoslovak Pres Husak resigned. **14** E German Stasi disbanded. **16** Huge violent demonstration against Romanian Pres Ceausescu in Timisoara. **20** US troops invaded Romania. **23** Fighting in Romania. **25** Ceausescus executed. **26** Ion Iliescu Pres of National Salvation Front government and Romania's provisional leader. **28** Alexander Dubcek Chairman of Czechoslovak Federal Assembly; Vaclav Havel, playwright and human rights activist, Pres until elections; Bulgarian demonstration for democracy; Lithuania launched USSR's 1st multiparty system; Latvia abolished Communist power monopoly.

THE CHANGING WORLD ORDER
1990

January 3 Manuel Noriega surrendered to US troops. **11** Independence rally in Vilnius; Armenian parliament voted itself the right to veto Soviet laws. **15** Bulgaria abolished Communist monopoly rule. **22** Yugoslavia's Communist Party voted to abolish Party's monopoly of power. **25** Hurricane-force winds battered S of England: 46 died.

February 1 New coalition government in Bulgaria **2** 30-year ban on ANC lifted. **5** Temporary Government of National Responsibility in E Germany. **7** Soviet Communist Party abolished monopoly rule. **11** Nelson Mandela freed after 25 years. **13** Conference of World War II allies and E and W Germany ("4 + 2") agreed German reunification formula.

March 6 Soviet parliament passed law sanctioning private property. **11** Lithuania's Supreme Council proclaimed independence. **18** Right-wing Alliance for Germany won E German General Election. **21** Namibian Independence celebrated. **23** Mongolia abolished Communist monopoly of power. **30** Estonian parliament proclaimed start of transition to independence. **31** Violence at massive anti-Community Charge demonstration in London.

April 11 Teesside Customs & Excise officers detained steel cylinders ("supergun") bound for Iraq. **15** Right-wing coalition formed Slovenian government. **19** Pres de Klerk rescinded 2 laws central to apartheid.

May 4 Latvia declared independence. **13** Baltic States Summit requested independence talks with Pres Gorbachev. **20** Romanian elections: NSF won huge victory. **27** First free elections in Poland for 50 years. **29** Boris Yeltsin elected Pres of Russian republic; Opposition League for Democracy, led by Aung San Suu Kyi, won Burmese elections.

June 1 Pres Bush and Pres Gorbachev signed accord on reduction of nuclear missiles. **7** Warsaw Pact Summit pledged radical transformation. **8** First free Czechoslovakian elections for 44 years: Russian parliament voted its laws to take precedence over those of USSR. **12** Russian Federation formally proclaimed sovereignty. **20** Chancellor of Exchequer John Major proposed new currency unit, the Ecu, backed by EMF. **22** Checkpoint Charlie in Berlin Wall removed.

July 6 NATO Summit agreed joint peace declaration with Warsaw Pact countries. **10** Pres Gorbachev re-elected Leader of Soviet Communist Party. **12** Boris Yeltsin resigned from Soviet Communist Party. **16** Ukraine issued declaration of sovereignty. **20** IRA bomb at Stock Exchange. **27** Belorussia declared itself a sovereign state within USSR. **30** Ian Gow MP killed by IRA bomb. **31** Estonia seceded from USSR.

A.D.
August 2 Iraqi forces invaded Kuwait. **6** Pretoria Minute: political prisoners freed, ANC hostilities suspended. **7** US ships, planes and troops in Gulf as part of multi- national defence force. **8** Iraq annexed Kuwait; Leader of Winnie Mandela's bodyguard sentenced to death for murder of teenage activist. **20** Western hostages in Kuwait held at military bases and potential targets. **24** Irish hostage Brian Keenan released. **31** E and W Germany signed unification treaty.

September 1 Boris Yeltsin demanded resignation of Soviet government. **4** Prime Ministers of N and S Korea met for the first time. **10** All Cambodian factions accepted peace formula to end civil war. **12** 4 Allied Powers of World War II signed Treaty handing back full sovereignty to single united German state. **26** Soviet parliament agreed bill on freedom of conscience and religious practice.

October 3 Germany celebrated reunification. **8** UK joined ERM. **24** Pakistan General Elections: Benazir Bhutto's PPP defeated. **25** Crash of Polly Peck International. **28** EC agreed 2nd stage of economic and monetary union: Britain alone in dissent.

November 1 Sir Geoffrey Howe resigned from Cabinet; Communist Party swept from power in Soviet Georgia. **9** Mary Robinson Ireland's first woman and youngest-ever President. **17** Pres Gorbachev presented constitutional reforms giving him increased powers and reinforcing Federal Council. **21** CSCE conference closed with signing of Charter of Paris for a New Europe. **22** Mrs Thatcher resigned. **25** Nationalist parties in Bosnia-Herzegovina won first free elections for 52 years. **27** John Major won Conservative leadership. **28** New Cabinet included Norman Lamont as Chancellor of Exchequer, Michael Heseltine Environment Secretary. **29** UN resolution to use force against Iraq.

December 2 Chancellor Köhl won German elections. **6** Saddam Hussein announced immediate release of all foreign hostages. **9** Lech Walesa won Polish Presidential election. **13** Oliver Tambo, ANC President, in S Africa after 30-year exile. **20** Soviet Foreign Minister Eduard Shevardnadze resigned.

1991

January 1 Fierce fighting in Mogadishu. **7** Soviet paratroopers in Baltic states. **8** Lithuanian PM Kashuleta Prunskiene resigned. **13** Soviet troops seized TV centre in Vilnius: 14 dead, thousands defended Parliament buildings: Boris Yeltsin and Baltic Presidents in UN appeal. **17** Huge air and missile attack on Iraq by US, British and Saudis, to liberate Kuwait in Operation Desert Storm. **18** Scud missile attacks on Israel. **19** Key Baghdad buildings damaged by missiles. **25** Iraq released millions of gallons of Kuwait oil into Gulf. **29** Nelson Mandela and Chief Buthelezi made peace.

February 1 Repeal of remaining S African apartheid laws. **7** IRA attack on Downing St. **10** Lithuanian referendum in favour of independence. **13** US missiles destroyed Baghdad bunker: 300 civilians killed. **20** Statue of Enver Hoxha toppled in Tirana: Pres Alia announced new government. **22** Iraqis set fire to Kuwait's oil installations. **24** Ground war for liberation of Kuwait began. **26** Kuwait City liberated. **27** Allied ceasefire in Gulf War.

March 3 Peace agreement between Allies and Iraq; Estonian and Latvian referendum in favour of independence. **4** S Iraq towns occupied by Shia Muslim resistance. **14** "Birmingham 6" released. **15** Kurdish guerrillas claimed control of Kurdistan. **17** Referendum on future of united USSR: minimal victory for Pres Gorbachev.

April 1 Kurdish revolt in N Iraq collapsed. **4** Refugee crisis on Turkish and Iranian borders. **9** Soviet Georgia declared independence. **15** European Bank for Reconstruction & Development launched. **23** New Council Tax unveiled to replace Poll Tax.

A.D.

May 5 Virtual civil war between Serbs and Croats. **13** Winnie Mandela found guilty on kidnap and assault charges. **19** Croatian referendum in favour of independence. **21** Rajiv Gandhi assassinated; Pres Mengistu of Ethiopia fled. **26** First-ever Presidential elections in USSR held in Georgia. **29** Ethiopian People's Revolutionary Democratic Front in control in Addis Ababa.

June 5 Pres Bendjedid of Algeria postponed elections, and dismissed government. **9** Mt Pinatubo in Philippines erupted. **13** Boris Yeltsin elected Russian Pres. **17** Congress (I) Party won Indian General Election; S Africa formally abolished apartheid. **25** Slovenia and Croatia declared independence. **26** "Maguire 7" convictions overturned.

July 1 Warsaw Pact disbanded. **4** UK–China agreement on new Hong Kong airport. **5** Bank of Commerce & Credit International (BCCI) collapsed. **6** ANC's first National Congress ended with Nelson Mandela as new Pres and democratically-elected National Executive. **20** Boris Yeltsin banned Communist Party in factories, offices and local government. **22** John Major launched Citizens' Charter.

August 8 British hostage John McCarthy released. **19** Pres Gorbachev deposed in dawn coup: Emergency Committee of 8 hardliners in control: Yeltsin denounced coup. **21** Estonia and Latvia declared independence: 3 killed outside Russian parliament: coup collapsed. Yeltsin assumed control of Soviet troops: Pres Gorbachev reinstated: Soviet troops withdrew from Lithuania. **24** Pres Gorbachev resigned as Communist Party leader, and dissolved Party organisation: Ukraine declared independence. **25** Armenia, Georgia and Belorussia declared independence. **26** Vukovar in E Croatia besieged by Serbs and Yugoslav troops. **28** Central Committee of KGB dissolved. **29** Soviet Parliament voted to curtail Pres Gorbachev's power. **30** Azerbaijan, Kirghizia and Uzbekistan declared independence.

September 3 Nagorno-Karabakh declared independence from Armenia. **5** Pres Gorbachev made sweeping constitutional changes. **9** Leningrad formally reverted to former name, St Petersburg; Macedonian citizens voted for independence. **15** Pro-democracy party won Hong Kong's first election. **24** British hostage Jackie Mann released. **26** Romanian government resigned. **30** Military coup in Haiti: Pres Aristide fled.

October 2 Dubrovnik besieged. **13** Communists ousted in Bulgarian multi-party elections. **30** Middle East peace conference in Madrid. **31** Pres Kaunda defeated in Zambia's 1st multi-party presidential election by Victor Chiluba.

November 5 Body of Robert Maxwell found in sea off Canary Is. **8** EC sanctions on Yugoslavia; Forcible repatriation of Vietnamese boat people. **18** Hostage Terry Waite released; Gen Aideed took control in Mogadishu. **25** "Tottenham 3" freed; Poland's 1st democratic Sejm for 50 years.

December 1 Ukrainian referendum in favour of independence. **4** Hostage Terry Anderson released; £600m missing from Mirror Group pension fund. **8** Leaders of Russia, Ukraine and Belorussia agreed new Commonwealth of Independent States, and declared USSR defunct. **10** Maastricht Summit agreed Treaty of European Union: Britain obtained exclusive opt-out clauses on single currency and social charter. **19** Australian Labor Party voted to replace PM Bob Hawke with Paul Keating, former Treasurer. **20** Opening of Convention for a Democratic S Africa (CODESA). **21** 8 former Soviet republics joined CIS. **25** Pres Gorbachev resigned as Pres of USSR. **26** Soviet parliament met for last time.

1992

January 1 New UN Secretary-General Boutros Boutros Ghali. **12** Algerian Higher Security Council cancelled elections and introduced martial law. **16** Mohammed Boudiaf returned to

A.D.

Algiers as Leader of Council of State. **27** Maxwell pension funds wound up with loss of millions of pounds. **30** Taoiseach Charles Haughey resigned.

February 6 Croatian Pres Tudjman accepted plan for UN peacekeeping force. **11** Albert Reynolds new Taoiseach. **19** N and S Korea declared end to 40-year confrontation. **29** Bosnia-Herzegovina referendum in favour of independence.

March 4 Algeria banned Islamic Salvation Front. **5** CODESA agreed outline of power-sharing interim government. **10** Eduard Shevardnadze Pres of Interim State Council to rule Georgia. **17** S African referendum in favour of Pres de Klerk's moves to end apartheid; UN peacekeeping troops in Croatia. **31** UN arms embargo on Libya.

April 3 Pres Alia of Albania resigned. **6** Fierce fighting in and around Sarajevo between Muslims and Serbs; EC recognised Bosnia. **9** General Election: Conservative majority of 21 and record-breaking 4th term of office. **10** IRA bombs in London: 3 dead. **11** Cabinet re-shuffle: Kenneth Clarke Home Secretary, Michael Heseltine Trade & Industry Sec, Malcolm Rifkind Defence Sec. **13** Neil Kinnock resigned Labour leadership. **27** Betty Boothroyd 1st-ever woman Speaker of Commons. **29** Los Angeles riots: 44 dead.

May 5 EC monitors withdrew from Sarajevo. **19** Serbian troops held 3,500 women and children hostage in Bosnia. **27** Mortar bombs in Sarajevo marketplace: 16 dead.

June 18 Kevin and Ian Maxwell charged with conspiracy to defraud. **20** Czech and Slovak political parties agreed to split Czechoslovakia into 2 separate states. **23** Yitzhak Rabin's Labour Party won Israeli General Election. **29** Pres Boudiaf of Algeria assassinated. **30** N Ireland Protestant leaders and Irish government met in 1st talks for 70 years.

July 9 Chris Patten sworn in as Governor of Hong Kong. **18** John Smith new Labour Party Leader. **20** Czechoslovak Pres Vaclav Havel resigned. **30** UN forces sent to Somalia.

August 3 Confirmation of Serbian detention camps where torture and killings had occurred. **10** Ban on Protestant Ulster Defence Association. **18** British troops in Iraq and Bosnia to protect UN aid convoys. **25** Serb bombardment destroyed National Library in Sarajevo: 90 dead. **27** Iraq accepted exclusion zone; Lord Owen new EC peace negotiator. **28** 3,000th sectarian death in N Ireland.

September 3 New Slovak constitution signed in Bratislava. **7** 28 ANC supporters shot dead by Ciskei troops as protest march crossed border. **9** Georgian forces and Abkhazia rebels agreed ceasefire. **11** £ close to ERM floor. **16** "Black Wednesday": £ withdrawn from ERM in de facto devaluation. **20** French referendum on Maastricht Treaty: narrow majority in favour. **21** EC Foreign Ministers agreed ratification of Maastricht Treaty. **24** National Heritage Minister David Mellor resigned.

October 5 £ at record low. **7** Sweeping plans for Hong Kong democracy. **13** Government and British Coal announced closure of 31 collieries. **15** 1st British troops in Croatia to support UN. **16** Pres Babangida declared Nigerian primary Presidential election void. **26** Last Russian troops left Poland. **30** IRA bomb in Whitehall.

November 3 Democrat Bill Clinton elected Pres of USA; GATT talks collapsed. **4** Government 3-vote majority in Maastricht debate. **11** Church of England General Synod voted narrowly in favour of ordination of women. **20** Windsor Castle fire.

December 2 German parliament won veto on EMU in Maastricht debate. **4** US troops in Somalia on food aid mission. **6** Swiss referendum against joining European Economic Area. **9** Prince and Princess of Wales separated. **12** EC Edinburgh Summit: deal saving Maastricht Treaty.

A.D.

1993

January 1 Inauguration of single European market; 2 new states, Czech Republic and Slovakia, came into being. **5** EC report confirmed rape of 20,000 Bosnian Muslim women by Serb forces. **13** Allied aircraft bombed air defence centres in S Iraq. **19** Iraq declared unilateral ceasefire: UN nuclear inspectors given clearance. **24** Croat troops seized Maslenica bridge connecting N Croatia with Adriatic. **26** Vaclav Havel 1st President of new Czech state.

February 12 S African government and ANC agreed plans for elected black and white interim government. **26** Terrorist bomb under World Trade Center, Manhattan.

March 8 Government defeated in Commons Maastricht debate. **13** Labor won record 5th term in Australian General Election. **16** VAT on domestic fuel in 2-stage plan announced in Budget. **20** IRA bombs in Warrington: 2 children dead. **25** Muslims and Croats signed full UN peace plan in New York. **26** UN Security Council voted to take over Somalia peacekeeping. **27** New Chinese Pres Jiang Zemin. **28** Right-wing landslide in French General Election.

April 2 State of Emergency in Azerbaijan. **4** Vancouver Summit: $1·6bn aid package to Russia. **8** UN admitted former Yugoslav republic Macedonia. **10** Chris Hani, Gen Sec of S African Communist Party and ANC leader, shot dead. **12** NATO enforced Bosnian "no fly" zone. **19** Waco siege ended: many dead. **24** IRA bomb in Bishopsgate. **25** Russian referendum: 58% backed Pres Yeltsin.

May 1 Sri Lankan Pres Premadasa assassinated. **4** Asil Nadir, former Chairman of Polly Peck, fled to N Cyprus. **18** Danish Maastricht Referendum: 56·8% in favour. **24** Eritrean independence. **27** Florence terrorist bomb: 6 dead, Uffizi museum damaged: Norman Lamont dismissed in Cabinet reshuffle: new Chancellor Kenneth Clarke.

June 6 1st democratic Latvian elections since 1931 won by centre-right alliance. **7** Bosnian government accepted "safe haven" plan. **11** US air strike against HQ of Gen Aideed. **13** 52 Bosnian Muslims killed in Serb rocket attack on Gorazde hospital.

July 3 Pres Clinton announced 1-year suspension of nuclear testing. **12** 10 Somalis killed in UN helicopter attack on Gen Aideed's control centre. **22** Government defeated in Maastricht vote.

August 2 Emergency meeting of EC Finance Ministers: *de facto* suspension of ERM. **4** Serb troops captured Mt Igman overlooking Sarajevo. **7** Buckingham Palace opened to public. **14** Serbs withdrew from Mt Igman. **18** Muslims, Serbs and Croats agreed to place Sarajevo under UN rule for 2 years, after 3-way division of Bosnia decided. **27** Muslims held UN convoy "hostage" in Mostar as protection against Croats. **29** Yasser Arafat won PLO executive committee support for peace plan giving Palestinians control of Gaza strip and Jericho.

September 9 PLO Chairman Yasser Arafat signed mutual recognition agreement with Israel. **13** Israel–PLO agreement signed at White House. **14** Jordan and Israel signed agreement. **21** Pres Yeltsin dissolved Russian parliament, and announced rule by decree: parliament swore in Speaker Alexander Rutskoi as Pres. **22** Pres Yeltsin supported by army, security forces, ministers, central bank and many world leaders. **24** US and Commonwealth lifted S African trade sanctions. **25** Russian Parliament (White House) telephones, power and hot water cut off. **29** Labour Party Conference passed John Smith's "One man one vote" motion.

October 4 Russian troops stormed White House: Alexander Rutskoi and other leaders surrendered: 170 dead. **12** Germany's highest court approved Maastricht Treaty. **19** Benazir Bhutto Pakistan's new PM. **25** Sinn Fein leader Gerry Adams

A.D.

banned from mainland Britain; Canadian General Election: landslide victory for Liberals.

November 1 European Union established as Maastricht Treaty came into force. **9** Stari Most, Mostar's celebrated 16th century bridge, destroyed by Croats. **17** Pres de Klerk and Nelson Mandela ratified S Africa's 1st democratic constitution; US Congress endorsed N American Free Trade Agreement (NAFTA).

December 7 Transitional Executive Council (TEC) inaugurated in Cape Town. **12** Vladimir Zhirinovsky's ultra-nationalist Liberal Democratic Party won most seats in Russian Election. **15** Downing St Declaration by John Major and Taoiseach Albert Reynolds on future of N Ireland; GATT talks agreement. **19** Ruling Socialist Party won Serbian General Election.

1994

January 5 Inkatha boycott of S African General Election. **9** Bosnia peace talks reopened with redrawn map. **13** District Auditor's inquiry charged Westminster City Council with gerrymandering. **17** Los Angeles earthquake; John Major revealed to have approved £234m aid to Malaysia for Pergau dam, linked to arms deal. **19** Serb-Croat pact to normalise relations. **30** US granted Gerry Adams visa for 2-day visit.

February 5 Mortar attack on Sarajevo market: 68 dead. **7** Parliamentary Private Secretary Stephen Milligan found dead. **10** NATO 10-day deadline to Bosnian Serbs to withdraw weapons from Sarajevo area or risk air strikes. **25** Jewish extremist settler shot dead 40 Arabs in Hebron mosque. **28** US jets shot down 4 Bosnian Serb aircraft, NATO's first-ever aggressive intervention.

March 1 Bosnian Muslims and Croats signed US brokered peace agreement. **9** IRA mortar attack on Heathrow airport. **22** PLO–Israel draft accord on armed presence to protect W Bank and Gaza Palestinians. **25** US troops left Somalia. **27** Italian General Election won by Silvio Berlusconi. **28** ANC security guards attacked Inkatha marchers carrying Zulu weapons: 30 dead. **31** State of Emergency in Natal and KwaZulu.

April 6 Presidents of Rwanda and Burundi died in rocket attack on plane. **7** Civil war in Rwanda: thousands dead, including PM. **10** NATO air strike on Serbian troops advancing on Gorazde. **11** 2nd NATO air strike on Bosnian Serb troops. **12** RPF (Rwandan Patriotic Front) Tutsi rebels captured Kigali: government fled. **17** Bosnian army's defence of Gorazde failed: UN-Serb agreement to restore peace. **19** Agreement brought Inkatha Freedom Party into S African Elections. **23** Western allies' troops began Berlin withdrawal. **24** Bosnian Serbs withdrew from Gorazde after NATO ultimatum. **26** New S African constitution came into force: long queues to vote in Elections.

May 2 Pres de Klerk conceded Election victory to Nelson Mandela: ANC won 63% vote. **3** 200,000 dead as Rwanda genocide continued. **4** Israel and PLO signed agreement to end 27-year occupation of Gaza and W Bank, initiating Palestinian self-rule. **6** Channel Tunnel officially opened. **9** Nelson Mandela elected Pres of S Africa. **12** Labour leader John Smith died. **13** Jericho under Palestinian control. **19** 1st Channel Tunnel freight service. **23** S Yemen declared independence. **27** Alexander Solzhenitsyn returned to Russia.

June 1 S Africa rejoined Commonwealth. **2** Helicopter crash on Mull of Kintyre killed 29 anti-terrorism experts. **12** European Election: Labour won 62 seats with 44% vote; Austrian referendum in favour of EU membership.

July 5 Yasser Arafat in Jericho: Palestine National Authority (PNA) sworn in; US, Russian and EU Foreign Ministers unveiled Bosnian peace plan in Geneva. **9** N Korean Pres Kim Il Sung died; G7 Naples Summit admitted Russia, effectively creating G8. **12** Commons inquiry into "cash for questions" and MPs' fees; Kim Jong Il to succeed

A.D.

father as N Korean Pres. **15** Emergency EU Summit endorsed Luxembourg PM Jacques Santer as new EC Pres. **16** 1st of 21 fragments of Comet Shoemaker-Levy 9 collided with Jupiter. **18** Hizbollah car bomb outside Jewish Centre in Buenos Aires: 100 dead; Israel-Jordan peace talks opened; EU brokered UK beef compromise with Germany. **20** Cabinet reshuffle: Michael Portillo Employment Sec, Jeremy Hanley Chairman of Conservative Party. **21** Tony Blair new Labour leader with 57% vote: John Prescott deputy leader. **25** King Hussein of Jordan and Israeli PM Rabin signed declaration ending 46-year conflict.

August 8 New Israel-Jordan border crossing near Eilat inaugurated; Yitzhak Rabin 1st Israeli PM to visit Jordan. **12** "Cradle to grave" NHS ended with abandonment of guaranteed care of elderly. **15** Venezuelan terrorist Carlos "the Jackal" arrested. **16** Republican Senators' delay tactics effectively killed US Health Bill. **26** 1st British patient received mechanical heart. **28** Sunday Trading Act came into force. **31** IRA declared ceasefire: UK government demanded evidence of permanence. Russian army left Latvia and Estonia.

September 12 Suicide pilot crashed light aircraft on White House lawn; Separatist PQ won control of Quebec provincial government. **16** Broadcasting ban on N Ireland extremists lifted. **28** 910 drowned in Baltic ferry disaster.

October 3 Channel Tunnel car service began. **4** At Labour Party conference Tony Blair announced replacement of Clause IV: "common ownership of means of production". **6** Labour Party conference narrowly reasserted backing for Clause IV. **13** N Ireland Loyalist paramilitary groups announced ceasefire. **16** Chancellor Kohl narrowly won 4th term. **19** Tim Smith N Ireland Minister, and later Neil Hamilton Minister at DTI, resigned over "cash for questions" affair. **21** John Major opened way to talks with Sinn Fein: bans on leaders lifted, border roads opened. **25** New body established under Lord Nolan to oversee standards in public life. **26** Israel-Jordan peace treaty signed.

November 8 Republican landslide victory in US midterm elections. **10** High Court ruled UK Pergau dam aid illegal; Saddam Hussein recognised Kuwait. **11** US abandoned Bosnia arms embargo. **14** UK National Lottery inaugurated. **17** Albert Reynolds resigned as Taoiseach. **18** Serb jets attacked UN "safe area" Bihac. **19** Bertie Aherne new Fianna Fail leader. **28** Government won Commons vote on European Finance Bill: Whip withdrawn from 8 Conservative abstainers; Serbs took Bihac; Norwegian referendum against EU membership. **29** Budget day: public spending cuts: VAT on fuel at 17·5% from April.

December 6 Government defeat on planned VAT increase on fuel; CSCE retitled Organisation for Security and Cooperation in Europe. **8** Chancellor of Exchequer's mini-budget to recoup £1bn lost by "VAT on fuel" defeat. **11** Russia invaded Chechnya. **18** Russian troops attacked Grozny.

1995

January 1 Austria, Finland and Sweden joined EU. **8** Sri Lankan government truce with Tamil guerrillas. **11** Pres Yeltsin assumed direct control of Russian armed forces. **12** Army to end Belfast daytime patrols. **17** Over 6,000 dead in Kobe earthquake. **18** Spanish Fishing Rights Bill narrowly passed after UK compensation doubled to £53m.

February 6 US space shuttle Discovery and Russia's Mir space station rendezvous. **10** £267m compensation agreement for Maxwell pension funds. **22** Joint Anglo-Irish document on N Ireland's future published. **26** 233-year-old Barings merchant bank collapsed.

March 2 Nick Leeson, Barings Bank financial trader involved in collapse, arrested in Frankfurt. **6** Spanish peseta and Portuguese escudo devalued after emergency meeting to realign ERM. **7** Dutch bank ING bought Barings in £1·6bn deal. **13** Tony

A.D.

Blair secured overwhelming National Executive support for new Clause IV. **20** Sarin nerve gas attack on Tokyo subway.

April 6 Scottish local elections result in the Conservatives failing to win control of any of the 29 new unitary authorities. **9** ZANU-PF win Zimbabwe general election. **19** Bomb outside a federal building in Oklahoma, USA kills 168; Gas attack in underground station in Yokohama, Japan. **21** FBI arrests Timothy McVeigh for Oklahoma bombing.

May 7 Chirac defeats Jospin in second round of French Presidential election. **11** Nolan Committee on Standards in Public Life publishes its first report. **13** Alison Hargreaves becomes the first woman to climb Mt Everest alone and without oxygen. **17** Chirac succeeds François Mitterrand as President of France; Alain Juppé new Prime Minister. **24** Death of Lord Wilson of Rievaulx.

June 2 Bosnian Serbs released UN hostages including 11 British soldiers. **14** Chechen rebels seize hundreds of hostages in a hospital in Budyonnovsk in southern Russia. **17** Russian forces attack the hospital freeing 200 hostages. **19** Last Russian hostages released by Chechens; EU Finance ministers set 1 Jan 1999 as date for single currency. **22** John Major resigns as leader of the Conservative Party.

July 4 John Major wins the leadership contest. **5** Cabinet reshuffle: Michael Heseltine the new Deputy Prime Minister. **10** Opposition leader Aung San Suu Kyi released after 6 years house arrest in Myanmar (Burma). **11** Bosnian Serbs capture Srebenica; USA restores full diplomatic relations with Vietnam. **13** All Muslims in Srebenica deported by Bosnian Serbs.

August 4 Croatian offensive into Serb-held Krajina. 100,000 troops advance on 3 fronts. **7** 150,000 Serb refugees flee Krajina after Croat victory. **11** President Clinton vetoes legislation to lift unilaterally the Bosnian arms embargo. **17** Alison Hargreaves, 1st woman to climb Everest alone, dies in an avalanche on K2. **18** Driest summer since 1659. **27** Rugby Union turns professional. **28** Bosnian Serb shelling of Sarajevo kills 35 in city centre; James Molyneaux resigns as UUP leader.

September 5 French nuclear test at Mururoa atoll. **6** Riots in Tahiti, after nuclear test. **8** David Trimble elected new leader of UUP. **10** NATO uses cruise missiles against the Bosnian Serbs. **24** Israel and PLO agree to extend self-rule to most of West Bank. **27** European Court of Human Rights condemned killing of 3 IRA terrorists by SAS in Gibraltar in 1988. **28** Publishers' Association ends Net Book Agreement (NBA).

October 1 Metrication Day; All pre-packed food to be sold in metric units. **2** 2nd French nuclear test in Pacific. **3** OJ Simpson released after a unanimous not guilty verdict. **5** 60-day cease-fire in Bosnia agreed in US-brokered deal. **7** Alan Howarth, Tory MP for Stratford-on-Avon, defects to Labour. **30** Quebec independence referendum results in a No vote; Quebec Premier Jacques Parizeau steps down.

November 1 Israeli PM Yitzhak Rabin assassinated in Tel Aviv. **10** Ken Saro-Wiwa and 8 other human rights activists executed in Nigeria. **11** Nigeria suspended from the Commonwealth. **19** Lech Walesa defeated in Polish Presidential elections. **21** Bosnian peace deal agreed in Dayton, Ohio.

December 1 Nick Leeson sentenced to 6½ years in prison in Singapore. **14** Bosnian peace agreement formally signed in Paris. **15** EU leaders agree to call the new single currency the Euro. **17** Communists come first in Russian parliamentary elections, winning 155 out of 450 seats. **19** Government loses the Fisheries vote in the House of Commons by 2 votes.

1996

January 8 François Mitterrand dies of cancer aged

A.D.
79. 21 Yasser Arafat elected as President of Palestine Authority.

February 9 IRA cease-fire expires as massive bomb explodes in South Quays, east London: 2 killed. 15 Scott Report on the Arms-to-Iraq Affair is published. 18 IRA bus bomb in Aldwych. 26 Government wins House of Commons' vote on the Scott Report by one vote. 28 Princess Diana formally agrees to a divorce.

March 2 John Howard becomes the new Australian PM as the Liberal-National Coalition wins a landslide victory in the general election. 3 José Maria Aznar wins the Spanish general election. 4 Northern Ireland proximity talks start at Stormont without Sinn Fein or the main Unionist parties. 13 Tom Hamilton kills 16 primary school children and their teacher in Dunblane, Scotland, before shooting himself. 19 President Nelson Mandela granted a divorce from Winnie; Bob Dole secures the Republican nomination. 20 The Government admits the possibility of a link between BSE in cows and CJD in humans.

April 18 Israeli bombing of UN refugee centre in south Lebanon kills 101; Islamic fundamentalists shoot 18 tourists dead in Cairo. 22 Italian general election won by Olive Tree alliance: new PM Romano Prodi. 28 Gunman Martin Bryant killed 35 tourists in Port Arthur, Australia.

May 2 Conservatives suffered heavy losses in local council elections. 9 Dame Shirley Porter ordered to pay £31 million surcharge for gerrymandering; National Party withdrew from the Government of National Unity in South Africa. 10 Congress (I) party lost the Indian general election. 31 Likud narrowly won the Israeli general election; Netanyahu new PM.

June 5 European Commission authorised partial lifting of ban on British beef. 10 All-party talks began at Stormont Castle, but Sinn Fein excluded. 14 Irish peace forum opened in Belfast. 15 IRA bomb caused extensive damage and 200 injuries in central Manchester.

July 3 Yeltsin won the Russian Presidential election. 13 Degree title granted to Prince and Princess of Wales. 18 228 killed as TWA jet exploded off Long Island, New York. 20 Centennial Olympic Games opened in Atlanta, Georgia. 27 Nail bomb in Centennial Park, Atlanta, killed 2, injured over 100.

August 1 Somali warlord General Aideed died. 21 The Globe Theatre reopened with the first production of Shakespeare there since 1642.

September 3 27 US cruise missiles fired on southern Iraq in Operation Desert Strike. 9 Pro-Iraqi KDP forces captured PUK stronghold of Sulaimaniya. 19 Kevin Maxwell freed after judge blocked a second trial. 27 Taliban forces capture Kabul; ex-President Najibullah executed.

October 1 Israeli PM Netanyahu and Palestinian leader Arafat met in Washington DC; MP Neil Hamilton admitted taking cash for questions. 4 Ministry of Defence admitted Gulf War troops were exposed to harmful chemicals. 16 Cullen report on Dunblane published: all handguns except smallest calibre (.22) pistols to be banned. 17 Yeltsin sacked National Security Adviser General Lebed.

November 5 President Clinton re-elected: Republicans retained both Houses of Congress; Benazir Bhutto dismissed as Pakistani PM. 17 President Milosevic annulled opposition victories in municipal elections: anti-government protests in Belgrade.

December 10 Government announced official inquiry into Gulf War syndrome; new coalition government in New Zealand: Jim Bolger remains PM. 11 Paymaster-General David Willetts resigned over cash for questions. 12 Labour win Barnsley East by-election: Government now in minority. 17 Tupac Amaru terrorists seized 430 hostages at Japanese embassy in Peru.

A.D.
1997
January 3 President Milosevic admitted defeat in Serbian municipal elections. 26 Violent protests in Albania after the collapse of a pyramid investment scheme.

February 3 Benazir Bhutto and Imran Khan defeated in Pakistani general election: Nawaz Sharif new PM. 5 O.J. Simpson found guilty in civil court case. 10 O.J. Simpson ordered to pay £15 million punitive damages. 19 Chinese Premier Deng Xiaoping died aged 92; 1st National Lottery draw on Wednesday. 21 Bridgewater Three freed after 18 years in jail. 22 Adult sheep (Dolly) successfully cloned by scientists.

March 2 Fighting in Vlore killed 12: state of emergency declared in Albania. 17 John Major called general election for 1 May. 19 Political row erupted over publication of the Downey Report into cash-for-questions.

April 6 BBC correspondent Martin Bell decided to stand on an anti-corruption ticket against Neil Hamilton in Tatton.

May 1 General election held in United Kingdom. Labour won landslide victory under Tony Blair. 2 Gordon Brown became Chancellor of the Exchequer; Robin Cook new Foreign Secretary; John Prescott is Deputy Prime Minister. John Major resigned as leader of the Conservative Party. 4 New Labour Government announces its intention of joining EU Social Chapter. 6 Bank of England given control of interest rates. 12 Russia and Chechnya signed peace treaty. 14 Author Laurie Lee died aged 82. 15 Trade union ban at GCHQ lifted. 16 President Mobutu fled Zaïre. 17 Rebels entered Kinshasa: Zaïre renamed Democratic Republic of Congo by new President, Laurent Kabila. 26 French PM Juppé resigned. 27 NATO-Russian co-operation charter signed in Paris.

June 1 Socialists won the French general election: Lionel Jospin new PM. 2 Liberal Party won Canadian general election; Timothy McVeigh found guilty of Oklahoma bombing. 10 Kenneth Clarke won first round of Tory leadership contest with 49 votes, Hague second with 41, Redwood third with 27: Lilley (24 votes) and Howard (23) withdrew. 11 MPs voted to ban all remaining handguns. 17 In second round, Clarke won 64 votes, Hague 62, Redwood 38: Redwood eliminated. 18 Amsterdam Treaty signed by EU leaders. 19 Hague won final round (92 votes to 70) to become youngest Tory leader since 1783.

July 1 Hong Kong handed over to Chinese rule; UK rejoined UNESCO; actor Robert Mitchum died aged 79. 2 Labour's first Budget, actor James Stewart died aged 89. 3 Downey report into cash-for-questions published: 5 former Tory MPs, including Neil Hamilton, criticised. 6 Orangemen parade in Drumcree led to rioting across N. Ireland. 15 Slobodan Milosevic elected as Yugoslavian President.

August 2 Author William Burroughs died aged 83. 25 Former E. German leader Egon Krenz jailed for Berlin Wall deaths. 26 South African Vice-President F W de Klerk retired. 31 Diana, Princess of Wales killed in car crash in Paris: her companion Dodi Fayed and driver Henri Paul also died.

September 5 Mother Teresa died aged 87. 11 Scotland voted Yes-Yes in dual referendum on a Scottish Parliament and its tax-raising powers. 16 Forest fires in Indonesia caused extensive smog across south-east Asia. 18 Referendum in Wales produced narrow vote (50·3% to 49·7%) in favour of Welsh Assembly; 7 tourists killed in bus bomb in Cairo. 19 6 killed in Southall rail crash. 26 Earthquakes in Italy damaged St Francis's Basilica, Assisi.

October 1 Fiji readmitted to the Commonwealth. 9 Romani Prodi resigned as Italian PM; 250 killed as Hurricane Pauline hit Acapulco. 13 Singer John Denver died in plane crash. 14 Piers Merchant resigned as Tory MP for Beckenham. 15

A.D.

Thrust broke the sound barrier on land (766·109 mph); author Harold Robbins died. **27** Dow Jones index fell 554 points; Chancellor committed UK to EMU after next election.

November 2 Iraq turned back UN nuclear weapons inspectors. **3** Jenny Shipley new PM in New Zealand. **4** Government decided to exempt Formula 1 from ban on tobacco sponsorship. **5** Republicans won decisive victory in mid-term Congressional elections. **8** Controversy over donation to Labour by Formula 1 lobbyist Bernie Ecclestone. **9** BBC launched 24-hour news channel. **13** Iraq expelled 6 US weapons inspectors: UN pulls out Inspection teams. **17** 58 tourists killed in massacre at Luxor temple; Windsor Castle reopened. **26** Hastings Banda of Malawi died aged 99.

December 9 Internal market scrapped in NHS reforms. **11** Gerry Adams at Downing St. for talks; *Britannia* decommissioned. **16** Beef-on-the-bone ban implemented. **18** Bill to create Scottish Parliament launched; Opposition leader Kim Dae-Jung won S. Korean presidential election.

1998

January 8 Currency crisis in Indonesia. **9** Mo Mowlam met with Loyalist leaders in Maze prison. **11** Ice storms in Canada left 3 million without power. **12** New British-Irish proposals for N. Ireland peace: cross-border council planned. **21** Sex scandal erupted after allegations of Clinton's affair with Monica Lewinsky.

February 8 Enoch Powell died aged 85. **13** Warmest February day on record (19·6C at Worcester). **16** Iraqi inspections crisis intensified. **19** UN Secretary-General Kofi Annan left on peace mission to Baghdad. **20** Sinn Fein suspended from N. Ireland peace talks: bomb blast in Moira.

March 1 Countryside March in London attracted 250,000 demonstrators. **5** Water discovered on the moon. **13** Private member's bill to ban hunting failed to get Government time in the Commons. **16** Dr Benjamin Spock died aged 94. **23** Pres Yeltsin sacked PM and cabinet.

April 1 Paula Jones sex case against Pres. Clinton dismissed by federal judge. **6** Mitchell draft settlement on N. Ireland published; UK and France ratified Nuclear Test Ban Treaty. **7** Unionists rejected Mitchell blueprint: Blair flew to Belfast for crisis talks. **8** Australian Senate rejected government's land rights' bill. **10** Peace agreement sealed in N. Ireland: new directly-elected assembly to be created. **15** Death of Pol Pot, Cambodian dictator. **17** Death of Linda McCartney (wife of Sir Paul McCartney).

May 2 Official birth of the 'Euro' at Brussels Summit; 11 EU countries have membership confirmed; Wim Duisenberg to take charge of European Central Bank. **7** Local elections in England; referendum in London approved creation of Mayor. **10** IRA prisoners temporarily released to attend Sinn Fein conference which voted for the Belfast Agreement. **11** India conducted three nuclear tests. **13** Frank Sinatra died aged 82. **15** LVF declared ceasefire. **21** President Suharto of Indonesia resigned. **22** Referenda on the Belfast Agreement in both parts of Ireland: 71% in Northern Ireland and 94% in the Republic in favour. **24** Pro-democracy parties won Hong Kong legislative elections; fighting in Kosovo escalated. **28** Pakistan conducted five nuclear tests.

June 2 Reports of Serbian massacres in Kosovo villages. **8** Nigerian President Abacha died. **18** Government announced introduction of minimum wage (£3·60ph) in April 1999. **22** House of Commons voted for equal age of consent for gay men. **25** Northern Ireland assembly elections held under PR.

July 1 David Trimble elected First Minister of Northern Ireland, Seamus Mallon as Deputy. **5** Stand-off between Orange marchers and police at Drumcree began. **7** Nigerian pro-democracy leader

A.D.

Chief Abiola died in jail. **8** Heavy rioting in Nigeria; Australian Senate finally passed government's land rights' bill. **22** House of Lords rejected gay age of consent clause: Government dropped it from bill. **26** President Clinton subpoenaed to appear before grand jury. **27** Cabinet reshuffle: Peter Mandelson and Alistair Darling promoted; former Pakistani PM Benazir Bhutto on trial for corruption. **28** Monica Lewinsky granted immunity from prosecution in return for testifying. **30** Court of Appeal overturned conviction of Derek Bentley, hanged in 1953. **31** UK ban on use of anti-personnel mines.

August 7 Bomb attacks on US embassies in Nairobi and Dar-es-Salaam: 240 dead. **8** Animal rights activists released 6,000 mink in Hampshire. **15** Massive bomb in Omagh, Tyrone, killed 28. **17** President Clinton testified to grand jury; in live television address he admitted to an 'inappropriate' relationship with Ms Lewinsky. **18** Splinter group the Real IRA admitted responsibility for Omagh bomb. **20** US missile attacks on Afghanistan and Sudan. **22** INLA announced ceasefire. **23** President Yeltsin sacked Russian cabinet: Chernomyrdin new PM.

September 3 Swissair plane crashed into sea off Halifax, Nova Scotia; 229 killed. **7** 'Real IRA' declares total cease-fire; William Hague calls ballot of party members over EU single currency question. **10** Historic meeting of David Trimble and Gerry Adams; preliminary details of Starr Report on President Clinton leaked to media. **11** Starr Report released on Internet: Yevgeni Primakov chosen as new Russian Prime Minister. **16** Microsoft becomes largest company in United States. **18** US Congressional Committee sanctions release of the 'Clinton Tapes'. **24** Britain to resume diplomatic relations with Iran. **25** Frenchman Benoit Lecomte became first person to swim the Atlantic (coming ashore at Quiberon in Brittany). **27** German elections: Chancellor Kohl defeated by Social Democrats under Schröder. **28** MCC voted to admit women members.

October 4 Kidnapping of 3 British workers and a New Zealander in Chechnya. **5** Result of Conservative Party ballot on Europe confirmed William Hague's position on single currency. **7** Official visit to China by Tony Blair. **8** House of Representatives voted 258–176 to institute impeachment proceedings against President Clinton. **13** Neill Report revolutionises funding of political parties in the United Kingdom. **15** Channel 4 acquires rights to show Test Match cricket. **16** Nobel Peace Prize awarded jointly to John Hume and David Trimble. **17** Arrest of former dictator of Chile, General Pinochet, at a private London hospital. **19** Terrorist bomb in Beersheba injured over 60; Middle East peace summit threatened. **23** Agreement reached at Maryland peace talks. **27** Arrival of President Menem of Argentina on official visit; abrupt resignation of Ron Davies, the Secretary of State for Wales, after 'lapse of judgement' on Clapham Common. **28** Arrest of General Pinochet overturned in the High Court. **29** Publication of report of Jenkins Commission on electoral reform.

November 4 Massive destruction by Hurricane Mitch in Central America. **8** Death of Lord Hunt (leader of 1953 Everest expedition). **13** Final warnings sent to Saddam Hussein in renewed Gulf Crisis. **14** Iraq complies with Western demands for inspection of sites. **23** EU ban on exports of British beef lifted.

December 8 Four Western hostages beheaded in Chechnya. **9** Home Secretary authorised Pinochet's extradition: Chile withdrew ambassador from UK. **11** House of Representatives passed two articles of impeachment against Clinton; Pinochet extradition hearing started. **12** Two more impeachment articles passed by Congress. **13** Lord Grade died aged 91. **15** House of Lords defeated European elections bill for 6th time: Parliament Act invoked; FA chief Graham Kelly resigned; pensions reforms unveiled. **17** Impeachment vote in Congress postponed; renewed bombing of Baghdad; Law Lords extradition ruling on Pinochet set aside. **19** Clinton

A.D.

impeached by House of Representatives on 2 counts: Speaker-elect Bob Livingstone resigned; bombing of Iraq halted. **23** Mandelson and Robinson both resigned from the Cabinet.

1999

January 3 Heavy snowfalls paralysed eastern USA. **4** Charlie Whelan, Gordon Brown's Press Secretary, resigned. **5** Flu epidemic caused NHS crisis. **7** US Senate sworn in for impeachment trial. **13** Global shares downturn sparked by Brazilian devaluation. **14** Impeachment prosecution case started, MEPs voted not to sack the European Commission. **16** Serb massacre of ethnic Albanians in Kosovo: 45 dead. **19** President Clinton's defence began; Jonathan Aitken pleaded guilty to perjury. **20** Paddy Ashdown announced resignation as Liberal Democrat leader; Lords reform unveiled. **22** International Olympic Committee shamed by bribes scandal. **25** Commons voted for equal age of consent for gay men.

February 1 Monica Lewinsky testified. **7** King Hussein of Jordan died, aged 63. **8** Dame Iris Murdoch died, aged 79. **10** Heaviest snowfalls in 50 years across the Alps: avalanche in Chamonix killed 12. **12** Clinton acquitted by Senate on both charges: 55–45 against perjury, 50–50 on obstruction of justice. **16** Kurdish leader Abdullah Ocalan abducted by Turkish agents in Kenya: worldwide Kurdish protests, Greek embassy in London occupied. **24** Lawrence Report published: Metropolitan Police criticised. **27** General Obasanjo won Nigerian presidential election.

March 5 Lord Denning died, aged 100; last *News at Ten* broadcast. **7** Stanley Kubrick died, aged 70. **9** Budget Day: basic rate of income tax down to 22p, starting rate of 10p introduced. **10** Prince of Wales visited Argentina. **11** Oskar Lafontaine resigned as German Finance Minister; Private Lee Clegg acquitted of murder. **12** Poland, Hungary and the Czech Republic joined NATO; Yehudi Menuhin died, aged 82. **13** Renewed Serb attacks in Kosovo; bombs killed 13 in Istanbul. **15** Report on corruption in the EU Commission released; Kosovo peace talks reopened. **16** EU Commission resigned en masse. **17** 6 IOC members expelled. **22** Over 100 killed in ethnic clashes in Borneo. **24** NATO forces attacked Serbia; fire in Mont Blanc tunnel killed 40; Romani Prodi named EU President.

April 1 3 US soldiers captured by Serbs. **3** NATO attacks on Belgrade. **5** NATO created refugee sanctuaries in Macedonia; Lockerbie suspects flown to Holland. **6** NATO rejected Serb ceasefire offer; bombing continued; Lockerbie suspects charged. **7** Refugee camps in Kosovo cleared by Serb forces. **8** NATO sent 8,000 troops to Albania. **10** Renewed violence in E Timor. **13** Serb attacks across Albanian border; Lords rejected equal age of consent for gays. **14** 64 killed in NATO bombing of refugee convoy. **15** Home Secretary authorised extradition of Gen Pinochet; Benazir Bhutto convicted of corruption. **17** Nail bomb in Brixton injured 50. **19** German Reichstag reopened; Turkish PM Ecevit resigned. **20** 15 killed in High School massacre in Littleton, Colorado. **22** Russia backed Serbian peace offer. **24** Nail bomb in Brick Lane injured 6. **25** First Kosovar refugees arrived in UK. **26** TV presenter Jill Dando murdered. **28** Serbian deputy PM Vuk Draskovic sacked; Sir Alf Ramsey died, aged 79. **30** Nail bomb at gay pub in Soho: 3 killed.

May 6 Voting for first Scottish Parliament since 1707 and new Welsh Assembly leaves Labour short of an overall majority in both polls. **7** Accidental bombing by NATO of Chinese embassy in Belgrade during Balkan conflict. **8** Death of actor, Dirk Bogarde. **11** House of Lords agrees to amendment providing for temporary reprieve of 92 hereditary peers until second stage of reform. **12** Lord Steel elected Presiding Officer of new Scottish Assembly; Alun Michael elected First Minister of Welsh Assembly; Russian Prime Minister, Yevgeny Primakov and his government dismissed by President Yeltsin. **13** Donald Dewar elected First Minister of Scottish Parliament, heading a Labour-Liberal Democrat coalition. **17** Ehud Barak

A.D.

became Prime Minister of Israel. **20** Rebellion of 67 Labour MPs in Commons' vote on welfare reform. **29** Democratically-elected President inaugurated in Nigeria; Nigeria rejoins the Commonwealth.

June 3 ANC returned to power in South African general election; Serbia accepts NATO peace plan. **5** Visit of Pope to Poland. **7** First democratic elections in Indonesia for over 40 years. **9** Serb generals sign peace deal with NATO commander, Sir Michael Jackson. **10** Elections to European Parliament marked by low turnout, Labour losses and increased representation for smaller parties. **12** British troops enter Kosovo, forming part of NATO peacekeeping force. **17** Death of Cardinal Hume. **18** Violence at anti-capitalist demonstration in City of London.

July 1 Formal opening of Scottish Parliament by the Queen; death of Joshua Nkomo, founder of the Zimbabwean African People's Union (ZAPU). **7** Resumption of full British diplomatic relations with Libya. Fighting in Russia on borders of Chechnya and Dagestan. **8** Proposals published to convert Post Office into a public limited company. **12** Dutch government voted to decriminalise euthanasia. **23** Death of King Hassan II of Morocco. **30** Referendum in East Timor votes for independence.

August 1 Ban on export of British beef lifted by European Union. **4** George Robertson, the Defence Secretary, appointed next Secretary-General of NATO. **9** Charles Kennedy elected leader of the Liberal Democrats. **16** Russian Duma approved Vladimir Putin as Prime Minister. **17** Devastating earthquake hits Turkey.

September 3 Forest fires rage in Brazil. **4** Israel and PLO sign new agreement; further withdrawal of Israel from West Bank. **7** Athens rocked by earthquake; over 30 people killed. **9** Publication of Patten Report on future of policing in Northern Ireland. **14** Extensive damage in Caribbean and United States caused by Hurricane Floyd. **20** Taiwan hit by devastating earthquake, leaving over 2,000 people dead; first UN peace-keeping troops arrived in East Timor, following massacres by pro-Indonesian militias. **27** 26 British tourists die in coach crash in South Africa; European Court of Human Rights rules that discrimination against gays in the British armed forces is unlawful.

October 5 Horrific train crash at Ladbroke Grove, outside Paddington, results in 31 deaths. **11** Return of Peter Mandelson to Cabinet, as Northern Ireland Secretary, in further reshuffle. **12** Military coup in Pakistan ousts discredited civilian government. **18** Pakistan suspended from Commonwealth following military coup. Arrival of President Jiang Zemin for state visit to Britain by leader of communist China. **20** Indonesian parliament selects Abdurrakhman Wahid as president after resignation of Habibie. **31** The 217 passengers and crew on an EgyptAir Boeing 767 feared dead after crashing into Atlantic on flight from New York to Cairo.

November 3 Revolt of 54 backbench Labour MPs over welfare reform proposals. **6** Referendum in Australia results in victory for monarchists; Rugby World Cup won by Australia, who defeat France. **12** Second major earthquake in Turkey; pop star Gary Glitter jailed after conviction over child sex pornography. **13** Lennox Lewis defeats Evander Holyfield to become part of heavyweight boxing legend. **25** Michael Portillo returned to Westminster in Kensington by-election. **26** General election in New Zealand won by Labour. **29** Historic steps towards power-sharing in Northern Ireland as new Executive is formed. **30** Riots in Seattle (and on a lesser scale in London) as World Trade Organisation gathering opens; Parliament confirms devolution of power to Northern Ireland (as of midnight on 1 December).

December 11 Death of the authoritarian Franjo Tudjman, President of Croatia, aged 77. **14** Panama Canal returned to Panama by USA, finally giving sovereignty to Panama. **17** Inaugural meeting of British-Irish Council. **19** Return of enclave of Macao to China marks final

A.D.

end of Portuguese empire in Asia; elections to Russian parliament show strong support for pro-government parties and disappointment for Communists. **20** Death toll in floods and landslides in Venezuela passes 5,000 (with thousands more missing). **25** Russian forces launch major assault on Grozny, the capital of Chechnya. **30** Knifeman stabs ex-Beatle George Harrison. **31** Resignation of Boris Yeltsin as President of Russia; Vladimir Putin became Acting President; global celebrations mark advent of the new millennium.

THE NEW MILLENNIUM

£000

January 1 Greenwich Electronic Time launched (new time standard for the Internet). **4** Alan Greenspan nominated to serve fourth 4-year term as head of the US Federal Reserve System. **12** Ban on gay men and women in UK armed forces ended. **21** Military coup in Ecuador. **26** Hans Blix appointed to supervise Iraqi weapons disarmament.

February 4 Lord Archer expelled from Conservative Party. **6** Russian troops take Grozny (capital of Chechnya). **9** Resignation of Alun Michael, First Secretary, Welsh Assembly. **11** Suspension of devolved government in Northern Ireland. **14** NASA spacecraft becomes first ever to orbit an asteroid (Eros). **17** Tuvalu to become 189th UN member state. **21** Violent riots in Kaduna (Nigeria) between Muslims and Christians.

March 2 UK drops extradition proceedings against former Chilean dictator Pinochet. **7** 'Super Tuesday' primaries confirm Al Gore and George Bush Jnr. as rival leading candidates. **12** Triumph for incumbent PM Aznar in Spanish elections. **18** Opposition wins presidency in Taiwan (after 50 years of Kuomintang rule). **26** Vladimir Putin elected President of Russia. **29** Two extra-solar planets discovered.

April 5 Yoshiro Mori elected Japanese PM. **6** Former Pakistani prime minister Nawaz Sharif sentenced to life imprisonment. **11** Right-wing historian David Irving loses libel lawsuit. **17** Israel announces withdrawal from Lebanon (effective from July).

May 4 Ken Livingstone wins first direct election for Mayor of London; Liberal Democrats win Romsey by-election. **7** Mikhail Kasyanov appointed Russian Prime Minister. **11** Opening of Tate Modern (art museum) in London. **18** Massive street protests in Belgrade. **20** Birth of Leo Blair; largest diamond mine in world opened in northern Botswana. **24** Last Israeli forces withdrawn early from Lebanon. **29** Former Indonesian President Suharto put under house arrest.

June 5 Bill Clinton first US President to address Russian parliament. **9** Protests in Argentina over austerity plan. **10** Death of President Assad of Syria; Millennium Bridge opens in London (only to be closed a week later for repairs). **13** First-ever visit of a South Korean President to North Korea. **15** Germany announces 20-year plan to close all nuclear power stations. **23** Cotonou Agreement between EU and developing countries.

July 2 Elections in Mexico end 71-year rule of Institutional Revolutionary Party. **17** Germany to pay compensation to those forced into slave labour under the Nazis. **19** 100th birthday celebrations of the Queen Mother. **25** Crash of Concorde on take-off from Paris.

August 3 Suharto formally charged with corruption. **12** Sinking of Russian nuclear submarine *Kursk* in Barents Sea.

September 4 French lorry drivers blockade fuel depots. **10** Second elections in Hong Kong under Chinese rule. **12** Same-sex marriages given equal status to heterosexual marriages in Holland. **15** Olympic Games open in Sydney. **24** Referendum in France votes to shorten presidential term to 5 years. **25** Disputed presidential election in Yugoslavia precipitates crisis; Milosevic refuses to

A.D.

accept Kostunica as victor. **28** Denmark votes to reject euro.

October 5 Popular uprising in Belgrade; revolution sweeps away Milosevic. **12** Terrorist attack on *USS Cole* in Aden, Yemen. **27** First performance of Wagner's music in Israel.

November 1 Yugoslavia re-admitted, as a new state, to UN. **7** Presidential election in USA results in prolonged deadlock (not resolved until Florida awarded to George Bush on 26 November). **13** Impeachment of President Joseph Estrada of the Philippines. **21** President Alberto Fujimori of Peru deposed. **27** Victory in Canadian general election for Jean Chrétien's Liberal Party.

December 6 Formal re opening of Great Court, British Museum. **9** Israeli PM Ehud Barak announces resignation. **16** Colin Powell nominated as next Secretary of State; 20,000th performance of *The Mousetrap*. **22** World Bank and IMF waive debts of 22 impoverished nations. **28** US Census reveals population now over 281 million.

2001

January 1 Greece adopts Euro (12th EU member to do so). **14** Portuguese president Jorge Sampaio re-elected. **23** Assassination of President Laurent Kabila of the Congo; resignation of Northern Ireland Secretary Peter Mandelson. **26** Devastating earthquake in Gujarat, India. **31** One of two Libyans on trial for Lockerbie bombing found guilty.

February 6 Israeli elections won by right-wing Likud under Ariel Sharon. **21** Foot and mouth outbreak discovered at Essex abattoir (start of devastating epidemic).

March 1 Foot and mouth outbreak spreads to Scotland and Ireland. **4** Switzerland referendum rejects talks to join EU. **8** Recovery of *Bluebird* (Donald Campbell's boat) from Coniston Water; Ariel Sharon, Israeli PM, announces 8-party coalition. **21** General election (and local elections) in Britain postponed because of foot and mouth outbreak.

April 10 Euthanasia legalised by Upper House of Dutch parliament. **26** First 15 'People's Peers' created by the Government.

May 1 Anti-capitalist protests by May Day demonstrators in London. **15** Fuel protestors demonstrate to urge cut in fuel tax. **26** Race riots in Oldham between whites and Asians. **30** Afghanistan refuses to extradite Osama Bin Laden, wanted for 1998 bombings of US embassies in Kenya and Tanzania.

June 7 General election returns Labour to power; Labour win 413 seats, Conservatives 166, Liberal Democrats 52. **8** Resignation of William Hague as Conservative leader. **11** Execution of Timothy McVeigh in Indiana for Oklahoma bombing. **17** Bulgarian elections won by party of ex-King Simeon II.

July 1 Resignation of David Trimble as First Minister in Northern Ireland. **5** Cease-fire in Macedonia with ethnic Albanian rebels. **8** Race riots in Bradford. **11** Organisation of African Unity (OAU) votes to become new African Union. **13** Beijing selected to host 2008 Olympics. **16** Russia and China sign treaty of friendship. **20** Anti-globalisation protests at G8 meeting in Genoa. **23** President Abdurrahman Wahid ousted in Indonesia; replaced by Megawati Sukarnoputri.

August 11 Devolved government restored in Northern Ireland. **13** Peace agreement signed in Macedonia. **23** USA announces withdrawal from ABM Treaty. **30** First free elections in East Timor to elect constituent assembly. **31** Peace agreement between Papua New Guinea and rebels on Bougainville.

September 5 Scientists report new evidence of a 'black hole' at centre of the Milky Way galaxy. **9** Assassination of Ahmad Shah Masoud, anti-

A.D.
Taleban leader in Afghanistan. **11** USA attacked in co-ordinated operation when two hijacked aircraft destroy the twin towers of the World Trade Centre; a third hits the Pentagon and a fourth crashes in Pennsylvania. Death toll of over 2,500 estimated. **13** Hundreds dead in Christian-Muslim violence in Jos, Nigeria. **17** Macedonia agrees to NATO force to maintain peace. **20** Department of Homeland Security to be created in USA (headed by Tom Ridge). **23** Voters in Poland reject Solidarity; success for former communists (now Democratic Left Alliance).

October 1 Swissair files for bankruptcy protection. **3** President Bush announces support for creation of a Palestinian state. **4** Rogue Ukrainian missile downs Russian airliner; 76 killed. Bangladesh elections result in victory for Khaleda Zia. **7** American and British planes attack Taleban positions in Afghanistan; bankrupt Railtrack re-organised. **16** Peace talks begin to end Congo civil war. **19** US ground troops in combat in Afghanistan.

November 3 Ruling party wins 9th consecutive election victory in Singapore. **4** Film version of *Harry Potter and the Philosopher's Stone* opens in UK. **6** David Trimble again heads power-sharing government in Ulster; Belgian airline Sabena goes bankrupt. **8** Resignation of Henry McLeish as First Minister in Scotland. **10** China becomes member of World Trade Organisation (WTO); Australian Prime Minister John Howard wins re-election. **13** Anti-Taleban forces take control of Kabul. **15** US Congress passes Aviation Security Bill. **17** First democratic legislative elections held in Kosovo are won by Albanian nationalists. **29** Death of former Beatle, George Harrison.

December 2 Largest corporate bankruptcy in US history as Enron collapses. **7** Kandahar abandoned by Taleban. **9** Outbreak of Ebola fever in Gabon confirmed. **13** Terrorist attack on Parliament House in New Delhi, India; formal US withdrawal from Anti-Ballistic Missile Treaty. **17** Resignation of Sr Guterres, Prime Minister of Portugal. **20** Resignation of Argentinean President Fernando de la Rúa after unrest on the streets. **21** India recalls its ambassador to Pakistan. **22** Hamid Karzai heads interim Afghan government.

2002

January 1 Euro becomes official currency of 12 EU member states. **10** Ancient cave paintings (*c.* 68,000 B.C.) in South Africa indicate earlier emergence of human art than previously thought. **11** First prisoners from Afghan war arrive in Guantanamo naval base in Cuba. **14** UK declared free of foot and mouth disease. **18** Israeli tanks surround Yasser Arafat's HQ in Ramallah. **28** Beginning of Doha Round of WTO talks. **29** 'Axis of evil' speech by President Bush identifies Iran, Iraq and North Korea.

February 5 Belgium apologises for its 1961 involvement in murder of Patrice Lumumba (first prime minister of Congo). **8** Winter Olympics open in Salt City. **9** Death of Princess Margaret. **13** Scottish Parliament outlaws foxhunting. **17** Rebels in Nepal kill 120. **19** Landslide in Bolivia kills 69 people. **22** UNITA leader Jonas Savimbi killed in Angola. Cease-fire signed in Angola. **27** Muslims set fire to train carrying Hindus in Gujarat; 58 killed.

March 3 Swiss referendum gives approval for UN membership. **8** Resignation over child abuse allegations of Bishop Anthony O'Connell in USA. **13** Re-election of President Mugabe in Zimbabwe widely condemned as blatant fraud. **14** Creation of five new cities in the UK: Preston, Newport, Newry, Lisburn and Stirling. **19** Zimbabwe suspended for one year from Commonwealth. **24** Israeli forces storm Yasser Arafat's compound in Ramallah; Arafat effectively imprisoned. **30** Death announced of the Queen Mother, aged 101.

April 1 Anti-Semitic violence in France; three synagogues set ablaze. **4** Israeli army completes re-occupation of West Bank. **11** Treaty signed creating permanent International War Criminals' Court at The Hague. US boycotts ceremony. **14** Presidential election in East Timor won by José

A.D.
Alexandre ('Xanana') Gusmâo. **17** Budget promises to double UK health spending over 10 years. **21** First round of presidential elections in France; National Front candidate, Jean-Marie Le Pen, secures second place.

May 1 Massive protests in Paris to denounce National Front leader, Le Pen. **3** Death of veteran Labour politician, Barbara Castle. **5** Victory for President Chirac in second-round of presidential contest. **6** Assassination of right-wing Dutch politician Pim Fortuyn. **10** Seven killed in Potters Bar rail crash; Court of Appeal rules that DNA evidence confirms James Hanratty was the 1962 A6 murderer. **17** Re-election of Bertie Ahern as Irish Prime Minister. **20** Formal independence for East Timor. **29** In Cabinet re-shuffle, Paul Boateng first black Cabinet member.

June 13 Hamid Karzai becomes Afghan leader. **14** Knighthood conferred on rock legend Mick Jagger. **24** New Middle East peace plan proposed by US President Bush.

July 3 First solo balloon flight around the world completed by Steve Fossett when he lands in Australian outback. **6** Assassination of Afghan Vice-President Haji Abdul Qadir. **7** HMS *Nottingham* damaged by rocks off East coast of Australia. **8** Winnie Mandela in court in South Africa on fraud charges. **9** Ban on marrying of divorcees lifted by Church of England. **11** Arrest of General Galtieri in Argentina on charges relating to murder of political opponents. **14** Major £92·5 billion 3-year UK public spending programme announced by Chancellor. **16** State of emergency declared in Argentina after anti-government protests. **19** Enquiry concludes 215 patients killed by jailed doctor Harold Shipman. **25** New Indian President, A P J Abdul Kalam. **30** Peace deal brokered by South Africa to end Congo civil war.

August 3 Outbreak of Legionnaire's disease at Barrow-in-Furness, Cumbria; 39 cases confirmed. **21** Bodies of missing schoolgirls Holly Wells and Jessica Chapman identified. **26** Earth Summit opened in Johannesburg.

September 24 6-year low for shares in UK. **27** Revelation by Edwina Currie of her affair with former PM John Major.

October 12 Terrorist attack on nightclub in Indonesian island of Bali leaves over 200 dead (89 of them Australian). **13** New world marathon record set by Paula Radcliffe (2 hrs, 17 mins, 18 secs). **26** Violent end to theatre siege in Moscow.

November 1 Intervention by the Queen halts trial of royal butler, Paul Burrell. **8** UN Resolution 1441 gives Iraq 'final chance' to disarm. **18** Resolution 1441 accepted by Iraq. **15** Death of Myra Hindley, the Moors murderer. **18** UN Inspectors arrive to resume work in Iraq. **19** Environmental disaster off Galicia from damaged oil tanker *Prestige*; riots in Nigeria in protest at forthcoming Miss World competition. **17** North Korea claims it has developed nuclear weapons.

December 2 UK government publishes dossier of Iraq human rights abuses. **5** Negotiations near agreement for peace deal in Sri Lanka. **7** 12,000 page Iraq dossier on arms denies it has any banned arms or weapons of mass destruction. **11** Peace deal brokered in Aceh.

2003

January 8 Blizzards sweep across UK; road and rail transport chaos. **10** North Korea withdraws from nuclear weapons treaty. **11** HMS *Ark Royal* heads UK task force to the Gulf. **18** Anti-war protests from San Francisco to Tokyo against war. **19** US offers Saddam Hussein immunity from prosecution if he leaves Baghdad and war is averted. **22** Controversial white paper on Higher Education proposes 'top-up' fees. **30** Further severe blizzards paralyse UK transport system.

February 1 Disintegration of US space shuttle on re-entry into earth's atmosphere. **11** Outbreak of SARS disease in China. **13** Ban on cigarette adver-

A.D.

tising comes into force. **15** Massive anti-war protest sees London's biggest-ever demonstration. **26** 121 Labour MPs in backbench revolt against war policy; 198 MPs support amendment arguing case for war not yet made.

March 16 Azores summit of USA, UK and Spain issues ultimatum. **19** UN Inspectors leave Iraq. **20** Second Gulf War begins with air strikes on Baghdad. **21** First Iraqi soldiers surrender at Umm Qasr. **22** US forces cross two key points on Euphrates River. **27** US orders 100,000 more troops to the Gulf. **29** First food aid arrives; Robin Cook condemns war as 'bloody and unnecessary'.

April 2 US forces take control of Karbala; advance troops storm 'red zone' around Baghdad. **4** Saddam International Airport near Baghdad seized by US 3rd Infantry Division. **6** Baath HQ destroyed as Royal Marines enter Basra. **14** Capture of Tikrit, Saddam Hussein's home town, marks end of Iraqi resistance. **29** First Palestinian PM, Mahmoud Abbas, sworn in. **30** US-backed 'road map' for peace in the Middle East published.

June 2 50th anniversary of the coronation of HM Queen Elizabeth II. **9** Gordon Brown announces that conditions have not been met for Britain to adopt the Euro. **24** President Putin arrives in London on first state visit by a Russian leader since 1874.

July 17 Tony Blair addresses joint session of US Congress. **18** Body of government weapons expert, Dr David Kelly, found in woods after apparent suicide. **22** Saddam Hussein's sons, Uday and Qusay, killed by US troops. **27** Comedian Bob Hope dies aged 100.

August 10 Temperatures reach a record 38·1°C (100·6°F) at Gravesend in Kent. **15** Libya accepts blame for Lockerbie bombing in 1988 and agrees to compensate victims' families. **19** Truck bomb destroys UN headquarters in Baghdad killing 23, including UN special representative, Sergio Vieira de Mello.

September 6 Palestinian PM, Mahmoud Abbas, resigns; Yasser Arafat nominates Ahmed Qurei. **11** Swedish Foreign Minister, Anna Lindh, is stabbed to death whilst shopping.

October 7 Arnold Schwarzenegger elected Governor of California. **15** China launches its first manned space flight. **19** Tony Blair admitted to Hammersmith Hospital with irregular heartbeat. **24** British Airways Concorde makes its last passenger flight. **29** Iain Duncan Smith resigns as Conservative Party leader after losing a vote of confidence.

November 5 Michael Howard becomes Conservative Party leader. **18** President Bush arrives in Britain for a 4-day state visit. **20** Two truck bombs hit British targets in Istanbul; Roger Short, UK consul-general, is amongst the dead. **22** England beat Australia 20–17 in the Rugby World Cup final in Sydney. **23** President Shevardnadze of Georgia resigns after three weeks of protests over claims of election-rigging. **26** Elections for Northern Ireland's National Assembly result in Dr Paisley's Democratic Unionists forming the largest party.

December 8 Commonwealth heads of government meeting in Nigeria agree to continue suspension of Zimbabwe; President Mugabe announces withdrawal from Commonwealth. **9** Britain's first toll motorway opens round Birmingham. **10** Angela Cannings has her conviction for murdering her three children quashed. **12** Paul Martin succeeds Jean Chretien as Canadian PM. **12** Saddam Hussein captured by US troops. **17** Ian Huntley convicted of the murder of Soham schoolgirls, Holly Wells and Jessica Chapman. **19** Announcement made that Libya is giving up weapons of mass destruction programmes.

2004

January 13 Serial killer Harold Shipman hangs himself in his cell at Wakefield prison. **28** Lord

A.D.

Hutton's report into the death of Dr David Kelly published; Gavyn Davies resigns as BBC chairman. **29** Greg Dyke resigns as BBC director-general. Cannabis downgraded from a class B to a class C (least harmful) banned substance.

February 3 Inquiry set up under Lord Butler into intelligence on Iraq and weapons of mass destruction. **5** Twenty-one Chinese migrant workers drown in Morecambe Bay.

March 11 Ten bomb blasts on Madrid commuter trains kill 191 people. **14** Socialists defeat the Popular Party in Spanish general election. **25** Tony Blair meets President Qaddafi in Tripoli. **29** NATO admits Bulgaria, Romania, Slovakia, Slovenia, Estonia, Latvia and Lithuania. Journalist and broadcaster Alistair Cooke dies aged 95.

April 2 Michael Grade appointed chairman of the BBC. **5** Thames Trains fined a record £2 million for their part in the Paddington rail disaster in 1999. **20** Tony Blair announces that there will be a referendum on the EU constitutional treaty. **24** In a referendum UN proposals for the reunion of Cyprus are approved in the Turkish sector but rejected by Greek Cypriots.

May 1 Estonia, Latvia, Lithuania, Czech Republic, Hungary, Poland, Slovakia, Slovenia, Malta and Cyprus become members of the EU. **14** Piers Morgan is sacked as *Daily Mirror* editor over the publication of fake photographs of British soldiers abusing Iraqi POWs. **19** Tony Blair hit by condoms containing purple flower thrown by protesters in the House of Commons.

June 5 Ronald Reagan dies aged 93. **10** Ken Livingstone re-elected as Mayor of London. **18** Agreement announced at Brussels Summit on a draft EU constitutional treaty.

July 1 Actor Marlon Brando dies aged 80. **14** Lord Butler's report into intelligence and Iraqi WMDs is published. **26** Democratic Convention opens in Boston; John Kerry and John Edwards nominated to run for president and vice-president.

August 13 The XXVIII Olympic Games open in Athens. **16** Boscastle in Cornwall is devastated by a flash flood following torrential rain. **22** Armed robbers steal Edvard Munch's painting *The Scream* from the Munch Museum in Oslo. **30** Republican Convention opens in New York; George Bush and Dick Cheney nominated to run for president and vice-president.

September 1 Terrorists seize control of a school in Beslan, North Ossetia; over 300 hostages killed when siege ends on 3 September. **15** Opponents of bill to ban hunting with dogs breach security and enter the House of Commons chamber. **30** Tony Blair announces he will serve a full third term if Labour wins the next election.

October 7 Car bomb attacks at three Egyptian resorts in the Sinai Peninsula, aimed at Israeli tourists, kill 34 people. **8** British hostage Kenneth Bigley murdered in Iraq. **9** In Australian general election PM John Howard's coalition government defeats Labour's Mark Latham. The Queen opens the controversial Scottish parliament building in Edinburgh. **9** In Afghanistan presidential election results in victory for Hamid Karzai. **26** Israeli parliament approves Ariel Sharon's plan for withdrawal of soldiers and settlers from Gaza Strip and parts of the West Bank. **29** At Rome Summit, EU member states sign a treaty providing for the introduction of the EU constitution when all 25 members have ratified it.

November 2 In elections in USA President Bush defeats the Democrat challenger John Kerry. **8** In Iraq US-led forces launch major operation to take rebel-held Falluja. **11** President Yasser Arafat dies in a Paris hospital. **16** Murder reported of British-born aid worker Margaret Hassan who was kidnapped in Iraq in October. **21** Presidential election in Ukraine results in victory for PM Viktor Yanukovich, but is later declared fraudulent.

December 15 David Blunkett resigns as Home

A.D.
Secretary; Charles Clarke appointed. **20** £26·5m stolen in armed robbery at the Northern Bank in Belfast: IRA accused. **26** Earthquake off the island of Sumatra creates tsunamis that kill over 225,000 along the Asian and East African coasts. In re-run of Ukrainian elections Viktor Yuschenko defeats Viktor Yanukovich.

2005

January 1 Freedom of Information Act comes into force. **9** Mahmoud Abbas elected President of the Palestinian Authority. In Sudan, peace agreement signed between the government and rebel forces led by John Garang. **30** In Iraq, elections held for National Assembly and provincial assemblies amidst intensified violence. **31** Alleged IRA involvement in murder of catholic Robert McCartney outside a pub in Belfast; McCartney family mounts campaign to bring killers to justice.

February 10 North Korea admits to having nuclear weapons. **16** Kyoto Protocol on climate change comes into force. **18** Act to ban hunting with dogs in England and Wales comes into force. **20** Spain becomes the first country to endorse the proposed EU constitution in a referendum.

March 11 Controversial Prevention of Terrorism Bill becomes law. **26** Former Prime Minister, Lord Callaghan, dies aged 92. **31** Robert Mugabe's ZANU-PF Party wins elections in Zimbabwe.

April 2 Pope John Paul II dies. **9** Prince Charles marries Camilla Parker Bowles. **15** Collapse of UK-owned car manufacturer MG Rover. **19** Cardinal Joseph Ratzinger of Germany elected to be the new Pope as Benedict XVI.

May 5 General Election returns Labour Party under Tony Blair for a third term. **29** In a referendum France rejects the proposed EU constitution. **31** French PM Jean-Pierre Raffarin resigns and Dominique de Villepin succeeds him.

June 1 Dutch reject the proposed EU constitution. **6** Government announces it will not proceed with bill for a UK referendum on EU constitution. **13** In California Michael Jackson is acquitted of child abuse. **19** Ugandan-born John Sentamu, Bishop of Birmingham, is appointed Archbishop of York, the first black holder of the post. **24** In Iran the ultra-conservative mayor of Tehran, Mahdi Ahmadinejad, is elected president.

July 6 London chosen to host the 2012 Olympic Games. **7** Suicide bombers explode three bombs on the London Underground and one on a bus; 56 dead. **8** G8 (Group of Eight) nations end their Summit in Scotland with pledge of action over African poverty and debt. **17** Former Prime Minister, Sir Edward Heath, dies aged 89. **21** Second attempt by terrorists to bomb London's transport system fails when devices do not explode. **22** Brazilian electrician, John Charles de Menezes, is mistaken for a terrorist and shot dead in London. **28** IRA announces an end to its armed campaign to achieve a united Ireland.

August 1 King Fahd of Saudi Arabia dies and is succeeded by his half-brother, Crown Prince Abdullah. **9** US space shuttle *Discovery* lands safely despite problems during its 14-day mission. **15** Israeli troops begin removing settlers from Gaza Strip and West Bank. **29** Hurricane Katrina strikes New Orleans, causing catastrophic flooding.

September 7 Hosni Mubarak re-elected as President of Egypt. **12** Israel completes evacuation of settlers and soldiers from the Gaza Strip. England draw fifth test match against Australia and regain the Ashes. **26** In Northern Ireland decommissioning of IRA weapons declared complete.

A.D.
October 8 Massive earthquake in Kashmir leaves over 87,000 dead and three million homeless. **15** Referendum in Iraq ratifies new constitution. **19** Trial of former president Saddam Hussein opens in Baghdad. **28** Rioting mainly by ethnic minorities in Paris suburbs followed by weeks of disturbances in cities across France.

November 2 David Blunkett resigns as Secretary of State for Work and Pensions over breaches in the ministerial code of conduct. **22** Angela Merkel formally elected by the Bundestag as first woman Chancellor of Germany. **24** New licensing laws come into force relaxing restrictions on licensing hours.

December 5 Civil Partnership Act providing for registered unions between same-sex couples comes into force. **6** David Cameron defeats David Davis to become Conservative Party leader at the age of 39. **11** Explosions at oil depot at Buncefield, Hemel Hempstead, result in largest fire in peacetime Europe. **15** In elections in Iraq the main Shiite bloc, the United Iraqi Alliance, wins 128 seats in the 275-member parliament. **17** At Brussels summit agreement on EU Budget involves cut in Britain's rebate.

2006

January 4 Israeli PM Ariel Sharon incapacitated by a stroke. **7** Charles Kennedy resigns as leader of the Liberal Democrats. **23** Canadian elections result in victory for Conservatives led by Stephen Harper. **25** In elections for Palestinian parliament militant Islamist group Hamas defeats Fatah party. **31** 100th member of the British forces to die in Iraq since the invasion is killed by a bomb.

February 3 Demonstrations take place outside the Danish Embassy in London, part of worldwide protest over cartoons showing the Prophet Mohammed originally published by a Danish newspaper in September 2005. **4** International Atomic Energy Agency votes to report Iran's nuclear programme to the UN Security Council; Iran announces intention to resume uranium enrichment. **7** Muslim cleric Abu Hamza jailed for seven years at the Old Bailey for inciting murder and racial hatred. **22** In Britain's biggest robbery £53 million stolen from Securitas depot at Tonbridge in Kent. Golden Mosque at Samarra in Iraq, one of the holiest Shiite shrines, blown up by insurgents.

March 2 Sir Menzies Campbell elected leader of the Liberal Democrats. **11** Former Serbian president Slobodan Milosevic, on trial for war crimes since 2002, found dead in his cell at The Hague. **24** Basque separatist organisation ETA declares a permanent ceasefire. **20** In Ukraine parliamentary elections result in defeat for President Yuschenko's Our Ukraine bloc. **28** In Israeli general election centrist Kadima Party led by Ehud Olmert emerges as the largest party. **29** The five permanent members of the UN Security Council, plus Germany, call on Iran to suspend its nuclear research within thirty days.

April 10 In Italian elections the centre-left led by Romano Prodi narrowly defeats Silvio Berlusconi's centre-right coalition. **11** Iran announces that it has successfully enriched uranium. **26** "Black Wednesday" for government as crisis mounts at Home Office, in NHS *etc.*

May 5 Local elections produce major setback for Labour (*see* **D13** and **C60**). **5** Major Cabinet changes: Charles Clarke sacked, Jack Straw demoted. Margaret Beckett first woman Foreign Secretary (*see* **D6**).

PART II. HISTORICAL GLOSSARY

A

Abdication. The term usually refers to the re-nunciation of the royal office by a reigning monarch. Both Edward II (1327) and Richard II (1399) were forced to abdicate, James II left the throne vacant without waiting for a formal deposition, and the abdication of Edward VIII was effected by the Declaration of Abdication Act, 1936. Since 1688 when Parliament de-clared James II to have abdicated, no monarch can abdicate without the consent of Parliament.

Angevin Dynasty includes the Plantagenet kings from Henry II to Richard II. The name came from Henry II's father, Geoffrey, Count of Anjou.

Annates were acknowledgments formerly paid to the Popes by way of fee or tax in respect of ecclesiastical preferment and consisted usually of a proportion of the income ("first-fruits") of the office. Introduced into England in the 13th cent.; annexed to the Crown under Henry VIII; transferred to a perpetual fund for the benefit of poorer clergy in 1704. See **Queen Anne's Bounty.**

Anschluss. See **Section L.**

Appeasement Policy. The name of the policy during 1937 and 1938 of yielding to the demands of Hitler and Mussolini in the hope that a point would be reached when the dictators would co-operate in the maintenance of peace. The policy culminated in the Munich Agreement (which was the subject of much criticism) after a series of concessions including the recognition of the Italian conquest of Abyssinia and the German annexation of Austria. The policy was finally demonstrated as futile when Hitler seized Czechoslovakia in March 1939.

Armada, Spanish, the naval expedition fitted out by Philip II of Spain in 1588 against England, commanded by the Duke of Medina Sidonia. It comprised 127 ships, was manned by 8,000 sailors and carried 19,000 soldiers and more than 2,000 cannon. Against this formidable force Elizabeth had only 80 ships, manned by 9,000 sailors, under Lord Howard of Effingham, under whom served Drake, Hawkins and Frobisher. The British Fleet awaited the Armada off Plymouth, and at Tilbury there was a con-siderable defensive land force under the com-mand of the Earl of Leicester. On 19 July the ships of the Armada were sighted off the Lizard, disposed in a crescent 11 km long from horn to horn. The excellent manoeuvring of the English, their fire-ships and a gale from the N.W. combined so effectively to cripple the Spanish ships that the Armada was scattered, reaching home via the North of Scotland. It was impossible to embark the army of Parma waiting in the Netherlands. Elizabeth had a medal struck bearing in Latin the inscription, "God blew and they were scattered".

Assassination, treacherous murder for political ends, usually of a ruler or distinguished person. Among the most notable: Julius Caesar, 44 B.C.; Thomas Becket, 1170; David Rizzio, 1566; Wil-liam the Silent, 1584; Henry IV of France, 1610; Jean Paul Marat, 1793; Abraham Lincoln, 1865; Alexander II of Russia, 1881; Archduke Francis Ferdinand of Austria, 1914; Mahatma Gandhi, 1948; President John F. Kennedy, 1963; Malcolm X, 1965; Dr. Verwoerd, 1966; Dr. Martin Luther King, 1968; Senator Robert Kennedy, 1968; Lord Mountbatten, 1979; John Lennon, 1980; Pres. Sadat, 1981; Indira Gandhi, 1984; Olof Palme, 1986; Rajiv Gandhi, 1991; Yitzhak Rabin, 1995; Pim Fortuyn (Dutch far-right politician), 2002; Sheikh Ahmed Yassin (founder of Hamas), 2004, and the Lebanese leader Rafik Hariri in 2005.

Austerlitz, Battle of, was fought near Brünn, in Moravia, on 2 December 1805. Napoleon defeated the Russians and Austrians under Kutuzov.

Auto-da-fe. See **Section L.**

B

Balance of Power was the doctrine in British policy whereby European groups should be so balanced as to prevent the emergence of a dominating Power. Thus the balance was maintained between the Triple Alliance (Germany, Austria and Italy) and the Triple Entente (Great Britain, France and Russia) and preserved peace from 1871 to 1914. After the first world war there was tentative support of Germany's recovery to counterweigh the possible French hegemony; but when Germany's power grew under Hitler leading to the second world war, Britain, France and Russia again became allies.

Barbarossa, the code-name for the German attack on the Soviet Union on 22 June 1941.

Bartholomew, Massacre of St., occurred in Paris on the night of 24 August 1572, when over two thousand Huguenots were massacred by order of the Catholic French Court.

Berlin Wall, construction formerly dividing Berlin. Symbol of the Cold War from 1961 to 1989.

Bill of Rights, or Declaration of Rights, was the document setting forth the conditions upon which the British throne was offered to William and Mary in 1688. This was accepted and ulti-mately became an Act of Parliament.

Black Death, the plague which swept across Europe in the years 1348-50, beginning in the ports of Italy, brought in by merchant ships from Black Sea ports. It was the worst scourge man has ever known; at least a quarter of the European population was wiped out in the first epidemic of 1348. It reached England in the winter of that year. The disease was transmitted to man by fleas from black rats, though this was not known at the time, the specific organism being *Bacillus pestis.* The disease continued to ravage Europe in recurrent outbreaks up to the late 17th cent. The epidemic in England in 1665 wiped out whole villages and one-tenth of London's population, then estimated at 460,000. Samuel Pepys wrote a grim account of it in his *Diary.* Recently, some studies have suggested the plague was caused by a virus (thus exonerating the rats!). See also **Labourers, English Statute of.**

Black Hole of Calcutta, the name given to the place where a captured British garrison was con-fined in 1756, during the struggle for India between the French and British. Into a confined space, about 6 m square, 146 persons were driven and only 23 were found alive the next morning. The authenticity of the story has been called into question.

Bloody Assizes, the assizes conducted in 1685 by George Jeffreys, Lord Chief Justice, at which participants in the Duke of Monmouth's rebellion against King James II were tried. They were marked by relentless cruelty.

Boer War lasted from 11 October 1899, when the Boers invaded Natal, to 31 May 1902, when the Treaty of Vereeniging ended hostilities. At first the operations of the British troops in Cape Colony were unsuccessful and disastrous reverses were sustained. Lord Roberts was then sent out as Commander-in-Chief, with Lord Kitchener as Chief-of-Staff, and from February 1900, when Kimberley was relieved and Cronje was compelled to surrender and Ladysmith and Mafeking were relieved, the even-tual military defeat of the Boers was inevitable by 1902.

Boston Tea Party, an incident which occurred on 16 December 1773, on board some tea-ships in Boston Harbour. High taxation imposed by the British Parliament under George III had caused bitter feelings, and instigated by popular meetings, a party of citizens, disguised as Indians, boarded the tea-ships and threw the tea overboard. This incident was a prelude to the American War of Independence (1775-83) which resulted in Britain's loss of her American colonies.

C

Capet, the family name of the royal house of France, founded by Hugh Capet in 987, with its collateral branches. The main line of the dynasty came to an end in 1328 with the death of Charles IV when the throne passed to the related house of Valois. The direct Valois line ended in 1498 with the death of Charles VIII. The first of the Bourbon line was Henry IV whose descendants ruled France (except during the Revolution and the Napoleonic era) until 1848.

Carbonari, members of a secret political society originating in Naples, and at one time very numerous. Their chief aim was to free Italy from foreign rule, and they exerted considerable influence in the revolutionary movements in the first half of the 19th cent. Their name comes from the charcoal-burners (carbonari).

Carolingians, dynasty of Frankish rulers founded in the 7th cent. The family was at its height when represented by Charlemagne. It ruled, with interruptions, until 987 when the Capetian dynasty succeeded.

Cavalier, a name adopted during the troubles of the Civil War to designate the Royalist party; it is also used generally in reference to a knightly, gallant or imperious personage.

Chouans, the name given to the band of peasants, mainly smugglers and dealers in contraband salt, who rose in revolt in the west of France in 1793 and joined the royalists of La Vendée. Balzac gives a picture of the people and the country in which they operated in his novel Les Chouans. They used the hoot of an owl as a signal—hence the name.

Commune of Paris has twice played a dramatic part in the history of France. In 1792 it was able, through its control of the administrative organisation of Paris, to override the National Assembly. In 1871, after the withdrawal of the Prussian troops, it tried to assert its authority. Public buildings were destroyed by members of the Commune and civil war raged during April and half May, but Government troops savagely suppressed the rising.

Concordat, an agreement of convention between the Pope and a secular government regarding ecclesiastical matters. The Concordat of Worms in 1122 between Calixtus II and the Emperor Henry V was famous as deciding a long struggle in regard to investiture. In 1801, Napoleon concluded a concordat with Pius VII defining the restored relations between the head of the Church and the French Roman Catholics.

Convention Parliaments, terms used to describe the Parliaments of 1660 (after the dissolution of the Long Parliament) and 1689, (summoned by William of Orange).

Corn Laws were statutes intended for the benefit of British agriculture, and restricted import and export of grain. From the 14th to the mid-19th cent. such laws were in force, and were often of a stringent nature. They became so oppressive and caused corn to reach so high a price that the poorer classes were plunged into distress. A powerful anti-corn law agitation was organised of which Cobden, Bright and Villiers were the leaders, and Sir Robert Peel in 1846, at the time of the Irish potato famine, carried through free trade. The repeal of the Corn Laws marked an important phase in the transformation of an agricultural to an industrial Britain.

Crimean War (1853–56). This war between Russia and the allied powers of Turkey, Britain, France and Sardinia, was connected with the Eastern Question (q.v.) and the desire of Russia for a port on the Mediterranean. Chief engagements were the Alma, Balaclava and Inkerman. Fighting virtually ceased with fall of Sevastopol in September 1855. The Treaty of Paris was signed 30 March 1856.

Crusades were military expeditions undertaken by some of the Christian nations of Europe with the object of ensuring the safety of pilgrims visiting the Holy Sepulchre and to retain in Christian hands the Holy Places. For two centuries nine crusades were undertaken: First, 1095–99, under Godfrey of Bouillon, which succeeded in capturing Jerusalem; Second, 1147–49, led by Louis VII of France, a dismal failure, which ended with the fall of Jerusalem; Third, 1189–92, in which Richard I of England took part, making a truce with Saladin; Fourth, 1202–4, led by French and Flemish nobles, a shameful expedition, resulting in the founding of a Latin empire in Constantinople; Fifth, 1217–21, led by John of Brienne; Sixth, 1228–29, under the Emperor Frederick II; Seventh, 1248–54, under St. Louis of France; Eighth, 1270, under the same leadership, but cut short by his death on an ill-judged expedition to Tunis; Ninth, 1271–72, led by Prince Edward of England, which accomplished nothing. Millions of lives were sacrificed in these enterprises which frequently degenerated into an orgy of killing against the followers of Islam.

The chief material beneficiaries were the Italian maritime cities; the chief spiritual beneficiary was the Pope.

D

Danegeld, tax imposed in England in Anglo-Saxon times to raise funds for resisting the Danes or to buy them off. Edward the Confessor abolished the tax, but it was revived by the Conqueror and subsequently retained, under another name, after the danger from the Danes was past. It is the basis of all taxation in this country.

Danelaw, the law enforced by the Danes in the kingdoms of Northumbria, East Anglia, and in the districts of the five (Danish) boroughs—lands grouped round Leicester, Nottingham, Derby, Stamford and Lincoln—which they occupied during the Viking invasions of the 9th and 10th cent. The country occupied was also called the Danelaw or Danelagh.

Dauphin, the title borne by the eldest sons of the Kings of France from 1349 to 1830.

D-Day, the allied invasion of Normandy on 6 June 1944 which began the liberation of France in World War II. Allied troops landed on the coast of Normandy between the river Orne and the Cotentin peninsula, in the largest ever seaborne invasion. Three divisions from the Canadian and British army landed on 'Gold', 'Juno', and 'Sword' beaches and two divisions of the American First Army at 'Omaha' and 'Utah' beaches. After a fierce battle on 'Omaha' a substantial beach-head—24 miles long and 4 miles deep—was established by nightfall.

Declaration of Independence was an act by which the American Congress, on 4 July 1776, declared the American colonies to be independent of Great Britain. "Independence Day" is a holiday in the United States.

Declaration of Rights. See Bill of Rights.

Diet, in German history an assembly of dignitaries or delegates called together to debate upon and decide important political or ecclesiastical questions. The most famous imperial Diets were those held at Worms (1521), Speyer (1529), and Augsburg (1530), all of which dealt with matters arising from the Reformation.

Doge, the chief magistrate in the old republics of Venice (697–1797) and Genoa (1339–1797, 1802–5).

Domesday Book was the famous register of the lands of England framed by order of William the Conqueror. According to Stowe, the name was derived from Domus dei, the name of the place where the book was deposited in Winchester Cathedral; though by others it is connected with doom in the sense of judgment. Its compilation was determined upon in 1085, in order that William might compute what he considered to be due to him in the way of tax from his subjects. William sent into each county commissioners to make survey. They were to inquire the name of each place, the possessor, how many hides of land were in the manor, how many ploughs were in demesne, how many homagers, villeins, cottars, serving men, free tenants, and tenants in soccage; how much wood, meadow, and pasture; the number of mills and fish ponds; what had been added to or taken away from the place; what was the gross value at the time of Edward the Confessor. So minute was the survey that the Saxon chronicler of the time reports "there was not a single hide, nor one virgate of land, nor even, it is shame to tell, though it seemed no shame to do, an ox, nor a cow, nor a swine was left that was not set down".

The record, which did not take in Northumberland, Cumberland, Durham and parts of Lancashire and Westmorland, was completed in 1086, and was comprised in two volumes—one a large folio, sometimes called the Little Domesday, which deals with Essex, Norfolk and Suffolk, the other a quarto, sometimes called the Great Domesday. The first is written on 384 double pages of vellum in one and the same hand, and in a small but plain character, each page having a double column. The quarto is written on 450 pages of vellum, but in a single column and in a large, fair character. The original is preserved in the Public Record Office at Kew. *See also* **Danegeld.**

Durbar, a term used in India from the Persian word *darbár* meaning "court" or "audience". The word was applied to great gatherings like Lord Lytton's durbar in 1877 and the Delhi durbar of 1911.

E

Eastern Front, the battlefront between Russia and Germany in both World Wars.

Eastern Question, a term formerly applied to the problems arising from the instability of the Ottoman Empire and its relations with the other nations of Europe. Later connected with other problems of the Near East such as the possession of Constantinople and rivalries in the Balkans.

East India Company was incorporated by Elizabeth in 1600. In 1613 the Company set up a factory at Surat, India, and in 1662 Bombay came under the Company's influence and developed into an important trading port. Dupleix wanted to establish French power in India and a struggle for supremacy took place. Clive gained the victory for England and thenceforward British dominion in India remained undisputed except by native princes. In 1772 Warren Hastings was appointed the first Governor-General and in 1784 Pitt's India Act established a Board of Control for the India Company. A great increase of trade resulted, and this rule continued down to 1858, when, as a result of the mutiny, the Crown assumed the sovereignty. British dominion ended in 1947.

F

Farmer-General, the name given to the financiers who in the days of the old French monarchy farmed certain taxes, contracting to pay the Government a fixed sum yearly, on condition that the unspecified taxes were collected and appropriated by themselves. The revolution of 1789 swept the Farmer-General away.

Fifth Column. When Franco, the Spanish dictator, revolted against the Spanish Republic in 1936 and attacked Madrid with four armies, his commander, General Mola declared that a group of fascists within the city was assisting the besiegers. The term is used to describe a body of spies behind a fighting front.

Fire of London, of 1666, extended from East to West, from the Tower to the Temple church, and northward to Holborn Bridge. It broke out in a baker's shop in Pudding Lane, and lasted four days, and destroyed 87 churches, including St. Paul's Cathedral, and many public buildings, among them the Royal Exchange, the Custom House and the Guildhall. In the ruins were 13,200 houses and 400 streets. About 100,000 people were made homeless yet in about 10 years all the houses had been rebuilt. The plague had not disappeared from London when the fire occurred.

Four Freedoms, a phrase coined by President Roosevelt in January 1941, embodying what should be the goal of the Allies. They were (1) Freedom of speech and expression; (2) Freedom of every person to worship God in his own way; (3) Freedom from want; (4) Freedom from fear.

Franco-German War (1870–71) was opened by a declaration of war by Napoleon III, but the Germans who were better prepared than the French, won victory after victory. On 12 September Napoleon with 104,000 men were made prisoners at Sedan, a republic was then proclaimed, and Paris sustained a four months' siege. In the end France ceded Alsace and part of Lorraine to Germany, who claimed a war indemnity of £200 million. Revenge for the loss of these territories was important in French politics.

Franklin, in feudal times a country landowner who was independent of the territorial lord, and performed many of the minor functions of local government, *e.g.* serving as magistrate.

G

Gabelle. French tax on salt, first levied in the 14th-century. Nobility, clergy and certain towns and provinces were exempt while elsewhere it was strictly imposed and proved both burdensome and unpopular. It was abolished in 1791.

Gavelkind, an old English custom of land tenure in Kent and other places in England, whereby on the death, intestate, of a property owner his property is subsequently divided equally among his children.

Geneva Convention, an agreement made by the European Powers at Geneva in 1864, establishing humane regulations regarding the treatment of the sick and wounded in war and the status of those who minister to them. All persons, hospitals, hospital ships are required to display the Geneva cross—a red cross on a white ground. A second conference held at Geneva in 1868 drew up a supplementary agreement. A major result of this Convention was the establishment of the Red Cross Society in 1870.

Gordon Riots of 1780 were an anti-popery agitation fomented by Lord George Gordon. Called also "No-Popery Riots".

Guelph and Ghibelline, italianised forms of the German words "Welf" and "Waiblingen", the names of two rival princely families whose conflicts made much of the history of Germany and Italy during the Middle Ages. The feuds between these two factions continued in Italy during the campaigns of Emperor Frederick I, and later developed into the fierce struggles of the 13th cent. between emperor and pope. In Italy the Ghibellines supported the side of the German emperors and the Guelphs the cause of the Pope. The present Royal Family of England and other Northern monarchies are descended by different routes from the Guelph George I, Duke of Brunswick-Lüneburg of the House of Hanover.

Gunboat diplomacy, the use of naval power to achieve foreign policy ends—invariably by a stronger against a weaker state—associated particularly with Lord Palmerston's second period at the Foreign Office from 1846 to 1851 and with American policy towards the Caribbean in the 20th century.

Gunpowder Plot was a conspiracy by a desperate band of Roman Catholics in the reign of James I to avenge the harsh treatment to which Catholics were subjected. Barrels of gunpowder were secreted in the vaults underneath the Houses of Parliament, and it was proposed to fire these when the King and his Ministers assembled on 5 November 1605. The plot was betrayed and Guy Fawkes and his co-conspirators were arrested and executed. The date serves to perpetuate the ancient custom of burning the effigy of Fawkes.

H

Habsburg (Hapsburg), the former ruling house of Austria, 1282–1918; held title of Roman Emperor, 1438–1806, except for 1740-5. The aggrandisement of the Habsburg family was mainly brought about by a series of fortunate marriages. In 1521 when the Habsburg power was at its zenith, Charles V divided his dominions into two branches—Austrian Habsburg and Spanish Habsburg. The Habsburg Danubian Monarchy dates from 1526 when the Hungarian and Bohemian crowns were united with the Austrian patrimony of the Habsburg. The union lasted 400 years.

The assassination of the heir to the Habsburg thrones, Francis Ferdinand, at Sarajevo in 1914, provoked the outbreak of the first world war. Francis Joseph's great-nephew, Charles, went into exile in 1918.

Hampton Court Conference, presided over at Hampton Court Palace by James I in 1604 and which brought about his authorised translation of the Bible, had an important bearing on the religious differences of the time. James refused to grant tolerations to the Puritans. This sowed the seeds of civil war. Following the conference three hundred English Puritan clergy were ejected from their livings.

Hanaper Office, a former Chancery office, deriving its name from the fact that its writs and papers were kept in a hanaper (hamper). The Chancellor's office thus came to be known as the Hanaper. The Comptrollers of the Hanaper were abolished in England in 1842.

Hanoverians, Royal dynasty which ruled Great Britain and Ireland, from 1714 to 1901. From the Brünswick-Luneburg branch of the Guelph family, they took their name from the German state of Hanover where they were Electors of the Holy Roman Empire. Their succession to the English, and later British, crown was secured by the 1710 Act of Settlement. In 1837 the crown of Hanover went to the uncle of Queen Victoria, Ernest, Duke of Cumberland and the personal union of the Hanoverian and British crowns ceased.

The British Hanoverian monarchs were George I (ruled 1714–27); his son George II (1727–60); George III, grandson of George II (1760–1820); his eldest son George IV (1820–30 and Prince Regent from 1812); William IV, third son of George III (1830–37) and Queen Victoria, granddaughter of George III (1837–1901).

Hanseatic League was a confederation of North German towns established about 1241 for purposes of mutual protection in carrying on international commerce. The League became so powerful that it was able to dominate the foreign trade of Norway, Sweden, Denmark, and even to some extent of London. A branch was established in London and had its guild hall in Cannon Street for hundreds of years. The League existed until the mid 17th cent.

Hamburg, Lübeck and Bremen are the only cities which, as free ports, still by commercial courtesy retain the name of Hanse towns. *Hansa* is Old High German for Association or Merchants' Guild.

Hearth-Money was a tax laid on hearths (in all houses paying the church and poor rates). Charles II introduced it in 1662, and it was repealed in the reign of William and Mary.

Heptarchy, a word derived from the Greek *hepta,* seven, and denoting the seven kingdoms (*archai*) into which Anglo-Saxon England was divided before 900. The seven were Kent, Essex, Sussex, Wessex, Mercia, East Anglia and Northumbria.

Holy Alliance, an alliance ostensibly for conserving religion, justice and peace in Europe, but used for repressing popular tendencies towards constitutional government. Formed by Alexander I of Russia, Francis I of Austria and Frederick William III of Prussia, at Paris on 26 September 1815. Subsequently joined by all the sovereigns of Europe, except the Pope and the King of England. It ended after the 1830 revolution in France.

Holy Roman Empire, the title traditionally given (although the term "Holy" does not appear in a document until 1157) to the revived Empire when the German king Otto I was crowned in Rome by Pope John XII in 962. It endured until Napoleonic times (1806) two years after Francis II had assumed the title of Emperor of Austria.

Hospitallers, Knights, were of the order of St. John of Jerusalem, at first devoted to the aid of the sick, but afterwards military monks, who became prominent figures in the Crusades of the 12th cent. They adopted the Benedictine black habit with the eight-pointed cross worn by the modern St. John Ambulance Brigade. In 1309 they took Rhodes, but were expelled by the Ottomans in 1522. In 1530 the emperor Charles V gave them the island of Malta, which as Knights of Malta, they held until 1798, when they were dislodged by Napoleon. The Knights still survive as a sovereign order, with headquarters in Rome. *See* **Templars** and **Teutonic Order.**

Huguenots, a name applied to the French Protestant communities of the 16th and 17th cent. Henry of Navarre, by the Edict of Nantes in

1598, granted them religious freedom, but more than a quarter of a century before—24 August 1572—thousands had been put to death in the massacre of St. Bartholomew. The revocation of the Edict of Nantes by Louis XIV in 1685 drove thousands into exile in England, Holland, Germany and America.

Hundred, the ancient divisonal name given to a portion of a county for administration or military purposes. It is supposed to imply the territory occupied by a hundred families; or the space of a hundred hides of land, or the capacity of providing 100 soldiers. Each hundred had its hundred court, with powers similar to those of a manor court, but this was abolished in 1867 by the County Court Act.

Hundred Days, the interval of time between Napoleon Bonaparte's entry into Paris after his escape from Elba and his departure after his abdication, extending from 20 March 1815 to 28 June. During this period occurred the battle of Waterloo (*q.v.*) on 18 June.

Hundred Years' War, a term applied to the almost incessant contest between England and France, lasting from 1338 to 1453, including such famous battles as Crécy, Poitiers and Agincourt, and engaging successively Edward III, Henry V and Henry VI, among English kings.

Huns, a fierce Asiatic race which swept over eastern Europe in the 4th cent. Under Attila about the middle of the 5th cent, they obtained control of a large portion of central and eastern Europe, forcing even Rome to pay tribute. Their defeat at Châlons-sur-Marne in 451 and the death of Attila in 453 ended their empire.

I

Impeachment, a special arraignment, usually before Parliament or other high tribunal, of a person charged with some offence against the State. The custom in England was for the impeachment to be made in the House of Commons, and the trial to be before the House of Lords. The first instance occurred in 1376 when Lord Latimer was impeached. With present parliamentary procedure, impeachment is no longer necessary, since the Cabinet is responsible for the individual actions of its ministers, who, acting as a team, must carry the Commons with them, or resign, when it falls to the Leader of the Opposition to form a new Cabinet. Other famous Impeachments were those of the Lord High Chancellor Francis Bacon (1621), Earl of Strafford and Archbishop Laud (1640), Warren Hastings (1788), the last being that of Lord Melville (1805). Under the constitution of the United States the President may be impeached by the House of Representatives and tried by the Senate. The first case was that of President Andrew Johnson who was saved from impeachment in 1868 by one vote. President Clinton became only the second president in US history to be impeached in December 1998. The trial ended in February 1999 with his acquittal.

Impressment, the forced seizure of persons for military service resorted to by many countries before the establishment of conscription. Press gangs forcibly recruited men for British warships especially during the Napoleonic wars, but such measures were abandoned after c 1850.

Indian Revolt (Mutiny). This turning-point in the history of modern India occurred in 1857–58. The ostensible cause was the serving out to the native troops of cartridges greased with animal fat, for contact with this was forbidden both by the Hindu and Muslim faiths. A rebellious feeling, however, had long been developing, and when the Sepoys at Meerut in May 1857 refused to obey the English officers, overpowered and put them to death, the revolt spread like wildfire. The rebels took Delhi and Lucknow, and for many months massacres and atrocities were committed. Order was re-established in the autumn of 1858 when the governing power was transferred from the East India Company to the Crown.

Indulgence, Declaration of, was the proclamation by which James II suspended the penal laws against Roman Catholics and Dissenters. It was issued in 1688, but the clergy as a body refused to obey, and the trial of the Seven Bishops and their acquittal by a jury followed. An invitation was thereupon sent to William of Orange to become King.

Industrial Revolution. The name, first given by Engels in 1844, to describe the radical changes that took place in Britain during c. 1730–1850 to transform a mainly agricultural country into one predominantly industrial. It began with the mechanisation of the textile industry (Hargreave's spinning jenny, 1764, Arkwright's water-frame, 1769, Crompton's mule, 1770, and Watt's steam-engine, 1785), with subsequent major developments in mining, transport and industrial organisation. It was based on Britain's rich mineral resources, particularly coal and iron ore. With the use of the steam-engine as power, industry became concentrated round the coalfields and the great new industrial towns developed—Birmingham, Manchester, Newcastle and Glasgow. Britain became supreme in constructional ironwork (Telford, George and Robert Stephenson).

Canals, bridges, railways and ships were built, and great advances were made in the practical application of scientific principles. Aided by colonial exploitation Britain became the most prosperous country in the world. The new industrial capitalists began to replace the country squires as ruling class. But the great accumulation of wealth at one pole of society was matched at the other by poverty and misery, for child labour, long working hours, low wages and slums were features of the industrial revolution in its infancy. As with all great technological developments, the industrial revolution produced related changes in all fields of social life—in politics, art, religion, morals etc.

Iron Curtain. In a speech at Fulton, USA, on 5 March 1946, Sir Winston Churchill used this phrase to describe the dividing line behind which, he said, lie all the capitals of the ancient States of Central and Eastern Europe—Warsaw, Berlin, Prague, Vienna, Budapest, Belgrade, Bucharest and Sofia. The Iron Curtain was symbolised by the Berlin Wall (dividing that city in half) and the rival military groupings of NATO and the Warsaw Pact. The dramatic changes in Eastern Europe since 1989 and the collapse of the Soviet Union in 1991 have ended all this as some former Communist countries look to membership of the EU and NATO.

Ironsides were Cromwell's special troopers, so called because of their solidity and firmness in battle.

Irredentists, a political party organised in Italy about 1878 with the object of incorporating within Italy neighbouring regions. Also a person, group or party advocating policies for the restoration to their country of territory formerly belonging to it but later lost.

J

Jacobins, a French revolutionary club or party, formed in 1789, and accustomed to meet at a Jacobin convent, hence the name. It became a controlling force in the Revolution, especially in the movement which led to the Terror. Robespierre was its chief spokesman.

Jacobites, adherents of the Stuart cause after the abdication of James II. First James himself, then his son (the Old Pretender) and later his grandson (the Young Pretender) tried to fan the flame of rebellion in Scotland and Ireland, but after the defeat at Culloden on 16 April 1746 the cause was lost. Also the name of the monophysite heretics of Syria, so named after their leader Jacobus Baradaeus in the 6th cent. A.D.

Janissaries, an élite band of Ottoman foot soldiers who acted as the Sultan's bodyguard. They were conscripts, raised by the "tribute of children" from conquered Christian countries, mainly Serbia and Albania. First recruited under Murad I (14th cent.). They were not allowed to marry. They gained great power under the Ottoman Empire. In 1826 the Sultan Mahmud II had them massacred.

K

Kaiser. Title of the German emperor, assumed by the kings of Prussia following German unification in December 1870.

Kamikaze. Japanese suicide-planes in World War II which, laden with bombs, were flown directly into Allied warships. The name derives from a legendary occasion in the 13th century when the fleet of Kublai Khan was destroyed by a typhoon while preparing for the invasion of Japan. The first kamikaze attacks were made in November 1944 on US warships in Leyte Gulf.

L

Labarum, the standard of Constantine the Great, adopted after his conversion to Christianity, marked with his seal and represented upon the coinage.

Labourers, English Statute of, was passed 1350–51, with the object of compelling labourers to accept a certain rate of wages and not leave their employers' service, the Plague having rendered labourers so scarce that they were in great demand and had been insisting on higher pay. These acts were bitterly opposed and led to the "Peasants' Revolt", headed by Wat Tyler.

Land League, an association formed in 1879, with Parnell as president, for compelling a reduction in the rents of land, and a reconstruction of the land laws in Ireland, and in case of non-compliance refusing to pay rent. For a time this League exercised great political influence and was an important aid to the Home Rule movement.

Leagues, or combinations of kings, countries, communities, have been frequent since the kings of Canaan united against the Israelites. Among the most famous leagues may be mentioned the Holy or Catholic League, which prevented the recognition of Henry IV as King of France until he became a Roman Catholic; and the League of Augsburg against Louis XIV of France in 1686.

League of Nations, was founded on 10 January 1920, with the object of promoting international peace and security. The original members were the signatories to the Peace Treaties at Versailles, and membership grew to fifty-three as new nations and ex-enemy States were admitted. Two notable absentees were the United States and Soviet Russia, the latter not being represented until 1934. Germany was a member from 1926 to 1933. The League had an Assembly which met at Geneva every year and a Council which met five or six times a year. The Permanent Court of International Justice (now under the UN) sits at The Hague. The League held its last Assembly at Geneva in April 1946. Its place was taken by the United Nations.

The International Labour Organisation, set up by the League of Nations, met in April 1944 at Philadelphia and resumed its work at Geneva under the UN in 1946.

Legion, a body of Roman troops, varying in numbers at different periods. A legion was divided into 10 cohorts, and every cohort into three maniples. Three legions composed the Roman army of occupation in Britain.

Lend-Lease. During the earlier phases of the second world war the bulk of British investments in the USA had to be either sold or pledged to Americans in payment for dollar supplies. After the United States entered the war this drain was stopped and Great Britain met the costs of American consumption in Great Britain, while the United States paid for British supplies from America. This arrangement was abruptly terminated on the ending of hostilities; and Great Britain and other belligerent countries found themselves without means of paying in dollars for indispensable American supplies, including the foodstuffs, materials and capital goods needed for economic reconstruction. In these circumstances Great Britain negotiated with the United States and also with Canada a large loan, which was used for buying dollar supplies and played an inportant part in helping the West European economies to maintain themselves and feed their people while they were carrying through the earlier stages of postwar reconstruction. These loans involved large charges for interest and amortisation in future years, but proved far too small to meet the dollar deficit for more than a short period. In face of this the USA launched the Marshall Plan.

Lettres de Cachet, sealed letters which the kings of France issued to their agents to secure the imprisonment of distrusted or disliked persons without trial. Abolished in 1789.

Levée, a State reception held by the Sovereign or his representative and attended by men only.

Levellers. *See Section J.*

Locarno, Treaty of, 1925, whereby Germany, France and Belgium undertook to maintain their present frontiers and to abstain from the use of force against each other. Hitler broke the pact by re-occupying the Rhineland.

Long Parliament (1640–60), marked the end of Charles I's 11-year attempt to govern without Parliament. It carried through what has come to be called "the English Revolution" and was the parliament of the civil war (1642–49).

Luddites, a combination of workmen formed in 1811, in a period of great distress, with the object of destroying the new textile machinery then being largely adopted, which they regarded as the cause of their troubles. Their first outbreak was at Nottingham, and was stated to have been started by a young apprentice named Ned Ludd.

Afterwards, serious Luddite riots occurred in various parts of the country, especially in West Yorkshire, where many people were killed, mills were destroyed and numbers of rioters were tried and executed. Charlotte Brontë used the period in her novel, *Shirley.*

M

McCarthyism, the term given to the wave of anti-Communist hysteria, associated with the name of Senator McCarthy (1908–57). The campaign lasted from early 1947 to late 1954.

Magna Carta was sealed by King John at Runnymede on 15 June 1215, in obedience to the insistent demands of the barons and has been confirmed many times by later monarchs. It was not a revolutionary document. It laid down what the barons took to be the recognised and fundamental principles for the government of the realm and bound king and barons alike to maintain them. Its main provisions were that no man should be punished without fair trial, that ancient libertics generally should be preserved, and that no demands should be made by an overlord to his vassal (other than those recognised) without the sanction of the great council of the realm.

Mahdi an Arab leader of great influence, invested with powers akin to those of a Messiah in the Mohammedan mind. The title was taken by Mohammed Ahmed, who overran the Egyptian Sudan, and in 1885 captured Khartoum.

Mamluks, commonly known as Mamelukes, were originally—in the 13th cent.—a bodyguard of Turkish and Circassian slaves in the service of the Sultan of Egypt, and attained such influence that in 1250 they were strong enough to appoint one of their own body to the throne of Egypt. After that a succession of Mamluk Sultans reigned down to 1517. Then the Turks annexed Egypt, and the Mamluks were taken into the service of the Beys. They again came to the front after Napoleon's conquest of Egypt, but in 1811 they were massacred by order of Mehemet Ali.

Maquis, name of the dense scrub in Mediterranean France and Corsica, providing good cover for bandits and outlaws. The French resistance movement, 1940-45, adopted the name Maquis.

Marprelate Tracts, seditious pamphlets written with great maliciousness by a group of Elizabethan puritans about 1586, and intended to discredit the episcopacy, caused a great sensation in their time, and led to the execution of their supposed author, John Penry.

Marston Moor. *See A61.*

Martello Towers, circular forts erected on the coasts of England, Ireland and the Channel Isles early in the 19th cent. as defences against the threatened Napoleonic invasion. So called from the circular fort at Mortella (Corsica), which resisted an English sea attack in 1794.

"Mary Rose". *See A61.*

Mau-Mau, a secret, violent, anti-European, movement among the Kikuyu tribe of Kenya, 1953–57. Mau-Mau was a symptom of insecurity and discontent; emergency powers were lifted in 1959, and reforms were instituted. Kenya attained independence in 1963 under Jomo Kenyatta.

"Mayflower", the name of the ship which in 1620 conveyed the Pilgrim Fathers, 101 in number, from England to America. *See Pilgrim Fathers.*

Merovingians, the name given to the family that ruled over France from about 500 to 750. Clovis was first of the line and Childeric the last. The "long-haired kings" have become the centre of much recent speculative history.

Middle Ages (*c.* A.D. 400–1500), usually considered to be the period between the decline and fall of the Western Roman Empire and the fall of Constantinople to the Turks in 1453. The period covers (*a*) an earlier part ending with the 12th cent. (sometimes called the Dark Ages) when science was dead, when theology was the main preoccupation, and when the language of the learned West was Latin; and (*b*) a later age of Arabian influence when alchemy and astrology (at that time indistinguishable from astronomy) were central interests, technology was advancing, and Greek learning was transmitted by Arab scholars.

Characteristic features of the mediaeval scene were monasticism (**Section J**), the Crusades (*q.v.*), Gothic art (*q.v.*), feudalism (**Section J**), and the supremacy of Islam in the field of learning. The period came to an end with the general decline of Christendom and the ushering in of the Renaissance (**Section J**). The term "Middle Ages" was coined by the 17th-cent. German historian Christoph Keller.

Millenary Petition was presented to James I in 1603, on behalf of nearly 1000 Puritan Ministers against certain of the rites and ceremonies of the Church of England. The Hampton Court Conference was the outcome of this petition.

Ming, the dynasty which ruled imperial China from 1368 to 1644 (before the Manchus took power).

Mogul. *See Mughal.*

Monroe Doctrine, a principle of American policy declining any European intervention in political affairs of the American continent, outlined by President Monroe in 1823. At the same time interference was disclaimed with existing European colonies in the Western Hemisphere. The American Civil War hampered the application of the doctrine for some time, but afterwards the United States firmly insisted on it.

Mughal, the dynasty founded by Babur in 1526 which ruled Muslim India until the 18th cent.

Munich Agreement. In September 1938 Mr. Neville Chamberlain and M. Daladier, British and French Premiers, reached agreement with Hitler at Munich for the dismemberment of Czechoslovakia, primarily for the benefit of Germany. Czechoslovakia itself was not consulted, nor Russia. Chamberlain declared on his return that he had secured "Peace in our Time".

N

Nantes, Edict of, was a decree promulgated by Henry IV of France in 1598, giving full freedom of worship to the Protestants of the country. It was the revocation of this edict in 1685 by Louis XIV that drove hundreds of thousands of French Huguenots abroad.

Naseby, Battle of. *See A61.*

National Assembly, the name taken by the body responsible for the opening stages of the French Revolution and subsequently by other sovereign bodies in France and elsewhere.

National Covenant, an oath and declaration subscribed to by the Scottish Presbyterians in 1638 to maintain their religion against Charles I.

NATO, the North Atlantic Treaty Organisation, established 4 April 1949. *See L77.*

Nazi. A member of the *Nationalsozialistische Deutsche Arbeiter Partie* (German National Socialist Workers' Party). The title was adopted by the former German Workers' Party at Munich in October 1920. The party's philosophy was similar to the romantic right-wing authoritarianism of Italian Fascism but after Hitler became leader he imposed his anti-semitic, racialist doctrines. The Nazi party expanded rapidly between 1930–32 due to the mass unemployment of the depression and on 30 January 1933 Hitler became Chancellor. In February 1932 party membership stood at two million. In 1945 the party disintegrated and it was outlawed by the constitution of the German Federal Republic.

New Deal. The measures taken by President Roosevelt in the USA in 1933 to overcome the great economic crisis which broke out at the end of 1929 and to restore the social security threatened by it. The measures were drawn up by a group of experts called a Brains Trust and they provided for recovery by a programme of public works, including large-scale construction of houses and large-scale assistance to farmers. Loans were granted and authorities formed to stimulate activities which reduced the workless from 17 millions to between 7 and 10 millions.

Nuremberg Trial. On 21 November 1945, an International Military Tribunal, consisting of one American, one British, one Russian and one French member, began the trial of twenty-four Nazi leaders. Twelve were condemned to hanging of whom ten were hanged on 16 October 1946. Goering committed suicide; Bormann is now dead; Papen, Schacht and Fritsche were acquitted. The rest received terms of imprisonment.

O

Octarch, the kings of the English heptarchy, Hengist (455) being the first, Egbert (800) the last.

Offa's Dyke. *See* **A61.**

Oléron Laws *or* **Judgments,** were a code of maritime laws, introduced into England in the reign of Richard I in the 12th cent. Oléron is an island off the west coast of France, opposite the mouth of the Charente.

Oriflamme, the name of the original banner of the abbey of St. Denis, and adopted by Louis VI as his standard. It remained the national emblem of France for three centuries. The flag was of red silk, the outer edge being cut in the form of flames.

P

Palatinate, a term formerly applied to two German regions, historically related, the Upper and Lower Palatinates. Now provinces of Bavaria.

Pale, the name given to the part of Ireland colonised by the English and comprising portions of the counties of Louth, Dublin, Meath and Kildare. The Anglo-Norman rulers were styled "Lords of the Pale".

Patricians, the aristocracy of ancient Rome.

Peasants' Revolt, term for the series of uprisings in England in 1381 in protest at the poll tax. In Kent, rebels led by Wat Tyler seized Rochester Castle. They then joined the men of Essex and entered the City of London on 13 June 1381, destroying various properties, including that of John of Gaunt, Duke of Lancaster (1340–99), who was widely blamed for the discontent.

The next day, King Richard II met the Essex bands at Mile End and agreed on a general pardon, the abolition of villeinage and various commercial and economic reforms. Meanwhile the Kentish men had seized the Tower of London and killed Simon Sudbury, Chancellor and Archbishop of Canterbury, and the Treasurer, Sir Robert Hales.

By September the government had recovered control of the country and the promises made by Richard during the crisis were never fulfilled.

Pilgrimage of Grace (1536), the rising in Lincolnshire and Yorkshire in the reign of Henry VIII against religious innovations and the dissolution of the smaller monasteries, which overlapped with discontents caused by taxation, rising prices, enclosures and land speculation. The insurrection was followed by many executions.

Pilgrim Fathers, the 101 English Puritans who,

after living some years in exile in Holland, to escape persecution in their own country, set sail for America in the *Mayflower*, 6 September 1620, landing at Plymouth, Mass., 4 December. They founded the settlement of Plymouth, and are regarded as the pioneers of American colonisation although 13 years earlier a small Virginian colony had been established.

Plantagenets, the kings who reigned in England between 1154 and 1485 and included the Houses of Lancaster and York. More correctly they are styled Angevins, from Anjou, of which Geoffrey, father of Henry II, was Count. His badge was a sprig of broom (*Planta genista*).

Pogrom. Russian word meaning "destruction". First used to describe the Czarist attacks on the Jews in 1881 in Russia. In 1938 Hitler ordered a general pogrom which led on to the holocaust.

Poitiers, Battle of, was fought on 19 September 1356, during the Hundred Years' War, when Edward the Black Prince gained a complete victory over John, King of France, who was taken prisoner and brought to London.

Pontifex, the title assigned in ancient Rome to members of the college of pontifices. "Pontifex maximus" was the official head of Roman religion. It was as "pontifex maximus" that Julius Caesar revised the calendar in 46 B.C., and when after the rise of Christianity the Popes took over the title the revision fell to them.

Potato Famine. Term for the disaster in Ireland in 1845 and 1846 when the failure of the potato crop led to a million deaths from starvation.

Potsdam Agreement was signed by Truman, Stalin and Attlee in August 1945. By this Agreement a Council of Foreign Ministers was established, representing the five principal Powers: China, France, Soviet Russia, the United Kingdom and United States of America, with the task of drawing up the peace treaties for submission to the United Nations. It laid down, *inter alia*, that German militarism and Hitlerism should be destroyed and that industrial power should be reduced. The Potsdam Agreement became a dead letter with the creation of a communist régime in the Russian zone of Germany, and marked the beginning of the "cold war".

Press-Gang, a body of sailors employed to impress men into naval service, frequently resorted to in England, especially during the Napoleonic Wars. Press gangs were not used after about 1850.

Prud'hommes (Prudent Men), **Councils of,** were French trade tribunals, of masters and workmen, formed to decide on disputes. Originally mediaeval, they were revived by Napoleon in 1806, and carried on by the Third Republic.

Q

Quisling, term which came into use during the second world war to denote traitor, collaborator or fifth-columnist. After Vidkun Quisling, who became head of the puppet government after the German invasion of Norway in 1940.

R

Reform Acts. The first was the great Reform Act of 1832, introduced by Lord John Russell and enacted under the Whig administration of Lord Grey. In addition to a sweeping redistribution of seats, this Act greatly extended the franchise but still left many people without the right to vote. The second Act, passed by Disraeli in 1867, by giving the vote to workers in towns, established household suffrage. A third Act, passed in 1884 under a Gladstone ministry, removed the distinction between borough and county franchise and enfranchised agricultural workers, thus giving the vote to all men over 21.

Women had to wait until 1918 to get the vote at the age of 30. The Representation of the People (Equal Franchise) Act, 1928, gave them the right to be registered as Parliamentary electors at the age of 21, thus making England into a true democracy. The Representation of the People Act, 1948, abolished the representation of the universities and the separate representation of the City of London and the business-premises vote. The Representation of the People Act, 1969, reduced the voting age to 18.

Roses, Wars of the (1455–85), between the rival houses of York and Lancaster, for the possession of the English crown, began in the reign of Henry VI and ended with the death of Richard III on Bosworth Field. The emblem or badge of the Lancastrians was the red rose and of the Yorkists the white rose. All rivalry between The Roses ended by the marriage of Henry VII, the Lancastrian, with the Princess Elizabeth, daughter of Edward IV, the Yorkist.

Roundhead. In the reign of Charles I and later, a Puritan or member of the Parliamentary party who wore his hair cut short. It was originally a term of derision applied by the Royalists, who usually wore ringlets. The Royalists were popularly known as Cavaliers.

Round Towers, high circular towers with conical roof and massive masonry walls, built during the early Middle Ages (c. 10th cent.). It is believed that they served as refuges and lookouts. These buildings are numerous in Ireland, and two remain in Scotland, at Brechin, which is attached to the church, and at Abernethy.

S

Salic Law was probably instituted in France in the 5th cent. for the purpose of excluding females from inheriting the Crown. The Bourbons introduced the same law into Spain, but this was abolished by decree in 1830 to enable Isabella II to succeed.

Sans-culottes (French = without knee breeches), a term applied by the aristocrats to the revolutionary leaders during the French Revolution who wore long trousers instead of knee breeches.

Sassanides were a dynasty of Persian rulers descended from Artaxerxes from 226 to 625.

Serfs, the name given to the peasants formerly existing in Russia, who answered to the condition of the feudal "villeins" of England. They were attached to the soil and were transferred with it in all sales or leases. Serfdom existed in Prussia until 1807 and in Russia until 1861.

Settlement, Act of, passed in 1701, assigned the Crown to the House of Hanover in case of Anne's death without children. The decision represented the determination of the squires and the Anglican Church never again to trust themselves to a Roman Catholic king. The ban on Roman Catholics ascending the English throne is now the subject of much debate.

Seven Years War was waged by Frederick the Great and England against Austria, France, and Russia, from 1756 to 1763. It resulted in the retention of Silesia by Prussia, the breaking of French power in India and the strengthening of the British Indian Empire.

Sicilian Vespers, the term applied to the terrible massacre of French people in Sicily in 1282. The French under Charles of Anjou were then in occupation of the island and had been guilty of many cruelties. It began at Palermo on Easter Monday at the hour of vespers and resulted in the expulsion of the French king and the introduction of Spanish rule.

Six Articles, The Statute of the, was passed in 1539 to compel adhesion to Roman Catholicism. Those who refused to subscribe to the Articles were treated as heretics. The Act was repealed in 1547.

South Sea Bubble, the name given to a series of financial projects which began with the formation of the South Sea Company in 1711 and ended nine years later in disaster after a mania of speculation. The idea behind the parent scheme was that the state should sell certain trading monopolies in the South seas in return for a sum of money to pay off the National Debt (which stood at £51,300,000 in 1719 when the scheme started). The idea fascinated the public, fabulous profits being dreamt of, and the price of the stock rose out of all proportion to the earnings of the Company. Many dishonest speculative ventures sprang up in imitation with the inevitable result that thousands were ruined. All classes had joined in the gamble and a Committee of Secrecy set up by the House of Commons in December 1720 to investi-

gate the Company proved that there had been fraud and corruption on a large scale. Sir Robert Walpole dealt with the crisis.

Spanish Armada. *See* Armada.

Spanish Civil War, 1936 to 1939. The war began with a revolt by the Fascist General Franco against the Republic which had succeeded the Monarchy in 1931. Germany and Italy aided the rebels who besieged Madrid for over 2 years. An International Brigade was formed to help the Republic, but the Spanish Government was faced by the greater part of the Army, and very effective assistance from Italy and Germany. Those powers seized the opportunity to have a curtain-raiser to the world conflict which they intended to precipitate. After a total loss of a million men the Fascists overpowered the Republic.

Star Chamber, an ancient tribunal of state in existence in 1487 and possibly earlier, charged with the duty of trying offences against the government, unfettered by the ordinary rules of law. It was in effect a Privy Council entrusted with judicial functions. Under Charles I the Star Chamber was used by the King and his party to persecute opponents; and in 1641 a Bill carried in both Houses abolished it.

States-General, national assembly in which the chief estates of the realm were represented as separate bodies. In France the states-general consisted of three orders, clergy, nobility and commons. Philip IV first summoned it in 1302 to support him in his quarrel with Pope Boniface VIII. While absolute monarchy was establishing itself it met rarely, and not at all from 1614 until 1789, when it was convoked as a last resort by Louis XVI. But when it met it declared itself the National Assembly which marked the beginning of the revolution.

Statute of Westminster, 1931. An Act of parliament which gave a basis of equality to the British Dominions. The Dominions as well as the United Kingdom were defined by the Balfour Memorandum of 1926 as "autonomous communities within the British Empire, equal in status, in no way subordinate one to another in any aspect of their domestic or external affairs, though united by a common allegiance to the Crown, and freely associated as members of the British Commonwealth of Nations". The Statute was the sequel. The Dominions are sovereign States governed solely by their own Parliaments and Governments.

Suffragette, member of the Women's Suffrage Movement who in the early part of the 20th century agitated to obtain the parliamentary vote. The movement ended in 1918, when women of 30 were given the vote. In 1928 a Bill was passed which granted equal suffrage to men and women. The leaders of the Women's Suffrage Movement were Mrs. Pankhurst and her two daughters, Sylvia and Dame Christabel, Mrs. Fawcett, Annie Kenney and others.

T

Taiping Rebellion, 1850–64, most famous of China's many peasant uprisings. It took place in Hunan (the province where Mao Tse-tung was born) and was savagely suppressed with the help of foreign powers.

Tallage, in Norman times, were taxes levied by the Crown upon lands of the royal demesnes. The levying of tallage was taken away in 1340.

Tammany, an organisation founded in New York (c. 1786) and formed from a benevolent society named after an Indian chief. It came to exert a powerful influence over political movements in that city. The leaders of the organisation used their power when their party was successful at the polls to appoint their nominee to every prominent office, and exacted bribes for concessions and privileges, and generally Tammany rule has meant wholesale corruption.

Tiers Etat, the lowest of the three estates of the realm as reckoned in France—nobility, clergy and commons (*tiers état*)—prior to the Revolution.

Tolpuddle Martyrs.. *See* A63.

Trafalgar, Battle of, was fought off Cape Trafalgar on 21 October 1805, between the British under Nelson and the French and Spanish under Villeneuve and

Gravina. It was a complete victory for the British, but Nelson (*see* **B44**) was killed.

Trebuchet. A giant siege engine used in medieval warfare.

Tudor Period extends from 1485 to 1603. The first Tudor sovereign was Henry VII, descended from Owen Tudor; then followed Henry VIII, Edward VI, Mary and Elizabeth, last of the line.

Turnpikes, privately-owned toll roads, run by trustees, which became increasingly common as a means of improving road transport in Britain from the late seventeenth century. Some produced opposition and rioting, though they are considered to have contributed substantially to improving journey times for passengers, mails, and goods.

U

Uhlan, a light cavalry soldier armed with lance, pistol, and sabre and employed chiefly as skirmisher or scout. Marshal Saxe had a corps of them in the French Army; and in the Franco-German war of 1870 the Prussian Uhlans won fame.

Union, Treaty of, was the treaty by which Scotland became formally united to England, the two countries being incorporated as the United Kingdom of Great Britain, the same Parliament to represent both, Scotland electing sixteen peers and forty-five members of the House of Commons. Uniformity of coins, weights, and measures was provided for, Scottish trade laws and customs were assimilated to those of England, and as regards religion and the practices of the law, Scotland was to continue as before. This Act was ratified on 1 May 1707.

V

Versailles, Treaty of. The Peace Treaty, 1919, ending the first world war. The first half was devoted to the organisation of the League of Nations. Among the territorial changes Germany ceded Alsace-Lorraine to France, Posen and the Corridor to Poland. Germany undertook to disarm, to abolish universal military service, to keep only a small army of 100,000 and a small navy. Her colonies were to be shared out among the Allies under League Mandates. Reparations were to be paid, but were gradually reduced and entirely ceased in 1932. Hitler took unilateral action against the Treaty especially in regard to rearmament and the annexation of Austria. Italy also resented the provisions of the Treaty.

Vienna Congress, sat at Vienna from September 1814 to June 1815, and settled the delineation of the territories of the various European nations after the defeat of Napoleon. The Treaty of Vienna which resulted gave Sri Lanka, Mauritius, Cape Colony, Heligoland, Malta and part of Guyana to England; Belgium, Holland and Luxemburg were united in the Kingdom of the Netherlands; Austria took Lombardy-Venetia; Russia took part of Poland; and Prussia, part of Saxony and the Rhenish province. Except for one or two changes the treaty was maintained virtually intact for over forty years.

W

Wapentake, the ancient name given in the northern counties to territorial divisions corresponding to the Hundreds of southern counties.

Warsaw Pact, Eastern European Mutual Assistance Treaty, signed in Warsaw on 14 May 1955 by Albania, Bulgaria, Czechoslovakia, East Germany, Hungary, Poland, Romania and the USSR. A Soviet response to West Germany's joining NATO in October 1954, it reaffirmed the USSR's hold over eastern Europe following agreement to withdraw all occupying forces from Austria. The treaty established a unified command structure controlled from Moscow and obliged all signatories to give armed help to any co-signatory who was attacked. Albania formally withdrew in September 1968. Their only joint military action was the occupation of Czechoslovakia in 1968. With the collapse of communism, the Pact ended on 1 July 1991.

Waterloo, Battle of, was fought on 18 June 1815. The Allies (British, German and Dutch) under Wellington and Blücher defeated the French under Napoleon, ending Napoleon's career.

Witan *or* **Witenagemot,** the name given to the king's council of "wise men" in Anglo-Saxon times, composed of the archbishops, bishops, abbots of the greater abbeys, earldormen and influential thanes.

PART III. SELECTED HISTORICAL TABLES

ENGLISH MONARCHS
(A.D. 827–1603)

Monarch	Accession	Died	Age	Reigned

I.—BEFORE THE CONQUEST.

SAXONS AND DANES

Monarch	Accession	Died	Age	Reigned
Egbert	827	839	—	12
Ethelwulf	839	858	—	19
Ethelbald	858	860	—	2
Ethelbert	858	865	—	7
Ethelred	865	871	—	6
Alfred the Great	871	899	50	28
Edward the Elder	899	924	54	25
Athelstan	924	939	45	15
Edmund	939	946	25	7
Eadred	946	955	32	9
Eadwig	955	959	18	3
Edgar	959	975	32	17
Edward the Martyr	975	978	17	3
Ethelred II ("the Unready")	978	1016	48	37
Edmund Ironside	1016	1016	27	Apr.–Nov.
Canute the Dane	1017	1035	40	18
Harold I	1035	1040	—	5
Hardicanute	1040	1042	24	2
Edward the Confessor	1042	1066	62	24
Harold II	1066	1066	44	Jan.–Oct.

II.—FROM THE CONQUEST TO THE PRESENT DAY.

NORMANS

Monarch	Accession	Died	Age	Reigned
William I	1066	1087	60	21
William II	1087	1100	43	13
Henry I	1100	1135	67	35
Stephen, Count of Blois	1135	1154	50	19

PLANTAGENETS

Monarch	Accession	Died	Age	Reigned
Henry II	1154	1189	56	35
Richard I	1189	1199	42	10
John	1199	1216	50	17
Henry III	1216	1272	65	56
Edward I	1272	1307	68	35
Edward II	1307	dep. 1327	43	20
Edward III	1327	1377	65	50
Richard II	1377	dep. 1399	34	22
Henry IV ⎫	1399	1413	47	13
Henry V ⎬ Lancaster	1413	1422	34	9
Henry VI ⎭	1422	dep. 1461	49	39
Edward IV ⎫	1461	1483	41	22
Edward V ⎬ York	1483	1483	13	Apr.–June
Richard III ⎭	1483	1485	32	2

TUDORS

Monarch	Accession	Died	Age	Reigned
Henry VII	1485	1509	53	24
Henry VIII	1509	1547	56	38
Edward VI	1547	1553	16	6
Jane	1553	1554	17	9 days
Mary I	1553	1558	43	5
Elizabeth I	1558	1603	69	44

THE BRITISH MONARCHY
(1603 to the present day)

Monarch	Accession	Died	Age	Reigned
STUARTS				
James I (VI of Scotland)	1603	1625	59	22
Charles I.	1625	beh. 1649	48	24
COMMONWEALTH DECLARED, MAY 19, 1649				
Oliver Cromwell, Lord Protector . . .	1653–8	—	—	—
Richard Cromwell, Lord Protector . .		1658–9	—	—
STUARTS (RESTORATION)				
Charles II	1660	1685	55	25
James II (VII of Scotland) .	1685	dep. 1688	68	3
Interregnum Dec. 11, 1688 to Feb. 13, 1689				
William III and Mary II	1689	1702	51	13
		1694	33	6
Anne.	1702	1714	49	12
HOUSE OF HANOVER				
George I	1714	1727	67	13
George II	1727	1760	77	33
George III	1760	1820	81	59
George IV	1820	1830	67	10
William IV	1830	1837	71	7
Victoria	1837	1901	81	63
HOUSE OF SAXE-COBURG				
Edward VII	1901	1910	68	9
HOUSE OF WINDSOR				
George V	1910	1936	70	25
Edward VIII	1936	Abd. 1936	77	325 days
George VI	1936	1952	56	15
Elizabeth II	1952			

SCOTTISH MONARCHS
(1034–1603)

Monarch		Accession	Died
Duncan I	Son of Malcolm II	1034	1040
Macbeth	Slew Duncan in 1040	1040	1057
Malcolm III (Canmore)	Son of Duncan I	1058	1093
Donald Ban	Brother of Malcolm Canmore	1093	—
Duncan II	Son of Malcom Canmore, by first marriage	1094	1094
Donald Ban	Restored	1094	1097
Edgar	Son of Malcolm Canmore, by second marriage	1097	1107
Alexander I	Son of Malcolm Canmore	1107	1124
David I	Son of Malcolm Canmore	1124	1153
Malcolm IV (the Maiden)	Son of Henry, eldest son of David I	1153	1165
William I (the Lion)	Brother of Malcolm the Maiden	1165	1214
Alexander II	Son of William the Lion	1214	1249
Alexander III	Son of Alexander II, by second marriage	1249	1286
Margaret, Maid of Norway	Daughter of Eric II of Norway, granddaughter of Alexander III	1286	1290
John Baliol	Grandson of eldest daughter of David, Earl of Huntingdon, brother of William the Lion	1292	1296
Robert I (Bruce)	Great-grandson of 2nd daughter of David, Earl of Huntingdon, brother of William the Lion	1306	1329
David II	Son of Robert I, by second marriage	1329	1371
Robert II (Stewart)	Son of Marjorie, daughter of Robert I by first marriage, and Walter the Steward	1371	1390
Robert III	(John, Earl of Carrick) son of Robert II	1390	1406
James I	Son of Robert III	1406	1437
James II	Son of James I	1437	1460
James III	Eldest son of James II	1460	1488
James IV	Eldest son of James III	1488	1513
James V	Son of James IV	1513	1542
Mary	Daughter of James V, by second marriage	1542	1587
James VI (ascended the Throne of England 1603)	Son of Mary, by second marriage	1567	1625

BRITISH PRIME MINISTERS

	Party	Served		Party	Served
George II, 1727–60			B. Disraeli	Conservative	1868
Sir Robert Walpole	Whig	1721–42	W. E. Gladstone	Liberal	1868–74
Earl of Wilmington	Whig	1742–3	B. Disraeli	Conservative	1874–80
Henry Pelham	Whig	1743–54	W. E. Gladstone	Liberal	1880–5
Duke of Newcastle	Whig	1754–6	Marquis of Salisbury	Conservative	1885–6
Duke of Devonshire	Whig	1756–7	W. E. Gladstone	Liberal	1886
Duke of Newcastle	Whig	1757–60	Marquis of Salisbury	Conservative	1886–92
			W. E. Gladstone	Liberal	1892–4
George III, 1760–1820			Earl of Rosebery	Liberal	1894–5
Duke of Newcastle	Whig	1760–2	Marquis of Salisbury	Conservative	1895–1901
Earl of Bute	Tory	1762–3			
George Grenville	Whig	1763–5	**Edward VII, 1901–10**		
Marquis of Rocking-	Whig	1766	Marquis of Salisbury	Conservative	1901–2
ham			A. J. Balfour	Conservative	1902–5
Earl of Chatham	Tory	1766–8	Sir H. Campbell-	Liberal	1905–8
Duke of Grafton	Whig	1766–9	Bannerman		
Lord North	Tory	1770–82	H. H. Asquith	Liberal	1908–10
Marquis of Rocking-	Whig	1782			
ham			**George V, 1910–36**		
Earl of Shelburne	Whig	1782–3	H. H. Asquith	Liberal	1910–15
Duke of Portland	Coalition	1783	H. H. Asquith	Coalition	1915–16
William Pitt	Tory	1783–1801	D. Lloyd George	Coalition	1916–22
Viscount Sidmouth	Tory	1801–4	A. Bonar Law	Conservative	1922–3
William Pitt	Tory	1804–6	S. Baldwin	Conservative	1923–4
Lord Grenville	Whig	1806–7	J. R. MacDonald	Labour	1924
Duke of Portland	Tory	1807–9	S. Baldwin	Conservative	1924–9
Spencer Perceval	Tory	1809–12	J. R. MacDonald	Labour	1929–31
			J. R. MacDonald	National	1931–5
George IV, 1820–30			S. Baldwin	National	1935–6
Earl of Liverpool	Tory	1812–27	**Edward VIII, 1936**		
George Canning	Tory	1827	**George VI, 1936–52**		
Viscount Goderich	Tory	1827			
Duke of Wellington	Tory	1827–30	S. Baldwin	National	1936–7
			N. Chamberlain	National	1937–39
William IV, 1830–7			N. Chamberlain	War Cabinet	1939
Earl Grey	Whig	1830–4	W. S. Churchill	War Cabinet	1940–45
Viscount Melbourne	Whig	1834	W. S. Churchill	Caretaker	1945
Sir Robert Peel	Tory	1834–5	C. R. Attlee	Labour	1945–51
Viscount Melbourne	Whig	1835–7	Sir W. S. Churchill	Conservative	1951–2
Victoria, 1837–1901			**Elizabeth II, 1952–**		
Viscount Melbourne	Whig	1837–41	Sir W. S. Churchill	Conservative	1952–5
Sir Robert Peel	Tory	1841–6	Sir A. Eden	Conservative	1955–7
Lord John Russell	Whig	1846–52	H. Macmillan	Conservative	1957–63
Earl of Derby	Tory	1852	Sir A. Douglas-Home	Conservative	1963–4
Earl of Aberdeen	Peelite	1852–5	H. Wilson	Labour	1964–70
Viscount Palmerston	Liberal	1855–8	E. Heath	Conservative	1970–4
Earl of Derby	Tory	1858–9	H. Wilson	Labour	1974–6
Viscount Palmerston	Liberal	1859–65	J. Callaghan	Labour	1976–9
Earl Russell	Liberal	1865–6	Mrs. M. Thatcher	Conservative	1979–90
Earl of Derby	Conservative	1866–8	J. Major	Conservative	1990–97
			A. Blair	Labour	1997–

PRESIDENTS OF THE UNITED STATES

The terms are for four years; only President F. D. Roosevelt
has served more than two terms.

	Party	Served		Party	Served
1. George Washington	Fed.	1789–97	23. Benjamin Harrison	Rep.	1889–93
2. John Adams	Fed.	1797–1801	24. Grover Cleveland	Dem.	1893–7
3. Thomas Jefferson	Rep.	1801–9	25. William McKinley*	Rep.	1897–1901
4. James Madison	Rep.	1809–17	26. Theodore Roosevelt	Rep.	1901–9
5. James Monroe	Rep.	1817–25	27. William Howard Taft	Rep.	1909–13
6. John Quincey Adams	Rep.	1825–9	28. Woodrow Wilson	Dem.	1913–21
7. Andrew Jackson	Dem.	1829–37	29. Warren G. Harding	Rep.	1921–3
8. Martin Van Buren	Dem.	1837–41	(died in office)		
9. William H. Harrison	Whig	1841	30. Calvin Coolidge	Rep.	1923–9
(died in office)			31. Herbert C. Hoover	Rep.	1929–33
10. John Tyler	Whig	1841–5	32. Franklin D. Roosevelt	Dem.	1933–45
11. James K. Polk	Dem.	1845–9	(died in office)		
12. Zachary Taylor	Whig	1849–50	33. Harry S. Truman	Dem.	1945–53
(died in office)			34. Dwight D. Eisenhower	Rep.	1953–61
13. Millard Fillmore	Whig	1850–3	35. John F. Kennedy*	Dem.	1961–3
14. Franklin Pierce	Dem.	1853–7	36. Lyndon B. Johnson	Dem.	1963–9
15. James Buchanan	Dem.	1857–61	37. Richard M. Nixon	Rep.	1969–74
16. Abraham Lincoln*	Rep.	1861–5	(resigned)		
17. Andrew Johnson	Dem.	1865–9	38. Gerald R. Ford	Rep.	1974–7
18. Ulysses S. Grant	Rep.	1869–77	39. James Carter	Dem.	1977–81
19. Rutherford B. Hayes	Rep.	1877–81	40. Ronald Reagan	Rep.	1981–9
20. James A. Garfield*	Rep.	1881	41. George Bush	Rep.	1989–93
21. Chester A. Arthur	Rep.	1881–5	42. William J. Clinton	Dem.	1993–2001
22. Grover Cleveland	Dem.	1885–9	43. George W. Bush**	Rep.	2001–

*Assassinated; **Re-elected, November 2004.

RULERS OF THE ROMAN WORLD
(from 753 B.C. to 363 A.D.)

The Kingdom

753	Romulus (Quirinus)
716	Numa Pompilius
673	Tullus Hostilius
640	Ancus Marcius
616	L. Tarquinius Priscus
578	Servius Tullius
534	L. Tarquinius Superbus

The Republic

509	Consulate established
509	Quaestorship instituted
498	Dictatorship introduced
494	Plebeian Tribunate created
494	Plebeian Aedileship created
444	Consular Tribunate organized
435	Censorship instituted
366	Praetorship established
366	Curule Aedileship created
362	Military Tribunate elected
326	Proconsulate introduced
311	Naval Duumvirate elected
217	Dictatorship of Fabius Maximus
133	Tribunate of Tiberius Gracchus
123	Tribunate of Gaius Gracchus
82	Dictatorship of Sulla
60	First Triumvirate formed (Caesar, Pompeius, Crassus)
46	Dictatorship of Caesar
43	Second Triumvirate formed (Octavianus, Antonius, Lepidus)

The Empire

27	Augustus (Galus Julius Caesar Octavianus)
14	Tiberius I
37	Gaius Caesar (Caligula)
41	Claudius I
54	Nero
68	Galba
69	Galba; Otho, Vitellius
69	Vespasianus
79	Titus
81	Domitianus

96	Nerva
98	Trajanus
117	Hadrianus
138	Antoninus Pius
161	Marcus Aurelius and Lucius Verus
169	Marcus Aurelius (alone)
180	Commodus
193	Pertinax; Julianus I
193	Septimius Severus
211	Caracalla and Geta
212	Caracalla (alone)
217	Macrinus
218	Elagabalus (Heliogabalus)
222	Alexander Severus
235	Maximinus I (the Thracian)
238	Gordianus I and Gordianus II; Pupienus and Balbinus
238	Gordianus III
244	Philippus (the Arabian)
249	Decius
251	Gallus and Volusianus
253	Aemilianus
253	Valerianus and Gallienus
258	Gallienus (alone)
268	Claudius II (the Goth)
270	Quintillus
270	Aurelianus
275	Tacitus
276	Florianus
276	Probus
282	Carus
283	Carinus and Numerianus
284	Diocletianus
286	Diocletianus and Maximianus
305	Galerius and Constantius I
306	Galerius, Maximinus II, Severus I
307	Galerius, Maximinus II, Constantinus I, Licinius, Maxentius
311	Maximinus II, Constantinus I, Licinius, Maxentius
314	Maximinus II, Constantinus I, Licinius
314	Constantinus I and Licinius
324	Constantinus I (the Great)
337	Constantinus II, Constans I, Constantius II
340	Constantius II and Constans I
361	Julianus II (the Apostate)
363	Jovianus

Note: In 364 the Empire was divided between the brothers Valentinian (in the West) and Valens (East).

MAJOR PLACE NAMES OF ROMAN BRITAIN

Andover	Levcomagus	Gloucester	Glevum
Bath	Aquae Sulis	Ilchester	Lindinus
Cambridge	Durolipons	Leicester	Ratae Coritanorum
Caernarvon	Segontium	Lincoln	Lindum
Canterbury	Durovernum	London	Londinium
Carlisle	Luguvalium	Manchester	Mamucium
Carmarthen	Moridunum	Northwich	Condate
Catterick	Cataractonium	Pevensey	Anderita
Chelmsford	Caesaromagus	Richborough	Rutupiae
Chester	Deva	Rochester	Durobrivae
Chichester	Noviomagus Regnensium	St. Albans	Verulamium
Cirencester	Corinium Dobunnorum	Silchester	Calleva Atrebatum
Colchester	Camulodunum	South Shields	Caer Urfa
Doncaster	Danum	Towcester	Lactodorum
Dorchester	Durnovaria	Wight, I. of	Vectis
Dover	Portus Dubris	Winchester	Venta Belgarum
Dunstable	Durocobrivae	Wroxeter	Viroconium Cornoviorum
Exeter	Isca Dumnoniorum	York	Eboracum

POPES
(Since 1800)

Pius VII	1800	Pius XI	1922
Leo XII	1823	Pius XII	1939
Pius VIII	1829	John XXIII	1958
Gregory XVI	1831	Paul VI	1963
Pius IX	1846	John Paul I	1978
Leo XIII	1878	John Paul II	1978
St. Pius X	1903	Benedict XVI	2005
Benedict XV	1914		

ARCHBISHOPS OF CANTERBURY
(Since the Reformation)

1533	Thomas Cranmer	1768	Hon. Frederick Cornwallis
1556	Reginald Pole	1783	John Moore
1559	Matthew Parker	1805	Charles Manners Sutton
1576	Edmund Grindal	1828	William Howley
1583	John Whitgift	1848	John Bird Sumner
1604	Richard Bancroft	1862	Charles Thomas Longley
1611	George Abbot	1868	Archibald Campbell Tait
1633	William Laud	1883	Edward White Benson
1660	William Juxon	1896	Frederick Temple
1663	Gilbert Sheldon	1903	Randall Thomas Davidson
1678	William Sancroft	1928	Cosmo Gordon Lang
1691	John Tillotson	1942	William Temple
1695	Thomas Tenison	1945	Geoffrey Francis Fisher
1716	William Wake	1961	Arthur Michael Ramsey
1737	John Potter	1974	Frederick Donald Coggan
1747	Thomas Herring	1980	Robert Runcie
1757	Matthew Hutton	1991	George Carey
1758	Thomas Secker	2002	Rowan Williams

ARCHBISHOPS OF YORK
(Since 1900)

1891	William Maclagan	1961	Donald Coggan
1909	Cosmo Gordon Lang	1975	Stuart Blanch
1929	William Temple	1983	John Habgood
1942	Cyril Garbett	1995	David Hope
1956	Arthur Michael Ramsey	2005	John Sentamu

ARMED FORCES: TRADITIONAL RANKS

The table below gives comparative rankings in the British armed forces. Radical plans to cut the number of ranks in the armed forces, put forward in a report by Sir Michael Bett in April 1995, were abandoned in 1996. The only proposal so far approved is to abolish the five star ranks – those of Admiral of the Fleet, Field Marshal and Marshal of the Royal Air Force.

Royal Navy	*Army*	*Royal Air Force*
1 Admiral of the Fleet	1 Field Marshal	1 Marshal of the RAF
2 Admiral	2 General	2 Air Chief Marshal
3 Vice-Admiral	3 Lieutenant-General	3 Air Marshal
4 Rear-Admiral	4 Major-General	4 Air Vice-Marshal
5 Commodore (1st & 2nd class)	5 Brigadier	5 Air Commodore
6 Captain	6 Colonel	6 Group Captain
7 Commander	7 Lieutenant-Colonel	7 Wing Commander
8 Lieutenant-Commander	8 Major	8 Squadron Leader
9 Lieutenant	9 Captain	9 Flight Lieutenant
10 Sub-Lieutenant	10 Lieutenant	10 Flying Officer
11 Acting Sub-Lieutenant	11 Second Lieutenant	11 Pilot Officer

THE BRITISH COMMONWEALTH

The Commonwealth of Nations is a free association of independent member nations and their dependencies. A short note on its evolution can be found on L18.

Country	Capital	Status	Joined
1. Antigua and Barbuda	St. John's	M	1981
2. Australia	Canberra	M	1931
3. The Bahamas	Nassau	M	1973
4. Bangladesh	Dhaka	R	1972
5. Barbados	Bridgetown	M	1966
6. Belize	Belmopen	M	1981
7. Botswana	Gaborone	R	1966
8. Brunei	Bandar Seri Begawan	M*	1984
9. Cameroon	Yaoundé	R	1995
10. Canada	Ottawa	M	1931
11. Cyprus	Nicosia	R	1961
12. Dominica	Roseau	R	1978
13. Fiji	Suva	R	1970
14. The Gambia	Banjul	R	1965
15. Ghana	Accra	R	1957
16. Grenada	St. George's	M	1974
17. Guyana	Georgetown	R	1966
18. India	New Delhi	R	1947
19. Jamaica	Kingston	M	1962
20. Kenya	Nairobi	R	1963
21. Kiribati	Tarawa	R	1979
22. Lesotho	Maseru	M*	1966
23. Malawi	Lilongwe	R	1964
24. Malaysia	Kuala Lumpur	M*	1957
25. Maldives	Male	R	1982
26. Malta	Valletta	R	1964
27. Mauritius	Port Louis	R	1968
28. Mozambique	Maputo	R	1995
29. Namibia	Windhoek	R	1990
30. Nauru	Nauru	R	1968
31. New Zealand	Wellington	M	1931
32. Nigeria	Abuja	R	1960†
33. Pakistan	Islamabad	R	1947*
34. Papua New Guinea	Port Moresby	M	1975
35. St. Kitts and Nevis	Basseterre	M	1983
36. St. Lucia	Castries	M	1979
37. St. Vincent and the Grenadines	Kingstown	M	1979
38. Samoa	Apia	M*	1970
39. Seychelles	Victoria	R	1976
40. Sierra Leone	Freetown	R	1961
41. Singapore	Singapore	R	1965
42. Solomon Islands	Honiara	M	1978
43. South Africa	Pretoria	R	1931**
44. Sri Lanka	Colombo	R	1948
45. Swaziland	Mbabane	M*	1968
46. Tanzania	Dodoma	R	1961
47. Tonga	Nuku'Alofa	M*	1970
48. Trinidad and Tobago	Port of Spain	R	1962
49. Tuvalu	Funafuti	M	1978(S)
50. Uganda	Kampala	R	1962
51. United Kingdom	London	M	1931
52. Vanuatu	Port Vila	R	1980
53. Zambia	Lusaka	R	1964
(Zimbabwe	Harare	R	1980)††

M = Monarchy under Queen Elizabeth, represented by Governor-General (except UK).
M* = Country with its own monarchy. Brunei is a Sultanate.
R = Republic.
(S) = Special Member.
* = Pakistan left in 1972, rejoining in 1989. It was suspended from 1999 to 2004.
** = South Africa left in 1961, rejoining in 1994.
† = Membership suspended from 1995 to 1999.
†† = Zimbabwe left the Commonwealth in 2003.

United Kingdom Overseas Territories

Anguilla
Bermuda
British Antarctic Territory
British Indian Ocean Territory
British Virgin Isles
Cayman Islands

Falkland Islands and Dependencies
(South Georgia, South Sandwich Islands)
Gibraltar
Montserrat
Pitcairn Islands Group
St. Helena and Dependencies (Ascension, Tristan da Cunha)
Turks and Caicos Islands

Territories of Member Countries

Australia Norfolk Island, Heard Island, McDonald Island, Cocos (Keeling) Islands, Christmas Island, Asmore and Cartier Islands, Coral Sea Islands   *New Zealand* Cook Islands, Niue, Tokelau Islands

The Channel Islands and the Isle of Man are dependent territories of the crown and do not form part of the United Kingdom. They have their own legislative assemblies and legal and administrative systems.

PART IV. HISTORICAL GUIDE TO BRITAIN

This new section in *Pears* provides a wide-ranging guide to a selection of places to visit relating to interesting people, events and developments in British history. The references at the end of each entry will provide more information about visiting a site: location, opening times, *etc*. The website addresses of the following organisations, which appear frequently in the text, are: National Trust – www.nationaltrust.org.uk; English Heritage – www.english-heritage.org.uk; National Trust for Scotland – www.nts.org.uk; Historic Scotland – www.historic-scotland.gov.uk; CADW: Welsh Historic Monuments – www.cadw.wales.gov.uk

A

Abbey Road, London NW8. A road in St John's Wood where EMI opened the first purpose-built recording studios in 1931. In the 1960s The Beatles made many hit records there and put it on the map in 1969 by calling the last album they recorded as a group *Abbey Road*. The pedestrian crossing that features on the album cover is just outside the studios. The studios opened to the public for the first time for a festival of films scored at Abbey Road in spring 2005. (www.abbeyroad.co.uk)

Abbotsford, Borders. Scottish baronial-style house on the River Tweed near Melrose, completed in 1824 for the novelist and poet, Sir Walter Scott. His study and library, containing some 9,000 rare books, are particularly atmospheric. (www.scottsabbotsford.co.uk) Scott is also commemorated by the Scott Monument, a Gothic spire designed by George Meikle Kemp, with a statue of Scott by Sir John Steell. It was inaugurated in 1846 in East Princes Street Gardens, Edinburgh. There are 287 steps to the top.

Alnwick Castle, Northumberland. Home of the Percy family, the Earls and Dukes of Northumberland, since 1309. Known as 'the Windsor of the North', it features as Hogwarts school in the Harry Potter films. (www.alnwickcastle.com) New gardens, created by the Duchess of Northumberland, containing features such as the impressive Grand Cascade, were opened in 2002. (www.alnwickgarden.com)

Althorp, Northamptonshire. Home of the Spencer family for more than 500 years. In 1997 a small island in the middle of the 'Round Oval' lake at Althorp was chosen as the final resting place of Diana, Princess of Wales, by her brother, Earl Spencer. There is an exhibition in the stable block commemorating her life and also her work. (www.althorp.com)

Antonine Wall, Falkirk. Roman defensive works, stretching 60 kms from the Clyde to the Firth of Forth, were begun in A.D. 142, in the reign of Emperor Antoninus Pius. The wall consisted of a turf rampart on stone foundations, with a timber palisade on top, a wide ditch in front and a Military Way running behind. By A.D. 180 the Romans had withdrawn to Hadrian's Wall. The best-preserved sections of ditch and rampart, together with the earthworks of Rough Castle fort, can be seen west from Falkirk, around Bonnybridge. (Historic Scotland)

Apsley House, London W1. The London residence of the Duke of Wellington at Hyde Park Corner ('Number 1, London'). The house contains many trophies of his military and political career. (English Heritage) Wellington is also associated with Stratfield Saye House and Walmer Castle, *see below*.

Avebury Stone Circles, Wiltshire. The principal circle, the largest in the world, dates from around 2500 B.C., and originally had 98 standing stones (only 27 now remain). With its surrounding ditch and outer bank, it covers 12 hectares. In 1986 Avebury was designated part of a UNESCO World Heritage Site, together with Stonehenge. There is a museum, named after Alexander Keiller who investigated the site in the 1930s. (National Trust)

B

Badbury Rings, Dorset. An Iron Age hill fort near Wimborne Minster, acquired by the National Trust in 1982. It consists of three concentric earth ramparts, enclosing an area planted with trees in the 18th century. It is one of the sites suggested for the battle of Mount Badon in the early 6th century when the Britons under Arthur won a great victory over the Saxons. (National Trust)

Balmoral Castle, Aberdeenshire. The estate was purchased by Prince Albert for Queen Victoria in 1852, and the new house was built in the Scottish baronial style in 1853–56. Since then it has been 'a favourite home to successive generations of the Royal Family.' The grounds and the largest room in the castle, the ballroom, are open to the public. (www.balmoralcastle.com)

Bannockburn, Stirling. Site of the battle on 24 June 1314 when King Edward II's army, attempting to relieve Stirling Castle, was heavily defeated by the Scots under Robert the Bruce. The traditional location of Robert the Bruce's command post is marked by the Borestone and a bronze equestrian statue of the Scottish King by Pilkington Jackson, unveiled in 1964. There is a Heritage Centre. (National Trust for Scotland)

Banqueting House, London SW1. All that remains of the great Whitehall Palace, destroyed by fire in 1698. It was designed by Inigo Jones and completed in 1622. The magnificent ceiling paintings were added by Rubens in the 1630s. In 1649 King Charles I was executed on a platform in front of the building. (www.banqueting-house.org.uk)

Barnet, Greater London. The battle of Barnet in the Wars of the Roses took place at Monken Hadley, just to the north of Barnet, on 14 April 1471. The Yorkists defeated the Lancastrians. The stone obelisk beside the A1000 road was erected in 1740, according to the inscription it marks the site of the battle where the Lancastrian leader, Warwick the Kingmaker, 'was defeated and slain.' (www.btlse.co.uk)

Bath, Bath & NE Somerset. Bath is an historical *tour de force* with the remains of the baths of Roman Aquae Sulis, the Abbey – the 'Lantern of the West' – and the magnificent architecture of the Georgian spa town. UNESCO recognised the city as a whole as a World Heritage Site in 1987. (www.visitbath.co.uk)

Battle Abbey, East Sussex. This was the site, about 10 kms north-west of Hastings, where Duke William's invading Norman army defeated King Harold's Anglo-Saxons on 14 October 1066. William founded Battle Abbey in 1070 to atone for the loss of life during his conquest of England. (English Heritage)

Beaulieu Abbey, Hampshire. A Cistercian Abbey was founded here in 1204. The Great Gatehouse became the home of the Montagu Family – Palace House – in 1538 after the Dissolution. In the grounds of Beaulieu Abbey one of the most influential features of life in the 20th century – the motorcar – is celebrated in the National Motor Museum, which opened to the public in 1972. (www.beaulieu.co.uk)

Beaumaris Castle, Isle of Anglesey. Construction of this, the last of King Edward I's Welsh castles, began in 1295. Not as impressive as Caernarvon or Harlech when viewed from a distance, it is probably the strongest and best-preserved concentric castle in Britain. It is one of the components of the Edwardian castles and town walls World Heritage Site, listed by UNESCO in 1987. (CADW)

Belfast, HMS, London SE1. The last survivor of the Royal Navy's heavy cruisers is moored by Tower Bridge and preserved as part of the Imperial War Museum. She was launched in 1938, and took part in convoy work, the battle of North Cape and the D-Day bombardment of Normandy. Exploring HMS *Belfast* gives an insight into what life was like in a great warship during the Second World War. (www.hmsbelfast.org.uk)

Berkeley Castle, Gloucestershire. A 12th-century castle that has been home to the Berkeley family since 1153. It is best known for the brutal murder of Edward II in 1327, and visitors can see the King's place of imprisonment. According to *1066 and All That*, 'horrible screams' were heard from the castle and the next day Edward was 'horribly dead'. (www.berkeley-castle.com)

Bignor Roman Villa, West Sussex. The villa, which lay close to Roman Stane Street, was discovered by a farmer ploughing his land in 1811. It was occupied from the 2nd to the 4th century, and was one of the largest in Britain, covering two hectares. It has some exceptional mosaics, including one that runs for 24 metres in all and is thought to be the longest in the country. (www.romansinsussex.co.uk)

Bladon, Oxfordshire. When Sir Winston Churchill died in 1965 he was buried with his parents in the churchyard of St Martin's, Bladon, on the south side of Blenheim Park. When Lady Churchill died in 1977, she was buried beside him. (www.blenheimpalace.com)

Blaenavon, Torfaen. This Welsh town was designated a World Heritage Site by UNESCO in 2000 on the grounds that it constituted an 'outstanding and remarkably complete example of a 19th century industrial landscape.' Centrepiece of this landscape today is the Big Pit colliery. It closed in 1980 and is now the National Mining Museum of Wales. Visitors can descend the 86 metres to the pit floor and be given a guided tour by a former miner. (www.nmgw.ac.uk)

Blenheim Palace, Oxfordshire. Home of the Dukes of Marlborough, and birthplace of Sir Winston Churchill in 1874. It was designed by Sir John Vanbrugh and presented to the first Duke to mark his victory over the French and Bavarians at Blenheim in 1704. The tapestries depicting Marlborough's victories are an outstanding exhibit. The Palace was designated a UNESCO World Heritage Site in 1987. (www.blenheimpalace.com)

Bletchley Park, Milton Keynes. Home of the Government Code and Cipher School in the Second World War and the 'birthplace of modern computing.' The team at Bletchley, including men such as Alan Turing, broke the German 'Enigma' machine ciphers and produced the top secret 'Ultra' information that helped to win the war. The whole operation remained secret until the 1970s. The Bletchley Park Trust was formed in 1992 and the site opened as a museum in 1994. (www.bletchleypark.org.uk)

Bodiam Castle, East Sussex. The castle was built by Sir Edward Dallingrigge in 1385 to defend the area against French raiders. It was bought by Lord Curzon in 1917, restored and given to the National Trust. Today, as the handbook says, it is 'the perfect example of a late-medieval moated castle.' (National Trust)

Boscobel House, Shropshire. The future King Charles II hid here, famously spending the day up an oak tree, after his defeat at the battle of Worcester in 1651. (English Heritage) Another of the royal fugitive's hiding places was a priest's hole at Moseley Old Hall, which was acquired by the National Trust in 1962.

Bosworth Field, Leicestershire. King Richard III was defeated and killed here by Henry Tudor on 22 August 1485, gaining the distinction of being the last English king to die leading his soldiers into battle. There is a Visitor Centre and battlefield trail on the site, which is run by Leicestershire County Council. On the website there is interesting material about the continuing debate over whether the battle actually took place somewhere else. (www.leics.gov.uk/country-parks-bosworth)

Brading Roman Villa, Isle of Wight. A 3rd century Roman villa, once at the heart of a prosperous farming estate. Discovered in 1879, it has some fine mosaics, including a head of Medusa surrounded by other classical mythological figures. (www.bradingromanvilla.org.uk)

Brantwood, Cumbria. The Victorian writer and artist, John Ruskin, lived in this house from 1872 to 1900. It lies on the eastern side of Coniston Water, and contains some of Ruskin's paintings, furniture and books. (www.brantwood.org.uk)

Bristol Temple Meads, City of Bristol. When Isambard Kingdom Brunel (*q.v.*) designed the Old Station at Temple Meads for the Great Western Railway in 1839, it was one of the first main line railway termini to be built in Britain. It remained in use until the 1960s. It is now a Grade I listed building, and since 2002 it has been the home of the British Empire and Commonwealth Museum. (www.empiremuseum.co.uk)

Broadlands, Hampshire. An elegant Palladian mansion on the banks of the River Test, which was the birthplace and home of the Victorian Prime Minister, Lord Palmerston. The house is particularly associated with a later resident, Lord Mountbatten. He opened the house to the public in 1979, only months before he was assassinated by the IRA. There is an exhibition telling the story of Mountbatten's career. (www.broadlands.net)

Brooklands, Surrey. The birthplace of British motorsport and aviation. The world's first motor-racing circuit was built here in 1907. Today many of the original buildings and the race-track form part of a museum, which has a fine collection of historic vehicles *etc*. (www.brooklandsmuseum.co)

Brownsea Island, Dorset. In 1907 Robert Baden-Powell held a camp on the island from which developed the Scouting and Guiding movement. The island is located in Poole Harbour and was acquired by the National Trust in 1962. Part of the island is leased to the Dorset Wildlife Trust as a nature reserve. (National Trust)

Buckingham Palace. *See* Section L.

Burghley House, Lincolnshire. The house was completed in 1587 for Sir William Cecil, later Lord Burghley, principal adviser and Lord High Treasurer to Queen Elizabeth I. The house has a large collection of art, porcelain and furniture. The 120-hectare deer park was landscaped by Capability Brown. Burghley is near the attractive old town of Stamford. (www.burghley.co.uk)

C

Cabinet War Rooms, London SW1. Work began in 1938 on creating emergency underground accommodation beneath government offices in Whitehall in anticipation of enemy bombing raids on London. Today visitors can see what became the nerve centre of the war effort during the Second World War, including the Map Room, Cabinet Room and also Churchill's bedroom. A fascinating Churchill Museum opened in 2005. (www.iwm.org.uk)

Cadbury Castle, Somerset. An Iron Age hill fort with massive earth ramparts covering 7 hectares. It is one of the leading candidates for the historical site of Arthur's headquarters, 'Camelot'. Extensive archaeological excavations in the 1960s showed that the site had been re-fortified in the Arthurian period, and revealed the remains of a large feasting hall. The site is known to have been a royal mint in the time of Aethelred the Unready. (www.time-scapes.co.uk)

Caerleon, Newport. Known to the Romans as Isca Silurum, this was an important Roman military base and headquarters of the 2nd Legion Augusta from A.D. 75 to 300. There are baths, a well-preserved amphitheatre and barrack blocks. (CADW). There is a Roman Legionary Museum. (www.nmgw.ac.uk)

Caernarvon Castle, Gwynedd. Work on the most impressive and costliest of Edward I's castles began in 1283 and continued for fifty years. The unusual polygonal towers, particularly the Eagle Tower, and the bands of coloured stone are said to have been inspired by Constantinople. Edward I created his son Prince of Wales here in 1301; the investiture of Prince Charles took place in 1969. It has formed part of a UNESCO World Heritage Site since 1987. (CADW)

Caerphilly Castle, Caerphilly. The castle's land and water defences cover some 12 hectares, making it the second largest castle in Britain after Windsor Castle. It was begun in 1268 by the King's son-in-law, Gilbert de Clare, and was one of the first concentric castles in the country. (CADW)

Cambridge University. *See* Section L.

Canterbury Cathedral. Kent. The Cathedral was founded by St Augustine, who arrived in Kent in A.D. 597 to convert the people to Christianity. Archbishop Lanfranc began building the present Cathedral in 1070. It became a place of pilgrimage after the murder of Archbishop Thomas Becket in 1170. The central tower, called Bell Harry Tower, dates from the late 15th century. In 1988 the Cathedral, together with the remains of St Augustine's Abbey and St Martin's Church, the oldest church in England still in use, were designated a World Heritage Site by UNESCO. (www.canterbury-cathedral.org)

Carisbrooke Castle, Isle of Wight. A castle with fortifications of many periods, ranging from the Norman motte surmounted by a 12th century shell keep, to the late 16th century artillery bastions. Charles I was held prisoner here in 1647–48. The original window that proved too narrow and foiled one of his escape attempts was replaced in the 19th century. (English Heritage)

Castle Howard, North Yorkshire. The house was constructed mainly between 1701 and 1712 for Charles Howard, 3rd Earl of Carlisle. It was the first building designed by playwright Sir John Vanbrugh, who went on to design Blenheim Palace. The façade is dominated by the dome, restored after a disastrous fire in 1940. There is an arboretum, called 'Kew at Castle Howard'; it opened to the public in 1999, and is a joint venture with the Royal Botanic Gardens at Kew. (www.castlehoward.co.uk)

Castlerigg Stone Circle, Cumbria. Near Keswick, this is thought to be one of the earliest stone circles in Britain. There are 38 stones in the circle, and a rectangle of 10 stones within it. The antiquarian, William Stukeley, popularised the linking of it with the Druids in the 18th century. John Keats visited the Circle in 1818, and in his poem *Hyperion* referred to it as 'a dismal cirque of Druid stones upon a forlorn moor.' (National Trust)

Chartwell, Kent. Sir Winston Churchill bought the house in 1922, and it was his family home until his death in 1965. The National Trust, which acquired the house in 1946, has left the interior and the gardens much as they were in Churchill's day. Many of Churchill's paintings and the brick walls he built himself can be seen. (National Trust)

Chatham Historic Dockyard, Kent. This was the site of an important Royal Dockyard on the River Medway from 1613 up to its closure in 1984. It covered 32 hectares and is said to be the most complete dockyard from the age of sail in the world. Over 400 Royal Navy ships were built there, including HMS *Victory*. Three historic warships are preserved there – HMS *Gannet* (1878), HMS *Cavalier* (1944) and HM Submarine *Ocelot* (1962) – together with the national collection of lifeboats. (www.chdt.org.uk)

Chatsworth, Derbyshire. A baroque mansion that is the family home of the Cavendishes, the Dukes of Devonshire. In addition to all that the house has to offer, the grounds have magnificent water features, including the early 18th century cascade and the Emperor Fountain, designed and constructed in the 1840s by Joseph Paxton (of Crystal Palace fame), who was the head gardener at Chatsworth. On an autumn day the view of the house from the bridge across the River Derwent, with the wooded hillside behind, is especially beautiful. (www.chatsworth.org)

Chedworth Roman Villa, Gloucestershire. The villa was one of the largest in the country, lying close to the Fosse Way in rich farming country. It was first excavated in 1864, and the site includes mosaics, bathhouses, hypocausts and a water shrine. (National Trust)

Cirencester, Gloucestershire. Known to the Romans as Corinium, this was the second largest city in Roman Britain after London. Sections of the walls can be seen, together with the remains of a 9,000-seater amphitheatre. (English Heritage) There are fine mosaics and sculptures in the Corinium Museum. (www.cotswold.gov.uk)

Cissbury Ring, West Sussex. This Iron Age hill fort lies on the South Downs to the north of Worthing and covers an area of 26 hectares. There is evidence of extensive mining of flint for making tools. (National Trust)

Claydon House, Buckinghamshire. The site has been the home of the Verney family since 1620. The present house was built in the 18th century. Florence Nightingale was the sister-in-law of the 2nd Baronet, Sir Harry Verney, and her bedroom and various mementoes have been preserved. (National Trust)

Clifton Suspension Bridge, Bristol. The bridge across the Avon Gorge was designed by Isambard Kingdom Brunel. The foundation stone was laid in 1831, but political and financial difficulties led to the abandonment of the project in 1843, with only the towers built. It was finally completed in 1864, five years after Brunel's death. At 214 metres, it had the longest suspended span in the world. There are guided tours of the bridge. (www.clifton-suspension-bridge.org.uk)

Colchester, Essex. The Roman city was known as Camulodunum. Relics of that period include the Balkerne Gate, the largest surviving Roman gateway in Britain. Colchester Castle, an important visitor attraction which now houses a museum with displays of Roman artefacts, was built by the Normans on the vaults of the Roman Temple of Claudius, and had the largest keep in Europe. (www.colchestermuseums.org.uk)

Conwy Castle, Conwy. The castle and town walls were built by King Edward I in 1283–87, and are today part of a UNESCO World Heritage Site. The town walls, with their 21 towers, are the best-preserved in Britain. The aerial photographs and artist's impressions in the CADW guidebook give a good idea of the whole site. (CADW)

Corfe Castle, Dorset. Before the present castle was built this was the site of the murder of King Edward the Martyr by his step-mother Elfryda in A.D. 978. In the Middle Ages it was a royal fortress, palace, treasury and prison. Held for the Royalists in the English Civil War, it withstood a siege in 1643, but was captured by treachery at the end of a second siege in 1646. It was then thoroughly 'slighted' on Parliament's orders, leaving us with one of the most impressive ruins in the country. (National Trust)

Coventry Cathedral, Coventry. The cathedral stands beside the remains of the 13th century St

Michael's Cathedral, which was destroyed by German bombers on the night of 14 November 1940. The new cathedral was designed by Sir Basil Spence and consecrated in 1962. It is notable for its Graham Sutherland altar tapestry, John Piper stained glass and Sir Jacob Epstein's bronze sculpture of St Michael subduing the devil. (www.coventrycathedral.org.uk)

Cragside, Northumberland. This Victorian mansion was designed by Richard Norman Shaw for the inventor, engineer and arms manufacturer, William Armstrong. It was the first house in the world to be lit by hydro-electricity. Armstrong landscaped the grounds, with woodlands and one of the largest rock gardens in Europe. It was acquired by the National Trust in 1977. (National Trust)

Culloden Moor, Highland. Site of the last major battle on British soil. On 16 April 1746 Prince Charles Edward Stuart led his clansmen to defeat at the hands of the Duke of Cumberland's Hanoverian forces, ending the Jacobite Rebellion. There is a Visitor Centre and a number of features on the battlefield, such as the Memorial Cairn, Cumberland Stone and the Graves of the Clans. The site is run by the National Trust for Scotland and their development plans can be explored on the Culloden Battlefield Memorial Project website (www.culloden.org)

Cutty Sark, London SE10. This famous tea clipper was built at Dumbarton on the Clyde in 1869. Her fastest time to London from the Far East round the Cape was 107 days in 1871. She opened to the public at Greenwich in 1957. The Lower Hold houses an impressive collection of merchant ship figureheads. (www.cuttysark.org.uk)

D

Deal Castle, Kent. A fine example of the coastal defences built by King Henry VIII in 1539–40. It is a castle for the artillery age, with a low profile and rounded bastions capable of mounting more than 100 guns. The cloverleaf design was already out of fashion when Henry built his castle at Southsea in Hampshire in 1545, incorporating angled rather than rounded bastions. (English Heritage)

Derwent Valley Mills, Derbyshire. The Derwent Valley, south of Matlock, is an important area for industrial archaeology. The Derwent Valley Mills were designated a UNESCO World Heritage Site in 2001. Cromford Mill, established by Sir Richard Arkwright in 1771, was the first water-powered cotton spinning mill. Historians refer to it as 'the true blueprint for factory production.' (www.derwentvalleymills.org)

Dover Roman Painted House, Kent. An unusual relic of Roman Britain, the painted house, which was discovered in 1970, is thought to have been built about A.D. 200 as a hotel for official visitors arriving in Britain. It has unique frescoes relating to Bacchus. The Roman name for Dover was Portus Dubris, and the remains of the pharos, a Roman lighthouse, can also be seen in Dover Castle. (www.romans-in-Britain.org.uk)

Dover Castle and Wartime Tunnels, Kent. The massive stone keep was built by King Henry II in the 1180s. The castle withstood – just – a lengthy siege by Prince Louis of France and rebel barons in 1216. Today the keep has displays relating to the siege and also to the arrival of Henry VIII's court in 1539. Dover Castle is also the site of tunnels that were the nerve centre for Admiral Ramsay to mastermind the Dunkirk evacuation in 1940. There is a statue of Ramsay, unveiled in 2000. (English Heritage)

Down House, Greater London. This early 18th century house at the village of Downe was Charles Darwin's family home from 1842 until his death in 1882. It was here that he wrote his revolutionary treatise, *On the Origin of Species by Means of Natural Selection*, published in 1859. (English Heritage)

Durham Castle and Cathedral, Durham. The castle and cathedral on their impressive site above the River Wear were designated a UNESCO World Heritage Site in 1986. The castle was begun by William the Conqueror in 1072, and was the residence of the Prince Bishops of Durham until the 1830s, when they made way for the newly-established university. The cathedral dates from the first half of the 12th century and was regarded by UNESCO as the largest and finest example of Norman architecture to be found in England. (www.durham.gov.uk)

E

Edgehill, Warwickshire. The first major battle of the English Civil War was fought to the south of Kineton on 23 October 1642. The result was inconclusive. There is a monument beside the Kineton-Banbury Road, but access to the battlefield is restricted as it lies on Ministry of Defence land. (www.battlefieldstrust.com)

Edinburgh Castle, City of Edinburgh. The Old Town, with the castle as its dominating feature, and the New Town, which dates from the 18th and 19th centuries, were together designated a World Heritage Site by UNESCO in 1995. The castle has been a royal residence since the 11th century, and the oldest surviving feature is St Margaret's Chapel, built in 1076. (www.Edinburgh.gov.uk)

Elstow, Bedfordshire. John Bunyan was born here in 1628. In neighbouring Bedford there is a John Bunyan Museum, and the sites of his home and the county gaol, where he wrote *Pilgrim's Progress*. There is also a statue of Bunyan, dating from 1874. (www.britainexpress.com)

Epworth Old Rectory, North Lincolnshire. The Queen Anne house where the founding fathers of Methodism, John and Charles Wesley, were brought up is preserved by the World Methodist Council as the home of the Wesleys, with items of family memorabilia and other relics on display. (www.epwortholdrectory.org.uk) Wesley's Chapel, House and Museum of Methodism are in City Road, London EC1. (www.wesleyschapel.org.uk)

Eton College, Windsor and Maidenhead. The College was founded by Henry VI in 1440, making it the second oldest in England after Winchester. The Chapel, which is one of the finest examples of Perpendicular architecture in England, was built between 1449 and 1482. The College's Museum of Eton Life illustrates the history and role of the College. (www.etoncollege.com)

Eyam, Derbyshire. The village has gone down in history because of an act of communal self-sacrifice in the 17th century. In 1665 cloth sent from London to the village tailor, George Vicars, brought the plague with it. The rector, William Mompesson, persuaded the villagers to quarantine themselves. 260 out of 350 inhabitants died over the next year. Eyam Museum tells the story, and the tombstones and memorial plaques show the impact of the plague on individual families. (www.eyammuseum.demon.co.uk)

F

Fishbourne Roman Palace, West Sussex. The palace, which was built A.D. 75–100, was discovered by workmen digging a new water main in 1960. The scale and quality of the palace, with a hundred rooms and some of the country's finest mosaic floors, has led to its being identified with Cogidubnus, a local British ruler and ally of Rome. The re-created Roman garden is a feature of the palace. (www.sussexpast.co.uk)

Flodden Field, Northumberland. An English army under the Earl of Surrey defeated the invading Scots, led by King James IV, south of the village of Branxton on 9 September 1513. James was killed. There is a large granite memorial cross on Piper's Hill, Branxton, where the English right wing formed up, and an exhibition at the nearby English Heritage property, Etal Castle. (www.flodden.net)

Fountains Abbey and Studley Royal, North Yorkshire. The ruins of the Cistercian abbey, founded in 1132, are the largest such remains in Europe. In the 18th century the Aislabie family made the abbey the focal point of their landscaped water gardens at Studley Royal. Also on the site are Fountains Mill, Fountains Hall, built 1598–1604 using stone from the abbey, and St Mary's Church, 'a masterpiece of the Victorian Gothic style' by William Burge. The whole assemblage was designated a UNESCO World Heritage Site in 1986. (www.fountainsabbey.org.uk)

G

Gad's Hill Place, Kent. Charles Dickens had admired this 18th century house to the north of Rochester as a boy and bought it in 1856. He lived there until his death in 1870. The house is now a school, but is open regularly to the public. Dickens sometimes wrote in a small Swiss chalet he had built in the garden, and this can be seen at Eastgate House in Rochester, formerly the Charles Dickens Centre. (www.medway.gov.uk)
Amongst many other Dickens-related sites in the country, the house where Dickens was born in 1812 is preserved as a museum in Portsmouth. (www.charlesdickensbirthplace.co.uk)

Glencoe, Highland. Glencoe is now a popular place for walking and climbing, but historically speaking it is notorious for the breach of hospitality that occurred on 13 February 1692 when Campbells and English troops quartered on the Macdonalds of Glencoe massacred 38 of their hosts. There is a National Trust for Scotland Visitor Centre. (National Trust for Scotland)

Glenfinnan, Highland. Here at the head of Loch Shiel on 19 August 1745 Prince Charles Edward Stuart raised his standard to mark the beginning of the Jacobite Rebellion. The Glenfinnan Monument, a tower with the figure of a highlander on top, was designed by James Gillespie Graham and erected in 1815 by Alexander Macdonald of Glenaladale. The inscription on the monument refers to the rebellion as 'that arduous and unfortunate enterprise' (National Trust for Scotland)

Grasmere, Cumbria. Dove Cottage at Grasmere was home to the poet, William Wordsworth, and his family from 1799 to 1808. The cottage and associated Wordsworth Museum are run by the Wordsworth Trust. (www.wordsworth.org.uk) Nearby Rydal Mount, overlooking Rydal Water, was Wordsworth's home from 1813 to his death in 1850. Wordsworth was a keen landscape gardener and the garden remains much as he designed it. (www.rydalmount.co.uk)

Great Britain, SS, City of Bristol. Designed by Isambard Kingdom Brunel and built in Bristol in 1843, this was the world's first iron, screw-propelled, ocean-going passenger ship. After being abandoned in the Falklands in 1886, she was eventually brought back in 1970 and carefully restored in the dock at Bristol where she was built. (www.ssgreatbritain.org)

Greenwich, London SE10. The Old Royal Observatory, built for King Charles II by Wren in 1675, is a good place to look down on all the historic buildings this site has to offer, including the Queen's House, designed by Inigo Jones in 1616, the Old Royal Naval College and the National Maritime Museum. 'Maritime Greenwich' was listed by UNESCO as a World Heritage Site in 1997, on the grounds that the historic buildings and the park symbolised 'English artistic and scientific endeavour in the 17th and 18th centuries.' (www.greenwichwhs.org.uk)

Grime's Graves, Norfolk. The largest Neolithic flint mines in Europe. It was given the name by the Anglo-Saxons, 'Grim' being a nickname for

Woden. With hard hats provided, visitors can descend by ladder into the workings. It is also a Site of Special Scientific Interest because of the range of flora and fauna to be found there. (English Heritage)

H

Hadrian's Wall. *See* **Section L**.

Hambledon, Hampshire. This was 'the cradle of English cricket' in the 18th century when the local club became the accepted authority on the game. There is a large stone memorial, erected in 1908, on nearby Broadhalfpenny Down, marking the site of the Hambledon Cricket Club's ground, *c*. 1750–87. The old pub opposite, The Bat and Ball, served as the club's pavilion and has a collection of cricket memorabilia on display. (www.hambledon-hants.com)

Hampton Court Palace, Greater London. Cardinal Wolsey began building the Palace in 1514, but it passed to Henry VIII when Wolsey fell from power and was a favourite royal residence for 200 years. Sir Christopher Wren carried out alterations for William and Mary at the end of the 17th century and the famous maze dates from 1690. (www.hampton-court-palace.org.uk)

Hardwick Hall, Derbyshire. Designed by Robert Smythson for Bess of Hardwick in the 1590s, its expanse of windows gave rise to the tag, 'Hardwick Hall, more glass than wall.' (National Trust) In the grounds are the ruins of Hardwick Old Hall, which was only just being completed when Bess began work on her prestigious new house. (English Heritage)

Hardy's Cottage, Dorset. The cottage where the novelist and poet, Thomas Hardy, was born in 1840 and wrote his early novels is at Higher Bockhampton, near Dorchester. It is owned by the National Trust, as is Max Gate, the house in Dorchester that Hardy designed and lived in from 1885 to his death in 1928. Also in Dorchester there is a statue of Hardy by Eric Kennington (1931) and a large Hardy collection, including a reconstruction of his study, at the County Museum. (www.dorsetcountymuseum.org)

Harlech Castle, Gwynedd. Although the sea in Tremadog Bay has now receded, this is still the most dramatically sited of Edward I's castles. It was completed by veteran castle builder, James of St George, in 1290. It has been part of a UNESCO World Heritage Site since 1986. (CADW)

Hatfield House, Hertfordshire. One of the largest Jacobean houses in England, it was built 1607–11 for King James I's Chief Minister, Robert Cecil, 1st Earl of Salisbury. In the grounds is the Great Hall of the Royal Palace of Hatfield where young Queen Elizabeth I spent some of her childhood. (www.hatfield-house.co.uk)

Haworth Parsonage, Bradford. This was the home of the Bronte family from 1820 to 1861. Its moorland setting 'had a profound influence on the writing of Charlotte, Emily and Anne Bronte.' It has been owned by the Bronte Society since 1928, and is known as the Bronte Parsonage Museum. (www.bronte.org.uk)

Hever Castle, Kent. This 13th century castle with its double moat has a special place in English history as the childhood home of Henry VIII's second wife, Anne Boleyn. In 1903 it was purchased and restored by the American millionaire, William Waldorf Astor, later the first Lord Astor of Hever. (www.hevercastle.co.uk)

Highgate Cemetery, London N6. The most impressive of seven large commercial cemeteries created around London in the mid-19th century. The West Cemetery opened in 1839 and the extension of the East Cemetery in 1854. At least 850 notable people are buried in the cemetery, but it is still probably most famous as the burial place of Karl Marx. (www.highgate-cemetery.org/index.asp)

Hod Hill, Dorset. An Iron Age hill fort, covering some 21 hectares. It was one of the hill forts captured by the future Emperor Vespasian. Excavations in the 1950s showed a concentration of ballista bolts around the south-eastern entrance, indicating the likely line of the Roman assault. The hill fort is unusual in that there are the ramparts of a Roman fort in the north-west corner. Nearby Hambledon hill fort is also worth the climb. (National Trust)

Holkham Hall, Norfolk. A classic Palladian mansion, in a beautiful setting near the Norfolk coast. It was designed by William Kent, and built 1734–64 for Thomas Coke, 1st Earl of Leicester. His great-nephew, Thomas William Coke, first pioneered the Norfolk four-course crop rotation system. (www.holkham.co.uk)

Holyroodhouse, Palace of, City of Edinburgh. Founded as a monastery in 1128, the Palace is the Queen's official residence in Scotland. It is situated at the opposite end of the Royal Mile from the Castle, against the backdrop of Arthur's Seat. Mary, Queen of Scots lived there 1561–67. The Queen's Gallery displays works of art from the Royal Collection. (www.royal.gov.uk)

Houghton Hall, Norfolk. A Palladian mansion built for Britain's first Prime Minister, Sir Robert Walpole, between 1722 and 1735. It was designed by James Gibbs, with interiors by William Kent. It is now the home of the Marquess of Cholmondeley. (www.houghtonhall.com)

Hughenden Manor, Buckinghamshire. Home of the Victorian Prime Minister and novelist, Benjamin Disraeli, Earl of Beaconsfield, from 1848 to his death in 1881. It still contains many of his possessions. Disraeli's grave can be seen in Hughenden churchyard and there is a monument erected to him by Queen Victoria in the church. (National Trust)

Huntingdon, Cambridgeshire. Oliver Cromwell was born here in 1599, and he was briefly its MP. He was educated at the local grammar school (as was Samuel Pepys), and this is now a Cromwell Museum. (www.cambridgeshire.gov.uk) Oliver Cromwell's House in Ely, where he lived 1636–47, can also be visited. (www.ely.org.uk)

I

Iona, Island of, Argyll and Bute. A small island off the south-west of the Isle of Mull. St Columba arrived from Ireland in A.D. 563 and established a monastery before setting out to convert Scotland to Christianity. It was destroyed by Norse raiders, but in 1203 St Mary's Abbey, a Benedictine foundation, was established. It was restored in the early 20th century. The Iona Community, an ecumenical Christian community, was founded in 1938. (Historic Scotland/National Trust for Scotland)

Ironbridge, Telford and Wrekin. The bridge across the River Severn was the world's first iron bridge. It was cast at Coalbrookdale by local ironmaster, Abraham Derby, and erected in 1779. It is the centrepiece of the Ironbridge Gorge UNESCO World Heritage Site (1986), where nine museums and historic sites tell the story of the major part played by the area in the Industrial Revolution. (www.ironbridge.org.uk)

J

Jane Austen's House, Hampshire. The house at Chawton where Jane Austen lived with her mother and her sister, Cassandra, from 1809 until shortly before her death in 1817. It was there that she wrote or revised her most famous novels. The house where she died in College Street, Winchester, is a private house but is marked by a plaque. She is buried in the nearby cathedral. (www.janeaustenmuseum.org.uk)

Jarrow, South Tyneside. St Paul's Monastery was founded in A.D. 681 and it was there that Britain's first historian, the Venerable Bede, completed his *Ecclesiastical History of the English People* in A.D. 731. There is a museum of early medieval Northumbrian history, called 'Bede's World', which includes displays of finds from excavations of the monastery. (www.bedesworld.co.uk)

K

Kedleston Hall, Derbyshire. Home of the Curzon family since the 12th century, the present Palladian mansion was designed by Robert Adam and completed in 1765. Probably the best-known occupant was the statesman, Lord Curzon, the 'most superior person', who was Viceroy of India 1899–1905 and also Foreign Secretary 1919–25. (National Trust)

Kenilworth Castle, Warwickshire. The mellow red sandstone remains are said to constitute the largest castle ruin in England. The castle was begun in the early 12th century, but probably its greatest moment of glory came in 1575 when Robert Dudley, Earl of Leicester, lavishly entertained Queen Elizabeth and her court for nineteen days. (English Heritage)

Kew Gardens. *See Section L.*

L

Lacock Abbey, Wiltshire. Medieval cloisters testify to the fact that this is a country house created out of the buildings of a nunnery following the Dissolution in the 1530s. In the 19th century it was home to the 'father of modern photography', William Henry Fox-Talbot, and a photographic museum describes his pioneering work. (National Trust)

Lichfield, Staffordshire. The house where Samuel Johnson was born in 1709 is now a museum which is devoted to his life and work. (www.lichfield.gov.uk/sjmuseum) Also open to the public is the 18th century town house in Gough Square, London EC4, where Dr Johnson compiled his famous dictionary, published in 1755. (www.drjh.dircon.co.uk)

Lincoln Castle and Cathedral, Lincolnshire. The cathedral, with its triple towers, dominates the city. It was built 1185–1280, after an earthquake destroyed the Norman cathedral. At 83 metres, the central tower is the highest in England. The castle, which faces the cathedral, was begun by William the Conqueror in 1086. One of the four surviving copies of the Magna Carta is on display. (www.lincolnshire.gov.uk)

Lindisfarne, Northumberland. One of the cradles of Christianity in Anglo-Saxon England. Settled by St Aidan in A.D. 635, Lindisfarne is especially associated with St Cuthbert and with the 8th century illuminated manuscript, the Lindisfarne Gospels, on display at the British Library. There are the sandstone ruins of the 11th century priory, dissolved by Henry VIII. The island's Tudor castle was converted into an Edwardian country house and garden by Edwin Lutyens and Gertrude Jekyll. (English Heritage/National Trust)

Liverpool Cathedrals, Liverpool. The Anglican and Catholic Cathedrals provide a fascinating contrast in 20th century church architecture. The gothic revival Anglican Cathedral is the largest in Britain. Designed by Sir Giles Gilbert Scott, it was begun in 1904, consecrated in 1924 but not finally completed until 1980. The ultra-modern Catholic Metropolitan Cathedral of Christ the King was designed by Frederick Gibberd, after an earlier Lutyen's plan had been abandoned on the grounds of cost, and completed in 1967. (www.liverpoolcathedral.org.uk) and see also (www.liverpoolmetrocathedral.org.uk)

Liverpool and the Beatles, Liverpool. The Beatles

made their debut appearance at the Cavern Club on 21 February 1961. In 1995 the National Trust acquired the boyhood home of Paul McCartney in Allerton, where he and John Lennon wrote many of their early songs. Then in 2002 the Trust acquired John Lennon's home, 'Mendips', in Woolton, and the two houses can now be visited. (National Trust)

Liverpool 'Maritime Mercantile City', Liverpool. The waterfront area of the City was recognised as a World Heritage Site by UNESCO in 2004 because of its role in the development of the British Empire and the world trading system, and as a pioneer in dock technology and port management in the 18th and 19th centuries. The focal point of the waterfront is the trio of buildings at the Pier Head – the Royal Liver Building, the Cunard Building and the Port of Liverpool Building. (www.liverpoolworldheritage.com)

Longleat, Wiltshire. One of the best examples of high Elizabethan architecture, Longleat was designed by Robert Smythson for Sir John Thynne in the 1570s. The 6th Marquess of Bath became the first stately home owner to open to the paying public on a regular basis in 1949, and the famous Safari Park with the Lions of Longleat opened in 1966. The 7th Marquess has added his own fantasy murals in the Private Apartments to the portfolio of other attractions. (www.longleat.co.uk)

Lord's Cricket Ground, London NW8. The ground of the Marylebone Cricket Club (MCC) was moved to this site in 1814 by a Yorkshireman, Thomas Lord. By the mid-19th century the MCC was the premier club and by the 20th century the governing body of the sport. There are tours and a museum, which displays the famous urn containing 'the ashes', reclaimed by England when they were victorious over Australia in the 2005 tests. (www.lords.org)

Lullingstone Roman Villa, Kent. The villa was built around A.D. 100 and enlarged over the next 300 years. Excavations began in 1949, and have revealed mosaics, an extensive bath complex and an early Christian chapel. (English Heritage)

M

Maiden Castle, Dorset. The best known of the country's Iron Age hill forts was the capital of the Durotriges. It covers 19 hectares, and the complex of earthworks protecting the eastern entrance is particularly impressive. It was stormed in A.D. 43 by the 2nd Legion Augusta under the future Emperor Vespasian. A skeleton with a Roman catapult bolt lodged in the spine was found during Sir Mortimer Wheeler's excavations in the 1930s and can be seen at the Dorset County Museum in Dorchester. (English Heritage)

Marston Moor, North Yorkshire. The largest battle of the English Civil War took place between Long Marston and Tockwith on 2 July 1644. The two-hour battle resulted in a decisive victory for the forces of Parliament and the Scots over the Royalists. There is a 1939 stone monument on the battlefield. (www.battlefieldstrust.com)

Mary Rose, City of Portsmouth. Henry VIII's favourite warship, *Mary Rose,* sank in the Solent on 19 July 1545 with a French invasion fleet in sight. Her remains were raised in 1982 and went on display at Portsmouth historic dockyard, together with hundreds of artefacts that form a unique 'Tudor time capsule'. (www.maryrose.org)

Menai Suspension Bridge, Isle of Anglesey. The bridge linking the Isle of Anglesey to the mainland was built by Thomas Telford to improve the London to Holyhead route and was opened in 1826. It had a central span of 176 metres and was the world's first large-scale iron suspension bridge. (www.anglesey-history.co.uk)

Mey, Castle of, Highland. The most northerly castle on the British mainland, it was originally built between 1566 and 1572. It was purchased by the Queen Mother in 1952. She restored the castle and the gardens, which are protected from the elements by a 3.5-metre high wall, known as the 'Great Wall of Mey.' The Castle of Mey is now open to the general public for part of the year. (www.castleofmey.org.uk)

Milton's Cottage, Buckinghamshire. A 16th century cottage at Chalfont St Giles, where John Milton came to live in 1665 to escape the plague in London. Although blind, Milton completed *Paradise Lost* and began work on *Paradise Regained* during his time at the cottage. There are four museum rooms and an attractive cottage garden. (www.miltonscottage.org)

N

Naseby, Northamptonshire. The most decisive battle of the English Civil War was fought on 14 June 1645 between Naseby and Sibbertoft. The Parliamentary forces under Cromwell and Fairfax defeated the Royalists under the King and Prince Rupert. There are two memorials to the battle – the Fitzgerald Obelisk, erected in 1823, and a 1936 monument. (www.battlefieldstrust.com)

New Lanark, South Lanarkshire. New Lanark was established as a cotton-spinning village on the Clyde in 1785 by philanthropist, David Dale. His son-in-law, Robert Owen, was mill manager 1800–25, and made improvements in working conditions, housing and education. The evidence at New Lanark today of Owen's pioneering work in developing a model industrial community led to its listing as a World Heritage Site by UNESCO in 2001. (www.newlanark.org)

Newstead Abbey, Nottinghamshire. The Abbey, which was originally founded in the 12th century, became the seat of the Byron family after the Dissolution in 1540. The poet Lord Byron inherited it in 1798, but financial problems led him to sell it in 1818. His apartments and related documents and artefacts can be seen at the Abbey today. (www.newsteadabbey.org.uk)

O

Offa's Dyke. Offa, King of the Mercians, had this earthwork constructed from about A.D. 785 to mark the western border of his kingdom. It stretched from Prestatyn in the north to the Severn Estuary in the south. Offa's Dyke Path is a British National Trail, 270 kms in length, which broadly follows the earthwork and was inaugurated in 1971. At about the midway point, at Knighton in Powys, there is a visitor centre run by the Offa's Dyke Association. One of the best-preserved sections lies to the north in the Clun area. (www.offasdyke.co.uk)

Orkney Islands. 'The Heart of Neolithic Orkney' was designated a World Heritage Site by UNESCO in 1999, on the grounds that it provided 'outstanding testimony to the cultural achievements of the Neolithic peoples of northern Europe.' The important Neolithic monuments include a large chambered tomb, two ceremonial stone circles and the settlement of Skara Brae, which was occupied from around 3100 to 2500 B.C. (Historic Scotland)

Osborne House. *See* Section L.

Oxford University. *See* Section L.

P

Peterloo Massacre, Manchester. The 'massacre' took place on 16 August 1819 when 60,000 people gathered on St Peter's Fields, Manchester, to demand parliamentary reform and the repeal of the Corn Laws. Magistrates decided to disperse the crowd, and 11 people were killed by the yeomanry cavalry. The episode is commemorated by a plaque on the former Free Trade Hall (now an hotel) that was later built on the site. (www.manchester2002-uk.com)

Plymouth Hoe, Devon. According to legend it was on Plymouth Hoe that Sir Francis Drake insisted on finishing his game of bowls before sailing to meet the Spanish Armada in 1588. The statue of Drake on the Hoe was unveiled in 1884. Buckland Abbey, to the north of Plymouth, was Drake's home and has been owned by the National Trust since 1948. (www.plymouthdata.info)

Portchester Castle, Hampshire. The Romans built a massive fort here at the end of the 3rd century, with 20 bastions and walls 6 metres high. Today it is the best-preserved of the Saxon Shore forts. In the 12th century Henry II built a square keep in the north-east corner. There is a good view of Portsmouth harbour from the top of the keep, although this has been somewhat superseded by the opening of Portsmouth's Spinnaker Tower in 2005. (English Heritage)

Portsmouth Historic Dockyard and Fortifications, City of Portsmouth. King Henry VII had the world's first dry dock built here in 1495–96, and Portsmouth grew into the country's premier naval base. It had to be protected, and fortifications of many periods are preserved at and around Portsmouth. One of the Victorian forts on Portsdown hill – Fort Nelson – appropriately displays the Royal Armouries' artillery collection. (www.hants.gov.uk/discover/navdef.html)

R

Richborough Roman Fort, Kent. Although the sea has now receded, this was once the main port of entry into Britain for the Romans, who called it Rutupiae. The foundations can be seen of a great monumental archway through which the Emperor Claudius is said to have ridden on an elephant when he visited Britain. The remains of the Saxon Shore fort and the amphitheatre date from the 3rd century. (English Heritage)

Rievaulx Abbey, North Yorkshire. Founded in 1131, this was the first Cistercian Abbey in the north of England and became one of the richest. It was dissolved by Henry VIII in 1538. (English Heritage) Above the abbey ruins are Rievaulx Terrace and Temples, a landscaped promenade laid out in the 18th century. (National Trust)

Rochester Castle, Kent. The square keep, which is 38 metres high, was built around 1127, and is an outstanding example of Norman military architecture. In 1215 King John besieged the castle, which was held by the rebel barons. He undermined and brought down one corner of the keep, but even then the defenders held out for another two months. (English Heritage)

Royal Pavilion Brighton, Brighton and Hove. It was built by John Nash for the Prince Regent, later King George IV, between 1815 and 1823. The Indian-style exterior and Chinese-inspired interiors make it one of the most 'exotically beautiful' buildings in Britain. Queen Victoria sold it to the town in 1850. (www.royalpavilion.org.uk)

Rufus Stone, Hampshire. A memorial near the village of Minstead in the New Forest, which is said to mark the place where the oak tree stood that was indirectly responsible for the death of King William II. An arrow shot by Sir Walter Tyrell, while out hunting with William Rufus on 2 August 1100, glanced off the tree and hit and killed the King. (www.new-forest-tourism.com)

Runnymede, Surrey. The riverside meadow where King John put his seal to Magna Carta on 15 June 1215 has been owned by the National Trust since 1931. The American Bar Association erected a Grecian-style temple to commemorate Magna Carta in 1957. Nearby are the Second World War Commonwealth Air Forces Memorial and the John F Kennedy Memorial. (National Trust)

S

St Albans, Hertfordshire. Known to the Romans as Verulamium, this was the third largest city in Roman Britain. Verulamium Museum tells the story of the Roman city, where the first British Christian martyr, St Alban, was executed around A.D. 250. (www.stalbansmuseums.org.uk) Nearby, the Roman Theatre, built in A.D. 140 with a stage rather than as an amphitheatre, is unique in Roman Britain. (www.romantheatre.co.uk)

St Ives, Cornwall. St Ives has been a popular location for artists since Victorian times. The Tate Gallery opened a branch overlooking Porthmeor Beach in 1993, focusing on the post-war modern movement. One of the leading figures was Barbara Hepworth, and there is now a museum and sculpture garden at the house where she lived 1949–75. (www.tate.org.uk)

St Paul's Cathedral. See **Section L**.

Salisbury Cathedral, Wiltshire. The foundation stone of the Cathedral was laid in 1220 when the clergy moved from the original settlement of Old Sarum. (English Heritage) The Cathedral was completed in 1258. In the first half of the 14th century the tower was raised and the spire added, making the total height 123 metres, the tallest in Britain. (www.salisburycathedral.org.uk)

Saltaire, Bradford. The philanthropic industrialist, Sir Titus Salt, founded this town on the River Aire as a model village for the workers in his factory, Salt's Mill, which was the largest in the world when it opened in 1853. As a 'complete and well-preserved industrial village of the second half of the 19th century', its importance was recognised as a World Heritage Site by UNESCO in 2001. (www.saltaire.yorks.com)

Sandham Memorial Chapel, Hampshire. There are many memorials to those who died in the First World War, but one of the most impressive is this red-brick chapel at the village of Burghclere. It was erected in the 1920s as a memorial to H W Sandham by his sister. It is famous for the murals by Stanley Spencer, which were inspired by his own experiences serving in the Royal Army Medical Corps in Salonika. (National Trust)

Sandringham, Norfolk. The estate was purchased by Queen Victoria in 1862 for her eldest son, Edward, and the new house was completed in the neo-Jacobean style in 1870. Sandringham opened to the public for the first time in 1977. The first car owned by a British monarch, a 1900 Daimler Phaeton, bought by the future King Edward VII in 1900, can be seen by visitors on display here. (www.sandringhamestate.co.uk)

Scapa Flow, Orkney Islands. The large sheltered anchorage was the main base of the Royal Navy's Home Fleet in the two world wars. The German High Seas Fleet scuttled itself there in 1919. In 1939 German submarine U-47 penetrated the defences and sank HMS *Royal Oak*, with the loss of 833 lives. The Churchill Barriers were built to increase security by Italian prisoners-of-war, who also created a chapel out of Nissen Huts. (www.orkneyheritage.com)

Seaford Martello Tower, East Sussex. Martello Tower No 74 at Seaford is an example of the chain of 103 Martello Towers built as a defence against invasion around the south and east coasts during the Napoleonic Wars. It was the last to be completed, and is now a local history museum. (www.martello-towers.co.uk)

Sedgemoor, Somerset. Site of the last battle on English soil, which was fought near the village of Westonzoyland on 6 July 1685. The Duke of Monmouth, illegitimate son of King Charles II, was defeated and later beheaded after this unsuccessful attempt to seize the throne. There is a memorial to those who died in the battle and those who were subsequently punished for taking part in the uprising. (www.battlefieldstrust.com)

Segontium Roman Fort, Gwynedd. The remains of a Roman fort at Caernarvon, established around

A.D. 78. Its strategic importance meant that it was manned until the end of the 4th century, longer than any other Roman fort in Wales. (National Trust/CADW)

Selborne, Hampshire. The pioneering naturalist, the Rev Gilbert White, lived in the house called 'The Wakes' at Selborne from 1729 to his death in 1793. He published his book, *The Natural History and Antiquities of Selborne*, in 1788. The house is also home to a museum devoted to the Oates family, especially Captain Lawrence Oates, who died in 1912 on Scott's Antarctic expedition. His family funded the purchase of the house and the subsequent opening of it to the public in 1955. (www.gilbertwhiteshouse.org.uk)

Silbury Hill, Wiltshire. An extraordinary artificial prehistoric mound, rising to a height of 40 metres. Archaeological investigations have so far failed to establish its original purpose. Soil erosion means that it is no longer possible to climb the mound. It is part of the Avebury/Stonehenge World Heritage Site, listed by UNESCO in 1986. (English Heritage)

Silchester, Hampshire. The site of the Roman town of Calleva Atrebatum. It had earlier been an Iron Age settlement, but it was abandoned after the Romans left and never reoccupied. Today it is possible to walk the 2·8 kms circuit of the town walls, built about A.D. 270, which are still 4 metres high in places. There are the remains of a large amphitheatre just outside the walls. The area within the walls, some 40 hectares in extent, contained some substantial buildings, but their remains are buried beneath pastureland to protect them. There are displays at Reading Museum. (English Heritage)

Stamford Bridge, East Riding of Yorkshire. Site of the battle by the River Derwent on 25 September 1066 when King Harold crushed an invasion by his brother, Tostig, and King Harold Hardrada of Norway, who both died. Three days later Duke William of Normandy landed at Pevensey. (www.battlefieldstrust.com)

Stirling Castle, Stirling. The castle was begun in the early 12th century, and has served as a fortress, royal residence, prison and barracks. Most of what can be seen today dates from the 15th and 16th centuries. It was besieged many times, and it was Edward II's attempt to lift a siege that ended in disaster at Bannockburn in 1314. (Historic Scotland)

Stonehenge. *See* **Section L**.

Stratfield Saye House, Hampshire. Home to the Dukes of Wellington since 1817. Plans to pull the old house down and build a 'Waterloo Palace', to emulate Blenheim Palace, were abandoned in 1821 on grounds of cost.
There is a Wellington Exhibition featuring the first Duke's massive funeral carriage. The grave of 'Copenhagen', the chestnut stallion Wellington rode at Waterloo, can be seen in the grounds. (www.stratfield-saye.co.uk)

Stratford-on-Avon, Warwickshire. The Shakespeare Birthplace Trust owns five houses associated with Shakespeare in and around Stratford-on-Avon. The centrepiece is the house where he was born in 1564. His tomb can be seen in Holy Trinity Church. The Shakespeare Memorial Theatre dates from 1932, replacing the Victorian theatre that burnt down. (www.shapespeare.org.uk)

Sudeley Castle, Gloucestershire. The castle was briefly home to King Henry VIII's sixth wife, Katherine Parr, after the King's death. She married Sir Thomas Seymour, but died in 1548 after giving birth to a daughter. During the English Civil War Prince Rupert made it his HQ and it was reduced to a ruin by parliamentary forces as a consequence. (www.sudeleycastle.co.uk)

Sutton Hoo, Suffolk. When one of a group of low grassy mounds above the River Deben near Woodbridge was excavated in 1939, an Anglo-Saxon ship burial containing priceless treasures was discovered. It is thought to have been the

burial of Raedwald, King of the East Angles, who died in A.D. 625. The site was given to the National Trust in 1998. A new Visitors' Centre, with an exhibition hall containing a full-size reconstruction of the ship burial, opened in 2002. (National Trust)

T

Tattershall Castle, Lincolnshire. The Great Tower, 34 metres high, is 'one of the masterpieces of medieval brickwork.' It was built 1434–46 for Henry VI's Lord Treasurer, Ralph, 3rd Baron Cromwell. The castle was restored by Lord Curzon before the First World War. (National Trust)

Tewkesbury, Gloucestershire. The scene of one of the most decisive battles of the Wars of the Roses, when the Yorkists under King Edward IV defeated the Lancastrians on 4 May 1471. After a Public Inquiry in 1998 plans for housing development on the Gastons, the field thought to have been at the heart of the battle, were turned down. (www.tewkesbury.org.uk/battlefield)

Tintern Abbey, Monmouthshire. This Cistercian Abbey on the River Wye was founded in 1131. It was dissolved by King Henry VIII in 1536, but much of the 13th century church has survived. In the late 18th century the romantic ruins attracted poets and artists, such as Wordsworth and Turner. (CADW)

Tolpuddle, Dorset. Here in 1834 six agricultural labourers were prosecuted for forming a trade union and transported to Australia. To mark the centenary of the Tolpuddle Martyrs, the TUC built six memorial cottages in 1934, and there is now a museum. The village green with the Martyrs' Tree, a sycamore beneath which the men gathered to meet, is owned by the National Trust. (www.tolpuddlemartyrs.org.uk)

Tower of London. *See* **Section L**.

Towton, North Yorkshire. A battle in the Wars of the Roses, which took place between Towton and Saxton on 29 March 1461. It was fought in a blizzard, and the Yorkists were victorious over the Lancastrians in one of the bloodiest battles on English soil. In 2005 the Towton Battlefield Society erected a new memorial to the dead of Towton. It is located in Saxton churchyard. (www.towton.org.uk)

U

Uffington White Horse, Oxfordshire. This stylised horse is probably the oldest chalk-cut hill figure in Britain. White Horse Hill forms part of the ancient Ridgeway Path and on top there is an Iron Age hill fort, Uffington Castle. Nearby is a mound called Dragon Hill where legend says St George killed the dragon. (National Trust)

V

Victory, HMS, City of Portsmouth. HMS *Victory* was laid down at Chatham Dockyard in 1759, and launched in 1765 as a 1st rate 104-gun ship-of-the-line. She was Nelson's flagship at the battle of Trafalgar on 21 October 1805, and the focal point of the bicentenary celebrations in 2005. She has been open to the public in dry dock at Portsmouth since 1928. (www.hms-victory.com)

W

Walmer Castle, Kent. One of Henry VIII's coastal defence forts of 1539–40, but probably more famous as the official residence of the Lord Warden of the Cinque Ports since 1708. The Duke of Wellington held the post for 23 years, and the armchair in which he died at the castle in 1852 is on display. (English Heritage)

Warrior, **HMS,** City of Portsmouth. Launched in 1860, she was the world's first iron-hulled armoured warship. Restored at Hartlepool, she has been on display at Portsmouth historic dockyard since 1987, providing a unique picture of life on a Victorian warship. (www.hmswarrior.org)

Warwick Castle, Warwickshire. The building of this castle began around 1068, but what can be seen today mainly dates from the 14th century, with much re-working from later periods. It was acquired by the Tussauds Group in 1978, and one of the features is a waxwork tableau of guests at a weekend house-party in 1898, including the Prince of Wales, later King Edward VII. (www.warwick-castle.co.uk)

West Kennet Long Barrow, Wiltshire. This chambered tomb dates from around 3250 B.C. The earth mound is built over giant stones and is 104 metres long. It is part of the Stonehenge/Avebury World Heritage Site listed by UNESCO in 1986. (English Heritage/National Trust)

Westminster Abbey. *See* **Section L.**

Whitby Abbey, North Yorkshire. The Abbey was founded by St Hilda in A.D. 657, and is best remembered in English history for the Synod of Whitby in A.D. 664, when King Oswy of Northumbria decided to follow the Roman rather than the Celtic church in matters such as the dating of Easter. Today's ruins are those of the 13th century Benedictine Abbey. The Whitby Abbey Cholmley House Visitor Centre opened in 2002. (English Heritage)

Wilton House, Wiltshire. Home of the Earls of Pembroke. The original Tudor house was rebuilt in the 17th century by Inigo Jones and his nephew, John Webb. The Double Cube Room is one of the finest extant state rooms in England. (www.wiltonhouse.com)

Winchester Cathedral, Hampshire. Work on the Cathedral began in 1079, and at 169 metres in length, it is the longest medieval church in Europe. It was originally built on marshland and it has the distinction of being saved from collapse by a diver, William Walker, who, between the years 1906 and 1912, replaced the rotting timber raft on which it rested by cement foundations. (www.winchester-cathedral.org.uk)

Windmill Hill, Wiltshire. A causewayed enclosure dating from around 2500 B.C., with three concentric rings enclosing 8 hectares, Windmill Hill has given its name to the culture of the Neolithic farmers who arrived in southern England from the continent 5000 years ago. It is part of the Avebury/Stonehenge World Heritage Site, listed by UNESCO in 1986. (National Trust)

Windsor Castle. *See* **Section L.**

Woburn Abbey, Bedfordshire. Originally a Cistercian Abbey, the Dukes of Bedford have lived here since 1547. As well as the treasures the house contains, the 1,200-hectare deer park has the largest breeding herd of rare Père David's deer in the world. (www.woburnabbey.co.uk)

Woolsthorpe Manor, Lincolnshire. This small 17th century farmhouse to the south of Grantham was the birthplace and family home of the scientist and philosopher, Sir Isaac Newton. He formulated some of his major works here during the plague years 1665–67 when Cambridge University was closed. The apple tree that inspired his theory of gravity is said to have been in the garden. (National Trust)

Worcester, Worcestershire. The site of the last battle of the English Civil War, which took place on 3 September 1651 and resulted in defeat for Prince Charles' army of Scots at the hands of Cromwell's New Model Army. A 15th century timber-framed building, the Commandery, was the Royalist headquarters, and now has displays interpreting the battle. (www.worcestercitymuseum.org.uk)

Wordsworth House, Cumbria. Georgian town house at Cockermouth where William Wordsworth was born in 1770. The house and garden have been recreated to suit the period when William and his sister, Dorothy, were growing up there. (National Trust)

Wroxeter, Shropshire. The Romans called their city here Viroconium Cornoviorum. It lay on Watling Street and was the fourth largest city in Roman Britain. The remains of the public baths, constructed A.D. 120–150, and particularly part of the original south wall of the basilica, are reminders of past glories. (English Heritage)

Y

York Minster. *See* **Section L.**

PROMINENT PEOPLE

Glimpses of some of the famous people in the history of the world. See also Section C (under individual countries) for major figures in world affairs and Section D for leading British politicians; Section P for musicians; Section M for many prominent literary figures; Section H for figures from the biblical world; and also Section Q for major figures in the history of the cinema. The section concludes with lists of winners of the Nobel Prizes.

PROMINENT PEOPLE

A

Abbas, Mahmoud (b. 1935), Palestinian leader who succeeded Arafat as head of Palestine Authority, 2005.

Abel, Sir Frederick (1826–1902). English military chemist, an authority on explosives. He and his friend James Dewar patented the propellant cordite (see Section L).

Abelard, Peter (1079–1142), one of the founders of scholastic moral theology, b. at Pallet (Palais) near Nantes. He lectured in Paris, where he was sought by students, though persecuted for alleged heresy. His main achievement was to discuss where others asserted. His love for Héloïse, a woman of learning, ended in tragic separation and in a famous correspondence.

Abercrombie, Sir Patrick (1879–1957), architect and town-planner. He was consulted on the re-planning of Plymouth, Hull, Bath *etc.* and produced a plan for Greater London, 1943.

Acton, 1st Baron (John Emerich Edward Dalberg Acton) (1834–1902), English historian. He planned the *Cambridge Modern History*.

Adam, Robert (1728–92), architect, one of four Scottish brothers. He developed a characteristic style in planning and decoration and his achievements in interior design include Hare-wood House, Yorks.; Osterley Park and Syon House, Middlesex; Kedleston Hall, Derbyshire; Luton Hoo, Bedfordshire; and Kenwood.

Adams, John (1735–1826), succeeded Washington as president of the USA. He was the first of the republic's ambassadors to England.

Adams, John Couch (1819–92), English mathematician and astronomer. He shared credit for the discovery of the planet Neptune (1846) with the French astronomer Leverrier, working independently.

Adams, John Quincy (1767–1848), 6th President of the USA, 1825–29; son of the 2nd President, John Adams. He had negotiated the peace treaty with Britain after the 1812 War.

Adams, Samuel (1722–1803), American revolutionary statesman, b. Boston. He advocated "no taxation without representation" as early as 1765; promoted the "Boston tea-party"; in 1776 signed the Declaration of Independence.

Adams, William (*c.* 1564–1620), navigator, b. Gillingham, Kent; the first Englishman to visit Japan. He found favour with the shogun Ieyasu, and an English and Dutch trading settlement was established till 1616.

Addams, Jane (1860–1935), American sociologist who founded Hull House, Chicago, in 1889.

Addison, Joseph (1672–1719), writer and Whig politician. He contributed to the *Tatler*, and was co-founder with Steele of the *Spectator*.

Adelard of Bath (*c.* 1090–*c.* 1150), English mathematician who translated into Latin the *Arithmetic* of Al-Kwarizmi and so introduced the Arabic numerals to the West.

Adenauer, Konrad (1876–1967), chancellor of the West German Federal Republic, 1949–63; founder of the Christian Democratic Party, 1945–66. To a defeated Germany he gave stable government and a place in the Western alliance. He promoted reconciliation with France.

Adler, Alfred (1870–1937), Austrian psychiatrist, founder of the school of individual psychology. An earlier pupil of Freud, he broke away in 1911, rejecting the emphasis on sex, regarding man's main problem as a struggle for power to compensate for feelings of inferiority. *See* Section J.

Adrian, 1st Baron (Edgar Douglas Adrian) (1889–1977), English physiologist. He shared with Sherrington the 1932 Nobel Prize for medicine for work on the electrical nature of the nerve impulse. O.M. 1942.

Adrian IV (Nicholas Breakspear) (d. 1159), pope 1154–59, the only English pope, b. near St. Albans. He crowned Frederick Barbarossa Holy Roman Emperor. Granted overlordship of Ireland to Henry II.

Aeschylus (524–456 B.C.), founder of Greek tragic drama. Of the many plays he wrote, only seven have come down to us, including *The Seven against Thebes*, *Prometheus Bound*, and a trilogy on Orestes.

Aesop (? 6th cent. B.C.), semi-legendary fabulist, originally a slave. The fables attributed to him probably have many origins.

Agassiz, Louis (1807–73), Swiss-American embryologist, author of *Lectures on Comparative Embryology*, intended for laymen, *Researches on Fossil Fishes*, and *Studies on Glaciers*. He was an opponent of Darwinian evolution.

Agricola, Gnaeus Julius (37–93), Roman governor of Britain, who subdued the country except for the Scottish highlands. His son-in-law Tacitus wrote his life.

Agrippa, Marcus Vipsanius (63–12 B.C.), Roman general.

Ahmad Khan, Sir Syed (1817–98), Indian educationist and social reformer who founded what is now the Aligarh Muslim University.

Airy, Sir George Biddell (1801–92), English mathematician who was astronomer royal for over 40 years, 1835–81. He set up a magnetic observatory at Greenwich.

Akbar, Jalal-ud-din Mohammed (1542–1605), Mogul emperor of India, son of Humayun. He extended the imperial power over much of India, stabilised the administration, promoted commerce and learning; and, though a Muslim, respected Hindu culture and tolerated Christian missions. His reign saw a flowering of culture.

Akhenaten, the name adopted by the heretic pharaoh **Amenhotep IV** (d. 1338 B.C.), who introduced a short-lived but influential religious and artistic reformation. He sought to convert his people from their polytheistic beliefs to a more compassionate religion based on the one supreme sun-god Aten (hence his name). His pacifism caused the temporary loss of most of Egypt's overseas territories. His wife was Nefertiti. He was succeeded by Tutankhamen, who gave in to the conservative priesthood.

Akihito (b. 1933), Emperor of Japan since 1989. Son of Hirohito (*q.v.*).

Alanbrooke, 1st Viscount (Alan Francis Brooke) (1883–1963), British field-marshal; chief of the imperial general staff 1941–46.

Alarcón, Pedro Antonio de (1833–91), Spanish novelist. His short story, *El Sombrero de tres picos* (The Three-Cornered Hat) became the subject of Falla's ballet and of Hugo Wolf's opera *Der Corregidor*.

Alaric I (376–410), Visigothic chief who, as first auxiliary to the Roman emperor Theodosius, later attacked the empire, sacking Rome in 410.

Alban, St. (d. *c.* 303), proto-martyr of Britain, converted by a priest to whom he had given shelter. He suffered under Diocletian at Verulam (now St. Albans), where in the 8th cent. King Offa of Mercia founded the abbey of that name.

Albert, Prince Consort (1819–61), son of the Duke of Saxe-Coburg-Gotha, married Queen Victoria in 1840. He helped the queen with political duties, projected the international exhibition of 1851, and in 1861 in a dispute with the United States advised a conciliatory attitude which averted war. He died of typhoid fever and is commemorated by the Albert Memorial in Kensington Gardens.

Albertus Magnus (Albert the Great) (1206–80), Dominican scholastic philosopher, b. Swabia. His interest in nature as an independent observer marked the awakening of the scientific spirit. Among his pupils was Thomas Aquinas.

Albright, Madeleine (b. 1937) American diplomat. Nominated first woman Secretary of State by President Clinton in December 1996. She served 1997–2001.

Alcibiades (*c.* 450–404 B.C.), Athenian general and statesman. Pupil and friend of Socrates, he was an egoist whose career brought Athens disaster. He was murdered in Phrygia.

Alcott, Louisa May (1832–88), American author of

books for girls, notably *Little Women*.

Alcuin (735–804), English scholar, who settled on the Continent and helped Charlemagne with the promotion of education.

Aldred (d. 1069), Saxon archbishop of York who crowned William the Conqueror.

Aldrich, Henry (1647–1710), English composer of church music, theologian and architect. He designed Peckwater quadrangle at Christ Church, the chapel of Trinity College, and All Saints' Church, Oxford, and wrote the "Bonny Christ Church bells."

Alekhine, Alexander (1892–1946), world chess champion, 1927–35, 1937–46. He was born in Moscow but later became a French citizen.

Alembert, Jean le Rond d' (1717–83), French mathematician, philosopher and encyclopaedist.

Alexander of Tunis, Earl (Harold Leofric George Alexander) (1891–1969), British field-marshal. Directed retreat at Dunkirk 1940, and Burma 1942; C.-in-C. Allied Armies in Italy 1943–4, Governor-general of Canada 1946–52.

Alexander II (1818–81), reforming Tsar of Russia, succeeded his father Nicholas in 1855. In 1861 he emancipated the serfs and in 1865 established provincial elective assemblies. Later his government became reactionary; he was assassinated by Nihilists; the pogroms followed.

Alexander the Great (356–323 B.C.), Greek conqueror. Educated by Aristotle, he succeeded his father Philip as king of Macedon in 336 B.C. He led the Greek states against Persia; and, crossing the Hellespont, he defeated Darius and sacked Persepolis. He captured Egypt and founded Alexandria. He penetrated to India. D. at Babylon.

Alexandra, Queen (1844–1925), daughter of Christian IX of Denmark, married the Prince of Wales (afterwards Edward VII) 1863.

Alfieri, Vittorio, Count (1749–1803), Italian poet and dramatist.

Alfonso the Wise (1221–84), king of León and Castile, known for his code of laws and his planetary tables. He caused the first general history of Spain to be written. Dethroned 1282.

Alfred the Great (849–99), king of Wessex who became a national figure. From the outset he had to repel Danish invaders. After years of effort he won the battle of Ethandun (Edington), and subsequently, probably in 886, made peace with Guthrum, leaving to the Danes the north and east. He built ships, was an able administrator, and promoted education, his own translations from the Latin being part of the earliest English literature.

Ali, Muhammad (b. 1942), one of the greatest heavyweight boxers. Born Cassius Clay. Adopted his new name on joining Black Muslim Movement.

Al-Kwarizimi (fl. c. 830), Persian mathematician said to have given algebra its name.

Allenby, 1st Viscount (Edmund Henry Hynman Allenby) (1861–1936), British general. Commanded in Palestine 1917–18, capturing Jerusalem on 9 December 1917.

Allende, Salvador (1908–73), Chilean radical leader, a Marxist democrat, who won the presidency 1970. He tried to bring social reform by democratic means but died in the 1973 coup.

Alleyn, Edward (1566–1626), great early actor and founder of Dulwich College and Alleyn's School.

Al-Mamun (813–33), caliph of Baghdad, son of Harun-al-Rashid. He built an observatory at Baghdad.

Ambedkar, Bhimrao Ramji (1893–1956), Indian politician. A leader of the Untouchables (and champion of the poor).

Amin (Dada), Idi (1925–2003), Ugandan dictator from 1971–79. His brutal dictatorship saw the expulsion of the Uganda Asians and the murder of countless thousands of fellow Ugandans.

Amis, Sir Kingsley (1922–95), novelist, poet and critic, whose first novel, *Lucky Jim* (1954), is a classic of English comic fiction. He won the Booker Prize for *The Old Devils* (1986). He was appointed CBE in 1981 and knighted in 1990. *See* **Section M**.

Ampère, André Marie (1775–1836), French physicist who propounded the theory that magnetism is the result of molecular electric currents. The unit of electric current is named after him.

Amundsen, Roald (1872–1928), Norwegian explorer, the first to navigate the north-west passage and to reach the south pole. Sailing in

the fishing smack *Gjoa*, he made the north-west passage in 3 years, 1903–6, and in 1911 sailed to the Antarctic in the *Fram*, reaching the pole on 14 December 1911, a month before his English rival Scott. His attempt to rescue Nobile after his crash in the airship *Italia* cost him his life.

Anacreon (c. 569–475 B.C.), Greek lyric poet.

Anand, Mulk Raj (1905–2004), the founding father of Indian literature in English. His classic novel, *Untouchable*, was inspired by Gandhi. The "Indian Dickens".

Anaxagoras (488–428 B.C.), Ionian philosopher who came to Athens 464 B.C. and inspired Pericles and the poet Euripides with his love of science. His rational theories outraged religious opinion.

Anaximander (611–547 B.C.), Miletan philosopher, pupil of Thales, the first among the Greeks to make geographical maps, and to speculate on the origin of the heavenly bodies. He introduced the sundial from Babylon or Egypt.

Anaximenes (b. c. 570 B.C.), the last of the Miletan school founded by Thales. For him the primal substance was air. He was the first to see the differences between substances in quantitative terms.

Andersen, Hans Christian (1805–75), Danish writer, especially of fairy tales such as *The Little Mermaid* and *The Ugly Duckling*. Also a performer, artist and considerable man of letters.

Anderson, Elizabeth Garrett (1836–1917), one of the first English women to enter the medical profession. She practised in London for many years. Sister of Millicent Garrett Fawcett.

Andrea del Sarto (1487–1531), Italian painter, b. Florence, the son of a tailor. Known as the "faultless painter," his chief works are the frescoes of the Annunziata at Florence and his Holy Families. He died of the plague.

Andrée, Salomon August (1854–97), Swedish explorer who attempted in 1897 to reach the north pole by balloon. In 1930 a Norwegian scientific expedition discovered the remains of the Andrée expedition on White Island.

Andrew, St. *See* **H5**.

Andrewes, Sir Christopher (1896–1988), British medical researcher. Prominent virologist. Helped discover the common cold virus.

Andropov, Yuri Vladimirovich (1914–84), Russian statesman. General Secretary of CPSU, 1982; State President, 1983–84.

Angelico, Fra (1387–1455), Italian painter. An exquisite colourist, Fra Giovanni (his Dominican name) painted especially religious frescoes, mainly at Florence and Rome.

Ångström, Anders Jöns (1814–74), Swedish physicist who studied heat, magnetism, and spectroscopy; hence the ångström unit used for measuring the wavelength of light.

Annan, Kofi (b. 1938) Ghanaian international civil servant. UN Secretary General, 1997–2006. Shared Nobel Peace Prize, 2001.

Anne, Queen (1665–1714), Queen of Gt. Britain and Ireland. A daughter of James II, she succeeded William III in 1702. The act of union with Scotland was passed in 1707. A well-intentioned woman without marked ability, she was influenced by favourites, at first by the Duchess of Marlborough, but in the main she was guided by Tory and high church principles (she established Queen Anne's Bounty to improve church finances). Her reign was notable for literary output and developments in science (Newton) and architecture (Wren, Vanbrugh).

Anning, Mary (1799–1847), pioneering palaeontologist who discovered early dinosaur fossils.

Anouilh, Jean (1910–87), French dramatist, whose plays include *Eurydice*, *Antigone*, *The Lark*, *Becket* and *The Fighting Cock*.

Anselm, St. (1033–1109), Italian scholar who succeeded Lanfranc as archbishop of Canterbury.

Anson, 1st Baron (George Anson) (1697–1762), English admiral who sailed round the world 1740–44, his squadron being reduced during the voyage from seven ships to one.

Antoninus Pius (86–161), Roman emperor, successor of Hadrian. In his reign, which was peaceful, the Antonine wall between the Forth and the Clyde was built to protect Britain from northern attack.

Antonius Marcus (Mark Antony) (c. 83–30 B.C.), Roman triumvir. He supported Caesar, and after the latter's death was opposed by Brutus and Cassius, and defeated by Octavian; committed suicide. His association with the Egyptian queen Cleopatra is the subject of Shakespeare's play.

Antony, St. (c. 251–356), early promoter of the monastic life. B. in Upper Egypt, he retired into the desert, where he was tempted, but attracted disciples and founded a monastery. Took part in the Council of Nicaea 325.

Apelles, 4th cent. B.C., Greek painter whose chief paintings, which have not survived, were of Alexander the Great holding a thunderbolt and of Aphrodite rising from the sea.

Apollinaire, Guillaume (Wilhelm Apollinaris Kostrowitzi) (1880–1918), French poet who invented the term *surrealism*.

Apollonius of Perga (fl. 220 B.C.), Greek mathematician of the Alexandrian school, remembered for his conic sections; introduced the terms *ellipse, parabola,* and *hyperbola.*

Apollonius Rhodius (fl. 250 B.C.), scholar and poet of Alexandria and Rhodes, librarian at Alexandria. His epic *Argonautica* is about the Argonaut heroes.

Appert, Nicholas (1752–1841), sometimes known as François Appert, invented the method of preserving animal and vegetable foods by means of hermetically sealed cans or tins, and paved the way for the creation of a vast world industry.

Appleton, Sir Edward Victor (1892–1965), English physicist, best known as the discoverer of the ionised region of the upper atmosphere which became known as the Appleton layer. His researches led to the development of radar. Nobel prizewinner 1947.

Aquinas, Thomas, St. (c. 1225–74), scholastic philosopher and Dominican friar of Italian birth, whose philosophico-theological system (called Thomism) is still accepted by Catholic ecclesiastics. He understood Aristotle well and interpreted his thought in accord with Christian teaching. His most important works are *Summa contra Gentiles* and *Summa theologica.*

Arafat, Yasser (1929–2004). The leader of the PLO (Palestine Liberation Organization). Shared Nobel Peace Prize for his efforts to secure agreement with Israel. Elected President, Palestine National Council, January 1996. A potent symbol of the Palestinian struggle for statehood.

Arago, Dominique François Jean (1786–1853), French astronomer and physicist, remembered for discoveries in electromagnetism and optics.

Archimedes (287–212 B.C.), Greek mathematician, b. Syracuse, son of an astronomer; remembered for his contributions to pure mathematics, mechanics, and hydrostatics, notably the Archimedean screw for raising water, the conception of specific gravity, the doctrine of levers, and the measurement of curved areas. He was killed by the Romans in the siege of Syracuse.

Argand, Aimé (1755–1803), Swiss physician, inventor of the lamp bearing his name, which was the first to admit a current of air to increase the power of the flame.

Ariosto, Ludovico (1474–1533), Italian poet, author of *Orlando Furioso.*

Aristides (d. c. 468 B.C.), Athenian general and statesman, called "the just"; fought at Marathon.

Aristippus (c. 435–356 B.C.), founder of the Cyrenaic school of philosophy. He taught that man should aim at pleasure, but held that the pleasant was identical with the good.

Aristophanes (c. 444–c. 385 B.C.), Greek dramatist and comic poet, who satirised Athenian life. Among his plays are *The Clouds* and *The Birds.*

Aristotle (384–322 B.C.), Greek philosopher, pupil of Plato, after whose death in 347 he left Athens to become tutor to the young prince Alexander of Macedon. Subsequently at Athens he established his famous school in the garden known as the *Lyceum,* where he lectured in the *peripatos* (cloister) which gave his school of philosophy its name *Peripatetic.* He took the whole field of knowledge as his subject, giving it unity, and providing a philosophy which long held its own.

Arkwright, Sir Richard (1732–92), English inventor. His "water frame" (run by water power), patented in 1769, was an early step in the industrial revolution. In 1790 he made use of Boulton and Watt's steam-engine.

Armstrong, Louis (c. 1898–1971), one of the greatest jazz trumpeters and singers. Nicknamed **Satchmo.**

Armstrong, Neil (b. 1930), US astronaut, the first man to set foot on the moon, 21 July 1969.

Arne, Thomas Augustine (1710–78), English composer, remembered for *Rule, Britannia!* (from a masque called *Alfred*), and for Shakespearean

songs such as *Where the Bee Sucks.* He also wrote operas (women singers appeared in *Judith* in 1761) and oratorios.

Arnold, Thomas (1795–1842), English headmaster, whose influence at Rugby (1828–42) gave it a high position among public schools. His son, **Matthew** (1822–88) was a poet, literary and social critic, and schools inspector. One of his famous poems is "Dover Beach," and his influential books include *Culture and Anarchy* (1869).

Arrhenius, Svante August (1859–1927), Swedish chemist, a founder of modern physical chemistry. Received 1903 Nobel prize for the theory of electrolytic dissociation (ionisation).

Artaxerxes, the name borne by several ancient Persian kings. The first Artaxerxes, son of Xerxes, reigned 464–424 B.C.; he was succeeded by Darius II 424–404 B.C., who was followed by Artaxerxes II, who reigned until 358 B.C. Artaxerxes III, the last to bear the name, was a treacherous man and was poisoned in 338 B.C.

Arthur (c. 500), fabled Celtic warrior, whose feats were first narrated in Geoffrey of Monmouth's *Historia* (c. 1135). In mediaeval times his legend developed an extensive literature, woven together by Sir Thomas Malory in his *Morte d'Arthur.*

Arthur, Chester (1829–86), 21st President of the United States (1881–85). Formerly Vice-President to his Republican predecessor James Garfield, his Administration was dominated by the question of civil service reform.

Arundel, Thomas (1353–1414), archbishop of Canterbury 1396, and for a time lord chancellor. An enemy of heresy, he persecuted the Lollards.

Ashdown, Lord ((Sir Paddy Ashdown) (b. 1941), Leader of the Liberal Democrats, 1988–99. MP, Yeovil, 1983–2001. High Representative, Bosnia, 2002–06.

Asimov, Isaac (1920–92), Russian-born American scientist and author, whose works include *The Intelligent Man's Guide to Science,* 1960; *Asimov's Guide to the Bible,* 1969–70.

Aske, Robert, (c. 1500–37), leader of the Pilgrimage of Grace 1536, directed against the Henrician Reformation; executed 1537.

Asoka (c. 269–232 B.C.), Indian emperor and upholder of Buddhism. At first he expanded his empire by conquest, but on being converted to Buddhism rejected war and aimed at the good of his people. He sent Buddhist missionaries as far as Sri Lanka and Syria. Art flourished.

Asquith, Herbert Henry, 1st Earl of Oxford and Asquith (1852–1928), Liberal prime minister 1908–16, having previously served under Gladstone. His government enacted social reforms including old-age pensions (1908) and unemployment insurance (1911), but as a war minister he had to give way to Lloyd George. He resigned leadership of his party in 1926.

Assad, Hafez al- (1930–2000), Syrian dictator. President of Syria after 1971. Succeeded by his son Bashar al-Assad in 2000.

Asser, a Welsh monk of the 9th cent., traditionally author of a life of King Alfred.

Astor, John Jacob (1763–1848), founder of the millionaire family. A native of Heidelberg, went to America, making a fortune in fur.

Astor, Viscountess (Nancy Witcher Astor, *née* Langhorne) (1879–1964), the first woman MP to take her seat in the Commons. An American by birth, wife of the 2nd Viscount Astor.

Atatürk, Kemal (1881–1938), maker of modern Turkey. A fine soldier, he defended the Dardanelles against the British in 1915 and drove the Greeks out of Turkey in 1922. President of the Turkish Republic, and virtually dictator, 1923–38.

Athanasius, St. (296–373), upholder of the doctrine of the Trinity against Arius, who denied the divinity of Christ. He was bishop of Alexandria. He is not now thought the author of the creed which bears his name.

Athelstan (895–940), grandson of Alfred the Great, was crowned king of England in 925, and was the first ruler of all England.

Attenborough, Sir David (b. 1926), British traveller and zoologist. Commentator in TV series *Life on Earth* (1979) and *The Living Planet* (1983). His latest TV series, *Planet Earth* (2006), received great acclaim. Created Companion of Honour (1996). Order of Merit (2005). His brother **Lord Attenborough** (b. 1923) is an actor, film producer and director.

Attila (406–53), invading king of the Huns from Asia. He defeated the Roman Emperor

Theodosius, and entered Gaul, but was defeated in 451 near Châlons-sur-Marne.

Attlee, 1st Earl (Clement Richard Attlee) (1883–1967), Labour prime minister 1945–51, having served as deputy to Churchill 1942–5. Called to the Bar in 1905. Lectured at the London School of Economics 1913–23. Parliamentary leader of his party 1935–55. His government helped to create a welfare society and granted independence to India.

Auchinleck, Sir Claude John Eyre (1884–1981), British field-marshal; G.O.C. North Norway 1940; C.-in-C. India 1941, 1943–7; Middle East 1941–2.

Auden, Wystan Hugh (1907–73), poet, b. in England. Naturalised an American. Succeeded C. Day Lewis as professor of poetry at Oxford 1956–61.

Auer, Leopold (1845–1930), Hungarian violinist who taught Mischa Elman and Jascha Heifetz.

Augustine of Canterbury, St. (d. c. 605), first archbishop of Canterbury. Sent from Rome in 597 by Gregory the Great to convert the English.

Augustine of Hippo, St. (354–430), one of the great Latin Fathers of the Church. Bishop of Hippo (in north Africa). Author of *Confessions* (400) and *The City of God* (412–27).

Augustus, Caius Octavianus (63 B.C.–A.D. 14), first Roman emperor. Great-nephew of Julius Caesar, he was for 12 years triumvir with Mark Antony and Lepidus; then reigned alone. His reign was notable for peace, and for writers like Horace and Virgil; hence Augustan age for a great period in literature (the title Augustus was given him by the Senate).

Aurelius, Marcus Antonius. *See* Marcus Aurelius Antoninus.

Auriol, Vincent (1884–1966), French politician. President of the Fourth Republic 1047–54.

Aurangzeb (1618–1707), Mogul emperor of India. Son of Shah Jehan, he obtained power by acting against his father and brothers. In his long reign the Mogul empire reached its fullest extent; but he estranged Hindus and Sikhs; and when he died his authority was in dispute and the Mogul empire broke up.

Austen, Jane (1775–1817), author of *Emma*, *Mansfield Park*, *Northanger Abbey*, *Persuasion*, *Pride and Prejudice*, and *Sense and Sensibility*. Though confining herself to the personal relations of the English middle classes, she combined artistry, accuracy, imaginative power, satiric humour, sense, and genuine feeling with the ability to create a range of living characters. She spent the first 25 years of her life at her father's Hampshire rectory. She was unmarried.

Austin, 1st Baron (Herbert Austin) (1886–1941), English motor manufacturer, pioneer of the small car—the 7-horsepower car—which he put on the market in 1921.

Avicenna (Ibn Sina) (c. 1000 1162), Arab physician, b. Seville. His chief work was the *Tasir*.

Averroës (Ibn Rushd) (1126–98), Arab philosopher, b. Cordova. He believed in the eternity of the world (not as a single act of creation as demanded by the current theology of Islam, Christianity and Judaism, but as a continuous process) and in the eternity of a universal intelligence, indivisible but shared in by all. He expounded Aristotle to his countrymen, but his teaching was modified by Neoplatonism.

Avicenna (Ali ibn-Sina) (980–1037), Arab philosopher and physician, of Bukhara. His *Canon of Medicine* attempted to systematise all medical knowledge up to his time.

Avogadro, Amedeo (1776–1856), Italian physicist, remembered for his hypothesis, since known as Avogadro's Hypothesis (*see* L12).

Avon, Earl of. *See* Eden, Anthony.

Awdry, Reverend Wilbert Vere (1911–97), Anglican clergyman who created *Thomas the Tank Engine*.

Ayckbourn, Sir Alan (b. 1939), leading British playwright. His first West-End success (1967) was *Relatively Speaking*. A master of farce (e.g. *Absurd Person Singular* (1973) and *Joking Apart* (1979).

Ayrton, William Edward (1847–1908), English electrical engineer, inventor of a number of electrical measuring instruments. His first wife, **Matilda Chaplin Ayrton** (1846–83), was one of the first woman doctors, and his second wife, **Hertha Ayrton** (1854–1923), became known for her scientific work on the electric arc and sand ripples and for her work for woman suffrage.

Ayer, A. J. (Alfred Jules Ayer) (1910–89), English philosopher, exponent of logical positivism. His writings include *Language, Truth and Logic* (1936).

Ayub Khan, Mohammed (1907–74), Pakistani military leader; president of Pakistan, 1958–69.

B

Babbage, Charles (1801–71), British mathematician. He designed an analytical engine, the forerunner of the modern digital computer.

Baber, Babar or Babur (Zahir ud-din Mohammed) (1483–1530), founder of the Mogul dynasty which ruled northern India for nearly three centuries; a descendant of Tamerlane.

Bach, Johann Sebastian (1685–1750), composer. B. at Eisenach, Germany, he was successively violinist, church organist, and chief court musician. It was as organist at the Thomaskirche, Leipzig, that he composed the St. Matthew and the St. John Passion and the B minor Mass. His work was in the school of the contrapuntal style (especially the fugue and the chorale); after his day it lost favour, but has now gained in popularity. *See* **Section P**.

Bach, Carl Philipp Emanuel (1714–88), 3rd son of the above, and one of the first experimenters in the symphonic and sonata forms.

Backhaus, Wilhelm (1884–1969), German pianist, who interpreted classical and romantic concertos.

Bacon, Francis, Lord Verulam (1561–1626), English deductive logic for the inductive method (*see* **Baconian method, Section J**); remembered for the impulse his writings gave to the foundation of the Royal Society (c. 1662). His chief work is the *Novum Organum*. His career as statesman under Elizabeth and James I was brought to an end by charges of corruption.

Bacon, Francis (1909–92), Dublin-born artist. A realist who depicted the complexity of human emotions (e.g. his *Study after Velazquez* of 1953).

Bacon, Roger (c. 1219/20–94), founder of English philosophy, advocate of the value of observation and experiment in science. He first studied arts at Oxford but when he returned from lecturing in Paris he devoted himself to experimental science, especially alchemy and optics. He became a Franciscan friar in 1257.

Baden-Powell, 1st Baron (Robert Stephenson Smyth Baden-Powell) (1857–1941), founder of Boy Scouts (1908) and Girl Guides (1910) to promote good citizenship in the rising generation; Chief Scout of the World 1921–41. As a young cavalry officer in the South African war he defended Mafeking.

Baer, Karl Ernst von (1792–1876), German natura list, b. Estonia, founder of the science of embryology. He discovered the mammalian ovum (1827). An opponent of Darwin's theory.

Baffin, William (1584–1622), British navigator and explorer who in 1616 discovered Baffin Bay.

Bagehot, Walter (1826–77), English economist and journalist, editor of *The Economist*. Among his works are *The English Constitution*.

Baird, John Logie (1888–1946), Scottish pioneer, inventor of the televisor and the noctovisor.

Baker, Sir Benjamin (1840–1907), English civil engineer. With Sir John Fowler he built the Forth bridge and the London Metropolitan railway. He designed the vessel which brought Cleopatra's Needle to London. In Egypt he was consulting engineer for the Aswan dam.

Baker, Sir Herbert (1862–1946), English architect. Designed the Bank of England, Rhodes House, Oxford, and, with Sir E. Lutyens, New Delhi.

Baker, Josephine (1906–75), black American revue artiste who galvanised Paris in the 1920s.

Bakst, Léon (1868–1924), Russian painter who designed scenery etc. for Diaghilev's ballets.

Baldwin of Bewdley, 1st Earl (Stanley Baldwin) (1867–1947), Conservative prime minister, 1923–4, 1924–9, and 1935–7. His handling of the crisis over Edward VIII's proposed marriage ended with the king's abdication.

Balfour, 1st Earl (Arthur James Balfour) (1848–1930), statesman and writer. He was Conservative prime minister 1902–5. As foreign secretary under Lloyd George, he was responsible for a declaration on Palestine.

Ball, John (d. 1381), English priest and a leader of the Peasants' Revolt, after which he was executed. The couplet *When Adam delved,* *and Eve span, Who was then the gentleman?* is attributed to him.

Balliol, John de (d. 1269), founder of Balliol College, Oxford; a regent for Scotland; sided with Henry III against his barons.

Balliol, John de (1249–1315), king of Scotland. Son of the above, he claimed the throne against Robert Bruce and was chosen by the arbitrator, Edward I of England, whose overlordship he acknowledged. Later, on renouncing homage, he was taken captive and d. in retirement. His son Edward Balliol (d. 1363) obtained the kingdom for a time, acknowledging Edward III of England and surrendering Lothian; but retired on an annuity, 1356.

Balzac, Honoré de (1799–1850), French novelist of wide influence, and author of over eighty novels to which he gave the covering title of *La Comédie Humaine*, depicting the appetites and passions of the new social class born of the revolution and Napoleon.

Bancroft, Sir Squire (1841–1926), Victorian actor-manager.

Banda, Hastings (1898–1997), brutal dictator of Malawi who steered his country to independence.

Bandaranaike, Solomon West Ridgway Dias (1899–1959), socialist prime minister of Ceylon from 1956 until his assassination. His widow, **Mrs Sirimavo Bandaranaike** (1916–2000), became the world's first woman premier in 1960. His daughter, **Chandrika Bandaranaike Kumaratunga**, (b. 1945) has been president of Sri Lanka since 1994.

Banks, Sir Joseph (1743–1820), an amateur scientist of wealth who accompanied Captain Cook on his expedition to the Pacific 1768–76.

Banting, Sir Frederick Grant (1891–1941), Canadian physician who with C. H. Best discovered insulin.

Bantock, Sir Granville (1868–1946), composer of songs, orchestral and choral music.

Barbarossa (Ital. = red beard), surname of two brothers who were Barbary pirates: **Uruz** (*c.* 1474–1518), was killed by Spaniards, and **Khaireddin** (*c.* 1483–1546) conquered Tunis for the Turks and died in Constantinople.

Barbirolli, Sir John (1899–1970), conductor of the Hallé Orchestra 1943–70; succeeded Toscanini as conductor of the New York Philharmonic Symphony Orchestra 1937–42.

Barbusse, Henri (1874–1935), French writer, author of the war novel *Le Feu*, which portrays the experience of the common soldier.

Barham, Richard Harris (1788–1845), English humorist, author of *The Ingoldsby Legends*, (under his pen-name of Thomas Ingoldsby). His best-known poem is *The Jackdaw of Rheims*.

Barker, Ronnie (1929–2005), acclaimed comic actor. Star of *The Two Ronnies*, *Porridge* and *Open All Hours*.

Barnard, Christiaan Neethling (1922–2001), South African surgeon who first pioneered heart transplant surgery. His first was carried out at Groote Schuur Hospital, Cape Town, in 1967.

Barnardo, Thomas John (1845–1905), founder of homes for orphan-waifs; devoted himself to the protection and care of destitute children.

Barrie, Sir James Matthew (1860–1937), Scottish author and dramatist. His novels include *A Window in Thrums*. Among his plays are *Dear Brutus*, *The Admirable Crichton*, and *Peter Pan* which gained great popularity with children.

Barrow, Isaac (1630–77), divine and mathematician, tutor of Sir Isaac Newton.

Barry, Sir Charles (1795–1860), architect of the houses of parliament at Westminster. The details were contributed by his assistant A. W. Pugin.

Barth, Karl (1886–1968), Swiss theologian, seen as a Protestant St. Thomas Aquinas.

Bartók, Béla (1881–1945), Hungarian composer. From an early age he was deeply interested in folk-song which inspired his researches into Hungarian and Rumanian peasant music. He left for America in 1940, where he lived precariously and apparently unhappily until the end of the war made a return possible, regrettably too late. *See* Section P.

Bartolommeo, Fra (di Paolo) (1475–1517), Italian painter. At first influenced by Savonarola. Some of his best work is at Lucca.

Bartolozzi, Francesco (1725–1815), Italian engraver, who settled in England and became a founder-member of the Royal Academy; noted for his stipple engravings.

Bashkirtseva, Maria Konstantinovna (1859–84), a Russian girl, achieved eminence as a painter in Paris, author of a famous diary.

Bassi, Agostino (1773–1856), Italian amateur microscopist who first suggested that infectious diseases might be caused by the invasion of the body by micro-organisms.

Bates, Sir Alan (1934–2003), leading actor whose career ranged from the "kitchen sink" theatre of the 1960s to brooding troubled portrayals from Chekhov and Hardy.

Batten, Jean Gardiner (1909–82), New Zealand airwoman who flew solo from England to Australia in 1934.

Baudelaire, Charles Pierre (1821–67), French poet of originality and sensitivity, best known for his *Les Fleurs du Mal*. His life was darkened by poverty and ill-health. A talented draughtsman.

Bax, Sir Arnold (1883–1953), composer and Master of the King's Musick 1942–52. One of his best-known works is the poem, *Tintagel* (1917).

Baxter, Richard (1615–91), noncomformist divine, b. Shropshire; author of many books on theology; imprisoned after the Restoration by Judge Jeffreys.

Bayard, Pierre de Terrail, Seigneur de (*c.* 1474–1524), French knight, known as the "chevalier sans peur et sans reproche." He fought in campaigns against Italy and fell at the battle of Romagnano.

Bayle, Pierre (1647–1706), French philosopher, author of the *Dictionnaire historique et critique* (1697). His sceptical views influenced Voltaire and the encyclopedists of the 18th cent.

Baylis, Lilian Mary (1874–1937), manager of the Old Vic from 1898 and of Sadler's Wells from 1931.

Bazalgette, Sir Joseph (1819–91), Victorian engineer, famous for building London's sewers.

Beardsley, Aubrey Vincent (1872–98), black-and-white artist, who published much work, some of it controversial (as in the *Yellow Book*).

Beatles, The (Sir Paul McCartney (b. 1942), John Lennon (1940–80), George Harrison (1943–2001), Ringo Starr (b. 1940)), a Liverpool pop group whose highly original and melodic songs held the attention of youth all over the world, especially during the period 1963–5 when they were in their prime. They parted in 1971. Lennon was shot dead in New York in 1980.

Beatty, 1st Earl (David Beatty) (1871–1936), British admiral; succeeded Jellicoe as commander of the Grand Fleet 1916–19. He fought the German fleet on 28 August 1914 in the Heligoland Bight, and on 31 May 1916 off Jutland.

Beaufort, Sir Francis (1774–1857), hydrographer of the navy, who introduced the wind scale (1805) which bears his name.

Beaumont, Francis (1584–1616), and **Fletcher, John** (1579–1625), joint authors of many plays, including *The Maid's Tragedy* and *Philaster*.

Beaverbrook, 1st Baron (William Maxwell Aitken) (1879–1964), British newspaper owner and politician, a Canadian by birth. He gave energetic service as minister of aircraft production 1940–1. He controlled the *Daily Express*, *Sunday Express*, and *Evening Standard*.

Becket, Thomas (1118?–70), saint and martyr. An able chancellor, 1155–62, on becoming archbishop of Canterbury he made the position of the church his first care; and, coming into conflict with Henry II, was murdered in Canterbury cathedral. His shrine became a place of pilgrimage.

Beckett, Samuel (1906–89), Anglo-Irish dramatist and novelist, b. Dublin. Plays include *Waiting for Godot*, *Endgame*, *Krapp's Last Tape*, *Happy Days*, *Not I*; novels include *The Nouvelles* (3 stories), the trilogy: *Molloy*, *Malone Dies*, *The Unnamable*, and *How It Is*. His work expresses man's isolation, bewilderment and suffering. Nobel Prize for Literature, 1969.

Becquerel, Antoine Henri (1852–1908), French physicist who in 1896 discovered radioactivity in uranium. Shared with the Curies the 1903 Nobel prize in physics.

Bede, the Venerable (673–735), English historian and scholar; lived at Jarrow. His chief work is his *Ecclesiastical History* to 731.

Beebe, (Charles) William (1877–1962), pioneer oceanographer. Co-inventor of the bathysphere.

Beecham, Sir Thomas (1879–1961), English conductor and impresario. Founded the London Philharmonic Orchestra in 1931; introduced into England the operas of Richard Strauss, Russian operas, and the Diaghilev ballet; championed the music of Delius.

Beecher, Henry Ward (1813–87), American preacher whose church was at Brooklyn.

Beerbohm, Sir Max (1872–1956), critic and caricaturist, master of irony and satire. His works include *Zuleika Dobson* and *A Christmas Garland*.

Beethoven, Ludwig van (1770–1827), composer. B. at Bonn (his father being a tenor singer at the Elector's court), at 17 he went to Vienna, was recognised by Mozart, and eventually settled there; he never married; gradually he became deaf. In the development from simplicity to complexity of musical treatment, he stands midway between Mozart and Wagner; but in him were uniquely combined the power to feel and the mastery of musical resources necessary to express his feelings. Between the years 1805 and 1808 he composed some of his greatest works: the oratorio *Mount of Olives*, the opera *Fidelio*, and the *Pastoral* and *Eroica* symphonies besides a number of concertos, sonatas, and songs. The symphonies, nine in number, rank as the greatest ever written. *See* Section P.

Begin, Menachem (1913–92), b. Brest-Litovsk; active in Zionist movement since youth; leader of Israeli Likud party; prime minister 1977–83. Made peace with Egypt (1979) but failed to solve Palestinian problem; took Israel into war in Lebanon (1982) which led to the end of his premiership.

Behring, Emil von (1854–1917), German bacteriologist, founder of the science of immunology. Nobel prizewinner 1901.

Behring, Vitus (1680–1741), Danish navigator who in 1728 discovered the strait which bears his name.

Belisarius (505–65), Roman general under Justinian who fought against the Vandals.

Bell, Alexander Graham (1847–1922), inventor, b. Edinburgh, emigrated to Canada in 1870, later becoming an American citizen. In 1876 he exhibited an invention which was developed into the telephone (though credit should more properly go to Antonio Meucci). He devoted attention to the education of deaf-mutes.

Bell, Gertrude Margaret Lowthian (1868–1926), the "uncrowned queen of Arabia," was a pioneer traveller in the Middle East.

Bellini, family of Venetian painters: **Jacopo** (*c.* 1400–70) and his two sons, **Gentile** (1429–1507), whose works include the *Adoration of the Magi* (National Gallery); and **Giovanni** (*c.* 1429–1516), brother-in-law of Mantegna, and teacher of Giorgione and Titian.

Belloc, Hilaire (1870–1953), versatile writer whose works include *The Bad Child's Book of Beasts, The Path to Rome, Hills and the Sea, Cautionary Tales*, and historical studies of Danton, Robespierre, and Richelieu. B. in France, he became a British subject in 1902.

Bellow, Saul (1915–2005), American novelist and short-story writer, author of *Adventures of Augie March, Henderson the Rain King, Mr. Sammler's Planet, Humboldt's Gift* etc. Nobel prize 1976.

Belzoni, Giovanni Battista (1778–1823), Egyptologist. B. at Padua, he settled in England in 1803. His first interest was in hydraulics, and for this purpose he went to Egypt to Mehemet Ali. There he explored Thebes, Abu Simbel, and one of the pyramids.

Benavente y Martínez, Jacinto (1866–1954), Spanish dramatist. Plays include *Los Intereses Creados* (Bonds of Interest). Nobel prizewinner 1922.

Benedict, St. (*c.* 480–*c.* 550), patriarch of western monasticism. B. at Nursia, and at first a hermit at Subiaco, he attracted numerous followers and grouped them in twelve monasteries. Later he went to Monte Cassino, where he formulated the widely-adopted Benedictine rule.

Benedict XVI (b. 1927), succeeded Pope John Paul II in 2005. Formerly Cardinal Ratzinger. At 78, the oldest pontiff to be elected since 1730. Seen as doctrinally conservative.

Benenson, Peter (1921–2005), human rights campaigner who founded Amnesty International (**L6**).

Benes, Eduard (1884–1948), Czechoslovak statesman; co-founder with Thomas Masaryk of the Czech Republic after the break-up of the Austro-Hungarian monarchy (1918).

Ben Gurion, David (1886–1973), Zionist leader. He helped organise the Jewish Legion in 1918, and became Prime Minister of Israel 1948–63.

Bennett, Alan (b. 1934), much-loved playwright. Born at Armley, Leeds, a butcher's son. His career highs include *An Englishman Abroad* and the *Talking Heads* series.

Bennett, (Enoch) Arnold (1867–1931), English author, who wrote of the pottery towns where he was brought up. His novels include *The Old Wives' Tale* and *Clayhanger*.

Bennett, James Gordon (1841–1918), proprietor of the *New York Herald*. He sent out Stanley on an expedition to find Livingstone.

Bennett, Sir William Sterndale (1816–75), English composer, pianist and teacher, best known for his oratorio *The Woman of Samaria*, songs and piano pieces. Founded the Bach Society.

Bentham, George (1800–84), British botanist. The 'quiet giant' of botany and horticulture who compiled many important works. Secretary of the Horticultural Society, 1829–40.

Bentham, Jeremy (1748–1832), utilitarian philosopher and writer whose main works are *Government* and *Principles of Morals and Legislation*.

Bentley, Richard (1662–1742), classical scholar who did pioneer work in textual criticism.

Benz, Karl (1844–1929), German engineer whose motor car produced in 1885 was one of the first to be driven by an internal combustion engine.

Beresford, 1st Viscount (William Carr Beresford) (1768–1854), British general. He fought under Wellington in the Peninsular War and reorganised the Portuguese army.

Berg, Alban (1885–1935), Austrian composer whose best-known work is the three-act opera *Wozzeck*, based upon a drama by Büchner.

Bergson, Henri Louis (1859–1941). French philosopher, exponent of the theory of creative evolution and the life force. Nobel prizewinner 1927. *See* Vitalism, Section J.

Bériot, Charles Auguste de (1802–70), Belgian violinist, whose wife was the operatic contralto Malibran. His son, **Charles Wilfrid de Bériot** (1833–1914) was a pianist who taught Ravel.

Berkeley, George (1685–1753), idealist philosopher and critic of Locke. His spiritual outlook led him to believe that reality exists only in the eye of God, though it can be revealed by religion. His chief works are *A New Theory of Vision* (1709) and *Principles of Human Knowledge* (1710). Of Irish birth, he became bishop of Cloyne.

Berlin, Irving (1888–1989), American composer of many popular songs; b. Mahilov (then in Russia, now Belarus).

Berlin, Sir Isaiah (1909–97), British philosopher, b. Riga; Chichele Prof. of Social and Political Theory at Oxford 1957–67. His works include *Karl Marx, The Hedgehog and the Fox*, and *The Age of Enlightenment*. O.M. (1971). One of the foremost liberal thinkers of the 20th century.

Berlioz, Hector (1803–69), composer. B. near Grenoble, the son of a doctor, his romantic sensibility, taste for the grand (as in his *Requiem*), and response to literary influence made him a prime figure in the French romantic movement. His works include the *Symphonie Fantastique*, and the operas *Benvenuto Cellini* and *Beatrice and Benedict*. *See* Section P.

Bernadotte, Count Folke (1895–1948), nephew of King Gustav of Sweden. U.N. mediator for Palestine 1947. Assassinated by Jewish terrorists.

Bernadotte, Jean Baptiste (1764–1844), a French commander who served under Napoleon, and in 1810 was chosen heir to the throne of Sweden. In 1818 he succeeded as Charles XIV.

Bernal, John Desmond (1901–71), physicist, b. Ireland. Prof. of Physics, Birkbeck College, Univ. of London, 1937–63, Prof of Crystallography, 1963–8. Author of *The Social Functions of Science, Science in History, The Origin of Life*. Lenin peace prize 1953.

Bernard, Claude (1813–78), French physiologist whose discoveries eventually paved the way for the work of Pavlov and Hopkins.

Bernard of Menthon (923–1008), patron saint of mountaineers. He founded Alpine hospices in the passes that bear his name.

Bernard, St. (1090–1153), abbot of Clairvaux, which became a chief centre of the Cistercian order. This order aimed at seclusion and austerity, and practised manual work. His writings had wide influence in Europe.

Berners-Lee, Sir Timothy. (b. 1955), computer pioneer, founder of the World Wide Web.

Bernhardt, Sarah (1844–1923), French tragedienne, b. Paris, daughter of Dutch jewess. She became a member of the Comédie Française after the siege of Paris. Her first performance in London was in 1879. Her successes included *Phèdre, La Dame* *aux Camélias, Fédora, Théodora,* and *La Tosca.*

Bernini, Gian Lorenzo (1598–1680), Italian baroque sculptor. Born Naples. Did much work in Rome, designing the piazza for St. Peter's.

Bernstein, Leonard (1918–90), Popular American composer, conductor and pianist. His scores included *Candide* (1956) and *West Side Story* (1957).

Berthelot, Marcellin Pierre Eugène (1827–1907), French chemist and politician. The first to produce organic compounds synthetically.

Berzelius, Jöns Jakob (1779–1848), Swedish chemist, founder of electrochemical theory. His work was concerned with the exact determination of atomic and molecular weights and he devised the present system of chemical symbols.

Bessemer, Sir Henry (1813–98), inventor of the process of converting cast-iron direct into steel. This revolutionised steel manufacture, reducing the cost of production and extending its use.

Best, Charles Herbert (1899–1978), Canadian physiologist, who with F. G. Banting discovered the use of insulin in the treatment of diabetes.

Best, George (1946–2005), footballing legend of the great Manchester United team of the 1960s (he appeared 464 times scoring 178 goals). An icon, despite his alcoholism.

Betjeman, Sir John (1906–84), English poet, author and broadcaster; Poet Laureate, 1972–84.

Bevan, Aneurin (1897–1960), British socialist politician, architect of the National Health Service which came into operation in 1948.

Beveridge, 1st Baron (William Henry Beveridge) (1879–1963), British economist who drew up the Beveridge Plan (1942), which formed the basis of the present social security services.

Bevin, Ernest (1881–1951), British trade union leader. He was assistant general secretary of the Dockers Union (his masterly advocacy of the London dockers' case in 1920 earned him the title of "the dockers' K.C."), later general secretary of the Transport and General Workers Union; Minister of Labour 1940–5, and Foreign Secretary 1945–51.

Beyle, Marie Henri. *See* **Stendhal.**

Bhave, Vinova (1895–1982), Indian reformer, leader of the Sarvodaya movement. A follower of Gandhi, in 1951 he began a walking mission to persuade landlords to help landless peasants.

Bichat, Marie François Xavier (1771–1802), French physiologist whose study of tissues founded modern histology. His theory was that life is "the sum of the forces that restrict death."

Biddle, John (1615–62), unitarian. He taught in Gloucester: was several times imprisoned for his controversial writings. He died of fever.

Binyon, Laurence (1869–1943), poet, art critic, and orientalist, who worked at the British Museum 1893–1933.

Birch, Samuel John Lamorna (1869–1955), English landscape painter in watercolour, known for his Cornish and Australian studies.

Birkbeck, George (1776–1841), founder of mechanics' institutes, first at Glasgow, later in London (the Birkbeck Institution developed into Birkbeck College, London University).

Birkenhead, 1st Earl of (Frederick Edwin Smith) (1872–1930), lawyer and politician; lord chancellor 1919–22; secretary for India 1924–8.

Bishop, Sir Henry Rowley (1786–1855), English composer who wrote *Home, sweet Home.*

Bismarck, Otto Eduard Leopold von, Prince Bismarck, Duke of Lauenburg (1815–98), Prusso-German diplomat and statesman, chief architect of the German empire. He was of Junker family. As Prussian ambassador at St. Petersburg (1859–62) and at Paris (1862), he learned to assess the European situation. He was recalled to Berlin by the king to become chief Prussian minister; and when the house of representatives would not pass a military bill he closed the house. He used a dispute over Schleswig-Holstein to bring about the defeat of Austria at Königgratz in 1866; and he provoked the Franco-Prussian war of 1870–1 when France was defeated at Sedan. Germany then became united under the military leadership of Prussia, with the king as emperor, instead of by the slower processes of democracy. He presided over the Berlin Congress of European powers in 1878. In 1884 he began a colonial policy. His authoritarian system was based on cautious and accurate assessment of power politics. This factor was not understood by

William II, who succeeded as emperor in 1888, and dismissed the "iron chancellor" in 1890.

Bizet, Georges (1838–75), properly **Alexandre César Léopold,** French composer, chiefly remembered for his opera *Carmen.*

Björnson, Björnstjerne (1832–1910), Norwegian poet, dramatist and novelist. His work provides an image of Norwegian life from the period of the sagas (*Kong Sverre*) to contemporary problems (*Over Aevne*).

Black, Sir James (b. 1924), Eminent British scientist. Discovered life-saving drug used to prevent heart attacks. Awarded Nobel Prize for Medicine, 1988.

Black, Joseph (1728–90), Scottish chemist. A professor first at Glasgow, later at Edinburgh, he was the first to undertake a detailed study of a chemical reaction. He laid the foundation of the quantitative science of heat and his discovery of latent heat was applied by Watt in improving his steam-engine.

Blackett of Chelsea, Baron (Patrick Maynard Stuart Blackett) (1897–1974), British physicist whose work on nuclear and cosmic ray physics gained him a Nobel prize in 1948; author of *Military and Political Consequences of Atomic Energy* (1948) etc. Numerous honours. O.M. 1967.

Blackmore, Richard Doddridge (1825–1900), English novelist and author of *Lorna Doone.*

Blackstone, Sir William (1723–80), English judge. His *Commentaries on the Laws of England* is a classic.

Blackwood, Algernon (1869–1951), English novelist and writer of short stories.

Blackwood, William (1776–1834), originator of *Blackwood's Magazine.*

Blair, Anthony Charles Lynton (b. 1953), Prime Minister since May 1997. Leader of the Labour Party since 1994 (following the death of John Smith). MP for Sedgefield since 1983. His 'New Labour' won a landslide victory in the 1997 general election. He became the youngest Prime Minister since 1812. Became the longest-serving Labour Prime Minister in February 2005. His 2001 election victory was followed by the invasion of Iraq which divided his party. Won historic third election victory, May 2005. *See* **Section C.**

Blair, Robert (1699–1746), Scottish poet, author of *The Grave.*

Blake, Robert (1599–1657), Parliamentary general and an admiral in the Cromwellian navy in the Dutch and Spanish wars.

Blake, William (1757–1827), English poet, mystic, and artist, son of a hosier in Carnaby market, Soho. A solitary and deeply religious man, he had a hatred of materialism. He produced his own books, engraving on copper plates both the text of his poems and the illustrations. His *Book of Job* is a masterpiece in line-engraving in metal, his poems range from the mystical and almost incomprehensible to the delightfully simple *Songs of Innocence.* He has been called "the great teacher of the modern western world." His art is in many ways reminiscent of that of the Spanish painter Goya.

Blankers-Koen, Fanny (1918–2004). The foremost woman athlete of the 20th cent. The most memorable champion of the 1948 Olympics.

Blanqui, Louis Auguste (1805–81), French revolutionary leader, master of insurrection. He invented the term "dictatorship of the proletariat," and his theories influenced Marx.

Blériot, Louis (1872–1936), French airman; the first to fly the English Channel from Calais to Dover, on 25 July 1909.

Bligh, William (1754–1817), sailor, b. Plymouth. He accompanied Cook 1772–4, and discovered breadfruit; but was in 1789 cast adrift from *HMS Bounty* by his mutinous crew. As governor of New South Wales (1806) he fought to suppress the rum traffic.

Blind, Karl (1826–1907), German agitator, b. Mannheim. He was active in the German risings of 1848, and imprisoned; but escaped and settled in England.

Bliss, Sir Arthur (1891–1975), English composer; Master of the Queen's Musick from 1953.

Bloch, Ernest (1880–1959), composer, whose music is characterised by Jewish and oriental themes.

Blondin, Charles (1824–97), French rope performer, who crossed the Niagara Falls on a tight-rope.

Blücher, Gebhard Leberecht von (1742–1819), Prussian general. He fought against Napoleon, especially at Lützen and Leipzig; and he completed Wellington's victory at Waterloo by his timely arrival.

Blum, Léon (1872–1950), French statesman, leader of the French Socialist Party. His efforts strengthened the growth of the Popular Front and the campaign against appeasement of Hitler. He held office only briefly and was interned in Germany 1940–5.

Blumlein, Alan Dower (1903–42), British electronics engineer and inventor, chiefly remembered for his fundamental work on stereophony.

Blunden, Edmund Charles (1896–1974), English poet and critic; professor of poetry at Oxford 1966–8.

Blunkett, David. *See* **D16**.

Blunt, Wilfrid Scawen (1840–1922), English poet and political writer who championed Egyptian, Indian, and Irish independence; imprisoned in 1888 for activities in the Irish Land League.

Blyton, Enid (1897–1968), enduringly popular writer of more than 700 children's books. A teacher in South London, she is perhaps best remembered for the 'Famous Five' books, the 'Secret Seven' adventures and, of course, her most famous creation, Noddy.

Boadicea (Boudicca), queen of the Iceni in eastern Britain, who fought against the Roman invaders, but was defeated in A.D. 61 and killed herself. Archaeologists tentatively identified her palace at Gallows Hill, Thetford, Norfolk.

Boccaccio, Giovanni (1313–75), Italian author, father of the novel. He is chiefly known for his *Decameron* (set in the neighbourhood of Florence during the plague), and for his life of Dante.

Boccherini, Luigi (1743–1805), Italian cellist and composer of chamber music.

Bode, Johann Ehlert (1747–1826), German astronomer remembered for his theoretical calculation (known as Bode's law) of the proportionate distances of the planets from the sun.

Boethius (480–524), Roman scientific writer who translated the logical works of Aristotle and provided the dark ages with some elementary mathematical treatises.

Bogarde, Sir Dirk. *See* **Section Q**.

Bohr, Niels Henrik David (1885–1962), Danish nuclear physicist whose researches into the structure of the atom gave him great authority in the world of theoretical physics. With Rutherford he applied the quantum theory to the study of atomic processes. Nobel prize 1922.

Boieldieu, François Adrien (1775–1834), French composer especially of operas, including *La Dame blanche*.

Boileau-Despréaux, Nicolas (1636–1711), French literary critic and poet, best known for his *Satires*.

Boito, Arrigo (1842–1918), Italian poet and composer; he wrote the libretti of *Otello* and *Falstaff* for Verdi.

Boleyn, Anne (1507–36), queen of Henry VIII and mother of Queen Elizabeth. She was maid-in-waiting to Catherine of Aragon and her successor when Catherine's marriage was annulled. She failed to produce a male heir and was beheaded on a charge of adultery.

Bolivar, Simón (1783–1830), South American revolutionary, called the Liberator, b. Carácas. He led independence movements in the northwest of South America against Spanish rule, aiming at a South American federation. He founded Grand Colombia (now Venezuela, Colombia, Panama, Ecuador). Revered as a Latin American hero.

Bonaventura, St. (1221–74), Franciscan theologian, b. Orvieto. His mystical theory of knowledge was in the Augustinian tradition.

Bondfield, Margaret Grace (1873–1953), as minister of Labour, 1929–31, she was the first woman to enter the cabinet and become a privy councillor.

Bondi, Sir Hermann (1919–2005), British mathematician, physicist and astronomer, b. Vienna: chief scientist to Min. of Defence, 1971–7.

Bone, Sir Muirhead (1876–1953), architectural draughtsman and etcher, b. Glasgow; excelled in dry-point and drawings of intricate scaffolding; official war artist in both world wars.

Bonhoeffer, Dietrich (1906–45), German Lutheran theologian who opposed Hitler. Executed by Nazis, 1945. He wrote *The Cost of Discipleship*.

Boniface, St. (680–754), apostle of Germany. B. at Crediton, Devon, his name being Wynfrith, he became a Benedictine monk, and went as missionary to Friesland, securing papal approval. He founded Fulda Abbey and became archbishop of Mainz, but was martyred.

Bonnard, Pierre (1867–1947), French painter of landscapes, still life, and nudes.

Booth, Edwin Thomas (1833–93), American Shakespearean actor, brother of John Wilkes Booth who assassinated President Lincoln.

Booth, William (1829–1912), founder and first general of the Salvation Army, b. Nottingham. In 1865, with the help of his wife, Catherine Booth, he began mission work in the East End of London, which led to the creation in 1878 of the Salvation Army (*q.v.*) on military lines. It developed branches in many parts of the world. His son Bramwell (d. 1929) and his daughter Evangeline were among his successors.

Boothroyd, Betty. *See* **D16**.

Borges, Jorge Luis (1899–1986), Argentine poet, critic, and short story writer. Some of his work has been translated into English, including *A Personal Anthology* and *Labyrinths*.

Borgia, Caesar (1476–1507), Italian general. The son of Pope Alexander VI, at 17 he was suspected of murdering his brother. He became captain-general of the church, and made himself master of Romagna, the Marches, and Umbria. Banished by Pope Julius II he met his death fighting in Spain.

Borlaug, Norman Ernest (b. 1914), American wheat scientist, responsible for the "green revolution" which transformed agriculture in less-developed countries. Awarded Nobel prize for peace 1970.

Borodin, Alexander Porfyrievich (1833–87), Russian composer who taught chemistry and founded a school of medicine for women. In a busy professional life he wrote two symphonies, two string quartets, the symphonic sketch *In the Steppes of Central Asia* and the opera *Prince Igor. See* **Section P**.

Borrow, George Henry (1803–81), English author, for many years agent for the British and Foreign Bible Society; he studied gypsy life and wrote of his experiences in *Lavengro, Romany Rye, Bible in Spain*.

Bose, Subhas Chandra (1897–1945), Indian nationalist leader; organised anti British Indian National Army; killed in a plane crash.

Boswell, James (1740–95), Scottish author of *The Life of Dr. Johnson*, with whom he spent some years. His own published journals and letters form an extensive literary collection.

Botha, Louis (1862–1919), South African soldier and statesman. In command of Transvaal forces 1899–1902 in the Boer war. Prime minister of the Transvaal in 1907, and first premier of the Union of South Africa in 1910.

Botticelli, Sandro (*c.* 1445–1510), Italian painter. He worked under Fra Lippo Lippi, and was influenced by Savonarola. His art is delicate and poetic. His *Birth of Venus* is in the Uffizi Gallery, Florence, and his *Mars and Venus* in the National Gallery. He illustrated Dante's *Inferno*.

Bottomley, Horatio (1860–1933), English politician, journalist, and notorious financier, who died in poverty after imprisonment for fraud.

Botvinnik, Mikhail (1911–95), Russian chess player: world champion 1948–57, 1958–60, 1961–3.

Boudicca. *See* **Boadicea**.

Boughton, Rutland (1878–1960), English composer of the opera *The Immortal Hour*, and writer on the history and philosophy of music.

Boult, Sir Adrian (1889–1983), famous conductor of the London Philharmonic Orchestra 1950–7, and of the BBC Symphony Orchestra 1930–50. Musical Director BBC 1930–42.

Boulton, Matthew (1728–1809), engineer who in partnership with James Watt manufactured steam-engines at his Soho works near Birmingham. He also minted a new copper coinage.

Bowdler, Thomas (1754–1825), issued for family reading expurgated editions of Shakespeare and Gibbon, hence the term "bowdlerise."

Boyce, William (1710–79), London organist and composer, who also collected the works of English church composers. He was master of the orchestra for George III.

Boyd Orr, 1st Baron (John Boyd Orr) (1880–1971), British physiologist and nutritional expert. Director-general, FAO, 1945–8. Nobel prize 1949.

Boyle, Robert (1627–91), English scientist who with Robert Hooke laid the foundations of the modern sciences of chemistry and physics. He established the law which states that the volume of a gas varies inversely as the pressure upon it, provided temperature is constant. His chief work is the *Sceptical Chymist* (1661).

Bradley, Omar Nelson (1893–1981), American general. In the second world war he commanded in Tunis, Sicily, and Normandy.

Bradman, Sir Donald George (1908–2001), Australian cricketer who captained Australia in test matches against England 1936–48. One of the greatest batsmen of all time.

Bragg, Sir William Henry (1862–1942), English physicist. He held the chair of physics at Adelaide, Leeds, and London, and was professor of chemistry at the Royal Institution 1923–42. Pres. Royal Society 1935–40.

Bragg, Sir William Lawrence (1890–1971), son of the above. He succeeded Rutherford at the Cavendish laboratory, Cambridge 1938–53, Dir. Royal Institution 1954–66. Shared with his father the 1915 Nobel prize for their fundamental work on X-rays and crystal structure.

Brahe, Tycho (1546–1601), Danish astronomer. At his island observatory at Uraniborg, provided by his sovereign, he carried out systematic observations which enabled Kepler to work out his planetary laws.

Brahms, Johannes (1833–97), composer. B. in Hamburg (son of a double-bass player). He was a friend of the Schumanns. *See* **Section P.**

Braille, Louis (1809–52), French educationist, who, as teacher of the blind, perfected his system of reading and writing for the blind. As the result of an accident when he was three years old he was himself blind.

Bramah, Joseph (1749–1814), English inventor of the safety-lock and hydraulic press which bear his name. He also invented the modern watercloset (1778) and a machine for printing the serial numbers on bank-notes.

Brancusi, Constantin (1876–1957). Romanian sculptor whose pure abstract forms and refined models changed the face of 20th century sculpture.

Brandes, Georg Morris Cohen (1842–1927), Danish literary critic who exerted a vitalising influence on literature and art.

Brandt, Willy (1913–92), first social democratic chancellor of the Federal Republic of Germany, 1969–74. His main achievements were the Moscow and Warsaw treaties (1972) the treaty between E. and W. Germany (1973) which recognised their sovereign existence and the Brandt Report setting out a world development programme. Resigned party leadership, 1987.

Brangwyn, Sir Frank (1867–1956), artist of Welsh extraction, b. Bruges; first worked for William Morris making cartoons for textiles; he excelled in murals and in etching.

Breakspear, Nicholas. *See* **Adrian IV.**

Brecht, Bertolt (1898–1956), German dramatist and poet, b. Augsburg, whose brilliant experimental theatre was characteristic of the period in Germany between the two world wars. A Marxist, he left Nazi Germany in 1933 and returned after the war to direct the Berliner Ensemble in E. Berlin and develop his influential techniques of production. His plays include *The Threepenny Opera* (with music by Kurt Weill), *Mother Courage* and *The Caucasian Chalk Circle*. He may be regarded as the most original dramatist of his time.

Brennan, Louis (1853–1932), inventor, b. Ireland. His inventions include a gyro-directed torpedo and a mono-rail locomotive.

Breton, André (1896–1966), French poet, founder of the surrealist literary movement in France and a close friend of Apollinaire.

Brewster, Sir David (1781–1868), Scottish physicist, noted for his research into the polarisation of light; invented the kaleidoscope. He helped to found the British Association for the Advancement of Science.

Brezhnev, Leonid Ilyich (1906–82), succeeded Khrushchev as First Secretary of the Soviet Communist Party in 1964. Under his leadership the Soviet Union achieved strategic parity with the USA, but the economy was put under strain.

Bridges, Robert (1844–1930), poet laureate 1913–30. He wrote *Testament of Beauty* (1929).

Bridgewater, 3rd Duke of (Francis Egerton) (1736–1803), founder of British inland navigation by his canal, to the design of James Brindley (*q.v.*) from Manchester to his coal mines at Worsley, later extended to join the Mersey at Runcorn.

Bridie, James (pseudonym of Osborne Henry Mavor) (1888–1951), Scottish author and dramatist. The first of his many successful plays was *The Anatomist*, produced in 1931. Other plays include *Tobias and the Angel*, *Jonah and the Whale*, *Mr. Bolfrey*, *Dr. Angelus*.

Bright, Sir Charles Tilston (1832–88), English telegraph engineer who supervised the laying of the British telegraph network and the Atlantic cables (1856–8).

Bright, John (1811–89), radical Quaker statesman and orator, b. Rochdale; friend of Cobden, with whom he promoted the movement for free trade.

Brindley, James (1716–72), English canal builder, b. Derbyshire, of poor parents, apprenticed as a millwright. He was employed by the Duke of Bridgewater (*q.v.*) and designed and constructed the Bridgewater canal, carrying it over the R. Irwell by an aqueduct, the first of its kind. He also built the Grand Trunk canal linking the Mersey with the Trent.

Britten, Baron (Edward Benjamin Britten) (1913–76), English composer, closely associated with the Aldeburgh festival. O.M. 1965. *See* **Section P.**

Broca, Paul (1824–80), French pathologist, anthropologist and pioneer in neuro-surgery. He localised the seat of speech in the brain and originated methods for measuring brain and skull ratios.

Broch, Hermann (1886–1951), Austrian novelist, author of the trilogy *The Sleepwalkers*.

Broglie, prominent family of Piedmontese origin; **Victor Maurice** (1647–1727), and **François Marie** (1671–1745) were marshals of France; **Louis Victor, Prince de Broglie** (1892–1987) received the Nobel prize for his work on quantum mechanics, and his brother **Maurice, Duc de Broglie** (1875–1960), also a physicist, is noted for his work on the ionisation of gases, radioactivity, and X-rays.

Brontë, Charlotte (1816–55), forceful novelist, daughter of an Anglican clergyman of Irish descent, incumbent of Haworth, Yorkshire. She published under a pseudonym *Jane Eyre*, which was at once successful and was followed by *Shirley* and *Villette*. Her sister **Emily** (1818–48) wrote poetry and also *Wuthering Heights*; and **Anne** (1820–49) wrote *Agnes Grey*.

Brooke, Rupert (1887–1915), English poet who died during the first world war, whose works, though few, showed promise and include the poems *Grantchester* and *The Soldier*.

Brougham and Vaux, 1st Baron (Henry Peter Brougham) (1778–1868), English legal reformer; advocate of Queen Caroline against George IV; helped to found London university.

Brown, Sir Arthur Whitten (1886–1948), together with Sir John Alcock (d. 1919) in 1919 made the first transatlantic flight, crossing from Newfoundland to Ireland in 16 hr. 12 min.

Brown, Gordon. *See* **D16.**

Brown, John (1800–59), American abolitionist. His action in inciting black slaves to rebel in 1859 led to the civil war. He was hanged after failing to hold the captured US arsenal at Harper's Ferry. Known as "Old Brown of Osawatomie" and regarded as a martyr.

Browne, Charles Farrer (1834–67), American humorist (used pseudonym Artemus Ward).

Browne, Hablot Knight (1815–82), English artist, the "Phiz" of many book illustrations, including many of Dickens's novels.

Browne, Sir Thomas (1605–82), author of *Religio Medici* and *Urne-Buriall*, was born in London and practised in Norwich as a physician.

Browning, Elizabeth Barrett (1806–61), English poet. Owing to an injury in childhood, she spent her youth lying on her back, but her meeting with Robert Browning, whom she married, brought a remarkable recovery. In her lifetime her works were more read than those of her husband. They include *Cry of the Children*, *Sonnets from the Portuguese*, and *Aurora Leigh*.

Browning, Robert (1812–89), English poet. Because of his involved style his reputation grew only slowly. In *Strafford* and *The Blot on the 'Scutcheon* he attempted drama also. He married Elizabeth Barrett and lived mainly abroad. His works include *Dramatis Personae* and *The Ring and The Book*.

Bruce, Robert (1274–1329), Scottish national leader against Edward I and Edward II of England. Crowned king in 1306. He defeated Edward II at Bannockburn in 1314.

Bruce, William Spiers (1867–1921), Scottish polar

explorer who led the Scottish national antarctic expedition in the *Scotia* 1902–4 and set up a meteorological station on the South Orkneys.

Bruch, Max (1838–1920), German composer and conductor, best known for his G minor violin concerto.

Bruckner, Anton (1824–96). *See Section P.*

Brueghel, Pieter (*c.* 1520–69), one of the greatest Flemish painters. His great originality and his pictures of peasant life can be seen in The Blind Leading the Blind (1568).

Brummell, George Bryan (1778–1840), "Beau Brummell," fashion leader and friend of the Prince Regent (George IV).

Brunel, Isambard Kingdom (1806–59), English civil engineer, son of **Sir Marc Isambard Brunel** (1769–1849), whom he assisted in building the Thames (Rotherhithe) tunnel. He was engineer of the Great Western Railway and built the ocean liners, the *Great Western*, the *Great Britain* (brought back from the Falkland Is. to Bristol in 1970), and the *Great Eastern*. His other works include the Clifton suspension bridge over the R. Avon at Bristol and the Royal Albert bridge over the R. Tamar at Saltash.

Brunelleschi, Filippo (1377–1446), Italian architect, b. Florence; he adapted the ideals of the Roman period. His work in Florence includes the Pitti Palace, the churches of San Lorenzo and San Spirito, and the cathedral dome.

Bruno, Giordano (1548–1600), Italian philosopher. A Dominican friar, he came to favour the astronomical views of Copernicus and was burnt at the stake.

Bruno, St. (*c.* 1032–1101), German monk, founder in 1084 of the Carthusian order at La Grande Chartreuse in the French Alps.

Brutus, Marcus Junius (85–42 B.C.), conspirator against Julius Caesar; later committed suicide.

Buchanan, George (1506–82), Scottish humanist who spent most of his life in France lecturing and writing Latin poems, plays, and treatises.

Buchner, Eduard (1860–1917), German chemist, remembered for his work on the chemistry of fermentation. Nobel prizewinner 1907.

Büchner, Georg (1813–37), German dramatist. Dying at 24, his limited output (principally *Dantons Tod* and the fragment *Wozzeck*) is marked by power and maturity.

Buddha. *See* Gautama, Siddhartha.

Budge, Sir Ernest Alfred Wallis (1857–1934), archaeologist who conducted excavations in Mesopotamia and Egypt.

Buffon, Georges-Louis Leclerc, Comte de (1707–88), French naturalist, author of the *Histoire naturelle* (44 vols., 1749–1804).

Bulganin, Nikolai Alexandrovich (1895–1975), Soviet leader 1955–8; defence minister 1947–9, 1953–5. Retired 1960.

Bull, John (*c.* 1562–1628), English composer; possibly the composer of *God save the Queen.*

Bülow, Hans Guido von (1830–94), German pianist and conductor. He married Liszt's daughter Cosima, who later left him to marry Wagner.

Bunsen, Robert Wilhelm (1811–99), German chemist, discoverer of the metals caesium and rubidium, and inventor of the Bunsen burner, battery, and pump. Made important observations in spectrum analysis.

Bunyan, John (1628–88), was originally a travelling tinker and is believed to have served in the Parliamentary army. He joined an Independent church in Bedford in 1655 and became a popular preacher. After the Restoration he was thrown into prison, and there wrote *The Pilgrim's Progress*. Of his 60 works, the best known after *Pilgrim's Progress* are *The Holy War*, *Grace Abounding*, and *Mr. Badman*.

Burckhardt, Jacob Christoph (1818–97), Swiss historian, author of *The Civilisation of the Renaissance in Italy*.

Burghley, 1st Baron (William Cecil) (1520–98), English statesman. He was Queen Elizabeth I's Secretary of State, 1558–72, and Lord High Treasurer, 1572–98.

Burke, Edmund (1729–97), Whig writer and political philosopher. B. in Dublin, he became secretary to Lord Rockingham and entered parliament in 1765. He advocated the emancipation (though not the independence) of the American colonies; and better administration in India; but was against the French revolution.

Burnett, Gilbert (1643–1715) bishop of Salisbury,

b. Edinburgh. He wrote a *History of his Own Times*, which deals with many events of which he had personal knowledge.

Burnet, Sir John James (1859–1938), architect, b. Glasgow. The north front of the British Museum (King Edward's galleries) is his work.

Burney, Fanny (Madame D'Arblay) (1752–1840), originator of the simple novel of home life. Daughter of the organist, Dr. Burney, she published *Evelina* in 1778, and this brought her into court and literary society. She also wrote *Cecilia* and *Camilla.*

Burns, Robert (1759–96), The bard of Scotland. The son of a cottar, his first poems published in 1786 were at once successful, and he bought a farm. The farm failed, but he had a post as exciseman, and continued to write simply with tenderness and humour. Among his best-known songs are *Auld Lang Syne*, *Scots wa hae*, *Comin' through the rye*, and *The Banks of Doon*. *Auld Lang Syne* is sung all over the world at countless functions. The "ploughman poet".

Burroughs, William (1914–97), novelist whose controversial work made him a cult figure.

Burton, Sir Richard Francis (1821–90), British explorer and orientalist, who made a pilgrimage to Mecca and Medina in 1853 disguised as a Moslem. He explored Central Africa and translated the *Arabian Nights* (16 vols.).

Burton, Robert (1577–1640), English cleric and scholar, author of *The Anatomy of Melancholy.*

Busby, Sir Matt (1909–94), legendary football manager who took Manchester United from tragedy to triumph.

Bush, George Herbert Walker (b. 1924), American politician. Vice-President of America, 1981–89. Elected 41st President, November 1988. Inaugurated, January 1989. First Vice-President to be elected President since Martin van Buren in 1836. His popularity soared in 1991 after the Gulf War, but quickly fell over domestic economic problems which contributed to his defeat in 1992.

Bush, George W. (b. 1946). President of the USA since January 2001. Son of **George Bush** (*see above*). Republican politician. Governor of Texas after 1995. His presidency has seen the war on terrorism and the 2003 invasion of Iraq. In November 2004 he was re-elected in a significant victory for the Republicans. *See* **Section C**.

Busoni, Ferruccio Benvenuto (1866–1920), pianist and composer of three operas (the last *Dr Faust*, unfinished at his death), much orchestral and chamber music, and works for the piano. *See Section P.*

Butler, Joseph (1692–1752), English bishop, remembered for his *Analogy of Religion*, published in 1736 in reply to deistic attacks.

Butler, Nicholas Murray (1862–1947), American educationist who shared with the sociologist Jane Addams the 1931 Nobel peace prize.

Butler, Baron (Richard Austen Butler) (1902–82), Conservative MP for Saffron Walden 1929–65. Brought in Education Act 1944; helped secure Conservative acceptance of the welfare state; held high office 1951–64. Life peerage 1965.

Butler, Samuel (1612–80), English verse-satirist, author of the poem *Hudibras* against the Puritans.

Butler, Samuel (1835–1902), English novelist and satirist, author of *Erewhon* and its sequel *Erewhon Revisited*. Other works include *The Fair Haven*, *Life and Habit*, and *Evolution Old and New*, in which he attacked Darwinism. His autobiographical novel *The Way of All Flesh* and his *Notebooks* were published after his death.

Butt, Clara (1872–1936), English contralto; made her début in London in 1892.

Butlin, Sir Billy (1899–1980), famous for promoting holiday camps (the first of which opened in Skegness in 1936).

Buxton, Sir Thomas Fowell (1786–1845), English social reformer; succeeded Wilberforce as leader of the anti-slavery group in parliament.

Buys Ballot, Christoph Henrich Diedrich (1817–90), Dutch meteorologist who formulated the law which bears his name (an observer with back to wind in northern hemisphere has lower pressure to left; in southern hemisphere to right).

Byrd, Richard Evelyn (1888–1957), American rear-admiral, explorer and aviator. He flew over the north pole, 1926; and in 1929 made the first flight over the south pole. He made other expeditions in 1925, 1933–5, 1939 and 1946.

Byrd, William (1543–1623), English composer of church music, sacred choral music, string music, vocal and instrumental music; and a founder of the school of English madrigalists. He was organist of Lincoln cathedral at 20 and later of Queen Elizabeth's chapel royal. See **Section P.**

Byron, 6th Baron (George Gordon Byron) (1788–1824), English romantic poet who influenced European literature and thought. At 20 he published *Hours of Idleness*, which was violently attacked by the *Edinburgh Review*. This provoked his sensational *English Bards and Scotch Reviewers*. His *Childe Harold's Pilgrimage* appeared in 1812. His married life was unhappy. He went to help the Greeks in their struggle for independence and died at Missolonghi.

C

Cable, George Washington (1844–1925), American author and social critic, b. New Orleans, whose writings reflect the racial problems of his day: *Ole Creol Days, The Silent South.*

Cabot, John (1425–c. 1500), Genoese explorer who settled in Bristol and sailed westwards under letters-patent from Henry VII of England in 1497. Discovered Newfoundland and Nova Scotia, believing them to be part of Asia, and may have reached the mainland of America before Columbus did. His son:

Cabot, Sebastian (1474–1557), was born in Venice, and in 1509 in search of a north-west passage to Asia sailed as far as Hudson Bay. Entered Spanish service in 1512, and spent several years exploring the Plate and Paraná rivers. Re-entered English service in 1548 and organised expedition to seek a north-east passage to India, which resulted in trade with Russia. English claim to North America is founded on the voyages of the Cabots.

Cabral, Pedro Alvarez (c. 1467–c. 1520), Portuguese navigator who discovered Brazil.

Cadbury, George (1839–1922), liberal Quaker philanthropist of Cadbury Bros., mainly responsible for the pioneer garden city of Bournville.

Cadogan, Sir Alexander (1884–1968), English diplomat who helped to draft the UN charter.

Caedmon, the first English Christian poet, lived in the 7th cent. and, according to Bede, was first a cowherd and later a monk at Whitby.

Caesar, Caius Julius (c. 101–44 B.C.), Roman general and writer. Under the declining republic, he was assigned in 61 the province of Gaul; in the course of pacifying it he invaded Britain (55 B.C.). Opposition in Rome to his career, mainly from Pompey, provoked him in 49 to the defiance of crossing the Rubicon with his army. He defeated Pompey, whom he pursued to Egypt, where he established Cleopatra as queen. At Rome he became dictator, and his reforms include the Julian calendar. He was murdered in 44. His career paved the way for Rome becoming an empire under his nephew Octavian.

Caine, Sir Michael. See Section Q.

Calderón de la Barca, Pedro (1600–81), Spanish dramatist, representative of contemporary Spanish thought, who also wrote court spectacles for Philip IV. Among his best-known works are *La Vida es Suenñl|o* and *El divino Orfeo.*

Callaghan, Lord (Sir James Callaghan) (1912–2005), Labour's fourth prime minister, 1976–9; parliamentary leader of the Labour Party, April 1976. MP, South Cardiff 1950–87; served as Chancellor of the Exchequer, Home Secretary, and Foreign Secretary in the Labour administrations, 1964–70, 1974–76. Succeeded by Foot as leader, 1980. Order of the Garter, 1987. The longest-lived of any former Prime Minister.

Callas, Maria (1923–77). Born New York as Maria Kalogéropoulos. A great operatic soprano.

Calvin, John (1509–64), French Protestant reformer and theologian. B. in Picardy, he broke with the Roman Catholic church about 1533, and subsequently settled in Geneva, where from 1541 he established a theocratic regime of strict morality. His theology was published in his *Institutes*; while, like Luther, he accepted justification by faith without works, he also believed in predestination. See **Section J.**

Camden, William (1551–1623), English antiquary and historian. His *Britannia* appeared in 1586.

Cameron, Sir David Young (1865–1945), Scottish etcher and landscape painter.

Cameron, David. See **D16.**

Cameron, Julia Margaret (1815–79), a pioneer photographer of genius whose work still has the power to amaze.

Cameron, Richard (1648–80), Scottish preacher who revolted in defence of the Solemn League and Covenant. Killed at Airds Moss (Ayrshire).

Cameron, Verney Lovett (1844–94), English explorer, the first to cross the African continent from east to west. He surveyed Lake Tanganyika. In 1872 went out to find Livingstone.

Camillus, Marcus Furius (4th cent. B.C.), Roman general. When the Gauls attacked in 387 B.C., he was made dictator and defeated them.

Camoltos, Luis Vaz de (1524–80), Portuguese poet, author of the epic *Os Lusiadas.*

Campbell, Colin, 1st Baron Clyde (1792–1863), Scottish general who was commander-in-chief in India during the Mutiny.

Campbell, Sir Malcolm (1885–1948), racing driver who held the land-speed record of 301 mile/h (1935) and water-speed record of 141·7 mile/h (1939). His son **Donald** held the water-speed record of 276·33 mile/h (1964); killed in 1967 at Coniston.

Campbell, Sir Menzies. See **D16.**

Campbell, Mrs. Patrick (Beatrice Stella Tanner) (1865–1940), English actress of beauty and wit, friend of G. B. Shaw.

Campbell, Thomas (1777–1844), Scottish poet, who at 22 published *The Pleasures of Hope.* His war poems include *Ye Mariners of England* and *The Battle of the Baltic.* He was one of the founders of University College, London.

Campbell-Bannerman, Sir Henry (1836–1908), Liberal statesman, prime minister 1905–8.

Camus, Albert (1913–60), French existentialist philosopher and writer, native of Algeria. Preoccupied with the themes of the Stranger and the Absurd. Author of the philosophical essay *Le Mythe de Sisyphe*, the plays *Caligula* and *The Price of Justice*, and the novel *L'Etranger.* Nobel prize 1957. Killed in car crash.

Canaletto (Antonio Canal) (1697–1768), Italian artist. B. at Venice, he painted views of his city. From 1746 to 1756 he worked mainly in London. Some of his work is in the National Gallery, and there is a collection at Windsor.

Canning, George (1770–1827), English statesman. He was an advocate of Catholic emancipation, and was the first to recognise the free states of South America.

Cannizzaro, Stanislao (1826–1910), Italian chemist who followed the work of Avogadro in distinguishing between molecular and atomic weights.

Canova, Antonio (1757–1822), Italian sculptor. He infused grace into the classical style.

Canton, John (1718–72), English physicist and schoolmaster, the first to verify in England Franklin's experiments on the identity of lightning with electricity. He was the first to demonstrate that water is compressible and produced a new phosphorescent body (Canton's phosphorus) by calcining oyster shells with sulphur.

Canute (Cnut) (c. 994–1035), king of the English, Danes and Norwegians. The son of a Danish king, after some years of fighting he established himself as king of England and ruled with wisdom.

Capablanca, José Raoul (1888–1942), Cuban chess player, world champion from 1921 to 1927.

Caractacus or **Caradoc**, a king in west Britain, who resisted the Romans in the first century. Captured, but freed by the emperor Claudius.

Caravaggio (Michelangelo Merisi da Caravaggio) (1573–1610), Italian painter of immense influence. His use of the effects of light and shadow were brilliant.

Carey, Lord (George Leonard Carey) (b. 1935), 103rd Archbishop of Canterbury, 1991–2002.

Carey, William (1761–1834), first Baptist missionary to India. Helped found Baptist Missionary Society (1792). He published 24 translations of the scriptures as well as compiling Indian dictionaries.

Carissimi, Giacomo (1604–74), Italian composer, b. near Rome. He introduced more instrumental variety into the cantata and oratorio, and brought the recitative to perfection. His *Jephtha* is still in print, and there are collections of his works at Paris and Oxford. See **Section P.**

Carlyle, Thomas (1795–1881), Scottish author. Of peasant stock, he went to Edinburgh university, but later lived mainly in England where he lectured. He married Jane Welsh. His individual views pervade his historical writing. His best-known works include *Sartor Resartus, Heroes and Hero Worship, Cromwell's Letters and Speeches*, and the *French Revolution*.

Carnegie, Andrew (1835–1919), philanthropist b. Dunfermline; emigrated to America 1848; after early struggles established the Carnegie iron works. He made munificent gifts to Free Libraries and other educational work.

Carnot, Lazare Nicolas Marguerite (1753–1823), French military engineer, prominent in the French revolutionary wars, 1792–1802. His son, **Sadi Carnot** (1796–1832), was a physicist and engineer who worked on the motive power of heat, establishing the principle that heat and work are reversible conditions.

Caroline, Queen (1768–1821), was married to George IV when he was Prince of Wales. They soon separated, but when he became king in 1820, she tried to assert her position. The question came before parliament. In spite of some public sympathy she was unsuccessful.

Carrel, Alexis (1873–1944), American surgeon who won the Nobel prize in 1912 for his success in suturing blood vessels in transfusion and in transplantation of organs. A Frenchman by birth, he returned to France in 1939.

Carroll, Lewis. *See* Dodgson, Charles Lutwidge.

Carson, Baron (Edward Henry Carson) (1854–1935), Irish barrister, solicitor-general for Ireland 1892; attorney general 1915; first lord of the admiralty 1916–17; member of the war cabinet 1917–18. He led a semi-militant organisation against Home Rule.

Carson, Rachel (1907–64), American biologist, remembered for *The Silent Spring*.

Carter, Howard (1873–1939), Egyptologist who was associated with Lord Carnarvon in discovering in 1922 the Tomb of Tutankhamen.

Carter, James Earl (b. 1924), American Democratic President 1977–81; former Governor of Georgia. His main achievements were the treaty between Israel and Egypt, the Panama Canal treaty, SALT II (though not ratified) and the settling of the release of American hostages held captive in Iran. Won 2002 Nobel Peace Prize.

Cartier, Jacques (1494 1557), French navigator, b. St. Malo, who explored Canada, especially the gulf and river of St. Lawrence.

Cartier-Bresson, Henri (1908–2004), legendary French photographer. He evolved concept of "the decisive moment".

Cartland, Dame Barbara (1901–2000), prolific authoress of 723 romantic novels.

Cartwright, Edmund (1743 1823), English inventor of the power-loom, and also of a wool-combing machine, important steps in the weaving side of the textile revolution.

Cartwright, John (1740–1824), brother of the above; reformer and agitator against slavery.

Caruso, Enrico (1873–1921), Italian tenor, b. Naples.

Carver, George Washington (1804–1943), Black American agricultural chemist of world repute.

Casabianca, Louis de (c. 1752–98), captain of the French flagship *L'Orient* at the Battle of the Nile. He and his ten-year-old-son died together in the burning ship.

Casals, Pablo (1876–1973), Spanish cellist and conductor, son of an organist, b. Vendrell, Tarragona. He exiled himself from Spain in 1938. Widely regarded as greatest-ever cellist.

Casanova de Seinfalt, Giacomo (1725–98), Italian scholar, diplomat and religious thinker whose reputation as a lover is much exaggerated.

Casement, Roger David (1864–1916), Irish nationalist. While in British consular service exposed abuses in Belgian Congo. Knighted 1911 (degraded 1916). Hanged after 1916 Easter Rising. His remains are in Glasnevin cemetary, Dublin.

Cash, Johnny (1932–2003), legendary country music singer, 'The Man in Black' whose rugged style spoke of man's dignity under pressure.

Cassin, René (1887–1970), French jurist. Principal author, UN Declaration of Rights of Man. Nobel Peace Prize, 1968.

Cassini, French family of Italian origin, distinguished for work in astronomy and geography. Through four generations (1671–1793) they were heads of the Paris Observatory.

Cassius, Caius Longinus, Roman general who opposed the dictatorship of Julius Caesar, and

took part in his murder. He died in 42 B.C. after being defeated by Mark Antony.

Casson, Sir Hugh (1910–99), famous architect who opened the Royal Academy to a wider audience. Architect of the Festival of Britain.

Castle, Baroness (Barbara Anne Castle) (1910–2002), Socialist politician who as Transport Secretary (1965–68) introduced the breath test. Later attempted to reform the trade unions with *In Place of Strife*. Campaigner for social justice.

Castlereagh, Viscount (Robert Stewart Castlereagh) (1769–1822), British minister of war and foreign secretary, who took a leading part in the Napoleonic wars. Committed suicide.

Castro, Fidel (b. 1927), Cuban revolutionary. After two unsuccessful attempts he succeeded in 1959 in overthrowing a police-state. He has initiated reforms in agriculture, industry, and education. His acceptance of Russian support led to the "missiles crisis" of 1962. The fall of Soviet communism has left his regime isolated.

Catherine, St. (4th cent.). Traditionally a virgin martyr in Alexandria, though not mentioned before the 10th cent. Legend represents her as tied to a wheel.

Catherine de' Medici (1519–89), Italian-born wife of Henry II and mother of three French kings (she was regent for Charles IX). Her antagonism to the Protestants may have led to the massacre of St. Bartholomew's day. She was able, and appreciated art and literature, but was unscrupulous and cruel.

Catherine of Aragon (1485–1536), first wife of Henry VIII of England, was daughter of Ferdinand and Isabella of Spain, and mother of Mary Tudor. After the Pope had refused to release Henry VIII from the marriage an English declaration of nullity was obtained (thus precipitating a movement towards the Reformation).

Catherine the Great (1729–96), Empress Catherine II of Russia. Daughter of a German prince, she married in 1745 the future Peter III, a weakling, later deposed and murdered. Intelligent, cultivated, autocratic, she proved a capable ruler. Her reign was marked by imperialist expansion and extension of serfdom.

Cato, Marcus Porcius (234–149 B.C.), Roman statesman and writer. His tenure of office as censor was characterised by austerity and conservatism. Advocated opposition to Carthage.

Catullus, Caius Valerius (c. 84–54 B.C.), Roman poet who wrote lyrics to Lesbia. His poems show sincere feeling and also Greek influence.

Cavell, Edith Louisa (1865–1915), English nurse in Brussels in 1914–15, who was executed by the Germans for helping Allied fugitives to escape.

Cavendish, Henry (1731–1810), English scientist, a contemporary of Black, Priestley, Scheele, and Lavoisier, remembered for his investigations into the nature of gases. He discovered hydrogen and the chemical composition of water. The Cavendish Laboratory is named after him.

Cavour, Camilio Benso di (1810–61), Italian statesman, who, as premier of Sardinia, helped to bring about the unification of Italy.

Caxton, William (1422–91), the first English printer and publisher, a man of wide-ranging abilities. He probably learnt the art of printing at Cologne (1471–2), setting up his own printing press at Westminster (1476). He printed Chaucer's *Canterbury Tales*, Malory's *Le Morte d'Arthur* and Aesop's *Fables*.

Ceauçescu, Nicolae (1918–89), Romanian communist leader. His dictatorship was ended by the 1989 revolution. Executed 25 December 1989.

Cecil of Chelwood, 1st Viscount (Robert Cecil) (1864–1958), English politician who helped draft the Charter of the League of Nations. Nobel prize for peace 1937.

Cecilia, St. (2nd or 3rd cent.), patron saint of music, often represented playing the organ.

Cellini, Benvenuto (1500–71), Italian sculptor and goldsmith. B. at Florence, he worked for some years in Rome. His bronze statue *Perseus with the head of Medusa* is at Florence. His life was adventurous and he wrote an *Autobiography*.

Celsius, Anders (1701–44), Swedish physicist and astronomer. Invented centigrade thermometer.

Ceresole, Pierre (1879–1945), Swiss founder of International Voluntary Service. Became a Quaker.

Cervantes, Saavedra Miguel de (1547–1616), Spanish novelist and dramatist, b. at Alcalá de Henares. He was injured at the battle of

Lepanto, and thereafter struggled to earn a livelihood from literature. His *Don Quixote* describes the adventures of a poor gentleman, confused in mind, who on his horse Rosinante with his squire Sancho Panza seeks adventures; it satirised chivalry, but is also a permanent criticism of life. Of his plays only two survive.

Cézanne, Paul (1839–1906), French painter, b. in Aix-en-Provence, the son of a wealthy banker and tradesman. He developed a highly original style, using colour and tone in such a way as to increase the impression of depth. He said that he wanted "to make of Impressionism something solid and durable, like the art of the Museums." Like Giotto, six hundred years before, he more than any other artist determined the course European painting was to take. *La Veille au Chapelet* and *Les Grandes Baigneuses* are in the National Gallery. He was a friend of Zola.

Chadwick, Sir Edwin (1800–90), English social reformer. Secretary of the Poor Law Board.

Chadwick, Sir James (1891–1974), English physicist, one of Rutherford's collaborators in the field of atomic research. Discovered the neutron in 1932, one of the main steps in the discovery of the fission process (and hence the atom bomb).

Chagall, Marc (1887–1985), Russian-born painter, b. at Vitebsk (now Belarus); the forerunner of surrealism.

Chamberlain, Joseph (1836–1914), English statesman. He began with municipal work in Birmingham. At first a Liberal under Gladstone, he became Conservative. He opposed Home Rule for Ireland, and was the first advocate of a partial return to protection.

Chamberlain, Neville (1869–1940), son of Joseph. He was prime minister 1937–40, when he appeased Hitler by the Munich agreement, 1938.

Chambers, Sir William (1726–96), British architect, b. Stockholm. He rebuilt Somerset House and designed the pagoda in Kew Gardens.

Champlain, Samuel de (1567–1635), French navigator who founded Quebec (1608), and discovered the lake known by his name.

Champollion, Jean François (1790–1832), French egyptologist, who found the key to the decipherment of hieroglyphics in the Rosetta stone (**L95**).

Chantrey, Sir Francis Legatt (1781–1841), English sculptor who left a fortune to the Royal Academy.

Chaplin, Sir Charles Spencer (1889–1977), first international screen star, with more than 50 years' achievement. B. in London, his mother was a music-hall singer and he made his début at five. In 1910 he went to the United States. *See* **Section Q**.

Chapman, George (1559–1634), Elizabethan poet, dramatist, and translator of the *Iliad* and *Odyssey*. His best-known play is *Bussy d'Ambois*.

Chapman, Sydney (1888–1970), English mathematician and geophysicist, who worked on the kinetic theory of gases, geomagnetism, and solar and ionospheric physics. An upper layer of the atmosphere and a crater on the moon are named after him.

Charcot, Jean Baptiste (1867–1936), French explorer, who in 1903–5 and 1908–10 commanded expeditions to the south polar regions. Charcot Island in the Antarctic is named after him.

Chardin, Jean Baptiste Siméon (1699–1779), French painter of still life and domestic scenes.

Chares (*c.* 300 B.C.), Greek worker in bronze from Rhodes, sculptor of the Colossus of Rhodes.

Charlemagne (742–814), Charles the Great. From being King of the Franks, he came to govern an empire comprising Gaul, Italy, and large parts of Spain and Germany, and was crowned Emperor by the Pope in Rome on Christmas Day, A.D. 800. His revival of the Western Empire was the foundation of the Holy Roman Empire (*q.v.*).

Charles, Jacques Alexandre César (1746–1823), French physicist, the first to use hydrogen gas in balloons and who anticipated Gay-Lussac's law on the expansion of gases.

Charles Edward (Stuart) (1720–88), the Young Pretender (*i.e.*, claimant of the English throne), grandson of James II, led an unsuccessful rising in 1745 and died in exile.

Charles (Philip Arthur George) (b. 1948), Prince of Wales, Duke of Cornwall and Rothesay, eldest son of Queen Elizabeth II; married Lady Diana Spencer, daughter of 8th Earl Spencer, 1981. A decree nisi ending the marriage was granted in 1996. Their eldest son is Prince William (b. 1982). In April 2005 he married Camilla Parker Bowles (who took the title Duchess of Cornwall).

Charles I (1600–49), King of England, Scotland, and

Ireland, succeeded his father James I in 1625. Personally sincere, and having an appreciation of art, he was yet ill-fitted to cope with the political problems of his time. His marriage with the French princess Henrietta Maria was unpopular. He supported Arch-bishop Laud's strict Anglicanism, and he also attempted to rule without parliament. Defeated in the Civil War which broke out in 1642, he spun out negotiations for a settlement till he was beheaded in 1649.

Charles II (1630–85), King of England, Scotland, and Ireland, son of Charles I; after the Civil War escaped to France, and returned in 1660 when the monarchy was restored. His religious sympathies were Roman Catholic and his personal life was amorous; but in political matters he was shrewd and realistic, and contrived not to "go on his travels" again. He promoted the development of the navy, but had to accept the laws enforcing religious conformity imposed by parliament.

Charles V (1500–58), Hapsburg ruler, succeeded his grandfather, Maximilian I, as emperor of the Holy Roman Empire, and as heir to Ferdinand and Isabella succeeded to the Spanish crown. His rivalry with Francis I of France led to prolonged war. He crushed a revolt of peasants in 1525. He presided in 1521 at the Diet before which Luther appeared, after which religious struggle continued in Germany till the Augsburg settlement of 1555. In that year he retired to a monastery in Spain.

Charles XII of Sweden (1682–1718), a brave but rash and ambitious general. He repelled Russian attacks at Narva in 1700, but subsequntly pursuing military adventure he was defeated by Peter the Great at Poltava in 1709; and on invading Norway was killed.

Chateaubriand, François René, Vicomte de (1768–1848), French writer and diplomat. In a varied career he was at first an emigré, and later served as diplomat under both Napoleon and Louis XVIII. He was a friend of Mme. Recamier.

Chatham, 1st Earl of (William Pitt) (1708–78), English statesman and orator. His energetic conduct of the Seven Years War was an important contribution to English victory and to acquisitions in Canada and India at the peace (1763), though by then he was out of office. In the dispute with the American colonies he upheld their right to resist imposed taxation, and collapsed while making a last speech on this dispute.

Chatterton, Thomas (1752–70), English poet who tried to pass off his writings as newly discovered ancient manuscripts. Killed himself at the age of 17.

Chaucer, Geoffrey (1340?–1400), English poet. His main work is *The Canterbury Tales*. *See also* **M5**.

Chaudhuri, Nirad Chandra (1897–1999), Indian author and broadcaster, who was resident in England after 1970. His best-known book is *Autobiography of an Unknown Indian* (1951). His other works include *A Passage to England* (1959). He was acclaimed world-wide, but spurned in India.

Chavez, Cesar (1927–93), Mexican-American (Chicano) trade union leader. Founded the National Farm Workers Association (later the United Farm Workers) in 1962 in California.

Chekhov, Anton (1860–1904), Russian dramatist and short-story writer, whose plays include *The Cherry Orchard, Uncle Vanya*, and *The Three Sisters*. His stories include *The Steppe, The Sleepyhead, The Post, The Student*, and *The Bishop*. A doctor, he was of humble origins.

Cheney, Richard (Dick) (b. 1941), US Republican Vice-President, 2001–. Defence Secretary, 1989–93.

Chernenko, Konstantin Ustinovich (1911–85) Soviet politician. Succeeded Andropov (*q.v.*) as General Secretary of the Communist Party, 1984–85.

Cherubini, Luigi (1760–1842), Italian-born musician, director of the Paris Conservatoire.

Cheshire, Lord (Group Captain Leonard Cheshire) (1917–92) War hero (most decorated World War II pilot) who founded the world-wide homes for the disabled. He married Sue Ryder (1923–2000).

Chesterfield, 4th Earl of (Philip Dormer Stanhope) (1694–1773), English statesman, whose *Letters* to his natural son, Philip Stanhope, are full of grace, wit, and worldly wisdom.

Chesterton, Gilbert Keith (1874–1936), English essayist, novelist and poet, who also wrote studies of Charles Dickens and Robert Browning. His works include *The Napoleon of Notting Hill* and *The Ballad of the White Horse*.

Chevalier, Albert (1861–1923), English music-hall comedian known for his coster sketches.

Chiang Kai-shek (1887–1975), Chinese general. He at first fought for Sun Yat-sen. After the latter's death (1925), as commander of the Kuomintang army, he attempted to unite China; but he was more anxious to defeat the Communists than to repel the Japanese in Manchuria in 1931. In 1949 retreated to Taiwan (Formosa).

Chichester, Sir Francis (1902–72), English seaman, who sailed his *Gipsy Moth IV* into Sydney harbour in 1966 after a 107-day voyage from Plymouth, and back again round the Horn.

Chingis Khan. *See* **Genghis Khan.**

Chippendale, Thomas (1718–79), designer of furniture, b. Otley, Yorks, son of a joiner. His designs are shown in *The Gentleman and Cabinet Maker's Director*, 1754.

Chirac, Jacques (b. 1932), French Gaullist politician, elected President of France, May 1995. Re-elected, 2002. Prime Minister, 1974–76 and 1986–88.

Chirico, Giorgio de (1888–1978), painter associated with the surrealist school, born in Greece of Italian parents.

Chomsky, Noam (b. 1928), American theoretical linguist whose *Syntactic Structures* revolutionised the field of linguistics.

Chopin, Frédéric François (1810–49), Polish pianist and composer, son of a French father and Polish mother. He has been called "the poet of the piano" because of the originality and delicacy of his playing. *See* **Section P.**

Chou En-lai (1898–1976), Chinese revolutionary statesman, administrator and diplomat. He organised revolt in Shanghai 1927, later formed close partnership with Mao Tse-tung, took part in the "long march" 1934–5, becoming prime minister of the new China in 1949.

Chrétien (Joseph Jack) Jean (b. 1934), Canadian Liberal politician and lawyer. Prime Minister for 10 years after 1993.

Christie, Dame Agatha (1890–1976), one of the greatest writers of detective novels. She created the Belgian detective Hercule Poirot and the inquisitive Miss Marple.

Chrysostom, St. John (*c.* 347–407), preacher. Chrysostom means golden-mouthed. First at Antioch, and later as patriarch of Constantinople, he was an eloquent teacher; but by outspokenness he lost the Empress Eudoxia's favour and died from ill-treatment.

Churchill, Lord Randolph Henry Spencer (1849–95), Conservative politician, who briefly held high office (as Leader of the House and Chancellor of the Exchequer). Father of Winston Churchill.

Churchill, Sir Winston Leonard Spencer (1874–1965), British statesman and author, son of the last-named. He entered parliament in 1900. He served as a junior officer with the British forces abroad; and during the Boer War he acted as war correspondent. His ministerial posts included Under Secretary for the Colonies 1905–8; President of the Board of Trade 1908–10; Home Secretary 1910–11; First Lord of the Admiralty 1911–15; Chancellor of the Duchy of Lancaster 1915; Minister of Munitions 1917; Minister of War 1918–21; Minister of Air 1919–21; Secretary of State for the Colonies 1921–2; Chancellor of the Exchequer 1924–9; First Lord of the Admiralty (again) 1939–40; Prime Minister and Minister of Defence 1940–5; Prime Minister 1951–5. His great achievement was as leader of the British people in the second world war. Also a prolific writer.

Cibber, Colley (1671 1757), a London actor and dramatist. His best comedies are *The Careless Husband* and *Love's Last Shift*.

Cicero, Marcus Tullius (106 43 B.C.), Roman orator and philosopher, many of whose letters and speeches survive. He held political office but was killed by the troops of the triumvirate.

Cid (El Campeador) (*c.* 1035–99), name given to the Spanish knight Rodrigo Diaz, a soldier of fortune who fought against Moors and Christians alike.

Cierva, Juan de la (1895–1936), Spanish engineer who invented the autogiro.

Cimabue, Giovanni (Cenni di Pepo) (1240–1302), early Florentine painter. His only certain work is the St. John in Pisa cathedral.

Cimarosa, Domenico (1749–1801), Italian composer. His best-known opera is *Il Matrimonio Segreto*. He held revolutionary views.

Cimon (*c.* 512–449 B.C.), Athenian statesman and general, son of Miltiades. He defeated the Persian fleet in 468. He worked for cooperation with other states, including Sparta.

Cipriani, Giambattista (1727–85), Italian painter of historical subjects who worked in London; a founder member of the Royal Academy.

Clare, John (1793–1864), Northamptonshire labourer who became a poet. *Poems Descriptive of Rural Life and Scenery*, and *The Village Minstrel* were among his publications. He died in the county lunatic asylum, but was a visionary poet of humble origins.

Clarendon, 1st Earl of (Edward Hyde) (1609–74), English statesman and historian. He was chancellor to Charles II, and his daughter married the future James II, but he fell and died in exile. He wrote a *History of the Rebellion*.

Clark, Baron (Kenneth McKenzie Clark) (1903–83), English art historian. He was director of the National Gallery 1934–45, Slade professor of fine arts at Oxford 1946–50, and chairman of the Arts Council 1953–60. O.M. 1976.

Clarke, Sir Arthur C. (b. 1917), science fiction writer, author of *2001: A Space Odyssey* (1968) (with various sequels) and *The Garden of Rama* (1991).

Clarke, Kenneth, *see* **D16.**

Clarkson, Thomas (1760–1846) devoted his life to the abolition of slavery and shares with Wilberforce credit for the passing of the Act of 1807 abolishing the British slave trade.

Claude Lorrain (Gelée) (1600–82), French landscape painter. B. near Nancy, he settled in Rome. A close student of nature, he excelled in depicting sunrise or sunset.

Claudius (10 B.C.–A.D. 54), Roman emperor. After the murder of Caligula, he was proclaimed emperor almost accidentally by the Praetorian Guard. He was a sensible administrator. In his time the empire was extended to include Britain, Thrace, and Mauretania. He was probably poisoned by his wife Agrippina.

Clausewitz, Karl von (1780–1831), German military expert whose *Vom Kriege*, expounding his theories on war, dominated Prussia in the 19th cent.

Cleisthenes (570–*c.*505 B.C.), Athenian constitutional reformer. Charged with redrawing the constitution of Athens after her occupation by Sparta in 510 B.C., he extended the work of Solon (*q.v.*). Henceforth all Athenians had equality of rights in the election of officials, regardless of wealth.

Clemenceau, Georges (1841–1929), French statesman of radical views; twice premier, 1906–9, 1917–20. He was a defender of Dreyfus.

Cleon (*c.* 495–429 B.C.) Athenian politician and demagogue, infamous for his extreme anti-Spartan position during the Peloponnesian War and his opposition to Pericles (*q.v.*).

Cleopatra (69–30 B.C.), daughter of Ptolemy XII, the seventh queen of Egypt by that name, a brilliant, ambitious woman. In 51 she became joint sovereign with her younger brother Ptolemy XIII. She was banished to Syria, but, obtaining the help of Caesar, regained the kingdom. She and Caesar became lovers, and in 47 she bore him a son Caesarion (later Ptolemy XV). After Caesar's murder she returned to Egypt. She met the triumvir Mark Antony and bore him twins; he deserted his wife and broke with his brother-in-law Octavian (later Augustus). Antony and Cleopatra were, however, defeated in 31 B.C.; Antony fell upon his sword, and Cleopatra killed herself with an asp bite.

Clinton, Bill (William Jefferson) (b. 1946), 42nd President of the United States, defeating George Bush in November 1992. President from 1993 to 2001. Born in Hope, Arkansas. A Rhodes Scholar at Oxford. Former Democrat governor of Arkansas. Became first Democrat since Roosevelt in 1936 to win reelection, but his second term was beset by scandal allegations, leading to impeachment (which he survived). His wife, Hillary Rodham Clinton, became the first former First Lady to be elected to the Senate (in November 2000).

Clive, 1st Baron (Robert Clive) (1725–74), English general who helped to lay the foundations of English power in India. B. near Market Drayton, he entered the service of the East India Company. He contemplated suicide, but Anglo-French rivalry, culminating in the Seven Years War, gave scope for his military powers in the siege of Arcot and the battle of Plassey. As a governor he showed administrative capacity.

Clovis (*c.* 465–511), Merovingian king of the Franks and a convert to Christianity. He defeated the Burgundians and West Goths, and fixed his court at Paris.

Clyde, Lord. See **Campbell, Colin.**

Cnut. See **Canute.**

Cobbett, William (1763–1835), English controversialist. He is known for his *Rural Rides*. Also published a weekly *Political Register* from 1802.

Cobden, Richard (1804–65), English advocate of free trade. The son of a Sussex farmer, he led agitation against the laws restricting import of corn, and they were repealed in 1846. He was impoverished by his public work and was helped by subscription.

Cochrane, Thomas, 10th Earl of Dundonald (1775–1860), British seaman, who crippled a French fleet in Biscay (1809), aided the liberation of Chile and Peru from Spanish rule (1819–22), of Brazil from Portuguese rule (1823–5), and assisted the Greeks in their independence struggle.

Cockcroft, Sir John Douglas (1897–1967), Cambridge nuclear physicist who shared with E. T. S. Walton the 1951 Nobel prize. They had worked together at Cambridge in the historic "atom-splitting" experiments beginning with the transmutation of lithium into boron. He helped develop British nuclear power.

Cockerell, Sir Christopher (1910–99), English inventor of the hovercraft. See **Hovercraft, Section L.**

Cocteau, Jean (1891–1963), French writer and artist in widely varied forms of art.

Cody, Samuel Franklin (1861–1913), American aviator, the first man to fly in Britain (1,390 ft. on 16 Oct. 1908). He became a British subject in 1909. Killed while flying.

Cody, William Frederick (1846–1917), American showman, known as "Buffalo Bill," whose Wild West Show toured America and Europe.

Coetzee, John M. (b. 1940) South African writer. Twice-winner of Booker Prize (*Life and Times of Michael K*, 1983; *Disgrace*, 1999). Nobel Prize for Literature, 2003. His most recent novel is *Slow Man* (2005).

Cohn, Ferdinand Julius (1828–98), German botanist, founder of the science of bacteriology.

Coke, Sir Edward (1552–1634), English legal author, judge, and rival of Francis Bacon. His legal works are his *Reports* and *Institutes*.

Colbert, Jean Baptiste (1619–83), French statesman under Louis XIV, who fostered new industries, encouraged commerce, reformed the finances and established the navy on a sound basis. A patron of literature, science, and art.

Cole, George Douglas Howard (1889–1959), English economist and political journalist, professor of social and political theory at Oxford, 1944–57. Among his writings are *The Intelligent Man's Guide through World Chaos*, and *A History of Socialist Thought* (5 vols.).

Coleridge, Samuel Taylor (1772–1834), English poet, critic, and friend of Wordsworth, with whom he published *Lyrical Ballads*. His poems include *The Ancient Mariner, Christabel*, and *Kubla Khan*.

Coleridge-Taylor, Samuel (1875–1912), English composer, the son of a West African doctor practising in London and an Englishwoman. He is best known for his Hiawatha trilogy.

Colet, John (c. 1467–1519), English humanist and divine, founded St. Paul's School (1512). As scholar and friend of Erasmus he helped to bring the new learning to England.

Colette (Sidonie Gabrielle Claudine Colette) (1873–1954), French author of the *Claudine* stories, *Chéri* and *La Fin de Chéri*.

Collier, John (1850–1934), English painter noted for his "problem" pictures.

Collingwood, 1st Baron (Cuthbert Collingwood) (1750–1810), British admiral whose ship, the *Royal Sovereign*, led the fleet to battle at Trafalgar. On Nelson's death assumed command.

Collingwood, Robin George (1889–1943), English philosopher, historian, and archaeologist, associated with Oxford from 1908 to 1941. His philosophical thought is best studied in *Speculum Mentis, Essay on Philosophical Method, Idea of Nature*, and *Idea of History*.

Collins, Michael (1890–1922), Irish politician and Sinn Fein leader. He successfully organised guerrilla warfare, and mainly negotiated the treaty with Britain in 1921, but was killed in a Republican ambush in the subsequent civil war.

Collins, William (1788–1847), English landscape and figure painter.

Collins, William Wilkie (1824–89), son of the above; one of the first English novelists to

deal with the detection of crime. He wrote *The Woman in White* and *The Moonstone*.

Colt, Samuel (1814–62), of Hartford, Connecticut, invented the revolver in 1835. It was used in the war with Mexico.

Columba, St. (521–97), founder of the monastery of Iona, b. Ireland. From the island shrine he made missionary journeys to the Highlands of Scotland. The founder of Christianity in Scotland.

Columbanus, St. (c. 540–615), Irish abbot who founded a number of monasteries in Europe.

Columbus, Christopher (c. 1451–1506), Italian navigator, b. Genoa, who, prevailing upon Ferdinand and Isabella of Spain to bear the expense of an expedition, in 1492 discovered the Bahamas, Cuba, and other West Indian islands. In 1498 he landed on the mainland of S. America.

Comenius, John Amos (1592–1670), Czech educationist and pastor, advocate of the "direct" method of teaching languages, of the use of pictures in education, and of equality of educational opportunity for girls.

Comfort, Alex (1920–2000), British sexologist whose books included *Sex and Society* (1963) and the best-selling *The Joy of Sex* (1972).

Compton, Arthur Holly (1892–1962), American physicist whose work on X-rays established what is known as the Compton effect (1923). While professor of physics at the university of Chicago (1923–45) he helped to develop the atomic bomb. Nobel prizewinner 1927.

Compton, Denis (1918–97), English cricketer. A postwar sporting idol and a most elegant batsman.

Compton, Karl Taylor (1887–1954), scientist-administrator, brother of the above.

Compton-Burnett, Dame Ivy (1884–1969), English novelist whose books include *Pastors and Masters, Men and Wives, A House and Its Head, etc.*

Comte, August (1798–1857), French philosopher, founder of positivism (q.v.).

Condé, Louis, Prince de (1621–86), French general who defeated Spain at Rocroi in 1643.

Confucius or K'ung Fu-tse (c. 551–478 B.C.), Chinese philosopher, founder of Confucianism (q.v.).

Congreve, William (1670–1729). Restoration dramatist, whose witty plays include *The Way of the World* and *Love for Love*.

Conrad, Joseph (1857–1924), English novelist of Polish birth, whose parents were exiled to Russia for political reasons. He became master mariner in the British merchant service, and began to write novels after 1884. His novels include *Almayer's Folly, Lord Jim, Nostromo*.

Conscience, Hendrik Henri (1812–83), Flemish novelist who wrote *The Lion of Flanders*.

Constable, John (1776–1837), English landscape painter, b. East Bergholt, Suffolk. Unlike his contemporary Turner, who journeyed over the Continent with his sketchbook, he found his scenes within a few miles of his home. His work was more popular in France than in England at the time and affected the Barbizon school and Delacroix. Examples of his work are in the National Gallery (*The Hay Wain, Flatford Mill*, and *The Cornfield*), the Victoria and Albert, and the Tate (*The Valley Farm*).

Constant, Jean Joseph Benjamin (1845–1902), painter of portraits and Oriental subjects.

Constantine (274–338), called "the Great," the first Christian Roman emperor. He was proclaimed at York by the army in 306. He stabilised the empire after a period of decline, and founded a new capital at Constantinople. A Christian council was held under his auspices at Nicaea in 325. Baptised on his death-bed.

Cook, James (1728–79), English navigator, son of an agricultural labourer. He entered the Royal Navy and gained a high reputation for his scientific skill. He made voyages of discovery to New Zealand and Australia in the ships under his command, *Endeavour, Resolution*, and *Adventure*. He anchored at Botany Bay in 1770 on his first voyage and gave it that name because of the interesting plants found on its shores. He also surveyed the Newfoundland coast. In an attempt to find the north-west passage he was murdered at Hawaii.

Cook, Robin. See **D16.**

Cook, Thomas (1808–92), pioneer of railway excursions and tourism. His first organised trip was from Leicester to Loughborough on 5 July 1841.

Cookson, Dame Catherine (1906–98), prolific authoress whose novels sold over 100 million copies.

The illegitimate daughter of an alcoholic mother.

Cooper, Sir Astley Paston (1768–1841), English surgeon and author of medical textbooks.

Cooper, James Fenimore (1789–1851), American novelist, who produced stirring stories of adventure, among them *The Spy, The Last of the Mohicans, The Pathfinder,* and *The Deerslayer.*

Cooper, Samuel (1609–72), English miniaturist, represented with his brother Alexander (d. 1660) in the Victoria and Albert Museum.

Copernicus, Nicolas (1478–1543), founder of modern astronomy, b. at Torun in Poland. He studied at Cracow and at a number of Italian universities before settling at Frauenburg in 1512 where he became canon of the cathedral. More of a student than a practical astronomer, he spent most of his private life seeking a new theory of the heavenly bodies. In his *On the Revolution of the Celestial Orbs,* he put forward the novel theory that the planets, including the earth, revolve round the sun.

Coppée, François Joachim (1842–1908), French poet, novelist and dramatist.

Coquelin, Benoit Constant (1841–1909), and **Coquelin, Ernest** (1848–1909), (Coquelin aîné et cadet), brothers, were leading lights of the French theatre.

Corelli, Arcangelo (1653–1713), Italian composer and violinist, who established the form of the concerto grosso. *See* Section P.

Corneille, Pierre (1606–84), French dramatist, who ranks with Racine as a master of classical tragedy. *Le Cid, Polyeucte,* and *Le Menteur* marked a new era in French dramatic production.

Cornwallis, 1st Marquess (Charles Cornwallis) (1738–1805), British general who commanded the British forces which surrendered to the Americans at Yorktown in 1781, thus ending the war of independence. He was twice governor-general of India.

Corot, Jean Baptiste (1796–1875), French landscape painter.

Correggio, Antonio Allegri da (1494–1534), Italian painter, b. Correggio. His style anticipates the baroque. His *Ecce Homo* is in the National Gallery.

Cortés, Hernando (1488–1547), Spanish adventurer, b. Medellin, Estremadura, who captured Mexico for Spain, crushing an ancient civilisation.

Coulton, George Gordon (1858–1947), scholar and historian of the Middle Ages. In his *Five Centuries of Religion* he sets forth his interpretation of monastic history in England.

Couperin, a family of French musicians who were organists at St. Gervais, Paris, from about 1650 till 1826. **François Couperin** (1668–1783), called "Couperin the Great," is the best known today for his harpsichord music.

Cousin, Victor (1792–1867), French educationist and philosopher, founder of the eclectic school.

Cousins, Samuel (1801–87), English mezzotint engraver of plates after Reynolds, Millais, Landseer, and Hogarth.

Cousteau, Jacques-Yves (1910–97), French underwater explorer, pioneer of aqualung diving. He opened up the oceans to exploration.

Couve de Murville, Maurice (1907–99), French diplomat; de Gaulle's foreign minister 1958–68.

Coverdale, Miles (1488–1568), one of the early English reformers, b. Yorkshire, later to become bishop of Exeter. He assisted Tyndale in translating the Pentateuch and completed his own translation of the Bible in 1535. The Psalms still used in the Prayer Book and many of the phrases in the authorised version of 1611 are from his translation.

Coward, Sir Noël (1899–1973), British playwright, actor, composer and composer. His first success (*The Young Idea,* 1923) was followed by a succession of witty plays and comedies. His popular songs included 'Mad Dogs and Englishmen'.

Cowdrey, Lord (Sir Colin Cowdrey) (1932–2000), English cricketer. Scored 42,719 runs in first-class cricket (and 107 centuries). First captained England, 1959. President of MCC, 1986–7.

Cowper, William (1731–1800), English religious poet. His work is characterised by simplicity and tenderness. His best-known poems are *John Gilpin* and *The Task.*

Cox, David (1783–1859), English landscape painter. A collection of his works is in the Birmingham Gallery and the Tate Gallery.

Crabbe, George (1754–1832), English poet of grim humour; author of *The Village* and *The Borough.*

Craig, Edward Gordon (1872–1966), son of Ellen Terry, producer and author of books on stagecraft.

Cranmer, Thomas (1489–1556), archbishop of Canterbury under Henry VIII, and Edward VI; an ardent promoter of the Reformation. On Mary's accession he at first consented to return to Catholicism, but when called upon to make public avowal of his recantation, refused, and was burnt at the stake.

Crichton, James (1560–82), Scottish adventurer who for his scholarly accomplishments was called "the admirable Crichton." Killed in a brawl.

Crick, Francis Harry Compton (1916–2004), English molecular biologist. With James D. Watson discovered the structure of DNA (1953). Jointly (with Watson and Maurice H. Wilkins) awarded 1962 Nobel Prize for Medicine and Physiology. Author of *The Astonishing Hypothesis: the Scientific Search for the Soul* (1994). Perhaps the greatest British scientist of the last century.

Cripps, Sir Stafford (1889–1952), British Labour statesman. As chancellor of the exchequer in postwar Britain, his programme was one of austerity.

Crispi, Francesco (1819–1901), Italian statesman, who aided Garibaldi and was later premier.

Crispin, St. (*c.* 285), martyr with his brother. By tradition they were Roman and became shoemakers, hence patron saints of shoemaking.

Croce, Benedetto (1886–1952), Italian philosopher and critic. His philosophy is expounded in the four volumes of *Filosofia dello Spirito* (which has been translated into English). He founded and edited *La Critica* in 1908. He was strongly opposed to fascism.

Croesus (d. *c.* 546 B.C.), last king of Lydia, reputed to be of immense wealth. Conquered and condemned to death by Cyrus, he was reprieved when Cyrus heard him recall Solon's saying "Call no man happy till he is dead."

Crome, John (1769–1821), English landscape painter, b. Norwich.

Cromer, 1st Earl of (Evelyn Baring) (1841–1917), British diplomat who, as British comptroller-general in Egypt from 1883 to 1907, did much to maintain order, improve the finances and promote development.

Crompton, Samuel (1753–1827), English inventor of the spinning-mule (1779), which substituted machinery for hand work. He was b. near Bolton, a farmer's son, and benefited little by his invention.

Cromwell, Oliver (1599–1658), Protector of the commonwealth of England, Scotland, and Ireland. B. at Huntingdon, he represented Huntingdon in parliament. When civil war broke out, he served under the Earl of Essex; and then reorganised the parliamentary army, winning victories at Marston Moor and Naseby. Tortuous negotiations with Charles I could not be brought to an end, and he promoted the king's trial and execution in 1649. He defeated the Scots at Dunbar. When continued difficulties beset government he became Protector in 1653, but was soon obliged to govern by major-generals. His handling of Ireland enhanced the difficulties of that country. An able general and a strong character, he was personally tolerant (an Independent), sincere and devout; but he was in the revolutionary's dilemma that there is no easy exit from a revolutionary situation.

Cromwell, Richard (1626–1712), son of the above, and his successor in the protectorate.

Cromwell, Thomas (1485–1540), English statesman, who succeeded Wolsey in the service of Henry VIII, and carried out the dissolution of the monasteries. Fell from favour and was executed.

Crookes, Sir William (1832–1919), English physicist who discovered the element thallium (1861) and invented the Crookes tube (1874) which was used by J. J. Thomson and others in their researches into the conduction of electricity in gases. He was also an authority on sanitation.

Cruikshank, George (1792–1878), caricaturist and book illustrator, whose work includes illustrations to *Grimm's Fairy Tales,* and *Oliver Twist.*

Cuéllar, Javier Pérez de (b. 1920), Peruvian diplomat. UN Secretary-General, 1982–end of 1991. Succeeded in negotiating Iran–Iraq ceasefire (1988) but failed to prevent Gulf War (1991).

Cummings, Bruce Frederick (1889–1919), English zoologist, better known however as the author of *Diary of a Disappointed Man* (1919) written

under the pseudonym W. N. P. Barbellion.
Cunard, Sir Samuel (1787–1865), founder of the Cunard line of steam ships. He was born in Nova Scotia, of a Welsh family of Quakers.
Cunningham of Hyndhope, 1st Viscount (Andrew Browne Cunningham) (1883–1963). British admiral in two world wars, b. Edinburgh. He served as C.-in-C., Mediterranean, 1939–42 and Feb.–Oct. 1943; naval C.-in-C. for the assault on North Africa 1942; and first sea lord 1943–6.
Curie, Marie Sklodowska (1867–1934), first great woman scientist, b. Poland. Her father was a professor of physics at Warsaw. She came to Paris to study at the Sorbonne and married **Pierre Curie** (1859–1906), professor of physics. Thus began a fruitful collaborative career that led to the discovery of radium for which they shared the 1903 Nobel prize for physics. In 1911 Mme Curie received the Nobel prize for chemistry. Pierre Curie was killed in an accident. See also Joliot-Curie.
Curzon of Kedleston, 1st Marquess (George Nathaniel Curzon) (1859–1925), statesman and administrator; viceroy of India 1898–1905; member of Lloyd George's war cabinet 1916–18; foreign secretary 1919–24.
Cuthbert, St. (c. 635–87), Celtic monk who became prior of Old Melrose (on the Tweed) and later of Lindisfarne. For a time he lived in seclusion on the Farne islands. Bede wrote his life.
Cuvier, Georges (1769–1832), French naturalist, noted for his system of classification of animals and his studies in comparative anatomy. His La Règne Animal (1819) became a standard work.
Cuyp, Albert (Aelbert) (1620–91), important Dutch landscape painter of sea and river views.
Cyprian, St. (d. 258), bishop of Carthage, and early Christian writer who was martyred.
Cyrano de Bergerac (Savinien de Cyrano) (1619–55), talented and original French satirist and writer. A colourful, almost mythical figure, who fought numerous duels. Forever identified by his large nose.
Cyrus (559–529 B.C.), Persian emperor. He founded the Achaemenid line, having defeated the Medes. By conquering Lydia and Babylonia, he controlled Asia Minor. He was a wise ruler, allowing the Jews to rebuild their temple.

D

Daguerre, Louis Jacques Mandé (1789–1851), French photographic pioneer, who invented the daguerrotype process. See Section L.
Dahl, Roald (1916–90), British author of Norwegian parentage. He wrote macabre, ingenious stories, including those in Kiss, Kiss (1960), and popular books for children, such as Charlie and the Chocolate Factory (1964). Some of his stories were dramatised for the TV series, Tales of the Unexpected.
Daimler, Gottlieb (1834–1900), German inventor, with N. A. Otto of Cologne, of the Otto gas engine. The Mercédès car, exhibited at Paris in 1900, was named after the daughter of Emile Jellinek, Austrian banker and car enthusiast.
Dalai Lama. See Section L.
Dale, Sir Henry Hallett (1875–1968), English physiologist. He shared the 1936 Nobel prize for medicine for his work on the chemical transmission of nerve impulses.
Dalhousie, 1st Marquess of (James Andrew Broun Ramsay) (1812–60), governor-general of India. He annexed the Punjab, opened the civil service to Indians and acted against suttee.
Dalton, John (1766–1844), English chemist and mathematician, a Quaker teacher of Manchester. In 1808 in the first number of his New System of Chemical Philosophy (1808–27) the modern chemical atomic theory was first propounded (i.e. that the atoms of the chemical elements are qualitatively different from one another).
Damien, Father (1840–89), Belgian missionary priest, originally named Joseph de Veuster, who led a fight to help lepers in Hawaii.
Damocles, 5th cent. B.C., Syracusan flatterer who pronounced the tyrant Dionysius the happiest of men. To illustrate the uncertainty of life, Dionysius invited him to a banquet, where a naked sword hung over his head by a hair. Hence the expression "Sword of Damocles" to

mean impending danger or threat.
Damrosch, Walter Johannes (1862–1950), American conductor and composer, b. Breslau, Prussia. He promoted musical development in the U.S., when conductor of the New York Symphony Society which his father, Leopold Damrosch (1832–1885) had founded in 1878.
D'Annunzio, Gabriele (1863–1938), Italian poet, dramatist and nationalist. In 1919 he led a raid on Fiume and seized it, but was eventually forced to surrender. His bodyguard wore the black shirt, later the uniform of the Fascists.
Dante Alighieri (1265–1321), Italian poet, a figure of world literature. He was b. at Florence in a troubled period. Though he saw her but once or twice, he loved a lady whom he called Beatrice, who is believed to have been Bice Portinari who married Simone di Bardi; she died in 1290, after which Dante wrote his Vita Nuova. His next work Convivio was philosophical. He joined the party of the Bianchi, attained municipal office, but was imprisoned and in 1301 fled. His Divina Commedia is a work of moral edification, replete with symbolism. He died at Ravenna.
Danton, Georges Jacques (1759–94), French revolutionary. To his eloquent lead in 1792 was largely due the defeat of the foreign forces attempting to quell the revolution. He was a member of the Committee of Public Safety, and sought to moderate the extremists, but was displaced by Robespierre and was executed.
D'Arblay. See Burney.
Darby, Abraham (1677–1717), member of the Quaker family of ironmasters of Coalbrookdale, Shropshire, who paved the way for the industrial revolution by developing iron metallurgy. His grandson **Abraham** (1750–91) built the first cast-iron bridge (1779) over the Severn at Coalbrookdale.
Darius I (548–486 B.C.), Persian king and founder of Persepolis. He extended the borders of the Persian empire beyond the Indus, and reorganised it into satrapies. He declared "God's plan for the earth is not turmoil but peace, prosperity and good government." On clashing with the Greeks, however, he was defeated at Marathon. **Darius II** was a natural son of Artaxerxes I and d. 405 B.C. **Darius III** (d. 331 B.C.) was the last of the Persian kings, and was defeated by Alexander and assassinated.
Darling, Grace Horsley (1815–42), English heroine who by putting off in a small boat from the lighthouse on one of the Farne islands, of which her father was keeper, saved the shipwrecked crew of the Forfarshire.
Darnley, Henry Stewart, Lord (1545–67), second husband of Mary, Queen of Scots (1565). He plotted the murder of her secretary Rizzio, and was subsequently himself murdered.
Darwin, Charles Robert (1809–82), English naturalist, b. Shrewsbury, one of the pioneers of experimental biology. After returning from his formative voyage round the world as naturalist on the Beagle (1831–6), he spent nearly twenty years building up evidence for his theory of evolution before publishing it in The Origin of Species (1859). In it he argued that the evolution of present-day morphology had been built up by the gradual and opportunistic mechanism of natural selection. See also T30.
Daudet, Alphonse (1840–97), French writer whose works include Lettres de mon Moulin, Robert Helmont, and Tartarin de Tarascon.
David (King of Israel). See Section H.
David I (1084–1153), King of Scotland. As uncle of Matilda, daughter of Henry I of England, he supported her claim to the English crown, but was defeated. In Scotland he promoted unity.
David II (1324–71), King of Scotland. He was son of Robert Bruce. In invading England he was captured at Neville's Cross, 1346.
David, Sir Edgeworth (1848–1934), Australian geologist who accompanied Shackleton's antarctic expedition, 1907–9, leading the party that reached the south magnetic pole.
David, Jacques Louis (1748–1825), French painter of classical subjects and an ardent republican.
David, St., patron saint of Wales who lived in south Wales in the 6th cent.
Davies, Sir Peter Maxwell. See P22.
Davies, Sir Walford (1869–1941), English organist, composer, and broadcaster on music.

Davies, William Henry (1871–1940), Welsh poet. He spent some years tramping in both England and America, and his work shows knowledge of and love for nature. He wrote *Autobiography of a Super-tramp.*

Davies, William Robertson (1913–95), Canadian writer whose works included *Rebel Angels* (1981) and *What's Bred in the Bone* (1985).

Da Vinci. *See* Leonardo.

Davis, David. *See* D16.

Davis, Jefferson (1808–89), American civil war leader. B. in Kentucky, he was made president of the Confederate States when the civil war broke out. After the war he was tried for treason, but discharged. He wrote *The Rise and Fall of the Confederate Government.*

Davis, John (c. 1550–1605), Elizabethan explorer and discoverer of Davis's Strait, the channel between the Atlantic and Arctic oceans. Invented the backstaff, or Davis's quadrant.

Davitt, Michael (1846–1906), Irish nationalist. The son of a peasant who later came to England, he joined the Fenians, and in 1870 was sentenced to penal servitude. On his release he helped to found the Land League in 1879; was again imprisoned; and wrote *Leaves from a Prison Diary.* He was subsequently returned to parliament.

Davy, Sir Humphry (1778–1829), English chemist, b. Penzance. Much of his work found practical application, e.g., the miner's safety lamp which still bears his name. His *Elements of Agricultural Chemistry* (1813) contains the first use in English of the word "element." Michael Faraday was his assistant at the Royal Institution.

Dawkins, (Clinton) Richard (b. 1941), Oxford biologist. Author of *The Selfish Gene* (1976), *The Blind Watchmaker* (1986), *Climbing Mount Improbable* (1996), *Unweaving the Rainbow* (1998), and *The Ancestor's Tale* (2004).

Day Lewis, Cecil (1904–72), poet and critic; professor of poetry at Oxford from 1951–6. He succeeded Masefield as poet laureate in 1968.

De Beauvoir, Simone (1908–86), feminist writer whose work *The Second Sex* is now the icon of feminism.

Debussy, Claude Achille (1862–1918), composer and leader of the French Impressionist school in music. Among his works are *Suite bergamasque*, containing the popular *Clair de lune*; *L'après-midi d'un Faune*, inspired by the poem of Mallarmé, and *La Mer*. He also wrote an opera *Pelléas et Mélisande*. Often described as 'the most French of all musicians'.

Defoe, Daniel (1660–1731), English political writer; also author of *Robinson Crusoe, Moll Flanders,* and a *Tour of Gt. Britain.* His *Shortest Way with Dissenters* brought him imprisonment.

De Forest, Lee (1873–1961), American inventor who was the first to use alternating-current transmission, and improved the thermionic valve detector by which wireless and sound films were made possible.

Degas, Edgar (1834–1917), French impressionist painter and sculptor. He painted subjects from everyday life—dancers, café life, the racecourse.

De Gasperi, Alcide (1881–1954), Italian politician who founded the Christian Democrat Party.

de Gaulle. *See* Gaulle, Charles de.

De Havilland, Sir Geoffrey (1882–1965), pioneer of civil and military aviation in Britain; designer of the famous Moth machines.

De Klerk, Frederik Willem (b. 1936), South African State President from 1989 to 1994. He launched a far-reaching reform process in South Africa. Shared Nobel Peace Prize, 1993, with Nelson Mandela. He retired from politics in 1997.

De Kooning, Willem (1904–97), one of the founding fathers of abstract expressionism in modern art.

Delacroix, Ferdinand Victor Eugène (1798–1863), French painter of the Romantic school.

De la Mare, Walter John (1873–1956), English poet and novelist whose work has a characteristic charm. Much of it was written for children.

Delane, John Thadeus (1817–79), editor of *The Times,* 1841–77, who did much to establish that paper's standing.

Delaroche, Paul (1797–1856), French historical painter.

Delibes, Clément Philibert Léo (1836–91), French composer of much graceful music, including operas, of which *Lakmé* is the best known, and ballets, among them *Coppélia.*

Delius, Frederick (1862–1934), English composer of German parentage. His music, highly idiosyncratic in idiom, was more readily re-

ceived in Germany than in England until promoted by Sir Thomas Beecham. *See* **Section P.**

Delors, Jacques, (b. 1925), French socialist politician. President, European Commission, 1985–95.

Deleuze, Gilles (1925–95), a key figure in poststructuralism. Author of *The Logic of Sense.*

Democritus (c. 470–c. 400 B.C.), one of the first scientific thinkers, pupil of Leucippus (fl. c. 440 B.C.). He took an atomic view of matter, denied the existence of mind as a separate entity, and counted happiness and inner tranquility as important moral principles. His attitude was not shared by his contemporary, Socrates, nor by Plato and Aristotle, but was accepted by Epicurus. The atomic theory thus passed into the background for many centuries.

Demosthenes (384–322 B.C.), Greek orator who, by his *Philippics,* roused the Athenians to resist the growing power of Philip of Macedon.

Dench, Dame Judi (b. 1934), outstanding and versatile actress of enduring popularity. C.H. (2005).

Deng Xiaoping (1904–97), Chinese politician, b. Szechwan; rehabilitated at Eleventh Party Congress (1977); effective leader of China in 1980s, target of May 1989 student revolt. Architect of the economic transformation of modern China. His career began with the Long March.

Denning, Lord (Alfred Denning) (1899–1999), English judge. Master of the Rolls, 1962–82. Conducted Profumo affair enquiry, 1963. Outspoken defender of individual liberties. O.M. (1997).

De Quincey, Thomas (1785–1859), English essayist and critic; friend of Wordsworth and Southey. He wrote *Confessions of an English Opium-eater.*

Derain, André (1880–1954), French artist, acclaimed for his Fauve pictures. Later influenced by Cézanne.

De Reszke, Jean (1853–1925) and **De Reszke, Edouard** (1856–1917), Polish operatic singers, the first a tenor, the second a baritone.

Derrida, Jacques (1930–2004). French philosopher who founded the philosophical school of "deconstruction". He had enormous influence on literary theory.

Derwentwater, 3rd Earl of (James Radcliffe) (1689–1716), leader of the English Jacobite movement. Defeated at Preston in 1715 and beheaded.

Descartes, René (1596–1650), French mathematician, pioneer of modern philosophy. Unconvinced by scholastic tradition and theological dogma, he sought to get back to why anything can be said to be true. The basis of his Cartesian philosophy is summed up in his own words, *Cogito, ergo sum* (I think, therefore I am).

Desmoulins, Camille (1760–94), French revolutionary. He represented Paris in the National Convention, and wrote witty and sarcastic pamphlets and periodicals. An ally of Danton and was executed with him.

Deutscher, Isaac (1907–67), Marxist historian, biographer of Stalin and Trotsky.

De Valéra, Eamon (1882–1975), Irish statesman, b. New York, son of a Spanish father and an Irish mother. He was imprisoned for his part in the Easter rising of 1916. He opposed the treaty of 1921; and in 1926, when the republican Fianna Fáil was founded, he became its president. Prime minister, 1937–48, 1951–4, 1957–9; president of the republic, 1959–73.

De Valois, Dame Ninette (1898–2001), Irish-born ballet dancer and choreographer. In 1931 she founded the Sadler's Wells Ballet School (now Royal Ballet School), of which she became director. *Autobiography* (1957).

Dewar, Donald. *See* D17.

Dewar, Sir James (1842–1923), chemist and physicist, a native of Kincardine. He succeeded in liquefying hydrogen, and invented the vacuum flask. The explosive cordite was the joint invention of himself and Sir Frederick Abel.

Dewey, John (1859–1952), American philosopher, psychologist, and educationist. A follower of William James and an exponent of pragmatism.

De Witt, Jan (1625–72), Dutch republican statesman, who carried on war with England and later negotiated the Triple Alliance, but was overthrown by the Orange Party and murdered.

Diaghilev, Sergei Pavlovich (1872–1929), ballet impresario and founder of the Russian ballet.

Diana, Princess of Wales (1961–97), born Diana Frances Spencer. Married **Charles,** Prince of Wales (q.v.) in 1981. Divorced 1996. Tragic death in car crash, 31 August 1997.

Dickens, Charles (1812–70), popular English novelist of the 19th cent., with enormous output and capacity for vivid story-telling. Of humble origin, he was extremely successful. His best-known works are perhaps *Pickwick Papers, Oliver Twist, A Christmas Carol* (this influenced the observance of Christmas), *Dombey and Son, David Copperfield, Little Dorrit,* and *Great Expectations.* His great-granddaughter, **Monica Dickens** (1915–92), wrote popular novels and autobiographical books.

Dickinson, Emily (1830–86), reclusive American poet whose writing has a mystic quality.

Dickinson, Goldsworthy Lowes (1863–1932), English author, an interpreter and upholder of the Greek view of life.

Diderot, Denis (1713–84), French man of letters, critic of art and literature, and editor of the *Encyclopédie* (1713–84).

Diemen, Anthony van (1593–1645), Dutch promoter of exploration. As governor-general in the Far East, he promoted Dutch trade and influence; and despatched Abel Tasman, who in 1642 discovered New Zealand and Van Diemen's Land (now Tasmania).

Diesel, Rudolf (1858–1913), German engineer, inventor of an internal combustion engine which he patented in 1893. *See also* **Section L.**

DiMaggio, Joe (1914–99), US baseball legend known as Joltin' Joe and The Yankee Clipper.

Diocletian (245–313), Roman emperor and persecutor of Christianity. He divided the empire under a system of joint rule; later abdicated.

Diogenes (412–322 B.C.), Greek cynic philosopher who lived in a tub and told Alexander to get out of his sunshine. He sought virtue and moral freedom in liberation from desire.

Dionysius the elder and younger, tyrants of Syracuse in the 4th cent. B.C.

Dionysius Exiguus (*fl.* 6th cent.), famous inventor of the Christian calendar. Known in English as Denis the Little.

Dirac, Paul Adrien Maurice (1902–84), English physicist who shared with Erwin Schrödinger the 1933 Nobel prize for their work on Heisenberg's theory of quantum mechanics. O.M. (1973).

Disney, Walter Elias (1901–66), American film cartoonist, creator of Mickey Mouse. He is known for his *Silly Symphonies, Snow White and the Seven Dwarfs,* and *Pinocchio.*

Disraeli, Benjamin, Earl of Beaconsfield (1804–81), British statesman and novelist who helped to form modern Conservatism in England. The son of Isaac (*q.v.*), he published his first novel at 21, and later *Coningsby* and *Sibyl,* which helped to rouse the social conscience. He entered parliament in 1837 and was prime minister 1868 and 1874–80, when he arranged the purchase of shares in the Suez canal. He was rival of Gladstone and friend of Queen Victoria.

D'Israeli, Isaac (1766–1848), father of Benjamin (*q.v.*) and author of *Curiosities of Literature.*

Dobson, Austin (1840–1921), English writer of light verse and of 18th cent. biography.

Dodgson, Charles Lutwidge (1832–98), English writer. Under the pseudonym Lewis Carroll, he wrote poems and books for children, including *Alice's Adventures in Wonderland.* In private life he was a lecturer in mathematics at Oxford.

Dolci, Carlo (1616–86), one of the last Florentine painters.

Doll, Sir Richard (1912–2005), epidemiologist who first demonstrated the link between smoking and lung cancer.

Dollfuss, Engelbert (1892–1934), Chancellor of Austria, 1932–34. Murdered during attempted Nazi coup.

Dominic, St. (1170–1221), founder of the Friars Preachers or Black Friars. B. in Castile, he and his followers sought to teach the ignorant. In 1216 they were formed into an order and vowed to poverty. The order spread widely.

Domitian (Titus Flavius Domitianus) (A.D. 51–96), Roman emperor, son of Vespasian. Emperor from A.D. 81. He ruled despotically, aroused the hatred of the senate, and was assassinated as a result of a palace conspiracy.

Donatello (Donato di Niccolò) (*c.* 1386–1466), Italian sculptor, b. Florence, son of Niccolò di Betto di Bardo. He was the founder of modern sculpture, producing statues independent of a background, designed to stand in the open to be viewed from all angles. Among his masterpieces are the statues of *St. George* and *David* (in the Bargello, Florence) and his equestrian *Gattamelata* in Padua, the first bronze horse to be cast in the Renaissance.

Donizetti, Gaetano (1797–1848), Italian composer. The best known of his sixty operas are *Lucia di Lammermoor, La Fille du Régiment,* and *Don Pasquale. See* **Section P.**

Donne, John (1572–1631), English metaphysical poet and preacher (dean of St. Paul's). His poems and sermons marked by passion, wit, and profundity of thought have received full publicity only in the present century. His writings include *Elegies, Satires, Songs and Sonnets, Problems and Paradoxes* and the *Holy Sonnets.*

Doré, Gustave (1833–83), French artist who painted scriptural subjects and illustrated Dante, Milton, and Tennyson.

Dostoyevsky, Feodor Mikhailovich (1821 81), Russian novelist, b. Moscow. As a result of his revolutionary activity he was sent to hard labour in Siberia. In his books, which include *Crime and Punishment, The Brothers Karamazov, The Idiot,* and *The Possessed,* he explored the dark places of the human spirit.

Douglas of Kirtleside, 1st Baron (William Sholto Douglas) (1893–1969), British airman; commanded Fighter command, 1940–2, Coastal command, 1944–5. A Labour peer.

Douglas, Norman (1868–1952), novelist and travel writer. A Scot, born in Austria, he settled on the Mediterranean. His works include *South Wind.*

Douglass, Frederick (*c.* 1817–95), prominent US abolitionist and statesman. Born a slave, he became a major force in the crusade against slavery. Later US minister to Haiti.

Doulton, Sir Henry (1820–97), English potter and the inventor of Doulton ware.

Dowden, Edward (1843–1913), English literary critic and Shakespearean scholar.

Dowding, 1st Baron (Hugh Caswell Tremenheere Dowding) (1882–1970), British airman; commanded Fighter Command in Battle of Britain.

Dowland, John (*c.* 1563–1626), English composer of songs with lute accompaniment. His son Robert was later Court lutenist to Charles I.

Doyle, Sir Arthur Conan (1859–1930), British writer, b. Edinburgh, creator of the detective Sherlock Holmes and his friend and foil, Dr. Watson. He was trained as a doctor but after 1890 devoted himself to writing.

Doyle, Richard (1824–83), humorous artist on the staff of *Punch.*

D'Oyly Carte, Richard (1844–1901), noted English theatrical manager, who built the Savoy theatre and there produced Gilbert and Sullivan operas.

Draco (7th cent. B.C.), Athenian lawmaker who redrew the constitution of Athens in 621 B.C. and substantially increased the penalties for debt, thus giving his name to very severe laws.

Drake, Sir Francis (*c.* 1540–96), English seaman. In 1577–80 he sailed round the world in the *Golden Hind.* In 1587 he destroyed a number of Spanish ships in Cadiz harbour; and under Lord Howard he helped to defeat the Spanish Armada in 1588.

Draper, John William (1811–82), American chemist, b. near Liverpool. He was the first, using Daguerre's process, to take a successful photograph of the human face (1840), and the moon.

Dreiser, Theodore (1871–1935), American novelist of austere realism. Author of *An American Tragedy.*

Dreyfus, Alfred (1859–1935), French victim of injustice. Of Jewish parentage, in 1894 he was accused of divulging secrets to a foreign power, and was sentenced by a military secret tribunal to imprisonment for life on Devil's Island in French Guiana. At a new trial in 1899 he was again found guilty. Efforts continued to be made on his behalf, and in 1906 he was entirely exonerated, restored to his rank in the army, and made a Chevalier of the Legion of Honour.

Drinkwater, John (1882–1937), English poet and playwright. His plays include *Abraham Lincoln,* and *Oliver Cromwell.*

Drummond, William, (1585–1649), Scottish poet and Royalist pamphleteer. Laird of Hawthornden.

Drury, Alfred (1857–1944), English sculptor, especially of statues of Queen Victoria.

Dryden, John (1631–1700), prolific English poet and dramatist, who also wrote political satire (*Absalom and Achitophel*). He was hostile to the revolution of 1688, and thereafter mainly translated classical writers, including Virgil.

Du Barry, Marie Jean Bécu, Comtesse (1746–93), mistress of Louis XV of France and guillotined by the revolutionary tribunal.

Dubček, Alexander (1921–92), Czech political leader. First Secretary, Communist Party, 1968–69. His reform programme (the 'Prague Spring') prompted the Russian invasion of August 1968. Restored to public life, 1989.

Du Chaillu, Paul Belloni (1835–1903), traveller in Africa, who in 1861 and 1867 published accounts of his explorations. A French-American.

Dufferin and Ava, 1st Marquess of (Frederick Temple Hamilton-Temple Blackwood) (1826–1902), British diplomat, writer, and governor-general of Canada and viceroy of India.

Dulles, John Foster (1888–1959), U.S. Secretary of State, 1953–9. A staunch Cold War warrior.

Dumas, Alexandre (1802–70), French romantic novelist, among whose major works are *The Three Musketeers*, *The Count of Monte Cristo*, and *The Black Tulip*. His remains were interned in the Pantheon in 2002.

Dumas, Alexandre (1824–95), French dramatist, son of above; author, *La Dame aux Camélias*.

Du Maurier, George (1834–96), contributor to *Punch* and author of *Trilby*.

Dummett, Professor Sir Michael (b. 1925), English philosopher. Succeeded Ayer as Wykeham Professor of Logic at Oxford University. Author of *Logical Basis of Metaphysics* (1990). Anti-racist.

Duncan Smith, Iain. See D17.

Dundee, 1st Viscount (John Graham of Claverhouse), (1648–89), Scottish soldier ("Bonnie Dundee"). Employed to suppress the covenanters, he was defeated at Drumclog, but victorious at Bothwell Brig. At the revolution of 1688 he supported James II, and was killed in the (victorious) battle of Killiecrankie.

Dundonald, Earl of. See Cochrane, Thomas.

Duns Scotus, John (c. 1265–1308), Scottish scholastic philosopher, b. at Maxton near Roxburgh, opponent of Thomas Aquinas. He joined the Franciscans, studied and taught at Oxford and Paris, and probably d. at Cologne. He challenged the harmony of faith and reason.

Dunstable, John (c. 1380–1453), the earliest English composer known by name. He was a contemporary of the Netherlands composers Dufay and Binchois. See Section P.

Dunstan, St. (908–88), reforming archbishop of Canterbury. He lived through seven reigns from Athelstan to Ethelred, and was adviser especially to Edgar. Under him Glastonbury Abbey became a centre of religious teaching.

Dupleix, Joseph François (1697–1763), French governor in India. He extended French influence and power in the Carnatic, but his plans were frustrated by his English opponent, Clive. He was recalled in 1754 and died in poverty.

Dürer, Albrecht (1471–1528), German painter and engraver. B. at Nuremberg, he was (like his Italian contemporary, Leonardo) a man of intellectual curiosity and scientific insight. His best work is in his copper engravings, woodcuts, and drawings; the former include *The Knight*, *Melancholia*, and *St. Jerome in his Study*. He was the friend of Luther and Melanchthon.

Durham, Earl of (John George Lambton) (1792–1840), governor-general of Canada after the disturbances of 1837, and in 1839 presented to parliament the *Durham Report*, which laid down the principle of colonial self-government.

Durrell, Gerald (1925–95). Zoo pioneer, conservationist and popular and gifted writer on animals. Author of *My Family and Other Animals*.

Duruflé, Maurice (1902–86), French organist, teacher and composer (e.g. *Three Dances for Orchestra*, 1939).

Duse, Elenora (1861–1924), Italian tragedienne.

Duval, Claude (1643–70), notorious highwayman who came to England from Normandy and was eventually hanged at Tyburn.

Dvořák, Antonín (1841–1904), Czech composer whose music is rich in folk-song melodies of his native Bohemia. In 1884 he conducted his *Stabat Mater* in London. His *New World* symphony was composed in New York, where he was head of the National Conservatoire (1892–5). See Section P.

Dylan, Bob (Robert Allen Zimmermann) (b. 1941). Performer and songwriter. One of the most influential and creative musicians in rock music.

Dyson, Sir Frank Watson (1868–1939), English

astronomer who was astronomer royal 1910–33, and astronomer royal for Scotland 1905–10.

Dyson, Sir George (1883–1964), English composer and writer. In *The New Music* he analysed the technique of modern schools of composition.

E

Earhart, Amelia (1898–1937), American air pioneer. First woman to fly the Atlantic alone. Disappeared in 1937 during a Pacific flight.

Eastlake, Sir Charles Lock (1793–1865), English painter of historical and religious works.

Eastman, George (1854–1932), American inventor of the roll photographic film and Kodak camera.

Easton, Florence (Gertrude) (1882–1955), English operatic soprano of great versatility. Repertoire of 88 roles. Last woman to sing with Caruso in 1920.

Eck, Johann von (1486–1543), German Catholic theologian and opponent of Luther.

Eddington, Sir Arthur Stanley (1882–1944), English astronomer (Greenwich observatory 1906–13; Cambridge observatory 1914–44). His works include *The Nature of the Physical World*.

Eddy, Mrs Mary Baker (1821–1910), American founder of the Church of Christ Scientist. Her *Science and Health with Key to the Scriptures* was published in 1875. See Christian Science, J9.

Edelinck, Gerard (1640–1707), Flemish engraver, b. Antwerp, the first to reproduce in print the colour, as well as the form, of a picture.

Eden, Robert Anthony, 1st Earl of Avon (1897–1977), British statesman. He entered parliament in 1923; became foreign secretary in 1935 (resigning in 1938 over Chamberlain's negotiation with Mussolini and rebuff to President Roosevelt); deputy prime minister in 1951; succeeded Sir Winston Churchill in 1955. His Suez policy divided the country. He resigned for health reasons in 1957. Earldom 1961.

Edgar (943–75), King of England 959–75. He was advised by Archbishop Dunstan.

Edgar Atheling (c. 1060 c. 1130), was the lawful heir of Edward the Confessor, but in the Norman invasion could not maintain his claim.

Edgeworth, Maria (1767–1849), Irish novelist, whose stories include *Castle Rackrent*, *The Absentee*, and *Belinda*.

Edinburgh, Duke of (Philip Mountbatten) (b. 1921), consort of Queen Elizabeth II. He relinquished his right of accession to the thrones of Greece and Denmark on his naturalisation in 1947 when he took the name of Mountbatten. The great-great-grandson of Queen Victoria.

Edison, Thomas Alva (1847–1931), American inventor of the transmitter and receiver for the automatic telegraph; the phonograph; the incandescent lamp (shared with the British inventor Swan); and many devices for the electrical distribution of light and power. From being a newsboy on the railway and later a telegraph clerk, he became a master at applying scientific principles to practical ends. He set up a laboratory at Menlo Park, New Jersey.

Edmund II (Ironside) (c. 990–1016), the son of Ethelred, king of the English, made a compact with Canute to divide England, but soon afterwards died.

Edward the Confessor (c. 1004–1066), English king who preceded the Norman Conquest and founded Westminster Abbey. He was canonised in 1161.

Edward the Elder (c. 870 c. 924), son of Alfred, succeeded him as king of the West Saxons in 899. He overcame the Danes and reoccupied the northern counties.

Edward I (1239–1307), King of England, succeeded his father Henry in 1272. Able and energetic, his legislation influenced the development of the land law, and he summoned parliamentary assemblies. A soldier, he conquered Wales, building castles, but could not maintain his hold on Scotland.

Edward II (1284–1327), succeeded his father Edward I as king of England in 1307 and was defeated by the Scots at Bannockburn. Weak and inept, he was murdered in 1327.

Edward III (1312–77), succeeded his father Edward II as king of England in 1327. Popular and ambitious he began the Hundred Years War with France. He fostered the woollen industry. Latterly he became senile.

Edward IV (1442–83), able but dissolute Yorkist leader whose reign (1461–70, 1471–83) brought about a revival in the power of the monarchy, in English sea power, and in foreign trade (in which he himself took part). Spent 1470–71, in exile. Began rebuilding of St. George's Chapel, Windsor. Patron of Caxton.

Edward V (1470–83), succeeded his father Edward IV at the age of 12 and was a pawn in the quarrels of baronial relatives. He and his brother were shut up in the Tower by his uncle, Richard, Duke of Gloucester, and there probably murdered, though proof has not been established.

Edward VI (1537–53), succeeded his father, Henry VIII, as king of England when in his tenth year. He was delicate and studious, and his government was carried on successfully by the Dukes of Somerset and Northumberland; while under Archbishop Cranmer the prayer book was issued. Named Lady Jane Grey his successor.

Edward VII (1841–1910), King of Great Britain and Ireland. The son of Queen Victoria, he married Princess Alexandra of Denmark in 1863, and succeeded his mother in 1901. Interested mainly in social life and in international contacts. He visited India in 1875.

Edward VIII (1894–1972), King of Great Britain, succeeded his father George V 1936, and abdicated later that year because of disagreement over his proposed marriage. He was created Duke of Windsor, and was governor of the Bahamas 1940–45. The Duchess of Windsor died in 1986.

Ehrlich, Paul (1854–1915), German bacteriologist, who at Frankfurt-on-Main carried out work in immunology. He discovered salvarsan for the treatment of syphilis. Nobel prizewinner 1908.

Eiffel, Alexandre Gustave (1832–1923), French engineer, one of the first to employ compressed air caissons in bridge building. Among his works are the Eiffel Tower (1887–9) and the Panama Canal locks.

Einstein, Albert (1879–1955), mathematical physicist whose theory of relativity superseded Newton's theory of gravitation. He was born in Ulm of Jewish parents, lived for many years in Switzerland, and held a succession of professorial chairs at Zurich, Prague, and Berlin. In 1921 he was awarded the Nobel prize for his work in quantum theory. He was driven by the Nazis to seek asylum in America and became professor at the Institute of Advanced Study at Princeton 1933–45. In August 1939 at the request of a group of scientists he wrote to President Roosevelt warning of the danger of uranium research in Germany and stressing the urgency of investigating the possible use of atomic energy in bombs. *See* **Relativity, Section T, Part II.**

Eisenhower, Dwight David (1890–1969), American general and statesman. He was C.-in-C. Allied Forces, N. Africa, 1942–3; and in the European theatre of operations, 1943–5; and was Republican President, 1953–61.

Eisenstein, Sergei Mikhailovich. *See* **Section Q.**

Eleanor (1246–90), Queen of Edward I. After her death in 1290 the king had memorial crosses erected at the twelve places where her body rested on its way from Grantham to Westminster.

Elgar, Sir Edward (1857–1934), English composer, specially of choral-orchestral works for festivals. His oratorios include *The Kingdom*, *The Apostles*, and *The Dream of Gerontius*; he also wrote the *Enigma Variations*, and the tone-poem *Falstaff*. He also composed symphonies and concertos. *See* **Section P.**

Elgin, 7th Earl of (Thomas Bruce) (1766–1841), British diplomat who, with the object of saving them, conveyed some sculptures from the Parthenon in Athens to the British Museum.

Eliot, George (1819–80), pen-name of Mary Anne (later Marion) Evans, b. Warwickshire. Her novels include *Adam Bede*, *The Mill on the Floss*, *Silas Marner*, *Middlemarch*, and *Daniel Deronda*. Her works show deep insight. She lived with the writer George Lewes from 1854 until his death 25 years later. (Although Lewes had been deserted by his wife it was not then possible to obtain a divorce.) She brought up his three children.

Eliot, Thomas Stearns (1888–1965), poet and critic. He was born in St. Louis, Missouri, and became a British subject in 1927. His poems include *Prufrock and Other Observations*, *The Waste Land*, *The Hollow Men*, *Ash Wednesday*, *Four Quartets*; his verse dramas *Murder in the*

Cathedral and *The Family Reunion*. He described himself as "classical in literature, royalist in politics, and Anglo-Catholic in religion". Nobel prizewinner 1948.

Elizabeth (1900–2002), Queen Consort of George VI, daughter of the 14th Earl of Strathmore. Before her marriage in 1923 she was Lady Elizabeth Angela Marguerite Bowes-Lyon. She died on 30 March 2002, having been a much loved figure for nearly 8 decades.

Elizabeth I (1533–1603), Queen of England, daughter of Henry VIII, succeeded her sister Mary in 1558. Politically and intellectually able and firm, though personally vain and capricious, she chose to serve her able men such as William Cecil; and her long reign was one of notability victory over the Spanish, and adventure in the New World; while the Church of England was established. It was however marred by the execution of Mary, Queen of Scots.

Elizabeth II (Elizabeth Alexandra Mary of Windsor) (b. 1926), Queen of Gt. Britain and N. Ireland, ascended the throne Feb. 1952 on the death of her father George VI. Her Consort, Prince Philip, Duke of Edinburgh (*q.v.*), is the son of Prince Andrew of Greece and a descendant of the Danish royal family. They have four children: **Charles, Prince of Wales** (*q.v.*), **Princess Anne** (b. 1950), **Prince Andrew** (b. 1960), and **Prince Edward** (b. 1964). Princess Anne was styled the Princess Royal in June 1987. She married Commander Tim Laurence in 1992, the first royal remarriage after a divorce since Henry VIII. Prince Charles and Princess Diana were divorced in 1996. In 1997 Diana was killed in a car crash. Prince Edward married Sophie Rhys-Jones in 1999 and took the title Earl of Wessex.

Ellis, Havelock (1859–1939), English writer whose *Studies in the Psychology of Sex* was influential in changing the public attitude towards sex.

Emerson, Ralph Waldo (1803–82), American poet and essayist, b. Boston, member of the transcendentalist group of thinkers. Among his best-known poems are *Woodnotes*, *Threnody*, *Terminus*, *Brahma*, *The Problem*.

Emin Pasha, the name adopted by **Eduard Schnitzer** (1840–92), a German explorer associated with Gen. Charles Gordon in the Sudan as a medical officer; and governor of the Equatorial Province 1878–89, when he was menaced by the Mahdi and rescued by Stanley.

Emmet, Robert (1778–1803), Irish patriot, led the rising of 1803, was betrayed, and executed.

Empedocles (*c.* 500–*c.* 430 B.C.), Greek philosopher, b. Agrigentum in Sicily, founder of a school of medicine which regarded the heart as the seat of life, an idea which passed to Aristotle, as did his idea that all matter was composed of four elements: earth, air, fire, and water.

Engels, Friedrich (1820–95), German socialist, son of a wealthy textile manufacturer, lifelong friend of Karl Marx, with whom he collaborated in writing the *Communist Manifesto* of 1848. Through him Marx acquired his knowledge of English labour conditions.

Epaminondas (*c.* 418–362 B.C.), Theban general who led the Boeotian League against Sparta in the early 4th cent. B.C. and even defeated her army at the battle of Leuctra in 371 B.C.

Epicurus of Samos (342–270 B.C.), refounded the atomic view of matter put forward by Democritus, and held that peace of mind comes through freedom from fear, the two main sources of which he regarded as religion and fear of death. *See* **Epicureanism, Section J.**

Epstein, Sir Jacob (1880–1959), sculptor, b. New York of Russian-Polish parents. His work includes *Rima*, in Hyde Park; *Day* and *Night* on the building of London Underground headquarters; *Genesis*, exhibited in 1931; *Lazarus*, in New College, Oxford; the *Madonna and Child* group in Cavendish Square, London; the figure of *Christ* in *Majesty* in aluminium in Llandaff cathedral; a sculpture for the TUC headquarters in London; and a bronze group for Coventry cathedral.

Equiano, Oluadah (1745–97), African slave who inspired Wilberforce to begin abolition campaign.

Erasmus, Desiderius (1466–1536), Dutch Renaissance humanist, who spent several years in England and was the friend of Dean Colet and Sir Thomas More. He aimed at ecclesiastical reform from within and scorned the cold scholastic teaching. He thus prepared the way for

Luther. His *Praise of Folly* is still widely read.

Erhard, Ludwig (1897–1977), German economist. Chancellor (1963–7) after Adenauer.

Essex, 2nd Earl of (Robert Devereux) (1566–1601), favourite of Queen Elizabeth I in her old age. Unsuccessful as governor-general of Ireland, he returned to England against the Queen's wish; plotted; and was executed.

Ethelbert, King of Kent at the close of the 6th cent., accepted Christianity on the mission of St. Augustine.

Ethelred II (*c.* 968–1016), King of England. Unable to organise resistance against the Danish raids, he was called the Unready (from Old Eng. uræd = without counsel).

Etty, William (1787–1849), English artist of historical and classical subjects.

Eucken, Rudolf Christoph (1846–1926), German philosopher of activism, which puts personal ethical effort above intellectual idealism. Nobel prizewinner 1908.

Euclid, Greek mathematician of the 3rd cent. B.C. Famous for his *Elements*.

Euler, Leonhard (1707–83), Swiss mathematician, remembered especially for his work in optics and on the calculus of variations. He was called by Catherine I to St. Petersburg, where he was professor, 1730–41, and by Frederick the Great to Berlin, 1741–66. He became blind but continued his work.

Euripides (480–406 B.C.), Greek tragic dramatist, who is known to have written about 80 plays of which 18 are preserved, including *Alcestis*, *Medea*, *Iphigenia*, and *Orestes*.

Eusebius (264–340), ecclesiastical historian. His *Ecclesiastical History* gives the history of the Christian church to 324. He also wrote a general history, *Chronicon*.

Evans, Sir Arthur John (1851–1941), English archaeologist, known for his excavations at Knossos in Crete and his discovery of the pre-Phoenician script.

Evans, Dame Edith Mary (1888–1976), English actress, whose celebrated roles included Millamant in *The Way of the World*.

Evans, Sir Geraint Llewellyn (1922–92), much-loved Welsh opera singer. Principal Baritone, Royal Opera House, Covent Garden, 1948–84.

Evans, Gwynfor (1912–2005), major figure in rise of Welsh nationalism. Won 1966 by-election in Carmarthen.

Evelyn, John (1620–1706), cultured English diarist who gives brilliant portraits of contemporaries. A book collector and librarian who wrote *Sylva*, a manual of arboriculture.

Eyck, Jan van (*c.* 1389–1441), Flemish painter, whose best-known work is the altarpiece in Ghent cathedral. His brother Hubert (*b.* 1070 1426) is associated with him.

Eysenck, Hans Jürgen (1916–97) was Professor of Psychology at the University of London Institute of Psychiatry. His many publications include *Know Your Own I.Q* (1962) and *Race, Intelligence and Education* (1971).

F

Fabius, the name of an ancient Roman family who played an important part in early Roman history. **Quintus Fabius Maximus Verrucosus** (d. 203 B.C.) saved Rome from Hannibal by strategic evasion of battle; hence his name *Cunctator* (delayer), and the term Fabian policy.

Fabre, Jean Henri Casimir (1823–1915), French naturalist, whose study of the habits of insects was recorded in his *Souvenirs entomologiques*.

Faed, name of two Scottish genre painters, **Thomas** (1826–1900), and **John** (1819–1902). A third brother, **James**, engraved their works.

Fahrenheit, Gabriel Daniel (1686–1736), German physicist, b. Danzig. He introduced *c.* 1715 the mercury thermometer and fixed thermometric standards.

Fairbairn, Sir William (1789–1874), Scottish engineer. In 1817 he took the lead in using iron in shipbuilding.

Fairfax, 3rd Baron (Thomas Fairfax) (1612–71), parliamentary general in the English civil war, and victor of Marston Moor. In 1650 he withdrew into private life.

Falconer, Hugh (1806–65), British botanist and

palaeontologist, b. Forres, Scot.; physician to East India Co.; introduced tea into India.

Falla de, Manuel (1876–1946), Spanish composer whose music is highly individual with a strong folk-song element. *See* **Section P.**

Fanon, Frantz (1925–61), West Indian psychoanalyst and revolutionary social philosopher.

Faraday, Michael (1791–1867), English experimental physicist, founder of the science of electromagnetism. He was the son of a Yorkshire blacksmith and at 13 became apprenticed to a bookseller in London. In 1813 he became laboratory assistant to Sir Humphry Davy at the Royal Institution, succeeding him as professor of chemistry in 1833. He set himself the problem of finding the connections between the forces of light, heat, electricity, and magnetism and his discoveries, translated by Maxwell (*q.v.*) into a single mathematical theory of electromagnetism, led to the modern developments in physics and electronics. He inaugurated the R.I. Christmas lectures for youngsters.

Farman, Henri (1874–1958), French aviation pioneer.

Farouk I (1920–65), King of Egypt, 1936–52. He was forced to abdicate after the 1952 coup.

Farrar, Frederick William (1831–1903), English clergyman, author of the schoolboy story *Eric*.

Faulkner, William (1897–1962), American novelist, whose series of novels, *The Sound and the Fury*, *As I Lay Dying*, *Light in August*, *Sanctuary*, depict the American South. Nobel prize 1949.

Fauré, Gabriel Urbain (1845–1924), French composer and teacher. His works include chamber music, nocturnes, and barcarolles for piano, an opera *Pénélope*, some exquisite songs, and *Requiem*. Ravel was among his pupils.

Fawcett, Millicent Garrett (1847–1929), educational reformer and leader of the movement for women's suffrage; one of the founders of Newnham College, Cambridge. Wife of the blind Liberal politician and economist, **Henry Fawcett** (1833–84) and sister of **Elizabeth Garrett Anderson**.

Fawkes, Guy (1570–1606), a Yorkshire catholic, who with Catesby and other conspirators planned the Gunpowder Plot. Though warned, he persisted and was captured and hanged.

Fénelon, François de Salignac de la Mothe (1651–1715), archbishop of Cambrai and author of *Telemachus*.

Ferdinand II of Aragon (1452–1516), who married Isabella of Castile, and with her reigned over Spain, saw the Moors expelled from Spain, equipped Columbus for the discoveries that led to Spain's vast colonial possessions, and instituted the Inquisition.

Ferguson, James (1710–76), Scottish astronomer who, from being a shepherd-boy, educated himself in astronomy, mechanics, and portrait painting.

Fermi, Enrico (1901–54), Italian nuclear physicist whose research contributed to the harnessing of atomic energy and the development of the atomic bomb. Nobel prizewinner 1938.

Feynman, Richard (Philips), (1918–88), American physicist, born of working-class Jewish parents. Helped develop the atomic bomb. Won Nobel Prize for Physics (1965) for work on quantum electrodynamics.

Fichte, Johann Gottlieb (1762–1814), German nationalistic and Romantic philosopher who paved the way for modern totalitarianism.

Field, John (1782–1837), Irish composer of nocturnes, pupil of Clementi and teacher of Glinka. His work served as a model for Chopin.

Fielding, Henry (1707–54), English novelist, author of *Tom Jones*, *Joseph Andrews*, and *Amelia*, as well as plays.

Fildes, Sir Luke (1844–1927), English painter and woodcut-designer.

Finsen, Niels Ryberg (1860–1904), Danish physician who established an institute for light therapy and invented the Finsen ultra-violet lamp. Nobel prizewinner 1903.

Firdausi, *pen-name* of Abu'l Kasim Mansur (940–1020), Persian poet, author of the epic *Shah-Nama* or Book of Kings.

Firth, Sir Raymond (1901–2002), eminent pioneering social anthropologist.

Fisher of Lambeth, Baron (Geoffrey Francis Fisher) (1887–1972), archbishop of Canterbury, 1945–61; Headmaster, Repton School, 1914–32.

Fisher, Herbert Albert Laurens (1865–1940), English historian and educational reformer.

Fisher, Sir Ronald Aylmer (1890–1962), British scientist who revolutionised both genetics and the philosophy of experimentation by founding the modern corpus of mathematical statistics.

FitzGerald, Edward (1809–83), English poet who translated the *Rubaiyát* of Omar Khayyam (1859).

Fitzroy, Robert (1805–65), British meteorologist, who introduced the system of storm warnings which were the beginning of weather forecasts.

Flammarion, Camille (1842–1925), French astronomer, noted for his popular lectures and books which include *L'Astronomie Populaire*.

Flamsteed, John (1646–1719), the first English astronomer royal, for whom Charles II built an observatory at Greenwich (1675) where he worked for 44 years.

Flaubert, Gustave (1821–80), French novelist, and creator of *Madame Bovary*. Other works were *Salammbô*, *L'Education sentimentale*, and *Bouvard et Pécuchet*.

Flaxman, John (1755–1826), English sculptor, b. York, employed as modeller by Josiah Wedgwood. He then took to monumental sculpture.

Flecker, James Elroy (1884–1915), English poet whose works include *Golden Journey to Samarkand*, *Hassan* (staged in London, 1923), and *Don Juan*, as well as many lyrics.

Fleming, Sir Alexander (1881–1955), Scottish bacteriologist who discovered the antibacterial enzyme lysozyme in 1922 and penicillin in 1928. Full recognition came during the war when Florey separated the drug now used from the original penicillin. Awarded Nobel prize jointly with Florey and Chain, 1945.

Fleming, Sir Ambrose (1849–1945), British scientist whose invention of the radio valve in 1904 revolutionised radio telegraphy and solved problems of radio-telephony. This eventually made possible high quality sound transmission, and thus led to broadcasting and television.

Fletcher, John (1579–1625), English dramatist who collaborated with Francis Beaumont (*q.v.*) in writing many pieces for the stage.

Flinders, Matthew (1774–1814), English navigator and explorer who made discoveries in and around Australia. He sailed through Bass Strait, so called in honour of his surgeon.

Florey, Baron (Howard Walter Florey) (1898–1968), British pathologist, b. Australia. Shared 1945 Nobel prize with Fleming and Chain for work on penicillin.

Fo, Dario (b. 1926), Italian playwright and performance artist, whose plays include *Accidental Death of an Anarchist* (1970) and *Can't Pay? Won't Pay!* (1974). Awarded Nobel Prize 1997.

Foch, Ferdinand (1851–1929), French general, b. Tarbes. In the first world war he halted the German advance at the Marne (1914), and was engaged in the battles of Ypres (1914 and 1915) and the Somme (1916). In 1918 he became supreme commander of the British, French, and American armies and dictated the terms of Allied victory.

Fokine, Michel (1880–1944), Russian dancer, choreographer to Diaghilev's company, and creator of *Les Sylphides*, *Prince Igor*, *Scheherazade*, *Firebird*, and *The Spectre of the Rose*.

Fokker, Anthony (1890–1939), Dutch aircraft engineer, b. Java. The Fokker factory in Germany made warplanes for Germany, 1914–18.

Fonteyn, Dame Margot (Mme. Roberto de Arias) (1919–91), prima ballerina of the Royal Ballet seen as the greatest ballerina of her age.

Foot, Michael (b. 1913), British journalist and politician; leader of the Labour Party 1980–83.

Ford, Gerald R. (b. 1913), American Republican President 1974–7; automatically succeeded Richard Nixon when he resigned.

Ford, Henry (1863–1947), founder of Ford Motor Company (1903), of which he was president until 1919, when he was succeeded by his son, **Edsel B. Ford** (1893–1943). He was the pioneer of the cheap motor car.

Forester, Cecil Scott (1899–1966), English novelist, author of the *Captain Hornblower* series.

Forster, Edward Morgan (1879–1970), English novelist, author of *The Longest Journey*, *A Room with a View*, *Howards End*, *A Passage to India*. O.M. 1969.

Foscari, Francesco (c. 1372–1457), Doge of Venice and victor over Milan.

Foster, Lord (Sir Norman Foster) (b. 1935), architect whose designs include the Berlin Reichstag, Chek Lap Kok airport in Hong Kong and the Millau Viaduct (world's tallest bridge). Life peerage, 1999.

Fourier, Charles (1772–1837), French socialist who propounded a system of associated enterprise which although utopian stimulated social reform.

Fourier, Jean Baptiste Joseph (1768–1830), French mathematical physicist. He played an active part in politics, holding administrative posts in Egypt and Isère, yet finding time for his own research, especially on the flow of heat.

Fowler, Sir John (1817–98), was the engineer of the first underground railway (the London Metropolitan) and with his partner Sir Benjamin Baker, of the Forth bridge.

Fox, Charles James (1749–1806), English Whig statesman. Son of the 1st Lord Holland, he entered parliament at 19. He held office only for brief periods between 1770 and 1806, but he upheld the liberal causes of the day (American independence, the French revolution, and parliamentary reform), and was one of the impeachers of Warren Hastings.

Fox, George (1624–91), founder of the Society of Friends, son of a Leicestershire weaver.

Foxe, John (1516–87), English martyrologist, author of *History of the Acts and Monuments of the Church* (better known as *Foxe's Book of Martyrs*).

Frampton, Sir George James (1860–1928), English sculptor of the Peter Pan statue in Kensington Gardens and the Edith Cavell memorial.

France, Anatole (1844–1924), French writer, especially of short stories. Nobel prize 1921.

Francis I (1494–1547), King of France. Brilliant but ambitious and adventurous, he fostered learning and art, and met Henry VIII at the Field of the Cloth of Gold. His rivalry with the Emperor Charles V involved prolonged war, especially in Italy (he was captured at Pavia, 1525). He persecuted the Protestants.

Francis of Assisi, St. (1181/2–1226), founder of the Franciscan Order. Son of a wealthy cloth merchant, in 1208 he turned from a life of pleasure to poverty and the complete observance of Christ's teaching. He and his friars went about preaching the gospel by word and example, and the brotherhood increased rapidly. He was canonised in 1228.

Francis, Sir Philip (1740–1818), English politician, reputed author of the *Letters of Junius*.

Franck, César Auguste (1822–90), composer and organist, b. at Liège in Belgium. *See Section P.*

Franco, Francisco (1892–1975), Spanish general and dictator. He led the Fascist rebellion against the Republican government (1936) and with German and Italian help ended the civil war (1939). He ruled Spain as a dictator.

Franklin, Benjamin (1706–90), American statesman. B. at Boston, he was at first a printer and journalist. He then took an interest in electricity, explained lightning as of electrical origin, and invented the lightning conductor. He was active in promoting the Declaration of Independence in 1773; he negotiated French support; and helped to frame the U.S. constitution.

Franklin, Sir John (1786–1847), English Arctic explorer. His expedition in the *Erebus* and the *Terror* to find the north-west passage ended disastrously, and all attempts to find survivors failed.

Franks, Baron (Oliver Shewell Franks) (1905–92), British academic, diplomat and banker; British ambassador to USA 1948–52; provost of Worcester College, Oxford 1962–76; chosen to head Falklands inquiry 1982. O.M. 1977.

Fraunhofer, Joseph von (1787–1826), optical instrument-maker of Munich, the first to map the dark lines of the solar spectrum named after him.

Frazer, Sir James George (1854–1941), Scottish anthropologist, author of *The Golden Bough*.

Frederick I (c. 1123–90). Holy Roman Emperor, nicknamed Barbarossa. A strong personality, he sought to impose his will on the city-states of northern Italy and the papacy, and was defeated at Legnano in 1176 but was more successful with a conciliatory policy (1183). He had also to contend with opposition at home. He died on the third crusade.

Frederick II (1194–1250), Holy Roman Emperor, grandson of the above, and son of the heiress of Sicily. Brilliant and enlightened, he attracted to his court its Jewish, Mohammedan, and Christian scholars; founded the university of Naples; was a patron of the medical school of

Salerno; wrote a treatise on falconry; and commissioned a code of laws. Politically he was less successful, having trouble with the Lombard cities, and being involved with the papacy especially as regards his delay in going on crusade; but after negotiations with the sultan of Egypt he actually was crowned king of Jerusalem.

Frederick II (the Great) (1712–86), King of Prussia. Having inherited from his father a well-drilled army, in 1740 he seized Silesia from Austria, and retained it through the resulting war and the Seven Years war. He also took part in the partition of Poland. An able administrator and and outstanding general he made Prussia powerful and strengthened its military tradition. He corresponded with Voltaire and he also played the flute.

French, Sir John, 1st Earl of Ypres (1852–1925), first British commander-in-chief in the first world war; replaced by Sir Douglas Haig in 1915.

Freud, Sigmund (1856–1939), psychiatrist and founder of psychoanalysis; b. Moravia, studied medicine in Vienna, where he lived until 1938 when the Nazi invasion of Austria sent him into exile in London where he died. His theories of the mind illumined the way we think about ourselves. His grandson, the artist Lucien Freud (b. 1911), was awarded the O.M. (1993).

Friedan, Betty (1921–2006), US feminist icon who wrote *The Feminine Mystique* (1963). Founder of National Organisation of Women (NOW). One of the most important feminist thinkers of her time.

Friedman, Milton (b. 1912), American economist. Leading proponent of monetarism. Strongly influenced Thatcherite monetary policy.

Friese-Greene, William (1855–1921), English inventor of the cinematograph. His first film was shown in 1890. He died in poverty.

Frink, Elisabeth (1930–93), English sculptor whose figurative work made her a much-loved artist.

Frobisher, Sir Martin (1535–94), first British navigator to seek the north-west passage from the Atlantic to the Pacific through the Arctic seas. He is commemorated in Frobisher's Strait. He also fought against the Spanish Armada.

Froebel, Friedrich Wilhelm August (1782–1852), German educational reformer, founder of the Kindergarten system.

Froissart, Jean (1337–1410), French author of *Chronicles* covering the history of Western Europe from 1307 to 1400.

Frost, Robert (1874–1963), American poet, author of *Stopping by Woods on a Snowy Evening*, *Birches*, *The Death of the Hired Man*, *After Apple-Picking*.

Froude, James Anthony (1818–94), English historian and biographer of Carlyle.

Fry, Christopher (b. 1907), English poet and dramatist of Quaker family; author of *The Lady's Not for Burning*, *Venus Observed*, *The Dark is Light Enough*, *Curtmantle*, *A Yard of Sun* and the religious play *A Sleep of Prisoners*.

Fry, Elizabeth (1780–1845), English Quaker prison reformer. She lived at Norwich.

Fry, Roger (1866–1934), English art critic and painter; introduced the work of Cézanne and the post-impressionists into England; author of *Vision and Design*.

Fuchs, Leonhard (1501–66), German naturalist whose compendium of medicinal plants was for long a standard work. He was professor of medicine at Tübingen and the genus *Fuchsia* is named after him.

Fuchs, Sir Vivian Ernest (1908–99), British geologist and explorer; leader of the British Commonwealth Trans-Antarctic Expedition 1957–8, the first to cross the Antarctic continent.

Fuller, Thomas (1608–61), English antiquarian and divine, author of *Church History of Britain*.

Fulton, Robert (1765–1815), American engineer who experimented in the application of steam to navigation, and in 1807 launched the *Clermont* on the Hudson.

Furniss, Harry (1854–1925), caricaturist, b. Wexford. He came to London as a young man, served on the staff of *Punch* and illustrated the works of Dickens and Thackeray.

G

Gaddafi, Colonel Muammar. *See Section C.*

Gade, Niels Vilhelm (1817–90), Danish composer.

While studying at Leipzig he met Mendelssohn, whom he succeeded as conductor of the Gewandhaus orchestra.

Gagarin, Yuri Alexeyevich (1934–68), Soviet cosmonaut, the first man to be launched into space and brought safely back (12 April 1961). Killed in an air crash.

Gainsborough, Thomas (1727–88), English landscape and portrait painter, b. at Sudbury in Suffolk. His portraits are marked by informality and grace.

Gaiseric or Genseric (c. 390–477), king of the Vandals, the ablest of the barbarian invaders of the Roman empire. He led his people from Spain into Africa, took Carthage, gained control of the Mediterranean and sacked Rome in 455.

Gaitskell, Hugh Todd Naylor (1906–63), Labour politician and economist. Chancellor of the Exchequer 1950–1; leader of the Labour Party 1955–63.

Galbraith, John Kenneth (1908–2006). Eminent professor of economics. b. Canada; his books include *The Affluent Society* (1958), *The Liberal Hour* (1960), *The New Industrial State* (1967), *The Age of Uncertainty* (1977). Ambassador to India 1961–3.

Galdós, Benito Pérez. *See Pérez Galdós.*

Galen, Claudius (131–201), physician, b. Pergamum (Asia Minor) of Greek parents. He systematised medical knowledge with his idea of purposive creation by the will of God; and thus discouraged original investigation. Many of his treatises survive, and his influence lasted for more than a thousand years.

Galileo Galilei (1564–1642), Italian scientist whose experimental-mathematical methods in pursuit of scientific truth laid the foundations of modern science. He became professor of mathematics at Pisa university when he was 25 and lectured at Padua for 18 years. He made a number of fundamental discoveries, e.g., in regard to the hydrostatic balance, thermometer, telescope, and foreshadowed Newton's laws of motion. He detected the four major satellites of Jupiter, the ring of Saturn, and the spots of the sun. He supported the superiority of the Copernican over the Ptolemaic theory, and was put under house arrest for so doing. He died the year Newton was born.

Galsworthy, John (1867–1933), English novelist and playwright, author of *The Forsyte Saga*, a series of novels dealing with the history of an upper middle-class family. Nobel prize 1932.

Galton, Sir Francis (1822–1911), founder of eugenics, cousin of Darwin. His early work *Meteorographica* (1863), contains the basis of the modern weather chart. He was an early advocate of using finger-prints for rapid identification, and was one of the first to apply mathematics to biological problems.

Galvani, Luigi (1737–98), Italian physician and physiologist, whose experiments at Bologna demonstrated the principle of animal electricity.

Gama, Vasco da (c. 1460–1524), Portuguese navigator. Discovered the sea route to India in 1498 by rounding the Cape of Good Hope.

Gandhi, Indira (1917–84), daughter of Nehru, succeeded Shastri in 1966 to become India's first woman prime minister. She suffered a defeat at the polls in 1977 but was spectacularly successful in 1980. Assassinated 1984. Succeeded by her son, Rajiv Gandhi, who was assassinated in 1991. His widow, Sonia, led the Congress Party to victory in May 2004.

Gandhi, Mohandas Karamchand (Mahatma) (1869–1948), Indian patriot, social reformer and moral teacher. From 1893 to 1914 he lived in South Africa opposing discrimination against Indians. In the movement for Indian independence after 1914 he dominated Congress, instituted civil disobedience, and advocated non-violence; and he sought to free India from caste. After independence he strove to promote the co-operation of all Indians but was assassinated on his way to a prayer meeting. His teaching of non-violence has had great influence.

Garbo, Greta (1905–90). See Section Q.

García, Manuel de Popolo Vincente (1775–1832), Spanish tenor, composer, and singing master. His son Manuel Patricio Rodriguez (1805–1906) was tutor to Jenny Lind. Both his daughters (Mme. Malibran and Mme. Viardot) were operatic singers.

García Lorca, Federico. *See Lorca.*

Garibaldi, Giuseppe (1807–82), Italian soldier and patriot, who with Mazzini and Cavour created

a united Italy. In 1834 he was condemned to
death for helping in a republican plot to seize
Genoa, but escaped to S. America. He returned
in 1848 to fight for Mazzini but was again forced
to flee. In 1851 he returned and gave his
support to Cavour, taking part in the Austrian
war of 1859. In 1860 with a thousand volunteers he freed Sicily, took Naples, and handed
over the Two Sicilies to Victor Emmanuel who
was proclaimed king.

Garrick, David (1717–79), English actor and
theatrical manager. Brought up at Lichfield,
he was taught by Samuel Johnson.

Garrison, William Lloyd (1805–79), American
philanthropist who worked to end slavery.

Gaskell, Mrs. Elizabeth Cleghorn (1810–65),
English novelist, author of *Mary Barton*,
Cranford, and a *Life of Charlotte Brontë*. She
was brought up by an aunt in Knutsford

Gates, Bill (William) (b. 1955), computer entrepre
neur and philanthropist. Co-founder of Microsoft.
The most generous donor in history.

Gaudí, Antoni (1852–1926), architect. Famous for
Church of the Holy Family, Barcelona.

Gaulle, Charles de (1890–1970), French general and
statesman, son of a headmaster of a Jesuit
school; first president of the Fifth Republic
1959–69. He fought in the first world war until
his capture in 1916. In the second world war he
refused to surrender (1940) and raised and led
the Free French forces, with headquarters in
England. He came to political power in
1958; allowed Algerian independence in 1962 in
face of an army and civilian revolt, initiated
closer ties with West Germany (Franco-German
treaty 1963), recognised Communist China,
withdrew from NATO, building his own nuclear
force, vetoed Britain's entry into the Common
Market (1963 and 1967); and based his government on personal prestige and use of the referendum in place of parliamentary approval. He
was taken by surprise by the 1968 rising and
resigned after losing the referendum in 1969.

Gauss, Karl Friedrich (1777–1855), German
mathematician. He spent most of his life at the
university of Göttingen where he set up the
first special observatory for terrestrial magnetism. He made major contributions to astronomy, mathematics, and physics. The unit of
magnetic induction is named after him.

Gautama, Siddhartha (Buddha, the enlightened) (c.
563–c.483 B.C.). B. near Benares, a rajah's son, he
gave himself up to the religious life and attracted
many disciples. Concerned with man's sorrow and
suffering, he planned a movement which could be
universally shared, in which kindness to others,
including animals, took a leading part. His
teaching is summarised in the "four noble truths"
and the "eightfold path" (*see* Buddhism, Section
J). After his death his teaching spread (with the
help of the King Asoka) over much of India and
through eastern Asia as far as Japan.

Gautier, Théophile (1811–72), French poet and
novelist, author of *Mademoiselle de Maupin*.

Gay, John (1685–1732), English poet, author of *The
Beggar's Opera* (set to music by Pepusch) and
Polly.

Gay-Lussac, Joseph Louis (1778–1850), French
chemist, who showed that when gases combine
their relative volumes bear a simple numerical
relation to each other and to the volume of their
product, if gaseous (1808), *e.g.*, one volume of
oxygen combines with two volumes of hydrogen
to form two volumes of water vapour.

Ged, William (1690–1749), Scottish printer who
patented stereotyping.

Geddes, Sir Patrick (1854–1932), Scottish biologist
and a pioneer in town and regional planning,
who invented the term conurbation.

Geikie, Sir Archibald (1835–1924), Scottish geologist. His brother **James** specialised in glacial
geology.

Geldof, Sir Bob (b. 1954), Irish singer and songwriter.
Initiator and organiser, Band Aid, Live Aid,
Live8 concerts for poverty relief.

Genghis (Chingis) Khan (1162–1227), Mongol conqueror. After years of struggle to make good his
succession to his father, he overran much of Asia
bringing devastation wherever he went. His original name was Temujin.

Geoffrey of Monmouth (1100–54), chronicler,
b. Monmouth, later bishop of St. Asaph. His
chronicle drew on his creative imagination.

George I (1660–1727), became King of Great
Britain in 1714 as descendant of James I. His
chief minister was Sir Robert Walpole. Himself personally undistinguished, his reign saw
political development; and in spite of the Jacobite threat (rising in 1715) it began a period of
dynastic stability.

George II (1683–1760), son of the above, succeeded
in 1727, and survived a more serious Jacobite
rising in 1745. His long reign helped the
development of constitutional government,
for he kept within the limitations of his powers
and capacity; and it saw the extension of
English power in India and North America.

George III (1738–1820), grandson of George II
reigned 1760–1820. Sincere and well-intentioned, but not politically able, he suffered from
mental illness due to intermittent porphyria.
His reign saw a clash with John Wilkes, the
rise of Methodism, and agrarian and industrial
revolution; also the loss of the American
colonies, the extension and the questioning of
English power in India (Warren Hastings), and
prolonged French wars.

George IV (1762–1830), eldest son of George III,
reigned 1820–30, having become Prince Regent
in 1812. Styled "the first gentleman of
Europe," he is remembered for his interest in
art and architecture. His reign was a time of distress and of demand for reform.

George V (1865–1936), was the second son of
Edward VII and Queen Alexandra. His elder
brother died in 1892 and, in 1901, on his father's
accession, he became heir to the throne. He joined
the Navy as a cadet in 1877. In 1893 he married
Princess Mary of Teck. He succeeded in 1910 and
discharged his office conscientiously. In 1932 he
began the royal broadcast on Christmas Day and
in 1935 celebrated his silver jubilee.

George VI (1895–1952), second son of George V,
was called to the throne in 1936 on the abdication of his elder brother, Edward VIII. His personal qualities gained wide respect. He married
Lady Elizabeth Bowes-Lyon (1900–2002) in 1923.

George, Henry (1839–97), American political
economist whose "single tax" on land values
as a means of solving economic problems is expounded in his *Progress and Poverty* (1879).

George, St., patron saint of England, adopted by
Edward III. He is believed to have been
martyred by Diocletian at Nicomedia in 303.

Gershwin, George (1898–1937). American jazz
pianist and song-writer, composer of *Rhapsody in
Blue* and the Negro folk-opera *Porgy and Bess.*
His brother **Ira** was a noted lyricist.

Gesner, Conrad (1516–65), Swiss naturalist, b.
Zurich. His magnificently illustrated volumes
describe animal and vegetable kingdoms.

Getty, Jean Paul (1892–1976), American oil magnate,
one of the richest men in the world. Founded J.
Paul Getty Museum at Malibu, California.

Ghali, Boutros Boutros (b. 1922), Egyptian politician. Secretary-General, United Nations, 1992–96.

Ghiberti, Lorenzo (1378–1455), Florentine sculptor
whose bronze doors, beautifying the baptistry
in Florence, were described by Michelangelo as
fit for the gates of paradise.

Ghirlandaio, Domenico (1449–94), Florentine
painter. Most of his frescoes are in Florence,
including the cycle of the life of the Virgin and
the Baptist in S. Maria Novella. Michelangelo
began his apprenticeship in his workshop.

Giacometti, Alberto (1901–66), Swiss sculptor and
painter, who worked mainly in Paris and
produced abstract symbolic constructions.

Giap, Vo Nguyen (1912–86), Vietnamese general
who defeated the French at Dien Bien Phu (1954)
and withstood American intervention in the Vietnam war which followed.

Gibbon, Edward (1737–94), English historian of the
Decline and Fall of the Roman Empire.

Gibbons, Grinling (1648–1720), English wood-
carver and sculptor, b. Rotterdam, was brought
to the notice of Charles II by Evelyn, the diarist.
The choir stalls of St. Paul's and the carving in
the Wren library at Trinity College, Cambridge,
are his work.

Gibbons, Orlando (1583–1625), English composer
of church music. *See also* **Section P.**

Gibson, Sir Alexander Drummond (1926–95).
Founder and music director of the Scottish Opera
Company. One of the foremost Scottish musicians.

Giddens, Lord (Anthony Giddens) (b. 1938).

Sociologist. Director, London School of Economics, 1997–2003. Author, *The Third Way* (1998) and a sequel *The Third Way and its Critics* (2000). Co-author (with Will Hutton) of *On The Edge: Living with Global Capitalism* (2000). Co-editor of *The New Egalitarianism* (2005).

Gide, André (1869–1951), French writer of many short novels in which he gives expression to his struggle to escape from his protestant upbringing (*Strait is the Gate*, *The Counterfeiters*). In his memoir *Si le grain ne meurt* he tells the story of his life up to his marriage.

Gielgud, Sir John (1904–2000), actor and director. His career spanned almost eighty years. Celebrated for his beautiful speaking voice, he was a versatile actor, whose most famous rôle was Hamlet. Knighted 1953; C.H. 1977; O.M. 1996.

Gilbert, Sir Alfred (1854–1934). English sculptor. His sculptures include *Eros* in Piccadilly Circus.

Gilbert, Sir Humphrey (1537–83), English navigator. He was knighted by Queen Elizabeth for service in Ireland. In 1583 he discovered Newfoundland, but was drowned the same year.

Gilbert, William (1540–1603), English physician to Queen Elizabeth. His book *On the Magnet*, published in Latin in 1600, was the first major contribution to science published in England.

Gilbert, Sir William Schwenck (1836–1911), English humorist and librettist, of the Gilbert and Sullivan light operas. First known as author of the *Bab Ballads*, from 1871 he collaborated with Sir Arthur Sullivan, his wit and satire finding appropriate accompaniment in Sullivan's music. Their operas include *H.M.S. Pinafore*, *Patience*, *Iolanthe*, *The Mikado*, *The Gondoliers*, and *The Yeomen of the Guard*.

Giles, Carl Ronald (1916–95), newspaper cartoonist. His work appeared after 1943 in the *Daily Express*.

Gill, Eric (1882–1940), English sculptor and engraver, whose works include the *Stations of the Cross* (Westminster Cathedral), *Prospero and Ariel* (Broadcasting House), *Christ Driving the Money-changers from the Temple* (Leeds Univ.)

Gillray, James (1757–1815), English caricaturist who produced over a thousand political cartoons.

Giotto di Bondone (1267–1337), Florentine artist. A pupil of Cimabue, he continued the development away from Byzantine tradition towards greater naturalism. His frescoes survive in the churches of Assisi, Padua, and Florence. He designed the western front of the cathedral at Florence and the campanile

Gissing, George Robert (1857–1903), English novelist whose works deal with the effect of poverty. The best known is *New Grub Street*.

Giulio Romano or **Giulio Pippi** (*c.* 1492–1546). Italian artist, was a pupil of Raphael. He was also an engineer and architect.

Gladstone, William Ewart (1809–98), English Liberal statesman. B. at Liverpool, he entered parliament in 1832 as a Tory and held office under Peel. From 1852 he served several terms as chancellor of the exchequer and was Liberal prime minister 1868–74, when his legislation included the education act of 1870, the ballot act, the disestablishment of the Church of Ireland and an Irish land act. In 1874 when Disraeli came to power, he temporarily withdrew, but made a come-back in 1879 with his Midlothian campaign. He was again prime minister 1880–5, 1886 and 1892–4; he carried a parliamentary reform act, but failed to win home rule for Ireland.

Glazunov, Alexander Constantinovich (1865–1936), Russian composer, pupil of Rimsky-Korsakov. The first of his eight symphonies was composed when he was 16.

Glendower, Owen (*c.* 1350–*c.* 1416), Welsh chief, who conducted guerrilla warfare on the English border. He figures in Shakespeare's *Henry IV*. His Welsh name is *Owain Glyndwr* or *Owain ap Gruffudd*.

Glinka, Mikhail Ivanovich (1804–57), Russian composer, first of the national school, best known for his operas, *A Life for the Tsar*, and *Russlan and Ludmilla*, based on a poem by Pushkin. See **Section P.**

Gluck, Christoph Wilibald (1714–87), German composer, important in the development of opera. He studied in Prague, Vienna and Italy, and his first operas were in the Italian tradition; but with *Orfeo ed Euridice* (1762) his style became more dramatic. There followed *Alceste, Armide,*

and *Iphigénie en Tauride*. See **Section P.**

Glyndwr. See **Glendower**.

Goddard, Robert Hutchings (1882–1945), American rocket pioneer who achieved (1926) the first rocket flight with a liquid-fuelled engine.

Gödel, Kurt (1906–78), eminent mathematician. Devised Gödel's proof, the vitally important proof of modern mathematics which declares that there will always exist statements that can be neither proven nor disproven in any mathematical system which has a finite number of axioms.

Godfrey of Bouillon (*c.* 1061–1100), Crusader on the first crusade. On capturing Jerusalem took title of protector of the Holy Sepulchre.

Godiva, Lady (1040–80), English benefactress. According to tradition, she obtained from her husband Leofric, Earl of Chester, concessions for the people of Coventry by riding naked through the town.

Godwin, Earl of the West Saxons (d. 1053), was the father of Edith, wife of King Edward the Confessor, and of Harold, last Saxon king.

Godwin William (1756–1836), English political writer and philosopher, author of *Political Justice* (which criticised many contemporary institutions) and a novel *Caleb Williams*. He married **Mary Wollstonecraft** (1759–97), author of *A Vindication of the Rights of Women*; and their daughter, **Mary Wollstonecraft Godwin** (1797–1851) wrote *Frankenstein* and married Shelley.

Goethe, Johann Wolfgang von (1749–1832), German poet and thinker. B. at Frankfurt-on-Main, his first notable work was a romantic play, *Götz von Berlichingen*, followed by a novel *Werthers Leiden*. In 1776 he became privy councillor to the Duke of Weimar, whom he served for many years. He had wide-ranging interests, and made discoveries in anatomy and in botany. Among his later writings are the play *Iphigenie* and the novel *Wilhelm Meister*. His best-known work is *Faust*.

Gogol, Nikolai Vasilievich (1809–52), Russian novelist and dramatist. His comedy, *The Government Inspector*, satirised provincial bureaucracy; and his novel, *Dead Souls*, deals with malpractice in the purchase of dead serfs.

Golding, Sir William (1911–93), novelist, whose imaginative and experimental fiction includes *Lord of the Flies* (1954) and *The Spire* (1964). Awarded the Nobel Prize for Literature (1983).

Goldsmith, Oliver (1728–74), Irish poet, dramatist and novelist. The son of a poor curate, he came to London in 1756, and eventually joined the circle of Dr. Johnson. Best known for his novel *The Vicar of Wakefield* and his play *She Stoops to Conquer*.

Golovine, Serge (1924–98), a supremely gifted French ballet dancer, equalled only by Nureyev.

Gombrich, Sir Ernst (1909–2001), the most eminent art historian of his time. Born in Vienna.

Goncourt, Edmond Louis Antoine Huot de (1822–96) and **Jules Alfred Huot de** (1830–70), French brothers, remembered for their *Journal des Goncourts*, an intimate account of Parisian society.

Góngora y Argote, Luis de (1561–1627), Spanish poet. In *Polifemo* and *Soledades* he attempted to express poetry in new forms.

Goodyear, Charles (1800–60), American inventor who discovered the art of vulcanising rubber.

Goossens, Sir Eugene (1893–1962), English conductor and composer of Belgian descent. His compositions include *Judith* and *Don Juan de Mañara*; brother of Léon, oboe virtuoso, and of **Sidonie** and **Marie Goossens**, harpists.

Gorbachev, Mikhail (b. 1931). Soviet politician. Succeeded Chernenko (*q.v.*) as General Secretary of the Communist Party, 1985. His accession marked the end of the "old-guard" leadership. Identified with policies of *glasnost* (openness) and *perestroika* (restructuring). President of the USSR, 1988–91. He presided over revolutionary changes both in Eastern Europe and Russia, but faced a growing crisis at home. The abortive coup in 1991 weakened his position, leading to the collapse of the USSR. Nobel Peace Prize, 1990.

Gordon, Charles George (1833–85), Scottish soldier. After service in the Crimea and China, in 1873 he was made governor of the Equatorial provinces of Egypt; and he was a notable governor of the Sudan, 1877–80. When a rising was led by the Mahdi, he was sent out in 1884 to the garrisons in rebel territory. Murdered by the Mahdi's forces on the palace staircase in Khartoum.

Gordon, Lord George (1751–93), agitator, led No-Popery riots in London in 1780.

Gorky, Maxim (Alexey Maximovich Peshkov) 1868–1936), Russian writer. From the age of ten he worked at many trades from scullion on a Volga steamboat to railway guard, while learning to write: see *My Childhood*. His early work was romantic. He spent many years abroad, but returned in 1928, a supporter of the Soviet regime. His later work is marked by social realism.

Gosse, Sir Edmund (1849–1928), English poet and critic, known for his literary studies of the 17th and 18th centuries; and for his memoir *Father and Son*.

Gounod, Charles François (1818–93), French composer, known for his operas *Faust* and *Roméo et Juliette*. His lyrical gifts are shown in earlier works, such as *Le Médicin malgré lui* and *Mireille*.

Gower, John (1325–1408), English poet of the time of Chaucer, author of *Confessio Amantis*.

Goya y Lucientes, Francisco José (1746–1828), Spanish painter and etcher b. nr. Saragossa. He became court painter to Charles III in 1786. His portraits are painted with ruthless realism; his series of satirical etchings (*Los Caprichos* and the *Disasters of War*) expose man's inhumanity and the cruelty of his day.

Gracchi, the brothers **Tiberius** (163–133 B.C.) and **Gaius** (153–121 B.C.) who, as Tribunes of the People, tried to reform the system of public landholding and liberalise the franchise at Rome, but were both killed when the Senate suppressed their followers.

Grace, William Gilbert (1848–1915). English cricketer who scored 54,896 runs, including 126 centuries, and took 2,876 wickets.

Graham, Billy (b. 1918), US evangelist who became world-famous for his campaigns.

Grahame, Kenneth (1859–1932), Scottish writer of books for children, including *The Golden Age*, *Dream Days*, and *Wind in the Willows*.

Grahame-White, Claude (1879–1959), the first Englishman to gain an aviator's certificate, 1909.

Grant, Ulysses Simpson (1822–85), American general of the civil war, and president of the United States from 1869 to 1876.

Granville-Barker, Harley (1877–1946), English dramatist, actor, and producer, who promoted the plays of Ibsen, Shaw, *etc*. His own works include *The Voysey Inheritance*.

Grass, Günter (b. 1927), German novelist and poet. Awarded 1999 Nobel Prize for Literature. His most famous novel is *Die Blechtrommel* (1959; translated as *The Tin Drum*, 1961).

Grattan, Henry (1746–1820), Irish statesman, who struggled for Irish legislative independence and for Catholic emancipation (though himself a Protestant) and parliamentary reform; but unsuccessfully.

Graves, Robert Ranke (1895–1985), English writer, author of *Goodbye to All That*, written after the first world war; and of *I Claudius* and *Claudius the God*; besides poetry.

Gray, Thomas (1716–71), English poet, author of *Elegy written in a Country Churchyard* and *Ode on a Distant Prospect of Eton College*.

Greco, El (Domenikos Theotokopoulos) (1541–1614), one of the most original painters of his time. The Greek (as he was known) was soon forgotten after his death but greatly influenced 20th century painters such as Picasso and Cézanne.

Greeley, Horace (1811–72), American newspaper editor, founder of the New York *Tribune* (1841).

Greenaway, Kate (1846–1901), English artist, who depicted children, especially in book illustrations.

Greene, Graham (1904–91), English novelist and journalist, whose novels (*The Power and the Glory*, *The Heart of the Matter*, *The End of the Affair*, *The Quiet American*, *Our Man in Havana*, *A Burnt-out Case*, *The Comedians*, *The Honorary Consul*), like his plays (*The Complaisant Lover*) and films (*Fallen Idol*, *The Third Man*) deal with moral problems in a modern setting. C.H. (1966), O.M. (1986). Widely regarded as one of the greatest English novelists.

Greer, Germaine (b. 1939). Feminist and writer. Born in Melbourne, Australia. Her most famous work is *The Female Eunuch* (1970) which exposed the misrepresentation of female sexuality by a male-dominated society. Other publications include *The Whole Woman* (1999) and *The Boy* (2003).

Gregory, St. (*c*. 240–332), converted King Tiridates of Armenia, so founding the Armenian church.

Gregory I (the Great), St. (*c*. 540–604), Pope 590–604, was the last great Latin Father and the

forerunner of scholasticism. The main founder of the temporal power and the political influence of the papacy, he also maintained the spiritual claims of Rome, enforcing discipline, encouraging monasticism, defining doctrine *etc*. He sent Augustine on a mission to England.

Gregory VII (Hildebrand) (*c*. 1020–85), Pope 1073–85. He strove for papal omnipotence within the church and for a high standard in the priesthood (especially by stamping out simony and clerical marriage). He also upheld the papacy against the Holy Roman Empire, and the emperor Henry IV did penance for three days in the snow at Canossa.

Gregory XIII (1502–85), Pope 1572–85; introduced the Gregorian calendar.

Gregory, James (1638–75). Scottish mathematician. He invented a reflecting telescope and was the first to show how the distance of the sun could be deduced by observations of the passage of Venus across the disc of the sun. Successive generations of the family reached distinction.

Grenville, Sir Richard (1541–91), English sea captain, who with his one ship engaged a fleet of Spanish war vessels off Flores in 1591, an exploit celebrated in Tennyson's ballad *The Revenge*.

Gresham, Sir Thomas (1519–79), English financier and founder of the Royal Exchange. Son of a Lord Mayor of London, he was an astute moneyfinder for four successive sovereigns, including Queen Elizabeth I. "Gresham's Law" is the statement that bad money drives out good.

Gresley, Sir (Herbert) Nigel (1876–1941), outstanding steam locomotive designer. His A4 class Pacific, *Mallard*, achieved the world speed record.

Greuze, Jean Baptiste (1725-1805), French artist, known especially for his studies of girls. His *Girl with Doves* is in the Wallace Collection.

Grey, 2nd Earl (Charles Grey) (1764–1845), British Whig statesman under whose premiership were passed the Reform Bill of 1832, a bill abolishing slavery throughout the Empire (1833), and the Poor Law Amendment Act, 1834.

Grey, Lady Jane (1537–54), Queen of England for a few days. The daughter of the Duke of Suffolk, she was put forward as queen by protestant leaders on the death of her cousin, Edward VI; but overcome by the legal claimant, Mary Tudor, and executed.

Grieg, Edvard Hagerup (1843–1907), Norwegian composer, b. Bergen. He presented the characteristics of his country's music with strong accentuation. He is best known for his incidental music to *Peer Gynt*.

Griffith, Arthur (1872–1922), the first president of the Irish Free State, 1921; founder of *Sinn Fein*.

Griffith, David Wark (1880–1948), American film producer, who introduced the close-up, and the flash-back, and developed leading actors.

Grimaldi, Joseph (1779–1837), British clown, "the father of modern clowning".

Grimm, the brothers **Jakob Ludwig Karl** (1785–1863), and **Wilhelm Karl** (1786–1859), German philologists and folk-lorists, best known for their *Fairy Tales*. Jakob published a notable philological dictionary, *Deutsche Grammatik*. The brothers also projected the vast *Deutsches Wörtebuch* which was completed by German scholars in 1961.

Grimond, Lord (Joseph) (1913–93), Leader of the Liberal Party, 1956–67.

Grimthorpe, 1st Baron (Edmund Beckett Denison) (1816–1905), horologist who invented the double three-legged escapement for the clock at Westminster, familiarly known as "Big Ben" (the name of the bell). Known as Sir Edmund Beckett.

Gromyko, Andrei Andrecvich (1909–89), Soviet diplomat and statesman. President, USSR, July 1985–88, Foreign Minister, 1957–85.

Grossmith, George (1847–1912), English actor. With his brother, **Weedon Grossmith,** he wrote *Diary of a Nobody*. His son, **George Grossmith** (1874–1935) was a comedian and introduced revue and cabaret entertainment into England.

Grote, George (1794–1871), English historian, author of a *History of Greece*.

Grotius (Huig van Groot) (1583–1645), Dutch jurist, the founder of international law. He was condemned to life imprisonment for religious reasons, but escaped to Paris, where he wrote *De Jure Belli et Pacis*.

Grouchy, Emmanuel, Marquis de (1766–1847), French general, who served under Napoleon; after Waterloo led defeated army back to Paris.

Grove, Sir George (1820–1900), English musicologist, author of *Dictionary of Music and Musicians*. By profession he was a civil engineer.

Guevara, Ernesto "Che" (1928–67), revolutionary hero, b. Argentina. He took part in the Cuban guerrilla war and became a minister in the Cuban government 1959–65. He was killed while leading a band of guerrillas against US-trained Bolivian troops. His remains were buried in Cuba in 1997.

Guido Reni (1575–1642), Italian painter of the Bolognese school whose works are characteristic of the Italian baroque of his period and include the *Aurora* fresco in the Rospigliosi palace at Rome, and *Crucifixion of St. Peter* (Vatican).

Guinness, Sir Alec. *See* **Section Q.**

Gustavus Adolphus (1594–1632), King of Sweden, the "Lion of the North." After a campaign in Poland he entered the Thirty Years' war in support of Swedish interests and Protestant distress, won the battle of Breitenfeld in 1631 and was killed in action the next year.

Gutenberg, Johann (*c.* 1400–68), German printer, b. Mainz, the first European to print with movable types cast in moulds. The earliest book printed by him was the Mazarin Bible (**L72**).

Guy, Thomas (1644–1724), English philanthropist. A printer, he made money by speculation; and in 1722 founded Guy's Hospital in Southwark.

Gwyn, Nell (*c.* 1650–87), English actress and mistress of Charles II by whom she had two sons. Of Hereford origin, she sold oranges in London and became a comedienne at Drury Lane.

H

Hadley, George (1685–1768). He developed Halley's theory of the trade winds by taking into account the effect of the earth's rotation and the displacement of air by tropical heat (1735).

Hadrian (76–138), Roman emperor. An able general, he suppressed revolts, and he was also a lover of the arts. He visited Britain *c.* A.D. 121 and built a protective wall between Wallsend-on-Tyne and Bowness-on-Solway.

Hafiz, pseudonym of **Shams ad-Din Mohammed** (d. *c.* 1388), Persian lyrical poet. His principal work is the *Divan*, a collection of short sonnets called *ghazals*. The sobriquet *Hafiz*, meaning one who remembers, is applied to anyone who has learned the Koran by heart.

Hague, William. *See* **D17**

Hahn, Otto (1879 1968), German chemist and physicist, chief discoverer of uranium fission.

Hahnemann, Samuel Christian Friedrich (1755 1843), German physician who founded homoeopathy (treatment of disease by small doses of drugs that in health produce similar symptoms).

Haig, Douglas, 1st Earl of Bermersyde (1861–1928), British field-marshal, b. Edinburgh. He replaced French as commander-in-chief in France, 1915–19, leading the offensive in August 1918; and after the war presided over the British Legion.

Haile Selassie I (1891–1975), Emperor of Ethiopia 1930–74. He spent the years of the Italian occupation 1936–41 in England. Deposed 1974.

Hailsham, Viscount. *See under* **Hogg.**

Hakluyt, Richard (1553–1616), English writer on maritime discovery. B. in Herefordshire, he spent some time in Paris. From 1582 (when *Divers Voyages* appeared), he devoted his life to collecting and publishing accounts of English navigators, thus giving further impetus to discovery.

Haldane, John Burdon Sanderson (1892–1964), biologist and geneticist, noted not only for his work in mathematical evolutionary theory but for explaining science to the layman. He emigrated to India in 1957. He was the son of **John Scott Haldane** (1860–1936), b. Edinburgh, who studied the effect of industrial occupations upon health.

Haldane, 1st Viscount (Richard Burdon Haldane) (1856–1928). British Liberal statesman. As war minister in 1905 he reorganised the army and founded the Territorials.

Hale, George Ellery (1868–1935), American astronomer, after whom is named the 200-inch reflecting telescope on Mount Palomar.

Halévy, Ludovic (1834–1903), French playwright, who collaborated with Henri Meilhac in writing libretti for Offenbach and Bizet.

Halifax, 1st Earl of (Edward Frederick Lindley Wood) (1881–1959), British Conservative politician; foreign secretary during the period of appeasement of Germany; as Lord Irwin, viceroy of India 1926–31.

Halifax, 1st Marquess of (George Savile) (1633–95), English politician of changeable views, who wrote *Character of a Trimmer*.

Hall, Sir Peter (Reginald Frederick) (b. 1930). Leading director of plays, films and operas. Director, National Theatre, 1973–88.

Hallam, Henry (1777–1859), English historian, best known for his *Constitutional History*. He was father of Arthur Hallam, friend of Tennyson.

Hallé, Sir Charles (1819–95), German-born pianist and conductor, who settled in Manchester and organised an orchestra of high-class talent. He married the violinist Wilhelmine Neruda.

Halley, Edmond (1656–1742), English astronomer royal 1720–42. He published observations on the planets and comets, being the first to predict the return of a comet (*see* **Section L**). He furthered Newton's work on gravitation, setting aside his own researches. He made the first magnetic survey of the oceans from the naval vessel *Paramour*, 1698–1700. His meteorological observations led to his publication of the first map of the winds of the globe (1686).

Hals, Frans (*c.* 1580–1666), Dutch portrait painter, b. at Mechlin. He is best known for his *Laughing Cavalier* in the Wallace Collection, and for portraits in the Louvre and at Amsterdam.

Hamann, Johann Georg (1730–88), German philosopher. Friend of Kant. An important counter-Enlightenment thinker.

Hamilton, Alexander (1755–1804), American statesman and economist. With Madison and Jay he wrote the *Federalist* (1787). As secretary of the Treasury (1789–95) he put Washington's government on a firm financial footing and planned a national bank. He was the leader of the Federalists, a party hostile to Jefferson. He was killed in a duel.

Hamilton, Emma, Lady (*née* Lyon) (*c.* 1765–1815), a beauty of humble birth who, after several liaisons, was married in 1791 to Sir William Hamilton, British ambassador at Naples. There she met Nelson, and later bore him a child, Horatia.

Hammarskjöld, Dag (1905–61), Swedish Secretary-General of the United Nations, 1953–61. He was killed in an air crash while attempting to mediate in a dispute between Congo and the province of Katanga. Posthumous Nobel peace prize.

Hammond, John Lawrence (1872 1949), English historian of social and industrial history, whose works (with his wife Barbara) include *The Town Labourer* and *The Village Labourer*.

Hampden, John (1594–1643), English parliamentarian and civil war leader. He refused to pay Charles I's ship money in 1636. When civil war broke out, he raised a regiment and was killed on Chalgrove Field.

Hamsun, Knut, pen-name of Knut Pedersen (1859–1952), Norwegian author who in his youth struggled for existence, visited America twice and earned his living by casual labour. *The Growth of the Soil* won him the 1920 Nobel prize. Other novels are *Hunger* and *Mysteries*.

Handel, George Frederick (1685–1759), German composer, son of a barber-surgeon to the Duke of Saxony; b. Halle, the same year as Bach; spent much of his life in England composing operas and oratorios. His operas, of which there are over 40, include *Atalanta*, *Berenice* and *Serse*, and his oratorios, of which there are 32, include *Saul*, *Israel in Egypt*, *Samson*, *Messiah*, *Judas Maccabaeus*, and *Jephtha*. Before he died he became blind and relied upon his old friend and copyist John Christopher Smith to commit his music to paper. *See* **Section P.**

Hannibal (247–182 B.C.), Carthaginian general. He fought two wars against Rome. In the first he conquered southern Spain. In the second he overran Gaul, crossed the Alps, and defeated the Romans in successive battles, especially at Cannae. Thereafter his forces were worn down by Roman delaying tactics; he was defeated by Scipio at Zama and later poisoned himself.

Hardicnut (Hardicanute) (1019–42), son of Cnut (Canute), and last Danish king of England.

Hardie, James Keir (1856–1915), Scottish Labour leader, one of the founders of the Labour party.

He first worked in a coal-pit; in 1882 became a journalist; and in 1892 was the first socialist to be elected to the House of Commons (for West Ham – South). He edited the *Labour Leader* 1887–1904. He was the first chairman of the parliamentary Labour party, 1906. A pacifist, he opposed the Boer war.

Hardy, Thomas (1840–1928), English novelist and poet, was trained as an architect and practised for some time, but became known in 1871 with *Desperate Remedies*. In 1874 his *Far from the Madding Crowd* was published. Following that came a series of novels, including *The Trumpet-Major, The Mayor of Casterbridge, Tess of the D'Urbervilles,* and *Jude the Obscure.* In 1908 he completed a dramatic poem, *The Dynasty,* whose central figure is Napoleon. *See* **M23**.

Hargreaves, James (1790–78), English inventor, b. Blackburn. His spinning-jenny was invented in 1764 and became widely used, though his own was broken by spinners in 1768 and his invention brought him no profit.

Harkness, Edward Stephen (1874–1940), American banker and philanthropist, who in 1930 founded the Pilgrim Trust in Gt. Britain.

Harley, Robert, 1st Earl of Oxford and Mortimer (1661–1724), English statesman and collector of MSS. He held office under Queen Anne, and brought a European war to an end with the treaty of Utrecht. After the Hanoverian succession he lived in retirement, and formed the MSS. collection, now in the British Museum, which bears his name.

Harold II (1022–66), last Saxon king of England, was son of Earl Godwin. He was chosen king in succession to Edward the Confessor. He had at once to meet a dual invasion. He defeated the Norwegian king at Stamford Bridge; but was himself defeated by William of Normandy at the battle of Hastings (fought at Battle 1066).

Harriman, William Averell (1891–1986), American public official. He was adviser to President Roosevelt and later presidents especially on Marshall Aid and foreign affairs.

Harris, Joel Chandler (1848–1908), American author, creator of Uncle Remus and Brer Rabbit.

Harrison, Frederic (1831–1923), English philosopher and lawyer, author of *The Meaning of History* and *The Philosophy of Common Sense.* He was president of the Positivist Committee.

Harrison, George. *See under* **Beatles.**

Harrison, John (1693–1776), "Longitude Harrison," English inventor of the chronometer, b. near Pontefract, Yorkshire, the son of a carpenter.

Harty, Sir Hamilton (1880–1941), composer and for some years conductor of the Hallé orchestra.

Harun al-Rashid (Aaron the Upright) (763–809), 5th Abbasid caliph of Baghdad. His court was a centre for art and learning, but he governed mainly through his vizier until the latter lost favour and was executed in 803. The *Arabian Nights* associated with him are stories collected several centuries later.

Harvey, William (1578–1657), English physician and discoverer of the circulation of the blood. B. at Folkestone, he studied at Padua while Galileo was there, and was physician to James I and Charles I. His treatise on circulation was published in Latin in 1628.

Hastings, Warren (1732–1818), English administrator in India. As governor-general of Bengal for the East India Company he revised the finances and administration and put down disorder. On his return to England he was impeached for alleged corruption, and, though acquitted, lost his fortune in his own defence. Later however he received a grant from the company.

Hauptmann, Gerhart (1862–1946), German dramatist and novelist. B. in Silesia. His play *The Weavers* deals with a revolt of 1844. Other works include *Die versunkene Glocke, Der arme Heinrich,* and *Rose Bernd.* Nobel prize 1912.

Havel, Vaclav (b. 1936) Czech playwright, dissident and statesman. Imprisoned, 1979–83. President of Czechoslovakia, December 1989–92. President of new Czech Republic, 1993–2003.

Havelock, Sir Henry (1795–1857), British general who helped to put down the Indian mutiny.

Hawke, 1st Baron (Edward Hawke) (1705–81), English admiral, who in 1759 defeated the French at Quiberon in a tremendous storm.

Hawking, Stephen William (b. 1942), British theoretical physicist. Lucasian Professor of

Mathematics, Cambridge University, since 1979. Author of *300 Years of Gravitation* (1987), *A Brief History of Time* (1988) and *The Universe in a Nutshell* (2001). Companion of Honour (1989). Sufferer from motor neurone disease.

Hawkins, Sir John (1532–95), English sailor and slave-trader. Born at Plymouth. In 1562 he was the first Englishman to traffic in slaves. Treasurer of the Navy, 1585–88. He helped to defeat the Spanish Armada in 1588, commanding the *Victory.* Died at sea off Puerto Rico, 12 Nov. 1595.

Hawthorne, Nathaniel (1804–64), American author. His works include *The Marble Faun, The Scarlet Letter* and *The House of the Seven Gables.*

Hayden, Matthew Lawrence (b. 1971) Australian cricketer who scored world record-breaking test innings of 380 in 2003 against Zimbabwe. His record was lost to Brian Lara in 2004.

Haydn, Franz Joseph (1732–1809), Austrian composer. He has been given the title "father of the symphony." Much of his life was spent as musical director to the princely Hungarian house of Esterhazy. In 1791 and again in 1794 he visited London, where he conducted his Salomon symphonies. His two great oratorios, *The Creation* and *The Seasons,* were written in old age. *See* **Section P.**

Hayek, Friedrich August (von) (1899–1992), Austrian economist. The 'father of monetarism.' Strongly influenced development of Thatcherite monetary policies. Shared Nobel Prize for Economics, 1974. C.H. (1984).

Hazlitt, William (1778–1830), English essayist and critic. His writings include *The Characters of Shakespeare's Plays, Table Talk,* and *The Spirit of the Age.* His grandson **William Carew Hazlitt** (1834–1913) was a bibliographer and writer.

Heaney, Seamus (b. 1939), Irish poet, whose works include *Death of a Naturalist* (1966) and *North* (1975). Professor of Poetry, Oxford University, 1989–94. Professor of Rhetoric and Oratory, Harvard University, USA. Awarded the Nobel Prize for Literature, 1995. His translation of the Anglo-Saxon epic poem *Beowulf* earned him the Whitbread Book of the Year award.

Heath, Sir Edward (1916–2005), British statesman, leader of the Conservative Party 1965–75; prime minister 1970–74; leader of the opposition 1965–70, 1974–75. In 1973 he took Britain into the EEC. Order of the Garter, 1992. "Father of the House" 1992–2001.

Hedin, Sven Anders (1865–1952), Swedish explorer of Central Asia; wrote *My Life as Explorer.*

Heenan, John Carmel (1905–76). English Roman Catholic Archbishop of Westminster 1963–76.

Hegel, Georg Wilhelm Friedrich (1770–1831), German idealist philosopher, b. Stuttgart, whose name is associated with the dialectic method of reasoning with its sequence of thesis —antithesis—synthesis. He studied theology at Tübingen with his friend Schelling. He taught philosophy at Jena, Nuremberg, Heidelberg, and Berlin. He produced an abstract philosophical system which was influenced by his early interest in mysticism and his Prussian patriotism. His doctrines were very influential in the 19th cent. *See also* **Dialectical Materialism, Section J.**

Heidenstam, Verner von (1859–1940), Swedish author and poet. Nobel prizewinner, 1916.

Heine, Heinrich (1797–1856), German lyric poet, b. Düsseldorf. He lived mostly in Paris.

Heisenberg, Werner (1901–76), German physicist, noted for his theory of quantum mechanics and the Uncertainty Principle. Nobel Prize, 1932.

Heller, Joseph (1923–99), US novelist, whose celebrated novel is *Catch 22* (1961).

Helmholtz, Herman von (1821–94), German physicist and physiologist. He published his *Erhaltung der Kraft* (Conservation of Energy) in 1847, the year that Joule gave the first clear exposition of the principle of energy. His pupil Heinrich Hertz discovered electromagnetic radiation in accordance with Maxwell's theory.

Heloïse (*c.* 1101–64), beloved of Abelard (*q.v.*). Her letters to him survive.

Hemingway, Ernest (1898–1961), American novelist of new technique and wide influence. His works include *A Farewell to Arms, Death in the Afternoon, For Whom the Bell Tolls, The Old Man and the Sea.* He committed suicide. Nobel prizewinner 1954.

Henderson, Arthur (1863–1935), British Labour

politician, b. Glasgow. He worked mainly for disarmament. Nobel peace prize, 1934.

Hendrix, Jimi (1942–70), pioneering rock guitarist, singer and songwriter. A key figure in the development of rock.

Henrietta Maria (1609–69), the daughter of Henry IV of France and wife of Charles I.

Henry, Joseph (1797–1878), American physicist and schoolteacher who independently of Faraday discovered the principle of the induced current. The weather-reporting system he set up at the Smithsonian Institution led to the creation of the U.S. Weather Bureau.

Henry I (1068–1135), King of England. The youngest son of William the Conqueror, he ascended the throne during the absence on crusade of his elder brother Robert of Normandy. His long reign brought order and progress, not entirely destroyed by the anarchy under his successor Stephen.

Henry II (1133–89), King of England. He was son of Matilda, daugher of Henry I, and Geoffrey Plantagenet, count of Anjou; and his lands stretched to the Pyrenees. He was a strong ruler to whom we largely owe the establishment of the common law system and permanent administrative reforms. His conflict with the Church led to the murder of archbishop Becket.

Henry III (1207–72), King of England, succeeded his father John in 1216. Himself devout and simple, his long reign was troubled by a partly factious baronial opposition.

Henry IV (1367–1413), grandson of Edward III and heir to the Duchy of Lancaster, became king of England in 1399. More solid and practical than his cousin Richard II, whom he had supplanted, he consolidated the government.

Henry V (1387–1422), son of Henry IV, succeeded his father as king of England in 1413. A successful commander, he renewed the French war and won the battle of Agincourt, but died young.

Henry VI (1421–71), son of Henry V, succeeded his father as king of England in 1422 as a baby. Gentle and retiring, he inherited a losing war with France. He founded Eton, and King's College, Cambridge. The Yorkist line claimed the crown from his (the Lancastrian) line, and the Wars of the Roses led to his deposition and death. Ruled 1422–61, 1470–71.

Henry VII (1457–1509), succeeded Richard III as king of England after defeating him in 1485. The first Tudor king, he was firm and shrewd, even avaricious; he built Henry VII's Chapel in Westminster Abbey, and encouraged John Cabot to sail to North America.

Henry VIII (1491–1547), King of England, succeeded his father Henry VII in 1509. A prince of the Renaissance, skilled in music and sports, he loved the sea and built up the navy. His minister Cardinal Wolsey fell when Henry, seeking divorce to obtain a legal heir, rejected papal supremacy and dissolved the monasteries. Ruthless and ostentatious, he executed Sir Thomas More and spent his father's wealth. The father of Edward VI, Mary I and Elizabeth I.

Henry IV of France (Henry of Navarre) (1553–1610). Prior to becoming king, he was the leader of the Huguenots; and although on being crowned he became a Catholic, he protected the Protestants by the Edict of Nantes. He then became a national king, but was later assassinated by Ravaillac, a religious fanatic.

Henry the Navigator (1394–1460), Portuguese promoter of discovery, son of John I. His sailors discovered Madeira and the Azores.

Henschel, Sir George (1850–1934), singer, composer, and conductor. B. in Breslau, he became a naturalised Englishman. Founder and conductor of the London Symphony Concerts (1886).

Hepplewhite, George (d. 1786), English cabinetmaker whose name is identified with the style which followed the Chippendale period.

Heraclitus of Ephesus (c. 540–475 B.C.), Greek philosopher. His discovery of a changing, more democratic, world influenced the philosophies of Parmenides, Democritus, Plato, and Aristotle, and later, of Hegel.

Herbert, George (1593–1633), the most purely devotional of English poets.

Hereward the Wake, the last Saxon leader to hold out against the Normans. His base in the fens was captured in 1071 but he escaped. His exploits were written up by Kingsley.

Herod the Great. See Herod Family, H11–12.

Herodotus (c. 485–425 B.C.), Greek historian, called by Cicero, the father of history. He travelled widely collecting historical evidence.

Herrick, Robert (1591–1674), English lyric poet. His poems include *Gather ye Rose Buds*, *Cherry Ripe*, and *Oberon's Feast*.

Herriot, Edouard (1872–1957), French Radical-Socialist statesman. A scholar, long-time mayor of Lyons. Three times prime minister.

Herschel, Sir John (1792–1871), British astronomer who continued his father's researches and also pioneered photography, a term introduced by him. One of his twelve children introduced fingerprints into criminology.

Herschel, Sir William (1738–1822), German-born astronomer who came to England from Hanover as a musician; father of the above. Unrivalled as an observer, and with telescopes of his own making he investigated the distribution of stars in the Milky Way and concluded that some of the nebulae he could see were separate star systems outside our own. He discovered the planet Uranus in 1781.

Hertz, Heinrich Rudolf (1857–95), German physicist, whose laboratory experiments confirmed Maxwell's electromagnetic theory of waves and yielded information about their behaviour.

Herzl, Theodor (1860–1904), founder of modern political Zionism, was b. Budapest. He convened a congress at Basle in 1897.

Hesiod (c. 735 B.C.), Greek poet, author of *Work and Days*, which tells of life in the country.

Heyerdahl, Thor (1914–2002), Norwegian anthropologist, famous for crossing the Pacific on the *Kon-Tiki* to demonstrate links between Peru and Polynesia.

Hildegard von Bingen, St. (1098–1179), medieval Benedictine nun, visionary and writer. The 'Sibyl of the Rhine'.

Hill, Octavia (1838–1912), English social reformer concerned with the housing conditions of the poor, a pioneer in slum clearance in London; founder (with Sir Robert Hunter and Canon Rawnsley) of the National Trust.

Hill, Sir Rowland (1795–1879), originator of the penny postal system. He was secretary to the Postmaster-General 1846–54, then chief secretary to the Post Office until 1864.

Hillary, Sir Edmund (b.1919), New Zealand mountaineer and explorer. Won world-wide fame when he and Sherpa Tenzing (d. 1986) were the first to reach the summit of Mt. Everest in 1953. Order of the Garter (1995).

Hindemith, Paul (1895–1963), German composer and viola player. He is associated with the movement in *Gebrauchsmusik*, which regarded music as a social expression. He incurred Nazi hostility and his later life was spent abroad. His numerous works include chamber works, songs, operas, ballet music, symphonies, and the oratorio *Das Unaufhörliche*. See also Section P.

Hindenburg, Paul von (1847–1934), German field-marshal. In 1914 he defeated the Rus sians at Tannenberg. In his old age a national hero, President of the German Reich, 1925–34.

Hinshelwood, Sir Cyril Norman (1897–1967), English chemist. He shared with Prof. Semenov of Russia the 1956 Nobel prize for chemistry for researches into the mechanism of chemical reactions. Pres. Royal Society, 1955–60.

Hippocrates of Chios (fl. c. 430 B.C.), Greek mathematician, the first to compile a work on the elements of geometry.

Hippocrates of Cos (fl. c. 430 B.C.), Greek physician, whose writings are lost, but who is believed to have established medical schools in Athens and elsewhere, and to have contributed towards a scientific separation of medicine from superstition. Seen as the ideal physician.

Hirohito, Emperor of Japan (1901–89), acceded to the throne in 1926. In 1946 he renounced his legendary divinity. Much controversy surrounds his role in Japanese aggression in the 1930s and his part in the Second World War.

Hirst, Damien (b. 1965), controversial contemporary artist who won the Turner Prize in 1995. His "pickled shark" launched the Britart movement.

Hitler, Adolf (1889–1945), German dictator, founder of National Socialism, b. in Austria, son of a customs official. He was in Vienna for 5 years with no regular work before going to Munich in 1913; enlisted in Bavarian infantry in 1914. In post-1918 Germany, he led the extreme-right

Nazi Party. He became Reich chancellor in 1933 and on the death of Hindenburg in 1934 Führer; and commander-in-chief *Wehrmacht* 1935.

Under Hitler, working class movements were ruthlessly destroyed; all opponents—communists, socialists, Jews—were persecuted and murdered. By terrorism and propaganda the German state was welded into a powerful machine for aggression. There followed the occupation of the Rhineland (1936), the annexation of Austria and Czechoslovakia (1938–9), the invasion of Poland and declaration of war by Great Britain and France (1939) and the invasion of Russia (1941). Final defeat came in 1945; on 30 April he committed suicide as the Russians closed in on Berlin.

Hobbes, Thomas (1588–1679), English philosopher who published *Leviathan* in 1651. He favoured strong government and supported the supremacy of the state, but his arguments aroused antagonism even among royalists. He was an enthusiast for scientific enquiry.

Hobhouse, Leonard Trelawney (1864–1929), English sociologist. His books include *The Theory of Knowledge, Morals in Evolution etc.*

Ho Chi-minh (1892–1969), leader of the Vietnam revolutionary nationalist party of Indo-China, which struggled for independence from France during and after the second world war. His main purpose was to weld together the nationalistic and communist elements in Vietnam. He fought to extend his control over South Vietnam, defying the United States.

Hockney, David (b. 1937), one of the most prominent British painters of the post-war generation. Born in Bradford, he moved to California in the 1960s. Companion of Honour.

Hodgkin, Sir Alan (1914–98), British biophysicist working in the field of nerve impulse conduction. He was one of the world's most eminent biophysicists. Nobel prizewinner, 1970; O.M. 1973.

Hodgkin, Dorothy Crowfoot (1919–94), the third woman to win the Nobel prize in chemistry, awarded in 1964 for her X-ray analysis to elucidate the structure of complex molecules, notably penicillin and vitamin B-12. She succeeded in 1969 in determining the crystalline structure of insulin. O.M. (1965).

Hofbauer, Imre (d. 1990), Hungarian-born artist, whose brilliance was portrayed in his compassionate studies of the down-trodden.

Hogarth, William (1697–1764), English engraver and painter, who satirised his time with character, humour, and power, especially in his *Harlot's Progress, Rake's Progress, Marriage à la Mode, Industry and Idleness*, and *The March to Finchley*.

Hogg, Quintin (1845–1903), educationist and philanthropist who purchased the old Polytechnic Institution in 1882 and turned it into a popular college providing education at moderate rates. His grandson, **Lord Hailsham** (1907–2001), was Lord Chancellor 1970–4, 1979–83, 1983–87.

Hokusai, Katsushika (1760–1849), Japanese landscape artist of the Ukiyo-e (popular school).

Holbein, Hans, the elder (*c.* 1465–1524), German painter, b. Augsburg, father of:

Holbein, Hans, the younger (1497–1543), German painter, b. Augsburg; settled in London 1532. He won the favour of Henry VIII, for whom he painted many portraits. He is also known for his series *The Dance of Death*.

Holden, Charles (1875–1960), British architect, designer of British Medical Association Building, London; Underground HQ; Senate House *etc.*

Holden, Sir Isaac (1807–97), British inventor of woolcombing machinery.

Hölderlin, Johann Christian Friedrich (1770–1843), German poet, friend of Hegel. His works include the novel *Hyperion* and the elegy *Menon's Laments for Diotima*. In his middle years his mind became unhinged.

Holford, Baron (William Graham Holford) (1907–75), British architect and town-planner.

Holmes, Dame Kelly (b. 1970), British athlete who took historic double at 2004 Olympics (800m and 1,500m titles).

Holmes, Oliver Wendell (1809–94), American author. His writings include *Autocrat of the Breakfast Table, The Professor of the Breakfast Table*, and *The Poet at the Breakfast Table*.

Holst, Gustave Theodore (1874–1934), British composer of Swedish descent whose compositions include *The Planets* suite, *The Hymn of Jesus*, an opera *The Perfect Fool* and a choral sym-

phony. An outstanding teacher. *See* **Section P.**

Holyoake, George Jacob (1817–1906), English social reformer and secularist. He wrote a history of the co-operative movement.

Holyoake, Keith Jacka (1904–83), New Zealand politician; prime minister 1960–72.

Home of the Hirsel, Lord (Alex Douglas-Home) (1903–95), British Prime Minister, 1963–64 (after renouncing his peerage as 14th Earl of Home). Foreign Secretary, 1960–63, 1970–74. Created Life Peer, 1974. His younger brother was the playwright **William Douglas-Home** (1912–92).

Homer (*c.* 700 B.C.), epic poet. He is supposed to have been a Greek who lived at Chios or Smyrna and has been regarded as the author of the *Iliad* and the *Odyssey*, though this is tradition rather than ascertained fact.

Hood, 1st Viscount (Samuel Hood) (1724–1816), British admiral who in 1793 was in command of the Mediterranean fleet and occupied Toulon.

Hood, Thomas (1799–1845), English poet. His poems include *The Song of the Shirt, The Dream of Eugene Aram* and *The Bridge of Sighs*. He was also a humorist and punster.

Hooke, Robert (1635–1703), English physicist. His inventions include the balance spring of watches. He was also an architect and drew up a plan for rebuilding London after the Great Fire. His *Diary* is published.

Hooker, Richard (1554–1600), English theologian, author of *Ecclesiastical Polity*. He was Master of the Temple, 1585–91. For his choice of words he was known as "Judicious Hooker".

Hope, Bob (**Leslie Townes**), (1903–2003), legendary entertainer. Born in Eltham, London, but raised in Ohio, USA. The quintessential comedian.

Hopkins, Sir Anthony. *See* **Section Q.**

Hopkins, Sir Frederick Gowland (1861–1947), English biochemist, pioneer in biochemical and nutritional research. He first drew attention to the substances later known as vitamins. Pres. Royal Society 1930–5. Nobel prize 1929.

Hopkins, Gerard Manley (1844–89), English poet of religious experience and of a novel style.

Hopkins, Harry (1890–1946), Franklin Roosevelt's personal assistant at foreign conferences, and in the New Deal and Lend-Lease.

Hopkinson, John (1849–98), English engineer. By developing the theory of alternating current and of the magnetic current in dynamos he paved the way to the common use of electricity.

Hoppner, John (1758–1810), English portrait painter, b. Whitechapel, of German parents.

Horace (Quintus Horatius Flaccus) (65–8 B.C.), Roman satirist and poet, son of a Greek freedman. He wrote *Satires, Epodes, Odes*, and *Epistles*. He fought on the republican side at Philippi, but became poet laureate to Augustus.

Horniman, Annie Elizabeth Fredericka (1860–1937), founder of the modern repertory system in England. Her father F. J. Horniman founded the Horniman Museum.

Hosking, Eric (1909–91), bird photographer. A highly skilled ornithologist and tireless champion of the grace and beauty of birds.

Hoskins, William George (1908–92), the great local historian of England and the English. Author of *The Making of the English Landscape* (1955).

Houdini, Harry (Erich Weiss) (1874–1926), American illusionist, son of a Hungarian rabbi. Famed for his escapes from handcuffs.

Housman, Alfred Edward (1859–1936), English poet, author of *A Shropshire Lad*; he was also a classical scholar. His brother Laurence (1865–1959) was a playwright and wrote *Little Plays of St. Francis* and *Victoria Regina*.

Howard, John (1726–90), English prison reformer. Imprisoned in France in wartime, he subsequently investigated English prisons, securing reforms; and later also continental prisons, dying in Russia of gaol fever.

Howard, Michael. *See* **D17.**

Howard of Effingham, 2nd Baron (Charles Howard) (1536–1624), afterwards Earl of Nottingham; commanded the fleet which defeated the Spanish Armada (1588), and took part in the capture of Cadiz (1596).

Howe, Elias (1819–67), American inventor of the sewing machine.

Howe, Julia Ward (1819–1910), American suffragette, author of *Mine eyes have seen the glory*.

Howe, 1st Earl (Richard Howe) (1726–99), British

admiral whose victories over the French in two wars included that off Ushant on 1 June 1794 ("the glorious first of June").

Hoyle, Sir Fred (1915–2001), popular but controversial astronomer who coined the term 'Big Bang' (but denied that it had happened).

Hua-Guofeng (b. 1922), b. Hunan, succeeded Mao Tse-tung as Communist Party Chairman, 1976–81.

Hubble, Edwin Powell (1889–1953), American astronomer, noted for his work on extragalactic nebulae. With the 100-inch telescope on Mount Wilson he detected the Cepheid variables. The Hubble space telescope is named after him.

Huddleston, Trevor (1913–98), Anglican archbishop who devoted his life to fighting apartheid.

Hudson, Henry (d. 1611), English navigator credited with the discovery of the Hudson river and Hudson Bay, where mutineers turned him adrift to die. He was on a voyage to find a passage by the north pole to Japan and China.

Hudson, William Henry (1841–1922), naturalist, b. Buenos Aires of American parents, naturalised in England (1900). His books include *The Purple Land*, *Green Mansions*, and *Far Away and Long Ago*. Hyde Park bird sanctuary was established in his memory.

Huggins, Sir William (1824–1910), astronomer who pioneered in spectroscopic photography.

Hughes, Ted (1930–98), English poet. Succeeded Sir John Betjeman as Poet Laureate in 1984. His early poems observed the natural world (as in the collection *The Hawk in the Rain*). O.M. (1998).

Hughes, Thomas (1822–96), English novelist, author of *Tom Brown's Schooldays*, which is based on Rugby school.

Hugo, Victor Marie (1802–85), French poet, dramatist, and novelist, who headed the Romantic movement in France in the early 19th cent. His dramas include *Hernani*, *Lucrèce Borgia*, *Ruy Blas*, and *Le Roi s'amuse*. Of his novels *Notre Dame* belongs to his early period, *Les Misérables*, *Les Travailleurs de la mer*, and *L'Homme qui rit* were written in Guernsey.

Humboldt, Friedrich Heinrich Alexander, Baron von (1769–1859), German naturalist and explorer whose researches are recorded in *Voyage de Humboldt et Bonpland* (23 vols., 1805–34), and *Kosmos* (5 vols., 1845–62). He is now regarded as the father of ecology.

Hume, Cardinal (George) Basil (1923–99) Catholic Benedictine monk. Abbot of Ampleforth, 1963–76, when he became Archbishop of Westminster. Awarded Order of Merit (1999), the first Catholic prelate to receive this honour.

Hume, David (1711–76), Scottish philosopher. His main works are *Treatise of Human Nature*, *Dialogues Concerning Natural Religion* and *Enquiry concerning Human Understanding*.

Hume, John. *See* D17.

Hunt, Holman (1827–1910), English artist, one of the founders of the Pre-Raphaellite movement. His pictures include *The Light of the World*.

Hunt, Baron (John Hunt) (1910–98), leader of the 1953 British Everest Expedition when Tenzing and Hillary reached the summit.

Hunt, Leigh (1784–1859), English poet and essayist. In 1813 he was fined and imprisoned for libelling the Prince Regent in *The Examiner*.

Hunter, Bob (1941–2005), Canadian pioneering environmental activist who co-founded Greenpeace. One of the first "eco-warriors".

Hus, Jan (1369–1415), Bohemian religious reformer. Strongly influenced by Wyclif, he urged reform both of abuses in the church and of doctrine. Sentenced to death or recantation, he suffered martyrdom on 6 July 1415. His death caused a civil war which lasted many years.

Hussein, King (1935–99), King of Jordan, 1952–99. A symbol of stability and the search for peace in the Middle East.

Hussein, Saddam (b. 1938), dictator of Iraq from 1979 to 2003. Launched the war with Iran in 1980 and the invasion of Kuwait, 1990. *See* Section C for the invasion of 2003 which ended his regime. He was captured on 13 December 2003.

Hutton, James (1726–97), an Edinburgh doctor who founded modern geological theory.

Hutton, Sir Leonard (1916–90), foremost English cricketer. Captained England 23 times, scoring 364 in 1938 against Australia.

Huxley, Aldous (1894–1963), English novelist, author of *Brave New World*.

Huxley, Sir Julian (1887–1975), biologist and writer,

grandson of T. H. Huxley and brother of Aldous; first director general of UNESCO 1946–8; a founder of the International Union for the Conservation of Nature and the World Wild Life Fund.

Huxley, Thomas Henry (1825–95), English biologist, b. Ealing. He started life as assistant-surgeon on H.M.S. *Rattlesnake* and during the voyage (1846–50) studied marine organisms. After the publication of Darwin's *Origin of Species* he became an ardent evolutionist. He coined the term "agnostic".

Huygens, Christian (1629–95), Dutch mathematician, physicist, and astronomer, son of the poet Constantijn Huygens (1596–1687); discovered the rings of Saturn, invented the pendulum clock, and developed the wave theory of light in opposition to Newton's corpuscular theory.

Hyde, Douglas (1860–1949), Irish scholar, historian, poet, and folk-lorist; first president of Ireland in the 1937 constitution, 1938–45.

Hypatia of Alexandria, most famous woman mathematician of antiquity. She excited the enmity of Christian fanatics. Murdered in A.D. 415.

I

Ibsen, Henrik Johan (1828–1906), Norwegian playwright and poet, who dealt with social and psychological problems and revolutionised the European theatre. His chief works are *Ghosts*, *The Wild Duck*, *The Master Builder*, *A Doll's House*, *Hedda Gabler* and the poetic drama, *Peer Gynt*.

Ingres, Jean Auguste Dominique (1780–1867), French historical and classical painter. His paintings include *La grande odalisque* in the Louvre.

Innocent III (c. 1160–1216), Pope 1198–1216. He asserted the power and moral force of the papacy over the Emperor Otto IV, Philip II of France, and John of England. He launched the fourth crusade, encouraged the crusade against the Albigensian heretics, and held the 4th Lateran council. His pontificate marks the zenith of the mediaeval papacy.

Ionesco, Eugene (1912–94), French playwright of the Absurd, b. Romania, whose plays include *The Bald Prima Donna*, *The Chairs* and *Rhinoceros*.

Iqbal, Sir Muhammad (1877–1938), poet-philosopher, b. Sialkot (Pakistan). He wrote both poetry and prose in Urdu, Persian, and English, and his work is marked by mystic nationalism.

Ireland, John (1879–1962), English composer, popularly known for his setting of Masefield's *Sea Fever*, but also a noted composer.

Irving, Sir Henry (1838–1905), English actor. At the Lyceum theatre from 1871, later with Ellen Terry, he gave notable Shakespearean performances, especially as Shylock and Malvolio. First actor to be knighted.

Irving, Washington (1783–1859), American essayist, whose works include *Tales of a Traveller* and *The Sketch Book*, also biographies.

Isabella of Castile (1451–1504), reigned jointly with her husband, Ferdinand II of Aragon, over a united Spain, from which the Moors and the Jews were expelled. During their reign the New World was discovered.

Isherwood, Christopher. *See* M30(1).

Ismail Pasha (1830–95), grandson of Mehemet Ali, was Khedive of Egypt. Under him the Suez canal was made, but his financial recklessness led to Anglo-French control.

Ismay, 1st Baron (Hastings Lionel Ismay) (1887–1965), British general who was chief of staff to Sir Winston Churchill in the second world war.

Ito, Hirobumi, Prince (1841–1909). Japanese statesman, four times premier, who helped to modernise his country. He was assassinated.

Ivan the Great (1410–1505) brought the scattered provinces of Muscovy under one control and put an end to Tartar rule.

Ivan the Terrible (1530–84), crowned as first Tsar of Russia in 1547, was an autocratic ruler who consolidated and expanded Russia.

J

Jackson, Andrew (1767–1845), American general who was twice president of the United States.

Jackson, Thomas Jonathan (1824–63), "Stonewall Jackson," was general on the Southern side in the American Civil War; killed at Chancellorsville.

Jacobs, William Wymark (1863–1943), English novelist, b. London, author of humorous sea and other stories.

Jacquard, Joseph Marie (1752–1834), French inventor whose loom provided an effective method of weaving designs.

Jagger, Sir Mick (Michael) (b. 1943), one of the legends of rock music. Formed the Rolling Stones (debut in 1962). The 'ultimate rock and roll rebel'.

Jahangir (1569–1627), 3rd Mogul emperor and patron of art.

James I (1566–1625), King of England (1603–25) and, as James VI, King of Scotland (1567–1625). He was the son of Mary Stuart and succeeded to the English throne on the death of Elizabeth I. His reign saw the Gunpowder Plot of 1605 and the publication of the Authorised Version of the Bible, but it also marked an increasingly critical attitude by the Puritans. Described as "the wisest fool in Christendom."

James II (1633–1701), King of England and, as James VII, King of Scotland (1685–8), was the younger son of Charles I. Personally honest, and an able admiral, he lacked political understanding; and when, having put down Monmouth's rebellion, he tried and failed to obtain better conditions for his fellow Roman Catholics, he was obliged in 1688 to flee the country.

James, Cyril Lionel Robert (1901–89), Trinidadian historian, literary critic, political theorist and cricket writer. Author of *Nkrumah and the Ghana Revolution* (1977) and *Spheres of Existence* (1980).

James, Henry (1843–1916), American novelist. He lived mainly in England. His work, noted for intellectual subtlety and characterisation, includes *The American, Daisy Miller, The Portrait of a Lady, What Maisie Knew, The Spoils of Poynton* etc.

James, William (1842–1910), American psychologist and philosopher, brother of Henry. He was a protagonist of the theory of pragmatism developed by his friend C. S. Peirce, and invented "radical empiricism." His major works are *The Principles of Psychology, The Will to Believe,* and *The Meaning of Truth.*

Janáček, Leoš (1854–1928), Czech composer and conductor, and student of folk music, b. in Moravia, son of a village schoolmaster, creator of a national style. His works include the opera *Jenufa. See Section P.*

Jaurès, Jean (1859–1914), French socialist leader and writer. Assassinated by nationalist fanatic, 1914.

Jefferies, Richard (1848–87), English naturalist of poetic perception, b. in Wiltshire, author of *Gamekeeper at Home* and *The Life of the Fields.*

Jefferson, Thomas (1743–1826), American president, 1801–9. He created the Republican Party, by which the federalists, led by Hamilton, were overthrown, and helped to draft the Declaration of Independence. He tried unsuccessfully to bring an end to slavery. He negotiated the Louisiana Purchase of 1803.

Jeffreys, 1st Baron (George Jeffreys) (1648–89), English judge who held the "bloody assize" after Monmouth's unsuccessful rebellion. In 1686 he was sent to the Tower and there died.

Jellicoe, 1st Earl (John Rushworth Jellicoe) (1859–1935), British admiral. He fought the indecisive battle of Jutland in 1916, after which the German fleet remained in harbour.

Jenkins, Lord (Roy Jenkins) (1920–2003), British politician, b. Wales; Pres. EEC Commission 1977–80; Home Sec. 1965–7; Chanc. of Exchequer 1967–70. Leader, SDP 1982–June 1983. Order of Merit (1993). Chaired Commission on Voting System, 1997–8. A highly influential statesman and architect of social reform.

Jenner, Edward (1749–1823), English physician, b. in Gloucs., pupil of John Hunter. His discovery of vaccination against smallpox (1798) helped to lay the foundations of modern immunology.

Jerne, Niels Kai (1911–94), Danish microbiologist and Nobel laureate.

Jerome, Jerome Klapka (1859–1927), English humorous writer, author of *Three Men in a Boat.*

Jerome, St. (c. 331–420), scholar who translated the Bible into Latin (the Vulgate).

Jesus Christ (c. 4 B.C.–A.D. 30). *See Section H.*

Jiang Zemin (b. 1926), Chinese politician. State President of China, 1993–2003. He continued the economic policies of the late Deng Xiaoping.

Jiménez, Juan Ramón (1881–1958), Spanish lyric poet. Nobel prizewinner 1956.

Jinnah, Mohammed Ali (1876–1948), Pakistani statesman. B. at Karachi, he became president of the Muslim League, and succeeded in 1947 in establishing the Dominion of Pakistan, becoming its first governor-general.

Joachim, Joseph (1831–1907), Hungarian violinist and composer.

Joan of Arc, St. (Jeanne d'Arc) (1412–31), French patriot, called the Maid of Orleans; of peasant parentage (she was b. at Domrémy), she believed herself called to save France from English domination; and by her efforts Charles VII was crowned at Rheims in 1429. Captured by the Burgundians and sold to the English, burned as a heretic, canonioed in 1920. Recent research has cast doubt on many events in her life.

Joffre, Joseph Jacques Césaire (1852–1931), French general. He was commander-in-chief of the French army in the 1914–18 war.

John, St., the Baptist. *See Section H.*

John, St., the Evangelist. *See Section H.*

John (1167–1216), youngest son of Henry II, was King of England from 1199. Able but erratic and arbitrary, he lost Normandy. Baronial opposition to him, under the influence of Archbishop Stephen Langton, acquired a national character, and in 1215 he was obliged to seal Magna Carta (*see* Section L).

John of Gaunt (1340–99), Duke of Lancaster, son of Edward III and father of Henry IV.

John XXIII (1881–1963), elected Pope in 1958, succeeding Pius XII, was formerly Cardinal Angelo Giuseppe Roncalli, patriarch of Venice. He sought to bring the Church closer to modern needs and to promote Christian unity.

John Paul II, (1920–2005), succeeded Pope John Paul I after his sudden death in 1978; formerly Cardinal Karol Wojtyla, archbishop of Cracow; first Pope to come from Poland. Assassination attempt made 1981. Presided over the Catholic Church during the fall of communism, but grew increasingly conservative with age. Pope John Paul declared more people saints (482), and travelled more widely, than any other previous pontiff.

John, Augustus (1878–1961), British painter and etcher, b. in Wales: noted for his portraits.

John, Sir Elton (b. 1947), born Reginald Kenneth Dwight. Rock singer and pianist. Knighted (1998) after his rendering of *Candle in the Wind* at funeral of Princess Diana.

Johnson, Amy (1904–41), was the first woman aviator to fly solo from England to Australia.

Johnson, Lyndon Baines (1908–73), President of the United States, 1963–9. He became president on Kennedy's assassination and followed a progressive policy at home, but his achievements were clouded by the war in Vietnam.

Johnson, Samuel (1709–84), English lexicographer and man of letters, b. at Lichfield. His *Dictionary* was published in 1755, and was followed by *Rasselas, The Idler* (a periodical), and *Lives of the Poets.* He was a focus of London literary life of his day. His biographer was James Boswell.

Joliot-Curie, Jean Frédéric (1900–58), and his wife **Irène** (1896–1956), French scientists who discovered artificial radioactivity. Nobel prizewinners 1935. Joliot-Curie was one of the discoverers of nuclear fission. **Irène** was the daughter of Pierre and Marie Curie. Both were communists, and both died from cancer caused by their work.

Jones, Ernest Charles (1819–69), English Chartist leader and poet.

Jones, Sir Harold Spencer (1890–1960), British astronomer royal, 1935–55. His major research was to determine the mean distance of the earth from the sun, 93,004,000 miles.

Jones, Inigo (1573–1652), architect of the English renaissance who studied in Italy and inspired the use of Palladian forms in England. His buildings include the banqueting hall in Whitehall and the queen's house at Greenwich. He also designed furniture and introduced the proscenium arch and movable scenery on the English stage.

Jonson, Ben (1573–1637), English poet and dramatist. His plays include *Every Man in his Humour, Volpone,* and *The Alchemist*; and his poems *Drink to me only with thine Eyes.* He also produced court masques.

Josephine, Empress (1763–1814), wife of Napoleon I, *née* de la Pagerie, she was previously married to the Vicomte de Beauharnais. She was divorced from Napoleon in 1809.

Josephus, Flavius (38–c. 100), Jewish historian, author of *History of the Jewish War.*

Joule, James Prescott (1818–89), English physicist, pupil of Dalton, who researched on electromagnetism and determined the mechanical equivalent of heat. *See* **Section L.**

Jowett, Benjamin (1817–93), English scholar. He translated Plato's *Dialogues,* and he was an influential Master of Balliol College, Oxford.

Jowitt, Earl (William Allen Jowitt) (1885–1957), British Labour politician and Lord Chancellor.

Joyce, James (1882–1941), Irish author, b. Dublin. His *Ulysses* gives a microscopic picture of a day in the life of two Irishmen, and flouted the conventions of his day. Other works include *Portrait of the Artist* and *Finnegans Wake.* He spent most of his life on the Continent. His acclaimed short stories include *Dubliners* (1914).

Julian the Apostate (331–63), Roman emperor who tried to restore paganism in the empire. He was killed in war against Persia.

Jung, Carl Gustav (1875–1961), Swiss psychiatrist. A pupil of Freud, he later formulated his own system of analytical psychology. *See* **Section J.**

Junot, Andoche (1771–1813), French general defeated by Wellington in the Peninsular War.

Jusserand, Jean Jules (1855–1932), French author and diplomat, who wrote on English literature and wayfaring life in the Middle Ages.

Justinian I (483–565), Roman emperor in the East. He and his wife Theodora beautified Constantinople, and his general Belisarius was successful in war. He codified Roman law.

Juvenal (60–140), Roman poet and Stoic, remembered for his *Satires.*

K

Kafka, Franz (1883–1924), German-speaking Jewish writer, b. Prague, whose introspective work, the bulk of which was not published till after his early death from tuberculosis, has had a notable influence on later schools, especially the surrealists. It includes the three novels *The Trial, The Castle,* and *America.*

Kālidāsa (c. A.D. 400), chief figure in classic Sanskrit literature. No facts are known about his life and date, but certain evidence places him in the 5th cent. Seven of his works survive: two lyrics, *Ritusamhara* (The Seasons), and *Megha-dūta* (Cloud Messenger), two epics, *Raghu-vamsa* (Dynasty of Raghu) and *Kumara-sambhava* (Birth of the War-god); and three dramas, *Sakūntala, Mālavikāgnimitra,* and *Vikramorvasīya.*

Kandinsky, Wasily (1866–1944) Russian-born painter, a leader of the *Blaue Reiter* group.

Kane, Bob (1915–98), American cartoonist who created Batman, the caped crusader.

Kant, Immanuel (1724–1804), German philosopher, author of *Critique of Pure Reason* (1781), *Critique of Practical Reason* (1788), and *Critique of Judgement* (1790). He came from a Pietist family of Königsberg, where he lectured, but the Prussian government forbade his lectures as anti-Lutheran. He was influenced by the writings of his neighbour Hamann (*see* **Romanticism, Section J**) and by Rousseau and Hume, and his own work was of immense influence in shaping future liberal thought. He believed in the freedom of man to make his own decisions and considered the exploitation of man as the worst evil.

Kapitza, Pyotr (1894–1984), Russian physicist who worked on atomic research with Rutherford at the Cavendish Laboratory, Cambridge, and returned to Russia in 1935. Nobel Prize for Physics, 1978.

Kauffman, Angelica (1741–1807), Anglo-Swiss painter, a foundation member of the Royal Academy and the first woman R.A.

Kaulbach, Wilhelm von (1805–74), German painter who illustrated the works of Goethe and Schiller.

Kaunda, Kenneth (b. 1924), African leader of international standing, son of Christian missionaries. He was president of Zambia, 1964–91.

Kean, Charles John (1811–68), English actor-manager son of Edmund. He married Ellen Tree. In the 1850s played with her in spectacular revivals at the Princess's Theatre, London.

Kean, Edmund (1787–1833), English tragic actor. He made his name as Shylock.

Keats, John (1795–1821), English poet who in his

short life produced poems notable for richness of imagination and beauty of thought. They include *Odes, Isabella,* and *The Eve of St. Agnes.*

Keble, John (1792–1866), English clergyman associated with the Tractarian movement (*See* **Section J**) and author of *The Christian Year.*

Keller, Helen Adams (1880–1968), American author and lecturer who overcame great physical handicaps (blind and deaf before the age of two) to live an active and useful life.

Kelly, Ned (1855–80), most famous of the Australian bushranger outlaws—to some a revolutionary martyr, to others a cold-blooded killer.

Kelvin of Largs, 1st Baron (William Thomson) (1824–1907), British mathematician and physicist, b. Belfast, known for his work on heat and thermodynamics, and contributions to electrical science and submarine telegraphy. In the domain of heat he stands to Joule as Maxwell stands to Faraday in the history of electrical science, both bringing pre-eminently mathematical minds to bear on the results of experimental discoveries. He introduced the Kelvin or Absolute scale of temperature and was one of the original members of the Order of Merit.

Kemble, Fanny (1809–93), English actress from a noted theatrical family, her father and uncle respectively being the actors Charles Kemble and John Philip Kemble, and her aunt, Mrs. Siddons.

Kempenfelt, Richard (1718–82), English admiral, who sank with his ship the *Royal George* together with 600 of the ship's company off Spithead when it capsized.

Kempis, Thomas à (1380–1471), name by which the German mystic Thomas Hammerken was known, was a monk of the Augustinian order, whose life was mainly spent at a monastery near Zwolle. The author of *The Imitation of Christ.*

Kennedy, Charles. *See* **Section D.**

Kennedy, John Fitzgerald (1917–63), President of the USA, 1961–3, the youngest and the first Roman Catholic to be elected; son of a financier. He had world-wide pre-eminence and gave the American people a sense of purpose to meet the challenges of a scientific age. He opposed racial discrimination and initiated a new era of East–West relations; but his foreign policy sowed the seeds of the Vietnam war. He and his brother **Robert** (1925–68) were assassinated, the latter while campaigning for the presidency in 1968. Robert Kennedy was Attorney General, 1961–64 and promoted the Civil Rights Act. The son of President Kennedy, **John F. Kennedy Jnr.** died in a plane crash in 1999.

Kent, William (1684–1748), English painter, furniture designer, landscape gardener, and architect, protégé of Lord Burlington, whose buildings include the great hall at Holkham and the Horse Guards, Whitehall.

Kenyatta, Jomo (1893 1978), African leader who became president of Kenya in 1964.

Kepler, Johann (1571–1630), German astronomer and mystic, for a short time assistant to Tycho Brahe whose measurements he used in working out his laws of planetary motion, which are: 1. Planets move round the sun not in circles, but in ellipses, the sun being one of the foci. 2. A planet moves not uniformly but in such a way that a line drawn from it to the sun sweeps out equal areas of the ellipse in equal times. 3. The squares of the period of revolution round the sun are proportional to the cubes of the distances. Newton explained these laws.

Kerensky, Alexander (1881–1970), Russian politician. Prime Minister of Provisional Government, July–November 1917. Rest of life in exile.

Kerouac, Jack (1922–58), American iconic novelist and poet. Champion of the Beat Generation. Born Lowell, Massachussetts of French-American parents.

Ketèlbey, Albert (1875–1959), British composer and conductor of many well-known compositions.

Keyes, 1st Baron (Roger John Brownlow Keyes) (1872–1945), British admiral who led the raid on Zeebrugge in 1918.

Keynes, 1st Baron (John Maynard Keynes) (1883–1946), British economist, who was a Treasury representative at the Versailles peace conference, and published his views in *The Economic Consequences of the Peace.* Author of *Treatise on Money* (1930) and *The General Theory of Employment, Interest and Money* (1936).

Khachaturian, Aram Ilich (1903–78), Armenian-born

composer who wrote the popular *Sabre Dance* and *Spartacus* (from which the Love Theme was used in TV's Onedin Line.)

Khomeini, Ayatollah (1900–89), Iranian religious leader. After 16 years in exile, returned to Iran in 1979 after the overthrow of the Shah. Architect of Islamic Republic of Iran. Virulently anti-Western.

Khrushchev, Nikita Sergeyevich (1894–1971), Russian statesman who became leader of the Soviet Union soon after the death of Stalin; first secretary of the Soviet Communist Party, 1953–64; effective leader, 1958–64. After the harsh years of the Stalinist régime he pursued a policy of relaxation in home and foreign affairs.

Kierkegaard, Sören (1813–55), Danish philosophical and religious thinker whose views have influenced existentialism. His main work is *Either–Or*

Kim Dae-jung (b. 1925), Korean politician. Survived assassination attempt, 1971 and repeated prison sentences. President, Republic of S. Korea 1997–2003. Nobel Peace Prize, 2000, for his "sunshine policy" of rapprochement with North Korea.

King, Mackenzie (1874–1950), prime minister of Canada, 1921–5, 1926–30, and 1935–48.

King, Martin Luther (1929–68), American clergyman and black civil rights leader; awarded the 1964 Nobel peace prize for his consistent support of the principle of non-violence in the black people's struggle for civil rights. Assassinated at Memphis, Tennessee.

King, Stephen (b. 1947), American writer of horror stories. Born Portland, Maine. His first novel *Carrie* established his world-wide reputation.

Kingsley, Charles (1819–75), English clergyman and novelist, author of *Hypatia*, *Westward Ho!*, *Hereward the Wake* and *The Water Babies.*

Kinnock, Lord (Neil Kinnock), (b. 1942), Labour politician. Leader of the Labour Party 1983–92. Reshaped the party for the 1992 election but resigned after Labour's fourth successive election defeat. EU Commissioner (with responsibility for Transport), 1995–9. Vice-President of the Commission, 1999–2004.

Kinsey, Alfred (1894–1956). Sexologist. Founder, Institute of Sex Research at Indiana University. His work led to more liberal attitudes to homosexuality, more relaxed divorce laws *etc*.

Kipling, Rudyard (1865–1936), British writer, b. Bombay. His vivid work portrays contemporary British rule in India and includes *The Light that Failed*, *Stalky and Co.*, *Kim*, and the *Barrack Room Ballads.* Among his books for children are the *Just So Stories*, *Puck of Pook's Hill* and the *Jungle Books.* Nobel prize 1907.

Kirchhoff, Gustav Robert (1824–87), German mathematical physicist, who with R. W. Bunsen discovered that in the gaseous state each chemical substance emits its own characteristic spectrum (1859). He was able to explain Fraunhofer's map of the solar spectrum. Using the spectroscope, he and Bunsen discovered the elements caesium and rubidium.

Kissinger, Henry (b. 1923), American Secretary of State 1973–7; inventor of shuttle diplomacy. Shared Nobel peace prize for 1973 with Le Duc Tho.

Kitchener of Khartoum, 1st Earl (Horatio Herbert Kitchener) (1850–1916), English general. In 1898 he won back the Sudan for Egypt by his victory at Omdurman. He served in the South African war. Secretary of State for War, 1914–16. He was drowned on his way to Russia.

Klee, Paul (1879–1940), Swiss artist, whose paintings are delicate dream-world fantasies.

Klemperer, Otto (1885–1973), German-born conductor, renowned as interpreter of the Beethoven symphonies. Expelled by the Nazis he became an American citizen and returned to Europe in 1946. He had been principal conductor of the Philharmonic Orchestra since 1959.

Kneller, Sir Godfrey (1646–1723), portrait painter, b. at Lübeck, who settled in England and was patronised by successive English sovereigns.

Knox, John (1514–72), Scottish reformer, b. near Haddington. While in exile at Geneva he was influenced by Calvin. On return to Scotland he was a leader of the reforming party against Mary, Queen of Scots. He wrote a *History of the Reformation in Scotland.*

Koch, Robert (1843–1910), German bacteriologist who discovered the bacillus of tuberculosis, and worked on cholera and cattle diseases.

Kodály, Zoltán (1882–1967), Hungarian composer and teacher. *See* **Section P.**

Kohl, Helmut (b. 1930), Chancellor of the Federal Republic of Germany until defeated in 1998. First Chancellor of re-united Germany after 1990. Narrowly re-elected Chancellor, 1994. A Christian Democrat who in November 1996 became the longest-serving Chancellor in German history (except for Bismarck). Since leaving office, plagued by financial scandals. *See* **Section C.**

Kokoschka, Oskar (1886–1980), Austrian portrait and landscape painter. Settled in England.

Korolyov, Sergei (1907–66), Russian space scientist, who designed the world's first earth vital lite, manned spaceship and moon rocket.

Kosçjuszko, Tadeusz (1746–1817), Polish patriot. After experience gained in America in the War of Independence, he led his countrymen against Russia in 1792 and 1794 in opposition to the partition of Poland.

Kossuth, Louis (1802–94), Hungarian patriot, who in 1848 led a rising of his countrymen against the Hapsburg dynasty, but had to flee to Turkey and later to England.

Kosygin, Alexei Nikolayevich (1904–80), succeeded Khrushchev in 1964 as chairman of the Council of Ministers of the USSR (prime minister).

Krebs, Sir Hans (1900–81), British biochemist, b. Germany. He became Professor of Biology at Oxford in 1954. Nobel prize 1953.

Kreisler, Fritz (1875–1962), Austrian violinist, who composed violin music and an operetta. He became an American citizen in 1943.

Krenek, Ernst (1900–91), Austrian–American composer of partly Czech descent, whose compositions include the jazz opera *Jonny spielt auf.*

Kropotkin, Peter, Prince (1842–1921), Russian anarchist, geographer and explorer, who was imprisoned for favouring the political action of a working men's association, but escaped to England. He wrote on socialistic and geographical subjects. Returned to Russia, 1917.

Kruger, Stephanus Johannes Paulus (1825–1904), Boer leader, who in 1881 was appointed head of the provisional government against Britain, and later president. When the war of 1899–1902 turned against the Boers, he vainly sought help in Europe.

Krupp, Alfred (1812–87), founder of the German gun factories at Essen. He began to make cast steel, and from 1844 specialised in armaments. The firm's factories made the Big Bertha guns which shelled Paris in 1918.

Krylov, Ivan Andreyevich (1768–1844), Russian writer of fables (the Russian La Fontaine.)

Kubelik, Jan (1880–1940), Czech violinist who at the age of 12 played in public.

Kublai Khan (1216–94), grandson of Genghis Khan, was the first Mongol emperor of China. He extended the Mongol empire by conquest, and lived in unparalleled splendour. His court was described by Marco Polo and is the subject of a poem by Coleridge.

Kubrick, Stanley. *See* **Section Q.**

Kuiper, Gerard Peter (1905–73), Dutch astronomer and founder of modern planetary astronomy. The Kuiper Belt is named after him.

L

La Fayette, Marie Joseph Paul Roch Yves Gilbert du Motier, Marquis de (1757–1834), French soldier and statesman. He fought for the colonists in the American War of Independence; and in the 1789 French revolution he proposed a declaration of rights and was commander of the National Guard till his moderation made him unpopular. When the monarchy was restored he was an opposition leader, and took part in the revolution of 1830. Recently, posthumously awarded American citizenship.

La Fontaine, Jean de (1621–95), French poet and fabulist, b. in Champagne, a friend of Molière, Boileau and Racine.

Lagerlöf, Selma (1858–1940), Swedish novelist and first woman member of the Swedish Academy. Nobel prizewinner 1909.

Lagrange, Joseph Louis, Comte (1736–1813), French mathematician, of Turin and Paris, whose interest in astronomy led him to distinguish two types of disturbance of members of the solar system, the periodic and the secular. He was called by Frederick the Great to Berlin to succeed Euler.

Lalande, Joseph Jerome LeFrançais de (1732–1807), French astronomer, author of *Traité d'astronomie.*

Lamarck, Jean Baptiste Pierre Antoine de Monet de (1744–1829), French biologist whose explanation of evolution was that new organs are brought into being by the needs of the organism in adapting to its environment and that the new characters acquired during its life-time can be passed on to the offspring through heredity, resulting in evolutionary change.

Lamb, Charles (1775–1834), English essayist, b. London. A clerk in the East India Office, he devoted his life to his sister Mary, who was of unstable mind. He is chiefly known for his *Essays of Elia,* and his letters, which have a blend of humour and tenderness.

Lambert, Constant (1905–51), English composer and critic, and conductor of Sadler's Wells ballet. His *Rio Grande* is in jazz idiom.

Landor, Walter Savage (1775–1864), English writer, b. Warwick, remembered for his *Imaginary Conversations* and poems.

Landseer, Sir Edwin (1802–73), English animal painter. He painted the *Monarch of the Glen* and designed the lions in Trafalgar Square.

Lane, Sir Allen (1902–70), English publisher who founded Penguin Books Ltd. in 1935.

Lane, Edward William (1801–76), English Arabic scholar, translator of the *Arabian Nights.*

Lanfranc (*c.* 1005–89), ecclesiastic. B. at Pavia, he became a prior in Normandy, and in 1070 an energetic archbishop of Canterbury.

Lang, Andrew (1844–1912), Scottish man of letters, whose output includes poems, fairy-tales *etc.*

Lang, 1st Baron (Cosmo Gordon Lang) (1864–1945), was archbishop of Canterbury, 1928–42.

Langland, William (1330?–1400?), English poet, author of *The Vision of Piers the Plowman.*

Langton, Stephen (1151–1228), archbishop of Canterbury. Adviser to the insurgent barons who induced King John to grant Magna Carta.

Lansbury, George (1859–1940), British Labour politician, founder of the *Daily Herald.* He improved London's amenities.

Lão Tsze (old philosopher) (*c.* 600 B.C.), traditional founder of Taoism in China. See **Section J.**

Laplace, Pierre Simon, Marquis de (1749–1827), French mathematician and astronomer, author of *Celestial Mechanics* (1799–1825). He believed that the solar system had condensed out of a vast rotating gaseous nebula.

Lara, Brian Charles (b. 1969), West Indies cricketer. Born Trinidad. An accomplished batsman who made the highest-ever score in test cricket (400 not out against England at Antigua in April 2004). In November 2005, overtaking Allan Border, he became the most prolific run maker in the history of test cricket.

La Rochefoucauld, François, Duc de (1613–80), French author of *Reflections and Moral Maxims.*

Larwood, Harold (1904–95), English cricketer, the most celebrated fast bowler of his time. At the centre of the 1932–3 'Bodyline' controversy.

Lasker, Emanuel (1868–1941), German chess player, world champion, 1894–1921.

Lassalle, Ferdinand (1825–64), German socialist who took part in the revolutionary movement of 1848 and organised workers movements.

Lassus, Orlandus (Lasso, Orlando di) (*c.* 1532–94), Flemish composer and choirmaster, contemporary of Palestrina, writer of *chansons,* madrigals, and sacred music. See **Section P.**

Latimer, Hugh (*c.* 1485–1555), English Protestant martyr, became bishop of Worcester in 1535, and was executed under Queen Mary.

Laud, William (1573–1645), archbishop of Canterbury and adviser to Charles I. His attempt to get conformity for his high church policy made him hated. He was impeached and beheaded.

Lauder, Sir Harry (1870–1950), Scottish comic singer who also wrote *Roamin' in the Gloamin'.*

Laval, Pierre (1883–1945), French politician who collaborated with the Germans, 1940–45.

Lavoisier, Antoine Laurent (1743–94), French chemist, b. Paris, was the first to establish the fact that combustion is a form of chemical action. We owe the word *oxygen* to him.

Law, Andrew Bonar (1858–1923), Conservative politician, prime minister 1922–3.

Lawrence, David Herbert (1885–1930), English poet and novelist, b. Notts., a miner's son. He tried to interpret emotion on a deeper level of con-

sciousness. His works, which have had wide influence, include *The White Peacock, Sons and Lovers, The Rainbow, Women in Love,* and *Lady Chatterley's Lover;* his plays had to wait half a century before coming to the stage in the 1960s.

Lawrence, Sir Thomas (1769–1830), English portrait painter.

Lawrence, Thomas Edward (1888–1935) (Lawrence of Arabia), British soldier who led the Arabs against the Turks in the war of 1914–18, and wrote *The Seven Pillars of Wisdom.*

Leacock, Stephen (1869–1944), Canadian humorist.

Leakey, Mary (1913–96), archaeologist and palaeoanthropologist, the matriarch of a distinguished family of environmentalists in East Africa.

Lean, Sir David. See Section Q.

Lear, Edward (1812–88), famous author of 'nonsense' verse (*e.g. The Owl and the Pussycat*).

Leavis, Frank Raymond (1895–1978), British critic, who edited *Scrutiny,* 1932–53, and whose works include *The Great Tradition, D. H. Lawrence, Novelist,* and *"Anna Karenina" and Other Essays.*

Leclerc, Jacques Philippe (Philippe, Comte de Hautecloque) (1902–47), French general. He led a Free French force in Africa in the second world war and liberated Paris in 1944.

Le Corbusier (1887–1965), pseudonym of Charles Édouard Jeanneret, Swiss architect, whose books and work (especially his Unité d'Habitation at Marseilles and the Punjab capital at Chandigarh) have influenced town-planning.

Le Duc Tho (1911–90), North Vietnamese politician. Chief negotiator at the Vietnam truce talks 1970–3.

Lee of Fareham, 1st Viscount (Arthur Hamilton Lee) (1868–1947), British politician who presented Chequers Court to the nation.

Lee Kuan Yew (b. 1923). First Prime Minister of Singapore, 1959–90. Helped establish prosperity of Singapore, but little opposition was tolerated.

Lee, Laurie (1914–97), poet and writer of autobiographical books about his Gloucestershire childhood and his experiences in Spain in the 1930s. *Cider with Rosie* (1959) has become a modern classic.

Lee, Robert Edward (1807–70), American confederate general in the Civil War, who made the surrender at Appomattox.

Lee, Sir Sidney (1859–1926), English critic. Joint editor of the *Dictionary of National Biography.*

Leech, John (1817–64), Humorous artist and political cartoonist who contributed numerous drawings to *Punch.* He illustrated Surtees's novels and Dickens's *A Christmas Carol.*

Lehár, Franz (1870–1948), Hungarian composer. Among his most popular operettas are *The Merry Widow* and *The Count of Luxembourg.*

Leibniz, Gottfried Wilhelm (1646–1716), German philosopher and mathematician, who invented the differential and integral calculus (1684) independently of Newton whose previous work on the same subject was not published until 1687. Leibniz's nomenclature was adopted.

Leicester, Earl of (Robert Dudley) (1533–88), English soldier, commanded English troops in the Netherlands, 1585–7, without much success, and in 1588 commanded forces assembled against the Armada. He was husband of Amy Robsart.

Leif Ericsson (fl. 1000), discoverer of Vinland on the north-east coast of America; b. Iceland, son of the Norse explorer, Eric the Red, who colonised Greenland.

Leighton, 1st Baron (Frederic Leighton) (1830–96), English painter whose works include *Paolo and Francesca.* He was also a sculptor.

Lely, Sir Peter (Pieter van der Faes) (1618–80), Dutch painter who settled in London and painted court portraits.

Lenin (Vladimir Ilyich Ulyanov) (1870–1924), Russian revolutionary leader and statesman. From 1893 to 1917 he worked underground in Russia and abroad for the revolutionary cause. During this time the Social-Democratic party was formed; within it developed an uncompromising revolutionary group, the Bolsheviks, and of this group Lenin was the leading spirit. In April 1917 he and his fellow exiles returned; after the November revolution he headed the new government having to face both war and anarchy. In 1921 his "new economic policy" somewhat modified the intensive drive towards planned industrialisation. He was born in Simbirsk (later Ulyanovsk) on the middle Volga. He died after his fourth stroke on 21 January 1924.

Leonardo da Vinci (1452–1519), Italian artist and man of science, son of a Florentine lawyer and a peasant. He described himself (when applying to Lodovico Sforza, Duke of Milan, for the post of city planner) as painter, architect, philosopher, poet, composer, sculptor, athlete, mathematician, inventor, and anatomist. His artistic output is small in quantity, and he is best known for his *Last Supper* in the refectory of Santa Maria delle Grazie in Milan and his *Mona Lisa* in the Louvre. He recorded his scientific work in unpublished notebooks written from right to left in mirror writing. The anatomy of the body (himself carrying out dissections), the growth of the child in the womb, the laws of waves, and the laws of flight, were all studied by him.

Leoncavallo, Ruggiero (1858–1919), Italian composer of the opera *Pagliacci*.

Leonidas was king of Sparta at the time of the invasion of Greece by Xerxes (480 B.C.), and who died defending the pass of Thermopylae.

Lermontov, Mikhail Yurevich (1814–41), Russian poet and novelist, exiled to the Caucasus for a revolutionary poem addressed to Tsar Nicholas I on the death of Pushkin. He has been called the poet of the Caucasus. His novel *A Hero of Our Time* was written at St. Petersburg. He lost his life in a duel.

Le Sage, Alain René (1668–1747), French author, b. in Brittany, who wrote *Gil Blas* and *Le Diable Boiteux*. He was also a dramatist and his plays include *Turcaret*.

Lesseps, Ferdinand, Vicomte de (1805–94), French engineer who while serving as vice-consul at Alexandria conceived a scheme for a canal across the Suez isthmus; the work was completed in 1869. He also projected the original Panama canal scheme, which failed.

Lessing, Gotthold Ephraim (1729–81), German philosopher, dramatist, and critic, noted for his work *Laokoon* and his play *Minna von Barnhelm*.

Leucippus (fl. 440 B.C.), Greek philosopher, founder with Democritus of atomism, a theory of matter more nearly that of modern science than any put forward in ancient times. One saying survives: "Naught occurs at random, but everything for a reason and of necessity."

Leverhulme, 1st Viscount (William Hesketh Lever) (1851–1925), British industrialist and philanthropist. He founded Lever Bros. which later became Unilever Ltd., and was a practical exponent of industrial partnership. He gave Lancaster House to the nation.

Leverrier, Urbain Jean Joseph (1811–77), French astronomer who, working independently of J. C. Adams of Cambridge, anticipated the existence of the planet Neptune.

Lévi-Strauss, Claude (b. 1908), French social anthropologist, b. Belgium, exponent of the theory of symbolic structures. The final vol. of his *Introduction to a Science of Mythology* about the myths and rituals of American Indians was published in 1981.

Lewis, Sinclair (1885–1951), American writer of novels satirising small-town life and philistinism. His works include *Main Street*, *Babbitt* and *Elmer Gantry*. Nobel prizewinner 1931.

Liaquat Ali Khan (1895–1951), leader of the Moslem League (1946) and first premier of Pakistan in 1947. He was assassinated.

Lie, Trygve (1896–1968), Norwegian politician. Secretary-General of the United Nations, 1946–52.

Lilburne, John (1614–57), agitator and pamphleteer, leader of the Levellers in Civil War.

Linacre, Thomas (c. 1460–1524), English humanist and physician, who translated Galen's works and founded the College of Physicians.

Lincoln, Abraham (1809–65), American president. Born in Kentucky, he became a lawyer and was returned to Congress from Illinois in 1846. He was a leader of the Republican party which was formed in 1856 to oppose slavery. He became president in 1861, in which year the Confederate States proposed to withdraw from the Union, and war broke out. The phrase "government of the people, by the people, for the people" comes from his Gettysburg speech of 1863. He was assassinated in 1865.

Lind, Jenny (1820–87), Swedish singer, popular in Europe, and known as the Swedish nightingale. She founded musical scholarships.

Lindbergh, Charles Augustus (1902–74), US aviator who completed the first solo non-stop flight across the Atlantic in the *Spirit of St Louis* (1927). The kidnapping of his baby son took place in 1932.

Linnaeus (1707–78), Swedish botanist, remembered for his system of defining living things by two Latin names, the first being its *genus*, and the second its *species*. His method is expounded in *Philosophia Botanica* (1751). In 1757 he was ennobled as Karl von Linné. He studied, taught and died at Uppsala.

Lippi, Fra Filippo (1406–69), Italian artist, b. Florence. Frescoes in Prato cathedral are his main work. His son **Filippino** (1457–1504) finished Masaccio's frescoes in the Carmine, Florence, and executed others, for instance in Santa Maria Novella.

Lippmann, Gabriel (1845–1921), French physicist who invented a capillary electrometer and was a pioneer in colour photography. Nobel prizewinner 1908.

Lippmann, Walter (1889–1974), American journalist of influence, writing for the New York *Herald Tribune*, 1931–62.

Lipton, Sir Thomas Johnstone (1850–1931), Scottish business man and philanthropist. B. Glasgow, he emigrated to America, but returned to Scotland and established extensive chain-stores for groceries. He unsuccessfully competed in yachting for the America's Cup.

Lister, Baron (Joseph Lister) (1827–1912), English surgeon, son of J. J. Lister (1786–1869), an amateur microscopist. He founded antiseptic surgery (1865) which greatly reduced mortality in hospitals.

Liszt, Franz (1811–86), Hungarian pianist and composer. His daughter Cosima became the wife of Hans von Bülow and later of Wagner.

Littlewood, Joan (1914–2002), theatre artist. One of the most influential modern theatre directors.

Litvinov, Maxim (1876–1952), Russian diplomat. Ambassador in London, then commissar for foreign affairs, and 1941–3 ambassador to the USA.

Livingstone, David (1813–73), Scottish explorer in Africa. He discovered the course of the Zambesi, the Victoria Falls and Lake Nyasa (now Lake Malawi), and roused opinion against the slave trade. He was believed lost, he was found by Stanley (q.v.) on 10 Nov. 1871.

Livingstone, Ken. *See* D17.

Lloyd-George of Dwyfor, 1st Earl (David Lloyd George) (1863–1945), Liberal statesman of Welsh origin. He was MP for Caernarvon, 1890–1944; and as chancellor of the exchequer he introduced social insurance, 1908–11. The war of 1914–18 obliged him to become a war premier (superseding Asquith), and he was subsequently one of the main figures at the peace conference. In 1921 he conceded the Irish Free State. His daughter, **Lady Megan Lloyd George**, was an MP for many years.

Lloyd-Webber, Lord (Sir Andrew Lloyd-Webber) (b. 1948), British composer. His musicals include *Jesus Christ Superstar* (1970), *Evita* (1978), *Cats* (1981), *Starlight Express* (1983), *Phantom of the Opera* (1986), *Sunset Boulevard* (1993), *Whistle Down the Wind* (1998), *The Beautiful Game* (2000), *Bombay Dreams* (2002) and *The Woman in White* (2004).

Locke, John (1632–1704), English liberal philosopher and founder of empiricism, the doctrine that all knowledge is derived from experience. His chief work in theoretical philosophy, *Essay Concerning Human Understanding*, was written just before the revolution of 1688 and published in 1690. Other writings include *Letters on Toleration*, *Treatises on Government*, and *Education*.

Locke, Matthew (c. 1621–77), English composer, born in Exeter. Composer-in-Ordinary to Charles II.

Lombroso, Cesare (1836–1909), Italian criminologist. His *L'uomo delinquente* was a major work.

Lomonosov, Mikhail Vasilievich (1711–65), Russian philologist and poet who systematised Russian grammar and orthography.

London, Jack (1876–1916), American author of adventure tales such as *Call of the Wild*.

Longfellow, Henry Wadsworth (1807–82), American poet, popular in his lifetime, author of *The Golden Legend* and *Hiawatha*.

Lope de Vega Carpio, Félix (1562–1635), Spanish writer of immense output. First a ballad-writer, he took to play-writing and founded the Spanish drama. The number of his plays is said to have been 1,500, but most are lost.

Lorca, Federico García (1899–1936), Spanish poet and dramatist of Andalusia. Among his works are *Llanto por Ignacio Sánchez Mejías*, an unforgettable lament on the death of a bull-fighter, and *Canción de Jinete* with its haunting refrain, "Córdoba, far away and alone." He was brutally murdered by Franco sympathisers .

Louis IX (1214–70), St. Louis, King of France. Of saintly character, he also carried out practical reforms. He died on crusade.

Louis XIV (1638–1715), King of France. A despotic ruler, builder of Versailles, he also dominated the Europe of his day; but he sowed the seeds of future trouble for France by his exhausting wars. He revoked the Edict of Nantes which had given religious freedom to the Huguenots since 1598. His reign, however, was a great period for literature.

Louis XV (1710–74), King of France. Extravagant and self-indulgent, his reign marked a declining period for the monarchy.

Louis XVI (1754–93), King of France. Well-meaning but incapable, he saw the outbreak of the French revolution of 1789, in which he and his queen Marie Antoinette were executed.

Louis, Joe (Joseph Louis Barrow) (1914–81), American Black boxer, who became world heavyweight champion in 1937, successfully defending his title 26 times.

Lovelock, James (b. 1919), British scientist best-known for the 'Gaia hypothesis' (which views the world as a single living entity). His recent books include *Homage to Gaia: The Life of an Independent Scientist* (2001) and *The Revenge of Gaia* (2006). Created Companion of Honour (2003).

Low, Archibald Montgomery (1888–1956), British scientist who worked in varied fields, *e.g.* wireless, TV, and anti-aircraft and anti-tank apparatus.

Low, Sir David (1891–1963), British cartoonist, b. New Zealand, associated with the *Evening Standard* and later the *Guardian*; creator of Colonel Blimp.

Lowell, Robert (1917–77), American poet, author of the verse play *The Old Glory*, and *Life Studies*, an autobiographical volume in verse and prose.

Lowry, L. S. (Laurence Stephen) (1887–1976), acclaimed painter of bleak urban landscapes (often in Salford).

Loyola, St. Ignatius (1491–1556), Spanish founder of the Jesuits, a missionary order working directly under the Pope.

Lucretius (99–55 B.C.), Roman poet, author of *De rerum natura*, a long philosophical poem advocating moral truth without religious belief.

Ludendorff, Erich (1865–1937), German general who directed German strategy in the first world war.

Lugard, 1st Baron (Frederick John Dealtry Lugard) (1858–1945), British colonial administrator in Africa, especially Nigeria, and exponent of the system of indirect rule through native chiefs.

Lukács, Georg (1885–1971), Hungarian writer, Marxist thinker and literary critic. Author of *History and Class Consciousness* (1923), *Studies in European Realism* (1946, Eng. tr. 1950), *The Historical Novel* (1955, Eng. tr. 1962)

Luther, Martin (1483–1546), German Protestant reformer. After spending time in a monastery, he was ordained priest (1507), and lectured at Wittenberg university. In 1517 he protested against the sale of indulgences; and when summoned before the Diet of Worms made a memorable defence. He was protected by the Elector of Saxony, and translated the Bible. *See* Lutheranism **(Section J)**.

Luthuli, Albert (1899–1967), African non-violent resistance leader, an ex-Zulu chief. Killed in train accident. Nobel prize for peace 1960.

Lutyens, Sir Edwin Landseer (1869–1944), English architect both of country houses and public buildings; designed the cenotaph, Whitehall; city plan and viceroy's house, New Delhi, British Embassy, Washington and Liverpool Roman catholic cathedral.

Luxemburg, Rosa (1870–1919), Polish-born German revolutionary leader. Major theoretician of Marxism. Imprisoned for opposition to First World War, 1915–18. Founded German Communist Party in 1918 with Karl Liebknecht, based on earlier Spartacist group. Opposed the nationalism of existing socialist groups. Brutally murdered by counter-revolutionary troops.

Lyell, Sir Charles (1797–1875), Scottish geologist, whose *Principles of Geology* (1830–33) postulated gradual geological change and helped to shape Darwin's ideas.

Lynn, Dame Vera (b. 1917), immensely popular singer, the 'Forces' sweetheart' immortalised in *We'll Meet Again* and *White Cliffs of Dover*.

Lysenko, Trofim (1898–1976), Russian biologist who maintained that environmental experiences can change heredity somewhat in the manner suggested by Lamarck.

Lytton, 1st Baron (Edward George Earle Lytton Bulwer-Lytton) (1803–73), English novelist and playwright, author of *The Last Days of Pompeii*.

M

Maathai, Wangari (b. 1940). Kenyan environmentalist and human rights campaigner. First African woman to be awarded Nobel Peace Prize (2004).

Macadam, John Loudon (1756–1836), Scottish inventor of "macadamising" system of road repair.

MacArthur, Douglas (1880–1964), American general. He defended the Philippines against the Japanese in the second world war, and was relieved of his command in 1951 in the Korean war.

MacArthur, Dame Ellen (b. 1976), English yachtswoman who in February 2005 completed the fastest solo round-the-world voyage.

Macaulay of Rothley, 1st Baron (Thomas Babington Macaulay) (1800–59), English historian, poet and Indian civil servant. His poems include *Lays of Ancient Rome*. In India he reformed the education system.

Macaulay, Zachary (1768–1838), anti-slavery agitator, father of the above.

Macbeth (d. 1057), Scottish king, married Gruoch, granddaughter of Kenneth, king of Alban. He was mormaer of Moray, succeeding Duncan in 1040 after killing him in fair fight. His reign of seventeen years was prosperous, but he was killed by Duncan's son, Malcolm, in 1057. Shakespeare's play is based on the inaccurate *Chronicle* of Holinshed.

MacDiarmid, Hugh (1892–1978), pseudonym of Christopher Murray Grieve, Scottish poet, leader of the Scottish literary renaissance; author of *A Drunk Man Looks at the Thistle*.

Macdonald, Flora (1722–90), Scottish Jacobite heroine who saved the life of Prince Charles Edward after the defeat at Culloden in 1746.

Macdonald, Sir John Alexander (1815–91), Canadian statesman, first prime minister of the Dominion of Canada.

MacDonald, James Ramsay (1866–1937), Labour politician of Scottish origin, premier 1924 and 1929–31; also of a coalition 1931–5. His action over the financial crisis of 1931 divided his party.

MacDonald, Malcolm (1901–81), son of above, held positions overseas in the Commonwealth, the last as special representative in Africa.

Machiavelli, Niccolò (1467–1527), Florentine Renaissance diplomat and theorist of the modern state. His book *The Prince* (1513), dedicated to Lorenzo, Duke of Urbino, is concerned with the reality of politics. His *Discourses* is more republican and liberal.

Mackail, John William (1859–1945), British classical scholar, translator of the *Odyssey*.

Mackenzie, Sir Compton (1883–1972), British writer, whose works include *Carnival, Sinister Street*, and a monumental autobiography.

McKinley, William (1843–1901), 25th President of the USA (1897–1901). A Republican, he presided over the Spanish-American War of 1898. Assassinated by an anarchist.

MacLean, Sorley (Somhairle MacGill-Eain) (1911–96), Gaelic poet. His collected poems, *Choille gu Bearradh (From Wood to Ridge)*, were published in 1989, and won the MacVitie Prize.

McLuhan, Herbert Marshall (1911–80), Canadian author of a number of books, *e.g. The Gutenberg Galaxy, The Mechanical Bride. See* **Section J**.

Macmillan, Harold. *See* Stockton, Earl of.

McMillan, Margaret (1860–1931), Scottish educational reformer, b. New York, and pioneer of open-air nursery schools.

Macneice, Louis (1907–63), British poet, playwright, and translator.

Macready, William Charles (1793–1873), British actor and manager, especially associated with Shakespearean roles.

Maeterlinck, Maurice (1862–1949), Belgian man of letters, whose plays include *La Princesse*

Maleine, *Pelléas et Mélisande*, and *L'Oiseau Bleu*. Nobel prizewinner 1911.

Magellan, Ferdinand (*c*. 1480–1521), Portuguese navigator, and commander of the first expedition (1519) to sail round the world.

Mahler, Gustav (1860–1911), Austrian composer and conductor; a writer of symphonies and songs, a classical romantic, much influenced by Anton Bruckner and Wagner. *See* **Section P.**

Mahavira, Vardhamana Jnatriputra (6th cent. B.C.), Indian historical (as opposed to legendary) founder of Jainism. *See* **Jainism, Section J.**

Mailer, Norman (b. 1923), U.S. novelist, whose novels include *The Naked and the Dead* (1948) and *The Executioner's Song* (1979).

Maintenon, Françoise d'Aubigné Marquise de (1005–1719), second wife of Louis XIV. Her first husband was the poet Scarron.

Major, Sir John (b. 1943), Prime Minister from 1990 to 1997. Leader of the Conservative Party, 1990–97. MP (Con.) Huntingdon, 1979–2001. Foreign Secretary, 1989. Chancellor of the Exchequer, 1989–90. His victory in the 1992 election heralded grave problems for his government . In 1995 he challenged his critics and won a leadership contest, but by late 1996 by-election losses (and defections) had produced a vulnerable administration. He was heavily defeated in 1997. Created Companion of Honour (1999) and awarded Order of the Garter, 2005.

Makarios III (1913–77), Greek Orthodox archbishop and Cypriot national leader. Deported by the British to the Seychelles in 1956, he returned in 1957. First President of Cyprus.

Malibran, Marie Félicité (1808–36), Spanish mezzo-soprano.

Malory, Sir Thomas (*c.* 1430–71), English writer. From earlier sources and legends of King Arthur and the Knights of the Round Table, he compiled the *Morte d'Arthur* printed by Caxton in 1485.

Malpighi, Marcello (1628–94), Italian physician and biologist. Founder of microscopic anatomy.

Malraux, André (1901–76), French novelist and politician. His works include *La Condition humaine*, *L'Espoir*, and *Psychologie de l'art* (tr. in 2 vols.), *Museum without Walls*, and *The Creative Act*. Served under de Gaulle.

Malthus, Thomas Robert (1766–1834), English clergyman and economist who in his gloomy essay *The Principle of Population* contended that population tends to increase faster than the means of subsistence and that its growth could only be checked by moral restraint or by disease and war. *See* **Malthusianism, Section J.**

Mandela, Nelson Rolihlahla (b. 1918), the President of South Africa, 1994–99, son of chief of Tembu tribe; imprisoned on political grounds 1964–90. His release from prison in February 1990 transformed the political scene in South Africa. Historic agreement (1993) with President De Klerk to form Government of National Unity after multi-party elections. Shared Nobel Peace Prize with De Klerk, 1993. The ANC victory in April 1994 paved the way for him to become President. Honorary Order of Merit, 1995. Stood down as ANC President, 1997.

Manet, Edouard (1832–83), French painter. His Impressionist pictures include *Olympia* and *Un bar aux Folies-Bergères* (the latter at the Courtauld).

Mann, Thomas (1875–1955), German writer who won world recognition at the age of 25 with his novel *Buddenbrooks*. His liberal humanistic outlook had developed sufficiently by 1930 for him to expose national socialism. He left Germany in 1933. Other works are *The Magic Mountain*, and the *Joseph* tetralogy. Nobel prizewinner 1929.

Mann, Tom (1856–1941), British Labour leader for more than fifty years.

Manning, Henry Edward (1808–92), English cardinal; archbishop of Westminster 1865–92. He was an Anglican before he joined Rome.

Mansfield, Katherine (Kathleen Beauchamp) (1890–1923), short-story writer, b. Wellington, New Zealand, whose work was influenced by the short stories of Chekhov. Her second husband was John Middleton Murry, literary critic.

Manson, Sir Patrick (1844–1922), Scottish physician, the first to propose that the malarial parasite was transmitted by the mosquito.

Manuzio, Aldo Pio (1450–1515), Italian printer, founder of the Aldine press in Venice which issued books famed for their type and bindings.

Manzoni, Alessandro (1785–1873), Italian novelist and poet, b. Milan. Author of historical novel *I Promessi Sposi* (The Betrothed).

Mao Tse-tung (Mao Zedong) (1893–1976), Chinese Communist leader. B. in Hunan, of rural origin. As a young man he worked as assistant librarian at Peking University. He understood how to win peasant support for a national and progressive movement. Attacked by Chiang Kai-shek, he led his followers by the "long march" to N.W. China, whence later they issued to defeat both Japanese and Chiang and proclaim a People's Republic in 1949, and later to promote the "great leap forward" of 1958–9 (the commune movement). He stood for an egalitarian democratic society, unhampered by, with revolutionary momentum. He promoted the "cultural revolution" (1965–9). *See* **Maoism, Section J.**

Marat, Jean Paul (1743–93), French revolution leader, largely responsible for the reign of terror, and assassinated by Charlotte Corday.

Marconi, Guglielmo Marchese (1874–1937), Italian inventor and electrical engineer who developed the use of radio waves. In 1895 he sent long-wave signals over a distance of a mile, and in 1901 received in Newfoundland the first transatlantic signals sent out by his station in Cornwall, thus making the discovery that radio waves can bend around the spherically-shaped earth. Nobel prizewinner 1909.

Marcus Aurelius Antoninus (121–180 A.D.), Roman emperor and Stoic philosopher of lofty character, whose *Meditations* are still read.

Marcuse, Herbert (1898–1979), political philosopher. B. Berlin, he emigrated to the U.S. during the Nazi regime. A critic of Western industrial society, he saw the student protest movement as the catalyst of revolution.

Maria Theresa (1717–80), Empress, daughter of the Hapsburg Charles VI. Able and of strong character, she fought unsuccessfully to save Silesia from Prussian annexation. She promoted reforms in her dominions. She married the Duke of Lorraine and had 16 children.

Marie Antoinette (1755–93), Queen of France, was daughter of the above and wife of Louis XVI; accused of treason, she and her husband were beheaded in the French revolution.

Marie Louise (1791–1847), daughter of Francis I of Austria, became the wife of Napoleon and bore him a son (Napoleon II).

Marius, Caius (157–86 B.C.), Roman general who defended Gaul from invasion; later civil war forced him to flee from Rome, and on his return he took terrible revenge.

Mark Antony. *See* **Antonius, Marcus.**

Markova, Dame Alicia (1910–2005), one of the greatest ballerinas of her time. Born Lilian Alicia Marks. A dancer of great technique and style.

Marlborough, 1st Duke of (John Churchill) (1650–1722), English general, victor of Blenheim, Ramillies, Oudenarde and Malplaquet. His wife, Sarah Jennings, was a favourite of Queen Anne.

Marley, Bob. *See* **P26(2).**

Marlowe, Christopher (1564–93), English dramatist and precursor of Shakespeare. His plays include *Dr. Faustus*, *Tamburlaine the Great*, *Edward II*, and *The Jew of Malta*. His early death was due to a tavern brawl.

Marryat, Frederick (1792–1848), English author of sea and adventure stories, including *Peter Simple*, *Mr. Midshipman Easy*, and *Masterman Ready*. A captain in the Royal Navy.

Marshall, George Catlett (1880–1959), American general. U.S. chief of staff 1939–45; originated the Marshall Aid plan. Nobel prize for peace 1953.

Martial, Marcus Valerius (*c.* 40–104), Roman poet, b. in Spain, remembered for his epigrams.

Marvell, Andrew (1620–78), English poet and political writer. He was Milton's assistant.

Marx, Karl (1818–83), German founder of modern international communism, b. Trier of Jewish parentage. He studied law, philosophy and history at the universities of Bonn and Berlin, and later took up the study of economics. In conjunction with his friend Engels he wrote the *Communist Manifesto* of 1848 for the Communist League of which he was the leader. Because of his revolutionary activities he was forced to leave the continent and in 1849 settled in London. Here, mainly while living at 28 Dean Street, Soho, he wrote *Das Kapital*, a deep analysis of the economic laws that govern modern society. In 1864 he helped to found the first International. He ranks as one of the most original and influential thinkers of modern times. He was buried in Highgate cemetery. See **Marxism, Section J.**

Mary I (1516–58), Queen of England, was daughter of Henry VIII and Catherine of Aragon. A Roman Catholic, she reversed the religious changes made by her father and brother, and about 300 Protestants were put to death. She married Philip of Spain.

Mary II (1662–94), Queen of England with her husband the Dutch William III. As daughter of James II, she was invited to succeed after the revolution of 1688 and expelled her father.

Mary Stuart, Queen of Scots (1542–87), daughter of James V of Scotland and Mary of Guise, she laid claim to the English succession. She was imprisoned in England by Elizabeth and beheaded. Her husbands were the dauphin of France (d. 1560), Lord Henry Stewart Darnley (murdered 1567) and Bothwell.

Masaryk, Jan Garrigue (1886–1948), Czech diplomat. The son of Thomas, he was Czech minister in London 1925–38, and foreign secretary while his government was in exile in London and after it returned to Prague, 1940–8.

Masaryk, Thomas Garrigue (1850–1937), Czech statesman and independence leader. He was the first president of Czechoslovakia, 1918–35.

Mascagni, Pietro (1863–1945), Italian composer of *Cavalleria Rusticana.*

Masefield, John (1878–1967), English poet. His best-known works are *Salt-Water Ballads* (as a boy he ran away to sea), and *Reynard the Fox.* He became poet laureate in 1930.

Maskelyne, John Nevil (1839–1917), English illusionist. He also exposed spiritualistic frauds.

Massenet, Jules Emile Frédéric (1842–1912), French composer of songs, orchestral suites, oratorios, and operas, e.g. *Manon* and *Thaïs.*

Massine, Léonide (1896–1979), Russian dancer, one of Diaghilev's choreographers.

Masters, Edgar Lee (1869–1950), American poet remembered for his *Spoon River Anthology.*

Matisse, Henri (1869–1954), French painter, member of a group known as *Les Fauves* (the wild beasts) for their use of violent colour and colour variation to express form and relief.

Matsys (Massys), Quentin (1466–1530), Flemish painter, b. Louvain, settled Antwerp; he worked at a time when Italian influence was gaining ground. His *Money-changer, and his Wife* is in the Louvre.

Matthews, Sir Stanley (1915–2000), first footballer to be knighted. He made 800 first-class appearances, 54 for England. Played in the legendary 1953 Cup Final (when Blackpool beat Bolton Wanderers 4–3). One of the greatest of all footballers.

Maugham, William Somerset (1874–1965), British writer, b. Paris. He practised as a doctor till the success of *Liza of Lambeth* (1897) followed by *Of Human Bondage.* He was a master of the short story and his work reflects his travels in the East. In both world wars he served as a British agent.

Maupassant, Guy de (1850–93), French writer whose novels and short stories show penetrating realism. His stories include *Boule de Suif,* *Le Maison Tellier,* and *La Parure.*

Mauriac, François (1885–1970), French writer whose novels deal with moral problems and include *Le Baiser au Lépreux* and the play *Asmodée.* Nobel prizewinner 1952.

Maurois, André (Emile Herzog) (1885–1967), French writer whose works include lives of Shelley and Disraeli.

Maxim, Sir Hiram Stevens (1840–1916), American inventor of the automatic quick-firing gun.

Maxton, James (1885–1946), Scottish Labour politician and pacifist; entered parliament 1922; chairman of ILP 1926–31, 1934–9.

Maxwell, James Clerk (1831–79), Scottish physicist. He wrote his first scientific paper at 15, and after teaching in Aberdeen and London became first Cavendish professor of experimental physics at Cambridge. His mathematical mind, working on the discoveries of Faraday and others, gave physics a celebrated set of equations for the basic laws of electricity and magnetism. His work revolutionised fundamental physics.

May, Peter (Barker Howard) (1929–94). English cricketer. The finest post-war batsman produced in Britain. A long-serving and successful captain.

Mazarin, Jules (1602–61), cardinal and minister of France was b. in Italy. In spite of opposition from the nobles, he continued Richelieu's work of building up a strong monarchy.

Mazeppa, Ivan Stepanovich (1644–1709), Cossack nobleman, b. Ukraine (then part of Poland, before E. Ukraine passed to Russia, 1667). He fought unsuccessfully for independence allying himself with Charles XII of Sweden against Peter I of Russia (Poltava, 1709). Byron wrote a poem about him.

Mazzini, Giuseppe (1805–72), Italian patriot. B. Genoa, he advocated a free and united Italy, and from Marseilles he published a journal, *Young Italy.* Expelled from the Continent, he took refuge in London in 1837. In 1848 he returned to Italy, and became dictator of the short-lived Roman republic, which was put down by French forces. His contribution to Italian unity was that of preparing the way.

Mbeki, Thabo Mvuyelwa (b. 1942), South African ANC politician who succeeded Nelson Mandela as President in 1999.

Mechnikov, Ilya (1845–1916), Russian biologist who discovered that by "phagocytosis" certain white blood cells are capable of ingesting harmful substances such as bacteria. He shared the 1908 Nobel prize for medicine.

Medawar, Sir Peter Brien (1915–87), British zoologist, author of *The Art of the Soluble* and *The Future of Man;* president of the British Association 1969. Nobel prizewinner 1960. O.M. 1981.

Medici, Florentine family of merchants and bankers who were politically powerful and who patronised the arts. **Cosimo the Elder** (1389–1464) was for over 30 years virtual ruler of Florence. His grandson, **Lorenzo the Magnificent** (1449–92), poet, friend of artists and scholars, governed with munificence. His grandson, **Lorenzo,** was father of **Catherine de' Medici,** Queen of France (*q.v.*). A later **Cosimo** (1519–74) was an able Duke of Florence and then Grand-Duke of Tuscany, which title the Medicis held until 1737.

Méhul, Etienne Nicolas (1763–1817), French operatic composer. *Joseph* is his masterpiece.

Meir, Golda (1898–1978), leading member of the Israeli Labour Party, her premiership included the Six Day and Yom Kippur wars.

Meitner, Lise (1878–1969), co-worker of Otto Hahn (*q.v.*) who interpreted his results (1939) as a fission process.

Melanchthon, Philip (1497–1560), German religious reformer, who assisted Luther, and wrote the first Protestant theological work, *Loci communes.* He drew up the Augsburg confession (1530).

Melba, Nellie (Helen Porter Mitchell) (1861–1931), Australian soprano of international repute.

Melbourne, 2nd Viscount (William Lamb) (1779–1848), English Whig statesman, was premier at the accession of Queen Victoria.

Mendel, Gregor Johann (1822–84), Austrian botanist. After entering the Augustinian monastery at Brünn he became abbot and taught natural history in the school. His main interest was the study of inheritance, and his elaborate observations of the common garden pea resulted in the law of heredity which bears his name. His hypothesis (published in 1866) received little attention until 1900.

Mendeleyev, Dmitri Ivanovich (1834–1907), Russian chemist, first to discover the critical temperatures. He formulated the periodic law of atomic weights (1869) and drew up the periodic table (*see* **Section T**), predicting the properties of elements which might fill the gaps. Element 101 is named after him.

Mendelssohn-Bartholdy, Felix (1809–47), German composer, grandson of Moses Mendelssohn, philosopher. He belongs with Chopin and Schumann to the early 19th cent. classic-romantic school, and his music has delicacy and melodic beauty. He was conductor of the Gewandhaus concerts at Leipzig for a time and often visited England. See **Section P.**

Menuhin, Lord (Yehudi Menuhin) (1916–99), famous violinist, b. New York of Russian Jewish parentage. He first appeared as soloist at the age of seven. He went on to become the greatest violinist of his age. Founded a School for musically gifted children. Order of Merit, 1987.

Menzies, Sir Robert Gordon (1894–1978), Australian Liberal statesman, P.M. 1939–41, 1949–66.

Mercator, Gerhardus (Gerhard Kremer) (1512–94), Flemish geographer who pioneered the making of accurate navigational maps. He worked out the map which bears his name in which meridians and parallels of latitude cross each other at right angles, enabling compass bearings to be drawn as straight lines.

Meredith, George (1828–1909), English writer, b. Portsmouth. His novels include *The Ordeal of Richard Feverel*, *The Egoist*, *Evan Harrington*, *Diana of the Crossways*, and *The Amazing Marriage*. Also a gifted poet.

Merkel, Angela (b. 1954). German Christian Democrat politician. First woman Chancellor of Germany, November 2005.

Mesmer, Friedrich Anton. *See* Mesmerism, Section J.

Mestrovlé, Ivan (1883 1902), Yugoslav sculptor of international repute. He designed the temple at Kossovo. He later lived in England, and examples of his work are in London museums.

Metastasio, Pietro (Pietro Bonaventura Trapassi) (1698–1782), Italian librettist who lived in Vienna and provided texts for Gluck, Handel, Haydn, and Mozart.

Metternich, Clemens (1773–1859), Austrian statesman and diplomat. Foreign Minister, 1809–48. Chancellor, 1812–48.

Michelangelo (Michelagniolo Buonarroti) (1475–1564), Italian painter, sculptor and poet. Of a poor but genteel Tuscan family, his first interest in sculpture came through his nurse, wife of a stone-cutter. He was apprenticed to Domenico Ghirlandaio. Like Leonardo, he studied anatomy, but instead of spreading his talents over a wide field, he became obsessed with the problem of how to represent the human body. In him, classical idealism, mediaeval religious belief, and renaissance energy met. Perhaps his most impressive work is the ceiling of the Sistine Chapel (a surface of about 6,000 square feet), the *Last Judgement* behind the chapel altar, his marble *Pieta* (St. Peter's) the statue of *David* (Academy, Florence), the great figure of *Moses* (San Pietro in Vincoli, Rome), and the four allegorical figures *Day*, *Night*, |*Dawn*, *Twilight* (intended for the tombs of the Medici family at San Lorenzo, Florence).

Michelet, Jules (1798–1874), French historian who wrote a history of France in 24 vols. and of the revolution in 7 vols.

Michelson, Albert Abraham (1852–1931), American physicist, b. Poland. He collaborated with E. W. Morley in an experiment to determine ether drift, the negative result of which was important for Einstein. Nobel prizewinner 1907.

Mickiewicz, Adam (1798–1855), Polish revolutionary poet, author of *The Ancestors* and *Pan Tadeusz*.

Mill, John Stuart (1806–73), English philosopher. A member of Bentham's utilitarian school, he later modified some of its tenets. His main work is *On Liberty*. *The Subjection of Women* supported women's rights. He also wrote *Principles of Political Economy*. He was godfather to Bertrand Russell.

Millais, Sir John Everett (1829–96), English artist, b. Southampton; in his earlier years a pre-Raphaelite (*Ophelia*). Later works include *The Boyhood of Raleigh* and *Bubbles*. He married Mrs. Ruskin after the annulment of her marriage.

Miller, Arthur (1915–2005), perhaps the greatest American dramatist of the 20th cent. His plays include *Death of a Salesman*, *The Crucible* etc.

Millet, Jean François (1814–75), French painter of rural life, sometimes in sombre mood; his works include *The Angelus*.

Millikan, Robert Andrews (1868–1954), American physicist, who determined the charge on the electron and discovered cosmic rays. Nobel prizewinner 1923.

Mills, Sir John (1908–2005), theatrical legend and Oscar winning actor. Knighted in 1976. He epitomised British charm and grit.

Milne, Alan Alexander (1882–1956), English humorist and poet. He remains popular.

Milner, 1st Viscount (Alfred Milner) (1854–1925), British administrator, especially in South Africa; author of *England in Egypt*.

Milošević, Slobodan (1941–2006), Serbian dictator. A ruthless manipulator of Serbian nationalism who brought disaster to the Balkans. Died while indicted as a war criminal.

Milstein, César (1927–2002) Argentinian-born molecular biologist. Joint Nobel Prize for Medicine, 1984.

Miltiades (d. 489 B.C.), one of the leaders of the Athenian army against the Persians at Marathon.

Milton, John (1608–74), English poet, author of *Paradise Lost*. B. in London, he wrote while still at Cambridge *L'Allegro*, *Il Penseroso*, *Comus*, and *Lycidas*. The Civil War diverted his energies for years to the parliamentary and political struggle, but during this period he defended in *Aereopagitica* the freedom of the press. After he had become blind he wrote *Paradise Lost* and a sonnet *On His Blindness*.

Minot, George Richards (1885–1950), who with W. P. Murphy discovered the curative properties of liver in pernicious anaemia. Shared Nobel prize 1934.

Mirabeau, Gabriel, Honoré Victor Riquetti, Comte de (1749–91), French revolutionary leader. His writings contributed to the revolution of 1789.

Miró, Joan (1893–1983), one of the great Spanish painters of the 20th century.

Mistral, Frédéric (1830–1914), French poet, and founder of a Provençal renaissance. His works include *Lou Trésor dóu Félibrige* and a Provençal dictionary. Nobel prizewinner 1904.

Mitchell, Reginald Joseph (1895–1937), British aircraft designer. Famous for developing the *Spitfire*.

Mithradates (c. 132–63 B.C.), King of Pontus, in Asia Minor; he was defeated by Pompey.

Mitterrand, François Maurice Marie (1916–96), French socialist politician, proclaimed fourth president of the Fifth Republic, 21 May 1981. Re-elected May 1988 for second 7-year term until 1995. The longest serving President of the Fifth Republic. He died of cancer in 1996.

Mobutu Sese Seko (1930–97), brutal and corrupt dictator of Zaïre (Congo), 1965–97.

Modigliani, Amedeo (1884–1920), Italian painter and sculptor, b. Livorno. His portraits and figure studies tend to elongation and simplification. He lived mainly in Paris.

Moffatt, James (1870–1944), Scottish divine who translated the Bible into modern English.

Mohammed (570–632), the founder of Islam (**J27**), the religion of the Muslims, received the revelation of the Koran (their sacred book), and the command to preach, at the age of 40. By his constant proc-lamation that there was only One God he gathered around him a loyal following, but aroused the hostility of other Meccans. The Muslims were forced to flee to Medina in 622, but grew sufficiently to return to Mecca in 630, and establish the Kaaba as the goal of the pilgrimage in Islam. *See* Islam, Section J.

Molière (Jean Baptiste Poquelin) (1622–73), French playwright. B. in Paris, he gained experience as a strolling player, and subsequently in Paris, partly in the king's service; he wrote an unsurpassed series of plays varying from farce as in *Les Précieuses ridicules* to high comedy. Among his plays are *Tartuffe*, *Le Misanthrope*, and *Le Bourgeois gentilhomme*.

Molotov, Vyacheslav Mikhailovich (1890–1986), Russian commissar for foreign affairs, 1939–49.

Moltke, Helmuth, Count von (1800–91), Prussian general and chief of staff (1858–88) during the period when Prussia successfully united Germany.

Mond, Ludwig (1838–1909), German chemist who in 1867 settled in England as an alkali manufacturer and in partnership with John Brunner successfully manufactured soda by the Solvay process.

Monet, Claude (1840–1926), French painter, leader of the Impressionists, the term being derived in 1874 from his landscape *Impression soleil levant*. He liked painting a subject in the open air at different times of day to show variation in light.

Monk, George, 1st Duke of Albemarle (1608–69), English general and admiral, whose reputation and moderation were mainly responsible for the return of Charles II in 1660.

Monmouth, Duke of (James Scott) (1649–85), English pretender, natural son of Charles II; centre of anti-Catholic feeling against succession of Duke of York (later James II). His troops, mostly peasants, were routed at Sedgemoor (1685) by John Churchill (later Duke of Marlborough). Beheaded on Tower Hill.

Monnet, Jean (1888–1979), French political economist, "father of the Common Market." He drafted the Monnet plan for French economic recovery.

Monroe, James (1758–1831), president of the USA. He propounded the doctrine that the American continent should not be colonised by a European power.

Montagu, Lady Mary Wortley (1689–1762), English writer. From Constantinople where her husband was ambassador she wrote *Letters* of which a complete edition was published 1965–7. She introduced England to the idea of inoculation against smallpox.

Montaigne, Michel de (1533–92), French essayist of enquiring, sceptical and tolerant mind.

Montcalm, Louis Joseph, Marquis de (1712–59), French general, who unsuccessfully commanded the French at Quebec against Wolfe.

Montesquieu, Charles-Louis de Secondat, Baron de la Brède et de (1689–1755), French philosopher. His works include *Lettres persanes*, a satire on contemporary life; and *De l'esprit des lois* giving his political philosophy. The latter was based largely, but to some extent mistakenly, on English practice, and its influence led the US constitution to separate the executive (President) from the legislature (Congress).

Montessori, Maria (1870–1952), Italian educationist, who developed an educational system based on spontaneity.

Monteverdi, Claudio (1567–1643), Italian composer who pioneered in opera. His chief dramatic work is *Orfeo* (1607). See Section P.

Montezuma II (1466–1520), Aztec emperor of Mexico when the Spanish under Cortés invaded.

Montfort, Simon de, Earl of Leicester (c. 1208–65), English statesman. He led the barons in revolt against the ineffective rule of Henry III, but he differed from other rebels in that he summoned a parliamentary assembly to which for the first time representatives came from the towns. He was killed at Evesham.

Montgolfier, the name of two brothers, **Joseph Michel** (1740–1810) and **Jacques Etienne** (1745–99), French aeronauts who constructed the first practical balloon, which flew 6 miles.

Montgomery of Alamein, 1st Viscount (Bernard Law Montgomery) (1887–1976), British field-marshal; commanded 8th Army, N Africa, Sicily, and Italy, 1942–4; C-in-C, British Group of Armies and Allied Armies in Northern France, 1944.

Montrose, Marquess of (James Graham) (1612–50), Scottish general. In the Civil War he raised the Highland clansmen for Charles I and won the battles of Tippermuir, Inverlochy, and Kilsyth; but was finally defeated and executed.

Moody, Dwight Lyman (1837–99), American revivalist preacher, associated with Ira D. Sankey, the "American singing pilgrim."

Moore, George (1852–1933), Irish novelist, author of *Confessions of a Young Man, Esther Waters,* and *Evelyn Innes.*

Moore, Henry (1898–1986), English sculptor in semi-abstract style, son of a Yorkshire coalminer. Examples of his work are to be seen all over the world, in the Tate Gallery, St. Matthew's Church, Northampton, the UNESCO building in Paris etc.

Moore, Sir John (1761–1809), British general, who trained the infantry for the Spanish Peninsular campaigns and conducted a brilliant retreat to Corunna, where he was mortally wounded after defeating the French under Soult.

Moore, Sir Patrick (b. 1923), astronomer whose great achievement has been to popularise his subject. Author of numerous books.

Moore, Thomas (1779–1852), Irish poet, author of *Irish Melodies, Lalla Rookh,* and *The Epicurean* (novel). He also wrote a life of Byron.

More, Sir Thomas (1478–1535), English writer and statesman. In 1529 he succeeded Wolsey as lord chancellor, but on his refusal to recognise Henry VIII as head of the church he was executed. His *Utopia* describes an ideal state. He was canonised in 1935 and has now been proposed as the patron saint of politicians.

Morgan, Sir Henry (c. 1635–88), Welsh buccaneer who operated in the Caribbean against the Spaniards, capturing and plundering Panama in 1671. Knighted by Charles II and made deputy-governor of Jamaica.

Morgan, John Pierpont (1837–1913), American financier who built a vast industrial empire.

Morita, Akio (1921–99), Japanese entrepreneur who co-founded the Sony empire (which produced Japan's first tape recorder, transistor radio etc.).

Morland, George (1763–1804), painter of rural life.

Morley, 1st Viscount (John Morley) (1838–1923), English biographer and Liberal politician. He held political office, but is mainly remembered for his lives of Gladstone, Cobden etc.

Morley, Thomas (c. 1557–1603), English composer of madrigals, noted also for his settings of some of Shakespeare's songs. He was a pupil of Byrd, organist of St. Paul's cathedral, and wrote *Plaine and Easie Introduction to Practicall Music* (1597) which was used for 200 years.

Morris, William (1834–96), English poet and craftsman. His hatred of 19th-cent. ugliness, his belief in human equality, and in freedom and happiness for all, combined to make him a socialist, and he accomplished much for the improvement of domestic decoration. He was a popular lecturer, founded the Socialist League and the Kelmscott Press.

Morrison of Lambeth, Baron (Herbert Morrison) (1888–1965), British Labour statesman. From being an errand-boy, he rose to become leader of the London County Council. Wartime Home Secretary. Deputy Prime Minister, 1945–51.

Morse, Samuel Finley Breese (1791–1872), American pioneer in electromagnetic telegraphy and inventor of the dot-and-dash code that bears his name.

Moss, Sir Stirling (b. 1929), legendary English racing driver who dominated the sport in the 1950s.

Motion, Andrew (b. 1952), poet, critic and biographer. Appointed Poet Laureate in 1999. His publications include books of verse and a life of Keats (1997).

Moulin, Jean (1899–1943) French resistance leader who died under Nazi torture.

Mountbatten of Burma, 1st Earl (Louis Mountbatten) (1900–79), British admiral and statesman. In the second world war he became chief of combined operations in 1942. As last viceroy of India, he carried through the transfer of power to Indian hands in 1947 and was the first governor-general of the dominion. His assassination by Irish extremists evoked horror.

Mozart, Wolfgang Amadeus (1756–91), Austrian composer. B. Salzburg, he began his career at four and toured Europe at six. In 1781 he settled in Vienna, where he became a friend of Haydn and where his best music was written. His genius lies in the effortless outpouring of all forms of music, in the ever-flowing melodies, in the consistent beauty and symmetry of his compositions, and in the exactness of his method. Among the loveliest and grandest works in instrumental music are his three great symphonies in E. flat, G minor, and C (called the "Jupiter"), all written in six weeks in 1788. Three of the greatest operas in musical history are his *Marriage of Figaro* (1786), *Don Giovanni* (1787), and *The Magic Flute* (1791). His last composition, written under the shadow of death, was the *Requiem Mass,* a work of tragic beauty. See Section P.

Mugabe, Robert Gabriel (b. 1924), first prime minister of independent Zimbabwe after 1980. His rule has become despotic. See Section C.

Muggeridge, Malcolm (1903–90), broadcaster and journalist who became an ardent Christian.

Müller, Sir Ferdinand (1825–96), German-born botanist who emigrated to Australia, where he was director of the Melbourne Botanical Gardens, 1857–73. He introduced the eucalyptus into Europe.

Müller, Friedrich Max (1823–1900), Philologist and orientalist. Born Dessau. A professor at Oxford.

Mulroney, (Martin) Brian (b. 1939), Prime Minister of Canada, 1984–93. First Conservative leader from Quebec in nearly 100 years.

Mumford, Lewis (1895–1990), American writer on town-planning and social problems. His works include a tetralogy: *Technics and Civilisation, The Culture of Cities, The Condition of Man,* and *The Conduct of Life; The Myth of the Machine,* and *The Urban Prospect.*

Munch, Edvard (1863–1944), Norwegian painter whose most characteristic work is *The Scream* (1913). He also painted *The Sick Child.*

Munnings, Sir Alfred (1878–1959), English painter, especially of horses and sporting subjects.

Murdoch, Dame Iris (1919–99). See M31.

Murdock, William (1754–1839), Scottish engineer and inventor, the first to make practical use of coal gas as an illuminating agent (introduced at the Soho works, Birmingham, 1800).

Murillo, Bartolomé Esteban (1617–82), Spanish painter, b. Seville, where he founded an Academy. His early works, such as *Two Peasant Boys* (Dulwich) show peasant and street life; his later paintings are religious, e.g., the *Immaculate Conception* in the Prado.

Murray, Gilbert (1866–1957), classical scholar of

Australian birth who settled in England. A teacher of Greek at the universities of Glasgow and Oxford, he translated Greek drama so as to bring it within the reach of a wide public.

Mussolini, Benito (1883–1945), Fascist dictator of Italy 1922–43. From 1935 an aggressive foreign policy (Abyssinia and Spain) was at first successful, and in June 1940 he entered the war on the side of Hitler. Defeat in North Africa and the invasion of Sicily caused the collapse of his government. He was shot dead by partisans while trying to escape to Switzerland.

Mussorgsky, Modest Petrovich (1839–81), Russian composer whose masterpiece is the opera *Boris Godunov* after the play by Pushkin. His piano suite *Pictures at an Exhibition* was orchestrated by Ravel. *See* Section P.

N

Naipaul, Sir Vidiadhur Surajprasad (b. 1932), Trinidadian novelist and writer, whose novels include *A House for Mr Biswas* (1961). Awarded the Booker Prize for *In a Free State* (1971). Nobel Prize for Literature, 2001.

Nanak (1469–1538), Indian guru or teacher, who tried to put an end to religious strife, teaching that "God is one, whether he be Allah or Rama." *See* Sikhism, Section J.

Nansen, Fridtjof (1861–1930), Norwegian explorer. In 1893 his north polar expedition reached the highest latitude till then attained—86° 14'. He was active in Russian famine relief, 1921. Nobel peace prize 1922.

Naoroji, Dadabhai (1825–1917), first Indian to be elected to House of Commons (for Finsbury, 1892–5). An influential critic of the Raj.

Napier, John (1550–1617), Scottish mathematician, b. Edinburgh, invented logarithms (published 1614) and the modern notation of fractions.

Napoleon I (Bonaparte) (1769–1821), French emperor and general, of Corsican birth (Ajaccio). Trained in French military schools, he became prominent in the early years of the revolution, with uncertainty at home and war abroad. In 1796 he became commander of the army in Italy and defeated the Austrians, so that France obtained control of Lombardy. He then led an expedition to Egypt but Nelson destroyed his fleet. After further Italian victories, he made a *coup d'état* in 1799, and in 1804 became emperor. Against continuing European opposition, he defeated the Austrians at Austerlitz, and his power in Europe was such that he made his brothers Joseph, Louis, and Jerome kings of Naples, Holland, and Westphalia; but in Spain he provoked the Peninsular War, and his armies were gradually driven back by the Spanish, helped by Wellington; while his invasion of Russia in 1812 ended in a disastrous retreat from Moscow; and in 1814 the Allies forced him to abdicate and retire to Elba. He emerged again in 1815 to be defeated at Waterloo and exiled to St. Helena. His government at home was firm and promoted some reforms (*e.g.*, legal codification), but the country was weakened by his wars. In Europe, in spite of the suffering caused by war, there was some spread of French revolutionary ideas, and equally a reaction against them on the part of authority. The imperial idea lingered in France, and Napoleon's remains were brought to Paris in 1840. He married first Josephine Beauharnais and second Marie Louise of Austria. Marie Louise was the mother of **Napoleon II** (1811–32).

Napoleon III (1808–73), son of Napoleon I's brother Louis. He returned to France in the revolution of 1848, and in 1851 came to power by a *coup d'état*. In his reign Paris was remodelled. His foreign policy was adventurous (the Crimean war, intervention in Mexico, war against Austria and Italy); but when he was manoeuvred by Bismarck into the Franco-Prussian war and defeated at Sedan he lost his throne and retired to England. His wife was Eugénie de Montijo.

Narayan, Rasipuram Kirshnaswamy (1906–2001), one of the greatest Indian novelists and short-story writers. Most of his writing was set in the fictional south Indian town of Malgudi.

Nash, John (1752–1835), English architect who planned Regent Street, laid out Regent's Park, enlarged Buckingham Palace, and designed Marble Arch and the Brighton Pavilion.

Nash, Paul (1889–1946), English painter and designer, official war artist in both world wars. Best-known pictures are *The Menin Road* of 1918 and *Totes Meer* of 1941.

Nash, Walter (1882–1968), New Zealand Labour politician; prime minister 1957–60.

Nasmyth, James (1808–90), Scottish inventor of the steam-hammer, which became indispensable in all large iron and engineering works.

Nasser, Gamal Abdel (1918–70), leader of modern Egypt and of the Arab world. He led the 1954 coup that deposed General Neguib. He became president of the Egyptian Republic in 1956 and of the United Arab Republic in 1958. His nationalisation of the Suez Canal in 1956 precipitated a short-lived attack by Britain and France, Israeli–Arab hostility led to the June war of 1967. He carried out reforms and constructed the Aswan High Dam.

Navratilova, Martina (b. 1956) Czech-born tennis player of outstanding ability. She won 18 Grand Slam singles, 37 Grand Slam doubles and 149 other championship singles titles.

Ne Win, General (1911–2002), Burmese dictator who reduced his country to ruin under his regime.

Needham, Joseph (1900–95), British biochemist, historian of science and orientalist. Author of the monumental *Science and Civilisation in China*.

Nefertiti (14th cent. B.C.), wife of the heretic Pharaoh Akhenaten. Traditionally considered the most powerful woman in Ancient Egypt.

Nehru, Pandit Jawaharlal (1889–1964), Indian national leader and statesman, first prime minister and minister of foreign affairs when India became independent in 1947. A leading member of the Congress Party, during which time he was frequently imprisoned for political activity. He played a part in the negotiations for independence. Under his leadership India made major advances. His daughter was **Indira Gandhi**, (*q.v.*).

Nelson, 1st Viscount (Horatio Nelson) (1758–1805), English admiral. Son of a Norfolk clergyman, he went to sea at 12 and became a captain in 1793. In the French revolutionary wars he lost his right eye in 1794 and his right arm in 1797. Rear-admiral in 1797, he defeated the French at Aboukir Bay in 1798. He was also at the bombardment of Copenhagen in 1801. In 1805 he destroyed the French fleet at Trafalgar, in which battle he was killed. His daring and decision made him a notable commander. He loved Emma Hamilton.

Nernst, Walther Hermann (1864–1941), German scientist who established the third law of thermodynamics that dealt with the behaviour of matter at temperatures approaching absolute zero. Nobel prizewinner 1920.

Nero, Claudius Caesar (A.D. 37–68), Roman emperor, the adopted son of Claudius. He was weak and licentious and persecuted Christians. In his reign occurred the fire of Rome.

Newcomen, Thomas (1663–1729), English inventor, one of the first to put a steam-engine into practical operation. In 1705 he patented his invention, the pumping-engine used in Cornish mines until the adoption of Watt's engine.

Newman, John Henry (1801–90), English priest and writer, who became a cardinal of the Roman church in 1879, and was a founder of the Oxford Movement. (*See* Section J) He is best remembered by his *Apologia pro Vita Sua* in which he described the development of his religious thought. He wrote *Lead, kindly Light*, set to music 30 years later by J. B. Dykes, and *The Dream of Gerontius*, set to music of Elgar.

Newton, Sir Isaac (1642–1727), English scientist, b. Woolsthorpe, Lincs. (the year Galileo died). He studied at Cambridge but was at home during the plague years 1665 and 1666 when he busied himself with problems concerned with optics and gravitation. Appointed to the Lucasian chair of mathematics at Cambridge in 1669 and remained there until 1696 when he was appointed Warden, and later Master of the Mint. He was a secret Unitarian and did not marry. His three great discoveries were to show that white light could be separated into a sequence of coloured components forming the visible spectrum; to use the calculus (invented by him independently of Leibniz) to investigate the forces of nature in a quantitative way; and to show by his theory of gravitation (for which Copernicus, Kepler and Galileo had prepared the way) that the universe was regulated by simple mathematical laws. His vision was set forth in the *Philosophiae Naturalis Principia Mathematica* of 1687, usually called the *Principia*. It was not until 200 years later that Einstein showed there could be another theory of celestial mechanics. Alongside his rationalism, Newton wrote on alchemy and was a religious zealot.

Ney, Michel (1769–1815), French general who served under Napoleon, especially at Jena, Borodino, and Waterloo.

Nicholas II (1868–1918), last emperor and Tsar of Russia, son of Alexander III. His reign was marked by an unsuccessful war with Japan (1904–5), and by the 1914–18 war. Ineffective and lacking ability, he set up a Duma in 1906 too late for real reform. Revolution broke out in 1917. He and his family were shot in July 1918. Canonised by Orthodox Church, 2000.

Nicholson, Sir William (1872–1949), English artist known for his portraits and woodcuts. His son, **Ben Nicholson**, O.M., (1894–1981) was a giant of English painting, with styles from Cornish landscapes to his controversial white minimalism.

Nicolson, Sir Harold (1886–1968), English diplomat, author, and critic. His works include *King George V* and *Diaries and Letters*. His wife was **Victoria Sackville-West** (1892–1962).

Niemeyer, Oscar (b. 1907), visionary modernist architect who designed Brasilia (capital of Brazil).

Niemöller, Martin (1892–1984), German Lutheran pastor who opposed the Nazi regime and was confined in a concentration camp. He was president of the World Council of Churches in 1961.

Nietzsche, Friedrich Wilhelm (1844–1900), German philosopher, in his younger years influenced by Wagner and Schopenhauer. His teaching that only the strong ought to survive and his doctrine of the superman are expounded in *Thus spake Zarathustra*, *Beyond Good and Evil* and *The Will to Power*.

Nightingale, Florence (1820–1910), English nurse and pioneer of hospital reform, who during the Crimean war organised in face of considerable official opposition a nursing service to relieve the sufferings of the British soldiers, who called her "the lady with the lamp." First woman appointed to Order of Merit (1907).

Nijinsky, Vaslav (1892–1950), Russian dancer, one of the company which included Pavlova, Karsavina and Fokine, brought by Diaghilev to Paris and London before the 1014–18 war. In *Les Sylphides*, *Spectre de la Rose* and *L'Aprèsmidi d'un Faune* he won supreme acclaim.

Nikisch, Arthur (1855–1922), Hungarian conductor of the Boston Symphony Orchestra, 1889–93. Piano-accompanist to Elena Gerhardt.

Nimitz, Chester William (1885–1966), American admiral, commanded in the Pacific 1941–5.

Nixon, Richard Milhous (1913–94), Republican president (for two terms) of the U.S., 1969–74. In foreign affairs he negotiated the withdrawal of American troops from S. Vietnam and began a process of reconciliation with China and détente with the Soviet Union. But at home the Watergate conspiracies brought disgrace and an end to his presidency. His resignation in August 1974 rendered the impeachment process unnecessary; he accepted the pardon offered by his successor, President Ford.

Nkomo, Joshua (1917–99), Zimbabwean statesman. Hailed as the 'Father of Zimbabwe' for his leadership of ZAPU which he founded in 1961. In post-independence Zimbabwe he was embroiled in bitter rivalry.

Nkrumah, Kwame (1909–72), Ghanaian leader, first premier of Ghana when his country achieved independence in 1957. Promoted the Pan-African movement; but unsound finance and dictatorial methods led to his overthrow in 1966.

Nobel, Alfred Bernhard (1833–96), Swedish inventor and philanthropist. An engineer and chemist who discovered dynamite, he amassed a fortune from the manufacture of explosives; and bequeathed a fund for annual prizes to those who had contributed most to the benefit of mankind in the fields of physics, chemistry, medicine, literature and peace.

Nolan, Sir Sidney Robert (1917–92), Australian artist and set designer. Best known for his works depict-

ing 19th cent. outlaw Ned Kelly. O.M. 1983.

North, Frederick (1732–92), favourite minister of George III who held the premiership from 1770 to 1782. (He held the courtesy title of Lord North from 1752.) The stubborn policies of George III led to the American war of independence.

Northcliffe, 1st Viscount (Alfred Charles Harmsworth) (1865–1922), British journalist and newspaper proprietor, b. near Dublin. He began *Answers* in 1888 with his brother Harold, (later Lord Rothermere). In 1894 they bought the *Evening News*, and in 1896 the *Daily Mail*. In 1908 he took over *The Times*.

Northumberland, John Dudley, Duke of (1502–53), English politician who attempted to secure for his daughter-in-law Lady Jane Grey the succession to the throne after Edward VI.

Nostradamus or **Michel de Notre Dame** (1503–66), French astrologer and physician, known for his prophecies in *Centuries*.

Novalis, the pseudonym of Baron Friedrich von Hardenberg (1772–1801), German romantic poet and novelist, whose chief work is the unfinished *Heinrich von Ofterdingen*.

Nuffield, 1st Viscount (William Richard Morris) (1877–1963), British motor-car manufacturer and philanthropist, and until he retired in 1952 chairman of Morris Motors Ltd. He provided large sums for the advancement of medicine in the university of Oxford, for Nuffield College, and in 1943 established the Nuffield Foundation.

Nureyev, Rudolf Hametovich (1938–93), the most celebrated ballet dancer of modern times. Born nr. Lake Baikal. Soloist, Kirov Ballet, Leningrad, 1958–61. Naturalised Austrian citizen, 1982. Ballet Director, Paris Opéra, 1983 89, Principal Choreographer, 1989–92.

Nyerere, Julius (1922–99), First premier of independent Tanganyika in 1961; and president. In 1964 he negotiated its union with Zanzibar.

O

Oates, Lawrence Edward (1880–1912), English Antarctic explorer. He joined Scott's expedition of 1910, and was one of the five to reach the south pole; but on the return journey, being crippled by frost-bite, he walked out into the blizzard to die.

Oates, Titus (1649–1705), English informer and agitator against Roman catholics.

Obote, Milton (1924–2005), Uganda politician. Twice President of his country, 1966–71 and 1980–85.

O'Casey, Sean (1880–1964), Irish dramatist. Plays include *Juno and the Paycock*, *The Silver Tassie*, *Red Roses for Me*, and *Oak Leaves and Lavender*.

Ockham (Occam), William of (c. 1270–1349), English scholar and philosopher and one of the most original thinkers of all time. He belonged to the Order of Franciscans, violently opposed the temporal power of the Pope, espoused the cause of nominalism and laid the foundations of modern theories of government and theological scepticism. *See* Ockham's razor, Section J.

O'Connell, Daniel (1775–1847), Irish national leader. A barrister, he formed the Catholic Association in 1823 to fight elections; his followers aimed at the repeal of the Act of Union with England, and formed a Repeal Association in 1840; but the formation of the Young Ireland party, the potato famine, and ill-health undermined his position and he died in exile.

O'Connor, Feargus (1794–1855), working-class leader in England, of Irish birth. He presented the Chartist petition in 1848.

O'Connor, Thomas Power (1848–1929), Irish nationalist and journalist, sat in parliament 1880–1929 and founded the *Star*.

Oersted, Hans Christian (1777–1851), Danish physicist who discovered the connection between electricity and magnetism.

Offa (d. 796), king of Mercia (mid-England), was the leading English king of his day, and built a defensive dyke (**A46**) from the Dee to the Wye.

Offenbach, Jacques (1819–80), German-Jewish composer, b. Cologne, settled at Paris. Known for his light operas, especially *Tales of Hoffmann*.

Ohm, Georg Simon (1787–1854), German physicist, professor at Munich, who in 1826 formulated the law of electric current–Ohm's law (*see* Section L).

Olivier, Baron (Laurence Kerr Olivier) (1907–89),

British actor and director, especially in Shakespearean roles. He also produced, directed, and played in films, including *Henry V*, *Hamlet*, and *Richard III*, and in television drama. In 1962 he was appointed director of the National Theatre (which opened in 1976) and in 1970 received a life peerage. O.M. 1981. His widow is Dame Joan Plowright.

Oman, Sir Charles William (1860–1946), English historian, especially of the Peninsular War.

Omar ibn al Khattab (581–644), adviser to Mahomet, succeeded Abu Bakr as 2nd caliph. In his reign Islam became an imperial power. He died at the hands of a foreign slave.

Omar Khayyám (*c.* 1050–1123), Persian poet and mathematician, called Khayyám (tent-maker) because of his father's occupation. His fame as a scientist has been eclipsed by his *Rubaiyat*, publicised by Edward FitzGerald in 1859.

O'Neill, Eugene Gladstone (1888–1953), American playwright who won success in 1914 with the oneact play, *Thirst*. His later plays include *Anna Christie*, *Strange Interlude*, *Mourning Becomes Electra*, *The Iceman Cometh*. Nobel prize, 1936.

Oppenheimer, J. Robert (1904–67), American physicist who was director of atomic-energy research at Los Alamos, New Mexico, 1942–5, when the atomic bomb was developed but in 1949 he opposed work on the hydrogen bomb on moral grounds.

Orchardson, Sir William Quiller (1835–1910), Scottish painter, b. Edinburgh, best known for his *Napoleon I on board H.M.S. Bellerophon* and *Ophelia*.

Origen (*c.* 185–254), Christian philosopher and Biblical scholar, who taught at Alexandria and Caesarea, and was imprisoned and tortured in the persecution of Decius, 250

Orpen, Sir William (1878–1931), painter of portraits, conversation pieces, and the 1914–18 war.

Ortega y Gasset, José (1883–1955), Spanish philosopher and essayist, known for his *Tema de Nuestro Tiempo* and *La Rebelión de Las Masas*.

Orwell, George (Eric Arthur Blair) (1903–50), English satirist, b. India, author of *Animal Farm*, *Nineteen Eighty-Four* and the earlier *Down and Out in Paris*.

Osborne, John (1929–94), playwright, was one of the "Angry Young Men" of the 1950s. His play *Look Back In Anger* (1956) marked a revolution in English theatre. His other plays include *The Entertainer* (1957), *Luther* (1961) and *Inadmissible Evidence* (1965).

Osler, Sir William (1849–1919), Canadian physician. Authority on diseases of the blood and spleen.

Ossietzky, Carl von (1889–1938), German pacifist leader after the first world war; sent by Hitler to a concentration camp. Nobel peace prize 1935.

Oswald, St (*c.* 605–42), won the Northumbrian throne by battle in 633 and introduced Christianity there.

Otto I (the Great) (912–73), founder of the Holy Roman Empire (he was crowned king of the Germans in 936 and emperor at Rome in 962). The son of Henry I of Germany, he built up a strong position in Italy (as regards the papacy) and in Germany where he established the East Mark (Austria).

Otto, Nikolaus August (1832–91). German engineer who built a gas engine (1878) using the fourstroke cycle that bears his name.

Ouida (Maria Louise Ramée) (1839–1908), English novelist of French extraction, whose romantic stories include *Under Two Flags*.

Ovid (43 B.C.–A.D. 18), Latin poet (Publius Ovidius Naso), chiefly remembered for his *Art of Love* and *Metamorphoses*. He died in exile.

Owen, Lord (David Owen). *See* D18.

Owen, Robert (1771–1858), Welsh pioneer socialist, b. Montgomeryshire. As manager, and later owner, of New Lanark cotton mills he tried to put his philanthropic views into effect; other communities on co-operative lines were founded in Hampshire and in America (New Harmony, Indiana) but although unsuccessful they were influential in many directions. He inaugurated socialism and the co-operative movement.

Owens, Jesse (1913–80), American black athlete whose 1936 Olympic triumph infuriated Hitler.

P

Pachmann, Vladimir de (1848–1933), Russian pianist gifted in the playing of Chopin.

Paderewski, Ignace Jan (1860–1941), Polish pianist and nationalist. He represented his country at Versailles and was the first premier of a reconstituted Poland. He died in exile.

Paganini, Niccolo (1782–1840), Italian violinist and virtuoso who revolutionised violin technique.

Pahlevi, Mohammed Riza Shah (1919–80), last Shah of Iran. Pro-Western ruler of Iran whose suppression of opposition helped precipitate an Islamic revolution. Went into exile, 1979.

Paine, Thomas (1737–1809), British radical writer and activist, b. Suffolk. Emigrated to America in 1774. Pamphlet, *Common Sense*, in 1776 advocated independence from Britain. First to use expression 'United States'. Returned to Europe in 1787, writing the *Rights of Man* in support of French Revolution. Elected member of French National Convention, 1792; imprisoned for opposing execution of King Louis XVI. Condemned in Britain for treason, he returned to the United States. Also wrote the deist *The Age of Reason*, 1794–5.

Palestrina, Giovanni Pierluigi da (*c.* 1525–94), Italian composer of unaccompanied church music and madrigals. *See* Section P.

Palgrave, Sir Francis (1788–1861), English historian and archivist, an early editor of record series. His son **Francis Turner Palgrave** (1824–97) was a poet and critic and edited *The Golden Treasury*; another son, **William Gifford Palgrave** (1826–88) was a traveller and diplomat.

Palissy, Bernard (*c.* 1510–89), French potter who discovered the art of producing white enamel, after which he set up a porcelain factory in Paris which was patronised by royalty.

Palladio, Andrea (1508–80), Italian architect, b. Padua, whose style was modelled on ancient Roman architecture (symmetrical planning and harmonic proportions) and had wide influence; author of *I Quattro Libri dell' Architettura*.

Palmer, Samuel (1805–81), English landscape painter and etcher, follower of Blake whom he met in 1824. *Bright Cloud* and *In a Shoreham Garden* are in the Victoria and Albert Museum.

Palmerston, 3rd Viscount (Henry John Temple) (1784–1865), English Whig statesman. At first a Tory, he was later Whig foreign secretary for many years, and prime minister 1855 and 1859–65. Pursued vigorous foreign policy.

Pancras, St. (d. 304), patron saint of children, was put to death at the age of fourteen in the persecution under Diocletian.

Panizzi, Sir Anthony (1797–1879), Italian bibliographer and nationalist. Taking refuge in England after 1821, he became in 1856 chief librarian of the British Museum, undertook a new catalogue and designed the reading room.

Pankhurst, Emmeline (1858–1928), English suffragette who, with her daughters Christabel and Sylvia, worked for women's suffrage, organising the Women's Social and Political Union.

Panufnik, Sir Andrzej (1914–91), Polish-born composer. His first major work, the *Graduation Concert* was performed in 1935. The first Pole to be knighted.

Paolozzi, Sir Eduardo Luigi (1924–2005), Scottish sculptor and pioneer of Pop Art. Knighted in 1989.

Papin, Denis (1647–1714), French physicist and inventor. He invented the condensing pump, and was a pioneer in the development of the steam-engine. Not being a mechanic, he made all his experiments by means of models.

Paracelsus (Theophrastus Bombastus von Hohenhelm) (1493–1541), Swiss physician whose speculations though muddled served to reform medical thought. He criticised the established authorities, Galen and Aristotle, and experimented and made new chemical compounds. His earliest printed work was *Practica* (1529).

Park, Mungo (1771–1806), Scottish explorer in west Africa, where he lost his life. He wrote *Travels in the Interior of Africa* (1799).

Parker, Joseph (1830–1902), English Congregational preacher, at what became the City Temple.

Parks, Rosa (1913–2005), the "mother of the US civil rights movement" who famously refused to yield her seat on a bus in Montgomery, Alabama, in 1955.

Parnell, Charles Stewart (1846–91), Irish national leader. To draw attention to Ireland's problems, he used obstruction in parliament. He was president of the Land League but was not implicated in crimes committed by some members. His party supported Gladstone, who became converted to Home Rule. His citation in divorce proceedings brought his political career to an end.

Parry, Sir William Edward (1790–1855), English explorer and naval commander in the Arctic, where he was sent to protect fisheries and also tried to reach the north pole.

Parsons, Sir Charles Algernon (1854–1931), English inventor of the steam-turbine, who built *Turbinia*, the first turbine-driven steamship in 1894.

Pascal, Blaise (1623–62), Frenchman of varied gifts, b. at Clermont-Ferrand. At first a mathematician, he patented a calculating machine. His *Lettres provinciales* influenced Voltaire. In 1654 he turned to religion. *See* Jansenism, **Section J.**

Pasternak, Boris Leonidovich (1890–1960), Russian poet and writer. B. Moscow, he published his first poems in 1931. For some years his time was spent in translating foreign literature, but in 1958 his novel *Dr. Zhivago*, which describes the Russian revolution and is in the Russian narrative tradition, was published abroad, though banned in the Soviet Union. He was awarded a Nobel prize but obliged to decline it.

Pasteur, Louis (1822–95), French chemist, b. at Dôle in the Jura, whose work was inspired by an interest in the chemistry of life. His researches on fermentation led to the science of bacteriology and his investigations into infectious diseases and their prevention to the science of immunology. The pathological-bacteriological import of his researches came about mainly through his disciples (Lister, Roux, and others) and not directly, though all founded on his early non-medical investigations on organisms of fermentation, etc., which were of great importance in industry, and fundamentally. He spent most of his life as director of scientific studies at the Ecole Normale at Paris. The Institute Pasteur was founded in 1888.

Patmore, Coventry (1823–96), English poet. *The Angel in the House* deals with domesticity. Later became a Roman catholic, and *The Unknown Eros* is characterised by erotic mysticism.

Patrick, St. (c. 389–c. 461), apostle of Ireland, was born in Britain or Gaul, and after some time on the continent (taken there after his capture by pirates) went as missionary to Ireland, where he fixed his see at Armagh. He wrote *Confessions.*

Patten, Lord. *See* D18.

Patti, Adelina (1843–1919), famous coloratura soprano, b. in Madrid of Italian parents.

Paul, St. *See* Section H.

Paul VI (Giovanni Battista Montini) (1897–1978), elected Pope in 1963. His encyclical *Humanae Vitae* (1968) condemned contraception.

Pauli, Wolfgang (1900–58), Austrian-born physicist who first predicted theoretically the existence of neutrinos. Nobel prize 1945.

Pauling, Linus Carl (1901–94), American scientist. Won 1954 Nobel Prize for Chemistry (for work on molecular structure). Won 1963 Nobel Prize for Peace (the only person to receive two Nobel Prizes outright).

Pavarotti, Luciano (b. 1935), Italian operatic tenor. Acclaimed for such roles as Rodolfo in *La Bohème*, the Duke of Mantua in *Rigoletto etc.*

Pavlov, Ivan Petrovich (1849–1936), Russian physiologist, known for his scientific experimental work on animal behaviour, particularly conditioned reflexes and the relation between psychological stress and brain function. Nobel prizewinner 1904.

Pavlova, Anna (1882–1931), Russian ballerina, b. St. Petersburg, excelling in the roles of *Giselle* and the *Dying Swan.*

Peabody, George (1795–1869), American philanthropist, a successful merchant who lived mainly in London. He promoted education and housing.

Peacock, Thomas Love (1785–1866), English novelist, b. Weymouth. His works included *Headlong Hall* and *Nightmare Abbey.*

Pearson, Lester Bowles (1897–1972), Canadian politician who served as minister for external affairs 1948–57, and prime minister 1963–8.

Peary, Robert Edwin (1856–1920), American arctic explorer, discoverer of the north pole (1909).

Peel, Sir Robert (1788–1850), English Conservative statesman, b. in Lancashire, son of a manufacturer. He first held office in 1811. With Wellington he enacted toleration for Roman catholics in 1829. As home secretary he reorganised London police. He developed a new policy of Conservatism, and in 1846, largely as a result of the Irish famine, he repealed the corn laws.

Peierls, Sir Rudolf (1907–95), Wykeham Professor of Physics at Oxford, 1963–74. A founding father of the atomic age.

Peirce, Charles Sanders (1839–1914), American physicist and philosopher, founder of the theory of pragmatism (described in **Section J**).

Pele (b. 1940), legendary Brazilian footballer. Real name Edson Arantes do Nascimento.

Penfield, Wilder Graves (1891–1976), Canadian brain surgeon, author of *The Cerebral Cortex of Man, Epilepsy and the Functional Anatomy of the Human Brain.* O.M.

Penn, William (1644–1718), English Quaker and founder of Pennsylvania. The son of Admiral William Penn, he persisted in becoming a Quaker, and on receiving for his father's services a crown grant in America he founded Pennsylvania. He wrote *No Cross, No Crown.*

Penney, Baron (William George Penney) (1909–91), British scientist. His nuclear research team developed the advanced gas-cooled reactor.

Pepys, Samuel (1633–1703), English diarist and naval administrator. His diary, 1660–69, was kept in cipher and not deciphered till 1825. It gives vivid personal details and covers the plague and fire of London. (The first complete version of the diary was issued in 1970.)

Perceval, Spencer (1762–1812), Prime Minister, 1809–12. Assassinated by a deranged bankrupt.

Pereda, José Maria de (1833–1906), Spanish regional novelist (around his native Santander).

Pérez Galdós, Benito (1843–1920), Spanish novelist and dramatist, who has been compared to Balzac for his close study and portrayal of all social classes, especially in the series of 46 short historical novels *Episodios nacionales.* His longer novels, *Novelas españolas contemporáneas,* some of which are translated, number 31.

Pergolesi, Giovanni Battista (1710–36), Italian composer, best known for his humorous opera *La Serva Padrona* and his *Stabat Mater.*

Pericles (c. 490 429 B.C.), Athenian statesman, general, and orator, who raised Athens to the point of its fullest prosperity, and greatest beauty, with the Parthenon, Erechtheum, and other buildings; but he died of plague following the outbreak of the Peloponnesian war.

Perkin, Sir William Henry (1838–1907), English chemist, b. London, who while seeking to make a substitute for quinine discovered in 1856 the first artificial aniline dye, mauve.

Perón, Juan (Domingo) (1895–1974), Argentinian populist politician. President, 1946–55. Returned in triumph from exile (1973). His second wife Eva (known as Evita) was idolized by the masses. His third wife Isabelita Péron, succeeded him as President on his death in 1974.

Perry, Frederick John (1909–95), the greatest player in the history of British lawn tennis. Last British player to win singles titles at Wimbledon (1934, 1935 and 1936).

Persius Flaccus Aulus (A.D. 34–62), Roman satirist and Stoic philosopher.

Perugino, Pietro (1446–1524), Italian artist. He worked in the Sistine Chapel at Rome and he taught Raphael.

Perutz, Max Ferdinand (1914–2002), British chemist. Nobel Prize, 1962 (with Sir John Kendrew). Founding father of the world-renowned Laboratory of Molecular Biology at Cambridge.

Pestalozzi, Johann Heinrich (1746–1827), Swiss educational reformer whose theories laid the foundation of modern primary education. He wrote *How Gertrude Educates Her Children.*

Pétain, Henri Philippe (1856–1951), French general and later collaborator. In the first world war he was in command at Verdun. Headed the pro-German Vichy regime in World War II.

Peter, St. *See* Section H.

Peter I, the Great (1672–1725), emperor of Russia. Son of Alexei, he succeeded his brother after some difficulty. He reorganised the army, and, after coming to Deptford to learn shipbuilding, he created a navy. To some extent he westernised Russian social life, and created a new capital at St. Petersburg (1703). In war with Charles XII of Sweden he was at first defeated, but later victorious at Poltava (1709). He married a peasant, Catherine, who succeeded him.

Peter the Hermit (c. 1050–1115), French monk who preached the First Crusade, originated by pope Urban II at the council of Clermont. He went on the crusade, but gave up at Antioch.

Petrarch, Francesco (1304–78), Italian poet, son of a Florentine exile. He is chiefly remembered for his poems *To Laura*, but he was also a scholar who paved the way for the Renaissance.

Petrie, Sir Flinders (1853–1942), British egyptologist who excavated in Britain after 1875, Egypt (1880–1924), and Palestine (1927–38).

Pevsner, Sir Nikolaus (1902–83), German-born architectural historian. Author of *The Buildings of England* (46 vols., 1951–74).

Phidias (5th cent. B.C.), Greek sculptor especially in gold, ivory and bronze, worked at Athens for Pericles. No certain examples of his work are extant, but the Elgin marbles in the British Museum may be from his designs.

Philip II of France (1165–1223), son of Louis VII. He went on the Third Crusade with Richard I of England, but in France is mainly remembered for firm government, the recovery of Normandy from England, and the beautifying of Paris.

Philip II of Macedonia (382–336 B.C.), a successful commander, made his the leading military kingdom in Greece. Father of Alexander the Great.

Philip II of Spain (1527–98), succeeded his father Charles V in Spain and the Netherlands, also in Spanish interests overseas. In the Netherlands his strict Roman catholic policy provoked a revolt which ended in 1579 in the independence of the United Provinces. He married Mary Tudor of England; and after her death sent the ill-fated Armada against Elizabeth in 1588.

Philip V of Spain (1683–1746), first Bourbon king, succeeded his great-uncle Charles II and was grandson of Louis XIV. His accession provoked European war.

Phillip, Arthur (1738–1814), first governor of New South Wales. Under his command the first fleet of 717 convicts set sail from Britain to Australia, and with the founding of Sydney in 1788 colonisation of the whole country began.

Phillips, Stephen (1868–1915), English poet who wrote verse dramas, *e.g. Paolo and Francesca.*

Piaf, Edith (1915–63), French singer and actress, renowned for her interpretation of the *Chanson.* Her real name was Edith Giovanna Gassion.

Piast, first Polish dynasty in Poland until the 14th cent. and until the 17th cent. in Silesia.

Piazzi, Giuseppe (1746–1826), Italian who discovered Ceres, the first of the asteroids to be seen by man.

Picasso, Pablo Ruiz (1881–1973) Spanish painter, b. Málaga; received his early training in Catalonia and settled in Paris in 1903. He and Braque were the originators of Cubism (*c.* 1909). His influence over contemporary art is comparable with that exercised by Cézanne (*q.v.*) over the artists of his time. Perhaps the best-known single work is his mural *Guernica,* expressing his loathing of fascism and the horrors of war.

Piccard, Auguste (1884–1962), Swiss physicist, noted for balloon ascents into the stratosphere and for submarine research. In 1960 his son **Jacques** made a descent of over 7 miles in the Marianas trench in the western Pacific in a bathyscaphe designed and built by his father.

Piggott, Lester (Keith) (b. 1935), outstanding jockey. Won the Derby 9 times, champion jockey 11 times. Rode 4,000th winner in Britain, 14 August 1982.

Pilate, Pontius. *See* Section H.

Pilsudski, Joseph (1867–1935), Polish soldier and statesman who in 1919 attempted by force to restore Poland's 1772 frontiers but was driven back. From 1926 he was dictator.

Pindar (522–443 B.C.), Greek lyric poet.

Pinero, Sir Arthur Wing (1855–1934), English dramatist whose plays include *Dandy Dick, The Second Mrs. Tanqueray* and *Mid-Channel.*

Pinochet, Augusto (b. 1915), Chilean dictator who led 1973 coup and presided over a brutal regime.

Pinter, Harold (b. 1930), British playwright, whose plays are notable for their spare dialogue, pauses, and sense of menace, *e.g.*, *The Birthday Party* (1957), *The Caretaker* (1959), *The Homecoming* (1965) and *No Man's Land* (1975). His many screenplays include *The French Lieutenant's Woman* (1981), from John Fowles's novel. Created CBE (1966) and a Companion of Honour (2002). Nobel Prize, 2005.

Pirandello, Luigi (1867–1936), Italian dramatist and novelist whose plays include *Six Characters in Search of an Author.* Nobel prize 1934.

Pissarro, Camille (1830–1903), French impressionist painter of landscapes; studied under Corot.

Pitman, Sir Isaac (1813–97), b. Trowbridge. Inventor of a system of phonographic shorthand.

Pitt, William (1759–1806), English statesman. Younger son of the Earl of Chatham, (*q.v.*) he entered parliament at 21 and became prime minister at 24 in 1783 when parties were divided and the American war had been lost. He rose to the position, and held office with scarcely a break till his death. An able finance minister, he introduced reforms, and would have gone further, but Napoleon's meteoric rise obliged him to lead European allies in a long struggle against France. He died worn out by his efforts.

Pius XII (1876–1958), elected pope 1939. As Eugenio Pacelli, he was papal nuncio in Germany and later papal secretary of state. It has been argued that he could have taken a stronger line against Nazi war crimes.

Pizarro, Francisco (*c.* 1478–1541), Spanish adventurer, b. Trujillo. After Columbus's discoveries, he conquered Peru for Spain, ending the Inca empire. He was murdered by his men.

Planck, Max (1857–1947), German mathematical physicist, b. Kiel, whose main work was on thermodynamics. In 1900 he invented a mathematical formula to account for some properties of the thermal radiation from a hot body which has since played an important role in physics. Nobel prize 1918. *See* **Quantum theory, Section L.**

Plato (427–347 B.C.), Athenian philosopher, pupil of Socrates, teacher of Aristotle. He founded a school at Athens under the name of the Academy, where he taught philosophy and mathematics. His great work is his *Dialogues,* which includes the *Republic,* the longest and most celebrated. His known writings have come down to us and constitute one of the most influential bodies of work in history.

Playfair, 1st Baron (Lyon Playfair) (1818–98), a far-sighted Victorian who stood for the greater recognition of science in national life. He forsook his profession as professor of chemistry at Edinburgh to enter parliament.

Plimsoll, Samuel (1824–98), English social reformer, b. Bristol. He realised the evil of overloading unseaworthy ships, and as MP for Derby he secured the Merchant Shipping Act, 1876 which imposed a line (the Plimsoll Mark) above which no ship must sink while loading.

Pliny the Elder (A.D. 23–79), Roman naturalist, author of a *Natural History.* He died of fumes and exhaustion while investigating the eruption of Vesuvius. His nephew, **Pliny the Younger** (A.D. 62–113), wrote *Letters* notable for the insight they give into Roman life.

Plotinus (*c.* 203–*c.* 262), Greek philosopher, was the founder of Neoplatonism, which had considerable influence on early Christian thought.

Plutarch (*c.* 46–120), Greek biographer, whose *Lives* portray 46 leading historical figures (in pairs, a Greek and a Roman whose careers were similar). Although based on myth his *Life of Lycurgus* about life in Sparta had a profound influence on later writers, *e.g.,* Rousseau and the romantic philosophers. He was educated at Athens but visited Rome.

Poe, Edgar Allan (1809–49), American poet and story-writer, b. Boston, Mass. His poems include *The Raven, To Helen,* and *Annabel Lee,* and his stories, often weird and fantastic, include *Tales of the Grotesque and Arabesque.*

Poincaré, Raymond Nicolas (1860–1934), French statesman. He was president 1913–20, and as prime minister occupied the Ruhr in 1923.

Pol Pot (1926–98) Evil dictator of Kampuchea (now Cambodia) and mass murderer.

Pole, Reginald (1500–58), archbishop of Canterbury, cardinal of the Roman church and antagonist of the reformation. He opposed Henry VIII's divorce and went abroad in 1532, writing *De Unitate Ecclesiastica*; as a result of which his mother, Countess of Salisbury, and other relatives were executed. Under Mary he became archbishop and died the year she did.

Polo, Marco (1256–1323), Venetian traveller, who claimed to have made journeys through China, India, *etc.*, visiting the court of Kubla Khan, and leaving an account of his travels.

Pompadour, Jeanne Antoine Poisson, Marquise de (1721–64), mistress of Louis XV of France. She exercised disastrous political influence.

Pompey (106–48 B.C.), Roman commander, who

cleared the Mediterranean of pirates, and became triumvir with Caesar and Crassus.

Pompidou, Georges Jean Raymond (1911–74), French administrator and politician who succeeded de Gaulle as president 1969.

Pope, Alexander (1688–1744), English poet, b. London, of a Roman catholic family, and largely self-educated. His brilliant satire was frequently directed against his contemporaries. He is remembered for *The Rape of the Lock*, *The Dunciad*, *Essay on Criticism*, and *Essay on Man*.

Popper, Sir Karl Raimund (1902–94), renowned philosopher of science, b. Vienna; author of *The Open Society and Its Enemies* (1945), *Conjectures and Refutations* (1963), *Objective Knowledge* (1972). He rejects the doctrine that all knowledge starts from perception or sensation and holds that it grows through conjecture and refutation.

Potter, Dennis (1935–94), television dramatist, wrote many innovative and stimulating plays. These included three six-part serials: *Pennies from Heaven* (1978), *The Singing Detective* (1986) and *Lipstick on your Collar* (1993).

Potter, Mary (1847–1913), only Englishwoman to found a religious nursing order, the Little Company of Mary (known as the "Blue Nuns").

Pound, Ezra Loomis (1885–1972), American poet and writer on varied subjects. Noted for his translations of Provençal, Latin, Chinese, French, and Italian poets.

Poussin, Nicolas (1593–1665), French painter. He lived in Rome 1624–40, 1642–65. His *Golden Calf* is in the National Gallery.

Powell, Colin (b. 1937). US Secretary of State, 2001–05 (the first black American to hold this office). General who won decisive victory in Gulf War but faced difficult decisions in war on terrorism.

Powell, (John) Enoch (1912–98), English politician, at first Conservative, later Ulster Unionist. A great parliamentarian and renowned orator, his rightwing views on immigration were unacceptable to the party leadership. He was also a Greek scholar.

Powys, John Cowper (1872–1964), English writer, best known for his novel *Wolf Solent* and his essays *The Meaning of Culture* and *A Philosophy of Solitude*. His brothers, **Theodore Francis** (1875–1953) and **Llewelyn** (1884–1939) were also original writers.

Prasad, Rajendra (1884–1963), Indian statesman, first president of the Republic of India, 1950–62.

Praxiteles (4th cent. B.C.), Greek sculptor, whose main surviving work is *Hermes carrying Dionysus*.

Preece, Sir William Henry (1834–1913), Welsh electrical engineer, associated with the expansion of wireless telegraphy and telephony.

Prescott, John. *See* D18.

Presley, Elvis (Aron) (1935–77). Legendary rock singer whose songs (Hound Dog, Love Me Tender *etc.*) sold millions. Buried at Gracelands, Memphis.

Prichard, James Cowles (1786–1848), English ethnologist who perceived that people should be studied as a whole. His works include *Researches into the Physical History of Mankind* and *The Natural History of Man*. He practised medicine.

Priestley, John Boynton (1894–1984), English critic, novelist, and playwright, b. Bradford. His works include the novels *The Good Companions*, *Angel Pavement*, and the plays *Dangerous Corner*, *Time and the Conways*, *I Have Been Here Before*, and *The Linden Tree*, O.M. 1977. He married the writer and archaeologist Jacquetta Hawkes (d. 1996) in 1953.

Priestley, Joseph (1733–1804), English chemist who worked on gases, and shared with Scheele the discovery of oxygen. A presbyterian minister, he was for his time an advanced thinker. In 1794 he settled in America.

Prior, Matthew (1664–1721), English poet. In early life he was a diplomat. He was a neat epigrammatist and writer of occasional pieces. His works include *The City Mouse and Country Mouse* and *Four Dialogues of the Dead*.

Pritchett, Sir Victor Sawdon, (1900–97) accomplished novelist, short-story writer and critic. His *Complete Short Stories* were published in 1990 and his *Complete Essays* in 1992. C.H., 1993.

Prokofiev, Serge Sergeyevich (1891–1953), Russian composer, whose music has a strong folk-song element, rich in melody and invention. He wrote operas such as *The Love of Three Oranges*, *The Betrothal in a Nunnery*, *War and Peace*; ballets: *Romeo and Juliet*, *Cinderella*; symphonies, chamber music, and the music for Eisenstein's films *Alexander Nevsky*, *Ivan the Terrible*.

Protagoras (c. 480–411 B.C.), Greek philosopher, chief of the Sophists, noted for his scepticism and disbelief in objective truth, and for his doctrine that "man is the measure of all things."

Proudhon, Pierre Joseph (1809–65), French socialist. In 1840 he propounded the view that property is theft. His main work is *Système des contradictions économiques* (1846).

Proust, Marcel (1871–1922), French psychological novelist, author of a series of novels known under the title of *A la recherche du temps perdu*.

Ptolemy of Alexandria (Claudius Ptolemaeus) (fl. A.D. 140), astronomer and founder of scientific cartography. In the *Almagest* he attempted a mathematical presentation of the paths along which the planets appear to move. His other great work was his *Geographical Outline*.

Puccini, Giacomo (1858–1924), Italian composer, b. Lucca, whose operas include *Manon Lescaut*, *La Bohème*, *Tosca*, *Madam Butterfly*, and *Turandot* (completed by a friend).

Pupin, Michael Idvorsky (1858–1935), physicist and inventor (telephony and X-rays).

Purcell, Henry (1659–95), English composer, b. Westminster, son of a court musician. He became organist of the chapel royal and composer to Charles II. His best works are vocal and choral. *See* **Section P.**

Pusey, Edward Bouverie (1800–82), English theologian, a leader of the Oxford or Tractarian movement with Keble and at first also with Newman, till the latter became Roman catholic.

Pushkin, Alexander (1799–1837), Russian writer, b. Moscow, whose place in Russian literature ranks with Shakespeare's in English. He wrote in many forms—lyrical poetry and narrative verse, drama, folk-tales and short stories. Musicians have used his works as plots for operas—the fairy romance *Russlan and Ludmilla* was dramatised by Glinka; the verse novel *Eugene Onegin* and the short story *The Queen of Spades* were adapted by Tchaikovsky, and the tragic drama *Boris Godunov* formed the subject of Mussorgsky's opera. He was inspired by the wild beauty of the Caucasus. He was killed in a duel defending his wife's honour.

Putin, Vladimir (b. 1952) President of Russia since January 2000 when he succeeded Yeltsin. A former KGB officer. *See* **Section C.**

Pym, John (1584–1643), English parliamentary leader in opposition to Charles I. He promoted the impeachment of Strafford and Laud.

Pythagoras (c. 582–500 B.C.), Greek philosopher, b. on the island of Samos, off the Turkish mainland, which he left c. 530 to settle at Croton, a Greek city in southern Italy. He was a mystic and mathematician, and founded a brotherhood who saw in numbers the key to the understanding of the universe.

Q

Quasimodo, Salvatore (1901–68), Italian poet of humanity and liberal views whose works include *La vita non e sogno*. Nobel prizewinner 1959.

Quesnay, François (1694–1774), French economist, founder of the physiocratic school. *See* **Section J.**

Quiller-Couch, Sir Arthur Thomas (1863–1944), Man of letters, b. Bodmin, known as "Q." Professor of English, Cambridge University, 1912–44.

R

Rabelais, François (c. 1495–1553), French satirist. At first in religious orders, he later studied medicine and practised at Lyons. His works are full of riotous mirth, wit and wisdom. The main ones are *Gargantua* and *Pantagruel*.

Rabin, Yitzhak (1922–95) Israeli defence chief and statesman. He was first Prime Minister from 1974–77. Again as Prime Minister he was an architect of the peace process. Assassinated in 1995.

Rachel, Elisa (Elisa Felix) (1821–58), Alsatian Jewish tragic actress (*e.g.* in Racine's *Phèdre*).

Rachmaninov, Sergey Vasilyevich (1873–1943), Russian composer and pianist, b. Nijni-Novgorod (now Gorki), best known for his piano music, especially his *Prelude*. *See* **Section P.**

Racine, Jean (1639–99), French tragic poet whose dramas include *Andromaque*, *Iphigénie* and *Phèdre*. An orphan, he was brought up by grandparents who sent him to Port Royal school where he acquired a love of the classics. In Paris he became a friend of Molière, whose company acted his first play, and of Boileau, with whom he became joint historiographer to Louis XIV. *Esther* and *Athalie* were written for Madame de Maintenon's schoolgirls.

Rackham, Arthur (1867–1939), English artist and book-illustrator, especially of fairy tales.

Radhakrishnan, Sir Sarvepalli (1888–1975), Indian philosopher and statesman; President of India 1962–7. He was at one time a professor at Oxford.

Raffles, Sir Thomas Stamford (1781–1826), English colonial administrator who founded a settlement at Singapore in 1819. He founded London Zoo.

Raikes, Robert (1735–1811), English educational pioneer, whose lead in the teaching of children at Gloucester on Sundays led to an extensive Sunday School movement.

Raleigh, Sir Walter (1552–1618), adventurer and writer. He found favour at the court of Elizabeth I, helped to put down the Irish rebellion of 1580, and in 1584 began the colonisation of Virginia, introducing potatoes and tobacco to the British Isles. At the accession of James I he lost favour and was sent to the Tower, where he wrote his *History of the World*. Released in 1615 to lead an expedition to the Orinoco, he was executed when it failed.

Ramakrishna (1836–86), famous Indian mystic.

Raman, Sir Chandrasekhara Venkata (1888–1970), Indian physicist whose main work has been in spectroscopy. For his research on the diffusion of light and discovery of the "Raman effect" he was awarded the 1930 Nobel prize.

Ramanuja (*fl.* A.D. 1125) Indian philosopher, the most revered teacher of the Vaishnava Hindus.

Rameau, Jean Philippe (1683–1764), French composer and church organist whose works on musical theory influenced musical development.

Ramkrishna Paramahamsa (1834–86), one of the great spiritual Hindu teachers of modern India.

Ramón y Cajal, Santiago (1852–1934), Spanish histologist who made discoveries in the structure of the nervous system. Shared 1906 Nobel prize.

Ramphal, Sir Shridath 'Sonny' (b. 1928), Guyanese statesman. Secretary-General of the Commonwealth, 1975 to 1990. First black Chancellor of a British university.

Ramsay, Sir William (1852–1916), Scottish chemist, and discoverer with Lord Rayleigh of argon. Later he discovered helium and other inert gases, which he called neon, krypton, and xenon. Nobel prizewinner 1904.

Ramsey, Arthur Michael (1904–88), archbishop of Canterbury, 1961–74, who worked for church unity.

Rand, Ayn (1905–82), Russian-born US novelist and philosopher who propagated the philosophy of Objectivism (*see* **J37**) through her novels.

Ranke, Leopold von (1795–1886), German historian, one of the first to base his work on methodical research. Author of a *History of the Popes*.

Raphael (Raffaello Santi) (1483–1520) of Urbino was the youngest of the three great artists of the High Renaissance. He was taught at Perugia by Perugino, and then at Florence he came under the influence of Leonardo and Michelangelo. Raphael's Madonnas, remarkable for their simplicity and grace, include the *Madonna of the Grand Duke* (Palazzo Pitti), the *Sistine Madonna* (Dresden) the *Madonna with the Goldfinch* (Uffizi), the *Madonna of Foligno* (Vatican), and the *Ansidei Madonna* (National Gallery). He painted the frescoes on the walls of the Stanza della Segnatura in the Vatican, and designed 10 cartoons for tapestries for the Sistine Chapel. After the death of Bramante, appointed architect for the rebuilding of St. Peter's.

Rasputin, Grigori Yefimovich (1869–1916), Russian peasant from Siberia, a cunning adventurer who at the court of Nicholas II exerted a malign influence over the Tsarina through his apparent ability to improve the health of the sickly Tsarevich Alexis. He was later murdered.

Rathbone, Eleanor (1872–1946), social reformer who championed women's pensions and in her book *The Disinherited Family* set out the case for family allowances.

Rattle, Sir Simon (b. 1955), foremost conductor. Music Director, City of Birmingham Symphony Orchestra, 1991–8. Appointed (1999) first British conductor of Berlin Symphony Orchestra.

Ravel, Maurice (1875–1937), French composer, pupil of Fauré, one of the leaders of the impressionist movement.

Rawlinson, Sir Henry Creswicke (1810–95), English diplomat and archaeologist. He made Assyrian collections now in the British Museum and translated the Behistun inscription of the Persian king Darius. He also wrote on cuneiform inscriptions and on Assyrian history.

Rawls, John (1921–2002), influential American philosopher concerned with justice. Author of *A Theory of Justice*.

Ray, John (1627–1705), English naturalist. A blacksmith's son, he went to Cambridge, travelled in Europe, and produced a classification of plants. He also wrote on zoology. *See* **T43**.

Rayleigh, 3rd Baron (John William Strutt) (1842–1919), English mathematician and physicist. He studied sound and the wave theory of light; and with Sir William Ramsay discovered argon. Nobel prizewinner 1904.

Read, Sir Herbert (1893–1968), English poet and art critic. His writings include *Collected Poems*, *The Meaning of Art* etc.

Reade, Charles (1814–84), English novelist. His chief work is *The Cloister and the Hearth*. He also wrote *Peg Woffington*, *It is Never too Late to Mend*, and *Griffith Gaunt*.

Reagan, Ronald (1911–2004). US President, 1981–89; former TV and film star, 1937–66. Governor of California, 1967–74. Won Republican victory, 1980. Re-elected in landslide victory, 1984. His popularity remained, helping ensure the election of George Bush (*q.v.*) as his successor.

Réaumur, René Antoine Ferchault de (1683–1757), French naturalist who invented a thermometer of eighty degrees, using alcohol.

Récamier, Jeanne Françoise (*née* Bernard) (1777–1849), French beauty and holder of a noted salon. Her husband was a banker.

Rees, Lord (Sir Martin Rees) (b. 1942). Eminent astronomer and scientist. Astronomer Royal since 1995. Master of Trinity College, Cambridge. President of the Royal Society.

Regnault, Henry Victor (1810–78), French chemist and physicist, who worked on gases, latent heat, and steam-engines.

Reith, 1st Baron (John Charles Walsham Reith) (1889–1971), Scottish civil engineer, first director-general of the BBC, 1927–38

Rembrandt (Rembrandt Harmenszoon van Rijn) (1606–69), Dutch painter and etcher, b. Leiden, a miller's son, one of the most individual and prolific artists of any period. His output includes portraits, landscapes, large groups, etchings, and drawings. He settled in Amsterdam establishing his reputation with *The Anatomy Lesson*, painted in 1632. In 1634 he married Saskia, a burgomaster's daughter. *The Night Watch* was painted in 1642; it was not well received and Saskia died the same year, leaving the infant Titus. The path from relative wealth to lonely old age is depicted in his self-portraits. Caring little for convention or formal beauty, his work is characterised by bold realism and spiritual beauty, by vitality and simplicity. His understanding of the play of colour and the effects of light can give his pictures a mystical beauty, as in the atmospheric painting *The Mill*. His figures, even for religious pictures, were taken from real life, the Jews in the etching *Christ Healing* from the Jewish quarter where he lived. He met the misfortunes of later life by withdrawing from society, but it was then that he produced his greatest works. *See* **N15**.

Renan, Ernest (1823–92), French writer who wrote on religious themes, especially a *Life of Jesus*.

Reni, Guido. *See* **Guido Reni**.

Rennie, John (1761–1821), Scottish civil engineer who built the old Waterloo and Southwark bridges. He also designed docks at London, Liverpool, Leith *etc.*; constructed Plymouth breakwater; made canals and drained fens.

Renoir, Pierre Auguste (1841–1919), French impressionist painter, b. Limoges. His works include portraits, still-life, landscapes, and groups, including *La Loge*, *Les Parapluies*, *La première Sortie*, *La Place Pigalle*. He was later crippled with arthritis.

Reuter, Paul Julius, Freiherr von (1816–99), German pioneer of telegraphic press service, who in 1851 fixed his headquarters in London.

Reymont, Vladislav Stanislav (1868–1925), Polish novelist, author of *The Peasants*. Nobel prize, 1924.

Reynolds, Sir Joshua (1723–92), English portrait painter, b. Plympton, Devon. His portraits, which include *Mrs. Siddons*, are remarkable for expressiveness and colour and he was a sympathetic painter of children. He was first president of the R.A. from 1768 till his death.

Rhodes, Cecil John (1853–1902), English empire-builder. B. at Bishop's Stortford, he went to South Africa for health reasons and there prospered at the diamond mines. He became prime minister of what was then Cape Colony and secured British power in what is now Zimbabwe and Zambia. He withdrew from politics after the failure of the Jameson Raid of 1895. He founded scholarships at Oxford for overseas students.

Ricardo, David (1772–1823), English political economist of Jewish descent. By occupation a London stockbroker, he wrote a major work, *Principles of Political Economy*.

Rice, Condoleezza (b. 1954), US Secretary of State since 2005. Former National Security Adviser.

Richard I (1157–99), succeeded his father Henry II as king of England in 1189. A patron of troubadours and a soldier (Lion-heart), he went on the third Crusade and took Acre, but could not recover Jerusalem from Saladin. On his return journey across Europe he was imprisoned and ransomed. He was killed in war with France.

Richard II (1367–1400), son of the Black Prince, succeeded his grandfather Edward III as king of England in 1377. Artistic and able, but erratic and egocentric, he personally at the age of fourteen met the Peasants' Revolt in 1381, making untenable promises. Latterly his rule became increasingly arbitrary, and he was deposed and imprisoned in 1399.

Richard III (1452–85), King of England (1483–5), younger brother of the Yorkist, Edward IV, is believed to have murdered his two nephews in the Tower. He was defeated and killed at Bosworth by the invading Earl of Richmond, who as Henry VII brought to an end the Wars of the Roses. Richard's character is disputed, but he was able and might have been a good ruler.

Richard, Sir Cliff (b. 1940) English singer, 'the first Knight of Pop'. Born Harry Webb in Lucknow, India. His first hit was '*Move It*' in 1958. He has had a number one hit in each of the last five decades.

Richards, Sir Gordon (1904–86), foremost English jockey who rode 4,870 winners. Knighted in 1953 after he won the Epsom Derby on *Pinza*.

Richardson, Sir Albert Edward (1880–1964), British architect, author of *Georgian Architecture*.

Richardson, Sir Owen Willans (1879–1959), English physicist who worked on thermionics or emission of electricity from hot bodies. Nobel prizewinner 1928.

Richardson, Sir Ralph David (1902–83), English actor who worked at the Old Vic, on the West End stage, and at Stratford-on-Avon, and appeared in films, including *South Riding*, *Anna Karenina*, and *The Fallen Idol*.

Richardson, Samuel (1689–1761), English author of *Pamela*, *Clarissa*, and *The History of Sir Charles Grandison*, exercised considerable influence on the development of the novel.

Richelieu, Armand Jean du Plessis, Duc de (1585–1642), French statesman, cardinal of the Roman church. As minister to Louis XIII from 1624 till his death, he built up the power of the French crown at home in central government, and by his military preparedness and active foreign policy gave France a lead in Europe.

Ridley, Nicholas (1500–55), English Protestant martyr, bishop of Rochester and later of London. He was burnt with Latimer.

Rienzi, Cola di (1313–54), Italian patriot, b. Rome, led a popular rising in 1347 and for seven months reigned as tribune, but had to flee, was imprisoned, and eventually murdered.

Rilke, Rainer Maria (1872–1926), German lyric poet, b. Prague. His work, marked by beauty of style, culminated in the *Duino Elegies* and *Sonnets to Orpheus*, both written in 1922, which gave a new musicality to German verse. His visits to Russia in 1899 and 1900 and his admiration for Rodin (who had been his wife's teacher) influenced his artistic career.

Rimbaud, Jean Nicolas Arthur (1854–91), French poet, b. Charleville, on the Meuse. In his brief poetic career (4 years from about the age of 16) he prepared the way for symbolism (*Bateau ivre*, *Les Illuminations*) and anticipated Freud (*Les déserts de l'amour*). He became intimate with Verlaine and at 18 had completed his memoirs. *Une saison en enfer*.

Rimsky-Korsakov, Nikolai Andreyevich (1844–1908), Russian composer whose works include the operas *The Maid of Pskov*, *The Snow Maiden*, *Le Coq d'or*, and the symphonic suite *Scheherezade*. He was a brilliant orchestrator and re-scored many works, *e.g.* Borodin's *Prince Igor*.

Rizzio, David (1533?-66), Italian musician and secretary of Mary, Queen of Scots. He was murdered in her presence at Holyrood by her jealous husband, Darnley.

Robbia, Luca Della (1400–82), Florentine sculptor who introduced enamelled terra-cotta work.

Roberts of Kandahar, 1st Earl (Frederick Sleigh Roberts) (1832–1914), British general. He took part in the suppression of the Indian Mutiny, in the Afghan war (relieving Kandahar), and when in command in South Africa in the Boer War he relieved Kimberley and advanced to Pretoria.

Robertson, Sir William (1860–1933), the first British soldier to rise from private to field-marshal.

Robeson, Paul (1898–1976), American Negro singer, b. Princeton, especially remembered for his singing of Negro spirituals, and his appearance in works ranging from *Showboat* to *Othello*.

Robespierre, Maximilien Marie Isidoire de (1758–94), French revolutionary. A country advocate, b. Arras, he was in 1789 elected to the States General and in 1792 to the Convention. He became a leader of the Jacobins, the more extreme party which came to power under stress of war and after the king's execution in 1793. In this crisis, the Committee of Public Safety, of which he was a member and which used his reputation as a cloak, sent many to the guillotine. He opposed the cult of Reason and inaugurated the worship of the Supreme Being. In the reaction from the reign of terror he was denounced, tried to escape, but was guillotined.

Robinson, Mary (b. 1944), President of Republic of Ireland, 1990–97 (1st woman President). Labour politician, lawyer and campaigner for women's rights. Served as UN High Commissioner for Human Rights, 1997–2002.

Robinson, William Heath (1872–1944), English cartoonist and book-illustrator, especially known for his humorous drawings of machines.

Rob Roy (Robert McGregor) (1671–1734), Scottish freebooter who helped the poor at the expense of the rich, and played a lone hand in the troubled times of the Jacobite rising of 1715.

Robsart, Amy (1532–00), English victim (it is believed) of murder. The wife of Robert Dudley, Earl of Leicester, she was found dead at Cumnor Place. Her death was used by Scott in *Kenilworth*.

Rockefeller, John Davison (1839–1937), American philanthropist, b. Richford, N.Y. He settled in Cleveland, Ohio, and with his brother William founded the Standard Oil Company, making a fortune. His philanthropic enterprises are carried on by the Rockefeller Foundation. **Nelson Rockefeller** (1908–79), Vice-Pres. of the United States 1974–7, was his grandson.

Rodin, Auguste (1841–1917), French sculptor, b. Paris. His best-known works include *Le Penseur*, *Les Bourgeois de Calais*, the statues of Balzac and Victor Hugo, and *La Porte d'Enfer*, a huge bronze door for the Musée des Arts Décoratifs, which was unfinished at his death.

Rodney, 1st Baron (George Rodney) (1719–92), English admiral, who served in the Seven Years War and the War of American Independence; in the latter war he defeated the French fleet under de Grasse.

Rogers, Lord (Sir Richard Rogers) (b. 1933), Architect of international repute. Creations include Lloyd's Building in London, the Pompidou Centre in Paris and the European Court of Human Rights building in Strasbourg.

Roland de la Platière, Manon Jeanne (1754–93), a leading figure in the French revolution. Her husband **Jean Marie** (1734–93), belonged to the more moderate or Girondist party, and when threatened escaped; but she was imprisoned and executed. She wrote *Letters* and *Memoirs*.

Rolland, Romain (1866–1944), French author, whose main work is a ten-volume novel, *Jean*

Christophe, the biography of a German musician, based on the life of Beethoven. Nobel Prize, 1915.

Rolls, Charles Stewart (1877–1910), with **Henry Royce** (1863–1933) the co-founders of Rolls-Royce car manufacturers (at Derby in 1907).

Romero y Galdames, Oscar (1917–80), Roman Catholic Archbishop of San Salvador. He was murdered in 1980 while preaching. Nobel Prizewinner.

Romilly, Sir Samuel (1757–1818), English lawyer and law-reformer, who aimed at mitigating the severity of the criminal law.

Rommel, Erwin (1891–1944), German Field-Marshal. He took part in the 1940 invasion of France, and was later successful in commanding the Afrika Korps till 1944. He committed suicide.

Romney, George (1734–1802), English artist, b. in Lancashire. He painted chiefly portraits, especially of Lady Hamilton, and lived mainly in London, but returned to Kendal to die.

Röntgen, Wilhelm Konrad von (1845–1923), German scientist who in 1895 discovered X-rays. Nobel prizewinner 1901.

Roosevelt, Franklin Delano (1882–1945), American statesman, a distant cousin of Theodore Roosevelt. During the first world war he held office under Wilson, and though stricken with poliomyelitis in 1921 continued his political career, becoming governor of New York in 1929 and U.S. president in 1933 (the first to hold office for more than two terms), till his death. A Democrat, he met the economic crisis of 1933 with a policy for a "New Deal" (*see* **Section A**). He strove in vain to ward off war. Towards other American countries his attitude was that of "good neighbour." After Pearl Harbor, he energetically prosecuted the war, holding meetings with Churchill and Stalin, and adopting a "lend-lease" policy for arms. He kept contact with his people by "fireside talks." His wife **Eleanor** (1884–1962) was a public figure in her own right.

Roosevelt, Theodore (1858–1919), American president. Popular because of his exploits in the Spanish–American war, he was appointed Republican vice-president in 1900, becoming president when McKinley was assassinated. Re-elected 1905. He promoted the regulation of trusts; and his promotion of peace between Russia and Japan gained the Nobel prize, 1906.

Rops, Félicien (1833–98), Belgian artist, known for his often satirical lithographs and etchings.

Ross, Sir James Clark (1800–62), Scottish explorer of polar regions, who accompanied his uncle Sir John, and himself discovered the north magnetic pole in 1831. He commanded the *Erebus* and *Terror* to the Antarctic (1839–43). His discoveries included the Ross ice barrier.

Ross, Sir John (1777–1856), Scottish explorer of polar regions, uncle of the above. He searched for the north-west passage and discovered Boothia peninsula.

Ross, Sir Ronald (1857–1932), British Nobel physician, b. India; discovered the malaria parasite.

Rossetti, Dante Gabriel (1828–82), English poet and painter, son of **Gabriele** (1783 1852), an exiled Italian author who settled in London in 1842. With Millais, Holman Hunt and others he formed the Pre-Raphaelite brotherhood which returned to pre-Renaissance art forms. His model was often his wife, Elizabeth Siddal. His poems include *The Blessed Damozel*. His sister **Christina Georgina** (1830–94) wrote poetry, including *Goblin Market*.

Rossini, Gioacchino Antonio (1792–1868), Italian operatic composer. See **Section P**.

Rostand, Edmond (1868–1918), French dramatist, whose *Cyrano de Bergerac* made a sensation in 1898.

Rostropovich, Mstislav (b. 1927), one of the greatest living cellists and conductors. Born in Baku, Azerbaijan.

Rotblat, Sir Joseph (1908–2005), Polish-born British physicist. Founder of the Pugwash Conferences. Shared 1995 Nobel Prize for Peace.

Rothenstein, Sir William (1872–1945), English portrait painter. His son, **Sir John** (1901–92), was an art historian and director of the Tate.

Rothschild, Meyer Amschel (1743–1812), German financier, founder of a banking family, b. Frankfurt. His five sons controlled branches at Frankfurt, Vienna, Naples, Paris and London (**Nathan Meyer**, 1777–1836). Nathan's son, **Lionel** (1808–79), was the first Jewish MP.

Roubiliac, Louis François (1695–1762), French sculptor who settled in London and carved a statue of Handel for Vauxhall gardens and one of Newton for Trinity College, Cambridge.

Rouget de Lisle, Claude Joseph (1760–1836), French poet, author of words and music of the *Marseillaise*, revolutionary and national anthem.

Rousseau, Henri (1844–1910), influential French "Sunday" painter, called "Le Douanier" because he was a customs official; self-taught, he was for long unrecognised as an artist of considerable talent and originality; he used the botanical gardens for his jungle scenes.

Rousseau, Jean-Jacques (1712–78), French political philosopher and educationist, b. Geneva, herald of the romantic movement. After a hard childhood he met Mme. de Warens who for some years befriended him. In 1741 he went to Paris where he met Diderot and contributed articles on music and political economy to the *Encyclopédie*. *La Nouvelle Héloïse* appeared in 1760, *Émile* and *Du Contrat Social* in 1762. *Émile* is a treatise on education according to "natural" principles and *Du Contrat Social*, his main work, sets forth his political theory. It begins, "Man is born free and everywhere he is in chains." Both books offended the authorities and he had to flee, spending some time in England. Later he was able to return to France. His views did much to stimulate the French Revolution.

Rowling, Joanne (b. 1965), the authoress of the best-selling Harry Potter novels which have captivated modern children. She writes as J.K. Rowling.

Royce, Henry, *see under* **Rolls, Charles Stewart.**

Rubens, Sir Peter Paul (1577–1640), Flemish painter. B. in exile, his family returned to Antwerp in 1587. He studied in Italy and visited Spain. His range was wide, his compositions vigorous, and he was a remarkable colourist. *Peace and War*, *The Rape of the Sabines*, and *The Felt Hat* are in the National Gallery.

Rubinstein, Anton Grigorovich (1829–94), Russian pianist and composer, who helped to found the conservatoire at St. Petersburg (Leningrad); as did his brother **Nicholas** (1835–81) at Moscow.

Rubinstein, Artur (1887–1982), Polish-born pianist of immense talent. He moved to the USA during World War II.

Rücker, Sir Arthur (1848–1915), English physicist, who made two magnetic surveys of the British Isles, 1886, and 1891.

Ruisdael, Jacob van (*c.* 1628–82), Dutch painter of landscapes, b. Haarlem. Several of his works are in the National Gallery, including *Coast of Scheveningen* and *Landscape with ruins*.

Rupert, Prince (1619–82), general, son of Frederick of Bohemia and his wife Elizabeth, daughter of James I of England. He commanded the Royalist cavalry in the English civil war, but was too impetuous for lasting success.

Rushdie, (Ahmed) Salman (b. 1947), controversial author of *The Satanic Verses* (1988 Whitbread Novel Award). Under death sentence (*fatwa*) by ayatollahs until lifted in 1998. He has also published *The Moor's Last Sigh* (set in his native Bombay) and, in 1994, *East, West* (a book of short stories), *The Ground Beneath Her Feet* (1999), *Fury* (2001) and *Shalimar the Clown* (2005).

Ruskin, John (1819–1900), English author and art critic, b. London. His *Modern Painters* in 5 volumes was issued over a period of years, the first volume having a strong defence of Turner. He helped to establish the Pre-Raphaelites. Other notable works include *The Seven Lamps of Architecture*, *The Stones of Venice* and *Praeterita*. *Unto this Last* develops his views on social problems, and he tried to use his wealth for education and for non-profitmaking enterprises. Ruskin College at Oxford is named after him. In 1848 he married Euphemia Gray, but in 1854 she obtained a decree of nullity and later married Millais.

Russell, 3rd Earl (Bertrand Arthur William Russell) (1872–1970), English philosopher, mathematician, and essayist, celebrated for his work in the field of logic and the theory of knowledge, and remembered for his moral courage, belief in human reason and his championship of liberal ideas. He published more than 60 books, including *The Principles of Mathematics* (1903). *Principia Mathematica* (in collaboration with A. N. Whitehead; 3 vols., 1910–13), *The Problem of Philosophy* (1912), *Mysticism and Logic* (1918), *The Analysis of Mind* (1921), *An Inquiry into Meaning and Truth* (1940) and *History of Western Philosophy* (1945). His *Autobiography*

(3 vols.) appeared 1967–9. He was the grandson of Lord John Russell. John Stuart Mill was his godfather. Nobel prize for literature 1950; D.M. 1949.

Russell, 1st Earl (John Russell), (1792–1878), English statesman, third son of the 6th Duke of Bedford. He had a large share in carrying the parliamentary reform bill of 1832. He was Whig prime minister 1846–52 and 1865–6.

Russell of Killowen, 1st Baron (Charles Russell), (1832–1900) British lawyer, b. Ireland; Lord Chief Justice 1894–1900. He defended Parnell.

Rutherford, 1st Baron (Ernest Rutherford) (1871–1937), British physicist, b. New Zealand, eminent in the field of atomic research. His experiments were conducted at Manchester and Cambridge. In 1911 he announced his nuclear theory of the atom and in 1918 succeeded in splitting the atom.

Ruysdael, Jacob van. See Ruisdael.

Ruyter, Michiel Adrianszoon de (1607–76), Dutch admiral who ranks with Nelson. He fought against England and in 1667 caused alarm by sailing up the Medway as far as Rochester and up the Thames as far as Gravesend. He was mortally wounded at Messina.

S

Sachs, Hans (1494–1576), German poet, b. Nuremberg. A shoemaker, he wrote over 6,000 pieces, many (including *Die Wittenbergische Nachtigall*) inspired by the Reformation.

Sachs, Julius von (1832–97), German botanist, founder of experimental plant physiology. He demonstrated that chlorophyll is formed in chloroplasts only in light.

Sadat, Mohammed Anwar El (1919–81), Egyptian statesman, President of Egypt 1970–81. His visit to Israel in Nov. 1977 was a bold and courageous move which led to the Camp David peace treaty with Israel. Assassinated 1981.

Sádi or Saadi (Muslih Addin) (c. 1184–1292), Persian poet, b. Shiraz, best known for his *Gulistan* (Flower Garden).

Sagan, Françoise (1935–2004), popular and controversial French author. Her most famous novel, *Bonjour Tristesse* (1954) was published when she was only 18.

Sainte-Beuve, Charles Augustin (1804–69), French critic, b. Boulogne. He studied medicine, abandoning it for journalism, and after attempting to write poetry, turned to literary criticism. His work reveals the wide range of his intellectual experience and includes *Causeries du lundi* and *Histoire de Port-Royal*.

Saint-Just, Antoine (1767–94), French revolutionary, a follower of Robespierre

St. Laurent, Louis Stephen (1882–1973), Canadian politician, prime minister 1948–57.

Saint-Saëns, Charles Camille (1835–1921), French composer, for 20 years organist at the Madeleine. His compositions include symphonic and chamber music and the opera *Samson et Dalila*, which was produced by Liszt at Weimar in 1877. See Section P.

Saint-Simon, Claude, Comte de (1760–1825), French socialist, who in his *L'Industrie* and *Nouveau christianisme* prepared the way for much later thought.

Saintsbury, George (1845–1933), literary historian and critic. Professor of Rhetoric and English Literature, Edinburgh University (1895–1915).

Sakharov, Andrei Dimitrievich (1921–89), Soviet nuclear physicist and human rights campaigner. Nobel prizewinner 1975.

Saladin (el Melik an-Nasir Salah ed-Din) (1137–93), sultan of Egypt and Syria and founder of a dynasty, who in 1187 defeated the Christians near Tiberias and took Jerusalem. This gave rise to the unsuccessful Third Crusade, in which Richard I of England joined. His great qualities were admired by his opponents.

Salam, Abdus (1926–96), theoretical physicist and mathematician of world stature. Pakistan's first Nobel Laureate.

Salazar, Antonio d'Oliveira (1889–1970), Portuguese dictator, having first been premier in 1932, a new constitution being adopted in 1933. He gave Portugal stability, but refused to bow to nationalism in Portuguese Africa and India.

Salimbene de Adamo (1221–c. 1228), mediaeval chronicler, b. Parma, whose vivid description

of life is embodied in his *Cronica*.

Salisbury, 3rd Marquess (Robert Arthur Talbot Gascoyne-Cecil (1830–1903), English Conservative statesman, prime minister 1885–6, 1886–92, 1895–1902, mainly remembered for his conduct of foreign affairs during a critical period.

Salk, Jonas (1914–95), developer of the first effective vaccine against poliomyelitis.

Samuel, 1st Viscount (Herbert Samuel) (1870–1963), British Liberal statesman of Jewish parentage.

Sand, George (1804–76), pseudonym of the French writer Aurore Dupin Dudevant. Her publications are extensive and varied, and include the novel *Mauprat*, rural studies, and an autobiography *Histoire de ma vie*. She was associated with Alfred de Musset and Chopin.

Sanger, Frederick (b. 1918), British scientist noted for his work on the chemical structure of the protein insulin. Nobel prizewinner 1958, and 1980.

Sankey, Ira David (1840–1908), American evangelist and composer, associated with Moody.

San Martin, José de (1778–1850), South American national leader in securing independence from Spanish rule to his native Argentina, Chile and Peru.

Santayana, George (1863–1952), American philosopher and poet, b. Madrid, of Spanish parentage. His books include *The Sense of Beauty*, *The Life of Reason*, and *The Realms of Being*.

Santos-Dumont, Alberto (1873–1932), Brazilian aeronaut who in 1898 flew a cylindrical balloon with a gasoline engine. In 1909 he built a monoplane.

Sappho of Lesbos (fl. early 6th cent. B.C.), Greek poetess, of whose love poems only three remained until a fourth was discovered in 2005.

Sardou, Victorien (1831 1908), French dramatist popular in his day. Sarah Bernhardt created famous parts in *Fédora*, *Théodora* and *La Tosca*; *Robespierre* and *Dante* were written for Irving.

Sargent, John Singer (1856–1922), American painter, b. Florence, who worked mainly in England, especially on portraits.

Sargent, Sir Malcolm (1895–1967), popular British conductor, who conducted the Promenade Concerts from 1950 till his death, and succeeded Sir Adrian Boult as conductor of the BBC Symphony Orchestra, 1950–7.

Sartre, Jean-Paul (1905–80), French existentialist philosopher, left-wing intellectual, dramatist, essayist and novelist. His major philosophical work is *L'Etre et le Néant* and his plays include *Les Mouches*, *Huis Clos*, *Crime passionel*, *La Putain respectueuse*, and *Les Séquestrés d'Altona*. He was awarded (though he declined it) the 1964 Nobel prize.

Sassoon, Siegfried (1886–1967), English poet and writer with a hatred of war. He is mainly known for *The Memoirs of a Foxhunting Man* the first part of the *Memoirs of George Sherston*.

Saul, King. See Section H.

Saunders, Dame Cicely (1918–2005), visionary founder of the modern hospice movement.

Savonarola, Girolamo (1452–98), Florentine preacher and reformer, a Dominican friar, who denounced vice and corruption not only in society but also in the Church itself, especially attacking Pope Alexander VI. He was excommunicated, imprisoned, and with two of his companions, hanged and burned. His passion for reform made him impatient of opposition and incapable of compromise, yet he was a notable figure and commands the respect of later ages. George Eliot's *Romola* portrays him.

Scarlatti, Alessandro (1659–1725), Italian musician who founded the Neapolitan school of opera. He composed over 100 operas, 200 masses, and over 700 cantatas and oratorios. His son Domenico (1685–1757) was a harpsichord virtuoso whose work influenced the evolution of the sonata. His later years were spent at the Spanish court in Madrid. See Section P.

Scarman, Lord (Leslie George Scarman) (1911–2005), Chairman, Law Commission. Author of Scarman Report on 1981 Brixton Riots.

Scheele, Carl Wilhelm (1742–86), Swedish chemist, discoverer of many chemical substances, including oxygen (c. 1773—but published in 1777 after the publication of Priestley's studies).

Schiaparelli, Giovanni Virginio (1835–1910), Italian astronomer, noted for having observed certain dark markings on the surface of the planet Mars which he called canals (recent close-range photographs show none).

B54

Schiller, Johann Christoph Friedrich von (1759–1805), German dramatist and poet, b. Marbach in Württemberg, began life as a military surgeon. His play *The Robbers* with a revolutionary theme was successful in 1782 in Mannheim. After a stay at Dresden, where he wrote *Don Carlos*, and at Jena, where he wrote a history of the Thirty Years War, he became the friend of Goethe and removed to Weimar, where he wrote *Wallenstein*, *Mary Stuart*, *The Maid of Orleans* and *William Tell*. He is a leading figure in the European romantic movement.

Schirrmann, Richard (1874–1961), German pioneer of youth hostels. A schoolmaster, in 1907 he converted his schoolroom during holidays to a dormitory. The Verband für deutsche Jugendherbergen was founded in 1913, and the International Youth Hostels Federation in 1932.

Schlegel, Friedrich von (1772–1829), German critic, b. Hanover, prominent among the founders of German Romanticism, whose revolutionary and germinating ideas influenced early 19th-cent. thought. His brother, **August Wilhelm** (1767–1845), made remarkable translations of Shakespeare, Dante, Calderon and Camões.

Schliemann, Heinrich (1822–90), German archaeologist, who conducted excavations at Troy and Mycenae. The subject of numerous biographies mostly based on his own writings which are now viewed with some scepticism.

Schmidt, Helmuth (b. 1918), German social democrat (SPD) statesman; succeeded Brandt as Chancellor of West Germany 1974–83.

Schnabel, Artur (1882–1951), American pianist of Austrian birth, regarded as a leading exponent of Beethoven's pianoforte sonatas.

Schoenberg, Arnold (1874–1951), Austrian composer of Jewish parentage who in 1933 was exiled by the Nazi regime and settled in America, teaching at Boston and Los Angeles. Among his works are the choral orchestral *Gurre-Lieder* and *Pierrot Lunaire*. *See Section P.*

Schopenhauer, Arthur (1788–1860), German philosopher, b. Danzig, important historically for his pessimism, and his doctrine that will is superior to knowledge. His chief work is *The World as Will and Idea*. He saw Hegel as a charlatan.

Schröder, Gerhard. (b. 1944), German Social Democrat. Chancellor of Germany, 1998–2005.

Schubert, Franz Peter (1797–1828), Austrian composer, b. Vienna, the son of a schoolmaster, and a contemporary of Beethoven. He wrote not only symphonies, sonatas, string quartets, choral music and masses, but also over 600 songs.

Schulz, Charles (1922–2000), the world's most popular cartoonist, creator of the *Peanuts* strip.

Schumann, Robert Alexander (1810–56), composer of the early 19th cent. German romantic school. He wrote much chamber music, four symphonies, a piano concerto, and choral music, but it is his early piano pieces and songs that give constant delight. His wife Clara (1819–96) was one of the outstanding pianists of her time.

Schweitzer, Albert (1875–1965), Alsatian medical missionary, theologian, musician and philosopher. He resigned a promising European career to found at Lambaréné in French Equatorial Africa a hospital to fight leprosy and sleeping sickness. Nobel peace prize 1952. O.M. 1955.

Scipio, Publius Cornelius (237–183 B.C.), Roman general in the second Punic War, known as Scipio Africanus the elder. **Scipio Africanus the younger** (185–129 B.C.) was an adoptive relative and an implacable opponent of Carthage.

Scott, Charles Prestwich (1846–1931), English newspaper editor. Under his editorship (1872–1929) the *Manchester Guardian* (now *The Guardian*) became a leading journal.

Scott, Sir George Gilbert (1811–78), English architect in the Gothic revival. He restored many churches and designed the Albert Memorial and the Martyrs' Memorial at Oxford.

Scott, Sir Giles Gilbert (1880–1960), English architect, grandson of above, designed the Anglican cathedral at Liverpool and planned the new Waterloo Bridge.

Scott, Robert Falcon (1868–1912), English antarctic explorer. He led two expeditions; one 1901–4 which discovered King Edward VII Land; and another 1910–12 which reached the south pole and found the Amundsen records; but while returning the party was overtaken by blizzards and perished just 11 miles from safety. *See also* Antarctic exploration, Section L. His son, **Sir Peter Scott** (1909–89), was an artist, ornithologist and pioneeer conservationist.

Scott, Sir Walter (1771–1832), Scottish novelist and poet, b. Edinburgh. He was educated for the law, but came to know and love the Border country and his interests were literary; and in 1802–3 he issued a collection of ballads, *Border Minstrelsy*. Poems such as *Marmion* and *The Lady of the Lake* followed. His novels appeared anonymously, beginning with *Waverley* in 1814; and continuing with *Guy Mannering*, *The Antiquary*, *Old Mortality*, *Rob Roy*, and *The Heart of Midlothian*. From 1819 he turned also to English history, with *Ivanhoe* and *Kenilworth*. In 1826 he became bankrupt, largely as the fault of his publishing partner.

Scriabin, Alexander (1872–1915), Russian composer and pianist, who relied to some extent on extra-musical factors such as religion, and in *Prometheus* tried to unite music and philosophy.

Seacole, Mary (1805–81), Jamaican businesswoman and nurse. Famous for her nursing of British soldiers in the Crimean War (1854–6), even though the War Office had rejected her help.

Seeley, Sir John Robert (1834–95), English historian, author of a life of Christ, *Ecce Homo.*

Segovia, Andrés (1894–1987), Spanish concert-guitarist. He adapted works by Bach, Haydn, Mozart *etc.* to the guitar.

Seifert, Richard (1910–2001), prolific but controversial architect who designed Centre Point (1966) and the NatWest Tower (1981), changing the London skyline.

Selfridge, Harry Gordon (1858–1947), American-born merchant who in 1909 opened a new style of department store in Oxford Street.

Semmelweis, Ignaz Philipp (1818–65), Hungarian obstetrician. Pioneered antiseptic methods, thus reducing the incidence of puerperal fever.

Sen, Amartya (b. 1933), Indian-born economist. Awarded 1998 Nobel Prize for Economics. Author of *Poverty and Famines* (1981). Master of Trinity College, Cambridge, 1998–2003.

Seneca, Lucius Annaeus (c. 4 B.C.–A.D. 65), Roman stoic philosopher who was a tutor to Nero, but lost favour and was sentenced to take his own life.

Senefelder, Alois (1772–1834), Bavarian inventor of lithography about 1796.

Senna, Ayrton (1960–94), Brazilian motor racing champion. The leading driver of his generation, he died in the 1994 San Marino Grand Prix at Imola.

Sentamu, John (b. 1949), Archbishop of York since 2005. First black archbishop in the UK. A strong supporter of human rights.

Severus, Lucius Septimius (146–211), Roman emperor, and a successful general. On a visit to Britain he suppressed a revolt, repaired Hadrian's Wall, and died at York.

Sévigné, Marie de Rabutin-Chantai, Marquise de (1626–96), French woman of letters. Her letters to her daughter Françoise written in an unaffected elegance of style give a moving picture of fashionable French society.

Sgambati, Giovanni (1841–1914), Italian pianist (pupil of Liszt), composer and teacher, who revived interest in classical instrumental music.

Shackleton, Sir Ernest Henry (1874–1922), British explorer, who made four antarctic expeditions; that of 1909 reached within 100 miles of the south pole. He died on his last expedition.

Shaftesbury, 7th Earl of (Anthony Ashley Cooper) (1801–85), English philanthropist largely responsible for legislation reducing the misery of the industrial revolution. He was for 40 years chairman of the Ragged Schools Union.

Shakespeare, William (1564–1616), England's greatest poet and dramatist, b. Stratford-on-Avon. Little is known of his career up to his eighteenth year, when he married Anne Hathaway. He came to London at the height of the English renaissance and soon became connected with the Globe theatre as actor and playwright. Thirty-eight plays comprise the Shakespeare canon. Thirty-six were printed in the First Folio of 1623 (the first collected edition of his dramatic works), of which eighteen had been published during his lifetime in the so-called Quartos. *Henry VI* (3 parts), *The Two Gentlemen of Verona, The Comedy of Errors, The Taming of the Shrew, Richard III, Titus Andronicus* and *Love's Labour's Lost* seem to have been the earliest, followed by *Romeo and Juliet, A Midsummer Night's Dream, Richard II* and *King*

John. Then followed *The Merchant of Venice*, *Henry IV* (2 parts), *Henry V*, *Much Ado About Nothing*, *The Merry Wives of Windsor*, and *As You Like It*. Then came some of his greatest plays: *Julius Caesar*, *Troilus and Cressida*, *Hamlet*, *Twelfth Night*, *Measure for Measure*, *All's Well that Ends Well*, *Othello*, *King Lear*, *Macbeth*, *Timon of Athens*, *Antony and Cleopatra* and *Coriolanus*. Shakespeare's career ended with *Pericles*, *Cymbeline*, *The Winter's Tale*, *The Tempest*, *King Henry VIII* and *The Two Noble Kinsmen* (often ascribed to him). In mastery of language, in understanding of character, in dramatic perception, and in skill in the use of ritual he has never been surpassed.

Sharon, Ariel (b. 1928), Israeli prime minister since March 2001. *See* Section C.

Sharp, Granville (1735–1813), English abolitionist of slavery. Founder of colony of Sierra Leone.

Shastri, Shri Lal Bahadur (1904–66), Indian politician who became prime minister of India after the death of Nehru in 1964. He died of a heart attack at the end of the Tashkent talks.

Shaw, George Bernard (1856–1950), Irish dramatist who conquered England by his wit and exposure of hypocrisy, cant, and national weaknesses, and whose individual opinions found expression in musical criticism, socialist pamphlets and plays. His plays include *Man and Superman*, *Heartbreak House*, *Back to Methuselah*, *Saint Joan*, *The Apple Cart*, and *Buoyant Billions*. In 1884 he joined the newly-born Fabian Society. Nobel prizewinner 1925.

Sheba, Queen of. *See* H24.

Shelley, Percy Bysshe (1792–1822), English poet, b. Horsham. He was a master of language and of literary form, and a passionate advocate of freedom and of new thought. Sent down from Oxford for his pamphlet *The Necessity of Atheism*, he came under the influence of William Godwin; and, after his first marriage came to an unhappy end, married the latter's daughter, Mary Wollstonecraft, herself a writer. In the same year began his friendship with Byron. His works include *The Revolt of Islam*, *The Masque of Anarchy* (an indictment of Castlereagh), *The Cenci* (a play on evil), and *Prometheus Unbound*, besides lyrics such as *To a Skylark* and *Ode to the West Wind*. He was accidentally drowned while sailing near Spezzia.

Shepard, Alan (1923–98). The first American (and the second man) to fly in space in 1961.

Sheppard, Hugh Richard (Dick) (1880–1937), Anglican clergyman and pacifist. He made St. Martin-in-the-Fields a centre of social service and also founded the Peace Pledge Union.

Sheraton, Thomas (1751–1806), English cabinetmaker, b. Stockton, whose *Cabinetmaker's Book* promoted neo-classical designs.

Sheridan, Richard Brinsley (1751–1816), British dramatist, b. Dublin. He was a brilliant writer of comedies, especially *The Rivals*, *The Duenna*, *The School for Scandal*, and *The Critic*. He acquired and rebuilt Drury Lane theatre which reopened in 1794, but was burnt down in 1809; and this, with his lack of business sense, brought him to poverty, in spite of his friends' efforts to help him. He was also in parliament.

Sherman, William Tecumseh (1820–91), American general, who served especially in the Civil War. He took part in the battles of Bull Run and Shiloh, was appointed in 1864 to the command of the southwest, and with 65,000 men marched across Georgia to the sea. In 1865 he accepted Johnston's surrender.

Sherrington, Sir Charles Scott (1857–1952), English scientist, an authority on the physiology of the nervous system. His research led to advances in brain surgery. His principal work is *Integration Action of the Nervous System* (1906). Shared with E. D. Adrian the 1932 Nobel prize.

Shirley, James (1596–1666), English dramatist. His tragedies include *The Traitor*, and his comedies *Hyde Park*. His death was hastened by the Great Fire.

Sholokhov, Mikhail Aleksandrovich (1905–84), Russian novelist, author of *And Quiet Flows the Don*. Nobel prizewinner 1965.

Shostakovich, Dimitri (1906–75), Russian composer whose music is complex, profound, and deeply significant of the Soviet age in which he lived. His works include operas, ballets, symphonies, chamber music, *etc. See* Section P.

Sibelius, Jean (1865–1957), Finnish composer imbued with national feeling. His works include seven symphonies, a violin concerto, and several tone poems, notably *Finlandia*, and some based on the poem *Kalevala*. *See* Section P.

Sickert, Walter Richard (1860–1942), British artist, b. Munich. He was influenced by Degas, and has himself influenced later painters. His *Ennui* is in the Tate Gallery.

Siddons, Sarah (1755–1831), English actress especially in tragic parts. She was daughter of the manager Roger Kemble.

Sidgwick, Henry (1838–1900), English philosopher who wrote *Methods of Ethics*, and who also promoted women's education, with the foundation of Newnham and Girton colleges at Cambridge.

Sidney, Sir Philip (1554–86), English poet and writer, best remembered for his *Arcadia*, *Apologie for Poetrie*, and *Astrophel and Stella*, all published after his death. Killed at the battle of Zutphen, where he passed a cup of water to another, saying "Thy necessity is greater than mine."

Siemens, Sir William (1823–83), German-born electrical engineer who settled in England and constructed many overland and submarine telegraphs. He was brother of **Werner von Siemens**, founder of the firm of Siemens-Halske.

Sienkiewicz, Henryk (1846–1916), Polish novelist and short-story writer; best known of his historical novels is *Quo Vadis?* Nobel prize, 1905.

Sikorski, Vladislav (1881–1943), Polish general and statesman, prime minister of the Polish government in exile (1939) and commander-in-chief of the Polish forces. Killed in an aircraft accident at Gibraltar.

Simpson, Sir James Young (1811–70), Scottish obstetrician who initiated the use of chloroform in childbirth.

Sinatra, Frank (1915–98), legendary singer and actor, a pre-eminent entertainment figure.

Sinclair, Upton (1878–1968), American novelist whose documentary novel *The Jungle* (1906) on the Chicago slaughter yards caused a sensation.

Singer, Isaac Merritt (1811–75), American mechanical engineer who improved early forms of the sewing-machine and patented a single-thread and chain-stitch machine.

Sisley, Alfred (1839–99), French impressionist painter of English origin, who painted some enchanting landscapes, *e.g. Meadows in Spring* (Tate Gallery). Influenced by Corot and Manet.

Sisulu, Walter (1912–2003), South African politician. Secretary-General of the ANC. One of Nelson Mandela's closest allies.

Sitwell, Edith (1887–1964), English poet, a great experimenter in verse forms. *Gold Coast Customs*, *Façade* (set to music by William Walton) and *Still Falls the Rain* are probably best known. She had two brothers, **Osbert** (1892–1969) and **Sacheverell** (1897–1988), both poets and critics.

Slessor, Mary (1848–1915), Scottish missionary (the 'Great Mother') in Calabar, Nigeria.

Slim, 1st Viscount (William Slim) (1891–1970), British soldier who rose from private to field-marshal. He commanded the 14th Army in Burma, was chief of the Imperial General Staff 1948–52, and governor-general of Australia 1953–60.

Sloane, Sir Hans (1660–1753), British collector, b. Ireland. He practised in London as a physician. His library of 50,000 volumes and his collection of MSS. and botanical specimens were offered under his will to the nation and formed the beginning of the British Museum.

Slowacki, Julius (1809–49), Polish romantic poet, a revolutionary; he lived in exile in Paris. His work includes the poetic dramas *Kordian*, *Balladyna* and *Lilli Weneda*, written in the style of Shakespeare; and the unfinished poem *King Spirit* which reveals his later mystical tendencies.

Smeaton, John (1724–92), English engineer; he rebuilt Eddystone lighthouse (1756–59), improved Newcomen's steam-engine, and did important work on bridges, harbours, and canals. He also invented an improved blowing apparatus for iron-smelting.

Smetana, Bedřich (1824–84), Czech composer, creator of a national style. He was principal conductor of the Prague National Theatre, for which he wrote most of his operas, including *The Bartered Bride* and *The Kiss*. Best known of his other compositions are the cycle of symphonic poems *My Country* and the string quartets *From My Life*. He became totally deaf in 1874, suffered a mental breakdown, and died in an asylum. See Section P.

Smiles, Samuel (1812–1904), Scottish writer, b. Haddington, in early life a medical practitioner, remembered for *Self Help* (1859), and his biographies of engineers of the industrial revolution.

Smith, Adam (1723–90), Scottish economist, b. Kirkcaldy. In Edinburgh he published *Moral Sentiments*. Later he moved to London, and his *Wealth of Nations* (1776) is the first serious work in political economy.

Smith, Sir Grafton Eliot (1871–1937), Australian anatomist who researched the mammalian brain. His works include *The Evolution of Man*.

Smith, John (1580–1631), English adventurer who in 1605 went on a colonising expedition to Virginia and was saved from death by the Red Indian Pocahontas.

Smith, John (1938–94), leader of the Labour Party, 1992-94. His much-respected, modernising leadership was ended by his untimely death. He is buried on the island of Iona.

Smith, Joseph (1805–44), American founder of the Mormons. He claimed that the *Book of Mormon* was revealed to him. In 1838 feeling against the Mormons culminated in a rising and Smith was murdered. He was succeeded by Brigham Young. See **Mormonism, Section J**.

Smith, Sydney (1771–1845), Anglican divine and journalist, who founded the *Edinburgh Review* and supported Catholic emancipation.

Smith, William (1760–1839), English surveyor and canal-maker, the first to map the rock strata of England and to identify the fossils peculiar to each layer.

Smith, Sir William Alexander (1854–1914), Scottish founder of the Boys' Brigade (1883), the oldest national organisation for boys in Britain.

Smith, William Robertson (1846–94), Scottish biblical scholar whose "Bible" contribution to the 9th edition of *The Encyclopaedia Britannica* resulted in an unsuccessful prosecution for heresy.

Smollett, Tobias George (1721–71), Scottish novelist whose work is noted for satire and coarse humour. His main novels are *Roderick Random*, *Peregrine Pickle*, and *Humphrey Clinker*.

Smuts, Jan Christian (1870–1950), South African statesman and soldier. B. in Cape Colony, during the Boer War he fought on the Boer side. He was premier of the Union 1919–24, 1939–48, and worked for cooperation within the Commonwealth and in the world, but his party was defeated in 1948 by Malan's Nationalists.

Smyth, Ethel Mary (1858–1944), English composer and suffragette. Her main works are operas (*The Wreckers* and *The Boatswain's Mate*) and a *Mass in D*.

Snow, Baron (Charles Percy Snow) (1905–80), English physicist and novelist, author of the essay *The Two Cultures and the Scientific Revolution*, and *Strangers and Brothers* (11 vols.).

Snyders, Frans (1597–1657), Flemish still-life and animal painter who studied under Breughel.

Soane, Sir John (1753–1837), English architect who designed the Bank of England. He left the nation his house and library in Lincoln's Inn Fields (Soane Museum). 'The architect's architect'.

Sobers, Sir Garfield (b. 1936), West Indies and Nottinghamshire cricketer who ranks as one of the greatest all-rounders. Knighted 1975.

Socinus or **Sozzini Laelius** (1525–62), Italian founder of the sect of Socinians, with his nephew **Faustus** (1539–1604). Their teachings resemble those of Unitarians.

Socrates (470–399 B.C.), Greek philosopher and intellectual leader, was the son of a sculptor of Athens. He distinguished himself in three campaigns (Potidaea, Delium, and Amphipolis). Returning to Athens, he devoted himself to study and intellectual enquiry, attracting many followers; through these, especially Xenophon and Plato, we know of his teachings, for he wrote nothing. In 399 B.C. he was charged with impiety and with corrupting the young, found guilty, and accordingly died by drinking hemlock; see Plato's *Apology, Crito*, and *Phaedo*.

Soddy, Frederick (1877–1956), English chemist, who in Glasgow about 1912 laid the foundation of the isotope theory. Nobel prizewinner 1921.

Solomon (King of Israel). See **Section H**.

Solon (638–558 B.C.), Athenian lawgiver, who in a time of economic distress cancelled outstanding debts, and introduced some democratic changes.

Solti, Sir Georg (1912–97), one of the great conductors of his time. Music director of Covent Garden and Chicago Symphony Orchestra.

Solzhenitsyn, Alexander Isayevich (b. 1918), Russian novelist, b. Rostov-on-Don; author of *One Day in the Life of Ivan Denisovich*, a documentary novel depicting life in one of Stalin's prison camps where he spent many years of his life. He was expelled from the Soviet Writers' Union in 1969, and from his country in 1974, returning in 1994. Nobel prize 1970. Elected to Russian Academy of Sciences, 1997. He has continued to criticize western materialism and Russian bureaucracy and secularization.

Somerset, Duke of (Edward Seymour) (1506 52), lord protector of England in the time of the young Edward VI, but he fell from power and was executed.

Soper, Lord (Donald Soper) (1903–98), Methodist preacher and campaigner for socialism.

Sophocles (495–406 B.C.), Athenian dramatist, who was awarded the prize over Aeschylus in 468. Of over a hundred plays of his, the only extant ones are *Oedipus the King, Oedipus at Colonus Antigone, Electra, Trachiniae, Ajax, Philoctetes.*

Sopwith, Sir Thomas (1888–1989), British designer of 'Sopwith Camel' biplane.

Sorel, Georges (1847–1922), French advocate of revolutionary syndicalism, author of *Reflections on Violence* (1905). The irrational aspects of his philosophy (derived from Bergson) appealed to Mussolini and the Fascists.

Soult, Nicolas Jean de Dieu (1769–1851), French general who fought under Napoleon in Switzerland and Italy, at Austerlitz, and in Spain.

Sousa, John Philip (1854–1932), American bandmaster and composer of some stirring marches.

Southey, Robert (1774–1843), English poet and historian. In 1803 he settled near Coleridge at Keswick, and in 1813 became poet laureate. His best work was in prose: histories of Brazil and of the Peninsular War; lives of Nelson, Wesley, *etc.*

Southwell, Robert (1561–95), English poet and Jesuit martyr, beatified 1920. His poems include *The Burning Babe.*

Spaak, Paul Henri (1899–1972), Belgian statesman and advocate of European Union. Secretary-general of NATO, 1957–61.

Spark, Dame Muriel (1918–2006), Scotland's most important modern novelist. Her most famous work is *The Prime of Miss Jean Brodie* (1961).

Spartacus (d. 71 B.C.), Thracian rebel. A Roman slave and gladiator in Capua, he escaped and headed a slave insurrection, routing several Roman armies, but was defeated and killed by Crassus.

Speke, John Hanning (1827–64), British explorer. In 1858 he discovered the Victoria Nyanza; in 1860 with J. A. Grant traced the Nile flowing out of it.

Spence, Sir Basil Urwin (1907–76), Scottish architect, mainly known for the new Coventry cathedral, for Hampstead civic centre and for university architecture. O.M. 1962.

Spencer, Herbert (1820–1903), English philosopher. B. Derby, he was at first a civil engineer, then a journalist (sub-editor of the *Economist*), when he wrote *Social Statics*. He coined the phrase (1852) "the survival of the fittest" and his *Principles of Psychology* (1855), published four years before Darwin's *Origin of Species*, expounded doctrines of evolution. Author of the ten-volume *Synthetic Philosophy.*

Spencer, Sir Stanley (1891–1959), English artist of visionary power. His two pictures of the *Resurrection* are in the Tate Gallery. He also painted Cookham regatta.

Spender, Sir Stephen (1909–95), poet and critic, first made his name as one of the politically committed poets of the 1930s. He was co-editor of *Encounter* 1953–67 and Professor of English, University College, London 1970–77.

Spengler, Oswald (1880–1936), German historicist who held that every culture is destined to a waxing and waning life cycle and that the West European culture was entering its period of decline. His principal work is *The Decline of the West*. His views prepared the way for national socialism.

Spenser, Edmund (1552–99), English poet, b. London and educated at Cambridge. His *Shepheards Calendar* appeared in 1579. In 1580 he went to Ireland as the lord deputy's secretary, and later acquired Kilcolman castle, where he wrote most of his main work, *The Faerie Queene*. His castle was burnt in an insurrection in 1598, when he returned to London. He is called "the poet's poet."

Spinoza, Baruch (1632–77), Dutch philosopher, b. Amsterdam, whose parents came to Holland from Portugal to escape the Inquisition. An independent thinker, his criticism of the Scriptures led to his being excommunicated from the synagogue. He supported himself by grinding and polishing lenses. He owed much to Descartes but was mainly concerned with religion and virtue. His philosophical theories are set out in the *Ethics* (published posthumously).

Spock, Dr Benjamin (1903–98). Paediatrician and child psychologist. Author of *Baby and Child Care* (1946).

Spofforth, Reginald (1770–1827), English writer of glees, including *Hail, Smiling Morn*.

Spurgeon, Charles Haddon (1834–92), English Baptist who preached at the vast Metropolitan Tabernacle, London, from 1861 (burnt down 1898).

Staël, Anne Louise, Baronne de Staël-Holstein (1766–1817), French writer. Daughter of the finance minister, Necker, she married the Swedish ambassador, and kept a salon. Her *Lettres sur Rousseau* appeared in 1788. After the revolution she lived partly abroad, partly in France, and after a visit to Italy wrote her novel *Corinne* (1807).

Stalin (Joseph Vissarionovich Djugashvili) (1879–1953), Soviet dictator who for nearly 30 years was leader of the Russian people. He originally studied at Tiflis for the priesthood, but became an active revolutionary and took part in the civil war after 1917. After Lenin's death, he ousted Trotsky and became the outstanding figure. He modernised agriculture on socialist lines by ruthless means, and his series of five-year plans from 1929 made Russia an industrial power. His regime carried out mass murder and the ruthless purges of the 1930s. On the German invasion in 1941 he assumed military leadership; and later attended Allied war conferences. After his death a gradual process of 'de-Stalinisation' began

Stanford, Sir Charles Villiers (1852–1924), Irish composer of instrumental, choral, operatic, and other music.

Stanley, Sir Henry Morton (1841–1904), British explorer, b. Denbigh. He fought for the Confederates in the American Civil War. He then became a correspondent for the *New York Herald*, was commissioned to find Livingstone, and did so in 1871 at Ujiji, and with him explored Lake Tanganyika. In 1879 he founded the Congo Free State. His works include *Through the Dark Continent* and an *Autobiography*.

Stark, Freya Madeline (1893–1993), British writer and explorer of the Arab world.

Stead, William Thomas (1849–1912), editor of *Pall Mall Gazette*. Campaigned against child prostitution.

Steel, Lord (Sir David Steel) (b. 1938), Liberal (Lib. Dem.) MP, 1965–97. Leader, Liberal Party, 1976–88. First Presiding Officer (Speaker) of Scottish Parliament, 1999–2003.

Steele, Sir Richard (1672–1729), British essayist, b. Dublin. He founded the *Tatler* (1709–11), to which Addison also contributed, and later the *Spectator* (1711–12) and the *Guardian* (1713).

Steen, Jan (1626–79), Dutch genre painter, b. Leiden, son of a brewer. *The Music Lesson* and *Skittle Alley* are in the National Gallery, the *Lute Player* in the Wallace collection.

Steer, Philip Wilson (1860–1942), English painter, especially of landscapes and of portraits.

Stefansson, Vilhjalmur (1879–1962), Canadian arctic explorer of Icelandic parentage; author of *Unsolved Mysteries of the Arctic*.

Stein, Sir Aurel (1862–1943), British archaeologist, b. Budapest. He explored Chinese Turkestan.

Steiner, Rudolf (1861 1925), founder of anthroposophy. *See Section J*.

Stendhal, pseudonym of Marie Henri Beyle (1783–1842), French novelist, b. Grenoble. He was with Napoleon's army in the Russian campaign of 1812, spent several years in Italy, and after the revolution of 1830 was appointed consul at Trieste, and afterwards at Civitavecchia. In his plots he recreates historical and social events with imaginative realism and delineates character with searching psychological insight. His main works are *Le Rouge et le Noir*, and *La Chartreuse de Parme*.

Stephen (1105–54), usurped the crown of England from Henry I's daughter in 1135; and, after anarchy, retained it till his death.

Stephen, Sir Leslie (1832–1904), English writer, critic, and biographer. He edited the *Cornhill Magazine* (1871–82), and the *Dictionary of National Biography* (1882–91). Father of Virginia Woolf.

Stephenson, George (1781–1848), English engineer; a locomotive designer, b. at Wylam near Newcastle, a colliery fireman's son. As enginewright at Killingworth colliery he made his first locomotive in 1814 to haul coal from mines. He and his son Robert built the *Locomotion* for the Stockton and Darlington Railway (1825), the first locomotive for a public railway. His *Rocket* at 30 miles an hour won the prize of £500 in 1829 offered by the Liverpool and Manchester Railway. He also discovered the principle on which the miners' safety lamp was based. First president of the Institution of Mechanical Engineers.

Stephenson, Robert (1803–59), English engineer, son of the above, engineered railway lines in England and abroad, and built many bridges including the Menai and Conway tubular bridges.

Sterne, Laurence (1713–68), English novelist and humorist. His main works are *Tristram Shandy* and *A Sentimental Journey*. He led a wandering and unconventional life, dying in poverty.

Stevenson, Adlai (1900–65), American politician, an efficient governor of Illinois, 1949–53; ambassador to the UN, 1960–5, and unsuccessful presidential challenger to Eisenhower 1952 and 1956.

Stevenson, Robert (1772–1850), Scottish engineer and builder of lighthouses, who invented "intermittent" and "flashing" lights.

Stevenson, Robert Louis (1850–94), Scottish author, b. Edinburgh. He suffered from ill-health and eventually settled in Samoa. His main works are *Travels with a Donkey*, *Treasure Island*, *Kidnapped*, *Dr. Jekyll and Mr. Hyde*, and *The Master of Ballantrae*.

Stiglitz, Joseph Eugene (b. 1943), American Professor of Economics. Author of such influential works as *Globalization and its Discontents* (2000), *The Roaring Nineties* (2003) *etc.* Nobel Prize for Economics, 2001.

Stinnes, Hugo (1870–1924), German industrialist who built up a huge coalmining, iron and steel, and transport business, and later entered politics.

Stockton, Earl of (Harold Macmillan) (1894–1986), British Conservative statesman, prime minister 1957 63; During his premiership came the crises of the Berlin Wall and the Cuban missiles (in which his personal diplomacy played an influential role), de Gaulle's veto to our entry into Europe, the signing of the Partial Test-Ban Treaty and his "wind of change" speech which hailed African independence. Created Earl of Stockton, 1984.

Stoker, Bram (Abraham Stoker) (1847–1912), Irish author of the horror story *Dracula* and *Personal Reminiscences of Henry Irving*.

Stokes, Sir George Gabriel (1819–1903), Irish mathematician and physicist to whom is due the modern theory of viscous fluids and the discovery that rays beyond the violet end of the spectrum (the ultra-violet rays) produce fluorescence in certain substances.

Stopes, Marie Carmichael (1880–1958), English pioneer advocate of birth control. Her *Married Love* appeared in 1918, and she pioneered birth control clinics.

Stoppard, Sir Tom (b. 1937), playwright, whose witty and linguistically inventive plays include *Rosencrantz and Guildenstern are Dead* (1966), *Jumpers* (1972), *Arcadia* (1993) and *The Invention of Love* (1997). Order of Merit (2000).

Stowe, Harriet Beecher (1811–96), American author of *Uncle Tom's Cabin* (1852), written to expose slavery.

Strachey, John St. Loe (1901–63), English Labour politician and writer. He held office 1945 51.

Stradivari, Antonio (1644–1737), Italian maker of violins, b. Cremona, first in his art.

Strafford, 1st Earl of (Thomas Wentworth) (1593–1641), English statesman. He supported Charles I with a "thorough" policy, both as president of the north and as lord deputy in Ireland, where he introduced flax. His efficiency made him a special target when parliament met, and he was impeached and executed.

Strauss, David Friedrich (1808–74), German theologian, whose *Life of Jesus* attempted to prove that the gospels are based on myths.

Strauss, family of Viennese musicians. **Johann Strauss** (1804–49), the elder, was a composer of dance music, who with Joseph Lanner established the Viennese waltz tradition. His son, **Johann Strauss** (1825–99), the younger, although not so good a violinist or conductor as his father, was the composer of over 400 waltzes, which include *The Blue Danube* and *Tales from the Vienna Woods*. Two of his brothers, **Josef Strauss** (1827–70) and **Eduard Strauss** (1835–1916) were also composers and conductors.

Strauss, Richard (1864–1949), German composer and conductor, the son of a horn player in the opera orchestra at Munich. He succeeded von Bülow as court musical director at Meiningen. His works include the operas *Salome*, *Elektra*, and *Der Rosenkavalier*, the symphonic poems *Don Juan*, *Till Eulenspiegel*, and *Don Quixote*, and many songs. *See* **Section P.**

Stravinsky, Igor (1882–1971), Russian composer and conductor, pupil of Rimsky-Korsakov. His ballets. *The Fire Bird* (1910). *Petrushka* (1911), representative of his early romantic style, and the revolutionary *The Rite of Spring*, which caused a furore in 1913, were written for the ballet impresario Diaghilev. He adopted a neo-classical style in later works, for example, in the ballets *Pulcinella* and *Apollo Musagetes* and the opera-oratorio *Oedipus Rex*. He brought new vigour and freedom to rhythm and younger composers have been much influenced by his music. He became a French citizen in 1934 and a US citizen in 1945. *See* **Section P.**

Straw, Jack. *See* **D18.**

Strindberg, Johan August (1840–1912), Swedish writer of intense creative energy. His work is subjective and reflects his personal conflicts. He produced some 55 plays as well as novels, stories, poems, and critical essays. *Lucky Peter*, *Gustav Adolf*, *Till Damascus*, *The Father*, *Miss Julie* are some of his plays.

Suckling, Sir John (1609–42), English poet, author of *Why so pale and wan?* He invented cribbage.

Sudermann, Hermann (1857–1928), German writer of plays and novels, including *Frau Sorge* (translated as Dame Care).

Suharto, General (b. 1921). Authoritarian president of Indonesia from 1968 to 1998.

Sukarno, Ahmed (1901–70). The founding father of Indonesia. An authoritarian president, 1950–68.

Sulaiman the Magnificent (1494–1566), sultan of Turkey, conqueror, and patron of art and learning, who dominated the eastern Mediterranean but failed to capture Malta.

Sulla (138–78 B.C.) Roman general, he supported the oligarchy of the Senate against the demagogues Marius (Julius Caesar's uncle) and Cinna and established himself dictator in 82 B.C.

Sullivan, Sir Arthur Seymour (1842–1900), famous composer, mainly known for the music he wrote for light operas with W. S. Gilbert as librettist, especially *The Pirates of Penzance*, *Patience*, *The Mikado*, *The Yeomen of the Guard* and *The Gondoliers*. He also wrote sacred music, some of which remains very popular. He and George Grove discovered Schubert's lost *Rosamunde* music.

Sully, Maximilien de Béthune, Duc de (1560–1641), French statesman, finance minister to Henry IV.

Summerson, Sir John (1904–92), the most distinguished British architectural historian of his generation. Recipient of Royal Gold Medal for Architecture (1976). Most often associated with John Nash and the Georgian period. Longest-serving Curator of Sir John Soane's Museum.

Sumner, Mary (1828–1921), founder of the Mothers' Union to help promote the virtues of family life.

Sun Yat Sen (1867–1925), Chinese revolutionary, idealist and humanitarian. He graduated in medicine at Hong Kong, but after a rising failed in 1895 he lived abroad, planning further attempts, which succeeded in 1911 when the Manchus were ousted and he became president.

Sutherland, Graham Vivian (1903–80), British artist. He painted the 80th birthday portrait of Winston Churchill for parliament, and designed the tapestry for Coventry cathedral. O.M. 1960.

Sutherland, Dame Joan (b. 1926), Australian operatic soprano who achieved international fame (*e.g.* in Handel's Samson).

Suu Kyi, Aung San (b. *c.* 1945), Opposition leader in Myanmar (Burma). Nobel Peace Prize, 1991.

Swan, Sir Joseph Wilson (1829–1914), British scientist who shares with Edison the invention of the incandescent electric lamp.

Swedenborg, Emanuel (1689–1772), Swedish author of *Arcana Coelestia*, *The Apocalypse Revealed*, *Four Preliminary Doctrines*, and *The True Christian Religion*. His works became the scriptures of his followers, the Swedenborgians.

Sweelinck, Jan Pieterszoon (1562–1621), Dutch organist and composer of sacred music. In his fugues he made independent use of the pedals, and prepared the way for Bach. *See* **Section P.**

Swift, Jonathan (1667–1745), English satirist, b. Dublin of English parents. He crossed to England in 1688 to become secretary to Sir William Temple, and took Anglican orders, but did not obtain promotion. His *Tale of a Tub* and *The Battle of the Books* appeared in 1704. At first active in Whig politics, he became Tory in 1710, writing powerful tracts such as *Conduct of the Allies* (1711). In 1714 he retired to Ireland as Dean of St. Patrick's. His devoted women friends followed him—Hester Johnson (d. 1728), the Stella of his *Journal*, and Esther Vanhomrigh (d. 1723), the Vanessa of his poetry. Here he wrote *Gulliver's Travels* (1726) and *The Drapier's Letters*.

Swinburne, Algernon Charles (1837–1909), English poet and critic. He first won attention with a play, *Atalanta in Calydon*, in 1865, followed by *Poems and Ballads*. Later followed *Songs before Sunrise*, *Bothwell*, and *Mary Stuart*.

Swithin, St. (d. 862), English saint, bishop of Winchester. Violent rain for 40 days fell in 971 when his body was to be removed on 15 July to the new cathedral (hence the superstition).

Symonds, John Addington (1840–93), English author who wrote on the Italian Renaissance.

Synge, John Millington (1871–1909), Irish poet and playwright, author of *Riders to the Sea* and *The Playboy of the Western World*.

T

Tacitus, Gaius Cornelius (*c.* 55–120), Roman historian. His chief works are a life of his father-in-law Agricola, and his *Histories* and *Annals*.

Taft, William Howard (1857–1930), 27th President of the United States (1909–13). A Republican, he supported the policies of his predecessor Theodore Roosevelt. He later served on the US Supreme Court as Chief Justice (1921–30), the only man ever to hold both offices.

Tagore, Rabindranath (1861–1941), Indian poet and philosopher who tried to blend east and west. Nobel prize 1913 (first Asian recipient).

Talbot, William Henry Fox (1800–77), English pioneer of photography which he developed independently of Daguerre. He also deciphered the cuneiform inscriptions at Nineveh.

Talleyrand-Périgord, Charles Maurice de (1754–1838), French politician and diplomat, led a mission to England in 1792 and was foreign minister from 1797 until 1807. He represented France at the Congress of Vienna.

Tallis, Thomas (*c.* 1510–85), English musician, with Byrd joint organist to the chapel royal under Elizabeth. He has been called the father of English Cathedral choral music.

Tamerlane (Timur the Lame) (1336–1405), Mongol conqueror. Ruler of Samarkand, he conquered Iran, Transcaucasia, Iraq, Armenia, and Georgia, and invaded India and Syria. He defeated the Turks at Angora, but died marching towards China. A ruthless conqueror, he was also a patron of literature and the arts. The line of rulers descended from him are the Timurids. He is the subject of a play by Marlowe.

Tarquinius: two kings of Rome came from this Etruscan family; **Lucius the Elder** (d. 578 B.C.); and **Lucius Superbus**, or the proud, (d. 510 B.C.) whose tyranny provoked a successful rising and brought an end to the monarchy.

Tartini, Giuseppe (1692–1770), Italian violinist, who wrote *Trillo del Diavolo*. He discovered the "third sound" resulting from two notes sounded together, a scientific explanation of which was later given by Helmholtz.

Tasman, Abel Janszoon (1603–59), Dutch navigator despatched by Van Diemen. He discovered Tasmania or Van Diemen's Land, and New Zealand, in 1642.

Tasso, Torquato (1544–95), Italian epic poet, b.

Sorrento, author of *Gerusalemme Liberata*. He also wrote plays, *Aminta* and *Torrismondo*.

Tawney, Richard Henry (1880–1962), British historian, b. Calcutta, pioneer of adult education, and leader of socialist thought—the first critic of the affluent society.

Taylor, Alan John Percivale (1906–90), English historian. Broadcaster, lecturer and radical. Author of such noted works as *English History, 1914–45* and *The Origins of the Second World War*.

Taylor, Sir Geoffrey Ingram (1886–1975), British scientist, noted for his work on aerodynamics, hydrodynamics, *etc.* O.M. 1969.

Taylor, Jeremy (1613–67), English divine, b. Cambridge, author of many religious works, of which the chief are *Holy Living* and *Holy Dying*.

Taylor, Zachary (1784–1850), 12th President of the United States (1849–50). Formerly commander of the American forces during the Mexican War of 1846–48, he opposed the extension of slavery into the western territories of the USA.

Tchaikovsky, Peter Ilyich (1840–93), Russian composer. His music is melodious and emotional and he excelled in several branches of composition. Among his works are the operas *Eugene Onegin* and *The Queen of Spades* (both from stories by Pushkin), symphonies, including the *Little Russian* and the *Pathétique*, ballets, including *Swan Lake*, *The Sleeping Beauty*, and *The Nutcracker*, the fantasies *Romeo and Juliet*, and *Francesca da Rimini*, the piano concerto in B flat minor, the violin concerto in D, and numerous songs. *See* Section P.

Tedder, 1st Baron (Arthur William Tedder) (1890–1967), British air marshal. From 1940 he reorganised the Middle East Air Force and later became deputy supreme commander under Eisenhower for the invasion of Europe.

Teilhard de Chardin, Pierre (1881–1955), French palæontologist and religious philosopher. He went on palæontological expeditions in Asia, but his research did not conform to Jesuit orthodoxy, and his main works were published posthumously, *The Phenomenon of Man* and *Le Milieu Divin*.

Telemann, Georg Philipp (1681–1767), German composer, b. Magdeburg. His vitality and originality of form are appreciated today after a long period of neglect. His works include church music, 46 passions and over 40 operas, oratorios *etc.*

Telford, Thomas (1757–1834), Scottish engineer, originally a stonemason. He built bridges (two over the Severn and the Menai suspension bridge), canals (the Ellesmere and Caledonian canals), roads, and docks.

Tell, William, legendary Swiss patriot, reputedly required by the Austrian governor Gessler to shoot an apple from his son's head, and the subject of a play by Schiller. The story is late, but the Swiss confederation did first arise in the 14th cent. with Schwyz, Uri, and Unterwalden.

Temple, Frederick (1821–1902), English divine. He was headmaster of Rugby, 1857–69, and archbishop of Canterbury, 1897–1902.

Temple, William (1881–1944), English ecclesiastic, son of above, was a leading moral force in social matters and a worker for œcumenism. He was headmaster of Repton, 1910–14, and became archbishop of Canterbury in 1942.

Temple, Sir William (1628–99), English diplomat and writer, was instrumental in bringing about the marriage of Princess Mary with William of Orange. Swift was his secretary.

Templewood, 1st Viscount (Samuel John Gurney Hoare) (1880–1959), British Conservative politician. He piloted the India Act through the Commons while secretary for India, 1931–5; and as foreign secretary he negotiated an abortive pact with Laval.

Teniers, David, the elder (1582–1649), and **the younger** (1610–94), Flemish painters of rural life and landscape. The elder lived at Antwerp and the younger at Brussels.

Tenniel, Sir John (1820–1914), English artist, principal cartoonist for *Punch* 1864–1901 and illustrator of Lewis Carroll's *Alice* books.

Tennyson, 1st Baron (Alfred Tennyson) (1809–92), English poet-laureate, b. Somersby, Lincs. A master of language, his publications extended over 60 years, mirroring much of his age. *In Memoriam* reflects his grief for his friend Arthur Hallam. Apart from his lyrics, his longer works include *The Princess*, *Maud*, *Idylls of the King*,

and *Enoch Arden*.

Tenzing Norgay Sherpa (1914–86), Nepalese sherpa. On his seventh Everest trip reached the summit with Edmund Hillary (*q.v.*) on 29 May 1953.

Terence, Publius Terentius Afer (*c.* 184–159 B.C.), a Latin poet and dramatist, an African (Berber), who rose from the position of a slave.

Teresa, Mother (1910–97), Albanian-born Catholic whose work in Calcutta won world-wide acclaim. Beatified, 2003.

Teresa, St. (1515–82), influential Spanish religious reformer and writer, b. Avila, a woman of boundless energy and spiritual strength. She entered the Carmelite order about 1534, established a reformed order in 1562 (St. Joseph's, Avila), and also founded, with the help of St. John of the Cross, houses for friars. Her writings include *The Way of Perfection* and *The Interior Castle*.

Terry, Ellen Alice (Mrs. James Carew) (1848–1928), English actress, especially in Shakespearean parts with Sir Henry Irving, and in the plays of her friend Bernard Shaw.

Tertullian Quintus (*c.* 160–220), Carthaginian theologian whose works, especially *Apologeticum*, have profoundly influenced Christian thought.

Tesla, Nikolai (1856–1943), Yugoslav physicist and inventor; went to America 1883; pioneer in high-tension electricity.

Tettrazzini, Luisa (1871–1940), Italian soprano, especially successful in *Lucia di Lammermoor*.

Tetzel, John (*c.* 1465–1519), German Dominican preacher, whose sale of indulgences for St. Peter's building fund provoked Luther.

Thackeray, William Makepeace (1811–63), English novelist, b. Calcutta, author of *Vanity Fair*, *Pendennis*, *Esmond*, *The Newcomes*, *The Virginians*, *Philip*, and *Lovel the Widower*. He edited the *Cornhill Magazine* from the first number in 1860, his most notable contributions being *Roundabout Papers*. He also wrote *Yellowplush Papers* and *The Book of Snobs* and lectured on *The English Humorists* and *The Four Georges*.

Thales of Miletus (*c.* 624–565 B.C.), earliest of the Greek scientists, he created a sensation by his prediction of an eclipse of the sun, which made visible at Miletus in 585 B.C. He saw water as the basis of all material things, and in his mathematical work enunciated natural laws.

Thant, Sithu U (1909–74), Burmese diplomat; secretary-general of the UN 1962–72.

Thatcher, Baroness (Margaret Hilda Thatcher) (b. 1925), leader of the Conservative Party 1975–90; prime minister, 1979–90; first woman to lead a western democracy; secured landslide victory, June 1983; MP (Finchley), 1959–92. Historic third successive election victory, June 1987. On 3 Jan 1988 became longest serving P.M. since Asquith. By 1990 she faced increasing unpopularity, reflected in a challenge to her leadership. Deserted by many in her party, she resigned on 28 November 1990. Created Baroness Thatcher of Kesteven, 1992. Order of the Garter (1995).

Themistocles (*c.* 523–458 B.C.), Athenian soldier and statesman. He fortified the harbour of Piraeus and created a navy, defeating the Persians at Salamis in 480 B.C. He prepared the way for later greatness, but fell from power and died in exile.

Theocritus (*c.* 310–250 B.C.), Greek poet, especially of pastoral subjects. His short poems came to be called *Idylls*.

Theodoric the Great (455–526), King of the East Goths, who conquered Italy. Himself an Arian, he practised toleration, and his long reign was peaceful and prosperous.

Theodosius the Great (346–95), Roman emperor of the East (the Empire being divided in 364). He was baptised as a Trinitarian, issuing edicts against the Arians, and after a judicial massacre at Thessalonica he did penance to (St.) Ambrose.

Theophrastus (*c.* 372–287 B.C.), Greek philosopher, who succeeded Aristotle as teacher at Athens and inherited his library. Best known for his botanical works and his *Characters* (moral studies).

Thesiger, Sir Wilfred (1910–2003), English explorer of Arabia's Empty Quarter.

Thierry, Augustin (1795–1856), French historian, known for his *History of the Norman Conquest*.

Thiers, Louis Adolphe (1797–1877), French statesman and historian. After a varied political career, he became president in 1871, helping to revive France after defeat. He wrote a history of the Revolution.

Thomas, Dylan (1914–53), Welsh poet, whose highly individual *Eighteen Poems* (1934) brought him instant recognition. There followed *Twenty-five Poems* and *Deaths and Entrances*. *Under Milk Wood*, a play for voices, has more general appeal.

Thompson, Sir D'Arcy Wentworth (1860–1948), Scottish zoologist whose *On Growth and Form* (1917) has influenced biological science.

Thomson, Sir George Paget (1892–1975), English physicist, son of Sir J. J. Thomson; author of *The Atom, Theory and Practice of Electron Diffraction, The Inspiration of Science.* Nobel prizewinner 1937.

Thomson, James (1700–48), Scottish poet who wrote *The Seasons* and *The Castle of Indolence.*

Thomson, James (1834–82), poet and essayist, b. near Glasgow. Wrote *The City Of Dreadful Night.*

Thomson, Sir Joseph John (1856–1940), English physicist and mathematician, leader of a group of researchers at the Cavendish laboratory, Cambridge. He established in 1897 that cathode-rays were moving particles whose speed and specific charge could be measured. He called them corpuscles but the name was changed to electrons. This work was followed up by the study of positive rays which led to the discovery of isotopes, whose existence had earlier been suggested by Soddy. Nobel prize 1906.

Thoreau, Henry David (1817–62), American essayist and nature-lover, who rebelled against society and lived for a time in a solitary hut. His chief work is *Walden.* He was a friend of Emerson.

Thorez, Maurice (1900–64), French communist leader from 1930 and after the second world war.

Thorndike, Dame Sybil (1882–1976), English actress. She made her début in 1904, and played in Greek tragedies, in the plays of Shakespeare and Shaw, and in Grand Guignol. Her husband was Sir Lewis Casson.

Thornycroft, Sir William Hamo (1850–1925), English sculptor, whose works include a statue of General Gordon in Trafalgar Square.

Thorpe, Sir Thomas Edward (1845–1925), English chemist who researched in inorganic chemistry and with his friend Arthur Rücker made a magnetic survey of the British Isles.

Thorwaldsen, Bertel (1770–1844), Danish sculptor. Works include the Cambridge statue of Byron.

Thucydides (*c.* 460–399 B.C.), Greek historian, especially of the Peloponnesian War in which he himself fought. He was not merely a chronicler, but saw the significance of events and tried to give an impartial account. The speeches attributed by him to leaders include the beautiful funeral oration of Pericles.

Tiberius, Claudius (42 B.C.–A.D. 37), Roman emperor who succeeded Augustus. His early reign was successful but his later years were marked by tragedy and perhaps insanity. He is the Tiberius of Luke 3.1.

Tiepolo, Giambattista (1696–1770), one of the greatest painters in Venetian history. A flamboyant Rococo artist.

Tillett, Benjamin (1860–1943), English trade-union leader, especially of a dockers' strike in 1889 and a transport-workers' strike in 1911.

Tillotson, John (1630–94), English divine, a noted preacher. Archbishop of Canterbury, 1691–94.

Tindal, Matthew (1655–1733), English deist, author of *Christianity as old as the Creation.*

Tintoretto (1518–94), Venetian painter whose aim it was to unite the colouring of Titian with the drawing of Michelangelo. His numerous paintings, mostly of religious subjects, were executed with great speed, some of them on enormous canvases. His *Origin of the Milky Way* is in the National Gallery. His name was Jacopo Robusti, and he was called Il Tintoretto (little dyer) after his father's trade.

Tippett, Sir Michael Kemp (1905–98), English composer whose works include the operas *The Mid-summer Marriage, King Priam,* and *Knot Garden,* and the song-cycles *Boyhood's End* and *The Heart's Assurance.* O.M. 1983. *See* Section P.

Titian (Tiziano Vecelli) (*c.* 1487–1576), Venetian painter. He studied under the Bellinis and was influenced by Giorgione, for example, in his frescoes at Padua. His mature style is one of dynamic composition and full colour, as in his *Bacchus and Ariadne* (National Gallery). Among his principal works are *Sacred and Profane Love* (Borghese Gallery, Rome), and some in the Prado. A giant of European painting.

Tito (Josip Broz) (1892–1980), Yugoslav leader, b. Kumrovec. In 1941 he organised partisan forces against the Axis invaders, liberated his country, and carried through a communist revolution. In 1945 he became the first communist prime minister and in 1953 president. He successfully pursued an independent line.

Titus (A.D. 39–81), Roman emperor, son of Vespasian, ended the Jewish war with the capture of Jerusalem. He completed the Colosseum.

Tizard, Sir Henry Thomas (1885–1959), English scientist and administrator. He was chairman of the Tizard Committee that encouraged the birth of radar before 1939. He was chief scientific adviser to the government, 1947–52.

Tocqueville, Alexis, Comte de (1805–59), French liberal politician and historian, author of *Democracy in America,* still relevant reading.

Todd, 1st Baron (Alexander Robertus Todd) (1907–97), Scottish biochemist, noted for his work on the structure of DNA. Nobel prizewinner 1957; Pres. Royal Society 1975. O.M. (1977).

Todd, Sir Garfield (1908–2002), Rhodesian missionary and statesman. As Prime Minister of Southern Rhodesia supported black rule.

Tolkien, John Ronald Reuel (1892–1973). Academic and writer. Professor of English language and literature at Oxford, 1945–59. Famous as creator of *The Hobbit* (1937), *The Lord of the Rings* (3 vols, 1954–5) and *The Silmarillion* (1977).

Tolstoy, Leo Nikolayevich, Count (1828–1910), Russian writer and philosopher, b. Yasnaya Polyana. Of noble family, he entered the army and fought in the Crimean War. Beginning with simple, natural accounts of his early life (*Childhood* and *Boyhood*), he proceeded to articles on the war, and so eventually to perhaps his best work, the long novel *War and Peace,* followed by *Anna Karenina.* Increasingly preoccupied with social problems, he freed his serfs before this was done officially, and refused to take advantage of his wealth. His later works include *The Kreutzer Sonata* and *Resurrection.*

Tonypandy, Viscount (George Thomas) (1909–97), Speaker of the House of Commons, 1976–83.

Tooke, John Horne (1736–1812), English politician and pamphleteer, was a supporter of Wilkes and later of Pitt. He was tried for high treason, but was acquitted.

Torquemada, Tomas de (1420–98), first inquisitor-general of Spain.

Torricelli, Evangelista (1608–47), Italian physicist, pupil of Galileo. He invented the barometer and improved both microscope and telescope.

Toscanini, Arturo (1867–1957), Italian conductor, b. Parma. He had a remarkable musical memory, and was at the same time exacting and self-effacing.

Toulouse-Lautrec, Henri de (1864–1901), French painter, whose pictures portray with stark realism certain aspects of Parisian life in the nineties, especially the *Moulin Rouge* series. Many are in the Musée Lautrec at Albi.

Tovey, Sir Donald Francis (1875–1940), English pianist and composer. His compositions include chamber music, a piano concerto, and an opera *The Bride of Dionysus;* and his writings *Essays in Musical Analysis.*

Toynbee, Arnold (1852–83), English historian and social reformer. The settlement Toynbee Hall was founded in his memory.

Toynbee, Arnold Joseph (1889–1975), nephew of above, English historian, known mainly for his 10-volume *A Study of History,* an analysis of many civilisations. He was for 30 years director of the Institute of International Affairs.

Tradescant, John (d. 1638) and **Tradescant, John** (1608–62), father and son who were pioneer gardeners and naturalists.

Traherne, Thomas (*c.* 1636–74), English religious poet; author of *Centuries of Meditations.*

Trajan (*c.* 53–117), Roman emperor, was a successful general and administrator. Born in Spain.

Tree, Sir Herbert Beerbohm (1853–1917), English actor-manager of the Haymarket theatre until 1897 when he built His Majesty's theatre. Sir Max Beerbohm was his half-brother.

Trenchard, 1st Viscount (Hugh Montague Trenchard) (1873–1956), British air-marshal. He served with the Royal Flying Corps in the first world war. The first air marshal of the RAF.

Trent, 1st Baron (Jesse Boot) (1850–1931), drug manufacturer, b. Nottingham. He built up the largest pharmaceutical retail trade in the world.

Trevelyan, George Macaulay (1876–1962), English historian, known for his *English Social History*.

Trevelyan, Sir George Otto (1838–1928), English liberal politician, father of above. He wrote a life of his uncle Lord Macaulay.

Trevithick, Richard (1771–1833), English mining engineer and inventor, b. near Redruth, Cornwall. His most important invention was a high-pressure steam engine (1801) and he is commonly (and rightly) acknowledged as the inventor of the steam locomotive for railways. *See* D18.

Trimble, Lord. *See* D18.

Trollope, Anthony (1815–82), English novelist. His early life was a struggle, the family being supported by his mother's writings. His own career was in the post office, but by strict industry he produced many novels especially portraying clerical life (the *Barchester* series) and political life (the Palliser Novels).

Trotsky, Leo (Lev Davidovich Bronstein) (1879–1940), Russian revolutionary, b. of Jewish parents in the Ukraine, one of the leaders of the Bolshevik revolution. As commissar of foreign affairs under Lenin he led the Russian delegation at the Brest-Litovsk conference. He differed from Stalin on policy, believing in "permanent revolution," according to which socialism could not be achieved in Russia without revolutions elsewhere, and was dismissed from office in 1925 and expelled from the Communist party in 1927. In 1929 he took up exile in Mexico where he was assassinated.

Trudeau, Pierre Eliott (1919–2000), Liberal prime minister of Canada 1968–79, 1980–84.

Truman, Harry S. (1884–1972), U.S. President, 1945–53. He inherited the presidency on Roosevelt's death in 1945 when he took the decision to drop the first atom bomb, and he won the election of 1948. He intervened in Korea and dismissed General MacArthur.

Tudjman, Franjo (1922–99), authoritarian President of Croatia, the father of modern Croat nationalism.

Tulsi Das (1532–1623), Indian poet whose master piece *Ram-Charit-Mānas* (popularly known as the *Ramayana* and based on the Sanskrit epic of *Valmiki*) is venerated by all Hindus.

Turenne, Henri de la Tour d'Auvergne, Vicomte de (1611–75), French commander who was successful in the Thirty Years' War.

Turgenev, Ivan Sergeyvich (1818–83), Russian novelist, friend of Gogol and Tolstoy, who spent part of his life in exile. His works include *Fathers and Children*, *Smoke*, and *Virgin Soil*.

Turing, Alan Mathison (1912–54), computer genius. Developed concept (1936) of Turing machine.

Turner, Joseph Mallord William (1775–1851), English landscape painter, b. London, a barber's son. He entered the Royal Academy and was at first a topographical watercolourist. Later he turned to oil and became a master of light and colour, achieving magical effects, especially in depicting the reflection of light in water. His works include *Crossing the Brook*, *Dido building Carthage*, *The Fighting Temeraire*, *Rain, Steam and Speed*. He also made thousands of colour studies. He encountered violent criticism as his style became more abstract which led to Ruskin's passionate defence of him in *Modern Painters*. He bequeathed his work to the nation.

Tussaud, Marie (1761–1850), Swiss modeller in wax who learnt from her uncle in Paris, married a Frenchman, and later came to England where she set up a permanent exhibition.

Tutankhamen (d. *c.* 1327 B.C.), Egyptian pharaoh of the 18th dynasty, son-in-law of Akhenaten, whose tomb was discovered by Howard Carter in 1922, with the mummy and gold sarcophagus intact. He died when he was 18, possibly murdered.

Tutu, Desmond Mpilo (b. 1931), South African Archbishop of Cape Town, 1986–96. Nobel Peace Prize, 1984. Outstanding opponent of apartheid.

Twain, Mark (Samuel Langhorne Clemens) (1835–1910), American humorist. His *Innocents Abroad* was the result of a trip to Europe. His works include *A Tramp Abroad*, *Tom Sawyer*, *Huckleberry Finn*, and *Pudd'nhead Wilson*.

Tweedsmuir, 1st Baron (John Buchan) (1875–1940), Scottish author of biographies, historical novels, and adventure stories, including *Montrose* and *Thirty-nine Steps*. He was governor-general of Canada 1935–40.

Tyler, John (1790–1862), 10th President of the United States (1841–45). Formerly Vice-President to his Whig predecessor William Henry Harrison; his Administration concluded with Great Britain the Webster-Ashburton Treaty of 1842 fixing the eastern border between the US and Canada.

Tyler, Wat (d. 1381), English peasant leader. He was chosen leader of the Peasants' Revolt of 1381 (due to various causes), and parleyed at Smithfield with the young king Richard II, but was killed.

Tyndale, William (*c.* 1494–1536), English religious reformer, translator of the Bible. He had to go abroad, where he visited Luther and his New Testament was printed at Worms. When copies entered England they were suppressed by the bishops (1526). His Pentateuch was printed at Antwerp, but he did not complete the Old Testament. He was betrayed, arrested, and executed. Unlike Wyclif, who worked from Latin texts, he translated mainly from the original Hebrew and Greek and his work was later to become the basis of the Authorised Version of the Bible.

Tyndall, John (1829–93), Irish physicist whose wide interests led him to research on heat, light, and sound, and on bacteria-free air and sterilisation. He discovered why the sky is blue (Tyndall effect) and pioneered popular scientific writing, *e.g.*, *Heat as a Mode of Motion*.

U

Ulbricht, Walter (1893–1973), East German statesman. Communist leader who ordered the building of the Berlin Wall.

Unamuno, Miguel de (1864–1936), Spanish philosopher, poet, essayist, and novelist, author of *El Sentimiento Trágico de la Vida* (The Tragic Sense of Life).

Undset, Sigrid (1882–1940), Norwegian novelist, author of *Jenny*, *Kristin Lavransdatter*, and *Olan Audunsson*. Nobel prizewinner 1928.

Unwin, Sir Raymond (1863–1940), English architect of the first garden city at Letchworth.

Updike, John (b. 1932), one of America's greatest novelists who writes on modern America and its morals. Author of *The Witches of Eastwick* and *Couples*.

Ursula, St., said in late legend to have been killed by Huns at Cologne with many companions while on pilgrimage. It arose from a 4th cent. inscription which simply referred to virgin martyrs

Usher, or Ussher, James (1581–1656), Irish divine who in 1625 became archbishop of Armagh. He placed the creation at 4004 B.C.

Ustinov, Sir Peter (1921–2004), gifted and much-loved raconteur, entertainer, actor and writer. An ambassador of laughter and understanding between peoples.

V

Valentine, St., was a christian martyr of the reign of the emperor Claudius II (d. A.D. 270). The custom of sending valentines may be connected with the pagan festival of Lupercalia.

Valéry, Paul (1871–1945), French poet and essayist, strongly influenced by the symbolist leader, Mallarmé. His poems include *La jeune Parque*, *Charmes*, and *Le cimetière marin*.

Vanbrugh, Sir John (1664–1726), English architect and playwright. His buildings include Blenheim Palace and his plays *The Provok'd Wife*.

Van Buren, Martin (1782–1862), 8th President of the United States (1837–41). Formerly Vice-President to his Democratic predecessor Andrew Jackson, he opposed the annexation of Texas to the US for fear of increasing the power of the South.

Vancouver, George (1758–98), British navigator who served under Captain Cook, also doing survey work, and who sailed round Vancouver island.

Vanderbilt, Cornelius (1794–1877), American merchant and railway speculator who amassed a fortune and founded a university at Nashville. His son, **William Henry Vanderbilt** (1821–85), inherited and added to it.

Van Dyck, Sir Anthony (1599–1641), Flemish painter, b. Antwerp. He studied under Rubens, travelled in Italy, and then settled in England with an annuity from Charles I. He excelled in portraits, especially of Charles I and Henrietta Maria, and of their court.

Vane, Sir Henry (1613–62), English parliamentary leader during the civil war period, though not involved in the execution of Charles I. He was executed in 1662.

Van Gogh, Vincent (1853–90), Dutch painter of some of the most colourful pictures ever created. With passionate intensity of feeling he painted without pause whatever he found around him—landscapes, still life, portraits; his was a truly personal art. His life was one of pain, and often despair, and in the end he committed suicide.

Vauban, Sebastien de Prestre de (1633–1707), French military engineer, whose skill in siege works (*e.g.*, at Maestricht 1673) was a factor in the expansive wars of Louis XIV. He protected France with fortresses and also invented the socket bayonet.

Vaughan Williams, Ralph (1872–1958), English composer, b. Gloucestershire. After Charterhouse and Cambridge he studied music in Berlin under Max Bruch and, later in Paris, under Ravel. He wrote nine symphonies besides a number of choral and orchestral works, operas (including *Hugh the Drover, Riders to the Sea*), ballets, chamber music, and songs. He showed great interest in folk tunes. *See* Section P.

Velasquez, Diego (*c.* 1460–1524), Spanish conquistador, first governor of Cuba.

Velasquez, Diego Rodriguez de Silva y (1599–1660), Spanish painter, b. Seville, especially of portraits at the court of Philip IV, and also of classical and historical subjects. He made two visits to Italy (1629–31, 1649–51), studying the Venetian painters, especially Titian, which hastened the development of his style. Among his masterpieces are *The Maids of Honour, The Tapestry Weavers* (both in the Prado), the Rokeby Venus and a portrait of Philip IV (both in the National Gallery), the landscape views from the Villa Medici (Prado) and *Juan de Pareja* (sold in London in 1970 for £2·25 million).

Venizelos, Eleutherios (1864–1936), Greek statesman, b. Crete. He became prime minister in 1910 and held this office intermittently. He promoted the Balkan League (1912), forced the king's abdication (1917), and brought Greece into the war on the Allied side, securing territorial concessions at the peace conference, but his expansionist policy in Turkish Asia failed.

Ventris, Michael (1922–56). Pioneering linguist who deciphered the Linear B script. Born Wheathampstead, Hertfordshire, he was killed in a road accident.

Verdi, Giuseppe (1813–1901), Italian composer, b. near Busseto in the province of Parma. His early works include *Nabucco, Ernani, I Due Foscari*, and *Macbeth*; a middle period is represented by *Rigoletto, Il Trovatore, La Traviata, Un Ballo in Maschera*, and *Don Carlos*; to the last period belong *Aida, Otello*, and *Falstaff* (produced when he was 80). *See* Section P.

Verlaine, Paul (1844–96), French poet, one of the first of the symbolists, also known for his memoirs and confessions. His works include *Poèmes saturniens, Fêtes galantes, Sagesse*, and *Romances sans paroles*. He was imprisoned for two years in Belgium for shooting and wounding his friend Rimbaud. He died in poverty in Paris.

Vermeer, Jan (1632–75), Dutch painter, b. Delft. His main paintings are of domestic interiors, which he makes into works of art, as in *Lady at the Virginals* (National Gallery). However, his tranquil images mask his own personal life of turmoil.

Verne, Jules (1828–1905), French writer of science fiction, including *Five Weeks in a Balloon, Twenty Thousand Leagues Under the Sea, Round the World in Eighty Days*.

Vernier, Pierre (1580–1637), French inventor of the small sliding scale which enables readings on a graduated scale to be taken to a fraction of a division.

Veronese, Paolo (1528–88), Italian painter of the Venetian school, whose works include *Marriage Feast at Cana in Galilee, The Feast in the House of Simon*, and *The Presentation of the Family of Darius to Alexander, His Adoration of the Magi* is in the National Gallery.

Veronica, St., legendary woman who was said to hand her kerchief to Christ on the way to Calvary, to wipe his brow, and his impression was left on the kerchief. In its present form her legend dates from the 14th cent.

Verwoerd, Hendrik Frensch (1901–66), South African politician, b. Amsterdam, exponent of the policy of apartheid; prime minister 1958–66. He was assassinated.

Vespasian, Titus Flavius (A.D. 9–79), Roman emperor. He was sent by Nero to put down the Jews and was proclaimed by the legions. He began the Colosseum.

Vespucci, Amerigo (1451–1512), Florentine explorer, naturalised in Spain, contractor at Seville for Columbus. He later explored Venezuela. The use of his name for the continent arose through a mistake.

Vico, Giambattista (1688–1744), Italian philosopher of history and of culture, b. Naples. His ideas were developed in his *Scienza nuova* (science of history) but it was not until our own day that his originality was fully recognised.

Victor Emmanuel II (1820–78), first king of Italy. King of Sardinia, he was proclaimed king of Italy in 1861 after the Austrians had been defeated and Garibaldi had succeeded in the south. Rome was added in 1870.

Victoria (1819–1901), Queen of the United Kingdom of Gt. Britain and Ireland and Empress of India, was granddaughter of George III and succeeded her uncle, William IV, in 1837. In 1840 she married Prince Albert of Saxe-Coburg-Gotha, who died in 1861. Conscientious, hard-working, and of strict moral standards, she had by the end of a long life (jubilees 1887 and 1897) won the affection and respect of her subjects in a unique degree. Her reign saw industrial expansion and imperial adventures. She is buried in the Royal Mausoleum at Frogmore (near Windsor).

Villeneuve, Pierre de (1763–1806), French admiral defeated by Nelson at Trafalgar and captured along with his ship, the *Bucentaure*.

Villon, François (1431–?1463), French poet, b. Paris, who lived at a turbulent time at the close of the Hundred Years War. After fatally stabbing a man in 1455 he joined the *Conquillards*, a criminal organisation. They had a secret language (the *jargon*) and it was for them that he composed his ballads. His extant works consist of the *Petit Testament* (1456), originally called *Le Lais*, and the *Grand Testament* (1461), masterpieces of mediaeval verse.

Virgil (Publius Vergilius Maro) (70–19 B.C.), Roman epic poet, b. at Andes near Mantua, he went to Rome to obtain redress for the military confiscation of his farm. He was patronised by Maecenas, and wrote his pastoral *Eclogues*, followed by his *Georgics*. His best-known work, the *Aeneid*, deals with the wanderings of Aeneas after the fall of Troy till his establishment of a kingdom in Italy.

Vivaldi, Antonio (*c.* 1675–1743), Venetian composer, violin master at the Ospedale della Pieta. His output of orchestral works was prolific and Bach arranged some of his violin pieces for the harpsichord. *See* Section P.

Volta, Alessandro (1745–1827), Italian physicist of Pavia, who, working on the results of Galvani, invented the voltaic pile, the first instrument for producing an electric current. It provided a new means for the decomposition of certain substances. His name was given to the volt, the unit of electrical potential difference.

Voltaire (François Marie Arouet) (1694–1778), French philosopher and writer. His first essays offended the authorities, and he spent the years 1726–9 in England, where he wrote some of his dramas. Returning to France, he published his *Philosophical Letters*, which aroused the enmity of the priesthood. At this juncture, the Marquise du Châtelet offered him the asylum of her castle of Cirey, and for the next 15 years he made this his home, writing there his *Discourses of Man, Essay on the Morals and Spirit of Nations, Age of Louis XIV*, etc. His most celebrated book was *Candide*, in which he attacked the theory of Optimism. His observations include "*pour encourager les autres*" (about Admiral Byng's execution) and its final message: "*il faut cultiver notre jardin.*"

Vondel, Joost van don (1587–1679), Dutch poet who lived at Amsterdam. Most of his dramas are on biblical subjects, and the two most famous are *Jephtha* and *Lucifer*.

Voroshilov, Klimentiv Efremovich (1881–1969), Soviet general who commanded the Leningrad defences in 1941. USSR president, 1953–60.

Vries, Adriaen de (1556–1626), Dutch Mannerist sculptor whose works include *Christ in Distress*.

Vyshinsky, Andrei Yanuarievich (1883–1954), Soviet jurist and diplomat; conducted the prosecution of the Moscow treason trials, 1936–8.

W

Wade, George (1673–1748), English general and military engineer who, after the rising of 1715, pacified the Scottish highlands, constructing military roads and bridges. In the 1745 rising Prince Charles' forces evaded him.

Wagner, Richard (1813–83), German composer, b. Leipzig. He achieved a new type of musical expression in his operas by the complete union of music and drama. He made use of the *Leitmotif* and was his own librettist. His originality (and involvement in the 1848 revolution) aroused opposition, and he was exiled for some years. But he was supported by loyal friends, including Liszt, the young King Ludwig of Bavaria, and Nietzsche. He began the music of the *Ring des Nibelungen* in 1853, but it was not until 1876 that the whole of the drama (Rheingold, Valkyrie, Siegfried, Götterdämmerung) was performed at Bayreuth under the conductor Hans Richter. Other operas are *The Flying Dutchman*, *Rienzi*, *Tannhäuser*, *Lohengrin*, *Tristan und Isolde*, *Die Meistersinger von Nürnberg*, and *Parsifal*, a religious drama. He married Liszt's daughter Cosima.

Walcott, Derek (b. 1930), West Indian poet and playwright, whose works include *Collected Poems 1948–1984* (1986) and *Omeros* (1990). He won the Nobel Prize for Literature (1992).

Waldheim, Kurt (b. 1918), Austrian diplomat; succeeded U Thant as secretary-general of the UN, 1972–81. President of Austria, 1986–92.

Walesa, Lech (b. 1943), Polish trade unionist. Shipyard worker in Gdansk. Leader of *Solidarity*. Awarded 1983 Nobel Peace Prize. President of Poland, 1990–95. Retired from politics, 2000.

Waley, Arthur (1889–1966), English orientalist, known for his translations of Chinese and Japanese poetry and prose. The first to bring the literature of those countries to the western world.

Walker, George (1618–90), hero of the siege of Londonderry in 1688, who kept the besiegers at bay for 105 days.

Wallace, Alfred Russel (1823–1913), British naturalist, b. Usk, Monmouth, joint author with Darwin of the theory of natural selection. In 1858, while down with illness in the Moluccas, he sent a draft of his theory to Darwin in England who was amazed to find that it closely agreed with his own theory of evolution which he was on the point of publishing The result was a reading of a joint paper to the Linnean Society.

Wallace, Edgar (1875–1932), English novelist and playwright, known for his detective thrillers.

Wallace, Sir Richard (1818–90), English art collector and philanthropist. His adopted son's wife bequeathed his collection to the nation (Wallace Collection, Manchester Square, London).

Wallace, Sir William (c. 1274–1305), Scottish patriot. He withstood Edward I, at first successfully, but was defeated at Falkirk, taken to London and brutally murdered. He is now a cultural icon.

Wallenstein, Albrecht von (1583–1634), German soldier and statesman during the Thirty Years War. An able administrator of his own estates, he sought the unity of Germany, but was distrusted and eventually assassinated.

Waller, Edmund (1606–87), English poet of polished simplicity, author of *Go, lovely rose*.

Wallis, Sir Barnes Neville (1887–1979), British scientist and inventor whose many designs include the R100 airship, the Wellington bomber, the swing-wing aircraft, and the "bouncing bomb" that breached the Ruhr dams in 1943.

Walpole, Horace, 4th Earl of Orford (1717–97), younger son of Sir Robert Walpole, English

writer, chiefly remembered for his *Letters*, his *Castle of Otranto*, and his "Gothic" house at Strawberry Hill.

Walpole, Sir Hugh Seymour (1884–1941), English novelist, b. New Zealand. His works include *Fortitude*, *The Dark Forest*, and *The Herries Chronicle*.

Walpole, Sir Robert, 1st Earl of Orford (1676–1745), English Whig statesman, who came to office soon after the Hanoverian succession and is considered the first prime minister.

Walter, Bruno (1876–1962), German–American conductor, especially of Haydn, Mozart, and Mahler.

Walter, John (1776–1847), English newspaper editor. Under him *The Times*, founded by his father **John Walter** (1739–1812), attained a leading position.

Walton, Izaak (1593–1683), English writer, especially remembered for *The Compleat Angler*, first published in 1653. He also wrote biographies of Donne, Hooker, and George Herbert. Known as the "father of angling".

Walton, Sir William Turner (1902–83), English composer, whose works include concertos for string instruments, two symphonies, two coronation marches, *Façade* (setting to Edith Sitwell's poem), and an oratorio, *Belshazzar's Feast*. O.M. 1967.

Warbeck, Perkin (1474–99), Flemish impostor, b. Tournai, who claimed to be the younger son of Edward IV with French and Scottish backing, but failed and was executed.

Warhol, Andy (1927–87), controversial pop artist and film-maker. The 'father of Pop Art'. Born in Pittsburgh, USA.

Warwick, Earl of (Richard Neville) (c. 1428–71), "the kingmaker." At first on the Yorkist side in the Wars of the Roses, he proclaimed Edward IV king; but later changed sides and restored the Lancastrian Henry VI. He was killed at Barnet.

Washington, Booker Taliaferro (1858–1915), American black educationist, author of *Up from Slavery*.

Washington, George (1732–99), first U.S. president. B. in Virginia, of a family which originated from Sulgrave, Northants., he served against the French in the Seven Years War. When the dispute between the British government and the Americans over taxation came to a head, he proved a successful general, and Cornwallis's surrender to him at Yorktown in 1781 virtually ended the war. In 1787 he presided over the Philadelphia convention which formulated the constitution, and was president 1789–97.

Watson, John Broadus (1878–1958), American psychologist, an exponent of behaviourism. *See* **Behaviourism, Section J**.

Watson-Watt, Sir Robert (1892–1973), Scottish physicist, who played a major part in the development of radar.

Watt, James (1736–1819), Scottish engineer and inventor, b. Greenock. He made important improvements to Newcomen's steam-engine by inventing a separate condenser (applying Black's discoveries (1761–4) on latent heat) and other devices based on scientific knowledge of the properties of steam. He was given support by Matthew Boulton, a capitalist, and settled down in Birmingham with him. He defined one horse-power as the rate at which work is done when 33,000 lb are raised one foot in one minute. He also constructed a press for copying manuscripts. The watt as a unit of power is named after him.

Watteau, Jean Antoine (1684–1721), French painter. He painted pastoral idylls in court dress. His works include *Embarquement pour Cythère* in the Louvre.

Watts, Isaac (1674–1748), English hymn-writer, author of *O God, our help in ages past*.

Watts-Dunton, Walter Theodore (1836–1914), English poet and critic, friend of Swinburne whom he looked after until his death in 1909.

Waugh, Evelyn (1902–66), English satirical writer, author of *Vile Bodies*, *The Loved One*, *Brideshead Revisited*, *Life of Edmund Campion*, *The Ordeal of Gilbert Pinfold*, and an autobiography, *A Little Learning*.

Wavell, 1st Earl (Archibald Percival Wavell) (1883–1950), British field marshal. He served in the first great war on Allenby's staff and in the second he commanded in the Middle East 1939–41, defeating the Italians; and in India 1941–3. He was viceroy of India 1943–7.

Webb, Matthew (1848–83), English swimmer, the first to swim the English Channel (1875).

Webb, Sidney James, Baron Passfield (1859–1947), and his wife **Beatrice,** née Potter (1858–1943), English social reformers and historians. They combined careful investigation of social problems (their books include *History of Trade Unionism* and *English Local Government*) with work for the future; they were members of the Fabian Society, launched the *New Statesman*, and helped to set up the London School of Economics. He held office under Labour.

Weber, Carl Maria Friedrich Ernst von (1786–1826), German composer, who laid the foundation of German romantic opera. His reputation rests principally on his three operas, *Der Freischütz, Euryanthe,* and *Oberon.* He was also an able pianist, conductor, and musical director. *See Section P.*

Webster, Daniel (1782–1852), American statesman and orator. He held office more than once and negotiated the Ashburton Treaty which settled the Maine–Canada boundary.

Webster, Noah (1758–1843), American lexicographer, who published an *American dictionary of the English language.*

Wedgwood, Dame Cicely Veronica (1910–97), English historian, author of *William the Silent, Thomas Wentworth, The Thirty Years' War, The King's Peace, The Trial of Charles I*; a member of the Staffordshire pottery family. O.M. 1969.

Wedgwood, Josiah (1730–95), English potter, who at his Etruria works near Hanley produced from a new ware (patented 1763) pottery to classical designs by Flaxman, and gave pottery a new impetus.

Wei Jingsheng (b. 1951), Chinese human rights campaigner. Imprisoned, 1979–93, for his political beliefs. Imprisoned again, 1995, then exiled.

Weill, Kurt (1900–50), German composer of satirical, surrealist operas, including *Die Dreigroschenoper* and *Mahagonny* (librettist Brecht). His wife, the Viennese actress **Lotte Lenya** (d. 1981) will be remembered for her singing of the Brecht songs and the interpretation of her husband's works. They left Europe for the United States in 1935.

Weingartner, Felix (1863–1942), Austrian conductor, also a composer and writer of a text book on conducting.

Weismann, August (1834–1914), German biologist. He worked on the question of individual variability in evolution, stressing the continuity of the germ plasm and rejecting the idea of inheritance of acquired characteristics.

Weizmann, Chaim (1874–1952), Israeli leader, b. Motol, near Pinsk (now in Belarus). He came to England in 1903 and taught biochemistry at Manchester. He helped to secure the Balfour Declaration (1917). In 1948 he became first president of Israel.

Welensky, Roland (Roy) (1907–91), Deputy Prime Minister and Minister of Transport of the Central African Federation, 1953–56. He then became Prime Minister and Minister of External Affairs. He remained Prime Minister until the break-up of the Federation in 1963.

Wellesley, Marquess (Richard Colley Wellesley) (1760–1842), British administrator. He was a successful governor-general of India, and was brother of the Duke of Wellington.

Wellington, 1st Duke of (Arthur Wellesley) (1769–1852), British general. B. in Ireland, he joined the army and gained experience in India. In the Peninsular War he successfully wore down and drove out the invading French. When Napoleon escaped from Elba, Wellington defeated him at Waterloo. Thereafter he took some part in politics as a Tory, but in the last resort was capable of accepting change.

Wells, Herbert George (1866–1946), English author. B. London, he was at first a teacher. He believed in progress through science, and became one of the most influential writers of his time. His long series of books includes romances of the Jules Verne variety (*The Time Machine, The Island of Dr. Moreau, The Invisible Man*), sociological autobiography (*Love and Mr. Lewisham, Kipps, Tono-Bungay, The History of Mr. Polly, Mr. Britling Sees it*

Through), and popular education (*Outline of History, The Science of Life, The Work, Wealth and Happiness of Mankind, The Shape of Things to Come, The Fate of Homo Sapiens*). He was a founder member of the Fabian Society.

Wells, Horace (1815–48), US dentist, the first to use laughing gas as an anaesthetic in dentistry (1844).

Wenceslaus, St. (907–929), Patron saint of the Czechs. A Christian ruler, murdered by his brother Boleslav on his way to Mass. The 'Good King' of the Christmas carol.

Wesker, Sir Arnold (b. 1932), English playwright best-known for such political and social dramas as *Chicken Soup with Barley* and *Chips with Everything.*

Wesley, Charles (1707–88), English hymnwriter. He was the companion of his brother John, and wrote over 5,500 hymns, including *Love divine* and *Jesu, lover of my soul.*

Wesley, John (1703–91), English evangelist and founder of Methodism (at first a nickname applied to friends of himself and his brother), b. at Epworth. After a trip to Georgia and after encountering Moravian influence, he began to teach on tour, covering in over 50 years more than 200,000 miles and preaching over 40,000 sermons. He made religion a live force to many ignorant folk of humble station who could only be reached by a new and direct challenge. He made a feature of the Sunday school and increased the use of music (the brothers' first hymnbook appeared in 1739). He did not plan separation from the Anglican church, though it was implicit in his ordination of a missionary, and it took place after his death. *See also* **Methodism, Section J.**

Westermarck, Edward Alexander (1862–1939), Finnish sociologist. His works include *History of Human Marriage, Origin and Development of the Moral Ideas,* and *The Oedipus Complex.*

Westinghouse, George (1846–1914), American engineer who invented an air-brake for railways (1868) called by his name, and pioneered the use of high tension alternating current for the transmission of electric power.

Westmacott, Sir Richard (1775–1856), English sculptor of Achilles in Hyde Park.

Wharton, Edith (1862–1937), American novelist and friend of Henry James. Her works include *House of Mirth* and *Custom of the Country.*

Whately, Richard (1787–1863), English archbishop of Dublin. He wrote treatises on *Rhetoric* and *Logic.*

Wheatstone, Sir Charles (1802–75), English physicist, one of the first to recognise Ohm's law. In 1837 he (with W. F. Cooke) patented an electric telegraph. He also introduced the microphone.

Wheeler, Sir Charles (1892–1974), English sculptor, especially on buildings. President, R.A., 1956–66.

Wheeler, Sir Mortimer (1890–1976), notable archaeologist who popularised his subject.

Whistler, James Abbott McNeill (1834–1903), American artist. B. at Lowell, he studied in Paris and settled in England. He reacted against the conventions of his day, and Ruskin's uncomprehending criticism of his work resulted in a lawsuit. Among his main works are studies of the Thames, and a portrait of his mother, now in the Louvre.

White, Sir George Stuart (1835–1912), British general. Defended Ladysmith in the Boer War.

White, Gilbert (1720–93), a father of English ecology. His book *The Natural History and Antiquities of Selborne,* was published in 1789.

White, Patrick (1912–90), Australian novelist whose books include *The Aunt's Story, Riders in the Chariot, The Solid Mandala* and *The Eye of the Storm.* Nobel prize 1973.

Whitefield, George (1714–70), English evangelist, b. Gloucester. He was at first associated with the Wesleys, but differed from them on predestination. His supporters built him a "Tabernacle" in London, and he had other chapels elsewhere. He founded no lasting sect.

Whitehouse, Mary (1910–2001), tireless campaigner against screen sex and violence.

Whitelaw, Viscount (William Whitelaw) (1918–99), Conservative. Deputy Prime Minister under Thatcher.

Whitgift, John (1530–1604), archbishop of Canterbury in the time of Elizabeth I (from 1583). His policy helped to strengthen Anglicanism.

Whitman, Walt (1819–92), American poet, b.

Long Island. He led a wandering life and did hospital work in the Civil War. He aimed at forming a new and free American outlook. His works include *Leaves of Grass*, *Drum Taps*, and *Democratic Vistas*.

Whittier, John Greenleaf (1807–92), American Quaker poet, b. Haverhill, Mass. He wrote against slavery (*Justice and Expediency*), turning to poetry after the Civil War, especially remembered for *Snow-bound*.

Whittington, Richard (*c.* 1358–1423), English merchant. Son of a Gloucestershire knight, he became a London mercer and was mayor of London 1398, 1406, 1419. The cat legend is part of European folklore.

Whittle, Sir Frank (1907–96), 'the father of jet flight'. The first flights of Gloster jet propelled planes with Whittle engines took place in 1941. O.M. (1986).

Whymper, Edward (1840–1911), English woodengraver and mountaineer. He was the first to climb the Matterhorn.

Wiesenthal, Simon (1908–2005), Nazi-hunter who devoted his life to bringing Nazi murderers to justice. The "conscience of the Holocaust".

Wilberforce, William (1759–1833), English philanthropist, b. Hull. He was the parliamentary leader of the campaign against the slave trade, abolished in 1807. He then worked against slavery itself.

Wilcox, Ella Wheeler (1855–1919), American writer of romantic sentimental verse.

Wilde, Oscar Fingall (1854–1900), Irish author and dramatist, son of a Dublin surgeon and leader of the cult of art for art's sake. His works include poems, fairy-tales, short stories, and witty plays—*Lady Windermere's Fan*, *A Woman of No Importance*, *An Ideal Husband*, and *The Importance of Being Earnest*. In a libel action he was convicted of homosexual practices and imprisoned for two years, when he wrote *The Ballad of Reading Gaol*.

Wilder, Thornton Niven (1897–1975), American author and playwright. Among his books are *The Bridge of San Luis Rey* and *Ides of March*.

Wilhelm, Kaiser. *See* William I, II *etc.*

Wilkes, John (1727–97), English politician. A Whig, he violently attacked George III in his paper the *North Briton*, and as a result of unsuccessful proceedings against him, general warrants were declared illegal. He was again in trouble for obscene libel; his defiance of authority brought him popularity, and he was four times re-elected to parliament but refused his seat, until his opponents gave way. He helped to establish freedom of the press.

Willcocks, Sir William (1852–1932), British engineer, b. India, who carried out irrigation works in India *etc.* He built the Aswan dam (1898–1902).

Willett, William (1856–1915), English advocate of "daylight savings," adopted after his death.

William I of England (1027–87), the "Conqueror," Duke of Normandy, claimed the English throne as successor to Edward the Confessor, and defeated Harold II at Hastings in 1066. An able commander and a firm ruler, he crushed Saxon resistance, especially in the north, transferred most of the land to his Norman followers, and drew England into closer relations with the continent, as did his archbishop Lanfranc. He ordered the Domesday survey.

William II of England (1056–1100), the Conqueror's son, surnamed Rufus, succeeded in 1087. Capricious and self-indulgent, his reign was troubled and he was shot (by accident or design) while hunting in the New Forest.

William III of England (1650–1702), King of England, Scotland, and Ireland (1689–1702), son of William II of Orange and Mary, daughter of Charles I. He married Mary, daughter of the Duke of York (later James II) while stadtholder of Holland. In 1688, when James had fled the country, he was invited to succeed and he and Mary became joint king and queen. The revolution of 1688 brought to England tolerance of Protestant worship, but William was mainly concerned with war against France, ended in 1697.

William IV of England (1765–1837), third son of George III, succeeded his brother George IV in 1830; called the "sailor king." The reform bill of 1832 and other reform measures were carried without obstruction from him.

William I of Germany (1797–1888), King of Prussia and first German emperor. He suc-

ceeded to the throne in 1861 and continued resistance to reform, appointing Bismarck as chief minister, and supporting him through the Austro-Prussian and Franco-Prussian wars. His personal character was simple and unassuming.

William II of Germany, the Kaiser (1859–1941), King of Prussia and German emperor from 1888, was grandson of William I and of Queen Victoria. He was intelligent but impetuous, and believed in military power. He dismissed Bismarck. In 1914 his support of Austria helped to precipitate European war, and the resulting defeat brought his abdication, after which he lived in retirement at Doorn in Holland.

William the Silent (1533–84), Dutch national leader. Prince of Orange, he led the revolt of the Protestant Netherlands against the rule of the Spanish Philip II. The union of the northern provinces was accomplished in 1579, and Spanish rule was renounced by 1584, in which year William was assassinated.

Williams, Sir Bernard (1929–2003), a brilliant and humane thinker, the outstanding moral philosopher of his age.

Williams, Eric (1911–81), the first Prime Minister of independent Trinidad and Tobago. He led his country to independence. His policy of "empirical socialism" saw his country prosper.

Williams, Sir George (1821–1905), founder of the Young Men's Christian Association.

Williams, Rowan (b. 1950), Archbishop of Canterbury, 2002–. An eminent theologian and profound thinker. Archbishop of Wales, 2000–02. Bishop of Monmouth, 1992–2000.

Willis, Ted (Lord Willis) (1914–92), socialist politician and playwright. His best-known play was *Woman in a Dressing Gown* (1962), and he created the TV series, *Dixon of Dock Green* (1953–75).

Wilson, Sir Angus (1913–91), British novelist and man of letters.

Wilson, Edmund (1895–1972), American critic, author of *Axel's Castle* (1931), *The Triple Thinkers* (1938), *The Wound and the Bow* (1941), *To the Finland Station* (1940), *The Shores of Light* (1952), *The Dead Sea Scrolls* (1955).

Wilson of Rievaulx, Lord (Sir Harold Wilson) (1916–95), British statesman, leader parl. Labour Party 1963–76; prime minister 1964–6, 1966–70, 1974–6. Entered parliament 1945 as member for Ormskirk; elected for Huyton 1950–83. Returned as Prime Minister on four occasions. Resigned March 1976. Founder of the Open University.

Wilson, Richard (1714–82), British landscape painter. Admired by Turner and Constable.

Wilson, Thomas Woodrow (1856–1924), American statesman. He was US president 1913–21, brought America into the first world war and advocated the League of Nations, but was not a successful negotiator at the peace conference and could not carry his country into the League. He introduced prohibition and women's suffrage.

Wingate, Orde Charles (1903–44), leader of the Chindit forces engaged behind the Japanese lines in Burma during the second world war.

Winifred, St., the 7th cent. patron saint of North Wales, said in late legend to have been killed by her rejected suitor, Prince Caradoc, but restored by her uncle.

Wiseman, Nicholas Patrick (1802–65), cardinal, b. in Spain of an Irish family. In 1850 on the restoration in England of the Catholic hierarchy he became first archbishop of Westminster.

Wittgenstein, Ludwig Josef Johann (1889–1951), Austrian linguistic philosopher whose main works were the *Tractatus Logico-Philosophicus* of his early period, much admired by Russell, and the *Philosophical Investigations*.

Wodehouse, Sir Pelham Grenville (1881–1975), English humorist, creator of Jeeves in the Bertie Wooster stories. He became a US citizen.

Wolf, Friedrich August (1759–1824), German scholar, a founder of scientific classical philology.

Wolf, Hugo (1860–1903), Austrian song-writer. In his settings of over 300 German lyrics, including many of Mörike and Goethe, he achieved union of poetry and music. *See* Section P.

Wolfe, James (1727–59), British general, b. Westerham. He showed early promise in the Seven Years' War, and was given command of the expedition against Quebec, which in spite of its strong position he captured, but lost his life.

Wolsey, Thomas (c. 1475–1530), English cardinal. A butcher's son at Ipswich, he entered the church, becoming archbishop of York and cardinal, while in the same year (1515) he became Henry VIII's lord chancellor. But in spite of his ability he was unable to secure papal sanction for the king's divorce from Catherine of Aragon, and fell from power and died.

Wood, Sir Henry Joseph (1869–1944), English conductor, founder of the Promenade Concerts which he conducted from 1895 till his death.

Woodcock, George (1904–79), trade union leader. TUC general secretary 1960–69; first chairman, Commission on Industrial Relations, 1969–71.

Woods, Donald (1933–2001), South African journalist whose friendship with Steve Biko inspired the film *Cry Freedom*.

Woods, Granville (1856–1910), black American inventor of induction telegraph system (1887). Known as the "Black Edison".

Woodsworth, James Shaver (1874–1942), Canadian politician, parliamentary leader of the Co-operative Commonwealth Federation.

Woodville, Elizabeth (1437–91), wife of Edward IV. Her daughter Elizabeth married Henry VII.

Woolf, Virginia (1882–1941), English writer, daughter of Sir Leslie Stephen and wife of Leonard Woolf with whom she founded the Hogarth Press. Her works include *To the Lighthouse*, *Mrs. Dalloway*, *The Waves*, *A Room of One's Own*.

Wollstonecraft, Mary (1759–97), feminist and writer. She was most famous for her work *A Vindication of the Rights of Women* (1792), a protest against the limited openings for women. See **Feminism, Section J**.

Wootton of Abinger, Baroness (Barbara Frances Wootton) (1897–1988), English social scientist.

Wordsworth, William (1770–1850), English poet, b. Cockermouth. He went to Cambridge, and in 1798 with Coleridge issued *Lyrical Ballads*, a return to simplicity in English poetry. He settled at Grasmere with his sister Dorothy (1771–1855), to whose insight his poems owe much. Among his best works are his sonnets and his *Ode on the Intimations of Immortality*, besides his *Prelude*.

Wren, Sir Christopher (1632–1723), English architect, b. Wiltshire. After the great fire (1666) he prepared an abortive plan for rebuilding London, but did in fact rebuild St. Paul's and more than fifty other city churches, including St. Stephen, Walbrook, and St. Mary-le-Bow. Other works include Chelsea Hospital, portions of Greenwich Hospital, the Sheldonian theatre, Oxford, and Queen's College library, Oxford. He had wide scientific interests (he was professor of mathematics at Gresham College, London, and professor of astronomy at Oxford) and helped to found the Royal Society.

Wright, (William Ambrose) Billy (1924–94), the golden-boy of post-war English football. A former captain of Wolves and England, he won 105 caps for England, captaining his country 90 times.

Wright, Frank Lloyd (1869–1959), American architect, initiator of horizontal strip and all-glass design. Buildings include the Imperial Hotel, Tokyo, and the Guggenheim Museum, New York.

Wright, Orville (1871–1948), American airman who with his brother Wilbur (1867–1912) in 1903 was the first to make a controlled sustained flight in a powered heavier-than-air machine, flying a length of 852 ft. at Kitty Hawk, N.C.

Wright, Richard (1908–60), black American novelist. Author of *Native Son* (1940) a pioneering novel of black revolt. A later work *The God That Failed* reflects his disillusion with communism.

Wyatt, James (1746–1813), English architect who built Fonthill Abbey.

Wyatt, Sir Thomas (1503–42), English poet (and diplomat) who introduced the sonnet from Italy.

Wyatt, Sir Thomas the younger (c. 1520–54), son of above, unsuccessfully led a revolt against Queen Mary on behalf of Lady Jane Grey.

Wycherley, William (1640–1715), English dramatist of the Restoration period. A master of satiric comedy, his plays include *Love in a Wood*, *The Plain Dealer* and *The Country Wife*.

Wyclif, John (c. 1320–84), English religious reformer. He taught at Oxford, later becoming rector of Lutterworth. He insisted on inward religion and attacked those practices which he thought had become mechanical. His followers, called Lollards, were suppressed, partly for political reasons. The Wyclif Bible, the first translation of the Latin Vulgate into English, was mainly the work of his followers at Oxford.

Wykeham, William of (1324–1404), English churchman. He held office under Edward III and became bishop of Winchester in 1367. He founded New College, Oxford, and Winchester School, and improved Winchester cathedral.

Wyllie, William Lionel (1851–1931), English marine painter of *The Thames Below London Bridge*.

Wyspianski, Stanislav (1869–1907), Polish poet, dramatist and painter. His plays include *The Wedding*, *Liberation*, and *November Night*.

X

Xavier, St. Francis (1506–52), "apostle of the Indies," b. at Xavero in the Basque country. He was associated with Loyola in founding the Jesuits, and undertook missionary journeys to Goa, Ceylon, and Japan.

Xenophon (444–359 B.C.), Athenian general and historian. He commanded Greek mercenaries under the Persian Cyrus, and on the latter's death safely marched the Ten Thousand home through hostile country. His chief works are the *Anabasis*, the *Hellenica*, and *Cyropaedia*.

Xerxes (c. 519–465 B.C.), King of Persia, was son of the first Darius. In 481 B.C. he started on an expedition against Greece when, according to Herodotus, he had a combined army and navy of over two and a half million men. He defeated the Spartans at Thermopylae, but his fleet was overcome at Salamis. He reigned from 485 to 465 B.C. and met his death by assassination.

Ximénes de Cisneros, Francisco (1436–1517), Spanish statesman and churchman. He became cardinal in 1507; carried out monastic reforms; and directed preparation of a polyglot bible, the *Complutensian*; but as inquisitor-general he was fanatical against heresy. He was adviser to Queen Isabella; in 1506 regent for Queen Juana. Attempted to conquer Oran.

Y

Yeats, William Butler (1865–1939), Irish lyric poet and playwright, b. near Dublin, a leader of the Irish literary revival. His plays were performed in the Abbey Theatre (which with **Lady Gregory** (1852–1932) he helped to found), and include *Cathleen Ni Houlihan*, *The Hour Glass*, and *Deidre*. A complete edition of the *Collected Poems* appeared in 1950.

Yeltsin, Boris Nikolayevich (b. 1931), Russian politician. President, 1990 to 1999, of the Russian Federation. At first an ally of Gorbachev (q.v.) then a rival. Yeltsin's role in opposing the August 1991 coup strengthened his power and undermined the old USSR. Architect of the Commonwealth of Independent States. He overcame the 1993 communist rising in Moscow.

Yonge, Charlotte Mary (1823–1901), English novelist. Influenced by Keble, she wrote novels which faithfully reflect some aspects of Victorian life; one such is *The Daisy Chain*. She also wrote historical fiction *e.g. The Dove in the Eagle's Nest*.

Young of Dartington, Lord (Michael Young) (1915–2002), an inspired innovator who helped create the Open University and the Consumers' Association.

Young, Brigham (1801–77), American Mormon leader, and president in 1844 after the founder's death. He was a main founder of Salt Lake City. He practised polygamy. See **Section J**.

Young, Francis Brett (1884–1954), English novelist, author of *My Brother Jonathan* and *Dr. Bradley remembers*.

Young, James (1811–83), Scottish chemist, b. Glasgow, whose experiments led to the manufacture of paraffin oil and solid paraffin.

Young, Thomas (1773–1829), English physicist, physician and Egyptologist, b. Somerset, of Quaker family. He established the wave theory of light and its essential principle of interference, put forward a theory of colour vision, and was the first to describe astigmatism of the eye. He was largely responsible for deciphering the inscriptions on the Rosetta stone.

Younghusband, Sir Francis Edward (1863–1942), English explorer and religious leader. He explored Manchuria and Tibet. He founded the World Congress of Faiths in 1936 (*see* **Section J**).

Ypres, 1st Earl of. *See* **French.**

Ysaÿe, Eugène (1858–1929), Belgian violinist and conductor, noted chiefly for his playing of the works of Bach and César Franck.

Yukawa, Hideki (1907–81), Japanese physicist, who received the 1949 Nobel prize for predicting (1935) the existence of the meson.

Z

Zadkiel (angel in rabbinical lore), pseudonym of two astrologers: **William Lilly** (1602–81) and **Richard James Morrison** (1794–1874).

Zadkine, Ossip (1890–1967), Russian-born sculptor who made play with light on concave surfaces.

Zaharoff, Sir Basil (1849–1936), armaments magnate and financier, b. Anatolia of Greek parents. He was influential in the first world war.

Zamenhof, Ludwig Lazarus (1859–1917), Polish-Jew who invented Esperanto. He was by profession an oculist.

Zatopek, Emil (1922–2000), Czech athlete, the greatest distance runner of the 20th century.

Zeno of Citium (?342–270 B.C.), philosopher, founder of the Stoic system. He left Cyprus to teach in Athens.

Zeppelin, Ferdinand, Count von (1838–1917), German inventor of the dirigible airship, 1897–1900. It was used in the first world war.

Zeromski, Stefan (1864–1925), Polish novelist, author of *The Homeless*, *The Ashes*, *The Fight with Satan.*

Zhao Ziyang (1919–2005), Chinese Communist leader. Advocate of economic reform. Ousted for moderate views after Tiananmen Square.

Zhukov, Georgi Konstantinovich (1896–1974), Soviet general, who led the defence of Moscow and Stalingrad and lifted the siege of Leningrad in the second world war. He accepted the German surrender in 1945.

Zhukovsky, Vasily Andreyevich (1783–1852), Russian poet and translator of German and English poets. For many years he was tutor to the future Tsar Alexander II.

Zola, Emile Edouard (1840–1902), French novelist, b. Paris, of Italian descent. His series, *Les Rougon-Macquart*, portrays in a score of volumes (the best known of which are perhaps *L'Assommoir*, *Nana* and *Germinal*) the fortunes of one family in many aspects and in realistic manner. He had the moral courage to champion Dreyfus.

Zorn, Anders Leonhard (1860–1920), Swedish sculptor, etcher, and painter.

Zoroaster (Zarathustra) (fl. 6th cent. B.C.), Persian founder of the Parsee religion. He was a monotheist, and saw the world as a struggle between good (Ahura Mazda) and evil (Ahriman). *See* **Zoroastrianism, Section J.**

Zoshchenko, Mikhail (1895–1958), Russian writer of humorous short stories, which include *The Woman who could not Read and other Tales* and *The Wonderful Dog and other Stories.*

Zosimus (fl. *c.* 300), the first known alchemist. He lived in Alexandria.

Zuccarelli, Francesco (1702–88), Italian artist of fanciful landscapes. He spent many years in London and was elected a founder member of the R.A. (1768).

Zuckermann, Baron (Solly Zuckermann) (1904–93), British biologist; chief scientific adviser to British governments; 1940–71. Author of *Scientists and War etc.* O.M. 1968.

Zwingli, Ulrich (1484–1531), Swiss religious reformer. He taught mainly at Zurich, where he issued a list of reformed doctrines, less extreme than those of Calvin.

Zwirner, Ernst Friedrich (1802–61), German architect who restored Cologne cathedral.

THE NOBEL PRIZES

The Background

The Nobel Foundation was established at the start of the last century to give effect to the wishes expressed by Alfred Nobel in his will. Alfred B Nobel (1833–96) was the inventor of dynamite and bequeathed $9,000,000 to the Foundation. The award of a Nobel Prize is accepted as the highest form of international recognition in the fields in which it is given: physics, chemistry, medicine, literature, peace and, since 1969, economics. The Royal Academy of Science in Sweden picks the prizewinners in physics, chemistry and economics. The medical faculty of Stockholm's Caroline Institute chooses the winner in the field of physiology or medicine. The Swedish Academy of Literature names the winner in the field of literature. The Norwegian parliament elects a committee of five persons to select the winner of the prize for peace. Currently the value of the prize is around £687,000. The first Nobel Prizes were awarded in 1901.

CHEMISTRY

This was first awarded in 1901. The following Britons received the award prior to 1945:

1904	Sir William Ramsay
1908	Ernest Rutherford
1921	Frederick Soddy
1922	Francis W. Aston
1928	Arthur Harden (with Hans von Euler-Chelpin (Ger, German-born)
1937	Walter N. Haworth (with Paul Karrer (Swi, Russian-born)

Winners since 1945 have been:

1945	Artturi I. Virtanen (Fin)
1946	James B. Sumner (USA)
	John H. Northrop (USA)
	Wendell M. Stanley (USA)
1947	Sir Robert Robinson (GB)
1948	Arne W. K. Tiselius (Swe)
1949	William F. Giauque (USA)
1950	Kurt Alder (Ger)
	Otto P. H. Diels (GDR)
1951	Edwin M. McMillan (USA)
	Glenn T. Seaborg (USA)
1952	Archer J. P. Martin (GB)
	Richard L. M. Synge (GB)
1953	Hermann Staudinger (GDR)
1954	Linus C. Pauling (USA)
1955	Vincent du Vigneaud (USA)
1956	Sir Cyril N. Hinshelwood (GB)
	Nikolai N. Semenov (USSR)
1957	Lord Todd (Alexander R. Todd) (GB)
1958	Frederick Sanger (GB)
1959	Jaroslav Heyrovsky (Cze)
1960	Willard F. Libby (USA)
1961	Melvin Calvin (USA)
1962	Sir John C. Kendrew (GB)
	Max F. Perutz (GB, Austrian-born)
1963	Giulio Natta (Ita)
	Karl Ziegler (GDR)
1964	Dorothy Crowfoot Hodgkin (GB)
1965	Robert B. Woodward (USA)
1966	Robert S. Mulliken (USA)
1967	Manfred Eigen (Ger)
	Ronald G. W. Norrish (GB)
	Sir George Porter (GB)
1968	Lars Onsager (USA, Norwegian-born)
1969	Derek H. R. Barton (GB)
	Odd Hassel (Nor)
1970	Luis F. Leloir (Arg, French-born)
1971	Gerhard Herzberg (Can, German-born)
1972	Christian B. Anfinsen (USA)
	Stanford Moore (USA)
	William H. Stein (USA)
1973	Ernst Otto Fischer (GDR)
	Geoffrey Wilkinson (GB)
1974	Paul J. Flory (USA)
1975	John W. Cornforth (GB)
	Vladimir Prelog (Swi, Yugoslavian-born)

1976	William N. Lipscomb Jr (USA)
1977	Ilya Prigogine (Bel, Russian-born)
1978	Peter Mitchell (GB)
1979	Herbert C. Brown (USA)
	Gerry Wittig (GDR)
1980	Frederick Sanger (GB)
	Paul Berg (USA)
	Walter Gilbert (USA)
1981	Roald Hoffman (USA)
	Kenichi Fukui (Jap)
1982	Aaron Klug (GB)
1983	Henry Taube (USA)
1984	R. Bruce Merrifield (USA)
1985	Herbert A. Hauptman (USA)
	Jerome Karle (USA)
1986	Dudley Herschbach (USA)
	Yuan T. Lee (USA)
	John C. Polanyi (Can)
1987	Donald J. Cram (USA)
	Charles J. Paderson (USA)
	Jean-Marie Lehn (Fra)
1988	Johan Deisenhofer (Ger)
	Robert Huber (Ger)
	Hartmut Michel (Ger)
1989	Thomas R. Cech (USA)
	Sidney Altman (USA)
1990	Elias J. Corey (USA)
1991	Richard R. Ernst (Swi)
1992	Rudolph Marcus (USA, Canadian-born)
1993	Michael Smith (Can, British-born)
	Kary Mullis (USA)
1994	George A. Olah (USA)
1995	Paul Crutzen (Hol)
	Mario Molina (USA)
	Sherwood Rowland (USA)
1996	Harold Croto (GB)
	Robert Curl (USA)
	Richard Smalley (USA)
1997	John Walker (GB)
	Paul Boyer (USA)
	Jens Skou (Den)
1998	John Pople (USA, UK born)
	Walter Kohn (USA)
1999	Ahmed Zewail (USA, Egyptian-born)
2000	Alan Heeger (USA)
	Alan MacDiarmid (USA)
	Hideki Shirakawa (Jap)
2001	Barry Sharpless (USA)
	William Knowles (USA)
	Ryoji Noyori (Jap)
2002	John Fenn (USA)
	Koichi Tanaka (Jap)
	Kurt Wietrich (Swi)
2003	Peter Agre (USA)
	Roderick MacKinnon (USA)
2004	Aaron Ciechanover (Isr)
	Avram Hershko (Isr)
	Irwin Rose (USA)
2005	Yves Chauvin (Fr)
	Richard Schrock (USA)
	Robert Grubbs (USA)

ECONOMICS

The Nobel Prize for Economics is the most recent of the Nobel Prizes, having been established in 1969.

Winners have been:

1969	Ragnar Frisch (Nor)
	Jan Tinbergen (Hol)
1970	Paul A. Samuelson (USA)
1971	Simon Kuznets (USA)
1972	Kenneth J. Arrow (USA)
	Sir John R. Hicks (GB)
1973	Vassily Leontief (USA) (Russian-born)
1974	Gunnar Myrdal (Swe)
	Friedrich A. von Hayek (Aut)
1975	Leonid V. Kantorovich (USSR)
	Tjalling C. Koopmans (USA) (Dutch-born)
1976	Milton Friedman (USA)
1977	Bertil Ohlin (Swe)
	James Edward Meade (GB)
1978	Herbert Simon (USA)
1979	Sir Arthur Lewis (GB) (St Lucien-born)
	Theodore W. Schultz (USA)
1980	Lawrence Klein (USA)
1981	James Tobin (USA)
1982	George J. Stigler (USA)
1983	Gerard Debreu (USA)
1984	Sir Richard Stone (GB)

1985	Franco Modigliani (USA, Italian-born)
1986	James M. Buchanan (USA)
1987	Robert M. Solow (USA)
1988	Maurice Allais (Fra)
1989	Trygve Haavelmo (Nor)
1990	Harry M. Markowitz (USA)
	William F. Sharpe (USA)
	Merton H. Miller (USA)
1991	Ronald H. Coase (GB/USA)
1992	Gary Becker (USA)
1993	Robert W. Fogel (USA)
	Douglass C. North (USA)
1994	John Nash (USA)
	Reinhard Selter (Ger)
	John Harsanyi (USA)
1995	Robert E. Lucas (USA)
1996	James Mirrlees (GB)
	William Vickrey (Can)
1997	Robert Merton (USA)
	Myron Scholes (USA)
1998	Amartya Sen (Ind)
1999	Robert Mundell (USA, Canadian-born)
2000	James J. Heckman (USA)
	Daniel L. McFadden (USA)
2001	Joseph Stiglitz (USA)
	George Akerlof (USA)
	Michael Spence (USA)
2002	Daniel Kahnemann (USA/Isr)
	Vernon Smith (USA)
2003	Robert Engle (USA)
	Clive Granger (GB)
2004	Finn Kydland (Nor)
	Edward Prescott (USA)
2005	Thomas Schelling (USA)
	Robert Aumann (USA/Isr)

LITERATURE

For the winners since 1980, and other literary prize-winners, *see* **M36**.

MEDICINE

The Nobel Prize for Medicine dates from 1901. Up to 1945 the following British persons were winners:

1902	Sir Ronald Ross
1922	Archibald V. Hill
1929	Sir Frederick G. Hopkins (joint)
1932	Edgar D. Adrian
	Sir Charles S. Sherrington
1936	Sir Henry H. Dale

Winners since 1945 have been:

1945	Sir Alexander Fleming (GB)
	Ernst B. Chain (GB, German-born)
	Sir Howard W. Florey (GB, Australian-born)
1946	Hermann J. Muller (USA)
1947	Carl F. Cori (USA, Czech-born)
	Gerty T. Cori (USA, Czech-born)
	Bernardo A. Houssay (Arg)
1948	Paul H. Müller (Swi)
1949	Walter R. Hess (Swi)
	Antonio Moniz (Por)
1950	Philip S. Hench (USA)
	Edward C. Kendall (USA)
	Tadeus Reichstein (Swi, Polish-born)
1951	Max Theiler (USA, S. African-born)
1952	Selman A. Waksman (USA)
1953	Hans A. Krebs (GB, German-born)
	Fritz A. Lipmann (USA, German-born)
1954	John F. Enders (USA)
	Frederick C. Robbins (USA)
	Thomas H. Weller (USA)
1955	Alex H. T. Theorell (Swe)
1956	André F. Cournand (USA, French-born)
	Werner Forssmann (Ger)
	Dickinson W. Richards Jr (USA)
1957	Daniel Bovet (Ita, Swiss-born)
1958	George W. Beadle (USA)
	Edward L. Tatum (USA)
	Joshua Lederberg (USA)
1959	Arthur Kornberg (USA)
	Severo Ochoa (USA, Spanish-born)
1960	Sir F. Macfarlane Burnet (Aus)
	Peter B. Medawar (GB, Brazilian-born)
1961	Georg von Békèsy (USA, Hungarian-born)

Year		Year	
1962	Francis H. C. Crick (GB) / James D. Watson (USA) / Maurice H. F. Wilkins (GB)	2001	Sir Paul Nurse (GB) / Tim Hunt (GB) / Leland Hartwell (USA)
1963	Sir John C. Eccles (Aus) / Alan L. Hodgkin (GB) / Andrew F. Huxley (GB)	2002	John Sulston (GB) / Robert Horvitz (GB) / Sydney Brenner (USA)
1964	Konrad E. Bloch (USA) / Feodor Lynen (Ger)	2003	Sir Peter Mansfield (GB) / Paul C. Lauterbur (USA)
1965	François Jacob (Fra) / André Lwoff (Fra) / Jacques Monod (Fra)	2004	Richard Axel (USA) / Linda Buck (USA)
1966	Charles B. Huggins (USA) / Francis Peyton Rous (USA)	2005	Barry Marshall (Aus) / Robin Warren (Aus)
1967	Ragnar Granit (Swe, Finnish-born) / Haldan Keffer Hartline (USA) / George Wald (USA)		

PEACE

The first Nobel Prize was awarded in 1901, five years after the death of Alfred Nobel, to Jean Henri Dunant, the Swiss founder of the Red Cross, and Frederic Passy, a French advocate of international arbitration.

1968	Robert W. Holley (USA) / Har Gobind Khorana (USA, Indian-born) / Marshall W. Nirenberg (USA)
1969	Max Delbrück (USA, German-born) / Alfred D. Hershey (USA) / Salvador D. Luria (USA, Italian-born)
1970	Julius Axelrod (USA) / Ulf von Euler (Swe) / Bernard Katz (GB)
1971	Earl W. Sutherland Jr (USA)
1972	Gerald M. Edelman (USA) / Rodney Porter (GB)
1973	Karl von Frisch (Aut) / Konrad Lorenz (Aut) / Nikolaas Tinbergen (GB, Dutch-born)
1974	Albert Claude (USA, Luxembourg-born) / Christian René de Duve (Bel) / George Emil Palade (USA, Romanian-born)
1975	David Baltimore (USA) / Howard Martin Temin (USA) / Renato Dulbecco (USA, Italian-born)
1976	Baruch S. Blumberg (USA) / D. Carleton Gajdusek (USA)
1977	Rosalyn S. Yalow (USA) / Roger C. L. Guillemin (USA, French-born) / Andrew V. Schally (USA)
1978	Werner Arber (Swi) / Daniel Nathans (USA) / Hamilton Smith (USA)
1979	Dr Hounsfield (GB) / Allan Cormack (USA)
1980	Baruy Benacerraf (Ven) / Jean Dausset (Fra) / George Snell (USA)
1981	Roger W. Sperry (USA) / David H. Hubel (USA) / Torsten N. Wiesel (Swe)
1982	Sune Bergstrom (Swe) / Bengt Samuelsson (Swe) / John R. Vane (GB)
1983	Barbara McClintock (USA)
1984	Cesar Milstein (GB, Argentinian-born) / Georges J. F. Kohler (Ger) / Niels K. Jerne (GB, Danish-born)
1985	Michael S. Brown (USA) / Joseph L. Goldstein (USA)
1986	Rita Levi-Montalcini (USA, Italian-born) / Stanley Cohen (USA)
1987	Susumu Tonegawa (Jap)
1988	Gertrude B. Elion (USA) / George H. Hitchings (USA) / Sir James Black (GB)
1989	J. Michael Bishop (USA) / Harold E. Varmus (USA)
1990	Joseph E. Murray (USA) / E. Donnall Thomas (USA)
1991	Edwin Neher (Ger) / Bert Sakmann (Ger)
1992	Edwin Krebs (USA) / Edmond Fischer (USA)
1993	Richard Roberts (GB) / Phillip Sharp (USA)
1994	Alfred G. Gilman (USA) / Martin Rodbell (USA)
1995	Edward B. Lewis (USA) / Christiane Nüesslein-Volhard (Ger) / Eric F. Wieschaus (USA)
1996	Peter Doherty (Aus) / Rolf Zinkernagel (Swi)
1997	Stanley Prusiner (USA)
1998	Robert Furchgott (USA) / Louis Ignarro (USA) / Ferid Murad (USA)
1999	Günter Blobel (USA, German-born)
2000	Arvid Carlsson (Swe) / Paul Greengard (USA) / Eric Kandel (USA)

Winners since 1945 have been:

1945	Cordell Hull (USA)
1946	Emily G. Batch (USA) / John R. Mott (USA)
1947	Friends Service Council (GB) / American Friends Service Committee (USA)
1948	no award
1949	Lord John Boyd Orr (GB)
1950	Ralph J. Bunche (USA)
1951	Léon Jouhaux (Fra)
1952	Albert Schweitzer (Fra, German-born)
1953	George C. Marshall (USA)
1954	Office of the UN High Commission for Refugees
1955	no award
1956	no award
1957	Lester B. Pearson (Can)
1958	Georges Pire (Bel)
1959	Philip J. Noel-Baker (GB)
1960	Albert J. Luthuli (SAf)
1961	Dag Hammarskjöld (Swe) (posthumous)
1962	Linus C. Pauling (USA)
1963	International Committee of the Red Cross / Red Cross Societies League
1964	Martin Luther King Jr (USA)
1965	United Nations Childrens Fund (UNICEF)
1966	no award
1967	no award
1968	René Cassin (Fra)
1969	International Labour Organization (ILO)
1970	Norman E. Borlaug (USA)
1971	Willy Brandt (FRG)
1972	no award
1973	Henry A. Kissinger (USA, German-born) / Le Duc Tho (NViet)
1974	Eisaku Sato (Jap) / Sean MacBride (Ire)
1975	Andrei D. Sakharov (USSR)
1976	Betty Williams (GB) / Mairead Corrigan (GB)
1977	Amnesty International
1978	Anwar el Sadat (Egy) / Menachem Begin (Isr)
1979	Mother Teresa of Calcutta (Alb)
1980	Adolfo Pérez Esquivel (Arg)
1981	Office of the UN High Commission for Refugees
1982	Alva Myrtal (Swe) / Alfonso Garcia Robles (Mex)
1983	Lech Walesa (Pol)
1984	Archbishop Desmond Tutu (SAf)
1985	International Physicians for the Prevention of Nuclear War
1986	Elie Wiesel (USA, Romanian-born)
1987	President Oscar Arias Sanchez (CoR)
1988	UN Peacekeeping Forces
1989	Dalai Lama (Tib)
1990	Mikhail Gorbachev (USSR)
1991	Aung San Suu Kyi (Mya)
1992	Rigoberta Menchu (Gua)
1993	F. W. de Klerk (SAf) / Nelson Mandela (SAf)
1994	Yitzak Rabin (Isr) / Yasser Arafat (Isr) / Shimon Peres (Isr)
1995	Joseph Rotblat (GB, Polish-born) / Pugwash Conferences
1996	Carlos Felipe Belo (Timor) / José Ramos-Horta (Timor)
1997	International Campaign to Ban Landmines / Jody Williams (USA)

1998	John Hume (UK)
	David Trimble (UK)
1999	*Médecins sans Frontières* (Fra)
2000	Kim Dae-jung (S Kor)
2001	Kofi Annan (Gha)
	United Nations
2002	Jimmy Carter (USA)
2003	Shirin Ebadi (Iran)
2004	Wangari Maathai (Ken)
2005	International Atomic Energy Agency
	Mohamed ElBaradei

PHYSICS

The first Nobel Prize for Physics was awarded in 1901 to Wilhelm C. Roentgen of Germany. Among the British recipients to be awarded the honour before 1945 were:

1904	Lord Rayleigh (John W. Strutt)
1906	Sir Joseph John Thomson
1915	Sir William H. Bragg
1917	Charles G. Barkla
1927	Charles T. R. Wilson (*joint award*)
1928	Owen W. Richardson
1933	Paul A. M. Dirac (*joint award*)
1935	Sir James Chadwick
1937	George P. Thomson (*joint award*)

Winners since 1945 have been:

1945	Wolfgang Pauli (USA)
1946	Percy Williams Bridgman (USA)
1947	Sir Edward V. Appleton (GB)
1948	Patrick M. S. Blackett (GB)
1949	Hideki Yukawa (Jap)
1950	Cecil F. Powell (GB)
1951	Sir John D. Cockcroft (GB)
	Ernest T. S. Walton (Ire)
1952	Felix Block (USA, Swiss-born)
	Edward Purcell (USA)
1953	Fritz Zernike (Hol)
1954	Max Born (GB, German-born)
	Walther Bothe (FRG)
1955	Polykarp Kusch (USA, German-born)
	Willis E. Lamb (USA)
1956	John Bardeen (USA)
	Walter H. Brattain (USA)
	William Shockley (USA)
1957	Tsung-Dao Lee (USA, Chinese-born)
	Chen Ning Yang (USA, Chinese-born)
1958	Paval A. Cherenkov (USSR)
	Ilya M. Frank (USSR)
	Igor J. Tamm (USSR)
1959	Owen Chamberlain (USA)
	Emilio G. Segrè (USA, Italian-born)
1960	Donald A. Glaser (USA)
1961	Robert Hofstadter (USA)
	Rudolf L. Mössbauer (FRG)
1962	Lev D. Landau (USSR)
1963	Maria Goeppert-Mayer (USA)
	J. Hans D. Jensen (FRG)
	Eugene P. Wigner (USA)
1964	Nikolai G. Basov (USSR)
	Aleksandr M. Prokhorov (USSR)
	Charles H. Townes (USA)
1965	Richard P. Feynman (USA)
	Julian S. Schwinger (USA)
	Sin-itiro Tomonaga (Jap)
1966	Alfred Kastler (Fra)
1967	Hans A. Bethe (USA, German-born)
1968	Luis W. Alvarez (USA)
1969	Murray Gell-Man (USA)
1970	Hannes O. G. Alfven (Swe)
	Louis E. F. Néel (Fra)
1971	Dennis Gabor (GB, Hungarian-born)
1972	John Bardeen (USA)
	Leon N. Cooper (USA)
	John R. Schrieffer (USA)

1973	Ivar Giaever (USA, Norwegian-born)
	Leo Esaki (Jap)
	Brian D. Josephson (GB)
1974	Antony Hewish (GB)
	Sir Martin Ryle (GB)
1975	L. James Rainwater (USA)
	Aage Bohr (Den)
	Ben Roy Mottelson (Den, USA-born)
1976	Burton Richter (USA)
	Samuel C. C. Ting (USA)
1977	John H. Van Vleck (USA)
	Philip W. Anderson (USA)
	Sir Nevill F. Mott (GB)
1978	Piotr Leontevich Kapitsa (USSR)
	Arno A. Penzias (USA, German-born)
	Robert W. Wilson (USA)
1979	Abdus Salam (GB)
	Sheldon Glashow (USA)
	Steven Weinberg (USA)
1980	James W. Cronin (USA)
	Val Fitch (USA)
1981	Nicolaas Bloemergern (USA)
	Arthur Schawlow (USA)
1982	Kenneth Wilson (USA)
1983	Subrahmanyan Chandrasekhar (USA)
	William Fowler (USA)
1984	Carlo Rubbia (Ita)
	Simon van der Meer (Hol)
1985	Klaus von Klitzing (Ger)
1986	Erns Ruska (Ger)
	Gerd Binnig (Ger)
	Heinrich Rohrer (Swi)
1987	Georg Bednorz (Ger)
	Alex Müller (Swi)
1988	Leon M. Lederman (USA)
	Melvin Schwartz (USA)
	Jack Steinberger (Ger)
1989	Norman Ramsey (USA)
	Hans Dehmelt (USA)
	Wolfgang Paul (Ger)
1990	Jerome Friedman (USA)
	Henry Kendall (USA)
	Richard Taylor (Can)
1991	Pierre-Giles de Gennes (Fra)
1992	Georges Charpak (Fra)
1993	Russell Huise (USA)
	Joseph Taylor (USA)
1994	Bertram N. Brockhouse (Can)
	Clifford G. Shull (USA)
1995	Frederick Reines (USA)
	Douglas Osheroff (USA)
1996	David Lee (USA)
	Robert Richardson (USA)
1997	Claude Cohen-Tannoudji (Fra)
	Steven Chu (USA)
	William Phillips (USA)
1998	Robert Laughlin (USA)
	Daniel Tsui (USA)
	Horst Störmer (Ger)
1999	Gerardus 't Hooft (Hol)
	Martinus Veltman (Hol)
2000	Zhores Alferov (Rus)
	Herbert Kroemer (USA)
	Jack Kilby (USA)
2001	Eric Cornell (USA)
	Carl Wiemann (USA)
	Wolfgang Ketterle (Ger)
2002	Raymond Davis Jnr (USA)
	Masatushi Koshiba (Jap)
	Riccardo Giacconi (USA)
2003	Anthony Leggett (GB)
	Alexei Abrikosov (Rus)
	Vitaly Ginzburg (USA)
2004	David Gross (USA)
	David Politzer (USA)
	Frank Wilczek (USA)
2005	Roy Glauber (USA)
	John Hall (USA)
	Theodor Haensch (USA)

BACKGROUND TO WORLD AFFAIRS

This section is in three parts. The first provides an up-to-date chronicle of political developments in Britain from 2001 to the local elections of May 2006. The second part provides a wide-ranging guide to events in important areas elsewhere in the world. The third part consists of a series of special topics. There are background articles in this edition on Iran, Venezuela, Belarus, Myanmar and the Central Asian Republics (with their new strategic importance).

TABLE OF CONTENTS

BACKGROUND TO WORLD AFFAIRS

This section is in three parts. The first outlines the political history of the United Kingdom since 2001. The second part provides a wide-ranging guide to events elsewhere in the world and takes stock of the changing patterns in international relations. The third section contains special topics on particular themes. The reader is invited to turn to **Section D** for further key facts and figures relating to the British political system.

I. SURVEY OF THE BRITISH POLITICAL SCENE

BRITISH POLITICAL EVENTS 1997–2006

Background Chronology: The Labour Government 1997–2001.

1997 Labour wins landslide victory; Hague replaces Major as Conservative leader; Bank of England given power to set interest rates; IRA renews ceasefire; Scotland and Wales vote for devolution; criticism of Royal Family following death of Princess of Wales; Labour backbench revolt over child benefit measures; Ecclestone Affair raises 'cash for access' concerns over donations to Labour.

1998 Good Friday Agreement backed in Ireland and Northern Ireland referendums; British and US missile attacks on Iraq; further concerns over political donations by Labour supporters; increased co-operation proposed between Labour and Liberal Democrats; Mandelson's first resignation from government.

1999 Single European currency established without Britain; gay consent age lowered to 16; Kennedy replaces Ashdown as Liberal Democrat leader; Macpherson Report raises issue of institutional racism; Lords reform compromise spares 92 hereditary peers; minimum wage introduced; anti-social behaviour orders introduced; Conservatives take 36 seats in European elections to Labour's 29; Northern Ireland power-sharing assembly established; Welsh Assembly and Scottish Parliament inaugurated; British aircraft bomb Yugoslavia.

2000 Millennium Dome opens to criticism; ban ends on gay men and women serving in armed forces; Northern Ireland assembly suspended; Labour setback in local elections; expelled Labour member Livingstone elected as London mayor; oil refineries blockade by farmers and lorry drivers in tax protest; Human Rights Act comes into force; Chancellor announces increased spending in three-year review; government rejects calls for rail renationalisation after series of accidents.

2001 Mandelson's second resignation; foot and mouth outbreak delays local elections; expansive budget increases spending on education and health; unemployment falls below a million for first time in 25 years; race riots in Oldham.

Labour's First Term: The Balance Sheet.

Labour's honeymoon had ended as the sense of hope that had greeted the 1997 victory faded. Labour could claim significant achievements, but these were balanced by a concern that the government, and Mr Blair in particular, were enmeshed in a culture of 'spin', with appearance dominating substance. Nevertheless, there was little doubt that Labour would return with a substantial majority as the Conservatives showed themselves unable to pose a plausible alternative. New Labour's timidity had disappointed many, but Mr Blair could legiti-mately claim that he had reduced Conservatism to a virtual irrelevance. Labour's supporters hoped that a second term might encourage the government to show a greater radicalism.

The 2001 Election Campaign.

Parliament was dissolved on 14 May, with the general election (and local elections in England and Wales) set for 7 June. With the result almost a foregone conclusion, as Labour's lead in the opinion polls held solid, the unveiling of the manifestos and the campaign generated little enthusiasm. Mr Blair manoeuvred carefully, playing to what Mr Blair saw as its strengths—education, health and economic competence—Mr Hague concentrated on rebuilding the Tory core vote that had collapsed so disastrously in 1997.

The Nominations.

A total of 3294 candidates stood for election (down from the record-breaking 3715 of 1997). The number of women candidates was significantly down (from 670 in 1997 to 631 in 2001). The Conservative and Labour parties each fielded 640 candidates, the Liberal Democrats 639. Over 400 candidates were put forward by the United Kingdom Independence Party (UKIP), while the Nationalists fought all seats in Wales and Scotland. The Greens fielded 145 candidates whilst left-wing challenges were mounted by the Socialist Alliance (100 candidates) and the Socialist Labour Party (114 candidates)

The Party Manifestos.

The Conservative manifesto pledged there would be no entry into the European currency during the lifetime of the next Parliament, a transparent attempt to paper over divisions that almost faltered in the face of Lady Thatcher's mid-campaign declaration that she would 'never' abandon the pound. The party promised to keep to Labour's spending commitments in popular areas such as health and education but nevertheless declared it could find £8 billion tax reductions. There were to be firmer law and order policies and stronger measures against asylum seekers. The Liberal Democrats, now arguably to the left of Labour, argued for increased taxation with a penny on the basic rate and a 50% band for people on over £100,000 a year, to fund increased recruitment to education and the NHS.

The Outcome.

In terms of seats won, the results were very similar to 1997. The Labour total fell slightly, the Conservatives made a net gain of just one seat, whilst the Liberal Democrats gained 8 to a total of 52. In Wales, Labour gained Anglesey (Ynys Mon) from Plaid Cymru which in turn gained the Carmarthenshire East and Dinefwr seat. Scotland saw only one change—a lone Conservative winning Galloway and Upper Nithsdale. In Northern Ireland the Ulster Unionists lost seats to both the

Democratic Unionists and to Sinn Fein, severely weakening David Trimble's position.

Overall, there was a swing from Labour to Conservative of 1·8 %, but the most marked feature of the election was the fall in turnout to 59·3 %. Another feature was a drop in the number of women MPs (from a record 121 in 1997 to 115 in 2001). The full election result was as follows:

	Seats	Gains	Losses	Total vote	% of vote
Lab	413	2	8	10,740,168	40·7
Con	166	9	8	8,354,460	31·7
LibDem	52	8	2	4,815,249	18·3
SNP	5	0	1	464,314	1·8
PC	4	1	1	195,892	0·7
Others	19	7	7	1,795,109	6·8

The Results Analysed.

For Labour, returning 413 MPs, the result was a remarkable triumph. Only 8 seats were lost, mainly suburban seats such as Romford and Upminster to the Conservatives. Other losses included Chesterfield to the Liberal Democrats and the Wyre Forest to an Independent (campaigning on local hospital closures). For the Conservatives, it was a night of almost unmitigated disaster. Only 9 seats were gained and 8 lost (mainly to the Liberal Democrats). Only one Conservative was returned in Scotland and none in Wales. The party failed to recover its hitherto safe seats lost in 1997 (such as Wimbledon or Torbay).

The Liberal Democrats had much to celebrate. Leading the party in his first election as leader, Charles Kennedy saw the tally of Liberal Democrat seats rise to 52 (the best result since the 1929 election when Lloyd George was leader).

For the Nationalists in Scotland, who lost one seat to the Conservatives, the election was a disappointment. Their total vote was well down (to 464,314). In Wales, however, Plaid Cymru achieved its best ever vote but its tally of seats remained the same at 4 (1 gain, 1 loss).

Minor parties in general fared badly. With 420 candidates, UKIP polled only 390,575 votes. The Greens, as well as a variety of socialist groupings, also made no impact.

The Resignation of William Hague.

Immediately the scale of the Conservative election defeat became apparent, William Hague announced his decision to resign as leader (a decision he had apparently made back in 1999). His resignation left the party not only with a potentially divisive leadership election but also in urgent need of redefining its policies and priorities.

The New Cabinet.

The second landslide Labour victory enabled the Prime Minister to undertake a major Cabinet reshuffle. Among the main changes, Jack Straw moved to the Foreign Office and David Blunkett to the Home Office. John Prescott remained as Deputy Prime Minister. In what was widely seen as a demotion, Robin Cook became Leader of the House of Commons. Margaret Beckett (one of a record seven women members of the Cabinet) was given the new post of Environment, Food and Rural Affairs. Promotion came to Estelle Morris who became Secretary of State for Education and Skills.

Two departures from the Cabinet were Chris Smith and Ann Taylor. The embattled Europe Minister, Keith Vaz, was replaced by Peter Hain, the former Energy Minister. Two surprises were the appointments of Harriet Harman as Solicitor-General and Alun Michael as Rural Affairs Minister.

The Legislative Programme.

There was little sign in the Queen's Speech in June of the government running out of steam. Legislation was proposed on further reform of the NHS, education and the House of Lords, on police powers and the complaints system, enforcement of business competition and increased encouragement for people on benefits to seek work. But, despite Labour's overwhelming election victory, there was continuing frustration over public services, particularly transport and health, which were felt to be in a worse condition than in 1997.

Victory for Iain Duncan Smith.

Media interest, however, concentrated on the Conservative leadership election, a long drawn out process that opened in June and continued into mid-September, when the party in the country chose Eurosceptic Iain Duncan Smith over the more publicly popular Kenneth Clarke. Michael Portillo, who had entered on a radical modernising programme, fell by the wayside.

Other Domestic Issues.

The Northern Ireland peace process stalled once more in July when First Minister David Trimble resigned in protest against the IRA's failure to meet his deadline for decommissioning weapons. Deadlock continued until 23 October when the IRA announced it would begin disarming, allowing the return of Mr Trimble and the Ulster Unionists to the Assembly.

July was marked by serious racial disturbances in Bradford, the culmination of three months of violence in northern English towns with large Asian populations. The events echoed riots in black areas in the 1980s and the causes were similar. On 12 July a former Commission for Racial Equality chairman reported that Bradford was divided on ethnic and religious lines, with segregation in education.

The Terrorist Aftermath.

The terrorist attacks in the United States played a dominant part in British politics during the year. On 11 September Mr Blair was due to face the Trades Union Congress with plans to outsource parts of the NHS to the private sector but instead returned to London. Mr Blair played a significant part in building an international coalition to support the United States in the 'war on terrorism', visiting many world capitals to weld the alliance. On 27 September he met leaders of Britain's two million Muslims to assure them that this was not a war against Islam. There were, however, attacks on Asians in British streets.

The Party Conferences.

The events muted the autumn party conferences. This had the advantage for Liberal Democrat leader Charles Kennedy of preventing discussion of the party's position in the political spectrum following its general election triumph. Labour's shortened conference avoided conflict over the role of the private sector in the public services and the government's asylum policies as Mr Blair gave an emotional speech on Britain's role in the world. The Conservatives showed little evidence that they had come to terms with their second election defeat.

Against the background of growing anger over the condition of the privatised railways, the Transport Secretary, Stephen Byers, announced on 7 October that Railtrack was going into administration and would be replaced by a non-profit company financed through bonds. There was, however, no evidence that what came next had been fully thought out as delays became worse rather than better. This was not helped by growing union militancy in the industry, something also rising in other areas.

Anti-Terrorist Measures.

The impact of 11 September on domestic politics became clear when the Home Secretary, David Blunkett, tabled emergency anti-terrorist measures in October including deportation of foreign suspects and the suspension of an article of the European Convention on Human Rights. The government was accused of taking the opportunity to extend police powers that had little connection with terrorism. Mr Blunkett dismissed fears as 'airy fairy' but came under pressure to dilute the legislation as 32 Labour backbenchers joined a cross-party revolt in November.

There were further problems for Labour when Scotland's First Minister, Henry McLeish, resigned after admitting he had received undeclared income.

House of Lords Reform.

In November the government published a white paper on the second stage of House of Lords reform. The remaining 92 hereditary peers would go. A fifth of the 600 members would be elected, 60 % nominated by political parties (in proportion to their share of the general election vote) and 20 % appointed by a commission. Law lords would continue to sit but representation of Church of England bishops would be reduced from 26 to 16 to allow access to other faiths and denominations. The proposals were attacked from all sides, with charges of 'cronyism'.

Over 100 Labour MPs pressed for more radical proposals and ministers, fearing a wider revolt, offered to listen. The Conservative leader further embarrassed the government on 13 January 2002 by proposing that the assembly should have only 300 members, with 80 % elected for 15 years on a rolling basis. Members should, he said, be affiliated to parties but retain their independence to enable them to resist government pressure. Mr Blair condemned the proposal on the grounds that a chamber too much like the Commons would lead to 'gridlock'.

Developing Problems.

The Chancellor, Gordon Brown, renewed the government's commitment to a publicly funded health service in his financial statement on 27 November, attempting to draw a contrast with Conservative policies. He promised more money for deprived areas and increased spending on the armed forces to meet the needs of the anti-terrorist campaign. But Mr Brown warned of significantly lower tax revenues in this and the following year.

On 10 December New Labour suffered its first defection as an anti-war MP crossed to the Liberal Democrats, somewhat illogically as they too supported the war against terrorism. On the following day the Cantle Report on the summer riots in Bradford, Oldham and Burnley was published. The report called on the government to take action to draw together divided communities, saying that people were living 'parallel' and 'polarised' lives, and made 67 recommendations covering education, housing regeneration, youth facilities and political leadership. It warned of the dangers of single-faith schools, something the government favoured

The Public Services.

Stung by criticism that he was neglecting domestic concerns in the wake of 11 September, Mr Blair turned to the public services in January 2002. He claimed they were improving but told a group of Labour backbenchers that failure to reform could cost the party the next election. Mr Blair was sensitive to a growing mood. Despite economic success there was dissatisfaction about what had once been described as public squalor amid private affluence. The collapse in the United States of the energy giant Enron in January raised questions about Labour's relations with big business. The party had accepted sponsorship from Enron. The Conservatives—who had also benefited from Enron money—took the opportunity to renew charges of 'sleaze' against the government.

Tensions within New Labour.

Mr Blair walked into further trouble with a speech on 3 February in which he denounced 'wreckers' resisting public service modernisation (taken by union leaders to refer to their members) at the very moment industrial militancy was growing. Labour won the Ogmore by-election on 15 February but with their 2001 majority halved as former supporters appeared disenchanted.

From mid-February Mr Blair faced one of the most uncomfortable periods of his career as his government drifted through a series of minor but debilitating crises. Mr Blair was accused of lobbying in favour of an Indian billionaire donor to Labour in his efforts to take over a Romanian steel company. The government's discomfort was increased by turmoil in the Transport and Local Government ministry, culminating in the resignation of a political aide and the dismissal of the chief press officer, followed by demands for Mr Byers to be sacked. By March there was growing backbench criticism of Mr Blair's support for an attack on Iraq. This seemed ever more likely after a meeting with President Bush in early April.

The year saw the paradox of a sense of disappointment and discontent with the government, and Mr Blair in particular, but little sign of Labour's poll lead falling significantly. The Conservatives, as

the main opposition party, and the Liberal Democrats, who hoped to seize that position, appeared incapable of making a breakthrough that would threaten the government.

Ministerial Resignations.

Mr Byers was forced to resign as transport secretary, weakened as much by an inadequate policy as his own failings. His successor effectively abandoned the 10-year transport plan. The resignation of the education secretary, Estelle Morris, involved the government's failure to meet numeracy and literacy targets and a fiasco over A-level marking, but also Cabinet arguments about higher education funding. Among other targets the government failed to meet were those on hospital waiting lists (despite increased NHS spending), violent crime, hard drug use and the expulsion of rejected asylum seekers. While the results of the pledge to halve child poverty in a decade were creditable, progress had slowed. Many targets were dropped in the comprehensive spending review.

Conservative Identity Crisis.

The intractable Conservative identity crisis continued. Mr Duncan Smith attempted to display a masterly ruthlessness by dismissing the party chairman in June for holding back the party's modernisation, replacing him with Ms Theresa May. At the party conference in October Ms May told members that some people saw them as the 'nasty' party while Mr Duncan Smith described himself as the 'quiet man' of politics. But rumours of moves against him gathered pace. In November Mr Duncan Smith admitted his own weakness by warning the party that it must 'unite or die'.

His work was not helped when Lord Heseltine called on the party in the Commons to oust their leader and replace him with Mr Clarke or Mr Portillo. Although the party was slowly developing new policies, it was tangled in a contradiction between trying to appear to be the champion of public services while retaining an instinct to cut taxes. The Liberal Democrats were unable to capitalise on the support they had won at the general election. Mr Kennedy, knowing that further advance depended on capturing Conservative seats, denied that his party would oppose the government from the left. He was convincing, however, in his attacks on the government's Iraq policy.

Renewed Trade Union Militancy.

With little effective opposition in parliament, the mood of discontent encouraged a turn to the left in trade union leadership elections, with the rejection of candidates seen as friendly to Mr Blair. Nowhere was a new sense of militancy more evident than in the series of firefighters' strikes that began in November and, after abortive negotiations (allegedly scuppered by the government), continued into 2003. Although their demand for a 40 % rise appeared excessive they had widespread public sympathy. The government's fear was that a firefighters' victory would prompt greater demands from an increasingly restive public sector workforce.

Polarisation in Northern Ireland.

Although the peace held in Northern Ireland, despite continuing Unionist anger at the IRA's failure to disarm and disband, allegations of Republican spying at Stormont in October forced the temporary abandonment of power-sharing as the British government re-imposed direct rule and suspended the Good Friday agreement institutions. The scene appeared set for an increasing polarisation, with the pro-peace process Ulster Unionists vulnerable to the more antagonistic Democratic Unionists in the longer term.

Problems for the Monarchy.

After an outflow of sympathy following the death of Princess Margaret and then of the Queen Mother at Easter, and an unexpectedly enthusiastic turnout for the Queen's golden jubilee celebrations, by the end of the year the Royal Family had returned to the grim position that had followed Princess Diana's death in 1997. In November embarrassing revelations emerged during and after the abandoned trials of two former butlers accused of theft. Once again the Royal Family, and the Prince of Wales in particular, appeared out of touch with modern life. Mr Blair's own family was similarly embarrassed in December when it was revealed that his wife had enlisted the help of a convicted fraudster, the companion of Mrs Blair's 'lifestyle adviser', in buying two flats. A tearful television appearance by Mrs Blair stemmed the affair, but Mr Blair's personal standing sustained some damage.

Mounting Economic Difficulties.

But the economy and the prospect of war with Iraq dominated politics. Britain remained stronger economically than most of her competitors but over the course of the year the domestic position weakened. One effect was a crisis in pensions, with final salary schemes increasingly phased out as the stock market fell. Manufacturing industry was weakening, while house prices and consumer spending soared unrealistically. Mr Brown's pre-budget report in November 2002 was the most difficult he had had to deliver since becoming chancellor. Growth had been slower than he had forecast. For this he blamed the downturn in the United States, Europe and Japan. His public spending plans remained unchanged and, consequently, the government would have to borrow more than he had expected. With national insurance contributions set to increase in April 2003, and the personal tax allowance frozen, the Conservatives were not slow to accuse the government of reverting to Labour type.

The Shadow of Iraq.

The possibility of war with Iraq threatened to be one of the most divisive issues Mr Blair had faced. He strenuously backed President Bush's call for an attack on Iraq if Saddam Hussein did not dismantle the weapons of mass destruction he was alleged to hold. The 'spin' placed on Mr Blair's policy was that he was attempting to restrain President Bush from any unilateral act and ensure that the United States acted through the United Nations. However, it proved a difficult balancing act, and one that strained relations with Britain's European partners. Only Mr Blair's emphasis on international action prevented an early revolt by Labour backbenchers.

As Iraq began to dominate politics and the government appeared unable to persuade a significant minority of public opinion to accept the case for an attack, Mr Blair came under intense pressure, with opinion polls showing falling popularity. The Conservatives— who backed the government's line—were, however, ill-placed to capitalise on this as Mr Duncan Smith's leadership came under inner-party attack.

Anti-War Protests.

On 15 February over a million protestors rallied in London as part of the international campaign against an apparently inevitable conflict. On 26 February, in the largest parliamentary revolt for over a century, 121 Labour backbenchers were among the 199 MPs supporting an amendment declaring the case for war not proven. The chancellor, Mr Brown, declared that the government would spend whatever was necessary to disarm Iraq. But on 9 March Cabinet tensions came into the open as international development secretary Ms Short threatened to resign if Britain became involved in an attack not sanctioned by the United Nations and accused the prime minister of recklessness. In the event, it was not Ms Short but Mr Cook, the leader of the House and a number of junior ministers who resigned on 17 March as it became clear the government was intent on war without United Nations support.

The following day the government secured a 419 to 149 majority on a motion endorsing an attack, but 139 Labour backbenchers backed an anti-war amendment. On 20 March British marines moved into southern Iraq.

The 2003 Iraq War.

For details of the campaign and the major events, *see* **Special Topic, C52.** With troops in action, opinion in the country on the war shifted towards the gov-

ernment, although significant opposition remained, not least on Labour's backbenches. But the appointment on 4 April of John Reid as leader of the House and Ian McCartney as party chairman was interpreted as a careful balancing act on the part of a prime minister who might seem vulnerable. Mr Reid was seen as a heavyweight able to enforce discipline, while Mr McCartney was a popular figure with the party grassroots and the trade union movement. With over 100 Labour backbenchers having declared their opposition to the government's policy to establish 'foundation' hospitals, Mr Blair faced further rebellion on the domestic front.

The April 2003 Budget.

As Allied forces continued to consolidate their hold on Baghdad, attention switched back on 9 April to domestic politics, with the presentation of the Budget (itself delayed and overshadowed by the Iraq war).

The Budget, as widely predicted, offered few surprises, with Mr Brown resorting to increased borrowing rather than any further major tax increases (although the duties on beer, wine and cigarettes were increased).

Resignation of Clare Short.

Conservative successes in the May local government elections gave Mr Duncan Smith a temporary respite from inner-party attacks. Meanwhile, on 12 May, International Development Secretary Clare Short resigned, after much hesitation that did little for her reputation. Ms Short criticised Mr Blair's increasing centralisation of power. Only a few days earlier, over 50 Labour rebels had opposed the government's proposals to introduce foundation hospitals, which they said were a first stage to privatising the NHS. In March over 130 Labour backbenchers had voted against the invasion of Iraq. The central political question over the course of the year was whether Mr Blair could survive as Labour leader. The election by the Transport and General Workers' Union of a left-wing general secretary, following left advances in Amicus and the rail union, held out the potential of union-government clashes and a divided party.

It proved to be the Chancellor, Mr Brown, who saved the government from the potentially embarrassing need to mount the promised referendum on whether Britain should join the European currency. He reported in June that the five tests had still not been passed, avoiding a vote that Mr Blair would in all likelihood have lost. A Cabinet reshuffle in the same month proved chaotic, as Mr Blair dismissed his former patron Lord Irvine as Lord Chancellor, prematurely abolished the office, and promoted his close friend Lord Falconer in his place.

The Death of Dr Kelly.

In July the Socialist Campaign Group convened a conference of left-wing MPs and union leaders to retrieve the party from New Labour, buoyed up by growing doubts over the legitimacy of the invasion of Iraq. But it was the suicide of government weapons expert Dr David Kelly on 18 July that would pose the greatest threat to Mr Blair. Dr Kelly had been named as the source of a BBC report alleging the government had knowingly exaggerated the threat from Iraq. Mr Blair denied any involvement in naming Dr Kelly and appointed a senior judge, Lord Hutton, to conduct an inquiry into the circumstances leading to Dr Kelly's death.

The Campbell Resignation.

The enquiry, and the evidence that emerged of how the government had conducted affairs, dominated the summer. There were suggestions that the Defence Secretary's position was vulnerable. In August Mr Blair's press secretary, Mr Campbell, resigned. Lord Hutton withdrew to write his report in September, fueling weeks of speculation. Given the atmosphere of suspicion and cynicism, it was perhaps not surprising that the Liberal Democrats captured Brent East from Labour in a by-election on 18 September, pushing the Conservatives into third place, sealing Mr Duncan Smith's fate and raising questions about Mr Blair's wisdom in holding an election at this point.

As the autumn conference season approached, Mr

Blair called union leaders to Downing Street in an attempt to prevent conflict over his public sector reform programme. Nevertheless, on 8 September the Trades Union Congress voted to block £40 million funding to the party and attacked the government for its policies on foundation hospitals, university top-up fees, long working hours and apparent favouritism to the wealthy. Mr Blair faced fewer alarms at the party conference, although a speech on the theme of 'Real Labour' by Mr Brown was inevitably interpreted as evidence of his willingness to offer a new kind of leadership. The conference rejected the government's proposals on foundation hospitals. Mr Blair promised greater concentration on domestic affairs and wider consultation.

The Fall of Duncan Smith.

Mr Duncan Smith's call for unity at the Conservative conference in October was followed a few days later by the announcement of a Parliamentary enquiry into his employment of his wife as a secretary. On 29 October Mr Duncan Smith lost a confidence vote among Tory MPs by 75 to 90. Mr Howard rapidly emerged as a unity candidate and on 4 November took the leadership unopposed, declaring he would lead the party from its centre. There was a rapid improvement in Conservative confidence. But an October reshuffle by Mr Kennedy of his leadership team, revealing a move to the right by the Liberal Democrats, suggested he saw Conservative voters as worth cultivating in a bid to become the main opposition party.

NHS Foundation Hospitals.

On 19 November the government's controversial foundation hospitals legislation was passed by only 302 votes to 285, reducing Labour's majority of over 160 to 17. But the Queen's Speech showed no diminution in Mr Blair's taste for challenging his party. At its centre was a new system of student finance, including variable tuition top-up fees. Labour had pledged not to do this in its 1997 and 2001 election manifestos and the issue was to prove dangerously divisive. Among other proposals were placing children of failed asylum seekers into care, establishing a Supreme Court to take over the judicial function of the House of Lords (from which the remaining hereditary peers were also to be removed), extending police powers in national emergencies, and measures to protect members of company pension schemes. A state visit by a closely-guarded President Bush at the end of November proved not to be the security problem that had been predicted.

Stalemate in Northern Ireland.

Meanwhile, although Northern Ireland remained at peace, hopes for further political progress stalled. With elections to the suspended Stormont postponed in May, progress was dashed in November when a deal between the Ulster Unionists and Sinn Fein collapsed in the face of dissatisfaction with the IRA's promises on arms decommissioning. Elections nonetheless went ahead, throwing the situation into greater turmoil. Dr Paisley's Democratic Unionist Party took 30 seats, Mr Trimble's Ulster Unionists taking 27. Sinn Fein returned with 24 seats, ousting the SDLP (with 18) as the voice of the nationalist community. Dr Paisley's refusal to contemplate power sharing with Sinn Fein shattered any prospect of a speedy return to devolved government.

Growing Doubts over Iraq.

The failure to find the weapons of mass destruction that had been Mr Blair's justification for invading Iraq undermined support for a war that, having been declared won in May, continued to smoulder dangerously. Lord Hutton's enquiry, ostensibly confined to the events surrounding Dr Kelly's death, had acted as a substitute for a thorough investigation into the government's war policy. The government argued that Saddam Hussein's capture in December, followed by Libya's promise to abandon the development of weapons of mass destruction, confirmed that the attack had been right. The war's opponents were building their hopes on Lord Hutton finding that Mr Blair had

lied, a charge the Tory opposition played upon and one that Mr Blair vigorously denied.

The Hutton Report.

As the vote on top-up fees and the publication of the Hutton Report approached, speculation mounted that Mr Blair's tenure in office was coming to an end. On 27 January 2004, with over 70 Labour MPs voting against tuition fees, the government saw its majority fall to a humiliating five as the Higher Education Bill was given a second reading by 316 votes to 311. Two days later Lord Hutton's report vindicated the government, making only minor criticisms over their handling of Dr Kelly, but thoroughly castigated the BBC, whose director general and chairman resigned. Whatever doubts there were about the conclusions Lord Hutton had reached, and opinion polls showed there were many, Mr Blair's position appeared secure. But the wider issue of the justification for war remained and Mr Blair was impelled to follow in President Bush's steps by setting up an enquiry into possible intelligence errors over Iraq's stocks of mass destruction.

Changes in Conservative Policy.

In February the Conservatives acknowledged the shift that Labour had achieved since 1997 by promising to put the protection of health and education before tax cuts. Mr Howard also declared the party would be less abrasive about Britain's relations with Europe. However, despite a growing Conservative confidence, the government's position seemed hardly dented by continuing popular concerns about Mr Blair's role in taking the country into the Iraq war. On 8 March the government suffered a serious defeat as the Lords delayed plans to create a Supreme Court and abolish the office of Lord Chancellor.

The March 2004 Budget.

With local and European elections due in June, and a general election expected in 2005, Mr Brown's 17 March Budget was political in emphasis, challenging the Conservatives with increased spending on health and education. Mr Brown delayed for another year any decision on entry into the European currency, and the referendum that would follow that decision.

The EU Referendum Debate.

With growing concerns about the situation in Iraq the question of trust continued to haunt the government. On 1 April the Immigration Minister was forced to resign after admitting 'unwittingly' misleading the Commons in a statement, in the process encouraging the mounting media scare campaign about immigration and asylum seekers. Mr Blair's announcement on 20 April that he would allow a referendum on a new European constitution, after months in which he had said it was unnecessary, was seen as either a humiliating retreat or an astute undermining of a possible Conservative election issue.

Middle East Criticisms.

Mr Blair's future as Labour leader was openly questioned as an unprecedented denunciation of his Middle Eastern policy by 52 former senior diplomats at the end of April was followed in May by revelations that Iraqi prisoners had been tortured by Coalition forces. Mr Blair declared he would lead his party to a third victory and opinion polls appeared to bear out his confidence in the party's longer term success. But the obstacle of the local and European elections remained to be surmounted.

"Super Thursday": The 10 June 2004 Elections.

Labour had much to defend in the June elections since many of the contests were in its metropolitan strongholds where the Liberal Democrats were hoping to make gains (buoyed by their success in the Brent East parliamentary by-election). With Iraq, Europe and rising petrol prices as campaign issues, political commentators were looking to see how the Muslim vote would fare and whether a strong BNP challenge would succeed (especially in such areas as

Yorkshire and the North East). The elections would also mark a very major test of Conservative fortunes under Michael Howard (with UKIP aiming to attract disaffected Conservatives).

The Eurosceptic Upsurge.

The local election results (discussed in detail on **D13**) were a near disaster for Labour, with the party in third place in terms of votes cast and with a swathe of once solid Labour councils lost (including Cardiff, Newcastle and Swansea.) The outcome of the European elections was bad both for Labour *and* the Conservatives. The real beneficiary was UKIP (the anti-EU United Kingdom Independence Party). In England, UKIP secured third place in terms of votes and took 12 seats (with around 17 % of the vote). The Liberal Democrats, although increasing their percentage vote and adding 2 to their tally of MEPs, were forced into fourth place. The far-right BNP, although winning no seats, took over 8 % of the vote in the Yorkshire and Humberside euro-constituency.

Draft EU Constitution.

On 18 June agreement was announced at the Brussels Summit on a draft EU Constitutional Treaty. Mr Blair claimed the constitution treaty was 'good for Britain and good for Europe' and that Britain's 'red lines' over issues such as taxation and defence had been protected. Opponents, riding a tide of Euroscepticism, disagreed strongly. The rejection of the constitution treaty by France and Holland in subsequent referendums, and the ensuing collapse of the July 2005 summit changed all this.

Growing Disillusion.

As the widely expected general election approached, there was growing disillusion with Mr Blair, not least over the Iraq war, combined with a continuing Labour lead in the opinion polls. Lord Butler's inquiry into pre-war intelligence, published in July 2004, criticised Mr Blair's style of government and cast doubt on the intelligence used to justify the attack on Iraq. Mr Blair's apology took the form of saying that he had acted rightly on what he now agreed was faulty information. In the subsequent House of Commons debate, 32 Labour backbenchers rebelled against the government. In by-elections, the Liberal Democrats captured Leicester South from Labour, who narrowly held Birmingham Hodge Hill.

Developments in 2004.

Mr Brown's spending review statement on 12 July confidently set out the government's proposals for the next three years, with overall spending rising by £61 billion to £340 billion in 2007-8. Over 100,000 civil service and other public sector posts were to be cut, in line with proposals made in the January 2004 Gershon Report. However, the Chancellor's personal position was undermined in September by Mr Blair's appointment of former health secretary Mr Alan Milburn as Labour election strategy co-ordinator, a role Mr Brown had seen as his own. Mr Blair went on to make it clear that he intended to serve a third term, a further rebuff to Mr Brown that was to have consequences in January 2005.

In a by-election at the end of September Labour held Hartlepool—vacated by Mr Mandelson on his appointment as a European Commissioner—while the Conservatives were pushed into fourth place by UKIP, further humiliating an already uneasy Tory leadership.

The Iraq Backcloth.

The Iraq Survey Group reported in October that Iraq had not possessed the weapons of mass destruction that had been Mr Blair's justification for the attack on Iraq. However, he was saved from an embarrassing defeat at the Labour Party conference when the leaders of the 'Big Four' trade unions, grateful for limited concessions Mr Blair had made at a summer meeting in Warwick, rallied round him. But as the news of violence and the murder of hostages in Iraq grew increasingly grim, opinion polls showed a growing lack of trust in the prime minister.

The 2004 Party Conferences.

The party conference season saw the first stages of what promised to be a long drawn out general election campaign. Mr Kennedy declared at the Liberal Democrats conference that three party politics was here to stay. The Conservatives offered a war on government waste and bureaucracy, opposition to the European Constitution, and held out a possibility of tax cuts. Labour promised security from crime and terrorism and opportunity for all. However, one of their policies—regional government—was given an early and decisive rejection in a referendum in the north-east of England.

The Legislative Priorities.

With what many saw as the diversion of the ban on fox hunting out of the way (the government invoked the Parliament Act to overcome House of Lords' resistance), the Queen's Speech on 23 November set out the government's priorities for the future. The speech was largely Home Office driven, with proposals to combat drug use, terrorism, organised crime and anti-social behaviour, and, most controversially, to introduce ID cards. Mr Blair said that security would go hand-in-hand with economic stability and improvements in public services. Mr Blunkett, the Home Secretary, denied a Liberal Democrat charge that the government was creating a 'climate of fear'.

Mr Brown said in his annual pre-budget report on 2 December that growth in 2004 had met his target of 3.25 % but that he was increasing government borrowing. Opponents claimed that the government would be forced to increase taxes or to borrow even more heavily. Mr Brown said he would not introduce a proposed fuel duty increase, would allocate £1 billion to hold council tax rises down, would devote a further £105 million to anti-terrorism measures, and increase paid maternity leave and nursery places.

Problems in Ulster.

Meanwhile, progress over the restoration of the Northern Ireland Assembly faltered in December as the Democratic Unionist Party remained dissatisfied with Sinn Fein's proposals on IRA disarmament. The Northern Ireland chief constable's charge that the IRA had carried out the largest ever bank robbery in the United Kingdom further undermined hopes of a settlement. On 2 February 2005 the IRA withdrew their commitment to decommission weapons, apparently as a bargaining gambit. The Republican crisis deepened with accusations of IRA involvement in a bar-room murder.

The Blunkett Resignation.

The turn of the year saw a series of dramatic events. On 15 December Mr Blunkett resigned following allegations that he had fast-tracked a visa application made by the nanny of his former lover. Mr Blunkett's position was not helped with the publication of a biography in which he criticised his Cabinet colleagues. Although evidence emerged of contacts by the Home Secretary's private office with the immigration service, despite earlier denials, Mr Blair declared that Mr Blunkett's integrity remained intact. Mr Charles Clarke was appointed in his place. On 16 December the House of Lords undermined a key plank of the government's anti-terrorism policy by ruling that the detention without trial of foreign terrorist suspects violated human rights laws. Finally, in January 2005, the long-running conflict between Mr Blair and Mr Brown over the Labour leadership burst into the open once more. In October 2004 Mr Blair had announced that he would serve a third term, breaking an earlier promise he was said to have made to Mr Brown that he would stand down before the next election. Mr Brown's response, according to a book by a journalist close to him, was to tell Mr Blair, 'There is nothing that you can say to me now that I could ever believe'. Mr Blair denied this, while Mr Brown was non-committal.

On 1 January 2005 the Freedom of Information Act came into force, giving a right of access to information held by public bodies, including central and local government, the police, schools and the National Health Service. Officials rejected opposition allegations that government departments had shredded papers in the run-up to implementation.

The Start of Electioneering.

The New Year saw a sharpening of the parties' pre-election positions. Mr Blair announced on 13 January that Labour's manifesto would be 'unremittingly New Labour', with an emphasis on individual prosperity and radically improved public services. On 17 January Mr Howard—somewhat embarrassed by the defection to Labour a day earlier of a former junior minister—promised a Conservative government would find savings of £35 billion, £23 billion of which would go to improved front-line services and £4 billion to tax reductions. Mr Kennedy declared that the Liberal Democrats now posed the real challenge to Labour, pointing to their opposition to the Iraq war, top-up fees and ID cards.

The Pre-Election Campaign.

As the pre-election campaign developed, with policy announcements from the three main parties, the Conservative emphasis on immigration, crime and the impact of the council tax on pensioners appeared to strike a chord. Iraq and terrorism continued to reverberate. In February three soldiers were convicted of abusing prisoners in Iraq and there were renewed questions about the advice on the legality of the war given by the Attorney General in 2003. The government was also forced into concessions in March on the terms of the Prevention of Terrorism Act following concerted opposition on civil liberties grounds from the Conservatives, the Liberal Democrats and a significant number of Labour backbenchers.

Mr Brown's budget on 16 March, with an emphasis on the retired and on young families, proved successful for Labour, underlining the government's record for economic competence, despite Conservative claims that a post election Chancellor would be forced into increasing taxes.

The Campaign Issues.

With the dissolution of Parliament on 11 April, the campaign proper opened following a short interlude for the Pope's funeral and the Royal wedding. The re-appearance of Mr Brown as an active campaigner underlined Labour's emphasis on economic success. The Conservatives opened strongly with a concentration on immigration, crime, tax and a distrust of Mr Blair, culminating in Mr Howard's denunciation of the prime minister as a 'liar' over Iraq. The Liberal Democrats campaigning on the 'real alternative', appeared to rest almost entirely on their opposition to the Iraq war.

The campaign failed to sparkle, not least because there was little of real substance dividing Labour and the Conservatives. They agreed on the main issues – support for globalisation, free trade and an independent Bank of England. Labour in office would devote all the expected annual economic growth of 2·5% to public spending: the Conservatives offered 0·5% for tax cuts but the rest on education and health. Under Labour's plans, public expenditure would account for 42% of the economy by 2001; under the Conservatives 40%. Of Europe there was, despite UKIP fielding 495 candidates, barely a word.

The 2005 Election Outcome.

But a dull campaign ended with Labour winning an historic third term, though with a significantly reduced majority, the Conservatives and Liberal Democrats making advances, and turnout edging up slightly over 2001.

	Seats	Gains	Losses	Total vote	% of vote
Lab	356	0	47	9,556,183	35·2
Con	197	36	3	8,772,598	32·3
LibDem	62	16	5	5,982,045	22·0
SNP	6	2	0	412,267	1·5
PC	3	0	1	174,838	0·6
Others	21	8	6	2,234,296	8·4

A Historic Victory?

Labour's third successive victory may well have been historic, but the majority was achieved with the support of hardly more than a third of those who voted. Labour's losses ranged from Blaenau Gwent, a rebellion against the imposition of a woman candidate, to Bethnal Green and Bow, where they were ousted by the anti-Iraq War Respect candidate (George Galloway). Support fell away not only among the anti-war liberal middle class, but also among working and lower middle class voters, notably where immigration was an issue.

The Conservative Disappointment.

The highly targeted Conservative campaign garnered a 33 seat increase but only barely shifted their share of the vote since 2001. Their victories were oddly haphazard, with Enfield Southgate (114 on the target list) and Reading East (108) coming over, but only 19 of the top 30 target seats. Many of the party's net gains arose from Labour defection to the Liberal Democrats rather than rising support for the Conservatives. The party had some success in suburban London, regaining Putney and Wimbledon, and outside with the capture of St Albans, Peterborough and Welwyn Hatfield, together with Guildford and Newbury from the Liberal Democrats.

The Liberal Democrat Achievement.

The Liberal Democrats, with the best results since 1923, seized Labour strongholds in Bristol, Cambridge and Manchester on anti-Iraq War and anti-tuition fee swings of up to 17%. But they secured only eight of their top 30 targets, but took Solihull (56 on their list) and Hornsey and Wood Green (77). Manchester Withington, which saw the surprise ousting of a former Labour minister, was 106. Four rural losses to the Tories clearly arose from voters' perception that the Liberal Democrats were to the left of Labour. Overall the Liberal Democrats took 12 seats from Labour while losing five to the Conservatives in return for only three gains.

Scotland, Wales and Northern Ireland.

In Scotland Labour lost five seats, though they remained the largest party with 41. The Liberals, who gained two seats, emerged with 11, while the Nationalists saw their total rise to six. The Conservatives took one seat. In Wales, Plaid Cymru were less successful, losing one seat as their number fell to three, Labour lost five seats, while the Liberal Democrats gained two and the Conservatives three. A remarkable result was the overturning of a huge Labour majority by a Labour dissident in Blaenau Gwent. But the most dramatic results were in Northern Ireland, where Mr Trimble resigned as Ulster Unionist Party leader after the loss by his party of five seats, including his own, The Democratic Unionist Party gained four seats, taking their total to nine. Sinn Fein gained one seat, increasing their number to five, while the SDLP remained at three seats. The fate of the peace process now hung in the balance unless an almost inconceivable power-sharing agreement could be reached between Sinn Fein and the DUP.

The Conservative Leadership.

Mr Howard's announcement on 6 May that he proposed to resign once the Conservatives had reformed their leadership selection procedures suggested a period of self-examination was imminent for the main Opposition party. The Liberal Democrats also felt the need for a re-evaluation of policies that had, despite their success, appeared to position them to the left of Labour and had, consequently, been unable to seduce Conservative voters. Any concerted criticism the government faced was as likely to come from its own backbenchers as from the two parties opposite.

The New Cabinet.

Mr Blair's Cabinet changes, though relatively minor, showed no sign of doubt in his mind that it was he who had won a third term. Mr Blunkett and Ms Hughes, who had been forced to resign in 2004, returned, one to the Cabinet and the other as a junior minister. Mr Blair's adviser on education was given a peerage and government office (one of a raft of peerages that made Labour the largest party in the House of Lords for the first time in its history). But an issue that had dominated politics remained –

not if Mr Blair would make way for Mr Brown, but when.

The Queen's Speech.

The Queen's Speech on 17 May set out 44 bills and two draft bills. These included a draft counter-terrorism bill, reform of incapacity benefit, an education bill, the controversial ID cards bill, an immigration and asylum bill, a return of proposals for legislation on incitement to religious hatred, and continuing NHS reform. Mr Blair declared that the proposals were 'quintessentially New Labour' and appealed to Labour backbenchers to unite behind the government's 'reform and respect' agenda. However, despite an apparent willingness to make concessions, and consult more widely, resistance seemed likely on the proposals for welfare and education reform.

The contents of the Queen's Speech were soon overshadowed by the political crisis which erupted in the EU after the rejection of the proposed constitution by both France and the Netherlands (see **C60**).

Terrorist Attacks on London.

On 7 July a series of terrorist attacks crippled the heart of London. Three underground trains, as well as a bus, were hit by the bombers. Casualties were high (with dozens confirmed killed or missing and over 700 injured). It was the worst terrorist outrage in the UK since Lockerbie and it also bore a marked similarity to the Madrid train bombings of March 2004.

The bombings overshadowed the G8 meeting in Gleneagles (where a pledge to double aid and help debt relief was agreed) and, more poignantly, ended the celebrations in the capital over the award of the 2012 Olympics to London.

In the tension that followed the July 2005 London bomb attacks, police killed a Brazilian whom they initially claimed was a terrorist suspect. The shooting became the subject of an Independent Police Complaints Commission inquiry. There was concern that the police were operating a hitherto unpublicised 'shoot to kill' policy. Mr Blair declared in August that new anti-terrorism legislation was planned as 'the rules of the game have changed'.

IRA Decommissioning of Arms.

There was positive news from Northern Ireland, where on 28 July the Provisional IRA announced an end to their armed campaign and appealed for renewed negotiations on power-sharing. Confirmation came in late September that all IRA weapons had been decommissioned, although not all sections of the community shared the optimism. Mr Blair could also claim success from his year as chairman of the G8 group of leading industrialised nations. In July he secured concessions from a reluctant United States on tackling African poverty through aid and debt cancellation and climate change.

The 2005 Party Conferences.

The autumn party conferences were dominated by the long drawn out Conservative leadership contest, with Mr Cameron making a significant mark and Mr Davis, until then the clear favourite, losing momentum. The Liberal Democrat conference saw open questioning of Mr Kennedy as leader and defeats on Post Office privatisation and Europe. Labour's conference was the first since Mr Blair had declared this to be his last term of office. Mr Brown set out his claim to the leadership and his loyalty to Mr Blair in a keynote speech, receiving in return Mr Blair's endorsement and that of most of the Cabinet. Mr Blair said he would use his final years of power to make irreversible reforms in the public sector. However, the leadership suffered four defeats, including a demand for more council house building and the restoration of the right to secondary industrial action. The contentious issue of Iraq remained on the sidelines.

Speculation over the Succession.

At the end of September Labour held Livingston in a by-election, but with a much reduced majority. Media interest concentrated on when precisely Mr Blair intended to hand over to Mr Brown and to

what extent Mr Blair's authority was ebbing away. On 2 November Mr Blunkett, Work and Pensions Secretary since the election, was forced to resign for a second time after breaking the ministerial code of conduct on paid work. On the same day the government's majority fell to one as Labour backbenchers rebelled in a vote on the Terrorism Bill.

A week later the government suffered a 31 vote defeat, its first ever, as Labour backbenchers rejected plans to hold terrorism suspects for 90 days without charge.

Education and Pensions.

Attention moved to an Education White Paper that had been launched in October. Mr Blair called in the foreword for a 'system of independent, non fee-paying schools, without unnecessary bureaucratic interference'. His Labour opponents, who were to include the former leader Lord Kinnock and (for a time) the present deputy leader Mr Prescott, feared this presaged selection by ability and a reduction in local democracy. Despite concessions, it remained to be seen whether the government could secure passage of a bill based on the White Paper.

The Turner Commission report on the future of pensions issued at the end of November proposed an increase in the retirement age, rising to 68 by 2050, and a more generous state pension, with less emphasis on means-testing. Mr Brown had voiced his doubts before the report was issued, but Mr Blair said nothing had been ruled out. Mr Brown's reputation as Chancellor suffered somewhat in December when he reduced his estimate of economic growth in 2005 from 3–3·5% down to 1·75%.

Victory for Cameron.

As the Conservative leadership contest reached its conclusion on 6 December, Mr Cameron defeated Mr Davis by a larger than expected margin, taking 134,446 votes to 64,398. Mr Cameron said he would offer 'a more compassionate Conservatism, right for our times and right for our country' (for a discussion of the 'New Conservatism', see **C59**). Mr Cameron's election appeared to be the final blow to Mr Kennedy's leadership of the Liberal Democrats. Mr Kennedy struggled in the face of growing criticism through December until he finally admitted he had a drink problem and resigned on 5 January 2006 (thereby precipitating a messy leadership election).

Growing Labour Difficulties.

Iraq and the 'war on terror', which had done much to undermine confidence in Mr Blair, returned as a major issue when on 7 December he denied to the Commons that he had any knowledge about the alleged torture of terrorist suspects in eastern European detention camps run by the United States' Central Intelligence Agency (CIA). Two weeks later he refused calls for an enquiry into whether CIA aircraft had used British airspace or airports to transport suspects to the camps. There was further concern over Iraq with the release of a video in February 2006 showing British troops ill-treating Iraqis.

The Dunfermline By-Election.

An opinion poll in late December gave the Conservatives their first lead since 2000 and suggested that two-thirds of voters believed the government was floundering. Over half were dissatisfied with Mr Blair as prime minister. Mr Blair's ability to press through with his reform programme became increasingly doubtful. On 31 January 2006 the government suffered two defeats in the Commons on a bill to outlaw religious hatred. On 9 February Labour lost Dunfermline and West Fife as the Liberal Democrats overturned a Labour majority of over 11,500.

The defeat was a blow to the party and to Mr Brown, who lived in the constituency and had campaigned strongly there.

Party Funding Controversies.

The government's problems intensified through March and April. A weakened Education Bill passed with Conservative support against continuing Labour backbench resistance. The aim of ending child poverty proved problematic and the health service faced a growing financial crisis, as staff redundancies mounted. No sooner had criticisms of the financial activities of the Culture Secretary's husband (with the added twist of his relationship with Italian prime minister Mr Berlusconi) abated, than links were alleged between contributions to Labour's funds and nominations to the House of Lords. Mr Blair neatly shifted the ground to a debate about the financing of all political parties, but there was a shadow on his reputation.

The 2006 Budget.

Mr Brown's largely uncontroversial March budget re-opened the question of the succession to Mr Blair. Commentators saw the Chancellor's speech as a challenge to the Conservatives on the balance between cutting tax and maintaining public spending and a foretaste of his own administration. He announced measures to help the poor and the elderly and to encourage private and business investment in energy saving. But at the centre of his budget was a promise to narrow the gap between the £8,000 a year spent on each private school pupil and the £5,000 average in state schools. In his response, Mr Cameron noted that Mr Brown had made no mention of the health service, a sign, he claimed, it was in trouble. But the date of Mr Blair's departure dominated the media, with Labour's performance in the May local elections seen as a possible determining key. Both the main opposition parties were fighting under new leadership, Sir Menzies Campbell having been chosen to head the Liberal Democrats.

In the Liberal Democrat leadership contest, Sir Menzies (Ming) Campbell had defeated Simon Hughes by 29,697 votes to 21,628 on a 72·5% turnout of party members.

Crisis for New Labour.

Labour's troubles intensified on the eve of the local elections. The Health Secretary was booed by nurses angered at redundancies and the Deputy Prime Minister was forced to admit he had had an affair with a civil servant. But more damaging was the revelation that the Home Office had persistently failed to ensure the deportation of foreign prisoners at the end of their sentences. The government faced debilitating charges of drift, sleaze and incompetence. This was all reflected in a very bad local election result for Labour and a marked Conservative revival (see **D13** for a summary and **C60** for a discussion of their significance).

The May Cabinet Reshuffle.

In the wake of Labour's failure at the May polls, Mr Blair shuffled his ministerial team, demoting Mr Straw from the Foreign Office and replacing him with Mrs Beckett and moving the peripatetic Dr Reid from Defence to the Home Office in place of Mr Clarke. (For a detailed list of the new Cabinet, see **D6**). Mr Prescott was stripped of departmental responsibilities but retained his title and salary. As pressure increased for Mr Blair himself to go, he indicated that he would give any successor time to settle in before a general election, which suggested he would leave office in 2007.

II. THE CHANGING WORLD SCENE

THE NEW EUROPE

THE EUROPEAN UNION.

Chronology of Key Events.

1951 France, Germany, Italy, Belgium, Luxembourg & the Netherlands (the Six) form European Coal and Steel Community (EC3C).
1957 The Six form the European Economic Community (EEC) under Treaty of Rome.
1962 Common Agricultural Policy established.
1963 President de Gaulle vetoes UK application to join EEC.
1973 UK, Ireland and Denmark join EEC (Greece 1981, Spain & Portugal 1986).
1989 Single European Act.
1991 Maastricht Treaty sets timetable for economic and monetary union.
1993 Single European Market comes into effect.
1995 Austria, Finland and Sweden join.
1997 Amsterdam Treaty prepares for membership enlargement to Eastern Europe.
1999 11 states adopt Euro as currency.
2000 Treaty of Nice increases centralised decision-making but allows national vetoes on tax and social security.
2004 Expansion of the EU (May) brings 10 new members. Draft EU Constitution agreed.

The Background.

The European Union, which now incorporates almost all of western and much of central Europe, has grown out of a rare marriage of political idealism and political realism nurtured by considerable pragmatism. It is a combination which has made the EU a dynamic force as Europe faces the new millennium, sidelining and absorbing earlier rivals.

The political idealism was focused, and largely remains focused, in the core continental states of western Europe—France, Germany and Italy. All three experienced defeat and occupation at some stage of the Second World War, and France and Germany had fought three wars in less than 80 years. The very concept of the nation state was perceived as flawed. The founding fathers of what was to become the European Union—Jean Monnet and Robert Schuman in France, Paul-Henri Spaak in Belgium, Konrad Adenauer in West Germany and Alcide de Gasperi in Italy—saw the future as lying rather in an ever closer integration of their peoples which would literally make another war impossible. They were also highly conscious of a very substantial common cultural heritage.

Realism and Idealism.

Political realism, however, was no less important than idealism. Integration was seen by Germany's neighbours as their surest defence against future German expansionism and by West Germany as its surest route to restored international respectability. It was also favoured by the Benelux countries (Belgium, Netherlands and Luxembourg), who feared nothing more than a renewed conflict between their two great neighbours. Moreover, the perceived threat from the Soviet Union prompted unification in the economic as much as in the military sphere and some were to see the future European institutions as NATO's economic and political arm in Europe.

These twin impulses of idealism and realism were, however, to be associated with considerable flexibility and pragmatism. There has never been a blueprint for European integration, let alone unity, and the organs of what is now the EU have evolved significantly in response to changing political pressures from the member states. The consistent thread has been the core belief that economic integration is the surest route to wider integration, with the creation of the single market being the keystone to the whole structure.

The First Practical Moves.

The first practical move towards integration was the creation of the European Coal and Steel Community (ECSC) in 1952, which pooled the Belgian, Dutch, French, Italian, Luxembourg and West German raw materials essential for waging traditional warfare, but the real birth of what is now the EU was heralded at the Messina Conference of 1955. Representatives of the six ECSC member states there agreed to establish the common market in goods, people and services which came into force as the European Economic Community in January 1958 following the signing of the Treaty of Rome the previous year.

The British Attitude.

To the considerable disappointment of many in the six states, the British held themselves aloof for reasons which remain familiar. The British did not feel "European", they had been neither defeated nor occupied in the Second World War, and they trusted their nation state, sympathising with the view of the then leader of the Labour Party, Hugh Gaitskell, that entry into the "common market" would be the end of a thousand years of history. Many felt more affinity with the United States or the Commonwealth, particularly perhaps on the right, and a number on the left suspected that the rules of the market would make it impossible to build socialism in Britain. Moreover, the British did not believe that the "common market" would work and instinctively saw moves towards European integration as a threat. They, therefore, actively promoted the European Free Trade Association as an alternative, but to no lasting avail. The "common market" did work, while the British economy comparatively lost ground. The European Economic Community proved an irresistible magnet to its neighbours, with the British themselves, together with Denmark and the Republic of Ireland, being in the first wave of new members in 1973. Greece joined in 1981, and Spain and Portugal in 1986. The former East Germany became a member on German unification in 1990. Austria, Finland and Sweden followed in 1995. Oil-rich Norway, remote Iceland, and traditionally neutral Switzerland were the only western European nations to remain outside.

The British Referendum.

Although the referendum on British membership of the European Community was conclusive, British motivation was essentially economic. There was little understanding of, or sympathy with, the concept of integration, and that situation has changed little in the last 30 years. Sir Edward Heath and the late Lord Jenkins of Hillhead remained the only two major political office holders to have given it consistent support. A further difficulty is that the British were, and are, ill at ease with the institutional framework of the Community, now Union, which reflects continental rather than UK practice. Their reserve is focused on the Commission, which is the EU's Brussels based civil service headed by, currently, 24 commissioners and a commission president, all nominated by the member states.

Although the Commission must swear loyalty to the Union as a whole, the most effective presidents are normally those who can rely on the political support of at least one major member state. The president (until November 2008) is José Manuel Durão Barroso of Portugal. The British commissioner is Peter Mandelson, who is in charge of trade policy. Former presidents are listed on D15.

The Commission was envisaged by the founding fathers as "the motor of the Community" and, in accordance with French practice, it promotes legislation on its own initiative as well as at the request of the other EU institutions. The relevant commissioners also represent and speak for the EU in international negotiations. It is often alleged that these characteristics make the Commission anti-democratic but such criticisms ignore the fact that the Commission has no power of decision. That power has largely lain with the council of ministers, whose membership reflects the topic under discussion (energy, environment, finance etc.) and is composed of the ministers of the member states, in consultation with the European Parliament.

The European Parliament.

The Parliament, which meets in Strasbourg and Brussels, is one of the original institutions of the Union, and was envisaged as its source of direct democratic legitimacy. Initially nominated, it has been directly elected since 1979, and it has grown steadily in significance. Since the enactment of the 1997 Treaty of Amsterdam it has shared the power of decision on a wide range of issues, including the environment, with the council of ministers. For all these advances it is yet to establish itself fully. Despite, and sometimes even because of, its real impact on many sectors of policy-making, it is suspect to many national governments, widely resented by other parliamentarians and a subject of general indifference for the public. Moreover, the latter problem seems to be growing worse. The turnout in the European elections of 2004 was the lowest on record.

Party Groupings.

The Parliament, like the Commission, operates in a fundamentally non-British way. A combination of differing national political traditions, the use of proportional representation, and in some countries very fluid political groupings, means that majorities have to be assembled issue by issue. There is no equivalent to the Westminster model whereby a disciplined majority provides and supports the government for a period of up to 5 years. Instead, there are usually about eight transnational groupings, of which the socialists have usually been the largest and the most organised. The British Conservatives work somewhat less readily with the continental Christian Democrats under the banner of the European People's Party, and the Liberals, the Greens, and the UK Independence Party participate in comparable groupings.

In June 2004 elections were held in the newly-enlarged EU for the 732-member Parliament. Of a total electorate of 350 million (the largest electorate in a democracy outside of India) only 44% voted. In the 10 new member states turnout was a mere 28·7%. With the exceptions of Spain and Greece the outcome of the election was a major (sometimes humiliating) setback for governing parties. Some groups advocating EU withdrawal did well (as in Sweden, Poland, the Czech Republic and Britain). However, the Centre Right (271 seats) remained the largest bloc at Strasbourg, with Socialists having 200 seats, Eurosceptics 128, Liberals 66, Greens 42 and a variety of Independents numbering 25.

The European Council.

The Treaty of Rome envisaged a balance between Commission, Parliament and council of ministers but it has been supplemented by the rapid growth in importance of the European Council, which brings together heads of government every six months. It is these summit meetings which determine the future direction of the EU and attempt to resolve the major tensions between member states and between sectoral policies. The chairmanship of the European Council and the council of ministers (the "presidency") is held by the member states for six month terms in rotation. Eurosceptic opinion often argues that the European Council, representing as it does the national governments alone, is the only legitimate form of European co-operation, and would abolish both the Parliament and the proactive role of the Commission. It seems unlikely, however, that other member states would ever agree to such a radical course of action.

Other Specialised Bodies.

The major institutions described are supported by a range of more specialised bodies of which the more important include the Economic and Social Committee in Brussels, which is a consultative body composed of employer, employee and public interest representatives, the European Investment Bank in Luxembourg and the Court of Auditors, also in Luxembourg, which conducts rigorous reviews of the effectiveness of EU programmes. The Commission is obliged to respond publicly and in writing to the Auditors' criticisms. The most important of the Luxembourg based institutions, however, is the European Court of Justice, which resolves conflicts between EU legislative acts and has the power to levy heavy fines on member states for non-compliance with EU legislation. The European Central Bank is discussed in **Section F**.

The New European Union.

For a discussion of recent events in the EU, including the 2004 enlargement and the dramatic referendum results in 2005 in France and the Netherlands, *see* **C56–8**.

FRANCE.

Chronology of Key Events.

1946 The Fourth Republic is established.
1951 Joins the European Coal and Steel Community.
1954 Relinquishes Indo-China following defeat at Dien Bien Phu; Algeria begins war for independence.
1956 Allies with Britain and Israel against Egypt during Suez events.
1957 Founder member of the European Economic Community.
1958 Fourth Republic collapses; de Gaulle establishes Fifth Republic.
1962 Algeria wins independence.
1968 Student riots and workers' strikes bring country close to revolution.
1969 De Gaulle resigns; Pompidou succeeds as president.
1974 Giscard d'Estaing becomes president.
1981 Socialist Mitterrand becomes president.
1986 'Cohabitation' between left president Mitterrand and right prime minister Chirac follows elections.
1988 Mitterrand re-elected.
1995 Chirac elected president.
1997 Socialist Jospin becomes prime minister.

Presidential Election Outcome.

The French Presidential elections of 2002 were won by President Chirac but politically dominated by a candidate whom he defeated: Jean-Marie Le Pen. In the first round, Chirac won fractionally less than one-fifth of the vote, but Prime Minister Jospin came third by half a percentage point to Le Pen, the leader of the National Front. The Communist Party, until 1981 a major force in French politics, virtually disappeared from the political map as its candidate, Robert Hue, won less than 4% of the vote (less than the percentages of two Trotskyite candidates). In the second round, Chirac won an overwhelming majority on the back of an unprecedented alliance of democratic voters on both right and left; he supplemented it shortly thereafter by winning a large majority in parliamentary elections.

The Advent of Raffarin.

Chirac chose as his Prime Minister Jean-Pierre Raffarin, a provincial politician with the common touch and without intimate, multiple, connections to the Parisian political and bureaucratic elites. Chirac and Raffarin have political room to advance the cause of public sector reform. Within that large subject, pensions policy has, if anything, become an even more severe a problem than in Germany and Italy; a consensus has emerged among policy analysts (though not among the voting public) that the inflation of health care costs needs to be contained. Raffarin has shown himself by instinct and practice a cautious politician: he has not needed his advisers to tell him of the intensity of resistance among the huge public sector work force to pension and health-care reforms that they think threaten their interests.

Developments in 2003.

Raffarin's standing was damaged in the summer and autumn of 2003 by the conjunction of three crises, two of them predictable and one not. Although his government was by no means knocked off course, political resistance to the first two (minor reforms of social security and public-sector pensions) harmed him more than they did the President. He also took the brunt of public anger at the govern-

ment's sluggish response to the unpredictably large number of deaths of elderly people in the extraordinary heat-wave that afflicted large parts of France in the summer. The impact of these three problems would have been diminished had the economy grown rapidly. But it did not: France's sluggish economic growth continued to feed through to the labour market where unemployment rates remained stubbornly high.

Public Spending Problems.

One strategic difficulty for France was that the EU's Stability and Growth Pact gave the government little freedom for manoeuvre on public spending to buy off disaffected groups. Although France (with Germany) effectively abrogated the terms of that Pact by the end of 2003, the government was in practice bound to adopt a fiscal policy tighter than the country's labour market or its political needs warranted.

Fifth Republic Presidents have tended to discern (often correctly) that their Prime Ministers' unpopularity threatens their own standing. Given that President Chirac's capacity to extract continuing political benefit from his opposition to the US-led war against Iraq would henceforth be slight, he had to guard his prospective public support by inoculating himself against the unpopularity of Raffarin.

The March 2004 Elections.

Against a background of nearly 10 per cent unemployment and a stagnant economy, the regional elections were hardly likely to deliver a pro-government vote. The outcome was a stinging defeat for President Chirac and Prime Minister Raffarin. The Socialist Party swept to victory in 20 of the 22 mainland regions, decimating the centre-right. Although Raffarin survived as Prime Minister, his longer-term political future now seemed bleak, with the June European elections adding to his difficulties.

The 2005 Referendum Crisis.

On 29 May, a referendum on the proposed EU constitution was held in France. By a margin of 55% to 45% the electorate rejected the constitution in a result that sent reverberations around Europe (*see* **C58**). Many factors lay behind this rejection – the unpopularity of the Raffarin government, high unemployment, a feeling that the proposed constitution was too 'Anglo-Saxon', a desire to deliver a protest vote to Chirac, opposition to the possibility of Turkish EU membership, and so forth.

The extreme left, many socialists and the parties of the extreme right were united in their opposition. Except for Paris, parts of Brittany and a few areas along the German border, nearly all of France was united in voting against.

The Referendum Consequences.

The result left President Chirac severely discredited. It also no doubt encouraged the Dutch in their own referendum a few days later to reject the treaty by a resounding majority (62% to 38%). It left the way forward for European integration in considerable doubt. More immediately, it led to the replacement of the highly unpopular Raffarin by a loyal Chirac ally, Dominique de Villepin (who was best known outside France for his outspoken opposition to the Iraq War).

Trade Union Discontent.

The new prime minister inherited a weakening economy, with a sharp slowdown in growth in the quarter to August 2005. Mr de Villepin's introduction of new labour laws to ease the dismissal of workers from small businesses provoked trade union opposition. On 1 September he promised to 'get France working again' with income tax cuts in 2006 and tax incentives for investment. But on 4 October transport and public sector workers mounted a widely supported general strike against the proposed labour reforms.

The State of Emergency.

The end of October saw events that questioned France's approach to cultural and religious diversity. On 27 October rioting began in the capital's working class, and largely Muslim, suburbs following the death of two youths allegedly fleeing from police. Within a week rioters had destroyed over 5,000 vehicles and many public and business premises. On 8 November, as the riots spread through other urban centres, the government declared a state of emergency, which remained in force until January 2006. As potential successors to President Chirac, both the prime minister and the interior minister, Nicolas Sarkozy, seized the opportunity to press their qualifications as candidates. Mr Sarkozy was accused of provocative language in his early comments, while Mr de Villepin appeared more measured.

In the midst of the riots, five million citizens bought shares in the newly-privatised electricity industry. On 10 November President Chirac said France had lessons to learn and acknowledged the part racial discrimination had played in extending the autumn disorder. Mr Sarkozy, whose initial firmness had won him significant backing, attempted to widen his support by urging the need for positive discrimination to ensure jobs for youths of immigrant origin.

Opposition Problems.

The Socialist opposition, meanwhile, remained confused following divisions over the party's stance in the May referendum. In November the party's members supported the platform of the moderate leader, François Hollande, by 54% for the 2007 presidential and general elections, giving former prime minister Laurent Fabius's more radical stance only 21%. But opinion polls suggested voters saw the Socialists as divided.

Widely supported student and union protests and strikes in March and April against a new labour contract making it easier to dismiss young workers revealed a growing malaise in the country's political temper and undermined Mr de Villepin's position as President Chirac called for compromise.

GERMANY.

1945 Defeated and occupied by Allies.
1948 British, French and US zones become Federal Republic of Germany and Soviet zone becomes German Democratic Republic.
1955 Cold War divisions solidify as East Germany joins the Warsaw Pact, West Germany the North Atlantic Treaty Organisation (NATO).
1957 West Germany is a founder member of the European Economic Community.
1961 East Germany builds the Berlin Wall to prevent flight of refugees.
1969 West German Social Democrat Chancellor Brandt attempts to improve East-West relations.
1973 West and East Germany become UN members.
1982 Christian Democrat Kohl becomes West German Chancellor.
1987 East German Chancellor Honecker pays official visit to West Germany.
1989 Berlin Wall dismantled.
1990 Germany unified under Chancellor Kohl.
1994 Kohl re-elected; all foreign troops leave Berlin.

The 2002 Election Outcome.

Chancellor Schröder's SDP-Green coalition won re-election in September 2002 with a tiny majority in one of the tightest election contests since the founding of the Republic in 1949. The SPD polled more strongly in the East, whilst the Green Party, buoyed by the popularity of Joschka Fisher, the Foreign Minister, increased its percentage share of the vote. The parties' shares of the vote and seats totals in the Bundestag were as follows:

Social Democrats (SPD) 38·5% (down 2·4% on 1998). 251 seats.
Christian Democrats/Christian Social Union (CDU/CSU) 38·5% (down 3·4% on 1998). 248 seats.
Greens 8·6% (up 1·9% on 1998). 55 seats.
Liberals (FDP) 7·4% (up 1·2% on 1998). 47 seats.
Ex-Communists (PDS) 4·0% (down 1·1% on 1998). 2 seats

The Results Analysed.

The results varied strongly by region—the CDU/CSU did exceptionally well in the mostly Catholic south and very poorly in the East; the SPD dominated the eastern *länder*; and the PDS gained its only two seats in Berlin. Schröder correctly calculated that he would gain votes by making plain his unwillingness to support US policy on Iraq and by campaigning for a renewal of the 'red-green' coalition with the Greens, thereby encouraging SPD supporters to use their second vote to support the Greens. That, coupled with his deft response to widespread heavy flooding in Germany in the summer of 2002, pushed the Greens comfortably over the 5% barrier and just enabled him to overcome the public's greater trust in the CDU/CSU's capacity to reduce unemployment.

Mounting Economic Problems.

In the six months after the election, Schröder gave little indication of having either the will or the guile to press forward with the reforms to the German labour market and welfare system that many commentators thought necessary for the revival of Germany's sluggish economy. The election results and his party base gave him little room for manoeuvre, a position made worse in February 2003 with poll defeats in Lower Saxony and Hesse.

"Agenda 2010" Reforms.

Chancellor Schröder's "Agenda 2010" reform package did not survive parliamentary scrutiny unchallenged or unchanged. Nevertheless, he saw his proposals for reforms to Germany's sclerotic labour markets, taxation, pensions, and social security through to enactment. Sceptical though many free-market critics were of the reforms' adequacy, 2003 might yet come to be regarded as a year of decisive change in the politics of German domestic policy reform. Symbols matter in politics, and these victories were symbolically powerful for altering the widespread assumption that German politicians who pursue reform are doomed to defeat. For Schröder personally, after a hugely difficult division with the United States over the invasion of Iraq, domestic political success was especially welcome.

SPD Leadership Change.

Against a background of a crushing defeat in state elections in Hamburg early in March (widely attributed to his social welfare reform), Schröder handed the leadership of the SPD to one of his most trusted aides, Herr Müntefering. But the electoral prospects of the SPD still seemed bleak—a fact confirmed by its disastrous performance in the June 2004 European elections.

Rising Unemployment.

Having surmounted in 2004 the challenge of legislating change, Chancellor Schröder faced in 2005 the different challenge of implementing it or, more accurately, of charting a course through public opinion which is indifferent at best, and hostile at worst, to the Hartz IV reforms. Their implementation in January 2005 resulted in a technical but politically unwelcome increase in unemployment above 5 million, and the reduction in cash benefits for welfare recipients. Against this difficult background, elections in March and May 2005 in Schleswig-Holstein and in Nord-Rhein Westphalia increased the political risks for the Chancellor.

Opposition Weaknesses.

A straw at which Schröder clutched was the weak condition of his principal opponents in the CDU/CSU. Just as his own SPD did poorly in *länder* elections in Saxony and Brandenburg (both states which were once in East Germany) in September 2004, so too did the CDU/CSU. Both were embarrassed by the surge in support for the extreme-right German People's Union (DVU) and the neo-Nazi National Democratic Party (NPD). The DVU won 6·1% of the vote in Brandenburg, and the NPD 9·2% in Saxony. Both parties won especially large shares of the vote among disaffected (and disproportionately unemployed) young voters. Whilst the

SPD did poorly in both elections, the CDU actually won smaller shares of the vote than it had done in the previous elections. To that extent, the SPD drew comfort from the twin facts that its own decline was less steep in these two cases than was the CDU/CSU's, and that it remained the largest party in Brandenburg.

Crisis for Schröder.

The continuing decline in support for the SPD reached a climax in the elections of 22 May in North-Rhine Westphalia. The vote, in Germany's most populous state, which had been in SPD control for 39 unbroken years, was a disaster for Schröder. The victorious Christian Democrats saw their support rise by 8% as the SPD registered its worst performance in 50 years. It led Schröder to call for the general election, scheduled for 2006, to be brought forward to autumn 2005 to end the political paralysis threatening to engulf Germany.

The 2005 Election Outcome.

With elections set for 18 September, there was a slither of good news for the government as unemployment fell slightly in August, while vigorous campaigning by Mr Schröder's SPD cut into the opinion poll lead of the CDU under Mrs Merkel. In the event, the CDU emerged marginally ahead of the SPD, at 226 seats to 222, with the Left Party (made up of former Communist and left-SPD supporters) winning a significant 54 seats, the liberal Free Democrats 61 and the Greens, Mr Schröder's former coalition partners, 51. On 10 October the CDU and SPD agreed to construct a 'grand coalition', with Mrs Merkel as Chancellor. The new government was formed on 12 November, receiving parliamentary approval on 22 November. Mrs Merkel became the first woman Chancellor and the first person from the former East Germany to hold the post.

The Merkel Agenda.

Mrs Merkel had promised to revive the economy, while her foreign policy position was more clearly aligned with the United States than her predecessor's. However, coalition with the SPD, whose members held a number of key government posts, including Labour, Foreign Affairs, and Finance, limited her room for manoeuvre. On 30 November Mrs Merkel said that her government would re-energise Germany as she announced increases in VAT and tax on higher incomes and the abolition of subsidies for first time house buyers. Mrs Merkel went on to play a balancing role in negotiations over the European Union budget in December, encouraging compromise between Mr Blair and President Chirac and suggesting that the exclusive Franco-German alliance was at an end.

An Insecure Coalition?

Mrs Merkel met President Bush in January 2006 and, despite her criticisms of some of the United States' actions in the anti-terrorism campaign, it was clear that the potential existed for a renewed closeness between the two countries. There were doubts, however, of how long the coalition with the SPD would survive.

ITALY.

1946 Republic proclaimed following a referendum.
1948 New constitution introduced; Christian Democrats begin long run of power.
1949 Joins NATO.
1951 Joins European Coal and Steel Community.
1955 Becomes a member of the United Nations.
1957 Founder member of the European Economic Community.
1963 Socialists join Christian Democrat led coalition under Moro.
1976 Communist Party makes election gains.
1978 A period of near civil war; Moro, architect of left-right unity, kidnapped and killed by the Red Brigades.

1980 Over 80 killed in far right bombing at Bologna.
1981 Cabinet resigns over P2 Masonic lodge scandal, opening of campaign against political corruption.
1983 Craxi becomes first post-war Socialist prime minister.
1984 Roman Catholicism ceases to be state religion under concordat with Vatican.
1991 Communist Party splits.
1992 Revelations of corruption involving all major political parties.
1994 Short-lived Freedom Alliance of Berlusconi's *Forza Italia*, the Northern League and neo-fascist National Alliance.
1995 Government of technocrats under Dini imposed austerity budget.
1996 Prodi becomes head of Centre-left Olive Tree alliance government.

The May 2001 Elections.

Berlusconi emerged from the 2001 elections as Prime Minister, and assembled a right-wing coalition government dominated by his own Forza Italia, with the support of the Northern League, and a conservative faction from within the former Christian Democratic Party. Partly in order to deflect anxieties among other EU leaders about Italy's policy towards her European partners, but mostly in response to pressure from the President and from business, he appointed as his Foreign Minister the highly-experienced Renato Ruggiero, former Director of the World Trade Organisation. Widely-respected though he was in other European capitals, Ruggiero lacked influence over Berlusconi and within the government more generally. He found himself unable to prevent or respond effectively to other ministers' public expressions of hostility to European initiatives (as in Berlusconi's own opposition to advanced plans for an EU-wide arrest warrant) and even to the Euro (about which Umberto Bossi, head of the Northern League, expressed doubts even as the currency was launched in the form of coins and notes). On 5 January 2002, Ruggiero resigned and Berlusconi declared that he would take the portfolio of Foreign Minister for himself.

Domestic Problems.

Foreign policy was not the only front on which Berlusconi had to fight. Following a long tussle between the government and the opposition, Carlo Taormina, a junior minister at the Ministry of the Interior, resigned. The immediate issue was Taormina's record and his vigorous attacks upon the supposed political bias of the judiciary. The wider context was that of the government's awkward relations with the judiciary in the face of what the latter regarded as government's assaults upon its independence—especially with regard to the government's attempts to limit retrospectively evidence gathered from abroad in prosecuting persons allegedly involved in fraud and financial corruption. The issue was highly sensitive given Berlusconi's own troubled past and the inquiries which continue into aspects of his business affairs.

The Murder of Biagi.

In March 2002, left-wing terrorists murdered Marco Biagi, a labour economist and adviser to the government. The event aroused considerable controversy, not least because of the attempts of Claudio Scajola, the Interior Minister, and Prime Minister Berlusconi himself, to exploit the event for their own purposes in the government's running confrontation with the trade unions over labour market reform. The incident illustrated both the febrile atmosphere of politics within the coalition government and the tendency of some of the politicians within it to speak and act rashly in order to advance their individual or their parties' interests at the expense of the government's.

Labour Market Reform.

Events in 2002 showed that trade union opposition to Berlusconi's policies of reform and his need to constrain the growing budget deficit was not implacable. Nor did unions present an entirely united front. As a result, the government secured union agreement to some aspects of labour market reform. Nevertheless, Berlusconi knew that the succession of elections in Italy from 2004 to 2006 meant that 2003 represented his last and best chance to secure major progress with his agenda for reform.

Conflicts with the Judiciary.

Berlusconi maintained his attacks upon the judiciary in 2003 amid opposition parties' continuing allegations that the Prime Minister was guilty of a conflict of interests between his vast media and financial services interests and his role in government. Berlusconi's apparent success in legislating to protect his media interests and even to extend his stakes into advertising met with opposition from President Ciampi who refused to sign the legislation into law on the ground of its alleged unconstitutionality.

Recent Developments.

The Prime Minister's own difficulties hampered him in his attempts to press on with the reform of pensions and reductions in taxation, just as they had damaged his professional reputation during Italy's accident-prone Presidency of the European Union from June to December 2003. Persisting slow rates of economic growth limited Berlusconi's freedom to reduce taxation (as he had promised to do), and he continued to face strong (if weakening) opposition from trade unions to his plans for pension reform. His political calculations were complicated both by European elections in 2004 and by the prospective return to Italian politics of Romano Prodi from his post as President of the European Commission. Prodi has the potential to provide a focus of centre-left opposition to Berlusconi who badly needs some domestic successes to bolster his public standing.

The Corruption Trial.

In December 2004, Berlusconi was finally found not guilty of corruption on one charge, and with the aid of the statute of limitations escaped judgement on another. However, Marcello Dell'Utri, an associate of the Prime Minister, was found guilty and sentenced to a prison term for having colluded with organized crime.

Developments in 2004.

The year 2004 was a difficult year for Berlusconi: the economy had continued to perform poorly; the coalition governing parties were badly defeated in a number of by-elections; whilst the European Parliament rejected the nomination of the conservative Catholic, Rocco Buttiglione, for Italy's slot on the European Commission. Buttiglione's defeat was attributable mostly to his conservative views about sexuality, but antipathy among many in Europe to the character of the Italian government also played its role.

The 2005 Crisis.

If 2004 had been a difficult year for Berlusconi, the opening months of 2005 were very much worse. The crisis was triggered by the heavy defeats for the Centre-Right in the spring regional elections. This led to the withdrawal in April of the smallest of the Coalition's partners from government — the Union of Christian Democrats (UDC) led by Marco Follini.

Berlusconi resigned, only to form a new government and avoid precipitating a general election. Berlusconi survived but his reputation was badly damaged.

The 2006 Election Background.

Mr Berlusconi's attention now focussed on elections due in 2006. In October 2005 the lower house of the legislature approved sweeping reforms to the voting system, including a return to an element of proportional representation. Deputies, many of whom refused to participate in the vote, accused Mr Berlusconi of seeking electoral advantage and said that the proposed changes would revive political instability. On 16 November the Senate gave final approval to the reforms, which also included devolution to the regions, a reduction in the number of deputies and senators, and a strengthening of the prime minister's powers.

The Ghost of Iraq.

The selection in a primary on 17 October of former European Commission president Romano Prodi as challenger ensured Mr Berlusconi would face a unified opposition. Aware of the continuing unpopularity of Italy's participation in the attack on Iraq, Mr Berlusconi declared at the end of October that he had attempted to dissuade President Bush from mounting the invasion. The main opposition parties said they would withdraw the 2,600 troops in Iraq immediately if they won office. The government attempted to defuse this as an issue by announcing in January 2006 that all troops would be home from Iraq by the end of the year.

Continuing Discontent.

Mr Berlusconi's prospects appeared bleak, bar a major upset in the opposition. The economy remained sluggish and on 25 November trade unions mounted a widely-supported general strike, the sixth in four years, in protest against public spending cuts. Having survived accusations of corrupt business practices, Mr Berlusconi faced fresh accusations of fraud and money-laundering in late 2005. Even his own coalition ally, foreign minister Gianfranco Fini, said he expected to become prime minister if his National Alliance won more seats than Mr Berlusconi's Forza Italia.

The Election Outcome.

The outcome of the April 2006 general election was the narrowest of victories for the coalition led by Romano Prodi. His majority in the Senate was wafer thin and Mr Berlusconi refused to concede defeat even when the courts made it clear he had lost. Italy was entering what seemed a period of political paralysis.

SPAIN.

Chronology.

1936–39 Spanish Civil War ends in Nationalist victory under Franco.
1955 Spain admitted to UN.
1959 ETA founded to campaign for independent Basque homeland.
1973 Prime minister Admiral Luis Carrero Blanco assassinated by Basque nationalists.
1975 Franco dies; monarchy restored with King Juan Carlos as head of state.
1977 First free elections since 1936.
1978 New constitution introduces a parliamentary monarchy.
1980 Basque country and Catalonia elect regional assemblies.
1981 Unsuccessful military coup attempt.
1982 Socialist government elected.
1986 Spain joins European Community.
1996 Jose Maria Aznar becomes prime minister of right-wing Popular Party/Catalan nationalist coalition.
1997 Demonstrations against rising Basque nationalist violence.
1998 ETA announces ceasefire.
1999 ETA talks with government collapse.
2000 ETA renews violence; landslide election victory for Popular Party.
2001 Spain and Britain agree to reach settlement on Gibraltar.
2002 Euro replaces peseta as currency.

The 2004 Elections.

The Socialists won the parliamentary election of 14 March 2004 held in the week following al-Qaeda's bombing of Madrid commuter trains. The government's attribution of responsibility for the mass killings to ETA angered a significant section of public opinion which inferred that the government's stance was explained not by the evidence (which the Spanish security services had doubted from the start) but by the calculation that public opinion would be more likely to rally to the government in the event that the bombings could be pinned on ETA rather than al-Qaeda. Adverse public reaction cut the Popular Party's support by nine percentage points in little more than a week, and boosted the standing of the PSOE.

Renewed Domestic Terrorism.

Mr José Luis Rodriguez Zapatero was sworn in as prime minister in April 2004 and the last Spanish troops left Iraq in May. However, much of 2005 was to be dominated by domestic terrorism from ETA, the militant Basque independence group. In February a car bomb exploded in Madrid, causing substantial injuries. Following Basque Nationalist Party losses in regional elections in April, the government offered negotiations if ETA disarmed. But on 25 May there was a further explosion in Madrid.

The Zapatero Agenda.

Meanwhile, in February 2005, voters approved the European Union constitution in a referendum by a large majority but on low turnout. The result became academic as France and the Netherlands voted against. In June the Cortes defied Catholic and conservative opinion by voting 187–147 to legalise gay marriage and to extend adoption and inheritance rights to homosexual couples. Mr Zapatero visited China in July and proposed an alliance between the two countries. In November Chinese President Hu Jintao returned the visit. More controversially, the government signed a $2 billion arms deal with Venezuela at the end of the month, despite objections from the United States.

Catalonian Autonomy.

There was a renewal of ETA terrorism in December, shortly after the largest ever trial involving alleged members opened in Madrid. In January 2006 proposals to extend the autonomy of Catalonia provoked a reminder of the military coup that had precipitated the 1936–39 Civil War. In November the Cortes had approved greater autonomy to the Catalan region. A general who asserted the army's constitutional right to intervene if the proposals endangered national unity was arrested and dismissed. The proposals had divided the ruling Socialists, who were trailing the opposition People's Party in opinion polls, and had undermined Mr Zapatero's position.

ETA declared a permanent ceasefire on 22 March, pledging to turn to democratic politics to achieve its aims in the Basque country.

POLAND.

The Resignation of Miller.

On 26 March 2004 the Prime Minister, Leszek Miller, announced he would resign after EU membership became effective. He was succeeded by Marek Belka.

The European Elections.

On an unprecedentedly low turnout, the European elections in 2004 resulted in a victory for the liberal-conservative opposition Civic Platform (PO) with 24.1% of the vote. The governing Democratic Left Alliance-Labour Union (SLD-UP) coalition lost exceptionally badly: its vote fell by more than 30 percentage points in September to just 9.4%. Parties hostile to the European Union did sufficiently well as to suggest that they will form a powerful voice in Polish politics over the medium-term but not so well as to threaten Polish membership of the EU.

Political Scandals.

Beset by quarrelling and jostling for advantage within and between the parties forming the coali-tion, the government lacked confidence at the beginning of 2005 in its capacity to continue its policy of public sector and fiscal reform. Allegations of corruption have for much of the post-communist period fed public distrust of Polish governments and politicians. It was a corruption scandal which brought down the government of Leszek Miller, and continuing investigations into corruption continue to drain public support from the governing parties (the former-communist Democratic Left Alliance (SLD) and smaller Labour Union (UP)). Public opinion polls show that more than four-fifths of those voters who supported the two parties at the 2001 general election no longer do so.

New Political Developments.

In early February 2005, the SLD decided against holding early parliamentary elections in May as it had earlier undertaken to do, but instead to hold them at the same time as presidential elections and the EU Constitutional Treaty referendum in the autumn. The delay increased the prospect that the required 50% of registered voters would turn out to vote in the referendum, but risked the EU Constitution falling victim to domestic political strife with the opposition parties gaining power partly on the strength of their opposition to the Treaty.

The 2005 Elections.

In the event, President Kwasniewski postponed the referendum on the EU constitution indefinitely following its rejection by French and Netherlands' voters. In elections to the 460 seat lower house (the Sejm) on 25 September voters shifted towards centre-right parties favouring deregulation and tax cuts. The Law and Justice Party (PjS) won 155 seats (up from 44), Civic Platform (PO) increased its representation from 65 to 133 seats, while the Democratic Left Alliance (SLD) slumped from 216 to 55. A minority government under PjS's Kazimierz Marcinkiewicz was sworn in as coalition negotiations began with PO.

Victory for Kaczynski.

In presidential elections on 23 October the PjS candidate, Lech Kaczynski, was chosen in preference to the PO's more overtly pro-market candidate by 54% to 46% in a run-off vote. Mr Kaczynski's success was seen as symbolizing a fear of too rapid free market reforms, with Mr Kaczynski promising to maintain welfare benefits in a country with almost 18% unemployment. President Kaczynski announced on 29 December that Poland would keep troops in Iraq until the end of 2006, overturning the previous government's proposed withdrawal.

THE CZECH REPUBLIC.

1993	Following 'velvet divorce' from Slovak Republic, Vaclav Havel elected President; privatisation programme introduced.
1996	Vaclav Klaus confirmed as head of coalition government in first general election.
1997	Klaus resigns following criticisms of economic policies; Social Democrat Milos Zeman forms minority government following inconclusive elections.
1998	Havel re-elected President.
1999	Joins NATO.
2002	Social Democrat Vladimir Spidla forms coalition government with Christian Democrats and Freedom Union.
2003	Klaus replaces Havel as President; referendum supports entry to EU.
2004	Joins EU; Stanislav Gross replaces Spidla at head of coalition government.

The Fall of Gross.

In a dramatic development in April 2005, Stanislav Gross announced he would resign as Prime Minister to make way for a new coalition government following the scandal concerning his purchase of a luxury home. He was succeeded by Jiri Paroubek, the Housing Minister under Gross.

EU Problems.

Following the results of the French and Netherlands' referendums on the European Constitution in 2005, Mr Paroubek announced the postponement of the Czech vote until at least 2007. On 5 September he announced that the country would not be able to enter the single European currency until 2010, later than his government had hoped, for economic and political reasons.

HUNGARY.

1949 Communist state declared; industry and agriculture comes under state control.

1956 Anti-Soviet uprising crushed; prime minister Nagy captured and later executed by Communists; Kadar becomes head of government.

1968 New Economic Mechanism introduces market socialism.

1988 Karoly Grosz replaces Kadar; opposition Hungarian Democratic Forum formed.

1989 Communist state collapses; transition to multi-party state begins.

1990 Centre-right coalition forms government; withdraws from Warsaw Pact.

1991 Soviet troops leave.

1994 Coalition of liberals and former Communists win elections.

1997 Joins NATO; EU membership negotiations begin.

1998 Viktor Orban leads centre-right coalition government.

2000 Peter Medgyessy forms centre-left coalition.

2003 Referendum approves joining EU on 46% turnout.

2004 Joins EU; Ferenc Gyurcsany replaces Medgyessy as prime minister.

Recent Events.

On 7 June 2005 Laszio Solyom, who was supported by the opposition, became President after the Socialists' candidate failed to win the backing of their coalition partners, the Free Democrats.

RUSSIA AND EASTERN EUROPE

RUSSIA.

The chronology below sets out the key dates from the disintegration of the former Soviet Union and the ending of communist rule until the elections of 1999. A detailed discussion of more recent events follows.

1991

Aug. Attempted hard-line coup in Moscow while Gorbachev on holiday in Crimea. Russian premier Boris Yeltsin defies coup and prepares to defend Russian parliament building with aid of loyal troops and populace. Coup collapses in face of popular resistance and declarations of independence by Republics. The leading plotters are arrested. Gorbachev returns to Moscow. Under pressure from Yeltsin, adopts sweeping reforms. Baltic states become independent states of Latvia, Estonia and Lithuania; Communist Party of Soviet Union dissolved, ending 74-year rule; Gorbachev resigns as General Secretary, retaining office of executive President of rapidly dissolving Soviet Union. Negotiates an association with ten Republics for a looser union with a common foreign and defence policy.

Dec. Leaders of Belorussia, Russian Federation and Ukraine declare that the Soviet Union is dead; in the Declaration of Minsk they proclaim new 'Commonwealth of Independent States' (CIS) with headquarters at Minsk in Belorussia. Formal resignation of Mikhail Gorbachev as President of the now defunct Soviet Union; the Russian flag replaces the Hammer and Sickle above the Kremlin; key EC states (and America) recognize independence of Russian Federation.

1992

Jun. Yegor Gaidar becomes premier of Russia.

Sept. Lithuania signs agreement with Russia for withdrawal of former Soviet troops.

Dec. Russian Congress blocks President Yeltsin's plans for a referendum on the powers of the President; also removes Yegor Gaidar as premier and replaces him with Viktor Chernomyrdin.

1993

Mar. President Yeltsin announces rule by decree and plan to hold a national referendum on 25 April. Move to impeach the President by Congress defeated.

Apr. Russian referendum gives vote of confidence to President Yeltsin and his economic policy.

Sept. President Yeltsin suspends parliament and calls for elections.

Oct. Suppression of rising against President Yeltsin's suspension of parliament.

1994

Jan. Reformers Gaidar and Fedorov leave Yeltsin government.

Dec. Russia gives ultimatum to breakaway Chechen Republic to disband army and free all prisoners; failure to reach agreement leads to major military assault on Chechen Republic.

1995

Jun. Russia and Ukraine finally settle dispute over Black Sea fleet.

Nov. President Yeltsin forced to relinquish control of four key ministries after suffering second heart attack.

Dec. Yeltsin resumes powers.

1996

Jan. Resignation of liberal Russian foreign minister Andrei Kozyrev.

Feb. President Yeltsin announces intention of seeking second term.

Jun. Success for Yeltsin in presidential elections.

1998

Mar. Dismissal of Chernomyrdin.

1999

Dec. Victory for Unity in elections.

The Yeltsin Resignation.

When Russia's voters went to the polls in mid-December, few anticipated that the entire shape of Russian politics would be altered less by the solidification of a pro-Kremlin bloc in the new Duma than the resignation at the year's end of Boris Yeltsin from the Presidency and his replacement as Acting President by Vladimir Putin. Yeltsin's decision had the effect, as Yeltsin intended that it should, of making Putin the overwhelming favourite to win the presidential election due on 26 March 2000.

The Advent of Vladimir Putin.

As he took office, Putin's intentions were clear in one respect only: he plainly sought a rapid and conclusive end to Russia's resumed war in Chechnya which Yeltsin had begun following his claim that three terrorist bomb attacks in Moscow in the late summer were the responsibility of Chechen Muslim rebels. The war against Chechnya, conducted largely beyond the reach of western television cameras, caused heavy casualties among Chechen civilians and left heavier Russian military casualties than the Ministry of Defence in Moscow acknowledged. It harmed Russia's reputation abroad, and placed those western governments who longed for a competent and non-corrupt Russian government in the awkward position of expressing displeasure at Russian brutality while indicating understanding for Russian anxieties about the terrorist threat which it perceived.

The Chechen War.

Putin's determination to win the war against the Chechens was not in doubt. In all other respects, however his friends and foes alike found Putin's intentions difficult to discern. The difficulty arose primarily from the opacity of his background in the KGB and its successor organization, the Federal Security Service. On one reading, he was a skilled bureaucrat; on another, he was merely an experienced and authoritarian, rather than an adept, bureaucrat. His public speeches showed a certain political skill in revealing different faces to different constituencies.

The Presidential Election.

These skills were enough to give the Presidency to Putin in his own right. He won the March 2000 presidential election on the first ballot with 52 per cent of the vote, easily dwarfing the 29 per cent achieved by the Communists. Russia, it seemed, had entered a new era.

Russia under Putin.

In his first year in office, Putin sought to assert national authority over the regions and Presidential authority over other centres of power both within government (notably over the bureaucracy and the legislature) and outside it (over the so-called oligarchs). After a year in power, the broad contours of Putin's Presidency were reasonably clear. His language was one of reform, both economic and political. But his actual object seemed to be the restoration of order rather than the building of a democracy. Moreover, where economic reform clashed with the imperatives of what Putin determined to be state interests, he typically gave the latter priority.

An Authoritarian President.

The means which Putin uses to achieve order are authoritarian. Both the object and the means may owe something to Putin's background in the state security apparatus; they certainly owe a great deal to Putin's networks in that apparatus as is apparent from the domination of his associates in the so-called Security Council—in effect, a cabinet of his immediate advisers and supporters. Media outlets which give platforms to inconvenient opposition voices now have no doubt about the seriousness of Putin's intent: whilst he is not acting to eliminate television dissent, he has certainly acted to quell it. The power of regional political leaders to resist the centre is much reduced, not least through the crippling of the Federation Council which previously gave them their institutional base of power at the centre. Henceforth, Putin's sway beyond Moscow will be enhanced both by his new power to suspend regional leaders and through his vicarious power over seven enlarged regions in the form of his own appointed subordinate officials charged with the maintenance of security (on Moscow's terms) and economic policy.

The Response to World Terrorism.

Of the responses to the terrorist attacks upon the United States (see **C**51), Russia's was among the more remarkable: President Putin offered visible political support; (mostly) hidden intelligence and logistical assistance; and the firmest rhetorical backing. As was the case elsewhere, Russia had powerful domestic reasons for supporting the United States, not the least of which was its desire to deflect American public criticism of its campaign against Chechen separatists. In the absence of a change of policy, Russia has little prospect of quelling human rights groups' criticisms of Russian actions in Chechnya. But the terrorist attacks upon New York and Washington pushed Russian policy on the question off US and European TV news programmes and newspapers; that has allowed US and European governments to trade off Russian support for a wider campaign against terrorism against a diminution in their criticisms of Russia's own anti-terrorist methods and purposes. (In fact, Russia's prospects of defeating Chechen rebels remain poor—with or without American understanding. Russian troops' ill-discipline confirms Chechen views of Russian values and purposes. Nor have Chechen fighters any significant prospect of defeating Russia. A negotiated standoff of some kind must come, as the United States is likely to continue privately to impress upon Putin.)

Media Repression.

The embarrassment which Russia's policy towards Chechnya causes western governments (which for reasons of geo-political stability, nuclear security, and economic reform wish to assist Putin) has ebbed as the cause of anti-terrorism has come to dominate the agenda of global politics. The embarrassment which Russia's repressive policy towards independent television stations causes has not. In short, no independent stations now remain: the Press Ministry shut the last remaining opposition national television station (TV-6) in January 2002. Russia is, formally, a democracy. But it is scarcely a liberal, and still less a pluralist, democracy.

Public Support for Putin.

President Putin maintained his extraordinary public support in 2002, but made less headway than he and his advisers wished in addressing the problems of public order, corruption, and the limited effectiveness of the state. The greatest public order challenge to the government came with a violent seizure of a Moscow theatre by armed Chechen terrorists that ended in the storming of the theatre by security personnel, the death of more than 120 of the hostages, and serious injuries to others. Public opinion polls show that Russian voters continued to regard Chechen rebels as beyond the pale and the Chechen crisis as having no negotiable outcome. Putin nevertheless gained from his personal decision to end the crisis by force because it underlined his key attraction to Russian voters—his decisiveness. Yet the limitations of Putin's policy were brutally exposed between Christmas and New Year in 2002 when two men drove two trucks packed with explosives into a Russian administrative office in Grozny. Detonating their explosives, they killed nearly one hundred people.

Corruption continued in 2002 to pose a grave threat to the quality of Russian democracy and its economy. A number of politicians and commentators observed that Russia needed public sector reform for reasons more fundamental than those of efficiency which prompted such reform in western economies.

The Iraq War.

Despite sharp policy disagreements with the United States and Britain over policy towards Iraq, Russia's relations with both countries in 2003 survived relatively unscathed. Part of the explanation lies in Russia having overriding interests in attracting western capital and in maintaining access to western markets. But part also lies in Russia being a relatively weak economic force and in its having only limited leverage over the west.

A More Stable Economy.

Despite its small GDP compared to the major western economies, Russia's economic policy is broadly stable and gives cause for some confidence about the country's potential. Yet Russia's political system continues to have the character of a nominal democracy with sharply authoritarian characteristics: whatever Russia has become more than a decade after the Soviet Union's collapse, it has become neither liberal nor pluralist. To that extent, Russia's development continues broadly to take the form that President Putin and those around him wish: Putin has not only not embraced the building of a pluralist state but has periodically made clear his disdain for it. Where Putin thinks that his interests are open to challenge, he has not hesitated to act. That is a key lesson of the arrest in November 2003 of the business tycoon Mikhail Khodorkovsky, boss of the Yukos conglomerate.

The 2003 Duma Elections.

Such events drew greater condemnation abroad than they do in Russia: the State Duma elections that took place shortly after Khodorkovsky's arrest resulted in the marginalisation of the two most numerous liberal parties and underlined Putin's dominance (though by no means unfettered command) of Russian politics. Putin's next electoral hurdle was the Presidential election in 2004.

The 2004 Presidential Election.

In February 2004, in a development reminiscent

of the Yeltsin era, Putin dismissed his entire government. The surprise choice for Prime Minister was Mikhail Fradkov, Russia's EU representative.

On 14 March, as widely expected, President Putin won a landslide presidential election victory, with around two-thirds of the votes cast. In distant second place was the Communist candidate, with a meagre 14·7% of the vote.

The Beslan Massacre.

Russia's exposure to Islamist terrorism arising from its policy towards Chechnya in particular and the Caucasus in general was brutally demonstrated in 2004 when more than three hundred people (including one hundred and fifty children) were killed in a school at Beslan in North Ossetia. The outrage followed terrorists taking the civilians hostage and laying explosives throughout the school, but were precipitated by Russian security forces' clumsy attempts to take the school. Supported by shocked Russian public opinion, President Putin presented the killings as Russia's "September 11", and imposed a more severe security policy.

Social Reform Policy.

January 2005 marked a new phase in Russia's reform of social policy. To supplement tiny state cash pensions, elderly Russians and others such as the disabled, and former soldiers in receipt of state payments, have long benefited from payments in kind such as free public transport and subsidized gas and electricity. Suspension of payments in kind from 1 January coupled with partial compensation through higher cash benefits provoked widespread protests by affected groups already living on the margins. Putin limited the political damage by blaming his ministers and advisers for the policy, and ordered that cash benefits be increased further to compensate the many who had lost out in the reforms.

Russia's economy remained strong in 2004. The economy grew vigorously at a rate of 6.5%; the balance of payments surplus remained strong; and foreign exchange reserves were strong, buoyed by high world oil prices. The prospects for the economy were nevertheless clouded by the government's destruction of Yukos, the oil conglomerate. Putin's action against Yukos, previously one of the most dynamic of the large Russian companies, did nothing to encourage business investment, especially from abroad.

Diplomatic Initiatives.

President Putin's talks with President Bush in September revealed clear disagreement on the response to Iran's alleged nuclear ambitions but agreement on the need to dissuade North Korea. There were efforts to consolidate relations with Asian neighbours. China in particular represented an important trading partner, with the volume of trade reaching an estimated $29 billion. Discussions appeared to resolve frontier issues and in August the two countries mounted a joint military exercise, partly intended to warn off the United States from envisaging too prominent a role in the region. In November President Putin led a delegation of business leaders to Tokyo to discuss growing economic links.

Events in Chechnya.

Chechnya, where Russia had been accused of human rights abuses, remained a flashpoint. In February 2005 the Chechen separatist leader, Aslan Maskhadov, announced a ceasefire and called on Russia to open negotiations, shortly before he was killed by Russian security forces. His successor announced the establishment of a Caucasus Front to widen anti-Russian action. Russia feared the regional impact of meeting demands for independence. In regional elections in November, United Russia took over half the seats and President Putin attended the opening session of the legislature. However, members of the security forces were killed almost daily in clashes with separatists.

The Imprisonment of Khodorkovsky.

In October President Putin backed off from a widely criticised reform that would have allowed him to abandon elections and appoint regional governors. But there were concerns that the imprisonment of Mikhail Khodorkovsky, former owner of a major oil company, for tax evasion in May had had as much to do with his financing of opposition parties as it had with his financial crimes. On a visit to Russia, United States Secretary of State Condoleezza Rice expressed concern about the lack of press freedom and growing centralisation of power. However, the government appeared confident that the country's pivotal position as an energy supplier would ward off significant criticism.

Growing International Criticisms.

Nevertheless, there were international criticisms of what appeared a further authoritarian step in December, when the Duma passed controversial legislation tightening state control over non-governmental organisations (NGOs) The government declared Western governments were using NGOs to encourage revolutions of the type recently seen in Ukraine. At the turn of the year Russia intensified pressure on Ukraine by raising the price of gas and then temporarily terminating supplies, with a knock-on effect on Western Europe. On 1 January 2006 Russia took over the chairmanship of the G8 group of the leading industrialised democracies, a step towards the restoration of the country's international prestige. But in February Russia came under pressure from its G8 partners to ratify an energy supply charter.

UKRAINE.

The 2004 Presidential Election.

Despite, and in part because of, the role played by Russian advisers to incumbent Prime Minister Viktor Yanukovich in the framing and conduct of his presidential campaign, the election (re-run after the Supreme Court had confirmed that the first was fraudulent) finally resulted in the victory of his opponent, the liberal Victor Yuschenko, with 52% of the vote in December 2004. The popular protests and massive demonstrations were nicknamed the 'Orange Revolution'.

The New Government.

Mr Yuschenko was sworn in as president in January 2005. In February, his nominee as prime minister, Yulia Tymoshenko, was approved as prime minister by the legislature. In March the government announced that Ukraine's peacekeeping force in Iraq would be withdrawn by October. But the political system was moving into crisis as the Orange Revolution failed to fulfil its promise. In September President Yuschenko's chief of staff resigned, alleging corruption among senior government officials. In an unravelling of the revolutionary coalition of 2004, President Yuschenko dismissed Ms Tymoshenko on 8 September, replacing her with Yuriy Yekhanurov.

Growing Domestic Difficulties.

As economic growth faltered, President Yuschenko promised in October that the country would regain stability within three months and pledged political reform that would devolve power to the prime minister and the legislature. The European Union granted Ukraine market economy status on 1 December, a move to increase trade, and supported a bid to join the World Trade Organisation. But at the end of December the country was thrown into crisis as Russia cut off gas supplies following a five-fold price increase. Russia's move was seen as a response to Ukraine seeking closer links with NATO and the European Union. Supplies were briefly interrupted but restored early in January 2006. There were criticisms of the agreement negotiated with Russia. On 11 January a motion to dismiss the prime minister was passed by 250–50 votes but rejected by President Yuschenko as unconstitutional.

Voters disappointed with President Yuschenko's achievements pushed his Our Ukraine bloc into third place in elections on 26 March 2006, behind Ms Tymoshenko, whom he had dismissed as prime minister, and, more significantly, Mr Yanukovich, who had been ousted in the 'Orange Revolution'. In April President Yuschenko began attempts to form an Orange coalition with Ms Tymoshenko's party.

BELARUS.

1991 Declares independence as the Soviet Union collapses.
1994 Alexander Lukashenko becomes president.
1996 Agreement on economic union signed with Russia; Lukashenko extends term in office.
1997 Pro-democracy demonstrations.
2000 Criticism of conduct of parliamentary elections; agreement with Russia on single currency by 2008.
2001 Lukashenko returned in widely criticised election.
2002 Rejects Russian proposals for union.
2004 Council of Europe criticised human rights abuses; EU imposes travel restrictions on senior officials.

Re-election of Lukashenko.

In October 2004, President Alyaksandr Lukashenko secured reelection and won a referendum to abolish the term-limits on the Presidency. Both the election and the referendum were fraudulent exercises, as neutral foreign observers (many of them subjected to harassment by state security forces) confirmed from their scrutiny of voting procedures at polling stations across Belarus. The government banned half of the candidates from opposition parties for parliamentary seats from standing, and prevented others from standing for office for the offence of arguing for the defeat of President Lukashenko's referendum proposal. Exercising almost total power within Belarus, the President is effectively the last of Europe's old dictators.

Recent Developments.

In January 2005 US Secretary of State Condoleezza Rice named Belarus as among the 'outposts of tyranny'. In October the country's last independent newspaper closed under government pressure. In November President Lukashenko and President Putin of Russia were presented with a draft re-unification constitution. However, there appeared little likelihood of movement while President Lukashenko remained in power. On 16 December the legislature brought forward presidential elections to March 2006 as the opposition united behind Alexander Milinkevich.

On 16 March President Lukashenko won a third term with 82·6% of the vote on a 92·6% turnout. His leading rival, Mr Milinkevich, who took 6%, denounced the elections as illegitimate, a view taken by the European Union and United States, both of which imposed sanctions on Belarus. It remained the case that however irregular the election, President Lukashenko's independent line had significant popular backing.

FORMER YUGOSLAVIA.

Chronology of Key Events.

1991-2 Yugoslavia confined to Serbia and Montenegro following breakaway of six former republics; civil war; UN Security Council votes to establish peacekeeping force.
1992 Federal Republic of Yugoslavia proclaimed by Serbia and Montenegro; sanctions and naval blockade imposed to end Yugoslav operations in Bosnia; Yugoslavia expelled from UN; Slobodan Milosevic elected President.
1995 Serbia, Croatia and Bosnia sign Dayton Accord to end war in Bosnia.
1998 Guerrilla war begins in predominantly Albanian Kosovo.
1999 NATO launches air attacks on Yugoslavia to force withdrawal from predominantly Albanian Kosovo; Serbian economy collapses; Montenegro proposes separation.
2000 Vojislav Kostunica takes office following revolt against Milosevic's refusal to accept election defeat; Milosevic arrested.
2001 Milosevic faces UN International Criminal Tribunal; sanctions lifted.
2002 Yugoslav Republic renamed Serbia and Montenegro, a loose union, with Svetozar Marovic as president.
2003 Serb prime minister Zoran Djindjic assassi-

nated; ultra-nationalist Socialist and Radical electoral revival in Serbia.
2004 Serb-Albanian ethnic clashes in Kosovo; former Yugoslav president Vojislav Kostunica becomes Serbian prime minister in centre-right coalition; Boris Tadic elected Serbian president.

Independence for Montenegro.

In February 2005 Montenegran leaders proposed breaking the union with Serbia to form separate republics, a proposal rejected by the Serb premier.

On 22 May 2006 Montenegro voted narrowly in favour of independence in a nation-wide referendum. Montenegro has thus become Europe's newest state and the disintegration of Yugoslavia has now been completed.

THE MIDDLE EAST

Note.

For a background chronology of events in the Middle East, *see* **Special Topic C54–6.**

ISRAEL.

Chronology of Key Events.

1948 State of Israel proclaimed, with Ben Gurion as prime minister; war with Arab neighbours.
1949 Defeat of Arabs sees Israel increase a third in area.
1956 Attacks Egypt with Britain and France.
1963 Eshkol succeeds Ben Gurion as prime minister.
1967 Defeats Egypt, Syria and Jordan in Six-Day War; occupies Sinai, Golan Heights, Gaza, West Bank and East Jerusalem; UN Resolution 242 demands withdrawal.
1969 Golda Meir becomes prime minister.
1973 Defeats Egypt and Syria in Yom Kippur War
1974 Rabin becomes prime minister.
1977 Begin defeats Rabin in general election, ending 29 years of Labour government; visit of Egyptian President Sadat opens peace negotiations.
1979 Camp David Agreement with Egypt.
1980 Jerusalem declared capital of Israel.
1982 Invades Lebanon to defeat Palestinian guerrillas.
1984 Labour leader Peres forms coalition with Likud.
1986 Shamir succeeds Peres as prime minister.
1987 Palestinian *intifada* (uprising) begins in occupied territories.
1993 Oslo Agreement outlines Palestinian autonomy in West Bank and Gaza on 'peace for land' principle.
1994 Peace treaty with Jordan.
1995 Oslo 2 Agreement; prime minister Rabin assassinated; succeeded by Peres.
1996 Palestinian terrorism threatens peace process; Natanyahu becomes prime minister.
1998 Wye River agreement on Israeli withdrawal from West Bank; Netanyahu abandons agreement alleging Palestinian failure to end terrorism.
1999 Labour-led coalition under Barak; 2000 deadline set for peace treaty.
2000 Peace talks collapse; second Palestinian *intifada* begins.
2001 Sharon becomes prime minister; renewed attacks on Palestinian territories.
2003 Withdrawals from parts of West Bank and Gaza; construction of security barrier through West Bank; Likud wins elections.
2004 Sharon proposes withdrawal from Gaza.

Key Developments.

In April 2004 Mr Sharon secured President Bush's backing for withdrawal from Gaza by the end of 2005. Mr Sharon proposed to pull military forces and 21 settlements out of the area and withdraw from four West Bank settlements. In May Mr Sharon's own Likud Party rejected his proposal and in June he dismissed two members of his cabinet as he manoeuvred to secure domestic support. There were demonstrations in July and September against the plan, but opinion polls showed widespread support in the country for the move.

The World Court Ruling.

On 1 July a court ruled that Israel's construction of a security barrier through the West Bank violated Palestinian human rights. The World Court followed this by calling the barrier a land grab, ordering its removal and payment of compensation to Palestinians. The government responded in September by announcing the expansion of settlements in the Jordan valley and the expropriation of 8,000 acres of land. Government papers revealed on 4 December that Israel envisaged that any future Palestinian state would be one of small enclaves surrounded by walls.

Withdrawal from Gaza.

On 26 October the Knesset voted 67–45 in favour of the withdrawal from Gaza and the northern West Bank, with seven abstentions. As 2004 ended, Mr Sharon further strengthened his position by reaching agreement with the Labour Party on a new coalition, with Mr Peres as deputy prime minister.

Israel made a conciliatory gesture of promising to release prisoners following the election of the new Palestinian Authority president in January 2005 but responded forcefully to continuing militant attacks. However, on 26 January it was announced that there had been preliminary discussions between Israeli and Palestinian officials.

On 6 February United States Secretary of State Rice told Israel "hard decisions" were necessary to advance the peace process. On 8 February Mr Sharon met Mr Abbas for talks in Egypt. Shortly after the Knesset approved the disengagement programme. Widespread hopes that moves towards peace might bear fruit were underlined by the government's relatively restrained response to a terrorist bombing in Tel Aviv. However, much depended on Mr Sharon's political survival.

Internal Opposition.

Mr Sharon pressed forward with the withdrawal, dismantling 21 Israeli settlements in Gaza and four in the West Bank in the face of protests from the settlers, demonstrations from the right, and the resignation of former prime minister Netanyahu from the cabinet in August 2005. The withdrawal was completed in October. However, Mr Sharon's approval of further West Bank settlements (despite President Bush's criticism in April 2005) and of the security barrier underlined his determination to retain the occupied West Bank.

Politics after Sharon.

Events then took a dramatic turn. Following the unexpected ousting of Mr Peres as Labour leader, his successor, Mr Amir Peretz, declared that the party would withdraw from the coalition, forcing elections in 2006. Facing a challenge to his leadership of Likud, on 21 November Mr Sharon announced the formation of a new centre party, Kadima, to which Mr Peres pledged his support, promising a realignment of Israeli politics. On 21 December Mr Netanyahu was elected leader of Likud. On 4 January 2006 Mr Sharon suffered a stroke. As Mr Sharon's life hung in the balance, Mr Ehud Olmert took over as acting prime minister and Kadima leader.

The 2006 Election.

In elections on 28 March Mr Olmert's centrist Kadima took 29 seats and the centre-left Labour Party 19, as the right-wing Likud trailed with 12 seats. A Kadima-Labour coalition government backed by smaller parties was clearly on the cards and negotiations opened in April.

EGYPT.

1952 Muhammad Najib deposed King Farouk; becomes president and prime minister in Free Officers' Movement coup.
1953 Republic declared.

1954 Nasser becomes prime minister; later president. Last British forces leave.
1956 Britain, France and Israel invade following Suez Canal nationalisation.
1958 Forms United Arab Republic with Syria (abandoned 1961).
1967 Defeated by Israel in Six-Day War.
1970 Sadat becomes president on Nasser's death; Aswan Dam completed.
1973 Yom Kippur war with Israel.
1978 Camp David Accords signed.
1979 Peace treaty with Israel; expelled from Arab League.
1981 Sadat assassinated by Islamic fundamentalists; succeeded by Mubarrak.
1989 Rejoins Arab League.
1995 Mubarrak survives assassination attempt; his National Democratic Party (NDP) wins over whelmingly in elections opponents declare rigged.
1998 Foreign tourists killed in Islamic terrorist attack.
1999 Mubarrak survives assassination attempt; returned to office in referendum with 95 % of vote.
2000 NDP retains majority in People's Assembly elections.
2002 Contacts with Israel suspended in support of Palestinians.
2003 Protests over US/British invasion of Iraq.

Developments in 2004.

Ahmed Nazif replaced Atef Obeid as prime minister on 9 July 2004, as the NDP government took further steps towards economic reform, reducing customs tariffs and attempting to curb bureaucracy. However, unemployment remained high. The NDP attempted to consolidate progress, with the slogan 'New Thought'. But opposition parties accused the NDP of stifling debate and operating through electoral fraud. The Popular Campaign for Reform, a recently formed umbrella group of human rights organisations, attempted to co-ordinate opposition. On 1 November the campaign issued a petition calling for constitutional reform, genuine elections and the repeal of the emergency laws in force since President Sadat's assassination in 1981.

Improved Climate with Israel.

The Interior Minister denied in October that al-Qaeda had played any part in terrorist attacks that month on Israeli tourists in the Sinai peninsula, linking them to Palestinian desperation over their plight in the occupied territories. There were, however, signs of improved relations with Israel, with agreement on the deployment of Egyptian troops on the Gaza border as a preliminary to Israeli withdrawal from the area.

On 14 December Egypt, Israel and the United States signed a trade agreement allowing free entry to the United States of joint Egyptian-Israeli products. The agreement followed an exchange of prisoners between Egypt and Israel and President Mubarrak's declaration that the Israeli prime minister, Mr Sharon, provided the Palestinians with their best hope for peace.

Muslim Brotherhood Arrests.

As the Muslim Brotherhood mounted demonstrations calling for democratic reform in May 2005, the parliamentary upper house approved measures for multi-party elections to the presidency. The opposition criticised the arrangements as fraudulent. At the end of the month dozens of Muslim Brotherhood members were arrested. The Brotherhood, founded in 1928, is the country's largest Islamist organisation.

The 2005 Elections.

In elections on 9 September, President Mubarrak, facing opposition for the first time, won a fifth term with 88·6 % of the vote. Turnout was 23 % and the major opposition groupings boycotted the poll. Ayman Nour of the Al-Ghad party took 7·3 % and Noaman Gomaa of the Wafd Party 2·8 %. Elections to the 454 People's Assembly were held in November and December. In the last Assembly the ruling National Democratic Party held over 90% of the seats. In the final announcement of results in December, the Muslim Brotherhood, running as independents, took 19% of seats, with the National Democratic Party winning over 70%. Observers questioned the poll's legitimacy. On 24 December Ayman Nour was sentenced to five years for alleged irregularities in the September presidential elections. The United States criticised the sentence's political motivation.

THE PALESTINIANS.

Chronology of Key Events.

1949 700,000 Palestinians become refugees from new state of Israel.
1964 Palestine Liberation Organisation (PLO) formed.
1965 Fatah (Movement for the Liberation of Palestine) begins guerrilla actions against Israel.
1967 Israeli victory in Six-Day War and occupations of Arab territory radicalise Palestinian resistance.
1968 PLO adopts demand for Palestinian homeland.
1969 Yasser Arafat elected PLO chairman.
1970 Black September aircraft hijackings; Jordan attacks Palestinian leadership.
1974 Arafat addresses UN; Arab summit declares PLO the 'sole and legitimate representative' of the Palestinians.
1982 Israel invades Lebanon to oust Palestinian guerrillas.
1987 First Palestinian intifada (uprising) in Israeli-occupied territories begins.
1988 Arafat rejects terrorism, accepts Israel's right to exist.
1990 Arafat loses Gulf states' support by backing Iraq's invasion of Kuwait.
1993 Arafat and Israeli prime minister Rabin agree on limited Palestinian self-rule in West Bank and Gaza.
1994 Arafat becomes head of Palestinian Authority in Gaza.
1995 Arafat and Rabin sign aborted agreement on West Bank.
1996 Palestinian suicide bombings in Israel undermine peace process; Arafat moves against Hamas militants.
1998 Arafat and Netanyahu sign Wye River agreement on phased Israeli West Bank withdrawal; Israel abandons, accusing Arafat of not meeting security promises.
1999 Arafat agrees with Israeli prime minister Barak on September 2000 deadline for peace treaty.
2000 US brokered peace negotiations at Camp David collapse; Palestinians begin second intifada following alleged provocation by Israeli opposition leader Sharon.
2001 Rising death toll in Israeli-Palestinian conflict.
2002 Arafat besieged by Israelis in presidential compound; Palestinian suicide bombings escalate.
2003 Arafat appoints Abbas (Abu Mazen) as prime minister under international pressure; Abbas resigns as Arafat refuses to relinquish security powers; Qurei (Abu Ala) succeeds; Palestinians accept US-backed 'road map' to peace.
2004 Increasing Palestinian dissatisfaction with Arafat and Palestinian Authority corruption; Arafat dies.

Mr Arafat's death in December 2004 marked the end of an era in Palestinian politics and was seen, rightly or wrongly, as opening a new opportunity for peace. For many years Arafat had personified the Palestinian struggle, ensuring the hopes of his people won international recognition. But Israel and the United States saw him as an obstacle to a settlement because of his unwillingness (or inability) to confront terrorism. In 1993 Mr Arafat had secured the establishment of the Palestinian National Authority, the first step towards statehood. But the final decade of his life was marked by aborted negotiations and upsurges of violence and counter-violence, culminating in Mr Arafat being held a virtual prisoner.

The Municipal Elections.

In municipal elections in the West Bank at the end of December 2004, over 140,000 Palestinian voters went to the polls in a virtual dress rehearsal for the election of Mr Arafat's successor. Fatah retained its traditional dominance, but the militant group Hamas revealed significant support. However, Mahmoud Abbas, the former prime minister, won a landslide victory in presidential elections held on 9 January 2005, taking 62% of the vote. His nearest rival, Mustafa Barghouti, took 21%. Hamas, which had boycotted the elections, said they were willing to co-operate with Mr Abbas.

Prospects for Peace.

It remained to be seen whether Mr Abbas's election would re-open the peace process. The immediate issues facing him were negotiations with Israel on the Gaza withdrawal, securing agreement with Hamas and Islamic Jihad, and confronting Mr Arafat's legacy of corruption and organisational disorder. On 17 January 2005 Mr Abbas ordered his security forces to prevent militant attacks on Israeli targets and an informal ceasefire followed. Local elections held in Gaza at the end of the month showed the strength of support for Hamas, as the militant group's candidates took two thirds of the seats, with a third going to Mr Abbas's Fatah. In February 2005 prime minister Ahmed Qurei appointed a new cabinet dominated by technocrats, removing many veterans and marking a break with the Arafat era. The Palestinian Authority condemned a terrorist attack in Israel in February and urged militant groups to formalise a ceasefire.

The March 2005 Ceasefire

Hamas (the Islamic Resistance Movement) and Islamic Jihad agreed to a ceasefire for the remainder of 2005 in March. Mr Abbas and Mr Sharon of Israel announced a mutual ceasefire at a summit in Egypt as preparations went ahead for Israel's withdrawal from Gaza. The Palestinian Authority, while welcoming the withdrawal, were not satisfied that it accorded in the longer term with a two-state agreement. Meanwhile, Israel transferred security control of a number of West Bank towns to the Palestinian Authority. On 5 May Fatah took half the seats and Hamas a third in municipal elections in Gaza and the West Bank.

With Israel's withdrawal from Gaza complete at the end of September, there were clashes between Hamas and Palestinian Authority security forces, as well as between Israel and Hamas, with air strikes in Gaza and the West Bank. On 20 October Mr Abbas, in a visit to Washington, urged President Bush to press Israel to halt construction of the West Bank security wall. Fatah's position appeared to be weakening as Hamas took over 70% of the vote in Nablus, a West Bank city hitherto a Fatah stronghold and there were renewed criticisms of Palestinian Authority corruption.

Sensational Victory for Hamas.

Elections held on 25 January 2006 saw the dramatic ousting of Fatah as Hamas took 76 seats to Fatah's 43. Ismail Haniya, a Gaza Strip leader, was appointed prime minister. As Hamas rejected calls to recognise Israel and accept the terms of past peace agreements, the European Union and the United States terminated direct aid to the Palestinian Authority in early April.

IRAN.

1935 Persia renamed Iran.
1941 Pro-German Shah ousted by Allies; replaced by son Mohammad Reza Pahlavi.
1950 Radical nationalist Mohammad Mossadeq becomes prime minister.
1951 Oil industry nationalised; power struggle between Shah and Mossadeq.
1953 Shah ousts Mossadeq with Western support.
1963 Shah begins "White Revolution" of land reform and social modernisation; uses secret police against opponents.
1973 Martial law imposed as resistance grows.
1979 Shah exiled; Islamic Republic declared under fundamentalist Ayatollah Khomeini.

1980 Government begins radical nationalisation programme; war with Iraq.

1988 War with Iraq ends.

1989 Ayatollah Khomeini dies; Ayatollah Khamenei becomes supreme leader; Ali Akbar Rafsanjani becomes president.

1995 US imposes trade sanctions, alleging Iran sponsors terrorism.

1997 Reformist Mohammad Khatami wins land-slide presidential election.

1999 Pro-democracy riots in Tehran.

2000 Reformists win parliamentary majority; conservatives attempt to thwart election result; judiciary bans reformist press.

Continuing Power Struggles.

President Khatami was re-elected for a second term in June 2001 with 77 % of the vote. The power struggle between reformists and conservatives continued. Ayatollah Khamenei postponed President Khatami's swearing in following a dispute over appointments to the conservative dominated Guardian Council. President Khatami was finally sworn in on 8 August.

The Freedom Movement Trial.

A further sign of the struggle between conservatives and reformists came on 11 November when 25 members of the liberal opposition Freedom Movement (which had been banned in March) went on trial for conspiracy to overthrow the government. The charges were criticised by President Khatami, human rights groups and reformist politicians. President Khatami went further on 22 December, calling on conservatives to respect the views of reformists and warned that the country's stability depended on democracy. But on 26 December three reformist deputies were imprisoned for insulting the conservative judiciary. Some deputies denounced the jailing as a coup against reform and called for a referendum on the court's powers.

The 'Axis of Evil' Speech.

On 15 January 2002 reformers were strengthened when supreme leader Ayatollah Ali Khamenei pardoned an imprisoned deputy following protests by Majlis members. United Nations secretary-general Kofi Annan praised the part Iran had played in the struggle in Afghanistan on 26 January but President Bush's speech in which he declared the country to be part of an 'axis of evil' at the end of the month angered both reformers and the clerical establishment. Thousands demonstrated in Tehran against the United States on 11 February. However, in March a spokesman said the government would not oppose discussions between deputies and American legislators.

American Relations with Iran.

But American criticisms continued. In April the Secretary of Defense accused Iran (along with Iraq and Libya) of financing suicide bombing attacks in Israel. In May the United States government said Iran was close to developing nuclear weapons. While Ayatollah Khamenei said negotiations would only be in America's interests, it remained clear that reformers still aspired to improved relations.

However, on 12 July President Bush said all engagement with President Khatami was over and declared his support for the Islamic revolution's opponents, accusing Iran on 28 August of harbouring al-Qaeda members. Iraq attempted to widen the breach when, on 29 September, the visiting foreign minister warned President Khatami that the United States threatened Islam as a whole, not just Iraq. But on 2 November the government announced the arrest of several hundred al-Qaeda suspects.

However, there were signs of improved relations internationally. In June European Union foreign ministers had agreed on trade discussions and there was an increasing closeness to Pakistan. On 20 December 2002 the World Bank announced its first investment in Iran since 1974.

The reformist cause was set back as President Khatami's allies suffered their worst electoral defeat for six years in local elections in March 2003. The elections were marked by high abstentions.

Despite the reformists' setback in the March 2003 elections, students mounted anti-clerical demonstrations in Tehran in June. But, as the low turnout in the elections had demonstrated, there was growing disillusion over the possibility of democratic change and disappointment at President Khatami's impotence.

Iran's Nuclear Programme.

Following the conclusion of the war in Iraq, Iran felt increasingly threatened by President Bush's accusations of nuclear ambitions and that it was harbouring terrorists. Russian technicians had begun building a nuclear reactor in 2002, despite US objections. In June the International Atomic Energy Agency (IAEA) demanded that Iran allow closer inspection of its nuclear facilities. The IAEA accused Iran of evading inspections. Iran insisted its programme was civilian and not aimed at developing weapons. The IAEA discovery in August of enriched uranium at a nuclear facility was followed by a UN ultimatum. In November, despite objections by hardliners, the government announced that it would allow total access to IAEA inspectors and end production of enriched uranium. On 18 December Iran signed the nuclear Non-Proliferation Treaty.

The February 2004 Elections.

Internal political divisions sharpened as the conservative Guardian's Council disqualified hundreds of reformist candidates (including 80 *Majlis* members) from elections due in February 2004. Reformist members responded by occupying the parliament building. The supreme leader, Ayatollah Ali Khamenei, appealed for calm and the Council appeared to be moderating its position. But on 26 January the Council rejected an attempt by opposition members of the *Majlis* to quash the ban. On 1 February over 120 reformists resigned and the main reform party, the Islamic Participation Front, said it would not take part in the elections.

With reformists calling for a boycott, turn-out at elections to the *Majlis* on 20 February was 50·6 %, significantly lower than the 67 % who voted in 2000. The conservative establishment, which won control of the *Majlis*, could take little comfort from what amounted to a contrived victory.

New Threats from America.

A second round of voting in May underlined continuing conservative power. Meanwhile, on 21 April President Bush threatened Iran over the country's alleged nuclear weapons development. Tension rose through the summer as the International Atomic Energy Agency criticised developments and in September passed a resolution requiring Iran to cease all uranium-enrichment activity. Initially defiant, the government announced a freeze on the enrichment programme in November as part of an agreement with the European Union. Iran denied further charges that the country was continuing production of weapons-grade uranium.

The government announced on 6 December that suspected al-Qaeda members had been tried and sentenced but gave no further details. The Supreme National Security Council had accused unnamed suspects of plotting terrorist activity in Iran. As disappointment continued with President Khatami's reforms, students interrupted a speech he was delivering at Tehran University with chants of 'Shame on you'. President Khatami responded by criticising hardliners who had closed newspapers and imprisoned dissidents.

Rising Military Tension.

As 2004 closed, Iran's military commander said forces were on standby to repel feared Israeli attacks on nuclear sites. He said a number of people had been arrested over the past year suspected of spying for Israel and the United States. An American publication reported that military planners had simulated an attack on Iran. On 15 January 2005 President Khatami rejected American criticisms of Iran's human rights record, pointing to the record of United States troops in Iraq. On 19 January Ms Rice, the incoming United States' Secretary of State, declared that Iran was one of the 'outposts of tyranny'

The 2005 Presidential Election.

On 24 June, in the second round of voting in the presidential election, the hard-line ultra-conservative Mayor of Tehran, Mahmoud Ahmadinejad, won a convincing victory with 62% of the votes cast. The defeat of the more moderate Mr. Rafsanjani sent alarm bells ringing in Israel and America, particularly over the nuclear ambitions of Iran. Liberals feared a return to the conservative, clerical values of the 1979 Islamic revolution.

Growing International Concerns.

President Ahmadinejad's success had been built on popular anger at corruption and the growing gap between rich and poor, but only 38% of those voting had supported his conservative line. Of more concern to international observers was his view that Iran should take a firmer line over nuclear development. In May the government had reached agreement with Britain, France and Germany on freezing activity. On taking office in August President Ahmadinejad rejected further European Union proposals and resumed uranium conversion. The United States reported that Iran could produce nuclear weapons within a decade. On 24 September the International Atomic Energy Authority (IAEA) reported that Iran had violated the Nuclear Non-proliferation Treaty.

The Mounting Crisis.

There was widespread international criticism when on 26 October President Ahmadinejad declared that Israel should be 'wiped off the map' and accused the West of ignoring Israeli crimes. On 2 November he replaced ambassadors in Europe who had been involved in earlier nuclear negotiations, underlining Iran's firmer stance. By mid-November it became clear that the purge of government posts was more far-reaching and President Ahmadinejad was accused of conducting a virtual *coup d'état*. But fears of economic sanctions or military action strengthened the country's conservatives. On 5 December the government approved proposals to build a second nuclear power plant. The removal of UN seals at a nuclear facility provoked a referral by the IAEA to the Security Council in early February 2006 but Iran said there was room for negotiation on a Russian compromise proposal. In April, the Iranian President announced that Iran had successfully joined the "nuclear club".

IRAQ.

1932 Gains independence from British control.
1958 General Karim Qasim overthrows monarchy.
1966 General Muhammad Arif becomes president.
1968 Arif is overthrown by General Ahmad Hasan al-Bakr.
1972 Signs Treaty of Friendship and Co-operation with Soviet Union; nationalises Iraq Petroleum Company.
1974 Grant of limited autonomy to Kurds rejected by Kurdistan Democratic Party.
1979 Saddam Hussein becomes president.
1980 War with Iran.
1988 War with Iran ends; Iraq uses chemical weapons against Kurds.
1990 Invades Kuwait.
1991 Defeated in Gulf War; UN safe haven established in north to protect Kurds; 'no flight' zone later set up in south.
1995 UN allows partial resumption of oil exports to buy medicine and food; referendum returns Saddam Hussein as president for seven years.
1998 Ends co-operation with UN supervision of weapons destruction; Britain and US launch bombing campaign.
2000 Rejects weapons inspection proposals; Iraq halts oil exports following dispute with UN.

The September 2001 Aftermath.

In the wake of the terrorist attack on the United States in September 2001 there were mixed messages on whether the Western coalition would attack Iraq after Afghanistan. At the end of October, the deputy prime minister, Tariq Aziz, said the United States was planning a missile attack on 300 Iraqi targets. The British government initially dismissed the possibility. But the US defence secretary did not rule it out while the secretary of state said Iraq faced attack if there was evidence linking the country to terrorism.

The Threat of War.

Iraq was dominated by the apparent inevitability of an attack by the United States and its allies. In March 2002 discussions opened between Iraqi representatives and United Nations (UN) secretary general Kofi Annan on the return of weapons inspectors, with foreign minister Naji Sabri asking the Security Council whether this would end threats of invasion. Talks between Iraqi representatives and the UN Monitoring, Verification and Inspection Commission (Unmovic) in May and July ended inconclusively as Iraq sought guarantees that sanctions would end.

The Return of UN Inspectors.

On 16 September Mr Sabri offered unconditional entry to UN inspectors but this was rejected by the United States which, instead, proposed a resolution to the Security Council which revised the inspectors' mandate and authorised the use of force if Iraq violated the resolution. President Bush warned that the United States would act alone if the United Nations did not. On 8 November the Security Council ordered Iraq to admit the inspectors to search at will and their arrival began shortly afterwards. On 7 December the government presented the UN with a 12,000 page dossier on all biological, chemical and nuclear weapons programmes. The United States said the dossier provided more evidence that Iraq was not complying with the UN resolution.

Meanwhile, in London on 17 December opposition exiles agreed on the principles and structures of a transitional government which would see Saddam Hussein be ousted or flee. Most seats on a 75-strong committee were allotted to the Shia-based Supreme Council of the Islamic Revolution in Iraq and Kurdish groups. Sunni Muslims, women and tribal leaders complained they had been largely excluded. Suggestions in January 2003 that war could be averted if Saddam Hussein went into exile were angrily rejected.

The Allied Attack on Iraq.

American and British coalition forces launched their attack on 20 March (*see* C52). Saddam Hussein's rule effectively ended with the entry of American troops into Baghdad on 7 April. But chaotic scenes of looting, and the breakdown in the country's infrastructure, demonstrated the coalition's failure of post-war planning. The United Nations lifted sanctions on 22 May and authorised the coalition to administer the country until an Iraqi government was in place. Paul Bremner, an American, was appointed civilian administrator. From the beginning the occupying forces, despite their claim to be carriers of democracy, faced protest demonstrations and armed resistance.

The Iraqi Governing Council.

On 13 July Mr Bremner appointed a 25-strong Iraqi Governing Council, though ultimate authority remained in his hands. The Council presented proposals to transfer policing from American troops to local militia. But moves towards the restoration of Iraqi government were slow as the security situation worsened. By early November, six months after the war had ostensibly ended, more American soldiers had died than were killed in the conflict itself. On 14 November 2003 the Council and Mr Bremner presented proposals for the establishment of a transitional assembly in May 2004 to prepare for the election of an interim government in June. The transfer of power would culminate in a general election at the end of 2005. Council President Jalal Talabani said the transitional body would be selected by consultation but on 26 November a leading Shiite cleric, Grand Ayatollah Ali al-Sistani, called for direct elections in June.

The Capture of Saddam Hussein.

On 13 December American troops captured Saddam Hussein. In January 2004 Shiites renewed their demands for early elections as the United States sought UN approval for their own proposals. A spirit of resistance against the occupying forces remained, as over 10,000 Iraqis continued to be imprisoned without trial and growing evidence emerged of ill-treatment of civilians. The World Bank estimated that $36 billion of reconstruction work was required, but little had begun because of the security situation.

On 26 February 2004 Ayatollah Ali al-Sistani renewed his call for elections to be held before the transfer of power to Iraqis on 30 June. But a United Nations report said this was unfeasible. On 1 March the US-appointed Iraqi Governing Council agreed on an interim constitution. A transitional government to be elected by early 2005 would draft a permanent constitution.

The Return of Sovereignty.

These developments came against the background of growing anti-coalition resistance, with mounting attacks on United States forces. In March 50 American soldiers were killed and in April over 100. However, civilian deaths far outweighed these and there was increasing Iraqi anger at the American occupation as the June deadline for the return of sovereignty to Iraq neared. On 1 June it was announced that the head of the US-appointed Governing Council, Ghazi al-Yawar, was to be president of the interim government until elections were held early in 2005. Iyad Allawi had been named as prime minister a few days earlier. On 28 June the USA formally returned sovereignty to Iraq amid an upsurge of bombings and abductions.

The Escalation of Violence.

The months following the transfer of sovereignty saw an increase rather than diminution of violence. This was hardly surprising, with the United States-led Coalition troops remaining in actual if not formal control. A poll in June showed that 92% of Iraqis viewed the Americans as 'occupiers' and only 2% as 'liberators'. An intelligence report foresaw the possibility of all-out civil war by the end of the year. In August United States Marines launched a three week offensive against Shiite militia in the holy city of Najaf.

There were uprisings in both Shiite and Sunni areas, and an increase in suicide bombings, the kidnapping and beheading of foreigners, and attacks on the already fragile Iraqi security forces. The former dictator Saddam Hussein made his first appearance in court in Baghdad, charged with crimes against Iraq and Kuwait. With much of the country under the control of what were described as 'insurgents', and Iraq's infrastructure still damaged, President Bush asked the United States Senate in September to divert $3.4 billion of the $18.4 billion promised reconstruction aid to increased security.

The Attack on Fallujah.

The United States' attack on Fallujah in November (accompanied by Shiite National Guards) was intended as a decisive blow against insurgency. Although the Americans claimed to have killed over 1,500 insurgents by the end of the month, there were no signs that the interim government's opponents were weakening.

Background to the 2005 Elections.

Violence intensified in the weeks before the 30 January elections. While the majority Shia population, comprising 60%, and the Kurds in the north of the country (17%) were enthusiastic, many Sunnis (the 20% of the population that had dominated Iraq under Saddam Hussein) were either boycotting the ballot or being intimidated into not voting.

The Election Outcome.

The Shia United Iraqi Alliance, backed by the country's leading cleric, Grand Ayatollah al-Sistani, took four million votes (48%) and was allocated 140 National Assembly seats. A Kurdish alliance came second with 2.2 million (26%), taking 75 seats. Supporters of the outgoing prime minister, Mr Allawi, won 1.2 million votes (14%), emerging with 40 seats. Sunni Muslims, who make up a fifth of the

population, largely boycotted the poll. A little over eight million of the 14 million registered voters turned out, signifying remaining doubts about the validity of an election held under foreign occupation and intractable problems in maintaining order.

By mid-March it had still proved impossible to form an administration as manoeuvring for position continued among politicians. The programme following the elections was for the National Assembly to formulate a new constitution by 15 August to be put to a referendum by 15 October. Fresh elections were to be held on 15 December and a government established by the end of 2005.

On 6 April 2005, after lengthy negotiations, the Kurdish leader, Jalal Talabani, was chosen as President of Iraq. His deputies were Ghazi al-Yawar, a Sunni Arab and the Shia finance minister, Adel Abdul Majdi.

Drafting a New Constitution.

There was no abatement in the insurgency following the formation of the government in May, with attacks reaching new heights. The continuing lack of security (and continuing corruption) frustrated reconstruction attempts, with limited progress on rebuilding the country's infrastructure. Oil output and power generation remained at pre-war levels. Following three months of negotiations, and a number of delays, drafting of a new constitution was completed in August. Sharing of oil revenues, the political role of Islam and the position of women remained contentious issues. In a referendum on 15 October 78% of voters (predominantly Shia and Kurds) supported the constitution, while 21% (mainly Sunni) rejected it. Turn-out was 63%. The trial of former president Saddam Hussein opened in October, with United Nations observers declaring the proceedings would not satisfy international standards of justice.

On 21 November Sunni, Shia and Kurdish leaders called for a specific date for the withdrawal of foreign troops. On 30 November President Bush told domestic critics of the occupation that pulling out troops before they had achieved their purpose played no part in United States' plans. However, there were suggestions in December that numbers could be cut from the present 160,000 to below 138,000.

Parliamentary Election Results.

Iraq voted for the first parliament since Saddam Hussein's overthrow on 15 December. The results, announced in January 2006, showed a country starkly divided between the Shia, Sunni and Kurdish regions. The United Iraqi Alliance, a grouping of Shia parties, took 128 of the 275 parliamentary seats, ten short of an overall majority. The Kurdish bloc took 53 seats and the main Sunni groups, the Accordance Front and the National Dialogue Front, 55. A secular nationalist grouping, led by the outgoing prime minister, Iyad Allawi, won 25 seats. On 22 January the United Iraqi Alliance appealed to other parties to work together in a government of national unity. Mr Ibrahim Jaafari was selected as prime minister by the Alliance on 12 February, an unpopular move with their Kurdish coalition partners.

As difficulties continued over forming a government following the December 2005 elections, a bomb attack on a Shia shrine in Samarra in February intensified sectarian violence, leading to growing fears that the country was descending into civil war. A more positive piece of news was the appointment of Jawad al-Maliki as Prime Minister in April.

SYRIA.

1970 Assad seizes power
1971 Assad elected president.
1973 War with Israel.
1974 Agreement signed with Israel.
1975 Assad offers Israel peace treaty in return for withdrawal from occupied territories.
1976 Intervenes in Lebanese civil war.
1980 Muslim Brotherhood assassination attempt on Assad.
1982 Army suppresses Muslim Brotherhood uprising; clashes with Israel in Lebanon.
1990 Joins the US-led coalition against Iraq.
1991 Holds abortive talks with Israel.

2000 Assad dies; succeeded by son Bashar.
2001 Becomes member of UN Security Council.

US Sanctions on Syria.

In May 2004, President Bush imposed economic sanctions on Syria, accusing the government of supporting terrorism and failing to prevent fighters entering Iraq. In October the United Nations called on Syria to withdraw 15,000 troops from Lebanon, the remainder of a force first deployed in 1976. The Syrian government claimed the troops were a stabilising factor and accused the United Nations of intervening in the country's relationship with Lebanon. Israel's prime minister, Ariel Sharon, declared on 2 December that peace talks could not be renewed while President Assad allowed the Palestinian militant groups Hamas and Islamic Jihad to operate in Syria. On 7 December 2004 the Syrian government announced the release of over 100 political prisoners, many thought to be Islamist militants, under presidential amnesty.

The government denied aiding terrorists in Iraq following a warning in January 2005 from the incoming American Secretary of State, Ms Condoleezza Rice, that Syria faced increased sanctions.

Withdrawal from Lebanon.

As tension increased over accusations of Syria's involvement in the assassination of a former Lebanese prime minister in February, the Iranian vice-president pledged support to Syria. However, at the end of the month Syria faced charges of having backed a Palestinian terrorist attack in Israel. In the face of international pressure Syria began a phased withdrawal of troops from Lebanon in March. The last Syrian troops withdrew from the country on 26 April 2005.

Recent Developments.

International suspicion continued over the part Syria might have played in the Lebanese prime minister's assassination. The suicide of the Syrian interior minister in October suggested a closer involvement than the government was prepared to admit. On 31 October the UN Security Council accused Syria of obstructing the investigation into the assassination and threatened economic sanctions. Early reports implicated Syrian intelligence. Meanwhile, Syrian security forces were involved in armed clashes with Islamic activists throughout the year, clearly to placate the United States. In May police cracked down on members of the banned Muslim Brotherhood in the capital Damascus. In September and again in December troops killed alleged Islamic militants. On 1 January 2006 the ruling Ba'ath party expelled former vice president Abdul Halim Khaddam, who had implicated President Assad in the assassination.

On 21 January President Assad said he was considering a programme of political reform, including legalising parties other than the Ba'ath party, encouraging popular participation in politics and giving the judiciary greater independence. His speech followed the early release of five leading political prisoners.

SAUDI ARABIA.

1982 Khalid succeeded by brother Fahd.
1990 Supports Gulf War against Iraqi invasion of Kuwait.
1992 Fahd announces mild democratic reforms.
1993 Consultative Council (Majlis al-Shura) comprising members selected by King inaugurated.
1995 Crown Prince Abdullah effective ruler following Fahd's stroke.
1996 Fahd resumes power; bomb attack on US base.
1997 Consultative Council enlarged.
2000 Amnesty International condemns treatment of women.
2001 Anti-terrorism and crime security pact with Iran signed.
2003 Following the Iraq war, the US announced a withdrawal of its forces from Saudi Arabia.

Increased Terrorist Threat.

The withdrawal of US troops had been an al-Qaeda demand but on 12 May 2003 suicide bombers killed 34 people, including eight Americans, in Riyadh. In July the US Congress alleged Saudi Arabia financed terrorist organisations and continued to harbour sympathisers. The government announced arrests of suspects in May and June. As terrorist incidents continued it was clear that the Saudi royal family itself was under threat, seen by opponents as Western puppets. On 9 November 17 died and many were injured in another suspected al-Qaeda bombing in Riyadh. Under growing pressure, King Fahd issued a decree on 30 November broadening the powers of the consultative council, the 120 member *Shura*.

The Khobar Attack.

A further Islamist militant attack at the end of May in which 22 people died in Khobar raised further questions about the regime's stability, triggering an oil price rise as al-Qaeda supporters appeared to be targeting the world's major exporter.

Continued Islamist Militancy.

Continuing terrorist attacks in 2004 showed the threat the ruling family continued to face from Islamist militancy and the tensions engendered by friendship with the United States. In June an American engineer was murdered by al-Qaeda and attacks culminated in December with the storming of the United States consulate. However, a month-long government amnesty offered to al-Qaeda members secured the surrender of one of the country's most wanted activists. On 16 December the London-based Movement for Islamic Reform in Arabia mounted anti-government demonstrations in Jeddah and Riyadh.

Slow Reform Progress.

The government's slow moves towards political reform continued, building on the establishment in the 1990s of the unelected 120-member national assembly, the Majlis al-Shura, but supporters of liberalisation were disappointed at the seeming popular apathy. Only 37% of eligible voters registered for elections to be held in Riyadh. Voting in other areas was due in March and April. However, voters could only elect half of council members and, despite earlier hopes, women remained excluded from balloting. In January an announcement was made that the Majlis al-Shura would expand to 150 members.

King Fahd and Crown Prince Abdullah, the country's effective ruler, took the opportunity of the hajj pilgrimage to Islam's holy places in Saudi Arabia, to urge Muslims on 20 January to reject terrorism and extremism.

In February 2005 there were elections to half the seats on Riyadh municipal council, the first ever in Saudi Arabia. Women were barred from voting and, in the event, less than a third of eligible voters turned out. Other elections were planned across the country in the course of the year.

The Accession of Abdullah.

On 1 August King Fahd, who had been monarch in name only since suffering a stroke in 1995, died. He was succeeded by his half-brother, Crown Prince Abdullah. The new monarch moved quickly to attempt to improve his country's image, declaring that he was determined to reduce oil prices and renewing his denunciation of Islamic extremism. On 11 November the World Trade Organisation approved the country's application for membership, following 12 years of negotiations. The need to open Saudi Arabia's protected economy to international competition and to cease participation in the Arab League's boycott of Israel led to concern on the part of religious leaders.

The country took what appeared to be a further step towards reform at the end of 2005 by allowing women to vote and run for election to seats in the Chamber of Commerce in Jeddah, the business capital.

SOUTH ASIA

INDIA.

1947 Gains independence from Britain.
1948 War with Pakistan over disputed Kashmir.

1951 Congress Party wins first elections under Jawaharlal Nehru.
1962 Defeated in border war with China.
1965 War with Pakistan over Kashmir.
1966 Indira Gandhi becomes prime minister.
1971 War with Pakistan.
1974 Explodes first nuclear weapon.
1975 Indira Gandhi declares state of emergency following conviction for electoral irregularities.
1977 Congress Party election defeat; Gandhi forms splinter Congress (I).
1980 Congress (I) wins election.
1984 Troops attack Golden Temple to eject Sikh militants; Gandhi assassinated by Sikhs; son Rajiv succeeds.
1987 Sends peacekeeping force to Sri Lanka; withdrawn 1990.
1989 Congress defeated in general election.
1991 Rajiv Gandhi assassinated; prime minister Rao begins economic reform
1992 Hindu-Muslim sectarian violence.
1996 Hindu nationalist Bharatiya Janata Party (BJP) largest single party following elections.
1998 BJP heads coalition government under Atal Behari Vajpayee; nuclear weapons tests.
1999 Clash with Pakistan over Kashmir.
2000 Continued clashes with guerrillas in Kashmir; long range missile test.

The 2004 Election.

In January 2004, an early election was called for April. But the results announced on 13 May saw an unexpected victory for Mrs Sonia Gandhi's United Progressive Alliance, which took 317 out of 543 Lok Sabha seats, the BJP-led coalition trailing with 138. The result was seen as a protest by the rural poor against their exclusion from the country's economic advances. Stung by nationalist criticism from the BJP, Italian-born Mrs Gandhi declined to take office as prime minister on 18 May, leaving the Sikh former finance minister Manmohan Singh as the new prime minister. It remained to be seen whether the new government could formulate a more inclusive programme.

Continuing Diplomatic Dialogue.

In September the foreign minister met his Pakistani counterpart to discuss the Kashmir dispute. Prime minister Manmohan Singh met Pakistan's President Musharraf at the United Nations on 24 September. India made an application, with Brazil, Germany and Japan, for a permanent seat on the Security Council. The Indian government responded to President Musharraf's appeal for a fresh approach to the Kashmir issue by asking on 26 October that proposals should be made through official channels rather than through journalists. However, on 12 November the prime minister ordered a reduction in Indian forces in Kashmir, though he warned that the army remained vigilant.
The prime minister refused to accept President Musharraf's suggestions of a redrawing of borders. However, by the end of the month there were hopes of progress as the prime minister met the Pakistani prime minister. On 3 December officials agreed to reopen a second rail link between the two countries. But there was disappointment over the failure of discussions between foreign ministry officials to reach any conclusion in late December.

The Tsunami Disaster.

Thousands were killed on India's south east coast and on the Andaman and Nicobar Islands by tidal waves triggered by an undersea earthquake off Indonesia on 26 December, with the state of Tamil Nadu being worst affected.
In April 2005 the leaders of India and Pakistan declared that peace was now "irreversible" and a wide-ranging agreement was signed on increasing trade, reopening road and rail links and on increasing a variety of cultural contacts.

Foreign Relations.

Talks between the Indian and Chinese prime ministers in April reached agreement on ending a 40-year border dispute and on trade relations. The keenness of Japan's prime minister, Mr Koizumi, to cement relations with India in April emphasised the country's pivotal position. In July prime minister

Manmohan Singh secured President Bush's agreement to work towards lifting the bar on civilian nuclear co-operation with India, enabling India to expand nuclear power development. The restriction had been in place since India's 1998 nuclear weapons tests.

Recent Developments.

As liberalisation of India's economy (the fourth largest in Asia) proceeded, millions of union members in transport and banking mounted a strike on 29 September against privatisation plans. The government's difficulty was that Communist parties in the ruling coalition also opposed further economic reform. India was the fastest growing major economy after China in 2005.
On 3 October India and Pakistan agreed to reduce tension by informing the other of missile test flights. While there was no progress on the Kashmir dispute, India's offer of $25 million aid following a major earthquake in October symbolised the continuing easing in relations between the two countries. The prime minister took over the foreign ministry following Natwar Singh's resignation for implication in the Iraq oil-for-food scandal. Seven MPs (including one from Congress, three from the opposition BJP) were suspended on 20 December following accusations of bribery. Further suspensions followed. On 29 December former prime minister and BJP founder Mr Vajpayee announced his retirement from politics. Two days later Mr Advani, the BJP president, stepped down, intensifying what appeared to be a developing crisis in the party.

Fighting Rural Poverty.

In February 2006 the government announced an ambitious programme to combat rural poverty, the National Rural Guarantee Scheme, which promised 60 million rural households 100 days work a year at a minimum wage or unemployment benefit. Congress had won office in 2004 on a pledge to improve the conditions of the poor.

SRI LANKA.

1948 Gains independence from Britain.
1956 Bandaranaike becomes prime minister.
1959 Bandaranaike assassinated; succeeded by his widow.
1965 United National Party wins elections.
1970 Mrs Bandaranaike returns to power.
1971 Student-led Marxist revolt.
1972 Changes name to Sri Lanka; Buddhism becomes country's religion.
1976 Liberation Tigers of Tamil Eelam (LTTE) formed in Tamil north and east of country.
1977 Tamil United Liberation Front gains all seats in Tamil area.
1983 Fighting begins between army and LTTE.
1985 First attempt at peace talks between government and LTTE fails.
1987 Government forces push LTTE back into northern city of Jaffna; offers limited local government to Tamils; Indian peacekeeping force deployed.
1988 Sinhalese JVP campaign against Indian involvement.
1990 Indian troops withdraw; escalating violence between army and separatists.
1991 LTTE implicated in assassination of Indian premier Gandhi.
1993 President Premadasa assassinated by LTTE.
1994 President Kumaratunga opens peace talks with LTTE.
1995 Peace talks collapse; major government offensive.
1996 State of emergency after LTTE bomb attacks in capital.
1997 Government offensive against LTTE.
1998 LTTE military successes.
1999 President Kumaratunga re-elected.
2000 President Kumaratunga's People's Alliance wins general elections; Norway offers mediation; government rejects LTTE ceasefire offer.
2002 Ceasefire agreed as preliminary to peace talks.

The Tsunami Catastrophe.

Thousands were killed in the regional disaster triggered by an undersea earthquake off Indonesia on 26 December, with the devastation of Sri Lanka's eastern coast. By early January 2005 there were bitter arguments over the extent of government assistance to Tamils in the former conflict areas, together with complaints about the deployment of troops in Tamil refugee camps. The United States Secretary of State said in a visit he hoped the crisis would help resolve the long-running conflict but, instead, tensions appeared to be heightening. On 19 January President Kumaratunga appealed for national unity as she announced a £1.8 billion reconstruction programme.

The 2005 Presidential Election.

The year 2005 saw a steady move towards a re-opening of conflict, despite the three year old ceasefire. On 12 August the foreign minister was killed by snipers. The Tamil Tigers denied responsibility and a week later the government and Tamil representatives agreed to re-open negotiations that had faltered in 2003. But presidential elections on 17 November threatened to undermine what little progress had been made. Prime minister Mahinda Rajapakse narrowly defeated opposition leader Ranil Wickramasinghe, taking 50·29 % of the votes to his 48·38 %. Mr Rajapakse had called in his campaign for firmness in negotiations and an 'honourable peace'.

Return to Violence?

On 21 November President Rajapakse appointed Ratnasiri Wickremanayake as prime minister. President Rajapakse offered to resume talks a week later but rejected Tamil demands for an independent state. Tamil leader Velupillai Prabhakaran threatened to renew the struggle if no settlement had been reached within a year. On 4 December the government blamed the Tamil Tigers for attacks in which nine soldiers died. President Rajapakse asked Norway to continue mediation efforts on 7 December. However, the head of the mediation mission warned that war appeared imminent. By mid-January 2006 over a hundred people had died in violence in the north east of the country but on 6 February the government and the Tamil Tigers announced they were meeting for talks at the end of the month.

PAKISTAN.

1947 Established as a Muslim state on the independence of India from Britain.
1948 First war with India over disputed Kashmir.
1956 Proclaimed an Islamic republic
1958 General Ayub Khan seizes power and proclaims martial law.
1960 Khan becomes president.
1965 War with India over Kashmir.
1969 Khan is succeeded by General Yahya Khan.
1971 War with India; East Pakistan secedes to establish Bangladesh.
1972 Zulfiqar Ali Bhutto becomes prime minister.
1977 Military coup by General Zia ul'Haq.
1985 Martial law lifted and political activity legalised.
1988 Zia killed in air crash; Benazir Bhutto's Pakistan People's Party wins elections.
1989 Bhutto dismissed for corruption; Nawaz Sharif succeeds.
1991 Islamic Sharia law incorporated into legal code.
1993 Sharif resigns as prime minister; Bhutto succeeds.
1996 Bhutto government dismissed for alleged corruption.
1997 Sharif's Pakistan Muslim League wins elections.
1998 Nuclear weapons tests.
1999 Clash with India over Kashmir; General Musharraf seizes power.
2000 Musharraf promises gradual restoration of democracy.

The 2002 Referendum.

In January 2002 General Musharraf promised to end three years of military rule with elections to be held in October. But in April he secured another five years in office by a referendum in which he was the only candidate. On 22 August he amended the constitution to ensure he could remain as president

and military commander-in-chief for another five years. No party won a clear majority in elections held on 10 October, but Islamic parties took power in two provinces bordering Afghanistan and there were marked nationwide successes for anti-American parties opposing the 'war on terrorism'. On 21 November, after six weeks of negotiations, the new parliament elected Zafarullah Khan Jamali, a Musharraf supporter, as prime minister. Mr Jamali's Pakistan Muslim League formed a fragile coalition with dissident members of former prime minister Benazir Bhutto's Pakistan People's Party and independents. In February 2003, in what President Musharraf called the final stage in the transition to democracy, the Pakistan Muslim League won most seats in elections to the Senate.

Developments in 2003.

In March 2003 security forces arrested what they claimed to be a close aide to al-Qaeda leader Osama bin Laden. At the end of April a further six members were arrested in Karachi. The difficulty of President Musharraf's role was shown by large demonstrations against the United States attack on Iraq. But in June President Bush offered President Musharraf $3 billion aid provided Pakistan continued its support in the war against terrorism and gave no help to North Korea in its nuclear weapons programme.

Peace Initiatives with India.

There were renewed tensions over Kashmir in March following the death of 24 Hindus, allegedly by Pakistan-backed Islamic militants. In May the government said Pakistan was ready to abandon its nuclear weaponry if India followed suit. Moves towards a settlement attempt were gathering pace and on 24 November India accepted a ceasefire offer made by Pakistan's prime minister Mr Jamali. On 2 December President Musharraf said he was prepared to withdraw troops from Pakistan-administered Kashmir if India did the same in her area. The cross-border rail service reopened on 20 December and on 5 January 2004 Mr Vajpayee and President Musharraf met for the first time in two years.

Internal Terrorism.

However, Pakistan had continued to experience internal terrorism. On 4 July 48 Shi'ites were killed in a suicide bomb attack on a mosque and in October riots followed the killing by gunmen of six Shi'ites in Karachi. President Musharraf himself narrowly escaped two assassination attempts in December, both allegedly the work of al-Qaeda. As part of his pledge that the country would return to civilian rule, President Musharraf said that he would resign from the military in 2004. In January he was confirmed as president until 2007 On 22 May the Commonwealth agreed to re-admit Pakistan, five years after membership had been suspended following the Musharraf coup. The move probably owed as much to the country's part in the 'war on terrorism' as it did to promises to restore civilian rule. On 26 June Chaudhry Shujaat Hussain became Prime Minister, replacing Zafarullah Khan Jamali. However, Chaudhry Shujaat Hussain himself resigned as prime minister on 25 August, to be replaced by former finance minister Shaukat Aziz.

The Campaign against Terror.

The campaign against terrorism continued, with the capture on 29 July of a Tanzanian believed to have been involved in the 1998 bombings of United States embassies in Africa. At the end of September security forces killed what they claimed was a high level al-Qaeda member who had been involved in two assassination attempts on President Musharraf. In a meeting with President Bush in December, President Musharraf stressed that resolving the Palestinian question was essential in the global fight against terrorism.

New Kashmir Initiatives.

On 25 October President Musharraf proposed radical moves to end the dispute with India over

Kashmir, including autonomy or division of the region. The opposition criticised his suggestion. The government expressed disappointment with India's response that a redrawing of borders was unacceptable. There were, however, discussions between the prime minister and his Indian counterpart, and on 3 December agreement was reached in principle to re-open a second rail link between the two countries.

Doubts over Musharraf.

Despite President Musharraf's earlier promise to step down as army commander, legislation passed on 1 November allowed him to retain his political and military positions. The opposition said this brought into question President Musharraf's commitment to a restoration of civilian rule. On 19 December there were protest demonstrations in Rawalpindi.

In mid-January 2005 there were renewed tensions over Kashmir following an exchange of fire. Pakistan denied responsibility. Mr Aziz, the prime minister, said at the end of the month he was planning to propose measures that would ease tensions with India. In April 2005 a wide-ranging agreement with India was signed.

Détente with Israel.

There was an unprecedented meeting on 1 September between the foreign ministers of Israel and Pakistan. The latter emphasised that this did not mean recognition of Israel was imminent but was a sign of the importance Pakistan attached to the withdrawal from Gaza. Although there was little sign of progress with India on the long-running Kashmir dispute, the two countries signed a security co-operation agreement on 3 October under which each would inform the other of missile test flights.

Recent Events.

While there was no progress over Kashmir, India's offer of $25 million aid following the 8 October earthquake symbolised the continuing easing in relations between the two countries. Over 80,000 people were killed and three million made homeless by the earthquake in the Kashmir region. On 4 November President Musharraf announced the postponement of a $25 million purchase of fighter aircraft from the United States to focus on reconstruction.

Events in January 2006 symbolised the difficulties Pakistan faced in the war on terror after 18 people died in an attack by United States aircraft on a village near the Afghan border aimed at al-Qaeda's deputy leader. Thousands of Pakistani citizens mounted anti-American protests while the prime minister, Shaukat Aziz, called the deaths unacceptable.

BANGLADESH.

1947 Gains independence from Britain; split into East and West.
1949 Awami League founded to campaign for East Pakistan autonomy.
1970 Awami League wins election victory in East Pakistan; government in West Pakistan refuses to accept result.
1971 East Pakistan declares independence as Bangladesh under Sheikh Mujibur Rahman; Pakistan troops defeated with Indian backing.
1974 State of emergency declared as unrest grows.
1975 Sheikh Mujib becomes president; assassinated in military coup; martial law imposed.
1977 General Zia Rahman becomes president; Islamic constitution adopted.
1979 Zia's Bangladesh National Party (BNP) wins elections.
1981 Zia assassinated in abortive military coup; Abdus Sattar succeeds.
1982 General Ershad leads military coup; constitution suspended.
1983 Ershad becomes president.
1986 Parliamentary and presidential elections; Ershad ends martial law.
1987 State of emergency following opposition demonstrations.

1988 Islam becomes state religion.
1990 Ershad resigns.
1991 Begum Khaleda Zia becomes prime minister.
1996 Awami League election victory; Sheikh Hasina Wajed becomes prime minister.
1997 Opposition BNP opens strike campaign against government.
2000 Tension with Pakistan over attitudes to 1971 independence war.
2001 Border clashes with India; Hasina hands power to caretaker authority.

Recent Developments.

In February 2004 Bangladesh held back from entering a free trade zone with India, Burma, Sri Lanka and Thailand for fear that lower tariffs would endanger manufacturing industries. The zone was due to come into operation in 2017 and Bangladesh promised to sign up by that date. Meanwhile, opposition agitation against the government continued with a further series of general strikes from February to April. In May a constitutional amendment reserved 45 parliamentary seats for women, to be selected by each party rather than directly elected. In continuing political violence, 20 were killed and hundreds injured in the bombing of an opposition Awami League rally in August. Party leader Sheikh Hasina blamed prime minister Khaleda Zia's government for the attack, which led to further disturbances. Having been named as the most corrupt country for four years in a row, the government launched a three-member Anti-Corruption Commission in November.

Bombings and Suicide Attacks.

In January 2005 two people were killed in a grenade attack at a rally of the opposition Awami League. In a protest general strike that followed, a police officer was killed and others injured. Nevertheless, in April the International Monetary Fund forecast economic growth of over 5%. On 17 August there were over 100 bomb explosions in 50 urban centres across the country, killing two people and wounding over 100. There were further bombings of courts in October. The government accused an outlawed Islamic group, Jamaat-ul-Mujahideen, which called for the establishment of Islamic law in Bangladesh. At the end of November a number of people were killed in what appeared to be suicide bombings in Chittagong and Gazipur. On 9 December there were country-wide demonstrations by Muslims against Islamic terrorism.

NEPAL.

1923 Britain formally recognises Nepal's independence.
1959 Multi-party constitution adopted.
1960 King Mahendra suspends parliament and political activity; monarch exercises sole power through non-party councils.
1972 King Mahendra dies, succeeded by Birendra.
1980 Non-party elections to national assembly allowed.
1985 Nepali Congress Party (NCP) begins civil disobedience campaign.
1986 New elections boycotted by NCP.
1990 King Birendra agrees to democratic constitution following agitation.
1991 NCP wins elections; Girija Prasad Koirala becomes prime minister.
1994 Koirala's government loses no-confidence motion; Communists win elections.
1995 Government dissolved; Maoist insurrection begins in rural areas.
1997 Period of political instability, with continual government changes.
1999 Koirala returns to office.
2001 Palace massacre of King Bihendra and family. Growing Maoist insurgency across Nepal.
2002 National strike and growing insurgency.

The government and Maoist rebels declared a ceasefire in January 2003 but political difficulties continued. In June the prime minister, Lokendra Bahadur Chand, was forced to resign under opposition pressure, to be replaced by Surya Bahadur Thapa. The rebels ended the ceasefire in August following the collapse of negotiations on the establishment of a constitutional assembly. The opposition demonstrated its strength in September when the country was brought to a halt in a three day general strike. On 15 November rebels killed a general in an ambush. There were protests in the capital on 30 January 2004 over King Gyanendra's refusal to relinquish the executive powers he had taken in 2002.

Blockade of Kathmandu.

In May the prime minister, Surya Bahadur Thapa, resigned after prolonged opposition demonstrations. King Gyanendra reappointed Sher Bahadur Deuba in his place. Maoist rebels mounted a siege of the capital Kathmandu in August, with the apparent hope of encouraging a rising. The blockade faltered after a week. The murder of 12 Nepalese hostages in Iraq provoked further violent protests and at the end of September 15,000 people demonstrated in Kathmandu demanding the restoration of parliament. Meanwhile, fighting continued between Maoist rebels and government forces, bringing the death toll since 1996 to over 9,000.

Human Rights Abuses.

In November the United States warned the government that future military aid depended on an improvement in the country's human rights record. On 9 December there were renewed protests in the capital as a royal advisory council held its first meeting. Demonstrators accused the king of attempting to institute an absolute monarchy. In December Maoists killed 20 government troops as a European Union delegation arrived urging peace talks. But on 27 December thousands demonstrated in the capital demanding peace talks.

The 2005 Royalist Coup.

On 31 January 2005 King Gyanendra mounted a coup, dismissing the government, placing the cabinet under house arrest, and declaring a state of emergency. The King's appointment of a hand-picked cabinet aroused international criticism.

Recent Events.

In April the Indian foreign minister urged King Gyanendra to restore democracy in Nepal. The country's largest political party, the centrist Nepali Congress, announced on 1 September that it favoured a republic. A European Union delegation said on 6 October that Nepal faced political collapse and urged a return to multi-party democracy. King Gyanendra announced shortly after that municipal elections would be held in February 2006 and parliamentary elections in April. In late November, following secret discussions in India, the country's main political leaders and Maoist insurgents agreed to press for a constituent assembly. Maoist forces declared a ceasefire as demonstrators rallied against the king in the capital, Kathmandu.

However, on 2 January 2006 the truce ended with bomb attacks in three towns and violent demonstrations against the government. With the main parties boycotting and the Maoists enforcing a general strike, even the government claimed a turn-out in the 8 February elections of only 20 %. Major aid donors questioned their legitimacy.

AFGHANISTAN.

Chronology of Key Events.

1919 Gains independence after third war against Britain.
1933 Zahir Shah becomes king.
1953 Prime minister Mohammed Daud heads reforming government until ousted in 1963.
1964 Power struggles follow introduction of constitutional monarchy.
1973 Republic declared following coup by Daud.
1978 Daud overthrown by left-wing People's Democratic Party; Islamic conservative revolt.
1979 Hafizullah Amin wins left power struggle in capital Kabul but is executed following Soviet invasion.
1980 Soviet Union installs Babrak Karmal as ruler; resistance from mujahedin groups backed by US, Pakistan, Saudi Arabia and Iran intensifies.

1985 Pakistan-based mujahedin forces unite.
1986 Najibullah replaces Karmal as head of government.
1989 Soviet Union withdraws; civil war intensified.
1992 Najibullah falls; rival militias compete for power.
1993 Mujahedin groups unite around President Burhanuddin Rabbani.
1996 Islamic fundamentalist Taliban forces capture Kabul; recognised as government by Pakistan and Saudi Arabia; Rabbani flees to join Northern Alliance.
1998 US bombs alleged bases of terrorist Osama bin Laden.
1999 UN embargo and sanctions imposed to secure trial of Osama bin Laden.

The Taliban Regime.

Western antagonism towards the Taliban regime intensified through 2000 and in January 2001 the United Nations imposed further sanctions to force them to hand over Osama bin Laden. There was, however, no lessening in Taliban intransigence. In March the government destroyed historic Buddhist statues in the face of international criticism. In May religious minorities were ordered to wear tags identifying them as non-Muslims. In September eight foreign aid workers were accused of promoting Christianity following months of tension between the Taliban and aid agencies.

The Invasion of Afghanistan.

The 11 September terrorist attack on the United States and the alleged links of the Taliban with those thought responsible, provided the opportunity to remove the government as a central part of the 'war against terrorism'. Following the onset of a prolonged bombing campaign by the United States and Britain, opposition forces seized Afghanistan's main cities in November. As Afghan groups met in Germany to agree on the form of an interim government, the final Taliban stronghold of Kandahar fell on 7 December, although the Taliban leader, Mullah Omar, was able to flee. On 22 December Pashtun royalist Hamid Karzai was sworn in as head of a 30-member interim government, with power shared between what were feared would revert to being competing factions.

In January 2002 the deployment of an 18-nation British-led International Security Assistance Force for Afghanistan was announced to underpin the interim government's authority. But limited to 5,000 troops and restricted to Kabul, there were questions about how effective the force would prove.

Although the former monarch, Zahir Shah, returned to Afghanistan on 8 April, the political situation remained dangerous and unstable.

Renewed Fighting.

Fighting continued throughout 2002 and 2003 and, despite a United States declaration on 1 May 2003, that there had been a transition from combat to reconstruction, President Karzai appeared to have little authority outside Kabul.

In November the government had submitted a draft constitution and on 14 December 500 delegates assembled to begin discussions intended to lead to its approval. Elections to a national assembly were planned for June 2004 to enable, commentators said, US President Bush to claim success before he faced the presidential election in November. The new constitution agreed on by the rival factions on 4 January 2004 provided for a strong presidency able to cement national unity in the continuing campaign against the Taliban and al-Qaeda forces.

Continued American Support.

President Karzai visited the United States in June and was given assurances of support by President Bush. At the end of the month, North Atlantic Treaty Organisation leaders agreed to expand their troops in the country from 6,500 to 10,000. However, on 9 July the electoral commission postponed parliamentary elections until April 2005.

The 2004 Presidential Elections.

As the October presidential election approached, there was little sign of a reduction in violence. At the end of July a major aid agency withdrew from the country, citing the government's failure to take action over the murder of five of its workers. In mid-August 21 people were killed in factional fighting in Herat province (the governor was dismissed in September). At the end of August seven died in an attack on an American security company. In September President Karzai survived a rocket attack on his helicopter, the most serious threat to his life since September 2002.

On 3 November Mr Karzai was declared the country's first directly elected president, with 55 % of the vote. At his inauguration on 7 December he warned that the Taliban remained a threat. Two deputies, representing the country's largest ethnic minorities, were also sworn in.

On 24 December a new cabinet was appointed, with some of the warlords prominent in the interim government being replaced by technocrats and reformers.

Continuing Military Problems.

In May 2005 President Bush declared that United States troops engaged in the anti-terrorist 'Operation Enduring Freedom' would remain under American command, despite President Karzai's request for more authority over their actions. In a reflection of growing concern over the continuing troop presence, China, Russia and a number of central Asian states asked the United States and coalition partners in July to set a withdrawal date.

The 2005 Parliamentary Elections.

Parliamentary elections postponed from 2004 were finally held on 18 September. In the six-month build-up over a thousand people were killed in the worst violence since 2001. Turn-out was low and allegations of widespread irregularities in the poll delayed release of the results until the end of the year. The majority of candidates stood as independents but President Karzai's supporters won over 50 % of seats. A third of members of the lower house are women. Meanwhile, on 12 December NATO announced expanded troop deployment, partly to combat the growing opium trade, while United States forces concentrated on the anti-terrorist action. International donors promised $2 billion further aid on 31 January 2006. British troops began their deployment in Helmand province in February.

THE FAR EAST

CHINA.

Chronology of Key Events.

1949 Chinese People's Republic proclaimed with Mao Zedong as Chairman of the Republic.
1950 Chinese troops intervene in Korean War against United Nations forces.
1951 China occupies Tibet.
1953 Main industries nationalised under first Five Year Plan.
1956 Mao's 'let a hundred flowers bloom' campaign raises disappointed hopes of intellectual freedom.
1958 Second Five Year Plan introduces 'Great Leap Forward' to industrialise China and build agricultural communes; widespread famine follows.
1960 China accuses Soviet Union of ideological 'revisionism'.
1962 War with India over border dispute.
1964 China explodes atomic bomb.
1966 Mao opens Cultural Revolution, encouraging Red Guards to attack his political opponents.
1969 Border clashes with Soviet Union.
1971 China joins the United Nations, replacing Taiwan (Nationalist China) as a permanent member of the Security Council.
1976 Mao dies; new Chairman and prime minister Hua Guofeng moves against Mao's widow, Jiang Qing, and her 'Gang of Four' allies.
1977 Economic pragmatism introduced; Jiang Qing expelled from party and imprisoned.
1978 China opens diplomatic relations with United States.

1979 China invades Vietnam; demonstrators in Beijing call for greater political freedom.
1983 Economic reformer Deng Xiaoping increases influence.
1984 Economic modernisation continues with weakening of collectivism in agriculture and industry.
1987 Zhao Zinyang replaces Hu Yaobang as prime minister in apparent backlash against reform.
1989 Increasing demands by students and workers for democracy culminate in Tiananmen Square massacre in Beijing; Zhao Zinyang replaced by Jiang Zemin in a party purge.
1990 Finance minister reports soaring unemployment and falling foreign investment.
1993 New constitution declares the establishment of a 'social market economy'; peasant riots over rising prices
1995 Five Year Plan calls for doubling gross national product by 2000.
1997 Deng Xiaoping dies. Hong Kong returned by Britain; increasing protests against unemployment and corruption; Party Congress sets programme for rapid privatisation of remaining state industries; US President Clinton criticises China's human rights record.
1998 China intensifies privatisation of state enterprises and the campaign against corruption; chief economic planner Zhu Rongji becomes prime minister; China and Europe hold first economic summit meeting; Taiwan rejects an offer of reunification with autonomy.
1999 Government slows economic reform in the face of soaring unemployment; there are mass arrests of dissidents in the run-up to the Republic's 50th anniversary; China agrees to join the World Trade Organisation; President Jiang declares China will complete the transition to a 'socialist market system' within a decade.

The Advent of Hu Jintao.

The 2002 congress ended with dramatic constitutional changes, the party being redefined as the 'vanguard of the working class and simultaneously the vanguard of the Chinese people', and the appointment of new leadership. Of the 356 central committee members, half had not served before. Six of the seven ruling politburo members, including President Jiang, retired. On 15 November vice president Hu Jintao, a former engineer, was announced as President Jiang's successor at the head of the party, with the certainty of succeeding him as President in March 2003. President Jiang retained his post of head of the military commission, an influential position overseeing the armed forces. By March 2003 (with Wen Jiabao chosen as Prime Minister) and Hu Jintao as President, China had new leadership at the helm. Almost immediately, the new leadership faced the SARS health crisis with all its implications for China.

The SARS Crisis.

In April the government admitted mishandling of the SARS outbreak, dismissing the health minister and the mayor of Beijing for attempting to cover up the seriousness of the situation. The World Health Organisation raised a warning against travel to Beijing in June and Hong Kong was declared free of the virus.

In June China and India reached agreement on the status of Sikkim and Tibet as part of a cross-border trade agreement. However, in Hong Kong 500,000 people demonstrated in protest against proposed anti-subversion legislation threatening heavy sentences for sedition and calls for secession. As demonstrations continued, two key officials resigned and in September the government announced that the legislation was being abandoned.

The Taiwan Question.

China took a further step forward as a major world power when in October it became only the third country to launch a person into space. On 19 October President Hu Jintao told US President Bush that China was willing to allow the market to set the value of its currency but ruled out any rapid moves that threatened stability. In November a prime minister warned Taiwan's President Chen Shui-bian that he was risking war if he attempted to declare the offshore island independent. President Bush issued an equally strong warning to Taiwan on 8 December. The matter appeared to be gaining momentum as an issue for elections to be held in Taiwan in 2004.

On 14 March the National People's Congress overwhelmingly agreed constitutional changes to protect private property for the first time since the 1949 revolution, signifying the final abandonment of the Communist project. Meanwhile, on 20 March Chen Shui-bian was narrowly re-elected president of Taiwan, which China continued to claim as part of its territory. The opposition, which claimed that an assassination attempt on the eve of the election had been contrived, rejected the result.

Hong Kong Local Elections.

On 26 April the government thwarted the hopes of the supporters of democracy in Hong Kong by ruling out universal suffrage in elections for the chief executive in 2007 and the legislature in 2008. Britain and the United States criticised China for breaking earlier pledges of autonomy for the region. There were mass demonstrations in favour of greater democracy in July but in local elections on 12 September pro-democracy candidates made only modest gains, taking 24 seats on the 60-seat legislative council.

In Taiwan, President Chen Shui-bian urged the United States to play a more active role in encouraging dialogue with China. The United States responded on 21 April by stressing a determination to defend the island from attack while warning Taiwan against declaring independence from the mainland. However, on 27 October President Chen Shui-bian claimed that Taiwan was a sovereign independent state. However, his party's defeat in parliamentary elections in December undermined his ambitions and he resigned as Democratic Progressive Party chairman on 14 December 2004.

The 2004 Leadership Changes.

At the Communist Party Central Committee's meeting on 19 September former president Jiang Zemin stood down as military chief, completing the full transfer of power to President Hu Jintao three years ahead of schedule. In a two week tour of Latin America in November, President Hu said China intended to invest £55 billion in the region over the coming decade, with £268 million going to Cuba. Meanwhile, relations with Japan remained strained, with the incursion into Japanese waters of a Chinese submarine in November.

Death of Zhao Ziyang.

The death on 17 January 2005 of former party leader Zhao Ziyang brought a reminder of the 1989 Tiananmen Square pro-democracy demonstrations. He had been held under house arrest after appearing sympathetic to the protestors in 1989. Security was tightened for fear that his death would provoke renewed demonstrations.

Relations with Japan.

Violent anti-Japanese protests in April showed a continuing strain in relations between the region's major powers. Commentators suggested that China's leaders were encouraging the demonstrations as a political safety valve. The protests, ostensibly against Japan's publication of school textbooks underplaying wartime atrocities in China, also symbolised a growing Chinese national assertiveness. A dispute over rights of access to gas and oil reserves in the East China Sea, and Japan's claims to a seat on the United Nations Security Council, exacerbated tensions. Talks between the Japanese foreign minister and his Chinese counterpart in Beijing on 17 April achieved nothing.

Developments in Foreign Affairs.

Despite continuing problems with Japan, China continued to consolidate wider relations. In April prime minister Wen Jiabao reached agreement on a long-running border dispute and increased trade co-operation with Indian prime minister Manmohan Singh. China went on to open free trade negotiations with Australia. In June President Hu Jintao visited President Putin in Russia and the two states mounted joint military exercises in August, partly

to warn the United States off too close an involvement in Central Asia. However, in July China joined the United States, Australia, India, Japan and South Korea in establishing an Asia-Pacific Partnership on Clean Development and Climate.

The Problem of Corruption.

A meeting of the ruling Communist Party Central Committee in October concentrated on addressing corruption and the growing gap between rich and poor, which had led to serious protests. The meeting announced a five-year plan to double the 2000 gross domestic product by 2010 but to do so in the context of improved social security. Any hopes there were of political reform were dashed by a government announcement on 20 October that the Communist Party would retain power under a 'democratic dictatorship' and postpone the introduction of elections.

The Public Order Problem.

There was similar disappointment in Hong Kong where the authorities unveiled government reforms in October that provoked a series of demonstrations demanding full democracy and a rejection of the proposals by the legislature. Meanwhile, there was renewed tension in relations between China and Taiwan, which China continued to claim. In March the National People's Congress approved a measure allowing 'non-peaceful means' to be used to prevent independence. President Chen Shui-bian of Taiwan's call for a referendum to establish a new constitution for the island in 2007 was condemned as provocative. On 1 January 2006 the Taiwan government said it was under growing military and economic pressure from China.

With growing social unrest representing the most significant threat to Communist Party rule, the government admitted in January 2006 that there had been a 6% growth in public order incidents arising from anger at corruption, economic inequality and land disputes.

JAPAN.

1945 Surrenders to Allies following atom bomb attacks.
1947 New constitution introduced.
1952 US military government ends.
1955 Liberal Democratic Party (LDP) begins over 30 years as ruling party.
1956 Joins UN.
1972 Opens diplomatic relations with China.
1989 Emperor Hirohito dies; Akihito succeeds.
1993 LDP loses power amidst bribery allegations and economic failure.
1994 Coalition government falls; LDP/Socialist led administration formed.
1996 Tension with United States over military bases in Okinawa; LDP forms minority government.
1997 Economic recession intensifies.
1998 LDP's Keicho Obuchi becomes prime minister.
2000 Yoshiro Mori succeeds Obuchi as prime minister; LDP-led coalition elected; Diet calls for review of pacifist constitution.
2001 Junichiro Koizumi succeeds Mori.

The Continuation of Scandal.

The year 2002 saw a continuation of the scandals that had debilitated Japanese politics. In March a Social Democratic Party Diet member resigned over alleged misuse of his state-paid secretary's salary. He was followed in April by former Liberal Democratic Party (LDP) secretary general Koichi Kato, who resigned following alleged tax evasion by one of his aides. In June a former LDP member was charged with bribery and perjury. Former foreign minister Makiko Tanaka resigned in August. Former House of Councillors president Yutaka Inoue resigned after allegations that one of his staff had accepted bribes. Mr Koizumi dismissed Financial Services Agency head Hakuo Yanagisawa in September following policy differences.

Mr Koizumi made a historic visit to North Korea on 17 September in an effort to restore relations. North Korea was seeking compensation for Japan's long occupation of Korea in the 20th century. During the visit North Korean leader Kim Jong Il admitted the abduction of 13 Japanese citizens in

1978, some of whom had died. Five were released on 15 October and the two leaders signed the Pyongyang Declaration.

The Long Economic Crisis.

Japan's decade-long economic crisis continued and Mr Koizumi's promises of structural reform remained unfulfilled. In October financial services minister Heizo Takenaka announced a new anti-deflation package, including nationalisation of faltering banks. But in November 2002 the stock market reached a new low. As company failures mounted, unemployment at 5.5% equalled the post-war record first reached in December 2001. Mr Koizumi's party rivals called for more government investment in public works projects. With the stock market at its lowest for 20 years Mr Koizumi said on 2 January 2003 that he was determined to revive the country's economy by accelerating the disposal of bad bank loans and overcoming deflation. He was echoed by the economics minister who declared reforms would gradually bear fruit in 2003 but that the economy depended on international developments, particularly in the United States.

Regional Problems.

As the regional crisis over North Korea's nuclear programme developed in early 2003, the prime minister, Mr Koizumi, met President Bush in May and agreed that a peaceful solution remained possible. He reached similar agreement with the South Korean president in June. The Iraq crisis had repercussions in July when the Diet passed legislation allowing the use of troops on reconstruction work in the country, the first such deployment outside Japan since World War Two. The plan aroused strong public opposition.

Domestic Events in 2003.

However, the economy and the government's reforms dominated events. On 20 September Mr Koizumi was confirmed as Liberal Democratic Party (LDP) leader with 60% support. Two days later he announced a sweeping cabinet reshuffle, appointing the reformist Sadakazu Tanigaki as finance minister.

On 10 October Mr Koizumi called an election for the 480 seat lower house. Although the governing coalition retained power on 9 November the result was no triumph for Mr Koizumi, whose LDP were returned with 237 (down from 247), the coalition emerging with a 244 seat overall majority. The opposition Democratic Party of Japan increased its seats from 137 to 177.

Overseas Troop Deployments.

The first of a projected one thousand non-combat troops were deployed in Iraq in February. In March 2004 three Japanese civilians were taken hostage by Islamist militants in Iraq. The refusal of the prime minister, Mr Koizumi, to accede to a demand to withdraw troops won popular support. The hostages were released unharmed. Mr Koizumi's Liberal Democratic Party (LDP) went on to win three Diet lower house by-elections, giving the governing coalition 279 out of the 480 seats. However, by July Mr Koizumi's position had weakened as his party suffered defeats in elections to the upper house, with the Democratic Party of Japan consolidating its position as a rival to the LDP.

Foreign Policy.

As the economy continued to stagnate, the government turned its attention to international affairs, launching an application in September for a permanent seat on the United Nations Security Council. Moves towards a reform of the country's pacifist constitution continued, under a combination of pressure from the United States and domestic fears of China and North Korea. In November Mr Koizumi met China's President Hu Jintao for the first time in over a year, in a bid to improve strained relations. On 10 December the government issued a revised defence policy setting out wider involvement in international peace-keeping. Relations with North Korea remained tense. In May Mr Koizumi had promised 250,000 tons of food aid in exchange for the return of five kidnapped citizens. But on 13 December 2004 assistance was frozen as

North Korea refused to co-operate with the investigation of the kidnappings.

The 2005 Elections.

Faced with opposition to his plans to privatise the post office from within his own Liberal Democratic Party (LDP), prime minister Junichiro Koizumi called a snap election for 11 September 2005 and went on to win a landslide victory. The LDP took 296 of the 480 lower house seats, up from 249 seats. The opposition Democratic Party of Japan (DJP) representation fell from 177 to 113 seats. The LDP's coalition partner, New Komeito, took 31 seats. Mr Koizumi had pledged to press on with wider privatisation proposals. A bill to take the post office out of public ownership was passed on 14 October. In a cabinet reshuffle Mr Koizumi appointed Shinzo Abe, the LDP deputy secretary general, as chief government spokesman, Heizo Takenaka as internal affairs minister and Taro Aso as foreign affairs minister. Sadakazu Tanigaki retained the finance ministry.

There was a renewal of tension with China and South Korea following a visit to a controversial war shrine in Tokyo by Mr Koizumi on 17 October. The following day China cancelled a planned visit by Japan's foreign minister, with South Korea following suit. In December China postponed an annual summit held with Japan and South Korea. On 7 December the government extended deployment of 500 troops in Iraq for a further year.

As 2006 opened political attention turned to the possible successor to Mr Koizumi.

KOREA.

1945 Korea is divided by the United States and the Soviet Union into southern and northern zones after being controlled by Japan for 40 years.

1950 North Korean attack on South Korea leads to United Nations military intervention.

1953 The Korean War ends in a stalemate; tense relations between north and south continue for two decades.

1972 Inconclusive discussions open between South and North Korea.

1991 North and South Korea agree on mutual recognition.

1994 Diplomatic progress is stalled on the death of North Korean dictator Kim Il Sung.

1995 Kim Jong Il succeeds his father as North Korean dictator; the country is devastated by famine.

1998 Newly elected South Korean president Kim Dae-jung launches a 'sunshine diplomacy' campaign to promote harmony between the two states; tension rises as North Korea begins missile tests over Japan.

1999 North Korea proposes discussions on unification; the United States lifts trade sanctions but expresses concern at missile development.

2000 Historic meeting of leaders of South Korea and North Korea.

In December 2003 the North Korean government had expressed willingness to participate in a new round of multi-national talks on its nuclear programme. Discussions held in Beijing in February 2004 involving North and South Korea, the United States, China, Japan and Russia were fruitless. At a further round in late June North Korea rejected an offer from the United States to provide energy aid and a security guarantee in return for an end to the nuclear programme. North Korea threatened to test a nuclear weapon. On 11 November the North Korean government refused to resume multi-national talks on nuclear weapons. US President Bush warned on 21 November that North Korea should end their weapons programme but President Roh of South Korea urged on 3 December that persuasion would achieve more than threats.

Relations with Japan remained tense as a dispute continued over the kidnapping by North Korea of Japanese citizens. In mid-January 2005 the North Korean government expressed a willingness to resume talks on the nuclear issue. However, on 19 January 2005 Ms Rice, the incoming United States'

Secretary of State, declared that North Korea was one of the 'outposts of tyranny' that required assistance in gaining freedom.

Diplomatic Moves.

Following North Korea's announcement in May 2005 that it had enough fuel to manufacture three nuclear weapons, negotiations resumed in Beijing in July with the ultimate aim of making the Korean peninsula a non-nuclear zone. In September North Korea promised to abandon its nuclear programme and to rejoin the Non-Proliferation Treaty at an unspecified time. However, in December talks stalled following clashes between United States and North Korean representatives in which North Korea was described as a 'criminal regime'.

Recent Developments.

Meanwhile, South Korea and the United States agreed in October 2005 to negotiate the resumption of the south's control over its armed forces in wartime, peacetime control having been handed over in 1994. In November North and South Korea agreed to field a single team at the 2008 Olympics, marking progress in economic and cultural exchanges. On 30 December the South Korean national assembly approved the withdrawal of 1,000 of the country's 3,200 troops in Iraq.

North Korean leader Kim Jong-il visited China for talks with President Hu Jintao early in January 2006, raising hopes of a resumption of the recently stalled nuclear negotiations.

BURMA (MYANMAR).

Chronology of Key Events.

1948 Burma, a British colony since 1886, becomes independent.

1962 Prime minister U Nu is deposed in a military coup led by General Ne Win; a long period of repression follows.

1988 Ne Win is overthrown in student-led riots but many are killed by the State Law and Order Restoration Council (SLORC) as it takes power; the country's name is changed to Myanmar.

1989 Opposition National League for Democracy (NLD) leader Aung San Suu Kyi is placed under house arrest.

1990 NLD wins a landslide victory in the first elections for 30 years; SLORC annuls the elections and retains power.

1991 Aung San Suu Kyi is awarded Nobel Peace Prize.

1995 Aung San Suu Kyi is released from house arrest but restrictions continue.

1996 There are widespread student demonstrations against the regime; all universities are closed.

1997 SLORC renames itself the State Peace and Development Council (SPDC) and attempts economic reform.

1998 NLD sets up a shadow parliament of members elected in 1990; opposition activists are arrested.

1999 The International Labour Organisation condemns the use of slave labour in Burma; the World Bank demands political and human rights reforms; the government intensifies long-running action against Karen National Union guerrillas on border with Thailand.

2000 Continued international condemnation of the regime.

2001 Major changes to ruling State Peace and Development Council.

The Arrest of Aung San Suu Kyi.

In April 2003 the opposition leader, Aung San Suu Kyi, criticised the government for its reluctance to engage in serious political dialogue. Following clashes between opposition National League for Democracy (NLD) and government supporters, she and leading NLD members were arrested on 30 May. There was renewed international criticism and in August a new prime minister, Khin Nyunt, was appointed. He pledged a restoration of democracy but gave no hint of timing. Aung San Suu Kyi was moved to house arrest following illness but declared

in November that she would not accept release until 35 NLD members still in custody were freed.

Developments in 2004.

In April, the government announced that the opposition National League for Democracy (NLD) leader Aung San Suu Kyi would be released from house arrest in May. However, on 14 May, with no sign of Ms Suu Kyi's release, the NLD and two smaller parties refused to participate. The replacement on 19 October of the prime minister, Khin Nyunt, by Lt. Gen. Soe Win, was taken as a sign that the military government intended to maintain the slow pace of reform. However, on 20 November the government released 4,000 prisoners, including a prominent dissident. On 23 November the government announced that the constitutional convention would reconvene in February 2005. However, two days later Ms Suu Kyi's house arrest was extended.

On 19 January 2005 Ms Rice, the incoming United States' Secretary of State, declared that Burma was one of the 'outposts of tyranny' that required assistance in gaining freedom.

Recent Events.

The ruling junta announced on 27 March that the country was moving towards democracy, but gave no details. In July the government released a number of political detainees, but over a thousand, including National League for Democracy (NLD) leader Ms Suu Kyi, remained under house arrest. The government agreed on 26 July not to take up the chairmanship of the Association of South East Asian Nations (ASEAN) to avoid a threatened Western boycott. Ms Suu Kyi's house arrest was extended for a further 12 months on 27 November. The NLD continued its boycott of the junta-inspired National Convention in Rangoon, a further session of which opened on 5 December, ostensibly to formulate a new democratic constitution. ASEAN criticised the government's human rights record on 12 December and called for Ms Suu Kyi's release as a preliminary to restoring democracy. The government adjourned the convention meeting on 31 January 2006.

INDONESIA.

1945 Indonesia declares independence from the Netherlands (recognised in 1949).

1957 President Sukarno introduces 'guided democracy', replacing the elected parliament with an appointed legislature.

1965 Thousands are killed as the Communist Party is banned following an attempted coup.

1966 General Suharto seizes power in an army coup and introduces a 'New Order'; he is elected president by a puppet People's Consultative Assembly in 1968.

1976 Occupation of the former Portuguese colony of East Timor provokes resistance; a separatist campaign begins in Aceh province.

1991 There is international condemnation of a massacre of East Timor demonstrators by Indonesian troops.

1996 Despite growing opposition, the ruling Golkar is returned to power with an increased majority.

1998 President Suharto resigns following intensifying opposition in the wake of economic crisis and is succeeded by President Habibie.

1999 Abdurrahman Wahid is elected President; East Timor referendum vote for independence provokes anti-separatist violence; separatist movements throughout Indonesia are increasingly active.

2000 Government threatened with financial scandal; corruption charges against Suharto fail; Irian Jaya separatists intensify campaign.

2001 Ethnic violence mounts; Wahid dismissed over corruption and incompetence charges; Sukarnoputri succeeds following clashes between rival supporters.

The April 2004 Elections.

In parliamentary and local elections in April 2004 President Megawati Sukarnoputri's PDI-P came a

poor second to Golkar, the party of former
President Sukharno. However, in the first round of
direct presidential elections on 5 July, it was the
Democrat Party candidate, former general Susilo
Bambang Yudhoyono, who took the lead, with
33·6% of the vote against President Megawati's
26·6%. In the run-off on 20 September, Mr
Yudhoyono (popularly known as SBY) defeated the
incumbent in a 61% to 39% landslide. The election
came in the wake of a 9 September terrorist attack
on the Australian Embassy in the capital Jakarta in
which nine people died and over 180 were injured.

The Advent of Yudhoyono.

In his inauguration on 20 October President
Yudhoyono promised a concerted campaign against
crime, corruption, terrorism and the separatist
movements in Aceh and Papua. Parliament
approved the extension of a state of emergency in
Aceh on 17 November. On 19 December President
Yudhoyono's position appeared strengthened when
his vice-president, Jusuf Kalla, was elected leader
of Golkar, the largest parliamentary party. This
promised to ease progress of his reform plans.

The Tsunami Catastrophe.

Thousands were killed and a million made homeless when a tidal wave resulting from an earthquake
off Sumatra devastated coastal regions on 26
December. The worst hit area was Aceh province,
already suffering from the long-running separatist
conflict. The government accused rebels of undermining relief work, while the Free Aceh Movement
(GAM), accusing the government of renewing a military offensive under cover of the disaster, appealed
for a truce as 2005 opened. At talks held in Finland
at the end of January, the government rejected
GAM's call for a referendum on Aceh's future.

Peace in Aceh.

On 22 February 2005 Free Aceh Movement (GAM)
separatists announced they were prepared to accept
peace proposals that involved autonomy rather
than outright independence. A Finnish mediator
announced on 16 April that GAM and Indonesian
government negotiators had made significant progress. The government lifted emergency rule in the
province on 19 May. The civil war, which had lasted
over 25 years and in which 15,000 people had died,
ended with the signing of a peace agreement on 15
August granting the province significant autonomy.
Government troops began withdrawing a week later
as GAM forces disarmed.

Reconciliation over East Timor.

Meanwhile, on 9 March Indonesia and East Timor
agreed to establish a commission to investigate
atrocities committed in East Timor in 1999. There
were signs of further reconciliation when President
Yudhoyono visited East Timor on 8 April. There
were also developments in Indonesia's international
relations. On 4 April Indonesia and Australia signed
an economic, trade and security agreement. President Bush announced at a meeting with President
Yudhoyono on 25 May that the United States
would allow the sale of defence equipment as a preliminary to restoring military links frozen because
of Indonesia's human rights abuses.

The country was once more a target for suicide
bombers on 1 October when there were attacks
at Jimbaran Bay and Kutu in Bali, the scene of a
previous incident in 2002. Over 20 people were
killed in a bombing thought to be the responsibility
of the Jemaah Islamiya group. By 31 December the
last Indonesian troops were withdrawn from Aceh.

AFRICA

Chronology of Events since 1957.

1957 Independence of Ghana under Nkrumah
begins era of European decolonisation.
1958 Guinea becomes independent.
1960 Independence of Nigeria, Cameroon, Togo,
Mali, Senegal, Belgian Congo, Somalia,

Dahomey (now Benin), Niger, Upper Volta
(now Burkina Faso), Ivory Coast, Chad Republic, Central African Republic, Congo
Brazzaville, Gabon, and Mauritania; black
South Africans massacred at Sharpeville;
African National Congress (ANC) banned.
1961 Angolan independence struggle against
Portugal begins; Sierra Leone and Tanganyika
(later Tanzania) become independent; South
Africa leaves Commonwealth; guerrilla resistance to apartheid regime begins.
1962 Uganda, Burundi and Rwanda gain independence.
1963 Organisation of African Unity formed;
Guinea-Bissau independence struggle against
Portugal begins; Kenya becomes independent.
1964 Malawi and Zambia gain independence;
Mandela sentenced to life imprisonment in
South Africa; Mozambique struggle against
Portugal begins.
1965 Gambia becomes independent; Southern
Rhodesia white regime declares illegal unilateral independence; Mobutu seizes power in
Congo (renamed Zaïre in 1971).
1966 African resistance to white Rhodesian regime
begins; South West Africa People's Organisation begins armed struggle against South
African occupation; Botswana and Lesotho
gain independence; Nkrumah ousted in Ghana
coup.
1967 Biafran secession begins civil war in Nigeria
(ends 1970).
1968 Emperor Haile Selassie of Ethiopia overthrown in military coup; Guinea-Bissau gains
independence.
1969 Amin seizes power in Uganda (ousted in 1979).
1975 Economic Community of West African States
formed; Angola, Mozambique and Cape Verde
gain independence; civil war breaks out in
Angola (ends 1994).
1976 Civil war in Mozambique (ends 1992); black
South African protestors killed in Soweto.
1980 Mugabe wins first free elections in Zimbabwe.
1981 Long-running civil war begins in Somalia.
1984 900,000 die in Ethiopian famine.
1989 Civil war begins in Liberia.
1990 Namibia gains independence from South
Africa; ban on black political organisations
ends in South Africa.
1991 Apartheid ends in South Africa.
1992 Rawlings wins first democratic elections in
Ghana.
1993 Southern African Development Community
established.
1994 Mandela becomes President in first South
African multi-racial elections; massacre of
Hutus by Tutsis in Rwandan civil war.
1996 Civil war breaks out in Zaïre (now Democratic
Republic of Congo).
1997 Kofi Annan becomes first black African
United Nations secretary general; Mobutu
ousted in Zaïre.
1998 Border war between Ethiopia and Eritrea;
United States bombs Sudan for alleged terrorist links.
1999 Obasanjo wins Nigerian presidential election.
2000 Kufuor wins presidential election in Ghana;
Islamic law (sharia) introduced in parts of
Nigeria.
2001 OAU dissolved, replaced by the African Union.
2002 Mugabe approves confiscation of white-owned
farms in Zimbabwe.
2003 Transitional government of national reconciliation formed in Congo Democratic Republic
(formerly Zaïre).
2004 Commission for Africa, a British initiative to
confront the continent's problems, holds first
meeting in Ethiopia.

ETHIOPIA.

1896 Defeats Italians at Adowa to retain independence.
1930 Haile Selassie becomes Emperor.
1936 Italy annexes Ethiopia (Abyssinia) and
retains control until 1941.
1952 Eritrea federates with Ethiopia; annexed in
1962.
1974 Serious famine; Haile Selassie overthrown in a
coup by Teferi Benti.

1977 Colonel Mengistu seizes power in a military coup; Benti killed; 'Red Terror' against opponents begins.
1978 Tigre People's Liberation Front begins autonomy campaign.
1985 Serious famine.
1987 New constitution; Mengistu elected president.
1991 Mengistu flees after capital captured by Ethiopian People's Revolutionary Democratic Front.
1993 Eritrea becomes independent from Ethiopia.
1994 Republic of Ethiopia established under new constitution.
1995 Negasso Gidada becomes president and Meles Zedawi prime minister.
1999 Border war with Eritrea.
2000 Serious famine; ceasefire with Eritrea.

Relations with Eritrea.

In February 2003 the Ethiopian government rejected Eritrean charges of a military build-up on the border. Almost 100,000 had been killed in a war that had ended in 2000. A dispute continued over control over the town of Badme. In March the United Nations accused Ethiopia of undermining the peace settlement. In September the United Nations said that peacekeeping efforts were at risk if Ethiopia and Eritrea did not settle the simmering border issue. Meanwhile, in July, neighbouring Somalia had accused Ethiopia of attempting to destabilise the country by arming warlords who opposed the transitional government.

The Spectre of Starvation.

The country sought increased international aid as a bad harvest led to fears in early 2003 that millions faced starvation. By September the government announced that the 20% of the population requiring humanitarian assistance appeared secure but that $40 million was still required to cope with the effects of drought. The prime minister, Meles Zenawi, nonetheless criticised International Monetary Fund pressure to intensify privatisation of state industries and to open up capital markets. He feared the effect on the country's development.

Developments in 2004.

In March 2004 the government began a programme to resettle over two million people from the highlands over the next three years. There were fears of a repetition of a previous badly organised project. In July the United Nations secretary general attempted to renew peace negotiations with Eritrea following Ethiopia's refusal to implement a border agreement. Over 4,000 United Nations peacekeepers remained deployed.
On 20 October Ethiopia's main international creditors agreed to cancel £110 million of debt to help promote growth, leaving £100 million outstanding. Following African Union intervention, prime minister Meles Zenawi announced on 25 November that although he considered the proposed border with Eritrea to be unjust he now proposed to accept it. But on 2 January 2005 the opposition mounted a demonstration against any agreement, declaring that the proposed border would be an issue for elections due in May.

The 2005 Elections.

Elections were held to the 548 seat House of Representatives on 15 May 2005. Prime Minister Zenawi's Ethiopian People's Revolutionary Democratic Front (EPRDF) retained a majority but opposition parties increased their representation. European Union observers criticised what they said was clear evidence of electoral fraud. In June there were clashes between anti-government demonstrators and police in which over 40 people were killed as opposition leaders and journalists were arrested for allegedly inciting violence. The main opposition Coalition for Unity and Democracy boycotted the opening of parliament on 10 October. Clashes between opposition protestors and the police continued through October and November. In November the government announced that detained opposition leaders and newspaper editors faced treason charges. This led to threats from Western donors to curtail aid.

Renewed Tension with Eritrea.

Meanwhile, tension rose on the border with Eritrea, threatening a resumption of the 1998-2000 war in which thousands had died. On 7 December Eritrea expelled United Nations peacekeepers, heightening the danger of clashes. As 2006 opened there were reports of troop movements on the border and on 10 January the United States offered to deploy a team to mediate. In late January Britain suspended direct aid to the government because of human rights violations.

ALGERIA.

1962 Gains independence from France.
1963 Ahmed Ben Bella elected first president.
1965 Houari Boumedienne overthrows Ben Bella.
1976 Boumedienne becomes president; introduces socialist constitution; National Liberation Front sole party.
1978 Chadli Bendjedid becomes military-backed president.
1986 Strikes and riots over unemployment.
1989 Opposition parties legalised; Islamic Salvation Front (FIS) established.
1991 FIS wins first round of elections.
1992 National People's Assembly dissolved; Higher State Council under Mohamed Boudiaf takes power; FIS clashes with troops; Armed Islamic Group formed; FIS banned; Boudiaf assassinated.
1995 Liamine Zeroual elected president.
1996 Referendum approves constitutional changes.
1997 Democratic National Rally wins elections.
1999 Abdelaziz Bouteflika elected president; government talks with FIS armed wing, the Islamic Salvation Army.
2000 Continuing violence; 100,000 killed since 1992.
2001 Berber Rally for Culture and Democracy leaves government following Berber/army clashes; government makes concessions.

Recent Events.

In January 2005 the government announced a further blow against the weakening Armed Islamic Group (GIA), with the arrest of its leader and the killing of his deputy. A report commissioned by the government revealed in March that security forces had been responsible for the disappearance of over 6,000 people during the 1990s civil war. On 29 September voters overwhelmingly supported government proposals for a general amnesty for an estimated 1,000 armed Islamist insurgents. The result, which was disputed by opponents, enabled President Bouteflika to proceed with a Charter for Peace and National Reconciliation to end a decade-long war in which 100,000 people had died.
In February 2006 US Defense Secretary Donald Rumsfeld said in Algiers that he intended to strengthen military and counter-terrorist cooperation with Algeria.

SUDAN.

Chronology of Recent Events.

1956 Sudan gains independence from Britain and Egypt.
1958 General Abbud ousts civilian government.
1962 Civil war begins in the south.
1964 Abbud overthrown; national government established.
1969 Ja'far Numayri leads military coup.
1972 South becomes self-governing region.
1978 Oil discovered in south.
1983 Numayri introduces *sharia* (Islamic law), provoking rebellion in the predominantly Christian and animist south.
1985 Numayri deposed; Transitional Military Council formed.
1986 Civilian coalition government established.
1989 Military coup.
1993 Omar al-Bashir becomes president.
1998 US bombs pharmaceutical factory in Khartoum.
1999 Bashir dissolves National Assembly; declares state of emergency; oil exports begin.
2000 Bashir returned in disputed elections.
2001 Sudan People's Liberation Army (SPLA) rebels in south threaten attack on oil workers;

Libya and Egypt mediate in civil war; US sanctions.

2002 SPLA begins negotiations with government.

2003 Bashir and SPLA leader John Garang meet for talks.

The Darfur Crisis.

As the civil war appeared to be drawing to a close, there were clashes in January 2004 between Arabs and the black African Sudan Liberation Army in the western region of Darfur, forcing thousands of refugees to flee to neighbouring Chad. In March United Nations officials accused the Arab pro-government 'Janjaweed' militia of slaughtering Africans in Darfur. Despite a ceasefire signed in April, fighting continued, the government claiming it had no control over the militia.

Denunciation of Genocide.

Meanwhile, the government and southern rebels moved closer to peace in the long-running civil war as they agreed on power-sharing and the division of oil-generated wealth. In July the United Nations called on the government to take action over the Darfur crisis, as additional pressure was imposed by the United States and the European Union. The US Secretary of State, Mr Powell, condemned the killings in Darfur as genocide in September as the United Nations accused the government of failing to adhere to a pledge made in July to disarm the militia. The United Nations threatened oil sanctions against Sudan and in October the African Union agreed to enlarge a peace-keeping force already deployed in the area.

Ending the Civil War.

On 31 December the government and rebels in the south reached agreement to end a civil war in which over a million had died. The peace agreement allocated half of the country's oil to the predominantly animist south and allowed autonomy and the right to secede after six years. In July 2005 Mr Garang, leader of the Sudan People's Liberation Army, was appointed vice-president in a power-sharing government. But at the end of the month he was killed in a helicopter crash, provoking rioting in Khartoum. His deputy, Salva Kiir, succeeded as the country's vice-president. A national unity government was sworn in on 22 September under President Omar al-Bashir, whose National Congress Party held half the 30 cabinet posts.

However, massacres continued in Darfur, as the Janjaweed militia continued their attacks on black Africans, despite the presence of a 6,000-strong African Union peacekeeping force. By the end of 2005 up to 400,000 people had been killed and over two million forced from their homes. On 13 January 2006 the United Nations announced plans to deploy troops as the African Union warned of a possible withdrawal.

NIGERIA.

1960 Nigeria becomes independent.

1963 Nigeria becomes a republic within the British Commonwealth.

1966 Civilian government overthrown in military coup by Major General Aguiyi Ironsi, who is then ousted by Colonel Yakuba Gowon.

1967 Biafra secedes, opening a three year civil war.

1970 Civil war ends with the surrender of Biafra.

1975 Gowon is overthrown in a bloodless coup by Brigadier Murkata Muhammed.

1976 Muhammed is assassinated and succeeded by General Olesegun Obasanjo.

1979 Nigeria returns to civilian rule under Shehu Shagari.

1983 Shagari is ousted by Major General Mohammadu Buhari.

1985 Buhari is overthrown by Major General Ibrahim Babangida.

1986 Babangida promises to restore civilian rule in 1990 but later postpones this to 1992.

1988 Rioting against the military government.

1989 Ban on political activity is lifted; two state-sponsored parties are formed.

1990 There is an unsuccessful coup against Babangida.

1992 The Social Democratic Party (SDP) wins legislative elections.

1993 SDP candidate Moshood Abiola elected President but military regime refuses to accept result; Babangida hands power to Ernest Shonekan as interim President but he is ousted by General Sani Abacha.

1995 Abacha promises restoration of civilian rule in 1998; Europe imposes economic sanctions following execution of Ken Saro-Wiwa.

1997 Multi-party municipal elections are held.

1998 Widespread boycott of legislative elections; Abacha dies in mysterious circumstances; his successor Olesegun Obasanjo promises to restore civilian rule.

1999 Obasanjo's People's Democratic Party (PDP) wins elections and Obasanjo becomes President; stability is threatened by growing ethnic conflict.

The 2003 Presidential Election.

In elections on 12 April President Obasanjo's People's Democratic Party won a majority in both the House of Representatives and the Senate over its nearest rival, Mr Muhammadu Buhari's All Nigeria People's Party (ANPP). Mr Obasanjo went on to defeat Mr Buhari in the presidential election a week later. However, ANPP charges that the elections were fraudulent posed questions about the stability of the country's democracy after the first civilian-run poll for 20 years.

Oil Industry Unrest.

In March ethnic clashes between the Ijaw and Itsekiri groups in the Niger Delta had cut oil production by 40%. In April oil workers seized offshore oil rigs in an industrial dispute, taking a hundred foreign hostages. The hostages were released in May. There were clashes between police and protestors during a general strike that began on 30 June over oil price increases. The strike ended on 8 July with the government agreeing to moderate the increases. Ending subsidies on fuel was a preliminary to privatising oil refineries to attract foreign investment. There were further clashes between ethnic groups in the Niger Delta area in August, once again threatening oil production.

Human Rights Accusations.

On 7 August a Nigeria peacekeeping force entered Monrovia, the Liberian capital, taking control of the port from rebel forces as part of the process to end the country's civil war. There was international criticism of the sentence to death by stoning under Islamic law of a woman accused of adultery. In September an appeal court acquitted the woman.

In December 2003, as Nigeria was hosting the Commonwealth conference, an American human rights organisation accused the government of abuses against opponents. The government declared the report was exaggerated.

In January 2004 the government faced a further general strike against a fuel tax increase which, the National Labour Congress said, would hit the poor. The strike was called off as the government obeyed a court order to suspend the rise. The government announced a renewed anti-corruption campaign on 24 January as five former officials appeared in court on bribery charges.

Election Irregularities.

The ruling People's Democratic Party won a sweeping victory in local government elections at the end of March 2004, though there were charges of widespread irregularities. On 18 May President Obasanjo declared a six-month state of emergency in Plateau state following further clashes in the long-standing conflict between Christians and Muslims, also suspending the local governor. The violence provoked retaliatory action in the north eastern state of Adamawa in June.

Niger Delta Discontent.

Meanwhile, the Nigeria Labour Congress called a general strike on 9 June to protest against a fuel price increase. A court declared the strike illegal on 11 June but in October there was a further four-day stoppage over price increases. The strikes raised fears for Nigeria's oil exports. In September a rebel group in the Niger Delta threatened to shut down production unless local people derived some benefit from sales.

On 20 November President Obasanjo declared, in his role as chairman of the African Union, that Africa's leaders would never again allow despotism or tyranny in the continent.

Recent Developments.

In February 2005 a national conference was held in the capital, Abuja, to prepare for constitutional reform. The opposition refused to attend, criticising the conference's powerlessness. General Gowon, a former military ruler, warned President Obasanjo not to revise the constitution to allow himself a third term in office when his mandate expired in 2007. The ruling People's Democratic Party (PDP) was reportedly divided over the succession. In September a PDP official urged Vice-President Abubakar to support President Obasanjo or resign. The government appeared to make serious moves against official corruption in 2005, with the dismissal of a number of ministers and the enforced resignation of the Senate speaker for bribery. In December the governor of Bayelsa state – a PDP member and supporter of Vice President Abubakar – was accused of fraud by the Economic and Financial Crimes Commission. Critics said that political rivalry lay behind many accusations.

Niger Delta Hostages.

In July international lenders wrote off two thirds of the country's $30 billion foreign debt. President Obasanjo reported that the government had recovered $470 million of looted state funds from Switzerland. In September trade union members demonstrated in Lagos in protest against a 30% rise in fuel prices following a reduction in subsidies. In January 2006 Movement for the Emancipation of the Niger Delta militants kidnapped four foreign oil workers to press demands for local people to have a greater share in wealth generated by oil. The hostages were soon released but there was little doubt that the campaign would continue. Support for constitutional changes announced by 36 state governors on 31 January heightened the possibility that President Obasanjo would run for a third term in 2007.

KENYA.

Chronology of Key Events.

1920 Crown colony of Kenya established.
1944 Kenyan African Union (KAU) formed to campaign for independence.
1947 Kenyatta becomes KAU leader.
1952 Mau Mau guerrilla action against British rule begins.
1953 Kenyatta imprisoned; KAU banned.
1960 Britain announced plans for majority rule; Kenya African National Union (KANU) formed.
1961 Kenyatta freed; becomes KANU president.
1963 Kenya independent; Kenyatta becomes prime minister.
1964 Kenya becomes a republic with Kenyatta as president and Odinga as vice-president.
1966 Odinga forms rival Kenya People's Union (KPU).
1967 'Africanisation' programme threatens position of Asians.
1969 Ethnic unrest following assassination of minister; KPU banned and Odinga arrested.
1978 Kenyatta dies; Moi succeeds.
1982 Kenya a one-party state.
1991 Newly formed opposition Forum for the Restoration of Democracy banned; government agrees to introduce a multi-party system under aid donor pressure.
1992 Moi re-elected as opposition splits into factions.
1994 Opposition forms United National Democratic Alliance.
1997 Demonstrations for reform; World Bank withholds credits; Moi re-elected.
1998 Over 200 dead in terrorist bomb at US Embassy.
1999 Moi announces anti-corruption campaign.
2002 Victory for Kibaki.

The New Constitution.

The country's new constitution dominated 2005. On 22 July parliament approved a draft by 102 votes to 61, with four cabinet members among the opponents. Critics said the proposed reforms, the first since Kenya gained independence from Britain in 1963, left too much power in the president's hands. In the run-up to a referendum on 21 November, a number of demonstrators were killed in clashes with the police. President Kibaki suffered a setback in the referendum as 58% of voters rejected his proposals. The vote revealed the country's ethnic divisions, with President Kibaki's Kikuyu tribe supporting the changes while the Luo tribe was prominent in opposing. Seven ministers rebelled to support the No campaign.

Recent Developments.

On 23 November President Kibaki dismissed his cabinet, appointing a new cabinet on 9 December after a number of nominees refused office. The opposition KANU called for immediate elections. The government was further undermined in January 2006 when the vice-president and two ministers were summoned to appear before the Kenyan Anti-Corruption Commission to explain their financial position. President Kibaki had been elected on a pledge to eradicate corruption. In February a number of ministers, including the Finance Minister, resigned following revelations by the chairman of the parliamentary public accounts committee, who had fled to Britain following threats to his safety.

CONGO (ZAÏRE until 1997).

1960 Congo gains independence from Belgium; there is immediate political upheaval.
1965 General Mobutu seizes power and rules as dictator; civil war continues until 1967.
1971 The country is renamed Zaïre.
1977 Anti-Mobutu forces unsuccessfully invade from Angola.
1990 President Mobutu promises democracy under international pressure.
1996 Zaïre is drawn into the Central African turmoil triggered by the Rwandan civil war.
1997 President Mobutu flees as rebels advance; long-term rebel leader Lauren Kabila takes power and the country is renamed the Congo.
1998 There is renewed civil war as rebel forces backed by Uganda and Rwanda advance, Angola, Zimbabwe and Namibia support Kabila.
1999 The combatants agree a ceasefire but violence soon resumes.

The Assassination of Kabila.

Another attempt was made in December 2000 to secure the withdrawal of outside troops in the country. The situation was thrown into crisis with the assassination on 16 January 2001 of President Kabila. In he succeeded two days later as interim leader by his son, Major General Joseph Kabila, his position confirmed by the unelected legislature. If the new president were to attempt to bring peace to his troubled country, how independent he could become of his father's outside backers remained open to question.

At the end of February the six countries and three rebel groups involved in fighting announced a withdrawal to defensive positions by 15 March under United Nations supervision. President Kabila meanwhile agreed to open negotiations with the country's internal opposition.

Steps Towards Peace.

As the ceasefire continued to hold, in July the United Nations praised the steps towards peace that had been made in the Congo. On 9 August President Kabila announced the establishment of a commission to secure national reconciliation and free elections. But on the same day the government accused Rwanda and Uganda of attempting to renew fighting despite their pledge to withdraw troops. At the end of the month talks opened in the Botswana capital, Gaborone and agreement was reached that an Inter-Congolese Dialogue would begin on 15 October 2001.

Violence in Eastern Congo.

However, there was fighting between Rwandan-backed rebels and government forces in the east of the country in September and in mid-October peace talks were close to collapse following the rejection of President Kabila's call for elections to precede the formation of a transitional government. The talks collapsed on 21 October as government delegates walked out after being accused by the Rwandan-backed Congolese Rally for Democracy of wanting the country to remain divided.

The South African Peace Talks.

At peace talks held in South Africa in April 2002, the government signed a power-sharing agreement with Ugandan-backed rebels but forces supported by Rwanda rejected the deal. However, in July President Kabila and the Rwandan president reached agreement on troop withdrawals. By October both Uganda and Rwanda claimed to have withdrawn the bulk of their forces. Talks on power-sharing between the government and the two main rebel groups were sponsored by the UN in October. On 17 December the four year civil war appeared to have ended when the government signed a peace treaty with the rebels. President Kabila was to remain president, sharing power in an interim government until elections were held in two and a half years. There were to be four new vice-presidents from the existing government, the Rwandan-backed Rally for Congolese Democracy, the Ugandan-backed Movement for the Liberation of the Congo and one representing other opposition groups. The new order was to be guaranteed by a UN force of 8,700.

New Power-Sharing Arrangements.

In May the last Ugandan troops left the east of the country but clashes were reported between rival militias. President Kabila announced the appointment of the new vice-presidents intended to lead a transitional administration, with representation for the government, the opposition and Ugandan and Rwandan backed militias. Meanwhile, the United Nations authorised the deployment of a 1,400 strong peacekeeping force in the north east. French troops arrived in June.

In July 2003 President Kabila inaugurated a power-sharing administration of 36 ministers that included 16 former rebels. Elections would take place in two years. In October there were reports of further clashes in the Ituri region but on 8 December soldiers from the two main rebel factions amalgamated with government troops to form a united army. There were fears, however, that the peace remained fragile.

Continuing Rebel Threats.

The situation remained unstable, with an apparent coup attempt in March 2004 and clashes in May and June between government forces and former members of the rebel Rally for Congolese Democracy in the east of the country. In August Burundi threatened to attack following allegations of Congolese participation in a massacre of Tutsi refugees. There was optimism at the end of November when 15 heads of state from the Great Lakes region signed a declaration proposing demobilisation of armed groups and a framework for development to secure economic stability.

On 23 November, following the deployment of a further 5,000 United Nations peacekeeping troops (bringing the total to 15,000), President Kabila reported that the country would be ready for elections within six months. However, in late December the government announced that 10,000 soldiers had been deployed to expel Rwandan forces, undermining hopes of a peaceful settlement. In January 2005 the United Nations reported that continuing clashes posed a serious threat to the possibility of holding elections in June. In mid-month workers struck in the capital following reports that the elections might be postponed till October.

The Constitution Referendum.

A referendum was held in December 2005 on a new constitution, the text of which had been agreed by the former warring factions and approved by the legislature in May. The constitution limited the president to two five-year terms and increased the number of provinces from ten to 26. Voters supported the proposals by 78% to 21% in what European Union observers described as a fair poll. However, violence continued as United Nations and Congolese troops clashed with rebel militia in the south east and north east.

Recents Events.

As 2006 opened medical observers in the country reported that 38,000 people a month were dying, with the majority falling victim to malnutrition and disease rather than violence. On 12 January the government set 30 July as the date for the country's first multi-party elections for 40 years.

SOUTH AFRICA.

Chronology of Recent Events.

1948 The National Party takes office on a programme of apartheid or 'separate development'.

1952 A 'defiance campaign' against apartheid is organised by the African National Congress (ANC).

1955 Black, Indian and Coloured organisations adopt a Freedom Charter calling for a multiracial South Africa; eviction of the black population from designated 'white' areas begins.

1958 Progress of apartheid intensifies with the election of President Verwoerd; process of establishing 'independent' black homelands begins.

1960 76 black demonstrators against the Pass laws are killed in the Sharpeville Massacre.

1961 ANC forms Umkhonto we Sizwe (Spear of the Nation) to wage armed resistance.

1964 Nelson Mandela and other ANC activists are imprisoned for life following the Rivonia treason trial.

1976 Demonstrations in Soweto open a new phase of anti-apartheid agitation in which over 1,000 people are killed.

1984 State of virtual civil war in black townships; international companies begin withdrawing from South Africa.

1986 President Botha declares that South Africa has 'outgrown' apartheid.

1989 President de Klerk succeeds Botha and promises reform.

1990 ANC leader Mandela is released from prison.

1994 Mandela is elected President in South Africa's first multi-racial elections and heads a government of national unity.

1996 South Africa adopts a new constitution; the white National Party withdraws from the government of national unity and goes into decline.

1998 Truth & Reconciliation Commission—established to investigate the causes and results of apartheid—issues report after two years of hearings.

1999 ANC strengthens its position in elections, taking 66% of the vote, enabling the party to amend the constitution; Thabo Mbeki succeeds Mandela as President.

The 2002 ANC Conference.

President Mbeki asserted his position at the opening on 17 December of the ANC's five-yearly conference that had been expected to see a showdown with the trade unions and the Communist Party over poverty and unemployment. President Mbeki accused critics of disloyalty and blamed civil servants for weaknesses in government policies. He said that his government would continue with privatisation and other market reforms but, echoing President Mugabe in neighbouring Zimbabwe, pointed to the fact that the bulk of the economy, including land, remained in white hands.

Developments in 2003.

On 10 April 2003 the government achieved the two thirds majority necessary to enable it to amend the constitution when nine members defected from other parties, giving the African National Congress (ANC) 275 seats in the 400 seat parliament. The Inkatha Freedom Party (IFP) condemned the defections as undemocratic. On 15 April the government agreed to pay $85 million reparations to the families of over 19,000 victims of apartheid.

In August, in the face of growing international criticism, President Mbeki reversed the government policy on combating the HIV-AIDS crisis, promising to supply drugs to prolong victims' lives. In November the health minister announced a country-wide treatment programme that would benefit five million people.

The 2004 Election Background.

As the 2004 parliamentary and presidential elections approached, the main opposition party, the Democratic Alliance (DA) formed an anti-ANC coalition with the IFP on 3 November. DA leader Mr Leon said this was intended to counter the danger of South Africa becoming effectively a one party state. IFP leader Mr Buthelezi criticised the government's record on unemployment, crime and poverty. The move came as the ANC faced internal problems, with a former prominent member having been convicted of corruption in an arms deal. Charges had been dropped against deputy leader Mr Zuma, a likely successor to President Mbeki.

Presenting the ANC's manifesto on 10 January 2004, President Mbeki promised a $15 billion infrastructure investment programme aimed at halving unemployment and poverty by 2014.

The Election Outcome.

The ANC took almost 70% of the vote in the 14 April elections, securing 279 of the 400 National Assembly seats. The predominantly white Democratic Alliance took 12% (50 seats) and the Inkatha Freedom Party 7% (28 seats). The New National Party, the dominant party of the apartheid era, won only 1·7%. President Mbeki, who was sworn in for his second term on 27 April, said he did not propose any constitutional changes, despite having the necessary two-thirds majority in the Assembly.

Public Sector Discontent.

A decade after the end of apartheid, the slow pace of black economic advance remained a crucial issue. In September thousands of public sector workers mounted the largest strike in South Africa's history to support a claim for higher pay and benefits. The strike ended with successful negotiations between the government and unions.

Charges of Cronyism.

On 18 November the Confederation of South African Trade Unions (COSATU) denounced the use of the government pension fund to buy telecoms shares for former government officials, ostensibly under the Financial Services Charter, which required companies to be a quarter black owned. COSATU said that so-called Black Empowerment appeared to be degenerating into cronyism rather than assisting black workers. Archbishop Desmond Tutu, a hero of the struggle against apartheid, said that millions of black South Africans were living in poverty while an elite benefited from the programme to boost black ownership. He said that 'kowtowing' within the ruling African National Congress was posing an obstacle to democracy. President Mbeki responded vigorously to Archbishop Tutu's attack, saying he had never been an ANC member and did not understand how the party functioned. There was, however, an acknowledgement by the government of popular dissatisfaction when it admitted that the pace of land reform was slow and promised to consider expropriation.

The death of former President Mandela's son of an AIDS-related illness in January 2005 aroused renewed criticisms of the government's attitude to the pandemic that was killing 600 people a day.

The ANC Crisis.

The crisis within the ruling ANC deepened in the course of 2005. In June President Mbeki dismissed his deputy, Jacob Zuma, as allegations were made of involvement in corruption. Mr Zuma, the favourite to succeed President Mbeki in 2009, remained one of the country's most popular politicians, particularly with the Confederation of South African Trade Unions (COSATU), which saw him as a champion of the poor and unemployed. On 17 August COSATU called for Mr Zuma's reinstatement as 100,000 gold miners struck for increased pay, bringing a crucial industry to a standstill.

Recent Developments.

Faced by continuing disappointment at the fruits of liberation, the government reiterated in September that it intended to redistribute a significant proportion of white-owned farm land. Over 80% of land remained in the hands of white farmers, who comprised only 10% of the population. In October the Commission on Restitution of Land Rights served an expropriation order on a white farmer who had refused an offer to buy his land.

As relations with the government deteriorated, COSATU attacked what the general secretary called President Mbeki's continuing failure over HIV/AIDS. Six million of the 40 million population were said to be infected. On 11 October Mr Zuma was charged with corruption. The crisis deepened in December when he was also charged with rape, which he denied.

In a further response to the government's growing unpopularity in the townships, President Mbeki announced a dramatic change in public spending policy in January 2006, proposing to allocate £37 billion to reduce the 25% unemployment rate and halve poverty by 2014.

The ANC emerged comfortably from local elections on 1 March, taking 66% of the vote on a 47% turnout, controlling five of the six major urban centres. The opposition Democratic Alliance took 15% and the Inkatha Freedom Party 7%.

ZIMBABWE.

Chronology of Recent Events.

1923 British colony of Southern Rhodesia is granted self-government under white rule.

1965 The white government illegally declares independence from Britain to avoid black majority rule.

1966 Guerrilla war against the white regime begins.

1977 The 'front line' African states step up support for liberation forces.

1979 The country is renamed 'Zimbabwe-Rhodesia' as a transitional government is established.

1980 The independent Republic of Zimbabwe is formed with resistance leader Robert Mugabe as prime minister.

1986 Mugabe's ZANU-PF wins an overwhelming majority in elections; he announces that he intends to create a one-party state.

1987 Mugabe becomes executive President with sweeping powers under a new constitution.

1990 Mugabe is re-elected as President and ZANU-PF wins the majority of seats in multi party elections.

1992 The Land Acquisition Act allows the confiscation of white-owned farms for redistribution.

1996 Mugabe is re-elected President following the withdrawal of opposition candidates; Zimbabwe formally abandons Marxism-Leninism as a state ideology.

1997 As popular discontent grows, Zimbabwe faces a wave of strikes; Mugabe threatens to confiscate 12.3 million acres of white-owned land.

1998 There is rioting in Harare and a nationwide general strike over unemployment and widespread economic breakdown; concern grows over Zimbabwe's increasing involvement in the Congo civil war.

1999 International aid donors withdraw their support for Zimbabwe; there are demonstrations against Mugabe's proposed constitutional reforms; trade union leader Morgan Tsvangirai launches a Movement for Democratic Change to contest elections due in 2000.

The Election Outcome.

The run up to the March 2002 presidential election was marked by growing intimidation and violence against MDC supporters from Mr Mugabe's ZANU-PF. Mr Mugabe rejected criticism as a British attempt to back the interests of white farmers against his land redistribution programme. Mr Mugabe won a fifth term as president with 1,685,212 votes while his MDC opponent Mr Tsvangirai—facing treason charges for allegedly plotting the president's assassination—took 1,258,401 votes. The conduct of the election polarised international and Commonwealth opinion. Somewhat to the surprise of some obervers, Zimbabwe's membership of the Commonwealth was suspended on 19 March 2002.

Following Zimbabwe's suspension from the Commonwealth in March, the European Union (EU) extended diplomatic sanctions on 22 July. Nevertheless, the EU agreed to a $34 million aid package in August.

Land Redistribution Campaign.

The land redistribution campaign continued. President Mugabe set 8 August as the deadline for the country's remaining white commercial farmers to leave their land. Two thousand defied the order and on 10 August President Mugabe told them to leave the country. By the end of the year, of the original 4,500 white farmers only 500 were left, the rest having returned to Europe or fled to neighbouring countries. Corruption ensured that the bulk of the country's 350,000 black agricultural workers did not reap the benefits of redistribution. Allocation depended on membership of the ruling ZANU-PF and the main beneficiaries appeared to be party officials and 'war veterans'. As famine swept southern Africa, seven million Zimbabweans faced starvation. Agricultural output—much of it export crops such as tobacco—fell by 70%. The country's ability to respond to the crisis was further undermined by the continuing AIDS epidemic.

The "War Cabinet".

On 26 August President Mugabe replaced his ministerial team with a 'War Cabinet' to confront what he described as British opposition. There was tension at the Earth Summit in South Africa where, on 2 September, President Mugabe denounced the British prime minister and his allies. But by November up to five million people were dependent on international food aid and there were allegations that supplies were only going to ZANU-PF supporters. A one day general strike called by the opposition National Constitutional Assembly on 10 December met with little support.

An Economy in Chaos.

As the situation deteriorated, with not only agriculture but also mining and manufacturing in chaos, President Mugabe blamed Britain and the dwindling white population at the ZANU-PF congress on 13 December. He threatened retaliation if the European Union sanctions continued. An attempt to secure 70% of the country's oil requirements from Libya collapsed in December when Zimbabwe was unable to supply beef, sugar and tobacco in exchange. On 13 January 2003 there were reports that senior ZANU-PF and military figures had proposed that President Mugabe should resign and an interim government be formed.

Mass Arrests and Repression.

President Mugabe had no intention of relinquishing power. A nationwide strike in March 2003 was followed by mass arrests. The presidents of South Africa, Malawi and Nigeria met in Harare on 5 May but proved unable to resolve the conflict between President Mugabe and Morgan Tsvangirai, leader of the opposition Movement for Democratic Change (MDC). Mr Tsvangirai was arrested on further treason charges in early June but released on bail on 21 June.

On 25 June US Secretary of State Colin Powell accused President Mugabe of tyranny and called for transition to a new government. But there were reports in late July that President Mugabe hoped to assure the succession of Emmerson Mnangagwa, who had allegedly been involved in the massacre of over 25,000 government opponents in Matabeleland in the 1980s.

A Deepening Crisis.

As inflation reached 525% and unemployment 70%, hundreds of trade union and civic activists were arrested in anti-government demonstrations in November. On 25 November the Commonwealth announced that President Mugabe would not be invited to the annual conference in December. As the conference voted to maintain Zimbabwe's

suspension, President Mugabe announced the country's withdrawal on 7 December.

As 2004 opened President Mbeki of South Africa announced that President Mugabe had agreed to negotiations with the opposition to end the economic and political crisis. Despite this, on 30 January the police prevented the opposition Movement for Democratic Change from presenting its proposals on rebuilding the country's economy at a meeting with diplomats and journalists.

On 3 March the USA imposed further sanctions after denouncing President Mugabe's determination to retain power regardless of the impact on his country.

Developments in 2004.

The year 2004 saw President Mugabe further consolidating his power while Zimbabwe's crisis deepened. The economy declined for a fifth consecutive year, bringing unemployment to over 70% while inflation averaged 200%. Life expectancy fell to 33 years as HIV/AIDS ravaged 25% of the population. It was estimated that three million people had fled the country. But in June the government announced a $200 million purchase of fighter jets and military vehicles from China, a move condemned by the opposition. The purchase ran parallel to increasing Chinese investment in Zimbabwe.

The 2005 Elections.

Opposition leader Morgan Tsvangirai was acquitted of treason charges in October but the Movement fort Democratic Change (MDC) said it would not run in parliamentary elections due in March 2005 unless the government introduced electoral reform and repealed oppressive security laws. But as the elections approached President Mugabe secured the appointment of the country's first female vice-president, who posed no immediate threat to his position, and legislation intensifying restrictions on the media and human rights groups.

The ruling ZANU-PF took 78 seats in the 1 April election, the opposition MDC 41 seats, and one independent was returned. President Mugabe's power to appoint a further 30 members gave his party a two thirds majority in the 150 seat legislature, allowing him to amend the constitution if he chose to do so. The election, though less violent than earlier contests, was criticised by international observers.

Operation Murambatsvina.

There was further international criticism in May 2005 when President Mugabe ordered the bulldozing of homes and businesses in Zimbabwe's urban centres in what he described as Operation Murambatsvina (Drive out rubbish). A United Nations report in July said that 700,000 had lost their homes or livelihoods. There were allegations that the areas selected had been those in which the opposition MDC had won support in the elections. On 2 August the government dropped the remaining treason charge against the MDC's leader, Morgan Tsvangirai.

Further Economic Decline.

At the end of August constitutional changes reintroduced the Senate, which had been abolished in 1987. In October the International Monetary Fund reported continued economic decline. Other reports estimated that 3·8 million people were starving in rural areas. At a United Nations conference in Rome on 17 October President Mugabe was applauded when he accused rich nations' farm subsidies of harming the poor. But in November the deputy agriculture minister admitted that much of the land redistributed since 2000 had gone to individuals with no farming experience and that this had led to food shortages.

Senate Elections.

The opposition MDC was thrown into crisis as Mr Tsvangirai urged members to boycott elections to the Senate in November 2005. In polling for 50 seats, President Mugabe's ZANU-PF won an overall majority, with a further six seats directly appointed by himself and another ten allocated to tribal leaders. Turnout was estimated at 15%. Mr Tsvangirai denounced the electoral process as discredited and called for non-violent mass resistance. On 2 December the government agreed to accept aid from the World Food Programme but rejected an offer of tents for those made homeless in May.

THE UNITED STATES

1960 Democrat Kennedy narrowly defeats Republican Nixon in presidential elections.
1961 Backs abortive Bay of Pigs invasion of Cuba; US imposes trade sanctions.
1962 Soviet Union removes weapons from Cuba following US pressure in 'Cuban Missile Crisis'.
1963 Kennedy assassinated; succeeded by Johnson.
1964 Gulf of Tonkin resolution allows Johnson to escalate Vietnam War; racial segregation is outlawed
1965 Watts Riots; Johnson attempts to build 'Great Society' with civil rights and welfare legislation.
1968 Growing opposition to intensifying Vietnam War; Martin Luther King and Robert Kennedy assassinated; Republican Nixon wins presidential election.
1969 Gradual withdrawal from Vietnam begins.
1970 Invasion of Cambodia.
1973 Nixon defeats Democrat McGovern in presidential election; Nixon makes historic visit to China; 'Watergate' scandal begins.
1973 Vice President Agnew resigns; replaced by Ford; Treaty of Paris ends US involvement in Vietnam.
1974 Nixon resigns; replaced by Ford.
1976 Democrat Carter defeats Ford in presidential election.
1978 Establishes diplomatic relations with China.
1979 Negotiates Camp David peace accord between Egypt and Israel.
1980 Republican Reagan defeats Carter in presidential election.
1981 Reagan survives assassination attempt.
1983 Invades Grenada; Reagan announces proposed 'Star Wars' strategic defence initiative.
1984 Reagan re-elected.
1986 Bombs Libya for alleged terrorist involvement; 'Irangate' scandal reveals illegal arms sales to Iran to fund war in Nicaragua.
1988 Republican Bush elected president.
1989 Invades Panama to oust president.
1991 Leads coalition to force Iraq from Kuwait.
1992 Signs treaty with USSR formally ending Cold War; Democrat Clinton defeats Bush in presidential election.
1994 Clinton's health care reforms rejected by Congress; Clinton faces corruption and sexual impropriety allegations.
1996 Clinton re-elected.
1998 Bombs Afghanistan and Sudan in response to terrorism and also Iraq; Clinton impeached; acquitted in 1999.
1999 Leads bombing of Yugoslavia; returns control of Panama Canal to Panama.
2000 Republican Bush defeats Democrat Gore in disputed presidential election.

The 2000 Presidential Election.

The 2000 US presidential election, which most Americans had written off as uninteresting or inconsequential prior to the vote in November, in the event produced the most remarkable and controversial result of the 20th century. A disputed outcome in the state of Florida between the Democratic candidate, Vice President Al Gore of Tennessee, and his Republican rival, Governor George W. Bush of Texas, led to a month of recounts and legal challenges until the unprecedented intervention of the US Supreme Court on 12 December in effect handed the presidency to Bush. Although Gore led the popular vote by some half a million, the Supreme Court's decision gave Bush victory in the Electoral College by 271 votes to 266, making this the first time since 1888 that the presidential victor had failed to win the popular vote.

The Events of September 2001.

The 11 September terrorist attacks on New York and Washington DC were to change the face of United States politics. Following the initial shock,

and an apparent unwillingness to consider why the country could be the target for an outrage of this kind, there was an outburst of patriotic fervour. President Bush promised the United States would 'hunt down and punish those responsible for this cowardly attack.'

On 14 September Congress approved the use by President Bush of 'all necessary and appropriate force' but stopped short of a full declaration of war. Congress also passed a $40 billion emergency anti-terrorist bill for increased military expenditure and $20 billion to reconstruct New York City. The result, however, was that the administration would be unable to meet its spending and tax commitments without eating into the social security budget.

The 'Patriot Act'.

The end of October saw passage of the 'Patriot Act', expanding government wire-tapping and internet surveillance powers, allowing the detention of foreign terrorist suspects and stronger moves against money laundering. A $100 billion economic stimulus plan for 2002—including further corporate and personal tax cuts—remained to be approved by the Senate.

Trial by Military Tribunal.

More controversial internationally was a directive signed by President Bush in November allowing suspected terrorists to be tried by military tribunals rather than in court. This raised the possibility of suspects being sentenced and executed in secret and was of particular concern when the United States denied detainees captured in Afghanistan and moved to Cuba the status of 'prisoner of war'. There were also questions about what had become known as the 'Bush doctrine', a speech in December rendering all 'rogue' states liable to attack, something that threatened—if acted upon—to commit the United States to unlimited and potentially destabilising conflict.

Developments in 2002.

Politics was dominated throughout 2002 by continuing fears of further terrorist attack, the economy and, above all, preparations for war against Iraq. There were concerns that the war on terrorism was faltering as the government warned that further incidents were almost inevitable. A number of suspects were arrested but a Congressional investigation pointed to ineffectiveness in the intelligence agencies and Democrat leaders expressed concern that the move against Iraq was acting as a distraction.

The Enron and WorldCom Scandals.

The spate of apparently unending business scandals that began in January undermined confidence in corporate America. Millions of shareholders saw their savings wiped away by accounting frauds at Enron and WorldCom and criminal investigations were launched into some of America's major companies. As stock markets tumbled, the economy faltered and public anger grew. The three most senior economic officials in the Bush administration, including the Treasury Secretary, were dismissed.

The November 2002 Mid-Term Elections.

Nonetheless, the November mid-term elections proved a triumph for President Bush, campaigning for the Republicans as a war leader. Barring a military or economic disaster, his prospects for re-election in 2004 appeared secure. In the Senate, the Republicans returned with 51 seats against 48 for the Democrats (plus one independent supporter). Republicans dominated the House of Representatives with 229 members to 204 Democrats. The Republicans were similarly successful in state legislative and gubernatorial contests.

The Department of Homeland Security.

President Bush moved quickly to capitalise on his strengthened position, pushing through the establishment of a $40 billion Department of Homeland Security combining 22 existing agencies. Other items on his agenda for the future included consolidating further tax cuts, reforming health care, opening up energy exploration, and appointing conservatives to the judiciary.

International Aspects.

There were also international implications in what was seen as a renewed mandate for President Bush. There had been early signs of a new American unilateralism. In March the imposition of a 30% tariff on steel imports had prompted complaints to the World Trade Organisation from the European Union and Japan. In July an International Criminal Court had been established in the face of opposition from the United States. The government now appeared to be in a stronger position to press the United Nations Security Council to take a firm line against Iraq This, as 2003 opened, was to dominate events. Although President Bush's policy had the backing of the majority of the American people, this remained conditional and there were signs that a serious anti-war movement might develop. But opinion hardened behind the President.

The Iraq War.

President Bush declared the main part of the war in Iraq concluded on 1 May 2003 but questions, and the cost, were to mount through the year. On 12 April Congress had approved $79 billion to pay for the conflict. But in September—as the tour of duty for troops in Iraq was extended—President Bush requested $87 billion for military and reconstruction programmes. On 4 November the Senate finally approved President Bush's proposals, taking expenditure on Iraq for the year to an estimated $130 billion.

Defense Secretary Rumsfeld admitted on 16 October that involvement in Iraq and Afghanistan would be a 'long, hard slog'. The government conceded on 7 July that President Bush had been wrong in his State of the Union message when he claimed Iraq had been attempting to buy uranium in pursuit of a nuclear weapons programme. President Bush maintained the war had been justified but in January 2004 the CIA's chief weapons inspector declared there was no evidence that biological, chemical or nuclear weapons existed in Iraq. On 2 February President Bush ordered an independent investigation into intelligence failures on the issue.

The 11 September Aftermath.

The aftermath of the 11 September events continued. A joint House of Representatives and Senate intelligence committee report on 24 July said that both the CIA and FBI had failed to take warnings of an imminent al-Qaeda attack seriously. President Bush refused to allow publication of a section of the report accusing Saudi Arabia of helping the terrorists. On 8 May the Republicans withdrew their demand for the Patriot Act, due to expire in 2005, to be made permanent. However, the Justice Department reported in July that the Act had led to widespread civil rights abuses.

The Tax Cuts Programme.

President Bush succeeded in his tax cuts programme, though with some modification. On 21 May the House of Representatives and the Senate approved a $350 billion cut over ten years (President Bush had originally sought $726 billion), with the greatest benefits going to the wealthy through dividend and capital gains reductions. There were also increases in the child tax credit. On 27 June Congress approved a $400 billion expansion in spending on Medicare. Democrats had opposed the programme, which would be run by private insurers with a government subsidy.

It became clear that the country was paying the price for the Iraq war, homeland security and an economic downturn when on 15 July the White House predicted a $455 billion federal budget deficit for the year. By January 2004 the projected deficit had increased to $520 billion, angering Republicans already dissatisfied with the administration's wavering economic record. Other domestic issues on President Bush's agenda included an end to the ban on research and development of nuclear weapons under five kilotons, agreed by the Senate on 20 May, and a loosening of environmental laws to allow refineries and power plants to modernise without the need to improve pollution controls, announced on 27 August.

Under pressure from the European Union and the World Trade Organisation, on 4 December President Bush removed $2.2 billion tariffs on steel imports imposed in 2002. The administration had been accused of hypocrisy in limiting free trade while advocating it throughout the world.

The California Governorship.

California continued its reputation for political eccentricity when on 7 October Austrian-born film actor Arnold Schwarzenegger ousted Governor Gary Davis in a recall vote. Republican Governor Schwarzenegger, who was sworn in on 17 November, found himself immediately grappling with an apparently intractable state budget deficit.

The 2004 Presidential Elections.

The 'Super Tuesday' primaries on 2 March saw Mr Kerry consolidate his lead for the Democratic nomination as he drove the final rival, Senator John Edwards, out of the race. The growing crisis in Iraq dominated politics, but Mr Kerry appeared unable to capitalise on the issue, remaining neck-and-neck with President Bush in early opinion polls. Mr Ralph Nader's determination to run as an independent could prove dangerous to the Democrats in a close-run contest in November.

Criticisms of Bush.

As the election approached there was much that the electorate could hold against President Bush. Despite signs of economic recovery, there were fewer jobs than at his inauguration in 2001; the value of the dollar had declined dramatically; but the trade deficit had soared to $600 billion; the domestic budget deficit had reached $440 billion. What had been intended as a lightning invasion of Iraq had become a war that, despite the formal handover of power in June, promised to be long drawn out and had become increasingly unpopular. Reports in July and September had been scathing in their analysis of the intelligence on which the invasion had been based.

The Election Outcome.

The November 2004 election results showed an almost evenly divided nation, with Mr Bush taking 58,941,293 votes (51%), giving him 274 Electoral College votes, and Mr Kerry 55,353,453 (48%), 252 Electoral College votes. A deeply polarised electorate gave the Independent candidate, Mr Nader, only 394,578 votes (0·3%). The Republicans gained four seats in the race for the Senate, taking their total to 55, the Democrats losing four to end with 44 seats. Republicans also dominated the House of Representatives. According to one poll the major issues dominating voters' choices had been 'moral values' (22%), the economy and jobs (20%), terrorism (19%) and Iraq (15%), while another suggested that fears of terrorism had been the most significant factor influencing voters. As with Mr Gore in 2000, Mr Kerry failed to take a single southern state.

The Republicans in Control.

President Bush declared that his aim was to unite the country on an agenda of security and prosperity. But his victory would give him the opportunity to reinforce the conservatism of the Supreme Court, opening the way to moves against legal abortion. Republican control of Congress would enable an overhaul of the tax system and the part-privatisation of social security. For the Democrats, the defeat demanded a period of internal debate on the party's values and purpose in the run-up to the 2006 mid-term elections.

The Advent of Condoleezza Rice.

Mr Rumsfeld, despite criticisms over war strategy and of abuses at the Abu Ghraib military prison in Iraq, remained Defense Secretary. Mr Powell was replaced at the State Department by Ms Condoleezza Rice, who was reputedly closer ideologically to President Bush.

The most controversial appointment was that of Mr Alberto Gonzales as Attorney General. Mr

Gonzales had justified torture of suspects in the war on terrorism, describing the Geneva Convention as 'quaint'. President Bush said in an interview in January that the November election victory had been an endorsement of his Iraq policy and that no-one involved in the decision to invade needed to be held accountable.

On 19 January 2005 Ms Rice condemned Cuba, Iran, North Korea, Zimbabwe, Burma and Belarus as 'outposts of tyranny' where the United States should bring freedom. President Bush's inauguration speech underlined his continuing determination to advance (but not necessarily impose) the United States' interpretation of liberty throughout the world. On 25 January the White House confirmed it intended to seek an extra $80 billion for operations in Iraq and Afghanistan from Congress, bringing spending on the war since 11 September 2001 to $300 billion.

The Second Term Agenda.

President Bush's State of the Union message on 2 February continued Ms Rice's theme. He warned Syria to end all support for terrorists and alleged that Iran was the world's 'primary sponsor of terrorism', calling on the Iranian people to stand up to the clerical regime. Despite what he saw as successful Iraqi elections, he refused to give a timetable for an end to the occupation. President Bush said a Middle East peace based on an independent Palestinian state was within reach and promised $350 million aid to the Palestinians. Domestically, President Bush stressed his determination to part-privatise the Federal pension system (though it now appeared that some Republicans would resist this) and promised to support a constitutional amendment banning gay marriage 'for the good of families, children and society'.

The 2005 Budget.

President Bush's $2,500 billion budget, which he put to Congress on 7 February, sought to confront the soaring deficit through, as had been expected, social security cuts, while increasing spending on defence and homeland security. Opponents promised strong resistance as the Senate Democratic leader contrasted reductions in benefits to the poor with tax cuts for the rich. President Bush was also expected to seek a further $80 billion for military operations in Afghanistan and Iraq.

Restoring Relations with Europe.

President Bush and Secretary of State Rice made what were seen as concerted efforts in February to restore relations with the European states that had opposed the attack on Iraq. Commentators differed over whether the United States was attempting to acknowledge the primacy of diplomacy or clearing the ground for future moves against Syria or Iran. There was, nonetheless, a general welcome for President Bush's new involvement with the Middle East peace process and his decisive backing for a Palestinian state. However, some ambiguity remained in the administration's international policy.

Disillusion with Bush.

Within months of the 2004 victory, President Bush's political capital appeared to be ebbing away as opinion polls reflected growing doubts about the war in Iraq, where the number of American dead reached 2,000 in the course of the year. The call by a respected Republican Representative on 17 November for an immediate withdrawal from Iraq was seen by many as an expression of the views of the senior officer class. President Bush remained confident, declaring in November that 'complete victory' remained the objective. But he could take little comfort from another foreign policy area, Latin America, where elections showed a significant shift to the centre-left. In November President Bush's hopes of constructing a Free Trade Area of the Americas were thwarted as several Latin American governments expressed concern over the possible effect on their economies, challenging the long-term trend of compliance with the wishes of the United States.

The Aftermath of Hurricane Katrina.

The administration faced criticism for the handling of a major domestic crisis, the aftermath of Hurricane Katrina, which struck the New Orleans region at the end of August, forcing millions from their homes, provoking a breakdown in order and revealing stark racial divisions. On 15 September President Bush accepted responsibility for a lack of preparedness, promising reconstruction and an improvement in social conditions and employment. Little progress appeared to have been made by early 2006. President Bush's attempts to fill Supreme Court vacancies drew attacks from his conservative base as well as liberals. He also failed to win the argument over his core policy of privatising the social security pension scheme and faced growing dissatisfaction as fuel prices soared.

Abuse of Power Allegations.

Accusations of corruption and abuse of power against prominent Republicans further undermined the administration. There were charges that re-building contracts in New Orleans had gone to companies with government connections. In September the Securities and Exchange Commission began investigating alleged insider trading involving the Senate majority leader. In the same month the House of Representatives majority leader resigned following indictment for alleged breach of election finance laws. In October Vice President Cheney's chief of staff was charged with perjury and obstruction of justice in a case involving the politically-motivated leak of a CIA officer's identity. Karl Rove, President Bush's chief adviser, was also alleged to have been implicated. In December a Republican member of the House of Representatives resigned after admitting accepting a $2·4 million bribe.

Recent Events.

The November 2005 elections saw a swing against Republicans as Democrats captured the governorships of Virginia and New Jersey. Opinion polls gave President Bush a new low of 36% in popular backing, with two thirds disapproving his Iraq policy and a majority believing the administration had manipulated intelligence to take the country to war.

On 18 December President Bush admitted that he had authorised covert wiretapping in the wake of the 2001 terrorist attacks. This followed widespread concerns over the policy of 'extraordinary rendition', with allegations that the United States exported terrorist suspects for interrogation under torture. As political pressure mounted and Democrat criticism of the administration's Iraq policy became more vigorous, Defense Secretary Rumsfeld suggested that troop levels could be reduced in 2006.

In his State of the Union message on 31 January 2006 President Bush warned that the United States must break what he called its addiction to oil and reduce the reliance on imports from the Middle East. He offered friendship to a free Iran, which he said was now held hostage by a repressive clerical elite and appealed to Hamas, victors in the Palestinian elections, to recognise Israel and reject terrorism. He insisted that the American-led coalition was winning the war in Iraq and rejected a hasty withdrawal.

CANADA

1867	Dominion of Canada established.
1931	Canada gains autonomy under Statute of Westminster.
1949	Founding member of NATO.
1964	New flag adopted as national sentiment grows.
1967	French President de Gaulle declares '*Vive le Quebec libre*' (Long live free Quebec).
1968	Liberal Pierre Trudeau becomes prime minister; *Parti Quebecois* (PQ) formed to campaign for Quebec independence.
1970	Quebec separatists kidnap British official.
1976	PQ wins elections in Quebec.
1980	Referendum rejects Quebec's independence.
1984	Progressive Conservative Mulroney becomes prime minister.
1992	Negotiations with US and Mexico on a North American Free Trade Agreement (NAFTA).
1993	Mulroney succeeded by Kim Campbell,

Canada's first female prime minister; NAFTA treaty ratified; Liberal Jean Chrétien becomes prime minister following elections.
1995 Quebec referendum narrowly rejects independence.
1997 Chrétien returned with reduced majority.
2000 Chrétien re-elected prime minister.

The June 2004 Elections.

Despite unanticipated political difficulties in the Spring of 2004 resulting from the so-called 'sponsorship scandal' concerning the award of contracts to politically supportive advertising agencies for work that was not actually done, Paul Martin led the Liberals to victory in the federal elections of 28 June. The results were as follows:

Party	Seats	Leader
Bloc Québécois	54	Gilles Duceppe
Conservative Party	98	Stephen Harper
Liberal Party	135	Paul Martin
NDP	20	Jack Layton
Other	1	na

Election Analysis.

Although their national popular vote fell by only four points from the election in 2000, the Liberals very nearly lost in 2004. Indeed, the result was the closest federal election in Canada in twenty-five years and obliges Prime Minister Martin to govern carefully. Of the four parties, however, only the Liberals have national presence. Its basis in cultural identity being both its greatest strength and greatest weakness, the Bloc Québécois is confined to a single province; the NDP's support lies primarily in British Columbia, Manitoba, and Ontario; whilst the newly-merged Conservatives' strength is ever more focused upon the western provinces.
Opposition divisions and vulnerabilities are the Prime Minister's greatest asset. After his reelection, he showed political imagination in reforming health care on politically consensual terms helpful to him. An early general election remains possible, but risky. Despite needing votes from elsewhere in the House of Commons for key legislation, the Liberals might well survive in government for some time without an overall majority.

The End of Liberal Rule.

Buffeted by corruption allegations, the Liberal government lost a no confidence vote by 171-133 on 28 November. In the ensuing general election campaign, an early opinion poll lead for the Liberals disappeared with reports that police were investigating new accusations of irregular finances involving the party. On 23 January 2006 12 years of Liberal rule ended, with the Conservatives, led by Stephen Harper, taking 124 seats, Mr Martin's Liberals 103, the Bloc Québécois 51, the New Democrats 29 and Independents one seat. Lacking an overall majority, Mr Harper was sworn in as leader of a minority government on 6 February.

LATIN AMERICA

Chronology of Recent Events.

1929 National Revolutionary Party (later the Institutional Revolutionary Party—PRI) formed in Mexico; retains power for 70 years.
1934 Mexican President Carderas introduces radical reform programme.
1937 Getulio Vargas seizes power in Brazil with military support; institutes authoritarian reformist regime.
1943 Military coup in Argentina; Brazil joins Allies in World War Two.
1945 Argentina declares war on Germany and Japan; Vargas ousted in Brazil.
1946 Peron elected Argentine president; re-elected in 1951.
1951 Former dictator Vargas elected Brazilian president.
1955 Military coup ousts Argentine President Peron.
1956 Period of economic growth in Brazil begins under President Kubitschek.
1959 Fidel Castro takes power in Cuban revolution.

1961 US backs Bay of Pigs invasion of Cuba; Cuba allies with USSR.
1964 Brazilian left-wing President Goulart ousted by military.
1966 General Ongania imposes military rule in Argentina.
1968 Student demonstrations violently suppressed in Mexico City.
1970 Allende becomes world's first democratically elected Marxist president in Chile; begins reform programme.
1973 General Pinochet ousts Allende in CIA-backed coup; establishes a dictatorship.
1974 Limited political activity restored to Brazil by President Geisel.
1976 General Videla seizes power in Argentina; regime wages 'Dirty War' against opponents.
1981 General Galtieri leads military coup in Argentina.
1982 Argentina invades Falklands (Malvinas); ejected by Britain.
1983 Civilian rule restored in Argentina.
1985 Neves elected as first civilian president in Brazil since 1964.
1988 New Brazilian constitution reduces presidential powers.
1989 Argentine President Menem introduces austerity programme; re-elected in 1995.
1993 Mexico joins Canada and US in North American Free Trade Agreement (NAFTA); Cuba introduces market reforms.
1994 Zapatista National Liberation Army (EZLN) rising begins in Mexico; Cardoso elected Brazilian president on pledge to stem inflation and introduce land reform.
1996 US trade embargo on Cuba made permanent.
1997 PRI loses parliamentary majority in Mexican elections.
1999 Centre-left President de la Rua elected in Argentina faces economic problems; Brazilian President Cardoso elected for a second term.
2000 PRI ousted in Mexican elections: Alliance for Change leader Fox becomes president; demonstrations and strikes in Argentina; indigenous population mounts protests at Brazil's 500th anniversary celebrations.
2001 Chilean court suspends human rights charges against Pinochet on health grounds. Left-wing Alejandro Toledo elected as President of Peru.
2002 Colombia elects centre-right Alvaro Uribe as President; Ecuador elects left-wing government of Lucio Gutierrez; Brazil elects left-wing President Ignacio Lula da Silva.
2003 Centre-right Carlos Mesa becomes Bolivian President; Nicanor Duarte Frutos elected centre-right President of Paraguay; centre-left Ricardo Lagos elected in Chile.
2004 Centre-left President Tabare Vazquez elected in Uruguay.

ARGENTINA.

Growing Economic Problems.

In March 2001 pressures on the country's economy forced a political crisis as left-wing ministers resigned in protest against an austerity package presented by the economy minister. The measures included a three year programme of spending cuts totalling $8 billion which, opponents said, would particularly harm the working class. President de la Rua met the crisis by forming a government of national unity and sought emergency powers on 19 March.
On 3 June the government announced it was partially deferring payment of the country's $128 billion debt. The economics minister, Domingo Cavallo, promised further reductions in public spending, including salaries and budgets, provoking a general strike in mid-July that brought Argentina to a standstill. The strike, significantly, was supported by some members of the governing coalition. Nevertheless, legislation was passed on 30 July reducing public salaries and pensions by up to 13%.

The Political Crisis Mounts.

As concern spread about the possible effect of Argentina's financial crisis on her neighbours, the issue dominated the Rio Group of Latin American leaders conference on 18 August. Four days later the International Monetary Fund (IMF) agreed to a

$8 billion loan, with conditions attached. As the country faced heavy loan repayments, President de la Rua's position was further weakened when elections in October gave the opposition Peronists control of the Chamber of Deputies and the Senate. In November President de la Rua met US President Bush in what would prove to be a fruitless attempt to avoid economic collapse. On 2 November President de la Rua announced a debt restructuring which was, effectively, a default on payment.

On 1 December Mr Cavallo imposed restrictions on withdrawals to prevent what was increasingly becoming a run on the banks. But the crisis deepened as on 5 December the IMF announced it would not be making that month's aid payment. As unemployment reached over 18%, public workers mounted another general strike on 13 December. The government's announcement on 18 December of a budget for 2002 including 20% spending reductions provoked rioting that led to the declaration of a state of siege.

On 20 December President de la Rua gave up the struggle, handing temporary power to Ramon Puerta. On 23 December Adolfo Rodriguez Saa, a Peronist, was sworn in as president but, failing to win support for proposed economic reforms and facing renewed street protests, he resigned on 30 December. Ramon Puerta resumed office, to be followed in rapid succession by Eduardo Camano and then, on 1 January 2002, by the Peronist former vice president Eduardo Duhalde, whom Mr de la Rua had defeated in the 1999 elections.

Declaration of Bankruptcy.

The country's debts now totalled $141 billion and on 2 January President Duhalde declared the country bankrupt, devalued the peso by 30% and blamed the free market policies of former President Menem for having destroyed the middle class and thrown millions into poverty. But demonstrations continued, with demands for fresh elections.

In the face of President Duhalde's criticisms of the disastrous effect for Argentina of policies it had imposed, the IMF declared on 11 January 2002 that it would offer no further aid until the government had formulated what it called a 'coherent' recovery programme. But at the end of the month the government faced renewed street protests.

On 3 February the government announced new measures to rescue the country's economy. As banks remained closed—despite a court ruling that this was unconstitutional—and trade union leaders called for renewed protests, President Duhalde announced that elections would be held on 14 September 2003. By April 2002 all banking and foreign exchange activity had come to a halt as President Duhalde admitted that Argentina's financial system was on the brink of collapse. Protests among the unemployed grew and in July two people were killed in violent demonstrations in Buenos Aires against the government and the International Monetary Fund (IMF). Under such rising pressure, President Duhalde announced that he was bringing elections forward from September to March 2003.

Government Frustration.

Against a background of over 20% unemployment and with half the population living below the poverty line, President Duhalde admitted that his government could do little more than tinker with an apparently unworkable system. In October it appeared unlikely that the IMF would resume aid withdrawn in December 2001 because of the government's inability to secure support for reform. On 14 November the government announced that Argentina would default on its World Bank debts, making only a token $79 million interest payment on the $805 million due. Finance minister Roberto Lavagna warned on 21 November that Argentina would be bankrupt by May 2003 without outside aid, although he said that production, having fallen by 15%, was showing signs of growth.

Developments in 2003.

The situation appeared more hopeful by mid-January 2003 as Argentina appeared close to an agreement with the IMF over the country's foreign debt. With around $5 billion due to be repaid in June, there were reports of an IMF offer to provide a three year breathing space if Argentina's eco-

nomic performance proved satisfactory over the next six months. There were signs of revival, with growth over three consecutive quarters and inflation under control.

The Advent of Nestor Kirchner.

Despite having a substantial lead over the Peronist candidate Nestor Kirchner in the first round of the presidential elections, Mr Menem abruptly withdrew on 15 May. Polls had made it clear that the former president stood little chance in the run-off due for 18 May and his departure left the way open for Mr Kirchner. The latter had promised rigorous reforms in his approach, with the judicial system and the armed forces as particular targets. He had pledged a repeal of the amnesty against prosecution for human rights abuses during the 'dirty war' conducted by the military dictatorship of 1976–83. On 25 July Mr Kirchner revoked a decree banning extradition of army officers. In August both Congress and the Senate voted to end the protection they had enjoyed from prosecution in Argentina.

The IMF Agreement.

There was some alleviation in the country's long-running financial crisis when, after having defaulted on a $3 billion loan repayment on 9 September, the government reached agreement the following day with the International Monetary Fund (IMF) on refinancing the total debt of $12.3 billion. However, in November Argentina defaulted on a further $800 repayment after the IMF had refused to grant further aid. The World Bank declared the country ineligible for new loans.

Developments in 2004.

The effects of Argentina's 2001 debt default continued to reverberate in 2004. An International Monetary Fund (IMF) report in July admitted that the role the fund had played had worsened the country's economic crisis but went on to blame the government for the default. President Kirchner blamed IMF policies for pushing 15 million people in Argentina into poverty. However, unemployment had fallen to below 13% from a high of 20%. On a state visit to Argentina in November, the Chinese president, Hu Jintao, promised increased trade and investment of over £11 billion over the coming decade.

The Return of Menem.

Former President Menem returned from his self-imposed exile in Chile in December after two international arrest warrants issued by a judge in April were cancelled. Mr Menem, whose period in office from 1989-99 had been marked by widespread corruption, still faced questioning about tax fraud and embezzlement but said he planned to stand in the 2007 presidential elections.

On 13 January 2005 the economy minister, Mr Lavagna, announced a proposed restructuring of the $103 billion debt to private creditors, offering to issue new bonds worth $42 billion. The government claimed this was the maximum the country could pay without triggering further economic problems.

Recent Developments.

In March 2005 President Kirchner said that restructuring of the country's debt had been a success and offered to exchange over $100 billion in defaulted bonds. President Kirchner saw some success in legislative elections held in October as his allies took 40 of the 72 Senate seats. However, with under a hundred seats in the lower house, his supporters failed to gain a majority, though they formed the largest single bloc. In November President Kirchner met President Chavez to discuss Venezuela's forthcoming entry into the Mercosur trade bloc. The two proposed the formation of a Latin American Investment Fund as a preliminary to an eventual South American Union. The Economy Minister credited with leading the country out of the 2002 recession, Roberto Lavagna, was replaced by Felisa Miceli in a cabinet reshuffle in November. In mid-December the government announced that it would pay a $10 billion debt to the International Monetary Fund three years early, saving $1 billion in annual interest payments.

BRAZIL.

Presidential Election Background.

As presidential elections approached in 2002 it was clear that however popular President Cardoso had been for bringing almost a decade of stability to what had once been a military dictatorship, his free market reforms had failed to bring prosperity. There were massive disparities in wealth distribution, with over a quarter of Brazilians living in poverty. The country was almost paralysed by debt and the currency was under pressure. In March Landless Peasant Movement members, angry at the slow pace of land reform, occupied President Cardoso's ranch. In July the country's currency reached a new low as financial markets feared a defeat of the centre-right in the coming elections.

The Triumph of Lula.

At the election in October the Workers' Party candidate, former metalworker Luiz Inacio Lula da Silva (popularly known as 'Lula') took 61% of the vote against Jose Serra, candidate of the ruling Brazilian Social Democratic Party. Mr da Silva was the first left-wing president elected since before the 1964-85 military dictatorship. He faced a difficult balancing act, promising to transform the lives of the poor, reform education and reduce corruption while at the same time meeting International Monetary Fund targets and not defaulting on the country's foreign debt. In the period before his inauguration on 2 January 2003 Mr da Silva constructed a diverse cabinet, including three Workers' Party ministers and the first black woman cabinet member. In his inaugural address, he promised that ending hunger would be his primary goal but appealed for consensus.

New Priorities in 2003.

On 4 January the government announced suspension of a $1 billion purchase of military aircraft to allow greater spending on its social programme. This was followed by President da Silva's announcement that his government intended to reform Brazil's expensive pensions system. Meanwhile, the currency had strengthened as it became clear that the new government remained committed to financial austerity.

Economic and Fiscal Austerity.

Elected on a pledge to improve the position of the poor through expanded social services, President da Silva made it clear from the beginning that fiscal austerity would be required to secure economic advance. His first target was to be the public sector pension scheme, operating with an annual $20 billion deficit. Legislation backing reform was approved in July and polls in August suggested he retained the support of the majority of the population.

At the end of June President da Silva met US President Bush in Washington, where both agreed on the need to conclude negotiations on the Free Trade Area of the Americas. President da Silva also made a week-long visit to five countries in Africa to underline Brazil's intention to mount an international campaign against poverty and hunger.

Growing Opposition.

But opposition appeared to be growing against the government's reform programme. In the months after his election the currency had increased 22% in value, the stock market thrived and interest rates fell in what was clearly a honeymoon. At the end of July, however, the strains were beginning to show as the currency and the market responded to growing public sector opposition to pensions reform and rising anger from the Landless Workers Movement, with its leader calling for a battle against the country's largest landowners. Unemployed urban workers began occupations of empty industrial plants. As public sector workers opened a campaign of strikes against pension reforms, President da Silva said the success of his government depended on carrying the changes through.

Free Trade Area of the Americas.

In January 2004 Brazil attended the Americas summit in Mexico at which there was agreement on establishing a Free Trade Area of the Americas by 2005, a demand made by the United States. Brazil had initially opposed the demand, with Venezuela. The final statement included at their insistence a commitment to promote development and combat poverty.

Renewed Land Occupations.

In April Landless Workers' Movement (MST) activists mounted a wave of farm occupations to force the government to keep to election promises of land reform. On 3 July President Luiz Inacio Lula da Silva (Lula) told the movement's leaders he remained committed to reform and called for patience. The MST demanded the settlement of a million landless people by 2006. In January 2005 the government admitted that only 81,000 families had been settled on land, far short of the 115,000 target.

Recent Developments.

In July 2004 there were demonstrations in the cities against the government's continuing conservative economic policy. As unemployment fell opinion polls suggested a majority of Brazilians supported President Lula's position. However, elections gave mixed messages. In the first round on 3 October his Workers' Party (PT) took most votes and controlled more cities than any other party. But there were significant losses in the second round on 31 October.

On a state visit in November China's President Hu Jintao offered up to £7 billion investment to improve the country's infrastructure, as well as guaranteeing greater access for Brazil's agricultural produce to the Chinese market. At the end of the month President Putin of Russia promised co-operation in Brazil's space programme, nuclear co-operation and trade development.

New Political Difficulties.

As 2004 ended President Lula faced problems as two allies, the Popular Socialist Party and the Brazilian Democratic Movement Party, withdrew from the governing coalition, with the latter threatening to field their own presidential candidate in elections due in 2006.

Pro-Market Reform Programme.

President Lula continued with pro-market reforms that, despite the introduction of a basic income for the poor, disappointed many of his followers. The public pensions system was partially privatised and public sector pensions cut. The 1988 constitution was amended to allow the establishment of an independent bank with control over interest rates. President Lula had prevented a substantial increase in the minimum wage. In May 2005 12,000 supporters of the Movement of Landless Rural Workers (MST) protested in Brasilia at the slow pace of land reform. President Lula had pledged to give land to over 400,000 families in his four-year term but the government admitted that less than 120,000 had been assisted.

Corruption Scandals.

President Lula promised on 7 June that his campaign against corruption would continue but on 16 June his chief of staff resigned following accusations of bribing political parties to join the Workers' Party alliance in Congress. A wave of resignations followed, including that of the party's leader. Although not directly implicated in the scandal, President Lula's popularity went into decline. In August the Workers' Party campaign manager admitted the party had used illegal money to finance the 2002 campaign. President Lula apologised and declared he would act firmly against all allegations but would press on with his reform programme, despite growing party divisions. In October Congress began hearings to expel 11 deputies involved in the vote-buying scandal. President Lula's former chief of staff, Jose Dirceu, was expelled on 1 December, despite his denials that there had been such a scheme. But in the face of continuing scandal the re-election of President Lula in elections due in October 2006 seemed increasingly doubtful.

VENEZUELA.

As 2003 opened, the position of the anti-globalist President Hugo Chavez seemed precarious. First elected in 1998, President Chavez won a further six years in power in 2000. In the course of a year his government passed 49 laws under powers enabling the National Assembly to be by-passed. President Chavez said the laws were intended to help the country's poor. But on 11 December 2001 millions demonstrated in the capital Caracas against the government's economic reforms, particularly a law allowing expropriation of large estates. His popularity had fallen from 80% to 30% in opinion polls. In February 2002 the currency lost a quarter of its value against the United States dollar following the end of exchange controls. President Chavez's appointment at the end of the month of a new board to the state oil monopoly met with opposition from managers who, with trade unions, called a general strike on 9 April. In ensuing clashes over 10 people died and armed forces commanders demanded his resignation.

The Renewed Crisis.

President Chavez resigned on 12 April and was placed in military custody. However, following mass demonstrations and the collapse of a military appointed interim government, President Chavez returned to office on 14 April. In October President Chavez said another plot to overthrow him had been discovered. A national strike demanded that he called early elections while senior military officers called for a civil disobedience campaign to oust him. An oil strike began in December 2002 to force his resignation. President Chavez, who had attacked the old political establishment and the Church, had proved incapable of narrowing the gap between rich and poor. On 10 January 2003 there were reports a group of 'friends of Venezuela' including Brazil, Mexico and Chile would attempt to defuse the crisis by developing proposals for early elections.

Internal Political Developments.

Anti-Chavez demonstrations continued, with clashes between the president's opponents and supporters. But in February 2003 the nine-week general strike was abandoned as the opposition proposed a recall referendum. President Chavez's claim in March that oil production was rising in the aftermath of the strike was rejected by the opposition. Oil provided over half of the government's revenues. In May the government and opposition appeared to have agreed to an Organisation of American States referendum plan. With President Chavez's poll support standing at 34%, the opposition delivered a 3·2 million signature petition backing the referendum in August, which the national election board rejected in September.

Popularity of Social Reform Programme.

President Chavez's popularity among the poor, who had benefited from his social reforms, remained solid and they feared the opposition would reverse them. On 2 December opposition leaders claimed to have collected over 3·6 million signatures. President Chavez accused them of irregularities. At the end of the month a leading Catholic accused the government of interfering in church affairs. In the past President Chavez had charged the Catholic hierarchy with backing the wealthy.

Tension was heightened when in January 2004 the United States warned of a possible terrorist attack on American interests in the capital, Caracas. President Chavez attended the Americas summit in Mexico in January 2004 at which there was agreement on establishing a free trade area throughout the continent by 2005, a demand made by the United States. A loose timetable had been agreed and President Chavez said this had been a victory for the free trade area's opponents in South America.

The 2004 Referendum.

On 10 February 2004 President Chavez devalued the peso, raising the revenue from oil but increasing inflation. The move came as the National Electoral Council was deciding whether sufficient signatures had been collected to force a referendum on President Chavez's continuation in office. The Council's rejection of thousands of signatures in March triggered demonstrations in which several people were killed. In June the Council ruled there were sufficient signatures. In a referendum on 15 August President Chavez survived by 57% to 42%. The Organisation of American States dismissed opposition charges of irregularities in the vote.

Land Reform Decree.

On 14 October eight civilians involved in the failed April 2002 coup against President Chavez were sentenced to terms of imprisonment. President Chavez had said that the coup had been encouraged by the United States. In 2002 the country's Supreme Court had ruled that there was insufficient evidence to try senior military officers allegedly involved in the attempt.

With his position strengthened by the referendum result, President Chavez signed a land reform decree on 11 January 2005, setting up a national land commission to break up large estates gradually and press forward with redistribution. Large landowners responded by threatening legal action against President Chavez.

A New Socialism?

President Chavez continued with what he described as 'socialism of the 21st century', pressing for greater involvement of workers in management in both the public and private sectors. In July 2005 President Chavez threatened to confiscate inactive private firms and to transform them into worker-controlled co-operatives. President Chavez's policies, and his close links with Cuba and Iran, attracted continuing criticism from the United States, which feared his growing influence in Latin America, strengthened by high oil prices. He warned in July, and again in October, that the United States might invade and called on Venezuelans to join a newly established militia.

Growing Anti-Americanism.

In the wake of Hurricane Katrina, President Chavez angered the United States government by providing aid to the victims of the crisis that followed the disaster. On 20 November thousands of Venezuelans demonstrated against the economic policies of President Bush and President Fox of Mexico, particularly attempts to establish a Free Trade of the Americas. President Chavez's accusation that President Fox was a lapdog of the United States led to a withdrawal of ambassadors by both countries. Venezuela and Spain concluded a $2 billion arms deal at the end of the month in the face of criticisms by the United States. President Chavez said the equipment was needed to deal with drug smuggling from neighbouring Colombia.

Recent Events.

Three opposition parties, including the main Democratic Action, announced on 29 November that they would boycott elections to an enlarged Congress. President Chavez's allies went on to take all 167 seats in December, giving the two-thirds majority required to amend the constitution. In February 2006 President Chavez warned again of the danger of invasion and responded to criticisms from British prime minister Blair by calling him a 'pawn of imperialism'.

AUSTRALASIA

AUSTRALIA.

Chronology of Key Events.

1901 Commonwealth of Australia established, unifying the country.

1931 Labour government defeated.
1941 War in Pacific closens relationship with United States.
1948 Australia encourages European immigration; over two million arrive in next three decades.
1950 Australian troops join UN force in Korean War.
1965 Australia sends troops to support US in Vietnam War.
1967 Aborigines given full citizenship following referendum.
1975 Dismissal of Whitlam's Labour government by governor-general calls relationship with Britain into question.
1986 Australian law becomes independent of British legal and parliamentary system under Australia Act.
1992 Citizenship Act removes obligation to swear oath of allegiance to British Crown.
1993 Labour wins elections under Keating; Native Title Act grants Aborigines compensation for lost land.
1996 Liberals form coalition with National Party under Howard.
1998 Liberal-National coalition re-elected with reduced majority; constitutional convention votes to replace monarchy with president elected by Parliament.
1999 Referendum vote to retain monarchy by 55 % to 45 %.
2000 Accused by UN human rights committee of discriminating against Aborigines.
2001 Howard re-elected in November elections.

The 2002 Bali Bombing.

The country suffered what the media called Australia's '11 September' when 89 of its citizens were killed in the terrorist bombing of a night-club in Bali, Indonesia, on 12 October. There were fears that an attack on Australia was imminent. Mr Howard, the prime minister, responded on 2 December by declaring his preparedness to take pre-emptive action against terrorists harboured in neighbouring countries. Indonesia, Thailand and the Philippines declared that such attacks would be contrary to international law.

Aboriginal Land Rights.

Aboriginal hopes that the government's recognition of their land rights in 1994 might bear fruit were undermined by a court judgment on 12 December that a group of Aboriginal people had no rights to the land from which their ancestors had been expelled in the 19th century. An Aboriginal spokesman said this was another example of 'white Australia' denying them their rights. There had been one successful case in September but a number of others had failed.

As 2003 opened there were further riots in asylum seekers' detention centres, causing over £2 million damage. Over 30 asylum seekers were imprisoned without charge as a result. The immigration minister blamed refugee support groups for encouraging disturbances.

Australia and Iraq.

In January 2003, despite public protests, the government moved troops to the Gulf in preparation for war in Iraq. As demonstrations mounted, the Senate passed a no confidence motion against the prime minister, Mr Howard, over his stance on Iraq. In the event, 2,000 Australian troops saw action in Iraq, with no casualties. Despite an opinion poll in July saying that two thirds of Australians believed the government had misled them over the war in Iraq, Mr Howard's personal standing remained firm with 65 % preferring him to 20 % for Labor opposition leader Mr Crean.

Developments in 2003.

The government's despatch of a 2,000 peacekeeping force in July to the Solomon Islands, which had degenerated into civil war, was greeted with strong local support and backed by New Zealand and Fiji. On 29 September Mr Howard carried out a major cabinet reshuffle, promoting the controversial immigration minister, Mr Ruddock, to attorney general. In June Mr Crean had beaten off a challenge from former leader Mr Beazley, but his

reprieve was short-lived. Growing unpopularity forced his resignation in November and on 2 December Mark Latham defeated Mr Beazley for the leadership by 47 votes to 45.

Intelligence Service Criticisms.

In March 2004 a parliamentary committee cleared the government of having lied about the threat posed by weapons of mass destruction in Iraq, against the background of the war's continuing unpopularity. In July a further report criticised the intelligence services for failings over Iraq and the Bali bombing, but rejected suggestions that the government had manipulated intelligence about Iraq.

The October 2004 Elections.

Following the announcement that Australia intended to pursue a missile programme to strengthen the country's defences, Mr Howard called elections for 9 October. Winning a fourth term for Mr Howard, the Liberal-led coalition returned with an increased parliamentary majority and control of the Senate. The extent of Labor's defeat led to criticism of the campaign mounted by the party's leader, Mr Latham. Mr Howard said that his key priorities were economic growth and national security. Mr Latham resigned as Labor leader on health grounds on 18 January 2005. He was succeeded by Mr Kim Beazley, who had led Labor to general election defeats in 1998 and 2001.

Diplomatic Agreements.

Mr Howard announced on 22 February 2005 that Australia would send a further 450 troops to Iraq. The year saw a round of international agreements. On 1 April Australia and NATO agreed on co-operation against terrorism and weapons proliferation. On 4 April a partnership agreement was signed with Indonesia as a preliminary to a new security treaty. President Yudhoyono and Mr Howard also agreed on economic and trade co-operation. Mr Howard and the president of Malaysia announced a proposed free trade agreement on 7 April. Mr Howard announced while visiting China that both countries would be negotiating a free trade agreement. On 28 July Australia, China, India, Japan, South Korea and the United States agreed on the establishment of an Asia-Pacific Partnership on Clean Development and Climate.

Recent Events.

The government announced in August that officials would be visiting European cities to encourage up to 20,000 skilled workers to immigrate. Clashes on beaches between white Australians and the Lebanese community in Sydney in December threatened a summer of racial tension.

NEW ZEALAND.

Chronology of Key Events.

1907 Becomes dominion within British Empire.
1947 Gains full independence from Britain.
1951 Joins Anzus Pacific security treaty with Australia and US.
1984 Labour government elected, prime minister Lange institutes sweeping economic reforms.
1985 Refuses entry to nuclear-powered or armed ships.
1986 US ends obligations under Anzus pact.
1989 Palmer replaces Lange as prime minister.
1990 National Party defeats Labour; Bolger becomes prime minister.
1993 National Party narrowly re-elected; proportional representation introduced.
1997 Shipley becomes first woman prime minister; National Party in coalition with New Zealand First.
1998 Government ordered to return land to its Maoris.
1999 Clark becomes prime minister following Labour election victory.

The 2002 General Election.

On 11 June Ms Clark called an early general election following the splintering of Labour's coalition partner, the Alliance Party. At this stage Labour, with a commanding opinion poll lead over the opposition National Party, campaigned on its successful economic policies and growing public spending. The National Party called for a rebuilding of the country's defences. As the campaign developed both parties lost support to smaller parties. In the election on 7 July Labour took 41 % of the vote, winning 52 seats in the 120 strong parliament, short of an overall majority. The National Party took 21 %, returning with only 27 seats. New Zealand First won 11 %, United Future 7 %, the Greens 6 % and the Progressive Coalition 2 %. Ms Clark went on to form a minority coalition government with the Progressive Coalition, counting for survival on United Future support in parliamentary votes.

Developments in 2003.

On 29 June 2003 the government declared its support for Australian proposals to deploy a peace-keeping force in the Solomon Islands and offered to provide 200 troops.

In August the Human Rights Commission reported that 70 % of the population believed Asian immigrants faced discrimination. Over the previous two decades over 200,000 Asians had entered the country. The right-wing New Zealand First Party, the third largest party, launched an anti-immigration campaign in December, calling for cuts in welfare payments to refugees and immigrants. The government, which had announced a pro-gramme to help immigrants find work, criticised the campaign, declaring that most immigrants made a positive contribution to the country. Meanwhile, a visit by China's President Hu Jintao in October concluded with an agreement to work on an

economic and trade treaty between the two countries.

The No Confidence Vote.

On 4 May 2004 Ms Clark narrowly survived a no confidence vote following a revolt by Maori members of her own Labour Party over proposals to nationalise beaches and the seabed. Maoris said this infringed ancestral rights granted by treaty with Britain in 1840. Ms Clark had already dismissed a minister, Tariana Turia, for her opposition to the proposed legislation.

The Civil Union Act.

Parliament passed controversial legislation on 9 December recognising civil unions between gay couples and between men and women who preferred not to marry. The Civil Union Act was passed by 65 votes to 55 and came into force in April 2005.

The 2005 Election.

In July 2005 Ms Clark called a general election for September, seeking a third successive term for her Labour-led administration. Labour faced a strong challenge from the National Party under Mr Don Brash, with attitudes towards the indigenous Maori population and taxation dominating the campaign. Labour took 50 seats in the 121 seat parliament, with 41 % of the vote, the National Party 49 seats, with 40 %. New Zealand First won seven seats, United Future three, the Maori Party four, with three seats going to two other parties. Ms Clark went on to form a coalition with New Zealand First, the United Future Party and the Progressive Party.

III. SPECIAL TOPICS

THE WAR ON TERRORISM

The Background.

Following the 11 September 2001 attacks, President Bush called for international support in what he described as a 'war on terrorism', a call echoed by prime minister Tony Blair. Osama bin Laden and his al-Qaeda group was accused of responsibility for the outrages. Although the group was said to be world-wide in scope, bin Laden was sheltering in Afghanistan and the Taliban government became the first target. President Bush warned, however, that a long war lay ahead.

Constructing an Alliance.

The initial task was the construction of an alliance against terrorism. Mr Blair was to play a central part in this, to such an extent that critics would suggest he had become the United States' 'foreign secretary'. NATO, for the first time in its 52-year history, invoked Article 5 of its charter, declaring that 11 September was an attack on all 19 member states.

The Role of Pakistan.

If the coming war were not to be seen as a conflict between Islam and the West, the support—or at least the acquiescence—of Muslim states was essential. Pakistan, bordering Afghanistan and the Taliban regime's closest friend, gave its backing in return for an easing of sanctions imposed in 1998 and the rescheduling of debts to the United States. Saudi Arabia and Iran condemned the attacks but refused access to air bases for use against Afghanistan. With the plight of the Palestinians a prime motivation for Islamic anger, there were moves to renew the Middle East process. President Bush and Mr Blair went as far as favouring the creation of a Palestinian state. Russia, too, with its own experience of conflict with Islamic militants, offered support and received concessions in return.

By the end of September the outline of what the United States intended was clear as the European Union was pressed to agree to the overthrow of the Afghan government and its replacement with a

United Nations sponsored administration. What remained less clear was whether the United States proposed actively to engage in a potentially bloody land war to further 'Operation Infinite Justice'.

The Afghan Refugee Crisis.

When it became inevitable their country would be a target, Afghans began fleeing, intensifying a refugee crisis on the borders with Iran and Pakistan and arousing fears of mass starvation among a people dependent on foreign aid. On 7 October the United States and Britain launched what President Bush called 'carefully targeted' bombing attacks on Kabul, the Taliban stronghold of Kandahar and al-Qaeda training camps. As the Taliban said the attacks had been ineffective and vowed to fight to the death, commentators warned that a land offensive could drag the United States into another Vietnam quagmire. The United States had so far deployed minimal special forces in Afghanistan.

The Northern Alliance.

The bombing campaign gave the opportunity for the opposition Northern Alliance to expand its long running conflict against the Taliban. On 22 October the United States confirmed that the air war was intended to ease the way for the Northern Alliance to overthrow the Taliban, though there appeared some reluctance to accept their occupation of Kabul in the power vacuum that would follow. However, on 25 October US defence secretary, Donald Rumsfeld, admitted the possibility that the war's initial objective—the capture or death of bin Laden —would not be achieved.

Growth of Anti-War Sentiment.

As the bombing continued—and the Taliban claimed increasing civilian casualties—there was a sense of unease about the shape the war was taking. There were the beginnings of an anti-war movement in Europe and the United States. What had been called a new type of war was, some critics said, another version of making the world safe for America's political and financial interests, above all the need for pliant governments in crucial oil-producing areas. Mr Blair pointed to the dangers of a confrontation between Islam and the West as he returned on 1 November from a disappointing mission to secure support in the Middle East. One element of this had been attacks on individual Muslims in the United States and Britain following the 11 September events.

The Taliban Collapse.

But then, to the surprise of many, Taliban power began to unravel. With almost half the country under Northern Alliance control, Herat fell on 12 November, opening the way to the capture of Kabul the following day. Memories were fresh of the last time the Northern Alliance had been in the city in 1996—they had left 50,000 dead as they retreated—and there were concerns about what would follow from their triumph and whether the country would degenerate into conflict between competing factions. Pakistan's General Musharraf declared that the Northern Alliance should have been restrained and called for the deployment of a United Nations peacekeeping force to prevent power falling into their hands.

As opposition advances continued, United Nations sponsored talks began in Bonn on 27 November in an effort to weld the various factions together in an interim government. At stake was billions of dollars in international aid for reconstruction and the establishment of stability in the region. On 5 December the factions reached agreement on the establishment of a 30-member interim executive council.

Developments in 2002.

As 2002 opened questions remained about United States policy. Bombing in the east of the country remained intense, with inevitable civilian casualties. None of al-Qaeda's leaders had been captured or killed. It remained to be seen whether Afghanistan's interim leader, Hamid Karzai, would feel impelled to call for a halt to enable reconstruction to begin. In the longer term, there were concerns about the implications of the 'Bush doctrine', a speech delivered in December in which President Bush suggested that 'rogue states' suspected of possessing weapons of mass destruction useful to terrorists remained open to attack, including Iraq, Iran, Sudan, Libya and North Korea. By late January 2002 there was increasing criticism—muted from governments, vociferous from human rights groups—over the refusal of the United States to accord prisoner of war status to detainees captured in Afghanistan.

The 'Axis of Evil'.

A widening of the war was implicit in President Bush's 29 January 'state of the union' message. Mr Bush denounced what he called an 'axis of evil' which, he said, included North Korea, Iran and Iraq. As accusations mounted that Iraq was still—having expelled United Nations monitors—developing weapons of mass destruction, it appeared by April 2002 that the world was being prepared for an attack on Iraq and the overthrow of Saddam Hussein, despite the threat this posed to the post-September anti-terrorist coalition.

The Problem of Iraq.

The problem facing President Bush was that the war on terrorism and a war against Iraq had no necessary logical connection and some thought the latter would undermine the effectiveness of the former, particularly in its impact on Islamic states. President Bush's original objective had been to hunt down the organisers of 11 September. But by June 2002 the leading al-Qaeda figures remained at large.

Weapons of Mass Destruction.

Attention now moved to the 'weapons of mass destruction' President Bush claimed that Iraq was developing in contravention of the 1990–91 Gulf War ceasefire and that posed a threat to the Middle East, Europe and America He attempted to link the two issues on 1 June by declaring that containment (President Clinton's policy) was not possible when dictators could deliver weapons of mass destruction and supply them to terrorists.

The Doctrine of 'Regime Change'.

Opponents suggested that America's real objective was 'regime change' that would establish a pliable government giving access to Iraq's massive oil reserves and reducing dependence on an increasingly unreliable Saudi Arabia. But there were also fears that ousting Saddam Hussein would lead to a fragmentation of Iraq that would trigger further crises of legitimacy throughout the Middle East.

Military Preparations.

By September, 2002 with an American military build-up under way on Iraq's borders, President Bush appeared more willing to work through the United Nations (UN) than take the unilateral action some allies had warned against. On 12 September he urged the UN to take steps to confront the 'grave and gathering danger' of Iraq. On 16 September Iraq, after earlier refusals, expressed willingness to allow weapons inspectors to return without conditions.

Continuing to attempt to link Iraq with terrorism, with no credible evidence, President Bush alleged on 7 October that al-Qaeda leaders had fled from Afghanistan to Iraq. Congress authorised President Bush on 10 October to use military force against Iraq and his domestic position was considerably strengthened by successes in the November Congressional elections. However, the effectiveness of the war against terrorism had been called into question by bombings in Pakistan and Kenya and the 12 October attack in Bali in which almost 200 people were killed.

UN Resolution 1441.

On 8 November the UN Security Council adopted Resolution 1441. Iraq was to declare all programmes to develop weapons of mass destruction by 9 December. The UN Monitoring, Verification, and Inspection Commission (UNMOVIC) and the International Atomic Energy Agency (IAEA) were to report on the results of their inspections on 27 January 2003. The United States had pressed for a resolution authorising war if Iraq failed to co-operate. France, Russia and China declared that it did not authorise the automatic use of force and that the United States and Britain had confirmed this to be their understanding. Iraq accepted the resolution on 13 November and inspectors were soon in place. On 7 December Iraq provided them with a 12,000 page dossier on the current state of its weapons programmes and declared there were no weapons of mass destruction in the country, but UNMOVIC chairman Hans Blix remained unconvinced.

The Road to War.

As 2003 opened the United States intensified its military presence in the Gulf. By mid-January there were 60,000 American troops in the region. Britain mobilised reservists and placed its forces on alert. There were around 150,000 American and up to 30,000 British troops in the region by the end of February.

The Attack on Iraq.

The American-British coalition attack opened on 20 March with bombing of Baghdad and central Iraq followed by the movement of American and British troops in the far south to secure oil fields and the port of Umm Qasr. France, China and Russia condemned the action. As the Americans moved north towards Baghdad, by-passing obstacles where resistance proved stronger than expected, British troops began a slow campaign to take Iraq's second city of Basra. Forecasts that the Iraqi people would rise against Saddam Hussein and that the regime's collapse would be speedy were confounded, as were fears that Turkey would invade from the north to curb Kurd ambitions. Coalition casualties were low, but many arose from 'friendly fire' incidents, while controversy grew over civilian casualties.

The Overthrow of Saddam Hussein.

On 3 April American forces reached the airport close to the capital and on 6 April Basra fell to

British troops. American forces began their decisive entry into Baghdad on 7 April. The Saddam regime had effectively ended. For recent events in Iraq, *see* C25–6.

Iraq and al-Qaeda.

President Bush declared the successful completion of the invasion of Iraq on 1 May. In the wake of the 11 September 2001 events President Bush had declared a 'war on terrorism', in the course of which Afghanistan and Iraq had been invaded. Afghanistan was attacked for harbouring Osama bin Laden and his al-Qaeda forces. If the move against Iraq had been in the context of a war on terrorism, its justification was less clear-cut. In the weeks leading up to the March invasion President Bush had implied, though was careful not to say directly, that there was a link between Saddam Hussein and 11 September. So successful had this been that on the eve of the war 45 % of Americans believed him to have been 'personally involved'.

The Iraq Aftermath.

Thousands of civilians were killed in the course of military action against Afghanistan and Iraq. In an Afghanistan liberated from the Taliban, the new government's writ hardly extended outside the capital, much of the country had returned to the rule of warlords, opium production had increased and al-Qaeda appeared to be functioning with relative impunity (with bin Laden still at large). In Iraq over 60 % of the population were still subsisting on food aid as 2004 opened, electricity and water supplies remained chaotic (partly through sabotage by those resisting the occupation), unemployment remained high and arguments about a handover of power by the occupying forces continued. An advanced Middle Eastern state, albeit a dictatorship, had become a shattered society. A prime justification for the invasion had been the danger presented by Iraq's 'weapons of mass destruction'. But at the end of January the Central Intelligence Agency's chief weapons investigator said there was no evidence that the regime had been in possession of biological, chemical or nuclear weapons.

The War on Terrorism: An Interim Balance Sheet.

How effective had the campaign against terrorism been? Critics had described the attack on Iraq as a diversion rather than a development. From May to November 2003 al-Qaeda was allegedly involved in terrorist attacks on Western interests in Tunisia, Pakistan, Indonesia, Saudi Arabia and Turkey. Atlantic flights were being cancelled in January 2004 for fear of hi-jacking. Al-Qaeda members were believed to be active in the resistance in Iraq, with the invasion having proved to be an encouragement rather than a deterrent to Islamist militancy. Only the chaos of the occupation of Iraq had, for the moment at least, dissuaded President Bush from following up his July 2003 threat to Syria and Iran about the unacceptability of harbouring and aiding terrorists. By the end of 2003 more United States troops had been killed in Iraq since 1 May than had died in the war itself. In October 2003 the United States Defense Secretary had reportedly noted that there had been 'mixed results' in the campaign against al-Qaeda and that the struggle in Afghanistan and Iraq would be a 'long, hard slog'. Saddam's capture in December was something of an empty triumph. Increasing United States casualties in Iraq in 2004 raised questions about the wisdom of President Bush's actions and the contribution they had made to an effective campaign against international terrorism.

Widespread Torture Allegations.

Evidence that emerged in May 2004 of widespread torture and mistreatment of Iraqi prisoners by American and, to a lesser extent British, forces raised stark questions about the moral basis of the Coalition's continuing occupation. On 16 June the 9/11 Commission in the United States concluded that, contrary to what President Bush had implied, there was nothing to show that Iraq had co-operated with al-Qaeda in terrorist attacks. On 9 July the Senate Intelligence Committee said that there was little, if any, evidence that Iraq had been constructing weapons of mass destruction.

Doubts on Total Victory.

President Bush himself admitted on 30 August that it was unlikely that the United States would ever be completely victorious in the war on terrorism. When Mr Annan, the United Nations secretary general, said on 15 September that the attack on Iraq had been illegal and in violation of the UN Charter, President Bush responded that the war was justified and that Iraq was moving towards stability. But as the January 2005 elections approached, violence in the country was mounting. In September American deaths in Iraq reached 1,000; there were no figures for Iraqi casualties.

Taunts from Bin Laden.

If the attacks on Afghanistan and Iraq had been intended to confront the terrorist threat, President Musharraf of Pakistan (an ally of President Bush) shattered any illusions on 6 December when he declared that Osama bin Laden was no nearer capture than he had been in 2001. He went further, saying that the war on terror had failed to address the causes of terrorism and had made the world a more dangerous place. Bin Laden taunted his enemies by releasing audio and video messages in April and October, the latter an obvious intervention in the United States presidential elections.

"Outposts of Tyranny".

Following the statement by Ms Rice, the incoming Secretary of State, on 19 January 2005 that Cuba, Iran, North Korea, Zimbabwe, Burma and Belarus were 'outposts of tyranny' to which the United States should bring freedom, it remained to be seen what further moves President Bush intended to take.

The continuing terrorist threat was again seen in the July 2005 attacks on London (*see* **C10**).

Renewed Doubts.

By late 2005 some commentators doubted the validity of the concept of a 'war on terrorism'. Indeed, in July 2005 White House officials had suggested re-branding the enterprise as a 'struggle against violent extremism'. The war itself had dominated President Bush's 2004 re-election campaign, but there was nothing to show how victory could be measured and when it might be achieved. While the re-branding exercise was being considered, only 34 % of Americans believed the war was being won. Persistent reports of al-Qaeda leaders being killed or captured, or that terrorist atrocities had been prevented, had an air of unreality.

A Strategy for Victory?

In October 2005 President Bush gave an address in Washington on what he saw as the nature of the enemy and the strategy for victory. He identified the foe as followers of Islamic radicalism, bound together by a shared ideology rather than a centralised command, an ideology that (like Communism) would collapse under its own contradictions. In his view, the United States and its allies were thwarting terrorist attacks before they occurred, denying weapons of mass destruction to outlaw regimes, preventing those regimes (such as Syria and Iran) from giving radical groups sanctuary, and denying terrorists the control of any nation (including Afghanistan, Iraq and Pakistan). President Bush pointed to Iraq's progress towards democracy since 2003 in the face of extremist attacks. He said the militants would be denied further recruits by the advance of democracy across the Middle East, identifying moves towards reform by Egypt and Saudi Arabia as signal successes.

Critics of Bush.

Critics of President Bush's analysis might suggest that anger at the United States' persistent support for Israel, the seizure of Iraq and Afghanistan, and the silence over Chechnya had been all too easy to channel into Islamic radicalism and that the latter was not a project for world domination. Might a reconsideration of America's foreign policy play as great a part in winning the struggle as military engagement? Or would that reconsideration in itself be interpreted as a defeat? A statement by Osama bin Laden broadcast in January 2006 made the latter all too likely. He warned that new attacks on the United States were in preparation but offered a long-term truce in exchange for withdrawal from Iraq and Afghanistan.

MAJOR TERRORIST ACTIONS
(since 11 September 2001)

Most of the actions below have been ascribed to Islamist terrorists, including al-Qaeda, the group responsible for the 11 September 2001 attacks on the United States. It remains open to question whether al-Qaeda is a centrally-directed organisation or a loose coalition of groups sharing a common aim. This chronology does not include the conflict between Israel and the Palestinians or events in Iraq.

2002
(April) 21 killed (including 14 German tourists) in bombing of a synagogue in Tunisia.
(May) 45 killed in bombings in Morocco; 15 killed (11 French) by car bomb in Pakistan.
(June) 12 killed in bombing at United States consulate in Pakistan.
(Oct.) Over 200 (89 of them Australians) killed in nightclub bombings in Bali; 41 died in theatre siege in Russia; one person killed in attack on a French oil tanker.
(Nov.) 15 killed in suicide attack on hotel in Kenya.

2003
(May) 34 killed (including 8 Americans) in suicide bomb attack in Saudi Arabia; 33 killed in bombings in Morocco; 50 killed in Chechnya suicide bombing.
(July) 14 killed by suicide bombers in Russia.
(Aug.) 12 killed in suicide bomb attack in Indonesia.
(Nov.) 17 killed in bombing in Saudi Arabia; 51 killed in bombings of synagogues and British consulate and bank in Turkey.

2004
(Feb.) 116 killed in explosion on ship in Philippines; over 35 killed in metro bombing in Russia.
(March) Over 200 killed in railway bombings in Spain.
(May) 22 killed in bombings of oil company office in Saudi Arabia; seven killed in Chechnya bombing.
(Aug.) Over 300 killed in siege in Russia; 90 killed in terrorist-related aircraft collision over Russia.
(Sept.) Nine killed by car bomb at Australian Embassy in Indonesia.
(Dec.) Nine killed in attack on United States consulate in Saudi Arabia.

2005
(July) Terrorists bomb London, hitting transport links. Worst casualties in UK since Lockerbie.

THE MIDDLE EAST: A NEW ERA?

WAR AND PEACE: A CHRONOLOGY.

1948 State of Israel proclaimed; war between Israel and its Arab neighbours; 700,000 Palestinian Arabs become refugees.
1956 Israel invades Sinai with British and French backing following Egypt's nationalisation of the Suez Canal.
1964 Palestinian Liberation Organisation (PLO) founded; it is reformed under Arafat in 1967.
1967 Israel captures Sinai, the Gaza Strip, the Golan Heights, the West Bank and East Jerusalem during 'Six Day War' against Egypt, Syria and Jordan; United Nations Resolution 242 orders Israel to withdraw from the occupied territories.
1972 Palestinians kill Israeli athletes at the Olympic Games as part of growing terrorist campaign.
1973 Egypt and Syria attack Israel in 'Yom Kippur War' but fail to recapture Sinai and the Golan Heights.
1978 Israel temporarily occupies southern Lebanon to protect her northern frontier; Israel agrees

to return Sinai to Egypt under 'Camp David Accord' between Egypt, Israel and the USA.
1982 Israel invades southern Lebanon to oust PLO guerrillas; Israeli-backed Christian militia in Lebanon massacres Palestinian refugees.
1983 Israel begins a phased withdrawal from most of southern Lebanon.
1987 Palestinian 'intifada' (uprising) mounted against Israeli occupation of the West Bank and Gaza; over 20,000 are killed or wounded.
1988 PLO leader Yasser Arafat renounces terrorism and recognises Israel as a state; US begins discussions with PLO.
1993 Following secret negotiations, the PLO and Israeli prime minister sign a declaration by which Israel recognises the PLO and agrees to give limited Palestinian autonomy in occupied Gaza and the West Bank.
1994 Israel and Jordan sign a peace treaty; Israel and the PLO agree on implementation of the 'Oslo Accords'; Israel will withdraw from 60% of Gaza and the West Bank town of Jericho; there is to be a five year negotiation on further withdrawals and the future of Jerusalem; Arafat becomes head of a new Palestinian National Authority in Gaza.
1995 Palestinian authority is extended over most of the West Bank under the Taba Agreement; Israel begins peace negotiations with Syria; talks are suspended following attacks by Palestinian terrorist group Hamas.
1996 Binyamin Netanyahu, an opponent of concessions, becomes Israeli prime minister; a ban on the construction of further Jewish settlements in Gaza and the West Bank is lifted.
1997 There are renewed terrorist attacks by the Palestinian group Hamas.
1998 Under US pressure, Netanyahu signs the Wye Accord agreeing to further Israeli withdrawals.
1999 Israel suspends the Wye Accord as Netanyahu's coalition splits over implementation; death of King Hussein of Jordan threatens delays; talks resume as Ehud Barak becomes Israeli prime minister and freezes further Jewish settlement around Jerusalem; Barak opens negotiations with Syria.
2000 Renewal of the intifada leads to escalating violence.

Victory for Sharon.

In elections on 6 February 2001, Mr Barak, taking 37·6% of the vote was comprehensively defeated by Mr Sharon, who won 62·4%. A slump in turnout—62% as opposed to over 78% in the 1999 Knesset elections—demonstrated Israeli Arab disenchantment with Labour. A resumption of the peace process remained on hold as Mr Sharon attempted to construct a coalition government. On 8 March he announced a broad but fragile coalition of left, right, ultra-nationalist and religious parties, an alliance that left little hope of rapid progress. Mr Sharon called on Mr Arafat to meet him to renew the peace process, on condition that the intifada was first ended. But there were fears that the turmoil of the past six months was pushing the Palestinian Authority to the point of collapse.

In May, as clashes continued (over 500 had died in the renewed intifada, the majority Palestinians), an international commission chaired by former United States Senator, George Mitchell, proposed a way forward. There was to be an immediate ceasefire, a cooling off period and then renewed negotiations. Mitchell called on the Palestinian leadership to act firmly against terrorism and for Israel to end the expansion of illegal settlements in the occupied territories, a step the government remained reluctant to take. Much of the impetus behind the peace process had been the commitment of President Clinton to find a resolution.

His successor, President Bush, initially held back from involvement but—as international criticism of Israel intensified, particularly over its use of American supplied warplanes against Palestinians—his government appointed a mediator at the end of May.

The Settlement Question.

Mr Sharon rejected Mr Mitchell's call for a freeze on Jewish settlement in the occupied territories, describing the settlers on 21 May as 'a vital national enterprise'. Following the death of 19 Israelis in a

Tel Aviv suicide bombing on 1 June 2001, Mr Arafat ordered an end to attacks in Israel. At talks on 13 June, President Bush's representative called on Israel to withdraw from recently occupied territory and for Mr Arafat to take firmer action against militants.

This pattern—violence interspersed by calls for peace—was to follow for the remainder of the year. At the end of June President Bush and Mr Sharon admitted disagreement over key issues but Mr Arafat won United States support, in principle, for a monitoring force to oversee a ceasefire. The assassination of Palestinian activists—described as 'targeted killings'—became official Israeli policy on 4 July, while Palestinian militants intensified suicide bombings. On 14 August Israel made its largest incursion into the Palestinian West Bank yet.

The Events of September 2001.

Following the attack on the United States on 11 September, Mr Sharon was accused of using the events to use greater force against what he described as Palestinian terrorists. On 17 September Mr Sharon said he would not sacrifice Israel's interests to meet the United States desire to secure Muslim support for a war coalition. But at the end of the month Israeli and Palestinian negotiators reached a short-lived agreement on a truce intended to renew the peace process. Aware of anger in Muslim states about the plight of the Palestinians, President Bush declared on 2 October that he supported the creation of a Palestinian state.

Escalating Conflict.

Hopes of progress ended with the assassination of a right-wing Israeli cabinet minister on 17 October by the Popular Front for the Liberation of Palestine (PFLP). Israel demanded that Mr Arafat should hand over the killers and outlaw militant groups or the Palestinian Authority would be treated as a terrorist state. The following day Israeli troops began occupying further areas of the West Bank. Mr Sharon refused an appeal from the European Union to resume negotiations. In November the United States Secretary of State despatched a peace mission. By the end of the year over 1,000 people had died in clashes.

The Slide to War.

As 2002 opened renewed efforts by United States and European peace envoys faltered when Israel captured a ship allegedly transporting weapons to the Palestinian Authority. A ceasefire called by Mr Arafat in December ended with an attack by Hamas on Israeli troops near the Gaza Strip on 9 January, calling his authority once more into question. Mr Arafat's announcement of the arrest of the PFLP leader on 15 January was intended as much to re-assert his leadership as it was to placate Israel and the United States. But commentators suggested Mr Sharon's plan was to see Mr Arafat ousted and for Palestinian territory to be broken up between competing warlords.

Negotiations behind the scenes between Israel's foreign minister, Shimon Peres, and Ahmed Qurela—a possible successor to President Arafat—raised cautious optimism in mid-February 2002. However, during March 2002, the situation deteriorated rapidly. Following a series of deadly suicide bombings, Israel responded with massive force. A major deployment of tanks and armoured cars made reprisal incursions into the West Bank. Ramallah, the location of Arafat's HQ, was attacked and blockaded. A string of Arab towns, from Nablus to Bethlehem, was entered by Israeli tanks. The Jenin refugee camp was partly razed to the ground (amid accusations of Israeli war crimes). An attempt to bring peace in April 2002 by US Secretary of State Colin Powell achieved little.

Pledges by Arafat.

On 15 May Mr Arafat promised reform and free elections to the Palestinian Assembly in an attempt to end criticism at home and abroad of his corruption-riddled administration. An envoy from President Bush urged Mr Arafat to reform his security forces to fight terrorism on 4 June. Mr Arafat dismissed half his cabinet on 9 June. President Bush made a long-awaited statement on

a revival of the peace process on 24 June. He said he supported a two-state solution but called on the Palestinians to reform, establish democracy and remove Mr Arafat. But he failed to call on Israel to withdraw from the West Bank and set no timetable for the establishment of a Palestinian state.

Nevertheless, two days later the Palestinian Authority announced presidential elections for January 2003. (These were later cancelled).

Suicide Bombings and Retaliation.

Palestinian suicide bombing attacks continued with, from Israel's viewpoint, half-hearted criticism from Mr Arafat. But it was Israel that faced charges of terrorism when, on 23 July, nine children were killed in an Israeli missile attack in which a Hamas leader died. On August 28 talks on a further Israeli withdrawal from Palestinian territory were suspended after clashes in the Gaza Strip. The United Nations Security Council demanded an Israeli withdrawal on 24 September. On 7 October 14 people were killed in Gaza during an Israeli operation against militants in the area. A militant group, Islamic Jihad, claimed responsibility for killing at least 15 Israelis in a bombing on 21 October. Once again, Mr Arafat condemned the attack. President Bush's envoy warned Palestinian leaders again on 24 October that there could be no negotiations on a Palestinian state until they acted decisively against terrorism.

The 2003 Election.

On 5 November Mr Sharon called elections following the collapse of his coalition government over spending on West Bank settlements. Mr Sharon's 6 December vision of a Palestinian state, a demilitarised state comprising less than half of the occupied territories and without Mr Arafat, was condemned by Palestinian leaders, who reiterated their demands for a return to the pre-1967 borders.

Following a further suicide bombing, the Israeli government imposed a travel ban to prevent Palestinian representatives attending a conference in London called by Mr Blair in a further effort to revive the peace process.

Mr Sharon's Likud was returned in the January 2003 Knesset elections with 40 seats, Labour with 19 seats and the secularist Shinui with 15. Labour refused to enter a national unity government, questioning Mr Sharon's sincerity about a peace settlement. On 27 February Mr Sharon announced a coalition government including two parties that opposed a Palestinian state. He warned that Israel would eventually have to make 'painful concessions' to secure peace in the region. On 8 March Mr Arafat, in response to both European Union and United States pressure to reform Palestinian administration, offered the post of prime minister to Mr Mahmoud Abbas. Mr Abbas had been a leading negotiator of the 1993 Oslo peace agreement. In a long awaited intervention President Bush declared on 14 March, with support from Mr Blair, that as soon as it had been demonstrated that the prime minister had real authority the United States would unveil a 'road map' for a Middle East settlement. The move was clearly an attempt to secure Arab acquiescence in the forthcoming attack on Iraq.

With the defeat of Iraq, and with Mr Arafat forced to accept a Prime Minister (Mr Mahmoud Abbas) the way was now clear for the much-heralded three-phase 'road map' proposed by the US President. Whether it could really lead to peace was questionable.

The Return to Bloodshed.

On 17 May the Palestinian and Israeli prime ministers met, with Mr Sharon agreeing on the need for a Palestinian state and Mr Abbas on the need to end terrorism. They re-affirmed their commitment at a meeting with President Bush on 5 June. But on 8 June, following criticism by the militant Hamas group of Palestinian concessions, three Islamic groups mounted a combined attack on Israeli soldiers, provoking an Israeli assassination attempt on a Hamas leader. A Palestinian suicide bomb attack followed.

As Israel began to withdraw from parts of the West Bank and Gaza and released Palestinian prisoners in July, the two prime ministers met again and Palestinian militants announced a temporary ceasefire. On 14 July Mr Abbas threatened to resign following criticism of his negotiations from President Arafat and there was further tension over the Israeli construction of a security barrier through the West Bank. In addition, Mr Sharon showed little willingness to curb Israeli settlement in Palestinian areas.

The End of the Ceasefire.

Continuing suicide bombings and Israeli attacks on Palestinian militants brought the peace process to a halt. On 24 August Hamas and two other groups formally ended what had become a ceasefire in name only. Then Mr Abbas's resignation as Palestinian prime minister on 6 September, and his replacement by Ahmed Qurei, seen as a more pliable supporter of President Arafat, marked an apparent waning of Palestinian hope. On 4 October a suicide attack provoked Israel to bomb a Palestinian camp in Syria the following day. The peace process was further weakened with Israel's announcement in October that it intended to expand both the barrier and the number of settlements on the West Bank. On 22 October the United Nations voted 144 to 4 against the barrier, with Israel and the United States voting in favour. In January 2004 Mr Arafat said hope was fading for a two-state solution to the conflict and blamed Israeli settlements and the security barrier. He offered new elections and said that he had authorised officials to meet the Israeli prime minister. Mr Sharon appeared to be moving closer to what he described as 'unilateral disengagement' from Palestinian areas. The militant Hamas and Islamic Jihad, meanwhile, offered a ceasefire in return for a Palestinian state encompassing the West Bank, Gaza and east Jerusalem. The peace process appeared effectively dead unless the United States was willing to intervene decisively and place pressure on both the Palestinians and the Israelis.

However, on 14 April President Bush abandoned any attempt at neutrality by supporting the proposal of the Israeli prime minister, Mr Sharon, to withdraw from Gaza while retaining control over the West Bank. President Bush said it was unrealistic to expect Israel to withdraw from territory occupied in 1967 or to allow the return of Palestinian refugees.

Developments in 2004.

The spiral of violence and counter-violence continued throughout 2004 with, it appeared, little hope for a revival of the peace process. Mr Sharon's proposal to withdraw from the Gaza Strip and the northern West Bank was a unilateral act that much Arab opinion saw as reducing rather than encouraging prospects for a negotiated settlement. However, other commentators suggested that such a withdrawal could create a new opportunity.

The Death of Arafat.

It was, however, the death of Mr Arafat on 11 November that prompted a fresh impetus. Israel had seen Mr Arafat as unwilling or unable to move decisively against Palestinian militants, though many argued that Israel had done little to help him in this. Within days of Mr Arafat's death, Mr Powell, the United States Secretary of State, visited Israel and the West Bank to attempt to resuscitate the peace process. On 14 December Mahmoud Abbas, Mr Arafat's eventual successor as President of the Palestinian Authority, declared that the four year armed uprising against Israel in the occupied territories had been a mistake and should end.

The Election of Abbas.

Mr Blair remained optimistic, declaring at the end of December that, following discussions with Israeli and Palestinian leaders, he would be holding a London conference in March 2005 on the political and economic reform of the Palestinian Authority. Israel made a conciliatory gesture of promising to release prisoners following Mr Abbas's election in January 2005. On 9 January Mr Blair said that President Bush would engage with the Middle East peace effort if the London conference succeeded in laying the groundwork for a viable Palestinian state.

As hopes grew that a decisive settlement was possible, Mr Abbas and Mr Sharon met for talks in Cairo in February. Mr Blair's London Conference on 1 March, though achieving little in itself, symbolised the new momentum.

Recent Developments.

There was little progress as far as negotiations were concerned in 2005. Mr Sharon won support within Israel for a withdrawal from settlements in the Gaza Strip and, to a far lesser extent, the West Bank. But the pull-out, which was concluded by September 2005, represented a unilateral act on Israel's part and, dramatic as it was, contributed little to prospects for a two-state solution to the region's problems. Indeed, many Palestinians feared Mr Sharon's intention was to weaken their position in the longer term.

On a visit to the area in November, the United States Secretary of State, Condoleezza Rice, repeated the administration's view that a viable Palestinian state could only enhance Israel's security but played down the possibility of a resumption of negotiations. The unlikelihood of further movement in the near future was underlined by the collapse of Israel's coalition government at the end of 2005 and the Hamas victory in Palestinian elections in January 2006 (see **C23**).

THE EUROPEAN UNION FROM ENLARGEMENT TO CRISIS

Within a few days in the early summer of 2005, the EU suddenly faced one of the most profound crises in its history. Turmoil ensued as first France and then the Netherlands rejected the proposed EU constitution.

One result of the crisis is that the EU is now being forced to face decisions on what "Europeanness" means, on where its final frontiers are to be drawn, and on what its fundamental purpose is in a globalising world.

The Fall of Communism.

Such questions did not arise with nearly so much force before the collapse of the Soviet bloc in 1990. However illogical in cultural and historic terms, the Iron Curtain represented an apparently definitive economic and political boundary to the east. The Turkish application submitted in 1987 could be left to others to decide in a rather indefinite future. The historic core of France, Germany and Italy was confident and prosperous and by 1991 laying the foundations of the common currency which was to fully materialise in 2002 as the euro. Some of the EU's more recent members, notably Britain and Denmark, remained comparatively aloof but not so as to seriously threaten the integrity of the whole. The demise of the Soviet bloc followed by the splintering of the Yugoslav Federation put all this in question. The EU decided very quickly that the countries of the former Soviet bloc should be offered the opportunity of joining, which most did in 2004. This was motivated by a mixture of generosity and a desire to roll back Russian influence while opportunity offered, but also by a desire in some countries, particularly Britain, to use enlargement as a means of diluting the European ideal of ever greater integration. An ever more confident and even aggressive Britain was increasingly returning to a vision of itself as a global trading nation, whose prime concern in Europe was to prevent the emergence of a united bloc which might threaten its freedom of action. It was a vision which the eighteenth century would have recognised, and was only modified by a much more recent close alliance with the United States. To the chagrin of many in Europe, the accession of Tony Blair to power in 1997, which was expected to produce a more "European"-minded Britain, has led in practice to an ever more "Atlanticist" Britain.

The Consequences of 2004.

The 2004 expansion, however, is having other consequences which may be less welcome to some other EU members. It has given considerable influence to a group of countries with little taste for

Turkish entry but with much enthusiasm for the admission of the Ukraine, which elected a new president at the beginning of 2005 who wants to open membership negotiations as soon as 2007. If the European idea is to have any cultural dimension at all, then the Ukraine clearly has a much more pressing claim than Turkey. If the Ukraine is a valid candidate, though, then why not Russia?

Cultural considerations, however, are being downplayed in many quarters. For Tony Blair, the fact that Turkey is a Muslim country which could plausibly become an EU member is a positive attraction. In his view, it could be a model of peace and democracy for the whole of the Middle East, and hopefully reduce the appeal of Islamic fundamentalism to the West's immigrant communities. For better or worse, it is a vision remote indeed from that of the fathers of the original European Community. For Giscard d'Estaing, chair of the EU constitutional convention, it would be "the end of Europe".

These different models for expansion may have other unintended and, for some, even unwelcome consequences. The admission of the Ukraine would reinforce the centrality of Germany to the new Europe, giving Berlin the opportunity to become its effective capital and conferring a new importance on the German language. Expansion to include Turkey, on the other hand, would place the spotlight on the Balkans. Bulgaria and Romania are both expected to join the EU in 2007 despite major problems of corruption, but Bosnia, Macedonia and Serbia all face a very uncertain future. Austria succeeded in October 2005 in persuading the EU to open membership talks with Croatia, as its price for agreeing to membership talks with Turkey.

An Unrecognisable EU?

Beyond all these strategic considerations are certain hard facts. On current trends, Turkey would be the largest country in the EU by 2020. The Ukraine is bigger than Poland and Russia is three times as large as the Ukraine. The admission of any of them, let alone all, would make the EU almost unrecognisable and perhaps hard to imagine except as the loosest of trading blocs. Some would see that as a disaster, others as a healthy development in a globalised world.

The Nice Summit.

It was at the Nice Summit in December 2000 that the EU seriously grappled with the political consequences of enlargement for the first time. Nevertheless, some changes were accepted without which enlargement would have meant paralysis. Qualified majority voting in the Council of Ministers was to be extended to 35 more areas, mostly minor but including the appointment of the president of the Commission. The number of votes available for both current and future member states has been changed by agreement to a potential total of 342 with 27 member states. 255 votes will be needed for a qualified majority, but there is also provision for a blocking minority of 88 votes.

The reallocation of votes protects the interests of the four larger member states—France, Germany, Italy and the UK—who will have 29 votes each, but a further, reserve provision confers a modest advantage on Germany with its appreciably larger population. The provision enables any member state to invoke a clause requiring the support of 62% of the EU population for any decision reached by a qualified majority vote. The importance of the provision may prove primarily symbolic in recognising united Germany's prime status in the EU of the twenty-first century, and it may actually contribute with other reserve provisions to making EU decision-making harder. Lastly, the larger member states agreed to forego from 2005 their right to nominate a second Commissioner, and each new member state will have a right to nominate a Commissioner until a total of 27 is reached.

Innovations to the EU.

As significant as these procedural changes, and perhaps in the longer term more significant, were two major innovations. The Nice Treaty authorised groups of eight or more member states to advance with closer integration, except on defence and military matters, provided other states have the right to join in later (enhanced co-operation), and the EU Charter of Fundamental Rights was formally proclaimed. Enhanced co-operation has long been resisted by those countries, notably the UK, fearful of being marginalised in a 'two-speed' Europe, but the logic of events, including non-participation in the euro, has made it virtually inevitable. The formal proclamation of the Charter of Fundamental Rights by the Commission, the Council and the Parliament was similarly unwelcome to the UK and some others who successfully insisted that it be non-binding, but again it seems inevitable that it will become a point of reference in EU law-making, particularly as continental European lawyers, when interpreting law, traditionally look at the spirit and not just at the letter.

The Achievements of Nice.

The results of the Nice Council are open to conflicting interpretations. In both tone and content it was a grave disappointment to the more federalist and integrationist-minded. It often took the line of least resistance, most obviously over the size of the Commission and the European Parliament, both of which many observers consider to be already too large. The ultimate membership of the states of the former Yugoslavia (except for Slovenia) was effectively overlooked, and the reform of the Common Agricultural Policy, deemed necessary to accommodate Poland's large agricultural sector, was similarly shelved.

On the other hand, it could be said that it was ever thus. Political realism, sometimes of a quite narrowly national kind, has always run in tandem with the idealism which so alarms the Eurosceptics. It is the logic of the single market, to which all subscribe, which ultimately is putting the nation state on the defensive, and which is likely to restore a higher profile to the Commission as the essential regulator.

Such internal considerations, however, do not alter the basic fact that Eastern Europe is very much poorer than western and integration will not occur, except on paper, unless that gap is narrowed. That again will not occur unless there is a major redistribution of funds and investment. The EU Commission has, however, put the overall accession costs for environmental infrastructure alone in the candidate states from central and eastern Europe at euro 80 110 billion (US$146 billion) at 1998 prices. The NATO attacks on Serbia greatly increased costs because the blocking of trade along the Danube and the destruction of trade links generally impoverished not only Serbia but all its neighbours including Bulgaria and Romania. The longer term implications for south-eastern Europe as a whole were incalculable—economically, politically and strategically.

Expanding the EU: The Copenhagen Summit.

The EU opened accession negotiations with the Czech Republic, Cyprus, Estonia, Hungary, Poland and Slovenia in 1998, and at the Helsinki summit in December 1999 it agreed to open negotiations with all the other applicants for membership as well, namely Bulgaria, Latvia, Lithuania, Malta, Romania, Slovakia and Turkey.

Those negotiations were complex but the EU decided at the Copenhagen summit in December 2002 that, except in the cases of Bulgaria, Romania and Turkey, they had advanced sufficiently to offer the candidate countries membership in 2004. Bulgaria and Romania may follow in, perhaps, 2007 and Turkey, to whose membership many groups are strongly opposed, in 2010.

It would then be a very different Union. With some 50 million citizens in Asian Turkey, it would no longer be exclusively European. It would have a sharply differentiated rather than a common cultural heritage. In that respect, it would have more in common with the big multi-cultural and multi-ethnic cities of western Europe, including London, than it would with many of the member states, a large number of which, notably Germany, define themselves in essentially ethnic terms. With a total population of more than 500 million, and the cultural diversity represented by more than 25 national languages, it would have more similarity in size and structure with India than any other contemporary political grouping.

On the other hand, experience suggests that profound attachment to a particular territory will remain characteristic of its peoples and that it will not become a cultural or ethnic "melting pot" like the United States. This very diversity and juxtaposition of cultures, many traditionally hostile, will make it particularly difficult to maintain a sense of common purpose and develop a sense of common citizenship. Without such a sense of citizenship, though, the European Parliament in particular will find it difficult to claim any form of democratic legitimacy.

Ensuing Problems.

The fully expanded Union would be held together primarily by a single market, regulated beyond the power of the individual states so as to guarantee competition on level terms and the fair distribution of prosperity, but flexible so as to recognise the very different conditions under which businesses and communities are operating. That single market is likely to be reinforced by a global move towards a small number of continental trading blocs and currencies with a power far beyond that available to virtually any single nation. On the other hand, it may be compromised by a contrary move towards much greater localism and self-sufficiency generated by concern over the environmental and resource implications of ever-expanding consumerism, with global warming and social dislocation as two of the more plausible sources of alarm.

There seems likely in any event to be continuing tension between the centralising and concentrating forces liberated by the single market and the probably related growth in cultural particularism familiar from England, Scotland and Wales, to look no further afield. The ability of the EU to absorb and bridge those opposing trends will probably determine its long-term success or failure.

The Proposed EU Constitution.

These wider practical and strategic considerations have a direct bearing on the seemingly unrelated issue of the EU constitution. Originally conceived as a means at one and the same time of codifying and simplifying the numerous agreements, practices and treaties which have accompanied the European Union since its foundation under the Treaty of Rome in 1957, and of allowing the Union to cope with the challenge of enlargement, a draft was produced in 2003 by a constitutional convention chaired by the former French president, Valéry Giscard d'Estaing. Initially considered at an acrimonious Summit in Brussels in December 2003 which collapsed under a dispute over national voting rights, it was finally adopted at a scarcely less acrimonious Summit on 18 June 2004.

Why Europe Disagrees.

The disagreements are not just between member states but within them. For some, including the UK government, it is essentially a tidying-up exercise which guarantees national interests. For others, it lays the foundations of a European superstate. Agreed provisions which have caused particular concern are the establishment of the EU as a legal entity in its own right, the primacy of EU law over national law including constitutions, the extension of EU jurisdiction to a wider range of activities, the loss of the veto in such sensitive areas as immigration, and the creation of an EU foreign minister and an EU diplomatic corps. On the other hand, there would for the first time be a process by which a country could leave the EU. The one provision which has received a general welcome is the creation of the new position of an elected president of the European Council, to replace the present six-month rotating system. The new president would be elected by the Council for a 2½ year term.

The Referendum Bombshells.

In mid-2005 the EU was suddenly thrown into turmoil by the referendum outcome in France and the Netherlands on the proposed EU constitution. On 29 May, France voted no by 55 % to 45 % (see **C17**). For France, one of the six founding members of the European Community, to vote no was a disaster. On 1 June the Netherlands rejected the proposed constitution by a landslide (62 % to 38 %). If the reasons for the Dutch rejection were perhaps different (many Dutch feared loss of sovereignty

and were angry at their level of EU Budget contributions), the consequences were the same. Europe, and the vision of European integration, was in turmoil.

Although the British presidency which took office in July 2005 succeeded in resolving the EU Budget crisis, the future direction of the EU was as unclear at the beginning of 2006 as it had been twelve months earlier.

THE CENTRAL ASIAN REPUBLICS

The Background.

The predominantly Muslim republics of Kazakhstan, Kyrgyzstan, Tajikistan, Turkmenistan and Uzbekistan gained their independence from the former Soviet Union in 1991. They form a geographical group south of Russia, east of the Caspian Sea, west of China and north of Iran and Afghanistan.

A New Strategic Importance.

The republics represent a potential flashpoint in relations between the United States, Russia and China. The United States presence in the region dates from the opening of the 'war on terror' in 2001 and the need to secure bases for operations in Afghanistan. In 2005 Russia and Uzbekistan signed a defence treaty. Uzbekistan formerly had, and Kyrgyzstan continued to provide, a base for United States forces. Russia too has a base in Kyrgyzstan, one in Tajikistan and has conducted joint military exercises with every republic but Turkmenistan. China has no bases, but with the western province of Xinjiang bordering Tajikistan and Kyrgyzstan shows increased interest in regional developments.

Regional Political Stability.

A major Russian concern is regional political stability, with a fear that threats not confronted will spill over into her territory. Russia sees itself as the prime guarantor of stability through the Shanghai Cooperation Organisation and the Collective Security Treaty Organisation, and hopes through its engagement to maintain great power status. In 2005 Russia supported the Uzbekistan President Karimov over the suppression of a rising in Andijan during May in which hundreds were killed. The United States criticised human rights in Uzbekistan and was asked to relinquish its airbase as a consequence. European troops deployed by NATO were also asked to leave. Kyrgyzstan saw a peaceful 'tulip revolution' in 2005, with alleged American involvement. The insistence of the United States on developing human rights and political reform in the republics has aroused some resentment among regional leaders.

Fears of Terrorism.

Russia, China and the United States have a shared interest in countering the possible growth of terrorism in the region and a shared fear of any of the republics becoming an al-Qaeda base, as Afghanistan was in the 1990s. But both Russia and China, who have also conducted joint military exercises, are wary of too strong an American influence in the area. Both have played a major part in encouraging the Shanghai Cooperation Organization, which includes Kazakhstan, Uzbekistan, Tajikistan, and Kyrgyzstan, as well as Russia and China.

Natural Resources.

Central Asia provides an important market for Russian and Chinese goods, but natural resources are at the centre of competition in the region, particularly between China and the United States. The United States sees the area's resources as an opportunity to meet its aim of reducing dependence on Middle Eastern oil, while China needs to fuel a rapidly growing economy. Kazakhstan's oil reserves are estimated at 26bn barrels, Uzbekistan's at 297m barrels, and Turkmenistan's at 273m barrels. Turkmenistan also has significant natural gas reserves. China has sought oil concessions in the area and is opening a pipeline to carry oil from Kazakhstan.

Chronology of Recent Events.

Kazakhstan

1991 Former Communist leader Nursultan Nazarbayev wins uncontested presidential elections.
1993 Wide-ranging privatisation begins.
1999 Nazarbayev re-elected in widely criticised presidential and parliamentary elections.
2001 Moves against opposition Democratic Choice begin.
2005 Democratic Choice ordered to dissolve; For A Just Kazakhstan movement formed; observers criticise elections in which Nazarbayev wins 91% of vote.

Kyrgyzstan

1991 Askar Akayev becomes president and is re-elected in 1995.
2000 International observers criticise conduct of Akayev's third election victory.
2002 Deaths and arrests in opposition demonstrations.
2005 Akayev resigns following mass protests; Kurmanbek Bakiev wins landslide victory.

Tajikistan

1991 Former Communist leader Rahmon Nabiyev elected president.
1992 Clashes between pro-government and Islamist and pro-democracy groups develop into civil war in which 20,000 die; Emomali Rahmonov becomes president.
1996 United Nations sponsors ceasefire between government and United Tajik Opposition.
1999 Rahmonov re-elected with 96% of the vote.
2004 Russian military base opened.
2005 People's Democratic Party landslide victory in widely criticised elections.

Turkmenistan

1991 Saparmurad Niyazov becomes president.
1993 Economic reform and encouragement of foreign investment in oil and gas.
1994 President Niyazov's term extended to 2004 in referendum.
1999 Legislature appoints Niyazov president for life.
2003 Russia signs long-term gas purchase deal.

Uzbekistan

1991 Islam Karimov elected president.
1994 Economic integration treaty with Russia.
2000 Karimov returned as president in internationally criticised election.
2001 US airbase opened; strategic partnership agreement signed with US.
2004 Islamic extremists blamed for wave of terrorism; opposition barred from participation in legislature elections.
2005 EU imposed sanctions following deaths of demonstrators in Andijan; US requested to close base.

A NEW CONSERVATISM?

The Background.

Following his convincing victory in the 2005 Conservative Party leadership contest, David Cameron declared he would offer "a more compassionate Conservatism, right for our times and right for our country". This had a ring of familiarity.

A previous new leader, Mr Hague, had said as the party digested the extent of Labour's 1997 general election victory, 'I'd like to tell you about a demo-

cratic, popular Conservatism that listens, that has compassion at its core.' By 2001 it was the Conservative core vote that Mr Hague was fighting to hold on to, claiming that Labour Britain was a 'foreign land', promising to save the pound and to put tax cuts before public services.

The Duncan Smith Leadership.

In turning to Mr Duncan Smith, Baroness Thatcher's preferred leadership candidate, after the 2001 defeat the party settled for a place on the right. Or at least the members in the country did; a majority of MPs would have preferred Mr Clarke. But in the Shadow Cabinet there was a realization that being marooned on the right was no place from which to win the prize of office. A leading frontbencher had the courage to say that the Conservatives were perceived as racist, homophobic and antagonistic to young people.

The Howard Leadership.

Mr Duncan Smith's replacement as leader by Mr Howard in 2004 had more to do with personality than policy, although even Mr Howard made a gesture towards 'compassionate conservatism', a slogan Mr Bush's Republicans had played with in the 2000 presidential contest. By the 2005 general election the Conservatives had reverted to what many saw as type, desperately playing the immigration card. The tactic may have warded off any threat from the outside right but achieved little in terms of seats. It took Mr Cameron to learn the lesson: tell the electorate you propose to do what they seem to want, not what the party wants.

A New Conservatism?

Mr Cameron's early interviews set out the mood of his new Conservatism. The party would return to the 'mainstream of British politics', would demand greater social responsibility from big business and no longer act as the City's mouthpiece. There would be a green agenda and concern for single parents. Even genuine asylum seekers would be welcomed. Mr Cameron was at pains to describe what his party was not: not racist, not homophobic, not Thatcherite. There was, he declared, such a thing as society. He invited Liberal Democrat voters (many of them disappointed Conservatives) to turn to him if they wanted to see the back of Labour.

Advantages of the New Leader.

Mr Cameron has a number of advantages. Young and almost unknown (as Mr Blair had been in 1994), he does not carry the baggage of the Conservative past and, for that reason, his claim to be a man for the 21st century has some plausibility. He emerged in the midst of a brewing Liberal Democrat crisis, which his arrival brought to a head and from which he benefited in the turmoil of the subsequent leadership struggle (*see* C10). There is a growing disappointment with Labour's achievements, and little sign that Mr Brown would be any different. Finally, the Conservatives may be desperate enough to accept almost anything that promises the possibility of office.

Critics of Cameron.

Not that Mr Cameron is without critics among Conservatives. One senior backbencher responded to his declaration that tax cuts would take second place to economic stability by asking what a Conservative government was for if not to tax people less. Lord Tebbit accused Mr Cameron of attempting to purge the memory of Thatcherism and said the centre ground he sought was a 'morass'. People would not vote at all if they could see no difference between the parties. Mr Cameron could take these tribal criticisms lightly.

Attacks by Labour.

Labour has found it as difficult to know how to respond to Mr Cameron as the Conservatives did when Mr Blair first came on the scene. Labour's deputy leader, Mr Prescott, launched the first direct attack, calling Mr Cameron an untrustworthy 'chameleon' with 'no substance'. He must have seen the irony in using the same criticisms that both right and left had thrown at his own leader. He may even have sensed with alarm that Labour was facing another man who understood that in an age of non-political politics, to have no substance, to travel light, is the safest way to woo the electorate.

The 2006 Local Elections.

The local elections of 4 May (*see* **D13** for their background) provided the first nationwide test of David Cameron's leadership and his success in wooing the electorate. On a very bad night for Labour, the Conservatives secured their best result since 1992, thereby comfortably confirming the leadership of David Cameron. The party secured around 40 per cent of the votes cast and took several key councils, especially in London. Its gains here included Croydon, Hammersmith and Fulham (where the party had not been in control since 1968) and Ealing. Outside London, Conservatives gained such councils as Winchester (where the local Liberal Democrat MP had been involved in a sex scandal), Chorley, Hastings and Coventry.

The Results Analysed.

There were, however, some less reassuring aspects of the Conservative performance. Many of Labour's losses of council seats had been as much the result of Liberal Democrat strength, especially in the North and in inner-city wards. As the list below shows, Conservative strength in some major northern towns remains very weak or indeed non-existent.

	LD	Lab	Con	Others
Liverpool	56	30	–	4
Newcastle	34	61	–	1
Hull	26	25	2	6
Sheffield	34	45	2	3
Manchester	34	61	–	1

Electoral Prospects.

The Conservatives thus face an uphill fight in many areas, particularly in the big cities outside London, and have still to fight off Liberal Democrat attacks (the Conservatives lost Richmond in southwest London on a large swing). Local elections are not, of course, very reliable pointers to a general election (particularly when a general election might well not come before 2009). Hence, although the Conservatives had cause to celebrate, more cautious political commentators were discussing the increasing likelihood of a "hung" parliament in 2009 or 2010.

POLITICAL COMPENDIUM

This compendium provides a compact reference work of key facts and figures for an understanding of modern British politics. It is fully revised each year to take account of the most recent political events. A Special Topic in this edition looks at the current civil liberties debate in Britain. Readers may wish to note that the preceding section, *Background to World Affairs*, provides a detailed account of the varying fortunes of the Labour Government under Tony Blair.

TABLE OF CONTENTS

POLITICAL COMPENDIUM

A. THE MONARCHY

The Queen is a constitutional monarch. In law she is the head of the executive, an integral part of the legislature, head of the judiciary, commander-in-chief of the armed forces and temporal head of the Church of England. In practice, the Queen's role is purely formal; she reigns, but she does not rule. In all important respects she acts only on the advice of her ministers. However, she still plays an important role symbolically as Head of State and Head of the Commonwealth. For a list of British monarchs, see **A49–50**.

B. GENERAL ELECTIONS

For electoral purposes the United Kingdom is divided into 646 constituencies (rising to 650 at the next General Election) each returning one MP to the House of Commons. Scotland now returns 59 MPs.

All British subjects and citizens of the Irish Republic are entitled to vote provided they are 18 years old and over and are included on the electoral register which is compiled annually.

The only exceptions are members of the House of Lords and those incapacitated through insanity or imprisonment (although certain relaxations of these rules are currently being proposed for less serious offenders).

Anyone who is entitled to vote and aged at least 21 (18 if current proposals become law) may stand as a candidate, the only exceptions being undischarged bankrupts, together with the holders of certain public offices.

All candidates have to pay a deposit of £500, which is forfeited unless they receive 5 % of the votes cast. In each constituency the winning candidate has (under the present voting system) only to obtain a simple majority.

General elections must be held every five years, but may occur more frequently either because no government can command a majority in the House of Commons or at the request of the Prime Minister. If a seat falls vacant between general elections a by-election is held on a date usually chosen by the party which previously held the seat. Elections are generally held on Thursdays.

General Elections, 1931–2005

VOTES CAST (thousands)

	Conservative	Labour	Liberal*	Communist	Plaid Cymru	SNP	Others
1931	12,320	6,991	1,509	75	2	21	293
1935	11,810	8,465	1,422	27	3	30	273
1945	9,988	11,995	2,248	103	16	31	752
1950	12,503	13,267	2,622	92	18	10	290
1951	13,745	13,949	731	22	11	7	177
1955	13,312	12,405	722	33	45	12	313
1959	13,750	12,216	1,639	31	78	22	125
1964	12,023	12,206	3,093	46	70	64	168
1966	11,418	13,095	2,328	62	61	128	171
1970	13,145	12,198	2,117	38	175	307	384
1974 (Feb.)	11,910	11,646	6,059	33	171	632	958
1974 (Oct.)	10,501	11,457	5,347	17	166	840	897
1979	13,698	11,532	4,314	17	133	504	1,024
1983	12,991	8,437	7,775	12	125	331	952
1987	13,761	10,030	7,340	6	124	417	859
1992	14,092	11,563	6,003	–	154	630	1,178
1997	9,590	13,550	5,243	–	161	622	2,440
2001	8,355	10,740	4,813	–	196	464	1,794
2005	8,772	9,556	5,982	–	174	412	2,234

* 1983 and 1987 figures for Liberals include the SDP total. Recent figures are for Liberal Democrats.
The Speaker has been regarded as a candidate of the party he represented before appointment.

SEATS WON

	Conservative	Labour	Liberal*	Communist	Plaid Cymru	SNP	Others (GB)	Others (NI)	Total
1931	521	52	37	0	0	0	3	2	615
1935	429	154	21	1	0	0	8	2	615
1945	213	393	12	2	0	0	16	4	640
1950	299	315	9	0	0	0	0	2	625
1951	321	295	6	0	0	0	0	3	625
1955	345	277	6	0	0	0	0	2	630
1959	365	258	6	0	0	0	1	0	630
1964	304	317	9	0	0	0	0	0	630
1966	253	364	12	0	0	0	0	1	630
1970	330	288	6	0	0	1	1	4	630
1974 (Feb.)	297	301	14	0	2	7	2	12	635
1974 (Oct.)	277	319	13	0	3	11	0	12	635
1979	339	269	11	0	2	2	0	12	635
1983	397	209	23	0	2	2	0	17	650
1987	376	229	22	0	3	3	0	17	650
1992	336	271	20	0	4	3	0	17	651
1997	165	419	46	0	4	6	1	18	659
2001	166	413	52	0	4	5	1	18	659
2005	198	356	62	0	3	6	3	18	646**

Others (NI): Ulster Unionists regarded as Conservatives 1929–70. The Speaker has been regarded as an MP of the party he or she represented before appointment.
* 1983 and 1987 figures for Liberals include SDP MPs. Since 1992 figures are for the Liberal Democrats.
** Polling in Staffordshire South was delayed until 23 June.

By-Elections 1945–29 June 2006

Parliament	Government	No. of By-elections	Changes	Con. +	Con. −	Lab. +	Lab. −	Lib./All.* +	Lib./All.* −	Others +	Others −
1945–50	Lab.	52	3	3	—	—	—	—	—	—	3
1950–51	Lab.	16	0	—	—	—	—	—	—	—	—
1951–55	Con.	48	1	1	—	—	1	—	—	—	—
1955–59	Con.	52	6	1	4	4	—	1	1	—	1
1959–64	Con.	62	9	2	7	6	2	1	—	—	—
1964–66	Lab.	13	2	1	1	—	1	1	—	—	—
1966–70	Lab.	38	16	12	1	·	15	1	—	3	—
1970–74	Con.	30	8	—	5	1	3	5	—	2	—
1974	Lab.	1	0	—	—	—	—	—	—	—	—
1974–79	Lab.	30	7	6	—	—	7	1	—	—	—
1979–83	Con.	29	6	1	4	1	1	4	1	—	—
1083–87	Con.	31†	6	—	4	1	1	4	—	1	1
1987–92	Con.	24	8	—	7	4	1	3	—	1	—
1092–97	Con.	18	9	—	8	3	—	4	—	2	1
1997–01	Lab.	17	2	—	1	—	—	1	—	1	1
2001–05	Lab.	6	2	—	—	—	2	2	—	—	—
2005–	Lab.	5††	1	—	—	—	1	1	—	—	—

* Liberal 1945–79; Alliance (Liberal and SDP) 1979–89, Liberal Democrat after 1990.
† Includes 15 by-elections held in Northern Ireland in January 1986 following Unionist resignations in protest at Anglo-Irish Agreement.
†† Since May 2005, only five by-elections have taken place. Labour has lost the Dunfermline and West Fife seat to the Liberal Democrats.

Electoral Reform

The Labour Government elected in May 1997 appointed the Commission on Voting Systems (chaired by Lord Jenkins) to examine changes to the electoral system. Jenkins recommended the AV-plus system (a refinement of the Alternative Vote in which a small top-up list of MPs with no specific constituencies would be elected according to their party's share of the vote in different areas). Other terms currently used are:

First past the post (FPTP): the current system used to elect MPs—whoever gets the most votes in a constituency wins, even if they secure a minority of all votes cast.

Alternative Vote (AV): a system whereby candidates are ranked by electors and redistributed until a candidate with 50% support emerges.

AV-plus: *(see above)*

Additional member system: The system now used for the Scottish Parliament and Welsh Assembly. Essentially FPTP with top-up list elected by proportional representation

Single Transferable Vote (STV): Multi-member seats elected by proportional representation—system favoured by Liberal Democrats.

TURNOUT AND PARTY SHARE OF VOTES CAST

Turnout (%)		Share of Poll (%)		
		Conservative	Labour	Liberal
1945	73	40	48	9
1950	84	44	46	9
1951	83	48	49	3
1955	77	50	46	3
1959	79	49	44	6
1964	77	43	44	11
1966	76	42	48	9
1970	72	46	43	8
1974 (Feb.)	78	38	37	19
1974 (Oct.)	73	36	39	18
1979	76	44	37	14
1983	73	42	28	26*
1987	75	42	31	23*
1992	78	42	34	18**
1997	72	31	43	17**
2001	59	32	41	18**
2005	61	33	36	22½**

* includes SDP figures.   ** Liberal Democrats

C. POLITICAL PARTIES

For their background, *see under* Conservatism, Liberalism and Socialism in **Section J**.

Party Leaders

Recent years have seen major changes in the way the political parties choose their leaders.

In 1993, Labour adopted a new democratic system for electing future leaders. This system was used to elect Tony Blair in 1994 after the death of John Smith. The Social and Liberal Democrat leader is elected by party members nationally (*see also* **C11**).

Changes to the method of electing a Conservative leader were proposed after the 1997 defeat. A new system was used to elect Iain Duncan Smith in September 2001. Two candidates (selected by Conservative MPs) were chosen by a ballot of all party members. In 2003, following the resignation of Iain Duncan Smith, Michael Howard was elected unopposed. Despite much debate, in 2005 two candidates chosen by Conservative MPs were voted for by party members. David Cameron beat David Davis (134,446 votes to 64,398).

Leaders *(as at 3 July 2006)*

Labour	Mr Tony Blair
Conservative	Mr David Cameron
Liberal Democrat	Sir Menzies Campbell

Conservative Party Leaders

1923–37	S Baldwin
1937–40	N Chamberlain
1940–55	(Sir) W Churchill
1955–57	Sir A Eden
1957–63	H Macmillan
1963–65	Sir A Douglas-Home
1965–75	(Sir) E Heath
1975–90	Mrs M Thatcher
1990–97	(Sir) J Major
1997–01	W Hague
2001–03	I Duncan Smith
2003–05	M Howard
2005–	D. Cameron

Labour Party Leaders

1906–8	J K Hardie
1908–10	A Henderson
1910–11	G Barnes
1911–14	J R MacDonald
1914–17	A Henderson
1917–21	W Adamson
1921–22	J Clynes
1922–31	J R MacDonald

1931–32	A Henderson
1932–35	G Lansbury
1935–55	C Attlee
1955–63	H Gaitskell
1963–76	H Wilson
1976–80	J Callaghan
1980–83	M Foot
1983–92	N Kinnock
1992–94	J Smith
1994–	A Blair

Liberal Party Leaders (since 1931)

1931–35	Sir H Samuel
1935–45	Sir A Sinclair
1945–56	C Davies
1956–67	J Grimond
1967–76	J Thorpe
1976–88	D Steel

Social and Liberal Democratic Party Leaders

1988–99	P Ashdown
1999–06	C Kennedy
2006–	Sir M Campbell

Party Officers
Conservative Party

Chairman of the Party Organisation
(appointed by the Leader of the Party)

1972–74	Lord Carrington
1974–75	W Whitelaw
1975–81	Lord Thorneycroft
1981–83	C Parkinson
1983–85	J Selwyn Gummer
1985–87	N Tebbit
1987–89	P Brooke
1989–90	K Baker
1990–92	C Patten
1992–94	Sir N Fowler
1994–95	J Hanley
1995–97	Dr B Mawhinney
1997–98	Lord Parkinson
1998–01	M Ancram
2001–02	D Davis
2002–03	Ms Theresa May
2003–05	{ Dr Liam Fox / Lord Saatchi
2005–	F Maude

Chairman of Conservative (Private) Members'
Committee (or the 1922 Committee)

1966–70	Sir A Harvey
1970–72	Sir H Legge-Bourke
1972–84	E du Cann
1984–92	Sir C Onslow
1992–97	Sir M Fox
1997–01	Sir A Hamilton
2001–	Sir M Spicer

Labour Party
General Secretary

1944–62	M Phillips
1962–68	A Williams
1968–72	Sir H Nicholas
1972–82	R Hayward
1982–85	J Mortimer
1985–94	L Whitty
1994–98	T Sawyer
1998–01	Ms M McDonagh
2001–04	D Triesman
2004–06	M Carter

Social and Liberal Democratic Party
President
(election by Party members)

1988–90	I Wrigglesworth
1990–94	C Kennedy
1994–98	R Maclennan
1998–00	Baroness Maddock
2000–04	Lord Dholakia
2004–	S. Hughes

D. PARLIAMENT

Parliament consists of the Queen, the House of Lords and the House of Commons. Over the centuries the balance between the three parts of the legislature has changed such that the Queen's role is now only formal and the House of Commons has established paramountcy over the House of Lords. Because of the party system the initiative in government lies not in Parliament but in the Cabinet. But Parliament, and especially the Commons, has important functions to play not only as the assembly to which the government is ultimately responsible but also in legitimising legislation, voting money and in acting as a body in which complaints may be raised.

House of Lords

Composition. The old House of Lords comprised c. 1,240 peers before its reform. These consisted of 26 bishops and archbishops, 10 Lords of Appeal, over 400 Life Peers and more than 760 hereditary peers. No new hereditary peers were created between 1964 and 1983. Since then, there were only 3: Viscounts Tonypandy (George Thomas) and Whitelaw, and the Earl of Stockton (Harold Macmillan). Less than 300 peers attended more than one-third of the Lords' proceedings, although 621 peers voted in the debate over Maastricht.

Reform. The current Labour Government has now implemented its initial plans for reform of the House of Lords, including legislation to strip hereditary peers of their voting rights. Some hereditary peers have been reprieved temporarily. A draft White Paper on the next stage of reform (*The House of Lords – Completing the Reform*) was published on 6 November 2001. However, in the vote in February 2003 MPs were unable to agree on the next stage of reform. Consequently, in September 2003 the Government announced plans for a fully appointed House of Lords (see C11) and the removal of the 92 last hereditary peers. Currently (2006) there are around 211 Conservative peers, 214 Labour and 74 Liberal Democrats. Crossbenchers number c. 180. The current number of peers in the Lords is c. 730.

The Speaker. Until 2006, the Lord Chancellor acted as Speaker of the House of Lords. The new post of Lord Speaker was first filled by election in June 2006. The Speaker sits on the Woolsack.

Functions. (1) *Legislation.* Some bills on subjects which are not matters of partisan controversy are initiated in the Lords. It also examines in detail many bills which originated in the Commons, but its part is limited by the Parliament Acts, under which it cannot require the Commons to agree to amendments nor delay a bill indefinitely.
(2) *Debate.* The Lords provides a forum for men and women, distinguished in most fields of national life, to discuss issues of importance free from the reins of party discipline.
(3) *Court of appeal.* The Lords is currently (2004) the highest court of appeal. Only the law lords participate in this. This function, however, will cease under current government proposals to create a new Supreme Court.

House of Commons

Composition. The size of the House of Commons is gradually increasing. At the last election (held in May 2005) there were 646 MPs elected to represent single-member constituencies (529 in England, 59 in Scotland, 40 in Wales and 18 in Northern Ireland).

The Speaker. Its proceedings are presided over by the Speaker, who is elected by MPs, at the beginning of each session. Miss Betty Boothroyd (the first woman Speaker) was elected in 1992. After her resignation in 2000, Michael Martin was elected amid calls for reform of the procedure to elect a Speaker (new rules will apply in future).

MPs sit on parallel rows of seats, known as benches, with those who support the government on one side of the chamber and the rest on the other side. Members of the government and the spokesmen of the Opposition are known as "frontbenchers"; other MPs are "backbenchers".

Functions. (1) Legislation. There are two types of legislation—*public acts*, most of which are introduced by the government, but which can also be introduced by individual MPs, and *private acts*, which confer special powers on bodies such as local authorities in excess of the general law and which are subject to special procedures.

All public legislation must pass through the following stages before becoming law:

First Reading. The bill is formally introduced.

Second Reading. The general principles of the bill are debated and voted.

Committee Stage. Each clause of the bill is debated and voted.

Report Stage. The bill is considered as it was reported by the committee, and it is decided whether to make further changes in individual clauses.

Third Reading. The bill, as amended, is debated and a final vote taken.

The Other House. The bill has to pass through the same stages in the other House of Parliament.

Royal Assent. The Queen gives her assent to the bill which then becomes law.

(2) Scrutiny of government activities. There are a number of opportunities for the opposition and the government's own back-benchers to criticise government policy. They can question ministers on the floor of the House; they can table motions for debate and speak in debates initiated by the government; and they can take part in one of the select committees set up to scrutinise government activity.

Committees. The House of Commons uses committees to assist it in its work in various ways. They are of two types:

Standing Committees. A standing committee is a miniature of the House itself, reflecting its party composition, and consists of between 20 and 50 MPs. Its function is to examine the Committee Stage of legislation. Usually seven or eight such committees are needed.

Select Committees. A select committee is a body with special powers and privileges to which the House has delegated its authority for the purpose of discovering information, examining witnesses, sifting evidence and drawing up conclusions which are then reported to the House. A few select committees are established *ad hoc*, but the majority are semi-permanent.

E. HER MAJESTY'S GOVERNMENT

Principal Cabinet Ministers (after the 5 May 2006 reshuffle)

Prime Minister, First Lord of the Treasury and Minister for the Civil Service	Mr Tony Blair
Deputy Prime Minister and First Secretary of State	Mr John Prescott
Chancellor of the Exchequer	Mr Gordon Brown
Leader of the House of Commons and Lord Privy Seal	Mr Jack Straw
Secretary of State for Constitutional Affairs and Lord Chancellor	Lord Falconer of Thoroton
Secretary of State for Foreign and Commonwealth Affairs	Ms Margaret Beckett
Secretary of State for the Home Department	Mr John Reid
Secretary of State for Environment, Food and Rural Affairs	Mr David Miliband
Secretary of State for International Development	Mr Hilary Benn
Secretary of State for Transport and Secretary of State for Scotland	Mr Douglas Alexander
Secretary of State for Health	Ms Patricia Hewitt
Secretary of State for Northern Ireland and Wales	Mr Peter Hain
Secretary of State for Defence	Mr Des Browne
Secretary of State for Work and Pensions	Mr John Hutton
Leader of the House of Lords and Lord President of the Council	Baroness Amos
Secretary of State for Trade and Industry	Mr Alistair Darling
Secretary of State for Education and Skills	Mr Alan Johnson
Secretary of State for Culture, Media and Sport	Ms Tessa Jowell
Chief Whip and Parliamentary Secretary to the Treasury	Ms Jacqui Smith
Minister without Portfolio (and Chair of the Labour Party)	Ms Hazel Blears
Chief Secretary to the Treasury	Mr Stephen Timms
Chancellor of the Duchy of Lancaster**	Ms Hilary Armstrong
Secretary of State for Communities and Local Government*	Ms Ruth Kelly

* Also Minister for Women. ** With responsibility for social exclusion.

The following also attend Cabinet meetings: Lord Grocott, Chief Whip (Lords) and Captain of the Gentlemen at Arms; Lord Goldsmith, Attorney General; Geoff Hoon, Minister for Europe and Ian McCartney, Minister of State for Trade; and Sir Andrew Turnbull, Secretary of the Cabinet and Head of the Home Civil Service.

Principal Ministers 1900–1951

	Prime Minister	Chancellor of the Exchequer	Foreign Secretary	Home Secretary	Leader of the House of Commons
1900–2	Marquis of Salisbury	Sir M Hicks-Beach	Marquis of Salisbury Marquis of Lansdowne	Sir M White-Ridley C Ritchie	A Balfour
1902–5	A Balfour	C Ritchie A Chamberlain	Marquis of Lansdowne	A Akers-Douglas	A Balfour
1905–8	Sir H Campbell-Bannerman	H Asquith	Sir E Grey	H Gladstone	Sir H Campbell-Bannerman
1908–16	H Asquith	D Lloyd George R McKenna	Sir E Grey	H Gladstone W Churchill R McKenna Sir J Simon Sir H Samuel	H Asquith
1916–22	D Lloyd George	A Bonar Law A Chamberlain Sir R Horne	A Balfour Earl Curzon	Sir G Cave E Shortt	A Bonar Law A Chamberlain
1922–23	A Bonar Law	S Baldwin	Earl Curzon	W Bridgeman	A Bonar Law
1923–24	S Baldwin	S Baldwin N Chamberlain	Earl Curzon	W Bridgeman	S Baldwin
1924	J R MacDonald	P Snowden	J R MacDonald	A Henderson	J R MacDonald
1924–29	S Baldwin	W Churchill	(Sir) A Chamberlain	Sir W Joynson-Hicks	S Baldwin
1929–35	J R MacDonald	P Snowden N Chamberlain	A Henderson Marquis of Reading Sir J Simon	J Clynes Sir H Samuel Sir J Gilmour	J R MacDonald
1935–37	S Baldwin	N Chamberlain	Sir S Hoare A Eden	Sir J Simon	S Baldwin
1937–40	N Chamberlain	Sir J Simon	A Eden Viscount Halifax	Sir S Hoare Sir J Anderson	N Chamberlain
1940–45	W Churchill	Sir K Wood Sir J Anderson	Viscount Halifax A Eden	H Morrison Sir D Somervell	C Attlee * Sir S Cripps A Eden
1945–51	C Attlee	H Dalton Sir S Cripps H Gaitskell	E Bevin H Morrison	C Ede	H Morrison C Ede

* Churchill deputed day to day business to Attlee.

Principal Ministers 1951– May 2006

Prime Minister		Chancellors	Foreign Secretary	Home Secretary	Leader of the House of Commons
1951–55	Sir W Churchill	R Butler	Sir A Eden	Sir D Maxwell-Fyfe G Lloyd George	H Crookshank
1955–57	Sir A Eden	R Butler H Macmillan	H Macmillan S Lloyd	G Lloyd George	R Butler
1957–63	H Macmillan	P Thorneycroft D Heathcoat Amory S Lloyd R Maudling	S Lloyd Earl of Home	R Butler H Brooke	R Butler I Macleod
1963–64	Sir A Douglas-Home	R Maudling	R Butler	H Brooke	S Lloyd
1964–70	H Wilson	J Callaghan R Jenkins	P Gordon Walker M Stewart G Brown M Stewart	Sir F Soskice R Jenkins J Callaghan	H Bowden R Crossman F Peart
1970–74	E Heath	I Macleod A Barber	Sir A Douglas-Home	R Maudling R Carr	W Whitelaw R Carr J Prior
1974–76	H Wilson	D Healey	J Callaghan	R Jenkins	E Short
1976–79	J Callaghan	D Healey	A Crosland D Owen	R Jenkins M Rees	M Foot
1979–90	Mrs M Thatcher	Sir G Howe N Lawson J Major	Lord Carrington F Pym Sir G Howe J Major D Hurd	W Whitelaw L Brittan D Hurd D Waddington	N St John-Stevas F Pym J Biffen J Wakeham Sir G Howe J MacGregor
1990–97	J Major	N Lamont K Clarke	D Hurd M Rifkind	K Baker K Clarke M Howard	J MacGregor A Newton
1997–	A Blair	G Brown	R Cook J Straw Ms M Beckett	J Straw D Blunkett C Clarke J Reid	A Taylor M Beckett R Cook J Reid P Hain G Hoon J Straw

Since 1979, there have been 13 or 14 select committees, each one scrutinising the work of one or two government departments (*e.g.* Agriculture, Foreign Affairs, Treasury and Civil Service); and various others including the following: European Legislation, Members' Interests, Parliamentary Commissioner for Administration, Privileges, Public Accounts, and Statutory Instruments.

Central Government

The executive work of central government is performed by the Prime Minister and the other ministers of the Crown. The power of executive action is not given to a government department as a corporate body but to the minister individually, who is responsible for the exercise of his duties legally to the Queen and politically to Parliament. For this reason, all ministers must be members of either the Commons or the Lords.

The Cabinet

At the head of the government structure is the Cabinet, which consists of the leading members of the majority party in the Commons, selected by the Prime Minister. Most Cabinet ministers are the heads of government departments, which are staffed by civil servants, but there are usually some without departmental responsibilities. Although legally ministers are individually responsible for the exercise of government powers, politically it is accepted that the Cabinet is collectively responsible for government policy. It thus acts as one man, and a minister who disagrees with the Cabinet must either resign or remain silent.

F. HER MAJESTY'S OPPOSITION

The leader of the largest party opposed to the government is designated Leader of Her Majesty's Opposition and receives an official salary. The leading spokesmen of the Opposition meet together as a committee and are generally known as the Shadow Cabinet (*see below*). A Conservative Shadow Cabinet, known as the Leader's Consultative Committee, is selected by the leader of the party.

Labour Shadow Cabinets, officially known as the Parliamentary Committee, are elected by the Parliamentary Labour Party, but the leader retains the right to invite members to take charge of particular subjects.

Leading Liberal Democrat spokespersons are listed below.

G. OTHER EXECUTIVE BODIES

A large number of semi-autonomous agencies have been established to carry out functions on behalf of the government, usually because a particular function is considered to be unsuitable for a normal government department. In this category are bodies such as the British Broadcasting Corporation and the Commission for Racial Equality which need to be insulated from the political process, and the former nationalised industries, most of which were managed by public corporations so as to secure managerial flexibility. Some public control over these bodies was maintained by means of various powers which ministers possessed.

H. THE CIVIL SERVICE

The civil service is the body of permanent officials who, working in the various departments, administer the policy of central government. In late 2004 it consisted of 554,110 full-time and part-time staff.

Over 80 % of the civil service work outside Greater London, mainly in the regional and local offices of departments such as Health, Work and Pensions, Education and Skills, Inland Revenue *etc*.

THE CONSERVATIVE SHADOW CABINET
(appointed in December 2005 by David Cameron)

Leader of the Opposition	Mr David Cameron
Shadow Chancellor	Mr George Osborne
Shadow Foreign Secretary	Mr William Hague
Shadow Home Secretary	Mr David Davis
Shadow Education Secretary	Mr David Willetts
Shadow Health Secretary	Mr Andrew Lansley
Shadow Defence Secretary	Dr Liam Fox
Shadow Leader of the Commons	Ms Theresa May
Shadow Trade and Industry Secretary	Mr Alan Duncan
Shadow Transport Secretary	Mr Christopher Grayling
Shadow Environment, Food and Rural Affairs Secretary	Mr Peter Ainsworth
Shadow Northern Ireland Secretary	Mr David Lidington
Shadow Chief Secretary to the Treasury	Ms Theresa Villiers
Shadow Work and Pensions Secretary	Mr Philip Hammond
Shadow Welsh Secretary	Ms Cheryl Gillan
Shadow Constitutional Affairs Secretary	Mr Oliver Heald
Shadow Culture, Media & Sport Secretary	Mr Hugo Swire
Shadow International Development Secretary	Mr Andrew Mitchell
Shadow Scottish Secretary	Mr David Mundell
Shadow Secretary for the Office of the Deputy Prime Minister	Ms Caroline Spelman
Leader in the House of Lords	Lord Strathclyde
Opposition Chief Whip	Mr Patrick McLoughlin
Chairman, Conservative Research Department	Mr Oliver Letwin
Party Chairman	Mr Francis Maude

PRINCIPAL LIBERAL DEMOCRAT SPOKESPERSONS
(after the March 2006 leadership election)

Leader of the Party	Sir Menzies Campbell
Deputy Leader (and Treasury)	Mr Vincent Cable
Foreign Affairs	Mr Michael Moore
Home Affairs	Mr Nick Clegg
Attorney General and Constitutional Affairs	Mr Simon Hughes
Health	Mr Steve Webb
Education and Skills	Ms Sarah Teather
Defence	Mr Nick Harvey
Environment	Mr Chris Huhne
Work and Pensions	Mr David Laws
Trade and Industry	Mr Ed Davey
Leader in the Lords	Lord McNally
Chief Whip	Mr Paul Burstow

The political head of each department is a minister, but, as he often has no previous experience of the field to which he is appointed and his tenure of office may be fairly short-lived, great responsibility falls on the shoulders of the permanent civil servants in his department. Civil servants remain largely anonymous and their relationship with their minister is a confidential one. They are non-political in the sense that they serve all political parties impartially.

Some lists of major heads of the civil service in the post-war period are given below.

Senior Civil Servants
Head of the Home Civil Service

1945–56	Sir E Bridges
1956–63	Sir N Brook
1963–68	Sir L Helsby
1968–74	Sir W Armstrong
1974–78	Sir D Allen
1978–81	Sir I Bancroft
1981–83	{ Sir R Armstrong { Sir D Wass
1983–88	Sir R Armstrong
1988–98	Sir R Butler
1998–02	Sir R Wilson
2002–05	Sir A Turnbull
2005–	Sir G O'Donnell

Head of the Diplomatic Service

1945–46	Sir A Cadogan
1946–49	Sir O Sargent
1949–53	Sir W Strang
1953–57	Sir I Kirkpatrick
1957–62	Sir F Hoyer Millar
1962–65	Sir H Caccia
1965–68	Sir S Garner
1968–69	Sir P Gore-Booth
1969–73	Sir D Greenhill
1973–75	Sir T Brimelow
1975–82	Sir M Palliser
1982–86	Sir A Acland
1986–91	Sir P Wright
1991–94	Sir D Gillmore
1994–97	Sir J Coles
1997–02	Sir J Kerr
2002–06	Sir M Jay
2006–	Sir P Ricketts

Permanent Secretary to the Treasury

1945–56	Sir E Bridges
1956–60	{ Sir N Brook { Sir R Makins
1960–62	{ Sir N Brook { Sir F Lee
1962–63	{ Sir N Brook { Sir W Armstrong
1963–68	{ Sir L Helsby { (Sir) W Armstrong
1968	{ Sir W Armstrong { Sir D Allen
1968–74	Sir D Allen
1974–83	Sir D Wass
1983–91	Sir P Middleton
1991–98	Sir T Burns
1998–02	Sir A Turnbull
2002–05	Sir G O'Donnell
2005–	N Macpherson

Secretary to the Cabinet

1938–47	Sir E Bridges
1947–63	Sir N Brook
1963–73	Sir B Trend
1973–79	Sir J Hunt
1979–88	Sir R Armstrong

1988–98	Sir R Butler
1998–02	Sir R Wilson
2002–05	Sir A Turnbull
2005–	Sir G O'Donnell

I. LOCAL GOVERNMENT

Background

Local government in the United Kingdom is the creation of Parliament. Its structure is laid down by Parliament, and local authorities may only exercise those powers which Parliament either commands or permits them to exercise. Their functions include responsibility for all education services, except further and higher education, most personal welfare services, housing, public health, environmental planning, traffic management and transport, in each case subject to some central government control.

Draft legislation in 2000 proposed a major shake-up of the running of town halls, opening up the prospect of directly-elected mayors with wide-ranging executive powers. The first directly-elected Mayors were voted for in May 2002.

Structure

The structure of local government varies in different parts of the country.

In London and the six metropolitan areas there was, after April 1986 (when the Greater London Council and the metropolitan county councils were abolished), a single-tier system with a few special bodies undertaking county-wide functions.

A referendum on the future government of London was held on 7 May 1998 when voters decided they wanted a new Greater London Assembly (GLA) and a directly elected Mayor. Londoners chose their first directly-elected Mayor on 4 May 2000 (electing the Independent candidate, Ken Livingstone). The second elections for the GLA were held in June 2004, when Ken Livingstone was re-elected (now standing as the Labour candidate).

Following the earlier review of local government proposed by the Conservative Government in 1991, many old councils have disappeared. Among authorities abolished were Avon, Humberside and Cleveland, all created in 1974.

Regional Assemblies

As a result of the Regional Assemblies (Preparations) Act, a referendum was held in north-east England on 4 November 2004. The outcome was a decisive rejection of a regional assembly, with 696,519 votes against an assembly (78%) and 197,310 for (22%). Turnout was around 48%. Future referendums on regional assemblies in England are now very unlikely to take place.

Wales and Scotland

In Wales, 22 all-purpose councils replaced the 8 counties and 37 district councils in 1996. Elections to these "shadow" councils first took place in 1995.

In Scotland, 29 single-tier authorities replaced the existing 2-tier structure after April 1996. These new authorities were first elected in April 1995. There are single-tier island councils in Orkney, Shetland and the Western Isles.

For a summary of the May 2006 local elections, see **D13**. See also **D12** for current control of metropolitan councils.

This list excludes Avon, Cleveland and Humberside which were abolished in April 1996. Since April 1995 the Isle of Wight has been a unitary authority, whilst Hereford and Worcester has been reorganised and Berkshire has lost its old status.

ENGLAND	Name	Political control in 2006	Number of districts	Administrative capital
Non-Metropolitan Counties	Bedfordshire	Con.	4	Bedford
	Buckinghamshire	Con.	5	Aylesbury
	Cambridgeshire	Con.	6	Cambridge
	Cheshire	Con.	8	Chester
	Cornwall	Lib Dem.	6	Truro
	Cumbria	NOM.	6	Carlisle
	Derbyshire	Lab.	9	Matlock
	Devon	Lib Dem.	10	Exeter
	Dorset	Con.	8	Dorchester
	Durham	Lab.	8	Durham
	East Sussex	Con.	7	Lewes
	Essex	Con.	14	Chelmsford
	Gloucestershire	Con.	6	Gloucester
	Hampshire	Con.	13	Winchester
	Hertfordshire	Con.	10	Hertford
	Kent	Con.	14	Maidstone
	Lancashire	Lab.	14	Preston
	Leicestershire	Con.	9	Leicester
	Lincolnshire	Con.	7	Lincoln
	Norfolk	Con.	7	Norwich
	Northamptonshire	Con.	7	Northampton
	Northumberland	Lab.	6	Morpeth
	North Yorkshire	Con.	8	Northallerton*
	Nottinghamshire	Lab.	8	Nottingham
	Oxfordshire	Con.	5	Oxford
	Shropshire	Con.	6	Shrewsbury
	Somerset	Lib Dem..	5	Taunton
	Staffordshire	Lab.	9	Stafford
	Suffolk	Con.	7	Ipswich
	Surrey	Con.	11	Kingston-on-Thames
	Warwickshire	NOM.	5	Warwick
	West Sussex	Con.	7	Chichester
	Wiltshire	Con.	5	Trowbridge
	Worcestershire	Con.	8	Worcester

NOM.—No overall majority.
* In North Yorkshire, the York City Council area was extended in April 1996 and the council became a unitary authority.

WALES

The following 22 new unitary authorities took up their duties on 1 April 1996.

Aberconwy and Colwyn	Merthyr Tydfil
Anglesey	Monmouthshire
Blaenau Gwent	Neath and Port Talbot
Bridgend	Newport
Caernarfonshire and Merionethshire	Pembrokeshire
Caerphilly	Powys
Cardiff	Rhondda, Cynon, Taff
Cardiganshire	Swansea
Carmarthenshire	Torfaen
Denbighshire	Vale of Glamorgan
Flintshire	Wrexham

SCOTLAND

The following 32 new unitary authorities took up their duties on 1 April 1996.

Aberdeenshire	Fife
Angus	Highland
Argyll and Bute	Inverclyde
Borders	Midlothian
City of Aberdeen	Moray
City of Dundee	North Ayrshire
City of Edinburgh	North Lanarkshire
City of Glasgow	Orkney Islands Council
Clackmannan	Perthshire and Kinross
Dumbarton and Clydebank	Renfrewshire
Dumfries and Galloway	Shetland Islands Council
East Ayrshire	South Ayrshire
East Dumbartonshire	South Lanarkshire
East Lothian	Stirling
East Renfrewshire	Western Isles Islands Council
Falkirk	West Lothian

	Name	Population	Political control (May 2006)
London	Barking & Dagenham	153,700	Lab.
	Barnet	319,400	Con.
	Bexley	220,000	Con.
	Brent	248,000	NOM.
	Bromley	295,600	Con.
	Camden	189,100	NOM.
	Croydon	333,800	Con.
	Ealing	297,000	Con.
	Enfield	262,600	Con.
	Greenwich	212,100	Lab.
	Hackney	193,800	Lab.
	Hammersmith and Fulham	156,000	Con.
	Haringey	216,000	Lab.
	Harrow	210,700	Con.
	Havering	230,900	Con.
	Hillingdon	247,700	Con.
	Hounslow	206,000	NOM.
	Islington	176,000	NOM.
	Kensington and Chelsea	159,000	Con.
	Kingston-on-Thames	141,800	Lib Dem.
	Lambeth	264,700	Lab.
	Lewisham	241,500	NOM.
	Merton	182,300	NOM.
	Newham	228,900	Lab.
	Redbridge	230,600	Con.
	Richmond-on-Thames	179,900	Lib Dem.
	Southwark	229,000	NOM.
	Sutton	175,500	Lib Dem.
	Tower Hamlets	176,600	NOM.
	Waltham Forest	220,000	NOM.
	Wandsworth	266,000	Con.
	Westminster	204,000	Con.
Greater Manchester	Bolton	265,000	NOM.
	Bury	181,000	NOM.
	Manchester	432,000	Lab.
	Oldham	221,000	Lab.
	Rochdale	207,000	NOM.
	Salford	229,000	Lab.
	Stockport	291,000	Lib Dem.
	Tameside	222,000	Lab.
	Trafford	218,000	Con.
	Wigan	313,000	Lab.
Merseyside	Knowsley	155,000	Lab.
	Liverpool	477,000	Lib Dem.
	St. Helens	180,000	NOM.
	Sefton	294,000	NOM.
	Wirral	334,000	NOM.
South Yorkshire	Barnsley	226,000	Lab.
	Doncaster	293,000	NOM.
	Rotherham	256,000	Lab.
	Sheffield	532,000	Lab.
Tyne & Wear	Gateshead	203,000	Lab.
	Newcastle-upon-Tyne	285,000	Lib Dem.
	North Tyneside	195,000	NOM.
	South Tyneside	157,000	Lab.
	Sunderland	298,000	Lab.
West Midlands	Birmingham	1,012,000	NOM.
	Coventry	304,000	Con.
	Dudley	312,000	Con.
	Sandwell	294,000	Lab.
	Solihull	200,000	Con.
	Walsall	265,000	Con.
	Wolverhampton	246,000	Lab.
West Yorkshire	Bradford	480,000	NOM.
	Calderdale	194,000	NOM.
	Kirklees	386,000	NOM.
	Leeds	725,000	NOM.
	Wakefield	317,000	Lab.

THE SCOTTISH PARLIAMENT
AND WELSH ASSEMBLY

Voting took place on 1 May 2003 for the second elections to the new Scottish Parliament and Welsh Assembly. In both Scotland and Wales, Labour had a commanding position at the 2001 General Election. Much attention was centred in 2003 on the performance of the Nationalists. Once again, Labour easily held off the Nationalist challenge. In Scotland, smaller parties did particularly well.

SCOTTISH PARLIAMENT				WELSH ASSEMBLY			
Party	Seats (1)*	Seats (2)**	Total	Party	Seats (1)*	Seats (2)**	Total
Labour	46	4	50	Labour	30	–	30
SNP	9	18	27	PC	5	7	12
Cons	3	15	18	Cons	1	10	11
Lib Dems	13	4	17	Lib Dem	3	3	6
Others	2	15	17	Others	1	–	1

*(1) Constituency seats won on 'First Past the Post' system.
**(2) 'Top-up' seats won under Proportional Representation.

THE 4 MAY 2006 LOCAL ELECTIONS

The Background

On 4 May 2006 voting took place for 4,360 of the 19,570 council seats in England in 176 of the 386 councils. For the first time since 2002 all 1,861 seats on the 32 London boroughs were up for election. A third of the seats in all 36 English metropolitan boroughs were also at stake in a contest seen as crucial for all three parties, with David Cameron and Sir Menzies Campbell facing their first national tests as party leader.

The Outcome

The outcome was a very bad night for Labour (though not quite the meltdown some had predicted) and a celebratory night for Conservatives (particularly against Labour in London) (see **C60**). Broadly, with 40% of the vote, this was the best

Conservative local election performance since 1992. Labour, on the other hand, lost control of such erstwhile citadels as Brent, Camden (Labour for 35 years), Hammersmith and Fulham and Tower Hamlets. Outside London Labour losses included Derby, Warrington, Stoke and Barrow-in-Furness.

The Liberal Democrats ended up much as they had started – a somewhat mixed result for their new leader (but they swept to victory in Richmond and their share of the national vote exceeded Labour). The Greens secured their first-ever councillor in Bristol and won several Norwich seats. The far-right BNP picked up seats in Barking and Dagenham, Sandwell and Stoke.

The final results gave the Conservatives a net gain of 316 seats, Labour a net loss of 319, the Liberal Democrats a gain of just 2, and Greens 20 net gains.

J. REDRESS OF GRIEVANCES

In the first instance most citizens who are aggrieved by the decision of a public body take up their complaint with the body concerned, either personally or in writing. If this does not satisfy them they have a number of options which vary according to the type of body and the nature of their complaint.

Central Government

1. MPs. MPs may be contacted by letter, and many of them hold regular surgeries in their constituencies. On receipt of a complaint they can write to the minister in charge of the department concerned or ask a question in Parliament. If the complainant alleges maladministration (e.g., arbitrary action, undue delay) this can be referred to the *Parliamentary Commissioner for Administration* (usually known as the Ombudsman). His powers and responsibilities are set out in the Parliamentary Commissioner Act 1967. In 1994 they were extended to include complaints arising from the Code of Practice on Access to Government Information.

Parliamentary Commissioner for Administration

(and Health Service Commissioner since 1973)

1967–71	Sir Edmund Compton
1971–76	Sir Alan Marre
1976–78	Sir Idwal Pugh
1979–85	Sir Cecil Clothier
1985–90	Sir Anthony Barrowclough
1990–96	Sir William Reid
1997–02	Sir Michael Buckley
2002–	Ms Ann Abraham

Parliamentary Commissioner for Standards

(established in 1995 after the Nolan Report)

1995–98	Sir Gordon Downey
1998–02	Ms Elizabeth Filkin
2002–	Sir Philip Mawer

2. Tribunals and Inquiries. In certain areas of government (e.g., social security), special tribunals exist to adjudicate on disputes between citizens and government. In others (e.g., planning) an inquiry can be set up. In both cases the machinery is less formal and more flexible than the ordinary courts.

3. Courts of Law. On certain restricted matters (e.g., that a public body has acted outside its lawful powers), citizens have recourse to ordinary courts.

Local Government

1. Councillors. Local councillors can be contacted in the same way as MPs. They can also refer complaints of maladministration to a *Commissioner for Local Administration* (or local Ombudsman). There are five commissioners, three in England and one each in Scotland and Wales, each investigating complaints in a particular part of the country.

2. Tribunals and Inquiries (as above).

3. Courts of Law (as above).

Other Bodies

1. National Health Service. Each health authority has its own complaints procedure subject to a national code of practice. Complaints, other than those involving the exercise of clinical judgement, may be taken to the *Health Service Commissioner*. Special procedures exist for complaints against doctors.

2. Privatised Industries. In former nationalised industries, independent regulatory bodies have been created (e.g. Ofwat for water, Ofgem for gas and electricity).

K. PRESSURE GROUPS

Large numbers of groups exist to exert pressure on government by direct consultation with ministers and civil servants, lobbying Parliament and general publicity campaigns. Some exist to defend interests such as labour, business or consumers; others promote particular causes such as the prevention of cruelty to children or the banning of blood sports. Of great importance in contemporary politics are the groups representing labour and business.

Trade Unions

In 1980, 49% of the workforce belonged to a trade union. This percentage has declined and by early 2006 there were around 6·5 million members of a trade union or staff association. Increasingly, unions are in discussions to form "super-unions". The proposed merger of the Transport and General Workers Union (T&G) with the GMB and Amicus, due to be completed in 2007, will create a union with c.2·6 million members.

For a further discussion of the role of trade unions, see **Section F Part I.**

The four largest unions are:

UNISON * (1,300,000 members)
Amicus** (935,000)
Transport and General Workers' Union (816,000)
General, Municipal, Boilermakers' and Allied Trades Union (GMB) (600,000)

* Formed in 1993 by the merger of NALGO, NUPE and COHSE.
** Formed from the MSF and AEEU in 2002.

Trades Union Congress (TUC)

The major unions, representing over 80% of total union membership, are affiliated to the Trades Union Congress, which is the federal body of the trade union movement, representing its views to government and others, and giving assistance on questions relating to particular industries.

TUC General Secretaries since 1946

1946–60	(Sir) V Tewson
1960–70	G Woodcock
1970–74	V Feather
1974–84	L Murray
1984–93	N Willis
1993–03	J Monks
2003–	B Barber

Business

The peak organisation representing British business is the *Confederation of British Industry*, formed in 1965. Its members now comprise over 11,000 individual enterprises and over 200 representative organisations (employers' organisations, trade associations etc.).

Business is also represented by large numbers of associations which promote the interests of individual industries and sectors.

Director-Generals of the CBI

1965–69	J Davies
1969–76	(Sir) C Adamson
1976–80	(Sir) J Methven
1980–87	(Sir) T Beckett
1987–92	(Sir) J Banham
1992–95	(Sir) H Davies
1995–00	(Lord) Adair Turner
2000–06	(Sir) Digby Jones
2006–	R Lambert

L. THE MEDIA

1. Principal Newspapers

The British are more committed to the reading of newspapers than any other country in Europe. Although newspaper sales are declining slightly, annual sales each day of national and regional newspapers are now (2006) around 17·7 million (and to these figures should be added the many millions of weekly papers and free newspapers). The free weeklies alone total over 24 million.

Ownership

The largest grouping is News International. Owned by Rupert Murdoch it possesses *The Sun*, *The Times*, the *Sunday Times*, and the *News of the World*. It also owns extensive interests in the US and Australia.

The Mirror Group follows with *The Mirror*, the *Sunday Mirror*, the *People* and the *Daily Record* (published in Scotland). It has sold its former interest in the company that runs *The Independent* and *Independent on Sunday*.

Northern and Shell is the owner of *The Express*, *Express on Sunday*, and *Daily Star*. Associated Newspapers owns the *Daily Mail*, *Mail on Sunday*, and large regional holdings, including the *Evening Standard* in London. Smaller companies are the Telegraph owning the *Daily Telegraph* and *Sunday Telegraph*; the Guardian owns *The Guardian*, *The Observer* and local newspapers; and Pearson which owns the *Financial Times*).

For a summary of papers and their proprietors, see below.

Paper	Proprietors
National Dailies	
The Express	Northern and Shell
Daily Mail	Associated Newspapers
The Mirror	Trinity Mirror
Daily Star	Northern and Shell
Daily Telegraph	Barclay Brothers
Financial Times	Pearson
Guardian	Guardian Media Group
Independent	Independent Newspapers
Sun	News International
The Times	News International
National Sundays	
Independent on Sunday	Independent Newspapers
Mail on Sunday	Associated Newspapers
News of the World	News International
Observer	Guardian Media Group
Express on Sunday	Northern and Shell
Sunday Mirror	Mirror Group
Sunday People	Mirror Group
Sunday Telegraph	Barclay Brothers
Sunday Times	News International
Daily Star Sunday	Northern and Shell

2. Broadcasting

Note: For a background article on television, *see* Section L.

British Broadcasting Corporation

Established in 1926 as a public service body and financed by licence fees paid by all owners of TV sets. It is directed (2006) by a board of governors appointed by the government. Major recent changes proposed include the abolition of the present structure of governors and a commitment to retain the licence fee for 10 years. From January 2007 a new BBC Trust replaces the current Board of Governors.

Its analogue services include BBC One, BBC Two, national and regional television, national, regional and local radio, BBC Radio 1,2,3,4 and 5 Live. Its digital services include CBBC, CBeebies, BBC Three, BBC Four, News 24 *etc.*

Chairman of the Board of Governors	Michael Grade
Director-General	Mark Thompson

Independent Television

There are now 15 independent regional TV licensees which comprise the ITV network. The ITC (Independent Television Commission) awards licences for a minimum of 10 years.

Ofcom

Ofcom, which began work in December 2003, brings together the work previously done by such bodies as the Broadcasting Standards Commission, the Radio Authority, Oftel, the Independent Television Commission *etc.*

It acts as a super-regulator for the communications industry. Its creation reflects the growing convergence of the modern technologies that allow the provision of TV, radio, telephone and the Internet. Its chairman is Lord Currie of Marylebone.

M. SCOTLAND, WALES AND NORTHERN IRELAND

The structure of government in Scotland, Wales and Northern Ireland differs from that in England.

Scotland

Most central government functions here were the responsibility of a single department, the Scottish Office, based in Edinburgh and represented in the Cabinet by the Secretary of State for Scotland. On many matters special Scottish legislation was enacted by Parliament and administrative structure (*e.g.* the local government system) and practice (*e.g.* the educational system) differ from that in England.

The Labour Government elected in May 1997 established a 129-member Scottish Parliament (following a 'Yes' vote on the issue on 11 September). Of those voting 74·3% voted in favour of a Scottish Parliament while 63·5% backed tax raising powers.

The Parliament, first elected on 6 May 1999, has devolved powers over such areas as education, health, law and local government. Foreign, defence, security and constitutional issues will remain at Westminster. The Scottish Parliament is able to increase or decrease tax by 3p. Some of the MPs are elected from a party list (*see also* **D**13). Donald Dewar became First Minister in 1999, to be succeeded after his untimely death in October 2000 by Henry McLeish. He in turn was replaced in November 2001 (following his resignation) by Jack McConnell.

Wales

The Welsh Office, based in Cardiff and represented in the Cabinet by the Secretary of State

for Wales, performed many central government functions in Wales but its responsibilities were narrower than its Scottish counterpart. In other respects too government in Wales resembled more closely that in England.

The Labour Government elected in May 1997 created a Welsh Assembly, following a very close referendum vote in favour. Of the 22 voting areas, 11 voted in favour, 11 voted against in the referendum on 18 September 1997 (the final figures were 'Yes', 559,419; 'No', 552,698; majority, 6,721). On a turnout of 50·1%, had voted in favour. A massive 'yes' vote in Carmarthenshire decided the outcome.

Northern Ireland

From 1921 until 1972 Northern Ireland was governed under the scheme of devolution embodied in the Government of Northern Ireland Act 1920. This created the Northern Ireland Parliament, generally known as Stormont after its eventual location. Executive powers were formally vested in the Governor of Northern Ireland, but were in effect performed by a Prime Minister and small cabinet, responsible to Stormont.

The onset of troubles in the province led the UK Government in 1972 to suspend the Government of Northern Ireland Act. After then, apart from a period of four months in 1974, Northern Ireland was ruled direct from Westminster, the powers of government being vested in the Secretary of State for Northern Ireland. This changed in 1999 with the return of devolved government. However devolved government has been suspended on frequent occasions (for three months in 2000, twice briefly in 2001 and most recently on 14 October 2002). *See also* **Section C**.

Most local government functions in the province are performed either by the Secretary of State or by special boards. There are, however, 26 elected district councils with limited functions, mainly in the environmental field.

N. BRITAIN IN EUROPE

For a background article on the European Union, its development and current issues, *see* **C**11–12.

Since joining the European Economic Community (now the European Union) in 1973, the United Kingdom has participated in the EU as follows:

Council of Ministers and Commission

The Council of Ministers is the main decision-making body within the Union, consisting of representatives of the 15 member states (12 before 1995), each government delegating one of its ministers according to the business under discussion. The principal UK delegate is the Secretary of State for Foreign and Commonwealth Affairs.

The Commission heads a large bureaucracy in Brussels which submits proposals to the Council of Ministers, implements its decisions, and has powers of its own to promote the Community's interests. Its members are appointed by agreement among the member states for 4-year renewable terms. Members are pledged to independence of national interests.

President of the Commission (from November 2004):
  Sr Durão Barroso

UK Commissioner (since November 2004):
  Mr Peter Mandelson

Former Presidents of the Commission

1958–66	Walter Hallstein (West Germany)
1966–70	Jean Rey (Belgium)
1970–72	Franco Malfatti (Italy)
1972–73	Sicco Mansholt (Netherlands)
1973–77	Francois-Xavier Ortoli (France)
1977–81	Roy Jenkins (UK)
1981–85	Gaston Thorn (Luxembourg)
1985–95	Jacques Delors (France)
1995–99	Jacques Santer (Luxembourg)
1999–04	Romano Prodi (Italy)

European Parliament

Apart from general powers of supervision and consultation, the Parliament, which meets in Luxembourg and Strasbourg, can dismiss the Commission and has some control over the Community Budget. Until 1979 it consisted of members nominated by the national parliaments of the member states. The first direct elections were held in June 1979, the second in June 1984, and the third in June 1989. The fourth elections were held in June 1994, when Britain elected 87 MEPs, 6 more than in 1989. Five extra seats were given to England and one to Wales.

The most recent elections were in June 2004, when Britain elected 78 MEPs (down from 87 due to the enlargement of the EU).

UK Seats Won, 1979–94

	1979	1984	1989	1994
Conservative	60	45	32	18
Labour	17	32	45	62
Liberals (Lib Dems)	0	0	0	2
Scottish Nationalist	1	1	1	2
Democratic Unionist	1	1	1	1
Official Unionist	1	1	1	1
Social Democratic and Labour	1	1	1	1

The 1999 and 2004 Elections

For the elections in June 1999 the European Parliament constituencies, which used to elect one member, were replaced by large multi-member constituencies (or regions). London, for example, became one constituency instead of the former ten. Electors voted not for an individual candidate but for a party list of candidates. These elections represented the first time proportional representation had been used nationwide.

In the elections of June 2004 the number of UK MEPs was reduced from 87 to 78 (owing to the enlargement of the EU). The results for 1999 and 2004 were:

Party	1999 Seats	2004 Seats
Conservative	36	27
Labour	29	19
Lib Dems	10	12
UKIP	3	12
Green	2	
Nationalist	4	3
Others	3	3

O. BRITAIN AND THE UN

Britain was one of the founding members of the United Nations Organization which was created in 1945. The UN now (2006) has 192 member states. (Montenegro having joined in 2006, leaving only the Vatican as an independent state which is not a UN member, but is currently considering whether to apply for full membership). Its principal organs, with headquarters in New York, are:

General Assembly in which each member state has one vote and which normally meets once a year in September;

Security Council which has five permanent members (China, France, Russia, UK, USA) and ten non-permanent members elected for a two- year term.

Also linked with the UN are various international organizations, including the International Court of Justice (based in the Hague), the International Labour Organization (based in Geneva), the Food and Agriculture Organization (based in Rome), the UN Educational, Scientific and Cultural Organization (based in Paris) and the World Health Organization (based in Geneva).

Secretary-General: Mr Kofi Annan (Ghana) (until end of 2006).

P. WHO'S WHO IN BRITISH POLITICS 1979–2006
(for MPs, present constituency only is given)

Ancram, Michael, b. 1945; MP (Con) Devizes since 1992 (MP earlier in Scotland); Minister of State, Northern Ireland Office, 1994–7; Shadow Constitutional Affairs Spokesman, 1997–8; Conservative Party Chairman, 1998–2001; unsuccessful leadership contender, 2001; Deputy Leader and Shadow Foreign Secretary, September 2001–05; Deputy Leader and Shadow Defence Secretary, May–Dec. 2005.

Ashdown, Lord, b 1941; MP (Lib) 1983–8, (SLD) 1988–2001 (Yeovil); Leader, Social and Liberal Democratic Party from 1988 to 1999. High Representative, Bosnia, 2002–05.

Baker, Lord, b. 1934; MP (Con) 1968–97 (Mole Valley); Secretary of State for the Environment 1985–6, for Education and Science 1986–9, Chancellor of Duchy of Lancaster and Chairman of the Conservative Party 1989–90; Home Secretary 1990–92.

Beckett, Margaret, b. 1943; MP (Lab) 1974–9 and since 1983 (Derby South); Deputy Leader 1992–4; Shadow Health Secretary, 1994–5; Trade and Industry, 1995–7. President of the Board of Trade and Secretary of State for Trade and Industry, 1997–8. Leader of the House of Commons, 1998–2001. Environment, Food and Rural Affairs Secretary, 2001–06; Foreign Secretary since May 2006.

Benn, Anthony Wedgwood, b. 1925; MP (Lab) 1950–83 (except for short period between father's death and renunciation of the family peerage) and 1984–2001 (Chesterfield); Minister of Technology 1966–70, Secretary of State for Industry 1974–5 and for Energy 1975–9; Member Labour Party NEC 1959–60 and 1962-93.

Blair, Tony, *see* Section B.

Blunkett, David, b. 1947; MP (Lab) since 1987 (Sheffield Brightside). Shadow spokesman on environment, 1988–92. Shadow Health spokesman 1992–5. Shadow Education and Employment spokesman, 1995–7. Secretary of State for Education and Employment, 1997–2001. Home Secretary, 2001–04 (resigned). Secretary of State for Work and Pensions, 2005 (May–November) (resigned)

Boothroyd, Baroness, b 1929; MP (Lab) 1973–2000 (West Bromwich & until 1974, then West Bromwich W (b). Speaker of the House of Commons 1992–2000. (As Betty Boothroyd, the first woman to be elected Speaker. Created Life Peer, 2000. O.M. (2005).

Brittan, Lord, b. 1939; MP (Con) 1974 89; Chief Secretary to the Treasury 1981–3, Secretary of State for Home Department 1983–5, and for Trade and Industry 1985–6; EEC Commissioner 1989–99. Vice-President, 1995–9.

Brown, Gordon, b. 1951; MP (Lab) since 1983 (Kirkcaldy and Cowdenbeath since 2005); Shadow spokesman on trade 1989–92; Shadow Chancellor, 1992–7. Appointed Chancellor of the Exchequer, May 1997, he has become the longest continuously serving Chancellor since Vansittart in 1823.

Callaghan, Lord, *see* Section B.

Cameron, David, b. 1969; MP (Con) Witney since 2001. Deputy Chairman, Conservative Party, 2003–04. Shadow Education and Skills spokesman, May–Dec 2005. Leader of the Conservative Party since 2005.

Campbell, Sir Menzies, b. 1941; MP (Lib, then Lib Dem) Fife North East since 1987. Spokesman on Foreign Affairs, 1997–2006. Deputy Leader, 2003–06. Leader of the Liberal Democrats, 2006–.

Carrington, Lord, b. 1919; Leader of Opposition in the Lords 1964–70 and 1974–9; Secretary of State for Defence 1970–4, for Energy 1974, and for Foreign and Commonwealth Affairs, 1979-82; Secretary-General of NATO 1984–8; Chairman Conservative Party Organisation 1972–4.

Clarke, Charles, b. 1950; MP (Lab) Norwich South since 1997; President, NUS, 1975–7; Minister without Portfolio and Chairman of the Labour Party, 2001–02; Secretary of State for Education and Skills 2002–04. Home Secretary, 2004–May 2006.

Clarke, Kenneth, b. 1940; MP (Con) since 1970 (Rushcliffe); Paymaster General 1985–7, Chancellor of the Duchy of Lancaster 1987–8, Secretary of State for Health 1988–90, for Education 1990–92. Home Secretary 1992–3, Chancellor of the Exchequer 1993–7. Defeated for Conservative leadership, 1997. Defeated again in 2001 and 2005.

Cook, Robin, (1946–2005); MP (Lab) 1974–2005 (Livingston); Shadow spokesman on Health 1987–92; Shadow Trade and Industry spokesman, 1992–4. Shadow Foreign Secretary, 1994–7. Foreign Secretary, 1997–2001. Leader of the House of Commons, 2001–03. Resigned, 17 March 2003.

Davis, David, b. 1948; MP (Con) Boothferry, 1987–97, Haltemprice and Howden since 1997. Minister of State, Foreign and Commonwealth Office, 1994–7. Chairman of the Conservative Party, 2001–02; Shadow Deputy Prime Minister, 2002–03; Shadow Home Secretary, 2003–.

Dewar, Donald, (1937–2000). MP (Lab) 1966–70 and 1978–2000 (Glasgow Garscadden). First elected to Shadow Cabinet 1984; Opposition Chief Whip 1995–7. Secretary of State for Scotland 1997–9; Chosen to lead Labour in Scottish Assembly, 1998. Scotland's First Minister 1999–October 2000.

Dobson, Frank, b. 1940; MP (Lab) since 1979 (Holborn and St. Pancras); Shadow spokesman on Transport and London, 1993–4. Shadow Environment spokesman, 1994 7. Shadow Spokesman for Health, 1997–9. Resigned to fight for post of Mayor of London (but lost election to Ken Livingstone).

Duncan Smith, Iain, b. 1954; MP (Con) Chingford 1992–7, Chingford and Woodford Green since 1997. Shadow Social Security spokesman, 1997–9. Shadow Defence Secretary, 1999–2001. Right-wing Eurosceptic who won 2001 leadership contest. First Roman Catholic to lead modern Conservative Party. Lost support of his party; resigned, Oct. 2003.

Edmonds, John, b. 1944; National Industrial Officer, General and Municipal Workers Union (later General, Municipal, Boilermakers and Allied Trades Union) 1972–85, General Secretary after 1985.

Foot, Michael, see Section B.

Fox, Liam, b. 1961; MP (Con) Woodspring since 1992. Co-Chairman, Conservative Party, 2003–05. Appointed Shadow Foreign Secretary, May 2005; Shadow Defence Secretary, Dec 2005.

Hague, William, b. 1961; MP (Con) since 1989 (Richmond, Yorks); Secretary of State for Wales, 1995–7, Became Leader of the Conservative Party, 1997, following election defeat of John Major, but resigned (8 June 2001) after his own election defeat. Shadow Foreign Secretary, Dec 2005–.

Hain Peter, b. 1950; MP (Lab) Neath since 1991; Minister of State, Foreign and Commonwealth Office, 1999–2000, 2001–02; Secretary of State for Wales, 2002 03; Leader of the House of Commons, Lord Privy Seal and Secretary of State for Wales, 2003–05; Secretary of State for Northern Ireland (and also Wales), 2005–.

Harman, Harriet, b. 1950; MP (Lab) since 1982 (Camberwell & Peckham); Shadow Health Secretary under Tony Blair. Secretary of State for Social Security, 1997–8. Solicitor-General 2001 05; Minister of State, Constitutional Affairs, 2005–.

Hattersley, Lord, b. 1932; MP (Lab) 1964–97 (Birmingham Sparkbrook); Secretary of State for Prices and Consumer Protection 1976–9; Shadow Home Secretary 1987–92; Deputy Leader 1983–92.

Healey, Lord, b. 1917; MP (Lab) 1952–92 (Leeds East); Secretary of State for Defence 1964–70, Chancellor of the Exchequer 1974–9; Deputy Leader 1980–3.

Heseltine, Lord, b. 1933; MP (Con) 1966–2001 (Henley); Secretary of State for the Environment 1979–83; for Defence 1983–6; for the Environment 1990–92. Secretary of State for Trade and Industry 1992–5; Deputy Prime Minister 1995–7.

Hewitt, Patricia, b. 1948; MP (Lab) Leicester West since 1997. General Secretary, National Council for Civil Liberties, 1974–83. Secretary of State for Trade and Industry, 2001–05; for Health, 2005–. At centre of problems over financing of the National Health Service.

Howard, Michael, b. 1941; MP (Con) since 1983 (Folkestone and Hythe); Secretary of State for Employment 1990–92, for the Enviroment, 1992–3. Home Secretary, 1993–7. Shadow Foreign Secretary 1997–9. Shadow Chancellor, 2001–03. Leader of the Conservative Party after November 2003. Announced he would resign as Leader, May 2005.

Howe, Lord, b. 1926; MP (Con) 1964–6 and 1970–92 (Surrey East); Solicitor-General 1970–2, Minister for Trade and Consumer Affairs 1972–4, Chancellor of the Exchequer 1979–83, Secretary of State for Foreign and Commonwealth Affairs 1983–9, and Leader of the House of Commons (and Deputy Prime Minister) 1989–90. Companion of Honour.

Hume, John, b. 1937; MP (SDLP) 1983–2005. Leader, Social Democratic and Labour Party, 1979–2001. MEP (SDLP) Northern Ireland, 1979–2004. Declined to stand for Irish Presidency, 1997. Shared 1998 Nobel Peace Prize (with David Trimble).

Hurd, Lord, b. 1930; MP (Con) 1974–97 (Witney); Minister of State, Foreign Office 1979–83, Home Office 1983–4, Secretary of State for Northern Ireland 1984–5, for Home Department 1985–9, and for Foreign and Commonwealth Affairs, 1989–95.

Jenkins, Lord, see Section B.

Joseph, Lord (Sir Keith Joseph), (1918–94). MP (Con) 1956–87 (Leeds South-East). Secretary of State for Social Services, 1970–4; for Industry, 1979–81; for Education and Science, 1981–6.

Kennedy, Charles, b. 1959; MP (Lib Dem) Ross, Skye and Lochaber since 2005. Previously SDP (then Lib Dem) MP for Ross, Cromarty and Skye, 1983–97; Ross, Skye and Inverness West, 1997–2005. President, Liberal Democrats, 1990–94. Leader of Liberal Democrats, 1999–2006 (Jan).

Kinnock, Lord, see Section B.

Lamont, Lord, b. 1942; MP (Con) 1972–97 (Kingston-upon-Thames); Financial Secretary, Treasury 1986–9, Chief Secretary 1989–90, Chancellor of the Exchequer, 1990–3.

Lawson, Lord, b. 1932; MP (Con) (Feb.) 1974–92 (Blaby); Financial Secretary to the Treasury 1979–81, Secretary of State for Energy 1981–3, Chancellor of the Exchequer 1983–9.

Letwin, Oliver, b. 1956; MP (Con) West Dorset since 1997. Spokesman on Constitutional Affairs, 1998–9; Treasury, 1999–2001. Shadow Home Secretary, 2001–03, Shadow Chancellor, 2003–05. Shadow Environment, Food and Rural Affairs Secretary, 2005–.

Lilley, Peter, b. 1943; MP (Con) since 1983 (St Albans, 1983–97, Hitchin and Harpenden since 1997). Trade and Industry Secretary, 1990–92; Secretary of State for Social Security, 1992–7. Leadership candidate, 1997; Deputy Leader of the Conservative Party 1998–9.

Livingstone, Ken, b. 1945; MP (Lab) 1987–2001 (Brent East). Leader, Greater London Council, 1981–6. Won election as Independent candidate for Mayor of London, May 2000. Re-admitted to Labour Party, January 2004. Re-elected Mayor (June 2004) as Labour candidate.

McConnell, Jack Wilson, b. 1960; MSP (Lab) Motherwell and Wishaw since 1999. Minister for Finance, Scottish Executive, 1999–2001. Confirmed as First Minister, 22 November 2001.

Major, Sir John, see Section B.

Mandelson, Peter, b. 1953; MP (Lab) Hartlepool, 1992–2004. Opposition Whip, 1994–7. Minister of State, Cabinet Office, 1997–8; Secretary of State for Trade and Industry, 1998. Resigned, December 1998. Secretary of State for Northern Ireland, 1999–2001. Second resignation, 24 January 2001. Appointed European Commissioner, 2004.

Martin, Michael, b. 1945; MP (Lab) Glasgow Springburn, 1979–2005; Glasgow North East, 2005–. Speaker since October 2000. The first Roman Catholic to hold the post since the Reformation.

Maude, Francis, b. 1953; MP (Con) since 1997 (Horsham) (earlier MP for Warwickshire North, 1983–92); Shadow Chancellor of the Exchequer 1998–2000; Shadow Foreign Secretary, 2000–2001. Appointed Chairman of Conservative Party, May 2005.

Mawhinney, Lord, b. 1940; MP (Con). 1979–2005 (Peterborough, then Cambridgeshire NW). Secretary of State for Transport, 1994–5. Chairman of the Conservative Party, 1995–7. Shadow Home Secretary, 1997–8.

May, Theresa, b. 1956; MP (Con) Maidenhead since 1997; first woman Chairman of the Conservative Party, 2002–03. Currently (2005) Shadow Secretary for Family and Culture, Media and Sport.

Michael, Alun, b. 1943; MP (Lab) Cardiff South and Penarth since 1987. Minister of State, Home Office, 1997–8. Secretary of State for Wales, 1998–9. First Minister, Welsh Assembly, 1999–February 2000. Rural Affairs Minister, June 2001–05.

Milburn, Alan, b. 1958; MP (Lab) Darlington, 1992–. Chief Secretary to the Treasury, 1998–9. Secretary of State for Health, 1999–2003. Chancellor of the Duchy of Lancaster, 2004–05.

Monks, John, b. 1945; official of Trades Union Congress. Deputy General Secretary, 1987–93, General Secretary since 1993. Retired in 2003.

Morgan, Rhodri, b. 1939; MP (Lab) 1987–2001 (Cardiff West). First Minister, Welsh Assembly, since 2000 (following resignation of Alun Michael).

Mowlam, Marjorie (1949–2005); MP (Lab) 1987–2001 (Redcar); Shadow Northern Ireland Secretary under Tony Blair. Secretary of State for Northern Ireland, 1997–9. Appointed Chancellor of the Duchy of Lancaster and 'Cabinet enforcer', 1999. Retired from Commons, 2001.

Osborne, George, b. 1971; MP (Con) Tatton since 2001. Appointed Shadow Chancellor, May 2005.

Owen, Lord, b. 1938; MP (Lab) 1966–81, (SDP, Ind. Soc. Dem. after 1990) 1981–92 (Plymouth Devonport); Secretary of State for Foreign and Commonwealth Affairs 1977–9; co-founder of Social Democratic Party 1981 and Leader 1983–7 and from 1988 until its dissolution in 1990. Co-Chairman, Peace Conference on ex-Yugoslavia, 1992–5. Created Companion of Honour, 1995.

Paisley, Rev. Ian, b. 1926; MP (Protestant Unionist 1970–4, Democratic Unionist since 1974) (Antrim North); MEP, 1979–2004; member of Stormont 1970–2, NI Assembly 1973–5, NI Constitutional Convention 1975–6, NI Assembly after 1982.

Patten, Lord, b. 1944; MP (Con) 1979–92 (Bath); Secretary of State for the Environment 1989–90; Chancellor of the Duchy of Lancaster, 1990–92; Chairman of the Conservative Party, 1990–92; Governor of Hong Kong, 1992–7. Created Companion of Honour 1998. EU Commissioner, 1999–2004. Chancellor of Oxford University, March 2003. Life Peerage, 2004.

Portillo, Michael Denzil Xavier b. 1953; MP (Con) Dec, 1984–97 (Southgate). Chief Secretary to the Treasury, 1992–5. Secretary of State for Defence, 1995–7. Defeated in 1997 election. Returned to parliament in Kensington and Chelsea by-election, November 1999. Shadow Chancellor of the Exchequer 2000–2001. Unsuccessful leadership candidate, 2001. Retired to backbenches. Left the Commons, 2005.

Prescott, John, b. 1938; MP (Lab) since 1970 (Hull East); Shadow spokesman on Transport, 1988–93; on Employment, 1993–4. Deputy Leader of the Labour Party, 1994–7. Deputy Prime Minister, and Secretary of State for Environment, Transport and the Regions, 1997–2001. Remained Deputy Prime Minister after 2001 and 2005 elections with title First Secretary of State (no departmental duties after May 2006).

Redwood, John, b. 1951; MP (Con) since 1987 (Wokingham). Secretary of State for Wales, 1993–5. Resigned to contest (unsuccessfully) the leadership against John Major (July 1995). Shadow Trade and Industry Secretary, 1997–2000. Shadow Deregulation Secretary, 2004–.

Reid, John, b. 1947; MP (Lab) Motherwell North, 1987–97, Hamilton North and Bellshill, 1997–2005; Airdrie and Shotts, 2005–; Secretary of State for Scotland, 1999–2001; Secretary of State for Northern Ireland, 2001–02; Chairman of the Labour Party and Minister without Portfolio, 2002–03. Briefly Leader of the House of Commons, 2003. Secretary of State for Health, 2003–05. Defence Secretary, 2005–06. Home Secretary, 2006–.

Ridley, Lord, 1929–93; MP (Con) 1959–92 (Cirencester and Tewkesbury); Secretary of State for Transport 1983–6, for the Environment 1986–9, and for Trade and Industry 1989–90.

Rifkind, Sir Malcolm, b. 1946; MP (Con) Edinburgh Pentlands, Feb 1974–97; Kensington and Chelsea since 2005; Secretary of State for Scotland, 1986–90; for Transport, 1990–92; for Defence, 1992–5; Foreign Secretary, 1995–7. Shadow Work and Pensions Secretary, 2005 (May–Dec).

Robertson, Lord, b. 1949; MP (Lab) Hamilton South, 1978–99. Secretary of State for Defence, 1997–9. Secretary-General of NATO, 1999–2003.

Salmond, Alex, b. 1954; MP (SNP) since 1987 (Banff and Buchan); Leader of SNP, 1990–2000. On left of party. Leader of SNP opposition in Scottish Parliament until 2000. Elected SNP Leader again, September 2004.

Short, Clare, b. 1946; MP (Lab) since 1983 (Birmingham Ladywood). Secretary of State for International Development, 1997–2003.

Smith, Lord, b. 1951; MP (Lab), 1983–2005 (Islington South and Finsbury); Shadow Social Security Secretary. National Heritage Secretary, 1997–2001. Office was renamed Department of Culture, Media and Sport.

Smith, John, see Section B.

Steel, Lord, see Section B.

Straw, Jack, b. 1946; MP (Lab) since 1979 (Blackburn); Shadow Home Secretary under Tony Blair. Home Secretary, 1997–2001. Foreign Secretary, 2001–06. Leader of the House, 2006–.

Swinney, John, b. 1964; MP (SNP) Tayside North, 1997–2001. MSP, Tayside North since 1999. Deputy Leader, SNP, 1998–2000. Leader, SNP, 2000–04.

Taylor, Baroness, b. 1947; MP (Lab) 1974–2005 (Dewsbury); President of the Council and Leader of the House of Commons, 1997–8; Chief Whip 1998–2001.

Tebbit, Lord, b. 1931; MP (Con) 1970–92 (Chingford); Secretary of State for Employment 1981–3, for Trade and Industry 1983–5, Chancellor of the Duchy of Lancaster 1985–7; Chairman of Conservative Party Organisation 1985–7.

Thatcher, Baroness, see Section B.

Trimble, Lord, b. 1944; MP (Ulster Unionist) from 1990 by-election to 2005 (Upper Bann). Leader of the Ulster Unionists after 1995. Chief Minister in Northern Ireland Assembly after 1998. Shared 1998 Nobel Peace Prize (with John Hume). Defeated in May 2005 election. Life Peerage, 2005.

Turnbull, Sir Andrew, b. 1945; Civil Servant; Principal Private Secretary to Margaret Thatcher, 1988–93; Permanent Secretary to the Treasury, 1998–2002; Secretary to the Cabinet and Head of the Home Civil Service, 2002–.

Walker, Lord, b. 1932; MP (Con) 1961–92 (Worcester); Secretary of State for the Environment 1970–2 and for Trade and Industry 1972–4, Minister of Agriculture 1979–83, Secretary of State for Energy 1983–7 and for Wales 1987–90.

Whitelaw, Viscount, see Section B.

Widdecombe, Ann, b. 1956; MP (Con) since 1997 (Maidstone and the Weald) (earlier MP for Maidstone, 1987–97); Minister of State, Employment, 1994–5; Minister of State, Home Office, 1995–7. Shadow Secretary of State for Health 1998–9. Shadow Home Secretary, 1999–2001.

Willetts, David, b. 1956; MP (Con) since 1992 (Havant); Paymaster-General, 1996; Shadow Secretary for Work and Pensions, 2001–03, 2004–05; Head of Policy Co-ordination, 2003–04. Currently Shadow Education Secretary (since Dec. 2005).

Williams, Baroness, b. 1930; MP (Lab) 1964–79, (SDP) 1981–3; Secretary of State for Prices and Consumer Protection 1974–6 and for Education and Science 1976–9; Member Labour Party NEC 1970–81; co-founder of Social Democratic Party 1981 and President 1982–8; joined SLDP, 1988. Leader, Liberal Democrats, House of Lords, 2001–04.

Q. GLOSSARY OF RECENT POLITICS

Anglo-Irish Agreement Agreement on Northern Ireland reached by Mrs Thatcher and the Irish premier Garret Fitzgerald on 15 November 1985. The Agreement recognised the right of the Northern Irish people to decide their own destiny but gave the Irish government a consultative role in the province's affairs through an Intergovernmental Conference where political, legal and security matters would be discussed. The Agreement was angrily received by the Protestant community and Unionist MPs subsequently boycotted the Commons in protest.

Asylum Seeker A person who applies for refugee status because he or she has, in the words of the 1951 United Nations Convention on Refugees, 'a well-founded fear of persecution' on the grounds of 'race, religion, nationality, membership of a particular social group or political opinion.' States that have signed the convention are obliged to grant refugee status to anyone who meets one of these five grounds. The Immigration & Asylum Act 1999, in force since April 2000, made it virtually impossible for asylum seekers to enter Britain legally.

Black Wednesday Heavy selling of the pound on the money markets in 1992 prompted the raising of the base rate twice on 16 September to 15%. When this failed to preserve sterling's value relative to the Deutschmark, Chancellor of the Exchequer Norman Lamont withdrew Britain from the Exchange Rate Mechanism (ERM) and effectively devalued the pound. Despite the longer term beneficial effect on the British economy, the crisis with its underlying impression of drift and weak leadership undermined the position of John Major and led to Norman Lamont's eventual resignation.

Brighton Bombing On 12 October 1984 a Provisional IRA bomb exploded at the Grand Hotel, Brighton, during the Conservative party conference, killing five people (including a Conservative MP), and seriously injuring Norman Tebbit and his wife.

Brixton Riots Rioting broke out on 11 April 1981 following an incident in the week-long "Operation Swamp" mounted by police against street crime but which the local black population saw as unnecessarily provocative. During three days of rioting black and white youths fought the police, burnt buildings and vehicles and looted the central shopping area. Further riots broke out in Toxteth, Southall, Handsworth, Manchester and a wide range of towns in July. There was further rioting in Brixton on 28 September 1985 (following the accidental shooting of a black woman by police) and again in 1995 after the death of a young black man in custody.

Broadwater Farm A local authority housing estate in Tottenham, North London, the scene of rioting on 6 October 1985 following the death of a black woman during a police raid. A police officer was killed during the clashes. Three black youths imprisoned for his murder were released in 1991 following successful appeals, one of many contemporary cases which called the police and judicial system into serious question.

Bruges Group Group formed following a speech in Bruges by Mrs Thatcher on 20 September 1988. The group supported her view set out in the speech that European co-operation should be restricted to an economic relationship between separate sovereign states rather than a thoroughgoing European union.

Citizens Charter An attempt to make public services more responsive to consumers' wishes, announced by Mr Major on 22 July 1991.

Clause 28 A Section of the 1988 Local Government Act inserted by Tory backbenchers which banned local authorities from promoting the acceptability of homosexuality in schools. The clause was seen by many lesbians and gay men as the beginning of an attack on their legal rights. Now repealed in Scotland. In July 2003 the House of Lords finally agreed to its repeal.

Delors Plan Proposal for European political and monetary union drawn up under Jacques Delors, President of the European Commission from 1985. The plan envisaged the creation of a European Monetary System, a central bank to exert greater influence and eventually control over national monetary policies. The plan was accepted in 1989 as the basis for future moves towards European Monetary Union but the plan's apparently inevitable progress towards European unity aroused resistance from Mrs Thatcher's government.

Downing Street Declaration Agreement on 15 December 1993 between Mr Major and Irish prime minister Albert Reynolds offering Provisional Sinn Fein participation in multi-party talks on the future of Ireland within three months of a permanent end to IRA terrorism. Although unification could not take place without Unionist agreement, the British government took a near-neutral stance on its possibility. The Declaration followed meetings between Sinn Fein president Gerry Adams and SDLP leader John Hume (and the revelation of previous secret contacts between the government and Sinn Fein). Hopes of immediate peace were disappointed but Provisional IRA announced a ceasefire on 31 August 1994. This ended in February 1996.

Dries Conservative Party members (and supporters of Mrs Thatcher) who favoured an economic policy of strict monetarism, lower taxation *etc.*

Essex Man Stereotypal South of England Conservative voter and Thatcher supporter in the 1980s, seen as a vulgar materialist racist. The expression (together with the sexist Essex Girl)— although first coined by Conservative journalist Simon Heffer—was used with superior disdain by the liberal middle classes.

Falklands Factor Britain's success in the Falklands War and her undoubted determination to win at all costs helped Mrs Thatcher—hitherto one of the most deeply unpopular of 20th century prime ministers—win an overwhelming victory in the 1983 general election and consolidated her power in the Conservative Party until 1990.

Falklands War Fought to restore the 2,000 population on the Falklands (Malvinas) Islands to British control following invasion by Argentine forces on 2 April 1982. A 6,000 strong military and naval task force crossed the Atlantic, landed on 21 May and captured the capital Port Stanley on 14 June, forcing the Argentine surrender.

GCHQ Government Communications Headquarters in Cheltenham which collected signals intelligence through a worldwide network of listening posts. The government banned GCHQ workers from union membership on 25 January 1984 following the allegedly disruptive effects of a civil service strike in 1981. Workers who refused to leave their union were dismissed. This ban was lifted in 1997 by the newly elected Labour Government.

Good Friday Agreement A stage in the Northern Ireland peace process, the agreement was signed on 10 April 1998 and contained sections on the internal structure of Northern Ireland (including an elected Assembly and power-sharing), the north's relations with the Republic of Ireland (including a number of North–South bodies), and relations between the Republic and the United Kingdom (which included a Council of the British Isles). There were additional sections on constitutional and human rights, decommissioning of weapons, security, policing and prisoners. The Agreement was put to a referendum in Northern Ireland and the Republic on 22 May 1998. Of those who voted, 94·39% supported the agreement in the Republic and 71·12% also voted for it in the north.

Grassroots Alliance Centre-left grouping (its full title is the Centre Left Grassroots Alliance) in the Labour Party formed to contest the party's National Executive Committee (NEC) elections against the leadership's preferred Members First. Grassroots Alliance candidates took four of the six constituency places in the 1997 NEC elections and three out of six in 1998. While not overtly 'Old Labour', the Grassroots Alliance tends to reflect the position of members who do not completely support the party establishment.

Greater London Authority (GLA) A strategic authority for London, partly a replacement for the Greater London Council abolished by the Conservative government in 1986. The 1998 Greater London Authority Act provided for an elected mayor and a 25-member GLA covering the 32 London boroughs (both ratified in a referendum held in May 1998). The GLA has a £3 billion annual budget and has responsibility for transport, the environment, planning, the police, fire services and economic regeneration. The first elections for mayor and GLA members – under a form of proportional representation – were held in May 2000. The second took place on 10 June 2004.

Greenham Common Base where Cruise missiles were deployed in 1983. Women protesting at their planned deployment began a vigil at the base perimeter on 12 December 1982 and a "peace camp" of protesters remained there until the missiles were withdrawn in 1989. The camp became a symbol internationally of anti-nuclear protest.

Maastricht Treaty signed on 10 December 1991 following a summit of European leaders setting out agreements reached on the Treaty of European Union. Leading a party deeply divided on Europe, Mr Major negotiated clauses allowing Britain to opt out of a single currency and the Social Chapter. The treaty was ratified by Parliament, despite a vigorous campaign for a referendum on the issue led in the House of Lords by Lady Thatcher.

Miners' Strike A bitter dispute in 1984–85, seen in part as the Conservative party's revenge for the 1974 strike which led to the fall of the Heath government. The NUM led by Arthur Scargill took action against what he claimed was a plan for massive pit closures. The NUM refused to hold a national ballot and this lost the support of the wider trade union leadership, as well as opening the way for a breakaway Union of Democratic Miners to continue working. Tactically, the miners suffered from opening their strike in the spring when coal stocks were high. The dispute was harshly fought, with much hardship among miners' families. Labour, led by Mr Kinnock, though sympathetic to the miners, distanced itself for fear of the impact on its electoral prospects. The miners' eventual defeat was followed by a massive closure programme.

Neill Report Report on the funding of political parties issued by the Committee on Standards in Public Life, chaired by Lord Neill of Buxton, in 1998. The Committee—established in 1994—had been asked to include party funding as part of its examination of conduct in public life in 1997. The report made a hundred recommendations, including maximum general election expenditure of £20 million for each party, full disclosure of all donations of over £5,000, an end to acceptance of donations from abroad, tax relief on individual donations up to £500 and procedures to allay concerns that large donors had been able to 'buy' honours. The Labour government introduced draft legislation based on Neill's proposals in July 1999.

Nolan Committee The Committee on Standards in Public Life set up in 1994 under the chairmanship of Lord Nolan following a series of "sleaze" events. One of its recommendations was the establishment of the office of Parliamentary Commissioner for Standards.

Opting Out Right of a school to leave local education authority control if a majority of parents and governors vote to do so, introduced in the 1988 Education Reform Act. The school is directly funded by central government and the governing body is responsible for spending and performance.

Private Finance Initiative (PFI) The Private Finance Initiative (PFI) was a creation of the Conservative government in 1992 and has been taken up by Labour. Under PFI, contractors pay for the construction costs of, for example, a hospital or a school, and then rent the finished project back to the public sector. This removes the need for the government to increase taxation. Critics of PFI say that it is more expensive in the long run to pay the private sector than for the government to finance construction and operation.

Privatisation *See* **Section L.**

Public Order Act 1986 The Act, which aroused criticism from civil liberties groups, created a new range of public order offences by extending police powers over marches and demonstrations, and creating for the first time statutory controls over open-air meetings and picketing. The Act made trespass a criminal offence.

Public Private Partnerships (PPP) Collaboration between public bodies, for example, local authorities or central government, and private business. PPP is at the centre of attempts by the Labour government since 1997 to revive public services and is based on the belief that private companies are more efficient and managerially effective than public bureaucracies. Advocates say that if privatisation represents a take-over of a publicly-owned asset, PPP is closer to a merger, with both sides sharing risks and reaping benefits. PPP is an important aspect of the Private Finance Initiative (PFI).

Scarman Report Lord Scarman was appointed to investigate the causes of the April 1981 Brixton riots and other disturbances. His report defended the measures police had taken but pointed to the need for more ethnic minority police officers, for the screening of recruits for racist attitudes and the dismissal of proven racist officers, greater consultation with local communities, more police on the beat, and the regulation of police search powers.

Scott Report The Report of Sir Richard Scott, published in 1996, into the 'Arms-to-Iraq' affair. The government narrowly survived a Commons vote on the Scott Report.

Section 28 *See under* **Clause 28.**

Sinn Fein Ban Order issued by Home Secretary Douglas Hurd on 19 October 1988 preventing the broadcasting of direct statements by representatives of Sinn Fein, the Ulster Defence Association and other organisations linked with terrorism. Actors were allowed to read transcripts of their comments, weakening the ban's effectiveness. The ban was lifted in September 1994 following the Provisional IRA ceasefire.

Social Chapter Section of the Treaty on European Union rejected by the Thatcher and Major governments. The seven Articles of the Chapter include: the improvement of living standards within a context of economic competitiveness; encouragement of health and safety at work, equality for women, and consultation of workers by employers; promotion of management-worker consultation by the European Commission; and European co-ordination of social policy. In May 1997 the new Labour Government took the first steps to join the Social Chapter.

Trafalgar Square Riot Violent demonstration against the widely unpopular poll tax (community charge) on 31 March 1990, the culmination of prolonged nationwide protests. Over 130 were injured, including 57 police, and 341 arrested in fighting and looting which spread through the centre of London. Mrs Thatcher, who was deeply committed to the tax, was replaced as leader in the autumn and plans to abolish the tax were later announced.

Westland Affair A government crisis which almost forced Mrs Thatcher's resignation as prime minister in 1986. On 13 November 1985 the ailing Westland Helicopters announced a rescue deal involving a US–Italian consortium. Defence Secretary Michael Heseltine favoured a deal with a European company. On 6 January 1986 a letter to Mr Heseltine from the Solicitor General Sir Patrick Mayhew warning him about his position was leaked to the press. Mr Heseltine resigned dramatically by walking out of a Cabinet meeting on 9 January. On 24 January Trade & Industry Secretary Leon Brittan resigned after allegations of his involvement in the leak. Only mishandling of a Commons debate by opposition leader Neil Kinnock prevented responsibility being attached to Mrs Thatcher.

West Lothian Question A key argument (named after the anti-devolution Labour MP Tam Dalyell who represented West Lothian) in the debates of the 1970s on devolution. In essence, Dalyell asked why an MP for a Scottish constituency could vote at Westminster on English issues, but an MP for an English constituency could not vote on Scottish issues. In the 1990s, devolution went ahead but the question was never satisfactorily answered. It has received renewed attention as the Blair government relied on Scottish Labour MPs over NHS reforms, top-up fees *etc.*

SPECIAL TOPIC

CIVIL LIBERTIES IN BRITAIN
THE CURRENT DEBATE

Introduction

Civil liberties represent a balance between the rights of the individual and the powers of the State. They include equality before the law, and freedom of conscience, opinion, association, movement and speech. Conflict arises when the machinery of the State, ostensibly overseeing society's broader concerns, attempts to shift the balance to satisfy interests of its own.

The issue has taken greater prominence because of government actions motivated by fears of 'international terrorism' in the wake of the 11 September 2001 attacks. Added to this in Britain has been Labour and Conservative anxiety about tabloid media charges that they are 'soft on crime'.

The Labour Record

Civil liberties campaigners have expressed mixed views about the Labour government's record on the issue. While acknowledging some potentially positive aspects, they have also remarked on what one commentator has described as the 'authoritarian populism' of the government and, in particular, the former Home Secretary David Blunkett.

ID Cards

Mr Blunkett's announcement in 2003 of the government's intention (though apparently hotly debated in Cabinet) to move towards compulsory identity cards (*see* L57) and a national database, encapsulated concern. He declared identity cards were an effective weapon against illegal immigration, misuse of the NHS by undeserving foreigners, terrorism and crime. His opponents, from both left and right, pointed to serious implications for individual liberty.

Launching the Identity Cards Bill in November 2004, Mr Blunkett said that the first cards would be issued on a voluntary basis in 2008. Parliament would then decide in 2011 or 2012 whether to make the ownership, though not the carrying, of cards compulsory.

Human Rights Act

On the positive side, Liberty, the leading civil liberties campaigning organisation, had praised the Human Rights Act 1998, which incorporated the European Convention on Human Rights into British law, making civil and political rights enforceable in the courts. In practice the government retains significant powers to deviate from the Convention in what it views as the 'national interest'.

The Race Relations (Amendment) Act 2000 was also welcomed for outlawing indirect racial discrimination by public bodies such as the police. Black and ethnic minorities, however, appear disappointed by the practical impact on their everyday lives.

Freedom of Information Act

Similarly, the Freedom of Information Act 2000, intended to guarantee the public right to information about government activity, proved weaker than Labour had promised in opposition, with ministers retaining substantial discretionary powers to withhold information. The Act came into force on 1 January 2005. The Data Protection Act 1998 gave individuals the right to access information held on them by private and public bodies.

Criminal Justice Proposals

On criminal justice, Labour's critics charge the government with extending Conservative legislation that they had criticised in opposition. The Conservative Criminal Justice and Public Order Act 1994, for example, removed a suspect's right to silence, allowing courts and juries to draw inferences when determining guilt. Labour was seen as taking this further in their proposals in the Criminal Justice Bill in 2003. The implications for civil liberties provoked resistance in both the Commons and the Lords.

Among the Bill's provisions were a limitation on the right to trial by jury, an easing of the double jeopardy rules preventing individuals being charged twice for the same crime, increased stop and search powers, a doubling to 14 days of the period a British terrorist suspect could be held without charge, and the admission of hearsay evidence in court on a person's character.

Opposition to the Proposals

Civil liberties campaigners argued that the removal of the individual's right to chose trial by jury in many cases, or allowing the court authorities to determine some trials as too complex for a jury, creates a two tier justice system. Abolishing double jeopardy in serious offences undermines a crucial principle and opponents claimed that a well-known defendant would be unlikely to get a fair second trial. Allowing previous convictions and even acquittals to be introduced in court would lead, opponents said, to a defendant being convicted for being likely to commit an offence rather than being the proved perpetrator.

Such was the level of opposition to the Bill that the government were able to pass it at the end of 2003 only after agreeing to concessions on their proposals for juries and the use of previous convictions in evidence.

Increased Police Powers

The Bill was part of a pattern of legislation that, campaigners argued, presents a growing threat to civil liberties. The Police Act introduced by the Conservatives in 1979 allows the police to enter property and install surveillance equipment if a chief constable believes this assists in action against serious crime. The property owner need not be a suspect. The incoming Labour government chose not to curtail this legislation.

Labour's Regulation of Investigatory Powers Act 2000 allows the police and other authorities to demand information from internet service suppliers about an individual's web browsing and e-mail contacts. Such information is intended to be of help in detecting or preventing crime, to assist national security or safeguard Britain's economic wellbeing. Civil liberties campaigners argue that enabling clandestine snooping on domestic e-mail represents a weakening of the presumption of innocence and the right to privacy.

A government attempt to enlarge these powers was defeated in 2002 but the following year Mr Blunkett announced his determination to increase the range of authorities entitled to access.

Football Disorder Act, 2000

The Football (Disorder) Act 2000 enables courts to ban potential hooligans from travelling, with no requirement for evidence that they have committed an offence. Police can prevent individuals leaving the country if there are 'reasonable grounds' to suspect they may become involved in violence or disorder at a football match. Civil liberties campaigners argue that this undermines both the presumption of innocence and the right of free movement.

Campaigners accuse the government of reacting unthinkingly to events (as over football disorder) or even manufacturing stunts. In 2002, for example, pilot schemes were set up allowing police to issue on-the-spot fines for anti-social behaviour, such as public drunkenness. In 2003 the government extended these powers with the Anti-Social Behaviour Act. Sections of the Health and Social Care Act 2001 allow the disclosure of confidential information on patients, a reaction to fears aroused by attacks by mentally ill individuals. The spread of close circuit television (CCTV) cameras on Britain's streets from the early 1990s increased surveillance, but opinion was divided over the system's effectiveness in reducing crime.

Counter Terrorism Legislation

Legislation to counter terrorism has generated further concern. The Terrorism Act 2000 replaced the Prevention of Terrorism Act 1974, initially introduced on a temporary basis by a previous Labour government in the face of Irish Republican terrorism. The 2000 Act defines terrorism broadly, including, for example, computer hacking or damage to property in a political cause. The government can proscribe an organisation without having to prove that members have committed a terrorist or, for that matter, any other offence.

Individuals can be convicted as terrorists for wearing clothing or emblems apparently connecting them with a proscribed organisation. In September 2003, protestors arrested at a London arms trade fair were charged under the Act. Police said they were prepared to use the Act to counter demonstrations against President Bush when he was visiting London in November 2003.

Concerns in the House of Lords

The Anti-Terrorism, Crime and Security Act 2001, rushed through Parliament in the wake of the 11 September attacks, allows the indefinite detention without trial of a foreign national designated by the Home Secretary as an international terrorist and a threat to national security; gives the police unrestricted access to confidential information held by government departments and public bodies, with no requirement to inform the individual being investigated; and allows the government wide powers to extend anti-terrorist or criminal justice legislation. Resistance in the House of Lords persuaded the government to limit the powers on access to confidential records and strengthened appeal rights against detention.

The government had used powers included in the Human Rights Act to waive Article 5 of the European Convention on Human Rights, which is intended to protect against arbitrary imprisonment. Britain—as Amnesty International pointed out—is the only European country that felt the need for such stringent legislation, despite the terrorist threat being repeatedly characterised as international in impact.

Within days of the Act becoming law in December 2001 eight people had been detained under its provisions. In October 2002 the Court of Appeal ruled that detention was legal.

However, following an appeal to the House of Lords in December 2004, this decision was reversed. In January 2005 the Home Secretary, Charles Clarke, announced that the provision would be extended to British citizens but that surveillance and house arrest would replace detention.

A draft Civil Contingencies Bill presented by the government at the end of 2003 was criticised by a committee of MPs and peers as threatening the 'dismantling of democracy'. The Bill, which was intended to extend the government's powers to counter terrorist attacks and deal with natural disasters, proposed enabling ministers to declare regional states of emergency There was particular criticism of provision to prevent the courts intervening on human rights grounds. The Civil Contingencies Act received Royal Assent in November 2004, with few amendments to the Bill having been accepted.

The Continuing Debate

Mr Blunkett ridiculed critics in 2002, pointing particularly to their objections to anti-terrorist legislation. He said that the government's actions on data protection, freedom of information and the Human Rights Act amounted to 'more protection for the British citizen against the State than anywhere else in the world.' In October 2004 Mr Kennedy, the Liberal Democrat leader, accused the government of undermining civil liberties by exploiting what he called a 'climate of fear' in the wake of the 11 September 2001 attacks. The government could argue that society has a right to live without the fear of crime and that it is the government's duty to secure that. Civil rights activists could respond, as Liberty did, that more convictions did not necessarily mean more justice. The government could argue that terrorism represents a threat to society requiring a determined response; civil rights activists could reply that in the longer term an unquestioning acceptance of the weakening of individual liberty poses a potentially greater threat.

Useful Contacts:

Liberty, 21 Tabard Street, London, SE1 4LA
www.liberty-human-rights.org.uk

Amnesty International, 99–119 Rosebery Avenue, London, EC1R 4RE
www.amnesty.org.uk

MONEY
MATTERS

This popular section provides a concise yet authoritative introduction to the complex problems of money, investment and taxation. There is help and guidance on such matters as house-buying, self-assessment, savings and insurance, as well as on making a will. Also included are details of the main tax rates set out in the March 2006 Budget and guidance on the new rules concerning pensions. Readers may also wish to refer to Section F for a wider background discussion of economic events.

TABLE OF CONTENTS

MONEY MATTERS

I. MONEY

1. SPENDING

Planning Your Expenditure.

Sometimes it is difficult to see just where all our money goes. Planning your expenditure can take time. However, it can be very worthwhile as it allows you to see how you are spending your money, where savings might be possible and how much is left over for other things.

The best way to plan and monitor your spending is to prepare a budget. The first step is to collect together all your household bills, bank statements, credit card statements, receipts and so on. This, of course, includes mortgage payments or rent, council tax, food, insurance, electricity, gas, water, other household expenses, telephone, motoring costs and travel to and from work. It should also include items such as presents, entertainment and holidays. The very act of adding these things up might give you some surprises as to just how much is being spent on some things and indicate possible savings.

As some of these expenditures vary over the year it is best to calculate the totals for the year. It is also a good idea to include something for unexpected expenses and emergencies. The annual total can then be divided into monthly or even weekly amounts. This shows how much has to be allowed for normal expenditure before there is money to spend on other things or to save.

A further stage is to go through all the items of expenditure looking for economies. It might be possible to move borrowings to lenders with lower interest rates. You might be able to do this with your mortgage loan as well but if you took out your mortgage before October 1995 this might affect the length of time you have to wait to get social security help with the mortgage interest in the event of redundancy or illness. Frequently there are savings to be made on household expenses, entertainment and other items. Certain things are also cheaper if they are bought on an annual basis – such as season tickets, insurance and car tax.

Setting Yourself Targets.

Some people find it helpful to set themselves particular targets. For example, you might aim to reduce your budget and keep it within a certain limit. This should not be too ambitious, just something that you can achieve without too much difficulty. It does not, of course, mean that you are making yourself worse off, just that you have greater control in deciding to move your money in the way you want to spend it. For instance, it might enable you to save for retirement or very large purchases that you might not otherwise be able to afford.

Planned saving can also be a helpful part of your budget in this respect. For example, you can have a regular sum of money transferred to a savings account and this can quietly accumulate until it is needed. Your budget can also be helped by paying many things by direct debit (*see* **E8**). This arrangement can spread the costs over monthly payments and some companies give a discount to customers who pay this way. However, you should still make sure you are not paying too much and see whether economies can be made.

2. SPENDING ECONOMICALLY

Many forms of expenditure are almost unavoidable. Thus the council tax and rent or mortgage payments cannot usually be avoided unless you move home. Nevertheless, in many other areas savings can be made.

As a general guide, the Consumers' Association publishes a monthly magazine *Which?* This provides a great deal of information about the price and quality of different products. Information about subscriptions to this magazine can be obtained from *Which?*, Subscription Department, PO Box 44, Hertford, SG14 1SH. Alternatively, it is available at libraries.

Utilities.

With increased competition between the suppliers of gas, electricity and telephone services you might be able to make significant savings by switching suppliers. This does not usually make an important difference to the service you receive, just the cost of it.

Food.

There are several points to remember when buying food. First of all, larger shops often sell goods at lower prices than smaller shops. As most people know, supermarkets often sell their own brands of many products. "Own brands" are, on average, cheaper than the brands of leading manufacturers. For example, on items such as peas, baked beans, soup and soup powder, own brands can be up to 15 per cent cheaper. On some lines, such as washing-up liquid, the savings can be even greater. There is no reason to suppose that own brands are inferior. They are commonly produced in the same place as the branded products. Often, the only difference is the packaging—and the price.

Other savings can be made with stores' special offers. Things like washing powder and toothpaste will be needed sooner or later; so it can make sense to buy these items when an offer is on, rather than waiting until you have run out.

When comparing prices, it is worth bearing in mind that the quantity varies as well. It is, therefore, better to compare the *unit cost* of products. This is the cost per gram or ounce. Packaging can easily make something look larger than it actually is.

Domestic Appliances.

Like food, the price of domestic appliances varies. Much of the variation depends on the number of extras. For example, a basic gas or electric cooker costs something in the region of £300. Such a cooker would serve a family quite adequately. If, however, you want a model with extras, then the cost can be £800 or more. A second important factor is where the appliance is sold. The price of the same model can vary considerably from place to place, so it is very worthwhile shopping around. There may also be a delivery charge. Discount warehouses are usually the cheapest place to buy appliances. The sales can also make a substantial difference to the price. Most appliances are likely to be cheaper in both winter and summer sales. Fridges are often particularly good bargains in winter sales, for obvious reasons. There is nothing inferior about domestic appliances sold in sales. Traders usually want to clear their premises for new lines. They also realise that January and the summer would otherwise be very lean times.

A particular question often arises as to whether to rent or to buy a television set. The advantages of renting are that repairs and service calls are included in the rent. If the set breaks down it is also likely to be repaired more quickly than if you owned a set. And if it cannot be fixed straight-away the rental company will provide a substitute until the original is repaired. On the other hand, it is generally true that it is cheaper to buy in the long run. This is true even if you buy the set on hire purchase. And if you decide to dispose of the set, you can always sell it. (Provided, of course, that any HP payments have been completed.)

Cars.

Cars are very expensive to buy and to run. It is quite common for the annual cost of running a car (including the drop in its secondhand value) to exceed £3,000. So it is worth thinking care-fully about whether or not to buy a car. It may be cheaper to use taxis. They also have the advantage of removing any worries about parking, maintenance and drunken driving.

If you do decide to buy a car, the initial invest-ment can be greatly reduced by buying a second-hand car. The value of most cars drops con-siderably in their first year. There are other advantages in buying second hand. A used car will have been run in and the teething troubles ironed out. However, if the car is more than three years old it must have an MOT (Ministry of Transport) test every year. The test is now very tough, so cars should be checked carefully before purchase.

If you do not get a guarantee from a reputable dealer you should consider having it examined by the AA or the RAC. They charge a fee for the service, but it may avoid a purchase you later regret. Alternatively, if faults are discovered it may enable you to negotiate a lower price.

Before setting out to buy a secondhand car it is sensible to study the market. Car price guides are widely available. They provide useful infor-mation on cars of different ages and condition. The two major sources of secondhand cars are professional dealers and private sellers. You are unlikely to get a bargain if you buy from a dealer, since they are very familiar with the value of used cars. If you buy privately you avoid the mark-up of the dealer, and so can expect to pay less. Even if you buy a new car, it can pay to ask for a dis-count, especially if you are paying cash. Dealers receive a sizeable discount on new cars. You may be able to persuade one to pass some of it on to you. Whatever sort of car you buy, new or old, you should give it a test drive. Even new cars are not immune from faults.

3. BORROWING

Under certain circumstances, it can be advan-tageous to borrow money. The biggest example in many peoples' lives is buying a house with the aid of a mortgage (see E11). On a much smaller scale most goods can be bought with the aid of credit. This does enable you to enjoy something without having to wait while you accumulate the cash to buy it outright. As prices rise, you may also be able to buy goods more cheaply through buying straightaway. And you save money buy-ing things like season tickets annually. But there are some disadvantages with borrowing. Some people might find easy credit too much of a tempt-ation and spend more than they can afford.

In addition, borrowing usually costs money. How much it costs depends on where the loan comes from. At the cheapest end of the scale are first mortgages. At the beginning of 2006 mortgage interest rates varied around 6 per cent and overdraft rates varied from 12 to around 18 per cent. The interest rate on personal loans was usually around 14 per cent. At the other end of the

scale are second mortgages, some hire-purchase arrangements and check trading. The rates of interest at the top end can be 30 per cent per year or even more. There are many sources of credit, so only the main ones will be discussed here.

Banks.

A flexible way of borrowing from a bank is to arrange an overdraft. This allows you to overdraw your current account up to a limit agreed with the bank manager. Overdrafts can be a relatively cheap way of borrowing since interest is charged only on the outstanding balance, but by being overdrawn you might incur higher bank charges. If you wish to overdraw regularly it may be worth comparing different banks' charges for overdrawn accounts. Unauthorised overdrafts should be avoided as they usually lead to higher interest and other charges.

With a personal loan you receive a lump sum and pay it back in regular instalments. This can make it easier to manage the repayments. Often the rate of interest will be fixed for the period of the loan. This is advantageous if interest rates rise during this time but not, of course, if interest rates fall. As with overdrafts, it may be worth shopping around to find the most favourable terms, and some building societies now offer personal loans as well.

Credit Cards.

Credit cards can be a convenient way of spreading the cost of purchases over a short period. They are also easy to use. When you buy something on credit the retailer will ask you to key in your Personal Identity Number (PIN). You can also draw cash from a bank displaying the appropriate sign. Every month you are sent a statement showing how much you owe. You then have to repay a certain mini-mum amount. If you wish to pay more, or clear all the debt, you can.

Credit cards can be cheap if you only need the borrowing facility for a short time, or if you normally pay all your bills in one go. For longer term loans it is usually cheaper to borrow the money in a different way, such as with a bank loan. It is also now possible for sellers to charge a higher price for credit card transactions. At the time of writing (2006) few retailers actually imposed higher charges, but if this becomes common it might be worth considering another form of payment.

Credit cards are now issued by a wide range of financial institutions. Originally cards were issued free of charge but many now have an annual fee. The rates of interest vary between cards and have fluctuated in recent years between 1·5 and 2·25 per cent per month but recently some credit cards have been offering cheaper rates. Some of the equivalent annual rates are as follows:

TABLE 1. *Credit Card Interest Rates*

Rate per month %	Equivalent rate per year %
1·50	19·5
1·75	23·1
2·00	26·8
2·25	30·6

Normally no interest is charged if the statement is paid off in full. For most cards, if only a part repayment is made, or if the payment arrives after the due date, there is no interest free credit period. On this basis, if you make a purchase just before the statement date and subsequently repaid the bal-ance in full, you may get about 20 to 35 days free credit. If, however, the purchase was made, say, three weeks before the statement, you could get up to 56 days free credit. For this reason, it can be use-ful to have two credit cards. If your statement dates differ, you can then use the card with the statement date furthest away. Credit cards can also be used overseas.

Other Cards.

There are several other cards. Affinity cards are credit cards which allow you to donate money to a worthy cause—for example 25p for every £100 spent. Store cards are operated in the same way as credit cards and sometimes offer special concessions. However the rate of interest charged is often higher than for credit cards and, of course, you can only use them in the issuer's shops. Charge cards, such as *American Express*, normally have no spending limits, but they do not offer extended credit and there is a charge for the card itself.

Hire Purchase.

Hire purchase is a form of credit but the rates of interest on hire-purchase agreements are generally higher than those charged on bank or credit-card loans. Salesmen sometimes quote "flat" rates of interest. This refers to the difference between the cash price and the cost if bought on credit. For example, suppose you could buy a cooker for £500 cash, or £625 payable in monthly instalments for one year. The extra cost of buying on credit is £125. This gives an annual flat rate of interest of 25 per cent on the £500 borrowed. But this is not the real rate of interest. The reason is that from the first month some of the capital has been repaid. In fact, the average amount borrowed throughout the year is just over £250. The true rate of interest on the balance outstanding (rather than the original loan) is over 40 per cent in this example. This calculation is known as the APR or annual percentage rate.

Insurance Companies.

If you have an insurance policy you may be able to borrow money from the insurance company on the strength of it. The policy would have to have a cash-in, or surrender value. The interest charged on such loans is often lower than other rates.

Second Mortgages.

These are loans that are secured on your home. As a result rates of interest may be lower than on some other forms of borrowing but your home is at risk if you fail to keep up the repayments.

4. SAVING

There are several reasons why people save. They include the need to meet unforeseen expenditures, to provide for retirement or simply to buy large items such as a car. It is normally cheaper to pay cash rather than to buy on hire purchase. Although many people save only when they have money left over from their various outgoings, it is better to plan savings. That is, budget your income and expenditure and to regard savings as part of your regular outgoings. This allows capital to be built up on a regular basis.

Before deciding where to invest these savings there are factors that you should consider. The first is whether to invest for short or long periods of time. It is generally true that long-term savings attract a higher rate of interest. However, there are usually financial penalties or constraints that will restrict your ability to draw on the money when required. This loss of *liquidity* is important, since you may require money immediately to meet unforeseen expenditures.

Real Rates of Interest.

Another consideration is the rate at which prices are increasing; that is the rate of inflation. The saver is particularly concerned with what goods or services money will buy in the future. The important rate of return of an investment is not the nominal or money rate of interest but the real rate of interest. If, for example, an investment offers a return of 5 per cent per annum and the rate of inflation is 3 per cent per annum, the real rate of interest is 2 per cent per annum. The individual requires 3 per cent per annum merely to maintain the purchasing power of the capital.

The real rate of interest is very important during periods of inflation because it may well be negative. For example, if the nominal rate of interest is 5 per cent per annum and the rate of inflation rises again, to say, 10 per cent per annum the real rate of interest is minus 5 per cent per annum. This

means that when the saver withdraws money in the future, it will not buy the same quantity of goods it would have when the investments were made.

Having considered these general points, we can now look at specific forms of investment.

National Savings and Investments.

These are schemes provided by the Government. A summary is shown in Table 2.

TABLE 2. *A Summary of National Savings Investments*

Investment	Features
Easy Access Savings Accounts	Instant access to savings
Investment Account Cash Mini ISA	One month's notice required
Fixed Interest Savings Certificates	Can invest for five years
Index-linked Savings Certificates	Tax-free and inflation-proof
Premium Savings Bonds	Chance to win a prize
Capital Bonds	Guaranteed interest
FIRST Option Bonds	Can invest for a year
Income Bonds	Regular income
Pensioners' Income Bonds	For those 60 and over
Children's Bonus Bonds	For children

National savings and investments are available through post offices. There are two main types of account, the 'easy access savings account' and investment accounts.

Easy Access Savings Accounts.

These accounts were introduced to replace the previous 'ordinary accounts' that dated back to Victorian times but were closed in 2004. Easy Access Savings Accounts can be opened by anyone aged eleven or over and can be held individually or jointly with one other person. The opening deposit must be £100 or more. After that money can be deposited or withdrawn as long as £100 remains in the account. The minimum deposit is £10 and this can be made at any post office, by telephone or by post and the maximum amount that can be saved is £2 million.

The minimum withdrawal is also £10 and up to £300 in cash can be withdrawn per day. Larger withdrawals can be arranged by telephone or post and the money paid into a bank or building society account. Higher rates of interest are paid on higher balances. The interest is taxable but tax is not deducted at source.

Investment Accounts.

Investment accounts can be opened by personal savers aged seven or over and can be held individually or jointly with someone else. An account may also be opened on behalf of a child under seven but withdrawals will normally be paid only to a parent or guardian until the child reaches seven.

The minimum amount needed to open an investment account is £20 and further deposits of £20 or more can be made up to a maximum of £100,000. Money can be withdrawn by giving one month's notice. It can be withdrawn without notice but this will result in the previous 30 days' interest being deducted. Withdrawals are arranged by post and the necessary form and envelope is available at post offices. Interest is paid at higher rates on higher balances and is taxable but tax is not deducted at source.

Cash Mini ISA.

Investment Savings Accounts (ISAs) are explained further on on **E7** and a cash mini ISA is offered by National Savings. It can be started with a deposit of £10. Additional deposits of £10 or over may then be made up to a total of £3,000 in each tax year (until 2010).

Fixed Interest Savings Certificates.

These certificates are issued with a guaranteed rate of interest for five years and there are now certificates for two years as well. They are available in the form of 'issues' each of which has its own rate of interest and maximum holding. This means that the maximum limit can be bought each time a new Issue is offered. At the time of writing (June 2006) the 83rd Issue of the five-year certificates guaranteed interest of 3·20 per cent compound if held for five years and the 33rd Issue of the two-year certificate paid 3·20 per cent.

To get the guaranteed rate of interest the certificates have to be held for the full term. If they are cashed in during the first year only the purchase price is repaid. If they are cashed in after the first year, the value of the certificates will be index-linked and interest paid for each full month they have been held.

The minimum investment is £100 and the maximum investment in an issue is £15,000. You can also reinvest any amount from matured National Savings Certificates on top of the £15,000.

You need not cash in Certificates when they reach maturity. In most cases, however, it will pay to do so. The General Extension Rate, the rate of interest currently paid on matured Certificates, is now well below most interest rates. Again anyone can hold certificates, including children under seven.

Tax-free Savings Certificates can be held in addition to Individual Savings Accounts (ISAs).

Index-Linked Savings Certificates.

These were originally known as "granny bonds' because when index-linked certificates were first issued they were only available to people over a certain age but this restriction no longer applies. These certificates are increased in line with the Retail Prices Index together with a guaranteed interest rate. They are available for periods of three or five years and repayments are tax-free.

The certificates are available in units of £100. You may buy up to £15,000 of the current issue in addition to any holdings you may have from previous issues. You may also reinvest from mature Savings Certificates over the £15,000 limit without any restriction.

Premium Bonds.

Premium Bonds are one of the most popular forms of national savings. No interest is earned as such on the bonds. Instead, you have a regular chance to win a cash prize each week and month.

All the prizes are tax free. However, before a bond is included in the draw it has to be held for one month following the month in which it was bought.

The winning numbers are generated by ERNIE (Electronic Random Number Indicator Equipment). The winning numbers are drawn entirely at random so that each bond has an equal chance of winning.

The size of the prizes varies from £50 to £100,000 and, since April 1994, there has been a monthly prize of £1,000,000 (twice a month since August 2005). Prizewinners are notified by post, so it is important to notify the Bonds and Stock Office of any change of address. The numbers of prize-winning bonds and a complete list of unclaimed prizes can be consulted at major post offices. In addition most daily newspapers publish the numbers of bonds which have won the larger prizes. If you fail to claim a prize at the time of the draw, this can be done later.

Premium Bonds can be bought at post offices, and banks. Any person over the age of 16 can buy bonds. A parent, grandparent or guardian can buy bonds on behalf of their children. For individuals aged 16 or over the minimum initial purchase is now £100 and the maximum holding is £30,000.

Capital Bonds.

Capital bonds are for people who wish to put some money away for a period of five years. They are available in multiples of £100 and the maximum amount held for all issues of capital bonds is £1 million. On each anniversary of the purchase interest is added and the rate of interest increases each year. The amount of interest is guaranteed over the period. At current rates (June 2006), the return is equal to 4·05 per cent compound. The bonds are repayable in full at the end of this period with all the interest due.

Although the interest is paid at the end of the five years, for income tax payers the interest is taxable each year. No further interest is earned after five years. Early repayment can be made after three months' notice is given but no interest is payable for repayments made in the first year.

Fixed Rate Savings Bonds.

This investment allows you to choose fixed rates of interest over set periods of time – currently one, three or five year terms. You can invest between £500 and £1 million in these bonds either individually or jointly with someone else. The rate of interest depends on the amount invested and the length of the set period of time.

Income Bonds.

These bonds provide a regular income from capital. The minimum investment is £500. Extra amounts can be invested in multiples of £500. The maximum holding is £1 million. The interest is paid on the fifth of each month and is taxable but tax is not withheld at source. Investments of £25,000 and over attract a higher rate of interest. Repayments may be obtained by giving three months' notice. The interest rate is adjusted from time to time.

Pensioners' Bonds.

The Pensioners' Guaranteed Income Bonds are designed for people of 60 and over who want a monthly income from their capital. The minimum investment is £500 and the maximum £1 million. The interest rate is fixed and there are now one, two and five year fixed rate bonds. The interest is paid on the 19th of each month directly into the investor's bank or building society account. Withdrawals can be made after 60 days notice and no interest is payable during this period.

Children's Bonus Bonds.

These are designed to be suitable gifts for children. They can be bought in units of £25 up to a maximum of £3,000 per child in the current issue. Before making such a gift, therefore, it is worth checking that it would not take the child's holding over the maximum. The bonds can be bought for any child under 16 and will continue earning interest until the child is 21. A bonus is added every five years. As nothing further is earned after the 21st birthday they should then be cashed in. All interest and bonuses are tax-free. The current issue (in June 2006) offered a guaranteed tax-free return of 3·85 per cent per annum compound when held for the first five years.

Guaranteed Equity Bonds.

National Savings and Investments offer a limited number of Guaranteed Equity Bond Issues from time to time and they are on sale for a limited period. The return on these bonds is linked to the performance of the stock market but guarantees that the original capital invested will be returned at the end of the investment period. These bonds have therefore offered gains (subject to an upper limit) from stock market investment without the risk of a loss.

Building Societies.

There are many building societies in the United Kingdom. Some of these are national, others local. All building societies are "mutual' organisations set up for the benefit of their investing and borrowing members. However, some of the former building societies such as the Abbey National and the Halifax have converted themselves into banks. There is no difference in the security of your money as between the small and large societies. If you want to be absolutely sure, you should choose one that has Trustee Status and is a member of the Building Societies Association.

For many years the interest rates quoted by building societies have been tax paid at the basic rate but non-taxpayers have not been allowed to claim the tax back. However the system was changed so that from 6 April 1991 non-taxpayers no longer have to suffer tax on the interest. Interest rates are higher for regular savings and the longer you are prepared to commit your money.

Banks.

Banks offer two main types of account, current and deposit. Current accounts are for everyday transactions and are discussed later (**E8**). Deposit accounts are more suitable for savings.

The rates of interest offered on deposit accounts do tend to change more quickly than those offered by other schemes. This is because the deposit rate is based on each bank's base rate which change as interest rates generally change. The deposit rate is usually between 4½ and 3 per cent below the base rate. The current rate offered by the various banks is usually on display at the bank branches. Interest is calculated on a daily basis. The interest is taxable, but in the past tax has not been deducted at source. However, from 6 April 1985, bank interest has been paid in the same way as building society interest. There is no minimum or maximum amount that can be deposited. If you want ready access to your savings, deposit accounts can be attractive for small amounts of money. But you should look at the rates offered by National Savings and Building Societies before choosing a bank deposit account.

Tax Exempt Special Savings Schemes (TESSAs).

Tax Exempt Special Savings Schemes (TESSAs) were introduced in January 1991 and investors could open new accounts until April 1999. The accounts ran for five years. At the end of the five years the saver received a bonus consisting of the money which would otherwise have gone in tax, provided that the capital had remained untouched.

Personal Equity Plans.

Personal equity plans (PEPs) were introduced on 1 January 1987 to provide a tax incentive for investing in shares. They were available for new investment until April 1999 when they were replaced by Individual Savings Accounts (ISAs).

Individual Savings Accounts (ISAs).

The Individual Savings Accounts (ISAs) are a tax-free way of saving that became available from April 1999 and replaced the previous TESSAs and PEPs. Existing TESSAs at April 1999 continued to run their course and when they matured the capital could be transferred into an ISA. Any continuing subscriptions and the maturing capital from a TESSA would not count against the annual subscription limit for a person's ISA account. Similarly PEPs in place in April 1999 can continue to be held outside ISAs but with the tax advantages.

Until April 2005 there were three types of ISAs – cash ISAs, stocks and shares ISAs and life insurance ISAs. However, in April 2005 the life insurance ISA was merged with the stocks and shares ISA. There are also Maxi ISAs and Mini ISAs. Maxi ISAs can include stocks and shares and cash. Mini ISAs can be cash ISAs or stocks and shares ISAs. For the tax year starting in April 2005 up to £7,000 can be invested in a Maxi ISA, of which no more than £3,000 may be in cash. For Mini ISAs in 2005/2006 up to £4,000 can be invested in a stocks and shares ISA and £3,000 in a cash ISA. The £7,000 annual limit on saving in Maxi ISAs will continue until 2010. Anyone who is resident for tax purposes in the UK can invest in an ISA provided they are aged 18 or over or 16 or over for cash ISAs.

The cash component of ISAs can be invested in cash accounts at banks and building societies or National Savings. For life insurance policies, up to £1,000 may be invested in a single premium policy. The rest can be invested in stocks and shares which qualified for TESSAs and PEPs, but not unlisted shares or those quoted on the Alternative Investment Market (AIM) since the ownership of such shares might already attract tax relief.

ISAs have to be run by authorised managers. Each person will be able to take out one ISA a year but can invest with a different manager the following year. Also, it is possible to move ISAs from one manager to another. Each year there is also a choice. The whole ISA can be placed with one manager. Alternatively separate managers may be chosen for Mini ISAs.

Gilt Edged Securities.

As well as raising taxes to finance its expenditure, the Government borrows from the general public. It does this by issuing gilt-edged stock. There are basically two types of stock, redeemable and irredeemable. Redeemable or dated stocks are those that the Government has agreed to repurchase on a certain date. Usually, two dates are given. This means that the Government cannot redeem them before the first date, but it must redeem them on or before the last date. Each stock has a par or face value of £100. This is the amount that will be repaid on redemption. An example of a redeemable stock is the 8 per cent Treasury Stock 2000–2006. Stocks that the Government is not committed to redeem are called irredeemable or undated stocks. The 2½ per cent consol introduced after the Second World War is an example.

Buying Costs of Gilts.

The cost of buying or selling securities will depend on whether you go through a stockbroker or through the Department for National Savings, Bonds and Stock Office. It is cheaper to use the National Savings Stock Office, although you can only deal in stocks that are on the National Stock Register. There is no limit to the total amount you may hold. Application forms may be obtained from Post Offices.

The interest or *coupon rate* on a stock is normally paid half-yearly. Some pay quarterly, which is particularly useful for old-age pensioners, for example. This is based on the nominal or par value. For example, the 8 per cent Treasury Stock pays £8·00 per year. However, the price that you pay for the stock will probably be less than par. The effective rate of interest or *running yield* will therefore be greater than 8 per cent.

Price Fluctuations of Gilts.

Prices of stocks fluctuate so that their yield keeps in line with interest rates generally. This presents the possibility of a capital gain or loss. However, it is generally true that as the stock approaches redemption, the closer the price will be to par, and the smaller the capital gain. The further away redemption is, the lower the price of the stock, and hence the greater will be the capital gain if the stock is held to redemption. Government securities are a very marketable investment. They can be sold quickly if need be. Also, stocks are free of capital-gains tax if in your possession for more than one year.

Shares.

For the more adventurous, there is the possibility of investing in shares on the stock market. Since share prices can fall as well as rise, it is advisable to "spread your risk." This means that you must have a varied and balanced collection of shares in your portfolio. To do this will require a lot of capital and knowledge of the market. So it is best to seek professional advice from a stockbroker or your bank manager. People with more limited means will be better advised to participate indirectly in the stock market (*e.g.* by unit trusts).

Unit Trusts and Investment Trusts.

Unit trusts sell "units" to investors and use the proceeds to buy shares. This allows the investor to spread the risk of his or her investment over all the shares the trust owns. Unit trusts are run by professional managers who can be expected to know more than many investors about the merits of different securities. The value of the units of a trust is worked out each day in line with the value of the fund's stock market investments. Two prices are quoted. The "offer' price is the price at which investors can buy units. The "bid' price is the price at which the managers will repurchase units. The offer price is higher than the bid price and the difference contributes towards the cost of running the trust. In addition, there is usually a small half-yearly or yearly charge. Units can be bought and sold directly from the managers.

Investment trusts are companies which invest in securities. Like unit trusts they enable investors to spread their investment risk. However, unlike unit trusts they have a fixed share capital. The shares in investment trusts are bought and sold in the same way as those of other companies, but some investment trusts also have savings schemes which can be taken out directly with the managers.

Life Assurance as Saving.

Life assurance policies provide an alternative method of saving regular amounts for long periods of time. The various policies are considered in the section on insurance. However one version which should be considered under the heading of saving is the tax-exempt life insurance policies sold by Friendly Societies (*see below*).

Friendly Societies: Tax Exempt Policies.

Friendly Societies are allowed limited tax relief on life insurance and endowment business and can therefore offer tax-free savings plans. In 1995 the general limit on a person's premiums was increased from £200 to £270 a year.

5. BANKS

Most people are familiar with the high street banks. These are the clearing banks and are known as the Big Four. They are the National Westminster (owned by the Royal Bank of Scotland), HSBC, Barclays and Lloyds TSB. A 'fifth force' emerged in 2001 with the merger of the Bank of Scotland and the Halifax (HBOS). In addition, there are a number of smaller banks, such as the Co-operative Bank. There is also the Girobank. Banks offer a variety of services, and we begin by considering current accounts.

Current Accounts.

A current account is a safe and easy way of making and receiving payments and is now offered by some building societies as well as banks. Many current accounts are operated free of charge if you stay in credit. If you go overdrawn or require additional services the charges vary considerably so it can be worth shopping around. To open an account you will have to supply samples of your signature, proof of identity and probably the names of two referees. These could be your employer and a friend with a bank account. To pay further amounts into your account, you simply fill in a paying-in slip provided by the bank. Some current accounts now attract interest but the rates are often very low indeed.

Making Payments.

With a current account you will receive a cheque book. This is used in making cash withdrawals from the bank or in making payments without using cash. A cheque is not money. It is merely a written instruction to the bank to pay an amount out of your account, to the person(s) named on the cheque. Cash can be obtained from your local branch. For cash from another you must make special arrangements or use a cheque card.

Cheque Cards.

Most retailers are reluctant to accept an unsupported cheque. This is because they do not know if you have sufficient money in your account for the bank to honour the cheque. And, of course, the cheque book may have been stolen. This problem is overcome by a cheque card. The card guarantees that the bank will honour cheques up to £50 or sometimes more regardless of the state of

the customer's account. You have to be a reliable and well-established customer before your bank will give you a cheque card. A cheque drawn on a cheque card cannot be stopped or cancelled.

Cash Cards.

Increasingly these cards can be used for more than just simply withdrawing cash from cash machines, for example checking the balance of the account or ordering statements. They are operated using your Personal Identification Number (PIN). This should be kept secret at all times and never written down where a thief could see it.

Debit Cards (Switch Cards, Connect Cards).

These are sometimes known as switch or connect cards and are the electronic version of cheques. Your card is swiped through a machine, you are asked to key in your PIN and the amount is then debited from your current account.

Standing Orders and Direct Debits.

There are other ways of making payments apart from cheques. If asked, the bank will automatically make regular payments from your account. These "standing orders" are useful for paying such things as insurance premiums, subscriptions and mortgage repayments.

Direct debits are slightly different from standing orders. In both cases you give your bank a written instruction to meet payments as they fall due. However, with direct debiting the recipient approaches your bank which then deducts the payment from your account. This can be convenient where the amount varies. The recipient has to tell you beforehand of the date and amount of payment. If you wish to cancel a direct debit instruction you should write to both your bank and the recipient.

Bankers' Drafts.

These are cheques which are payable by a bank itself and are therefore a very acceptable means of payment. They can be useful in buying expensive items when a personal cheque may not be so acceptable. Once a bankers' draft has been used to pay for something, it cannot then be cancelled through the bank.

Telephone Banking.

The first full telephone banking service was set up in 1989 and this facility has since been introduced by other high-street banks. It has the convenience of operating a bank account by telephone from home or elsewhere and some banks charge calls at the local rate. The main banking services are normally accessible in this way.

Internet Banking.

This is also known as *online banking* or *'e-banking'* and allows banking transactions to be conducted electronically using the Internet. As with telephone banking it is now possible to use the Internet to conduct a wide range of transactions.

Other Services.

In addition to the services mentioned, banks provide a whole range of other services. These include lending (considered in the section on Borrowing), deposit accounts (considered in the section on Saving), travel facilities, advice on investment, insurance and taxation, safe custody of items and many more.

Girobank.

The National Giro was set up by the Government to provide a low-cost current-account bank service. When Giro started it was considerably cheaper to run compared with a current account at a bank. However, the difference is now small. In 1990 it was bought by the Alliance and Leicester Building Society and in 2003 it was renamed the Alliance and Leicester Commercial Bank.

6. INSURANCE

Insurance is a contract to pay a premium in return for which the insurer will pay compensation in certain eventualities, for example, fire or theft. In effect, insurance is a means of sharing certain risks. The traditional forms of insurance are general insurance and life assurance (called "assurance" because the cover is given against the occurrence of an event which is inevitable.)

Life Assurance.

Life assurance provides a capital sum to your estate in the event of your death. Some policies also combine a savings element so that you receive a lump sum if you survive the period. These are called endowment policies. As a general point, it is just as important that you do not overburden yourself with life assurance as it is to have some form of cover. If you have to give up or surrender your policy before it matures there are usually severe financial penalties. There are three basic types of life assurance: term assurance, whole-life assurance and endowment assurance. All forms of life assurance used to attract tax relief. However, this was changed in the Budget of 13 March 1984 so that the tax relief does not apply to policies taken out after that date.

Term Assurance.

This type of policy provides life assurance for a fixed period of time. Should you die during the term of the policy your estate will receive the sum assured. However, if you survive the period you receive nothing. There are variations on the basic type of term policy. A *decreasing term* policy, for example, is often necessary if you have a mortgage. The sum assured decreases as you pay off the mortgage.

Other types of policies include level and convertible term policies. With *level term* policies the sum assured remains fixed throughout the term of the policy. A *convertible term* policy has the additional option of being able to convert it to another kind of policy later on, if you so desire. Term policies provide the cheapest form of life cover.

Whole-Life Assurance.

With this type of policy you are normally required to pay the premiums for the whole of your life-time. Like term assurance, the sum assured is paid out to your estate only on your death. Whole-life policies can either be with or without profits. A with-profits policy will be more expensive, since the sum received on your death will be the sum assured plus a share in the profits made by the company. Having to keep up the premiums after your retirement can be a problem, so *limited payment* policies are available. Premiums are paid until you reach a specific age, although life cover continues until your death. The premiums will be higher than for a straight whole-life policy.

Endowment Assurance.

Both whole-life and term policies normally provide benefit only on your death. With an endowment policy, benefit is still provided should you die before the maturity date of the policy. But if you survive this period you will receive the sum assured. Like whole-life policies, these policies can be with or without profits. Although the more expensive, with-profits endowment policies are the most popular form of life assurance in this country. However, the proportion of the premium used to provide death cover is small. This is because the chances of dying before the maturity date are usually low. Thus, the bulk of the premiums is used by the company to build up the capital sum on maturity.

Endowment policies are often used in conjunction with loans for house purchase, school fees and for providing for retirement. As well as with-profits investment policies, life assurance companies offer other investment policies. These include equity linked contracts, property bonds and policies linked to building societies. With unit-linked contracts the bulk of the premium is used to purchase units in a unit trust. Property bonds are similar (with investment in property).

General Insurance.

As mentioned earlier, this provides cover for an eventuality that may never happen. The types of general insurance considered here are for house and possessions, motor vehicles, sickness and medical insurance.

Insuring your House and Possessions.

If you are buying a house on a mortgage the bank or building society will insist that it is insured. The sum that you will have to insure your house for may be more than what you paid for it. This is because the insurance value will be related to the cost of rebuilding the house. It is therefore important to adjust the amount for which the house is insured periodically to keep pace with inflation. Alternatively, you can take out policies which are "index-linked." Although most policies give the same kind of cover, there is no standard house insurance. So you should check to see if your policy covers all eventualities. This is particularly important if your area is prone to such events as flooding or subsidence.

Unless you have a combined policy, the contents of your home and other possessions will not be covered by your house insurance. In the past insurance companies have reimbursed the purchase cost of articles, less a charge for wear-and-tear. However, you can get policies that do not make this deduction.

House and Possessions.

If you are a tenant living in rented accommodation you should only buy policies that cover the contents of the house and leave the landlord to buy insurance for the buildings. For owner-occupiers, it is best to buy a combined policy of house and possessions. This has the advantage that it will be generally cheaper than buying two separate policies.

Motor Insurance.

Motor insurance is compulsory by law. However, only a basic minimum is compulsory, and many people prefer to take out more comprehensive policies. Insurance companies offer two main types of policy; third party and comprehensive insurance.

Third-Party Motor Insurance.

The additional cover provided by this type of policy is the cost of repairing the other driver's car. Also, if you incur legal costs in dealing with a claim, these will be reimbursed if your insurer approves your actions. Since third-party insurance does not cover damage to your car, it is only suitable if your car is fairly old. "Third party, fire and theft" will cover you if your car is burnt out or stolen, but not if it is damaged in an accident.

Comprehensive Motor Insurance.

If your car is relatively new and hence more valuable, then you should consider a comprehensive policy. The most important additional benefit of such a policy is cover for loss or accidental damage to your car.

Sickness and Medical Insurance.

There has been some concern that the National Health Service and National Insurance schemes might not always be adequate to cover needs in the case of illness. Private Medical Insurance can provide cover for some illnesses but it is important to realise that no scheme covers the cost of every possible treatment. The cover is usually designed for 'acute illnesses' that are treatable and not 'chronic illnesses' such as multiple sclerosis. Other common exclusions include treatment for mental illness, alcoholism and drug abuse, infertility and cosmetic surgery.

'Pre-existing conditions', that is health problems existing when the insurance policy is started, are also likely to be excluded or subject to special arrangements such as a higher premium. Different policies have different levels of cover and, of course, different levels of premiums so it is worth shopping around for the most suitable one.

Buying Insurance.

Because of the bewildering variety of policies available it is often best to seek professional advice when buying insurance. This can be obtained from an insurance broker or your bank.

7. BUYING A HOUSE

Buying a house is very often preferable to renting a home. Your own house provides you and your family with a secure home. A house is also one of the soundest investments available to most people. In addition, a house can be a useful asset. For example, if you wish to move elsewhere the house can always be sold and the proceeds used to buy a home elsewhere. A house can be particularly valuable on retirement. With the mortgage paid off the retired owner can choose from a number of possible courses of action. He or she could continue living in it rent free. If the house proved too large for retirement part of it could always be let out to provide some additional income. Alternatively, the owner could move to a smaller home and the difference in the value of the two houses would provide a useful capital sum.

For many people there is no satisfactory alternative to buying a home. Most people are unlikely to be offered council accommodation. Furthermore, a home owner is likely to find it much easier to move than a council tenant. Councils are often reluctant or unable to offer new accommodation when their tenants wish to move; whereas an owner occupier can always sell his house and buy another elsewhere.

Accommodation rented privately also has its disadvantages. Reasonably priced rented accommodation is often difficult to find. Tenants sometimes pay nearly as much, or even more, in rent than they would have to pay for a mortgage on property. Finally, rents are likely to rise as inflation continues. Mortgage repayments on the other hand, although they fluctuate from time to time, are related to the original loan and not to the current value of the property.

The Costs.

The basic drawback of buying a house is the cost of buying and selling. The costs can include solicitor's and surveyor's fees and (in the case of selling) an estate agent's fee. If the mortgage is a high proportion of the value of the house, the lender may make an additional charge. Normally there will be the costs of .... in a new home the cost of curtains is one example. These costs clearly mean that it is not advantageous to buy a home if you expect to move in the near future.

An obstacle for many people is cash. One hundred per cent mortgages are uncommon, and the buyer has to find the difference between the mortgage offered and the price of the house. There are also the other fees mentioned above. The position may be illustrated with an example. Mr. and Mrs. Smith agree to buy a house for £160,000. The Smiths' building society is prepared to lend them 95 per cent of the value of the property. In this case, the loan would be £152,000 which leaves the Smiths £8,000 to find. On top of the £8,000, the Smiths have to pay a valuation fee to the bank or building society. The valuation fee is related to the value of the property so that the higher the value, the higher the fee. It may be possible to arrange for the surveyor making the valuation for the lender also to produce a house buyer's report for the buyer. A combined fee of £700 is shown in the example but it is possible, of course, to have a more detailed survey done if you wish.

Stamp Duty.

If the price of the house or flat exceeds £125,000 stamp duty land tax (SDLT) also has to be paid (though there are some concessions in disadvantaged areas). Normally the rate of SDLT for residential property is 1 per cent where the amount paid is between £125,000 and £250,000, 3 per cent where it is over £250,000 and up to £500,000 and 4 per cent on properties over £500,000. Note that duty is levied on the total price of the house, and not just the excess over £125,000. So, for example,

the stamp duty on a £160,000 house would be £1,600. Finally, the Smiths receive a solicitor's bill for £1,200. The solicitor's charge will depend partly on the value of the house, and partly on how much work the solicitor has to do to transfer the house from the seller to the buyer.

In this example, therefore, the Smiths need at least £11,500 of their own money. Frequently the amount of money needed will be greater than this. For example, if the Smiths' mortgage were limited to 90 per cent of the value of the house they may have had to find at least £19,500.

It should also be borne in mind that more money is needed to furnish the house. A first-time buyer needs almost everything from curtains to a cooker, and from doormats to a dinner service. Not all of these things need to be bought straight away. So it can be seen that, unless one is likely to move in the near future, buying a house can be a sensible decision. The key thing is to save up a reasonable sum of money towards these costs.

Choosing a House.

Given the price of houses, selecting your future home is clearly not a decision to be rushed. Possibly the first thing to do is to work out how much you can afford to pay. If you need a mortgage, building societies and other lenders will give you a rough indication of the maximum amount they will lend. They cannot give a precise figure, however, because the amount a society will lend depends not only on your income but also the house itself. There is more on this below. The next stage is to decide where you would like to live. If you are not familiar with the area it pays to spend time studying a map in detail. That way you soon get an idea of the proximity of each area to your work, to the nearest shopping centre and so on. It is also worth thinking carefully about the type of house you want. You may, of course, be influenced by what is available. Nevertheless, if you have a fairly clear idea of what you want a lot of time can be saved by eliminating houses that are obviously unsuitable. Features to think about include whether you want a house, bungalow or flat; the number of bedrooms you require and the type of garden you need.

Checking the House Market.

The next move is to find out as much as possible about the current state of the home market. Estate agents are always delighted to deluge prospective home buyers with details of many properties. Many of them might be unsuitable for you, but they will begin to give you an idea of the .... price or different houses. You may also change your mind about the sort of house you want. Estate agents are not the only source of information about houses for sale. Houses are often advertised privately, usually in the local newspaper. And because the seller will be saving hundreds of pounds in estate agent's fees, you might be able to buy a house advertised privately for less than one handled by an agent.

There are several other considerations that should be borne in mind. For example, if you are likely to have to move within a few years you may wish to buy a house which is relatively easy to resell. Such a house might be a fairly modern three-bedroomed semi-detached house which is close to shops and schools: rather than a "character" property in a remote area.

Home Information Pack.

The Government is introducing regulations requiring those selling a residential property to produce a Home Information Pack. The basic idea is to improve home buying by the provision of a copy of standard documents and information for prospective buyers. Although legislation to introduce the pack was first introduced in the Homes Bill in 2000, implementation has been delayed for a number of reasons. At the time of writing some of the final details had still to be decided.

Buying a House.

The process of buying a house should not be rushed. In fact, at this stage it is well to have two or three properties in mind. This reduces the disappointment should you fail to get your first choice. It also puts you in a better bargaining position over the price of the house. There is nothing sacred about the asking price. Sellers will often ask for a bit more than they think they will probably get. So, depending on the state of the market, it can often pay to offer less than the advertised price.

The "Subject to Contract" Stage.

When a price is agreed, make it "subject to contract." Neither party is formally bound to the agreement until the contracts are actually exchanged. Before that happens there are a number of things to be done. First of all you will probably want a solicitor. It is not absolutely necessary to use a solicitor, but unless you are familiar with the procedure it is usually advisable to do so. If you need a mortgage the next thing to do is to give full details of the house you intend to buy to your building society or bank manager. He or she will then arrange to have the property surveyed and valued. The purpose of this is to safeguard the building society's money by making sure that the house is a good investment. When the building society is ready it will inform you how much it is prepared to lend on the house. Your solicitor should then be instructed to complete the remaining formalities.

The Exchange of Contracts.

As soon as the solicitors are satisfied about the technicalities of the purchase the next stage is the signing and exchange of contracts. The contract is usually prepared in duplicate with one copy to be signed by the buyer and one by the seller. The buyer is normally expected to pay a deposit of 10 per cent of the purchase price when contracts are exchanged. The exchange of contracts legally commits both parties to the purchase. This commitment stands regardless of what happens thereafter. This is why it is important for you or your solicitor or both to find out as much as possible about the property before the contract is signed. The contract will contain a number of details, including the date on which the deal will be completed. The date is usually a few weeks ahead and allows both parties to make final arrangements before the house is actually handed over. On the completion date the balance of the purchase money is paid, and the purchaser can take possession of the house.

The length of time between finding a home of your choice and taking possession can vary considerably. It depends on the number of complications involved. If everything goes well it would probably take between eight and ten weeks to buy the house. Such is the process of buying a home. However for many people the major consideration is the mortgage. It is therefore worth describing mortgages in greater detail.

Mortgages.

A "mortgage" is a technical term meaning that certain rights over one's property are given to someone else as security for a loan. In other words, if you buy a house with a loan you give a mortgage as security. In everyday usage, however, a mortgage refers just to the loan, even though the property is still used as security. Even if you can afford to pay cash, it is often worthwhile buying a house with the aid of a mortgage. As inflation continues the value of money declines, and so the real value of the mortgage also declines. As a result, the mortgage repayments will not tend to rise in line with inflation.

It is true that interest rates fluctuate and that when they rise your mortgage repayments will rise as well. But sooner or later the rate of interest will fall again. In addition, when interest rates rise it is sometimes possible to extend the repayment period, rather than increase the monthly repayments. The most common types of mortgage are repayment mortgages and endowment mortgages. In recent years many lenders have been offering attractive discounts to new borrowers. These can be very advantageous but be aware of any conditions such as penalties for repaying the mortgage early.

Repayment Mortgages.

Repayment mortgages are usually the most straightforward. They are repaid in equal monthly instalments. Each payment consists partly of interest and partly of a repayment of capital. In the early years the repayments consist almost entirely of interest. As the loan is paid off, the interest element declines.

In the past, there was some tax relief on mortgage interest, but it was removed completely from April 2000.

Interest-only Mortgages.

With these mortgages only the interest is paid during the term of the loan and some other arrangement is made for repaying the capital at the end of the term.

Endowment mortgages used to be the most popular mortgage of this type. An endowment mortgage is an interest-only mortgage linked to an endowment policy intended to produce sufficient funds to repay the loan and sometimes an additional capital sum as well. However the advantages of endowment mortgages are now much less than they used to be and such policies can fail to produce sufficient funds even to repay the loan.

Another option is *Individual Savings Account (ISA) mortgages.* With this arrangement the borrower pays into an ISA (*see* **E7**) with the intention of accumulating enough to repay the loan at the end of the term. ISAs replaced Personal Equity Plans (PEPs) in 1999 and PEP mortgages taken out under that scheme can continue through an ISA.

Pension mortgages involve payments into a personal pension scheme (including stakeholder pensions). The aim is that the tax-free lump sum payable on retirement can be used to repay the loan. Although payments into a personal pension scheme attract considerable tax relief, this is an inflexible way of repaying a loan. It is quite possible that a person's housing and pension needs may change over the long periods of time involved and such an arrangement ceases to be appropriate. There is still much to be said for the simplicity of a repayment mortgage described above.

Getting a Mortgage.

The majority of mortgages have been supplied by building societies but in recent years banks have become an important source of mortgages. Some insurance companies also provide mortgages, but this is only a minor source of loans. Some employers, such as banks, will provide their employees with loans at favourable rates.

The first thing to do is to plan ahead. As we have seen, you will probably need to put up a substantial sum of money of your own, so you should start saving as soon as possible. It can be advantageous to save by investing in a building society. When mortgage funds are in short supply societies are likely to consider their own investors before casual applicants. Building societies have fairly strong preferences about the sort of property they are prepared to lend on. For example, they are often very reluctant to lend on older property. Many building societies are also reluctant to lend on flats. Nevertheless, the lending policies of building societies differ, so if you are turned down by one society, try another. It can also help to ask people who are likely to have close contacts with building societies. Estate agents, your solicitor or bank may each be able to suggest a possible source.

How Much Can Be Borrowed?

As stated above, the amount an individual can borrow partly depends on the value of the house concerned. But it also depends on the financial status of the borrower. Lenders have to safeguard their investors' money and are careful not to lend more to anyone than they are likely to be able to repay. A person with a secure career may therefore be treated more favourably than a person whose future earnings are uncertain. Again, different societies have different policies. None the less, it is very rare for building societies to lend more than two and a half times or three times your annual income. Most building societies will also take a spouse's income into account, but for a smaller proportion. For example, suppose you went to a lender which was prepared to lend up to three times your annual earnings plus an amount equal to your spouse's annual income. If you earn £30,000 and your spouse £20,000, the lender would then be prepared to lend you up to £110,000:

Your income	£30,000	Maximum loan	£90,000
Spouse's income	£20,000	Maximum loan	£20,000
		Combined Limit	£110,000

The extent to which your spouse's income is taken into account depends on the lender.

Re-mortgaging.

Re-mortgaging refers to changing either the type of mortgage or the lender in order to get a better deal. In recent years there has been a great deal of competition between lenders and it can be possible to save a significant amount of money by switching mortgages. However, anyone contemplating such a change should always compare all the advantages and disadvantages of the alternatives. For example, some mortgages may charge an attractively low rate of interest for a period but this may be followed by a higher rate later and penalties for those who wish to change their mortgages again.

II. TAXES

Taxation permeates almost every aspect of financial life. In addition, the entire subject is exceedingly complex, and the tax system is altered or amended at least once a year.

For reasons which are largely historical, taxes are often divided into *direct* and *indirect* taxes. Direct taxes are paid to the Inland Revenue. There are four main types of direct taxation:

1. Income tax
2. Capital gains tax
3. Inheritance tax (formerly Capital transfer tax)
4. Corporation tax

It could also be argued that National Insurance Contributions are a form of tax and they are also described below.

Indirect taxes are collected mainly by the Customs and Excise. They include:

1. Value added tax
2. Customs and excise duties
3. Car tax
4. Stamp duties

Stamp duties are, however, the responsibility of the Inland Revenue.

In terms of the amount of revenue raised, income tax is by far the most important tax. It is also the tax most likely to affect the average taxpayer directly.

8. INCOME TAX

If you are resident in the United Kingdom tax is levied on your income whether it originates in the UK or from overseas. Even if you are not resident, tax is still levied on any income you have which originates in the UK. Tax is charged for each year of assessment; that is the year from 6 April to the following 5 April.

Income Subject to Tax.

Most types of income are taxable, including the following:

Income from employment. This includes wages, bonuses, commission, tips and benefits in kind, such as the private use of the company's car.

Income from self-employment, business, professions and vocations.

Interest, dividends and annuities.

Rent.

Pensions.

Income not Subject to Tax.

A few types of income are not subject to tax. The main groups are:

Interest on National Savings Certificates and increases in the value of Index-Linked National Insurance Certificates. Also, interest from the Save-As-You-Earn scheme is exempt and also income from Individual Savings Accounts (ISAs).

Social security benefits that are not taxable include attendance allowance, child benefit, Christmas bonus for pensioners, disability living allowance, disability working allowance, invalidity pension, maternity allowance, mobility allowance, one parent benefit, severe disablement allowance, sickness benefit (but not statutory sick pay) and youth training scheme allowance.

Educational grants and awards.

Compensation for loss of employment—up to £30,000.

War widows' pensions.

Wound and disability pensions.

Any wins from gambling, including Premium Bond prizes.

Profit-related pay, within certain limits.

Rent under the 'rent a room' scheme up to £4,250.

Personal Allowances and Rates of Tax.

Almost everyone is entitled to at least one personal allowance which may be deducted before tax is levied on the remainder of a person's income. The allowances for 2005/2006 and 2006/2007 are shown in Table 3.

The basic personal allowance is available to individuals generally and there are two levels of higher personal allowances for taxpayers aged 65 or more as shown in Table 3. These higher personal allowances are reduced if total income exceeds a certain limit (£19,500 in 2005/2006 and £20,100 in 2006/2007). The allowance is reduced by £1 for every £2 that limit is exceeded until it reaches the level given to people under 65.

TABLE 3. *Personal Allowances Against Gross Income in 2005/06 and 2006/07*

	2005/2006	2006/2007
	£	£
Personal allowance	4,895	5,035
Personal allowance age 65–74	7,090	7,280
Personal allowance age 75 and over	7,220	7,420
Married couple's allowance age less than 75 and born before 6 April 1935	5,905	6,065
Married couple's allowance age 75 and over	5,975	6,135
Blind person's allowance	1,610	1,660

The married couple's allowance for couples was abolished from 6 April 2000 except for taxpayers born before 6 April 1935. The additional personal allowance and widow's bereavement allowance have also been withdrawn from April 2000. The rate of relief for the continuing married couple's allowance is 10 per cent.

TABLE 4. *The Rates of Income Tax in 2005/2006 and 2006/2007*

| | Taxable Income | |
	2005/2006	2006/2007
	£	£
Starting rate – 10 %	1–2,090	1–2,150
Basic rate – 22 %	2,091–32,400	2,151–33,300
Higher rate – 40 %	over 32,400	over 33,300

Income from saving is taxed at 20 per cent unless the taxpayer is liable for higher rate tax or is liable for tax at the starting rate.

9. ASSESSMENT AND COLLECTION

The administration of income tax is the responsibility of the Inland Revenue. In practice, the job is divided into two parts: assessment and collection. The "assessments" for tax are the responsibility of inspectors of taxes in over 700 tax offices spread throughout the country. When an individual's tax has been assessed the information is then passed to a collector of taxes who actually sends out the bill. If you receive a tax bill which you think is wrong you should contact the inspector. The collector has no power to amend the bill, his or her job is to collect the amounts decided between you and the inspector.

For historical reasons, income is divided into six groups known as "schedules." These are:

1. **Schedule A:** Income from property.

2. **Schedule B:** Income from commercial woodlands. Schedule B was finally abolished in 1988.

3. **Schedule C:** Certain interest and annuities paid out of public revenue.

4. **Schedule D:** Income from trades, businesses and professions. Also included are interest, rents and income not covered by other schedules.

5. **Schedule E:** This is the schedule that affects most people as it covers wages and salaries. It also deals with pensions.

6. **Schedule F:** Dividends and other distributions made by companies.

Pay-As-You-Earn.

By far the largest schedule is Schedule E. Nearly all Schedule E income is taxed through the Pay-As-You-Earn (PAYE) system. PAYE is the method used to deduct tax from wages, salaries and some pensions. In order to keep the deductions as accurate as possible, PAYE is operated on a cumulative basis. This means that your earnings, tax paid and so on are accumulated throughout the tax year. This is how it works.

At the beginning, or before the start of the tax year, your tax-free allowances are added up. The total is then converted into a code number. For example, if your allowances came to £5,000 your code might be 500L where the 500 represented the £5,000 and the L represented your entitlement to the basic personal allowance. The suffixes P, V and Y are used for taxpayers born before 6 April 1935 and entitled to one of the higher personal allowances.

The suffix T is used to take account of other fac-

tors or the taxpayer asked the tax office not to use one of the other codes. Suffix K is used where the value of the perks from your job is greater than your personal allowances. This enables the excess to be collected through the PAYE system. If your current code number is different from the previous one the tax office will send you a "Notice of Coding." This will show the allowances the tax office has taken into account and how your code number has been calculated. If you do not receive a notice of coding you may request one. You should always check to see that you have received your full entitlement to allowances. Your code number is also sent to your employer so he knows how much tax to deduct from your earnings. It is worth noting that the higher your code, the lower the tax deducted from your pay.

A Typical Example.

It may be of interest to work through a simple example of PAYE operating. Suppose that a person's allowances for the year amount to £5,200, and the appropriate code is issued to his employer. The principle is that the annual allowances are divided by the number of pay periods in the year. If an individual is paid weekly, therefore, his allowances are divided by 52. In our example the individual would be granted £100 worth of allowances each week. This weekly allowance is then accumulated as the tax year progresses. Hence in, say, week 26 of the tax year the individual would be entitled to £2,600 worth of allowances. At the same time, the PAYE system accumulates the amount of earnings received. This enables the amount of tax to be deducted to be calculated accurately. Suppose the individual in our example earned £140 in Week 1 of the tax year. The employer knows from the code number that the person's allowances for that week amount to £100. The employer then deducts this £100 from the £140 gross pay, which leaves £40 of "taxable pay". The next stage is to calculate the tax due on £40.

Calculating the Tax.

To assist him or her in this process, the employer has two sets of tax tables. The first table converts code numbers into weekly or monthly allowances. After these allowances have been deducted from gross pay the second set of tables is used to calculate the tax due on the remaining pay. In the example, there is £40 of taxable pay, so with a tax rate of, say, 30 per cent, £12 would be deducted in tax. Suppose that the wage in the second week was also £140. Because of the cumulative feature, the value of the allowances would now be £200, (£100 for the second week, plus £100 for the first week). Cumulative pay would now be £280. After deducting the allowances, taxable pay is now £80. The second set of tables would now show a total of £24 due in tax. £12 ("cumulative tax paid") was deducted in week 1. The amount of tax due in week 2, therefore, is a further £12 (£24 minus £12 deducted in week 1). This process then continues for the rest of the tax year.

Advantages of PAYE.

PAYE has a number of advantages. These include accurate deductions of tax. The system can also repay tax during the year if the employee's pay falls substantially. Repayments occur when the value of the allowances accumulates faster than gross pay. The system does not always work in this way. For example, suppose you fail to send your tax return back to the tax office. You may find that you are then put on the Emergency Code (E). This code only gives your allowances equal to the single person's allowance, so if you are entitled to more you will have too much tax deducted. This, of course, provides you with an incentive to sort out your tax affairs with the Inland Revenue. In addition, a taxpayer who becomes unemployed will not normally receive any rebate due until after either he or she ceases to claim unemployment or supplementary benefit, or the end of the tax year. Also, rebates cannot usually be paid if a person is on strike.

Sometimes you may find that you have been put on what is known as a "week 1" basis. This means that tax is being deducted from your pay on a *non-cumulative* basis. In other words, every week is treated as though it were the first week of the tax year. One of the main results of the "week 1" basis is that it prevents tax repayments being made automatically if, say, your income falls through unemployment.

How to Check your Code Number.

As you can see from the above explanation, your code number is the factor that determines the amount of tax that is deducted from your pay. You can check your code number by examining your Notice of Coding. You should compare the allowances and expenses you claimed on your tax return with the ones listed on the Notice. One item which might appear on the Notice of Coding is "Tax unpaid for earlier years." This is to enable the tax office to collect outstanding tax by lowering the value of your code. The tax will then be collected slowly over the tax year rather than in one lump sum.

Appeals.

When your tax for the year is assessed you will be sent a Notice of Assessment. This is often not considered necessary if you are taxed under PAYE and your tax situation is straightforward, though you can still ask for one.

If you receive a Notice of Assessment which you think is wrong you must appeal within 30 days of the date appearing on the Notice. Appeals made after 30 days are normally allowed only if you can provide a satisfactory explanation such as being in hospital or abroad, and can show that the appeal was made without unreasonable delay. Most appeals are settled directly with the inspector. If you and the inspector cannot agree, then the case goes before the Commissioners of Income Tax. There are two types of Commissioners: the General Commissioners and the Special Commissioners. The General Commissioners are unpaid and recruited from members of the public. They sit with a clerk who provides advice on tax law. The Special Commissioners are professional civil servants who are experts in tax matters. It is often said that if your appeal is based on common sense, rather than the intricacies of tax law, you may do better to go to the General Commissioners. Each party pays its own costs for hearings before the Commissioners. If, however, the case is taken on to the High Court, or further, the loser usually pays the costs.

10. SELF-ASSESSMENT

Self-assessment was introduced for those receiving income tax returns from 1997. It is a different way of calculating and paying tax which has been used in many other countries for some time. The main difference with the previous system is that a greater responsibility is placed on taxpayers to keep records, to complete their tax returns properly and to send them back on time. For taxpayers who are late there are penalties.

Self-assessment tax returns contain different schedules which apply to different sorts of income received by taxpayers. They are designed to allow taxpayers to be able to work out their own tax. There is also a guide which should be read carefully before completing the return.

With self-assessment, the process is stricter than before. Not all taxpayers are required to complete a tax return but they should all keep the necessary records to enable them to do so if required. If taxpayers receive income or capital gains which should be taxed and have not been, they are required to inform the Inland Revenue within six months of the end of the tax year, that is by 5 October. Most tax returns are sent out in April each year. If taxpayers wish the Inland Revenue to calculate their tax for them they should submit their returns by 30 September. If the taxpayer does the calculation the return does not have to be submitted until 31 January.

The Deadline.

If the tax return is not submitted by 31 January then a fixed penalty of £100 is applied. If the return is still outstanding six months later a further penalty of £100 becomes due. The Inland Revenue is able to ask the Commissioners of Income Tax to apply further penalties of up to £60 a day where they feel it is necessary. Interest is charged on overdue tax. There is also a 5 per cent penalty for tax outstanding at the end of February and another 5 per cent on any tax still outstanding by 31 July.

Some Basic Advice.

It is very worthwhile keeping a tax file containing all the information relevant to your tax affairs. The whole process of completing a tax return is much simpler if you keep all the relevant documents close together. These documents include items such as: P60 (from your employer); dividend advice slips; receipts for expenses. You may also be asked by the inspector to submit detailed records supporting expense claims. A second point is to keep a copy of your return. A photocopy is perhaps the best method of doing this. Alternatively, you can keep a separate record of what you put in the return as you go along.

Keeping a copy of your return has two advantages. First of all it will help you deal with any questions the inspector may have about your return. Secondly, it will enable you to complete your next return more easily. The tax office usually compares your latest tax return with your previous one to see if you have forgotten something. So it is better if you spot any omissions first. If you get into difficulties with your return, you can always telephone or write to the tax office whose address appears on the front of the form. If you wish to call personally, most tax offices are open for public enquiries between 10 am and 4 pm. But remember to take your tax file with you. It does not matter if you wish to make a personal call and your tax office is hundreds of miles away. This is often the case with Londoners and people who work for large nationwide companies. You can always call at a local office and in London there are special PAYE enquiry offices. (Their addresses are in the telephone directory.) Most enquiries can be handled without recourse to your official file. If the file is needed, the Inland Revenue can arrange to have it sent to a local office.

11. CAPITAL GAINS TAX

When you dispose of an asset or possession you may make a capital gain or a capital loss. An asset is property of any kind. It includes both property in the United Kingdom and property overseas. You are considered to have disposed of an asset if you sell it, lose it, exchange it or give it away. However, the transfer of a possession between a husband and wife who are not separated is not considered to be a disposal.

Tax-free Gains.

The following assets are exempt from the tax:

Your home (but *see below*).

Personal possessions, household goods and other chattels, provided that each item is worth £6,000 or less at the time of the disposal. A set of goods, for example a pair of vases, is counted as one item. (*Chattels* means tangible, movable property.)

Animals, private cars, caravans and boats. Also other chattels which are wasting assets; that is assets expected to last 50 years or less.

Life assurance policies.

National Savings Certificates, British Savings Bonds and Save-As-You-Earn.

British government stocks if owned for more than one year or inherited. This exemption has been extended to corporate bonds (*e.g.*

debentures) which are issued after 13 March 1984 and held for at least twelve months.

British money.

Foreign currency obtained for personal or family expenditure.

Winnings from betting or from Premium Bonds.

Gifts to charities.

Gifts to certain institutions such as the National Trust and the British Museum.

Your Own Home.

When you sell your house any capital gains you make will normally be exempt from tax. From 1980/81 onwards this exemption has applied (within certain limits) if you let part of your home. However, there are a number of circumstances in which you may get only partial exemption. For example, if you use part of your home for business you may not be allowed full exemption from capital gains tax. These circumstances are described in more detail in the Inland Revenue publication CGT1, *Capital Gains Tax—An Introduction*. You should enter any gains from the disposal of your house on your tax return in case they are not wholly exempt.

Capital Losses.

Your capital gains can be reduced by deducting allowable losses. An allowable capital loss is usually one which would have been taxable if it had been a gain. For example, a loss on an item which is exempt, such as your car, would *not* be considered an allowable loss. If your losses exceed your gains in the tax year you can carry the balance forward to set against gains in future years. You can also deduct allowable expenditure from your capital gains (or add them to your capital losses). Allowable expenditure includes the costs of acquiring or disposing of an asset; for example, commission, conveyancing costs and advertising. It also includes expenditure which increases the value of the asset, such as improvements to property.

Working Out Your Gain.

Normally your capital gain (or loss) is the amount you receive when disposing of the asset *minus* the original amount you paid for it. If you give the asset away, the market value at the time of disposal is used instead. The same method is used if you were originally given the asset, or if you inherited it.

Shares.

If you buy batches of the same share at different prices the cost of each share is considered to be the average cost. For example, suppose you purchase 100 shares in a company for £200. Three months later you buy a further 100 of the same shares for £300. You would then have a total of 200 shares which cost you £500. The average cost is, therefore, £2·50 per share. When you sell all or some of these shares the calculation of your gain or loss will be based on this average cost.

The Rates of Capital Gains Tax.

From its introduction in 1965 to 1988, capital gains tax was levied at a flat rate of 30 per cent. From 6 April 1999 capital gains have been charged at an individual's income tax rate for savings income, currently 20 per cent (or 40 per cent). However the tax is only applied to a person's gains over £7,200 for 2000/2001, £7,500 for 2001/2002, £7,700 for 2002/2003, £7,900 for 2003/2004, £8,200 for 2004/2005, £8,500 for 2005/2006 and £8,800 for 2006/2007. Gains accruing prior to April 1982 are exempt.

12. INHERITANCE TAX

Inheritance tax emerged from the remains of the previous capital transfer tax in March 1986. Capital transfer tax applied to transfers of capital made both during life and on a person's death.

Capital transfer tax had replaced the old estate duty which was imposed on property passing at death, and gifts made within 7 years before death. The position has now turned full circle because, essentially, inheritance tax, like the old estate duty, is levied on transfers between individuals made on the death of the donor, or up to 7 years before death.

The Tax.

Inheritance tax is payable on transfers made on or after 18 March 1986 on transfers made at death or in the years preceding death. Certain gifts, most of which are listed below, are exempt from tax. All other gifts which are not exempt and which are made within 7 years of death are taxable as soon as the total amount of taxable transfers exceeds the threshold for tax. For 2005/2006 the threshold for tax was £275,000. For 2006/2007 the threshold was £285,000 and £300,000 for 2007/2008. Rates for 2008/2009 are £312,000 and for 2009/2010 £325,000.

Furthermore, there are rules, similar to those operated under estate duty, which apply where the donor continues to enjoy some benefit from a gift even after it has been "given away". For example, this might apply where a person gives his or her home to the children, but continues to live in it. If this happens, for the purpose of inheritance tax, the gift will normally be treated as if it had been given on the date such enjoyment finally ceases.

The method of valuing assets largely continues on from the previous capital transfer tax and estate duty. Assets are usually valued at the price they would fetch on the open market at the time of the transfer.

The value of the estate on death will be taxed as the top slice of cumulative transfers in the 7 years before death. (For capital transfer tax the cumulation period was 10 years.)

Tax Relief.

From 2001/2002 the tax has been levied at a single rate of 40 per cent on transfers over the legal threshold. However, where gifts are made between individuals more than 3 years before the death of the donor the rate of tax is reduced by the relevant percentage given in Table 5. Different rules apply to gifts into and out of trust, discretionary trust charges and gifts involving companies.

TABLE 5. *Relief for Lifetime Transfers*

Years between gift and death	Percentage of full charge
0–3	100
3–4	80
4–5	60
5–6	40
6–7	20
Over 7	0

Exempt Transfers.

Certain transfers are eligible for exemption in much the same way as they were under capital transfer tax, including the following:

Transfers up to £3,000 in any one year (unused relief may be carried forward for one year only).

Small gifts of up to £250 to any one recipient in any tax year.

Gifts made as part of normal expenditure.

Marriage gifts as follows:

Parents	£5,000 each
Grandparents	£2,500 each
Bride and groom	£2,500 to each other
Other people	£1,000 each

Transfers between husband and wife if the recipient is domiciled in the United Kingdom.

Gifts to charities and political parties. A "political party" is defined as one with two MPs, or one MP and not less than 150,000 votes for its candidates at the last general election.

Gifts for national purposes, *etc.* For example, gifts to the National Trust, National Gallery, universities and museums are exempt.

Other Relief.

There is also some relief for business assets, agricultural land and shares which represent a controlling interest in a company. In addition, a certain amount of relief is available for minority shareholdings in unquoted companies.

Administration and Collection.

The responsibility for the administration of inheritance tax lies with the Inland Revenue, and the procedures for assessment, appeals and penalties are similar to those for income tax. As with the previous capital transfer tax, the responsibility for dealing with Inland Revenue enquiries about transfers made before death lies with the personal representatives of the deceased. Where a person's death creates tax liability on gifts previously made, the main responsibility for the tax falls on the recipient, but with recourse to the donor's estate if necessary.

13. VALUE ADDED TAX

Value Added Tax (VAT) is levied on most goods and services at a rate of 17·5 per cent. For most people it is simply included in the selling price. Anyone with a business over a certain threshold must register with HM Revenue and Customs.

The way VAT works is that it is charged at each stage of production but businesses may deduct any VAT they have been charged on their inputs. There are some concessions in the form of a reduced rate of VAT, zero-rating and exemption.

Reduced Rate.

A reduced rate of VAT applies to the following groups of goods and services:

Supplies of domestic fuel or power.
Installation of energy-saving materials.
Grant-funded installation of heating equipment or security goods or connection of gas supply.
Women's sanitary products.
Children's car seats.
Residential conversions.
Residential renovations and alterations.
Contraceptives

Zero-Rating.

Goods and services that are "zero-rated" are in principle subject to VAT but the rate applying to them is zero. This means that while VAT is not charged on these goods, businesses can still recover VAT paid on their own purchases. The effect of this arrangement is that zero-rated goods and services should be entirely free of tax. The groups of items treated in this way are:

Food of a kind used for human consumption and animal feeding stuffs but not "meals out", hot takeaway food and drink, ice cream, confectionary, beverages, pet foods *etc.*
Sewerage services and water.
Books etc.
Talking books for the blind and handicapped and wireless sets for the blind.
Construction of buildings *etc.*
Protected buildings.
International services.
Transport.

Caravans and houseboats.
Gold.
Bank notes.
Drugs, medicines, aids for the handicapped etc.
Imports, exports, etc.
Charities etc.
Clothing and footwear for young children and protective equipment.

Exempt Supplies.

Exempt goods and services are not subject to VAT, even in principle. A business cannot take any credit for VAT paid on the supplies used to produce exempt goods. Exemption is therefore less advantageous than zero-rating, but if a good falls into both categories it is zero-rated. Exempt items include:

Land.
Insurance.
Postal services.
Betting, gaming and lotteries.
Finance.
Educational.
Health and welfare.
Burial and cremation.
Subscription to trade unions, professional and other public interest bodies.
Sport, sports competitions and physical education.
Works of art etc.
Fund-raising events by charities and other qualifying bodies.
Cultural services etc.
Supplies of goods where input tax cannot be recovered.

More comprehensive definitions of the groups of goods and services that are subject to a reduced rate, zero-rating or are exempt are available from HM Revenue and Customs.

14. NATIONAL INSURANCE CONTRIBUTIONS

There are four classes of National Insurance contribution. Class 1 relates to employees and is paid by both employers and employees. Class 2 is payable by the self-employed. Class 3 is voluntary and is to help people protect their entitlement to the basic state pension if they do not pay enough Class 1 or Class 2 contributions. Class 4 contributions are paid by the self-employed in addition to Class 2, but they do not count towards National Insurance benefits.

Contribution Rates.

For 2006/2007 the Class 1 contribution is paid by employees at a rate of 11 per cent of earnings between £97 and £645 per week and 1 per cent on earnings above £645. There is also an employers' Class 1 contribution. Class 2 contributions are levied on those with self-employment earnings over the small earnings exemption of £4,465 at a rate of £2·10 per week in 2006/2007. The Class 3 contribution is £7·55 a week in 2006/2007. Class 4 is payable by those with self-employed earnings at a rate of 8 per cent between the lower profits limit of £5,035 and the upper profits limit of £33,540 in 2006/2007 and 1 per cent on profits above £33,540.

There is some further discussion of the highly complex subject of National Insurance contributions in Section F.

III. MISCELLANY

THE COUNCIL TAX

The council tax was introduced in April 1993. The tax is based on property but there is also a personal element. The property element is assessed using a system of banding which is constructed around average property values. Every home in Britain is allocated to one of eight bands according to its value. Properties in the same band in a local authority area are assessed to tax on the same basis. The tax levied on homes in the highest band is limited to two and a half times the amount levied on homes in the lowest band.

Special Discounts.

The assessment to tax begins with the assumption that each home contains two adults, so that households of three or more adults are not charged extra. However a personal element remains in that single adult households receive a discount of 25 per cent of the basic charge. Discounts are also extended to students. If the first or second adult in a household is a student, a student nurse or Youth Training trainee, he or she is entitled to a personal discount. So, for example, in a household of students and no other adults, two 25 per cent discounts are available.

For individuals with a second home, the tax should be reduced by two personal discounts so that only half the usual charge would apply.

People on low incomes may be entitled to Council Tax Benefit. The claim form for Income Support also includes a claim form for Council Tax Benefit. For those not claiming Income Support a claim form should be available from the Council, or Regional Council in Scotland.

Current Valuation.

The value of each home for the purposes of council tax is the value on 1 April 1991. This is worked out on the basis of the amount the home could have been sold for on the open market if it had been sold on 1 April 1991. Each home is put in one of the eight bands shown below. The amount of council tax payable is then calculated on the basis of the band in which your home is placed.

COUNCIL TAX VALUATION BANDS

Band	£
A	Up to 40,000
B	40,001–52,000
C	52,001–68,000
D	68,001–88,000
E	88,001–120,000
F	120,001–160,000
G	160,001–320,000
H	Over 320,000

Appeals.

It is not possible, of course, to appeal against the amount of council tax your council decides to raise. However, there are some grounds for appeal. One of these is where there has been a *material change* in the value of the home. This may arise, for example, because part of the dwelling has been demolished. There is no appeal on the grounds that there has been a general movement in house prices. A leaflet entitled "Council Tax—How to Appeal" should be available from your local council.

PENSIONS TAX SIMPLIFICATION

The Background.

From 6 April 2006 the different tax rules applying to different pensions arrangements have been replaced with a new set of rules applying to all schemes.

If a pension scheme agrees there are no limits to the amount that can be paid into a pension there are still limits to the tax relief available. However these limits are often higher than they were before and there is more scope for paying into more than one pension – for example having both an occupation pension and a personal pension.

Tax Relief Rules.

From April 2006 UK taxpayers can get tax relief on pension contributions of up to 100 per cent of their UK earnings. Any contributions from employers do not count against the available tax relief. However there is an upper limit in the form of an annual allowance – which has been initially set at £215,000 for the year 2006/07. If the value of a person's pension rights or their contributions (plus any employer contributions) exceed the annual allowance, the excess is taxed at 40 per cent. There is also a lifetime allowance (LTA) which has been initially set at £1·5 million for 2006/07. If a person's pension savings exceed this they may be taxed on the amount over £1·5 million. The "Lifetime Allowance charge" is set at 25 per cent for additional savings taken as a pension and 55 per cent if it is taken as a lump sum.

These limits are therefore too high to affect most people. Non-taxpayers can also benefit as the Revenue and Customs will add £28 for every £100 contributed to a pension fund up to a maximum contribution of £3,600 per tax year.

Other Key Changes.

Some of the other rules are also changing. By 6 April 2010 every pension scheme must have an age limit of at least 55 as the earliest age at which a pension can be taken. There are different rules for those retiring because of serious ill health or because they had the right to retire before age 55 at 6 April 2006.

The new rules also allow individuals to carry on working and take some or all of their pension. This may allow greater flexibility in planning and managing pensions towards complete retirement. However pensions must be taken by the age of 75 though there are a number of ways of doing this.

Pensions continue to be subject to income tax though most schemes offer a tax-free lump sum in addition to the pension. If they choose, all pension schemes can now offer such a lump sum of up to 25 per cent to members when they first draw their pension.

Small Pension Funds.

There are provisions where individuals have small pension funds. If the total value of a person's pension savings (in all schemes if they have more than one) is £15,000 or less and the pension scheme allows it, he or she may be able to take the entire fund as a lump sum. Of that amount, 25 per cent would be tax-free and the rest taxed as income. If this is done with respect to a pension already in payment than all of it would be fully taxable as income.

MAKING A WILL

Introduction.

Making a will might seem to be an uncomfortable experience since it is often difficult to imagine life without ourselves present. However, you need to make a will if you want to decide how your possessions are distributed after your death. It might also save those nearest to you a great deal of trouble later on. This can still be true even if you do not consider yourself to be well off. Furthermore, it is sensible to review your will from time to time as your family and financial circumstances change.

Your Estate.

If you die without making a will you are said to have died 'intestate'. After your death your possessions (known as your 'estate') are divided according to legal rules. Briefly, if you are married and your possessions are worth less than a certain amount (£125,000 in 2001) they all go to your spouse, whether or not there are children. If your estate is worth more than that, it becomes more complicated. For example, if there are children they will get a share. If you do not have a husband or wife then all your property goes equally to the children. If you die intestate without a spouse or children then it goes to your parents and if they are dead to your brothers and sisters and so on. If there is nobody alive to inherit under these rules, the estate would normally go to the Crown.

Making a Will Yourself.

You can make a will yourself if you do not wish to use a solicitor. Convenient forms can be obtained from a stationer or you can produce the document yourself. Preparing a will yourself, however, should be done with great care. If it is badly done or misleading it may not achieve the result you intended and it can lead to expensive court cases after your death if there is a dispute. It is therefore worth considering using professional help.

You can make a valid will if you are at least 18 years old and also of 'sound mind'. Your will should appoint executors who, after your death, will be responsible for dealing with your affairs. It is common to ask a spouse or close relative to act as executor and an executor of a will can also be a beneficiary of the estate. It is common to appoint two executors but not strictly necessary.

You should state any wishes you have regarding your funeral and so on. After that you should be as clear as possible how you would like your possessions to be distributed among the beneficiaries. If anything is unclear it could, of course, lead to arguments later on. The will must be signed in the presence of two witnesses who should then also sign.

The witnesses do not need to see the contents of your will – they are merely witnessing that you signed it. A person who has been left anything in the will should not be a witness. Also, a husband or wife should not act as a witness.

Altering a Will

Later alterations should not be made to the will itself. A simple alteration can be made by a codicil. This is a supplement that amends part of the will. It should be signed in the same way as the will itself though the two witnesses do not have to be the same as the original two. For more complex alterations, it is often easier to make a new will.

Although most people do not have sufficient possessions for their estate to attract Inheritance Tax, you should be aware of that tax and it is described on **E15**.

BACKGROUND TO ECONOMIC EVENTS

The aim of this section is to help the ordinary reader (as well as the student) to follow economic events as they happen, and to understand the controversies that accompany them. The section looks not only at the major debates on economic policy but also at recent trends in the global economy. Topics covered in the developing world range from poverty in Africa to the rise of China and India as major new economic powers.

TABLE OF CONTENTS

BACKGROUND TO
ECONOMIC EVENTS

This section is divided into four parts. **Part I** gives a brief description of the most important problems of economic policy. **Part II** is concerned with a more detailed survey of the British economy and the way in which it operates. In the course of this survey, the specialised terms used by economists are explained, and the attempt is made to present an intelligible summary of the information, facts and figures relevant to an understanding of economic events. There are five main sub-sections: International Trade and Payments; Employment, Production, and Industry; Incomes, Wages, and Prices; Money, Banking, and Finance; and Economic Aspects of the Public Services.

Part III outlines the main economic problems faced by the less developed countries, and the economic policies of Britain and other developed countries towards the less developed world. Some suggestions for further reading are given at the end of **Parts II and III. Part IV** is written as shortly before publication as possible, and contains a survey of recent developments in the British economy.

I. CENTRAL PROBLEMS OF ECONOMIC POLICY

Why Economists Disagree.

On some of the most important issues Economics is in a state of disarray. Economic problems are in general as serious as they have ever been, yet the economics profession is no less divided now than in the past on the diagnosis of the problems and on the prescriptions for economic policy. Why is this the case?

Economic relationships are complicated and changeable, and normally difficult to measure. Economists cannot conduct rigorous experiments in the way that natural scientists do. Everything is happening at once in an economy, and the influence of any one variable is not easy to isolate, even with the use of sophisticated statistical techniques. This is one reason why economists disagree, and why they should always bear in mind the limitations of their knowledge.

It is important to distinguish between *positive* and *normative* economics, *i.e.*, between consideration of how the economy actually works and of how it ought to be made to work. Even if economists were unanimous in their understanding of the economy, different economists might nevertheless prescribe conflicting policies because they made different moral or political judgements. For instance, macroeconomic policy prescriptions might depend crucially on the relative strength of one's dislike for the two evils of inflation and unemployment. But disagreement among economists is not only about goals and objectives. In macroeconomics, the "Keynesian consensus" which held sway in the 1950s and 1960s gave way in the 1970s and 1980s to a variety of different schools of thought. This development reflected changes in the economy and the emergence of new and more pressing economic problems: a rise in the rates of inflation and unemployment and a fall in the rate of economic growth. The accepted analysis and prescriptions were found wanting. At the simplest level, the disputing schools divided into the *New Keynesians*, on the one hand, and the *Monetarists*, or *New Classical* school, on the other.

Economics and Politics.

The two major political parties in Britain were, in the 1980s, committed to extreme and radically different approaches to the solution of Britain's economic problems. The Conservative Government, in office 1979–97, placed its faith in *laissez faire* economics, in the efficient operation of market forces, and in Monetarist policies. The Labour Party did not accept that the uncontrolled play of market forces would be beneficial, and it favoured Keynesian reflation and an expansion of state activity and state control. In part, these different approaches were based on differences in economic analysis. However, much of the disagreement was really based on differences in objectives, or on ideological considerations. Policies based on ideology or slogans can be dangerous. A great disservice is done by those who claim to have simple answers to what in reality are complex problems.

The General Elections of 1997 and 2001 were unusual in that the two main contending parties did not offer distinctly different economic policies to the electorate. The advent of "New Labour" in 1997, the search for the middle ground by the Conservatives in opposition, the political consensus that inflation must be curbed and controlled, and the relative success of economic policy-making over the last decade, have all made macroeconomic management a less contentious and more technical matter.

Are Economists Useful?

Given their disagreements and the limitations of their knowledge, can economists perform a useful function? In the 1985 Reith Lectures, concerned with the influence of economic ideas on economic policy, David Henderson complained about the influence of what he called *do-it-yourself economics*. Over wide areas of policy the judgements of politicians and their officials, as also public opinion in general, are guided by beliefs and perceptions about the workings of the economy which owe little or nothing to the economics profession. The amateurs have not been driven from the field, and they have still been in control of policy.

According to Henderson, do-it-yourself economics is based on peoples' intuitions and tends to be interventionist: politicians like to be active and to be seen to be active. These intuitions rarely extend beyond the immediate effects of the intervention, whereas professional economists analyse the less obvious, indirect and often unintended effects of interventions, which take place through the response of market forces. To give a simple example, rent controls appear to tackle the ill-effects of housing shortage but, by deterring investment in housing, they may exacerbate the shortage. Or mortgage interest tax relief may be electorally popular, but the economist's approach is to trace its consequences through to the end of the chain—higher house prices, losers as well as gainers, and less resources for non-housing. The professional approach is generally more quantitative than that of the amateur. Economists *can* often be useful, but their advice is ignored more frequently by policy-makers than that of, say, lawyers or engineers.

The Objectives of Policy: Avoiding Unemployment.

The central issues of economic policy concern certain desirable objectives. One important objective is the avoidance of unemployment. Between 1919 and 1939, mass unemployment was Britain's most urgent problem: unemployment caused waste, hardship and poverty. For a long time after 1945, the maintenance of full employment was accepted as a primary objective of economic policy by all political parties. Until the late 1960s less than 2 per cent of the labour force was unemployed.

Unemployment can be either *cyclical* or *structural*. Cyclical unemployment, arising from a lack of demand in the economy, can be tackled by policy measures to increase total spending in the economy. Structural unemployment arises from a misallocation of resources. In the 1970s and 1980s it grew as redundancies rocketed in the increasingly uncompetitive manufacturing sector, *e.g.*, motor and engineering industries, and in declining industries such as steel and coal.

With the emergence in the 1970s and 1980s of new and greater problems of inflation, the commitment to full employment first faltered and then was withdrawn. The concern that has daunted Governments in recent years is that expansionary policies to eliminate cyclical unemployment might fuel a spiral of inflation. Between 1983 and 1986, and again in 1993, unemployment in Britain exceeded the figure of 3 million, or 10 per cent of the labour force.

The Objectives of Policy: Controlling Inflation.

A second objective of economic policy has been the cure of inflation. In the 1960s retail prices increased on average by 4·4 per cent per annum; in the 1970s by no less than 14 per cent per annum; in the 1980s by 6·6 per cent per annum; and in the 1990s by 3·5 per cent per annum. Inflation can be harmful in various ways. It is associated with an arbitrary redistribution of purchasing power. Prices rise for everyone but some groups in society are better able to protect themselves against inflation. The feeling that particular groups are falling behind is a source of much unrest and discontent. Moreover, the general economic uncertainty that inflation brings can become a threat to economic prosperity.

Theories of Inflation.

Two main explanations have been advanced to account for inflation. The first stresses the role of excess demand or spending power in the economy. Such *demand-side* theories are put forward by Monetarists, who point to increases in the money supply in generating demand, and by Keynesians who recommend restrictive monetary and fiscal policies to curb excess demand, when it arises. The second explanation stresses the role of excessive increases in costs, *e.g.*, wage costs or imported raw material costs, in raising prices. Such *supply-side* theories imply, for instance, that policies may be needed to restrain the power of trade unions to raise wages. Neither explanation precludes the other: both demand and supply factors are likely to have contributed—with different strengths at different times—to inflation. Moreover, adherents of both views recognise that, once expectations of continued inflation become entrenched, these expectations themselves sustain and fuel the inflation.

Policy Against Inflation.

In the 1990s the old divisions gave way to a consensus view that, whatever the causes of inflation, the best way of controlling it is by means of interest rate policy to regulate the level of demand in the economy. In 1997 the Bank of England was given the task of determining interest rates, without reference to Government, with the objective of targeting inflation, *i.e.* raising interest rates when inflation is heading above the target level set by Government and lowering them when it is below. The new policy arrangements have proved to be successful: over the eight years 1997–2005 the retail price index rose by only 2·5 per cent per annum.

The Objectives of Policy: Promoting Growth.

A third objective of economic policy is the fostering of economic growth. Successive British Governments in the post-war period have tried to raise the growth rate—the most important long run determinant of the standard of living. Britain's living standards have risen gradually in the post-war period, but more rapidly prior to the first oil shock (by 2·5 per cent per annum over the period 1948–73) than after it (by 1·6 per cent per annum over the period 1973–2000). The long run British growth rate compares unfavourably with that achieved by most other industrial countries.

The Determinants of Growth.

The determinants of economic growth are not well understood, but most economists would agree that in order to raise the growth rate it is necessary to encourage the community to save, and businesses to invest, a higher proportion of the national income. In a fully employed economy the source of increased output is higher productivity, *i.e.*, output per worker. There is a danger, however, that higher productivity growth will be achieved at the expense of employment, as was partly the case in Britain in the 1980s: reported employment stagnated over the 1980s and increased by 6 per cent over the 1990s.

A constraint on the achievement of the above objectives has been the need to maintain balance in international payments. The British balance of payments position was precarious, so that unfavourable turns of events have precipitated economic crises. The expansion in the late 1970s of North Sea oil production, and the resulting confidence of foreign investors, transformed the British balance of payments. But this created new problems, particularly the adverse effect of the ensuing high exchange rate on manufacturing, our traditional export sector and an important employer of labour.

The emergence of vast international flows of funds in the 1980s and 1990s meant that the balance of payments increasingly depended on interest rate policy. The balance of payments no longer figured centrally in government policies.

The Inter-Relationship of Economic Problems.

The achievement of each of the objectives briefly described above is extremely complex. The difficulties are further aggravated by the fact that the problems are inter-related in such a way that measures which are helpful for one objective can make others more difficult to achieve. For example a reduction of purchasing power could curb inflation but also raise unemployment and retard economic growth.

The trade-off between the objectives of low unemployment and low inflation has met with different government responses at different times. The Conservative Government in office after 1979 was determined to get inflation down and paid little heed to the short run effects of its policies on unemployment and economic growth. In 1980 the Government faced the high inflation rate of 18 per cent and an unemployment rate of 6 per cent. By 1987 it had got the inflation rate down, to below 4 per cent, but unemployment had risen to 10 per cent.

The Labour Government in office since 1997 has also given priority to targeting inflation but this policy has not yet required high unemployment. In 2005 the inflation (excluding mortgage interest payments) and unemployment figures were 2·3 and 4·7 per cent respectively. However, if there were an oil crisis—for instance as the result of a Middle East war—inflation targeting and the consequent rise in interest rates could bring about high unemployment and economic stagnation.

There are other examples of a conflict in policy objectives. For instance, while the advent in the 1970s of a floating exchange rate helped to correct the balance of payments, a depreciating pound in turn fuelled inflation. The defence of a fixed exchange rate can force interest rates higher and higher, with unhelpful deflationary effects on the economy—as happened to Britain in the early 1990s.

Trends in the World Economy.

In the mid-1970s, after 30 years of rapid growth and unprecedented prosperity for the major Western economies, the prospects for continued growth became much less favourable. The main cause was the remarkable increase in the price of oil in 1973 and again in 1979, a fuel on which the Western economies had become heavily dependent. This produced a strong burst of inflation and gave rise to an unprecedented balance of payments problem and world recession. The period from the mid-1970s to the mid-1990s was one of relatively slow world economic growth. Since then the pace of economic advancement has risen: over the period 1995–2004, income per capita grew annually by 3·0 per cent in the countries in transition, 2·1 per cent in advanced economies, and no less than 3·5 per cent in developing countries. This was also a period in which inflation was generally brought down to low levels—the result of making the control of inflation through monetary policy the cornerstone of economic policy in the major economies.

II. SURVEY OF THE BRITISH ECONOMY

1. INTERNATIONAL TRADE AND PAYMENTS

International Trade.

(i) Imports and Exports.

In 2000 the United Kingdom bought from abroad goods to the value of £218 billion (thousand million), or about £3,650 per head. Food accounted for 8 per cent of this total, and basic materials, fuels and chemicals for 17 per cent. The great majority of imports (74 per cent) were manufactures. The most important manufacturing imports were machinery and transport equipment: electrical machinery represented no less than 23 per cent of the total imports and road vehicles another 11 per cent. All this can be seen in the table. The table also shows the remarkable similarity in the composition of exports and imports.

There are three main determinants of the level of British imports. One is the competitiveness of British with foreign producers. Britain imports those commodities which—at the ruling exchange rate between the pound and foreign currencies—can be bought more cheaply from foreign than from home producers. Secondly, the level of imports depends on the extent to which free trade is prevented by tariffs on imported goods or by other devices. Thirdly, as total incomes in the economy expand, there is a general increase in the demand for goods and services including imports. Therefore imports can be expected to vary with the total incomes in the country, known as the *national income*.

UNITED KINGDOM IMPORTS AND EXPORTS, 2000

Imports of goods	£ million	Percentage of total
Food, drink, and tobacco	18,049	8·3
Basic materials	5,827	2·7
Fuels	9,955	4·6
Chemicals, oils and fats	21,091	9·7
Manufactures of materials	29,279	13·4
Machinery and transport equipment	99,192	45·5
Miscellaneous manufactures	32,796	15·0
Other	1,847	0·8
TOTAL IMPORTS	218,036	100·0
Exports of goods		
Food, drink, and tobacco	9,897	5·3
Basic materials	2,446	1·3
Fuels	17,087	9·1
Chemicals, oils and fats	25,075	13·4
Manufactures of materials	22,661	12·1
Machinery and transport equipment	87,638	46·7
Miscellaneous manufactures	21,167	11·3
Other	1,685	0·9
TOTAL EXPORTS	187,656	100·0

Whereas in 1970 imports amounted to 20 per cent of national income, in 2000 the proportion was 26 per cent. The main reason for this rise is the liberalisation of trade among countries over recent decades.

Since the exports of one country must be the imports of another, the same factors in reverse—foreign competitiveness, access to foreign markets, and the level of foreign incomes—determine the level of British exports. In 2000 these amounted to over £188 billion of which 72 per cent were manufactures.

In the past, Britain gained from trade by exporting manufactures, in which she had a *comparative advantage*, in return for food and raw materials, which she was not suited to produce. Increasingly—with the growth of trade and specialisation among the major economies—Britain gains from trade by exporting those manufactures in which her producers specialise and importing other manufactures. Among the main manufacturing exports are cars and commercial vehicles, tractors, aircraft and aircraft engines, finished steel, various forms of machinery, woollen fabrics, man-made fibres, and chemicals; among the main manufactured imports are wood products, aluminium, newsprint, cars, and aircraft.

(ii) The Terms of Trade and the Volume of Trade.

The value of trade can be separated into two components, price and volume. The ratio of the average price of exports to that of imports is known as the *terms of trade*; and a rise in the price of exports relative to imports indicates an improvement in the terms of trade.

Superficially it would appear that any improvement in the terms of trade raises the value of British exports relative to imports. However, faster inflation in Britain, leading to a more rapid increase in export prices, would harm rather than help the balance of payments. Similarly, inflation in Britain makes it more difficult to compete with imports.

The relevant concept that economists use is the *price elasticity of demand*, i.e. the percentage fall in demand for a product in response to a percentage rise in its price. If this elasticity exceeds one, the value (price times volume) of exports falls as their price rises.

(iii) Trade Competitiveness.

The main determinant of trading success is competitiveness: a country's costs of production in relation to its competitors' costs. A country's competitiveness is harmed by domestic inflation of costs and prices, and helped by depreciation of the external value of its currency, i.e. of its *exchange rate*. There are various measures of trade competitiveness. One is the *index of relative export prices* (UK export prices divided by a weighted average of competitors' export prices, all expressed in United States dollars). Another is the *index of import price competitiveness* (the ratio of an import-weighted index of UK producer prices of domestic sales of manufactures to the average price of imports of manufactures).

The Balance of Payments.

A detailed examination of recent movements in the British *balance of payments* is made in **Part IV**. Here we explain the underlying concepts and the terms used.

(i) The Balance of Visible Trade.

The *balance of (visible) trade* is the difference between exports and imports of goods. It is said to be in *surplus* if exports exceed imports and in *deficit* if imports exceed exports.

The table shows the geographical pattern of British trade in 2000. There is a trade surplus with some countries and a deficit with others. However, these are unimportant: all that counts is the ability to finance an overall net deficit. The European Union accounts for no less than 54 per cent of total UK trade (exports plus imports). Within the EU, Britain's main trading partners are Germany (12 per cent), France (9 per cent), the Netherlands, Belgium and Ireland, in that order. The United States accounts for 14 per cent of British trade. A growing source of trade, particularly of imports, are the newly industrialising countries of Asia (7 per cent), including Hong Kong, Singapore, Taiwan, South Korea and China.

(ii) The Balance on Current Account.

The chronic deficit in the balance of visible trade has in normal years been offset by a surplus in the *balance of invisible trade*. This relates to international transactions in services as opposed to goods. The main components are: net receipts from non-residents for services such as shipping, civil aviation, tourism, insurance, and financial services; net receipts of gifts and grants made to this country; net receipts of interest, dividends, and profits earned on overseas investment.

(iii) Capital Flow.

The capital account of the balance of payments contains net private investment abroad (being the difference between investment abroad by United Kingdom residents and investment in the United Kingdom). There are also large, short-term capital flows, sometimes referred to as *monetary movements*. These include bank lending and borrowing—trade credits, changes in sterling reserves held by foreign governments, and Euro-dollar transactions. Such funds can be highly volatile, moving out of a currency if there is a risk of its depreciation and into it if there is a chance of appreciation or if other currencies are suspect.

Therefore, monetary movements can accentuate a surplus or deficit in the other items of the balance of payments. They are also dependent on relative rates of interest at home and abroad, being attracted to financial centres which offer high interest rates.

(iv) Foreign Exchange Reserves.

A deficit on current plus capital account can be financed through an increase in liabilities, *i.e.* by government borrowing from abroad, or by a reduction in assets, *e.g.*, a depletion of the official foreign-exchange reserves. The official reserves are used to finance payments abroad which cannot be financed in any other way: they are a last line of defence in international trade.

The book-keeping identity of international payments and receipts requires that the flow of goods and services on current account should be precisely offset by the total *net transactions in assets and liabilities*. However, not all such transactions can be accurately recorded. There is generally an unrecorded capital flow, known as the *balancing item*. In some years the balancing item is so large that it actually exceeds the current account balance.

Correcting a Deficit.

If an imbalance in international payments persists, the deficit cannot be met indefinitely from official financing. At some stage the Government must take action to remove the deficit. What action can it take? There are a number of alternatives available, each with its advantages and disadvantages, and economic

THE PATTERN OF BRITISH TRADE, 2000

£ billion	Exports to	Imports from	Trade balance
European Union	107·6	111·2	−3·6
of which:			
France	18·5	18·2	0·3
Belgium	10·3	11·6	−1·3
Netherlands	15·1	15·1	0·0
Germany	22·7	27·7	−5·0
Ireland	12·3	9·5	2·8
Spain	8·3	6·0	2·3
Italy	8·4	9·4	−1·0
Sweden	4·2	4·9	−0·7
United States	29·4	28·5	0·9
Canada	3·5	4·0	−0·5
Japan	3·7	10·2	−6·5
Australia	2·7	1·5	1·2
Oil exporting countries	6·1	4·3	1·8
India	2·1	1·7	0·4
South Africa	1·4	2·6	−1·2
Switzerland	3·1	5·5	−2·4
Russia	0·7	1·5	−0·8
Hong Kong	2·7	5·9	−3·2
China	1·5	4·8	−3·3
South Korea	1·4	3·4	−2·0
Singapore	1·6	2·4	−0·8
Taiwan	1·0	3·6	−2·6
TOTAL	187·7	218·0	−30·3

opinion is by no means unanimous on the choice of policy. Let us consider each of these alternatives in turn.

(i) Variation of the Exchange Rate.

The *exchange rate* is the ruling rate of exchange of pounds for dollars or other currencies. It determines the value of British goods in relation to foreign goods. Under the post-war Bretton Woods arrangements (*see* **F8-9**), Britain and other countries maintained a constant value of their currencies in terms of gold, permitting only very minor fluctuations of the exchange rate about its par value. However, persistent balance of payments deficits or surpluses caused occasional adjustments of the official exchange rate, the response to persistent deficit being *devaluation* and to persistent surplus *upvaluation*.

In 1972 the major countries adopted a system of fluctuating exchange rates. However, exchange rates are often not permitted to fluctuate entirely freely, *i.e.*, so that the market supply and demand for foreign exchange are continuously equated. While some monetary authorities permit the foreign exchange market to influence the exchange rate they are prepared in the national interest to intervene in the market (by buying or selling their currency) and so to keep the exchange rate within bounds. Given some flexibility in the exchange rate, a tendency for a deficit to arise is thus met by a *depreciation* of sterling and an incipient surplus by *appreciation*.

If the pound depreciates in terms of other currencies (which are paid for in pounds) become cheaper to foreigners and British imports (paid for by purchasing foreign currency) become more expensive to holders of pounds. In this way a fall in the value of the pound can improve the British balance of payments position by encouraging exports and discouraging imports.

But there are certain disadvantages attached to depreciation. The prospect of depreciation results in a speculative outflow of capital funds: and one fall may be taken as a sign that there will be a further fall in the future. Moreover, the rise in the price of imports of raw materials and consumption goods results in higher costs and prices and then in wage demands to maintain the British standard of living. It is possible that inflation will in this way neutralise the beneficial effects of depreciation.

The probable effect of a depreciation in Britain

THE PATTERN OF WORLD TRADE, 2000

Exports from/to	Developed countries	Developing countries	Ex-communist countries	World total
Developed countries	47·2	14·7	2·2	65·1
Developing countries	17·4	11·8	0·4	30·7
Ex-communist countries	2·4	0·7	1·0	4·1
World total	67·0	27·2	3·6	100·0

is initially to *worsen* the balance of trade, because the sterling price of imports is likely to be raised by more than that of exports. After about six months the effect of the depreciation on quantities —curbing imports and expanding the volume of exports—dominates, and the balance of trade improves. However, the improvement is maintained only if fiscal and monetary policies can prevent the fall in sterling from feeding through to domestic prices and costs and so both neutralising the gain in competitiveness and exacerbating inflation.

The Fortunes of Sterling.

The pound was devalued from £1 = $4·0 in 1949, when an official exchange rate of £1 = $2·8 was established, and again in 1967, to a rate of £1 = $2·4. In 1972 the value of sterling in relation to other currencies was allowed to *float*. With widespread floating, an *effective exchange rate* is now calculated, which shows the value of sterling in relation to a bundle of other currencies, with each currency receiving a weight according to the extent of trade with Britain. This rate followed a strong downward trend in the face of rapid inflation until 1977, and then recovered until 1980 due mainly to the advent of North Sea oil. Thereafter, the value of sterling tended to decline, reflecting the generally faster rate of inflation in Britain than in most of her trading partners, until the early 1990s, since when it has risen.

Britain became a member of the *Exchange Rate Mechanism* (ERM) from October 1990 until sterling was forced out by speculation in September 1992. Membership of the ERM required effectively fixing sterling (within narrow bands) to the *European Currency Unit* (ECU), so relinquishing the exchange rate as a policy variable. At the start of 1999 exchange rates of most currencies within the European Union were fixed irreversibly against a single currency, the *Euro*. Whether Britain should join this monetary union will be a major issue in the coming years (*see* **F57**).

(ii) Foreign Exchange Controls.

In the past, foreign exchange controls were used by governments to avoid or correct payments imbalances. Governments have moved away from controls because of the revolution in information technology. The explosion in the way in which funds can be transferred and intermediation of all kinds can take place makes such controls increasingly impractical for any reasonably sophisticated economy.

(iii) Import Controls and Tariffs.

Import controls impose limitations on the quantity or value of goods which are permitted to enter a country; *tariffs* are duties levied on imported goods so that the price of those goods to consumers in a country is higher than the price received by the foreigners supplying the goods. In the early post-war years, Britain maintained strict import controls over a wide range of goods.

All countries impose tariffs. However, their rights to do so are closely circumscribed by the rules of the *World Trade Organisation* (WTO), which works towards free trade in goods and services, especially through a reduction in tariffs. The disadvantage of introducing import controls or tariffs to correct a deficit in the balance of payments is that the benefits of free trade are lost. Moreover, there is always the possibility of retaliation by trading partners.

Britain's powers to impose tariffs and quotas on imports were removed by membership of the European Union, since this requires free trade within the Union and a common external tariff.

(iv) Deflation.

For much of the post-war period, the UK balance of payments was far from secure. As a result, domestic economic policies were much influenced by balance of payments considerations. By ruling out devaluation and trade restrictions, the authorities had to fall back on *deflation* of the economy to correct periodic deficits. In other words, the Government took measures to discourage demand and so cut back incomes and employment. In this way, the authorities secured a fall in demand for imports. Deflation is a painful method of correcting a deficit: not only does it have a direct effect on the level of incomes and employment, but it is also liable to slow down the rate of growth of the economy. This can happen because deflation can weaken the incentive to expand productive capacity by investing.

Deflation need not be the conscious policy. When inflation is high and the balance of payments weak, deflation may result from policies to raise domestic interest rates in order to protect sterling against speculative outflows of capital. This is a good description of British economic policy in the early 1990s.

International Trade Flows.

We can divide the world into three trading groups: the industrial countries (mainly OECD), the developing countries and the ex-communist countries. The matrix of the world exports presented in the table (above) shows that the industrial countries accounted for no less than 65 per cent of world exports, 47 per cent being exports to countries within that group. Trade within the European Union represented 23 per cent of the world total. No less than 80 per cent of industrial countries' exports were manufactured goods. The developing countries exported 31 per cent of the world total. Trade between the developed and the developing countries amounted to 32 per cent of the total. The ex-communist countries were still not much integrated into the world economy.

A breakdown of world exports by commodity in 2002 shows the predominance of manufactures—accounting for 78 per cent of the total. Machinery and transport equipment made up more than half of manufactures. Agricultural food and raw materials accounted for 12 per cent of world exports and minerals for 10 per cent, most of which was oil.

The International Monetary System.
(i) The International Monetary Fund.

The *International Monetary Fund* (IMF) was set up at Bretton Woods in 1944 with the object of working towards free trade at stable exchange rates. Under the original agreement establishing the Fund, members agreed to make their currencies convertible into other currencies and gold at fixed rates of exchange, and agreed not to impose exchange or import controls without the permission of the Fund.

The function of the Fund is to make foreign-exchange resources available to members which run into balance of payments difficulties. Each member country has a deposit (called its quota), paid partly in foreign exchange and partly in its own currency, with the Fund. In return, it is granted certain automatic drawing rights, which entitle it to borrow foreign currencies from the Fund. The Fund has power to make larger loans, and to grant standby credits to be drawn on if required. Before the Fund will make such loans and credits available it has to be satisfied that the borrowing country is taking appropriate action to correct its macroeconomic disequilibrium. The relations between the IMF and the developing countries are examined on **F48–9**.

(ii) International Money.

Gold played a central role in the international monetary system during the 1950s and 1960s. Central banks were prepared to buy and sell gold at a fixed price in terms of their currencies, and gold was exchanged among them in settlement of imbalances. The price of gold was held for many years at $35 per fine ounce. However, this fixed price in the face of rising costs of gold production meant that gold supply could not increase rapidly enough to provide the international liquidity needed to finance expanding world trade, and gold gradually lost its monetary role.

The domestic currency of the United Kingdom is not backed by gold: on a ten-pound note the Governor of the Bank of England promises to pay the bearer on demand the sum of ten pounds—merely another note! Yet, within Britain, there is complete confidence in the currency, because it is generally acceptable and so convertible into goods and services. Just as gold no longer backs the domestic currency, there is no need for gold in settlement of international payments. All we need is a generally acceptable international currency, i.e., one in which all countries have confidence. Only very limited steps towards the creation of an international currency—the issue by the IMF of small quantities of *special drawing rights* (SDRs)—have been made.

(iii) Foreign Exchange Reserves.

Surplus countries are prepared to hold short-term debt in foreign currencies—so earning a rate of interest—confident that their future trading deficits can be financed by payment of these currencies. They can perform their function only if there is confidence that they can be converted into other currencies and hence into goods and services at current exchange rates.

After World War Two the dollar replaced the pound as the main reserve currency, used in settlement of international payments. The United States ran a large and persistent payments deficit during the 1950s and 1960s, made possible by the willingness of the creditor countries to build up their dollar balances. But there is necessarily a limit to such a process. The deficits produced periodic fears that the dollar would be devalued; and this resulted in speculation against the dollar, and contributed to the breakdown of the Bretton Woods system.

Under the present system of flexible exchange rates, in which the major currencies—the dollar, the euro, the yen and the pound—can float, i.e. their prices against other currencies vary flexibly according to market supply and demand, the need for foreign exchange reserves is much reduced.

(iv) International Capital Markets.

There are now vast sums of money that are moved between international financial centres according to which centre offers the greatest safety and the highest rate of interest. For instance, foreign governments, corporations and individuals hold balances in sterling (e.g. Treasury bills, short term loans and bank accounts). The size of the funds held in sterling will depend on the rate of interest in London in relation to other financial centres and on expectations about the exchange rate between sterling and other currencies.

The sensitivity of capital flows to the rate of interest means the Government has the power to protect the balance of payments against an adverse balance of trade. For instance, high interest rates protected the UK's huge current account deficit in the early 1990s. However, that episode also reveals the limitations of this policy variable. Eventually, in September 1992, speculators expected that the pound would have to fall and, through capital flight, precipitated its collapse (see **F51**).

2. EMPLOYMENT, PRODUCTION, AND INDUSTRY

Population.

In 2004 the population of the United Kingdom was estimated to be 59·8 million—50·1 m. in England 2·9 m. in Wales, 5·1 m. in Scotland and 1·7 m. in Northern Ireland. Since 1961 the population has increased by over 12 per cent. This increase is partly accounted for by the birth rate exceeding the death rate. The size of population is also affected by the net migration rate. Since the early 1980s there has been a small positive net inflow into the UK. Between 1981 and 1991 this inflow averaged 43,000 per annum. In the following 10 years the figure increased to 114,000 per annum. In recent years net immigration has been still higher. In 2003 it was 151,000 and in 2002 153,000. In the previous three years it had ranged from 162,000 to 172,000.

The official forecast of the population of the United Kingdom in the year 2011 is 61·9 million. But prediction of future trends is difficult. For instance, it depends on immigration and emigration policies, the effect of improving medical services on the average length of life, trends in the age at which people marry, advances in techniques of birth control, and attitudes towards desirable family size. This projection is based on the belief that the birth rate will slightly exceed the death rate, and that there will be net migration into the UK. It is also projected that the birth rate will continue to fall.

The Labour Force.

Of the total population only some are of *working age*, i.e., between the minimum school leaving age of 16 (15 before 1973) and retiring age—65 years for men and 60 for women. Of course, not all those of working age do work and not all those above working age have retired. In 2005 the labour force was 30·1 million. Of men aged between 16 and 64, 83·4 per cent were in the labour force. The equivalent figure for women aged between 16 and 59 was 70·2 per cent. The labour force is defined to include not only those who are gainfully employed (as employees or self-employed) but also the unemployed who are looking for work and those on work related government training programmes. Students and housewives are excluded unless they do some work for cash. One feature of the past decade or so has been a fall in the proportion of adult males going out to work. It is caused by an increasing number of students and others undergoing full-time training and by more people retiring or leaving the labour market early. Those factors also affected the proportion of women going out to work, but they have been more than offset by a rising participation of married women, particularly in part-time work.

Most of the labour force work for wages and salaries as employees. In late 2005 3·7 m. were employers or self-employed, 24·9 m. were employees, 0·2 m. were on work-related government training programmes or in unpaid family work, and 1·7 m. were recorded as unemployed. Half the population who are at work have to produce not only for themselves but also for the rest of the population who are either not in the labour force or who are unemployed.

The table (**F11**) shows the industries in which people work. As an economy develops there is a tendency for employment in the primary sector to decline as the production industries expand. As an economy gets richer still, the proportion of income spent on services increases, and employment in the service sector consequently rises whilst the proportion of the workforce in production industries declines. Thus, in the early 1950s services accounted for only about one third of total employment; whereas by 2003 the proportion had risen to over 80 per cent. The distribution of men and women differs across industries. There is a preponderance of men in manufacturing and in construction and a preponderance of women in other services.

Employment and Unemployment.

To some extent official unemployment figures are misleading, in that certain individuals may not record themselves as being out of work and will thus appear to drop out of the working population. Until 1982 the official unemployment figure was calculated on the number registered as available for work. Registration was a prerequisite for claiming unemployment benefit. Individuals not eligible for such benefits—particularly married women—often did not register as unemployed even if they still wished to work. Their only incentive for doing so was if they felt that the authorities would help them find a job. Further, the count did not include those who were temporarily stopped or working short time. Since late 1982 the official unemployment figures have been calculated according to the number actually claiming benefit, for which registering as available for work is no longer essential. Those under 18 are now not included in the unemployment figures, as they are assumed to be on a government scheme, to have a job, or to have remained in full-time education. The above are not the only changes that have been introduced in the last two or so decades in the way that unemployment is measured. For example, older workers tend not to get included in the count, whilst many believe that the special employment and training measures (see **F15–16**) artificially deflate the unemployment figure. So much concern has been expressed about the quality of the claimant count figures that the Government has introduced an alternative set of unemployment figures derived from the Labour Force Survey.

Trends in Unemployment.

Using the claimant count for reasons of historical comparison, in 2005 an average of 0·86 million persons—2·8 per cent of the working population—were unemployed in the UK. In most post-war years until the late 1960s the average was lower than 1·5 per cent. This contrasts with an average of nearly in 1937, the best year of the 1930s, of 11 per cent, and with a maximum of 22 per cent at the bottom of the slump in 1932. The low unemployment of the post-war years was not maintained from the late 1960s. Unemployment grew to reach almost one million in early 1972. It then started to fall back with the general economic recovery, only to start rising again from late 1074 as the economy moved back into recession. Unemployment peaked in 1986 but fell sharply between then and the first half of 1990. The figures began to rise rapidly again as the economy entered recession, topping 2 million by Spring 1991 and continuing to rise until early 1993, since when there has been a sustained fall until 2005.

Until the late 1960s 1–1·5 per cent unemployment was somewhere near the practicable minimum. Some unemployment is more or less inevitable. A seasonal rise in unemployment in the winter must be expected, e.g., in seaside towns, and for this reason unemployment in January is higher than in June. Moreover, some unemployment is bound to be involved in job-changing and as the composition of output changes. Finally there is a core of people who are simply unemployable. "Full employment" means that there should be about as many jobs vacant as there are workers looking for jobs. A large excess of vacancies is evidence of inflationary pressure in the labour market. It means that the employers needing workers to meet the demands for their products will have to compete with each other by bidding up wages.

Minimum Level of Unemployment.

Most commentators feel that the practicable minimum level of unemployment increased from the late 1960s. By minimum they mean that any attempt to reduce unemployment below it, by injecting monetary demand, would be likely to cause increasing inflation or a deteriorating balance of trade. After its prolonged rise, the equilibrium rate of unemployment fell in the 1990s, but it remains higher than in the early 1960s.

Many possible reasons were advanced for the increase in the "equilibrium rate of unemployment" until the early 1990s.

One explanation was that as the fixed costs (like National Insurance) of employing workers went up, so employers were more careful to economise on labour. Another possible explanation was that the level of social security benefits on a whole was too high, causing people to demand an unrealistically high wage before accepting a job. Whilst the above factors, particularly the burden of National Insurance contributions, may well have played a role at times, it is unlikely that they were persistently important.

Structural Unemployment.

Many of the unemployed had skills which were redundant in an economy where the structure of industry was changing. Hence there could well have been an excess demand for some skills even when many people were without work. As well as skill mismatch of this sort, there could have been geographical mismatch—that is the distribution of the population failing to coincide with the distribution of job vacancies.

However, there is grave disagreement amongst economists about the importance of such mismatch explanations. No-one denies that there was a severe degree of mismatch in the British economy; the doubt concerns the extent to which it increased over time. Similar disagreement attends the claim that technological advance, reducing the need for labour, was a major factor. Interestingly many industrialists would put this as a prime explanation. Most economists would be inclined to disagree with them. They would put greater stress on a too rapid growth of real wages (that is wages compared to prices), causing employers to try to produce a given amount of output with smaller quantities of labour.

Experience of the 1980s.

The experience of the late 1980s when a surge in output and then a sharp drop in unemployment contributed to a renewed increase in inflation and to a dramatic worsening of the balance of trade suggests that the equilibrium rate of unemployment had not fallen despite the supply-side reforms of the 1980s. Though unions were weaker, competition between employers for a limited stock of suitable workers, as well as a pervasive belief that rising real wages were important for motivating staff, may be amongst the more important explanations of why the real wage and the equilibrium rate of unemployment remained high. Also of importance was the UK's failure to much improve its relatively inadequate performance (by international standards) in vocational education and training. Recently some commentators have laid stress on two other structural characteristics: the lack of coordinated wage bargaining and the lack of a time limit on social security benefits for the unemployed. Also prominent in contemporary debate is the contention that demand for unskilled labour is threatened by cheap labour in the Third World competing effectively in the production of standardised products. Some also argue that the increased use of high technology by many firms is destroying the demand for less skilled workers.

Causes of Unemployment.

Whatever the relative importance of these explanations, there is little doubt that the major cause of the rise in unemployment in the early 1980s was deficiency of aggregate demand for British goods. This in turn is was partly the consequence of restrictive government policies, and partly of our loss of international competitiveness. There is, however, dispute as to how much of this reduction in demand was necessary to stabilise inflation. Indeed there were some who thought that much of the fall in inflation rates in the early 1980s was the consequence of a massive slowdown in the rate of increase in world commodity prices and the consequentially slower growth of import prices. Equally there are those who believe that even if it was necessary in the above sense, it contributed to increasing the rate of equilibrium unemployment—because some of the workers who lost their jobs became hard to re-employ. Partly this was because of the effect of joblessness on their own attitudes and skills, and partly because of the perceptions of employers as to their worth. It may also have been difficult for the unemployed to "compete" with the employed by "bidding down" wages, since the latter may have great bargaining power vis a vis their employers for whom their departure would represent a major waste of training expenditure.

Changes in Unemployment.

A combination of the changes in the way unemployment was calculated, and the rapid expansion of demand in the second half of the decade, meant that recorded unemployment fell steadily between early 1986 and mid 1990. Thereafter, the emerging recession in the UK economy pushed unemployment back up, and at an accelerating rate. By the first quarter of 1991, unemployment was increasing by about 80,000 per month. Much to the surprise of many, unemployment started to fall slowly from early 1993. This came much earlier than had happened in the aftermath of earlier recessions. Though much of the increase in employment came in the form of part-time work, it is probably the case that the labour market was also witnessing the reversal of an unusually rapid shedding of labour during the recession. By late 2003 unemployment had fallen to 835,000. This prolonged fall in unemployment represented a very different experience from some other major European economies (notably France and Germany) since the early 1990s. Clearly buoyant demand played an important role, but most commentators also stress developments on the supply side. In particular they emphasise two factors. The first is the tougher administration of the social security system which now puts much greater pressure on the unemployed and inactive to return to work rather than claim out-of-work benefit. The second is the diminished power of trade unions. A question that has to be asked about the second of these explanations is why the weakening of unions did not apparently impact upon the economy earlier than it in fact did.

Regional Unemployment.

Extreme variations in regional unemployment were not a general feature of the post-war period: only in Northern Ireland was unemployment persistently very high. Nevertheless, regional inequalities existed and were magnified in absolute terms in the 1980s.

In early 2006 the proportion of all workers unemployed in the UK was 2·9 per cent. Even within the more fortunate regions there are pockets of high unemployment. These are concentrated particularly in the inner areas of large cities, but also elsewhere. For example, Scotland had an unemployment rate of 3 per cent, but in Kirkcaldy it was 6·1 per cent. The unemployment rate in the West Midlands was 3·3 per cent, but in Birmingham it was 5·8 per cent. Unemployment rates in Hackney and Tower Hamlets were 5·7 per cent, but in Greater London as a whole 3·5 per cent.

The Pattern of Regional Unemployment.

One of the main reasons for the traditional regional pattern of unemployment used to be that certain industries and services, in which big changes had been taking place, tended to be grouped in specific regions. Most of our early industrial centres had to be established close to coal, iron ore, and adequate water supplies. But employment in many long-established industries has been declining. Such industries include textiles, mining and quarrying, shipbuilding, and agriculture. On the other hand new and growing industries, and their related head offices, were concentrated in Greater London, the South East, and the Midlands. The growth of services, too, centred on the areas where industry was booming and population was increasing. In the absence of government intervention, it was thought that the process would tend to become cumulative, and regional inequalities would grow rather than diminish. The 1970s saw an interesting change. The West Midlands, traditionally after the South-East, the most prosperous area of the country, was severely hit by the particular impact of the recession on engineering, and appeared as one of the regions with higher than average unemployment. This remained the case until recently despite the fact that in the mid 1980s the West Midlands began to benefit from the ripple effect of the boom in the South East and as firms began to relocate some of their activities from the crowded South-East to areas where the labour market was less tight.

The Disadvantaged Regions.

Other bad areas of unemployment saw little or no improvement in their relative position during the

---

DISTRIBUTION OF EMPLOYEES BY INDUSTRY, UNITED KINGDOM 2005
(Percentages of all employees)

Distribution, hotels, catering and repairs	23
Manufacturing	11
Transport and communication	6
Construction	7
Financial and business services	20
Agriculture	2
Energy and water supply	<1
Public administration, education and health	25
Other services	6

UNEMPLOYMENT AND VACANCIES
(United Kingdom, thousands)

	Unemployment.† (Annual Average)	Vacancies. (Annual Average)	Unemployment as a percentage of total labour force.
1974	615	298	2·0
1976	1,359	122	4·1
1978	1,383	210	4·4
1980	1,665	143	4·8
1982	2,917	111	9·4
1984	3,160	157	10·6
1986	3,293	188	11·1
1988	2,370	248	8·2
1990	1,627	174	5·4
1992	2,702	117	9·2
1994	2,630	158	8·8
1996	2,119	227	7·0
1998	1,356	296	4·6
2000	1,088	358	3·6
2002	947	n.a.	3·1
2003	933	n.a.	3·0
2004	854	n.a.	2·8
2005	861	n.a.	2·8

† Prior to October 1982 the unemployment count consisted of those people registered at Jobcentres who were unemployed (the registrant count). From October 1982 the unemployment count consisted of those claiming unemployment-related benefits.

PERCENTAGE OF WORKERS UNEMPLOYED, BY REGIONS, EARLY 2006

North East	3·3
North West	2·8
Yorkshire and the Humber	2·9
East Midlands	2·4
West Midlands	3·3
East	2·0
London	3·5
South East	1·7
South West	1·7
Wales	2·7
Scotland	3·0
N. Ireland	2·8

period of strong economic growth 1986–1988, the worst affected regions remaining Northern Ireland, Scotland, Wales, the North and the North West. This may have been linked to an additional factor—the relative concentration of unemployment in inner city areas in particular regions. Unemployment in the inner cities grew more rapidly than elsewhere from the 1960s, and seems to have been the result of limited growth of firms there together with only a slow emergence of new enterprise. When the economy slowed down in 1989 and entered recession in 1990 and 1991, a different pattern of regional unemployment started to emerge. In contrast to the recession of the early 1980s, the downturn affected service industries before manufacturing, so the initial rise in unemployment was heavily concentrated in the South East and in other regions where service industries predominate, such as East Anglia. Some commentators christened this the "yuppie recession". This had the effect of substantially narrowing regional variations in unemployment. Traditionally both Scotland and Wales exhibited higher unemployment than the UK average. However the early 1990s recession hit them less badly than many other areas of the UK. This was true even strongly of Northern Ireland. For a while unemployment in Scotland and Wales was little different from the national average.

The Table (**F11**) shows that in early 2006 the West Midlands, the North East and Scotland were experiencing unemployment which was significantly above the national average. Thus regional dimensions to unemployment do remain, but they are less striking than they once were. As a dramatic illustration of this, the Table (**F11**) shows that unemployment in London was higher than in any of the individual regions, thus underlining the large city element of the problem.

Regional Planning.

There are essentially two ways of tackling the problem of regional imbalances; taking jobs to the people or bringing people to the jobs. In so far as the latter alternative is chosen, the Government should encourage the mobility of labour, e.g., through retraining schemes or rehousing subsidies. However, the migration of population may damage community life in the denuded areas, and cause congestion, housing shortages, and overcrowding in the booming regions. The Government can create employment opportunities in the relatively depressed regions in various ways. It can try to induce expanding firms to set up new establishments in these regions by offering tax incentives or grants; it can authorise additional expenditure on public works by accelerating road-building programmes—to provide additional employment; it can place orders for the goods it needs—e.g., defence contracts—where work is required. It can also use physical controls on expansion in the better-off areas; between 1947 and 1981 factory building over a particular size required the granting of an *Industrial Development Certificate*.

(i) Labour's Policy in the 1960s.

On taking office in October 1964, the Labour Government made regional planning the responsibility of its Department of Economic Affairs. Britain was divided into eight regions, with the intention of producing a plan for each region.

Fiscal incentives to locate industry in the depressed regions were given, e.g., the cash grants provided in 1966 for new plant and machinery in manufacturing were at twice the national rate in the Development Areas. Buildings also received cash grants in Development Areas, in Intermediate Areas (where regional depression existed but in not such an acute form), and in Special Development Areas (where depression was most acute). By contrast, office building in London and some other cities was strictly limited. To encourage the mobility of labour, the Government introduced redundancy compensation and achieved some expansion in both public and private training facilities. In 1967 regional differentials in the selective employment tax were also introduced. This was known as the Regional Employment Premium (REP).

(ii) Policy in the 1970s.

In 1970 the incentive to invest in the Develop-

ment Areas was affected by the Conservative Government's replacement of cash grants (except on buildings) by a system of initial allowances against tax. Whereas cash grants had been 40 per cent of investment in plant and machinery in Development Areas and 20 per cent in other areas, there was now a 100 per cent initial allowance in Development Areas and 60 per cent initial allowances in other areas.

In 1972 the Government introduced 100 per cent allowances throughout the country on all investment in plant and machinery; the preferential treatment of investment in Development Areas was therefore ended. Instead *regional development grants*, in the form of cash payments towards investment in plant, machinery and buildings, were introduced. The Government also proposed in four years to triple expenditure on retraining facilities, and to pay a worker who had undergone retraining a housing grant if he moved house to take a new job; and also a grant to any worker in an assisted area who moved house to take a new job. It should be remembered, however, that strong measures were necessary merely to replace the Labour Government's system of cash grants, and the REP which it was planned to phase out in 1974. Though, in the event, REP was retained by the incoming Labour Government, it was finally replaced by more selective measures in 1977.

(iii) Conservative Policy in the 1980s and 1990s.

In July 1979, the new Conservative Government announced some changes to be introduced over the 1979–83 period. The extent of the assisted areas would be gradually reduced, so as to cover 25 per cent instead of 40 per cent of the employed population and some areas were "down-graded". Industrial Development Certificate procedures were abolished in 1981.

It was also felt that in a slack labour market, regional policy was more likely to re-allocate geographically a given number of jobs rather than increase them in net terms. Alongside regional policy, therefore, were introduced measures on inner city decay (a problem even in non-assisted areas such as the South East), rural development and derelict land. In his March 1980 Budget the Chancellor announced proposals to establish about half a dozen "Enterprise Zones". These were small sites (of no more than 500 acres) with problems of economic and physical decay. The Zones were an experiment to test how far industrial and commercial activity could be encouraged by the most usual of certain fiscal burdens and by the removal or streamlined administration of statutory or administrative controls. By January 1996 there were 7 such zones. Although the government did not envisage extending the scheme massively, enterprise zones were seen to be an effective way of tackling particular local problems. Simplified Planning Zones were also designed to assist urban development.

Urban Development Corporations.

In 1981 the Government set up two Urban Development Corporations (UDCs), one in London's Docklands and the other in Merseyside. The aim of the UDCs was to reclaim and develop derelict land for housing, commercial and recreational purposes. By early 1992 the London Docklands UDC had received over £1,300 million in Government aid and had obtained over £9 billion in private sector funding commitments. The London Docklands is the site for one of the largest single office developments in Europe. From 1987 ten more UDCs were established in Birmingham, the West Midlands, Bristol, Leeds, Central Manchester, Greater Manchester, Sheffield, Teesside, Tyne and Wear, and Plymouth. All the UDCs were abolished in 1998. In 1988 the Government also announced an Action For Cities programme to improve co-operation between Government departments, private enterprise and local authorities in order to rejuvenate derelict inner city areas. Task Forces operated under this regeneration banner. City Grant (introduced in 1981) encouraged private sector initiatives in the inner cities. In 1991 the Government launched a further scheme—"City Challenge" Abolished in 1998, this had provided Government funding for 'particularly imaginative' local authority schemes.

In 1983 the Government introduced a Green Paper on regional policy. The suggestion was for a tighter and more selective approach, with aid being directed more at job creation, at small firms and at the services. But even a non-interventionist Government concluded that "wage adjustments and labour mobility cannot be relied upon to correct regional imbalance in employment opportunities". By the end of 1984 there were only two types of assisted areas in Britain—development and intermediate. In 1993 the development and intermediate areas were re-defined, as they were in 2000. The British Government now directs its assistance to be in conformity with EU law. Objective 1 areas are those whose GDP is less than 75 per cent of the EU average. The UK areas involved are Cornwall and the Isles of Scilly, Merseyside, South Yorkshire and West Wales and the Valleys. The Scottish Highlands and Islands and Northern Ireland are "transitional" Objective 1 areas. Objective 2 areas are ones which face structural difficulties. In the UK these account for 14 million people.

Regional Assistance.

Throughout the assisted areas help was available mainly through Regional Selective Assistance (RSA). This was available for help to "create and safeguard jobs; help attract international investment; improve regional and local competitiveness; and help areas adversely affected by the impact of economic change". The value of RSA grants in Great Britain rose from £250·8 million in 2001/2002 to £294·6 million in 2002/2003. England accounted for 36·6 per cent of these, Wales for 42·8 per cent and Scotland for 20·6 per cent. According to the Industrial Development Act Annual Report 2004/2005, 28·2 per cent of RSA grants went to England, 35·8 per cent to Scotland and 25·5 per cent to Wales. The Government also introduced an Enterprise Grant Scheme, which provided assistance to small and medium sized enterprises in assisted areas. A Regional Coordination Unit was also introduced, in order to draw together the various strands of regional help and assistance. Until recently in England, policy and help was delivered through English Partnerships and the Rural Development Commission. Similar roles were played in Scotland by Scottish Enterprise and Highlands and Islands Enterprise; in Wales by the Welsh Development Agency; and in Northern Ireland by the Department of Economic Development.

Regional Development Agencies.

The Labour Government established 9 Regional Development Agencies. The RDAs took over the work of English Partnerships, the Rural Development Commission and the Government Offices for the Regions. The RDAs have charge of the Single Regeneration Budget. Eighty per cent of the funds are for schemes in the most deprived areas.

In Scotland the Scottish Executive Enterprise, Transport and Lifelong Learning Department now has overall responsibility for economic development. A similar role is performed in Northern Ireland by Invest Northern Ireland, an agency of the Department of Enterprise, Trade and Investment.

In 2004, the English Government replaced Regional Selective Assistance and Enterprise Grants with Selective Finance for Investment in England. This is very much in line with the Conservative Government's distrust of general regional assistance which was confirmed by its decision in 1988 to abolish automatic regional grants. All assistance for the regions is now selective.

Meanwhile a number of policies are in place to encourage urban renewal generally and inner city unemployment in particular. A key role is being played by English Partnerships (EP). As the Government puts it, EP "seeks to create new jobs and investment through sustainable economic regeneration and development." In 1999 urban regeneration companies (URCs) were formed. By 2006 23 URCs had been announced, 21 in England and one each in Wales and Northern Ireland.

EU Regional Funds.

There are four funds—the Regional Development Fund, the Social Fund, the Agricultural Guidance and Guarantee Fund and the Financial Instrument for Fisheries Guidelines. The first of these funds is available only to Objective 1 and 2 areas. The

Social Fund can operate outside these areas. For 2000–06 the UK will receive more than $10bn from the four funds combined.

National Income: GDI and GDP.

Gross domestic income (GDI) is the sum total of incomes received for the services of labour, land, or capital in a country. Gross domestic product (GDP) is the money value of all the goods and services produced in the country. So as to avoid double-counting, only the *value added* at each stage of production is included: firms' purchases of goods and services from other firms are excluded. The revenue from selling the GDP is either paid out to the hired factors of production—labour, land, and capital—or retained in the form of profits. Therefore, provided it is calculated net of taxes on goods produced, GDP must equal GDI. To estimate gross national income (GNI) from GDI it is necessary to add the net income—such as profits and interest—received from abroad. If an allowance is made for wear and tear of the nation's capital equipment, *i.e.*, for *capital consumption*, we arrive at net national income, better known as the *national income*.

In 2004 the gross national income of the United Kingdom was £1,189,623 million, implying a national income per head of nearly £20,000. In 1955 the corresponding figure had been about £380 per head. However, only part of the increase in value was due to an increase in the quantity of goods and services produced; some of the increase simply reflected a rise in prices. It is important to calculate changes in the volume of output—known as *real output*—as well as changes in its value. Real output is calculated by the statistical device of constructing an index number. This is done by calculating the volume of goods and services provided in each year and then valuing these goods and services at the prices found in one particular year. Thus between 1955 and 2004 the money value of gross national product per head rose by nearly 5,000 per cent, whereas real per capita incomes only trebled, and the difference represented a rise in prices.

The Quality of Life.

National income per head is an indicator of the standard of living. However, this measure is necessarily a crude one. For instance, it cannot take into account changes in the distribution of income between rich and poor, nor in the length of the working week or year.

It may also conceal important changes in the "quality of life", *e.g.*, in our physical environment. This is affected by such things as traffic congestion, noise-, water- and air-pollution. Between 1961 and 2006 the number of car miles travelled on British roads more than quadrupled. Movement of civil aircraft over Britain increased even more. On the more positive side, the air in our cities became less polluted by smoke, sulphur dioxide, lead and other industrial emissions.

However, concern about emissions from motor vehicles continued. Tougher requirements for car emission systems have reduced this source of pollution. Overall air quality has improved in the last decade. The main air pollutant is now ground level ozone in addition to road traffic, electricity production is a major problem in this regard. Water quality has also improved in the last decade. About 95 per cent of the UK river network is now classified as being "good" or "fair" in chemical quality. There has also been sustained improvement in the quality of our coastal bathing waters.

Complaints about noise were noticeably higher in the 1980s than before, and were even higher by the early 2000s. An increasing concern in recent times has been the disposal of the ever-greater amounts of waste produced by a wealthy economy. Still the most common form of disposal is landfill, but there are obvious limits as to the feasibility of this practice. Hence the emphasis on recycling schemes.

Anti-Pollution Policy.

In recent years environmental concerns have moved increasingly from the national to the international level. In particular the issue of global warming has become important. *See* **Section Y.**

There had been growing public concern with environmental issues, and an awareness that the Conservative government's "laissez faire" approach to industrial policy might have prevented progress being made on issues such as carbon dioxide emissions from power stations. In answer to its critics, the government pointed to co-operation with international bodies such as the EC and the OECD in developing laws on pollution control. It also published a White Paper in September 1990 entitled "This Common Inheritance" which set out a policy framework for the 1990s. The paper was widely criticised by environmentalists as lacking substance, since it failed to support measures such as a carbon tax.

The Environmental Protection Act of 1990 announced the phasing in of a so-called integrated system of pollution control. Various agencies in this process (*e.g.* the National Rivers Authority and Her Majesty's Inspectorate of Pollution) were merged to form the Environment Agency in 1996. There were similar bodies for Scotland and Northern Ireland. At the beginning of 1994, BS7750 was published. This was described by the Government as "the world's first standard for environmental management systems'.

The UK Government announced that it was committed to a strategy of sustainable development, phraseology first arising from the "earth summit" in Rio de Janeiro in 1992. In 1997 the new Labour Government merged the Departments of Environment and Transport in the hope that this would enable a more integrated approach to environmental issues. At the Kyoto summit in 1997 the British Government committed itself to targets for the reduction of emissions of six greenhouse gases. The most recent international conference at the end of 2005 saw the UK in the vanguard of further measures to reduce the pace of climate change, but lack of cooperation from the US and China was notable. Early in 2006 the Government launched its UK Climate Change Programme.

In 1999 the Government announced a revised approach to sustainable development which added social aims to environmental ones. In 2000 a new pollution control system, known as Pollution Prevention Control, was launched.

The UK government has claimed that the reduction of greenhouse gas emissions in the last decade represents a major success for policy. However, some influential environmental economists would disagree.

Industrial Production.

It is fairly easy to measure output in the main manufacturing industries, and in many of the other industries producing goods. It is much more difficult to do so for the service industries. The output of a doctor or a lawyer is not easily measured. So each month the Office for National Statistics calculates the *index of industrial production* covering the main production industries. Industrial production is thus an early indicator of economic trends, but historically it is prone to fluctuate more than the other components of GDP.

Manufacturing industry accounts for most industrial production. Within manufacturing the following industries expanded rapidly in the three decades after World War II—chemicals, including drugs, plastics, cosmetics and detergents, coal and petroleum products, including oil refining, and instrument and electrical engineering. The slowest growing, and sometimes declining, manufacturing industries were textiles, clothing, leather and shipbuilding, which were losing their markets to cheaper competitors. Those industries in which demand stagnated tended to be the industries in which output per employee, *i.e.*, productivity, had stagnated.

International Comparisons.

In the 1960s and 1970s Britain's GDP grew less rapidly than that of almost any other major Western country. The British economy was also characterised by a relatively slow growth of output per head, *i.e.*, productivity. Britain fell behind many of the European countries in terms of income per head.

Many explanations of Britain's poor performance were suggested, and there is by no means agreement on this matter among economists. However, until recently there was general consensus that relatively slow productivity growth was the main culprit rather than an inadequate growth of capital and labour. The factors most often

blamed were poor management, an inadequate and inefficient industrial relations system and low investment in training and research. Commentators differed in the relative importance they assigned to these different explanations, but agreed that low investment in physical plant and machinery was likely to have been the consequence rather than the primary cause of low growth. However in the last few years some economists have started to put renewed stress on the importance of capital and labour inputs. They argue that traditional analysis has under-estimated the effect of investment in either capital or labour. This is because new investment embodies technical progress which increases productivity, and additionally there are knock-on effects on the rest of the economy which are hard to measure but nevertheless very real. For example, if a business spends money on developing a new product, the very existence of this new product creates opportunities for others. Think of the peripheral products and services which have relied on the development of cheap home computers.

Endogenous Growth Theories.

Economists who argue in this manner have developed so-called endogenous growth theories. They have contended that, when a business invests in physical equipment or in training or in research and development, it creates potential opportunities not just for itself but for others. By this mechanism investment can have a substantial impact on productivity.

The performance of the British economy in the mid- to late-1980s was much better relative to other countries than was the case in the 1970s. Growth in total output averaged about 2·5 per cent per annum in the period 1980–88, compared to a European average of less than 2·0 per cent in the same period.

Sceptics who believed that there had been no real underlying improvement were proved at least partly correct. The period of rapid growth in 1986–88 finally ended because it met the UK's traditional constraints of inflation and balance of payments weakness. The policy tightening invoked to cope with these depressed the UK economy and kept growth well below the European average in the period 1989–94.

Investment.

In 2003 gross investment in real assets amounted to £179,810 million in the United Kingdom. This was about 16 per cent of GNP. The net addition to the nation's stock of capital assets was only about one third of total investment, the rest being needed to offset the wastage of assets already in use, *i.e.*, to make good the *capital consumption*.

There are four main kinds of investment: plant and machinery, vehicles, dwellings, and other new buildings and works. In 2003 the four categories accounted for 31, 9, 23 and 37 per cent respectively. Investment may also be analysed by the purpose for which it is used. Social services such as education and health take a small proportion of total investment. Distribution and other service industries take a large proportion. Manufacturing investment is low in relation to the contribution of manufacturing to output. There is evidence that the quality of investment undertaken has shown a marked improvement in recent years.

Increasing Investment.

Historically, the proportion of total output invested—the *investment ratio*—has been lower in Britain than in other countries with faster growth rates of output and productivity; and there is reason to believe that a higher proportion would have improved the growth rate to a certain extent. This was seen in the mid 1980s when a sharp acceleration in productivity growth was associated with a recovery of investment (particularly in manufacturing) from the very depressed levels of the early 1980s. But in a fully employed economy it is not possible to increase investment expenditures without curtailing other forms of expenditure, notably private and public consumption. This curtailment would have to be brought about by increasing taxation or encouraging people to save or by pruning public services. Yet the very act of restricting private consumption may induce private firms to *reduce* their investment expenditures. For society as a whole, increasing investment involves a choice between the loss of current consumption and the ensuing gain of future consumption.

In 2005 about 90 per cent of total investment in the United Kingdom was carried out in the private sector, and the remaining 10 per cent by public authorities and by the public corporations. Governments do possess various policy measures by which to influence private investment but private investment is volatile and highly dependent on businessmen's expectations, especially their expectations about the future growth of their markets.

It is no easy matter to raise the British investment ratio. Even in the sustained growth of the mid and late 1980s, investment rates were particularly high only for two or three years.

The Finance of Investment.

Any business is allowed to charge as a cost the depreciation of its assets. Normal depreciation allowances used to be based on the original cost of the asset and on its expected useful life. In a time of price inflation depreciation allowances calculated in this way will not provide sufficient finance to permit the replacement of assets at higher prices, and accountants have been slowly moving towards the concept of depreciation allowances being based on replacement costs.

Government Policy Towards Investment.

Governments have adopted certain fiscal devices to encourage replacement and net investment. Soon after the war initial allowances were introduced. Under this system firms were permitted to charge against profits in the first year of its life 20, or at times 40, per cent of the cost of any new equipment, and the investment amounted to a loan of the tax saved in the first year, repaid over the life of the asset. In 1954 initial allowances for machinery were replaced by a system of investment allowances, under which a firm could charge against profits 20 per cent of the cost of any new machine, with the difference that all ordinary depreciation allowances were still chargeable. So the investment allowance was a grant, not a loan, of the saved tax. In 1966, initial and investment allowances on new plant and machinery in three sectors—manufacturing, mining, and shipping—were replaced by cash grants. Other plant and machinery and industrial building received higher initial allowances. In 1970 the Conservative Government reintroduced initial allowances in place of investment grants but in 1972 tried to encourage investment by granting free depreciation; *i.e.* 100 per cent allowance in the first year. The details of capital allowances changed from time to time over the following decade, but in the 1984 Budget a more radical change was announced. By 1986 first year allowances were scrapped, to be replaced by an annual allowance of 25 per cent and lower rates of Corporation Tax. In 1988–89 the Corporation Tax rate was reduced to 35 per cent, with a lower rate for small companies.

Response to Recession.

In response to the serious recession, the March 1991 Budget made a retrospective reduction in the Corporation Tax rate of 1% for the financial year 1990–91, and cut Corporation Tax by a further 1% to 33% for 1991–92 and beyond. The Spring 1998 Budget cut the rate to 30 per cent, and to 20 per cent for small companies. The small company rate was cut still further in the 2002 Budget—to 19 per cent. This leaves British rates of company taxation well below the European norm. Companies with annual profits of less than £10,000 pay no tax. Beyond this amount they pay on a sliding scale, hitting 19 per cent at £50,000. The tax rate than remains at 19 per cent until profits hit £300,000. Beyond this figure the rate rises on a sliding scale, hitting 30 per cent at profits of £1·5 million. In addition, tax relief is provided for various forms of investment.

Apart from Government help, companies rely mainly on retained profits to fund investment. Other sources of company finance are borrowing in

financial markets and the issue of company shares. As compared to many other countries, in Britain a relatively high proportion of external investment funds are raised by equity issue rather than by direct borrowing. Much public investment must be financed by the Treasury, except for relatively small amounts raised by public corporations on the financial markets. The 1979 Conservative Government announced its intention to seek private capital for some public investment projects, *e.g.* roadbuilding—a path followed by subsequent Labour administrations. The Government also maintained a new stress on helping small firms. This had been given particular impetus by the report of the Wilson Committee and by differentially favourable tax treatment. The 1989 Enterprise Initiative continued this theme of assistance to small firms—by, for example, state-funded consultancy help. Traditionally, investment measures were concerned with reducing the cost of capital. Many people believed that investment could be increased more effectively if more steps were taken to encourage a high and stable demand for output.

Labour Subsidies.

Initially Government subsidies were employed primarily as incentives for investment, particularly in a regional context. A 1972 Act, however, gave wide powers to the Government to offer financial assistance in almost any form to almost any enterprise, provided the assistance was "in the public interest". The Labour Government in 1974 greatly increased subsidisation, aimed mainly at maintaining employment. These subsidies consisted chiefly of direct assistance to industries both within and outside the assisted areas and labour subsidies in the form of temporary employment and job creation schemes, aimed particularly at young people. Thus there was a new emphasis on subsidies which cheapened the cost of labour. Some of the schemes, like the Temporary Employment Subsidy, were pure subsidies in this sense. Others combined the subsidy element with measures to increase either the mobility or training of workers, the Youth Opportunities Programme for instance. The new Conservative Government cut back on such schemes soon after its election in 1979, but did continue an emphasis on training, with the Youth Training Scheme (later, Youth Training), which was extended in 1986.

New Subsidies.

Two other major subsidies were introduced. The Community Programme encouraged sponsoring agencies or individuals to set up projects of community value to utilise unemployed labour. The Government provided a cash grant for each person employed, and paid their wage which was supposed to be equivalent to the going rate for the job in the area. A second subsidy was the Enterprise Allowance Scheme, which provided a small weekly payment to the unemployed set up their own business. Subsequently, this was effectively replaced by the Business Start-Up Scheme. Until 1985 the Government had a fourth scheme (the Young Workers' Scheme), which paid employers to take on youths to gain work experience.

In 1986 and 1987 the Government shifted to more overt job subsidies, including the Job Start Scheme whereby a worker taking a job paying less than a specified minimum was paid the balance by the State. Other schemes were however phased out, including the New Workers Scheme (designed to encourage the young to accept low-paid employment) and the Job Release Scheme (which subsidised early retirement). Job-Sharing schemes however remained in place for longer.

By 1989 all training schemes for unemployed adults had been amalgamated under an umbrella Employment Training Scheme (later, Employment Training).

Training.

An emphasis on training is now a major part of the Government's supply strategy for the labour market. There had long been criticism of the British training effort. It was said that the school system was ill attuned to the needs of industry, that not enough young people continued with education or full-time training after the minimum school-leaving age. The old apprenticeship system was justly accused of being too rigid and of forming skills often inappropriate to changing technology. Financing of industrial training was thought to be insufficient. There was inadequate provision for the retraining of adults—so necessary in a changing world.

In some respects matters had been getting worse. The recession of the early 1980s, for example, decimated training recruitment. As a consequence of Government policy, most of the old Industrial Training Boards were disappearing, without adequate substitutes being found.

Changing Policy Towards Training.

Although training was the focus of much attention, the main outcomes—Youth Training and Employment Training— were regarded by many as merely cosmetic devices to hide unemployment. The main criticisms of training programmes included lack of finance and a failure to address the key problem that arises under private sector provision of training, namely that unless an employer can guarantee that an employee stays in the firm for a considerable period of time, then the employer's return from the training investment is less than society's. The consequence is that if left to their own devices private employers will "under- invest". Meanwhile there had been some progress in the area of youth training and vocational education. The school curriculum was made more vocationally directed. The 1988 Education Act introduced a National Curriculum which, along with the switch from "O" Levels to GCSE, was intended to improve the vocational orientation of secondary education. More generally, the National Council for Vocational Qualifications was introducing a standard set of national qualifications to replace the myriad previously available. Some YT schemes were excellent whilst some industries were developing better alternatives to the old apprenticeship system.

The 1988 Employment Act.

The 1988 Employment Act incorporated all the employment training schemes for adults under the Employment Training Initiative. This was workplace-based and was supported by a significant number of large employers. The scheme was designed to provide training for twelve months. Despite support from many employers, the scheme was criticised widely in the trade union movement where it was regarded as another means of attracting cheap labour and artificially reducing the official unemployment register. More generally there were some doubt about the quality of training being offered by some of the firms in the scheme.

Training and Enterprise Councils.

As well as introducing the Employment Training Scheme, the 1988 Employment Act also brought substantial changes in structure of responsibility for training. At the local level, training was overseen by a network of Training and Enterprise Councils (TECs). Each TEC was an independent company, with two-thirds of its board being comprised of local employers. The reason for majority representation for businesses in TECs was said by the Government to be that local industry had the best insight into local skills needs. One difficulty was that the government laid down fairly rigid rules about the seniority of the businessmen serving on TECs and this caused recruitment difficulties in some areas. It was doubtful whether increased employer involvement in TECs would, in itself, make any difference to Britain's poor record in the area of skills compared to other countries. A deficiency in education and training is now widely blamed for the UK's bad industrial record and for the emergence of skills shortages at relatively high levels of unemployment. Meanwhile tentative steps were taken to encourage individuals to take more responsibility for their own training decisions. Pilot schemes of Training Credits were introduced which were meant to give people the power to shop around for good training, whilst the 1991 Budget introduced tax relief for personal training expenditures.

These credits were intended to give access to a new Modern Apprenticeship scheme. Meanwhile in 1993 Employment Training and Employment Action

were replaced by two new schemes—Training for Work and Jobplan Workshops. Much progress was made. More people were undergoing training and achieving qualifications, but the general view was that the UK still lagged behind. Much of the training taking place was at a relatively low level.

The Conservative Government had a set of official targets both for foundation and lifelong learning. At the same time increasing stress was placed on helping and encouraging firms to become Investors in People (IIP).

Labour Government Policy.

The new Labour Government put, if anything, even greater emphasis on education and training. The term 'the learning society' became the common currency of public discussion. Yet the substance of policy initially changed little. Youth training continued to be subsidised via Modern Apprenticeships and, at a lower level, via National Traineeships. Adult training was subsidised via a Training for Adults, which had replaced Training for Work. Subsequently the main adult programme became Work-Based Learning, available to those who had been unemployed for 6 months or more. Loans were also available to small firms to help them with training. Two new initiatives were announced— Individual Learning Accounts and the University of Industry. Both initiatives emphasised the role of individuals rather than the employer, and to an extent placed government subsidy and decision taking into their hands. However, a more fundamental question remains unanswered. The thrust of policy continues to be to solve the UK's VET problems by increasing the *supply* of skills. But it may be that the problem is that employers do not demand skill. Many commentators believe that too many British producers are producing low specification goods (the basic version of a good) with low-skill production methods. In other words the country is getting the VET performance that its employers want. Only if substantial numbers of them change their product strategies will VET improve.

National Learning and Skills Council.

In 2001 the TECs were abolished. A National Learning and Skills Council was established, with local offices. The new body subsumed the functions not only of the TEC National Council but also of the Further Education Funding Council. Whilst this dealt with skills issues on a geographical basis the Government also decided to introduce them on a control basis, establishing a range of sector skills councils under the umbrella of the Sector Skills Development Agency.

The Government also reformed the Modern Apprenticeship system. National Traineeships were re-labelled Foundation Modern Apprenticeships aiming at NVQ2 level qualifications. Modern Apprenticeships themselves acquired the prefix "Advanced", but still aimed at NVQ3. Sixteen and seventeen year olds are also entitled to paid time off work to study for NVQ2. Subsequently the two levels were re-named yet again as Apprenticeships and Advanced Apprenticeships.

Monopoly and Competition.

A trend to increasing size and increasing capitalisation has been going on now for many decades, and in the process it has changed the face of British industry. In the early 19th century the typical firm was the owner-managed textile mill. Then in the 1860s and 1870s came the discovery of cheap methods of making steel, with the consequential immense growth in the engineering industries. Most of the chemical industry is still newer, and there are many entirely 20th century industries such as aircraft, electronics and bio-technology.

In the capital-intensive industries the big firm predominates. In some it has become almost a monopoly; in others the pattern is of a few firms, all large. In 2004, of the world's largest 500 companies, 36 were UK-owned. Of the top 10 UK companies, four were banks and there were three each in the oil and gas sector and in pharmaceuticals and biotechnology. BP is the biggest UK company. Vodaphone is the largest telecommunications services company in the world, whilst Glaxo SmithKlein is the world's fourth largest pharmaceutical and biotech company.

The UK has two of the world's biggest banks—HSBC and the Royal Bank of Scotland.

The extent of *concentration* of British industry—according to measures such as the proportion of the output of an industry produced by the largest three firms—has increased since 1945. There are about 4 million businesses in Britain. Over 3,000 of them employ more than 500 people, but they account for 37 per cent of employment and 40 per cent of turnover. Concentration increased particularly rapidly in the 1960s. There were two possible reasons. The first was the natural growth of already large firms; the second was because of merger activity. This latter factor has been the more important in Britain. Although evidence is scanty, there is some suggestion that for a while in the mid 1970s, concentration stopped increasing, and it may even have fallen a little. From the late 1980s there was a massive increase in merger activity. The last twenty years have witnessed a sustained increase in cross-border mergers, peaking in 2000. For example, in 2000 acquisitions abroad by British companies were at a record level, involving £181·3 billion. The two largest were the acquisition of Mannesmann by Vodaphone, and the acquisition of Atlantic Richfield by BP. However, in 2001–03 acquisitions abroad fell sharply, reflecting a general fall in merger and acquisition activity.

The Changing Nature of Competition.

Competition goes on, but it has changed its form. Competition used to be largely by price. Now it is also by advertising and by variations in the quality and other features of the product—detergents and motor cars being good examples. In many industries, groups of firms producing similar products entered into agreements which had the effect of restricting competition, for example through schemes for price-fixing. The effect was to increase the price to the consumer and to reduce the amount of output available. Some authorities have estimated that the total "welfare" loss because of this was relatively small, and have argued that our major concern should be over the dangers of large corporations having substantial political power because of their size, and over their using this power to force the Government into unwise decisions about, for example, subsidising inefficient management.

Domestic monopolies are also limited by foreign competition, and by the discipline of "potential cross entry"—that is, the possibility that a powerful firm may be attracted into a new sector by the sight of very high profits. The British industrial scene has nevertheless changed substantially, not only with the emergence of very large and powerful domestic firms, but also with the extensive presence of foreign-owned multinationals. Finally, however, it is worth remembering the words of the Nobel Prize winning economist, Sir John Hicks, that the greatest return to a monopolistic existence is a quiet life. In other words, firms will try not to make "too large" profits for fear of attracting new competition. An interesting question, however, is how far the stock market "disciplines" firms into maximising their profits. If they do not, the argument goes, dividends will be low, investors will sell their shares whose price will go down, thus rendering the firm liable to be taken over.

Regulation of Competition and Monopoly.

(i) Restrictive Trade Practices.

The Restrictive Trade Practices Acts of 1956 and 1968 outlawed many of the main forms of restrictive agreements preventing competition. Collective price-fixing was declared to be illegal unless an industry could show that the practice brought substantial benefit to the public. Collective price-fixing was the system under which a central association for the industry laid down minimum prices at which members might sell. Usually such a system was backed by arrangements for collective boycotts, under which members of the association would refuse to sell goods to wholesalers or retailers who broke the rules. Collective boycotts were also found in industries without collective price-fixing, one common purpose being to make sure that retailers did not sell a manufacturer's products below his recommended price. This form of collective resale price maintenance was also outlawed by the Acts.

Under the Acts any restrictive agreements of

several specified kinds had to be registered with the Registrar of Restrictive Practices. He then had to decide whether there was a *prima facie* case for the discontinuation of the agreement, and, if he thought there was, the case was referred to a Restrictive Practices Court, containing both judicial and lay members. For an agreement to be upheld, the agreeing parties had to prove to the Court that the agreement conferred some substantial benefit on the public which out-weighed any injury it did to the public. A 1976 Act extended this legislation to cover service agreements.

(ii) Resale Prices Act.

The Act of 1956 permitted individual manufacturers to enforce *resale price maintenance* (rpm) for their own products. Few suppliers would want the publicity of enforcing rpm through the courts, but they could still put some commercial pressure on price-cutters, *e.g.*, by offering less favourable terms or by refusing them supplies. The Resale Prices Act of 1964 prohibited all methods of enforcing minimum resale prices. However, goods which had been registered in due time with the Registrar of Restrictive Practices or had been approved by the Restrictive Practices Court, were exempted, temporarily in the former case and permanently in the latter. For rpm to be approved by the Court, it had to be shown that some ensuing benefit to customers (*e.g.*, of increased quality or more retail outlets) outweighed any detriment. With the exception of books and until 2001 some pharmaceuticals, where rpm was still not unlawful, rpm has largely been replaced by "recommended" retail prices, which are in effect maximum prices.

(iii) The Monopolies Commission.

The Restrictive Practices Acts left untouched those industries in which one firm is dominant: these remained the responsibility of the Monopolies Commission. This was an independent administrative tribunal, established in 1948, with powers to investigate and decide whether a monopoly (defined in terms of market share) was contrary to the "public interest."

(iv) Monopolies and Mergers Act.

The Monopolies and Mergers Act of 1965 strengthened control over monopolies and mergers. With regard to monopolies, the Government wished to provide itself with legal powers of enforcement: previously monopolies had been expected to comply voluntarily with the findings of the Monopolies Commission. The Act also permitted the Government to refer a merger or a proposed merger to the Monopolies Commission in cases where the merger would lead to monopoly (defined as control of at least one third of the market) or would increase the power of an existing monopoly, or where the value of the assets taken over exceeded £5 million (now £70 million). The 1965 Act was repealed in 1973 and replaced by the Fair Trading Act. The rules governing referral to the Monopolies Commission were changed. In 1989, the decision to refer a merger to the Monopolies Commission, and the criteria by which the commission examined the public interest, became less rigidly defined. Considerations of formal market share were probably less important than, for example, the existence of barriers to entry. The Companies Act of 1989 also introduced a number of changes aimed at improving procedures for merger control: a voluntary procedure for pre-notification of proposed mergers which would allow rapid approval; provision for the companies involved to accept statutory undertakings which might obviate the need for a full investigation by the Commission; and the temporary prohibition on dealing in one another's shares in the case of a merger referred to the Commission.

In interpreting the public interest, the Monopolies Commission had to weigh up the negative aspects (of large size, high prices, reduced product choice and restricted entry for new firms into the market) against the benefits of greater resources for product innovation and lower costs due to synergy.

(v) The Fair Trading Act.

The 1973 Fair Trading Act placed the previously

dispersed responsibilities for overseeing competition policies in the hands of a civil servant—the Director General of Fair Trading. The Monopolies Acts of 1948 and 1965 were repealed and replaced by rather more comprehensive rules. Monopoly was now defined as control of one quarter of the market instead of one third. For the first time local monopolies were made subject to control. Also "complex monopolies" were made subject to investigation—that is situations where no one firm had 25 per cent of the market, but where several of them collaborated to restrict competition. The Director General of Fair Trading—as well as the Department of Trade and Industry—was enabled to refer monopoly situations to the Monopolies Commission; though it was still only the Department which could make references on mergers. Additionally the Director General took over the functions of the Registrar of Restrictive Practices and responsibility for general consumer protection, and set up a new body to assist in that aim—the Consumer Protection Advisory Committee.

In 1978 the Labour Government published a review of its general policy which recommended a more neutral policy towards mergers and that greater stress should be put on competition.

(vi) The Competition Act.

In 1980 the new Conservative Government introduced a Competition Act which strengthened the powers of the authorities to deal with practices which limited competition in both the public and private sectors. Procedures were also speeded up considerably. There was a new power to refer nationalised industries and other public bodies for investigation of their efficiency, costs, services to consumers, and possible abuse of monopoly position. Perhaps the most celebrated case of applying the authorities' new legislation involved the UK Stock Exchange. In return for a pledge from the Government not to prosecute, the Stock Exchange abolished the restrictive practices which governed entry into the stockbroking profession, and separate the broking from the market-making functions in the stock market—the so-called "Big Bang" in the City of London. Self-regulation for the City was enshrined in the Financial Services Act of 1986. Of increasing importance were EC provisions, Articles 85 and 86, which relate to anti-competitive practices which affect trade between member states.

(vii) The Enterprise Initiative and Companies Act, 1989.

Under this Act the main reason for referring mergers became their likely effect on competition (see (iii) above). Though "public interest" referrals remained, the Government would intervene only rarely. Generally, it was claimed, the "market" would look after the public interest. When judging the impact of a merger on competition, due regard was given to foreign competition and also to potential entrants. The latter represents a particular fashion among modern industrial economists, who argue that many apparently monopolistic or oligopolistic industries may in fact be constrained to behave in a relatively competitive manner by the possibility that other firms might be attracted into their sector by high profits. Accordingly Monopolies Commission hearings were increasingly concerned with the existence or otherwise of "barriers to entry". Mergers policy was not, however, without its critics, many of whom believed that the criteria for referral were too lax, particularly compared to general practice in Europe. In 1993 the Government announced that it intended to take tougher measures against anti-competitive practices. In 1992 the Cadbury Committee, on the management of companies, provided a code of best practice for company boards.

(viii) The Competition Act of 1998.

This new legislation is concerned with anti-competitive agreements and the abuse of dominant positions. The main enforcer is the Director General of Fair Trading. The new law is more closely aligned with EU legislation. A new Competition Commission has been established, to replace the Monopolies and Mergers Commission. The Government announced consultations about taking sterner action against restrictive practices in the legal, architecture and accountancy professions.

(ix) The Enterprise Act of 2002.

This piece of legislation reinforced the 1998 Act on various fronts. It strengthened competition law and the framework for enforcing consumer rights. Perhaps most importantly, it extended the range of issues which could be referred to the Competition Commission. As a consequence of this legislation the Competition Commission now has three broad sets of tasks: to investigate mergers; to investigate markets (in place of the former monopoly references); and the regulation of the main regulated industries. The Office of Fair Trading is normally the body which refers cases to the Competition Commission and has more general responsibilities for consumer protection.

(x) Industrial Structure.

Mergers may lead to monopoly and to the abuse of monopoly power. But it would be wrong to presume that mergers are always bad: mergers—by facilitating research and other economies of large-scale production—may increase industrial efficiency. For this reason the *Industrial Reorganisation Corporation* (IRC) was set up in 1966 under Government auspices. Its functions were to promote industrial reorganisation in the interests of industrial efficiency, e.g., by enabling industries to achieve economies of scale or by reorganising inefficiently managed firms. It assisted firms in agreed regroupings and could intervene to encourage a particular takeover which, in its estimation, was in the public interest. However its objective in making loans was to "prod" and not to "prop" inefficient firms. It supported mergers in electronics, trawling, nuclear power, mechanical engineering, and other industries. In 1970 the Conservative Government decided to wind up the IRC. However, some of the proposed functions of the National Enterprise Board, set up in 1975, were similar to those performed by the IRC. The 1979 Conservative Government initially streamlined the NEB, and subsequently amalgamated it with the National Research and Development Corporation to form the British Technology Group.

Nationalised Industries.

After the extensive privatisation of industries and utilities undertaken during the last decade, the Nationalised Industries now account for less than 1 per cent of GDP. Postal Services, the underground operations of the old London Transport, British Nuclear Fuels and the Civil Aviation Authority are the most significant concerns which remain, at least partly, in public ownership. Consignia was established in 2001 to take on the operations of the Post Office. In the following year, it changed its name yet again. Today Royal Mail Holdings remains publicly owned and operates through Royal Mail, Parcelforce and a retail operation.

Even this tiny rump of the public sector is changing fast. The Government is actively working on public-private partnerships, which will introduce a large element of private sector finance and ownership.

For example, day-to-day air traffic control has been taken from the CAA and put in the hands of National Air Traffic Services Limited (NATS). NATS is a consortium comprising the Government, seven UK airlines and the BAA. The CAA is still responsible for safety and also regulation of NATS' charges.

Early Nationalisation.

Nationalisation was a central feature of the policies of the post-Second World War Labour Government. With the exception of steel—denationalised 1951–53 and re-nationalised in 1967—nationalisation was for a long time not extended into manufacturing industry. The post-1974 Labour Government nationalised the shipbuilding and aerospace industries, and established the British national Oil Corporation and the National Enterprise Board with wide powers to take holdings in private industry. Under the 1979 Conservative Government the post-war trend towards greater public ownership of industry was reversed.

A 1967 White Paper, amended in 1978, dictated that as well as achieving specified financial targets, nationalised industries should earn a target rate of return on their investments and price according to the marginal cost of a service.

With respect to pricing, it was government policy that subsidies could be made for some services which were justified on social grounds, *e.g.*, grants to British Rail to continue unremunerative rail services. The 1979 Conservative Government was much more vigorously reluctant to continue this approach.

The post-1979 Government challenged the whole concept of running publicly-owned industries even where a natural monopoly quite clearly existed, and launched a massive campaign of privatisation. To counter monopoly forces prices are regulated to ensure that they reflect general inflation adjusted for changes in the industry's underlying cost structure. One difficulty is that prices may nevertheless be set too high because the regulator (for example, Ofcom for the telecommunications industry) relies heavily on information which is provided by the industry itself. Restructuring of the industry may help overcome this difficulty, since this makes available several sources of information from the component firms and thus allows sensible comparisons to be made. This was one of the motives behind privatising electricity and water as area boards. The Government has also sought to introduce competition in the provision of public services. For example, local authorities are now obliged to put services such as refuse collection out to public tender. Many traditional civil service functions were put out to Agencies. Following the 1988 Education Act schools could effectively compete for pupils and as of April 1991 hospitals were essentially competing for patients referred through general practitioners.

Labour's Reforms.

The present Labour Government, in reforming the administration of the NHS, has removed the short-term nature of internal markets, though internal competition remains. Similarly, changes to the structure of the educational system retain large elements of competition.

3. INCOMES, WAGES, AND PRICES

Personal Income.

National income is a measure of the total income accruing to the residents in a country in return for services rendered (*see* **F13**). It therefore consists of the sum of wages, salaries, profits, and rents having allowed for depreciation. But not all this income accrues to persons, *e.g.*, companies do not distribute all their profits to shareholders and some nationalised industries earn profits. This is part of national income but not of *personal income*. On the other hand, some personal incomes are not payments for services rendered. Such incomes are called *transfer incomes* to emphasise that their payment

SOURCES OF HOUSEHOLD INCOME
1992 AND 2002

(As percentage of total)

	1992	2002
Wages and salaries . . .	65	68
Self-employment . . .	9	8
Investments . . .	6	3
Annuities and pensions . .	6	7
Social security benefits . .	13	12
Other sources . . .	2	1

does not add to the national income, but only transfers income from one agent to another. Included in this category are retirement pensions, child benefit and student grants.

Personal Disposable Income.

Not all personal income is available for spending. In 2003 the State took 31 per cent of household income in *income taxation*, Social Security contributions, which being compulsory are in effect a form of tax, and in contributions to pension schemes, council tax and other deductions. The remaining 69 per cent of income—called *household disposable income*—was available for spending. However, not all disposable income need be spent on consumer goods and services; income can instead be saved. There are many possible motives for saving, *e.g.*, to meet future contingencies, for a future purchase such as a house or car, for retirement, or for the income to be derived from saving. Saving as a fraction of personal disposable income fluctuated in the range 4·5 to 6·15 per cent in the late 1960s. By 1975 it had reached 8·5 per cent. It remained high thereafter, and peaked at about 11·7 per cent in 1980. It then fell and was only 3·9 per cent in 1988 although it recovered rapidly to a level of 11·5 per cent in 1992. Thereafter it fell slightly to reach 9·3 per cent in 1997, and fell more dramatically to 5·7 per cent in 1998, to 5·2 per cent in 1999 and to 5·0 per cent in 2000. In recent years it was 6·5 per cent in 2001, 5·3 per cent in 2002 and 5·7 per cent in 2003. In the autumn of 2004 it stood at 5·7 per cent. Many explanations of this varying savings ratio have been advanced—historically it has often been higher, the higher the rate of inflation. In the mid-1980s the fall in savings was related to rapid growth in the value of personal sector wealth, particularly in housing. Finally it has often been related to the perceptions of economic security prevalent at any given time.

The recovery of the ratio in the early 1990s seems to be closely linked to the high level of uncertainty generated by the recession, and also with the fall in the real value of the personal sector's assets relative to its debt. This latter phenomenon was intimately linked to the temporary decline in house prices.

Types of Personal Income.

The table (opposite) shows sources of household income. Over the post-war period, the share of self-employment income and incomes from property fell while that from wages and salaries and from social security benefits tended to rise. During the 1980s and early 1990s, however, income from self-employment increased a little, in line with a larger share of the self-employed in the labour force. The share of income from annuities and pensions is also tending to grow along with the expansion of privately funded occupational pension schemes.

Inequality of Income.

In 2002–03 the top 20 per cent of income recipients (defined as households rather than individuals) received half of all original income, whilst the bottom 40 per cent received only a tenth. Thus Britain is far from being an egalitarian society. For the first three decades after the Second World War inequality diminished. But from the mid-1970s and through the 1980s there was an increase in inequality. There has certainly been little narrowing since the early 1990s and possibly some further increase in the dispersion of original income.

Taxes on income are of course progressive, rising as income increases. This progressivity was reduced through the 1980s as higher rates of income tax were lowered. By the beginning of 1992 there

PERCENTAGE SHARES OF ORIGINAL, DISPOSABLE AND
FINAL HOUSEHOLD INCOME, 2002–03

	Quintile groups of households				
	Bottom Fifth	Next Fifth	Middle Fifth	Next Fifth	Top Fifth
Original Income	3	7	15	25	50
Disposable Income	8	12	17	23	41
Final Income	6	12	16	23	43

was a standard rate of 25 per cent and just one higher rate of 40 per cent. The Budget of that year introduced an additional lower band of 20 per cent. Subsequent Budgets lowered the standard rate to 24 and then 23 per cent. From April 2000 it was 22 per cent. In 1999 the lower band of 20 per cent was abolished, and replaced by one of 10 per cent in the case of earned income. The 20 per cent rate remains for income from savings.

The table (**F19**) shows the shares of disposable income. This is original income minus direct taxes and plus cash benefits. We can see that the effect is redistributive. In 2002–03 the share of the bottom three fifths of the distribution was 37 per cent, as compared to 25 per cent of original income. Allowing for the effects of indirect taxation and benefits in kind produces final income. As the table shows the net effects of these adjustments is mildly regressive.

Thus the direct tax burden somewhat squeezes the distribution of incomes. But until the mid 1970s the narrowing dispersion of incomes before tax was of greater importance in making Britain rather more egalitarian than taxation policy. Between the mid-1970s and the early 1990s, however, inequality of pre-tax incomes increased, whilst the tax benefit system as a whole became less redistributive. As with original income this trend appears to have largely, but not entirely, halted in the last few years.

Income and Spending Power.

In various ways figures for incomes alone underestimate the degree of inequality in British society. First, incomes are incomes as defined for income tax purposes. Any allowed expenses are excluded; and for the self-employed and the higher ranks of management the expense allowance now adds substantially to spending power. Second, if one buys an asset which then rises in value one gains extra spending power. Such capital gains can be very important to the wealthy in periods of boom in ordinary share prices, land prices and house prices. Yet only in 1965 did capital gains become taxable and even then the rate of tax on capital gains was low in relation to the rate on additional income. From 1988, capital gains have been taxed at the individual's or corporation's higher rate of tax, although there is a larger tax-free allowance. The 1998 Budget introduced lower rates for long-term gains. Similar concessions for long-term business gains were announced in the 2000 and 2002 Budgets.

Inequality of Wealth.

Spending power depends not only on income and capital gains but also on the sheer amount of capital owned. The ownership of capital in Britain have to be estimated indirectly from information arising in connection with the payment of death duties, supplemented by information from capital transfer tax (from 1986 inheritance tax) returns and therefore cannot always be relied upon. An alternative method is to estimate the stock of wealth by working back from information on investment income, but this approach is also prone to error. It appears from the table that the most wealthy 1 per cent of the population own 23 per cent of all wealth, whilst 56 per cent of all wealth is owned by the richest 10 per cent. Even more strikingly, the poorer half of the population own only 6 per cent of total wealth.

WEALTH OF INDIVIDUALS, 2002

Percentage of wealth owned by:	
Most wealthy 1 per cent of population	23
,, ,, 5 ,, ,, ,, ,,	43
,, ,, 10 ,, ,, ,, ,,	56
,, ,, 25 ,, ,, ,, ,,	74
,, ,, 50 ,, ,, ,, ,,	94

It should be emphasised, however, that the data refer to *individuals* rather than to *households*: this can give a misleading impression if, for example, the assets of married couples are generally registered in the name of one of the marriage partners rather than as jointly-owned assets. Nevertheless, it is fair to conclude from the data that the disparity of wealth is considerably greater than

AVERAGE GROSS HOURLY PAY OF FULL-TIMERS BY MAJOR OCCUPATIONAL GROUP,
Great Britain, April 2005, £ per hour

	£ per hour
Managers and Senior Officials .	19·90
Professional Occupations . .	19·50
Associate Professional and Technical Occupations .	13·96
Administrative and Secretarial .	9·16
Skilled Trade Occupations .	9·84
Personal Service Occupations .	7·60
Sales and Customer Services .	6·75
Process Plant and Machine Operatives	8·72
Elementary Occupations . .	6·96
All Occupations . . .	12·55

AVERAGE GROSS WEEKLY PAY OF FULL-TIMERS: FIVE HIGHEST PAID AND FIVE LOWEST PAID,
Great Britain, April 2003, £ per week

	£ per week
Directors and chief executives of major organisations . . .	2,406·7
Corporate managers and senior officials	1,957·4
Medical practitioners . . .	1,278·5
Financial managers and chartered secretaries	1,235·5
Solicitors, lawyers, judges and coroners	928·8
Shelf fillers	253·6
Kitchen and catering assistants .	241·3
Waiters and bar staff . . .	236·5
Hotel porters	228·7
Retail cashiers and check-out operators	205·4

that of income. Moreover, there is a natural tendency for the inequality of wealth to grow because the higher income groups tend to save a higher proportion of their income and so to accumulate capital more readily. The Government, by capital transfer tax, tried but largely failed to neutralise this tendency.

Capital transfer tax (CTT) was introduced in 1974. Until then only transfers of wealth on death or shortly before death were taxable, and redistribute Inheritance, but did something to redistribute wealth. The 1986 Budget effectively abolished CTT for gifts *inter vivos*, the tax (renamed inheritance tax) applying on death or transfers made in the 7 years preceding death.

Wages and Salaries.

About 50 per cent of personal income was paid to employees in the form of wages and salaries. In April 2005 average gross weekly earnings for full-time men were £569·0 and for full-time women were £436·1. The first table above shows earnings for different broad occupational groups, whilst the second table is concerned with more narrowly defined occupations, listing the five best paid and the five worst paid.

Earnings by Occupation.

Different occupations command different pay, as the table shows. The structure of pay reflects in part the amount of responsibility which the different jobs entail. The differentials reflect also the ease of entry into various occupations. This in turn depends on the degree of specialised knowledge, skill or talent required, and in a few cases it depends on the extent to which artificial barriers to entry have created scarcity. The structure of pay is also influenced, of course, by the degree of organisation and bargaining strength of workers in different occupations. Finally, the relative strengths of demand for different types of worker is important, as is the force of custom.

Within the lower level occupations the difference between skilled, semi-skilled and unskilled pay narrowed over the post-war years. This was most marked during the war, in the years immediately after the war and between 1970 and 1976 when skilled workers were often granted the same flat rate advances as unskilled. The 15 years from the mid-1970s witnessed a reversal of such narrowing and indeed substantial widening. These years also saw a widening of the gap between manual and non-manual pay. Since the early 1990s there has been much more stability.

Earnings by Industry.

There are significant differences in earnings among industries. These are associated with the bargaining strength of different groups of workers, with the prosperity of the industry, and with the average skill levels required in production. Manufacturing industries as a whole pay relatively well. Public administration (including local government) is a low-wage sector.

Earnings by Sex.

There are very significant earnings differences within each industry between men and women. There are two possible reasons why women are paid less than men. One is that they are crowded into lower-paying occupations. The second is that they may have lower pay than men within the same occupation. Either form of disadvantage could be the result of discrimination or of women possessing inferior productive characteristics. In practice it is a very difficult distinction to make. Equal opportunities and equal pay legislation attempts to reduce discrimination. The Equal Pay Act (1970) obliged a firm to pay men and women, who are doing the same job, the same wage by the end of 1975. In 1972 women in manual occupations had median earnings which were about half those of men. By 1978 this figure had risen to over 60 per cent. In 2005 women working full-time had weekly earnings which were 77 per cent of their male counterparts. By contrast the comparable figure for part-timers was 92 per cent.

These changes are explained by the impact of the Act, by flat rate general increases agreed under incomes policies in the 1970s, and by trade union bargaining policy. There have been renewed initiatives against sexual discrimination. In particular, in 1984 an amendment to the Equal Pay Act insisted that as well as paying men and women doing the same job the same rate of pay, parity of pay should also apply to jobs of equal value. The Equal Opportunities Commission supports positive actions which employers might take to improve the lot of women in employment. Recently this has contributed to a catch-up for women in areas of the retail trade. A number of "equal pay for work of equal value" claims have been made under the 1984 Act and taken to the European Court of Human Rights.

Recently the Equal Opportunities Commission has expressed concern about slow progress towards parity of pay for women in the last decade or so. The figures quoted above suggest that this is indeed a problem for full-time workers.

Overtime and Short-time.

The earnings of any individual worker depend on many factors, and are often well above the basic wage rate payable for a *standard working week*. They include overtime earnings; and over-time working is still common. Nor is overtime confined to male manual employment; it is found, for example, in office work and even in some of the professions like medicine and accountancy. The working week is composed of standard hours and overtime hours. Its length has diminished since before the war, although the standard week has been more significantly reduced.

In most industries, for manual workers it was cut from 48 to 44 hours soon after 1945. A 42-hour week was introduced between 1960 and 1962, and there was a movement towards a 40-hour standard working-week in the late 1960s. Subsequently there were pressures from unions, notably in engineering industries, to reduce the standard week below 40 hours, and indeed this has happened in many sectors. In much of the chemical industry, for example, it is often as low as 35 hours. The standard working week tends to be slightly less for white collar workers than for manual workers. Notwithstanding these developments total hours worked have

increased for many people since the early 1980s. The consequence is that working hours are now longer in the UK than in continental Europe. In 2005 on average they were 40·6 hours per week for full-time men and 37·5 hours per week for full-time women. An interesting recent development has been an increase in unpaid overtime—a phenomenon reflecting one dimension of work intensification in Britain.

Earnings and Rates.

Overtime is not, however, the main reason why earnings exceed basic wage-rates. One reason is payment by results, the system of payment under which the worker's wage depends partly on output or performance. A common form is still the piecework system, under which pieceworkers are paid a fixed low rate per hour for each hour worked plus a fixed piecework price for each operation performed; but some employers tend to prefer schemes under which the bonus payment is related to the output or some other measure of the performance of a larger group or to that of a whole factory. Individual merit-related pay has become fashionable, particularly in white-collar work. An example of such a scheme would be that each employee is given a cost of living increase each year plus an additional amount based on merit, as judged by an annual assessment. This principle has been extended further in some large firms, where employees receive performance-related bonuses according to whether or not they have met pre-determined targets.

Wage Determination.

In Britain there were 7·4 million trade union members in 195 unions in 2003. Most of these unions are very small, the majority of them having less than 2,500 members. But 4 have memberships over 500,000. Union membership has fallen from its peak of 13·3 million in 1979. Until 1997, each successive year had seen a fall in union membership from its 1979 peak. Since 1997 the decline has slowed. The proportion of employees who are union members is nowadays only about 26 per cent as compared to about 53 per cent in 1979. The main job of unions is collective bargaining with employers. The structure and scope of collective bargaining changed significantly in the 1980s. Until the beginning of that decade in most industries most employers belonged to associations which bargained collectively on their behalf. Some big firms, however, preferred to remain outside the associations, and strike their own bargain with the unions. Before the war many firms tried to encourage the formation of Company Unions, *i.e.*, of unions confined to employees of a single firm; but this became very uncommon. In some lowly paid trades minimum wages were fixed by Wages Councils set up by the Department of Employment; and representatives of the workers and employers, and independent members, met together to reach agreement on the settlement to be recommended to the Minister. But over most of industry the aim of collective bargaining was to reach voluntary agreement, and the Department of Employment intervened only when no agreement is reached. In 1974 the Labour Government set up the *Advisory Conciliation and Arbitration Service* (ACAS) to provide independent arbitration services.

Development of Plant Bargaining.

After the Second World War plant bargaining developed as an increasingly important supplement to industry-wide bargaining in many sectors of the economy. Initially this was largely informal bargaining, with shop-stewards (unpaid lay trade union officials at the plant level) negotiating with management about, for example, special rates for working new machines. It is this which to a large degree was responsible for the growing gap between wage rates and earnings. The Donovan Commission, which was set up to inquire into the state of industrial relations and which reported in 1968, also saw it as a major cause of many of Britain's industrial relations problems, such as a high level of strike activity. Realising that it was impossible to put the clock back, the Commission recommended that plant bargaining procedures should be formalised, giving, for instance, proper channels for the resolution of wage disputes. In the 1970s there was

WAGES AND PRICES, 1960–2005
(1955 = 100)

	Weekly earnings	Index of retail prices	Real earnings
1960 . . .	130	114	114
1965 . . .	175	136	129
1970 . . .	250	169	148
1975 . . .	540	313	173
1980 . . .	997	611	163
1985 . . .	1,537	865	178
1990 . . .	2,321	1,154	201
1995 . . .	2,957	1,364	217
2000 . . .	3,659	1,556	235
2002 . . .	3,992	1,609	248
2003 . . .	4,160	1,656	251
2004 . . .	4,338	1,706	254
2005 . . .	4,529	1,754	258

indeed an increase in *formal* plant negotiations, with many plants setting their own wage rates and using national agreements purely as a minimum benchmark. This development probably improved the climate of industrial relations. In the mid-1970s some companies, especially in manufacturing, which had been concerned about the administrative cost as well as about the leapfrogging effects of plant agreements, had moved to single company bargains.

Decentralisation of Bargaining.

Thus in the years up to the 1980s there had been increasing decentralisation of bargaining. This continued apace during the 1980s with active Government encouragement. The national multi-employer bargaining declined considerably in significance and ultimately disappeared altogether. At the same time pay setting in many companies was becoming more decentralised to profit and cost centres. Simultaneously the range of issues over which bargaining took place diminished, whilst even pay setting became more individualised.

It has always been the case, and still is, that more people are covered by collective bargaining than are union members. In 1979, when union density was 53 per cent, 78 per cent of the workforce was covered by a collective agreement. Today only 35 per cent of the workforce is covered. Such has been the decline of unionism that increasingly large numbers of workers find that a collective bargain has little, if any, role to play in the determination of their pay. This is particularly true in the growing service sector and in small firms. The traditional heartlands of union influence are the public sector and the declining manufacturing industries. Although instances of formal de-recognition have been relatively few, even in these areas the influence of collective bargaining has waned. There has been a deliberate move to "individualise" the determining of pay; and here new fashions in payments systems, like merit pay, have played a large role.

Strikes.

The strike has alwasy been the unions' weapon of last resort. Most unions maintain strike funds in order to support their members when they call them out on strike; but these funds are small, and strike pay is usually very much below normal wages. So unions cannot afford to call strikes irresponsibly, and major official strikes are relatively uncommon.

Before the 1980s most strikes were neither large nor official. An official strike is one called by a union, usually by decision of the national executive, and is typically the result of collective bargaining about wages. But unofficial strikes called by local leaders were often about other matters. Few of the big unofficial strikes which plagued the docks were about wages; rather they reflected job insecurity and the poor state of labour relations in that industry. Much the same was true of the frequent strikes in ship-building, many of them caused by demarcation disputes concerning which jobs should be done by which type of skilled worker. Other strike-prone industries were mining and vehicles. In most industries there have always been very few strikes, and they have tended to be concentrated in the larger plants.

Frequency of Strikes.

From the mid-1950s the number of strikes in Britain increased, except in coal mining. In 1969 and 1970 there was a huge jump in both the number of stoppages and working days lost. After that industrial disputes fell to a more normal level, and indeed by the early 1980s were at an historically very low intensity. When unemployment fell sharply in 1988 and 1989, the number of strikes did not increase disturbingly. Thereafter there was a further reduction in strike activity, only for 1996 to show a slight resurgence. In that year there were 223 stoppages and 1,299,000 working days lost. In 2000 there were 207 stoppages involving 182,000 workers and causing the loss of 499,000 working days. In 2001 there were 174 stoppages involving 163,700 workers and causing the loss of 510,000 working days. In 2002 there were 146 stoppages involving 943,000 workers, causing the loss of 1,323,000 working days. The large number of working days lost was mainly due to the fire fighters' strikes. In 2003 there were 133 stoppages involving the loss of 499,000 working days, whilst in 2004, 905,000 days were lost as a result of 130 strikes. In 2005 only 157,000 days were lost in 116 strikes.

The 1971 Industrial Relations Act.

In its Industrial Relations Act of 1971 the Conservative Government laid down new laws for the regulation of industrial relations and for the curbing of strikes. However, the Act was repealed by the incoming Labour Government in 1974, which itself brought in several new pieces of legislation, including the Trade Unions and Labour Relations Act, the Employment Protection Act, and the Trade Unions and Labour Relations (Amendment) Act. As well as increasing legal protection for the individual employee and extending trade union immunities and rights, this legislation was concerned to improve industrial relations practice. The belief behind the legislation was that this could be done by machinery which ensured, for example, that employers formally recognised unions for collective bargaining purposes and that unions had greater access to information to enable them to negotiate about issues (such as a firm's investment plans) which previously ignorance had precluded them from doing.

With the election of a Conservative Government in 1979, the direction of legislation altered again. The 1980 Employment Act introduced measures to moderate the closed shop, provide funds for secret union ballots about important issues such as industrial action, and to limit picketing to only the establishments at which strikes were taking place. A further Act in 1982 intensified pressure on the unions. In particular it introduced further measures against existing closed shops and increased the liability of unions for the actions of their members. In 1984 came the Trade Union Act concerned with union democracy. In this unions were denied immunity if strikes took place without ballots, voting members of union executives had to be elected, and periodic ballots on the political use of union funds were required. In 1988 a further piece of legislation was passed by Parliament, which, inter alia, made it illegal for unions to discipline members who refused to obey a strike call, even a legal one. Such legislative developments were likely to reduce unions' ability to call and prosecute strikes, and possibly also to diminish the scope for local union leaders to have a decisive impact on strike decisions. The legislative process continued. A new Employment Act, passed in the final months of 1990, made further reforms to the closed shop and to the rules governing both secondary and unofficial industrial action.

The Act amended the Employment Act of 1980, making unions liable for the actions of all their officials, including their workplace representatives, during an industrial dispute. The 1990 Act also effectively outlawed the pre-entry closed shop by making it unlawful to refuse to employ someone on the grounds of union membership or lack of it. Much of the legislation was consolidated in the Trade Union and Labour Relations (Consolidation) Act of 1992.

The 1993 Act.

In 1993 the Trade Union Reform and Employment Rights Act was enacted. It finally abolished Wages Councils, whose scope had been much reduced by legislation in 1986. Strike ballots had to be postal, and industrial action was only legal after a period of notice had been given. Two other provisions were of greater significance. First, henceforth workers would be able to decide for themselves which union to join. This provision was expected to diminish the ability of the TUC to regulate competition amongst its member unions, and weaken its power still further. Second, workers would have to periodically re-affirm their willingness to have their subscriptions automatically deducted from their pay. This was intended to eliminate any tendency for people to remain members of a union through inertia.

The Employment Relations Acts of 1999 and 2004.

The Labour Government has softened some aspects of the Conservative legislation. It has introduced provisions for the recognition of unions by employers. The law now also requires consultation when redundancies are planned and protection for employees when businesses are transferred to new ownership. Individual rights have also been somewhat enhanced, for example the "qualifying period" for unfair dismissal rights has been reduced to one year, whilst unfair dismissal provisions have been extended to cover workers on strike.

However, this softening of the law in the last 8 years makes relatively minor adjustments to the legislation introduced by the Thatcher and Major governments. This means that unions are far more legally constrained than could have been envisaged in the 1960s and 1970s.

Prices and Real Incomes.

Prices rose very rapidly (by over 30 per cent) between 1949 and 1953, and earnings only just kept ahead in this period. But after that *real earnings* (*i.e.*, the command which money earnings have over goods and services) rose quite steadily until the early 1970s. Since then real earnings have increased more spasmodically.

In the calculation of real wages it is usual to make use of the *index of retail prices*, commonly called the cost-of-living index. The index is calculated monthly by the Department of Employment, and it naturally has an influence on the course of wage negotiations.

Over the last forty years or so the allocation of consumers' expenditure amongst different items has altered substantially. Of growing importance in household budgets were housing and transport and vehicles, whilst of diminishing importance was food. As people grow richer they spend a smaller proportion of their income on food. Nor have price changes been the same for all types of goods and services. For example, during the same long period, prices of fuel and light went up by more than the average whilst those for clothing, drink and durable household goods rose by less.

Calculation of Retail Price Index.

The general retail price index is calculated by weighting each of the commodity price indexes by the proportionate importance of that com-

modity in total expenditure in a particular year, and then summing all the indexes, *i.e.*, the general index is a *weighted average* of its constituent indexes. A different pattern of expenditure would mean a different set of weights, and hence a different cost-of-living index. For instance, the poor—and particularly pensioners—spend a higher proportion on the basic necessities; food, fuel and light, and housing. It is possible that the cost-of-living rose more for the poor than for these rich over these years.

The cost-of-living index has not risen evenly in Britain. There were spurts of rapid inflation in the periods 1950–52 and 1954–56, followed by a decade of relatively little inflation (averaging under 3 per cent per annum). After 1967, however, the rate of inflation accelerated, rising progressively from 2·5 per cent per annum between 1966 and 1967 to 7·0 per cent between 1971 and 1972.

The Causes of Inflation.

(i) Import Prices.

Prices charged in the shops are determined by a great many factors, over many of which the Government has little or no control. First among these is the price of imports. Prices of imported food and raw materials are determined in the world markets, in which Britain is only one of many purchasers. Prices in raw material and food markets can fluctuate wildly. Big increases in commodity prices occurred during the Korean war, in the early 1970s and again in 1979. The sharp increases in the prices of primary commodities contributed to British inflation at these and other times, but for most of the post-war period the rise in import prices was less rapid than domestic inflation even allowing for unfavourable exchange rate movements which push up the price of imports in sterling terms.

The main source of domestic inflation was the tendency for the incomes of factors of production (wages, profits and other incomes) to rise faster than real output.

(ii) The Influence of Demand.

An explanation of domestically generated inflation is that it arises not so much from increased costs as from demand pressures increasing prices and profits. If there is an increase in aggregate demand for goods and services in the economy, how does the economy respond? If it is operating at less than full employment, producers are able to expand their production to meet the additional demand. But if full employment has already been achieved, it is the price level and not production which rises. Given an excess demand for goods and services, there is competitive bidding for the limited supplies and producers are able to sell at higher prices. A more sophisticated version of this argument recognises that full employment cannot be precisely defined: rather, there are degrees of more or less unemployment. Bottlenecks appear in different firms and industries at different stages; so that any increase in demand is met by an increase in both prices and production. But the lower the rate of unemployment, the more the responses take the form of price increases.

A variant of this approach is the so-called *quantity theory of money*, in which inflation is seen as a response to an increase in the supply of money; there is too much money chasing too few goods. The theory dates back at least to David Hume, but it was generally discredited as a result of the writings of Maynard Keynes in the 1930s. However, it was revived by Milton Friedman and has received some measure of acceptance among economists, especially in the United States.

The great shortages during and immediately after the war would no doubt have generated rapid demand inflation had it not been for rationing and price controls; and the spurt of inflation between 1954 and 1956 was associated with a very high pressure of demand. On the other hand, inflation has occurred even in periods of relatively high unemployment. Moreover, the method by which most firms price their products is on the basis of their costs; so that most prices are not directly sensitive to the pressure of demand. A more plausible mechanism by which demand might influence prices indirectly is through its effect on wages. In fact, there has been a lively debate as to the extent to which wages are influenced by the pressure of demand as opposed to being relatively independent of it. There is, however, general agreement that wages were the main driving force behind prices for much of the post-war period.

(iii) Wages and Inflation.

When employers grant a wage increase, they will immediately consider whether they should increase their prices to cover their increased wage-costs. As it is common practice for firms to fix the selling prices of their products by first calculating the direct cost of labour and of materials, and then adding on a percentage to cover overhead costs and profits, they will tend to want to raise their prices not only to cover the cost of the wage advance, but also to cover their percentage addition. Moreover, in deciding whether or not their customers will stand for such increases, firms will be influenced by the knowledge that their competitors have to pay the increased wages too, and will probably therefore be raising their prices. So industry-wide wage advances—and changes in costs of materials—are particularly likely to be passed on to the consumer; and, as wage-earners are also consumers, to generate further demands for wage advances to cover the increased prices.

Once this spiral gets going, it is very hard to stop it. In general, the requirement is that wage earnings should not rise faster than productivity (output per man). But as in some industries productivity is very slow to rise, and as it would often be unfair and impracticable (leading to the loss of good employees) to exclude their workers from participating in any general rise in the standard of living, this requirement means that in industries with a rapid growth of productivity wage advances should be kept well below the rate of rise of productivity. For two reasons this is rather difficult. First, rising productivity often raises the wages of some workers in these industries automatically, because they are paid by results or through some incentive scheme. The rise of wages from this source takes the form of a tendency on the part of earnings in these industries to rise faster than basic wages. Second, employers in the rapidly-growing industries have far less reason to resist demands for wage increases than those in slowly-growing industries. Indeed, they are quite likely to bid up wages in order to obtain and motivate labour rather than to try to hold down wages.

There are therefore major problems in preventing a faster rise in wages than in productivity, with its consequence of rising prices. And once a wage-price spiral has started, the problems become more acute because workers and employers become accustomed to substantial annual advances in money wages.

(iv) The Phillips Curve.

Even if wage behaviour is primarily responsible for inflation, the pressure of demand may still be important. If unemployment is low or falling rapidly, and unfilled vacancies high, there is competitive bidding among employers to obtain or retain their workers. Moreover, with the economy booming the bargaining strength of trade unions increases: employers are more willing to concede wage demands. These possibilities have led economists to postulate—and indeed to measure—the so-called *Phillips Curve* relationship: the lower the level of unemployment, the faster the rate of increase in money wages. Such a relationship has been found to exist in the British economy over some periods. But it is dangerous to postulate "general laws" in economics: in the 1970s inflation increased despite high and growing unemployment and governments in most Western countries were confronted with a phenomenon known as stagflation. Clearly, changes in the cost-of-living, expectations for the future, Government policies and the degree of militancy of trade unionists can all have a significant influence on wage behaviour; and the level of demand may at times be relatively unimportant.

Worker Expectations.

There are many schools of thought attempting to explain developments from the late 1960s, but it is possible to discern two general approaches. The first is that trade unions behaved reactively. In other words, they responded in their wage demands to their expectations about prices and Government policies. A restrictive monetary policy might help moderate inflation, in that it might directly reduce prices and it might affect expectations. The second school of thought was that unions, as well as responding to their perception of the events they faced, acted in a more initiatory way—to fulfil, for example, aspirations (developed perhaps over a long period of time) about what their real earnings, and therefore their share of the national cake, should be. In striving to realise these aspirations, they might be relatively unaffected by concern over rising unemployment. A likely explanation was that unions felt unconcerned about relatively minor variations in the unemployment rate, safe in the knowledge that Government was committed to the maintenance of full employment. In the mid-1970s such a commitment was quite explicitly abandoned. That, together with the experience of very high unemployment in the 1980s might, it was argued, tighten the demand constraint in more prosperous future times. No longer, it was argued, would unions or workers be able to count on being "protected from the consequences of their own actions". Many economists, therefore, were surprised at the persistence of quite high wage inflation during the very high unemployment of the mid-1980s.

Modern Approaches to Inflation.

Modern approaches to inflation suggest that workers (or unions) have a "target" real wage and at the same time there is a "feasible" real wage which the economy can afford. Only when the two are equal will inflation be stable. At any given time there is a unique level of unemployment (or economic activity) at which the two will be consistent. If the Government attempts to run the economy at lower levels of unemployment, there will be a wage-price spiral of the sort already described, and as a consequence increasing inflation. Both the target wage and the feasible wage are determined by the underlying structures of the labour and product markets (*e.g.* the power of the unions, or the effectiveness of training, or basic productivity performance) as well as by the attitudes of workers and employers. Thus it is the supply-side which determines the level of unemployment at which it is safe to run the economy.

The more unhealthy the supply-side, the higher this level of unemployment will be. Hence the modern stress on supply-side reform.

The Effects of Inflation.

British Governments have been concerned about inflation mainly because of its effects on British competitiveness, and hence on the balance of payments. If our costs rise relative to competitors' costs, British exporters find it more difficult to compete in foreign markets if they raise their prices; and if they keep prices down in order to compete, this implies their having to accept lower profit margins on exports than on sales in the home market, and so discourages exporting. Alternatively, this lack of competitiveness might be reflected in falling exchange rates, although membership of the ERM from the autumn of 1990 until the autumn of 1992 limited the scope for currency changes. Depreciation by itself is not necessarily a bad thing, but the danger is that it can start a spiral. An initial depreciation causes price inflation to increase at home, which causes further wage increases, which leads to further depreciation, and so on. The result could be hyperinflation. This clearly has a major efficiency cost, since it will cause people to economise on the use of money in conducting their transactions.

Inflation can have other harmful consequences. It often produces a redistribution of income, with the strong gaining at the expense of the weak, *i.e.*, the poorly organised workers and the pensioners. In inflationary conditions income gains can appear to result not so much from work or sacrifice as from ingenuity and speculation and the exercise of economic and political power. Inflation can breed insecurity and industrial unrest. Among businessmen it increases uncertainty, reduces investment and hence growth. Finally, it causes a redistribution of income away from lenders to borrowers unless interest rates remain positive in real terms, as they are at present. What is clear is that the costs of inflation are significantly greater the more unanticipated it is.It is also clear that its interaction with the tax system can have real consequences—particularly for the corporate sector.

Government Policy against Inflation.

There are several possible methods of attack on the inflationary spiral of wages and prices. Their usefulness will depend on the causes of the inflation. One policy appropriate to most inflations, and also helpful to other objectives of economic policy, is to achieve a faster rate of productivity growth. The faster the growth of average productivity the faster can average incomes rise without an increase in average prices. Comprehensive and detailed government control of wages, except as an emergency policy, was thought for a long time to be impractical for political and institutional reasons, as was comprehensive and detailed control of prices. Experience suggested that such detailed policy, except as a temporary general "freeze", would be very difficult to operate and, if successful, would involve a major loss of flexibility in the economy. At the other extreme, general exhortations to unions to exercise restraint on wages, and to manufacturers to exercise restraint on prices, were thought to have little effect. After 1974 more people began to think that a semi-permanent incomes policy might in fact be a viable policy tool.

Control of Purchasing Power.

The Government can attempt to regulate inflation by controlling purchasing power through its monetary and fiscal policies, the nature of which will be examined below. There is a danger that curbing demand also curbs the growth of output and productivity in the economy; so conflicting with other objectives of economic policy. Moreover, there is no certainty that inflation is sensitive to the rate of unemployment over the politically acceptable range of unemployment.

A further option is to try to impose an external inflationary discipline by linking the exchange rate to that of a low-inflation currency, removing the option of devaluation and thereby imposing a constraint upon employers' ability to pass on cost increases without loss of external competitiveness. By entering the ERM in October 1990 the Government effectively chose this option. After leaving the ERM in the autumn of 1992, the Government had to search for an alternative strategy. The policy which has emerged is based on the belief that inflation is influenced by monetary policy. However this influence takes time. Therefore a 12 or 24 month view of underlying inflation is taken and interest rates are set accordingly. Interest rates control the demand for and therefore the supply of money—on the assumption that the financial system produces more or less the quantity of money demanded. This interest rate policy is made an open one through the operation of the Monetary Policy Committee (MPC) of the Bank of England.

On taking office in 1997 the Labour Government placed the setting of the base rate in the hands of this Committee of experts. Its deliberations are open. It is believed that this openness is an important indicator to the general public of the government's determination to maintain inflation at very low levels. The Government's target is 2 per cent per annum.

4. MONEY, BANKING AND FINANCE

Economic Objectives and Demand Management.

The various economic objectives—full employment, balance of payments equilibrium, the control of inflation, *etc.*—which, as mentioned in **Part I**, have been shared by all post-war British Governments, are all to a greater or a lesser extent dependent for their attainment upon the type of *demand management* policy pursued by the government. By this is meant the policy, or set of policies, with which the government seeks to regulate the total level of expenditure on goods and services. The latter is the sum of consumption and investment expenditure by both the private sector (firms and consumers) and the public sector (the government and the nationalised industries). If the resulting level of aggregate demand for output is greater than the amount which can be produced with the economy's resources the result will be shortages leading to

inflation and/or an increased demand for imports. If the level of demand is not high enough, on the other hand, the result will be a waste of resources, *i.e.*, workers will be unemployed and capital equipment will be underutilised. Hence it is crucial for the government to keep the pressure of demand at an appropriate level by regulating the various types of expenditure making up the total.

Fiscal and Monetary Policy.

One way in which the government can attempt to regulate demand is by fiscal policy, *i.e.*, the regulation of taxes and public expenditure. If the government believes, for example, that the level of demand is too high, it may seek to reduce it by raising taxes whilst leaving public expenditure unchanged, thereby reducing its *budget deficit (i.e.*, the excess of public spending over tax revenue). Since the private sector's expenditure plans are financed partly out of its after-tax income and partly out of borrowing, an increase in taxes will generally reduce private sector expenditure, so that total expenditure then falls if public expenditure is held constant. Conversely, the government can cut taxes or increase public spending if it wants to expand the economy by increasing total expenditure.

However, fiscal policy of this type is not independent of *monetary policy, i.e.*, the regulation of interest rates or the stock of money in the economy. For example, if the government increases public spending it has to pay for the various resources which this involves. The finance may come from additional taxes, but if the government does not raise taxes the extra expenditure then has to be paid for in one of two ways: either the government increases its borrowing from the private sector by issuing government stock in return for money to pay for public expenditure; or the government prints new money for this purpose. In the latter case the supply of money is increased; in the former case interest rates will generally be increased, since the private sector will probably require higher interest rates if it is to be induced to lend extra funds to the government.

Old Economic Controversies.

The operation of monetary and fiscal policies used to be an active area of controversy among economists, with a division of opinion between *Keynesian* and *monetarist* economists. Keynesians emphasised the use of fiscal policy and argued for activist policies, with frequent manipulation of tax and spending levels in order to seek to maintain economic activity at high levels, with a view to maintaining low levels of unemployment.

Monetarists, by contrast, emphasised the use of monetary policy, favoured the use of simple policy rules which would be maintained unchanged over time, and believed that low inflation, rather than low unemployment, should be the principal policy objective.

Keynesian views were dominant in the 1950s and 1960s, but gradually gave way to monetarism during the 1970s. In the 1980s and 1990s many of these old controversies lost force amongst professional economists, though the labels "Keynesian" and "monetarist" continue to feature in popular commentaries on economic events. Few economists would want to revert to old-style Keynesianism. On the other hand, experience has taught that simpler monetarist prescriptions do not always work well in practice: for instance, the pursuit of low inflation often involves prolonged periods of high unemployment.

The Ricardian Approach.

Both monetarists and Keynesians agree that changes in the size of the government's budget deficit have significant effects on the economy—their disagreements concern the nature of the effects. A third school of thought, often called "Ricardian", argues in contrast that budget deficit changes may have little impact—in some circumstances no impact at all—upon economic activity. This approach gained many adherents in the 1970s and 1980s. It concentrates on the future effects, as well as the immediate impact, of a change in the budget deficit. If the government reduces taxes while holding its spending level constant, and increases its borrowing in order to replace the lost tax revenue, this new borrowing will have to be repaid, with interest, some time in the future.

Thus new borrowing in 2004, using government bonds with a 5-year redemption period, will have to be repaid in 2009. The Ricardian approach argues that when the repayment falls due this will require taxes to be raised. The Ricardian approach goes on to argue that the prospect of future tax increases is forseen by consumers at the time when the cut in taxes takes effect, and that consumers save the resulting increase in their current disposable incomes in order to be able to meet the anticipated extra tax bill in the future. Consequently, Ricardians argue, tax cuts do not stimulate economic activity because they do not generate increases in demand. The same argument applies in reverse.

Ricardian Arguments.

The Ricardian approach thus argues that changes in budget deficits have little or no impact on economic activity, because they induce offsetting changes in savings, whereas both Keynesian and monetarist theories predict that the main impact is on current spending. The difference reflects the Ricardian assumption that consumers are willing, and able, to work out the future implications of current policy changes and to take account of both present and future effects in deciding on their current behaviour. Some economists argue that, in practice, most people are not sufficiently well informed nor sophisticated to pay much attention to the future implications of current tax changes. Other economists argue that, even if people are able to make sophisticated calculations, there is so much uncertainty about the future course of events that people are likely to discount them very heavily. Yet another complication is that if the repayment of current borrowing is sufficiently delayed, the burden may fall on future generations rather than on current tax payers.

Whilst all these arguments suggest reasons why changes in the size of the budget deficit are likely to lead at least to some change in the pressure of demand, and not simply to changes in savings, the Ricardian view has nonetheless become quite influential. This is partly because studies in many countries, but especially America, suggest that the impact of budgetary changes on demand pressure is often less strong than would be predicted by simple Keynesian ideas. In addition, Ricardian ideas have become quite influential in financial markets, which now routinely assess the longer term prospects for fiscal policy, as well as its immediate impact.

The Definition of "Money".

Money plays a central role in any modern economy: without it, all but the simplest buying and selling transactions would become difficult or impossible, since people would then have to use barter. In a barter economy goods are traded directly, so that anyone wishing to obtain, say, food has to pay for it by providing the food producer with some good or service which he requires. The obvious difficulty is that this relies on a "double coincidence" of wants: if the prospective food purchaser cannot supply anything which the food producer wants, the transaction cannot take place. Hence barter only works well in very simple economies with a limited range of goods and with a high degree of self sufficiency. It cannot operate in an economy with a significant range of goods and services, and with specialisation of production. In these circumstances money is the essential oil which lubricates the economic process: an individual can buy a range of goods with the money earned from his job, instead of having to trade products directly.

Most people probably have a clear idea of what they understand by "money", and might be surprised to find that its precise definition is a source of difficulty for, and sometimes disputes among, economists. There is no difficulty about the basic concept: economists agree that the appropriate definition of "money" is *anything which is generally acceptable as a means of payment*. Problems arise in attempting to apply this general definition to particular "financial assets". These constitute legal entitlements to particular streams of income, for example in the form of interest payments, dividend payments, *etc.* Thus cash, bank accounts, building society accounts, government bonds, gilt-edged securities, and company share certificates are all examples of "financial assets".

Types of Financial Assets.

Most people probably loosely think of "money" and "financial assets" as one and the same thing, but to an economist this is not the case because, whilst some financial assets clearly satisfy the economist's definition of money, others equally clearly do not. More troublesome, the boundary between the two types of financial assets is not fixed by any objective criterion but instead can, and does, vary over time and across countries.

Three examples illustrate the general idea. First, someone who owns a financial asset such as a share certificate probably thinks of it as "money", but such an asset does not meet the economist's definition: consider going into a shop and trying to make a purchase with a company share certificate! If someone needs to use his savings in company shares to make a purchase, he first has to sell the shares and pay the proceeds into his bank account. He can then make the purchase by drawing a cheque on the strength of the additional money in his bank account. Thus, bank deposits constitute "money" but share certificates do not.

Changing Building Society Status.

A second example is provided by the changed status of building societies within the United Kingdom. Until the early 1980s building society accounts did not satisfy the definition of "money" because in general they could not be used to make purchases. Since then, however, financial deregulation has altered the functions of many financial institutions. Traditionally, building societies provided loans for house purchase but did not provide cheque accounts, whilst the reverse was the case for banks. During the 1980s this compartmentalisation broke down, with banks increasingly trying to move into the building societies' territory, and building societies in turn trying to steal the banks' business. Indeed, many of the traditional building societies effectively disappeared. In 1989 the Abbey National converted from a mutually-owned building society into a bank owned by shareholders with shares tradable on the Stock Exchange, and during the 1990s many of the other former building societies made similar conversions. The result was that building society accounts now had to be included in measures of "money" if these were to correspond to sensible definitions of the "means of payment."

A third example is the growing importance of the Internet as a vehicle for doing business. As payments over the Internet become more important, so it is quite likely that arguments will develop for widening practical definitions of money to include Internet-located means of payment.

Although this definitional issue may appear arcane, it is of great practical importance because the amount of money (as the economist defines it) in the economy crucially affects the pressure of demand for goods and services and thus, the level of economic activity. Governments seek to manipulate economic activity by aggregate demand management, and for this purpose they require a clear definition and understanding of the monetary aggregates which they target as a part of this process.

Measuring the Money Supply.

In the United Kingdom, the starting point for practical measures of the money supply is the "wide monetary base", known as M0. This includes cash in circulation outside banks, together with banks' own cash holdings (both within individual banks, and their cash deposits at the Bank of England). Clearly cash is only a small part of the total available means of payment. M1 is defined as M0 plus current bank accounts (sight deposits), and M3 is equal to M1 plus bank saving accounts. Until the change in status of building society accounts in the 1980s, M3 was regarded as a reasonable measure of the total money supply. As building society accounts became more important in this context, so measures of money supply which incorporated them came to be used. M4 equals M3 plus building society time deposits.

Money supply measures sometimes distinguish between retail and wholesale bank deposits. The former are deposits made in the main high street banks at the standard rate of interest. The latter are one-off deals at negotiated rates of interest, typically involving large deposits by corporate bodies. This distinction is contained in the measure M2, which is equal to M4 minus wholesale deposits in banks and building societies; M2 is also known as "retail M4".

Policy-makers currently focus on M0 and M4. By contrast, M3 was the main policy target until the mid-1980s. The accompanying table shows data for M0, M2 and M4 for recent years.

£billion	1999	2001	2003
M0	31·0	35·1	39·9
M2	553·4	645·6	740·5
M4	812·8	941·5	1132·0

The Liquidity Spectrum.

One way in which economists seek to classify the range of financial assets is in terms of their varying degrees of *liquidity*. This concept measures the speed with which an asset can be sold, and the predictability of the price at which it can be sold. The concept of liquidity thus stems from the economist's definition of money as the means of payment. Consider someone with savings held in non-money assets whose circumstances unexpectedly alter in such a way that he needs to cash in these assets in order to finance some urgent item of spending. If this sale can be completed quickly, and if the amount of money which it realises is relatively predictable—in other words, if the assets are highly liquid—then he is unlikely to suffer any significant financial embarrassment. Such embarrassment is more likely if either the sale takes a long time, or the amount of money realised is not predictable (so that a forced sale may occur at very unfavourable price), *i.e.*, if the asset is *illiquid*.

Illiquid Financial Assets.

An example of an illiquid financial asset is a company share certificate: the certificate can be sold very quickly, but the price is unpredictable because share prices can and do fluctuate widely in unpredictable ways. Many real assets are highly illiquid. *e.g.* selling a house takes a long time and the sale price is not very predictable. In this respect more illiquid assets are also more risky because they offer less insurance against the risk of unfavourable contingencies. By definition, money (as the economist defines it) is perfectly liquid.

Economists often speak of "near-money" financial assets. These are assets which, although not generally acceptable as means of payment, are easily changed into money with minimal uncertainty about the sale price. Various forms of government saving instruments fall into this category, as did building society accounts in earlier times.

Liquidity and Expenditure.

The existence of a large spectrum of financial assets, and the tendency for the "near money" boundary to shift over time, emphasises the practical difficulty of controlling the money supply. If "money" and various forms of "near money" are in practice very close substitutes for one another, attempts by the government to control the money supply may be self defeating, because whatever the precise definition of "money" which is used, some liquid assets will be excluded, and the financial sector may then negate the effects of the controls by shifting towards greater use of other assets, not included in the definition and therefore not subject to control. This problem is often known as "Goodhart's Law", named after Charles Goodhart, formerly an economic adviser at the Bank of England. Goodhart's Law states that as soon as the government attempts to regulate any particular set of financial assets, these become unreliable as indicators of economic trends. The basic reason is that financial institutions can relatively easily devise new types of financial assets, and this allows them to negate the effects of controls on particular types of assets, based on particular definitions of the money supply. There is very little which the government can do to prevent it.

Indirect Control of Money Supply.

One response by policy-makers during the 1980s was to try to control the money supply indirectly, by fixing interest rates, instead of attempting to

control it directly. The principle behind this idea is that the demand for money varies inversely with interest rates. Higher interest rates tend to reduce the demand for money because they increase the *opportunity cost* of holding money, i.e. the amount of interest income which is sacrificed by keeping funds in money (which traditionally does not pay interest) instead of in some other financial asset on which interest is paid. If the monetary authorities reduce the money supply, the resulting shortage of money will tend to drive interest rates upwards as people try to sell other financial assets (so driving the price of these assets down, and driving up the interest rates payable on them) in order to build up their money balances. Faced with difficulties in controlling the money supply, however, the monetary authorities in the UK tended during the 1980s to reverse this procedure, pushing interest rates up in the expectation that this would reduce the demand for money and that the supply of money would then fall in line. The difficulty with this approach was similar to that with direct control of the money supply. Rapid changes in the financial sector have tended to make the relationship between interest rates and money demand difficult to predict. For example, most banks in the UK started to offer interest payments on current accounts during the 1980s. By thus reducing the opportunity cost of holding money, this had the effect of increasing the demand for money at each level of interest rates.

Problems of Indirect Control.

More generally, attempting to control the money supply by using interest rates is an indirect procedure which relies to a considerable extent upon factors beyond the government's control. The largest component of the money supply is deposits at the main banks. If interest rates are to be used to control the money supply, changes in interest rates have to be able to induce changes in the level of bank deposits. The mechanism involved is as follows. If interest rates rise, this will tend to reduce the demand for bank loans and overdrafts, since the cost of servicing these debts is increased. The resulting fall in bank borrowing reduces the pressure of demand for goods and services—since some of this is financed by borrowing—and this in turn reduces sales and raises receipts. This fall in receipts means that less money is deposited with banks; at this point the objective of reducing money supply by reducing bank deposits is achieved. However, whilst this mechanism is clear in principle, in practice its weak link is the relationship between interest rates and the demand for bank loans. In the early 1980s, for example, when interest rates were raised to what were then record levels, the demand for bank loans proved surprisingly resilient. One reason for this may have been the problems experienced by many industrial companies, which found their cash flow positions squeezed between depressed sales revenue and relatively buoyant labour costs. For many firms, bank loans represented a possible way of easing these cash flow problems. The demand for loans remained relatively strong, even in the face of high interest rates.

Consequences of High Interest Rates.

In practice, if interest rates are kept sufficiently high for a sufficiently long period of time, the demand for loans is likely to fall eventually, with consequent downward pressure on the money supply and on aggregate demand. The problem for policy-makers is in judging the appropriate level of interest rates in the context of such delayed reactions. If initial increases in rates have little or no immediate effect, there is a strong temptation to raise rates further—indeed, to continue raising them until the money markets respond. However, the danger is that rates will be raised much too far, so that the market response, when it comes, will be far stronger than planned or desired. Economists sometimes illustrate this by the analogy of someone pulling one end of a piece of elastic, in order to pull towards them a heavy weight which is attached to the other end. Initial gentle tugging does not move the weight, and there is a temptation to pull harder and harder. The end-result is that the person doing the pulling is likely to be hit in the face when the pressure reaches the point at which the weight is catapulted forwards.

The National Debt and Government Borrowing.

The *National Debt* is a measure of the total indebtedness of the government, excluding local authorities. The table below shows how it has varied over time. Although the absolute size of the National Debt has risen steadily, this simply reflects inflation: as a proportion of national income the National Debt has fluctuated, rising sharply after each of the two World Wars—both of which saw borrowing on a massive scale by the government to finance the war effort—but falling slowly but steadily for 20 years up to 1975. From 1975 to the mid-1980s the proportion altered little; in the second half of the 1980s, it fell sharply; in the early 1990s it rose again; since then it has fallen slightly.

THE NATIONAL DEBT IN SELECTED YEARS

	The National Debt (£bn.)	The National Debt as a percentage of national income
1900	0·6	31·9
1914	0·7	25·6
1921	7·6	147·7
1938	7·8	150·6
1946	23·0	259·6
1975	46·4	49·0
1990	199·0	35·0
2002	434·5	42·0

The government borrows in several different ways. First, the issue of new bank-notes is a form of borrowing: as seen above it can be used to finance a budget deficit. Second, it borrows from foreign governments. Third, it also borrows from companies through tax reserve certificates, whereby-company taxes are paid at the later date when the taxes become legally due. Fourth, it borrows from private individuals through the various forms of national savings, *e.g.*, Post Office accounts.

These four types of borrowing result in *non-marketable debt, i.e.*, an individual who has a Post Office account cannot sell it in the market to another individual. Two other types of borrowing—gilt-edged securities and Treasury Bills— result in *marketable debt, i.e.*, an individual who owns gilt-edged securities can sell them in the market to someone else. In practice, most gilt- edged and all Treasury Bills are held by institutions—banks, discount houses, etc.—rather than by private individuals. However, whereas Treasury Bills, representing short-term (usually three months) loans to the government are liquid assets (*i.e.*, they can quickly be cashed at a predictable price), gilt-edged are illiquid. They represent promises to repay a certain sum of money at a specified future date. At any time prior to repayment gilt-edged can be traded, and there is a large market for such trading in which the market price (as opposed to the fixed repayment price) varies widely.

Interest Rates and Debt Financing.

As already seen, such variations in gilt-edged market prices cause changes in interest rates on all financial assets. Aside from the effects on aggregate demand, interest rate changes themselves have a large impact upon the financing of the National Debt, and hence upon overall public expenditure. For example, if restrictions on the growth of the money supply cause interest rates to rise, this increases the interest charges which the government has to pay on its existing debts.

At one time some commentators and policy-makers used to argue that the solution to this problem was to keep interest rates low, if necessary by repeated increases in money supply. Economists have long since realised, however, that this policy does not work and that it is actually potentially counterproductive. In particular, persistent monetary expansion in excess of the economy's long term growth rate is likely to raise, rather than lower, interest rates in the longer term. The reason is that persistent monetary expansion in excess of the economy's ability to expand output creates inflationary pressure. Inflation in turn reduces the attractiveness of holding gilt-edged stock, because the future purchasing power of its fixed interest payments is eroded. This lowers demand for gilt-

edged stock, which pushes its price down and thus forces its effective rate of interest up. This continues until the effective interest rate has risen sufficiently to compensate investors for the effects of inflation, which in turn leads to interest rates elsewhere in the economy increasing, as banks, building societies and other financial institutions seek to maintain their competitiveness against gilt-edged stock.

Real and Nominal Rates.

There is thus an important distinction between *real* and *nominal* interest rates. The nominal rate—the rate currently payable in the market—equals the real rate plus the expected inflation rate. Persistent monetary expansion is likely to push up the nominal interest rate; the faster the inflation rate, the higher the nominal interest rate. Evidence from many countries is broadly consistent with this prediction. However, market rates do not normally alter by precisely the amount of any change in the inflation rate, at least in the short run; thus, real interest rates tend to alter when the inflation rate alters, though over time this effect normally lessens.

One point to note is that *nominal* interest rates can be very misleading as a guide to *real* interest rates which, as explained above, are equal to nominal rates minus the expected rate of inflation. In the 1970s nominal rates were very high but for most of the time the rate of inflation was even higher, so that real interest rates were negative. This was particularly marked in 1975–76, when nominal rates reached a then record high level of around 16 per cent. At the time, however, inflation was running at around 25 per cent, implying real interest rates of around minus 9 per cent—a record *low* level.

The same applied in reverse in the 1980s. Nominal interest rates fell to lower levels than in the 1970s, but inflation fell faster, so that by 1986 nominal interest rates of around 12 per cent coexisted with inflation of around 5 per cent, implying real interest rates of plus 7 per cent—a record *high* level. Thus changes in nominal interest rates cannot be taken as a good guide to changes in the real cost of borrowing.

Inflation and National Debt Financing.

The distinction between real and nominal interest rates also substantially qualifies the earlier point about the effect of inflation on the financing of the National Debt. The latter consists mainly of debts which are fixed in money value. Hence, persistent inflation erodes their real value in terms of purchasing power. This substantially offsets the increased burden of interest payments when higher inflation raises nominal interest rates. In effect, the government loses through higher inflation in terms of interest payments, but gains in terms of the erosion of the real burden of its debts.

International Influences on Interest Rates.

Another substantial complication in considering interest rates concerns the relationship between interest rates in Britain and in other countries. The removal of exchange controls in 1979, and the much greater degrees of competition and openness in foreign exchange markets which emerged in the 1980s, mean that changes in interest rates in other countries, especially Germany, have come to play a major role in determining British rates. Institutions such as pension funds, insurance companies, and large industrial companies which have substantial amounts of money to invest are now easily able to move money between alternative assets in different currencies. Consequently, if interest rates in Germany rise above those in Britain there will normally be a large movement of funds out of assets such as British government bonds, denominated in sterling, and into German marks in order to take advantage of the higher rates of return. The same applies if interest rates rise in other important financial centres such as Tokyo. Since selling of sterling assets implies a reduced demand for sterling and increased demand for other currencies, this tends to push down the exchange rate of sterling against other currencies. If the British government is reluctant to see a fall in the exchange rate it will then be forced to allow a rise in British interest rates in order to prevent it.

The ERM Commitment.

These international linkages became even more important when, in October 1990, the government finally decided that the UK should join the Exchange Rate Mechanism (the ERM) of the European Monetary System (see **F56**). This involved a commitment to hold the pound within an agreed band of values against all other ERM currencies. This meant that interest rate policies became subordinate to the exchange rate. If, for example, the sterling exchange rate moved close to the bottom of its band, the UK government would be required to take offsetting action, the most likely such action being an increase in interest rates.

The German mark was then the strongest currency in the ERM, so that Britain's entry was interpreted by many commentators as effectively fixing the pound's value to that of the mark. This still further emphasised the importance of international influences on domestic UK interest rates. Indeed, some people opposed Britain's entry to the ERM on precisely these grounds.

This argument was put increasingly strongly as the UK plunged into a very severe recession in 1991 and 1992. Critics argued that it was illogical to keep real interest rates at record high levels—as was the case for almost the whole of 1991—during a deep recession. In effect, they argued, Britain's interest rates were being decided according to the needs of the German rather than the British economy. Many of the critics felt vindicated when, after Britain left the ERM in September 1992, rates were rapidly reduced by 3 percentage points. On the other side of the argument, however, it was pointed out that, whether inside or outside the ERM, Britain was inescapably part of a highly integrated world economy, and that cuts in British interest rates would depress the exchange rate and so generate inflationary pressures. The current controversy over whether or not Britain should adopt the euro reflects much the same contrasting views.

The Commercial Banks.

If the government does adopt monetary targets, its main need is to find ways of influencing the behaviour of the commercial banks, known in England as the clearing banks. For as seen above, the main component of the money supply is the deposits of the clearing banks.

The latter earn profits by borrowing at low or zero rates of interest—anyone holding a bank account is in effect making a loan to his bank—and lending out part of the resulting funds at higher interest rates. In normal circumstances—i.e., unless there is a run on the banks—not all deposits will be withdrawn at once; therefore the banks need keep only a small proportion of their deposits in the form of cash.

The commercial banks can "create" money because of their ability to accept deposits far in excess of their cash and liquid asset holdings; as economists would say, because they operate under a fractional reserve system. If a bank provides an overdraft facility to a customer who then draws cheques on the facility, the recipients of these cheques pay the proceeds into their bank accounts which are thereby enlarged; and this represents an increase in the money supply, since the enlarged accounts can be used to finance additional transactions. Thus any increase in the banks' cash and liquid asset holdings allows them to expand loans, overdrafts, etc.—and thereby the money supply—by a multiple amount.

The government can control the money supply by controlling the components of banks' cash and liquid asset holdings. A reduction in the latter can be engineered by open market operations, which involve the Bank of England's selling more gilt-edged than it otherwise would; this reduces the banks' liquidity since, as already seen, gilt-edged are not regarded as liquid assets, so that their purchase involves a drain of liquidity from the banks. At the same time, as already seen, it will generally involve a rise in interest rates.

Financial Deregulation.

When the Thatcher government took office in 1979 it embarked on a series of measures to reduce the degree of government control over and regulation of the financial sector of the economy. Its general philosophy here, as in other economic contexts, was to increase the importance of market

forces and reduce the role of the government. The first, and in some ways the most dramatic change was the removal, in October 1979, of all the remaining foreign exchange controls.

Two further changes proved to have very important effects. In October 1983 the Building Societies Association ended its previous practice of recommending a common mortgage rate for all mortgage lenders. In future each lending institution was left free to choose its own rate. The main effect was to encourage new institutions to enter the housing finance market. The latter was also significantly affected when, in December 1986, the Bank of England withdrew its "guidance" on mortgage lending by financial institutions, thus leaving the market entirely unregulated. The main consequence was that the supply of credit, especially for housing finance, was sharply increased.

The Stock Exchange.

Whilst short-term credit is mostly provided by banks and Finance Houses, long-term borrowing by companies is undertaken through the Stock Exchange. Firms in the private sector of the economy issue three main types of security on the Stock Exchange. *Debenture Stock* is simply a fixed-interest loan. *Preference Stock* is a fixed-interest loan with provisions for waiving the interest if no profits are earned. The most important type, representing the great majority of holdings, are *Ordinary Shares*. The owner of an Ordinary Share is, legally, a part-owner of the company concerned, with a right to participate in any net profits which it makes (though he has no legal right to any particular level of dividend or interest payment).

In contrast to government stock, a significant proportion of Ordinary Shares is owned by private individuals. However, an increasing proportion is owned by insurance companies and pension funds, which have grown in importance as private superannuation schemes have become more widespread.

The attraction of Ordinary Shares to the investor wanting an outlet for his savings is that because they represent a part ownership of the firm concerned, their prices and dividends are likely to rise as the value of the firm increases. This is so whether the firm's value increases in real terms, because it is expanding, or simply in money terms, because of general inflation. Thus Ordinary Shares generally represent a reasonable "hedge" against inflation—unlike fixed-interest securities such as gilt-edged.

The Big Bang.

In October 1986 several major changes occurred in the organisation of the Stock Exchange. These had been under active discussion and planning for several years, but because they were all formally introduced simultaneously, they became known as the *Big Bang*. The main changes consisted of alterations in the structure and ownership of firms operating in the stock market, removal of restrictions on charging for financial services, and new forms of regulation of activity.

Traditionally, stock market firms had been divided into "jobbers" and "brokers". The former were responsible for the trading of shares on the floor of the stock market, whilst the latter dealt with clients and provided business for the jobbing firms: clients wishing to buy or sell shares were not allowed to deal directly with jobbers. The market imposed what was known as the "single capacity" restriction: no firm was allowed to be both a jobber and a broker. It also imposed strict limits on the ownership of all member firms: they were required either to be partnerships, or to be limited companies with a maximum limit on the amount of capital which could be owned by non-member firms (i.e. firms not actually operating in the market). In addition, the market operated fixed minimum commission rates on share deals.

Internationalisation of Financial Markets.

Although this structure had worked well in earlier years, during the 1970s and 1980s it started to become increasingly inappropriate. The main catalyst for change was the growing *internationalisation of financial markets*. This was itself the result of several forces. Technological developments were making it very easy for financial firms to obtain virtually instant information, at very low cost, about assets in any currency and any country. Simultaneously, firms needing finance, especially the large multinationals operating throughout the world, were becoming increasingly willing to consider finance from any source. In addition, the abolition of UK exchange controls in 1979 meant that UK financial institutions rapidly acquired a much more diversified range of assets and interests, and needed to deal regularly in markets throughout the world, and also to compete within the UK against foreign based financial firms. Their ability to do so was heavily constrained by the traditional arrangements: minimum commission requirements restricted competition, the single capacity arrangement was unwieldy, and the limits on outside capital ownership meant that most of the firms were undercapitalised in terms of the scale of risks which they needed to run in global operations.

Consequences of Big Bang.

The Big Bang swept away most of the old restrictions. It allowed "single capacity" firms to operate, ended minimum commission rates, and removed restrictions on the entry and the ownership of firms. The main result was a series of mergers between and takeovers of old-established stock market firms. After Big Bang, most of the firms operating in the market were merely parts of, or subsidiaries of, much larger financial conglomerates, many of them foreign owned. These large firms felt that they could raise their overall profitability by operating in the UK stock market, though for many of them this was only one part of a large range of financial activities. Big Bang effectively recognised that the London stock market, like other stock exchanges around the world, could no longer be organised so as to supply finance for solely UK-based firms: instead, it was now a part of a global market for finance.

Financial Regulation.

It was recognised that these new arrangements would require *regulation* in order to protect the interests and retain the confidence of clients. This was particularly the case since the liberalisation of financial markets coincided with a growth in demand for financial services of various kinds. For instance, in the late 1980s an increasing number of people began to consider investing in personal pension plans, instead of relying on state pensions or on group occupational pensions. Thus, the financial services sector was becoming an increasingly important part of the economy.

A key difficulty is that many individuals who seek, and require, financial services are much less well informed about financial matters than the firms who supply such services. The danger is that some firms may seek to make use of this asymmetry of information in order to exploit their clients. If this happens, confidence in the overall financial services market may decline, with adverse effects for everyone, including firms seeking to do business in a legitimate fashion. In order to address this problem, the 1986 Financial Services Act provided an initial framework. Regulatory powers were delegated to the *Securities and Investment Board* (SIB), whose members were appointed by the government and the Bank of England. The SIB had the power to authorise firms as "fit and proper" to operate in the stock market, and in the provision of various other financial services.

Problems with Pensions.

A number of problems emerged which illustrated the need for—and the difficulty of—financial regulation. The "mis-selling of pensions" problem arose when financial institutions persuaded a large number of individuals to switch away from their existing company and occupational pension schemes and instead to take out new personal pensions. It soon emerged that they had been given seriously misleading advice. As a result many had abandoned pension schemes which were well suited to their needs and had transferred to new and inferior schemes. A second scandal arose following the death of Robert Maxwell in 1987. Soon after his death it was discovered that Maxwell had expropriated the pension funds of some of his employees, transferring the money to other companies controlled by him.

These two scandals illustrated the difficulty posed by asymmetric information on the two sides of the market. A different sort of problem was illustrated by the collapse of Barings Bank in 1992, following unsupervised trading in derivative securities by one of its employees. The increasing complexity of modern financial markets, and financial instruments, posed a serious difficulty of regulating the activities of individual firms, or their employees.

The Financial Services Authority (FSA).

When Labour was elected to power in 1997 one of the first actions of the Chancellor, Gordon Brown, was to introduce an enhanced framework for financial regulation. Its centrepiece was the new *Financial Services Authority* (FSA). This inherited the powers of the Securities and Investment Board, but the FSA was given wider responsibilities. First, the banking regulatory duties previously undertaken by the Bank of England were transferred to the FSA. Second, the functions of various previously self-regulating bodies were also transferred: these included bodies responsible for building societies, retail investment, and securities and derivatives. The Labour government believed that the various difficulties which the financial services industry had experienced justified the creation of a single, high-profile, regulatory body with powers over the whole industry. The FSA's brief was to maintain public confidence in, and promote public understanding of, the financial services industry, to protect consumers, and to combat financial crimes.

Monetary Policy in Britain.

By the second half of the 1970s monetarist ideas had become the dominant influence upon policy making. This happened in two stages. The first occurred in the autumn of 1976 when Britain applied to the IMF for large credit facilities. One of the requirements which the IMF imposed as a condition of granting these facilities was that the Government should lay down, and stick to annual *monetary targets, i.e.,* target annual growth rates in sterling M3. Successive governments adopted this approach for the next ten years.

The adoption of monetary targets in turn meant that the *public sector borrowing requirement* PSBR became a target, rather than a consequence, of policy. The PSBR is the combined deficit of the central government, local authorities and public corporations. It has to be financed by a combination of borrowing (from the private sector or from abroad) and increasing the money supply. Since domestic borrowing will push up interest rates, any government which has a monetary target and which is also unwilling to tolerate rises beyond a certain point in interest rates, will be compelled to limit the size of the PSBR. This has to be done by a combination of tax rises and cuts in public spending. Thus targets for monetary growth carry implications for the government's tax and expenditure policies.

The second, and decisive, stage in the growth of monetarist influence was the election of a Conservative government in May 1979. The new government came into office committed to a monetarist approach to economic policy; several of its leading members declared themselves converts, to a greater or lesser extent, to the teachings of Professor Friedman, and rejected the Keynesianism of earlier post-war years.

Doubts about Monetarism.

By the end of 1981 the experience since 1976, and more especially since 1979, had begun to erode support for monetarist ideas, at least in their simple form. One area of doubt concerned the actual ability of the government to control money supply, however defined. A second argument revived the traditional Keynesian emphasis upon wider measures of liquidity: some economists, led by Nobel prize winner Professor James Meade, argued that the government should abandon monetary targets and instead set targets for the growth of *money national income*—the volume of output multiplied by its average price level—and should use a variety of fiscal instruments for this purpose, with monetary policy being used mainly to influence interest rates and the exchange rate.

The Demise of Monetary Targeting.

In the course of the 1980s these criticisms gathered force. Despite its clear commitment to steady reductions in the growth rate of the money supply as a central part of its anti-inflation policy, Mrs. Thatcher's government persistently failed to achieve its monetary targets. Moreover its main target— £M3—became very volatile and, apparently, increasingly unreliable as a guide to underlying economic trends. By the middle of the 1980s it was clear that the government was attaching steadily less weight to formal monetary targets, and the 1987 Budget announced the end of £M3 as a target. This was certainly a substantial change from the period 1979–83, when £M3 was overwhelmingly the main policy instrument of macroeconomic policy. Many of the difficulties experienced in monetary targeting reflected the problems discussed earlier, and summarised in "Goodhart's Law", also mentioned earlier.

This modification of the Government's views was matched by changes in the views of many Keynesian economists. The traditional Keynesian view that money does not matter, which dominated policy making for some twenty years after 1945, had been discarded by almost all the government's critics (some of whom pointed out Keynes himself had never argued that money was unimportant). Most economists accepted that there was sufficient evidence from the experience of the British economy in recent years to indicate that excessive expansion of the money supply was bound to lead to rises in inflation and nominal interest rates and was therefore harmful.

Confusion in Policy-Making.

The abandonment of monetary targetting in the second half of the 1980s coincided with what, in retrospect, appears to have been a considerable loss of cohesion in economic policy-making. Up to the mid-1980s the Thatcher governments, despite the various criticisms mentioned, had maintained a consistent approach to policy, with the defeat of inflation always the main priority and the use of monetary targets within the Medium Term Financial Strategy the main policy instrument. In the second half of the decade neither of these features was so clear cut. Whilst the Government continued to maintain that control of inflation was still the main priority, its actions suggested some modification.

Two episodes of policy making in particular illustrated these apparent changes. In 1986, £M3 exceeded its target by a large amount. The Government's response, as already mentioned, was to abandon £M3 as a target in the following year, thus ignoring the potential inflationary implications. This policy was justified by the Chancellor at the time on the grounds that £M3 had become too volatile to be a useful policy indicator.

The 1988 Episode.

A similar policy episode occurred in 1988. By this time the Government was using M0 as its only formal monetary indicator. However, at the same time the Government had become increasingly preoccupied with exchange rate targets, and at the time the Chancellor was seeking to prevent the exchange rate of the pound from rising above three D-marks. To achieve this aim he was prepared to accept increases in M0 above the target range. The Government in effect abandoned its monetary target for an exchange rate target.

This emphasis on exchange rate targeting had emerged partly in response to pressure from companies engaged in large amounts of international trade, for whom volatile and unpredictable exchange rates had become an increasingly important problem. These firms argued in favour of policies aimed at stabilising exchange rates so as to make trading conditions more predictable. Many economists and policy makers were sympathetic to this view. However, economists emphasised that a policy of fixing or controlling the exchange rate was incompatible with one of monetary targetting. If the Government fixes the exchange rate it then has to allow the money supply to vary by whatever amounts are required to maintain the exchange rate target. However, it seemed that this point was not clearly grasped by the British Government, with the result that the clarity which

had characterised policy making in the early 1980s was lost.

Consequences of ERM Entry.

When the Government took the decision to enter the Exchange Rate Mechanism of the European Monetary System in October 1990, it seemed that the confusion in policy-making had been resolved. Once again the Government had a clear strategy: all other policies were now subordinate to the requirement to maintain the sterling exchange rate within its agreed ERM bands, and this in turn was designed to re-emphasise the central importance of controlling inflation. However, the financial markets gradually lost confidence in the willingness or ability of the government to maintain the agreed exchange rate, and the resulting speculative pressure forced the pound out of the ERM again in September 1992. For the next few months, confusion about policy re-emerged in an even sharper form. The Government appeared to have no clear view about either the ultimate objectives of policymaking, or the appropriate policy tools. Gradually, however, a new view emerged which gave greater weight to encouraging growth in economic activity, whilst still stressing the importance of the inflation objective. The new emphasis on growth reflected the seriousness of the recession in which the economy had been trapped for the previous two years. The Government committed itself to adjusting taxes, public spending and interest rates in ways designed to give the economy the best possible chance of recovery. This marked a considerable shift of emphasis from policy-making in the 1980s.

The New Labour Government.

As the Government's economic policy evolved in the 1990s, the Labour opposition was also altering its stance. Following its fourth successive general election defeat in 1992, many of its traditional commitments to high levels of public expenditure, and associated tax rates, were modified or abandoned. This was especially the case following the sudden death of the Labour leader, John Smith. With Tony Blair as the new leader, and Gordon Brown as the Shadow Chancellor, the Labour Party was now firmly under the control of its "modernising" wing, and the result was a sharp shift in its economic policy stance. The reduced emphasis on taxes and public spending was matched by an abandonment of its traditional commitment to nationalisation, and a new commitment to private enterprise.

The Monetary Policy Committee.

These changes narrowed the gap between Labour and the Conservatives, and probably helped to achieve the large Labour majority in the May 1997 election. Within a few days of the election, however, the new Chancellor, Gordon Brown, produced a major surprise—and a fundamental change in the operation of monetary policy—when he announced that he proposed to give the Bank of England independent control of interest rates. For the previous 50 years such decisions had been made by elected politicians. Under the Chancellor's proposals the decisions would in future be made by a newly constituted *Monetary Policy Committee* (MPC) of the Bank of England. The MPC would consist of the Governor of the Bank, three other Bank officials, and four independent economists to be appointed by the Chancellor. The Committee was to meet monthly and to decide on interest rates at each such meeting by majority vote, with the Governor having a casting vote, with its minutes subsequently being published. Under the proposals the government specified an inflation target, and the MPC's duty was then to choose interest rates in a way which it judged would be consistent with achieving the target over time.

Bank of England Independence.

Many economists had long advocated giving the Bank independent control of interest rates, and the new Chancellor's move was widely welcomed in economic and financial circles. The basic justification underlying the idea was that it would be likely to increase the *credibility* of the Government's commitment to low inflation and to sound financial policies. This was because if politicians have control of interest rates, they face temptations to use this control for electoral purposes to over-expand the economy, especially in the run-up to elections, regardless of the adverse longer term implications for the inflation rate. Bank officials, by contrast, face no similar temptations. International comparisons of countries suggest a clear tendency for those countries with relatively independent central banks to have relatively low inflation rates.

Work of the MPC.

The MPC rapidly gained credibility for its commitment to low inflation, and although arguments continued about the exchange rate, there was a widespread acceptance that the new policy-making regime was an improvement on the previous one. The new consensus was emphasised when, following Labour's re-election in the 2001 general election, the Conservative opposition officially endorsed the MPC and Bank of England independence as the appropriate basis for monetary policy.

Under this policy-making regime the MPC and the Bank of England have *instrument independence*, but not *goal independence*. In other words, the final goal (policy objective) is chosen by the government rather than by the MPC, but the latter has freedom to determine the policies (instruments) which it judges to be appropriate to achieve this objective. The basic policy target, which has been maintained unchanged since 1997, is an annual inflation rate of 2·5 per cent, using RPIX as the measure of inflation. RPIX is the retail price index, excluding the impact of mortgage interest payments.

Use of RPIX rather than the unadjusted RPI is justified on the grounds that if inflation threatens to increase beyond the government's policy target, the appropriate policy for the MPC is to raise interest rates. Any rise in interest rates, however, increases the cost of mortgage interest payments and thus puts upward pressure on the unadjusted RPI. If the latter were the policy target, therefore, there would be an awkward internal contradiction in that the MPC's anti-inflation policy instrument would itself put upward pressure on the chosen measure of the inflation rate. Use of RPIX avoids this contradiction.

Inflation Forecasting.

In practice it is impossible to ensure that the inflation target can always be precisely achieved. The MPC's target is therefore expressed in terms of an acceptable band of inflation rates, with a one point margin of error on either side of the target. In the event that the rate turns out to exceed 3·5 per cent or fall below 1·5 per cent, the MPC is required to write an open letter to the Chancellor explaining why this has happened, and specifying the actions it plans to take in order to bring inflation back within the required range.

Policy-making has to be forward-looking. Policy decisions made today have no impact on today's inflation rate, which reflects past decisions. Rather, today's decisions are likely to affect the inflation rate up to two years ahead. Consequently, the MPC's decisions are based upon forecasts of inflation for about two years into the future. These forecasts contain a "best estimate" together with margins of error. If the best estimate of future annual inflation suggests that it is likely to fall well below the central objective of 2·5 per cent, then the MPC will normally consider cutting interest rates unless there are strong reasons not to do so; and conversely for an estimate well above 2·5 per cent. Because of the margin of error, decisions can be mistaken, and because inflation responds only slowly to changes in policy, such mistakes cannot instantly be corrected. Thus, inflation targeting is necessarily an inexact science.

The Repo Market.

If the MPC's inflation forecasts cause it to decide to alter interest rates, it announces the decision at the end of its monthly meeting. The announcement rapidly leads to a general change in interest rates throughout the economy. Banks follow the lead of the MPC because they know that the MPC's decision signals a change in the interest rate at which the Bank of England will lend them money.

Moreover, the Bank can force the private banks to borrow from it by its use of open market opera-

tions—buying or selling government securities—which regulate the amount of high powered money which the banks hold. Thus, if the MPC signals an increase in interest rates, the private banks know that they will shortly have to pay higher rates on loans from the Bank of England, so they in turn raise the rates which they charge to their customers.

The main instrument through which the Bank of England lends to the private banks is a *repo* (or sometimes a *reverse repo*.) "Repo" is short for "sale and repurchase agreement." Under a repo agreement, a private bank sells an agreed amount of long term government securities to the Bank of England in exchange for a credit in its account held with the Bank. It simultaneously agrees to buy back the securities at a future date, for more than the amount of the initial sale. The difference between the selling and buying price is the interest rate—the repo rate—on the deal.

Effectively, the Bank of England makes a secured loan to the private bank, the security being the long term asset which it holds for the duration of the loan. If the MPC wishes to increase interest rates throughout the economy, the means of so doing is to increase the repo rate on two-week repo deals. Reverse repos work on the same principle, but in the opposite direction: the Bank of England borrows from, rather than lends to, the commercial banks.

5. ECONOMIC ASPECTS OF THE PUBLIC SERVICES

The Cost of Public Services.

In 2004–05, total public expenditure was £486·6 billion, over £6,500 per head. Of this the bulk (about 75 per cent) was spent by central government, and the remainder by local authorities and public corporations. From 1960 public expenditure rose as a proportion of GDP to a peak in 1982–83 when it reached nearly 49 per cent. It then declined.

In 1991, public spending's share in national income rose quite sharply as the recession and higher levels of unemployment pushed up expenditure on social security. After Mr. Major became Prime Minister there was also greater emphasis on public spending programmes such as health. Nevertheless, from 1993 government current spending as a proportion of GDP declined slightly, reflecting a recovering economy. By 2004–05 total government spending as a proportion of GDP was about 41 per cent.

Central Government collects in revenue considerably more than it spends itself, but transfers funds to the local authorities, to the National Insurance Fund, and to the public corporations. In the last 25 years the expenditure of the public sector as a whole has generally exceeded its revenue, the difference being met by net borrowing. However, the buoyancy of privatisation receipts and the process of "real fiscal drag"— where tax allowances keep pace with inflation but not the rise in earnings so that tax payments as a percentage of earned incomes go up—provided some offset. There was a financial deficit in each year of the 1980s until 1988 when there was a surplus. There was also a surplus in the following year, but then the Government started to move back into deficit as the recession pushed up spending, depressed tax revenues and curbed the Government's scope for further privatisations.

Improving Public Finances.

Strong economic growth started to improve the state of government finances. By 1997 net borrowing was £15·7 billion as compared to a staggering £51 billion in 1993. In 1998 the government moved into a surplus which has continued until recently. Even so the ratio of government debt to GDP will remain high. The problem any Government faces is clear. The welfare state is expensive. Good economic climes remove some of this expense in that unemployment falls and private incomes rise. But the country remains with a large dependent population, partly because of widespread poverty and partly because of demographic forces increasing the retired as a proportion of the population. Add to that the expenditure burden of servicing existing public debt, and it is easy to see that the problem is a difficult one. Improved government finances have allowed some repayment of debt. In the last three years or so debt has started to rise again and in 2004–05 stood at 41·4 per cent of GDP.

Not all categories of public expenditure have expanded at the same rate. Over the period from 1984, for example, expenditure on public order and safety, social security, health and education increased faster than the total; expenditure on agriculture and on housing and community amenities fell behind the total.

Public Housing.

Expenditure on public housing (net of sales) amounted to less than 1 per cent of public expenditure in 2005. This is in marked contrast to the centrality of public sector housing in the post-war period until the late 1970s. Housing expenditure consists of two quite different items. There is the capital cost of building new houses or of improvement grants and the like. There is also a recurrent cost, in the form of subsidies. April 1990 saw new financial arrangements for public sector housing, and a number of Government subsidies were consolidated into a Housing Revenue Account Subsidy in 1998–99. Direct subsidies to rents fell sharply. The Government's aim was to divert subsidies from the property to the person, via the housing benefit system.

Post-War Subsidies.

For most of the post-war period governments provided a substantial subsidy to public sector housing, either in the form of help for new building, or as a direct subsidy to rents. The mix depended very much on the priorities of the day. From 1972 to 1975 there was a "fair rent" system, which then gave way to a system designed to subsidise the construction of new dwellings and improvements to the existing housing stock. The whole direction of policy for public sector housing was altered by the Housing Act of 1980. Since then subsidies have been much more carefully controlled. The result is that council rents have risen substantially in real terms. At the same time, private ownership has been encouraged e.g. through the sale of council houses. Between 1979 and 2000, over 2 million council houses are estimated to have been sold. The Housing Act of 1988 further eroded the role of local authorities in the provision of housing by allowing public sector tenants to change their landlord if the authority in question was deemed to be unsatisfactory, and housing associations and other registered social landlords have become significant providers of new housing in the subsidised rented sector. Such organisations now own and manage well over one million homes in England. If registered with the Housing Corporation or equivalent bodies in Scotland and Wales, they can qualify for government support. There have been a variety of initiatives (not least in the 1996 Housing Act) to enable/encourage Housing Associations and also private sector concerns to take over responsibility for local authority housing.

The Housing Market.

Government housing policy must be seen in terms of the housing market as a whole. In 2004 there were 25·3 million dwellings in Great Britain, 70 per cent being owner-occupied, 20 per cent council or housing association houses, and the other 10 per cent privately rented. The importance of owner-occupation has grown and that of private renting has declined: in 1960 they had accounted for 42 per cent and 32 per cent of the total respectively. One of the main aims of the 1988 Housing Act was to stimulate the private rented sector by deregulating rents on new private sector lettings. On an international comparison, owner occupation is more common in the UK than in the EU as a whole. Of the 15 EU countries, only Ireland, Spain, Italy, Greece and Luxembourg have high owner occupation rates. It should also be noted that the pattern of tenure varies quite significantly across different parts of the UK—owner occupation ranges from 63 per cent in Scotland to 76 in South-West England.

The switch to owner-occupation in the UK is largely the result of Government policy. Rent controls meant that there was little incentive to build houses for renting, nor even to maintain existing rented houses, although the 1988 and 1996 Housing Acts were intended to remove some of the disincentives to private rental. On the other hand, in the past, Government has given considerable tax advantages to owner-occupiers. Owner-occupied

houses are exempt from the capital gains tax introduced in 1964, and owner-occupiers used to be able to also obtain tax relief on mortgage-interest payments on a principal of up to £30,000. However, this £30,000 limit for relief was unchanged from March 1983, in spite of very rapid house price inflation.

Changing Tax Position.

Until August 1988 unmarried owner-occupiers could claim tax relief on multiples of £30,000, depending on the number sharing. Thereafter relief was restricted to £30,000 per property. In the March 1991 Budget mortgage interest relief was restricted to the basic rate of income tax; previously higher rate tax payers could claim relief on interest payments at their highest marginal rate of income tax. Since the abolition of the Schedule A tax in 1961—whereby owner-occupiers paid tax on the rental income imputed to their houses—this tax relief on interest payments could only be justified as an inducement to home-ownership; but it was also a considerable subsidy to owner-occupiers, who tend to be the relatively well-off. From 1994 mortgage interest relief was limited to 20 per cent. From April 1995 it was further limited to 15 per cent and from April 1998 to 10 per cent. The 1999 Budget announced the complete abolition of mortgage interest relief from 2000.

Public Sector Housebuilding Peak.

The year 1953 was a peak for public sector housebuilding in the United Kingdom when 256,000 council dwellings were completed. There was a trough in 1961 (119,000), a peak in 1967 (204,000) and a subsequent fall to 108,000 in 1973. Since the mid 1970s there has been a steady decline in the construction of public dwellings. In 1993 only about 40,000 were completed and by the end of the 1990s only about 25,000 per year were being completed. Local authorities now play only a minor role in the provision of new dwellings, but they and other registered social landlords still have an important role to play in renting out property. By contrast, the number of private dwellings completed rose steadily from 63,000 in 1953 to a peak of 222,000 in 1968. Thereafter the number fell back to an annual average of slightly less than 200,000 in the early 1970s, and still further to an average of about 130,000 in the early 1980s. There were further rises in 1983 to about 148,000, and to a peak of 200,000 in 1988 before a fall to 159,260 in 1991. Since then the figure has averaged about 150,000 per annum. The total number of dwellings completed reached a peak of 414,000 in 1968, and fell to 270,000 in 1974. Since then, the best year has been 1976 (315,000), and the worst 1992 (171,000). In 2001–02 c. 180,000 houses were completed, in 2002–03, 183,449, in 2003–04, 190,000 and in 2004–05, 206,000.

House Price Inflation.

Over the 15 years 1955–70 the rate of inflation in the price of houses averaged 5 per cent per annum: somewhat faster than the rise in the cost of living. After 1970 there was a great surge in house prices: between December 1970 and December 1972 the average rise was no less than 30 per cent per annum. There are various reasons for this remarkable inflation. Partly it reflected the rapid acceleration of general inflation; in such times it is sensible to hold one's wealth in the form of assets which will appreciate in value. It also reflected the decline in house-building after 1968, and a slowing-down in the rate at which building land became available. The precise timing of the inflation resulted from the sudden and large increase in the availability of building society mortgages. And as the inflation grew, so optimistic expectations helped to raise house prices still further. By 1974 the rate of increase had slowed down considerably. It subsequently slowed even further. In 1978 and 1979 prices started to accelerate again, slackening off in 1980, only to start accelerating again at the end of 1982. This rise was sustained through to 1988, but 1989 through to early 1991 saw sharp falls in house prices, particularly in areas such as the South East and East Anglia where house price inflation had accelerated rapidly in the previous two years. By 1990 the housing market slowdown was evident in all regions, and nationally house prices fell by 5 per cent. Further declines were registered in 1991 and

1992, but the pattern varied from region to region. By 1996 a slow, but general recovery in house prices was underway. By and large this continued and in 1999 was accelerating alarmingly in some regions of the country (especially London). By early 2000 house price inflation had started to slow only to pick up again in early 2001. In 2002 house prices increased by 14 per cent. This meant that the average house cost twice as much as 10 years before. In 2003 house prices rose by a further 15·7 per cent, and in 2004 by 11·8 per cent.

Current Housing Needs.

The number of dwellings comfortably exceeds the number of households. Yet the picture is not as rosy as this implies. The regional distribution of supply and demand is not equally spread. The measured number of households understates the number of "units" needing accommodation—a married couple, for example, living in someone else's house.

Much accommodation is substandard in one way or other. In 1990 housing renewal areas were established in England and Wales to cover, inter alia, renovation and redevelopment of substandard housing. These complemented housing action areas in Scotland and Northern Ireland, which had authority to channel funds for redevelopment where at least half the housing stock did not meet "statutory tolerable" standards. In spite of such initiatives, the above factors, together with personal financial and social problems, mean that a worrying number of people are homeless. Thus in 2004–05 121,000 households were accepted as homeless by the local authorities in England. The problem was particularly acute in London.

A Government strategy for the homeless in England, Coming in From the Cold, was published in 1999. Similar initiatives were declared for elsewhere in the UK. In December 2002, the Government issued a policy statement, The Way Forward for Housing. Amongst its proposals was a new Starter Home Initiative to help first time buyers in expensive areas. It also proposed assistance with housing costs for the unemployed who need to move house to secure work as well as reform of Housing Benefit. Greater controls on landlords were envisaged.

Subsequently many initiatives were announced. In 2003 The Sustainable Communities Plan put particular emphasis on trying to ensure affordable homes in the south east of England, and on renewing the housing stock in low demand areas of the country. In 2004 the Key Worker Living programme was introduced to help workers move to jobs in areas where housing costs were high. The Housing Act of 2004 was concerned to improve the standards of the existing housing stock, to control the activities of private sector landlords and to improve the procedures for the buying and selling of houses.

The Barker Review.

In the following year the Barker Review of Housing Supply was concerned with the increasing problem of the affordability of housing for those on modest incomes, particularly for first-time buyers. The Review pointed out that over the previous 30 years the number of households had increased by 30 per cent while the level of house building had fallen by 50 per cent. It went on to argue that "the market was not sufficiently responding to housing demand and that as a result house price increases were the highest in Europe". In response the Government announced a commitment to ensure the building of at least 150,000 per year. It promised to explore partnerships with the private sector to promote shared equity and ownership schemes and to increase the amount of social housing.

Education.

Educational expenditure accounted for about 14 per cent of public expenditure in 2005. It had increased over the previous 25 years for two reasons. First the number of full-time pupils had grown. Second the more expensive sectors—secondary schools and universities—expanded most rapidly. For example, in 2002–03 there were 4·0 million students in state secondary schools as opposed to 3·2 million in 1961, although the 2002–03 figure was well below the comparable total for 1981 of 4·6 million. This reflects changing demographics. Falling

birth rates meant that the secondary school population reached a peak in the mid-to-late 1970s, after which it fell. Higher education subsequently started to see the impact of these declining birth rates.

Even so, there were about 1·4 million full-time students in higher education in 2002–03, compared with a total of 456,800 in 1970–71. A further 1·0 million part-timers were in higher education and 4·8 million students in further education. The proportion of young people entering higher education rose from one in eight to one in five by 1990. The Government's target had been for the total to rise to one in three by 2000. The autumn of 1993 saw a record entry which effectively met that target. In other words there has been a massive increase in participation in higher education. Today about 40 per cent of the relevant age cohort in England and Wales are in higher education; and the rate is even higher in Scotland. This contrasts with an age participation rate of around 6 per cent in the mid 1960s.

It was generally recognised that education can be an economic investment for the future just as much as capital formation in, say, machinery or roads. There is a "private return" on "investment in education", which takes the form of higher earnings over the lifetime of the person educated; and there is a "social return" on public resources devoted to education being the greater contribution to the national product which trained and educated people can make. Both the 1974 Labour and 1979 Conservative Governments considered longer term policies for education. The key theme of a consultative White Paper in 1977 was the need to attune school curricula to the employment needs of school-leavers, and to encourage stronger ties between schools and industry. This has been a recurrent theme. Questions about longer term educational requirements were initially subsumed under the post-1979 Conservative Government by debate on the relative merits of private and public sector education. There was also a renewed emphasis on making the later years of school education more directly related to labour market requirements.

The Introduction of Markets into Education.

In 1985 in a White Paper entitled "The Development of Higher Education into the 1990s", the Government also considered ways of improving the contribution of higher education to economic performance. Thus the links between full-time education and job training were being intensified. The system of National Vocational Qualifications (and their school counterparts, GNVQs) was intended to unify academic and vocational credentials.

Such themes were continued in the 1988 Education Reform Act. It proposed the introduction of a National Curriculum, the establishment of City Technical Colleges and giving business greater representation on the new University Funding Council than it had had on the University Grants Committee. Many of the provisions of the 1988 Education Reform Act remained highly controversial, particularly those which related to the National Curriculum and what were perceived to be over-rigid prescription of its content. Many commentators saw the Act as increasing central government's control over education—for example, LEAs lost control of the Colleges of Further Education and of the former Polytechnics, while schools could choose to opt out of Local Authority control in favour of administration by central government if a majority of parents and governors so desired. At the same time the Act emphasised the theme of intensified competition in the provision of education. Schools now had to compete for pupils and universities for funding. In schools this was known as the policy of "open enrolment". The theme of greater competition was also evident in the higher education sector, where the "binary divide" between universities and polytechnics was ended. All such establishments are now funded by the Higher Education Funding Council.

The Dearing Report.

The Dearing Committee reported on the future of higher education in 1997. Amongst the matters it considered was the size of the university sector. The problem was that the number of graduates being produced was increasing faster than the number of traditional graduate jobs. The question had to be asked, therefore, as to how productively some of our graduates were being used; and whether resources might not, with social profit, be diverted to other elements of the education system. Unfortunately, Dearing failed to consider adequately this important issue.

The new Labour Government changed funding arrangements for university students. A small proportion of the fee is now paid by the student, whilst he or she is now totally responsible for his or her own living expenses. The only exception is for those whose families are in receipt of welfare benefits. One of the declared reasons for this change was that private rates of return were thought to be higher than social rates of return. In 1998 the new Labour Government announced a new framework for the organisation of schools. Essentially this continued the theme of markets, but in part restored the position of LEAs. Rigorous inspection of schools continues to be conducted by OFSTED. So intent is the Labour Government on increasing staying-on rates in full time education beyond 16 that it introduced Educational Maintenance Allowances across England in 2004. Depending on parental income students may be entitled to an allowance of between £10 and £30 per week.

In the autumn of 2000 the Government introduced an important reform of sixth form work in schools. The A level syllabuses were altered and simultaneously new Advanced Subsidiary level qualifications were introduced. This latter corresponded to half an A level. The aim of the reform was to broaden the range of studies undertaken. GNVQ at level 3 is being replaced by vocational A levels, whilst vocational GCSEs are being introduced.

The 2002 Education Act.

The Education Act of 2002 stresses, *inter alia*, more flexible curricula for schools, more autonomy for schools that are performing well, measures to increase standards and more business involvement in schools. Early in 2004 the DfES also announced its intention to change the basis of some elements of higher education funding. This would involve allowing universities to charge modest "top-up" fees (to a maximum of £3,000) from 2006, and making the "pay-back" terms for student loans more generous. Meanwhile, at the school level, the Government has announced its intention to establish at least 53 Academies by 2007. These establishments would be to replace existing schools that were facing difficulties or where there was excess demand from prospective pupils. Private and voluntary sector sponsors, as well as "faith groups", are meant to be involved. The Academies will cater for secondary age children.

Introduction of Trust Schools.

A 2005 White Paper announced the introduction of trust schools. Under this scheme schools could opt out of direct local authority control, though they would still be reliant on local authority finance. The controversial idea seems to be that greater parental and external involvement would help to drive up standards. Unlike the Academies, where private finance was involved, private finance would not be expected in trust schools. Also in 2005 a white paper was published on the reform of further education. The basic thrust of these reforms was an attempt to ease and to subsidise access of second chance learners, and to make what FE Colleges offered more attuned to the needs of local business.

Social Security.

In 1988 the Social Security system underwent considerable change and there have been further changes since then. In what follows we first describe the old system, before turning to the new.

There were two forms of social security: *National Insurance* and *Supplementary Benefits*. The former was non-means tested. They were designed to be exactly what the name indicated—insurance for when an individual met circumstances implying a loss of income, be that circumstance old age, unemployment or sickness. By contrast the latter were means tested, and were designed to keep people out of poverty. As such under the original Beveridge scheme, they were meant to be a safety net for the unfortunate few. The majority were to be covered by the insurance element. Formidable financing difficulties meant that this ideal was never achieved and supplementary benefits attained an unwanted prominence in the British social security system.

(i) National Insurance.

Under this scheme employees received rights to unemployment benefit, sickness benefit, retirement pensions, widows' benefits, injury and disablement benefits. For those below pensionable age, the major national insurance benefit available was unemployment benefit. Weekly rates were laid down for each benefit. The basic rate was increased according to the number of dependants. In 1966 an earnings-related supplement was introduced for unemployment benefits paid to persons between 18 and 65 (men) or 60 (women): the supplement being related to earnings in the previous tax year. The maximum total benefit, including increases for dependants, amounted to 85 per cent of earnings. This, together with tax rebates, meant a higher income out of work for a very few people. In 1982 the earnings-related unemployment supplement was withdrawn, whilst unemployment benefit became taxable.

By far the most important benefit was and still is the retirement pension, paid as of right to contributors on retirement. Individuals may increase their rate of pension by staying on at work after the minimum retiring age of 65 for men and 60 for women. In 2006 basic retirement pensions were £84·25 per week for single persons and £134·75 for a married couple. In accordance with European legislation, measures have been introduced to make the state pension age 65 for both men and women. The change will be phased in over ten years, starting from 2010.

(ii) The Financing of National Insurance.

Some benefits are conditional upon the payment of National Insurance contributions which most of the adult population have to pay. For employees, both employer and employee pay a contribution. The self-employed also pay contributions of smaller size than the sum of the employer's and employee's contribution, but they were not entitled to unemployment benefit. As a result of the 1985 and 1989 Budgets, employers' and employees' national insurance contributions were cut for the lowest paid workers, in order to increase the incentives to work and to hire more labour. At the same time, while a maximum earnings limit for employees' contributions remains, the upper-earnings limit on employer's contributions has been abolished. In the 1989 Budget the structure of National Insurance payments was altered. Previously, the rate went from zero to more than 9 per cent once an individual hit the lower earnings limit. This meant that someone moving just above the lower limit for National Insurance contributions could face a marginal tax rate in excess of more than 100 per cent which was clearly a major disincentive. Although such traps have by no means been eradicated, National Insurance contributions were charged at 2 per cent on earnings below the lower earnings limit once that limit has been reached, and thereafter at 10 per cent until the upper earnings limit. From April 1999 there were further reforms. Individuals had no longer to pay contributions on earnings below the lower limit, whilst the system for employer contributions was much simplified and their liability to pay contributions at all for lower paid workers was removed.

Aspects of the National Insurance Scheme.

The National Insurance Scheme is an odd mixture of insurance and tax. The levels of contributions, when the scheme started in 1948, were fixed on the actuarial principle that contributions by or on behalf of an individual plus a specified State contribution should on average suffice to pay for the benefits to which he was entitled. But the scheme did not allow for inflation and a rising standard of living. In particular a succession of increases granted in the rate of pensions helped to put an end to this actuarial probity. As the post-war period wore on two other forces put strains on the National Insurance system. These were a major increase in longevity, with a consequential increase in the burden of pension payments, and an increase in unemployment. Instead the principle became established that the rate of contributions in each year, together with a transfer from the Government, should equal the total benefits paid out in that year. Expenditure on non-contributory benefits is covered by general revenues.

(iii) Reform of Pensions.

There are about eleven million pensioners in Britain. At least a third of these are kept out of poverty only by receiving other benefits. Recently the Government introduced the Minimum Income Guarantee for people aged 60 or over. In October 2003 it was replaced by the Pension Credit. In April 2006 this topped up weekly income to at least £114·05 for a single person and to £174·05 for a couple.

Many of the remainder find their living standards considerably reduced from when they were working. This is because the existing state retirement pension is inadequate. There are some occupational pension schemes which offer a better income. Over 10 million people are now receiving benefits from such schemes. Many other individuals now also contribute to personal pensions. However, like personal savings, many of the schemes tend to have only limited safeguards against inflation unless they are index-linked. There are also often substantial losses involved in changing jobs.

A scheme for graduated pensions was introduced for employees in 1961. Under the scheme there were two kinds of employees—*ordinary* and *contracted-out*. In the case of contracted-out workers, their employer (on whom the decision whether to contract out rested) had to institute a private superannuation scheme that gave at least as favourable terms as the new State scheme, including the provision that rights under the scheme should be transferable up to the limits of the State scheme. Transferability was the guarantee that the individual did not lose his pension rights when he changed his job. In practise transferability was never really achieved.

The Conservative Government announced its proposals for reform in a White Paper published in 1971. It considered that the costs of earnings-related benefits would be too great; instead it favoured earnings-related contributions for basically flat-rate pensions. In addition it wished to encourage contracting out, so that almost all employees would also be members of a private occupational pension scheme, in which pensions would be related to past contributions. The Government recognised that it would have to ensure that occupational pension rights were transferable between jobs.

Problems of Pension Funding.

The difficulty of funding an adequate state pension when the number of pensioners is rising relative to the size of the workforce has led to a withdrawal from the goals for pensions laid down in the 1970s. These goals were for a two-tier pension. The bottom tier was a common flat-rate for everyone. The top tier was earnings-related—that is, a fixed proportion of the pensioner's previous earnings. Because of the flat-rate element, a low earner would be able to expect a pension which was a higher percentage of his working income than that obtained by a higher earner. Contributions to the scheme would be earnings related. The pensions would be fully protected against inflation, and women would enter the scheme on the same footing as men. There was an obvious emphasis on the need to protect women from poverty in retirement, after the death of the husband. There would be a maximum pension entitlement and a maximum contribution. For this reason among others, the Government planned to encourage new and improved occupational schemes, to exist alongside the state scheme. It was hoped that the scheme would come to full maturity by 1998, this long delay reflecting the formidable difficulties in financing the plan. In the meantime fully earnings-related contributions started in 1975, and minor earnings-related benefit in 1979. These replaced flat-rate National Insurance payments and graduated pension contributions. In the event, funding problems meant that the earnings-related component had less impact than was intended.

Transferability of Pensions.

A renewed concern in the early 1980s was with a particular aspect of occupational pensions—their transferability from job to job. Someone who left an occupational scheme had the choice of either leaving his pension rights at his old employer, and receiving a deferred pension at retirement age, usually unadjusted for inflation between his departure and retirement; or, if his old and new employers both agreed, transferring the fund, from which effectively the pension is paid, to his new employer, usually at great loss to himself. Governments have attempted to introduce the full transferability of pension rights from job to job.

The advantage to the government of a shift into private pension schemes is that it will reduce the impact of demographic change, namely the cost of supporting a larger retired population relative to that of working age. Both private and state schemes are now operating on a fully funded basis i.e. the individual pays for his or her future pension entitlement, which contrasts with the "pay as you go" system in operation in many countries where pension payments are funded by current contributions.

Intense concern has started to be expressed about whether the State can continue to maintain its present pension system. The essential problem increasingly was seen to be the non-means tested component. Many commentators were starting to argue that eventually the bulk of pension payments would have to be means-tested. Meanwhile in the last couple of years some private company pension schemes have come under pressure. Many of these are based on final year or years' salary. This is fine if the stock market is healthy because the relevant fund is growing enough to keep pace with the demands made upon it. But in a depressed stock market, as at present, major strains are placed on the necessary funding.

The other common form of private pension is known as a money purchase scheme. Both the employee and employer make contributions, which are invested. The value of the investment is typically converted into an annuity when the individual reaches retirement age. The collapse of stock markets has threatened this form of pension too.

Mounting Pension Problems.

So concerned has the Government become with the potential problems of income in old age and with the potential funding burden on the State that, in the autumn of 2002, it published a major consultation document. This document stated baldly that a significant proportion of the labour force was likely to suffer major, and probably unacceptable, falls in income after retirement if things continued as at present. The State, through its minimum income guarantee, could do little more than keep people out of dire poverty. If people wanted to do better than that, they had to make private provision. At least 25 per cent of the current workforce was at risk. Only two things could improve the situation—working longer or saving more. The Government had many suggestions. For example, it intended to intensify schemes to bring more men over 50 back into the labour market—the labour force participation rate of men between that age and 65 is currently only just over 70 per cent. However, it was clear that there were no easy solutions to an increasingly worrying problem.

In 2006, in the wake of the Turner Report, the government outlined plans to raise the pension age to 66 from 2024, 67 from 2034 and 68 from 2044. Pensions would be linked to earnings from 2012 "if affordable".

(iv) Poverty in Britain.

Despite the existence of social protection there are many people in Britain whose income falls below that which the Government regarded as adequate. If people in this position "are not required to be available for work", they are supported from Government revenues by means of *income support*, formerly *supplementary benefits*, and before 1966 known as *National Assistance*. It was a fault of the National Insurance Scheme that so many have required this assistance. In 2002 about one third of pensioners received extra financial help on top of the state pension as well as getting extra help with rent and Council Tax. Of families whose head was in work, about 1·2 million families received Working Families Tax Credit, whilst well over half of the male unemployed were wholly dependent on additional state support. A Treasury Report, published in 1999, concluded that 12 million people in the UK were in poverty. A more recent report by Oxfam suggests a figure of 13 million. However, one achievement of the present Labour Government has been a reduction of the number of children living in poor households.

Until 1996 anyone who was out of work for more than a year lost entitlement to unemployment benefit and became reliant on supplementary payments through what was the supplementary benefit system and is now income support (*see* (v) *below*). From 1996 all unemployed benefit recipients were transferred to a single benefit (the Jobseeker's Allowance), regardless of duration of unemployment. In contrast to unemployment benefit, Jobseeker's Allowance also attracts means tested payments.

A major fault with the earlier supplementary benefits scheme was that they could not be paid to those in employment whose earnings were below the benefit level, and if such persons became unemployed they could claim benefits only up to their normal earnings level. The *Family Income Supplement* was introduced in 1971 to alleviate hardship amongst low earners, but it has been estimated that only half of those eligible claimed FIS. The take-up of the new Family Credit (subsequently replaced by Working Families Tax Credit) payment was initially even lower.

(v) The Reform of Social Security.

In 1985 the Government issued a White Paper detailing reforms of the whole social security system. The basis of dissatisfaction was three-fold. First, the system was a complex and costly one to run. Second, it worked in such a way as to help some who, on official definitions of poverty, did not need assistance; whilst, conversely, it failed to provide it for some who did. Third, it created unemployment benefit traps, supplementary benefit traps and poverty traps. These imply that people who are unemployed or employed on low pay might be deterred from taking employment or taking jobs with higher pay, because the combined effects of the tax and benefit system mean that the consequential increase in their net income is negligible. Behind their proposed reforms was the concern about future financing difficulties, and a wish to make the system simpler. The main elements of the new system were introduced in April 1988.

On pensions, it was originally proposed to retain basic pensions, but to abolish earnings related pensions (SERPS). Instead, greater stress was to be placed on occupational pension schemes. Substantial political pressures caused a change of mind, and SERPS was retained, albeit in a modified form (*see* (iii) on **F36**). Universal child benefit was retained. But for low earnings families, FIS was replaced by *Family Credit*, paid through the pay packet. As compared to FIS it allowed a smoother tapering of payments as original income increased. For those not in work, supplementary benefits were replaced by *"income support"*, which was intended to be simpler and to involve a smaller range of payments. Benefits were at a lower rate for the under-25s and at a higher rate for pensioners. An additional sum is paid for each dependent child, as it is for single parents and the long-term sick and disabled. Beyond these, there are no additional payments. There was also a new simplified scheme for housing benefits. Unemployment benefit, the maternity allowance (in revised form) and sickness benefit survived the 1988 review, but maternity and death grants were abolished. Substantial changes were made in provisions for widowhood.

The "Twin Pillars" Philosophy.

The Government's catchphrase for these reforms was "the twin pillars": state help combined with encouragement for private provision. Returning to the three major complaints about the previous system, certainly the revised one was cheaper to administer. It probably directed the benefits more accurately. It may also have alleviated the worst incentive traps, but in substantially improving the lot of some in this respect, it worsened it for more. Indeed, the scheme was not a major departure, and fell far short of more radical proposals for a combined tax and benefit credit system.

In 1996 benefits for the unemployed were replaced by the Jobseekers' Allowance. In the previous year Invalidity Benefit and Sickness Benefit (after a limited period of eligibility) were replaced by the much more strictly tested Incapacity Benefit. In October 1999, Family Credit was replaced by the *Working Families' Tax Credit*, which provides more generous in-work incentives.

Also in 1999 came the Welfare Reform and Pensions Act. This heralded the introduction of "stakeholder pensions" and pension sharing for divorced couples. It also proposed a single "gateway" to the benefit system for those below pension age and a new structure of benefits for those with disabilities or long-term illness. Stakeholder pensions represent an attempt to extend the provision of company pensions.

In April 2003 Working Families Tax Credit was replaced by Working Tax Credit, which effectively extends the benefits of the former to people on low incomes without children.

In the summer of 2001, as part of a general reorganisation of government, a new department—the Department for Work and Pensions—was established. Inter alia this takes on all responsibilities for welfare payments.

Expenditure on social protection in the UK is slightly less than the average for the EU as a whole, lagging behind Luxembourg, Denmark, Sweden, the Netherlands, Germany, Austria, France and Belgium. An important reason for this is that our pension provisions are relatively ungenerous.

Public Revenue.

In the table below we show government revenue and expenditure. No less than 63 per cent of the total public revenue comes from social security contributions and taxes on income. Taxes on expenditure account for about 35 per cent of the total. Two commodities in particular are heavily taxed: alcoholic drink and tobacco. These commodities are singled out partly for social reasons and partly because—in economists' jargon—the demand for them is *inelastic; i.e.*, the public reduces its consumption of drink and tobacco only slightly in response to a rise in their price. Indirect taxation—taking the form of excise duties and purchase taxes (value added tax after 1973)—used to be spread very unevenly over different sorts of expenditure. The introduction of Value Added Tax in 1973 tended to even out the incidence of indirect taxes on different goods and services, though tobacco, drink and motoring continued to be hit.

Until 1989 in Scotland, and 1990 in England and Wales, the major method of collecting local taxes was through rates. A rateable value was assessed for each commercial or domestic property, corresponding roughly to its size, imputed rental value, and amenities. Each year, the appropriate local authority decided at what rate in the pound to tax this rateable value. On the dates mentioned above, the government substantially altered the local tax system for private households in an ostensible effort to broaden the tax base for the domestic element. Instead of local taxes being paid on the basis of property ownership, each adult paid a flat rate charge or poll tax.

PUBLIC SECTOR FINANCIAL BALANCE AND BORROWING REQUIREMENT, 2004–05 (£ billion)

Current expenditure	452·6
Gross investment	30·7
Total managed expenditure	486·6
Total current receipts	447·1
Public sector net borrowing	39·5
Public sector net debt (% of GDP)	35·0

SOURCES OF GOVERNMENT RECEIPTS

Taxes on income	283·0
Taxes on expenditure	154·5
Other current receipts	9·6

The Poll Tax Controversy.

Although some minor adjustment was made to allow for personal circumstances, the tax was highly regressive and its introduction was very controversial. Part but not all of the objections related to the government's under-estimate of the burden of local government revenue which could fall on the personal sector. Local authorities were no longer allowed to set rates on the business sector—these were charged uniformly by central government and the proceeds were then distributed to local authorities on some notional calculation of need. The large burden of local authority taxation falling on persons, particularly in previously low-rated areas, was tackled by an increasingly bureaucratic system of rebates. The first year of the poll tax in England and Wales merely served to demonstrate its unpopularity and its inefficiency in high collection costs. In order to defray the political consequences of the poll tax, the March 1991 Budget included a provision to reduce poll tax bills in 1991–92 and beyond, financed by a rise in the VAT rate from 15% to 17·5%.

Even this failed to overcome objections to a tax which created far more losers than gainers, and in April 1991 the government announced plans to revert to a property-based system of local taxation, retaining only vestigial elements of the poll tax principle that all should contribute something to the cost of local services. The Government proposed that the new "Council Tax" would be a property tax banded according to the size of dwelling, thus reintroducing an element of progressivity. The Council Tax came into existence in 1993–94.

The Budget.

Each year the Chancellor of the Exchequer announces his Budget for the coming fiscal year. The most important and most difficult task in drawing up the Budget is to decide on the size of deficit or surplus to aim for. The deficit is the excess of public expenditure over public revenue; and it has to be financed by borrowing or by printing money. A large deficit is normally reflationary; sometimes that may be required to get the economy out of recession. A small deficit—and even more, a surplus—is deflationary, and is a means of holding a demand-pull inflation in check. In 1998 the Government announced new mechanisms for controlling public expenditure. Perhaps the most important element of the reforms was to allow Departments to carry over money from one year to the next.

In 1970 there was a small surplus, and thus the net borrowing requirement was negative. After that the borrowing requirement became large and positive, peaking in the recessionary years 1979–82. In the 1980s more favourable economic circumstances and the one-off receipts from major privatisations enabled the public sector accounts to swing into surplus. By 1991 the public finances had once again deteriorated markedly and were in deficit by some £8·8 billion. This deterioration was caused by a combination of much slower economic growth, difficulties with the privatisation programme, and a significant increase in government expenditure. The last of these was largely due to much higher public sector pay awards. A surplus is not itself indicative of a very tight fiscal policy, any more than a deficit automatically implies an expansionary stance. To assess the true fiscal stance, one must adjust the surplus/ deficit for the effects of inflation, privatisation receipts, and the stage of the economic cycle, i.e. the level of unemployment. Therefore it was particularly worrying that from 1991 the deficit continued to increase, to £30bn in 1992 and £43bn in 1993, despite the recovery in the domestic economy. This could have fuelled demand led inflation. Thereafter the deficit started to fall back, initially slowly and then

more rapidly. By 1998 a surplus had started to emerge. Subsequently the surplus fell back and, by 2003, the public finances were moving into deficit.

The calculation of the precise deficit or surplus needed is a chancy business; for the level that is required depends on the amount of saving and on the amount of spending out of credit that people intend to do—and this is not easily predictable. It also depends on the change in the foreign balance. Nor can the Chancellor be sure his figures are right: estimating next year's revenue, and even next year's expenditure by the Government is difficult enough, but he needs to estimate also the likely trends of private income and expenditure, without really reliable information as to what they were in the past year.

Importance of Fiscal Policy.

In spite of such problems, fiscal policy—running deficits when economic activity is low, and small ones or surpluses when it seems to be excessively high—remains an important method through which the economy can be kept on an even keel. Indeed, it can be argued that the role of fiscal policy was enhanced by membership of the EMS Exchange Rate Mechanism (ERM). Even after withdrawal from ERM, the level of interest rates is now largely determined by the need to preserve sterling's value on the foreign exchanges, meaning that the only domestic policy tool over which the government has any direct control is the fiscal stance. If and when the UK enters EMU, fiscal policy could become important because, as under ERM, there be no national control of monetary policy.

However, since fiscal stance can have monetary consequences, the EMU countries have devised rules that limit the freedom of individual countries even with respect to overall fiscal stance. How limiting such rules will in fact turn out to be is uncertain, and there has been much recent concern about the extent to which the French and German governments have broken them.

6. SOURCES OF STATISTICS: SOME FURTHER READING

The non-specialist will find that most of the statistics needed are given in the *Annual Abstract of Statistics*, published every year by The Stationery Office (TSO). This comprehensive document includes figures on population, social conditions, education, labour, production, trade and balance of payments, national income and expenditure, etc.

Fuller information on labour matters is given in *Labour Market Trends* and on financial matters in the *Bank of England Quarterly Bulletin*. These two periodicals include discussions on the statistics presented. *Social Trends* contains articles and detailed statistics on social, cultural and economic conditions in Britain. A sourcebook on the EU is *Basic Statistics of the Community*, annual (Eurostat).

For an analysis of developments in the economy see the *National Institute Economic Review*, a private publication issued by the National Institute for Economic and Social Research. The quarterly *Oxford Review of Economic Policy* (Oxford University Press) contains up-to-date articles on aspects of the economy.

For a comprehensive introduction to the British economy the reader is referred to Peter Curwen, *Understanding the UK Economy* (Macmillan).

III. THE LESS DEVELOPED ECONOMIES

Income Levels.

Two-thirds of the world's population live in dire poverty—a poverty which can scarcely be imagined by those accustomed to the standards of living attained in the relatively few developed countries of the world. The orders of world inequality may be seen from the table comparing annual gross national products per capita. The alleviation of poverty is widely recognised as the most important economic—and indeed political—task for the world community.

What is a Less Developed Country?

There are no less than 140 countries that are referred to as "less developed" or "developing" or "poor" countries. There is a great diversity among them, and yet they have a number of features in common. Foremost is their poverty, but even poverty is not universal: some of the oil-producing countries such as Saudi Arabia, Kuwait and Libya have achieved very high levels of income per capita while retaining many of the other characteristics of less developed countries.

Most of the developing countries are primarily agricultural economies, with the bulk of the population engaged in *subsistence agriculture*. For many millions of peasant farmers the primary objective is to produce enough food for their family to subsist. India is a classic example, with no less than 64 per cent of its one billion people dependent on agriculture for a living. Most less developed countries have only a small industrial sector as yet: it is rare for the output of the manufacturing sector to exceed 25 per cent of the gross domestic product. The main exceptions to this rule are the successful exporters of labour-intensive manufacturing goods, such as Malaysia, Thailand, China and Mexico. Many of the less developed countries lack the necessary ingredients for successful industrialisation—capital, skills and entrepreneurship.

The developing countries vary enormously in size—from the teeming masses of India and China to scores of countries with less than a million people. The development problems and possibilities facing large and small countries are very different. The small size of most developing economies forces them to concentrate on the production of one or two primary products for world markets. Their high degree of specialisation and heavy dependence on exports and imports makes these economies dangerously vulnerable to the vagaries of world trade and the world economy.

Apart from their poverty, the less developed countries have other economic characteristics and problems in common. However, it is dangerous to generalise because there are also important differences. In particular, they vary in their degree of development and in their potential for development. A semi-industrialised, urbanised country such as Argentina has little in common with an utterly backward country such as Chad, and the economic prospects for an oil-rich country such as Venezuela are far brighter than for a country with few natural resources such as Tanzania.

International Comparisons of Income.

The table below sets out the income per capita in the low-income, middle-income and high-income countries of the world, and in particular countries within each category. The first column shows *gross national product* (GNP) per capita in 2002, in dollars converted at the currency exchange rates of that year. The second column shows GNP per capita in dollars converted at *purchasing power parity* (PPP) rates.

GROSS NATIONAL PRODUCT PER CAPITA BY GROUPS OF COUNTRY AND SELECTED COUNTRIES, 2002, $ PER ANNUM

	at exchange rates	at PPP rates
Low-income developing countries	430	2,040
of which: Sierra Leone	140	490
Tanzania	280	550
Nigeria	290	780
Bangladesh	360	1,720
India	480	2,570
Middle-income developing countries	1,840	5,630
of which: China	940	4,300
Thailand	1,980	6,680
South Africa	2,600	9,870
Brazil	2,850	7,250
Mexico	5,910	8,540
South Korea	9,930	16,480
High-income countries	26,310	27,590
of which: Spain	14,430	20,460
UK	25,250	25,870
Singapore	20,690	23,090
Japan	33,550	26,070
USA	35,060	35,060

Figures of national income per capita converted at currency exchange rates can be a misleading guide to relative living standards of different countries.

Exchange rates tend in the long term to equate the prices of goods and services that enter into international trade, but trade imbalances and short term capital flows cause them to depart from this purchasing power parity in the short term, and exchange rates do not take account of non-traded activities. In particular, the prices of labour-intensive goods and services which do not enter international trade tend to be lower in poor than in rich countries.

Accordingly, it is better to estimate GNP per capita in PPP dollars, which have the same purchasing power over domestic GNP as US dollars have over US GNP. The average ratio of GNP at PPP rates to GNP at currency exchange rates is 4·7 to 1 in low-income developing countries, 3·1 to 1 in middle-income developing countries, and 1·05 to 1 in the industrial countries. Thus, at currency exchange rates, the ratio of GNP per capita in high-income countries to that in developing countries was 22 to 1 whereas, in PPP dollars, it was 7 to 1. World disparities in living standards are indeed vast, but they are not as vast as the use of currency exchange rates would imply.

Population Growth.

Many developing countries are experiencing an unprecedented population explosion: annual rates of increase of between 2 and 3 per cent—which double population in as little as 35 and 24 years respectively—are experienced. This is a phenomenon of the last five decades. Death rates have fallen sharply in response to improved health services and modern methods of control, *e.g.*, immunization programmes and the eradication of malaria through DDT spraying. On the other hand, birth rates have been kept up by such factors as the tradition, social prestige, religion, and a lack of facilities for family planning.

The table below indicates that over half the world's population lives in Asia, and that the developed regions account for under a quarter of the total. The developed countries show slower rates of population growth than Africa, Latin America and Asia. The figures of population density may easily be misleading, since they take no account of the nature of the area, *e.g.*, deserts are included. But it is clear that Asia is more densely populated than Africa or Latin America. The low population density of Europe as a whole conceals the high figure (166) for western Europe.

POPULATION SIZE, GROWTH AND DENSITY BY REGION

	Population 2001 (m)	Growth rate 2000–05 (% p.a.)	Density 2001 (per sq km)
North America	319	1·0	15
Europe	728	−0·1	33
Oceania	31	1·2	4
Africa	814	2·2	27
Latin America	528	1·4	26
Asia	3,728	1·3	117
of which:			
India	1,027	1·6	310
China	1,272	1·0	136
World Total	6,148	1·2	45

Life Expectancy.

Although death rates have fallen in the developing countries, especially infant mortality, life expectancy is generally low in the poorest countries. Thus, for instance, the expectation of life at birth in 2000 was below 50 years in many countries of Africa, including Botswana, Zimbabwe, Kenya, Malawi, Ethiopia, South Africa and Sierra Leone, and some in Asia, including Afghanistan. Life in these countries is all too short.

Life expectancy is related to income per head. In most of the developed countries life expectancy at birth is about 77 years, being 77 in the United States, 78 in the United Kingdom and Germany, and 82 in Japan in 2000. However, the average length of life depends also on the quantity and quality of medical provision and the degree of income inequality about the mean: life expectancy reached

70 years in some of the poorest countries, including China, Malaysia and Sri Lanka. Life expectancy is an important indicator of the "quality of life".

The Population Problem.

In many developing countries there is population pressure on the land, and many people want more land for farming. Population density is a hindrance in agricultural economies, but not necessarily in industrial economies: because it is industrialised and has accumulated much capital, Western Europe can support at a high standard of living a population more concentrated even than that of Asia.

As a result of rapid population growth the pressure of population on the land has increased. The consequences have been far more serious in countries such as Bangladesh (with a population density of 954 people per square kilometre in 2000) or India (305 per sq km) than in Zambia (14 per sq km) or Brazil (20 per sq km). In those countries with abundant land the expanding population can spread into unused areas; but as land becomes increasingly scarce, increasingly unproductive land must be brought into cultivation and soil erosion and loss of fertility become major problems. A substantial increase in output is required to prevent a fall in per capita income as population grows, and an even greater increase is required if living standards are to be improved.

Taking all developing countries as a group, per capita food production rose by 1·6 per cent per annum in the 1980s and 2·4 per cent per annum in the 1990s. However, for the group of 50 least developed countries the corresponding figures were −0·7 and 0·3 per cent respectively.

Even in those countries with plenty of land a rapid increase in population can have harmful effects. For instance, it diverts scarce investment resources away from directly productive investments such as factories and irrigation projects so as to meet the needs of the expanding population for more schools, hospitals, housing, cities and other public services.

Family Planning Programmes.

In many African and the poorer Latin American countries the rate of population growth appears to be constant, but in the more developed parts of Latin America and much of Asia there are signs that the growth rate has peaked and is now declining. The annual rate of growth of population in the 1990s averaged 2·0 per cent in the low-income developing countries and 1·2 per cent in the middle-income developing countries; it was as high as 2·6 per cent in sub-Saharan Africa.

The different experiences may reflect differences in government policies: in 1980 a quarter of less developed countries had no official family planning programme. The success stories include India, where in the late 1990s, 48 per cent of married women used contraceptives and the female fertility rate fell from 5·0 to 3·2 between 1980 and 1998, China (84 per cent contraceptive use and a fall from 2·5 to 1·9 per cent), Brazil (77 per cent use and a fall from 3·9 to 2·3 per cent), and South Africa (56 per cent use and a fall from 4·6 to 2·8).

The successful cases show what can be done, but private incentives and attitudes still favour large families in many poor societies: simply providing facilities for family planning may not be enough. In Pakistan, for instance, contraceptive use was 28 per cent and the fertility rate was still as high as 4·9 in 1998. In Ethiopia, use was only 8 per cent and the fertility rate (6·4 per cent) had not fallen over the 18-year period.

Problems of Agriculture.

There are many millions of peasant farmers throughout the developing world eking out a subsistence from the soil. The margin between what can be produced and what is required to support life is narrow: the failure of crops because of drought, floods or pests can lead to famine unless food is quickly supplied from outside the area affected.

Agricultural production may be held back by a shortage of land, or by the use of primitive tools and methods of cultivation (which may in turn be due to a lack of farming knowledge and skills or to a lack of funds for investment in land improvement or equipment), or by an unjust system of land tenure which deprives the farmer of in-

centive to raise production. Perhaps all these problems must be tackled simultaneously.

The Green Revolution.

A technology has been developed which can increase the yields from foodgrains by 50 per cent or more in tropical areas. This technology is commonly thought to have caused a *green revolution*. It consists of high-yielding seeds, largely for wheat and rice. Not only are the yields per acre higher but also shorter cropping cycles permit multiple cropping. The new technology economises on land and, being labour-intensive, provides more farm employment. The introduction of high-yielding cereals is important in the emergence of India and Pakistan into the ranks of solid economic achievers.

However, we cannot assume that it is going to solve the problem of foodgrain shortage in the poorer countries. To be effective, some of the new seeds require substantial inputs of fertiliser and of water; in many areas expensive irrigation is important to their success. Moreover, the fact that fertiliser and water are complementary inputs has meant that the green revolution has caught on—and been encouraged by governments—among the larger, more prosperous farmers in the better-watered, more prosperous regions. Unless governments ensure that the benefits of the green revolution are widely spread, the net effect might even be to harm small peasant farmers by increasing the competition from large farmers.

Land Reform.

There are many forms of land tenure in less developed countries. In black Africa communal or tribal ownership of land is common, with members of the community or tribe receiving rights to use the land individually. In parts of Asia and Latin America, there is private ownership of land, which—particularly where the land is densely populated—has often led to great inequality of land ownership. In some cases land tenure is characterised by absentee landlords and sharecropping tenants. The development of large estates produces a class of landless labourers.

The need for land reform varies according to the circumstances. In most cases the main argument is for greater social justice. In some cases it may be possible also to expand production by redistributing land more evenly or by giving land to share-cropping tenants and so improving their incentives. On the other hand, large farmers may have access to technology, skills and capital which small farmers lack: there is a danger that greater equity will be achieved only at the expense of efficiency. Hence the need to ensure that land reform is accompanied by a package of measures, *e.g.*, education, training and advice, and credit for fertiliser, tools and land improvements.

Few governments have succeeded in implementing serious land reform programmes. The main reason is that the system of land tenure in a country often reflects the balance of political power: land reform invariably faces political opposition from entrenched interests. By the same token, a successful land reform may alter the balance of political power so as to facilitate broad-based development.

Exports of Primary Products.

Many developing countries export primary products (foodstuffs, industrial raw materials or minerals) and import manufactured goods, especially the capital goods (plant, machinery and vehicles) required for development. This international division of labour has operated to the disadvantage of the developing countries in recent decades. The world demand for their primary products has increased only slowly. This is because people spend just a small part of their additional income on food (*e.g.*, tea, coffee, chocolate), because synthetic substitutes have been developed for many raw materials (*e.g.*, rubber, cotton, jute), because developed countries protect their own agriculture (*e.g.*, sugar) and because demand in the developed countries has moved towards commodities with low raw material content (*e.g.*, from heavy industries to services).

In consequence, the general trend has been for the prices of primary products to fall in relation to those of manufactured goods. Oil is a special case (see **F52**). The terms of trade of the developing countries worsened by 2·3 per cent per annum over the 1980s and by 0·8 per cent per annum over the 1990s (see **F6**). Unsatisfactory prices of primary commodities have contributed to the shortage of foreign exchange which restricts investment expenditure in many poor countries.

Economic Instability.

The prices of various primary products tend to fluctuate violently from one year to another. Many developing economies depend heavily on the exports of one or two commodities. For instance, copper is the most important export product in Chile, cotton in Egypt, copper in Zambia, sugar in Cuba, cocoa in Ghana, tin in Bolivia and diamonds in Botswana. Fluctuations in the world price of its main export cause instability in the export revenues of a country, and this in turn can produce fluctuations in income throughout its domestic economy.

Even the oil-producing developing countries, whose problems are in many ways quite different, have faced problems of economic instability. The governments of these countries have had to decide how best to use their oil revenues to promote economic and social development without overturning their societies. The political events in Iran during the 1980s were closely related to the economic boom which oil produced.

Problems of Industrialisation.

In those developing economies where there is population pressure on the land, alternative employment has to be created in industry or services. Even in countries with a surplus of land, if there is heavy dependence on one or two primary products, industrialisation provides a means of diversifying the economy.

But industrialisation is not an easy course. Because the margin between agricultural production and food consumption is narrow, the surplus from the agricultural sector exchangeable for the products of other sectors *e.g.*, industry and services—is small; *i.e.*, the demand for the goods and services produced by other sectors is low. A second constraint on industrialisation is imposed by competition from abroad; new industries in an unindustrialised country have to compete with established industries in industrial countries, which have the advantage of experience, a trained labour force and markets big enough for them to reap all the potential economies of large-scale production.

Industrialisation Strategies.

One means of overcoming the small size of market is to export manufactures to the developed countries. Developing countries with cheap labour are likely to have a comparative advantage in the manufacture of relatively labour-intensive commodities. A number of less developed countries have had remarkable success in following this strategy. Among their successful activities are textiles, clothing and labour-intensive components of electronic equipment.

A means of overcoming competition from the industries of the developed countries is by nurturing an infant industrial sector behind tariff walls—which is how the United States and Germany developed their industries in the face of British competition in the nineteenth century. A number of developing countries have adopted this strategy. However, it has its drawbacks. Sometimes the "infants" never grow up, and vested interests press for continued protection. Import-substituted industrialisation often means that raw materials or semi-processed goods are imported for local processing. There is a danger that fluctuations in export proceeds will periodically curtail imports of necessary intermediate goods. The under-utilisation of capital in the manufacturing sector because of foreign exchange shortages has frequently occurred in countries such as Pakistan, Tanzania and Ghana.

The Newly Industrialising Countries.

The remarkable success of a handful of developing countries—the *newly industrialising countries* (NICs)—in exporting manufactured goods raises the questions: why were they successful, and can others do the same?

The most successful NICs—known as the "Asian Tigers"—are Hong Kong, South Korea, Taiwan and Singapore. As a group they exported manufactures equal to 10 per cent of world exports of manufactures in 2000.

Example of South Korea.

South Korea is perhaps the most successful of the NICs. After a period in which government pursued a policy of industrialisation through import substitution, the policy was changed in the 1960s to one of promoting exports of labour-intensive manufactures. This was achieved by devaluing the currency in order to encourage export industries in which the country would have a comparative advantage, and liberalising imports to discourage inefficient industrial production. In 1962 South Korea exported manufactures worth $10 million; in 1990 their value was $64,000 million and in 2000 $150,000 million. Between 1962 and 1990 the proportion of the labour force employed in industry rose from 10 to 30 per cent, manufacturing production rose by 17 per cent per annum, and GNP per capita rose by 7 per cent per annum. The labour-intensive nature of industrialisation, as well as its speed, helped to alleviate poverty through the market: first employment and later, as labour became scarce, also real wages rose rapidly.

South Korea benefited from its trading relationships with Japan and its close ties with the United States in finding markets for its products. It has a well educated labour force: 91 per cent of the relevant age group in 2000 were enrolled in secondary school, which was higher than any other developing country. Industrialisation may also have benefited from stable autocratic government and a beleaguered sense of national purpose. In part the initial Korean success represents the harnessing of cheap labour in almost free trade conditions for exporters. However, the government also played an active role, *e.g.* it both generated high savings and successfully directed savings into the favoured sectors. It will take much more than policies of *laissez faire* for other developing countries to be able to emulate South Korea.

Outward-Oriented Industrialisation Policies.

The success of the NICs has led many policy advisers to press for more outward-oriented industrialisation policies. The policy advice is gradually to dismantle the system of protection of import-substituting industries and to devalue the currency in order to provide incentives to export manufactures. It is argued that competition in world markets will act as a spur to domestic efficiency and help to divorce economic activities from domestic political processes.

The traditional view has been that few developing countries could succeed in breaking into world markets for manufactures. However, potential access to the markets of industrialised countries is far better than it used to be, and broadly-based progress has been made. In 1970 manufactures accounted for 27 per cent of the exports of the developing countries, but in 2000 for 62 per cent. If the NICs constitute the "first division", a "second division" of countries has expanded manufacturing exports rapidly, including India, China, Pakistan, Thailand, Turkey, Malaysia, Colombia, Brazil and Mexico. In 1998 manufacturing accounted for 52 per cent of the exports of low income developing countries (dominated by China and India), and for 71 per cent of the total in the case of the middle-income developing countries.

Unemployment and Underemployment.

Unemployment and underemployment occur on a very considerable scale in both the rural and the urban areas of developing countries. Consider first the rural case. Because farm work is normally shared, underemployment—disguised unemployment—is more common than open unemployment. People work for only a part of the day or year. Where land is scarce, underemployment is chronic: people would like to work more if only they had more land. Unless the yield from the land can be raised, growth in population causes greater underemployment and reduces income per head on the

F42

land. Where land is abundant, underemployment is a seasonal phenomenon. People are fully employed in the busy season—harvesting and planting—but underemployed at other times of the year.

Urban Unemployment.

In the towns open unemployment is common with people queueing for *formal sector* jobs at the job centres and at the factory gates. Rates of urban open unemployment well in excess of 10 per cent are often recorded, *e.g.*, in Ethiopia, Colombia, Zimbabwe, Trinidad, West Bank and Gaza, South Africa and Sri Lanka. Few developing countries can afford unemployment benefits, so that job-seekers remain openly unemployed only until their savings are used up or support by their relations is withdrawn. Then they have to scrape out a subsistence in the urban *informal sector* while waiting and hoping for something better. Underemployment is rife in the easily entered traditional sector activities such as petty trading, hawking, beer brewing, fetching and carrying. A shoe-shiner may be on the streets for ten hours a day but have only a couple of customers. The more people enter these activities, the further average income per worker is depressed. In many less developed countries this self-employment in the informal sector accounts for the majority of urban workers.

Migration to the Cities.

Urbanisation is proceeding at an unprecedented pace in much of the developing world. Over the 21 years 1980–2001 the total urban population of the developing countries as a whole grew by 90 per cent, *i.e.* by more than one billion people. The table illustrates the pace of urbanisation in a number of developing countries.

URBAN POPULATION AS A PERCENTAGE
OF TOTAL POPULATION IN SELECTED
DEVELOPING COUNTRIES, 1980 AND 2001

	1980	2001
Developing countries	32	42
of which: Ethiopia	10	16
Nepal	7	12
Uganda	9	15
Kenya	16	34
Nigeria	27	45
India	23	28
China	20	37
Zimbabwe	22	36
Argentina	83	88
Turkey	44	66
Philippines	35	59
Malaysia	42	58
Colombia	73	75
Brazil	67	82
South Africa	48	58
High-income countries	73	78
of which: United Kingdom	89	90
Australia	86	91

Rural people are often drawn to the cities at a rate well in excess of the capacity of the cities to absorb them productively. The reason for this migration might be economic or social. The economic explanation runs in terms of an income differential between the urban and the rural areas. Relatively unskilled wages in the formal sector of the economy—often governed by minimum wage legislation or trade union bargaining—can be well above the incomes to be derived from peasant agriculture. People go to the town in search of formal sector wage jobs, although they may actually end up under- employed in the low-income informal sector. Rural–urban migration may be a social phenomenon: rural people are attracted by the facilities and "bright lights" of the cities. The recent expansion of education in many countries may also play a part, since a high proportion of the migrants are school leavers.

Whatever the reasons, the consequences are socially harmful and politically explosive. Shanty towns and slums proliferate in the cities and their outskirts; poverty, disease and crime flourish.

In 1950 there were only two urban agglomerations in the world with more than 10 million inhabitants, New York and London. In the year 2000

there were some 25 such cities, of which 20 were in the developing world and the largest was Mexico City with a population approaching 30 million.

Employment Creation.

In many developing countries, the objective of creating productive employment has received growing priority. For various reasons the growth of formal sector employment has been tardy and has lagged behind the growth of output. One reason is that the formal sector normally uses capital equipment and technology which is imported from the developed countries. This means that, even in countries with cheap and abundant labour, the most profitable techniques of production are often capital-intensive, so that the amount of scarce investment funds required to equip a worker is high. There is some danger that the establishment of capital-intensive factories may actually harm existing labour-intensive production. For instance, sandals can be made by small cobblers using local leather (or old car tyres) or by a large plant using imported plastic materials: a new factory employing a few machine operators might displace many more traditional craftsmen who have no alternative employment opportunities.

Governments, by encouraging or discouraging particular forms and areas of investment, have the power to influence the growth of employment. In the rural areas the encouragement and organisation of labour-intensive developmental or community projects can assist in harnessing the one abundant resource which almost all developing countries possess: unskilled labour.

Human Capital.

Many developing countries are faced with the dual problem of unskilled labour surpluses and scarcities of skilled and educated labour. The problem has been very acute in some of the previously colonised countries of Africa. To give an extreme example: at the time of its independence in 1964, Zambia had only 100 Zambian university graduates and 1,200 secondary school graduates in a population of 3·5 million. In such countries the great shortage of educated and skilled people enabled them to earn high incomes— with the result that there was a very unequal distribution of income. And even in countries where surpluses have developed, the existence of an international market for professional people such as doctors and engineers helps to keep up their earnings: these countries suffer from a "brain drain" to the developed world.

Economic development is not just a matter of physical capital accumulation: it requires also an increase in *human capital*, *i.e.* in skilled and educated labour. Not only more knowledge but also new habits and attitudes—*e.g.*, attitudes towards risk-taking, hard work and thrift. Education—of the right sort and with suitable content—is generally acknowledged to be important for development, although the benefits of education cannot be quantified at all precisely.

Educational Policy.

The table (**F43**) shows enrolment ratios (the percentage of children in the relevant age-group enrolled in education) at the primary and secondary educational levels for selected developing countries in 2001. There is a strong tendency for enrolment ratios to increase with the income per head of a country. Educational provision remains extremely low in most of the least developed countries, particularly beyond the primary level. On the other hand, there are developing countries whose problem is now surplus rather than shortage of educated labour. Such cases are common in Asia, *e.g.* India and the Philippines.

As the table shows, by no means all countries had achieved universal primary education by 2001. In some countries this was due to financial costs and constraints, and in others to lack of parental demand, especially in the case of female education.

Economists are able to estimate the *private rate of return to education*, *i.e.* the benefit accruing to the individual in the form of additional income over the working life, expressed as a percentage return on the individual's "investment" in education. In many developing countries the returns to investment in human capital are higher than the returns to investment in physical capital. In the past the returns were highest at the primary educational level; increasingly they are now highest at the (often subsidised) tertiary level.

Enrolment ratios increased rapidly in most countries between 1980 and 2000. The high financial returns accruing to the educated have generated powerful pressures for the expansion of state education, to which governments have often acceded.

Economists have attempted to estimate not only the *private* but also the *social* rate of return to education, *i.e.* the benefit accruing to society as a whole from the devotion of resources to education. In many countries, and at various educational levels, the social return is high enough to justify educational expansion. Much of the recent success of the East Asian NICs has been attributed to their early investment in the quantity and quality of education.

In other countries the social rate of return is now very low. Some governments have found that it is easier to expand an educational system than it is to expand an economy, and shortages have given way to surpluses. The response to surplus may take various forms: unemployment of the educated, or displacement of the less educated from their jobs, so pushing the unemployment down the educational ladder, or pressures on government to create unnecessary jobs for the educated in the public service. In this last case—previously true of Egypt, for example—scarce resources are doubly wasted.

Economic Aid.

The main industrial countries—organised as a 21-member *Development Assistance Committee* (DAC)—have provided economic aid to the developing countries. The total net flow of economic assistance to the developing countries was $220 billion in 2001. Roughly $150 billion of this was net private investment and $70 billion official aid from governments. Over one sixth each of the net *official development assistance* (ODA) was contributed by Japan and the United States; the other principal donors were Germany, Britain, France and the Netherlands, in that order. Net private investment is volatile and cannot be relied upon. The provisional figure for 2003 is only $130 million.

EDUCATIONAL ENROLMENT RATIOS AND
ADULT LITERACY RATE IN DEVELOPING
COUNTRIES, 2001

	Age-group enrolment ratio (%)		Adult literacy rate (%)
	Primary	Secondary	
All developing countries	82	60	75
Least developed countries	60	31	53
Niger	30	5	17
Mozambique	54	9	45
Tanzania	47	5	76
Ethiopia	47	13	40
Bangladesh	89	43	41
Ghana	58	31	73
Egypt	93	79	56
South Africa	89	57	86
Vietnam	95	62	93
Brazil	97	71	87
Malaysia	94	88	88
Trinidad and Tobago	92	71	98
Philippines	93	53	95
South Korea	99	91	98

The DAC nations have accepted three aid targets. One is that the net flow of private and official resources combined should exceed 1 per cent of each country's gross national product. In 2002, only 4 out of 22 countries achieved this percentage, including Britain. The second target is that net ODA should exceed 0·7 per cent of GNP; 5 countries managed this in 2002. The third target, more generally achieved, concerns the "grant element"—the extent to which ODA contains an element of grant as opposed to commercial loans.

The flow of resources from the DAC countries to the developing countries grew in real terms and,

expressed as a proportion of GNP, it rose from 0·55 per cent in 1988 to a peak of 1·81 per cent in 1998 but then fell to 1·35 per cent in 2002: private capital is volatile and unreliable. Net ODA fell, from 0·33 to 0·23 per cent, over the years.

Forms of Aid.

Aid to the developing countries takes many forms, it serves many purposes and it is given for many reasons. Less developed countries need aid to provide finance for development projects; to provide foreign exchange with which imports for development purposes can be bought; and to provide the trained manpower and technical knowledge they lack. The motives of the donor are not always humanitarian. "Aid" can take a military form; it can be used to prop up an incompetent or unjust government, or to buy political support. Nor is aid always beneficial to the recipient country. It may be wasted on ill-conceived or prestige projects, or cause the government simply to relax its own efforts. Concern over donors' motives and instances of waste have led some people to react against aid-giving. However, the correct remedy is not to cut off aid but rather to prevent its misuse.

Financial aid is not always enough. Many developing countries need technical assistance in planning their development, to ensure that development possibilities are exploited and that scarce resources are used to best advantage. Hence the many schemes for providing experts by individual countries and by the technical agencies of the United Nations, such as the Food and Agriculture Organisation (FAO), the World Health Organisation (WHO), the International Labour Organisation (ILO), the United Nations Educational, Scientific and Cultural Organisation (UNESCO), and so on. Hence also the schemes for educating and training people from the developing countries.

Foreign Direct Investment.

One possible form of assistance is *Foreign Direct Investment (FDI)* by firms from developed countries. These investments—setting up branch factories, for example—are concentrated in those projects which appear profitable to the investor. However, it has been questioned whether private investment constitutes aid to less developed countries. Its opponents argue that the benefits can be weak: foreign-owned firms repatriate high profits and avoid tax by means of royalty payments to the parent company or unrealistic pricing of their transactions with the parent company; and these firms deter local enterprise. Supporters of foreign investment point to the high political risks which necessitate high profits in order to attract investors to developing countries, and question whether resources are available for any alternative path to development. A form of compromise which has become common in developing countries is a partnership arrangement between multinational companies and government or private firms in the host country.

FDI has increased greatly in recent years: it is a sign of the *globalisation* of diverse economies. In 1980 their capital stock representing past FDI inflows amounted to 10 per cent of the GDP of the developing economies; in 2000 it was 30 per cent. In 2001 the developing countries attracted $205 billion of FDI inflows, 28 per cent of the total world inflow. The largest recipient was China, with $47 billion; the 50 "least developed countries" attracted only $4 billion. The inflow into developing countries reached $233 billion in 2004.

British Aid.

In 2002 Britain's total ODA was £3,282 million, equal to £52 per head of population and 0·31 per cent of the GNP. Government aid may be divided into multilateral and bilateral aid. Multilateral aid (a third of the total) is given through the medium of the international development institutions: bilateral aid is given directly to the developing countries. Almost all British ODA takes the form of grants, and the rest is loans.

Aid takes the form not only of financial but also of technical assistance. Government expenditure on technical assistance amounts to 60 per cent of bilateral aid. 45 per cent of British ODA went to the 50 poorest countries of the world in 1999–00, and 44 per cent to sub-Saharan Africa. The countries receiving most UK aid in 1999–00 were India, Uganda, Bangladesh, Tanzania, China and Ghana. However, it is the micro-states which often fare best in per capita terms.

All British official aid is channelled and co-ordinated by the *Department for International Development* (DFID). In addition there are various private associations concerned with promoting development, such as Oxfam, Save the Children and Voluntary Service Overseas. £195 million was chan-nelled by DFID through these *non-governmental organisations* (NGOs) in 1999–00.

The World Bank.

The International Bank for Reconstruction and Development (IBRD), known as the *World Bank*, is an agency of the United Nations established in 1945. It has the primary function of making funds available to assist developing countries. Member nations agreed to subscribe quotas—fixed in much the same way as the quotas for the IMF—to the Bank. In fact, the major part of the Bank's resources are borrowed—on the security of the quo-tas—in financial centres.

Loans are made to finance specific projects and the Bank will normally make a loan only if it is satis-fied that the investment will yield a revenue suf-ficient to enable the payment of interest on the loan, and the repayment of the sum lent. It is clear that some projects of great benefit cannot be financed in this way, because they would not yield returns quickly or large enough to meet the Bank's require-ments for interest and repayment. Accordingly, its offshoot, the *International Development Association* has the power to make loans at low rates of interest and with more generous repayment conditions.

Trade Reform: The Birth of GATT.

An important development in recent decades that has benefited the world economy in general and the developing economies in particular, is the negoti-ated move towards greater freedom of trade. In 1947, when the *General Agreement on Tariffs and Trade* (GATT) was born, average tariff levels were 38 per cent. In 1962, they stood at 17 per cent. In seven successive rounds of trade negotiations— the most important of which were the Tokyo Round and the Uruguay Round—by 1995 tariffs were down to only 4 per cent on average.

The World Trade Organisation.

The *World Trade Organisation* (WTO) is the inter-national body, based in Geneva, that arranges and promotes trade among countries. It was established in 1995, as a successor to the GATT. It administers multilateral trade agreements, acts as a forum for trade negotiations, and seeks to resolve trade dis-putes. It promotes trade without discrimination—the only notable exception being free trade areas and customs unions. It is as much concerned with trade in services and in ideas (intellectual property) as with trade in goods.

The three most sensitive trade issues facing the WTO are agriculture, textiles and clothing, and dumping. In the case of agricultural products, which are subject to heavy *non-tariff barriers* (NTBs), quotas were converted into equivalent tariffs, which would in turn be reduced over six years of imple-menting the Uruguay Round.

The Doha Round.

At the 2001 Doha conference, the WTO members agreed to launch the Doha Development Agenda. This would include multilateral negotiations to reduce trade-distorting policies and to safeguard the interests of poor countries: some poor countries might lose from global trade reforms. Progress after 2001 was slow because of the conflicting interests. OECD countries' protection of agriculture through tariffs, non-tariff barriers, and subsidies is a key issue. The negotiations, still ongoing in 2006, should be judged by their ability to offer developing country farmers better access to the markets of developed countries.

End of the Multifibre Arrangement.

The Multifibre Arrangement was a longstand-ing method of protecting industrial countries against the textile and clothing exports of develop-ing countries by means of NTBs. Being labour-intensive and low-tech, this industry is particularly vulnerable to competition based on low wages. The quotas expired at the start of 2005.

Immediately Chinese exports rocketed dramati-cally; and Indian producers could be expected to respond as well. Producers in the developed coun-tries, such as the US and the EU, were undercut and factory closures loomed. Their remaining advantages—faster responses to orders and high quality products—offered much smaller markets. However, not only the developed countries were affected. Some of the smaller developing countries, such as Lesotho, Kenya and Sri Lanka, whose exports had been protected by the quota system, also faced tougher competition.

Inequality Within Countries.

In some less developed countries economic growth has been achieved without any apparent improve-ment in the lot of the masses. The majority of the people are engaged in agriculture in the rural areas, whereas much of the development has taken place in industry and services in the urban areas. A minority of people have benefited—industrialists, bureaucrats, educated and skilled workers, organ-ised labour in the modern sector of the economy—but the poor living in the urban slums, often in open or disguised unemployment, and the enormous numbers in the rural areas have been little affected by development. In many countries the fruits of development have not been widely spread. It is a common criticism that development policies have been biased towards industry and towards the cities, and that rural people in agriculture have been neglected. This outcome may be a reflection of the uneven distribution of political power within a developing country.

The growth of GNP per capita as a goal of development has been questioned. Governments have shown increasing concern for poverty, employ-ment creation and social equity. Many donors, including DFID, have modified their aid policies to try to reach the poor.

Poverty.

This growing concern with poverty has led to the collection of representative data on household income and expenditure levels. Some governments set national poverty lines to assist policy-making, and international agencies have introduced common standards, such as $1 per day per capita measured in *purchasing power parity* (see **F39**). Of the 70 de-veloping countries for which this measure is avail-able, 12 have more than half their population below that poverty line. These are Burkino Faso, the Central African Republic, Chad, Gambia, Nicaragua, Ethiopia, Uganda, Mali, Niger, Nigeria, Sierra Leone and Zambia. Poor but relatively egali-tarian countries like China and Sri Lanka have low figures, and some highly unequal societies, such as Mexico and South Africa have more poverty than their middle-income developing country status warrants.

Progress in World Poverty Alleviation.

Accepting the poverty standard of $1 a day, has recent progress been made in reducing world poverty? Comparisons can be drawn between 1990 and 2001 from the table below.

In the world as a whole, the number of people in extreme poverty fell by 130 million, and the propor-tion fell from 28 to 21 per cent. However, this

PEOPLE LIVING ON LESS THAN $1 A DAY,
ABSOLUTE NUMBER AND PERCENTAGE,
1990 AND 2001

	Million		Per cent	
	1990	2001	1990	2001
World	1,218	1,089	27·9	21·1
of which East Asia	472	271	29·6	14·9
South Asia	462	431	41·3	31·3
Latin America	49	50	11·3	9·5
Africa	227	313	44·6	46·3

progress is entirely due to the remarkable rate of economic growth in China (*see* **F45–6**). Here poverty was cut from 375 to 212 million. Elsewhere in the world the absolute number of poor rose by 33 million. The incidence of extreme poverty fell by 201 million in East Asia and by 31 million in South Asia but rose by 86 million in sub-Saharan Africa. By 2001, 46 per cent of African people were poor by this criterion. Despite the overall progress, in 2001 no less than 1,089 million people—the world's bottom billion—remained in abject poverty.

Basic Needs.

A direction in which international thinking has moved is towards the acceptance of a *Basic Needs* strategy of development. Essentially the aim is to alleviate absolute poverty, *i.e.*, to meet minimum standards of food, shelter, clothing and safe drinking water, and to satisfy certain other basic human needs. It is proposed that these standards be reached not so much by means of welfare transfers as by enabling the poor to help themselves through productive employment. The minimum standards are inevitably subjective, there are economic and political obstacles to the fulfilment of basic needs, and the approach does not translate easily into specific policies. Nevertheless, the basic needs strategy has an impact on the priorities both of aid agencies and of recipient governments.

Human Development.

There is a growing emphasis in developing countries and in the donor community on *human development, i.e.* the notion that development of peoples' *capabilities* to improve and control their lives is an important end in itself. For instance, in addition to helping people to raise their incomes, being better informed, in better health and having a greater say in local affairs are regarded as good in themselves. This has led to greater emphasis on basic health and basic education services, as ways of improving peoples' lives.

There are indicators of the quality of life other than income. One is the prevalence of child nutrition. Of the 90 reporting developing countries in 2001, 13 had more than 40 per cent of their children under five who were malnourished: Afghanistan, Bangladesh, Cambodia, Eritrea, Ethiopia, India, Laos, Mali, Nepal, Niger, North Korea, Tajikistan and Yemen.

Another indicator is the mortality rate of children under five. In 2001 it exceeded 20 per cent (one in five) in Afghanistan, Angola, Chad, Democratic Republic of Congo, Liberia, Mali, Niger, Sierra Leone, Somalia and Zambia.

The UN Human Development Index.

The United Nations has developed and published a *human development index* (HDI) which goes beyond income to include also life expectancy and educational enrolments. The ranking of some countries on the HDI differs considerably from their income ranking: some governments are more concerned with the broad notion of human development than others.

In 2002 Norway, Sweden, Australia and Canada, in descending order, had the highest value of the Human Development Index, with the US in eighth and the UK in twelfth place. At the other end of the scale was a series of African countries, with Niger and Sierra Leone at the bottom. The developing countries whose HDI most exceeded their GDP per capita were Costa Rica, Cuba, Jamaica, Sri Lanka, and some of the former communist countries of Eastern Europe.

Many traditional, poor societies display a high degree of *gender bias*. Women occupy subservient positions in society and in the family. This is often apparent from the unequal distribution of resources within the household, for instance greater spending on the health and education of boys than of girls. Take health: as a result of excess female mortality, 7 per cent of girls under 5 are "missing" in China, and 4 per cent in India. In Africa, male adult illiteracy is 35 per cent but the female figure is 54 per cent; the difference is even larger in South Asia. The modernisation of an economy generally reduces gender discrimination but governments can accelerate the process, for instance by ensuring gender equality before the law or by subsidising girls' schooling.

The Causes of Famine.

In the last couple of decades food production in many of the poorest countries has done little more than keep pace with the growth of population. Several have become net food importers, and this trend is likely to continue.

Famine is by no means always simply the result of a fall in food production which affects all people in the area uniformly. In the 1974 Bangladesh famine and the terrible Ethiopian famines, those who suffered most were respectively the landless, who normally exchange labour for food, and pastoralists, who normally exchange cattle for food grains. The landless, losing their source of earnings because farmers no longer hired labourers, and pastoralists, seeing the prices of their emaciated beasts fall as more and more were marketed, could no longer buy food: these were the people who starved.

Inequality Among Countries.

Not all less developed countries have fared equally well in recent years. In particular there appears to be a tendency for disparities among less developed countries to widen. The countries which have performed well tend to be semi-industrialised and able to respond to opportunities for exporting manufactures to the developed countries, or to be well endowed with mineral or oil resources. Growth success stories include Chile, Botswana, Thailand, China, South Korea, Taiwan, Malaysia, Vietnam and Singapore. Some of these are on the way to becoming self-reliant economically: they are known as the *newly industrialising countries* (NICs).

The poorest countries—50 of which were designated the *least less developed countries* (LLDC's)—are experiencing the greatest difficulty in escaping from the vicious circle of poverty. A growing recognition of their problem has led the DAC countries to reallocate aid in favour of the least developed countries, and to offer aid on more concessionary terms to these countries.

The East Asian Economic Miracle?

East Asia has a record of high and sustained economic growth over the last quarter-century. Much of this is due to the performance of Japan, the "Gang of Four" (Hong Kong, Korea, Singapore and Taiwan) and a few other successful "Tiger" economies, including, Malaysia and Thailand. What are the reasons for their success? What can other countries learn from their experience?

Most of them share a number of characteristics which point to the explanation. First, most have extremely high ratios of investment in physical capital to GDP, assisted by high saving rates. Rapid capital accumulation, then, is a necessary condition for rapid economic growth, but it may not be a sufficient condition. It, too, needs to be explained. A second common feature was rapid accumulation of human capital: educational participation rates were high even in the 1960s, and subsequently rose. Economic growth was probably also assisted by a decline in population growth rates. Fourth, these countries have created a business-friendly environment, and have generally sought foreign technology and investment.

A fifth general feature was good economic management, which tended to be in the hands of bureaucrats, insulated from political influence and interest groups. It would be wrong to claim that these are free market economies: in several, government interventions to accelerate the pace of development have been pervasive. In particular, they have promoted exports in various ways: they have all adopted outward-orientated industrialisation policies.

Successful Economic Reform in China.

China is another country in East Asia that has performed remarkably well in recent years. The average annual growth rate of real income per capita in China over the period 1985–2003 was no less than 8 per cent. The reasons for its success are rather different from those for other East Asian countries. In 1976, when Mao died, it was a communist country with central planning and in which politics, rather than economics, was in command. Today it is in many respects a market economy in which the role of the state, previously all-pervasive, is rapidly diminishing. The economic reforms in China proceeded steadily in a way which brought greater prosperity to almost everyone. The successful reforms in China are to be contrasted with Eastern Europe and the old USSR.

Reforming Chinese Agriculture.

In 2003 China contained no fewer than 1,300 million people, of whom 770 million (59 per cent) live in rural areas. The economic reforms began in the rural areas. Under Mao agriculture was collectivised and the peasants lacked incentives: farm production stagnated. The new leadership permitted the peasants to disband their communes and restore household production on family farms. Farm production grew by 8 per cent per annum between 1978 and 1984, as peasants responded to new opportunities and higher prices for their products.

There was a second transformation of the Chinese countryside: the growth of rural industry, owned collectively by villages or privately. By 2003 rural industry employed 150 million people. It contributed greatly to the absorption of surplus labour on the land.

Reforming Urban China.

The urban reforms began in 1984. Although it had grown rapidly, industry—mainly state-owned—in urban China was inefficient. Enterprises had no autonomy within the centralised planning system. Prices and production were determined by the state, all output was sold to the state and all profits handed over to the state. The reforms took the form of decentralising decisions and introducing market sales and market prices alongside the state plan: gradually the market came to dominate the plan, and far more consumer goods were produced as the market for them expanded. By 2003, 89 per cent of urban households had a refrigerator, 94 per cent a washing machine, and there were 130 colour television sets per 100 households. Assisted by foreign investment and technology and by low labour costs, both rural and urban industry were increasingly able to export manufactures to the developed economies.

Chinese Economic Progress.

The remarkable rate of economic growth has reduced poverty substantially. In 1990 70 per cent of the Chinese population were estimated to be under the poverty line of $2 a day. In 2003 the estimate was 37 per cent. Over the same period, those under the very low poverty line of $1 a day fell from 32 to 13 per cent.

How has China managed to achieve such a high growth rate? Its success is partly due to the smooth transition from socialist planning to a market system but partly also to the integration into the world economy. It was a gradualist process of reform—and not a Big Bang as in the former USSR—described as "crossing the river by feeling the stones". The process required continued political stability, and this was achieved by a combination of political repression and the significantly widespread sharing in rising prosperity.

The Opening Up of China.

From being one of the most closed economies in the world, China has opened up remarkably. This enabled it to take advantage of its one abundant resource, labour. China's comparative advantage in trade lies in low-wage labour-intensive manufacturing. Labour-intensive goods could be traded for capital-intensive and technology-intensive goods. Exports grew tenfold in real terms over the period 1980–2003.

China was able to respond to the new trade opportunities for various reasons. One was the proximity of the Chinese business diaspora in East Asia. Another was the fact that the "Asian Tigers" (Hong Kong, Taiwan, Singapore and South Korea) which had led East Asian industrialisation were now becoming high-wage economies, and were vacating the labour-intensive export industries in favour of more sophisticated production, so leaving a gap for China. Recently China has been receiving the largest annual volume of net foreign direct investment (FDI) ever to a single economy. The inflow of FDI rose to the equivalent of 5 per cent of China's GDP,

amounting to over $50 billion a year. FDI is important because it helps China to develop a set of industrial and technological capabilities. The previous tight constraints on resources and on technology are being loosened.

China's Virtuous Circle of Growth.

Underpinning the high growth rate has been a remarkably high rate of capital accumulation. The investment rate has exceeded 35 per cent of GDP in recent years. This requires a high rate of domestic saving but, most important, it depends on business confidence. The Chinese economy has got into a virtuous circle of high saving, high investment, and high growth, in which buoyant expectations are self-fulfilling.

Will China be the Next Economic Superpower?

If recent trends continue, China will become the largest economy in the world withing a couple of decades. It will become the next economic superpower. The key question is: can rapid growth be maintained? Or could there be some shock to the Chinese economy which would destroy the virtuous circle of high confidence and high growth?

One threat comes from the flawed nature of the Chinese financial system. The banks (all state-owned) used to be merely conduits for the distribution of public funds; they did not apply the normal criteria of creditworthiness to their loans. With many state-owned enterprises making losses on account of marketisation, the Chinese banking system has a very high proportion of non-performing loans (representing 50 per cent of GDP). Especially when the banking system is opened up to foreign competition, due in 2006 under the WTO Agreement with China, the government may have to bail out loss-making Chinese banks in order to shore up confidence.

Rising Inequality in China.

Another threat to China's continued rapid growth is that of political instability. There are inevitably political tensions surrounding economic reform, with its losers as well as its gainers. Economic inequality has risen very rapidly, in many dimensions: between urban and rural China (the urban-rural income gap has widened), among regions (the coastal provinces have prospered more than the interior), and among households. The labour market has helped some people—those with human capital—and harmed others—in particular the many redundant workers from loss-making enterprises. A wealthy entrepreneurial class has formed very rapidly. There are many complaints of corruption in the still semi-marketised economy. These rising inequalities can be expected to generate a good deal of social discontent which, in the absence of democracy, the political system has to repress. Should discontent boil over at some point, economic progress could be threatened. There is little sign as yet of political change to match the economic transformation.

The Unshackling of the Indian Economy.

The Indian economy has long been shackled by poor economic policies. Industrialisation was inward-looking, and enterprises were hamstrung by pervasive bureaucratic controls and restrictions. In recent years, however, the Indian government espoused more market-friendly and outward-oriented policies, and the private sector responded to the new opportunities. Whereas growth in income per capita over the period 1970–1995 was weak, over the years 1990–2003 it averaged over 4 per cent per annum and rising.

Like China, India's comparative advantage lies in low-wage labour-intensive exports of manufactures, but it has taken the lead in exporting business services, such as software development and call centres. India is now more welcoming to foreign direct investment than in the past. The prospects are that India will follow China in growing rapidly on the basis of strong export performance.

Do China and India Pose a Threat to Other Developing Countries?

The breakneck industrialisation and burgeoning

exports of manufactures in China and India have two opposing effects on the growth prospects of other developing countries. On the one hand, their success poses a threat to other countries attempting to export labour-intensive manufactures. On the other hand, their growing demand for raw materials and energy will boost the markets for suppliers of products such as metals, oil, coal, and industrial crops. The terms of trade of natural resource-intensive countries—and there are several in Africa —should improve.

Economic Stagnation in Africa.

Africa has become the area of the world that presents the greatest economic problem. Income per head in Sub-Saharan Africa has fallen since 1980. There are various reasons not associated with natural phenomena. First, population growth has continued to rise and now stands at 2·5 per cent per annum. Second, the terms of trade of the region deteriorated in the 1980s and again in the 1990s. Third, in 2004, Africa's external debt was 46 per cent of its GDP, making the region the most heavily indebted of all; and debt service obligations were 12 per cent of export revenues, but not all were actually paid, so that arrears accumulated. Both the level and the efficiency of investment have fallen. Fourth, drought hit many countries of Africa in the 1980s and 1990s, including the Sahel, Eastern Africa and Southern Africa. This has not only produced great human suffering but it has also created problems of economic recovery and development. Fifth, parts of Africa are in the grip of an HIV/AIDS epidemic (*see below*).

With the World Bank forecasting a further fall in living standards, Africa is the focus of aid donors' attention. Some of Africa's problems are within the control of their governments, and aid agencies have increasingly made their aid to African countries conditional on the reform of economic policies. This involves a strategy requiring less government intervention, more reliance on market forces and more grass-roots development, and emphasising the development of institutional and human capacities to provide the enabling environment for growth.

Malaria and Economic Development.

Malaria has been and remains one of the greatest scourges of humanity. Whereas its incidence has fallen elsewhere in the world, it is a particularly devastating health problem in sub-Saharan Africa, where there are 650 million infections a year. To some observers, the economic retardation of Africa can be substantially explained by malaria. Not only does it have a direct effect on productivity but it also scares off foreign investors and traders.

There are several strategies for addressing the problem—draining standing water, spraying with pesticides, and using netting at night, as well as drugs. *Chloroquine* is cheap and widely used, but the malaria parasite is becoming resistant to it. The new *Artemesin* drug (based on a traditional Chinese herbal medicine) is effective but expensive. The limited purchasing power of the market keeps it costly and limits investment in improvements by the major pharmaceutical companies. There is a case for international subsidisation: public sector investment in research and development of anti-malarial drugs as part of donor aid programmes.

The HIV/AIDS Pandemic.

The HIV/AIDS pandemic poses a serious threat to many developing countries. Although it is a world-wide phenomenon, the majority of sufferers live in developing countries, many of which are too poor to provide treatment and ill-equipped to cope with the harmful effects on their economies. The first cases were recognised in the early 1980s, and by 1990 some 10 million people were infected. Since then that number has more than quadrupled, to about 42 million in 2002. Moreover, the disease has already killed 22 million people and left 13 million orphans in its wake.

HIV/AIDS in Africa.

HIV/AIDS is crippling parts of Africa. Roughly one in three adults is infected in Botswana, Lesotho, Swaziland and Zimbabwe, and one in five in Namibia, South Africa and Zambia. It is estimated to have reduced life expectancy by roughly 30 years in several countries of southern Africa. In 2004 there were in Africa 25 million people living with HIV/AIDS, and 2·3 million deaths from the disease.

The Economic Consequences of HIV/AIDS.

HIV/AIDS destroys more than lives. By incapacitating and killing adults in the prime of their lives, it throws economic development off course. For instance, business investment is deterred, and education and health services suffer. In 1998 Zambia lost 1,300 teachers to the disease—equivalent in number to two-thirds of the teachers trained that year. HIV/AIDS has severe effects in peasant agriculture: the illness of an adult means that farmwork suffers, money must be found for health care, and children are taken out of school. Communities begin to break down.

Policies Against HIV/AIDS.

The spread of the disease depends not only on the response of individuals and families but also on government policies. These can take the form of educational campaigns, including the targeting of sex workers, counselling and screening services, and provision of safe blood supplies, condoms and drugs. Medicines are now available that can at least postpone further development of the disease. Uganda is one African country to have begun to reverse a serious epidemic, and there are signs that Zambia is in the process of reversal. However, several governments have appeared to be in denial.

HIV/AIDS elsewhere in the Developing World.

Although Sub-Saharan Africa accounts for the majority of cases, the disease is spreading rapidly in other regions. China, India and the Russian Federation—all with huge populations—are at risk of seeing their infection rates soar. About 7 million people are infected in these three countries: in Africa 7 million cases exploded into 25 million in a decade.

HIV/AIDS in the Developed Countries.

The infection rate is far lower than in poor countries. The proportion of adults aged 15–49 living with HIV/AIDS in 2001 was 0·61 per cent in the US, 0·10 per cent in the UK, 0·30 per cent in the OECD as a whole, 1·00 per cent in developing countries, and 9·00 per cent in Sub-Saharan Africa.

Whereas in Africa the disease affects men and women equally, in western countries it is concentrated among gay men. For instance, in the United States 80 per cent of the sufferers were men.

Developed countries have the resources to combat the disease. For instance, in Britain the cumulative reported cases of AIDS up to 2002 was 18,000 but the peak reporting year was back in 1996. HIV/AIDS causes suffering everywhere, but it is in the developing countries that it threatens social and economic disaster.

Growing Indebtedness.

The external indebtedness of the developing countries grew rapidly in the 1970s and 1980s. Many developing countries failed to adjust fully to the worsened economic and trading conditions after the oil crisis of 1973, preferring instead to borrow heavily. After the second oil crisis in 1979–80, the world economy went into prolonged recession. Many developing countries were squeezed between stagnating foreign exchange earnings and heavy foreign exchange commitments. This precipitated two problems: a *debt crisis* for certain heavily indebted developing countries and the need for *stabilization policies* among a broader group of developing countries.

It was the more successful developing countries which attracted lending: Brazil and Mexico together accounted for 40 per cent of the private debt. A measure of the strain on developing countries is provided by the ratio of debt and of debt servicing (annual interest and amortisation payments) to annual foreign exchange earnings from exports. These ratios had reached 133 per cent and 18 per cent respectively in 1983. This precipitated the debt crisis, in which a general default on debts was widely feared.

Countries became increasingly dependent on new loans to service the old, and private banks were reluctant to provide these. In all the major cases a rescheduling of debt repayments was arranged, usually in conjunction with IMF programmes. However, the formal procedures for managing debt problems were overtaken by informal actions, such as the suspension of debt servicing.

The debt crisis peaked in 1986, and thereafter it was eased by the acceleration of world economic growth, by debt reduction initiatives for the poorest countries, and by debt write-offs. For debtors, the problem represented economic hardship, a dampening of investment, and social and political discontent. In 2003 interest on debt and amortisation payments took up 18 per cent of the export proceeds of developing countries.

The IMF and Stabilization Policies.

Many developing countries have run into serious balance of payments problems in recent years. Many seek temporary financial assistance from the International Monetary Fund (see **F8–9**).

As a condition of its larger loans the IMF generally requires a country to accept a series of *stabilization* measures. The typical stabilization package contains the following policies: a devaluation to assist the balance of payments, monetary and credit restrictions and reduced government budget deficits to reduce demand and curb inflation, and, more generally, the elimination of restrictions such as import controls and interest rate regulations in order to harness market forces.

The wisdom of such a package in a developing country is much disputed among economists. It is most obviously the correct remedy when the problem is one of general excess demand in the economy. However, when the problem arises from an extraneous shock, such as a fall in the world price of a major export or a financial crisis, the IMF's remedies may prove to be inappropriate. Credit restrictions and cuts in government spending may depress the economy, reducing output and employment. This may temporarily alleviate the immediate problems of inflation and balance of payments deficit, but the effect on long run economic growth may be negative.

It is for these reasons that critics accuse the IMF of doctrinairely and narrowly focussing on monetary variables and ignoring structural problems and developmental objectives. The IMF, on the other hand, often sees itself as a handy scapegoat for unpopular measures made inescapable by domestic economic mismanagement.

The Country-led Approach to Aid.

In recent years the imposition of conditionality by donor countries has been on the wane. The UK Department for International Development (DfID) has moved instead towards a *country-led approach* to aid policy. It is now central to the UK's aid programme.

The policy is that DfID should not tell countries what to do. Instead it bases its country strategy on the recipient country's plans. Aid is then forthcoming provided only that there is confidence in the plans. The argument in favour of the new approach is that a policy is more likely to be successful if the government of the developing country itself has "ownership" of that policy. However, this aid strategy is more likely to be successful in states with relatively good governance than in poorly governed, fragile states.

To give an example of the policy at work: in 1999 only 50 per cent of Tanzania's children went to primary school but in 2005 the figure was over 90 per cent. The elected government of Tanzania chose to expand educational opportunities and, on account of the country-led approach, was able to use aid money to abolish school fees.

Inflation in Developing Countries.

Inflation in developing countries is often high, and it is generally higher than in the OECD group. Several Latin American countries like Brazil, Argentina, and Bolivia, but also some African countries such as Ghana and Zimbabwe, have experienced bouts of hyperinflation. High inflation can be a response—sometimes acting as a "safety valve"—to such problems as heavy debt servicing, the collapse of exports, or a fall in real incomes. Inflation

can be volatile because developing countries are prone to suffer shocks to their economies. Once established, however, inflation can feed on itself by changing expectations and behaviour. In the period 1987–96 the average inflation rate in developing countries was 57 per cent per annum (generally well into double figures but also elevated by a few hyperinflations) whereas in the period 1997–2005 it was down to 8 per cent per annum.

Inflation Targeting.

Inflation targeting—a framework for monetary policy that commits the central bank to achieving low inflation—has enjoyed considerable success in Britain and other industrial countries in helping to maintain macroeconomic and price stability.

Inflation targeting is an alternative to monetary targeting or exchange rate targeting. Many less developed countries have in the past used exchange rate targeting, but now must pursue more flexible exchange rate arrangements: the increasing mobility of capital in recent years makes it difficult to maintain fixed exchange rates. Monetary targeting has also fallen into disrepute because of the weak short term relationship between "money" (in its various definitions) and inflation.

A number of the more advanced developing countries—including Brazil, Chile, Colombia, Mexico, South Africa and Thailand—have followed the numerous developed countries that have adopted inflation targeting. This policy is more difficult for less developed countries because their economies, exchange rates and inflationary pressures are more volatile, but it has so far appeared to be successful in securing macroeconomic stability.

The State versus the Market.

The role that the state should play in economic development has become a major issue. In past decades the governments of most developing countries have been extremely interventionist. The presumption was that markets do not work well in underdeveloped economies and that the state can improve on the market outcome by directly allocating resources. However, many countries lacked the skilled manpower required to make the economic bureaucracy efficient, and the economic powers taken by the state were often an invitation to corruption. By the end of the 1980s there was a widespread feeling that the pendulum had swung too far in favour of the state.

The 1990s have seen a move towards greater reliance on the market in many developing countries. In the words of John Maynard Keynes, "the important thing for government is not to do things which individuals are doing already, and to do them a little better or a little worse; but to do those things which at present are not done at all." In many developing countries there is a case for privatising state-owned enterprises and for doing away with price controls, import quotas, high tariffs, heavy production subsidies and the like. At the same time, governments need to do more in those areas where markets alone cannot be relied upon, such as investing in health, nutrition, education, family planning and poverty alleviation, and building an efficient infrastructure within which private enterprises can flourish.

Improving the Investment Climate.

Governments of developing countries are generally much more supportive of private enterprise nowadays than they were in the past. How best can they encourage private investment? The World Bank conducted a survey of 26,000 firms in 53 developing countries. It found that the following four factors were regarded as the greatest impediments to investment, each mentioned by over 70 per cent of respondents. First came policy uncertainty, followed by, in order, macroeconomic instability, tax rates, and corruption. It is clear, therefore, that good governance is essential if a country is to achieve and maintain a good investment climate.

Structural Adjustment Policies.

The process whereby developing economies are redirected towards improved balance of payments, debt reduction, more openness to the world economy, less government intervention and greater use of markets, has come to be known as *structural adjustment*. It is being promoted by international donors and resisted by domestic vested interests. Many governments have accepted the need for structural adjustment; time will tell whether rhetoric becomes reality.

Much of the World Bank's lending in recent years has taken the form of *Structural Adjustment Loans*, providing funds to the government of a developing country on condition that it implements agreed structural adjustment policies. Supporters seek to justify such lending in terms of its results; opponents see it as an infringement of national sovereignty.

The evidence suggests that only where the national government itself makes a serious commitment to reform—assuming "ownership" of the structural adjustment policy—is there a good prospect of its success. There is now a tendency to give more aid to those governments that have shown that commitment, *i.e.* to reward policy success rather than mere intent. In Africa two successfully reforming countries, Ghana and Uganda, are benefiting accordingly.

Globalization of Financial Markets.

One of the policy reforms pressed for by the IMF and the World Bank, and eagerly adopted by many developing country governments, was the liberalization of financial markets. There was a substantial increase in private capital flows to developing countries in the 1990s, reflecting financial liberalization and the welcoming stance of host governments. Net capital inflows into developing countries as a group decreased from an annual average of $115 billion in the five years 1993–97 to $40 billion in the subsequent five years 1998–2002, essentially because of a flight of portfolio investments and private loans. By contrast, the annual net FDI component grew, the corresponding figures being $88 billion and $134 billion respectively.

Emergent stock markets flourished for a time in such countries as Argentina, Chile, Thailand, Malaysia and Taiwan, but investors were easily frightened.

In principle, capital inflows are good for the developing countries, encouraging investment and accelerating economic growth. However, they also carry dangers, as the examples of Mexico in 1994, when capital flight from the peso provoked a crisis, East Asia in 1997–98, and Argentina in 2001 show.

The East Asian Financial Crisis.

Many of the East Asian countries suffered a serious financial crisis in 1997 and 1998. The crisis began in Thailand but it spread rapidly to engulf South Korea, Malaysia, Indonesia, and the Philippines. Other major developing economies of the region—China, Taiwan and Singapore—were shaken but relatively unscathed.

There were common roots to the crisis, although the reversal of market sentiment became infectious. Financial liberalization produced a wave of investment in the region, funded from both local and foreign sources. Some of the investment was ill-conceived, and some politically influenced (hence the term "crony capitalism"). The investment boom in turn contributed to worsening current accounts on the balance of payments, which were anyway suffering from the tying of currencies to the appreciating US dollar.

By 1997 there was sufficient concern to set off a capital flight, which in turn fed on itself. Currencies depreciated very sharply. For instance, between July 1997 and February 1998 the Indonesian rupiah fell by three-quarters of its value against the US dollar, and the Thai baht, the South Korean won, and the Malaysian ringgit by 40 per cent or more. This increased the burden of debt, and of debt servicing, denominated in terms of foreign currency, and so further destroyed confidence.

The countries in crisis received support from the IMF and the World Bank, on condition that they introduced policies of monetary and fiscal restraint to stabilize their economies and rectified the weaknesses of their financial systems. The hope was that these policies, together with their depreciated currencies, would restore their export competitiveness in world markets. Indeed, the affected economies began to pick up in 1999, and rapid growth resumed in 2000.

Environmental Issues.

To be economically sustainable development must also be environmentally sustainable. Much of the population increase of recent years has occurred in environmentally fragile regions of the world. Desertification, deforestation, soil depletion through over-use of fragile land, and pollution are issues of growing concern.

Environmental degradation can contribute to famine (as in Ethiopia) and to devastating flooding (as in Bangladesh). Population pressures, poverty, inadequate systems of land tenure and the growing need for fuelwood lead to the cutting or burning of forests and the clearing of new land. Problems of pollution have become critical in many of the urban agglomerations of the developing world. Sanitation, clean water and clean air are important aspects of the quality of life, and these require that government plays an active role.

The world's most polluted cities are located in poor countries. Using the criterion of more than 100 micrograms per cubic metre of air, there are nine such cities in China (including Beijing, Chongqing, and Tianjin), five in India (including Calcutta and Delhi), and one each in Egypt (Cairo) and Indonesia (Jakarta).

Protecting the Global Commons.

An important subset of environmental problems is global in scope. No individual country can address them by acting alone. As in the case of a small community over-exploiting its common resources, so the global community is at risk if no collective action is taken. Examples are global climate change (requiring control of air pollution and of deforestation) and threats to biodiversity (requiring protection of species). Climate change can raise sea level and threaten low-lying areas and agricultural production. For instance, a one-metre rise in sea level would cut Bangladesh's rice production in half. The control of overfishing the seas was tightened by the extension of exclusive fishing zones to stretch 200 miles off the coastline of many countries but there are problems of enforcement. These issues are also discussed in **Section Y**.

The Economics of Climate Change.

Economic growth increases living standards but poses multiple threats to the natural environment, of which climate change ("global warming") has emerged as the most serious. Indeed, many politicians and scientists identify it as the single most critical issue facing humanity.

Global warming results from the emission of "greenhouse gases" (carbon dioxide (CO_2), methane, *etc.*) as a by-product of economic activity. Their build-up in the atmosphere traps heat and warms the earth's surface. The most authoritative scientific analysis, by the United Nations Intergovernmental Panel on Climate Change, predicts a rise in average surface temperatures of up to 5.8°C by 2100, and continuing subsequent rises, if current trends in global economic activity continue.

The Threshold Effects.

Some resulting costs (*e.g.* loss of marginal agricultural land) are certain to occur but are only a small fraction of global real income. This has led some analysts to dismiss climate change as a trivial problem. There is a growing scientific consensus, however, that this view is wrong because of the risk of *threshold effects*, whereby once the temperature rise crosses a threshold, the costs may dramatically increase.

For example, beyond a critical surface temperature the West Antarctic Ice Sheet may collapse, and this and similar threshold effects would cause a rise in sea levels sufficient to overwhelm many of the world's largest cities and create hundreds of millions of destitute environmental refugees in both rich and poor countries. Ultimately such effects could cause the global breakdown of human society.

To prevent such problems requires a massive reduction in the world's emission of greenhouse gases, especially CO_2. This can be achieved if the world as a whole makes a large-scale switch from reliance for energy on oil and coal to use of renewable energy (*e.g.* wind or solar power, or—more controversially—nuclear power). If renewables cannot provide sufficient energy, then the only other option is a substantial reduction in global economic activity (and thus a reduced need for CO_2-producing energy).

Addressing the Problem.

There is no market mechanism that will ensure that such global economic changes occur: substantial intervention by policy-makers is essential. Moreover, action by individual national governments cannot address the global nature of the problem: co-ordinated international action is needed. The world's first major attempt at this—the Kyoto Protocol—illustrates the formidable obstacles. The United States (the single biggest source of greenhouse gases) has refused to support it, and two other major potential sources, China and India, are not even covered by the Protocol. The latter's provisions in turn only scratch the problem's surface. Ultimately, enormous changes in the world economy may be required, involving the localisation of economic activities. This could be implemented via global carbon rationing, or a punitive global carbon tax.

There is no sign that the world is even near to serious consideration of such revolutionary changes. This is not surprising since those who would have to implement them—current generations of global citizens, via their elected representatives—would incur all the costs and reap none of the benefits, all of which would go to future generations. There are few if any historical precedents for political action embodying such a degree of inter-generational altruism.

Environmental Policies.

Environmental dangers are greater in poor countries which can little afford to invest in environmental protection and resource management. Their governments often find it difficult to monitor, regulate and control environmental pollution. Rather than attempt to regulate, it may be better to levy taxes on polluting equipment (e.g. combustion machinery) or fuels (e.g. petrol) according to the expected level of pollution. If, as in large cities, household use of energy is a major contributor to pollution, the types of fuel and equipment which reduce pollution might be subsidised and those that increase it might be taxed.

In the 1990s the OECD nations began to give greater emphasis to environmental improvements in their aid policies. A Global Environmental Facility was established by donors to assist developing countries to undertake investment projects which would protect the global environment. These would include protection of the ozone layer, affected by chlorofluorocarbon (CFC) and other gas emissions, limiting "greenhouse" gas emissions (such as carbon dioxide and methane) that contribute to global warming, protecting biological species against extinction and protecting international waters against pollution (e.g. waste pollution and oil spills). Recognising the global advantages of such projects, the international donors are willing to offer this aid on concessional terms.

The United Nations Conference on Environment and Development, otherwise known as the Earth Summit, was held in Rio de Janeiro in 1992. It failed to produce specific commitments concerning the environment, but it helped to change attitudes and emphasis. For instance, principles were agreed on control of greenhouse gases.

Millennium Development Goals.

At the Millennium Summit in 2000 world leaders set seven goals for the international community to meet by 2015. These add up to an ambitious agenda for reducing poverty and improving the quality of life.

There were eight specific goals: to eradicate extreme hunger and poverty; achieve universal primary education; promote gender equality; reduce child mortality; improve maternal health; combat HIV/AIDS, malaria and other diseases; ensure environmental sustainability; and create a global partnership for development.

The World Summit on Sustainable Development, held in Johannesburg in 2002, was largely a talking shop aiming to change attitudes. Nevertheless, it set targets for improving the living conditions of the world's poor, including environmental targets, in line with the Millennium Development Goals.

Some Suggestions for Further Reading.

For an introduction to the subject the reader is referred to Michael Todaro, Economic Development (Longman). William Easterly, in The Elusive Quest for Growth (MIT Press) gives an entertaining iconoclastic account of development fashions and policies. For a critique of globalisation, see Joseph Stiglitz, Globalisation and its Discontents (Allen Lane). Jeffrey Sachs, in The End of Poverty, puts the case for helping the poor. An interesting comparison of African and Asian development is made in N. and S. Thompson, The Baobab and the Mango Tree (Zed Books).

An interesting quarterly publication of the IMF and the World Bank, Finance and Development, is available free of charge; applications should be sent to Finance and Development, IMF Building, Washington, DC 20431, USA.

IV. RECENT DEVELOPMENTS IN THE BRITISH ECONOMY

1. INTERNATIONAL DEVELOPMENTS

THE BRITISH BALANCE OF PAYMENTS.

The balance of payments problem has dominated events in the British economy until recent years and may do so again. It is therefore important to understand why the balance of payments has been a problem; and to see its effects on economic policy. The balance of payments and its components are explained on F6–8. The balance of payments in the period 1999–2005 is shown in the table on F51.

The 1970s.

The early 1970s witnessed a remarkable inflation in the prices of various primary products in world markets. This unprecedented jump in primary commodity prices stemmed from the sharp and well-synchronised expansion of the major industrial economies during 1972 and 1973.

An event of great importance was the decision of the Arab oil-producing states, taken in October 1973, to restrict oil supplies and to raise oil prices. The restriction of supplies was initiated as a short-run political weapon in the Arab–Israeli conflict; but it revealed a potential for obtaining higher prices which had not previously been exploited by the Organisation of Petroleum Exporting Countries (OPEC). Alternative sources of energy could not be developed—and thus the demand for oil could not be curtailed—or even its growth retarded—for some years. However, maintenance of high prices depended on the ability of the OPEC group to restrict oil supplies to the market despite the incentive of each individual country to take advantage of the high prices by expanding its sales.

In the wake of the oil crisis the world economy duly moved into severe recession. To this the British economy was no exception. During 1975 the rate of inflation in Britain was some 15 per cent above the average for the OECD countries: sterling depreciated sharply.

The "oil deficit" in the balance of payments, huge in the mid-1970s, slowly declined as North Sea oil production expanded, and was transformed into an "oil surplus", becoming as large as £5·5 billion in the mid-1980s, and then declining. The exploitation of North Sea oil was a mixed blessing. Through its strengthening of the balance of payments and consequent raising of the exchange rate, it harmed the manufacturing sector. The problems of structural adjustment, of which rising unemployment was a symptom, brought a social cost.

THE UK BALANCE OF PAYMENTS 1999–2005
(£ BILLION)

	1999	2000	2001	2002	2003	2004	2005
Exports of goods	166	187	191	187	189	191	210
Imports of goods	195	221	231	233	236	251	276
Visible balance	−29	−33	−41	−46	−47	−60	−66
Invisible balance	5	9	17	28	28	37	34
Current balance	−24	−24	−24	−18	−19	−23	−32
Capital account	24	24	24	18	19	23	32
of which: capital account	1	2	1	1	1	2	2
financial account	21	25	22	9	17	8	25
errors and omissions	2	−3	1	8	1	13	5

The 1980s.

Increased demand for sterling was met in part by the willingness of the monetary authorities to let the exchange rate rise. This was partly due to North Sea oil production, its direct effect on the balance of payments and its indirect effect on foreign confidence in the British economy. Also important were the high interest rates engendered by the incoming Thatcher Government's restrictive monetary policy.

The appreciation of sterling helped to curb domestic inflation by keeping down the sterling price of imports (an imported good selling for $1 could now be bought for fewer pence). However, it also had a harmful effect on the manufacturing sector and on competitiveness (an exported good costing £1 would now have to be sold at a higher dollar price to cover costs). The current account surplus fell after 1982, reflecting a lagged adjustment to the unfavourable competitiveness of British products, and it deteriorated sharply from 1986 onwards. The main reason for this was an upswing in the economy—the so-called "Lawson boom"

The Effects of Entry to the EMS.

In 1990 the decision was finally taken to make Britain a fuller member of the *European Monetary System* (EMS) by entering the *Exchange Rate Mechanism* (ERM) (*see* **F56**). The economy was already in difficulties, with inflation high and the current account deficit worsening. These difficulties were compounded by the relatively high level of sterling at which Britain entered the ERM. This curbed trade competitiveness, so depressing the economy. The need to maintain sterling within the permitted ERM band required the authorities to keep interest rates above German levels. German rates were rising and this prevented the government from reducing interest rates by as much as the recession warranted.

Black Wednesday.

German interest rates rose further in 1992, reflecting German reunification. Despite the severity of the economic recession in Britain, the current account remained in deficit. The markets lost confidence in the ability and commitment of the British Government, faced with weak international competitiveness and a depressed economy, to defend the pound within the EMS. Speculation fed on itself and, despite heavy (and costly) financial support by the Bank of England and the Bundesbank, the Government was defeated by the markets on *Black Wednesday*, 16 September. The pound dropped sharply, depreciating by some 16 per cent.

The old policy had failed, mainly because the government had joined the EMS at an over-valued rate for sterling. It hastened to invent a new policy regime. Unemployment had reached 10 per cent and was still rising: it was decided to place greater emphasis on overcoming the recession. Indeed, some commentators regarded Black Wednesday as heaven-sent: the markets had saved the government from its self-imposed straitjacket.

Response to Devaluation.

The pound was worth 2·82 deutschmarks in August 1992 and 2·36 deutschmarks in February 1993. The Treasury bill rate fell from 9·9 to 5·5 per cent over the same period, and other interest rates came down as well. The improved competitiveness provided a boost for producers, and lower interest rates eased the burden on mortgage-holders and encouraged investors. At last there was the prospect of an end to economic contraction.

In the four quarters after the devaluation there was an 11 per cent improvement in British competitiveness: the inflationary impact of the devaluation was very limited because of the extremely depressed state of the economy. With a lag, exports began to rise rapidly. The economy also began to recover.

For the next four years Britain benefited from export-led growth in the wake of the enforced devaluation of sterling.

Sterling Appreciation.

During 1996 the value of sterling began to appreciate sharply: by 10 per cent against a basket of currencies from April to November. This reflected confidence in the British economy relative to its European partners, together with higher interest rates in Britain and their expected rise, as pressed for by the Bank of England. The pound—nearly back to its level before the 1992 enforced devaluation—became overvalued.

The balance of payments on current account moved from surplus to balance in 1998, and the deficit rose to no less than £24 billion in 1999. This deterioration reflected the overvaluation of the pound, caused by the policy of maintaining higher interest rates in Britain than in its main trading partners. Interest rates are determined by the Bank of England's *Monetary Policy Committee* (MPC), whose brief is to control the rate of inflation (*see* **F31–2**).

The Pound and the Euro.

When the euro was created at the start of 1999, the pound remained too high: a binding to the euro at the rate that then prevailed would have threatened British growth and prosperity. The subsequent appreciation of sterling against the euro (by 12 per cent in the course of the year), reflecting the higher interest rates in Britain, increased that threat. The pound was steady against the euro during 2000 but fell sharply against the rising dollar. Nevertheless, the real effective exchange rate for sterling (1995 = 100), which had been 131 in 1998, averaged 143 in 2002 and (despite the appreciation of the euro) was as high as 133 in late 2005. This is reflected in the continuing current account deficit (£18 billion in 2002, £19 billion in 2003, £23 billion in 2004 and £32 billion in 2005).

THE INTERNATIONAL ECONOMIC SYSTEM.

The international monetary system is explained on **F8–9**. The main problems facing the international economic system in the 1970s were world inflation and the international imbalance caused by the increased price of oil, and the resultant threat to economic growth. Subsequently the main problems were international debt, world recession and tardy economic growth. We trace the issues and events as they unfold.

Introduction of Flexible Exchange Rates.

The United States ran a large and persistent

payments deficit in the 1950s and 1960s. This was initially financed through the willingness of foreigners to run up dollar balances. However, distrust of the dollar grew. Massive speculation forced the United States government to devalue the dollar in 1973, and the EC countries agreed that their currencies would float against the dollar. The international monetary system had entered a new era of flexible exchange rates. The Bretton Woods system, which had operated throughout the post-war period, had come to an end. No longer would countries be required to maintain fixed exchange rates subject only to periodic realignment in response to fundamental disequilibrium in their balance of payments.

The Oil Crises.

The price of oil rose from $3·5 to $9·3 a barrel between 1973 and 1974. The oil-producing countries ran a vast current account surplus, which meant a corresponding deficit for the oil-importing countries as a group. Such a transformation in the international balance of payments was unprecedented in its scale and speed. It involved a massive transfer of purchasing power from consumers to producers of oil. Since only a small part of the additional oil revenue was spent, this had a severe deflationary effect on the world economy.

The less developed countries sustained large deficits in the wake of the oil price increase. The deposits made by oil-producers in western banks gave these banks an opportunity to lend on a much enlarged scale. Private lending to developing countries increased greatly; this sowed the seeds of the debt crisis of the 1980s (see **F47-8**).

The price of oil doubled over the course of 1979, rising from $13 to $25 a barrel. This was due to the halving of Iranian oil production after the revolution in Iran, and to a scramble for oil stocks by the consuming countries. In 1980, assisted by the outbreak of war between Iran and Iraq, the OPEC oil price soared. The higher oil price led again to higher inflation and an increased balance of payments deficit in the industrial countries. Both the restrictive monetary policies which were then introduced and the high interest rates which they generated had a depressing effect on the major economies.

The Oil Market.

The two great increases in the price of oil occurred in 1973–74 and 1979–80. Could the oil cartel maintain the price at its high level? World production of crude oil in 1985 was at the same level (21 billion barrels)as it had been in 1974. However, OPEC production was down to below 6 billion barrels. Saudi Arabia was unwilling to continue withholding production so that other members—such as expansionist Libya, war-torn Iran and Iraq and heavily indebted Nigeria—could exceed their quotas: Saudi production expanded rapidly. Market forces took over. The spot price of oil collapsed, from just under $30 a barrel at the beginning of December 1985 to $10 a barrel in April 1986. The cartel had fallen apart. The oil market was virtually a free-for-all.

Early in 1999 the average OPEC price was $11 a barrel. However, it more than doubled in the course of the year, to around $25 a barrel, as the OPEC members once more tried to restrict production (by some 1·5 million barrels a year). The price rise put pressure on world inflation and therefore, through the response of governments, it slowed down economic growth: 2001 and 2002 were years of world recession. The price rose to well over $30 a barrel in March 2003 in anticipation of war against Iraq. Oil prices rose very sharply again (to around $40) in early summer 2004 on fears of terrorism in Saudi Arabia. In the face of rising demand (especially from China which was scouring the world for oil supplies) and slowing supply (for instance, the effects of the Katrina hurricane damage), the price exceeded $50 during 2005, and the expectation was that it would rise rather than fall.

The oil price had thus risen five-fold since the start of 1999, and had doubled since 2003. That posed a threat to the growth of the global economy, via the effect of increased fuel costs on the inflationary outlook and the consequent interest rate policies of "inflation-targeting" central banks. Their restriction of demand could be expected to dampen growth prospects. For instance, the International Monetary Fund, in its *World Economic Outlook*, in September 2005 projected OECD annual economic

growth to fall from its 2004 recovery of 3·3 per cent to about 2·5 per cent in 2005 and in 2006.

Was the attack of the United States and its allies against Iraq motivated by a concern to expand and control Iraq's oil production, as some critics have claimed? Although implausible, it is a view that is inherently difficult to prove or refute. Underlying such a claim, however, is the recognition that world economic prosperity is dependent on maintaining a low and stable oil price, and thus on the geopolitics of the Arab world.

Projecting World Energy Demand.

How is the global energy situation likely to evolve in future years? The *International Energy Authority* (IEA) in its annual *World Energy Report* has made projections for 25 years ahead. If governments stick with current policies, energy demand will be almost 60 per cent higher in 2030. However, if they adopt a set of more energy-efficient and environmentally-friendly policies, the increase in demand is expected to rise by some 50 per cent—about 10 per cent less. This reduction will come mainly from oil savings through greater fuel efficiency and alternative-fuel vehicles.

A World Economy Constrained by Energy?

Most of the increase in demand for energy will occur in the rapidly growing developing countries like China and India. Fossil fuels—coal and oil—will continue to dominate the energy mix. Global demand for oil is projected to grow by 1·6 per cent per annum, and it is likely that this growth in demand can be met by all producers, largely in the Middle East. However, energy-related carbon dioxide emissions are expected to grow in line with energy demand. Here lies the danger: it is the likely effect of these emissions on global warming that will either force serious reform of world energy policies or threaten the projected growth rate of the world economy (see **F49-50**).

World Financial Crisis, 1987.

A global financial crisis occurred in October 1987. The most fundamental cause was a loss of confidence in the economic policies of the US Government. No significant action had been taken to reduce the Federal budget deficit—action which would be needed to eliminate the trade deficit.

The budget deficit and tight monetary policy increased US interest rates. This posed a threat to equity prices, which had risen during the year on a speculative wave. Market operators became increasingly sceptical that the dollar could be supported in the face of the US trade deficit.In October the markets panicked, share prices plummeted and, as funds left the US, the dollar depreciated sharply. Stock exchanges around the world fell sharply.

The financial crisis led to fears that it would cause world-wide economic recession if business confidence was shaken and investment dried up. As a precaution, governments in various countries responded to the deflationary impetus by adopting more expansionary fiscal and monetary policies, hoping thereby to lower interest rates. In fact, the fears proved groundless and an excessive boom ensued. Then, when inflationary pressure built up, governments raised interest rates and economic growth was reined in. There was serious economic recession in the advanced economies in the early 1990s.

ANNUAL AVERAGE GROWTH
RATES OF REAL GDP IN THE ADVANCED
ECONOMIES, 1986–2005

1986–95	1996–2005	1996	1997	1998	1999
3·0	2·8	3·0	3·4	2·7	3·5

2000	2001	2002	2003	2004	2005
3·9	1·2	1·5	1·9	3·3	2·5

World Economic Recession, 2001–03.

The rise in the world oil price after 1999 put pressure on world inflation and therefore, through the response of governments, it slowed down economic growth. Another contributory factor was the stock market crash of 2000 and its subsequent decline. Over-optimism and "herd behaviour" had produced a remarkable stock market boom around the world, led by the IT sector. Setting dot-com share prices at 100 in 1995, at the end of 1998 they were 180 in the US and 160 in Europe. By the start of 2000 speculation had raised shares to 550 in the US and 600 in Europe. The eventual recognition that shares were overvalued precipitated a crash: by January 2001 they were 250 in the US and 220 in Europe.

These factors combined to produce a severe economic recession in all the major economies: the United States (*see* **F53–4**), Europe (*see* **F57**) and Japan (**F53**). We see from the table (**F52**) that economic growth in the advanced economies was only 1·2 per cent in 2001, 1·5 per cent in 2002 and 1·9 per cent in 2003. They began to emerge from recession in 2004 (3·3 per cent) but this revival appeared to falter (2·5 per cent) when the world oil price rose to about $50 a barrel at the start of 2005. The world economy remains very sensitive to the oil market.

Exchange Rate Arrangements.

In 2005 the following exchange rate arrangements were in operation. Some currencies, including the pound, the dollar and the yen, were independently floating. Other currencies had "managed floats", *i.e.*, floating subject to a policy of periodic government intervention. Many developing countries pegged their currencies to those of major trading partners, such as the dollar, or to some currency composite of their own choice.

The table below shows both recent exchange rates against sterling and the movement of the *real effective exchange rate* of the major currencies since 2000. Each is measured against a basket of other currencies and adjusted for changes in costs to obtain a measure of competitiveness. We see that, between 2000 and 2005, the pound depreciated in real terms by 4 per cent and the dollar by 9 per cent, the euro rose by 18 per cent, and the yen fell by 31 per cent.

Over a period of several years, movements in exchange rates and in prices tend to offset each other. This long run tendency is known as *purchasing power parity* (PPP) (*see* **F39**). However, it is only a weak tendency when there are large flows of short term funds.

EXCHANGE RATES, NOVEMBER 2005

	Exchange rate against sterling, (£1 =)	Index of effective exchange rate, (2000 = 100)
Sterling	1·00	90
US dollar	1·73	91
Euro	1·47	118
Japanese yen	205·87	69

Volatility of the Foreign Exchanges.

The movements in the 1970s towards greater flexibility of exchange rates helped to correct international imbalances. The early 1980s was a period in which governments made a virtue out of their reduced control over financial markets. It also coincided with a world-wide shift in the political climate away from a belief in the efficiency of central control towards a greater reliance on the allocative forces of competition. Fairly "clean" floating of currencies (with little central bank intervention) was adopted, and exchange rate policies were not pursued.

The burgeoning and integration of financial markets make control of short term capital flows very difficult and give rise to the possibility of exaggerated and destabilising movements in international exchange rates. Exchange rates became more responsive to expectations about currency revaluation and to interest rate arbitrage than to underlying current account imbalances. By the 1990s, the inadequacies of this system—the volatility and economic irrationality of the behaviour of currencies—were more apparent, and the threat it poses to the international economy more appreciated. Examples of the havoc that short term capital flows can cause are provided the East Asian financial crisis of 1997 (*see* **F49**) and Argentina's financial crisis of early 2002. Having tied the peso to the US dollar during

the 1990s, Argentina was forced by the collapse of confidence in its fiscal and debt management to depreciate its currency sharply.

The Successful Performance of Japan prior to 1990.

Japan's economy outpaced all the major industrial economies until the 1990s. Over the period 1965–89 annual growth of real income per head was no less than 4·3 per cent. The current account surplus was consistently above 2 per cent of GNP, partly offset by an outflow of long term capital, and the yen continued to appreciate in value. The Tokyo stock market rose inexorably—by over fourfold between 1982 and 1989.

By 1990 Japan's national income per capita (expressed in purchasing power parity) was 10 per cent higher than Britain's, and its total GNP was 55 per cent that of the United States. Japan, with its population of 124 million, had become an economic superpower. Its success was bound up with the hard work and thriftiness of its people.

Japan's Vicious Circle.

In 1990 signs emerged that Japanese economic confidence and expectations were faltering. Despite a continuing current account surplus, the yen depreciated. The Nikkei share index fell sharply and interest rates were raised. Speculative buying of shares and land was probably the culprit. The high level of share prices in relation to company profits strengthened the incentive to move capital abroad, and this realisation triggered the fall in the yen and in shares.

While the yen recovered, asset prices did not. Between the end of 1989 and the end of 1992 share prices were halved. The fall in the prices of their assets placed the Japanese banks in financial jeopardy. The economy slowed down from a growth rate of 5 per cent in 1990 to a mere 1·1 per cent per annum over the period 1991–2001. The fear of a financial crisis sapped the economy. Recorded unemployment rose to a record 5 per cent in 2001.

At the roots of Japan's problems since the bubble burst were its failure to address the excess stocks of capital and debt created in the bubble years and its slow pace of adjustment to globalisation and technological change. The Japanese economy appeared to be trapped in a vicious circle. Business confidence was low. The banking system remained vulnerable.

The government attempted to stimulate the economy with a zero interest policy and a fiscal expansion. The economy stagnated in both 2001 and 2002. A tardy recovery began in 2003, and gained pace in the next two years when growth reached 2·5 per cent per annum. Assisted by a decline in the yen in 2005, it seemed that the era of deflation was ending and that Japan might at last escape from its vicious circle.

The US Economic Boom of the 1990s.

The United States economy enjoyed a substantial boom during the Presidency of Bill Clinton. The rate of economic growth during the 1990s averaged 3·2 per cent per annum, and indeed it exceeded 4 per cent after 1996. Moreover, employment expanded impressively and the unemployment rate fell. The US success may well have been due to its taking the lead in the introduction of the *new economy*. There are three features of the new economy: rapid technological progress in the computer and communications industry, the internationalisation of the economy, and financial innovations, *e.g.* in providing venture capital. These features have enabled information technologies to be disseminated rapidly and have stimulated a wide range of new activities. The rate of growth of labour productivity in the US outstripped both its historical rate and productivity growth in the other major economies.

In the latter half of the 1990s the US stock market boomed remarkably, led by the new technology sector. The Dow Jones index rose by no less than 130 per cent between 1995 and 2000. Many American households own shares: their capital gains sparked a consumption boom. Moreover, the high demand for shares enabled investors to obtain cheap finance. However, there was a danger that the stock market boom would be excessive and that the bubble would burst. And so it proved. In response to rising interest rates and energy costs, confidence in the stock market faltered and then collapsed. Share prices fell dramatically early in 2001, especially new technology stocks.

US Economic Difficulties after 2000.

The stock market collapse appeared to precipitate a serious recession in the US economy. Economic growth fell from 3·7 per cent in 2000 to only 0·8 per cent in 2001, and it was 1·9 per cent in 2002. Moreover, severe macroeconomic imbalances began to emerge. The US authorities pursued an expansionary fiscal policy and a lax monetary policy to ward off recession. A budget surplus of 1·3 % of GDP in 2000 ballooned into a budget deficit of no less than 3·7 % of GDP in 2005. By contrast, short-term interest rates remained below European levels. The current deficit account of the US balance of payments, already in deficit in 2000 because of the economic boom, actually increased—to 6·1 % of GDP in 2005.

Will the Dollar Collapse?

It was inevitable that the dollar would fall if and when US macroeconomic policy came to lose credibility. From 2000 to the end of 2005, the dollar depreciated in nominal terms against a trade-weighted basket of currencies by 14 per cent—mainly against the euro and sterling. The United States was able to borrow from the rest of the world and in this way offset its persistent and rising current account deficit and finance its budget deficit.

The main purchasers of securities were central banks, particularly the Asian countries, like China and Japan, with large trade surpluses. Would their governments be willing to go on not only holding but also accumulating dollar reserves?

The US experience of 1987 (see **F52**) and its continuing macroeconomic imbalances suggest that at some point the creditors will lose confidence. However, the central banks would then face the dilemma that, if they were to start selling dollars, a collapse of the dollar could ensue, and they would then suffer a capital loss on their remaining reserves. The future of the dollar remains uncertain.

The adjustment required to correct the imbalance in the US economy will pose problems for other economies. For instance, the appreciation of the euro will tend to depress demand in Europe, and the need for higher interest rates to protect the dollar against further speculation will tend to slow down economic growth in the United States and beyond. Although temporarily warding off economic recession, the increasing public debt of the United States will harm investor and consumer confidence in the long term, again threatening economic growth.

The North American Free Trade Area.

The *North American Free Trade Area* (NAFTA) was established in 1994. It is a free trade area of the United States, Canada and Mexico, creating a common market with roughly the same population and income as the European Union.

The moves towards NAFTA began in the mid-1980s, partly as a response to the success of the European Community. The goals of NAFTA are to eliminate barriers to trade and investment and to improve regional co-operation. The United States favours the expansion of NAFTA to include other countries in the Americas; a likely contender being Chile.

Economic Reform in Eastern Europe.

Over 40 years of centrally planned economic systems left a legacy of stagnating economies with major structural and macroeconomic problems. Output per head remains well below that of the EU countries. The remarkable political revolution that took place in almost all of Eastern Europe in 1989 and 1990 provided the opportunity and the challenge to introduce an economic revolution, with the dismantling of central planning and the introduction of market economies.

The problems of transition are considerable, as the new governments inherited large fiscal deficits, rapid inflation, polluted environments and heavy external indebtedness. For instance, in 1989 debt exceeded $1,000 per capita in Bulgaria, the GDR, Hungary and Poland. The new electorates had high expectations of rapid economic improvement, but

the move to market prices involved large price changes and associated changes in incomes and vast transfers of resources, including the closing down of unprofitable activities.

Between 1990 and 1994, real GDP in the transition economies of Eastern Europe and the former Soviet Union fell by no less than a third. Over the same period prices rose by a remarkable 1800 per cent! Among the impediments to development were corruption, the capture of policy by vested interests, and the lack of institutions such as secure property rights.

Economic Progress through Reform.

By the late 1990s those economies that had advanced furthest to a market economy—including Poland, Albania, the Czech and Slovak Republics, Hungary and Slovenia—had turned the corner and were enjoying strong economic growth. Output in Russia, however, was no higher in 1999 than it had been in 1995. The Russian economy began to grow rapidly (in excess of 5 per cent per annum) only in 1999. In 2003 and 2004 its growth exceeded 7 per cent per annum, the driving force being its exploitation of natural resources such as gas, exported to Europe.

The transition economies as a whole managed to grow on average by some 4·6 per cent per annum over the period 2000–2003, and the figure was even higher in the *Commonwealth of Independent States* (the former USSR). Indeed, economic and political progress in some of the Eastern European countries had been so good that some were admitted to the European Union in May 2004 (see **F57–8**).

GLOBALISATION.

The Integration of Financial Markets.

There is a growing worldwide integration of financial markets. Financial intermediation has become a footloose industry with only limited ties to particular national markets or stock exchanges. Borrowers and lenders in different countries are brought together often by intermediaries based in a third country. The major currencies are traded in most financial centres and dealing continues around the clock.

Much of this change is due to technological innovations in communications. The declining cost of communication has meant that arbitrage is now possible at only very small price differentials, and companies throughout the world are alive to the advantages of scanning money and currency markets on a worldwide basis to meet their requirements at least cost. The consequent competitive pressures have meant that those markets have become more integrated.

Markets for Risk.

Economic life is full of uncertainties and risks. Some individuals or companies dislike taking risks and are willing to pay to avoid them; others are willing to take risks in search of gain. Markets therefore develop in which risk is bought and sold like any other commodity. The most well-known are insurance markets. For instance, by pooling the risks of many customers, insurance companies can offer house insurance on terms that are attractive to most house-owners.

If the insurers are not as well informed as their customers, insurance markets may not work. For instance, if companies selling private health insurance cannot know about the health of individual customers and they therefore charge everyone the average premium, this can drive the healthy out of the market and push up the premiums. The healthiest of the remaining customers always have an incentive to withdraw, and so the market can collapse. This is an argument for having a national health service without permitting anyone to opt out of paying contributions.

Markets for Derivatives.

The explosive growth of *derivatives* since the 1980s has been one of the most profound innovations in financial markets since the introduction of limited liability equity markets early in the nineteenth century. For a price, the amount and type of market risk associated with almost any combination of assets and liabilities can now be tailored to suit the needs of market participants.

A *derivative* market is a particular form of market for risk. A derivative is a tradable contract based on (or derived from) something which is actually marketed, such as a commodity (*e.g.* wheat, oil) or a financial asset (*e.g.* a currency, a share, or a share index). Instead of buying or selling the commodity or financial asset itself, the derivative is traded.

Futures and Options.

The most common derivatives are *futures* and *options*. A future obliges each party to the contract to fulfil it in the future. It is an obligation to buy, or to sell, (say) cocoa at some future date. An option is a similar contract to trade in the future, but it allows the choice of fulfilling the contract or letting the option to do so lapse.

Both futures and options provide ways of avoiding risk. If an exporter will need to sell its dollar proceeds in three months' time, it can sell dollars forward at a fixed price, so transferring the risk of a fall in the dollar to the market. Alternatively, it can, for a premium, take out an option to sell dollars forward. If the dollar falls, the option is used; if it rises, the producer can take advantage of the price rise by selling the dollars in the *spot* (*i.e.* actual) market.

Professional investment managers use derivatives to hedge against risk, *i.e.* to sell risk in the sense of buying risk protection. A derivative can offer the same exposure to a market as the underlying commodity or share, but more quickly and at much lower initial outlay and cost. There is no need to own the commodity or asset. Herein lies a danger: derivatives can also be used to buy risk, *i.e.* to speculate in pursuit of big but risky profits.

Globalisation and IT.

Globalisation is the result of the fall in the costs of and barriers to doing business across countries. The *information technology* (IT) revolution has lowered communication costs, especially over long distances, for instance the cost of rapidly accessing and processing information and ideas from anywhere in the world. The table below gives an idea of the speed with which the capacity for electronic commerce has grown in recent years. Over the 1990s there was an explosive increase in personal computers and in Internet use, which has facilitated globalisation. A side-effect of the emergence and expansion of the Internet is the increased use of English, and this too has been a force for globalisation.

GROWTH IN CAPACITY FOR ELECTRONIC COMMERCE IN THE WORLD, 1991–2001

millions	1991	2001	2001 (1991=100)
Telephone main lines	545	1,000	183
Cellular phones	16	400	2,500
Personal computers	123	450	365
Personal computers with Internet access	5	300	6,000

In 2001 there were 52 internet users per 100 people in South Korea, 50 in the United States, 47 in Canada, 38 in Japan, 33 in the UK, 4 in Mexico, 2·6 in China, 0·7 in India and 0·1 in Nigeria.

Globalisation and Trade.

In addition to the fall in communication and information costs, other changes have accelerated globalisation. One is a fall in transport costs, which has facilitated the movement of goods and people. Another is the reduction in tariff and non-tariff barriers to the movement of goods, services and financial capital. This is in turn due to the growing international consensus about the benefits of trade and financial liberalisation, given authority by the World Trade Organisation (*see* **F44**) and other international bodies.

We see the growing importance of trade in the world from the following figures. Between 1990 and 2000 the value of world exports rose by 70 per cent; over the same period the value of world GDP rose

by 40 per cent (both in current prices). Exports as a proportion of GDP increased from 15 to 19 per cent. Over roughly the same period exports of IT goods rose from 7·5 to 11 per cent of total exports.

Globalisation of Financial Capital.

The fall in communication costs and policies of liberalising capital markets has produced a rapid increase in capital movements, both short and long term. For instance, the daily turnover of foreign exchange on world markets increased by 150 per cent between 1989 and 1998.

Private direct investment across international boundaries, known as *foreign direct investment* (FDI) leaped from $192 billion in 1990 to $1,400 billion in 2000. This reflected the boom in stock markets and in the world economy, privatisation policies, and the opening up of China.

FDI fell to $650 billion in 2002, due to tumbling stock markets and world economic slowdown, but recovered to $730 billion in 2004. The United States was then the largest gross recipient, followed by the United Kingdom and then China. There were 70,000 transnational corporations with 690,000 affiliates abroad. Ranked by foreign assets, General Electric (US) was the biggest transnational corporation, with Vodaphone (UK) second.

The Assessment of Globalisation.

The globalisation of trade has benefited consumers by reducing costs and increasing competition among suppliers. The globalisation of finance and capital has led to more efficient resource allocation and greater competition. However, there are also costs of globalisation, at least for some people or countries. Concerns about the losers appear to be the reason for the rather inarticulate public protests against globalisation at times of international meetings, such as the annual meetings of the IMF and the summit meetings of EU countries.

Trade competition can generate insecurity among workers; workers are more easily substitutable now that production is more mobile. Increased trade may create unemployment for, and lower the wages of, unskilled workers in advanced economies.

There is more foreign currency turnover each day than there are official foreign exchange reserves in the world: monetary authorities are less well equipped to defend currencies in the face of speculative attacks. Some have inadequate supervisory and monitoring regulations to manage foreign capital flows, as the East Asian crisis of 1997 revealed (*see* **F49**).

The use of electronic commerce means that tax authorities have difficulty in dealing with audit trails, offshore banking, transfer pricing and jurisdictional issues. The IT revolution has unleashed "fiscal termites" gnawing away at the foundations of the tax system. Without reforms, governments stand to lose tax revenues.

Finally, some of the poorer countries may be unable to cope with and benefit from globalisation. For instance, although the return on investment in Africa is relatively high, Africa has failed to attract commensurate private capital flows, possibly owing to inadequacies in its infrastructure, governance, legal framework and human capital. Africa's share was reduced from 2·8 to 1·7 per cent of world exports between 1983 and 2002. International inequalities will grow if globalisation marginalises the poorest countries.

Globalisation and British Wages.

One of the most remarkable changes in the world economy has been the rise of the *newly industrialising countries* (NICs) (*see* **F41**). They have greatly expanded their exports to the industrialised economies. Their success is based mainly on their efficient use of low-wage labour to produce labour-intensive manufactures.

Economic theory predicts that when there is an increase in trade between two regions with different endowments, and different prices, of capital and labour, these prices will tend to equalise. Thus as a result of the increase in British imports from low-wage countries, unskilled wages should tend to fall in relative terms. This is precisely what has happened in Britain over recent years. The ratio of non-manual to manual wages rose from 1·2 in 1979 to 1·8 in 2000. The increase in imports from the NICs may also have contributed to the growth of unemployment among relatively unskilled manual workers. Expressed as a percentage rate, this is considerably higher than that for the labour force as a whole.

We should recognise, however, that increased imports from low-wage countries are not the only likely influence on unskilled wages. New technology often substitutes capital and skilled labour for less skilled labour. The demise of incomes policy and the decline in trade union membership may also have helped to widen the distribution of wages in Britain.

The Growth of Outsourcing.

Outsourcing is the term used for the transfer of production to countries where the costs are lower. The outsourcing of labour-intensive production of manufactures is a long-standing and well-developed practice, especially by multinational companies. However, the outsourcing of services is a more recent phenomenon. British use of call centres and computing services in India is a well-known example. It has been made possible by improvements in the ease and cost of communications.

Is Outsourcing a Threat?

Outsourcing attracts disapproval in developed countries because it is held responsible for job losses. However, the outsourcing of services to lower-wage countries can alternatively be seen as one of the gains from trade, by which all parties can benefit. There are losers only if the displaced workers cannot be readily absorbed into other employment. Outsourcing has not yet gone very far. In 2003 imports of business services represented only 0·4 per cent of GDP in the US and 1·0 per cent in the UK, and business services represented 2·5 per cent of GDP in India. Moreover, the US and the UK are also exporters of business services. There is no evidence that outsourcing has harmed the UK economy.

THE EUROPEAN UNION.

The *European Community* (EC), now called the *European Union* (EU), was set up by the Treaty of Rome, ratified in 1958. It consisted of six full members—Belgium, France, Holland, Italy, Luxembourg, and Western Germany. For a background discussion, *see* **C11–13, C56–8**.

The United Kingdom acceded as a full member of the EC in 1973. Economic ties with the Community strengthened over the ensuing years. In 2002 no less than 57 per cent of British trade was with the EU.

Economic Arrangements of the EU.

The EU forms a common market with no tariffs or trade controls within it and a Common External Tariff (CET). There is a Common Agricultural Policy (CAP), which is maintained by a system of variable import levies setting *threshold prices* on imports of agricultural products from outside the Union, and by means of *intervention prices* at which agricultural products of the EU are purchased. The EU has a large Budget required mainly for supporting the CAP, *i.e.*, for subsidising farmers. There is free movement of both goods and labour within the Union, and a certain degree of fiscal harmonisation.

It is in the British interest that the CAP—with its heavy support of farmers—be reformed. EU funds are available to protect farmers by buying excess food and building up stocks of food if the free market price falls below the intervention price. As a result "food mountains" have developed. Various attempts have been made to cut the subsidy by gradually reducing the prices paid to farmers. However, reform of the CAP runs up against vested interests: progress is slow.

The European Monetary System.

The *European Monetary System* (EMS) was introduced in 1979. A currency was permitted to float within a narrow band on either side of the par rate between the currency and any other member's currency. Central bank intervention was required to keep the currency within the band. The difference in inflation rates among countries in the EMS necessitated periodic currency realignments. Initially

Britain resisted joining on account of London's role as a financial centre and because, Britain being a net oil exporter, the British balance of payments was likely to move inversely to that of other EU countries as the world price of oil fluctuated.

Nevertheless, events were pushing Britain towards full membership of the EMS, involving entry to the *Exchange Rate Mechanism* (ERM). The ERM required member countries to keep their exchange rates fixed within narrow bands and to adopt domestic monetary policies to achieve this target.

British Entry to the ERM.

In October 1990 John Major, then Chancellor of the Exchequer, announced that Britain would join the ERM. The exchange rate was set at a rate of £1 – 2·95 deutschmarks. It is interesting to note that the disagreement between the Prime Minister, Margaret Thatcher, her Chancellor of the Exchequer, Nigel Lawson, and her Deputy Prime Minister, Sir Geoffrey Howe, which led eventually to the resignation of all three of them, was related to the dispute over entry to the EMS. To many members of the public this seemed an obscure technical issue, but underlying the technicalities were important points of substance, relating to the most effective policies to control inflation and to maintain national sovereignty.

Towards Economic Integration.

The *Single European Act* was introduced in 1986 to establish a free internal market in the Community. This was defined as an area without frontiers in which the free movement of goods, persons, services and capital is ensured. The single market involved the end of exchange controls, common financial services and technical standards, and mutual recognition of professional qualifications.

The Act circumscribed the powers of member countries to impose a veto in all but sensitive issues. It also made provision for what is called "cohesion", which means reducing the gap between rich and poor regions of the Community. The Act could be seen as a small step in the direction of a federal Europe.

The Treaty of European Union.

At a summit meeting held in Maastricht in December 1991, leaders of the Community member states—the *European Council*—agreed on a draft Treaty of European Union (the *Maastricht Treaty*). European economic and monetary union was now a gradual but irreversible commitment. It will become a single currency by 1999, administered by a single independent central bank.

John Major, now Prime Minister, signed the Treaty but secured concessions: Britain would not be required to participate in a social policy agreement, intended to provide a charter of social rights for workers. Britain's opposition to the Social Charter was based on grounds of cost and of ideology, *e.g.* it would "restore trade union practices that the government had spent much of the last twelve years eliminating".

The British Government eschewed a referendum but managed to secure ratification of the Treaty in Parliament. The Community became the *European Union* on 1 November 1993.

Crisis in the Community, 1992.

There was an upheaval in the EMS in 1992. High interest rates in Germany posed problems for the countries with weak currencies and depressed economies. In particular, there was speculation against the lira and the pound. On 13 September, the lira was devalued 7 per cent by agreement, and on 17 September the pound was forced out of the EMS by speculation, despite massive supportive intervention (*see* **F51**). Britain thereafter stayed out of the ERM.

EMU 1999.

At Maastricht in 1991 certain *convergence criteria* were laid down as a condition for *European Monetary Union* (EMU) in 1999. They concerned inflation, the fiscal situation, interest rates and exchange rates. Each joining country's inflation rate should not be greater than those of the three lowest-inflation countries by more than 1·5 per cent per annum. The ratio of the budget deficit to GDP should not exceed 3 per cent, and the ratio of government debt to GDP should not exceed 60 per cent. Long term interest rates should be within two percentage points of those in the three lowest-inflation countries. Finally, each joining country must have maintained ERM parity within the normal margins for at least two years. The argument was that, unless these conditions were satisfied, the tensions among divergent economies would be too great to withstand the permanent locking of exchange rates that was implicit in the creation of the new currency, the *Euro*.

The *Euro* was created on 1 January 1999, and it replaced national currencies on 1 January 2002. There were twelve EMU members: Germany, Greece, France, Italy, Netherlands, Belgium, Luxembourg, Ireland, Portugal, Spain, Finland and Austria. Denmark, Sweden and the United Kingdom stayed out.

There is some danger that countries have entered EMU without having achieved adequate convergence. If, in the face of any future shocks to the European economy, this proved to be the case, it would generate serious economic and political strains within the monetary union. The choice would then have to be made between less economic integration and closer political integration in order to solve the problems.

The Growth and Stability Pact.

Member states, led by Germany, were concerned that countries within EMU would lack fiscal discipline. As a safeguard against this danger, a *Growth and Stability Pact* was concluded in June 1997. It prescribed sanctions against countries that breach the Maastricht budget deficit ceiling (3 per cent of GDP). In principle, the Pact applies to all European Union members but only countries in the Euro area can be fined. Such penalties would also assist fiscal policy coordination among member states.

There is a counter-argument, however. It is that governments need more, not less, fiscal autonomy in pursuing their macroeconomic objectives once they cede power over monetary policy to the *European Central Bank* (ECB). The fiscal rules might thus be put to the test by governments held responsible by their electorates for achieving national prosperity and growth.

Economic Stresses in the EU.

Along with other advanced economies, the EU was in recession from 2001 to 2003. The German economy was particularly badly affected: it grew by 0·8 per cent in 2001, 0·1 per cent in 2002, and not at all in 2003; and only weakly (by 1·6 per cent) in 2004. The underlying problem was poor export performance—the result of weakened competitiveness—and weak business confidence, which deterred investment.

The Growth and Stability Pact Under Strain.

Both Germany and France exceeded the maximum government budget deficit (3 per cent of GDP) permitted by the Growth and Stability Pact. In 2003 their deficits were −3·8 and −4·1 per cent respectively, and exceeded −3·0 per cent again in 2004 despite the fiscal tightening that both countries announced. Germany and France were able to stave off the threat of European Commission fines for which they were liable under the Pact. Their tactics were resented by the smaller member states. However, it is arguable that this fiscal laxity was appropriate in order to help extract Euroland from its economic recession.

In early 2005, the Growth and Stability Pact was reformed by member governments, despite opposition from the European Central Bank. More flexibility was introduced: the rules would now be applied on a case-by-case basis.

Economic Prospects for the Euro Area.

Unemployment in Euroland averaged no less than 9 per cent in 2004. The poor growth performance of the Euro area is probably due to the high value of the euro weakening competitiveness, the conservative monetary policies of the inflation-conscious ECB, and the fiscal limitations (albeit now somewhat relaxed) imposed by the Growth and Stability Pact. Moreover, the outlook would be worse if the new German government were to raise VAT by 3 percentage points in 2007, as it proposed to do. Were the ECB then to lift interest rates so as to offset the inflationary effect, on one estimate this would reduce the growth rate of the Euro area in 2006 and 2007 from 2·0 to 1·8 per cent per annum.

Should Britain join EMU?

In 2000 Britain faced an important choice: whether to join EMU and, if so, when? Public opinion, business opinion and professional economists were divided on this issue, as were the main political parties. In 1999 a poll of voters found only 20 per cent of people to be in favour, another found 50 per cent of companies in favour, and a third 64 per cent of economists in favour. The British government's position was that entry would require a positive referendum result. It is clear that the issue is a political as well as an economic one: monetary union is very likely to require, and to generate, closer political union.

The government laid down five tests to be satisfied before putting the choice to the electorate: there should be sustainable convergence between Britain and other EU members, there should be sufficient flexibility to cope with economic change, and the effects on investment, the financial services sector, and employment should be favourable. In a sense, these tests will be satisfied when the government says so. A key issue, however, will be the exchange rate. In November 2005 the euro stood at €1·47 = £1. Locking into the euro at that rate might pose a problem of competitiveness for British producers, as did Britain's entry to the EMS in 1990.

The other main danger is that the government would lose adequate control of the economy once monetary policy had been handed over to the European Central Bank in Frankfurt. As against these dangers, a common currency could bring the potential benefits of more trade and more competition and the resultant cheaper goods and services.

Tax Policy in the EU.

The European Union adopted *value added tax* (VAT) as the main indirect tax, and has allowed member countries to set their own rates. The normal VAT rate in Britain (17·5 per cent) is lower than in Denmark and Sweden (25 per cent) but higher than in Spain (16 per cent). As the internal market became a reality, differences in indirect taxes began to divert business. Harmonisation of taxes, expecially indirect taxes, became EU policy.

When indirect tax is expressed as a proportion of GDP, Britain is at the EU average (14 per cent in 1997), but the range was from 19 per cent in Denmark to 11 per cent in Spain. The case for harmonising direct taxes is not so strong, and there remains a wide range (over 20 per cent in Sweden and Denmark, 15 per cent in the UK, and 10 per cent in Portugal in 1997). There are no EU plans to harmonise social security contributions, varying from 19 per cent of GDP in France, 7 per cent in the United Kingdom (the third lowest), to 2 per cent in Denmark.

The average overall tax burden in the EU was 42 per cent of GDP in 1997. Along with Ireland, the United Kingdom was relatively lightly taxed. However, Europe's taxation is high by comparison with its main competitors, the United States and Japan.

Expansion of the Union.

Greece joined the Community in 1981, and Spain and Portugal in 1986. East Germany was incorporated in 1990. In 1994 the electorates of Austria, Finland and Sweden voted to join, and the Norwegians voted narrowly against. The three countries entered the Union in 1995. The Treaty on Economic Union provides that any European state whose system of government is democratic may apply to become a member of the Union.

Ten countries joined the European Union in May 2004. These were three Baltic countries (Estonia, Latvia and Lithuania) two Mediterranean islands (Cyprus and Malta) and five countries in central Europe (Czech Republic, Hungary, Poland, Slovakia and Slovenia). Other candidates knocking at the door were Bulgaria, Romania and Turkey.

The ten new members add another 105 million

people to the Union. However, their incomes per head are considerably lower than those of the existing members, ranging in 1995 from 18 per cent of the mean in Latvia to 59 per cent in Slovenia. Their entry would bring the political benefit of greater stability in Europe, but there would be economic costs for the existing members. Unless the CAP were reformed, its cost would be greatly increased. Expansion would also widen economic inequality among member states and so require larger regional budgetary transfers, and it would probably retard economic and monetary integration within the Union.

In 2006 negotiations for the entry of Bulgaria and Romania were well-advanced, and those for the more contentious case of Turkey were beginning.

2. INTERNAL DEVELOPMENTS

The Post-1945 Era.

Since the end of World War Two, the British economy has experienced mixed fortunes. Throughout the 1950s and 1960s, economic growth was relatively rapid by historic standards, and unemployment very low. The Prime Minister in the late 1950s, Harold Macmillan, won a General Election in 1959 with the slogan "you've never had it so good". There were also problems, however. Inflation persisted, and gradually increased to levels which, by the mid-1970s, had become unacceptable. Balance of payments crises periodically forced governments to deflate the economy. The share of public spending in total national income rose, and with it the share of incomes paid in taxes; there was continued argument about whether or not this was acceptable. A further cause for concern was that Britain's growth rate was less than that of many competitor countries. Over time, therefore, the country's relative position gradually worsened.

Thatcherism.

In the 1970s economic growth dried up, and the problems of inflation, balance of payments deficits and rising government expenditure all intensified. There was a widespread feeling in the country that a change of emphasis was needed, and this led to the election of Margaret Thatcher as Prime Minister in 1979. Mrs. Thatcher promised, and delivered, many changes. She broke the inflationary psychology which had taken hold in the 1970s, though at the cost of a large and prolonged rise in unemployment. She reduced the powers of trade unions, whose aggressive behaviour had contributed to the country's inflationary problems and had also seemingly held back productivity advances. She privatised many previously state-owned industries, and in this and other ways sought to reduce the share of public spending in national income.

Mrs. Thatcher's changes were initially highly controversial but many of them subsequently won wider acceptance within the country. There were problems, however. The sharp rise in unemployment put pressure on the public finances, with the result that Mrs. Thatcher made little headway with her aim of cutting the share of public spending in national income. This aim was itself a source of some problems, producing a squeeze on resources for essential public services such as health and education. Over the years of Mrs. Thatcher's leadership, the feeling also grew that her policies were in some respects unnecessarily divisive. The sharp widening of income inequality during the 1980s typified the problem: whilst average incomes grew quite fast, those on relatively low incomes experienced virtually no rise at all. These problems gradually eroded her support, and in 1990 she was removed as Prime Minister and replaced by John Major.

The 1990s.

At the start of the 1990s the economy was plunged into a steep recession, as the government was forced to deflate the economy in order to remove the effects of what, with hindsight, had been the over-expansionary policies of the late 1980s. The government also had to raise taxes in order to remove a substantial deficit in the public finances, itself partly a product of the recession but also of over-optimistic cuts in taxes in the late 1980s.

Not surprisingly, the combination of tax increases and a steep recession made Mr. Major's government very unpopular, especially since the government had won the 1992 General Election on promises of steady economic growth and tax cuts. Further unpopularity resulted when, in September 1992, government was forced to pull the pound out of the European Exchange Rate Mechanism into which it had entered two years previously. The government had made ERM membership the centrepiece of its economic policy. When it was forced to abandon the policy, it lost its reputation for economic competence. Mr. Major's government never recovered from this, and was heavily defeated in the 1997 elections.

During the 1997 election campaign there was naturally much debate about the government's economic record, after nearly 18 years in power. The government claimed to have transformed the economy; its critics argued that economic performance had been poor, with the country losing ground internationally. The evidence suggests that extreme judgements on either side of the argument are difficult to justify. In terms of income and productivity growth, the country's performance, compared with other industrial economies, improved somewhat during the 1980s and 1990s compared with earlier decades. However, critics could argue that there was still much ground to make up, with average productivity levels in the mid-1990s still some 20 per cent below those in Germany. The country's unemployment and inflation performance remained poor. To some extent this reflected poor performance in the European Union generally, but both the USA and Japan could point to a better performance over those 18 years. Overall, such international comparisons pointed to a slight strengthening of the British economy in relation to its competitors, but there remained a gap between Britain and the strongest economies.

The 1997 Labour Government.

The new Chancellor, Gordon Brown, came to office with various plans and commitments. His most spectacular initial act was the wholly unexpected decision to transfer power to determine interest rates away from the Chancellor to the newly established Monetary Policy Committee of the Bank of England.

With hindsight this initial decision was a fundamental one. It gave instant credit that the new government's claim that its priority was to establish economic stability, by removing short term political calculation as an influence over interest rates and monetary policy. Although there were some early teething problems with the new system, these soon disappeared, leading to general acceptance across the political landscape that the change was sensible and should become permanent.

Redistribution and Welfare-to-Work.

Two other priorities for the new government also soon emerged. The first was a commitment to helping those on relatively low incomes, with the aim of stopping, and to some extent reversing, the trends of the previous two decades, which had seen a sharp widening of income inequality and a serious deterioration in the relative position of those on the lowest incomes. This group had hardly shared at all in the general rise in real incomes during the 1980s and 1990s.

Mr Brown's commitment to addressing this problem took two main forms. The first involved straightforward redistribution, through a series of tax and spending measures. The second addressed a specific, and important, source of poverty, namely the low incentives for some people of working age to seek jobs rather than remaining unemployed. Mr Brown sought to shift people in this position away from welfare and into work by redesigning the structure of taxes and benefits so as to ensure that those taking jobs saw a worthwhile increase in their net incomes.

State Pension Linked to Earnings or Prices?

The implementation of these aims involved some difficult choices. For example, many of those on the lowest incomes were elderly and were dependent on the state pension as their only, or principal, income source. This pension had at one time been linked to average earnings, but during the 1980s it had been decided to break this link, and instead to link the pension to the index of retail prices. In the intervening years average earnings had risen substantially more than prices—reflecting economic growth—with the result that the purchasing power of the state pension had declined significantly compared with that of average earnings. In effect, breaking the link with earnings meant that pensioners were no longer sharing in the proceeds of economic growth.

Many people had opposed the decision of the Thatcher government to break the link, and in the light of Mr Brown's intention to help those on low incomes they argued that he should restore it. However, he refused to do so on the grounds that this would be a wasteful way of trying to combat poverty, because a substantial proportion of pensioners were not badly off. This reflected the growth of occupational and personal pensions, causing many retired people no longer to be primarily dependent on the state pension. Mr Brown argued that to restore the state pension's link to earnings would be very costly over time, and that much of this extra outlay would be wasteful, going to people who did not need the extra income. He argued instead that help should be targeted on those pensioners with few resources over and above the state pension.

Poverty Alleviation versus Incentives.

Such issues illustrated the difficulty of designing cost-effective measures to alleviate poverty. Another illustration was provided by the welfare-to-work objectives. To increase the incentives for people with relatively low earning power to take jobs rather than remain unemployed and rely on welfare payments, The Government needed to design measures that provided benefits conditional on being in work. However, this potentially risked the same problem as that posed by the proposal to reintroduce the link between pensions and earnings: generalised benefits payable to all those in work would be wasteful because they would go to higher paid people as well as to those with low earning power. To avoid this again required a form of means testing, this time by "tapering" benefits i.e. making benefit entitlement inversely related to earnings, with entitlement falling to zero beyond an upper threshold.

Whilst this ensured effective targeting, it also reduced the incentives for those already in work but on low incomes to try to better themselves, e.g. by acquiring additional training or qualifications aimed at raising their earning power. The problem for such people was that they would secure little benefit from such efforts, since much of the extra income would be offset by a loss of benefits. In effect, tapering of benefits meant that such people faced very high marginal tax rates. This again illustrated the complications involved in trying to alleviate poverty: whilst targeted benefits offered a cost-effective method, they were by no means problem-free.

Public Service Problems.

The second priority for the new Labour government concerned public services. There was a widespread feeling in the Labour party that the public services had been starved of funding by the Thatcher and Major governments and that the quality of the services had deteriorated as a result. Mr Brown came into office determined to reverse this trend.

Just as in the case of his desire to narrow inequalities, however, so also in this case there were problems in achieving his objectives. In the run-up to the 1997 election Mr Blair had promised that Labour would not increase either the basic or the higher rates of income tax if elected. As with some of its other promises, this had been designed to increase voter confidence that a Blair-led Labour government would behave differently from earlier Labour governments. The problem that Mr Blair's promise created, however, was a serious one. To fund significant increases in public expenditure required additional tax revenue, and one obvious way of achieving this—raising standard or higher rates of income tax—was ruled out for the whole of Labour's first term of office. (Indeed, Mr Blair repeated the promise in Labour's campaign for re-election in 2001, thus continuing to rule it out for his second term.)

Moreover, Mr Brown was keen to introduce a new, lower, rate of income tax on the first slice of income, in order to help those on lower incomes, and duly did so in 1999; this further reduced the revenue from income tax.

"Stealth Taxes".

To meet the need for additional tax revenue Mr Brown therefore had to look elsewhere. For example, in his first budget he introduced graduated rates for Stamp Duty, payable as a percentage of the purchase price of houses. Progressively higher rates were introduced on the purchase of more expensive properties. In later budgets this principle was extended, with the higher rates being increased, and additional higher rates on the most expensive properties being introduced. This provided a substantial new source of tax revenue, especially as a result of the sustained rapid increase in house prices: with the tax bands being held constant, ever larger proportions of house purchasers found themselves paying Stamp Duty at higher rates.

Some of these, and other tax increases, were labelled "stealth taxes" by some of the Chancellor's critics. They argued that Mr Brown was attempting to raise tax revenue in ways that the voters would not notice, rather than using high profile methods such as increases in income tax rates or in Value Added Tax rates. To the extent that this was an influence on Mr Brown's policy decisions, the very fact that his critics started to focus attention on it probably negated their point, since tax increases can hardly remain unnoticed if their imposition becomes a focus for public debate. Mr Brown might in any case have mounted the defence that many of his critics were also just as vocal in their criticisms of the poor quality of some core public services, perhaps implying an element of inconsistency or even hypocrisy on the critics' part: it is hard to object to poor quality public services if one also objects to the tax increases needed to fund an improvement in quality.

Problems with Stealth Taxes on Pension Funds.

The Chancellor encountered problems with some of his so-called stealth taxes. For example, in his first budget in 1997 he abolished dividend tax credits for pension funds. This seemed a good illustration of a stealth tax: although its implications were noted at the time with some concern by economists, it had little immediate impact and therefore went largely unnoticed by most voters. However, the measure rebounded during Labour's second term. The tax change reduced the effective rate of return on pension schemes. When combined with the fall in equity prices at the turn of the century, this led to a very substantial fall in the profitability of many such schemes, leading many companies to re-evaluate their pension policies.

Many company pension schemes in the UK had traditionally been *defined benefit* schemes, whereby the size of final pension is governed mainly by length of service and by salary at retirement. Such schemes were valued by those belonging to them because they were largely insulated from stock market fluctuations. Throughout the 1990s the persistent rises in equity prices meant that most businesses could easily meet their commitments to such schemes. The sharp falls after 1999 drastically altered the picture. Companies began to find that the returns on their pension fund investments were no longer sufficient to meet their commitments. Faced with the choice of either increasing pension contributions, or altering the schemes, many companies chose the latter option, closing their defined benefit schemes to new employees (and in a few cases, also to existing employees who already belonged to the schemes.) Typically, companies proposed instead to switch to *defined contribution* schemes. The basic principle of these schemes is that pension benefits are determined by the returns on the pension fund investments, rather than by rules relating to final salary or length of service. Thus, they expose the members of such schemes to stock market risks, and in this respect shift the risk away from companies and move the risk towards individuals.

Other Problems with Stealth Taxes.

Although the Chancellor's abolition of tax credits on pension fund income was by no means the only cause of problems with pensions, it was clearly one contributory factor. As such it perhaps illustrated the "law of unintended consequences" the tendency for actions taken with one purpose in mind to have unpredicted impacts in other contexts. The use of stealth taxes produced some other instances of this. For example, from 1997 onwards Mr Brown set out to raise excise duty on road fuel by substantially more than the rate of inflation. He had two main aims in mind: to raise additional tax revenue, and to contribute towards environmental protection by seeking to discourage vehicle use, the latter being one of the major sources of climate change and global warming.

The resulting rise in the cost of road transport, when combined with a squeeze on farmers' revenue from some crop and animal products, caused increasing resentment in some farming communities, leading to widespread civil disobedience in 2000, with farmers, supported by other affected groups such as lorry drivers, blockading roads in protest against high excise duties and resulting high petrol prices. Faced with these protests the government backed down, and scrapped plans for projected further increases in fuel excise duties.

Council Taxes.

Yet another example of largely unintended consequences was the growing protests during Labour's second term about very rapid rises in council taxes. These taxes are levied by local authorities to finance locally organised activities such as schools, retirement homes, and refuse collection. The costs of many these activities increased by substantially more than the rate of inflation during Labour's second term, partly reflecting the government's determination to improve their quality. At the same time the government's difficulties in raising tax revenue meant that it was unable to increase its contribution to the costs of locally provided services by the same proportionate amount. Consequently many local councils found themselves forced to raise council taxes by much more than the rate of inflation in order to fill the gap between the government's service quality objectives and its provision of funding support.

In a sense such council tax rises could also be viewed as stealth taxes because, although highly visible, the government could argue that it was not responsible. In practice this argument did not work well because many voters clearly blamed the government.

Alternative Funding Methods for Public Services.

Such problems led the government to consider other ways of financing public services. One possibility that emerged during its second term was that of co-payments, whereby users of public services pay part of the cost directly if they can afford to do so. Ideas that were floated included charging patients for appointments with doctors, and for catering costs during hospital stays. Another—university tuition fees—became one of the major political controversies during the government's second term.

The Funding of Higher Education.

The funding of universities provided the government with a major dilemma. It wanted to increase the proportion of school leavers going into higher education towards 50 per cent, and for this and other reasons was keen to channel additional resources into the country's universities. However, the acute difficulties that it was experiencing in generating enough tax revenue to fund even its existing level of public spending commitments meant that it ruled out providing all the increased university funding through tax revenue. The government therefore proposed a co-payment scheme, with the cost of university degree programmes being met partly by tax revenue and partly by the consumers of the programmes, *i.e.* students.

Not surprisingly this proved to be controversial, with critics arguing that some people with the ability to benefit from going to university would be deterred from doing so. The government's critics, however, had some problems of their own since it was common ground among all sides to the debate that additional funding was needed for the university sector. The critics therefore had to explain how they proposed to achieve this if they ruled out co-payments.

The only specific alternative suggested was an increase in general taxation, perhaps targeted on those with very high incomes. The difficulty with this alternative, however, was that there were many other strong claims on any increase in tax revenue, making it unlikely that all or even most of the revenue would actually find its way into the universities. By contrast, co-payments in the form of increased student tuition fees would be earmarked for university use.

The Funding of Health Care.

The possible use of co-payments extended beyond the case of universities, to include various aspects of health care. Some people argued that the country might learn from the experience of some of the continental European countries, and require individuals to fund part of their health care through private insurance schemes. The government rejected this approach, but some of its critics argued that in countries such as France and Germany the quality of health care was superior to that in Britain because these countries devoted a significantly larger fraction of their national income to health care, with most of the difference between their levels and the lower British level being accounted for by private insurance top-ups of basic state provision.

The argument revolved around how to channel more resources into a public service from which consumers appeared to want improved quality whilst simultaneously being reluctant to see their taxes increase.

Public Spending.

Such arguments about public spending, and how to fund it, continued to dominate economic and political discussion throughout Labour's second term. The Chancellor had maintained the Conservatives' tough controls on public spending during his first two years in office, but this was contrary to his longer term aim—central to traditional Labour party thinking—of seeking to improve the quality of public services. From 2000 onwards successive annual budgets oversaw a significant growth in spending, especially in the "front line" education and health services. Some of this extra spending could be met without any increase in tax rates, because continuing economic growth meant buoyant tax revenue. However, by no means all the extra spending could be funded like this. Some of it came from increases in "stealth taxes", and some of it was planned to come from savings in other areas of public spending.

Increased taxes continued to be a source of controversy, though there seemed to be some understanding on the part of voters that it would be difficult to secure improvements in the quality of services without them. Savings in other areas of spending were also a source of debate, with critics arguing that, for example, reductions in the number of civil servants might seem like painless economies but, in the longer term, would cause damaging deterioration in the quality of support services. By contrast, other critics feared that the planned savings would not materialise, and that as a result the Chancellor would lose control of the public finances, with overall spending rising much faster than tax revenue.

The 2005 Budget and the General Election.

These arguments continued in the discussion of Mr Brown's March 2005 Budget, and in the ensuing general election. In his Budget the Chancellor announced no substantial new policy initiatives, but expressed confidence that his broad strategy of spending and taxation was sustainable. He also re-emphasised some of the continuing themes that had been important throughout his tenure as Chancellor: for example, the welfare-to-work programme, and targeted and means-tested benefits. The Budget contained some detailed measures that were widely interpreted as election bribes, for example one-off payments to people aged over 65 to help them meet their council tax payments. Although it was easy to be cynical about such proposals, Mr Brown was not alone in seeking to bribe the voters, since the main opposition parties had also proposed policies aimed at reducing retired voters' local taxation liabilities. Similar "bidding wars" for voter support affected other parts of the tax system: for example, both Mr Brown's Budget, and the Conservative opposition election proposals, involved increases in thresholds for payment of inheritance taxes.

The General Election Arguments.

In the general election, debate about economic policy was somewhat muted, for two reasons. First, and unusually for a British general election, a foreign policy issue—the Iraq war and its aftermath—emerged as a leading issue, and many voters clearly felt more strongly about this than about any domestic policy issues. Second, the differences among the main political parties were limited. All accepted the framework of policy-making laid down by Mr Brown right at the start of his tenure as Chancellor, with an independent Bank of England being responsible for interest rate and monetary policy decisions.

Although there were fierce arguments at the margins of debate about public spending (for example, about the extent to which elderly people needing nursing care should have to fund it themselves, rather than it being financed out of tax revenue) there was no great divide among the main parties about levels of taxation and public spending. Although many leading Conservatives instinctively favoured a much smaller public sector, and correspondingly lower taxes, they were conscious that voter sentiment was not sympathetic to cutbacks in front line public services, and this limited their ability to present a radically different economic policy.

The 2006 Budget.

Labour won the election, albeit with a much reduced majority of seats in Parliament, and on the basis of support from only just over one third of those who voted. Mr Brown continued as Chancellor, and presented his tenth Budget in March 2006. The Budget contained relatively few strategic developments though there was a wealth of detail.

The Budget Backdrop.

The Budget was set against a backdrop of positive forecasts for the future growth of the economy. Mr Brown predicted annual growth of between 2 and 2·5 per cent in 2006, rising to between 2·75 and 3·25 per cent in 2007 and 2008. On the basis of his growth forecasts, the Chancellor predicted annual public sector borrowing of £37 billion during 2006, falling to £36 billion in 2007 and £30 billion in 2008. His forecasts were generally thought to be on the optimistic side among private forecasters in the City of London, but they were roughly in line with those of the Bank of England. Those predicting slower growth based their forecasts mainly on a projected slowdown in world economic growth. Some of the Chancellor's critics pointed out that each of his previous five Budgets had been based on growth forecasts that turned out to be too optimistic.

The critics pointed to other difficulties. They noted that economic growth had fallen, and unemployment had risen, during 2005, and they argued that this was a domestically generated problem. Mr Brown was adamant that this was only a temporary blip in what he continued to present as a sustained period of exceptionally good economic performance. He attributed the slowdown in growth in 2005 to increased oil prices and to a slowdown in the housing market, both of these being events which he expected would be only temporary. He also argued that the economy's labour market was much more flexible than at the time of previous oil price shocks, and that this would prevent oil price rises from being translated into an inflationary spiral of wage and price increases.

Doubts on Continued Growth.

Mr Brown's critics also argued that some of the economic growth experienced during his tenure as Chancellor resulted from trends which could not be sustained. They pointed to growth in consumer spending, in government spending and in the current account balance of payments deficit, as three contributors to growth which could not continue indefinitely. The critics had a point: consumer spending and public spending cannot persistently outstrip overall economic growth, and neither can the current account deficit grow without limit. The implication was that there would need to be a structural shift in the economy—towards investment and exports—for sustainable growth to continue. The critics argued that the Chancellor had not addressed himself seriously to such structural issues.

Mr Brown pointed out that he had budgeted for much slower future growth in public spending for the years up to 2010 than during the period from 2000 to 2005. He readily agreed with his critics that during these years there had been rapid growth in public expenditure, but disagreed with them that this was a matter for criticism, arguing that a substantial boost to public spending was required to repair what he believed to be a cumulative shortfall following a period of underinvestment in essential public services. Some of his critics nevertheless objected that he had not accompanied the extra spending with reforms in public services, leading much of the extra spending to be applied wastefully rather than productively.

Mr Brown argued that his record over nearly nine years as Chancellor was very strong. Britain had outperformed the Eurozone consistently since 1997, and the average annual growth rate of around 2·8 per cent since 1997 comfortably exceeded the annual average of 2·1 per cent during the 18 years of Conservative government between 1979 and 1997.

The Budget and Education.

The Budget did not seek to engineer any strategic changes in policy. Much attention therefore focused on some of the Budget's more detailed proposals. One feature was the priority given to schools, in the form of an additional £34 billion of spending over the next five years. The Chancellor's aim was to raise the level of spending per pupil in state schools to the same level as in the country's private schools. He pointed out that this figure stood at some £8,000 in private schools compared with £5,000 in state schools. Much of the gap in spending could be accounted for by a much lower pupil-teacher ratio in private schools; Mr Brown hoped that the additional spending would fund additional teacher recruitment in the public sector, allowing its ratio to fall towards the private sector's.

The Budget and the Environment.

The growing perception that global climate change represented an unprecedented threat to the future of human civilisation (see **F**49–50) meant that much attention was focused on the extent to which the Budget might affect the country's ability to curb its carbon emissions. The Chancellor announced a number of measures aimed at the issue. He provided £50 million to help fund new micro-generation technologies, aimed at trying to decentralise energy supplies, reducing dependence on traditional large scale power plants. An objection to these plants is that a high proportion of the heat energy that they produce is wasted, whereas smaller scale combined heat and power plants might be able substantially to reduce wastage, thus generating the same amount of usable energy with much lower carbon emissions. Mr Brown also provided additional funds for domestic insulation.

At the international level he proposed discussions on establishing a new large-scale World Bank fund to finance renewable energy projects in developing countries. A final significant measure was that the Climate Change Levy, which had been kept at a fixed level since its introduction in 2002, was increased in line with inflation.

Environmental Critics.

While most of these measures were welcomed by environmental groups, they were sceptical that the measures were sufficiently significant to address the scale of the climate change problem. The critics fastened on an admission by the government, in the week following the Budget, that it would fail to meet its self-imposed target for reducing carbon emissions in 2010. They argued that much tougher measures were urgently needed. Many critics put particular emphasis on the transport sector, where carbon emissions had grown rapidly. They objected to plans for expansion of airports, and to the continued absence of taxation on aviation fuel. They also argued for much higher taxation on cars emitting large amounts of carbon dioxide, and for more government help to encourage investment in alternative transport technologies.

Other Budget Measures.

Other measures announced by the Chancellor included increases in the thresholds for stamp duty and inheritance tax. The stamp duty threshold directly affected those buying houses. The government, however, renewed its commitment to trying to help first-time purchasers, for example through schemes for shared equity purchase. The Chancellor announced a doubling of the amount paid into Child Trust Funds, and an above inflation increase in child tax credits. Mr Brown re-emphasised his strong commitment to combating child poverty, though he admitted that the government had missed its own targets for reducing the number of children living in poverty. He also announced tough targets for public sector pay, aiming for job cuts in several government departments and for below-inflation pay increases for many groups of employees.

A Budget for Continuity.

Overall, the Budget did not signal any significant change in the government's economic strategy or in its medium term forecasts for the economy. Although there were arguments about the Chancellor's judgement, these were mainly marginal rather than fundamental differences of view, and few mainstream politicians advocated a substantially different economic strategy. The most fundamental arguments were increasingly between, on the one hand, mainstream politicians who saw continued economic growth as the fundamental objective of policy, and on the other hand, a small but growing minority who argued for a completely different set of priorities, based on the need to combat global climate change by moving to an economy with much lower carbon emissions.

BIBLICAL GLOSSARY

This section provides an easy to use treasure-house of information about the biblical world. It presents a concise and valuable guide to the people, places and events which have had so much influence on the course of history (with a note on the history of the Bible itself and the Apocrypha).

THE LAND OF PALESTINE

N.B. This map does not represent Palestine as it was at any one period of history. It shows most of the Palestinian locations mentioned in the text from whatever period.

BIBLICAL GLOSSARY

THE BIBLE

Introduction

There is a sense in which the Bible is part of every person's heritage. Though it is sometimes claimed that we are now living in a post-Christian era, the marks of a Christian culture are part of our everyday experience: the great cathedrals of our cities, the parish churches and village chapels of our countryside. At the root of this culture is the revelation of God offered by the Bible.

It is not, however, an easy book. The modern reader has to bridge a major time-gap of at least 2,000 years (often much more) and enter into an alien culture if he is to become familiar with the biblical world. It is astonishing how many Christians have succeeded in making this transition with little or no help, and found that the Bible can still speak across the barriers of time and space. But today it should not be necessary for anyone to read the Bible unaided. During the 20th century our understanding of the way the biblical writers worked, of the cultural back ground against which their lives were set, and of the wider historical, social and religious background of the surrounding nations all increased enormously.

Composition of the Bible

The Bible includes the Hebrew sacred Scriptures (Old Testament) and those held sacred by the Christians (New Testament). The Old Testament—the prehistoric portion—consists of 39 books, and is divided into three parts: (1) the Law, (2) the Prophets, (3) Miscellaneous Writings. The Old Testament was written in Hebrew except for parts of Ezra and Daniel, which were in Aramaic.

It was not until the 9th century A.D. that a complete Hebrew text was made, the so-called Massoretic text. Before that the main versions were the Alexandrian Greek translation (Septuagint) made in the 2nd cent. B.C. and St. Jerome's Latin Vulgate of the 4th cent. A.D. (It was Jerome who used the Latin word "testament" (formed from *testis* = a witness).) Portions were translated into the Anglo-Saxon in the 8th cent. and the Venerable Bede put the greater part of St. John's gospel into English, but it was not until 1535 that a complete, printed English version appeared—the Coverdale Translation.

The Authorised Version

The Authorised Version dates from 1611 in the reign of James I, and its beautiful phraseology has given it a lasting appeal. The Revised Version dates from 1885. *The New English Bible*, with the Apocrypha, was published in 1970. It is a new translation in plain English prose of the earliest Hebrew, Aramaic, and Greek manuscripts. The finding of the Dead Sea Scrolls (*see* **H24**) has added to our knowledge of Scripture.

The Apocrypha

These "hidden writings" are the books which were included in the Septuagint (Greek) and Vulgate (Latin) versions of the Old Testament but excluded from the sacred canon at the Reformation by the Protestants on the grounds that they were not originally written in Hebrew nor regarded as genuine by the Jews. The books include: 1 and 2 Esdras, Tobit, Judith, additions to Esther, Wisdom of Solomon, Ecclesiasticus, Baruch, Song of the Three Holy Children, History of Susannah, Bel and the Dragon, Prayer of Manasses, 1 and 2 Maccabees. The term is usually applied to the additions to the Old Testament, but there are also numerous Christian writings of the same character. The apocryphal First Book of Enoch (the seventh patriarch in the Book of Genesis) was used at first in the Christian Church and is still accepted in Ethiopia.

ABBREVIATIONS USED IN GIVING BIBLICAL REFERENCES

Acts	Acts	Isaiah	Is	Nehemiah	Neh
Amos	Amos	James	Jas	Numbers	Num
Chronicles	Chr	Jeremiah	Jer	Obadiah	Obad
Colossians	Col	Job	Job	Peter	Pet
Corinthians	Cor	Joel	Joel	Philemon	Phlm
Daniel	Dan	John	Jn	Philippians	Phil
Deuteronomy	Deut	Jonah	Jon	Proverbs	Prov
Ecclesiastes	Ecc	Joshua	Josh	Psalms	Ps
Ephesians	Eph	Jude	Jude	Revelation	Rev
Esther	Esth	Judges	Judg	Romans	Rom
Exodus	Ex	Kings	Kgs	Ruth	Ruth
Ezekiel	Ezek	Lamentations	Lam	Samuel	Sam
Ezra	Ezra	Leviticus	Lev	Song of Songs	Song
Galatians	Gal	Luke	Lk	Thessalonians	Thes
Genesis	Gen	Malachi	Mal	Timothy	Tim
Habakkuk	Hab	Mark	Mk	Titus	Tit
Haggai	Hag	Matthew	Mt	Zechariah	Zech
Hebrews	Heb	Micah	Mic	Zephaniah	Zeph
Hosea	Hos	Nahum	Nah		

A

Aaron. The elder brother of Moses, he was appointed by God to be Moses' spokesman in the negotiations with the Egyptian Pharaoh for the release of the Jews (Ex 4:14). After the exodus, in Moses' absence, he made a golden calf for the people to worship (Ex 32:1-6). In spite of this lapse, tradition regards him as Israel's first High Priest (Ex 29:1-7).

Abednego. One of three young men who, according to the book of Daniel, survived being thrown into a blazing furnace for refusing to worship a gold statue set up by King Nebuchadnezzar (Dan 3:1-27).

Abel. The second son of Adam and Eve, he was killed by his elder brother Cain out of jealousy because God found Abel's offering of a lamb more acceptable than his offering of grain (Gen 4:1-8). The story probably reflects a feeling among traditionalists that the Jews had been corrupted by the agricultural civilisation of Canaan, and were less acceptable to God than when they had been shepherds.

Abiathar. When his father Ahimelech was killed by Saul for his unwitting involvement in David's escape, Abiathar fled to join David's outlaw band (1 Sam 22:16-23). He subsequently became David's High Priest, but was banished by Solomon because he supported Adonijah in the struggle for succession to the throne (1 Kgs 1:5-7, 26-27).

Abijah. King of Judah (915-913 B.C.).

Abner. Saul's commander-in-chief. After Saul's death he supported Ishbosheth, his only surviving son, as king of Israel, but soon became disenchanted with him. He was negotiating with David to transfer the allegiance of the northern tribes to him when he was murdered by David's commander, Joab, in pursuance of a family quarrel (2 Sam 3:6-27).

Abraham. Abraham, originally known as Abram, is regarded as the father of the Jewish people. While there are doubtless legendary elements in the stories told of him, there is no reason to question his historical existence, probably in the period 2000-1800 B.C. Through the stories of Abraham run two complementary themes: God's promises and Abraham's faith. God promises to Abraham that he will have numerous descendants, that they will occupy the land of Canaan and that they will be a source of blessing to all mankind (Gen 12:1-3). Abraham responds to these promises with faith, shown in his willingness to set out for the promised land not knowing where he is being led, and to sacrifice his son Isaac when he thinks that this is what God requires. Neighbouring peoples (e.g. the Moabites) still practised child sacrifice a thousand years later, and this story, as well as indicating Abraham's faith, reflects the early understanding of the Jews that God did not require human sacrifice.

Absalom. David's third son. After his sister Tamar had been raped by his elder half-brother Amnon, he plotted revenge and eventually had Amnon killed (2 Sam 13). As a result he had to flee to the small state of Geshur which his grandfather ruled. After three years he was permitted to return at the instigation of David's general, Joab, who probably felt that Amnon had only got his due punishment. He then proceeded to plot against his father, sowing seeds of discontent among the northern tribes especially (2 Sam 15:1-6) and finally raised an army to march on Jerusalem. David withdrew across the Jordan, gained time to organise loyal forces and crushed the rebels. In the decisive battle Absalom was killed by Joab, even though David had expressly instructed that he should not be harmed (2 Sam 18:6-15).

Acts of the Apostles. The book is clearly a sequel to Luke's gospel, being addressed to the same person, Theophilus, and referring to an earlier work which described "the things that Jesus did and taught from the time he began his work until the day when he was taken up to heaven." It is invaluable for the insight it gives into the first thirty years of the Christian church. Peter and Paul are the leading personalities in the book, yet the theme is not one of human heroes but of God at work among the community of believers through the gift of the Holy Spirit.

The somewhat surprising ending, with Paul under house arrest in Rome, has led many to wonder whether the work was unfinished or a third volume planned, yet in some ways this is a most fitting conclusion—Paul in spite of everything proclaiming the good news at the very heart of the Roman empire.

Adam. The name is simply the Hebrew for "man". Adam is therefore to be thought of not as the first man in a historical sense but as the symbolic prototype of all mankind.

Adonijah. The fourth son of David. As the eldest surviving son by the time his father reached old age, he expected to succeed to the throne and had himself declared king by Abiathar and Joab before David's death. David, however, nominated Solomon to succeed him and Solomon soon found occasion to accuse Adonijah of treachery and have him put to death (1 Kgs 1:5-53, 2:13-25).

Agrippa. See **Herod Family**.

Ahab. King of Israel (869-850 B.C.). The son of Omri, who arranged his marriage to Jezebel, daughter of the king of Tyre, as part of his policy of friendly relations with Phoenicia. His chief fault was his failure to curb the excesses of his wife, who was determined to supplant the worship of Yahweh with the worship of her own god, Baal Melkart. He ignored the advice of the prophet Micaiah to go to battle against the Syrians at Ramoth-Gilead, where he was fatally wounded by an arrow.

Ahaz. King of Judah (735-715 B.C.). Ahaz came to the throne at a moment of crisis. King Pekah of Israel and King Rezin of Damascus had formed an allegiance against the powerful Assyrians, and were threatening to attack Judah if she did not join them. In desperation, and against the advice of Isaiah, he appealed to the Assyrians for help. This he received, but at the cost of becoming an Assyrian vassal. He is criticised by the biblical historians for taking part in idolatrous practices, and is even said to have sacrificed his own son (2 Kgs 16:1-4).

Ahaziah. (1) King of Israel (850-849 B.C.). The son of Ahab, within two years of coming to the throne he fell from a balcony and never recovered from his injuries (2 Kgs 1:2).
(2) King of Judah (842 B.C.). The son of Jehoram, he had the misfortune to be visiting his father's namesake, Jehoram king of Israel, at the time of Jehu's rebellion in which he was killed (2 Kgs 9:27-28).

Ahijah. A prophet from Shiloh who predicted the division of the kingdom after Solomon's death by tearing his robe into twelve pieces and giving ten of them (representing ten tribes) to Jeroboam, later to be the first king of the breakaway state of Israel (1 Kgs 11:29-40).

Ahimelech. The priest at Nob who unwittingly assisted David's escape from Saul by giving him food and a sword. He was subsequently killed by Saul together with all other priests at Nob.

Alexandria. Though only mentioned four times in the Bible (all the references being in Acts), Alexandria had a large Jewish community almost from its foundation in 332 B.C. by Alexander the Great, and it was here that the Septuagint, the Greek translation of the Old Testament, was made during the third and second centuries B.C.

Amalekites. A nomadic people who lived in the desert regions to the south of Israel. They attacked the Israelites during their march from Egypt to the promised land, and were later attacked and defeated by both Saul and David (1 Sam 15:1-9, 30:1-20).

Amaziah. King of Judah (800-783 B.C.). After succeeding in regaining territory earlier lost to the Edomites, Amaziah got into an unnecessary and disastrous quarrel with King Jehoash of Israel from which he emerged the clear loser. He was eventually assassinated at Lachish, whence he had fled, having heard of a plot against his life (2 Kgs 14:1-19).

Ammonites. A trans-Jordanian tribe frequently at war with the Israelites. It was in action against the Ammonites that Saul proved his powers of leadership (1 Sam 11:1-15), and although David seems to have established good relations with King Nahash of Ammon, his son insulted David's envoys and bitter hostilities ensued. David ultimately took the Ammonite crown, but only after a long struggle (1 Sam 10:1-11:1, 13:26-31).

Amon. King of Judah (642–640 B.C.). The son of the hated Manasseh, he was soon assassinated because he continued in his father's idolatrous ways.

Amos. The first of the great reforming prophets of the eighth century B.C., we know relatively little about the man himself as opposed to what he taught. A herdsman and grower of figs from Tekoa in Judah, he prophesied in the cities of Israel to which he perhaps travelled to sell his produce. His prophetic career may have lasted as little as a few months sometime during the period 760–750 B.C.

Amos was appalled by a society in which an affluent minority exploited the poverty-stricken majority. Loans would be made to the poor, and when they were unable to repay them, their houses and land would be seized, or their children sold into slavery to pay off the debt. The use of false weights and measures by the merchants was commonplace, and bribery in the courts ensured that no case against them would ever succeed. Yet these same merchants made lavish sacrifices to God at the national shrines of Gilgal and Bethel.

The message of Amos is uncompromising, and needs to be balanced by the words of later prophets who saw the possibility of redemption as well as judgement. His importance is immense, as the man who proclaimed with a new clarity the incompatibility of worshipping God and exploiting one's fellow men.

Ananias. (1) A member of the early church who sold some property and gave part of the proceeds to the church, but claimed to have given all. Peter accused him of lying to God, and he fell down dead (Acts 5:1–6).

(2) A Christian in Damascus who, in response to a vision, went and baptised Saul following his conversion (Acts 9:10–19).

(3) The Jewish High Priest before whom Paul appeared after his arrest in the temple at Jerusalem (Acts 23:1–5).

Andrew, St. The brother of Simon Peter and one of the first disciples. His feast day is 30 November. Patron Saint of Scotland.

Annas. Though he had retired from the High Priesthood before the time of Jesus' trial, Annas continued to exercise influence through his son-in-law and successor, Caiaphas.

Antioch. (1) The capital of the Roman province of Syria and an important centre of early Christianity. It was here that disciples were first called Christians, and it was this church that sent Paul and Barnabas out on the first missionary journey (Acts 13:1–3).

(2) A city in Pisidia (part of Asia Minor) visited by Paul on his first missionary journey (Acts 13:13–52).

Apocalypse. Prophetic description of the end of the world from the Greek word meaning "revelation".

Apocrypha. *See* **Introduction**, **H3**.

Apollos. A Jew from Alexandria who proclaimed the gospel in Ephesus but only knew about John's baptism as opposed to Christian baptism in the Holy Spirit. After Prisca and Aquila had explained Christianity more fully to him he went on to Corinth where, unfortunately, opposing factions developed according to whether they "followed" Apollos or other teachers (Acts 18:24–28, 1 Cor 1:12–13)

Apostles. The twelve apostles who were disciples of Jesus were: Simon Peter and Andrew (his brother), James and John (sons of Zebedee), Philip, Bartholomew, Thomas, Matthew, James, Thaddaeus, Simon, and Judas Iscariot. After the Ascension Matthias was chosen to take the place of Judas. St. Paul was the leading apostle in the mission to the Gentiles, though he was not one of the twelve. St. Barnabas has also been called an apostle.

Apostolic Fathers were the immediate disciples or followers of the apostles, especially such as left writings behind. They included Barnabas, Clement of Rome, Ignatius of Antioch, Hermas, Papias of Hieropolis and Polycarp.

Aquila. A Jew who, with his wife Prisca, was expelled from Rome by an edict of Claudius and settled in Corinth. Here they welcomed Paul, and later worked with him in Ephesus (Acts 18:1–4, 24–26).

Aramaeans. *See* Syrians.

Areopagus. An open space in Athens, often used for public debates, and where Paul addressed the Athenians (Acts 17:16–34).

Ark of the Covenant. An ornate wooden chest believed to contain the stone tablets on which the ten commandments were written. It accompanied the Israelites throughout their nomadic wanderings and was then kept at Shiloh during the early years of the occupation of Palestine. Brought by the Israelites to encourage them in battle against the Philistines at Aphek, it was in fact captured, but the Philistines soon returned it, attributing a series of disasters to its presence. David brought it to Jerusalem, where Solomon eventually enshrined it in the temple. It is presumed to have remained there until the temple was destroyed by the Babylonians in 586 B.C.

Artemis. A Greek goddess identified with the Roman Diana. Her temple at Ephesus was famous, though the worship there seems to have been based on an earlier fertility cult.

Asa. King of Judah (913–873 B.C.).

Ascension. Although this is the word normally used to describe Jesus' departure from the earth, its significance is metaphorical rather than literal. It signifies the return of Jesus to God, and the taking up again of the power and authority he voluntarily laid down in order to share the human nature (Acts 1:6–11).

Ashdod. One of the five Philistine city-states.

Asher. (1) The eighth son of Jacob, his second by Zilpah, Leah's slave-girl.

(2) The tribe of Asher which occupied fertile land along the coastal plain north of Mount Carmel.

Ashkelon. One of the five Philistine city-states.

Assyria. A major power to the north-east of Israel for over two centuries. As early as 853 B.C. Ahab had to meet the threat of an Assyrian invasion, though it was not until the accession of Tiglath-pileser III to the Assyrian throne in 745 B.C. that Assyria took a dominating role in the affairs of Palestine. By 721 B.C. the northern kingdom of Israel had become an Assyrian province and the southern kingdom of Judah was paying heavy tribute. An attempt by Hezekiah to become independent from Assyria in 705 B.C. was punished by an invasion in which all the fortified cities of Judah except for Jerusalem itself were taken and destroyed. Judah remained subservient to Assyria until the Assyrian empire began to break up under pressure from the Medes and the Babylonians *c.* 630 B.C.

Athaliah. Queen of Judah (842–837 B.C.). The wife of Jehoram, king of Judah and mother of Ahaziah, who succeeded him. When Ahaziah lost his life in Jehu's rebellion, Athaliah seized the throne and put to death all male members of the royal family except for Joash, one of Ahaziah's sons who was hidden by his aunt. After six years in hiding he was proclaimed king by forces acting on the instructions of Jehoiada the priest, and Athaliah was killed.

Athens. Visited by Paul on his second missionary journey. The sermon he preached there (Acts 17:16–34) is notable for its attempt to speak to Greek thinkers in terms they would find familiar, but his success appears to have been slight, and Athens was never an important centre of Christianity.

Atonement, Day of. The most solemn day of fasting in the Jewish calendar. The High Priest went into the most sacred part of the temple (the only day of the year on which this was permitted) to make a special offering in expiation of the sins of the people. These sins were symbolically transferred to a goat (the "scape-goat") which was then driven out into the wilderness.

B

Baal. The Hebrew word means simply "master", "owner" or "husband", and it was used as a general term for foreign gods, but especially for the Canaanite fertility god. Although the debased sexual practices associated with the worship of this god were fiercely condemned by Hebrew writers, it was probably through contact with Canaanite religion that the people of

Israel came to view their own God as creator and lord of the world of nature.

Baasha. King of Israel (900–877 B.C.), and involved in a border dispute with Asa, king of Judah.

Babel, Tower of. The significance of the story is mythological rather than historical. Partly it is an attempt to explain the variety of human languages, but it also reflects a view long held in certain sectors of Israelite society that man's close relationship with God was broken once he began to build cities and become, in his own eyes, self-sufficient.

Babylonians. When the Babylonians and Medes destroyed Assyria they divided her empire between them, with the Babylonians taking the southern portion. They therefore took over from the Assyrians the dominating role in Palestinian affairs from 605 B.C. Rebellions against Babylonian overlordship in 598 B.C. and 589 B.C. were disastrously unsuccessful, the latter resulting in the destruction of Jerusalem and its temple and the exile of many of its people in 586 B.C. (the Babylonian Captivity). In 538 B.C. the exiles were permitted to return to Jerusalem when Babylon was taken by Cyrus.

Baptism. The origins of baptism are obscure. John the Baptist baptised as a sign of repentance (Mk 1:4–5), and the Jews are known to have used a form of baptism as a means of entry to the Jewish faith for non-Jews, though it is uncertain whether or not this custom was established before John started baptising. There is no record of Jesus baptising anyone, yet it seems to have been established as the mode of entry into the Christian church from earliest times (Acts 1:38). Baptism was first administered to adult believers, or sometimes to whole families on the conversion of the head of household (Acts 16:33), and from this seems to have sprung the practice of baptising infants of Christian parents.

Barabbas. According to an established custom of releasing a prisoner at Passover time, Pilate set free Barabbas in preference to Jesus on the insistence of the crowd (Jn 18:38–40).

Barnabas. A prominent member of the early church, invariably exerting an influence for good at crucial moments. He was the first to befriend Paul in Jerusalem after his conversion (Acts 9:26–27). Sent by the Jerusalem church to report on work among the Gentiles which had begun in Syrian Antioch, he made a favourable recommendation, remained himself to continue the work and brought Paul to join him (Acts 11:19–26). He was Paul's companion the first missionary journey (Acts 13:1–3), but did not accompany him on the second journey for uncharacteristic reasons. Paul did not want to take John Mark, who had failed them on the first journey, while Barnabas wanted to give him a second chance. Significantly Paul was later to become reconciled to John Mark, thus confirming Barnabas' judgement (2 Tim 4:11).

Bartholomew. One of the twelve disciples. See **Nathaniel.**

Baruch. Acted as scribe to Jeremiah and read out a message from Jeremiah in the temple precincts at a time when Jeremiah himself had been banned from speaking there (Jer 36:1–8).

Bathsheba. The wife of Uriah, an officer in King David's army. Because she was expecting a child by David, he gave orders that Uriah be left in an exposed position during the fighting against the Ammonites, and he was killed. Bathsheba's child died in infancy, but she subsequently bore Solomon (2 Sam 11:2–12:25).

Beersheba. A town on the southernmost border of Judah: hence the expression "from Dan to Beersheba" to mean the whole of Israel.

Bel and the Dragon is the title of certain supplementary chapters to the "Book of Daniel" of an apocryphal character. First appeared in the Septuagint, but the Jewish Church did not accept it as inspired. In 1546 the Council of Trent declared it to be canonical.

Belshazzar. The last king of Babylon before its capture by the Persian monarch Cyrus in 539 B.C. Mentioned in the Bible only in the book of Daniel, particularly in the dramatic story of his downfall recorded in the fifth chapter.

Benjamin. (1) The twelfth son of Jacob, his second by Rachel, who died giving birth to him.

(2) The tribe of Benjamin, occupying a relatively small area just north of Judah.

Bernice. The sister of Herod Agrippa II, she heard with him Paul's defence of his conduct before the Roman governor Festus.

Bethany. A village just outside Jerusalem, the home of Lazarus, Martha and Mary. Here Jesus stayed on his final visit to Jerusalem.

Bethesda. A pool in Jerusalem believed to have healing properties, particularly when the waters were disturbed. The scene of one of Jesus' healing miracles in John 5:1–9.

Bethlehem. A town in Judah, some five miles south of Jerusalem and known from before King David's time. Chiefly famous as the birthplace of Jesus, although some scholars now believe it more likely he was born in or near Nazareth.

Bible. See **H3.**

Bildad. The second of Job's three "comforters".

Booths. See **Tabernacles.**

C

Caesarea. A city on the Palestinian coast built by Herod the Great and named after Caesar Augustus. The Roman governors of Palestine had their residence in Caesarea, and it was here that Paul was tried before Felix and Festus, spending the intervening two years under arrest (Acts 24:1–26:32).

Caiaphas. The High Priest during the time of Jesus' ministry, who presided at his examination before the Jewish Council.

Cain. See **Abel.**

Cana. A village in Galilee where Jesus attended a wedding celebration and, according to John 2:1–11, turned water into wine.

Canaanites. The people who occupied the territory subsequently taken over by the people of Israel. Their civilisation was materially more advanced than that of the people of Israel, but morally they lagged far behind and their cultic practices are condemned by biblical writers. Around 1800 B.C. they invented the alphabet.

Capernaum. A little frontier town by the Sea of Galilee which for a time was the centre of Jesus' ministry. It was here that he called Matthew (Mt 9:9) and performed a number of healings including the centurion's servant (Lk 7: 1–9).

Carmel. The culmination of a spur branching westwards from the main north–south mountain range of Palestine and almost reaching the coast. It was the scene of Elijah's confrontation with the prophets of Baal (1 Kgs 18:19–40).

Chaldeans. See **Babylonians.**

Christ. See **Jesus** and **Messiah.**

Christian. A nickname, first used in Syrian Antioch (Acts 11·26), which gradually became the normal way of describing a follower of Christ. Elsewhere in the New Testament, Christians are referred to as followers of "the Way", Nazarenes or simply the saints.

Chronicles, Books of. These books give an account of the history of the Jews from the death of Saul to the return from the exile. They are therefore largely a retelling of events already recorded by earlier authors in the books of Samuel and Kings. The purpose of the chroniclers seems to have been to reassure their people of God's care for them in spite of the adversities recently suffered, and this leads them to present an unjustifiably rosy view of Israel's history (e.g. glorifying David's reign and glossing over his weaknesses). Consequently most scholars prefer to rely on the earlier and more sober accounts in Samuel and Kings, but, treated with caution, the information in Chronicles provides a useful supplement to the earlier records.

Colossians, Letter to the. As far as is known, Paul himself never visited Colossae, but the church there had been founded by Epaphras, a close associate of Paul (Col 1:7). Perhaps he felt some responsibility for the Colossian Christians because of this. The letter was probably written during Paul's imprisonment in Rome and appears to be a response to reports of false teachers in Colossae. These teachers suggest that there is a special kind of knowledge (over and above the knowledge of Christ) which is necessary for salvation, and they advocate an ascetic way of life. Paul's reply stresses that Christ alone is all-sufficient for the needs of his readers.

Commandments. There are, of course, many commandments in the Bible, but the ten commandments which God is said to have given to Moses on Mount Sinai have a special place. They are seen as the basis of God's agreement with the people of Israel and, significantly, combine religious and social obligations. *See also* **Decalogue, H8.**

Corinth. Strategically situated at a major junction of trading routes, Corinth in New Testament times was a wealthy city which not even Athens could match in importance among the cities of Greece. It also had an evil reputation, however, because of its notoriously lax moral standards. Both its importance and its depravity may have commended it to Paul as a place to preach the Christian gospel. He spent 18 months there about A.D. 50 (Acts 18:1–18), and made at least one further visit, possibly two. His letters to the church at Corinth show that he was passionately concerned about its welfare.

Corinthians, Letters to the. Although Paul's correspondence with the Corinthians is collected into two letters in the New Testament, most scholars are agreed that they include parts of four separate communications summarised below:

(1) A letter of warning against pagan influences, a fragment of which appears in 2 Corinthians 6:14–7:1 and which is referred to in 1 Corinthians 5:9–13.

(2) The letter now known as 1 Corinthians.

(3) An extremely severe letter partly preserved in 2 Corinthians 10–13.

(4) A much more relaxed letter, perhaps showing relief that the severe letter had had the desired effect, and preserved in 2 Corinthians 1–9.

The letters afford valuable insights into the problems which faced a small Christian community set in a pagan environment, and into the relationship between Paul and a church which nearly drove him to distraction because of its waywardness and the depth of his concern for it.

Cornelius. A Roman centurion whose baptism by Peter represented an important step in the progress of the Christian church from a Jewish sect to a universal faith (Acts 10).

Covenant. The concept of the covenant—an agreement between God and man—is implicit throughout the Old Testament. The first explicit reference comes in the story of Noah where God makes a covenant to save Noah and his family from the impending flood and subsequently agrees never again to send such a flood upon the earth. God then makes a covenant with Abraham to establish his descendants as a chosen people, though it should be noted that they are chosen to bring God's blessing to all nations (Gen 12:3). It is however, the covenant made at Sinai after the exodus that is regarded as the most important. In this covenant God offers the people of Israel a special place in his plans if they will serve him alone and obey his commandments (Ex 19:5–6). Again it is noteworthy that the people of Israel are to serve God as priests, *i.e.* as people who mediate the knowledge of God to others.

Covenant, Book of the. In 622 B.C. during the course of repairs on the temple, a scroll was discovered which is described as the Book of the Covenant. When this was brought to King Josiah he realised that his people had failed to live up to God's demands, and set in motion the most far-reaching religious reforms ever known in Judah. These included the suppression of all pagan cults, an edict that in future sacrifice could only take place in the temple in Jerusalem, and the re-institution of the Passover which had apparently not been celebrated for many years (2 Kgs 22:3–23:23). The close similarities between these measures and instructions contained in the book of Deuteronomy suggest that the Book of the Covenant was in fact the first edition of Deuteronomy. It is thought to have been written by pious Jews during the long and evil reign of Manasseh (687–642 B.C.) as a re-statement and amplification of the covenant with Moses. Not daring to

publish it openly at the time, they hid it in the temple, hoping that it would later be discovered and acted upon.

Creation. There are two creation stories in the Old Testament, a primitive version which nevertheless has considerable charm starting at Genesis 2:4, and the more familiar version with which Genesis begins, but which is actually later in origin. *See also* **Genesis.**

Cross. The supreme symbol of the Christian faith because it represents the depths of suffering Jesus was prepared to embrace in order to save mankind by inaugurating God's Kingdom upon earth. Crucifixion was the normal method of execution for those who did not possess Roman citizenship, and because the wounds inflicted were not in themselves very serious, a strong man could take days to die. According to Mark 15:44, Pilate was surprised that Jesus had died within hours.

Cyrenius. *See* **Quirinius.**

Cyrus (c. 559–530 B.C.). The Persian king who overthrew the Babylonian empire and allowed the exiled Jews to return to their homeland.

D

Damascus. An ancient city, the capital of Syria. In the Old Testament, in fact, Damascus and Syria are synonymous. It was on his way to Damascus to persecute the Christian community there that Paul had his conversion experience.

Dan. (1) The fifth son of Jacob, his first by Bilhah, Rachel's slave-girl.

(2) The tribe of Dan, occupying a small area north of Judah and west of Benjamin.

(3) The city of Dan in the far north of Israel: hence the expression "from Dan to Beersheba" meaning the whole of Israel.

Daniel. Almost certainly written between 167 and 164 B.C., Daniel is one of the last of the books of the Old Testament chronologically. At this time the Greek ruler Antiochus Epiphanes was attempting systematically to destroy the Jewish religion. The book was written to encourage the resistance movement with stories of Daniel and his friends, who refused to compromise in religious matters during the Babylonian captivity some four hundred years earlier. The second half of the book contains obscure visions which appear to predict the ultimate downfall of pagan empires and the triumph of the people of God.

David. King of Israel from about 1000 to about 960 B.C. It is not clear whether David first came to Saul's attention as a skilled musician able to soothe him in his depressions (1 Sam 16:17 23) or as the shepherd boy who killed the Philistine champion Goliath (1 Sam 17:12–51). In either case he soon showed his military skill, and before long was receiving adulation greater than Saul himself (1 Sam 18:7). Saul's insane jealousy forced David to flee from his court and become an outlaw, eventually offering his services, and those of the 600 men who had joined him, to the Philistines as a way of keeping out of Saul's clutches (1 Sam 27:1–4).

Whilst nominally a Philistine vassal, David attacked traditional enemies of Israel such as the Amalekites, and distributed his booty among the tribe of Judah, thus indicating that his change of allegiance was a temporary expedient (1 Sam 30:1–31). When Saul was killed in battle David was initially accepted as king of Judah (2 Sam 2:4), but the northern tribes were ruled by Saul's son, Ishbosheth, until he was assassinated by two of his officers (2 Sam 4:5–8).

As king of all Israel David rapidly subdued the Philistines (2 Sam 5:17–25), and soon turned his attention to the Ammonites, who had insulted his ambassadors (2 Sam 10:1–5). During the Ammonite war he successfully beat off a Syrian attack and subsequently annexed much Syrian territory. He also conquered the Moabites and the Edomites east of the Jordan. In the end he ruled an empire stretching some 725 kilometres from north to south and 185 kilometres from east to west.

David was not just a brilliant military tactician however. He was a statesman who understood the need for national unity and the crucial part to be played by his people's religion in achieving this. He established his capital in Jerusalem because it was close to the boundary between Judah and the northern tribes, and did not actually belong to any of the tribes, being still in the hands of the Jebusites. This was presumably to avoid inter-tribal jealousy. Although he did not build a temple, he brought the ark of the covenant to Jerusalem, thus establishing it as a religious centre and not just an administrative capital.

David's later years were marred by struggles among his sons to gain the throne, and he seems to have been uncharacteristically weak and indecisive in dealing with them.

Dead Sea Scrolls. *See* **Scrolls**.

Deborah, Song of. It this hymn of triumph over the enemy commander, Sisera, was composed at the time of the events, as seems likely, it dates from before 1100 B.C. and is therefore one of the oldest fragments of literature in the Old Testament (Judg 5:2–31).

Decalogue, the name given to the Ten Commandments of the Old Testament. There are two versions of them, differing in detail: Exodus xx. 2–17 and Deuteronomy v. 6–21. They are of Hebrew origin and are recognised by Jews and Christians as the divine law given by God to Moses on Mt. Sinai. Most of them are prohibitions in contrast to the beatitudes (pronounced by Christ in the Sermon on the Mount) which are positive, *e.g.*, Blessed are the merciful.

Dedication, Feast of. A feast to commemorate the rededication of the temple following its desecration by the Greek ruler Antiochus Epiphanes in 168 B.C.

Deluge, a flood, commonly applied to the story of Noah and the Ark in the Bible. A similar tradition can be found in the mythology of many ancient peoples.

Demetrius. A silversmith of Ephesus who stirred up trouble for the Christian community because the success of Christianity was affecting the trade of those who made silver models of the temple of Artemis (or Diana), the local goddess (Acts 19:23–41).

Deuteronomy. *See* **Covenant, Book of the.**

Devil. Contrary to popular opinion, the devil has a very minor role in the biblical writings. In the book of Job, Satan is counsel for the prosecution at the court of God, and therefore not a figure of evil as such. At the beginning of Jesus' ministry the devil appears in the role of tempter (Lk 4:1–13) and elsewhere as the adversary of God (1 Jn 3:8).

Diana. *See* **Artemis.**

Dispersion (Greek *Diaspora*), over a period of centuries many Jews left Palestine for a variety of reasons. Some left in times of famine to seek food elsewhere, some fled from invading armies or were forcibly exiled, others went voluntarily to set up business in the major centres of commerce. By New Testament times these Jews of the Dispersion outnumbered those in Palestine, and there were few cities round the eastern Mediterranean without a sizeable Jewish colony. It is no accident that some of the most important figures in the early church—Stephen, Philip, Barnabas and Paul, for example—were Jews of the Dispersion, for their circumstances made them less fettered by tradition and more open to new thinking.

Dorcas. A Christian woman who lived in Joppa and was renowned for her good deeds among the poor. According to Acts 9:36–42 Peter restored her to life after she had died.

E

Ecclesiastes. A strange book to find in the Bible because of its apparently unrelenting pessimism. The burden of the author's message seems to be that there is no fulfilment to be found in human existence.

Edomites. Recognised as relations of the Jews because of their alleged descent from Esau, the Edomites were nevertheless often in conflict with the people of Israel. Their territory extended from the southern end of the Dead Sea

to the Gulf of Aqaba, and was of importance because of its copper mines and because it afforded access to African trade routes via the Red Sea. David conquered the Edomites and Solomon made full use of the strategic advantages thus gained, but they gradually reasserted their independence and were never again completely subjugated by the people of Israel.

Egypt. Although the influence of Egypt on Palestinian affairs was less dramatic than that of the Mesopotamian empires of Assyria and Babylonia, it was far more persistent. From very early times the story of the Jews is linked with Egypt, and the great event of Jewish history is the escape from Egyptian captivity. During the period when Assyria and Babylon were at the height of their power, Egypt used the Palestinian states to foment trouble against them, promising assistance if they rebelled against their Mesopotamian overlords. The promised assistance did not always materialise, however, and when it did it was inadequate. After the destruction of the temple by the Babylonians in 586 B.C. a considerable number of Jews sought refuge in Egypt, and it was in Egypt during the third and second centuries B.C. that the Greek translation of the Old Testament was made. References to Egypt in the New Testament are far fewer, though Joseph and Mary are said to have fled there to protect their child from the wrath of Herod.

Ekron. One of the five Philistine city-states.

Elah. King of Israel (877–876 B.C.).

Eli. The priest who brought up Samuel.

Elihu. A young man who, after Job's three "comforters" had failed to persuade him of the error of his ways, made another attempt to do so (Job 32).

Elijah. A prophet from Tishbe in Gilead, Elijah is rightly considered one of the great figures of the Old Testament. He was the supreme champion of Israel's God at a time when Jezebel was trying to substitute the worship of her own god, Baal Melkart. This epic struggle is epitomised by the confrontation between Elijah and the prophets of Baal on Mount Carmel (1 Kgs 18:19–40). While many different interpretations of this story have been offered, ranging from the absolutely literal to the purely legendary, there can be no doubt whatever that the conflict it represents was real. Apart from this, however, the Elijah stories contain many pointers towards a more complete understanding of God. On Mount Horeb (Sinai) he realised that God was to be found in the quiet reflection rather than in dramatic natural events, and God's instructions he received there showed that God's power extended beyond Israel to the surrounding nations (1 Kgs 19:8–16). The encounter with King Ahab over Naboth's vineyard (1 Kgs 21:1–24), while not proclaiming anything new, is a forceful restatement of God's concern with social justice, and clearly anticipates the work of Amos.

Eliphaz. The first of Job's three "comforters" (Job 4).

Elisha. Though he is inevitably linked with his master and predecessor Elijah, Elisha is a very different character. More miraculous incidents are recorded about Elisha, yet many of them are trivial, e.g. recovering an axe-head from the river Jordan (2 Kgs 6:1–7), and the effect is to diminish rather than enhance his stature. Whereas Elijah was a largely solitary figure spending long periods in the wilderness, Elisha associated freely with the communities of prophets and lived in the capital city, Samaria, for at least part of his career. Though not always in sympathy with the kings of Israel, he advised them in military matters. He added little or nothing to the understanding of God achieved by Elijah, but some of the ways in which he exemplified that understanding are notable, e.g. the breadth of concern shown in the healing of Naaman, the commander of the Syrian army (2 Kgs 5:1–19).

Elizabeth. The mother of John the Baptist and a relative of Mary, mother of Jesus.

Emmanuel. The name, meaning "God with us", is in fact used in a prophecy of Isaiah to King Ahaz during a time of crisis. Isaiah says that a young woman will conceive and bring forth a son, whom she will name Emmanuel. He is saying, in effect, that in nine months' time the situation will have improved so much that parents will give their children a name expressive of God's care for his people. Though the immediate prophecy, therefore, refers to events in the immediate future, it is not surprising that Christians should have seen in these words the foreshadowing of God's presence with his people in Christ (Mt 1:22–23).

Enoch, Book of. See Aprocrypha, H3.

Epaphras. An associate of Paul who founded the church at Colossae (Col 1:7).

Epaphroditus. A Christian from Philippi who was sent by the Philippian church to render assistance to Paul during imprisonment, probably in Rome. While with Paul he had a serious illness and Paul thought it best to send him back home possibly taking the letter to the Philippians with him (Phil 2:25–30).

Ephesians, Letter to the. Although apparently written by Paul, there is considerable doubt as to the authorship of this letter. It was not uncommon in those times for a follower of a great teacher to write in the teacher's name and, far from being considered fraudulent, this was regarded as a mark of respect. The style of writing is not quite as in Paul's other letters, themes are introduced which appear nowhere else in his correspondence, and there is a remarkable absence of personal greetings considering that Paul had spent two years in Ephesus. If the author were not Paul, however, he was clearly well acquainted with Paul's writings, especially the letter to the Colossians, parts of which are quoted almost verbatim. The first part of the letter emphasises the unity of Christian believers, whose common life in Christ overrides all human distinctions, and the glory of the church which, whatever its human weaknesses, is Christ's body. The second part of the letter draws out the implications of this view of the church for practical living.

Ephesus (in Asia Minor). The capital of the Roman province of Asia and an important trading centre, Ephesus was famous for its temple of Artemis (Diana). It had a substantial Jewish population, and soon became an important centre of Christianity. Paul visited Ephesus as he returned from his second missionary journey (Acts 18:19–21) and subsequently spent two years there (Acts 19:1–10).

Ephraim. (1) Although he was Joseph's second son, he received from Jacob his grandfather the blessing normally due to the eldest, and established an important tribe (Gen 48:17–19).

(2) It appears that Joseph never had a tribe named after him, but he gave rise to two of the tribes of Israel, named after his sons Manasseh and Ephraim. The tribe of Ephraim occupied fertile land running down to the Mediterranean coast north of Dan and Benjamin and south of Manasseh. Its significance in the affairs of Israel was such that the northern kingdom was often referred to as Ephraim.

Epicureans. A school of Greek philosophers with whom Paul debated in Athens (Acts 17:18).

Epiphany, a Christian festival celebrated on 6 January, originally an old solstice festival, celebrating the birth of light.

Esau. The first-born son of Isaac, he sold the birthright which was his by tradition to his younger brother, Jacob, for a bowl of soup. He is regarded as the ancestor of the Edomites.

Essenes. See Section J.

Esther. Dated between 150 and 100 B.C., the book of Esther describes how a Jewish heroine of that name became queen to the Persian king, Xerxes, and was able to save her people from the evil plotting of one Haman. The book makes no mention of God at all, and it appears to have gained its place in the Old Testament purely as an expression of nationalist sentiments. The deliverance from Haman is still celebrated by Jews in the feast of Purim.

Eve. Adam's partner (Gen 2:21–24, 3:20). As Adam should be thought of as a symbolic prototype of mankind, so is Eve the typical woman rather than the first woman.

Exile. The term usually refers to the exile of the leading Jewish people in Babylon between 586 and 538 B.C., though there had been an earlier deportation in 597 B.C. This experience was of great importance to the Jews for a number of

reasons. They had to learn how to worship God without the temple and without sacrifice, and so it was here that forms of worship developed which were based on the recollection of the way God had led them throughout their history. This in turn stimulated interest in writing down their history, and it was during the exile that much of the editorial work on the historical books of the Old Testament was done. On the negative side, the Jews became more exclusive during the exile because of fears that intermarriage would result in the loss of their religious and national identity. The Jews, therefore, emerged from the exile purified but also hardened in a way that was not entirely to the good.

Exodus. The name given to the escape of the people of Israel from Egypt, an escape always seen as the supreme symbol of God's concern for them and an event still celebrated annually by Jews in the feast of the Passover. While some allowance has to be made for exaggeration of the incidents leading up to the escape, there is no reason to doubt the essential historical truth of the account. It appears that, originally having gone to Egypt because of famine in Palestine, the Jews had become slave-labourers working on Egyptian building projects. They were freed from this oppression about 1250 B.C. under the leadership of Moses with the assistance of a remarkable sequence of events known as the plagues of Egypt (Ex 7:14–12:36). The pursuing Egyptian army fell into a panic as their chariots sank in the waters of a shallow swamp, successfully crossed on foot by the Israelites, in the area of the Suez canal today. Whatever our interpretation of these events, the people of Israel ascribed them to God.

Exodus, Book of. As its name implies the book of Exodus tells the story of the Jews' escape from Egypt, but it contains much else of importance besides. It includes the account of God's covenant with the people of Israel at Sinai based on the ten commandments. It also gives instructions about the construction of the ark and of the tent in which it is to be housed, as well as directions concerning worship.

Ezekiel. Ezekiel is probably the most difficult of the major prophets for the modern reader to come to grips with. Among the Jews deported to Babylon in the first exile of 597 B.C., his call to be a prophet came in Babylon and the whole of his prophetic ministry was carried out there, though his prophecies are directed to his people in Jerusalem as well as to the exiles. Many of the messages of Ezekiel are in the form of symbolic visions of great complexity; in fact, Ezekiel has been called "the father of apocalyptic", a kind of visionary writing represented elsewhere in the Bible by the books of Daniel and Revelation. The Old Testament book stresses the responsibility of the individual before God, rather than the people as a corporate body (Ezek 18:1–4), looks forward to the restoration of his people (Ezek 37:1–14) and presents a vision of the future temple and its worship (chapter 40 onwards). This interest in ritual, the result of his priestly status (Ezek 1:1) is in sharp contrast to earlier prophets who tend to condemn ritual, or at least the insincerity of ritual without righteousness.

Ezra. A lawyer who led a party of exiles to Jerusalem from Babylon about 460 B.C. (Ezra 7:1–9) and played a major role in the re-establishment of the worship in the temple. Unfortunately he shows the hard-line tendencies some of the Jews developed in exile, to the extent of insisting that Jews who had married foreign wives should get rid of them and their children. The book of Ezra relates events from the first return of exiles in 538 B.C. up to those in which Ezra himself was involved. It is not clear how much of the book is the work of Ezra.

F

Fathers of the Church were early writers who laid the foundations of Christian ritual and doctrine. The earliest were the Apostolic Fathers (q.v.). The Four Fathers of the Latin Church were

St. Ambrose, St. Jerome, St. Augustine and St. Gregory the Great. The Four Fathers of the Greek Church were St. Basil, St. Gregory Nazianzen, St. John Chrysostom and St. Athanasius.

Felix. The Roman governor of Judaea from about A.D. 52 to 58, he had a Jewish wife and was apparently well informed about the Christian way (Acts 24:22–25). He kept Paul in custody for two years, having no cause to condemn him but unwilling to release him for fear of opposition from the Jewish leaders (Acts 24:27).

Festivals. *See* separate entries under **Dedication, Feast of; New Year; Passover; Tabernacles, Feast of; Weeks, Feast of.**

Festus. The Roman governor of Judaea who succeeded Felix about A.D. 58. He seems to have behaved with absolute correctness in his dealings with Paul, and would probably have set him free had not Paul taken the matter out of his hands by appealing to Caesar.

G

Gabriel. The literal meaning of the name is simply "man of God". In Jewish tradition one of seven archangels, he is said to have announced the birth of John the Baptist to Zechariah (Lk 1:5–20) and of Jesus to Mary (Lk 1:26–38).

Gad. (1) Jacob's seventh son, his first by Zilpah, Leah's slave-girl.
(2) The tribe of Gad, holding territory east of the Jordan, north of that occupied by Reuben.

Galatia. The ancient kingdom of Galatia was in central Asia Minor, but the Roman province of the same name included a much larger area reaching down to the Mediterranean coast. Paul visited several towns within the Roman province on his first missionary journey.

Galatians, Letter to. One of the earliest of Paul's letters, probably written in *c.* A.D. 54, though some scholars would date it to A.D. 49, making it the first of all his surviving letters. It was written, almost certainly, to the churches Paul founded in the Roman province of Galatia on his first missionary journey, and is unusual in being addressed to a group of churches rather than a single church. The purpose in writing is very clear: Paul has been told that there are people going round the churches claiming that circumcision and the acceptance of the Jewish law is a necessary part of Christianity. Paul writes with the utmost urgency and vigour to refute these claims. He himself had been a Pharisee and knew that the attempt to satisfy God by perfect obedience to the law was impossible. It was faith in Christ which had liberated him from that futile pursuit, and the last thing he wanted was to see anyone persuaded into taking up something he had only discovered by long and painful experience to be of no value.

Galilee. The area west of the Sea of Galilee (actually an inland lake some 20 km long) where Jesus was brought up and spent much of his ministry. In the time of Jesus it formed the northern part of the Roman province of Galilee and Peraea, governed by Herod Antipas.

Gallio. The proconsul of the Roman province of Achaia before whom Paul was accused during his eighteen-month stay at Corinth (Acts 18:12– 17). An inscription from Delphi establishes that Gallio was in Corinth by A.D. 52, probably having been appointed the previous year. It is implied (though not definitely stated) in Acts that Paul's trial took place soon after Gallio's arrival, and if this is accepted it fixes Paul's ministry in Corinth within a year or so, providing a useful fixed point in the chronology of the early church.

Gamaliel. A well-known Jewish teacher who numbered Paul among his pupils (Acts 22:3), and who argued in the Jewish Council against trying to stamp out Christianity on the grounds that history would show whether it was a movement from God or a worthless novelty (Acts 5:34–40).

Gath. One of the five Philistine city-states.

Gaza. The southernmost of the five Philistine city-states.

Gedaliah. When Zedekiah, the last king of Judah, was taken in chains to Babylon in 586 B.C., the Babylonians appointed Gedaliah as governor. Though in his brief spell of office he seems to have acted with wisdom and humanity, he was soon assassinated by supporters of the royal house who regarded him as a traitor (2 Kgs 25:22–26).

Gehazi. Elisha's servant, condemned by Elisha for accepting gifts against his instructions from the healed Syrian commander, Naaman (2 Kgs 5:19–27).

Genesis. As the name implies, the first book of the Bible. Chapters 1–11 contain the acounts of the creation and the stories of Adam and Eve, Cain and Abel, Noah and the tower of Babel. These stories, though they may have some basis in historical fact, are important mainly for their mythological value. They are to be seen as parables, conveying in a vivid and often entertaining way, the convictions of their authors on immensely important matters—the nature of God, the nature of the universe and the nature of man. From chapter 12 onwards, with the entrance of Abraham into the story, the book is dealing with historical figures, however much allowance may have to be made for the inevitable legendary accretions acquired during centuries of handing down by word of mouth.

Gentiles. The word usually translated as Gentiles means literally "the peoples" or "the nations", i.e. the peoples other than the people of Israel. The Bible shows ambivalent attitudes among the Jews towards Gentiles. The covenants with Abraham and Moses both stress that the people of Israel are to be a blessing to "the nations", but during and following the exile the fear of religious and ethnic absorption made the Jews increasingly exclusive. Even in the early church there was a long and sometimes acrimonious debate before the mission to the Gentiles was accepted by all as an inevitable implication of Christian belief. It was this crucial decision which made Christianity a universal faith and no longer just a sect within Judaism.

Gethsemane. An olive grove on the western slopes of the Mount of Olives, facing Jerusalem across the Kidron valley, it was apparently Jesus' custom to go there with his disciples to avoid the crowds, and it was there that he was arrested (Mk 14:32–52).

Gibeah. A town some 7 km north of Jerusalem which was Saul's capital throughout his reign.

Gideon. Before the monarchy was established, the people of Israel relied on inspired leaders, known as judges, to raise armies and cope with enemy aggression as the need arose. Gideon was one such leader, renowned for his victory over the Midianites (Judg 7:1–22).

Gilgal. (1) A town on the west bank of the Jordan, just north of the Dead Sea, where the people of Israel first entered the "promised land" and Saul was later proclaimed king.
(2) A settlement north of Bethel where there was a community of prophets in the time of Elijah and Elisha (2 Kgs 2:1, 4:38).

God. The existence of God is never discussed in the Bible; it is simply assumed from start to finish. But if the biblical authors never question God's existence, they do question what sort of God he is and, as one would expect of a varied group of writers working over a period of many centuries, they do not all arrive at the same conclusion. Samuel believed that God demanded the total destruction of Israel's ancient enemy the Amalekites, severely criticised Saul because he had spared the life of Agag the Amalekite king, and himself cut him to pieces (1 Sam 15:1–33). The writer of 2 Kings 2:23–24 believed that God had punished some boys who had made fun of Elisha by causing them to be mauled by bears. Clearly these are primitive views of God.

In spite of these relics of an early religion, however, the Bible as a whole presents a remarkably unified view of God, with most of the key concepts established at quite an early date in Israel's history. The "otherness" of God is expressed in the idea that no man could look upon the face of God and live (Ex 33:20) or that anyone who touched the ark, representing God's presence, would be struck dead (2 Sam 6:6–8). Later on these primitive attempts to express belief in a God whose ways are unsearchable, whose powers are unlimited, whose holiness is literally aweful, and who is as far removed from man as the heavens are from the earth, find nobler expression in such passages as the call vision of Isaiah (Is 6:1–8) and many of the Psalms. But the God of the Bible, though far removed from man in his wisdom, power and purity, is never remote. From the very earliest stories in the Bible he is a God who involves himself in the life of men, both making demands on them and caring for them. What he demands from men is justice in their dealings with each other. The ten commandments (Ex 20:1–17) form the basis of the moral code by which men are to live, and it is significant that even the king is subject to these demands and open to criticism for failure (1 Kgs 21:17–19) unlike other monarchs of the day who were a law unto themselves. What he offers men is a constant concern for their welfare, seen at an early stage in the exodus and expressed most movingly among Old Testament writers by the prophet Hosea, who daringly compares God to a faithful husband whose love for his wife does not waver in spite of her infidelity. So the thinkers of the Old Testament prepared the way for one whose moral demands reached new and frightening heights in the commandment to "love your enemies and do good to those who hate you".

Golgotha. The name of the place where Jesus was crucified, the word means "skull". Whether this is a reference to the shape of the hill or an indication that executions had long been carried out there is uncertain, as is the location.

Goliath. A Philistine warrior of enormous stature supposedly killed by David, though 2 Samuel 21:19 says that it was Elhanan who killed Goliath, and it seems possible that tradition transferred this exploit to David.

Gomorrah. One of five cities described in Genesis 14:3 as occupying the valley of Siddim. The location is not quite certain, but is thought to be covered now by the southern part of the Dead Sea. Notorious for its wickedness, the city was destroyed by burning sulphur according to Genesis 19:24–25.

Gospels. Those key portions of the New Testament which deal with the life, death, resurrection and teachings of Christ. They are the gospels of Matthew, Mark, Luke and John, all probably compiled in the later part of the 1st cent. The first three are called the *synoptic gospels* because of their general unity of narrative. Mark was probably the first to be written and John the last, and it is to Mark that scholars have turned for the most reliable source of the life of Jesus.

The word *gospel* comes from two Anglo-Saxon words *gode* (good) and *spell* (tidings), a translation of the Greek *evangelion* = evangel, evangelist.

Greeks. Apart from its literal meaning, the word is often used in the New Testament as a general word for non-Jews. Thus in Romans 1:16 Paul says that the gospel is the saving power of God for "the Jew first but the Greek also". Some modern versions use the translation "Gentile" when this is the sense intended.

H

Habakkuk. A prophet whose ministry coincided with the rise to power of the Babylonians in the closing years of the seventh century B.C. The Old Testament book views the ascendency of the Babylonians as an act of God, but nevertheless questions how God can countenance such ruthless people, and declares that they are doomed, whereas "the righteous shall live by faith" (Hab 2:4).

Hagar. The slave-girl of Abraham's wife Sarah. When it seemed that Sarah would never have a child, Hagar was given to him to bear his children, and gave birth to Ishmael (Gen 16:1–4, 15). After the birth of Sarah's own son, Isaac, she sent Hagar and Ishmael away, but God promised Abraham that Ishmael would become the father of a nation (Gen

21:9–20).

Haggai. A prophet who prophesied about 520 B.C. some twenty years after the first Jews had returned from the exile to Jerusalem. He said that the reason for the poor harvests the people were getting was their failure to make a start on rebuilding the temple, and encouraged them to begin the rebuilding programme.

Haman. The villain of the book of Esther, an official at the Persian court who schemed to bring about the destruction of the Jews.

Hannah. The mother of Samuel, she was childless for many years and therefore considered to be out of favour with God. She made a promise that if God granted her a son she would dedicate him to the service of his sanctuary at Shiloh (1 Sam 1:1–28).

Hazael. An army officer who came to the Syrian throne shortly before 840 B.C. by suffocating the ruling monarch, Benhadad, in his bed. Elijah had been instructed to anoint Hazael king of Syria, but had not been able to do so before his death. Elisha is said to have told Hazael that he would become king, though he did not apparently anoint him (2 Kgs 8:7–15). Hazael was to be a scourge to Israel throughout his long reign, and it is significant that the people of Israel were prepared to see even an enemy who oppressed them as God's appointed agent.

Hazor. A large town in the far north of Israel, one of those which Solomon specially fortified and made into a garrison town for his chariot forces (1 Kgs 9:15–19).

Hebrew. The language in which the Old Testament was written. Over the last fifty years, archaeological work has brought to light a vast quantity of texts in Hebrew or closely related Semitic languages, and this has greatly increased our knowledge.

Hebrews, Letter to the. Although traditionally ascribed to Paul, it has long been recognised that this is not one of Paul's letters, being quite unlike Paul's writing in both style and content. The main theme of the letter is an interpretation of the significance of Jesus' life and teaching based on the concept of priesthood—Jesus as the supreme mediator between God and man. It is most famous for its eleventh chapter on the nature of faith. The obviously Jewish outlook of the writer has led most commentators to assume that the letter was destined for a community of Jewish Christians, as the title implies, but even this has been questioned and it has to be said that authorship, destination and circumstances of writing remain conjectural.

Hebron. A city in the territory of Judah, it was David's capital for a time before the northern tribes accepted him as king and he established Jerusalem as the new religious and administrative centre.

Hermon. At over 2,800 m., Mt Hermon is the highest point in Palestine and also represents the far north-eastern frontier of Israel at the height of her power. It is considered by some to be the scene of the transfiguration because of its proximity to Caesarea Philippi.

Herod Family. Four Herods of four different generations are mentioned in the New Testament, in addition to Philip, who was also a member of the family. Herod the Great ruled the whole of the territory of the Jews (under Roman authority) from 40 to 4 B.C. He was the Herod ruling at the time of the birth of Jesus (which was incorrectly calculated when the Christian calendar was established: hence the anomaly of Jesus' birth taking place "before Christ"). Although suspicious and intolerant by nature, he kept his country free from conflict for 35 years, which was no mean achievement. On his death, his kingdom was divided between his three sons, Archelaus, Herod Antipas and Philip. Archelaus, however, was deposed in A.D. 6 and his territory came under the direct rule of a Roman governor. Herod Antipas, the Herod who had John the Baptist killed and before whom Jesus was tried, continued to rule Galilee and Peraea until his banishment in A.D. 39. Philip ruled Ituraea and Trachonitis until his death in A.D. 34. The territories of both Herod Antipas and Philip passed to Herod Agrippa I, who persecuted the Church and had James put to death (Acts 12:2). He himself died in A.D. 44 and was succeeded by

Herod Agrippa II, the king before whom Paul appeared in Acts 25.

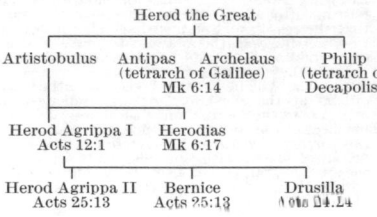

Herod the Great

| Artistobulus | Antipas (tetrarch of Galilee) Mk 6:14 | Archelaus | Philip (tetrarch of Decapolis) |

Herod Agrippa I   Herodias
Acts 12:1   Mk 6:17

Herod Agrippa II   Bernice   Drusilla
Acts 25:13   Acts 25:13   Acts 24:24

Herodias. Originally the wife of Philip (not the tetrarch) she was subsequently married to his half-brother Antipas. It was John the Baptist's objection to this marriage which brought about his imprisonment and eventual death (Mk 6:14–29).

Hezekiah. King of Judah (715–687 B.C.). Hezekiah came to the throne as a vassal of Assyria as his father, Ahaz, had been. The Assyrian ruler, Sargon II, was having difficulties elsewhere in his empire, however, and Hezekiah soon removed Assyrian religious objects from the temple, a step he might have hesitated to take but for the temporary Assyrian weakness. He also attacked the old Canaanite places of worship which were still used, and broke a bronze serpent allegedly made by Moses before which incense was burned. The exact extent of his religious reforms is uncertain, but it is clear that they were far-reaching. In spite of his removal of Assyrian cult objects from the temple, Hezekiah did not join other small Palestinian states, led by the Philistine city of Ashdod, in rebellion against the Assyrians in 713 B.C., perhaps because Isaiah opposed the enterprise. In 705 B.C., however, when Sargon II died, Hezekiah did refuse tribute to Assyria.

Facing troubles elsewhere, it was 701 B.C. before the new king Sennacherib was able to move against Judah. When he did, he devastated 46 of Judah's fortresses and, in the words of his own inscription, shut up Hezekiah in Jerusalem "like a bird in a cage". What happened at this point is not clear. 2 Kings 18:14–16 says that Sennacherib demanded vastly increased tribute and Hezekiah meekly agreed. 2 Kings 18:17–19:37, however, relates how Hezekiah defied Sennacherib and the Assyrian had to return home, for his army had been cut down by some mysterious agency. No attempt to reconcile these conflicting statements is entirely satisfactory, and this has led some scholars to suggest that the account of Hezekiah's successful defiance relates to a second invasion about 688 B.C. There is no corroborative evidence for this however.

Hinnom. A deep valley south-west of Jerusalem where child sacrifice was carried out according to Jeremiah 7:30–34. It is not clear from Jeremiah when this occurred (at no time was it a normal feature of Jewish religion), but it may have been during the long and evil reign of Manasseh (687–642 B.C.).

Hittites. A people referred to many times in the early period of Old Testament history from the time of the patriarchs to the establishment of the monarchy. It is now known that they ruled a considerable empire, centred on Asia Minor and achieving its maximum influence between 1400 and 1200 B.C. They defeated Pharaoh Rameses II at the Battle of Kadesh, 1299 B.C.

Hosea. Hosea prophesied in the northern kingdom of Israel shortly after Amos (i.e. from about 750 B.C. onwards) during a period of political anarchy which was eventually to lead to the end of Israel as an independent kingdom in 721 B.C. His prophetic message is coloured throughout by his own experience of marriage, though the facts about his marriage are disputed, the evidence being ambiguous on many points. The most commonly accepted view is that his wife Gomer was unfaithful to him and eventually left him to become a prostitute. Falling upon hard times, she was sold into slavery, from which Hosea bought her back, attempting to reform her by keeping her in seclusion for a period of time. Such a view certainly accords well with Hosea's daring portrayal of God as the faithful and persistent lover who will not abandon his faithless wife Israel. Although Hosea's message is therefore supremely hopeful, being based on the constant love of God for his people, it is not lacking in stern warnings of judgement, for the concept of God's love does not exclude the possibility of corrective punishment and Hosea is utterly appalled by the idolatry and unrighteousness of his people. Yet even God's judgement is seen as something positive, as a necessary step towards the re-establishment of a relationship between God and his people which is based on faithfulness on both sides.

Hoshea. King of Israel (732–724 B.C.). The last king of Israel, Hoshea came to the throne by the assassination of his predecessor Pekah. It was a period of Assyrian domination and for a while Hoshea wisely remained subservient to his Assyrian masters. When the capable Assyrian ruler Tiglath-pileser III died in 727 B.C., however, Hoshea made an alliance with Egypt and withheld tribute. The new Assyrian king Shalmaneser V, attacked and overran Israel, taking Hoshea captive in 724 B.C., though the capital city, Samaria, held out against the Assyrians until 721 B.C. Thereafter Israel was an Assyrian province.

I

Iconium. A city in the Roman province of Galatia visited by Paul and Barnabas on Paul's first missionary journey (Acts 13:51–14:6).

Immanuel. See **Emmanuel.**

Isaac. The son of Abraham and Sarah, he was nearly sacrificed to God until God showed Abraham that he did not require child sacrifice (Gen 22:1–14). His wife Rebecca bore him twin sons, Esau and Jacob, whose descendants became the Edomites and the people of Israel respectively.

Isaiah. It has long been recognised that the book of Isaiah is the work of three major prophets, often known for convenience as first, second and third Isaiah.

First Isaiah, also sometimes called Isaiah of Jerusalem, prophesied from "the year that King Uzziah died" (c. 742 B.C.) until at least the end of the eighth century B.C., and his work occupies chapters 1–39 of the book which bears his name. It has been said that Isaiah was more of a statesman than a prophet because of the close interest he took in Judah's affairs, and especially her foreign policy. Thus, when King Ahaz was threatened by Pekah of Israel and Rezin of Syria, Isaiah advised against taking panic measures because he believed the threat would be short-lived. Ahaz, however, ignored his advice, appealed to Assyria for help and became an Assyrian vassal for the remainder of his reign.

Later Isaiah was to warn King Hezekiah against becoming involved in rebellion against Assyria led by the Philistine city-state of Ashdod, and this time his advice was heeded. He also constantly spoke out against reliance on Egyptian help against the Assyrians. But to call Isaiah a statesman rather than a prophet is to ignore the religious foundations of his political advice. He believed in a God whose control of history was absolute. He also believed that his people's difficulties were the result of their failure to put their trust in God and to meet his moral demands in their social life. For him, therefore, the way to solve their problems was to put these things right. Political intrigues and alliances with foreign nations were not only worthless but diverted attention from the real issues. For much of his career Isaiah regarded the Assyrians as instruments of God's judgement, and consequently argued that resistance to them was futile, but towards the end of his life he encouraged King Hezekiah in defying them, perhaps feeling that his people had now received sufficient punishment and certainly believing that the arrogance of the Assyrians must in its own time come under God's judgement.

Second Isaiah, the author of chapters 40–55 of the prophetic book, was a prophet of the exile. Like the earlier Isaiah he had a profound belief in the utter sovereignty of God, and expresses this in some of the most beautiful and exalted language in the Old Testament. His most important contribution to religious thought, however, comes in the sections which speak of a suffering servant of the Lord. These passages are enigmatic, and it is not clear whether Isaiah was speaking of a past, present or future figure. What is important is the insight—quite astonishing in his time—that a man who set himself to serve God faithfully might be despised, reviled and rejected and that God might somehow bring healing to his people through such a person. Whatever Isaiah himself intended, it is hardly surprising that Christians equate the suffering servant with Christ.

Third Isaiah, responsible for chapters 56–66, mostly addresses people back in Jerusalem after the exile, offering them encouragement through his belief in a God who keeps his promises. It may seem strange to us that the work of three different prophets, living at different times, should have been combined in this way in one book under one name, yet the book does show a fundamental unity of outlook, especially in its proclamation of God's sovereignty. It seems possible that the first Isaiah left behind a group of disciples which continued in existence long after his death, a group which included the two later authors and which was responsible for the editing of the book of Isaiah as we know it.

Ishbosheth. The only one of Saul's four sons to survive his final tragic battle against the Philistines, Ishbosheth was accepted as king by the northern tribes while Judah proclaimed David as its king (2 Sam 2:8–11). David carefully avoided open confrontation with Ishbosheth while constantly weakening his position by diplomatic pressure. Abner, Saul's general, soon defected and Ishbosheth was later murdered in his bed by two of his officers (2 Sam 4:5–7).

Ishmael. The son Abraham had by Hagar, Sarah's slave-girl, when it seemed that Sarah herself would have no children (Gen 16:1–4, 15). After Sarah had Isaac, Hagar and Ishmael were driven out (Gen 21:9–20).

Israel. In the first instance this is the name given to Jacob by his mysterious opponent in the wrestling match at Peniel (Gen 32:22–28). His descendants therefore became the children of Israel, or simply Israel. When, after Solomon's reign, the northern tribes rebelled against his son Rehoboam, the term was reserved for the northern kingdom as opposed to the southern kingdom of Judah. Sometimes the term "all Israel" is used of the undivided kingdom to distinguish this usage from the later use for the northern kingdom only.

Issachar. (1) The ninth son of Jacob, his fifth by Leah.

(2) The tribe of Issachar which occupied a fairly small area west of the Jordan and south of the Sea of Galilee.

J

Jabesh-Gilead. A town just east of the Jordan which Saul delivered from the Ammonites (1 Sam 11:1–11). In gratitude the men of Jabesh-Gilead rescued the bodies of Saul and his sons from the Philistines and took them back to give them a decent burial (1 Sam 31:11–13).

Jacob. One of twin brothers, Jacob nevertheless had no claim on his father's property or the special blessing reserved for the eldest son because he was the second from his mother's womb. However, he first got his brother, Esau, to agree to sell his birthright (Gen 25:29–33) and then tricked his blind father Isaac into giving him the blessing (Gen 27:1–29). He fled from his father's wrath to his uncle Laban, in whom he met someone almost as crafty as himself. He served Laban for seven years for his

younger daughter Rachel, only to find after his marriage that he had been given the elder daughter Leah (Gen 29:15–26). He then had to serve another seven years for Rachel. Nevertheless, Jacob prospered with Laban and returned a wealthy man to be reconciled with Esau (Gen 33:1–4). He ended his days in Egypt as the guest of his eleventh son, Joseph (Gen 47:11–12). The stories of Jacob which do not gloss over his failings, show a man who is often self-centred and careless about God in his early years, but who comes to see that God has plans for him and has in fact been caring for him throughout his life.

Jahweh. *See* **Yahweh.**

James. (1) One of the three disciples who were with Jesus on the mount of transfiguration (Mk 9:2–9). The brother of John and a son of Zebedee, he was later killed by Herod Agrippa I (Acts 12:1–2).

(2) Another disciple, the son of Alphaeus, of whom nothing more is known (Mk 4:18).

(3) The brother of Jesus who apparently became an apostle after a special resurrection appearance to him (1 Cor 15:7, Gal 1:19) and subsequently became leader of the Jerusalem church (Acts 15:13–21).

James, Letter of. Though some have identified the author as James the brother of Jesus, this can only be speculation, nor is there any clear indication to whom the letter was first addressed. It is a set of practical instructions on how to live the Christian life, and its emphasis on deeds (as opposed to Paul's emphasis on faith) led Luther to dismiss it as "a letter of straw". In reality, however, there is no conflict; for both James and Paul righteousness is a product of faith.

Jebusites. The original inhabitants of Jerusalem, they were not conquered by the people of Israel when they occupied Canaan but remained as an independent city-state. David took the city, however, by sending his men along a water tunnel, and established his capital there (2 Sam 5:6–10).

Jehoahaz. (1) King of Israel (815–801 B.C.). The son of Jehu, Jehoahaz was an ineffective ruler and spent the whole of his reign under Syrian domination.

(2) King of Judah (609 B.C.). The unfortunate Jehoahaz succeeded his father Josiah who had been killed in battle with the Egyptians. He was almost immediately deposed by the Egyptians in favour of his brother Eliakim, who took the throne-name Jehoiakim.

Jehoash. King of Israel (801–786 B.C.). A strong ruler who regained from Syria all the territory lost by his father Jehoahaz, and who also defeated King Amaziah of Judah after being provoked into a quarrel he did not seek.

Jehoiachin. King of Judah (598–597 B.C.). Jehoiachin came to the throne when a Babylonian army was already on the march against Jerusalem because of his father Jehoiakim's rebellion. Within three months he surrendered the city and was taken into exile where he spent the rest of his life.

Jehoiakim. King of Judah (609–598 B.C.). Placed on the throne by the Egyptians after they had killed his father Josiah in battle and deposed his elder brother Jehoahaz, Jehoiakim remained a vassal of Egypt until 605 B.C. when the Egyptians were routed by the Babylonians. He transferred his allegiance to Babylon, but in 601 B.C. another battle between the Egyptians and Babylonians on the Egyptian frontier resulted in the withdrawal of the Babylonian armies to reorganise. Interpreting this as weakness, Jehoiakim rebelled. In December 598 the Babylonians marched against him, and in the same month Jehoiakim died, possibly by assassination (this may be implied by Jeremiah 22:18, 36:30). Jeremiah, himself forced into hiding by Jehoiakim, is scathing in his criticism of the king as one who callously exploited the people and shed much innocent blood.

Jehoram. (1) King of Israel (849–842 B.C.). A son of Ahab, he actually succeeded his brother Ahaziah, who died after a short reign leaving no sons. During his reign the Moabites successfully rebelled against him, and the war against Syria, in which Ahab had lost his life, dragged on. It was while recovering from wounds received in the Syrian war that he was killed in Jehu's coup.

(2) King of Judah (849–842 B.C.). Like his contemporary and namesake in Israel, Jehoram of Judah lost territory to his enemies in Edom and also on the Philistine frontier. He was married to Ahab's sister (or possibly daughter) Athaliah, who was to seize the throne after the death of their son Ahaziah.

Jehoshaphat. King of Judah (873–849 B.C.). A capable ruler who allied himself with Omri and Ahab, his contemporaries in Israel, to subjugate enemies across the Jordan and, with rather less success, keep the Syrians at bay. In 2 Chronicles 19:4–11 we are told of a reform of the judicial system he carried out, and it seems from 2 Kings 3:14 that Elisha held him in considerable respect.

Jehu. Jehu was anointed king while serving as commander of Jehoram's army by one of the prophets acting on Elisha's instructions (2 Kgs 9:1–10). He promptly killed Jehoram, who was recovering from wounds in Jezreel, King Ahaziah of Judah who had the misfortune to be visiting him at the time, and the evil Jezebel who, as queen mother, still exercised considerable influence. He went on to exterminate every surviving member of the royal family and the worshippers of Baal. In so doing he broke the alliance with Judah, on which Israel's defence against her enemies largely depended, and deprived the nation of many of its leading figures. In spite of the ferocity of his coup, he was unable to withstand the aggression of Hazael, king of Syria, and lost all his territory across the Jordan.

Jephthah. One of the inspired leaders of Israel known as judges, before the days of the monarchy. He defeated the Ammonites, having made a vow to sacrifice the first living thing he met on his return if God gave him victory. In consequence he was compelled to sacrifice his own daughter (Judg 11:1–39).

Jeremiah. Jeremiah was called to be a prophet as a young man about 630 B.C. and prophesied until after the fall of Jerusalem to the Babylonians in 586 B.C. His long prophetic ministry therefore spanned the last years of Judah as an independent kingdom. His early prophecies paint a terrifying picture of impending disaster (Jer 5:23–31) which, in the short term at least, never materialised and made Jeremiah feel that God had made a laughing stock of him (Jer 20:7). Among the many fascinations of the book of Jeremiah are the frankness of the prophet's conversations with God and his reflections on how to distinguish true prophecy from false. When Josiah carried out the great religious reforms in 622 B.C. Jeremiah supported them and thus aroused the anger of his family, who were priests at Anathoth just outside Jerusalem and probably objected to the ban on sacrificial worship except in the temple (Jer 11:1–8,21). Although a supporter of the reforms initially, Jeremiah soon saw their limitations or even dangers: because the external forms of Judah's religion had been regularised people might become complacent, failing to realise that what God really required was a change of heart. It was this that led Jeremiah to speak of a new covenant written in men's hearts (Jer 31:31–34). From Jehoiakim's time onwards Jeremiah became increasingly unpopular because of his insistence that the presence of the temple would not save the Jews from the Babylonians, contrary to the accepted doctrine that God would never permit his city to be taken or his temple destroyed (Jer 26:1–11). During the siege of Jerusalem he was imprisoned and nearly killed as a traitor because he constantly advocated surrender and was suspected of deserting to the Babylonians (Jer 37:11–38:13). When Jerusalem finally fell, Jeremiah was permitted to remain rather than being taken into exile on the express instructions of King Nebuchadnezzar (Jer 39:11–14). After the murder of the newly appointed governor, Gedaliah, Jeremiah was taken against his will to Egypt by the remaining officials who fled there. Here he ended his days. In spite of the almost unrelieved tragedy of his life, Jeremiah was not without hope. At the height of the siege of Jerusalem he bought a plot of land from a kinsman as a symbol that people would one day have the confidence to engage in business again (Jer 32:1–15), and he wrote a letter to the first group of exiles, taken to Babylon in 597 B.C., declaring that the future of the nation was in their hands and that God had plans for their welfare (Jer 29:1–14).

Jericho. A very ancient city a few miles west of the Jordan, it was the first stronghold to be captured by Joshua after crossing the river. In Elijah's time it was the home of a company of prophets (2 Kgs 2:4–5), and in the gospels it is the setting for the healing of blind Bartimaeus and the rehabilitation of Zacchaeus (Lk 18:35–19:9).

Jeroboam I. King of Israel (922–901 B.C.), Jeroboam first appears as one of Solomon's officials in charge of forced labour. Told by the prophet Ahijah that he would receive ten of the twelve tribes of Israel, he became a marked man and had to flee to Egypt to escape Solomon's wrath (1 Kgs 11:26–40). After Solomon's death he returned to lead the northern tribes in their revolt against Rehoboam, and became the first king of the northern kingdom (1 Kgs 12:1–20). He established a capital at Shechem initially, but later moved to Tirzah, which remained the capital until the reign of Omri. Clearly he could not have his people going to the Jerusalem temple to worship, since the cult there celebrated amongst other things, God's eternal covenant with the house of David. He therefore established two rival centres at the ancient shrines of Dan and Bethel, and in each of them placed a golden calf. The significance of these animals is not in fact clear, but the biblical writers assume that they were idols and the name of Jeroboam is always associated by them with idolatry (1 Kgs 12:26–30).

Jeroboam II. King of Israel (786–746 B.C.). Long-lived and capable, in human terms Jeroboam II must be judged one of the most successful kings the northern kingdom ever had. The biblical record gives few details but states that he "restored the border of Israel from the entrance to Hamath as far as the Sea of Arabah" (2 Kgs 14:25). It appears from this that his north-eastern border stood where it had been in Solomon's time. The books of Amos and Hosea give a vivid picture of social conditions during Jeroboam's reign, a picture of great prosperity, but prosperity confined to a fortunate minority who cared little for the fate of the masses.

Jerusalem. An ancient city originally occupied by the Jebusites but captured from them by David. It made an ideal capital because of its military strength, because it was near the border between Judah and the northern tribes who were now being brought together again under David's rule, and because it did not actually belong to any of the tribes, having remained as an independent enclave until David took it. As time went on it acquired a mystical significance as the city of God, with the temple as his dwelling-place. This mystique was partly, though not entirely, destroyed by the experience of the exile, which showed that Israel's faith could survive without Jerusalem and its temple.

Jesse. The father of David (1 Sam 16:1).

Jesus. Without doubt more words have been written about Jesus than any other figure in history, and the debate still continues, not only about the historical facts but about their significance. It is impossible in a short article to do justice to the complexity of the issues arising from the life of this man, but the main facts of his public ministry may be stated with some certainty.

The existence of Jesus, as a religious leader put to death by the Romans at the instigation of the Jewish authorities, is attested by the contemporary Jewish historian Josephus. For the details of his life and teaching we have to rely mainly on the four gospels written some 35 to 65 years after his death. The earliest of these, Mark, does not record the birth of Jesus and the birth stories contained in Luke and Matthew are important more for their symbolic value than for their contribution to our historical knowledge. They do establish the date of Jesus' birth as about 4 B.C. (the obvious anomaly is due to the fact that when the

Christian calendar was established much later the date of Jesus' birth was miscalculated).

Virtually nothing is known about his life until he was nearly thirty when he received baptism from John the Baptist and was confirmed in his conviction that God had entrusted him with a special mission and he retired to the wilderness to reflect upon it (Lk 3:21–22, 4:1–13). When he returned he declared his manifesto in the synagogue at Nazareth using some words of Isaiah, "to bring good news to the poor, to proclaim liberty to the captive and recovery of sight to the blind, to set free the oppressed, and to announce that the time has come when God will save his people". He proceeded to put this manifesto into practice in both words and actions. Jesus believed that the Kingdom of God foreshadowed in the Old Testament was about to be realised and his teaching was to prepare people for that Kingdom which he described in his parables. "Unless a man has been born again he cannot see the Kingdom of God" (Jn 3:3). Wherever he went he healed the sick. Whether these were miracles in the sense that normal physical laws were set aside is, of course, open to question, but they are such an integral part of the gospel records that they cannot be ignored. It seems clear that Jesus was able to heal people who could not otherwise be healed in his day, and drove himself to exhaustion in doing so, thus demonstrating in practice the love of God he preached. Inevitably this made him popular, in the end embarrassingly so, for the people came to have expectations of him which he had no intention of fulfilling (Jn 6:14–15). As it became clear that he was not going to lead his countrymen in throwing off the yoke of Roman rule, disillusionment set in.

It had also become clear that alongside the tremendous assurance of God's unwavering love Jesus set demands far harder to meet than those of the Old Testament. What other teacher had ever required that they should love their enemies and do good to those who hated them (Mt 5:43–48)? The religious authorities had never shared the popular enthusiasm for Jesus, partly because of his disregard for sabbath rules (Mk 2:23–3:6) but even more so because the note of authority in his teaching put them to shame and seemed to imply a special relationship with God (Mk 2:1–12). Jesus, well aware that their net was closing in around him, set out for Jerusalem for the final confrontation (Lk 9:51). Here, having failed to trap him by any legal method the authorities arrested him by night with the connivance of Judas (Mk 14:43–46), condemned him in their own court on the charge of blasphemy (Mk 14:55–64) and rushed him before the Roman governor on charges of political subversion (Mk 15:1–5). Within hours he was dead, executed by crucifixion (Mk 15:24–37). Yet not long afterwards his followers, who had gone to ground after his arrest, were boldly proclaiming his message regardless of the risks and declaring that death had been unable to hold him fast (Acts 2:22–24). In all the inevitable questioning over the resurrection of Jesus one fact seems beyond dispute: that his disciples were prepared to stake their lives on its reality.

Jethro. A Midianite priest whose daughter Zipporah was married to Moses (Ex 2:16–22). He also advised Moses on the setting up of a judicial system after the exodus (Ex 18:13–26).

Jezebel. A Phoenician princess who was married to Ahab, probably as part of his father Omri's policy of friendly relations with the Phoenicians for trade purposes. She was a fanatical devotee of the Phoenician Baal Melkart and made strenuous efforts to introduce his worship to Israel, equally strenuously opposed by Elijah (1 Kgs 18:19–40). Her involvement in Naboth's unjust execution (1 Kgs 21:1–15) shows a completely despotic view of the king's rights. She outlived Ahab and continued to exercise an evil influence as queen mother during the reigns of his sons Ahaziah and Jehoram until killed in Jehu's rebellion.

Jezreel. A city which seems to have been used as a second capital by the kings of Israel about the time of Ahab. It was here that Jehoram

went to recover from his wounds received in the Syrian wars and where he was killed, together with Jezebel, in Jehu's coup (2 Kgs 9:14–35). Hosea named his first child Jezreel as a symbol of judgement on the house of Jehu for its unnecessary brutality (Hos 1:3–4).

Joab. David's commander-in-chief and a considerable influence upon him. It was he who persuaded David to accept Absalom back from exile (2 Sam 14:1–24), though after Absalom's death he took David to task for showing excessive grief over his rebellious son rather than gratitude to those who had been loyal to him (2 Sam 19:1–8). As David's life drew to a close Joab backed Adonijah as his successor, but David nominated Solomon, who subsequently had Joab killed (1 Kgs 1:5–6, 2:28–34).

Joash. King of Judah (837–800 B.C.). The only son of Ahaziah to escape Athaliah's slaughter, he was kept in hiding for six years and then proclaimed king at the age of seven on the instructions of Jehoiada the priest (2 Kgs 11:1–11). Under Jehoiada's influence he made repairs to the temple, but according to Chronicles 24:17–22 he showed a very different character once Jehoiada was dead. Certainly he must have aroused the hatred of his subjects, as he was eventually assassinated.

Job. The book of Job is a protest against the commonly accepted view that God rewards the good with prosperity and punishes the wicked with suffering. It postulates the case of a man who had led a blameless life (Job's personal code of conduct described in chapter 31 is astonishing in its closeness to the ideals later proclaimed by Jesus) who nevertheless suffers every conceivable disaster from the death of his children to painful and disfiguring illness. The major part of the book consists of dialogue between Job and three of his friends (later joined by a fourth). The friends try to convince Job that he must have done something to deserve his misfortunes, while Job continues to protest his innocence and cannot accept this explanation of his suffering. The book does not arrive at any specific answer to the problem of innocent suffering but rejects facile solutions, declaring in majestic poetry that God is far greater than human understanding can encompass.

Joel. The book of Joel tells us nothing about the author except his father's name, and there is no clear indication when he lived, though a date in the fifth or fourth century B.C. is likely. The prophet regards a severe infestation of locusts as a sign of God's judgement on his people, and calls them to repent. He looks forward to a time when God will pour out his spirit on every one, men and women young and old alike, a passage quoted by Peter on the first Whit Sunday.

John. (1) John the Baptist. A kinsman of Jesus, he was also his forerunner, preaching repentance to all who would listen and baptising them in the Jordan as a symbol of the new way of life to which they committed themselves (Lk 3:3–14). Jesus accepted baptism from John but then embarked on a very different kind of ministry. It is clear, however, that the two men regarded each other with the greatest respect (Lk 7:18–28). John was imprisoned by Herod Antipas for criticising his marriage to his half-brother's wife Herodias, and it was Herodias who eventually engineered his execution (Mk 6:17–28).

(2) The brother of James, a son of Zebedee and one of the inner group of disciples who were with Jesus on the mount of transfiguration. Though the identification between John and "the disciple whom Jesus loved" in John's gospel is not certain, it is widely assumed. In the early days of the Christian church he was a prominent leader with Peter (Acts 3:1–10, 4:1–21) but we hear relatively little of him afterwards. His connection with the writing of the fourth gospel is problematic (see next entry).

John, Gospel of. The fourth gospel is clearly different from the other three even to the casual reader. To name only the most obvious difference, whereas the teaching of Jesus in the first three gospels is in the form of short pithy sayings or vivid parables, in John it appears as long philosophical discourses. The gospel is not therefore so much an account of the life of Jesus as an interpretation of its significance. But although the author has deliberately and freely recast the teaching of Jesus into a more explicitly theological form, this does not mean that he is not concerned with the historical truth; indeed, the leading British New Testament scholar of recent times has argued that in some respects the historical information in the fourth gospel is superior to that in the other three. The author then was a man of great intellectual stature who had long reflected on the significance of Jesus, and was capable of expressing his conclusions in a form more akin to Greek philosophical writing than traditional Jewish teaching, but who was also in contact with a good historical source independent of the other three gospels. John the disciple of Jesus, with his humble background as a Galilean fisherman, seems an unlikely author, but may well have been the source of the author's historical information.

John, Letters of. The three letters of John show many similarities with the fourth gospel in their vocabulary, style and thematic content, but there are some difficulties in ascribing them to the same author. If they were not by the author of the fourth gospel they were certainly written by someone thoroughly steeped in his way of thinking. The first letter is concerned with a form of false teaching which claims that there is a special way of knowing God open only to the initiated, that Jesus was not truly a physical person and that morality, having nothing to do with actions in the physical world has nothing to do with religion. In opposing this heresy John insists on the physical reality of Jesus and declares that knowing God is inseparable from loving others. Whereas the first letter appears to be a "circular" for general dissemination among the churches, the second is addressed to "the dear lady and her children"—probably a local church. It is much shorter but deals with the same false teaching. The third letter is addressed to an individual, Gaius, encouraging him and warning him against one Diotrephes.

Jonadab. The son of Rechab, he seems to have been the real founder of the Rechabites who tried to maintain the way of life of their forefathers, living in tents rather than houses and not planting crops or vineyards or drinking wine. Apart from this the only information we have on Jonadab is that he helped Jehu in his seizure of the throne (2 Kgs 10:15–17).

Jonah. The book of Jonah is in effect a short story, making a very important point in a humorous way. The essence of the story is Jonah's reluctance to preach to the people of Nineveh, the Assyrian capital, in case they listen to him and consequently enjoy the benefits of God's favour! His attempt to flee to a distant place out of God's reach is foiled by a storm and the great fish which conveniently deposits him on the Palestinian shore once more. Realising that he has no option but to do as God has told him, he goes and preaches to the people of Nineveh, who, as he had feared, repent of their evil and turn to God. Jonah consequently sulks over God's failure to punish them for their previous sins until God shows him how unreasonable his attitude is. The book is thus a witty but serious appeal to the Jews to broaden their conception of God and to rejoice in his concern for other nations. In spirit it comes close to several of the parables of Jesus, e.g. the parable of the prodigal son and his elder brother who refuses to rejoice over the return of the lost one.

Jonathan. One of the four sons of Saul whose reckless daring was largely responsible for a victory over the Philistines at the pass of Michmash (1 Sam 14:1–23). He is best known, however, for his unwavering friendship with David which survived his father's intense jealousy and David's ultimate exile (1 Sam 19:1–7, 20:1–42). He was killed, together with his father and two other brothers, in battle against the Philistines (1 Sam 31:1–4).

Joppa. A port on the Palestinian coast where Peter was staying when he had his vision showing him that there was no distinction between Jew and Gentile in God's sight (Acts 10:9–23).

Joram. See Jehoram.

Jordan. The river Jordan runs north-south from the foot of Mount Hermon to the Dead Sea through a rift valley which is below sea level for the greater part of its length. It forms a natural division between the central highlands of Palestine to the west and the plateau of the Transjordanian desert to the east. As well as being a natural barrier it is also a psychological one, the crossing of the Jordan having the same sort of significance for the people of Israel as the crossing of the Rubicon for Julius Caesar—a decisive step on the road to conquest.

Joseph. (1) The eleventh son of Jacob, his first by Rachel. A precocious child who provoked the enmity of his brothers, he was taken and sold as a slave in Egypt by Ishmaelite or Midianite traders. Not only is the story confused on this point but also as to whether he was sold to the traders by his brothers or rescued by the traders from a pit where his brothers had left him (Gen 37:12–35). After various vicissitudes in Egypt he gained high office by his power to interpret dreams, and in this position he was able both to help and test his brothers incognito when they came seeking corn in time of famine (Gen 41:1–45:14). Eventually he brought his father and brothers to live in Egypt (Gen 47:11–12). While there is no reason to doubt that the Joseph stories have a historical basis, they may well have been embellished in order to drive home the theological point made in Joseph's words to his brothers when he revealed his identity: "so it was not really you who sent me here but God" (Gen 45:8). Joseph gave rise to two of the tribes of Israel named after his sons Ephraim and Manasseh.

(2) The husband of Mary. Information on Joseph is sparse. He was a descendant of David (Mt 1:20), and worked as a village carpenter in Nazareth (Mt 13:55). He is not mentioned after the visit to Jerusalem when Jesus was twelve (Lk 2:41–51), and it seems a reasonable supposition that he had died before Jesus began his public ministry. This has led to the tradition, not necessarily true, that he was much older than Mary.

(3) Joseph of Arimathea. A rich Jew who was a member of the Jewish Council but who sympathised with Jesus and his cause. After Jesus' execution he requested the body from Pilate and had it buried in his own rock-hewn tomb (Mk 15:42–46).

Joshua. The book of Joshua takes the middle from Moses' succession and records the invasion and settlement of Canaan by the people of Israel under his leadership. While it includes some very early material, the book has been extensively edited and did not reach its final form until centuries after the events it describes. It is generally considered that the picture it presents is a simplified one, representing the invasion of Canaan as a single co-ordinated campaign with Joshua as commander-in-chief. In fact, the likelihood is that the occupation was far more haphazard, with some of the tribes at least acting independently and Joshua commanding only the most successful part of the invasion forces. In particular there are indications in Joshua 15:13–14 and Judges 1:11–21 that the southern tribes of Judah, Simeon and Benjamin may have operated in isolation from the main body with a man called Caleb as their leader. The most famous incident in the conquest is undoubtedly the battle of Jericho, and controversy still rages on what actually happened on this occasion (Josh 6:1–20). In spite of the unresolved historical questions, the character of Joshua emerges clearly—a man of simple faith who believed that God had given the land of Canaan to the people of Israel and would continue to support them if they remained true to him.

Josiah. King of Judah (640–609 B.C.). Josiah is chiefly remembered for the great religious reform he carried out in 622 B.C. following the discovery in the temple of a Book of the Covenant which made him realise how far short his people had fallen from the standards God demanded. He closed down all pagan altars and, in order to prevent irregularities, decreed that sacrifice could only be offered in the temple in Jerusalem. These measures were extended even to parts of the old northern kingdom of

Israel, indicating the degree of freedom Josiah enjoyed due to the preoccupation of the Assyrians with survival against the Medes and Babylonians. He also reinstated the celebration of the Passover which had apparently lapsed (2 Kgs 23:1–23). In 609 B.C. the Egyptians marched through Judah on their way to render assistance to the beleaguered Assyrians, preferring to maintain a weakened Assyria in power than to face a strong Babylon. Josiah tried to stop them and was killed in battle at Megiddo.

Jotham. King of Judah (742–735 B.C.). The son of Uzziah, Jotham ruled as co-regent with his father for some years as his father had contracted "leprosy" (*i.e.* a disfiguring skin disease, not necessarily leprosy as it is known today), and could not carry out public duties. Little is said about Jotham except that he continued the good work of his father, building the upper gate of the temple. At the end of his reign he was under pressure from Pekah of Israel and Rezin of Syria to join an anti-Assyrian coalition, but this problem was left to his successor Ahaz.

Judaea. Like many names which denote an area, the term Judaea is used differently at different times. Its most common usage, however, is to denote the Roman province of Judaea, the area of southern Palestine which from A.D. 6 onwards came under the rule of a Roman governor rather than a member of the Herod family. It was this province which was governed by Pontius Pilate and later by Felix and Festus.

Judah. (1) The fourth son of both Jacob and Leah.
(2) The tribe of Judah which occupied a large area to the west of the Dead Sea and as far as the Egyptian frontier.
(3) The name of the southern kingdom after the northern tribes had broken away under Jeroboam I. While its boundaries coincided roughly with the old tribal area of Judah, it also included most of the territory of Benjamin.

Judas. (1) Judas, son of James, a disciple of Jesus about whom nothing else is known.
(2) Judas Iscariot, the disciple of Jesus who betrayed him. John 12:4–6 states that he was in charge of the common purse used by the disciples and stole from it, but apart from that there is little information on him prior to his act of betrayal. After betraying Jesus for 30 pieces of silver (Mt 26:14–16) he returned the money and committed suicide (Mt 27.3–5). His motives will always remain a matter of speculation. The most charitable view is that he was trying to force Jesus into a position where he would have to perform a dramatic miracle to save himself, thus convincing the sceptics, and he never anticipated that Jesus would let himself be killed.

Judas, Gospel of. An ancient Coptic manuscript, found in the 1970s in Egypt. Hailed as an authentic copy of a lost Gospel and portraying Judas, not as a traitor, but as carrying out Christ's plan.

Jude, Letter of. A short letter warning of the dangers of false teaching and the judgement which will befall those who distort the Christian message. Though it has been suggested on the basis of Mark 6:3 that the author was one of the brothers of Jesus, this is by no means certain.

Judge. The term is used in several senses in the Old Testament, including the modern sense of one who arbitrates in a legal dispute or enforces the law. There is, however, an important special use of the term to describe men like Gideon, Jephthah and Samson who exercised leadership among the tribes of Israel, especially in times of danger, during the period between the settlement of Canaan and the establishment of the monarchy. Their authority was regarded as God-given and was entirely personal, *i.e.* it did not extend to their sons. In many ways they acted as kings, but for a long time the establishment of a recognised monarchy was resisted on the grounds that it would be a denial of God's sovereignty (Judg 8:22–23).

Judges, Book of. This book deals with the history of the people of Israel during the period of the Judges, *i.e.* from the death of Joshua until shortly before the anointing of Saul as Israel's first king. It contains some material (*e.g.* the song of Deborah in chapter five) which is con-

temporaneous with the events described, and therefore of enormous historical value, though like all the historical books of the Old Testament it was not edited into its final form until centuries later. Much of the book is concerned with the battles for survival against hostile tribes, but as in all the writings of the Old Testament the uniting theme is a theological one, tracing in Israel's history a recurring cycle of disobedience, oppression, repentance *etc.*

K

Kenites. A tribe which lived in southern Palestine and, unlike many of the surrounding tribes enjoyed friendly relations with the people of Israel, perhaps because they had religious affinities with them. Moses' father-in-law, Jethro, was a Kenite (Judg 1:16) and the Rechabites who long persisted as an ascetic group among the people of Israel appear to have been closely connected with the Kenites (1 Chr 2:55).

Kidron. A stream running through a deep valley to the east of Jerusalem and separating the city from the Mount of Olives.

Kings, Books of. The two books of Kings are the major source for nearly 400 years of the history of the people of Israel, from the accession of Solomon around 960 B.C., through the division of the kingdom on Solomon's death and the end of the northern kingdom after the fall of Samaria in 721 B.C., to the destruction of Jerusalem and the exile of the leading people by the Babylonians in 586 B.C. Like all the historical books of the Old Testament, it is a composite work containing material of different ages and not reaching its final form until centuries after some of the incidents described. Many of the major events recorded, however, can be confirmed by archaeological evidence from other sources, *e.g.* the Moabite stone, an inscription of Mesha, king of Moab, which describes relations between his people and the northern kingdom of Israel about the time of Jehoram and, except in minor details, agrees with the biblical record. The interest of the authors of Kings was not in history as an academic exercise, however, but history as it revealed the hand of God, and the kings of Israel and Judah are therefore judged by their loyalty to Yahweh, and the fortunes of their people are related to this. On this criterion all the kings of Israel are judged to have failed, but among the kings of Judah, Uzziah, Hezekiah and Josiah especially are regarded as good kings.

L

Laban. Jacob's uncle and the father of Leah and Rachel.

Lachish. An important city and stronghold about 50 km south-west of Jerusalem. Against both the Assyrians in 701 B.C. and the Babylonians in 587 B.C. it proved its defensive strength, in the latter campaign holding out longer than any other city except Jerusalem itself. Important archaeological finds have been made there, including the Lachish letters written in the heat of the Babylonian invasion.

Lamentations, Book of. Traditionally known as the Lamentations of Jeremiah, there is in fact no evidence to connect them with the prophet. The book is a collection of fine poems mourning the devastation of Jerusalem in 586 B.C. The third chapter expressed hope for the future, however, and the fifth is a prayer for mercy.

Laodicea. A city of Asia Minor near Colossae. The church there is referred to in Revelation 3:14–22 and criticised for its lukewarmness. There is particular irony in the author's claim that the church is blind, for Laodicea was famed for an eye ointment made there. It appears from Colossians 4:16 that Paul wrote a letter to Laodicea, though he never visited it as far as is known.

Last Supper. *See* Lord's Supper.

Lazarus. (1) The brother of Martha and Mary whom, according to John 11:17–44, Jesus raised to life again.

(2) The poor beggar in Jesus' parable of the rich man and Lazarus (Lk 16:19–31).

Leah. The elder daughter of Laban and first wife of Jacob. She bore six of Jacob's twelve sons.

Levi. (1) The third son of both Jacob and Leah.
(2) See **Matthew**.

Levites. It appears that the descendants of Levi never possessed any tribal territory of their own but were dispersed among the other tribes. At an early stage, by a process which is far from clear, they were associated with the priesthood, and it became the custom that only Levites could be priests, although not all Levites were. Later the term was used for an order of temple assistants with lower status than priests, as in the parable of the good Samaritan.

Leviticus. As the name of the book implies it is almost entirely concerned with Levitical or priestly duties (see above), the offering of worship and sacrifice, the maintenance of ritual purity and the proper response to God's holiness. To the modern reader who does not accept the need for physical sacrifice as part of worship, much of it may appear irrelevant or even repugnant, yet it represents a real desire to give to God the respect properly due to him, and it is not completely taken up with obscure ritual instructions, for it includes the words quoted with approval by Jesus, "love your neighbour as you love yourself " (Lev 19:18).

Lord's Prayer. This brief prayer, given by Jesus in response to a request from his disciples (Lk 11:1), is highly characteristic of his thought. It first places God at the centre of the worshipper's life and only then concerns itself with human needs, asking only for the basic physical requirements of food and the spiritual necessities of forgiveness and strength under testing.

Lord's Supper. The name given both to the last meal Jesus had with his disciples and to its reenactment by the Christian community subsequently. The earliest account of the meal occurs in 1 Corinthians 11:23–26, and it is clear from the fact that Paul was instructing the Corinthian church in the proper celebration of the Lord's Supper that it was an established part of Christian worship by the mid-fifties A.D. Accounts are also given in the first three gospels. While John does not describe the meal itself, his treatment of the feeding of the five thousand is given strong sacramental overtones (Jn 6:25–58) which suggest a knowledge of the Lord's Supper. It is impossible to reconstruct with certainty the exact words of Jesus on this occasion, but it seems clear that he linked the breaking of bread and sharing of wine with his approaching sacrifice and ultimate triumph, and also with the new covenant (or new relationship) between God and man foreseen by Jeremiah (Mk 14:22–25).

Lot. A nephew of Abraham who journeyed with him to Canaan. Eventually they had to separate because their herds were too big to remain together, and Lot chose the plain of the Jordan near the Dead Sea as his territory. Escaping from the destruction of Sodom and Gomorrah his wife is said to have looked back and been turned into a pillar of salt (Gen 19:26).

Luke. Luke is referred to only three times in the New Testament, but is of special interest as being almost certainly the author of the third gospel and the book of Acts (see below). Only one of the references, that in Colossians 4:14, gives any information other than his name. Here he is spoken of as "our dear doctor", and since Paul has earlier named three people as the "only Jewish converts who work with me" it follows that Luke was a Gentile.

Luke, Gospel of. The question of the authorship of this gospel is closely linked to that of Acts, which is clearly a sequel to the gospel, being addressed to the same person Theophilus. The author of Acts sometimes uses the first person plural, showing that he was present himself for certain parts of the story, including Paul's crossing from Troas to Philippi on his second missionary journey and his voyage to Rome as a prisoner. It seems likely, therefore, that he would be among the people Paul names as his co-workers in his letters and, by a process of elimination, Luke emerges as the strongest candidate. Since there is also a tradition going back to the second century that Luke was the author of the third gospel this seems a near certainty. About half the material in Luke's gospel comes from Mark (in those days copying another author's work, far from being considered unethical, was regarded a mark of respect), and some of the remainder comes from a collection of the sayings of Jesus which Matthew evidently used as well. Luke had other sources of his own, however, and it is to him that we owe the preservation of some of Jesus' best-loved parables including those of the good Samaritan and the prodigal son. He also gives us the story of Zacchaeus and the account of the two disciples on the road to Emmaus. He lays special emphasis on Jesus' concern for Gentiles and outcasts.

Lydia. A resident of Philippi and dealer in the purple-dyed cloth for which that area was famous, she was Paul's first convert there and opened her house to him and his companions .

M

Macedonia. A Roman province including parts of northern Greece, Albania and Serbia with Philippi as its chief city. It was here that Paul first preached in Europe (as opposed to Asia Minor) in response to a vision of a man of Macedonia asking for his help (Acts 16:9–12).

Magi, the 'wise men' from the East who presented gifts to the infant Jesus at Bethlehem. Only tradition suggests there may have been three and may have been kings.

Magnificat, the hymn of the Virgin Mary, given in Luke 1, 46 beginning in the Vulgate with the words "Magnificat anima mea Dominum" ("My soul doth magnify the Lord").

Malachi. The book of Malachi clearly comes from some time after the reconstruction of the temple following the Babylonian exile. A probable date would be the first half of the fifth century B.C. The prophet takes his people to task for their laxity in the worship of God and their failure to obey the terms of God's covenant. He warns of God's judgement but also speaks of his saving power (Mal 4:2–3).

Malta. Paul was shipwrecked and spent the rest of the winter here on his journey to Rome.

Manasseh. (1) The elder of Joseph's two sons.
(2) The tribe of Manasseh, which occupied a large area on both banks of the Jordan to the north of Ephraim.
(3) King of Judah (687–642 B.C.). Regarded as the worst king in Judah's history, he actively promoted Assyrian and other pagan religious practices, sacrificed his own son and "killed so many innocent people that the streets of Jerusalem were flowing with blood" (2 Kgs 21:16).

Manna. The name of the food which God is said to have provided for the people of Israel during their wanderings in the wilderness (Ex 16:1–31). It is thought to have been a secretion formed by insects feeding on the scrublands of the desert.

Mark. The house of John Mark's mother, Mary, appears to have been the headquarters of the Jerusalem church (Acts 12:12). Paul and Barnabas took him to work with them in Antioch (Acts 12:25) and subsequently on the first missionary journey (Acts 13:5). He left them at Perga to return to Jerusalem, however, and this led to Paul refusing to take him on his second journey, with the consequence that Barnabas took him to Cyprus instead (Acts 15:36–40). It is clear from Colossians 4:10 and other references that Mark later became a close associate of Paul, and we are also told here that he was Barnabas' cousin. See also below.

Mark, Gospel of. There is a tradition dating back to A.D. 135 that the second gospel was written by Mark on the basis of Peter's memories of the life and teaching of Jesus. It seems probable that Mark collected these reminiscences shortly before Peter's death in Nero's persecution of A.D. 64 and published his gospel in Rome soon afterwards. While the identification of this Mark with John Mark cannot be absolutely certain, it seems highly likely, since John Mark knew Peter from the early days in Jerusalem. The view that the gospel is based on the firsthand information of an eye-witness is borne out by the many vivid details it contains—details often omitted by Luke and Matthew when they later used Mark's work as a basis for their own. They had other material to include and economised on unnecessary detail. Mark's gospel is of special value, therefore, as the one with most direct links with the events described.

Martha. The sister of Mary and Lazarus, who gave Jesus hospitality at her home in Bethany just outside Jerusalem (Lk 10:38–41, Jn 11:1).

Mary. (1) The mother of Jesus. Our knowledge of Jesus' mother is very limited. The birth stories present her as a pious girl, open to God's bidding. Luke's account of the visit to Jerusalem when Jesus was twelve shows her anxious and somewhat uncomprehending of her unusual son (Lk 2:41–51), and it is later suggested (Mk 3:21) that she may have attempted to restrain Jesus in his public ministry. John records that she was present at the crucifixion, and that Jesus entrusted her to the "beloved disciple". By this time she must have been old by current standards and may well have died soon after.

(2) The sister of Martha and Lazarus, who was praised for her sense of priorities in listening to Jesus (Lk 10:38–41).

(3) Mary Magdalene. A woman whom Jesus cured of "seven demons" (Lk 8:2), and who became one of those who travelled with Jesus and his disciples ministering to their needs. She was present at the crucifixion, was among a group which discovered the empty tomb and was a witness of the resurrection (Mk 15:40, 16:1, Jn 20:11–18). The tradition which identifies her with the sinful woman of Luke 7:37 is wholly without foundation.

(4) The mother of James and Joseph. Another woman who followed Jesus to Jerusalem, witnessed his crucifixion and saw the empty tomb (Mk 15:40, 47, 16:1).

(5) The mother of John Mark (Acts 12:12).

Massorah, a collection of criticisms on the Hebrew text of the Scriptures and rules for its correct interpretation.

Matthew. Also called Levi, Matthew was a tax collector before becoming one of the twelve disciples (Mt 9:9–13, cf. Mk 2:13–17).

Matthew, Gospel of. It is highly unlikely that the author of the gospel was the disciple Matthew, since he draws heavily on Mark for much of his material, and this would have been unnecessary for an eyewitness of the events. Like Luke, he also uses a collection of the sayings of Jesus in addition to some material of his own (e.g. the parable of the sheep and the goats). It is clear that the author was a Jewish Christian who was concerned among other things to stress the continuity between the Christian church and the old community of the people of Israel. Significantly, Matthew traces the ancestors of Jesus back to Abraham, whereas Luke traces them back to Adam, the symbolic father of the whole human race, and Matthew frequently states that events occurred in order to fulfil Old Testament prophecies. He arranges most of his material in five sections, possibly a conscious imitation of the Pentateuch (the five books of teaching which begin the Old Testament and have a special status among the Old Testament writings for Jews). Each section begins with a narrative and continues with the teaching of Jesus. It is the teaching of the first main sections in chapters 5–7 which constitutes the so-called Sermon on the Mount.

Megiddo. A city of strategic importance controlling the pass through the Carmel ridge from the coastal plain on the south to the Plain of Esdraelon on the north side. It was fortified by Solomon, and it was here that King Josiah lost his life in battle against the Egyptians.

Melchizedek. A king and priest who gave hospitality to Abraham (Gen 14:18–20) and who is referred to by the author of Hebrews as a forerunner of Christ, himself a priest-king.

Menahem. King of Israel (745–738 B.C.). Menahem secured the throne by the murder of his predecessor Shallum and a bloody struggle against his opponents. He gave tribute to the Assyrian ruler Tiglath-pileser III, hoping both to forestall any Assyrian designs on his territory and gain support to keep him in power. He raised the money by unpopular taxation.

Mephibosheth. A crippled son of Jonathan who was befriended by David (2 Sam 9:1–13),

though he later entertained hopes of gaining the throne as the only remaining descendant of Saul (2 Sam 16:3). Perhaps because this was by now a totally unrealistic hope, David chose to overlook the matter (Sam 19:24–30).

Mesha. The king of Moab during Jehoram's reign, he succeeded in regaining much territory from Israel, according to an ancient inscribed stone known as the Moabite stone (see below). This is consistent with 2 Kings 3:27, which implies that after a highly successful campaign against Mesha, the Israelite forces were unnerved by Mesha's sacrifice of his son and withdrew, having failed to bring the rebel into subjection.

Meshach. One of the three young men who, according to the book of Daniel, survived being thrown into a blazing furnace for refusing to worship a gold statue set up by King Nebuchadnezzar (Dan 3:1–27).

Mesopotamia. The fertile area between the rivers Tigris and Euphrates. It was from here that Abraham came. It was also the land of the Assyrians and Babylonians.

Messiah. The Hebrew word means "anointed one" and therefore implies kingship. "Christ" is the Greek equivalent. The concept of a Messiah has a complex background, but essentially it was born out of Israel's calamitous history and a sense of disillusionment with her leaders. As a result of these factors the hope grew up of a future leader who would truly be God's representative and would consequently restore his people to the position of power and prosperity they enjoyed under David and Solomon. The balance between his spiritual and political functions seems to have been viewed differently by different groups, however, which may well explain why Jesus was apparently prepared to accept the title from his disciples (in a spiritual sense) while forbidding its general use for fear of misunderstanding.

Micah. A contemporary of Isaiah prophesying in the southern kingdom of Judah towards the end of the eighth century B.C., Micah pronounces God's judgement on his people for their failure to establish a just society and declares that not even the temple will be spared in the general destruction (Mic 3:12). His book is best known for its simple but searching statement of God's requirements: to do what is just, to show constant love and to walk in humble fellowship with God (Mic 6:8). Many scholars consider that the more hopeful elements in the book of Micah are later editorial insertions, and on this view Micah must be considered primarily as a prophet of judgement like Amos before him in the northern kingdom.

Micaiah. A prophet who, in contrast to the 400 court prophets, predicted disaster for King Ahab if he went to take Ramoth-Gilead from the Syrians (1 Kgs 22:1–35).

Miletus. A port near Ephesus. Paul called the leaders of the Ephesian church to meet him here on his last journey to Jerusalem, and warned them against false teachers (Acts 20:17–38).

Miriam. The elder sister of Moses, she is referred to as a prophetess when she leads the women of Israel in a song and dance of triumph after the crossing of the sea on the escape from Egypt.

Moabite Stone, a stone of the 9th cent. B.C. containing the earliest known inscription in Phoenician characters, and discovered in the highlands of Moab in 1868. It is now in the Louvre, Paris. It records the campaign between Moab and Israel (c. 850 B.C.) (2 Kings 3:27).

Moabites. Occupying land east of the Dead Sea, the Moabites were generally hostile to the people of Israel. David conquered them, but they reasserted their independence in the period of weakness after the division of the kingdom, only to be subjugated again later by Omri. They were finally led to independence by Mesha while Jehoram was king of Israel.

Molech. A Canaanite god whose worship involved child-sacrifice. King Manasseh apparently worshipped him (2 Kgs 21:6), but Josiah desecrated the site of these sacrifices to prevent them happening again (2 Kgs 23:10).

Mordecai. The cousin and foster-father of Queen Esther (Esth 2:6–7).

Moses. If Abraham is the father of the Jewish race, Moses is the founder of Jewish religion. This does not mean, however, that the religion he established had no antecedents, but it was under Moses that it achieved its definitive form. While it is admittedly difficult to disentangle fact from legend in many of the stories of Moses, there is no reason to doubt their essential historical basis as recollections of the great leader who took the people of Israel from slavery in Egypt to the threshold of the promised land, and in the process firmly established their religious traditions. At the centre of Moses' religion is the concept of the covenant, an agreement between God and the people of Israel whereby God gives them a special position of responsibility in his plans and they pledge him their loyalty and obedience. This obedience is to be expressed not only in worship but also in behaviour towards others as laid down in the ten commandments.

N

Naaman. Commander of the Syrian army, cured of "leprosy" by Elisha (2 Kgs 5:1–19).

Naboth. Owner of a vineyard adjoining King Ahab's palace, he was put to death on false evidence at Jezebel's instigation so that Ahab could take the property in the absence of an heir (1 Kgs 21:1–16).

Nadab. King of Israel (901–900 B.C.). Assassinated within two years of his accession by Baasha whilst fighting the Philistines at Gibbethon (1 Kgs 15:27).

Nahum. The book is a poem exulting in the fall of the Assyrian capital Nineveh, which is seen as an example of God's judgement on a nation which had long taken for granted its dominant position and gave no thought to the suffering of its subject peoples. Nineveh fell in 612 B.C.

Naphtali. (1) The sixth son of Jacob, his second by Bilhah, Rachel's slave-girl.
(2) The tribe of Naphtali, occupying territory to the north and west of the Sea of Galilee.

Nathan. A prophet who advised David not to build a permanent temple in Jerusalem and rebuked him for his misconduct with Bathsheba. Nevertheless, he backed Bathsheba's son, Solomon, in the struggle for succession. It was largely through him that David was eventually persuaded to declare himself in Solomon's favour (1 Kgs 1:11–40).

Nathanael. Often identified with Bartholomew, since John omits all mention of Bartholomew but names Nathanael as one of the disciples. Brought to Jesus by Philip (who is linked with Bartholomew in the other gospels), Jesus referred to him as "a true Israelite in whom there is nothing false" (Jn 1:47).

Nativity. There are three nativity festivals of the Church: Christmas, 25 December, festival of birth of Christ; birthday of the Virgin Mary (8 Sept.); and St. John the Baptist (24 June).

Nazareth. The home of Joseph and Mary, and the place where Jesus lived until he began his itinerant ministry. Until then this small Galilean town was of no importance and is not even mentioned in the Old Testament.

Nazirite. A person dedicated to God's service and following an ascetic rule of life involving abstinence from alcohol and refusal to cut hair amongst other things. Samson was a Nazirite and John the Baptist may have been.

Nebuchadnezzar. The Babylonian ruler (605–562 B.C.) under whose orders Jerusalem was taken and destroyed and the people exiled in 586 B.C. By the standards of his day he was not excessively ruthless, and it could be argued that only the intransigence of the Jews compelled him to treat them with severity.

Nehemiah. A Jewish exile who became cupbearer to the Persian king Artaxerxes and was allowed by him to go to Jerusalem as governor about 445 B.C. in order to accelerate reconstruction of the nation's life. The book of Nehemiah relates how he overcame opposition to get the walls of Jerusalem rebuilt. It also tells how Ezra read the law aloud to the people and got them to enter into an agreement to keep it. While it seems that the two men worked together on the re-establishment of the nation's religious and economic life, the relationship between them is not entirely clear.

New Year. Originally the Jewish New Year began in the autumn, but during the exile the Babylonian New Year starting in the spring was adopted. The autumn New Year was still maintained for cultic purposes, however, and there has been much speculation, based on strong but circumstantial evidence mainly from the Psalms, over the possibility that the autumn New Year was the occasion of a major religious festival celebrating and renewing the covenant.

Nicene Creed, a summary of the principles of Christian faith, first issued in 325 by the Council of Nicaea (summoned by the emperor Constantine the Great) for the purpose of thwarting the Arian heresy and asserting the godhead of Christ. Date of Easter fixed at Council of Nicaea.

Nicodemus. A member of the Jewish Council who sympathised with Jesus and came to see him by night—presumably fearful of associating with him openly (Jn 3:1–12). He objected to the Council condemning Jesus without giving him a chance to defend himself (Jn 7:50–51) and helped Joseph of Arimathea to give Jesus a decent burial (Jn 19:39–42).

Nineveh. The capital of Assyria until its destruction by the combined forces of the Medes and Babylonians in 612 B.C. It was legendary for its size and sinfulness (Jon 1:2).

Noah. While the story of Noah may have a historical basis, its primary value lies in what it says about God. It shows God as one who does not fully carry out the judgement which man's sinfulness deserves, but in his generosity makes a new start possible. *See also* **Deluge.**

Numbers, Book of. The name of the book refers to two censuses of the people of Israel recorded in it, one just before they left Mount Sinai and the other about a generation later. The book covers the history of the people of Israel from the exodus until just before the crossing of the Jordan and lays down various rules for everyday life and worship.

O

Obadiah. (1) A high official under King Ahab who tried to protect loyal worshippers of Yahweh against the persecution of Queen Jezebel.
(2) A prophet who wrote sometime after the fall of Jerusalem in 586 B.C., condemning the Edomites for taking advantage of Judah's plight to settle old scores, and predicting final victory for the people of Israel.

Omri. King of Israel (876–869 B.C.). Although Omri is only given six verses in the books of Kings (1 Kgs 16:23–28), and is condemned for leading his people into idolatry, he was a capable ruler who in a relatively short reign established good relations with both Judah and the Phoenician states, subjugated enemies east of the Jordan and built a new capital, Samaria.

Onesimus. A runaway slave who was converted by Paul and sent back to his master Philemon, bearing with him the letter of that name.

P

Palestine. Derived from "Philistine", the name originally referred only to the southern part of the coastal plain around the Philistine cities, but it came to be used for the whole of the area bordering the eastern Mediterranean from the Lebanon southwards to the Egyptian frontier and across to the desert land of Transjordan.

Paraclete (the Holy Ghost, or Comforter), the name used in the English translations of St. John's Gospel, and adopted by Abelard to designate the convent in Champagne founded by him, of which Héloïse became the abbess.

Passover. A festival celebrated in spring by a special meal. Originally it probably derived from a custom of sacrificing the first lamb of the new season, but it became associated with the deliverance from slavery in Egypt, and it is as a way of remembering this that it has been celebrated ever since. It is followed by a week of eating unleavened bread, also in memory of the escape from Egypt.

Paul. We know more about Paul than about any other leader of the early church, our information coming both from Acts and his own letters. Born in Tarsus in Asia Minor, he was brought up in strictest Jewish tradition and studied under the renowned teacher, Gamaliel. He considered it his duty to persecute the Christian community, and was present at the stoning of Stephen, whose saintly behaviour towards his executioners almost certainly sowed the first seeds of doubt in his mind. These doubts culminated in a shattering conversion experience as he travelled to Damascus to continue his persecution of the Christians there. It was not until many years had elapsed, however, that Paul emerged as the leading figure in the mission to the Gentiles, and he did so at the instigation of Barnabas, who sent for him to help in the work at Antioch. Soon the church decided to send Paul and Barnabas on a missionary journey which took them first to Cyprus and then into the Roman province of Galatia. By this time some of the Jewish Christians were becoming alarmed at the large number of Gentile converts, and on their return they went to a gathering in Jerusalem to thrash out questions of policy with regard to the admission of Gentiles to the church. Here, Paul, more aware than anyone else of the futility of the Jewish law, strongly resisted the imposition of Jewish customs on Gentile converts, and appears to have won, though the argument was to rumble on for many years.

Soon he undertook a second missionary journey with Silas, in the course of which he founded the first church in Europe at Philippi and stayed for eighteen months in Corinth. On a third journey he spent two years in Ephesus before revisiting the churches founded earlier during his second journey. On a visit to Jerusalem at the end of his third journey he was arrested by Roman guards during a disturbance in the temple courtyard when Jews alleged that he had taken Trophimus, a Gentile from Ephesus, into the temple. After two years' imprisonment during which he was neither condemned nor declared innocent, Paul appealed to Caesar and was duly sent to Rome. We are told in Acts 28:30 that he was there for two years, presumably waiting for his accusers to present a case against him, and this may imply that he was then released, since the rule was that a case must be presented within two years. But this is not certain, and tradition has it that he died, together with Peter, in Nero's persecution of A.D. 64.

From about the year A.D. 50 onwards Paul wrote numerous letters, mainly to churches he had founded, but occasionally to churches he had not visited himself, and some of these letters form a substantial part of the New Testament. Some have accused Paul of complicating the simple gospel preached by Jesus, yet the church today may owe its very existence to Paul's clear understanding that Christianity could not just remain an offshoot of Judaism, but must become a universal religion.

Pekah King of Israel (737–732 B.C.). Seizing the throne by assassinating his predecessor, Pekah immediately entered an anti-Assyrian coalition with his Syrian neighbour Rezin. Together they made threats against Ahaz, king of Judah, who soon appealed to the Assyrians for help. In 733 B.C. Tiglath-pileser III attacked Israel, capturing many cities and deporting much of the population. It was possibly only Pekah's assassination by Hoshea, who promptly surrendered, which saved Israel from further destruction.

Pekahiah. King of Israel (738–737 B.C.). Assassinated after a short period by Pekah, probably because of discontent with his policy of submission to Assyria.

Pentateuch. The first five books of the Old Testament, having special significance for the Jews as the Torah, the basis of Jewish law.

Pentecost. See Weeks, Feast of.

Peter. The undisputed leader of the disciples, and of the Christian church during its earliest days. A Galilean fisherman, he was brought to Jesus by his brother Andrew and quickly became one of the inner group of disciples. He showed his leadership in his declaration of faith in Jesus as the Christ at Caesarea Philippi, and it was here that Jesus added the name Peter (the rock) to his original name Simon. After Jesus' arrest he denied all knowledge of him, but it could be

argued that he was only exposed to this temptation because he had had the courage to follow Jesus to the High Priest's house. He was the first disciple to enter the empty tomb and preached the first Christian sermon on the day of Pentecost. He was also instrumental in paving the way for Gentiles to enter the church through the baptism of the Roman centurion Cornelius and his subsequent defence of this action (Acts 10:1–11:18). It is unfortunate, though understandable, that the emphasis in the second half of Acts on the work of Paul leave us in ignorance as to the subsequent development of Peter's ministry. Tradition has it that he founded the church in Rome, and died there in Nero's persecution of A.D. 64.

Peter, Letters of. There is considerable doubt whether either of these letters is by the disciple Peter, or indeed whether they are by the same author. The first letter is written to encourage Christians in Asia Minor who are suffering or are likely to suffer, for their Christian faith. If this were written during a specific period of persecution it would almost certainly have been that under the Roman emperor Domitian (A.D. 81–96), since Nero's persecution does not appear to have extended far beyond the capital, and this would rule out authorship by Peter if he had died in A.D. 64. The second letter, which shows a detailed knowledge of the letter of Jude, is a general warning against false teachers. Many scholars date it as the latest document in the New Testament, around the second century.

Pharaoh. The title of the kings of Egypt. The Pharaohs under whom the people of Israel served as forced labourers have not been identified with certainty, but the likelihood is that the Pharaoh at the time of the exodus was Rameses II (reigned 1304–1237 B.C.).

Pharisees. One of the chief sects within Judaism at the time of Jesus. The movement started as an attempt to bring everyday life more closely into conformity with the law of Judaism, so that religious observance became an integral part of daily living. Jesus would hardly have quarrelled with this aim, but the effect had been to emphasise trivial details and lose sight of basic principles. It was this, and the sense of self-righteousness so often engendered, that Jesus criticised in the Pharisees.

Philemon, Letter to. A short personal letter from Paul to a member of the church at Colossae. Onesimus, Philemon's slave, had run away to Rome, where he came into contact with Paul. Paul would have liked to keep him as he was proving so useful, but felt bound to return him to Philemon, begging Philemon to welcome him back not just as a slave but as a Christian brother.

Philip. (1) Ruler of Ituraea and Trachonitis (4 B.C.–A.D. 34). See **Herod family.**

(2) One of the twelve disciples about whom little is known, although John's gospel gives him slightly greater prominence than the other three (Jn 1:43–46, 12:20–22, 14:8–9).

(3) One of the seven deacons appointed to organise the distribution of resources in the system of sharing goods adopted by the early church in Jerusalem (Acts 6:1–6). In fact, he quickly became a notable evangelist, working among the Samaritans and also in southern Palestine, where he converted an Ethiopian official travelling home, before settling in Caesarea, where he still lived nearby thirty years later (Acts 8:4–40, 21:8).

Philippi. A city of Macedonia where Paul first preached in Europe (Acts 16:12).

Philippians, Letter to the. Unlike many of Paul's letters, the letter to the church at Philippi does not seem to have been written with any particular object in mind—to combat false teaching (Galatians) or pave the way for a possible future visit (Romans). It is simply keeping in touch with old friends, for the church at Philippi had apparently been the first to give Paul financial support so that he could be a full-time missionary without the necessity of plying a trade (Phil 4:15–16). Although he warns the Philippian Christians to be on their guard against any attempt to impose Jewish customs on them (Phil 3:2–7), he seems confident of their ability to maintain their Christian life against any opposition it encounters. The whole atmosphere of the letter is one of gratitude, joy and peace, all the more remarkable as Paul was in prison and possibly close to death as he wrote (Phil 1:20–24).

Philistines. A people who came from Crete or the Aegean islands to settle on the coastal plain of Palestine about the same time that the people of Israel were entering Canaan from the east. They were organised in five main city-states and were a serious threat to the Israelites because of their iron weapons (Israel being still in the Bronze Age), their use of chariots and their military form of government. After the period of acute antagonism which was brought to a close by David's unchallengeable superiority, they lived relatively peacefully apart from occasional incidents until, sometime after the exile, the Philistines disappeared as an independent entity. They were a more cultured people than previously thought.

Phoenicia. A term used to describe the coastal area north of Mount Carmel which is now the Lebanon. It was never a kingdom as such, but included a number of city-states, of which Tyre was the most important. The Phoenicians were seafarers and traders and times of prosperity in Israel often hinged upon good relations with Phoenicia, as in Solomon's reign.

Pilate, Pontius. The Roman governor of Judaea at the time of Jesus' execution, he does not seem to have handled the admittedly difficult task of governing the Jews particularly well. All the gospels represent him as resisting the death sentence on Jesus, however, and only passing it under Jewish pressure. John implies that the Jews had some kind of hold over Pilate: possibly because of previous blunders he could not afford to antagonise the Jews again. In fact, he was recalled to Rome *c.* A.D. 36, tried and imprisoned.

Priest. In the early period of Jewish religion there were no priests. The head of the family would perform any religious functions necessary. Samuel, however, is said to have condemned Saul for offering sacrifice, thereby usurping his proper function (1 Sam 13:8–14). This suggests that by now a specific priestly role was recognised. It was with the construction of the temple and the development of more elaborate rituals that a priesthood became essential, though it was the offering of sacrifice which remained the primary function.

Prisca. *See* **Aquila.**

Prophet. What marks a person out as a prophet has been much debated. The prophets of Baal on Mount Carmel present an extremely unedifying spectacle as they dance and cut themselves to invoke the power of their god (1 Kgs 18:26–29), yet there were prophets in Israel whose behaviour was not dissimilar (1 Sam: 10:10–13). There is clearly a vast gulf between such people and men of the calibre of Amos, Hosea or Jeremiah. The one thing they have in common is their enthusiasm for God. It is possible to trace the gradual transition from these primitive prophets who expressed themselves in emotional outbursts to the great religious thinkers of later times but to sum up the difference in terms of emotions against intellect (or any other pair of contrasting qualities) is an over-simplification. Possibly the best short definition of a prophet is "one who is convinced that God has something to say through him". Although prophets were expected to have knowledge of future events, this is not an essential part of the Hebrew concept of prophecy.

Proselyte. One who was not a Jew by birth but who, by circumcision and a form of baptism, had become a Jew by faith.

Proverbs, Book of. This is basically a collection of short sayings offering advice on how to act in everyday situations, but, as with all the biblical writings, it emphasises an important theological belief—that all true wisdom comes from God and is based on respect for him. The sayings are ascribed to Solomon, who may indeed be responsible for some of them, but the compilation of the book took place centuries after his death and incorporated much later material.

Psalms, Book of, for many years attributed to David, but present-day scholars are of the view that the psalms were written by a series of authors at different times and for different purposes, and that few, if any, were written by David. The Holy Scriptures contain 150.

It is a truism to say that the Psalms are the hymn book of the Old Testament, yet it is only recently that the implications of this obvious truth have been explored. If the Psalms were collected for use in corporate worship, we need to ask for each Psalm, "On what sort of occasion would these have been appropriate sentiments to express?" In recent years this approach has led to some interesting conclusions about the worship of the people of Israel, and greatly illuminated the Psalms themselves. For the ordinary reader, however, the attraction of these poems remains what it has always been—their expression of a very wide range of human emotions within an overall context of faith in God.

Publius. The chief official (his exact status is unclear) on Malta where Paul was shipwrecked. Paul cured his father of a fever (Acts 28:7–10).

Q

Quirinus (Cyrenius). Described by Luke as the governor of Syria at the time of Jesus' birth, though if this took place in the reign of Herod the Great, Luke is wrong on this point. He later had two terms of office as governor of Syria, but at this time commanded the Roman army there.

R

Rabbah. The Ammonite capital, captured by David. It was during the siege of Rabbah that David arranged for Uriah to be left exposed to the enemy, in order to marry his wife Bathsheba (2 Sam 11:14–17).

Rabbi. Sometimes translated "teacher", but implying rather more than this. It is a respectful title, suggesting that the one who uses it accepts the authority of the one to whom it is used. In John's gospel Jesus is addressed in this manner several times.

Rachel. Laban's younger daughter and Jacob's second wife, though she was his first choice. She bore him Joseph and Benjamin.

Rahab. A prostitute of Jericho who concealed two spies sent by Joshua, and was subsequently spared when the other inhabitants were slaughtered (Josh 1:1–21, 6:22–25).

Rameses. An Egyptian city where Israelite slave labour was used, and from which the people of Israel started out on the exodus. It was on the eastern edge of the Nile delta, and is generally identified with a city earlier known as Avaris and later as Tanis.

Ramoth-Gilead. A town on the border between Israel and Syria which was the scene of bitter fighting between these traditional enemies. It was here that Ahab died, and that Jehoram received the wounds from which he was recovering at the time of Jehu's coup.

Rebecca. The sister of Laban, wife of Isaac, and mother of the twins Esau and Jacob.

Rechabites. The descendants of Rechab, about whom we know nothing except that he was the father of Jonadab, who laid down the rules of the Rechabite community. He insisted that they lived in tents and refrained from alcohol, thus trying to protect them against the corrupting influences of Canaanite civilisation. Jeremiah commends the Rechabites for their faithfulness to these principles, in contrast to the lack of faithfulness found elsewhere among the people of Israel (Jer 35:1–17).

Red Sea. The name translated as "Red Sea" in older versions of the Bible is not always to be equated with the Red Sea as known today. References in the exodus story may be to a shallow inland lake in the region now cut through by the Suez Canal, and in 1 Kings 9:26 the reference is to the Gulf of Aqaba, rather than the Red Sea itself.

Rehoboam. King of Judah (922–915 B.C.). The son of Solomon, Rehoboam refused to listen to the grievances of his people at the beginning of his reign and as a consequence was faced with rebellion by the ten northern tribes under Jeroboam's leadership. Rehoboam was unable to prevent the division and soon gave up any attempt to reassert his authority over Israel.

He lost nearly all his foreign territory, was invaded by the Egyptians and had to ransack his treasury to pay the tribute demanded.

Resurrection. It is quite clear from the book of Acts that the resurrection of Jesus was the central theme of early Christian preaching. It is equally clear that those who proclaimed the resurrection in this way stood a considerable risk of sharing the fate of their leader. It follows that they must have been absolutely certain in their own minds of the truth and importance of their claims. Because these claims are admittedly extraordinary, it is natural that people should have sought explanations in terms of natural causes, but no such explanation has proved entirely satisfactory. In any case, an extraordinary event is needed to explain the transformation in the behaviour of the disciples. Among those who believe in the resurrection it is, of course, possible to find a wide variety of interpretations as to what exactly took place.

Reuben. (1) The first-born son of both Jacob and Leah.

(2) The tribe of Reuben, which occupied an area on the eastern shore of the Dead Sea between Ammonite and Moabite territory.

Revelation, Book of. Without doubt the most difficult book in the New Testament for modern readers because its thought-forms and imagery are so remote from those to which we are accustomed. Written during a time of persecution, probably that of the emperor Domitian in the last decade of the first century, it declares in highly metaphorical language that the stage of human history is set in the context of an eternal scheme of things, in which God reigns supreme. Whatever their present sufferings, ultimate victory is assured to those who put their trust in Jesus. The writer describes himself as John, and some scholars have identified him with the disciple John, but there is no solid evidence for this. There is no question of the writer being the author of John's gospel or the letters of John.

Rezin. King of Syria (about 740–732 B.C.). An ally of Pekah, king of Israel, against the Assyrians. Together they threatened to attack Judah if King Ahaz would not join their coalition. Rezin was killed by the Assyrians when they finally took his capital, Damascus.

Romans. The Roman empire provides the context in which the events of the New Testament took place. Many Jews hated the Romans, and there were frequent misguided attempts at rebellion which culminated in the revolt of A.D. 66 and the eventual destruction of Jerusalem by the Romans in A.D. 70. In spite of occasional persecution, Roman rule was generally helpful to the spread of Christianity through its good communications and political stability.

Romans, Letters to the. Paul's letter to the Romans was written to an already flourishing church which he did not know personally. Its purpose was apparently to pave the way for further missionary work in the western Mediterranean, using Rome as a base. Paul seems to feel it necessary to lay before the Roman church the gospel that he preaches, and this letter provides the most coherent statement of his theology that we possess. Its great emphasis is on faith in Jesus as the sole necessity for reconciliation with God.

Rome. The capital of the Roman empire, a church seems to have been established there at an early but unknown date. Tradition says it was founded by Peter, but there is no biblical evidence for this. Paul spent two years there under arrest and, again according to tradition, died there with Peter in Nero's persecution.

Ruth. The book of Ruth is one of the gems of the Old Testament. It tells how Ruth, the Moabite widow of an Israelite husband, decides to accompany her widowed mother-in-law, Naomi, back to her home town of Bethlehem. In so doing Ruth accepts Israel's God as her own. Boaz, a kinsman of Naomi, notices Ruth gleaning the remains of his barley field and ultimately marries her, and they give birth to Obed, David's grandfather. The story is a parable (as is suggested by the names of the chief characters, all of them symbolic), but may rest on a historical fact, for much of the point of the story depends on Ruth being David's great-grandmother, and

if this were made up the point would be lost. The book is essentially a plea for tolerance of mixed marriages, and as such it shows a liberality of outlook matched in the Old Testament only by the book of Jonah. Attempts to date the book have proved very difficult, but the most likely period is shortly after the exile, when the Jewish community was becoming more exclusive.

S

Sabaoth, a Hebrew word, meaning an army or host, and applied sometimes to the Supreme Being, *e.g.*, "the Lord of Hosts" (Rom. ix. 29).

Sabbath. The observance of the sabbath as a day of rest and worship goes back at least to the time of Moses, yet it was only during the exile that it came to assume the importance it has had ever since for Jews. Deprived of temple worship, and living among aliens, strict sabbath observance became the identifying characteristic of a good Jew. By Jesus' time the number of rules about the sabbath was enormous, and while Jesus clearly supported the principle of the sabbath, he would not let his work be hindered by such petty rules. This became one of the major sources of friction between him and the Pharisees.

Sacrifice. Although the Jews came to realise at an early stage that God did not require human sacrifice (Gen 22:9–14), animal sacrifice continued to be part of their worship until the destruction of Herod's temple by the Romans. Many of the prophets questioned the value of the practice, however, declaring that what God really wanted was justice and compassion in all men's dealings with their fellows.

Sadducees. A major party within Judaism at the time of Jesus. They were mainly of priestly background and, because many of them occupied positions which depended on the good will of the Romans, they generally favoured a conciliatory approach. Unlike the Pharisees, many of whom commanded respect by their conscientiousness, the Sadducees were liked by no one.

Salome. One of the women who had followed Jesus from Galilee to Jerusalem, watched the crucifixion and saw the empty tomb.

Samaria. Originally the name referred to the new capital city built by Omri, king of Israel. It was increasingly used, however, as another term for the northern kingdom as a whole. After the kingdom had ceased to exist it denoted an area corresponding to the central part of the old kingdom.

Samaritan. An inhabitant of Samaria. The Jews considered Samaritans to be excluded from their ranks because, following the deportation of many Samaritan citizens by the Assyrians in 721 B.C. and the establishment of people from other parts of the Assyrian empire on their soil, many mixed marriages had taken place. Since the northern kingdom had always been considered idolatrous by southern Jews, this put them both religiously and socially beyond the pale.

Samson. A Nazirite, and one of the most famous of the judges. He seems to have had more valour than discretion, however, and provoked the Philistines needlessly (Judg 15:1–6). He paid for this unnecessary bravado with his life (Judg 16:4–30).

Samuel. Samuel was the last great leader of Israel before the establishment of the monarchy, and a unique figure combining the functions of prophet, priest, judge and even ruler. Undoubtedly the most significant part of his work was the creation of the monarchy, but unfortunately the role he played in this is far from clear. There are two conflicting accounts interwoven in 1 Samuel. One represents Samuel privately anointing Saul as king on God's instructions, and later arranging for a public acclamation of his kingship when he has proved himself in battle. The other suggests that the people demanded a king against Samuel's advice and that only under protest did he arrange a system for choosing a king by lots. Whatever his initial attitude, his support for Saul was soon withdrawn when Saul offered sacrifice instead of waiting for Samuel to do it (1 Sam 13:8–14) and failed to destroy totally the Amalekites according to Samuel's instructions (1 Sam 15:13–23). It seems clear that Samuel came to regard Saul as one who was usurping God's position, and his hostility did much to break the man who, willingly or otherwise, he had created king.

Samuel, Books of. The two books of Samuel cover an epoch-making period in Israel's history. They trace the development of a loose confederation of tribes, without any established form of government, into a considerable empire under a dynastic ruler. Like all the historical books, they contain material from a variety of sources, some much closer to the events than others. We are fortunate, however, to have in 2 Samuel 9–20 (and continuing in 1 Kings 1–2) a continuous source which is widely recognised as the finest piece of history writing of its time from anywhere in the world. The author deals with the reign of David in such a way that he can only have been a close associate of the king himself. Not only does he describe in detail David's conversations with his advisers, but he does it so vividly that the characters of the major participants are laid open to scrutiny. He is quite remarkable in his absence of bias. He paints a sympathetic portrait of David but does not gloss over his failings, and neither condemns nor attempts to justify his more questionable activities.

Sanhedrin. A council meeting under the High Priest at Jerusalem which had ultimate authority in religious and legal matters except for the power to pass the death penalty. This was why the Jews had to take Jesus before Pilate. The stoning of Stephen appears to have been a flagrant violation of this restriction. How and when the Sanhedrin was established is uncertain, but it came to an end with the destruction of Jerusalem in A.D. 70.

Sarah. Wife of Abraham and mother of Isaac. One of a number of women in the Bible whose child was seen as a special mark of God's favour because it came late in life.

Saul. (1) As the first king of Israel shortly before 1000 B.C., Saul faced a near impossible task, and his undoubted courage in battle was not an adequate qualification. The people of Israel wanted a king to defend them from their enemies, especially the Philistines, but they were not yet ready to give up their tribal independence, or support a permanent army as opposed to a constantly changing collection of volunteers. So he occupied an uncomfortable position in which more was expected of him than of the judges of old, but without any constitutional means of exercising his authority. When Samuel, a powerful influence on public opinion, withdrew his support, Saul clearly felt exposed and vulnerable, and the popularity of the young hero David increased his sense of insecurity. When David fled from his jealousy, helped unwittingly by the priest Ahimelech, Saul's slaughter of Ahimelech and his household was widely regarded as unjust, and must have alienated the priesthood. Thereafter much of his time and energy was diverted into hunting down David when it could have been more usefully employed in other ways. His final battle was an act of desperation, meeting the Philistines on level ground at the foot of Mount Gilboa, where their chariots gave them a decisive advantage. In the early years of his reign he seems to have enjoyed success, however, ejecting the Philistines from the central mountain range and, temporarily at least, being sufficiently free from the Philistine threat to strike at other enemies across the Jordan and far to the south. When he died there seems to have been no move to dispense with a king, so in spite of his ultimate failure, he seems to have achieved the acceptance of the monarchy by his people, paving the way for his successors.

(2) The Hebrew name by which Paul was known before his conversion. He may have taken the Roman form of his name to signify that he was "a new man in Christ", or possibly in order to identify himself with the Gentiles.

Scapegoat. A goat on which the sins of all the people were symbolically laid before driving it out into the wilderness. This happened annu-

ally on the Day of Atonement (Lev 16:20–22).

Scribes. The scribes were the professional interpreters of the law from the exile onwards. Many of them were also Pharisees, and the two are often linked in the New Testament.

Scripture. The term can be applied to any body of writings, but in the New Testament (where it is sometimes used in the plural) it invariably refers to the Old Testament. The use of the term by Christians to signify the Bible as a whole naturally came later.

Scrolls, Dead Sea. A collection of about 500 documents, the first of them discovered in 1947, from caves near the Dead Sea. Written between 170 B.C. and A.D. 70, some of them relate to the life of the ascetic community to which they belonged and others are parts of the Old Testament. Surprisingly the most ancient manuscripts of the Old Testament previously known were mediaeval, yet the differences in the text are mostly insignificant.

Sennacherib. The king of Assyria who invaded Judah in 701 B.C., destroyed 46 of its fortified cities and shut up Hezekiah "like a bird in a cage" (to use the words of his own inscription). He did not take Jerusalem, but it is not clear whether this was because of a disaster in the Assyrian camp or because Hezekiah accepted his punitive terms of surrender.

Septuagint. The Greek translation of the Old Testament, so called because of a tradition that it was made by 72 scribes. The Latin *septuaginta* actually means 70, and hence the use of LXX as an abbreviation.

Seven Champions of Christendom, were St. George of England, St. Andrew of Scotland, St. Patrick of Ireland, St. David of Wales, St. James of Spain, St. Denis of France, and St. Antony of Italy.

Seven Churches of Asia, referred to in the Revelation of St. John, were those of Ephesus, founded by St. Paul in 57, Smyrna, Pergamos, Thyatira, Sardis, Philadelphia (Lydia) and Laodicea (Phrygia), all in W. Asia Minor.

Shadrach. One of three young men, who according to the book of Daniel, survived being thrown into a blazing furnace for refusing to worship a gold statue set up by King Nebuchadnezzar.

Shallum. King of Israel (745 B.C.). He came to the throne by assassinating his predecessor and died in the same manner a month later.

Shaphan. The high official of King Josiah who took the Book of the Covenant from the temple and read it to him (2 Kgs 22:3–10). His family later protected Jeremiah, particularly during Jehoiakim's reign.

Sheba, Queen of. Sheba, in the Arabian peninsula, was a trading nation. The visit of the Queen of Sheba to Solomon (1 Kgs 10:1–10, 13) was probably what would now be called a trade mission, with Solomon offering copper in exchange for spices.

Shechem. A town with ancient religious connections, since Jacob is said to have built an altar there (Gen 33:18–20). Centrally situated on the borders of Ephraim and Manasseh, it was the first capital of the northern kingdom.

Shiloh. A town where the tabernacle was taken after the occupation of Canaan and which became the site for a permanent temple, the central sanctuary for the confederation of Israelite tribes before the monarchy (1 Sam 1:3). Jeremiah refers to the destruction of this temple, most probably by the Philistines.

Sidon. Next to Tyre, the most important city of Phoenicia and a good port. Jesus passed through its territory on at least one occasion.

Silas. Sent with Paul and Barnabas to present the findings of the Council of Jerusalem to the church at Antioch, he subsequently became Paul's companion on the second missionary journey (Acts 16:22–41). Probably to be identified with the Silvanus mentioned in some of Paul's letters.

Siloam. The name of a pool within the city walls of Jerusalem, fed from a spring outside by a tunnel some 620 m long. The tunnel was cut by Hezekiah (2 Chr 32:30) and still exists.

Simeon. (1) The second son of Jacob and Leah.

(2) The tribe of Simeon which originally possessed territory south of Judah but was then absorbed into its neighbour.

Simon. (1) *See* Peter.

(2) **Simon the Zealot,** one of the twelve dis-

ciples, whose name suggests that he started at least with very different political ideals from Jesus (Mk 3:18).

(3) **Simon the Pharisee.** The man with whom Jesus was eating when a sinful woman anointed him (Lk 7:36–47).

(4) **Simon of Cyrene.** The man who was compelled to carry Jesus' cross (Mk 15:21).

(5) **Simon Magus.** A miracle-worker in Samaria who, when he saw the effects of the Holy Spirit on a group of converts Peter and John had laid hands on, tried to buy this power from them (Acts 8:9–24).

Sinai. The peninsula between the Gulf of Suez and the Gulf of Aqaba which was the first objective on the exodus from Egypt. Mount Sinai (also called Horeb) has not been identified with certainty. If the giving of the law was accompanied by volcanic activity, as elements of the account suggest, a site on the eastern side of the Gulf of Aqaba (and therefore not on the Sinai peninsula at all) is more likely.

Smyrna. An important city on the Aegean coastline of Asia Minor. The book of Revelation (Rev 2:8–11) refers sympathetically to the church there and its steadfastness under persecution, but we know little else about it.

Sodom. A city of evil reputation, probably to be located in an area now covered by the southern part of the Dead Sea. The city was destroyed by burning sulphur (presumably a volcanic disturbance) according to Genesis 19:24–25.

Solomon. King of Israel (*c.* 960–922 B.C.). Solomon is traditionally regarded as a wise king, yet by the end of his reign his subjects were seething with discontent, and it would have taken a man of exceptional ability to win back their loyalty. Rehoboam, his son, was not such a man, and so the great empire of Solomon was reduced almost overnight to two insignificant states. For this Solomon must take much of the blame. His reputation for wisdom is not without foundation, however. Inheriting a large and relatively peaceful empire from his father, David, he was never in serious danger from enemies, though he strengthened his defences and added chariots to his army just in case.

Solomon was thus able to concentrate on economic policy and proved a genius at exploiting his position across a number of major trade routes as well as developing the copper mines south of the Dead Sea. The wealth generated by this economic development went into building his own palace and its ancillary buildings and the first temple. He allowed himself to get carried away by the splendour of his own designs, however, and got into such debts that not even heavy taxation could pay them and he had to give away territory to his neighbour Hiram, king of Tyre, in payment for the supply of cedar wood (1 Kgs 9:10–11). These measures, together with the system of forced labour introduced to man the copper mines and the building projects, were exceedingly unpopular. So was his marriage to foreign wives (often in pursuance of trade agreements) and his tolerance of their pagan religions. Less obviously the reign of Solomon saw the beginnings of an insidious trend towards the concentration of power in the hands of a small number of people, which led ultimately to the kind of social injustice so fiercely condemned by the prophets. That Solomon was clever is beyond dispute; whether he was wise may be debated.

Sosthenes. The leader of the synagogue at Corinth who was beaten by the Jews (Acts 18:17). The reason for this is not stated. Possibly he had shown sympathy towards Christianity, since a Sosthenes is associated with Paul in the writing of 1 Corinthians.

Stephen. Appointed originally as one of the seven administrators of the charitable work of the Jerusalem church (Acts 6:1–6), Stephen soon showed himself a powerful advocate of the Christian faith. He was brought before the Jewish Council on charges of denigrating the temple and denying the necessity for the law of Moses, and was illegally executed by stoning, the traditional Jewish method (Acts 6:8–60).

Stoics. Members of a Greek school of philosophers who believed in the suppression of the emotions so as to remain unaffected by life's

adversities. Paul debated with the Stoics in Athens (Acts 17:18).

Stoning. The method of execution among the Jews, and the prescribed penalty for 18 crimes. The accusers were required to throw the first stone (Deu 17:5–7, *see* John 8:7 for Jesus' reaction to this rule).

Sychar. According to John 4:5–6 the site of Jacob's well. Usually identified with Shechem.

Synagogue. The development of synagogue worship was a response to three things: the law forbidding sacrifice except in the Jerusalem temple, the destruction of the temple in 586 B.C. and the dispersion of the Jews. As a result, the offering of sacrifice could no longer be a regular way of worship and a non-sacrificial form of worship had to be developed. This was based on the reading and exposition of the Law, interspersed with psalms and prayers, and it set the pattern for later Christian worship.

Synoptists. The writers of the first three Gospels whose narratives in the main agree, though Matthew and Luke add material not found in Mark; all three differ from John's Gospel.

Syrians. Also known as Aramaeans, these people were Israel's immediate north-eastern neighbours. At one time forming several small kingdoms, they gradually coalesced into a single state which was frequently at war with Israel. Syria became a province of Assyria after the destruction of Damascus, the capital, in 732 B.C.

T

Tabernacle. The name given to the "tent of meeting", the place where Moses met with God and which represented God's presence among his people. An elaborate structure, it was in effect a travelling temple.

Tabernacles, Feast of. Known also as the Feast of Booths, the festival was both a celebration of the grape harvest and a recollection of the wilderness wanderings, symbolised by people living in temporary shelters (booths) through out the week.

Tarsus. A city in Asia Minor which was the home of Paul. It had a large Jewish population, but was also noted for its Greek philosophers, and it was this dual attachment that equipped Paul especially to be a missionary to the Gentiles.

Temple. There were three successive temples in Jerusalem. Solomon's temple, the first, was destroyed by the Babylonians in 586 B.C. After the exile a second temple was built, but due to the circumstances of the time this seems to have been a relatively poor affair. Then in 19 B.C. Herod the Great began work on the third temple, a large and imposing structure in every way. Though substantially complete by Jesus' time the finishing touches were not added until about A.D. 60. Ten years later it was destroyed by the Romans.

Ten Commandments. *See* Commandments.

Tertullus. A Roman or Romano-Jewish lawyer whom the Jewish Council employed to present the case against Paul before Felix (Acts 24:1–9).

Tetrarch. Both Herod Antipas and Philip were known as tetrarchs because they each received roughly a quarter of Herod the Great's kingdom (the other half going to Archelaus).

Thaddeus. One of the twelve disciples (Mk 3:18), known in Luke as Judas, son of James.

Thessalonians, Letters to the. The two letters of Paul to the Thessalonians are the earliest writings in the New Testament unless, as some scholars think, Galatians came earlier. They were written from Corinth, within a short time of each other, about A.D. 52. Amongst other things they show that the church at that time still expected the second coming of Christ in a literal form quite shortly, and that this expectation had led to undesirable behaviour such as refusal to work any more. Although Paul's correspondence with the Corinthians two to three years later shows that he still thought in terms of a second coming then, it is not a theme which occurs in his later letters.

Thessalonica. The capital of Macedonia in northern Greece, the city was visited by Paul during his second missionary journey (Acts 17:1–9) and presumably on the short tour he made of the Greek churches following his ministry in Ephesus (Acts 20:1-6).

Thomas. One of the twelve disciples well characterised in John's gospel, where he appears as loyal but slow to learn. His confession of Jesus as "My Lord and my God" after the resurrection identifies Jesus with God more clearly than any other statement in the gospels, however (Jn 20:28).

Tiglath-pileser III. King of Assyria (745-727 B.C.). It was Tiglath-pileser who established the Assyrian dominance of Palestine which was to last well over a century. It was to him that Ahaz of Judah appealed for help against Israel and Syria, both of which were invaded and devastated.

Timothy. Born of a Jewish mother and Greek father, Timothy was a native of Lystra. When Paul revisited the city at the start of his second missionary journey he asked Timothy to join him. From this time onwards he was constantly with Paul, or working elsewhere under Paul's oversight, and only three of the letters ascribed to Paul do not mention him.

Timothy, Letters to. There are difficulties in ascribing to Paul the two letters to Timothy. The style is not quite like Paul's, and the more formal organisation of the church suggests a later period. The most probable view is that they do contain fragments of personal notes written by Paul to Timothy, but that these have been used by a later author as the basis for general advice to church leaders. Similar considerations apply to the letter to Titus, which is often linked with the two letters to Timothy under the title of the Pastoral Letters.

Titus. A companion and co-worker of Paul, he seems to have been particularly involved in Paul's correspondence with Corinth, carrying his letters and acting as his representative (2 Cor 7:7, 8:16-17).

Titus, Letter to. See Timothy, Letters to.

Tongues, Speaking with. An outpouring of incomprehensible sounds which often accompanied a state of religious excitement in New Testament times, and still occurs in some churches today. The implication that the disciples actually spoke in foreign languages on the day of Pentecost is probably intended as a way of symbolising the universal relevance of the gospel. Paul warned against giving undue emphasis to this gift of the Spirit (1 Cor 14).

Tower of Babel. See Babel, Tower of.

Tribes of Israel. Traditionally descended from the twelve sons of Jacob, the number remained twelve in spite of some changes. The descendants of Joseph in fact formed two tribes, named after his sons Ephraim and Manasseh, whereas Simeon quickly became absorbed into Judah.

Tyre. The principal city of Phoenicia, and the centre of a city-state. The kings of Tyre were often on good terms with the kings of Israel, and the two nations traded to their mutual advantage (1 Kgs 5:1-11).

U

Unclean Foods. By long established tradition the Jews did not eat (and still do not eat) certain foods which were ritually unclean. This, and the fact that every meal was seen as a family religious occasion, meant that Jews rarely sat down at table with Gentiles. When Jewish and Gentile Christians began to associate with one another this was one of the difficulties they had to face (Rom 14:14-15).

Unleavened Bread. See Passover.

Ur. The home town of Abraham, sited in the southern part of the fertile flood-plain of the Tigris-Euphrates river system.

Urim and Thummim. Two objects used by a priest to determine God's will. It is not known how they were used, but the technique was probably to ask specific questions, to which the objects, on being thrown like dice, would then give a "yes" or "no" answer (1 Sam 14:41).

Uzziah. King of Judah (783-742 B.C.). Long-lived, capable and with the welfare of his people at heart, Uzziah was one of the better kings of Judah. He repaired and strengthened the defences of Jerusalem, re-equipped his army

(with slings for hurling stones among other things), attacked the Philistine cities and recaptured from the Edomites the important port of Elath on the Gulf of Aqaba (2 Chr 26:1-15). Towards the end of his reign he was stricken by a skin disease and his public duties were taken over by his son Jotham.

W

Weeks, Feast of. Also known as Pentecost, the feast came at the end of the wheat harvest and later was associated with the giving of the Law on Sinai. It was during this feast that the apostles received the gift of the Holy Spirit (Acts 2:1-4).

Wisdom Literature. A name applied to books such as Proverbs, Job and Ecclesiastes which discuss philosophical issues or offer practical advice for living. There is a parallel literature from other middle-eastern civilisations, but the Hebrew literature is unique in its emphasis on the knowledge of God (and not merely academic knowledge but the knowing that comes from a relationship) as the basis of all wisdom.

Y

Yahweh. The proper name of the God of Israel was written as YHWH, there being no vowels in Hebrew. How it would have been pronounced (in fact it was considered too sacred ever to be spoken aloud) is a matter of speculation, but modern opinion favours Yahweh. Jehovah is an earlier attempt to render the same name.

Z

Zacchaeus. A tax collector of Jericho who became a follower of Jesus and generously compensated all those he had previously cheated (Lk 19:1-10).

Zadok. He appears to have been High Priest jointly with Abiathar during David's reign, but when Abiathar was banished by Solomon for supporting Adonijah in the rivalry for succession, Zadok became the sole High Priest.

Zebulun. (1) The tenth son of Jacob, his sixth by Leah.
(2) The tribe of Zebulun which occupied a fairly small area of northern Israel surrounded by Manasseh, Issachar, Naphtali and Asher.

Zechariah. (1) King of Israel (746-745 B.C.). The son of Jeroboam II, he was assassinated by Shallum.
(2) A prophet who wrote chapters 1-8 of the book of Zechariah about 520 B.C. His prophecies look forward to the restoration of the temple and the new age about to dawn. Chapters 9-14 are from a later period.
(3) The father of John the Baptist.

Zedekiah. King of Judah (597-586 B.C.). The uncle of his predecessor Jehoiachin, he was placed on the throne by the Babylonians when Jehoiachin surrendered to them in 597 B.C. and was deported. In 589 B.C. Zedekiah himself rebelled and so precipitated the final crisis in the history of Judah. After Jerusalem fell in 586 B.C. he fled, but was captured, and after watching all his sons killed he was blinded and taken in chains to Babylon.

Zephaniah. A contemporary of Jeremiah, Zephaniah threatened a day of judgement against his people, primarily because of their unfaithfulness in worshipping other gods, but also he looked forward to repentance and restoration.

Zimri. King of Israel (876 B.C.). After assassinating his predecessor Elah, Zimri ruled for only seven days before committing suicide in order to avoid being murdered by Omri.

Zion. Originally just the name of one of the hills on which Jerusalem is built, it came to be a symbolic term indicating the dwelling-place of God and associated with the belief that he would always protect Jerusalem.

Zophar. The third of Job's "friends" (Job 11).

CLASSICAL MYTHOLOGY

This popular section gives a brief introduction to the myths and legends of Greece and Rome in an easily referable form. Great artists and writers throughout the ages have enriched their work by reference to these endearing tales of the classical world and some knowledge of them is indispensable to the full appreciation of our art and literature.

CLASSICAL MYTHOLOGY

A

Abas. In Greek mythology either (1) the son of Celeus and Metanira. His mockery of Demeter (*q.v.*) as she drank resulted in his being turned into a lizard, or
(2) the twelfth king of Argolis who owned a magic shield from which he derived authority. He was the father of Acrisius (*q.v.*) and Proetus (*q.v.*).

Abderus. *See* The friend of Heracles (*q.v.*) in whose care Heracles left the mares of Diomedes (*q.v.*). The horses ate him and Heracles founded Abdera, a coastal town in Thrace, in his honour.

Absyrtus (or **Apsyrtus**). Half brother of the sorceress Medea (*q.v.*). When Aëtes pursued Jason (*q.v.*) and Medea, in order to recover the golden fleece, Medea slew the boy, cut his corpse into pieces and tossed the pieces into the sea. Because Aëtes stopped his ship to collect the pieces of his son for burial Jason and Medea were able to escape.

Abyla. *See* **"Pillars of Hercules"**.

Acamas. Son of Theseus (*q.v.*) and Phaedra (*q.v.*), brother of Demophon (*q.v.*). He went to Troy (*q.v.*) with Diomedes (*q.v.*) to demand the return of Helen (*q.v.*). He and his brother also rescued their grandmother Aethra, who had been Helen's slave, when Troy fell.

Acastus. Son of Pelias King of Iolcos and one of the Argonauts (*q.v.*). When Medea (*q.v.*) caused his father's death he banished her and Jason (*q.v.*). Showed hospitality to Peleus (*q.v.*) but suspecting him of advances towards his wife he left Peleus to die at the hands of the Centaurs (*q.v.*). Later Peleus returned to slay the couple. Acastus was the father of Laodamia (*q.v.*).

Acestes. In Roman mythology a chieftain of Trojan descent who had settled in Sicily prior to the arrival of Aeneas (*q.v.*).

Achelous. A great river god, the son of Oceanus (*q.v.*) and Tethys (*q.v.*). By defeating Achelous Heracles (*q.v.*) won the hand of Deianeira (*q.v.*) daughter of Oeneus (*q.v.*).

Acheron. A real river of Epirus flowing into the Ionian Sea. Part of it is an underground which may account for its position in Greek mythology. Here it is the "river of grief " which flows in the underworld of the dead.

Achilles. A Greek warrior who is the principal character of the *Iliad*. The son of Peleus (*q.v.*) King of the Myrmidones at Phthia in Thessaly and Thetis (*q.v.*) one of the Nereids (*q.v.*). As a baby his mother dipped him in the Styx (*q.v.*) making him invulnerable save for his heel, by which she held him. He was educated in the arts of war and hunting, and in morality, by Cheiron (*q.v.*). His mother, knowing that he would die at Troy (*q.v.*) tried to prevent him joining the Greek expedition there by disguising him as a girl and sending him to the court of Lycomedes, King of Scyros. Here Lycomedes' daughter Deidamia, bore him a son, Neoptolemus (*q.v.*). Odysseus (*q.v.*) learned of this subterfuge and visited Lycomedes' court disguised as a merchant. While the king's daughters and the disguised Achilles were surveying his wares he suddenly produced swords which Achilles eagerly clasped, thus revealing himself. Achilles proved himself the most formidable warrior at Troy. At Tenedos on the way to Troy he killed King Tenes and his father Cycnus and by raiding Aeneas' (*q.v.*) cattle prompted him to join the Trojan forces. In the tenth year of the war Achilles quarrelled with Agamemnon (*q.v.*) over the captive girl Briseis and withdrew from the fighting. However he loaned his armour to Patroclus, his cousin and friend who was slain by Hector (*q.v.*). His death prompted Achilles to cease sulking in his tent and to return to the fray. Thetis gave him new armour made by Hephaestus (*q.v.*) and wearing this he slew Hector. He also killed Penthesilea (*q.v.*) and the

Greek Thersites (*q.v.*). After killing Memnon (*q.v.*) Achilles was shot in his vulnerable ankle at a battle near the Scaean gate (*q.v.*) Odysseus and Ajax (*q.v.*) recovered his body and argued over his armour.

Acis. In later Greek legend the young son of Faunus (*q.v.*) and a river nymph. He loved the sea-nymph Galatea (*q.v.*) and was killed by his jealous rival Polyphemus (*q.v.*). According to Sicilian tradition he was then turned into the river of the same name which runs at the foot of Mount Etna. This tradition first appears in the writing of Theocritus (*q.v.*) and later in Ovid's (*q.v.*) "Metamorphoses". It inspired paintings by Poussin and Claude and the opera *Acis and Galatea* by Handel.

Acrisius. Son of Abas (*q.v.*), twin brother of Proetus (*q.v.*) and King of Argos. Warned by an oracle that the son of his daughter Danaë (*q.v.*) would kill him he had her locked up in a brazen tower. But this was to no avail because Zeus (*q.v.*) visited her and fathered Perseus (*q.v.*), Acrisius then cast mother and son adrift on the sea, locked in a chest. Years later Perseus returned to Argos causing Acrisius to flee to Larissa. However Perseus, visiting Larissa to take part in the games, accidentally killed him with a discus.

Acropolis. In general terms a high citadel found in all Greek cities. The best known acropolis is that at Athens which was first inhabited around 2000 B.C. From time immemorial it was dedicated to Athene (*q.v.*).

Actaeon. Mythical huntsman and grandson of Cadmus (*q.v.*) of Thebes. Artemis (*q.v.*) turned him into a stag, torn to pieces by his own hounds because he inadvertently spied her bathing. The story is recounted in Ovid's (*q.v.*) "Metamorphoses" and recalled in the works of Titian, Veronese, Poussin, Rembrandt, Gainsborough and Parmigiano.

Admetus. King of Pherae in Thessaly and husband of the beautiful Alcestis (*q.v.*). Apollo (*q.v.*) offered to allow Admetus to avoid death if one of his family would die in his place. All offered herself but according to legend either Persephone returned her or Heracles (*q.v.*) rescued Alcestis from Hades (*q.v.*). This forms the theme of one of Euripedes' best known plays and Gluck's opera *Alceste* (in which Apollo not Heracles saves her).

Adonis. A Syrian deity associated with the mystery of vegetation. He was a beautiful Cypriot youth, the son of Myrrha and her father. For this incest Myrrha was turned into a tree. Nine months later Adonis was born from the bark of the tree, taken up by Aphrodite (*q.v.*) and placed in the care of Persephone (*q.v.*). He spent alternate parts of the year with Persephone and Aphrodite who loved him. He was killed by a boar sent by Artemis (*q.v.*). Shakespeare's *Venus and Adonis* is based on Ovid's (*q.v.*) version of the tale while Shelley's elegy on the death of Keats, *Adonais*, derives its title from Bion's *Lament for Adonis*. Adonis was painted by Titian, Veronese and Poussin.

Adrastus. Son of Talaus and King of Argos. An oracle told him that his offspring would be a lion and a boar and in accordance with this he gave his daughter Argia to Polynices (*q.v.*) and her sister to Tydeus (*q.v.*) who bore images of these animals on their shields. He attempted to restore Polynices to his throne at Thebes (*see* **Seven against Thebes**). He survived this adventure—some say due to his magic horse Arion (*q.v.*)—and led a second expedition (of the Epigoni, *q.v.*) against Thebes, dying of grief when he heard that his son Aegialeus had fallen in the attack.

Aeacides. The descendants of Aeacus (*q.v.*).

Aeacus. Son of Zeus and Aegina and King of the Myrmidones. The Myrmidones were originally ants, transformed into men by Zeus at the request of Aeacus. He aided Poseidon (*q.v.*) and Apollo (*q.v.*) in the construction of the walls of Troy. He had two sons, Peleus (*q.v.*) and Telamon (*q.v.*) by his wife Endeis. He was also the father of Phocus (q.v.) by a Nereid. Aeacus later exiled Peleus (future father of Achilles) for the murder of Phocus. A model of virtue and piety, Aeacus was made one of the three judges of the Underworld.

Aeaea. In the Odyssey the island home of Circe (q.v.).

Aedon. In Greek mythology the wife of Zethus, king of Thebes. She was jealous of Niobe, wife of Zethus' brother Amphion (q.v.). In trying to murder Niobe's son she killed her own son Itylus by mistake. In pity Zeus (q.v.) turned her into a nightingale whose song still mourns Itylus.

Aegaeon. Alternative name for Briareus (q.v.).

Aegeus. King of Athens and father of Theseus (q.v.) by Aethra (q.v.) daughter of Pittheus king of Troezen. She brought Theseus up secretly at her father's court, during which time Aegeus married Medea (q.v.). When Theseus finally returned to his father's court Medea fled. Before Theseus went to slay the Minotaur (q.v.) he and Aegeus agreed that he would hoist a white sail when returning to Athens to signal his success. On returning Theseus forgot to do this and Aegeus seeing a black sail on his son's ship supposed him dead and, in grief threw himself into the sea, henceforth called the Aegean.

Aegisthus. The son of Thyestes (q.v.) by his daughter Pelopia. Pelopia exposed the baby but it was rescued by her husband Atreus (q.v.) who believed it to be his own son. Atreus was king of Mycenae and when Thyestes, an enemy, returned in later years he ordered Aegisthus to kill him. But father and son recognised each other and Aegisthus killed Atreus. Thyestes became king of Mycenae but Atreus had had two sons by Acrope, Menelaus (q.v.) and Agamemnon (q.v.). Agamemnon expelled Thyestes and reclaimed his father's throne. While Agamemnon was at Troy (q.v.) Aegisthus seduced his wife Clytemnestra (q.v.) and helped her murder him on his return. These two murderers of Agamemnon now ruled Mycenae. But at the urging of his sister Electra (q.v.) (whom Aegisthus would have liked to kill and whom he forced to marry a peasant) Agamemnon's son Orestes (q.v.) and his friend Pylades (q.v.) returned from exile in Phocis and with Electra's help avenged their father, slaying Aegisthus and Clytemnestra.

Aeneas. The Trojan hero regarded by the Romans as their ancestor. The son of Anchises (q.v.) and Aphrodite (q.v.). Led the survivors of the Trojan War to Italy. The lover of Dido. See under Aeneid.

Aeneid. Virgil's (q.v.) unfinished epic poem. In 12 volumes, it is written to honour Rome, to increase the prestige of Augustus (by recalling the deeds of his supposed ancestor) and to foretell prosperity to come. It describes Aeneas' (q.v.) wanderings after Troy fell, recounting his stay in Carthage and love for Dido (q.v.) the funeral games of his father Anchises (q.v.) in Sicily, a journey to the Underworld to visit his dead father's spirit and his arrival at the mouth of the Tiber where he landed on the Latin shore. Here he fought wars with the Latins and their allies before finally defeating Turnus the Rutulian prince and uniting the races by marrying Lavinia the Latin princess. He founded Lavinium, named in her honour.

Aeolian Isles. The present Aeolian Isles are off the North East of Sicily, forming part of the Liparia group. They are mentioned in the Odyssey.

Aeolus. In Greek mythology (1) the son of Helen and ruler of Thessaly, believed to be the brother of Dorus and Xuthus (q.v.) and the ancestor of the Aeolians or Aeolic Greeks, i.e. those inhabiting Aeolis.
(2) The son of Poseidon (q.v.) and ruler of the Aeolian isles (q.v.). Zeus (q.v.) made him guardian of the winds. He gave Odysseus (q.v.) a bag of winds which his men let loose and which blew the ship off course.

Aeschylus. See Section B.

Aetolus. Legendary conqueror of Aetolia. The son of Endymion (q.v.) king of Elis, he was banished across the Corinthian Gulf after accidentally killing Apis in a chariot race.

Agamemnon. Son of Atreus (q.v.) and Aerope, brother of Menelaus (q.v.) and king of Mycenae. He married Helen's (q.v.) half-sister Clytemnestra (q.v.) and commanded the Greek forces at Troy (q.v.). Before the Greek fleet could leave Aulis to sail for Troy he had to sacrifice his daughter Iphigenia (q.v.). At Troy he quarrelled with Achilles (q.v.) when he seized Briseis from Achilles. He did this because Apollo (q.v.) had forced him to return Chryseis to her father, the Trojan Chryses (q.v.).

On his return to Mycenae he was murdered by Aegisthus (q.v.) and Clytemnestra. Clytemnestra attacked him with an axe while he was bathing. This occurred despite the warning given to Agamemnon by Cassandra (q.v.) whom he had brought back from Troy as his mistress. He was avenged by his children Orestes (q.v.) and Electra (q.v.). The story inspired Aeschylus' (q.v.) trilogy Orestia.

Aganippe. A fountain at the foot of Mt. Helicon, sacred to the Muses (q.v.) who are sometimes called Aganippides. It inspired those who drank from it. The fountain of Hippocrene, also sacred to the Muses, was known as Aganippis.

Agathyrsans. In the Aeneid (q.v.) a tribe in Thrace.

Aglaia. "The bright one": one of the Graces (q.v.).

Aides or Aidoneus. Hades (q.v.)

Ajax. (Greek Aias) In Greek legend two Ajaxes appear. The first was the son of King Telamon of Salamis. He killed Teuthras King of Teuthrania, an ally of Troy (q.v.) and took his daughter Tecmessa. At Troy he fought all day with Hector (q.v.) and at the end of the duel they exchanged gifts, Hector giving him a sword. With Menelaus (q.v.) he rescued the body of Patroclus (q.v.) and with Odysseus (q.v.) killed Glaucus and rescued the body of Achilles. Homer (q.v.) says the pair quarrelled over the armour and that Odysseus killed him. Later, when Odysseus summoned the spirits of the dead Ajax held aloof. But Sophocles (q.v.) in his Ajax calls on another tradition in which Ajax, disappointed at not being given the Palladium (q.v.) of Troy when the city fell, went mad, killing the Greek sheep under the delusion they were his rivals before impaling himself on the sword Hector had given him. The other Ajax was the son of Oileus, king of the Locrians. He was courageous but blasphemous. When Troy was sacked he dragged Cassandra (q.v.) from the altar of Athene (q.v.) where she sought refuge and gave her to Agamemnon (q.v.). On his return to Greece Poseidon (q.v.) saved him from shipwreck in a storm sent by Athene. Taking shelter on a rock he boasted himself more powerful than the goddess. She commanded Poseidon to crack the reef with his trident and Ajax drowned.

Alba Longa. The Latin city founded by Ascanius (q.v.) in the Alban Hills. In fact, as well as legend, Alba was the mother city of Rome which was probably founded as one of her western outposts. Alba was capital of the Latin League, a confederation of Latin states, but was eventually supplanted by Rome.

Alcaeus. See Alcmene.

Alcestis. Daughter of Pelias (q.v.) and the only one of his daughters not to follow Medea's (q.v.) advice and boil him alive. Married Admetus (q.v.) and was devoted to him.

Alcides. Another name for Heracles (q.v.) whose grandfather was reputed to be Alcaeus.

Alcinous. King of the mythical Phaeacians of the isle of Scheria. A grandson of Poseidon (q.v.), he married Arete his own sister. Father of the beautiful Nausicaa (q.v.). He entertained Odysseus and gave him a ship. He was also said to have entertained the Argonauts and refused to return Medea to her father. Scheria has been identified with Corfu.

Alcmaeon. In myth the son of Amphiaraus (q.v.) and Eriphyle (q.v.). One of the Epigoni (q.v.).

Alcmene. The wife of Amphitrion (q.v.) son of Alcaeus. Her brothers had been slain by the Taphians and she would not consummate her marriage until Amphitrion avenged them. While he was away warring with the Taphians Zeus (q.v.) appeared in his likeness and fathered Heracles (q.v.) upon her. Hermes (q.v.) was ordered to make the dawn in order that Zeus might take his time—an amusing situation which has appealed to Plautus, Molière and Dryden. Later that night the real Amphitrion returned and fathered Iphicles (q.v.). In his Amphitryon 38 Jean Giraudoux claims 37 versions of the tale have preceded him. On the death of Amphitrion Alcmene married Rhadamanthus (q.v.).

Alcyone or Halcyone. (1) Leader of the Pleiades (q.v.), daughter of Atlas (q.v.) and Pleione.
(2) The daughter of Aeolus (q.v.) and wife of Ceyx. When Ceyx was lost at sea she drowned herself in sorrow. The sympathetic gods turned the pair to kingfishers which supposedly bred during the winter solstice. Then Aeolus forbids the wind to blow leaving the Aegean calm while they build and sit on their nest. This is the time of year

called the "Halcyon days". The story is told in Ovid's (q.v.) "Metamorphoses" and Chaucer's "Book of the Duchess".

Alecto. One of the Erinnyes (q.v.).

Alexander the Great. See Section B.

Amalthea. The she-goat which nursed the infant Zeus in the Dictaean cave in Crete. As a reward she was placed among the stars as Capricorn while one of her horns which had broken off became the Cornucopia, or horn of plenty.

Amazons. Mythical race of female warriors at one time believed by the Greeks to live in Thrace or Asia Minor. As the Greeks' knowledge of the world grew, so the homeland of the Amazons was held to be more distant. In the Iliad (q.v.) Priam (q.v.) is said to have warred with them, though they came to the aid of Troy (q.v.). Achilles (q.v.) slew their queen Penthesilea (q.v.). Heracles (q.v.) fought with them and seized the girdle of the queen Hippolyte (q.v.) while Theseus (q.v.) carried off either Hippolyte or Antiope (q.v.). Theseus' act caused the Amazons to invade Attica but Theseus defeated them in the streets of Athens. In antiquity it was thought they amputated their right breast (Greek mazos) in order to hold a bow better.

Ambrosia. The food of the Olympians which gave immortality.

Ammon. The Egyptian god Amun was known to the Greeks from the 7th century B.C. when they came into contact with his cult at the Siwa oasis. They identified him with Zeus. Alexander the Great consulted the oracle of Zeus and Ammon was recognised as the son of Zeus by the priests of the oracle. A legend grew up that Alexander was begotten by Ammon in the form of a snake.

Amphiaraus. See Seven Against Thebes.

Amphion. Twin brother of Zethus, sons of Zeus (q.v.) and Antiope (q.v.). Antiope was married to Lycus King of Thebes who divorced her. She was cruelly treated by his second wife Dirce. The twins were raised by herdsmen on Mt. Cithaeron. When they reached manhood they avenged their mother by killing Zethus and tying Dirce to the horns of a wild bull. The fountain into which her body was thrown henceforth bore her name. The twins now took possession of Thebes and built the fortifications below the Cadmea. Amphion, who had been given a lyre by Hermes (q.v.) played so skilfully that the stones moved into place of their own accord. They ruled jointly, Zethus marrying Thebe who gave her name to the city, and Amphion marrying Niobe (q.v.).

Amphitrion. Son of Alcaeus, husband of Alcmene (q.v.) and father of Iphicles (q.v.). Foster father of Heracles (q.v.). When Heracles killed his teacher Linus with Linus' own lyre, Amphitrion sent him away to keep cattle. Later he would be killed helping Heracles defeat the Minyans.

Amphitrite. The daughter of Nereus (q.v.) leader of the Nereids (q.v.). Persuaded by Delphinos to accept Poseidon (q.v.) (Delphinos was rewarded by having his image placed amongst the stars as the Dolphin). By Poseidon she was mother of Triton (q.v.). Her hatred of Scylla (q.v.), Poseidon's daughter by another, led her to turn Scylla into a monster with six barking heads and twelve feet.

Amphitroniades. Another name for Heracles (q.v.) whose putative father was Amphitrion (q.v.).

Amyclae. One of the most sacred sites in the Peloponnese, a sanctuary a few miles from Sparta consecrated to Hyacinthus (q.v.).

Anchises. A cousin of Priam (q.v.). For his piety he was allowed to sleep with Aphrodite (q.v.) who bore him Aeneas. When Troy (q.v.) fell Aeneas carried his father (now blind) through safety through the Dardanian gate of the city. He died in Sicily and was buried at Eryx. In the Aeneid (q.v.) he appears among the blessed spirits of the dead to foretell Rome's greatness. Aeneas carrying his Father is an early work of Bernini.

Ancus Martius. The legendary fourth king of Rome who succeeded Tullus Hostilius. A grandson of Numa Pompilius (q.v.) he ruled from 640 to 616 B.C. He was very religious but also succeeded in defeating the Latins. He was succeeded by Tarquin the Elder.

Andromache. A Trojan princess, wife of Hector (q.v.) and by him mother of Astyanax. When Troy fell her son was thrown from the city walls, despite her spirited defence of him with a pestle. She was carried off to Epirus by Neoptolemus (q.v.) and here married his brother in law Hellenus and

became joint ruler. She also had a son by Neoptolemus and was threatened by his jealous wife Hermione (see Racine's Andromaque). Her days were ended at Pergamum, the city founded by her and Neoptolemus' son, Molossus. In historic times the Molossi claimed descent from Molossus and Neoptolemus.

Andromeda. See Cassiopeia.

Antaeus. A Libyan giant, son of Poseidon (q.v.) and Ge (q.v.). An invincible wrestler until Heracles (q.v.), realising he drew his strength from his mother, held him in the air and squeezed him to death. He is featured in a painting by Pollaiuolo in Florence.

Antenor The wisest of the Trojans. Priam (q.v.) sent him to reclaim Hesione from Telamon after Heracles (q.v.) sacked Troy (q.v.). He advised the Trojans to return Helen (q.v.) to Menelaus (q.v.) but they refused. His hatred for Deiphobus (q.v.) led him to help the Greeks steal the Palladium (q.v.). The husband of Theano and father of Laocoön (q.v.). After Troy fell he and his wife went to Italy and founded either Venice or Padua.

Antigone. Daughter of Oedipus (q.v.) and Jocasta (q.v.) she accompanied her father into exile (recalled in Sophocles' Oedipus at Colonus). After his death she returned to Thebes where her brother Eteocles (q.v.) and Polynices (q.v.) were warring on each other. Both perished in battle and her uncle Creon (q.v.) seized power. Because Polynices had fought against his own country Creon refused him burial. Antigone defied Creon and buried her brother with full rites and was imprisoned in a cave for doing so. Here she hung herself, and her betrothed, Creon's son Haemon, committed suicide in despair. The story and the ethical principles it raises are the basis of Sophocles' Antigone. In his work of the same name Anouilh reconsiders the arguments involved.

Antilochus. Son of Nestor (q.v.) a valiant Greek warrior at Troy (q.v.). Too young to sail from Aulis when the expedition began he arrived later. Slain by Memnon (q.v.) while defending his father.

Antinous. See Odysseus.

Antiope. (1) An Amazon, sister of Hippolyte (q.v.). According to some legends she was carried off by Theseus (q.v.), perhaps with the aid of Heracles (q.v.) and bore him Hippolytus (q.v.).
(2) A Theban princess who bore Amphion (q.v.) and Zethus to Zeus (q.v.) who visited her in the form of a satyr (q.v.). Her father exposed the children on Mt. Cithaeron. She was badly treated and imprisoned by Lycus and his wife Dirce (Lycus was either her husband, who divorced her to marry Dirce, or her uncle). She later freed and avenged by her twin sons. Titian, Correggio and Watteau have all painted Zeus visiting Antiope as a satyr.

Aphaia. A goddess worshipped in Aegina and identified with the Cretan Britomartis.

Aphrodite. The goddess of love, desire and procreation, known to the Romans as Venus. She sprang from the seed of Uranus (q.v.), rising naked from the sea at Paphos in Cyprus. However, Homer (q.v.) holds her to be the daughter of Zeus (q.v.) and Dione, and makes her the wife of Hephaestus (q.v.). She was not faithful to Hephaestus, but bore children by Ares (q.v.), Poseidon (q.v.), Dionysus (q.v.), and Hermes (q.v.), She loved the mortals Adonis (q.v.) and Anchises (q.v.) by whom she bore Aeneas (q.v.), and tempted Paris (q.v.) to desert Oenone. It was to her that Paris gave the golden apple of discord, she being the "fairest" goddess. In return she promised him the most beautiful woman in the world. Around her waist she wore a magic girdle which made her beautiful and irresistibly desirable.

Apis. The sacred bull of Memphis which the Egyptians worshipped as a god.

Apollo. Son of Zeus (q.v.) and the mortal Leto; twin brother of Artemis (q.v.). As a child he killed the she-dragon Python on Mt. Parnassus and took over her role as the oracle at Delphi. Hence he was sometimes known as the Pythian or as Loxias "the Ambiguous". He was also a symbol of light and was known as Phoebus or "shining". Apart from being god of prophecy he was a god of song and music, having been given the lyre by Hermes (q.v.). He was the leader of the Muses (q.v.) and was sometimes called Musagetes. He could be a destroyer (he is always portrayed with bow and arrows) and sent plagues amongst the Greeks at Troy, but was also protective against evil and was father of Asclepius (q.v.). When Zeus slew Asclepius he retaliated by slaying the Cyclopes (q.v.)

and was punished by being sent as a servant to Admetus (*q.v.*) of Pherae in Thessaly. Prior to this Zeus had sent him as a bondsman to King Laomedan whom he helped to build the walls of Troy. This was punishment for his part in a conspiracy (led by Hera, Poseidon and himself) against Zeus. He loved Hestia (*q.v.*) but also seduced the nymph Dryope and attempted to seduce Daphne. When Daphne protested she was turned into a laurel tree. Amongst mortal women he at one time loved Cassandra (*q.v.*). With his sister Artemis he shot the giant Tityus, whom the jealous Hera sent to violate Leto; it was he who shot the vulture which tormented Prometheus and he also helped Paris (*q.v.*) shoot Achilles (*q.v.*). He was identified with the sun-god by later writers but in Homer (*q.v.*) he and Helios (*q.v.*) are quite distinct.

Arachne. A Lydian maiden who competed with Athene (*q.v.*) at a weaving contest. When she won the angry goddess forced her to hang herself before turning her into a spider and her weaving into a cobweb.

Arcadia. Green but mountainous region, isolated in the centre of the Peloponnese. Its inhabitants were primitive shepherds and peasants.

Arcas. The son of Zeus (*q.v.*) and Callisto (*q.v.*) who gave his name to Arcadia (*q.v.*).

Ares. The son of Zeus (*q.v.*) and Hera (*q.v.*) and the god of war. Associated with Mars, by the Romans. He was disliked by all the gods save Hades (*q.v.*) and Eris (*q.v.*) because of his love of battle for its own sake. He loved Aphrodite (*q.v.*), and Hephaestus (*q.v.*) once caught the pair in an invisible net exposing them to the ridicule of the other gods. The father of Penthesilea (*q.v.*) by Otrere. He was once defeated by Heracles (*q.v.*), was wounded by Diomedes (*q.v.*) and imprisoned for 13 months (till Hermes (*q.v.*) released him) in a brazen vessel by the Aloeidae (*q.v.*). Athene (*q.v.*) got the better of him on several occasions. He once stood trial on the site of the Areopagus.

Arethusa. A river and a river goddess of southern Greece. She was pursued under the sea to Sicily by the river god Alpheus. In Sicily she was identified with Artemis and a cult of Artemis Arethusa flourished at Syracuse.

Argo. A fifty-oared ship built for Jason (*q.v.*) by Argus. In its prow Athene (*q.v.*) fitted an oracular beam.

Argonauts. The heroes who sailed with Jason (*q.v.*) in the Argo (*q.v.*) to fetch the golden fleece from Colchis. Their ranks included Heracles (*q.v.*), Orpheus (*q.v.*) Castor and Polydeuces (*q.v.*) Echion, Idas (*q.v.*) and Lynceus (*q.v.*). The voyage was an adventurous one and after dallying at Lemnos they passed through the Hellespont and reached Mysia. Here Hylas (*q.v.*) was lost and Heracles stayed to look for him. At some point the Sirens (*q.v.*) were passed with the help of Orpheus (*q.v.*) and at Bebrycos Polydeuces (*see* **Castor**) slew Amycus. In Thrace they rid Phineus (*q.v.*) of the Harpies (*q.v.*) and in return were told how to navigate the Symplegades (*q.v.*).

Argus. (1) The builder of the Argo (*q.v.*).
(2) A hundred-eyed giant set by Hera (*q.v.*) to watch Io (*q.v.*).
(3) The faithful hound of Odysseus (*q.v.*).

Ariadne. The daughter of Minos (*q.v.*) and Pasiphae (*q.v.*). She helped Theseus (*q.v.*) but he abandoned her at Naxos when Dionysus (*q.v.*) fell in love with her. He married her and gave her a crown of seven stars which became a constellation after her death.

Arimaspi. A mythical people of the Scythian steppes said to be neighbours of the Hyperboreans. They had one eye and constantly fought a group of griffins for the gold they guarded. Herodotus (*q.v.*) tells of a poem by Aristeas, a priest of Hyperborean Apollo, about them. Aristeas is clearly a *shaman*, able to separate body and soul and to be in two places at once. Aeschylus (*q.v.*) refers to them when describing Io's (*q.v.*) wanderings.

Arion. A fabulous horse, the offspring of Demeter (*q.v.*) and Zeus (*q.v.*). Demeter had taken the form of a mare and Zeus raped her in the form of a horse. She also gave birth to the nymph Despoena and possibly Persephone (*q.v.*) at the same time as Arion. It saved Adrastus (*q.v.*) at the siege of Thebes.

Aristaeus. The son of Apollo (*q.v.*) and a Lapith (*see* Lapithae) girl Cyrene. A minor deity, the protector of cattle, fruit trees and bee-keepers. Virgil (*q.v.*) makes Cyrene a nymph and says that Aristaeus fell in love with Eurydice who died of a snake bite she received while fleeing from him. In punishment all his bees were killed. Cyrene sought the advice of Proteus (*q.v.*) and Aristaeus made sacrifices of cattle to placate the nymphs. Nine days later he found fresh swarms in the carcasses.

Aristophanes. *See* **Section B.**

Artemis. The daughter of Zeus (*q.v.*) and Leto (*q.v.*) twin sister of Apollo (*q.v.*). Her Roman counterpart was Diana. She was often conflated with Hecate (*q.v.*) and Selene (*q.v.*), the moon goddess. A goddess of the chase and protectoress of children and young animals. She was also treated as a mother or earth goddess in the Asian tradition and was worshipped orgiastically at Ephesus. She was generally portrayed with a bow and arrows, made by Hephaestus (*q.v.*) and like Apollo could spread the plague and death. With her arrows she punished impiety (*e.g.* Niobe). A virgin who sternly protected her own chastity, she was known to punish unchastity in others *e.g.* Callisto (*q.v.*).

Ascanius. The son of Aeneas (*q.v.*) and Creusa, who escaped from Troy (*q.v.*) with his father. Another tradition makes his mother the Latin princess Lavinia. He succeeded his father as king and made Alba Longa (*q.v.*) his capital.

Asclepius or Aesculapius. The son of Apollo (*q.v.*) and Coronis, a god of healing whose worship spread to Rome after a plague in 293 B.C. He was taught healing by Cheiron the centaur (*q.v.*). Once he brought a dead man back to life and Zeus (*q.v.*) punished him, killing him with a thunderbolt. At Apollo's request he was placed among the stars.

Asopus. A river god, the son of Oceanus (*q.v.*) and Tethys (*q.v.*). The father of Evadne, Euboea and Aegina.

Astraeus. A Titan (*q.v.*) and by Eos the father of the beneficent winds. According to other traditions he also fathered the stars.

Astyanax. The son of Hector (*q.v.*) and Andromache (*q.v.*). He was a sensitive child frightened by the plume of his father's helmet. When Troy (*q.v.*) fell Andromache struggled to protect him but Neoptolemus (*q.v.*) threw him from the city walls. Another tradition says she took him to Neoptolemus' court in Epirus.

Atalanta. The Boeotian Atalanta was the daughter of Schoeneus and wife of Hippomenes, the Arcadian Atalanta, the daughter of Iasus and Clymene and wife of Milanion. Similar tales were told of her in both traditions. She was exposed by her father and suckled by a bear sent by Artemis (*q.v.*) with whom she was sometimes identified. She became a famous huntress and hunted the Calydonian Boar (*q.v.*). Though vowed to virginity she bore Meleager (*q.v.*) a son. She refused to marry any suitor except he who beat her in a foot race. Hippomenes (or Milanion) did this by placing three golden apples, gifts from Aphrodite (*q.v.*) in her path, causing her to stop and collect them.

Athamas. The son of Aeolus and king of Orchomenus in Boeotia. He loved Ino (*q.v.*) who bore him Learchus and Melicertes, but Hera (*q.v.*) forced him to marry Nephele who bore him Phrixus and Helle (*q.v.*). Hera drove him mad because he sheltered Dionysus (*q.v.*) and he killed Learchus. Ino flung herself into the sea with Melicertes and both became sea deities. Ino became Leucothea and Melicertes became Palaemon. Athamas fled to Thessaly.

Athene or Athena. Identified with Minerva by the Romans. The daughter of Zeus (*q.v.*) and Metis (*q.v.*). Though it was foretold she would be a girl, an oracle said that if Metis bore another child it would be a son who would depose Zeus. He then swallowed Metis and later suffered a terrible headache near Lake Triton. Hermes (*q.v.*) knew the cause and persuaded Hephaestus (*q.v.*) to cleave Zeus' skull. Out sprang Athene fully armed. She was the goddess of wisdom and patron of arts and crafts, a protectress of agriculture and also a warrior. Moreover, she was a virgin (*see* Pallas). She disputed possession of Athens with Poseidon (*q.v.*): he offered the city the horse, Athene the olive which was judged to be the better gift. Henceforth she was patron of the city which was a centre of her cult. Her epithet "glaucopis" meant "bright-eyed" or "owl-faced" and in the *Odyssey* (*q.v.*) she assumed the form of a bird. Athenian coins bore an owl and the saying "Owls to Athens" meant the same as "Coals to Newcastle". She was worshipped on the Acropolis. A defender of all heroes who worked for the good of mankind, *e.g.* Heracles (*q.v.*).

Atlantiades. Another name for Hermes (*q.v.*) whose mother Maia was the daughter of Atlas (*q.v.*).

Atlantis. A legendary island said to be to the west of the Pillars of Hercules (q.v.). Its inhabitants, once powerful and virtuous, became wealthy and degenerate and were conquered by the Athenians. Later the island sank beneath the ocean in a day and a night. It may be that the island Plato speaks of in *Timaeus* was part of Crete or some other island which suffered when a volcano on Suntorini (ancient Thera) erupted.

Atlas. A Titan (q.v.) the son of Iapetus and Clymene and brother of Prometheus (q.v.) and Epimetheus. For his part in the Titanomachia (q.v.) he was condemned to carry the sky on his shoulders and stood holding it far to the west of the Pillars of Hercules (q.v.). For a brief time Heracles (q.v.) shouldered his burden. It is said Perseus (q.v.) turned him to stone with Medusa's (q.v.) head and he was identified with Mt. Atlas in North-West Africa. The father of Calypso (q.v.) and the Pleiades (q.v.).

Atreus. *See* **Thyestes.**

Attis. A god of vegetation whose cult originated in Phrygia and involved a festival of death and resurrection in the Spring. A consort of Cybele (q.v.) according to one tradition he castrated himself in a religious frenzy and became head of her college of eunuch priests.

Augeas. A king of Elis with more sheep and cattle than any other man. Heracles (q.v.) was given the task of cleansing his filthy stables (the Augean stables) which had not been cleared for many years. Heracles promised to cleanse them in a day in return for one tenth of the cattle. He did so by diverting the rivers Peneius and Alphaeus through them but Augeas refused to pay him. Heracles later invaded Elis, killed Augeas, his sons and their allies the Moliones and destroyed the city of Pylus which had also helped Augeas. One tradition says he spared Augeas.

Aurora. The Roman goddess of the dawn, associated with the Greek Eos (q.v.).

Autolycus. The son of Hermes (q.v.) and Chione, father of Anticleia and thus grandfather of Odysseus (q.v.). Also grandfather of Sinon (q.v.). He was renowned for trickery, cunning and theft.

Aventine. One of the hills of Rome and the southernmost. It was close to the Tiber, was outside the pomerium and was associated with the "plebians".

Avernus, Lake. The modern Lago di Averno near Naples, thought to be an entrance to the Underworld. This is how Aeneas (q.v.) was told to enter Hades (q.v.). Agrippa linked it with the Lucrine Lake while building the harbour of Portus Julius.

B

Bacchae. The female followers of the cult of Bacchus or Dionysus whose worship was characterised by wine-induced frenzies of a mystic nature. At the height of such frenzies they believed themselves to be at one with the god. Also known as Bacchantes, Maenads and Thyiads.

Bacchoi. Male equivalent of the Bacchae.

Bacchus. Latin name for Dionysus (q.v.).

Bassaris. A Bacchante (*See* **Bacchae**).

Baucis. *See* **Philemon.**

Bellerophon. Son of Glaucus (q.v.) King of Corinth. He killed one Bellerus and fled to Tiryns where Anteia, wife of the King Proetus falsely accused him of trying to seduce her. Proetus sent him to his father-in-law Iobates with a letter requesting Iobates to kill the bearer of it. Reluctant to kill a guest Iobates sent him to kill the Chimaera (q.v.). Capturing Pegasus (q.v.) with a golden bridle given to him by Athene (q.v.) he was able to accomplish the task. He was then sent to fight the Amazons (q.v.) and again triumphed. On his return to Tiryns he survived an ambush set by Iobates and finally persuaded the king of his innocence. Iobates made him his heir. One tradition says Bellerophon presumed to rise to Olympus on Pegasus but Zeus sent a gadfly which stung the horse. Pegasus threw Bellerophon to earth but itself entered Olympus.

Belus. One of Poseidon's (q.v.) sons and father of Danaus (q.v.), Cepheus (q.v.) and Aegyptus.

Biton and Cleobis. Sons of a priestess of Hera (q.v.) in Argos who drew their mother's chariot several miles to the goddess's temple when no oxen could be found. Their mother asked Hera to bestow on them the best of gifts for mortals, and they died in their sleep in the temple.

Boeotia. Region of northern Greece; the capital city was Thebes.

Bona Dea. A Roman fertility goddess. Only women worshipped her. Cicero (q.v.) recounts an occasion when his opponent Clodius (q.v.), disguised as a woman, entered an annual nocturnal ceremony of her worshippers over which the chief magistrate's wife presided.

Boreas. The Roman Aquilo; the north wind in Greek mythology. Son of Astraeus (q.v.) and Eos (q.v.) and brother of the other beneficent winds Zephyrus (q.v.), Notus (q.v.) and Eurus (q.v.). In Athens who destroyed Xerxes' (q.v.) fleet. He carried off Oreithyia, daughter of Erechtheus king of Athens who bore him two sons Zetes (q.v.) and Calais (q.v.) and two daughters, Chione and Cleopatra, wife of Phineus.

Brauron. Site on the east coast of Attica. Centre of a cult of Artemis (q.v.). It was believed the locals had killed a she-bear, an animal sacred to the goddess, and that she demanded they worship her on the site, and that girls between the ages of 7 and 11 serve her and live in her temple. Also believed to be the burial place of Iphigenia (q.v.) after her sacrifice at Aulis.

Briareus or **Aegaeon.** One of the Hecatoncheires (q.v.).

Briseis. *See* **Achilles.**

Brontes. One of the Cyclopes (q.v.).

Brutus, Lucius Junius. According to a Roman tradition accepted by Livy (q.v.) the liberator of Rome from the Etruscan kings following the rape of Lucretia (q.v.). Also the first Roman consul in 509 B.C. He ordered the execution of his own sons when they became involved in a conspiracy to restore the monarchy.

C

Cacus. In Roman tradition this fire-breathing giant and his sister Caca were children of Vulcan (q.v.) who lived on the Palatine hill (q.v.), although Virgil in book 8 of the *Aeneid* (q.v.) makes it the Aventine (q.v.). Virgil tells how Cacus stole the cattle of Geryon (q.v.) from Hercules (q.v.) who pursued Cacus back to his cave, tracking him by the cattle's mooing. There he slew Cacus. This event has been portrayed in a painting by Poussin and a statue by Bandinelli in the Signoria, Florence.

Cadmus. Son of Agenor, king of Phoenicia and grandson of Poseidon (q.v.). When Zeus (q.v.) carried off his sister Europa (q.v.) he went to look for her but was told by the Delphic oracle (*see* Apollo) to relinquish the search and to follow a magical cow. Where the cow lay down he was to found a city. The place where it sank became the site of the Cadmea, the citadel of Thebes. Here Cadmus slew the dragon guarding the spring of Ares and on her advice sowed its teeth. The Sparti (q.v.) sprang up. Cadmus married Harmonia (q.v.) and their wedding was attended by the gods. Their children included Autonoe, Ino, Semele (q.v.) Agave Polydoros (q.v.) and Illyrius. In old age Cadmus, who had introduced the use of letters to Greece from Phoenicia, gave up his throne to his grandson Pentheus and went to reign in Illyria. Later he and Harmonia were received into Elysium (q.v.) in the form of serpents.

Caeneus. Originally the nymph Caenis turned into a man at her own request by Poseidon (q.v.). Accompanied the Argonauts (q.v.) and hunted the Calydonian Boar (q.v.). Invulnerable to normal blows he was killed by the Centaurs (q.v.) in their battle with the Lapithae (q.v.) when they buried him beneath a pile of trees. His soul left the body as a bird and in the Underworld again became female.

Calais. Twin brother of Zetes. Winged sons of Boreas (q.v.) and Oreithyia, they accompanied the Argonauts (q.v.) and drove off the Harpies (q.v.), tormenting Phineus (q.v.) husband of their sister Cleopatra.

Calchas. A renegade Trojan seer who helped the Greeks at Troy (q.v.). He foretold that Troy would not fall without Achilles' (q.v.) presence and that the sacrifice of Iphigenia (q.v.) was necessary to secure a favourable wind. It was he who advised Agamemnon to return the girl Chryseis to her father the Trojan priest Chryses. This caused Agamemnon to seize Briseis and sparked the quarrel with Achilles. Calchas later died of grief when surpassed in prophecy by Mopsus, a mysterious mythical figure who was also said to have sailed with the Argonauts (q.v.).

Caliope. See Pillars of Hercules.

Calliope. See Muses.

Callirhoë. Daughter of the river god Achelous (q.v.) and wife of Alcmaeon (q.v.). Alcmaeon gave her the necklace and robe of Harmonia (q.v.).

Callisto. Daughter of Lycaon (q.v.). One of Artemis' (q.v.) huntresses. She bore Arcas (q.v.) to Zeus (q.v.) who sought to conceal their affair from Hera (q.v.) by turning Callisto into a bear. Realising the ruse Hera had the bear hunted down but Zeus saved her and placed her amongst the stars as Arctos. Others say that Artemis turned her into a bear and Arcas hunted her. In this version Callisto became the Great Bear constellation and Arcas the Little Bear.

Calydonian Boar. A savage boar which Artemis (q.v.) sent to ravage Calydon because its king, Oeneus (q.v.) had not offered her proper sacrifice (see also Atalanta and Meleager). Pausanias (q.v.) tells of a story of long tusks found at Tegea, seen by Augustus and taken to Rome.

Calypso. A nymph of Ogygia who tended Odysseus (q.v.) there for eight years until Zeus (q.v.) ordered her to send him home to Ithaca. The name means "hidden" and she may have been a death goddess. At one point she offers the hero eternal youth, but he refuses, preferring real life. She bore him two sons.

Camilla. The Roman equivalent of an Amazon (q.v.) —a female warrior.

Capaneus. See "Seven Against Thebes".

Capricorn. See Amalthea.

Cassandra. Daughter of Priam (q.v.) and Hecuba and twin of Helenus. She was given the gift of prophecy by Apollo (q.v.) but when she disappointed him he decreed that no one would ever believe her prophecies. Several times her important warnings went unheeded, e.g. against Paris (q.v.) going to Sparta, and against the wooden horse (q.v.). She was taken as a slave by Agamemnon (q.v.) when Troy (q.v.) fell and became his mistress. She was murdered with him by Clytemnestra (q.v.).

Cassiopeia. The wife of Cepheus and mother of Andromeda. Her boast that Andromeda was more beautiful than the Nereids (q.v.) caused Poseidon (q.v.) to send a monster to ravage the kingdom. Only the sacrifice of Andromeda could prevent this. Perseus (q.v.), who found her chained naked to a rock by the sea, offered to save her if she would become his wife. Cepheus and Cassiopeia agreed to this and Perseus slew the beast. Her parents then attempted to renege on their promise, claiming Andromeda was promised to another. At her wedding to Perseus the other suitor and his followers attempted to seize the bride but Perseus turned them all to stone with the head of Medusa (q.v.). The images of Cepheus and Cassiopeia were set amongst the stars by Poseidon.

Castalian Spring. Sacred spring on Mt. Parnassus, near the site of the Delphic oracle. Here the young girl Castalia drowned herself to avoid Apollo's (q.v.) advances.

Castalides. A name for the Muses (q.v.).

Castor and Polydeuces. (Latin "Pollux") The "Dioscuri". The twin "Sons of Zeus", brothers of Helen (q.v.) and the sons of Leda (q.v.) the wife of Tyndareus of Sparta. One tradition says that they were born from an egg, like Helen, after Zeus had visited Leda in the form of a swan. Others say only Polydeuces was Zeus' son and that Castor being the son of Tyndareus was a mere mortal. Castor was a famous horse tamer and Polydeuces a great boxer. Sailing with the Argonauts (q.v.) Polydeuces slew Amycus son of Poseidon (q.v.) who lived on the isle of Bebrycos. Amycus was a renowned boxer who killed travellers by challenging them to a boxing match. They also hunted the Calydonian boar (q.v.). The Dioscuri fought a mortal battle with their cousins the twins Idas and Lynceus Zeus then killed Idas but Polydeuces begged to die with his brother. However Zeus decided they should live alternate days with the gods and under the earth. Their image was placed amongst the stars as Gemini. Poseidon gave them power over the wind and waves and they became protectors of seafarers. They were said to have appeared on horseback to help the Romans against the Latins in the battle of Lake Regillus in 484 B.C., after which their cult was adopted at Rome.

Centaurs. A race of savage creatures, half-man, half-horse which inhabited the woodlands and mountains, particularly those of Thessaly. They were the offspring of Ixion and a cloud. In Homer (q.v.) the centaurs appear as representatives of primitive desires, fighting, drinking and womanising, but later they are only portrayed as turning to violence when drunk. When they tried to abduct Deidamia (q.v.) from her wedding, they became involved in a famous battle with their neighbours the Lapithae (q.v.).

Centimani. See Hecatoncheires.

Cephalus. Husband of Procris who was carried off by Eos (q.v.). Eos released him but Procris, suspicious of the time he spent hunting, followed him into the woods. Hearing him praying for a breeze she supposed it to be his mistress (the Roman equivalent of Eos was Aurora, the Latin for breeze aura). Moving closer she was struck by his spear, which never missed, and killed. The story is told by Hesiod and Ovid and inspired paintings by Poussin and Claude.

Cepheus. King of Tegea and one of the Argonauts (q.v.). He and most of his 20 sons were killed helping Heracles (q.v.) fight Hippocoon.

Cerberus. A huge and savage dog, the offspring of Echidne (q.v.) and Typhon (q.v.) which guarded the entrance to Hades (q.v.). He is usually said to have had three heads, but Hesiod gives him fifty. His back was covered with serpents' heads and he had a snake for a tail. Heracles (q.v.) dragged him from the Underworld; Orpheus (q.v.) charmed him with music when seeking Eurydice while Aeneas (q.v.) drugged him with a cake of honey and narcotics, hence "a sop to Cerberus".

Cercyon. A son of Hephaestus (q.v.) reigning near Eleusis. Here he challenged all travellers to a wrestling match and killed them, until he challenged Theseus (q.v.) and was killed himself.

Ceres. Ancient Italian corn-goddess worshipped in a temple on the Aventine. Games and a spring festival, the Ceriala, were held in her honour. She was associated with Demeter (q.v.) from an early date and her daughter Proserpina with Persephone (q.v.).

Ceryneian Hind. A creature with brazen feet and golden antlers. One of Heracles' (q.v.) tasks was to catch it alive. He pursued it for a year and caught it without shedding blood by pinning its forelegs together with an arrow.

Chalybes. Mythical inhabitants of north Asia Minor said by some traditions to have invented iron working.

Chaos. In Greek creation myth Chaos was the infinite space existing before creation. From Chaos sprang Ge (q.v.), the Earth.

Charities. Also called the Gratiae or Graces by the Romans. They were originally divinities of nature. In the Iliad (q.v.) only one Charity is personified, Charis, wife of Hephaestus (q.v.). Later the three Graces appear, Aglaia, Thalia and Euphrosyne, friends of the Muses (q.v.) with whom they inhabited Mt. Olympus.

Charon. The surly ferryman who transported the dead across the Styx (q.v.) to Hades (q.v.). He only transported them if they had received the correct funeral rite and if their relatives had placed a small coin, his fare, under the tongues. However Heracles (q.v.) forced his passage and Orpheus (q.v.) charmed his with his lyre. Amongst the Etruscans (q.v.), as in modern Greek folklore, he was regarded as a synonym or figure of death. Virgil (q.v.) portrays him with unkempt white hair and eyes of fire in the 6th book of the Aeneid.

Charybdis and Scylla. Two monsters guarding the Straits of Messina. Charybdis swallowed the sea and vessels on it, three times a day, regurgitating what she swallowed each time. Opposite was Scylla, the daughter of Poseidon (q.v.) by a mortal, whom the jealous Amphitrite (q.v.) turned into a monster with six barking heads and twelve feet. Odysseus (q.v.) was forced to pass between the two evils and the equally undesirable choice between the pair has become proverbial.

Cheiron. Also called Chiron. A centaur (q.v.). A son of Cronus (q.v.) and Philyra, hence he is sometimes referred to as Philyrides. Unlike his fellow centaurs a wise and kindly being who learnt music, medicine, hunting and prophecy from Apollo (q.v.) and Artemis (q.v.). This learning he imparted to numerous heroes including Achilles (q.v.), the Dioscuri (q.v.), Jason (q.v.) and Peleus (q.v.). An immortal, he was accidentally wounded by the poisoned arrow of his friend Heracles (q.v.). In pain he longed for death. By surrendering his immortality he was relieved of life and suffering and placed among the stars as Sagittarius.

Chimeira. A monster with a lion's head, goat's body and a serpent for a tail. It could breathe fire. The offspring of Echidne (q.v.) and Typhon (q.v.), though some say it was begot by the Sphinx (q.v.) and Orthrus (q.v.). It was killed by Bellerophon (q.v.) while ravaging Lycia. The beast gave us the word "chimera" or fanciful notion.

Chryseis. (Cressida) Daughter of the Trojan seer and priest of Apollo (q.v.). Chryseis was captured by Agamemnon (q.v.) who refused to ransom her. Apollo then sent a plague on the Greek camp and when Calchas (q.v.) explained the cause Agamemnon released her. He then seized Briseis thus causing the quarrel with Achilles (q.v.) The medieval *Roman de Troie* tells how Troilus loved her, but she left him for Diomedes (q.v.). This is the basis of Chaucer's *Troilus and Criseyde* and Shakespeare's *Troilus and Cressida*.

Chrysippus. The son of Pelops (q.v.), murdered by his half-brother Atreus (q.v.) and Thyestes (q.v.) at the instigation of his step-mother Hippodameia (q.v.).

Chthonius. See **Spartii**.

Circe The daughter of Helios (q.v.) and Perse. A sorceress living on the island of Aeaea (Virgil (q.v.) identifies it with Circeii in Campania (q.v.)). She turned Odysseus' (q.v.) men into swine but he resisted by use of the herb "moly" given to him by Hermes (q.v.). Having forced her to restore his men he stayed a year with her and she advised him on his trip to the Underworld and return to Ithaca. She had a son, Telegonus by him and later married his son by Penelope (q.v.), Telemachus (q.v.). In the *Argonautica* of Apollonius of Rhodes she purifies Jason (q.v.) and Medea (q.v.) of murder on their return from Colchis. She was worshipped in Campania in the form of Feronia.

Cisseus. Father of Hecabe (q.v.).

Claros. Site of a shrine and oracle of Apollo (q.v.) to the south of Smyrna.

Cleobis. See **Biton**.

Clio. See **Muses**.

Cloacina. Ancient Roman divinity of "purification", later identified with Venus.

Cloelia. A Roman girl, legendary for having escaped from Porsenna (q.v.) when taken hostage and swimming back to Rome across the Tiber.

Clotho. One of the Fates (q.v.). She pulled the Limbs of Pelops (q.v.) from the cauldron in which they were to be boiled, thus enabling his restoration to life.

Clytemnestra. Daughter of Tyndareus (q.v.) and a half-sister of Helen (q.v.) and Castor and Polydeuces (q.v.). Wife of Agamemnon (q.v.) by whom she bore Orestes (q.v.), Iphigenia (q.v.) and Electra (q.v.). While Agamemnon was at Troy (q.v.) she began an affair with Aegisthus (q.v.) and on his return the pair murdered him. She was killed by Orestes. Her murder of Agamemnon should be seen in the context of his infidelity with Cassandra (q.v.) and others and his sacrifice of Iphigenia. This is how Strauss views the matter in his opera *Elektra*.

Cocles. The "one-eyed", a nickname of Horatius (q.v.) who kept the bridge across the Tiber.

Cocytus. The river of wailing in Hades (q.v.).

Coeus. One of the Titans (q.v.).

Cornelia. Mother of the "Gracchi", daughter of Scipio Africanus and a model of what Romans of the Republic thought a matron should be. On the deaths of her sons she withdrew to Misenum and her home became a centre of culture. She appears in Plutarch's (q.v.) *Lives* of her sons and he tells us that when a visitor asked to see her jewels she presented her sons saying "These are my jewels".

Coronis. Thessalian princess made pregnant by Apollo (q.v.) but who fell in love with an Arcadian youth. Learning of this from a crow, Apollo sent Artemis (q.v.) to kill her. The unborn child was snatched from her and given to Cheiron (q.v.) to rear. The child was Asclepius (q.v.).

Corybantes. Priests of Rhea (q.v.) or Cybele (q.v.) in Phrygia and Asia Minor. Known for their dancing and performance of wild rites to the sound of drums and cymbals.

Corydon. Common Arcadian shepherd's name but in Virgil's (q.v.) second *Eclogue* the shepherd

Corydon laments his "faithless Alexis". From this Corydon has become a symbol of homosexual love.

Creon. A "ruler" or "prince" and the name often given to subsidiary characters in Greek legend, e.g. the brother of Jocasta (q.v.) who succeeds Oedipus (q.v.). See also **Jason**.

Cretan Bull. A magnificent white bull sent by Poseidon (q.v.) to Minos (q.v.) for sacrifice. Minos' wife Pasiphaë (q.v.) so admired the bull she had Daedalus (q.v.) construct a hollow cow for her to get inside. She then mated with the bull and later bore the Minotaur (q.v.). Minos also admired the bull and rather than sacrifice it, substituted another bull. The original bull escaped to ravage Crete until captured by Heracles (q.v.) and taken to Eurystheus (q.v.). Eurystheus freed it and it ravaged Greece until captured by Theseus (q.v.) at Marathon (q.v.) and sacrificed to Athene (q.v.).

Creusa. Feminine equivalent of Creon. The most famous is the daughter of Priam (q.v.), first wife of Aeneas (q.v.) and mother of Ascanius. She was lost in the escape from Troy (q.v.) when the city fell. When Aeneas looked for her he met only her ghost who bid him go forward to meet his destiny.

Croesus. Last king of Lydia who in the mid-6th century B.C. amassed a great fortune. His wealth is proverbial. Regarded as a model of piety for his gold offerings to Apollo (q.v.) at Delphi (q.v.). He met Solon and tried to persuade him to admit that Croesus was the happiest of men. Solon refused, saying that no man could be considered happy till his life had ended. The Delphic oracle told him that a great empire would fall if he invaded Persia. His own did. The Persian king Cyrus ordered him to be burnt alive but he called on Solon's name and told Cyrus of Solon's sayings. Cyrus pardoned him and made him an adviser. A later tradition says Apollo saved him and carried him to the land of the Hyperboreans.

Crommyum, Sow of. Wild sow slain by Theseus (q.v.).

Cronus. The son of Uranus (q.v.) and Ge (q.v.). The youngest of the twelve Titans (q.v.). When Ge stirred the Titans to revolt against Uranus she gave Cronus a flint sickle with which he castrated his father. Having deposed Uranus, Cronus reigned supreme and consigned the Cyclopes (q.v.) and the Hecatoncheires (q.v.) to Tartarus (q.v.). He married his sister Rhea (q.v.) and by her was father of Hestia (q.v.), Demeter (q.v.), Hera (q.v.), Poseidon (q.v.), Hades (q.v.) and Zeus (q.v.), Mindful of a curse by Uranus and Ge that he too be deposed by his own son, he swallowed each child at birth. But Rhea gave him a stone to swallow instead of Zeus and later gave him an emetic forcing him to regurgitate his other children. They now joined Zeus in a war on Cronus and the Titans. The Cyclopes aided them and gave Zeus the thunderbolt, Poseidon the trident and Hades a helmet of darkness or invisibility. Cronus was defeated and the Titans were consigned to Tartarus.

Cupid or **Amor**. Roman god of love, identified with the Greek Eros (q.v.).

Curetes. Priests of Rhea (q.v.) who drowned the cries of the infant Zeus (q.v.) as he lay in the Dictaean Cave by the clashing of their weapons. This prevented Cronus (q.v.) finding and devouring him. They were half-divine and in later times were conflated with the Corybantes (q.v.) who were also believed to be half-divine. All became part of Dionysus' ritual.

Cybele. The mother goddess of Phrygia where she and her lover Attis (q.v.) were worshipped in orgiastic rites and purification ceremonies including bathing in the blood of a sacrificed bull. Her symbol was a black stone and this was brought to Rome from Pessinus in 204 B.C. However it was only during the reign of Claudius that Roman citizens were allowed to serve as her priests and the oriental eunuchs serving her cult were always frowned upon. Her worship is described by Lucretius (q.v.) in book 2 and Catullus in his *Attis*. The artists of the classical world portray her with a crown of towers, a libation dish and tambourine, flanked by lions to show her control of wild nature.

Cyclops. Generally known to the Greeks as one-eyed giants living in a distant country, perhaps Sicily. In Homer (q.v.) the Cyclops Polyphemus is a man-eating son of Poseidon (q.v.), made drunk and blinded by Odysseus (q.v.) and his men whom he had captured and meant to eat. Hesiod (q.v.) refers to three Cyclops but describes them as Titans (q.v.). The three (Brontes, Steropes and Arges) were sons of Ge (q.v.) and Uranus (q.v.) who made weapons for Zeus (q.v.), Poseidon and Hades (q.v.) (see **Cronus**). Other traditions make them skilled craftsmen helping Hephaestus (q.v.) at his Sicilian forge. They were also builders of cities including Athens and the walls of Tiryns.

Cyllenius. Another name for Hermes (q.v.) who was said to have been born on Mt. Cyllene in southern Greece.

Cycnus. "The Swan", a mythical king of Liguria who loved Phaeton (q.v.) and was turned into a swan.

Cynthia. A name given to Artemis (q.v.). She and Apollo (q.v.) were thought to have been born on Mt. Cynthus in Delos and were thus referred to as Cynthia and Cynthus.

Cyrene. In myth the mother of Aristaeus (q.v.) by Apollo (q.v.) who carried her to Libya where she gave her name to the city of Cyrene.

Cythera. An island off the south-east coast of Greece noted for its sanctuary of Aphrodite (q.v.). She was thus referred to as "the Cytherean".

D

Dactyli. Greek equivalent of the Roman Chalybes (q.v.) the mythical beings who lived on Mt. Ida in northern Asia Minor and invented iron-working.

Daedalus. Mythical Athenian craftsman. His jealousy of his nephew Perdix or Talos, who was said to have invented the saw, caused him to throw Perdix from Athene's (q.v.) temple on the Acropolis (q.v.). Having thus committed murder he fled to Crete. Here he arranged the liaison between Pasiphaë (q.v.) and the Cretan Bull (q.v.) which produced the Minotaur (q.v.). Then, to conceal what had transpired from Minos (q.v.) he built the famous labyrinth to hide the Minotaur. When Minos discovered the truth he imprisoned Daedalus and his son Icarus in the labyrinth. Pasiphaë released them and Daedalus invented wings which, when attached to their shoulders by wax, enabled him and his son to fly. However Icarus flew too near to the sun, the wax melted, and he fell to his doom in the Icarian sea. Daedalus reached Cumae and then went to Sicily. The King Cocalus welcomed him and when Minos arrived in pursuit Cocalus daughters helped Daedalus kill him. In Sicily Daedalus was credited with many wonderful buildings including a honeycomb of gold for Aphrodite's (q.v.) temple on Mt. Eryx. His name has become synonymous with ingenuity and skill, hence "Daedal" and "daedalian" in the English language.

Damocles, Member of the court of Dionysius I, tyrant of Syracuse. Cicero tells how the tyrant had him eat a sumptuous dinner while a sword was suspended by a hair over his head. This illustrated the luxurious but precarious life style of the tyrant and "the sword of Damocles" has become proverbial.

Danaë. A princess of Argos, daughter of King Acrisius (q.v.). An oracle told the king that Danaë's son would kill him so he imprisoned her in a brazen tower. Zeus (q.v.) visited her in a shower of gold and fathered Perseus (q.v.). Acrisius cast them adrift in a box and they came to Seriphos. They were found by the fisherman Dictys and taken to the king Polydectes. He wished to marry Danaë and so, to get Perseus out of the way, sent him to fetch the head of Medusa (q.v.). Danaë was saved from Polydectes' advances when Perseus returned and, showing the head, turned him to stone.

Danai. A general name used by Homer for the Greeks assembled at Troy. It was meant to perpetuate the memory of a common ancestor, Danaus (q.v.).

Danaus. A king of Libya and the father of 50 daughters, the "Danaides". His brother Aegyptus, who had 50 sons, wanted a mass marriage, but Danaus fled with his daughters to Argos where he became king. Eventually Aegyptus' sons followed and demanded the "Danaides". Danaus agreed but gave each daughter a weapon with which they slew their husbands on the wedding night. All, that is, save Hypermestra who spared Lynceus. Lynceus killed Danaus and became king of Argos. In the Underworld the Danaides were condemned to carry water in sieves for ever. The story is told by Pindar (q.v.) and the Danaides form the chorus in Aeschylos' (q.v.) *Suppliants*.

Daphne. The daughter of the river god Peneus or Ladon. A nymph pursued by Apollo (q.v.). To escape him she prayed either to her father or to the Earth to be turned into a laurel tree, which she was. Apollo made himself a laurel wreath as consolation and it became the prize at the Pythian Games held in his honour.

Daphnis. The son of Hermes (q.v.) and a nymph. She abandoned the infant but he was raised by Sicilian shepherds. Pan (q.v.) taught him the pipes and he was the originator of pastoral poetry. Later he was unfaithful to a nymph who loved him and in revenge she blinded him. His father ordered both the fountain of Daphnis near Syracuse in his honour.

Dardanus. The son of Zeus (q.v.) and the Pleiad (q.v.) Electra. He founded Dardania on land given to him by Teucer. He was grandfather of Tros, great grandfather of Ilus (q.v.) and Ganymede (q.v.). Hence an ancestor of the Trojans who were sometimes called Dardanids, Dardans or Dardonians. Roman legend sometimes envisages him migrating to Dardania from Italy.

Deianeira. The daughter of Oeneus, king of Calydon and the wife of Heracles (q.v.) who won her hand by defeating the river god Achelous (q.v.). She bore him a son Hyllus. After accidentally killing Eunomus, Heracles took her and Hyllus into voluntary exile. When they came to cross the River Evenus the centaur (q.v.) Nessus offered to transport her on his back. However he tried to rape her and was killed by Heracles. As he lay dying he told her to take his blood as it was a charm which would keep Heracles in love with her. Later Heracles won Iole, daughter of Eurytus King of Oechalia, in an archery contest. When Eurytus refused to surrender Iole Heracles invaded Oechalia and defeated him. He then ordered Deianeira to send him a white shirt which he was to wear at a thanksgiving sacrifice to Zeus (q.v.). Deianeira, jealous of Iole, dipped the shirt in the blood of Nessus. But the blood was poisonous and when Heracles donned the shirt it burned his body and attempts to pull it off tore pieces of flesh from the hero. In agony he ordered Hyllus to build a funeral pyre on which he would find quick death and release from the pain. He also had Hyllus marry Iola. Deianeira, horrified at the result of her action, hanged herself. The story forms the plot of Sophocles' *Women of Trachis*.

Deidamia. The maiden who fell in love with Achilles (q.v.) and bore him Neoptolemus (q.v.).

Deiphobus. See **Helen** and **Helenus**.

Delis, Delius. Epithets of Artemis (q.v.) and Apollo (q.v.) who were born on Delos (q.v.).

Delos. Site of the important Ionian shrine of Apollo (q.v.). Here he was known as Phoebus ("the shining") or Lycius. When the jealous Hera (q.v.) pursued Leto (q.v.) she sought asylum where she could give birth to Apollo, her son by Zeus (q.v.). Delos, which was so poor it could lose nothing to Hera's wrath, accepted her.

Delphi. Site of Apollo's (q.v.) Dorian shrine and the most famous centre of his worship. Here he took his prophetic role having replaced Python. The oracle, located near the Castalian spring, was supposed to contain the omphalos or navel store of the Earth. A priestess, the Pythia, sat on a tripod chewing the intoxicating laurel leaf and voicing his utterances. Intoxicating vapours also issued from a chasm in the shrine. In this role Apollo was known as Loxias "the Ambiguous". (See **Croesus**). The priests of the shrine were not incorruptible and were known to take sides, e.g. with Sparta against Athens and with Philip of Macedon against Greece. The oracle had greatest influence during the period of overseas colonisation when its advice on location of colonies was always sought. The oracle encouraged Rome to defy Hannibal but was looted by Sulla. Nero visited it and Hadrian tried in vain to revive its prestige. Its decline came with the advance of Christianity and the growing interest in astrology as a means of prophecy. The temples at Delphi were sacked by Alaric in A.D. 396. Apollo's temple with its inscribed maxims "Know thyself" and "Nothing in excess" had stood on the highest point of Mt. Parnassus and had housed the sepulchre of Bacchus (q.v.) who was also worshipped at Delphi.

Demeter. The counterpart of the Roman Ceres, a

Greek corn-goddess responsible for the fertility of the earth. The daughter of Cronus (q.v.) and Rhea (q.v.) she became mother of Persephone (q.v.) or Kore ("the maiden") by her brother Zeus (q.v.). A 7th century B.C. Homeric *Hymn to Demeter* tells how Hades (q.v.) carried off Persephone from Eleusis twelve miles from Athens (Ovid says she was taken while gathering poppies in Sicily). Demeter scoured the earth for her until Helios (q.v.) told her what had occurred. She then shunned Olympus (q.v.) and wandered the earth, forbidding it to bring forth fruit and therefore threatening famine. Zeus finally agreed that Persephone could leave Hades provided she had not eaten in the Underworld. Hades agreed to let her go but tempted her into eating a pomegranate. She thus had to spend half a year with him in the Underworld and half with Demeter. Demeter again made the earth fertile but turned Ascalaphus, who had seen and reported Persephone eating the pomegranate, into an owl. She punished those who had been unkind to her during her wandering (*see* Abas) but rewarded those who had treated her hospitably. She taught Triptolemus, another son of Celeus (q.v.) the art of agriculture and gave him an ear of corn whose virtues he revealed to his fellow men. The Eleusian Festival was held in Demeter's honour from the 6th century B.C. and there was an annual procession from Eleusis to Athens. Those who spoke Greek were initiated into the mysteries of her cult. The Thesmophoria, a celebration of the foundation of laws, was held in her honour in many cities.

Demophon (1) The son of Theseus (q.v.) and Phaedra (q.v.) brother of Acamas (q.v.). He helped rescue his grandmother Aethra who had been Helen's (q.v.) slave, when Troy (q.v.) fell. Phyllis, a Thracian princess, loved him and committed suicide when he left her to visit Athens. She was then transformed into a tree.

(2) The son of Celeus and Metaneira. Demeter (q.v.) tried to reward the pair for their kindness to her by making Demophon immortal. To achieve this he had to be suspended above a fire, but Metaneira cried out thus breaking the spell and he perished.

Deucalion. The son of Prometheus (q.v.), husband of Pyrrha and father of Hellen. He was thus the ancestor of the Greeks. When Zeus (q.v.) decided to flood the earth in order to destroy mankind they escaped in an ark which finally made land on Mt. Parnassus. The couple prayed to Themis (q.v.) that mankind be restored and were told to scatter their mother's bones behind them. They took this to mean stones, the skeleton of Mother Earth. The rocks Deucalion scattered became men; those Pyrrha scattered became women.

Diana. Italian goddess of woods, women, childbirth and later, by association with the Greek Artemis (q.v.), the moon. Her cult was originally centred on the volcanic Lake Nemi at Aricia. The lake was known as Diana's mirror. The priest here, known as the rex, was always a runaway slave who had murdered his predecessor. A temple of Diana, said to have been founded by Servius Tullius also stood on the Aventine.

Dictaean Cave. A cave on Mt. Dicte in Crete, the reputed childhood home of Zeus (q.v.). Hence he was known as Dictaeus.

Dictys. (1) The sailor who found Perseus (q.v.) and his mother Danaë (q.v.) adrift at sea in a chest.

(2) A Cretan said to have accompanied Idomeneus (q.v.) to the Trojan war. His diary of the war was supposedly buried near Cnossos and found in the reign of Nero.

Dido. A daughter of the king of Tyre originally called Elissa. Her husband Sychaeus was murdered but with a few followers she escaped to Libya and founded Carthage. Local legend said she burnt herself on a funeral pyre to avoid marrying Iarbas, a native king. The Roman version, given in the *Aeneid* takes Aeneas (q.v.) to Carthage where Dido's unrequited love for him results in her death. Aeneas abandons her to fulfil his destiny as ancestor of Rome.

Didyma. A great sanctuary of Apollo (q.v.) at Miletus.

Dindyma. Mountain in Asia Minor and a centre of the Cybele's (q.v.) cult.

Diomedes. (1) A king of the Bistones in Thrace who possessed man-eating mares. A labour of Heracles (q.v.) was to bring them to Eurystheus (q.v.). This he did by stealing them and beating off

his pursuers. But while he was busy fighting, the mares devoured his friend Abderus. Heracles founded the city of Abdera in his honour. Eurystheus freed the horses on Mt. Olympus (q.v.) where wild beasts devoured them.

(2) The son of Tydeus, king of Argos. One of the Epigoni (q.v.). He also went to Troy (q.v.) and was a companion of Odysseus (q.v.). With Odysseus he sailed to fetch Achilles (q.v.) and later Neoptolemus (q.v.). He encouraged Agamemnon (q.v.) to sacrifice Iphigenia (q.v.) and helped Odysseus capture the Trojan spy Dolon. He wounded Aeneas (q.v.) and Aphrodite (q.v.) as she saved the Trojan. He also wounded Ares. He returned from Troy to find his wife had been unfaithful and went to settle in Daunia in Italy. Here he married Euippe, daughter of king Daunus. He was buried on one of the Diomedan islands.

Dionysus. The Roman Bacchus. Also called Bromius "the Boisterous". The son of Zeus (q.v.) and Semele, a mortal, Zeus visited her in the guise of a mortal but when she was six months pregnant the jealous Hera (q.v.) came to her as an old woman. She advised Semele to demand her lover appear in his true form. Zeus unwillingly agreed to do so and Semele was consumed by fire. The unborn child was sewn up in Zeus' thigh to be born as Dionysus. The child was given into the care of Athamas and Ino. He was disguised as a girl but Hera learned the truth and drove Athamas mad, causing him to kill his own son. Hermes (q.v.) then took Dionysus to Mt. Nysa in India where he was raised by nymphs. Zeus placed their images in the stars as the Hyades. Here he was taught the use of the vine by his tutor Silenus and his satyrs and here he invented wine. As an adult he journeyed through India, Egypt, Syria and Asia accompanied by a wild following of Maenads or Bacchae and Satyrs. As he went he founded cities and taught cultivation of the vine. When he reached Thrace, Lycurgus, king of the Edones, opposed him but was driven mad by Rhea (q.v.) and slew his own son. His people then had him torn apart by horses. King Pentheus of Thebes also opposed Dionysus and was torn apart by crazed Bacchae whose ranks included his mother and sisters. Entranced they took him for a wild animal. Sailing to Naxos Dionysus was captured by pirates for sale as a slave. He became a lion and turned the oars to serpents. Ivy grew on the mast. The terrified pirates jumped overboard and became dolphins. At Naxos he married Ariadne (q.v.) whom Theseus (q.v.) had deserted. He was eventually received into Olympus as a god, replacing Hestia (q.v.). He fetched his mother to Olympus from the Underworld and she was henceforth known as Thyone. Dionysus was the god of wine and intoxicating herbs like ivy and laurel. He was also the god of tillage and law giving. He was worshipped at Delphi (q.v.) and in the spring festival, the Great Dionysia. In Rome the mysteries of his cult were a closely guarded secret. His followers worshipped him in communal wine-induced frenzies and the ritual involved sacrifice of animals, flagellation and a mystical marriage of novices with the god.

Dioscuri. *See* Castor and Polydeuces.

Dirce. *See* Antiope.

Dis or Orcus. Hades (q.v.).

Dodona. Site of an oracle of Zeus (q.v.) in north west Greece near modern Janina. It was associated with the union of Zeus and Dione, a minor goddess. The oracle centred on an oak and messages were transmitted by the rustling branches and cooing of pigeons nesting in it. The priests were "Selloi" who slept on the ground and walked barefoot. It was visited by Croesus (q.v.) and Alexander the Great offered the sanctuary a large sum of money.

Dryope. The daughter of King Dryops. Apollo (q.v.) seduced her and she was carried off by the Hamadryads (nymphs of trees).

E

Echidne. A mythical creature, half-woman, half-serpent. Mother by Typhon (q.v.) of the Chimaera (q.v.), Sphinx (q.v.), Cerberus (q.v.), Hydra (q.v.), Nemean Lion, Orthrus (q.v.), and Ladon. Slain by Argus.

Echion. A son of Hermes (*q.v.*). An Argonaut (*q.v.*) who took part in the hunt of the Calydonian boar (*q.v.*).

Echo. A nymph who occupied Hera's (*q.v.*) attention by incessant talk while Zeus (*q.v.*) enjoyed himself with the other nymphs. In punishment Hera deprived her of the power of speech except to repeat the words of others. Echo loved Narcissus who refused her. Heart-broken she pined away to nothing, only her voice remaining. Artemis (*q.v.*) punished Narcissus for his heartlessness by making him fall in love with his own reflection. Desparingly he committed suicide and was turned into a flower.

Egeria. An Italian goddess or nymph whose worship was connected with that of Diana (*q.v.*). She was associated with water. It was believed she advised Numa Pompilius (*q.v.*) especially on religious matters and Livy tells us they met in a sacred grove near Rome.

Eileithyia. A goddess of childbirth whom the Greeks associated with Artemis (*q.v.*) and the Romans with Juno (*q.v.*).

Elatus. The father of Caeneus and one of the Lapithae (*q.v.*).

Electra. (1) A Pleiad (*q.v.*).

(2) The daughter of Agamemnon (*q.v.*) and Clytemnestra (*q.v.*). Treated as a slave by her mother and Aegisthus (*q.v.*) she later helped her brother Orestes (*q.v.*) and his friend Pylades (*q.v.*) avenge their father and married Pylades. This is the basis of Euripedes' *Electra* and Strauss's *Elektra*. Freud gave the name "Electra complex" to female fixation on the father, the opposite of the "Oedipus complex".

Electryon. The son of Perseus (*q.v.*) and Andromeda (*q.v.*). King of Mycenae and father of Alcmene (*q.v.*) wife of Amphitrion (*q.v.*).

Eleusis. A sacred site twelve miles west of Athens facing Salamis. Here Celeus received Demeter (*q.v.*). Games and an oracle were found there. A cult involving "Mysteries" was centred there and administered by two families, the Eumolpidae and Kerykes. Ceremonies were held twice a year in Spring and Autumn and initiation to the mysteries, of which we know little, was open to all men, Greek or not, free or slave, who had not committed murder.

Elissa. *See* **Dido.**

Elpenor. One of Odysseus' (*q.v.*) crew who fell off the roof of Circe's (*q.v.*) palace while sleep-walking and broke his neck. When Odysseus visited the Underworld his shade begged for cremation and a burial mound in which his ear was to be planted.

Elysium. A blessed abode of the dead, placed by Homer near the Underworld but not in Hades (*q.v.*). The virtuous went here after death. It was a land of warmth never knowing cold or snow. Later it was associated with "Fortunate Isles" holding "Elysian Fields" which were believed to be far to the west, beyond the Pillars of Hercules (*q.v.*).

Empusae. Daughters of Hecate (*q.v.*). They were demons with the haunches of an ass who wore brazen slippers. Able to turn themselves into cows, bitches or young maidens, as the latter they lay with young men and sucked their blood as they slept.

Enceladus. A son of Ge (*q.v.*). One of 24 giants (*q.v.*) with serpents' tails whom Alcyoneus led in an assault on Olympus (*q.v.*). Buried under Mt Etna in Sicily as a punishment.

Endymion. Either a shepherd of Caria or an Aeolian youth who became king of Elis. As he slept in a cave Selene (*q.v.*) the moon saw him and descended to kiss him. Captivated by his looks she made him fall into a dreamless everlasting sleep so that she could always gaze upon him. His son Aetolus conquered Aetolia.

Enipeus. A river god, beloved of Tyro (*q.v.*).

Eos. The goddess of the dawn, the Romans identified her with Aurora (*q.v.*). The daughter of Hyperion (*q.v.*) and Theira and sister of Helios (*q.v.*). She drove the chariot of Helios each morning to announce his arrival and traversed the sky with him as Hemera before landing in the west as Hespera. The wife of Astraeus and by him mother of the stars and all the winds save the east. She carried off several handsome youths including Orion (*q.v.*) Cephalus (*q.v.*), and Tithonus to whom she bore Memnon (*q.v.*). She requested Zeus (*q.v.*) to make Tithonus immortal but forgot to ask for eternal youth and as he aged he shrank to a cicada.

Epaphus. The son of Zeus (*q.v.*) and Io who ruled Egypt and was said by some to be the sacred bull of Egypt, Apis (*q.v.*).

Epeius. A cowardly son of Panopeus who built the Trojan Horse.

Ephialtes. One of the 24 giants (*q.v.*) led by Alcyoneus. (*See also* **Otus**).

Epidaurus. Site of a famous sanctuary of Asclepius (*q.v.*) built in the 6th century B.C. Here pilgrims could see the tomb of the god.

Epigoni. Descendants of the "Seven against Thebes" (*q.v.*) who also attacked the city ten years after their fathers had done so. They were assembled by Adrastus (*q.v.*) and their ranks included his own son Aegialeus, Diomedes son of Tydeus, Sthenelus son of Capaneus and Eradne and Therseander. Like his father Polynices (*q.v.*) Therseander bribed Eriphyle (*q.v.*) into persuading Alcmaeon into joining the assault on Thebes. Aegialeus died at the walls of the city but the Theban prophet Teiresias advised the citizens to leave the city at night as he had foreseen the Argives (*i.e.* the Epigoni), capturing an empty city. He died next morning drinking from the well of Tilphussa. Adrastus died of grief hearing of his son's death while the remaining Epigoni were left holding an empty city. Alcmaeon went home to take revenge on Eriphyle (*q.v.*).

Erebos. A deep chasm in the Underworld.

Erebus. "Darkness", the son of Chaos (*q.v.*) and father of Aether and Hemera by "Night", his sister. Some traditions hold that the Fates (*q.v.*) were daughters of Erebus and Night and that they held sway even over Zeus (*q.v.*).

Erechtheus. Son of Pandion and grandson of Erichthonius (*q.v.*) with whom he is sometimes confused or identified. Both were reared by Athene (*q.v.*) and were associated with serpents. Both were mythical kings of Athens. When the Eleusians led by Eumolpus, a son of Poseidon (*q.v.*), invaded Athens, Erechtheus was told by an oracle to sacrifice his daughter Otonia. He did so and her sisters Protogonia and Panora also sacrificed themselves. He slew Eumolpus and was slain by lightning from either Poseidon or Zeus (*q.v.*).

Erichthonius. A son of Hephaestus (*q.v.*) by Athene (*q.v.*). The child was concealed in a chest by the normally chaste Athene and entrusted to the daughters of Cecrops of Athens who were forbidden to open it. However they did so and finding a serpent inside went mad and leaped to their death from the Acropolis (*q.v.*). Erichthonius eventually succeeded Cecrops as King of Athens and was grandfather of Erechtheus. It was said Erichthonius was the founder of the Panathenaean games in honour of Athene and that he was the first man to harness a team of four horses to a single chariot.

Eridanus. An Italian river god, later thought to be the River Po.

Erigone. The daughter of Icarius. Led to her father's grave by his faithful pet hound Maera, she hanged herself from the tree beneath which he lay.

Erinnyes. Three daughters of Mother Earth whom she conceived by the blood of Uranus (*q.v.*) when Cronus (*q.v.*) castrated him. They personified the conscience and were powerful divinities who punished crimes of sacrilege, especially matricide. They pursued Alcmaeon (*q.v.*) and drove Orestes (*q.v.*) mad and into exile. These winged creatures had serpent hair and lived in the Underworld. Their names were Alecto, Magaera and Tisiphone. Orestes was acquitted by Athene (*q.v.*) of matricide following his defence by Apollo (*q.v.*). To pacify the Erinnyes Athene gave them a grotto at Athens where they received libations and sacrifices. Henceforth they were euphemistically referred to as the Eumenides or "kindly ones".

Eriphyle. The sister of Adrastus (*q.v.*) and wife of the seer Amphiarus. Mother of Alcmaeon (*q.v.*). Polynices (*q.v.*) bribed her into persuading Amphiarus into joining the Seven Against Thebes (*q.v.*) despite the seer's prophecy that only Adrastus would survive their expedition. She received the necklace of Harmonia (*q.v.*) for this. Later Thersander bribed her with the magic robe of Harmonia into persuading Alcmaeon to join the Epigoni (*q.v.*). On returning from Thebes Alcmaeon slew her for her selfish deceit.

Eris. A female divinity personifying Quarrels and Strife for the Greeks.

Eros. The Greek god of love, identified with the Roman Cupid (*q.v.*) or Amor. A son of Aphrodite (*q.v.*), whom he often accompanied, by either her father Zeus (q.v.) or Hermes (q.v.). His half-brother was Anteros, son of Aphrodite and Ares (q.v.) who personified mutual love. It was only from the 4th century B.C. onwards that he came to be represented as a winged boy firing arrows of love which could wound both men and gods. (See **Psyche**).

Erymanthian Boar. A giant wild boar from Mt. Erymanthus which was ravaging the region of Psophis until captured by Heracles (q.v.). Whilst performing this task he was given wine made by Dionysus (q.v.) by the centaur Pholus. A dispute broke out with other centaurs, eager as ever for their share of the drink, and in the resulting battle Heracles accidentally wounded his friend Cheiron (q.v.). He caught and chained the boar in a snow drift and delivered it to Eurystheus (q.v.) before going to join the Argonauts (q.v.).

Erysichthon. Son of Triopas. He was punished with an insatiable hunger by the goddess Demeter (q.v.) for felling trees in one of her sacred groves.

Eryx. Mythical Sicilian hero. A son of Venus (q.v.) and a renowned boxer. The mountain near modern Trapani is named after him.

Eteocles. See **Seven Against Thebes.**

Etruscans. See **Section L.**

Eumneus. Born of royal birth but given to Phoenician slave traders, Eumneus' story is told in Book 15 of the *Odyssey*. He became Odysseus' (q.v.) faithful swineherd.

Eumolpus. "The good singer", son of Poseidon (q.v.) and Chione. Chione threw him into the sea at birth but Poseidon saved him and he was raised at the court of King Tegyrius of Thrace before becoming a priest of Demeter (q.v.) and Persephone (q.v.) at Eleusis. Here he initiated Heracles (q.v.) into the mysteries and taught the hero the lyre. He later made war on Athens and was slain by Erechtheus (q.v.). His descendants became hereditary priests of the Eleusian mysteries.

Euphorbus. Son of Panthous, a Trojan who wounded Patroclus (q.v.) before he was slain by Hector (q.v.).

Euphrosyne. One of the Charities or Graces (q.v.).

Euripides. See **Section B.**

Europa. Daughter of Agenor and Telephassa and a grand-daughter of Poseidon (q.v.). While she was on the sea-shore Zeus (q.v.) appeared in the form of a white bull and when she jumped on his back carried her off to Crete where he fathered three sons on her, Minos (q.v.), Rhadamanthus (q.v.) and Sarpedon (q.v.). The Cretan king married her and adopted the children. Zeus gave her a necklace fashioned by Hephaestus (q.v.) which rendered the wearer irresistibly beautiful.

Eurystheus. A grandson of Perseus (q.v.). He was conceived shortly after Heracles (q.v.) but when Zeus (q.v.) boasted that Heracles would rule the House of Perseus, Hera (q.v.) in her jealousy extracted a promise from Zeus that the next son born to the House of Perseus would be its ruler. She then delayed the birth of Heracles until after that of Eurystheus. Later, after Heracles had slain his children in a fit of madness he was told by the oracle to serve Eurystheus in order to be cleansed of guilt. Eurystheus, a cowardly and contemptible creature, set him twelve labours. After Heracles' death he decided to expel the Heracleidae (q.v.) or descendants of Heracles from Greece but they sheltered at Athens. Eurystheus attacked the city but was resisted by Theseus (q.v.), Iolaus (q.v.) and Hyllus (q.v.). An oracle demanded the sacrifice of one of Heracles' children and Macaria slew herself. Eurystheus was then defeated and slain by Alcmene.

Eurus. The South-East wind, son of Astraeus (q.v.) and Eos.

Euryale. One of the Gorgons (q.v.).

Eurydice. The wife of Orpheus (q.v.). She died from a snake bite and Orpheus followed her to the Underworld. Hades (q.v.) delighted by Orpheus' lyre playing allowed him to take her back to life provided he did not look back. Unfortunately at the gates of the Underworld the anxious Orpheus could no longer resist the temptation to gaze on her beauty nor acquiesce in her accusations of indifference. He turned round to see her and she was lost to him.

Eurytus. See **Deianeira.**

Euterpe. Muse of music and lyric poetry.

Evadne. The daughter of Iphis and wife of Capaneus who killed herself on the funeral pyre of the Seven against Thebes (q.v.).

Evander. A mythical king of Arcadia who settled in Italy on the future site of Rome.

Evenus. The father of Marpessa. When Idas carried her off he drowned himself in the river which henceforth bore his name.

F

Fates. The personifications of impersonal destiny who sometimes seem to control even Zeus (q.v.), at others merely to perform his will. The concept developed of three Molrae (*Latin Parcae*) daughters of Zeus and Themis (q.v.), or of Erebus (q.v.) and Night. The first, Clotho, spins the thread of life, Lachesis measures it, and Atropus cuts it. With Hermes (q.v.) they composed the Alphabet.

Faunus. An Italian god of the flocks, herds and wild countryside, later identified with Pan (q.v.). In this context he was half-human, half-goat and lived in Arcadia (q.v.). He had a shrine on the Palatine Hill. He is sometimes regarded not as one god but as numerous spirits of the woods or "fauns".

Faustulus. A kindly shepherd who, with his wife Acca Larentia, raised Romulus (q.v.) and Remus (q.v.). His name relates to Faunus (q.v.) and his wife's to Lares (q.v.) respectively the pastoral god of Latium and the tutelary deities of the Roman home. Up to Cicero's time Romans proudly pointed to a hut on the Palatine which was said to be that where Faustulus raised Romulus but, embarrassingly, a hut with similar claims also stood on the Capitol.

Fidius. Dius Fidius was a name for Jupiter (q.v.) as guarantor of Good Faith.

Flora. Italian goddess of flowers and the spring, worshipped at Rome from the mid 3rd century B.C. Ovid tells us the April festival in her honour, "Ludi Florales" was one of drunken boisterousness. As an earth nymph called Chloris she was pursued by Zephyr (q.v.) and changed into Flora whose breath spread flowers across the fields. The scene has been a subject for Botticelli, Titian and Poussin.

Fortuna. Roman goddess identified with Tyche (q.v.).

Fortunate Isles. See **Elysium.**

G

Gaea or Ge. The "Earth" who sprang from Chaos (q.v.). She was mother of Uranus (q.v.), the heavens, and Pontus the sea. By Uranus she was mother of the Hecatoncheires (q.v.), the Cyclopes (q.v.), the Titans (q.v.) and Themis (q.v.). When Uranus condemned the Cyclopes to Tartarus (q.v.) she instigated rebellion by the Titans and gave Cronus (q.v.) the flint sickle with which he castrated Uranus. From the blood which fell on her she bore Erinnyes (q.v.) and from the blood which fell into the sea came Aphrodite (q.v.). By Tartarus she was mother of Typhon (q.v.). She gave Hera (q.v.) a tree of golden apples which was guarded by the Hesperides (q.v.). The Romans identified her with their own earth goddess Tellus.

Gaetulians. A mythical savage tribe which the Romans placed in North Africa.

Galatea. (1) A sea nymph who loved the Sicilian shepherd Acis (q.v.). She was pursued by the Cyclops Polyphemus and to escape him threw herself into the sea off Sicily. She turned Acis into a river.

(2) See **Pygmalion.**

Ganymede. The most handsome of youths, the son of Tros (q.v.) and Callirhoë. Zeus (q.v.) loved the youth and taking the form of an eagle carried him off to become cup-bearer of the gods, leaving Tros two white horses in compensation. A subject for Correggio, Rubens, and Rembrandt.

Garamantians. Mythical North African tribe appearing in the *Aenead* (q.v.).

Ge. See **Gaea.**

Geryon. A three-bodied monster living on the island of Erythia far to the west of the known world.

Here he kept cattle guarded by Eurytion, son of Ares (q.v.) and Orthrus (q.v.). Heracles (q.v.) was sent to steal the cattle by Eurystheus (q.v.) and on his way to Erythia erected the "Pillars of Hercules" (q.v.), before sailing, on a boat provided by Helios (q.v.), to the island. He overcame Eurytion, Orthrus and Geryon and fetched the cattle to Eurystheus.

Giants (Gigantes). (1) The sons of Ge (q.v.) and Uranus (q.v.), twenty-four giants with serpents' tails who, to avenge the imprisonment of their brothers the Titans (q.v.), attacked the gods on Mt. Olympus (q.v.). Their leader was Alcyoneus and their ranks included Porphyrion, Ephialtes, Pallas, Minas, Enceladus and Polybotes. The gods finally triumphed due to the help of Heracles (q.v.) and the giants were buried under various volcanoes in punishment.

(2) In another version two giants, Ephialtes and Otus, the sons of Iphimedeia and Poseidon (q.v.), but called the Aloeidae after the name of Iphimedeia's husband Aloeus, attacked Olympus. At an early age the two imprisoned Ares (q.v.), then swearing to rape Hera (q.v.) and Artemis (q.v.) they stacked Mt. Pelion on top of Mt. Ossa in order to climb to the heavens. But Artemis lured them to Naxos and disguised as a doe leapt between them and they slew each other by accident. In Hades (q.v.) they were tied by vipers to a pillar back to back.

Glauce. Or Creusa, daughter of Creon. For her Jason (q.v.) forsook Medea (q.v.) and in revenge the sorceress sent Glauce a garment which enveloped her in flames and also killed Creon.

Glaucus. (1) King of Corinth, son of Sisyphus and Merope and father of Bellerophon (q.v.). He fed his horses on human flesh but Aphrodite (q.v.) caused them to devour Glaucus himself because he mocked her.

(2) His great-grandson, the grandson of Bellerophon who fought for the Trojans and was slain by Ajax (q.v.).

(3) The son of Minos (q.v.) and Pasiphaë (q.v.) who was drowned in a barrel of honey. The seer Polyides found the corpse and was entombed with the boy for failing to restore him. Both were saved when a serpent revealed a magic herb which resurrected Glaucus.

(4) A Boeotian fisherman who pursued Scylla (q.v.) and was turned into a sea god on eating a magic herb.

Golden Age. A concept of Hesiod's who lists four ages of man in his Works and Days: golden, silver, bronze and iron. Horace, Virgil, and Ovid also refer to it. A tranquil time when Cronus (q.v.) ruled as the ideal king.

Golden Bough. A gift Aeneas (q.v.) had to take to Proserpina (q.v.) before he could enter the Under world. Also associated with the cult of Diana (q.v.) at Aricia where a runaway slave had to break the bough from a sacred tree before killing the priest and taking his place. Subject of a painting by J. W. M. Turner.

Gordian Knot. Gordius was a peasant who was acclaimed king of Phrygia by the inhabitants when he appeared in a wagon. An oracle had prophesied that the new king would appear thus. In thanksgiving he dedicated the cart to Zeus (q.v.) in the acropolis of Gordium. An oracle prophesied that he who untied the complex knot joining the yoke and pole would rule all Asia. It was eventually severed by Alexander the Great

Gorgons or **Gorgones.** Three beautiful sisters, Medusa (q.v.), Stheno and Euryale, daughters of Phorcys and Ceto. Medusa slept with Poseidon (q.v.) in a temple of Athene (q.v.) and was transformed into a winged monster with serpent hair and brazen claws by the goddess as punishment. She could turn those who looked on her to stone. The Gorgons were sisters of the Graeae (q.v.). See also Perseus.

Graces (also **Gratiae**). See **Charities.**

Graeae. Sisters of the Gorgons (q.v.) who lived on Mt. Atlas. The three old women possessed only one eye and one tooth which they shared, passing them from one to the other. Perseus (q.v.) stole the eye and thus forced them to reveal the whereabouts of Medusa (q.v.) and also of the Stygian nymphs who gave him the winged sandals, magic wallet and helmet of Hades (q.v.) which Hermes (q.v.) said he needed in order to slay Medusa.

Gyes or **Gyges.** One of the Hecatoncheires (q.v.).

H

Hades. (1) The son of Cronus (q.v.) and Rhea (q.v.) brother of Zeus (q.v.) and Poseidon (q.v.). The Cyclopes (q.v.) gave him a helmet of darkness which made him invisible. When he and his brothers threw lots for their kingdoms Hades won the Underworld, home of the dead. His name was later extended to his realm itself. He was one of the few gods to like Ares (q.v.) and Hermes (q.v.) was his herald, conducting the shades of the dead to the Underworld. Because his name was too dread to mention he was often called "Pluto" (q.v.). No favours were expected of him so no temples were dedicated to him. He abducted Persephone (q.v.) and also chased the nymph Minthe (whom the jealous Persephone turned into a mint plant) and Leuce, who was turned into a white poplar.

(2) His realm, the Underworld, land of the dead. Its deepest reaches were called Tartarus (q.v.). Hades and Persephone ruled over it. Persephone was accompanied by Hecate (q.v.). There were five rivers in Hades, the Styx, Acheron, river of woe, Phlegethon, river of flame, Lethe, river of forgetfulness and Cocytus river of wailing. Three judges Minos (q.v.), Aeacus (q.v.) and Rhadamanthus (q.v.) decided on what would happen to souls, sending the evil for punishment, the virtuous to Elysium (q.v.) and those who had led indifferent lives to the drab asphodel fields.

Harmonia. The daughter of Ares (q.v.) and Aphrodite (q.v.) and the wife of Cadmus (q.v.). The gods attended their wedding and Aphrodite gave her the necklace which Zeus (q.v.) had given to Europa (q.v.). It had been made by Hephaestus (q.v.) and conferred irresistible beauty on the wearer. Athene (q.v.) gave her a robe which conferred divine dignity on its possessor. The couple had three children, Autonoe, Ino and Semele (q.v.). After Cadmus had resigned his throne to Pentheus (q.v.) the couple left Thebes and were eventually, in the form of serpents, received in Elysia (q.v.). The necklace and robe were later used to bribe Eriphyle.

Harpalyce. A mythical princess of Thrace, a fierce warrior and huntress.

Harpies (Greek "snatchers"). Originally spirits of the wind, in Homer they appear to carry people off to their death. Later they are portrayed as winged monsters with women's heads and claws, sent by the gods to torment mortals. They snatched and carried off people for their food.

Hebe. A personification of the Greek word for youth, the daughter of Zeus (q.v.) and Hera (q.v.). She was cupbearer to the gods until replaced by Ganymede (q.v.). Her Roman counterpart was Juventas. She married Heracles (q.v.) after his apotheosis.

Hecabe or **Hecuba.** The second wife of Priam (q.v.) who bore him 19 sons including Hector (q.v.) and Paris (q.v.). By Apollo (q.v.) the mother of Troilus (q.v.). Taken as a slave by Odysseus (q.v.) when Troy (q.v.) fell. Priam had entrusted their youngest son Polydorus, plus much gold, to Polymester, king of the Thracian Chersonese. He had murdered Polydorus and thrown his body into the sea. When Odysseus took her to the Thracian Chersonese she found the body, killed Polymester and his two sons, and escaped in the form of a bitch, Maera.

Hecate. An ancient goddess, later closely associated with Artemis (q.v.). Originally she was venerated by women, she was powerful in Heaven, Earth and the Underworld. But primarily she was seen as a goddess of the Underworld and companion of Persephone (q.v.). She was represented holding torches and accompanied by wolves. She was most formidable at the full moon with which she was associated. A practitioner of sorcery her image was worshipped at crossroads where she was portrayed with three heads or three bodies.

Hecatoncheires. The sons of Ge (q.v.) and Uranus (q.v.), three 100-handed giants called Cottus, Gyges or Gyges and Briareus or Aegaeon.

Hector. The eldest son of Priam (q.v.), Trojan hero of the Trojan War. Husband of Andromache (q.v.) and father of Astynax. He fought the great Ajax (q.v.) until nightfall when the two exchanged gifts. He slew Patroclus and in turn was slain by Achilles (q.v.) who dragged his body round the walls of Troy (q.v.). Priam begged for the corpse and his funeral is the closing scene of Homer's *Iliad*. A chivalrous warrior.

Helen. The daughter of Leda (*q.v.*) by Zeus (*q.v.*), hatched from an egg, and the sister of Clytemnestra (*q.v.*), Castor and Polydeuces (*q.v.*) (known as the Dioscuri). She was raised at the court of Leda's husband, Tyndareus of Sparta. As a child she was abducted by Theseus (*q.v.*) and Pirithous (*q.v.*) but being too young to marry, was left with Theseus' mother Aethra. The Dioscuri rescued her and Aethra became her slave. The most beautiful of women she had many suitors who swore to defend her chosen husband, Menelaus (*q.v.*). She was taken by Paris (*q.v.*) to Troy (*q.v.*) thus causing the Trojan war (*q.v.*) and "launching a thousand ships" (of the Greeks who went to reclaim her). When Paris died Helenus (*q.v.*) and Deiphobus quarrelled for her, the latter torcibly marrying her. By then she was homesick for Sparta and when Odysseus (*q.v.*) entered Troy in disguise told him so and gave him information useful to the Greek cause. When Troy fell Deiphobus was killed and mangled by Odysseus and Menelaus, but when Menelaus chased her, sword drawn, to punish her, she calmed him by baring her breast. In the *Odyssey* she was reconciled to Menelaus and became a domesticated and faithful wife. She bore him a daughter, Hermione. It appears that Helen may have been a pre-Greek goddess associated with birds and trees. Various tales are told of her. Stesichorus says that only her phantom went to Troy: the real Helen went to Egypt. Another legend says that at her death she was carried off to live eternally with Achilles (*q.v.*) on a "white isle". Others suggest that her mother was not Leda but Nemesis (*q.v.*).

Helenus. The son of Priam (*q.v.*) and Hecabe (*q.v.*), twin of Cassandra (*q.v.*) and a prophet. He quarrelled with his brother Deiphobus over Helen (*q.v.*) and when the latter forcibly married her fled Troy (*q.v.*) and was captured by Odysseus (*q.v.*). Calchas (*q.v.*) had said that only Helenus knew the secret oracles of how Troy would fall. He told Odysseus that the city would be taken in the summer if a bone of Pelops (*q.v.*) were brought to the Greeks, if Neoptolemus (*q.v.*) joined them, and if the Palladium (*q.v.*) were stolen. These things were done. After the war he was taken by Neoptolemus and prophesied a safe route home for him. When Neoptolemus settled in Epirus he gave part of the kingdom to Helenus who married Andromache (*q.v.*).

Helicon. A mountain in Boeotia (*q.v.*) sacred to Apollo (*q.v.*) and inhabited by the Muses (*q.v.*) who were thus called respectively Heliconides and Heliconides.

Helios. Equates to the Roman "Sol", a Titan later identified with Hyperion and Apollo (*q.v.*), though some traditions make him the son of Hyperion and Theia. A sun-god, his chariot was drawn across the sky each day by four horses and at night he returned to the east floating on the stream of Ocean, which surrounded the earth, in a large cup. The husband of Rhode by whom he had seven sons and a daughter, Pasiphaë. He was father of Phaeton (*q.v.*) by Clymene and of Circe (*q.v.*) by Perse. He reputedly saw all, but missed Odysseus' (*q.v.*) men stealing his cattle. When he shone too brightly Odysseus (*q.v.*) fired an arrow at him. Admiring the hero's boldness he lent him his cup or boat with which to travel to Erythia. It was he who told Demeter (*q.v.*) that Hades (*q.v.*) had abducted Persephone (*q.v.*).

Hellas, Hellenes, Hellenism. The Greeks of the classical period termed themselves Hellenes and their country Hellas (in contrast to Homer's "Achaeans"). They traced their common descent from Hellen (*q.v.*) an eponymous hero. In modern times Hellenism refers to the culture flourishing in Greece, the Aegean isles, the Ionian coast of Asia Minor and Magna Graecia between the first Olympiad in 776 B.C. and the death of Alexander the Great in 323 B.C.

Hellen. Eponymous ancestor of the Greeks or Hellenes (*q.v.*), the son of Pyrrha and Deucalion (*q.v.*). His sons were Aeolus, Dorus and Xuthus.

Hephaestus. One of the Olympian gods, the son of Zeus (*q.v.*) and Hera (*q.v.*). The god of fire and metal work, known to the Romans as Vulcan (*q.v.*). He was hated by Hera because he was lame and she threw him down from Olympus and he landed in the sea where Thetis (*q.v.*) and Eurynome cared for him. Nine years later Hera

accepted him back but Zeus, angry with him for taking Hera's side in a quarrel, again cast him down. He was a day falling and landed on Lemnos. On returning to Olympus he sought to keep the peace between Zeus and Hera. The other gods always laughed at his lameness. His workshop was said to be on Olympus or else in Sicily, where the Cyclopes (*q.v.*) helped him in his labours. He made palaces for all the gods, the necklace of Harmonia (*q.v.*), the armour of Achilles (*q.v.*) and a wide variety of other wonderful articles. He was married either to Charis or to Aphrodite (*q.v.*) who deceived him with Ares (*q.v.*).

Hera. The Roman Juno, daughter of Cronus (*q.v.*) and Rhea (*q.v.*), sister and wife of Zeus (*q.v.*). A pre-Hellenic goddess, originally having power over all living things and vegetable life, she gradually lost these functions and eventually was only the goddess of marriage and childbirth. She was the mother of Ares (*q.v.*), Hephaestus (*q.v.*), Hebe (*q.v.*) and Ilythia (*q.v.*) by Zeus. Her virginity was renewed annually by bathing in a magical spring near Argos. Though she was the goddess of marital fidelity she had difficulty controlling the amorous adventures of her own husband (who had wooed her in the form of a cuckoo) and was violently jealous of his many affairs and cruel to her rivals and their offspring, *e.g.* Semele, Leto, Alcmene and Heracles. She once led a conspiracy against Zeus in which Poseidon (*q.v.*) and Apollo (*q.v.*) participated. Zeus was enchained and when he was freed he punished her by suspending her from the sky by the wrists with an anvil on each ankle. She helped Jason (*q.v.*) but was opposed to the Trojans because Paris (*q.v.*) did not give her the apple of discord. Her name means simply "lady".

Heracleidae. The children of Heracles (*q.v.*). Eurystheus (*q.v.*) attempted to expel them from Greece but failed.

Heracles. A hero who later became a god, a figure popular all over Greece and in Italy where the Romans knew him as Hercules. The son of Alcmene (*q.v.*) and Zeus (*q.v.*) and half-brother of Iphicles (*q.v.*). Alcmene fearing Hera's (*q.v.*) jealousy exposed him but by mistake Hera nursed him. After he had been returned to his mother Hera sent two snakes to kill him in his cradle, but he strangled them. He was taught to fight by Castor (*q.v.*), to play the lyre by Eumalpus, to wrestle by Autolycus (*q.v.*) and the art of archery by Eurytus. Linus also tried to teach him to play the lyre but, when he censured his awkward pupil, Heracles killed him with his own instrument. Amphitrion (*q.v.*) then sent him to keep cattle. At the age of 18, after a 50 day banquet he killed a huge lion on Mt. Cithaeron because it had been ravaging the herds of Amphitrion and Thespius. He did this with a wild olive club and later wore the pelt everywhere, though some other sources say he wore the pelt of the Nemean lion. In reward Thespius gave him his 50 daughters. At Thebes he defeated the Minyan heralds of Orchomenus who had come to demand tribute. Creon, king of Thebes, rewarded him by giving him his daughter Megara or Megera who bore him several children. His half-brother Iphicles married Creon's youngest daughter. Hera now made him mad and he killed his own children and two of Iphicles'. At Delphi the Pythia (*q.v.*), calling him Heracles for the first time, sent him to serve, for 12 years, his wretched cousin Eurystheus (*q.v.*) in order to purify himself of the murder. At the end of that time he would become immortal. With his nephew Iolaus (*q.v.*) as companion he embarked on 12 labours set by Eurystheus. These were to fetch the pelt of the Nemean lion, to kill the Hydra of Lerna (*q.v.*), to capture alive the Ceryneian Hind (*q.v.*), to capture alive the Erymanthian Boar (*q.v.*), to cleanse the stables of Augeas (*q.v.*), to drive off the Stymphalian Birds (*q.v.*), to capture the Cretan Bull (*q.v.*), to fetch the horses of Diomedes (*q.v.*), to fetch the girdle of Hippolyte (*q.v.*), to steal the cattle of Geryon (*q.v.*), to fetch the golden apples of the Hesperides (*q.v.*) and to bring back Cerberus (*q.v.*). After capturing the Erymanthian Boar he had joined the Argonauts (*q.v.*) but his squire Hylas was spirited off by the Naiads (*q.v.*) while fetching water at Cios in Mysia and Heracles left the expedition to search for him. Having completed his service for Eurystheus he returned to Thebes and here gave Megara to Iolaus. But Hera again drove him mad and he killed Megara and her children. Some traditions say he also killed himself and his family. He now desired to marry Iole daughter of his friend Eurytus of Oechalia and won her in an archery contest. But Eurytus refused to surrender her because Heracles had slain his own children. The incident ended in Heracles killing Iphitus (q.v.) but he later seized Iole. To purify himself of this murder he went to serve Omphale (q.v.). After serving her he and Telamon saved Hesione, daughter of Laomedon (q.v.) and sacked Troy (q.v.). Heracles gave Hesione to Telamon and ransomed Priam (q.v.). Next he made war on Augias and Neleus (q.v.) and then on Hippocoon who had helped Neleus. In this he was assisted by Cepheus (q.v.) and he restored Tyndareus (q.v.). At this time he seduced the priestess Auge, daughter of Aleus king of Tegea, who bore him a son, Telephus. Now he married Deianeira (q.v.) who inadvertently caused his death. As Heracles ascended his funeral pyre, to be burned alive he gave his bow and quiver to Philoctetes (q.v.) who kindled the flame but thunderbolts demolished the pyre and he was carried on a cloud to Olympus. Here he was reconciled to Hera (q.v.) and married Hebe (q.v.), himself becoming an immortal. Numerous other legends concerning Heracles exist. We are told he rescued Alcestis (q.v.), helped the gods defeat the Giants (q.v.), defeated Antaeus (q.v.) and, when the Delphic Oracle would not give him an answer seized the sacred tripod and struggled with Apollo (q.v.) for it. Xenophon tells us that before beginning his adventures Heracles was confronted by two beautiful women, one offering a life of ease, the other of service to mankind and he had to choose between the two. Other writers tell of him having to choose between two roads offering similar alternatives to the women. From a mighty and boisterous hero the picture of Heracles gradually developed into a morality tale of selfless service and fortitude eventually rewarded and for this reason the Stoic philosophers of Rome idealised him.

Hercules. See Heracles.

Hermaphroditus. The son of Hermes (q.v.) and Aphrodite (q.v.) who refused the advances of the nymph Salmacis. Her request that their bodies be joined in one was then granted by the gods. The name gives us the word "hermaphrodite", a being with the characteristics of both sexes.

Hermes. The Roman Mercury. Originally a god of fertility. The son of Zeus (q.v.) and Maia, daughter of Atlas (q.v.). He was born on Mt. Cyllene (hence he was sometimes referred to as Cyllenius). While still hours old he left the cradle and stole Apollo's (q.v.) cattle. He invented the lyre by stringing a tortoise shell with cow-gut and gave it to Apollo. This calmed Apollo's wrath and the two became friends. Zeus made him messenger of the gods and gave him his winged sandals (the Alipes), broad-brimmed hat (the Petasus) and herald's staff (caduceus) originally entwined with two white ribbons, later represented as entwined snakes. He conducted the souls of the dead to Hades (q.v.) and in this role was known as Psychopompus. The patron of travellers, traders and thieves and the father of Autolycus the thief, by Chione, and of Echion herald of the Argonauts (q.v.). He was the father of Pan (q.v.) by Penelope (q.v.) and a companion of the Muses (q.v.). He helped the Fates compose the alphabet, invented the musical scale, weights and measures and olive cultivation. A god of dice games. As herald he was eloquent and in Acts ch. XIV St. Paul, who spoke in tongues more than any man, is mistaken for him.

Hermione. The daughter of Helen (q.v.) and Menelaus (q.v.). Betrothed by Tyndareus (q.v.) to Orestes (q.v.) but given to Neoptolemus (q.v.) by Menelaus.

Hero. A priestess of Aphrodite (q.v.) at Sestos. Her lover Leander (q.v.) used to swim the Hellespont each night to see her but drowned when a storm extinguished the light she used to guide him. She then drowned herself. The subject of a play by Marlowe and paintings by Rubens and Turner.

Herodotus. See Section B.

Heroes. To the Greeks a hero was the son of a mortal or divinity who was essentially superior to other men. They were venerated and received sacrifices because they were believed to help the living. Thus Theseus (q.v.) was supposed to have helped the Athenians at Marathon. "Heroic poetry" was epic poetry, telling of their deeds.

Hesiod. See Section B.

Hesperides. "The daughters of evening" who lived in a land at the end of the world, far to the west. These maidens guarded a tree belonging to Hera (q.v.) which bore golden apples. They were assisted by a dragon, Ladon. Ge (q.v.) had given the tree to Hera on her wedding day. On the advice of Prometheus (q.v.) Heracles (q.v.) (who had been sent to get the apples by Eurystheus (q.v.)) persuaded Atlas (q.v.) to fetch three apples while he shouldered Atlas' burden. Atlas then refused to take the sky back on his shoulders but Heracles tricked him into doing so. On his return journey Heracles slew Antaeus (q.v.). Eurystheus gave the apples back to Heracles and he passed them to Athene to return to the Hesperides.

Hesperus. The evening star, the Greek form of the Latin vesper or evening.

Hestia. The sister of Zeus (q.v.) and Hera (q.v.), the goddess of the hearth worshipped by every family. Though Poseidon (q.v.) and Apollo (q.v.) tried to seduce her she swore to Zeus always to remain a virgin. The Romans worshipped her counterpart, the goddess Vesta (q.v.).

Hippodamia. (1) The daughter of Oenomaus, king of Elis. An oracle said he would die at the hands of his son-in-law so he challenged all her suitors to a chariot race. Victory meant they could marry Hippodamia, defeat meant death. His horses were the gifts of his father Ares (q.v.). However Pelops (q.v.) engineered his death and married Hippodamia.
(2) The wife of Pirithous (q.v.). When a drunken centaur (q.v.) abducted her on her wedding day the battle between the Lapithae (q.v.) and Centaurs occurred.

Hippolyte. A queen of the Amazons (q.v.) and sister of Antiope. Heracles (q.v.) had to fetch her golden girdle for Eurystheus. At first he was well received but Hera (q.v.) stirred the Amazons against him and in the fight he slew Hippolyte and took the girdle. Returning home he saved Laomedon's (q.v.) daughter Hesione. Another legend says Theseus (q.v.) abducted Hippolyte who bore him the son Hippolytus (q.v.).

Hippolytus. The son of Theseus (q.v.) and the Amazon Hippolyte (q.v.) or her sister Antiope (q.v.). When Theseus married again to Phaedra (q.v.), sister of Ariadne (q.v.), Phaedra fell in love with her stepson and committed suicide when he refused her. She left a note falsely accusing Hippolytus. Theseus prayed to Poseidon (q.v.) who was under an obligation to him, that Hippolytus would die the same day. Poseidon then sent a sea-monster which scared the youth's horses and he was dragged to death behind his chariot.

Homer. See Section B.

Horae. The "hours", three daughters of Zeus (q.v.) and Themis (q.v.) and tutelary goddesses of nature and the seasons. They were bound to the soil and promoted fertility. Thus they were important and are involved in solemn oaths. However they rarely appear except in attendance on other gods and have no "adventures".

Horatii. Three Roman brothers whose tale is told by Livy. In the mid 7th century B.C. while Rome was ruled by Tullus Hostilius the city of Alba Longa (q.v.) was destroyed and its population transferred to Rome. According to legend the Horatii challenged the three Alban champions, the Curatii, to a sword battle. Two Horatii were killed but the third slew all the Curatii. On returning to Rome he met his sister, who had been engaged to one of the Curatii, weeping. He stabbed her to death. After ceremonies of expiation Tullus acquitted him of murder.

Horatius Cocles. Another of the Horatii family, the "one-eyed" (Cocles). In the 6th century B.C. he held the Etruscans at bay on the wooden Sublican bridge into Rome until it was pulled down beneath him. He then swam the Tiber to safety. The subject of a Lay by Macaulay.

Hyacinthus. A Peloponnesian youth loved by Apollo (q.v.) who was killed when the jealous Zephyrus (q.v.) diverted a discus to hit him. From his blood sprang the "hyacinth" flower. He had a shrine at Amyclae in Laconia and a three-day festival, the Hyacinthia, was held in his honour at Sparta.

Hyades. Nymphs who cared for Dionysus (q.v.) as a child on Mt. Nysa. Zeus (q.v.) placed their images in the sky as the "rain stars", part of the constellation of Taurus which rises at midnight in the rainy season.

Hydra of Lerna. The "water snake", offspring of Echidne (q.v.) and Typhon (q.v.) and raised by

Hera (*q.v.*). It was a monster with the body of a dog and 9 serpent heads. Heracles (*q.v.*) was sent to kill it by Eurystheus (*q.v.*). It lived at the source of the River Amymone in the swamp of Lerna. As Heracles lopped off a head two more grew. He also had to crush a giant crab which Hera placed among the signs of the zodiac. Finally he crushed the Hydra's heads with his club and Iolaus (*q.v.*) burned them to stop them regrowing. He dipped his arrows in the beast's blood thereby making them poisonous.

Hygeia. The wife or daughter of Asclepius (*q.v.*), a goddess of health.

Hylas. *See* Heracles.

Hyllus. The son of Heracles (*q.v.*) and Deianeira (*q.v.*). He conducted Heracles to his funeral pyre. Either he or Iolaus (*q.v.*) defeated Eurystheus (*q.v.*) Eventually he was slain by Echemus, king of Tegea.

Hymen. God of weddings.

Hyperboreans. A mythical race living far to the north, behind Boreas (*q.v.*) i.e. at the place where the north wind originates. Apollo (*q.v.*) spent time with them before going to Delphi and spent the winter months with them. A Hyperborean soothsayer, Olen, installed Apollo's oracle at Delphi. Their land was supposed to have perpetual sunshine and was a land of plenty, an earthly paradise where men lived in peace and ease on the fruits of the earth. Herodotus tells us that one of their priests, Aburis, travelled the world on a golden arrow and never needed to eat. He places their land in Southern Russia.

Hypenor. One of the Spartii (*q.v.*).

Hyperion. A Titan (*q.v.*) and sun-god, father of Helios (*q.v.*), Selene (*q.v.*) and Eos (*q.v.*), the sun, moon and dawn. In Keats' poem he is the last of the old gods to be deposed, the young Apollo (*q.v.*) taking his place.

Hypermestra. *See* Danaus.

Hypnus. The god of sleep.

I

Iacchus. Alternative name for Dionysus (*q.v.*) used in the Eleusian mysteries where he was regarded as the son of Zeus (*q.v.*) and Demeter (*q.v.*), not Semele (*q.v.*).

Iapetus. A Titan (*q.v.*), father of Prometheus (*q.v.*), Atlas (*q.v.*) and Epimetheus.

Iasion. Or Iasius or Iasus, the son of Zeus (*q.v.*) and Electra (*q.v.*), lover of Demeter (*q.v.*) who bore him a son Pluton. Zeus in his jealousy slew him with a thunderbolt.

Icarius. Father of Erigone. An Athenian to whom Dionysus (*q.v.*) taught cultivation of the vine and who gave wine to a band of shepherds. Mistaking drunkenness for witchcraft they slew him.

Icarus. *See* Daedalus.

Idaea. A nymph, mother of Teucer (*q.v.*) by Scamander (*q.v.*) of Crete.

Idas. The twin of Lynceus and a son of Poseidon (*q.v.*). He abducted Marpessa in a chariot given to him by Poseidon and fought Apollo (*q.v.*) for possession of her. Given the choice by Zeus (*q.v.*) she chose Idas. He and Lynceus took part in the voyage of the Argonauts (*q.v.*) and the hunt of the Calydonian boar (*q.v.*) and were killed in battle with their cousins the Dioscuri (*q.v.*).

Idomeneus. King of Crete who contributed 100 ships to the expedition against Troy (*q.v.*). Virgil adds that on his return from Troy he was caught in a storm and vowed to sacrifice the first person he met to Poseidon (*q.v.*) in return for safe passage. This proved to be his son and the sacrifice brought a pestilence on Crete. Idomeneus was banished to Calabria in Italy.

Ilia. A priestess of Vesta (*q.v.*) also called Rhea Silvia. The mother of Romulus (*q.v.*) and Remus.

Iliad. Homer's epic poem on the siege of Troy (*q.v.*). Although it hints at earlier and later events it covers only a period of weeks in the tenth year of the war, recounting Achilles' (*q.v.*) quarrel with Agamemnon (*q.v.*), the death of Patroclus (*q.v.*) and the death of Hector (*q.v.*). It ends with Achilles returning Hector's (*q.v.*) body to Priam (*q.v.*). Although many gods and heroes appear, Achilles and Hector are the main protagonists.

Ilioneus. An old and venerated Trojan who accompanied Aeneas (*q.v.*).

Ilithyiae. Daughters of Hera (*q.v.*) who helped women

in childbirth. Later only one goddess, Ilithyia, is mentioned in this connection.

Ilus. (1) The son of Tros (*q.v.*) and father of Laomedon (*q.v.*). An ancestor of the Trojans.
(2) Original name of Ascanius (*q.v.*) son of Aeneas (*q.v.*) and Creusa.

Inachus. The first king of Argos, son of Oceanus (*q.v.*) and Tethys. A river was named after him.

Ino. The daughter of Cadmus (*q.v.*) and Harmonia (*q.v.*), sister of Autonoe, Agave, Polydoras, Illyrus and Semele. She helped to rear Dionysus (*q.v.*) and her husband Athamas (*q.v.*) was punished for it by Hera (*q.v.*) who drove him into madness and the murder of his own children. Ino, Autonoe and Agave were Bacchae (*q.v.*) and they slew Pentheus, the son of Agave and heir to Cadmus, for opposing the worship of Dionysus. Ino committed suicide (*see* Athamas) and became a sea deity.

Io. The daughter of Inachus, Zeus (*q.v.*) loved her and turned her into a white heifer to deceive the jealous Hera (*q.v.*). He did not succeed in this and Hera set the hundred-eyed Argus to watch the heifer. But Hermes (*q.v.*) at Zeus' command cut off his head and placed his eyes in the tail of the peacock. He also sent a gadfly whose sting caused Io to wander the earth till she reached Egypt. On her wanderings she gave her name to the Ionian sea and to the Bosphorus ("ford of the cow"). In Egypt Zeus restored her to human form and she bore him a son, Epaphus, an ancestor of Danaus (*q.v.*).

Iobates. *See* Bellerophon.

Iolaus. Son of Iphicles (*q.v.*) and nephew of Heracles (*q.v.*) to whom he was charioteer and constant companion. He helped Heracles kill the Hydra (*q.v.*) and perform his other labours and in return Heracles gave him his wife Megara. He also sent Iolaus as the leader of his sons by the daughters of Thespius to settle in Sardinia.

Iolcus. The kingdom of Jason's (*q.v.*) father Aeson, usurped by his half brothers Pelias and Neleus.

Iole. *See* Deianeira.

Ion. The son of Xuthus and Creusa, brother of Achaeus. In Euripides' play *Ion* he is the son of Creusa and Apollo (*q.v.*) who is carried off to Delphi (*q.v.*), as a baby but is eventually restored to Creusa and adopted by Xuthus. The eponymous ancestor of the Ionian Greeks.

Iphicles. (1) One of the Argonauts (*q.v.*).
(2) The son of Amphitrion (*q.v.*) and Alcmene (*q.v.*) a night younger than Heracles (*q.v.*). The father of Iolaus (*q.v.*). He married the youngest daughter of Creon of Thebes when Heracles married Megara.

Iphigenia. The daughter of Agamemnon (*q.v.*) and Clytemnestra (*q.v.*), sacrificed by her father at Aulis to get a favourable wind for the Greek fleet sailing to Troy (*q.v.*). Euripides cites another tradition in which Artemis (*q.v.*) substituted a doe for Iphigenia at the last moment and carried her off to Tauris. Later Orestes (*q.v.*) found Iphigenia on the Tauric Chersonese and brought her home to Greece.

Iphitus. A son of Eurytus who argued that his father should deliver Iole (*see* Deianeira) to Heracles (*q.v.*). But in a rage Heracles slew him and though purified for the murder was told by an oracle to sell himself into slavery and give the proceeds to Iphitus' family.

Irene. The daughter of Zeus (*q.v.*) and Themis (*q.v.*), goddess of peace and one of the Horae (*q.v.*). The Romans identified her with Pax.

Iris. The personification of the rainbow and, in later myth, a messenger of the gods, particularly Hera (*q.v.*).

Isis. An Egyptian goddess, wife of Osiris and mother of Horus. In Hellenistic times she became one of the most important deities of the Mediterranean world, her cult arriving in Rome by the time of Augustus. Here the features of her worship, Egyptian priests, processions, initiation ceremonies *etc.* were described by Apuleius in his *Golden Ass*. One of her temples is preserved at Pompeii.

Ismene. The daughter of Oedipus (*q.v.*) and Jocasta (*q.v.*). She followed her father and her sister Antigone (*q.v.*) into exile.

Issa. The daughter of Macareus and his sister Canace, beloved by Apollo (*q.v.*).

Isthmian Games. Quadrennial games held at Corinth in honour of Poseidon (*q.v.*).

Ithaca. The island home of Odysseus (*q.v.*), one of the Ionian islands.

Itys, Itylus. *See* **Procne.**

Iulus. A name used for Ascanius (*q.v.*) by Virgil to indicate the descent of the Julian clan from Aeneas (*q.v.*).

J

Janus. A god of beginnings or new ventures, worshipped at Rome. He had a flamen (sacred priest) and was very important but the origin and nature of his worship is obscure. He had two faces and may represent the assimilation of an eastern god and an Etruscan deity. Also associated with doorways and thresholds.

Jason. Son of Aeson, rightful king of Iolcus who was usurped by his half-brothers, Pelias and Neleus. The infant Jason was smuggled out of Iolcus and reared by Cheiron (*q.v.*) while Pelias expelled Neleus and ruled alone. When Jason returned to claim his birthright Pelias sent him to fetch the Golden Fleece from Colchis. This was the fleece of the ram on which Phrixus (*q.v.*) had escaped and which he had given to Aëtes, king of Colchis. Its presence was the cause of Colchis' prosperity and it hung from an oak tree in the grove of Ares (*q.v.*) where a dragon guarded it. After numerous adventures Jason and his Argonauts (*q.v.*) arrived at Colchis and Aëtes promised Jason the fleece if he could yoke two fire-breathing bulls with brazen feet made by Hephaestus (*q.v.*), and sow the grove of Ares with dragons' teeth left by Cadmus of Thebes (*q.v.*). Medea (*q.v.*) the sorceress gave him a fire-proof lotion which allowed him to complete the task and when her father Aëtes refused to give up the fleece, charmed the dragon to sleep while Jason stole it. Pursued by Aëtes the couple escaped when Medea murdered her half-brother Absyrtus and dropped pieces of his corpse into the sea, causing Aëtes to stop and collect them. They were purified for the murder by Circe (*q.v.*). At Iolchus Pelias had forced Aeson to commit suicide and in revenge Medea persuaded Pelias' daughters to boil their father alive pretending it would restore his youth. The couple were banished because of this and went to Corinth. Here Jason abandoned Medea for Glauce (*q.v.*) whom Medea killed. Jason took his own life though one tradition holds he was killed by the falling prow of the Argo (*q.v.*).

Jocasta. Daughter of Menoeceus, wife of Laius king of Thebes and mother of Oedipus (*q.v.*). When her unwitting incest with Oedipus brought a plague on Thebes Menoeceus sacrificed himself in answer to an oracle demanding the life of one of the Sparti (*q.v.*) i.e. a descendant of the "sown men". Jocasta hanged herself when she learned the truth of her marriage to Oedipus.

Jove. Alternative name for Jupiter (*q.v.*).

Juno. Italian goddess of womanhood and childbirth, associated by the Romans with the Greek Hera (*q.v.*) and regarded as the consort of Jupiter (*q.v.*).

Jupiter. Originally an Italian sky-god, later regarded by the Romans as *Dies Pater*—"Father Day", god of the day. Later still identified with Zeus (*q.v.*). His cult was introduced to Rome by the Etruscans and the temple to Jupiter Optimus Maximus (Best and Most High) stood on the Capitol. His *flamen*, the *flamen* Dialis was the most important of the college. He was guarantor of the *imperium* and city of Rome and triumphs were an act of Jupiter worship. Worshipped in various capacities as *Stator* (he who founds or maintains), *Teretrius* (he who strikes), *Ultor* ("Avenger") and *Tonans* ("Thunderer").

Juturna. (1) An Italian goddess of springs and streams.
(2) The sister of Turnus (*q.v.*).

Juventas. Italian goddess identified with Hebe (*q.v.*).

L

Labdacus. Mythical king of Thebes; a descendant of Cadmus (*q.v.*) and an ancestor of Oedipus (*q.v.*).

Lachesis. One of the Fates (*q.v.*).

Laelaps. A fleet-footed hound given to Procris by Cephalus (*q.v.*).

Laertes. The king of Ithaca, father of Odysseus (*q.v.*) by Anticleia, daughter of the thief Autolycus. While Odysseus was at Troy (*q.v.*) Penelope's (*q.v.*) suitors forced him to retire to the country.

Laestrygones. A race of giant cannibals ruled by Lamus. At Telepylos, their capital city, Odysseus (*q.v.*) lost all but one of his twelve ships to them. Homer says their summer nights were so short that shepherds going out with their flocks in the morning met those returning at sunset. Traditionally located in eastern Sicily or at Formiae in central Italy.

Laius. *See* **Oedipus.**

Lamia. One of the Empusae (*q.v.*), daughter of Belus.

Lamus. *See* **Laestrygones.**

Laocoön. A Trojan prophet, son of Antenor and a priest of Apollo (*q.v.*) and Poseidon (*q.v.*). He warned the Trojans against the Wooden Horse (*q.v.*) and flung a spear at it. However he had angered Apollo by breaking his vows of celibacy and the god now sent two sea serpents which crushed him and his two sons. A famous group of statues depicting the scene, carved in Rhodes *c.* 25 B.C., now stands in the Vatican museum. The Trojans disastrously drew the wrong conclusion *viz.* that his death was punishment for striking the horse.

Laodamia. The daughter of Acastus and wife of Protesilaus of Thessaly, the first Greek ashore at Troy (*q.v.*) though he knew from an oracle that the first Greek to land would die. Homer says he left his wife mourning and his house unfinished but Catullus, Virgil and Ovid follow another tradition in which she begged the gods that Protesilaus might return to life for three hours. When he died a second time she committed suicide. Wordsworth's poem *Laodamia* takes the tale as its subject.

Laodice. (1) A daughter of Priam (*q.v.*), sister of Cassandra (*q.v.*) and wife of Helicaon. When Troy (*q.v.*) fell the earth swallowed her.
(2) Alternative name for Electra (*q.v.*), Agamemnon's (*q.v.*) daughter.

Laomedon. The son of Ilus (*q.v.*), king of Troy (*q.v.*) and father of Hesione and Priam (*q.v.*). Apollo (*q.v.*) and Poseidon (*q.v.*) helped him build the walls of Troy and he refused to pay them. Poseidon then sent a sea monster to devour Hesione but Heracles (*q.v.*) saved her. Laomedon then refused to pay Heracles the agreed white horses left by Zeus (*q.v.*) in exchange for Ganymede (*q.v.*). Heracles and Telamon then sacked Troy and slew Laomedon and all his sons save Priam (*q.v.*).

Lapis Niger. Black marble paving in the Roman Forum said to cover the tomb of Romulus (*q.v.*).

Lapithae or **Lapiths.** Mythical tribe of Thessaly, governed by Pirithous, son of Ixion (*q.v.*) and thus half-brothers to the Centaurs (*q.v.*). At the wedding of Pirithous and Hippodamia, attended by Theseus (*q.v.*) a centaur tried to abduct the bride and a famous battle between the Lapithae and Centaurs ensued. It is described by Ovid and is depicted in the Parthenon and the frieze of Apollo's (*q.v.*) temple at Bassae. It is also the subject of a sculptured frieze by Michelangelo

Lares. Originally fertility gods, worshipped by the Romans privately in the home and semi-publicly at crossroads. They were represented as youths with handfuls of fruit who wandered the farmstead incessantly whirling round and round. They kept away maleficent demons and ensured the prosperity of the family home. Each month they received offerings of oat cakes, milk, honey and flowers. Generally associated with the Penates, the spirits who guarded the household stores. Together the guardians of the hearth and home.

Larissa. A city in Thessaly near modern Volos. Reputed birthplace of Achilles (*q.v.*) hence his nickname "the Larissaen".

Lars Porsenna. Legendary Etruscan chief whom Livy tells us besieged Rome on behalf of the exiled Tarquinius Superbus. Lars means "overlord" and he is probably a symbol of Etruscan suzerainty over Rome. (*See* **Horatius Cocles**).

Latinus. Eponymous king of the Latini or Latins in Italy. Hesiod makes him the son of Odysseus (*q.v.*) and Circe (*q.v.*). Virgil makes him the son of Faunus (*q.v.*). Livy and Virgil portray him as opposing the settlement of Aeneas (*q.v.*) and the Trojans in Italy but then agreeing Aeneas should marry his daughter Lavinia. He next helps Aeneas fight Turnus king of the Rutuli, to whom Lavinia had been promised. Livy says he died in battle and Aeneas became king of the Latins; Virgil that he survived to celebrate the marriage and uniting of Latins and Trojans.

Leander. Mythical youth who drowned while swimming to meet Hero (*q.v.*).

Leda. Daughter of Thestius and wife of Tyndareus king of Sparta. Seduced by Zeus (*q.v.*) in the form of a swan she gave birth to two eggs, from one of which hatched Helen (*q.v.*) and Polydeuces (*q.v.*) from the other, Castor (*q.v.*) and Clytemnestra (*q.v.*). One tradition says that Helen was the daughter of Nemesis (*q.v.*) who left the egg for Leda to incubate.

Lemnos. A small island at the mouth of the Hellespont, home at one time of a primitive people known to the Greeks as the Pelasgi. Hephaestus (*q.v.*) was said to have landed on the island when Zeus (*q.v.*) hurled him out of heaven and supposedly had a forge here.

Lethe. "Forgetfulness", one of the rivers of the Underworld whose waters induced amnesia in those who drank of them. Virgil holds that here souls forgot their past prior to reincarnation and Ovid says that it flowed round the "cave of sleep". *See also* Niobe.

Leto. Known to the Romans as Latona. The daughter of the Titans (*q.v.*) Coeus and Phoebe and the mother of Apollo (*q.v.*) and Artemis (*q.v.*) by Zeus (*q.v.*). While she carried the unborn gods the jealous Hera (*q.v.*) forced her to wander the earth until she finally gave birth to them at Ortygia, henceforth called Delos (*q.v.*). Hera sent the giant Tityus (*q.v.*) to rape her but her children slew him with their arrows. *See also* Niobe.

Leuce. A nymph loved by Hades (*q.v.*) who turned her into a white poplar tree.

Leucippus. (1) King of Messenia whose daughters Hilaera and Phoebe were abducted by the Dioscuri (*q.v.*) and whose brothers Idas (*q.v.*) and Lynceus (*q.v.*) fought to save them.
(2) The son of Oenomaus who loved Artemis (*q.v.*) To be near her he disguised himself as a nymph but when Apollo (*q.v.*) advised the nymphs to bathe naked he was discovered and torn to pieces by them.

Leucothea. Originally Ino, daughter of Cadmus (*q.v.*) and wife of Athamas who helped Zeus (*q.v.*) save Dionysus (*q.v.*) at the death of Semele (*q.v.*). In revenge Hera (*q.v.*) drove her mad and she leapt into the foaming sea to become the sea deity Leucothea—"the white goddess". In this role she helped Odysseus (*q.v.*) land on Scheria. Her son was Palaemon, a minor sea god.

Liber Pater. An ancient Italian god of the vine, early identified with Bacchus (*q.v.*) by the Romans.

Lichas. The herald of Heracles (*q.v.*) who took the shirt of Deineira (*q.v.*) to him. In his agony Heracles took him by the ankle, swung him round three times and threw him into the Euboean Sea. A lump of human shape which henceforth bore his name.

Linus. (1) The son of Psamathe of Argos and Apollo (*q.v.*). Fearful lest her father learn of her liaison with the god she exposed the baby who was reared by shepherds but later killed by her father's hounds. When her distress revealed her secret her father condemned her to death but Apollo sent a plague to the city which only abated when the Argives propitiated mother and son with dirges called *linoi*.
(2) The son of a Muse who was so gifted musically that the jealous Apollo killed him.
(3) Heracles' (*q.v.*) music tutor whom Heracles slew in a rage with his own lyre.

Lotophagi. ("The Lotus eaters"). A mythical people living on lotus fruit which induced trances and forgetfulness and made the eater lose any desire to return home. They gave the fruit to Odysseus' (*q.v.*) men. Herodotus placed them in western Libya, possibly the island of Jerba.

Luceres. One of the original three tribes into which Rome was divided and which were believed to date back to Romulus (*q.v.*). The other tribes were the Ramnes and Tities.

Lucifer. The "light bringer", the name given to the planet Venus which can be seen before dawn. In the evening sky the Greeks called it Hesperus.

Lucretia. Wife of Tarquinius Collatinus whose rape by Sextus, son of Tarquinius Superbus led her to stab herself in shame. Junius Brutus then swore by her spirit to expel the Tarquins which he did. The story is told by Livy and Ovid and inspired Shakespeare's poem *The Rape of Lucrece* and Brit-

ten's opera *The Rape of Lucretia*. A subject also for Titian, Botticelli, Tintoretto and Veronese.

Lucretius. *See* **Section B.**

Lycaon. A mythical character who tricked Zeus (*q.v.*) by feeding him human flesh. Zeus killed him and all his sons save Nyctinus by lightning or turned them into wolves, hence Lycanthropy.

Lycomedes. The king of Scyros who murdered Theseus (*q.v.*). It was to his court that Thetis (*q.v.*) sent Achilles (*q.v.*), and Lycomedes' daughter Deidamia bore Achilles his son Neoptolemus (*q.v.*).

Lycurgus (1) Mythical king of Thrace who was made blind and mad for opposing the worship of Dionysus (*q.v.*).
(2) Mythical founder of the Spartan constitution and military regime, first mentioned by Herodotus and subject of a *Life* by Plutarch. Some traditions say the Pythia at Delphi gave him the constitution, others that he devised it while in Crete. In Sparta he was worshipped as a god.

Lynceus. (1) *See* Danaus.
(2) Twin of Idas (*q.v.*) noted for his keen eyesight.

Lyrnessus. City near Troy (*q.v.*) sacked by Achilles (*q.v.*).

M

Macareus. *See* Issa.

Macaria. *See* Eurystheus.

Machaon. The son of Asclepius the physician (*q.v.*).

Maenads. *See* Bacchae.

Maia. The daughter of Atlas (*q.v.*) and Pleione, eldest of the Pleiades (*q.v.*) and the most beautiful. By Zeus (*q.v.*) the mother of Hermes (*q.v.*). The Romans identified her with spring and as a nature goddess gave her name to the month of May.

Manes. "The good ones", the Roman name for the spirits of the dead, regarded as a collective divinity, *Di Manes*. On certain days they could leave the Underworld and were capable of great mischief. Thus they demanded propitiatory ceremonies at funerals and on set days when the head of the house, the *paterfamilias*, would go into the night and cast boiled beans to them. The Roman poets applied the term also to the gods of the Underworld and to the Underworld itself.

Marpessa. *See* Idas. The daughter of the river god Evenus.

Mars. Roman god of war, at one time also associated with agriculture. Later completely identified with Ares (*q.v.*).

Marsyas. A Phrygian, in some traditions a silenus (*q.v.*), who found the flute invented and discarded by Athene (*q.v.*). He challenged Apollo (*q.v.*) to a music contest, judged by the Muses (*q.v.*). Apollo won and had him flayed alive. The tears of the woodland spirits and animals which wept for him formed the river Meander.

Medea. The niece of Circe (*q.v.*) and daughter of Aëtes of Colchis some say by Hecate (*q.v.*). She loved Jason (*q.v.*) and helped him steal the Golden Fleece, murdering her half-brother in their escape. Having cut a goat in pieces, boiled them and pulled forth a lamb she persuaded the daughters of Pelias to boil him, causing his death. When Jason left her for Glauce (*q.v.*) she caused her death and slew her sons by Jason. She then escaped in a chariot drawn by winged serpents to Athens. Here she married Aegeus (*q.v.*). When Theseus (*q.v.*) returned she tried to poison him to secure the succession of her own son Medus (*q.v.*) but Aegeus recognised Theseus and saved him. She fled to wander the earth: some say she returned to Colchis and was reconciled to her father, others that she went to Asia Minor where her son gave his name to the Medes. She became an immortal.

Medus. Son of Medea (*q.v.*) and Aegeus (*q.v.*) eponymous ancestor of the Medes.

Medusa. *See* Gorgons. Slain and beheaded by Perseus (*q.v.*) as she slept. From her corpse sprang forth the fully grown Pegasus (*q.v.*) and the warrior Chrysaor.

Megaeia. One of the Erinnyes (*q.v.*).

Megara or **Megaera.** The eldest daughter of Creon of Thebes. Wife of Heracles (*q.v.*) and bore him several children. Later married Iolaus (*q.v.*) though one tradition says Eurystheus tried to kill her and Heracles instead killed Eurystheus. In revenge Hera (q.v.) drove Heracles mad and he killed Megara and his children.

Melampus. Son of Amythaon, a seer who introduced the worship of Dionysus (q.v.) to Greece. He and his brother Bias cured the women of Argos (including the daughter of the king, Proctus) of madness and received two thirds of his kingdom in reward.

Meleager. The son of Oeneus and Althaea. The Fates (q.v.) told his mother he would only die when a certain brand, which was on the fire, was burned. She extinguished and hid it. Meleager was one of the Argonauts (q.v.) and organised the hunt of the Calydonian Boar (q.v.). He fell in love with Atalanta who joined the hunt and having killed the boar himself gave her the hide on the pretext she had touched it first. This set the hunters quarrelling and in the dispute he killed his uncles, brothers of Althaea. She cursed their murderer, not realising the truth, and when she learned the Erinnyes (q.v.) were persecuting him because of the curse burned the brand and committed suicide. Her daughters (save Gorge and Deianeira) were turned into guinea-hens by Artemis. The son of Meleager and Atlanta was Parthenopaeus.

Melpomene. The Muse of Tragedy.

Memnon. The son of Eos (q.v.) and Tithonus, half-brother of Priam (q.v.). The king of Ethiopia who helped the Trojans and killed many Greeks. Achilles (q.v.) met him in single combat while Zeus (q.v.) weighed their fates in the balance. Achilles slew him but Zeus answered his mother's request that he be honoured by having the birds called *Memnonides* rise above his funeral pyre, then fall as a sacrifice. They annually visited his tomb on the Hellespont though one tradition says he survived the war and ruled five generations in Ethiopia before becoming an immortal. The Greeks assumed many monuments, which they called *Memnonia*, were dedicated to him including a huge statue in Egyptian Thebes.

Menelaus. Son of Atreus, younger brother of Agamemnon (q.v.) and husband of Helen (q.v.). When her father chose him from amongst many suitors he made the others swear to help him in any misfortune. He was thus able to summon the Greek forces for the war on Troy (q.v.). At one stage in the war he fought a duel with Paris (q.v.) to decide the war and was winning until Aphrodite (q.v.) carried Paris off. Because he failed to sacrifice to Athene (q.v.) he took eight years to return from Troy to Sparta.

Menoeceus. (1) See Jocasta.

(2) See Seven against Thebes.

Mentor. Friend and adviser of Odysseus (q.v.) who was too old to go to Troy (q.v.) and remained at Ithaca to watch over Odysseus' interests. Athene (q.v.) took his form to guide Telemachus' (q.v.) search for his father. The name is now synonymous with a trusted counsellor.

Mercury. The Roman equivalent of Hermes (q.v.).

Merope. A Pleiad. Wife of Sisyphus.

Metis. Counsellor of the young Zeus (q.v.) and his first wife. Mother of Athene (q.v.). Herself the daughter of Oceanus (q.v.) and Tethys.

Midas. Son of Gordius. See **Gordian Knot.** His hospitality to Silenus (q.v.) led Dionysus (q.v.) to grant him any wish: he wished that all he touched would turn to gold. When even his food became gold he begged to be relieved of his gift—and was—by bathing in the River Pactolus which was henceforth rich in gold. When he judged Pan (q.v.) a better musician than Apollo (q.v.) the latter gave him asses' ears which he hid under his hat. Only his barber knew, but when his barber told a hole in the ground, reeds grew from it which, via the wind, revealed his secret to the world.

Milanion. Husband of Atalanta (q.v.).

Miletus of Crete. The son of Aria and Apollo (q.v.), a beautiful youth over whom Minos (q.v.) and his brothers Rhadamanthus (q.v.) and Sarpedon quarrelled. Miletus chose Sarpedon and to escape Minos' jealousy they fled to Asia Minor where Miletus founded the city Miletus which bore his name.

Minerva. Etruscan goddess of wisdom, the arts and crafts. The Romans identified her with Athene (q.v.).

Minos. The son of Zeus (q.v.) and Europa (q.v.), brother of Rhadamanthus (q.v.) and Sarpedon (q.v.). Ruler of Crete and supported in this by Poseidon (q.v.) who gave him a magnificent white bull. See **Cretan Bull.** He gave Crete her laws and defended the island with the aid of Talos, a brazen

giant with a bull's head. He pursued the nymph Britomartis for nine months but she leapt into the sea. Artemis (q.v.) deified her and the two shared the epithet Dictynna. While besieging Nisa, the port of Megara, Scylla, the daughter of the king Nisus fell in love with Minos and cropped her hair on which Nisus' life depended. She let Minos into the city but he was repulsed by her parricide and deserted the girl who swam after his ship. According to one tradition her father's spirit in the form of an eagle seized her and she was transformed into the Ciris bird; according to another tradition Minos drowned her and she became a fish. Minos married Pasiphaë (q.v.) who bore him Ariadne (q.v.), Androgeos and Phaedra. When Androgeos won all the events at the Panathenaic games Aegeus (q.v.) had him murdered and in revenge Minos extracted a tribute of seven Athenian youths and maidens who were devoured by the Minotaur (q.v.). He was killed by the daughters of Cocalus of Sicily while pursuing Daedalus (q.v.) and became one of the three judges of the Underworld.

Minotaur. Offspring of Pasiphaë (q.v.) and the Cretan Bull (q.v.) which had the head of a bull and body of a man. It lived in a labyrinth devised by Daedalus (q.v.) where it devoured the maidens and youths of Athens delivered in tribute to Minos (q.v.). It was slain by Theseus (q.v.).

Minyans or **Minyae.** Prehistoric inhabitants of Boeotia (q.v.) and Thessaly whose reputed ancestor was Minyas.

Misenus. Trumpeter of Aeneas (q.v.) who was drowned by a Triton (q.v.) and buried in the Bay of Naples at the port which then bore the name Misenum (the modern Capo Miseno). From the time of Agrippa Misenum was a major Roman naval station.

Mithras. An Iranian deity whose worship was developed in Persia and spread throughout the Middle East. Known to the Greeks from the time of Herodotus his worship spread to Rome under the Republic and from the 2nd century A.D. spread throughout the empire. Mithras was linked with astrology and appears to have been linked with the sun following a fight with the sun-god. But the core of his cult was that man or the soul had fallen from grace and that Mithras could bring redemption and thus eternal life. Very popular with the Roman legions. Mithras was the one serious contender with Christianity for religious supremacy. His ritual involved seven stages of initiation and secret ceremonies conducted in underground caves or artificial subterranean chambers such as that found in London. These temples were called mithraea.

Mnemosyne. "Memory", the daughter of Uranus (q.v.) and by Zeus (q.v.) the mother of the Muses (q.v.).

Moirae or **Moerae.** See **Fates.**

Monoecus. "The lone dweller", Latin name for Heracles (q.v.) who was said to have dwelt alone for a time in the region of modern Monte Carlo.

Mopsus. The son of Apollo (q.v.) and Manto, daughter of Teiresias. When he beat Calchas (q.v.) in prophecy Calchas died of grief.

Morpheus. The Greek *Hypnos*. The son of the god of "Sleep". A god who sends dreams and visions of human form. In Ovid's *Metamorphoses*, Sleep sends him to Alcyone (q.v.) in the form of her dead husband.

Musaeus. A mythical poet who succeeded Orpheus (q.v.), the first poet.

Muses or **Musae.** The daughters of Zeus (q.v.) and Mnemosyne (q.v.) who presided over the arts and sciences. Originally three in number, Hesiod later names nine. Clio was muse of history, Euterpe of lyric poetry and music, Thalia of comedy, Melpomene of tragedy, Terpsichore of song and dance, Erato of mime, Polyhymnia or Polymnia of the hymn, Calliope of epic poetry and Urania of astronomy, though the attributions vary.

Myrmidons or **Myrmidones.** Tribe of southern Thessaly which provided Achilles' (q.v.) contingent at Troy.

Myrtilus. The son of Hermes (q.v.). The charioteer of Oenomaus whose death he caused by removing the lynch pin of his chariot and substituting a wax replica. He did this because Pelops (q.v.) had bribed him with the promise of half his kingdom, but instead Pelops flung him into the sea. He cursed the House of Pelops as he died and his father placed him amongst the stars.

N

Naiads or **Naiades**. Fresh-water nymphs in Greek mythology. They carried off Hylas (*q.v.*).

Narcissus. *See* Echo.

Nauplius. A king of Euboea who lured ships returning from Troy (*q.v.*) to their doom on the promontory of Caphareus by lighting misleading fires.

Nausicaa. Daughter of Alcinous, king of the Phaeacians who found Odysseus (*q.v.*) after a shipwreck while playing ball with her friends on the beach. She looked after him and her father gave him a ship.

Nectar. The drink of the Greek gods which conferred immortality.

Neleus. Twin of Pelias (*q.v.*), sons of Poseidon (*q.v.*) and the nymph Tyro. The twins were exposed by their mother but reared by a horse breeder. When Tyro married Cretheus, king of Iolcus, he adopted the boys who were thus half-brothers of Aeson. Pelias then later seized the kingdom, imprisoned Aeson and expelled Neleus who went to Pylus with Bias and Melampus and became its king. He and all twelve of his sons bar Nestor (*q.v.*) were killed by Heracles (*q.v.*) for aiding Augias (*q.v.*) in his war against Heracles.

Nemesis. Greek goddess, daughter of Oceanus. Originally she was envisaged as allotting to men their share of happiness and unhappiness, thereby chastening the over-fortunate. Later she was portrayed as the punisher of crime, the goddess of retribution. Some say she laid the egg from which Helen (*q.v.*), Clytemnestra (*q.v.*) and the Dioscuri (*q.v.*) were born. She had a sanctuary at Rhamnus from around 430 B.C.

Nemi. A lake in the Alban mountains, site of a sanctuary and sacred wood of Diana (*q.v.*).

Neoptolemus. Also called Pyrrhus, a son of Achilles (*q.v.*) and Deidamia. Odysseus (*q.v.*) and Diomedes (*q.v.*) persuaded his grandfather Lycomedes to let him go to Troy (*q.v.*) after his father's death. He was one of the Greeks inside the Wooden Horse. He slew Polites, the son of Priam (*q.v.*) and Hecuba (*q.v.*) before their eyes. He killed Priam at the altar of Zeus, smashed the skull of Astyanax (*q.v.*), Hector's (*q.v.*) child, and sacrificed Polyxena, Priam's daughter, on his father's tomb. He was given Andromache (*q.v.*) but back in Greece married Hermione (*q.v.*) with the blessing of Menelaus (*q.v.*) despite her prior betrothal to Orestes (*q.v.*). When their marriage proved barren he went to Delphi (*q.v.*) to consult the oracle and was slain either by Orestes or the priests of Apollo (*q.v.*).

Nephele. A phantom conjured up by Zeus (*q.v.*) to deceive Ixion. She later married Athamas.

Neptune. Italian sea-god whom the Romans identified with Poseidon (*q.v.*).

Nereids or **Nereides**. Fifty beautiful sea nymphs, the daughters of Nereus (*q.v.*) and Doris, of whom the most famous were Amphitrite (*q.v.*) and Thetis (*q.v.*).

Nereus. An ancient and benevolent sea god, the son of Pontus (the sea) and Ge (*q.v.*). Husband of Doris, the daughter of Oceanus (*q.v.*) by whom he was father of the Nereids (*q.v.*).

Nero. *See* Section B.

Nessus. *See* Deianeira.

Nestor. King of Pylos, only one of Neleus' (*q.v.*) twelve sons spared by Heracles. He participated in the Calydonian Boar (*q.v.*) hunt and the battle of Lapithae (*q.v.*) and Centaurs (*q.v.*). The oldest of the Greeks at Troy (*q.v.*) he was famous for his eloquence and wisdom. The father of Antilochus, a friend of Achilles (*q.v.*) and one of the bravest Greeks at Troy. Nestor was the only Greek to return home without mishap.

Nike. Goddess of Victory, not only in war but in musical and athletic competitions in Hesiod's *Theogony*, the daughter of the Titan Pallas and Styx. A minor deity, later envisaged not as one goddess but as several spirits, represented as young girls with wings who flew across the heavens to carry the crown to the victor. Zeus honoured Nike for helping the Olympian gods in the Titanomachia (*q.v.*). She was sometimes identified with Athene (*q.v.*).

Niobe. Daughter of Tantalus, sister of Pelops (*q.v.*) and wife of Amphion (*q.v.*) by whom she had seven sons and seven daughters (according to Ovid, Homer makes it six of each). She boasted of being superior to Leto (*q.v.*) who only had two children and in revenge Apollo (*q.v.*) slew her sons and Artemis (*q.v.*) her daughters. She wept for nine days and nights and Zeus (*q.v.*) then turned her into a stone on Mt. Sipylus.

Nisus. *See* Minos.

Nomius. "The pasturer", a name given to Pan (*q.v.*), Apollo (*q.v.*) and Hermes (*q.v.*) in their roles as protectors of flocks and pastures.

Notus. The south-west wind, known to the Romans as Auster. The son of Astraeus (*q.v.*) and Eos (*q.v.*).

Numa. The name of two Italian warriors in the *Aeneid*.

Numa Pompilius. Legendary king of Rome. The second king, successor of Romulus (*q.v.*) he was said to have ruled between 717 and 673 B.C. Said to be of Sabine (*q.v.*) origin he reorganised Roman religion under the guidance of Egeria (*q.v.*). He was said to have been initiated into the mysteries of Pythagoras, an obvious anachronism as he predates Pythagoras' 6th century visit to Italy, but his reputed religious reforms signify a new strand in Roman religion, a disinterested search for knowledge as opposed to inspired action. He founded the cult of Janus (*q.v.*), organised the priests in *collegia* and established the flamens, and reorganised the Salii whose war dances in honour of Mars (*q.v.*) reflected a very ancient Italic rite. He also appointed the Pontifex Maximus, a high priest with responsibility for ensuring religious rites were properly performed and for preventing the growth of undesirable foreign cults. He also reformed the Roman calendar to achieve the maximum coincidence of lunar and solar cycles.

Numicius. A sacred river in Latium between Ardea and Lavinium.

Numitor. The grandfather of Romulus (*q.v.*) and Remus (*q.v.*).

Nymphae or **Nymphs.** Minor deities, the spirits of nature. These daughters of Zeus (*q.v.*) were semi-mortal and were generally benevolent, though they could be malevolent particularly to unresponsive lovers. Each was the tutelary deity of a rock, tree, cave or fountain and was better known to the local peasants than the great gods of Olympus (*q.v.*). Lavishly decorated monumental fountains (a "*nymphaeum*") were dedicated to the nymphs by both Greeks and Romans.

Nysa, Mt. Mountain in Libya where, according to tradition, Dionysus (*q.v.*) was raised.

O

Oceanides. Sea nymphs (*q.v.*) of the ocean, daughters of Oceanus (*q.v.*). Hesiod says they were 40 in number.

Oceanus. One of the Titans (*q.v.*), the son of Ge (*q.v.*) and Uranus (*q.v.*). The only Titan not to revolt against Uranus (*q.v.*). In Aeschylus' *Prometheus Bound* he preaches submission to the authority of Zeus (*q.v.*). He was seen originally as the river encircling the world from which all rivers and seas sprang. He is thus depicted as the rim on Achilles' (*q.v.*) shield. The husband of Tethys and by her father of, among others, Metis.

Odysseus. The hero of Homer's *Odyssey*, itself the model for James Joyce's *Ulysses*, Ulysses being the Roman name for him. The son of Laertes, king of Ithaca, and Anticleia, daughter of the wily thief Autolycus. However, one tradition makes him the son of Sisyphus (*q.v.*). He married Penelope (*q.v.*). Warned by an oracle not to go to Troy (*q.v.*) he feigned madness when the heralds arrived by sowing salt, but when Palamedes placed his son Telemachus (*q.v.*) before the plough he was forced to disclose his sanity and join the expedition. Later, at Troy, he avenged himself by having a letter signed in Priam's (*q.v.*) hand placed in Palamedes' tent. The letter was found and Palamedes was stoned to death. But Odysseus himself tricked Achilles (*q.v.*) into revealing his true identity and joining the expedition. At Troy Odysseus and Diomedes (*q.v.*) entered the city at night to kill Rhesus the Thracian and steal his white horses, because it was prophesied that if they drank of the Scamander (*q.v.*) Troy would not fall. He quarrelled with Ajax (*q.v.*) over the armour of Achilles and some say he killed him. He captured Helenus and from him learned the secret oracles which told how Troy would fall. In accordance with these he stole the Palladium of Athene (q.v.). It was also Odysseus who devised the stratagem of the Wooden Horse. When Troy fell he took Hecuba (q.v.) as a slave. His journey home lasted ten years and involved many adventures. He first went to Cicones to procure jars of sweet wine and then visited the Lotophagi (q.v.). After leaving them he landed in Sicily where he blinded Polyphemus the Cyclops (q.v.). Next he visited Aeolus (q.v.) and as a result was blown off course and lost all his ships save one at Telepylos. In this he reached Aeaea, land of Circe (q.v.) and on her advice sought the aid of Teiresias, a dead seer in the Underworld. In the land of the Cimmerians he summoned Teiresias' shade, and also those of his mother and former comrades, though Ajax (q.v.) held aloof. Then, with Circe's counsel he navigated the Scylla and Charybdis (q.v.) and neutralised the spell of the Sirens (q.v.) by blocking his crew's ears with wax but having himself tied to the mast that he might hear their song. At Thrinacia his men slaughtered the cattle of Helios (q.v.) and were punished by Zeus (q.v.), all but Odysseus dying in a subsequent shipwreck. He drifted to Ogygia on flotsam, where he spent eight years with the nymph Calypso (q.v.). On a raft he made land at Scheria, was found by Nausicaa (q.v.) and given a ship to Ithaca (q.v.). Here he was recognised by Eumaeus (q.v.) despite his disguise as a beggar. He found Laertes (q.v.) in the country and Penelope (q.v.) besieged by suitors. This drunken and unruly crew were headed by one Alcinous, their most persistent member. Penelope had kept them at bay by promising to marry one of them when she had finished weaving a robe for Laertes: a robe she unpicked each night. But betrayed by her servants she was now being forced to choose a husband. Meanwhile Telemachus (q.v.) who had sailed away to find Odysseus returned to find him with Laertes and they plotted revenge. Still dressed as a beggar Odysseus entered the palace and was recognised only by his nurse Eurycleia and his faithful hound Argus which died on seeing his long lost master. Penelope now announced she would marry the suitor who could fire Odysseus' bow. Only he was able to bend and string it. The suitors having failed Odysseus strung the bow and with Telemachus slew the suitors. The *Odyssey* ends when Athene (q.v.) reconciles the hero and the kinsmen of the suitors who were seeking revenge. Teiresias had prophesied that Odysseus had to set out on another journey to appease Poseidon (q.v.) for the blinding of his son Polyphemus and would then live to an old age until death came from the sea.

One tradition tells how Telegonus, Odysseus' son by Circe came looking for his father, landed and began plundering for supplies. Odysseus and Telemachus gave battle and Telegonus killed Odysseus, not recognising his father. He also took Telemachus and Penelope to Aeaca where he himself married Penelope.

Odyssey. See under **Odysseus.**

Oedipus ("Swollen-foot"). The son of Laius, king of Thebes, and Jocasta (q.v.). The Delphic oracle said Laius would be killed by his son so he had the baby exposed on Mt. Cithaeron with a nail driven through its feet—hence "Oedipus". But he was found by a shepherd and raised by Polybus, king of Corinth, as his own son. As an adult Oedipus learned from the oracle that he would kill his own father and marry his own mother and believing himself the son of Polybus, left Corinth. He met Laius on the road and killed him in a quarrel. Laius had been on his way to Delphi to seek advice on ridding Thebes of the Sphinx (q.v.). This Oedipus did and was made king by the Thebans. He married Jocasta and they had four children, Eteocles (q.v.), Polynices (q.v.), Antigone (q.v.) and Ismene (q.v.). When Thebes suffered a plague because of their incest Oedipus contacted the seer Teiresias and learned whose son he was. When she heard the truth Jocasta hanged herself and Oedipus blinded himself with the pins from her dress. With Antigone and later Ismene he went into exile at the grove of the Eumenides (see **Erinnyes**) at Colonos in Attica. Here he was received by the gods, having first cursed the sons who had neglected him, saying they would divide their kingdom by the sword.

Oeneus. King of Pleuron and Calydon, husband of Althaea and father of Tydeus (q.v.), Meleager (q.v.), Gorge and Deineira (q.v.). His realm was seized by his nephews but his grandson Diomedes (q.v.) avenged him and put Andraemon, husband of Gorge, on the throne. He accompanied Diomedes to the Peloponnesus where he was killed by two nephews who had escaped Diomedes. Deineira (q.v.) married Heracles (q.v.).

Oenomaus. A son of Ares (q.v.), king of Elis. An oracle said he would be killed by his son-in-law. Therefore he challenged all his daughter's suitors to a chariot race and if they won they would marry his daughter Hippodameia: if they lost they were put to death. His own chariot was drawn by wind-born horses, a gift of Ares. He was murdered by Myrtilus at the instigation of Pelops (q.v.).

Oenone. A nymph who loved Paris (q.v.). He deserted her for Helen (q.v.) and when he was wounded by Philoctetes (q.v.) she refused to help him. Then, in remorse at his death, she committed suicide.

Oileus. One of the Argonauts (q.v.), and father of Ajax (q.v.).

Olympia. A small province in the western Peloponnesus, isolated from the centre and east of the Peloponnesus by high mountains. The site of a major sanctuary of Zeus (q.v.) whose worship replaced that of an early female divinity in the 9th century B.C. However, it was not till about 470 B.C. that a magnificent temple was built to Zeus. From 776 B.C. though, the Olympic games had been celebrated at Olympia in honour of Zeus. These quadrennial contests were international in character and an international truce accompanied their celebration. The prestige of the games was great and from 776 Greek chronology was based on the games, an "Olympiad" being a four-year cycle. Hence Olympiad 12, 1 denoted the 1st year in a four-year period after 11 previous Olympiads. If the number of Olympiads is multiplied by 4 and deducted from 776 we have our date e.g. $11 \times 4 = 44$, subtracted from 776 is 732 B.C.

Olympius. A term for any deity or muse inhabiting Olympus and not the Underworld.

Olympus, Mt. The highest peak in Greece on the borders of Thessaly and Macedonia. Its 2075 m are almost inaccessible and it was not climbed until 1913. It was believed to be the home of the twelve Olympian gods.

Omphale. Queen of Lydia and widow of Tmolus who purchased Heracles (q.v.) as a slave. He served her for three years and one tradition says he dressed as a woman and swapped clothes with Omphale during this period.

Ops. Roman goddess of plenty, a consort of Saturn (q.v.) and the personification of abundance.

Orcus. The Roman name for Hades (q.v.) and for his realm.

Orestes. The son of Clytemnestra (q.v.) and Agamemnon (q.v.). As a child he was smuggled out of Mycenae by his sister Electra (q.v.) when Clytemnestra and Aegisthus (q.v.) seized power. He took refuge at the court of king Strophius in Phocis, becoming a close friend of Pylades (q.v.), the king's son. When of age he, Pylades and Electra killed Aegisthus and Clytemnestra, and Orestes was punished for his matricide by the Erinnyes (q.v.). He fled to the Acropolis of Athens and embraced the image of the goddess. Athene (q.v.) then summoned the Areopagus to judge his case. Apollo (q.v.), whose oracle had encouraged his crime, defended him on the grounds that fatherhood was more important than motherhood. Athene's casting vote found him innocent. Another tradition says Apollo told him he could be free of the Erinnyes by fetching the statue of Artemis (q.v.) from the Tauric Chersonese. Orestes and Pylades went to Tauris and were seized by the natives for sacrifice to Artemis. But it transpired that his sister Iphigenia (q.v.) was the priestess and she helped them steal the statue and return to Greece. They met Electra and went on to Mycenae where Orestes killed Aegisthus' son and became king. Later he slew his rival Neoptolemus (q.v.) and married his cousin Hermione.

Oreithyia. See **Boreas.** He turned her into a wind.

Orion. A giant, son of Poseidon (q.v.) who was a renowned hunter and very handsome. He loved Merope, daughter of Oenopion of Chios and was promised her hand in return for ridding Chios of wild animals. This he did but Oenopion would not give up Merope which led Orion to seduce her. Oenopion, with the help of his father Dionysus, blinded Orion who was told by the oracle he could only recover his sight by going to the east and gazing on the sun as it rose. This he did with the help of Hephaestus (q.v.) and once there Eos (q.v.) fell in love with him and Helios (q.v.) restored his sight. Later he joined Artemis (q.v.) in a hunt. Apollo (q.v.) angry at his boasting that he would kill all the wild beasts and afraid he would seduce Artemis contrived his death at the unwitting hands of Artemis. She placed his image in the stars, his constellation rising with the sun at the autumnal equinox.

Orpheus. The son of king Oeagrus of Thrace and Calliope (q.v.). The Greeks regarded him as the first great poet. He could enchant the beasts and trees with his lyre, a gift from Apollo (q.v.). After returning from the voyage of the Argonauts (q.v.) he married Eurydice (q.v.) His grief at losing her after redeeming her from Hades (q.v.) led to a failure to honour Dionysus (q.v.) at a Bacchanalia and he was torn to pieces by Bacchae (q.v.) The muses buried the pieces at the foot of Mt. Olympus (q.v.) save his head which was thrown into the River Hebrus still singing. The head and his lyre eventually floated to Lesbos (q.v.) and were finally placed amongst the stars at the request of Apollo and the Muses. *See also* **Orphism, Section J.**

Orthrus. A giant two-headed dog, the offspring of Typhon (q.v.) and Echidne (q.v.) and, some say, the father of the Sphinx (q.v.) and Chimaera (q.v.). It was set to watch the oxen of Geryon (q.v.) and was slain by Heracles (q.v.).

Ortygia (1) Port of Syracuse in Sicily.
(2) Port of Delos (q.v.), birthplace of Artemis (q.v.).

Otus and **Ephialtes.** Twin sons of Iphimedeia and Poseidon (q.v.), named Aloeidae after their mother's later husband Aloeus. At an early age they imprisoned Ares (q.v.) and later swore to rape Hera (q.v.) and Artemis (q.v.). In a vain effort to achieve this they placed Mt. Pelion on top of Mt. Ossa and attacked Heaven. But Artemis induced them to seek her at Naxos. Here she leapt between them in the form of a doe and they accidentally slew each other. In Tartarus (q.v.) their shades were tied back to back by bonds of vipers. **Ovid.** *See* **Section B.**

P

Palaemon. A sea god, the son of Athamas and Ino who was originally named Melicertes.
Palamedes. *See* **Odysseus.**
Pales. Italic deity of flocks and herds, worshipped on the Palatine.
Pallas (1) ... ... god ... hero worshipped in Sicily and mentioned in the *Aeneid* (q.v.).
Palinurus. "Wind Astern", the helmsman of Aeneas. He managed the ship between the Scylla and Charybdis (q.v.) and in the storm off the coast of Carthage but later fell asleep and into the sea. He was cast ashore but murdered by local tribesmen. His shade begged Aeneas for carriage across the Styx (q.v.) so it could be at rest, but the Sibyl refused as he had not been properly buried. However she promised him a shrine, Capo Pulinuro in Lucania near modern Salerno.
Palladium. A mythical statue of Athene given to Dardanus (q.v.) by Zeus (q.v.) to ensure the protection of Troy. By one tradition it was stolen by Odysseus (q.v.) and Diomedes (q.v.). By another Aeneas (q.v.) saved it and brought it to Rome where it saved the city several times in its early years.
Pallas. (1) A title of Athene (q.v.) given to her by the Achaens. Pallas, Kore and Parthenos signify a virgin, maiden or girl.
(2) One of the 24 Giants (q.v.) who rebelled against Zeus (q.v.).
(3) A brother of Aegeus (q.v.). *See also* **Theseus.**
(4) An ancestor of Evander (q.v.).
(5) Evander's son who went to follow Aeneas (q.v.).
Pan. A god, half-man, half-goat, said by some to be a son of Zeus (q.v.) by others to be the son of Hermes (q.v.) and Penelope with whom he inhabited Arcadia. He was a patron of shepherds and herdsmen and a lover of mischief. When not frolicking with the nymphs he liked to startle peasants and flocks inspiring "panic". He loved and

pursued Syrinx whose flight from him resulted in her being transformed into a reed from which he made a seven-piped flute, the syrinx. He also seduced Selene (q.v.). Sometimes identified with the Roman Faunus (q.v.).
Pandarus. A Trojan archer who broke a truce by shooting at the Greeks. In Chaucer's *Troilus and Criseyde* and Shakespeare's *Troilus and Cressida* he is Cressida's uncle and the lovers' go-between. The word "pandar" is derived from his name for this reason.
Pandora. "All gifts", the first woman fashioned and given life by Hephaestus (q.v.) and Athene (q.v.). Zeus (q.v.) sent her to punish man after Prometheus (q.v.) had given him fire. She married the brother of Prometheus, Epimetheus. Her curiosity led her to open a box which it was forbidden to touch, and from it sprang all the evils and diseases which beset mankind. Only hope was left at the bottom of the box.
Parcae. The Roman equivalent of the "Fates" or Horae.
Paris. Son of Priam (q.v.) and Hecuba (q.v.) who dreamed during her pregnancy that she would bring forth a blazing firebrand. As a child he was exposed on Mt. Ida. Raised by shepherds he was named Paris or sometimes Alexander ("defender of men") because of his courage. He loved and deserted Oenone (q.v.) which eventually caused his death. Promised the fairest of women by Aphrodite (q.v.) if he gave her the apple of discord, he did as she bade. Reunited with his parents he then left for Sparta whence he seduced Helen (q.v.) thus starting the Trojan War. At one point in the war Aphrodite saved him from death in a duel with Menelaus. He shot the arrow which slew Achilles (q.v.) at the Scaean Gate but was himself mortally wounded by Philoctetes (q.v.).
Parnassus, Mt. 2461 m peak in the Pindus range, north-east of Delphi (q.v.). Home of Apollo (q.v.) and the Muses (q.v.) hence the name "Montparnasse" for the hill in Paris on which centred the university and cultural life of that city. On the original's slopes was also the Corycian Cave, a centre of the Bacchae (q.v.).
Parthenon. *See* **Section L.**
Parthenos. *See* **Pallas.**
Parthenope. A nymph whose body was said to have washed up at Neapolis (Naples) around 600 B.C. She gave her name to the short-lived Parthenopean Republic of Naples established by Napoleon in 1799.
Parthenopeus. *See* **Seven Against Thebes.**
Parthenos. *See* **Pallas.**
Pasiphaë. Daughter of Helios (q.v.) and Persë, and wife of Minos (q.v.). Mother of the Minotaur (q.v.) by the Cretan Bull (q.v.) and of many children, including Ariadne (q.v.), Glaucus and Phaedra, by Minos.
Patroclus. Cousin and bosom companion of Achilles (q.v.) with whom he lived at the court of Peleus (q.v.) while in exile for an accidental murder. Slain by Hector (q.v.) while wearing Achilles' armour, his death persuaded Achilles to re-enter the Trojan War.
Pausanias. Spartan king who intervened to moderate Lysander's arrogant attitude towards Athens and other Greek cities after the Peloponnesian War.
Pegasus. Winged horse, offspring of Poseidon (q.v.) and Medusa (q.v.). It was captured by Bellerophon (q.v.) at the fountain of Pirene and helped him slay the Chimaera (q.v.). It struck Mt. Helicon with its hoof and brought forth the spring of Hippocrene, sacred to the Muses.
Peleus. The son of Aeacus, king of Aegina. With his brother Telamon he killed their half-brother Phocus and the two were expelled to Phthia in Thessaly by Aeacus. Here Eurytion purified them of murder. They took part in the Calydonian Hunt when they accidentally killed Eurytion. They then fled to the court of Acastus (q.v.) of Iolcis. Zeus (q.v.) married him to Thetis (q.v.) though he himself loved Thetis. This was because the oracle foretold that her son would be greater than his father. Their son was Achilles (q.v.). All the gods save Eris (q.v.) were invited to the wedding and in revenge she cast the Apple of Discord. Peleus later ruled the Myrmidones at Phthia.
Pelias. *See* **Jason.**
Pelicles. Son of Peleus *i.e.* Achilles (q.v.).
Peloponnesus. The "island of Pelops" (q.v.), the large southern peninsular of mainland Greece, attached to northern Greece by the Corinthian isthmus.
Pelops. Son of Tantalus (q.v.) king of Lydia. Tantalus cut him in pieces and served him to the gods at a meal. Only Demeter (q.v.) grieving for Persephone

(*q.v.*) did not realise and she ate Pelops' shoulder. Zeus (*q.v.*) restored him to life by having Hermes (*q.v.*) boil him in a pot. Demeter gave him an ivory shoulder, said to be the birthmark of his descendants. His shoulder blade was later taken to Troy (*q.v.*) by the Greeks as the oracle said this was necessary if the city were to fall. He married Hippodamia.

Pelorus. One of the Sparti (*q.v.*).

Penates. Roman deities of the home, confused from early times with the *genius* and the Lares. Eventually a wide variety of deities, *e.g.* Mars, Mercury, Venus, were regarded as "*di Penates*" that is, "guardians of the hearth".

Penelope. The wife of Odysseus (*q.v.*), usually seen as a symbol of fidelity. One tradition in the Peleponnesus made her adulterous and the mother of Pan (*q.v.*) by Hermes (*q.v.*) or by all of her many suitors.

Peneus. The son of Oceanus (*q.v.*) and Tethys. A river god and father of Daphne (*q.v.*) and Cyrene (*q.v.*). Identified with the River Peneus in Thessaly.

Penthesilea. Daughter of Otrere and Ares (*q.v.*), queen of the Amazons (*q.v.*) who helped the Trojans. Slain by Achilles (*q.v.*) they fell in love as she died and he later mourned her. When the wretched Thersites mocked his grief Achilles slew him which caused his kinsman Diomedes (*q.v.*) to throw her corpse into the Scamander. It was retrieved and honourably buried.

Pentheus. Grandson of Cadmus (*q.v.*) and king of Thebes. The subject of Euripedes' *Bacchae*. He refused to allow Dionysus (*q.v.*) into the city but the god, in disguise, persuaded him to dress as one of the Bacchae (*q.v.*) and watch their orgies. He was then torn to pieces by the Bacchae, led by his own mother who was in a trance.

Perdix (or **Talos**). See **Daedalus**.

Periclymenus. The son of Neleus (*q.v.*) and brother of Nestor (*q.v.*). An Argonaut (*q.v.*) he could assume any form he chose. Slain by Heracles (*q.v.*).

Periphetes. A giant residing at Epidaurus who murdered travellers with an iron club. Slain by Theseus (*q.v.*) who henceforth carried his club.

Perse. The daughter of Oceanus (*q.v.*). Wife of Helios (*q.v.*) to whom she bore Circe (*q.v.*), Pasiphaë (*q.v.*), Aeetes and Perses (*q.v.*).

Persephone. Daughter of Zeus (*q.v.*) and Demeter (*q.v.*). She spent the winter months with Hades (*q.v.*) when nothing grew and with Demeter she spent the fertile months. Thus she was a goddess of vegetation. She was also queen of the Underworld and was a symbol of death. Known to the Romans as Proserpina. Her companion in the Underworld was Hecate (*q.v.*).

Perses. The son of Helios (*q.v.*) and Perse (*q.v.*) father of Hecate (*q.v.*).

Perseus. Grandson of Acrisius (*q.v.*) king of Argos and the son of Zeus (*q.v.*) and Danae (*q.v.*). Raised at the court of Polydectes who sent him to fetch the head of Medusa (*q.v.*). Hermes (*q.v.*) gave him a sickle with which to do this and told him how, via the Graeae (*q.v.*) he could procure Hades' (*q.v.*) helmet of invisibility, winged sandals and a magic wallet to help him in the task. Once he had the head he petrified the Titan Atlas (*q.v.*) with it. He then flew to Aethiopia where he found Andromeda (*see* **Cassiopeia**). Returning to Seriphos he slew Polydectes, made Dictys (*q.v.*) king and returned to Argos. He went on later to exchange the kingdom of Argos for that of his cousin Megaperthes of Tiryns.

Phaebus ("Shining") A name used for Apollo (*q.v.*) at Delos (*q.v.*) where he was associated with Artemis (*q.v.*).

Phaedra. The daughter of Minos (*q.v.*) and wife of Theseus (*q.v.*) to whom she bore Acamas and Demephon. See also **Hippolytus**.

Phaeton. The son of Helios (*q.v.*) and Clymene. Helios let him drive the chariot of the sun across the sky but he lost control of it and was killed by a thunderbolt from Zeus (*q.v.*) for almost setting the world on fire. He fell into the River Po and his sisters who mourned him were turned into poplar or alder trees and their tears into amber.

Phalanthus. Mythical founder of Tarentum in Italy.

Philemon. The husband of Baucis. This old Phrygian couple once received Zeus (*q.v.*) and Hermes (*q.v.*) with great hospitality.

Philoctetes. The son of Poecas, nephew of Protesilaus, and companion of Heracles (*q.v.*). He lit Heracles funeral pyre and received his bow and arrows. On the way to Troy (*q.v.*) one of the poisoned arrows wounded him, or he was bitten by a snake on the island of Tenedos. The smell of the wound became so offensive that on the advice of Odysseus (*q.v.*) he was left on Lemnos. Later an oracle revealed that Troy would not fall till the bow and arrows of Heracles were brought to the Greeks and Odysseus and Diomedes (*q.v.*) fetched him to Troy. Here either Machaon or Podalirius, the sons of Asclepius (*q.v.*) cured him of his wound. He slew Paris (*q.v.*) and later settled in Italy.

Philomela. See **Procne**.

Phineus. King of Salmydessus in Thrace and the son of Agenor. He first married Cleopatra, then Idaca who falsely accused her stepsons of improper advances. Phineus imprisoned them and was made blind and pursued by the Harpies (*q.v.*). Eventually the Argonauts (*q.v.*) whose ranks included Zetes and Calais, Cleopatra's brothers, slew the Harpies. Phineus freed the stepsons and told Jason (*q.v.*) what course to set.

Phlegethon ("Blazing"). A river of the Underworld called the "river of flames" by Plato. The shades of those who had committed crimes of violence against their kin were roasted in it until they received forgiveness.

Phlegyas. A king of the Lapithae (*q.v.*) who burnt Apollo's (*q.v.*) shrine at Delphi and was punished for it in the Underworld by having to sit beneath a huge rock which was liable to fall at any time.

Phocis. Small mountainous province of northern Greece which held the oracle of Delphi.

Phocus. See **Peleus**.

Phoebe ("Bright"). In early myth the daughter of Heaven and Earth and mother of Leto (*q.v.*). Later identified with Artemis (*q.v.*) the moon-goddess.

Phoenix ("Red"). (1) Companion and tutor of Achilles (*q.v.*) who tried to reconcile him with Agamemnon (*q.v.*).

(2) The brother of Cadmus (*q.v.*) and Europa (*q.v.*), eponymous ancestor of the Phoenicians.

(3) A mythological Egyptian bird which died on a funeral pyre every 500 years before rising again from the ashes.

Phorcys. A sea-god, the father of Echidne (*q.v.*), Ladon, the Gorgons (*q.v.*) and the Graeae (*q.v.*).

Phrixus and Helle. Brother and sister, the children of Athamas king of Aeolia. Their stepmother, Ino (*q.v.*), had engineered their sacrifice by Athamas out of jealousy but they escaped on a flying ram with a golden fleece sent by Zeus (*q.v.*). Helle fell off into what was henceforth the Hellespont, but Phrixus reached Colchis and sacrificed the ram to Zeus (*see* **Jason**). The ram's image was placed amongst the stars as Aries.

Phyllis. See **Demophon**.

Picus. An ancient Italian god represented as a woodpecker *i.e.* "*picus*".

Pierides. A name applied to the Muses (*q.v.*). It was derived from the inhabitants of Pieria, on the south coast of Macedonia, who were noted for their worship of the Muses

Also a name for nine daughters of Pierus king of Macedonia who were defeated in a contest by the Muses and turned into birds.

Pillars of Hercules. Two pillars, Calpe and Abyla, erected on either side of the straits of Gibraltar by Heracles (*q.v.*).

Pilumnus. An ancient minor Italian god, "the spearman".

Pindar. See **Section B**.

Pirithous. Son of Ixion (*q.v.*) and Dia, companion of Theseus (*q.v.*) and king of the Lapithae (*q.v.*). He led the fight on the Centaurs (*q.v.*). On the death of his wife Hippodamia he and Theseus abducted the young Helen (*q.v.*) of Troy. She fell by lot to Theseus who, in return and despite misgivings, promised to help Pirithous abduct a daughter of Zeus (*q.v.*) for himself. They attempted to abduct Persephone (*q.v.*) from the Underworld but Hades (*q.v.*) chained them to a rock. Heracles (*q.v.*) later freed Theseus but Pirithous was left to suffer torment for his sins.

Pleiades. The seven daughters of Atlas (*q.v.*) and Pleione and companions of Artemis (*q.v.*). Zeus (*q.v.*) turned them into doves and placed their image in the stars to save them from the attentions of Orion (*q.v.*) who pursued them for five years. A group of seven poets in 3rd century B.C. Alexandria also called themselves the Pleiad.

Plutarch. See **Section B**.

Pluto. (1) A Roman name for Hades (*q.v.*), "the rich one" who owns the riches of the earth itself.

(2) A nymph who was mother of Tantalus (*q.v.*) by Zeus (*q.v.*).

Podarces. (1) *See* **Priam.**

(2) Son of Iphiclus, leader of the Thessalians who fought at Troy (*q.v.*).

Polites. A son of Priam (*q.v.*) and Hecabe (*q.v.*), slain before their eyes by Neoptolemus (*q.v.*).

Pollux. The Roman name for Polydeuces. *See* **Castor.**

Polydeuces. *See* **Castor.**

Polydorus. (1) The son of Cadmus (*q.v.*) and Harmonia and ancestor of Oedipus (*q.v.*) and other great Theban kings.

(2) The youngest son of Priam (*q.v.*) and Hecabe (*q.v.*).

Polymnia. *See* **Muses.**

Polynices. The son of Jocasta and Oedipus (*q.v.*), brother of Eteocles (*q.v.*), Antigone (*q.v.*) and Ismene (*q.v.*). *See also* **Seven Against Thebes.** When Creon refused to allow his burial Antigone (*q.v.*) disregarded the order and buried the corpse.

Polypemon. Also known as Procrustes, "the stretcher". A robber who tied travellers to a bed and if they were too tall he cut off their legs; if too short he put them on a rack. Theseus (*q.v.*) did the same to him.

Polyphemus. *See* **Cyclopes and Galatea.**

Polyxena. The daughter of Priam (*q.v.*) and Hecuba (*q.v.*) beloved by Achilles (*q.v.*) whose shade requested her sacrifice by Neoptolemus (*q.v.*) after Troy's (*q.v.*) fall. This is the theme of Euripides' *Hecabe.*

Pomona. An Italian goddess of tree-fruits (*poma*) *e.g.* apples. She was a minor deity but had her own priest and sanctuary near Rome. Ovid links her with Vertumnus, an Etruscan god with the power to change his shape. He was god of the changing seasons and the ripening fruits of autumn, and also of money changing. *Vertere* means "change" in Latin. He loved Pomona and pursued her disguised as a harvester, vine-dresser, herdsman and old woman, but only won her when he appeared as himself. His statue stood in the Vicus Tuscus, a busy street of brothels and shops named after him as an Etruscan.

Pontus. The sea, offspring of Ge (*q.v.*) the earth.

Pontus Euxinus. The "Hospitable Sea", the Greek name for the Black Sea. The name was an attempt to flatter and placate a hostile sea which was much feared by sailors.

Porphyrion. *See* **Giants.**

Porsenna. *See* **Lars Porsenna.**

Portunus. A Roman sea-deity associated with harbours.

Poseidon. The Roman Neptune, the god of earthquakes, and later of the sea. The eldest son of Cronus (*q.v.*) and Rhea. When he and Zeus (*q.v.*) and Hades (*q.v.*) cast lots for their realms he won the sea and had an underwater palace near Aegae in Euboea. Here he kept horses with brazen hoofs and gold manes who drew his chariot across the sea. Its passage calmed the sea. Poseidon created the horse and invented the bridle. As a horse he raped Demeter (*q.v.*) who was disguised as a mare. Their offspring was the horse Arion and the nymph Despoena and, some say, Persephone (*q.v.*). He resented Zeus (*q.v.*) and helped Hera (*q.v.*) and Apollo (*q.v.*) enchain him. In punishment Zeus made him a servant of Laomedon (*q.v.*) and he built the Neptunilia Pergama, the walls of Troy. He helped the Greeks at Troy but hated Odysseus (*q.v.*) who blinded Polyphemus (*q.v.*). He disputed the possession of Athens with Athene (*q.v.*) and lost, but Zeus gave him the Isthmus of Corinth instead. Here the Isthmian games were held in his honour. He married Amphitrite (*q.v.*). By mortal women he had many children including Pegasus (*q.v.*) and the Aloeidae (*q.v.*). He is usually portrayed with a trident which he used to shake the earth.

Priam. The son of Laomedon (*q.v.*) and husband of Hecuba (*q.v.*). Originally called Podarces his name was changed to Priam *i.e.* "ransomed" because Heracles (*q.v.*) spared him and sold him to Hesione (*q.v.*) his sister. He had fifty sons and fifty daughters, nineteen of whom were by Hecuba and included Hector (*q.v.*), Paris (*q.v.*), Helenus (*q.v.*) and Cassandra (*q.v.*). He begged Achilles (*q.v.*) to return Hector's body. Eventually slain at the altar of Zeus (*q.v.*) by Neoptolemus (*q.v.*).

Priapus. The son of Dionysus (*q.v.*) and Aphrodite (*q.v.*). A fertility god whose worship spread from the Hellespont to Greece and later Rome, though he was never taken seriously. He was often por-

trayed in the form of a red-faced scarecrow with a large detachable phallus and in this role was used to scare birds. The phallus became a truncheon to ward off other intruders. He was also a protector of cultivated gardens and a god of sailors. In Petronius' *Satyricon* he pursues the hero Encolpius and makes him impotent. Horace and Martial write of him lightheartedly and 85 obscene poems about him – *"priapeia'* - exist of unknown authorship. His sacrificial animal was the donkey, a symbol of lust.

Procne. The daughter of Pandion, king of Athens. Pandion gave her to Tereus in return for his assistance and they had a son Itys. But Tereus wanted her sister Philomela. He made Procne a slave and tore out her tongue, then seduced Philomela saying Procne was dead. Procne could only alert her sister and be free by stitching a message to her robe. Once free she slew Itys, cooked pieces of the corpse and fed it to Tereus. When Tereus learnt what had happened he chased the sisters with an axe but the gods turned him into a hawk, Procne into a swallow and Philomela a nightingale though some traditions say it was Philomela who lost her tongue and became a swallow.

Procris. Daughter of Erectheus of Athens and the wife of Cephalus. Eos (*q.v.*) who also loved Cephalus showed him that Procris was easily seduced in return for gold. Procris then fled to Crete and lived for a time with Minos (*q.v.*). On returning to Athens disguised as a youth she brought with her a hound and spear, gifts from Artemis (*q.v.*), which never missed their quarry. Cephalus so wanted the gifts that the couple were reconciled. But Procris suspected Cephalus of having an affair with Eos and followed him on a hunt where he accidentally killed her with the spear.

Procrustes. *See* **Polypemon.**

Proetus. The son of Abas (*q.v.*) king of Argolis. His twin brother Acrisius (*q.v.*) expelled him and he fled to Lydia where he married Anteia (also called Stheneboea) daughter of king Iobates (*see* **Bellerophon**). He later returned to Argolis and forced Acrisius to give him half the kingdom. He ruled from Tiryns whose huge walls he built with the aid of the Cyclopes (*q.v.*). Eventually gave two thirds of his kingdom to Melampus (*q.v.*) and Bias.

Prometheus. A Titan (*q.v.*) and the brother of Epimetheus (*q.v.*) or "afterthought" and Atlas (*q.v.*). Sometimes said to be the maker of mankind. He supported Zeus (*q.v.*) against his brother Titans but stole fire from Olympus and gave it to men. This angered Zeus who took revenge on man through Pandora (*q.v.*) and punished Prometheus by chaining him to a rock in the Caucasus. Here an eagle tore at his liver each day. The liver was renewed daily and Prometheus suffered this torment until Heracles (*q.v.*) rescued him.

Proserpina. Roman counterpart of Persephone (*q.v.*).

Proteus. A sea god and a subject of Poseidon (*q.v.*). He had the power of prophecy and could change his form. He would avoid prophecy by changing form until tightly gripped; then he appeared in his true shape and spoke the truth. Said to live on the isle of Pharos in the Nile Delta. Menelaus (*q.v.*) mastered him while returning from Troy (*q.v.*) and forced him to reveal the way to Sparta.

Psyche. In Greek literature, the "soul" personified, often portrayed as a butterfly. As the centre of emotion she was tormented by *"eros"*. Her beauty made Aphrodite (*q.v.*) jealous and she sent Eros (*q.v.*) to torment her. Instead he fell in love with her though he would not let her see him or disclose his identity. But at the bidding of her two sisters she sought to discover who he was. For the first time she saw him, holding a candle above him as he slept, but hot wax fell on him. He woke and left her to seek him. After many trials she found him, became immortal and was united with Eros for ever.

Pygmalion. (1) The king of Tyre and brother of Dido (*q.v.*).

(2) The king of Cyprus who made and fell in love with a maiden's statue. Aphrodite (*q.v.*) answered his prayers and gave the statue life as the girl Galatea. They married and had two sons, Paphus and Metharme. In some versions the tale he is a sculptor. The basis of Shaw's *Pygmalion* and the musical *My Fair Lady.*

Pylades. Husband of Electra (*q.v.*). *See also* **Orestes.**

Pyramus and Thisbe. The lovers in a tale by Ovid which he heard in the East. Living in Babylon they are forbidden to meet but converse through a chink in a wall. They arrange a meeting at the tomb of Ninus but Thisbe, arriving first, was chased away by a lion and dropped her veil. Finding this, Pyramus thought her dead and committed suicide. She returned and slew herself on his sword. Since that time the nearby mulberry has borne fruit the colour of blood. This is the basis of Bottom's tale in Shakespeare's *A Midsummer Night's Dream*.

Pyrrhus. Another name for Neoptolemus.

Pythia. The priestess of Apollo (*q.v.*) at Delphi (*q.v.*).

Python. A she-dragon of Mt. Parnassus who controlled the oracle at Delphi (*q.v.*). The boy Apollo (*q.v.*) slew her and the Pythia (*q.v.*) took over her task of giving voice to oracles.

Q

Quirinus. A very ancient Roman deity whose cult was centred on the Quirinal. The Romans eventually forgot his original character and he was identified with Mars (*q.v.*) in classical times, though Romulus (*q.v.*) was also supposed to have adopted the name after his deification.

R

Rape of the Sabine Women. An episode recounted by Livy and Ovid to explain the intermarriage of the Roman settlers and natives. Romulus (*q.v.*) and his followers invited the surrounding tribes to celebrate a festival in the Circus Maximus then carried off the native girls. War broke out but the Sabine women, who had been well treated, intervened to restore peace. The event has been the subject of paintings by Poussin and Rubens and of a group of statues by Giovanni da Bologna.

Remus. *See* **Romulus.**

Rhadamanthus. The son of Zeus (*q.v.*) and Europa (*q.v.*), brother of Minos (*q.v.*) and Sarpedon (*q.v.*). Once the ruler of part of Crete but Minos forced him to flee to Boeotia (*q.v.*). Famed for his wisdom and justice he was made one of the judges of the Underworld after his death. He married Alcmene (*q.v.*) on the death of Amphitrion (*q.v.*).

Rhea. (1) A Titaness, daughter of Ge (*q.v.*) and Uranus (*q.v.*). *See* **Cronus.**
(2) *See* **Romulus.**

Rhesus. A Thracian king who helped the Trojans. An oracle said that if his magnificent snow-white horses ate the grass of the Trojan plain and drank of the River Scamander Troy would not fall. Diomedes (*q.v.*) and Odysseus (*q.v.*) raided his camp, slew him, and stole the horses.

Rhodos/Rhode. The daughter of Poseidon (*q.v.*), wife of Helios (*q.v.*).

Rome. The "eternal city" sited on the banks of the Tiber. Traditionally founded in 753 B.C. (year 1 of the Roman calendar) by Romulus (*q.v.*). It only really became a city in the 6th century under the Tarquins. Under the Republic it had a population of two or three hundred thousand, of 450,000 by the time of Augustus and 1,000,000 under the Antonines, though the population was occasionally reduced by wars, fires and plagues.

Romulus. The legendary founder of Rome (*q.v.*), twin brother of Remus and together the sons of Rhea or Rhea Silvia. She was the daughter of Numitor, king of Alba Longa (*q.v.*) who was deposed by his brother. Her uncle compelled her to become a Vestal Virgin (*q.v.*) but she bore Romulus and Remus, according to her, by Mars (*q.v.*). Her uncle then imprisoned her and threw the babies into the Tiber. The shepherd Faustulus (*q.v.*) found a wolf suckling them and reared them. When they reached manhood they returned to Alba Longa, restored Numitor to the throne and set off to found a city of their own. They went to the site of Rome and decided to consult the gods. Romulus chose the Palatine Hill, his childhood home, as the centre of the city, Remus the Aventine (*q.v.*). The gods favoured Romulus, sending him an extraordinary omen of twelve vultures, Remus only six. Thus Romulus was given the honour of founding Rome which he did by ploughing a furrow around the Palatine. As he commenced building the city wall Remus derisively jumped over it, a quarrel ensued and Romulus slew him. Romulus took in fugitives in order to populate the city, found them wives by the "Rape of the Sabine women" (*q.v.*) and reigned for forty years before disappearing in a whirlwind on the Campus Martius. He was deified and identified with the Sabine god Quirinus (*q.v.*).

Rubicon. *See* **Section L.**

S

Sabines. A branch of the Samnite race and one of the Sabellian peoples who occupied the Etruscanised area on the middle valley of the Tiber around Falerii. To the south of Rome they held the mountainous land between Rome and Campania. They were a constant threat to early Rome and the tradition that one Titus Tatius, a Sabine prince, was offered joint rule by Romulus (*q.v.*) may indicate a period of Sabine occupation or domination of Rome.

Sabinus. A mythical Sabine king.

Salmoneus. The son of Aeolus (*q.v.*) and brother of Sisyphus (*q.v.*). The founder of Salmone. His pride led him to emulate the thunder and lightning of Zeus (*q.v.*) who slew him and crushed his city with a thunderbolt.

Sarpedon. The son of Zeus (*q.v.*) and Europa (*q.v.*), brother of Minos (*q.v.*) and Rhadamanthus (*q.v.*). The three brothers quarrelled over the love of the youth Miletus (*q.v.*). Sarpedon went to Asia Minor and became king of the Lycians after helping king Cilix of Cilicia defeat them. Zeus allowed him to live three generations and he helped Troy (*q.v.*) in the Trojan war. Patroclus (*q.v.*) slew him.

Saturn. From *Satus* i.e. "sown". Ancient Mediterranean god of agriculture, possibly of Ligurian origin and particularly revered in Sardinia (*q.v.*) and Africa (*q.v.*). Later identified with Cronus (*q.v.*) who supposedly emigrated to Italy after being deposed by Zeus (*q.v.*). Here he presided over a mythical "Golden Age". His temple in Rome was consecrated in 497 B.C. and housed the state treasury. His festival, the Saturnalia, was celebrated near the winter solstice, originally on 17 December but from the 4th century A.D. on New Year's Day. During the celebrations complete licence was given, slaves took the place of their masters, presents were given, a "Lord of Misrule" appointed and merrymaking and disorder of every kind was rife. It may be that in primitive times his worship involved the sacrifice of humans because in classical times rush dummies in human shape (*argei*) were flung into the Tiber each year on 15 May in his honour.

Satyrs. Young spirits of wildlife, the woods and hillsides. Sons of Hermes (*q.v.*) closely associated with Dionysus (*q.v.*). They were possessed by lechery and a love of wine and embodied the fertile force of nature. Usually they were personified with pointed ears, horns and a tail like Pan's (*q.v.*).

Scaean Gate. The "left hand", the gate in the walls of Troy (*q.v.*) where Achilles (*q.v.*) fell.

Scamander, River. River in Asia Minor near Troy (*q.v.*), originally called the Xanthus. Its name was changed when the mythical Scamander (*q.v.*) of Crete founded a colony in Phrygia and jumped into the river.

Scamander. One-time king of Crete, father of Teucer (*q.v.*) by the nymph Idaea and therefore an ancestor of the Trojans.

Sciron. A robber who dwelt on the border of Attica and Megara. He preyed on travellers and forced them to wash his feet on the Scironian rock. He then kicked them off the rock into the sea to be eaten by a giant turtle. Theseus (*q.v.*) slew him.

Scylla. (1) *See* **Minos.**
(2) *See* **Charybdis.**

Scyrus. Aegean isle, half-way between Lesbos and Euboea and off the major trade routes. It was of no importance save in legend: here Achilles (*q.v.*) was hidden by Lycomedes. It was also here that Lycomedes threw Theseus (*q.v.*) from a rock while the hero was in voluntary exile from Athens after giving the city its first constitution. In 470 B.C. Cimon expelled the local populace in order to install Athenian colonists. At the same time he found the reputed body of Theseus and took it back to Athens amidst great pomp.

Selene. Eastern goddess whom the Greeks identified with Artemis (*q.v.*) and the Romans with Diana (*q.v.*) or the older moon goddess Luna. Both also identified her with Hecate (*q.v.*) and thus the moon became associated with sorcery.

Semele. *See* Dionysus.

Semiramis. The wife of Ninus. These two were the mythical founders of Ninus or Nineveh.

Seven Against Thebes. Oedipus (*q.v.*) cursed his sons for neglecting him, saying they would divide their kingdom by the sword. To avoid this Eteocles and Polynices agreed to rule in turn but Eteocles then refused to give up the throne when his term expired. Polynices sought the help of Adrastus (*q.v.*) king of Argos and married his daughter Argia while her sister married Tydeus son of Oeneus of Calydon who was in exile because of a murder he had committed. Amphiaraus the seer (brother-in-law of Adrastus) prophesied death for all who marched on Thebes save Adrastus. But on the advice of Tydeus, Polynices bribed Eriphyle into persuading Amphiaraus to join them. These four were joined by Capaneus, Hippomedon and Parthenopaeus. The seven were initially successful but Teiresias (*q.v.*) prophesied that a Theban royal prince must sacrifice himself to save the city and Menoeceus did so. The fortunes of the seven now waned. Zeus (*q.v.*) killed Capaneus with a thunderbolt as he stormed the city walls. Tydeus was wounded by Melanippus but Athene (*q.v.*) intended to save him with an elixir from Zeus. But Amphiaraus, who had a grudge against him, persuaded him to drink the brains of Melanippus which so disgusted Athene she let him die. Hippomedon and Parthenopaeus were also slain. Polynices now fought a duel with Eteocles to settle the matter and both were mortally wounded. Amphiaraus was swallowed up by the earth and only Adrastus survived. *See also* **Antigone** and **Epigoni.**

Seven Hills of Rome. The Quirinal, Viminal, Esquiline, Caelian, Capitoline, Palatine and Aventine.

Seven Kings of Rome. Traditionally said to be Romulus, Numa Pompilius, Tullus Hostilius, Ancus Martius, Tarquinius Priscus, Servius Tullius and Tarquinius Superbus.

Seven Sages of Greece. Usually held to be Thales of Miletus, Bias of Priene, Solon, Chilo of Sparta who brought the bones of Orestes (*q.v.*) to Sparta, Periander of Corinth, Pittacus of Mytilene, a democrat, contemporary of Solon and opponent of Alcaeus, and Cleobulus of Rhodes.

Sibyl (Sibylla). A priestess and prophetess who uttered oracles. Localised in several places the term came to be used generically of many sibyls and Varro lists ten. The most famous was at Cumae in Campania and she told Aeneas (*q.v.*) how to enter the Underworld. Ovid says she was seven generations old when Aeneas met her and that Apollo (*q.v.*) had granted her request to live as many years as there were grains in a handful of sand. But she had forgotten to seek eternal youth and was now withered with age. In Petronius' *Satyricon* she hangs in a bottle and when asked what she wants replies "I want to die".

Sibylline Books. A Roman tradition tells how a sibyl (*q.v.*) offered Tarquinius Priscus nine prophetic books which he refused to buy at the price. She destroyed three and he still refused them; she burnt three more and he took the remaining three at the price demanded for the nine. Special priests kept them and they were consulted only when the Senate authorised it in time of need. In 83 B.C. the originals were destroyed by fire but replaced by new ones. Many later additions were made including Jewish and Christian forgeries and fourteen still exist. They were last consulted in the 4th century A.D. and shortly afterwards Stilicho had them burnt. The original books instructed the Romans to convey the sacred stone of Cybele to Rome.

Sigeum. Part of Troy (*q.v.*). Hence the Dardanelles were known as the "straits of Sigeum".

Sileni, Silenus. Scholars distinguish between *sileni* and satyrs (*q.v.*) but the two are very similar and the Greeks themselves seem to have made no distinction. They are regarded as companions of Dionysus (*q.v.*) and have pointed ears, flat noses and the tail of a horse or goat. By the 6th century B.C. one of their number, Silenus, stands out from his fellows for his wisdom and is sometimes said to have been the tutor of Dionysus. His special

knowledge comes from wine drinking and like his fellows he is usually drunk. An old man with horse-ears and tail he proves a good raconteur when captured, though something of a comic drunkard.

Silvanus. Ancient Italian god, a protector of uncultivated land.

Sinis or **Sinnis.** A robber of the Corinthian Isthmus who killed travellers by tying them to the tops of fir trees tied to the ground and then releasing the trees. Theseus (*q.v.*) slew him in the same fashion.

Sinon. A cousin of Odysseus (*q.v.*) and grandson of Autolycus the thief. When the Greeks pretended to leave Troy (*q.v.*) he remained in camp and persuaded the Trojans that the wooden horse was a gift in atonement for the theft of Athene's Palladium (*q.v.*). Once the horse was inside Troy he signalled the Greek fleet to return.

Sirens. In Homer two sisters who lure sailors to their death by their singing. Odysseus (*q.v.*) and the Argonauts (*q.v.*) withstood their fatal charms, the latter because Orpheus (*q.v.*) outsang them. They have been associated with the modern Galli islands. In non-Homeric tradition their number varies and they are portrayed as having the bodies of birds and heads of either sex. Some say they were daughters of Ge (*q.v.*) and companions of Persephone (*q.v.*) who escorted the dead to the Underworld. They were said to feed on the dead. Later they are given the heads of beautiful women and sing to console the dead they escort. Finally they lose their funerary and evil nature and develop fishes' tails like mermaids.

Sisyphus. The son of Aeolus and husband of the Pleiad Merope who bore him Glaucus. He was an ancestor of Bellerophon (*q.v.*) and also seduced Anticleia, mother of Odysseus (*q.v.*) and may have been his father. The founder of Ephyra (later Corinth) and an infamous rogue and knave he was condemned in the Underworld perpetually to push a large stone, uphill, only to see it always roll down, hence the term "labour of Sisyphus" to denote a futile task.

Sophocles. *See* Section B.

Spartii. "The sown men" who sprang up when Cadmus (*q.v.*) sewed the dragon's teeth. They were fully armed and fought amongst themselves until only five remained, Echion, Udaeus, Chthonius, Hyperenor and Pelorus. These helped Cadmus build the Cadmea, citadel of Thebes, and were ancestors of the Thebans. The title was also given to their descendants. Cadmus saved some of the teeth and Jason (*q.v.*) had to sow these to get the Golden Fleece.

Sphinx. A fabulous monster with a human head and the body of a lion. In Egyptian mythology where it originates it could be of either sex but in Greek myth is a female and lives north of Thebes. It was the offspring of Echidne (*q.v.*) and Typhon (*q.v.*) or possibly Orthrus (*q.v.*) and the Chimaera (*q.v.*) and plagued Thebes by strangling and devouring all who could not answer her riddle: what walks on four legs at dawn, two at noon and three in the evening? Oedipus (*q.v.*) answered correctly that it was man who first crawls, then walks upright and finally uses a stick in old age. The sphinx then leapt from her rock and was dashed to pieces.

Stentor. Greek herald in the Trojan war who supposedly had a voice equal to that of fifty men. He died after Hermes (*q.v.*) beat him in a shouting match. His name gives us the word "stentorian" meaning extremely loud.

Steropes. One of the Cyclopes (*q.v.*).

Sthenoboea. Another name for Anteia. *See* **Bellerophon.**

Sthenelus. (1) A king of Mycenae, the son of Perseus (*q.v.*) and Andromeda (*q.v.*). The husband of Nicippe by whom he was the father of Alcinoe, Medusa (*q.v.*) and Eurystheus (*q.v.*).

(2) The son of Capaneus and Evadne, a companion of Diomedes (*q.v.*) and one of the Epigoni (*q.v.*). One of the Greeks in the Wooden Horse (*q.v.*).

(3) A Trojan and companion of Aeneas (*q.v.*).

Stheno. One of the Gorgones (*q.v.*).

Strymon. River in Thrace, believed by the Greeks to be the home of the crane.

Stymphalian Birds. Monsters inhabiting Lake Stymphalus, a marshy area in northern Arcadia. They were huge birds with bronze beaks and claws that ate human flesh. They used their feathers as arrows. The birds were sacred to Ares (*q.v.*) but Heracles (*q.v.*) startled them with bronze castanets provided by Athene (*q.v.*) and shot them. Some say they flew to the Black Sea and were found there by the Argonauts (*q.v.*).

Styx. The river of "hate" in the Underworld and flowing several times around its perimeter. When dipped in it Achilles (*q.v.*) was made invulnerable. Ghosts could only cross it if they paid Charon (*q.v.*) to ferry them across and for this purpose a coin was placed beneath the tongue of corpses. On its far bank was Cerberus (*q.v.*). Aristophanes (*q.v.*) and others describe it as a marsh rather than a river though Herodotus (*q.v.*) identifies it with a trickle from the rock near Pheneus. Generally it was associated with the cascade on Mt. Chelmos further west whose cold waters stain the rock black. Plutarch and Arrian say Alexander the Great was poisoned by water from here brought to him in a mule's hoof.

Sul or Sulis. A Celtic deity identified with Minerva (*q.v.*) by the Romans. The patron of Aquae Sulis.

Symplegades. Floating islands, like icebergs, at the entrance to the Bosphorus. They clashed together and crushed ships. Jason (*q.v.*), on the advice of Phineus, let loose a dove which made them recoil and as they did so the Argo (*q.v.*) slipped between them. Henceforth they remained stationary.

Syrinx. An Arcadian nymph. *See* **Pan.**

T

Talaus. The father of Adrastus (*q.v.*).

Talos. (1) A mythical brazen giant with a bull's head said to protect Crete.

(2) *See* **Daedalus.** Another name for Perdix.

Tantalus. A wealthy king, the son of Zeus (*q.v.*) and the nymph Pluto. The father of Pelops, Broteas and Niobe. He was favoured by Zeus and was invited to Olympian banquets but stole nectar (*q.v.*) and ambrosia (*q.v.*) and revealed Zeus' secrets. He received the golden dog made by Hephaestus (*q.v.*) for Rhea (*q.v.*) (which had watched Zeus' cradle) from Pandareus. This incensed the gods but Tantalus denied having seen it. Pandareus was then put to a miserable death and his daughters were abducted by the Harpies (*q.v.*). His numerous other crimes included serving Pelops (*q.v.*) as a meal to the gods. For this he was punished in the Underworld, either by being placed beneath a huge rock which constantly threatened to fall and crush him or by being placed in a lake the waters of which receded whenever he tried to drink, while above his head were boughs of fruit "tantalisingly" behind his reach.

Tarchon. Legendary ancestor of the Etruscan "Tarquins" who lead a group of emigrants from Lydia to Italy and there founded Tarquinii and other Etruscan cities. He became an ally of Aeneas (*q.v.*).

Tarpeia. The daughter of Tarpeius, commander of the Roman garrison on the Capitol during the Sabine (*q.v.*) wars shortly after Rome's foundation. Her story is told by Livy. She treacherously offered to show the way into the citadel if the Sabine chief Tatius would give her that which his men "wore on their shield arms". By this she meant gold torques but instead the Sabines crushed her to death with their shields. The tale is an attempt to account for the name of the Tarpeian Rock (*q.v.*).

Tarpeian Rock. A precipice on the south-west corner of the Capitol from which traitors and other condemned criminals were thrown to their death. The last victim was an equestrian implicated in a conspiracy against Claudius in 43 A.D.

Tartarus. (1) Another name for Hades (*q.v.*) though in Homer it refers to the deepest reaches of the Underworld, a place of punishment to which the Titans (*q.v.*) and Centimani (*q.v.*) were consigned by Cronus (*q.v.*).

(2) Also the name of a son of Ge (*q.v.*) who was father, by his mother, of the monster Typhon (*q.v.*).

Teiresias or Tiresias. A blind Theban prophet, who, while young, had come upon Athene (*q.v.*) bathing in the nude. She had therefore blinded him but in compensation gave him the gift of prophecy. He revealed to Oedipus (*q.v.*) the truth of his incest. He helped Thebes against the Seven (*q.v.*) then died after drinking from the well of Tilphussa.

Odysseus (*q.v.*) consulted his shade in the land of the Cimmerians.

Telamon. The son of Aeacus and brother of Peleus (*q.v.*). After the two murdered their half-brother Phocus, his father expelled him to Salamis where he married Glauce and later succeeded her father as king. Next he married Periboea of Athens and she bore him Ajax (*q.v.*). A friend of Heracles (*q.v.*) and with him sacked Troy (*q.v.*). He carried off Hesione who bore him Teucer and his refusal to return her to her brother Priam (*q.v.*) was one cause of the Trojan war.

Telchines. Mythical beings, artists in metal work who made a sickle for Cronus (*q.v.*) and the trident for Poseidon (*q.v.*). They raised the infant Poseidon. At times they were destructive and interfered with the weather. They annoyed Zeus (*q.v.*) who drowned a number of them in a flood, and Apollo (*q.v.*) who took the form of a wolf to savage them.

Telemachus. *See* **Odysseus.**

Telephassa. The mother of Europa (*q.v.*) and Cadmus (*q.v.*) by Agenor.

Telephus. The son of Heracles (*q.v.*) and Auge (a priestess and daughter of Aleus, king of Tegea). Abandoned as a child, the Delphic oracle later directed him to the court of king Teuthras in Mysia where he found his mother married to Teuthras. He later succeeded Teuthras and married Laodice, daughter of Priam (*q.v.*). When the Greeks on their way to Troy (*q.v.*) landed in Mysia he repulsed them, but Dionysus (*q.v.*) caused him to trip on a vine and Achilles (*q.v.*) wounded him. An oracle told him he could only be cured by the one who wounded him while the Greeks were told they could not take Troy without his help. He therefore went to Achilles who cured the wound with rust from his spear and in return Telephus showed the Greeks the route to Troy.

Tempe. A vale in Thessaly where Apollo (*q.v.*) pursued Daphne (*q.v.*) and was purified of the killing of Python.

Tenedos. Small island off the coast of Asia Minor, south west of Troy (*q.v.*). Here Achilles (*q.v.*) slew king Tenes (*q.v.*) and his father Cyncus and here Philoctetes (*q.v.*) was wounded.

Tenes. The son of Apollo (*q.v.*) though reputed to be son of Cycnus, king of Colonae in Troas. His stepmother attempted to seduce him and, when he refused her, made false accusations against him. Cycnus then put Tenes and his sister Hemithea into a chest and cast it adrift at sea. It washed up on the isle of Leucophrys where Tenes became king and gave his name to the island, Tenedos (*q.v.*).

Tereus. *See* **Procne.**

Terpsichore. The muse of song and choral dance, portrayed with a lyre and plectrum.

Teucer. (1) The son of Scamander (*q.v.*) and the nymph Idaea. He gave the land to Dardanus (*q.v.*) on which Dardanus built Dardania. An ancestor of the Trojans.

(2) The son of Hesione and Telamon, half brother of Ajax (*q.v.*) behind whose shield he fought at Troy (*q.v.*).

Teucri. Name for the Trojans derived from that of their ancestor Teucer (*q.v.*).

Teuthras. *See* **Telephus.** The father of the girl Tecmessa. Ajax (*q.v.*) raided the Thracian Chersonese, slew him and abducted Tecmessa.

Tethys. A Titaness, mother of Oceanus (*q.v.*) and Metis.

Thalia. (1) Muse of comedy

(2) One of the Charities (*q.v.*).

Thebe. The wife of Zethus, who gave her name to Thebes.

Themis. A Titaness, the daughter of Ge (*q.v.*) and Uranus (*q.v.*) and sister of Cronus (*q.v.*). The wife of Zeus (*q.v.*) before Hera (*q.v.*), she bore him the Horae (*q.v.*) and Moerae (*q.v.*). She determined religious rites, instituted laws and was the first to distinguish between that which was permitted and that which offended the divine order. Hence she became the personification of justice and represented the incarnation of divine law.

Therseander. *See* **Epigoni.**

Theocritus. *See* **Section B.**

Thersites. A low-minded, ugly and mean spirited wretch amongst the Greek forces at Troy (*q.v.*). He accused Agamemnon (*q.v.*) of prolonging the war to serve his own interest until Odysseus (*q.v.*) beat him into silence.

Theseus. The son of Aethra, a princess of Troezen, by Aegeus (*q.v.*) though one tradition says Poseidon (*q.v.*) fathered him in the form of a bull.

Aegeus left her after seducing her but showed her a rock under which he had hidden his sword and sandals. Theseus was raised secretly by his mother at her father's court, and when he reached adolescence lifted the rock to claim Aegeus' sword and sandals. With these he set off for Athens and on the way had many adventures, slaying the wild sow of Crommyum, Sciron (q.v.), Periphetes (q.v.), Cercyon and Procrustes (q.v.). Arriving at Athens Aegeus recognised the sword and sandals and accepted him as his son despite the plots of Medea (q.v.). Theseus then scattered the Pallantides, fifty nephews of Aegeus and the sons of Pallas who hoped to claim the throne themselves. Next he captured the Cretan Bull (q.v.). But his greatest task was to go voluntarily to Crete to slay the Minotaur (q.v.). As one of the tribute demanded by Minos (q.v.) he was to be sacrificed to the monster but Minos' daughter Ariadne fell in love with him and gave him a sword with which to slay the beast and a thread by which he could retrace his steps through the massive labyrinth in which it lived. The couple then fled to Naxos where he left Ariadne and where she was loved by Dionysus (q.v.) whose sacred island it was. Aegeus tragically killed himself on Theseus' return and the hero then became king of Athens. Either alone or with Heracles (q.v.) he invaded the land of the Amazons and carried off either Antiope or Hippolyte. The Amazons attacked Athens but Theseus defeated them in the middle of Athens. By the Amazon queen he became father of Hippolytus (q.v.). Later he married Phaedra and was father by her of Acamas and Demophon (q.v.). A close friend of Pirithous (q.v.), the two shared many adventures. Eventually he returned again to Athens but was ousted by Menestheus and retired to Scyros where, for some reason he was murdered by Lycomedes. Unlike Heracles, Theseus was not worshipped throughout the Hellenistic world but was very much an Athenian hero and his reputed bones were brought to the city from Scyros in historical times. He is said to have gathered the villages of Attica into one state by the process of *synoecismus*.

Thetis. A Nereid (q.v.) who was raised by Hera (q.v.) and remained attached to her. Zeus (q.v.) and Poseidon (q.v.) desired her but it was foretold that her son would be greater than his father. She was thus forced to marry a mortal, Peleus (q.v.), but only after she had tried to avoid him by changing her shape, becoming various animals including a lion. Their wedding on Mt. Pelion was attended by all the gods save Eris (q.v.). They had a number of children who were killed when Thetis tried to make them immortal by throwing them into the fire. Peleus snatched their seventh child, Achilles (q.v.), from her as she tried yet again. Instead she dipped him in the Styx (q.v.). Angry at not giving birth to an immortal she left Peleus to live with her sister Neireids. She cared for Hephaestus (q.v.) when Zeus threw him into the sea, and for Dionysus (q.v.) though she and Briareus (q.v.) freed Zeus when the other gods enchained him.

Thoas. The son of Andraemon king of Calydon who took forty ships to Troy (q.v.) and was one of the Greeks in the Wooden Horse (q.v.).

Thyades. *See* Thyia.

Thyestes. The son of Pelops (q.v.) and Hippodamia and brother of Atreus, ancestor of the illustrious Atridae family. He and Atreus murdered their half-brother Chrysippus and fled to Mycenae. Here Atreus seized the kingdom and banished Thyestes. Thyestes had seduced Atreus' second wife Aerope and he now tricked Atreus into killing Pleisthenes, his son by his first wife. In revenge Atreus lured Thyestes to Mycenae, slew his three sons and served them to him. Thyestes unknowingly ate them. Not surprisingly he cursed the house of Atreus on learning the truth. The Delphic oracle told Thyestes he could get revenge by fathering a son on his own daughter Pelopia, a priestess at the court of Threspotus of Sicyon. He raped her and Atreus later married her, believing her to be the daughter of Threspotus. He raised Thyestes' son Aegisthus (q.v.) as his own.

Thyia. The first woman to worship and sacrifice to Dionysus (q.v.). She gave her name to the Attic women who participated in the orgies of Dionysus at Parnassus, the Thyiades. These women were also called Thyades, "raging women", a similar name but of different origin.

Thyone. *See* Semele.

Thyrsus. A wand carried by the Maenads, covered with ivy wreaths and surmounted by a fir cone.

Tiryns. City reputedly founded by Proetus (q.v.) and built with the help of the Cyclopes (q.v.). The actual site is a mound 300 yd long on the Gulf of Argolis. It was first inhabited in the 3rd millennium B.C. and held a chief's residence and town. Around 1600 B.C. a larger palace was built and ramparts constructed. In the 14th and 13th centuries the rampart was rebuilt and enlarged. Its impressive ruins remain.

Tisiphone. One of the Eumenides (q.v.).

Titanesses. Sisters of the Titans (q.v.), daughters of Ge (q.v.) and Uranus (q.v.) Their numbers included Rhea (q.v.), Themis (q.v.), Tethys and Mnemosyne.

Titanomachia. The ten-year war, waged in Thessaly by Zeus (q.v.) and the Olympian gods against Cronos (q.v.) and the Titans (q.v.) led by Atlas (q.v.). Ge (q.v.) promised Zeus (who had usurped his Titan father Cronos) victory if he would free the Cyclopes (q.v.) and Hecatoncheires (q.v.) from Tartarus (q.v.). He did and the Cyclopes gave him the thunderbolt, Hades (q.v.) a helmet which conferred invisibility and Poseidon a trident. The three overcame Cronos and the Hecatoncheires stoned the other Titans who were defeated and consigned either to Tartarus or an island far to the west. Here the Hecatoncheires guarded them. Atlas was made to carry the sky as punishment but the Titanesses (q.v.) were spared. The war is the basis of Keats' *Hyperion*.

Titans. The sons of Ge (q.v.) and Uranus (q.v.). There were twelve of them though the lists given of their names are inconsistent. The most often named are Cronus (q.v.), Oceanus (q.v.), Hyperion, Iapetus and Atlas (q.v.). Brothers of the Titanesses (q.v.). When Uranus consigned the Cyclopes (q.v.) to Tartarus (q.v.) Ge persuaded Cronos and his brother Titans to depose Uranus. The Titans were in turn deposed in the Titanomachia (q.v.).

Tithonus. The son of Laomedon and Strymor and a half-brother of Priam (q.v.). By Eos (q.v.) the father of Memnon (q.v.). Eos begged Zeus (q.v.) to make him immortal, which he did, but forgot to ask for perpetual youth. Tithonus grew older and older until Eos tired of looking on him, turned him into a cicada and locked him in a cage.

Tities. One of the three primitive tribes of Rome.

Tityus. A giant son of Ge (q.v.) sent by Hera (q.v.) to violate Leto (q.v.) but Artemis (q.v.) and Apollo (q.v.) slew him with their arrows. In Hades (q.v.) he was pegged to the ground (he covered nine acres) while two vultures picked at his liver.

Tleopolemus. A son of Heracles (q.v.) who settled in Argos and later Rhodes.

Triptolemus. *See* Demeter.

Triton. The son of Poseidon (q.v.) and Amphitrite (q.v.) though sometimes several tritons are spoken of. He was a merman, his upper body being human, the lower fish. He blew a shell-trumpet, the concha, to calm the waves and Ovid tells us that he blew the concha to order the waters to recede after the Flood. (*See* Deucalion).

Troilus. A young son of Priam (q.v.) slain by Achilles (q.v.). His romance with Cressida is a medieval invention.

Trojan War. The ten-year siege of Troy (q.v.) and its eventual sack by Greek forces under Agamemnon (q.v.). The combined forces sought to restore Helen (q.v.) to Menelaus (q.v.). The story of the war is told in Homer's *Iliad* where Achilles (q.v.) is the major hero of the Greeks and Hector (q.v.) of the Trojans. According to Homer the war was ended by the Wooden Horse (q.v.) concocted by Odysseus (q.v.). The war is usually placed by tradition as occurring in the 12th century B.C. The war is not a purely mythical episode. Archaeological evidence from the site of Troy shows that the city occupying the seventh stratigraphical layer was destroyed by fire, though probably in the 14th century B.C. Archaeology also confirms the *Iliad's* description of the main towns in Trojan civilisation together with its picture of the Greek people and army.

Trophonius and **Agamedes.** Sons of Erginus who built a temple for Apollo (q.v.) at Delphi. They were rewarded by living merrily for six days and dying in their sleep on the seventh. Trophonius later had an oracle of his own at Lebadeia in Boeotia. Here, according to Pausanias, the questioner underwent a complex initiation, was dressed as a sacrificial victim and (carrying a honey-cake to placate the Underworld divinities) descended into a pot-hole. An underground stream swept him along some distance before he was returned to the light having heard invisible speakers in the cavern. Not surprisingly the questioner would look dazed and dejected and it became common to speak of a gloomy person as one who had been consulting Trophonius.

Tros. (1) The grandson of Dardanus (*q.v.*) and father of Ilus (*q.v.*) and Ganymede (*q.v.*). An ancestor of the Trojans, he gave his name to Troy (*q.v.*). (2) A small town absorbed by the city of Troy (*q.v.*).

Troy. Also called Ilium, a city of Asia Minor near the sea not far from the straits of the Dardanelles. From its position the inhabitants could watch the sea traffic between the Aegean and Sea of Marmara. Many traders off-loaded cargo and used the land route to bypass the dangerous straits. Hence in the late 3rd millennium B.C. Troy became very prosperous from trade, a prosperity which returned at various periods in the 2nd millennium. In 1870 the German Heinrich Schliemann, an amateur archaeologist, sought the site near modern Hissarlik in Turkey. He found it and later excavations have distinguished nine strata of occupations, the richest dating from 2200 B.C. and the 7th showing signs of destruction by fire (*See* **Trojan War**). From the 14th century B.C. the site was of little importance until the Roman occupation when, as Ilium Nevum, it played a large part in provincial life. Homer's Troy had probably absorbed three neighbouring towns, Tros (*q.v.*), Dardania and Ilium and the names of three tribes, Ilians, Trojans and Dardanians are represented in the myths of its foundation.

Tyche or **Tuche.** The Roman "Fortuna", and always more popular in Rome. A daughter of Zeus (*q.v.*) and the goddess of luck who bestowed or denied gifts to men according to her whims. She often accompanied Pluto (*q.v.*). She is portrayed juggling a ball, symbolising the instability of fate, or with a rudder to guide men's affairs.

Tydeus. Son of Oeneus and Calydon, husband of Deipyle. After committing a murder in his youth he fled to the court of Adrastus (*q.v.*). *See* **Seven Against Thebes.**

Tyndareus. The brother of Hippocoon who deposed him as king of Sparta, but Heracles (*q.v.*) reinstated him. Helen (*q.v.*) was brought up at his court (she was his wife Leda's (*q.v.*) child by Zeus (*q.v.*)). Helen married Menelaus (*q.v.*) who succeeded Tyndareus. Tyndareus had had all the Greek nobles who sought Helen's hand swear an oath to defend her chosen husband. This was the reason why the Greeks allied in support of Menelaus in the Trojan War (*q.v.*). Tyndareus also helped Agamemnon (*q.v.*) expel Thyestes (*q.v.*) and regain his throne.

Typhon. The monstrous offspring of Ge (*q.v.*) and Tartarus (*q.v.*), whose eyes could expel fire and whose limbs ended in snakes' heads. He attacked Olympus and the gods fled to Egypt disguised as animals, Zeus (*q.v.*) as a ram, Apollo (*q.v.*) as a cow, Dionysus (*q.v.*) as a goat, Hera (*q.v.*) as a white cow, Artemis (*q.v.*) as a cat, Aphrodite (*q.v.*) as a fish, Ares (*q.v.*) as a boar and Hermes (*q.v.*) as an ibis. Athene (*q.v.*) did not flee and persuaded Zeus to fight. In a great struggle Zeus was saved by Hermes and Pan (*q.v.*) and then defeated Typhon with his thunderbolts. He was then buried under Mt. Etna. By Echidne (*q.v.*) Typhon was father of a variety of monsters.

Tyro. A nymph, the mother of Pelias (*q.v.*) and Neleus (*q.v.*) by Zeus (*q.v.*) and of Aeson by Cretheus. The grandmother of Jason (*q.v.*).

U

Udaeus. One of the Spartii (*q.v.*).

Ulysses. The Roman name for Odysseus (*q.v.*).

Urania. The Muse of Astronomy.

Uranus. The Sky, offspring of Ge (*q.v.*) the earth and brother of Pontus, the sea. The father by Ge of the Hecatoncheires (*q.v.*), the Cyclopes (*q.v.*) and the Titans (*q.v.*). He threw the rebellious Cyclopes into Tartarus (*q.v.*). Ge then persuaded the Titans to rise against their father and avenge their brothers. She gave Cronos (*q.v.*) a flint sickle with

which he castrated Uranus. The blood of Uranus which fell to earth produced the Erinyes and the blood which fell into the sea produced Aphrodite (*q.v.*). Uranus was deposed but cursed Cronos that his own children depose him.

V

Venus. Originally an Italian deity whose name meant "beauty" or "charm", she was a goddess of vegetable rather than animal fertility. She became identified with Aphrodite (*q.v.*) by way of Aphrodite's cult at Mt. Eryx in Sicily, said to have been founded by Aeneas (*q.v.*) on the death of Anchises (*q.v.*). In 217 B.C. Venus Erycina was given a temple at Rome and became completely associated with Aphrodite taking on her functions and attributes. She was patron goddess of Sulla and Pompey. In the imperial cult she played a very important role as the Julian family claimed descent from Aeneas and therefore Aphrodite. In this context she was Venus Genetrix, creator of all things, the universal mother and life giver.

Vesta. A primitive Roman goddess of the hearth, the counterpart of Hestia (*q.v.*). She was worshipped in each Roman house and officially in a circular temple in the Forum. The temple held a fire, said to have come from Troy (*q.v.*) which could never be allowed to go out. It was tended by the Vestal Virgins (*q.v.*). Her cult was purely Italian and never spread to the provinces.

Vestal Virgins. A college of priestesses of the cult of Vesta (*q.v.*). There were originally four of them, later six and finally seven. Candidates for the college were chosen at between six and ten years of age; both their parents had to be alive and they underwent a prolonged special training. They served for thirty years under the control of the Pontifex Maximus and during all this period had to remain virgins. The punishment for unchastity was burial alive. However they were highly honoured and had great privileges. For instance they could save from execution any criminal they met on the way to his death. They lived in a large residence near the temple of Vesta. The sacred fire of Vesta was tended by Vestal Virgins up to the 4th century A.D.

Victoria. The Roman goddess of victory, corresponding to the Greek Nike (*q.v.*).

Virgil. *See* **Section B.**

Vulcan. The Roman god of fire, identified with Hephaestus (*q.v.*) and sometimes called Mulciber, "the smelter". His name gives us the word "volcano".

W

Wooden Horse of Troy. The "Trojan Horse", a stratagem devised by Odysseus (*q.v.*) which ended the Trojan War (*q.v.*). The Greeks had Epeius, son of Panopeus, build a large wooden horse. Athene (*q.v.*) helped him and it bore an inscription dedicated to her. Then twenty-three or more Greeks including Odysseus, Neoptolemus (*q.v.*), Sthenelus and Thoas hid inside it. The rest of the Greek force then burnt their camp and put to sea leaving only the wily Sinon (*q.v.*) to trick the Trojans into dragging the horse into Troy. (*See also* **Laocoön**). Inside the city Helen (*q.v.*) patted the horse and called out the names of those she suspected were inside it, but she was accompanied by the Trojan prince Deiphobus and Odysseus stopped the Greeks answering. At night the Greek fleet returned, Sinon let the men out of the horse, the gates of Troy were opened and the city was sacked.

X

Xenophon. *See* **Section B.**

Xuthus. The son of Hellen and husband of Creusa, the daughter of Erectheus, king of Athens. By her the father of Achaeus and Ion. On the death of

Erectheus Xuthus was asked to determine which of the king's sons should succeed him. He chose Cecrops and was expelled to Achaia by the other heirs. Euripedes (*q.v.*) makes Ion the son of Apollo (*q.v.*) and Creusa.

Z

Zagreus. A son of Zeus (*q.v.*). He was torn apart and eaten by Titans (*q.v.*) except for his heart which Athene (*q.v.*) saved. He is sometimes identified with Dionysus (*q.v.*).

Zephyrus. The son of Astraeus and Eus. He was the west wind, originally imagined, like all winds, in the form of a horse. The father of Xanthus and Balius, the talking horses of Achilles (*q.v.*) which Poseidon (*q.v.*) had given to Peleus (*q.v.*) as a wedding gift. The husband of Iris (*q.v.*). He deflected the discus which killed Hyacinthus (*q.v.*). His Roman counterpart was Favonius.

Zetes. *See* **Calais.**

Zethus. *See* **Amphion.**

Zeus. The son of Cronos (*q.v.*) and Rhea (*q.v.*). He deposed his father and defeated the Titans (*q.v.*). Then he and his brothers Hades (*q.v.*) and Poseidon (*q.v.*) cast lots for their kingdoms and Zeus won the sky. The earth was common to all. Zeus was the king of the gods and was identified with Jupiter by the Romans. He was the father of men. In early legend his consort is Dione, but his consort on Mt. Olympus (*q.v.*) is the jealous Hera (*q.v.*). He first married Hetis who bore him Athene (*q.v.*) and his second wife was Themis (*q.v.*) who bore him the Horae and Maerae. Hera bore him Ares (*q.v.*), Hebe (*q.v.*) and Hephaestus (*q.v.*). His sister Demeter (*q.v.*) bore him Persephone (*q.v.*) and Eurynome bore him the Charities (*q.v.*) while by Mnemosyne he was father of the Muses (*q.v.*). By mortal women he was father of Hermes (*q.v.*), Apollo (*q.v.*) and Artemis (*q.v.*) and Dionysus (*q.v.*). Given the thunderbolt by the Cyclopes (*q.v.*) he was known as the thunderer.

IDEAS &
BELIEFS

This section explains many of the ideas and beliefs that have dominated our history during the centuries. The arrangement is alphabetical and the subjects range from a world-wide spectrum of religious and philosophical terms to the major political ideologies which have shaped contemporary thought. A new Special Topic in this edition examines some of the New Religious Movements that have flourished in recent years.

IDEAS AND BELIEFS

This section explains many of the ideas and beliefs which people have held at different periods in history. Beliefs may be true or false, meaningful or totally meaningless, regardless of the degree of conviction with which they are held. Since man has been moved to action so often by his beliefs they are worth serious study. The section throws a vivid light on human history.

Man has always felt a deep need for emotional security, a sense of "belonging". This need has found expression in the framing of innumerable religious systems, nearly all of which have been concerned with man's relation to a divine ruling power. There is also to be found in man an irresistible curiosity which demands an explanation of the world in which he finds himself. This urge to make the world intelligible takes him into the realm of science where the unknown is the constant challenge. Science is a creative process, always in the making, since the scientist's conjectures are constantly being submitted to severe critical tests. Basic scientific ideas are discussed in **Section T**, while major economic theories are to be found in **Section F**.

A

Abortion is the ending of the life of a foetus after conception and before birth. Is this ever morally right? After 1967 there was a liberalization of abortion laws throughout Europe, but opponents have not given up the argument, making abortion a bitter ethical issue. The Roman Catholic church in particular is strongly opposed to it. Defenders of abortion argue that an embryo is very different from us and that there is little difference between an early abortion and contraception. Opponents focus on the later stages of pregnancy. They talk of 'the unborn child' and claim that abortion is the deliberate killing of an innocent human being and in the same category as murder. So the debate is often about drawing the line as to where one becomes a human being or person. The debate is particularly acrimonious in the USA.

Activists, those in a political movement who insist on taking active steps towards their objectives rather than merely putting forward a programme. Lately activism has become an increasingly common facet of political life. This is probably because the undeniably rapid social changes which are taking place across the world at the moment are not generally being followed by appropriate shifts in political structures and ideals.

Acupuncture, a unique medical system originating in China and based on the established therapeutic effects of implanting fine gold needles in specific parts of the body. The site of needle implantation is decided according to traditional texts. The apparent lack of any logical relationship between the implantation sites and any known physiological or anatomical systems within the body once caused acupuncture to be held in low regard by Western medicine. Indeed it was certainly true that acupuncture and other similar practices tended to flourish in parts of the world where orthodox medicine has made little progress or where doctors and trained staff are scarce. Recent years however have seen a curious and unexpected revival of interest in acupuncture in Europe and America. Chinese medicine has now used acupuncture for over 2000 years. In Britain there is now a growing number of acupuncturists registered with the British Acupuncture Council. Increasingly the British Medical Association (BMA) is endorsing acupuncture as studies show its beneficial effects are similar to Western medicines.

Adlerian Psychology. In 1911 the Viennese psychoanalyst Alfred Adler (1870–1937) together with his colleague Carl Gustav Jung broke with their friend Sigmund Freud over disputes concerning the latter's theoretic approach to psychoanalysis. Jung and Adler were themselves shortly also to part company, each to set up and develop his own "school" of psychoanalysis. Adler's system of psychotherapy is based on the idea, not of sex as a driving force as in the case of Freud, but on the concept of "compensation" or a drive for power in an attempt to overcome the "inferiority complex" which he held to be universal inhuman beings. The child naturally feels inferior to adults, but bullying, making him feel insignificant or guilty or contemptible, even spoiling, which makes him feel important within the family but relatively unimportant outside, increases this feeling. Or the child may have physical defects: he may be small or underweight, have to wear glasses, become lame, be constantly ill, or stupid at school. In these ways he develops a sense of inferiority which for the rest of his life he develops a technique to overcome.

This may be done in several ways: he may try to become capable in the very respects in which he feels incompetent—hence many great orators have originally had speech defects; many painters poor eyesight; many musicians have been partially deaf; like Nietzsche, the weakling, he may write about the superman, or like Sandow, the strong man, be born with poor health.

On the other hand he may overdo his attempt and overcompensate. Hence we have the bully who is really a coward, the small man who is self-assertive to an objectionable degree (Hitler, Napoleon, Stalin, and Mussolini were all small men) or the foreigner who like three of these men wanted to be the hero of his adopted country—Hitler the Austrian, Napoleon the Italian, Stalin the Georgian.

But what about the man who can do none of these things, who continues to fail to compensate? He, says Adler, becomes a neurotic because neurosis is an excuse which means "I could have done so-and-so but . . ." It is the unconscious flight into illness—the desire to be ill. Adler's treatment involves disclosing these subterfuges we play on ourselves so that we can deal with the real situation in a more realistic way. Adlerian psychoanalysis still attracts supporters, but its golden days were when the founder was at the head of the movement in the USA, when his views were considered to provide a more "acceptable" theory of the mind than the controversial theories of Freud with their strong sexual orientation.

Adventists, a group of American religious sects, the most familiar being the Seventh-Day Adventist Church, which observes Saturday as the true Sabbath. With (2004) more than 5 million members throughout the world, it shares with other Adventists a belief in the imminent second coming of Christ (a doctrine first widespread in the USA during the early decades of the 19th cent. when the end of the world was predicted by William Miller for 1843, then for 1844). Modern Adventists content themselves with the conviction that the "signs" of the Advent are multiplying, the "blessed event" which will solve the world's ills. Believers will be saved, but the sects differ as to whether the unjust will be tortured in hell, annihilated, or merely remain asleep eternally.

Agnosticism. See **God and Man.**

Albigenses, also known as Cathars. French heretical sect (named after the town of Albi in Provence) which appeared in the 11th cent. to challenge the Catholic Church on the way true Christians should lead their lives. They followed a life of extreme asceticism in contrast to the local clergy and their faith was adopted by the mass of the local population, especially in Toulouse. Condemned as heretics by Pope Innocent III, the sect was exterminated in the savage Albigensian Crusade (1208–29), initially led by Simon de Montfort. (In his thoroughness, de Montfort also succeeded in destroying the high culture of the Troubadours.)

Alchemy, ancient art associated with magic and astrology in which modern chemistry has its roots. The earliest mention of alchemy comes from ancient Egypt but its later practitioners attributed its origins to such varied sources as the fallen angels of the Bible, to Moses and Aaron, but most commonly to Hermes Trismegistus, often identified with the Egyptian god Thoth, whose knowledge of the divine art was handed down only to the sons of kings (cf. the phrase "hermetically sealed"). Its main object was the transmutation of metals. Egyptian speculation concerning this reached its height during the 6th cent. in the Alexandrian period. Brought to Western Europe by the Moslems, one of its most famous Arab exponents was Jabir (c. 760–c. 815), known to the Latins as Geber, who had a laboratory at Kufa on the Tigris. One school of early Greek philosophy held that there was ultimately only one elemental matter of which everything was composed. Such men as Albertus Magnus (1206–80) and Roger Bacon (1214–94) assumed that, by removing impurities, this *materia prima* could be obtained. Although Bacon's ideas were in many ways ahead of his time, he firmly believed in the philosopher's stone, which could turn base metals into gold, and in an elixir of life which would give eternal youth.

Alternative Medicine includes treatments such as acupuncture (**J2**), osteopathy, aromatherapy and yoga. In Britain nearly 6 million people make use of such treatments. *See also* **Homoeopathy.**

Amish. *See* **Mennonites.**

Anabaptists. *See* **Baptists.**

Analytical Psychology, the name given by Carl Gustav Jung (1875–1961) of Zürich to his system of psychology, which, like Adler's (*see* **Adlerian Psychology**), took its origin from Freud's psychoanalysis from which both diverged in 1911. Briefly, Jung differed from Freud: (1) in believing that the latter had laid too much emphasis on the sexual drive as the basic one in man and replacing it with the concept of *libido* or life energy of which sex forms a part; (2) in his theory of types: men are either extrovert or introvert (*i.e.* their interest is turned primarily outwards to the world or inwards to the self), and they apprehend experience in four main ways, one or other of which is predominant in any given individual—sensing, feeling, thinking, or intuiting; (3) in his belief that the individual's unconscious mind contains not only repressed materials which, as Freud maintained, were too unpleasant to be allowed into awareness, but also faculties which had not been allowed to develop—*e.g.,* the emotional side of the too rational man, the feminine side of the too masculine one; (4) in the importance he attaches to the existence of a collective unconscious at a still deeper level which contains traces of ancient ways of thought which mankind has inherited over the centuries. These are the *archetypes* and include primitive notions of magic, spirits and witches, birth and death, gods, virgin mothers, resurrection, *etc.* In the treatment of the neuroses Jung believed in the importance of (*a*) the present situation which the patient refuses to face; (*b*) the bringing together of conscious and unconscious and integrating them.

In the 1940s and 1950s interest in Jung's ideas waned, at least in academic circles, as the emphasis among experimental psychologists shifted closer and closer to the "hard" scientific line. This was also true in the field of psychoanalysis where the Jungian as opposed to the Freudian point of view became progressively less popular. At the present time this trend is beginning to reverse, and while Jung's offbeat views on astrology, telepathy, *etc.*, are still unfashionable, a reappraisal of the significance of his views on the nature of the unconscious is taking place and many psychologists feel that his contribution to our understanding of the nature of human mental processes has been greatly underrated.

Anarchism, a political philosophy which holds, in the words of the American anarchist Josiah Warren (1798–1874), an early follower of Robert Owen, that "every man should be his own government, his own law, his own church." The idea that governmental interference or even the mere existence of authority is inherently bad is as old as Zeno, the Greek Stoic philosopher, who believed that compulsion perverts the normal nature of man. William Godwin's *Enquiry Concerning Political Justice* (1793) was the first systematic exposition of the doctrine. Godwin (father-in-law of Shelley) claimed that man is by nature sociable, co-operative, rational, and good when given the choice to act freely; that under such conditions men will form voluntary groups to work in complete social harmony. Such groups or communities would be based on equality of income, no state control, and no property: this state of affairs would be brought about by rational discussion and persuasion rather than by revolution.

The French economist Proudhon (1809–65) was the first to bring anarchism to the status of a mass movement. In his book *What is Property?* he stated bluntly that "property is theft" and "governments are the scourge of God". He urged the formation of co-operative credit banks where money could be had without interest and goods would be exchanged at cost value at a rate representing the hours of work needed to produce each commodity. Like Godwin, he disapproved of violence but, unlike Marx, disapproved of trade unions as representing organised groups.

In communistic anarchism these ideas were combined with a revolutionary philosophy, primarily by the Russians Michael Bakunin (1814–76) and Peter Kropotkin (1842–1921) who favoured training workers in the technique of "direct action" to overthrow the state by all possible means, including political assassination. In 1868 anarchists joined the First International which broke up a few years later after a bitter struggle between Bakuninists and Marxists. Subsequently small anarchist groups murdered numerous political figures.

Anarchism and communism differ in three main ways: (1) anarchism forms no political party, rejects all relationship with established authority, and regards democratic reform as a setback; (2) communism is against capitalism, anarchism against the state as such; (3) both have the final goal of a classless society, but anarchism rejects the idea of an intermediate period of socialist state control accepted by communism. Philosophical anarchists, such as the American writer Henry David Thoreau (1817–62), were primarily individualists who believed in a return to nature, the non-payment of taxes, and passive resistance to state control; Thoreau thus strongly influenced Gandhi as did the Christian anarchist Tolstoy.

Although active in the 1917 Russian Revolution, where it opposed Bolshevik dictatorship, anarchism has had little effective political influence. Its most notable achievement was in the anarcho-syndicalist trade union, the CNT, which had mass support in parts of Spain and which developed agricultural and industrial workers' control in the early stages of the 1936–9 civil war. There was a revival in the 1960s student movement, particularly in the 1968 French events, and the anti-capitalist and anti-globalisation movement of recent years has shown renewed interest. *See also* **Syndicalism.**

Anglicanism. *See* **Church of England.**

Anglo-Catholicism. To Queen Elizabeth I the Church of England was that of the "middle way" in which human reason and commonsense took their place beside Scripture and Church authority. The extent to which these various factors are stressed creates the distinctions between "high" and "low" church.

Anglo-Catholics tend to reject the term "Protestant" and stress the term "Catholic" and, although few accept the infallibility of the

Pope some Anglo-Catholic churches have introduced much or all of the Roman ritual and teach Roman dogmas. The ordination in March 1994 of the first women priests to the Anglican ministry caused over 200 former Anglican clergy (many of them married) to be received into the Catholic Church. *See* **Catholicism, Tractarianism.**

Animal Rights. *See* **Anti-vivisection** (*below*).

Animism. To early man and in less developed societies the distinction between animate and inanimate objects was not always obvious—it is not enough to say that living things move and non-living things do not, for leaves blow about in the wind and streams flow down a hillside. In the religions of early societies, therefore, we find a tendency to believe that life exists in all objects from rocks and pools to seas and mountains. This belief is technically known as *animalism*, which differs from *animism*, a somewhat more sophisticated view which holds that natural objects have no life in themselves but may be the abode of dead people, spirits, or gods who occasionally give them the appearance of life. The classic example of this, of course, is the assumption that an erupting volcano is an expression of anger on the part of the god who resides in it.

Anthropomorphism, the attribution of human form, thoughts or motives to non-human entities or life forms from gods to animals. At one end this can be summed up in the once widespread image of God as a "white-bearded old gentleman sitting on a cloud." At the other end is the very common tendency to invest domestic animals and pets with man-like wishes and personalities. At both extremes the belief could be seriously misleading. Firstly, it could be very unwise to assume that God, if he exists, necessarily thinks as humans do and has human interests at heart. Secondly, we shall learn very little about animal behaviour if we look upon them as mere extensions of our own personality, and we do them less than justice if we see them simply as human beings of diminutive intelligence.

Anthroposophy, a school of religious and philosophical thought based on the work of the German educationist and mystic Rudolf Steiner (1861–1925). Steiner was originally an adherent of Madame Blavatsky's theosophical movement (*cf* Theosophy) but in 1913 broke away to form his own splinter group, the Anthroposophical Society. Steiner was much influenced by the German poet and scientist, Goethe, and believed that an appreciation and love for art was one of the keys to spiritual development. One of the first tasks of his new movement was the construction of a vast temple of arts and sciences, known as the Goetheanum, to act as the headquarters of the society. This structure, which was of striking and revolutionary architectural style, was unfortunately burnt down in 1922 to be replaced by an even more imaginative one which today is one of the most interesting buildings of its kind in the world.

Anthroposophy, which continued to expand following its founder's death, is well-established in various parts of the world with specialised, and often very well equipped, schools and clinics which propagate the educational and therapeutic theories of the movement. These, which include the allegedly beneficial powers of music, coloured lights, *etc.*, have made an increasing impact on modern educational ideas, but the schools have acquired a reputation for success in the training of mentally handicapped children. Today there are more than 750 Steiner schools worldwide, many clinics and homes for the handicapped, adult education centres, an international management consultancy, and several hundred thousand acres under biodynamic cultivation without the use of chemical pesticides, herbicides, or fertilizers. Interesting work continues to be done, in pharmacology, botany, mathematics and physics, and architecture. New banking systems, operating rather like credit unions, have arisen (Mercury in Britain, Prometheus in New Zealand).

Anticlericalism, resentment of priestly powers and privileges, traceable in England to Wyclif's insistence in the 14th cent. on the right of all men to have access to the Scriptures. The translation of the Bible into the common tongue was a great landmark in the history of

the Bible and the English language. Wyclif's principles were condemned by the Roman Church of his time but were readily accepted during the Reformation. Tudor anticlericalism arose from motives ranging from a greedy desire to plunder the riches of the Church to a genuine dislike of the powers of the priesthood whose spiritual courts still had the right to decide on points of doctrine or morals in an age when the layman felt he was well able to decide for himself. In innumerable ways the Church was permitted to extort money from the laity. It is generally agreed, says Trevelyan, that the final submission of church to state in England was motivated quite as much by anticlericalism as by Protestantism. The rise of the Reformed churches in England satisfied the people generally and anticlericalism never became the fixed principle of permanent parties as happened in France and Italy.

Anti-Globalisation is either scepticism of the existence of globalisation (*see* **J22**), or opposition to globalisation. Scepticism of globalisation rejects the view that globalisation is new and intrinsically different, and points to the long history of global trade, exchange of ideas and culture, and international treaties and laws. Such sceptics also point to the continued importance of nation states as many groups continue to strive for nationhood, and global free trade struggles with national protected markets and economic subsidies. Opponents regard globalisation as a cloak for the expansion of western, and particularly American economic, political and social power. Some opponents promote an alternative form of globalisation where solidarity and cooperation defeat private capital and western strategic interests. Such has been the motivation of the anti-globalisation protests in London, Seattle and Genoa in recent years.

Antisemitism, a term which gained currency about the middle of the 19th century to those who were anti-Jewish in their outlook. Although this attitude was prevalent for religious reasons throughout the Middle Ages, modern antisemitism differed (*a*) in being largely motivated by economic or political conditions, and (*b*) in being doctrinaire with a pseudo-scientific rationale presented by such men as Gobineau (1816–82) and Houston Stewart Chamberlain (1855–1927), and later by the Nazi and Fascist "philosophers".

It was evident in Russia and Hungary with the pogroms of 1882. It was later to spread south and westwards where, in France, the Dreyfus case provided an unsavoury example in 1894. Thousands of Jews from Eastern Europe fled to Britain and America during this period; for in these countries antisemitism has rarely been more than a personal eccentricity. During the Second World War the murder of six million Jews by the Nazis and their accomplices led to a further exodus to various parts of the world and finally to the creation of the state of Israel.

The individual Jew-hater makes unconscious use of the psychological processes of projection and displacement: his greed or sexual guilt is projected on to the Jew (or Black or Catholic) because he cannot bear to accept them as his own emotions, and his sense of failure in life is blamed on his chosen scapegoat rather than on his own inadequacy.

But there are also causes too and politicians in some lands are well versed in the technique of blaming unsatisfactory conditions (which they themselves may have in part produced) upon minority groups and persuading others to do the same. Historically, the Jew is ideally suited for this role of scapegoat; (1) in the Middle Ages when usury was forbidden to Christians but not to Jews, the latter often became moneylenders incurring the opprobrium generally associated with this trade; (2) many trades being closed to Jews, it was natural that they concentrated in others, thus arousing suspicions of "influence" (*i.e.* Jews are felt to occupy a place in certain trades and professions which far exceeds their numerical proportion to the population as a whole); (3) even with the ending of ghetto life, Jews often occupy *en masse* some parts of cities rather than others and this may lead to resentment on the part of the original inhabitants who begin to feel themselves dispossessed; (4) Jews tend to form a closed society and incur the suspicions attached to all closed societies within which social contacts are largely limited to members; marriage outside the group is forbidden or strongly disapproved of, and the preservation, among the orthodox, of cultural and religious barriers tends to isolate them from their fellow citizens. Since 1990, with the political changes in Russia and Eastern Europe, neo-fascists have begun a resurgence of anti-semitism. Anti-semitism, perhaps the oldest form of racism, is still with us.

Anti-Slavery International, the world's oldest human rights organisation (founded in 1839). It is the successor to the British and Foreign Anti-Slavery Society. Slavery was abolished in the British Empire in 1839. *See* **Special Topic, L119–120.**

Anti-vivisection, opposition to scientific experimentation upon live animals based, according to its supporters, both on the moral grounds of the suffering imposed, and also on the grounds that many doctors and scientists of repute have rejected the value of information gained in this way. It is true that the protagonists of the movement during its early days in the mid-19th cent. included a number of eminent physicians and surgeons. Many people today remain deeply concerned about the moral problems of vivisection, even though without animal experiments we would be unable to test out new drugs for safety before using them on human beings. There are in Britain many active anti-vivisection societies. Much of their work is co-ordinated through the British Council of Anti-Vivisection Societies. In Britain, experiments on live animals are covered by the 1986 Animals (Scientific Procedures) Act. It is estimated that worldwide 200 million animals are killed in experiments each year. Many people would like the number of experiments on animals reduced and the law changed to prohibit any experiments in which there is any risk of inflicting suffering. Recent years have seen an upsurge in support for organisations whose objective is to lessen the suffering of animals. The most militant group is the Animal Liberation Front.

On the more general question of cruelty to animals, a new Animal Welfare Bill is currently (2006) before Parliament, designed to replace the 1911 Protection of Animals Act

Apartheid. An Afrikaans word meaning "apartness", which refers to the policy of total racial discrimination between black and white South Africans by successive governments of that country from 1948 until the early 1990s when the system was dismantled. At its height, apartheid was an inhuman system which denied even the most basic human rights to the Africans.

In January 2000 a far-reaching Equality Bill was introduced in South Africa which sought finally to end the legacy of apartheid.

Arianism, formed the subject of the first great controversy within the Christian Church over the doctrine of Arius of Alexandria (d. 336) who denied the divinity of Christ. The doctrine, although at first influential, was condemned at the Council of Nicaea (325), called by the Emperor Constantine, at which Arius was opposed by Athanasius, also of Alexandria, who maintained the now orthodox view that the Son is of one substance with the Father.

Arius was banished but the heresy persisted until the 7th cent., especially among the barbarians, the Goths, Vandals and Lombards. Disbelief in the divinity of Christ has formed part of the doctrine of many sects since (*e.g.*) **Unitarianism** (*q.v.*).

Arminianism. A theological movement in Christianity, based on the teachings of the Dutch theologian Jacob Harmensen (or Hermansz) (1560–1609), whose name was Latinised as Jacobus Arminius. He reacted against the Calvinist doctrine of predestination. His followers formulated his three main beliefs as: divine sovereignty was compatible with real freewill in man; Christ died for all men (and not only the elect); and all who believe in him can be saved. Arminianism had an important influence on John Wesley and through him on Methodism.

Asceticism. The practice of self-discipline of both mind and body in order to achieve a spiritual ideal or goal. From the Greek *askein*, to practise or exercise. The term originally referred to the training carried out by athletes. The concept was

then transformed into the idea of training for wisdom. This view is clearly articulated in Plato, who argued that one must free oneself from the desires of the body in order to achieve full spiritual insight. Since all religions exalt the soul over the body, the spiritual over the material, and eternal life over this world, they all have traces of asceticism. In many of them, there are adherents who have gone beyond self-denial to self-punishment. Important features of ascetic movements are celibacy, abdication of worldly possessions, abstinence and fasting. Some ascetics have dispensed with washing, or have isolated themselves in deserts or mountains. Extreme ascetics have resorted to self-laceration, wearing iron devices under their clothes, flagellation, even castration

Asceticism has been very important in Christianity, most notably in the monastic movement (*see* **Monasticism**), though practices varied widely among monks, from the extravagant austerity of Egyptian hermits to the work-oriented community life of the Benedictines. Since the rise of Protestantism, however, extreme austerity has been less favoured. Hinduism also has a strong tradition of asceticism, and there are elements in Buddhism and Islam.

Assassins, a sect of Muslim Shi'ites, founded by the Persian Hasan i Sabbah (*c.* 1090), which for more than two centuries established a rule of terror all over Persia and Syria. The coming of the Mongols in 1256 destroyed them in Persia and the Syrian branch suffered a similar fate at the hands of the then Mamluk sultan of Egypt, *c.* 1270. It was a secret order, ruled over by a grand master, under whom the members were strictly organised into classes, according to the degree of initiation into the secrets of the order. The devotees, belonging to one of the lower groups, carried out the actual assassinations under strict laws of obedience, and total ignorance of the objects and ritual of the society. It is believed that these devotees were given ecstatic visions under the influence of hashish, whence the term *hashshashin,* which became corrupted to "assassin".

Associationism. In psychology, the Associationist school of the 19th cent. accepted the association of ideas as the fundamental principle in mental life. It was represented in Britain by the two Mills and Herbert Spencer, in Germany by J. F. Herbart (1776–1841). To these, mental activity was nothing but the association of "ideas" conceived of as units of both thought and feeling—the emotion of anger or the perception of a chair were both "ideas"—and apart from them the self did not exist. Personality was simply a series of these units coming and going, adding to or cancelling each other out, in accordance with rigid scientific laws.

Astrology was once the best available theory for explaining the course of human life and bears much the same historical relationship to astronomy as alchemy does to chemistry

Originally it was divided into two branches: (1) **Natural Astrology** which dealt with the movements of the heavenly bodies and their calculations, and (2) **Judicial Astrology** which studied the alleged influence of the stars and the planets on human life and fate. It was the former that developed into modern astronomy; the latter was, and remains, a myth.

Astrology owes most to the early Babylonians (or Chaldeans) who readily accepted the idea that divine energy is manifested in the movements of the sun and planets. Gradually this concept became enlarged and the relative positions of the planets both in relation to each other and to the fixed stars became important together with the idea of omens—that, if a particular event occurred whilst the planets were in a particular position, the recurrence of that position heralded a recurrence of the same sort of event. Soon the planets became associated with almost every aspect of human life. They were bound up with the emotions, with parts of the body, so that astrology played quite a large part in medicine up to late mediaeval times. Not only was the position of the planet to be considered but also the particular sign of the zodiac (or house of heaven) it was occupying, and it was believed possible to foretell the destiny of an individual by calculating which star was in the ascendant (*i.e.* the sign of the zodiac nearest the eastern horizon and the star which arose at that precise moment) at the time of his birth. Astrology was popular among the Egyptians, the Romans (whose authorities found the Chaldean astrologers a nuisance and expelled them from time to time), and during the Middle Ages when astrologers were often highly respected.

Atheism. See **God and Man.**

Atlantis, a mythical empire supposed to have lain somewhere between Europe and America and a centre of advanced civilisation before it was inundated by some great natural catastrophe in preChristian times. Plato made use of the myth. Some believe the myth was based on the eruption of Santorini. Some recent research suggests a location near the Straits of Gibraltar.

Atomism. In philosophy, the atomists were a group of early Greek thinkers, the most important of whom were Leucippus (fl, c. 440 B C) and his younger contemporary Democritus (c. 400–370 B.C.). Prior to these men, although it had been agreed that matter must be composed of tiny ultimate particles and that change must be due to the manner in which these mingled or separated from each other, it was supposed that there existed different types of particle for each material—e.g. for flesh, wood, hair, bone. The atomists taught that atoms were all made of a single substance and differed only in the connections (pictured as hooks, grooves, points, etc.) which enabled them to join each other in characteristic ways. Theirs was the first move towards modern atomic theory and a predecessor of the modern concept of chemical linkages.

Aum Shinrikyo. See **J61.**

Authoritarianism, a dictatorial form of government as contrasted with a democratic one based on popular sovereignty. Its alleged advantages are the avoidance of the delays and inefficiency said to be characteristic of the latter.

Automatism, the production of material, written or spoken in "automatic" fashion—i.e., apparently not under the conscious or volitional control of the individual. This psychologically perplexing phenomenon has occurred from time to time throughout the history of literature and art, and while it has occasionally produced work of great merit (much of William Blake's poetry, Coleridge's "Kubla Khan", etc.) the bulk of it is indifferent and often simply rubbish. Spiritualists claim that the work is produced under the direct guidances of the spirit world, and their argument has attracted considerable attention through the compositions of the pianist Rosemary Brown who, with little or no academic background in musical theory, has produced a number of "original" piano pieces allegedly composed by Beethoven, Mozart, etc., from the astral plane. While few music critics doubt Mrs. Brown's honesty and integrity, most consider her work to be clever pastiche and barely comparable in quality to the masterworks of the dead composers. Nevertheless automatism wants some explaining, and most psychologists today defer judgement, taking the view that it serves to remind us of the fund of material which lies in the unconscious mind, and which is prone to pop up from time to time without warning.

Rather similar is the case of Matthew Manning, a young English student who produced clever and artistically intriguing drawings and sketches, allegedly guided by the hands of famous dead artists.

Ayurveda (Sanskrit, the Science of Life), a philosophy based on divine Hindu writings, which seeks to prolong both physical and spiritual life and health.

B

Baconian Method, the use of the inductive (as opposed to the deductive or Aristotelian) method of reasoning as proposed by Francis Bacon in the 17th cent. and J. S. Mill in the 19th cent. Deduction argues from supposedly certain first principles (such as the existence of God or Descartes's "I think, therefore I am") what the nature of the universe and its laws *must* be,

whereas the only means of obtaining true knowledge of the universe, in Bacon's view, was by the amassing of facts and observations so that when enough were obtained the certain truth would be known in the same way that a child's numbered dots in a playbook joined together by a pencilled line create a picture. However, this is not the way science progresses in practice. Bacon had underrated the importance of hypothesis and theory and overrated the reliability of the senses. In discussing the scientific tradition, Sir Karl Popper in his book, *Conjecture and Refutations*, says: "The most important function of observation and reasoning, and even of intuition and imagination, is to help us in the critical examination of those bold conjectures which are the means by which we probe into the unknown." Two of the greatest men who clearly saw that there was no such thing as an inductive procedure were Galileo and Einstein.

Bahá'í Faith. Although its origins lie within Islam, the Baha'i movement today considers itself to be the fourth branch of the Western Monotheistic Tradition. Believing that God's revelation to mankind did not end with the Prophet Muhammad, Baha'is revere two further figures, Bab and Baha'u'lla. It was begun in 1844 by a Persian Muslim, Mirza Ali Muhammad, who pronounced himself to be Bab, 'The Gate', who would be a forerunner for a greater prophet. Upon his execution in 1850, one of his closest followers Mirza Husayn-Ali Nuri, also known as Baha'u'lla, 'The Glory of God' took over the community and in 1863 announced that he was the promised one. Baha'is revere the holy writings of both figures and believe them to be the first-hand writings of God's own messengers.

The fundamental beliefs of the faith relate to God sending a messenger in every generation to bring together the teachings of those who have gone before. It prides itself on inclusion, having no priesthood or liturgy and a structure based on gender and race equality as well as absolute democracy. Although at times plagued by internal disputes, it claims that the message of Baha'u'lla is for the whole of mankind. An emphasis is placed on the education of all, traditional family values and healthy living, including the recommendation of vegetarianism.

Baptists, a Christian denomination whose distinctive doctrines are that members can only be received by baptism "upon the confession of their faith and sins" and that "baptism is no wise appertaineth to infants." Baptism is therefore by total immersion of adults. Modern Baptists base their doctrines upon the teaching of the Apostles and some hold that the Albigenses (q.v.) maintained the true belief through what they regarded as the corruption of the Roman Church in mediaeval times. On the other hand any connection with the Anabaptist movement during the Reformation is rejected and the beginning of the modern Church is traced to John Smyth, a minister of the Church of England who in Amsterdam came under the influence of the Arminians (q.v.) and Mennonites. Smyth died in 1612 when the first Baptist church in England was built at Newgate.

This, the "General" Baptist Church, rejected Calvinistic beliefs and held the Arminian doctrine of redemption open to all, but some years later a split occurred with the formation of the "Particular" Baptist Church which was Calvinist in doctrine. In 1891 the two bodies were united in the Baptist Union and today the sect is spread throughout the world, notably in the United States. There are (2006) less than 150,000 Baptists in Great Britain.

The Anabaptist movement began in Zurich, Switzerland, in 1525, when Conrad Grebel, Felix Manz and Jörg Blaurock, their hearts moved by their failure to live according to the Gospel, decided to give their lives to following Christ's teaching, whatever the cost. The movement spread widely in Switzerland, Germany and Holland in the 16th century, and its followers suffered martyrdom by fire, water and the sword for the sake of their faith. They met with further condemnation and persecution because of the excesses of a violent and radical group, known as the Münster Anabaptists, whom they disowned.

The wider movement was non-violent and stood for baptism on confession of faith, love to one's enemies and obedience to the Spirit of Christ's Sermon on the Mount. This movement is the spiritual precursor of several of the Peace Churches of today: the Hutterians (named after their founder, Jakob Hutter), the Mennonites (after Menno Simons), and, later, the Amish.

The most radical of these groups is that of the Hutterian Brethren, who live, work, and hold their goods in common like the first Christians.

Beat Generation, a term first used by the American writer Jack Kerouac (1922–69), author of *The Town and the City* and *On the Road*, to define various groups spread across the face of the country, but notably in New York and San Francisco, who, belonging to the post-war generation, represented various rebellious attitudes to authority.

Behaviourism, a school of psychology founded in 1914 by J. B. Watson (1878–1958), an animal psychologist at Johns Hopkins University, Baltimore. Its main tenet was that the method of introspection and the study of mental states were unscientific and should be replaced by the study of behaviour. When animals or human beings were exposed to specific stimuli and their responses objectively recorded, or when the development of a child, as seen in its changing behaviour, was noted, these alone were methods which were truly scientific. Watson contributed an important idea to psychology and did a great deal towards ridding it of the largely philosophical speculations of the past. But he also went to absurd extremes, as in his view that thought is nothing but subvocal speech, consisting of almost imperceptible movements of the tongue, throat, and larynx (*i.e.*, when we think, we are really talking to ourselves), and his further opinion that heredity is, except in grossly abnormal cases, of no importance. He claimed that by "conditioning", the ordinary individual could be made into any desired type, regardless of his or her inheritance.

The work of Ivan Pavlov had begun about 1901, but was unknown in America until about ten years later, and it was through another Russian, Vladimir Bekhterev, that the concept of "conditioning" was introduced into the country. Bekhterev's book *Objective Psychology*, describing his new science of "reflexology", was translated in 1913 and played a great part in the development of Behaviourist ideas. The conditioned reflex became central to Watson's theory of learning and habit, formation (*e.g.*, he showed that a year-old child, at first unafraid of white rats, became afraid of them when they came to be associated with a loud noise behind the head).

Finally all behaviour, including abnormal behaviour, came to be explained in terms of conditioned responses; these were built up by association on the infant's three innate emotions of fear, rage, and love, of which the original stimuli were, for the first, loud noises and the fear of falling; for the second, interference with freedom of movement; and for the third, patting and stroking.

Because of its considerable theoretical simplicity and its implicit suggestion that human behaviour could be easily described (and even modified or controlled), Pavlovian psychology appeared very attractive to the Communist regime in Russia, and before long it became the "official" dogma in universities and research laboratories. Whereas in America and Western Europe its severe limitations became gradually apparent, in the former USSR these were ignored or disguised for ideological reasons with the inevitable outcome that Soviet psychology failed to evolve and, at one stage, seemed to be no more than a pallid offshoot of physiology. In non-Communist countries simple Watsonian behaviourism evolved into more sophisticated studies of animal learning, largely pioneered by the Harvard psychologist, Skinner. These techniques, which have shown that animals, from monkeys to rats, may be taught to solve a remarkable range of physical problems (such as pressing complex sequences of buttons or levers to escape from a cage) have themselves turned out to be rather disappointing in terms of advancing our general understanding of the workings of the human and animal brain. There is a growing feeling among psychologists that the real keys to the understanding of mankind will only be found through the study of man himself, and not his simpler animal cousins. *See also* **Gestalt Psychology.**

Benthamism. *See* **Utilitarianism.**

Bermuda Triangle, an area of sea, bounded by Bermuda, Florida and Puerto Rico where unexplained disappearances of aircraft and ships have led to many fanciful theories. Natural phenomena are the most likely explanation.

Bioethics, the application of ethics (**J58**) to such fields as the biological sciences, medicine, health-care *etc.* as well as the debate on which policies should be approved by government in these areas.

Biopsychology, the study of the biological and physiological bases of behaviours and psychological processes. It is considered to be a branch of neuroscience and includes the study of: the structure and development of the nervous system; the effects of hormones and other chemicals on neural activity; the effects of drugs, surgery and electrical manipulation on the central nervous system; and the genetics and heritability of behavioural traits.

Bolshevism. When the Russian Social Democratic Party at a conference held in London in 1903 split over the issue of radicalism or moderation, it was the radical faction headed by Lenin which polled the majority of votes. The Russian for majority is *bolshinstvo* and for minority *menshinstvo*; hence the radicals became known as Bolsheviks and the moderates as Mensheviks. Bolshevik was sometimes used (wrongly) in a derogatory way to include all communists (after the Bolshevik seizure of power in Russia in 1917). *See* **Communism, Marxism.**

Brahma Kumaris. *See* **J59.**

Brahmanism. A religion of ancient India which evolved out of the Vedas about 1000–800 B.C. and is still powerful today. It provides the orthodox core of traditional Hinduism. Characteristics of the faith were elaborate ceremonies, material offerings, animal sacrifice, a dominant priestly caste (the Brahmins), and a development of the idea of Brahman as the eternal, impersonal Absolute Principle. *See also* **Hinduism.**

Branch Davidians. *See* **J61.**

Buchmanism. *See* **Moral Re-Armament.**

Buddhism, one of the great Oriental religions. It arose against the background of Brahmanism in north India in the 6th cent. B.C., its founder being the Sakyan prince Siddhattha Gotama, known as the Buddha or "Enlightened One". Distressed by the problem of human suffering from which even death allowed no escape—since Buddha accepted a doctrine of a cycle of lives—he left his palace and his beloved family to become a religious mendicant and ascetic, studying for six years the beliefs of Brahmin hermits and self-torturing recluses. After this long search he sat down under a tree (the Banyan tree, which became known as the Bo-tree or tree of enlightenment because of his enlightenment) and finally came to understand the cause and release from suffering. The result of his meditations are enshrined in the "four noble truths" which are: (1) that all living is itself suffering; (2) suffering is caused by desire; (3) suffering ceases when desire is eradicated; (4) that it can be destroyed by following the "noble eightfold path" whose steps are: right views; right thought; right speech, plain and truthful; right conduct, including abstinence not only from immorality and the taking of life, whether human or animal; right livelihood, harming no one; right effort, always pressing on; right awareness of the present; and lastly, right meditation. The more man acquires merit by following these rules in his chain of lives, the sooner is *Nirvana* attained; he loses his individuality, not by annihilation, but "as the dewdrop slips into the shining sea," by merging with the universal life.

Buddhism teaches a way of liberation through ethics and meditation. In many Buddhist nations no word exists for the concept of an Almighty God, which was neither affirmed nor denied by Buddha himself but simply ignored. Nor did Buddha claim to be other than a man, although prayers were made to Buddha, ritual developed, sacred relics preserved under stupas, and the belief in a succession of Buddhas introduced; the sacred writings (*Tripitaka*) are divided into three parts; *Suttanta*, *Abhidhamma* and *Vinaya*. *Suttanta* are mostly teachings in everyday language, *Abhidhamma* are teachings using the analytical method and the *Vinaya* is the monastic rule for monks. They were gathered by devotees at various councils—the first held after the death of Buddha at the age of 80, a third at the order of King Asoka in 244 B.C. The founder himself wrote nothing.

Buddhism spread to Sri Lanka, Nepal, Tibet, Mongolia, Indo-China, Myanmar (Burma), Thailand, China, and Japan, although on the whole losing influence in India. In Tibet, Buddhism developed into Lamaism (*q.v.*). In Sri Lanka, Burma, Thailand *etc.*, it persisted in its pure form (the Theravada), while in China and Japan it developed into the Mahayana. Today (2006) there are *c.* 370 million Buddhists world-wide, with around 152,000 in Britain. Fragments of the oldest known Buddhist manuscript (the religion's equivalent to the Dead Sea Scrolls) were discovered by the British Library in 1996.

Bushido, the traditional code of honour ot the Samurai or Japanese military caste corresponding to the European concept of knighthood and chivalry. Bushido evolved in the 12th cent. Even today it is a potent influence among the upper classes, being based on the principles of simplicity, honesty, courage, and justice which together form a man's idea of personal honour.

C

Cabala, originally a collection of Jewish doctrines about the nature of the Universe, supposedly handed down by Moses to the Rabbis, which evolved into a kind of mystical interpretation of the Old Testament. Students of the history of religious belief have found its origins to be in fact extremely obscure, and some aspects appear to have been lifted from ancient Egyptian sources. Skilled Cabalists hold that the system contains a key to biblical interpretation based on the numerical values of the words and letters of the Scriptures which reveal hidden depths of meaning behind the allegorical Old Testament stories. This 'received' teaching is now enjoying a major revival (*e.g.* in the USA).

Calvinism, the branch of Protestantism founded basically (although preceded by Zwingli and others) by Jean Chauvin (1509–64), who was born in Noyon in Picardy. John Calvin, as he is usually called, from the Latin form of his name, Calvinius, provided in his *Institutions of the Christian Religion* the first logical definition and justification of Protestantism, thus becoming the intellectual leader of the Reformation as the older Martin Luther was its emotional instigator. The distinctive doctrine of Calvinism is its dogma of predestination which states that God has unalterably destined some souls to salvation to whom "efficacious grace and the gift of perseverance" is granted and others to eternal damnation. Calvinism, as defined in the Westminster Confession, is established in the Reformed or Presbyterian churches of France, Holland, Scotland, *etc.*, as contrasted with the Lutheran churches, and its harsh but logical beliefs inspired the French Huguenots, the Dutch in their fight against Spanish Catholic domination, and the English Puritans. The rule set up under Calvin's influence in Geneva was marred by the burning at the stake of the anatomist Servetus for the heresy of "pantheism", or, as we should say, Unitarianism.

Perhaps its greatest single influence outside the Church was the result of Calvinist belief that to labour industriously was one of God's commands. This changed the mediaeval notions of the blessedness of poverty and the wickednesss of usury, proclaimed that men should shun luxury and be thrifty, yet implied that financial success was a mark of God's favour. In this way it was related to the rise of capitalism either as cause or effect. Max Weber, the German sociologist, believed that Calvinism was a powerful incentive to, or even cause of, the rise of **capitalism** (*q.v.*): Marx, Sombart, and in England, Tawney, asserted the reverse view—that Calvinism was a result of developing capitalism, being its ideological justification.

Capitalism is an economic system under which the means of production and distribution are owned by a relatively small section of society which runs them at its own discretion for private profit. There exists, on the other hand, a propertyless class of those who exist by the sale of their labour power. Caplitalism arose towards the end of the 18th cent. in England where the early factory owners working with small-scale units naturally approved of free enterprise and free trade. But free enterprise has no necessary connection with capitalism; by the beginning of this century monopolies were developing and state protection against foreign competition was demanded. Capitalism is opposed by those who believe in socialism (*q.v.*), first, for the moral reasons that it leads to economic inequality and the exploitation of labour and the consuming public, and that public welfare rather than private profit should motivate the economic system, secondly, for the practical reason that capitalism has led to recurrent economic crises. Any major world economic crisis led to great hopes on the part of Marxists and Communists that capitalism was involved in its final death throes.

Cartomancy, the art of fortunes or predicting the future by playing cards or by the Tarot pack.

Caste System. *See* **Hinduism.**

Cathars. *See* **Albigenses.**

Catholic Reformation. *See* **Counter-Reformation.**

Catholicism. For those who are not Roman Catholics the term "Catholic" has two separate meanings. The more general refers to the whole body of Christians throughout the world, the more specific refers to a particular view of Christianity. In this latter sense the Church of England, the Orthodox Eastern Churches, and others consider themselves "Catholic" meaning that (*a*) they belong to Christ's Church as organised on an accepted basis of faith and order; (*b*) they insist on the necessity of "liturgical" worship through established forms (*e.g.*, baptism, holy communion); (*c*) they emphasise the continuity of Christian tradition by the use of ancient creeds (*e.g.*, the Apostles' Creed, the Nicene Creed) and regard the ministry as a succession (Apostolic succession) deriving from early practice. In this sense there is thought to be no necessary contradiction between Catholicism and Protestantism regarded as a renewal of the Church in the 16th cent. by an appeal to the Scriptures as interpreted by the early Fathers of the Church. This definition obviously excludes Quakers, Christian Scientists, and many Nonconformist sects. *See also* **Roman Catholic Church.**

Characterology, the attempt made over many centuries to classify people into personality types on the basis of physical or psychological characteristics. The first attempt was made by Hippocrates in the 5th cent. B.C. who classified temperaments into the *sanguine* (or optimistic), the *melancholic*, the *choleric* (or aggressive), and the *phlegmatic* (or placid).

Theophrastus, a pupil of Aristotle, described, with examples, thirty extreme types of personality (*e.g.* the talkative, the boorish, the miserly, *etc.*); these were basically literary and imaginative but about the same time "physiognomy" arose which attempted to interpret character from the face.

Physiognomy subsequently became of importance again during the Renaissance and there are still those today who believe in it in spite of the fact that, broadly speaking, there is no connection whatever between facial features and personality (*i.e.* although it may be possible to tell from the features that a man is an idiot or some extreme abnormal type and some idea of character may be obtained from an individual's characteristic facial expressions, it is not possible to tell (as Johann Lavater, the bestknown physiognomist of the late 18th cent. believed) from the shape of the nose, height of the brow, or dominance of the lower jaw, whether anyone is weak, intellectual or determined). The old contention of the 19th cent. Italian criminologist Cesare Lombroso that criminals show typical facial characteristics was convincingly disproved by Karl Pearson when he found that 3,000 criminals showed no major differences of features, carefully measured from a similar number of students at Oxford and Cambridge.

It has, however, been noted that people in general tend to be intellectual or emotional, inward- or outward-looking, and this observation is reflected in the classification of the Scottish psychologist, Alexander Bain (d. 1903), into intellectual, artistic, and practical; Nietzsche's Apollonian and Dionysian types; William James's "tender" and "toughminded"; and C. G. Jung's introvert and extrovert.

Some connection has been found between temperament and body-build. The German psychiatrist Ernst Kretschmer (1888–1964) showed that manic-depressive patients and normal people who are extroverted and tend to alternate in mood (as do manic-depressives to an exaggerated degree) were usually short and stout or thick-set in build; schizophrenics and normal people, who both show shyness, serious or introverted reactions, were usually tall and slender. The former of "pyknic" body-build are "cyclothyme" in temperament, the latter with "schizothyme" temperament are of two bodily types—the tall and thin or "asthenic" and the muscularly well-proportioned or "athletic". The American Sheldon has confirmed these observations on the whole and gone into further details. According to him the basic body types are: (1) *endomorphic* (rounded build), corresponding to Kretschmer's pyknic, normally associated with the *viscerotonic* temperament (relaxed, sociable); (2) *mesomorphic* (squarish, athletic build), normally associated with the *somatotonic* temperament (energetic, assertive); and (3) *ectomorphic* (linear build) normally associated with the *cerebrotonic* temperament (anxious, submissive, restless).

Glandular and metabolic factors have considerable effect on human personality and also, to some extent, on physique. It is not too surprising, therefore, to find an association between body build (or "somatotype" as Sheldon termed it) and general mood. However, Sheldon's original clear-cut categories of body-type are no longer looked upon as reliable indicators of personality.

Charismatic, the evangelical, 'New Church' Christian movement that has broken away from the traditional Church. The 'house church' movement is part of this rapidly-growing movement, which started in Britain with the 1987 'March for Jesus'.

Chartism, a socialistic movement in England (1837–55) which attempted to better the conditions of the working classes. Named after "The People's Charter" of Francis Place (1838), its programme demanded: (1) universal manhood suffrage; (2) vote by ballot; (3) equal electoral districts; (4) annual parliament; (5) payment of members; (6) abolition of their property qualifications. Chartism was supported by the Christian socialists (*q.v.*), J. F. D. Maurice (1805–72), and Charles Kingsley (1819–75) with certain qualifications. The movement, the first mass organisation of the industrial working class, had considerable influence on the evolution of socialist ideas in England. It is worth noting that its demands—with the exception of the unworkable "annual parliament"—have largely been met today, though at the time they were thought by many to be both outrageous and impossible. The movement failed at the time from internal divisions.

Chauvinism, a term applied to any excessive devotion to cause, particularly a patriotic or military one. The word is derived from Nicholas Chauvin whose excessive devotion to Napoleon made him a laughing-stock.

Chirognomy, the study of the shape of the hands and fingernails.

Chirology, the subject concerned with the hand as an indicator of psychological and medical significance. Chirology derives from an Oriental tradition concerning mental and physical healing and spirituality and as such encompasses many associated arts and studies of direct relevance to modern day living. Palmistry in the main is a crude folk art and does not attempt to understand or clarify its own teachings.

The Cheirological Society was founded in 1889 by Katherine St. Hill to promote the systematic study of the hand as a serious subject worthy of scientific attention bereft of superstition and fakery. It still exists today and has members throughout the world.

Chiromancy, the study of lineal formations of the hand.

Chiropractic, the art of manipulation of the joints, in particular the spine, as a means of curing disease. Some qualified doctors employ its principles and, as with its near-neighbour osteopathy, it seems on occasions to be a useful complement to medical treatment.

Christadelphians, The Christadelphians (or Brothers of Christ) were founded in 1848 by an English doctor, John Thomas, who, having been saved from a shipwreck on his emigration to America, vowed to devote his life to the service of Christ. In 1849, believing that the Last Days had begun, he published Elpis Israel, 'The Hope of Israel' promising the restitution of the nation. It was not designed however to be a replacement for the Bible which Christadelphians regard as inerrant and the sole source of revelation. Congregationalist in background, Thomas also advocated local ecclesiastical authority, but went further in rejecting the need for a priesthood. Critical of other Christian Churches in their approach to the interpretation of the Bible and the nature of Christ, they are neither Trinitarian nor Unitarian in their dogma.

Christadelphians believe strongly in Christ's atoning work, but regard evil as a human failing rather than as the work of a supernatural power. Moreover, they do not believe in the traditional concepts of heaven, hell or the immortality of the soul, believing rather in a millenialist approach to the resurrection of the faithful upon earth. Although previous predictions have proved inaccurate, Christadelphians still feel strongly that the world is in its latter days.

Christianity, the religion founded by Jesus Christ whose teaching is found in the New Testament's four Gospels. Simple as His creed may seem it soon became complicated by the various ways in which Christians interpreted it, and the differences within the early Church are reflected in the numerous Councils held to define truth from heresy. The Eastern Church of the Byzantine Empire from the 5th cent. onwards had differed in various ways from the See of Rome and by 1054 the breach became permanent. The 16th cent. Reformation was the other great break in the unity of the Church and once Protestantism had given in effect the right to each man to interpret the Scriptures in his own way, the tendency to fragmentation increased so that, by 1650, there were no fewer than 180 sects, mostly dogmatic and intolerant towards each other. Today there are many more, some of which are mentioned in this section under the appropriate headings. Nevertheless there are signs today that the trend of disunity is being reversed. The modern ecumenical movement, which has its roots in the great missionary movement of the 19th cent., aims to bring about a reunion of Christendom by uniting Christians throughout the world on the simple basis of the acceptance of Jesus Christ as God and Saviour, *i.e.*, on the basis of Christian fellowship. The movement finds expression in the World Council of Churches (*q.v.*). The Christian life is expressed in the words of Christ: "Thou shalt love the Lord thy God with all thy heart and thy neighbour as thyself."

For many it is the humanitarian side of Christianity that has meaning today; to accept responsibility for others, as well as for oneself.

Christian Science. Founded around 1866 by Mary Barker Eddy, Christian Science is noted for its belief in the power of spiritual healing practised and inaugurated by Christ Himself. It uses as its key text along with the Bible, 'Science and Health with Key to the Scriptures,' although this has undergone substantial revisions over time. Literature forms a very important part of the life of Christian Scientists, and compulsory purchase of reading material is an important Church practice. The worship follows the 'Church Manual' laid down by Mrs. Eddy in 1895 and many statutes of church organisation still refer to her direct authority. Claiming to be a reinstitution of primitive Christianity, it regards evil and suffering as non-existent, and healing occurs by believing through prayer that the illness does not exist.

Christian Science uses the term healing to refer to all the 'ills' which befall mankind, and they argue that moral regeneration goes hand in hand with physical restoration. Members make a commitment to refrain from harming their bodies to the extent of avoiding tea and coffee, and abstain from non-marital sexual relationships. Non-trinitarian in nature, Christian Scientists believe that the Christ-spirit has been present in good men and women down the ages.

Christian Socialism, a movement launched in 1848, a year of revolutions throughout the continent, by a group in England designed to commit the church to a programme of social reform. The leaders, notably J. F. D. Maurice, Charles Kingsley (both Anglican clergymen), and John Ludlow were deeply moved by the wretched conditions of the British working class and the two priests had, indeed, given active support to the Chartist movement (*q.v.*). However, all insisted that socialism in its existing forms ignored the spiritual needs of mankind and must be tempered with Christianity. Tracts were written to expose the sweated industries, the consequences of unrestrained competition and the evils following the enclosure system; but, more concretely, Christian socialism fostered co-operative workshops and distributive societies based on those of the Rochdale pioneers, organised a working-man's college, and set up elementary classes for education. It also supported the emerging trade-union movement.

The traditions of Christian socialism have been carried on by the Fabian Society, by adherents of Guild Socialism, and by individuals who reject Marx's teaching of revolutionary change and seek methods of political action.

Church of England. There is some evidence of possible continuity with the Christianity of Roman Britain, but in the main the Church derives from the fusion of the ancient Celtic church with the missionary church of St. Augustine, who founded the See of Canterbury in A.D. 597. To archbishop Theodore in 673 is ascribed its organisation in dioceses with settled boundaries, and in parishes. St. Augustine's church was in communion with Rome from the first, but the Church of England was not brought within papal jurisdiction until after the Norman conquest, and was at no time under the complete domination of Rome.

It remains (at least in one sense) the Catholic Church of England without break of continuity, but during the Reformation the royal supremacy was accepted and that of the pope repudiated. It is the Established Church (*i.e.*, the official church of the realm), crowns the sovereign, and its arch-bishops and bishops in the House of Lords can act as a kind of "conscience of the state" at every stage of legislation. The Church is organised in two ecclesiastical provinces (Canterbury and York) and 43 dioceses. Its traditional forms of worship are embodied in the Book of Common Prayer, but the Alternative Service Book of 1980 is also widely used. A new service book, *Common Worship*, was introduced in 2000. The 39 articles (*see also* **Tractarianism**) embody its main tenets.

In 1992, the General Synod finally accepted the ordination of women priests. The first 32 women priests were ordained on 12 March 1994 in Bristol Cathedral. The first 42 Anglican women priests in Scotland were ordained in the Scottish Episcopal Church in December 1994. By 1997, 10% of Anglican clergy were women.

The first women priests in Wales were ordained in 1997, whilst in 1996 the Movement for the Ordination of Women was reformed to campaign for Anglican women bishops. The first Anglican woman Provost was appointed (to Leicester Cathedral) in 2000. In February 2005 the Synod began to take the first real steps for women to become bishops by 2010.

In 1997 the General Synod formally agreed to unity talks with the Methodists. More recently, controversy surrounded the decision in 2002 by the Church of England to relax its ban on divorcees remarrying in Church (although remarriage of divorcees was previously forbidden, in practice all 43 dioceses allowed remarriage in certain circumstances). All these continuing problems faced Dr Rowan Williams, the current Archbishop of Canterbury who succeeded Dr. Carey in 2002.

The crisis in Anglicanism reached a new height in 2003, caused by three events: the nomination (and subsequent withdrawal) of the gay Dr Jeffrey John as Bishop of Reading; the election of the openly gay Canon Gene Robinson as Bishop of New Hampshire by the Episcopal Church of America; and the same-sex blessings authorised in New Westminster, Canada. An emergency conference of the 38 primates held at Lambeth Palace in October 2003 established a commission to investigate these issues, narrowly avoiding schism. The ensuing Windsor Report urged moderation and restraint. The failure of the February 2005 Anglican "summit" in Northern Ireland left the Church still facing possible schism.

The **Anglican Communion** comprises 38 self-governing churches (or provinces) spread across 164 countries which are in communion with the Church of England. All the bishops of the Anglican Communion meet every ten years in the Lambeth Conference (first held in 1867), over which the Archbishop of Canterbury by custom presides as *primus inter pares*. At the 1968 Conference observers and laymen were admitted for the first time. The 1998 Lambeth Conference (attended by 798 bishops) strongly supported the traditionalists over homosexuality issues. The 2008 Lambeth Conference will be held in Canterbury.

Church of Jesus Christ of Latter Day Saints. *See* **Mormons.**

Church of Scotland, the established national church of Scotland, presbyterian in constitution, and governed by a hierarchy of courts—the kirk-sessions, the presbyteries, the synods, and the General Assembly. Its congregations have declined rapidly in recent years (from 1,133,000 in 1971 to around 600,000 in 2006). *See* **Presbyterianism.**

Clairvoyance. *See* **Telepathy.**

Collectivism. The theory of the collective ownership or control of all the means of production, and especially of the land, by the whole community or state, *i.e.* the people collectively, for the benefit of the people as a whole. The term has also acquired a broader sense, to denote the view that the individual is subordinate to the social collectivity. An influential expression of collectivist ideas can be found in Rousseau's *Du contrat social* (1762). It is an important theme in Hegel and Marx, and has been expressed in such movements as socialism, communism and fascism. Collectivism is to be contrasted with individualism (*q.v.*).

Colonialism. Colonialism refers to the kind of imperialism practised by European countries in for example Africa and S.E. Asia, where the colonised country was allowed to have partially autonomous legal and social institutions, while the mother country retained supreme power, and the colonial community had social and political rights denied to the natives. "Neo-colonialism" means the cultural and economic infiltration of developing countries by manipulation of market forces. *See also* **Imperialism.**

Communism, ideally refers to the type of society in which all property belongs to the community and social life is based on the principle "from each according to his ability, to each according to his needs." There would be public ownership of all enterprises and all goods would be free.

Since no such society as yet exists, the word in practice refers to the attempt to achieve such a society by initially overthrowing the capitalist system and establishing a dictatorship of the proletariat (Marx identified the dictatorship with a democratic constitution). Communists believe that their first task is the establishment of socialism under which there remain class distinctions, private property to some extent, and differences between manual and brain workers. The state is regulated on the basis "from each according to his ability, to each according to his work". Lenin applied Marx's analysis to the new conditions which had arisen in 20th-cent. capitalist society. Marxism–Leninism develops continuously with practice since failure to apply its basic principles to changed circumstances and times would result in errors of dogmatism. Mao Tse-tung worked out the techniques of revolutionary action appropriate to China; Che Guevara the guerrilla tactics appropriate to the peasants of Latin America. His counsel "It is not necessary to wait until conditions for making revolution exist; the insurrection can create them", was the opposite of Mao Tse-tung's "Engage in no battle you are not sure of winning", and Lenin's "Never play with insurrection". A fundamental principle of communism is the class struggle between oppressed and oppressing classes and between oppressed and oppressor nations. Maoism, for example, held that it was a mistake to lay one sided stress on peaceful transition towards socialism otherwise the revolutionary will of the proletariat becomes passive and unprepared for the tasks ahead.

In Russia the civil war developed *after* the revolution; in China the communists fought their civil war *before* they seized power; the Yugoslav partisans won their own guerrilla war *during* their stand against the fascist powers—differences which had important political consequences. Russia suffered three decades of isolationism and totalitarian suppression ("an isolated and besieged fortress") before the advent of Gorbachev heralded a new openness (*glasnost*) in Soviet politics.

Following the collapse of the Soviet Union, only Cuba, North Korea and China remain under Communist Party control and even China is restoring the role of private ownership in the economy, while retaining the party's political dominance. *See* **Maoism, Marxism** and **Trotskyism**.

Confucianism. Confucius (Latinised form of K'ung-Fo-tzu) was born in 551 B.C. in the feudal state of Lu in modern Shantung province. He was thus a contemporary of Buddha, although nobody could have been more dissimilar. Where Buddha was metaphysical in his thought, Confucius was practical; Buddha was original, Confucius had hardly an original idea in his head; Buddha wanted to convert individuals to an other-worldly philosophy. Confucius wanted to reform the feudal governments of his time, believing that in this way their subjects would be made happier. Other religions have in their time, been revolutionary; Confucius was a conservative who wanted to bring back a golden age from the past. The only respect in which Confucius agreed with the Buddha was that neither was particularly interested in the supernatural.

Much of his time was spent in going from the court of one feudal lord to another trying to impress them by his example. For he suffered from the curious belief that the example set by the ruler influences his subjects. He made much of etiquette, trembling and speaking in low tones and behaving with "lofty courtesy" to his inferiors. Promoting the idea of "the golden mean", he was not impressed by heroic deeds or unusual people, and was greatly displeased when he heard that a truthful son had reported that his father had stolen a sheep: "Those who are upright", he said, "are different from this; the father conceals the misconduct of the son, and the son conceals the misconduct of the father." One feels that Confucius would have felt not at all out of place in an English public school. Virtue brings its own reward in this world, ceremonial is important, politeness when universal would reduce jealousy and quarrels; "reverence the spirits but keep them far off." Destiny decides to what class a man shall belong, and as destiny is but another name for Nature prayer is unnecessary, for once having received his destiny, a man can demand and obtain from Nature what he chooses, his own will decides.

Congregationalists, the oldest sect of Nonconformists who hold that each church should be independent of external ecclesiastical authority. They took their origin from the Brownists of Elizabeth's days. Robert Browne (*c.* 1550–*c.* 1633), an Anglican clergyman, who had come to reject bishops, was forced with his followers to seek refuge, first in Holland and then in Scotland where he was imprisoned by the Kirk. In later life he changed his views and is disowned by Congregationalists because of his reversion to Anglicanism. His former views were spread by Henry Barrow and John Greenwood who, under an Act passed in 1592 "for the punishment of persons obstinately refusing to come to church" (and largely designed for the suppression of this sect), were hanged at Tyburn. They had preached (*a*) that the only head of the church is Jesus Christ; (*b*) that, contrary to Elizabethan doctrine, the church had no relationship to the state; (*c*) that the only statute-book was the Bible whereas the

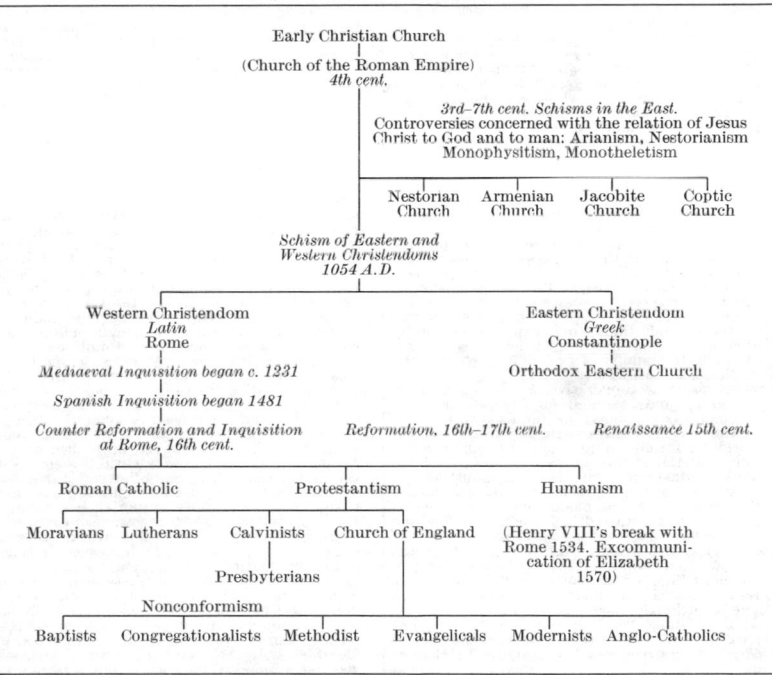

Early Christian Church

(Church of the Roman Empire)
4th cent.

3rd–7th cent. Schisms in the East.
Controversies concerned with the relation of Jesus
Christ to God and to man: Arianism, Nestorianism
Monophysitism, Monotheletism

| Nestorian Church | Armenian Church | Jacobite Church | Coptic Church |

*Schism of Eastern and
Western Christendoms
1054 A.D.*

Western Christendom
Latin
Rome

Mediaeval Inquisition began c. 1231

Spanish Inquisition began 1481

*Counter Reformation and Inquisition
at Rome, 16th cent.*

Eastern Christendom
Greek
Constantinople

Orthodox Eastern Church

Reformation, 16th–17th cent.   *Renaissance 15th cent.*

| Roman Catholic | Protestantism | Humanism |

(Henry VIII's break with
Rome 1534. Excommuni-
cation of Elizabeth
1570)

Moravians Lutherans Calvinists Church of England

Presbyterians

Nonconformism

Baptists Congregationalists Methodist Evangelicals Modernists Anglo-Catholics

Articles of Religion and Book of Common Prayer were mere Acts of Parliament; (d) that each congregation of believers was independent and had the power of choosing its own ministers. The body fled once more to Holland and were among the Pilgrims who set sail in the *Mayflower* for America in 1620 whilst those who remained were joined by Puritans fleeing from Charles I. They became free once more to live in England under the Commonwealth only to be repressed again under Charles II. Finally full liberty of worship was granted under William III. In 1833 the Congregational Union of England and Wales was formed which had no legislative power. It issued a Declaration of Faith by which no minister was bound; he was responsible to his own church and to nobody else.

The sect is widespread both in Britain and the USA where it is held in special honour because of its connection with the Pilgrim Fathers. In 1972 the Congregational Church in England and Wales and the Presbyterian Church of England united to form the United Reformed Church. Those who did not join comprise the Congregational Federation.

Conservatism, is sceptical of rationalism as the lodestar of politics and social life. Conservatives instead prefer the inherited wisdom of tradition and history, regarding the persistence of values and institutions through time as a good pragmatic reason to justify their authority. Edmund Burke crystallised conservatism in his *'Reflections on the Revolution in France'* which argued that society was an organic unity with a naturally hierarchical relationship between its parts. A similar opposition to rationalism in politics was expressed in the 20th century by Michael Oakeshott. Oakeshott argued that socialism's rational approach to political problems ignored the style of human relationships that were ordered more by experience, tradition, wisdom, and prudence.

Contemporary conservative politics has been dominated more by neoliberalism (q.v.) than traditional conservative values. Contemporary conservatives share an opposition to social democratic values and bureaucratic state institutions, but favour a view of society as a free market rather than an organic unity.

Consumerism. Traditionally, an individual's identity and role in society was seen as determined by what they produced. Being a miner, a farmer, or an office clerk would contribute greatly to the nature of a person's income, social class, and opportunities. Increased prosperity, wider social and geographical mobility, and more pervasive markets have allowed for consumption to be a more important and dominant feature of the identity of persons and societies. The proliferation of choice and products, combined with relentless advertising, has allowed consumerism to pervade all areas of life and society: toddlers and children are important consumers in contemporary markets.

Consumerism has also encroached on politics, and not simply in the promotion of political parties as brands and products. Parents and the sick are encouraged to see health and education as products to be consumed in a competitive market place. Successive governments have justified this on the grounds that people expect choice in all areas of life, and that competition for consumers improves the quality of products, whether toasters, health, or education.

Cooperativism. A cooperative is an organization owned by and operated for the benefit of its members, who may be either workers or customers. They have been set up all over the world, for farming, purchasing of equipment and raw materials, and in wholesaling, retailing, banking, insurance and housing industries. In most cooperatives the members receive a share of the net earnings. The modern consumer cooperative movement started in Rochdale in 1844 and developed rapidly in the second half of the 19th century, mostly in the industrial areas of Northern England and Scotland. It spread quickly through northern Europe. Development in the USA and Latin America came later in the 20th century.

Coptic Church, the sect of Egyptian Christians who, holding "Monophysite" opinions (*i.e.*, refusing to grant the two natures, God and Man, of Christ), were declared heretical by the Council of Chalcedon in 451. They practise circumcision and have dietary laws. Their language is a direct descendant of ancient Egyptian. Like the Armenians, they are regarded as an heretical branch of Eastern Christianity. Their religious head is the patriarch of Alexandria.

Counter-Reformation. A movement in the 16th and 17th centuries in Europe, by which the Roman Catholic church reformed itself, defined its doctrines, strengthened its discipline and halted the advance of Protestantism. The Council of Trent (1545–1563) aimed at removing abuses within the church and defining Catholic thought in the debate with Protestantism. New, more active religious orders were founded, in particular the Jesuits (1534). The greater control exercised over church doctrine was seen in the setting up of the Inquisition and an Index of Prohibited Books. Some historians now prefer the term Catholic Reformation to Counter Reformation.

Creationism. The theory which attributes the origin of matter, the different species of plants and animals, *etc.*, to "special creation" by a supreme being or deity. Creationists thus accept that the Book of Genesis is a literal description of the beginning of the world. It is this doctrine which fundamentalist Christians have opposed to the evolutionary theories of Darwin, which have come to be accepted by most scientists since the publication of *The Origin of Species* in 1859. An attempt was made in the 1980s in the United States to have creationism taught alongside evolution, but failed in the US Supreme Court.

A second slightly older meaning of the term is in reference to the theory that God creates a soul for every being born.

Cynics, a school of philosophy founded in the time of Alexander the Great by Diogenes. Choosing to live like a dog by rejecting all conventions of religion, manners, or decency, and allegedly living in a tub. Diogenes unwittingly brought on his school the title "Cynic," meaning not "cynical", as the word is understood today, but "canine". His teacher, Antisthenes, who had been a disciple of Socrates, decided, after the latter's death, that all philosophy was useless quibbling and man's sole aim should be simple goodness. He believed in a return to nature, despised luxury, wanted no government, no private property, and associated with working men and slaves. Far from being cynics in the modern sense, Diogenes and Antisthenes were virtuous anarchists rather like old Tolstoy.

D

Dalits. See **Untouchables**.

Daoism. See **Taoism**.

Deism. See **God and Man**.

Demonism, Demons, and the Devil. Demons are ethereal beings of various degrees of significance and power which are believed to be implicated in men's good, but especially evil, fortune. They are common to most cultures. From the anthropological point of view the demon arose as a widespread concept in the following ways: (1) as a psychological projection into the outer world of man's own good or evil emotions and thoughts; (2) as a survival of primitive animism (q.v.), thus spirits are believed to haunt places, trees, stones, and other natural objects; (3) when by warlike invasion the gods of the vanquished become the devils of the conquerors (as when the Jews occupied Canaan); (4) as a primitive belief that spirits of the dead continue after death to hover near their former habitation, and not always entirely welcome to the living; (5) the conception of a supreme source of evil (the Devil or Satan) which took shape among the Jews during their sojourn in Babylon under the influence of Zoroastrianism (q.v.), a religion in which the struggle between the two spirits, Good and Evil, reached its height in the imagination of the ancient world.

The Satan of the Old Testament was first regarded as one of God's servants (in the Book of Job he goes up and down the earth to see whether God's commands are obeyed), but when the Jews returned from their captivity he had become identified with Ahriman, the spirit of evil, who was in continual conflict with Ahursa Mazda, the spirit of good. The primitive mind ascribed both good and evil to one power alone; the division into God and the Devil, priest and witch, belongs to a higher stage of civilisation. The worship of evil itself, or of its personification in Satan, is a curious practice which seems to have developed hand-in-hand with Christianity and to have received steady support from a small but measurable minority. Many of the ceremonies involved in Satanism or in the so-called Black Mass appear to have been no more than opportunities for sexual excesses of one kind or another—such indulgences being traditionally barred to devout Christians.

Determinism and Free-will. The question of whether man is, or is not, free to mould his own destiny is one which has exercised the minds of philosophers since Greek mythology conceived of the Fates as weaving a web of destiny from which no man can free himself. Socrates emphasised that man could through knowledge influence his destiny whilst ignorance made him the plaything of fate; Plato went further in pointing out that man can, and does, defeat the purposes of the universe and its divine Creator. It is our duty to live a good life, but we can live a foolish and wicked one if we chose. Aristotle wrote "Virtue is a disposition or habit involving deliberate purpose or choice". If this were not so morality would be a sham.

The Problem for Theology. The last of the great philosophers of Antiquity and one of the great influences in moulding Catholic theology was Plotinus (c. 204–70). Soul, he taught, is free, but once enmeshed in the body loses its freedom in the life of sense. Nevertheless, man is free to turn away from sensuality and towards God who is perfect freedom; for even when incarnated in matter the soul does not entirely lose the ability to rescue itself. This conception was carried over into the beliefs of the early Christian Apologists because it appeared to be in line with the teaching of Jesus that He had come to save man from sin. Sin implies guilt, and guilt implies the freedom to act otherwise; furthermore an all-good God cannot be responsible for the sin in the world which must be man's responsibility and this again implies freedom. Pelagius (c. 355–c. 425), a Welsh priest, not only believed in free-will but questioning the doctrine of original sin, said that when men act righteously it is through their own moral effort, and God rewards them for their virtues in heaven. This belief became fairly widespread and was declared a heresy by the Church, being attacked notably by St. Augustine (354–430), a contemporary of Pelagius, who believed in predestination—that, since the sin of Adam, God had chosen who in all future history would be saved and who damned. This represents one tradition in Christianity: the determinism which leads to Calvinism (q.v.).

St. Thomas Aquinas (1227–74), the greatest figure of scholasticism and one of the principal saints in the Roman Catholic Church, compromised between the two positions in the sense that, believing man to be free, he yet held that Adam's sin was transmitted to all mankind and only divine grace can bring salvation. But even when God wishes to bestow this salvation, the human will must cooperate. God foresees that some will not accept the offer of grace and predestines them to eternal punishment.

The Problem for Philosophy. With the Renaissance, thinkers began to free themselves from the domination of the Church and so study the world objectively and freely without preconceptions. But the more man turned to science, the more he discovered that the world was ruled by apparently inexorable laws and, since the scientist must believe that every event has a cause, he was led back to determinism. Man as part of the universe was subject to law too and all that existed was a vast machine. Francis Bacon (1561–1626) separated the fields of religion and science but left man subject completely to the will of God. Thomas Hobbes (1588–1679) was a rigid determinist and materialist although, having had trouble with the church in France whence, as a royalist, he had fled, he took care to announce that the Christian God is the Prime Mover.

Modern philosophy begins with René Des-

cartes (1596–1650), a Frenchman who tried to reconcile the mechanical scientific universe of his time with the spiritual need for freedom. He did this by separating completely mind and body; the former, he said, is free, the latter completely determined. But, by admitting that the will can produce states of body, he was left with the problem of how this could happen—a problem which the so-called Occasionists solved to their own satisfaction by stating that the will is free and God so arranges the universe that what a person wills happens. Baruch Spinoza (1632–77), a Dutch Jew whose independence of thought had led to his excommunication from the Amsterdam Synagogue in 1656, was a complete determinist. He asserted that God and Nature are one, everything that happens is a manifestation of God's inscrutable nature, and it is logically impossible that things could be other than they are. Thus both Hobbes and Spinoza were determinists for entirely opposed reasons. The former as a materialist, the latter because he believed in the absolute perfection and universality of God. Yet the great religious mystic and mathematician Blaise Pascal (1623–62) held that, no matter what reason and cold logic may indicate we *know* from direct religious experience that we are free. John Calvin (1509–64) and Martin Luther (1483–1546) were both determinists. *See* **Calvinism, Lutheranism.**

Locke and Hume. To the British philosophers, John Locke (1632–1704) and David Hume (1711–76), free-will was related to personality. Locke believed that God had implanted in each individual certain desires and these determine the will; the desires are already there, but we use our will to satisfy them. Hume argued that a man's behaviour is the necessary result of his character and if he had a different character he would act otherwise. Accordingly, when a man's actions arise from his own nature and desires he is free. He is not free when external events compel him to act otherwise (e.g., if he strikes another because his own nature is such he is free as he is not if he is compelled to do so against his desire). Leibnitz (1646–1716), although as a German metaphysical philosopher holding very different general views, said much the same thing—that choice is simply selecting the desire that is strongest. But most of the 18th cent. thinkers after Voltaire, with the great exceptions of Rousseau and the later German philosophers Kant, Fichte, Schopenhauer, and Hegel, who were initially influenced by him, accepted determinism. Rousseau (1712–78) began to stem the tide by his declaration that man is a free soul striving to remain free and only prevented from being so by society and the cold science which stifles his feeling heart. Once again the will became important as Kant (1724–1804) asserted that belief in freedom is a moral necessity although it cannot be proved by reason; the moral nature of man shows that there is a "transcendental" world beyond the senses where freedom applies. Fichte and Schelling found freedom in the Absolute ego or God, of whom each individual was part and thus also free. Hegel (1770–1831) saw the whole universe as evolving towards self-awareness and freedom in man although this could only be fully realised in a society that makes for freedom. Even God himself only attains full consciousness and self-realisation through the minds of such individuals as are free. This is the goal of the dialectical process. (*See* **Dialectical Materialism.**)

The Scientist's View. For the scientist the law of cause and effect is a useful hypothesis since, by and large, it is necessary for him to assume that all events are caused. Nevertheless the modern tendency is to think in terms of statistical probability rather than relentless mechanistic causality, and, although the free-will problem does not concern the scientist as such, it is clear that freedom and determinism (assuming the terms to have any meaning at all) are not necessarily opposed. In sociology, for example, we *know* that certain actions will produce certain results upon the behaviour of people in general, e.g., that raising interest rates will discourage business expansion. But this does not mean that Mr. Brown who decides in the circumstances not to add a new wing to his factory is not using his free-will. Even in the case of atoms, as Dr. Bronowski has pointed out, the observed results of allowing gas under pressure in a cylinder to rush out occur because most of the atoms are "obeying" the scientific "law" relating to such situations. But this does not mean that some atoms are not busy rushing across the stream or even against it—they are, but the general tendency is outwards and that is what we note. Lastly, the modern philosophical school of Logical Analysis would probably ask, not whether Free-will or Determinism is the true belief, but whether the question has any meaning. For what scientific experiment could we set up to prove one or the other true? The reader will note that some of the philosophers mentioned above are using the words to mean quite different concepts.

Dialectical Materialism, the combination of Hegel's dialectic method with a materialist philosophy produced by Karl Marx (1818–83) and his friend Friedrich Engels (1820–95). It is the philosophical basis of **Marxism** (q.v.) and **Communism** (q.v.) "Dialectic" to the ancient Greek philosophers meant a kind of dialogue or conversation, as used particularly by Socrates, in which philosophical disputes were resolved by a series of successive contradictions: a thesis is put forward and the opposing side holds its contradiction or antithesis until in the course of argument a synthesis is reached in which the conflicting ideas are resolved.

From Thesis through Antithesis to Synthesis. Hegel in the 19th cent. put forward the view that this process applies to the course of nature and history as they strive towards the perfect state. But to him, as to the Greeks, the conflict was in the field of ideas. The "universal reason" behind events works through the ideas held by a particular society until they are challenged by those of another which supersedes them and in turn, usually by war, becomes the agent of universal reason until the arrival of a new challenger. Hegel therefore regarded war as an instrument of progress and his Prussian compatriots found no difficulty in identifying their own state as the new agent of progress by universal conquest. Feuerbach, Lassalle, and other early socialists were impressed by some of Hegel's ideas: *e.g.,* that societies evolved (with the assumption that finally their own ideal society would be achieved) and that truth, morals, and concepts were relative so that a society that was "good" at one time was not necessarily so at another.

However, Marx and Engels in effect turned Hegel upside-down, accepted his dialectic but rejected his belief that ideas were the motive force. On the contrary, they said, ideas are determined by social and economic change as a result of materialistic forces. (*See* **Calvinism,** where it is pointed out that the Marxist view is not that Calvin changed men's economic ideas but rather that a developing capitalism unconsciously changed his.) The historical materialism of Marxism purports to show that the inexorable dialectic determines that feudalism is displaced by capitalism and capitalism by creating a proletariat (its antithesis) inevitably leads to socialism and a classless society. The state, as a tool of the dominant class, withers away. Dialectical materialism is applied in all spheres. As a philosophy there is little to be said for it save that it has shown us the close dependence of man's thoughts upon material and social conditions. But as a battle-cry it wielded immense power over the minds of men. *See also under* **Marxism.**

Dianetics. *See* **Scientology.**

Diggers, one of the many sects which flourished under the Commonwealth (others were the Muggletonians, the Levellers, the Millenarians, and the Fifth Monarchy Men), so-called because they attempted to dig (*i.e.* cultivate) untilled land. Gerrard Winstanley, a profoundly religious man, and leader of the Diggers, believed in the economic and social equality of man and castigated the clergy for upholding the class structure of society. In his book *The True Leveller's Standard Advanced* (1649) he wrote: "Every day poor people are forced to work for fourpence a day, though corn is dear. And yet the tithing priest stops their mouth and tells

them that "inward satisfaction of mind' was meant by the declaration "the poor shall inherit the earth'. I tell you, the Scripture is to be really and materially fulfilled. You jeer at the name "Leveller'; I tell you Jesus Christ is the Head Leveller".

Divine Light Mission. *See* **J61.**

Doukhobors, a religious sect of Russian origin, founded by a Prussian sergeant at Kharkov in the middle of the 18th cent., and now mainly settled in Canada. Like many other sects they belong to that type of Christianity which seeks direct communication with God and such bodies tend to have certain traits in common, such as belief in the "inner light", opposition to war and authority in general, and often ecstasies which show themselves in physical ways such as shaking, speaking in strange tongues (glossolalia), and other forms of what to the unbeliever seem mass hysteria. Liturgy, ritual, or ceremony is non-existent. The Doukhobors were persecuted in Tsarist Russia, but in 1898 Tolstoy used his influence to have them removed to Canada in what is now Saskatchewan.

Dowsing. *See* **Radiesthesia.**

Dreamtime, in Australian aboriginal mythology, the period of time when mystic beings shaped the natural environment. Some of these mystic beings took human form. Human life was created by the great fertility mother. To the aborigines, these mystic beings are spiritually alive today. Alternative names for this period are *World Dawn* or *The Dreaming.*

Druidism, the religion of Celtic Britain and Gaul of which Druids were the priesthood. They were finally wiped out by the Roman general Suetonius Paulinus about A.D. 58 in their last stronghold, the island of Anglesey. There are two sources of our present beliefs in Druidism:

(1) the brief and factual records of the Romans, notably Pliny and Julius Caesar, which tell us that they worshipped in sacred oak groves and presumably practised a religion doing reverence to the powers of nature.

(2) the beliefs put forward by William Stukeley, an amateur antiquarian who from 1718 did valuable work by his studies of the stone circles at Stonehenge and Avebury. However, influenced by the Romantic movement, he later put forward the most extravagant theories which unfortunately are those popularly accepted by those without archaeological knowledge today. Stonehenge and Avebury were depicted as the temples of the "white-haired Druid bard sublime" and an attempt was made to tie up Druidism with early Christianity, above all with the concept of the Trinity. In fact, these circles have no connection with the Druids. They may have made ceremonial use of them but recent evidence suggests that the megalithic stones at Stonehenge belong to a Bronze Age culture (2100–1600 B.C.). Nor have Druidism and Christianity any relationship.

Druse, an offshoot of Islam, with around 300,000 followers in the Lebanon and *c.* 500,000 around the world.

Dualism, any philosophical or theological theory which implies that the universe has a double nature, notably Plato's distinction between appearance and reality, soul and body, ideas and material objects, reason and the evidence of the senses, which infers that behind the world as we perceive it there lies an "ideal" world which is more "real" than that of mere appearance. In religions such as Zoroastrianism and the Gnostic and Manichaeism heresies, it was believed that the universe was ruled by good and evil "principles"—in effect that there was a good God and a bad one. In psychology, dualism refers to the philosophical theories which believe mind and body to be separate entities. The opposite of dualism is monism which asserts the essential unity of the substance of the universe.

An essential problem in the dualistic view lies in the question as to how and where the two separate and distinct properties of the universe interact. Where, for example, does the "mind" actually mesh with the physical mechanics of the brain and body—where does the ghost sit in his machine? Descartes decided that mind and body must interact somewhere and he selected the pineal gland (an apparently functionless part of the brain) as the spot. But this did nothing to explain how two *totally different* aspects of nature can possibly influence each other, today most philosophers and psychologists reject dualistic views of life and personality as posing more problems than they solve. *See also* **Psychology, Occam's Razor**.

E

Ecumenism, a world movement which springs from the Christian belief that all men are brothers and that the Christian Church should be re-structured to give reality to the belief. Christ's church exists not to serve its own members, but for the service of the whole world. Some see the answer in a united church of a federal type (unity in diversity), others in an organic structure with one set of rules. The period since the convening of the Second Vatican Council by Pope John has been one of prolonged discussion among Christian theologians with the aim of promoting Christian unity. *See* **World Council of Churches**.

Education. Education was no great problem to primitive man, but as societies became more complex people began to ask themselves such questions as: *What* should young people be taught? *How* should they be taught? Should the aim of their education be to bring out their individual qualities or rather to make them good servants of the state?

The first teachers were priests who knew most about the traditions, customs, and lore of their societies and thus the first schools were in religious meeting places. This was notably true of the Jews who learned from the rabbis in the synagogue.

The Greeks. We begin, as always, with the Greeks whose city-states, based on slavery, educated men (not women) for the sort of life described in Plato's *Dialogues*—the leisured life of gentlemen arguing the problems of the universe at their banquets or in the market-place. This made it necessary to learn debate and oratory (or rhetoric) especially for those who proposed to take up politics. The Sophist philosophy taught the need to build up convincing arguments in a persuasive manner, to learn the rules of logic and master the laws and customs of the Athenians, and to know the literature of the past so that illustrations might be drawn from it. These strolling philosophers who taught for a fee were individualists showing the student how to advance himself at all costs within his community.

Socrates had a more ethical approach, believing that education was good in itself, made a man happier and a better citizen, and emphasised his position as a member of a group. His method of teaching, the dialectic or "Socratic" method, involved argument and discussion rather than overwhelming others by rhetoric and is briefly mentioned under **Dialectical Materialism** (*q.v.*). Today this method is increasingly used in adult education where a lecture is followed by a period of discussion in which both lecturer and audience participate; for psychologists have shown that people accept ideas more readily when conviction arises through their own arguments.

Socrates' pupil Plato produced in his book *The Republic* one of the first comprehensive systems of education and vocational selection. Believing that essentially men have very different and unequal abilities he considered that in an idealistic or utopian society they should be put into social classes corresponding to these differences, and suggested the following method: (1) For the first 18 years of a boy's life he should be taught gymnastics and sports, playing and singing music, reading and writing, a knowledge of literature, and if he passed this course sent on to the next stage; those who failed were to become tradesmen and merchants. (2) From 18–20 those successful in the first course were to be given two years of cadet training, the ones thought incapable of further education being placed in the military class as soldiers. (3) The

remainder, who were to become the leaders of society, proceeded with advanced studies in philosophy, mathematics, science, and art. Such education was to be a state concern, state supported and controlled, selecting men and training them for service in the state according to their abilities.

Plato's pupil Aristotle even suggested that the state should determine shortly after birth which children should be allowed to live and destroy the physically or mentally handicapped; that marriage should be state-controlled to ensure desirable offspring. However, in their time the leisured and individualistic Sophists held the field and few accepted the educational views of Plato or his pupil.

Rome. The Romans were not philosophers and most of their culture came from Greece. Administration was their chief aptitude and Quintilian (A.D. *c.* 35–*c.* 95) based his higher education on the earlier classical tuition in public speaking, but he is important for emphasising the training of character and for his humanistic approach to the method of teaching that caused his *Institutio oratoria* to be influential for centuries later—indeed one might almost say up to the time of the great Dr. Arnold of Rugby. Education, he believed, should begin early but one must "take care that the child not old enough to love his studies does not come to hate them" by premature forcing; studies must be made pleasant and interesting and students encouraged by praise rather than discouraged when they sometimes fail; play is to be approved of as a sign of a lively disposition and because gloomy, depressed children are not likely to be good students; corporal punishment should never be used because "it is an insult as you will realise if you imagine it yourself". The world became interested not in *what* he taught but *how* he taught it; he was the pioneer of humanistic education and character-training from Vittorino d. Feltre (1378–1446) of Mantua, through Milton and Pope who commended his works to the modern educationists who have studied their pupils as well as their books.

The Middle Ages: *The Religious View.* With the development of Christianity education once more became a religious problem. The earliest converts had to be taught Christian doctrine and were given instruction in "catechumenal" schools before admission to the group, but as the religion came increasingly into contact with other religions or heresies a more serious training was necessary, and from these newer "catechetical" schools, where the method used was the catechism (*i.e.*, question and answer as known to all Presbyterian children today), the Apologists arose among whom were Clement of Alexandria and the great Origen. From this time education became an instrument of the church and in 529 the Emperor Justinian ordered all pagan schools to be closed.

As typical of the best in mediaeval education we may mention St. Benedict (*c.* 480 *c.* 547) of Monte Cassino. There, in southern Italy, a rule was established which became a part of monastic life in general. Monastic schools were originally intended for the training of would-be monks, but later others were admitted who simply wanted some education; thus two types of school developed one for the *interni* and the other for *externi* or external pupils. Originally studies were merely reading in order to study the Bible, writing to copy the sacred books, and sufficient calculation to be able to work out the advent of holy days or festivals. But by the end of the 6th cent. the "seven liberal arts" (grammar, rhetoric, dialectic, arithmetic, geometry, music, and astronomy) were added.

The Renaissance. The close of the Middle Ages saw the development of two types of secular school. One came with the rise of the new merchant class and the skilled trader whose "guilds" or early trade unions established schools to train young men for their trades but ultimately gave rise to burgher or town schools; the other was the court school founded and supported by the wealthy rulers of the Italian cities—Vittorio da Feltre (mentioned above) presided over the most famous at Mantua.

These Renaissance developments are paralleled in northern Europe by the Protestant reformers who, having with Martin Luther held that everyone should know how to read his Bible in order to interpret it in his own way, were logically committed to popular education, compulsory and universal. In theory this was intended for biblical study, but writing, arithmetic, and other elementary subjects were taught and Luther said that, even if heaven and hell did not exist, education was important. In this sense, universal education is a Protestant conception.

Views of Philosophers. From this period onwards people were free to put forward any ideas about education, foolish or otherwise, and to create their own types of school. Of English philosophers who theorised about, but did not practise, education we may mention the rationalist Francis Bacon (1561–1626) who saw learning as the dissipation of all prejudices and the collection of concrete facts; the materialist and totalitarian Hobbes (1588–1679) who, as a royalist, believed that the right to determine the kind of education fit for his subjects is one of the absolute rights of the sovereign power or ruler; the gentlemanly Locke (1632–1704) whose ideal was a sound mind in a sound body to be attained by hard physical exercise, wide experience of the world, and enough knowledge to meet the requirements of the pupil's environment. The end result would be one able to get on with his fellows, pious but wise in the ways of the world, independent and able to look after himself, informed but reticent about his knowledge. Classics and religious study were not to be carried to excess, since Locke held that these subjects had been much overrated in the past.

Jean-Jacques Rousseau (1712–78), a forerunner of the Romantic movement (*q.v.*), despised society and its institutions, put emotion at a higher level than reason. His book *Emile* describes the education of a boy which is natural and spontaneous. Society, he holds, warps the growing mind and therefore the child should be protected from its influences until his development in accordance with his own nature is so complete that he cannot be harmed by it. During the first 4 years the body should be developed by physical training; from 5 to 12 the child would live in a state of nature such that he could develop his powers of observation and his senses; from 13 books would be used and intellectual training introduced, although only in line with the child's own interests, and he would be given instruction only as he came to ask for it. Moral training and contact with his fellows to learn the principles of sympathy, kindness, and helpfulness to mankind would be given between 15 and 20. Girls, however, should be educated to serve men in a spirit of modesty and restraint. His own five children he deposited in a foundling hospital.

Summary. Broadly speaking, then, there have been four main attitudes to education: (1) religious, with a view to a life beyond death; (2) state-controlled education, with a view to uniform subservience to authority; (3) "gentlemanly" education, with a view to social graces and easy congress in company; (4) the "child-centred" education, which attempts to follow the pupil's inner nature. It is unnecessary to mention the ordinary method of attempting to instil facts without any considerable degree of co-operation between pupil and teacher in order that the former may, with or without interest, follow some occupation in adult life; for this the philosophers did not consider. Today there remain the two fundamental principles: education for the advantage of the state and its ideology or education for individual development and freedom.

Four educationists of the modern period who have influenced us in the direction of freedom were Johann Pestalozzi of Switzerland (1746–1827) who, by trying to understand children, taught the "natural, progressive, and harmonious development of all the powers and capacities of the human being"; Friedrich Froebel (1782–1852) of Germany, the founder of the Kindergarten who, like Pestalozzi, was influenced by Rousseau but realised the need to combine complete personal development with social adjustment; Maria Montessori (1869–1952) whose free methods have revolutionised infant teaching; John Dewey (1859–1952) who held that the best interests of the group are served when the individual develops his own particular talents and nature.

Egalitarianism. The doctrine that human beings are, in an important sense, equal and that it is desirable to remove inequalities by social and political means. It was part of the famous slogan of the French Revolution: "Liberty, Equality, Fraternity". There has been much debate, however, as to what extent human beings are, in fact, equal. Critics of equality as a political ideal argue that it conflicts with other more valuable ideals or social values, and that the different kinds of equality are not compatible.

Elan Vital. *See* J61.

Eleatics, the philosophers of Elea in ancient Greece who, at the time when Heraclitus (*c.* 535–475 B.C.) was teaching that change is all that exists and nothing is permanent, were asserting that change is an illusion. Of the three leaders of this school, Xenophanes asserted that the universe was a solid immovable mass forever the same; Parmenides explained away change as an inconceivable process, its appearance being due to the fact that what we see is unreal; and Zeno (the best-known today) illustrated the same thesis with his famous argument of the arrow which, at any given moment of its flight, must be where it is since it cannot be where it is not. But if it is where it is, it cannot move, this is based, of course, on the delusion that motion is discontinuous.

Elitism. A political theory, largely drawn from the writings of V. Pareto (1848–1923). Power in a society will always be exercised by a minority (the elite) which takes the major decisions. An elite gains its dominant position through possessing certain resources or qualities valued in that particular society, *e.g.* priests or soldiers or senior state officials. Elites normally aim to continue their domination, but are not always capable of doing so and become displaced by another elite. If elite rule is inevitable then there can be no hope of an egalitarian, socialist society. This analysis of the importance of elites has been very influential. Some sociologists have extended the theory in recent years to argue that in all developed countries there is a plurality of competing elites within different systems of control. Such systems are politics, trade union organisations, cultural and educational institutions.

Empiricism. While not a single school of philosophy, empiricism is an approach to knowledge which holds that if a man wants to know what the universe is like the only correct way to do so is to go and look for himself, to collect facts which come to him through his senses. It is, in essence, the method of science as contrasted with rationalism (*q.v.*) which in philosophy implies that thinking or reasoning without necessarily referring to external observations can arrive at truth.

Empiricism is typically a British attitude, for among the greatest empirical philosophers were John Locke, George Berkeley, and David Hume. *See* **Rationalism.**

Encyclopedists. The writers (all men) who contributed to the *Encyclopedie* published in France from 1751 to 1772. The work's full title was *Encyclopedie, ou dictionnaire raisoné des sciences, des arts et des metiers.* It was designed as a synoptic description of all branches of human knowledge, and is perhaps the most characteristic work of the Enlightenment (*q.v.*). The *Encyclopedie* was inspired by Chambers' *Cyclopedia, or a universal dictionary of arts and sciences* published in London in 1728. The project began in 1745, with Denis Diderot and Jean d'Alembert as editors. The latter resigned in 1758, leaving Diderot to shoulder most of the work. In 1772 the project reached 28 volumes; between 1776 and 1780 7 supplementary volumes were published.

Besides Diderot and d'Alembert and many obscure writers, Voltaire, Rousseau and d'Holbach contributed. The work was a showcase for representatives of new schools of thought in all branches of intellectual activity. The work was tolerant, liberal, and also innovative in giving attention to trades and mechanical arts. In its scepticism, its emphasis on being scientific, and its criticism of superstition and contemporary social institutions, the *Encyclopedie* had immense influence.

Enlightenment. A European intellectual movement of the 18th century. Enlightenment thinkers aimed to bring clarity, order and reason, in a word, *light* to regions where formerly there had been mystery, superstition and blind authority, that is, darkness. Man would become enlightened by knowledge and progress to greater happiness and freedom. The movement affected the arts, the sciences, political and social life.

The Enlightenment was prepared by the rise of science from the 16th century on. In particular, the success of Newton (1642–1727) in encapsulating the laws that govern the motion of the planets gave great hopes in man's capacity to attain extensive understanding. According to the German philosopher Kant (1724–1804) the motto of the Enlightenment was "Have courage to use your own understanding". Scientific knowledge was the ideal. If something was held to be true, it had to be based on dispassionate rational investigation. This overrode any claim to knowledge based on authority. One great source of authority was the Christian church, which was widely criticised by Enlightenment thinkers (*e.g.* in Voltaire's *Candide*); another was the despotism and arbitrary power of many states at the time. Although there is now a tendency to be sceptical about the Enlightenment and the power of reason, the belief in human progress through increased knowledge has been one of the most powerful ideas of the last 250 years.

Environmentalism. *See* **Section Y**.

Epicureanism. The two great schools of the Hellenistic period (*i.e.* the late Greek period beginning with the empire of Alexander the Great) were the Stoics and Epicureans, the former founded by Zeno of Citium (not to be confused with Zeno the Eleatic) (*q.v.*), the latter by Epicurus, born in Samos in 342 B.C. Both schools settled in Athens, where Epicurus taught that "pleasure is the beginning and end of a happy life." However, he was no sensualist and emphasised the importance of moderation in all things because excesses would lead to pain instead of pleasure and the best of all pleasures were mental ones. Pleasures could be active or passive but the former contain an element of pain since they are the process of satisfying desire not yet satiated. The latter involving the absence of desire are the more pleasant. In fact, Epicurus in his personal life was more stoical than many Stoics and wrote "when I live on bread and water I spit on luxurious pleasures." He disapproved of sexual enjoyment and thought friendship one of the highest of all joys. A materialist who accepted the atomic theory of Democritus, he was not a determinist, and if he did not disbelieve in the gods he regarded religion and fear of death as the two primary sources of unhappiness.

Epiphenomenalism. *See* **Mind and Body**.

Epistemology. *See* **J58**.

Erastianism, the theory that the state has the right to decide the religion of its members, wrongly attributed to Erastus of Switzerland (1524–83) who was believed to have held this doctrine. The term has usually been made use of in a derogatory sense—*e.g.* by the Scottish churches which held that the "call" of the congregation was the only way to elect ministers at a time when, about the turn of the 17th and 18th cent., they felt that Episcopalianism was being foisted on them. "Episcopalianism" (*i.e.* Anglicanism) with its state church, ecclesiastical hierarchy, and system of livings presented by patrons was to them "Erastian" in addition to its other "unscriptural practices."

Essenes, a Jewish sect which, during the oppressive rule of Herod (d. 4 B.C.), set up monastic communities in the region of the Dead Sea. They refused to be bound by the scriptural interpretations of the Pharisees and adhered rigorously to the letter of Holy Writ, although with additions of their own which cause them by orthodox Jews today to be regarded as a break-away from Judaism. Among their practices and beliefs were purification through baptism, renunciation of sexual pleasures, scrupulous cleanliness, strict observance of the Mosaic law, communal possession, asceticism.

Akin in spirit, though not necessarily identical with them, were the writers of Apocalyptic literature preaching that the evils of the present would shortly be terminated by a new supernatural order heralded by a Messiah who would reign over a restored Israel. The casting out of demons and spiritual healing formed part of these general beliefs which were in the air at that time. The sect has an importance far beyond its size or what has been known about it in the past since the discovery from 1947 onwards of the Dead Sea Scrolls (*see* **Scrolls, Section H**) of the Qumran community occupying a monastery in the same area as the Essenes and holding the same type of belief. These scrolls with their references to a "Teacher of Righteousness" preceding the Messiah have clear relevance to the sources of early Christianity and have given rise to speculations as to whether Jesus might have been influenced by views which, like His own, were unacceptable to orthodox Jews but in line with those of the Dead Sea communities. Scholars now think that early Christianity was not a sudden development but a gradual one which had its predecessors.

Ethical Church, a movement typical of 19th cent. rationalism which attempted to combine atheism (or at any rate the absence of any belief in a God which was inconsistent with reason or based on revelation) with the inculcation of moral principles. Prayers were not used and ordinarily the service consisted in the singing of edifying compositions interspersed with readings from poems or prose of a similar nature by great writers holding appropriate views. It terminated in a talk on an ethical or scientific theme. Conway Hall (built 1929) in Red Lion Square, London, belongs to the South Place Ethical Society, founded by Moncure Conway who preached at their Unitarian chapel in South Place, Finsbury, 1864–97.

Ethics. *See* **J58**.

Ethnocentrism, the exaggerated tendency to think the characteristics of one's own group or race superior to those of any others.

Eugenics, a 19th-cent. movement largely instigated by the British scientist and mathematician, Sir Francis Galton. Galton argued that many of the most satisfactory attributes of mankind—intelligence, physical strength, resistance to disease, *etc.*—were genetically determined and thus handed down in the normal process of inheritance. From this he reasoned that selective mating of physical "superior" individuals, and its converse, the controlled limitation on the breeding of criminals or the insane, would lead inevitably to a progressive improvement in the overall standards of the human race. In their simplest form these proposals are incontestable, though they do of course introduce marked restrictions on the choice of the individual for marriage and procreation. Worse yet is the way in which the argument can be misapplied or elaborated—as it was in Nazi Germany—to include the sterilisation of alcoholics, confirmed criminals and even epileptics.

In 1997 it was revealed that extensive sterilisation of mentally-handicapped people had been carried out until the 1970s in Norway and Switzerland.

Euthanasia (mercy killing), the term applied to the painless killing of those (especially the old) suffering from unbearable pain and an illness for which there is no cure. In Britain, attempts in Parliament to introduce its legalisation have failed but in 1993 Holland voted to tolerate euthanasia governed by tight guidelines. Under these procedures, euthanasia is tolerated when the patient is conscious, suffers an incurable disease paired with intolerable pain and clearly requests a "soft death". The World Right to Die Organisation now has thriving branches worldwide.

Legislation permitting voluntary euthanasia was passed in the Northern Territory of Australia in 1995 and the world's first legal euthanasia took place in 1996. In 1997 the Liberal Democrats became the first major party in Britain to debate legalisation and there is increasing pressure in the UK for reform of the law to make it legal to assist a terminally ill person if they wish to die. In 2001 the Dutch government decriminalised mercy killing by passing new legislation. Belgium followed the Dutch example in May 2002. Switzerland also allows assisted suicide for the terminally ill. France is following a similar path (and euthanasia is legal in Oregon in the USA).

Evangelicalism, the belief of those Protestant sects which hold that the essence of the Gospel consists in the doctrine of salvation by faith in the atoning death of Christ and not by good works or the sacraments; that worship should be "free" rather than liturgical through established forms; that ritual is unacceptable and superstitious. Evangelicals are Low Churchmen. Nowadays, a new breed of evangelical Christianity is flourishing as a result of the Alpha course and the conservative Reform group. They have a powerfully ally in the Anglican Church in Africa, which preaches a hardline reading of the Bible.

Evangelism, the preaching of the Gospel, emphasising the necessity for a new birth or conversion. The evangelistic fervour of John Wesley and George Whitefield (*see* Methodism) aroused the great missionary spirit of the late 18th and 19th cent. George Fox, founder of the Society of Friends (*q.v.*), was also an evangelist. Evangelists can be Low, High, or Middle Churchmen.

Evolutionary Psychology, an approach that aims at understanding the relationship between psychological processes, behaviours and the evolutionary mechanisms that have shaped human physiology. It studies the ways in which the survival value of certain behaviours and cognitive abilities may have resulted in current human psychology.

Existentialism, a highly subjective philosophy which many people connect with such names as Jean-Paul Sartre (1905–80) or Albert Camus (1913–60) and assume to be a post-war movement. However, existentialism stems from Sören Kierkegaard (1813–55), the Danish "religious writer"—his own description of himself—in such works as *Either/Or, Fear and Trembling,* and *Concluding Unscientific Postscript.* Between the two world wars translations of Kierkegaard into German influenced Martin Heidegger's great work *Being and Time* and the other great existentialist Karl Jaspers; it has strongly influenced modern Protestant theology notably in Karl Barth, Reinhold Niebuhr, and Paul Tillich and beyond that field the French philosopher Gabriel Marcel, the Spanish writer Unamuno in his well-known *The Tragic Sense of Life,* and Martin Buber of Israel in his *I and Thou.* We have it on Heidegger's authority that "Sartre is no philosopher" even if it is to his works that modern existentialists often turn.

Existentialism is extremely difficult for the non-metaphysically-minded to understand, it deals, not with the nature of the universe or what are ordinarily thought of as philosophical problems but describes an attitude to life or God held by the individual. Briefly, its main essentials are: (1) it distinguishes between *essence, i.e.,* that aspect of an entity which can be observed and known—and its *existence*—the fact of its having a place in a changing and dangerous world which is what really matters; (2) existence being basic, each self-aware individual can grasp his own existence on reflection in his own immediate experience of himself and his situation as a free being in the world; what he finds is not merely a knowing self but a self that fears, hopes, believes, wills, and is aware of its need to find a purpose, plan, and destiny in life; (3) but we cannot grasp our existence by thought alone; thus the fact "all men must die" relates to the essence of man but it is necessary to be involved, to draw the conclusion as a person that "I too must die" and experience its impact on our own individual existence; (4) because of the preceding, it is necessary to abandon our attitude of objectivity and theoretical detachment when faced by the problems relating to the ultimate purpose of our own life and the basis of our own conduct; life remains closed to those who take no part in it because it can have no significance; (5) it follows that the existentialist cannot be rationalist in his outlook for this is merely an escape into thought from the serious problems of

existence; none of the important aspects of life—failure, evil, sin, folly—nor (in the view of Kierkegaard) even the existence of God or the truth of Christianity—can be proved by reason. "God does not exist; He is eternal," was how he expressed it; (6) life is short and limited in space and time, therefore it is foolish to discuss in a leisurely fashion matters of life and death as if there were all eternity to argue them in. It is necessary to make a leap into the unknown, *e.g.,* accepting Christ (in the case of the Christian existentialist) by faith in the sense of giving and risking the self utterly. This means complete commitment, not a dependence on arguments as to whether certain historical events did, or did not, happen.

To summarise: existentialism of whatever type seems to the outsider to be an attitude to life concerning itself with the individual's ultimate problems (mine, not yours); to be anti-rationalist and anti-idealist (in the sense of being, as it seems to the believer, practical) in effect it seems to say "life is too short to fool about with argument, you must dive in and become committed" to something. Sartre who called himself an "atheist existentialist" was apparently committed to the belief that "hell is other people," but for most critics the main argument against existentialism is that it often rests on a highly specialised personal experience and, as such, is incommunicable.

Existential Psychology, a rather diffuse movement in modern psychology with no specific founder but with a number of figures who, perhaps against their will, acquired leader status. One of the key figures was the British psychiatrist, R. D. Laing (1927–89), whose radical views on psychotherapy were counted as being heretical by the vast majority of his medical colleagues. Laing held that many so-called neurotic and psychotic conditions are essentially not "abnormal" and merely represent strategies by which an individual may adjust to environmental and personal stress. Instead of attempting to suppress or eliminate the psychosis in the traditional manner, one should lead the patient through it thus allowing the individual's "unconscious plan" for his own adjustment to be fulfilled.

Exorcism, the removal or ejection of an evil spirit by a ritual or prayer. It is easy to forget that the concept of insanity as representing a disorder of the brain is fairly recent in origin. Tragically, many of the symptoms of severe forms of mental disorder induce such an apparent change in the personality of the individual as to suggest that an alien individual has indeed taken over their body, and this belief is still common in many parts of the world.

Most religious systems have developed some ritual or set of rituals for expelling these so-called demons.

F

Fabian Society. In 1848 (the year of *The Communist Manifesto* by Marx and Engels) Europe was in revolt. In most countries the workers and intellectuals started bloody revolutions against the feudal ruling classes which were no less violently suppressed; hence on the continent socialism took on a Marxist tinge which to some extent it still retains. But at the same time England was undergoing a slow but non-violent transition in her political and industrial life which led the workers in general to look forward to progress through evolution. Marxism never became an important movement in England even though it took its origin here. There were many reasons for this: the agitation of the Chartists (*q.v.*); the reforms of Robert Owen; the religious movement led by the Wesleys; the Co-operative societies; and the Christian socialists.

Furthermore legislation stimulated by these bodies had led to an extension of the franchise, remedial measures to correct some of the worst abuses of the factory system, recognition of the trade unions, *etc.*

This was the background against which the

Fabian Society was founded in 1884 with the conviction that social change could be brought about by gradual parliamentary means. (The name is derived from Quintus Fabius Maximus, the Roman general nicknamed "Cunctator," the delayer, who achieved his successes in defending Rome against Hannibal by refusing to give direct battle.) It was a movement of brilliant intellectuals, chief among whom were Sidney and Beatrice Webb, H. G. Wells, G. B. Shaw, Graham Wallas, Sidney Olivier, and Edward Pease. The Society itself was basically a research institution which furnished the intellectual information for social reform and supported all contributing to the gradual attainment by parliamentary means of socialism.

The Webbs's analysis of society emphasised that individualist enterprise in capitalism was a hang-over from early days and was bound to defeat itself since socialism is the inevitable accompaniment of modern industrialism; the necessary result of popular government is control of their economic system by the people themselves. Utopian schemes had been doomed to failure because they were based on the fallacy that society is static and that islands of utopias could be formed in the midst of an unchanging and antagonistic environment. On the contrary, it was pointed out, society develops: "The new becomes old, often before it is consciously regarded as new." Social reorganisation cannot usefully be hastened by violent means but only through methods consonant with this natural historical progression—gradual, peaceful, and democratic. The Fabians were convinced that men are rational enough to accept in their common interest developments which can be demonstrated as necessary; thus public opinion will come to see that socialisation of the land and industries is essential.

The Society collaborated first in the formation of the Independent Labour Party and then with the more moderate Labour Party and the trade unions and Co-operative movement. But in general it disapproved of independent trade union action since change should come from the government and take political form. The class-war of Marx was rejected and so too was the idea of the exclusive role of the working class —reform must come from the enlightened co-operation of all classes. With the advent of a new century, Fabians are now considering weakening their commitment to collective ownership.

Faith Healing, the belief and practice of curing physical and mental ills by faith in some super-natural power, either allegedly latent in the individual or drawn in some way from God.

Falangists. The Fascist Party of Spain founded in 1933 by José Antonio Primo de Rivera, son of the man who was dictator of the country from 1923 to 1930. The Falange was the only political party allowed in Spain during the Franco era. *See* **Fascism** (below).

Falun Gong, Chinese mystic healing movement, attacked by the Beijing government as an 'evil and dangerous cult'. Led by the US-based Li Hongzhi, it is banned in China. The movement, with *c.* 70 million members, is based on the ancient mystical and healing principles of *qigong*.

Fascism. From the end of mediaeval times with the opening up of the world, the liberation of the mind and the release of business enterprise, a new spirit arose in Europe exemplified in such movements as the Renaissance, the Reformation, the struggle for democracy, the rise of capitalism, and the Industrial Revolution. With these movements there developed a certain tradition, which, in spite of hindrances and disagreement or failures, was universally held by both right- and left-wing parties however strongly they might fail to agree on the best means of attaining what was felt to be a universal ideal.

The hard core of this tradition involved: belief in reason and the possibility of human progress; the essential sanctity and dignity of human life; tolerance of widely different religious and political views; reliance on popular government and the responsibility of the rulers to the ruled; freedom of thought and criticism; the necessity of universal education; impartial justice and the rule of law; the desirability of universal peace. Fascism was the negation of every aspect of this tradition and took pride in being so. Emotion took the place of reason, the "immutable, beneficial, and fruitful inequality of classes" and the right of a self-constituted élite to rule them replaced universal suffrage because absolute authority led to action rather than talk. Contrary opinions are not allowed and justice is in the service of the state; war is desirable to advance the power of the state; racial inequality made a dogma. Those who belong to the "wrong" religion, political party, or race are outside the law.

The attacks on liberalism and exaltation of the state derive largely from Hegel and his German followers; the mystical irrationalism from such 19th cent. philosophers as Schopenhauer Nietzsche, and Bergson; from Sorel (*see* **Syndicalism**) came the idea of the "myth", and an image which would have the power to arouse the emotions of the masses and from Sorel also the rationale of violence and justification of force. But these philosophical justifications of fascism do not explain why it arose at all and why it arose where it did—in Italy, Germany, and Spain. These countries had one thing in common—disillusionment. Germany had lost the 1914–18 war, Italy had been on the winning side but was resentful about her small gains. Spain had sunk to the level of a third-rate power, and people were becoming increasingly restive under the reactionary powers of the Catholic Church, the landed aristocracy, and the army. In Marxist theory, fascism is the last fling of the ruling class and the bourgeoisie in their attempt to hold down the workers.

Italian Fascism. The corporate state set up by Benito Mussolini in Italy claimed to be neither capitalist nor socialist, and after its inception in 1922 the Fascist Party became the only recognised one. Its members wore black shirts, were organised in military formations, used the Roman greeting of the outstretched arm, and adopted as their slogan "Mussolini is always right". Membership of the Party was not allowed to exceed a number thought to be suited to the optimum size of a governing class and new candidates were drawn, after strict examinations, from the youth organisations. The Blackshirts, a fascist militia, existed separately from the army and were ruled by Fascist Headquarters.

At the head of government was Mussolini, "Il Duce" himself, a cabinet of fourteen ministers selected by him and approved by the King to supervise the various functions of government, and the Grand Council or directorate of the Fascist Party, all the members of which were chosen by the Duce. Parliament, which was not allowed to initiate legislation but only to approve decrees from above, consisted of a Senate with life-membership and a Chamber of Fasci and Corporations composed of nominated members of the Party, the National Council of Corporations, and selected representatives of the employers' and employees' confederations. Private enterprise was encouraged and protected but rigidly controlled; strikes were forbidden, but a Charter of Labour enforced the collaboration of workers and employers whose disputes were settled in labour courts presided over by the Party. All decisions relating to industry were government-controlled (*e.g.*, wages, prices, conditions of employment and dismissal, the expansion or limitation of production), and some industries such as mining, shipping, and armaments were state-owned.

Italian fascism served as a model in other countries, notably for the German National Socialist Party (the Nazis) and also in Spain and Japan. Most European nations between the wars had their small Fascist parties, the British version led by Sir Oswald Mosley being known as the British Union which relied on "strong-arm tactics", marches and violence. The Public Order Act of 1936 was passed to deal with it. Although fascism in all countries has certain recognisable characteristics, it would be wrong to think of it as an international movement taking fixed forms and with a clearly thought-out rationale as in the case of communism.

Although classical fascism ended with the defeat of Germany in 1945 there have been persistent revivals in Italy, France, in Germany following reunification, and in Russia and the Balkans after the collapse of Communism. Fascism won significant electoral support in France and Austria in the 1990s. Modern fascist parties, the British National Party in Britain, for example, or the National Front in France, concentrate more on the tensions caused by mass immigration into Europe rather than formulating any coherent economic and social policies. See **Falangists, Nazism**.

Fatalism. See **Determinism**.

Federalism, belief in the desirability of a political unit consisting of several smaller units, usually termed states, involving a central government and regional or state governments. The states or provinces devolve certain powers over themselves and their citizens to the larger unit, such powers being embodied in a written constitution which can only be amended with the consent of a fixed percentage of the states. The constitution specifies the powers devolved to the federal or central government and the restrictions placed on its interference in the internal affairs of the states.

Given the possibility of disputes as to the spheres of competence of federal and state governments, machinery such as a 'supreme court' is established to interpret the constitution. Examples of federations include the USA, Canada, Australia, India and Germany.

Federalists. US party which in the early days of American independence in the late 18th century, favoured a concentration of power in the central government. Their opponents, the anti-federalists (later the Democrats) were supporters of the rights of individual states.

Feminism. Feminism is an expression which emerged in the mid-19th century. It is an international movement (there was, for example, a feminist congress in Paris in 1890), which aimed at ending female inequality in male-dominated societies. In early 20th century Britain feminism sought political advance through a militant campaign for women's suffrage. This, and the part played by women in World War One, made it impossible for a male elite to deny women the right to vote. But in each country it became increasingly clear to women that the political process alone left many of their needs unsatisfied, if not unrecognised. However, in post-World War Two Britain, legislation made a gesture towards outlawing discrimination against women at work with the 1970 Equal Pay Act and the 1975 Sex Discrimination Act.

Activist feminism, the "Women's Liberation Movement" of the 1960s and 1970s (primarily in America and Europe as well as Britain), centred on questions of sexuality and the right of women to make choices, for example, over when (and whether) to become pregnant. The contraceptive pill appeared to open up sexual choice for women and to liberate them from traditional responsibilities for home, family and the welfare of children. In practice, it appeared to many women that the pill (as well as having physical side-effects) merely relieved men from a recognition of their own responsibility. The 1967 Abortion Act in Britain implied an acceptance of a woman's right to control her own reproduction, a right which has been systematically but unsuccessfully challenged since.

As western economies faltered in the late 1970s a recurring problem for the movement was consolidating the small gains that had been made. But the women's movement achievements cannot be measured by tangible results alone. A central aspect of the movement was "consciousness-raising", helping women recognise the social roots of their individual oppression. In their analysis of sexual stereotyping, late 20th century feminist writings—for example, Betty Friedan's *The Feminine Mystique* (1963) and Germaine Greer's *The Female Eunuch* (1970)—encouraged a change in some women's expectations. These writers, and many like them, enabled a new generation of women to challenge the dominant decision-making role of men and to demand acceptance of the principle of equality between the sexes. Dale Spender's *Man Made Language* (1980) pointed to the ways in which the "sexist" structure of language internalised the perpetuation of male dominance. A simple, but not superficial, result of this is the acceptance of the abbreviation "Ms" rather than "Mrs" or "Miss" on the grounds that the latter presupposed that a woman's identity depended on her marital status.

Although feminism as a movement was loosely structured—there were, for example, early on, differing emphases between socialists, black women, working class women, and lesbians, based on their own experiences—the movement became increasingly fragmented during the 1980s. Some women, who were now building individual careers, distanced themselves from agitation and thought little more could be achieved by collective action. Single-issue pressure groups evolved, focusing on campaigns for change in particular areas.

The Greenham Common Women's Peace Camp which began in the mid-1980s as a protest against the deployment of Cruise missiles in Britain, was able to develop from this into an exemplary feminist action which reverberated internationally. Self-organisation among miners' wives in the 1984-85 strike proved similarly effective.

The irony of "classical" feminism is that it became a concern of the generation that came to maturity in the late 1960s. Their children—and their younger sisters—had absorbed the earlier failures and successes and moved on. By the 1990s, for what became the older generation, there was a view that the earlier movement had implanted unrealistic expectations in women (particularly those with domestic responsibilities), the "double burden" of maintaining a career and home. This led at a time of growing recession and unemployment to an anti-feminist campaign or "backlash", not only among men (which was to be expected) but also among some women who described themselves as post-feminists. Susan Faludi, speaking for a younger generation in *Backlash: The Undeclared War Against Women* (1991) documents a process which has as a common thread the attempt to force women back into the home and a return to "traditional" family life. However, a significant recognition of the altered balance between the sexes came with the October 1991 House of Lords decision that rape within marriage was an offence.

The mid-1990s saw a new emphasis placed by political parties on the role of the family and its reputed breakdown as the root of many of the problems confronting Western society. This was interpreted by some as an attempt to reverse the social and economic advances achieved by some women in the past half century. Working mothers, for example, were accused of neglecting their prime duty as home-makers, although the research evidence presented was often contradictory.

Feng Shui, a Chinese philosophy whose basic principles seek to change the environment with colours, objects and placement of furniture to counteract negative energy and encourage a flow of positive energy.

Fetichism, originally a practice of the peoples of West Africa and elsewhere of attributing magical properties to an object which was used as an amulet, for putting spells on others, or regarded as possessing dangerous powers. In psychology the term refers to a sexual perversion in which objects arouse sexual excitement.

Feudalism. The feudal system took its origins from Saxon times and broadly speaking lasted until the end of the 13th cent. It was a military and political organisation based on land tenure, for, of course, society throughout this period was based almost entirely on agriculture. The activities of men divided them into three classes or estates. The First Estate was the clergy, responsible for man's spiritual needs; the Second was the nobility, including kings and emperor as well as the lesser nobles; the Third was composed of all those who had to do with the economic and mainly agricultural life of Europe. The praying men, the fighting men and administrators, and the toilers were all held to be dependent on each other in a web of mutual responsibilities.

The theory of feudalism, although it by no means always worked out in practice, was as follows: the earth was God's and therefore no man owned land in the modern sense of the word. God had given the pope spiritual charge of men, and secular power over them to the emperor from whom kings held their kingdoms, and in turn the dukes and counts received the land over which they held sway from the king. Members of the Second Estate held their lands on the condition of fulfilling certain obligations to their overlord and to the people living under them, so when a noble received a fief or piece of land he became the vassal of the man who bestowed it. To him he owed military service for a specified period of the year, attendance at court, and giving his lord counsel. He undertook to ransom his lord when he fell into enemy hands and to contribute to his daughter's dowry and at the knighting of his son. In return the lord offered his vassal protection and justice, received the vassal's sons into his household and educated them for knighthood.

The system was complicated by the fact that large fiefs might be subdivided and abbots often governed church lands held in fief from nobles. The serf or toiling man dwelt on the land of a feudal noble or churchman where he rendered service by tilling the soil or carrying out his craft for his manorial lord in return for protection, justice, and the security of his life and land. He was given a share in the common lands or pastures from which he provided for his own needs. In the modern sense he was not free (although at a later stage he could buy his freedom) since he was attached to the soil and could not leave without the lord's permission. On the other hand he could neither be deprived of his land nor lose his livelihood. Feudal tenures were abolished in England by statute in 1660, although they had for long been inoperative. In Japan a feudal system existed up to 1871, in Russia it lasted until 1917.

Fideism. A term applied to religious doctrines which hold that the intellect or reason of man is incapable of attaining knowledge of divine matters and that religious faith is the way to truth.

Flying Saucers. In June 1947 a US private pilot, Kenneth Arnold, reported seeing a series of wingless objects flying through the air at a speed which he estimated at thousands of miles an hour. The UFO phenomenon had been born. Initially the American Air Force launched an official enquiry—Project Bluebook—to attempt to solve the mystery of these "unidentified flying objects" or "UFOs," which folded in 1969 after hesitantly concluding that the sightings were probably misinterpretations of natural phenomena. A CIA report in 1997 confirmed that over half of all the UFO sightings were actually American spy planes on secret missions (most UFO sightings happened during the paranoia of the Cold War).

The advent of the new century has seemingly consigned UFOs to history. The paranormal journal *Fortean Times* has declared the science of Ufology dead and the world's oldest UFO society (the British Flying Saucer Bureau) has suspended its activities.

Fourierism *See* **Utopianism.**

Freemasonry, a widespread, influential secret organisation of English origin. Although it can be traced back to the Middle Ages when itinerant working masons in England and Scotland were organised in lodges with secret signs for the recognition of fellow-members, modern freemasonry first arose in England in the early decades of the 18th cent. On 24 June 1717 four London lodges came together at the Goose and Gridiron Ale House in St Paul's Churchyard to form the first Grand Lodge in the world. Freemasons' Hall was opened in 1776.

With its clubs for discussion and social meetings (women were excluded) it met a need and became a well-known feature of English life. The movement quickly spread abroad to places which had direct trade links with England. The graded lodge structure, the social prestige conferred by membership, the symbolism, ritual and ceremony, and the emphasis on mutual help had a lasting appeal.

Membership used to bring definite business and social advantages, particularly in small communities where the leading middle- class figures were generally members. Recently this advantage has markedly declined and freemason lodges nowadays tend to be little more than worthy charitable organisations. Indeed, hundreds of masonic lodges now face closure because of a drastic membership decline. Fear of secret societies has given freemasonry many opponents; it was con-

demned by the Roman Catholic Church, banned by Fascist dictators, and denounced by the Comintern. A statement from the Congregation for the Doctrine of the Faith in 1981 reminded Catholics that under Article 2335 of the Code of Canon Law they are forbidden under pain of excommunication from joining masonic or similar associations. Recently, there have been calls for Freemasons who are members of, for example, the judiciary to declare their membership openly.

Freudian theory. *See* **Psychoanalysis.**

Friends, The Society of. *See* **Quakers.**

Fundamentalism originated in 19th century America as an opposition to the liberalising trend in theological practice. Fundamentalists rejected the attempt to interpret ancient scripture to make it more relevant to modern society, and argued for a return to a literal reading of the Bible. In the 1960s, such Christian fundamentalists, repulsed by the breakdown in traditional moral and social practices, began organising politically. Groups such as the Christian Coalition and the Moral Majority became powerful within American politics, and campaigned against abortion and gay rights, and promoted traditional family structures.

The label has now been attached to many other groups who also oppose modern liberal social and political values, and who appeal to a strict literal reading of religious texts or moral values. Such wide usage is probably unhelpful as it may include fundamentalist Muslims inspired by the ideology of Sayyid Qutb (such as Osama Bin Laden). This confuses a rejection of modernity and a literal reading of a religious text with an attempt to achieve political goals at any cost. Christian fundamentalists on the right in America are clearly not fundamentalist in this fashion.

Friends of the Western Buddhist Order. *See* **J59.**

G

Game Theory, an approach to understanding human and animal behaviour which takes the view that psychological insight is best gained by studying the decisions which all living things make constantly and which govern the course of their lives. It proposes that life is basically a strategic game following complex rules which can probably only be understood by a study of the "decision units" as and when they occur. Because one is dealing with highly variable animals controlled by highly complex brains, and not with simple clockwork or electro-mechanical systems, the study of the rules which operate in the game of life is enormously complicated and thus game theory has quickly taken off into advanced mathematics. Game theory, incidentally, can be used to apply to individual action or to the behaviour of groups.

Gay Movement, term for the campaign to remove legal and other discrimination from homosexual men and lesbian women and to allow them to lead their lives to the full in our society. Its first large-scale manifestation was in America in the 1970s, paralleled in Britain with organisations such as the Gay Liberation Front and, more recently, OutRage. Although much discrimination remains, many people now accept that the sexual orientation of a person should not be a ground for any form of discrimination. Issues such as gay priests, and the onset of AIDS, have continued to ensure that "gay rights" remains a controversial area. In a vote in the Commons in March 1999 on the question of equalising the age of consent (there was then a higher minimum age of consent for male homosexual acts than for heterosexual) a majority of 281 to 82 was in favour, but the House of Lords again rejected the reform in April 1999. Eventually the law was changed in December 2000. Gay people have often received support from the European Court of Human Rights. The government announced the lifting of the ban on gays in the armed forces on 12 January 2000. New legislation proposes to remove existing laws against buggery, gross indecency and discrimination at work as well as giving new legal rights to gay couples (so they have the same rights—and responsibilities—as heterosexual couples). Controversy over the appointment of gay priests as bishops has divided the Church.

In Holland, the Dutch Senate has now legalised same sex marriages and given such couples the right to adopt Dutch children. Other countries (such as Canada and Belgium) have followed. In London, the GLA set up a London Partnerships Register in September 2001 for the official registration of same sex relationships. Adoption by gay couples became legal in Britain in 2002. Under the Civil Partnership Act, effective from December 2005, gay couples can enter into 'civil partnership registrations' at register offices. Parts of America (e.g. Texas) remain strongly against any form of gay partnerships and the issue is highly controversial.

Gestalt Psychology. In the latter half of the 19th cent. it became evident to psychologists that in principle there was no good reason why "mental" events should not be just as measurable and manageable as "physical" ones. Intensive studies of learning, memory, perception, and so on were therefore undertaken and the beginnings of an empirical science of psychology were underway.

In the early part of the 20th cent. the experiments of Pavlov (see **Behaviourism**) and his co-workers suggested that the behaviour of an animal, or even men, might ultimately be reduced to a descriptive account of the activities of nervous reflex loops—the so-called conditioned reflexes.

With the subsequent publication of Watson's important book on Behaviourism in 1914 it looked as though the transfer of psychological studies from the field of philosophy to that of science could now take place. Actually the over-simplified picture of cerebral and mental pictures which Behaviourism offered was rather comparable to the billiard ball view of the universe so fashionable in Victorian science.

Just as Behaviourism implied that there was a fundamental building block (the conditioned reflex) from which all mental events could be constructed, so Victorian physics assumed that the entire universe could be described in terms of a vast collection of atoms pushing each other around like billiard balls. The development of nuclear physics was to shatter the latter dream and at the same time a challenge to the naïve "reflex psychology" came from the Gestalt experimental school.

The founders of this school were Max Wertheimer, Kurt Koffka and Wolfgang Köhler, three young psychologists who in 1912 were conducting experiments—notably in vision—which seemed to expose the inadequacies of the behaviourist position. The Pavlov–Watson view, as we have said, implied that complex sensory events were no more than a numerical sum of individual nervous impulses. Wertheimer's group proposed that certain facts of perceptual experiences (ruled out of court as subjective and therefore unreliable by Watson) implied that the whole (*Gestalt*) was something more than simply the sum of its parts. For example, the presentation of a number of photographs, each slightly different, in rapid series gives rise to cinematographic motion. In basic terms, the eye has received a number of discrete, "still" photographs, and yet "motion" is perceived. What, they asked, was the sensory input corresponding to this motion? Some processes within the brain clearly *added* something to the total input as defined in behaviourist terms. An obvious alternative—in a different sense modality—is that of the arrangement of musical notes. A cluster of notes played one way might be called a tune; played backwards they may form another tune, or may be meaningless. Yet in all cases the constituent parts are the same, and yet their relationship to one another is evidently vital. Once again the whole is more than the sum of the parts.

The implications of all this appeared to be that the brain was equipped with the capacity to organise sensory input in certain well-defined ways, and that far from being misleading and scientifically unjustifiable, human subjective studies of visual experience might reveal the very principles of organisation which the brain employs. Take a field of dots, more or less randomly distributed; inspection of the field will soon reveal certain patterns or clusters standing out—the constellations in the night sky are a good illustration. There are many other examples, and Wertheimer and his colleagues in a famous series of experiments made some effort to catalogue them and reduce them to a finite number of "Laws of Perceptual Organisation" which are still quoted today.

Ghosts, belief in ghosts is one of the most common features of supernatural and mystical philosophy. At its roots it is based on the assumption that Man is essentially an individual created of two separate and distinct substances, mind and body. Most religious systems hold to this dualistic view (see **Dualism**). The discarnate spirit is normally assumed to progress to some other realm whereupon it loses contact with the mortal world. Occasionally, however, for one reason or another, the spirits may not progress and may become trapped and unable to escape the material world. Traditionally this is supposed to occur when the death of the individual is precipitated by some great tragedy. Serious scientific interest in ghosts has now waned rapidly.

Globalisation. In modern times the nation state has provided a structure for political, economic, and social relationships. Globalisation describes the collapse of the importance of the nation state in these relationships. The ability to communicate, travel, trade, and organise on a global scale, with ease and speed, allows political institutions, corporations, and social movements to thrive unconstrained by the legal and geographical boundaries of nation states.

As examples of globalisation, proponents point to global capital markets and vast free trade areas which allow multinational companies to produce and sell worldwide, the Internet and international travel which enables social movements to pursue causes independent of particular territories, and the International Criminal Court and World Trade Organisation as political and legal structures superior to national and regional polities. However, the nature and very existence of globalisation is hotly disputed (see **Anti-globalisation**). Readers may also wish to refer to **Section F** for economic aspects of globalisation.

Gnosticism. Among the many heresies of early Christianity, especially during its first two centuries, was a group which came under the heading of Gnosticism. This was a system or set of systems which attempted to combine Christian beliefs with others derived from Oriental and Greek sources, especially those which were of a mystical and metaphysical nature, such as the doctrines of Plato and Pythagoras. There were many Gnostic sects, the most celebrated being the Alexandrian school of Valentius (fl. c. 136–c. 160). "Gnosis" was understood not as meaning "knowledge" or "understanding" as we understand these words, but "revelation." As in other mystical religions, the ultimate object was individual salvation; sacraments took the most varied forms. Many who professed themselves Christians accepted Gnostic doctrines and even orthodox Christianity contains some elements of Gnostic mysticism. It was left to the bishops and theologians to decide at what point Gnosticism ceased to be orthodox and a difficult task this proved to be. Two of the greatest, Clement of Alexandria and his pupil Origen, unwittingly slipped into heresy when they tried to show that such men as Socrates and Plato, who were in quest of truth, were Christian in intention, and by their lives and works had prepared the way for Christ. Thus they contradicted Church doctrine which specifically said *Extra ecclesiam nulla salus*—outside the Church there is no salvation.

God and Man. The idea of gods came before the idea of God and even earlier in the evolution of religious thought there existed belief in spirits (see **Animism**). It was only as a result of a long period of development that the notion of a universal "God" arose, a development particularly well documented in the Old Testament. Here we are concerned only with the views of philosophers, the views of specific religious bodies being given under the appropriate headings. First, however, some definitions.

Atheism is the positive disbelief in the existence of a God. **Agnosticism** (a term coined by T. H. Huxley, the 19th cent. biologist and contemporary of Darwin) signifies that one cannot know whether God exists or not. **Secularism**

(prominent from the 1850s) pursued "a philosophy of life which ignores theology". **Deism** is the acceptance of the existence of God, not through revelation, but as a hypothesis required by reason. **Theism** also accepts the existence of God, but, unlike Deism, does not reject the evidence of revelation (*e.g.*, in the Bible or in the lives of the saints). **Pantheism** is the identification of God with all that exists (*i.e.*, with the whole universe). **Monotheism** is the belief in one God, **Polytheism** the belief in many (*see also* **Dualism**).

Early Greek Views. Among the early Greek philosophers, Thales (*c.* 624–565 B.C.) of Miletus, in Asia Minor, Anaximander (611–547 B.C.), his pupil, and Anaximenes (b. *c.* 570 B.C.), another Miletan, were men of scientific curiosity and their speculations about the origin of the universe were untouched by religious thought. They founded the scientific tradition of critical discussion. Heraclitus of Ephesus (*c.* 540–475 B.C.), was concerned with the problem of change. How does a thing change and yet remain itself? For him all things are flames—processes. "Everything is in flux, and nothing is at rest." Empedocles of Agrigentum in Sicily (*c.* 500–*c.* 430 B.C.) introduced the idea of opposition and affinity. All matter is composed of the so-called four elements—*earth*, *water*, *air*, and *fire*—which are in opposition or alliance with each other. All these were materialist philosophers who sought to explain the working of the universe without recourse to the gods.

Socrates, Plato, and Aristotle. Socrates (470–399 B.C.) was primarily concerned with ethical matters and conduct rather than the nature of the universe. For him goodness and virtue come from knowledge. He obeyed an "inner voice" and suffered death rather than give up his philosophy. He believed in the persistence of life after death and was essentially a monotheist. Plato (427–347 B.C.) was chiefly concerned with the nature of reality and thought in terms of absolute truths which were unchanging, logical, and mathematical. (*See* **Mind and Matter.**) Aristotle (384–322 B.C.) took his views of matter not from Democritus (atomic view) but from Empedocles (doctrine of four elements), a view which came to fit in well with orthodox mediaeval theology. Matter is conceived of as potentially alive and striving to attain its particular form, being moved by divine spirit or mind (*nous*). (An acorn, for example, is matter which contains the form "oak-tree" towards which it strives.) Thus there is a whole series from the simplest level of matter to the perfect living individual. But there must be a supreme source of all movement upon which the whole of Nature depends, a Being that Aristotle describes as the "Unmoved Mover", the ultimate cause of all becoming in the universe. This Being is pure intelligence, a philosopher's God, not a personal one. Unlike Plato, Aristotle did not believe in survival after death, holding that the divine, that is the immortal element in man, is mind.

Among the later Greek thinkers the Epicureans were polytheists whose gods, however, were denied supernatural powers. The Stoics built up a materialist theory of the universe, based on the Aristotelian model. To them God was an all-pervading force, related to the world as the soul is related to the body, but they conceived of it as material. They developed the mystical side of Plato's idealism and were much attracted by the astrology coming from Babylonia. They were pantheists. The Sceptics were agnostics.

From Pagan to Christian Thought. Philo, "the Jew of Alexandria," who was about 20 years older than Jesus, tried to show that the Jewish scriptures were in line with the best in Greek thought. He introduced the *Logos* as a bridge between the two systems. Philo's God is remote from the world, above and beyond all thought and being, and as His perfection does not permit direct contact with matter the divine *Logos* acts as intermediary between God and man. Plotinus (204–70), a Roman, and the founder of Neoplatonism, was the last of the great pagan philosophers. Like Philo, he believed that God had created the world indirectly through emanations—beings coming

from Him but not of Him. The world needs God but God does not need the world. Creation is a fall from God, especially the human soul when enmeshed in the body and the world of the senses, yet (*see* **Determinism**) man has the ability to free himself from sense domination and turn towards God. Neoplatonism was the final stage of Greek thought drawing inspiration from the mystical side of Plato's idealism and its ethics from Stoicism.

Christianity: The Fathers and the Schoolmen. It was mainly through St. Augustine (354–430), Bishop of Hippo in North Africa, that certain of the doctrines of Neoplatonism found their way into Christianity. Augustine also emphasised the concept of God as all good, all wise, all knowing, transcendent, the Creator of the universe out of nothing. But, he added, since God knows everything, everything is determined by Him forever. This is the doctrine of predestination and its subsequent history is discussed under **Determinism**.

In the early centuries of Christianity, as we have seen, some found it difficult to reconcile God's perfection with His creation of the universe and introduced the concept of the *Logos* which many identified with Christ. Further, it came to be held that a power of divine origin permeated the universe, namely the Holy Spirit or Holy Ghost. A theory had to be worked out to explain the relationships of these three entities whence arose the conception of the Trinity. God is One; but He is also Three: Father, Son (the *Logos* or Christ), and Holy Ghost.

This doctrine was argued by the Apologists and the Modalists. The former maintained that the *Logos* and the Holy Spirit were emanations from God and that Jesus was the *Logos* in the form of a man. The Modalists held that all three Persons of the Trinity were God in three forms or modes: the *Logos* is God creating, the Holy Spirit God reasoning, and God is God being. This led to a long discussion as to whether the *Logos* was an emanation from God or God in another form; was the *Logos* of like *nature* with God or of the same *substance*? This was resolved at the Council of Nicaea (325) when Athanasius formulated the orthodox doctrine against Arius (*q.v.*): that the one God is a Trinity of the same substance, three Persons of the same nature—Father, Son, and Holy Ghost.

St. Thomas Aquinas (1227–74), influenced greatly by Aristotle's doctrines, set the pattern for all subsequent Catholic belief even to the present time. He produced rational arguments for God's existence: *e.g.*, Aristotle's argument that, since movement exists, there must be a prime mover, the Unmoved Mover or God; further, we can see that things in the universe are related in a scale from the less to the more complex, from the less to the more perfect, and this leads us to suppose that at the peak there must be a Being with absolute perfection. God is the first and final cause of the universe, absolutely perfect, the Creator of everything out of nothing. He reveals Himself in his Creation and rules the universe through His perfect will. How Aquinas dealt with the problem of predestination is told under **Determinism**.

Break with Mediaeval Thought. Renaissance thinkers, free to think for themselves, doubted the validity of the arguments of the Schoolmen but were unwilling to give up the idea of God (nor would it have been safe to do so). Mystics (*see* **Mysticism**) or near-mystics such as Nicholas of Cusa (*c.* 1401–64) and Jacob Boehme (1575–1624) taught that God was not to be found by reason but was a fact of the immediate intuition of the mystical experience.

Giordano Bruno held that God was immanent in the infinite universe. He is the unity of all opposites, a unity without opposites, which the human mind cannot grasp. Bruno was burned at the stake in 1600 at the instigation of the Inquisition (a body which, so we are told, never caused pain to anyone since it was the civil power, not the Inquisition, that carried out the unpleasant sentences) for his heresy.

Francis Bacon, who died in 1626, separated, as was the tendency of that time, science from religion. The latter he divided into the two categories of natural and revealed theology.

The former, through the study of nature, may give convincing proof of the existence of a God but nothing more. Of revealed theology he said: "we must quit the small vessel of human reason . . . as we are obliged to obey the divine law, though our will murmurs against it, so we are obliged to believe in the word of God, though our reason is shocked at it."

Hobbes was a complete materialist and one feels that his obeisance to the notion was politic rather than from conviction. However, he does mention God as starting the universe in motion; infers that God is corporeal but denies that His nature can be known.

From Descartes Onwards. Descartes (1596-1650) separated mind and body as different entities but believed that the existence of God could be deduced by the fact that the idea of him existed in the mind. Whatever God puts into man, including his ideas, must be real God is self-caused, omniscient, omnipotent, eternal, all goodness and truth. But Descartes neglected to explain how mind separate from body can influence body, or God separate from the world can influence matter.

Spinoza (1632-77) declared that all existence is embraced in one substance—God, the all-in-all. He was a pantheist and as such was rejected by his Jewish brethren. But Spinoza's God has neither personality nor consciousness, intelligence nor purpose, although all things follow in strict law from His nature. All the thoughts of everyone in the world, make up God's thoughts.

Bishop Berkeley (1685-1753) took the view that things exist only when they are perceived, and this naturally implies that a tree, for example, ceases to exist when nobody is looking at it. This problem was solved to his own satisfaction by assuming that God, seeing everything, prevented objects from disappearing when we were not present. The world is a creation of God but it is a spiritual or mental world, not a material one.

Hume (1711-76), who was a sceptic, held that human reason cannot demonstrate the existence of God and all past arguments to show that it could were fallacious. Yet we must believe in God since the basis of all hope, morality, and society is based upon the belief. Kant (1724-1804) held a theory similar to that of Hume. We cannot know by reason that God exists, nor can we prove on the basis of argument anything about God. But we can form an idea of the whole of the universe, the one Absolute Whole, and personify it. We need the idea of God on which to base our moral life, although this idea of God is transcendent, *i.e.*, goes beyond experience.

William Damon (1842-1910), the American philosopher (*see* **Pragmatism**), held much the same view: God cannot be proved to exist, but we have a will to believe which must be satisfied, and the idea works in practice. Hegel (1770-1831) thought of God as a developing process, beginning with "the Absolute" or First Cause and finding its highest expression in man's mind, or reason. It is in man that God most clearly becomes aware of Himself. Comte (1798-1857), the positivist, held that religion belongs to a more primitive state of society.

Good and Evil.

Early Philosophers' Views. The early Greek philosophers were chiefly concerned with the laws of the universe, consequently it was common belief that knowledge of these laws, and living according to them, constituted the supreme good. Heraclitus, for example, who taught that all things carried with them their opposites, held that good and evil were like two notes in a harmony, necessary to each other. "It is the opposite which is good for us". Democritus, like Epicurus (*q.v.*), held that the main goal of life is happiness, but happiness in moderation. The good man is not merely the one who *does* good but who always *wants* to do so: "You can tell the good man not by his deeds alone but by his desires." Such goodness brings happiness, the ultimate goal. On the other hand, many of the wandering Sophist teachers taught that good was merely social convention, that there are no absolute principles of right and wrong, that each

man should live according to his desires and make his own moral code. To Socrates knowledge was the highest good because doing wrong is the result of ignorance: "no man is voluntarily bad."

Plato and Aristotle, although differing in many other respects, drew attention to the fact that man is composed of three parts: his desires and appetites, his will, and his reason. A man whose reason rules his will and appetites is not only a good but a happy man; for happiness is not an aim in itself but a by-product of the good life. Aristotle, however, emphasised the goal of self-realisation, and thought that if the goal of life is (as Plato had said) a rational attitude towards the feelings and desires, it needs to be further defined. Aristotle defined it as the "Golden Mean"—the good man is one who does not go to extremes but balances one extreme against another. Thus courage is a mean between cowardice and foolhardiness. The later philosophers Philo and Plotinus held that evil was in the very nature of the body and its senses. Goodness could only be achieved by giving up the life of the senses and, freed from the domination of the body, turning to God, the source of goodness.

Christian Views. St. Augustine taught that everything in the universe is good. Even those things which appear evil are good in that they fit with the harmony of the universe like shadows in a painting. Man should turn his back on the pleasures of the world and turn to the love of God. Peter Abelard (1079-1142) made the more sophisticated distinction when he suggested that the wrongness of an act lies not in the act itself, but in the intention of the doer: "God considers not what is done but in what spirit is it done; and the merit or praise of the agent lies not in the deed but in the intention." If we do what we believe to be right, we may err, but we do not sin. The only sinful man is he who deliberately sets out to do what he knows to be wrong. St. Thomas Aquinas agreed with Aristotle in that he believed the highest good to be realisation of self as God has ordained, and he also agreed with Abelard that intention is important. Even a good act is not good unless the doer intended it to have good consequences. Intention will not make a bad act good, but it is the only thing that will make a good act genuinely good.

In general, Christianity has had difficulties in solving the problem of the existence of evil; for even when one accepts that the evil men do is somehow tied up with the body, it is still difficult to answer the question; how could an all-good God create evil? This is answered in one of two ways: (*a*) man was given free-will and chose to sin (an answer which still does not explain how sin could exist anywhere in the universe of a God who willed everything; (*b*) by denying the reality of evil as some Christians have chosen to do (*e.g.*, Christian Science *q.v.*). The Eastern religions, (*see* **Zoroastrianism**), solved the problem in a more realistic way by a dualism which denied that their gods were the creators of the whole universe and allowed the existence of at least two gods, one good and one evil. In Christianity there is, of course, a Devil, but it is not explained whence his evil nature came.

Later Philosophic Views. Hobbes equated good with pleasure and evil with pain. They are relative to the individual man in the sense that "one man's meat is another man's poison." Descartes believed that the power to distinguish between good and evil given by God to man is not complete, so that man does evil through ignorance. We act with insufficient knowledge and on inadequate evidence. Locke, believing that at birth the mind is a blank slate, held that men get their opinions of right and wrong from their parents. By and large, happiness is good and pain is evil. But men do not always agree over what is pleasurable and what not. Hence laws exist and these fall into three categories: (1) the divine law; (2) civil laws; (3) matters of opinion or reputation which are enforced by the fact that men do not like to incur the disapproval of their friends. We learn by experience that evil brings pain and good acts bring pleasure and, basically, one is good because not to be so would bring discomfort.

Kant (*see* **God and Man**) found moral beliefs

to be inherent in man whether or not they can be proved by reason. There is a categorical imperative which makes us realise the validity of two universal laws: (1) "always act in such a way that the maxim determining your conduct might well become a universal law; act so that you can will that everybody shall follow the principle of your action; (2) "always act so as to treat humanity, whether in thine own person or in that of another, in every case as an end and never as a means."

Schopenhauer (1788–1860) was influenced by Buddhism and saw the will as a blind impelling striving, and desire as the cause of all suffering. The remedy is to regard sympathy and pity as the basis of all morality and to deny one's individual will. This is made easier if we realise that everyone is part of the Universal Will and therefore the one against whom we are struggling is part of the same whole as ourselves.

John Stuart Mill and Jeremy Bentham were both representatives of the Utilitarian school, believing that good is the greatest good (happiness) of the greatest number (see **Utilitarianism**). Lastly, there is the view held mostly by political thinkers that good is what is good for society in general (see **State and Man**). See also **Ethics, J58**.

Guild Socialism, a British form of syndicalism (q.v.) created in 1906 by an architect, A. J. Penty, who was soon joined by A. R. Orage, S. G. Hobson, and G. D. H. Cole. The guild socialists advocated a restoration of the mediaeval guild system as was being recommended by the French syndicalists whose programme involved a return to direct economic action, a functional industrial structure, return of craftsmanship, and distrust of the state. Guild socialists believed that value was created by society as a whole rather than by individuals singly, and that capitalist economists had recommended the acquisition of wealth without emphasising the social responsibilities which wealth should bring. The trade unions were to be organised to take over and run their own industries after nationalisation.

Thus guild socialists were not only against capitalism but also against state socialism in which the state took over the control of industry. Political authority was held to be uncongenial to human freedom and therefore nothing was to be gained by the substitution of state bureaucracy for capitalist control.

The National Guilds League, formed in 1915, advocated abolition of the wages system, self-government in industry and control by a system of national guilds acting in conjunction with other functional democratic organisations in the community. This body was dissolved in 1925, but the theories of guild socialism have undoubtedly influenced British socialism.

H

Hare Krishna. See **J60**.
Hasidism (**Chasidism**). From the Hebrew *hasid*, pious or faithful one. A Jewish mystical movement which began in Poland in the 18th century, and which spread widely, first through Eastern Europe and then into Western Europe and America. The movement was founded by Israel ben Eliezer (1700–60), who came to be known as the Ba'al Shem Tov ("Master of the Good Name"). It was originally opposed to the authority of the rabbis and traditional Jewish practices. According to Hasidism, true religion comes not from study of the sacred texts but from purity of heart, prayer and observance of the commandments. The movement was also characterized by ecstatic forms of worship. Its present day followers are ultra-conservative orthodox Jews.
Heaven's Gate. See **J61**.
Hedonism. From Greek *hedone*, pleasure. The theory of ethics in which pleasure is regarded as the chief good, or proper end, of action. This is sometimes called ethical hedonism and is thus distinguished from psychological hedonism, which is the theory that behaviour is primarily motivated by the pursuit of pleasure and the avoidance of pain. Psychological hedonism can of course be employed to support ethical hedonism.

This view, that only pleasure is ultimately good, has been held by many distinguished

philosophers, including Epicurus, Locke, Hobbes, Hume, Bentham and Mill. In the case of the last two, it is closely associated with utilitarianism (q.v.). Although the term "pleasure" suggests physical enjoyments, hedonists have taken it to include intellectual pleasures also. They also argue that many things beside pleasure, such as virtue and knowledge, are desirable in that they produce pleasure.

Heresy, originally meant a sect or school of thought holding views different from others (e.g., Pharisees and Sadducees within Judaism). Later it came to mean beliefs contrary to orthodox teaching (e.g., Arianism, Jansenism, Pelagianism).

Hermeneutics. Originally, the study of the general principles of biblical interpretation. The term came into philosophy in the late 19th century to refer to a more general study of interpretation, namely the interpretation of the significance of human actions, utterances, products etc.

Hermeticism (or **Hermetism**). Philosophies based on the Hermetic writings, also called the Hermetica, works on occult, theological and philosophical subjects ascribed to the Egyptian God Thoth (referred to in Greek as Hermes Trismegistos, Hermes the thrice-greatest). This collection, written in Latin and Greek, dates from 2nd–3rd centuries A.D. It reached Europe, from the Arabs, in the late 15th century, and had some influence during the Renaissance. It continues to fascinate modern devotees of magic and astrology.

The term also has a literary sense. It refers to an Italian poetic movement of the 20th century, characterized by brevity and obscurity.

Hinduism, the religion and social institutions of the great majority of the people of India. Hinduism has no fixed scriptural canon but its doctrines are to be found in certain ancient works, notably the *Veda*, the *Brahmanas*, the *Upanishads*, and the *Bhagavad-gita*.

The dark-skinned Dravidians invaded India between c. 3250 and 2750 B.C. and established a civilisation in the Indus valley. They were polytheists who worshipped a number of nature-gods; some elements of their beliefs persisted into Hinduism. They were subdued by light-skinned Indo-European speakers who invaded from Asia Minor and Iran about 1500 B.C. The language of these people was Vedic, parent of Sanskit in which their religious literature (the Vedas) came to be written after many centuries of oral transmission.

The *Veda* or Sacred Lore has come down to us in the form of mantras or hymns of which there are four great collections, the best-known being the *Rig-Veda*. These Vedic Aryans worshipped nature-deities, their favourites being Indra (rain), Agni (fire), and Surya (the sun). Their religion contained no idolatry but became influenced by the beliefs of the Dravidians. Sacrifice and ritual became predominant in a ceremonial religion.

As a reaction a more philosophic form arose (c. 500 B.C.) with its scriptures in the *Upanishads*. At its highest level known as Brahmanism belief is in a subtle and sophisticated form of monotheism (Brahman is an impersonal, all-embracing spirit), but there is a tolerant acceptance of more primitive beliefs. Thus Vishnu (a conservative principle) and Siva (a destructive principle) grew out of Vedic conceptions. The two great doctrines of Hinduism are *karma* and transmigration. The universal desire to be reunited with the absolute (*atman* or Brahman) can be satisfied by following the path of knowledge. Life is a cycle of lives (*samsara*) in which man's destiny is determined by his deeds (*karma*) from which he may seek release (*moksa*) through ascetic practices or the discipline of Yoga (q.v.). Failure to achieve release means reincarnation—migration to a higher or lower form of life after death—until the ultimate goal of absorption in the absolute is reached.

In the great Sanskrit epic poems *Ramayana* and *Mahabharata* the deity takes three forms, represented by the divine personalities of Brahma, Vishnu, and Siva. There are also lower gods, demi-gods, supernatural beings, and members of the trinity may even become incarnate, as Vishnu became identified with Krishna, one of the heroes of the *Mahabharata* and the well-known *Bhagavad-gita*.

The ritual and legalistic side of Brahmanism is the caste system based on the elaborate codes of the *Law of Manu*, according to which God created distinct orders of men as He created distinct species of animals and plants. Men are born to be Brahmans, soldiers, agriculturists, or servants, but since a Brahman may marry a woman from any of these castes, an endless number of sub-castes arise.

Hinduism has historically shown great tolerance for varieties of belief and practice. Ideas pleasant and unpleasant have been assimilated: fetishism, demon-cults, animal-worship, sexual cults (such as the rites of *Kali* in Calcutta). Today, as would be expected in a country which is in the throes of vast social change, Hinduism itself is changing. Under the impact of modern conditions new ideas are destroying old beliefs and customs. A militant political Hinduism is now threatening the cohesion of India, fanned by the Bharatiya Janata Group (BJP) which extols Hindu fundamentalism. There are (2000) c. 635,000,000 Hindus worldwide (560,000 in Britain). The Hindu temple in Neasden, north London, is the largest place of Hindu worship outside India. See *also* Jainism and Sikhism.

Homoeopathy, an alternative branch of medicine whose motto *Similia Similibus Curantur* (like cures like) sums up its particular approach to therapy. In essence the homoeopathists claim that a disease can be treated by administering quite minute doses of a substance which produce symptoms (in the healthy person) similar to those induced by the disease itself. The founder and populariser of this unusual approach to medicine was the German Samuel Hahnemann who was born in 1775, a friend of the physician Mesmer who propagated hypnotherapy. Hahnemann lived to see his ideas spread across the civilised world (despite the grave theoretical difficulties implicit in the question of how the very minute dosages actually achieve any result at all). Recent years have seen a major growth in public demand for homoeopathy. However, one risk of relying solely on homoeopathy is that a patient may be deprived of life-saving medicines.

The amount of research being carried out in homoeopathy by medical doctors, physicists, molecular biologists, *etc.*, is phenomenal; furthermore, two real milestones occurred in the UK when papers on homoeopathy were published in *The Lancet* in 1988 and in the *British Medical Journal* in 1989. Since then the subject has attracted more and more interest but scientists in contrast remain convinced sceptics.

The Government has proposed a new watchdog to regulate the alternative medicine industry and all practitioners will be required to register.

Homosexuality. *See* Gay Movement.

Humanism, the term applied to (1) a system of education based on the Greek and Latin classics; and (2) the vigorous attitudes that accompanied the end of the Middle Ages and were represented at different periods by the Renaissance, the Reformation, the Industrial Revolution, and the struggle for democracy. These include: release from ecclesiastical authority, the liberation of the intellect, faith in progress, the belief that man himself can improve his own conditions without supernatural help and, indeed has a duty to do so. "Man is the measure of all things" is the keynote of humanism. The humanist has faith in man's intellectual and spiritual resources not only to bring knowledge and understanding of the world but to solve the moral problems of how to use that knowledge. That man should show respect to man irrespective of class, race or creed is fundamental to the humanist attitude to life. Among the fundamental moral principles he would count freedom, justice and tolerance.

Hussites, the followers of John Hus, the most famous pupil of John Wyclif. He was the rector of Prague University and, although it is now by no means certain that his beliefs were heretical, he was condemned to death for heresy and burnt at the stake in 1415 at Constance whither he had come with a safe conduct issued by the Emperor Sigismund of Hungary. The latter based his action on the doctrine that no faith need be kept with heretics, but it is obvious that the main objection to Hus was his contempt for authority of any kind. After their leader's death, the Hussites became a formidable body in Bohemia and Moravia. They took up arms on behalf of their faith, their religion being strongly imbued with political feeling (hostility to Germanism and to the supremacy of the Roman Church). Their religious struggles for reform led to the Hussite Wars during which the movement splintered into several groups.

Hutterites. *See* Mennonites.

Hypnotism. *See* Mesmerism.

I

I Ching, the Chinese "Book of Changes" which is supposed to provide a practical demonstration of the truths of ancient Chinese philosophy. The method consists of casting forty-nine sticks into two random heaps, or more simply, of tossing three coins to see if there is a preponderance of heads or tails. The coins are cast six times whereupon the head tail sequence achieved is referred to a coded series of phrases in the book, which are supposed to relate in some way to the question held in the mind when the sticks or coins are being cast. The phrases are without exception vague, and platitudinous remarks such as "Evil people do not further the perseverance of the superior man," *etc.*, abound.

Consequently it is not difficult to read into such amorphous stuff a suitable "interpretation" or answer to one's unspoken question. The I Ching was once a great fad in Europe and America.

Idealism, in philosophy, the belief that there is no matter in the universe, that all that exists is mind or spirit. *See* Mind and Matter and Realism.

Illuminati, a secret society founded in 1776 by Adam Weishaupt, a Bavarian professor of canon law at Ingolstadt, in an attempt to combat superstition and ignorance by founding an association for rational enlightenment and the regeneration of the world. "He tried to give the social ideals of the Enlightenment realisation by conspiratorial means" (J. M. Roberts, *The Mythology of the Secret Societies*, 1972). Under conditions of secrecy it sought to penetrate and control the masonic lodges for subversive purposes. Among its members were Goethe and Schiller. The Order spread to Austria, Italy and Hungary but was condemned by the Catholic Church and dissolved in 1785 by the Bavarian government.

Immortality. The belief in a life after death has been widely held since the earliest times. It has certainly not been universal, nor has it always taken a form which everyone would find satisfying. In the early stages of human history or prehistory everything contained a spirit (*see* Animism) and it is obvious from the objects left in early graves that the dead were expected to exist in some form after death. The experience of dreams, too, seemed to suggest to the unsophisticated that there was a part of man which could leave his body and wander elsewhere during sleep.

It will be helpful to classify the various types of belief which have existed in philosophical thought regarding this problem: (1) There is the idea that, although *something* survives bodily death, it is not necessarily eternal. Thus most primitive peoples were prepared to believe that man's spirit haunted the place around his grave and that food and drink should be set out for it, but that this spirit did not go on forever and gradually faded away. (2) The ancient Greeks and Hebrews believed for the most part that the souls of the dead went to a place of shades there to pine for the world of men. Their whining ghosts spent eternity in a dark, uninviting region in misery and remorse. (3) Other people, and there were many more of these, believed in the transmigration of souls with the former life of the individual determining whether his next life would be at a higher or lower level. Sometimes this process seems to have been thought of as simply going on and on, by others (*e.g.*, in Hinduism and Buddhism) as terminating in either non-sentience or union with God but in any case in annihilation of the self as self. Believers in this theory were the Greek philosophers Pythagoras, Empedocles, Plato (who believed that soul comes from God and strives to return to God, according to his own rather confused notions of the deity. If it fails to free itself completely from the body it will sink lower and lower from one body to another.) Plotinus held similar views to Plato, and many other religious sects in addition to those mentioned have believed in transmigration. (4) The belief of Plato and Aristotle that if souls continue to exist after death there is no reason why they should not have existed before birth (this in part is covered by (3)), but some have pointed out that eternity does not mean "from now on," but the whole of the time before and after "now"—nobody, however, so far as one knows, held that *individual* souls so exist. (5) The theory that the soul does not exist at all and therefore immortality is meaningless: this was held by Anaximenes in early Greek times; by Leucippus, Democritus, and the other Greek atomists; by the Epicureans from the Greek Epicurus to the Roman Lucretius; by the British Hobbes and Hume; by Comte of France; and William James and John Dewey of America. (6) The thesis, held notably by Locke and Kant, that although we cannot prove the reality of soul and immortality by pure reason, belief in them should be held for moral ends. (For the orthodox Christian view *see* **God and Man, Determinism and Free-will.**)

From this summary we can see that many philosophies and religions (with the important exceptions of Islam and Christianity) without denying a future life do deny the permanence of the individual soul in anything resembling its earthly form (*see* **Spiritualism, Psychic Research**).

Imperialism, the practice by a country, which has become a nation and embarked upon commercial and industrial expansion, of acquiring and administering territories, inhabited by peoples usually at a lower stage of development, as colonies or dependencies. Thus the "typical" imperialist powers of the mid-19th cent. and earlier were Britain, France, Belgium, Holland, Spain and Portugal, whilst Germany, Italy, and Japan, which either did not have unity during this period or adequate industrial expansion, tried to make good their weakness in this direction by war in the late 19th cent. The term "imperialism" is not easy to define today (although often enough used as a term of abuse). There is economic imperialism exerted, not through armies, but through economic penetration. There is what may be described as ideological imperialism, *e.g.,* the anti-communist crusade that led America (in the name of freedom) into a disastrous and widely-condemned war in Vietnam; the dogmatism that led the former Soviet Union into the invasion of Czechoslovakia, Israel into occupying neighbouring lands and (some have argued) America into the occupation of Iraq.

Individualism. The doctrine that the single person is the basic unit of political analysis. The term covers all political and social philosophies that place a high value on the freedom of the individual. It is believed that the interests of the individual are best served by allowing him maximum freedom and responsibility. Society is seen as a collection of individuals. So individualism opposes controls over the individual, especially when they are exercised by the state. The most extreme form is anarchism, but all individualists believe that government interference should be kept to a minimum. It is opposed to collectivism (*q.v.*). The term was originally used critically, to refer to egoism as a matter of principle.

Intelligent Design, a movement which opposes Darwin's theory of evolution. Similar to *Creationism* (*q.v.*) it argues that parts of the Universe were made by an intelligent agent rather than by an undirected process. It is gaining support in the USA.

International Church of Christ. *See* **J60.**

Iridology, the study of the iris of the eye to secure information about the health of the body.

Irrationalism. An attitude that puts emotion and passion before reason.

Islam, the religion of which Mohammed (570–632) was the prophet, the word signifying submission to the will of God. It is one of the most widespread of religions. Its adherents are called Muslims. Islam came later than the other great monotheistic religions (Judaism and Christianity) and drew its inspiration mainly from Judaism and Nestorianism. Mohammed accepted the inspiration of the Old Testament and claimed to be a successor to Moses, but recognised Jesus only

as a prophet.

The sacred book of Islam is the Koran. Its revelations are contained in 114 *suras* or chapters: all but one begin with the words: "In the name of Allah, the Merciful, the Compassionate." It is written in classical Arabic, and Muslims memorise much or all of it. Its ethical teachings are high. Like orthodox Judaism Islam is a literal-minded religion lived in everyday life. No Muslim is in any doubt as to exactly how he should carry on in the events of his day. He has five duties: (1) Once in his life he must say with absolute conviction: "There is no God but Allah, and Mohammed is His Prophet". (2) Prayer preceded by ablution must be five times daily—on rising, at noon, in mid-afternoon, after sunset. and before retiring. The face of the worshipper is turned in the direction of Mecca. (3) The giving of alms generously, including provisions for the poor. (4) The keeping of the fast of Ramadan, the holy month, during which believers in good health may neither eat nor drink nor indulge in wordly pleasures between sunrise and sunset. (5) Once in his life a Muslim, if he can, must make the pilgrimage to Mecca.

In addition, drinking, gambling, and the eating of pork are forbidden and circumcision is practised. Polygamy is permitted, although decreasing; sexual relations outside marriage are disapproved of; marriage is only with the wife's consent; and divorce may be initiated by either husband or wife. A great advantage in the spread of Islam has been its lack of race prejudice.

Mohammed's main achievements were the destruction of idolatry, the welding of warring tribes into one community, the progress of a conquest which led after his death to the great and cultured empire which spread throughout the Middle East into north Africa, north India, and ultimately to Spain. That it did not spread all over Europe was due to the Muslim defeat by Charles Martel at Poitiers in 732.

During the 1980s, militant Islam became a major political force in Iran (under Ayatollah Khomeini). Islamic fundamentalism became, in the 1990s, a growing political force in, for example, Algeria, Egypt, Afghanistan, Pakistan and much of central Asia. The most extreme form of fundamentalism was the Taleban regime in Afghanistan until its overthrow. There are (2006) nearly 2,000,000,000 Muslims in the world.

Britain's total Muslim population (2001 Census) numbered 1·54 million, with 70 % under the age of 25. There are over 1,200 mosques and numerous prayer centres thoughout Britain. The first was established at Woking in Surrey in 1890. The Central Mosque in Regent's Park, London has the largest congregation in Britain while other centres include Bradford, Oldham, Leeds, Leicester and Glasgow.

The largest mosque in Britain (the Baitul Futuh mosque in Morden) was completed in 2003. The largest mosque in the western world is in Dearborn, Michigan, USA.

J

Jainism. The Jains are an Indian sect, largely in commerce and finance. Their movement founded by Vardhamana, called Mahavira (the great hero), in the 6th cent. B.C. arose rather earlier than Buddhism in revolt against the ritualism and impersonality of **Hinduism** (*q.v.*). It rejects the authority of the early Hindu Vedas and does away with many of the Hindu deities whose place is largely taken by Jainism's twenty-four immortal saints; it despises caste distinctions and modifies the two great Hindu doctrines of *karma* and transmigration. Jain philosophy is based on *ahimsa*, the sacredness of all life, regarding even plants as the brethren of mankind, and refusing to kill even the smallest insect. The first Jain temple in the Western world opened in 1988 in Leicester. Of an estimated 3,900,000 Jains world-wide, there are *c* 3,700,000 in India. Jainism claims 30,000 devotees in Britain (2005).

Jansenism, the name given by the Roman Catholic Church to the heresy of Cornelius Jansen (1585–1638), a Dutch-born professor of theology at

Louvain, derived from his work *Augustinus*, published after his death. He proposed that without special grace from God, the performance of his commandments is impossible, that man has no free will, and that most human beings are condemned to damnation. The movement based on these ideas was very influential in France in the 17th century.

Jehovah's Witnesses. One of the best known offshoots of mainstream Christianity, Jehovah's Witnesses are renowned for their doorstep witness. Founded in the second half of the nineteenth century in Pittsburgh by Charles Taze Russel, and taking their name from a passage in Isaiah 43, they are strongly millenialist, and put much emphasis on the return of Christ and his heavenly rule upon earth. Various attempts to set a specific date since 1874 have proved unsuccessful, however. Russel, rejecting the notion of a Hell, put a focus on the nothingness of death until the Second Coming or Rapture. At this point the 144,000 or 'little flock' will rule with Christ in Heaven, whilst other Jehovah's Witnesses, the 'great crowd' will be ruled on Earth.

They support their beliefs based on the Bible, in particular their own version, The New World Translation. They emphasise the Judaic name for God, Jehovah and regard him as God alone. They reject the Trinity, and regard Jesus Christ as God's first creation and therefore inferior, and the Holy Spirit as another way of expressing God's power in action. They believe in upholding what they regard as the universal elements of the Mosaic Law, and are well known for their rejection of blood transfusions as non-biblical. They regard all other religions and denominations as false, rejecting in particular strongly hierarchical church organisation, despite criticisms of authoritarianism themselves. At the heart of the movement lies directed Bible study supported by its huge publishing wing, the Watch Tower Bible and Tract Society.

Jesus People, one of the early revivals of interest in the teaching and personality of Jesus Christ which featured from the 1960s as part of the American "Hippy" scene. The Jesus People or Jesus Freaks, as they were sometimes called, were generally white but not necessarily of an orthodox Christian background. The cult developed in California.

Jihad, the Islamic term is best translated 'to struggle to the utmost'. In the West it has become synonymous with a holy war.

Judaism, the religion of the Jews, the oldest of the great monotheist religions, parent of Christianity and Islam, the development of which is presented in the Old Testament. The creed of Judaism is based on the concept of a transcendent and omnipotent One True God, the revelation of His will in the *Torah*, and the special relation between God and His "Chosen People." The idea of Incarnation is rejected, Jesus is not recognised as the Messiah. The *Torah* is the Hebrew name for the Law of Moses (the Pentateuch) which, Judaism holds, was divinely revealed to Moses on Mount Sinai soon after the exodus of the Israelites from Egypt (1230 B.C.).

Many critics today deny the Mosaic authorship of the first five books of the Bible and believe them to be a compilation from four main sources known as J(Jahvist), E (Elohist), D (Deuteronomist) and P (Priestly Code), distinguished from each other by the name used for God, language, style, and internal evidence. From the historical point of view an important influence on Judaism may have been the monotheism of Akhenaten, the "heretic" Pharaoh (note, for example, the striking resemblance between Psalm 104 and Akhenaten's "Hymn to the Sun").

Talmud. The Talmud is a book containing the civil and canonical laws of the Jews and includes the *Mishna*, a compilation from oral tradition written in Hebrew, and the *Gemara*, a collection of comments and criticisms by Jewish rabbis, written in Aramaic. There are in fact two Talmuds: the one made in Palestine (the Jerusalem Talmud), finished at the beginning of the 5th cent B.C., and the other made in Babylon, completed at the end of the 6th cent B.C.

Judaism at the beginning of the Christian era had a number of sects: (1) the Pharisees (whose views include the first clear statement of the resurrection of the just to eternal life and the future punishment of the wicked) who held to the *Torah* and the universality of God; (2) the Sadducees, the upper class of priests and wealthy landowners, to whom God was essentially a national God and who placed the interests of the state before the *Torah*; they rejected ideas of resurrection and eternal life; (3) the Essenes (*q.v.*) who were regarded as a puritanical break-away movement by both parties. The views of the Pharisees prevailed.

Jewish Philosophers. Jewish writing continued through the years and some books were added to the *Torah*, among them the Three Major Prophets and certain books of the Twelve Minor Prophets. There were also the Apocalyptic writers who were unorthodox in their preaching of a divinely planned catastrophic end to the world with a "new Heaven and a new earth," preceded by a divine Messiah, and a future life—all of which beliefs influenced early Christianity. Judah Halevi of Toledo (c. 1085–c. 1140) and Moses Maimonides of Cordova (1135–1204) were the great Jewish philosophers.

Modern movements in Judaism stem from the Enlightenment, notably with Moses Mendelssohn in the 18th cent. who accepted, as was the tendency of the period, only that which could be proved by reason. He translated the Pentateuch into German thus encouraging German Jews to give up Yiddish and Hebrew for the language of the land and thereby preparing them for their vast contribution to Western civilisation. One of his disciples, David Friedländer (d. 1834) instituted "reform" Judaism. He wanted to eliminate anything that would hamper the relationships of Jews with their neighbours or tend to call in doubt their loyalty to their adopted state. A similar movement in America (1885) called for the rejection of dietary laws, the inauguration of Sunday services, and the repudiation of Jewish nationalism.

Between "reform" and orthodoxy there arose the conservative movement which, in England, includes prayers in English in the service, does not segregate men and woman in the synagogue, and translates the Law in a more liberal way. Judaism is essentially a social and family religion which, more than almost any other concerns itself with the observances of every aspect of daily life. As in Islam (*q.v.*) details are laid down in the most minute way for the behaviour of the orthodox.

The home is the main Jewish institution. Circumcision takes place eight days after birth, and a boy becomes a man for religious purposes at his Bar Mitzvah at the age of thirteen.

Among festivals are Passover, recalling the Exodus; Rosh Hashanah (the Jewish New Year), the anniversary of the Creation and the beginning of ten days of penitence ending with Yom Kippur (the Day of Atonement), a day of fasting spent in the synagogue; Purim, celebrating the deliverance of the Jews from Haman; and Chanukah, celebrating their victory against the Syrians under their leader Judas Maccabeus. A new and semireligious festival is the Yom Haatzmaut, the anniversary of the birth of the state of Israel.

Countries with the largest Jewish populations are the USA (5,280,000), Israel (5,230,000) and France (521,000). The 2001 Census showed 267,000 in Britain. There are nearly 15 million Jews world-wide.

There are currently divisions in Judaism over the role women can play in Jewish religious life.

K

Kabbala. *See* **Cabala.**

Khalsa, the sacred brotherhood of the Sikhs (*q.v.*).

Ku Klux Klan. After the American Civil War (1861–65) southern conservatives and ex-Confederate leaders began to fear (as they had every reason to do) both Black and poor White rule. Taxes were rising owing to radical legislation and the tax-burdened and disenfranchised planters finally took to illegal means to achieve their ends by trying to effect an alliance with the poor White and small farmer through appealing to his anti-Black prejudice.

Hence the Ku Klux Klan was formed in 1866

as a secret society by a small group of Confederate veterans in Tennessee with the intention of frightening Blacks by dressing in ghostly white robes in the guise of the spirits of dead soldiers. But the movement spread like wild-fire throughout the South encouraged by small farmers and planters alike. General Nathan Bedford Forrest was appointed "Grand Wizard" of the Klan "empire" and in every community armed Klansmen riding at night horsewhipped "uppity" Blacks, beat Union soldiers, and threatened carpet-bag politicians (*i.e.*, fortunehunters from the North). Soon several similar organisations arose, many of which did not stop at torture, burning property, and murder.

The Klan was a vicious and contemptible organisation in which former Southern leaders trying to regain control deliberately set poor and middle-class Whites against the Blacks by appeal to race prejudice. Congress struck back with laws and intervention of Federal troops, and after a large number of convictions in South Carolina much of the violence stopped.

After the 1914–18 war the movement, dormant since 1900, revived as a sadistic anti-Black, anti-Jewish, anti-Catholic society, spreading to the north as well as the south. By 1926, the Klan began to subside once more. While it revived again in the mid-1960s, it soon fell back. The terrorist attack of 11 September 2001 has seen some extreme groups receive renewed support.

Koran (Quran). *See* Islam.

L

Lamaism, the religion of Tibet. Its beliefs and worship derive from the Mahayana form of Buddhism which was introduced into Tibet in 749. The emphasis laid by its founder on the necessity for self-discipline and conversion through meditation and the study of philosophy deteriorated into formal monasticism and ritualism.

The Dalai Lama, as the reincarnated Buddha, was both king and high priest, a sort of pope and emperor rolled into one. Under him was a hierarchy of officials in which the lowest order was that of the monks who became as numerous as one man in every six or seven of the population. The main work carried out by this vast church state was the collection of taxes to maintain the monasteries and other religious offices. Second in power to the Dalai Lama was the Panchen or Tashi Lama believed to be a reincarnation of Amitabha, another Buddha.

The last Dalai Lama fled to India in 1959 when the Chinese entered his country. For a brief period following his departure, the Panchen Lama surprised the Western world by publicly welcoming the Communist invasion, but he later renounced the regime and the suppression of Lamaism in Tibet continued unchecked.

Latter-day Saints. *See under* Mormons.

Levellers, an English military-politico-religious party prominent in the Parliamentary Army about 1647 which stood for the rights of the people. *See* Diggers.

Liberalism. The Liberal Party is the successor to the Whigs (a nickname derived from *Whiggamore*, used in the 17th cent. for Scottish dissenters) of the 18th and 19th cents. Under Gladstone's two great ministries (1868–74; and 1880–85), and again under Campbell-Bannerman and Asquith (1906–14) much reforming legislation was enacted. The Asquith–Lloyd George split of 1916, and the advent of Labour as a major party after 1918, caused the Liberals to be relegated as a much smaller, third party. In the decade after 1945, there were times when the Liberal Party barely survived. But revivals have since occurred under the leadership of Jo Grimond (1962), Jeremy Thorpe (1974), David Steel (1979) and Paddy Ashdown (from 1988 to 1999).

Liberal philosophy is moderately radical and progressive in terms of social reform. But the party strongly disapproves of state control or any form of monopoly, private or public. The main

proposals favoured by the party are co-ownership in industry, proportional representation, greater protection of individual liberties, and a strong commitment to Europe.

Many younger members of the party hold views to the left of official party policy. The phenomenon of "community politics" owed much to these younger and more radical Liberals. The 1987 election setback heralded a merger ("democratic fusion") between the Liberals and their SDP Alliance partners. The new Social and Liberal Democratic Party (SLD) was formed in 1988. The first leader of the new party was Paddy Ashdown, MP for Yeovil.

After 1997 it pursued a policy of 'constructive opposition' to the Labour Government. Charles Kennedy became the new leader of the party in 1999. In his first election as leader, in June 2001, the party secured 52 seats,. In May 2005 it won 62 seats, its best performance since 1923.

Libertarianism is the view that the moral and material benefit of individuals is best served by a society devoid of government except for the enforcement of rights to life and property. In this way libertarianism differs from anarchism, which argues for the abolition of all authority and government. Famous contemporary libertarians, such as Hayek and Nozick, argue that the pursuit of social justice by the state endangers individual liberty, and threatens tyranny. They argue for a society which operates much like an ideal market where a natural equilibrium of individuals' interests will provide for each person's needs.

Libertarianism's affection for the market has influenced neoliberalism (*q.v.*). Libertarians disagree with modern liberals on the importance of social justice. Liberals argue that there is a moral duty to seek greater equality, and they embrace democratic institutions as appropriate structures through which to promote social justice. Libertarians need to explain either why social justice is not important, or how it can be achieved without democratic political institutions.

Literary Theory. Modern literary theory is concerned with ways in which meaning is constructed and with ideological influences. It challenges received notions of imagination and inspiration, moral significance, and the personality of the author. Its origins lie partly in semiology and formalism, which concentrate on the actual words and structure of a literary text.

Marxism is also important in the works of such critics as Georg Lukács and Louis Althusser. Later approaches include structuralism and post-structuralism. Feminism has become an increasingly significant form of criticism. Other theories are New Historicism, which examines social and cultural contexts, and Reader-Response Criticism, which analyses readers' constructions of meaning.

Logical Positivism, a school of philosophy founded in Vienna in the 1920s by a group known as "the Vienna circle": their work was based on that of Ernst Mach, but dates in essentials as far back as Hume. Of the leaders of the group, Schlick was murdered by a student, Wittgenstein came to Britain, and Carnap went to America following the entry of the Nazis. Briefly the philosophy differs from all others in that, while most people have believed that a statement might be (*a*) true, or (*b*) false, logical positivists consider there to be a third category; a statement may be meaningless. There are only two types of statement which can be said to have meaning: (1) those which are tautological, *i.e.*, those in which the statement is merely a definition of the subject, such as "a triangle is a three-sided plane figure" ("triangle" and "three-sided plane figure" are the same thing); and (2) those which can be tested by sense experience. This definition of meaningfulness excludes a great deal of what has previously been thought to be the field of philosophy; in particular it excludes the possibility of metaphysics.

Thus the question as to whether there is a God or whether free-will exists is strictly meaningless for it is neither a tautological statement nor can it be tested by sense experience.

Lollards, a body of religious reformers and followers of Wyclif who were reviled and persecuted in the reign of Richard II. The name "Lollard" comes from a Flemish word meaning "mutterer"— a term of contempt used to describe the sect.

Under Henry V, determined efforts were made to crush the Lollards. Their leader, Sir John Oldcastle, was burnt at the stake (December 1417).

Low Church, term formerly applied to those Anglicans most sympathetic to Protestant non-conformity (*i.e.*, the opposite of the High Church Anglo-Catholics).

Luddites. *See* **A45**.

Lutheranism. The Reformation had a long history before it became, under Luther and Calvin, an accepted fact. The mediaeval Church had held (as the Catholic Church holds today) that the sacraments were the indispensable means of salvation. Since these were exclusively administered by the clergy, any movement which attacked clerical abuses was forced by sheer necessity to deny the Church's exclusive control of the means of salvation, before it could become free from dependence on a corrupt priesthood. Hence the Albigenses and the Waldenses (*qq.v.*), the followers of John Hus and Wycliff (*see* **Anticlericalism**), were bound to deny the authority of the Church and emphasise that of the Bible. Luther began his movement primarily in order to reform the Church from its gross abuses and the famous ninety-five theses of 1517 were not primarily theological but moral complaints dealing with the actual behaviour of the clergy rather than Church beliefs.

Luther began with the support of the peasants who were genuinely shocked at the abuse of indulgences and other matters, but ended up by being supported by the noblemen who wanted to destroy the power of the pope over the German states and looked forward to confiscating the lands and property of the Church. When the peasants wanted the reform of actual economic abuses relating to the feudal system, Luther took the side of the nobles against them. The contemporary movement in Switzerland led by Ulrich Zwingli had no such secular support, and Zwingli was killed in 1531.

Martin Luther (1483–1546) was the son of a miner in Eisleben in Saxony, entered the order of Augustinian Friars in 1505, and later taught at the newly founded university of Wittenberg. After the publication of the theses the real issue so far as the Church was concerned was whether he was willing or not to submit to the authority of his superiors; Luther refused to compromise with his conscience in the famous words: "Here I stand; I can do no other." In a further statement Luther recommended the formation of a German national church, the abolition of indulgences and other means whereby Rome obtained money from Germany, and an end to the celibacy of the clergy. For this he was naturally excommunicated.

His teaching was based on the German translation of the Bible, but he was by no means a fundamentalist: *e.g.*, he denied that the Book of Hebrews was written by Paul, would have nothing to do with the Apocrypha, and regarded the letter of James as "an epistle of straw." The Scriptures were open to all and could be interpreted by private judgment enlightened by the Spirit of God.

Like Calvin, Luther was a predestinarian and determinist, but he was also a conservative and soon became alarmed about the position taken by many extremists once the Reformation was under way. He had really wanted the Church to reform itself, but when he alienated Rome he had perforce to rely more and more on the secular powers which finally resulted in the state-church form which became pronounced in Prussia and later elsewhere. Whereas Calvin wished the Church to be at least the equal of the State and in some respects its superior, Luther's rebellion resulted in the reverse, a state-controlled episcopalianism.

In 1999 the Lutheran World Federation and the Vatican agreed a historic "Common Statement" on the doctrine of justification. *See* **Calvinism, Presbyterianism**.

Lycanthropy, the belief that men may, by the exercise of magical powers or because of some inherited affliction, occasionally transform into wolves. The so-called werewolf is an important feature of mid-European folklore and much the same can be said of the were-tigers and were-bears of Africa and the Far East. Man's fear of werewolves can be seen in prehistoric rock carvings dating back 30,000 years.

M

McLuhanism. According to Marshall McLuhan (1911–80), a Canadian, and former professor of English at Toronto, the *way* people communicate is more important than *what* they communicate, hence his famous slogan, "the medium is the message." There have been two great landmarks in human understanding since we learnt to speak and write: the invention of the printed book and the present electronic revolution. The printed word took us step by step along the linear, logical path to understanding; television comes at us from all directions at once and now electronic circuitry has overthrown the regime of 'time' and 'space'.

McLuhan's importance lies in alerting us to the present clash between two great technologies, the literate and the electromagnetic, and in his vision, beyond the present chaos, of a world drawn tighter together in a "global village" where identity will merge in collectivity and we shall all be able to co-operate for the common good.

Magic, a form of belief originating in very early days and based on the primitive's inability to distinguish between similarity and identity. The simplest example would perhaps be the fertility rites in which it is believed that a ceremony involving sexual relations between men and women will bring about fertility in the harvest. Or the idea that sticking pins in an image of an individual will bring about harm or even death to the real person. Magic is regarded by some as a form of early science in that man in his efforts to control Nature had recourse to magical practices when the only methods he knew had failed to bring the desired results. It filled a gap. By others magic is regarded as an elementary stage in the evolution of religion. It can be said to have served a purpose there too. Yet magic differs from religion, however closely at times it may come to be related with it in this important respect: religion depends upon a power *outside and beyond* human beings, whereas magic depends upon nothing but the casting of a spell or the performance of a ceremony.

The idea that "like produces like" is at the roots of imitative magic. It follows that an event can be compelled by imitating it. One engages in swinging, not for pleasure, but to produce a wind as the swing does; ball games are played to get rainy weather because the black ball represents dark rainclouds; other ball games, in which one attempts to catch the ball in a cup or hit it with a stick, represent the sexual act (as some gentlemen at Lords may be distressed to hear) and bring about fertility; in medicine until a few centuries ago herbs were chosen to cure a disease because in some respects their leaves or other parts looked like the part of the body affected. *See* **Witchcraft** and **Demonism**.

Malthusianism, the theory about population growth put forward by the Rev. Thomas Malthus (1766–1834) in *An Essay on Population* (1798). His three main propositions were (1) "Population is necessarily limited by means of subsistence." (2) "Population invariably increases where means of subsistence increase unless prevented by some very powerful and obvious checks." (3) "These checks, and the checks which repress the superior power of population, and keep its effects on a level with the means of subsistence, are all resolvable into moral restraint, vice and misery." In other words, no matter how great the food supply may become, human reproductive power will always adjust itself so that food will always be scarce in relation to population; the only means to deal with this is by "moral restraint" (*i.e.*, chastity or not marrying), "vice" (*i.e.*, birth-control methods), or misery (*i.e.*, starvation).

More specifically, Malthus claimed that while food increases by arithmetical progression, population increases by geometrical progression. It is true that these gloomy predictions did not take place in Malthus's time largely owing to the opening up of new areas of land outside Europe, the development of new techniques in agriculture, the growth of international trade to poorer areas, the increased knowledge of birth-control, and developments in medical science which reduced the misery he had predicted. Furthermore, we now know that as a society becomes industrialised its birthrate tends to fall. Growth in the world's population has increased from about 465 million in 1650 to pass 6,000 million in 1999. *See also* **Section Y** for world population trends.

Manichaeism, an Asiatic religion which developed from Zoroastrianism (*q.v.*) and shows the influence of Buddhism (*q.v.*) and Gnosticism (*q.v.*), being founded by Mani, a Persian who was born in Babylonia, *c.* 216 A.D. Mani presented himself to Shapur I as the founder of a new religion which was to be to Babylonia what Buddhism was to India or Christianity to the West. His aspiration was to convert the East and he himself made no attempt to interfere directly with Christianity although he represented himself as the Paraclete (the Holy Ghost or "Comforter") and, like Jesus, had twelve disciples. His success in Persia aroused the fury of the Zoroastrian priests who objected to his reforming zeal towards their religion and in 276 Mani was taken prisoner and crucified.

Of Mani's complicated system little can be said here, save that it is based on the struggle of two eternal conflicting principles, God and matter, or light and darkness. Although its founder had no intention of interfering with the West, after his death his followers soon spread the religion from Persia and Mesopotamia to India and China. It reached as far as Spain and Gaul and influenced many of the bishops in Alexandria and in Carthage where for a time St. Augustine accepted Manichaeism. Soon the toleration accorded it under Constantine ended and it was treated as a heresy and violently suppressed.

Yet it later influenced many heresies, and even had some influence on orthodox Catholicism which had a genius for picking up elements in other religions which had been shown to appeal to worshippers provided they did not conflict unduly with fundamental beliefs.

Maoism is the branch of communism in China that was shaped by one of the most remarkable statesmen of modern times, Mao Tse-tung (1893-1976). He set the pattern of revolution for poor peasant societies despite the traumas of the "Great Leap Forward" and the Cultural Revolution. Although Marxist theory guided the Chinese communists in their struggle for liberation from the old, bourgeois and feudal China, it was interpreted in a manner peculiar to China and developed to fit into the Chinese way of life and the "thoughts" of Chairman Mao. As early as 1926 Mao had pointed out that the Chinese proletariat had in the peasantry its staunchest and most numerous ally.

The struggles of 1925-49 (the Long March of the Red Army, the Anti-Japanese War, the Civil War against Chiang Kai-shek) were the foundations on which present-day China has been built. Maoism is against authoritarianism and for self-reliance; against bureaucracy and for revolutionary momentum; against rivalry between individuals and for common effort. Great efforts have been made to remove poverty, ignorance, corruption and disease from China. Mao taught that struggle is necessary for the revolution to endure. "Running water does not go stale and door-hinges do not become worm-eaten," Mao reminded his comrades. "We must," he said, "make every comrade understand that the highest criterion for judging the words and deeds of the communists is whether they conform with the best interests and win the support of the broadest masses of the people."

The decades since the death of Mao Tse-tung have seen a huge shift towards the modernisation of China and the introduction of capitalism.

Maronites, Christian sect which appeared in Syria in the 6th cent. They are the largest Christian group in Lebanon. The Maronite patron saint is the Syrian monk Maron (d. *c* 410). The Maronites retain ancient Eastern rites.

Marxism. The sociological theories founded by Karl Marx and Friedrich Engels on which modern communist thought is based. Marx and Engels lived in a period of unrestrained capitalism when exploitation and misery were the lot of the industrial working classes, and it was their humanitarianism and concern for social justice which inspired their work. Marx wrote his *Communist Manifesto* in Brussels in 1848 and in his great work, *Das Kapital* (1867), he worked out a new theory of society. Marx showed that all social systems are economically motivated and change as a result of technical and economic changes in methods of production. The driving force of social change Marx found to be in the struggle which the oppressed classes wage to secure a better future.

Thus in his celebrated theory of historical materialism he interpreted history in terms of economics and explained the evolution of society in terms of class struggle. (*See* **Dialectical Materialism**.) "In the social production of their means of existence," he wrote, "men enter into definite and unavoidable relations which are independent of their will. These productive relationships correspond to the particular stage in the development of their material productive forces." Marx's theory of historical materialism implies that history is propelled by class struggle with communism and the classless society as the final stage when man will have emancipated himself from the productive process. Marx was the first to put socialism on a rational and scientific basis, and he foretold that socialism would inevitably replace capitalism. His prophecy, however, came to realisation not in the advanced industrial countries as he had envisaged but in Russia and China. *See* **Communism**.

Materialism. Any theory that tends to the view that only matter or material objects exist and that everything else, notably minds and mental experiences, can be described in material terms. Materialism is thus opposed to dualism or idealism and, in general, to any belief in God, in disembodied spirits *etc*. There is much contemporary philosophical debate as to whether "consciousness" is not a name for something mysterious, but simply a way of talking about the brain. *See also* **Mind and Matter**.

Mechanism. As a theory, the view that everything happens mechanically, that natural phenomena are to be explained by reference to certain laws of nature applied to the behaviour of matter in motion. Through the influence of science, there is a strong tendency in Western thought to compare the universe or parts of it, even human beings, to machines. It is a view closely connected with materialism.

Mennonites, a Christian sect rejecting infant baptism. Named after Menno Simons (1496-1559). Its members reject military service and refuse to hold public office. Hutterites share their beliefs. The Amish, based from the 1700s in Pennsylvania, are a splinter group from the Mennonites.

Mesmerism, a rapidly vanishing name to denote the practice of hypnosis, which owes its popularity, though not its discovery, to the Austrian physician, Anton Mesmer (1733-1815). Mesmer's contribution was the realisation that a large number of what we would today call psychosomatic or hysterical conditions could be cured (or at least temporarily alleviated) by one or another form of suggestion. Mesmer himself relied on the idea of what he called "animal magnetism," a supposedly potent therapeutic force emanating from the living body which could be controlled by the trained individual.

Mesmer used wands and impressive gadgetry to dispense the marvellous force and he effected a remarkable number of cures of complaints, hitherto looked upon as incurable or totally mysterious in origin—the most typical of these being hysterical blindness, paralysis or deafness, nervous skin conditions, and so on. Hypnosis, which is a valid if very poorly understood psychological phenomenon even today, would probably have been developed much further had not efficient general anaesthetics such as ether, nitrous oxide, *etc.*, been discovered, thus greatly diminishing its role as a pain reliever in surgery. Mesmer, who was three parts charlatan, never really troubled to think deeply about the cause of his undoubted success. The first man to treat hysteria as a formal class of illness and who made a scientific attempt to treat it with hypnosis was Ambrose Liébeault (1823–1904). He and his colleagues Hippolyte Bernheim (1840–1919) believed: (*a*) that hysteria was produced by suggestion, and particularly by autosuggestion on the part of the patient, and (*b*) that suggestion was a normal trait found in varying degrees in everyone. These conclusions are true, but as Freud showed later are far from being the whole truth.

Messianism. Most varieties of religious belief rely on the assumption that the deity is a supernatural being either permeating the universe or dwelling in some other sphere, and normally inaccessible to man. Where divine intervention is necessary, the deity is traditionally believed to nominate a human being—in the case of Christianity, for example, Jesus is believed to be the actual son of God. Messianic cults introduce a novel variant on the traditional theme. In these a human being is held to be God himself. He may either nominate himself for this role, relying on his own personality or native talent to acquire the necessary following, or for one reason or another large numbers of people may alight on one individual and declare him the Messiah. While it might seem that beliefs of this kind would be confined to earlier epochs in man's recorded history, this is in fact not the case. In the past century, and even within recent decades, a number of individuals have been held by groups to be actually divine.

To simple people the idea that God is to be found on earth and that one may even be personally introduced to him, is an obviously attractive one. The trouble is that all self-styled gods to this present date have eventually disappointed their supporters by performing that most human of acts—dying.

Metapsychology. Not to be confused with parapsychology (*q.v.*). The branch or off-shoot of psychology which goes beyond empirical and experimental studies to consider such philosophical matters as the nature of mind, the reality of free-will and the mind/body problem. It was originally used by Freud as a blanket descriptive term denoting all mental processes, but this usage is now obsolete.

Methodism, the religious movement founded by John Wesley in 1738, with the aim of spreading "scriptural holiness" throughout the land. Up to that time Wesley had been a High Churchman but on a visit to Georgia in the United States he was much impressed by the group known as Moravians (*q.v.*), and on his return to this country was introduced by his brother Charles, who had already become an adherent, to Peter Böhler, a Moravian minister in England. Passing through a period of spiritual commotion following the meeting, he first saw the light at a small service in Aldersgate in May 1738 "where one was reading Luther's preface to the Epistle to the Romans" and from this time all Wesley's energies were devoted to the single object of saving souls.

Soon Whitefield, a follower with Calvinist views, was preaching throughout the country and Charles Wesley was composing his well-known hymns; John's abilities at this time were taken up in organising the movement described as "People called Methodists." They were to be arranged in "societies" which were united into "circuits" under a minister, the circuits into "districts" and all knit together into a single body under a conference of ministers which has met annually since 1744. Local lay preachers were also employed and to maintain interest the ministers were moved from circuit to circuit each year. These chapel services were not originally meant to conflict with the Church of England of which Wesley still considered himself a member. They were purely supplementary, and it used to be the custom (before the Methodists began to count themselves as Nonconformists) for Methodists to attend Church in the morning and Chapel in the evening.

The class-meeting was the unit of the organisation where members met regularly under a chosen leader to tell their "experiences" upon which they were often subjected to severe cross-examination. At the end of every quarter, provided their attendances were regular, they received a ticket of membership which entitled them to come to monthly sacramental services. If attendance was inadequate the name was removed from the list, without appearance on which nobody was deemed a member. The price of the ticket was "a penny a week and a shilling a quarter" but Wesley was not interested in receiving money from anyone who was not utterly devoted to the cause.

The Work of Wesley. John Wesley introduced four other innovations, some of which were regarded by Churchmen who had previously been willing to commend his efforts in bringing religion to the poorer classes as dangerous: (1) He started the Sunday-school scheme and afterwards enthusiastically supported that of John Raikes, often regarded as the founder of the idea; this was of immense importance in the days before the Education Acts. (2) He reintroduced the Agapae or "love feasts" of the early Church which were fellowship meetings deepening the sense of brotherhood of the society. (3) He began to copy the open-air meetings of the eloquent Whitefield and soon unwittingly produced the most extraordinary results, finding that his sermons led to groans, tears, fainting fits, and all sorts of emotional expression. Even his open-air lay speakers produced like results and these came to be associated with Methodism and gave significance to the proud Anglican claim that *their* services would be "without enthusiasm." (4) After some hesitation he ventured to consecrate Dr. Thomas Coke, who was being sent as a missionary to America, as a bishop of his church. In addition to Wesley's religious work he was a great educator of the common man. Thus he introduced the cheap book and the church magazine, publishing books of any sort which he thought would edify and not harm even when the views expressed were different from his own—*e.g.*, Thomas à Kempis's *Imitation of Christ* and works of history, biography, science, and medicine in some cases written by himself. In this way the movement with its cheap books and reading rooms had an influence far beyond its actual membership. Both the Anglican Church and the Evangelical movement of Wilberforce and others profited from Wesley's work.

Later Schisms. Methodism, especially after Wesley's death in 1791, began, like other movements, to develop schisms. These were the long-standing differences which the Baptist movement (*q.v.*) had shown too between Arminian and Calvinist sections—*i.e.*, between those who did and those who did not accept the doctrine of predestination. In the case of the Methodists, this led to a complete break in 1811. Then there were differences associated with the status of the laity, or the relationship of the movement with the Anglican Church. The "Methodist New Connection" of 1797 differed only in giving the laity equal representation with the ministers but the more important break of the Primitive Methodists in 1810 gave still more power to the laity and reintroduced the "camp-meeting" type of service. In 1815 the Bryanites or "Bible Christians" were formed, and a further schism which was even brought before the law courts was ostensibly over the foundation of a theological college. The real reason, of course, was that the ministers were becoming more Tory, whilst the laity were becoming more Radical. Finally in 1932, at a conference in the Albert Hall in London, the Wesleyan Methodists, the Primitive Methodists, and the United Methodists became one Church, the Methodist Church.

Adult Methodist membership has fallen recently, but it remains the third largest Christian church in England.

During 1998, Methodists began the first formal steps towards talks with Anglicans about reunion (a process which could be completed by 2010). Earlier attempts to unite with the Anglicans in 1969 and 1972 ended in failure. Methodists and Anglicans are now working on a joint 'covenant' to prepare for unity. A recent Methodist report called for the creation of

Methodist bishops. Such a move would help pave the way for union with the Church of England. The Methodist Church has separately agreed to bless gay couples "married" under the civil partnership law.

Millenarianism. The belief in a future "millenium", that is, the thousand year reign of Christ on earth. The idea however has pre-Christian roots and is reflected in Jewish and Islamic thought. It is not part of orthodox Christianity, but many sects in the 19th century, like the Plymouth Brethren and Adventists, espoused millenarianism. The idea has since broadened to mean any theory with an expectation of some transforming change: not only the Kingdom of God, but also the just society, harmony among peoples *etc.*

Mind and Matter.
Early peoples could see that there is a distinction between those things which move and do things by themselves and others, such as stones, which do not. Following the early state of **Animism** (*q.v.*), in which spirits were believed to have their abode in everything, they began to differentiate between matter or substance and a force which seems to move it and shape it into objects and things. Thus to the Greek Parmenides (fl. *c.* 475 B.C.), who was a philosopher of pure reason, thought or mind was the creator of what we observe and in some way not quite clear to himself it seemed that mind was the cause of everything. This is perhaps the first expression of the movement known as Idealism which says, in effect, that the whole universe is mental—a creation either of our own minds or the mind of God. But from Anaxagorus (488–428 B.C.) we have the clearer statement that mind or *nous* causes all movement but is distinct from the substance it moves. He does not, however, think in terms of individual minds but rather of a kind of generalised mind throughout the universe which can be used as an explanation of anything which cannot be explained otherwise. This is the position known as Dualism (*q.v.*) which holds that both mind and matter exist and interact but are separate entities.

Most people in practice are dualists since, rightly or wrongly, mind and body are thought of as two different things: it is the "commonsense" (although not necessarily the true) point of view. Plato in a much more complex way was also a dualist although he held that the world of matter we observe is in some sense not the genuine world. The real world is the world of ideas and the tree we see is not real but simply matter upon which mind or soul has imprinted the idea of a tree. Everything that exists has its corresponding form in the world of ideas and imprints its pattern upon matter. Mind has always existed and, having become entangled with matter, is constantly seeking to free itself and return to God.

Plato's pupil Aristotle had a much more scientific outlook and held that, although it was mind which gave matter its form, mind is not *outside* matter, as Plato had thought, but *inside* it as its formative principle. Therefore there could be no mind without matter and no matter without mind; for even the lowest forms of matter have some degree of mind which increases in quantity and quality as we move up the scale to more complex things.

So far, nobody had explained how two such different substances as matter and mind could influence each other in any way, and this remains, in spite of attempts to be mentioned later, a basic problem in philosophy.

Two later ideas, one of them rather foolish and the other simply refusing to answer the question, are typified by the Stoics and some members of the Sceptic school. The first is that only matter exists and what we call mind is merely matter of a finer texture, a view which as an explanation is unlikely to satisfy anyone; the other, that of some Sceptics, is that we can know nothing except the fleeting images or thoughts that flicker through our consciousness. Of either mind or matter we know nothing.

Renaissance Attitude. Christian doctrines have already been dealt with (*see* **God and Man, Determinism and Free-will**), and the past and future of the soul is dealt with under

Immortality. Nor need we mention the Renaissance philosophers who were really much more concerned about how to use mind than about its nature. When they did consider the subject they usually dealt with it, as did Francis Bacon, by separating the sphere of science from that of religion and giving the orthodox view of the latter because there were still good reasons for not wishing to annoy the Church.

17th-cent. Views: Hobbes, Descartes, Guelincx, Spinoza, Locke, Berkeley. Thomas Hobbes in the 17th cent. was really one of the first to attempt a modern explanation of mind and matter even if his attempt was crude. As a materialist he held that all that exists is matter and hence our thoughts, ideas, images, and actions are really a form of motion taking place within the brain and nerves. This is the materialist theory which states that mind does not exist.

Thus there are three basic theories of the nature of mind and body: idealism, dualism, and materialism, and we may accept any one of the three. But, if we accept dualism, we shall have to explain precisely the relationship between body and mind. In some of his later writings Hobbes seems to suggest that mental processes are the effects of motion rather than motion itself; *i.e.*, they exist, but only as a result of physical processes just as a flame does on a candle. This theory of the relationship is known as *epiphenomenalism.*

Descartes, the great French contemporary of Hobbes, was a dualist who believed that mind and matter both exist and are entirely different entities; therefore he had to ask himself how, for example, the desire to walk leads to the physical motion of walking. His unsatisfactory answer was that, although animals are pure automatons, man is different in that he has a soul which resides in the pineal gland (a tiny structure in the brain which today we know to be a relic of evolution with no present function whatever). In this gland the mind comes in contact with the "vital spirits" of the body and thus there is interaction between the two. This theory is known as *interactionism*, and since we do not accept its basis in the function of the pineal gland, we are simply left with the notion of interaction but without the explanation of how it takes place.

One of Descartes's successors, Arnold Guelincx, produced the even more improbable theory of *psychophysical parallelism* sometimes known as the theory of the "two clocks". Imagine you have two clocks, each keeping perfect time, then supposing you saw one and heard the other, every time one points to the hour the other will strike, giving the impression that the first event causes the second, although in fact they are quite unrelated. So it is with the body and mind in Guelincx's view, each is "wound up" by God in the beginning in such a way as to keep time with the other so that when I have the desire to walk, purely unrelated physical events in my legs cause them to move at the same time. A variety of this theory is *occasionism*, which says that whenever something happens in the physical world, God affects us so that we *think* we are being affected by the happening.

The trouble about all these theories is (a) that they really explain nothing, and (b) that they give us a very peculiar view of God as a celestial showman treating us as puppets when it would surely have been easier to create a world in which mind and matter simply interacted by their very nature. Spinoza, too, believed in a sort of psychophysical parallelism in that he did not think that mind and body interacted. But since in his theory everything is God, mind and matter are simply two sides of the same penny.

John Locke, another contemporary, thought of the mind as a blank slate upon which the world writes in the form of sensations, for we have no innate or inborn ideas and mind and matter do interact although he does not tell us how. All we know are sensations—*i.e.*, sense impressions. Bishop Berkeley carried this idea to its logical conclusion: if we know nothing but sensations, we have no reason to suppose that matter exists at all. He was, therefore, an idealist.

18th cent. Views: Hume, Kant. David Hume went further still and pointed out that, if all we know are sensations, we cannot prove the existence of matter but we cannot prove the existence of mind either. All we can ever know is that ideas, impressions, thoughts, follow each other. We do not even experience a self or personality because every time we look into our "minds" all we really experience are thoughts and impressions. Hume was quick to point out that this was not the same as saying that the self did not exist; it only proved that we cannot know that it does.

Kant made it clear that, although there is a world outside ourselves, we can never know what it is really like. The mind receives impressions and forms them into patterns which conform not to the thing-in-itself but to the nature of mind. Space and time, for example, are not realities but only the form into which our mind fits its sensations. In other words our mind shapes impressions which are no more like the thing in itself than the map of a battlefield with pins showing the position of various army groups at any given moment is like the battlefield. This, of course, is true. From physics and physiology we know that the sounds we hear are "really" waves in the air, the sights we see "really" electromagnetic waves. What guarantee do we have that the source is "really" like the impression received in our brain? Kant was the leader of the great German Idealist movement of the 18th cent. which in effect said: "why bother about matter when all we can ever know is mental?"

19th and 20th cent. Views. The Englishman Bradley, and the Frenchman Henri Bergson in the 19th and early 20th cent. both held in one form or another the belief that mind in some way creates matter and were, therefore, idealists, whereas Comte, the positivist (*q.v.*), and the Americans William James and John Dewey, held that mind is a form of behaviour. Certain acts (*e.g.*, reflexes) are "mindless" because they are deliberate; others which are intended may be described for the sake of convenience as "minded" (*i.e.*, purposeful). But like the majority of modern psychologists—insofar as they take any interest in the subject—they regarded mind as a process going on in the living body. Is there any reason, many now ask, why we should think of mind as being any different in nature from digestion? Both are processes going on in the body, the one in the brain the other in the stomach and intestines. Why should we therefore regard them as "things"?

Mithraism, a sun-religion which originated in Persia with the worship of the mythical Mithra, the god of light and of truth. It was for two centuries one of early Christianity's most formidable rivals, particularly in the West since the more philosophical Hellenic Christianity of the East had little to fear from it. (Arnold Toynbee has described Mithraism as "a pre-Zoroastrian Iranian paganism—in a Hellenic dress"; Manichaeism as "Zoroastrianism—in a Christian dress".) Mithraism was a mystery faith with secret rites known only to devotees. It appealed to the soldiers of the Roman Army which explains its spread to the farthest limits of the Roman empire and its decline as the Romans retreated. The religion resembled Zoroastrianism (*q.v.*) in that it laid stress on the constant struggle between good and evil and there are a number of parallels with Christianity. *e.g.*, a miraculous birth, death, and a glorious resurrection, a belief in heaven and hell and the immortality of the soul, a last judgment. Both religions held Sunday as the holy day of the week, celebrated 25 December (date of the pagan winter solstice festival) as the birthday of the founder; both celebrated Easter, and in their ceremonies made use of bell, holy water, and the candle.

Mithraism was to reach its height about 275 A.D. and afterwards declined both for the reason given above and, perhaps, because it excluded women, was emotional rather than philo-

sophical, and had no general organisation to direct its course. Yet even today traces of the religion remain and antiquarians are familiar with the image of the sun-god and the inscription *Deo Soli Mithrae, Invicto, Seculari* (dedicated to the sun-god of Mithra, the unconquered).

Mithraism enjoyed a brief revival in the 1950s when workers excavating the foundations of the skyscraper, Bucklersbury House in the City of London, found the remains of a Roman Mithraic temple.

A campaign to save the temple as a national monument resulted in its now being on open display on a site in front of the skyscraper.

Modernism. The term has two main connotations:

1. A movement in the Roman Catholic church, *c.* 1890–1910. The 19th century stress on science and the application of scientific methods in fields like history, psychology and philosophy, raised serious problems for traditional Catholic doctrine. The Modernists sought to reinterpret orthodox church teaching in the light of this modern knowledge. The movement was condemned as heresy in 1907.

2. The term is more frequently used to refer to the "modern" movement in all the arts in the period *c.* 1900–30, though defining the period it covers is only one of the problems in describing the movement. It is generally seen as an artistic response to the changes which undermined the securities on which 19th century art and literature were founded. Modernism is marked by a greater ambition for works of art themselves. As well as being novels, or paintings, or music, *etc.*, they were increasingly considered, by artists and critics alike, as representing a theoretical programme, attempts to make the audience see or understand the world in a different way. So modernist characteristics include an increased self-consciousness of the artist, and formal experiment employing a wide variety of technical innovations.

In literature the prime works of modernism are T. S. Eliot's *The Waste Land* and James Joyce's *Ulysses*; the most important painters include Picasso and Matisse; and among composers Schoenberg and Stravinsky stand out.

Mohammedanism. *See* Islam.

Monasticism. When in the 4th cent. A.D. Constantine in effect united state and church there were naturally many who hastened to become Christians for the worldly benefits they expected it to bring in view of the new situation. But there were others who, in their efforts to escape from wordly involvement, went into the deserts of North Africa and Syria to live as hermits.

In these regions there grew up large communities of monks whose lives of renunciation made a considerable impression on the Christian world. They were men of all types but the two main groups were those who preferred to live alone and those who preferred a community life. Among the first must be included St. Anthony, the earliest of the hermits, who was born in Egypt *c.* 250 and who lived alone in a hut near his home for fifteen years and then in the desert for a further twenty. As his fame spread Anthony came forth to teach and advocate a life of extreme austerity, until by the end of his life the Thebaid (the desert around Thebes) was full of hermits following his example. (Not unnaturally, he was constantly assailed by lustful visions which he thoughtfully attributed to Satan.) In the Syrian desert St. Simeon Stylites and others were stimulated to even greater austerities and Simeon himself spent many years on the top of a pillar in a space so small that it was only possible to sit or stand.

The first monastery was founded by Pachomius of Egypt *c.* 315 and here the monks had a common life with communal meals, worship, and work mainly of agricultural type. In the Eastern part of the Empire St. Basil (*c.* 360) tried to check the growth of the extreme and spectacular practices of the hermits by organising monasteries in which the ascetic disciplines of fasting, meditation, and prayer, would be balanced by useful and healthy activities. His monasteries had orphanages and schools for boys—not only those who were intended for a monkish life. But the Eastern Church in general continued to favour the hermit life and ascetic extremes.

The monastic life was introduced to the West

by St. Athanasius in 339 who obtained its recognition from the Church of Rome and St. Augustine introduced it into North Africa beyond Egypt. The movement was promoted also by St. Jerome, St. Martin of Tours, who introduced it into France, and St. Patrick into Ireland. The monastery of Iona was founded by St. Colomba in 566. But it must be remembered that the Celtic Church had a life of its own which owed more to the Egyptian tradition than to Rome. Unlike the more elaborate monasteries of the Continent those of the early Celtic Church were often little more than a cluster of stone bee-hive huts, an oratory, and a stone cross. It had its own religious ceremonies and its own art (notably its beautifully carved crosses and the illuminated manuscripts such as the Lindisfarne Gospel (c. 700) and the Irish Book of Kells dating from about the same time). The Scottish St. Ninian played a major part in introducing Egyptian texts and art to Britain where, mixed with Byzantine influences and the art of the Vikings, it produced a typical culture of its own.

Strangely enough, it was the Celts who played almost as large a part in preserving civilisation in Europe during the Dark Ages as the Italians have since. It was St. Columbanus (c. 540-615) who founded the great monasteries of Annegray, Luxeuil, and Fontaine in the Vosges country, St. Gall in Switzerland, and Bobbio in the Apennines. So, too, it was the Anglo-Saxon Alcuin (c. 735-804) who was called from York by Charlemagne to set up a system of education throughout his empire; the most famous of the monastic schools he founded was at Tours. Among those influenced by him was the philosopher John Scotus Erigena.

Meanwhile from the south, as the disintegrating Roman empire became increasingly corrupt, St. Benedict of Nursia (c. 480-c. 543) fled the pleasures of Rome to lead a hermit's life near Subiaco. Here he founded some small monasteries, but c. 520 made a new settlement, the great monastery of Monte Cassino in southern Italy, where he established a "Rule" for the government of monks. This included both study and work and emphasised that education was necessary for the continuance of Christianity. As his influence spread his Rule was adopted by other monasteries, and schools became part of monastic life. Outside the Roman Catholic Church, both Eastern Orthodox and Anglican Christians owe much to the monastic movement.

Monasticism, of course, is not peculiar to Christianity and forms a major aspect of Buddhism, especially in the form of Lamaism (q.v.) in Tibet.

Monophysitism, a heresy of the 5th cent. which grew out of a reaction against Nestorianism (q.v.). The majority of Egyptian Christians were Monophysites (Mono-physite = one nature)—i.e. they declared Christ's human and divine nature to be one and the same. This view was condemned at the Council of Chalcedon (A.D. 451) which pronounced that Jesus Christ, true God and true man, has two natures, at once perfectly distinct and inseparably joined in one person and partaking of the one divine substance. However, many continued to hold Monophysite opinions, including the Coptic Church (q.v.), declaring the Council to be unoecumenical (i.e. not holding the views of the true and universal Christian Church).

Montanism, a Phrygian form of primitive Puritanism with many peculiar tenets into which the early Christian theologian Tertullian (c. 150-c. 230) was driven by his extremist views that the Christian should keep himself aloof from the world and hold no social intercourse whatever with pagans. The sect had immediate expectation of Christ's second coming and indulged in prophetic utterance which they held to be inspired by the Holy Ghost but which their enemies put down to the work of the Devil.

Moonies. See under Unification Church, J62.

Moral Philosophy. See Ethics, J58.

Moral Re-Armament, a campaign launched in 1938 by an American evangelist of Lutheran background, Frank N. D. Buchman (1878-1961), founder of the Oxford Group Movement, and at first associated with the First Century Church Fellowship, a fundamentalist Protestant revivalist movement. On a visit to England in 1920 Buchman preached "world-changing

through life-changing" to undergraduates at Oxford, hence the name Oxford Group. Two of the Group's most typical practices were group confession of sins openly and the "quiet time" set aside during the day to receive messages from the Almighty as to behaviour and current problems. In the eyes of non-Groupers the confession (often of trivial sins) appeared to be exhibitionist and there was felt to be a certain snobbery about the movement which made it strongly conscious of the social status of its converts.

The Oxford Group gave way to Moral Re-Armament, the third phase of Buchmanism. MRA is open to all. Its starting point is the readiness of each person to make real in their own life the changes they wish to see in society. A commitment to search for God's will in daily life forms the basis for creative initiative and common action. Absolute moral standards of honesty, purity, unselfishness and love help to focus the challenge of personal and global change.

The peak of public interest in MRA was probably reached in the 1950s. The phrase "moral rearmament" was coined by the English scientist W. H. Bragg and appropriated by Buchman.

Moravian Church, a revival of the Church of the "Bohemian Brethren" which originated (1457) among some of the followers of John Hus. It developed a kind of Quakerism that rejected the use of force, refused to take oaths, and had no hierarchy. It appears to have been sympathetic towards Calvinism but made unsuccessful approaches to Luther. As a Protestant sect it was ruthlessly persecuted by Ferdinand II and barely managed to survive. However, in the 18th cent. the body was re-established by Count Zinzendorf who offered it a place of safety in Saxony where a town called Herrnhut (God's protection) was built and this became the centre from which Moravian doctrine was spread by missionaries all over the world. Their chief belief (which had a fundamental influence on John Wesley—see Methodism) was that faith is a direct illumination from God which assures us beyond all possibility of doubt that we are saved, and that no goodness of behaviour, piety, or orthodoxy is of any use without this "sufficient sovereign, saving grace".

Mormons, or Latter-day Saints. Better known as the Mormon religion, their its origins in New York State in the 1820s, the Church of Jesus Christ of Latter Day Saints now has more than 11 million members worldwide. Although there is much dispute over the details, the movement was founded by Joseph Smith who at the age of 14 asked God which denomination of Christianity was the true one. In a vision, he was told that all were wrong and that he should wait a few years. In 1823, he had another vision of the angel Moroni who directed him to dig up golden plates buried in a hillside. Smith began to translate the text in 'reformed Egyptian hieroglyphs' using special eye-glasses, dictating it to his wife from behind a curtain. The first edition of the 'Book of Mormon: Another Testament of Jesus Christ' was published in 1830. It focuses on two migrations of mysterious Jewish tribes to America, one of whom, the Nephites were visited by Christ after his resurrection. The last of the tribe were the prophet Mormon and his son Moroni who were responsible for the creation of the golden tablets.

Although continuous revelation remains an important element of doctrine, it can come only from the Presidents of the Church, who have followed Smith. His own authority and power in the early progress of the movement was questioned, leading to dissension and eventually to Smith's murder in 1844. His successor was Brigham Young, who in 1847 led the breakaway to the Great Salt Lake Valley which is now in Utah. Mormons continued to attract hostile criticism however, largely owing to their belief in polygamy which was later abandoned. Of importance for Mormons is the belief that the new Jerusalem will be built in America. They also have an unorthodox belief in the Trinity which claims that both God the Father and God the Son have bodily forms. A further key belief is in the pre-existence of souls which come from God who lives with his family on a planet near the star Kolob.

Although Mormons worship in churches, many of their most important rites take place in Temples, and are said to have links with Masonic practices. Special clothing is worn and admission reserved for certain members in order to ensure sacredness. This relates to the very complex system of hierarchy and government within the Church. Mormons have very strict views about morality and oppose the use of any stimulants. Members are encouraged to give two years free service to the Church, which is often spent abroad in missionary work.

Muggletonians, one of the many sects which arose during the Commonwealth but, unlike most of the others (**Levellers** (q.v.), **Diggers** (q.v., Fifth Monarchy Men, and the Millenarians) which tended to have a strongly political aspect, this was purely religious. Founded by two journeymen tailors, Lodowick Muggleton and John Reeve, who interpreted the Book of Revelation in their own peculiar way, it was decided that Reeve represented Moses, and Muggleton, Aaron. They also believed that the Father, not the Son, had died on the cross (an ancient heresy) but added the strange statement that He left Elijah in control during His period on earth. Rejecting the doctrine of the Trinity, they also asserted that God has a human body.

Multiculturalism. Liberal democracy concentrates on the rights, obligations, and welfare of individuals. Critics argue that this focus on individuals ignores the special needs and identities of groups. Multiculturalism is the view that the state should acknowledge the importance of identity conferring groups, and create a legal and political order in which the multiplicity of groups in any society are allowed to practice their own distinct cultures within the boundaries of mutual respect. Such groups may be based on ethnicity, gender, sexuality, language, or religion.

Multiculturalists may also support special exemptions or privileges for groups, on the grounds that their identity and interests would otherwise be threatened. Examples include recent debates about the wearing of religious clothing in state schools and positive discrimination in the workplace. Opponents of multiculturalism argue that this destroys the shared unity and values of society. Liberals also regard multiculturalism as a nefarious obstruction on the rights of individuals to choose their own identity, and not have it prescribed by others.

Mystery Religions. See **Orphism.**

Mysticism, a religious attitude which concerns itself with direct relationship with God, "reality" as contrasted with appearance or the "ultimate" in one form or another. All the higher religions have had their mystics who have not always been regarded without suspicion by their more orthodox members, and, as Bertrand Russell points out, there has been a remarkable unity of opinion among mystics which almost transcends their religious differences. Thus, characteristic of the mystical experience in general, have been the following features; (1) a belief in insight as opposed to analytical knowledge which is accompanied in the actual experience by the sense of a mystery unveiled, a hidden wisdom become certain beyond the possibility of doubt; this is often preceded by a period of utter hopelessness and isolation described as "the dark night of the soul"; (2) a belief in unity and a refusal to admit opposition or division anywhere; this sometimes appears in the form of what seem to be contradictory statements: "the way up and the way down is one and the same" (Heraclitus). There is no distinction between subject and object, the act of perception and the thing perceived; (3) a denial of the reality of time, since if all is one the distinction of past and future must be illusory; (4) a denial of the reality of evil (which does not maintain, e.g., that cruelty is good but that it does not exist in the world of reality as opposed to the world of phantoms from which we are liberated by the insight of the vision).

Among the many great mystics have been Meister Eckhart and Jakob Boehme, the German religious mystics of the 13th and 16th cent. respectively, Acharya Sankara of India, and St. Theresa and St. John of the Cross of Spain. Mystical movements within the great religions have been: the Zen (q.v.) movement within Buddhism;

Taoism in China; the Cabalists and Hasidim in Judaism; and the Sufis within Islam.

N

Nation of Islam. See **J62.**

Nationalism. Devotion to one's nation and its interests. Politically, this is translated into the theory that each nationality should be organised in a sovereign state. Nationalism first developed in Western Europe with the consolidation of nation states, and brought about the reorganization of Europe in the 19th and 20th centuries, e.g. the unification of Italy, the rise of Germany. At first, nationalism was liberal and democratic in tone, but it has also been associated with national expansion at the expense of other nations, and was an essential element of Fascism. In the 20th century it was important in the political awakening of Asia and Africa against colonialism. In Europe, the collapse of Communist regimes led to a resurgence of nationalism (e.g. Serbia).

Natural Law, the philosophical doctrine which states that there is a natural moral law, irrespective of time and place, which man can know through his own reason. Originally a product of early rational philosophy, the Christian form of the doctrine is basically due to St. Thomas Aquinas who defined natural law in relation to eternal law, holding that the eternal law is God's reason which governs the relations of all things in the universe to each other. The natural law is that part of the eternal law which relates to man's behaviour. Catholic natural law assumes that the human reason is capable of deriving ultimate rules for right behaviour, since there are in man and his institutions certain foundations produced by God's reason which man's reason can know to be correct and true. Thus, the basis of marriage, property, the state, and the contents of justice are held to be available to man's natural reason. The rules of positive morality and civil law are held to be valid only insofar as they conform to the natural law, which man is not only capable of knowing but also of obeying.

Protestant theologians criticise this notion. Thus Karl Barth and many others hold that sinful and fallen man cannot have any direct knowledge of God or His reason or will without the aid of revelation. Another theologian Niebuhr points out that the principles of the doctrines are too inflexible and that although they are the product of a particular time and circumstance, they are regarded as if they were absolute and eternal. In fact, as most social scientists would also agree, there is no law which can be regarded as "natural" for all men at all times. Nor does it seem sensible to suppose that all or even many men possess either the reason to discern natural law or the ability to obey it; whether or not we accept man's free-will (and not all Protestant sects do), we know as a fact of science that people are not always fully responsible for their actions and some not at all.

Such basic human rights as freedom of speech and religion, and freedom from fear and want, derive from natural law as later developed by John Locke.

Naturalism. 1. In general, the view that what is studied by the human sciences is all that there is, and that there is no need to go beyond or outside the universe for any explanation.

2. In ethics, the view that value terms can be defined in terms of neutral statements of fact, or derived from such statements.

Nazism, the term commonly used for the political and social ideology of the German National Socialist Party inspired and led by Hitler. The term *Nazi* was an abbreviation of *National-sozialistische Deutsche Arbeiterpartei*. See **A45.**

Neocolonialism. See **Colonialism.**

Neoconservatism. Whilst sharing such traditional conservative values as patriotic pride, opposition to bureaucratic welfare states, and belief in free trade, neoconservatives differ from traditional conservatives in their views on foreign policy. Particularly strong in American politics, neoconservatives argue that liberal democracy is inherently vulnerable to threats from extreme political ideologies which seek global domination. In order to protect liberal democracy, such states must pursue a policy of military empowerment and intervention against perceived threats. Consequently, neoconservatism's defining feature is the view that liberal democracy must be promoted and protected aggressively in foreign policy. Traditional conservatism, at least in America, tended towards an isolationist foreign policy. Neoconservatives feared such isolationism would lead to appeasement of totalitarianism and increased vulnerability from militarily strong expansionist ideologies, such as Soviet Communism.

Neoconservatives argue that there is a moral obligation on liberal democracies to spread their freedoms around the globe, and that such promotion is the best way to secure the national interest of liberal democratic states.

Neo-Fascism. See **Fascism, J19.**

Neoliberalism. Traditionally, liberalism has prioritised the freedom of the individual and argued that private property is the greatest bulwark against curtailment of an individual's freedom by others. In the late 20th century, neoliberalism developed in response to a perceived assault on individual freedoms that resulted from the pursuit of social justice by social democratic states.

Neoliberals regarded progressive taxation, redistributive fiscal policies, extensive welfare provision, and state ownership of industry as illegitimate and inefficient uses of state power. They criticised particularly the moral and economic dependency encouraged by extensive welfare provision, and argued that welfare discouraged individuals from work and from taking responsibility for the security and prosperity of themselves and their families. Neoliberals such as Thatcher and Reagan argued that the role of the state should be restricted to protecting the freedoms and private property of individuals. Consequently, neoliberals privatised state owned industries and utilities, reduced taxation and public spending, and withdrew welfare support and other redistributive policies. Neoliberalism has come to dominate western electoral politics, and is now promoted in developing nations by such bodies as the IMF, WTO, and World Bank.

Neoplatonism. Movement begun by Plotinus' interpretation of Plato and carried forward by various philosophers of the next three centuries and which had some influence in the Renaissance, Plotinus (205–270) saw reality as hierarchically ordered in a graded series from the divine to the material; man, who contains some part of the divine, longs for union with the highest level. Subsequent Neoplatonists include Porphyry, Iamblichus and Philoponus. (See also **Determinism** and **Free-will** and **God and Man**)

Nestorian Heresy. The 5th cent. of the Christian Church saw a battle of personalities and opinions waged with fanatical fury between St. Cyril, the patriarch of Alexandria, and Nestorius, patriarch of Constantinople. Nestorius maintained that Mary should not be called the mother of God, as she was only the mother of the human and not of the divine nature of Jesus. This view was contradicted by Cyril (one of the most unpleasant saints who ever lived) who held the orthodox view. In addition to his utter destruction of Nestorius by stealthy and unremitting animosity Cyril was also responsible for the lynching of Hypatia, a distinguished mathematician and saintly woman, head of the Neoplatonist school at Alexandria.

As if this were not enough Cyril took pains to stir up pogroms against the very large Jewish colony of Alexandria. At the Council of Ephesus (A.D. 431) the Western Bishops quickly decided for Cyril. This Council (reinforced by the Council of Chalcedon in 451) clarified orthodox Catholic doctrine (see **Monophysitism**).

Nestorius became a heretic, was banished to Antioch where he had a short respite of peace, but later, and in spite of his age, was dragged about from one place to another on the borders of Egypt. Later the Nestorian church flourished in Syria and Persia and missions were sent to India and China.

New Age, a quasi-religious movement, based on a millennarian mysticism, astrology and ecology.

New Labour. See **Third Way.**

New Religious Movements. See **J59–62.**

Nihilism, the name commonly given to the earliest Russian form of revolutionary anarchism. It originated in the early years of Tsar Alexander

II (1818–81), the liberator of the serfs, who, during his attempts to bring about a constitutional monarchy, was killed by a bomb. The term "nihilist", however, was first used in 1862 by Turgenev in his novel *Fathers and Children.* See **Anarchism.**

Nominalism. Early mediaeval thinkers were divided into two schools, those who regarded "universals" or abstract concepts as mere names without any corresponding realities (Nominalists), and those who held the opposite doctrine (**Realism**) that general concepts have an existence independent of individual things. The relation between universals and particulars was long a subject of philosophical dispute.

The first person to hold the nominalist doctrine was probably Roscelin or Roscellinus in the late 11th cent., but very little is known of him and none of his works remains except for a single letter to Peter Abelard who was his pupil. Roscelin was born in France, accused twice of heresy but recanted and fled to England where he attacked the views of Anselm, according to whom Roscelin used the phrase that universals were a *flatus voci* or breath of the voice.

The most important nominalist was the Englishman William of Ockham in the 14th cent. who, once and for all, separated the two schools by saying in effect that science is about things (the nominalist view) whereas logic, philosophy, and religion are about terms or concepts (the Platonic tradition).

Nonconformism, the attitude of all those Christian bodies, which do not conform to the doctrines of the Church of England. Up to the passing of the Act of Uniformity in 1662 they were called "puritans" or "dissenters" and were often persecuted. The oldest bodies of nonconformists are the Baptists, Independents, and (in England) the Presbyterians; the Methodists, although dating from 1738, did not consider themselves nonconformists until some time later. The Presbyterians are, of course, the official Church of Scotland where it is the Anglicans (known as "Episcopalians") who are technically the nonconformists.

O

Objectivism, a philosophy developed by American novelist, Ayn Rand. The briefest summary of Objectivism given by Miss Rand was simply, *"Follow reason"*, but that is rather too terse. Objectivism begins with reality as objective, absolute and independent of any mind perceiving it. Consciousness is the faculty of perceiving that which exists, and therefore, existence precedes consciousness. Human conceptual, volitional consciousness (reason) is man's unique means of survival. Ayn Rand upheld reason as the only means to knowledge with logic as its method. Man should live solely by the guidance of his reason.

Ockham's Razor, the philosophical maxim by which William of Ockham, the 14th cent. Franciscan has become best-known. This states in the form which is most familiar: "Entities are not to be multiplied without necessity" and as such does not appear in his works. He did, however, say something much to the same effect: "It is vain to do with more what can be done with fewer." In other words, if everything in some science can be interpreted without assuming this or that hypothetical entity, there is no ground for assuming it.

Optimism. Originally the doctrine propounded by Leibniz (1646–1716) that the actual world is the "best of all possible worlds", being chosen by the Creator out of all the possible worlds which were present in his thoughts as that in which the most good could be obtained at the cost of the least evil. This view was memorably mocked by Voltaire in *Candide.*

Opus Dei. See **J62.**

Orangemen, members of a society formed in Ulster back in 1795 to uphold Protestantism. Their name is taken from King William III, Prince of Orange, who defeated James II at the Battle of the Boyne (1690), hence the numerous banners depicting "King Billy on the Boyne" carried in procession on 12 July each year. The Unionist Party of Northern Ireland (the ruling political party from 1921 to 1972) is largely maintained by the Orange Order. The Order also has branches in many English-speaking countries.

Original Sin, in Christian doctrine, the corruption that is born with us, as a result of Adam's fall.

Orphism. The Greeks in general thought very little of their gods, regarding them as similar human beings with human failings and virtues although on a larger scale. But there was another aspect of Greek religion which was passsionate, ecstatic, and secret, dealing with the worship of various figures among whom were Bacchus or Dionysus, Orpheus, and Demeter and Persephone of the Eleusinian Mysteries. Dionysus (or Bacchus) was originally a god from Thrace where the people were primitive farmers naturally interested in fertility cults. Dionysus was the god of fertility who only later came to be associated with wine and the divine madness it produces. He assumed the form of a man or a bull and his worship by the time it arrived in Greece became associated with women (as was the case in most of the Mystery Religions) who spent nights on the hills dancing and drinking in order to stimulate ecstasy; an unpleasant aspect of the cult was the tearing to pieces of wild animals whose flesh was eaten raw. Although the cult was disapproved of by the orthodox, it existed for a long time.

This primitive and savage religion in time was modified by that attributed to Orpheus whose cult was more spiritualised, ascetic, and substituted mental for physical intoxication. Orpheus may have been a real person or a legendary hero and he, too, is supposed to have come from Thrace, but his name indicates that he, or the movement associated with him, came from Crete and originally from Egypt, which seems to have been the source of many of its doctrines. Crete, it must be remembered, was the island through which Egypt influenced Greece in other respects. Orpheus is said to have been a reformer who was torn to pieces by the Maenad worshippers of Dionysus. The Orphics believed in the transmigration of souls and that the soul after death might obtain either eternal bliss or temporary or permanent torment according to its way of life upon earth. They held ceremonies of purification and the more orthodox abstained from animal food except on special occasions when it was eaten ritually. Man is partly earthly, partly heavenly, and a good life increases the heavenly part so that he may become one with Bacchus and be called a "Bacchus".

The religion had an elaborate theology. As the Bacchic rites were reformed by Orpheus, so the Orphic rites were reformed by Pythagoras (c. 582–c. 507 B.C.) who introduced the mystical element into Greek philosophy, which reached its heights in Plato. Other elements entered Greek life from Orphism. One of these was feminism which was notably lacking in Greek civilisation outside the Mystery Religions. The other was the drama which arose from the rites of Dionysus. The mysteries of Eleusis formed the most sacred part of the Athenian state religion, and it is clear that they had to do with fertility rites also, for they were in honour of Demeter and Persephone and all the myths speak of them as being associated with the supply of corn to the country.

Christianity, just as it accepted elements of Gnosticism and Mithraism, also accepted elements from the Mystery Religions as they in turn must have done from earlier cults. The miraculous birth, the death and resurrection the sacramental feast of bread and wine, symbolising the eating of the flesh and drinking of the blood of the god, all these are common elements in early religions and not just in one. None of this means that what we are told about Jesus is not true, but it surely does mean: (a) that Christianity was not a sudden development; (b) that the early Church absorbed many of the elements of other religions; (c) that perhaps Jesus Himself made use of certain symbols which He knew had a timeless significance for man and invested them with new meaning.

Orthodox Eastern Church. There are two groups of Eastern churches: (1) those forming the Orthodox Church dealt with here which include the ancient Byzantine patriarchates of Constantinople, Alexandria, Antioch, and Jerusalem, and the national churches of Russia, Greece, Serbia, Bulgaria, Romania, etc. (although Orthodox communities exist all over the world and are no longer confined to geographical areas); (2) the churches which rejected Byzantine orthodoxy during various controversies from the 5th to the 7th cent., notably the Coptic church (q.v.) and the Armenian church. Although all Orthodox churches share the same doctrine and traditions they are arranged as national independent bodies each with its own hierarchy. They do not recognise the pope, and the primacy of the patriarch of Constantinople is largely an honorary one. Although claiming to be the One Holy, Catholic, and Apostolic Church its alleged infallibility rests on universal agreement rather than on any one individual, and agreement over the faith comes from the Scriptures interpreted in the light of the Tradition.

The latter includes dogmas relating to the Trinity, Christology, Mariology, and Holy Icons; the testimony of the Fathers (St. Athanasius, St. Basil, St. John Chrysostom, St. Cyril of Alexandria, etc.); the canons or rules as formulated by the Councils and the Fathers.

The Orthodox Church did not take part in the great Western controversies about the Bible, nor, of course, in the Reformation. Attempts have been made to improve relations between Rome and Constantinople: the two Churches agreed in 1935 to retract the excommunications cast on each other in A.D. 1054, which formalised the Great Schism. After the fall of communism in Russia, the Orthodox Church flourished in the 1990s. In England, the first purpose-built Orthodox Cathedral has been constructed in west London. In 1999 Pope John Paul II visited Romania, the first papal visit to a mainly Orthodox country in almost 1,000 years.

Oxford Group. See **Moral Re-Armament.**

Oxford Movement. See **Tractarianism.**

P

Pacifism. The belief that, because violence and the taking of life is morally wrong, war and the employment of organized armed forces cannot be justified. The word first came into use to describe movements advocating the settlement of disputes by peaceful means. Since the First World War the word has been used to describe the refusal of individuals to undertake military service. The first pacificists were minority Christian groups like the Quakers and Plymouth Brethren. In the present century the movement has broadened and many democratic nations allow their citizens to abstain from fighting on grounds of principle, often described as "conscientious objection".

Paganism, a form of worship which has its roots in the ancient nature religions of Europe. Pagans reverence the sanctity of the Earth, its people and other life forms. Paganism is still a living religion, the main forms of which include Wicca (witchcraft), Druidry, Asatru and Shamanism.

The Pagan Federation was founded in 1971 to provide information and to counter misconceptions about Paganism. There are over 100,000 practising pagans in Britain (mainly Druids).

Pan-Africanism, the perception by people of African origins and descent that they have interests in common. The fight against economic exploitation and for equality has been an important unifying theme.

Pantheism. See **God and Man.**

Panpsychism. Literally, "all-soul-ism", the view that everything that really exists in the world is a mind or consciousness. To be distinguished from "hylozoism", which claims that everything is alive. Panpsychic views can be found in Leibniz and Schopenhauer, and in the 20th century philosopher A. N. Whitehead (1861–1947).

Papal Infallibility. The basis of papal infallibility is (a) that every question of morals and faith is not dealt with in the Bible so it is necessary that there should be a sure court of appeal in case of doubt, and this was provided by Christ when he established the Church as His Teaching Authority upon earth; (b) ultimately this idea of the teaching function of the Church shapes the idea of papal infallibility which asserts that the Pope, when speaking officially on matters of faith or morals, is protected by God against the possibility of error. The doctrine was proclaimed in July 1870.

Infallibility is a strictly limited gift which does not mean that the Pope has extraordinary intelligence, that God helps him to find the answer to every conceivable question, or that Catholics have to accept the Pope's views on politics. He can make mistakes or fall into sin, his scientific or historical opinions may be quite wrong, he may write books that are full of errors. Only in two limited spheres is he infallible and in these only when he speaks officially as the supreme teacher and lawgiver of the Church, defining a doctrine that must be accepted by all its members. When, after studying a problem of faith as carefully as possible, he emerges with the Church's answer—on these occasions it is not strictly an answer, it is *the* answer.

Historically speaking, the Roman Catholic Church of the early 19th cent. was at its lowest ebb of power. Pope Pius IX, in fear of Italian nationalism, revealed his reactionary attitude by the feverish declaration of new dogmas, the canonisation of new saints, the denunciation of all modern ideals in the Syllabus of Errors, and the unqualified defence of his temporal power against the threat of Garibaldi. It is not too much to say that everything regarded as important by freedom-loving and democratic people was opposed by the papacy at that time. In 1870, after a long and protracted struggle, the Vatican Council, convened by Pius IX, pronounced the definition of his infallibility. Döllinger, a German priest and famous historian of the Church, was excommunicated because, like many others, he refused to accept the new dogma. There was clearly a connection between the pronouncement of the Pope's infallibility and his simultaneous loss of temporal power.

After the humanism of the Second Vatican Council (1962–5) Pope Paul's encyclical *Humanae Vitae* (1968), condemning birth control, came as a great disappointment to the many people (including theologians, priests, and laymen) who had expected there would be a change in the Church's teaching. The Church's moral guidance on this controversial issue, however, does not involve the doctrine of infallibility. (The Roman Catholic Church teaches that papal pronouncements are infallible only when they are specifically defined as such.) There is similarly to be any immediate softening of the Church's line on infallibility.

This was made clear in July 1973 when the Vatican Sacred Congregation for the Doctrine of the Faith published a document strongly reaffirming papal infallibility. The document also reminded Catholics of their obligation to accept the Catholic Church's unique claims to authenticity.

Parapsychology, the name given to the study of psychical research (*q.v.*) as an academic discipline, and chosen to denote the topic's supposed status as a branch of psychology. The impetus behind parapsychology came from the psychologist William MacDougall who persuaded Duke University in North Carolina, USA, to found a department of parapsychology under J. B. Rhine. Throughout the 1930s and 40s the work of Rhine and his colleagues, who claimed to have produced scientific evidence for the existence of ESP, attracted world-wide attention. Increasing reservations about the interpretation of Rhine's results and an apparent lack of any readily repeatable experiments gradually eroded scientific confidence in the topic.

Parsees. *See* Zoroastrianism.

Pavlovian Theory. *See* Behaviourism.

Pelagianism. The Christian doctrine that each person has responsibility for ensuring his own salvation, apart from the assistance of divine grace. Its name is derived from Pelagius, a British lay monk who came to Rome about 400 A.D. and attacked Augustine's view that moral goodness is only possible through divine grace. Pelagius argued that if men and women were not held to be responsible for their actions, there would be nothing to restrain them from sin. His emphasis on free will and the essential goodness of human nature suggested an optimism that was at odds with doctrines of original sin. Augustine attacked

Pelagius' views as heretical, a judgement that was confirmed by the church in 417, when Pelagius was excommunicated.

Pentecostalism, a religious movement within the Protestant churches, holding the belief that an essential feature of true Christianity is a vigorous and profound spiritual or mystical experience which occurs after, and seemingly reinforces the initial conversion.

The origins of modern Pentecostalism lie in the occasion on 1 January 1901 when a member of a Bible College in Topeka, Kansas, one Agnes N. Ozman, spontaneously began to speak in an apparently unknown language at one of the College's religious meetings. This "speaking in tongues" was assumed to be evidence of her conversion and "spirit baptism", and became a feature of most Pentecostal meetings in due course.

The movement spread very rapidly across America, particularly in rural communities, and also was a strong feature of Welsh religious life in the early part of the century. Pentecostal services are enthusiastic and rousing with a strong emphasis on music and participation on the part of the congregation. Pentecostalism is evangelistic in nature and is gaining in strength at the present time. Two of the leading Pentecostal groups in Britain are the Assemblies of God and the Elim Pentecostal Church. There are also a growing number of Black Pentecostal churches. *See* **Weeks, Feast of (H26)**.

People's Temple. *See* **J62**.

Peronism, a political movement begun in the late 1940s in Argentina. It followed the teaching of Juan Perón and his wife Eva.

Personality Cult. Political phenomenon whereby a leader, usually the head of state, is elevated above his colleagues to a position where he is seen as responsible for all the nation's or party's achievements but none of its failures. Such elevation is achieved by a massive propaganda exercise including posters and statues of the leader, the naming of towns after him, *etc.* Joseph Stalin (1879–1953) set the pattern as Soviet leader but others have followed, for example Adolf Hitler of Germany, Mao Tse-Tung in China and Kim Il-sung in North Korea. Such cults appear to flourish only in totalitarian régimes.

Pessimism. Philosophically this refers to the doctrine associated with Arthur Schopenhauer (1788–1860), that in this world everything tends to evil, that the amount of pain is greater than the amount of pleasure. Of course, pessimistic ideas have a long history. As the Greeks said: "Call no man happy until he is dead." They are also present in the teachings of eastern and western religions, which emphasize the corruptness of this world and the possibility of happiness only in a hereafter. Schopenhauer's pessimism had a strong influence on Nietzsche, and through him on existentialism (*q.v.*).

Peyotism. A religious movement among North American Indians centred around the *peyote*, a part of the cactus which produces hallucinogenic effects.

Phrenology, a psychological "school" founded in 1800 by two Germans, Franz Josef Gall and Johann Gaspar Spurzheim. Gall was an anatomist who believed there to be some correspondence between mental faculties and shape of the head. He tested these ideas in prisons and mental hospitals and began to lecture on his findings, arousing a great deal of interest throughout both Europe and America, where his doctrines were widely accepted.

Phrenology became fashionable, and people would go to "have their bumps read" as later men and women of fashion have gone to be psychoanalysed. Roughly speaking, Gall divided the mind into thirty-seven faculties such as destructiveness, suavity, self-esteem, conscientiousness, and so on, and claimed that each of these was located in a definite area of the brain. He further claimed that the areas in the brain corresponded to "bumps" on the skull which could be read by the expert, thus giving a complete account of the character of the subject. In fact, (*a*) no such faculties are located in the brain anywhere, for this is simply not the way the brain works; (*b*) the faculties described by Gall are not pure traits which cannot be further analysed and are based on a long outdated psychology; (c) the shape of the brain bears no specific relationship to the shape of the skull. Phrenology is a pseudo-science; there is no truth in it whatever. But, even so, like astrology, it still has its practitioners.

Physiocrats. A French school of economic thought during the 18th cent., known at the time as *Les Economistes* but in later years named physiocrats by Du Pont de Nemours, a member of the School. Other members were Quesnay, Mirabeau, and the great financier Turgot. The physiocrats held the view, common to the 18th cent., and deriving ultimately from Rousseau, of the goodness and bounty of nature and the goodness of man "as he came from the bosom of nature". The aim of governments, therefore, should be to conform to nature; and so long as men do not interfere with each other's liberty and do not combine among themselves, government ments should leave them free to find their own salvation. Criminals, madmen, and monopolists should be eliminated. Otherwise the duty of government is *laissez-faire, laissez passer.*

From this follows the doctrine of free trade between nations on grounds of both justice and economy; for the greater the competition the more will each one strive to economise the cost of his labour to the general advantage. Adam Smith, although not sharing their confidence in human nature, learned much from the physiocrats, eliminated their errors, and greatly developed their teaching.

Physiognomy. See **Characterology.**

Pietism, a movement in the Lutheran Church at the end of the 17th cent.—the reaction, after the sufferings of the thirty years' war, of a pious and humiliated people against learning, pomp and ceremony, and stressing the importance of man's personal relationship with God. The writings of Johann Georg Hamann (1730–88) who came from a Pietist family of Königsberg influenced Kierkegaard. The Pietist movement was one root of the great Romantic movement of the 18th cent.

Platonism. Philosophical ideas that are inspired by the writings of Plato, usually embracing his belief in a realm of unchanging and eternal realities (specifically, abstract entities or universals) independent of the world perceived by the senses. Most working mathematicians are Platonists, in the sense that they believe that mathematical objects like numbers exist independently of our thought and hence that mathematical statements are true or false independently of our knowledge of them.

Pluralism. (1). In philosophy, any metaphysical view that the world must consist of more than one or two basic kinds of entity; these latter views would be called Monism or Dualism. Pluralists, such as William James, think of themselves as empiricists, reaffirming plain facts of experience against metaphysical extremists and pointing to the irreducible variety of things.

(2). In political thought, it refers to the autonomy enjoyed by disparate groups or institutions within a society and also to the belief that such an arrangement for the distribution of political power should exist. As such it provides an alternative to collectivist doctrines, which may coerce the individual, and individualistic doctrines, which fail to provide an understanding of the individual's role in society. Pluralism is widely regarded as an ideal, but there is much argument as to how pluralism is to be interpreted in detail and how it is to be applied effectively within a modern society.

Plymouth Brethren, a religious sect founded by John Nelson Darby, a minister of the Protestant Church of Ireland, and Edward Cronin a former Roman Catholic, in 1827. Both were dissatisfied with the lack of spirituality in their own and other churches and joined together in small meetings in Dublin every Sunday for "the breaking of bread". Soon the movement began to spread through Darby's travels and writings and he finally settled in Plymouth, giving the popular name to the "Brethren". Beginning as a movement open to all who felt the need to "keep the unity of the Spirit", it soon exercised the right to exclude all who had unorthodox views and split up into smaller groups. Among these the main ones were the "Exclusives", the Kellyites, the Newtonites,

and "Bethesda" whose main differences were over problems of church government or prophetical powers. Some of these are further split among themselves.

Today, the majority of Brethren belong to the "Open Brethren" assemblies and, unlike the "Exclusives" hold that the Lord's Supper (a commemorative act of "breaking the bread" observed once a week) is for all Christians who care to join them. Baptism is required and Brethren believe in the personal premillennial second coming of Christ.

Poltergeist, allegedly a noisy type of spirit which specialises in throwing things about, making loud thumpings and bangings, and occasionally bringing in "apports", i.e., objects from elsewhere. Most so-called poltergeist activities are plain frauds, but the others are almost invariably associated with the presence in the house of someone (often, but not always a child) who is suffering from an adolescent malaise or an epileptic condition. The inference is that those activities which are not simply fraudulent are either due to some unknown influence exuded by such mentally disturbed people, or that they are actually carried out by ordinary physical means by such people when in an hysterical state—i.e., unconsciously. The second hypothesis is much the more probable. See **Psychic Research.**

Polytheism. See **God and Man.**

Populism. A form of politics which emphasizes the virtues of the common people against politicians and intellectuals, who are distrusted as devious and selfish. "The will of the people" can provide sufficient guidance to the statesman. It is not restricted to any one political view and can manifest itself in left, right or centrist forms.

Positivism, also known as the **Religion of Humanity,** was founded by Auguste Comte (1798–1857), a famous mathematician and philosopher born in Montpellier, France. His views up to the end of the century attracted many and it would have been impossible throughout that time to read a book on philosophy or sociology that did not mention them, but today his significance is purely of historical interest. In his *Cours de Philosophie Positive* (1830) he put forward the thesis that mankind had seen three great stages in human thought: (1) the theological, during which man seeks for supernatural causes to explain nature and invents gods and devils; (2) the metaphysical, through which he thinks in terms of philosophical and metaphysical abstractions; (3) the last positive or scientific stage when he will proceed by experimental and objective observation to reach in time "positive truth".

Broadly speaking, there is little to complain of in this analysis; for there does seem to have been some sort of general direction along these lines. However, Comte was not satisfied with having reached this point and felt that his system demanded a religion and, of course, one that was "scientific". This religion was to be the worship of Humanity in place of the personal Deity of earlier times, and for it he supplied not only a Positive Catechism but a treatise on Sociology in which he declared himself the High Priest of the cult. Since, as it stood, the religion was likely to appear somewhat abstract to many, Comte drew up a list of historical characters whom he regarded as worthy of the same sort of adoration as Catholics accord to their saints. The new Church attracted few members, even among those who had a high regard for Comte's scientific work, and its only significant adherents were a small group of Oxford scholars and some in his own country. Frederic Harrison was the best-known English adherent and throughout his life continued to preach Comtist doctrines in London to diminishing audiences.

Postmodernism. Given that "modernism" (q.v.) is a term difficult to define, "postmodernism" is an even more elusive concept, though a very fashionable one for describing contemporary art. The modernist tradition of formal and stylistic experiment, added to our increased knowledge of the history of Western and non-Western arts, has provided a vast range of styles, techniques and technologies for the artist to choose from. This extension of choice has simultaneously created uncertainty about their use. If no one or few styles have any authority, then the artist picks and chooses with little commitment, and so tends towards pastiche, parody, quotation, self-reference and eclecticism. The post-modern style is to have no settled style. But it is always dangerous to try and pin down an artistic movement that is still taking place.

Pragmatism, a typically American school of philosophy which comes under the heading of what Bertrand Russell described as a "practical" as opposed to a "theoretical" philosophy. Whereas the latter, to which most of the great philosophical systems belong, seeks disinterested knowledge for its own sake, the former (*a*) regards action as the supreme good, (*b*) considers happiness an effect and knowledge a mere instrument of successful activity.

The originator of pragmatism is usually considered to have been the psychologist William James (1842–1910) although he himself attributed its basic principles to his life-long friend, the American philosopher, Charles Sanders Peirce (1839–1914). The other famous pragmatist is John Dewey, best-known in Europe for his works on education (for although American text-books on philosophy express opinions to the contrary, few educated people in Europe have taken the slightest interest in pragmatism and generally regard it as an eccentricity peculiar to Americans). James in his book *The Will to Believe* (1896) points out that we are often compelled to take a decision where no adequate theoretical grounds for a decision exist; for even to do nothing is to decide. Thus in religion we have a right to adopt a believing attitude although not intellectually fully convinced. We should believe truth and shun error, but the failing of the sceptical philosopher is that he adheres only to the latter rule and thus fails to believe various truths which a less cautious man will accept. If believing truth and avoiding error are equally important, then it is a good idea when we are presented with an alternative to believe one of the possibilities at will, since we then have an even chance of being right, whereas we have none if we suspend judgment. The function of philosophy, according to James, is to find out what difference it makes to the individual if a particular philosophy or world-system is true: "An idea is "true" so long as to believe it is profitable to our lives" and, he adds, the truth is only the expedient in our way of thinking . . . in the long run and on the whole of course". Thus "if the hypothesis of God works satisfactorily in the widest sense of the word, it is true". Bertrand Russell's reply to this assertion is: "I have always found that the hypothesis of Santa Claus "works satisfactorily in the widest sense of the word'; therefore "Santa Claus exists' is true, although Santa Claus does not exist." Russell adds that James's concept of truth simply omits as unimportant the question whether God really *is* in His heaven; if He is a useful hypothesis that is enough. "God the Architect of the Cosmos is forgotten; all that is remembered is belief in God, and its effects upon the creatures inhabiting our petty planet. No wonder the Pope condemned the pragmatic defence of religion."

Predestination. *See* **Calvinism.**

Presbyterianism, a system of ecclesiastical government of the Protestant churches which look back to John Calvin as their Reformation leader. The ministry consists of presbyters who are all of equal rank. Its doctrinal standards are contained in the *Westminster Confession of Faith* (1647) which is, in general, accepted by English, Scottish, and American Presbyterians as the most thorough and logical statement in existence of the Calvinist creed. The Church of Scotland is the leading Presbyterian church in the British Isles.

The Reformation in Scotland was preceded by the same sort of awareness of the moral corruption of the Roman Church as had happened elsewhere, but for a variety of political and emotional reasons the majority of the Scottish people (unlike the English who had been satisfied with the mere exchange of Crown for Pope) were determined on a fundamental change of doctrine, discipline, and worship, rather than a reform of manners.

The Scottish preachers had learned their Protestantism not from Luther but from Calvin and their leader John Knox had worked in Geneva with Calvin himself and was resolved to introduce the system into Scotland. In 1557 the "Lords of the Congregation" signed the Common Band (*i.e.*, a bond or covenant) to maintain "the blessed Word of God and his congregation" against their enemies, and demanded the right to worship as they had chosen. However, the real date of the Scottish Reformation is August 1560 when Mary of Guise (the regent for Mary Queen of Scots who was not yet of age) died and the Estates met to settle their affairs without foreign pressure; the *Scots Confession* was drawn up and signed by Knox and adopted by the Estates.

The ideas on which the Reformed Kirk was based are found in the *Scots Confession*, the *Book of Discipline*, and the *Book of Common Order*, the so-called Knox's liturgy. Knox's liturgy, the same as that used in Geneva but translated into English, was used until Laud's attempt to force an Anglican liturgy on the Kirk led to an abandonment of both in favour of "free prayers."

The Presbyterian tradition includes uncompromising stress upon the Word of God contained in the Scriptures of the Old and New Testaments as the supreme rule of faith and life, and upon the value of a highly trained ministry, which has given the Church of Scotland, a high reputation for scholarship and has in turn influenced the standard of education in Scotland. The unity of the Church is guaranteed by providing for democratic representation in a hierarchy of courts (unlike the Anglican Church, which is a hierarchy of persons). The local kirk-session consists of the minister and popularly elected elders (laymen). Ministers, elected by their flocks, are ordained by presbyters (ministers already ordained). Above the kirk-session is the court of the presbytery which has jurisdiction over a specified area; above that the court of synod which rules over many presbyteries; and finally the General Assembly which is the Supreme Court of the Church with both judicial and legislative powers, and over which the Moderator of the General Assembly presides. The function of the elders is to help the minister in the work and government of the kirk.

The episcopacy set up by James VI and I, and maintained by Charles I was brought to an end by the Glasgow Assembly (1638), but General Assemblies were abolished by Oliver Cromwell and at the Restoration Charles II re-established episcopacy. The Covenanters who resisted were hunted down, imprisoned, transported, or executed over a period of nearly thirty years before William of Orange came to the throne and Presbyterianism was re-established (1690).

In 1972 the Presbyterian and Congregationalist Churches in England were merged to form the United Reformed Church. *See* **Church of Scotland, Calvinism.**

Protestant, the name first applied to those who favoured the cause of Martin Luther and who protested against the intolerant decisions of the Catholic majority at the second Diet of Speyer (1529), revoking earlier decisions of the first Diet of Speyer tolerating the Reformers in certain cases (1526).

In general the name "Protestant" is applied to those Churches which severed connection with Rome at the time of the Reformation. The essence of Protestantism is the acceptance by the individual Christian of his direct responsibility to God rather than to the Church. *See also* **Lutheranism, Presbyterianism, Calvinism.**

Psychiatry, a branch of medicine concerned with the treatment of psychological problems and mental illness. It uses drugs and psychotherapeutic techniques.

Psychic Research is a general term for the various approaches to the scientific investigation of the paranormal, in particular supposed extrasensory powers of the mind, but also manifestations such as ghosts, poltergeists, spiritualistic phenomena, *etc.* In recent years the word parapsychology has also come into use, particularly for the investigation of ESP (extrasensory perception) in a laboratory setting, but it is really part of psychic research as the subject's fascinating history reveals.

For all recorded history, and no doubt very much earlier, man has been puzzled at his apparent ability to perceive features of the universe without the use of the normal senses—mind-to-mind contact, dreams about the future which come true, *etc*. He has also been intrigued by the notion that in addition to the natural world of people and things, there exists in parallel, a *supernatural* world of ghosts, spirits and other similar strange manifestations.

Belief in such oddities has been tremendously widespread. Of course, until the 19th cent. or thereabouts such phenomena, while bizarre, unpredictable and possibly frightening, were not at odds with man's view of himself and his world as revealed through basic religious beliefs. Man was supposed to be in essence a supernatural being with eternal life, and the world was seen as the happy hunting ground of dynamic evil forces which could intervene directly in the lives of humans. The rise of material science in the 19th cent. however began to shake the orthodox religious frame-work, and as a result in due course scientists began to question the basis of all supernatural powers and manifestations, putting forward the reasonable argument: "if such things *are* real then they should be demonstrable in scientific terms—like all other aspects of the universe are."

The Society for Psychical Research.

Once having advanced this argument, the next step was to carry it to its conclusion and set about the systematic investigation of the phenomena to see whether they *did* conform in any way to the immensely successful framework of 19th cent. science, and from this step psychic research was born. In fact one can date its origins rather precisely—to 1882 when a group of scholars formed the Society for Psychical Research in London—an organisation which still exists today. The first experiments in this slightly eccentric field of science were haphazard and tended to be confined to spiritualistic phenomena such as table tapping, mediumistic messages, ectoplasmic manifestations, *etc.*, which were having a great wave of popularity among the general public at the time. In fact what one might term as the first phase of psychic research—it has gone through three phases in its history—was really heavily tied up with Spiritualism.

Before ridiculing it for this, it is only fair to point out that many of the most eminent figures of the time—the great physicists Sir Oliver Lodge and Sir William Crookes, Alfred Russell Wallace, co-discoverer with Darwin of the theory of evolution by natural selection, the brilliant author and creator of Sherlock Holmes, Sir Arthur Conan Doyle, and many others—became convinced Spiritualists as the result of their early experiments. Nevertheless, despite the ardent support of such intellectual giants, medium after medium was in due course detected in fraud— sometimes of the most blatant kind—and the majority of scientists gradually became more critical and less likely to be taken in by even the subtlest of trickery. As a result, interest slowly shifted from the séance room to a different realm, and as it did so the first phase of psychic research drew to a close.

The second phase was, broadly speaking, the era of the ghost hunter. With the idea of spirits materialising in laboratories seeming intrinsically less and less credible, scientists began to study what struck them at the time to be basically more "plausible" matters—haunted houses, poltergeist phenomena and so on. For some reason the idea of a house dominated by a psychic presence as the result of some tragic history seemed (at the turn of the century) *somehow* scientifically and philosophically more acceptable than did the old spiritualist notions about direct communication with the spirit world. The key figure in the "ghost hunting" era was Harry Price, an amateur magician who became the scourge of fraudulent mediums, but who staked his name and credibility on the authenticity of the alleged poltergeist phenomena at Borley Rectory in Suffolk, which became world famous through his book, *The Most Haunted House in England*.

The ancient rectory's catalogue of ghosts and marvels allegedly witnessed by numerous "reliable witnesses" seemed irrefutable. Unfortunately investigations by the Society for Psychical Research after Price's death made it seem certain that Price was responsible for faking some of the Borley phenomena himself, and with these disclosures scientifically "respectable" ghost hunting took a nasty tumble. Thus, with an increasingly critical attitude developing among scientists, haunted houses and poltergeists gradually began to shift out of favour to usher in the third phase of psychic research.

Developments in the USA.

The date of the commencement of this phase can be identified as 1927 when the Parapsychology Laboratory at Duke University in North Carolina was formed by Dr. J. B. Rhine. Here the emphasis was on laboratory studies along the traditional lines of experimental psychology; spirit forms and poltergeists were ignored in favour of the routine testing of literally thousands of people for telepathy, precognition (the ability to see into the future), etc., almost always involving card tests which could be rigidly controlled and the results statistically analysed. By the 1940s Rhine was claiming irrefutable evidence of telepathy achieved by these means, but once again critical forces began to gather and it was pointed out that results obtained in Rhine's laboratory rarely seemed to be replicable in other scientists' laboratories in different parts of the world. In fact the failure of ESP experiments of this kind to be easily repeatable has turned out to be crucial and has led to a growing scepticism on the part of uncommitted scientists who now question whether psychic research and parapsychology have really advanced our understanding of the world of the paranormal in any way.

Current Developments.

To sum up the topic one could say that in a curious way, while the third phase of psychic research is now drawing to a close, the evidence suggests that a fourth phase is appearing, and that this may well feature a return to the study of the more sensational and dramatic phenomena reminiscent of the Victorian séance room. If this is so, over a century after its foundation the wheel will have turned full circle and psychic research will be back where it started, without in the opinion of most scientists, having solved any of the basic questions which it had set out to answer. *See* **Parapsychology, Poltergeist, Telepathy, Spiritualism.**

Psychoanalysis, an approach to the study of human personality involving the rigorous probing, with the assistance of a specially trained practitioner, of an individual's personal problems, motives, goals and attitudes to life in general. Often, and quite understandably, confused with psychology (of which it is merely a part), psychoanalysis has an interesting historical background and has attracted the interest of philosophers, scientists and medical experts since it emerged as a radical and controversial form of mental therapy at the turn of the century. The traditionally accepted founder is the great Austrian Sigmund Freud, but he never failed to acknowledge the impetus that had been given to his own ideas by his talented friend, the physiologist Joseph Breuer, who for most of his working life had been interested in the curious phenomena associated with hypnosis. Breuer had successfully cured the hysterical paralysis of a young woman patient and had noticed that under hypnosis the girl seemed to be recalling emotional experiences, hitherto forgotten, which bore some relationship to the symptoms of her illness. Developing this with other patients Breuer then found that the mere recalling and discussing of the emotional events under hypnosis seemed to produce a dramatic alleviation of the symptoms—a phenomenon which came to be known as *catharsis*. Breuer also noticed another curious side-effect, that his women patients fell embarrassingly and violently in love with him, and he gradually dropped the practice of "mental catharsis", possibly feeling that it was a bit too dangerous to handle. This left the field clear for Freud, whose brilliant mind began to search beyond the therapeutic aspects of the topic to see what light might be thrown on the nature of human personality and psychological mechanisms in general. The most important question concerned the "forgotten" emotional material which turned up, apparently out of the blue, during the hypnotic session. Freud rightly saw that this posed problems for the current theories of memory, for how could something once forgotten (a) continue to have an effect on the individual without his being aware of it, and (b) ultimately be brought back to conscious memory again. It must be remembered that at this time memory was considered to be a fairly simple process—information was stored in the brain and was gradually eroded or destroyed with the passage of time and the decay of brain cells. Once lost, it was believed, memories were gone for ever, or at best only partially and inaccurately reproducible. Furthermore, human beings were supposed to be rational (if frequently wilful) creatures who never did anything without thinking about it (if only briefly) beforehand and without being well aware of their reasons for so doing.

The Genius of Freud.

It was within this framework that Sigmund Freud had his great insight, one which many people believe to be one of the most important ideas given to mankind. This was simply the realisation that the human mind was not a simple entity controlling the brain and body more or less at will, but a complex system made up of a number of integrated parts with at least two major subdivisions—the conscious and the unconscious. The former concerned itself with the normal round of human behaviour, including the larger part of rational thought, conversation, etc., and large areas of memory. The latter was principally devoted to the automatic control of bodily functions, such as respiration, cardiac activity, various types of emotional behaviour not subject to much conscious modification and a large storehouse of relevant "memories" again not normally accessible to the conscious mind. Occasionally, Freud proposed, an exceedingly unpleasant emotional or otherwise painful event might be so troublesome if held in the conscious mind's store, that it would get shoved down into the unconscious or "repressed" where it would cease to trouble the individual in his normal life. The advantages of this mechanism are obvious, but they also brought with them hazards. With certain kinds of memory, particularly those involving psychological rather than physical pain—as for example a severe sexual conflict or marital problem—repression might be used as a device to save the individual from facing his problem in the "real" world, where he might be able ultimately to solve it, by merely hiding it away in the unconscious and thus pretending it did not exist. Unfortunately, Freud believed, conflicts of this kind were not snuffed out when consigned to the basements of the mind, but rather tended to smoulder on, affecting the individual in various ways which he could not understand. Repressed marital conflicts might give rise to impotence, for example, or perhaps to homosexual behaviour. Guilt at improper social actions similarly repressed might provoke nervous tics, local paralysis, etc, etc. Following this line of reasoning, Freud argued that if the unwisely repressed material could be dredged up and the individual forced to face the crisis instead of denying it, then rapid alleviations of symptoms and full recovery should follow.

To the great psychologist and his growing band of followers the stage seemed to be set for a dramatic breakthrough not only in mental therapy but also in a general understanding of the nature of human personality. To his pleasure—for various reasons he was never too happy about hypnosis—Freud discovered that with due patience, skill and guidance an individual could be led to resurrect the material repressed in his unconscious mind in the normal, as opposed to the hypnotic, state. This technique, involving long sessions consisting of intimate discussions between patient and therapist became known as psychoanalysis, and it has steadily evolved from its experimental beginnings in the medical schools and universities of Vienna to being a major system of psychotherapy with a world-wide following and important theoretical connotations. Psychoanalysis, as practised today, consists of a number of meetings between doctor and patient in which the latter is slowly taught to approach and enter the *territory* of his subconscious mind, and examine the strange and "forgotten" material within. A successful analysis, it is claimed, gives the individual greater insight into his own personality and a fuller understanding of the potent unconscious forces which are at work within him.

Freud's initial ideas were of course tentative, and meant to be so. He was however a didactic and forceful personality himself, unwilling to compromise on many points which became controversial as the technique and practice of psychoanalysis developed. The outcome was that some of his early followers, notably the equally brilliant Carl Jung and Alfred Adler, broke away to found their own "schools" or versions of psychoanalysis. Jungian analysis, practised by the followers of C. G. Jung is an important aspect of psycho-analysis.

All psychoanalysts, Freudian and Jungian, must have a lengthy training analysis by a training analyst from a recognised institute. This is not restricted to individuals qualified in medicine or psychology. Today, psychoanalysis is coming under increasing scrutiny, and its claims are being treated with a good deal of reservation. Notable antagonists include the English psychologist Professor H. J. Eysenck. Analysts respond by saying that their system is closer to an art than a craft and not amenable to routine scientific experiment.

The controversy will no doubt continue for some time to come, but whatever its validity as therapy, the basic ideas behind psycho-analysis—notably the reality and power of the unconscious mind—are beyond question and have given human beings definite and major insights into the greatest enigma of all—the workings of the human mind.

Psychology is the study of people: how they think, how they act, react and interact. Psychology is concerned with all aspects of behaviour and the thoughts, feelings and motivation underlying such behaviour. Modern psychology is thus the science of human behaviour and experience. *See* **Adlerian Psychology, Biopsychology, Evolutionary Psychology, Gestalt Psychology** etc.

Psychotherapy, a method aimed at alleviating mental and emotional suffering through a specialised relationship between therapist and patient. The whole range of psychotherapies is represented on the National Register, which is compiled by the UK Council for Psychotherapy. This incorporates eight different models, each one of which holds in common a theory about the human mind, a concept of the development of the individual, and a theory of change.

Puritans were a separate sect before the accession of Edward VI, but did not become prominent till the reign of Elizabeth. Afterwards they split up into Independents and Presbyterians, and the influence of Oliver Cromwell made the former supreme. Since the Revolution the word has been replaced by "Nonconformist" or "Dissenter", but, of course, Roman Catholics in England and Protestant Episcopalians in Scotland are just as much Nonconformists or Dissenters as Baptists or Methodists.

Pyramidology, a curious belief that the dimensions of the Great Pyramid at Giza, if studied carefully, reveal principles of fundamental historical and religious significance. The perpetrator of this was a Victorian publisher, John Taylor, who discovered that if you divide the height of the pyramid into twice the side of its base you get a number very similar to *pi*—a number of considerable mathematical importance. Later discoveries in the same vein include the finding that the base of the pyramid (when divided by the width of a single casing stone) equals exactly 365—number of days in the year.

Many books have been written on the interpretation of the dimensions of the pyramid, none of which has any scientific or archaeological validity. Pyramidology is simply a classic example of the well-known fact that hunting through even a random array of numbers will turn up sequences which appear to be "significant"—always provided that one carefully selects the numbers one wants and turns a blind eye to those that one doesn't!

Pyrrhonism, a sceptical philosophy which doubts everything. (*See* **Scepticism**)

Pythagoreanism. The school of thought initiated by the followers of Pythagoras. It is to be distinguished from Pythagoras himself, whose own doctrines are difficult to determine. The Pythagoreans believed that at its deepest level, reality is mathematical in nature, that is, all things can be ultimately reduced to numerical relationships. Their theory of number was applied to music theory, acoustics, geometry and astronomy. The doctrine of the "harmony of the spheres" seems to have started with them: certain parameters characterizing the planets are related to one another "harmoniously" by a mathematical rule. The revolution of each planet produces a distinct tone, and the whole set corresponds to the notes of a scale.

They also held a doctrine of metempsychosis: the soul transmigrates through successive reincarnations to union with the divine.

Q

Quakers, (**Religious Society of Friends**), a religious body founded in England in the 17th cent. by George Fox (1624–91). The essence of their faith is that every individual person has the power of direct communication with God who will guide him into the ways of truth. This power comes from the "inner light" of his own heart, the light of Christ, Quakers meet for worship avoiding all ritual, without ordained ministers or prepared sermons; often there is silence until someone is moved by the Holy Spirit to utter his message.

In the early days Quakers gave vent to violent outbursts and disturbed church services. Friends had the habit of preaching at anyone who happened to be nearby, their denunciation of "steeple-houses" and references to the "inner light," their addressing everyone as "thee" and "thou," their refusal to go beyond "yea" and "nay" in making an assertion and refusing to go further to taking an oath, must have played some part in bringing about the savage persecutions they were forced to endure.

Many emigrated to Pennsylvania, founded by William Penn in 1682, and missionaries were sent to many parts of the world. The former violence gave way to gentleness. Friends not only refused to take part in war but even refused to resist personal violence. They took the lead in abolishing slavery, worked for prison reform and better education. As we know them today Quakers are quiet, sincere, undemonstrative people, sometimes given to a somewhat serious turn of mind. The former peculiarities of custom and dress have been dropped and interpretation of the Scriptures is more liberal.

Quakers refuse to take part in warfare, but they are always ready to help the victims of war. In Britain the Quakers have (2006) over 17,500 adult members. There are *c* 214,000 worldwide.

Quietism, a doctrine of extreme asceticism and contemplative devotion, embodied in the works of Michael Molinos, a 17th cent. Spanish priest, and condemned by Rome. It taught that the chief duty of man is to be occupied in the continual contemplation of God, so as to become totally independent of outward circumstances and the influence of the senses. Quietists taught that when this stage of perfection is reached the soul has no further need for prayer and other external devotional practices. Similar doctrines have been taught in the Muslim and Hindu religions. *See* **Yoga.**

Quran (Koran). *See* **Islam.**

R

Racism, the doctrine that one race is inherently superior or inferior to others, one of the bases of racial prejudice. It has no connection whatever with the study of race as a concept, nor with the investigation of racial differences, which is a science practised by the physical anthropologist (who studies physical differences), or the social anthropologist (who studies cultural differences).

Radiesthesia, the detection, either by some "psychic" faculty or with special equipment, of radiations alleged to be given off by all living things and natural substances such as water, oil, metal, *etc.* The word radiesthesia is in fact a fancy modern name for the ancient practice of "dowsing," whereby an individual is supposed to be able to detect the presence of hidden underground water by following the movements of a hazel twig held in his hands. Dowsers, or water diviners, as they are sometimes called, claim also to be able to detect the presence of minerals and, hard though it may seem to believe, have actually been hired by major oil companies to prospect for desert wells—though without any notable success. Dowsers are still employed to locate water for farms or to locate underground pipes and cables.

There is an important link between radiesthesia and the pseudo-science of *radionics,* which holds that the twig or pendulum can be superseded by complicated equipment built vaguely according to electronic principles.

The originator of radionics seems to have been a Dr. Albert Abrams who engaged in medical practice using radionic devices in America in the 1920s and 1930s.

Ramadan. The ninth month of the Islamic calendar during which the Prophet received his first revelations from God. Mohammed had traditionally spent this month fasting and praying, but now it is a compulsory duty for Muslims to fast between the hours of sunrise and sunset, known as *Sawm.* This fast extends to food, drink, cigarettes, chewing gum and sexual relations. Its purpose is to concentrate the heart on God without distraction and to develop self-control. It is traditionally broken each day with *iftar,* some dates and water, following the Prophet's example. A later meal will then follow. Whilst it is a duty, certain groups will be excused including the aged and those under twelve years of age. Pregnant or nursing mothers as well as travellers are temporarily excused with the understanding that fast days will be made up at a later date. Following the lunar calendar Ramadan moves forward in relation to each season and, as such, *Sawm* can be a very testing experience for Muslims during the height of summer.

Ranters, a fanatical antinomian (holding the doctrine that Christians are not bound to keep the law of God) and pantheistic sect in Commonwealth England. The name was also applied to the Primitive Methodists because of their noisy preaching.

Rastafarianism, a Caribbean religious movement which took root in Jamaica in the 1930s following the teachings of Marcus Garvey who set up the "Black Star Liner" for the repatriation of Africans abroad. Rastafarians look to Ethiopia as their spiritual home since that country was the one part of Africa not to be colonised permanently (it was invaded by Mussolini in the 1930s). Reggae is their music. Many Rastafarians smoke marijuana as a spiritual act. Coffee, milk and alcohol are usually avoided.

Rationalism is defined as "the treating of reason as the ultimate authority in religion and the rejection of doctrines not consonant with reason." In practice, rationalism had a double significance: (1) the doctrine as defined above, and (2) a 19th cent. movement which was given to what was then known as "free-thought," "secularism," or agnosticism—*i.e.,* it was in the positive sense anti-religious and was represented by various bodies such as the Secular Society, the National Secular Society, and the Rationalist Press Association (founded in 1899).

In the first sense, which implies a particular philosophical attitude to the universe and life, rationalism is not easy to pin down although, at first sight, it would appear that nothing could be simpler. Does it mean the use of pure reason and logic or does it mean, on the other hand, the use of what is generally called the "scientific method" based on a critical attitude to existing beliefs? If we are thinking in terms of the use of pure reason and logic then the Roman Catholic Church throughout most of its history has maintained, not that the whole truth about religion can be discovered by reason, but as St. Thomas Aquinas held, the basis of religion—*e.g.* the existence of God—can be rationally demonstrated. Nobody could have made more use of logic than the schoolmen of the Middle Ages, yet not many people today would accept their conclusions, nor would many non-Catholics accept St. Thomas's proofs of the existence of God even when they themselves are religious. The arguments of a First Cause or Prime Mover or the argument from Design on the whole leave us unmoved, partly because they do not lead up to the idea of a *personal God*, partly because we rightly distrust logic and pure reason divorced from facts and know that, if we begin from the wrong assumptions or premises, we can arrive at some very strange answers.

If the existence of a Deity can be proved by reason, then one can also by the use of reason come to the conclusions, or rather paradoxes, such as the following: God is by definition all good, all knowing, all powerful—yet evil exists (because it if does not exist then it cannot be wrong to say "there is no God"). But if evil exists, then it must do so either because of God (in which case He is not all good) or in spite of God (in which case He is not all powerful).

Arguments of this sort do not appeal to the modern mind for two historical reasons: (1) many of us have been brought up in the Protestant tradition which—at least in one of its aspects—insists that we must believe in God by faith rather than by logic and in its extreme form insists on God as revealed by the "inner light"; (2) our increasing trust in the scientific method of observation, experiment and argument. Thus, no matter what Aristotle or St. Thomas may say about a Prime Mover or a First Cause, we remain unconvinced since at least one scientific theory suggests that the universe did not have a beginning and if scientific investigation proved this to be so, then we should be entirely indifferent to what formal logic had to say.

The secularist and rationalist movements of the 19th cent. were anti-religious—and quite rightly so—because at that time there were serious disabilities imposed even in Britain by the Established Church on atheism or agnosticism and freedom of thought. They are of little significance now because very little is left, largely thanks to their efforts, of those disabilities.

Finally, although most people are likely to accept the scientific method as the main means of discovering truth, there are other factors which equally make us doubt the value of "pure" logic and reason unaided by observation. The first of these is the influence of Freud which shows that much of our reasoning is mere rationalising—*e.g.*, we are more likely to become atheists because we hated our father than because we can prove that there is no God. The second is the influence of a movement in philosophy which, in the form of logical positivism or logical analysis, makes us doubt whether metaphysical systems have any meaning at all.

Today, instead of asking ourselves if Plato was right or wrong, we are much more likely to ask whether he did anything but make for the most part meaningless noises. Religion is in a sense much safer today than it ever was in the 19th cent. when it made foolish statements over matters of science that could be *proved* wrong; now we tend to see it as an emotional attitude to the universe or God (a "feeling of being at home in the universe," as William James put it) which can no more be proved or disproved than being in love.

Realism is a word which has so many meanings, and such contradictory ones, in various spheres, that it is difficult to define. We shall limit ourselves to its significance in philosophy. In philosophy, "realism" has two different meanings, diametrically opposed. (1) The most usual meaning is the one we should least expect from the everyday sense of the word—*i.e.*, it refers to all those philosophies from Plato onwards which maintained that the world of appearance is illusory and that ideas, forms, or universals are the only true realities, belonging to the world beyond matter and appearance—the world of God or mind. In early mediaeval times St. Thomas Aquinas was the chief exponent of this doctrine which was held by the scholastics as opposed to the Nominalists (*q.v.*). (2) In its modern everyday meaning "realism" is the belief that the universe is real and not a creation of mind, that there is a reality that causes the appearance, the "thing-in-itself" as Kant described it. Material things may not really be what they appear to be (*e.g.* a noise is not the "bang" we experience but a series of shock-waves passing through the atmosphere), yet, for all that, we can be sure that matter exists and it is very possible (some might add) that mind does not.

Reformation, the great religious movement of the 16th cent., which resulted in the establishment of Protestantism. John Wyclif (d. 1384), John Hus (d. 1415) and others had sounded the warning note, and when later on Luther took up the cause in Germany, and Zwingli in Switzerland, adherents soon became numerous. The wholesale vending of indulgences by the papal agents had incensed the people, and when Luther denounced these things he spoke to willing ears. After much controversy, the reformers boldly propounded the principles of the new doctrine, and the struggle for religious supremacy grew bitter. They claimed justification (salvation) by faith, and the use as well as the authority of the Scriptures, rejecting the doctrine of transubstantiation, the adoration of the Virgin and Saints, and the headship of the Pope. Luther was excommunicated. But the Reformation principles spread and ultimately a great part of Germany, as well as Switzerland, the Low Countries, Scandinavia, England, and Scotland wore won over to the new faith.

In England Henry VIII readily espoused the Reformation, his own personal quarrel with the Pope acting as an incentive. Under Mary there was a brief and sanguinary reaction, but Elizabeth gave completeness to the work which her father had initiated. *See* **Lutheranism, Calvinism, Presbyterianism, Baptists,** *etc.*

Relativism. Theories or doctrines that truth, morality *etc.* are relative to situations and are not absolute. The view that all truth is relative is associated with Scepticism (*q.v.*). In the area of morality, it is the view that there are no absolute or universal criteria for ethical judgements. This view is often a reaction to the differences in moral belief between different societies. It is objected against relativism that there must be standards by which to measure the correctness of judgements or beliefs.

Religious Society of Friends. *See* **Quakers.**

Renaissance, the revival of art and letters, under the influence of classical models, which began in Italy in the 14th century. It is a term which must be used with care for the following reasons: (1) Although it was first used in the form *rinascita* (re-birth) by Vasari in 1550 and people living at that time certainly were aware that something new was happening, the word had no wide currency until used by the Swiss historian Jacob Burckhardt in his classic *The Civilization of the Renaissance in Italy* (1860). (2) The term as used today refers not only to art in its widest sense but to a total change in man's outlook on life which extended into philosophical, scientific, economic, and technical fields. (3) Spreading from Italy there were renaissance movements in France, Spain, Germany, and northern Europe, all widely different with varying delays in time. As the historian Edith Sichel wrote: "Out of the Italian Renaissance there issued a new-born art; out of the Northern Renaissance there came forth a new-born religion. There came forth also a great school of poetry, and a drama the greatest that the world had seen since the days of Greece. The religion was the offspring of Germany and the poetry that of England."

The real cause of the Renaissance was not the fall of Constantinople, the invention of printing, or the discovery of America, though these were phases in the process; it was, quite simply, money. The birth of a new merchant class gave rise to individualist attitudes in economic affairs which prepared the way for individualism and humanism. The new wealthy class in time became patrons of the arts whereas previously the Church had been the major patron and controller. Thus the artist became more free to express himself, more respected, and being more well-to-do could afford to ignore the Church and even, in time, the views of his patrons.

It is true that art continued to serve to a considerable extent the purposes of faith, but it was judged from the standpoint of art. Mediaeval art was meant to elevate and teach man: Renaissance art to delight his senses and enrich his life. From this free and questing spirit acquired from economic individualism came the rise of modern science and technology; here Italy learned much from the Arab scholars who had translated and commented upon the philosophical, medical, and mathematical texts of antiquity, while denying themselves any interest in Greek art and literature. Arabic Latin versions of Aristotle were in use well into the 16th cent. The Byzantine culture, though it had preserved the Greek tradition and gave supremacy to Plato, had made no move forward. But the Greek scholars who fled to Italy after the fall of Constantinople brought with them an immense cargo of classical manuscripts. The recovery of these Greek masterpieces, their translation into the vernaculars, and the invention of printing, made possible a fuller understanding of the Greek spirit.

It was the bringing together of the two heritages, Greek science, and Greek literature, that gave birth to a new vision. But it was not only Aristotle and Plato who were being studied but Ovid, Catullus, Horace, Pliny and Lucretius. What interested Renaissance man was the humanism of the Latin writers, their attitude to science, their scepticism.

The period c. 1400-1500 is known as the **Early Renaissance.** During this time such painters as Masaccio, Uccello, Piero della Francesca, Botticelli, and Giovanni Bellini were laying the foundations of drawing and painting for all subsequent periods including our own. They concerned themselves with such problems as anatomy, composition, perspective, and representation of space, creating in effect a grammar or textbook of visual expression. The term **High Renaissance** is reserved for a very brief period when a pure, balanced, classical harmony was achieved and artists were in complete control of the techniques learned earlier. The High Renaissance lasted only from c. 1500 to 1527 (the date of the sack of Rome), yet that interval included the earlier works of Michelangelo, most of Leonardo's, and all the Roman works of Raphael.

Ritualism, a tendency which, during the 19th cent., developed in the High Church section of the Church of England to make use of those vestments, candles, incense, etc. which are usually regarded as features of the Church of Rome. Since some opposition was aroused, a Ritual Commission was appointed in 1904 to take evidence and try to find some common basis on which High and Low Church could agree with respect to ceremonial. The report of 1906 in effect recommended the giving of greater powers to bishops to suppress objectionable practices.

Although they are often associated together, it is worth while pointing out that there was no special connection between the Oxford Movement or Tractarians (q.v.) and Ritualism because Pusey disliked ritual and even Newman, who eventually went over to Rome, held simple services at his church of St. Mary's.

Roman Catholic Church, the Christian organisation which acknowledges the Pope as the lawful successor of St. Peter, the apostle appointed by Christ to be the head of His Church. The reforming impulse at the Second Vatican Council (1962-5), summoned by Pope John, set in train movements towards religious unity and the reform and modernisation of the Church. Pope Paul made changes in the government and liturgy of the Church but refused to allow birth control, the marriage of priests or a greater role for women.

A historic meeting took place in 1982 between Rome and Canterbury when Pope John Paul II made the first papal visit to Britain. The 1993 papal encyclical, *Veritatis Splendor*, forcefully restating the Catholic opposition to artificial birth control, reopened Catholic divisions on this issue. The English text of the Catechism of the Catholic Church, the first complete survey of Roman Catholic teaching since the 16th century, was published in 1994. Pope John Paul's book, *Crossing the Threshold of Hope* was published the same year. In 1995 the Pope's encyclical *Evangelium Vitae* (Gospel of Life) repeated his attacks on abortion, euthanasia, suicide and *in vitro* fertilisation. Many liberal Roman Catholics were unhappy with the more conservative pronouncements of the Pope (such as the document *Ad Tuendam Fidem*, On the Defence of Faith) published in 1998.

During his pontificate, Pope John Paul canonised more saints than any Pope in history, but his pontificate was over-shadowed by widespread child abuse in some dioceses.

Some Anglicans (opposed to women priests) have moved to join the Catholic Church. The resignation in September 1996 of the Bishop of Argyll reinforced the growing debate on celibacy in the priesthood (the celibacy rule dates from 1139). In March 2000 the Pope sought a historic pardon for the sins of the Church (the *mea culpa*). With the death of Pope John Paul II in April 2005 the Roman Catholic Church entered a new era. Over recent years, weekly attendance at Sunday Mass in England declined from 1·7 million in 1989 to 1,041,000 in 1999. Entrants to the priesthood are also declining. The most important Catholic countries (by numbers) are Brazil (c. 150 million), Mexico (94 million), the Philippines (66 million) and the USA (also 66 million). (*See also* **Papal Infallibility.**)

Romantic Movement or **Romanticism** is the name given not so much to an individual way of thinking but to the gradual but radical transformation of basic human values that occurred in the Western world round about the latter part of the 18th cent. It was a great breakthrough in European consciousness and arose through the writings of certain men living during the half-century or more following, say, 1760. It arose when there was a revolution in basic values—in art, morals, politics, religion, etc. The new view was of a world transcending the old one, infinitely larger and more varied.

To understand the Romantic movement it is necessary first to take note of the climate of thought preceding the great change; then to account for its beginning in Germany where it did (*see* **Pietism**) during the latter part of the 18th cent., and finally to appraise the writings of those men whose ideas fermented the new awakening. Briefly, the shift was away from French classicism and from belief in the all pervasive power of human reason (the Enlightenment) towards the unfettered freedom that the new consciousness was able to engender. What mattered was to live a passionate and vigorous life, to dedicate oneself to an ideal, no matter what the cost (*e.g.,* Byron).

The ideas of the Enlightenment (*e.g.,* Fontenelle, Voltaire, Montesquieu) had been attacked by the Germans Hamann and Herder and by the ideas of the English philosopher Hume, but Kant, Schiller, and Fichte, Goethe's novel *Wilhelm Meister*, and the French Revolution all had profound effects on the aesthetic, moral, social, and political thought of the time. Friedrich Schlegel (1772-1829) said: "There is in man a terrible unsatisfied desire to soar into infinity; a feverish longing to break through the narrow bonds of individuality." Romanticism undermined the notion that in matters of value there are objective criteria which operate between men. Henceforth there was to be a resurgence of the human spirit, deep and profound, that is still going on.

Rosicrucians, a mystical society founded in the 16th cent. by Christian Rosenkreuz which attempted to forge a theoretical link between the great Egyptian religions and the Church of Rome, drawing rituals and philosophy from both camps. The Society did not long survive the death of its founder (he managed to reach the age of 106 incidentally) but has been revived in succeeding centuries by a series of rivalling factions. Perhaps the most famous of these is the Rosicrucian Order which has become well-known in the Western world as a result of its heavy advertising in the popular press. Founded by the American H. Spencer Lewis, this offers a simple and good-natured doctrine preaching the Brotherhood of Man, the reincarnation of the soul and the immense latent potential of the human mind.

S

Sabbatarianism, the belief held by those Christians who regard the first day of the week as the Sabbath and wish to respect it as a holy day according to the 4th Commandment. Sabbatarianism became a principal characteristic of Presbyterianism (q.v.).

Observance of the Sabbath has declined in recent years along with the general fall in church attendance and the advent of sporting, leisure and now shopping, gaming and more relaxed licensing laws on the Sabbath.

Salafism, a form of Sunni Islam.

Salvation Army. The religious movement which in 1878 became known by this name arose from the Christian Mission meetings which the Rev. William Booth and his devoted wife held in the East End of London for the previous thirteen years. Its primary aim was, and still is, to preach the gospel of Jesus Christ to men and women untouched by ordinary religious efforts. The founder devoted his life to the salvation of the submerged classes whose conditions at that time were unspeakably dreadful. Originally his aim had been to convert people and then send them on to the churches, but he soon found that few religious bodies would accept these "low-class" men and women. So it was that social work became part of their effort. Practical help like the provision of soup-kitchens, accompanied spiritual ministration.

Soon, in the interests of more effective "warfare" against social evils, a military form of organisation, with uniforms, brass bands, and religious songs, was introduced. Its magazine *The War Cry* gave as its aim "to carry the Blood of Christ and the Fire of the Holy Ghost into every part of the world.'

General Booth saw with blinding clarity that conversion must be accompanied by an improvement of external conditions. Various books had earlier described the terrible conditions of the slums, but in 1890 he produced a monumental survey entitled *In Darkest England and the Way Out.* From that time forward the Army was accepted and its facilities made use of by the authorities. Today (2005) the Army's spiritual and social activities have spread to over 94 countries across the world; every one, no matter what class, colour, or creed he belongs to, is a "brother for whom Christ died." Within Britain there are now (2006) over 1,700 officers (i.e. ordained ministers). In September 2002 the Salvation Army elected Commissioner John Larsson as its new world leader.

Scepticism. From the Greek, *skepsis*, enquiry or questioning. The philosophical attitude of doubting claims to knowledge. It springs from observations that the senses are unreliable, that the best methods often fall short of reaching the truth, and that experts often disagree. Sceptical attitudes emerge early in ancient Greek philosophy, but were only systemized into a school of thought by Pyrrhon Elis (c. 360–c. 272 B.C.). The Greek Sceptics proposed *epoche*, or suspension of belief, and aimed at *ataraxia*, tranquility of mind.

Scepticism is a recurring theme in Western philosophy, for example in Montaigne (1533–92) and Bayle (1647–1706). The most powerful sceptical thinker of the modern age is David Hume (1711–76). His arguments throw doubt upon induction, the notion of causality, the identity of the self and the existence of the external world. The term is also associated with Descartes (1596–1650), though Descartes himself is not a sceptic. It refers to his "method of doubt", which attempted to put knowledge upon a sure foundation by suspending Judgement on any proposition whose truth could be doubted, until one can be found that is absolutely certain. This secure point is the famous "I think therefore I am".

Scholasticism. From the time of Augustine to the middle of the 9th cent. philosophy, like science, was dead or merely a repetition of what had gone before. But about that time there arose a new interest in the subject, although (since by then Western Europe was entirely under the authority of the Catholic Church) the main form it took was an attempt to justify Church teaching in the light of Greek philosophy.

Those who made this attempt to reconcile Christian beliefs with the best in Plato and Aristotle were known as "schoolmen" and the philosophies which they developed were known as "scholasticism." Among the most famous schoolmen must be counted John Scotus Erigena (c. 800–c. 877), born in Ireland and probably the earliest; St. Anselm, archbishop of Canterbury (1033–1109); the great Peter Abelard whose school was in Paris (1079–1142); Bernard of Chartres, his contemporary; and the best-known of all, St. Thomas Aquinas of Naples (1225–74), who was given the name of the "Angelic Doctor."

The philosophies of these men are discussed under various headings (**God and Man, Determinism and Free-will**), but being severely limited by the Church their doctrines differed from each other much less than those of later philosophical schools. However, one of the great arguments was between the orthodox Realists (q.v.) and the Nominalists (q.v.) and a second was between the Thomists (or followers of St. Thomas Aquinas) and the Scotists (followers of John Duns Scotus—not to be confused with John Scotus Erigena). The two latter schools were known as the Ancients, whilst the followers of William of Occam, the Nominalist, were known as the Terminalists. All became reconciled in 1482 in face of the increasing threat from humanism of which the great exponent was Erasmus of Rotterdam (1466–1536).

Scientology, an applied religious philosophy dealing with the study of knowledge, which through the application of its technology, claims to bring about desirable changes in the conditions of life. The word Scientology comes from the Latin word Scio (knowing in the fullest meaning of the word) and the Greek word Logos (study of). Developed and founded by author, philosopher and humanitarian L. Ron Hubbard (1911–86). Scientology purports to explain all of life's difficulties and contradictions in terms of occurrences in past lives. These mental blocks are removed so the individual can return to the deified state from which he came many incarnations ago.

Until the late 1960s the worldwide headquarters was in East Grinstead, Sussex. This is now the UK headquarters. Scientology ® is a registered trademark.

Secularism. See **God and Man** and **Rationalism**.

Semiology, Semiotics. These two words are now used almost interchangeably. The original sense of semiotics was the study of signs and sign-using behaviour, and was propounded by the American philosopher Peirce (1839–1914). Semiotics was divided into three branches: syntactics, the study of grammar; semantics, the study of meaning, and pragmatics, the study of the purposes and effects of meaningful utterances. Under the influence of the French linguist de Saussure (1857–1913) the term has broadened to the study of any means by which human beings communicate, not only through language, but also through gestures, clothes, objects, advertisements etc. Societies have a multiplicity of language-like "codes" by which objects like cars and buildings have cultural meanings over and above their functions.

Shakers, members of a revivalist group, styled by themselves "The United Society of Believers in Christ's Second Appearing," who seceded from Quakerism in 1747 though adhering to many of the Quaker tenets. The community was joined in 1758 by Ann Lee, a young convert from Manchester, who had "revelations" that she was the female Christ; "Mother Ann" was accepted as their leader. Under the influence of her prophetic visions she set out with nine followers for "Immanuel's land" in America and the community settled near Albany, capital of New York state. They were known as the "Shakers" in ridicule because they were given to involuntary movements in moments of religious ecstasy. Central to their faith was the belief in the dual role of God through the male and female Christ: the male principle came to earth in Jesus; the female principle, in "Mother Ann." The sexes were equal and women preached as often as men at their meetings which sometimes included sacred dances—nevertheless the two sexes, even in dancing, kept apart.

Their communistic way of living brought them economic prosperity, the Shakers becoming known as good agriculturists and craftsmen, noted for their furniture and textiles. After 1860, however, the movement began to decline and it is now virtually extinct.

Shamans, the medicine men found in many primitive societies who used their magical arts to work cures, and protect the group from evil influences. The *shaman* was a man apart and wore special garments to show his authority.

Shiites or Shia, a Muslim sect in Iran (Persia), opposed by the orthodox Sunnites who see them as heretics. The dispute, which came almost immediately after the death of the Prophet and led to bitter feuding, had little to do with matters of doctrine as such but with the succession. After Mohammed's death, there were three possible claimants: Ali, the husband of his daughter Fatima, and two others, one of whom gave up his claim in favour of the other, Abu Bakr. The orthodox selected Abu Bakr, who was shortly assassinated, and the same happened to his successor as Ali was passed over again.

The Shiites maintain that Ali was the true vicar of the Prophet, and that the three orthodox predecessors were usurpers.

In Iraq, the majority Shiites have enjoyed a revival of influence since the fall of Saddam Hussein (under whose regime they were oppressed). They are dominant in Iran. Elsewhere Shia now (2006) number 60 % of the population in Iraq, 60 % in Bahrein, 40 % in Lebanon, 30 % in Kuwait and 12 % in Saudi Arabia.

Shintoism, literally means "teaching of the Gods". It is a native Japanese religion, with a strong bias towards ancestor worship and the divine powers of natural forces. Unusual in that it had no recognised founder nor written dogma, Shintoism permeated Japanese life in a most vigorous way until the defeat of the country at the hands of the Allied Powers in 1945. In the 1500 years of its existence the Shinto religion produced tens of thousands of unique and beautiful shrines throughout Japan. Vast numbers of these were destroyed by bombing in the war.

Shintoism was disestablished by the US occupying forces in 1945 and Hirohito "abdicated" his divine powers.

The first written record of Shinto beliefs and customs was completed in A.D. 712.

Sikhism. The Sikh community of the Punjab, which has played a significant part in the history of modern India, came into being during a period of religious revival in India in the 15th and 16th cent. It was originally founded as a religious sect by Guru (teacher) Nanak (1469–1538) who emphasised the fundamental truth of all religions, and whose mission was to put an end to religious conflict. He condemned the formalism both of Hinduism and Islam, preaching the gospel of universal toleration, and the unity of the Godhead, whether He be called Allah, Vishnu, or God. His ideas were welcomed by the great Mogul Emperor Akbar (1542–1605). Thus a succession of Gurus were able to live in peace after Nanak's death; they established the great Sikh centre at Amritsar, compiled the sacred writings (the *Adi Granth*), and improved their organisation as a sect.

But the peace did not last long, for an emperor arose who was a fanatical Muslim, in face of whom the last Guru, Govind Singh (1666–1708), whose father was put to death for refusal to embrace Islam, had to make himself a warrior and instil into the Sikhs a more aggressive and warlike spirit.

A number of ceremonies were instituted by Govind Singh; admission to the fraternity was by special rite; caste distinctions were abolished; hair was worn long; the word singh, meaning lion, was added to the original name. They were able to organise themselves into 12 *misls* or confederacies but divisions appeared with the disappearance of

a common enemy and it was not until the rise of Ranjit Singh (1780–1839) that a single powerful Sikh kingdom was established, its influence only being checked by the English, with whom a treaty of friendship was made. After the death of Ranjit Singh two Anglo-Sikh wars followed, in 1845–46, and 1848–49, which resulted in British annexation of the Punjab and the end of Sikh independence. In the two world wars the Sikhs proved among the most loyal of Britain's Indian subjects. The partitioning of the sub-continent of India in 1947 into two states, one predominantly Hindu and the other predominantly Muslim, presented a considerable problem in the Punjab, which was divided in such a way as to leave 2 million Sikhs in Pakistan, and a considerable number of Muslims in the Indian Punjab.

Although numbering less than 3 per cent. of the population the Sikhs are a continuing factor in Indian political life. Demands for Sikh independence led to the storming by Indian troops of the Golden Temple at Amritsar on 6 June 1984. In October 1984, Mrs. Gandhi was assassinated by Sikh extremists. There are c. 450,000 Sikhs in Britain (2006).

The largest Sikh temple outside India was opened in Southall in March 2003. There is a pioneering World Sikh University based in Harrow. There are over 24m. Sikhs world-wide.

Socialism, is a form of society in which men and women are not divided into opposing economic classes but live together under conditions of approximate social and economic equality, using in common the means that lie to their hands of promoting social welfare. The brotherhood of man inspires the aims of socialism in foreign, colonial, social, and economic policies alike.

The word "socialism" first came into general use in England c. 1834 in connection with Robert Owen's "village of cooperation" at New Lanark. About the middle of the 19th cent., Charles Kingsley and others established a form of Christian socialism, and William Morris, John Burns, and others founded a Socialist League in 1886.

With the development of trade unions the socialist movement took a more practical trend. Fabianism (*q.v.*) associated in its early days with the names of Beatrice and Sidney Webb and George Bernard Shaw, aimed at the gradual reorganisation of society by creating intelligent public opinion by education and legislation. The British Labour Party believed in peaceful and constitutional change to socialism by democratic methods based upon popular consent. The Labour Government of 1945–51 initiated a major period of social reform and public ownership and remains perhaps the greatest reforming government of the 20th century.

Though beset by economic difficulties, the 1964–70 Labour Government continued a policy of radical reform. The minority Labour Government (of February–October 1974) and the subsequent administration continued this process, particularly in the area of state intervention in industry. The election defeats of 1979, 1983 and 1987 inevitably led to a questioning of the future direction the party should take and, under the leadership of Neil Kinnock, the party became (in effect) a modernised social democratic party. It fought the 1992 election on this platform but went down to its fourth consecutive defeat. Under John Smith (until his untimely death in 1994) and subsequently under Tony Blair, the party continued its modernisation policy.

The Party's 1997 election manifesto effectively buried its commitment to socialism. Some socialists, unhappy with these changes, formed the Socialist Labour Party in May 1996. Its leading figure was Arthur Scargill. The outcome of the May 1997 election seemingly vindicated the Blairite approach as the party captured 418 seats, a greater tally than ever before. The party repeated its electoral success in the 2001 election.

In the 2005 general election Labour secured an historic third term in power, but lost many votes to the Liberal Democrats.

Soka Gakkai, Japan's largest religious organisation with 10 million followers. Founded in 1930 as the lay arm of a venerable Buddhist sect.

Solipsism. The theory that nothing really exists but oneself and one's mental states. No philosopher has deliberately held this view, but it is often seen to follow from certain views, for example, the belief that all one can know is oneself and one's immediate knowledge. It is philosophically interesting in that though the theory is intrinsically absurd, it is difficult to refute. Ludwig Wittgenstein (1889–1951) argued that the fact that we have a language (in which to express this solipsism) depends on the existence of a mind-independent external world.

Spiritualism is a religion which requires to be distinguished from psychical research (q.v.) which is a scientific attempt carried on by both believers and non-believers to investigate psychic phenomena including those not necessarily connected with "spirits"—e.g., telepathy or clairvoyance and precognition. As a religion (although for that matter the whole of history is filled with attempts to get in touch with the "spirit world") Spiritualism begins with the American Andrew Jackson Davis who in 1847 published *Nature's Divine Revelations*, a book which is still widely read. In this Davis states that on the death of the physical body, the human spirit remains alive and moves on to one or another of a considerable range of worlds or "spheres" where it commences yet another stage of existence. Since the spirit has not died, but exists with full (and possibly even expanded) consciousness, there should be no reason, Davis argues, why it should not make its presence known to the beings it has temporarily left behind on earth. In 1847, the year of the publication of Davis's book, two young girls, Margaret and Kate Fox, living in a farmhouse at Hydesville, New York, began apparently to act as unwitting mediums for attempts at such between-worlds communication. The girls were the focus for strange rappings which it was alleged defied normal explanation and which spelt out, in the form of a simple alphabetical code, messages from the spirits of "the dead." The Fox sisters were later to confess that they had produced the raps by trickery.

In the late 19th cent. Spiritualism went into a phase of expansion and for various reasons attracted the attention of many scientists.

Today many find it astonishing that people of such brilliance should find the phenomena of the seance room of more than passing interest, but the commitment of the Victorian scientists is understandable if we realise that Spiritualists, after all, claim to do no more than demonstrate as fact what all Christians are called on to believe—that the human personality survives bodily death. Furthermore, at the time of the late 19th cent. peak of Spiritualism, much less was known about human psychology and about the great limitations of sensory perception in typical seance conditions, when lights are dimmed or extinguished and an emotionally charged atmosphere generated. Today the most striking phenomena of the seance room the alleged materialisation of spirit people and the production of such half-spiritual, halfphysical substances as ectoplasm—are rarely if ever produced at Spiritualist meetings. Some say that the most probable explanation for this is that too many fraudulent mediums have been caught out and publicly exposed for the profession to be worth the risks.

The movement today, which still has a large and often articulate following, now concentrates on the less controversial areas of "mental mediumship," clairvoyance and the like, or on the very widespread practice of "spirit healing." Where people are not deliberately deluded by bogus mediums acting for monetary reward (a practice which largely died out with the "death" of ectoplasm) Spiritualism probably has an important role to play in the life of many people whose happiness has been removed by the death of a much loved relative or spouse. It does not deserve the violent attacks that are often made on it by clergy who allege that Spiritualists are communicating not with the souls of the departed but with the devil or his emissaries. *See* **Greater World Spiritualists.**

Stalinism. The methods and policies associated with Joseph Stalin (1879–1953), leader of the USSR from 1929 until his death. This form of despotism consisted of the concentration of power in his own hands, and the ruthless suppression of dissent in any form, plus a "cult of personality", which used every means of propaganda to present Stalin as a wise and benevolent ruler.

State and Man. Most of the early civilisations such as those of Egypt and Babylonia were theocratic, that is to say, they were arranged in a hierarchy with, at the peak, a king who was also an incarnation of the god. It is with the rise of the city states of ancient Greece that the problem really began to be discussed.

The Greek Approach. The early pre-Socratic philosophers Democritus and the Pythagorean school for example, held that the individual should subordinate himself to the whole; they had no doubt that the citizen's first duty was to the state. The Greeks until the time of Plato were not really thinking in terms of individual rights, nor had they given much thought to what form the state should take—they simply accepted it. The first great attempt to describe the ideal state is to be found in Plato's *The Republic* which is referred to elsewhere (*see* **Education**). His pupil Aristotle did not try to form a utopia but made many comments on the nature of government. Thus, while agreeing that the state was more important than any individual person, he distinguished between good and bad states, and pointed out that to the extent that the state does not enable its citizens to lead virtuous and useful lives it is evil. A good constitution must recognise the inequalities between human beings and confer on them rights according to their abilities: among these inequalities are those of personal ability, property, birth, and status, as freeman or slave. The best forms of rule were monarchy, aristocracy, and democracy; the worst forms—tyranny, oligarchy (or rule of a powerful few), and ochlocracy (or mob-rule). The later Greek thinkers of Hellenistic times held two opposed points of view. The Epicureans (q.v.) taught that all social life is based upon self-interest and we become members of a group for our own convenience; therefore there are no absolute rights and laws—what is good is what members decide at that time to be good, and when they change their minds the law must change too. Injustice is not an evil in any god-given sense; we behave justly simply because if injustice became the general rule, we ourselves should suffer. The Stoics (q.v.), on the other hand, held that the state must dominate the individual completely and everyone must carry out, first and foremost, his social duties and be willing to sacrifice everything for it; but the state of the Stoics was no narrowly national one, but one that strove to become a universal brotherhood.

The Christian Approach. The orthodox Christian view is expressed in St. Augustine's book *The City of God*. Here it is held that the church, as the worldly incarnation of the City of God, is to be supreme over the state, and the head of the church is to be supreme over secular rulers. In addition it must be recognised that, whilst the secular ruler can make mistakes, the church does not, since it is the representative of God's kingdom on earth.

The Secular State. During the Renaissance (q.v.) people began to think for themselves and the results of their cogitations were not always pleasant; for it was during this time that many rulers, petty and otherwise, were seeking absolute authority. Two notable thinkers at this stage were Niccolo Machiavelli (1469–1527) in Italy and Thomas Hobbes (1588–1679) in England, where, of course, the Renaissance arrived later in history. Both supported absolute monarchy against the former domination of the church. The name of Machiavelli has become a by-word for any behaviour that is cunning and unscrupulous, but he was not really as bad as he is usually painted. It is, indeed, true that in his book *The Prince* he showed in the greatest detail the methods by which a ruler could gain absolute control and destroy civic freedom, but this despotism was intended as merely a necessary intermediate stage towards his real idea which was a free, united Italian nation wholly independent of the church. Hobbes was a materialist whose thesis was that man is naturally a ferocious animal whose basic impulse is war and pillage and the destruction of whatever stands in his way to gain his desires. But if he allowed himself to behave in this way his life would be "nasty, brutish, and short" so he creates a society in which he voluntarily gives up many of his rights and hands them over to a powerful ruler in his own interest. But having done this he must obey; even when the ruler is unjust, as he has no right to complain because anything is better than a return to his natural state. The religion of the king must be the religion of the people and the only things no ruler has the right to do is to cause a man to commit suicide or murder or to make him confess to a crime.

Views of Locke: Live and Let Live. John Locke (1632–1704) disagreed with these views. Man is naturally peaceful and co-operative and therefore social life comes readily to him. He sets up an authority in order to preserve the group and that is why laws are made; but the function of the state is strictly limited to maintaining the public good and beyond this men are to be left free. Therefore absolute power and the doctrine of the Divine Right of Kings were wrong because power ultimately rests with the people who have the right to make and break governments. It is also wrong that those who make the laws should be able to execute them. This is the important British doctrine of the separation of powers between the legislature and the executive which is regarded as one of the bases of democracy.

Rousseau's Social Doctrine. The only other views we need consider here are those of Jean-Jacques Rousseau (1712–78) and Herbert Spencer (1820–1903), since the views of the two important intervening figures, Hegel and Karl Marx, are dealt with elsewhere (see **Dialectical Materialism**) and after Spencer we come to a stage where political philosophy begins to merge with sociology and the social sciences. Rousseau is a puzzling figure. On the one hand he has been hailed as the prophet of freedom and on the other as the father of modern totalitarianism. His book *Social Contract* (1762) begins with the words: "Man is born free, and everywhere he is in chains." He says that he is in favour, not merely of democracy, but of direct democracy in which everyone has to give his assent to all measures as in the Greek city-states and in Geneva, of which city he was a citizen. (This method is still in force in respect of some measures in the Swiss cantons.) Natural society is based on a "social contract" or mutual agreement and Rousseau speaks of a "return to nature" which would ensure the sovereignty of the people at all times. Thus far, he seems to agree with Locke but soon we find that he is more akin to Hobbes, since (as the twentieth century showed) nothing is more tyrannical than the absolute rule of all the people. (Public opinion is more Hitlerian than Hitler.) As it turns out, then, the "social contract" consists in "the total alienation of each associate, together with all his rights, to the whole community" and "each of us puts his person and all his power in common under the supreme direction of the general will." Rousseau admired direct democracy in the small city-state, but if his doctrine is applied to large states, then the "general will" becomes absolute. It is in this sense that he is regarded as the forerunner of totalitarianism. Herbert Spencer is quoted only as an example of the inappropriate application of a biological theory to social issues. Influenced by Darwin's thesis of natural selection, he saw in society a struggle in which the fittest survived and the less fit perished. Each individual had the right to preserve himself, but in the case of human beings this depended upon group life in which, to some extent, each individual is limited by the rights of others. But this should not go too far, and he condemned the socialism of J. S. Mill which (a) would give over-much protection to the unfit, and (b) would give the state powers which it has no right to since the best government is the least government. In accordance

with Darwinism free competition was essential. **State Capitalism.** Lenin's description of the compromise made with financial interests in 1918 to ensure Communist survival, while simultaneously reinforcing central control over the economy. More recently, a pejorative description of Soviet socialism in which a privileged bureaucracy is said collectively to dominate economic life with the same relationship to the working class as employers under private capitalism.

Stoics, the followers of Zeno, a Greek philosopher in the 4th cent. B.C., who received their name from the fact that they were taught in the Stoa Poikile or Painted Porch of Athens. They believed that since the world is the creation of divine wisdom and is governed by divine law, it is man's duty to accent his fate. Zeno conceived virtue to be the highest good and condemned the passions. (*See* **God and Man, State and Man, Determinism and Free will.**)

Structuralism.
1. **Psychology.** The name of a school of thought whose influence has not lasted. It sought to investigate the structure of consciousness through the analysis, by introspection, of simple forms of sensation, thought, images, *etc.* and then find out how these components fitted together in complex forms. The school, which is mainly identified with Edward Titchener (1867–1927), discounted the value of analysing the significance of mental experience, and of examining the functions of the mind.
2. **Linguistics.** The theory that language is best described in terms of its irreducible structural units in morphology (the study of word structure) and phonology (the study of sound systems).
3. **Social Sciences.** Theories or methods of analysis characterised by a preoccupation, not simply with structures, but with such structures as can be held to underlie and generate the phenomena under observation. To use a distinction of the linguist Noam Chomsky (b. 1928), the concern is with deep structures rather than surface structures. The main influences on the movement have been the theories of the French anthropologist Claude Levi-Strauss (b. 1908). According to him, universal patterns of cultural and social systems are products of the invariant "deep" structure of the human mind. He believed that structural similarities underlie all cultures and that an analysis of the relationships between cultures could provide insight into innate and universal principles of human thought.
Structural analysis has also been applied to literary theory, *e.g.* by the French critic Roland Barthes (1915–80). *See under* **Literary Theory.**

Subjectivism. In moral philosophy, the belief that all moral attitudes are merely a matter of personal taste. According to this an assertion like "Abortion is wrong" does not express an objective truth but means that the speaker or, more broadly, his society, or people in general, disapprove of abortion.

Sufism. A mystical movement within Islam. It started as a reaction against the legalistic approach of early Islam, seeking to establish a more personal relationship with Allah, or God. The objective of Sufism is perfection of the individual and union with God. Sufi orders were first established in the 12th century and some are still thriving today. Sufism has been very important in the history of Islamic faith and had a great influence on Muslim love poetry, and created a genre of mystical love poetry.

Suicide. *See* **Euthanasia.**

Sunnites, the orthodox sect of Islam as contrasted with the Shiites or Shia (q.v.).

Surrealism. *See* **Section N.**

Swedenborgianism. The Church of the New Jerusalem, based on the writings of Emanuel Swedenborg (1688–1772), was founded by his followers eleven years after his death. The New Church is essentially a movement bearing the same relationship to Christianity as Christianity does to Judaism. Swedenborg's many works include the 12-volume *Arcana Caelestia* (*Heavenly Secrets*) (1749–56).

Synchronicity, an attempt by the psychologist, Carl Gustav Jung, to explain the apparently significant relationship between certain events in the physical universe which seem to have no obvious "causal" link. This rather involved concept is easily understood if one realises that almost all scientific and philosophical beliefs are based on the notion that the continuous process of change which is taking place in ourselves and in the universe around us is dependent upon a principle known as causality. We can express this another way by saying that an object moves because it has been pushed or pulled by another. We see because light strikes the retina and signals pass up the nervous system to the brain. A stone falls to the ground because the earth's gravity is pulling it towards its centre, *etc.*, *etc.* For all practical purposes every event can be looked upon as being " caused" by some other prior event and this is obviously one of the most important principles of the operation of the universe. Jung, however, felt that there is a sufficiently large body of evidence to suggest that events may be linked in a significant (*i.e.*, non-chance) way without there being any true causal relationship between them. The classic example he held to be the supposed predictive power of astrology by which there appears to be a relationship between the stellar configurations and the personality and life-pattern of individuals on earth. Jung was scientist enough to realise that there could be no causal connection between the aspect of the stars and the lives of people billions of miles from them, yet felt the evidence for astrology was strong enough to demand an alternative non-causal explanation. The trouble with synchronicity, which has not made much impact on the world of physics or of psychology, is that it is not really an explanation at all but merely a convenient word to describe some puzzling correspondences. The real question, of course, is whether there really are events occurring which are significantly but not *causally* linked, and most scientists today would hold that there were probably not.

Syndicalism, a form of socialist doctrine which aims at the ownership and control of all industries by the workers, contrasted with the more conventional type of socialism which advocates ownership and control by the state. Since syndicalists have preferred to improve the conditions of the workers by direct action, *e.g.*, strikes and working to rule, rather than through the usual parliamentary procedures, they have been closely related to anarchists (*q.v.*) and are sometimes described as anarcho-syndicalists.

Under syndicalism there would be no state; for the state would be replaced by a federation of units based on functional economic organisation rather than on geographical representation. The movement had bodies in the United Kingdom, where guild socialism (*q.v.*) was strongly influenced by its doctrines, in France, Germany, Italy, Spain, Argentina, and Mexico, but these gradually declined after the first world war. Fascism (*q.v.*) was also strongly influenced by the revolutionary syndicalism of Georges Sorel.

T

Talmud. See **Judaism.**

Tantra. 1 *Tantric Buddhism.* Tantra refers to a series of ritual texts said to have been first transmitted by the Buddha himself. The tantras speak of the evocation of various gods, the pursuit of magical powers, the use of chants, and the attainment of enlightenment through meditation and yoga. Tantric theory and practice is a development within the Mahayana Buddhist tradition. It died out in India but moved to Tibet. The most famous tantra is the *Tibetan Book of the Dead.*

2. *Tantric Hinduism.* Within Hinduism tantra refers to a group of Sanskrit texts not part of the orthodox Veda (*see* **Hinduism**). These are concerned with acquiring spiritual power and liberation in life, through practices aiming at purifying the body and controlling one's mental processes.

Taoism is still one of the great Eastern creeds. Its alleged founder, Lao-tze, is said to have been born in Honan about 604 B.C.; he is also said to be the author of the bible of Taoism, the *Tao-te-ching,* or in English *The Way of Life,* and to have disapproved of Confucius. This, if true, would hardly be surprising; for Taoism is eminently a mystical religion recommending doing nothing and resisting nothing, whereas

Confucianism (*q.v.*) is eminently a practical code of living and its founder insisted on intervening in everything to do with social life. But the truth as revealed by modern scholarship is rather different. We are told that the poems of the *Tao-te-ching* are anonymous and probably originated among recluses in lonely valleys long before the time of Confucius; they were collected and given form at some time late in the 3rd cent. B.C. and their authorship attributed to Lao-tze. It is entirely possible that no such peson ever existed (unlike Confucius, who certainly did), but if there were such a man he appears to have used a pseudonym since "Lao" is not a surname but an adjective meaning "old" and it was customary to attribute important works to old men on account of their supposed wisdom. Lao-tze simply means "the old philosopher", and although the *Tao-te-ching* is one of the most remarkable and instructive books ever written it is as anonymous as the Border Ballads.

It is apparent that the religion learned both from the ancient Chinese mystics and from Brahmanism: *Tao*, the Way, is impalpable, invisible, and incapable of being expressed in words. But it can be attained by virtue, by compassion, humility, and non-violence. Out of weakness comes true strength whereas violence is not only wrong but defeats its own ends. There is no personal God and such gods as men imagine are mere emanations of *Tao* which gives life to all things. *Tao* is Being. Works are worthless and internal renunciation is far better than anything that follows from the use of force because passive resistance convinces the other from within that he is in error, whereas violence only compels the external appearance of conviction whilst inwardly the individual is as before. "It is wealth to be content; it is wilful to force one's way on others."

Later Lao-tze became a divinity and indeed one of a Trinity each worshipped in the form of idols (which the founder had hated). Soon there was worship of the forces of nature: the stars, the tides, the sun and moon, and a thousand other deities among whom Confucius was one. The purest mysticism and wisdom had been utterly corrupted by contact with the world.

Telepathy and Clairvoyance. Telepathy is the alleged communication between one mind and another other than through the ordinary sense channels. Clairvoyance is the supposed faculty of "seeing" objects or events which, by reason of space and time or other causes, are not discernible through the ordinary sense of vision. Such claims have been made from time immemorial but it was not until the 20th century that the phenomena were investigated scientifically. The first studies were undertaken by the Society for Psychical Research, which was founded in 1882 with Professor Henry Sidgwick as its first president. Since then it has carried out a scholarly programme of research without – in accordance with its constitution—coming to any corporate conclusions.

It would be odd if some scientists were not interested in ESP because of the enormous weight of anecdotal evidence which has built up over centuries to support it. The weakness of the scientific as opposed to the casual evidence is however exemplified by the failure of ESP researchers to produce a reliable "repeatable" experiment.

Terrorism. A form of political violence used against governments, groups or individuals with the purpose of creating a climate of fear in which the aims of the terrorists may be fulfilled. The term derives from the "Reign of Terror" in the French Revolution. In the 20th century it is most closely associated with the violence of small political movements of both the extreme left and right, attempting to overthrow existing political institutions.

It has often been used as part of nationalist movements seeking to remove colonial governments, as in the expulsion of Britain from Kenya and France from Algeria. There is also what is known as "*state terrorism*", as practised by totalitarian regimes such as Hitler's Germany and Stalin's Soviet Union. Today fears are growing of *bio-terrorism* (*e.g.* the possible use of deadly germ and bacterial warfare by a country such as Iraq).

Theism. See **God and Man.**

Theosophy (Sanskrit *Brahma Vidya* = divine

wisdom), a system of thought that draws on the mystical teachings of those who assert the spiritual nature of the universe, and the divine nature of man. It insists that man is capable of intuitive insight into the nature of God. The way to wisdom, or self-knowledge, is through the practice of **Yoga** (*q.v.*). Theosophy has close connections with Indian thought through Vedic, Buddhist, and Brahmanist literature. The modern Theosophical Society was founded by Mme H. P. Blavatsky and others in 1875, and popularised by Mrs. Annie Besant.

Third Way (New Labour). Social democratic political parties suffered successive defeats at the hands of neoliberal conservatives throughout the 1980s and 1990s. New Labour/Third Way politics attempted to apply and adapt traditional social democratic values to this hostile political landscape. Third Way politicians such as Bill Clinton and Tony Blair accepted the policies of privatisation, low taxes, and reduced welfare provision, and have in many cases extended neoliberal policies to areas of public services untouched by Thatcher and Reagan. Whilst rejecting increased progressive taxation, Third Way/New Labour politicians have attempted to promote social justice by spending the fruits of stable growing neoliberal economies on health, education, and anti-poverty measures. This increase in public spending has redistributed wealth in some areas of society at unprecedented levels, for example child poverty in the UK. Increasingly, Third Way/New Labour policies have changed the role of the state from owner and direct provider, to regulator and enforcer of central government's targets.

Traditional social democrats argue that Third Way/New Labour politics ignores the value of equality in social justice, and neoliberal conservatives argue that Third Way/New Labour public spending is parasitic on their economic reforms and legacy of growth.

Tory, a name given in 1680 by English Protestants to those who did not wish to exclude a Catholic heir from the succession to the throne of Charles II. It then remained the name of one of the two great political parties (*see* **Whigs**) until 1832, when the Tory Party restyled itself the Conservative Party. The term now denotes a supporter or member of the Conservative Party.

Totalitarianism. Totalitarian government is one which tolerates only one political party, to which all other institutions are subordinated, and which usually demands the complete subservience of the individual to the government. The Italian dictator Mussolini coined the term in the 1920s to describe the new fascist state of Italy, and the word has become synonymous with absolute and oppressive single-party government, as in Nazi Germany or Soviet Russia. *See also* **Stalinism.**

Totemism. A totem is an animal, plant or object with which a social or religious group feels a special affinity and which is often considered to be the mythical ancestor of the group. The totem is worshipped or esteemed by members of the group or clan bearing its name. Totemism is the form of social organization consisting of such clans. Membership of the clan is inherited and lifelong; but marriage is usually with a partner outside the totemic clan. Totem poles (as erected by North American Indians) are a way of representing the clan's guardian spirit. Totemism has been important in the religion and society of many less developed peoples.

Tractarianism, a Catholic revival movement, also known as the **Oxford Movement** (not to be confused with the so-called Oxford Group), which had its beginnings at Oxford in 1833. The leaders included the Oxford high churchmen E. B. Pusey, J. Keble and J. H. Newman.

Through the *Tracts for the Times* (1833–41), a series of pamphlets which were sent to every parsonage in England, they sought to expose the dangers which they considered to be threatening the church from secular authority. The immediate cause of the movement was the Reform Act (1832) which meant that the state was no longer in the safe keeping of Tories and Churchmen but that power was falling into the hands of Liberals and Dissenters. They advocated a higher degree of ceremonial in worship nearer the Roman communion. In *Tract 90* (the last) Newman showed how the

Thirty-nine Articles themselves, which were regarded as the bulwark of Protestantism, could be made to square with Roman doctrine. It was obvious which direction the movement was taking and the romanizing tendency was widely resented. In 1845 Newman went over to Rome. Pusey and Keble persisted in their efforts to secure recognition of Catholic liturgy and doctrine in the Anglican Church. Catholicism of the Anglican type (*i.e.*, Catholic in ritual, ceremony, and everything save submission to the Pope) is termed Anglo-Catholicism (*q.v.*).

Transcendental Meditation, popularised in the West by the Maharishi Mahesh Yogi, who achieved sensational worldwide publicity by his "conversion" of the Beatles. This is a simple meditational system which it is claimed is an aid to relaxation and the reduction of psychological and physical stress. It is a technique which can be taught in a relatively short, concentrated period of time, provided that someone trained by the Maharishi is the teacher. The pupil or would-be meditator is given a *mantra*—letting his thoughts flow freely while sitting in a comfortable position. Very many claims are made on behalf of the system. As with most cults, religious and occult systems, there is an initial psychological benefit to anyone who becomes deeply involved. Nevertheless, apart from this simple "participation-effect", there is some evidence that the body's autonomic functions (heart rate, respiratory cycle, brain waves, *etc.*) can be modified by certain individuals including yogis. The TM movement in Britain is based at Mentmore Towers in Buckinghamshire. The movement recruits heavily on campuses in America, but has been the subject of many complaints by parents.

Transcendentalism. 1. A term used to refer to the transcendental idealism of Immanuel Kant (1724–1804). *See* **Mind and Matter.**

2. A movement established in the United States in the 1830s, much influenced by German idealism and Platonism, which included Ralph Waldo Emerson (1803–82) and Henry Thoreau (1817–62) among its members. Transcendentalism's characteristic belief was in the supremacy of insight over logic and experience for the revelation of the deepest truths. It tended towards mysticism, pantheism and optimism about the progress of the spirit. Although the movement's followers believed that true reform must come from within the individual, they took part in contemporary reform movements.

Transcendentalism itself faded with the coming of the American Civil War, but it had a strong influence on the writings of Whitman, Emily Dickinson and Hawthorne.

Transubstantiation, the conversion in the Eucharist of the bread and wine into the body and blood of Christ—a doctrine of the Catholic Church.

Trinity. The Christian doctrine that God exists in three persons, all co-equal, and indivisible, of the same substance—God the Father, God the Son (who became incarnate as Jesus), begotten of the Father, and God the Holy Ghost, proceeding from Father and Son. The system denying the Trinity is Unitarianism (*q.v.*).

Trotskyism, a form of communism supporting the views of Leon Trotsky, the assumed name of Lev Bronstein (1879–1940) who, in 1924, was ousted from power by Stalin and later exiled and assassinated in Mexico. Trotsky held that excessive Russian nationalism was incompatible with genuine international communism and that Stalin was concentrating on the economic development of the Soviet Union to an extent which could only lead to a bureaucratic state with a purely nationalist outlook. After the Hungarian uprising in 1956, which was ruthlessly suppressed by the Soviet Armed Forces, a wave of resignations from Western Communist parties took place, many of the dissidents joining the Trotskyist movement. Trotsky laid emphasis on the idea of 'permanent revolution' and his supporters formed the Fourth International.

U

Ufology. *See* **Flying Saucers.**

Uniates, the Eastern Orthodox Churches which are in full communion with the Roman Catholic

Church, recognise the authority of the Pope and in faith and doctrine are totally Catholic. However, they retain their traditional liturgies and separate canon law and permit their priests to marry. The Pope visited Ukraine's Uniates in 2001.

Unification Church. *See* **J62.**

Unitarianism has no special doctrines, although clearly, as the name indicates, belief is in the single personality of God, *i.e.*, anti-trinitarian. This general statement, however, can be interpreted with varying degrees of subtlety. Thus unitarian belief may range from a sort of Arianism which accepts that, although Christ was not of divine nature, divine powers had been delegated to him by the Father, to the simple belief that Christ was a man like anyone else, and his goodness was of the same nature as that of many other great and good men. Indeed, today many Unitarians deny belief in a personal God and interpret their religion in purely moral terms, putting their faith in the value of love and the brotherhood of man. The Toleration Act (1689) excluded Unitarians but from 1813 they were legally tolerated in England. Nevertheless attempts were made to turn them out of their chapels on the ground that the preachers did not hold the views of the original founders of the endowments. But this ended with the Dissenting Chapels Act of 1845. In America no such difficulties existed, and in the Boston of the 19th cent. many of the great literary figures were openly unitarian in both belief and name: *e.g.*, Emerson, Longfellow, Lowell *etc.*

United Reform Church. *See* **Presbyterianism.**

Untouchables (Dalits), the lowest caste in Hindu society. *See* **Hinduism.**

Utilitarianism, a school of moral philosophy of which the main proponents were J. S. Mill (1806–73) and Jeremy Bentham (1748–1832). Bentham based his ethical theory upon the utilitarian principle that the greatest happiness of the greatest number is the criterion of morality. What is good is pleasure or happiness; what is bad is pain. If we act on this basis of self-interest (pursuing what we believe to be our own happiness), then what we do will automatically be for the general good. The serious failing of this thesis is (1) that it makes no distinction between the quality of one pleasure and another, and (2) that Bentham failed to see that the law might not be framed and administered by men as benevolent as himself. J. S. Mill accepted Bentham's position in general but, seeing its failings emphasised (1) that self-interest was an inadequate basis for utilitarianism and suggested that we should take as the real criterion of good the social consequences of the act; (2) that some pleasures rank higher than others and held that those of the intellect are superior to those of the senses. Not only is the social factor emphasised, but emphasis is also placed on the nature of the act.

Utopias. The name "utopia" is taken from two Greek words meaning "nowhere" and was first used in 1516 by Sir Thomas More (1478–1535) as the title of his book referring to a mythical island in the south Pacific where he sited his ideal society. Since then it has been used of any ideal or fanciful society, and here a few will be mentioned. (The reader may recall that Samuel Butler's 19th cent. novel, describing an imaginary society in New Zealand where criminals were treated and the sick punished, was entitled *Erewhon* which is the word "nowhere" almost in reverse.) Not all utopias were entirely fanciful—*e.g.*, Robert Owen's and François Fourier's beliefs, although found to be impractical, were, in fact, tried out.

Sir Thomas More. More wrote at a time when the rise of the wool-growing trade had resulted in farming land being turned over to pasture and there was a great wave of unemployment and a rise in crime among the dispossessed. More began to think in terms of the mediaeval ideal of small co-operative communities in which class interests and personal gain played a decreasing part, a society which would have the welfare of the people at heart both from the physical and intellectual points of view. His utopia was one in which there was no private property, because the desire for acquisition and private possessions lay at the root of human misery. There was, therefore, only common ownership of land and resources. Each class of worker was equipped to carry out its proper function in the economic scheme and each was fairly rewarded for its share in production so that there was neither wealth nor poverty to inspire conflict. Nobody was allowed to idle, until the time came for him to retire when he became free to enjoy whatever cultural pleasures he wished, but since the system was devoid of the waste associated with competition, the working day would be only six hours.

There was to be compulsory schooling and free medical care for everybody, full religious toleration, complete equality of the sexes, and a modern system of dealing with crime which was free from vindictiveness and cruelty. Government was to be simple and direct by democratically-elected officials whose powers would be strictly limited and the public expenditure kept under close scrutiny. It will be seen that More was far in advance of his age, and to most democratically-minded people in advance of an earlier utopia, Plato's *Republic*, which is described under the heading of Education.

James Harrington. James Harrington published his book *The Commonwealth of Oceana* in 1656 and offered it to Oliver Cromwell for his consideration but without tangible results. Better than any other man of his time Harrington understood the nature of the economic revolution which was then taking place, and, like More, saw the private ownership of land as the main cause of conflict. He put forward the theory that the control of property, particularly in the shape of land, determines the character of the political structure of the state; if property were universally distributed among the people the sentiment for its protection would naturally result in a republican form of government.

The Commonwealth of Oceana was a society "of laws and not of men"—*i.e.*, it was to be legally based and structured so as to be independent of the good or ill-will of any individuals controlling it. Thus there must be a written constitution, a two-house legislature, frequent elections with a secret ballot, and separation of powers between legislature and executive—all today familiar features of parliamentary democracy, but unique in his time.

Saint-Simon. The utopias of the late 18th and 19th cent. come, of course, into the period of the industrial revolution and of laissez-faire capitalism. Individual enterprise and complete freedom of competition formed the outlook of the ruling class. Naturally the utopias of this period tended to have a strongly socialist tinge since such theories are obviously produced by those who are not satisfied with existing conditions. Saint-Simon's *New Christianity* (1825) is one such, and by many, Claude Henri, Comte de Saint-Simon (1760–1825) is regarded as the founder of French socialism.

His book urged a dedication of society to the principle of human brotherhood and a community which would be led by men of science motivated by wholly spiritual aims. Production property was to be nationalised (or "socialised" as he describes the process) and employed to serve the public good rather than private gain; the worker was to produce according to his capacity and to be rewarded on the basis of individual merit; the principle of inheritance was to be abolished since it denied the principle of reward for accomplishment on which the society was to be founded. Saint-Simon's proposals were not directed towards the poorer classes alone, but to the conscience and intellect of all. He was deeply impressed with the productive power of the new machines and his scheme was, first and foremost, intended as a method of directing that power to the betterment of humanity as a whole.

Fourier. François Marie Charles Fourier (1772–1837), although by conviction a philosophical anarchist who held that human beings are naturally good if allowed to follow their natural desires, was the originator of what, on the face of it, one would suppose to be the most regimented of the utopias. It consisted of a system of "phalanxes" or co-operative communities each composed of a group of workers and technicians assured of a minimum income and sharing the surplus on an equitable basis.

Agriculture was to be the chief occupation of each phalanx and industrial employment planned and so carefully assigned that work would become pleasant and creative rather than burdensome. One of his ideas was that necessary work should receive the highest pay, useful work the next, and pleasant work the least pay. The land was to be scientifically cultivated and natural resources carefully conserved. Most of the members' property was to be privately owned, but the ownership of each phalanx was to be widely diffused among members by the sale of shares. Such "parasitic and unproductive" occupations as stockbroker, soldier, economist, middle-man and philosopher would be eliminated and the education of children carried out along vocational lines to train them for their future employment.

The strange thing was that Fourier's suggestions appealed to many in both Europe and the USA and such men as Emerson, Thoreau, James Russell Lowell, and Nathaniel Hawthorne strongly supported them. An American Fourier colony known as Brook Farm was established and carried on for eight years.

Robert Owen. Robert Owen (1771–1858), a wealthy textile manufacturer and philanthropist, established communities founded on a kind of utopian socialism in Lanarkshire, Hampshire, and in America. Of his New Lanark community an American observer wrote: "There is not, I apprehend, to be found in any part of the world, a manufacturing community in which so much order, good government, tranquillity, and rational happiness prevail." The workers in Lanark were given better housing and education for their children, and it was administered as a co-operative self-supporting community in Scotland. Later in life Owen returned to sponsoring legislation that would remove some of the worst evils of industrial life in those days. But he lived to see few of his reforms adopted.

V

Vedanta. An ancient system of Indian thought. It is expressed in commentaries on the *Brahma Sutras.* A key figure is Shankara (788– 820 A.D.) who founded what is known as Advaita Vedanta.

Vegans, *see under* **Vegetarianism.**

Vegetarianism, a way of life practised by those who abstain from meat. Strict vegetarians (Vegans) also exclude all animal products (*e.g.* butter, eggs milk) from their diet as well as "hidden" animal products such as gelatin and rennet (an enzyme used to make cheese).

Vitalism, the philosophical doctrine that the behaviour of the living organism is, at least in part, due to a vital principle which cannot possibly be explained wholly in terms of physics and chemistry. This belief was held by the rationalist thinker C. E. M. Joad (1891–1953) and is implicit in Henri Bergson's (1859–1941) theory of creative evolution. It was maintained by Bergson that evolution, like the work of an artist, is creative and therefore unpredictable; that a vague need exists beforehand within the animal or plant before the means of satisfying the need develops. Thus we might assume that sightless animals developed the need to become aware of objects before they were in physical contact with them and that this ultimately led to the origins of organs of sight.

During the 20th century a form of vitalism described as "emergent evolution" was put forward. This theory maintains that when two or more simple entities come together there may arise a new property which none of them previously possessed. Today biologists would say that it is the *arrangement* of atoms that counts, different arrangements exhibiting different properties, and that biological organisation is an essentially dynamic affair.

W

Wahabis, members of an Arabian sect of Islam which originated in the teaching of Muhammad

Ibn Abd-al-Wahab, born at the end of the 17th cent. He was deeply resentful of Ottoman rule which, in addition to its tyranny, had brought about innovations in the religion which Muhammad regarded as a perversion of its original form. He proceeded to reform Islam to its earliest conditions and impressed his beliefs on Mohammed Ibn Saud, a sheikh who spread them with the aid of his sword.

Under the successors of Ibn Saud the power of the Wahabis spread over much of Arabia where it is dominant today in Saudi Arabia. Its particular characteristic is that it refuses to accept symbolic or mystical interpretations of the words of the Prophet and accepts quite literally the teaching of Islam. It is, in fact, a type of Muslim fundamentalism. Although crushed by the Ottomans in 1811 15, the movement remains an important element in Islam.

Partly in reaction to what it sees as the decadence and immorality of the West, and partly as a result of Saudi oil wealth, it now wields increasing influence.

Waldenses, a movement also known as "The Poor Men of Lyons," founded by Peter Waldo of that city about the same time, and in the same part of southern France, as the Albigenses (*q.v.*) with whom, however, they had nothing in common. Their main belief was a return to Apostolic simplicity, based on reading the Bible in their own language; their doctrines were somewhat similar to those of the Mennonites and the Quakers. However, they did not wish to separate themselves from the Church and were originally protected by several Popes until the Lateran Council of 1215 excluded them mainly for the crime of preaching without ecclesiastical permission. From this time they were subjected to persecution, yet maintained some contact with the Church until the Reformation when they chose to take the side of the Protestants. Situated mainly on the sides of the Alps, half in Piedmont and half in France, they were persecuted or not according to the contemporary political convenience of the Dukes of Savoy, and the major attempt to destroy them called forth Oliver Cromwell's intervention and the famous sonnet of Milton. The sect survived, and still exists, having been granted full equality of rights with his Catholic subjects by Charles Edward of Piedmont in 1848.

Wandjina, the ancestral spirit beings of the Aboriginal people in Western Australia. They can be found depicted on cave walls and rock shelters.

Weathermen, Far left group whose aim was to overthrow the American political system. The group's name was borrowed from the lyrics of songwriter Bob Dylan. Its membership was drawn from the well-educated, and it committed specific and well-planned acts of violence.

Whig. In 1680, a term derisively applied to politicians who sought to exclude Roman Catholics from succession to the throne, it thereafter became the name of the political party opposed to the Tory (*q.v.*) party. At first dominated by the nobility, it represented those forces which hoped to limit the power of the monarch and to increase the power of Parliament. The Whigs (the governing party in 1868 under Gladstone) formed an element in the emerging Victorian Liberal Party.

Witchcraft, the exercise of supposedly supernatural powers for evil purposes (black magic). It has a history dating back to classical times (*e.g.* the enchantress Medea in Greek mythology). Accounts of witchcraft were widespread in the medieval period.

Draconian opposition to its practices by the Church led to scores of witch trials, ruthless persecution and torture. Between 1400 and 1750 it is estimated over 100,000 people, the vast majority women, were prosecuted for witchcraft in Europe and colonial America.

Many innocent people perished, especially after the promulgation of the bull *Summis desiderantes* by Pope Innocent VIII in 1484. In 1494 the *Malleus Maleficarum* (Hammer of Witches) codified the ecclesiastical rules for detecting acts of witchcraft.

One early authority, Dr. Murray, points out that there have been two theories about witchcraft: (1) that there were such things as witches, that they possessed supernatural powers and that the evidence given at their trials was substantially correct; (2) that the witches were simply poor creatures who deluded themselves into believing that they had certain powers or, very often, were tortured into admitting things.

She herself accepts a third theory: that there were such beings as witches, that they really did what they admitted to doing, but that they did not possess supernatural powers. They were in fact believers in the old religion of pre-Christian times and the Church took centuries to root them out. That there existed "covens" of witches who carried out peculiar rites Dr. Murray has no doubt whatever. The first to show that the majority of so-called witches were people suffering from mental illness was the physician Johann Weyer of Cleves (1515–88). His views were denounced by the Catholic Church.

Today (2006) it is now known that the victims of the famous Salem witch trials in North America were suffering from ergot poisoning, which was mistaken for witchcraft. Three centuries later they have finally been exonerated. In the 1990s, the Catholic Church established a commission in the Czech Republic to review the notorious Šumperk witch trials of 1679 (when 100 people were burnt alive in Moravia). It is a sign of changing attitudes.

Few people realise how deeply the notion of witchcraft is implanted in our minds. For example, the Witchcraft Act was not repealed in Britain until the 1950s. In the Australian State of Victoria it was not legalised until 2005!

Women's Liberation Movement. *See under* **Feminism.**

World Congress of Faiths, an inter-religious movement which aims to break down barriers between faiths. The first step was taken by the world's parliament of religions held in Chicago in 1893; similar gatherings were held subsequently at intervals in Europe; but the actual organisation was formed in 1936 by Sir Francis Younghusband; and now an annual conference is held and educational activity carried on.

World Council of Churches, a union of Christian Churches from over 100 countries (including the Churches of the Protestant, Anglican, and Orthodox traditions, but excluding the Roman Catholic Church), engaged in extending Christian mission and unity throughout the world. This modern ecumenical movement stems from the great World Missionary Conference held at Edinburgh in 1910. The World Council was founded in 1948 and meets for consultation from time to time. The 8th Assembly met in Harare, Zimbabwe, in 1998 but was overshadowed by doubts over the future for the council. Back in 1981, the Salvation Army resigned in protest at the movement's involvement in African liberation.

World Federalism, the extension of the principle of federalism (already an established political system in such countries as Canada, Germany, Switzerland and the USA) to a world, international order, to prevent wars and to tackle *global* issues on a *global* basis. The Association of World Federalists campaigns for this objective.

Y

Yin and Yang, the two basic forces in ancient Chinese thought. Yang is associated with masculinity, heat, light, creation *etc.*, yin with femininity, coldness, dark, passivity *etc. See also* **Confucianism, Taoism.**

Yoga, a Hindu discipline which teaches a technique for freeing the mind from attachment to the senses, so that once freed the soul may become fused with the universal spirit (*atman* or Brahman), which is its natural goal. This is the sole function of the psychological and physical exercises which the Yogi undertakes, although few ever reach the final stage of *Samadhi* or union with Brahman which is said to take place in eight levels of attainment. These are: (1) *Yama*, which involves the extinction of desire and egotism and their replacement by charity and unselfishness; (2) *Niyama*, during which certain rules of conduct must be adopted, such as cleanliness, the pursuit of devotional studies, and the carrying out of rituals of purification; (3) *Asana*, or the attainment of correct posture and the reduction to a minimum of all bodily

movement (the usual posture of the concentrating Yogi is the "lotus position" familiar from pictures); (4) *Pranayama*, the right control of the life-force or breath in which there are two stages at which the practitioner hopes to arrive, the first being complete absorption in the act of breathing which empties the mind of any other thought, the second being the ability almost to cease to breathe which allegedly enables him to achieve marvellous feats of endurance; (5) *Pratyahara* or abstraction which means the mind's complete withdrawal from the world of sense; (6) *Dharana* in which an attempt is made to think of one thing only which finally becomes a repetition of the sacred syllable OM; (7) *dhyana*, meditation, which finally leads to (8) *Samadhi* the trance state which is a sign of the complete unity of soul with reality.

Yoga is very old, and when the sage Patanjali (*c.* 300 B.C.) composed the book containing these instructions, the *Yoga Sutras*, he was probably collecting from many ancient traditions. Some of the claims made by Yogis seem, to the Western mind, frankly incredible; but in the West Yoga methods have been used at the lower levels in order to gain improved self-control, better posture, and improved health.

Yom Kippur, the Day of Atonement, the final day of repentance begun at Rosh Hashanah, and the holiest day in the Jewish calendar. It is referred to as the Sabbath of Sabbaths and is typified by twenty-five hours of fasting. Prior to this is a feast with festival candles. Each individual must attempt to confess not only their sins to God, but ask forgiveness from others on the eve of Yom Kippur.

An important part of the *teshuvah* or repentance is the general confession in the synagogue. Readings will tell of the ancient atonement involving a scapegoat in Leviticus; Deuteronomy 30, and the prophetic book of Jonah. The message of all is God's infinite capacity to forgive even those who are undeserving. The last service of the day will end with the opening of the Shema, 'Hear O Israel, the Lord is our God, The Lord is One', and the triumphant cry of Elijah, 'The Lord, He is God'. The last act will be the blowing of the shofar to bring the fast to a close.

Z

Zen Buddhism, a Buddhist sect which is believed to have arisen in 6th cent. China but has flourished chiefly in Japan. The sect places absolute faith in a person's own inner being. Apparently the intention is that, so far from indulging in inward meditations or such practices as the Yogi uses, the student must learn to act spontaneously, without thinking, and without self-consciousness or hesitation.

This is the main purpose of the *koan*, the logically insoluble riddle which the pupil must try to solve. One such is the question put by master to pupil: "A girl is walking down the street, is she the younger or the older sister?" The correct answer, it seems, is to say nothing but put on a mincing gait, to *become* the girl, thus showing that what matters is the experience of being and not its verbal description. Another *koan* is "What is the Buddha?" "Three pounds of flax" is attributed to T'ungshan in the 9th cent. and a later authority's comment is that "none can excel it as regards its irrationality which cuts off all passages to speculation." Zen, in effect, teaches the uselessness of trying to use words to discuss the Absolute.

Zen came to Japan in the 13th cent., more than five centuries after Confucianism or the orthodox forms of Buddhism, and immediately gained acceptance whilst becoming typically Japanese in the process. One of the reasons why it appealed must have been that its spontaneity and insistence on action without thought, its emphasis on the uselessness of mere words, and such categories as logical opposites, had an inevitable attraction for a people given to seriousness, formality, and logic to a degree which was almost stifling. Zen must have been to the Japanese what nonsense rhymes and nonsense books, like those of Edward Lear and Lewis Carroll, were to the English intellectuals. Lear's limericks, like some of the *koans*, end up with a line which, just at the time when one expects a point to be made, has no particular point at all, and *Alice in Wonderland* is the perfect example of a world, not without logic, but with a crazy logic of its own which has no relationship with that of everyday life. Therefore Zen began to impregnate every aspect of life in Japan, and one of the results of its emphasis on spontaneous action rather than reason was its acceptance by the Samurai, the ferocious warrior class, in such activities as swordsmanship, archery, Japanese wrestling, and later Judo and the Kamikaze dive-bombers. But much of Japanese art, especially landscape gardening and flower-arrangement, was influenced similarly, and Zen is even used in Japanese psychiatry.

The very strict life of the Zen monks is based largely on doing things, learning through experience; the periods of meditation in the Zendo hall are punctuated by sharp slaps on the face administered by the abbot to those who are unsatisfactory pupils. Dr. Suzuki denies that Zen is nihilistic, but it is probably its appearance of nihilism and its appeal to the irrational and spontaneous which attracts the Western world at a time when to many the world seems without meaning and life over-regimented.

However, it has influenced such various aspects of Western life as philosophy (Heidegger), psychiatry (Erich Fromm and Hubert Benoit), writing (Aldous Huxley), and painting (Die Zen Gruppe in Germany).

Zionism, a belief in the need to establish an autonomous Jewish home in Palestine which, in its modern form, began with Theodor Herzl (1860–1904), a Hungarian journalist working in Vienna. Although Herzl was a more or less assimilated Jew, he was forced by the Dreyfus case and the pogroms in Eastern Europe to conclude that there was no real safety for the Jewish people until they had a state of their own. The Jews, of course, had always in a religious sense thought of Palestine as a spiritual homeland and prayed "next year in Jerusalem," but the religious had thought of this in a philosophical way as affirming old loyalties, not as recommending the formation of an actual state. Therefore Herzl was opposed both by many of the religious Jews and, at the other

extreme, by those who felt themselves to be assimilated and in many cases without religious faith. Even after the Balfour Declaration of 1917, there was not a considerable flow of Jews to Palestine, which at that time was populated mainly by Arabs. But the persecutions of Hitler changed all this and, after bitter struggles, the Jewish state was proclaimed in 1948. Today Zionism is supported by the vast majority of the Jewish communities everywhere. In the 1990s, a major exodus of Jews from Russia (made possible by the demise of the Soviet Union) introduced a new phase in the history of Zionism.

Zoroastrianism was at one time one of the great world religions. Under the Achaemenidae (*c.* 550–330 B.C.) Zoroastrianism was the state religion of Persia. Alexander's conquest in 331 B.C. brought disruption but the religion flourished again under the Sassanian dynasty (A.D. *c.* 226–640). With the advance of the Muslim Arabs in the 7th cent. Zoroastrianism finally gave way to Islam. A number of devotees fled to India there to become the Parsees (literally meaning "Persians in India"). In Iran itself a few scattered societies remain, perhaps numbering around 30,000 followers.

The name Zoroaster is the Greek rendering of Zarathustra, the prophet who came to purify the ancient religion of Persia. It is thought that he lived at the beginning of the 6th cent. B.C. He never claimed for himself divine powers but was given them by his followers.

The basis of Zoroastrianism is the age-long war between good and evil, Ahura Mazda heading the good spirits and Ahriman the evil ones. Morality is very important since by doing right the worshipper is supporting Ahura Mazda against Ahriman, and the evil-doers will be punished in the last days when Ahura Mazda wins his inevitable victory.

The sacred book of this religion is the *Avesta*. If Zoroastrianism has little authority today, it had a very considerable influence in the past. Its doctrines penetrated into Judaism (*q.v.*) and, through Gnosticism, Christianity. The worship of Mithra by the Romans was an impure version of Zoroastrianism. Manichaeism (*q.v.*) was a Zoroastrian heresy and the Albigensianism of mediaeval times was the last relic of a belief which had impressed itself deeply in the minds of men.

SPECIAL TOPICS

INTRODUCTION TO PHILOSOPHY

What is Philosophy?

In everyday speech the term 'philosophy' is often used informally to refer to general principles (as in a person's 'philosophy of life'), and this idea of generality also helps to define Philosophy as an intellectual, academic discipline. The philosopher is concerned with the fundamental structures and assumptions underlying particular areas of human knowledge and endeavour. As specialist branches of knowledge have developed, subjects which at one time would have been considered part of philosophy (such as the natural sciences and, more recently, psychology) have taken on their own identities. Philosophers have, however, continued to explore the conceptual foundations of these subjects—for example, philosophers of science debate such topics as the nature of scientific method and the status of scientific laws. If one phrase can summarise what philosophy is about, it might be 'the study of concepts'.

The Philosophical Tradition

The philosophical tradition in the West stretches back to the ancient Greeks. In the 20th century there has been a sharp division between the predominantly analytical approach of English-language philosophy and the more speculative attitude associated with 'continental philosophy' (although these labels involve an oversimplification—important influences on the development of analytical philosophy came from Austria, with Wittgenstein and the Vienna Circle). There now seems to be a greater willingness on the part of philosophers on both sides of this divide to learn from each other. It should also be noted that many non-Western cultures (those of China and India, for example) have their own rich philosophical traditions, and Western philosophers have begun to take a serious interest in these.

There are many areas of philosophy which could have been included in the brief account which follows—political philosophy, philosophy of language, philosophy of mind, philosophy of science, philosophy of mathematics, philosophy of religion. Some material relevant to these can be found elsewhere in the Ideas and Beliefs section. Those areas chosen illustrate the range of concerns in the subject, focusing as they do on reason (Logic), fundamental issues of facts about and knowledge of the world (Metaphysics, Epistemology), and questions of value (Ethics, Aesthetics).

Logic

Logic is the study of argument and reasoning. It deals with such concepts as proof, implication, inference, entailment, contradiction. Crucially, it is not the *content* of an argument but its *form* which interests the logician, not its *truth* but its *validity*. Traditionally an argument can be presented in the form of a syllogism with premisses and a conclusion, for example: 'All men are mortal' (premiss 1); 'Socrates is a man' (premiss 2); 'therefore Socrates is mortal' (conclusion). This is a valid argument, because it is not possible for the premisses to be true and the conclusion false—such is the definition of validity. It so happens that this particular argument in fact has true premisses and a true conclusion, but that is not the point. It is quite possible to have a valid argument consisting entirely of untrue statements: 'All swans are green; Socrates is a swan; therefore Socrates is green.' It is still the case in this example that *if* the premisses were true the conclusion *could not* be false. What both examples have in common is their form: 'All As are B; x is an A; therefore x is B', and it is this which guarantees their validity. It is one form of valid argument, but not the only one.

Now consider this argument: 'All men are mortal; Socrates is mortal; therefore Socrates is a man.' All the constituent statements are true but the argument is invalid (because the first premiss does not say that *only* men are mortal), as are all arguments

of the form 'All As are B; x is B; therefore x is an A'. (To see this more clearly, substitute 'swans/swan' for 'men/man', and you have an argument whose premisses are true and its conclusion false.) It is an example of a *fallacy*. (Fallacious reasoning is not infrequent in public life, and the ability to spot a fallacy is perhaps one of the more useful contributions that the study of logic can make to the formation of a politically sophisticated electorate!)

Inductive Logic

So far we have considered *deductive* logic, but much of our everyday reasoning is *inductive*. While deduction is concerned with logical necessity, induction involves types of reasoning in which the conclusions are strongly supported but not strictly implied by their premisses—reasoning which moves from evidence to a conclusion. An example might be: 'Five minutes ago when I passed the bus stop 30 people were waiting; now when I pass it no-one is waiting; therefore the bus has come and picked them up.' This is sensible reasoning, based upon experience and probability, but it is not deductively valid. (Incidentally, many of Sherlock Holmes's so-called deductions are actually inductive.) Induction is the typical procedure of the sciences (*see* **Baconian Method**).

Other topics covered in the study of logic include: quantification (the logic of the terms 'all', 'some', 'none'); names and descriptions, sense and reference; necessity and possibility; and paradoxes.

The Study of Logic

Historically the study of logic has developed in three periods in particular: in the 4th and 3rd centuries B.C. in ancient Greece (Aristotle, generally considered the founder of logic, being the major figure here, though important contributions were also made by a group of philosophers based at Megara and by the Stoics); in medieval times, especially at the Universities of Paris and Oxford, with such thinkers as Peter Abelard, Duns Scotus and William of Ockham; and in the 20th century beginning with the work of Gottlob Frege and Bertrand Russell around the turn of the century.

Modern logic (sometimes called mathematical logic) with its apparatus of symbols and its ability to deal with arguments of enormous complexity is a highly specialised discipline. It has found its most powerful practical application in the development of computing and information processing.

Metaphysics

Metaphysics is a central area of philosophy. It deals with fundamental questions regarding the ultimate nature of reality—questions lying beyond the purview of the natural sciences. For Aristotle, it was the investigation of 'being *qua* being'.

Characteristic metaphysical topics include ontology (what there is, the categories of existence), substance and properties (how does an apple 'as such' relate to its qualities of colour, flavour, texture, shape?), universals (why are two different things both apples? what do all green things have in common?), causation, personal identity. If some of these seem obscure, it should be pointed out that any kind of abstract reflection on the concepts which we use in relation to ourselves and the world can very easily give rise to metaphysical questions.

Personal Identity and Causation

To take two examples from the above list: (i) *personal identity* and (ii) *causation*. (i) What is a person? What is the 'I' to which sentences like 'I am tall', 'I am thinking', 'I can play the piano' refer? In what sense am I the same person now that I was 30 years ago? Questions of bodily continuity, consciousness, and memory are obviously involved here. Bearing in mind how important the concept of a person is in our moral and legal concerns, it is evident that these issues do relate to practical problems.

(ii) We use the concept of 'cause' all the time: 'the

moon causes the tides', 'the application of heat caused the water to boil', 'what was the cause of the accident?', 'what were the causes of World War I?'. But we do not in any given case observe x causing y: we observe x *followed* or *accompanied* by y. Is there then anything more to the concept of cause than the idea of regular, consistent correspondence? Does 'x causes y' simply *mean* that on all occasions where the circumstances are the same, x is followed or accompanied by y? David Hume, in *An Enquiry concerning Human Understanding* (1748), questioned the notion of cause as 'necessary connection': 'We cannot attain any definition, which may point out that circumstance in the cause, which gives it a connexion with its effect. We have no idea of this connexion; nor even any distinct notion what it is we desire to know, when we endeavour at a conception of it. We may, for example, that the vibration of this string is the cause of this particular sound. But what do we mean by that affirmation? We either mean, *that this vibration is followed by this sound, and that all similar vibrations have been followed by similar sounds*: Or, *that this vibration is followed by this sound, and that upon the appearance of one, the mind anticipates the senses, and forms immediately an idea of the other*. We may consider the relation of cause and effect in either of these two lights; but beyond these, we have no idea of it.'

Metaphysics: System or Description?

Metaphysics is often thought of as highly speculative—as involving the building of 'systems' by pure thought rather than on the basis of observation. Certainly this seems to be the case with, for example, Plato, the 17th-century Rationalists (Descartes, Spinoza, Leibniz) and later continental thinkers such as Hegel. This runs against the grain of the dominant empiricist, analytical tradition of English-language philosophy. However, in the last half-century, metaphysics has undergone something of a revival in the English-speaking world. The term 'descriptive metaphysics' (used by P.F. Strawson in his influential book *Individuals*, 1959) characterises the approach: not a speculative venture, but the application of rigorous analysis to elucidate the basic conceptual framework by which we understand and relate to the world.

Epistemology

Epistemology, or theory of knowledge, has been one of the principal areas of investigation throughout the history of Western philosophy. It deals with questions of knowledge, truth, belief, evidence and justification. Some of the main concerns of epistemology can be summarised as: the *definition*, the *basis*, and the *content* of knowledge.

Knowledge, in the sense of factual knowledge, has often been defined as 'justified true belief' (a definition which in essentials goes back to Plato's *Theaetetus*). My knowledge that Paris is the capital of France has three elements: (1) my *belief* that Paris is the capital of France; (2) the *truth* of the proposition that Paris is the French capital (I could not be held to *know* a false proposition, *e.g.* that Berlin is the capital of France, however strongly I might believe it); (3) a satisfactory *justification* of my belief (I might correctly believe that Paris is the capital of France, but if that belief were the result of, say, hypnotic suggestion, it would not count as knowledge). The third element, justification, has particularly been the subject of debate.

The Justification of Belief

Frequently, when asked to justify a belief, we appeal to other beliefs: my belief about the French capital is based upon beliefs about the existence of a large city called Paris, the governmental and constitutional arrangements of France, and so on. These beliefs in turn depend upon yet other beliefs. Is there a stopping-point in this process? To answer this question, the approach called *foundationalism* looks to an unassailable, 'self-evident' foundation which requires no further justification, finding it perhaps in *sense-perception*. In contrast, *coherentism* asserts that belief in a true proposition is justified by its forming part of a coherent system with other true beliefs—it is the coherence of the system as a whole which provides the justification.

What can I truly be said to *know*? My claims to knowledge take in such varied propositions as:

'2+2=4'; 'Paris is the capital of France'; 'The cat was sitting on the mat 15 minutes ago'. The sceptic might be happy with the first of these, but would question whether the other two count as knowledge. Characteristically the sceptic seeks the same level of certainty about the facts of the external world as seems to be available for statements in mathematics or logic—and not surprisingly, cannot find it. Statements about the external world are justified by different criteria from those of mathematics; but this does not mean that they lack justification. The value of epistemology lies not in attempting the hopeless task of 'proving' beyond any doubt that there 'really is' an external world of which I can have knowledge, but in the clarification of concepts and the critical analysis of claims and arguments about what is and can be known. In these tasks, however, an attitude of scepticism can be a useful starting-point. *See also* **Scepticism, Solipsism**.

Ethics

Ethics, or Moral Philosophy, is concerned with such issues as good and bad, right and wrong, obligation and responsibility; in short, with all aspects of human action and behaviour considered from the standpoint of *value*.

Three main types of ethical theory are often identified: *consequentialist ethics, deontological ethics* and *virtue ethics*. Although oversimplified, this categorisation provides a useful way into the subject. Consequentialism judges the goodness of an action by its results—the best known consequentialist theory is probably **Utilitarianism** (*q.v.*). The deontological view, classically represented by Immanuel Kant, is concerned with the nature of the act itself and the maxim which it embodies, and with concepts such as duty. Virtue ethics, whose history goes back to Aristotle, starts not from the act but from the agent, and emphasises the formation of the virtuous character. A simple illustration might be the morality of truth-telling: a consequentialist approach would judge the value of telling the truth by its consequences; a deontological argument would consider whether truth-telling is an obligation *per se*; virtue ethics would examine honesty as a desirable feature of a person's character.

Metaethics

Moral philosophers also concern themselves with the broad concepts and terminology of ethical theory—this aspect of the subject is sometimes called Metaethics. To pursue the above example: how is one to understand a sentence like 'truth-telling is good'? Is it in some way an objective statement of fact, which can be true or false? If so, on what grounds could we determine its truth or falsity? Or is it not really a factual statement at all, but an expression by the speaker of his/her approval of truth-telling? If so, why should it have any force for the rest of us?

Applied Ethics

At the other end of the scale from these rather abstract matters is the rapidly developing field of Applied Ethics—the practical application of ethical theory to actual moral problems arising in today's society. The current willingness of moral philosophers to engage with issues such as animal rights, abortion, the environment and the implications of genetic science is to be welcomed after a period in the mid-20th century when the analysis of moral language seemed to dominate the subject excessively in the English-speaking world.

Aesthetics

Aesthetics is the branch of philosophy concerned with the nature of art and the human response to art. Some aestheticians, for example Kant, have also applied the concept of aesthetic experience to the appreciation of beauty in the natural world.

Philosophical reflection on the arts goes back to Plato and Aristotle, but aesthetics emerged as a distinct field of enquiry in the 18th century, the term itself being coined by Alexander Baumgarten in his *Reflections on Poetry* (1735). He defined aesthetics as a study of sensory perception and its resultant feelings, considered as one branch of the study of knowledge—'the science of sensible knowledge'. This definition came to refer specifically to a methodological approach to the study of taste and of beauty. Baumgarten derived the term from the Greek *aisthanomai* ('to perceive') and this connection of aesthetics with the way humans experience in a sensory capacity, and the emotions which result from the experience, remains at the core of all subsequent theories.

The Definition of 'Art'

The development of this branch of philosophy coincided with the notion that there exists a category of 'the fine arts', which included painting, sculpture, poetry, music and dance. The definition of art and the debate as to what is to count as 'art' continue to be central issues in aesthetics. Attempts to classify artworks in terms of specific features such as form, expression, intention or representation look to the art object itself for a definition; an alternative approach to defining art can be sought by reference to human responses to the art object. Since the category of fine arts became established, new forms and media such as photography, film, television and computer art have developed, and many writers have sought to include them under the heading 'art'; this is an aspect of the continual process of redefining the category of artworks as a whole.

Aesthetic Value

The term *aestheticism* had its roots in late 18th- and early 19th-century German theory with such writers as Kant, Schiller and Goethe; it carries the implication that art is an end in itself, to be judged not by non-aesthetic criteria but in terms of 'aesthetic value'. This leads to the idea that criticism is not just a matter of individual taste but requires disinterested contemplation of the artwork at an 'aesthetic distance' The notion of 'art for art's sake' also led, in the Romantic period, to the conception of 'the artist' as being outside moral or political standards of judgement. Modern aesthetic argument, on the other hand, questions the assumption that the value of art should be independent of moral or political criteria; some theorists argue for the elimination of 'aesthetic value' altogether as a criterion for judgement and dispute the autonomy of the 'fine arts'. In addition, many non-Western cultures do not recognise an autonomous concept of 'art' or those features which Western philosophy uses to classify works of art. An increasing interest in issues outside the Western tradition therefore challenges our most basic concepts of the artwork and prompts constant rethinking of the question 'what is art?'

NEW RELIGIOUS MOVEMENTS

Introduction

The term new religious movement (NRM) refers mainly to any group or belief system which has emerged in the twentieth century. They are mostly to be found in the Developed World. Many are breakaway sects from the Western Monotheistic Tradition, or developments of Eastern Religions and philosophies, and might be described as 'splinter groups'. Others are imbued with Paganism, Spiritualism, Psychology or even elements of Science Fiction and show few similarities to mainstream established religion. What must be remembered is that this broad classification refers to a huge diversity of alternative religions.

The term 'cults' is often used as a description for NRMs. This has become popularist and negative as a synonym, and is used widely in the media and by groups who are opposed to the alleged abuses of some NRMs. It is estimated that there are around five hundred New Religious Movements active in the United Kingdom, and four times as many in the United States. Japan, however, is at the centre of the growth in new religions where it is believed that there are up to forty thousand emerging groups.

Common Features

There are several features which might well be apparent in a New Religious Movement (at least in some of the less scrupulous). It may use coercion in order to attract members, and indoctrination of its belief system in order to retain them. It may have at its basis a sense of elitism, exclusivity, or divine ordination. It may have a charismatic, self-appointed leader who may claim divinity and may require absolute and unquestioning authority. It is likely to be self-funding, and may use dubious methods in order to raise membership or funds. These features, however, are far from universal and may be totally anathema to many new religious movements. As a grouping they are more likely to be observed in NRMs which have no direct links to established religions.

Owing to the breadth and sensitive nature of this topic, this article neither claims to be comprehensive, nor to make judgements on the groups mentioned. It does however provide a glimpse into some of the most famous individual New Religious Movements both past and present.

Brahma Kumaris

Brahma Kumaris World Spiritual University is largely a meditation movement which caters for women, Brahma being the Creator within the Hindu Trimurti and 'kumaris' meaning young woman. Its founder was Dada Lekh Raj, a Hindu man who was born into a poor family, but after a successful career as a jeweller, had a profound religious experience in 1936 at the age of sixty. His visions gave him a new insight into the human condition, the soul, the nature of God and of the future destruction of the earth by mankind. He held meetings under the name Om Mandli, 'The Gathering of Om', the sacred Hindu sound and symbol, which were mostly attended by women.

Under the direction of their founder, the women took charge of the organisation and began to assert their independence from traditional society, rejecting arranged marriages in favour of celibacy and asceticism. Although linked to the main Hindu teachings of karma and reincarnation, Brahma Kumaris focus on dealing with the problems living in the present. Indeed, their meditation occurs with eyes open, seeking calm and tranquillity from focusing on the 'third eye' of another person. Recognised globally for their impact on community and humanitarian issues, one of the key beliefs of the movement is 'When we change, the world changes'.

Friends of the Western Buddhist Order

The FWBO was set up in 1967 by an English Buddhist monk Sangharakshita who, born Dennis Lingwood, had become a Buddhist at the age of 16 and travelled to India during World War 2. The story of his experiences has become part of FWBO legend, and details his absconding from the army and his exposure over twenty years to the great teachers of the three main schools of Buddhism, of which his path is a synthesis. Followers are able to take from any of the traditions those teachings which best apply to their spiritual growth in the West. The centres focus on meditation, one form of which is 'the development of unlimited friendliness.' They also place an emphasis on charitable giving and on 'Right Livelihood' ethical employment. Problems have arisen over the individual governance of centres, as well as its liberal attitudes towards homosexuality in the past. All of the Friends' activities are single sex based, which has at times led to accusations of gender bias and misogynism stemming from Sangharakshita's teaching that men are more spiritually advanced than women.

ISKON (Hare Krishna)

The International Society for Krishna Consciousness was founded by His Divine Grace Bhaktivedanta Swami Prabhupada shortly after his arrival in the United States in 1965, and is one of the best known and most visible new religious movements. He had been charged by Bhakti Siddhanta, the leader of the Hindu revivalist Gaudiya Mission to take Krishna consciousness to the West (although it took 26 years for him to begin his mission). The movement reached Britain in 1968, and was heavily sponsored by its links with Beatles' guitarist George Harrison. As in America, ISKON immediately found a following with young people and became associated with those who had been involved in the hippie drug culture of the Sixties. At the centre of ISKON lies Prabhupada's translation of the Bhagavad Gita, the central section of the epic Sanskrit poem, the Mahabarata.

ISKON regard Krishna as the original and most important *avatar* or appearance of the god Vishnu and follow a monotheistic form of Hinduism known as Vaishnavism, or Vishnu worship. Krishna is not only the sustaining force of the universe, but can be described as the Supreme Godhead. ISKON focuses on devotion to Krishna as a young man, and on the chanting of his mantra, repeating his name accompanied by cymbals and drums in order to reach a blissful and loving understanding of God in this life.

A great emphasis is placed on the individual's response to God, and as such whilst many devotees shave their heads, they retain a pigtail as a symbol of their own identity.

Followers who enter the *ashram* or communities lead a very ascetic lifestyle which includes a ban on sex unless on a restricted basis for procreation within marriage. Followers are directed to find their pleasure through spiritual activity. Although the presence of ISKON is much less noticeable today, they run a charity Food for Life which distributes free vegetarian food around the globe. Although some are still critical of ISKON's conversion tactics, lack of gender equality and the movement's history of bad publicity following the 'deviations' and abuses of power of some senior officials, ISKON regards itself as a progressive organisation which has adapted to change and dealt with controversy since the death of Prabhapada in 1977.

International Church of Christ

An offshoot of The Church of Christ, an established evangelical denomination in the United States to which the ICOC now has no ties, this organisation has attracted much attention in recent years. It was founded by Kip McKean, an evangelist who had enjoyed much success as part of a Florida-based Crossroads mission team. He set up his own church, the Boston Church of Christ in 1979. Its first activity outside the United States was the 'planting' of the London Church of Christ in 1982. The Church is strongly evangelical, and believes that salvation is strictly to be found within its walls. Christians who join must be re-baptised into an ICOC Church. The Church specifically targets students. The mission of the Church is to 'seek and save the lost', and believes that a great deal of love and attention should be given to members. New members are often offered accommodation by the Church and all members follow a programme known as 'discipling' or 'shepherding' whereby a younger member is closely linked to a more experienced member throughout the Church hierarchy. There have been disagreements about the level of obedience required, and the level of the authority that personal pastors hold.

The Church regards itself as a family, and spiritual accountability is important. Forgiveness for sin is closely related to discipline for unrepentant sinners, and the Church has again been criticised for its writing of 'sin lists' on members' behaviour. The salvation and spiritual welfare of every member is of paramount importance to the ICOC, so breaking of contact with the Church can be problematic and lengthy.

Jesus Fellowship Church (Jesus Army)

A very well publicised movement, the Jesus Army began in the late 1960s when Noel Stanton, a Baptist minister and some members of his small Northamptonshire church were baptised with the Holy Spirit and began to be able to speak in tongues, heal and preach with new conviction. Although it has been expelled from the Evangelical Alliance, it regards itself as a mainstream branch of reformed, evangelical and charismatic Christianity, and follows orthodox Christian belief. Around a quarter of members live in communities which provide them with jobs and accommodation. All members are regarded as equal, and the assets belong to the community. Each house within the community operates a 'common purse' arrangement of pooled income, and strict accounts are kept.

The communities are serious and ascetic, with no television or radio and even Christian festivals are not observed owing to their pagan origins. Children are strictly disciplined, and corporal punishment is used in some forms. Celibacy is highly valued. All relationships have to be approved by the Church authorities, and married couples adopt the use of separate beds. The Jesus Fellowship Church also follows traditional gender roles in terms of status and Church leadership. Unlike many NRMs, the Jesus Army accepts members into their communities only over the age of 21 and following a probationary period of two years. They are, however, a visible presence on city streets, and are involved in evangelising and a wide form of social care particularly amongst the homeless and those suffering from drug or alcohol abuse.

New Kadampa Tradition

Deriving from the Tibetan Buddhist tradition, this organisation is well known for controversy, not least opposition from mainstream Buddhists including His Holiness the Dalai Lama. It was officially founded in 1991 by Geshe Kelsang Gyatso after he severed links with an existing Mahayana Buddhist centre of which he had been spiritual director. It takes its name from an influential eleventh century school, and advocates the integration of all of the Buddha's teachings with the special teachings of the Kadampas known as the 'Stages of the Path'. It claims not to reinvent, but to make Buddhism appropriate for the needs and state of the modern world, although much study is based on the writings of Geshe Kelsang himself.

The movement is critical of the Dalai Lama for what they see as an unnecessary authority, and for his adoption of teachings from all four Tibetan schools rather than simply the 'pure' tradition of the Kadampas. A further dispute relates to the worship in the NKT of the protector deity Dorje Shugdan whom some Buddhists regard as unpredictable, dangerous and as a source of bad publicity for the Tibetan Buddhist cause.

Universal Church of the Kingdom of God

Founded in Rio de Janeiro by Edir Macedo in 1977, this charismatic evangelical church is well-known for its strong financial power known as prosperity theology or seed-faith giving whereby the more a member gives to God, the more He will return to them. Miracles, exorcisms and faith-healings are also prominent facets of the Church's hugely attended services. Known as 'deliverance ministry', the movement emphasises its ability to free members from malignant spirits which take a variety of forms from disease to substance misuse. Although little is known about the organisation owing to their desire to avoid publicity, some critics have commentated on allegations that leaders have been involved in financial irregularity, lavish spending and sexual promiscuity. It continues to face adverse attention in Brazil and the United States, but is growing in the UK, where it purchased London's Rainbow Theatre as a base in 1995.

Vineyard

Begun in 1982 in the USA, as an offshoot of the Calvary Chapel Movement whose message had been directed to Sixties hippies, Vineyard has an emphasis on gifts of the spirit such as prophecy, healing and speaking in tongues. It was founded by former Righteous Brothers keyboardist John Wimber and another Calvary pastor Kenn Gulliksen, and has attracted members through its balance of lively and contemplative musical worship.

It is best known however, for its recent disassociation with one of its churches. The Toronto Airport Vineyard Church has attracted much attention for its practise of the Toronto Blessing during services. First beginning in 1994, it occurs at the climactic point of worship where people spontaneously burst into tears, produce laughter, shouting, unknown language and in particular, fall to the floor in a state of spiritual unconsciousness, 'slain by the spirit'. It has been 'exported' to churches around the globe by those who have experienced it. It has been heavily criticised for its hysteria and lack of meaning, as well as being a tool of social conditioning. The Toronto Blessing has been performed in London's famous but criticised evangelical Anglican Church, Holy Trinity, Brompton.

Aum Shrinrikyo

The Supreme Truth Society or Aum Shrinrikyo

was founded officially in 1987 in Japan by partially sighted Shoko Asahara who had changed his name following a spiritual enlightenment. Although primarily Buddhist, it contained elements of Hinduism in Shiva worship and Christian Apocalyptic teaching. Its aim was to free its followers through knowledge from the impending destruction of the Earth, transferring negative energy to positive. Politically and legally astute, Asahara successfully won several lawsuits early on to protect his organisation, following attacks from members' families who were sceptical of the need for adherents to break all social ties.

Following increasing pressure from the Japanese government and press which rendered the organisation politically powerless, Asahara began to prepare for the end and ordered the building of nuclear shelters, increasing the organisation's isolation. A chemical weapons programme was developed to protect the group and sarin attacks took place on prominent judges and lawyers. In March 1995 the Tokyo subway attack was directed at civilians which promted a rapid response from the government including the arrest of Asahara himself. In 1999, the organisation accepted responsibility for the attack, offering a public apology and compensation. Although it still exists in some form, the group has vowed to change and disassociated itself with Asahara, whilst still following some of his teachings. He remains in prison charged with several counts of murder, kidnap and subverting justice.

Branch Davidians

A splinter group from Seventh Day Adventism, the organisation was first founded by Victor Houteff whose apocalyptic interpretations of the books of Daniel and Revelation caused his expulsion from the movement, known originally as the Shepherd's Rod, and later after their migration from Los Angeles to Waco, as the Davidian Seventh-day Adventists. Following his death and the failure of the Second Coming to materialise in 1959, various fragmentations occurred, one led by Benjamin Roden known as the Branch Davidians. In 1986 there was a tense struggle for power within the movement eventually bringing to power Vernon Howell, who changed his name to David Koresh, after the legendary kings of Israel and Persia.

The main tenets of the group continued to be Saturday worship and a belief in the imminent return of Christ, but this latter belief was hastened by Koresh who viewed himself as the messenger of the Apocalypse, with the power to break the Seventh Seal described in the Book of Revelation. He was regarded as supremely authoritative in the movement for his charisma, biblical knowledge and powerful preaching. His followers spent much time in the construction of the ranch at Mount Carmel in Waco, including an underground shelter, and Koresh gave himself the right to sleep with any female in the community, some as young as twelve.

Increasingly isolated from the outside world, the compound was raided by the Bureau of Alcohol, Tobacco and Firearms in February 1993, looking for illegal weapons. Following unexpected resistance and the failure of questionable 'hastening' methods, the FBI used tanks and CS gas to bring the siege to an end. The stockpile of weapons in the compound exploded, killing over eighty of the community. Only nine members survived. The FBI's involvement in the tragedy continues to be questioned.

Elan Vital (Divine Light Mission)

Originally known as the Divine Light Mission, set up by Shri Hans Ji Maharaj in Delhi in 1960, this movement came to prominence when it was taken over by his son, eight year old Prem Pal Singh Rawat in 1966. At 13, as Guru Maharaj Ji, he embarked on a world tour, married his American secretary at 16, and lived what some critics have described as a luxury lifestyle. He soon dropped the eastern influences, favouring more universal teachings for a global audience, changing the name to Elan Vital in 1983. Unlike some NRMs where leaders crave absolute power, Maharaji renounced his status as Lord of the Universe, stopped communal living, reduced the authority of spiritual leaders and decentralised the structure of the organisation. He did, however, in 1987, take on sole responsibility for the teaching of the Knowledge. This refers to the state of true joy experienced through complete understanding of self, and is focused on this one life,

rather than on subsequent lives or states.

There is little doctrine, and the emphasis lies on developing subjectively through four forms of meditation, appealing more to the emotional rather than the intellectual. Although non-theistic, references are made to the god within. Elan Vital makes much of claiming that its teachings are free of charge, does not consider itself a religion as such, and exists in the UK as an educational charity.

Heaven's Gate

This doomsday movement is well known for the death of 39 of its members in San Diego, California in 1997. Founded by Marshall Herff Applewhite or Do in 1975, the teaching focused on a form of Gnostic dualism whereby human beings contained a divine spirit trapped within a bodily prison which sought release. Through Applewhite's teaching which combined elements of New Age spirituality with science fiction, members could progress through stages of development towards freedom. The message centred on a group of extra-terrestrials who came to earth from the Kingdom of Heaven 2000 years ago. One of these was Do who on his second mission began to disseminate the beliefs.

There was also a highly significant apocalyptic motif which led to the mass assisted suicide. In particular they emphasised a passage in the Book of Revelation which described witnesses who were killed, remained dead for three and a half days, and were then revived and 'taken up'. Members lived celibate monastic lifestyles and Do amongst them submitted to voluntary castration in preparation for their next existence. On the approach of Comet Hale-Bopp in March 1997, cult members believed that behind it was travelling an alien spacecraft. Through 'Scientific Remote Viewing' they were able to make contact, and believed that the craft had come to take their spirits away. In video tapes, they documented their pleasure at their approaching salvation. Not all members had the courage to take their lives, but all who did were adults including Applewhite himself who seem to have acted of their own volition with no external pressure.

Although Applewhite's teachings are still distributed by some, not least because the organisation used the Internet as a business and recruitment tool, the movement is no longer significantly active.

Order of the Solar Temple

Over a period of three years between 1994 and 1997, over seventy people belonging to the Solar Temple committed suicide in Switzerland, France and Canada. It was founded in 1984 in Quebec by Luc Jouret, a charismatic homeopathist, absorbing the Foundation Golden Way led by Joseph Di Mambro. It was broadly Masonic, combining Neo-Templar esotericism with the highly secret teachings of the Rosicrucian Order. Di Mambro convinced members that in a previous life he had been a member of the fourteenth century Knights Templar. The Order of the Solar Temple was the inner sanctum of the organisation. Like many Masonic orders, its members came from the upper strata of society.

Tensions erupted over leadership, and claims that Di Mambro faked spiritual experiences during ceremonies and invented mythology and authority for the group. He claimed that his daughter had been divinely conceived, and was the spiritually important 'cosmic child'. Moreover, members were arrested for attempting to buy illegal weapons, and the group were heavily implicated in the murder of a family whose baby they believed to be the Antichrist. Their teachings focused on the Apocalypse due in 1994, and much of the group's imagery was associated with fire and death. It was this which led them to arson as one means of suicide alongside poison, narcotics and shooting. They believed that at the End Time, they would reunite with the Source, linked to the star Sirius, and be given invisible solar bodies. The organisation continues to operate in Canada and worldwide.

The Unification Church (Moonies)

Better known to outsiders as the Moonies, the Unification Church is part of a larger organisation now known as the Family Federation for World Peace and Unification. Its founder was the Reverend Sun Myung Moon, who in 1936 at the age of 16, had a vision of Christ who told him to further God's Kingdom on Earth. Following intensive personal prayer and study, he began preaching in 1945. Following release from Communist imprisonment in North Korea, he founded the Unification Church in 1954. The group continue to be anti-communist and have been linked to several right-wing politicians around the globe. They have significant business interests and own the *Washington Times* amongst other companies. Moon himself has been prosecuted for tax evasion and is criticised for the scale of his personal fortune. The Church also has a charity wing, the International Relief Friendship Foundation and sponsors many cultural enterprises.

In 1959, the Church expanded abroad, using young people to raise the profile, finances and recruitment by selling flowers and candles on the street. The Church was particularly accused of 'love-bombing' new recruits into full membership. Amongst its main tenets is the authority of Moon's own publication *Discourse on the Principle* or *Divine Principle* as equal to the Bible. One key principle is the understanding of the Fall in which Eve has sex with the fallen angel Lucifer and then with Adam in repentance. It is this abuse of love which caused mankind's separation from God. Jesus was sent to restore the ideal family, the Church's Trinity of God, Man and Woman, by having a family rather than in death and resurrection. His failure required the resending of the Messiah, Moon himself, to establish the perfect marriage, although he has had between two and four wives.

Despite these claims, the Church believes that neither Jesus nor Moon is God, but that they are prophets. Mass arranged marriages with partners selected by Moon have become the hallmark of the movement, although they are not legally binding. Ritual dictates how love should be made in the initial days of marriage, symbolically re-establishing God's plan.

People's Temple

This NRM is famed for being responsible for the largest mass suicide in American religious history. In November 1978, 918 members of the People's Temple Christian Church under the leadership of James 'Jim' Warren Jones died. In 1954, aged 23, Jones began to preach at a local Pentecostal Tabernacle in Indianapolis, but following disputes over his recognition of African Americans, he left to found his own church. It was designed to be a utopian blend of Pentecostal Christianity with Communism.

Jones himself claimed to be the Messiah and to have the gifts of prophecy and healing. He practised a form of indoctrination on new members known as 'catharsis' involving confessional and public physical punishment. Loyalty tests also involved signing documents claiming to have committed various illegal, often sexual, acts. Jones forced both men and women to have sex with him, although he claimed to be the only true heterosexual. Through infidelity, he hoped to achieve absolute fidelity to himself alone and to create a multiracial society. Indeed, it was the Church's anti-racist stance which brought it most early attention and forced the group to move around until eventually they fled to land in Guyana with the support of the black minority socialist government.

The agricultural commune became known as Jonestown and here Jones exchanged worship for politics. There was much dispute about conditions there and Concerned Relatives, an organisation which had been set up to combat the Church, lobbied the State Department to visit the compound and release those who wished to leave. California Congressman Leo. J Ryan headed the delegation.

Despite lengthy and positive exchanges, on his departure, members of the community opened fire killing Ryan and four others. Despite plans to flee to the Soviet Union, Jones claimed that the end had come, and that 'revolutionary suicide' was the only answer. Members were injected in their sleep, or drank from a vat of potassium cyanide, mixed with tranquilisers and sedatives. Jones himself died from a gunshot wound. An autopsy failed to resolve whether or not it was self-inflicted.

Nation of Islam

The origins of the Nation of Islam (NOI) can be traced back to Noble Drew Ali, born Timothy Drew, who set up the Moorish Science Temple of America in 1926 on the principle that the black people of the United States could only be united by Islam. In 1930, Master Fard Muhammed, claiming to be Drew's reincarnation, set up the Lost-Found Nation of Islam preaching freedom, equality and the idea that America's blacks were a lost tribe of Muslims known as the Shabazz.

Upon Fard's disappearance in 1934, the movement was taken over by the Honourable Elijah Muhammad who was responsible for much of the theology of the movement, as well as its opposition to the Second World War, for which he was imprisoned until 1946. They have a distinct mythology which regards black people as the original races, and white people as the creation of an evil scientist named Yakub. Based on an interpretation of Ezekiel's eschatological vision, at the end time the black races will have a final victory over their oppressors.

In the 1950s the well known civil rights activist Malcolm X became a prominent member but his emphasis on traditional Islam as opposed to radical new Black Islam led to his assassination by NOI members in 1965. This led within the next decade, to a major examination of the movement, in particular by Wallace D. Muhammad, the son of Elijah Muhammad. He changed the name to the American Muslim Mission, linking it to more mainstream Islam, and dropped many of the racially exclusive policies.

The gap which this left was exploited by Louis Farrakhan, a senior NOI member, who broke with Wallace Muhammad in 1978, and re-founded the Nation of Islam. Farrakhan turned his organisation increasingly militant once more, reinstating a strict dress code, and the personal security force known as the Fruit of Islam. The Million Man March in Washington D.C. in 1995 notably raised the profile of the movement, although subsequently Farrakhan was denied entry to Britain on the grounds that his visit would incite racial tension.

Opus Dei

This ultra orthodox Roman Catholic movement was founded in 1928 by a Spanish priest, Monsignor Josemaria Escriva de Balaguer y Albas, and has increasingly found media attention in recent years. It has been heavily criticised for its authoritarian attitudes towards its members and is regarded by some as a church within a church, with a significant amount of Vatican power. Critics view it in almost cultic terms emphasizing accounts of self-mortification, gender separation, youth recruitment and the inability to break ties with the movement. It has also been challenged over its zealous desire to canonize its founder. Its strong membership amongst the clergy as well as the support of Pope John Paul II has given it much credibility, and many regard it as a way to live out their Catholic faith through receiving spiritual support and by understanding better the doctrines of the Church.

It considers itself to be in total agreement with Catholic teachings. Unlike the rest of the Church, it has no official geographical boundaries, and is united through membership. Around a third of members are 'numeraries' who live apart in single gender communities and take vows of celibacy. Although their income does not go directly to Opus Dei, they make serious financial commitments to the work of the Catholic Church. Other 'associates' live celibate lives outside residences, although some members may be married and live within the wider community.

GAZETTEER OF THE WORLD

An index and guide to the maps with up-to-date descriptive matter. Each year the Gazetteer is amended to record recent place name changes, new boundaries and frontiers, as well as revised population figures as they become available. The section concludes with a glossary of modern geographical terms.

GAZETTEER OF THE WORLD

Physical Features.

In using the gazetteer the reader should note that it is impossible to make absolutely correct measurements of geographical phenomena. For example, measurement of height of land above sea-level depends, in the first instance, upon the definition of the elusive concept of sea-level itself. This is constantly changing and so an arbitrary value of *mean sea-level* is normally used, but the value adopted varies from country to country. As a result, height above sea level has inbuilt inconsistencies and inaccuracies. Similarly, the length of a river will depend upon the scale of the survey from which measurements are made. Large-scale maps and aerial photographs can show in great detail the sinuous course of rivers, whereas a map on a smaller scale must reduce the amount of information shown and thereby the apparent length.

Definition of Urban Area.

An even more difficult problem of measurement relates to the definition of the urban area of a town or city. It is possible to define the extent of urban areas in three major ways, by using (1) the administrative area, (2) the physically built-up area, and (3) the socio-geographic, metropolitan area. This latter concept is in many ways the most meaningful for it relates to the notion that a city exerts a strong influence over the population resident beyond its administrative or built-up boundary. For example, the city may provide employment opportunities or shopping and entertainment facilities for a population resident some distance away from it. In order to define "city" in these terms some means of measuring the degree of connection between it and its surrounding hinterland (the city-region) must be found and, needless to say, there is considerable disagreement among workers in this field as to what are the most suitable criteria to use. Different criteria produce different definitions and even the most recent measurements are soon obsolete.

The population figures given in the gazetteer normally relate to the city's administrative area. In the case of some large cities two figures are given—(1) for the administrative city, and (2) for the more extensive metropolitan area which surrounds and includes the administrative city. In cases in which this figure is more meaningful or in which recent population figures for the administrative area are not available, only the population for the metropolitan area of a city or town is given.

Place Names.

Where there have been recent changes in place names, the new name is used with the old name in brackets and a cross reference from old to new. The adoption of new names increased in the 1990s with the fall of communism. Towns and cities have abandoned their Soviet names (*e.g.* Leningrad is now St. Petersburg). Elsewhere change continues. Zaïre has reverted to Congo. New provinces (such as Gauteng and Mpumalanga) have been created in South Africa, where Pretoria has now been renamed Tshwane. New states have been established within Nigeria. In India, Bombay has become Mumbai, Calcutta has become Kolkata. In 2003 Yugoslavia formally changed its name to Serbia–Montenegro (and in 2006 Montenegro and Serbia became separate independent republics).

Industries.

In many countries (not least Britain) old industries are gradually fading away. Because the gazetteer aims to be in part a historical guide, mention of these industries has been retained (even though the factories may have closed).

Population Figures.

Total population figures from a census count are no longer regarded as necessarily more accurate than estimates arrived at by other methods. The useful-ness of censuses lies rather in the additional information which they provide. Even so, some countries like the Netherlands have given up censuses altogether. The gazetteer therefore no longer distinguishes between census figures and estimates but reliable figures from whatever source. For smaller towns, population figures below 20,000 are not usually given here.

New Cities.

To celebrate the Millennium, three places were granted city status. These were Inverness, Wolverhampton and Brighton & Hove. Five more cities were created to mark the 2002 Golden Jubilee. These were Preston, Newport (in Gwent), Stirling and, in Northern Ireland, Lisburn and Newry. In the previous 40 years, the only cities to be created were Swansea (1969), Derby (1977), Sunderland (1992) and, in 1994, Armagh and St. Davids.

Census 2001.

The last official census in the United Kingdom took place on 29 April 2001 (the census is normally held at 10-year intervals, the previous census being in 1991). For summary details, *see* **K163**.

Local Government Reorganisation.

The eight counties of Wales were replaced on 1 April 1996 by 22 unitary authorities and the 12 regions of Scotland by 32 unitary authorities. Thirteen English unitary authorities were also created on that date, with a further 13 being created on 1 April 1997. The process was completed on 1 April 1998.

It is very difficult within the confines of short entries to make clear the complexity of these changes. In Scotland, for example, the name Angus has now been used for a historic county (until 1974), for a local government district within the Tayside Region (until 31 March 1996), and for a new unitary authority from 1 April 1996. On each occasion the area denoted by the name has changed. The new unitary authority called City of Dundee is not the same as the burgh of Dundee nor the same as the local government district of Dundee which it replaces.

International Time-Table (GMT).

The following table gives times around the world.

Place	Time h	Place	Time h
Adelaide	21 30	Malta	13 00
Amsterdam	13 00	Mauritius	16 00
Ankara	14 00	Melbourne	22 00
Athens	14 00	Montreal	07 00
Auckland (NZ)	24 00	Moscow	15 00
Beijing	20 00	Nairobi	15 00
Belgrade	13 00	New York	07 00
Berlin	13 00	Oslo	13 00
Bombay	17 30	Ottawa	07 00
(Mumbai)		Panama	07 00
Brisbane	22 00	Paris	13 00
Brussels	13 00	Perth (WA)	20 00
Budapest	13 00	Prague	13 00
Buenos Aires	09 00	Quebec	07 00
Cairo	14 00	Rangoon	18 30
Calcutta	17 30	Rio de Janeiro	09 00
(Kolkata)		Rome	13 00
Cape Town	14 00	San Francisco	04 00
Chicago	06 00	St. John's (NF)	08 30
Copenhagen	13 00	Singapore	20 00
Gibraltar	13 00	Stockholm	13 00
Helsinki	14 00	Sydney	22 00
Hobart	22 00	Tehran	15 30
Hong Kong	20 00	Tokyo	21 00
Istanbul	14 00	Toronto	07 00
Jerusalem	14 00	Vancouver	04 00
London	12 00	Vienna	13 00
Madeira	12 00	Winnipeg	06 00
Madrid	13 00	Yokohama	21 00

ABBREVIATIONS USED IN THE GAZETTEER

GEOGRAPHICAL NAMES

Ala. = Alabama
Ark. = Arkansas
Atl. Oc. = Atlantic Ocean
B.C. = British Columbia
BEF = British Expeditionary Forces
Brit. = British
Cal. = California
CERN = European Centre for Nuclear Research
Col. = Colorado
Conn. = Connecticut
Del. = Delaware
Eng. = England
E.U. = European Union
Fla. = Florida
Fr. = French
Ga. = Georgia
Ill. = Illinois
Ind. = Indiana
Kan. = Kansas
Ky. = Kentucky
La. = Louisiana

Land = prov. (Germany)
Mass. = Massachusetts
Md. = Maryland
Me. = Maine
Mich. = Michigan
Minn. = Minnesota
Miss. = Mississippi
Mo. = Missouri
Mont. = Montana
NATO = North Atlantic Treaty Organisation
N.C. = North Carolina
N.D. = North Dakota
Neth. = Netherlands
N.H. = New Hampshire
N.J. = New Jersey
N.M. = New Mexico
N.S.W. = New South Wales
N.T. = Northern Territory (Australia)
N.Y. = New York
N.Z. = New Zealand
Okla. = Oklahoma

OPEC = Organization of Petroleum Exporting Countries
Ore. = Oregon
Pac. Oc. = Pacific Ocean
Penns. = Pennsylvania
R.I. = Rhode Island
R.o.I. = Republic of Ireland
S.C. = South Carolina
Scot. = Scotland
S.D. = South Dakota
SHAPE = Supreme Headquarters, Allied Powers, Europe
Tenn. = Tennessee
U.K. = United Kingdom
U.N. = United Nations
USA = United States of America
Va. = Virginia
Vt. = Vermont
Wash. = Washington
W.I. = West Indies
Wis. = Wisconsin
Wyo. = Wyoming

OTHER ABBREVIATIONS

a. = area
admin. = administrative
agr. = agriculture
alt. = altitude
anc. = ancient
arch. = archaeological
a.s.l. = above sea-level
ass. = associated
auth. = authority
aut. rep. = autonomous republic
bdr. = border
bdy. = boundary
bldg. = building
bor. = borough
C. = cape
c. = city; circa, c. = about
can. = canton
cap. = capital
cas. = castle
cath. = cathedral
C.B. = county borough
ch. = chief
cm = centimetres
co. = county
col. = colony
colly. = colliery
comm. = commercial
conurb. = conurbation
cst. = coast
ctr. = centre
cty. = country
dep. = department
dist. = district
div. = division
E. = east or easterly
elec. = electrical
engin. = engineering
esp. = especially
exp. = exports

F. = firth
Fed. = Federation
fed. = federal
fish. pt. = fishing port
fortfd. = fortified
G. = Gulf
gen. = general
G.N.P. = gross national product
gr. = great, group
gtr. = greater
ha = hectares
hgst. = highest
I. = island
impt. = important
inc. = including
indep. = independent
inds. = industries
industl. = industrial
Is. = Islands
km = kilometres
km² = square kilometres
L. = lake
l. = length
lgo. = large
l. gov. = local government
lgst. = largest
lt. = light
m = metres
machin. = machinery
M.B. = metropolitan borough
met. a. = metropolitan area
met. co. = metropolitan county
mftg. = manufacturing
mkg. = making
mkt. = market
mm = millimetres
mnfs. = manufactures
mng. = mining

mtn. = mountain
mun. = municipality
N. = north or northerly
nat. = national
non-met. co = non-metropolitan county
nr. = near
p. = population
par. = parish
penin. = peninsula
pref. = prefecture
prin. = principal
prod. = product
prot. = protectorate
prov. = province
pt. = port
R. = river
rep. = republic
residtl. = residential
rly. = railway
S. = south or southerly
shipbldg. = shipbuilding
sm. = small
spt. = seaport
st. = state
sta. = station
sub. = suburb
t. = town
terr. = territory
tr. = trade
trib. = tributary
U.D. = urban district
unit. = unitary
univ. = university
v. = village
W. = west or westerly
wat. pl. = watering place
wkg. = working
wks. = works
wkshps. = workshops

A

Aachen (Aix-la-Chapelle), t., N. Rhine-Westphalia, **Germany**; anc. spa t. in coal-field dist.; industl., route ctr.; contains tomb of Charlemagne; p. (2002) 245,778.

Aalen, t., Baden-Württemberg, **Germany**; on R. Kocher; iron, textiles, lens mkg.; p. (2002) 66,559.

Aalst (Alost), t., E. Flanders, **Belgium**, 24 km N.W. Brussels; industl., comm. ctr. at rly. junc.; agr. tr.; p. (1991) 76,380.

Aarau, t., cap. of Aargau can., **Switzerland**.

Aare, R., **Switzerland**; flows through Brienz and Thun Ls., thence into Rhine; Aare gorges above Meiringen; lgst R. wholly in Switzerland, 290 km long.

Aargau, can., N. **Switzerland**; occupies lower Aare R. valley; agr. in valleys, wooded uplands; cap. Aarau; a. 1,404 km²; p. (1000) 496,300.

Aba, t., **Nigeria**, N.E. of Pt. Harcourt; mkt., palm oil processing; p. (1992) 270,500.

Abaco, Gt., I., **Bahamas, W.I.**; sheltered harbours, yachting; exp. crayfish.

Ābādān, c., **Iran**; spt., major oil terminal and refining ctr. on A.I. in Persian G.; permanently damaged by Iraqi air attack; now closed (1980); p. (1991) 84,774.

Abashiri, t., N. cst. Hokkaido, **Japan**; impt. fishing base; p. (1990) 44,416.

Abbeville, t., N. **France**; on R. Somme; connected with Paris and Belgium by canals; sugar-milling, carpets, biscuits, beer; p. (1999) 24,578.

Abbots-Langley, v., Herts., **Eng.**; birthplace of Nicholas Breakspeare (Pope Adrian IV).

Abenrå, spt., S.E. Jutland, **Denmark**; at head of A. fjord and admin. ctr. of S. Jutland prov.; vehicles, clothing, food processing; p. (1990) 21,463.

Abeokuta, t., **Nigeria**; cap. Ogun st.; N. of Lagos; palm oil, textiles; p. (1992) 386,800.

Abercarn, t., Caerphilly, **Wales**; tinplate, knitting pins; former colliery t.; p. (1991) 14,069.

Aberdare, t., Rhondda, Cynon, Taff, **Wales**; on R. Cynon; wire cables; former coal-mng.; p. (1991) 29,040.

Aberdare Range, mtns., Nat. Park, **Kenya**; rise to 4,000 m; form a section of E. rim of Gr. Rift Valley; equable climate attractive to white settlers; camphor forests, fruit and pastoral agr. at higher alts.

Aberdeen, royal burgh, unit. auth. created in 1996, formerly part of Grampian, E. **Scot.**; between mouths of Rs. Dee and Don; impt. fishing pt.; established itself as centre of rapidly growing N. Sea oil ind.; "granite-city"— much granite used in central bldgs.; univs., cath.; p. (2002) 184,788 (c.), (2002) 209,270 (unit. auth.).

Aberdeen, t., S.D., **USA**; ctr. for wheat and livestock region; p. (1990) 24,927.

Aberdeenshire, E. **Scot.**, unit. auth. created in 1996, incorporating historic co. which became part of Grampian in 1974; bordered N. and E. by N. Sea; inc. cstl. ts. of Fraserburgh, Peterhead and Stonehaven; p. (2002) 227,280.

Aberfeldy, burgh, Perth and Kinross, **Scot.**; in Strath Tay, 6 km below Loch Tay; mkt.; salmon and trout fishing resort; p. (2002) 1,895.

Abergavenny, t., Monmouthshire, **Wales**; on R. Usk; scene of massacre of Welsh chiefs; light engin., concrete prods.; cattle mkt.; cas.; p. (1991) 14,092.

Aberlour, Charlestown of, burgh, Moray, **Scot.**; on R. Spey, 19 km S. of Elgin; p. (2002) 785.

Abernethy, burgh, Perth and Kinross, **Scot.**; on R. Tay, once cap. of Pictish Kings; p. (2002) 945.

Abertillery, t., Blaenau Gwent, **Wales**; collieries, tinplate; p. (1991) 11,680.

Aberystwyth, t., Ceredigion, **Wales**; on Cardigan Bay at mouth of R. Ystwyth, resort; cas., univ.; Nat. Library of Wales; p. (1991) 11,154.

Abidjan, c., replaced as cap. of **Côte d'Ivoire** by Yamoussoukro but remains seat of government; pt.; exp. palm oil, cocoa, copra, hardwood, rubber; oil refining at Vridi nearby; p. (2000) 3,305,000 (met. a.).

Abilene, t., Texas, **USA**; univ.; agr. processing, oil refining; p. (1996) 108,476.

Abilene, t., on Smoky Hill R., Kansas. **USA**; childhood home of Eisenhower; p. (1980) 6,572.

Abingdon, t., Vale of White Horse, Oxon., **Eng.**; mkt. t. on R. Thames; leather gds.; mediaeval and Georgian bldgs.; p. (2001) 36,010.

Abingdon, t., Va., **USA**; timber inds., agr. processing and tr., tobacco; tourist ctr.

Abinger Hammer, v., Surrey, **Eng.**; former centre of Weald iron industry.

Abkhazia, aut. rep., **Georgia**; borders Black Sea; sub-tropical crops, tourism; cap. Sukhumi; a. 8,599 km²; p. (2004) 250,000.

Abo. *See* Turku.

Abomey, t. anc. cap., former Kingdom of Dahomey, now **Benin**; former slave mkt.; cotton; p. (2002) 114,800.

Abovyan, t., **Armenia**; 16 km from Yerevan; new model t. founded 1963; p. (1990) 58,700.

Aboyne and Glentanner, par., Aberdeenshire, **Scot.**; on R. Dee nr. Ballater; Highland games, resort; p. (2002) 2,202.

Abraham, Plains of, nr. Quebec, **Canada**; Wolfe's victory over French under Montcalm, 1759.

Abram, t., Gtr. Manchester, **Eng.**; engin.; p. (1991) 11,482.

Abrantes, t., **Portugal**, on Tagus R.; French won battle here in Napoleonic Wars, 1807, dist. of Santarém; p. (1991) 5,980.

Abruzzo, region, central **Italy**; high limestone plateaux, narrow cstl. plain bordering Adriatic; poor agr., livestock; methane; a. 8,513 km²; p. (1992) 1,255,549.

Abu Dhabi, I., emirate, lgst. of **United Arab Emirates**; S.E. Arabian pen.; rich oil reserves; a. 207,200 km²; p. (2000) 927,000.

Abuja, new t., **Nigeria**; became cap. of Nigeria in 1991; built from oil revenue; building slowing down with fall in oil prices; p. (1992) 305,900 (Federal Capital Territory).

Abu Qir, v. on A. Bay, **Egypt**; site of anc. Canopus; Battle of the Nile fought in the Bay 1798; offshore gasfield linked by pipeline to fertiliser plants near Alexandria.

Abu Simbel, Nile Valley, **Egypt**; anc. temples carved out of solid sandstone, one to Rameses II and the other to his Queen; saved from waters of Lake Nasser.

Abydos, anc. t. of Phrygia, Asia Minor, in present **Turkey**; resisted Philip of Macedon; famed for story of Leander and Hero.

Abydos, ruined c., Upper **Egypt**; celebrated for its temple of Osiris.

Abyssinia. *See* Ethiopia.

Acapulco de Juárez, spt., Pac. cst., **Mexico**; major modern resort in bay surrounded by steep mtns.; exp. agr. prods.; struck by Hurricane Pauline (1997); p. (1990) 592,187.

Accra, c., cap. of **Ghana**; spt.; univ.; airpt.; consumer gds.; p. (2000) 1,976,000 (c.).

Accrington, t., Hyndburn, Lancs., **Eng.**; 32 km N. of Manchester; former cotton ctr.; textile machin., more diversified new inds.; p. (2001) 35,203.

Aceh, prov., **Indonesia**; cap. Banda Aceh; local pop. seeking indep.

Achill I., Mayo, **R.o.I.**; mtnous.; agr., fishing, tourism at Dugort and Keal; major gas find offshore (1999) in Corrib field; a. 148 km²; (1991) 46,200.

Acireale, spt., Sicily, **Italy**; cath.; sulphur springs, p. (1991) 46,200.

Aconcagua, mtn., Andes, **Argentina**; highest peak of Western Hemisphere, alt. 6,956 m.

Aconquija, Nevada de, mtn. range, in E. Andes, N. **Argentina**; rises from Chaco lowland to 5,500 m.

A Coruña. *See* La Coruña.

Acre. *See* "Akko.

Acre, st. W. **Brazil**; isolated within Amazon basin; rubber estates; producer of coagulated rubber; cap. Rio Branco; a. 153,170 km²; p. (1991) 1,125,000.

Acton. *See* Ealing.

Adamawa Highlands, **Nigeria**; rise to over 5,490 m; stock rearing.

Adam's Bridge, chain of sandbanks, 35 km long, in Palk Strait, between **India** and **Sri Lanka**; construction of rail causeway mooted.

Adana, t., **Turkey**; on Seijhan R.; ctr. for fruit and cotton, impt. exp. from Turkey; cas.; cap. of A. prov.; 4th. t. of Turkey; Yumurtalik Free Trade Zone (1987); p. (1990) 972,318, 1,934,907, (prov.).

Adapazari, t., **Turkey**; rly. junction; silk, linen; highgrade concentrate from low-grade iron ore deposits in Camdagi a.; p. (1993) 298,000.

Adda, R., N. **Italy**; flows through L. Como to R. Po.; agr. in wide valley above L. Como; 240 km long.

Addis Ababa, c., cap. of **Ethiopia**; at 2,440 m in central highlands; terminus of Djibouti rly., ctr. of coffee tr., main concentration of inds. in Ethiopa; consumer gds., food processing; new cotton mill (1981); admin. ctr.; univ., palaces; p. (2000) 2,640,000 (met. a.).

Adelaide, c., spt., cap. of S. **Australia;** on alluvial plain of R. Torrens with Mount Lofty Range to E. and Gulf St. Vincent to W.; growth based on wheat, wool and fruit but heavy inds. since war (nearby coal and iron); cars, electrical goods, textiles, chems., oil refining; p. (1993) 1,071,100.

Adélie Land (Terre Adélie), Antarctica; French terr. and dependency of Réunion.

Adelsberg, t., **Yugoslavia.** See **Postojna.**

Aden, spt., economic and commercial cap. of **Yemen;** former Brit. col.; bay behind headlands of Aden t. and Little Aden, excellent anchorage; p. (1987) 417,366.

Aden, G. of W. **Arabian Sea;** one of most impt. shipping lanes in world; pts. of Aden, Berbera, Djibouti; length 880 km, width 480 km at mouth.

Adige, R., N. **Italy;** upper course forms impt. routeway through Alps between Italy and N.; flows via Verona to Adriatic; 360 km long.

Adirondack, mtns., **USA;** hgst. peak Mt. Marcy (1,630 m), average height 1,200 m; scenically attractive, ski resorts, sanatoria, iron-ore deposits.

Adlington, t., Lancs., **Eng.;** nr. Chorley; former cotton spinning t.; p. (1991) 8,556.

Admiralty Is., 27 km of sm. coral Is., one lge. I., S.W. **Pac. Oc.;** part of Papua New Guinea; forms part of Bismarck Archipelago; anc. civilisation; pearl fishing, coconuts; ch, t. Lorengau.; a. 2,072 km².

Adria, mkt. t., Rovigo, **Italy;** formerly on cst., now 22 km inland, old Etruscan c.; p. (1991) 21,200.

Adrianople. See **Edirne.**

Adriatic Sea, branch of the Mediterranean, between Italy and Balkan Peninsula; forms G. of Venice on the N.; chief trading pts., Venice, Trieste, and Ancona on the N.; Brindisi and Dürres on the S.; a. 134,680 km², 720 km long.

Adullam or Aidelma, Judean c. of Canaanite origin, S.W. Jerusalem, **Israel,** where David hid in cave from Saul.

Adur, l. gov. dist., West Sussex, **Eng.;** lower A. valley and ts. of Shoreham-by-Sea and Southwick; p. (2001) 59,627.

Adwick le Street, t., South Yorks, **Eng.;** coal; home of George Washington's family; p. (1991) 10,288.

Adygeyskaya (Adygei), aut. region, **Russia;** in foothills of Caucasus; mainly agr. and lumbering; cap. Maykop; a. 7,599 km²; p. (1989) 432,000.

Adzharskaya, aut. rep., **Georgia;** borders Turkey; mtnous.; sub-tropical crops; cap. Batumi; a. 2,849 km²; p. (1990) 382,000.

Aegades, gr. of rocky Is. off W. cst. of Sicily, **Italy;** ch t, Favignana on I. of that name

Aegean Is., between **Greece** and **Turkey;** called the Grecian Archipelago, inc. Crete, Cyclades, Sporades, and Dodecanese; a. 3,901 km².

Aegean Sea, branch of the Mediterranean; studded with Is., between Greece and Turkey; connected through the Dardanelles with Sea of Marmara and thence through the Bosporus Strait with the Black Sea; rich cultural history; coral sponge fishing; recent oil finds contested between Greece and Turkey; length 640 km, width 320 km.

Afan. See **Port Talbot.**

Afars and Issas. See **Djibouti.**

Afghanistan, rep. (1973), former kingdom, Asia; land locked, lies N. and W. of Pakistan; cap. Kabul; comm. ctrs. Kabul, Kandahar; mtnous.; ch. Rs., Kabul and Helm; intense summer heat, severe winter cold, scanty rainfall; ethnic variety, Pashtuns, Ghilzays, Uzbeks and Tadzhiks; many hill tribes; languages Pashtu and Farsi; religion Islam; geography causes fragmented settlement and slow economic progress; many severe droughts; 75 percent depend on agric.; heavily dependent on irrigation; wheat staple crop, also cotton, rice, maize; sheep, goats, horses; handicraft inds. (carpets and weaving) more impt. than modern inds.; mineral resources but poor transport hinders development; no rly.; hydroelectr. at Asadabad; invaded by Russian troops, Dec. 1979 but withdrew Feb.1989; subsequent civil war; extremist Taliban regime and training centres for terrorism;

life expectancy, 43 yrs (2004); a. 647,500 km²; p. (2004) 28,513,677. Allied aircraft attack, 2001; Taliban regime overthrown; US military forces occupy capital.

Africa, third lgst. continent contains 22 per cent of world's land a. but only 11 per cent of p.; diverse physical and cultural conditions; plateaux interrupted in N. and S. by steeply folded, sharply eroded mtn. ranges and by mtn. massifs of Sahara and E. Africa; climate and vegetation vary from hot desert to equatorial rain forest and from Mediterranean woodland to tropical savannah; sparse but ethnically varied p., concentrated mainly along N.W. Mediterranean cst., Nile valley, cst. of W. Africa and N.E. of L. Victoria; little urbanisation; economic development hindered by colonial legacy and neo-colonial international companies, poorly developed transport network, poor soils, inadequate rainfall and fluctuating prices of primary prods. on world mkt.; petroleum deposits providing revenue for devel. in few ctys.; those ctys. without oil severely handicapped by high cost of imports; schemes like Volta R. multipurpose development and the Cabora Bassa dam designed to alleviate this poverty; continent contains 40 per cent of world hydroelectric potential and is storehouse of non-energy producing minerals, but many exported in unprocessed form; agr. predominant economic activity, except in industl. enclaves of Egypt, Zimbabwe and S. Africa; popltn. growth threatened by AIDS epidemic; a c. 30,365,000 km²; p. (2003) 850,000,000.

Agadir, spt., S. cst. **Morocco;** wrecked by earthquake, 1960; new t. built S. of former c. in a. of greater geological stability; p. (1994) 365,965.

Agana, cap of **Guam;** reconstructed after 1945; p. (1990) 4,800 (exc. armed forces).

Agen, t., cap. of Lot-et-Garonne, **France;** mkt t.; aqueduct and bridge over Garonne R.; fruit tr. and processing; p. (1999) 30,165.

Agincourt (Azincourt), v., Pas-de-Calais, **France;** famed for battle in 1415 between English, led by Henry V and French under d'Albert.

Agra, c., Uttar Pradesh, **India;** on Jumna R., 184 km S.S.E. of Delhi; formerly cap. of Mogul Empire; famous Taj Mahal mausoleum; univ.; p. (1991) 892,000.

Agrigento, t., S. Sicily, **Italy;** spt., exp. sulphur, salt. Formerly Girgenti, founded Akragas, c. 580 B.C., famous for its temples; birthplace of Empedocles; p. (1996) 475,669.

Aguascalientes, st., **Mexico;** on central plateau at 1,800 m; agr.; mineral springs; cap. A.; a. 6,472 km²; p. (1990) 719,650.

Aguascalientes, t., cap. of A. st. **Mexico;** alt. over 1,800 m; 416 km N.W. of Mexico City; wide range of local inds.; hot springs; p (1990) 506,384.

Agulhas, C., rocky projection, 160 km E. of C of Good Hope, most southerly point of **Africa.**

Ahmadabad, temporary cap. of Gujarat, **India;** Jain temple, mosques; univ.; impt. textile ctr.; oilfield at Nawagam nearby; p. (1991) 2,877,000.

Ahmadnagar, c., Maharashtra, **India;** admin. ctr.; old Bahmani cap.; lge. tr. in cotton and silk gds.; p. (1991) 181,339 (c.).

Ahrewady. See **Irrawaddy.**

Ahvāz (Ahwāz), c., cap. of Khuzestan prov., **Iran;** airpt.; oil, aluminium, steel pipes; new steel plant; p. (1994) 828,000.

Aigues-Mortes, t., Gard dep., **France;** on Rhône delta; canal ctr., once spt , now 5 km from Mediterranean; salt works; much of mediaeval t. preserved; tourism; p. (1999) 6,012.

Aiguille d'Arves, mtn., Dauphiné Alps, S.E. **France;** 3 rock needles; lgst. alt. 3,511 m.

Aiguille du Midi, mtn., Mt. Blanc massif, S.E. **France;** rock needle, funicular rly.; alt. 3,845 m.

Aiguille Verte, mtn., Mt. Blanc massif, S.E. **France,** rock needle overlooking Chamonix; alt. 4,130 m.

Ailefroid, mtn., Dauphiné Alps, S.E. **France;** double summit; alt. 3,962 m.

Ailsa Craig, rocky I., S. Ayrshire, **Scot.;** alt. 340 m; gannetry; puffins returned to breed after 50 years (2002).

Ain, dep., **France;** in Jura; mainly agr., famous for pigs and poultry; a. 5,822 km²; p. (1999) 515,184.

Ain, R., **France;** trib. of R. Rhône, flows S.S.W. from Jura; hydroelectric power; 194 km long.

Airdrie, burgh, N. Lanarkshire, **Scot.;** 19 km E. of Glasgow; iron inds., brick and concrete wks., steel tubes, pharmaceutics; p. (2002) 36,326.

Aire, R., West Yorks., **Eng.**; trib. of Ouse; major valley for power production; length 112 km.

Aisne, dep., **France**; borders Ardennes; forested; mainly agr., sugar-beet; sm. textile ts.; cap. Laon; a. 7,423 km²; p. (1990) 537,500.

Aisne, R., N.E. **France**; navigation improved by regularisation; 240 km long.

Aitolia and Akarnania, Greece; mtnous. prov. on N. side G. of Patras; arable cultivation on cstl. plain; cap. Missolonghi; a. 5,390 km²; p. (1991) 228,180.

Aix-en-Provence, t., Bouches-du-Rhône, **France**; 29 km N. of Marseilles; old cap. of Provence; thermal springs; cultural and comm. ctr.; agr., inds.; p. (1999) 133,818.

Aix-la-Chapelle. See Aachen.

Aix-les-Bains, health resort, Savoy, **France**; p. (1982) 23,534.

Ajaccio, spt., Corse-du-Sud, Corsica, **France**; timber, flour, olive oil, tobacco; tourism; birth-place of Napoleon; p. (1990) 59,318.

Ajman, emirate, one of United Arab Emirates; p. (1995) 118,800.

Akhaia, prov., **Greece**; impt. currant producing a.; livestock; inc. pt. of Patras; a. 3,134 km²; p. (1991) 300,078.

Akhisar, t., **Turkey**; anc. Thyatira; p. (1990) 74,000

Akita, pref., **Japan**; a. 11,663 km²; contains Japan's lgst. oilfield and copper mine; mtns. and fertile lowlands; p. (1990) 1,227,000.

Akita, c., **Japan**; cap. Akita pref.; old cas. t., pt; oil refining ctr.; p. (1990) 302,359.

'Akko (Acre), c., spt., **Israel**; famous for sieges during Crusades; withstood Napoleon for 61 days in 1799; pt. functions now assumed by Haifa; p. (1994) 45,300.

Akmola. See Astana.

Akmolinsk. See Tselinograd.

Akola, t., Maharashtra, **India**; p. (1991) 328,000.

Akosombo, pt. and new t. S. of L. Volta; **Ghana**; textile factory being built; planned p. 50,000.

Akron, c., Ohio, **USA**; lge. rubber mftg. ctr.; maize, mills, woollens, machin., chemicals; univ.; p. (2000) 217,074 (c.), 657,575 (met. a.).

Aktyubinsk, t., N.W. **Kazakhstan**; at S. end of Ural mtns.; ferro-alloys, engin., lignite, elec. power, chemicals, copper; p. (1990) 261,100.

Akureyri, t., N. **Iceland**; herring fishery, food processing; 2nd. t. of Iceland; p. (1993) 14,799.

Akyab, See Sittwe.

Alabama, st., **USA**; cap. Montgomery, ch. pt. Mobile; "cotton st.", cattle-rearing; fertilisers, chemicals, mng.; lgst. c. Birmingham; settled 1702; admitted to union 1819; st. flower camelia, st. bird yellowhammer; much destruction by Hurricane Katrina (2005); a. 133,667 km²; p. (2002) 4,486,508.

Alagôas, st., N.E. **Brazil**; hot, dry cattle rearing a., poor st. with low living standards; cap. Maceió; a. 28,640 km²; p. (1991) 2,512,515.

Alameda, spt. Cal., **USA**; on I. in San Francisco Bay; impt. naval and air base; pt. inds.; p. (1996) 76,042.

Aland Is. (Ahvenanmaa), group belonging to **Finland** at entrance of G. of Bothnia; a. 1,481 km²; p. (1993) 25,102.

Alaska, Arctic st., **USA**; separated from other sts.; bought from Russia (1868); mtnous.; furs, timber, salmon; major oil and natural gas discoveries on N. slope have led to controversial major drilling plans; growing evidence of global warming with increased vegetation; pipeline from Prudhoe Bay to Valdez; lgst. c. Anchorage; admitted to union 1959; st. flower forget-me-not, st. bird Willow Ptarmigan; cap. Juneau (planned cap. at Willow South never built); a. 1,518,776 km²; p. (2002) 643,986. Caribou herds threatened by oil drilling.

Alaska G. of, S. cst. A., **USA.**; semi-circular G. with precipitous csts.; oil in Cook Inlet and Controller B.; a. 5,000 km².

Alaska Highway, from Dawson Creek, B.C., **Canada**, to Fairbanks, Alaska, **USA**; 2,443 km long; built for second world war programme; main supply base and H.Q., Edmonton, Alberta.

Alaska Range, mtn. massif, S.A., **USA**; extends in arc of 640 km; separates S. cst. and N. tundra; S.E. flowing glaciers; many peaks over 3,000 m; Mt. McKinley, 6,182 m.

Alava, Basque prov., N. **Spain**; ch. t. Vitoria; viticulture; a. 3,043 km²; p. (1998) 284,600.

Albacete, prov., S.E. **Spain**; stock-raising; a. 14,864 km². p. (1998) 358,600.

Albacete, t., cap. of A. prov., **Spain**; agr., mkt.,

fruit, saffron; p. (1991) 134,584.

Alba-Iulia, t., **Romania**; on R. Mures, formerly Carisburgh; union of Transylvania with Romania proclaimed here 1918; p. (1992) 71,254.

Albania, rep., S.E. Europe; lying along Adriatic, adjacent to Serbia and Greece; food ch. ind.; petroleum reserves and refining, hydroelectric power, coal, chrome ore, copper, iron ore; first external rail link opened (1986); fastest growing p. in Europe; virtual anarchy, 1997; huge influx of Kosovo refugees, 1999; cap. Tirana; a. 27,529 km²; p. (2004) 3,544,808.

Albano, crater L., **Italy**; tourist attraction 24 km S.E. of Rome; steep sides; a. 8 km².

Albany, c., cap. of N.Y., st., **USA**; R. pt. on Hudson R., admin, and industl. ctr.; p. (1990) 101,082 (c.), 874,000 (met. a. with Schenectady-Troy).

Albany, t., W **Australia**; pt. on King George Sound; founded (1826) as penal col.; first white settlement in W. Australia, established to counter Fr. settlement of W.; p. (1991) 11,186.

Albert, L. See Mobutu Seso, L.

Alberta, prov., W. **Canada**; part of prairies; Rockies in W.; wheat, livestock, feed crops; coal less impt. with development of rich oil and gas resources; chemicals, timber; cap. Edmonton; a. 661,188 km²; p. (1996) 2,696,825.

Albertville. See Kalemie.

Albi, t., cap. of Tarn dep., **France**; cath., industl. and comm. ctr.; p. (1990) 48,707.

Ålborg, c., cap. of N. Jutland prov., **Denmark**; spt. on S. side of Lim fjord; shipping, cement, textiles; airpt.; p. (1990) 155,019.

Albula Alps, mtn. range, Rhaetian Alps, E. **Switzerland**; summits intersected by low passes; inc. several impt. Dolomitic peaks.

Albuquerque, t., N.M., **USA**; on Rio Grande; alt. 1,525 m.; univ.; food prod., engin.; resort; p. (2000) 448,607 (met. a.).

Albury-Wodonga, t., N.S.W., Vic., **Australia**; regional urban growth ctr. (1974) on Murray R.; p. (1991) 63,600.

Alcalá de Henares, t., **Spain**; nr. Madrid; univ.; birthplace of Cervantes; p. (1998) 163,800.

Alcamo, t., Sicily, **Italy**; nr. ruins of anc. Segesra; p. (1991) 42,600.

Alcatraz, I., Cal., **USA**; San Francisco Bay; former prison.

Aldabra Is., Seychelles Rep.; 400 km N.W. of Madagascar; leased (1971–1985) to Royal Society for wildlife research (unique animal and plant species).

Aldan, R., E. Siberia, **Russia**; flows from Stanovoy Range to Lena R. via Tommot gold-mng. dist.; coal in lower course; 2,682 km long.

Aldeburgh, spt., Suffolk **Coast** **Suffolk**, **Eng.**; famous for annual music festival; p. (1991) 2,654.

Aldermaston, Berkshire, **Eng.**; atomic weapons research ctr.

Alderney, I., dependency of **Guernsey**; horticulture, tourism; a. 794 ha; p. (1994) 2,375.

Aldershot, t., Rushmoor, Hants., **Eng.**; bricks; lge. military camp; p. (2001) 58,170.

Aldridge, t., West Midlands, **Eng.**; plastics, packing cases; expanded t.; p. (1991) 16,862.

Alençon, t. cap. of Orne dep., **France**; textiles; p. (1990) 31,139.

Aleppo, c., **Syria**; 2nd. c. of Syria; in limestone hills; univ.; mkt and textile ctr.; p. (1993) 1,494,000.

Alessandria, t., N. **Italy**; rly. ctr. on Tanaro R.; engin.; p. (1996) 433,300.

Ålesund, spt. on Giske I., W. **Norway**, fishing, fish processing; airpt. on I. to N.; p. (1990) 23,741.

Aletsch, glacier, **Switzerland**; in Bernese Alps; lgst. in Europe; length 24 km.

Aletschhorn, mtn., Bernese Alps, **Switzerland**; alt. 4,198 m.

Aleutian Is.; Bering Sea, Alaska, **USA**; chain of over 150 Is. formed from partially submerged peaks of volcanic A. mtn. range; on earthquake belt; U.S. air base.

Alexander Archipelago, S.E. Alaska, **USA**; dense I. system; fjord scenery; well populated; furs, lumbering, fishing; a. 33,670 km².

Alexandria (El Iskandariyah) ch. pt. and prov., **Egypt**; founded by Alexander the Great, 332 B.C.; floating dock; exp. cotton, wheat, rice, gum; second lgst. c. in Africa; new steel plant at El Dikhelia; pt. being expanded and new pt. at Dikhelia; linked to offshore gas field; rapid growth, second lgst. c. in Africa; p. (2000) 4,113,000 (met. a.).

Alexandria, c., spt., Va., **USA**; on Chesapeake Bay; indust. t.; p. (1996) 117,586.

Alfreton, t., Amber Valley, Derbys., **Eng.**; mkt. t.; formerly coal mng.; hosiery, knitwear; p. (2001) 22,302.

Algarve, prov., anc. kingdom, **Portugal**; in extreme S. of cty; tourism, fishing, fruit.

Algeciras, spt., **Spain**; W. of Gibraltar on A. Bay; nearby Campo de Gibraltar scheme for social and economic development; p. (1991) 101,365.

Algeria, indep. st. (1962), N. Africa; former French colony; fertile cstl. plain borders Mediterranean Sea where cereal, wine, fruit and olive production and incr. mkt. garden prods. for exp.; Land reform (1980) encouraging livestock; afforestation to prevent N. spread of Sahara; exp. of high grade iron ore, phosphates, petroleum and natural gas are financing ambitious industrialisation plans; incr. tourism; new roads link Saharan oilfields to cst.; cap. El Djezair; 60 per cent of p. under 19; a. 2,373,994 km²; p. (2004) 32,129,324. Civil war since 1992 against Muslim fundamentalists.

Algiers. See El Djezair

Alicante, spt., cap of A. prov., **Spain**; wine, fruits; oil refinery; p. (1998) 272,400, 1,389,000 (prov.).

Alice Springs, t., N.T., **Australia**; ch. t., of desert a.; major cattle raising ctr.; natural gas nearby; growth of winter tourism; new rly. link to Darwin now opened; p. (1991) 24,678.

Aligarh, t., Uttar Pradesh, **India**; 128 km S.E. of Delhi; univ.; p. (1991) 481,000.

Alkmaar, t., **Netherlands**; impt. cheese mkt. on N. Holland canal; p. (1994) 92,962.

Allahabad, t., Uttar Pradesh, **India**; at confluence of Jumna and Ganges Rs.; univ.; Hindu pilgrimage ctr.; p. (1991) 806,000 (c.).

Allegheny Mtns., USA; part of Appalachian system, inc. several parallel ranges; water-shed between Atlantic and Mississippi R. drainage; forested, tourism; average alt. 1,500 m.

Allegheny R., Penns., N.Y., **USA**; rises in A. mtns., flows to Ohio R.; Pittsburg met. a. on lower reaches where R. entrenched 120 m below plateau making urban development difficult; used for coal and oil transport; 520 km long.

Allen, Bog of, R.o.I.; peat bogs, peat cutting, culti vation; a. 958 km².

Allentown, t., Penns., **USA**; coal, textiles, cement; p. (1990) 105,090 (c.), 687,000 (met. a.).

Alleppey (Alappuzha), spt., Kerala, S. **India**; on sand split; coconut prods; p. (1991) 265,000.

Allerdale, l. gov. dist., Cumbria, **Eng.**; cstl. dist. inc. Workington, Maryport, Cockermouth and Keswick; p. (2001) 93,492.

Alliance, t., Ohio, **USA**; iron, steel, engin.; p. (1990) 23,400.

Allier, dep., **France**, N. of Massif Central; coal and iron mng.; mineral springs, wine, wheat; a. 4,786 km²; p. (1990) 357,700.

Alloa, sm. burgh, Clackmannan, **Scot.**; on N. bank of R. Forth; bricks, tiles, glass, distilling; p. (2002) 18,989.

Alma-Ata, See Almaty.

Almada, t., **Portugal**; on R. Tagus estuary opposite Lisbon; Salazar bridge (opened 1966) links it with Lisbon; p. (1991) 22,212.

Almaty, t., **Kazakhstan**; in foothills of Tien-Shan mtns.; univ.; comm. agr., and ind. ctr., food processing, machin., printing; p. (1997) 1,248,000. Capital city (until 1995).

Almeria, spt. on G. of A., S.E **Spain**; cap. A prov.; cath.; exp. grapes, oranges; p. (1998) 168,000, 505,500 (prov.).

Alnwick, t., l. gov. dist., Northumberland, **Eng.**; cas.; mkt. t.; p. (2001) 31,029 (dist.), (1991) 7,419 (t.).

Alor Setar, t., cap. of Kedah, W. **Malaysia**; on main W. cst. road and rly.; p. (1991) 165,100.

Alost. See Aalst.

Alpes-de-Haute-Provence (Basses-Alpes), dep., S.E. **France**; mtnous., infertile a. bordering Italy; olives, wines; cap. Digne; a. 6,988 km²; p. (1990) 130,900.

Alpes-Maritimes, dep., S.E. **France**; ceded by Italy in 1860; ch. t. Nice; olives, wines, fruit; a. 3,737 km²; p. (1999) 1,006,281.

Alps, hgst. mtns. in **Europe**; 960 km long, inc. 1,200 glaciers; separates S. and central Europe, forming a climatic divide; major tourist a., winter sports; hydroelec. power; main peaks Mont Blanc (4,814 m), Mont Rosa (4,641 m), Matterhorn (4,509 m); melting permafrost now threatens Alpine communities.

Als, I., S. **Denmark**; in the Little Belt, a. 337 km²; linked to Jutland by bridge; p. (1990) 50,744.

Alsace-Lorraine, region, E. **France**; bordered to E. by W. Germany and Rhine R; incorporated into Germany at time of unification (1871), returned to France by Treaty of Versailles (1919); impt. iron-ore and iron and steel inds. in Lorraine; regional aid for economic development; well wooded; p. (1999) 1,732,082 (Alsace) See Lorraine.

Alsdorf, t., N. Rhine-Westphalia, **Germany**; 16 km N. of Aachen; p. (1994) 46,750.

Altai Mtns., Mongolia, **Russia**; border China; steppes and glaciers; silver and mercury; multi-purpose R. project at Kamenna-Obi; ctr. of Russian atomic ind, at Ust Kamenogorsk; stock-rearing; average alt. 3,000 m, highst. alt. 4,656 m at Tabun Bogdo.

Alta, R., N. **Norway**; scene of major new h.e.p. sta. fiercely opposed by Lapp residents.

Altamura, caves, N. **Spain**; prehistoric shelters, paintings of animals (Magdalenian).

Altamura, t., Apulia, **Italy**; at foot of Apennines; wines, wool; cath.; p. (1991) 57,900.

Altdorf, t., cap. of Uri can., **Switzerland**; rubber gds., wood workings; statue of William Tell and Tell Theatre; p. (1990) 8,150.

Altenahr, t., N. Rhine-Westphalia, **Germany**; site of anc. cas. of Counts von der Marck; metals, wine; p. (1999) 23,400.

Althorp, (Northants), seat of Earl Spencer; burial place of Princess Diana (1997).

Altrincham, mkt. t., Trafford, Gtr. Manchester, **Eng.**; engin.; residtl.; p. (2001) 40,695.

Alva, burgh, Clackmannan, **Scot.**; at S. foot of Ochil Hills, 5 km N. of Alloa; woollens, printing, fruit and fish canning; p. (2002) 5,181.

Alvsborg, co., S.W. **Sweden**; cap. Vänersborg; a. 11,394 km²; p. (1992) 445,921.

Alwar, c., Rajasthan, **India**; in hilly agr. region; former cap. of A. princely st.; fort, palace; p. (1991) 205,086.

Amagasaki, c., **Japan**; nr. Osaka; chemicals polyethylene; iron and steel; oil refining; p. (1990) 498,998.

Amalfi, spt., **Italy**; on G. of Salerno; tourist resort; former maritime republic; fisheries; p. (1990) 5,600.

Amapá, fed. terr., N. **Brazil**; on equator; tropical rain forest; a. 137,423 km²; p. (1991) 380,000.

Amārah, Al, pt., **Iraq**; on left bank of R. Tigris 400 km below Baghdad; Arab t. and agr. mkt. at R. crossing; p. (2002 est.) 340,000.

Amārapura, t., **Myanmar**; on R. Irrawaddy 10 km. S.W. of Mandalay; former cap.; craft inds.

Amarillo, t., Texas, **USA**; oil refining, creameries, meat packing; p. (1990) 169,588.

Amasya, t. and prov., **Turkey**; on Yesil-Cekerek R.; tr. ctr.; p. (1997) 70,200, (1990) 357,191 (prov.).

Amazon, gr. R., S. **America**; drains lgst. a. and carries more water than any other R. in world; main Andean headstreams Huarco Ucayali and Marañón from Peru unite to flow across Brazil to Atl. Oc., receiving waters of many Rs. inc. the Madeira; lgst. rain forest in world but rapidly disappearing; ocean steamers penetrate to Iquitos, Peru, c. 3,680 km from mouth; a. drained c. 6 mil lion km² of sparsely populated cty., mostly in Brazil; length 6,448 km; basin inc. 40% of S. America; ocean pt. Belém.

Amazonas, lgst. st., of **Brazil**; isolated; tropical rain forest; tree prods.; vast mineral reserves; cap. Manáus; a. 1,595,823 km²; p. (1996) 2,390,000.

Amazonas, fed. terr., **Venezuela**; cap. Puerto Ayacucho on Orinoco R., isolated, tropical rain forest; a. 181,300 km²; p. (1990) 55,700.

Amazonia, Peru, Colombia, Brazil; a. covered by Amazon R. and its tribs. and the surrounding lowland; thickly forested; underdeveloped.

Ambato, c., **Ecuador**; S. of Quito, on slope of Mt. Chimborazo; alt. 2,702 m; textiles, canned fruits, leather gds.; p. (1990) 124,166.

Amberg, t., Bavaria, **Germany**; mediaeval walled t. on R. Vils; specialist steels, textiles; p. (2002) 44,217.

Amber Valley, l. gov. dist., Derbys., **Eng.**; S. of co., nr. Notts.; inc. Alfreton, Ripley, Heanor and Belper; p. (2001) 116,471.

Ambleside, tourist ctr., Cumbria, **Eng.**; N. of L. Windermere; p. (1991) 2,905.

Amboise, t., Indre-et-Loire dep., **France**; 24 km E. of Tours; famous cas, and prison; p. (1999) 11,466.

Ambon, I., Moluccas, **Indonesia**; spices, coconuts; religious riots (1999); a. 818 km²; p. (1995) 313,000.

America, the lands of the Western hemisphere, comprising the continents of North and South

America, separated by narrow Isthmus of Panama; most N. point over 14,400 km from C. Horn, the extreme S. point. *See also* **North**, **South**, and **Central America**.

American Samoa, Is, E.N.E. Fiji under US rule; a. 197 km²; p. (2004) 57,902.

Amersfoort, c., Utrecht, **Neth.**; walled c. on R. Eem; rapid growth of light inds.; p. (1994) 110,117.

Amersham, t., Bucks., **Eng.**; radio isotopes; lt. inds., 17th cent. mkt. hall; p. (2001) 21,470.

Ames, t., Iowa, **USA**; Iowa State Univ. of Science and Technology and many fed. and st. institutes; p. (1996) 47,698.

Amiens, c., cap. of Somme dep; major textile ctr. of **France**, on R. Somme; cath.; p. (1990) 136,234 (c.), 156,120 (met. a.).

Amindivi, Is, Arabian Sea; joined with Laccdive & Minicoy Is to form Lakshadweep, Union territory, **India**.

Amirante Isles, gr. of islands in the Indian Oc. belonging to **Seychelles**.

Amlwch, t., Isle of Anglesey, **Wales**; N. cst. resort; pt.; oil terminal; p. (1991) 3,519.

Amman, c., cap. of **Jordan**; N.E. of Dead Sea; site of biblical Raboth Ammon; textiles, cement, tobacco; airpt.; univ.; p. (2000) 1,430,000.

Ammanford, t., Carmarthenshire, **Wales**; brick mkg.; p. (1991) 12,106.

Amoy. *See* **Xiamen**.

Ampthill, Mid Beds., **Eng**; mkt. t.; p. (1991) 6,230.

Amravati, c., Maharashtra, **India**; cotton ctr., univ.; p. (1991) 422,000.

Amritsar, c., Punjab, N.W. **India**; Golden Temple sacred to Sikhs. Massacre of Indian nationalists by troops under British control, 1919; p. (1991) 709,000.

Amroha, t., Uttar Pradesh, **India**; pilgrimage ctr.; p. (1991) 137.061.

Amsterdam, spt., cap. of **Netherlands**; at junction of R. Amstel and the IJ; built on 96 Is. joined by 300 bridges, harbour at terminus of N. Sea canal can hold 1,000 ships; two univs., Royal Palace, Bourse; extensive tr.; exp. dairy prod., sugar, tobacco; shipbldg., diamond polishing, aeronautical, marine, elec. machin., oil refining; p. (1998) 718,200.

Amu Darya (Oxus), R., marks boundary between **Turkmenistan**, **Uzbekistan** and **Afghanistan**; flows from Pamir mtns. to Aral Sea; Kara- and Ksyl-Kum deserts on either bank; rich in fish; 1,395 km long.

Amur (Heilong Jiang), major R. of E. **Asia**; flows from Mongolia between N.E. China and E. Siberia into Pac. Oc. opposite Sakhalin I.; with tribs. Argun and Ussuri forms lgst. R. frontier in world; crossed by Trans-Siberian rly. at Khabarovsk; 2,827 km long.

Anaconda, t., Mont., **USA**; one of lgst. copper mines in world; p. (1996) 10,093.

Anaheim, t., Cal., **USA**; tourism; Disneyland; p. (2000) 328,014 (c.), 2,411,000 (met. a.).

Anahuac, plateau, **Mexico**; average alt. 2,000 m; surrounded by higher cty. inc. volcano Popocatapetl (5,456 m); contains Mexico City heartland of Aztec Mexico; a. c. 3,900 km².

Anatolia (Asia Minor), penin. approx. coextensive with Turkey bounded by Black Sea (N.), Mediterranean (S.), Aegean (W.).

Anching. *See* **Anqing**.

Anchorage, t., Alaska, **USA**; timber, salmon fishing and canning; earthquake 28 Mar. 1964; spt.; airpt.; p. (2000) 260,283.

Ancona, spt., central **Italy**; on the Adriatic Sea; founded by Dorians, 1500 B.C.; sugar refineries, shipbldg., petrochemicals; p. (1992) 100,701.

Andalucía. *See* **Andalusia**.

Andalusia, region, covering southern **Spain**; Córdoba, Seville, Jaén and Granada, ctrs. in Moorish times; irrigation for wines *etc*; p. (1998) 7,236,000.

Andaman and Nicobar Is., Bay of Bengal; constituted a union terr., **India**, 1956; hilly remnants of drowned mtn. chain; tribal people now outnumbered by displaced Tamils from Sri Lanka, resettled by India; devastated by tsunami, 2004; a. 8,327 km²; p. (2001) 356,300.

Anderlecht, t., residtl. and industl. sub. of Brussels, **Belgium**; p. (1991) 87,880.

Andermatt, v., Uri, **Switzerland**; at foot of Mt. St. Gotthard; tourist ctr., winter health resort.

Andes, gr. volcanic mtn. system, S. **America**; extends over 6,400 km from N.-S.; physical and climatic divide rising to over 6,000 m; densely populated; high tropical plateaux; rich in minerals;

hgst. peak, Aconcagua (6,965 m).

Andhra Pradesh, st. S.E. **India**; cap. Hyderabad; inc. valleys of lower Godavari and Krishna Rs.; sugar, rice; a. 275,278 km²; p. (2001) 75,727,500.

Andizhan, c. **Uzbekistan**; once residence of Khans of Khokan; industl. ctr.; in irrigation a.; cotton, silk; oilfields; p. (2000) 300,000 (est.).

Andorra, sm. mtn. st., E. Pyrenees; under joint suzerainty of French President and Bishop of Urgel (Spain until 1993; now virtually indep.); livestock, wines, tobacco; tourism; alt. 900–3,000 m; a. 495 km²; p. (2004) 69,865.

Andover, mkt. t., Test Valley, Hants., **Eng.**; prehistoric earthwks.; expanded t.; p. (2001) 37,955.

Andria, t., S Italy, Roman remains, cath., palaces, p. (1991) 90,100

Andropov. *See* **Rybinsk**.

Andros, lgst. I., **Bahamas**; sponges, sisal, hemp; a. 5957 km²; p. (1990) 8,155.

Angara, R., Siberia, **Russia**; trib. of Yenisey; navigable almost its entire length., rises nr. and flows through L. Baykal; length 2,080 km; hydro-electric power.

Angel Falls (Salto del Angel), waterfall, **Venezuela**; nr. Ciudad Bolívar; 980 m drop.

Angers, t., cap. of Maine-et-Loire dep., **France**; on R. Maine; mkt. t. for local produce, fruit, vegetables, Anjou wines, Cointreau; textiles; cath., cas.; p. (1999) 151,150.

Angkor, c., **Cambodia**; jungle-covered ruins of c. from Khmer civilisation; discovered 1860.

Anglesey. *See* **Isle of Anglesey**.

Angola, Rep. of (former Portuguese province), interior forms part of central African plateaus, bounded by transitional escarpments in W. which face on to narrow coastal plain; rainfall diminishes from N.-S. with consequent crop zoning; coffee, cotton, oil palm in N., corn, peanuts, sisal in drier interior, cattle in S., semidesert in S.E.; economy dependent upon primary inds., especially agr.; coffee major exp., produced on plantations; newly discovered oilfields; diamonds in remote N.E. Luanda dis.; iron-ore mng. impt. at Cassinga; little mftg.; hydroelectric scheme on Cuarza R.; pts. on natural harbours impt. transhipment points for land-locked central African ctys.; indep. 1975, followed by civil war between rival guerrilla groups; ceasefire agreed, April 2002; cap. Luanda; a. 1,246,375 km²; p. (2004) 10,978,552.

Angoulême, mftg. t., cap. of Charente dep., **France**; on R. Charente; cognac, paper; cath.; suffered during Huguenot wars; p. (1999) 43,132.

Angren, t., **Uzbekistan**; E. of Tashkent; lgst. ctr. of lignite mng. in central Asia; p. (1990) 133,200.

Anguilla, I., Leeward Is., W.I.; dry climate, thin limestone soil; exp. cotton, salt; a. 91 km²; reverted to Brit. Crown after secession from St. Kitts–Nevis ass. st. 1967; status of separate Brit. dependency and withdrawal from St. Kitts–Nevis ass. statehood 1980; p. (2004) 13,008.

Angus, E.Scot., unit. auth. created in 1996, reinstating most of historic co. which became part of Tayside in 1974; bordered E. by N. Sea; inc. ts. of Arbroath, Forfar and Montrose; p. (2002) 108,130.

Anhui (Anhwei), prov., E. central **China**; in delta region of Chang Jiang; a. 140,686 km²; cap. Hefei; soya-beans, rice, tea, coal and iron; p. (1994) 59,380,000.

Aniakchak, volcano, S.W. Alaska, **USA**; rich variety of flora and fauna on crater floor; alt. 1,384 m.

Anjou, former prov. of **France**; mainly S. of lower R. Loire; ch. t. Angers.

Ankara, c., cap. of **Turkey** since 1923; alt. 1,037 m; univ., cultural and admin. ctr.; p. (1990) 2,541,000, 3,236,626 (prov.).

'Annaba, spt., dep., N. **Algeria**; on fertile plain; fertiliser factory supplied by phosphates from Djebel-Onk; iron and steel complex; p. (2002 est.) 240,000 (t.), 620,000 (dep.).

Annam, region, **Vietnam**; formerly within French Union; divided by 17th parallel bdy. (1957); a. 147,560 km²; ch. t. Hué.

Annamese Cordillera, cstl. mtn. range, **Laos**, **Vietnam**; N.-S. watershed between Mekong and S. China Sea; rising to 2,000 m in Ngoc Linh; forested; inhabited by hill tribes.

Annan, royal burgh, Dumfries and Galloway, **Scot.**; on R. Annan, 3 km from its mouth in Solway F.; Chapelcross reactor sta.; p. (2002) 8,389.

Annapolis, c., cap. of Maryland, **USA**; naval academy; p. (1996) 33,234.

Annapolis Valley, Nova Scotia, **Canada;** famous fruit growing a., especially for apples.

Annapurna, massif, **Nepal;** part of Himalayas; many glaciers in W. and N.W.; alt. 8,080 m.

Ann Arbor, c., Mich., **USA;** on the Huron; univ. of Michigan.; motor lorries, farm implements, scientific instruments; p. (1990) 109,592 (c.), 283,000 (met. a.).

Annecy, t., **France;** dep. of Haute-Savoie; at lower end of beautiful L. Annecy; textiles, paper, watches; resort; p. (1999) 50,271.

Ansbach, t., Bavaria, **Germany;** machin., metallurgy, furniture indus.; rly. ctr.; p. (1994) 39,200.

An-shan, c., Liaoning, N. **China;** at foot of Qian Shan, 96 km S.W. of Shenyang; lgst. iron and steel complex in China (fully automated steel plant), elec., chemical and locomotive ind.; p. (1994) 1,251,700.

Antakya (Antioch), anc. c., S. **Turkey;** on R. Orontes; cap. of Hatay prov., major Roman cap. and early ctr. of Christian culture; p. (1990) 124,400.

Antalya, c., S.W. **Turkey;** freeport (1986) with shallow harbour from which Paul and Barnabas sailed to Antakya; p. (1990) 353,149, 1,132,211 (prov.).

Antananarivo (Tananarive), cap. of **Madagascar;** ctr. of commerce and communications; airpt.; lge meat preserving factories, plastics, radios, car assembly, shoes, knitted gds.; rice mills; univ.; p. (2000) 1,507,000.

Antarctica, plateau continent within A. circle; snow-covered, extensive ice sheets and glaciers; volcanoes and Is.; alt. 2,000–3,000 m; dependencies of UK, Australia, N.Z., France, Norway but a. S. of 60° S reserved for peaceful international scientific research. Antarctica is the world's highest continent. Growing tourist numbers (15,000 in 2000). *See also* **Section L.**

Antarctic Ocean, parts of Pac., Atl. and Indian Oceans, S. of 60° S.; cold and dangerous; no mammalian life other than whales.

Antibes, t., Alpes-Maritimes, N. of Cap d. A., S.E. **France;** spt. on Fr. Riviera; exp. oranges; flowers for perfume mnfs.; resort; Roman remains; p. (1990) 70,688.

Antigua, anc. c., **Guatemala;** 32 km W. of Guatemala c.; former cap., destroyed by earthquake 1773; comm. ctr. in coffee dist.; notable colonial ruins; UN World Heritage site; tourism; p. (1994) 16,400.

Antigua and Barbuda, Leeward gr., W.I.; aut. st. in ass. with Gt. Britain; indep. 1981; semi-arid limestone; 75 per cent p. in N.E.; sugar, cotton, tourism; cap. St. Johns; a. (inc. Barbuda and Redonda) 440 km²; p. (2004) 68,320.

Antilles, Greater and **Lesser,** archipelago enclosing Caribbean Sea and G. of Mexico, **W.I.;** complex political structure, tropical climate and crops; a. c. 259,000 km².

Antioquia, mtnous. dep. **Colombia;** colonial mng.; agr. now more impt.; one of major p. clusters in Colombia inc. dep. cap. Medellin; a. 65,791 km²; p. (1992) 4,467,914.

Antofagasta, spt., **Chile;** cap., comm. and industl. ctr. of A. region; exps. copper from Chuquicamata; situated in desert, water supply 240 km by aqueduct from Andes; p. (1992) 226,749, 407,409 (prov.).

Antony, t., Hauts-de-Seine, **France;** brick wks., toys; sub. of Paris; p. (1999) 59,819.

Antrim, former co.; l. gov. dist., N. **Ireland;** fertile lowland a., arable agr.; borders L. Neagh in S.W. and A. mtns. in N.E.; p. (2001) 48,366.

Antrim, mkt. t., N. **Ireland;** on Lough Neagh; linen, nylon; p. (1991) 20,878.

Antsiranana, (Diego Suarez), t., extreme N. of **Madagascar;** oxygen plant; Fr. naval base.

An-tung. *See* Dandong.

Antwerp, (Anvers), low-lying prov., N. **Belgium;** grain, flax; a. 2,859 km²; p. (1993) 1,619,613.

Antwerp, (Anvers), spt., **Belgium;** on Scheldt R., 88 km from sea; major transit pt. for EU; competes with Rotterdam; oil pt., refineries; diamonds; Gothic cath.; of artistic and historic interest; p. (1993) 465,102.

Anuradhapura, anc. cap., **Sri Lanka;** ctr. of Buddhism; comm. ctr of irrigated rice-growing a. in dry zone; p. (1995 est.) 40,000.

An-yang, c., Henan prov., **China;** coal, cotton ind.; former cap. of Shang dynasty; p. (1994) 458,000.

Anzhero-Sudzhensk, t., S.W. Siberia, **Russia;** nr. Tomsk; coal mng., mng. equipment pharmaceutics; p. (1989) 108,000.

Aoraki, mtn. *See* Cook, mtn.

Aomori, spt., N. Honshu, **Japan;** on A. Bay; cstl. tr. of timber, fish with Hokkaido; S. outlet of Seiken Tunnel between Honshu and Hokkaido; cap. of apple-growing A. prov.; p. (1990) 287,813.

Aosta, t., cap. of Val d'Aosta, N. **Italy;** in valley of Dora Baltea at node of trans-Alpine routes; iron inds.; Mont Blanc road tunnel links to Chamonix, Switzerland, opened 1964; cath., p. (1991) 36,100.

Aotearoa, Maori name for New Zealand.

Apapa, spt., sub. of Lagos, **Nigeria;** on mainland opposite I. on which Lagos is situated; modern pt. terminus of W. Nigerian rly. system; exp. agr. prods.; imports industl. prods.

Apeldoorn, c., Gelderland, **Netherlands;** holiday resort; royal summer palace of Het Loo; p. (1994) 149,449.

Apennines, mtn. "backbone" of **Italy;** rich in minerals inc. Carrara marble; cultivation on lower slopes; earthquakes, in S.; barrier to E.–W. communications; hgst. alt. 2,916 m, (Gran Sasso d'Italia); length N.–S. 1,280 km; width 120 km.

Apia, spt., N. Upolu, cap. of **Samoa;** exp. agr. prods.; p. (1999) 38,000.

Apolda, t., Erfurt, **Germany;** ball-casting and museum; p. (1994) 26,500.

Appalachian Mtns., parallel ranges between Atl. Oc. and Mississippi basin, stretching for 2,560 km from Me. to Ala., **USA;** afforestation, hydroelec. power, coal in N., iron ore in S.; region of human poverty; average alt. 900 m; Mt. Mitchell 2,039 m.

Appenzell, can., N.E. **Switzerland;** divided into the half-cans. Appenzell Inner-Rhoden, a. 174 km², cap. Appenzell; and Appenzell Ausser-Rhoden; textiles, agr.; a. 243 km², cap. Herisau; p. (1990) 65,100.

Appenzell, picturesque t., cap. of A. can., **Switzerland;** on R. Sitter; lace, embroidery.

Appian Way, anc. Roman highway; runs from Rome to Campania and S. **Italy.**

Appleton, c., Wis., **USA;** industl. c. in rich dairy dist.; p. (1990) 65,695 (c.), 315,121 (met. a. with Oshkosh-Neenah).

Apulia. *See* Puglia.

Aqaba, t., **Jordan's** only spt. at head of G. of A., 88 km from Israeli Elat.; exp. phosphates, imports petroleum; p. (1996 est.) 52,000.

Aqaba G., Red Sea, between **Sinai Peninsula** and **Saudi Arabia;** impt. Biblical waterway; few natural harbours, Dahab, Elat, Aqaba main pts; Elat ctr. of mng. a., and airpt.; length 160 km, width 24 km.

Aquila (L'Aquila), t., cap. of Abruzzo prov., **Italy;** on R. terrace of R. Aterno; mkt. and sm. inds. ass. with local farming; holiday resort; cath.; p. (1991) 66,800.

Aquitaine, region, S.W. **France;** inc. deps. Dordogne, Gironde, Landes, Lot-et-Garonne, Pyrénées-Atlantique; to W. and S.W. of Central Massif, to N of Pyrenees, bordered on W. by Atl. Oc.; warm, wet, oceanic climate; rich agr lowland, inc. Landes, reclaimed sandy area; ch. t. Bordeaux, Toulouse; p. (1999) 2,905,847.

Arabia, peninsula, S.W. **Asia;** mainly desert plateau, lying between Red Sea and Persian Gulf; inc. Saudi Arabia, South Yemen, North Yemen, Oman, United Arab Emirates, Kuwait, Bahrain, Qatar; coffee, dates, gums, horses, camels; E. Arabia rich in oil reserves; a. 2,590,000 km²; p. 8,000,000.

Arabian Desert, E. Egypt; between R. Nile and Red Sea; alt. approx. 350–2,000 m; a. 207,200 km².

Arabian Mtns., ridge along W. and S.W. csts. of **Arabia;** volcanic, hgst. peaks in Yemen Arab Rep.; average alt. 1,500 m, rising to over 3,500 km.

Arabian Sea, N.W. part of Indian Oc., tr. in Arab dhows; width 2,880 km.

Aracaju, spt., cap. of Sergipe st., **Brazil;** sugar, soap, textiles, tanneries; p. (1996) 426,600.

Arad, new t. (1962) **Israel;** in Negev desert, nr. Beersheba; inds. to be based on gasfields at Zohar and Kanaim; chemicals.

Arafura Sea, N. of Australia, S.W. of Papua-New Guinea, and E. of Timor.

Aragua, sm. upland cstl. st., **Venezuela;** lies in densely populated industl. agr., urban and political region of cty.; tropical climate; good road network; cap. Maracay in fertile Aragua valley; a. 7,014 km²; p. (1991) 1,120,100.

Araguaia, R., **Brazil;** trib. of Tocatins R.; splits

into 2 parts in middle course to form Banaral I.; rapids; length 1,800 km.

Arak, t., **Iran**; mkt. and agr. processing ctr. for surrounding region on Trans-Iranian rly.; carpets; p. (1994) 379,000.

Aral Sea (Aral'skoye More), inland sea with no outlet, **Uzbekistan/Kazakhstan**; fed by Amu-Dar'ya and Syr Dar'ya Rs.; sparse p. on shore but attempts to develop agr.; a. 63,805 km².

Aran Is.; Galway, **R.o.I.**; inc. anc. religious ctr. and I. of Inishmore; fishing; agr.; a. 47 km².

Arandjelovac, t., Serbia, **Serbia and Montenegro**; industl. a. based on local sources of refractory clays; tourist resort.

Aranjuez, t., **Spain**; 18th cent. planned t. on R. Tagus; mkt. gardens; strawberries, asparagus; p. (1990) 38,200.

Ararat, volcanic mtn., **Turkey**; supposed resting place of Noah's Ark.; 5.168 m.

Ararat, t., Victoria, **Australia**; former gold rush t. on W. Highway and ctr. for Grampians; p. (1986) 8,015.

Aras (Araxes) R., flows from Bingöl Dağlari mtns. (**Turkey**) to Caspian Sea forming long sections of **USSR–Iran** frontier; valley in rich fruit growing a.; home of anc. civilisation; length 880 km.

Araucania, region., **Chile**; cap. Temuco; concentration of A. Indians, especially in Rio Tolten valley; a. 31,761 km²; p. (1992) 774,959.

Arbroath, royal burgh, Angus, **Scot.**; engin., textiles, fishing pt.; holiday resort; p. (2002) 22,785.

Arcachon, t., Gironde, S.W. **France**; on S. side of Bassin d'Arcachon, Bay of Biscay; fish. pt., oysters; resort; p. (1990) 12,200.

Arcadia, region of anc. **Greece** in Peloponnesus; tradition of pastoral agr. in dry a.; ch. c. was Megalopolis; p. (1991) 105,309.

Arctic Ocean, almost landlocked sea extending from N. Pole to Atl. Oc.; flora and fauna of scientific interest; a. 14,089,600 km².

Ardabil, anc. c. in fertile agr. a., Azerbaijan, **Iran**; tr. and route ctr.; carpets; p. (1994) 330,000.

Ardal, t., **Norway**; on Sogne fiord; site of aluminium wks.

Ardèche, dep., S. **France**; Cevennes Mtns.; olives, wine, silk, minerals; cap. Privas; a. 55,530 km²; p. (1999) 286,010.

Ardennes, hilly wooded region, **Belgium**, N. **France**, **Luxembourg**, rising to over 600 m; infertile; heavy fighting in both world wars.

Ardennes, dep., N.E. **France**; farming, woollens, iron; cap. Mézières; a. 5,250 km²; p. (1999) 290,047.

Ardglass, sm. t., Down, **N. Ireland**; one of N.I.'s impt. fishing pts; p. (1991) 1,651.

Ardnacrusha, Clare, **R.o.I.**; power sta. on R. Shannon, 5 km N. of Limerick; p. (1991) 570.

Ardrishaig, sm. spt., Argyll and Bute, **Scot.**; on Loch Gilp, at entrance to Crinan Canal; p. (2002) 1,283.

Ardrossan, burgh, N. Ayrshire, S.W. **Scot.**; resort and spt. on Firth of Clyde; oil storage, ship-bldg., road bitumen, engin.; p. (2002) 10,952.

Ards, l. gov. dist., **N. Ireland**; formerly part of Down; N. of Strangford L.; main t. New-townards; p. (2001) 73,244.

Arecibo, spt., N. cst. **Puerto Rico**; sited in rich agr. a.; local hydroelec. power; site of major observatory. p. (1990) 93,385.

Arendal, spt. **Norway**; on Skagerrak; wood pulp, aluminium, shipping; p. (1990) 24,985.

Arequipa, c., **Peru**; cap. of A. prov. and former Inca c.; impt. wool mkt.; alpaca wool inds.; growth point for prov. industl. development; copper mng. nearby; earthquakes frequent; p. (1993) 916,806 (prov.), 619,156 (c.).

Arezzo, c., cap. of Arezzo prov., Tuscany, **Italy**; hill site in basin within Apennines at junc. of valley routes; in mediaeval times ctr. of learning and the arts; birthplace of Petrarch and Vasari; Gothic cath.; mkt. for silk, wine, olives; p. (1996) 316,735.

Argenteuil, t., Val-d'Oise, **France**; N.W. sub. of Paris; industl. inds. and suburbs; p. (1999) 93,823.

Argentina, fed. rep., S. America; 2nd. in a., 3rd. in p. of S. American sts.; p. predominantly of European origin and highly urbanised; varied relief and climate, inc. Andes, tropical N., Chaco, Pampas, Patagonia in S.; agr. less impt. internally than other S. American sts., yet provides most of exp., inc. meat, wool, wheat, maize, cotton; petroleum, natural gas; cap. Buenos Aires; new cap. to be built on fringe of Patagonia to

decentralize power from Buenos Aires; econ. and polit. turmoil, 2002; a. 2,797,109 km²; p. (2004) 39,144,753.

Argos, c. of anc. **Greece**; N.E. Peloponnesus; leading c. in 7th cent. under King Pheidon; p. (1991) 78,884.

Argostólion, cap. of Cephalonia I., **Greece**; ship-bldg.; earthquake 1953; p. (1991) 6,750.

Argyll and Bute, W. Scot.; unit. auth. created in 1996, incorporating most of historic co. of **Argyllshire** which became part of Strathclyde in 1974; rural a. N.W. of Glasgow conurb.; p. (2002) 91,030.

Arhus, c., **Denmark**; prin. spt. on E. cst. Jutland; admin. ctr. of A. prov.; Gothic cath.; univ.; comm. and industl. ctr.; pt. processing inds., oil refining; p. (1992) 202,140.

Arica, spt., N. **Chile**, free zone; exp. tin, copper, sulphur mainly from Bolivia; rly. to La Paz and oil pipeline connects to Sica-Sica in Bolivia; p. (1992) 169,217.

Ariège, dep., S. **France**; Pyrenees in S., fertile lowland in N.; livestock, fruit, iron, copper; cap. Foix; a. 4,900 km²; p. (1999) 137,138.

Arizona, st., **USA**; home of Apache Indians; much desert, rainfall increasing to E.; many lge. irrigation schemes for cotton, grain, fruit, vegetables; inc. Col. Plateau and Grand Canyon to N.; copper, lead mng. and refining; prin. ts. Phoenix (cap.), Tucson; huge meteorite crater nr. Winslow; admitted to union 1912; st. flower Saguaro Cactus blossom; st. bird cactus wren; a. 295,024 km²; p. (2002) 5,456,453.

Arkansas, st., **USA**; highland in N.W., inc. Ozark, Ouachita mtns., lowland in S.E. where Arkansas R. and Mississippi alluvium; humid climate; cotton cultivation; bauxite, coal, petroleum; admitted to union 1836; st. flower Apple Blossom, st. bird Mockingbird; cap. Little Rock; a. 137,534 km²; p. (2002) 2,710,079.

Arkansas, R., **USA**; rises in Rockies, trib. of Mississippi; completion (1971) of 704 km waterway (17 dams and locks), opening Okla. and Ark. to sea; flows through impt. agr. a.; several major cs. on banks; length 2,334 km.

Arkhangel'sk, c., major spt., **Russia**; on E. side Dvina estuary, White Sea; lge. harbour kept open in winter by ice breakers; fishery head-quarters; inds. from local softwood resources; engin.; hydroelec. power; p. (1989) 416,000.

Arklow, t., spt., Wicklow, **R.o.I.**; fisheries, pottery; fertiliser plant under construction; resort; p. (1991) 8,000.

Arlberg, Alpine pass, 1,803 m; main western entry to Austria; rly. tunnel 10 km long; road tunnel (1979) 14 km long.

Arles, t., Provence, S. **France**; on Rhône delta; anc. Roman t.; historic bldgs. and monuments; Roman amphitheatre painted here; p. (1990) 52,593.

Arlington, t., Texas, **USA**; aircraft, missiles; rapid expansion; p. (2000) 332,969.

Arlington, t., Va., **USA**; Arlington National Cemetery contains tombs of the Unknown Soldier and President Kennedy; p. (1996) 175,334.

Arlon, t., cap. of Luxembourg prov., **Belgium**; p. (1991) 23,420.

Armadale, burgh, W. Lothian, **Scot.**; 16 km S.W. Linlithgow; p. (1991) 8,958.

Armagh, former co.; l. gov. dist., **N. Ireland**; lowland in N. rising to over 450 m adjoins R.o.I. border; mainly rural; p. (1991) 51,817.

Armagh, c., **N. Ireland**; caths.; linen, whiskey; p. (1991) 14,265.

Armenia, CIS, former rep. USSR; former a divided between Turkey, Russia, Iran; mineral inds.; sub-tropical agr.; hydroelec. stas. under constr.; earth-quake 1988; disturbances 1989; cap. Yerevan; a. 30,821 km²; p. (2004) 2,991,360.

Armenia, t., Colombia; coffee; earthquake devastation (1999); p. (1992) 212,310.

Armentières, mftg. t., Nord, **France**; base of British operations against Lille in first world war; textiles; p. (1999) 25,267.

Armidale, t., N.S.W., **Australia**; univ.; ctr. of New England wool producing dist.; p. (1991) 21,600.

Arnhem, c., cap. of Gelderland prov., **Neth.**; on R. Neder-Rhine; lge. tin smelter; lt. inds. using rubber and rayon; p. (1994) 133,670 (c.), 311,755 (met. a.).

Arnhem Land, N. part of N.T., **Australia**; an aboriginal reserve; nat. park; a. 96,089 km².

Arno, R., central **Italy**; flows past Florence and Pisa into Mediterranean; Val d'Arno is the fruitful valley of the R.; length 120 km.

Arnold, t., Gedling, Notts., **Eng.**; almost continuous with Nottingham; hosiery, brick mkg.; p. (2001) 37,402.

Arnsberg, c. N. Rhine Westphalia, **Germany**; mftg. on R. Ruhr; p. (1999) 78,600.

Arnstadt, t., Erfurt, **Germany**; on R. Gera, 16 km S. of Erfurt; artificial silk, leather gds., engin.; p. (1989) 29,665.

Aroostook, dist., New England, **USA**; produces 12 per cent of USA potatoes.

Arran, I., N. Ayrshire, **Scot.**; in Firth of Clyde; contains many summer resorts; p. (1991) 4,474.

Arras, t., cap. of Pas-de-Calais dep., **France**; historic cap. of Artois; renowned for tapestry; agr. mkt.; brewing, textiles, metal inds.; almost destroyed in first world war; p. (1990) 42,715(t.), 79,607 (met. a.).

Árta, prov., Epirus, **Greece**; agr. area; Pindhos range; p. (1991) 78,884.

Arthur's Seat, famous hill, Edinburgh, **Scot.**; 251 m.

Artois, former prov. of N. **France**; now mainly with dep. of Pas-de-Calais.

Aru Is., gr., **Indonesia**; S.W. of W. Irian; fertile; sago, rice, sugar, coconuts, tobacco; a. 8,402 km²; p. 18,139.

Aruba, I., Leeward Is., **W.I.**; closure of oil refinery (1985) which provided employment and one-third gov. receipts; shipping; guano; voted for indep. (1977) internal self-government granted 1986; a. 176 km²; p. (2004) 71,218.

Arun, l. gov. dist., West Sussex, **Eng.**; W. section of S. Downs and ts. of Arundel, Littlehampton and Bognor Regis; p. (2001) 140,759.

Arunachal Pradesh, new union terr. (1972), N.E. Assam, **India**; formerly N.E. Frontier Agency; in Himalayas bordering Tibet and Burma; tribal p.; cap. Itanagar; a. 81,424 km²; p. (2001) 1,091,100.

Arundel, t., Arun, West Sussex, **Eng.**; mkt. t. on Arun R.; Arundel Castle, seat of Duke of Norfolk; p. (1991) 3,033.

Arusha, t., **Tanzania**; S.W. of Mt. Meru; mkt. for coffee; H.Q. of E. African Common Market; airpt. at 1,388 m (W. of t.).

Aruwimi, R., **Congo**; trib. of R. Congo; route of Stanley's famous forest march in 1887; 902 km long.

Arvika, t., N. of L. Vänern, **Sweden**; agr. machin. and implements, pianos, organs.

Asahikawa, c., Hokkaido, **Japan**; on Ishikari R.; industl., comm. and rly. ctr. for gr. agr. region; p. (1990) 359,069.

Asansol, t., W. Bengal, **India**; in Damodar valley; rly. junc.; coal mng., iron, steel; p. (1991) 262,000.

Ascension I., part of Brit. col. **St. Helena**, 1,216 km to S.E.; volcanic; ch. settlement Georgetown; nesting place of sooty tern; Brit. earth satellite sta. (1966); airstrip known as Miracle Mile; some arable and pastoral agr.; some tourist growth; a. 88 km²; p. (1993) 1,117.

Aschaffenburg, t., Bavaria, **Germany**; pt. on R. Main and Trans-European waterway; cas.; synthetic fibres, scientific-based inds.; p. (2002) 68,361.

Ascoli Piceno, cath. c., central **Italy**; cap. of A.P. prov.; lies in wooded hills; agr. inds.; (1991) 53,600.

Ascot, v., Berks., **Eng.**; racecourse at Ascot Heath.

Ashanti, admin. region, central **Ghana**; formerly powerful native st.; timber, cocoa; growing importance of gold mines (15% Ghana's exp.); new mines opened 1984; cap. Kumasi; a. 24,390 km²; p. (1990) 2,490,000.

Ashbourne, t., Derbys. Dales, **Eng.**; nr Dovedale; mkt. t.; quarrying, milk processing, antique shops; p. (1991) 6,300.

Ashburton, t., Teignbridge, Devon, **Eng.**; old mkt. t., S. gateway to Dartmoor; anc. stannary t.; p. (1991) 3,564.

Ashburton, t., S. Island, **N.Z.**; ctr. of gr. wheat growing dist.; p. (1996) 15,598.

Ashby-de-la-Zouch, t., North West Leics., **Eng.**; hosiery; p. (1991) 10,595.

Ashdod, pt., **Israel**; new modern deepwater pt. on Med. cst., 32 km S. of Jaffa.

Ashdown Forest, East Sussex, **Eng.**; heath and woodland; site of former iron industry.

Asheville, c., N.C., **USA**; economic and cultural ctr. of mtnous. region; winter resort; glass; p. (1996) 64,067.

Ashfield, l. gov. dist., Notts., **Eng.**; comprises Sutton-in-Ashfield, Hucknall and Kirkby-in-Ashfield; p. (2001) 111,387.

Ashford, t., l. gov. dist., Kent, **Eng.**; mkt. t., rly. works, site of international station at northern end of channel tunnel; p. (2001) 102,661 (dist.), (2001) 58,936 (t.).

Ashgabat, c., cap. of **Turkmenistan**; in foothills of Kopet-Dag mtns.; textiles, clothing, food processing; univ.; p. (2000) 520,000.

Ashikaga, c., Honshu, **Japan**; cultural ctr.; old silk-weaving ctr.; anc. school with library of Chinese classics; p. (1990) 167,687.

Ashington, t., Wansbeck, Northumberland, **Eng.**; coal mng., p. (2001) 27,335.

Ashkhabad. *See* Ashgabat.

Ashtabula, t., Ohio, **USA**; pt. on L. Erie handling iron ore, coal; many inds.; p. (1990) 21,600.

Ashton-in-Makerfield, t. Gtr. Manchester, **Eng.**; nr. Wigan; former coal mng.; p. (2001) 28,505.

Ashton-under-Lyne, t., Tameside, Gtr. Manchester, **Eng.**; textiles, lt. engin., rubber, tobacco; p. (2001) 43,236.

Asia, largest continent, extends over nearly one-third of the land surface of the earth; chief mtn. ranges, Himalayas, Kunlun, Tien Shan, Altai, Tibetan plateau; ch. Rs., Ob, Yangtze, Yenisey, Lena, Amur, Hwang-ho, Mekong; deserts, Arabia, Thar, Takla Makan, Gobi; some very fertile valleys and plains; climate very varied, extreme in N., monsoonal in S. and E.; gold, coal, oil, iron, manganese, antimony, tin; principal countries in Asia: Turkey in Asia, Israel, Jordan, Iran, Iraq, Afghanistan, India, Pakistan, Sri Lanka, Myanmar (Burma), China, Vietnam, Indonesia, Thailand, Malaysia, South Korea, North Korea, Japan, Bangladesh, Cambodia, Laos, Philippines, Syria, Lebanon, Taiwan, and Russian Asia; industrialisation greatest in Japan, China, Korea, India, and former Russian Asia; a. c. 44,614,000 km²; p. (2003) 3,823,000,000.

Asia Minor. *See* Anatolia.

Asir, dist., S.W. **Saudi Arabia**; desert cstl. plain with parallel R. mtns.

Asmara, c., cap. of **Eritrea**; alt. 2,226 m; on rly.; textiles, matches, soap, brewing; p. (1999) 514,000.

Asnières, t., sub. N.W. Paris, Hauts-de-Seine, **France**; regattas; p. (1990) 72,250.

Aspra Spitia, t. central **Greece**; new industl. t. close to Andikira Bay; aluminium wks.

Aspull, t., Gtr. Manchester, **Eng.**; nr. Wigan; former coal mng.; p. (1991) 4,765.

Assam, st., **India**; on Brahmaputra R.; valley enclosed by mtns.; forested; extensive tea plantations; rice, cotton, coal; oil development at Rudrasagar; former cap. Shillong; since 1956 4 new sts. carved out – Nagaland (1963), Meghalaya, Manipur, Tripura (1972), and union terrs. of Arunachal Pradesh and Mizoram (1972); a. (1972) 121,973 km²; p. (2001) 26,638,400.

Assen, t., prov. cap. Drenthe, **Neth.**; route ctr.; food processing; p. (1994) 52,268.

Assisi, t., Umbria, central **Italy**; birthplace of St. Francis; cath. and old cas.; damaged by earthquake (1997); p. (1991) 24,600.

Assyria, gr. anc. empire, northern plain Mesopotamia (Iraq), cap. Nineveh; drained by R. Tigris; now mainly pastoral farming a.)

Astana, c., new cap. of **Kazakhstan** (since 1995), transport ctr.; mftg.; p. (1990) 311,900.

Asti, t., **Italy**; route, industl., comm. ctr.; cath.; sparkling wines; p. (1996) 209,798.

Astrakhan', c., **Russia**; major air and sea pt. on delta of R. Volga, 80 km from Caspian Sea; handles petroleum, timber; lge. fishing fleet; caviar; food and pt. processing inds.; astrakhan fur; cap. A. oblast; univ.; p. (1989) 509,000.

Asturias, region and former kingdom, N.W. **Spain**; S. of Bay of Biscay; now Oviedo prov.; isolated from rest of Spain by Cantabrian mtns.; coal mng; p. (1998) 1,082,000.

Asunción, c., cap. of **Paraguay**; at confluence of Rs. Paraguay and Pilcomayo; 25 per cent of p. of Paraguay in and around A.; admin., industl., comm. ctr.; cath.; p. (2000) 1,262,000 (met. a.).

Aswan, t. and prov., Upper **Egypt**; on Nile at first cataract; anc. name Syene. Aswan dam built 1902, 5 km S. of t., to control Nile flood; lge. cement plant; univ. proposed; p. (1986) 191,461 (t.), (1991) 925,000 (prov.).

Aswan High Dam (107 m high) opened 1971, on R. Nile, **Egypt**, 6 km S. of old Aswan dam, has harnessed R. to bring electricity and irrigation to hundreds of vs. and prevent Nile's flood from being lost into Mediterranean. *See also* Nile.

Asyût, major c. and prov. of Upper **Egypt**; nr. A. dam on Nile R.; anc. Lycopolis; noted pottery, wood, ivory carving; caravan tr. ctr.; cap, of A. prov.; p. (1996) 343,500 (c.), 2,802,000 (prov.).

Atacama, region **Chile;** cap. Copiapo; a. 75,705km²; p. (1992) 230,786.

Atacama Desert, N. Chile; arid coastal tract rich in nitrates; one of world's driest deserts.

Atami, t., Honshu, **Japan;** on Sagami Bay; seaside hot-spring resort; p. (1990) 47,291.

Ataturk Dam, on R. Euphrates, **Turkey.** Sixth largest in world when completed.

Atbarah, t., **Sudan;** at confluence of Atbara R. with Nile; heavy inds.; international airpt.; p. (1993) 87,900.

Atbarah R., or **Black Nile, Ethiopia** and **Sudan;** trib. of Nile; provides irrigation water for Sudan; length 1,264 km.

Athelney, hill, formerly encircled by marsh nr. Taunton, Somerset, **Eng.;** between the Rs. Tone and Parret; King Alfred's hiding-place.

Athens (Athinai), c., can of Greece, on plain of Attica, admin., economic and cultural ctr.; varied mnfs., notably textiles; anc. c. of Greek art and learning; Acropolis and many splendid temples; univ.; airpt; underground rly. opened (2000); hosted 2004 Olympics; p. (1999) 748,100 (c.), 3,110,000 (met. a.).

Athens, t., Ga., **USA;** univ.; cotton gds., lumber; p. (1996) 89,405.

Athens, t., Ohio, **USA;** univ.; coal, lt. inds.; p. (1990) 21,300.

Atherstone, t., North Warwicks., **Eng.;** N. of Coventry; mkt. t., footwear, granite quarrying; p. (1991) 10,677.

Athlone, t., Westmeath, **R.o.I.;** on R. Shannon; radio sta.; textiles; p. (1991) 15,400.

Atholl, dist., N. Perth and Kinross, **Scot.;** extensive deer forests and grouse moors.

Athos, peninsula, Khalkidhiki, N.E. **Greece;** Mt. Athos (2,034 m) at S. tip, known as Holy Mountain, home of monastic community; ch. t. Karves.

Atitlán L., S.W. **Guatemala;** volcanic; famed for beauty; dense p. on shore; maize, fishing; a. 137 km².

Atlanta, c., st. cap. Ga., **USA;** univ.; cotton, paper, farm implements, printing, clothing; p. (2000) 416,474 (c.), 2,833,511 (met. a.).

Atlantic City, c., N.J., **USA;** summer resort, convention c.; p. (1990) 37,986 (c.), 319,000 (met. a.).

Atlantic Ocean, 2nd lgst ocean; a. est. 82,440,000 km²; connected to Pac. Oc. by Panama Canal; central ridge of volcanic activity runs S. from Iceland to Antarctic, some peaks emerging as Is. mainly in N. (*e.g.* Azores, Ascension, Tristan da Cunha); S, mainly a barren waste of water; chief deeps: Milwaukee Deep (9,225 m) nr. Bahamas and Nares Deep (8,531 m) nr. Puerto Rico.

Atlas, mtn. range, N.W. **Africa;** extends 2,400 km through Morocco, Algeria, to Tunisia; formed of several chains; mineralised, roads across passes; long been home of Berber tribes; average height 2,500–3,000 m; hgst. peak Jebel Toubkal, 4,141 m.

Attica, (Attiki), dep., **Greece;** agr., serving cap. Athens; a. 3,761 km²; p. (1991) 3,523,407.

Attleboro, c., Mass., **USA;** founded (1669) by immigrants from English Attleborough (Norfolk); jewellery, silverware.

Attock, t., **Pakistan;** on Indus R. between Peshawar and Islamabad; oil wells, oil refining; impt. crossing of R. Indus.

Atyrau, (Guryev) c., **Kazakhstan;** pt. on R. Ural at entrance to Caspian Sea; oil refining; pipe-line to Orsk; p. (1990) 151,400.

Aube, dep., N.E. **France;** arid, infertile chalk in ctr. and N.W.; wooded and fertile S.E.; drained by Seine and A. Rs.; cap. Troyes; a. 6,024 km²; p. (1999) 292,020.

Aubervilliers, t., Seine-St. Denis, **France;** sub. of Paris; industl.; p. (1990) 67,836.

Auburn, t., N.Y., **USA;** shoes, woollens, farm implements; st. prison; p. (1990) 31,300.

Auch, t., cap. of Gers dep., **France;** agr., mkt., tr. in Armagnac brandy; agr. processing; p. (1999) 21,838.

Auchterarder, burgh, Perth and Kinross, **Scot.;** 24 km S.W. of Perth; health resort on S. slopes of Vale of Strathearn; woollen inds.; p. (2002) 3,945.

Auchtermuchty, burgh, Fife, **Scot.;** at S. foot of Lomond Hills, 40 km N.E. of Alloa; distilling (now closed down); p. (2002) 2,010.

Auckland, spt., c., N.I., **N.Z.;** lgst. c. in N.Z.; seat of government 1845–64; univ.; extensive tr. and shipping; sawmills, sugar refinery, shipbldg., glass; steelwks. projected 40 km S. of A., in Waikato iron sand a.; p. (1991) 315,668 (c.), 855,571 (urban a.).

Aude, dep., S. **France;** mtnous.; fertile N., salt from S. cstl. lagoons; drained by A. R. to Mediterranean; cap. Carcassonne; a. 6,340 km² p. (1999) 309,639.

Audenshaw, t., Gtr. Manchester, **Eng.;** metals, leather, pharmaceuticals; p. (1991) 13,173.

Aughrim, v., Galway, **R.o.I.;** battle (1691) between William III and James II.

Augsburg, c., Bavaria, **Germany;** at confluence of Rs. Lech and Wertach; cath'; theological institute; major industl. ctr., textiles, engin.; route ctr.; p. (2002) 257,836.

Augusta, t., (Sicily), **Italy;** on E. cst. peninsula; gd. harbour used as naval base; fishing; lubricants; p. (1991) 34,200.

Augusta, c., Maine, **USA;** state capital and commercial centre on Kennebec River; p. (1996) 20,441.

Augusta, c., Georgia, **USA;** pt.; on Savannah R. and boundary with S.C.; cotton, cotton-seed oil, chemicals, foundries; p. (1990) 44,600 (c.), 397,000 (met. a.).

Aulnay-sous-Bois, t., Seine-St. Denis, **France;** residtl. sub. of Paris; p. (1999) 80,018.

Aurangabad, t., admin. ctr., Maharashtra, **India;** textiles, grain tr.; p. (1991) 573,000.

Aurès, mtn. massif, **Algeria;** Berber stronghold.

Aurignac, v., Haute-Garonne, S. **France;** at foot of Pyrenees; caves, paleolithic remains; p. (1999) 978.

Aurillac, t., cap., mkt. t. for dep. of Cantal, **France;** cheeses, umbrellas, leather goods; p. (1999) 30,552.

Auschwitz. *See* Oswiecim.

Aussig. *See* Usti Nad Labem.

Austin, st. cap., Texas, **USA;** educational and artistic ctr., st. univ.; food processing; major airpt.; p. (2000) 656,562 (c.), 782,000 (met. a.).

Australasia, div. of **Oceania;** inc. Australia, Tasmania, N.Z., New Guinea and neighbouring archipelagos.

Australia, Commonwealth of, lgst. I., smallest continent in world; forms part of Australasia; Cook took possession for Britain 1770; Commonwealth proclaimed 1901; fed. of N.S.W., Victoria, Queensland, S.A., W. Australia, Tasmania; inc. also Cap. Terr. (Canberra) and N.T.; p. and inds. concentrated around cst. and in st. caps.; 41 per cent live in Gtr. Sydney and Melbourne; agr. economy (sheep, wheat, dairying) giving way to mineral inds. esp. in W.A. where lge. and diverse deposits abound; offshore petroleum deposits; N. cst. tropical, interior dry, S.E. cst. more moderate, Mediterranean climate in S.W.; mtns. in E. form Gr. Dividing Range separating E. cst. from interior, where plains drained by Murray-Darling and L. Eyre R. systems (used for hydroelec. power and irrigation); referendum (1999) voted against republic; cap. Canberra; a. 7,682,300 km²; p. (2004) 19,913,144.

Australian Alps, form S. part of Gr. Dividing Range, between E. cst. and interior, **Australia;** extend for 320 km.; contain highst. mtns. in Australia; Mount Kosciusko (2,228 m.); snow melt vital for irrigation of S.E.; popular tourist and naturalist a.

Australian Antarctic Territory, part of Antarctica; between 145° E. and 160° E. and S. of 60° S. excluding Adélie Land; research stas. of Mawson, Davis and Casey.

Australian Capital Territory, fed. terr. surrounding Canberra, seat of Fed. Govt. of **Australia;** also inc. a. around Jervis Bay, originally planned to serve as pt. p. (1993) 299,400.

Austria, rep., Europe; after long and glamorous history under the Habsburgs, instability between Austria and Hungary a cause of first world war; forcibly incorporated in German Reich, 1938, liberated 1945, recovered indep. 1955; almost entirely within Alps; drained mainly by Danube; continental climate; magnificent scenery generates a major tourist ind. but much food must be imported; forests and timber inds.; mineralised, iron-ore of Styria; hydro-elec.; inds. located in ts.; cap. Vienna; joined EU 1995; farright election gains (1999); a. 83,898 km²; p. (2004) 8,174,762.

Austria, Lower, st., **Austria;** impt. agr. a.;

cap. Vienna; a. (excluding Vienna) 18,384 km²; p. (excluding Vienna) (1993) 1,505,266.

Austria, Upper, st., **Austria**; oil, gas, iron & steel, aluminium mftg.; cap. Linz; a. 11,980 km²; p. (1993) 1,373,317.

Auvergne, old prov. and present region of **France**; inc. deps. **Allier, Cantal, Haute-Loire, Puy-de-Dôme**; part of Massif Central; volcanic scenery; ch. t. Clermont-Ferrand; p. (1990) 1,321,200.

Auvergne Mtns., mtns., central **France**; in N.W. of Central Massif; highest peak Puy de Sancy in Mt. Dore, 1,887 m; volcanic landscape.

Auxerre, t., cap. of Yonne dep., **France**; comm. and industl. ctr.; wine; tr.; Gothic cath.; p. (1999) 37,777.

Ava, c., **Myanmar**; on the Irrawaddy R.; former cap.; many pagodas, now ruins; bridge over R.

Avebury, v., Wilts,. **Eng.**; mediaeval v. outside Neolithic circle and avenues, nr. Silbury Hill; lgst. prehistoric structure in England.

Aveiro, t., **Portugal**; on Vouga estuary, connected to sea by canal; fish. pt. salt from lagoons; p. (1991) 35,200.

Avellaneda, industl. sub. of Buenos Aires, **Argentina**; hides, wool; p. (1991) 346,600.

Avellino, t., cap. of A. prov., **Italy**; on motorway from Naples to W.; monastery; sulphur mng. and refining; hats; p. (1996) 441,675.

Aversa, t. **Italy**; in fertile plain of Campania; agr. and route ctr.; p. (1991) 54,030.

Aveyron, dep., **France**; on S.W. rim of Central Massif, inc. Causses limestones; extensive forests; grain, dairying, sheep; coal; cap. Rodez; a. 8,767 km²; p. (1999) 263,784.

Aviemore, t., Highland, **Scot.**; on R. Spey, 19 km S.W. of Grantown; winter sports; p. (2002) 2,397.

Avignon, t., cap. of Vaucluse, dep., **France**; anc. Roman t. at crossing of R. Rhône; Provençal tourist ctr.; diversified inds. inc. wine tr.; p. (1999) 85,730.

Avila, t., cap. of A. prov., **Spain**, in Old Castile; univ., cath.; mediaeval architecture; birth-place of St. Teresa; p. (1991) 45,000, (1998) 167,800 (prov.).

Avon, R., Wiltshire/Bath and N.E. Somerset/Bristol, **Eng.**; flows from Cotswolds to enter Bristol Channel at Avonmouth; spectacular limestone gorge between Bristol and the sea; length 128 km.

Avon, R., Warwicks, **Eng.**; flows past Stratford-on-A., to reach Severn R. at Tewkesbury; fertile agr. valley; string of ts. along course; length 152 km.

Avon, R., Wilts./Hants./Dorset, **Eng.**; flows past Salisbury into English Channel at Christchurch; length 112 km.

Avonmouth, outport of Bristol, at mouth of R. Avon, **Eng.**; docks; seed crushing, petrol refinery, non-ferrous metal and chemical plants.

Avranches, t., Manche, **France**; Normandy mkt. t.; cider and dairy produce; p. (1993) 9,500.

Awe, Loch, Argyll and Bute, **Scot.**; 13 km N.W. of Inveraray, bordered by Ben Cruachan; length 40 km; salmon and trout fishing; hydroelec. sta. at Cruachan.

Axholme, Isle of, flat lowland a., N. Lincs., **Eng.**; W. of Trent R.; drained by Vermuyden in 17th cent.

Ayacucho (Huamanga.) c., and prov., **Peru**; founded by Pizarro in 1539; lies in equable fertile valley; p. (1993) 492,507 (prov.), 105,918 (c.).

Aydin, t., **Turkey**; anc. Tralles; rly. and agr. tr. ctr. for surrounding a.; p. (1990) 106,600 (c.), 824,816 (prov.).

Ayers Rock. See **Uluru**.

Aylesbury, co. t., Aylesbury Vale, Bucks., **Eng.**; mkt. t.; expanded t.; p. (2001) 69,021.

Aylesbury Vale, l. gov. dist., Bucks., **Eng.**; a. in N.W. of co. inc. Aylesbury and Buckingham; p. (2001) 165,748.

Aylesford, mkt. t., Kent, **Eng.**; N.W. Maidstone; p. (2001) 24,244.

Ayr, royal burgh, S. Ayrshire, **Scot.**; pt. on F. of Clyde, 48 km S.W. of Glasgow; Burns born nearby; p. (2002) 46,431.

Ayrshire, historic co., W. **Scot.**; now divided into E., N., and S. Ayrshire.

Aysen, reg. Chile; cap. Coihaique; a. 108,997 km²; p. (1992) 82,017.

Aysgarth, v. Richmondshire, North Yorks., **Eng.**; on R. Ure in Wensleydale; famous waterfalls.

Ayutthaya, t., **Thailand**; former cap., on Menam Chao Phraya R. delta; ruins; p. (1990) 61,200.

Azarbaijan, E. and W., provs., N. **Iran**; border Azabaijan and Turkey; cap. (E.A.) Tabriz; cap. (W.A.) Rezayeh; p. (2002) 3,379,000 (W) and 2,768,000 (E).

Azerbaijan, CIS, former rep. USSR; Transcaucasia, rep.; Caucasus and Lesser Caucasus separated by hot dry irrigated steppe; major oil boom, 1990s; disturbances 1989; endemic corruption; 86,661 km²; p. (2004) 7,868,385.

Azores, gr. of physically and climatically attractive Is. in mid-Atlantic about 1,440 km W. of Lisbon, **Portugal**; partial indep. by regional gov. (1977); volcanic; fruit, wine; ch. spts: Ponta Delgada, Horta, Angra do Heroismo; U.S. air bases on Terceira I.; a. 2,569 km²; p. (1991) 241,600.

Azov Sea (Azovskoye More), Ukraine/**Russia**; joins Black Sea by Kerch strait; receives Don R.; fisheries; a. 36,000 km².

Azraq Desert Nat. Park, **Jordan**; first Jordanian nat. park around oasis of Azraq, 96 km E. of Amman; a. 3,900 km².

B

Baalbek, c., **Lebanon**, S.W. Asia; old Heliopolis; ruins; tourism.

Bab-el-Mandeb, strait connecting Red Sea and Indian Oc.; dangerous but impt. shipping lane; length 32 km, width 27 km.

Babergh, l. gov. dist., S. Suffolk, **Eng.**; inc. Sudbury and Hadleigh; p. (2001) 83,461.

Babylon, anc. cap. of Babylonian Empire, in Euphrates valley about 96 km S. of Baghdad, **Iraq**.

Bacau, t., E. **Romania**; on R. Bistrita; oil, saw-milling, textiles; p. (1992) 204,495.

Bacolod City, t., Negros, **Philippines**; sm. pt.; exp. sugar; p. (1995) 402,000.

Bacton, v., Norfolk, **Eng.**; terminal for S. gasfields in N. Sea; p. (1991) 1,435 (with Walcott).

Bacup, t., Rossendale, S.E. Lancs., **Eng.**; 32 km N. of Manchester; textiles, felts, footwear; p. (1991) 13,682.

Badagri, t., W. of Lagos, **Nigeria**; on the Bight of Benin; formerly a gr. slave pt.; coir sacks.

Badajoz, lgst. prov., **Spain**; gr. reclamation scheme in progress; a. 21,624 km²; p. (1998) 663,800.

Badajoz, c., cap. of B. prov., W. **Spain**, in Estremadura; anc. fortress c.; transit tr.; p. (1991) 129,737.

Badalona, c. nr. Barcelona, **Spain**; shipbldg.; p. (1991) 206,120.

Baden, t., **Switzerland**; health resort, mineral springs; p. (2000) 15,900.

Baden-Baden, t., Baden-Wurttemberg, **Germany**; fashionable spa; p. (2002) 53,084.

Baden-Württemberg, *Land*, **Germany**; created 1952; bounded by Rhine in W., drained by Neckar and Donau R. systems; mtnous, inc. Black Forest and Swabian Jura; received much immigrant ind. from E. Europe, so encouraging prosperous and diversified industl. structure; several impt. industl. regions centred on Mannheim, Karlsruhe, and cap. Stuttgart; a. 35,750 km²; p. (2005) 10,700,000.

Bad Lands, S.D., **USA**; stretches of infertile badly eroded soil.

Badrinath, mtn. and t., Uttar Pradesh, **India**; pilgrim shrine of Vishnu.

Badulla, t., **Sri Lanka**; tea; anc. t.; rly. terminus; ctr. of tea estates; p. (1995) 35,000.

Badwater, salt pool, Cal., **USA**; 85 m below sea-level, lowest point in N. America.

Baeza, t., S. **Spain**; anc. Moorish c.; olives, wine; p. (1991) 15,270.

Baffin B., between Greenland and Canada; joined to Atl. Oc. by Davis Strait, to Arctic Oc. by Nares Strait; open 4 months per year; B.I., in W., ctr. of Arctic research and communications; length 1,120 km, width 100–650 km.

Baghdad, c., cap. of **Iraq**; anc. c. on R. Tigris; terminus Baghdad rly.; airport; univ.; textiles, gum, bricks, tiles, metal inds.; heavy fighting in 2003 war; p. (2000) 4,797,000.

Baghdad, prov. or liwa, **Iraq**; between Iran and Syrian Desert; inc. some of the most fertile lands in the Tigris and Euphrates valleys; p. (2000) 6,211,200.

Baghlan, t., **Afghanistan;** new industl. t. in ctr. of sugar producing a.; alt. 518 m.

Bagnolet, t., Seine-St. Denis, **France;** sub. of Paris; famous for "plaster of Paris" from local gypsum; textiles; p. (1999) 32,511.

Bagshot, t., Surrey Heath, Surrey, **Eng.;** heath of same name; historically old postal town, 42 km S.W. of London; residtl.; p. (1991) 5,190.

Baguio, Luzon, N.W. of Manila, summer cap. of **Philippines,** alt. 1,500 m; p. (1990) 183,102.

Bahamas, indep. st. (1973) within Brit. Commonwealth, W.I.; more than 700 coral atolls; subtropical climate; valuable tourist tr.; exp. crayfish; lashed by Hurricane Floyd, 1999; cap. Nassau; a. 11,406 km²; p. (2004) 299,697.

Bahawalpur, t., **Pakistan;** former cap. of B. princely st.; impt. bridging point over Sutlej R.; p. (1998) 403,400.

Bahia, st., **Brazil;** cap. Salvador; cattle, cacao, sugar, coffee, tobacco; oil, extensive mineral deposits; a. 560,139 km²; p. (1991) 11,801,810.

Bahía Blanca, spt., **Argentina;** industl. ctr., oil refining; prin. shipping point of S.; exp. oil, grain, wool, hides; p. (1991) 271,467.

Bahrain, indep. st. (1971) in Persian G.; low sandy Is. linked by road causeway to Saudi Arabia (1985); springs allow cultivation of dates; oil wells, oil and aluminium refining; trading ctr., declining importance of agr. as incr. salinity of traditional water supplies; cap. Manamah; airpt. at Muharraq; a. 678 km²; p. (2004) 677,886. This includes 235,108 non-nationals.

Baia, historic v., Campania, **Italy;** beautifully situated on Bay of Naples; celebrated Roman pleasure resort.

Baia-Mare, t., N.W. **Romania;** on Somesul R., in region mining copper, lead, zinc, gold, silver; mtn. resort; p. (1992) 148,815.

Baikal L. *See* **Baykal L.**

Baildon, t., West Yorks., **Eng.;** nr. Bradford; moorland resort; p. (1991) 15,385.

Baja, t., **Hungary;** impt. bridging point of R. Danube in Gr. Plain; p. (1997) 38,000.

Baja California. *See* **Lower California.**

Bakar, pt., **Croatia** (formerly Yugoslavia); S. of Rijeka; new pt. and oil harbour.

Bakersfield, c., Cal., **USA;** ctr. of oil prod. and refining; aircraft assembly; p. (2000) 247,057 (c.), 543,000 (met. a.).

Bakewell, t., Derbys Dales. **Eng.;** tourist ctr. Peak District; agr., mng.; p. (1991) 3,818.

Bakhchisaray, t., Crimea, **Ukraine;** old cap. of Tartar Khans; copper, leather; p. (1990) 25,700.

Bakhuis Gebergte mtns., W. **Suriname;** major aluminium complex based on local power and bauxite.

Baku, cap. of **Azerbaijan;** pt. on Caspian Sea; univ.; new oil boom in 1990s; oil pipeline connects with Tbilisi and Ceyhan (opened 2005); shipbldg.; p. (2000) 1,936,000 (met. a.).

Bala, t., Gwynedd, N. **Wales;** mkt. town; tourism; p. (1991) 1,922.

Bala, L., Gwynedd, N. **Wales;** drained by the Dee.

Balaklava, pt., S. Crimea, **Ukraine;** scene of the charge of the Light Brigade (1854).

Balaton, L., lgst. in **Hungary;** a. 596 km²; long history of settlement in a.; shores forested; vineyards; tourism.

Balbriggan, spt., Dublin, **R.o.I.;** p. (1991) 7,700.

Baldock, t., North Herts., **Eng.;** on N. edge of Chiltern Hills and Gr. N. Road; hosiery, malting, lt. engin.; p. (1991) 9,232.

Baldwin, t., N.Y., **USA;** on S. Long I.; fisheries.

Balearic Is., in Mediterranean Sea, **Spain;** inc. Majorca, Minorca, Ibiza, Formentera; limestone scenery and mild climate encourage tourism which has swamped Moorish influence; agr.; ch. t. Palma; a. 5,014 km²; p. (1998) 796,500.

Bali, I. off Java, **Indonesia,** in Lesser Sundas; equable climate, fertile soil, luxurious vegetation; p. mainly engaged in agr.; noted native dancers; terrorist bomb carnage, 2002; second terrorist attack (2005); a. (inc. Lombok) 10,196 km²; p. (2001) 3,050,000.

Balikesir, t. and prov., **Turkey;** rly. junc.; ctr. of fertile agr. region; p. (1990) 973,314. (prov) 172,570 (t.).

Balikpapan, t., Kalimantan, **Indonesia;** new oil refinery; p. (1995) 416,200.

Balkan Mtns., **Bulgaria;** fine alpine meadows, forested; tourism based on Sofia; average alt. 900–1,200 m, hgst. point Botev Peak, 2,377 m.

Balkan Peninsula, the easternmost of the three gr. southern peninsulas of Europe, between the Adriatic and Ionian seas on the W., and the Black Sea, Sea of Marmara and the Aegean Sea on the E., with an area of, roughly, 500,000 km²; includes Turkey, Serbia, Montenegro, Croatia, Slovenia, Bosnia, Bulgaria, Albania, Macedonia and Greece; ch. mtns.: Rodopi, Pindhus, Balkan; ch. Rs.; Danube, Maritsa, Vardar; ch. Ls.; Scutari, Okhrida.

Balkh. *See* **Wazirabad.**

Balkhash, t., **Kazakhstan;** on N. shore of L.B.; smelting, esp. local copper; vermiculite deposits nearby, salt; p. (1990) 87,400.

Balkhash, L., Kazakhstan; receives Ili R., but has no outlet; salt water; fishing, salt-panning; a. 17,301 km².

Ballachulish, v., Highland, **Scot.;** on S. shore of Loch Leven, N.E. of Oban; tourism; ferry across Loch Linnhe; new road bridge; p. (2002) 615.

Ballarat, t., Victoria, **Australia;** 117 km N.W. of Melbourne, former gold-field dist.; mkt. ctr.; fine examples of 19th century architecture; 2 caths.; p. (1991) 64,980.

Ballater, burgh, Aberdeenshire, **Scot.;** on R. Dee, 59 km S.W. of Aberdeen; tourist resort, mineral wells; nr. the royal Highland residence of Balmoral; p. (2002) 1,446.

Ballina, t., spt., Mayo, **R.o.I.;** agr. machin. salmon fishing; p. (1991) 6,714.

Ballinasloe, t., Galway and Roscommon, **R.o.I.;** agr. ctr.; cattle mkt.; terminus of Grand Canal; p. (1991) 5,600.

Ballybunion, resort, Kerry, **R.o.I.;** at mouth of R. Shannon; p. (1991) 1,300.

Ballycastle, spt., mkt. t., Moyle, **N. Ireland;** abbey and cas. ruins; seaside resort; p. (1991) 4,005.

Ballyclare, t., Newtownabbey, **N. Ireland;** paper, linen, dyeing, asbestos-cement prod.; p. (1991) 7,108.

Ballymena, mkt. t., l. gov. dist., **N. Ireland;** on R. Braid; linen and dyeing; p. (2002) 28,112 (t.), 58,610, (dist.).

Ballymoney, mkt. t., l. gov. dist., **N. Ireland;** 64 km N.W. of Belfast; linen; p. (2001) 26,894 (dist), 7,818 (t.).

Ballyshannon, spt., Donegal, **R.o.I.;** at mouth of R. Erne; salmon fishery; resort; hydroelectric power plant; p. (1991) 2,840.

Balmoral Cas., Aberdeenshire, **Scot.;** royal residence, on R. Dee, 13 km W. of Ballater.

Baltic Sea, an arm of Atl. Oc., opens into N. Sea by narrow channels between Denmark and Sweden; joined to Arctic by White Sea Canal; low, dune-backed cst.; shallowness, tendency to freeze hinders shipping; a. 414,000 km².

Baltic White Canal. *See* **Volga Baltic Waterway.**

Baltimore, industl. c., spt., Md., **USA;** fine harbour nr. head of Chesapeake B.; pt. processing and diversified inds.; steel wks. at Sparrow's Point; educational, cultural ctr., seat of Johns Hopkins univ.; many fine bldgs. despite disastrous fire of 1904; p. (2000) 651,154 (c.), 2,382,172 (met. a.).

Baltoro Glacier, Karakoram Mtns., **Pakistan;** drains into tribs. of Indus; alt. 3,532 m.

Baluchistan, prov. (revived 1970), **Pakistan;** S. of Afghanistan; largely desert and rugged barren mtns.; cap. Quetta; cereals, potatoes, fruits, dates; new oil and natural gas discoveries; a. 137,011 km²; p. (1998) 6,511,000.

Bamako, cap. c. of **Mali;** impressive site at foot of escarpment on R. Niger; admin. and agr. tr. ctr.; R. pt.; univ.; main industl. ctr. of Mali; p. (2000) 1,131,000.

Bamberg, c., Bavaria, **Germany;** cath.; textiles, elec., leather and engin. inds.; impt. R. pt. on Trans-European waterway; p. (2002) 69,396.

Bamburgh, t., Northumberland, **Eng.;** former cap. of Bernicia and Northumbria; cas.; birthplace of Grace Darling.

Banaba I. *See* **Ocean I.**

Banagher, v., Offaly, **R.o.I.;** impt. crossing of R. Shannon; p. (1991) 1,420.

Banant, terr., Vojvodina, N. **Serbia;** major source of petroleum, natural gas, vineyards, but economically backward.

Banbridge, t., l. gov. dist., **N. Ireland;** on Bann R.; linen; p. (1991) 11,448 (t.), 33,482 (dist.).

Banbury, mkt. t., Cherwell, Oxford, **Eng.;** 128 km from London; aluminium ind., furniture, printing, ladies' wear; expanded t.; old livestock market closed (1998); p. (2001) 43,867.

Banchory, burgh, Aberdeenshire, **Scot.;** on R. Dee, 27 km S.W. of Aberdeen; p. (2002) 6,034.

Banda Is., volcanic gr. in Moluccas, in Banda Sea

Indonesia; nutmegs and mace; a. 103 km².

Bandama, R., Ivory Coast; major power and irrigation scheme at Kossou Dam; length c. 320 km.

Bandar. *See* **Masulipatnam.**

Bandar Abbās, spt., S. **Iran;** airport; oil exploration; deepwater harbour; p. (1994) 384,000.

Bandar-e-Büshehür (Bushire), spt., S.W. **Iran;** on Persian G., Iran's major pt.; petrochem. complex project; p. (1996) 143,600.

Bandar Khomeynī, spt., **Iran,** on Persian G., terminus of rly. from Tehran; petrochemical plant.

Bandar Seri Begawan, t., cap. of **Brunei;** 20 km from mouth of Brunei R.; airport; p. (1999) 85,000.

Bandjarmasin, c., cap. of Kalimantan, **Indonesia;** pt. on Martapura R., nr. confluence with Barito R.; tr. ctr.; oil, timber, rubber, printing plant; p. (1995) 535,000.

Bandung, c., W. **Java, Indonesia;** industl. and tourist ctr.; tech. institute; radio sta. at nearby Malabar; p. (1995) 2,368,000.

Banff Nat. Park, Canada; first Canadian Nat. Park; in Rocky Mtns.; variegated scenery, many tourist facilities; a. 6,695 km².

Banff, royal burgh, Aberdeenshire, **Scot.;** on Moray F. at mouth of R. Deveron; fisheries; tourism; p. (2002) 3,991.

Banffshire, historic co., E. **Scot.** now divided between Aberdeenshire and Moray.

Bangalore, c., Karnataka, **India;** well-planned c., former Brit. military sta. and admin. H.Q.; route ctr.; textiles, engin.; high tech. industries (India's Silicon Valley); p. (2004) 5,700,000.

Bangka (Banka), I., between Sumatra and Kalimantan, **Indonesia;** tin; a. 11,942 km²; p. (1990) 626,950.

Bangkok (Krung Thep), cap. c., **Thailand;** pt. on Menam Chao Phraya R., 32 km from sea; built originally round canals; major industl. ctr.; royal palace, univ.; p. (1999) 7,133,000.

Bangladesh (East Pakistan), indep. sov. st., S. Asia; within Commonwealth (1972); occupies former Indian prov. of E. Bengal and E. part of Ganges delta; dense rural p. engaged in intensive farming of rice and jute; illiteracy 80 per cent; poor internal communications hinder devel.; exp. textiles; susceptible to flooding and cyclones; major floods 1998; cstl embankment project; open warfare between India and Pakistan (Dec. 1971) resulted in creation of indep. st.; cap. Dacca; a. 142,776 km²; p. (2004) 141,340,476.

Bangor, t., North Down, **N. Ireland;** spt. on S. shore of Belfast Lough, 16 km N.E. of Belfast; lt. inds.; carpets, hosiery; seaside resort; p. (1991) 52,437.

Bangor, t., Gwynedd, **Wales;** pt. on S. shore of Menai Strait; cath., univ. college; lt. engin.; tourist ctr.; p. (1991) 12,330

Bangui, c., cap. of **Central African Rep.;** pt. on R. Ubangi, airpt ; p. (1999) 622,000.

Bangweulu, L., **Zambia;** 240 km long, 128 km wide, contains 3 islands. Dr. Livingstone died at Iliala, on S. shore of this L., in 1873.

Banja Luka, t., Bosnia-Herzegovina, formerly Yugoslavia; caths., mosques; recent industl. development; cellulose; rly. junc.; p. (1991) 142,644.

Banjul (Bathurst), c., cap. of **Gambia;** pt. at mouth of Gambia R., exp. groundnuts; airport; p. (1999) 229,000.

Banks I., Canada, Arctic Oc.; separated by McClure Strait from Melville I.

Banks Peninsula, dist. on E. cst. of S.I., **N.Z.;** feature of Canterbury cst.; p. (1991) 7,639.

Banks Strait, separating Furneaux Is. from Tasmania, **Australia.**

Bann, Upper and Lower R., **N. Ireland;** rises in Mtns. of Mourne, and flows through Lough Neagh to Atlantic nr. Coleraine; length 144 km.

Bannockburn, moor, t. nr. Stirling, **Scot.;** Bruce's victory over Edward II on 23–24 June, 1314 established Scotland's independence; p. (2002) 7,396.

Banská Bystrica, region, **Slovakia;** copper and silver mng.; a. 9,230 km²; p. (1990) 87,000.

Banstead, Surrey, **Eng.;** dormitory t.; l. gov. dist. with Reigate; p. (1994) 118,300 (dist.), (2001) 38,664 (t.) (with Tadworth).

Bantam, t. and dist., W. **Java, Indonesia;** suffered severely from fever and volcanic eruption; former pt. and sultanate; cattle rearing.

Bantry Bay, Cork, **R.o.I.;** Atlantic inlet; natural harbour situated mainly by oil-storage depot.

Baoding (Paoting), c., Hebei prov., **China;** on main rly. to Beijing; p. (1994) 519,000.

Baoji (Paoki), c., Shaanxi prov., **China;** ctr. of arable agr. a.; cotton weaving; nearby gorge on Huang-He used for multi-purpose dams; p. (1994) 379, 000.

Baotou (Paotow), c., Mongol Zizhiqu (Inner Mongolia), **China;** on left bank of Huang-He, on road and rly. routes to E. China; terminus of caravan routes through Gobi Desert and Tarim basin to Turkestan; tr. in non-perishable livestock prods., cereals; modern steel ind.; p. (1994) 1,033,000.

Bar, spt., Dalmatian cst., **Montenegro;** terminal of Belgrade-Bar rly.

Baracaldo, t., N.E. **Spain;** rapidly growing industl. t. on Bilbão estuary; p. (1991) 105,170.

Baranovichi, c., **Belarus;** admin. ctr. of agr. dist.; impt. rly. ctr.; p. (1996) 172,000.

Barataria Bay, S.E. Louisiana, **USA;** 56 km S. of New Orleans; ctr. of shrimp ind., petroleum extraction; picturesque stilt vs.; a. 466 km².

Barauni, t., N. Central Bihar, **India;** oil refining; oil pipelines to Gauhati, and Kanpur and from Haldia; p. (1991) 12,500.

Barbados, I., indep. sovereign st. (1966), within Brit. Commonwealth, W.I.; fertile soils; economy based on intensive agr. supporting dense p.; sugar, molasses, rum; fishing; tourism; cap. and spt. Bridgetown; moves towards becoming a republic; a. 429 km²; p. (2004) 278,289.

Barbary Coast, gen. name applied to Mediterranean cst. of N. Africa between Strait of Gibraltar and C. Bon.

Barberton, t., Ohio, **USA;** S.W. of Akron; tyre mftg.; p. (1990) 27,600.

Barberton, t., Mpumalanga, **S. Africa;** developed from 19th cent. gold rush; ctr. of rich agr. dist.

Barbican, dist., City of London, **Eng.;** inc. major housing scheme to attract p back into c.; cultural amenities.

Barbizon, v., nr. forest of Fontainebleau, **France;** haunt of painters, especially those ass. with the Barbizon school; p. (1999) 1,490.

Barbuda, I., Leeward Gr., **Antigua and Barbuda;** sea-island cotton; a 161 km²; p. (1991) 1,400.

Barcellona, t., N.E. cst., Sicily, **Italy;** mkt. t.; p. (1991) 40,540.

Barcelona, c., cap. of B. prov., major spt. of **Spain;** industl. and comm. ctr., textiles and varied inds.; exp. agr. prod. inc. cork; cath., univ.; p. (1998) 1,505,600, 4,666,300 (prov.).

Barcelona, t., N. **Venezuela;** cap. of Anzoátegui st.; agr. tr.; brewing; adjoins Puerto la Cruz on Caribbean cst.; joint p. (1990) 106,061.

Barcoo Creek. *See* **Cooper's Creek.**

Barents Sea, part of Arctic Oc., E. of Spitzbergen to N. Cape; impt. cod fisheries; oil potential; short Rs. to be diverted from Sea to Volga to carry water to Karakum Desert.

Bargoed, t., Caerphilly, S. **Wales;** p. (1991) 14,979.

Bari, c., cap. of B. prov., Apulia, **Italy;** spt. on Adriatic handling agr. prods.; agr. processing inds., oil refinery; p. (1992) 342,129.

Barinas, t., cap. of B. st., **Venezuela;** cattle, oil in surrounding Llanos; p. (1990) 152,853 (t.), 456,246 (prov.).

Barisal, t., **Bangladesh;** nr. Tetulia at mouth of Ganges; river pt.; gr. damage and loss of life from cyclone 1965; p. (1991) 163,481.

Barking and Dagenham, outer bor., E. London, **Eng.;** on Rs. Roding and Thames; diversified inds. inc. huge Ford motor wks.; p. (2001) 163,944.

Bar-le-Duc, t, cap. of Meuse dep., **France,** in picturesque Ornain valley; many fine old houses; varied inds.; p. (1999) 16,944.

Barletta, t., spt., **Italy;** diversified pt. processing inds.; wine tr.; p. (1991) 89,530.

Barmouth, t., Gwynedd, **Wales;** pt. on Cardigan Bay; chemicals; resort; p. (1991) 2,306.

Barnard Castle, Teesdale, Durham, **Eng.;** mkt. t.; woollens, penicillin; cas.; p. (1991) 6,084.

Barnaul, t., W. Siberia, **Russia;** route ctr. in cotton-growing dist. nr. industl. Kuznetsk Basin; varied inds.; p. (1989) 602,000.

Barnet, former U.D., Herts., **Eng.;** now outer bor., Greater London; comprising Finchley, Hendon, Barnet, East Barnet and Friern Barnet; p. (2001) 314,019.

Barnsley, t., met. dist., South Yorks., **Eng.;** machin., plastics; carpets; tourism centred on old industrial heritage; p. (2001) 218,063 (dist.), (2001) 71,599 (t.).

Barnstaple, North Devon, **Eng.;** mkt. t., pt. on

R. Taw; seaside resort; p. (1991) 27,691.

Baroda (Vadodara), t., Gujarat, **India**; univ.; palaces, Hindu temples; natural gas pipeline from Ankleshwar; oil refining nearby at Jawaharnagar; heavy water plant; p. (1991) 1,126,800.

Barquisimeto, t., **Venezuela**; well built c.; comm. ctr. for fertile agr. a.; p. (1990) 602,622.

Barra Is., Outer Hebrides, Western Isles, **Scot.**; lighthouse on Barra Head; p. (1991) 1,244.

Barranquilla, t., **Colombia**; major spt. nr. mouth of Magdalena R.; impt. industl. ctr.; international airpt.; p. (1992) 1,018,763.

Barrow-in-Furness, spt., l. gov. dist., Cumbria, **Eng.**; iron and steel ind.; shipbldg., submarines; p. (2001) 71,980 (dist.), (2001) 47,194 (t.).

Barrow I., W. **Australia**; since 1067 one of Australia's richest oilfields.

Barrow Point, most N. headland in Alaska, **USA**.

Barry, pt., Vale of Glamorgan, **Wales**; rapid growth in 19th cent. as outport of Cardiff; modern light inds., replacing coal and tinplate inds.; p. (1991) 49,887.

Bartlesville, t., Okla., **USA**; oil refining, metal inds.; p. (1990) 34,300.

Barton-on-Humber, mkt. t., N. Lincs., **Eng.**; anc. Eng. pt.; S. site of Humber Bridge; p. (1991) 9,422.

Basel, c., cap. of B. can., 2nd. t. of **Switzerland**; cath., univ.; burial place of Erasmus; comm., industl. rly. ctr. at head of barge navigation on R. Rhine; p. (1990) 171,000 (c.) 358,500 (met. a.).

Basel, can., **Switzerland**; divided into 2 half cantons; (1) B.—Stadt; in immediate vicinity of B.c.; cap. B.; a. 36 km²; p. (est. 1990) 191,800; (2) B.—Land; on N. Jura slopes; watchmaking; cap. Liestal; a. 427 km²; p. (1990) 230,000.

Bashkir (Bashirskaya) aut. rep. occupying Belaya R. basin in S.W. Urals, **Russia**; impt. mng. and metal inds., inc. major oilfield; arable agr.; cap. Ufa; a. 143,486 km²; p. (1989) 3,943,100.

Basildon, t., l. gov. dist., Essex, **Eng.**; new t. 1949; light inds.; old town (Upper Basildon) on the lower R. Thames; p. (2001) 165,668 (dist.), (2001) 99,876 (t.).

Basilicata, region, S. **Italy**; comprising provs. of Potenza and Matera, mtnous. in W., drains to G. of Taranto; arable agr.; a. 9,984 km²; p. (1992) 610,821.

Basingstoke, t., part of l. gov. dist. of **Basingstoke and Deane,** N. Hants., **Eng.**; 80 km W. of London; expanded t.; engin., light inds.; p. (2001) 152,573 (dist.), (2001) 90,171 (t.).

Basle. See Basel.

Basotho ba Borwa (S. Sotho), former Bantu Terr. Authority, **S. Africa**.

Basque Provs., N. **Spain**; comprise 3 provs.: Alava, Guipuzcoa and Vizcaya where Basque language spoken; regional parliam't to 100 provs. in Spain to help off separatist moves (1980); lgst. t. Bilbao; p. (1998) 2,100,000.

Basra, t., **Iraq**; cap. of B. prov.; R. pt., 64 km from mouth of Tigris R., on main rly. from Baghdad; exp. agr. prods.; heavy fighting in 2003 war; p. (2002 est.) 1,337,600.

Bas-Rhin, dep., E. **France**; N. part of Alsace; extends to Rhine rift valley, inc. Vosges Mtns.; impt. agr. dist.; many industl. ts.; cap. Strasbourg; a. 4,791 km²; p. (1990) 953,100.

Bass Strait, Australia; between Victoria and Tasmania; length 320 km; width 224 km.

Bassano del Grappa; cap. of Vicenza prov., on R. Brenta, **Italy**; light and craft inds.; cath.; p. (1991) 38,900.

Basse-Normandie, region, N. **France**; inc. deps. Calvados, Manche, Orne; ch.t. Caen; p. (1999) 1,420,889. See Normandy.

Bassenthwaite, L., L. Dist., Cumbria, **Eng.**; most N. of lge. Ls.; drained to Solway Firth by R. Derwent; length 6 km, width 1·6 km.

Basses-Alpes. See Alpes-de-Haute-Provence.

Basses-Pyrénées. See Pyrénées-Atlantique.

Basse-Terre, I., cap. of Guadeloupe, **Fr. W.I.**; pt.; p. (1990) 14,107.

Basseterre, t., **St. Kitts I., W.I.**; cap. St. Kitts-Nevis-Anguilla ass. st.; pt.; sugar refining; p. (1994) 12,600.

Bassetlaw, l. gov. dist., N. Notts., **Eng.**; lge. a. based on Worksop and East Retford; p. (2001) 107,713.

Bastia, c. spt., cap. Haute Corse, N.E. Corsica, **France**; agr. and inds.; growing tourist centre; p. (1990) 38,728

Basutoland. See Lesotho.

Bataan, peninsula and prov., W. Luzon, **Philip**-

pines; mtnous.; inc. t. of Balanga; timber inds., oil refining; p. (1990) 425,803.

Batangas, prov. and spt., S.W. Luzon, **Philippines**; oil refining; agr. tr.; p. (1990) 184,970.

Batavia. See Djakarta.

Bath, c., Bath and N.E. Somerset, **Eng.**; Roman baths, hot springs, medicinal waters; fine Regency architecture; univs.; elec. engin., metal inds.; p. (1991) 85,20.

Bath and North East Somerset, unit. auth. created in 1996, formerly part of Avon, **Eng.**; bordered by Mendips in S.; p. (2001) 169,040.

Bathgate, burgh, W. Lothian, **Scot.**; coal mng.; automobile ind.; p. (2002) 15,068.

Bathurst, t., N.S.W., **Australia**; former gold t., reliant on wool and wheat; diversifying with secondary inds.; with Orange to form site of major inland c. of 200,000; p. (1991) 24,680.

Bathurst, t., off cst. of N.T., **Australia**; separated from Melville I. by Apsley Str.; aboriginal reserve; cypress pine milling.

Bathurst, t., N.B., **Canada**; pt. on Nipisiguit Bay; salmon fishing; local mng.; p. (1991) 15,890.

Bathurst. See Banjul.

Bâtinah, Al, fertile coastal plain, **Oman**, Arabia; produces early-ripening dates famous for flavour.

Batley, t. West Yorks., **Eng.**; heavy woollens, shoddy; p. (2001) 49,448.

Batna, t., dep., N. **Algeria**; p. (2002 est.) 270,700 (t.), 1,018,300 (dep.).

Baton Rouge, st. cap., La., **USA**; on Mississippi; major tr. ctr.; univ.; oil refining, chemical plants; badly hit by Hurricane Katrina (2005); p. (2000) 227,818 (c.), 528,000 (met. a.).

Battambang, prov., **Cambodia**; N.W. of Phnom-Penh; rice growing, cotton mill; p. (1994) 566,000.

Battersea, dist., London, **Eng.**; S. of R. Thames; famous park; lge. power sta. now disused; part of Wandsworth.

Batticaloa, t., cap. of E. Prov., **Sri Lanka**; on E. cst.; comm. ctr.

Battle, t., Rother, East Sussex, **Eng.**; battle of Hastings 1066; abbey; p. (1991) 5,253.

Battle Creek, t., Mich., **USA**; on Kalamazoo R.; engin., local cereal prod.; p. (1996) 53,430.

Batu Arang, t., **Malaysia**; ctr. of only worked coalfield in Malaya; 45 km from Kuala Lumpur.

Bauchi, state, **Nigeria**; cap. Bauchi; ctr. of Jos plateau; tin-mng. ctr.; p. (1991) 4,294,413.

Bauld, C., northernmost part of Newfoundland, **Canada**.

Bauru, t., São Paulo st., **Brazil**; comm. ctr.; food inds.; p. (1996) 293,900.

Bavaria (Bayern), (qv), **Germany**; mtnous., bounded by Alps, inc. Böhmerwald, Fichtelgebirge, Franconian Forest; main Rs. Danube and Main; fertile agr. valleys; forestry and agr.; economic life concentrated in ts., esp. cap. Munich, now a focus of p. immigration; rural beauty attracts tourist tr.; celebrated beer; a. 70,220 km²; p. (2005) 12,388,000.

Bavarian Alps, mtn. range, **Germany**, along Austrian border; Zugspitze (2,969 m) highest mtn.

Bavarian Forest. See Böhmerwald.

Bawdwin, t., **Myanmar**; in Shan plateau; impt. mng. ctr.; wolfram, lead, zinc, silver, rubies.

Bayamo, t. **Cuba**; early settlement; agr. & rly. ctr.; p. (1990) 125,021.

Bayamón, t., **Puerto Rico**; in fertile valley; oil refining; p. (1990) 220,262.

Baybay, t., Leyte, **Philippines**; impt. comm. pt.; p. (1990) 82,281.

Bay City, t., Mich., **USA**; comm. pt. nr. head of Saginaw B.; fishing; pt. processing inds.; p. (1990) 38,940.

Bayelsa, new st. (since 1996) in south of **Nigeria**. Created from Rivers. Headquarters at Yenagoa. Oil wealth

Bayeux, t., Calvados, **France**; mkt. t.; cath., museum, Bayeux tapestry; p. (1990) 15,100.

Baykal, L. (Ozero Baykal), Siberia, **Russia**; sixth largest fresh-water L. in world; basin forms deepest depression in world (1,616 m); many pts. around shores but frozen Nov.–May; skirted by Trans-Siberian rly.; sturgeon, salmon; tourism; UNESCO World Heritage Site; a. 35,483 km².

Bayonne, t., Pyrénées-Atlantique, S.W. **France**; cath.; noted for invention of bayonet; Basque Museum; p. (1999) 39,895.

Bayonne, t., N.J., **USA**; 10 km from New York; chemicals, oil refining; dry docks; p. (1996) 60,499.

Bayreuth, t., Bavaria, **Germany**; home of Wagner; famous musical festivals; p. (2002) 74,519.

Beachy Head, chalk headland, S.W. of Eastbourne, East Sussex, Eng.; 175 m high. Major cliff fall into sea, January 1999.

Beaconsfield, t., South Bucks., Eng.; residtl; home of Edmund Burke; p. (1991) 12,282.

Beardmore Glacier, Antarctica; one of world's lgst. glaciers; over 176 km in length.

Bear I. (Björnöya I.), **Norway**; in Arctic Oc., 208 km S. of Spitzbergen; cod fisheries.

Bearsden, burgh, E. Dunbartonshire, **Scot.**; residtl.; p. (2002), 27,967.

Beas (Bias), R., Punjab, **India**; trib. of Sutlej R.; part of irrigation scheme.; marked limit of Alexander's advance into India, 327 B.C.

Beauce, region, central **France**; flat limestone plateau; arid, few surface streams; thin layer of loam (limon) permits agr.; impt. wheat growing a. ("the granary of France"); p. mainly grouped in vs.

Beaufort Sea, off N. Alaska, **USA**; part of Arctic Oc.

Beaujolais, France; in upper Rhône valley, N.E. Massif Central; wine-growing dist.

Beaulieu, v., Hants, **Eng.**; on Beaulieu R.; Cistercian abbey; car museum.

Beauly, t., Highland, **Scot.**; on Beauly R.; ruined priory; p. (2002) 1,164.

Beaumont, t.; 2nd. pt. of Texas, **USA**; ctr. of petrochemical inds.; p. (1990) 114,323 (t.), 361,000 (met. a. with Port Arthur).

Beaune, t., Cote d'Or, **France**; mediaeval walled t.; ctr. of wine tr.; p. (1999) 21,922.

Beauvais, agr. mkt. t., cap. of Oise dep., N. **France**; cath.; Gobelin tapestry removed to Paris; p. (1999) 55,411.

Bebington, Wirral, Merseyside, **Eng.**; part of pt. of Liverpool; soap, chemicals, engin.; p. (2001) 57,066.

Becancourt, t., Quebec, **Canada**; on S. bank of St. Lawrence; integrated steel mill projected.

Beccles, Waveney, Suffolk, **Eng.**; mkt. t. on R. Waveney S. of Broads; resort, agr. inds.; p. (1991) 10,337.

Bechuanaland. *See* **Botswana.**

Beckum, t., N. Rhine-Westphalia, **Germany**; cement, chalk, engin. wks.; p. (1999) 38,200.

Beddington and Wallington. *See* **Sutton.**

Bedford, co. t. and l. gov. dist., **Eng.**; on R. Ouse, 80 km N. of London; gen. engin., inc. marine and elec., bricks, aero research; Bunyan imprisoned; p. (2001) 147,911 (dist.), (2001) 82,488 (t.).

Bedfordshire, non-met. co., **Eng**; crossed by Chilterns; agr., mkt. gardening, brickmkg cement, vehicles, engin.; p. (2001) 381,572.

Bedford Level, once over 162,000 ha. of peat marsh in S. Fenland, **Eng.**; first successful draining initiated by Earl of Bedford 1634.

Bedlington, t., Wansbeck, Northumberland, **Eng.**; nr. Blyth; former coal mng.; electronics; p. (1991) 15,431.

Bedloe's I., or **Liberty I.**, N.Y. harbour, **USA**; on which the statue of Liberty stands.

Bedworth, t., Warwicks., **Eng.**; l. gov. dist. with Nuneaton; nr. Coventry; coal mng., limestone quarrying, engin., textiles; p. (2001) 30,001.

Beerenberg, mtn., Jan Mayen I., **Norway**, Arctic Oc.; one of lgst. volcanic cones in world; glaciated; alt. 2,546 m.

Beersheba, t., **Israel**; ctr. for development of the Negev; p. (1992) 128,400.

Beeston and Stapleford, Broxtowe, Notts, **Eng.**; sub. of Nottingham; engin., drugs, telephones; p (2001) 66,683.

Behera, prov., **Egypt**; Nile delta; cap. Damandur; a. 10,129 km²; p. (1991) 3,730,000.

Beijing (Peking), c. and mun., cap. of **China**; cultural ctr. and c. of gr. architectural beauty; for hundreds of years seat of Chinese emperors (Mongol, Ming, Manchu); formerly surrounded by walls; Imperial and Summer palaces; seat of govt.; univ.; Catholic cath. reopened (1985); many sm. factories producing a very wide range of goods, esp. chemicals, computers, textiles, synthetic fibres, machin., precision instruments, printing, publishing; route ctr., rly. junc.; new airpt. (largest in world); a. 8,770 km²; p. (2001) 10,840,000.

Beira, spt., **Mozambique**; airpt; rly. runs inland to Harare (Zimbabwe) and Blantyre (Malawi); exp. sugar, maize, cotton; oil pipeline to Umtali; p. (1990) 299,300.

Beirut, c., cap. of **Lebanon**; pt. on Mediterranean; anc. Phoenician c., now busy shipping and mercantile ctr.; silk, wool, fruits; 4 univs.; p. (2000) 2,055,000.

Beisan (Bet She'an), t., **Israel**; in Jordan valley,

c. 90 m below sea-level; archaeological finds date from 1500 B.C.; rebuilt since 1948 by Israelis.

Bejaia (Bougie), spt., dep., N. **Algeria**; impt. tr. ctr.; exp. wood, hides; oil pipeline connection to Hassi-Messoud; p. (2002 est.) 164,200 (t.), 947100 (dep.).

Belarus, CIS, former rep. USSR; cap., Minsk; low-lying; timber; agr. on drained marshes; peat; 209,790 km²; p. (2004) 10,310,520.

Belau, *See* **Palau, Rep. of**

Belém, spt., cap. of Pará st., **Brazil**; comm. ctr., ch. pt. of Amazon basin, entrepôt for riverside settlements, exp. forest prod. inc. jute, cocoa and cotton; inds. dominated by food processing and textiles; steel works; univ.; p. (1996) 1,142, 300.

Belfast, l. gov. dist., cap. of N. **Ireland**; pt. on Belfast Lough; once Britain's lgst. single shipyard, now all closed; linen mnf., rope, tobacco, distilling, aircraft, fertilisers, computers; oil refinery on E. side of harbour; univ.; Stormont Castle; p. (2001) 277,391.

Belfort, t., cap. of Belfort dep., E. **France**, in Alsace; fortress t. between Jura and Vosges; heavy inds., rly. wks., cotton ind.; elec. engin.; p. (1999) 50,403.

Belfort (**Territoire de**), dep., **France**; ch. t. Belfort; a. 608 km²; p. (1990) 134,100.

Belgaum, t., Karnataka, **India**; cotton; alt. 760 m; Jain temples; p. (1991) 326,000.

Belgium, kingdom, W. Europe, comprises 9 admin. provs.; low-lying except in Ardennes in S.E.; very high density of p., intensive agr. and highly industl.; severe social and economic problems have resulted from decline of Sambre- Meuse coalfield and associated heavy engin. inds., similar difficulties in textile inds. in N.W.; industl. expansion on Kempenland coalfield in N.E. and around Brussels, Antwerp, and Ghent; heavily dependent upon foreign tr. for economic survival; member of EU; major spt. of Antwerp competing with Rotterdam for hinterland; 2 language groups: Flemish (Dutch dialect) in N., French dialect in S. (Walloon a.); univs. at Brussels, Ghent, Liège, Louvain; cap. Brussels; a. 30,445 km²; p. (2004) 10,348,276.

Belgorod, t., **Russia**, N.W. of Kharkov, on N. Donets R.; rly. junc. in agr. region; p. (1989) 300,000.

Belgrade (Beograd), c., cap of **Serbia**; inland pt. on Danube at mouth of Sava R.; industl., admin. and cultural ctr.; univ.; airport; bombed by NATO, 1999; popular uprising, 2000; p. (2000) 1,482,000.

Belize, indep rep. (1981), Central America; formerly Brit. Honduras; almost totally underdeveloped; heavy rainfall, hurricanes; tropical forest; only 15 percent of land is cultivated; economy hit by fall in world sugar prices; recent sale of 13 percent of land a. to clear tropical forest for citrus production; 20 per cent unemployed; lowest p. density in Central America, now can Belmopan; a. 22,962 km²; p. (2004) 272,945.

Belize City, c., former cap. of **Belize**; almost devastated by hurricane 31 Oct. 1961; cap. moved to Belmopan 80 km further inland; spt.; p. (1996) 47,700.

Bellary, c., Karnataka, **India**; fort; cotton processing and tr.; p. (1991) 245,391

Bell Bay, pt., Tasmania, **Australia**; on bank of Tamar R.; modern pt. and aluminium refinery (1950s) for processing Queensland bauxite; ferry terminal; now part of Launceston.

Bell I., Newfoundland, E. **Canada**; in Conception Bay, 32 km N.W. of St. Johns; impt. Wabana iron-ore deposits outcrop on N.W. cst., smelted on Pictou coalfield, Nova Scotia; a. 31 km².

Belleville, pt., L. Ontario, **Canada**; agr. processing; white marble nearby; cement; light inds.

Belleville, t., Ill., **USA**; industl. ctr., domestic prod., coal; air force training school; p. (1990) 42,800.

Belleville, t., N.J., **USA**; machin., chemicals; p. (1990) 34,200.

Bellinzona, t., **Switzerland**; on R. Ticino; 22 km N. of Lugano; three castles built on hills dominating t.; rly. engin.; tourism; p. (1993) 17,100.

Bell Rock (Inchcape I.), rock and lighthouse 19 km S.E. of Arbroath, Scot.

Belluno, t., cap. of B. prov., Venezia, N. **Italy**; route ctr. at S. foot of Dolomites; cath.; engin.; p. (1996) 211,996.

Belmopan, new inland cap., **Belize**; p. (1997) 6,800.

Belo Horizonte, c., cap. of Minas Gerais st. **Brazil**; impt. inland c.; ctr. rich agr. and mng. region; steel mills, food inds., textiles, diamond cutting; oil pipeline from Guanabara; univ.; one of the fastest growing c. in Brazil, especially since building of Fiat factory; p. (1996) 2,091,800.

Belorussia. *See* **Belarus.**

Belper, mkt. t., Amber Valley, Derbys., **Eng.**; hosiery, textiles, oil wks., iron foundries; p. (2001) 21,938.

Belsen, v., 24 km N.W. of Celle, **Germany**; notorious second world war concentration camp.

Belterra, t., dist., Pará st., N.E. **Brazil**; nr. confluence of Tapajós and Amazon Rs; site of Fordlandia scheme.

Beltsy, t., **Moldova**; on trib. of Dniester R.; agr. ctr., food processing; p. (1990) 164,800.

Belvoir (pronounced Beaver), **Vale of,** Melton Leics., **Eng.**; clay vale, cattle, sheep; Stilton cheese; recent development of coalfield.

Bembridge, v., E. cst., I. of Wight, **Eng.**; resort, p. (1991) 3,397.

Benares. *See* **Varanasi.**

Benbecula I., Outer Hebrides, Western Isles, **Scot.**; between Is. of N. and S. Uist; airpt. in N.; fishing; p. (1991) 1,803.

Bendigo, c., Victoria, **Australia**; former goldmng. dist., gold rush 1851; mng. ceased 1955; primary prods.; impt. egg producing ctr.; p. (1991) 57,427.

Benevento, c., Campania, **Italy**; cap. of B. prov. which contains many Roman remains; cath.; agr. processing; p. (1996) 295,803.

Benfleet, t., Castle Point, Essex. **Eng.**; residtl.; p. (2001) 48,539.

Bengal, Bay of, part of **Indian Oc.** washing E. shores of India and W. shores of Burma, receives waters of Rs. Krishna, Ganges; Brahmaputra, Irrawaddy.

Bengbu (Pengpu), c., Anhui, **China**; on Kwo-Ho 168 km. NW of Nanjing; on Tianjin–Nanjing rly; p. (1994) 712,000.

Benghazi (Benghezi), c. **Libya**; spt. and airpt. on G. of Sirte; univ.; former Greek Hesperides; p. (1994) 750,000.

Benha, t., **Egypt**; impt. mkt. t., rail and road ctr. in heart of cultivated a. of Nile delta 48 km N. of Cairo; airpt.

Beni, dep. **Bolivia**; drained by R. Mamoré; rubber, cattle; a. 213,564 km².

Benin City, t., **Nigeria**; cap. of Benin st.; former notorious slave ctr.; p. (1992) 207,200.

Benin, People's Republic of, (Dahomey), indep. st. (1960), West Africa; former French Colony; high standard of education reflected in heavy government sector and low level of productive activity in the economy; staple foods of groundnuts, palms, coffee, cocoa; intensive farming in fertile Terre de Barre; land held collectively; full potential of drier N. not yet exploited; concern about desert encroachment; oil found offshore from main pt. Cotonou; inds. process many prods.; joint Benin-Nigeria inly much tropical rain (N and S.; dependence on Nigeria; many joint industl. projects; cap. Porto Novo; a. 112,622 km²; p. (2004) 7,250,033.

Beni Suef, t. and prov., **Egypt**; on Nile, 96 km S. of Cairo; ctr. of fertile agr. a.; carpets, cotton; p. (1996) 172,000 (t.), 1,860,200 (prov.).

Ben Lawers, mtn., Perth and Kinross, **Scot.**; by Loch Tay; arctic and alpine flora; alt. 1,215 m.

Ben Macdhui, mtn., Aberdeenshire, **Scot.**; Cairngorm gr.; second highest peak in Brit. Is.; alt. 1,310 m.

Ben Nevis, mtn., Highland, **Scot.**; volcanic; hgst. peak in Brit. Isles; alt. 1,342 m.

Benoni, t., Gauteng, **S. Africa**; gold mng. ctr.; engin.; p. (1991) 288,600.

Bensheim, t., Hesse, **Germany**; ctr. of fruit and wine dist. on E. edge Rhine valley; textiles, paper, metallurgy; p. (1994) 36,700.

Bentley with Arksey, t., South Yorks., **Eng.**; p. (2001) 33,968.

Benton Harbor, t., Mich., **USA**; midway along E. cst. L. Michigan; p. (1990) 12,800.

Benue R., Nigeria-Cameroon; rises in Adamawa mtns.; forms ch. trib. of Niger R.; R. pts. and agr. tr.; length 1,392 km.

Ben Wyvis, mtn., Highland, **Scot.**; nr. Dingwall; alt. 1,046 m.

Benxi (Penki), c., Liaoning prov., **China**; metallurgical ctr.; p. (1994) 805,000.

Ben-y-Gloe, mtn., Glen Tilt, Perth and Kinross, **Scot.**; alt. 1,120 m.

Beograd. *See* **Belgrade.**

Beppu, c., Kyushu, **Japan**; hot spring resort; p. (1990) 130,323.

Berbera, pt., **Somalia**, on G. of Aden; exp. livestock from pastoral hinterland; deep- sea pt.

completed 1969; airport; p. (2002 est.) 213,400.

Berchtesgaden, v., **Germany**; mtn. resort 24 km S. of Salzburg; Hitler's mtn. retreat; tourism; potash.

Berck-Plage, resort, Pas-de-Calais, **France**, on Eng. Channel; p. (1990) 14,700.

Berdyansk, c., **Ukraine**; pt. on Sea of Azov; agr. ctr.; machin.; health resort; p. (1990) 133,500.

Bere Regis, mkt. t., Dorset, **Eng.**; Saxon royal residence; p. (1991) 1,767.

Berezina, R., **Belarus**; trib. of Dnieper; forms part of Baltic-Black Sea waterway; 608 km long.

Bergama, t., **Turkey**; anc. Pergamos, ruins; morocco leather inds.; agr. tr.; p. (1997) 46,100.

Bergamo, c., Lombardy, **Italy**, 54 km N.E. Milan; cath. and academy, silk industry; historic hill town; p. (1992) 114,930.

Bergen, spt., W. cst. **Norway**; univ.; most impt. comm. pt. in kingdom; shipping, fishing; mftg. inds.; birthplace of Grieg; p. (2000) 194,000.

Bergen op Zoom, t. N. Brabant, **Neth.**; sugar refining. engin.; p. (1993) 47,546.

Bergerac, t., Dordogne, S.W. **France**; impt. bridge over Dordogne R.; mkt. for wines and luxury foods; anc. Huguenot stronghold; p. (1999) 26,090.

Bergisches Land, terr., N. Rhine-Westphalia, **Germany**; specialised iron and steel prod.; chemicals machin.; inc. ts. of Solingen, Remscheid, Velbert, Wuppertal.

Bergisch-Gladbach, t., N. Rhine-Westphalia, **Germany**; 11 km E. of Cologne, paper, metallurgy, textiles; p. (2002) 105,569.

Berhampur (Brahmapur), t., Orissa, **India**; admin. and educational ctr.; p. (1991) 210,600.

Bering Current (Okhotsk Current, or **Oyashio),** ocean current, N. **Pac. Oc.**; flows through Bering Strait from Arctic, along E. cst. of Kamchatka and Japanese Is. Hokkaido, Honshu; relatively cold; moderate summer temperatures along csts. causes fogs.

Bering Sea, part of N. **Pac. Oc.** between Aleutian Is. and B. Strait; fishing; a. 2,274,020 km².

Bering Strait, narrow sea which separates Asia from N. America, and connects Bering Sea with Arctic Oc.; 58 km wide at narrowest part.

Berkeley, v., Gloucs., **Eng.**; nr. R. Severn, 24 km N. of Bristol; scene of murder of Edward II; nuclear power-sta. decommissioning.

Berkeley, c., Cal., **USA**; univ.; chemicals; now inc. in San Francisco; p. (1990) 102,724.

Berkhamsted, Dacorum, Herts., **Eng.**; mkt. t.; chemicals; cas. ruins, 17th cent. school; birthplace of William Cowper the poet; p. (1991) 18,044.

Berkshire, former co., **Eng.**; chalk lowland inc. Inkpen Beacon, White Horse Hills; drained by Thames and tribs.; residtl.; electronics, biscuits; dairying; Windsor Gr. Park; Ascot racecourse.

Berlin, c., cap. of re-unified **Germany**; on Spree R.; formerly divided into 4 occupied zones 1945; Soviet (E. Berlin), British, American, French (W. Berlin); W. Berlin formed isolated enclave within E. Germany; focal point of escape attempts from E. to W. led to construction of "Berlin Wall", destroyed 1989; W. Berlin major industl. ctr. aided by American and W. German capital; educational, cultural and tourist ctr.; E. Berlin, former cap. of E. Germany, rebuilt as showpiece with high-rise housing, elect. manfs. machin; Reichstag and govt. ministries returned to Berlin, 1999; p. (2002) 3,289,000. (c.), 4,101,213 (met.a.).

Bermuda, Brit. gr. coral Is. (360 in no. of which 20 are inhabited) N. Atlantic; about 1,120 km E. of S.C.; Hamilton, on Long I. is the ch. t.; Brit. and US air and naval stas.; favourite winter resort for Americans; inds. attracted by tax incentives; no surface water; total a. 54 km²; p. (2004) 64,935.

Bern, c., cap. of B. can. and fed. cap. **Switzerland**; on Aare R.; cath., univ.; textiles, musical instruments, chocolate; H.Q. of Postal Union; bear pit; p. (2000) 941,100 (met. a.).

Bern, can., **Switzerland**; fertile valleys, dairying; watches; hydroelectric power; plans for separate can. in Jura reg.; a. 6,881 km²; p. (1990) 945,600.

Bernard, Great St., one of the Alps in the S. of the Valais, **Switzerland**; highest point 3,390 m; height of mtn. pass between Italy (Aosta) and Switzerland (Martigny), 2,477 m; famous hospice for travellers in monastery on mtn.; road tunnel completed 1962.

Bernard, Little St., one of Graian Alps, Savoy, S. of Mt. Blanc, France; pass traversed by Hannibal 218 B.C.

Bernese Oberland (Berner Alpen), alpine region, Switzerland; 35 peaks over 3,000 m inc. Finsteraarhorn and Jungfrau; tourist a. inc. resorts of Interlaken and Grindelwald.

Bernina Alps, Switzerland; alt. 4,050 m.

Berri, oilfield, **Saudi Arabia**; 72 km N.W. of Ras Tannura; the field extends offshore.

Berwickshire, historic co., S. **Scot.**, now part of Borders.

Berwick-upon-Tweed, l. gov. dist., Northumberland, **Eng.**; spt. on mouth of Tweed; border t., changed between Eng. and Scot. 15 times in history; fishing, lt. engin., tweeds, knitwear; cas. ruins; p. (2001) 25,949 (dist.), (1991) 13,544 (t.).

Besançon, t., cap. of Doubs dep., **France**; cath., observatory, univ.; farm implements, textiles; watch- and clock-making; birthplace of Victor Hugo; p. (1999) 117,304.

Beskids, W. and E., **(Beskidy Zachodnie)**, mtn. range, **Poland, Slovakia**, E. Europe; northern range of Carpathian mtn. system, seldom exceeds alt. 1,200 m, many passes; forested; tourism; length 352 km.

Bessarabia, terr., ceded to USSR by Romania 1940, and now part of **Moldova**; agr. region.

Bethany (El Azarieh), v., on Mt. of Olives 6 km W. of Jerusalem.

Bethel, anc. c., the modern Beitin, **Jordan**; 16 km N. Jerusalem.

Bethesda, t., Gwynedd, **Wales**; slate, lt. engin; p. (1991) 3,558.

Bethlehem, t. 9 km S.W. Jerusalem, according to Matthew and Luke birthplace of Christ; mainly Muslim pop. since 1948; p. (1995 est.) 32,000.

Bethlehem, t., Penns., **USA**; 80 km N. of Philadelphia; iron-wks.; univ.; p. (1996) 70,245.

Bethnal Green, dist., London, **Eng.**; in E. End of London, now in Tower Hamlets.

Béthune, t., Pas-de-Calais, **France**; rail and canal ctr. for coalfield; mkt. t.; p. (1990) 25,261 (t.), 259,679 (met. a.).

Betws-y-coed, t., Conwy, **Wales**; waterfalls; tourism.

Beuthan. See Bytom.

Beverley, mkt. t., E. Riding of Yorks., **Eng.**; famous minster (13th cent.); agr. processing; p. (2001) 29,110 (t.).

Beverly Hills, t., Cal., **USA**; sub. of Los Angeles; home of many film celebrities; many retail centres; p. (1990) 32,000.

Bewdley, Wyre Forest, Worcs., **Eng.**; mkt. t. on R. Severn; birthplace of Stanley Baldwin, residtl.; p. (1991) 9,009.

Bexhill-on-Sea, t., Rother, East Sussex, **Eng.**; resort; p. (2001) 39,451.

Bexley, former bor., W. Kent; now outer bor., Greater London, **Eng.**; inc. Sidcup, Crayford and Erith; p. (2001) 218,307.

Béziers, t., Hérault, **France**; ctr. of wine, brandy tr. and inds.; chemicals; p. (1990) 70,996.

Bezwada. See Vijayawada.

Bhadravati, t., Karnataka, **India**; steel; p. (1991) 149,000.

Bhagalpur, t., Bihar, **India**; agr. tr. ctr. on R. Ganges; p. (1991) 253,000.

Bhamo, t., Upper **Myanmar**; on Irrawaddy; inland limit of steam boats; mkt. ctr.; ruby mines

Bhandara, cap. of Bhandara dist., Maharashtra, **India**, 48 km E. of Nagpur; cotton cloth, brass mftg.; p. (1991) 71,800.

Bharuch, t., Gujarat, **India**; world's lgst. stream urea fertiliser plant; nearby oilfield.; p. (1991) 133,102

Bhatpara, t., W. Bengal, **India**; on R. Hooghly; industl. t.; jute, engin.; p. (1991) 316,000.

Bhaunager, t., Gujarat, **India**; pt. on G. of Cambay; exp. cotton, oilseeds; p. (1991) 402,000.

Bhilai, t., Madhya Pradesh, **India**; steel plant; rails and rly. sleepers; p. (2000) 398,800.

Bhim-Gora, sacred pool, place of Hindu pilgrimage, Uttar Pradesh, **India**.

Bhopal, c., cap. of Madhya Pradesh, **India**; impt. tr. ctr.; varied inds.; prehistoric cave paintings nearby; 2,000 killed in world's worst chem. accident (1984); p. (1991) 1,063,000.

Bhubaneswar, t., cap. of Orissa, **India**; 29 km from Cuttack; admin. ctr.; Hindu temples, pilgrimage ctr.; p. (1991) 412,000.

Bhutan, kingdom, indep. mtn. st., E. Himalayas; heavy monsoon rain, rich tropical vegetation. valuable forests; N.–S. ridges and valleys

result in semi-closed communities; first motor link with India opened 1962; undef. border w. Tibet to N. and W.; cap. Thimphu; a. c. 46,620 km²; alt. 7,558 m (Kula Kangri); p. scattered and nomadic (2000) 877,000. Insurgents active along Indian border.

Biafra, Bight of. See Bonny, Bight of.

Biala Podlaska, t. and prov., E. **Poland**; wool, furniture; p. (1995) 56,271 (t.), 309,394 (prov.).

Bialystok, t. and prov., **Poland**; nr. Grodno; major industl. ctr.; rly. ctr.; p. (1995) 277,768 (t), 700,088 (prov.).

Biarritz, t., Pyrénées-Atlantique dep., **France**; on Bay of Biscay; seaside resort; p. (1990) 28,900.

Biberach, t., Baden-Württemberg, **Germany**; on R. Kinzig; spa; wood, metal and engin. inds ; p. (1994) 30,600.

Bicester, Cherwell, Oxford, **Eng.**; anc. mkt. t., N.E. of Oxford; priory (1182) now in ruins; p. (2001) 31,113.

Biddulph, t., Staffs. Moorlands, Staffs., **Eng.**; coal mng., machin., textiles, furniture; residtl.; p. (1991) 16,725.

Bideford, Torridge, N. Devon, **Eng.**; pt. on estuary R. Torridge; mkt.; resort; p. (1991) 14,328.

Biel (Bienne), t., Berne, **Switzerland**; nr. Lake B.; watches; impt. industl. ctr.; p. (1990) 52,736.

Bielefeld, t., Rhine-Westphalia, **Germany**; ch. ctr. of linen industry; machin., bicycles; p. (2002) 323,373.

Biella, t., Vercelli, **Italy**; textiles; p. (1991) 48,300.

Bielsko-Biala, t., and prov., S. **Poland**; textiles, engin.; p. (1995) 180,657 (t), (1989) 895,400 (prov.).

Bies-Bosch, reclaimed fenland area between N. Brabant and S.W. **Neth.**; sugar refining, dairying; a. 142 km².

Biggar, sm. burgh, S. Lanarkshire, **Scot.**; 213 m alt. in Southern Uplands; p. (2002) 2,098.

Biggin Hill, London Borough, Bromley, **Eng.**; nr. Orpington; famous airfield of Battle of Britain; p. (1991) 14,107.

Biggleswade, t., Mid Beds., **Eng.**; in valley of R. Ivel, 14 km S.E. of Bedford; ctr. of fruit-growing and mkt. gardening dist.; hydraulic machin. tools, hosiery, caravans; p. (1991) 12,350.

Big Horn Mtns., Wyo. and Mont., **USA**; Rockies; favourite film location; attractive agr. valleys; highest alt., 3,600 m.

Bihac, t., **Bosnia-Herzegovina**, formerly Yugoslavia; on R. Una; industl; timber processing.

Bihar, st., N.E. **India**; in Ganges basin; hilly; bulk of p. in agr. N.; irrigation; minerals in S.E.: coal, iron, mica; steelwks. at Jamshedpur, oil refining at Barauni; cap. Patna, admin. ctr. Ranchi; a. 173,882 km²; p. (2001) 82,878,300.

Bihar, t., Bihar, **India**; within middle Ganges valley nr. Patna; p. (1991) 201,323.

Biisk, c., Siberia, **Russia**; ctr. of rich agr. a.; meat packing, textiles.

Bijagós, Archipelago dos (Bissagos Is.), off W. cst. **Guinea-Bissau**; c. 14 Is.; coconuts, rice; ch. t. Bolama on Bolama I.; a. 1,554 km².

Bijapur, t., Karnataka, **India**; cotton tr. and inds.; ruins; former cap. of B. kingdom; p. (1991) 186,939.

Bikaner, t., Rajasthan, **India**; in Thar desert; on former caravan route; wool tr., bldg. stone, handicrafts; p. (1991) 416,000.

Bikini, atoll, Pac. Oc.; atomic-bomb tests (1946).

Bilaspur, t., Madhya Pradesh, **India**; silks, cottons.

Bilbao, spt., N. **Spain**; cap. Basque prov. of Viscaya; formerly famous for rapier making; iron ore, smelting; pipeline from Ayoluengo oilfield; new Guggenheim Museum opened, 1997; European City of Culture, 2001; p. (1998) 358,500

Billingham, t., Stockton-on-Tees, **Eng.**; on N. of Tees estuary; petrochemical plant; p. (2001) 35,592.

Billings, t., Mont., **USA**; agr. tr. ctr. in irrigated a.; sulphur plant; p. (1996) 91,195.

Billingsgate, London, **Eng.**; old river-gate and wharf, formerly ch. fish mkt. of England; now moved to Isle of Dogs.

Bilma (Kawar), oasis t., **Niger**; on caravan route from Tripoli to Agadès and L. Chad.

Billiton I. See Belitung.

Biloxi, t., Miss., **USA**; fishing, tourist ctr.; US Coast Guard air base; devastated by Hurricane Katrina (2005).

Bingen, t., Rhineland Palatinate, **Germany**; at S. entrance to Rhine gorge; wine; beautiful scenery; tourism; p. (1999) 24,800.

Bingham Canyon, t., N. Utah, USA; silver, gold, lead; major open pit copper mine.

Binghamton, N.Y., USA; on Susquehanna R.; boot factories, aircraft components, cameras; p. (1990) 53,008 (t.), 264,100 (met. a.).

Bingley, West Yorks., Eng.; mkt. t. on R. Aire 26 km N.W. of Leeds; textiles, engin., agr.; p. (1991) 19,585.

Bintan I., lgst. island of Riouw archipelago, Indonesia; bauxite, tin.

Biobio, reg. Chile; cap. Conception; a. 36,939 km²; p. (1992) 1,729,920.

Biratnagar, t., S.E. Nepal, in the Tarai; jute, sugar, cotton milling, stainless steel.

Birbhum, dist., W. Bengal, India; cap. Suri; healthy climate; rice, sugar; mnfs. silk, cotton; a. 4,550 km²; p. (1991) 2,556,100.

Birkenhead, Wirral, Merseyside, Eng.; spt. on R Mersey, opposite Liverpool; handles industl. goods; heavy and pt. processing indo.; shipbldg.; p. (2001) 83,729

Birmingham, c., met. dist., West Midlands, Eng.; industl. cap. Midlands, second lgst. c. Gt. Britain; metal inds.; motor vehicles, components and accessories (Longbridge once known as 'car city'); univs., cath.; new Bull Ring (2003); p. (1995) 1,017,500 (dist.), (2001) 977,087 (c.).

Birmingham, t., Ala., USA; coal, iron, limestone, steel, aircraft, chemicals, textiles; p. (2000) 242,820 (t.), 907,810 (met. a.).

Birnam, v., Perth and Kinross, Scot.; location of Birnam Wood in *Macbeth*; former royal forest; p. (2002) 1,005 (with Dunkeld).

Birobidzhan, or Jewish aut. oblast, Russia; in Khabarovsk terr.; agr., timber and wheat. inds.; a. 35,988 km²; cap. Birobidzhan City; p. (1989) 82,000.

Birr, t. Offaly, R.o.I.; mkt. t. on Brosna R.; observatory; p. (1991) 4,050.

Bisbee, t., Arizona, USA; very rich copper deposits, gold, silver, lead; p. (1990) 6,300.

Biscarosse, Landes dep., France; 72 km S.W. Bordeaux; rocket and missile testing range projected; p. (1999) 9,313.

Biscay, Bay of, stormy a. of Atl. Oc., W. of France and N. of Spain, from Ushant to C. Ortegal; the Roman Sinus Aquitanicus; heavy seas.

Bisceglie, t., Apulia, Italy; spt. on E. cst. 35 km N.W. of Bari; tr. in wine and olives; light inds.; cath.; p. (1991) 47,400.

Bishkek, (Frunze), c., cap. of Kyrgyzstan; univ.; engin., textiles, meat-packing; p. (1999) 619,000.

Bishop Auckland, t., Wear Valley, Durham, Eng.; palace of Bishop of Durham; iron, lt. engin.; former coal mng.; p. (2001) 24,764.

Bishopbriggs, sm. burgh, E. Dunbartonshire, Scot.; p. (2002) 23,118.

Bishop Rock, isolated rock, lighthouse, Scilly Is., Eng.; 58 km S.W. of Land's End, Cornwall; regarded internationally as E. end of transAtlantic ocean crossing.

Bishop's Stortford, t. East Herts., Eng.; mkt. t. on Stort R.; light inds.; Norman cas.; p. (2001) 35,325.

Biskra, t., dep., Algeria; a. 109,729 km², p. (2002 est.) 190,800 (t.), 657,000 (dep.).

Bismarck, t., st. cap. N.D., USA; on Missouri R.; agr. mkt. ctr.; p. (1996) 53,514.

Bismarck Archipelago, volcanic gr., S.W. Pac. Oc., off New Guinea, admin. by Australia.

Bisotūn, t., Iran; in ruins; monuments to Darius I (the Great).

Bissagos Is. See Bijagós, Achipelago dos.

Bissau, t., cap of Guinea-Bissau; former ctr. of slave tr.; airpt.; plans to expand harbour; p. (1999) 274,000.

Bitola, t., Macedonia, formerly Yugoslavia; varied mnfs., recent industl. development; mosques; p. (1994) 77,800.

Bitonto, t., Apulia, on E. cst. 11 km N.W. of Bari; Italy; cath.

Bitterfeld, t. Saxony, Germany; lignite mng., engin. chemicals; p. (1989) 20,017.

Bitter Lakes, Isthmus of Suez, Egypt, utilised by Suez Canal.

Biwa-ko, lgst. lake in Japan, S. Honshu; 101 m a.s.l.; canal to Kyto provides hydroelectric power; superb scenery, historical associations; a. 675 km².

Biysk or Bisk, c., Altai terr., Russia; pt. on Biya R.; terminus of branch of Turk-Sib. rly.; p. (1989) 233,000.

Bizerte, c., N. Tunisia; pt. and naval sta. on Med.; the anc. Hippo Zaritus; fishing, oil refining, steel wks., tyres; p. (1994) 98,900.

Björnborg. See Pori.

Blaby, t. and l. gov. dist., Leics., Eng.; sm. a. S.W. of Leicester; p. (2001) 90,252 (dist.), (1991) 6,538 (t.).

Black Belt, coastlands of Mississ. and Ala., USA, where black soil prairie land is good for cotton.

Blackburn, t., l. gov. dist., Lancs., Eng.; once major cotton weaving ctr.; engin., lt. inds.; p. (2001) 137,470 (dist.), (2001) 105,085 (t.).

Black Country, Midlands, Eng.; formerly impt. iron-working and coal-mng. dist. mainly in S. West Midlands; now area of light engineering.

Blackdown Hills, Devon and Somerset, Eng., sandstone hills rising over 005 m.

Black Forest. See Schwarzwald.

Blackheath, open common, S.E. London, Eng.; mustering place of Wat Tyler's (1381) and Jack Cado's (1450) revolutionary peasants; now main attraction of expensive residtl. a.; a. 108 ha.

Black Hills, mtns. between S.D. and Wyo., USA; highest., Horney Peak, 2.208 m; form part of Nat. Park.

Black Mtn., Powys and Carmarthenshire, S. Wales; rises to 802 m; sandstone plateau; moorland; valleys used for reservoirs.

Black Mtns., Powys, S. Wales; rise to 811 m at Waun Fâch.

Blackpool, t., l. gov. dist., Lancs., Eng.; on cst. of Fylde dist.; one of major Brit. resorts; (16 million visitors annually); p. (1995) 153,600 (dist.), (2001) 142,283 (t.). Blackpool Illuminations began in 1879.

Black Prairie, region Texas, USA; extends 560 km S.W. from Ouachita Mtns. to Austin; contains very fertile Black Waxy and Grande Prairie sub-regions; cotton growing; ch. ts., Dallas, Fort Worth, Austin; a. 77,700 km².

Blackrod, t., Gtr. Manchester, Eng.; nr. Chorley; former cotton weaving; p. (1991) 5,681.

Black Sea, bordered by 6 sts., Ukraine, Russia, Georgia (N. and E.), Turkey (S.), Bulgaria, Romania (W.); receives waters of Danube, Dniester, Dnieper, Don. Bug; stagnant and lifeless below 150 m; fisheries in N. and W.; oil exploration by Turkey; suffering heavily from pollution; a. 424,760 km² (exc. Sea of Azov).

Blacksod Bay, cst. of Mayo, R.o.I.

Black Volta, R., rises in Burkina Faso, flows E. and S. into L. Volta, Ghana; length c. 1,200 km.

Blackwater, R., N. Ireland; rising in Dungannon, it forms border with R.o.I.; enters L. Neagh; 80 km long.

Blackwater, R., R.o.I.; flows from Knockanefune to enter Atl. Oc. at pt. and town of Youghal; chain of sm. ts. on course; 144 km long.

Blackwood, t., Caerphilly, S.E. Wales; N. of Abercarn; p. (1991) 14,466.

Blaenau Ffestiniog, t., Gwynedd, N. Wales; at head of Vale of Ffestiniog, 14 km E. of Porthmadog; consists of Ffestiniog and Blaenau Ffestiniog; slate quarries; pumped-storage hydroelec. sta. (1963); cement; narrow gauge rly.; p. (1991) 4,546.

Blaenau Gwent, S. Wales, unit. auth. created in 1996 from former l. gov. dist.; inland valley a. inc. Ebbw Vale and Abertillery; p. (2001) 70,084.

Blaenavon, t., Torfaen, Wales; former coal mng. a., UNESCO World Heritage Site; p. (1991) 6,066.

Blagoveshchensk, t., E. Siberia, Russia; on Chinese bdr. and R. Amur; wat. pl.; engin., sawmilling, flour milling; on Trans-Siberian rly.; p. (1989) 206,000.

Blair Atholl, v., Perth and Kinross, Scot.; tourist resort; cas.; seat of Duke of Atholl.

Blairgowrie and Rattray, burgh, Perth and Kinross, Scot.; at foot of Scot. Highlands; mkt. t. in Strathmore fruit growing dist.; p. (2002) 7,965.

Blakeney, v., N. Norfolk, Eng.; nr. sand spit; yachting; wild fowl.

Blandford or Blandford Forum, North Dorset, Eng.; on R. Stour; pastoral mkt. t. since 13th cent.; p. (1991) 8,880.

Blantyre, c., Malawi; in Shire Highlands; linked by rail to Beira (Mozambique); comm. ctr.; timber processing; p. (1998 est.) 2m.

Blantyre, v., S. Lanarkshire, Scot.; Lower B. birthplace of David Livingstone; p. (2002) 17,328.

Blarney, v., 6 km N.W. Cork, R.o.I.; cas. and Blarney stone; p. (1991) 2,040.

Blasket Is., Kerry. R.o.I.; rocky Is.; lighthouse.

Blaydon, t. N.E. Eng.; former coal mng.; p. (1991) 15,510.

Bled, glacial L., Slovenia (formerly Yugoslavia); tourism.

Blekinge, co. S. Sweden; cap. Karlskrona; a. 2,909

km²; p. (1992) 151,266.

Blenheim, t., S.I., **N.Z.**; fruit; p. (1991) 23,637 (urban a.).

Blenheim, v., **Germany**; scene of battle (1704) when English and Austrians under Marlborough defeated the French and Bavarians; **Blenheim Palace**, Woodstock, Oxon. **Eng.**; named in honour of this victory.

Blessington, L., Wicklow, **R.o.I.**; glacial L., now serves as reservoir for Dublin.

Bletchley, Milton Keynes, **Eng.**; expanded t.; p. (2001) 47,176.

Bletchley Park, Bucks, **Eng.**; wartime code-breaking centre (cracked Enigma cipher). Now high-tech museum.

Blida. *See* El Boulaïda.

Bloemfontein, t., cap. Free State prov., **S. Africa**; on plateau, alt. 1,393 m; route and tr. ctr.; univ.; p. (1991) 300,000 (met. a.).

Blois, t., cap. of Loir-et-Cher dep., **France**; historic t. on Loire R.; Renaissance château; wines; p. (1990) 51,549.

Bloomington, t., Ill., **USA**; comm. ctr. and industl. t. in rich agr. and coal-mng. a.; univ.; p. (1990) 52,000.

Bloomington, t., Ind., **USA**; electronic equipment, furniture, structural glass; univ.; p. (1996) 66,479.

Bloomsbury, dist., London, **Eng.**; fashionable dist. with many squares; famous literary history; inc. Brit. Museum, Univ. of London.

Blue Grass, dist., Ky., **USA**; area where blue grass abundant; horse breeding.

Blue Mountains, t., N.S.W., **Australia**; tourist ctr.; new t. (1947).

Blue Mtns., Jamaica; famous for coffee; dense forest; tourism; average alt. 900–1,200 m, rising to 2,294 m in Blue Mtn. peak.

Blue Nile (Bahr-el-Azraq), R., rises in tablelands of Ethiopia, joins the White Nile at Khartoum; its seasonal flooding provides the bulk of water for irrigation in Sudan and Egypt.

Blue Ridge Mtns., S. Penn., Ga., **USA**; inc. Shenandoah valley; superb scenery, resorts; average alt. 600–1,200 m, rising to 1,737 m in Grandfather Mtn.

Blumenau, mkt. t., Santa Catarina st., **Brazil**; butter, sugar.

Blyth., spt., Northumberland, **Eng.**; on former coalfield; part of l. gov. dist. of Blyth Valley; p. (2001) 81,265 (dist.), (2001) 35,691 (t.).

Bo, t., Sierra Leone; gold; p. (2002 est.) 81,000.

Boa Vista, t., R. pt., cap. Roraima st., **Brazil**; p. (1996) 154,200.

Bobbio, t., Emilia-Romagna, **Italy**, in northern Apennines; ctr. European cultural life, 9th–12th cent.; St Columban founded monastery, 612; p. (1901) 3,900.

Bobigny, N.E. sub of Paris, cap. of Seine-St. Denis dep., **France**; varied inds.; p. (1990) 44,841.

Bochum, t., N. Rhine-Westphalia, **Germany**; heart of Ruhr iron and steel ind.; known since 9th cent.; Univ. of Ruhr; p. (2002) 390,087.

Bodensee (**L. Constance**), S.W. **Germany** and Switzerland; 72 km long, 14 km wide.; R. Rhine flows through; fruit and horticulture.

Bodmin, co. t., North Cornwall, **Eng.**; on S.W. flank of Bodmin moor; china clay, lt. engin.; p. (1991) 12,553.

Bodmin Moor, upland, N.E. Cornwall, **Eng.**; lower slopes cultivated, higher slopes used for sheep pastures; average alt. 300 m, highest point, Brown Willy, alt. 419 m; major ctr. of china clay quarrying.

Bodø, t., Norway; nr. Lofoten Is.; spt.; fish processing; N. rly. terminus; p. (1990) 30,252.

Bodrum, t., on Aegean cst., **Turkey**; anc. Halicarnassus; 15th cent. Crusader castle; fishing.

Boeotia, region of anc. **Greece**; scene of many battles; Thebes was the ch. c.; home of Hesiod and Pindar; p. (1991) 134,034.

Bogda Ula, massif, Sinkiang, **China**; forms N. perimeter of Turfan depression; 240 km wide, average alt. 4,000 m, rising to 5,479 m in Turpanat Targh.

Bognor Regis, t., Arun, West Sussex. **Eng.**; residtl.; seaside resort; p. (2001) 62,141.

Bogota, cap. and lgst. c. of **Colombia**; in E. Cordilleras, 2,745 m a.s.l.; univ., nat. observatory, colonial architecture; political, social and financial ctr. of rep.; p. (2000) 6,290,000 (met. a.).

Bo Hai (Pohai), G. of, N. **China**; together with G. of Liaotung forms shallow expanse of water almost cut off from Yellow Sea by Liaotung and Shan-

dong peninsulas; receives water and silt from Huang He; a. approx. 38,900 km².

Bohemia, historic region, former kingdom, Czech **Rep.**; plateau drained by R. Elbe; borders W. Germany; agr. dist.; minerals inc. lignite, graphite; textiles, sugar, pottery.

Böhmerwald (Bohemian Forest), forested range of mtns. between **Czech Rep.** and Bavaria, **Germany**; 240 km long; alt. 1,479 m at Aber; region of poor soils; sm. farms; some mng. and quarrying.

Bohol I., prov. **Philippines**; maize, coconuts, rice; a. 3,864 km²; p. (1990) 948,315.

Boise, t., cap. of Idaho, **USA**; financial ctr.; timber mills; hot springs; p. (1990) 125,738.

Boksburg, t., Gauteng, **S. Africa**; industl., former coal-mng.

Bolan Pass, Baluchistan, **Pakistan**; pass from Pakistan to Afghanistan; summit 1,800 m.

Boldon, t., Tyne and Wear, **Eng.**; coal mng.; p. (1991) 12,420.

Boliden, t., N. **Sweden**; impt. deposits of copper and arsenic.

Bolivia, inland rep., S. America; land-locked, 9 deps.; caps. Sucre (judicial), La Paz (admin.); much US investment but discouraged by nationalism from late 1960s; relief makes transport difficult; moves towards gaining access to cst. via internat. corridor; forests; savannahs; agr. in backward conditions; embryonic industl. devel. suffered from political instability; much social protest against military rule, return to democracy 1982; rubber, quinine, cattle, hides; ch. exp. gas and tin; petroleum; mafia cocaine tr.; exp. illegal narcotics; language Spanish; a. 1,331,661 km²; p. (2004) 8,724,156.

Bologna, c., N. **Italy**; cap. of B. prov. on N. flank of Apennines; impt. route ctr. commanding road and rly. across Apennines to Florence; preserved and restored in Arcadian style by Communist admin.; univ., service t.; p. (1992) 401,308.

Bolsena, L., Latium region, **Italy**; occupies lge. extinct volcanic crater in S. of Tuscan Hills 96 km N.W. of Rome; a. (approx.) 129 km²; p. (1991) 4,100.

Bolsover, t., l. gov. dist., Derbys., **Eng.**; limestone; textiles; cas.; Hardwick Hall 6 km to S.; p. (2001) 71,766 (dist.), (1991) 11,743 (t.).

Bolton, t., met. dist., Gtr. Manchester, **Eng.**; cotton, textiles, engin.; univ.; p. (2001) 261,037 (dist.), (2001) 139,403 (t.).

Bolton Abbey, North Yorks. **Eng.**; ruined Augustinian Priory.

Bolzano, t., Trentino-Alto Adige **Italy**; on R. Isarco at S. approach to Brenner Pass; resort; p. (1991) 98,200.

Boma, t., **Congo**; pt. on estuary of R. Congo; exp. timber, cocoa, palm prods., bananas; p. (1991) 246,207.

Bombay. *See* Mumbai.

Bône. *See* Annaba.

Bo'ness, burgh, Falkirk, **Scot.**; spt. on Firth of Forth, 6 km E. of Grangemouth; foundries, timber yards; p. (2002) 13,961.

Bonifacio, spt., Corse du Sud, Corsica, **France**; opposite Sardinia on Strait of Bonifacio; p. (1993) 2,700.

Bonin Is., Pac. Oc., **Japan**; 15 Is., volcanic; 960 km S. of Tokyo; a. 103 km².

Bonn, c., **Germany**; at confluence of Rs. Sieg and Rhine; univ.; former seat of W. German parliament; birthplace of Beethoven; founded in Roman times; varied inds. inc. printing, publishing; p. (2002) 306,016 (c.), 878,742 (met.a.).

Bonnet a l'Eveque, mtn., **Haiti**; sheer sides, flat top; site of La Ferrière fortress, alt. 900 m.

Bonneville Dam, Ore., Wash., **USA**; across R. Columbia 64 km above Portland (Ore.), provides irrigation to valleys on Columbia-Snake Plateau; locks permit navigation and provide hydroelectric power.

Bonneville Salt Flats, Utah, **USA**; remains of anc. lake; world automobile speed test, 1937–47.

Bonny, Bight of (Bight of Biafra until 1975), **W. Africa**; bay lying E. of the G. of Guinea between the Niger and C. Lopez.

Bonnyrigg and Lasswade, burgh, Midlothian, **Scot.**, 11 km S.E. of Edinburgh, p. (2002) 14,457.

Boothia, peninsula on Arctic cst., **Canada**; separated from Baffin I., by G. of B.

Bootle, t., Sefton, Merseyside, **Eng.**; on E. side of entrance to Mersey estuary; dockside inds. inc. tanning, ship-repairing; tin plant; p. (2001) 59,123.

Bophuthatswana, indep. Bantu Terr. (1977) never recognised by UN, re-incorporated in S. Africa 1994.

Borås, t., S. **Sweden**; on R. Viske, nr. Göteborg; ctr. of textile and clothing inds.; p. (1992) 102,840.

Bordeaux, spt., cap. of Gironde, **France**; nr. mouth of R. Garonne; cath., univ.; exp. wines, liqueurs, sugar, potatoes, pit props; oil refining nearby; p. (1999) 215,148.

Borders, unit. auth., created in 1996 from former Region, **Scot.**; occupies E. half of Southern Uplands; hilly cty. drained by R. Tweed and tribs.; rural a. interspersed by mkt. and mill ts.; p. (2002) 107,400.

Bordighera, t., Italy; Riviera winter resort.

Borehamwood, t., Herts., **Eng.**; lt. engin., computers, film studios; p. (2001) 31,172.

Borislav, t., **Ukraine**; formerly Polish (1919–39); oilfield, natural gas; richest ozocerite deposits in Europe; oil pipeline links to Drogobych and Dashava; p. (1990) 40,700.

Borisov, t., **Belarus**; defeat of Napoleon, 1812; chemicals, sawmills; p. (1990) 146,800.

Borlänge, t., **Sweden**; iron, paper, engin. and chemical wks.; p. (1992) 47,300.

Borneo, lgst. I. in Malay archipelago and 3rd lgst. in world; high mtn. range extends from ctr. to N. rising to 4,180 m; low-lying swamp in S.; politically divided into Kalimantan (Indonesian B.), Sabah and Sarawak (E. Malaysia) and Brunei; jungle-covered and underdeveloped; scattered tribes inc. Dyaks; few nodes of development around oilfields (Sarawak and Brunei); much recent clearance of virgin rain forest; new settlement in Barito valley (Kalimantan); a. 738,150 km²; p. (1990) 9,103,000.

Bornholm, I. in Baltic Sea, **Denmark**; mostly granite with poor soils; cattle rearing; kaolin; tourism and fishing impt.; cap. Rønne; a. 543 km²; p. (1990) 45,784.

Borno, state, **Nigeria**; S.W. of L. Chad; former Moslem st.; a. 132,090 km²; p. (1991) 2,596,589.

Borobudur, Java, **Indonesia**; gr. Buddhist temple; ruins now restored.

Borrowdale, valley, Cumbria, **Eng.**; tourist resort; former graphite mines.

Boscastle, spt., Cornwall, **Eng.**; resort; pilchard fishing; sm. harbour built for slate exp.; devastating flood, 16 Aug. 2004.

Bosnia-Herzegovina, rep., formerly part of Yugoslavia; mtnous., forested, watered by R. Sava and tribs.; one-fourth cultivated; tobacco, cereals, fruit; cattle, sheep, pigs; mineral deposits; civil war in early 1990s; cap. Sarajevo; a. 51,199 km²; p. (2004) 4,007,608.

Bosporus or **Strait of Constantinople (Karadeniz Bogázi)**, between Black Sea and Sea of Marmara; suspension bridge, 1 to link Europe and S.W. Asia, opened 1973; badly polluted by sewage from Istanbul and oil spillage from shipping.

Boston, t., l. gov. dist., Lincs., **Eng.**; sm. pt. on Witham R., agr. mkt., fruit and vegetable canning; p. (2001) 55,750 (dist.), (2001) 35,124 (t.).

Boston, c., st. cap. Mass., **USA**; fine harbour and leading pt. at head of Boston Bay; cultural, comm. and financial ctr., impt. mkt. for fish and wool; 3 univs.; leading c. in 19th cent.; varied inds. inc. leather, rubber, textiles, shoes and elec. gds.; p. (2000) 589,141 (c.), 2,871,000 (met. a.).

Bosworth or **Market Bosworth**, t., Leics., **Eng.**; battle between Richard III and Henry VII, 1485; see Hinckley.

Botany Bay, N.S.W., **Australia**; inlet of Tasman Sea on E. cst., site of landing of James Cook, 1770; 8 km S. of Sydney; resort; first settled by Brit. in 1787; old penal colony; deep-water pt. (1961) for oil tankers supplementary to Pt. Jackson.

Bothnia, G. of, N. of Baltic; between Finland and Sweden; shallow sea, many Is.

Botswana, Rep. of, indep. sov. st. within Brit. Commonwealth (1966), Southern Africa; stretches from Orange R. to Zambesi R., and merges in W. with Kalahari desert; land locked; depends on rly. link to Zimbabwe and S. Africa; coal produced since 1980 to reduce dependence on S. Africa; minerals located but few mined; diamonds since 1971 (50 percent of exp.); copper, nickel; limited livestock agr.; potential arable land of Okavango chobe swamp; few inds.; AIDS epidemic now very widespread; cap. Gaborone; a. 582,000 km²; p. (2004) 1,561,973.

Bottrop, t., N. Rhine-Westphalia, **Germany**; once a

sm. t., now ctr. of Ruhr coal basin; p. (2002) 120,780.

Bouches-du-Rhône, dep., S. **France**; covers Rhône delta and inc. the Camargue and Crau; lagoon cst.; mainly agr. but inc. industl. complex ass. with cap. of Marseilles; a. 5,270 km²; p. (1999) 1,832,848.

Bougainville, I. seceded from **Papua New Guinea** to form Rep. of N. Solomons; secessionist conflict still continues; granted autonomy (2002); major reserve of copper in Panguna valley; new mng. ts. of Anewa Bay and Panguna; forested; a. 10,619 km².

Bougie. See Bejaia.

Boulder, t., Col., **USA**; gold- and silver-mng. dist.; univ.; resort; p. (1990) 83,312 (t.), 225,339 (met. a. with Longmont).

Boulder City, t., Nevada, **USA**; nr. Hoover Dam. gr. engin. project; model t., ctr. for Nat. Park services; p. (1996) 14,249.

Boulogne-Billancourt, S.W. sub. of Paris, **France**; car, aircraft inds.; p. (1990) 101,971.

Boulogne-sur-Mer, t., Pas-de-Calais dep., **France**; on English Channel; comm. and fish. pt.; Channel port; pt. inds.; p. (1999) 44,862.

Bounty I., N.Z., S. Pac. Oc.; uninhabited guano covered I.

Bourg-en-Bresse, t., cap. of Ain dep., **France**; route ctr., varied inds.; p. (1990) 42,955

Bourges, t., cap. of Cher dep., **France**; cath., univ.; industl. and transit ctr.; p. (1999) 72,626.

Bourget, L., Savoie, **France**; tourist a.

Bourgogne, region, E. **France**; inc. deps Côte-d'Or, Nièvre, Saône-et-Loire, Yonne; upland region draining to the north-west into the Paris basin and to the south-east via the Saône into the Rhône; ch. t. Dijon; p. (1999) 1,609,356.

Bourne, t., South Kesteven, Lincs., **Eng.**; home of Hereward the Wake; also home of Raymond Mays, racing driver; agr. machin. printing; p. (1991) 8,777.

Bournemouth, t., Dorset; **Eng.**, unit. auth. created in 1997, formerly part of Hampshire; on S. cst., E. of Poole Harbour; seaside resort; univ; conference ctr.; p. (2001) 163,444 (former dist.), (1991) 155,488 (t.).

Bournville, garden sub. founded by George Cadbury (1897), 6 km S.W. of Birmingham **Eng.**; chocolate and cocoa wks.

Bourton-on-the-Water, v., Gloucs. **Eng.**; tourist ctr.; p. (1991) 2,239.

Bow or **Stratford-le-Bow**, Tower Hamlets, E. London, **Eng.**; 5 km from St. Paul's.

Bow Fell, mtn., Cumbria, **Eng.**; nr. hd. of Borrowdale, 6 km N.W. of Wm. Water alt. 903 m.

Bowland, Forest of, W. offshoot of Pennines, Lancs., **Eng.**; between Rs. Lune and Ribble; now designated area of outstanding natural beauty; reservoirs.

Bowness, v., Cumbria, **Eng.**; W. end of Hadrian's Wall.

Bowness, t., Cumbria, **Eng.**; on L. Windermere; tourist ctr.

Box Hill, nr. Dorking, Surrey, **Eng.**; E. of R. Mole gap through N. Downs; chalk; wooded, fine views; alt. 233 m.

Boyne, R., R.o.I.; flows to Irish Sea; Battle of the Boyne (1690) fought at Oldbridge, 5 km W. of Drogheda; salmon fishing; 128 km long.

Boyoma Falls (Stanley Falls), on Upper Congo R., **Congo**; nr. equator; originally named after the explorer.

Bozrah, c. of anc. Edom, probably modern Buseira (Jordan), S.E. of Dead Sea.

Brabant, prov., **Belgium**; S. section of former Duchy; fertile and wooded; many breweries; mnfs., linen, cloth, paper, lace; cap. Brussels; a. 3,281 km²; p. (1993) 2,262,896.

Brabant, North. See Noord Brabant.

Brač, I., Adriatic Sea, off coast of **Croatia**; lgst. of Dalmatian Is.; tourism, fishing; a. 393 km².

Brackley, t., South Northants., **Eng.**; flour milling, brewing; former prosperous wool tr.; p. (1991) 9,113.

Bracknell, t., part of l. gov. dist. of Bracknell Forest, Berks., **Eng.**; on Thames Valley terrace, 16 km S. of Windsor; new t. designated 1949 to meet overspill needs from London; engin., plastics; major redev. of town centre planned; p. (2001) 109,617 (dist.), (2001) 70,795 (t.).

Bradford, c., met. dist., West Yorks., **Eng.**; 14 km W. of Leeds; comm. ctr. of wool-textile inds.; impt. for worsted; engin. and chem. inds.; univ.; birthplace of Delius and J. B. Priestley; p. (2001) 467,665 (dist.), (2001) 293,717 (c.).

Bradford-on-Avon, t., West Wilts., **Eng.**; on the Bristol Avon; former ctr. of wool ind.; major Roman remains currently being excavated; p. (1991) 8,815.

Braemar, dist. in Grampians, Aberdeenshire, **Scot.**; containing Balmoral estate.

Braeriach, mtn., Aberdeenshire, **Scot.**; alt. 1,296 m.

Braga, t., cap. of B. dist., N.W. **Portugal;** agr. tr. ctr.; religious ctr.; cath.; p. (1991) 86,300.

Bragança, t., cap. of B. dist., N.E. **Portugal;** agr. tr.; p. (1991) 15,600.

Brahmapur. See Berhampur.

Brahmaputra, one of longer Rs. in **Asia;** flows for much of its length through Himalayas and Assam; called Tsangpo in Tibet; fertile agr. valley subject to flooding and silting; 2,880 km long.

Brăila, t., **Romania;** R. pt. on Danube, nr. Galati; grain tr., boatbldg., reed processing; p. (1992) 234,706.

Braintree, t., Mass., **USA;** elec. machin., rubber gds., glassware; p. (1990) 33,800.

Braintree, t., l. gov. dist., Essex, **Eng.**; on Blackwater; rayon mftg., metal windows, engin.; p. (2001) 132,179 (dist.), (2001) 42,393 (t.).

Brakpan, t., Gauteng, **S. Africa;** gold mng.; p. (1980) 79,800 (dist.).

Brampton, t., Ontario, **Canada;** noted for its greenhouses; p. (1991) 234,445.

Brandenburg, Land, cap. Potsdam; **Germany,** pop. (2005) 2,580,000.

Brandenburg, t., **Germany;** on R. Havel; cath.; tractors, textiles, machin.; p. (2002) 76,351.

Brandon, t., Manitoba, **Canada;** on Assiniboine R., W. of Winnipeg; comm. ctr. wheat a.; agr. equipment oil refining; p. (1991) 38,567.

Brandon, t., Suffolk, **Eng.**; ctr. of Breckland; expanded t.; p. (1991) 7,804.

Brandon and Byshottles, ts., former U.D., Durham, **Eng.**; former coal-mng. a.; p. (1991) 9,162.

Brandywine Creek, R., Penns., **USA;** Americans defeated by British 1777; length 32 km.

Brantford, t., Ontario, **Canada,** on Grand R., S.W. of Hamilton; leading mnf. t.; farm implements, cycles, bus and truck parts; p. (1996) 100,238.

Brasilia, cap. of **Brazil,** Goiás st., 960 km N.W. of Rio de Janeiro; ch. of many cities designed to open up interior of rep.; modern architecture; inaugurated 1960; p. (2000) 1,990,000.

Brasov, t., **Romania;** at foot of Transylvanian Alps; aircraft, engin., lge. German and Hungarian p.; p. (1992) 323,835.

Bratislava, c., cap. of **Slovakia;** pt. on Danube 48 km below Vienna; univ.; industl. and comm. ctr.; textiles, chemicals; engin., oil refining, linked to Mozyr', Belarus, by oil pipeline; p. (1999) 460,000.

Braunschweig. See Brunswick.

Bray, t., Wicklow, **R.o.I.**; on Irish Sea cst.; popular resort; p. (1991) 26,950.

Brazil, Federative Republic of, S. America; a. 8,512,035 km², 5th lgst. cty. in world, exceeded in size only by Russia, China, Canada and USA, covers variety of land and climate; in S., gr. Brazilian plateau, in N., Amazon R. basin (thickly forested); leading industl. nation of Latin America; agr.; coffee, cotton, sugar, cocoa, rubber, fruits, hardwoods; rapid exploitation of rainforests now at crisis level; cattle-raising; vast mineral reserves inc. manganese, iron, gold, diamonds; admin. through 22 sts., 4 terrs., and Fed. Dist.; cap. Brasilia; lgst. industl. ctr. São Paulo and Belo Horizonte, many multinational companies, inc. car mftg., chems., construction materials; p. mainly White, Negro, Indian, Mestizo; Portuguese official language; p. concentrated in coastal belt, leaving vast a. of interior relatively underdeveloped; oil shortages led to use of sugar alcohol for cars; incr. finds of oil (second largest oil reserves in S. America); p. (2004) 184,101,109.

Brazos, R., Texas, **USA;** flows through agr. and industl. Young Co. via Waco to industl. Brazosport; length 1,520 km.

Brazzaville, c., cap. of **Congo Rep.;** connected by rly. with the Atlantic at Pointe-Noire; R. pt. under construction; airport; p. (2000) 1,234,000.

Brechin, royal burgh, Angus, **Scot.**; on S. Esk; cath.; whisky; p. (2002) 7,199.

Breckland, dist., S.W. Norfolk, N.W. Suffolk, **Eng.**; chalk overlain by glacial sands; heathland and coniferous plantations; l. gov. dist., inc. Thetford, Swaffham and East Dereham; p. (2001) 121,418.

Brecknockshire, historic co., S. **Wales,** now part of Powys.

Brecon (Brecknock), t., Powys, **Wales**; on R. Usk; agr. ctr.; p. (1991) 7,523.

Brecon Beacons, mtns., S. **Wales;** 8 km S. of Brecon; highest peak 888 m; sandstone moorland; Nat. Park.

Breda, c., N. Brabant prov., **Neth.**; mnf. ctr.; machin., foundries, canneries, refineries; historic t., 13th cent. cath.; p. (1994) 129,125 (c.), 165,729 (met. a.).

Bredbury and Romiley, ts., Gtr. Manchester, **Eng.**; paper, engin., dyeing, textiles; p. (2001) 28,167.

Bregenz, t., cap. of Vorarlberg, **Austria;** on Bodensee; hydroelec. power; textiles; resort nr. Bregenz Forest; p. (1991) 27,236.

Breidha Fjord, lge. inlet, W. cst. Iceland.

Bremen, Land, **Germany;** a. 404 km²; cap. Bremen; p. (2005) 660,000.

Bremen, c., cap. of Land B., **Germany;** old t. on right bank of Weser R., 64 km from N. Sea; new t., founded 17th cent., on left bank; leading pt., industl. and comm. ctr.; former member of Hanseatic League; p. (2002) 540,950 (c.), 849,800 (met.a.).

Bremerhaven, c., Bremen, **Germany;** outport of Bremen at mouth of R. Weser; docks; impt. passenger and fish. pt.; shipbldg.; united with Wesermünde 1941; p. (2002) 118,701.

Bremerton, t., Wash., **USA;** on Puget Sound; naval dockyard; elec. equipment; p. (1990) 38,100.

Brendon Hills, Somerset, **Eng.**; extension of Exmoor, rising to over 400 m.

Brenner Pass, lowest Alpine pass from Bolzano (**Italy**) to Innsbruck (**Austria**); used by road and rail; frequent meeting place of Mussolini and Hitler (1940–2).

Brent, outer bor., Greater London, **Eng.**; inc. Wembley and Willesden; p. (2001) 263,464.

Brenta, R., N. **Italy;** rises in picturesque Alpine valley; forestry, silk, tourism; flows to Adriatic Sea; navigable in lower course; length 180 km.

Brentford and Chiswick. See Hounslow.

Brentwood, bor., l.gov.dist., Essex, **Eng.**; residentl.; new R.C. cath. (1991); p. (2001) 68,456 (dist.).

Brescia, c., cap. B. prov., Lombardy, N. **Italy;** industl. ctr.; iron, steel, engin., textiles; many historic bldgs.; p. (1992) 192,883.

Breslau. See Wrocław.

Bressay I., Shetland Is., **Scot;** p. (1991) 352.

Brest, naval pt., Finistère dep., N.W. **France;** base of French Atlantic fleet; used by Germans as fortfd. submarine base 1940–4; exp. agr. prods.; impt. industl. ctr.; p. (1999) 149,584.

Brest (Brest-Litovsk), c., **Belarus;** nr. Polish border; route ctr. and agr. mkt.; timber, food-processing, textiles. Captured by Germans in 1915. Treaty of Brest-Litovsk signed with Soviet Russia 1918; p. (1990) 268,800.

Bretagne. See Brittany

Bretton Woods, resort, N.H., **USA;** site of US monetary and financial conference, 1944, leading to establishment of the International Monetary Fund and the World Bank.

Brezhnev. See Naberezhnyye Chelny

Briançon, t., Hautes-Alpes, **France;** in upper Durance R. valley; winter sports; p. (1982) 11,851.

Bridgend, t., unit. auth. created in 1996 from former l. gov. dist. of Ogwr, S. **Wales;** industl. trading estate; iron, stone, paper; former coal mng. a.; p. (1991) 35,841 (t.), (2001) 128,645 (unit. auth.).

Bridge of Allan, burgh, Stirling, **Scot.**; 3 km N. of Stirling; p. (2001) 5,046.

Bridgeport, c., Conn., **USA;** on Long Island Sound; impt. industl. c.; firearms, hardware, elec. equipment, metal products; p. (1996) 137,990.

Bridgetown, t., spt., cap. **Barbados;** deepwater harbour, comm. ctr.; exp. sugar, molasses, rum; tourism; p. (1999) 133,000.

Bridgewater Canal, Worsley–Manchester–Runcorn, Gtr. Manchester and Cheshire, **Eng.**; crosses ship canal by means of Barton swing bridge; 61 km long.

Bridgnorth, sm.t., l. gov. dist., Shrops., **Eng.**; cas.; aluminium prods; light inds; n. terminus, Severn Valley Rly; p. (2001) 52,497, (dist.).

Bridgwater, t., Sedgemoor, Somerset, **Eng.**; on R. Parrett, 16 km from Bristol Channel; engin., wire rope, cellophane; p. (1991) 34,610.

Bridlington, t., E. Riding of Yorks., **Eng.**; on Bridlington Bay, S. of Flamborough Head; fishing; seaside resort; p. (2001) 33,589.

Bridport, West Dorset, **Eng.**; mkt. t.; seaside resort; p. (1991) 11,667.

Brie, region, Marne and Seine-et-Marne deps., France; low, level plateau of limestones and clays, S.E. of Paris; loam (limon) cover and plentiful water supply encourage agr.; grains, sugar-beet, fruit, dairy cattle; famous cheese; densely populated.

Brienz, t., **Switzerland**; resort on L. Brienz; wood carving.

Brierley Hill, t., West Midlands, **Eng.**; on W. edge of Black Cty.; cut glass, castable metal gds., firebricks, roofing and tiling, iron and steel.

Brigg, mkt. t., N. Lincs., **Eng.**; ctr. of agr. dist. between Lincoln Heights and Wolds; p. (1991) 5,768.

Brighouse, t., Calderdale, West Yorks., **Eng.**; on R. Calder, 5 km S.E. of Halifax; textiles and engin.; p. (2001) 32,360.

Brightlingsea, t., Tendring, Essex, **Eng.**; on R. Colne; oysters, boatbldg., yachting, p. (1991) 7,441.

Brighton, c., unit. auth. created in 1997, formerly part of East Sussex, **Eng.**; 80 km S. of London on S. cst.; seaside resort and residtl. t.; Royal Pavilion (1817), univs.; lt. inds.; Brighton & Hove created Millennium City, 2000; p. (1995) 156,200 (former dist.), (2001) 134,293 (t.).

Brindisi, c., Apulia, S. **Italy**; spt. on Adriatic cst., sea and air connections to Middle E.; cath.; cas.; wine, olive oil, silk, petrochemicals; oil refining; p. (1996) 413,338.

Brisbane, t., cap. of Queensland, **Australia**; third c. of A., set on winding B. river, 20 km from attractive sandy cst.; caths., univ.; consumer goods, processing of primary prods.; severe flooding 1974; rapid growth in past 30 years; p. (1993) 1,421,600 (met. a.).

Brisbane Water, t., N.S.W., **Australia**; N. of Broken Bay; rapid growth with electrification of commuting rly. to Sydney.

Bristol, c., unit. auth. created in 1996, formerly part of Avon, **Eng.**; pt. on R. Avon 14 km from Bristol Channel; outport at Avonmouth; cath., univs.; docks; aircraft engin., tobacco, paint, printing and lt. inds.; new British Empire & Commonwealth Museum (2002); p. (2001) 380,615 (unit. auth.), (1991) 407,992 (c.).

Bristol, t., Conn., **USA**; foundries, ball bearings, clocks, bells; p. (1996) 59,619.

Bristol Channel, arm of Atl. Oc. between S. cst. of Wales and Somerset and Devon, **Eng.**; noted tidal bores.

British Antarctic Territory, Brit. col., created 1962; consists of all land and Is. S. of lat. 60° S. and between 20° and 80° W. longitude; comprising Graham Land peninsula, S. Shetlands, S. Orkneys and smaller Is., excluding S. Georgia and S. Sandwich Is.; a. 1,222,500 km².

British Columbia, W. prov. separated from rest of Canada by Rockies, borders Pac. Oc.; little lowland; parallel N.W.–S.E. ranges of Rockies crossed by Rs. Fraser, Columbia, Kootenay and Peace; vast coniferous forest and hydroelec. resources; salmon fishing on cst.; mng.; p. concentrated in S.W. around Vancouver; a. 948,600 km²; p. (1996) 3,724,500.

British Honduras. See Belize.

British Indian Ocean Territory. See Chagos Is.

British Is., archipelago, N.W. Europe; comprising 2 lge. Is. of Great Britain and Ireland and 5,000 sm. Is.; a. 315,029 km².

British Solomon Is. See Solomon Is.

British Virgin Islands (BVI). See Virgin Islands.

Brittany (Bretagne), region, N.W. France; inc. deps. Côtes-du-Nord, Finistère, Ille-et-Vilaine, Morbihan; penin. between Eng. Channel and Bay of Biscay; contrast between productive cst. lands (fishing, early vegetables, tourism) and barren moorland interior; economically depressed; p. (1999) 2,904,863.

Brive-la-Gaillarde, t., Corrèze dep., **France**; regional mkt. in fertile basin on edge of Central Massif; p. (1990) 52,677.

Brixham, S. Devon, **Eng.**; incorporated in Torbay; fishing; resort; p. (1991) 15,865.

Brno (Brünn), c., **Czech Rep.**; cap. of Moravia; finely situated at confluence of Svratka and Svitava Rs., 109 km N. of Vienna; industl. and communications ctr. with mnfs. of machin., precision tools, textiles; annual tr. fair; p. (1990) 391,000.

Broadstairs, Thanet, Kent, **Eng.**; seaside resort; 5 km N.E. of Ramsgate; p. (1991) 22,118.

Broads, The, Norfolk, **Eng.**; series of Ls. formed by mediaeval turf cutting in lower alluvial reaches of Rs. Bure, Waveney, and Yare; yachting, fishing, tourism; lge. part forms **Broadland**, l. gov. dist., p. (1995) 112,500.

Brockton, c., Mass., **USA**; S. of Boston; lge. shoe and leather ind., machin.; annual tr. fair; p. (1996) 92,324 (met. a.).

Broken Hill, t., N.S.W., **Australia**; major mng. (silver, lead, zinc) ctr. in arid W. of st.; p. (1991) 23,300.

Bromberg. See Bydgoszsz.

Bromley, outer bor. of London, **Eng.**; inc. Beckenham, Orpington, Penge, and Chislehurst; p. (2001) 295,532.

Bromsgrove, t. and l. gov. dist., Worcs., **Eng.**; mkt. t., 21 km S.W. Birmingham, wrought ironwk., lt. engin.; p. (2001) 87,837 (dist.), (2001) 20,937 (t.).

Bromyard, Worcs., **Eng.**; sm. mkt. t.; p. (1991) 3,117.

Bronx, The, one of the five bors. of New York City, **USA**; connected by bridges to bor. of Manhattan; residtl. with parks, zoological and botanical gardens, colleges and professional schools; p. (1990) 1,203,789.

Brooklyn, bor., N.Y. City, **USA**; linked with Manhattan bor. by Brooklyn, Manhattan, and Williamsburgh suspension bridges across East R.; and with Staten I. by Verrazano-Narrows bridge (longest in world); mainly residtl. with much mftg. and comm.; p. (1990) 2,291,604.

Brooks Range, mtns., N. Alaska, **USA**; forms N. section of Rocky Mtns.; Inuit p.; Arctic climate, flora and fauna; alt. 2,000 m rising to 2,818 m (Mt. Michelson).

Brora, t., Highland, Scot.; on E. cst., 19 km N.E. of Dornoch Firth; Harris Tweed ind.; tourism.

Brownhills, t., West Midlands, **Eng.**; former mng. t.; expanded t.; p. (1991) 18,159.

Brownsville, t., Texas, **USA**; pt. on Rio Grande nr. Mexican border; livestock, sugar-cane, fruit processing, chemicals; p. (1996) 132,091 (t.), (1990) 260,000 (met. a. with Harlingen).

Broxbourne, t., l. gov. dist., Herts., **Eng.**; on gravel terrace to W. of R. Lea; ctr. of very intensively cultivated dist.; lt. inds.; p. (2001) 87,054 (dist.).

Broxtowe, l. gov. dist., Notts., **Eng.**; made up of Beeston and Stapleford and Eastwood; p. (2001) 107,570.

Bruay, t., Pas-de-Calais, **France**; coal mng.; p. (1990) 25,450.

Bruges. See Brugge.

Brugge (Bruges), c., cap. of W. Flanders prov., N. Belgium; mediaeval t. (now UNESCO World Heritage Site) connected by canal to its outer pt. Zeebrugge; univ.; impt. mkt. for grain, cattle, horses; engin., ship-repairing, elec. gds., glass mkg., textiles, lace; p. (1993) 116,871.

Brunei, indep. st. (1984), N. Borneo; enclave of Sarawak; Brit. protectorate after 1888; thriving economy based on Seria and offshore oil and gas fields; oil and gas provide 95 per cent of exp.; need to diversify as reserves dwindle and prices fall; 80 percent of food is imported; agr. therefore being encouraged since only 15 per cent of land is cultivated; cap. Bandar Seri Begawan; a. 5,765 km²; p. (2004) 365,251.

Brünn. See Brno.

Brunswick (Braunschweig), c., Lower Saxony, **Germany**; on R. Oker; formerly cap. of st. of Brunswick, now a comm. and industl. ctr.; mnfs. inc. canning, tinplate, optics, pianos, lorries; p. (2002) 245,516.

Brussels (Bruxelles), cap. of Belgium and of prov. of Brabant; impt. comm., industl. and cultural ctr.; varied mnfs.; inc. pharmaceuticals, electronic equipment, machine tools; lge. oil refinery at Feluy; noted for carpets and lace; occupied by the Germans 1914–18, 1940–4; univ.; mediaeval and Renaissance monuments; H.Q. of EU; p. (2000) 1,120,000.

Bryansk, c., cap. of B. oblast, **Russia**, on Desna R.; rly. junc.; a fortress until 19th cent.; sawmilling, engin., textiles, chemicals, steel; oil pipeline from Kuybyshev; p. inc. Bezhitsa (1989) 452,000.

Brynmawr, t., Blaenau Gwent, **Wales**; former coal mng. a.; industl. estate; p. (1991) 14,581.

Brzeg (Brieg), t. Opole, **Poland**; on R. Oder; German until 1945; textiles, leather, chemicals; p. (1989) 38,504.

Bucaramanga, c., N. central Colombia, 900 m a.s.l. in E. highlands of Andes; ctr. of coffee-growing dist.; cigar and cigarette mkg.; p. (1992) 349,403.

Buchan Ness, c., nr. Peterhead, E. Scot.

Bucharest (Buckresti), cap. and lgst. c. of Romania; "Little Paris," on the Dambovita, trib. of Danube; cath., univ.; textiles, chemicals, pharmaceuticals, oil refining, engin.; 20 per cent industl. output of rep.; badly damaged by earthquake (1977); p. (1999) 2,011,000.

Buckfastleigh, t., S. Devon, **Eng.**; wool, quarrying; nearby Benedictine abbey on site of mediaeval Cistercian abbey; p. (1991) 2,786.

Buckhaven and **Methil**, burgh, Fife, **Scot.**; on N. Side of Firth of Forth, 13 km N.E. of Kirkcaldy; coal; p. (2002) 16,391.

Buckie, burgh, Moray, **Scot.**; boat- and yacht-bldg.; fisheries; p. (2002) 8,059.

Buckingham, Aylesbury Vale, Bucks., **Eng.**, mkt. t. on R. Ouse, 24 km N.W. of Aylesbury; home of the Independent University; p. (1991) 10,168.

Buckinghamshire, non-met. co., **Eng.**; crossed by Chilterns and Vale of Aylesbury; rural and wooded, dairy farming; co. t. Aylesbury; mnfs. chiefly in High Wycombe; lace mkg. and furniture; p. (2001) 479,026.

Buckley, t., Flintshire, **Wales**; p. (1991) 17,753.

Budapest, cap. and lgst. c. of Hungary; stands on both banks of Danube (Buda on right, Pest on left); attractive townscape; univ.; varied mnfs., inc. steel, textiles, chemicals, engin., motorbuses, oil refining; employs 40 per cent industl. workers of Hungary; p. (2000) 1,825,000.

Budaun, t., Uttar Pradesh, **India**; agr. processing; ruins; p. (1991) 116,695.

Bude. See **Stratton and Bude.**

Budel, t., N. Brabant, S. **Neth.**; 19 km S. of Eindhoven; major zinc smelter project; p. (1991) 11,926.

Budge-Budge, t., W. Bengal, **India**; on lower Hooghly R.; hemp, rice; p. (1991) 73,400

Budleigh Salterton, East Devon, **Eng.**; resort; birthplace of Raleigh; p. (1991) 3,759.

Buena Park, c., Cal., **USA**; agr. processing mkt.; oilfields; p. (1996) 71,999.

Buenaventura, spt., **Colombia**; lumber yards, tanning, fish canning; p. (1993) 218,300.

Buenos Aires, c., cap. of Argentina; B.A. now contains one third of A.'s p.; ch. spt. at head of Rio de la Plata, on E. edge of Pampa; connected to Uruguay, Paraguay, and Brazil by gr. R. system; industl. and tr. ctr. for outlying regions; p. (2000) 2,000,000 (city), 12,560,000 (met. area).

Buenos Aires, prov., **Argentina**; cap. La Plata, agric.; p. (1991) 12, 594,974.

Buffalo, c., N.Y., **USA**; pt. on L. Erie; focus of communications on Gr. Ls. has encouraged many heavy inds.; diversified lt. inds.; univ.; p. (2000) 292,648 (c.), 969,000 (met. a.).

Bug, R., **Ukraine**; known as S. or Ukrainian B.; flows from Volyno-Podolsh upland to Black Sea; navigable in lower course; 853 km long.

Bug, R., the western Bug rises in **Ukraine**, not far from the southern Bug and flows N. to join the Vistula below Warsaw; forms bdy. between Poland and Ukraine; 774 km long.

Buganda, prov., **Uganda**, E. Africa; located W. of L. Victoria largely at alt. between 1,300 and 1,800 m; intensive cultivation, cotton (ch. comm. crop), plantains, millets; cap. Kampala.

Builth Wells, t., Powys, **Wales**; on upper course of R. Wye; medicinal springs; p. (1991) 2,474.

Buitenzorg. See **Bogor.**

Bujumbura, t., cap. of Burundi; pt. on L. Tanganyika; varied mds.; airpt.; p. (1999) 321,000.

Bukavu, t., **Congo**; cement, quinine processing; p. (1993) 236,000.

Bukhara (Bokhara), t., **Uzbekistan**; in Amu-Dar'ya valley at W. foot of Tien Shan; agr. mkt. at W. terminus of anc. caravan route from China; modern route ctr.; local natural gas, textiles; p. (1990) 227,900.

Bukoba, t., **Tanzania**; pt. midway along W. shore of L. Victoria; exp. coffee, rice and other foodstuffs to L. pts. in Kenya and Uganda.

Bulawayo, t., **Zimbabwe**; impt. rly. ctr.; major ctr. of commerce and heavy engin., airpt.; p. (1992) 620,936.

Bulgaria, Rep. of, S.E. Europe; in E. Balkans, bounded by Black Sea in E., and by Danube R. in N. which separates it from Romania; Rodopi range in S.W.; Maritsa R. basin forms central lowland a.; sharp climatic contrasts between winter and summer; fertile lowland areas organised into lge.-scale cooperative farms producing grain; impt. exp. tr. in agr. prods., inc. fruit, vegetables, tobacco; rapidly increasing industl. output; mineral and oil resources; popular tourist a. on Black Sea cst.; awaiting EU membership; cap. Sofia; a. 110,911 km²; p. (2004) 7,517,973.

Buncrana, mkt. t., Donegal, **R.o.I.**; salmon fishing; seaside resort; p. (1991) 4,400.

Bungay, Waveney, Suffolk, **Eng.**; mkt. t. on R. Waveney; printing, leather gds.; p. (1991), 3,393.

Bungosuido Channel, **Japan**; E. entrance into Inland Sea.

Bunzlau. See **Boleslawiec.**

Buraimi, oases lying between **Oman** and **United Arab Emirates**; rich in oil.

Buraydah (Buraida), t. Nejd., **Saudi Arabia**; oasis; tr. ctr.; p. (1988) 184,000.

Burbank, c., Cal., **USA**; airpt.; aeroplanes, film studios; p. (1990) 93,650.

Burdwan (Bardhaman), t., W. Bengal, **India**; agr. processing and tr. ctr. in Damodar valley close to Raniganj coalfield; p. (1991) 245,000.

Bure, R., Norfolk, **Eng.**; lower course forms part of Norfolk Broads; joins Yare at Yarmouth; 93 km.

Burgas, c., **Bulgaria**; spt. and comm. ctr. on Black Sea; ch. exp. pt. for rep.; pt. for oil tankers under construction; p. (1990) 204,915.

Burgenland, prov., **Austria**; bordered on E. by Hungary; low-lying in N., agr.; hilly in S.; cap. Eisenstadt; a. 3,962 km²; p. (1991) 273,541.

Burgess Hill, t., Mid Sussex, West Sussex, **Eng.**; bricks, tiles; p. (2001) 29,388.

Burghead, burgh, Moray, **Scot.**; fish pt., resort; p. (2002) 1,640.

Burgos, c., N. **Spain**; cap. of B. prov.; anc. cap. of Castile and cap. of Franco's regime 1936–9; cath; home of the Cid; tourism, varied inds.; p. (1998) 162,000.

Burgos, prov., Old Castile, **Spain**; cap. B.; a. 14,050 km²; p. (1998) 346,400.

Burgstädt, t., Saxony, **Germany**; textiles, machin.; p. (1994) 12,000.

Burgundy, former kingdom and prov., N.E. **France**; composed largely of upper valley of R. Saône; famous vineyards; strategic position on route leading between plateau of Vosges and Jura Mtns., from Rhône valley to Rhine valley.

Burhanpur, t., Madhya Pradesh, **India**; anc. walled Mogul c.; textiles, brocades; p. (1991) 172,710.

Burkina Faso, (Upper Volta), W. Africa; landlocked st. under Fr. rule until 1960; savana and low hills, hot and dry desert in N.; p. concentrated in S. and dependent on nomadism and subsistence agr.; many migrate to Ivory Coast and Ghana for work; soil erosion and desert encroachment reduce potential; poorest cty. in Africa; low life expectancies; dependent on aid; much emigration; cap. Ouagadougou; a. 274,123 km²; p. (2004) 13,574,820.

Burlington, t., S. Ontario, **Canada**; on L. Ontario, sub., N.E. of Hamilton; in fruit-growing a.; industl.; tourism; p. (1991) 129,572.

Burlington, t., Iowa, **USA**; on bluffs of Missisippi R.; machin.; agr. implature; p. (1990) 27,208.

Burlington, t., Vt., **USA**; on L. Champlain; pt. of entry and ch. industl. and comm. t. in st.; mnfs.; p. (1996) 38,306.

Burma. See **Myanmar, Union of**

Burnham Beeches, Berks./Bucks., **Eng.**; part of anc. forest acquired 1879 for public use; a. 243 ha.

Burnham-on-Crouch, t., Essex, **Eng.**; pt., yachting, boat-bldg.; p. (1991) 7,067

Burnham-on-Sea, t., Sedgemoor, Somerset, **Eng.**; on Bridgwater Bay; resort; p. (1991) 19,588.

Burnie, spt., Tasmania, **Australia**; pulp and paper mills; impt. mineral pt (tin); p. (1991) 20,483.

Burnley, t., l. govr. dist., Lancs., **Eng.**; textiles, engin., car accessories; p. (2001) 89,542 (dist.), (1991) 47,661 (t.).

Burntisland, royal burgh, Fife, **Scot.**; on F. of Forth; p. (2002) 5,667.

Burray, one of the Orkney Is., **Scot.**; p. (1991) 363.

Burrinjuck, t., N.S.W., **Australia**; on Murrumbidgee R., N. of Canberra; site of impt. dam providing irrigation in Riverina (dist.)

Burry Port, t., Carmarthenshire, **Wales**; p. (1991) 8,508.

Bursa, c. and prov., N.W. **Turkey**; noted for its textiles; cap. of anc. Bithynia (3rd cent. B.C.) and later of Ottoman empire; mosques; p. (1990) 1,603,137 (prov.), 775,388 (t.).

Burslem. See **Stoke-on-Trent.**

Burton-on-Trent, t., East Staffs., **Eng.**; brewing, malting, rubber gds.; p. (2001) 43,784.

Burundi, rep., E. central Africa; high plateau on N.E. shore of L. Tanganyika; tropical climate. irregular rainfall; economy based on agr., inc. subsistence crops of manioc. sweet potatoes, and cash crops of cotton, coffee; coffee major exp.; one of poorest states in world; sm. mftg. inds. developing, but no rlys.; home of ruling Tutsi and rebel Hutu; cap. Bujumbura; a. 27,834 km²; p. (2004) 6,231,221.

Bury, t., met. dist., Gtr. Manchester, **Eng.;** on R. Irwell to S. of Rossendale Fells; cotton, textiles; birthplace of Robert Peel; p. (2001) 180,608 (dist.), (2001) 60,718 (t.).

Buryat (Buryatskaya), aut. rep. **Russia;** borders L. Baykal; mtnous., forested; lge. mineral deposits; cap. Ulan Ude; a. 350,945 km²; p. (1989) 1,038,300.

Bury St. Edmunds, St. Edmundsbury, Suffolk, **Eng.;** old mkt. t., on R. Lark, abbey ruins; farm implements, sugar-beet processing; expanded t.; p. (2001) 36,218.

Bushey, t., Hertsmere, Herts., **Eng.;** residtl.; p. (1991) 16,488.

Dushir. *See* Bandar-e-Būshchr.

Busto Arsizio, t., Varese prov., N. **Italy;** 30 km. N.W. of Milan; cotton milling ctr., iron, steel, rayon, textile machin.; p. (1991) 77,100.

Bute, I, Argyll and Bute, **Scot;** p. (1991) 7,375.

Buteshire, historic co., W. Scot., now divided between Argyll and Bute and N. Ayrshire.

Butte, t., Mont., **USA;** mng. t. (copper, zinc. silver, manganese, gold, lead, arsenic); also a farming ctr.; p. (1990) 33,340.

Buttermere, L., Cumbria, **Eng.**

Butt of Lewis, promontory with lighthouse; Lewis, Hebrides, **Scot.**

Buxton, t., High Peak, Derbys., **Eng.;** spa; limequarrying; Opera House; p. (2001) 20,836.

Bydgoszez, prov., **Poland;** cap. B.; drained by Rs. Vistula, Brda, and Notec; formerly called Pomorze; salt and lime deposits aid chemical inds.; a. 20,800 km²; p. (1995) 1,130,880.

Bydgoszcz (Bromberg), c., N. central **Poland;** on R. Brda; R. pt., rly. ctr.; elec. equipment, machine tools, timber mnfs.; p. (1995) 385,764.

Bytom, c., S.W. **Poland;** formerly in Prussian prov. of Upper Silesia; ctr. of Katowice mng. a.; p. (1995) 227,606.

C

Cabinda, enclave, **Angola;** separated by Congo R. estuary from Angola; tropical climate encourages thick forest cover; tropical crops; offshore oil production; uranium; a. 7,236 km²; p. (1992) 152,100.

Cabot Strait, entrance of G. of St. Lawrence between C. Breton I. and Newfoundland, **Canada.**

Cáceres, c., and cap. of C. prov., W. Central III Estremadura, above Tagus valley; mkt. t. lies below the old t. topping the hill; p. (1990) 14,000; (1998) 405,600 (prov.).

Cachar, dist., Assam, **India;** tea-growing ctr.; a. 6,961 km².; p. (1991) 987,200.

Cachoeira, t., Bahia, **Brazil;** historic c.; p. (1991) 28,300.

Cádiz, maritime prov., S.W. **Spain;** cap. Cádiz; a. 7,321 km²; p. (1998) 1,107,500.

Cádiz, c., cap. of C. prov., S.W. **Spain;** in Andalusia; pt. on Bay of C.; fortress t., naval base; exp. sherry, cork, fruit, olive oil, tunny fish; univ., cath.; one of the most anc. ts. in Europe, built by Phoenicians, *c.* 1100 B.C.; p. (1998) 143,100.

Caen, c., cap. of Calvados dep., **France;** church and abbey, tomb of William the Conqueror; univ.; iron-ore mng. and processing; severely damaged in second world war; p. (1999) 113,594.

Caerleon, t., Newport, **Wales;** on R. Usk, 5 km N.E. of Newport; Roman Isca Silurum remains; agr. machin., tools, bricks; p. (1991) 8,931.

Caernarfon, t., Gwynedd, N. **Wales;** pt. on S. shore of Menai strait; cas.; birthplace of Edward II; bricks, plastics; p. (1991) 9,695.

Caernarvonshire, historic co., N.W. **Wales;** now part of Gwynedd.

Caerphilly, t., unit. auth. created in 1996 from former l. gov. dists. of Islwyn and Rhymney Valley, S. **Wales;** cas.; lt. inds.; former coal mng. a.; p. (1991) 28,481 (t.), (2001) 169,519 (unit. auth.).

Caesar Mazaca, anc. c., Asia Minor; residence of the Cappadocian Kings; the modern Kayeri, **Turkey.**

Caesarea Palestinae, old c., **Israel,** 32 km S. Mt.

Carmel; cap. of Herod the Great.

Cagliari, cap. and ch. pt. of Sardinia, **Italy;** univ., cath.; p. (1992) 180,309.

Cahir, t., Tipperary, **R.o.I.;** on R. Suir; anc. cas. and abbey; salmon fishing; p. (1991) 2,050.

Cahors, t., cap. of Lot dep., **France;** comm. ctr.; many historic bldgs., inc. cath., palace; distilleries, shoe factory; p. (1999) 20,003.

Cairngorm, mtns., Moray, Aberdeenshire and Highland, **Scot.;** rise to 1,310 m (Ben Macdhui); form part of Highlands; nat. nature reserve of arctic flora and fauna; winter sports; opened in 2003 as Scotland's second National Park, the largest in the UK.

Cairns, spt., Queensland, **Australia;** on Trinity Bay, bulk sugar terminal; resort for Barrier Reef; cyclone damage (2000); p. (1991) 86,227 (met. a.).

Cairntoul, mtn., Aberdeenshire, **Scot.;** alt. 1,294 m.

Cairo (El Qâhira), c., cap. of Egypt and prov.; on E. bank of Nile, at head of delta; lgst. c. in rep.; univ.; mosques, palace; fortress of Babylon in old c.; rapid growth with rural depopulation p. (2000) 10,552,000 (met. a.).

Caistor, t., West Lindsey, Lincs., **Eng.;** site of Roman camp in Lincs. Wolds; p. (1991) 2,502.

Caithness, historic co., N. Scot., now part of Highland.

Cajamarca, c., cap. of C. dep., **Peru;** in mtn. valley, 2,745 m; impt. in Inca times; p. (1993) 1,259,808 (prov.), 92,447 (t.).

Calabar, spt., S.E. **Nigeria;** cap. Cross River st.; exp. palm oil, kernels, rubber, ivory, cement; p. (1992) 157,800.

Calabria, region, extreme S.W. **Italy;** mtnous. pen.; highest point Mt. Pollino 2,234 m; ch. R. Crati; cap. Catanzaro; p. (1992) 2,074,763.

Calais, spt., Pas-de-Calais, N.E. **France;** crosschannel ferry pt. opposite to and 33·6 km distant from Dover; nearby Sangatte exit of Channel Tunnel; p. (1999) 77,311.

Calama, oasis, Antofagasta prov., N. **Chile;** in Atacama desert at foot of Andean Cordillera; water from R. Loa supplies Antofagasta and used for irrigation locally; p. (1992) 120,602.

Calatafimi, t., Sicily, **Italy;** Garibaldi defeated Neapolitans, May 1860; p. (1991) 7,600.

Calcutta. *See* Kolkata.

Calderdale, met. dist., West Yorks., **Eng.;** chief t. Halifax; also inc. Todmorden, Brighouse, Hebden Royd, Ripponden and Sowerby Bridge; p. (2001) 192,405.

Calder Hall, Cumbria, **Eng.;** first full-scale nuclear power sta. in world (1956); now closed.

Caldey, I., off Pembroke, Dyfed, **Wales;** lighthouse; Trappist monastery.

Caledonian Canal, from Inverness to Fort William, **Scot.,** connecting North Sea with Atl. Oc.; 100 km long; opened 1822.

Calgary, ch. t., Alberta, **Canada;** ctr. of ranching cty.; lumber mills, tanneries, oil refining, flour milling; p. (1996) 821,628.

Cali, c., cap. of Valle del Cauca dep., W. **Colombia;** 1,068 m on Cauca R.; comm. and transport ctr. for rich agr. a.; p. (1992) 1,624,401.

Calicut (Kozhikode), t., Kerala, **India;** first pt. reached by Vasco da Gama (1498); gave its name to calico cloth; p. (1991) 420,000 (t.).

California, st., W. **USA;** admitted to Union 1850; st. flower golden poppy, st. bird California Valley quail; mtnous., forested, fertile valleys; subject to earthquakes from San Andreas fault; rich in minerals, oil, natural gas, gold, silver, copper; fruits; film ind.; high-tech industries in "Silicon Valley"; attractive climate and scenery; cap. Sacramento; ch. pt. San Francisco, lgst. c. Los Angeles; most populous st. in USA; a. 411,014 km²; p. (2002) 35,116,033.

California Current, E. Pac. Oc.; flows N. to S. along cst. of Ore. and Cal., **USA;** relatively cold water; reduces summer temp. and causes fog in cst. a. especially nr. San Francisco.

California, G. of, arm of Pac. Oc., N.W. **Mexico;** 1,120 km long; same rift as Imperial and Coachella valleys in S.E. Cal.

Callander, burgh, Stirling, **Scot.;** mkt. t. on R. Teith, 24 km N.W. of Stirling; "the gate of the Highlands", tourism; p. (2002) 2,754.

Callao, c. and prov., W. **Peru;** pt. of Lima; sheltered harbour; impt. container port; sacked by Drake in 16th cent.; p. (1993) 639,729 (prov.), 359,768 (c.).

Calne, North Wilts., **Eng.;** mkt. t. on Marden R.

Caltagirone, t., Catania, Sicily, **Italy**; cath.; majolica ware; p. (1991) 36,900.

Caltanissetta, t., cap. of C. prov., Sicily, **Italy**; cath.; agr., sulphur ctr.; p. (1991) 61,300.

Calvados, dep., N.E. **France**; low-lying cty. and damp climate aid dairying; butter and cheese prods.; apple orchards produce Calvados brandy; cap. Caen; a. 5,690 km²; p. (1999) 647,252.

Cam (Granta), R., Cambridge, **Eng.**; trib. of R. Ouse; flows through the "backs" at Cambridge; 64 km long.

Camagüey, c., **Cuba**; comm. ctr. in rich agr. region; cattle, sugar-cane; p. (1990) 125,021.

Camargue, delta dist., Bouches-du Rhône, **France**; at mouth of R. Rhône; famous col. of flamingoes; gypsies; bull-rearing; a. 777 km².

Camberley, t., Surrey, **Eng.**; Royal Military Staff College, Royal Military Academy; p. (2001) 47,123 (with Frimley).

Cambodia, State of (Kampuchea), S.E. Asia; between Thailand and Vietnam; former ass. st. of Fr. Union; cap. Phnom Penh on Mekong R.; mainly agr., rice, rubber, maize, pepper, kapok, livestock; Tonle Sap impt. for fishing; car assembly, cigarette mkg., textiles, plywood, paper, tyres,cement; oil refinery nr. Kompong Som; ravaged by civil war; a. 181,300 km²; p. (2004) 13,363,421.

Camborne, t., Cornwall, **Eng.**; 18 km S.W. Truro; old tin and copper mines; engin., radio-television assembly; textiles, chemicals; p. (1991) 35,915 (inc. Redruth).

Cambourne, planned £450m. new town near Cambridge.

Cambrai, t., Nord dep., **France**; on R. Scheldt; textiles (gave its name to cambric), agr. processing; suffered in both world wars; p. (1999) 33,738.

Cambrian Mtns., Wales; collective name for mtns. of N. and Central Wales inc. Snowdonia and Cader Idris.

Cambridge, univ. c., co. t., l. gov. dist., Cambridgeshire, **Eng.**; on Cam R.; famous univ. with residtl. colleges; leading ctr. of high-tech and research-based inds.; p. (2001) 120,650 (dist.).

Cambridgeshire, non-met. co., **Eng.**; low-lying, sloping from E. Anglian Heights in S.E. to Fens in N.; crossed by Rs. flowing to Wash; rich soils aid intensive agr. and mkt. gardening; inc. former cos. of Huntingdon, Peterborough and Isle of Ely; ch. t. Cambridge; p. (2001) 552,658.

Cambridge, c., Mass., **USA**; 5 km from Boston; seat of Harvard Univ. and MIT; mftg.; impt. research ctr.; now inc. in Boston met. a.; p. (1996) 93,707.

Camden, inner bor., N. London, **Eng.**; inc. Hampstead, Holborn, and St. Pancras; major redevelopment of Kings Cross area; p. (2001) 198,020.

Camden, c., N.J., **USA**; pt. of entry on Delaware R., opposite Philadelphia; comm., mftg. and residtl.; iron foundries, chemicals, shipbldg.; p. (1996) 84,844; inc. in Philadelphia met. a.

Camerino, t., central Italy; in Apennines; univ. cath.; the anc. Camerium; p. (1991) 7,300.

Cameroon, United Rep. of, unitary st. (1972) W. Africa; on G. of Guinea; fed. cap. Yaoundé; dependence on primary exports of coffee and cocoa now reduced by rapid incr. in petroleum production since 1977; growing industrial sector, logging threatens environmental destruction; a. 475,500 km²; p. (2004) 16,063,678.

Cameroon Mtn., volcano, massif, Cameroon; cstl-mtn., hgst. in W. Africa; last eruption 1959; alt. 4,072 m.

Campagna di Roma, Latium, **Italy**; former malarial coastal plain around Rome; now reclaimed and used for pasture.

Campania, region, S. **Italy**; comprising provs. Avellino, Benevento, Caserta, Naples, Salerno; admin. and comm. ctr. Naples; high p. density; fertile; intensive agr.; p. (1992) 5,668,895.

Campbeltown, royal burgh, spt., Argyll and Bute, **Scot.**; distilling, fishing; planned ctr. for construction of off-shore oil platforms; p. (2002) 5,144.

Campeche, spt., S.E. **Mexico**; on G. of Campeche; gives its name to prov. (a. 56,099 km²; p. (1990) 528,824); clothing; exp. timber, sisal hemp; p. (1990) 172,208.

Campinas, t., **Brazil**; 88 km N. of São Paulo; coffee; machin.; rubber gds.; p. (1996) 908,000.

Campine or Kempenland, region in Limburg and Antwerp provs., **Belgium**; concealed coalfield in

heathland a.

Campobasso, t., cap. of C. prov., S. **Italy**; agr. ctr.; cutlery; 15th cent. cas.; p. (1996) 239,227.

Campo Belo, t., Minas Gerais st., **Brazil**; impt. cattle ctr. nr. L. formed by Furnas Dam on Rio Grande; p. (1996) 47,350.

Campo Grande, c., cap. Mato Grosso de Sul st. **Brazil**; p. (1996) 598,200.

Campos, c., Rio de Janeiro st., **Brazil**; ctr. for rich agr. region; sugar refining; p. (1991) 388,640.

Campos do Jordão, t., **Brazil**; alt. 1,699 m; health resort, known as the Switzerland of Brazil; p. (1996) 36,000.

Campsie Fells, range of hills, Stirling/E. Dunbartonshire, **Scot.**; highest point, 578 m.

Canada, indep. st., within Commonwealth; occupies N. part of N. America; enclave of Alaska (USA) in N.W.; second lgst. cty. in world, consisting of 10 provs., 3 terrs.; coastal mtns. and Rockies in W., interior plains in ctr., Hudson Bay lowlands in N., plateau a. of Quebec and Newfoundland in E.; many Is. off Arctic cst.; continental climate, severe in interior but moderated on csts.; less than 8 per cent of total land a. classified as cultivated land but agr. prods. (especially wheat) very valuable exp.; enormous forest resources but many economically inaccessible; fur trapping in N., impt. fishing inds. on both Pac. and Atl. csts.; considerable mineral resources; lgst. world producer of asbestos, silver, nickel, zinc.; major oil and gas resources in Alberta; one of most urbanised ctys. in world; p. concentrated along E.-W. axis in S. parts of W. provs. and along Gr. Ls. and St. Lawrence lowland; economy highly integrated with USA; 80 per cent of mftg. inds. based on US investment and 78 per cent of external tr. with USA; major cultural differences between English and French communities; strong separatist movements in Quebec; both nat. languages official (30 per cent p. speak French); cap. Ottawa; a. 9,976,185 km²; p. (2004) 32,507,874.

Canada Dam, Bihar, **India**; on R. Mayurakshi, 256 km from Calcutta.

Canadian Coast Range, mtns., B.C., W **Canada**; penetrated by deep inlets (fjords) with very little cst. plain; crossed only by R. Skeena in N., R. Fraser in S.

Canadian Shield (Laurentian Shield), **Canada**; vast region of hard anc. rock surrounding Hudson Bay, deeply eroded by ice, and lake covered; mng. and forestry.

Canaries Current, ocean current, flows S along N.W. coast of Africa from El Dar-el-Beida to C. Verde; relatively cold and has very marked cooling effect on Saharan coastlands.

Canary Is., or Canaries, N. Atl. Oc.; gr. of 7 volcanic Is. belong to Spain, 96 km off cst. Africa; desires independence; inc. Tenerife (the lgst. I.), Gran Canaria, La Palma, Gomera, Hierro, Fuerteventura, Lanzarote; dry sunny climate and impressive volcanic landscape encourage tourism; intensive, irrigated agr. for bananas, tomatoes, oranges and vegetables; cap. Las Palmas, the "Fortunate Isles" of myths; a. 7,272 km²; p. (1998) 1,630,000.

Canberra, cap. **Australia**; midway between Melbourne and Sydney, lgst. inland c.; rapid growth since cap. established (1912); half work-force employed in government; spacious planned c. centred around L. Burley Griffin, reliant on high car ownership; p. (1997) 309,500.

Candia. See Iráklion.

Canea. See Khaniá.

Cancún, Yucatan, **Mexico**; booming holiday destination, known as 'Mexican Riviera'.

Canna, sm. I., Hebrides, Highland, **Scot.**; basaltic pillars.

Cannanore (Kannur), t., Kerala, **India**; exp. timber, coconuts; p. (1991) 464,000.

Cannes, spt., dep. Alpes-Maritimes, **France**; 32 km S.W. Nice; famous resort; perfumes; airpt.; annual spring international film festival; p. (1999) 67,260.

Cannock Chase, upland a., Staffs., **Eng.**; close to Midlands conurb.; forms l. gov. dist. based on Cannock t.; p. (2001) 92,126 (dist.), (2001) 65,022 (t.).

Canopus, c. of anc. Egypt; 19 km E. of Alexandria; here bdy. between Asia and Africa was drawn; Aboukir nr. ruins of temple of Serapis.

Cantabrians (Sierra de Cantabria), mtns., N. Spain; stretch from Pyrenees to C. Finisterre; form barrier between sea and central plateau; thick vegetation on lower slopes; coal, iron, hydroelec. power; hgst. peak Peña Ubiña (2,673 m).

Cantal, dep., S.E. **France;** volcanic a., part of Massif Central; hgst. peak Plomb du Cantal (1,859 m); difficult agr., sparse p.; cap. Aurillac; a. 5,778 km²; p. (1999) 150,755.

Canterbury, c., l. gov. dist., Kent, **Eng.;** at foot of N. Downs on R. Stour; univ.; cath. founded A.D. 597 by St. Augustine; famous shrine of Thomas Becket; p. (2001) 135,278 (dist.), (2001) 43,552 (t.).

Canterbury, region, rich grazing and wheat-growing dist., on merged alluvial fans, S.I., **N.Z.;** ch. t. Christchurch; ch. pt. Lyttelton; p. (1991) 442,392.

Can-tho, t., **Vietnam;** on Mekong R. delta, tr. ctr.; rice, fish; p. (1992) 216,000.

Canton. See Guangzhou.

Canton R. See Zhujiang.

Canton, c., Ohio, **USA;** iron and steel, pulleys, hydraulic presses; p. (1990) 84,161 (c.), 394,106 (met. a.).

Canvey I., Castle Point, Essex, **Eng.;** fronting the Thames; expanded t.; resort; radio components, bookbinding, iron and wire wks., oil storage; oil refinery; liquid gas terminal; p. (2001) 37,479.

Cape Breton I., Nova Scotia, **Canada;** coalmng., steelwks; farming, timber, fishing; ch. t. Sydney; discovered in 1497 by John Cabot; a. 9,324 km²; p. (1996) 117,849.

Cape Canaveral, E. Fla., **USA;** formerly Cape Kennedy; barrier I. separating Banana R. lagoon from Atl. Oc.; military base for testing missiles.

Cape Coast, t., **Ghana;** pt. of G. of Guinea, 96 km S.W. of Accra; cap. of Gold Coast until 1876; exp. cacao; cas.; p. (2002 est.) 77,400.

Cape Cod, low sandy penin., Mass. Bay, **USA;** resort; fishing, boat bldg.; encloses C. C. Bay where Pilgrim Fathers first arrived in America 1620.

Cape Horn, Chile, most southerly point of S. America.

Cape Kennedy. See Cape Canaveral.

Cape of Good Hope, S. Africa; famous headland, S. of Cape Town; 305 m high.

Capernaüm, in time of Christ impt. place in Palestine, on N. shore of L. Galilee; the modern Tell Hum (Israel).

Cape Town, c., cap. of Western Cape prov, **Rep. of S. Africa;** spt. on Table Bay, 48 km N. of C. of Good Hope; communication by rail direct with Zimbabwe, Transvaal, Natal, Free State *etc.*; docks; cath.; univ.; exp. wool, gold, diamonds; oil refinery at Milnerton 10 km N.E., p. (2000) 2,993,000 (met. a.).

Cape Verde, most W. part of **Africa;** site of Dakar, cap. of Senegal.

Cape Verde, Is., archipelago off W. cst. Africa; former Portuguese col.; 15 volcanic Is. and islets, divided into two grs.; windward and leeward; a. 4,040 km²; cap. Praia; agr. sugar, fruit-growing; São Vicente fuelling sta. for navigation to S. America; indep. achieved 1975; plans to develop infrastructure; plans for irrigation and reafforestation projects; p. (2004) 415,294.

Capraia, I., 26 km E. of Corsica, belonging to **Italy;** volcanic; part of Genoa prov.

Caprera, I., off N.E. cst. Sardinia, **Italy;** Garibaldi buried here.

Capri, I. and tourist resort in Bay of Naples, **Italy;** famous Blue Grotto; celebrated in times of Augustus and Tiberius; wines; a. 10 km²; p. (2000 est.) 15,000.

Capua, t., Campania, S. **Italy;** on Volturno R.; founded by Etruscans, impt. ctr. under Roman rule, sacked by Gaiseric; modern t. 5 km N. of site of anc. Capua; cath., Roman bridge; p. (1991) 18,800.

Caracas, c., cap. of **Venezuela;** in mtn. valley 921 m a.s.l.; 13 km inland from its pt. La Guaira; modern c.; contains 12 per cent of p. of rep.; cath., univs.; oil, textile mills, sugar refining; p. (2000) 3,153,000.

Caradon, l. gov. dist., Cornwall, **Eng.;** a. between Tamar and S. cst.; inc. Looe, Saltash and Liskeard; p. (2001) 79,649.

Carbon County, N. Utah, **USA;** contains immense reserves of gd. coking coal suitable for blast furnaces; not yet developed.

Carbonia, t., Sardinia, **Italy;** built 1937–8 nr.

lignite and barytes a.; p. (1991) 32,900.

Carcassonne, c., cap. of Aude dep., S. **France;** historic citadel guarding impt. routeway from Aquitaine to Rhône valley; old c. divided from new by Aude R.; tourism; UNESCO World Heritage Site; p. (1990) 44,991.

Cardamom Hills, Kerala, S. **India;** highland formed where W. and E. Ghats meet; rise to over 2,400 m; hgst. land of Indian penin.; rainfall less seasonal than most of India; "China" tea plantations on middle slopes.

Cardiff, c., cap. of **Wales,** unit. auth. created in 1996 from former l. gov. dist.; at mouth of R. Taff on Bristol Channel, formerly one of world's gr coal-shipping pts.; unlvs. cath., cas.; docks at Barry, iron and steel wks., flour mills; freeport (1984) to help redevelopment of docks; home of Millennium Stadium; location of Welsh Assembly; new Wales Millenium Centre; p. (1991) 272,129 (c.), (2001) 305,353 (unit. auth.).

Cardigan, sm. t., Ceredigion, S. **Wales;** at mouth of Teifi R.; former pt., now mkt. ctr.

Cardiganshire. See Ceredigion.

Caribbean Sea, part of Atl. Oc., between W.I. and Central and S. America; warm sea, entirely within tropics; a. 19,425 km².

Cariboo Range, mtns., B.C., W. **Canada;** mass of anc. crystalline rocks inside the gr. bend of R. Fraser; widespread occurrence of lode and alluvial gold; mainly above 1,500 m; hgst. point Mt. Sir Wilfred Laurier (3,584 m).

Carinthia (Karnten), prov., **Austria;** cap. Klagenfurt; contains hgst. mtn. in Austria, Grossglockner, alt. 3,801 m; many Ls.; p. (1991) 552,421.

Carlisle, c., l. gov. dist., Cumbria, **Eng.;** on Eden R.; pt. and route ctr.; Norman cas.; cath.; textiles, plasterboard, flour, bacon, biscuits, metal boxes; p. (2001) 100,739 (dist.), (2001) 71,773 (c.).

Carlow, co., S.E. Leinster, **R.o.I.;** arable agr. and livestock; co. t. Carlow; a. 896 km²; p. (1991) 40,900.

Carlow, co. t., Carlow co., **R.o.I.;** cath.; mkt., agr. processing; p. (1991) 14,020.

Carlsbad, t., N.M., **USA;** tourist resort; impt. potash deposits; p. (1990) 24,950.

Carlsbad Caverns National Park, N.M., **USA;** in foothills of Guadalupe mtns.; limestone caves; a. 18,600 ha.

Carlton, t., Gedling, Notts., **Eng.;** 3 km N.E. Nottingham; hosiery; p. (2001) 48,493.

Carmarthen, t., Carmarthenshire, **Wales;** on Towy R.; impt. agr. ctr.; cas. ruins; p. (1991) 13,524.

Carmarthenshire, S.W. **Wales,** unit. auth. created in 1996 from former l. gov. dists. of Carmarthen, Dinefwr and Llanelli, reinstating historic co. split up in 1974; stock rearing and fattening; industl. in S.E.; p. (2001) 172,842.

Carmiel, t., N. **Israel;** new t. built between Acre and Safad, in the Galilean hills.

Carmona, t., **Spain;** Roman walls and necropolis.

Carnac, sm. t., Brittany, N.W. **France;** famous for its megalithic monuments; p. (1999) 4,444.

Carnarvon, t., W. **Australia;** on R. Gascoyne; NASA tracking sta.; p. (1991) 6,900.

Carnoustie, burgh, Angus, Scot.; on N. Sea; 10 km S.W. of Arbroath; resort; p. (2002) 10,561.

Carpathian Mtns., range, **E. Europe;** arc of mtns. extending from Slovakia into Ukraine and Romania; major European range; 1,288 km long; contains oilfields.

Carpentras, t., Vaucluse, **France;** on R. Auzon; antiquities; sweetmeats; p. (1990) 25,500.

Carpi, t., central **Italy;** 16 km N. of Modena; cath.; food processing; p. (1991) 60,700.

Carrantuohill, mtn., Kerry, **R.o.I.;** 1,041 m, loftiest in all Ireland.

Carrara, t., Massa Carrara, central **Italy;** famed for white marble used by Michelangelo; p. (1991) 67,200.

Carrick, l. gov. dist., Cornwall, **Eng.;** stretches across penin. and surrounds Fal estuary; inc. Truro, Penryn and Falmouth; p. (2001) 87,865.

Carrickfergus, t., l. gov. dist., **N. Ireland;** pt. on N. shore of Belfast Lough; textiles, nylon fibres, tobacco inds.; p. (2001) 37,659 (dist.), 22,786 (t.).

Carrick-on-Shannon, co. t., R. D., Leitrim, **R.o.I.;** on flat land in Upper Shannon valley; p. of t. (1991) 1,900.

Carrick-on-Suir, mkt. t., Tipperary, **R.o.I.;** leather prods.; N.W. of Waterford; p. (1991) 5,140.

Carron, v., Falkirk, **Scot.;** nr. Falkirk; site of first ironwks. in E. Lowlands of Scot; p. (2002) 5,398.

Carron, Loch, inlet, W. cst., Highland, **Scot.**; followed by rly. from Dingwall to Kyle of Lochalsh.

Carse of Gowrie, Perth and Kinross, **Scot.**; fertile coastal dist. between Perth and Dundee, S. of Sidlaw Hills; soft fruits, especially raspberries.

Carsington, reservoir opened May 1992, S. Derbyshire.

Carson City, cap. Nevada, **USA**; smallest st. cap. at 1,427 m; tourist ctr.; p. (1996) 47,237.

Carstenz Mtns., Irian Jaya, **Indonesia**; major copper and base metal deposits and mng.; slurry pipeline to pts. on Tipoeka R.

Cartagena, spt., cap. dep. Bolívar. **Colombia**; shares with Barranquilla tr. from Magdalena R. valley; platinum, coffee, chemicals, textiles, fertilisers, oil refinery; drugs summit 1990; founded 1588; p. (1993) 728,800.

Cartagena, c., Murcia prov., S.E. **Spain**; on Mediterranean; spt. and naval base; cath.; shipbldg., metalwkg.: p. (1998) 175,600.

Cartago, c., Costa Rica; former cap.; 1,504 m at foot of volcanic Mt. Irazu; coffee, fruits; subject to earthquakes; p. (1998) 32,600.

Cartago Basin, Meseta Central, **Costa Rica**; alt. 5,000 ft.; a. of early Spanish settlement.

Carter Fell, mtn., a summit of the Cheviot hills, on the Eng./Scot. border, 554 m.

Carthage, anc. c., N. **Africa**; on Bay of Tunis; destroyed by Romans 146 B.C.; site is sub. of Tunis.

Casablanca. *See* El Dar-el-Beida.

Casale Monferrato, t., Piedmont, **Italy**; on R. Po; cath.; cement.

Cascade Range, USA and Canada; extends N. and S. through B.C., Wash., and Ore. between Rocky Mtns. and Pac. cst.; timber resources, hydroelec. power; hgst. peak Mt. Rainier, 4,395 m.

Cascade Tunnel, longest rly. tunnel in N. America, Wash., **USA**; carries trunk rly. from Spokane to Seattle through Cascade Mtns.; length 12·5 km,

Caserta, t., **Italy**; on N.E. edge of plain of Campania; impt. route ctr. and agr. mkt.; cath.; palace; p. (1991) 69,000.

Cashel, mkt. t., Tipperary, **R.o.I.**; anc. seat of kings of Munster; ruins of cath. on Rock of Cashel; p. (1991) 2,300.

Casiquiare, R., and canal, **Venezuela**; joins Orinoco to the Rio Negro, a trib. of the Amazon.

Caspian Sea, salt lake, **Kazakhstan, Turkmenistan, Russia, Azerbaijan** and **Iran,** between Europe and Asia; lgst. inland sea in world; a. 386,400 km² but shrinking; 28 m below sea level; maximum depth 975 m; fed by R. Volga; agr. and dense p. on S. shore; pts.; Astrakhan, at mouth of Volga, Baku (oil ctr.).

Casquets, dangerous rocks, 11 km W. of Alderney, Channel Is., **Eng.**; lighthouse.

Cassino, t., Frosinone, **Italy**; in Apennines, on Rapido R.; t. and nearby monastery (Montecassino) destroyed 1944, now rebuilt; p. (1991) 32,790.

Castel Gandolfo, t., central **Italy**; in Alban Hills; papal summer residence; tourist centre; p. (1991) 13,500.

Castellammare del Golfo, spt., N.W. Sicily, **Italy**; wat. pl., tuna fishing.

Castellammare di Stabia, t., Campania, **Italy**; on Bay of Naples, at foot of Vesuvius; historic arsenal and dockyards; mineral springs; cath.; resort; p. (1991) 68,200.

Castellón de la Plana, prov., **Spain**; on Mediterranean, part of anc. Valencia, mainly mtns. a. 6,679 km²; cap. Castellón; p. (1998) 461,700.

Castellón de la Plana, t., **Spain**; on plain inland from Mediterranean cst.; varied agr. inds.; oil refining; p. (1998) 137,700.

Castelnaudary, t., Aude dep., **France**; in strategic gap between Central Massif and Pyrenees; captured by Black Prince 1355; mkt. for cereals; pottery; p. (1999) 10,753.

Castelo Branco, t., **Portugal,** prov. cap. Beira Baixa; agr. mkt. t.; p. (1981) 21,300.

Castelvetrano, agr. t., W. Sicily, **Italy**; wine mkg.; p. (1991) 32,000.

Castile, region in the high plateaux of central **Spain**; former kingdom; divided into Old Castile in N. (Avila, Burgos, Logroño, Santander, Segovia, Soria) and New Castile in S. (Ciudad Real, Cuenca, Guadalajara, Madrid, Toledo). Its dialect became the standard language of Spain.

Castlebar, cap. Mayo, **R.o.I.**; mkt. t.; p. (1991) 7,650.

Castlecary, v., N. Lanarkshire, **Scot.**; sta. on Roman wall; silica, fire clay deposits.

Castle Donington, t., Leicestershire, **Eng.**; East Midlands airpt; power sta. (now demolished); p. (1991) 6,007.

Castle Douglas, burgh, Dumfries and Galloway, **Scot.**; nr. R. Dee; nearby cas.; stock mkt.; p. (2002) 3,671.

Castleford, t., West Yorks., **Eng.**; 16 km S.E. of Leeds at confluence of Rs. Aire and Calder; coal mng., chemical, glass, and clothing mnfs, flour milling, brick mkg.; p. (2001) 37,525.

Castle Morpeth, l. gov. dist., Northumberland, **Eng.**; based on Morpeth; p. (2001) 49,001.

Castle Point, l. gov. dist., Essex, **Eng.**; comprises Canvey I. and Benfleet; p. (2001) 86,608.

Castlereagh, l. gov. dist., N. **Ireland**; inc. S.E. outskirts of Belfast; p. (2001) 66,488.

Castleton, v., Derbys., **Eng.**; on Hope R.; tourist ctr. for the Peak District; nearby fluorspar mines.

Castletown, t., **Isle of Man**; former cap.; pt., cas. tower; p. (1991) 3,152.

Castres, t., Tarn, **France**; on R. Agout; former Huguenot stronghold; cath.; textiles, soap, earthenware; p. (1990) 46,300.

Castries, t., cap. **St. Lucia,** Windward Is., **W.I.**; fine harbour; p. (1999) 57,000.

Castrop-Rauxel or **Kastrop Rauxel,** t., N. Rhine-Westphalia, **Germany**; part of Ruhr conurb.; industl.; coal, cement, tar prod., tiles, brandy; p. (2002) 78,471.

Catalonia, region, N.E. **Spain**; ch. industl. a.; comprises 4 provs.; Barcelona, Gerona, Lérida, Tarragona; cap. Barcelona; hilly, drained by Ebro R.; cereals, olive oil, wines; textiles, cars; hydroelec. power stas.; nuclear power sta. projected; a. 32,185 km²; p. (1998) 6,148,000.

Catamarca, t., cap. of Catamarca prov., N.W. **Argentina**; in Andean foothills 128 km S. of San Miguel de Tucumán; ctr. of irrigated oasis producing vines, apricots, cherries, cotton; thermal springs; p. (1991) 132,626 (t.), 264,234 (prov.).

Catanduanes, I., prov. off S. Luzon, **Philippines**; hilly, fertile; rice, corn, cotton, hemp, coconuts; a. 1,429 km²; p. (1990) 187,000.

Catania, c., Sicily, **Italy**; cap. of C. prov.; pt. on E. cst. at foot of Mt. Etna; rebuilt several times after earthquakes and volcanic eruption; cath., univ., cas.; p. (1992) 329,898.

Catanzaro, t., S. **Italy**; univ.; service ctr., regional cap. of Calabria; p. (1991) 96,600.

Catastrophe, C., S. extremity of Eyre Peninsula, S. **Australia.**

Caterham and **Warlingham,** ts., former U.D. Tandridge, Surrey, **Eng.**; on N. Downs; residtl.; p. (2001) 31,649.

Cathay, anc. name for China and E. Tartary.

Catskill Mtns., N.Y., **USA**; gr. in Appalachians, W. of Hudson R., well wooded; resort for p. of N.Y. c.; alt. c. 900 m.

Cauca, dep., **Colombia**; cap. Popayán; a. 30,191 km²; p. (1993) 1,127,700.

Caucasia, region between Black Sea and Caspian, occupied by parts of **Russia, Georgia, Azerbaijan** and **Armenia** divided by Caucasus Mtns. into N. or Cis-Caucasia and S. or Trans-Caucasia.

Caucasus (Bol'shoy Kavkaz), mtns., separate **Russia** from **Georgia** and **Azerbaijan**; run from Black Sea to Caspian Sea; divided into 3 ranges; hgst. summits Mt. Elbruz (5,631 m) and Kasbek (5,047 m); many lofty passes and glaciers; total l. c. 1,520 km.

Cancun, t., off Yucatan penin., **Mexico**; developing tourist ctr.; airpt.

Causses, Les, limestone plateau, Aveyron, Tarn deps., S. **France**; on S.W. flank of Central Massif; caverns, gorges of Rs. Lot and Tarn; sheep provide milk for Roquefort cheese; alt. 900–1,800 m.

Cauvery, R., S. **India**; rises in W. Ghats, flows into Bay of Bengal through Karnataka and and Tamil Nadu; length 640 km; lge. irrigation and hydroelec. power project.

Cava de' Tirreni, t., Salerno, **Italy**; summer resort; textiles; p. (1991) 52,500.

Cavan, inland co., **R.o.I.**; agr. a. with many Ls.; depopulation; borders Ulster; a. 1,932 km²; p. (1991) 52,800.

Cavan, ., co. t., Cavan, **R.o.I.**; 115 km S.W. Belfast; mkt.; cath.; p. (1991) 5,250.

Cavite, spt., Luzon, **Philippines**; walled t.; oil

refining nearby; p. (1990) 91,641.

Cavour Canal, irrigation canal. Piedmont and Lombardy regions, N. **Italy**; links R. Po nr. Chivasso with R. Ticino 16 km N.E. of Novara; provides water for 101,000 ha of rice-fields and meadow-land; length 128 km.

Cawnpore. *See* **Kanpur.**

Caxias do Sul, t., Rio Grande do Sul, **Brazil**; wines; p. (1991) 290,930.

Cayambe, volcanic mtn., Andes, **Ecuador**; alt. 5,958 m.

Cayenne, c., cap of French **Guiana**, at mouth of Cayenne R.; exp. gold; gave its name to Cayenne pepper; p. (1990) 41,659.

Cayman Is., W.I.; consists of Grand Cayman, cap. George Town; Little Cayman; and Cayman Brac.; turtle and shark fishing; 5th largest banking sector in world; tourism; a. 259 km²; p. (2004) 43,103.

Ceará, st., N. **Brazil**; stretches from Brazilian Plateau to Atl. cst.; poor cattle rearing a. with many droughts; cap. Fortaleza; a. 148,078 km²; p. (1996) 6,803,600.

Cebu, one of Visayan Is., prov. **Philippines**; mtnous.; forested; coal, oil, gold; coconuts, maize; 4,408 km²; p. (1990) 2,645,735.

Cebu, c., Cebu I., **Philippines**; tr. ctr. of Visayan Is.; pt. for abaca and copra; p. (1995) 662,000.

Cedar Falls, t., N. Iowa, **USA**; on Cedar R.; p. (1990) 34,298.

Cedar Mountain, hill, Va., **USA**; here Stonewall Jackson defeated Banks in Civil War (second battle of Bull Run, 1862).

Cedar Rapids, c., Iowa, **USA**; distribution and rly. ctr. for agr. a.; p. (1996) 113,482.

Celaya, mkt. t., Guanajuato, **Mexico**; rly. junc.; ctr. of rich farming a.; many inds.; sweet-meats; p. (1990) 315,577.

Celebes. *See* **Sulawesi.**

Celle, t., Lower Saxony, **Germany**; on R. Aller; cas. was residence of dukes of Brunswick-Lüneburg until 1705; oil refining, machin., textiles; p. (2002) 71,949.

Celtic Sea, a. bounded by S. Ireland, Wales, Cornwall and Brittany; rich natural gas deposits 48 km S.W. of Kinsale.

Central African Republic, indep. st., former empire until 1979; within Fr. Community, Equatorial Africa; formerly Fr. colony of Ubangi-Shari; land-locked upland plateau covered by savannah grassland; S.W. forest zone likely to develop with proposed rail link with Transcameroon rly.; cotton, diamonds; cap. Bangui; a. 622,984 km²; p. (2004) 3,742,482.

Central America, stretch of land between Mexico and S. America, from the Isthmus of Tehuantepec to that of Panama; includes Guatemala, Honduras, Mexico, Nicaragua, Salvador, Costa Rica, Panama, Belize; tropical climate; forests, savannahs.

Central Asia, usually applied to regions between 30° and 40° N. lat. and 55° and 85° E. long.; the land between China and Afghanistan and the Caspian, consisting of Kazakhstan, Tajikistan, Turkmenistan, Uzbekistan and Kyrgyzstan.

Central Clydeside Conurbation, conurb., **Scot.**; based on Glasgow and includes other urban areas (Bearsden, Milngavie, Clydebank, Cumbernauld, Kilsyth, East Kilbride, Eastwood, Hamilton, Monklands, Motherwell, Renfrew and Strathkelvin); p. (1993) 1,619,960.

Central Valley, Cal., **USA**; valleys of Rs. San Joaquin and Sacramento; main agr. a. of Cal.; vast scheme for irrigation, hydroelec. power, flood control and protection of wildlife.

Centre, region, France; inc. deps. Cher, Eure-et-Loir, Indre, Indre-et-Loire, Loir-et-Cher, Loiret; region based on the upper Loire and its tributaries; agr; vineyards; ch. ts. Orleans, Tours; p. (1999) 2,440,333.

Cephalonia (Kefalliniá), lgst. of Ionian Is., **Greece**; mtnous. with fertile valleys; impt. harbours of Argostólion and Lexourion; site of massacre of Italian troops by German military (1941); currant production; a. 751 km²; p. (1991) 32,474.

Ceram. *See* **Seram.**

Ceredigion, W. **Wales**, unit. auth. created in 1996 from former t. and prov. dist., reinstating historic co. of **Cardiganshire** disbanded in 1974; upland a. drained by the Teifi and Ystwyth Rs.; ch. t. Aberystwyth; p. (2001) 74,941.

Cérignola, t., Apulia, **Italy**; agr. ctr.; Spanish victory over French in the Italian wars 1503; p. (1991) 55,050.

Cernauti. *See* **Chernovtsy.**

Cerro de Pasco, t., Pasco dep., **Peru**; mng. ctr. at 4,403 m; univ.; copper, gold, lead, zinc; p. (1991) 62,749.

Cerro Rico, mtn., **Bolivia**; in Andes, W. of Potosi; alt. 4,782 m; rich silver, tin, tungsten ores.

Cesena, t., Emilia-Romagna, **Italy**; flourished in Renaissance times; cath., Malatesta library; agr. mkt. t.; p. (1981) 89,640.

České Budějovice (Budweis), t., **Czech Rep.**; on R. Vitava, 128 km S. of Prague, major industl. ctr.; pencils, porcelain, brewing, anthracite; p. (1990) 99,000.

Cesky Těšín, t., **Czech Rep.**; on Olse R., trib. of Oder; part of former t. of Teschen on Czech side of frontier with Poland; coal mng.

Cessnock-Bellbird, t., N.S.W., **Australia**; coal mng. declining since 1968; ctr. for Hunter Valley vineyards; p. (1991) 17,930.

Ceuta, spt., **Spanish N. Africa**, naval base; opposite to and 26 km from Gibraltar; cath.; the anc. Abyia, one of the Pillars of Hercules; p. (1994) 71,900.

Cevennes, mtns., S. **France**; separating basins of Rhône, Loire, and Tarn; highest point Mt. Mézenc, alt. 1,767 m.

Ceylon. *See* **Sri Lanka.**

Chaco, prov., N. **Argentina**; farming and prairie land; cap. Resistencia; a. 99,632 km²; p. (1991) 839,677.

Chad, indep. st. within Fr. Community, Equatorial Africa; landlocked, focus of trans Sahara and Equatorial tr. routes; N. frontier (Aouzou Strip) rich in minerals and occupied by Libya; valuable uranium and oil reserves but no exploitation; severe droughts (1982–3) reduced cattle and restricted arable crops; cash crops of cotton and ground nuts; cap. Ndjamena; a. 1,282,050 km²; p. (2004) 9,538,544.

Chad, L., lge. sheet of water bordering **Nigeria, Niger, Chad** and **Cameroon**; a. 129,500 km² when in flood; varies in extent with season, and is drying up; shallow, many Is., lies between the wooded region of the Sudan and the steppes leading to the Sahara desert; joint project for devel. by neighbouring ctys.

Chadderton, t., Gtr. Manchester, **Eng.**; engin., chemicals, textiles; p. (2001) 33,001.

Chagos Is., 5 coral Is., Indian Oc.; since 1965 the **British Indian Ocean Territory**; fine harbour in Diego Garcia.

Chainat, t., **Thailand**; on Menam Chao Phraya; major barrage for hydroelec. power and flood control.

Chalcis, t., **Greece**; resort for Athens; joined to mainland by swing bridge; p. (1991) 51,600.

Chalfont St. Giles, v., Bucks., **Eng.**; in London commuter belt; home of the poet Milton; p. (1991) 4,987.

Châlons-sur-Marne, t., cap. of Marne dep., N.E. **France**; comm. and industl.; cath., churches; p. (1990) 51,533.

Châlon-sur-Saône, t., Saône-et-Loire dep., E. **France**; R. pt., comm. ctr. for Burgundy; historic t.; p. (1990) 56,259.

Chambal, R., trib. of R. Jumna, rising in Vindhya hills, Madhya Pradesh, **India**; major power, irrigation and industl. scheme; agr. in lower valley causing soil erosion, major soil conservation projection; 880 km long.

Chambéry, t., cap. of Savoie dep., S.E. **France**; leather gds.; tourism; p. (1990) 55,603 (t.), 102,548 (met. a.)

Chambord, v., Loir-et-Cher dep., **France**; on R. Cosson, trib. of Loire; Renaissance château; p. approx. 200.

Chamonix, t., Haute-Savoie, **France**; at foot of Mont Blanc, in valley of R. Arve; winter sports ctr., road tunnel links to Aosta; p. (1990) 10,100.

Champagne, former prov. now incorporated in **Champagne-Ardenne** region, France; inc. deps. Ardennes, Aube, Marne, Haute-Marne; famous for its champagne wine; wheat, sheep; Ardennes hilly and heavily wooded; ch. t. Reims; p. (1990) 1,347,800.

Champaign, t., Ill., **USA**; close to Urbana; univ.; foundries; food processing; p. (1996) 64,002.

Champigny-sur-Marne, t., Val-de-Marne dep., **France**; E. sub. of Paris; varied inds.; p. (1990) 79,778.

Champlain Canal, N.Y., USA; follows gap between Adirondack Mtns. and Green Mtns. occupied by Hudson R.; links Albany with L. Champlain and allows through barge traffic between New York and St. Lawrence valley.

Champlain, L., USA; N. frontier of N.Y. st.; discharges by Richelieu R. into St. Lawrence; flanked by trunk route from New York to Montreal; forms link between Hudson R. and St. Lawrence waterway; a. 1,126 km².

Chanda, t., Nagpur, Maharashtra, India; anc. temples.

Chandausi, t., Uttar Pradesh, India; cotton, hemp; rly. ctr.; p. (1991) 82,700.

Chandernagore (Chandannagar), t., W. Bengal, India; on Hooghly R., N. of Kolkata (Calcutta); founded by French 1686; p. (1991) 122,400.

Chandigarh, union terr. (1966) and former cap. of both Punjab and Haryana sts., India; new c. designed by Le Corbusier to replace former cap. Lahore, now in Pakistan; to be sole capital of Punjab on plateau at foot of Himalayas, S.W. of Simla, (now postponed because of Sikh unrest); univ.; a. of terr. 114 km², p. (1991) 511,000 (c.), (2001) 900,900 (terr.).

Changchun, c., Jilin, China; rly. ctr.; univ.; China's biggest motor vehicle plant, machine tools; now important film production centre; p. (1994) 1,810,000.

Changnacheri, t., Kerala, S. India; tea, cotton-spinning, silk; p. (1991) 52,400.

Changbai Shan, mtns.; form bdy. between China and N. Korea; drained by Rs. Yalu and Tumen; hgst. point Pai-t'ou-shan, 2,442 m.

Chang Jiang (Yangtse Kiang), R., China; rises in plateau in Xizang Zizhiou (Tibet) and flows E. to E. China Sea nr. Shanghai; one of China's major Rs.; crosses "Red Basin" of Sichuan, a deep gorge above Yichang and finally a broad level plain; many lge. cs. on its banks inc. Yichang, Nanjing, Wuhan, Zhenjiang, Chongqing; major water control project; navigable by ocean-going vessels for 2,880 km. to Yichang; total length 5,600 km.; longest river in Asia.

Changsha, c., cap. of Hunan prov., China; pt. on Xiang Jiang; univ.; tea, rice, antimony; p. (1994) 1,198,000.

Changzhou (Changchow), c., Jiangsu, China; in valley of Chang Jiang, on Grand Canal 112 km S.E. of Nanjing; mkt. for intensively cultivated dist.; silk; p. (1994) 683,000.

Channel Is., gr. of self-governing Is. belonging to the Brit. Crown off N.W. cst. France, of which the lgst. are Jersey, Guernsey, Alderney, and Sark; part of the old duchy of Normandy; vegetables, flowers, fruit, granite; two famous breeds of dairy cattle; tourist resort; impt. banking and insurance ctr. encouraged by low taxes; retirement ctr.; a. 194 km²; p. (1991) 138,800.

Chantilly, t., Oise, France; famous racecourse; formerly famous for lace and porcelain; p. (1999) 10,834.

Chao Phraya. See Menam Chao Phraya.

Chapala, t. and L., Mexico; chiefly in Jalisco st.; attractive site and climate encourage tourism; pastoral agr. on shores; a. 1,080 km²; p. (1990) 35,414.

Chapelcross, nr. Annan, Dumfries and Galloway, Scot.; AEA nuclear power sta., producing electricity for nat. grid.

Chapel-en-le-Frith, mkt. t., High Peak, Derbys., Eng.; brake-linings; p. (1991) 8,715

Chapra, t., Bihar, India; on Ganges R.; ctr. of former saltpetre and indigo tr.; p. (1991) 136,877.

Chard, mkt. t., Somerset Eng.; lace, engin., shirt and cotton mftg.; p. (1991) 10,770.

Chardzhou, t., Turkmenistan; inland pt. on Amu-Dar'ya R.; shipyards, textiles, chemicals; major oil refinery project; p. (1990) 163,700.

Charente, dep., S.W. France; cap. Angoulême; ctr. of distilling tr.; cognac; a. 5,970 km²; p. (1999) 339,568.

Charente, R., S.W. France; rises W. of Limoges and flows into Bay of Biscay below Rochefort; valley slopes beyond Angoulême produce celebrated grapes from which brandy is made at Cognac and Jarnac.

Charente-Maritime, dep., S.W. France; cap. La Rochelle; borders Bay of Biscay; wine, wheat; oysters, pilchards; a. 7,229 km²; p. (1999) 557,269.

Charleroi, t., Hainaut, Belgium; on R. Sambre;

former coal mng.; glass; p. (1993) 207,045.

Charleston, c., spt., S.C., USA; industl. and comm. ctr. on Atl. cst. founded 1670; scene of onset of Civil War; p. (1990) 80,414 (c.), 506,875 (met. a.).

Charleston, t., cap. W. Va., USA; on Kanawha R.; in bituminous coal dist.; chemicals, glass, tools, oil, natural gas, lumber, coal processing; p. (1996) 56,098.

Charlotte, c., N.C., USA; key rly. junc.; machin., chemicals, textiles; p. (2000) 540,828 (c.), 1,162,093 (met. a. with Gastonia-Rock Hill).

Charlotte Amalie, t., cap. of Virgin Is. of USA; on St. Thomas I.; excellent natural harbour; former coaling sta.; p. (1990) 12,330.

Charlottesville, t., Va., USA; on Rivanna R.; in apple-growing region; univ.; textiles; Monticello nearby, home of Jefferson; textiles; p. (1990) 40,340.

Charlottetown, t., ch. pt. Prince Edward I., Canada; originally named after Queen Charlotte, consort of George III; univ.; p. (1996) 57,224.

Charnwood Forest, upland dist., Leics., Eng.; to W. of Soar valley, 19 km N.W. of Leicester; composed of anc. rocks; stone-crushing; largely forests; alt. 180–275 m; forms l. gov. dist. of Charnwood inc. Loughborough and Shepshed; p. (2001) 153,462.

Charters Towers, t., N. Queensland, Australia; fine bldgs. remain from 1872 gold rush; ctr. of agr. dist.; p. (1994) 9,020.

Chartres, t., cap. of Eure-et-Loir dep., France; mkt. for cereals from Beauce region; famous Gothic cath.; p. (1999) 40,431.

Châteauroux, t., cap. of Indre dep., France; 96 km S.E. of Tours, on R. Indre; agr. ctr.; woollens, pottery; p. (1999) 49,628.

Chateau Thierry, t., Aisne, France; on R. Marne; mkt. t.; cas.; p. (1990) 15,800.

Châtellerault, t., Vienne, France; 64 km S. of Tours on R. Vienne; cutlery, metallurgical and aeronautical engin. Descartes lived here; p. (1999) 34,126.

Chatham, t., Rochester upon Medway, Kent, Eng.; on estuary of R. Medway; lt. inds.; famous naval dockyard established by Henry VIII; now planned to become heritage site; p. (1996) 67,068.

Chatham, c., Ont., Canada; on extinct L. plain on R. Thames; agr. prods.; p. (1991 43,600.

Chatham Is., N.Z. dependency, S. Pac. Oc.; volcanic Is.; sheep rearing and fishing; a. 963 km²; p. (1991) 760.

Chatsworth, Derbys., Eng.; on R. Derwent; seat of the dukes of Devonshire.

Chattanooga, c. Tenn., USA; on Tennessee R.; univ.; rly. ctr.; cottons; iron, steel, chemicals, paper, metals; p. (1990) 152,466 (c.), 433,204 (met a.).

Chatteris, Fenland, Cambridge, Eng.; mkt. t.; p. (1991) 7,261.

Chaudière Falls, on Ottawa R., above Ottawa, Canada; hydroelec. sta.

Chauk, t., Myanmar; on R. Irrawaddy; ctr. of oilfield; oil refining; fertilisers.

Chaumont, t., cap. of Haute-Marne dep., France; on R. Marne; gloves, leather; p. (1990) 28,900.

Chautauqua, L., N.Y. st., USA; summer resort; vineyards.

Chaux-de-Fonds, La, t., can. Neuchâtel, Switzerland; ctr. of watchmkg. ind.; p. (1990) 36,272.

Cheadle, t., Staffs. Moorland, Staffs., Eng.; metal mnfs.; former coal-mng. a.; p. (1991) 10,833.

Cheadle and Gatley, ts., Gtr. Manchester, Eng.; textile finishing and bleaching, engin.; residtl.; p. (2001) 57,507.

Cheboksary, c., cap. of Chuvash aut. rep., Russia; R. pt. on Volga; agr. ctr.; hydroelec. plant; p. (1989) 420,000.

Chechen Republic, rep. Russia, formerly known as Checheno - Inguish rep; declared independence 1991; conflict with Russia, 1996 and since 1999; a. 19,300 km²; cap. Grozny; p. (2000) 1·3m (disputed); mainly Islamic.

Cheddar, v., Somerset, Eng.; famous limestone caves and gorge in Mendips; cheese, strawberries; p. (1991) 4,484..

Chefoo. See Yantai.

Cheju (Quelpart), I. and prov., off S. Korea, E. China Sea; extinct volcano Mt. Halla, 1,968 m; p. (1990) 515,000.

Chekiang. See Zhijiang.

Che-ling Pass, on bdy. between Guandong and Hunan, S. China; historic route across Nanling mtns., now followed by Wuhan to Guangzhou trunk rly.; alt. 300 m.

Chelm, t. and prov., E. **Poland;** nr. Lublin; cath.; flour-milling; p. (1995) 69,070 (t.) 249,890 (prov.).

Chelmsford, co. t., l. gov. dist., Essex, **Eng.;** 48 km N.E. London; cath.; agr. mkt.; p. (2001) 157,072 (dist.), (2001) 99,962 (t.).

Chelsea, dist., London, **Eng.;** fashionable residtl. dist. *See* **Kensington.**

Cheltenham, t., l. gov. dist., Gloucs., **Eng.;** spa; educational ctr.; precision instruments; birthplace of Gustav Holst; p. (2001) 110,013 (dist.), (1991) 91,301 (t.).

Chelyabinsk, t., **Russia;** major industl. ctr. on Miass R., Siberian lowlands; steel wks.; metallurgy, machin.; on natural gas pipeline from Gazli gasfield; p. (1989) 1,142,000.

Chelyuskin, Cape, most N. point in Asia, in Krasnoyarsk Terr., **Russia;** named after Russian navigator who discovered it in 1742.

Chemnitz, c., Saxony, **Germany;** leading industl. ctr.; cotton, woollens, machin., cars, furniture, chemicals, engin.; nr. lignite mines; p. (2002) 255,798.

Chemulpo. *See* **Inchon.**

Chenab, R., W. Punjab, **Pakistan;** one of "five rivers" of Punjab; rises in Himalayas, flows S.W. into R. Sutlej; dams at Marala and Khanki; c. 1,440 km long.

Chengchow. *See* **Zhengzhou.**

Chengdu (Chengtu), c., cap. of Sichuan prov., **China;** telecommunications centre, oil refinery; chemicals, electronics, textiles, machin.; p. (1994) 1,933,000.

Chennai (Madras), c., cap. of Tamil Nadu st., **India;** spt. on Bay of Bengal, on Coromandel cst.; cath., univ.; comm. and mftg. ctr.; textile mills, tanneries, potteries, chemical plants; oil refinery; new film industry; p. (2000) 6,650,000. Formerly known as Madras.

Chepstow, mkt. t., Monmouthshire, **Wales;** on R. Wye, 3 km above confluence with R. Severn; ruined cas.; p. (1991), 9,461.

Chequers, official residence of Brit. prime ministers, 3 km S. of Wendover, Bucks., **Eng.;** gift of Lord Lee of Fareham.

Cher, dep., **France;** cap. Bourges; crossed by Cher R.; a. 7,301 km²; p. (1990) 321,600.

Cher, R., central **France;** rises in Central Massif, joins Loire below Tours; length 320 km.

Cherbourg, spt., Manche, **France;** N. cst. of Contentin peninsula; opposite to and 128 km dist. from Portsmouth; naval arsenal, shipbldg.; metals, ropes, fishing; p. (1999) 25,381.

Cherepovets, c., **Russia;** on Rybinskoye reservoir of R. Volga; steel, engin., sawmills, shipbldg.; p. (1989) 310,000.

Cheribon. *See* **Tjirebon.**

Cheriton, dist. near Folkestone, Kent, **Eng.;** Channel Tunnel, linked to Sangatte, Calais, France opened 1994.

Cherkassy, t., **Ukraine;** nr. Kiev, on reservoir formed by Dnieper R.; sugar, engin., sawmilling; p. (1990) 297,200.

Chernobyl, Ukraine; site of world's worst nuclear accident (1986).

Chernovtsy, t., **Ukraine;** univ.; Greek cath.; wheat, dairy produce, textiles, engin., chemicals; p. (1990) 257,300.

Cherrapunji, t., Assam, **India;** in Khasi Hills; reputed wettest place in world, average annual rainfall 12,700 mm.

Chertsey, t., Runnymede, Surrey, **Eng.;** on S. bank of R. Thames, 6 km below Staines; residtl.; p. (1991) 10,016.

Cherwell, l. gov. dist., Oxon., **Eng.;** stretches from Banbury to Bicester; p. (2001) 131,785.

Cherwell, R., trib. of Thames, nr. Oxford, **Eng.;** length 48 km.

Chesapeake Bay, inlet on Atl. cst., **USA;** extending 320 km from mouth of Susquehanna R. to C. Charles; shellfish ind.; bridge-tunnel (opened 1964) spans entrance to Bay; p. of c. (2000) 199,184.

Chesham, t., Bucks., **Eng.;** in heart of Chiltern Hills; printing, textiles, lt. engin.; residtl; p. (2001) 20,357.

Cheshire, non-met. co., N.W. **Eng.;** lowland a. drained by Rs. Dee and Mersey, bounded by Pennines in E.; dairying and mkt. gardening; chemical ind. based on salt deposits around Northwich; heavy inds. in and around Warring-

ton; attracting many high technology inds.; much of co. residtl. for Liverpool and Manchester; cap. Chester; p. (2001) 673,788.

Cheshunt, t., Herts., **Eng.;** in Lea valley, 11 km S. of Hertford; bricks, mkt. gardening, horticulture; p. (2001) 55,275.

Chesil Bank, Dorset, **Eng.;** shingle ridge enclosing the Fleet lagoon running from I. of Portland to Bridport.

Chester, c., l. gov. dist., Cheshire, **Eng.;** at head of estuary of R. Dee; cath., anc. walls and old timbered houses; Roman c. of Deva site of legionary barracks; engin., metal goods; univ.; p. (2001) 118,210 (dist.), (2001) 80,121 (c.).

Chester, t., Penns., **USA,** on Delaware R. S.W. Philadelphia; called Uppland by Swedish settlers 1643, renamed by William Penn, pt. of entry; shipbldg.; p. (2000) 36,900.

Chesterfield, mkt. t., colly. dist., l. gov. dist., Derbys., **Eng.;** on Rother R.; 13 km S. of Sheffield; variety of heavy inds.; 14th cent. church with crooked spire; p. (2001) 98,845 (dist.), (2001) 70,260 (t.).

Chesterfield Inlet, arm of Hudson Bay, **Canada;** 400 km by 40 km.

Chester-le-Street, t., l. gov. dist., Durham, **Eng.;** clothing, confectionery, sand wkg.; p. (2001) 53,692 (dist.), (2001) 36,049 (t.).

Cheviot Hills, range between **Scot.** and **Eng.;** hgst. summit, the Cheviot, 816 m.

Cheyenne, t., cap. of Wyo., **USA;** cattle-ranching dist.; rly. ctr.; p. (1996) 53,729.

Chhatisgarh, st., **India;** new st. created 1997 from E. sect. of Madhya Pradesh, p. (2000) 20,796,000.

Chiana, Val di, valley, central **Italy;** separates Tuscan hills from central Apennines; occupied by upper course of R. Arno, middle course of R. Tiber; followed by main route from Florence to Rome.

Chiang Mai, c., cap of C. prov., and 3rd c. of **Thailand;** rly. terminus on Ping R.; tr. ctr.; teak; univ.; p. (1991) 161,541.

Chiapa, R., flows N. from **Guatemala** through **Mexico** to G. of Campeche; impt. routeway in lower course; length 320 km.

Chiapas, Pac. st., **Mexico;** mtnous., forested; bananas, tobacco, sugar and cocoa; cattle; oil reserves; close associations with Guatemala; cap. Tuxtla Gutiérrez; a. 74,408 km²; p. (1990) 3,203,915.

Chiasso, frontier t., S. **Switzerland;** rly. sta. on Italian border.

Chiayi, c., co., W. central **Taiwan;** p. (1995) 261,749 (c.), 565,172 (co.).

Chiba, c., cap. of C. pref. **Japan;** part of Keihin conurb. on Tokyo B.; tr. ctr., giant shipyard, oil refining, aluminium, chemicals, iron and steel; airpt.; p. (2000) 887,000.

Chicago, c., Ill., **USA;** on S. shore of L. Michigan; economic heart of Mid-West; comm. ctr. called "The Loop"; immense tr. by rail and Gr. Ls.; univs.; grain mills, meat packing plants, iron and steel wks., major iron-ore mkt., electronic equipment, furniture; lgst. airport in world; p. (2000) 2,896,016 (c.), 6,070,000 (met.a.).

Chichester, t., l. gov. dist., West Sussex, **Eng.;** on S. cst. plain, 18 km W. of Arundel; cath.; p. (2001) 106,450 (dist.), (2001) 27,477 (t.).

Chickamauga Creek, USA; branch of Tennessee R. above Chattanooga; Civil War battles; site of Nat. Park.

Chickerell, E. Dorset, **Eng.;** 5 km N.W. of Weymouth; East Fleet, a sea-fed tidal estuary, lies to the west of the village.

Chiclayo, c., Lambayeque dep., **Peru;** mkt. ctr. for irrigated desert a. between Andes and Pac. Oc. producing mainly rice and sugar; p. (1993) 411,536.

Chicoutimi, t., Quebec, **Canada;** pt. on Chicoutimi R.; lumber, pulp, paper; hydroelectric power; p. (1991) 62,670 (t.), (1996) 160,454 (met. a. with Jonquière).

Chiemsee, L., lge. lake nr. Munich, **Germany.**

Chieti, t., cap. of C. prov., S. **Italy;** cath.; anc. Teate Marrucinorum; Europe's lgst. glass plant, using methane from Abruzzi field; p. (1981) 54,927.

Chigrik, t., **Uzbekistan;** new t. (1963) 34 km S. of Tashkent.

Chigwell, t., Epping Forest, Essex, **Eng.;** on borders of Epping Forest; Hainault Estate now incorporated in Redbridge, Greater London; resdtl.; p. (1991) 10,332.

Chihli, Gulf of. *See* **Pohai.**

Chihuahua, lgst. st. in **Mexico;** dry climate

impedes agr.; mng., cotton, cattle, Chihuahua dogs; a. 247,024 km²; p. (1990) 2,439,954.

Chihuahua, c., cap. Chihuahua st., **Mexico**; univ., cath.; ctr. silver-mng. ind.; p. (1990) 530,487.

Chikchi, peninsula, **Russia**; world's first Arctic nuclear power sta. being built.

Chikugo, t., N. Kyushu, **Japan**; lgst. coal mines in country; p. (1990) 43,835.

Chilaw, t., **Sri Lanka**; ctr. of coconut plantations.

Chile, rep., S. America; extends between Andes and Pac. for 4,160 km to C. Horn, E. to W. 400 km; Atacama desert; Spanish language; Roman Catholic; similar climate to that of Argentina but lacks space for extensive agr., dairying, sheep, wool; ch. exp. nitrates, copper, iron-ore, coal, iodine, petroleum, paper; cap. Santiago; ch. pt. Valparaíso; earthquake 1960, hgst. recorded magnitude; domestic and foreign protests against human rights abuses of government; a. 738,494 km²; world's lgst. producer of copper; p. (2004) 15,823,957.

Chillán, t., Chile; destroyed 1939 by one of world's worst recorded earthquakes; since rebuilt; agr. and comm. ctr.; p. (1992) 158,731.

Chilpancingo de los Bravos, t., cap. of Guerrero st., **Mexico**; ctr. of pre-Aztec culture; univ.; p. (1990) 136,243.

Chiltern, l. gov. dist., Bucks., **Eng.**; inc. part of C. Hills and Chesham and Amersham; p. (2001) 89,228.

Chiltern Hills, chalk escarpment, Oxon., Bucks., Beds., and Herts., **Eng.**; cut by no. of impt. gaps used by main communications; sheep and barley; hgst. point 276 m nr. Wendover.

Chimborazo, mtn., **Ecuador**; 6,286 m; Andes; extinct volcano, first explored by von Humboldt (1802), first scaled by Whymper (1880).

Chimkent (Shymkent), t., **Kazakhstan**; in W. foothills of Tien Shan; nearby oasis fed by Arys R.; major industl. ctr.; lead smelting; p. (1990) 400,900.

China, People's Republic of, Asia; Third lgst. cty. of world; ancient conservative civilisation overthrown by long civil war and establishment of communist régime (1949); lge. p. crowded on cultivable valleys of Hwang-ho (Yellow R.), Yangtze and Si-kiang in E.; rest of cty. either mtnous. (plateau of Tibet) or desert (Sinkiang); rapid economic growth following onset of communist régime; agr. organised on commune basis, becomes increasingly intensive in S. where climate is less extreme; vast mineral resources, esp. iron ore and coal, many underdeveloped; mineral fuels major export; recent industl. growth; heavy inds. at Wuhan, Baotou and in N.E. (Manchuria); special economic zones to attract foreign investment; poor communications except in E.; increasingly self-sufficient in petroleum; 1984 economic reform liberalised state planning system to allow mkt. forces; consumer goods and services to be expanded; cap. Beijing; now accounts for 9.8% of total world energy consumption; second highest CO_2 emissions in world; massacre of student protesters, Tiananmen Square (1989); Hong Kong returned (1997) and Macao (1999); new threat from growing spread of HIV; affected badly by SARS virus, 2003, a. 9,596,961 km²; p. (2005) 1,300,000,000.

China Sea, part of W. Pacific between Korea and Philippines; divided by the narrow Formosa Strait into two areas; E. China Sea, inc Yellow Sea, and S. China Sea.

Chinandega, mkt. t., cap. of C. dep., **Nicaragua**; sugar refining; p. (1990) 84,300.

Chincho. See Jinzhou.

Chinghai. See Qinghai.

Chinkiang. See Zhenjiang.

Chinon, t., Indre-et-Loire, central **France**; on R. Vienne, industl.; ruined cas., once a royal residency; nuclear power sta.; p. (1993) 8,960.

Chinqui, volcano, **Panama**; 3,480 m.

Chinwangtao. See Qinhuangdao.

Chioggia, spt., cath. t., N. **Italy**; on I. in G. of Venice; fishing; p. (1991) 53,200.

Chios (Khios) I., in Aegean Sea, **Greece**; mainly agr.; wines, fruits and figs; supposed birthplace of Homer; p. (1991) 52,184.

Chippenham, North Wilts., **Eng.**; mkt. t. on R. Avon; rly. signal and brake equipment, bacon curing, tanning; p. (1991) 25,961.

Chipping Campden, v., Gloucs., **Eng.**; in Cotswold Hills; formerly impt. for woollens; tourism; p. (1991) 1,741..

Chipping Norton, mkt. t., Oxford, **Eng.**; nr. Banbury;

formerly impt. for woollens; p. (1991) 5,386.

Chipping Sodbury, mkt. t., S. Gloucs., **Eng.**; 13 km N.E. of Bristol; p. (1991) 31,973.

Chiricahua Mtns., Arizona, **USA**; form part of Coronado Nat. Forest; long inhabited by Apache Indians; spectacular volcanic scenery; alt. 2,987 m.

Chirk, t., Wrexham, **Wales**; on R. Cleriog, S. of Wrexham; slate, former coal mng. a.; cas.; p. (1991) 4,264.

Chisinau (Kishinev), c., cap. of **Moldova**; on Byk R., trib. of Dniester; cath., univ.; industl., comm. ctr. in rich farming a.; tourism; p. (1999) 655,000.

Chislehurst. See Bromley.

Chistyakovo. See Torez.

Chita, c., rly. ctr., Siberia, **Russia**; on upper R. Ingoda, 640 km E. of L. Baykal; coal, engin., chemicals, sawmilling; p. (1989) 366,000.

Chittagong, c., **Bangladesh**; main pt. on Karna-fuli R., nr. Bay of Bengal; exp. jute, tea; oil refining; steel mill; hydroelec. power; p. (1991) 1,363,998.

Chittaranjan, t., West Bengal, **India**; new t. on Barakhar R., in steel ctr. of Damodar valley; rly. locomotive wks.; p. (1991) 47,200.

Chkalov. See Orenburg.

Cholula, anc. c. of Puebla prov., **Mexico**; Aztec temple, pyramid of Cholula, and other remains.

Chomo Lhari, mtn., Tibet, China and Bhutan; sacred to Buddhists; part of Himalayas; alt. 7,319 m.

Chongqing (Chungking), c., S.E. Sichuan prov., **China**; on Chang Jiang; comm. ctr. of W. China chosen 1983 as centre for experimental economic reforms; ctr. of rich agr. dist. of Red Basin of Sichuan; coal, iron and steel, heavy machin.; lorries, vans, chemical fertilisers; textiles; former treaty pt.; p. (1994) 3,870,000.

Cho Oyu, mtn., between Nepal and Tibet, **China**; sixth hgst. in world; alt. 8,225 m.

Chorley, t., l. gov. dist., N. Lancs., **Eng.**; on W. flank of Rossendale Fells, 11 km S.E. of Preston; cotton, engin.; expansion as new t. with Leyland; p. (2001) 100,449 (dist.), (2001) 33,424 (t.). See **Central Lancashire.**

Chorleywood, t., Three Rivers, Herts., **Eng.**; nr. Watford; p. (1991) 9,025.

Chorrilos Pass, **Argentina**; in E. cordillera of Andes at alt. 4,470 m; used by rly. from San Miguel de Tucumán to Antofagasta.

Chorzów (Królewska Huta), t., Katowice, **Poland**; coal, iron and steel, chemicals, engin.; p. (1995) 125,826.

Chota Nagpur, plateau, Madhya Pradesh, **India**; produces lac; impt. mng. ctr.; bauxite, mica.

Chou Kou Tien, site nr. Beijing, **China**; discovery of fossil bones of Beijing (Peking) man (*Sinanthropus pekinensis*).

Christchurch, t., l. gov. dist., Dorset, **Eng.**; on S. cst. 8 km E. of Bournemouth; holiday resort, aircraft, lt. inds.; p. (2001) 44,865 (dist.), (1991) 36,379 (t.).

Christchurch, c., Canterbury region, S.I., **N.Z.**; lgst. c. of S.I.; comm. ctr. for lamb, wool, and grain; cath., univ.; airpt; nickname, the "Garden City"; p (1991) 292,858 (c), 307,179 (met. a.).

Christianshåb, Danish settlement on Disko Bay, **W. Greenland**; meteorological sta.; p. (1990) 1,712.

Christmas I., in Indian Oc., external terr. of **Australia** since 1958; a. 140 km², healthy climate, phosphate deposits, p. (1994) 2,500.

Christmas I., lge. coral atoll in Pac. Oc., one of Line Is.; discovered by Cook 1777; a. 135 km²; nuclear test site, 1957-64.

Chu, R. Kazakhstan; rises in Tien Shan flows N.W for 800 km into inland drainage basin; Chumysh Dam provides hydroelectricity and water for cultivation of cotton, sugar-beet, citrus fruits.

Chuanchow. See Quanzhou.

Chubut, prov., **Argentina**; cap. Rawson; p. (1991) 357,189.

Chuchow. See Zhuzhou.

Chudleigh, mkt. t., Devon, **Eng.**; on R. Teign; stone quarrying.

Chu-kiang. See Zhujiang.

Chula Vista, t., Cal., **USA**; agr., aircraft; p. (1990) 135,163.

Chungking See Chongqing.

Chuquibamba Mtns. (alt. c. 6,400 m), Peru.

Chuquicamata, t., N. **Chile**; 3,050 m in Andes; lgst copper mine in world.

Chuquisaca, dep. **Bolivia**; oil, agr.; cap. Sucre; a. 51,524 km²; p. (1992) 306,360.

Chur (Coire), t., cap. Graubünden, **Switzerland**; in valley of upper Rhine; historic bldgs.; fruit, wine, tourist ctr.; p. (1990) 30,975.

Church, Hyndburn, sub. of Accrington, Lancs., **Eng.**; engin.; p. (1991) 4,277.

Churchill, R., formerly Hamilton R., flows into Hamilton inlet, cst. of Labrador, **Canada**; magnificent waterfall, Churchill Falls with lge. hydroelec. scheme.

Church Stretton, mkt. t., Shrops., **Eng.**; tourism; p. (1991) 3,435.

Chusan I. *See* **Zhousan**.

Chuvash, aut. rep., **Russia**; in middle Volga valley; arable agr., lumbering, food processing; a. 18,407 km²; p. (1989) 1,338,000.

Cibao, lowland a., **Dominican Rep.**, Central America; extends along N. side of Cordillera de Cibao for 180 km; 16–56 km wide; early a. of Spanish settlement; E. part called Vega Real; richest agr. a. of Hispaniola; cacao, tobacco, maize; dense p.; ch. t. Santiago.

Cicero, t., Ill., **USA**; adjoins Chicago; electrical appliances, hardware; p. (1996) 70,915.

Cienfuegos, t., **Cuba**; sugar, tobacco; picturesque; nuclear power sta.; p. (1990) 123,600.

Cieszyn, t., Bielsko-Biala prov., **Poland**; part of former Teschen on Polish side of frontier with Czech Republic; p. (1995) 37,264.

Cimpina, t., **Romania**, in Walachia; petroleum ctr.; oil pipeline links to Ploiesti and Constanta on Black Sea.

Cincinnati, c. Ohio, **USA**; route and comm. ctr. on terraces of Ohio R.; food processing and many varied inds.; univs.; p. (2000) 331,285 (c.), 1,452,645 (met. a.).

Cinderford, t., Gloucs., **Eng.**; former ctr. of coalmng. a. of Forest of Dean; new lt. industl. estate; p. (1991) 9,566.

Cinque Ports, confederation of anc. **Eng.** pts. on cst. of Kent and Sussex; original 5: Sandwich, Dover, Hythe, Romney, Hastings; Winchelsea, and Rye added later.

Cirencester, t., Cotswold, Gloucs., **Eng.**; Roman Corineum; former woollen t.; famous parish church; p. (1991) 15,221.

Citta di Castello, walled t., **Italy**; in upper Tiber valley; impt. in Roman times; Renaissance cath., palaces; p. (1991) 37,450.

Citta Vecchia (**Mdina**), c., central **Malta**; former cap.; Roman remains; cath.

Ciudad Bolivar, c., Bolivar st., **Venezuela**; pt. on Orinoco R.; formerly called Angostura; coffee, cattle; ctr. of new industl. development on lower Orinoco; p. (1990) 225,846.

Ciudad del Este, t., **Paraguay**; rapidly growing t. close to Itaipú Dam on Parana R.; p. (1992) 133,893.

Ciudad Guayana, c., Bolivar st., **Venezuela**; spt. on R. Orinoco; heavy inds. ctr.; p. (1990) 453,050.

Ciudad Juarez, c., **Mexico**; comm. ctr. on USA border; agr. processing; tourism; p. (1990) 797,679.

Ciudad Obregón, t., Sonora, Mexico; on Yaqui R.; ctr. of irrigated land a.; p. (1990) 220,000.

Ciudad Real, c., cap. of Ciudad Real prov., **Spain**; mkt. t. founded 1255; textiles; p. (1990) 58,200.

Ciudad Real, prov., central **Spain**; mostly at 600 m; covering la Mancha dist.; agr.; cap. C.R.; a. 19,741 km²; p. (1998) 479,500.

Ciudad Rodrigo, old fortress t., Salamanca prov., **Spain**; strategic position nr. Portuguese bdy.; in Peninsular War fell to Fr. (1810) and captured by Wellington (1812); p. (1990) 16,000.

Civitavecchia, t., Latium, **Italy**; pt. for Rome on Tyrrhenian cst., 48 km N. of mouth of R. Tiber; p. (1991) 51,200.

Clackmannan, t., central **Scot.**, unit. auth. created in 1996, reinstating historic co. of **Clackmannanshire** which became part of Central Region in 1974; bordered S.W. by R. Forth; ch. t. Alloa; p. (2002) 3,450 (t.), (2002) 47,930 (unit. auth.).

Clacton-on-Sea, t., Tendring, Essex, **Eng.**; on E. cst. 19 km S.E. of Colchester; seaside resort; lt. inds.; residtl.; p. (2001) 51,284.

Clairvaux, v., Aube, **France**; Cistercian abbey.

Clamart, t., Hauts-de-Seine, **France**; sub. of S.W. Paris; p. (1999) 48,575.

Clapham, S. London rly. junction; busiest station in Britain.

Clare, co., Munster, **R.o.I.**; cstl. co. bounded in S. and E. by R. Shannon; mainly agr. and tourism; inc. cliffs of Moher; Shannon airpt. and tax-free industl. development scheme; co. t. Ennis; a. 3,351 km²; p. (1991) 90,920.

Clare I., Clew Bay, Mayo, **R.o.I.**; p. (1986) 140.

Clarence Strait, between Melville I. and Darwin, N.T., **Australia**.

Clarksville, t., Tenn., **USA**; on Cumberland R.; tob-

acco mkt.; p. (1990) 75,494 (t.), 169,439 (met. a.).

Clay Cross, t., Derbys., **Eng.**; former ctr. coal mng. (first developed by George Stephenson 1838) iron, engin.; p. (2001) 20,754 (with North Wingfield).

Clayton-le-Moors, t., Hyndburn, Lancs., **Eng.**; nr. Blackburn; textile machin., cotton and blanket weaving, bristles, soap; p. (1991) 6,961.

Clear C., southernmost point of Ireland, Clear I., **R.o.I.**; off S.W. cst. of Cork.

Cleare, c., Alaska, **USA**; site of ballistic missile early warning sta.

Clearwater, t., Fla., **USA**; citrus fruit, flowers, fish; resort; p. (1990) 98,784.

Cleator Moor, t., Cumbria, **Eng.**; former colly. t.; p. (1991) 6,410

Cleckheaton t., West Yorks., **Eng.**; nr. Bradford; woollens, blankets, asbestos; p. (2001) 26,796.

Cleethorpes, t., N.E. Lincs., **Eng.**; 5 km S. of Grimsby; resort; p. (2001) 31,853.

Clerkenwell, industl. dist., London, **Eng.**; immediately N. of the City; noted for jewellry.

Clermont-Ferrand, c., cap. Puy-de-Dôme dep. central **France**; in Auvergne; rubber tyres, chemicals, food inds.; Gothic cath., Romanesque church; p. (1990) 140,167 (c.), 254,416 (met. a.).

Clevedon, t., N. Somerset, **Eng.**; at mouth of R. Severn; seaside resort; quarrying, bricks, footwear; p. (1991) 21,670.

Cleveland, c., Ohio, **USA**; impt. Gr. Ls. pt. handling iron ore and coal which support a major iron and steel ind.; oil refining, food processing, many varied inds.; univ.; p. (2000) 478,403 (c.), 1,831,122 (met. a.).

Cleveland Hills, North Yorks., Redcar and Cleveland, **Eng.**; part of N. York Moors; once mined for iron ore, impt. potash deposit.

Clichy, t., Hauts-de-Seine, **France**; N.W. sub. of Paris; oil refining, aircraft, automobile components; p. (1999) 50,154.

Clifton, sub., Bristol, **Eng.**; on R. Avon; mineral springs; famous suspension bridge.

Clinton, t., Iowa, **USA**; on Mississippi R.; iron and steel, machin.; p. (1990) 29,201.

Clitheroe, t., Ribble Valley, Lancs., **Eng.**; in Ribble valley; mkt. t. for rural a.; limestone quarrying nearby; p. (1991) 13,548.

Clonakilty, t., Cork, **R.o.I.**; nr. Bandon; sm. harbour; agr. prods.; p. (1991) 2,800.

Cloncurry, t., Queensland, **Australia**; rly junction and air terminal in ctr. of copper field; uranium nearby; p. (1991) 2,300.

Clones, mkt. t. on Ulster border, Monaghan, **R.o.I.**; rly. ctr.; p. (1991) 2,350.

Clonmacnoise, v., Offaly, R.o.I.; ecology. Hist. ruins.

Clonmel, t., Tipperary, **R.o.I.**; on R. Suir; mkt. ctr., fairs; cider, footwear; p. (1991) 15,600.

Clowne, t., Derbys., **Eng.**; coal mng.; p. (1991) 7,234.

Cluj-Napoca, c., **Romania**; in Transylvania on Somesul R.; univs., historic bldgs.; industl. ctr.; p. (1999) 333,000.

Clutha R., R. of S.I., **N.Z.**; hydroelec. power; 320 km long; gives name to district.; p. (1991) 18,303.

Clwyd, R., Denbighshire, N. **Wales**; flows into Irish Sea at Rhyl; length 48 km.

Clydach, t., Swansea, **Wales**; on R. Tawe, 8 km N.E. Swansea; steel wks., nickel refineries.

Clyde, R., central **Scot.**; flows through industl. belt into Firth of C.; Glasgow, Greenock, Clydebank main pts.; hydroelec. stas.; twin-road tunnel under R. in Glasgow (Whiteinch–Linthouse) completed 1963; 170 km long.

Clydebank, t., W. Dunbartonshire, **Scot.**; on Clyde adjoining Glasgow; tyres, biscuits; p. (2002) 29,858.

Clyde, Firth of, stretches from Dumbarton to Ailsa Craig, **Scot.**; Bute, Arran, Gr. and Little Cumbrae ch. Is.; 102 km long.

Coahuila, st., **Mexico**; 3rd st. of Mexico; lies S. of Texas, bordering Rio Grande valley; main coal deposits; mnfs. impt.; irrigated agr.; cap. Saltillo; a. 142,611 km²; p. (1990) 1,971,344.

Coalbrookdale, v., Shrops, **Eng.**; old coal and iron mines; home of iron master Abraham Darby. *See* Bridges, Section L.

Coalville, t., North West Leics., **Eng.**; nr. Ashby-de-la-Zouch; former coal mng., engin., elastic webbing; p. (2001) 32,124.

Coast Range, mtns., **USA**; along Pac. cst.; wooded ranges causing rain shadow to E. valleys; alt. up to 600 m.

Coatbridge, burgh, N. Lanarkshire, **Scot.**, 16 km E. of Glasgow; coal, iron and steel, prefabricated houses, tubes engin.; p. (2002) 41,170.

Coatzacoalcos (Puerto Mexico), spt., **Mexico**; on G. of Campeche; oil refinery; chemicals, fertilisers; p. (1990) 232,314.

Cobalt, t., Ont., **Canada**; silver, cobalt, arsenic, nickel; p. (1991) 1,500.

Cobán, t., **Guatemala**, mkt. t.; coffee and Peruvian bark tr.

Cóbh (Queenstown), c., Cork, **R.o.I.**; spt. on Great I. in Cork Harbour; lge. docks; H.Q. of Royal Cork Yacht Club; resort; p. (1991) 8,220.

Coburg, t., Bavaria, **Germany**; old cas.; wickerwork, furniture, metal, machines, toy inds.; p. (2002) 42,798.

Cochabamba, dep., **Bolivia**; E. of Andes; lgst. p. concentration of Bolivia in C. basin; a. 65,496 km²; p. (1992) 1,110,200.

Cochabamba, c., cap. of C. dep., **Bolivia**; second lgst. c. in rep.; alt. 2,559 m; univ., cath.; oil refining, shoes, rubber tyres, fruit-canning, modern milk plant; hydroelectric power; p. (1992) 404,102.

Cochin. *See* Kochi.

Cockenzie and Port Seton, small burgh, E. Lothian, **Scot.**; two fishing pts. on F. of Forth; p. (2002) 5,499.

Cockermouth, t., Allerdale, Cumbria, **Eng.**; slate, shoe mftg., plywood, concrete prods.; birthplace of Wordsworth; p. (1991) 7,702.

Cockpit Country, upland a., W. **Jamaica**; classic karst landscape forming rugged upland; some cultivation in hollows; a. 500 km²; alt. 300–800 m.

Coco, R., **Honduras** and **Nicaragua**; flows to Caribbean Sea through economically impt. valley; agr., forestry, mng., potential as routeway; 480 km long.

Cocos (Keeling) Is., 27 coral atolls, Indian Oc.; since 1955 terr. of **Australia** purchased by Australia (1978) to ensure democracy; strategic position S.E. of Sri Lanka, radio and cable sta. German cruiser *Emden* destroyed by Australian cruiser *Sydney* on N. Keeling I. in 1914; uninhabited until 1826; developed by Clunies Ross family for coconut prod.; controlled emigration since 1948 to solve problem of overpopulation; voted to integrate with Northern Territory, Australia (1984); a. 13 km²; p. (2004) 629.

Cognac, t., Charente, **France**; cognac, bottles; p. (1999) 19,534.

Coihaique, t. **Chile**; cap. Aysen region; p. (1992) 43,140.

Coimbatore, t., Tamil Nadu, **India**; commands Palghat Gap; varied inds. benefit from local hydroelec. power; p. (1991) 816,000.

Coimbra, t., **Portugal**; cath., oldest univ. in Portugal; wine-growing; earthenware mfns.; p. (1991) 96,140.

Colchester, t., l. gov. dist., Essex, **Eng.**; pre-Roman t. of Camulodunum on R. Colne; univ.; lt. inds., engin., oyster fisheries; pt.; p. (2001) 155,796 (dist.), (2001) 104,390 (t.).

Cold Harbour, v., Va., **USA**; battles between Grant and Lee 1864.

Coldstream, t., Borders, **Scot.**; on Eng. border; agr. machin., knitwear; p. (2002) 1,813.

Coleraine, t., l. gov. dist., **N. Ireland**; pt. on R. Bann, 6 km from sea; univ.inen, acrilan mftg., distilling; p. (2001) 56,315 (dist.), 50,438 (t.).

Coleshill, t., North Warwickshire, **Eng.**; lurgi gasification plant; p. (1991) 6,324.

Colima, mkt. t., **Mexico**; on Colima R. in fertile valley; univ.; agr. processing; p. (1990) 116,155.

Colima, st., **Mexico**; on Pac. cst.; cap. Colima; pt. Manzanillo; cotton, sugar, rice, coffee; a. 5,203 km²; p. (1990) 424,656.

Colima, volcano (48 km N.E. of c.), **Mexico**, alt. 3,869 m.

Coll, I. off cst. of Mull, Argyll and Bute, **Scot.**; agr., lobster fishing; p. (1991) 172.

Collie, t., W. **Australia**; impt. coal deposits supply power for much of W. Australia; p. (1991) 7,700.

Collingwood, t., Ont., **Canada**; on Georgian Bay, L. Huron; shipbldg., steel.

Colmar, t., cap. Haut-Rhin dep., **France**; ctr. of Alsace textile ind.; attractive mediaeval t.; mkt. for vineyards; p. (1999) 65,153.

Colne, t., Pendle, E. Lancs., **Eng.**; cotton mnfs., felts; p. (2001) 20,118.

Colne, R., **Eng.**; trib. of Thames rising in Chilterns.

Cologne (Köln), c., N. Rhine–Westphalia, **Germany**; on Rhine at N. end of Rhine gorge; cath., univ.; impt. R. pt., route and comm. ctr., eau-de-

Cologne, electro-technical ind., machin., metallurgy, paper, chemicals, cars, oil refining, textiles; p. (2002) 967,940 (c.), 1,823,475 (met.a.).

Colombes, t., Hauts-de-Seine dep., **France**; sub. of Paris on R. Seine; p. (1999) 76,667.

Colombia, rep., N.W. S. America; cap. Bogotá; Andes contain most of p.; the savannahs (llanos) to S.E. are almost uninhabited; industl. employment growing; increasingly indep. of USA sphere of influence; agr. impt.; coffee, (50 percent of exports), bananas; major oil reserves discovered (1985), some exp.; rapidly expanding coal production in 1990s; eruption of Nevado del Ruiz (1985) Mount Galeras (1993); centre of drugs trade, a. 1,139,592 km²; p. (2004) 42,310,775.

Colombo, c., cap. of **Sri Lanka**; on W. cst.; univ.; impt. pt. (artificial) built by British; exp. tea, rubber, coconuts; p. (1999) 690,000.

Colón, t., **Panama**; at Atl. end of Panama Canal; free tr. zone; comm. and industl. ctr.; oil refining nearby; p. (1990) 140,908.

Colonsay, I., Inner Hebrides, Argyll and Bute, **Scot.**; 13 km long; ecclesiastical antiquities; p. (1991) 349.

Colorado, st., **USA**; admitted to Union 1876; st. flower Rocky Mtn. Columbine, st. bird Lark Bunting; hgst. st. in USA; in the Rockies extending up to 4,401 m (Mt. Elbert), no land below 1,000 m; drained by headwaters of Rs. Arkansas and Colorado; major stockrearing a.; many minerals esp. uranium, radium and molybdenum; cap. Denver; a. 270,000 km²; p. (2002) 4,506,542.

Colorado, plateau, Arizona, Utah, Col., N.M., **USA**; arid upland with spectacular scenery, inc. Grand Canyon; alt. 1,500–3,300 m.

Colorado, major R. of W. **USA**; drains 8% of USA; formed by confluence of Green and Grand Rs.; spectacular canyons inc. Grand Canyon; hydroelec. power from many dams inc. Hoover Dam; irrigation supplies intensive horticultural a. in S. section and consequent rapid decrease in volume to a sm. stream in lower course; length 2,320 km.

Colorado, R., rises N.W. Texas, **USA**; flows to G. of Mexico; irrigation and power; 1,552 km long.

Colorado Desert, Cal., **USA**; inc. Imperial Valley, a fertile irrigated a.

Colorado Springs, t., Col., **USA**; 102 km S. Denver; resort; p. (2000) 281,140 (t.), 360,890 (met. a.).

Columbia, t., Mo., **USA**; st. W. St. Louis; st. univ.; flour, lumber; p. (1996) 76,756.

Columbia, t., st. cap. S.C., **USA**; in ctr. of rich farming a.; textiles, clothing; burned down in Civil War 1865; p. (1990) 98,052 (t.), 453,331 (met. a.).

Columbia, District of (D.C.); area on east bank of Potomac R.; coterminus with c. of Washington, cap. of USA; a. 179 km²; p. (1990) 606,900.

Columbia, R., major R. of western N. **America**; rises in Rocky Mtns., B.C., flows though Washington, **USA**; power sources, inc. Grand Coulee Dam, Bonneville Dam; deepwater harbour at mouth; length 2,240 km.

Columbus, c., Ga., **USA**; at head of navigation on Chattahoochee R.; industl. and shipping ctr ; textile mills, food-processing; cotton-ginning machin., p. (1996) 182,828.

Columbus, t., Ind., **USA**; engin.; leather gds.; p. (1990) 31,800.

Columbus, c., st. cap. Ohio, **USA**; rly. ctr.; st. univ., machin , paper, aircraft machin., chemicals; p. (2000) 711,470 (c.), 1,377,410 (met. a.).

Colwyn Bay, t., Conwy, N. **Wales**; on cst. 10 km E. of Llandudno; seaside resort; p. (1991) 29,883.

Comayagüela, c., former cap. of **Honduras**; twin c. of Tegucigalpa from which it is separated by Choluteca R.; both cs. administered together as Central Dist.

Combe Martin, v., Devon, **Eng.**; 8 km E. of Ilfracombe; seaside resort; p. (1991) 2,453.

Commonwealth of Independent States, a community of independent states, successor to USSR; members Russia, Ukraine, Belarus, Armenia, Azerbaijan, Georgia; Moldova, Kazakhstan, Kirghizia, Tajikistan, Turkmenistan, Uzbekistan.; cap. Minsk.

Como, c., N. **Italy**; at foot of Alps, on L. Como; oranges, olives; textiles; cath.; p. (1991) 87,060.

Como, L., N. **Italy**; beautiful mtn. scenery, tourism, villas; a. 145 km².

Comodoro Rivadavia, spt., Chubut prov., **Argentina**; on San Jorge G., 880 km S.W. of Bahia Blanca; military zone; univ.; ch. source of oil in Argentine; oil refining.

Comorin, C., most S. point of **India.**

Comoros, Indian Oc.; in Mozambique channel, midway between Africa and Madagascar; cap. Moroni; total a. 2,170 km²; turtle fishing; vanilla, copra, sisal, timber, perfume plants; Mayotte Is. remained French at indep.; ongoing struggle for indep. by Anjouan Is.; p. (2000) 578,000.

Compiègne, t., Oise, **France;** sugar mills, rope; Armistice signed between Allies and Germany 1918; Fr. surrendered to Hitler 1940; resort; p. (1999) 41,300.

Compton, t., Cal., **USA;** residtl. for Los Angeles; heavy engin., glass, oil refining; p. (1996) 91,700.

Conakry, c., cap. of **Rep. of Guinea;** impt. pt. on offshore islet; exp. iron-ore and alumina; experimental fruit gardens; p. (2000) 1,824,000 (met. a.).

Concepción, c., cap. Biobio region, **Chile;** shipping ctr. through its pt. Talcahuano; univ.; comm. and cultural t.; severe earthquakes 1939 and 1960; nr. to coalfield; p. (1992) 330,448.

Concepción, t., cap. of C. prov., **Paraguay;** main comm. ctr. for Chaco, pt. on R. Paraguay; p. (1992) 35,300.

Concord, t., Cal., **USA;** residtl. and comm. ctr. in San Francisco met. a.; p. (1990) 111,348.

Concord, t., Mass., **USA;** literary ctr.; textiles; p. (1990) 17,080.

Concord, t., st. cap., N.H., **USA;** on Merrimack R.; granite, machin., textiles; p. (1996) 37,021.

Concordia, t., **Argentina;** pt. on Uruguay R.; exp. agr. prod.; p. (1991) 138,905.

Coney I., t., N.Y., **USA;** on Long I., 8 km long, comprises Manhattan Beach, Brighton Beach, W. Brighton, and W. End.

Congleton, t., l. gov. dist., E. Cheshire, **Eng.;** on S.W. margin of Pennines; once impt. for silk; p. (2001) 90,655 (dist.), (2001) 25,400 (t.).

Congo, Dem. Rep. of (formerly Zaïre), Central Africa; comprises 11 regions (caps. in brackets): Bas-Congo (Matadi), Bandundu (Bandundu), Equateur (Mbandaka), Haut-Congo (Kisangani), Kinshasa (Kinshasa), Maniema (Kindu), North Kivu (Goma), South Kivu (Bukavu), Shaba (Lubumbashi), Kasai Oriental (Mbuji-Mayi), Kasai Occidental (Kananga); lies in vast basin of Congo R., mtns. on E. and S. borders; climate equatorial in N., tropical in S.; agr. exp. inc. palm oil, coffee, but economy based on mng., diamonds (Kasai), cobalt, non-ferrous metals (Shaba), major world producer of copper; radium deposits nr. Lubumbashi; extensive navigation on Congo R.; main pt. Matadi on estuary linked by rail to cap. Kinshasa; endemic civil war; a. 2,345,457 km²; p. (2004) 58,317,930.

Congo, People's Rep. of the, indep. st. within Fr. Community. Equatorial Africa; cap. Brazzaville; a. 342,000 km²; p. (2004) 2,998,040.

Congo, gr. R. of **Equatorial Africa;** numerous tribs., drains 3,885,000 km²; navigable from sea to Matadi for ocean steamers, from Matadi to Pool Malebo interrupted by rapids and falls, again navigable to Boyoma Falls; proposed power project to be lgst. in Africa; estuary 11–16 km wide; c. 4,800 km long.

Conisborough, t., South Yorks., **Eng.;** limestone, bricks, tiles; p. (1991) 16,031.

Coniston, t., Ont., **Canada;** on rly. 13 km E. of Sudbury; nickel smelting; t. built by and for nickel-mng. company.

Coniston Water, L., Cumbria, **Eng.;** focus of tourism in L. Dist.; 8-8 km long.

Conjeeveram. See **Kanchipuram.**

Connacht, prov., **R.o.I.;** inc. Galway, Mayo, Sligo, Leitrim, Roscommon; mtnous in W.; farming, fishing; a. 17,775 km²; p. (1991) 423,000.

Connah's Quay, t., Flintshire, **Wales;** lt. engin.; p. (1991) 14,443.

Connecticut, R., New Eng., **USA;** middle course forms fine agr. land; investment in navigation, irrigation and flood control; 566 km long.

Connecticut, st., New England, **USA;** one of original 13 sts.; admitted to Union 1788; st. flower mountain Laurel, st. bird robin; humid climate; arable agr.; diversified inds.; many natural harbours on cst.; cap. Hartford; lgst. c. Bridgeport; a. 12,973 km²; p. (2002) 3,460,503.

Connemara, mtns., dist., **R.o.I.;** Co. Galway; many lakes and bogs; tourist resort.

Consett, t., Derwentside, Durham, **Eng.;** on edge of Pennines, 16 km S.W. Newcastle; iron, steel closed (1980), coal mng.; p. (2001) 20,659.

Constance (Konstanz), c., Baden–Württemberg, Germany; on Bodensee; cath.; textiles, machin., chemicals, elec. inds.; route ctr.; p. (1994) 79,500.

Constance, L. See **Bodensee.**

Constanta, ch. spt. S.E. **Romania;** on Black Sea; oil pipeline to Ploiesti and Cimpina; Danube-Black Sea canal (1984) shortens route of Trans-European waterway to Black Sea; exp. petroleum, wheat; cement, chemicals.; p. (1999) 340,000.

Constantine. See **Qacentina.**

Constantinople. See **Istanbul.**

Conwy, spt., N. **Wales;** mediaeval walled t. at mouth of R. Conwy; sm. seaside resort; cas.; quarrying, lt. engin.; unit. auth. created in 1996 from former l. gov. dists. of Aberconwy and Colwyn; inc. Conwy Valley and coastal resorts of Conwy, Llandudno and Colwyn Bay; p. (1991) 3,627 (t.), (2001) 109,596 (unit. auth.).

Cook, mtn., alt. 3,753 m; hgst. point in S. Alps. and **N.Z.;** 3 peaks. Now called Aoraki Mt. Cook.

Cook Inlet, S. cst. Alaska, **USA;** oil pipeline connects oilfields of Granite Point with marine terminal at Dritt R.

Cook Is., Brit. gr. (Rarotonga lgst.) in S. Pac., annexed to **N.Z.** 1901; internal self-govt. 1965; bananas, oranges, copra; a. 241 km²; p. (2004) 21,200.

Cookstown, mkt. t., l. gov. dist., **N. Ireland;** cement wks.; p. (2001) 32,581 (dist.), 9,842 (t.).

Cook Strait, channel between N. and S. Is. of **N.Z.;** 24–29 km wide; undersea cable completed 1965.

Cooma, t., N.S.W., **Australia;** mkt. t.; tourist ctr. for Kosciusko Nat. Park; H.Q. of Snowy Mts. Authority; p. (1991) 7,400.

Coonoor, t., Tamil Nadu, **India;** in Nilgiri Hills; sanatorium c. 1,800 m a.s.l.; p. (1991) 48,000.

Cooper Creek (Barcoo), intermittent R., central Australia; rises in Warrego Range, Gr. Dividing Range, flows S.W. into marshes of L. Eyre; provides water for livestock in semi-arid region; 1,408 km long.

Copeland, l. gov. dist., Cumbria, **Eng.;** cstl. a. N. of Barrow and inc. Whitehaven and Millom; p. (2001) 69,318.

Copenhagen (København), ch. spt., cap. of **Denmark;** on E. cst. of Sjaelland I.; royal palace, univ. library; naval sta.; freeport; steel, metal, textiles, clothing, breweries; p. (2000) 1,388,000 (met. a.).

Copiapó, t., cap. of Atacama region, **Chile;** copper- and iron-mng. ctr.; p. (1992) 100,946.

Coquimbo, region **Chile;** cap. La Serena; a. 40,656 km²; p. (1992) 502,460.

Coquimbo, spt., **Chile;** exp. iron. copper, and manganese ores; p. (1992) 122,872.

Coral Sea, Pac Oc., extends from the New Hebrides to Australia.

Coral Sea Islands Territory, Fed. terr., **Australia;** scattered Is., E. of Gr. Barrier Reef, off Queensland cst.; possibility of oil exploration.

Corbridge, t., Northumberland, **Eng.;** on R. Tyne, nr. Hexham; 17th cent. bridge; Roman t. nearby; p. (1991) 2,719.

Corby, t., l. gov. dist., Northants., **Eng.;** 11 km N. of Kettering; new t.; former steel wks., clothing, lamps; p. (2001) 53,174 (dist.), (2001) 49,222 (t.).

Córdoba, t. and prov., central **Argentina;** univ.; cultural and comm. ctr.; exp. wheat, cattle, lumber; health resort; local hydroelec. power from La Vina; p. (1991) 1,208,713 (c.), 2,766,683 (prov.).

Córdoba, t., Veracruz, **Mexico;** mkt. t. in coffee growing a.; p. (1990) 150,428.

Córdoba, prov., Andalusia, **Spain;** cap. Córdoba; olives, vines, livestock; a. 13,724 km²; p. (1998) 767,200.

Córdoba, c., Andalusia, **Spain;** cap. of C. prov., on Guadalquivir R.; cath. first built as a mosque in 8th cent.; tourist ctr.; p. (1998) 310,000.

Corfu (Kérkira), most N. of Ionian Is., **Greece;** traversed by mtns. but largely lowland producing olive oil, figs, wine, oranges; a. 637 km²; p. (1991) 107,592 (prov.).

Corinth (Kórinthos), t., cap. Corinthia prov., **Greece;** at end of Isthmus of C.; occupies site 5 km from anc. classic c. destroyed by earthquake in 1858; raisins, wine; p. (2002 est.) 32,900 (t.), 155,100 (prov.).

Corinth Canal, ship canal, S. **Greece;** traverses Isthmus of Corinth, links G. of Corinth and Ionian Sea with Saronic G. and Aegean Sea; opened 1893; length 5·6 km, depth 8 m.

Corinto, ch. spt., N.W. **Nicaragua;** handles 50 per cent of cty's tr.; exp. hides, sugar, coffee; p. (1995) 17,000.

Cork, co., **R.o.I.;** lgst. and most S.; mtns.;

dairying, brewing, agr., fisheries; cap. Cork; a. 7,485 km²; p. (1991) 410,370.

Cork, spt., Cork, **R.o.I.**; at mouth of R. Lee; cath., univ.; woollens, butter, cattle, brewing; p. (1991) 174,000.

Cornwall, t., Ont., **Canada**; on St. Lawrence R.; H.Q. of Seaway Authority; p. (1996) 62,183.

Cornwall and Isles of Scilly, non-met. co., S.W. **Eng.**; penin. bordering Atl. Oc. and Eng. Channel; granite moorlands supply kaolin; formerly tin mining; mild maritime climate encourages tourism, dairying, and mkt. gardening; many small fishing vs.; co. t. Bodmin; p. (2001) 501,267.

Corocoro, t., La Paz dep., **Bolivia**; at alt. c. 4,000 m in central Andes, 80 km S. of La Paz; impt. copper-mng. ctr.

Coromandel Coast (**Carnatic region**), cst. of Tamil Nadu, **India**; where earliest European settlements established; extensive a. of flat land built up by R. Cauvery.

Coronation Gulf, arm of Beaufort Sea; extreme point N. Canadian mainland; discovered by Franklin.

Corpus Christi, c., Texas, **USA**; cotton, oil refining, chemicals; resort; p. (2000) 277,454 (c.), 350,000 (met. a.).

Corréze, dep., S. central **France**; part of Massif Central, mostly over 600 m; cap. Tulle; a. 5,884 km²; p. (1990) 237,900.

Corrib, Lough, Galway and Mayo, **R.o.I.**; drained by Corrib R. into Galway Bay; impt. brown trout fishery; a. 176 km².

Corrientes, t. and prov., **Argentina**; agr. tr. ctr. on Paraná R.; univ.; cattle, sugar, rice, cotton; river navigation reduces isolation; p. (1991) 258,103 (t.), 795,594 (prov.).

Corryvreckan, strait and whirlpool between Jura and Scarba Is., Inner Hebrides, **Scot.**; whirlpool caused by tidal movement over variable sea bed.

Corse du Sud. See Corsica.

Corsica (**Corse**), I., **France**; in Mediterranean Sea; violent history in 16th and 17th cent.; high granite peaks (Monte Cinto), mtn. torrents, fertile plains; inland and sea fishing; rapid growth of tourism with little benefit to indigenous Corsicans; split into 2 deps. (1975); Haute Corse, cap. Bastia (1990) 131,600, Corse-du-Sud, cap. Ajaccio (1990) 118,800; special status granted, 1982; growing autonomist agitation; home rule referendum, July 2003; a. 8,721 km²; p. (2003) 260,000.

Corsicana, t., Texas, **USA**; site of first oil drilling in USA; p. (1990) 22,900.

Cortona, t., Tuscany, **Italy**; nr. Perugia; Roman remains, cath.; p. (1991) 22,600.

Corunna. See La Coruña.

Coryton, t., Essex, **Eng.**; on Thames, oil refining; oil pipeline to Stanlow refinery.

Cos (**Kos**), I., Dodecanese, **Greece**; in Aegean Sea, second lgst. of gr.; gave name to Cos lettuce; birthplace of Hippocrates; p. (1991) 21,334.

Cosenza, c., S. **Italy**; ctr. for figs, oranges, olive oil, wine; cath., univ., cas.; p. (1991) 86,660.

Costa Brava, region, Catalonia, **Spain**; tourism.

Costa del Sol, region, Málaga cst., **Spain**; tourism.

Costa Rica, rep., Central America; over half p. in equable Meseta Central; cap. San José; forests, volcanic mtns.; agr. 10 per cent G.N.P.; coffee, bananas, cacao; high literacy and living standards; a. 50,009 km²; p. (2004) 3,956,507.

Côte d'Azur, France; Mediterranean littoral E. of Rhône R.; inc. resorts of Nice, Cannes, Monte Carlo, and St. Tropez.

Côte d'Ivoire (**Ivory Coast**), rep., on G. of Guinea, formerly a Fr. overseas terr.; hot, humid climate; coastal lagoons, interior plateau (300–1,200 m); economy based on subsistence agr. although an impt. coffee and timber producer; world's third lgst. coffee producer; half p. relies on coffee as principal source of income; underdeveloped mineral resources; poorly developed rail network but extensive road system; new pt. at San Pedro; Pt. Bouet outport of former cap. Abidjan; new cap. Yamoussoukro (1983); revolt by sections of army, 2002; a. 322,481 km²; p. (2004) 17,327,724.

Côte d'Or, dep., E. **France**; heart of anc. Burgundy, traversed by R. Saône; cap. Dijon; wines, livestock, iron and steel; a. 8,783 km²; p. (1999) 506,387.

Cotentin, peninsula, N. **France**; 80 km long; Cherbourg, at its extremity, 128 km from Portsmouth.

Côtes-d'Armor, dep., N. Brittany, **France**; rugged cst. and Is. and mild climate encourage tourism; mkt. gardens along cst.; many fishing ts.; cap. St. Brieuc; a. 7,218 km²; p. (1999) 542,123.

Cotonou, pt., **Benin Rep.**; new artificial pt.; fishing; lt. inds.; offshore oilfields; p. (1992) 536,800.

Cotopaxi, volcano, (alt. 5,982 m) in the Andes of Ecuador, nr. Quito; loftiest active volcano in the world; recent eruptions have caused great damage to Ecuador.

Cotswold, l. gov. dist., Gloucs., **Eng.**; lge a. covering C. Hills and inc. Cirencester and Northleach; p. (2001) 80,376.

Cotswold Hills, W. **Eng.**; limestone escarpment; Gloucs., Oxon.; once famous for woollens; source of Thames and tribs.; highest point Cleeve Cloud, 309 m; tourism.

Cottian Alps, mtn. range on border of **France** and **Italy** crossed by Hannibal; craggy; max. alt. 2,844 m (Monte Viso).

Coulsdon and Purley. See Croydon.

Council Bluffs, t., Iowa, **USA**; on Missouri R. nr. Omaha; rly. ctr.; farm implements, paper, machin.; p. (1996) 55,569.

Courtrai. See Kortrijk.

Coventry, c., met. dist., West Midlands, **Eng.**; 29 km E.S.E. of Birmingham; former ctr. of cycle, motor cycle, motor car and aircraft engines, engin.; tools; chemicals; projectiles, textiles; cath.; univ.; p. (2001) 303,475.

Covilhã, t., **Portugal**; cloth factories; winter sports; p. (1991) 22,030.

Covington, t., Ky., **USA**; on R. Ohio, opp. Cincinnati; machin., furniture; p. (1990) 43,264.

Cowbridge, t., Vale of Glamorgan, S. **Wales**; nr. Cardiff; p. (1991) 3,682.

Cowdenbeath, burgh, Fife, **Scot.**; 8 km N.E. of Dunfermline; coal; p. (2002) 11,627.

Cowes, resort and pt., I. of Wight, **Eng.**; on estuary of R. Medina; regattas and yacht bldg.; hovercraft; p. (1991) 16,335.

Cowra, t., N.S.W., **Australia**; famous wheat dist. and site of state experimental farm; p. (1991) 8,400.

Craców. See Kraków.

Cradle, Mt., mtn., Tasmania, **Australia**; alt. 1,546 m; Nat. Park.

Craigavon, c., l. gov. dist., **N. Ireland**; new "city in a garden" under construction, 16 km long, merging Portadown and Lurgan, linked by motorway, to provide major base for ind.; p. (2001) 80,671 (dist.), 9,201 (c.).

Crail, royal burgh, Fife, **Scot.**; cstl. resort; p. (2002) 1,695.

Craiova, c., S. **Romania**, in Wallachia; tr. ctr.; agr. processing, textiles, engin., chemicals; p. (1992) 303,520.

Cramlington, t., Northumberland, **Eng.**; 13 km N. of Newcastle; new t.; p. (2001) 28,653.

Cranborne Chase, Wilts., **Eng.**; chalk upland of over 275 m; extension of Salisbury Plain.

Cranbrook, mkt. t., Kent, **Eng.**; hops and grain; former weaving t.; p. (1991) 3,522.

Crater L., Ore., **USA**; in Nat. Park, is a body of water 600 m deep and 9·5 km across, set in a crater of an extinct volcano, c. 2,400 m high; varied flora and fauna on shore.

Craters of the Moon, dist., Idaho, **USA**; Nat. Monument of volcanic craters and cones; a. 192 km².

Crau, La, region, Bouches-du-Rhône dep., S.E. **France**; dry, pebbly area E. of Rhône delta; winter pasture for sheep.

Craven, dist., central Pennines, **Eng.**, relatively low limestone plateau, alt. mainly below 240 m; drained by R. Ribble to S.W., R. Aire to S.E.; sheep rearing in valleys, cattle for fattening, root and fodder crops; forms l. gov. dist. based on Skipton and Settle; p. (2001) 53,620.

Crawley, t., l. gov. dist., West Sussex, **Eng.**; on N.W. flank of Weald, 14 km S. of Reigate; new t. (1947); engin., pharmaceuticals, metal, leather, wooden goods; p. (2001) 99,744 (dist.), (2001) 100,547 (t.).

Crayford. See Bexley.

Creag Meagaidh, mtn., Highland, **Scot.**; alt. 1,128 m.

Cree, R., Dumfries and Galloway, **Scot.**; flows into Wigtown Bay.

Crema, industl. and agr. t., N. **Italy**; S.E. of Milan; cath.; p. (1991) 33,240.

Cremona, t., cap. of C. prov., Lombardy, N. **Italy**; famed as a ctr. of learning and later for mnf. of violins and violas; revived in last 20 years; birthplace of Stradivari; cath.; on new Milan-Adriatic Waterway; p. (1991) 74,100.

Creswell Crags, Derbyshire, **Eng.**; limestone gorge and world-famous prehistoric cave paintings; home to Ice Age people.

Crete (**Kríti**), I., E. Mediterranean, lgst. I. of

Greece; cradle of Minoan civilisation between 1600 and 1400 B.C.; mild climate; sm. a. of cultivable land; few minerals; part of Greece since Balkan Wars (1913); cap. Iraklion; birthplace of El Greco; a. 8,379 km²; p. (1991) 540,054 (admin. reg.).

Créteil, t., cap. Val-de-Marne dep., **France**; light inds.; p (1999) 82,140.

Creuse, dep., in Massif Central, **France**; soil infertile, harsh climate, limited agr.; a. 5,605 km² p. (1999) 124,447.

Crewe, t., Cheshire, **Eng.**; 32 km S.E. of Chester; lge. rly. wks.; impt. rly. junc.; aircraft and refrigerator wks., clothing, engin., motor vehicles; expanded t.; part of l. gov. dist. of **Crewe and Nantwich**; p. (2001) 111,007 (dist.), (2001) 67,683 (t.).

Crewkerne, mkt. t., Somerset, **Eng.**; 13 km S.W. of Yeovil; leather gds.; grammar school (1499); p. (1991) 7,142.

Cricklade, t., N. Wilts., **Eng.**; on R. Thames, 13 km N.W. of Swindon; fortified Saxon township; p. (1991) 3,808.

Crieff, t., Perth and Kinross, **Scot.**; on R. Earn; summer resort; p. (2002) 6,579.

Crimea (**Krym**) **Peninsula**, juts into Black Sea, **Ukraine**; wheat, tobacco, fruit; campaign 1854–55 between Russia and Allied Forces of Turkey, Britain, France, and Sardinia was chiefly fought out here (Alma, Balaclava, and Sevastopol); tourism, demands for independence (1992).

Crinan Canal, across peninsula of Argyll and Bute, S.W. **Scot.**; connects Loch Gilp with Atl. Oc.; 14 km long.

Croaghpatrick, mtns., May, **R.o.I.**; 766 m.

Croatia, formerly part of Yugoslavia, recognised as independent by EC, 1991; stretches from Istria on Adriatic cst. to Dinaric Alps; crossed by Drava and Sava Rs.; traditional agr. being replaced by new inds.; impt. aluminium wks. based on local bauxite; chemicals, shipbldg.; impt. oilfields; cap. Zagreb; applied for EU membership, 2003; a. 56,524 km²; p. (2004) 4,496,869.

Crocodile R. *See* **Limpopo**.

Cromarty, burgh, Highland, **Scot.**; N.E. cst. of Black Isle; offshore oil platforms at Nigg, C. Firth; p. (2002) 719.

Cromer, t., North Norfolk, **Eng.**; on N. cst. of E. Anglia; seaside resort; p. (1991) 7,267.

Cromford, v., Derbys., **Eng.**; Richard Arkwright's first waterpowered mill (1771); cotton; p. (1991) 2,426 (with Matlock Bath). Cromford Mills now World Heritage Site.

Crook and Willington, ts., former U.D., Wear Valley, Durham, **Eng.**; varied inds. to replace coal mng.

Crosby, t., Sefton, Merseyside, **Eng.**; on Liverpool Bay 5 km N. of Bootle, Seaforth container pt.; residtl.; seaside resort; p. (2001) 51,789.

Cross R., rises in Cameroon Highlands, flows W. and S. into G. of Guinea at Calabar; useful inland waterway; 640 km long.

Cross River, state Nigeria, cap. Calabar; agric., cement, oil; a. 27,237 km²; p. (1991) 1,865,604.

Cross Fell, mtn., Cumbria, **Eng.**; on E. border of co.; alt. 894 m; highest point of the Pennines.

Crotone, t., S. **Italy**; pt. on E. cst. Calabria; electro-chemicals and metallurgical inds.; on site of anc. Crotona founded as Greek col.; home of Pythagoras; p. (1991) 59,000.

Crowland, t., Lincs., **Eng.**; mkt. t. in the Fens, on R. Welland; 8th-cent. abbey ruins; p. (1991) 3,172.

Crows Nest Pass, B.C., Alberta, **Canada**; southernmost pass across Canadian Rocky Mtns.; used by rly. from Medicine Hat to Syokane (USA); summit, 1,360 m.

Croydon, residtl. t., **Eng.**; now outer bor., Greater London; inc. Coulsdon and Purley; lt. inds.; major office ctr.; new tramlink network; p. (2001) 330,587.

Crummock Water, L. Dist., Cumbria, **Eng.**; ribbon L.

Csongrad, mkt. t., agr. dist., **Hungary**; at junc. of Rs. Tisza and Körös; p. (1991) 19,850.

Cuba, I., indep. rep., W.I.; cap. Havana; lies within tropics; highly fertile although half land a. is mtnous.; exp. sugar, nickel, tobacco, rum, citrus fruits; revolution (1959) reoriented economic and political connections away from USA towards USSR; excellent health care and education; 88 per cent of cultivated land in state farms or cooperatives; recent attempts to diversify economy but sugar still 75 per cent of exp; a. 114,494 km²; p. (2004) 11,308,764.

Cubatão, t., **Brazil**; N.E. of Santos; rapidly growing t. from industl. expansion; hydro-electric, oil refinery, petro-chems., new integrated steel wks. to aid vehicle ind. of São Paulo; p. (1996) 94,500.

Cuckmere, R., Sussex, **Eng.**; passes through S. Downs in beautiful gap; length 37 km.

Cúcuta, t., cap. of Norte de Santander, **Colombia**; close to Venezuelan border; nr. oilfield; destroyed by earthquake, 1875; new planned t.; p. (1992) 450,318.

Cuddalore, spt., Tamil Nadu, **India**; nr. Pondicherry; exp. oilseeds, cottons; p. (1991) 144,561.

Cuddapah, t., Andhra Pradesh, **India**; cotton, cloth factories, millet, rice; p. (1991) 121,422.

Cudworth, South Yorks., **Eng.**; p. (1991) 11,715.

Cuenca, t., cap. of Azuay prov., 3rd. c. of **Ecuador**; in fertile agr. basin of Andes; sugar, tyres, flour mills, Panama hats; p. (1990) 194,981.

Cuenca, agr. and mng. prov., central **Spain**; furniture, leather, paper; a. 17,063 km²; p. (1998) 199,100.

Cuenca, t., cap of C. prov., **Spain**; on gorge above R. Júcar; mkt. t.; famed in mediaeval times for silver and cloth mnfs.; p. (1990) 43,200.

Cuernavaca, t., cap. of Morelos st., central **Mexico**; anc. Indian t. captured by Cortes; tourist resort; univ.; p. (1990) 281,752.

Cuiabá, t., cap. of Mato Grosso st., **Brazil**; ctr. pastoral a.; gold and diamonds produced; galena deposit nearby; p. (1996) 443,100.

Cuillin Hills, mtns., I. of Skye, **Scot.**; attaining 992 m in Sgurr Alasdair.

Culloden Moor, 10 km E. of Inverness, **Scot.**; defeat of Prince Charles Edward Stuart's highlanders by Duke of Cumberland's forces (1746).

Culross, royal burgh, Fife, **Scot.**; belongs to Nat. Trust; abbey.

Culver City, t., Cal., **USA**; sub. of Los Angeles; lge. motion-picture plant; electronic equipment, machin., chemicals, tools; p. (1990) 38,800.

Cumaná, c., N.E. **Venezuela**; pt. on Caribbean; European settlement since 1510; exp. coffee, cacao; sardine canning; airpt.; p. (1990) 212,492.

Cumberland, historic co., N. **Eng.**; now part of Cumbria non-met. co.

Cumberland Gap, Ky., **USA**; ch. break in high E. wall of Cumberland plateau; gives access from upper Tennessee valley to Cumberland and Ohio valleys; impt. route in colonisation of Ky.

Cumberland Plateau, mtn. region, Ky., Tenn., Ala., **USA**; forms S.W. zone of Appalachian mtn. system terminating abruptly towards Tennessee valley to E., Cumberland valley to W.; drained W. by tribs. of Cumberland and Ohio Rs; composed of horizontal sandstones overlying coal; thinly populated by farming communities except where mng. ts. occur in valleys cut back to coal; mng. ts. 500–900 m.

Cumberland R., Tenn. and Ky., **USA**; trib. of Ohio R., rises in C. plateau; upper course forested; crosses coal-mng. a. and fertile agr. valley; part of Tenn. Valley Authority scheme; hydroelec. power; 1,104 km long.

Cumbernauld, new t. (1955), N. Lanarkshire, **Scot.**; to house 50,000 overspill from Glasgow; mnfs. of adding machines rapidly declining with use of computers; p. (2002) 49,664.

Cumbrae, Gt. and Little, Is. in F. of Clyde, off cst. of N. Ayrshire, **Scot.**; p. (1991) 1,393.

Cumbria, non-met. co., N.W. **Eng.**; centred on L. Dist. where rugged glaciated scenery encourages tourism, sheep farming, forestry and water storage; Cumberland coalfield on W. cst. and declining heavy inds. being replaced by new lt. inds.; ch. ts. Carlisle and Barrow; p. (2001) 487,607.

Cumbrian Mtns., L. Dist., Cumbria, **Eng.**

Cumnock, t., E. Ayrshire, **Scot.**, hilly dist. S. of Glasgow; p. (2002) 9,358.

Cundinamarca, dep., **Colombia**; contains many Andean Ls. and the fed. cap Bogotá; a. 23,585 km²; p. (1992) 1,658,751 (excluding Bogota).

Cunene. *See* **Kunene R.**

Cuneo, prov., **Italy**; a. 7,433 km²; p. (1981) 548,452.

Cuneo, t., cap. of C. prov., Piedmont, **Italy**; mkt. for prod. of surrounding a.; withstood many sieges under the rule of house of Savoy; p. (1991) 55,800.

Cupar, royal burgh, Fife, **Scot.**; on R. Eden, W. of St. Andrews; p. (2002) 8,506.

Curaçao, I., Neth. **Antilles**, off N. cst. Venezuela; major ctr. for refining and trans-shipping Venezuelan oil; threatened closure (1985) offset for 5 years to avoid economic collapse (provides 25 percent of C. income); picturesque Dutch architecture in cap. Willemstad; a. 544 km²; p. (1994) 149,376.

Curepipe, t., central **Mauritius;** health resort; p. (1993) 76,133.

Curicó, t., Chile; agr. and comm. ctr.; earthquake 1928; p. (1992) 103,919.

Curitiba, c., cap. of Paraná st., **Brazil;** univ.; industl. and comm. ctr. at c. 900 m; coffee, maté, chemicals, pharmaceutical and forest prods., foodstuffs; p. (1996) 1,465,700.

Curragh, plain, Kildare, **R.o.I.;** turf; racecourse.

Curtis I., Queensland, **Australia;** low volcanic I.; wooded; cattle.

Curzola. See **Korčula.**

Cuttack, t., Orissa st., **India;** on Mahanadi R., long famous for gold and silver filigree work; p. (1991) 403,000.

Cuxhaven, spt., Lower Saxony, **Germany;** outport of Hamburg at the mouth of R. Elbe; fine harbour; p. (2002) 53,168.

Cuyahoga Falls, t., Ohio, **USA;** industl. and residtl.; p. (1990) 48,950.

Cuzco, dep., **Peru;** inc. Central Cordilleras, reaching c. 5,800 m; tropical climate; agr. varies with alt.; minerals; cap. C.; a. 144,304 km²; p. (1990) 1,041,800.

Cuzco, t., cap. of C. dep., S. **Peru;** in Andes at alt. 3,418 m in valley of Urubamba R.; once cap of Incas; sacked by Francisco Pizarro 1533; cath., ruins of Inca fortress; tr. ctr. for agr. prod.; p. (1993) 1,028,763 (prov.), 255,568 (t.).

Cwmbran, t., Torfaen, **Wales;** in valley of Afon Lwyd, 8 km N. of Newport; new t. (1949); motor accessories, wire, elec. prods., bricks, tiles, pipes.

Cyclades (Kirkádhes), gr. of about 220 Is., **Greece;** rugged and barren csts, conceal sheltered agr. valleys; ch. t. and pt. Hermoupolis; a. 2,650 km²; p. (1991) 94,005.

Cyprus, Rep. of, I., indep. state, E. Mediterranean, 64 km S. of Turkey; N., inc. main pt. of Famagusta, occupied by Turkey from 1974; indep. st. of Turkish Rep. of Cyprus declared (1983) but only recognised by Turkey; varied cst., limestone hills in N., forested mtns. in S., central plains of Messarois in which cap. Nicosia is situated; agr. employs 30 per cent of p.; many irrigation schemes also aid soil and water conservation; land reform programmes to reduce fragmentation of holdings; copper in Troodos mtns. but asbestos of increasing importance; lt. inds. and tourism helping to restructure economy but agr. provides over 50 per cent of exp., inc. wine, citrus fruit, vegetables; split of cty. by Attila line into 2 separate parts N. dependent on aid from Turkey but S. developing rapidly since 1974; EU member since 2004; unsuccessful attempts by UN to reunify island, a. 9,251 km²; p. (2004) 775,927.

Cyrenaica, prov., **Libya;** impt. region in anc. times; Greek col. 7th cent. B.C., Roman prov. 1st cent. B.C., captured by Arabs A.D. 642, part of Ottoman Empire 16th cent.; animal grazing, dates, oilwells; a. 854,700 km².

Czechoslovakia, former federal republic consisting of two nations of equal rights; landlocked country linked to sea by Elbe, Oder and Danube; socialist planned economy with coal, iron and steel; division into **Czech Republic** and **Slovakia** took place on 1 January 1993.

Czech Republic, western part of former Czechoslovakia, cap. Prague; 8 administrative regions; privatisation programme; EU member since 2004; a. 78,864 km²; p. (2004) 10,246,178.

Czernowitz. See **Chernovtsy.**

Czestochowa, c. and prov., S. **Poland;** on Warta R.; rly. and industl. ctr.; iron and steel, textiles; celebrated religious ctr.; monastery; p. (1995) 259,538 (c.), 782,061 (prov).

D

Dacca (Dhaka), c., cap. of **Bangladesh;** on Buriganga R., old channel of Ganges; jute, muslin, paper mnfs.; medical radioisotope ctr.; univ.; p. (2000) 12,317,000 (met. area).

Dachau, t., Bavaria, **Germany;** paper, elec. gds., brewing; concentration camp during last war; p. (1999) 37,000.

Dachstein, mtn., Salzkammergut, **Austria;** alt.

2,998 m.

Dacorum, l. gov. dist., Herts., **Eng.;** a. of Chilterns inc. Tring, Berkhamsted and Hemel Hempstead; p. (2001) 137,799.

Dadra and Nagar Haveli, union terr., **India;** admin. ctr. Silvassa; a. 490 km²; p. (2001) 220,500.

Dagenham, dist. former M.B., **Eng.;** now forms part of Greater London bor. of Barking; on N. bank of R. Thames with river-side Ford motor works.

Dagestan, Caucasian aut rep., **Russia;** mtnous.; cap. Makhachkala; cotton, orchards and vineyards; machin., engin. oil; growing demands for indep.; 50,246 km²; p. (2005) 2,500,000.

Dagupan, c., Pangasinan, Luzon, **Philippines;** on Lingayen Bay; comm. ctr.; p. (1990) 122,247.

Dahlak Archipelago, Eritrea; in Red Sea; only 2 Is. inhabited; noted for pearl fishing.

Dahomey. See Benin, People's Rep. of.

Dakar, spt., cap. of **Senegal,** W. Africa; S.E. of C. Verde behind Gorée I. on Atl. cst.; exp. groundnuts; some industl. development; free tr. zone, international airport; univ. and medical ctr.; p. (2000) 2,079,000.

Dakhla, oasis, Libyan Desert, **Egypt;** 272 km S.W. of Asyût; dates, olives; stage on caravan route from Cyrenaica to Upper Egypt; site of New Valley Project for irrigation.

Da Lat (Dalat), t., Vietnam; 224 km N.E. Ho Chiminh City; in Annamite hills; nuclear reactor (1963); airport.

Dalbeattie, burgh, Dumfries and Galloway, **Scot.;** granite, dairy prod., gloves; p. (2002) 4,289.

Dalby, t., Queensland, **Australia;** 1961 oil strike of Moonie oilfield; rich volcanic soils aid grain and beef production.

Dalgety, t., on Fife cst., **Scot.;** new t. proposed; p. (2002) 10,011.

Dalian, spt., Liaoning prov., **China;** seafood cultivation; shipbldg., heavy engin., elec., chemical inds., fully mechanised pt. and another being built; designated development zone in cty.'s new open door policy; p. (1994) 1,855,000.

Dalkeith, burgh, Midlothian, **Scot.;** 10 km S.E. of Edinburgh; mkt. t.; p. (2002) 11,566.

Dallas, c., Texas, **USA;** in cotton- and grain-growing a.; machin., aircraft, petroleum prod.; univ.; scene of assassination of President Kennedy (1963); p. (2000) 1,188,580 (c.), 2,553,362 (met. a.).

Dalmatia, region of **Croatia,** N.E. Adriatic cst.; high Karst plateaus; olive oil, wine; tourism; contains many resorts; a. 12,732 km².

Daltonganj, t., Jharkhand, **India;** on R. Koel; coal, cement; p. (1991) 56,300.

Dalton-in Furness, t., Cumbria, **Eng.;** limestone quarrying, textiles; abbey ruins; p. (1991) 7,550.

Daman (Damão), spt., Union Territory **India;** 160 km N. Bombay; fishing, ship-bldg., cotton; former Portuguese settlement; p. (1991), 62,101 (t.), (2001) 158,100 (terr.).

Damanhûr, t., Egypt; on W. margin of Nile delta, 40 km S.E. of Alexandria; mkt. for local agr. produce; p. (1996) 212,200.

Damascus (Arabic **Esh-Sham**), cap. c., **Syria;** 91 km S.E. of its pt. Beirut; claims to be oldest continuously inhabited c. in world; metal-wk., glass, cement; univ.; p. (2000) 2,335,000.

Dambovita (Dimbovita), R., **Romania;** rises in Mt. Omul (Transylvanian Alps), flows S. through Bucharest to R. Danube, via impt. oilfields; 320 km long.

Damodar, R., Bihar, **India;** flows through India's major coalfields; valley forms ch. industl. a. of India; multipurpose scheme for hydroelectric power, irrigation and flood control.

Dampir Strait, channel between Irian Jaya and Waigeo I.

Danakil Land (Dankalia), coastal desert a., mainly in **Ethiopia,** but partly in **Djibouti.**

Da-nang (Tourane), c., S. **Vietnam;** ch. pt. of Annam on S. China Sea; exp. agr. prod.; p. (1992) 383,000.

Danao, c., Cebu, **Philippines;** rice and sugar dist.; p. (1990) 73,358.

Dandenong, t., Victoria, **Australia;** virtually suburb of Melbourne; growing industl. ctr.

Dandong (Antung), c., Liaoning, **China;** pt. on Yalu R., 24 km. from mouth; Chinese frontier sta. on main rly. from China into N. Korea; mkt. for agr. prod.; lumbering; p. (1994) 551,000.

Dannemora, t., Sweden; 40 km N.E. of Uppsala; iron ore worked since 1579.

Danube (Donau), R., second longest R. in Europe; rises in Black Forest, Germany, and flows

E. into Black Sea; forms comm. highway; Iron Gate hydro-electric and navigation project inaugurated by 1978; major rise in pollution causing concern with conservationists; linked by canals with Main, Rhine and Oder; completion of Rhine-Main-Danube canal and Danube-Black Sea canal (1984) created Trans-Europe Waterway of 3,500 km.; Vienna, Budapest, Belgrade, and other lge. cs. on its banks; 2,706 km long.

Danzig. See **Gdansk**.

Darbhanga, t., Bihar, **India**; rice, oil-seeds, grain, sugar tr.; univ.; p. (1991) 218,391.

Dardanelles, strait between European and Asian **Turkey**, connecting Aegean Sea with Sea of Marmara; (the anc. Hellespont), 64 km long.

Daresbury, v., Cheshire, **Eng.**; birthplace of C. L. Dodgson (Lewis Carroll).

Dar-es-Salaam, spt., former cap. of Tanzania; univ.; textile mill projected; oil refining, pipeline to Ndola, Zambia; naval base and Tanzam rly. built with Chinese aid; p. (2000) 2,347,000.

Darfur, prov., W. **Sudan**; mainly plain, with livestock-raising; current civil war causing humanitarian disaster, refugees fleeing to Chad; a. 196,555 km².

Darien, region, **Panama**; tortoiseshell, pearls, gold, but agr. is basis of economy; cap. La Palma; a. 15,540 km²; p. (1990) 43,382.

Darien, Gulf of, inlet of Caribbean Sea; separates Colombia and Panama.

Darjeeling, hill t., W. Bengal, **India**; tea, quinine; Himalayan resort; original name, Darling; tea plantations now facing crisis; p. (1991) 73,100.

Darlaston, t., West Midlands, **Eng.**; nuts, bolts, fabricated steel mnfs., drop forgings, car components; pig iron plant closed.

Darling Downs, plateau, S.E. Queensland, **Australia**; rich agr. region, fertile black soils aid wheat growing; ch. t. Toowoomba.

Darling R., N.S.W., **Australia**; longest trib. of the Murray, forming part of the Murray-Darling Rs. scheme for irrigation and flood control; 2,723 km long.

Darlington, t., unit. auth. created in 1997, formerly part of Durham, **Eng.**; bridge bldg., woollen yarn mnf., engin., rly. wagons, steel wks.; p. (2001) 97,838 (former dist.), (2001) 86,082 (t.).

Darmstadt, c., Hesse, **Germany**; cas.; comm. ctr.; metallurgical prods., paper, machin., radio, chemicals, plastics; p. (2002) 138,457.

Dart, R., Devon, **Eng.**; rises in Dartmoor, flows S. into English Channel at Dartmouth; picturesque estuary; 74 km long.

Dartford, t., l. gov. dist., Kent, **Eng.**; S. side of Thames estuary; Dartford-Purfleet road tunnel (1963); road bridge (1991); engin., chemicals, quarrying, paper; nr. Bluewater shopping complex; p. (2001) 85,911 (dist.), (2001) 56,818 (t.).

Dartmoor, high granite plateau, S.W. Devon, **Eng.**; rough moorland; sheep, cattle, and wild ponies; granite tors; Nat. Park; tourism; granite quarries, reservoirs; prison at Prince-town; china clay (Lee Moor) now extends into Nat. Park; discovery of tungsten, lgst. deposit in W. Europe but conflicts with conservation; a. 583 km²; hgst. point High Willays, 622 m.

Dartmouth, spt., S. Devon, **Eng.**; on W. of estuary of R. Dart; Royal Naval College; pottery; yachting, holiday resort; p. (1991) 5,676.

Dartmouth, industl. spt., sub. of Halifax, Nova Scotia, **Canada**; oil refining; p. (1991) 67,798.

Darvel, burgh, E. Ayrshire, **Scot.**; on R. Irvine, 13km E. Kilmarnock; birthplace of Sir Alexander Fleming, discoverer of penicillin; p. (2002) 3,361.

Darwen, t., N.E. Lancs., **Eng.**; on flank of Rossendale Fells, 5 km S. of Blackburn; tile and glaze bricks, paint, wallpaper, plastics; p. (2001) 31,570.

Darwin, c., cap. N.T., **Australia**; pt. and regional ctr., invigorated in the 1950s by nearby uranium mng. (Rum Jungle); devastated by cyclone 1974, rebuilding complete by 1979; international airpt.; closer to Singapore than Sydney; trans-Australia rly. link to Adelaide, completed 2004; p. (1993) 77,900.

Daryal Gorge, Caucasus, **Georgia**; deep gorge (1,800 m) cut by Terek R.; identified as the classical Caspian or Iberian Gates from which distances were reckoned.

Datia, t. Madhya Pradesh, **India**; stone-walled, palaces; p. (1991) 64,500.

Datong (**Tatung**), c., Shanxi prov., **China**; impt. coal-field; diesel locomotives; p. (1994) 845,000.

Daugavpils, t., **Latvia**; on Dvina R.; textiles, engin.,

rly. repair wks., food prods.; p. (1991) 129,000.

Dauphiné Alps, mtn. range, S.E. **France**; 24 peaks over 3,050 m.

Davangere, t., Karnataka, S. **India**; on 600 m plateau in Indian Penin.; p. (1991) 266,000.

Davao, c., Mindanao, **Philippines**; pt. for sugar; p. (1995) 1,006,000.

Davenport, t., Iowa, **USA**; on Mississippi R. where it is spanned by bridges to Rock Island, Molise and East Molise; rly., comm. and industl. ctr.; p. (1990) 95,300 (t.), 351,000 (met. a. with Rock Island-Moline).

Daventry, t., l. gov. dist., Northampton, **Eng.**; 14 km S.E. of Rugby; boot-mkg., lt. engin.; radio-transmission sta.; expanded t.; p. (2001) 71,838 (dist.), (2001) 21,731 (t.).

David, t., cap. of Chiriqui prov., **Panama**; timber coffee, cacao, sugar, p. (1990) 102,678.

Davis Strait, channel between Greenland and Baffin I., N.W. Terr., **Canada**; connects Atl. Oc. with Baffin Bay; navigable.

Davos-Platz and **Dörfli**, ts., Grisons, **Switzerland**; Alpine winter resorts; annual World Economic Forum at Davos; alt. 1,478 m; p. (1990) 10,960.

Dawley, t., The Wrekin, Shrops., **Eng.**; on S.E. flank of the Wrekin; ironwks., pipe, cement, roadstone, asphalt and brick wks., engin.; part of Telford new t. (1963).

Dawlish, t., Teignbridge, S. Devon, **Eng.**; on S. cst. between estuaries of Rs. Exe and Teign; seaside resort; flower tr.; p. (1991) 9,648.

Dawson, sm. t., Yukon Terr., **Canada**; on Yukon R., nr. Klondike goldfields.

Dayton, c., Ohio, **USA**; on Great Miami R.; univ.; aircraft, elec. machin., rubber gds.; p. (1990) 182,044 (c.), 951,270 (met. a. with Springfield).

Daytona Beach, t., Fla., **USA**; resort; shipping, ctr.; motor speed trials; p. (1996) 65,203 (t.), (1990) 371,000 (met. a.).

De Aar, t., rly. junc., Eastern Cape Prov., **S. Africa**; 500 m. from Cape Town; rlys. from N.W. (Luderitz, Walvis Bay) and S.E. (Pt. Elizabeth, E. London) join Cape Town to Johannesburg trunk rly.; p. (1991) 25,400.

Dead Sea, salt-water L. between **Israel** and **Jordan**; surface 392 m below level of Mediterranean; a. 881 km², length 76 km, greatest width 15 km, greatest depth 399 m; receives waters of Jordan; high mineral content, very saline; Israeli plans to link to Mediterranean Sea by underground canal to generate hydro-electric power. Dead Sea now shrinking at an alarming rate. Plans for canal to link with Red Sea.

Deal, anc. pt., E. Kent, **Eng.**; on S.E. cst., 11 km N.E. Dover; opposite Goodwin Sands; seaside resort; p. (2001) 29,248.

Dean, Forest of. See **Forest of Dean**.

Dearborn, t., Mich., **USA**; birthplace of Henry Ford; largest mosque in the Western world (Islamic Center of America); p. (1996) 91,418.

Death Valley, depression, Cal., **USA**; N. of Mojave Desert, 240 km N.E. of Los Angeles; completely arid; floor covered with saline deposits; tourist attraction; depth of valley floor 84 m below sea-level.

Debre Markos, t., cap. of Gojam prov., **Ethiopia**; vegetable oil extraction; p. (1994) 49,300.

Debrecen, t., **Hungary**; 183 km E. of Budapest; univ.; ctr. of pastoral dist.; fairs; pharmaceutics, medical instruments, furniture; ctr. of Calvinism; p. (1997) 210,000.

Decatur, t., Ala., **USA**; steel textiles; industl. development after establishment of Tenn. Valley Authority; p. (1996) 53,797.

Decatur, t., Ill., **USA**; on Sangamon R.; industl.; rly. engin.; food processing; univ.; p. (1990) 83,885 (t.), 117,206 (met. a.).

Deccan, The, upland of S. **India**, bounded by the Narbada and Kistna Rs.; coincides with Maharashtra st.; area of very fertile lava soils; impt. cotton-growing region.

Dee, R., N. Wales and Cheshire, **Eng.**; 144 km long; lge. silted estuary, use for water storage planned.

Dee, R., Aberdeenshire, Scot.; picturesque, tourism; 139 km long.

Dehiwala-Mt Lavina, t., **Sri Lanka**; on cst. S. of Colombo; p. (1995) 192,000.

Dehra Dun, t., Uttaranchal, **India**; important scientific research ctr.; sawmills; p. (1991) 368,000.

Delaware, st., **USA**; admitted to Union 1787, popular name First State; st. flower Peach Blossom, st. bird Blue Hen Chicken; low-lying a. of Atl. cst. plain; agr., lumber; fertilisers, minerals, leather, chemicals, machin.; cap. Dover; ch. pt. Wilmington; a. 6,138 km²; p. (2002) 807,385.

Delaware Bay, inlet, Atl. cst., **USA;** drowned estuary of R. Delaware, extends 128 km inland from C. May into heart of highly industl. a. of Philadelphia.

Delaware, R., flows between N.Y. st., **USA** along the Penns. border, through N.J. to Delaware Bay; 504 km long.

Delft, c., pt., S. Holland, **Neth.;** on Schie R. (canalised), nr. Rotterdam; technical univ.; ceramics (delft-ware), tool mftg., precision instruments; 13th cent. Old church and 15th cent. New church; p. (1994) 91,941.

Delhi, c., cap. of **India;** on watershed between Rs. Indus and Ganges; made up of Old Delhi with walls, palace, and fort, and New Delhi with admin. ctr.; univ.; new Metro now open (2003); p. (2000) 11,700,000 (met. a.).

Delhi, union terr., **India;** hot and arid region between Indus valley and alluvial plain of Ganges; irrigation to support agr.; New Delhi and Old Delhi ch. ctrs.; a. 1,497 km²; p. (2001) 13,782,800.

Delitzsch, t., Saxony, **Germany;** 26 km E. of Halle; sugar, chemicals; p. (1989) 27,894.

Delmenhorst, t., Lower Saxony, **Germany;** nr. Bremen; jute, woollens, linoleum, foodstuffs; p. (2002) 76,284.

Delphi, anc. Phocis, central **Greece;** N. of G. of Corinth; famous for Delphic oracle on Mt. Parnassus.

Del Rio, t., Texas, **USA;** pt. of entry on Rio Grande; mkt. for agr. a.; grapes; exp. wool; border t., bridge to Mexico; p. (1990) 30,700.

Demavend, dormant volcano, Iran; hgst. peak in Elburz range, c. 5,673 m.

Demerara, co., **Guyana;** between Essequibo and Demerara Rs.; exp. sugar, molasses, rum.

Demerara, R., **Guyana;** drains N. to Atl Oc.; bauxite transport.

Denbighshire, N. **Wales,** unit. auth. created in 1996 from former l. gov. dists. of Glyndŵr and Rhuddlan, reinstating part of historic co. split up in 1974; inc. cst. t. of Prestatyn and Rhyl and inland rural a.; p. (2001) 93,065.

Denbigh, t., Denbighshire, **Wales;** in Vale of Clwyd, 16 km S. of Rhyl; cas.; tourism; dairy prods.; birthplace of Stanley the explorer; p. (1991) 8,529.

Denby Dale, t., West Yorks., **Eng.;** 13 km W. of Barnsley; woollen textiles; earthenware pipes; p. (1991) 2,282.

Den Helder. *See* Helder.

Denholme, t., West Yorks., **Eng.;** nr. Bradford; dairying, textiles; p. (1991) 2,295.

Denizli, t., **Turkey;** 75 km S.E. of Izmir; gardens — "the Damascus of Anatolia"; nr. site of Laodica; p. (1990) 190,360, 750,882 (prov.).

Denmark, kingdom, N.W. Europe; part of Scandinavia; member of EU; consists of Jutland peninsula, is. of Djaelland, Fyn Falster, Lolland, and Bornholm, and 400 smaller is., between N. Sea and Baltic; emphasis on dairy agr.; producing butter, eggs, and bacon; increasing industrialisation; referendum (2000) voted against joining Eurozone; cap. Copenhagen; a. 42,932 km²; p. (2004) 5,413,392.

Denny and Dunipace, burgh, Falkirk, Scot.; 10 km W. of Falkirk; steel castings, precast concrete; p. (1991) 13,481.

Dent du Midi, mtn. gr., Vaud can., S.W. Switzerland; rises to 10,694 ft. in Haut Cime.

Denton, t., Gtr. Manchester, **Eng.;** nr. Manchester; felt-hat mkg.; p. (2001) 26,866.

Denton, mkt. t., Texas, **USA;** univs.; food processing; p. (1996) 73,483.

Denver, c., cap. of Col., **USA;** on E. slope of Rockies, on South Platte R.; univs.; oil, electronic equipment, mng. machin., livestock, canning; tourism; p. (2000) 554,636 (c.), 1,622,980 (met. a.).

Deoghar, t., Jharkhand, **India;** temples, place of pilgrimage; p. (1991) 76,400.

Deptford. *See* Lewisham.

Dera Ghazi Khan, t., **Pakistan;** on W. bank of Indus R.; silk, brass; p. (1998) 108,100.

Dera Ismail Khan, t., **Pakistan;** on Indus R.; admin. ctr., caravan ctr.; p. (1998) 90,400.

Derby, c., unit. auth. created in 1997, formerly part of Derbys., **Eng.;** on R. Derwent; general engin., aero-engines, man-made fibres; Toyota car plant; p. (2001) 229,407 (unit. auth.).

Derbyshire, non-met. co., **Eng.;** much of a. occupied by Pennines and Peak Dist. Nat. Park.; coalfield and industl. a. in E.; forms part of Manchester met. a. in N.W.; p. (2001) 734,585.

Derbyshire Dales, l. gov. dist., Derbys., **Eng.;** Pennine

a. inc. Matlock, Bakewell and Ashbourne; p. (2001) 69,469.

Derg, Lough, in basin of R. Shannon, **R.o.I.;** separating Galway and Clare from Tipperary.

Derg, L., Donegal, **R.o.I.,** with cave on I. visited by pilgrims; known as "St Patrick's Purgatory".

Derry.; l. gov. dist., N. **Ireland;** borders R.o.I. and L. Foyle; Sperrin Mtns. in S.; p. (2001) 105,066.

Derry. *See* Londonderry.

Derwent, lgst R. of Tasmania, **Australia;** flows to Storm Bay via Hobart; hydroelec. power; 190 km long.

Derwent, R., Derbys., **Eng.;** trib. of R. Trent; length 96 km.

Derwent, R., North Yorks, **Eng.;** trib. of R. Ouse; length 91 km.

Derwentside, l. gov. dist., Durham, **Eng.;** inc. Consett, Stanley and surrounding a.; p. (2001) 85,074.

Derwentwater, L., Cumbria, **Eng.;** 5 km long.

Desaguadero, R., **Bolivia;** outlet of L. Titicaca; used for irrigation; 320 km long.

Desborough, t., Northants., **Eng.;** boot and shoe mnfs., iron mng.; p. (1991) 7,351.

Des Moines, c., cap. of Iowa st., **USA;** in heart of corn belt; transport and industl. ctr.; univ.; p. (2000) 198,682 (c.), 393,000 (met. a.).

Des Moines, R., Iowa, **USA;** trib. of Mississippi rising in Minn.; 880 km long.

Desna, R., main trib. of Dnieper R., **Russia/Ukraine;** navigable below Bryansk; 1,184 km long.

Des Plaines, t., Ill., **USA;** sub. of Chicago on Des Plaines R.; p. (1996) 54,836.

Dessau, t., Saxony - Anhalt, **Germany;** at confluence of Mulde and Elbe Rs.; cas.; machin., rly. carriages, paper, sugar, chemicals; route ctr.; p. (2002) 80,965.

Detroit, ch. c., pt., Mich., **USA;** busy comm. and industl. ctr.; univ.; gr grain mart; and ctr. of the Ford motor-car wks., aeroplanes, military tanks, synthetic diamonds, pharmaceutics, tools, chemicals, steel; lgst exporting t. on Great Lakes; p. (2000) 951,270 (c.), 4,382,000 (met. a.).

Detroit, R., channel between L. St. Clair and L. Erie (40 km) separates st. of Mich., **USA,** from Ontario, **Canada;** carries more shipping than any other inland waterway in the world.

Deux-Sèvres, dep., Poitou-Charentes, **France;** cap. Niort; a. 6,053 km²; p. (1990) 346,000.

Deva, t. cap. Hunedoara prov. W. central **Romania;** agr., tourism; castle; p. (1990) 82,313.

Deventer, t., Overijssel, **Neth.;** on IJssel R.; indstl. ctr., Hanse t. in Middle Ages; p. (1994) 69,079.

Devil's Island (I. du Diable), I., Atl. Oc. off **Fr. Guiana;** former penal settlement where Dreyfus was confined in 1894. From 1852 to 1938 it saw 70,000 prisoners enter its gates.

Devizes, Kennet, Wilts., **Eng.;** mkt. t., on Kennet and Avon canal at foot of Marlborough Downs; bricks, tiles, bacon-curing; p. (1991) 13,205.

Devon, non-met. co., S.W. Eng.; between English and Bristol Channels; attractive cstl. scenery, Nat. Parks of Dartmoor and Exmoor encourage tourism; mixed farming; modern lt. inds.; major ctrs. of p. at Plymouth, Torbay, Exeter; p. (2001) 1,059,000.

Devonport, spt., N. Tasmania, **Australia;** pt. for fruit dist. of R. Mersey; mnfs. primary prods.; Mersey-Forth power project p. (1991) 24,622.

Devonport, suburb of Auckland, **N.Z.;** naval base and dockyard.

Dewsbury, t., West Yorks., **Eng.;** on R. Calder, 13 km from Leeds; heavy woollens, shoddy, coalmng.; dyewks.; p. (2001) 54,341.

Dezful, t., Iran; mkt. ctr.; oil fields nearby; p. (1994) 202,000.

Dhahran, spt., **Saudi Arabia;** main oil pt. of S.A.; College of Petroleum and Minerals.

Dhanbad, t., Jharkhand, **India;** lead, zinc, tools, radio assembly, fertilisers; p. (1991) 151,789, (t.), 815,000 (met. a.).

Dhanushkodi, t., Tamil Nadu, **India;** on I. in Palk Strait; ferry pt. for passenger traffic from India to Sri Lanka.

Dhar, t., Madhya Pradesh, **India;** cultural and tr. ctr.; p. (1991) 48,900.

Dharmsala, hill sta., Himachal Pradesh, **India;** 160 km N.E. of Amritsar; sanatorium; c. 1,800 m; imposing mtn. scenery.

Dharwad, t., Karnataka, **India;** 112 km E. of Goa; univ.; cotton mnf.; p. (1991) 527,000.

Dhaulagiri, mtn. peak, 8,172 m, **Nepal,** 4 summits in Himalayas.

Dhulia, t., Khandesh dist., Maharashtra, **India;**

cotton ind.; rly. ctr.; p. (1991) 278,000.

Diamante, R., Mendoza prov., **Argentina;** rises in Andes, flows E. to R. Salado; irrigates oasis of San Rafael; 320 km long.

Dibrugarh, t., Assam, **India;** former terminus of rail communications from Calcutta; p. (1991) 125,667.

Didcot, sm. t., Oxon, **Eng.;** 16 km S. of Oxford; Grand Prix engin.; rly. ctr.; p. (2001) 25,231.

Diego Garcia, I., **Brit. Indian Oc. Terr.;** Anglo-American naval communications ctr.: c. 1,000 islanders evacuated to Mauritius, 1966–71, now successful in demands to return home. Major US military base.

Diego Suarez. *See* Antsiranana.

Dien Bien Phu, site of battle in **Vietnam** (Nov. 1953) which resulted in disastrous French defeat.

Dieppe, pt., Seine-Maritime, **France;** 56 km N of Rouen; fisheries, shipbldg., machin.; cross-Channel ferry; p. (1999) 34,651.

Digboi, N E. Assam, **Ludia;** oil fields and refinc[y] v.

Digne, t., cap. of Alpes-de Haute-Provence, **France;** nr. Aix; cath.; p. (1990) 17,425.

Dijon, c., cap. Côte-d'Or, E. **France;** the Roman Divonense castrum; route ctr.; Seine-Saône watershed; wine tr.; industl. ctr.; univ., cath.; p. (1999) 149,841.

Dili, t., cap. of E. Timor. Destroyed by pro-Indonesia militia, 1999; major spt; p. (1996) 62,000.

Dimitrovgrad, t., **Bulgaria;** founded 1947; fertilisers, chemicals, superphosphate plant.

Dimitrovo. *See* Pernik.

Dinajpur, t., **Bangladesh;** comm. ctr.; univ.; p. (1991) 126,189.

Dinan, t., Brittany, **France;** mediaeval t. above Rance R.; hosiery, brewing; holiday resort; p. (1990) 12,870.

Dinant, t., Namur, **Belgium;** on R. Meuse: mkt. t., tourist resort; exported copperware (*dinanderie*) in Middle Ages; cath., citadel (1040); p. (1991) 12,180.

Dinapur, t., Bihar, **India;** on Ganges R., nr. Patna; p. (1991) 126,189.

Dinard, t., Brittany, **France;** resort, especially for English; p. (1990) 10,340.

Dinaric Alps, mtn. range, extending 640 km along Adriatic; from **Albania** to **Italy;** hgst. peak Durmitor, 2,515 m.

Dindigul, t., Tamil Nadu, **India;** 40 km S. of Tiruchirapalli; cigars; p. (1991) 182,477.

Dingle B., Kerry, **R.o.I.;** long inlet of sea on Atl. cst.

Dingwall, royal burgh, Highland, **Scot.;** at head of Cromarty F.; rly. junction; cattle mkt., admin. ctr.; distilling, handloom weaving; p. (2002) 5,026.

Diomede Is., two barren granitic islets in Bering Strait between Alaska and Siberia; accepted bdy. between Russian and US terr.

Disko U., off W. cst. of **Greenland** in Baffin Bay; contains harbour of Godhavn, cap. N. Greenland; rendezvous for whalers; shrimp beds; a. 8,288 km².

Dismal Swamp, morass, S. Va. and N.C., **USA;** contains L. Drummond and extends 50–65 km S. from nr. Norfolk.

Diss, South Norfolk, **Eng.;** mkt. t. on R. Waveney, 45 km S.W. of Norwich; p. (1991) 6,538.

Distaghil, major peak, Gr. Karakoram, N. Kashmir, **Pakistan;** two summits connected by a ridge, max. alt. 7,890 m.

Distrito Federal, federal dist., **Brazil;** 19 admin. regions inc. cap. c. of Brasilia; Parque Nacional de Brasilia; a. 5,815 km².

Ditchling Beacon, 10 km N. of Brighton, East Sussex, **Eng.;** hgst point of South Downs, 248 m.

Diu, spt., I., off S. cst. of Mumbai; Union Territory, **India;** oil nearby at Kayakov; p. (1991) 39,485.

Diwānīyah, Ad, t., **Iraq;** cap. D. prov.; on Baghdad–Basra rly.; p. (2000 est.) 419,000.

Diyarbakir, c., cap. of D. prov., central **Turkey;** on Tigris R.; comm. and mnf. ctr.; flour and rice mills; the anc. Amida, old walls, gates, citadel; p. (1990) 371,038 (t.). 1,094,996 (prov.).

Djajapura (Sukarnapura), t., cap. of Irian Jaya, **Indonesia;** on Humboldt B., an inlet of Pac. Oc.

Djakarta. *See* Jakarta.

Djambi, dist., and t., Sumatra, **Indonesia;** on E. cst. plain 160 km N.W. of Palembang; univ.; field; a. (dist.) 44,924 km².

Djerba, t. and I., **Tunisia**, at S. entrance to G. of Gabès, joined to mainland by causeway; olives, textiles, pottery; a. 510 km²; p. (2000) 128,600.

Djibouti, c. cap. of Djibouti; rly. terminus; main pt. free pt. (1981), container terminal (1985); p. (2000) 450,000.

Djibouti, **Rep. of,** indep. st. (1977) N.E. Africa; former French Somaliland, renamed Fr. Terr. of Afars and Issas 1967; extends inland from straits of Bab-el-Mandeb; economy based on trade through international pt. of D.; plain, mainly below 180 m; hot, dry climate; shark and mother-of-pearl fisheries; little cultivable land; a. 23,051 km²; p. (2000) 638,000.

Dneprodzerzhinsk, t., **Ukraine;** W. of Dnepropetrovsk on Dnieper R.; iron and steel, engin., chemicals; hydroelec. sta. nearby; p. (1990) 283,600.

Dneproges (abbrev. Dnieper hydroelectric sta.), **Ukraine;** nr. Zaporoz'ye, on Dnieper: lgst dam and power sta. in Europe; destroyed by Germans, rebuilt 1944–9.

Dnepropetrovsk, c., **Ukraine;** on R. Dnieper; univ.; impt. rly. and industl. ctr., using iron ore (from Krivoy Rog), coal (Dombas), manganese (Nikopol) and electric power from Dnieper dam; heavy machin., chemicals; p. (1990) 1,186,700.

Dneprostroy. *See* Zaporoz'ye.

Dnieper (Dnepr), gr. R. of **Russia, Belarus, Ukraine;** 3rd longest R. of Europe; rises in Valdai hills, flows into Black Sea, 2,240 km long; connected by canals to Baltic; tribs. inc. Berezina, Pripet, Desna, Orel, Samara; since erection of Dneproges dam navigable almost entire length.

Dniester (Dnestr), R., **Ukraine, Moldavia;** rises in Carpathians and flows into the Black Sea; 1,403 km long.

Dobrich, t., N.E. **Bulgaria;** comm. and agr. ctr. of Dobruja; food-processing, textiles, furniture, agr. machin.; named **Tolbukhin** in honour of Russian soldier who took it from Germans, 1944; renamed Dobrich, 1991; p. (1990) 115,786.

Dobruja, historic region, S.E. **Europe;** along Black Sea cst., S.E. Romania, and N.E. Bulgaria; mainly agr.; ch. pt. Constanta.

Dobšiná, t., **Slovakia;** cave containing ice-field p. 0·8 ha; asbestos, iron ore; p. (1991) 4,600.

Docklands, expanding area of former docks, E. London; commercial and office devt; expensive housing; light railway; Canary Wharf tallest blg. in London.

Dodecanese (S. Sporades), gr. of some 20 Greek Is. (originally 12) in S. Aegean Sea; most impt. are Rhodes, Cos, and Leros; Italian 1912–46; p. (1991) 163,476.

Dodoma, cap. of **Tanzania** since 1974; at geographical ctr. of T. in rural a.; p. (1994) 215,000.

Dodworth, t., South Yorks., **Eng.;** nr. Barnsley.

Dogger Bank, sandbank in N. Sea, between England and Denmark; depth varies from 6 to 37 m; valuable fishing ground.

Dogs, I. of, riverside dist., formed by bend in the R. Thames off Greenwich, London, **Eng.;** Millwall and India docks.

Doha, t., cap. of **Qatar;** spt. on E. of Qatar peninsula, Persian Gulf; internat. airpt., deep sea pt.; contains 80 per cent of p.; p. (1999) 391,000.

Dôle, t., Jura, E. **France;** on R. Doubs, nr. Dijon; industl. ctr.; anc. cap. of Franche-Comté, ceded to France in 1678; birthplace of Pasteur; p. (1999) 24,949.

Dolgarrog, Gwynedd, **Wales;** site of hydroelectric sta.

Dolgellau, t., Gwynedd, **N. Wales;** agr., quarrying, timber, p. (1991) 2,396.

Dollar, burgh, Clackmannan, **Scot.;** at foot of Ochil Hills; p. (2002) 2,877.

Dolomites, gr. of limestone mtns., S. Tyrolese Alps, N.E. **Italy;** tourist dist.; peaks assume fantastic forms; principal peak Marmolada 3,355 m.

Dominica, **Commonwealth of,** W.I.; indep. st. (1978); most N. of Windward Is.; 25 per cent under cultivation; volcanic soils highly suitable for bananas; N.-S. mtn. range has spectacular volcanic scenery; cap. Roseau; a. 751 km²; p. (2004) 69,278.

Dominican Rep., rep., W.I.; shares I. of Hispaniola with Haiti; comprises Nat. Dist. (inc. cap. Santo Domingo) and 25 admin. provs.; mtnous. with sub-tropical climate; in path of tropical cyclones; badly devastated by hurricane (1979); comm. economy mainly agr.; transport system geared to exp. of sugar (now declining with U.S. quotas on imports); decline in tobacco sales causing farmers to abandon production; govt. investment in agr. and mng.; oil refining at Nigua; exp. bauxite; 48,430 km²; p. (2004) 8,833,634.

Domodossola, frontier t., Piedmont, N. **Italy;** nr. Alpine tourist resort in Toce valley, nr. Simplon; p. (1991) 18,900.

Don, R., South Yorks., **Eng.;** trib. of R. Ouse,

112 km long.
Don, R., Aberdeen/Aberdeenshire, **Scot.**; flows into N. Sea nr. Aberdeen; salmon; 131 km long.
Don, major R. of southern **Russia;** falls into Sea of Azov below Rostov, its ch. pt.; navigable to Voronezh; ch. trib., Donets; access to Volga by Don-Volga canal; fisheries; 1,955 km long.
Donauwörth, t., W. Bavaria, **Germany;** bridge t. on N. bank of Danube at Wörnitz confluence; p. (1989) 17,546.
Donbas, industl. region, **Ukraine;** in valleys of Rs. Donets and lower Dnieper; about 23,300 km²; important coalfield; adjoins Krivoy Rog iron-fields; many lge. industl. ts.
Doncaster, t., met. dist., South Yorks., **Eng.;** on Don R., 27 km N.E. of Sheffield; only Harworth colliery remains; tractors, nylon mftg.; racecourse; new Robin Hood airport, 7 mile S.E. of town; p. (2001) 286,866 (dist.), (2001) 67,977 (t.).
Donegal, spt., Co. Donegal, **R.o.I.;** on W. cst. on Donegal Bay; tweeds, carpets; p. (1991) 2,200.
Donegal (Tirconnail), co., N.W. **R.o.I.;** fishing poor agr.; cloth, hydroelectric power; co. t. Lifford; a. 4,830 km²; p. (1991) 128,100.
Donets, R., rises in uplands of central **Russia;** N.E. of Belgorod, flows S.E. to join R. Don; crosses Donets coalfield; length 1,040 km. *See* Donbas.
Donetsk (Stalino), t., **Ukraine;** industl. ctr. of Donets coal basin; iron, steel, engin., chemicals; p. (1990) 1,116,900.
Dongola (Dunqulah), t., **Sudan;** on left bank of Nile above Third Cataract; Old D. was 120 km to S.
Dong Ting (Tung Ting), lge. L., Hunan, **China;** receives water from Xi Jiang and Yuan Rs., drains N. to Chang Jiang; surrounded by flat intensively cultivated land; rice, sugar; size varies with season; max. (in late summer) 6,500 km².
Donzère-Mondragon, Vaucluse, **France;** site of Rhône barrage supplying hydroelectric power; p. (1999) 4,379.
Dora Baltea, R., N. **Italy;** rises in Mt. Blanc, flows E. and S. through Val d'Aosta to R. Po at Chivasso; impt. routeway from N. Italy to Switzerland (through Gr St, Bernard Pass) and France (through Little St. Bernard Pass), 152 km long.
Dorchester, co. t., West Dorset, **Eng.;** mkt. t. on R. Frome; lime, agr., engin.; Roman remains; nearby prehistoric Maiden Castle; linked with the name of Thomas Hardy; p. (1991) 15,037.
Dordogne, dep., S.W. **France;** cap. Périgueux; crossed by Dordogne R.; fertile valleys; p. (1999) 388,333.
Dordogne, R., S W **France;** rises in Central Massif, joins Garonne to form Gironde, vineyards; upper reaches used for hydroelectric power.
Dordrecht, c., nr. Rotterdam, **Neth.;** on R. Merwede; met. a. with Zwijndrecht; timber, shipbldg., sea-planes; p. (1994) 113,394 (c.) 213,074 (met. a.).
Dorking, t., Mole Valley, Surrey, **Eng.;** on R. Mole to S. of gap through N. Downs; mkt., residtl.; lt. inds.; p. (1991) 15,658.
Dornoch, burgh, Highland, **Scot.,** N. of Dornoch F.; resort; p. (2002) 1,206.
Dorset, non-met. co., S. **Eng.;** borders English Channel along attractive cliffed cst. formed by E.-W. limestone ridges; Portland stone quarried; many tourist resorts; mkt. ts. serve agr. interior; p. (2001) 390,980.
Dorset Heights, hills, extend E. to W. across cen tral Dorset, **Eng.;** chalk; pastoral farming, sheep; some cultivation where soil is deep enough; rise to 250-275 m.
Dorsten, t., N. Rhine-Westphalia, **Germany,** on R. Lippe; coal, iron; p. (2002) 81,293.
Dortmund, c., N. Rhine-Westphalia, **Germany;** on Dortmund-Ems Canal; industl. ctr. and pt. of Ruhr; coal, iron, steel; p. (2002) 589,240.
Dortmund-Ems Canal, N. Rhine-Westphalia, **Germany;** links Dortmund on Ruhr coalfield with R. Ems 8 km above Lingen; 144 km long.
Douai, t., Nord, **France;** nr. Lille on Scarpe R.; coal, iron and engin. wks.; bell founding, arsenal; p. (1990) 44,195 (t.), 199,562 (met. a.).
Douala, spt., **Cameroon;** rly. to Yaoundé; exp. hardwoods; p. (2000) 1,670,000.
Doubs, dep., E. **France;** traversed by Jura range and R. Doubs; industl. agr.; watchmkg., motor vehicles; cap. Besançon; a. 5,315 km²; p. (1999) 498,444.
Douglas, t., cap. of Isle of **Man;** 120 km W. of Liverpool, **Eng.;** spt; resort; nearby freeport (1983) gaining from low tax rate; p. (1991) 22,214.
Douglas Point, on shore of L. Huron, Ont., **Canada;** nuclear power sta.
Dounreay, Highland, **Scot.;** fast-breeder nuclear

reactors. Closure of reprocessing plant announced (1998).
Douro, R., **Portugal** and **Spain;** enters Atl. Oc. below Oporto; known as Duero R. in Spain; l. 776 km; famous port wine a.
Dove, R., Derbys. and Staffs., **Eng.;** trib. of Trent; flows through beautiful dales; 77 km long.
Dovedale, valley, Derbys., **Eng.;** steeply sloping limestone ravine of R. Dove; tourism.
Dover, packet pt., l. gov. dist., Kent, **Eng.;** Cinque pt.; nearest spt. to France, the Strait of D. being only 34 km wide; ch. pt. for Continent; cas.; p. (2001) 104,566 (dist.), (2001) 34,087 (t.).
Dovey, R., **Wales;** flows from Cambrian Mtns. and enters Cardigan Bay by a wide estuary.
Down, former co.; l. gov. dist., **N. Ireland;** borders Strangford Lough and Dundrum Bay; agr. and fisheries; p. (2001) 63,828.
Downham Market, t., West Norfolk, **Eng.;** on R. Ouse; flour-milling, malting, sheet-metal wks.; p. (1991) 5,841.
Downpatrick, t., Down, **N. Ireland;** on R. Quoile; linen; p. (1991) 10,113.
Downs, natural harbour of refuge for shipping between Kent cst. and Goodwin Sands in the English Channel.
Drachenfels, mtn. peak of the Rhine, **Germany;** the steepest of the Siebengebirge range, nr. Königswinter; alt. 325 m; ascended by lt. rly.; famous cave of legendary dragon.
Drakensberg, mtn. chain between Natal and Free State, **S. Africa,** and Lesotho; extending 800 km from Gt. Fish R. to Olifants R.; hgst. peak Mont-aux-Sources 3,283 m; rly. crosses range by Van Reenen Pass.
Drammen, spt., **Norway;** nr. Oslo, on the Drammen R.; shipyard; exp. timber, wood-pulp, paper; p. (1990) 58,717.
Drancy, t., Seine-St. Denis, **France;** N.E. sub of Paris; p. (1999) 62,262.
Drava (Drau), R., trib. of Danube, **Austria** and **Yugoslavia;** flows from the Tyrol across Carinthia and Styria, joining Danube nr. Osijek; length 720 km; used for hydroelec. power.
Drax, West Yorks., **Eng.;** thermal elec. power sta. linked to Selby coalfield.
Drenthe, prov., **Neth.;** on German frontier; cap. Assen; a. 2,663 km²; p. (1994) 451,409.
Dresden, c., **Germany;** R. pt. on Elbe, 80 km E. of Leipzig; cap. Saxony *Land*; impt. route ctr.; engin., chemicals, optical and photographic apparatus, porcelain, glass, brewing; fine art collections; scientific research; oil pipeline from Schwedt under construction; severe flooding 2002; p. (2002) 478,631 (c.), 681,953 (met.a.).
Drin, R., N. **Albania;** rises in Montenegro and flows through deep gorges into Adriatic; hydro-elec. power; 288 km long.
Drina, R., trib. of Sava R.; **Montenegro;** forming boundary between Montenegro and Bosnia-Hercegovina; source of hydroelec. power; 480 km long.
Dröbak, spt., S.E. **Norway;** winter pt. for Oslo.
Drobeta-Turnu Severin, c., S.W. **Romania;** R pt. on Danube below Iron Gate cataracts; grain, salt, petroleum tr., shipbldg.; p. (1992) 115,526.
Drogheda, spt., Louth, **R.o.I.;** considerable tr. in agr. produce, salmon, etc.; stormed by Cromwell in 1649; p. (1991) 24,700.
Drogobych, t., **Ukraine;** 64 km S.W. of Lvov; ctr. of lge. oilfields, refineries; mftg.; p. (1990) 78,500.
Droitwich, t., Wychavon, Worcs., **Eng.;** brine baths; lt. inds., expanded t.; p. (2001) 22,585.
Drôme, dep., S.E. **France,** traversed by Alps and watered by Rs. Rhône, Drôme, and Isère; cap. Valence; agr., forestry, sericulture, textile ind.; a. 6,560 km²; p. (1990) 414,100.
Dromore, mkt. t., Banbridge, **N. Ireland;** on Lagan R.; linen; p. (1991) 3,434.
Dronfield, t., North East Derbys., **Eng.;** between Chesterfield and Sheffield; edged tools, engin. and agr. implements; p. (2001) 21,177.
Droylsden, t., Gtr. Manchester, **Eng.;** sub. of Manchester; chemicals; textiles; p. (2001) 23,172.
Drumochter Pass, Grampian Mtns., **Scot.;** carries main Perth to Inverness rly. and main road from Glen Garry into valley of R. Spey; highest alt. reached by any main rly. in Gt. Britain, 453 m.
Dschang, t., **Cameroon;** quinine processing; bauxite mng.; p. (2000 est.) 38,000.
Dubai (Dubayy), emirate, one of **United Arab Emirates,** Arabian Gulf; recently developed as free pt. (modelled on Singapore); p. (1995) 674,101.
Dubbo, t., N.S.W., **Australia;** busy road, rail, air

junction in rich agr. dist.; p. (2000) 1,100,000.

Dublin, co., **R.o.I.;** co. t. Dublin; a. (inc. c. of Dublin) 922 km²; p. (2000) 1,100,000.

Dublin (Irish *Baile Átha Cliath*), C.B., cap. of **R.o.I.;** co. t. Co. Dublin; at mouth of R. Liffey; ctr. of govt., commerce, ind., and culture; cath., univ., Abbey Theatre; brewing, distilling, food processing; Swift was buried here; p. (2000) 985,000 (met. a.).

Dubrovnik (Ital. Ragusa), t., **Croatia** (formerly Yugoslavia); impt. pt. on Adriatic; retains much of its mediaeval architecture but damaged in civil war, 1991; tourism; airport; now UNESCO World Heritage Site; p. (1991) 49,700.

Dubuque, t., Iowa, **USA;** pt. on Mississippi R.; varied inds. inc. meat-packing; p. (1996) 57,312.

Dudley, t., met. dist., West Midlands, **Eng.;** cas.; engin.; cables, chains; p. (2001) 305,155 (dist.), (2001) 194,010 (t.).

Duisburg, c., N. Rhine-Westphalia, **Germany;** R. pt. on E. bank of Rhine at confluence with R. Ruhr, 16 km N. of Düsseldorf; iron and steel inds., machin., textiles, chemicals, pt. inds., route and R. tr. ctr.; p. (2002) 512,030.

Dukeries. *See* Section L.

Dukinfield, t., Tameside, Gtr. Manchester, **Eng.;** 10 km E. of Manchester; textiles, engin., rope and twine; p. (1991) 17,917.

Duluth, t., Minn., **USA;** at W. end of L. Superior; gr. tr. in grain, timber and iron ore; natural gas pipeline into the Mesabi Iron Range; p. (1996) 83,699.

Dulwich, residtl. sub. in bor. of Southwark, Greater London, **Eng.;** village character with lge. park and public school.

Dumbarton, royal burgh, W. Dunbartonshire, **Scot.;** on N. bank of R. Clyde, 19 km below Glasgow; shipbldg., valve and tube-mkg., iron and brassware; p. (2002) 20,527.

Dum-Dum, t., W. Bengal, **India;** ammunition; impt. airpt.; p. (1991) 149,965 (N.), 232,811 (S.).

Dumfries, royal burgh, Dumfries and Galloway, **Scot.;** on R. Nith, 16 km from Solway F.; p. (2002) 31,146.

Dumfries and Galloway, unit. auth. created in 1996 from former Region, S. **Scot.;** occupies W. half of Southern Uplands; drained by S. flowing rivers to Solway F.; sparse rural p.; p. (2002) 147,310.

Dumfriesshire, historic co., S. **Scot.;** now part of Dumfries and Galloway.

Dunaujváros, t., **Hungary;** new t. built from v. of Dunapentele; iron and steel wks.; paper inds., engin. p. (1997) 57,000.

Dunbar, royal burgh, E. Lothian, **Scot.;** sm. fishing pt.; Cromwell's victory 1650; p. (2002) 6,354.

Dunbartonshire, historic co., central **Scot.;** now divided between Argyll and Bute, W. Dunbartonshire, E. Dunbartonshire and N. Lanarkshire.

Dunblane, mkt. burgh, Stirling, **Scot.;** on Allan Water, 8 km from Stirling; Gothic cath. now used as par. church; scene of horrific school massacre, 1996; p. (2002) 7,911.

Dundalk, t., cap. of Co. Louth, **R.o.I.;** harbour, rly. ctr.; engin., footwear, tobacco, brewing; p. (1991) 30,060.

Dundee, c., spt., royal burgh, unit. auth. created in 1996, formerly part of Tayside, E. **Scot.;** on F. of Tay, 80 km N. Edinburgh; jute mnf. (ended 1999); engin., computers, refrigerators, clocks, watches, preserves, linoleum; publishing., univ.; p. (2002) 154,654 (c.), (2002) 144,180 (unit. auth.).

Dundonald, t. E. of Belfast, **N. Ireland,** p. (1991) 12,943.

Dunedin, c., Otago, S.I., **N.Z.;** univ.; wool and dairy produce; named after the old name of Edinburgh; p. (1991) 116,577.

Dunfermline, royal burgh, Fife, **Scot.;** 22 km E. of Alloa; linen, rubber prods., synthetic fibre; birthplace of Charles I and Andrew Carnegie; cap. of Scot. 1057–93; p. (2002) 39,229.

Dungannon, mkt. t., l. gov. dist., **N. Ireland;** linen, bricks; p. (1991) 9,190 (t.), (2001) 47,735 (dist.).

Dungeness, headland of shingle, Kent, **Eng.;** 16 km S.E. of Rye; two Magnox nuclear power stas.; linked by power cable to France 1961.

Dunkeld, t., Perth and Kinross, **Scot.;** on R. Tay at entrance to Strathmore; cath.; ecclesiastical ctr. in 9th century; tourist resort; p. (2002) 1,005 (with Birnam).

Dunkirk (**Dunkerque**), spt., Nord dep., **France;** strong fort; gd. harbour and tr.; fisheries, shipbld., oil refining; steel mill; scene of evacuation of B.E.F. 1940; p. (1990) 71,071 (c.), 192,852 (met. a.).

Dun Laoghaire (**Kingstown**), t., Dublin, **R.o.I.;** spt., fishing; ferry to Eng.; p. (1991) 55,540.

Dunoon, burgh, Argyll and Bute, **Scot.;** on N. side of F. of Clyde, anc. cas.; resort; p. (2002) 9,058.

Duns, burgh, Borders, **Scot.;** agr. and allied inds.; mkt. t.; cas.; p. (2002) 2,594.

Dunsinane, hill, Perth and Kinross, **Scot.;** nr. Perth; alt. 309 m; referred to by Shakespeare in *Macbeth.*

Dunstable, t., South Beds., **Eng.;** on N. edge of Chiltern Hills, 6 km W. of Luton; motor vehicles, engin., cement, rubber, and plastic gds.; p. (2001) 50,775.

Duque de Caxias, t., **Brazil;** Brazil's largest oil refinery, petro-chemicals; Alfa-Romeo car plant; p. (1996) 712,400.

Durance, R., S.E. **France;** trib. of Rhône; rapid current, 347 km long; provides irrigation and hydroelec. power.

Durango, c., cap. of D. st., **Mexico;** cath.; silver, gold, copper, iron-ore; p. (1990) 414,015.

Durango, st., N.W. **Mexico;** mng., agr., cotton, wheat; a. 109,484 km²; p. (1990) 1,352,156.

Durban, c., S. **Africa;** on Durban Bay; ch. comm. c. of Natal; exp. coal, manganese, wool, hides; oil and sugar refining, chemicals, textiles, engin.; oil pipeline to Johannesburg; univ.; main pt. and seaside resort; new name eThekwini; p. (1996) 2,120,000.

Düren, t., N. Rhine-Westphalia, **Germany;** on R. Ruhr 37 km S.W. of Cologne; rly. ctr.; iron and steel wks., vehicles; p. (2002) 92,292.

Durgapur, t., W. Bengal, **India;** site of barrage on Damodar R.; p. (1991) 426,000.

Durham, c., co. t., l. gov. dist., Durham, N.E. **Eng.;** sited within a meander of R. Wear; cath., cas., univ.; pipe organ mftg., confectionery; p. (2001) 87,709 (dist.), (2001) 42,939 (c.).

Durham, non-met. co., N.E. **Eng.;** between Rs. Tyne and Tees; stretches from attractive Pennine moorland in W. to coalfield and industl. a. with many sm. ts. in E.; borders the N. Sea; p. (2001) 493,470.

Durham, t., N.C., **USA;** tobacco ind., textiles; univ.; p. (1996) 149,799.

Durrës (**Durazzo**), ch. spt., **Albania;** on Adriatic; pt. for Tirana; tobacco ind., plastics; tourism; p. (1991) 86,900.

Dursley, t., Gloucs., **Eng.;** 21 km S.W. of Gloucester; engin., agr. machin.; 18th cent. mkt. house; p. (1991) 13,331.

Dushanbe, c., cap. of **Tajikistan;** univ.; industl. and agr. ctr.; rly. junc.; earlier called Stalinabad; 1989 ethnic unrest; p. (2000) 520,000.

Düsseldorf, c., cap. of N. Rhine-Westphalia, **Germany;** on R. Rhine, 32 km N. of Cologne; admin. and cultural ctr., art and medical academies; iron, steel, machin., soap, cars, paper, chemical inds.; impt. trans-shipment pt.; p. (2002) 570,765 (c.), 1,315,736 (met.a.).

Dust Bowl, region, **USA;** name applied to great plains on E. flank of Rocky Mtns.; subject to severe soil erosion by wind, particularly in drought years (1933, 1936) due to destruction of natural vegetation by over-grazing or by excessive ploughing.

Dutch Guiana. *See* Suriname.

Dutch Harbour, t., Unalaska I., Aleutian gr., N. Pac. Oc.; strategic American naval base.

Dzaudzhikau. *See* Ordzhonikidze.

Dzerzhinsk, c., **Russia;** R. pt. of Oka; chemicals (fertilisers, explosives); world's most chemically-polluted city; p. (1989) 602,000.

Dzhalil, t., **Russia;** new t. 48 km N.E. of Almetyevsk to serve new oilfield there.

Dzhambul, c., **Kazakhstan;** on Talas R. and on Turk-Sib rly.; chemicals, food-processing; p. (1990) 310,900.

Dzungaria, inland basin, Xinjiang prov., N.W. **China;** lies between Tien-Shan highlands and Altai mtns.; former historic kingdom of Zungaria.

E

Ealing, outer bor., Greater London, **Eng.;** comprising former bors. of Acton, Ealing, and Southall; univ.; p. (2001) 300,948.

Earl's Court, residtl. a., London, **Eng.;** Bor. of Kensington and Chelsea, contains E.C. exhibition hall.

Earn, R., Perth and Kinross, **Scot.;** issues from

Loch **Earn** (10 km long) and flows into Tay R.; 74 km long.

Easington, l. gov. dist., Durham, Eng.; colly. closed 1993; now part of Peterlee new t.; p. (2001) 93,993.

Easington, v., E. Riding of Yorks., Eng.; nr. Hull; natural gas terminal; p. (1991) 7,593.

East Anglia, comprises Norfolk and Suffolk, Eng.; former Anglo-Saxon kingdom; one of Britain's most productive agr. regions.

East Anglian Heights, hills, extend S.W. to N.E. across N.E. Hertfordshire, N. Essex, and S.W. Suffolk, Eng.; chalk overlain by glacial clays and sands; smooth, rolling surface; region of lge. farms and lge. fields, mixed farms mainly grain; rarely exceed 180 m.

East Ayrshire, unit. auth. created in 1996, formerly part of Strathclyde, W. Scot.; ch. t. Kilmarnock; p. (2002) 119,740.

East Bergholt, v., Suffolk, Eng.; birthplace of Constable.

Eastbourne, t., l. gov. dist., East Sussex, Eng.; on S. cst. to E. of Beachy Head; seaside resort; p. (2001) 89,667 (dist.), (2001) 106,562 (t.).

East Cambridgeshire, l. gov. dist., Cambs., Eng.; a. N.E. of Cambridge inc. Ely; p. (2001) 73,214.

East Cape, extreme E. point of **N.Z.**; named by Cook on his first voyage in 1769.

East Chicago, t., Ind., **USA**; L. Michigan; iron and steel wks., oil refining; p. (2000) 32,400.

East Dereham, t., Breckland, Norfolk, Eng.; 22 km W. of Norwich; agr. implements; p. (1991) 12,974.

East Devon, l. gov. dist., Devon, Eng.; Exmouth, Sidmouth and Seaton on cst. and inland ts. Honiton and Ottery St. Mary; p. (2001) 125,520.

East Dorset, l. gov. dist., Dorset, Eng.; rural a. based on Wimborne Minster; p. (2001) 83,786.

East Dunbartonshire, unit. auth. created in 1996, formerly part of Strathclyde, central Scot.; lies immediately N. of Glasgow; p. (2001) 107,310.

Easter Island (Rapa Nui), S. Pac. Oc., 3,760 km W. of Chile; various theories to explain origin of gigantic statues; severe fall in population in 17th cent.; p. (1992) 2,770.

Eastern Cape, coastal prov., **Rep. of S. Africa**; rocky coast, hills, mountains, tropical and temperate forests, mangroves, grassland, karoo bushland, many endemic species; fruit, tourism, motor-vehicle manufacture, shipping, agriculture, dairy products, tea, coffee, sheep, angora wool, maize, sorghum, timber, fisheries; cap. Bisho; a. 169,580 km²; p. (1996) 6.482 m.

East Grinstead, t., West Sussex, Eng.; in ctr. of Weald, 14 km W. of Tunbridge Wells; famous hospital for plastic surgery; p. (2001) 26,222.

East Ham. See Newham.

East Hampshire, l. gov. dist., Hants., Eng.; stretches from Alton to Petersfield; p. (2001) 109,274.

East Hertfordshire, l. gov. dist., Herts., Eng.; lge a. inc. Ware, Bishop's Stortford, Hertford and Sawbridgeworth; p. (2001) 128,919.

East Indies, name commonly applied to Is. between S.E. Asia and N. Australia, variously known as Malay archipelago, Malaysia, Indonesia.

East Kilbride, t., S. Lanarkshire, Scot.; 11 km S.S.E. of Glasgow; new t. 1947; lge. agr. machin., aero engines, engin., elec. prods., seawater distillation plant; knitwear, clothing; p. (2002) 79,796.

East Lansing, t., Mich., **USA**; residtl.; univ.; p. (2000) 46,500.

Eastleigh, t., l. gov. dist., Hants., Eng.; rly. engin., many new inds.; p. (2001) 116,169 (dist.), (2001) 52,894 (t.).

East Lindsey, l. gov. dist., Lincs., Eng.; lge. a. on E. cst. inc. Louth, Mablethorpe, Horncastle, Skegness and Alford; p. (2001) 130,447.

East London, spt., Eastern Cape Prov., **S. Africa**; at mouth of Buffalo R.; holiday resort; trading ctr.; inds. inc. car assembly, textiles, engin.; titanium deposits nearby; p. (1991) 270,000.

East Lothian, E. Scot., unit. auth. created in 1996, incorporating most of historic co. which became part of Lothian in 1974; lies E. of Edinburgh, bordered N.E. by N. Sea, S.W. by Lammermuir Hills; p. (2002) 90,750.

East Northamptonshire, l. gov. dist., Northants., Eng.; stretches from Oundle to Irthlingborough, Rushden, Raunds and Higham Ferrers; p. (2001) 76,550.

East Orange, t., N.J., **USA**; residtl. sub. of New York; p. (1996) 70,534.

East Pakistan. See Bangladesh.

East Point, t., Ga., **USA**; textiles, fertilisers; p. (2000) 39,600.

East Providence, t., Rhode I., **USA**; textiles, machin.; p. (2000) 48,700.

East Renfrewshire, unit. auth. created in 1996, formerly part of Strathclyde, W. Scot.; lies immediately S.W. of Glasgow; p. (2002) 89,630.

East Riding of Yorkshire, unit. auth. created in 1996, formerly part of Humberside, Eng.; lge. a. N. of the R. Humber inc. Holderness Peninsula and ts. of Beverley and Bridlington; p. (2001) 314,113.

East River, tidal strait about 26 km long and 180–1,200 m wide; separates the bors. of Manhattan and Bronx from the bors. of Queens and Brooklyn, N.Y., **USA**.

East St. Louis, t., R. pt., Ill., **USA**; on Mississippi R.; lge stockyards, meat-packing, aluminium, chemicals; p. (2000) 31,540.

East Staffordshire, l. gov. dist., Staffs., Eng.; stretches from Uttoxeter to Burton-on-Trent; p. (2001) 103,770.

East Sussex, non-met. co., S.E. Eng.; mainly rural, urban growth on cst., where resorts, retirement and dormitory ts. for London, inc. Hastings and Eastbourne; crossed by S. Downs in S. terminating at Beachy Head, Ashdown Forest in N.; p. (2001) 492,324.

East Timor, indep. state since 2002; former Port. terr. until 1975; sovereignty claimed by Indonesia and territory seized by force; atrocities against local population; referendum on independence (30 Aug 1999) followed by massacres; UN intervention; withdrawal of Indonesian forces; mtnous; cap. Dili; a. 14,693 km²; p. (2004) 1,019,252 (est.).

Eastwood, t., Broxtowe, Notts., Eng.; birthplace of D. H. Lawrence; coal; p. (1991) 19,363.

Eau Claire, t., Wis., **USA**; on Chippewa R.; agr. mkt.; univ. food processing, varied mnfs.; p. (1996) 58,872.

Ebbw Vale, t., Blaenau Gwent, **Wales**; 27 km N.W. of Newport; coal, iron, tinplate, bricks, pipes, precast concrete; end of steel-making, 2002; p. (1991) 19,484.

Ebonyi, new st. (since 1996) in S. of **Nigeria**. Capital, Abakaliki. Merger of Abia and Enugu.

Ebro, ch. R. of N.E. **Spain**; flows to Mediterranean from Cantabrian Mtns.; feeds hydroelectric plants, irrigation, esp. around Zaragoza; 928 km long.

Eccles, Gtr. Manchester, Eng.; 6 km W. of Manchester; chemicals, oil refining, engin.; p. (2001) 36,610.

Echo L., Tasmania, **Australia**; used to store water for hydroelectric power.

Echuca, t., Victoria, **Australia**; major inland pt. on Murray R. in mid 19th century; in 1970s original pt. and bldgs. restored; p. (1991) 9,400.

Écija, t., Seville, **Spain**; olive oil, wine, pottery; the Roman Astigi; p. (1991) 36,700.

Ecrins, mtn. peak, S.E. **France**; hgst. point of massif du Pelvoux and Dauphiné Alps; alt. 4,106 m.

Ecuador, rep., S. America; on equatorial Pac. cst., bounded by Colombia to N. and Peru to W. and S.; inc. Galapagos Is. in Pac. Oc.; lowland to E. and W. of central Andes; climate temperate in Andes and hot and humid in lowlands; comm. economy mainly agr. with impt. exp. of bananas, coffee, cocoa; petroleum impt. (68 per cent of exports); pipeline across Andes to pt. of Esmeraldas; attempts to control illegal narcotics exp.; major pts. Guayaquil and Manta; official language Spanish; cap. Quito; a. inc. Galapagos Is. 454,752 km²; p. (2004) 13,212,742.

Edam, t., N. Holland, **Neth.**; on cst. IJsselmeer; cheese, tool mftg.; p. (1993) 25,242.

Eday, I., Orkney Is., **Scot.**; the Ocelli of Ptolemy; p. (1991) 166.

Eddystone, rock with lighthouse, Eng. Channel; S.W. of Plymouth.

Edea, t., pt., **Cameroon**; aluminium smelting based on nearby hydroelectric power plant; p. (2000 est.) 90,000.

Eden, Vale of, fertile belt in Cumbria, Eng.; between barren hills of Pennines and L. Dist.; occupied by R. Eden; mkt. ts. Appleby and Penrith; forms l. gov. dist. Eden, inc. Penrith, Alston and Appleby; p. (2001) 49,777.

Eder, R., Germany; joins Fulda R. S. of Kassel; Eder dam lgst. in Germany.

Edessa (Edhessa), t., N.E. **Greece**; agr. tr. ctr.; the anc. Ægae, burial place of Macedonian kings; p. (1991) 16,050.

Edgehill, ridge, 24 km S. of Warwick, **Eng.**; scene of first battle of civil war, 1642.

Edinburgh, c., cap. of **Scot.**, unit. auth. created in 1996, formerly part of Lothian; royal burgh on F. of Forth; univs., cas.; palace (Holyrood); caths., printing, publishing, brewing, electronics equipment, rubber prods.; Edinburgh Festival in August; UNESCO's first world City of Literature (2004); Leith, with docks is joined to E.; p. (2002) 430,082 (c.), (2002) 452,194 (unit. auth.).

Edirne, t. and prov., **Turkey**; in Thrace, on R. Maritsa; comm. ctr. with tr. in wine, tobacco, silk; the anc. Adrianople, named after emperor Hadrian; cap. of Ottoman sultans 1366-1453; p. (1985) 86,909, (1990) 404,599 (prov.).

Edmonton, c., cap. of Alberta, **Canada**; fast growing c. (119 km²) on both sides of N. Saskatchewan R.; high-level bridge links Strathcona; major military ctr.; univ.; international air ctr.; oilfields and farming; p. (1996) 862,597.

Edremit, t., Balikesir, N.W. **Turkey**; cereals, opium; silverwk., p. (1997) 51,800.

Edward, L., on frontier of Uganda and Zaïre, one of the sources of R. Nile; occupies Gr. Rift Valley; alt. c. 900 m, 70km long, breadth 51km; salt, fishing, wildlife.

Eger, t., N.E. **Hungary**; mkt. t. in wine producing region; mediaeval fortress t.; p. (1997) 59,000.

Egersund, pt., S. cst. **Norway**; fishing; mentioned in Norwegian sagas.

Egham, t., Runnymede, Surrey, **Eng.**; on R. Thames, nr. Staines; contains field of Runnymede; residtl.; p. (2001) 27,667.

Egmont, mtn., N.I., **N.Z.**; extinct volcano; alt. 2,501 m. Maori name is Mt. Taranaki.

Egremont, mkt. t., Cumbria, **Eng.**; 10 km S. of Whitehaven; limestone; former iron ore mng.; p. (1991) 6,581.

Egypt, Arab Republic of, indep. st., N.E. corner Africa; member of Federation of Arab Reps.; 96 per cent a. is desert except Nile valley and delta where 95 per cent of p. live; agr. depends on annual rise of Nile waters and irrigation; cereals, sugarcane, vegetables, fruit; cotton main cash crop; phosphates; oilfield in Sinai and recent finds offshore in G. of Suez and in Western Desert; nat. gas since 1974; 6 oil refineries; major port development on Red Sea to handle mineral exp.; textiles account for ⅓ of manuf. output; cap. Cairo; Aswan High Dam has produced problems; (1) silting up of reservoir (L. Nasser) behind dam; (2) reduction in fertilising silt deposits in lower Nile valley; (3) erosion of Nile delta itself; (4) reduction of fish p. in E. Med.; a. 999,740 km²; p. (2004) 76,117,421.

Eider, R., **Germany**; separates Holstein from Schleswig; flows into N. Sea; 125 m. long.

Eiger, mtn., one of the hgst. peaks of the Bernese Oberland, **Switzerland**; infamous for steep N. wall; alt. 3,978 m.

Eigg, I., Inner Hebrides, Highland, **Scot.**; 24 km S.W. of Mallaig; basaltic rocks on cst.; rises to 393 m; p. (1991) 141.

Eilat, new spt., Negev, **Israel**; on G. of Aqaba; growing tourist tr.; copper at Timna; oil pipeline from Ashdod (1970).

Eindhoven, c., N. Brabant, **Neth.**; electronic equipment, motor vehicles; technical univ.; p. (1994) 196,130 (c.), 393,326 (met. a.).

Eire. See **Ireland, Republic of.**

Eisenach, t., Erfurt, **Germany**; on R. Hörsel, at foot of Thuringian forest; ctr. of Werra potash field; cars, machin., textiles; birthplace of J. S. Bach; p. (2002) 44,242.

Eisenerz Alps, mtn. range, **Austria**; most N. range of Alps, overlooking Danube valley between Linz and Vienna; impt. iron-ore deposits; alt. from 1,800-2,700 m.

Eisleben, t., Saxony - Anhalt, **Germany**; machin., copper and silver-mng. ctr.; birthplace of Luther; p. (1999) 22,400.

Ekibastuz, t., **Kazakhstan**; 120 km S.W. of Pavlodar; ctr. of rapidly developing mng. a. coal, gold, metals; p. (1990) 137,000.

Ekiti, new st. (since 1996) in south of **Nigeria**. Created from Ondo. Capital, Ado-Ekiti.

El Aaiun, (Laayoune) t., **Western Sahara**; main pt. for exp. of phosphates; p. (1994) 136,950.

El Alamein, v., **Egypt**; in Libyan Desert 96 km S.W. of Alexandria, scene of Allied victory, second world war; oilfield nearby; terminal nr. Sidi Abd el-Rahman.

Elan, R. Powys, **Wales**; rises on S.E. sides of Plynlimon, flows into R. Wye; lower valley contains series of 4 lge. reservoirs, capacity 45,460

million litres; ch. source of water for Birmingham.

Elâzığ, t. and prov., E. **Turkey**; dam and hydroelec. project at Keban, 48 km to N.W. at confluence of E. and W. branches of Euphrates; p. (1990) 498,225 (prov.), 218,121 (t.).

Elba, I., off Tuscan cst., **Italy**; iron ore, wine, marble, salt; ch. t. Portoferraio; Napoleon's first exile here; a. 363 km².

Elbe (Labe), R., in Czech Rep. and Germany; rises in Riesengebirge and flows into N. Sea at Cuxhaven; navigable for 840 km of total l. of 1,160 km; connected with Rhine and Weser Rs. by Mittelland canal.

Elbasan, town in cent. **Albania**.

Elbert, mtn., Col., **USA**; hgst. peak of Rocky Mtns. in USA, 4,401 m.

Elblag or **Elbing**, spt. and prov., N. **Poland**, shipbldg., machin., vehicles; p. (1995) 128,706 (t.), 491,079 (prov.).

El Boulaïda (Blida), t., dep., **Algeria**; agr. ctr.; citrus fruits; p. (2000 est.) 177,000 (t.), 875,000 (dep.).

Elbruz Mt., Caucasus, **Russia**; hgst. in Europe (5,636 m), over-topping Mont Blanc by 822 m; twin volcanic peaks.

Elburz, mtn. range, N. **Iran**; bordering on Caspian Sea; hgst. peak, Demavend, 5,642 m.

Elche, t., Alicante, **Spain**; palm groves; oil, soap, footwear; p. (1998) 191,700.

El Dar-el-Beida (Casablanca), c., **Morocco**; pt. on Atl. Oc.; artificial harbour; fish canning, textiles; exp. phosphate; p. (1994) 2,940,600.

Eldorado, radium mine, N.W. **Terr.**, **Canada**; on E. shore of Gr. Bear Lake nr. Arctic Circle; produces 40 per cent of world's radium, sent to Pt. Hope, Ontario, for refining.

El Djezair (Algiers), dep., pt., cap. c. of **Algeria**; old t. surmounted by 16th cent. Casbâh (fortress); univ.; exp. wine, citrus fruit, iron ore; oil refining at Maison Carrée; airpt. at Maison Blanche, 16 km E. of c.; p. (2000), 1,885,000 (met. area).

Elektrénai, t., **Lithuania**; new township nr. Vievis, at site of thermal power sta. (1990) 15,800.

Elektrostal, t., **Russia**; 56 km E. of Moscow; steel, engin.; p. (1989) 152,000.

Elephanta I., Bombay Harbour, **India**; Brahmanic caves with monolithic carvings.

El Ferrol, spt., **Spain**; on N.W. cst.; birthplace of Franco; fortfd., fishing; p. (1990) 86,300.

Elgin, royal burgh, Moray, **Scot.**; pt. Lossiemouth; whisky; ruins anc. cath.; p. (2002) 20,829.

El Giza, t. and prov., **Egypt**; on Nile, sub. of Cairo; nr. pyramids of Khufu (Cheops), Khafra (Chephren), and the Sphinx; film ind.; p. (1990) 2,156,000 (t.) (1991) 4,182,000 (prov.).

Elgon Mt., extinct volcano, bdy. of **Kenya** and **Uganda**; 4,300 m; cave dwellings on slopes.

Elie and Earlsferry, burgh, Fife, **Scot.**; summer resort.

Elisabethville. See **Lubumbashi.**

Elizabeth, c., N.J., **USA**; univ.; sewing machines, oil refining, cars, aircraft components; now inc. in Newark; p. (1996) 110,149.

Elk I., Nat. Park, **Canada**; animal reserve, tourism.

Elk Mtns., W. Col., **USA**; highest point Castle Peak, 4,305 m.

Elland, t., West Yorks., **Eng.**; on R. Calder, 5 km S.E. of Halifax; textiles; p. (1991) 14,232.

Ellesmere, mkt. t., Shrops., **Eng.**; nearby lake; tourism; p. (1991) 2,967.

Ellesmere I., extreme N. of Arctic **Canada**; barren uninhabited; a. 106,200 km².

Ellesmere Port, t., N.W. Cheshire, **Eng.**; on Manchester Ship Canal and 14 km S.S.E. of Liverpool; metal mftg., paper, engin., oil refineries; cars; expanded t.; forms part of l. gov. dist. of Ellesmere Port and Neston; p. (2001) 81,672 (dist.), (2001) 66,265 (t.).

Ellice Is. See **Tuvalu I.**

Elliott Lake, t., N. Ont., **Canada**; ctr. of uranium mines; p. (1991) 14,000.

Ellis I., N.Y. harbour, **USA**; served as ch. immigration ctr.; 1943.

Ellon, burgh, Aberdeenshire, **Scot.**; on R. Ythan; p. (2002) 8,754.

El Mahalla el Kubra, t., **Egypt**; N. of Cairo on Nile delta; textile ctr.; p. (1996) 395,400.

Elmbridge, l. gov. dist., Surrey, **Eng.**; close to Gtr. London; inc. Esher, Walton and Weybridge; p. (2001) 121,936.

Elmira, t., N.Y., **USA**; rly. gds., farm implements; burial place of Mark Twain; p. (1990) 33,724.

El Misti, mtn., S. **Peru**; dormant volcano with snow cap; alt. 5,846 m.

El Paso, c., Texas, **USA**; on E. bank Rio Grande opposite Ciudad Juárez (Mexico); natural gas distribution, oil refining, metallurgy; tourism; p. (2000) 563,662 (c.), 592,000 (met. a.).

El Salvador, rep., on Pac. cst. of Central America; bounded by Guatemala to W. and Honduras to N. and E.; comprises 14 administrative departments; temperate volcanic uplands, hot humid coastal lowlands; comm. economy mainly agr., especially coffee, also developing comm. fisheries and iron and steel ind.; electric power from dam across Lempa R.; well-developed transport system, inc. Pan-American Highway; pt. at Acajutla and airport at Ilopango; member of Central American Common Market; protracted guerrilla warfare during much of the 1980s; cap. San Salvador; a. 21,331 km²; p. (2004) 6,587,541.

Elsinore. See **Helsingør**.

Elstow, v., Beds., **Eng.**; the birthplace of John Bunyan.

Elstree, t., Hertsmere, Herts., **Eng.**; 6 km W. of Barnet; residtl.; films, lt. engin., silk hosiery; p. (1991) 2,196.

Eluru, t., Andhra Pradesh, **India**; cotton, carpets, hosiery, oil; p. (1991) 212,918.

Elvas, mkt. t., **Portugal**; on Guadiana R.; plums, olives, jams; cath.; once strongly fortfd.; p. (1991) 13,420.

Ely, c., Cambridge, **Eng.**; on S. fringe of Fens; mkt., cath.; agr. ctr.; p. (1991) 10,329.

Ely, I. of. See **Cambridgeshire**.

Emden, t., Lower Saxony, **Germany**; impt. N. Sea pt. nr. mouth of R. Ems and on Dortmund-Ems and Ems-Jade canals; exp. coal and iron from Ruhr; shipyards, fisheries; p. (2002) 51,185.

Emilia-Romagna, region, N. **Italy**; S. of Po R.; divided into 8 provs.; fertile agr. a.; a. 22,124 km²; p. (1992) 3,920,223.

Emmental, dist., **Switzerland**; dairy produce, especially cheese.

Empoli, t., Tuscany, **Italy**; on R. Arno; textile mnfs., glass; p. (1991) 43,500.

Emscher, R., **Germany**; rises in Sauerland, flows W. through heart of Ruhr coalfield to enter R. Rhine at Hamborn; canalised for most of its course; highly polluted; 88 km long.

Encarnación, pt., cap. of Itapuá dep. S.E. **Paraguay**; on Paraná R.; exp. timber, maté, tobacco, cotton, hides; p. (1992) 56,300.

Enderby Land, Australian terr., S. of C. of Good Hope, **Antarctica**.

Enfield, outer bor., Greater London, **Eng.**; comprising Edmonton, Enfield, and Southgate; p. (2001) 273,559.

Enfield, t., Conn., **USA**; mftg.; p. (2000) 42,200.

Engadine, **Switzerland**; upper valley of Inn R., health resort; ch. t. St. Moritz; Swiss Nat. Park.

Engels. See **Pokrovsk**.

England, southern and lgst. political div. of U.K.; bounded by Wales on W., by Scot. on N. and separated from continent of Europe by English Channel and North Sea, highly industl., circa 80 per cent of p. live in urban areas; major trading nation through main pts. London, Liverpool, Southampton; increasing contrast between prosperous S. and depressed N. and W.; very varied geology and topography produce contrasts in landscape, matched by climatic variability; increasingly attractive as tourist area although urban and agr. pressures on rural countryside cause concern in such a densely populated cty.; excellent road and rail network; rich and varied cultural heritage and historic bldgs.; cap. London; p. (2004) 50,100,000.

Englewood, t., Col., **USA**; sub. of Denver; glasshouses; p. (2000) 31,700.

English Channel (La Manche), narrow sea separating England from France; extends from Strait of Dover to Land's End in Cornwall; length 480 km, greatest width 248 km.; now crossed by Channel Tunnel See **Cheriton**.

Enham-Alamein, Hants., **Eng.**; rehabilitation ctr. for disabled ex-service men; 4 km N. of Andover; lt. inds.

Enid, t., Okla., **USA**; univ.; ironwks., farm implements; wheat mkt.; p. (2000) 47,050.

Enna (Castrogiovanni), t., Sicily, **Italy**; sulphurmines; famous for its connection with the Proserpine legend; p. (1991) 28,300.

Ennepetal, t., N. Rhine–Westphalia, **Germany**; t. created 1949 with merging of Milspe and Voerde; iron, machin.; p. (1994) 34,400.

Ennerdale Water, L., Cumbria, **Eng.**

Enniscorthy, mkt. t., Wexford, **R.o.I.**; cath.; p. (1991) 7,700.

Enniskillen, t., Fermanagh, **N. Ireland**; brewing, nylon mftg., meat processing; IRA bomb outrage, 8 Nov. 1987; p. (1991) 11,436.

Enschede, c., Overijssel, **Neth.**; textile ctr.; technical univ.; with Hengelo forms met. a.; p. (1994) 147,624 (c.), 254,063 (met. a.).

Ensenada, t., **Mexico**; spt., exp. cotton; fishing and fish processing; p. (1990) 260,905.

Entebbe, t., **Uganda**; on L. Victoria; univ.; cotton ginning; airport; p. (1991) 41,638.

Entre Rios, prov., **Argentina**; between Paraná and Uruguay Rs.; wheat, linseed, livestock; cap. Paraná; a. 76,216 km²; p. (1991) 1,020,257.

Enugu, cap. of E. prov., **Nigeria**; coal; cloth mill; p. (1992) 286,100, (1991) 3,161,295 (state).

Epernay, t., on S. bank of Marne, **France**; champagne ctr.; p. (1990) 27,740.

Ephesus, anc. Ionian c., in what is now **Turkey**, S. of Izmir; sacked by Goths A.D. 262; excavations.

Epinal, t., cap. of Vosges dep., **France**; on Moselle R.; textiles, printing, liqueur; p. (1990) 39,480.

Epirus, dist., N.W. **Greece**; a. 9,552 km²; p. (1991) 339,210.

Epping Forest, Essex, **Eng.**; forest a. N.E. of London free to public (opened by Queen Victoria 1882); formerly part of royal hunting forest; also l. gov. dist., inc. Chigwell, Waltham Abbey and Ongar; p. (2001) 120,896.

Epsom and Ewell, ts., l. gov. dist., Surrey, **Eng.**; 29 km S.W. of London; residtl., racecourse; p. (2001) 67,059 (dist.), (2001) 64,493 (ts.).

Epworth, v., N. Lincs., **Eng.**; birthplace of John Wesley; p. (1991) 3,359.

Equatorial Guinea, unitary state, W. Africa; former Spanish col.; indep. 1968; comprises 2 provs.; Rio Muni (mainland and Is. of Corisco, Elobey Grande, Elobey Chico) and Biako (Is. of Biako and Pagalu); narrow coastal plain and dissected upland plateau (600 m); economy almost entirely based on agr. and timber; new oil wealth; cap. Malabo on Biako I.; a. 28,051 km²; p. (2005) 536,000.

Erbil, t., **Iraq**; comm. ctr.; rly. terminus; p. (2000 est.) 830,000.

Erebus, mtn., active volcano, Victoria Land, **Antarctica**; alt. 4,027 m.

Erewash, l. gov. dist., Derbys., **Eng.**; a. close to Nottingham inc. Ilkeston and Long Eaton; p. (2001) 110,099.

Erfurt, c., **Germany**; on Gera R.; cap. Thuringia Land; cath., ctr. of mkt. gardening and seed-growing dist., textiles, machin., foodstuffs, footwear, radios, heavy engin.; p. (2002) 200,126.

Ericht, Loch, Scot.; in central Grampians; 25 km long; hydroelec. scheme.

Erie, c., N.W. Penns., **USA**; pt. on L. Erie; coal, iron, grain, petroleum; machin., domestic appliances; p. (1990) 108,718 (c.), 276,000 (met. a.).

Erie Canal. See **New York State Barge Canal**.

Erie, one of Great Lakes (the shallowest), N. America, separating Canada from USA; 386 km long, 48-91 km wide, polluted waters; petroleum resources.

Erith, former M.B., Kent, **Eng.**; on Thames estuary; plastics, paints, varnishes, timber, concrete; now inc. in London bor. of Bexley.

Eritrea, indep. st. N.E. Africa (1993); formerly prov., Ethiopia; tobacco, cereals, pearl fishing; secessionist rebellion crushed (1978); severe drought 1982-3; new war with Ethiopia (2000); cap. Asmara. a. 124,320 km²; p. (2004) 4,447,307.

Erivan. See **Yerevan**.

Erlangen, t., Bavaria, **Germany**; univ.; textiles, elec. and precision engin., gloves; p. (2002) 101,912.

Ernakulam, dist., Kerala, **India**; cotton, coffee, hides; p. (1991) 1,141,000.

Erne, R., **N. Ireland/R.o.I.**; links Ls. in Cavan and Fermanagh; 115 km long.

Erode, t., S. Tamil Nadu, **India**; on R. Cauvery; p. (1991) 159,232.

Erzgebirge (Ore Mtns.), mtn. range along border of Czech Rep. and **Germany**; reaching highest peak in Mt. Klinovec (1,240 m); uranium; tourism.

Erzurum, t., **Turkey**; agr. ctr. on fertile plateau c. 1,890 m a.s.l.; formerly of gr. strategic importance; univ.; earthquake (1983); p. (1990) 297,544. (t.), 848,201 (prov.).

Esbjerg, spt., **Denmark**; W. cst. of Jutland; export harbour on N. Sea cst.; exp. agr. prod.; fishing; airport; p. (1990) 81,504.

Eschwege, t., Hesse, **Germany**; cas.; machin., textiles, leather, cigars, chemicals; p. (1986) 22,900.

Eschweiler, t., N. Rhine–Westphalia, **Germany**; N.W. of Aachen; lignite mng., steel, iron metallurgy; p. (2002) 55,257.

Esfahān (Isfahan, anc. Aspadana), c., central **Iran**; prov. cap.; historic, picturesque c. noted for carpets and metal ware; tourism, airpt.; new steel mill; impt. oil refining ctr.; p. (1994) 1,221,000.

Esher, t., Elmbridge, Surrey, **Eng.**; on R. Mole, residtl.; Sandown Park racecourse; p. (2001) 50,344.

Eshowe, health resort, **S. Africa**; 64 km from Tugela R.; p. (1994) 13,400.

Esk, R., Borders, **Scot.**; Cumbria, **Eng.**; attractive agr. valley; flows into Solway F. from confluence of Black and White Esk Rs.; 37 km long.

Eskilstuna, t., **Sweden**; on R. of same name; iron, steel, machin., machin tools; p. (1992) 89,584.

Eskişehir, t. and prov., **Turkey**; W. of Ankara, anc. Dorylaeum; rly. ctr.; p. (1990) 415,831 (t.), (1990) 641,087 (prov.).

Esmeraldas, prov., **Ecuador**; cap. E. on R. of same name; cacao, tobacco; a. 14,152 km²; p. (1990) 306,628.

Esmeraldas, pt., **Ecuador**; bananas, timber, tobacco, cacao, rubber; gold mines nearby; terminal of petroleum pipeline from Oriente; p. (1990) 98,558.

Esneh. *See* **Isna**.

Espirito Santo, st., **Brazil**; sugar, cotton, coffee, fruits, lumber, thorium; cap. Vitória; a. 40,883 km²; p. (1996) 2,786,100.

Espiritu Santo, I., **Vanuatu**; volcanic I., lgst. of gr.; depopulation.

Essaouira (Mogador), spt., **Morocco**; cereals, almonds, gum-arabic, crude oil; p. (1994) 433,681.

Essen, c., N. Rhine–Westphalia, **Germany**; gr. industl. c., ctr. of Ruhr conurbation; coal, steel (Krupp), electric power, engin.; canal links with Dortmund–Ems and Mittelland canals and with Rhine; minster severely damaged in second world war; p. (2002) 591,889 (c.), 5,823,685 (met.a.).

Essequibo, R.; flows N. from Brazilian border draining half **Guyana**.

Essex, non-met. co., **Eng.**; bounded on S. by Thames, on E. by N. Sea; co. t. Chelmsford; on London clay and chalk; agr.; wheat, barley, sugar-beet; mkt. gardens; S.W. of co. forms part of Greater London with mftg. subs.; oil refineries at Shell Haven; civil nuclear power sta. at Bradwell; p. (2001) 1,310,835.

Esslingen, t., Baden–Württemberg, **Germany**; on R. Neckar; mach. and rly. shops; textiles, chemicals, leather gds.; Liebfrauen church (1440); p. (2002) 90,905.

Essonne, dep., **France**; S. of Paris; cap. Evry; a. 1,810 km²; p. (1990) 1,170,984.

Eston, t., Redcar and Cleveland, **Eng.**; 5 km E. of Middlesbrough; shipbldg. and repairing; p. (2001) 32,788 (with South Bank).

Estonia (Estoniya), former USSR constituent rep.; borders on Baltic, G. of Finland, G. of Riga; lowland with many Ls.; farming and dairying, fishing; oil deposits; hydroelec. power; mainly Lutheran; univ.; EU member since 2004; cap. Tallinn; a. 45,610 km²; p. (2004) 1,341,664.

Estoril, wat. pl. and thermal spa, **Portugal**; N. side of Tagus estuary; holiday resort; p. (1991) 24,850.

Estremadura, region, S.W. **Spain**; on the border of Portugal; largely plateau, alt. 450–900 m.; heathy moorland; sheep; less arid conditions than in remainder of central Spain allow olives, vines, cereals; irrigation in valleys of Tagus, Guadiana; p. (1998) 1,070,000.

Etang de Berre, lagoon, Bouches-du-Rhône, S.E. **France**; E. of Rhône delta; traversed by Rhône–Marseille canal; salt pans; oil refineries in a.; approx. a. 260 km².

Étaples, t., Pas-de-Calais, **France**; seaside resort; p. (1990) 11,400.

Etawah, t., Uttar Pradesh, **India**; textiles; p. (1991) 124,027.

eThekwini. *See* **Durban**.

Ethiopia (Abyssinia), indep. st. N.E. Africa; temperate climate as a result of high plateau terrain; coffee most impt. comm. crop, but poor communications inhibit economic development; low per capita income and rapid growth of p.; potential for hydro-electric power is lge., one sta. open on Awash R.; mftg. dominated by textiles; severe drought began in 1970s and con-

tinued in 1980s; renewed drought, 2000; cap. Addis Ababa; monarchy abolished 1975; a. 1,221,900 km²; p. (2004) 67,851,281.

Ethiopian Highlands, mtns., **Ethiopia**; rise over 4,500 m; source of headwaters of tribs. of R. Nile.

Etna, volcano, N.E. Sicily, **Italy**; most recent eruptions 1971, 1979, 1992 and 2001; alt. 3,276 m. It is Europe's largest active volcano.

Eton, t., Berks., **Eng.**; on N. bank of R. Thames opposite Windsor; public school, founded by Henry VI; p. (1991) 1,974.

Etruria, anc. dist., **Italy**; now forms Tuscany; home of the Etruscans and part of the Roman empire by 400 B.C.

Etruria, t., Stoke, **Eng.**; part of Stoke-on-Trent; seat of Josiah Wedgwood's potteries (1769).

Euboea (Evvoia), lgst. of Greek Is., Aegean Sea; mtnous. (Mt. Delphi 1,746 m), vines and olives in lowlands, sheep and goats in highlands; a. 3,904 km²; p. (1991) 209,132.

Eucumbene Dam and **L.**, N.S.W., **Australia**; major storage of Snowy Mtns. hydroelectric scheme; holds eight times as much water as Sydney harbour.

Eugene, c., Ore., **USA**; univ.; mkt. ctr. for rich agr. and lumbering region; fruit-canning, sawmilling; headquarters of Willamette National Forest; p. (1990) 112,669 (c.), 283,000 (met. a. with Springfield).

Euphrates, lgst. R. in S.W. **Asia**; rises in Armenian uplands and joined by the Tigris enters Persian G. as the Shatt-al Arab; anc. ctr. of civilisation; modern irrigation, navigation, high dam opened 1973 and Ataturk Dam (1981) part of multi-purpose project; 2,848 km long.

Eure, dep., Normandy, **France**; agr., fruit, livestock, textiles; cap. Evreux; a. 6,037 km²; p. (1999) 540,550.

Eure-et-Loir, dep., N. **France**; mainly agr.; cap. Chartres; a. 5,934 km²; p. (1999) 407,842.

Europe, continent; W. peninsula of Eurasian land mass; no well-defined bdy. with Asia but line normally accepted runs along Ural Mtns. to Caspian Sea and Caucasus to Black Sea, Sea of Marmara and Dardanelles; after Australia, Europe is smallest continent in a., but contains 11 per cent of world's p. and even more of world's economic activity; climate varies from Arctic to Mediterranean and from temperate maritime to severe continental; major physical features inc. Alps, Pyrenees in S., Baltic Shield in N.; many European countries now included within European Union (EU) which has expanded rapidly; old division of East and West has disappeared. Major concentration of p. and economic activity within Golden Triangle (*q.v.*); total a. c. 10,360,000 km²; p. (2000) 728,000,000 (inc. Eur. Russia).

Euro-port, name of the post-war expansion of the port of Rotterdam, Neth., capable of handling 100,000 tonne oil-tankers; oil refining centre.

Euxine Sea. *See* **Black Sea**.

Evansville, c., Ind., **USA**; on Ohio R.; shipping and comm. ctr. for agr. region; coal mng.; p. (1990) 116,646 (c.), 279,000 (met. a.).

Eveneki National Area, Siberia, **Russia**; forest and tundra covered; home of Eveneki people; cap. Tura; a. 740,740 km²; p. (1989) 24,800.

Everest, Mt. (Chomolungma = Goddess Mother of the World), Himalayas, on frontier of **Nepal** and Tibet, **China**; alt. 8,850m; hgst. mtn. in the world; Hillary and Tenzing first to reach summit in 1953; within Nepal Nat. Park. Height declining due to global warming.

Everett, t., Wash., **USA**; on Puget Sound; harbour; comm. ctr.; timber; tourism; p. (1996) 81,028.

Everglades, Fla., **USA**; subtropical a.; extensive marshes; home of Seminole Indians; lge. scale drainage since 1905; restoration plan launched (2000) to save its endangered ecosystem.

Evesham, mkt. t., Wychavon, Worcs., **Eng.**; on R. Avon, in Vale of Evesham, 24 km S.E. of Worcester; fruit ctr.; tourism; p. (2001) 22,179.

Evian, c., Haute-Savoie, **France**; G8 Summit held here, 2003; tourism; water imp. p. (1999) 25,047.

Évora, t., cap. of Upper Alentejo prov., S. **Portugal**; mkt. for agr. prod.; cath.; p. (1991) 38,900.

Évreux, t., cap. of Eure dep., **France**; mkt. ctr.; p. (1999) 51,183.

Evros, prov., **Greece**; borders Bulgaria and Turkey; a. 4,191 km²; p. (1991) 143,791.

Evry, t. cap. of Essone dep., **France**; new cathedral inaugurated, April 1996.; p. (1990) 45,854.

Exe, R., Somerset and Devon, **Eng.**; rises on

Exmoor, flows S. via Exeter to English Channel at Exmouth; 86 km long.

Exeter, l. gov. dist., cath. c., co. t., Devon, Eng.; former Roman Isca; E. of Dartmoor on R. Exe; mkt. t.; univ.; aircraft components; airport; p. (2001) 111,076 (dist.).

Exmoor, Somerset and Devon, Eng.; sandstone moorland, deep wooded valleys; Nat. Park.

Exmouth, t., East Devon, Eng.; on estuary of R. Exe; holiday resort.

Eye, mkt. t., Mid Suffolk, Eng.; 29 km N. of Ipswich; anc. church.

Eyemouth, burgh, Borders, Scot.; on E. cst. 14 km N. of Berwick; fishing; p. (2002) 3,383.

Eyre Lake, 2 shallow salt lakes in northern S. Australia; 12 m below sea level; receives water from flash flooding, sometimes dry; a. 7,800 km².

Eyre Peninsula, S. Australia; between Gr. Australian Bight and Spencer G.; iron-ore deposits; a. 51,800 km².

F

Fabriano, t., Marches, Italy; in Apennines; cath.; paper mills; p. (1991) 28,700.

Faenza, t., Ravenna, Italy; at foot of Apennines; majolica, textiles; p. (1991) 54,100.

Failsworth, t. Gtr. Manchester, Eng.; N.E. of Manchester; textiles, elec. gds.; p. (1991) 20,160.

Fairbanks North Star, t., Alaska, USA; univ.; sawmilling; mng.; p. (1990) 77,720.

Fairfield, t., Conn., USA; chemicals, automobile parts; univ.; p. (2000) 57,300.

Fair I., midway between Shetland and Orkney, Scot.; bird sanctuary; famous for brightly patterned, hand-knitted articles; p. (1991) 67.

Faisalabad c. W. Punjab, Pakistan; univ. cotton chemicals, fertilizers; p. (2000) 2,232,000.

Faiyum (El Faiyûm), t. and prov. Egypt; oasis nr. L. Karun (anc. L. Moeris), fertilised by Nile water and silt; cereals, sugar-cane, fruits, cotton; p. (1996) 261,000 (t.), 1,989,900 (prov.).

Faizabad, t., Uttar Pradesh, India; mkt. t.; sugar refineries; p. (2001) 145,000.

Falaise, t., Calvados, France; birthplace of William the Conqueror; p. (1999) 8,428.

Falaise de l'Ile de France, low S.E.-facing escarpment, 80 km S.E. and E. of Paris, France; overlooks Champagne Pouilleuse; ch. vine-growing district for champagne-wine ind. of Reims and Epernay.

Falcón, st., Venezuela; bordering Caribbean Sea; cap. Coro; p. (1990) 632,513.

Falconara Marittima, t., Italy, nr. Ancona; spt.; oil refining, shipbldg.; p. (1991) 30,100.

Falkirk, burgh, unit. auth. created in 1996, formerly part of Central Region, Scot.; 16 km S.E. of Stirling, bordered N.E. by F. of Forth; foundries, bricks, chemical, aluminium wks., concrete, timber yards; battles 1298 and 1746; p. (2002) 32,379 (t.), (2002) 145,560, (unit. anth.).

Falkland, burgh, Fife, Scot.; 5 km S. of Auchtermuchty; mkt.; p. (2002) 1,183.

Falkland Is., Brit. Crown col., S. Atl., comprises E. and W. Falkland and adjacent Is.; known as Malvinas and claimed by Argentina; sheep rearing (for wool); cap. Stanley on E. Falkland I.; invasion by Argentina led to Falklands War (1982); airpt. opened (1985) capable of taking long range aircraft; major offshore oil reserves; a. 12,173 km²; p. (2004) 2,967.

Falkland Is. Dependencies, S. Atl.; inc. Is. of S. Orkney and S. Shetland; now form part of Brit. Antarctic Terr.

Fall River, c., Mass., USA; on Mt. Hope Bay; pt. of entry; clothing, rubber gds., food prods., paper; p. (1996) 90,865.

Fallujah, c. Iraq, known as 'City of Mosques'; Mainly Sunni pop.; uprising, 2004; pop. 300,000 (2003).

Falmouth, t., Carrick, Cornwall, Eng.; on W. side of estuary of R. Fal. 16 km S. of Truro; sheltered harbourage; offshore oil supply base; seaside resort; fisheries, ship repairing, mng., quarrying, lt. engin.; cas.; new Maritime Museum opened, 2002; pt.; p. (1991) 20,297.

Famagusta, t., spt., Cyprus; on E. cst.; resort; anc. crusade pt.; p. (2000 est.) 22,000.

Fareham, t., l. gov. dist., Hants., Eng.; at N.W. corner of Portsmouth Harbour; p. (2001)

107,977 (dist.), (2001) 56,160 (t.).

Farewell (Kap Farvel), C., southernmost tip of Greenland.

Farewell, C., most N. point S.I., N.Z.

Fargo, t., N.D., USA; rly. ctr. and R. pt.; grain, farm machin.; p. (1996) 83,778.

Faringdon, mkt. t., Vale of White Horse, Oxon., Eng.; Faringdon Folly; p. (1991) 5,235.

Farnborough, t., Rushmoor, Hants., Eng.; Aldershot military camp; Royal Aircraft Establishment; p. (2001) 57,147.

Farne Is., gr. of islets off Northumberland cst., Eng.; bird sanctuary; National Trust.

Farnham, t., Waverley, Surrey, Eng.; at N. foot of N. Downs, 16 km W. of Guildford; mkt.; p. (2001) 36,298.

Farnworth, t., Gtr. Manchester, Eng.; nr. Bolton, textiles, engin., paper; p. (2001) 25,264.

Faro, spt., cap. of Algarve prov., Portugal; cork, figs, oranges; p. (1991) 32,000.

Faroe Is., 320 km N.W. of the Shetlands; cap. Thórshavn (Strömö I.); Danish possession but not member of EU; impt. fisheries; now seeking independence; rich gas and oil deposits nearby; a. 1,399 km²; p. (2004) 46,662.

Farrukhabad, t., Uttar Pradesh, India; on Ganges R.; gold, lace, brass wk.; p. (1996) 3,817,000.

Fars, prov., S. Iran; agr.; cap. Shīrāz; p. (1996) 3,817,000.

Fastnet, lighthouse in Atl. Oc., 7·2 km S.W. C. Clear, Irish cst.

Fatima, v., W. Portugal, nr. Leiria; R.C. pilgrimage.

Fatshan See Foshan.

Faversham, pt., Swale, N.E. Kent, Eng.; at head of F. creek; mkt.; fruit, hops, bricks, brushes, engin.; p. (1991) 17,070.

Fawley, t., Hants., Eng.; on W. shore Southampton Water; lge. oil refinery with pipeline to Staines and Heathrow Airpt.

Fayetteville, t., N.C., USA; agr. processing; p. (1996) 79,631 (t.), (1990) 275,000 (met. a.).

Featherstone, t., West Yorks., Eng.; p. (1991) 10,496.

Fécamp, sm. spt. on cst. of Normandy, France; fishing, tourism, 12th cent. abbey; p. (1999) 20,987.

Fedchenko, glacier, Tajikistan; in Pamir mtns; 80 km long; one of longest in world.

Feira de Santana, t., Bahia, Brazil, inland mkt. t.; p. (1991) 405,700.

Feldberg, highest peak in Black Forest, Germany; alt. 1,495 m.

Feldkirch, t., Vorarlberg, Austria; on Swiss frontier; p. (1991) 26,743.

Felixstowe, pt., Suffolk Coastal Suffolk, Eng.; container pt.; seaside resort; p. (2001) 29,349.

Felling, Tyne and Wear, Eng.; Tyneside mftg. dist.; p. (2001) 34,196.

Feltham. See Hounslow.

Fenland, l. gov. dist., Cambs., Eng.; agr. a. in N. of co. inc. Wisbech, Chatteris, March, Whittlesey and North Witchford; p. (2001) 83,519.

Fens, The, low-lying dist. around the Wash, Eng.; artificial drainage first begun in 17th cent.; impt. agr. dist.; root crops, wheat, fruit, bulbs; a. 3,367 km².

Ferghana, region, Uzbekistan; deep basin at W. end of Tien Shan Mtns.; drained W. by R. Syr Dar'ya; semi-arid but extensive irrigation system allows intensive cultivation of cotton, citrus fruits, silk, rice; ch. ts. Kokand, Namangan.

Ferghana, c., Uzbekistan; hydroelectric power, petroleum refining, textiles; p. (1990) 197,800.

Fermanagh, former co.; l. gov. dist., N. Ireland; bisected by R. Erne and lakes; stock raising, dairying; p. (2001) 57,527.

Fernando de Noronha, i., fed. terr., N.E. cst. Brazil; penal settlement and met. sta.; cap. Vila dos Remédios; a. 26 km²; p. (1996) 1,336.

Fernando Po. See Bioko.

Ferrara, c., N. Italy; nr. head of Po delta; cath., univ., palaces; mkt. for fertile plain; silk, hemp, wine; oil refinery nearby; petrochemicals; birthplace of Savonarola; p. (1992) 137,099.

Ferro (Hierro), most S. of the Canary Is.; a. 275 km²; cap. Valverde; chosen by Ptolemy (A.D. 56) for his prime meridian and used by French scientists in 17th cent.; reckoned as exactly W. 20 ° of Paris.

Ferryhill, v., Durham, Eng.; 8 km S. of Durham, in gap through limestone ridge which separates Wear valley from Tees valley; commands main N. to S. route along lowland E. of Pennines; p. (1991) 11,610.

Fertile Crescent, an arc of fertile land from the Mediterranean Sea, N. of the Arabian Desert, to Persian G.; home of some very early civilisations and migrations.

Fez (Fès), c., **Morocco;** lies inland 160 km E. of Rabat; one of the sacred cities of Islam; univ. attached to mosque (one of lgst. in Africa); comm. ctr.; p. (1994) 772,000.

Fezzan, prov., S.W. **Libya;** desert plateau with numerous wells and inhabited oases.

Ffestiniog. See **Blaenau Ffestiniog.**

Fianarantsoa, t., **Madagascar;** rice mills, meat preserves; p. (1990) 124,489.

Fichtelgebirge, mtn. range, N.E. Bavaria, **Germany;** rising to 1,051 m in Schneeberg; beautiful forested slopes.

Fiesole, t., Tuscany, **Italy;** on summit of wooded hill overlooking Florence and the Arno; rebuilt; 11th cent. cath.; p. (1991) 15,100.

Fife, E. Scot., unit. auth. created in 1996, reinstating historic co. which became Region in 1974, occupies a. between Tay and Forth estuaries; industl. dist. based originally on coalfields; Longannet colliery remains; p. (2002) 350,700.

Fiji, S.W. Pac. Oc., former Brit. col., gained independence in 1970; comprises around 330 Is.; tropical climate; agr. basis of economy, especially sugar and processed fish; gold an impt. exp.; forestry and tourism developing; forms centre of communications in S.W. Pac. Oc.; fast-growing (now 46 per cent) Indian population; international airport at Nadi, ch. pt. and cap. Suva; a. 18,272 km²; cosmopolitan p. (2004) 850,000. Rejoined Commonwealth, 1997. Military coup, 2001.

Filton, Bristol, **Eng.;** aircraft wks.

Finchley. See **Barnet.**

Findhorn, v., Moray, **Scot.;** resort; 12th cent. abbey; remains of port washed away in 1702 now rediscovered; p. (2002) 885.

Fingal's Cave, Staffa I., Inner Hebrides, W. **Scot.;** basaltic columns.

Finger Lakes, gr. of narrow glacial Ls., N.Y., **USA;** picturesque resorts and state parks.

Finistère, dep. N.W. **France,** in Brittany; cap. Quimper; fishing, tourism; a. 7,071 km²; p. (1999) 852,176.

Finland, rep., N. Europe; part of Scandinavia; low-lying plateau severely eroded by ice to form 60,000 Ls.; economy based on timber (forests cover 72 per cent of a.); world's leading exporter of pulp and paper; increasing importance of metal and engin. inds.; cap. Helsinki; joined EU 1995; a. 360,318 km²; p. concentrated in S.; p. (2004) 5,214,512.

Finland, G. of, E. arm of Baltic Sea, between Finland and Russia.

Finnart, Argyll and Bute, **Scot.;** crude oil terminal situated in Loch Long, N.W. Glasgow; pipeline to Grangemouth.

Finnmark, most N. co., **Norway;** inhabited by Lapps; whale fisheries; lge. copper deposits discovered nr. Reppan fjord; a. 48,125 km²; p. (1990) 74,590.

Finsbury. See **Islington.**

Finsteraarhorn, highest peak in Bernese Oberland, **Switzerland;** 4,277 m.

Finucane I., pt., W. **Australia;** deepwater pt. to ship iron ore and new t. projected.

Firenze. See **Florence.**

Firozabad, t., Uttar Pradesh, **India;** glassware; agr. tr; p. (1991) 215,128.

Firozpur, t., Punjab st., N.W. **India;** rly. t.; admin. ctr.; p. (1991) 61,142.

Fishguard, spt., Pembrokeshire, **Wales;** on S. of Cardigan Bay; ferry connection to Rosslare (Ireland); p. (1991) 2,679.

Fitzroy, R., W. **Australia;** flows into King Sound; dry in winter; irrigation; 560 km long.

Fiume. See **Rijeka.**

Flag Fen, nr. Peterborough; major Bronze Age site.

Flamborough Head, promontory of Yorks. cst., **Eng.;** steep chalk cliffs; lighthouse; anc., Brit. earthwork (Danes' dyke).

Flanders, region between R. Scheldt and cst., crossed by Franco-Belgian frontier; Dunkirk, Lille ctrs. of French F.; Belgian F. divided into 2 provs., E. and W., p. (1993) 1,116,244 and 1,344,263 respectively; caps. Bruges and Ghent.

Fleet, t., Hart, Hants., **Eng.;** 6 km N.W. of Aldershot; p. (2001) 32,726.

Fleetwood, spt., Wyre, Lancs., **Eng.;** at mouth of Wyre, Morecambe Bay; deep-sea fish. pt.; fish processing; lge. chemical plant nearby; p. (2001) 26,841.

Flensburg, spt., Schleswig-Holstein, **Germany;** on Baltic, close to Danish border; shipbld., machin., rum distilleries, fishing; p. (2002) 84,480.

Flevoland, prov., **Neth.;** estab. 1986; p. (1994) 253,699.

Flinders Range, chain of mtns., S. **Australia;** extending 400 km N.E. from head of Spencer G., reaching 1,190 m in St. Mary's Peak; named after Matthew Flinders; uranium ore at Mt. Painter.

Flint, t., Flintshire, **Wales;** viscose textile yarn, cas. ruins; p. (1991) 11,737.

Flint, t., Mich., **USA;** motorcars, aircraft engines; p. (1990) 140,761 (t.), 430,000 (met. a.).

Flintshire, N.E. **Wales,** unit. auth. created in 1996 from former l. gov. dists. of Alyn and Deeside and Delyn, reinstating part of historic co. split up in 1974; inc. ts. of Buckley, Connah's Quay, Flint and Mold; p. (2001) 148,594.

Flodden, v. Northumberland, **Eng.;** on R. Till; battle between James IV of Scot. and the English under the Earl of Surrey 1513.

Flora, t., **Norway;** new t. 136 km N. of Bergen.

Florence (Firenze), c., Tuscany, **Italy;** on R. Arno; univ.; leather-work; famous for art treasures, cath. and churches; ruled by Medici 1421-1737; birthplace of Dante and Machiavelli; the 'cradle of civilisation'; severely affected by floods 1966; p. (1992) 397,434.

Flores, I., most northwesterly of Azores gr.; Portuguese; cap. Santa Cruz; French ballistic missiles tracking sta.; a. 142 km².

Flores, I., Indonesia; mtnous.; volcanic, densely forested; a. 22,973 km².

Florianópolis, spt., cap. of Santa Catarina st., **Brazil;** comm. ctr., fishing; p. (1996) 268,500.

Florida, st., **USA;** Sunshine St.; admitted to Union 1845; st. flower Orange Blossom, st. bird Mockingbird; between Atl. Oc. and G. of Mexico; low-lying, swampy, inc. Ever-glades; sea resorts on Atl. cst.; citrus fruit and subtropical agr.; agr. processing; cap Tallahassee; a. 151,670 km²; p. (2002) 16,713,149; hgst. percentage of p. over 65 in USA (18.3). Hit by hurricane Georges, 1998.

Florida Keys, archipelago, **USA;** extends in an arc from S.E. cst. Florida W.S.W. to Key West in G. of Mexico; fishing resorts.

Florida Strait, between Florida and Bahama Is.; course of Gulf Stream from G. of Mexico.

Florina. See **Phlorina.**

Flushing. See **Vlissingen.**

Fly, lgst. R. of **Papua New Guinea;** flows S.E. from Victor Emmanuel Range to G. of Papua; 1,280 km long.

Fochabers, v., Moray, **Scot.;** nr. mouth of Spey; tourist resort; food canning; p. (2002) 1,499.

Focsani, t., **Romania;** at foot of Transylvanian Alps; wine and grain ctr.; p. (1992) 101,296.

Foggia, cath. c., S. **Italy;** rly. ctr. and mkt. ctr. for plain of Apulia; site of cas. of Frederick II; p. (1992) 155,674.

Foix, t., cap. of Ariège dep., S. **France;** historic t.; p. (1999) 9,109.

Foligno, t., central **Italy;** in Apennines, on Topino R.; cath., textiles, paper; p. (1981) 52,484.

Folkestone, t., Shepway, Kent, **Eng.;** seaside resort; p. (2001) 45,273.

Fonseca, Gulf of, Honduras; lgst. indentation along Pac. cst. of Central America; sm. pt. of Amapala, US naval base, and new deepwater pt.

Fontainebleau, t., Seine-et-Marne, **France;** on R. Seine, 56 km S.E. Paris; in former royal forest; magnificent palace; p. (1999) 15,944.

Fontenoy, v., **Belgium;** nr. Tournai; scene of battle (1745) when the French under Marshal Saxe inflicted defeat on the English and their allies.

Foochow. See **Fuzhou.**

Fordlandia. See **Belterra.**

Foreland, N. and S., two headlands on E. cst. Kent, **Eng.;** between which are the Goodwin Sands and Pegwell Bay; lighthouses; sea battle between de Ruyter and Monk (1666).

Forest Heath, l. gov. dist., Suffolk, **Eng.;** part of Breckland inc. Mildenhall and Newmarket; p. (2001) 55,510.

Forest Hills, residtl. a., central Queen's bor., N.Y., **USA;** national and international matches played at West Side Tennis Club.

Forest of Dean, Gloucs., **Eng.;** between Wye and

Severn Rs.; former Royal Forest; Forestry Commission plantations; former coal mng. a.; tourism; new lt. industl. estates; forms l. gov. dist.; p. (2001) 79,982.

Forfar, royal burgh, Angus, Scot.; jute, linen; p. (2002) 13,208.

Forlì, c., Emilia-Romagna, central Italy; route ctr. in Appennine foothills; felt, textiles, footwear; p. (1992) 109,080.

Formosa, t. and prov., N. Argentina; bordering on Paraguay; timber; cap. Formosa; a. 72,067 km²; p. (1991) 148,074 (t.), 398,413 (prov.).

Formosa. See Taiwan.

Forres, royal burgh, Moray, Scot.; on Findhorn R. nr. Moray F.; agr., forestry, engin., distilleries; cas.; p. (2002) 8,967.

Forst, t., Brandenburg, Germany; on R. Neisse; E. section of t. Polish since 1945; textiles; p. (1989) 26,313.

Fortaleza, c., cap. of Ceará st., Brazil; in the dry Sertão reg. of the N.E.; terminus of cattle droving route; growth resulting from planned industl. development to revitalise region; p. (1996) 1,967,400.

Fort Collins, t., Col., USA; ctr. of rich farming a.; grain, sugarbeet, livestock; univ.; p. (1990) 87,758 (t.), 186,136 (met. a.).

Fort de France, cap. of Martinique, Fr. W.I.; landlocked harbour; exp. sugar, rum; comm. ctr.; Fr. naval base; p. (1990) 101,544.

Forth, R., Scot.; formed by two headstreams rising to N. of Ben Lomond which meet nr. Aberfoyle; takes meandering course to Alloa, whence it expands into Firth of Forth; 165 km long.

Forth, Firth of, lge. inlet, E. cst. of Scot.; submerged estuary of R. Forth; navigable by lge. vessels for 64 km inland to Grangemouth, other pts., Leith, Rosyth (naval), Bo'ness; l. (to Alloa) 80 km; the Forth rly. bridge (1890) spans the F. at Queensferry; road bridge (1964).

Forth and Clyde Canal, Scot.; links F. of Forth at Grangemouth and F. of Clyde at Glasgow; not completely navigable; 61 km long.

Fort Johnston, t., S. Malawi, on L. Malombe; new t., 1966; tobacco; airpt.

Fort Knox, Ky., USA; nation's gold bullion depository; military air-base.

Fort Lamy. See Ndjamene.

Fort Lauderdale, c., Fla., USA; on Atl. cst. N. of Miami; lge. marina; citrus fruits, mkt. garden prod.; holiday resort; p. (2000) 152,400.

Fort Myers, t., Fla., USA; on G. of Mexico; resort; Edison experimented here; p. (2000) 48,200.

Fortrose, t., royal burgh, Ross and Cromarty, Scot.; on S. cst. of Black Isle, on Moray F.; p. (2002) 1,174.

Fort Smith, c., Ark., USA; on Arkansas R.; mkt. ctr. for agr. a.; varied mnfs., inc. furniture, glass; coal and zinc mined nearby; p. (1990) 72,708 (c.), 142,083 (met. a.).

Fort Victoria, (Masvingo), t., Zimbabwe, agr. and mng. ctr.; cattle, historic ruins in Zimbabwe Nat. Park; p. (1992) 51,750.

Fort Wayne, c., Ind., USA; at confluence of 2 headstreams of Maumee R.; rly. repair shops; elec. machin. and domestic appliances, originally a Fr. fort; p. (2000) 205,727 (c.), 364,000 (met. a.).

Fort William. See Thunder Bay.

Fort William, burgh, Highland, Scot.; nr. head of Loch Linnhe, at base of Ben Nevis; aluminium factory; pulp- and paper-mill at Corpach; p. (2002) 9,908.

Fort Worth, c., Texas, USA; rly. and comm. ctr. on Trinity R.; livestock and grain mkt.; oil refining, meat packing, oilfield equipment; p. (2000) 534,694 (c.), 1,332,053 (met. a. with Arlington).

Fort Yukon, trading sta. on Yukon R., N.E. Alaska, USA.

Fotheringhay, v., Northampton, Eng.; on R. Nene; Mary Queen of Scots beheaded (1587) in F. Castle.

Foulness I., S. Essex, Eng.; at mouth of R. Crouch; owned by Min. of Defence; site of projected third London airport at Maplin, now abandoned; projected container and oil pt.

Fountains Abbey, ruined 12th cent. Cistercian abbey, North Yorks., Eng.; nr. Ripon.

Fowey, sm. spt., Cornwall, Eng.; nr. mouth of R. Fowey; exp. kaolin; resort; fishing; p. (1991) 1,939.

Foyers, Falls of, Highland, Scot.; E. of Loch Ness, nr. Fort Augustus; aluminium wks., the first hydroelectric plant erected in Britain (1896).

Foyle, Lough, inlet, N. Ireland; between Donegal (R.o.I.) and Londonderry; outlet of R. F.; Londonderry t. at head of inlet.

Foynes Is., R.o.I.; oil terminal on N. side, E. of Battery Point.

Foz do Iguaçu, t., Paraná, Brazil; highway (coffee road) from Paranaguá; rapid growth with opening of Itaipú Dam; p. (1996) 231,600.

Framingham, t., Mass., USA; 32 km W. of Boston; lt. inds.; p. (2000) 66,900.

Framlingham, mkt. t., Suffolk, Eng.; N.E. of Ipswich; cas.

Francavilla Fontana, t., Apulia, Italy; rly. junc.; agr. tr.; p. (1991) 34,000.

France, rep., W. Europe; bounded by 3 seas; Eng. Channel, Atl. Oc., Mediterranean; variety of climate and relief; leading agr. cty. of Europe; 75 per cent under cultivation; exps. grain, fruit, vegetables, wine; industl. expansion since second world war; lgst. inds. inc. iron and steel, motor vehicles, aircraft, engin., textiles, chemicals; tourism impt.; EU member; cap. Paris; 96 deps.; excessive social, economic, and political concentration around Paris promotes description of France as "Paris and the French Desert"; recent attempts to break this down using framework of 21 economic planning regions; a. 550,634 km²; p. (2004) 60,424,213.

Franceville, t., Gabon, Equatorial Africa; on R. Ogooué; lined to Libreville as part of the Trans-Gabon rly. project; manganese mines opened 1962; founded by De Brazza.

Franche-Comté, region E. France bordering Switzerland; inc. deps. Doubs, Jura, Haute-Saône, Territoire de Belfort; mainly mountainous and wooded but industrial round cht. ts. Belfort, Besançon; p. (1999) 1,116,421.

Frankfurt-am-Main, c., Hesse, Germany; local point in Rhine-Main urban region; rly. ctr., transit pt.; machin., cars, chemicals, elec. engin.; publishing; airport; cath., univ.; birthplace of Goethe; p. (2002) 641,076 (c.), 1,896,741 (met.a).

Frankfurt-an-Oder, c., Brandenburg, Germany; agr. ctr., R. pt., rail junc.; machin., chemicals; E. part of t. (Slubice) Polish since 1945; p. (2002) 70,308.

Frankischer (Franconian) Jura, plateau with steep N.-facing edge, S.E. of Germany; runs 128 km S.W. from Fichtelgebirge; drained by Reg nitz and Altmühl Rs.

Franklin, dist., N.W. Terr., Canada; comprising the Is. of Arctic Canada from Banks I. to Baffin I., including Boothia Peninsula and Melville Peninsula; sparsely populated; furs; a. 1,434,943 km².

Františkovy Lázne (Franzensbad), famous spa, W. Bohemia, Czech Rep.; 445 m a.s.l., between the Erzgebirge and the Fichtelgebirge.

Franz Josef Land (Zemlya Frantsalosifa), Russia; archipelago in Arctic Oc. N. of Novaya Zemlya; a. 20,720 km²; mainly ice covered.

Frascati, t., Italy; 19 km S.E. of Rome; summer resort; wine; famous villas and arch. remains; nuclear research ctr.; p. (1991) 20,100.

Fraser I. (Great Sandy I.), Queensland, Australia; low sandy I., timber reserve and Nat. Park; concern over ecology caused discontinuation of mineral sand exp. (1977).

Fraser, R., B.C., Canada; rises at c. 1,800 m on W. slopes Rocky Mtns.; famous salmon fisheries; routeway; Vancouver nr. delta; 1,360 km long.

Fraserburgh, spt., burgh, Aberdeenshire, Scot.; the largst shellfish pt. in Europe; p. (2002) 12,454.

Frauenfeld, t., cap. of Thurgau can., Switzerland; 11th cent. cas.; textiles; p. (1993) 20,300.

Fray Bentos, t., cap. of Río Negro dep., Uruguay; pt. on R. Uruguay 80 km from mouth; meatprocessing; p. (1996) 22,600.

Fredericia, t., pt., E. Jutland, Denmark; major rly. junc.; textiles, silver and electroplated gds., fertilisers; oil refinery; p. (1990) 46,072.

Fredericton, c., cap. of N.B., Canada; on St. John R.; univ., cath.; timber, shoes, plastics; p. (1996) 78,950.

Frederikshavn, fish. pt., N. Jutland, Denmark, on Kattegat; p. (1990) 35,500.

Frederikstad, t., Norway; at mouth of Glomma R.; ctr. of pulp and paper-producing ind.; electrotechnical inds., shipbldg., fish canning; p. (1990) 50,170.

Frederiksvaerk, t., Sjaelland, Denmark; impt. iron

and steel wks.; p. (1990) 17,941.

Free State, central, land-locked prov., **Rep. of S. Africa**; Vaal River in the north and Orange River in the south, mountains, semi-desert, prairie, veld; fruit, sunflowers, horticulture, vegetables, wheat, asparagus, soya, sorghum, seeds, gold, coal, diamonds, bentonite, chemicals; cap. Bloemfontein; a. 129,480 km²; p. (1996) 2.634 m.

Freetown, c., cap. of **Sierra Leone**; pt. on Atl. Oc.; one of lgst. natural harbours in world; humid, oppressive climate; exp. diamonds, palm oil; food processing, oil refining; fishing; much fighting (1999) in civil war; p. (1999) 822,000.

Freiberg, t. Saxony, Germany; S.W. of Dresden, at foot of Erzgebirge; mng. academy (silver discovered 12th cent.); metallurgy, textiles, glass, porcelain; p. (2002) 45,228.

Freiburg im Breisgau, c., Baden-Württemberg, Germany, in Black Forest, cath., univ., cultural ctr; tourism; p. (2002) 208,294.

Freital, t. Saxony, Germany; S.W. Dresden; glass, uranium ore processing; coalmines nearby; p. (1994) 38,200.

Fréjus, t., Var dep., S.W. **France**; cath., Roman ruins; resort on Fr. Riviera; p. (1990) 42,600.

Fréjus, Col de, Alpine pass, **France** and **Italy**, 2,083 m, under which runs the Mont Cenis tunnel (13·6 km).

Fremantle, spt., W. **Australia**; at mouth of Swan R., 19 km S.W. from Perth, principal pt. in W. Australia and first Australian pt. of call for mail steamers; part of Perth met. a.; giant industl. complex at Kwinana; p. (1991) 23,834.

French Equatorial Africa, formerly included Gabon, Congo (Brazzaville), Ubangi-Shari and Chad, sts. which are now independent.

French Guiana (Guyane), Fr. Overseas dep., on N. cst. of **S. America**, between Surinam to W. and Brazil to S. and E.; tropical climate; little developed and thinly populated; ch. ctr. of p. and spt. at cap. of Cayenne; economy based on agr., especially sugar and forestry; some gold and bauxite mng.; a. 90,650 km²; p. (2004) 191,309.

French Polynesia, Fr. overseas terr., in S. Pac. Oc., comprising several archipelagos; Society Is., Marquesas Is., Tubuai Is., Tuamotu Is., and Gambier Is.; increased autonomy since 1977; cap. Papeete; a. 4,002 km²; p. (2004) 266,339.

French Somaliland. *See* **Djibouti**.

French Southern and Antarctic Terrs., Fr. overseas terr., comprising several grs. of Is. and Antarctic terr. of Adélie Land; a. 409,220 km²; no permanent p.

Freshwater, sm. t., I. of Wight, **Eng.**; at W. end of I., 13 km W. of Newport; resort; p. (1991) 7,317 (with Totland).

Fresno, c., Cal., **USA**; ctr. of vast irrigated fruit-growing dist.; p. (2000) 427,652 (c.), 667,000 (met. a.).

Fribourg (Freiburg), c., cap. of F. can., **Switzerland**; between Berne and Lausanne; viaduct and bridges; cath., univ.; p. (1990) 34,722.

Fribourg (Freiburg), can., **Switzerland**; mainly dairy farming; cereals, sugarbeet, cheese; a. 1,671 km²; p. (1990) 207,800.

Friedrichshafen, t., **Germany**; on Bodensee; machin., boat bldg., motors; resort; p. (2002) 57,538.

Friendly Is. *See* **Tonga**.

Friern Barnet. *See* **Barnet**.

Friesland, prov., N. **Neth.**; cap. Leeuwarden; dairying, horses, cattle; natural gas on Ameland I.; a. 3,432 km²; p. (1994) 607,016.

Frimley and Camberley, ts., Surrey Heath, former U.D., Surrey, **Eng.**; 5 km N. of Farnborough; lt. engin., plastics; military training ctr.; p. (1991) 46,120.

Frinton and Walton, Tendring, Essex, **Eng.**; on E. cst., 8 km N.E. of Clacton; seaside resort.

Frisches Haff, shallow freshwar lagoon, Baltic cst. of Poland; 85 km long, 6–18 km broad.

Frisian Is., chain of Is. stretching from Den Helder to Jutland, along csts. of Neth., Germany, and Denmark; ch. Is. are Texel, Vlieland, Terschelling, Ameland (West Fr. Is.), Nordeney, Borkum (East F. Is.), Sylt, Föhr, Rømø (North Fr. Is.); severe erosion; Sylt now half size it was 500 years ago.

Friuli-Venezia Giulia, aut. reg. (created 1963), N.E. **Italy**; comprising 3 provs. Udine, Gorozia, Trieste; p. (1992) 1,195,055.

Frobisher Bay, inlet in S. Baffin I., N. **Canada**, extending 320 km between Cumberland Sound and Hudson Strait.

Frome, mkt. t., Mendip, Somerset, **Eng.**; on R.

Frome, 18 km S. of Bath; p. (1991) 23,159.

Frome, R., Dorset, **Eng.**; flows from N. Dorset Downs into Poole Harbour.

Frontignan, t., Hérault, S. **France**; oil refining; pipeline under sea from Sète; produces muscat; p. (1990) 16,300.

Frunze. *See* **Bishkek**.

Frýdek-Místek, t., **Czech Republic**; on R. Ostravice on opposite banks; timber, textiles; p. (1990) 66,000.

Fuerteventura, I., Canary gr.; a. 1,717 km².

Fujayrah, emirate, one of **United Arab Emirates**, Persian G.; p. (1995) 76,300.

Fujian (Fukien), prov., **China**; cap. Fuzhou; intensive agr., rice and sugar-cane; shellfish raised along cst.; a. 123,103 km²; p. (1990) 30,610,000.

Fujiyama, extinct volcano, **Japan**; 96 km S.W. of Tokyo; pilgrim resort; hgst. peak of Japan; alt. 3,780 m.

Fukui, c., cap. of F. pref., central Honshu, **Japan**; synthetic fibres, paper; old silk weaving ctr.; p. (1990) 252,743.

Fukuoka, c., N. Kyushu, **Japan**; pt. on Hakata Bay; univ. ctr., old cas. t.; textiles, dolls, shipbldg.; p. (2000) 1,341,000.

Fukuyama, c., S. Hokkaido, **Japan**; p. (1990) 365,612.

Fulda, t., Hesse, **Germany**; nr. Kassel; on R. Fulda; palace, abbey; textiles, metallurgy, rubber; route ctr.; p. (2002) 62,819.

Fulham. *See* **Hammersmith**.

Funchal, cap. of **Madeira Is.**; pt., winter resort; cath.; p. (1991) 110,000.

Fundy, Bay of, inlet between Nova Scotia and New Brunswick, **Canada**; lge. tidal range of 21 m.

Furness, dist., Cumbria, **Eng.**; between Morecambe Bay and the Irish Sea.

Fürstenwalde, t., Brandenburg, **Germany**; on R. Spree; metallurgy, leather, tyres; p. (1989) 35,658.

Fürth, t., Bavaria, **Germany**; nr. Nürnberg; toy and glass inds.; p. (2002) 111,257.

Fusan. *See* **Pusan**.

Fuse, t., Honshu, **Japan**; machin., textiles, chemicals; now part of Higashiosaka.

Fushimi, c., Honshu, **Japan**; sub. of Kyoto; p. (1990) 280,276.

Fushun, c., Liaoning, N. **China**; at foot of Changbai Shan, 35 km N.E. of Shenyang; major industl. ctr.; possesses world's thickest bituminous coal seam (127 m) worked by deep and opencast mines; oil refinery based on local oil shales; steelwks., chemicals; electronics; timber inds.; diversification planned; p. (1994) 1,246,000.

Futa, La, pass, Tusco-Emilian Apennines, N. **Italy**; used by main road from Bologna to Florence; alt. 903 m.

Fuxin (Fuzin), c., Liaoning, N. **China**; ctr. of lge. coalfield; p. (1994) 665,000.

Fuzhou (Foochow), c., cap. of Fujian prov., **China**; at mouth of Min R., major comm. and industl. ctr.; diverse light inds.; became impt. with tea exp.; former treaty pt.; p. (1994) 952,300.

Fylde, W. Lancs., **Eng.**; low plain behind coastal sand dunes; pig- and poultry-rearing dist.; ch. t. Blackpool; l. gov. dist. excluding Blackpool; p. (2001) 73,217.

Fylingdales, ballistic missile early warning sta. on N. Yorks. moors, Eng.

Fyn, I., **Denmark**; in Baltic Sea; a. 3,419 km²; cap. Odense; dairying, sugarbeet; p. (1990) 426,106.

Fyne, Loch, on Argyll and Bute cst., W. **Scot.**; an arm of F. of Clyde; offshore oil platform construction; 64 km long.

G

Gabès, spt., **Tunisia**; on G. of Gabès, 320 km S. of Tunis; dates, henna, wool; p. (2000) 106,600.

Gabon, rep., W. Africa; Cameroon to N., Congo to S. and E.; tropical climate, hot, humid; much tropical rain forest; forestry main ind. but mng. increasingly impt.; petroleum exp. creating increasing prosperity; manganese at Moanda (S.), iron-ore at Mekambo (N.E.); communications geared mainly to mng. areas; major pls. Libreville (cap.), Port Gentil; Trans-Gabon rly. project to promote exploitation of timber; first part opened 1979; intense forest cover makes internal air services very impt.; airport at Libreville; a. 266,770 km²; p. (2004) 1,355,246.

Gaborone (Gaberones), cap. **Botswana**; formerly

sm. v.; chosen as cap. for new rep., bldg. began 1964; p. (1998) 192,800.

Gadag-Betgeri, t., Karnataka, India; cotton and silk weaving; p. (1991) 134,051.

Gaeta, t., naval pt., Italy; on promontory on shore of G. of Gaeta; the anc. Caietae Portus; cath.; p. (1991) 22,300.

Gaillard Cut, excavated channel, Panama; carries Panama Canal through Culebra Mtn. from L. Gatun to Pac. Oc.; 11 km long.

Gainesville, t., Fla., USA; univ.; mkt. gardening; electronics, wood prod.; p. (1990) 84,770.

Gainsborough, t., West Lindsey, Lincs., Eng.; on R. Trent; agr. implements, milling, packing and wrapping machin.; mkt.; George Eliot's St. Ogg's in *Mill on the Floss*; p. (1991) 19,704.

Gairdner, salt L., S. Australia; a. 4,766 km².

Galapagos, volcanic Is., Pac. Oc.; 960 km W. of Ecuador (to whom they belong) on equator; flora and fauna peculiar to each I.; visited by Darwin 1835; rapid development of ecotourism; a. 7,428 km²; p. (1994) 12,000.

Galashiels, burgh, Borders, Scot.; on Gala Water, 3 km above confluence with R. Tweed; tweeds, woollens; p. (2002) 14,361.

Galati or **Galatz**, c., E. Romania; major inland pt. on lower Danube; cath.; p. (1999) 328,000.

Galicia, historic region, S.E. Poland and W. Ukraine.

Galicia, region, N.W. Spain; comprising provs. La Coruña, Lugo, Orense, and Pontevedra; p. (1998) 2,725,000.

Galilee, northern div. of Palestine in Roman times, containing the ts. Cana, Capernaum, Tiberias, Nazareth; scene of Christ's ministry; now Israel.

Galilee, Sea of (Lake Tiberias), also known as L. Gennesaret; Biblical associations; 207 m below level of Med.; level still (2000) falling; Israel plans to draw water from L. to irrigate Negev; a. 166 km².

Gallarate, t., Italy; nr. Milan; textiles; p. (1991) 45,000.

Galle, c., pt. on S.W. cst. of Sri Lanka; exp. tea, rubber, coconut oil; suffered from competition with Colombo after construction of modern harbour there; p. (2000 est.) 89,000.

Gallego, R., N.E. Spain, rises in Pyrenees, flows S. to R. Ebro at Zaragoza; provides irrigation around Zaragoza; valley used by main rly. across Pyrenees from Pau to Zaragoza; 176 km long.

Gallipoli. See Gelibolu.

Galloway, anc. dist. S.W. Scot.; now part of Dumfries and Galloway.

Galloway, Mull of, the extremity of the Rinns of G., the most southern pt. of Scot.

Galston, burgh, E. Ayrshire, Scot.; on R. Irvine, nr. Kilmarnock; p. (2002) 5,000.

Galveston, c., spt., Texas, USA; on I. in Bay at entrance to G. of Mexico; gr. cotton and sulphur pt with lge. exp. of agr. prod.; mills, foundries, food-processing, chemicals; univ., resort; scene of worst hurricane disaster in USA, 1900; p. (1990) 59,070 (c.), 217,000 (met. a. with Texas City).

Galway, co., Galway Bay, Connacht, R.o.I.; fishery, cattle, marble quarrying; a. 6,351 km²; p. (1991) 180,400.

Galway, co. t. and cultural ctr. Galway, R.o.I.; univ.; spt., fishing, sawmills, textiles, printing; p. (1991) 50,900.

Gambia, The, W. Africa, on Atl. Oc.; comprises St. Mary's I. (on which is Banjul, the cap.) and narrow mainland enclave (average width 32 km) extending 320 km inland astride R. Gambia, hot all year, summer rain, but savannah inland; agr. is basis of economy, esp. groundnuts; economic aid from Taiwan, communications developed around Banjul (spt. and airpt.); union with Senegal (1982), dissolved 1989; one of Africa's smallest sts.; new on-shore and off-shore oil discoveries; a. 11,295 km²; p. (2004) 1,546,848.

Gambia, R., Gambia, rises in Futa Jalon Plateau, flows N. and W. into Atl. Oc. at Banjul; forms main means of communication through Gambia, 1,120 km long.

Gambier Is., Fr. Polynesia, S. Pac. Oc., 4 coral Is.; a. 31 km².

Gand. See Ghent.

Gandhinagar, new cap. of Gujarat, India; on Sabarmati R., 21 km N. of Ahmadabad; under construction; p. (1991) 123,359.

Ganges (Ganga), sacred R. of India; rises in Himalayas and flows to Bay of Bengal via alluvial cones at foot of Himalayas and by several delta mouths, on one of which stands Calcutta; navigable for lge. ships from Allahabad; delta alone larger than Eng. and Wales; flood plain and delta very fertile and densely populated; removal of irrig. water by India causes friction with Bangladesh; agreement over division of water at Farraka barrage reached (1978); 2,400 km long.

Gangtok, sm. t., cap. of, Sikkim st; India; E. Himalayas; agr. tr. ctr.; carpets.

Gansu (Kansu), prov., N.W. China; borders Inner Mongolia; cap. Lanzhou; pastoral agr., wheat, cotton, tobacco; coal reserves; rich iron ore deposits; attemps to break down isolation by attracting foreign investment; major oil discovery (2004); a. 391,507 km²; p. (1994) 23,520,000.

Gard, dep., S. France; in Languedoc on Mediterranean; cap. Nîmes; vines, olives, sericulture; a. 5,879 km²; p. (1999) 622,581.

Garda, L., between Lombardy and Venezia, Italy; variety of scenery, winter resort; a. 370 km²; greatest depth, 346 m.

Gardéz, t., Afghanistan; alt. 2,287 m; ctr. of comm. and transport; p. (2000 est.) 101,000.

Garforth, t., West Yorks., Eng.; coalmng., lt. inds.; p. (1991) 15,250.

Garigliano, R. and dist., S. central Italy; where Liri R. joins Gari R. below Cassino; nuclear power plant.

Garonne, R., S.W. France; rises at foot of Mt. Maladetta (Pyrenees), flows via Toulouse and agr. valley, and enters Gironde estuary 32 km below Bordeaux; 720 km long.

Garrigue, region, Languedoc, S. France; low limestone hills, run N.E. to S.W., W. of Rhône delta; semi-arid; Mediterranean vegetation to which region gives name; winter pasture for sheep; olives; Montpellier, Nîmes located on S. flank.

Gary, c., Ind., USA; on S. shore of L. Michigan; producer of steel, tinplate, cement; p. (1990) 116,646 (c.), 605,000 (met. a. with Hammond).

Gascony, anc. prov., S.W. France; now comprises deps. along Atl. cst. and Pyrenees; Landes, Gers, Hautes-Pyrenees, and parts of Lot-et-Garonne, Tarn-et-Garonne, Haute Garonne, Gironde, and Ariège. Battleground in Hundred Years War.

Gateshead, t., met. dist., Tyne and Wear, Eng.; on R. Tyne opposite Newcastle; engin., food processing, pumps, paper; pt.; Millennium Bridge (2000); Baltic Gallery (opened 2002); p. (2001) 191,151 (dist.), (2001) 78,403 (t.).

Gatwick, West Sussex, Eng.; 40 km S. London; first airport in world where trunk road, main rly. line and air facilities combined in one unit.

Gaul (Lat. *Gallia*), embraced the lands inhabited by Celtic peoples in Roman times, covering what is now modern France (Gaul proper), Belgium, N. Italy, and parts of Germany, Neth., and Switzerland. South of the Alps was known as Cisalpine Gaul, north of the Alps as Transalpine Gaul.

Ganri-Sankar, mtn. in Himalayas, Nepal and Tibet, China; 56 km W. of Mt. Everest; alt. 7,149 m.

Gauteng, land-locked prov., Rep. of S. Africa; agricultural land, internationally important wetlands; dairy products, vegetables, fruit, meat, eggs, flowers, maize, sunflowers,gold, finance; cap. Johannesburg; a. 17,010 km²; p. (1996) 7.35 m.

Gävle, spt., Sweden; timber, textiles, steel, porcelain; p. (1992) 89,194.

Gävleborg, co., Sweden; ch. t., Gävle; a. 18,544 km²; p. (1992) 289,190.

Gaya, t., Bihar, India; Buddhist pilgrim ctr.; cottons, silks; p. (1991) 292,000.

Gaza Strip, coastal a. under Egyptian admin. since 1949; occupied by Israeli troops, Nov. 1956–March 1957, and 1967–Sept. 2005; Jewish settlements removed; limited Palestinian self-rule; ch. t. Gaza; first international Palestinian airport opened (1998); p. (2004) 1,324,991.

Gaziantep, t. and prov., Turkey; S.W. of Malatya; mkt.; p. (1990) 573,968 (t.), 1,140,594 (prov.).

Gazli, Uzbekistan; 96 km N.W. of Gukhara; natural gas field; pipeline to Chelyabinsk opened 1963; destroyed by major earthquake (1976); p. (1990) 8,900.

Gdansk (Danzig), c., and prov., N. Poland; Baltic pt.; on branch of Vistula; annexed to Germany 1939, massacre of POWs, 1945; restored to Poland 1945; shipbldg., machin., chemicals, metals;

Gdansk, Gdynia and Sopot admin. as single c. (Trójmiasto = tricity). Birthplace of famous Solidarity movement; p. (1995) 462,830 (c.), 1,452,227 (prov.). Shipyards closed (1997).

Gdynia, spt., Gdansk, **N. Poland**; competes with spt. of Gdansk for Polish hinterland; impt. comm., rly. and industl. ctr.; part of the Trójmiasto; p. (1995) 251,400.

Gedling, l. gov. dist., Notts., **Eng.**; Basford, Carlton and Arnold and N.E. outskirts of Nottingham; p. (2001) 111,787.

Geelong, c., Victoria, **Australia**; spt. on Corio Bay (part of Pt. Phillip Bay); expanding comm. and industl. ctr.; improved pt. facilities in 1960s, bulk grain terminal; p. (1993) 151,900 (met. a.).

Gejiu (Kokiu), t., Yunnan prov., **China**; leading tin-mng. ctr. of China.

Gela, t., S. Sicily, **Italy**; in cotton-growing a.; petrochemicals, p. (1991) 61,300.

Gelderland, prov., **Neth.**; E. and S. of Utrecht prov., a. 5,022 km²; cap. Arnhem; cereals, tobacco, cattle rearing, p. (1994) 1,851,402.

Geleen, with Sittard, met. a. Limburg. prov., N.E. of Maastricht **Neth.**; p. (1993) 34,123 (c.), (1994) 185,278 (met. a.).

Gelibolu (Gallipoli), pt. and penin. on the Dardanelles, **Turkey**; scene of unsuccessful landing by British and Anzac troops 1915; 176 km long.

Gelsenkirchen, t., N. Rhine–Westphalia, **Germany**; in Ruhr conurb. on Rhine–Herne canal; coal, ironwks., glass, chemicals, oil refining; p. (2002) 276,740.

Geneva, c., cap. of G. can., **Switzerland**; at exit of Rhône from L. Geneva; cath., univ.; former H.Q. of League of Nations; H.Q. of ILO, WHO, and Red Cross; watchmkg., jewellery, elec. gds., optical instruments; tourist resort; birthplace of Rousseau; p. (1990) 167,200 (c), 376,000 (canton).

Geneva (L. Léman), L., S.W. corner of **Switzerland**; forms a gr. crescent of water, source of poetic inspiration; 371 m a.s.l.; a. 578 km².

Génissiat, France; site of gr. barrage and hydroelec. power sta. on Rhône below Geneva.

Genoa (Genova), c., ch. pt. **Italy**; cath., univ., palaces; handles one-third of Italy's foreign tr.; pt. and airpt. expansion, shipyards, steelwks., engin., textiles, tanning; p. (1992) 667,563.

George Town, cap., **Cayman Is.**; pt.; offshore banking.

Georgetown (Demerara), c., cap. of **Guyana**; on Demerara R.; exp. sugar, cocoa, coffee, timber, gold, diamonds, bauxite; airpt. nearby; botanical gardens; p. (1999) 275,000.

George Town. *See* Penang.

Georgia, st., S.E. **USA**; one of 13 original sts.; admitted to Union 1788; st. flower Cherokee Rose, st. bird Brown Thrasher; on Atl. cst.; rising to Appalachians; impt. arable agr.; cotton and *tobacco inds.; major source of kaolin cla; b.* Atlanta (cap.), Savannah; a. 152,489 km²; p. (2002) 8,560,310.

Georgia (Gruziya), former USSR constituent rep.; rich agr., fruit, tobacco, grain; mng. inc. manganese, gold, oil; several hydroelectric power plants; coastal and mtn. resorts; active Jewish community; ethnic unrest 1989; popular uprising (the 'Rose Revolution'), 2003; cap. Tbilisi; a. 69,671 km²; p. (2004) 4,693,892.

Gera, c., cap. of G. admin. dist., **Germany**; on White Elster R.; woollens, printing; lignite mined nearby; p. (2002) 109,926.

Geraldton, spt., W. **Australia**; N. outlet for wheat belt; also exps. wool and manganese; early tomatoes; super phosphate; p. (1991) 20,587.

Germany, reunified 3 October 1990 after partition into Democratic Rep. (E. Germany) and Federal Republic (W. Germany) since 1948; N. half part of N. European Plain; rises in S. to Bavarian Alps; 2nd lgst. trading nation of world; mainly industl. with core in Ruhr conurb.; motor vehicles, chemicals, precision engin.; member of EU; tourism; 16 admin. dists. (*Länder*); cap. Berlin (seat of parliament, govt. to be decided); faced economic problems after reunification; a. 357,041 km²; p. (2004) 82,424,609.

Gers, dep. S.W. **France**; cap. Auch; grain, vines, brandy; a. 6,291 km²; p. (1990) 174,600.

Gersoppa Falls, Sharavati R., Karnataka, **India**; hgst. cascade 253 m; hydroelec. power.

Getafe, t. Madrid prov. C. **Spain**; agric. ind., geog. centre of Spain; p. (1998) 143,600.

Gezira, dist., **Sudan**, N.E. Africa; between Blue and White Niles; c. 12,173 km² capable of irrigation provided by Blue Nile at Sennar Dam; lge-scale growing of high-quality cotton; total a. c. 20,200 km².

Ghadames (Ghudamis), oasis, Sahara Desert, **Libya**; at point where Tunis, Algeria, Libya converge 480 km S.W. of Tripoli.

Ghaghara (Gogra), sacred R., **India**; trib. of Ganges, rises in Tibet, flows through Uttar Pradesh; lge. catchment a. but poorly developed floodplain; 960 km long.

Ghana, rep., W. Africa; indep. st., member of Brit. Commonwealth; tropical monsoon climate, but rainfall decreases inland; badly affected by Sahelian drought; S. Ghana more developed than N.; agr. basis of comm. economy and cocoa (of which Ghana is world's lgst producer) 60 per cent of all exp. by value; Volta R. scheme produces power from main dam at Akosombo and an aluminium smelter plant began production in 1967; reservoir decreasing with drought in Sahel reducing power production, oil refining and production, communications network based on Accra and Takoradi on cst., and inland ctr. of Kumasi; development of road network vital for expansion of comm. agr.; 3 univs.; tourism now third largest component of economy, pts. at Takoradi and Tema; cap. Accra; a. 238,539 km²; p. (2004) 20,757,032.

Ghardaia, dep., Algeria; N. of Sahara; includes Mzab valley; p. (1987) 215,955.

Ghats, mtn. ranges which border the Deccan plateau in S. India. The **Eastern Ghats** are broken by many Rs. and rise only to 1,362 m in Northern Circars. The **Western Ghats** form an almost unbroken range, reaching 2,672 m in Dodabetta in Nilgiri hills; rainfall extremely heavy; forests.

Ghaziabad, t., Uttar Pradesh, **India**; on R. Jumna opposite Delhi; p. (1991) 454,000.

Ghazipur, t., Uttar Pradesh, **N. India**; on Ganges, E. of Varanasi; p. (1991) 76,500.

Ghazni, mtn. t., E. **Afghanistan**; once cap. of empire of Mahmud, c. A.D. 1000; now mkt. t.

Ghent, c., cap. of E. Flanders prov., **Belgium**; pt. at confluence of Rs. Scheldt and Lys; cath., univ.; textiles, steel, plastics, chemicals; oil refinery; p. (1993) 229,828.

Giant's Causeway, basaltic columns on promontory of N. cst. of Moyle, **N. Ireland**.

Gibraltar, City of, Brit. terr. at W. entrance to Mediterranean; rocky I., 426 m, joined to Spain by sandy isthmus; few natural resources; economy depends on tourism, old Admiralty dockyard, services to shipping, and entrepôt tr.; Spanish govt. lays claim to terr.; new talks with Spain over terr. began, Nov. 2001; referendum (2002) rejected joint sovereignty; a. 6·5 km²; p. (2004) 27,833.

Gibraltar, Strait of, connects Mediterranean with Atl.; 13·6 km wide; of strategic importance for 24-mile rail tunnel to link with N. Africa.

Gifu, t., Central Honshu, **Japan**; cas.; fans, lanterns, textiles; tourism for cormorant fishing; p. (1990) 410,318.

Gigha, I, Argyll and Bute, **Scot.**; off W. cst. of Kintyre; 10 km by 3 km.; p. (1991) 143. Island bought by inhabitants (2001).

Gila, R., N.M. and Arizona, **USA**; trib. of R. Colorado; used for irrigation in Imperial valley; 1,040 km long.

Gilan, prov., N.W. Iran; on Caspian Sea, bounded by frmr. USSR; sub-tropical climate; agr., inc. cotton and rice; cap. Rasht; p. (1996) 2,241,900.

Gilbert Is. *See* Kiribati.

Gilgit, dist., Kashmir, **India**; mtnous., exceeding 6,000 m on N. and W.; with Ladakh links India with Tibet.

Gillingham, t., l. gov. dist., Kent, **Eng.**; 3 km E. of Chatham; on R. Medway; naval and military establishments, cement, lt. inds.; p. (1995) 95,800, (1991) 94,923 (t.).

Gippsland, dist., S.E. Victoria, **Australia**; between Dividing Range and cst.; main brown coal field supplying local power plants; intensive dairying and also mkt. gardens for Melbourne; p. (1992) 169,760.

Girgenti. *See* Agrigento.

Girona, c., cap. of G. prov., **Spain**; cath.; textiles, p. (1990) 70,900 (c.), (1998) 543,200 (prov.).

Gironde, dep., S.W. **France**; vineyards, grain, fruit, wines; cap. Bordeaux; a. 10,723 km²; p. (1999) 1,286,309.

Gironde, estuary, S.W. **France**; formed by junc.

of Rs. Garonne and Dordogne; navigable to Pauillac and Bordeaux.

Girvan, burgh, S. Ayrshire, **Scot.**; on F. of Clyde, 29 km S.W. of Ayr; summer resort; p. (2002) 6,992.

Gisborne, c. and dist., spt., N.I., **N.Z.**; on Poverty Bay, 96 km N.E. of Napier; freezing-wks.; fishing; p. (1991) 44,361 (dist.).

Giuba, R. *See* **Juba** R.

Giurgiu, t., **Romania**; pt. on Danube; opposite Ruse, Bulgaria; linked by oil pipelines with Ploiesti; p. (1992) 74,236.

Givors, t., Rhône dep., **France**; on Rhône R. 16 km S. of Lyons; mnfs. inc. glass; oil refining near by at Feyzin; p. (1990) 19,800.

Glace Bay, t., Cape Breton I., Nova Scotia, **Canada**; coal; harbour; p. (1991) 19,501.

Glacier National Park, Mon., **Canada**; mtn. scenery, resorts; a. 1,349 km².

Glacier National Park, Mon., **USA**; Rocky mtns., picturesque; a. 4,040 km².

Gladbeck, t., N. Rhine–Westphalia, **Germany**; N. of Essen; coalmng; p. (1999) 78,700.

Gladstone, t., Queensland, **Australia**; pt. exports coal to Japan; alumina plant (1973), oil storage; p. (1991) 33,447.

Glamis, v., Angus, **Scot.**; G. cas. childhood home of Queen Elizabeth the Queen Mother, and featured in Shakespeare's *Macbeth*.

Glamorgan, historic co., S. **Wales**, now divided into 8 unit. auths. inc. Cardiff and Swansea.

Glamorgan, Vale of. *See* **Gwent, Plain of**.

Glarus, can., **Switzerland**; E. of Schwyz; a. 684 km²; sheep, cheese, cottons; p. (1990) 167,200.

Glarus, t., cap. of can. G., **Switzerland**; on R. Linth, nr. Wessen; p. (1990), 5,500.

Glasgow, c., burgh, unit. auth. created in 1996, formerly part of Strathclyde, W. **Scot.**; on R. Clyde; leading spt. and 3rd lgst. c. in Gt. Britain; major problems of urban renewal; ctr. of industl. belt; shipbldg., iron and steel, heavy and lt. engin., electronics equipment, printing; univs., cath.; p. (2002) 629,501 (c.), (1995) 618,430 (unit. auth.).

Glas Maol, mtn., Angus, **Scot.**; part of the Braes of Angus; alt. 1,068 m.

Glastonbury, t., Somerset, **Eng.**; on R. Brue, ruins of 10th century abbey; nearby prehistoric lake villages; p. (1991) 7,747.

Glatz. *See* **Klodzko**.

Gleiwitz. *See* **Gliwice**.

Glen Affric, Highland, **Scot.**; 48 km S.W. of Inverness; drained E. to Moray F.; hydroelectric scheme.

Glencoe, Highland, **Scot.**; S.E. of Ballachulish; scene of massacre of MacDonalds 1692.

Glendalough, Wicklow, **R.o.I.**; scenic valley with Ls. and monastic ruins; tourism.

Glenelg, t., S. **Australia**; on St. Vincent G.; sub. of Adelaide; first free settlement in Australia.

Glen Garry, Perth and Kinross, **Scot.**; used by Perth to Inverness rly. on S. approach to Drumochter Pass.

Glen More, Scottish valley traversed by Caledonian Canal from Fort William to Inverness.

Glenrothes, t., Fife, **Scot.**, new t. (1948); electronics; p. (2002) 36,679.

Glen Roy, Highland, **Scot.**; 24 km N.E. of Fort William; remarkable terraces, remains of series of glacial lakes.

Glittertind, mtn., Opland co., S. **Norway**; highest peak in Scandinavia; alt. 2,483 m.

Gliwice (**Gleiwitz**), c., S.W. **Poland** (since 1945); coal mng. and steel ctr. of Katowice region; machin., chemicals; p. (1995) 214,612.

Glomma (**Glommen**), R., S. **Norway**, lgst. R. in Scandinavia; flows to Skaggerak; timber inds.; hydroelec. power; 400 km long.

Glossop, t., High Peak, Derbys., **Eng.**; at foot of Pennines; paper, food-canning, textile finishing; mkt.; p. (2001) 32,219.

Gloucester, cath. c., l. gov. dist., **Eng.**; on R. Severn; the Roman Glevum; cath., on site of Benedictine abbey; aircraft mftg. and repair; engin., nylon; p. (2001) 109,885 (dist.), (1991) 114,003 (c.).

Gloucester, t., Mass., **USA**; pt. at head of G. Harbour; resort, fish-processing; p. (2000) 30,270.

Gloucestershire, non-met. co., W. **Eng.**; situated around lower Severn basin, Cotswolds, Forest of Dean; sheep, dairy and fruit farming; major ctrs. of p. at Gloucester and Cheltenham; p. (2001) 564,559.

Glynde, v., Sussex, **Eng.**; nearby Tudor manor and opera house of Glyndebourne.

Gmünd. *See* **Schwäbish-Gmünd**.

Gniezno (**Gnesen**), c., W. **Poland**; E. of Poznan; first cap. of Poland (11th cent.); cath.; p. (1995) 70,977.

Goa, **India**; former Portuguese enclave; statehood conferred 1987; cap. Panaji; iron pyrites, manganese, coconuts, fish, spices, cashew nuts, salt; tourism incr. impt., ecological concerns; a. 3,693 km²; p. (2001) 1,344,000.

Gobi, steppes and stony or sandy desert, **China** and **Mongolia**; divided into two principal divs.; Shamo in Central Mongolia, and the basins of the Tarim, E. Turkestan; l. about 2,400 km (E. to W.), breadth 800–1,120 km; average elevation 1,200 m; crossed by impt. Kalgan–Ulan Bator highway.

Godalming, t., Waverley, Surrey, **Eng.**; 6 km S.W. of Guildford; first public supply of elec. 1881; Charterhouse School; p. (2001) 21,514.

Godavari, sacred R., **India**; rises in W. Ghats, flows E. across Deccan through gap in E. Ghats to Bay of Bengal; forms lge. delta; irrigation and hydroelec. power; c. 1,440 km long.

Godesberg, Bad, t., N. Rhine–Westphalia, **Germany**; part of Bonn; spa; meeting place of Chamberlain and Hitler 1938.

Godhavn, Danish settlement, Disco I., W. of **Greenland**; arctic research sta.; fish processing; p. (1990) 1,164.

Godthåb (**Nuuk**), t., admin. ctr., **Greenland**; first Danish col. 1721; sm. pt.; fish processing; p. (1990) 12,687.

Godwin-Austen Mt. *See* **K2**.

Gogmagog Hills, Cambs., **Eng.**; low chalk upland, S. of Breckland; traces of Roman entrenchment.

Gora. *See* **Ghaghara** R.

Goiânia, t., cap of Goiás st., **Brazil**; comm. and industl. ctr.; p. (1996) 998,500.

Goiás, st., central **Brazil**; mtnous, forested; stock-raising, tobacco; gold, diamonds; cap. Goiânia on Vermelho R.; a. 642,061 km²; p. (1996) 4,501,500.

Gökçeada I. (**Imbroz I.**), off W. **Turkey**, in Aegean Sea at entrance to Dardanelles; a. 280 km².

Golconda, fort and ruined c., nr. Hyderabad, S. **India**; famous for its legendary diamond troves.

Gold Coast, City of, Queensland, **Australia**; 40 km catl. a. inc. 18 townships, named 1959; rapid tourist devel. inc. Surfer's Paradise; p. (1993) 300,200.

Golden Gate, strait between San Francisco Bay and Pac. Oc., Cal., **USA**; spanned by Golden Gate Bridge, opened 1937.

Golden Triangle, a. of Britain and Europe roughly bounded by Birmingham, Frankfurt, and Paris; economic core a. of **W. Europe**.

Golden Vale, dist., Limerick, Tipperary, **R.o.I.**; drained W. to Shannon and E. to Suir; rich farming a., beef and dairy cattle, pigs.

Gold River, t., B.C., **Canada**; on W. cst. of Van couver I. at junc. of Heber and Gold Rs.; new t. 1967; p. (2000) 1,750.

Golspie, t., Highland, **Scot.**; p. (2002) 1,404.

Gomal Pass, a pass in Sulaiman ranges, **Pakistan**, leading from Indus valley to Afghanistan.

Gombe, new st. (since 1996) in north of **Nigeria**. Created from Bauchi. Headquarters at Gombe.

Gomel', c., S.E. **Belarus**; on R. Sozh, trib. of Dnieper; R. pt., agr. ctr.; engin., chemicals, clothing inds.; p. (1990) 506,100.

Gomera, I., **Canaries**; 21 km S.W. Tenerife; cap. San Sebastian.

Gondar, t. N.W. **Ethiopia**; N. of L. Tana; old capital; airport; p. (1994) 112,250.

Goodwin Sands, dangerous sandbanks off E. cst of Kent, **Eng.**; shielding the Down roadstead.

Goodwood, v., West Sussex, **Eng.**; racecourse and motor racing; home of Dukes of Richmond.

Goole, t., **Eng.**; second pt. of Hull on Humber; shipbldg., flour milling, fertilisers, alum and dextrine mftg.; p. (1991) 19,410.

Goonhilly Downs, Cornwall, **Eng.**; satellite communications sta. of Post Office.

Gorakhpur, t., Uttar Pradesh, **India**; on Rapti R., N. of Varanasi; grain, timber; fertilisers; univ.; p. (1991) 506,000.

Gori, t., central **Georgia**; at confluence of Bolshoy, Liakhvi, and Kura Rs.; birthplace of Stalin; p. (1990) 69,600.

Goring Gap, Berks./Oxon., **Eng.**; where R. Thames cuts through Chilterns and Berkshire Downs.

Gorizia (**Görz**), c., cap. of Gorizia prov., N.E. **Italy**; on Slovenia border; cas.; agr. mkt., fruit, wine; textile machin.; p. (1991) 38,500.

Gorki or **Gorky**. *See* **Nizhniy Novgorod**.

Görlitz, t. Brandenburg, **Germany**; on W. Neisse on Polish border; lignite mines; textile mills; mystic Jacob Boehme lived here; p. (2002) 60,264.

Gorlovka, t., **Ukraine**; in Donets Basin; coal, chemicals, engin.; oil pipeline connects with Grozny oilfields; p. (1990) 337,900.

Gorno-Altai, aut. region, S.E. Altai terr., **Russia**; in Altai mtns. on Mongolian border; cap. Gorno-Altaisk; forested, pastoral agr., mng. (gold, manganese, mercury); a. 92,567 km; p. (2000) 204,800.

Gorno-Altaisk, t., **Russia**; cap. of Gorno-Altai aut. region; nr. Chuya highway to Mongolia; food-processing of agr. prod. from region; p. (2000) 52,200.

Gorno Badakhshan, aut. region, S.E. **Tajikistan**; in Pamirs, bordered by China and Afghanistan; mng. (gold, mica, salt, limestone); livestock; cap. Khorog; a. 63,688 km²; p. (1990) 164,300.

Gornyy Snezhnogorsk, t., **Russia**, new t. in Siberia Arctic on R. Hantaiki, 56 km W.N.W. Komsomolsk; tin-mng

Gorseinon, t., **Swansea**, S. **Wales**; nr. Loughour estuary, 6 km N.W. of Swansea; former steelwks., zinc refineries; p. (1991) 18,917.

Gorzów Wielkopolski (**Landesberg an der Warthe**), c., Gorzow prov. W. **Poland** (since 1945); industl. ctr.; lignite mines; p. (1995) 124,932 (c.), 509,868 (prov.).

Gosainthan (**Xixabangma Feng**), mtn. massif, Nepal–Tibet (**China**) border; part of Himalayas; rises to 8,091 m.

Gosforth, t., sub. to Newcastle upon Tyne, Tyne and Wear, **Eng.**; p. (2001) 23,620.

Goslar, t., Lower Saxony, **Germany**; mng. ctr. at foot of Harz mtns.; tourism; p. (2002) 44,123.

Gosport, t., l. gov. dist., Hants., **Eng.**; naval depot W. of Portsmouth to which it is linked by ferry; marine engin.; p. (2001) 76,415 (dist.), (2001) 69,348 (t.).

Göta, R., **Sweden**; flows from L. Vänern to the Kattegat; also canal connecting L. Vänern with the Baltic; the G. Canal provides a popular tourist trip from Stockholm to Göteborg.

Göteborg or **Gothenburg**, c., cap. of Göteborg and Bohus, S.W. **Sweden**; at mouth of R. Göta on Kattegat; second c. in Sweden for commerce and ind.; univ.; shipbldg., oil refining; deepwater tanker terminal; p. (1992) 433,811 (t.), 747,849 (co.).

Gotha, t., Erfurt, **Germany**; iron, machin., engin., musical instruments, textiles, porcelain, printing, cartography; p. (2002) 47,922.

Gotham, v., Notts., **Eng.**; gypsum mng. and plaster wks; p. (1991) 1,638.

Gothenburg. See **Göteborg**.

Gotland, I. in the Baltic, **Sweden**; many historic bldgs.; cap. Visby; tourism; a. 3,173 km²; p. (1992) 57,578.

Göttingen, t., Lower Saxony, **Germany**; univ.; scientific instruments, pharmaceutics, film studios; p. (2002) 123,822.

Gottwaldov. See **Zlin**.

Gouda, t., S. Holland, **Neth.**; on R. IJssel, 18 km from Rotterdam; cheese, candles, ceramics, pipes; p. (1994) 69,917.

Gough I., Atl. Oc. dependency of **St. Helena**; breeding ground of the great shearwater; guano.

Goulburn, t., N.S.W., **Australia**; commands route across Gr. Dividing Range; in agr. dist. W. of Sydney; cath.; wool, shoes; p. (1992) 155,100 (met. a.).

Goulburn Is., N.T., **Australia**; 2 sm. Is. off N. cst. of Arnhem Land; Methodist Mission sta.

Gourock, burgh, Inverclyde, **Scot.**; on F. of Clyde, 3 km W. of Greenock; ferry to Dunoon; resort; p. (2002) 11,511.

Gove Peninsula, N.T., **Australia**; N.E. extremity of Arnhem Land; giant bauxite and alumina production complex (1968); model t. of Nhulunbuy.

Gower, peninsula, Swansea, **Wales**; tourism.

Gozo, I. in Mediterranean, belonging to **Malta**; the anc. Gaulos; surrounded by perpendicular cliffs; a. 67 km²; p. (1990) 26,064.

Grado-Aquileia, t., Friuli-Venezia Giulia, N.E. **Italy**; pleasure resort and former Roman spt.; early Christian mosaics and antiquities; Grado joined to mainland by bridge.

Graham Land, part of **British Antarctic Territory**; mtnous., icebound; discovered 1832.

Grahamstown, t., Eastern Cape Prov., S. **Africa**; univ. cath.; p. (1991) 19,800.

Graian Alps, mtns. between Savoie, **France**, and Piedmount, **Italy**; hgst. point Gran Paradiso,

4,063 m.

Grain Coast, name formerly applied to cst. of **Liberia**, W. Africa; "grain" refers to spices.

Grammichele, t., E. Sicily, **Italy**; 37 km S.W. of Catania; planned settlement after 1968 earthquake; p. (2000 est.) 14,200.

Grampians, mtns. of **Scot.**; forming natural bdy. between Highlands and Lowlands; inc. Ben Nevis, the hgst. peak (1,344 m), the Cairngorms and Schiehallion.

Granada, t., W. **Nicaragua**; on L. Nicaragua; in rich agr. region; distilling, soap, furniture; p. (1995) 74,400.

Granada, c., cap. of G. prov., S. **Spain**; in Andalusia, at foot of Sierra Nevada; formerly cap. of Moorish kingdom of G.; univ., cath., famous 14th cent. Alhambra; tourism; first mosque since 1492 opened in 2003; p. (1998) 241,500.

Granada, prov., S. **Spain**; traversed by Sierra Nevada; wheat, olives, textiles, liqueurs, paper; a. 12,530 km², p. (1998) 801,200.

Gran Chaco, extensive lowland plain, **Argentina**, **Paraguay**, and **Bolivia**, between Andes and Paraguay-Paraná Rs.; hot, wet, swampy region with forests containing quebracho trees, a source of tannin; potential for petroleum.

Grand Banks, submarine plateau, extending S.E. from Newfoundland, **Canada**; a. 1,295,000 km²; impt. cod fisheries.

Grand Canal, canal, N. **China**; c. 1,600 km long from Tianjing to Hangzhou; built between A.D. 605–18 and 1282–92; rebuilt for navigation and flood control.

Grand Canary, I., **Canaries**; cap. Las Palmas; tomatoes, bananas, potatoes; tourism; extinct volcanoes.

Grand Cayman I., **Cayman Is.**, W.I.; a. 220 km²; coconuts; cap. Georgetown; p. (1999) 37,100.

Grand Combin, mtn., **Switzerland**; part of Pennine Alps nr. Italian border; alt. 4,320 m.

Grand Coulee Dam, Wash., **USA**; on Columbia R., 176 km below Spokane; one of lgst. concrete dams in world, producing 1,924 mW hydroelec. power; reservoir (Franklin D. Roosevelt Lake) recreational a.; supplies irrigation water to 4,900 km² between Rs. Columbia and Snake.

Grand Falls, t., Newfoundland, **Canada**; newsprint; falls provide hydroelectric power; p. (1991) 14,693 (with Windsor).

Grand Island, t., Nebraska, **USA**; cattle and grain t.; p. (2000) 42,900.

Grand Prairie. See **Black Prairie**.

Grand Rapids, c., Mich., **USA**; on Grand R.; furniture mkg., car and aircraft parts, chemicals, paper; p. (2000) 197,800 (c.), 688,000 (met. a.).

Grand R., Mich., **USA**; enters L. Mich. at Grand Haven, navigable to Grand Rapids; hydroelec. power; 400 km long.

Grand Turk, I., cap. of **Turks and Caicos** Is.; p. (1990) 3,761.

Grange, t., South Lakeland, Cumbria, **Eng.**; on N. cst. of Morecambe Bay; popular summer resort.

Grangemouth, burgh, Falkirk, **Scot.**; on F. of Forth; shipbldg. and repair, marine engin., oil refining, projected oil tanker terminal; petroleum prods., chemicals, pharmaceutics; electronics and elec. ind.; oil pipeline to Finnart; p. (2002) 17,771.

Granite City, Ill., **USA**; iron and steel, tinplate, rly. engin., chemicals; p. (2000) 31,300.

Gran Sasso d'Italia, rugged limestone highlands, Abruzzi e Molise, central **Italy**, in highest part of Apennines, rising to 2,923 m in Monte Corno; Mussolini was rescued from here by German paratroopers 1943; Aquila at foot of Gran Sasso winter sports ctr.

Grantham, t., S. Kesteven, Lincs., **Eng.**; on Witham R.; tanning, agr. machin., engin., brewing, malting, expanded t.; birthplace of Margaret Thatcher; p. (2001) 34,592.

Grantown-on-Spey, burgh, Highland, **Scot.**; on R. Spey; resort; p. (2002) 2,166.

Grasmere, v., Cumbria, **Eng.**; at head of Grasmere L.; home of Wordsworth.

Grasse, t., Alpes-Maritimes dep., S.E. **France**, in Provence in hills above Cannes; perfumers; birthplace of Fragonard; p. (1999) 43,722.

Graubünden. See **Grisons**.

Graudenz. See **Grudziadz**.

's-Gravenhage. See **Hague**.

Graves, Pointe de, N. point of Médoc peninsula,

France; in famous wine dist.

Gravesend, spt., Gravesham, Kent, **Eng.**; S. bank R. Thames facing Tilbury; pilot sta. for Port of London; paper, cement; oil refinery projected; p. (2001) 53,045.

Gravesham, l. gov. dist., Kent, **Eng.**; based on Gravesend and surrounding dist.; p. (2001) 95,717.

Graz, c., cap. of Styria, **Austria**; on R. Mur at foothills of Alps; second lgst. c.; univs. (3); cath.; machin., iron and steel, rly. wks.; p. (1991) 232,155.

Great Altai, range of mtns., lying mainly in **Outer Mongolia** but also in Western Siberia, **Russia**; rising to 4,200 m.

Great Artesian Basin, Central **Australia**; underlies plains of Queensland, N.S.W., S. **Australia**; supplies water for cattle and sheep stations; too saline for use in some a. and too hot in others (cooling towers necessary); a. 2 million km.²

Great Atlas (Haut Atlas), mtn., N.W. **Africa**; alt. c. 2,000 m; part of the Atlas mtns.

Great Australian Bight, gr. cstl. indentation s. of Nullarbor Plain, **Australia**.

Great Barrier Reef, coral reef barrier off N.E. cst. of **Australia**; 1,600 km long, 120–160 km from cst.; currently being eaten away by the star fish, *Acanthaster planci*; much marine pollution; many reef Is. form Nat. parks; World Heritage area since 1981.

Great Basin, high plateau region between the Wasatch and Sierra Nevada mtns., **USA**; inc. most of Nevada, parts of Utah, Cal., Idaho, Ore., Wyo.; drainage ctr. Great Salt Lake; a. 543,900 km²; much desert; sparse p.

Great Bear Lake, lge. L., N.W. Terr., **Canada**; c. 280 km long; a. 36,260 km²; outlet through Great Bear R. to Mackenzie R.

Great Belt (Store Bælt), strait. **Denmark**; separates Fyn I. from Sjaelland I.; sinuous shape makes navigation difficult; rly. ferry at narrowest point (18 km) between Nyborg and Korsør; 64 km long; proposed bridge.

Great Britain. *See* **England, Scotland, Wales, British Isles.**

Great Dividing Range, mtn. system, E. **Australia**; extends, under different local names, from Queensland to Victoria and separates E. cst. plains from interior; reaches max. alt. in Mt. Koskiusko (2,228 m), in Australian Alps, on bdy. between Victoria and N.S.W.

Great Driffield, t., E. Riding of Yorks, **Eng.**; on Yorks. Wolds 21 km N. of Beverley; p. (1991) 9,463.

Great Dunmow, mkt. t., Uttlesford, Essex, **Eng.**; on R. Chelmer; 16 km N.W. of Chelmsford.

Greater Manchester, former met. co., pt., N.W. **Eng.**; lge. urban a. centred on major comm. ctr. of M., with former cotton spinning ts. to N., inc. Bolton, Bury and Rochdale; dormitory ts. to S.; former concentration on textile mftg. now reduced and inds. diversified; major industl. estate at Trafford Park; p. (2001) 2,482,328.

Great Falls, c., Mont., **USA**; on Missouri R.; lgst. c. in st.; mkt. for irrigated farming a.; ctr. of hydroelectric power, called the "electric city"; copper- and oil-refining, flour mills; p. (1996) 57,758.

Great Fisher Bank, submarine sandbank in N. Sea; 320 km E. of Aberdeen, 160 km S.W. of Stavanger; valuable fishing-ground; depth of water, from 45–75 m.

Great Gable, mtn., Cumbria, **Eng.**; alt. 899 m.

Great Grimsby, spt., N.E. Lincs., **Eng.**; on S. bank of R. Humber; major distant waters fish. pt.; food-processing; p. (2001) 87,574.

Great Harwood, t., Hyndburn, Lancs., **Eng.**; 8 km N.E. of Blackburn; textiles, aero-engin.; p. (1991) 10,562.

Great Lake, Tasmania, **Australia**; lgst. freshwater L. in Australia.

Great Lakes, N. **America**; 5 freshwater Ls.; Superior, Michigan, Huron, Erie, Ontario; glacial genesis; frozen 4 to 5 months in winter; traffic in cereals, iron, coal, etc.; major ctr. of heavy inds.; resorts; serious pollution; a. 248,640 km².

Great Plains, lowland a. of central **N. America**; extending E. from Rocky mtns., and S. from Mackenzie to S. Texas.

Great Rift Valley, geological fault system extending from S.W. Asia to E. Africa, 4,800 km in l.; inc. L. Tiberias (Sea of Galilee), Jordan

valley, Dead Sea, G. of Aqaba, Red Sea, and chain of Ls., notably L. Rudolf and L. Malawi; a branch runs through Ls. Tanganyika, Mobutu and Edward; used for geothermal power.

Great Salt Lake, shallow salty L., N. Utah, **USA**; in Great Basin plateau of N. America; remnant of L. Bonneville; alt. 1,286 m; varies in size and depth; receives Bear, Jordan and Beaver Rs.; many Is., no outlet.

Great Sandy Desert, W. **Australia**; mostly sand-hills, stony in ctr.; one of A. 3 great deserts.

Great Slave Lake, N.W. Terr., **Canada**; a. 28,490 km²; 496 km long; drained by Mackenzie R.; navigable.

Great Smoky Mtns., Tenn., **USA**; with Blue Ridge mtns. form E. zone of Appalachian mtn. system; hgst peak Clingmans Dome 2,026 m; largely preserved as Nat Park.

Great Torrington, t., Torridge, Devon, **Eng.**; on R. Torridge; mkt., processing of agr. prod.; p. (1991) 4,073.

Great Wall of China, wall built in N. **China** along S. edge of Mongolian plateau to keep out invading Mongols; length 2,400 km; begun in Ch'in dynasty by Shih Huang Ti, c. 228 B.C.; present form dates from Ming dynasty (1368–1644).

Great Yarmouth, pt., l. gov. dist., Norfolk, **Eng.**; at mouth of R. Yare; holiday resort; fish and food processing plants; base for N. Sea gas; p. (2001) 90,810 (dist.), (2001) 58,032 (t.).

Greece, rep., S.E. Europe; mtnous. peninsula, between Mediterranean and Aegean Sea, inc. many sm. Is. to S., lgst. Crete; inds. increasingly impt. but agr. prods. still ch. exp. (tobacco, olive oil, cotton, citrus fruit, wine); only 25 per cent a. cultivable; economy also helped by lge. merchant fleet and tourism; deposed king in exile; executive power held by military junta 1967–74; 10th member of EU (1981); territorial disputes with Turkey over Aegean islands and tension over Cyprus; cap. Athens; a. 132,561 km²; p. (2004) 10,647,529.

Green Bay, c. E. Wisconsin, **USA**; oldest settlement in Wisconsin at mouth of R. Fox; p. (1996) 102,076.

Greenland, I., between Arctic Oc. and Baffin Bay; lofty ice-capped plateau; peopled by coastal settlements of Inuits; fisheries; whale oil, seal skins; lge. uranium deposits, potential for petroleum; first onshore drilling (1984) in Scoresby Land; some coal, lead, zinc; US base at Thule; part of Danish kingdom; internal self-government 1979; growing calls for indep.; cap. Nuuk (Godthåb); a. 2,175,600 km² of which 1,833,720 km² are under a permanent ice-cap; ice-cap now receding; second lgst. island in world; p. (2004) 56,384.

Greenland Sea, Arctic Oc., between Greenland and Spitzbergen; ice-covered.

Greenock, spt., burgh, Inverclyde, **Scot.**; on S. shore of F. of Clyde, 40 km W. of Glasgow; container facilities, shipbldg.; sugar refining, woollens, chemicals, aluminium casting, tin-plate inds.; birthplace of James Watt; p. (2002) 45,467.

Green River, Wyo., Utah, **USA**, rises in Wind R. Range (major watershed in Rockies); flows via spectacular scenery to Colorado R.; impt. routeway; 1,168 km long.

Greensboro', c., N.C., **USA**; cotton, tobacco, chemicals; regional financial ctr.; educational institutes; p. (2000) 223,891 (c.), 942,000 (met. a. inc. Winston-Salem-High Point).

Greenville, t., S.C., **USA**; univ.; industl. and comm. ctr.; textile mills, farm prod. processing; p. (1990) 58,282 (t.), 641,000 (met. a. with Spartanburg).

Greenwich, inner bor., London, **Eng.**; inc. most of former bor. of Woolwich on S. bank of R. Thames; famous for its hospital, observatory (now moved to Cambridge) and R.N. College (now closed); univ.; longitudes conventionally calculated from Greenwich meridian; site of Millennium Exhibition and Village; new community planned on Greenwich peninsula; maritime Greenwich now World Heritage Site; p. (2001) 214,403.

Greenwich Village, lower Manhattan, N.Y. city, **USA**; bohemian quarter.

Greifswald, spt., Mecklenburg - West Pomerania, **Germany**; on Baltic inlet; shipbldg., textiles, wood inds.; p. (1999) 57,700.

Grenada, W.I., most S. of Windward Is.; inc. Southern Grenadine Is.; known as the "spice islands" as major exp. is nutmeg; cloves and vanilla also grown; sugar and sugar prods.;

cotton-ginning; US invasion 1983, troops left 1985. cap. St. George's; former Brit. col., achieved indep. 1974; Pt. Salinas airport opened (1984); a. 344 km²; p. (2004) 89,357.

Grenadines, gr. of over 100 sm. Windward Is., W.I., attached to **Grenada** and **St. Vincent and the Grenadines**.

Grenoble, c., cap of Isère dep., S.E. **France**; on Isère R. at foot of Alps; univ.; thriving cultural and scientific ctr.; impt. hydroelectric ctr.; science-based inds., joint Franco-German nuclear research reactor; gloves, paper, cement, liqueurs; tourism based on skiing; p. (1999) 151,887.

Gretna (Green), v., Dumfries and Galloway, Scot.; on Eng. border; famous as place of runaway marriages until 1940; p. (2002) 2,705.

Greymouth, spt., S.I., **N.Z.**; on W. cst. at mouth of Grey R.; ch. t. prov. of Westland; grew with gold mng., now coal and timber; p. (1991) 10,600.

Grimaldi, caves, N.W. **Italy**; remains of prehistoric man, late Paleolithic, found there.

Grimsby. See **Great Grimsby**.

Gris-Nez, C., N.E. **France**; nearest point on Fr. cst. to Dover.

Grisons (Graubünden), can., E. **Switzerland**; region of glaciers and magnificent peaks; ch. resorts Davos, Arosa, St. Moritz; Swiss Nat. Park; lgst. can.; sparse p.; ctr. Romansch language; a. 7,112 km²; p. (1990) 169,000.

Grodno, c., W. **Belarus**; pt. on Neman R.; a Polish t. until 1939; machine parts, cloth; historic bldgs.; p. (1990) 277,000.

Groningen, c., cap. of G. prov., **Neth.**; univ.; impt. trading ctr.; p. (1994) 170,535 (c.), 210,269 (met. a.).

Groningen, prov., N.E. **Neth.**; agr. and dairying; major natural gas deposits at Slochteren; a. 2,157 km²; p. (1994) 556,607.

Groote Eylandt, I., G. of Carpentaria; off cst. of N.T., **Australia**; aboriginal reserve; manganese ore-mng.

Grosseto, t., cap. of G. prov., Tuscany, **Italy**; cath.; agr. mkt.; severely affected by floods 1966; p. (1991) 71,300.

Gross Glockner, mtn. (3,801 m) and pass (2,370 m), **Austria**, part of Hohe Tauern range; hgst. peak in Austria. cap. Chechersop.

Grozny, t., cap. Chechen rep. **Russia**; on R. Terek; naphtha wells, refinery, engin.; starting point of oil pipelines to Makhachkala, Tuapse and Gorlovka; fell to Russian attack 1995; p. (1989) 400,000.

Grudziadz (Graudenz), t., on R. Vistula, Torun prov., **Poland**; mftg.; p. (1995) 102,948.

Grünberg. See **Zielona Góra**.

Gruyères, dist., can. Fribourg, **Switzerland**; cheese.

Gruziya. See **Georgia**.

Guadalajara, c., cap. of Jalisco st., W. **Mexico**; c. 1,500 m high; impt. industl. and comm. ctr.; textiles, agr. processing, traditional pottery and glassware; cath.; gas pipeline from Salamanca; health resort; p. (1990) 2,846,720.

Guadalajara, c., cap. of G. prov., **Spain**; on Henares R., N. of Madrid; palace of Mendoza family; battle in Spanish Civil War, March 1937, fought nearby; p. (1990) 63,600 (c.), (1998) 159,300 (prov.).

Guadalcanal, volcanic I., Pac. Oc.; lgst. of Solomon Is.; jungle and mtns.; exp. copra; ch. t. Honiara.

Guadalquivir, R., S. **Spain**; flows through Andalusia via Seville to Atl.; c. 560 km long; hydroelec. plants; agr.

Guadalupe Hidalgo, place of pilgrimage, N.W. Mexico City, **Mexico**; basilica and shrine; treaty ending Mexican-U.S. war signed here 1848.

Guadarrama, Sierra de, mtn. range, central **Spain**; rugged, forest covered; affects Madrid's climate; reaches 2,431 m.

Guadeloupe, overseas dep. France, **W.I.**; comprises most S. of Leeward gr., Basse-Terre, Grande-Terre, Marie-Galante and other Is.; economy based on sugar exports to France; rapidly rising p. aggravates process of econ. development; attempts to develop tourism and food-processing inds.; ch. comm. ctr. and pt. Pointe à Pitre (Grande Terre); cap. Basse-Terre; a. 1,748 km²; p. (2004) 444,515.

Guadiana, R., forms part of Spanish and Portuguese frontier; flows into G. of Cádiz; Estremadura valley reclamation scheme; 816 km long.

Guam, I., U.S. air and naval base in W. Pac.; developing tourist ind.; free-port and tax incentives aid investment; ch. t. Agaña; a. 541 km²; p. (2004) 166,090.

Guanajuato, st., central **Mexico**; average elevation 1,800 m; mng. (silver, gold, tin, copper, iron, lead,

opals); a. 30,572 km²; p. (1990) 3,980,204.

Guanajuato, cap. of G. st., **Mexico**; 1,990 m high in gorge; resort; p. (1990) 113,580.

Guangdong (Kwantung), prov., S. **China**; on S. China Sea; cap. Guangzhou; occupied by delta of Xijiang and its confluents; Hong Kong in estuary; tropical monsoon climate; densely p. on R. plains and valley slopes; intensive farming of rice, sugar, fruits; 2 Special Economic Zones to encourage foreign investment; a. 221, 308 km²; p. (1994) 66,910,000.

Guangzhou (Canton), c., cap. Guangdong prov., S. **China**; industl. and educational ctr.; mnfs. inc. steel, ships, paper, cement; univ.; former treaty pt. and major spt. of S. China but site on Zhujiang R. delta results in silting and expensive harbour wks., hence Chinese interest in Hong Kong; ctr. of revolutionary movement from days of Sun Yat-Sen; p. (1994) 3,114,000.

Guang Zhuang (Kwangsi Chuang), aut. region, S. **China**; borders on Vietnam; cap. Nanning; drained by Xijiang and trits., ther most imbt. crop; timber; home of the Zhuang people (over 7 million); a. 221,321 km²; p. (1994) 44,550,000.

Guantánamo, c., S.E. **Cuba**; sugar, coffee, bananas, cacao; pt. at Caimanera on G. Bay; controversial US detention centre; p. (1990) 200,381.

Guaporé, R., **Brazil**; rises in Mato Grosso st., forms Brazil-Bolivia bdy. before joining the Mamoré; length 1,440 km.

Guarulhos, c., **Brazil**; N.E. of São Paulo; mechanical and electrical engin.; benefits from rapid industl. growth of São Paulo; p. (1996) 972,800.

Guatemala, rep., Central America; straddles Central American isthmus; interior mtnous. with temperate climate; coastal lowlands hot and humid; economy based on agr., coffee accounting for half exp.; timber exploitation, food processing; two oil refineries; trades mainly with USA, ch. pts. Puerto Barrios, San José, Santo Tomas de Castilla; prolonged civil war, peace accord 1996; cap. Guatemala City; a. 108,889 km²; p. (2004) 14,280,596.

Guatemala City, c., cap. of G. rep.; cath., univ.; fruit and vegetable mkts.; coffee tr.; remains Mayan civilisation; partially destroyed by earthquake (1976); p. (2000) 3,242,000 (met. a.).

Guayaquil, ch. pt., **Ecuador**; cap. of Guayas prov. on Guayas R., nr. Bay of G.; univ., cath.; sawmills, foundries, machin., brewing, oil refinery; p. (2000) 2,293,000 (met. a.).

Guayas, prov., **Ecuador**; cst. lowlands; plantations for coffee, cocoa, bananas, rice; cap. Guayaquil; p. (1990) 2,515,146.

Guelph, t., Ont., **Canada**; on Speed R.; univ.; mkt. ctr. in rich farming a.; cloth, elec. equipment; p. (1996) 105,420.

Guernica, sm. t., Vizcaya prov., **Spain**; bombed by Germans in 1937 in Spanish Civil War (famous painting by Picasso).

Guernsey, I., Channel Is., between cst. of France and Eng.; tomatoes, grapes (under glass), flowers, cattle, tourist resort, t. and ch. spt. St. Peter Port; banking; a. 6,335 ha; p. (2004) 65,031.

Guerrero, st., S. **Mexico**; cst. mtnous.; cereals, cotton, coffee, tobacco; cap. Chilpancingo; ch. pt. Acapulco; a. 64,452 km; p. (1990) 2,622,067.

Guiana Highlands, plateau, S. **America**; extend c. 1,440 km from E. to W. across S. parts of Venezuela, Guyana, Surinam, Fr. Guiana; steep sides, rounded tops c. 900 m but rise to 2,852 m in Mt. Roraima; chiefly composed of crystalline rocks rich in minerals.

Guienne, former prov., **France**, partly coincides with the Aquitaine basin (q.v.); controlled by England 1154-1451.

Guildford, co. t., l. gov. dist., Surrey, **Eng.**; 48 km S.W. London; on gap cut by R. Wey through N. Downs, cath., univ.; vehicles, agr. implements, lt. inds.; residtl., cas.; p. (2001) 129,701 (dist.), (2001) 69,400 (t.).

Guilin (Kweilin), c., Guangxi, **China**; on R. Li; univ.; textiles, sugar refining, timber; noted for its beautiful setting; p. (1994) 399,000.

Guinea, rep., W. Africa; climate hot and humid on cst. but temperate in higher interior; 95 per cent p. engaged in agr., but bauxite dominates exp. from deposits at Boké, (world's second largest producer); hydroelectric dam and aluminium smelter at Konkouré; pt. at Kamsar for mineral exp.; major spt. at cap. Conakry; a. 245,861 km²; p. (2004) 9,246,462.

Guinea, gen. name for W. African coastlands from Senegal to Angola.

Guinea-Bissau, formerly Portuguese Guinea, W. Africa; indep. 1974; cap. Bissau; poor econ. infrastructure; no manf. inds.; depends on agr. of rice, ground-nuts and stock raising; cst. edged by mangroves; offshore oil potential; a. 36,125 km²; p. (2004) 1,388,363.

Guinea, Spanish. See **Equatorial Guinea**.

Guinea Current, ocean current, flows W. to E. along Guinea cst., diverted away from cst. in Bight of Benin by C. Three Points.

Guinea, Gulf of, arm of Atl. Oc. formed by gr. bend of cst. of W. Africa between Ivory Coast and Gabon; Bight of Benin and Bight of Bonny are inner bays.

Guipúzcoa, smallest prov. **Spain**; cap. San Sebastian; on B of Biscay and French border; a. 1,997 km²; p. (1998) 676,400.

Guisborough, t., Redcar and Cleveland, **Eng.**; at foot of Cleveland Hills; former ctr. of iron mng.; 12th cent. abbey ruins; p. (1991) 18,156.

Guiyang (Kweiyang), c. and cap., Guizhou prov., **China**; univ.; comm. and industl.; coal; iron and steel, chemicals; p. (1994) 1,131,000.

Guizhou (Kweichow), inland prov., S.W. **China**; upland a. with p. concentrated in valley urban areas; cap. Guiyang; cereals, tung oil; forestry; coal, mercury; a. 176,480 km²; p. (1994) 33,800,000.

Gujarat, st., **India**; cap. Gandhinagar.; oil development in Cambay area; fertiliser plant projected; devastated by earthquake, 2001; communal violence, 2002; a. 187,115 km²; p. (2001) 50,597,000.

Gujranwala, c. **Pakistan**; N. of Lahore; power plant, engin.; p. (1998) 1,217,600.

Gujrat, t., Rawalpindi, **Pakistan**; agr. ctr., handicraft inds.; p. (1981) 154,000.

Gulbarga, t., Karnataka, **India**; cotton, flour, paint; (1991) 304,000.

Gulf Stream, warm current of the Atl. Oc., issuing from G. of Mexico by Fla. Strait.

Guntur, c., Andhra Pradesh, **India**; on E. cst. N. of Madras; cotton mkt.; p. (1991) 273,000.

Guryev. See **Atyrau**.

Gütersloh, t., N. Rhine–Westphalia, **Germany**; nr. Bielefeld; silk and cotton inds.; famous for its Pumpernickel (Westphalian rye bread), machin., furniture, publishing, metallurgy; p. (2002) 95,459.

Guwahati, t., **India**; temporary cap. of Assam being developed in E. suburb of Dispur; univ.; silk, cotton, lace, oil refinery; pipeline from Barauni; p. (1991) 577,591.

Guyana, rep., N. cst. S. America; former Brit. col.; largely covered by dense jungle, p. concentrated on narrow coastal belt; economy based on agr., especially sugar and rice; forestry inds. limited by lack of transport; impt. bauxite deposits; high birth rate creates social and economic problems, especially on overpopulated coastal belt; ethnic tension (1998); airport at Timehri; univ. at Turkeyen; cap. Georgetown; a. 214,970 km²; p. (2004) 705,803.

Gwalior, t., Madhya Pradesh, **India**; adjoins Lashkar (q.v.); dominated by rock of Gwalior with Jain sculptures; p. (1991) 691,000.

Gwent, Plain of (Vale of Glamorgan), lowland dist., S. **Wales**; lies S. of moorland of S. Wales coalfield, extends E. into Monmouthshire; fertile soils; mixed farming except in industl. areas of Cardiff, Barry.

Gwynedd, N.W. **Wales**, unit. auth. created in 1996 from former l. gov. dists. of Arfon, Dwyfor and Meirionnydd; mtnous. a. except cst.; sparse p. inland where hill farming; inc. Snowdonia Nat. Park, Lleyn Penin., and ts. of Bangor and Caernarfon; p. (2001) 116,843.

Gyandzha, (Kirovabad) c., W. **Azerbaijan**; on Gyandzha R.; industl. ctr.; textiles, agr. implements, wine; copper and manganese mines; aluminium plant; p. (1990) 281,000.

Győr, t., **Hungary**; at confluence of Rs. Raba and Danube; cath.; textile ctr., rolling stock, chemicals, machine tools; p. (1997) 127,000.

H

Haarlem, c., cap. of N. Holland prov., **Neth.**; nr. N. Sea cst.; tulip-growing, textiles, printing; 15th cent. church; p. (1994) 150,213 (c.), 214,152 (met. a.).

Hackney, inner bor., N.E. London, **Eng.**; incorporates former bors. of Shoreditch and Stoke Newington; furniture, clothing, p. (2001) 202,824.

Haddington, burgh, E. Lothian, **Scot.**; on R. Tyne, 26 km E. of Edinburgh; woollen mnf.; grain mkt., corn mills, lt. engin., hosiery; p. (2002) 8,851.

Hadhramaut, governorate, **Yemen**; ch. pt. and c. Al Mukalla; fertile coastal valley; frankincense, aloes, tobacco, shawls, carpets; p. (1986) 537,095.

Hadleigh, t., Babergh, Suffolk, **Eng.**; mkt.; flourmilling; p. (1991) 6,595.

Hadrian's Wall, part of frontier barrier, N. **Eng.**; stretching across Tyne–Solway isthmus, 118 km long. See **Roman Walls, Section L**.

Hagen, t., N. Rhine-Westphalia, **Germany**; N.E. of Wuppertal; iron, steel, chemicals, textiles, paper; p. (2002) 202,060.

Hagerstown, t., Md., **USA**; machin., furniture, chemicals, aircraft; p. (1990) 35,445.

Hagersville, t., Ont., **Canada**; gypsum producer.

Hague, The, or **'s-Gravenhage** or **Den Haag**, c., S. Holland, **Neth.**; seat of government; permanent court of international justice; admin. ctr.; urban inds., machin. and metal wares; engin., printing; now home of International War Crimes Tribunal; p. (1998) 442,800.

Haifa, c., ch. spt., **Israel**; on Bay of Acre at foot of Mt. Carmel; terminus of Iraq oil pipeline; oil refining and heavy inds.; p. (1992) 251,000.

Haikou (Hoihow), c., ch. pt. of Hainan I., Guangdong prov., **China**. p. (1994) 365,000.

Hail, t., and oasis, Nejd, **Saudi Arabia**; p. (1992) 176,800.

Hailsham, mkt. t., Wealden, East Sussex, **Eng.**; 8 km N. of Eastbourne; p. (1991) 18,426.

Hainan, I., S. cst. of **China**; densely wooded; monsoon climate; seafood cultivation; sugarcane, rubber, peanuts, sesame main crops; recent industrial development; food processing, cement, electronics; a. 36,193 km²; p. (1994) 6,910,000.

Hainaut, prov., **Belgium**; adjoining N.E. border of France; industl. and agr.; coal- and iron-mines; a. 3,719 km²; p. (1993) 1,285,934.

Haiphong, c., ch. pt., **Vietnam**; on Red R. delta; comm. and trading ctr.; cotton, thread, soap, glass, enamel ware, fish-canning; former naval base of Fr. Indo-China; p. (1992) 783,000.

Haiti, rep., W.I., W. third of I. of Hispaniola; tropical climate modified by alt.; agr. basis of economy; coffee accounts for 45 per cent exp.; irrigation scheme in Artibonite valley; unexploited mineral resources, some bauxite mng. and exp.; sm.-scale inds.; well-developed road network and international shipping services; cap. Port-au-Prince; corrupt Duvalier dictatorship ousted in 1986; anti-government coup, 2004; a. 27,713 km²; p. (2004) 7,656,166.

Hakodate, c., S. Hokkaido, **Japan**; Seikan rail tunnel to Honshu (Aomori) opened 1988; fishing pt.; fish food processing; p. (1990) 307,251.

Halberstadt, t., Saxony - Anhalt, **Germany**; cath., metallurgy, rubber inds., engin., sugar refining; rly. junc.; p. (1989) 46,851.

Halden, t., S.E. **Norway**; wood-pulp, paper, footwear, cotton spinning; nuclear research reactor; p. (1990) 20,134.

Haldia, pt., W. Bengal, **India**; nr. mouth of R. Hooghly; satellite pt. for Calcutta to handle coal, ore, grain; oil pipeline to Barauni; refinery; p. (1991) 100,347.

Hale, t., Trafford, Gtr. Manchester, **Eng.**; residtl.; p. (1991) 15,868.

Halesowen, t., S.W. of Birmingham, West Midlands, **Eng.**; weldless tubes, elec. gds., stainless steel forgings, engin.; p. (2001) 55,273.

Halesworth, t., Suffolk, **Eng.**; on R. Blyth, 14 km S.W. of Beccles; p. (1991) 4,575.

Halifax, spt., cap. of Nova Scotia, **Canada**; univ.; naval sta. and dockyard, open in winter; machin., iron foundries, footwear, oil refining, food-processing; scene of explosion of munitions ship (1917); p. (1996) 332,518.

Halifax, t., Calderdale, West Yorks., **Eng.**; on E. flanks of Pennines; carpets, textiles, machine tools; cast iron wks.; p. (2001) 83,570.

Halland, co. S.W. **Sweden.**; cap Halmstad; a. 5,448 km²; p. (1992) 261,172.

Halle, c. Saxony - Anhalt **Germany**; on R. Saale; univ.; lignite and potash mined nearby; engin., chemicals, p. (2002) 243,045.

Hallstatt, v., Upper **Austria**; in the Salzkammergut; early Iron Age culture type site.

Halmahera, I., **Indonesia**; mtnous., active volcanoes, tropical forests; spices, pearl fisheries, sago, rice; religious riots (1999); a. 17,218 km².

Halmstad, spt., Kattegat, **Sweden**; iron and steel wks., machin. engin., cycles, textiles, leather, jute, wood-pulp; p. (1992) 81,084.

Hälsingborg. *See* Helsingborg.

Halstead, t., Essex, **Eng.**; on R. Colne, N.W. of Colchester; rayon weaving; p. (1991) 9,775.

Halton, unit. auth. and t., Cheshire, **Eng.**; surrounds Mersey R. and inc. Runcorn and Widnes; p. (2001) 118,208 (unit. auth.).

Haltwhistle, mkt. t., Tynedale, Northumberland, **Eng.**; on R. South Tyne; former coal-mng. dist.; p. (1991) 3,773.

Hama, c., N. **Syria**, on R. Orontes; the anc. Hamath, ctr. of Hittite culture; food tr., rural inds.; p. (1993) 229,000.

Hamadān, t., **W. Iran**; alt. *c*. 1,800 m; the anc. Ecbatana, cap. of Media; carpets, pottery; air port.; tomb of Avicenna; p. (1994) 406,000.

Hamamatsu, c., S. Honshu, **Japan**; on cst. plain 96 km S.E. of Nagoya; ctr. of impt. cotton mftg. region; textiles, dyeing, musical instruments, motor cycles; p. (1990) 534,624.

Hamble, Hants, **Eng.**; popular yachting ctr.; p. (1991) 3,229.

Hambleton, t. and l. gov. dist., North Yorks., **Eng.**; inc. Northallerton, Bedale and Thirsk; p. (2001) 84,111 (dist.), (1991) 1,566 (t.).

Hamburg, c., *Land* H., **Germany**; astride R. Elbe, nr. N. Sea; 2nd. lgst. German c. and ch. pt.; freeport since 1189; pt. to be extended by reclaiming Is. of Neuwerk and Scharhörn; diversified tr. inc. liner traffic, barge traffic down Elbe, entrepôt goods; major pt. processing inds., airpt., univ.; cultural and musical ctr.; heavily bombed in second world war; p. (2002) 1,726,363 (c.), 2,515,468 (*Land*).

Hämeenlinna (Tavastehus), c., cap. of Häme co., S.W. **Finland**; L. pt.; tourist ctr.; birthplace of Sibelius; p. (1993) 44,176.

Hameln (Hamelin), t., Lower Saxony, **Germany**; pt. on R. Weser; iron, textiles; scene of legend of the Pied Piper; p. (2002) 59,052.

Hamhung, c., **N. Korea**; industl. and comm. ctr., oil refinery; p. (1981) 775,000.

Hamilton, spt., cap. of **Bermuda**; tourism. comm. and service ctr.; p. (1994) 1,100.

Hamilton, c., and L. pt., S.E. Ont., **Canada**; at W. end of L. Ont.; univ.; varied metallurgical mnfs.; p. (1991) 318,499 (c.), (1996) 624,360 (met. a.).

Hamilton, c. ctr. of major pastoral region; N.I., **N.Z.**; on Waikato R.; univ.; p. (1991) 101,448 (c.), 148,625 (urban. a.). Moves to rename city Waikato.

Hamilton, burgh, S. Lanarkshire, **Scot.**; in Clyde valley, 16 km S.E. of Glasgow; admin. ctr.; elec. prods., carpet mftg., cottons, woollens, knitwear; Rudolf Hess landed near Duke of Hamilton's estate 1941; p. (2002) 48,546.

Hamilton, t., Ohio, **USA**; on Great Miami R.; industl. ctr.; mnfs. metal prods., paper, machin.; p. (1990) 61,368 (t.), 291,000 (met. a. with Middletown).

Hamm, t., N. Rhine-Westphalia, **Germany**; on R. Lippe, in Ruhr conurb.; rly. marshalling yards, iron and steel foundries; p. (2002) 183,805.

Hammerfest, spt., **Norway**; world's most N. t., on Kvalöya I.; fishing.

Hammersmith and Fulham, Thames-side inner bor., London, **Eng.**; inc. former bor. of Fulham; industl., residtl.; p. (2001) 165,242.

Hammond, c., N.W. Ind., **USA**; on Grand Calumet R., nr. Chicago; originally slaughtering and meat-pkg. ctr., now ch. mnfs., petroleum and steel prods., soap; p. (1996) 80,081.

Hampshire, non-met. co., S. **Eng.**; inc. Hampshire basin of chalk covered in clay and sand; inc. infertile heath and New Forest; lt. inds.; tourism, seaside resorts; co. t. Winchester; p. (2001) 1,240,103.

Hampstead, inc. in Greater London, **Eng.**; hilltop v. with nearby heathland. *See* Camden.

Hampton, Thames-side t., Richmond upon Thames, London, **Eng.**; Hampton Court Palace; Hampton Wick E. of H. Court.

Hampton, t., S.E. Va., **USA**; oldest English community in US; fishing, oyster and crab packing; p. (1990) 133,793.

Han, R., Hubei, **China**; rises in S.W. Shaanxi prov.; flows E. to join Chang Jiang at Wuhan; ch. trib. of Chang Jiang; 1,280 km long.

Han, R., S. **China**; forms rich agr. delta nr. Shantou; *c*. 400 km long.

Hanau, t., Hesse, **Germany**; on Rs. Mein and Kinzig; jewellery ctr., rubber and non ferrous metals inds.; birthplace of Jakob and Wilhelm Grimm, Paul Hindemith; p. (2002) 88,801.

Hanchung. *See* Hanzhong.

Hangzhou (Hangchow), c., cap. of Zhejiang prov., E. **China**; picturesque setting at head of H. Bay; former treaty pt., now silted up; silk weaving, chemicals, jute cloth; tourism; p. (1994) 1,185,000.

Hankou, c., Hubei, **China**; at junc. of Han and Chang Jiang, 960 km from mouth of Yangtze but accessible to ocean-going ships; ch. comm. and mnf. ctr. of central China; former treaty pt., now part of Wuhan conurb.; machin., chemicals, cigarettes, silk. *See* **Wuhan.**

Hanley. *See* Stoke-on-Trent.

Hannibal, t., Mo., **USA**; on Mississippi R.; shoes, cement, metal gds.; boyhood home of Mark Twain; p. (2000) 17,800.

Hanoi, c., cap. of **Vietnam**; on Red R.; old Annamese fort, now modern comm. ctr.; univ.; cotton, silks, tobacco, pottery; superphosphate and magnesium phosphate nearby; bricks, concrete, rubber; p. (2000) 3,734,000.

Hanover (Hannover), c., cap. of Lower Saxony, **Germany**; route ctr.; iron, textiles, machin., paper, biscuits, cigarettes, cars, rubber-processing, chemicals; p. (2002) 516,415 (c.), 996,586 (met. a.).

Hanyang. *See* Wuhan.

Haora. *See* Howrah.

Happy Valley-Goose Bay, sm. t., Labrador, **Canada**; on Churchill R., international airpt.

Hapur, t., W. Uttar Pradesh, **India**; tr. in sugar, timber, cotton, brassware; p. (1991) 146,262.

Harar, (Harer), t., cap. H. prov., **Ethiopia**; unique African hilltop t. with medieval walls, towers and gates; anc. c. of Islamic learning; overlooks Rift Valley; brewery; p. (1994) 76,400.

Harare (formerly Salisbury), c., cap. of **Zimbabwe**; admin. and industl. ctr. in agr. region with gold and chrome mines nearby; tr. in agr. prods., inc. tobacco; clothing, furniture, fertilisers; univ., airpt.; p. (2000) 1,752,000.

Harbin (Haerhpin), c., cap. of Heilongjiang prov., **China**; rly. on Sunghua Jiang; tr. and comm. ctr. of N.E. China; exp. soyabeans; food-processing, machin., paper-mills, oil refining, hydro-turbines, textiles; former treaty pt.; p. (1994) 2,505,000.

Harborough, l. gov. dist., S. Leics., **Eng.**; based on Market Harborough and Lutterworth; p. (2001) 76,559.

Hardanger Fjord, W. cst. **Norway**; 120 km long; magnificent scenery; tourism.

Hardt Mtns., **Germany**; northward continuation of Vosges on W. of Rhine rift valley; formerly forested, now largely cleared for pasture; hgst. points reach just over 600 m.

Haridwar, c., Uttaranchal, **India**; on R. Ganges; gr. annual fair and pilgrimage; nearby dam.

Hargeisa, t., **Somalia**; comm. ctr. of livestock-raising region; airport; p. (1987) 400,000.

Har Homa, controversial Israeli settlement bordering Arab East Jerusalem.

Haringey, outer bor., Greater London, **Eng.**; comprising former bors. of Hornsey, Tottenham, and Wood Green; p. (2001) 216,507.

Hari-Rud, R., N. **Afghanistan** and **Iran**; the anc. "Arius"; length 1,040 km; (*Rud* = river).

Harlech, t., Gwynedd, **Wales**; on Cardigan Bay 16 km N. of Barmouth; farming; cas.; seaside resort; p. (1991) 1,233.

Harlem, upper Manhattan, N.Y. city, **USA**; residtl. and business section of c. with lge. black p.; depressed economic a. with much poverty.

Harlem, R., N.Y., **USA**; separates Manhattan I. from bor. of Bronx; with Spuyten Duyvi Creek forms waterway 13 km long from East R. to Hudson R.

Harlow, t., l. gov. dist., Essex, **Eng.**; in valley of R. Stort, 35 km N.E. of London; new t. (1947); spreads S.W. from nucleus of old mkt. t. of H.; engin., glass, furniture mkg., metallurgy; p. (2001) 88,296.

Harpenden, t., Herts., **Eng.**; in Chiltern Hills, 8 km N. of St. Albans; Rothamsted agr. experimental sta.; residtl.; p. (2001) 28,452.

Harris, S. part of Lewis I., Outer Hebrides, Western Isles, **Scot.**; and several sm. Is.

Harrisburg, c., cap. of Penns., **USA**; on Susquehanna R.; iron and steel ind.; machin., cigarettes, cotton gds.; p. (1990) 588,000 (met. a. with Lebanon-Carlisle).

Harrogate, t., l. gov. dist., North Yorks., Eng.; in valley of R. Nidd, 22 km N. of Leeds; spa; favoured a. for retirement; p. (2001) 151,336 (dist.), (2001) 85,128 (t.).

Harrow, outer bor., Greater London, Eng.; public school; camera mftg.; p. (2001) 206,814.

Harsprånget, t., Norrbotten, Sweden; lge. hydroelectric plant.

Harstad, ch. t., Lofoten Is., N.W. Norway; herring ind., woollen gds.; p. (1990) 32,327.

Hart, l. gov. dist., N.E. Hants., Eng.; comprises Fleet and Hartley Wintney; p. (2001) 83,505.

Hartebeestpoort Dam, S. Africa; on R. Crocodile (Limpopo), 40 km W. of Pretoria; supplies water for cultivation, under irrigation, of cotton, maize, tobacco.

Hartford, c., cap. of Conn., USA; comm. and insurance ctr.; univ.; sm. arms, typewriters, elec. machin., aircraft engin., ceramics; Mark Twain lived here; p. (1990) 139,739 (c.), 768,000 (met. a.).

Hartlepool, spt., unit. auth. created in 1996, formerly part of Cleveland, Eng.; on E. cst., 5 km N. of Tees estuary; shipbldg., lt. inds.; timber, iron and steel inds., pipe making; advanced gascooled reactor nuclear power sta; p. (2001) 88,511 (unit. auth.), (2001) 86,075 (t.).

Harwell, v. Oxon., Eng.; 19 km S. of Oxford; Atomic Energy Authority nuclear power research establishment; p. (1991) 2,236.

Harwich, spt., Tendring, Essex, Eng.; on S. cst., of estuary of R. Stour; ferry port for Belgium, Neth., Denmark; docks, container facilities, naval base; p. (2001) 20,130.

Haryana, st. India; formed 1966 from Hindispeaking areas of Punjab; former cap. Chandigarh; Hindu speaking a. transferred from Chandigarh (1986); a. 45,584 km²; p. (2001) 21,083,000.

Harz Mtns., range, Germany; between the Weser and the Elbe; highest peak the Brocken; ch. t. Goslar; forested slopes; rich in minerals; tourism.

Haslemere, t., Waverley, Surrey, Eng.; nr. Hindhead; mkt., residtl., lt. inds.; p. (1991) 12,218.

Haslingden, t., Rossendale, Lancs., Eng.; on Rossendale Fells, 5 km S. of Accrington; heavy industl. textiles, waste-spinning; p. (1991) 15,024.

Hasselt, t., prov., Limburg, Belgium; mkt. t.; gin distilleries; p. (1993) 67,080.

Hastings, t., l. gov. dist., East Sussex, Eng.; on S. cst., midway between Beachy Head and Dungeness; seaside resort; Cinque Port; cas.; Norman victory over Saxons, 1066; p. (2001) 85,029 (dist.).

Hatay (Sanjak of Alexandretta), prov. and t., S. Turkey; comprising Antioch (now Antakya) and its pt. Alexandretta (now Iskenderun), ceded to Turkey from France 1939; p. (1990) 1,109,754 (prov.), 118,443 (t.).

Hatfield, t., Welwyn and Hatfield, Herts., Eng.; 30 km N. of London; new t. (1948) which grew around old t. of Bishops Hatfield; aircraft inds. (closed 1994); computers; univ.; p. (2001) 32,281.

Hathras, t., Aligarh dist., Uttar Pradesh, India; sugar, cotton, carved work; p. (1991) 113,285.

Hatteras, Cape, promontory on I. and cays off N.C., USA; stormy region, marked by lighthouse.

Haugesund, spt., S. Norway; on S.W. cst., 35 m. N. of Stavanger; ch. ctr. of herring fishery; canning inds.; p. (1995) 29,100.

Houraki Gulf, arm of Pac. Oc., E. cst. N.I., N.Z.; forming entrance to harbour of Auckland; Nat. Park; gives name to dist.; p. (1991) 16,921.

Haute Corse. See Corsica.

Haute Garonne, dep., S. France; in Languedoc, cap. Toulouse; a. 6,366 km²; p. (1999) 1,046,519.

Haute-Loire, dep., France; mainly in Massif Central; cap. Le Puy; cattle, fruit, vineyards; a. 4,999 km²; p. (1999) 209,190.

Haute-Marne, dep., France; mainly in Champagne; metallurgical inds.; a. 6,268 km²; p. (1990) 204,100.

Haute-Normandie, region N. France; inc. deps. Eure, Seine-Maritime; ch. t. Rouen; p. (1990) 1,737,200. See Normandy.

Hautes-Alpes, dep., France; mtnous.; on Italian border; sheep; cap. Gap; a. 5,641 km²; p. (1999) 121,357.

Haute-Saône, dep., France; inc. part of Vosges mtns.; mainly agr.; cap. Vesoul; a. 5,372 km²; p. (1999) 229,690.

Haute-Savoie, dep., France; borders on Italy and Switzerland; reaches highest alt. in Mont Blanc; cap. Annecy; winter sports; a. 4,595 km.; p. (1999) 631,210.

Hautes-Pyrénées, dep., S. France; rises in S. to steep peaks of Pyrenees, forming bdy. with Spain;

Basques live on both sides of border; cap. Tarbes; Lourdes place of pilgrimage; a. 4,533 km²; p. (1999) 222,365.

Haute-Vienne, dep., France; entirely in Massif Central; cap. Limoges; cattle-raising; a. 5,488 km²; p. (1999) 353,421.

Haut-Rhin, dep., E. France; in lower Alsace; cap. Colmar; ch. industl. t. Mulhouse; a. 3,507 km²; p. (1999) 707,837.

Hauts-de-Seine, dep., France; W. of Paris; cap. Nanterre; a. 176 km²; p. (1999) 1,425,555.

Havana (La Habana), c., cap. of Cuba; ch. pt. of W.I., with lge. harbour; cigars, tobacco, sugar, rum, coffee, woollens, straw hats, iron-ore; oil refining on outskirts of c.; p. (2000) 2,256,000 (met. a.).

Havant, t., l. gov. dist., Eng.; at foot Portsdowns Hill, 10 km N.E. of Portsmouth; p. (2001) 116,849 (dist.), (2001) 45,435 (t.).

Havel, R., Germany; rises in Neubrandenburg L. region; flows to Elbe R.; partially canalised nr. Berlin; 354 km long.

Haverfordwest, t., Pembrokeshire, Wales; 10 km N.E. of Milford Haven; agr. mkt.; Norman cas.; p. (1991) 13,454.

Haverhill, t., St. Edmundsbury, Suffolk, Eng.; expanded t.; textiles; p. (2001) 22,010.

Haverhill, t., Mass., USA; industl.; shipping containers; p. (1990) 394,000 (met. a. with Lawrence).

Havering, outer bor., E. London, Eng.; inc. Hornchurch and Romford; p. (2001) 224,248.

Havirov, t. Czech Republic, S.E. of Ostrava; mnfs., mng.

Hawaii, I., N. central Pac. Oc.; lgst. of Hawaiian gr.; three gr. volcanic mtns., Mauna Kea (4,208 m), Mauna Loa (4,172 m), Hualalal (last erupted, 1801); ch. pt. Hilo (devastated by tidal wave, 1946); lava deserts, bamboo forests; sugar-cane, cattle, coffee; tourism; deep-sea fishing; p. (2000) 148,700.

Hawaii, st., Pac. Oc., admitted 1959 as 50th st. of USA; st. flower Hibiscus, st. bird Nene; chain of coral and 1959 as 50th st. of USA; chain of coral and volcanic Is.; cap. Honolulu on S.E. cst. of Oahu I.; tourism; ctr. of international shipping routes; sugar, pineapples; a. 16,638 km²; p. (2002) 1,244,898.

Hawarden, t., Flintshire, N. Wales; steel plant; home of Gladstone.

Hawick, burgh, Borders, Scot.; on R. Teviot, 28 km S.W. of Kelso; hosiery, tweed, and woollens; p. (2002) 14,573.

Hawke's Bay, region, N.I., N.Z.; on E. cst.; cap. Napier; a. 11,033 km²; p. (1991) 139,479.

Hawkesbury, R., N.S.W. Australia; impt. waterway flowing into Broken Bay; spectacular gorges.

Haworth, t., West Yorks., Eng.; nr. Keighley; home of the Brontës; p. (1991) 4,956.

Hawthorne, t., S.W. Cal., USA; residtl.; in gasand oil-producing a., aircraft; p. (1996) 72,942.

Hay-on-Wye, t., Powys, Wales; on R. Wye; cas.; mkt.; large number of book shops; p. (1991) 1,407.

Hay, R., Alberta, Canada; flows into G. Slave Lake; 560 km long.

Haydock, t., Merseyside, Eng.; coal mng.; inc. H. Park racecourse; p. (1991) 16,705.

Hayes and Harlington. See Hillingdon.

Hayling Island, resort, Hants., Eng.; E. of Portsmouth; p. (1991) 14,054.

Hayward, t., Cal., USA; fruit-canning, poultry; p. (1990) 111,498.

Haywards Heath, residtl. t. West Sussex, Eng.; p. (2001) 29,110.

Hazel Grove and Bramhall, subs. of Stockport, Ctr. Manchester, Eng.; p. (2001) 38,724.

Hazleton, t., Penns., USA; anthracite region; textiles, iron and steel mnfs.; p. (2000) 23,300.

Headingley, sub., Leeds, West Yorks., Eng. mainly residtl.; county cricket ground. Vote (1997) to move to new ground near Wakefield.

Heanor, t., Amber Valley, Derbys., Eng.; 11 km N.E. of Derby; hosiery, pottery, prefabricated timber bldgs. mftg.; p. (2001) 22,620.

Heathrow, London airport, Eng.; 24 km W. of central London, S. of M4 motorway; on Piccadilly tube line; fast rail link to Paddington; new Terminal 5 given approval (Nov. 2001).

Hebburn, t., Tyne and Wear, Eng.; on R. Tyne 6 km below Gateshead; shipbldg., engin.; p. (1991) 18,183.

Hebei (Hopeh), prov., N.E. China; part of N. China plain; bounded on N. by Great Wall; cap. Shijiazhuang; wheat, kaoling, cotton, coal mng., a. 194,250 km²; p. (1994) 63,660,000.

Hebrides or **Western Isles, Scot.**; grouped as Outer and Inner Hebrides; ch. t. Stornoway, Lewis. Depopulation in Outer Hebrides.

Hebron, t., 26 km. S.W. of Jerusalem.

Heckmondwike, t., West Yorks., **Eng.**; wool textiles; p. (1991) 9,855.

Hedon, t., E. Riding of Yorks., **Eng.**; former spt.; p. (1991) 6,646.

Heerenveen, t., Friesland prov., N. **Neth.**; bicycles; p. (1993) 38,728.

Heerlen, t., Limburg, **Neth.**; 22 km E. of Maastricht; coal mng.; with Kerkrade, met. a.; p. (1994) 95,794 (c.), 270,118 (met. a.).

Heidelberg, c., Baden–Württemberg, **Germany**; on R. Neckar, nr. Mannheim; celebrated univs., cas.; tobacco, wood, leather; p. (2002) 141,509.

Heidenheim, t. Baden–Württemberg, **Germany**; N.E. of Ulm; textiles, machin., metallurgy, furniture; p. (2002) 50,963.

Heilbronn, t., R. pt., Baden–Württemberg, **Germany**; engin., vehicles, foodstuffs; p. (2002) 120,163.

Heilongjiang (Hellungkiang), prov., N.E. **China**; separated from Russia by Amur and Ussuri Rs.; mtnous.; crossed by Songhua R. in central plain; maize, soyabeans, millets; opencast coalmines; gold; cap. Harbin; a. 466,200 km²; p. (1994) 35,570,000.

Hejaz, W prov., **Saudi Arabia**; mainly desert; poor communications; ch. t. Mecca; a. 388,500 km².

Helder (Den Helder), t., N. **Holland, Neth.**; on strait between peninsula and I. of Texel; naval base; p. (1994) 61,024.

Helena, st. cap., Mont., **USA**; grew up as gold- and silver-mng. t.; bricks, pottery; resort; p. (1996) 27,982.

Helensburgh, t., Argyll and Bute, N. **Scot.**; on the Clyde; resort; p. (2002) 14,626.

Helford, R., Cornwall, **Eng.**; oysters, tourism.

Helicon, mtn. gr., **Greece**; abode of classical muses.

Heligoland (Helgoländ), sm. I., N. Sea; off mouth of Elbe; ceded by Britain to Germany 1890 in return for Zanzibar.

Hellespont. See Dardanelles.

Helmand or **Helmund,** R., **Afghanistan**; flows c. 1,360 km from mtns. of Kabul to Hamun-i-Helmand swamp on Iranian border; cultivation in valley; major irrigation project.

Helmond, t., N. Brabant, **Neth.**; on Zuid-Willemsvaart (canal); textiles; p. (1994) 72,293.

Helmsley, mkt. t., Ryedale, North Yorks., **Eng.**; cas.

Helmstedt, t., Lower Saxony, **Germany**; E. of Brunswick; on E. German border; textiles, machin.; p. (1994) 26,700.

Helsingborg (Hälsingborg), spt., Malmöhus, **Sweden** industl. ctr.; train ferry to Elsinore, Denmark; p. (1992) 110,614.

Helsinger, t., spt., **Denmark**; shipbldg.; setting of Shakespeare's *Hamlet*; p. (1990) 56,701.

Helsinki or Helsingfors, c., cap. of **Finland**; spt., on G. of Finland; harbour ice-bound Jan. to Apr.; channel opened by ice-breakers; cultural ctr., univ.; timber, textiles, carpets; exp. mainly timber prods.; p. (2000) 1,167,000 (met. a.).

Helston, mkt. t., Kerrier, Cornwall, **Eng.**; on R. Cober, 13 km W. of Falmouth; tourist ctr.; famous for festival of floral dance (8 May); fishing, soup-canning; p. (1991) 8,505.

Helvellyn, mtn., L. Dist., Cumbria, **Eng.**; severely eroded by ice; alt. 951 m; sharp ridge of Striding Edge.

Helwan, t., **Egypt**; 24 km S. of Cairo; sulphur springs; iron and steel complex, recently expanded (1982); fertilisers, cement; car assembly; p. (1986) 328,000.

Hemel Hempstead, t., Dacorum, Herts., **Eng.**; new t. (1947), on S. slopes of Chilterns; scientific glass, elec. engin., cars; p. (2001) 83,118.

Henan (Honan), prov., Central **China**; traversed by Huang He; cap. Zhengzhou; densely p. in fertile E.; mainly agr.; wheat, cotton; new AIDS problem; a. 167,172 km²; p. (1994) 90,050,000.

Hengelo, t., Overijssel, **Neth.**; industl. ctr.; cattle mkt.; metals, textiles; p. (1994) 77,514.

Hengyang, c., Hunan, **China**; on Xiang Jiang in foothills to S. Chang Jiang plain; on main Guangzhau-Beijing rly.; lead and zinc mines nearby; p. (1994) 543,000.

Hénin-Beaumont, t., Pas-de-Calais, **France**; on coalfield; p. (1990) 24,500.

Henley-on-Thames, t., South Oxfordshire, Oxon., **Eng.**; 8 km N.E. of Reading; mkt. gardening, brewing; annual regatta since 1839; Henley Bridge built 1786; p. (2005) 10,000.

Hensbarrow, upland a., Cornwall, **Eng.**; granite; kaolin-mng. dist., kaolin exp. by sea from Fowey; rises to over 300 m; a. 70 km².

Herakleion. See Iráklion.

Herāt, c., cap. of H. prov., N.W. **Afghanistan**; on Hari Rud R.; of historic and strategic importance, has been called "the key of India"; crude petroleum and chrome-ore nearby; tr. ctr.; textiles; p. (1990) 187,000.

Hérault, dep. S.W. **France**; in Languedoc; agr.; cap. Montpellier; govt.-sponsored tourist developments along shores of Mediterranean; a. 6,221 km²; p. (1999) 896,571.

Herculaneum, anc. c., S. **Italy**; 6 km E. of Naples; buried along with Pompeii by eruption from Vesuvius A.D. 79; rediscovered 1709; site of modern Resina and Portici.

Hereford and Worcester, non-met. co. (until 1998), **Eng.**; crossed by Wye and Severn valleys, separated by Malvern Hills; mainly agr.; beef, dairy and fruit farming; major ts. Hereford and Worcester; p. (1995) 694,300. Worcs. and Hereford separated in 1998.

Hereford, c., l. gov. unit. auth., **Eng.**; on R. Wye; cath.; mkt.; tiles, engin., timber, cider and preserves; furniture, brass-ware; p. (2001) 56,373 (c.).

Herford, t., N. Rhine–Westphalia, **Germany**; on R. Werra; cotton, flax, furniture, cigars, confectionery, metallurgy; p. (2002) 65,097.

Herm, sm. I., dependency of **Guernsey**, English Channel; 6 km N.W. Sark and N.E. of Guernsey; remarkable shell-beach; a. 130 ha.

Hermon, Mount (Jebel esh Sheikh), mtn., in Anti-Lebanon range, on **Syria–Lebanon** bdy., nr. Israel; alt. 2,862 m.

Hermosillo, c., cap. of Sonora st., N.W. **Mexico**; on San Miguel R.; oranges; agr. and mng. ctr.; p. (1990) 449,472.

Hermoupolis or **Hermopolis,** t., Syros I., **Greece**; cap. of Cyclades; Aegean pt. and comm. ctr.; p. (1991) 13,000.

Herne, t., N. Rhine–Westphalia, **Germany**; pt. on Rhine-Herne canal; industl. t. of Ruhr conurb.; p. (2002) 174,018.

Herne Bay, t., Kent, **Eng.**; on cst., 19 km W. of Margate; p. (1991) 31,861.

Herstmonceux, v. nr. Hastings, Sussex, **Eng.**; cas.; frmr. site of Royal Greenwich Observatory (now Science Centre).

Hertford, co. t., East Herts., **Eng.**; on R. Lea, 32 km N. of London; pharmaceutics, flour milling, rolling stock, diesels, brewing; p. (2001) 24,460.

Hertfordshire, non-met. co., **Eng.**; borders Greater London on S.; ch. ctr. St. Albans; drained by Rs. Thames and Lea; intensive agr., lt. inds.; new ts. Welwyn, Stevenage, Hatfield, Hemel Hempstead; p. (2001) 1,033,977.

's-Hertogenbosch, t., **Neth.**; on Rs. Dommel and Aa; cap. of N. Brabant prov.; cath.; cattle mkt.; industl. development; p. (1994) 95,448 (t.), 197,380 (met. a.).

Hertsmere, l. gov. dist., Herts., **Eng.**; a. close to London, inc. Bushey, Elstree and Potters Bar; p. (2001) 94,450.

Hesse, Land, Germany; part of former Prussian prov. Hesse-Nassau; mainly upland; inds. at Frankfurt, Kassel, Darmstadt; wine produced along Rhine valley; cap. Wiesbaden; tourism; a. 21,103 km²; p. (2005) 6,090,000.

Hetch Hetchy Dam, Cal., **USA**; on R. Toulumne upstream from San Joaquin R.; ch. source of irrigation for middle San Joaquin valley; supplies water and generating power to San Francisco.

Hetton, t., Tyne and Wear, **Eng.**; 8 km N.E. of Durham; coal-mng. dist.; p. (1991) 13,538.

Hexham, mkt. t., Tynedale, Northumberland, **Eng.**; on R. Tyne, 32 km W. of Newcastle; priory; p. (1991) 11,008.

Heysham. See Morecambe and Heysham.

Heywood, t., Gtr. Manchester, **Eng.**; 5 km E. of Bury; chemicals, engin.; p. (2001) 28,024.

Hialeah, t., Fla., **USA**; sub. of Miami; racecourse; p. (2000) 226,419.

Hidalgo, st., central **Mexico**; mtnous. with fertile valleys in S. and W.; cap. Pachuca; mng.; maguey (type of lily), tobacco, cotton, coffee; a. 20,868 km²; p. (1990) 1,880,632.

Higashiosaka, c., **Japan**; E. of Osaka; formed from amalgamation of Fuse, Kawachi, Hiraoka and many sm. ts.; p. (1990) 518,251.

Higham Ferrers, mkt. t., East Northants, **Eng.**; 5 km E. of Wellingborough; footwear and leather dressing; p. (1991) 5,345.

Highgate, residtl. dist., N. London, **Eng.**;

hilltop v. in bor. of Haringey. Famous cemetry whose 50,000 graves include Karl Marx and the scientist Michael Faraday.

Highland Park, t., Mich., **USA**; sub. of Detroit; grew up with expansion of motor-car ind.; p. (2000) 16,750.

Highland, N. **Scot.**, unit. auth. created in 1996 from former Region and part of Strathclyde; inc. I. of Skye and Inner Hebrides; rugged mtns. inland; p. concentrated around cst.; off- shore oil development; stock raising, forestry, tourism; p. (2002) 208,140.

High Peak, l. gov. dist., Derbys., **Eng.**; a. of Pennines inc. New Mills, Glossop, Whaley Bridge and Buxton; p. (2001) 89,433.

High Willhays, hgst. summit, Dartmoor, Devon, **Eng.**; 621 m.

High Wycombe, t., Bucks., **Eng.**; 13 km N. of Maidenhead; furniture, paper-mkg., egg processing; in London commuter belt; p. (2001) 77,178.

Hildesheim, t., Lower Saxony, **Germany**; at foot of Harz mtns.; cath.; machin., farm implements, textiles, ceramics; p. (2002) 103,717.

Hillah, Al, mkt. t., **Iraq**; on R. Euphrates; nr. anc. Babylon; food tr. rugs, leather; p. (1985) 215,249.

Hillerod, t., **Denmark**; admin. ctr. of Frederiksborg prov.; p. (1990) 33,388.

Hillingdon, outer bor. Greater London, **Eng.**; comprising Hayes and Harlington, Ruislip and Northwood Yiewsley, W. Drayton, and Uxbridge; p. (2001) 243,006.

Hilo, t., **Hawaii**; pt. of entry and main tr. and shipping ctr. of I.; tourism; Mauna Loa volcano nearby; p. (1996) 37,808.

Hilversum, t., **Neth.**; nr. Utrecht; radio broadcasting ctr.; noteworthy modern architecture; p. (1994) 84,213 (t.), 102,369 (met. a.).

Himachal Pradesh, st., N.W. **India**; bounded by Tibet on E.; forested mtns., cultivated valleys; cap. Shimla (Simla); a. 56,019 km²; p. (2001) 6,077,200.

Himalayas, vast chain of mtns. along N. border of India, between the Indus and Brahamaputra Rs., and lying in Pakistan, India, Nepal, Sikkim, Bhutan, and China; made up of several parallel-ranges inc. the Siwaliks, the Hindu Kush, and the Karakorams; crossed by passes, mainly in W.; 2,560 km long; hgst. peak Mt. Everest, 8,854 m.

Himeji, c., S. Honshu, **Japan**; mkt. ctr. on shore of Inland Sea, 48 km W. of Kobe; iron and steel ind., heavy engin.; oil refining; p. (1990) 454,360.

Hinckley, mkt. t., Leics., **Eng.**; hosiery, cardboard boxes, dye-wks., engin.; with Market Bosworth forms l. gov. dist. of Hinckley and Bosworth; p. (2001) 100,141 (dist.), (2001) 43,246 (t.).

Hindenburg. See Zabrze.

Hindhead, t. and hill common, Surrey, nr. Haslemere, **Eng.**; p. (1991) 7,473 (t.).

Hindiya Barrage, dam, **Iraq**; across R. Euphrates, 48 km above Al Hillah; provides flood control and irrigation in a. between Shatt al Hillah and R. Euphrates.

Hindley, t., Gtr. Manchester, **Eng.**; 3 km S.E. of Wigan; paint, rubber; p. (2001) 23,457.

Hindu Kush, mtn. range, mainly in N.E. **Afghanistan**; hgst peak Tirich Mir (7,755 m) in Chitral dist., **Pakistan**; Salang tunnel (opened 1964) with 2-lane motor highway cuts H.K. at height of 3,300 m, runs 240 m below mtn. top, 3·2 km.

Hindustan, former name of part of N. **India** between Himalayas and Vindhya ranges.

Hinkley Point, Somerset, **Eng.**; two nuclear power-sta., one Magnox, one advanced gas-cooled reactor.

Hiroshima, c., S.W. Honshu, **Japan**; on delta of Ota R.; first c. to be destroyed by atomic bomb (6 Aug. 1945); since rebuilt; motor vehicles, ship-bldg.; p. (1990) 1,085,705.

Hirschberg. See Jelenia Góra.

Hispaniola, second lgst. I. of **W.I.**; lies between Cuba and Puerto Rico; divided between Haiti (Fr.-speaking) and Dominican Rep. (Spanish-speaking); complex relief, climate, and vegetation, but strong cultural differences make international bdy. a sharp divide; a. 76,498 km².

Hitchin, t., North Herts., **Eng.**; in gap through Chiltern Hills, 56 km N. of London; lt. engin., tanning, chemicals, distilling; mkt.; p. (2001) 33,352.

Hjälmaren Lake, central **Sweden**; drained into L. Malaren by Esk R.; linked by canal to Arboga; a. 474 km².

Hjörring, c., Jutland, N. **Denmark**; biscuit and clothing wks.; p. (1990) 34,558.

Hobart, cap. and ch. pt. of Tasmania, **Australia**;

on R. Derwent; univ.; fruit exp.; mostly light inds.; zinc; cadmium, superphosphates, textiles; p. (1993) 193,200.

Hoboken, t., N.J., **USA**; on Hudson R. above Jersey City, opp. N.Y. to which it is linked by subway and ferry; pt. for ocean commerce; industl. ctr.; p. (1990) 33,397.

Ho Chi Minh City (Saigon), c., spt., **Vietnam**; former cap. of S. Vietnam; on Saigon R. to E. of Mekong Delta; tree-lined boulevards; cath., univ., modern airport; comm. ctr.; exp. rice, rubber; food processing; p. declining rapidly since reunification of Vietnam; p. (2000) 4,615,000.

Höchst, t., Hesse, **Germany**; industl. sub. of Frankfurt-on-Main; site of German chemical ind.

Hoddesdon, t., Herts., **Eng.**; in Lea valley, 6 km S. of Ware; food processing; p. (2001) 35,235.

Hodeida (Al Hudaydah), t., **Yemen**; on Red Sea; pt. and naval base; exp. dates, hides, coffee; p. (1994) 298,500.

Hof, t., Bavaria, **Germany**; on R. Saale; textiles, iron, machin., porcelain, glass, brewing; p. (2002) 50,654.

Hofei or Hefei, c., cap. of Anhui prov., **China**; rice-growing a.; cotton and silk, iron and steel; p. (1994) 866,800.

Hofuf (Al Hufuf), t., El Hasa, **Saudi Arabia**; dates, wheat, fruit; textiles, brass- and copper-ware; oil-fields nearby; p. (1992) 225,800.

Hog's Back, Surrey, **Eng.**; steep chalk ridge; alt. 154 m.

Hohe Tauern, Alpine range, Tyrol, **Austria**; rugged crystalline rocks; highest point Gross Glockner, 3,801 m; traversed by rly. tunnel 8 km long.

Hohhot (Huhehot), c., Nei Mongol (Inner Mongolia), **China**; diesel engines; woollen mill; p. (1994) 683,000.

Hoihow. See Haikou.

Hokkaido, lge. I., **Japan**, N. of Honshu; colder than other Is.; less dense p.; temperate agr.; skiing; tunnel link with Honshu to aid economic development; a. 88,775 km²; p. of pref. (1990) 5,643,647.

Holbeach, mkt. t., S. Lincs., **Eng.**; in Fens, 11 km E. of Spalding; brewing; ctr. of bulb-growing dist.; p. (1991) 6,088.

Holborn. See Camden.

Holderness, peninsula, E. Riding of Yorks., **Eng.**; between R. Humber and N. Sea; agr.

Holguin, t., N.E. **Cuba**; comm. ctr.; sugar, tobacco, coffee, cattle; exps. handled by pt. Gibara; p. (1990) 228,052, (1990) 927,700 (dep).

Holland. See Netherlands.

Holland, N. See Noord Holland.

Holland, Parts of. See Lincolnshire.

Holland, S. See Zuid Holland.

Hollandia, former name of cap. W. Irian, **Indonesia**; renamed Kota Baru by Indonesia, then Sukarnapura, now Djaiapura.

Holloman, t., N.M., **USA**; atomic and space research ctr.; site of 1st. man-made atomic explosion.

Hollywood, t., Fla., **USA**; seaside resort on Atl. cst.; cement, furniture; p. (1996) 127,894; part of Fort Lauderdale met. a.

Hollywood, sub. of Los Angeles, Cal., **USA**; ctr. of film industry.

Holmesdale, Vale of, Kent, E. Surrey, **Eng.**; extends along foot of N. Downs escarpment; drained by Rs. Mole, Darent, Medway, Len, Stour; heavy clay soils; ch. ts. Dorking, Reigate, Sevenoaks, Maidstone, Ashford, which have grown up in gaps through hills to N. and S. of Vale; length 96 km, average width 2 km.

Holmfirth, t., West Yorks., **Eng.**; 8 km S. of Huddersfield, textiles, engin.; p. (2001) 22,690.

Holt, mkt. t., N. Norfolk, **Eng.**; 8 km S.W. of Sheringham; 16th-cent. school; p. (1991) 2,972.

Holt, t., Wrexham, **Wales**; on R. Dee, 11 km S. of Chester; cas. ruins.

Holyhead, spt., Isle of Anglesey, **Wales**; on Holyhead I.; mail packet sta. for Ireland; lt. engin., woodwkg., clocks; site for aluminium smelter; p. (1991) 11,796.

Holy I. (Lindisfarne), off cst. of Northumberland, **Eng.**

Holy I., Scot., in F. of Clyde, nr. I. of Arran.

Holy I., off cst. of Isle of Anglesey, **Wales.**

Holyoke, t., Mass., **USA**; on Connecticut R., above Springfield; paper, machin.; p. (2000) 39,800.

Holywell, mkt. t., Flintshire, N. **Wales**; woollen, rayon and paper inds.; p. (1991) 7,531.

Holywood, spt., North Down, **N. Ireland**; on S. shore of Belfast Lough; seaside resort; p. (1991) 9,252.

Homburg (Bad Homburg), c., Hesse, **Germany;** famous spa; p. (1999) 51,900.

Home Counties, term applied to the geographical counties adjoining London, *i.e.,* Middlesex, Surrey, Essex, and Kent; sometimes Hertfordshire, Buckinghamshire, and Berkshire are included, and occasionally Sussex.

Homs, t., **W. Syria;** on R. Orontes in fertile plain; anc. Emesa; steel plants, fertilisers, lt. inds.; pipeline from Kirkūk oil fields; p. (1993) 537,000.

Honan. *See* Henan.

Honda, old Spanish t., **Colombia;** on Magdalena R., at rapids; former comm. ctr.

Honduras, rep., straddles Central American isthmus with longest cst. on Caribbean; comprises 18 deps. inc. offshore Bay Is.; coastal lowlands hot and humid, more temperate in interior highlands which rise to over 2,000 m; agr. basis of economy, especially American-owned banana plantations; bananas almost half exp., some mng.; rlys. oriented to banana-producing areas to facilitate exp., nationalised forests; land reform; devastated in 1998 hurricane; cap. Tegucigalpa; 5 airports.; a. 111,958 km², p. (2004) 6,823,568.

Honduras, British. *See* Belize.

Hong Kong, former Brit. Crown Col., S.E. cst. **China,** comprises Hong Kong I., Kowloon peninsula and New Territories; road and rail tunnels link H.K. with Kowloon; deepwater harbour of Victoria; industl. development rapid since second world war yet few natural resources; exp. clothing, toys, electronics, watches; dense p. increased by immigration from China and Vietnam; returned to Chinese sovereignty 1 July 1997 with status of special admin. reg.; capitalist system to remain for 50 years; new airport (Chep Lap Kok) opened, July 1998; a. 1,068 km², p. (2004) 6,855,125.

Honiara, t., cap. of **Solomon Is.;** on Guadalcanal I.; p. (1999) 68,000.

Honiton, t., East Devon, **Eng.;** on R. Otter, 26 km E. of Exeter; mkt.; trout-fishing; formerly lace making; p. (1991) 7,859.

Honolulu, c., cap. of **Hawaii;** on Oahu I.; social and comm. ctr. and ch. pt. of archipelago; gd harbour; univ.; airport; fruit-canning, sugar-processing; tourism; p. (2000) 371,657 (c.), 836,000 (met. a.).

Honshu, lgst. I. of **Japan;** contains most of p. along E. cst. in 320 km industl. belt; Seikan tunnel links I. to Hokkaido; a. 230,300 km²; p. (1990) 99,254,000.

Hooghly, R., arm of Ganges R., **India;** flows into Bay of Bengal; used in jute-milling and navigable as far as Kolkata (Calcutta); 256 km long.

Hooghly Chinsura, t., W. Bengal, **India;** on Hooghly R.; rice-milling; p. (1991) 151,806 (part of Kolkata (Calcutta) met. a.).

Hook of Holland (Hoek van Holland), spt., **Neth.;** port with ferry connections to Harwich, Eng.

Hoorn, old fishing t., N. Holland, **Neth.;** on IJsselmeer, 39 km N. of Amsterdam; cattle mkts.; birthplace of Jan P. Coen, founder of Batavia; p. (1994) 60,979.

Hoover Dam, USA; on Colorado R.; used for irrigation (parts of Cal., Arizona, and Mexico), flood control and hydroelectric power; Lake Mead, 184 km long, 2–13 km wide, one of world's lgst. man-made Ls.

Hopeh. *See* Hebei.

Horbury, t., West Yorks., **Eng.;** nr. Wakefield; p. (1991) 9,186.

Horeb. *See* Sinai.

Hormuz, Strait of, between Persian G. and G. of Oman.

Horncastle, mkt. t., E. Lindsey, Lincs., **Eng.;** at confluence of Rs. Bain and Waring at foot of Lincoln Wolds; mkt.; vegetable-processing; p. (1991) 4,994.

Hornsea, t., E. Riding of Yorks., **Eng.;** on E. cst., N.E. of Hull; seaside resort; p. (1991) 7,573.

Hornsey. *See* Haringey.

Horsens, t., **Denmark,** E. Jutland; on inlet of Kattegat; industl. and comm. ctr.

Horsforth, t., West Yorks., **Eng.;** in Aire valley N.W. of Leeds; cloth, tanning, lt. engin.; p. (1991) 18,593.

Horsham, t., l. gov. dist., West Sussex, **Eng.;** on R. Arun at W. end of forested dist. of the High Weald; agr.; timber, engin., chemicals; Shelley's birthplace; impt. commuting centre; p. (2001) 122,088 (dist.), (2001) 47,804 (t.).

Horta, t., cap. of H. dist., **Azores;** on Fayal I.; excellent harbour and base for transatlantic flights; p. (1991) 4,900.

Horten, spt., **Norway;** nr. Oslo; naval base; shipbldg., mftg. inds.; p. (1990) 16,043.

Horwich, t., Gtr. Manchester, **Eng.;** on W. edge of Rossendale Fells, N.W. of Bolton; rly. t.; engin.; rly. workshops closed (1983); p. (1991) 18,017.

Hospitalet de Llobregat, t., **Spain;** sub. of Barcelona, in Llobregat valley; p. (1998) 248,500.

Hotan (Khotan), c., S.W. Xinjiang, **China;** in fertile H. oasis at base of Kunlun Shan; silk, carpets, jade-ware; on anc. Silk Road; early ctr. of Buddhism; visited by Marco Polo 1274.

Hot Springs, c., Ark., **USA;** in Ouachita mtns. S.W. of Little Rock; Nat. Park since 1832; health resort; p. (1996) 36,255.

Houghton-le-Spring, t., Tyne and Wear, **Eng.;** S.W. of Sunderland; former coal mng.; p. (2001) 36,746.

Hounslow, outer bor., Greater London, **Eng.;** inc. former bors. of Brentford and Chiswick, Heston and Isleworth, Feltham and Hounslow; rubber goods; p. (2001) 212,341.

Housatonic, R., W. Mass., Conn., **USA;** falls attracted early Puritan settlement and industrialisation; dairy farming; 240 km long.

Houston, c., spt., S. Texas, **USA;** on Galveston Bay; gr. pt., lgst. c. of S.; univ.; oil refineries, oilfield machin., steel, chemicals, paper, processing, milling and assembling plants; NASA's manned space flight ctr. and lunar science institute; p. (2000) 1,953,631 (c.), 3,301,937 (met. a.).

Houston Ship Canal, Texas, **USA;** links Houston to head of shallow Galveston Bay and continues through bay to deep water; provides site for heavy inds.; opened 1915; total length 72 km.

Hove, t., Brighton and Hove, **Eng.;** on S. cst., contiguous with Brighton; residtl.; holiday resort; p. (2001) 72,335.

Howrah (Haora), c., W. Bengal, **India;** on W. bank of Hooghly R., in met. a. of Kolkata (Calcutta); p. (1991) 197,000.

Hoylake, t., Wirral, Merseyside, **Eng.;** on N. cst. of Wirral peninsula; residtl.; golf course; p. (2001) 25,524.

Hradec Králové, t., **Czech Rep.;** at confluence of Elbe (Labe) and Orlice Rs.; industl. ctr.; mnfs. machin., precision instruments; 14th-cent. cath. and town hall; p. (1990) 101,000.

Huainan (Hwainan), c., Anhui prov., central **China;** ctr. of China's ch. coal mng. region; p. (1994) 769,000.

Huai He (Hwai-ho), R., **China;** flows E. between N. China plain and lower Chang Jiang; subject to disastrous floods; since 1950 flood control and irrigation canal to sea; 1,224 km long.

Huamanga. *See* Ayacucho.

Huambo. *See* Nova Lisboa.

Huancayo, t., cap. of Junin dep., **Peru;** in high valley of Andes, *c.* 3,300 m; textiles; p. (1993) 258,209.

Huang Hai (Hwang-hai or **Yellow Sea),** arm of Pac. Oc. between Korea and China; branches into Gs. of Bo Hai and Liaotung; shallow sea rapidly infilling; named after yellow silt from Huang He; length 960 km, greatest width 640 km.

Huang He (Hwang Ho), R., **China;** the Yellow R., rises in Kunlun Shan; flows *c.* 4,800 km. into G. of Bo Hai; cuts through Shaanxi in a deep gorge; filled with yellow silt (loess) from this a.; floods frequently and changes course (once entered sea S. of Shandong); in lower part forms fertile plain; now part of multipurpose scheme for hydro-electric power, irrigation and flood control; lgst. dam in China opened at Liuchia in 1975; flow now (1999) reduced to a trickle in parts; threat of major catastrophe; 4,640 km long.

Huangshi (Hwangshih), c., Hubei prov., **China;** main iron and steel ctr. of central China, built since 1950; p. (1994) 538,400.

Huarás or **Huaráz,** cap. of Ancash dep., **Peru;** on Santa R., *c.* 3,000 m; mainly agr., some mng.; avalanche 1941 killed 6,000 inhabitants; p. (1993) 66,888 (predominantly Indian).

Huascarán, extinct volcano, Peruvian Andes, nr. Huarás, 6,773 m high; avalanche 1970 killed 20,000 people.

Hua Shan (Tsinling Shan), mtn. range, central **China;** rises to over 1,830 m; watershed between Huang He and Chang Jiang basins; impt. climatic divide between temperate N. China and tropical S. China.

Hubei (Hupeh), prov., central **China;** N. of the Chang

Jiang; many Ls. and Rs.; rice, wheat, cotton; iron ores; Wuhan is major industl. ctr. of prov. and central China; cap. Wuhan; a. 186,363 km²; p. (1994) 56,560,000.

Hubli, c., Karnataka, **India;** E. of Goa; textiles, rly. engin.; p. (1991) 648,000.

Hucknall, t., Ashfield, Nottingham, **Eng.;** hosiery, coal; p. (2001) 29,188.

Huddersfield, t., West Yorks., **Eng.;** on edge of Pennines, 16 km S. of Bradford; wool, textiles, chemicals, engin.; univ.; birthplace of Labour leader, Harold Wilson; p. (2001) 146,234.

Hudson, R., N.Y., **USA;** flows from Adirondacks to N.Y. harbour; with valley of Mohawk R. makes gr. highway of tr. between Great Ls. and N.Y.; scenic; hydroelec. power; 560 km long.

Hudson Bay, gr. inland sea, **Canada;** communicates by Hudson Strait with Davis Strait (Atl. Oc.); ice-free mid-July to Oct.; salmon, cod; a. 1,398,600 km².

Hué, c., **Vietnam;** on Hué R., 16 km from S. China Sea; pt. and tr. ctr.; former cap. of Annam; royal palace; p. (1992) 219,000.

Huelva, coastal prov., S.W. **Spain;** copper mng., vine- and olive-growing, stock-raising, fisheries, brandy distilling; a. 10,117 km²; p. (1998) 454,000.

Huelva, c., cap. of Huelva prov., **Spain;** pt. on G. of Cadiz; oil refining, chemicals, food processing; exp. of minerals from nearby Rio Tinto; p. (1998) 140,000.

Huesca, c., cap. of H. prov., N.E. **Spain;** at foot of Pyrenees on R. Isuela; cath.; agr. ctr.; wine and timber tr. with France; p. (1990) 42,800, (1998) 205,000 (prov.).

Hugh Town, cap. of the Scilly Isles, **Eng.;** on St. Mary's I.

Huhehot. See **Hohhot.**

Hula L. See **Waters of Merom.**

Hull or **Kingston upon Hull,** c., unit. auth. of Kingston upon Hull created in 1996, formerly part of Humberside, **Eng.;** major spt. of UK; at influx of R. Hull in estuary of Humber; originally laid out by Edward I; lge. docks; premier distant water fishing pt.; inds. inc. oil-extracting, flour milling, sawmilling, chemicals, engin.; univs.; p. (2001) 243,589 (unit. auth.).

Humber, estuary of Rs. Ouse and Trent, **Eng.;** fine waterway; 2-13 km wide, 61 km long; Humber bridge opened (1981), longest single span suspension bridge in Britain.

Humboldt, R., N. Nevada, **USA;** rises in Ruby Mtns., flows for 480 km before disappearing by evaporation and percolation; impt. 19th cent. routeway.

Humboldt Bay, inlet, Cal., **USA;** nuclear experimental breeder reactor.

Humboldt Current. See **Peru Current.**

Hunan, prov., central **China;** S. of the Chang Jiang; hilly in S. and W.; rice, wheat, beans; rich mineral resources, inc. mercury, tin, tungsten; cap. Changsha; Mao Tse-tung came from Hunan peasant stock; a. 205,589 km²; p. (1994) 63,050,000.

Hunedoara, dist., **Romania;** iron mining, cap. Deva; a. 7,016 km²; p. (1992) 547,993.

Hungary, rep., E. Europe; bounded by Ukraine, Slovakia, Romania, Serbia, and Austria; lies in basin of middle Danube (Duna), with plain in E. and Carpathian mtns. in W.; mainly agr.; exp. meat, fruit, vegetables to EU; inds. increasingly impt. and now account for over 50 per cent of income; member of NATO and (since 2004) EU; substantial Romany minority; cap. Budapest; a. 93,012 km²; p. (2004) 10,032,375.

Hunstanton, t., West Norfolk, **Eng.;** S.E. shore of Wash; seaside resort; p. (1991) 4,634.

Hunter, R., N.S.W., **Australia;** rises in Liverpool range of Gr. Dividing Range, flows S. and E. into Tasman Sea at Newcastle; world famous grape growing and wine producing reg.; coal exp.; c. 400 km long; p. (1992) 539,100 (dist.).

Hunterston, N. Ayrshire, **Scot.;** civil nuclear power sta.; integrated iron and steel wks., engin. of oil platforms and oil terminal planned.

Huntingdon, t. located in the historic co. of **Huntingdonshire,** E. **Eng.,** now l. gov. dist. within Cambs. on R. Ouse; expanded t.; canning, engin., processed rubber, confectionery; birthplace of Cromwell and home of the poet Cowper; p. (2001) 156,954 (dist.), (2001) 20,600 (t.).

Huntly, burgh, Aberdeenshire, **Scot.;** at confluence of Rs. Bogie and Deveron; agr. mkt.; angling resort; p. (2002) 4,412.

Huntsville, c., Ala., **USA;** textiles; rocket research

ctr.; p. (1990) 159,789 (c.), 238,912 (met. a.).

Hupeh. See **Hubei.**

Huron, L., between **Canada** and **USA;** one of the Gr. Ls. of the St. Lawrence basin; a. 59,596 km²; 330 km long.

Huyton with Roby, Knowsley, Merseyside, **Eng.;** sub. of Liverpool; p. (2001) 54,766.

Hwai-ho. See **Huai He.**

Hwainan. See **Huainan.**

Hwang-hai. See **Huang Hai.**

Hwang-ho. See **Huang He.**

Hwangshih. See **Huangshi.**

Hyde, t., Tameside, Gtr. Manchester, **Eng.;** on R. Tame, 11 km S.E. of Manchester; paints, chemicals, food-processing; p. (2001) 31,253.

Hyderabad, ch. c., Andhra Pradesh, **India;** on R. Musi; walled t. and impt. comm. ctr.; univ., nuclear fuel fabrication plant; p. (2000) 6,840,000.

Hyderabad, c., **Pakistan;** 5 km W. of Indus; 144 km N.E. of Karachi; old cap. of Sind; univ.; noted for silk, gold and silver embroidery; now varied mnfs.; dam at nearby Kotri; p. (1998) 1,150,000.

Hyndburn, l. gov. dist., Lancs., **Eng.;** inc. Colne Valley ts. of Accrington, Great Harwood, Rishton, Clayton-le-Moors, Church and Oswaldtwistle; p. (2001) 81,496.

Hythe, sm.t., Shepway, Kent, **Eng.;** on S. cst., 5 km W. of Folkestone; Cinque pt.; military canal passing through t., used for boating.

I

Iasi (Jassy), c., **Romania;** former cap. of Moldavia; in fertile agr. region; univ., cath.; cultural ctr.; textiles, plastics, chems.; p. (1999) 348,000.

Ibadan, c., cap. Oyo st.; S.W. **Nigeria;** univ.; ctr. of rich agr. a., between the savannah and forest regions; p. mainly Yoruba; crafts, small inds.; p. (1992) 1,295,000.

Ibagué, c., cap. of Tolima dep., **Colombia;** transport ctr.; cotton, tobacco, sugar, leather gds.; p. (1992) 334,078.

Ibarra, t., **Ecuador;** alt. 2,226 m at foot of Imbabura volcano; on Pan-American highway; p. (1990) 80,991.

Iberian Peninsula, S.W. peninsula of Europe; containing sts. of **Spain** and **Portugal;** lge. a. of high tableland; interior isolation and regionalism; a. 593,250 km².

Ibiza, I., Balearic gr. in W. **Mediterranean;** Spanish, cath., tourism; over 700,000 UK visitors annually.

Icel. See **Mersin.**

Iceland, rep., N. Atl. Oc.; volcanic I. with ice-covered plateaux; glacier fields cover 13,000 km²; only 1 per cent of a. cultivated; cold climate; hot house cultivation using thermal springs; economy dependent on fishing and fish-processing inds., high standard of living; tourism increasingly impt.; 7 admin. dists.; cap. Reykjavik; a. 102,846 km²; p. (2004) 293,966.

Ichang. See **Yichang.**

Ichinomiya, c., S.E. Honshu, **Japan;** anc. Shinto shrine; textiles, pottery; p. (1990) 262,434.

Ichow. See **Lin-i.**

Icknield Way, prehistoric route running from near Avebury, Wilts., **Eng.;** along the Berkshire Downs, Chilterns and East Anglian Heights into Norfolk, crossing the Thames at Streatley.

Idaho, st., **USA;** Gem State; admitted to Union 1890; St. flower Syringa, St. bird Mountain Bluebird; one of the Rocky Mtn. sts.; rich in minerals; agr. mainly in irrigated Snake R. valley; cap. Boise; a. 216,413 km²; p. (2002) 1,341,131.

Idaho Falls, c., Idaho, **USA;** on Snake R.; food-processing, lumbering; silver, lead, and gold mines nearby; nuclear experimental breeder reactor; p. (1996) 48,079.

Idle, t., West Yorks., **Eng.;** in Aire valley, 5 km N. of Bradford; woollens.

Ife, t., **Nigeria;** ctr. of the cacao tr.; univ.; p. (1992) 268,600.

Ifni, enclave, S. **Morocco;** ceded by Spain to Morocco (1969); cap. Sidi Ifni; a. 1,500 km².

Iglesias, t., Sardinia, **Italy;** N.W. of Cagliari; mng. for lead, pyrites, zinc; p. (1991) 30,100.

Iguaçu, R., trib. of Paraná; mostly in Brazil; famous falls where Argentina, Brazil, and Paraguay meet, height 20 m higher than Niagara; hydroelec. power potential.

Ijmuiden, c., N. Holland, **Neth.**; on cst. at mouth of N. Sea canal; fishing; gasification plant, major iron and steel plant.

Ijsselmeer (Lake Ijssel), freshwater reservoir, **Neth.**; formerly Zuider Zee; separated from N. Sea by Wieringen–Friesland Barrage; active land reclamation in progress; Wieringermeer drained 1930, N.E. Polder 1942, E. Flevoland 1957, S. Flevoland 1968, Markerwaard to remain undrained; when reclamation complete a. of Neth. will have increased by some 6 per cent.; ch. c. on inlet (IJ) Amsterdam.

Ilchester, t., Somerset, **Eng.**; on R. Yeo; N.W. of Yeovil; birthplace of Roger Bacon; p. (1991) 1,733.

Ile-de-France, region, **France**; inc. deps. Paris, Seine-et-Marne, Yvelines, Essonne, Hauts-de-Seine, Seine-Saint Denis, Val-de-Marne, Val-d'Oise; the most populous region of France, centred on Paris; p. (1999) 10,938,912.

Ilesha, t., **Nigeria**, tr. ctr., cotton weaving; p. (1992) 342,400.

Ilford. *See* Redbridge.

Ilfracombe, t., North Devon, **Eng.**; sm. pt. on cst. of Bristol Channel; resort; p. (1991) 10,429.

Ili, R., **Central Asia**; rises in Tienshan, China, and flows into L. Balkhash; Russia.; c. 1,200 km long.

Iligan, c., Mindanao, **Philippines**; integrated steel mill; cement; p. (1995) 273,000.

Ilkeston, t., Erewash, Derbys., **Eng.**; W. of Nottingham, iron, engin., locknit fabrics, needles, plastics; p. (2001) 37,270.

Ilkley, t., spa, West Yorks., **Eng.**; on R. Wharfe, N.W. of Leeds; local mkt.; p. (1991) 13,530.

Illawarra, dist., N.S.W., **Australia**; forming belt of land between S. tableland and cst.; very fertile; dairy farming; coal seams; ch. ts., Kiama, Wollongong, Bulli, Gerringong; p. (1992) 355,100.

Ille-et-Vilaine, dep., N.W. **France**; on English Channel; a. 6,990 km², agr.; cap. Rennes; p. (1999) 866,904.

Illimani, one of the high peaks of the Cordillera Real, Andes, **Bolivia**, 6,461 m, E. of La Paz.

Illinois, st., **USA**; Prairie State; admitted to Union 1818; St. flower Native Violet; St. bird Cardinal; in Middle West; named after its principal R., a lge. trib. of Mississippi; many Rs.; cap. Springfield, metropolis Chicago; rich agr.; fuel and mineral resources; major coal-mng. st.; inds. inc. meat-processing, farm implements; a. 146,076 km²; p. (2002) 12,600,620.

Illinois, R., Ill., **USA**; glacial valley; long history of settlement; impt. routeway; 437 km long.

Illyria, region stretching along Adriatic Sea from Trieste in N. to **Albania** in S. and inland as far as Rs. Danube and Morava.

Ilminster, t., Somerset, **Eng.**; 16 km S.E. of Taunton; cutstone, concrete, collars, radio valves; p. (1991) 4,162.

Iloilo, c., cap. of I. prov., Panay, **Philippines**; ctr. of rly. network; impt. pt. exp. sugar, rice, copra, hemp; p. (1995) 334,000.

Ilorin, t., N. **Nigeria**; on Lagos–Kano rly.; agr. and caravan ctr.; p. (1992) 430,600.

Imbroz. *See* Gökçeada I.

Immingham, pt., N.E. Lincs., **Eng.**; on the Humber, N.W. of Grimsby; lge. docks; new deep-sea oil and coal terminals; chemical engin., refinery nearby at Killingholme; p. (1991) 12,278.

Imola, t., **Italy**; S.E. of Bologna; cath.; glass, pottery; p. (1991) 62,600.

Imperia, t., **Italy**; on G. of Genoa; sm. pt. olive-growing ctr.; resort; p. (1991) 40,700.

Imperial Valley, S. Cal., **USA**; extends 48 km S.E. from Salton Sea to Mexican bdy.; mainly below sea-level; hot, arid climate; irrigation from Colorado R. chiefly by All-American Canal nr. Yuma; total irrigated a. 405,000 ha; principal crops, fruit, dates, tomatoes, cotton, and dairy prod.

Imphal, cap. of Manipur, **India**; in rice-growing basin in hills of Assam nr. Burma bdy.; p. (1991) 201,000.

Inari L., extensive L., Lappi, **Finland**; outlet into Barents Sea; hydroelec. power; a. 1,774 km².

Ince-in-Makerfield, t., Gtr. Manchester, **Eng.**; nr. Wigan; engin.; p. (1991) 10,554.

Inchon, c., **S. Korea**; on Yellow Sea; pt. for Seoul; exp. soyabeans, rice; textile ctr., steel mill, glass, diesel engines; new airport to serve Seoul; p. (1990) 1,818,293.

Independence, c., Mo., **USA**; E. of Kansas; oil refining; agr. machin.; p. (1996) 110,303.

India, rep., indep. st. (since 1947), S. Asia; second cty. of world by p.; 28 sts. and 7 union terrs.; peninsula bounded by Himalayas in N. extends in wide plateau to Indian Oc. in S.; most of p. concentrated in Indo-Gangetic Plain; unpredictable monsoon climate; heavy dependence on agr.; 70 per cent of p. farmers; few cash crops except cotton (the Deccan), tea (Himalayas), and jute (W. Bengal); 854 languages and dialects impede economic development; strong caste system; new inds. expanding rapidly; chems., engin. electronics; rapid spread of HIV (2nd largest in world); cap. New Delhi; main pts. Bombay (Mumbai), Calcutta (Kolkata), a. 3,268,580 km²; p. (2004) 1,065,000,000.

Indiana, st., **USA**; 'Hoosier State'; admitted to Union 1816; St. flower peony; St. bird Cardinal; in Middle West, bounded by Mich., Ohio, Ill. and sep. from Ky. by Ohio R.; agr.; coal, limestone, petroleum; steel, metal prods., machin., food prod.; cap. Indianapolis; a. 93,994 km²; p. (2002) 6,159,068.

Indianapolis, c., cap. of Ind., **USA**; on White R.; univ.; rly. ctr.; meat-packing, jet engines, aircraft parts, chemicals, pharmaceutics; p. (2000) 791,926 (c.), 1,249,822 (met. a.).

Indian Ocean extends from S. of Asia and E. of Africa to the C. of Good Hope and C. Leeuwin in Australia, separated from the Pacific by the Malay Archipelago and Australia; a. 75,990,600 km². Scene of devastating 2004 tsunami.

Indo-China, S.E. Asia; federation in Fr. Union until end of hostilities July 1954; consisted of Vietnam, Cambodia, and Laos.

Indo-Gangetic Plain, India, Bangladesh and **Pakistan**; name applied to flat land created by the Indus and Ganges basins; densely populated a.

Indonesia, rep., S.E. Asia; former Neth. E. Indies; made up of many sm. Is. straddling equator for over 4,800 km; many Is. in W. volcanic and E. coral; geothermal energy supply being developed; lgst. Is. inc. Java, Sumatra, Kalimantan (S. Borneo), Sulawesi, and Irian (W. New Guinea); mostly underdeveloped except Java; intensive agr. employs 55 per cent of p.; rapidly developing oil and gas industry but falling oil revenues (70 per cent of exports); near to econ. and financial collapse, 1997; self-sufficient in rice, stored surpluses; 63 per cent p. on Java, Madura and Bali Is.; planned decentralisation to other Is.; devastation of Sumatra by tsunami, 2004; cap. Jakarta; a. 1,907,566 km²; p. (2004) 238,452,952.

Indore, c., Madhya Pradesh, **India**; nr. valley of Narbada R.; comm. ctr.; cotton-mills; p. (1991) 1,092,000.

Indre, dep., central **France**; agr. and industl.; cap. Châteauroux; a. 6,905 km²; p. (1999) 231,155.

Indre-et-Loire, dep., central **France**; drained by Indre and Loire Rs.; vineyards, orchards; cap. Tours; a. 6,156 km²; p. (1999) 554,174.

Indus, R., **Pakistan**; rises in Tibet, flows through Kashmir, Punjab, Sind, to Arabian Sea; 5 tribs. Jhelum, Chenab, Ravi, Beas, Sutlej, form one of world's major R. systems, now used extensively to irrigate the Punjab and the Sind; impt. cotton, wheat, and sugar dist.; hydroelec. power; supported Indus valley civilisation 3000–1500 B.C.; 2,880 km long.

Ingleborough, mtn., near Settle, North Yorks., **Eng.**; underground caves, stalactites; made of limestone and millstone grit; alt. 724 m.

Inglewood, t., S. Cal., **USA**; sub. of Los Angeles; chinchilla farms; furniture, lt. engin., aircraft parts; p. (1990) 109,602.

Ingolstadt, t., Bavaria, **Germany**; on Danube, nr. Munich; cas.; machin., cars, tobacco, oil refining; pipeline from Genoa; transalpine oil pipeline from Trieste, through N.E. Italy and Austria to I.; p. (2002) 117,311.

Ingushetia, rep. within **Russian Federation**; Islamic; brief war with Ossetia (1992).

Inishmore, lgst. of Aran gr., Galway, **R.o.I.**; fishing.

Inland Sea, Japan; between Honshu on N. and Shikoku and Kyushu on S.; sheltered sea with many Is.; ch. spts. Osaka, Amagasaki, Kōbe, Okayama, Hiroshima, Kure; Nat. Park; a. c. 9,500 km².

Inn, R., traversing **Switzerland**, the Tyrol, **Austria** and Bavaria; enters R. Danube at Passau; hydroelec. plants; 512 km long.

Innerleithen, burgh, Borders, **Scot.**; on R. Tweed; 8 km S.E. of Peebles; woollen cloth and knitwear;

mineral springs; p. (2002) 2,586.

Inner Mongolia (Nei Mongol), Chinese aut. region, N.E. **China;** stretches along S. border of Republic of Mongolia; vast steppelands, sparse p.; st. farms for animal husbandry; peat beds; milk-processing; cap Hohhot; a. 1,177,518 km²; p. (1994) 22,170,000.

Innsbruck, c., cap. of the Tyrol, W. **Austria;** on R. Inn; commands N. approach to Brenner Pass; univ.; tourism; fortfd. 12th cent.; p. (1991) 114,996.

Inowroclaw, t., N. **Poland;** prov. Bydgoszcz; rock-salt. iron pyrites; agr. prod.; p. (1989) 76,497.

Insterburg. *See* Chernyakhovsk.

Inter-American Highway, section of Pan-American Highway system, from Mexico to Panama.

Interlaken, t., Bernese Oberland, Berne, **Switzer-land;** on R. Aare between Ls. Thun and Brienz; tourist resort.

Intracoastal Waterway, USA; toll-free waterway along Atl. and Gulf of Mexico csts.; completed 1949 using bays, rivers and canals; 4,960 km long.

Inveraray, burgh, Argyll and Bute, **Scot.;** nr. head of Loch Fyne; herring fishing; p. (1991) 512.

Inverbervie, burgh, Aberdeenshire, **Scot.;** on E. cst., 13 km S. of Stonehaven; linen; p. (2002) 2,094.

Invercargill, c., S.I., **N.Z.;** on S.E. cst.; sawmills, freezing wks.; aluminium smelter; served by Bluff Harbour; p. (1991) 56,148.

Inverclyde, unit. auth. created in 1996, formerly part of Strathclyde, W. **Scot.;** on F. of Clyde, inc. Gourock and Greenock; p. (2002) 83,600.

Invergordon, burgh, spt., Highland, **Scot.;** on N. side of Cromarty F., 19 km N.E. of Dingwall; former naval pt.; whisky distillery; p. (2002) 3,890.

Inverkeithing, royal burgh, Fife, **Scot.;** on F. of Forth, nr. Dunfermline; shipbreaking, papermkg., quarrying; p. (2002) 5,412.

Inverkip, par., v., Inverclyde, **Scot.;** 10 km S.W. of Greenock; par. contains Gourock; resort; p. (2002) 1,598.

Inverness, c., royal burgh, Highland, N.E. **Scot.;** on Moray F.; distilling, lt. engin.; tweeds; sm. pt. for general cargo; tourism; created a Millennium City, 2000; p. (2002) 40,949.

Inverness-shire, historic co., N.W. **Scot.,** now part of Highland.

Inverurie, royal burgh, Aberdeenshire, **Scot.;** on R. Don, 22 km N.W. of Aberdeen; rly. ctr., mkt. t.; tourism; p. (2002) 10,882.

Inyokern, t., E. Cal., **USA;** naval ordnance research sta.

Ioannina (Janina), t., Epirus, **Greece;** nr Albanian frontier; agr. tr.; embroidery; univ.; p. (1981) 44,829, (1991) 157,214 (reg.).

Iona, I., off cst. of Mull, Argyll and Bute, **Scot.;** early Scottish Christian ctr.; restored abbey; St. Columba's burial place; anc. burial place of Scottish kings; p. (1991) 130.

Ionian Is., gr. in Mediterranean, belonging to **Greece;** comprising Corfu, Paxos, Levkas, Cephalonia, Zakinthos, Ithake; severe earthquake 1953; total a. 1,948 km²; p. (1991) 193,734.

Ionian Sea. Mediterranean; between Greece and E.; Italy and Sicily on W.

Iowa, st., **USA;** Hawkeye St.; admitted to Union 1846, 3t. flower Wild Rose, St. bird Eastern Goldfinch; in Middle West; prairie cty., watered by Mississippi and Missouri; rich farm land; maize, oats, and other grains; hogs, pigs; process-ing of farm prod.; flood control, reforestation; diverse inds.; cap. Des Moines; a. 145,791 km²; p. (2002) 2,936,760.

Iowa City, c., S.E. Iowa, **USA;** former st. cap. (1839–56); univ.; p. (1996) 60,923.

Ipoh, c., cap. of Perak st., N.W. **Malaya,** tin-mng. ctr.; Chinese rock temples; p. (1991) 468,800.

Ipswich, co. t., l. gov. dist., Suffolk, **Eng.;** pt. on estuary of R. Orwell; increasingly impt. container pt.; exp. timber, grain and malt; birthplace of Cardinal Wolsey; diesel engines, gen. engin.; p. (2001) 117,069 (dist.).

Iqaluit, cap., Nunavut region, **Canada;** pop. 5,000.

Iquitos, t., N.E. **Peru;** on Amazon, 3,680 km from mouth; comm. ctr.; exp. timber, cotton; sawmills, oil refining; p. (1993) 274,759.

Iráklion (Candia or Herakleion), t., cap. of Crete, **Greece;** impt. spt. on G. of I., arm of Aegean Sea; at foot of terraced hill slopes; wine, olive oil, fruit, fishing; tourism; p. (1991) 115,124.

Iran, former kingdom, Islamic st. (1979), S.W. **Asia;** known as Persia until 1935; interior plateau at c. 900 km, ringed by mtn. ranges of up to c. 5,500 m; much of a. is desert; settled agr. limited to

Caspian plain; heavy dependence on oil; oilfields centred on Abādān; pipeline to Iskenderun (Turkey) on Mediterranean cst. started (1986) as alterna-tive exp. route; high quality carpets exported, confrontation with US over nuclear policy; Shia Muslims 89 per cent of pop.; Sunni Muslim 10 per cent; cap. Tehran; a. 1,626,520 km²; p. (2004) 69,018,924.

Irapuato, c., central **Mexico;** agr. tr. and processing; iron-founding; p. (1990) 362,471.

Iraq, rep., S.W. **Asia;** the anc. Mesopotamia; domin-ated by 2 Rs., Tigris and Euphrates; much of a. desert and semi-desert but presence in S. and centre enables settled agr. for barley, wheat, dates, and tobacco; only outlet to sea at N.W. end of Persian G.; oil principal source of wealth; main oilfield at Kirkūk; main oil pt. at Basra; pipe-lines to Lebanon and Syria; new inds. based on oil; 14 provs.; cap. Baghdad; a. 435,120 km²; p. (2004) 25,374,691. For the 2003 war and subse-quent insurgency, *see* Section C.

Ireland, I., W. of Gt. Britain, separated by Irish Sea; divided politically into R.o.I. (Eire) and N. Ireland (Ulster, part of U.K.); ch. physical features, L. Neagh in N.E., Ls. of Killarney in S.W.; Rs. Shannon, Boyne, Blackwater; mtns. of Mourne, Wicklow, and Kerry; mild moist climate; called "emerald isle"; pastoral agr., especially dairying; tourism; a. 83,937 km²;

Ireland, Republic of, indep. st., W. Europe; comprises 26 of 32 cos. making up I. of Ireland; member of EU; ring of highlands surround central lowland basin, much of which is peat-covered; economy based on agr., especially dairying; exps. butter, cheese, bacon; new govt.-encouraged inds.; mineral resources; tourism; cap. Dublin; a. 68,894 km²; p. (2004) 3,969,558.

Irian Jaya (formerly Dutch New Guinea, later W. Irian), prov., **Indonesia;** part of Indonesia, 1963; inaugurated as prov., 1969; primitive agr. of rice, poultry, cocoa; few oil deposits; cap. Djajapura; growing calls for independence from Indonesia; greater autonomy (2001); a. (inc. Ternate) 412,784 km²; p. (1990) 1,641,400.

Irish Sea, Brit. Is.; between Gt. Britain and Ireland, connecting N. and S. with Atl. Oc.; 320 km long; 80–224 km wide; greatest depth 840 m; a. 18,130 km².

Irkutsk, c., cap. of I. oblast, **Russia;** on Angara R. in E. Siberia; on Trans-Siberian rly., 64 km W. of L. Baykal; univ.; engin., sawmilling, petroleum refining, chemicals, hydroelec. power sts.; p. (1989) 626,000.

Irlam, t., Gtr. Manchester, **Eng.;** orig. tar, soap, glycerine, margarine; over-spill p.

Ironbridge, t., Shrops., **Eng.;** scene of Darby's iron ind.; derives name from first cast-iron bridge (1779) which here crosses Severn; now inc. in Telford new t.; p. (1991) 2,184.

Iron Country, Utah, **USA;** vast reserves of iron ore; undeveloped due to inaccessibility.

Iron Gate (Porlile de Fier), Romania; famous rapids in R. Danube; Romanian Yugoslavian hydroelectric and navigation project, 1964–71.

Irrawaddy, R., **Myanmar;** flows S. to Bay of Bengal; navigable for lge. steamers 1,440 km; irriga-tion wks.; major Asian rice bowl; 2,000 km long.

Irvine, royal burgh, N. Ayrshire, **Scot.;** nr. mouth of R. Irvine; new t. (1966); cas.; hosiery, lt. engin., bottle wks.; chemicals; lorry plant closure announced (1999); p. (2002) 33,090.

Irwell, R., Gtr. Manchester, **Eng.;** flows through Manchester to the Mersey via Manchester Ship Canal; 48 km long.

Isar, R., **Austria** and W. **Germany;** rises in Austrian Tyrol, flows N.E. to Danube; hydro-electric power stas. below Munich; 261 km long.

Isarco, R., N. **Italy;** rises nr. Brenner Pass, flows S. into R. Adige at Bolzano; 80 km long.

Isdud, anc. c. of the Philistines. *See* Ashdod.

Ise (Ujiyamada), t., Honshu, **Japan;** sacred c. of Shintoism; p. (1990) 104,162.

Ise Bay, inlet, S. Honshu, **Japan;** flanked by ch. textile mftg. a. of cty. with 5 million people centred on Nagoya; 64 km long, 24–32 km wide.

Iseo, L., N. **Italy;** E. of Bergamo; 124 km².

Isère, dep., S.E. **France;** drained by Rs. Isère and Rhône; cap. Grenoble; mtnous.; cereals; wine, butter, cheese; iron, coal, lead, silver, copper; gloves, silks; a. 8,231 km²; p. (1999) 1,092,049.

Isère, R., S.E. **France;** rises in Graian Alps, flows W. into R. Rhône nr. Valence; used to generate hydroelec. power; used, with trib. R. Arc, by main rly. from France to N. Italy through Mt. Cenis (Fréjus) tunnel.

Isfahan. See **Esfahān.**

Ishimbay, c., Bashkir aut. rep. **Russia;** on R. Belaya; ctr. of Ishimbay oilfields; pipelines to Ufa, Orsk, and Shkaparo.

Isis, R., headstream of R. Thames, **Eng.;** so named around and above Oxford.

Iskenderun (Alexandretta), spt., S. **Turkey;** recent modernisation for new Iran/Turkey rly.; new steel wks.; p. (1990) 175,998.

Islamabad, new cap. of **Pakistan,** to N. of Rawalpindi below Himalayas; nuclear power stas.; p. (1998) 530,000.

Islay, I. Inner Hebrides, Argyll and Bute, **Scot.;** farming, dairying, distilleries; p. (1991) 3,538.

Isle of Anglesey, N.W. **Wales,** separated from mainland by Menai Straits; former stronghold of Druids, attacked by Romans A.D. 61; mainly agr. and tourism; unit. auth. created in 1996 from former l. gov. dist., reinstating historic co. disbanded in 1974; p. (2001) 66,829.

Isle of Grain, Kent, **Eng.;** flat promontory at confluence of Thames and Medway, once separated from mainland by a tidal estuary; lge oil refinery; pipelines to Walton-on-Thames and Heathrow Airport.

Isle of Man, Brit. dependency, Irish Sea; high plateau N.E. to S.W.; ch. t. Douglas; old cap. Castletown; admin. according to own laws; tourism; growing Manx identity; reintroduction of Manx Gaelic into schools; a. 572 km²; p. (2004) 74,655.

Isles of Scilly, archipelago, l. gov. dist., 45 km. S.W. of Land's End, Cornwall, **Eng.;** early flowers and vegetables benefit from mild winter climate; tourism; p. (2001) 2,153.

Isle of Wight, unit. auth. created in 1995, **Eng.;** English Channel, separated from Hampshire by Spithead and the Solent; crossed by chalk hills, terminating in the Needles; holiday resort; ch. ts. Newport, Ryde, Cowes; p. (2001) 132,731.

Islington, inner bor., London, **Eng.;** N. of City; incorporates Finsbury; univ.; residtl.; clocks, precision engin.; p. (2001) 175,797.

Ismailia (Ismā'īlīya), t. and prov., **Egypt;** at mid-point of Suez Canal on L. Timsah; rail connections with Cairo, Suez, Port Said; declined during canal closure; p. (1996) 254,500 (t.), 715,000 (prov.).

Israel, rep., S.W. Asia; occupies narrow corridor between Jordan valley and Mediterranean Sea; extends S. into the Negev desert (half a. of rep.); Mediterranean climate enables cultivation of early fruits and vegetables, especially citrus fruits; special feature of agr. is cooperative settlements (Kibbutz); main factor limiting agr. development is availability of water; diamonds hgst. exp. earner; most highly industrialised cty. of S.W. Asia, especially for textiles and clothing; petroleum of increasing impt.; tourism; Jewish rep. since 1948; until then part of the mandate Palestine; surrounded by Arab sts.; controversial settlements on occupied land; cap. Jerusalem; a. 20,850 km²; nat. a. in dispute, particularly since wars of 1967 and 1973; p. (2002) 6,199,008.

Istanbul (Constantinople), ch. spt., former cap., **Turkey;** on Golden Horn peninsula on European cst. at entry of Bosporus into Sea of Marmara; divided into old "Stamboul" on S. side, and dists. of Galata and Beyoglu (Pera) on N.; the anc. Byzantium; magnificent mosque of Sta. Sophia; univ.; industl. and comm. ctr.; tourism; p. (2000) 9,451,000 (met. a.).

Istria, peninsula, N. Adriatic, **Croatia** (formerly Yugoslavia); ch. c. Pula; agr., olives, vines, oranges, maize; p. Yugoslav and Italian; a. c. 5,200 km².

Itabira, t., Minas Gerais st., **Brazil;** on Brazilian Plateau, 96 km N.E. of Belo Horizonte; lgst. deposits of iron ore in Brazil; p. (1996) 95,200.

Italy, rep., S. Europe; peninsula extending into Mediterranean; inc. 2 main Is. of Sicily and Sardinia; bounded by Alps to N.; central spine of Apennines; Mediterranean climate; contrast between industrialised N. and less developed agr. S.; member of EU; agr. impt., especially in Po basin; tourism attracted by Roman and Renaissance art and architecture and by climate; inds. based on hydroelectric power in N., inc. elec. engin., motor vehicles and textiles, centred at Milan and Turin; 19 admin. regions; cap. Rome; a. 301,049 km²; p. (2004) 58,057,477.

Ithaca, t., N.Y., **USA;** on Cayuga L.; seat of Cornell Univ.; elec. clocks; machin.; p. (2000) 29,300.

Ithake, one of the Ionian Is., **Greece;** a. 96 km²; ch. t. Ithake; severe earthquake, 1953.

Itzehoe, t., Schleswig-Holstein, **Germany;** founded by Charlemagne; wood, cement, machin.; p. (1999) 34,300.

Ivanovo, t., **Russia;** N.E. of Moscow; textiles, iron and chemical wks.; peat-fed power stas.; p. (1989) 481,000.

Iviza. See Ibiza.

Ivory Coast. See Côte d'Ivoire.

Iwaki, t., Honshu, **Japan;** ctr. of apple producing dist., p. (1990) 355,817.

Iwo, t., **Nigeria;** nr. Ibadan; tr. ctr.; fmr. cap. of Yoruba kingdom; p. (1991) 125,600.

Izhevsk, (Ustinov), c., cap. of Udmurt aut. rep. **Russia;** steel ctr., engin., p. (1989) 635,000.

Izmail, c., **Ukraine;** in Bessarabia, on Danube delta, nr. Romanian border; former Turkish fortress; p. (1990) 94,100.

Izmir (Smyrna), c., **Turkey;** at head of G. of I., Anatolia; exp. figs, raisins, tobacco, carpets, rugs; anc. and historic c.; ch. comm. ctr. of the Levant; Nemrut Free Trade Zone (1987); ambitious industl. project, refinery and chem. complex (1972–86); univ.; p. (1990) 2,319,188 (t.), 2,694,770 (prov.).

Izmit, c., **Turkey;** E. end of Sea of Marmara; cereals, tobacco, oil refinery and polythene plant; major earthquake, 1999; p. (1990) 254,800.

J

Jabalpur (Jubbulpore), c., Madhya Pradesh, **India;** rly. ctr.; ordnance wks.; p. (1991) 742,000.

Jackson, t., cap. of Miss., **USA;** comm. and industl. ctr.; p. (2000) 184,300.

Jacksonville, c., Fla., **USA;** pt. on St. John's R.; impt. ctr. on Atl. cst.; chemicals, shipbldg. and repair, printing, lumber, cigar mftg.; tourism; p. (2000) 735,617.

Jacobabad, t., Sind, **Pakistan;** driest and hottest place in Indian sub-continent; p. (1981) 80,000.

Jacui, R., S. **Brazil;** rises in S. edge of Brazilian Plateau, enters Atl. Oc., through lagoon, Lagoa dos Patos; 560 km long.

Jadotville. See Likasi

Jaduguda, Bihar, **India;** uranium mine and mill to supply India's growing nuclear power production.

Jaén, t., cap. of prov. of Jaén, **Spain;** in foothills of Andalusian mtns.; cath.; olive oil, wine, chemicals; p. (1991) 105,545, (1998) 645,800 (prov.).

Jaffna, spt., N. **Sri Lanka;** on J. peninsula; second t. of rep.; p. (1995) 135,000.

Jaipur, c., cap. of Rajasthan, **India;** univ.; fine fabrics, jewellery; tourism; old cap. Amber is 8 km away; p. (1991) 1,458,000.

Jajce, t., Bosnia-Herzegovina, formerly Yugoslavia; at junc. of Rs. Vrbas and Pliva (hydroelectric power); Fed. People's Rep. of Yugoslavia declared here by Tito (1943).

Jakarta, (Batavia), c., cap. of **Indonesia,** N.W. Java; comm. ctr.; textiles; exps. rubber, tea; printing; airport; p. (2000) 11,018,000.

Jalalabad, c., E. **Afghanistan;** on Kābul R., nr. Khyber Pass; univ.; agr. tr. ctr.; p. (1988) 55,000.

Jalgaon, t., Maharashtra, **India;** in Tapti R. valley nr. Bhusawal; p. (1991) 242,193.

Jalisco, st., **Mexico;** on Pac. Oc.; traversed by Sierra Madre; well timbered, agr.; minerals; tourism; a. 80,876 km²; p. (1990) 5,287,987.

Jalón, R., **Spain;** rises in Iberian Mtns., flows N.E. into R. Ebro nr. Zaragoza; valley forms main rly., road route from Madrid to Ebro valley.

Jamaica, rep., W.I.; member of Brit. Commonwealth; mtnous.; Blue Mtn. range runs E. to W. and rises to 2,258 m; tropical climate modified by alt.; economy based on agr. and mng.; major exp. crops sugar and bananas; major world producer of bauxite (recent contraction) and alumina; tourist ind. expanding; member of Caribbean Free Trade Association; 25 per cent unemployment; major pts. Kingston, Montego Bay, Pt. Antonio; international airpt.; univ. at cap. Kingston; a. 11,424 km²; p. (2004) 2,713,130, of which 22 per cent are in Kingston.

James, R. Va., **USA;** hydroelec. power in upper reaches, wide estuary in lower course; outlet to Chesapeake Bay; 544 km long.

James Bay, S. arm of Hudson Bay, **Canada;** c. 480 km long, 224 km wide.

Jamestown, spt., cap. of St. Helena I.; flax; p. (1992) 1,500.

Jamestown, t., dist., Va., USA; nr. mouth of James R., where first English permanent settlement was founded 1607.

Jammu, t., J. and Kashmir, India; winter cap. of st.; univ., fort, palace; p. (1991) 206,000.

Jammu and Kashmir, st., N.W. India; traversed by ranges of Himalayas; wheat and rice; 1972 agreement divided state between India and Pakistan; renewed conflict, 2002; cap. Indian sector Srinagar, cap. Pakistani sector Muzaffarabad; devastating earthquake, 2005; total a. 222,823 km²; p. (2001) 10,069,900.

Jamnagar, t., Gujarat, India; on G. of Kutch; p. (1991) 342,000.

Jamshedpur, c., Jharkhand, India; W. of Calcutta; major industl. ctr. of rep.; Tata iron and steel wks.; engin.; p. (1991) 461,000.

Jämtland, co. W. Sweden; cap. Ostersand; a. 49,857 km²; p. (1992) 135,910.

Janina. See Ioánnina.

Japan, E. Asia; 4 main Is., Honshu (lgst.), Hokkaido, Shikoku, Kyushu; mtnous.; 18 active volcanoes; subject to earthquakes; only 17 per cent of land cultivable; intensive and mechanised agr.; rice, fruits, vegetables; few animals; inds. highly developed and based on imports of raw material and export of finished prods.; rapid industrialisation since second world war; economic growth has been rapid, but major financial crisis (1997); rapid technological innovation; inds. inc. shipbldg., motor vehicles, textiles, steel, electronics, chemicals; cap. Tokyo, world financial ctr.; a. 370,370 km²; p. (2004) 127,333,002 (inc. Okinawa and Ryuku Is.).

Japan Current. See Kuroshio.

Japan, Sea of, portion of Pac. Oc. between Korea, Russia and Japan.

Jari, new t., Amazonia, Brazil; ambitious project of timber and pulp plant in the rain forest; not as successful as hoped.

Jaroslaw, t., Przemysl., prov., S.E. Poland; on R. San; food-processing; founded 11th cent.; impt. tr. ctr. 16th cent.; p. (1995) 41,834.

Jarrow, t., South Tyneside, Tyne and Wear, Eng.; on S. bank of Tyne, 11 km below Gateshead; grew up as shipbldg. ctr.; in depression; hunger march to London 1936; new inds; steel and tube wks., oil storage; die-castings; home of the Venerable Bede; p. (2001) 27,526.

Jaunpur, t., Uttar Pradesh, India; mkt. t.; ctr. of Muslim learning and architecture in 15th cent.

Java, I., Indonesia; most developed of Indonesian Is.; traversed E. to W. by forested volcanic mtns.; fertile volcanic soils aid intensive rice cultivation; over-populated; contains 70 per cent of cty.'s p. yet only 8 per cent of land a.; exps. inc. coffee, rubber, sugar, copra, teak; noted for silver craft and batik work (anc. craft of fabric decoration); a. 130,510 km²; p. (1990) 107,525,500.

Javari, R., forms bdy. between Peru and Brazil. trib. of R. Amazon.

Jebel Aulia, v., Sudan; S of Khartoum; dam across White Nile R.

Jedburgh, royal burgh, Borders, Scot.; on Jed Water, S.W. of Kelso; tweeds, woollens, rayon; abbey ruins; p. (2002) 4,090.

Jeddah. See Jiddah.

Jefferson City, st. cap. Mo., USA; on Missouri R.; univ.; comm. and processing ctr. of agr. a.; shoes, tiles, farm implements; p. (2000) 39,600.

Jelenia Góra (Hirschberg), t. and prov., S.W. Poland (since 1945), formerly in Lower Silesia; mftg.; spa; p. (1995) 95,513 (t.), 524,171 (prov.).

Jemappes, t., Belgium; 5 km W. of Mons; industl., Fr. victory over Austria 1792; battle of Mons 1914.

Jena, c., Germany; on R. Saale, 72 km S.W. of Leipzig; univ., observatory; optical glass-ware, precision instruments; leading cultural ctr. late 18th and early 19th cent.; defeat of Prussians by Fr. 1806; p. (2002) 101,157.

Jerez de la Frontera, t., Spain; in Andalusia, 22 km N.E. of Cádiz; in fertile agr. a.; sherry; p. (1998) 181,600.

Jericho, v., Jordan Valley, Jordan; one of oldest towns in the world (6000 B.C.).

Jersey, lgst. of Channel Is., 21 km W. of Fr. cst.; potatoes, tomatoes, cauliflowers, flowers, fruit. cattle; tourist resort; banking; ch. t. St. Helier; a. 117 km²; p. (2004) 90,502.

Jersey City, c., N.J., USA; E. of Newark, on Hudson R.; comm. and industl. ctr.; diverse

inds.; p. (2000) 240,055 (c.), 553,000 (met. a.).

Jerusalem, c., Israel and Jordan; 811 m a.s.l.; between Dead Sea and Mediterranean; the "Holy City" of the Jews and the sacred c. of the Christians and Muslims; Israeli western sector and Arab eastern sector declared by Israeli parliament (1980) united c. and cap.; modern mftg.; p. (1997) 591,400 inc. E. Jerusalem.

Jesselton. See Kota Kinabalu.

Jhang Maghiana, t., Pakistan; textiles; mkt.; on R. Chenab; p. (1998) 292,300.

Jhansi, c., Uttar Pradesh, India; ctr. rly. ctr.; mkt.; p. (1991) 313,000.

Jharia, t., Bihar, India; ctr. of most impt. coalfield in India; p. (1991) 69,600.

Jharkhand, st., India, new st. created 1997 from S. sect. of Bihar; p. (2000) 26,909,400.

Jhelum, R., W. Punjab, Pakistan; most W. of the five Rs. of the Punjab; forms Vale of Kashmir in upper course; Mangla Dam under Indus Waters Treaty, completed 1967.

Jhelum, c., Pakistan; on Jhelum R.; p. (1998) 145,800.

Jiangsu (Kiangsu), coastal prov., China; on Yellow Sea; low lying a. N. of Chang Jiang delta; rich agr., dense p.; cotton, sericulture, tea, sugar, fish (many Ls.); cap. Nanjing; a. 109,000 km²; p. (1994) 68,310,000.

Jiangxi (Kiangsi), prov., S.E. China; in basin of navigable Gan R. which drains through L. Poyang to Chang Jiang; ch. cs. Shanghai, Zhenjiang, Wuxi, Nanchang (cap.); rice, wheat, tea, cotton; tungsten, coking coal, kaolin; a. 172,494 km²; p. (1994) 38,930,000.

Jiddah or Jeddah, c., admin. cap., Hejaz, Saudi Arabia; on Red Sea, pt. of Mecca; pilgrims; steel mill and oil refinery; new King Faisal Port nearby; univ. (with Mecca), new rly. link planned to Riyadh; p. (2000) 1,810,000.

Jihlava, t., Moravia, Czech Rep.; on Jihlava R.; 519 m a.s.l.; timber, grain, textiles; Prague Compactata signed here 1436; p. (1991) 51,800.

Jilin (Kirin), prov., N.E. China; N. of Korea and Liaotung peninsula; crossed by Songhua R.; in fertile Manchurian plain; impt. industl. a.; soya beans, grain, lumber, coal, gold, lead; cap. Changchun; a. 186,998 km²; p. (1994) 25,150,000.

Jilin (Kirin), or c., Jilin, N.E. China; former prov. cap.; on Songhua R., at outlet of Songhua reservoir; impt. position on rly. from Changchun to coastal pts.; chemical fertilisers, steel, oil refinery; p. (1994) 1,120,000.

Jimma, t., Ethiopia; ch. prod. Jimma coffee; connected by road with Addis Ababa; Agricultural Technical School; p. (1994) 88,900.

Jinan (Tsinan), c., cap of Shandong prov., China; on S. bank of Huang He, 160 km. from G. of Bo Hai; agr. ctr.; textiles, foodstuffs, chemicals, trucks; univ; p. (1994) 1,659,900.

Jinja, t., Uganda; on N. shore of L. Victoria where Nile drains from L. over Ripon Falls; (now submerged by the construction of Owen Falls dam 2.4 km downstream); cotton mnts., copper smelting; rly. to Kampala; p. (1991) 60,979.

Jinsha. See Shashi.

Jinzhou (Chinchö), c., Liaoning prov., China; cement, glass, bricks, tiles, paper, wood and pulp, oil; p. (1994) 610,300.

João Pessoa, t., cap. of Paraíba st., Brazil; through its pt. Cabedelo expts. cotton, sugar, minerals; industl. expansion; p. (1991) 497,214.

Jodhpur, t., Rajasthan, India; ctr. of Thar desert; old fortress t.; p. (1991) 668,000.

Jogjakarta, c., Java, Indonesia; univ., cultural ctr.; handicrafts; citadel with palace; p. (1990) 412,100.

Johannesburg, c., Gauteng Prov., S. Africa; univ.; gold-mng. ctr. of Witwatersrand; diamond cutting, engin., textiles, chemicals; oil pipeline from Durban; p. (2000) 2,335,000 (met. a.).

John o' Groat's House, place nr. Duncansby Head, Highland, Scot.

Johnston Atoll, two sm. Is. 1,150 km S.W. of Hawaii, belonging to USA; p. (2004) 396.

Johnstone, burgh, Renfrewshire, Scot.; on R. Black Cart, nr. Paisley; machine tools, textiles, iron and brass foundry; p. (2002) 16,468.

Johnstown, sm. industl. t., Penns., USA; on Conemaugh R.; coal-mng. and steel ctr.; machin.

Johore, st., Malaysia; at S. end of Malaya; forested; cap. Johor Baharo; rubber, rice, copra, pineapples; tin, iron, bauxite; a. 18,985 km²; p. (2000 est.) 2,650,000.

Joina Falls, Mali; dam projected for hydroelectric power and irrigation under auspices of Organisation of Riparian States of R. Senegal (Guinea, Mali, Mauritania, Senegal).

Joliet, c., Ill., **USA**; on Des Plaines R., S.W. of Chicago; R. pt.; coal and limestone nearby; rly. engin., oil refining; p. (1990) 76,836 (c.), 390,000 (met. a.).

Joliette, t., Quebec, **Canada**; textile mills, paper, tobacco-processing; p. (1991) 17,400.

Jönköping, t., cap. of J. co., **Sweden**; safety-matches, textiles, footwear; p. (1992) 112,802 (t.) 309,867 (co.).

Jonquière, t., S. Quebec, **Canada**; paper and pulp mills; p. (1991) 57,933. See Chicoutimi.

Jordan, kingdom, S.W. Asia; bounded by Israel, Syria, Saudi Arabia, and Iraq; consists of high plateau (600 m), Jordan valley, and hill cty. to W. of R. Jordan; only 25 per cent of a. sufficiently humid for agr., much is migratory herding of animals and subsistence agr., sm. mineral wealth; only outlet to sea Aqaba, pt. on G. of Aqaba; only one single-track rly.; new rail link built to Al-Hara phosphate mines, now major exp.; dependant on oil imports; cap. Amman; W. Bank of R. Jordan occupied by Israeli forces after June 1967; a. 101,140 km²; p. (2004) 5,611,202.

Jordan, R., **Israel** and **Jordan**; flows S. from Anti-Lebanon along sinuous course, mostly below sea-level to Dead Sea; its rapidly and variant depth render it unnavigable, and no t. of any importance has ever been built on its banks; Jesus was baptised in its waters; contemporary strife over use for irrigation; 368 km long.

Jos, t., central **Nigeria**; on Bauchi Plateau, 96 km S.W. of Bauchi; impt. tin mines; steel rolling mill; serious religious clashes (2001); p. (1992) 185,600.

Jostedalsbre, icefield, W. **Norway**, lgst. icefield of European mainland; a. 881 km²; rises to 2,043 m.

Jotunheimen, mtn. region, central **Norway** hgst. in Scandinavia; Galdhopiggen 2,470 m, Glittertind 2,482 m.

Juan Fernández, two rocky volcanic Is., S. **Pac. Oc.**, belonging to **Chile**; a. 98 km²; the buccaneer Alexander Selkirk marooned here 1704–9 gave idea for Defoe's *Robinson Crusoe*. Now renamed **Robinson Crusoe Is**.

Juan les Pins, resort, Alpes-Maritimes dep., S.E. **France**.

Juba (**Giuba**), R., **Somalia**; narrow fertile valley, imp. agr. a.; 872 km long.

Jucar, R., E. **Spain**; rises in Montes Universales, and flows to Mediterranean; irrigation and hydroelec. power; 400 km long.

Judaea, div. of Palestine in the Roman period.

Juggernaut. See Puri.

Julfa (**Jolfa**), c., N. **Iran**; on northern frontier, customs and transit ctr. on overland route from Europe.

Julian Alps, mtn. range, **Slovenia** (formerly Yugoslavia) and **Italy**; hgst. peak 2,865 m.

Julianehåb, t., S.W. **Greenland**; N.W. of C. Farewell; tr. ctr., fish. pt.; p. (1990) 3,543.

Jülich, t., N. Rhine–Westphalia, **Germany**; nuclear reactor; p. (1999) 32,600.

Jullundur (**Jalandhar**), c., Punjab, **India**; rly. ctr.; st. cap. until Chandigarh was built; p. (1991) 520,000.

Jumna, R., N. **India**; ch. trib. of R. Ganges; rises in the Himalayas and flows past Delhi and Agra to Allahabad; 1,376 km long.

Junagadh, t., Gujarat, **India**; agr. tr. and food-processing; industl. ctr.; formerly cap. of principality of J.; p. (1991) 130,484.

Jundiai, t., São Paulo st., **Brazil**; industl. ctr.; nr. São Paulo; p. (1996) 293,200.

Juneau, c., cap. of Alaska, **USA**; at foot of Chilkoot mtns., lumbering; fisheries; gold settlement (1881); p. (1996) 29,756. See Willow South.

Jungfrau, peak, Bernese Oberland, **Switzerland**; height 4,161 m; electric rly. from Kleine Scheidegg to Jungfraujoch.

Jura, dep., E. **France**; named from mtn. range on Franco-Swiss border; agr. and pastoral; cap. Lons-le-Saunier; a. 5,053 km²; p. (1999) 250,895.

Jura, I., Argyll and Bute, **Scot.**; off W. cst.

Jura, mtn. range, **Switzerland** and **France**; folded parallel ranges separated by deep R. valleys; hgst. peak Crêt de la Neige, 1,724 m; 240 km long, breadth 48–64 km.

Jura, canton, **Switzerland**; between Berne and Basle in a strong French speaking dist. in Jura Mtns; p. (1990) 65,700.

Juruá R., lge. trib. of Amazon; rises in E. **Peru**

and flows through Acre and Amazonas sts., **Brazil**; over 3,200 km long.

Juyjuy, prov., N.W. **Argentina**; p. (1991) 512,329.

Jylland (**Jutland**), peninsula region, **Denmark**; intensive agr. and poultry farming; sandy heath in W.; more fertile clay in E. used for dairying; a. 29,554 km²; p. (1990) 2,378,348.

K

K2 or **Godwin-Austen Mt.**, peak (8,611 m) in Karakoram between Tibet and Sinkiang, **China**, after Everest highest in world; summit reached by Italian exp. Desio 1954; also named Chobrum.

Kabardino-Balkaria, aut. rep., Transcaucasia, **Russia**; cap. Nalchik; livestock, lumber, wheat, fruit; non-ferrous metals; hydro-metallurgy plant; mainly Islamic; a. 12,432 km²; p. (2005) 900,000.

Kabinda. See Cabinda.

Kâbul, c., cap. of **Afghanistan**; on Kâbul R. S. of Hindu Kush; 2,104 m a.s.l.; univ.; comm. and cultural ctr.; textiles, leather, timber inds.; p. (2000) 2,590,000 (met. area).

Kâbul, R., flows from Hindu Kush through gorges in Khyber Pass to Indus; site of dam for hydro-elec. power and irrigation; length c. 480 km.

Kabwe (**Broken Hill**), **Zambia**; comm. and mng. ctr.; lead, zinc, cadmium, silver; p. (1989) 210,000.

Kachchh, peninsula, Gujarat st., N.W. **India**; bounded on N. by Pakistan; largely barren except for fertile strip along Arabian Sea; p. (1991) 1,252,500.

Kachin State, semi-aut. st., **Myanmar**; comprising former Myitkyina and Bhamo dists.; home of Kachins; a. 89,042 km²; p. (2000 est.) 1,300,000.

Kaduna, t., N. **Nigeria**; cap of Kaduna st.; rly. junc.; aluminium wks.; spinning and weaving; new oil refinery; conflict between Moslems and Christians, 2000; p. (1992) 309,600 (t.), (1991) 3,969,252 (state).

Kaffa, region, **Ethiopia**; mtnous., forested; natural habitat of coffee plant.

Kagoshima, c., at S. end of Kyushu I., **Japan**; pt. on K. Bay; univs.; cas.; porcelain, silk and cotton clothing, food-processing, publishing; rocket launching site at Uchinoura; p. (1990) 536,685.

Kahoolawe, I., **Hawaii**; a. 117 km²; uninhabited.

Kaieteur Falls, waterfall, **Guyana**; where R. Potaro leaves Guiana Highlands; among world's hgst. falls (226 m).

K'ai-feng, c., Henan, **China**; nr. S. bank of Huang He; one of the most anc. cities in China; cottons, chemicals; p. (1994) 535,300.

Kaikoura, dist., S.I., **N.Z.**; on E. cst., 128 km N.E. of Christchurch; in this region are the Kaikoura ranges, in which the hgst. peaks are Tapuaenuku (2,887 m) and Alarm (2,867 m); p. (1991) 3,711.

Kailas (**Kang-ti-ssu Shan**), range and peak, S.W. Tibet, **China**; unclimbed sacred mtn.; source of Indus, Ganges, Sutlej and Zangbo (head-stream of Brahmaputra).

Kainji Dam, Nigeria; power sta. transmission system and river transportation on R. Niger.

K'ai-ping, t., Hebei, N. **China**; second lgst. coal-mng. a. (Kailan mines) in China; coal exported through Qinhuangdao.

Kairouan, holy c. of Moslems, **Tunisia**; 128 km S.S.E. of Tunis; founded A.D. 670; mosque; p. (1994) 102,600.

Kaiserslautern, c., Rhineland-Palatinate, **Germany**; nr. Mannheim; iron, textiles, machin., tobacco, wood; p. (2002) 99,794.

Kaiser Wilhelm's Land, Australian dependency, **Antarctica**.

Kakamega, t., **Kenya**; E. Africa; 48 km N. of Kisumu; ctr. of gold-mng. dist.

Kalahari Desert, region of semi-desert, southern **Africa**; between Orange and Zambesi Rs.; mainly in **Botswana**; alt. 1,128 m; a. 51,800 km²; inhabited chiefly by Bushmen; new Trans-Kalahari highway completed (1998).

Kalamata, t., Peloponnesus, **Greece**; nr. Sparta; figs, currants, flour-milling, cigarette mftg.; p. (1991) 43,800.

Kalamazoo, c., Mich., **USA**; industl. and comm. ctr. in farming a.; paper, pharmaceuticals; fish hatchery nearby; p. (1996) 77,460.

Kalewa, t., **Myanmar**; at confluence of Irrawaddy and Chindwin Rs.; coal deposits.

Kalgan See Zhangjiakou.

Kalgoorlie, t., W. **Australia;** gold mng. ctr. in arid region adjacent to "Golden Mile" auriferous reef; nickel mng.; p. (1991) 26,079 (inc. Boulder).

Kalimantan (Indonesian Borneo); straddles equator; sparse p.; poor soils; lge. areas of swamp; plans for reclamation; coal, oil, diamonds, gold in sm. quantities; rice, pepper, copra; violent ethnic clashes, 2001; a. 539,461 km²; p. (1990) 8·7 m.

Kalinin. See **Tver.**

Kaliningrad (Königsberg), c., **Russia,** former cap. of E. Prussia; on R. Pregel, linked by canal to outer pt. Pillau; univ., cath.; shipbldg., machin., wood-pulp, chemicals, exp. agr. prods.; Kant lived here all his life; p. (1989) 401,000.

Kalisz, t. and prov., **Poland;** on R. Prosna; industl. ctr., textiles; oldest Polish t. mentioned in 2nd cent. A.D. by Ptolemy; p. (1995) 106,842 (t.), 721,540 (prov.).

Kalmar, co. and t., spt., S. **Sweden;** on I. in Kalmar Sound; cath., cas.; matches, food inds., shipbldg.; p. (1992) 56,863 (t.), 241,912 (co.).

Kalmuk (Kalmytskaya), aut. rep., **Russia;** on Caspian Sea; harsh and infertile steppe; pastoral agr.; cap. Elista; a. 75,887 km²; p. (1989) 322,600.

Kalyan, spt., Maharashtra, **India;** nr. Bombay; bricks, tiles; p. (1991) 1,015,000.

Kama, R., **Russia;** ch. trib. of Volga which it joins below Kazan; rises in foothills of Urals; lge. hydro-electric sta. at Perm; navigable; 2,016 km long.

Kamaishi, t., spt., N.E. Honshu, **Japan;** serves Kamaishi-Sennin iron-ore field, lgst. worked deposits and reserves in Japan; impt. iron and steel ind; p. (1990) 52,484.

Kamakura, t., Honshu, **Japan;** on shore of Sagami Bay; tourism; p. (1990) 174,307.

Kamaran I., Red Sea, **Yemen;** formerly under Brit. occupation, 1915–67; a. 57 km².

Kamchatka, peninsula, E. Siberia, **Russia;** volcanic ranges; geothermal power sta.; mineral wealth, fisheries on cst.; climate cold, wet and foggy; closed to foreigners until 1991; cap. Petropavlovsk.

Kamenets-Podolskiy, t., **Ukraine,** on Smotrich R.; lt. inds.; old fortress t.; p. (1990) 103,300.

Kamensk-Uralsk, c., **Russia;** aluminium, iron, steel, engin.; p. (1989) 208,000.

Kamet, Himalayan peak, on border of **India** and Tibet, **China;** 7,761 m; highest mtn. climbed (Smythe, 1931) until 1953 (Everest).

Kamloops, t., B.C., **Canada;** on Thompson R.; formerly Fort Thompson; on transcontinental rlys.; suppl ctr. for mng. and grazing dist.; fruit and livestock mkts.; p. (1990) 64,011.

Kampala, c., cap. of **Uganda;** univ., ch. comm. ctr.; lt. inds., coffee-processing; p. (2000) 1,212,000.

Kampot, prov., **Cambodia;** on G. of Siam; ctr. of pepper ind.; p. (1998) 524,000.

Kampuchea, Democratic. See **Cambodia.**

Kan, R. See **Gan Jiang.**

Kananga (Luluabourg), c., cap. of Kasai Occidental prov., **Congo;** on Lulua R.; comm. and communications ctr. in cotton-growing a.; p. (1991) 371,862.

Kanazawa, c., Honshu, **Japan;** in Kana plain, on Sea of Japan; machin., silk and cotton textiles; landscape gardens; No theatre; p. (1990) 442,868.

Kanchenjunga, mtn., on Nepal-Sikkim bdy., N.E. **India;** third highst. mtn. in world, 8,585 m.

Kanchipuram (Conjeeveram), t., Tamil Nadu, S. **India;** on plain S.W. of Madras; pilgrimage ctr.; textiles; p. (1991) 144,955.

Kandahar. See **Qandahar.**

Kandy, c., **Sri Lanka;** in mtns. in ctr. of I.; 120 km from Colombo; univ. at sub. of Peradeniya; resort in hot season; tea, cocoa, p. (2001) 110,000.

Kangaroo I., lgst. I. off S. **Australia** cst.; tourists attracted by spectacular granite scenery and varied flora and fauna.

Kano, c., N. **Nigeria;** trading centre for whole of Sudan region; impt. airport and rly. terminus; groundnut ctr.; p. (1992) 699,900 (c.), (1991) 5,632,040.

Kanpur (Cawnpore), c., Uttar Pradesh, N. **India;** on R. Ganges; impt. mftg. ctr.; textiles, chemicals, leather goods, foodstuffs; p. (1991) 1,879,000.

Kansas, st., **USA;** called the "sunflower state"; prairie; farming, maize, wheat; cattle, dairying, pigs; coal, petroleum, natural gas, lead, meat packing, flour milling, aircraft, chemicals, machin.; admitted to Union 1861; st. flower sunflower, st. bird Western Meadowlark; cap. Topeka; a. 213,095 km²; p. (2002) 2,715,884.

Kansas, R., Kan., **USA;** trib. of Missouri R., con-fluence at Kansas City; vegetable growing in valley; periodic flooding; 272 km long.

Kansas City, Kansas and Mo., **USA;** at confluence of Kansas and Missouri Rs.; univ.; gr. livestock mart, car and aircraft assembly, steel prods., meat-packing, food processing; p. (2000) 149,767 (Kansas) 441,545 (Mo.); 1,566,280 (joint met. a.).

Kansu. See **Gansu.**

Kant, t., **Kyrgyzstan;** 19 km E. of Frunze; to be expanded to industl. c.; proposed p. 100,000.

Kaohsiung, spt., co., **Taiwan;** on S.W. cst.; industl. ctr., road and rly. terminus; oil refining, aluminium wks.; p. (1995) 1,423,821 (c.) 1,191,258 (co.).

Kaolack, inland pt., **Senegal;** 112 km up Saloum R.; groundnut ctr., integrated textile complex; p. (1992) 179,894.

Kara-Bogaz-Gol, lge. shallow bay, **Turkmenistan;** an arm of Caspian Sea; rapid evaporation allows huge quantities of salt from Caspian to be deposited along its shores (world's lgst. source of Glauber's salt); a. 18,130 km².

Karacheyevo-Cherkesskaya, aut. region, **Russia;** in Greater Caucasus; cap. Cherkessk; livestock; grain; coal, lead, zinc; a. 14,095 km²; p. (1989) 415,000.

Karachi, c., **Pakistan;** on Arabian Sea, nr. Indus delta; former cap. of Pakistan; univ.; spt., air ctr.; oil refining, industl. gases, steel mill, natural gas from Sui; nuclear power sta.; p. (2000) 11,790,000.

Karaganda, c., **Kazakhstan;** on impt. coalfield developed since 1926; supplies industl. ctrs. of Urals; iron and steel wks., power sta.; p. (1990) 613,200.

Kara-Kalpak, aut. rep., N.W. **Uzbekistan;** inc. Ust-Urt plateau, Kyzyl-Kum desert; irrigated agr.; cap. Nukus; a. 165,553 km²; p. (1990) 1,244,700.

Karakoram Range, part of Himalayas between **Kashmir** and **China;** many lofty peaks, inc. K2; Karakoram highway linking Pakistan with Xinjiang prov. of China, opened 1971.

Kara-Kum, sand desert, **Turkmenistan;** E. of S.E. shore of Caspian Sea; to be irrigated with water diverted from Rs. which flow to Barents Sea. a. 349,650 km²; canal 1,440 km long across desert.

Kara Sea, Arctic Oc.; E. of Novaya Zemlya; navigation to and from Siberian pts. July–Sept.

Karbala, c., **Iraq;** N.W. of Al Hillah; ctr. of pilgrimage; sacred c. of Moslem Shiite sect; p. (2000 est.) 540,000.

Karelian, aut. rep., **Russia;** between Kola peninsula and Finland; lake-covered, coniferous forests; cap. Petrozavodsk; rich in timber, minerals, precious metals; granite and mica quarried; paper and pulp milling; a. 179,408 km²; p. (1989) 790,200.

Karelian Isthmus, Russia, strategic route between Finland and Russia; impt. for defence of St. Petersburg (Leningrad).

Kariba Dam, in Kariba gorge of Zambesi R., on **Zimbabwe–Zambia** border; operated jointly by the two govts.; one of lgst. dams in world with vast artificial lake supplying hydroelectric power to Zimbabwe and the copperbelt of Zambia; badly polluted with use of DDT in tsetse and malaria control; involved resettlement of Batonka peoples; completed 1960.

Karkonosze. See **Riesengebirge.**

Karl-Marx-Stadt. See **Chemnitz.**

Karlový Vary (Carlsbad), t., Bohemia, **Czech Rep.;** on R. Ohre; hot mineral springs; health resort; porcelain; p. (1991) 56,200.

Karlskoga, t., **Sweden;** E. of L. Vänern; seat of Bofors armament wks.; iron and steel, explosives, chemicals; p. (1990) 31,100.

Karlskrona, spt., S. **Sweden;** on Baltic Sea; main naval sta.; lighting fixtures, china; p. (1992) 59,390.

Karlsruhe, c., Baden-Württemberg, **Germany;** road and rly. ctr.; outport on Rhine; chemicals, engin., elec., tobacco inds., oil refining; nuclear reactor; oil pipeline to Lavera, nr. Marseilles; p. (2002) 279,578 (c.), 590,718 (met.a.).

Karlstad, t., **Sweden;** on N. shore L. Väner; ironwks., engin., machin.; p. (1992) 77,290.

Karnak, t., **Egypt;** on Nile, E. of Luxor; site of the anc. Thebes; ruined temples.

Karnataka (Mysore), st., S.W. **India;** borders Arabian Oc.; inc. W. Ghats where high rainfall and hydroelec. power; rainfall decreases to E.; cap. Bangalore; a. 192,203 km²; p. (1991) 44,977,201.

Karpathos, I., Dodecanese, **Greece;** Aegean Sea; between Rhodes and Crete; p. (2000 est.) 6,400.

Karroo, S. Africa; high plateau, scrub-covered; irrigated by Verwoerd dam on Orange R.

Kars, t. and prov., N.E. **Turkey;** in Armenia, alt. c. 1,800 m, in strategic position nr. Soviet border; p. (1997) 93,000 (t.), 323,000 (prov.).

Karst, dist., **Slovenia** (formerly Yugoslavia); in Dinaric Alps; gives name to limestone landforms which are well developed here.

Karvina, t., **Czech Rep.;** on Polish border; ctr. of Ostrava-Karvina coalfield; p. (1990) 70,000.

Kasai, R., **Angola** and **Congo,** Central Africa; rises in Bihé Plateau (Angola) and flows over 1,920 km into R. Congo 192 km above Kinshasa; alluvial diamond mng. at Chicopa.

Kasai, former prov., **Congo;** agr.; impt. source of industl. diamonds; attempted secession 1960; now divided into E. Kasai (cap. Mbuji-Mayi), and W. Kasai (cap Luluabourg)

Kashi (Kashgar) c., Xinjiang, prov., **China;** on anc. imperial silk route through central Asia; growth rapid with irrigation, visited by Marco Polo 1275, p. (1994) 190,000.

Kashmir. See **Jammu and Kashmir.**

Kassala, t., N.E. **Sudan;** ctr. of cotton-growing dist.; p. (1993) 234,000.

Kassel, t., Hesse, **Germany;** on R. Fulda; cas.; machin., vehicles, science-based inds.; route ctr.; p. (2002) 194,748.

Kastamonu, t., N. **Turkey;** cap. of K. prov.; ctr. of dist. rich in minerals; textiles, copper gds.; p. (1997) 59,100.

Katanga. See **Shaba.**

Katmai, Mount, S. Alaska, **USA;** active volcano with crater L.; alt. 2,135 m.

Katmandu (Kathmandu), cap. of **Nepal;** on Vishnumati R., 120 km from Indian frontier; highway to Kodari; hydroelec. sta.; brick and tile wks.; many famous palaces and temples; p. (1995) 533,000.

Katoomba, t., N.S.W., **Australia;** holiday resort at 1,017 m in the Blue Mountains; since 1947 part of City of Blue Mtns.; p. (1991) 16,900 (inc. Wentworth Falls).

Katowice, prov., S. **Poland;** in Upper Silesia; cap. K.; mng. and industl. a. drained by Warta R.; a. 9,516 km²; p. (1995) 3,933,000.

Katowice, c., S. **Poland;** cap. of K. prov.; impt. iron-mng. and industl. ctr.; heavy machin. chemicals; p. (1995) 354,218.

Katrine, Loch, Stirling, **Scot.;** beautiful woodland and moorland scenery; source of Glasgow water supply; scene of Scott's *Lady of the Lake*; 13 km long, c. 1·6 km wide.

Katsina, t., **Nigeria;** nr. Niger border; agr. tr. ctr., groundnuts, cotton; rural craft inds.; steel rolling mill; Hausa cultural ctr.; p. (1992) 186,900, (1991) 3,878,344 (state).

Kattegat, arm of N. Sea linked with Baltic; separates **Denmark** (Jutland) from **Sweden;** 64–112 km wide.

Kaunas (Kovno), c., **Lithuania;** on R. Nemen; R. pt. and comm. ctr.; univ.; 11th cent. c.; metal gds., chemicals, textiles, hydroelec. power; Jewish p. (circa 30 per cent) exterminated during German occupation 1941–4; p. (1990) 429,700.

Kavalla, c., E. Macedonia, **Greece;** on Bay of Kavalla; processes and exp. tobacco; the anc. Neapolis; p. (1991) 58,600.

Kawasaki, S. sub. Tokyo, Honshu, **Japan;** pt. for import of industl. raw materials; heavy inds.; p. (2000) 1,250,000.

Kayah State, semi-aut. st., **Myanmar;** on Thai border; forested plateau; tungsten mines; teak; a. 11,730 km²; p. (2000 est.) 241,000.

Kayseri, c. and prov., **Turkey;** S.E. of Ankara; textiles, carpets, food tr.; anc. Hittite c.; p. (1990) 943,484 (prov.), 461,415 (c.).

Kazakstan, (Kazakhstan), CIS, former USSR constituent rep., located in central Asia; cap. Akmola; steppe with stock-raising; lge. desert areas being made fertile by irrigation; plans to divert Ob R.; grain in N.; coal at Karaganda; asbestos at Dzhetygara; minerals inc. metaborite (richest boron mineral); major oil discoveries (esp. Kashagan field); vast gas reserves in Karachaganak field; atomic power sta. to W. of Caspian Sea; cosmodrome at Leninsk, E. of Aral Sea; 9th largest country in world; a. 2,778,544 km²; p. (2004) 15,143,704.

Kazan, c., **Russia;** cap. of Tatar aut. rep.; pt. on Volga; impt. tr. ctr. for E. Russia, Turkestan Bokhara and Iran; cath., univ. (where Tolstoy and Lenin were educated); engin., chemicals, synthetic rubber, textiles, paper, oil refining; natural gas pipeline to Minnibayevo; p. (1989) 1,094,000.

Kazanluk, t., central **Bulgaria;** in region famous for attar of roses.

Käzerün, t., S.W. **Iran;** ctr. of agr. dist.

Kazvin or **Qazvin,** c., N.W. **Iran;** transit tr.; carpets, textiles; p. (1983) 244,265.

Kearsley, sm. t., Gtr. Manchester, **Eng.;** chemicals.

Keban Dam, S.E. **Turkey;** at confluence of the E. and W. branches of Euphrates.

Kecskemet, c., central **Hungary;** fruit-canning and wine-distilling from locally grown prods.; 4th cent. c.; p. (1997) 105,000.

Kedah, st., **Malaysia;** on Strait of Malacca, N.W. Malaya; rice, rubber, coconuts, tungsten; cap. Alor Star; a. 9,479 km²; p. (2000 est.) 1,650,000.

Kediri, t., E. Java, **Indonesia;** food processing; p. (1995) 261,000.

Keeling Is. See **Cocos Is.**

Keelung, c., N. **Taiwan;** on E. China Sea; naval base and ch pt.; exp. agr prods., chemicals; gold sul. phur, copper mined nearby; p. (1995) 368,173.

Keighley, t., West Yorks., **Eng.;** in Aire valley, 24 km N.W. of Leeds; engin., woollen and worsteds; p. (2001) 49,453.

Keihin, vast conurb. of Tokyo, Yokohama and Kawasaki, **Japan.**

Keith, burgh, Moray, **Scot.;** mkt. t. in agr. dist.; p. (2002) 4,491.

Kelantan, st., **Malaysia;** one of most fertile areas on E. cst. Malaya; cap. Kota Bharu; rice, coconuts, rubber; a. 14,815 km²; p. (2000 est.) 1,300,000.

Kells or **Ceannanus Mor,** mkt. t., Co. Meath, **R.o.I.;** notable for monastic remains and illuminated Book of Kells, now in library of Trinity College, Dublin; p. (1991) 2,200.

Kelso, burgh, Borders, **Scot.;** at confluence of Rs. Teviot and Tweed; p. (2002) 5,116.

Kemerovo, c., **Russia;** S.E. of Tomsk; coalmng. ctr.; chemicals, textiles, plastics; p. (1989) 520,000.

Kempten, t., Bavaria, **Germany;** nr. Bodensee; Benedictine abbey; p. (2002) 61,505.

Kendal, l. gov. dist., Cumbria, **Eng.;** mkt. ctr.; tourism; p. (2001) 28,030.

Kenilworth, t., Warwicks., **Eng.;** 6 km S.W. of Coventry; mkt.; ruined cas.; p. (2001) 22,218.

Kenitra. See **Mina Hassan Tani.**

Kennet, l. gov. dist., Wiltshire, **Eng.;** stretches from Marlborough to Devizes; p. (2001) 74,838.

Kennet, R., Wilts. and Berks., **Eng.;** trib. of R. Thames; followed by main rly. London to W. of Eng.; 70 km long.

Kennington, dist., in London bor. of Lambeth, **Eng.;** inc. the Oval cricket ground, home of Surrey C.C.

Kensington and Chelsea, Royal Borough of, inner bor., W. London, **Eng.;** mainly residtl.; contains Kensington Palace and Gardens; p. (2001) 158,919.

Kent, non-met. co., **Eng.;** intensive agr., mkt. gardening, orchards, hops; "Garden of England"; crossed by N. Downs and Weald; industl. zone bordering Thames and Medway estuaries; tourist resorts and cross-channel ferry pts. on cst.; London commuter hinterland; co. t. Maidstone; p. (2001) 1,329,718.

Kentucky, E. central st., **USA;** in W. foothills of Appalachians and crossed by tribs. of Mississippi; "Bluegrass" st.; mainly agr.; some coal; cap. Frankfort; lgst. c. Louisville, at falls of Ohio R.; hydroelec. power; tourism; admitted to Union 1792; st. flower Goldenrod, st. bird Cardinal; a. 104,623 km²; p. (2002) 4,092,891.

Kentucky, R., Ky., **USA;** flows from Cumberland plateau to Ohio R.; length 400 km.

Kenya, rep., E. Africa; member of Brit. Commonwealth; comprises 7 provs.; straddles equator but climate modified by alt.; marked contrast between sparsely populated and arid N. and well-developed S. where upland climate has attracted the European p.; economy based on prod. and processing of arable and pastoral prods., inc. dairy prod.; relatively well developed cooperative African farming; 80 per cent of p. earn living on the land; most industl. of E. African cty., mostly exp. orientated; growth in exp. of cement and fluorspar; tourism incr. impt; ch. spt. Mombasa, airports at Nairobi and Mombasa; famous for big game; major problem of HIV infection; univs.; cap. Nairobi; a. 582,646 km²; p. (2004) 32,021,856.

Kenya, Mt., volcano, **Kenya;** just S. of equator; snow-covered; alt. 5,197 m; 2nd hgst. peak in Africa; Nat. Park.

Kephallenia. See **Cephalonia.**

Kerala, st., **India**; cap. Trivandrum; plantations producing rubber, tea, pepper; higher proportion of literacy than in any other st.; a. 38,855 km²; p. (2001) 31,838,600.

Kerch, c., **Ukraine**; in Crimea, commanding K. strait connecting Black Sea and Azov Sea; spt. and industl. ctr.; metallurgical plant, iron and steel mills, shipbldg., fisheries; iron-ore, vanadium, natural gas nearby; p. (1990) 176,300.

Kerguelen, archipelago, S. **Indian Oc.**; part of Fr. Antarctic terr.; whaling, fishing; famous for K. cabbage (*Pringlea antiscorbutica*).

Kérkira. *See* **Corfu**.

Kermadec Is., volcanic gr. Pac. Oc.; 960 km N.E. of N.Z.; a. 34 km²; met. sta. on Sunday I. (Raoul I.) (lgst. of gr.); annexed to **N.Z.** 1887; inhabited only by scientists.

Kerman, region, S.E. **Iran**; mtnous., much desert land; agr.; carpet-weaving; coal and iron-ore mng. being developed; recent copper find; irrigation scheme projected; p. (1996) 2,004,300.

Kermān, c., S.E. **Iran**; prov. cap.; carpet-weaving ctr.; textile mftg.; airpt.; mediaeval mosques; p. (1996) 385,000.

Kermānshāh, (Qahremānshahr) t., N.W. **Iran**; cap. of Kermānshāhān prov.; agr., comm. and route ctr.; airpt.; oil refinery; p. (1996) 693,000.

Kern, R., E. Cal., **USA**; one of most impt. power-generating Rs. in st.

Kerrier, l. gov. dist., Cornwall, **Eng.**; a. inc. Lizard penin. and Helston; p. (2001) 92,517.

Kerry, coastal co., Munster, **R.o.I.**; deeply indented cst.; cap. Tralee; tourism; a. 4,703 km²; p. (1991) 121,900.

Kerulen, R., N.E. **Mongolia and China**; flows parallel to edge of Gobi Desert; a. designated for economic development; 1,256 km long.

Keswick, Allerdale, Cumbria, **Eng.**; on Greta R.; at N. end of L. Derwentwater; tourist ctr.; mkt.; pencils; p. (1991) 4,836.

Kettering, l. gov. dist., mkt. t., Northants., **Eng.**; nr. Wellingborough; footwear; iron mng.; p. (2001) 81,844 (dist.), (2001) 51,063 (t.).

Kew, dist., London bor. of Richmond upon Thames, **Eng.**; contains Kew botanical gardens.

Keynsham, t., Bath and N.E. Somerset, **Eng.**, expanded t.; p. (1991) 15,193.

Key West, c., Fla., **USA**; on I. c. 240 km from mainland; naval sta., coastguard base; cigar-mftg.; tourism; p. (2000) 25,500.

Khabarovsk, c., **Russia**; cap. of K. terr., E. Siberia, on Amur R.; cath.; oil refining, aircraft engin., wood and paper inds., pipeline links with oilfields in N. Sakhalin; transport ctr. of Far East; p. (1989) 601,000.

Khaniá, or Canea, c., Crete, **Greece**; in sheltered bay on W. cst.; historic sites; p. (1991) 50,100.

Khanty-Mansi, admin. div., **Russia**; in W. Siberian lowland; sparse p.; cap. KhantyMansiisk (at confluence of Ob' and Irtysh Rs.); natural gas; a. 556,850 km²; p. (1989) 1,282,400.

Kharagpur, c., W. Bengal, **India**; industl., scientific research ctr.; rly. junc.; p. (1991) 265,000.

Kharg, I., Persian Gulf, **Iran**; oil terminal for supertankers, 48 km from mainland; repeated Iraqi air attacks resulted in floating terminal at Sirri island and plans for replacement terminal.

Khar'kov, c., **Ukraine**; impt. industl. ctr. in Donets coal region; cap. of K. region; univ., cath.; rly. ctr.; extensively rebuilt after second world war; p. (1990) 1,618,400.

Khartoum, c., cap. of the **Sudan**; at confluence of Blue and White Niles; univ.; famous siege under Gordon 1884–5; p. (2000) 2,731,000 (met. a.).

Khashm el Girba, t., **Sudan**; new t. on Atbara R., between Khartoum and Ethiopian border; for p. of Wadi Halfa inundated by Aswan L.; sugar refinery.

Khasi Hills, Meghalaya, N.E. **India**; form abrupt S. edge to middle Brahmaputra valley; very heavy monsoon rains on S.-facing slopes; lower slopes forested; middle slopes impt. tea-growing region; rise to over 1,800 m.

Kherson, c., **Ukraine**; 24 km up R. Dnieper from Black Sea; sea and R. pt., rly. junc.; grain, oil refining, engin., textiles, shipbldg; founded by Catherine the Great as fortress t.; p. (1990) 361,200.

Khingan, Gr. and Little, mtn. ranges, Inner Mongolia and Heilongjiang prov., N.E. **China**; rich timber resources; rise to over 1,800 m.

Khios or **Chios**, I., **Greece**; in Aegean Sea; wines, figs, fruits; marble; cap. Khios; supposed

birthplace of Homer; p. (1991) 52,200.

Khiva, c., N.W. **Uzbekistan**; in oasis nr. Kara-Kum desert; cottons, carpets; anc. c.; p. (1990) 40,600.

Khmel'nitskiy (Proskurov), c., **Ukraine**; on R. Bug; machin. tools, textiles, food inds.; p. (1990) 241,000.

Khmer Republic. *See* **Cambodia**.

Khor Abdulla, **Iraq**; in Persian G. nr. Basra; deepwater oil-loading island terminal.

Khorāsan or **Khurasan**, prov., N.E. **Iran**; sparsely p.; agr.; wool; turquoises; cap. Mashhad; new proposals to divide prov.; p. (1996) 6,047,700.

Khorramshahr, spt., S.W. **Iran**, leading pt. on Persian G.; increased in importance in second world war when harbour facilities expanded; handles major part of foreign trade; main exp. dates; linked by pipeline to oilfields and by road and rail to Ahvāz and Tehran.

Khotan. *See* **Hotan**.

Khudzhand, **(Leninabad)**, c., **Tajikistan**; on Syr Dar'ya R., S. of Tashkent; silks, cottons, fruit-preserving; hydroelectric power sta.; p. (1990) 163,100.

Khulna, c., **Bangladesh**; in low-lying a. in W. Ganges delta; p. (1991) 545,849.

Khunjerab Pass, Kashmir, **India**; 5,000 m. pass in Karakoram Range; links Sinkiang (China) with Pakistan and Middle East; new metal route opened (1982) making shorter route to W. for China and took 20 years to build.

Khuzestan, prov., W. **Iran**; frontier Iraq; leading petroleum ctr.; lge. dams; cap. Ahvāz; p. (1996) 3,746,800.

Khyber Pass, pass in Hindu Kush mtns., between Pakistan and Afghanistan; followed by route from Peshawar to Kabul; historically most famous route into India, used by many invaders, inc. Alexander the Great.

Kiamusze. *See* **Jiamusi**.

Kiangsi. *See* **Jiangxi**.

Kiangsu. *See* **Jiangsu**.

Kicking Horse Pass, mtn. pass (1,628 m), over Rocky Mtns., B.C., **Canada**; used by Canadian Pac. rly.

Kidderminster, t., Wyre Forest, Worcs., **Eng.**; on R. Stour 6 km above its confluence with R. Severn; carpets, engin., sugar-beet refining, textile machin., elec. vehicles, drop forgings; p. (2001) 55,348.

Kidsgrove, t., "Potteries," Stoke, **Eng.**; 5 km N.W. of Stoke-on-Trent; chemicals, metal wks., rayon, silk and nylon spinning, precast concrete, ceramics; p. (2001) 28,724.

Kidwelly, Carmarthenshire, **Wales**; mkt. t.; sm. harbour; cas.; p. (1991) 2,664.

Kiel, spt., cap. of Schleswig-Holstein, **Germany**; univ.; Baltic naval pt.; shipbldg. and allied inds., elec. gds., textiles, fishing; p. (2002) 232,242.

Kiel Canal (North Sea–Baltic Canal or **Kaiser-Wilhelm-Kanal) Germany**; connects Elbe estuary on North Sea with Baltic; 98 km long; opened 1895, reconstructed 1914; internationalised 1919 by Treaty of Versailles; repudiated by Hitler 1936.

Kielce, c. and prov., central **Poland**; in Swieto-krzyskie mtns.; cath.; route ctr.; agr. machin., chemicals; minerals quarried in prov.; founded 12th cent.; p. (1995) 213,701 (c.), 1,135,046 (prov.).

Kielder, reservoir, Northumberland, **Eng.**; one of lgst. man made lakes in Europe.

Kiev (Kiyev), c., cap. of **Ukraine**; on R. Dnieper; leading cultural, industl. and comm. ctr.; cath., univ.; machin., textiles; in a. of rich mineral deposits; natural gas pipeline runs from Dashava; historic c., once cap. of Muscovite empire; home of Kiev Opera House; p. (2000) 2,670,000.

Kigali, cap. of **Rwanda**; comm. ctr.; airport; new tungsten and iron foundries; p. (1999) 369,000.

Kigoma, t., W. **Tanzania**, pt. on E. shore of L. Tanganyika; W. terminus of Central rly. to Dar-es-Salaam.

Kii, peninsula, **Japan**; highland area and inlet of same name, S. Honshu.

Kilauea, crater, 1,112 m high, on S.E. slope of Mauna Loa, **Hawaii**, one of lgst. active craters in world; over 3 km in diameter.

Kildare, inland co., Leinster, **R.o.I.**; dairying, cereals; co. t. Naas; a. 1,694 km²; p. (1991) 122,700.

Kildare, mkt. t., cap. of Kildare, **R.o.I.**; cath.; close by is the famous racecourse, the Curragh of Kildare; p. (1991) 4,200.

Kilimanjaro, volcanic mtn., N. **Tanzania**; hgst. peak in Africa, 5,895 m; snows melting with global warming; international airpt. at 894 m on Sanya Plain; Nat. Park.

Kilindini, spt., **Kenya**; adjoins Mombasa; the finest harbour on E. cst. of Africa.

Kilkenny, inland co., Leinster, **R.o.I.**; cap. Kilkenny; pastoral farming, black marble; a. 2,062 km²; p. (1991) 73,600.

Kilkenny, t., cap. of Kilkenny, **R.o.I.**; on R. Nore; local mkt., caths., cas.; p. (1991) 8,500.

Killaloe, v., Co. Clare, **R.o.I.**; crossing point for R. Shannon; cath.; p. (1991) 950.

Killarney, t., Kerry, **R.o.I.**; local mkt.; tourist ctr. for the Ls. of K.; p. (1991) 7,300.

Killarney, Lakes of, Kerry, **R.o.I.**; Lower, Middle, and Upper, celebrated for their beauty; tourist resorts; Muckross on Middle L. site of anc. abbey.

Killiecrankie, Pass of, **Scot.**; on R. Garry; at S. approach to Drumochter Pass; used by main rly. Perth to Inverness; scene of battle 1691.

Killingworth, t., Tyne and Wear, **Eng.**; 6 km N.E. of Newcastle; new t.; proposed p. 20,000.

Kilmarnock, burgh, E. Ayrshire, **Scot**; on R. Irvine, 17 km N.E. of Ayr.; p. (2002) 43,588.

Kilo-Moto, goldfield, **Congo**; in N.E. of st., 80 km W. of L. Kasenyi; linked by motor road to R. Congo (Kisangani) and L. Kasenyi.

Kilrenny and Anstruther, t., Fife, **Scot.**, at entrance to F. of Forth; fishing, hosiery, oilskin mnfs; p. (1991) 3,154.

Kilrush, sm. spt., U.D., Co. Clare, **R.o.I.**; on R. Shannon; p. (1991) 2,750.

Kilsyth, burgh, N. Lanarkshire, **Scot.**; at S. foot of Campsie Fells, 16 km W. of Falkirk; p. (2002) 9,816.

Kilwinning, burgh, N. Ayrshire, **Scot.**; 8 km E. of Ardrossan; p. (2002) 15,908.

Kimberley, t., B.C., **Canada**; on R. Kootenay; site of Sullivan mine, silver, lead, zinc; ores smelted at Trail; p. (1991) 6,500.

Kimberley, t., cap., Northern Cape Prov., **S. Africa**; diamond-mng. (ended 2005); asbestos, manganese, cement, engin.; founded 1871; p. (1991) 167,000.

Kinabalu, Mount, Sabah, **Malaysia**; in Crocker mtns.; hgst. peak in Borneo, alt. 4,104 m.

Kincardineshire, historic co., E. **Scot.**, now part of Aberdeenshire.

Kinder Scout, mtn., N. Derbys., **Eng.**; hgst. point of the Peak dist.; alt. 637 m.

Kineshma, c., **Russia**; on Volga, N.W. of Gorki; pt. for Ivanovo industl. a.; textiles; dates from early 15th cent.; p. (1989) 105,000.

King George's Sound, W. **Australia**; nr. Albany; fine harbour and bay.

Kinghorn, t., Fife, **Scot.**; on F. of Forth, 5 km S. of Kirkcaldy; p. (2002) 2,835.

Kingsbridge, t., South Hams, S. Devon, **Eng.**; at head of Kingsbridge estuary, 16 km S.W. of Dartmouth; mkt.; p. (1991) 5,258.

King's Lynn, spt., West Norfolk, **Eng.**; at mouth of Gr. Ouse; docks; fishing base; agr. machin., canning, chemical fertilisers, shoes; expanded t.; part of l. gov. dist. of King's Lynn and West Norfolk; p. (2001) 40,921 (t.), (2001) 135,345 (dist.).

Kingston, t., Ont., **Canada**; E. end of L. Ontario; univ., military college; p. (1996) 143,416.

Kingston, spt., cap. of **Jamaica**; ch. comm. ctr. for J.; landlocked harbour; agr.-processing; univ.; p. (1999) 655,000.

Kingston upon Hull. See **Hull.**

Kingston upon Thames, former M.B., Surrey, **Eng.**; now The Royal Borough of Kingston-upon-Thames, outer bor. of Greater London; inc. bors. of Malden and Coombe and Surbiton; residtl. with Richmond Park, Hampton Court, Bushey Park nearby; aircraft parts; univ.; p. (2001) 147,273.

Kingstown, spt., cap. of **St. Vincent**, W.I.; cath., botanic gardens; p. (1999) 28,000.

Kingswood, t., S. Gloucs., **Eng.**; nr. Bristol; elec. vehicles, motor cycles, boots, brushes, tools; school founded by John Wesley; p. (1991) 60,192 .

Kington, sm. mkt. t., Hereford, **Eng.**; 19 km W. of Leominster.

Kinki, dist., S.W. Honshu, **Japan**; agr., industl. and comm. complex centred on Osaka, Kyoto, and Kōbe; p. (1990) 22,207,000.

Kinlochleven, v., Highland, **Scot.**; at head of Loch Leven; hydroelec. power sta.; aluminium smelting; p. (2002) 897.

Kinross, burgh, Perth and Kinross, **Scot.**; on Loch Leven, 26 km N.E. of Alloa; textiles; resort; p. (2002) 4,681.

Kinross-shire, historic co., E. **Scot.**, now part of Perth and Kinross.

Kinsale, t., Cork, **R.o.I.**; sm. fish pt. on K.

harbour; tourism; natural gas field; p. (1991) 1,800.

Kinshasa (Leopoldville), c., cap. of **Congo**; above the cataracts on R. Congo; univ.; textiles, shoes; founded by Stanley 1887; p. (2000) 5,064,000.

Kintyre, peninsula, Argyll and Bute, **Scot.**; terminates in Mull of Kintyre; 67 km long, 16 km wide.

Kioga (Kyoga), L., **Uganda**; on R. Nile midway between L. Victoria and L. Mobuto Seso.

Kirghizia (Kyrgyzstan), CIS, former USSR constituent rep.; S.W. of Siberia; mtnous. cty., in Tienshan and Pamir systems; livestock breeding; mineral resources, food processing; Russians constitute 12 % of population; cap. Frunze; a 196,581 km²; p. (2004) 5,081,429.

Kiribati (Gilbert Is), indep. st. (1979), former Brit. col., central Pac. Oc., chain of coral Is. across equator; economy based on phosphate mng. and copra, cap. Bairiki on the island of Tarawa; Ellice Is separated 1976 and renamed Tuvalu; a. 956 km²; p. (2004) 100,798.

Kirin. See **Jilin.**

Kirkburton, t., West Yorks., **Eng.**; S.E. of Huddersfield; woollens; p. (1991) 4,121.

Kirkby, t., Knowsley, Merseyside, **Eng.**; p. (2001) 40,006.

Kirkby in Ashfield, t., Ashfield, Notts., **Eng.**; 16 km N.W. of Nottingham; p. (2001) 27,067.

Kirkbymoorside, t., Ryedale, North Yorks., **Eng.**; nr. Vale of Pickering; mkt.-place; sailplanes, gliders; p. (1991) 2,650.

Kirkcaldy, royal burgh, Fife, **Scot.**; spt. on N. side of F. of Forth; linoleum, engin.; birthplace of Adam Smith; p. (2002) 46,912.

Kirkcudbright, royal burgh, Dumfries and Galloway, **Scot.**; on R. Dee at influx into K. Bay, S.W. of Dumfries; agr. ctr., hosiery; cas., abbey; p. (2002) 3,447.

Kirkcudbrightshire, historic co., S. **Scot.**, now part of Dumfries and Galloway.

Kirkenes, t., Finnmark prov., N.E. **Norway**; on S. arm of Varanger fjord, nr. Russian border; pt. for iron-mng. dist.

Kirkham, sm. t., Kirklees, Lancs., **Eng.**; textiles.

Kirkintilloch, burgh, E. Dunbartonshire, **Scot.**; on Forth and Clyde Canal; engin.; p. (2002) 20,281.

Kirklees, met. dist., West Yorks., **Eng.**; comprises Huddersfield, Dewsbury, Batley, Spenborough, Colne Valley, Meltham, Holmfirth, Denby Dale, Kirkburton, Heckmondwike and Mirfield; p. (2001) 388,567.

Kirkstone Pass, mtn. pass, Cumbria, **Eng.**; used by main road between Ullswater and Windermere Lakes.

Kirkūk, t., **Iraq**; most imp. centre of Iraqi oil industry; p. (2000 est.) 720,000.

Kirkwall, royal burgh, Mainland I., Orkney Is., **Scot.**; cath.; p. (1991) 6,469.

Kirov. See **Vyatka.**

Kirovabad. See **Gyandzha.**

Kirovograd. c., **Ukraine**; on Ingul R.; cap. of K. oblast; agr. ctr.; engin.; p. (1990) 274,200.

Kirriemuir, burgh, Angus, **Scot.**; on N. margin of Strathmore, 8 km W. of Forfar; jute-weaving; birthplace of J. M. Barrie; p. (2002) 5,693.

Kirtland, t., N.M., **USA**; atomic and space research sta.

Kiruna, t., N. **Sweden**; inside Arctic Circle, N.W. of Luleå; linked by rly. to Narvik (Norway); impt. deposits of iron ore; p. (1990) 20,500.

Kisangani (Stanleyville), t., **Congo**; on R. Congo nr. Boyoma Falls; airpt.; univ.; p. (1991) 373,397.

Kishinev. See **Chisinau.**

Kislovodsk, c., **Russia**; in N. Caucasus; famous spa; p. (1989) 114,000.

Kismayo, t., **Somalia**; new deep-water harbour; airpt.; p. (2000 est.) 200,000.

Kisumu, spt., cap. of Nyanza prov., **Kenya**; at head of Kavirondo G. on L. Victoria; handles bulk of cotton from Buganda and coffee from N. Tanzania for transhipment E. by rail; lge. brewery; p. (2000 est.) 270,000.

Kitakyūshū, c., N. Kyushu, **Japan**; one of Japan's lgst. muns. on merging (1963) of ts. Moji, Kokura, Tobata, Yawata, and Wakamatsu; sixth c. to enjoy special aut. rights; p. (2000) 1,011,000.

Kitchener, c., Ont., **Canada**; agr. machin., tyres, hardware, agr. processing; p. (1991) 168,281 (c.).

Kithira. See **Cerigo.**

Kitimat, t., B.C., **Canada**; lge. aluminium smelter powered by hydroelectricity from diversion of

R. Fraser trib. through the Rockies; p. (1991) 11,300.

Kitwe, t., **Zambia;** contiguous to mng. township of Nkana, ctr. of copperbelt; p. (1989) 495,000.

Kiukiang. *See* **Jiujiang.**

Kivu, L., on border of **Congo** and **Rwanda;** in highlands of Gr. Rift Valley; natural gas discoveries; 1,473 m high, 96 km long.

Klagenfurt, t., cap. of Carinthia, **Austria;** winter sports ctr.; varied mnfs.; p. (1991) 89,502.

Klaipeda (Memel), c. **Lithuania;** ice-free spt. on Baltic Sea; exp. timber, textiles, chemicals, paper; p. (1990) 206,200.

Klamath, mtns., N. Cal., S.W. Ore., **USA;** beautiful ranges containing Nat. Park and Indian reserve; hgst. alt. Mt. Eddy, 2,757 m.

Klerksdorp, t., Gauteng, **S. Africa;** gold, diamonds; p. (1991) 321,500.

Klondike, R., Yukon, **Canada;** sm. trib. of Yukon in gold-mng. region; gold rush 1896; 160 km long.

Klyuchevskaya Sopka, one of 18 active volcanoes, **Russia;** in N.E. Siberia, on Kamchatka peninsula; alt. 4,748 m.

Knaresborough, t., North Yorks., **Eng.;** 5 km N.E. of Harrogate; mkt.; p. (1991) 13,380.

Knighton, t., Powys, **Wales;** on R. Teme; mkt.; p. (1991) 2,972.

Knob Lake. *See* **Schefferville.**

Knossos, ruined c., cap. of anc. Crete, **Greece;** S.E. of Iráklion; ctr. of Cretan bronze age culture, 1800 B.C.; archaeological source of knowledge about the Minoans.

Knottingley, t., West Yorks., **Eng.;** on R. Aire, 19 km S.E. of Leeds; engin., glass, tar distilling, chemicals; coal mng; p. (1991) 14,690.

Knowsley, met. dist., Merseyside, **Eng.;** comprises Kirkby, Prescot and Huyton with Roby; p. (2001) 150,459.

Knoxville, c., Tenn., **USA;** univ.; livestock and tobacco mkt.; textiles, marble, plastics, chemicals, aluminium; p. (1990) 165,121 (c.), 605,000 (met. a.).

Knutsford, t., N.E. Cheshire, **Eng.;** mkt.; home of Mrs. Gaskell, author of *Cranford*; p. (1991) 13,352.

Kōbe, c., spt., Honshu, **Japan;** at E. end of Inland Sea; 5th c. of Japan; developed as pt. for Osaka and Kinki plain; iron and steel, shipbldg., rubber; major earthquake January 1995; p. (2000) 1,493,000.

Koblenz (Coblenz), t. Rhineland-Palatinate, **Germany;** at confluence of Rs. Rhine and Moselle; fine buildings; wine, paper, machin., leather, ceramics; p. (2002) 107,730.

Kochi (Cochin), spt., Kerala, **India;** on Malabar cst.; exp. coconut oil, tea; oil refining; silting pt.; p. (1991) 564,000.

Kōchi, plain and c., Shikoku, **Japan;** early vegetables, double rice cropping; p. (1990) 317,000.

Kodiak I., lgst. of Is. of Alaska, **USA;** 144 km long; forested mtns ; fur-trading, salmon-fishing, canning; earthquake 1964; p. (1990) 7,677.

Kōfu, basin and c., Honshu, **Japan;** rice, vine-yards, orchards, silk, wine; p. (1990) 200,630.

Kohat, t., **Pakistan;** on trib. of Indus; military t.; cement wks.; p. (1998) 125,300.

Koh-I-Baba Mtns., Afghanistan; spur of the Hindu Kush; highest point 5,380 m.

Kokand, t., **Uzbekistan;** in the Ferghana Valley; mftg. ctr., textiles, chemicals; p. (1990) 175,700.

Kokiu. *See* **Gejiu.**

Koko-Nor. *See* **Qinghai Hu.**

Kokura. *See* **Kitakyūshū.**

Kola Peninsula, peninsula, **Russia;** extension of Lapland; rich mineral deposits; hydroelectric plants and missile base.

Kolar Gold Fields, t., Karnataka, **India;** prod. 95 % of India's gold; p. (1991) 155,000 (met. a.).

Kolarovgrad. *See* **Shumen.**

Kolding, c., at head of Kolding fjord, Jutland, **Denmark;** spt. and fishing base; lt. inds.; p. (1990) 57,285.

Kolhapur, c., Maharashtra, S.W. **India;** cap. of former princely st. of K.; bauxite; anc. Buddhist ctr.; p. (1991) 406,000.

Kolkata (Calcutta), c., cap. of W. Bengal st., **India;** pt. on Hooghly R., lgst. c. in rep. and one of most densely populated areas of world; vast tr. from Ganges plain; univ.; jute-mills, textiles, chems., engin.; exp. jute, cotton, sugar-cane, rice, tea, coal; p. (2000) 12,920,000. Renamed Kolkata (1999).

Köln. *See* **Cologne.**

Kolomna, c., **Russia;** on Moskva R., nr. confluence with Oka R.; industl. ctr.; engin., locomotives, machin., synthetic rubber; p. (1989) 162,000.

Kolwezi, c., S. Shaba, **Congo;** comm. ctr. for mng. dist. (cobalt and copper); p. (1991) 544,497.

Kolyma, R., N.E. Siberia, **Russia;** flows into Arctic Oc., via Kolyma goldfields; navigable in summer; basin largely covered with tundra, sparsely p.; 2,560 km long.

Komi, aut. rep., **Russia;** wooded lowland, pastoral agr.; coal from Pechora basin, oil at Ukhta and Troitsko-Pechorsk; mng. now ch. economic activity; cap. Syktyvkar, lumber ctr.; a. 415,799 km²; p. (1989) 1,250,800.

Komi-Permyak, admin. div., **Russia;** forestry, cellulose, paper; cap. Kudymbar; a. 31,080 km²; p. (1989) 158,500.

Kompong Som (Sihanoukville) c., **Cambodia;** deepwater pt. on G. of Thailand; linked to Phnom Penh by modern highway; oil refining.

Kommunarsk (Voroshilovsk), t., **Ukraine;** 40 km S.W. of Lugansk; ctr. of iron, steel and coking inds.; p. (1990) 125,700.

Komsomolsk, c., **Russia;** built by volunteer youth labour, after 1932; heavy industl. development; oil refining; pipeline connects with oilfield in N. Sakhalin; p. (1989) 315,000.

Konin, t. and prov., C. **Poland;** brown coal, rlwy, aluminium; p. (1995) 82,655 (t.) 479,090 (prov.).

Konstantinovka, industl. t., **Ukraine;** in heart of Donbas industl. region, 61 km N. of Donetsk; heavy engin., iron and steel, zinc smelting; p. (1990) 107,700.

Konya, c., **Turkey;** cap. of K. prov.; agr. tr. ctr.; mnfs. textiles, carpets, leather gds.; the anc. Iconium, fortress of the Hittite empire; p. (1990) 543,460 (c.), 1,750,303 (prov.).

Kooland I., W. **Australia;** rugged I. with iron-ore deposits worked since 1960 and exp. to Japan.

Koolyanobbing, mng. t., W. **Australia;** high-grade haematite and limonite ores mined since 1961 and t. constructed as residential and service ctr.

Kootenay or **Kootenai,** R., flows from B.C., **Canada,** through Montana and Idaho, **USA,** into K. L., draining it by narrow channel into Colombia R.; beautiful scenery; 720 km long.

Kopparberg , co. C. **Sweden;** cap. Falun; a. 28,350 km²; p. (1992) 290,245.

Korat Plateau, E. **Thailand;** headwaters of Mekong tribs.; cattle-rearing; tr. ctr. Korat.

Koroë (Koritsa), t., S.E. **Albania;** in infertile basin at 854 m nr. Greek border; mkt.; cultural ctr.; p. (1991) 67,100.

Korea, Democratic People's Republic of (N. Korea), occupies N. part of Korean peninsula (N. of 38th parallel), E. Asia; bounded on N. by China and Russia; continental climate; cold dry winters, hot humid summers; predominantly mtnous. with many uninhabited offshite Is., all inds. nationalised and collective agr.; rapid mechanisation, agr. employs 43 per cent working p ; development emphasis on mng. resources of coal, iron-ore and on growth of heavy inds.; most industl. resources located in N. Korea; rapid incr. in industrialisation; international airport at cap. of Pyongyang; longest surviving hard-line Communist ruling dynasty in Asia; widespread famine in mid-1990s; a. 121,248 km²; p. (2004) 22,097,553.

Korea, Rep. of (S. Korea), occupies S. part of Korean peninsula (S. of 38th parallel); climate resembles N. Korea's, topography less rugged; massive US aid revitalised economy after Korean war and Korea acquired one of world's largest foreign debts; 20 per cent work-force engaged in agr.; undergoing rapid industrialisation; textiles, electronics, shipbldg., vehicles; iron and steel ind. at Pusan; major debt and financial crisis, 1997; irrigation and power project (1971–81) for 4 Rs.—Hangang, Naktangang, Kum-Gang, and Yongsan-Gang; cap. Seoul; new cap. planned for Yongi-Kongju; a. 98,992 km²; p. (2004) 48,598,175.

Korea Bay, Yellow Sea; between N. Korea and North-East China (Manchuria).

Koriyama, Honshu, **Japan;** textiles, chemicals; p. (1990) 314,642.

Kortrijk (Courtrai), t., W. Flanders prov., N.W. **Belgium;** textiles; 13th cent. Notre Dame church; battle of the Spurs 1302; p. (1993) 76,264.

Koryak, admin. div., N.E. Siberia, **Russia**; sparse p.; a. 393,680 km²; p. (1989) 39,900.

Kos, I. See **Cos**, I.

Kosciusko, Mount, N.S.W., in Australian Alps; highest peak in **Australia**; 2,228 m; Nat. Park popular for skiing.

Košiče, c., S.E. **Slovakia**; lies in fertile basin; major industl. ctr.; heavy inds., iron and steel plant; agr.-processing; univ., Gothic cath.; mediaeval fortress t.; p. (1990) 236,000.

Kosovo-Metohija, aut. region, S.W. **Serbia**, **Serbia**; mtnous., fertile valleys; stock raising, forestry; overwhelmingly Albanian p. causing agitation for independence; Serb repression led to war and ethnic cleansing (1999); NATO KFOR peace-keeping troops; under UN and NATO administration since 1999; ch. t. Priština; a. 10,352 km²; p. (1991 est.) 2 m.

Kostroma, c., cap. of K. oblast, **Russia**; at confluence of Volga and Kostroma; in flax growing a.; textiles, engin.; p. (1089) 278,000.

Koszalin (**Koslin**), c. and prov., N.W. **Poland**; nr. Baltic cst.; paper mills, textiles, building materials; p. (1995) 111,667 (c.), 520,914 (prov.).

Kota, t., Rajasthan, **India**; on R. Chambal; textiles; two nuclear reactors and heavy water plant; p. (1991) 537,000.

Kota Kinabalu (**Jesselton**), t., cap of Sabah, **Malaysia**; on W. cst.; main rubber pt.; rly. terminal; p. (1991) 208,484.

Kotka, spt., S.E. **Finland**; on G. of Finland, at mouth of Kymi R.; major exp. pt. for timber, paper, pulp; p. (1993) 56,267.

Kotor, spt., S. **Montenegro**; on Bay of K., inlet of Adriatic; cath.; tourism.

Kotri, t., **Pakistan**; on R. Indus, opposite Hyderabad; barrage N. of the t., to help irrigate Sind.

Kottbus. See **Cottbus**.

Koulikoro, t., **Mali**, W. Africa; on upper course of R. Niger; mkt. for groundnuts, gumarabic, sisal; linked by R. to Timbuktu and Gao; 1,216 km from Dakar.

Kowloon, peninsula, S.E. **China**; on mainland opposite Hong Kong I.; pt. installations; major industl. and tr. ctr.; part of Hong Kong zone.

Kozáni, dep., Macedonia, **Greece**; cap. K.; mainly agr.; a. 6,143 km²; p. (1991) 150,386.

Kozhikode. See **Calicut**.

Kra Isthmus, neck of land between B. of Bengal and G. of Thailand, linking Malay peninsula with continent of Asia.

Kragujevac, t., central **Serbia**; on both banks of Lepenica R.; cath.; arsenal and garrison; route ctr., developing agr. and industl. ctr.; p. (1991) 146,607.

Krakatoa (**Rakata**), volcanic I., Sunda strait, **Indonesia**; between Java and Sumatra; greater part disappeared in violent eruption 1883; impt. site for biol. study.

Kraków (**Cracow**), c. and prov., S. **Poland**; pt. on Vistula; cultural ctr., univ. (Copernicus matriculated here); many historic monuments; inc. c. of Nowa Huta lgst. iron and steel ctr. of rep.; machin., chemicals, farm implements; p. (1995) 745,435, (c.), 1,239,775 (prov.).

Kramatorsk, c., **Ukraine**; in Donets basin; heavy engin., metallurgy; p. (1990) 199,300.

Krasnodar Territory, region, **Russia**; extends from Sea of Azov and Black Sea to N.W. end of Caucasus; contains Kuban steppe and Maikop oilfields; fertile black soil; main pt. Tuapse; many health resorts; p. (1989) 5,052,900.

Krasnodar, c., cap. of K. region, **Russia**; R. pt. Kuban R.; ctr. of industl. and agr. region; p. (1989) 621,000.

Krasnoyarsk Territory, extensive region, **Russia**; extends across Siberia to Arctic Oc.; traversed by Yenisey and tribs.; minerals, grain from Minusinska basin and timber from coniferous forests; cap. K.; a. of labour camps in Stalin era; p. (1989) 3,605,500.

Krasnoyarsk, c., cap. of K. terr., E. Siberia, **Russia**; on Trans-Siberian rly. at crossing of Yenisey R.; hydroelectric sta.; industl. ctr.; local copper and iron-ore deposits; ctr. for grain and timber; p. (1989) 913,000.

Krefeld, t., N. Rhine–Westphalia, **Germany**; chemicals, steel, machin., textiles, soap; former ctr. of silk inds.; p. (2002) 239,559.

Kremenchug, c., **Ukraine**; on R. Dnieper; timber, engin., textiles; hydroelectric sta.; oil refining; p. (1990) 238,000.

Krems, mkt. t., **Austria**; on R. Danube; fruit processing; founded in 10th cent. as imperial fortress; p. (1991) 22,829.

Kreuznach, Bad, t., Rhineland Palatinate, **Germany**; on R. Nahe; metallurgy, leather, optical and chemical inds.; viticulture, mineral baths; p. (1994) 42,950.

Krishna (**Kistna**), R., S. **India**; rises in W. Ghats, flows E. across Deccan plateau into Bay of Bengal; lower valley and delta under intensive rice cultivation; densely populated; 1,360 km long.

Kristiansand, spt., S. **Norway**; on Skagerrak; shipbldg.; ships, timber, paper, pulp, fish; electro-metallurgy; p. (1990) 54,267.

Kristianstad, c., cap. of K. prov., **Sweden**; on Helge R.; its pt. Ahus is on Baltic; foodprocessing, clothing, machin.; founded 1614 as fortress; p (1982) 71,708 (t.), 282,593 (co.).

Kristiansund, spt., W. cst. **Norway**; built on 3 Is.; trawler fleet base, exp. dried fish, heavily damaged in second world war; since rebuilt; p. (1990) 17,093.

Krivoy Rog, c., **Ukraine**; on R. Ingulets; ctr. of ch. iron-mng. a. of USSR; p. (1990) 717,400.

Krk, I., N. Adriatic Sea, off **Croatia**; S. of Rijeke; agr.; tourism; ch. t., K.; p. 14,500.

Krkonose. See **Riesengebirge**.

Kronoberg, co. S. **Sweden**; cap. Växjö; a. 8,459 km²; p. (1992) 178,961.

Kronshlot (**Kronstadt**), spt., on I. of Kotlin, **Russia**; at head of G. of Finland, nr. St. Petersburg; Baltic pt. and naval base; scene of naval mutiny which precipitated the Russian revolution; founded by Peter the Great 1710.

Kroonstad, t., Free State., **S. Africa**; on R. Vals; rly. junc.; engin., milling; p. (1991) 110,950.

Krosno, t. and prov., S.E. **Poland**; R. Wislok; oil centre; p. (1995) 49,416 (t.), 506,025 (prov.).

Kruger Nat. Park, N.E. Gauteng, **S. Africa**; game reserve; a. 20,720 km².

Krugersdorp, t. Witwatersrand, **S. Africa**; gold mng., uranium, manganese; p. (1991) 196,200.

Kuala Lumpur, c., fed. terr., **W. Malaysia**; old cap. of Fed. of Malaysia and of Selangor st.; univ.; ctr. of rubber and tin dist.; outport Port Kelang; new Sepang airport, 1998; p. (2000) 1,378,000.

Kuangchow. See **Guangzhou**.

Kuantan, main t. on E. cst. **W. Malaysia**; linked to Kuala Lumpur; tin mng; p. (1991) 201,300.

Kuching, c., cap. of Sarawak, **Malaysia**; pt. on Sarawak R.; gold discovered nearby at Bau; p. (1989) 157,000.

Kufra, oasis, **Libya**; dates, barley; on caravan route.

Kuldja. See **Yining**.

Kumamoto, c., W. Kyushu, **Japan**; 3rd c. of K.; cas., univs.; food inds.; business ctr.; p. (1990) 579,305.

Kumasi, c., cap. of Ashanti region, **Ghana**; univ., aerodrome; road and rly. junc.; ctr. of cocoaproducing a.; bauxite nearby; jute bags; p. (1996) 420,000.

Kumayri (**Leninakan**), c., **Armenia**; nr. Turkish border; textiles, engin., rug-mkg.; earthquake 1988; p. (1990) 122,600.

Kumba Konam, t., Tamil Nadu, **India**; on Cauvery delta; silks, cotton; sacred Hindu c.; p. (1991) 139,483.

Kunene (**Cunene**), R., **Angola**; scheme to channel water from Angola to S.W. Africa; 1,200 km long.

Kun Lun (**Kwen Lun**), mtn. ranges, Xizang Zizhiou (Tibet), **China**; extend 2,900 km E. from Pamirs along N. edge of high plateau of Xizang Zizhiou; drained N. into inland drainage basin of Lop Nor; alt. often exceeds 5,400 m; rising to 7,729 m.

Kunming, c., cap. of Yunnan prov., S.W. **China**; univ.; comm. and cultural ctr., noted for its scenic beauty; iron and steel, milling and boring machin., textiles, chemicals; p. (1994) 1,240,000.

Kuopio, t., **Finland**; on L. Kalki; timber inds.; tourism; p. (1993) 83,097.

Kura, R., rises in Turkey, chief R. of Transcaucasia, **Russia**; flows into Caspian Sea; agr., fishing, hydroelec. power; 1,504 km long.

Kurdistan (**Country of the Kurds**), includes parts of E. Turkey, Armenia, N.E. Iraq, and N.W. Iran; attempts at autonomy.

Kure, c., S.W. Honshu, **Japan**; spt. and naval base; engin.; shipbldg.; p. (1990) 216,723.

Kurgan, c., **Russia**; on Tobol R.; impt. junc. on Trans-Siberian rly.; tr. in cattle and foodstuffs; agr. engin.; p. (1989) 356,000.

Kuria Muria Is., 5 barren Is. in Arabian Sea off cst. of Oman; admin. by U.K. until 1967 now ceded to **Oman.**

Kurile Is., chain of volcanic Is., N. Pac., **Russia;** extend from Kamchatka to Hokkaido; mainly mtnous.; sulphur, hunting, fishing; Japan claims sovereignty over 4 Is. (Kunashiri, Etorofu, Shikotan, Habomai); a. 15,592 km².

Kurisches Haff (Kurštu Martos), shallow lagoon, Baltic cst. of **Lithuania;** receives water of R. Niemen; narrow entrance to Baltic Sea at N. end of lagoon commanded by pt. of Klaipeda (Memel); length 92 km, maximum width 32 km.

Kurische Nehrung, sandspit, Baltic Sea; almost cuts off Kurisches Haff from Baltic Sea; 88 km long.

Kurnool, t., Andhra Pradesh, **India;** agr. comm. ctr.; p. (1991) 236,800.

Kuroshio (Japan Current), ocean current, flows N.E. along Pac. cst. of Kyushu, Shikoku and S. Honshu, relatively warm water, exerts slight warming influence on this cst. in winter.

Kursk, c., cap. of K. oblast, **Russia;** on Tuskor R.; rly. junc.; in fertile fruit-growing a.; engin., textiles, synthetic rubber; p. (1989) 424,000.

Kurume, t., W. Kyushu, **Japan;** on Chikugo plain; comm. ctr.; p. (1990) 228,300.

Kushiro, spt., S.E. Hokkaido, **Japan;** exp. lumber; local coal; fishing; p. (1990) 205,640.

Kustanay, c., **Kazakhstan;** on Tobol R.; agr.-processing, lt. inds.; p. (1990) 228,400.

Kütahya, t., cap. of K. prov., central **Turkey;** agr. mkt. ctr.; ceramics; chemical complex; p. (1990) 135,432 (t.), 578,020 (prov.).

Kutaisi, c., **Georgia;** on R. Rion (hydroelectric plant); chemicals, textiles, mng. equipment; big coal deposits being mined; mkt. gardening a.; p. (1990) 236,400.

Kut-al-Amara, t., cap. of K. prov., **Iraq;** on R. Tigris; agr. tr. ctr.; p. (2000 est.) 375,000.

Kutch, Rann of, desert region covered with salt, but flooded during monsoons; nine-tenths belongs to India; one-tenth to Pakistan.

Kuwait, indep. Arab st., S.W. Asia; under Brit. protection until 1961; invaded by Iraq, August 1990; lies at head of Persian G.; inc. mainland and 9 sm Is.; mainly desert with a few oases; imports most of food requirements; possesses 13 per cent of the proved world reserves of oil; heavily dependent on oil and natural gas exports; fresh-water scarce; one of hgst. incomes per capita in world, but most of p. remains poor; a. 24,235 km²; p. (2004) 2,257,549.

Kuwait, c., cap. of **Kuwait;** pt. with natural harbour on Persian G.; univ.; p. (1995) 28,900.

Kuybyshev. *See* **Samara.**

Kuzbas (Kuznetsk Basin), industl. region, Siberia, **Russia;** lies S. of Trans-Siberian rly. in upper valleys of Rs. Ob and Tom; coal, iron and steel mftg., heavy metallurgical ind.; ch. ts., Novosibirsk, Novokuznetsk, Kemerovo, Leninsk-Kuznetsky.

Kwangsi Chuang. *See* **Guang Zhuang.**

Kwantung. *See* **Guangdong.**

Kwanto Plain, S.E. Honshu, **Japan;** lgst. a. of continuous lowland in Japan, extends 128 km inland from Tokyo; plain devoted to intensive rice cultivation; higher, drier terraces under mulberry, vegetables, tea, tobacco; very dense rural p.; lge. number of urban ctrs., inc. Tokyo, Yokohama; a. 13,000 km²

KwaZulu-Natal, coastal prov., **Rep. of S. Africa;** forms east coast from Port Edward to the border with Mozambique; sub-tropical coastline, savannah, mountains, forests; tourism, coal, sugar-cane, timber, steel, meat-processing, agriculture, fruit, vegetables, dairy products; cap. Pietermaritz-burg; a. 92,100 km²; p. (1996) 8·417 m.

Kweichow. *See* **Guizhou.**

Kweilin. *See* **Guilin.**

Kweiyang. *See* **Guiyang.**

Kwinana, new t. (1952), pt., W. **Australia;** oil refinery and steel plant, alumina reduction, integrated steelwks.; p. (1991) 13,500.

Kyle of Lochalsh, v., Highland, **Scot.;** at entrance to Loch Alsh, facing S. end of I. of Skye; terminus of rly. across Highlands from Dingwall; ch. pt. for ferries to N.W. cst., I. of Skye, Outer Hebrides; p. (2002) 739.

Kymi, R., **Finland;** rises in L. Päijänne, flows to G. of Finland; many Ls., timber transport.

Kyoto, c., Honshu, **Japan;** cultural and religious ctr., without lge.-scale inds.; former cap. 794–1868; univ.; shrines, old Imperial palace; p. (2000) 1,849,000.

Kyrgyzstan. *See* **Kirghizia.**

Kyushu, most S. of 4 major Is. of **Japan;** mtnous.; coal mng. in Chikugo basin; heavy inds.; agr. on coastal lowlands; joined to Honshu by bridge and rly.; a. 42,007 km²; p. (1990) 13,296,000.

Kyustendil, t., **Bulgaria;** in foothills of Osogovo mtns.; lge. lead and zinc deposits; combined plant for mng. and ore dressing projected.

Kzyl Orda, R. and t., **Kazakhstan;** lge. dam to irrigate rice plantations; p. of t. (1990) 155,500.

L

Laaland I. *See* **Lolland I.**

Labrador, mainland a. of prov. Newfoundland and Labrador, **Canada;** separated from I. by Strait of Belle I.; barren, severe climate; impt. cod fisheries; iron ore reserves nr. Quebec bdy.; Churchill R. power project; cap. Battle Harbour; a. 292,219 km².

Labrador City, t., Newfoundland and Labrador, **Canada;** new t. built 1965, nr. Wabush L..

Laccadive, coral Is., Arabian Sea; about 320 km off Malabar cst. joined with Minicoy and Amindivi Is. to form union terr. Lakshadweep, **India.**

Lachine, c., Quebec, **Canada** now part of gter. Montreal; on Montreal I. where St. Lawrence R. leaves St. Louis L.; iron and steel, wire, rope; Lachine canal by-passes rapids; p. (1986) 34,906.

Lachlan, R., N.S.W., **Australia;** main trib. of R. Murrumbidgee; irrigation; 1,472 km long.

La Coruña (A Coruña), spt., cap. of La Coruña prov., N.W. **Spain;** fishing; p. (1998) 243,100 (c.), 1,106,000 (prov.).

Ladakh, reg., of the Upper Indus, **India,** and N. E. **Pakistan;** bordering Tibet; ch. t. Leh; isolated and remote; alt. 3,600 m.

Ladoga (Ladozhskoye), L., St. Petersburg, **Russia;** a. 18,389 km²; (lgst. in Europe); drained to G. of Finland by R. Neva; fishing; link in new deepwater canal between White and Baltic Seas.

Ladybank, burgh, Fife, **Scot.;** 8 km S.W. of Cupar; p. (2002) 1,487.

Ladysmith, t. KwaZulu/Natal, **S. Africa;** cotton mills; siege by Boers 1899–1900; p. (1980) 105,020 (dist.).

Lagôa dos Patos, L., **Brazil;** drained by Rio Grande do Sul; 224 km long.

Lagôa Mirim, L., on bdy. between **Brazil** and **Uruguay;** drains N.; 176 km long.

Lagos, spt., former cap. of **Nigeria;** unhealthy and congested; cap. recently moved to Abuja; gd. natural harbour; exp. cocoa, groundnuts, palm oil and kernels, timber, hides and skins, cotton, rubber, crude oil; mnfs. textiles, confectionery, chemicals, car assembly; univ.; p. (1992) 1,347,000, (1991) 5,685,781 (state).

La Grande Chartreuse, limestone region between Chambery and Grenoble, **France;** famous monastery and liqueur.

La Grande Rivière, N. Quebec, **Canada;** major hydroelec. scheme; mineral and timber inds.

Laguna, dist., Durango st., **Mexico;** former L. bed irrigated by Rs. Nazas and Aguanaval; ch. cotton-growing region in Mexico; ch. t., Torréon; a. 259,000 km²

Lahore, ch. c., **Pakistan;** univ., cath., temples, mosques; textiles, pottery, carpets, industl. gases; atomic research ctr.; second c. of Pakistan; p. (2000) 6,040,000.

Lahti, t., S. **Finland;** wood, plywood, brewing, textiles; p. (1993) 94,160.

Lake Champlain, N.Y., **USA;** forms lowland a. for main routes between Montreal and N.Y.

Lake Charles, c., La., **USA;** spt. at mouth of Calcasieu R.; connected to G. of Mexico by channel; exp. oil, chemicals, rice, cotton; p. (1996) 71,445.

Lake District, almost circular mtnous. a., Cumbria, **Eng.;** 17 major and many smaller Ls. formed by glacial erosion and deposition; increasing tourist pressure on Nat. Park as motorways improve accessibility.

Lakeland, c., Fla., **USA;** citrus fruit ctr.; holiday resort; p. (1990) 70,576 (c.), 405,000 (met. a. with Winter Haven).

Lakeview, t., Ont., **Canada;** thermal elec. power plant projected; to be lgst. in world.

Lakshadweep, union terr., **India;** made up of Laccadive, Minicoy and Aminidivi Is; coir, coconuts; a. 32 km.²; p. (2001) 60,600.

La Laguna, second lgst. t., former cap. Tenerife, Canary Is; p. (1991) 116,500.

La Linea, t., **Spain;** on isthmus connecting Gibraltar with mainland; p. (1991) 61,600.

La Mancha, plain, Ciudad-Real prov., S. **Spain;** in shallow depression on central plateau, alt. between 450–900 m, drained by headstreams of R. Guadiana; semi-arid climate with hot summers, cold winters; salt deposits; Merino sheep, esparto grass; Spain's lgst. grape-growing region.

Lambaréné, t., **Gabon;** site of Schweitzer's hospital on Ogooué R.

Lambayeque, prov., N.W. **Peru;** ctr. of irrigated dists.; sugar, cotton, tobacco; cap. Chiclayo, ch. pt. Pimental; a. 11,948 km²; p. (1993) 920,795.

Lambeth, inner bor., London, **Eng.,** L. palace, residence of Archbishop of Canterbury; p. (2001) 267,785.

Lammermuir Hills, E. Lothian, **Scot.,** highest peak Lammer Law, 529 m.

Lampang, t., **Thailand;** modern sugar plant; p. (1980) 42,301.

Lampedusa, lgst. of Pelagi Is., between Malta and Tunisian cst., belonging to **Italy;** barren limestone; a. 21 km²; p. (1981) 4,792.

Lampeter, t., Ceredigion, S. **Wales;** on R. Teifi; mkt.; univ. college; p. (1991) 1,989.

Lamu, t., **Kenya;** impt. historical and tourist ctr. on Indian Ocean.

Lanark, royal burgh, S. Lanarkshire, **Scot.;** in Clyde valley 35 km S.E. of Glasgow; hosiery; ctr. of mkt. gardening a.; nr. New Lanark model t. built by Robert Owen; p. (2002) 8,253.

Lanarkshire, historic co., central **Scot.;** now divided between Glasgow, N. and S. Lanarkshire.

Lancashire, non-met. co., N.W. **Eng.;** major growth of p. in 19th cent. based on prod. of cotton and coal; main industl. ctrs. now outside co. in Merseyside and Gtr. Manchester met. cos.; Pennines in E.; extensive lowland in W.; admin. ctr. Preston; p. (2001) 1,134,974.

Lancaster, c., co. t., l. gov. dist., Lancs., **Eng.;** 10 km up R. Lune; cas., univ.; linoleum, vinyl, clothing; p. (2001) 133,914 (dist.), (2001) 45,952 (t.).

Lancaster, c., Penns., **USA;** agr. ctr., tobacco mkt.; stockyards; mnfs. linoleum, watches; birthplace of Robert Fulton; p. (1995) 53,597.

Lanchow. See Lanzhou.

Landau, t., Rhineland-Palatinate, **Germany;** on R. Queich; cigar mftg., wine, iron ind.; here the carriages called landaus were first made; p. (2002) 41,089.

Landes, dep., S.W. **France;** on Atl. cst.; agr., vineyards, resin; cap. Mont-de-Marsan; a. 9,334 km²; p. (1990) 306,000.

Landes, Les, region, Aquitaine, S.W. **France;** fringes Bay of Biscay from Pointe de Grave to Biarritz; coastal sand dunes and lagoons backed by low, flat plain of alternate sandy tracts and marsh; reclaimed by drainage and afforestation, now over half a. covered by pine forests; turpentine, timber; oilfield.

Land's End, extreme S.W. point of **Eng.** on Cornish cst.

Landshut, t., Bavaria, **Germany;** on R. Isar; cas.; elec. inds., glass, metallurgy, textiles, coal; rly. junc.; p. (2002) 59,513.

Landskrona, spt., **Sweden;** on the Sound; shipping and tr. ctr.; agr.-processing; on nearby I. of Ven; Tycho Brahe built his observatory; p. (1983) 35,656.

Langdale Pikes, L. Dist., **Eng.;** 2 peaks Harrison Stickle (733 m), Pike o'-Stickel (709 m); popular rambling and climbing a.; 5 km W. of Grasmere.

Langebergen, mtns., **S. Africa;** 240 km E. to W. parallel to S. cst. of Africa; form barrier to access from cst. plain to Little Karroo, broken across by valley of R. Gouritz; max. alt. exceeds 1,370 m.

Langkawi, group of 104 islands off n. coast of peninsular Malaysia; new tourist development.

Langres, t., Haute-Marne, **France;** cath., mediaeval fortifications; famous for its cutlery; birthplace of Diderot; p. (1999) 9,586.

Languedoc, former prov. now incorporated in **Languedoc-Roussillon** region, S. **France;** inc. deps. Aude, Gard, Hérault, Lozère, Pyrénées-Orientales; major govt. sponsored investment in chief inds., along Mediterranean cst.; mono-cultural vine prod., irrigation scheme to aid agr. diversification; p. (1990) 2,115,000.

Lannemezan, region, Aquitaine, S.W. **France;** belt 80 km wide stretches over 160 km along foot of Pyrenees W. of Toulouse; consists of immense deltas of glacial gravel deeply cut by tribs. of Rs. Garonne and Adour; valleys liable to severe floods in summer, intervening plateau dry, bare; scantily populated.

Lansing, c., cap of Mich., **USA;** on Grand R. at confluence with Cedar R.; automobiles, chemicals; p. (1990) 127,321 (c.), 433,000 (met. a. with E. Lansing).

Lanzarote, I., **Canary Is.;** volcanic mtns.; developing tourist ind.; cochineal; cap. Arrecife.

Lanzhou (Lanchou), c., cap. of Gansu prov., **China;** on Huang He; tr. ctr.; oil refining, gaseous diffusion plant, woollen mills, coal mng. nearby; p. (1994) 1,295,600.

Laoighis or **Leix Co.,** Leinster, **R.o.I.;** mtns. and bog; inland pasture and tillage; cap. Port Laoighise (Maryborough); a. 1,720 km²; p. (1986) 53,284.

Laon, t., cap. of Aisne dep., **France;** on rocky height above plain; historic fortress t.; cath.; p. (1999) 26,265.

Laois. See Laoighis.

Laos, People's Democratic Rep. of, S.E. Asia; kingdom until 1975; bordered by China, Vietnam, Cambodia, Thailand and Burma; formerly part of Fr. Indo- China; under-developed and isolated cty.; considerable mineral resources but only tin exploited; disrupted by civil war, drought, crop pests; economic ctr. is Mekong valley, scene of recent Mekong R. Development Project; elsewhere thickly forested mtns.; 70 per cent of p. engaged in subsistence agr. for dry rice; now produces rice surplus; main exp., hardwoods; no rlys.; royal cap. Luang Prabang, admin. cap. Vientiane; a. 231,399 km²; p. (2004) 6,068,117.

La Pampa, prov., central **Argentina;** p. (1991) 259,996.

La Paz, dep., **Bolivia;** traversed by Andes; de facto cap. La Paz, legal cap. Sucre; cocoa, coffee, rubber, tin-mng. at Catari; a. 105,377 km²; p. (2000) 1,480,000.

La Paz, c., **Bolivia;** seat of govt.; comm. ctr.; copper, alpaca wool, cinchona, textiles; highest cap. c. in world; p. (1992) 711,036.

Lapland, terr., N. **Europe,** in Norway, Sweden, Finland and Russia, extending from Norwegian cst. to White Sea; mainly mtn. and moorland, with many lakes; Lapps are nomadic pastoralists with reindeer herds; iron-ore at Kiruna and Gällivare; a. 336,700 km²; p. of Swedish Co. of L. (1983) 118,819.

La Plata, c., spt., **Argentina;** cap. of Buenos Aires prov., univ.; mftg. ctr.; iron and steel, oil refining, refrigerated meat prods.; p. (1991) 542,567.

La Plata, Rio de. See Plata, Rio de la.

Laptev Sea (Nordenskjöld Sea), inlet of Arctic Oc.; between Severnaya Zemlya and New Siberian Is., **Russia.**

Laramie, t., Wyo., **USA;** univ.; industl. ctr. for cattle and timber region; rly. engin.; p. (1990) 26,687.

Laredo, t., Texas, **USA;** frontier t. on Rio Grande; smuggling; ctr. of Chicanos; p. (1990) 122,899.

Largo, v., Fife, **Scot.;** fishing, holiday resort; birthplace of Alexander Selkirk.

Largs, burgh, N. Ayrshire, **Scot.;** on F. of Clyde opposite Is. of Bute and Cumbrae; seaside resort, fishing; battle 1263 defeating last attempt by Norsemen to conquer Scot.; p. (2002) 11,241.

La Rioja, t. and prov., N.W. **Argentina;** a. 92,331 km²; p. (1991) 103,727 (t.), 220,729 (prov.).

Larissa, dep., Thessaly, **Greece;** inc. infertile basin of R. Pinios; cap. Larissa; ch. pt. Volos; p. (1991) 112,777 (c.), 270,612 (dep.).

Larnaca, spt., **Cyprus;** the anc. Citium; grain, cotton, fruit; oil refinery; growing tourist ctr.; p. (1997) 106,000.

Larne, spt., l. gov. dist., **N. Ireland;** at entrance to Larne Lough; cross channel service to Stranraer; tourism; p. (2001) 30,832 (dist.), 17,525 (t.).

La Rochelle, spt., cap. of Charente-Maritime dep., **France;** on Atl. cst.; its deepwater pt. is La Pallice; cath.; fishing pt.; chemicals, food-processing; tourism; p. (1999) 76,584.

La Roche-sur-Yon, t., cap of Vendée dep., **France;** on R. Yon; built by Napoleon I; p. (1990) 48,518.

Larvik, spt., **Norway;** S.W. of Oslo; seaside resort; engin., pulp, stone; former whaling pt; p. (1990) 20,594.

Las Cruces, t., N.M., **USA**; on Rio Grande R.; irrigated agr.; univ.; p. (1996) 74,779.

La Serena, c., cap. of Coquimbo prov., **Chile**; 14 km inland from its pt. Coquimbo; cath.; resort; p. (1992) 120,336.

Lashio, t., **Myanmar**; on R. Salween; rly. terminus; Burma road links with China; ctr. of silver-lead mines.

Lashkar, c., Madhya Pradesh, central **India**; modern industl. t., adjoining Gwalior.

Las Palmas, prov., Canary Is., **Spain**; inc. Gran Canaria, Lanzarote, Fuerteventura and smaller Is.; intensive irrigated agr. of bananas, tomatoes, potatoes; tourism encouraged by climate and volcanic landscape; a. 4,053 km²; p. (1998) 850,000.

Las Palmas, c., N.E. Gran Canaria, ch. pt. of Canary Is.; exp. agr. prods.; cath.; p. (1998) 352,600.

La Spezia, spt., Liguria, N.W. **Italy**; on Bay of Spezia; ch. Italian naval sta., arsenal and docks; maritime inds., elec. machin., olive oil, oil refining; p. (1992) 100,458.

Lassen Peak, Nat. Park, Cascade Range, Cal.; only active volcano in **USA**.

Lasswade. See **Bonnyrigg and Lasswade**.

Las Vegas, c., Nevada, **USA**; noted for its gambling casinos (Nevada legalised gambling in 1931); ranching and mng. a.; p. (2000) 478,434 (c.), 741,000 (met. a.).

Latacunga, t., **Ecuador**; at about 2,740 m in Andean basin, not far from Cotopaxi volcano; anc. Inca t.; ctr.; p. (1990) 39,882.

Latakia, spt., **Syria**; exp. tobacco, olive oil, sponges; p. (1993) 293,000.

Latina (**Littoria**), c., cap. of Latina prov., in Latium central **Italy**; in ctr. of reclaimed a. of Pontine marshes; mkt. ctr., on which planned road system converges; built since 1932; nuclear power sta. nearby; p. (1981) 93,738.

Latin America, the Spanish-, Portuguese- and Fr.-speaking countries of N. America, S. America, Central America, and the W.I., inc. the reps. of Argentina, Bolivia, Brazil, Chile, Colombia, Costa Rica, Cuba, Dominican Republic, Ecuador, Salvador, Guatemala, Haiti, Honduras, Mexico, Nicaragua, Panama, Paraguay, Peru, Uruguay, and Venezuela; sometimes Puerto Rico, Fr. W.I., and other Is. of the W.I. are included, and occasionally also comprises Belize, Guyana, Fr. Guiana, and Surinam.

Latium (**Lazio**), region, central **Italy**; between Apennines and Tyrrhenian Sea, comprising provs. of Rome, Frosinone, Latina, Rieti, Viterbo; a. 17,182 km²; p. (1992) 5,162,073.

Latrobe Valley, one of most impt. economic a. in Victoria, **Australia**; major brown coal and electric power production; secondary inds. attracted by cheap power.

Latvia, former constituent rep., USSR; dairying, stock-raising, forestry; EU member, 2004; cap. Riga; spts. Ventspils, Liepaya; a. 66,278 km²; p. (2004) 2,306,306.

Launceston, t., Tasmania, **Australia**; at head of Tamar estuary, inc. Bell Bay where many heavy inds.; p. (1991) 93,347.

Launceston, t., North Cornwall, **Eng.**; agr. mkt.; quarrying, lt. engin.; p. (1991) 6,466.

Laurencekirk, burgh, Aberdeenshire, **Scot.**; agr. ctr. in the Howe of Mearns; p. (2002) 1,808.

Laurion or **Laurium**, pt. on Attic peninsula, **Greece**; lead, manganese, zinc, and silver mines; silver mined 5th cent. B.C.

Lausanne, c., cap. of Vaud can., **Switzerland**; nr. L. Geneva; cath., univ.; impt. rly. junc.; seat of Swiss high courts of justice; tourism; p. (1990) 123,200 (c.), 262,900 (met. a.).

Lauterbrunnen, Alpine valley, Bern can., **Switzerland**; famous for its waterfalls, the highest of which is Staubbach 299 m; winter sports ctr.

Laval, t., cap. of Mayenne dep., **France**; Mayenne R. divides old and modern parts; cotton, paper, machin., marble; cas., church; p. (1999) 50,947.

Lavenham, sm. t., Suffolk, **Eng.**; a ctr. of the wool tr. in 15th cent., still preserves its mediaeval character.

Lawrence, t., Mass., **USA**; on Merrimac R., N.W. of Boston; textiles, paper, footwear, engin.; p. (1990) 394,000 (met. a. with Haverhill).

Lazio. See **Latium**.

Lea or **Lee**, R., **Eng.**; rises in Chiltern Hills nr. Luton, flows S. and E. into R. Thames through industl. zone of N.E. London; valley to become a regional park; mkt. gardening a.; 74 km long.

Leamington (**Royal Leamington Spa**), t., Warwicks.,

Eng.; on R. Leam, trib. of Avon, 3 km N.E. of Warwick; fashionable spa; engin. inds.; p. (2001) 61,595.

Leatherhead, t., Mole Valley, Surrey, **Eng.**; on R. Mole to N. of gap through N. Downs; residtl.; p. (2001) 42,885.

Lebanon, mtn. range, **Lebanon**, extending to cst. of Syria; snow-capped most of year; highest peak Timarum, 3,214 m; famous in anc. times for cedar forests.

Lebanon, rep., S.W. Asia; at E. end of Mediterranean Sea; bordered by Syria to N. and Israel to S.; narrow coastal strip backed by mtnous. interior; free mkt. a., with economy based on transit tr.; most of p. involved in tourism, finance and commerce; oil refining based on imports; cap. Beirut; strife-torn by civil war, now being rebuilt; Israeli withdrawal from S. of country, May 2000; a. 8,806 km²; p. (2004) 3,777,218.

Le Bourget, t., N.E. of Paris, **France**; airpt.; p. (1982) 11,021.

Lebowa Territory, former Bantu Terr., **S. Africa**; home of N. Sotho and Ndebele peoples.

Lecce, c., Apulia, S. **Italy**; agr. and route ctr. with ceramic and glass inds.; anc. Greek col.; baroque churches and palaces; p. (1992) 100,508.

Lecco, t., **Italy**; in Lombardy, on L. Como; iron and copper wks., agr.-processing, cheese.

Lech, R., rises in Austria and flows past Augsburg in Bavaria, **Germany**, to join Danube; 283 km long.

Ledbury, t., Hereford, **Eng.**; at W. foot of Malvern hills; fruit preserving, tanning; 17th cent. mkt. hall; birthplace of John Masefield; p. (1991) 6,216.

Leeds, c., met. dist., West Yorks., **Eng.**; on R. Aire; at E. margin of Pennines; univs.; lge. clothing ind., varied engin. mnfs., paper and printing; with Bradford forms conurb. of W. Yorks., p. (2001) 715,402 (dist.), (2001) 443,247 (c.).

Leek, mkt. t., Moorlands, Staffs., **Eng.**; 18 km N.E. of Stoke-on-Trent; silk mnfs., butter; p. (1991) 18,167.

Lee-on-the-Solent, t., Hants., **Eng.**; on the Solent, p. (1991) 7,259.

Leeuwarden, c., cap. of Friesland prov., **Neth.**; noted cattle mkt.; rly. junc.; p. (1994) 87,464.

Leeuwin, C., S.W. point of **Australia**; notorious storms; Nat. Park (1971).

Leeward Is., W.I., northern gr. of Lesser Antilles archipelago; so-called because winds in this a. generally blow from E.; inc. Virgin Is. of US; Fr. I. of Guadaloupe, Dutch Is. of St. Eustatius and Saba, and Brit. Leeward Is. (Montserrat, Virgin Is., and former cols. of Antigua, St. Kitt-Nevis, Anguilla).

Lefkosia. See **Nicosia**.

Leganes, t., Madrid prov., C. **Spain**; mineral springs, electronics; p. (1998) 173,200.

Legazpi, c., cap. of Albay prov., **Philippines**; spt. in S.E. Luzon; linked by rly. with Manila; p. (1990) 121,116.

Leghorn. See **Livorno**.

Legionowo, t., **Poland**; on outskirts of Warsaw; nr. artificial L. in R. Bug valley; p. (1995) 50,589.

Legnano, t., Lombardy, **Italy**; N.W. of Milan; textiles, machin.; p. (1981) 49,308.

Legnica (**Liegnitz**), c. and prov., S.W. **Poland** (since 1945); on Katzbach R., in rich agr. region; p. (1995) 107,968 (c.), 523,125 (prov.).

Leh, cap. of Ladakh, Kashmir, **India**; isolated t. in Himalayas on caravan route to Tibet, p. (1991) 8,700.

Le Havre, spt., Seine-Maritime dep., N. **France**; at mouth of Seine on English Channel; shipbldg., engin., chemicals, ropes, cottons, oil refining; pipeline to Grandpuits; p. (1999) 190,650.

Leicester, c., unit. auth. created in 1997, formerly part of Leics., **Eng.**; on R. Soar; univs. (Leicester and De Montfort); footwear, hosiery, knitwear, etc. now declined; major shopping complex at Fosse Park; new Walker football stadium; National Space Science Centre; Roman remains; p. (2001) 296,000 (unit. auth.).

Leicestershire, non-met. co., **Eng.**; mainly rural, low-lying Midland co., but inc. Charnwood Forest; mixed agr., sm. coalfield; hosiery and footwear inds.; p. (2001) 609,578.

Leiden or **Leyden**, c., S. Holland prov., **Neth.**; on Oude Rijn; famous univ.; printing; textiles, medical equipment; gr. weaving ctr. in Middle Ages; revolt against Spanish rule

1573–4; birthplace of Rembrandt; p. (1994) 114,892 (c.), 194,051 (met. a.).

Leigh, t., Gtr. Manchester, **Eng.;** 8 km S.E. of Wigan; textiles; p. (2001) 43,006.

Leighton Buzzard, t., South Beds., **Eng.;** at N.E. end of Vale of Aylesbury; tiles, engin., sand quarrying; p. (2001) 32,753 (inc. Linslade).

Leinster, S.E. prov., **R.o.I.;** bulk of recent Irish p. increase; a. 19,637 km²; p. (1986) 1,852,649.

Leipzig, c. Saxony, **Germany;** comm., industl., and cultural ctr. at junc. of Rs. Pleisse, Elster, and Parthe; famous univ.; inds. inc. publishing, steel, textiles, chemicals, machin., cars; tr. fairs; Bach was organist at Thomaskirche; birthplace of Leibnitz and Wagner; p. (2002) 493,052.

Leiston-cum-Sizewell, t., Suffolk Coastal, Suffolk, **Eng.;** on cst. 6 km E. of Saxmundham; imp. nuclear power sta.; p. (1991) 5,950.

Leith, t., Edinburgh **Scot.,** shipbldg., timber whisky; outport for Edinburgh.

Leith Hill, Surrey, **Eng.;** nr. Dorking; alt. 294 m, Lower Greensand crest.

Leitmeritz. See Litoměřice.

Leitrim, co., Connacht, **R.o.I.;** agr.; cap. Carrick-on-Shannon; a. 1,588 km²; p. (1986) 27,035.

Leix. See Laoighis.

Leixões, the modern harbour of Oporto, **Portugal.**

Le Locle, t., Neuchâtel, **Switzerland;** ctr. of watch-mkg. ind.; p. (1986) 10,900.

Léman L. See Geneva, L.

Le Mans, t., cap. of Sarthe dep., N.W. **France;** cath.; linen, ironmongery, chemicals, motor cars, aeroplanes; motor-racing; p. (1999) 145,901.

Lemnos, Greek I., Aegean Sea, **Greece;** 64 km S.W. of Dardanelles; ch. t. Kastro (the anc. Myrina); tobacco, wine; a. 466 km²; part of Lesvos dep.

Lena, one of gr. Siberian Rs., **Russia;** rises in Oc.; navigable; 4,480 km long.

Leninabad. See Khudzhand.

Leninakan. See Kumayri.

Lenin Dam (Dnieper Dam). See Zaporozh'ye.

Leningrad. See St. Petersburg.

Leninogorsk. See Ridder.

Lenin Peak (Mt. Kaufmann); Trans-Altai Range, **Tajikistan-Khirghizia;** adjoining glacier; 7,132 m.

Leninsk-Kuznetski, t., Russia; in W. Siberia on Inya R.; coalfield in Kuznetsk basin; heavy engin., power sta.; p. (1989) 134,000.

Lenkoran, c., pt. Azerbaijan; on Caspian Sea, nr. Iranian border; rice, citrus fruits, tea, fisheries.

Lennoxtown, t., E. Dunbartonshire, **Scot.;** aluminium wks.; p. (2002) 3,773.

Lens, t., Pas-de-Calais dep., N. **France;** industl. ctr. in coal a.; p. (1999) 36,214.

Leominster, mkt. t., Hereford, **Eng.;** 19 km N. of Hereford; once famed for woollen ind.; enormous Saxon rotunda uncovered; p. (1995) 41,200 (dist.), (1991) 9,453 (t.).

León, c., central **Mexico;** at c. 1,700 m; comm., agr. and mng. ctr. (gold, copper, silver, lead, tin); textiles, leather; p. (1990) 872,453.

León, c., cap. of León dep., N.W. **Nicaragua;** cath., univ.; ctr. for agr. and industl. prods.; footwear, textiles; p. (1992) 172,000.

León, cap. of L. prov., N.W. **Spain;** gothic cath.; craft inds.; p. (1998) 139,800, 506,400 (prov.).

Léopoldville. See Kinshasa.

Lepontine Alps, Switzerland–Italy; alt. over 3,300 m.

Le Puy, t., cap. of Haute Loire dep., **France;** lace, liqueurs; cath. sited on old volcanic plug; tourism; p. (1990) 23,434.

Lérida, t., cap. of L. prov., **Spain;** on R. Segre; 2 caths.; textiles, leather, glass; p. (1998) 112,200 (t.), 358,000 (prov.).

Lerwick, t., Shetland Is., **Scot.;** on Mainland; fishing; p. (2002) 6,830.

Lesbos. See Lesvos.

Les Causses. See Causses, Les.

Les Landes. See Landes, Les.

Leslie, burgh, Fifeshire, **Scot.;** 11 km N. of Kirk-caldy; paper, bleaching; p. (2002) 2,998.

Lesotho (Basutoland), kingdom, southern Africa; surrounded by Rep. of S. Africa; at head of Orange R. and enclosed by Drakensberg mtns.; economy mainly agr., especially pastoral farming; exp. livestock, wool, mohair, diamonds; 50 per cent revenue from UK grants; poor communications; many workers migrate to S. Africa; inds. encouraged by tax concessions becoming increasingly impt.; Highlands Water Project started (1986) to export water from Orange R. to S. Africa and generate hydro-electr. from 6 dams; major AIDS problem; cap. Maseru; a.

30,344 km²; p. (2004) 1,865,840.

Lesser Antilles. See Antilles.

Lesvos (Lesbos, Mytilene), I., off Turkey, Aegean Sea, belonging to **Greece;** highest point 939 m; agr., antimony, marbles; cap. Mytilene; a. 1,601 km²; p. (1991) 103,700 (dep.).

Leszno, t. and prov., W. **Poland;** engin., distilling, tobacco; p. (1995) 61,295 (t.) 396,627 (prov.).

Letchworth (Garden City), t., North Herts., **Eng.;** at foot of Chiltern Hills, 3 km N.E. of Hitchin; first garden c., founded by Sir Ebenezer Howard 1903; engin., office equipment; expanded t.; p. (2001) 32,932.

Lethbridge, c., Alberta, **Canada;** in foothills of Rockies; ctr. of lge. coal-mng. dist. and of irrigated wheat-growing a.; p. (1996) 63,053.

Le Touquet-Paris Plage, fashionable resort, W. cst. **France;** S. of Canche estuary.

Letterkenny, t., Co. Donegal, **R.o.I.;** on Lough Swilly; tourist ctr.; p. (1986) 6,691.

Levant, French and Italian name for E. cst. of Mediterranean.

Leven, burgh, Fife, **Scot.;** on N. side of F. of Forth; resort; p. (2002) 8,051.

Leven, Loch, Perth and Kinross, **Scot.;** ass. with escape of Mary Queen of Scots from Castle I. 1568.

Leverkusen, t., N. Rhine–Westphalia, **Germany;** on R. Rhine, N. of Cologne; iron, machin., textiles, chemicals; p. (2002) 160,829.

Levkás or **Santa Maura,** one of Ionian Is., off W. **Greece;** wine, olive oil, currants; p. (1991) 20,900.

Lewes, t., l. gov. dist., East Sussex, **Eng.;** on R. Ouse at N. entrance to gap through S. Downs; mkt., cas., printing, light inds.; p. (2001) 92,177 (dist.), (1991) 15,376 (t.).

Lewis, I., Outer Hebrides, Western Isles, **Scot.;** fishing, tweeds; construction of world's biggest onshore wind farm planned; ch. t. Stornoway; p. (1991) 21,731 (with Harris).

Lewisham, inner bor., London, **Eng.;** inc. Deptford; residtl.; industl.; p. (2001) 248,922.

Lewiston, sm. t., Maine, **USA;** power for textile mill supplied by waterfall since early 19th cent.

Lexington-Fayette, c., Ky., **USA;** in heart of Blue Grass region; univ.; ch. tobacco mkt. and horse-breeding ctr. of USA; p. (2000) 260,512 (c.), 348,000 (met. a.).

Lexington, t., Mass., **USA;** nr. Boston; residtl.; first battle in war of independence 19 Apr. 1775; p. (1980) 29,479.

Leyden. See Leiden.

Leyland, t., Lancs., **Eng.;** 8 km S. of Preston; motor vehicles, rubber; p. (2001) 37,103. See Central Lancashire.

Leyte, one of Visayan Is., **Eng.;** central **Philippines;** maize, abaca, rice; Japanese fleet defeated by US in battle of Leyte Gulf 1944; a. 7,213 km²; p. (1990) 1,368,510.

Leyton. See Waltham Forest.

Lhasa (Lasa), c., cap. of Tibet, **China;** "forbidden" c.; Buddhist ctr., temple, monasteries, shrines; caravan tr. in carpets, silk, lace, gold, tea; pharmaceutical factory, turbine pumps, fertilisers; much hotel bldg. and restoration of Buddhist sites to encourage tourism; rly. to Golmud (700 miles) opened Oct. 2005; p. (1994) 118,000.

Lhotse, mtn., Tibet, **China–Nepal;** 4th hgst. mtn. in world; alt. 8,506 m.

Lianyungang, spt., Jiangsu, **China;** impt. fishing and tea centre; rapid industrial development, esp. mineral processing, chemicals and motors; univ.; attracting foreign investment as "open" c. under China's new economic policy; p. (1994) 401,100.

Liaoning, prov., N.E. **China;** inc. lower course and delta of Liao-ho; part of N.E. China (formerly called Manchuria); maize, millets, soyabeans; lge. mineral reserves of coal and iron ore; cap. Shenyang; a. 150,220 km²; p. (1994) 40,070,000.

Liaoyang, c., E. Liaoning prov., N.E. **China;** in fertile valley of Liao-ho; cotton-growing; textile mills; p. (1994) 541,300.

Liberec, t., Czech Rep.; on R. Neisse; univ.; textiles, chemicals, tr. ctr.; p. (1990) 104,000.

Liberia, rep., W. Africa; founded (1847) by free slaves from USA; tropical climate; few cash crops, inc. rubber and cocoa; rich iron deposits provide main exp.; world's lgst. merchant fleet as result of "flag of convenience"; endemic civil war; cap. and ch. pt. Monrovia; a. 99,068 km²; p. (2004) 3,390,635.

Libertador, reg. **Chile;** cap. Rancagua; a. 16,456 km²; p. (1992) 688,385.

Libreville, c., cap. of **Gabon**; pt. on G. of Guinea; exp. tropical hardwoods, rubber, cacao; Trans-Gabon rly. project to link L. to Booué to promote timber exploitation; p. (1999) 523,000.

Libya, (**Great Socialist People's Libyan Arab Republic**) (since 1977), rep., N. Africa; on Mediterranean cst.; desert conditions prevail; radical attitude towards oil companies as oil accounts for 99 per cent of exp. earnings and forms basis of new-found wealth; petro-chemical inds.; over half working p. are foreigners; most of p. engaged in subsistence agr. (nomadic pastoralism); most food and mnfs. imported; cap. Tripoli; a. 1,759,537 km²; p. (2004) 5,631,585.

Libyan Desert, part of the Sahara, **Africa**.

Licata, t., Sicily, **Italy**; spt.; sulphur-processing; p. (1981) 40,050.

Lichfield, c., l. gov. dist., Staffs., **Eng.**; cath.; agr. and lt. inds.; expanded t.; birthplace of Dr. Samuel Johnson; p. (2001) 93,232 (dist.), (2001) 28,435 (c.).

Lickey Hills, gr. of hills, Hereford and Worcs., **Eng.**; 6 km S.W. of Birmingham; reveal anc. rocks underlying younger sediments; rise to 292 m, largely wooded.

Liechtenstein, principality, between Austria and Switzerland; official language German; econ-omy based on sm.-scale inds. and tourism in picturesque Alpine scenery aided by mild climate; wine; cap. Vaduz; a. 161 km²; p. (2004) 33,436, one-third foreign born.

Liège (**Luik**), industl. c. and prov., E. **Belgium**; on R. Meuse nr. confluence of Ourthe; cath., univ.; conurb. inc. Herstal, Bressoux, Ougrée, Angleur, Grivegnée; metallurgy, armaments, vehicles, chemicals, textiles, glassware, tyres; p. (1993) 196,632 (c.), 1,011,368 (prov.).

Liepaja (**Libau**), c., **Latvia**; ice-free pt. on Baltic Sea, second to Riga; shipyards, steel-wks., paper mills, chemicals; exp. timber, grain; p. (1991) 114,900.

Liffey, R., **R.o.I.**; rises in Wicklow Mtns. and enters Irish Sea at Dublin.

Liguria, region, N.W. **Italy**; inc. provs. of Genoa and Porto Maurizio; a. 5,411 km²; p. (1992) 1,667,896.

Ligurian Sea, Mediterranean; N. of Corsica.

Likasi (**Jadotville**), t., **Congo**; ctr. for copper mng. and refining; p. (1991) 279,839.

Lille, c., cap. of Nord dep., N. **France**; on R. Deûle; mftg., comm. and cultural ctr.; former cap. of Fr. Flanders (1668); textiles (the term lisle derived from earlier spelling of city's name), metallurgy, engin.; univ., art museums; p. (1999) 182,228.

Lilongwe, c., main ctr. of Central Region, **Malawi**; replaced Zomba as cap. 1975; p. (1998 est.) 1 m.

Lima, c., cap. of **Peru**; 13 km from its pt. Callao; dominates comm., industl. and social life of cty.; cath., univ., imposing architecture; seaside subs. Miraflores, Barranco, Chorillos; shanty ts. on out-skirts; p. (1998) 7,443,000.

Limassol, t., S. **Cyprus**; spt. on Akrotiri Bay; new artificial harbour; ctr. of admin. dist.; wine, agr.-processing; exp. foodstuffs; tourism. p. (1997) 183,000.

Limavady, t., l. gov. dist., **N. Ireland**; mkt.; linen; p. (2001) 32,422 (dist.), 10,350 (t.).

Limbe. See Blantyre-Limbe.

Limbourg, prov., N.E. **Belgium**; bordering Neth.; mainly agr.; coal-mng. in Campine region; cap. Hasselt; a. 2,409 km²; p. (1993) 763,565.

Limburg, prov., S.E. **Neth.**; bordering on Belgium and W. Germany; drained by R. Maas; former coalmng.; new inds. to relieve unem-ployment; a. 2,191 km²; p. (1994) 1,125,187.

Limeira, t., São Paulo, **Brazil**; ctr. of orange cultivation; hats, matches; p. (1996) 230,300.

Limerick, co., Munster, **R.o.I.**; agr., livestock, fishing; a. 3,385 km²; p. (1986) 164,569.

Limerick, cap. of Limerick, **R.o.I.**; spt. at head of Shannon estuary; bacon, tanning, shipbldg.; p. (1986) 56,279.

Limmat, R., **Switzerland**; trib. of R. Aare; flows through c. of Zürich; 128 km long.

Lim Fjord, shallow strait, Jutland, **Denmark**; links N. Sea with Kattegat; contains I. of Mors.

Limoges, c., cap. of Haute-Vienne dep., **France**; to N.W. of Central Massif; anc. t., celebrated in middle ages for goldsmith's work, later for enamel ware and porcelain; cath.; p. (1999) 133,591.

Limón, spt., **Costa Rica**; on Caribbean; oil refining nearby; p. (1984) 67,784 (dist.).

Limousin, region and former prov., central **France**; to W. of Auvergne; inc. deps. Corrèze, Haute-

Vienne, Creuse, plateau, average alt. 300 m, composed of old crystalline rocks; exposed damp climate; infertile, some pastoral agr.; kaolin; ch. t.; Limoges; p. (1990) 722,900.

Limpopo or **Crocodile R.**, **S. Africa**, Mozambique, and **Zimbabwe**; lower R. forms a fertile valley 1,600 km long. Major flooding (2000).

Limpopo, prov., **South Africa**. New name for old Northern Province (q.v.)

Lincoln, c., co. t., l. gov. dist., Lincs., **Eng.**; on R. Witham in gap through Lincoln Edge; impt. Roman t.; cath., cas.; heavy engin., iron foundries, bricks, lime, seed milling, malting; univ campus; p. (2001) 85,595 (dist.).

Lincoln, c., cap. of Nebraska, **USA**; univ.; educational ctr.; grain and cattle mkt.; flour mills, agr. machin., cars, chemicals, rubber gds.; univ.; p. (2000) 225,581.

Lincoln Edge, limestone ridge, Lincs. and N. Lincs., **Eng.**; runs N. from Ancaster through Lincoln to Humber; narrow ridge with steep scarp slope to W., broken by R. Witham at Lincoln; iron-ore deposits worked in N. nr. Scunthorpe; sheep, barley; rarely exceeds 90 m alt.

Lincolnshire, non-met. co., **Eng.**; between the Humber R. and the Wash; fertile soil on low-lying fenland; intensive agr., arable crops, bulbs, mar-ket gardening; food processing; formerly divided into 3 admin. parts: Holland, Kesteven, and Lindsey; p. (2001) 646,645.

Lincoln Wolds, low plateau, Lincs. and N. Lincs., **Eng.**; runs N. 72 km from Wash to Humber; chalk covered with glacial deposits; mixed farming, grains, roots, sheep; lge. farm units; scantily populated; rise to approx. 135 m.

Lindau, t. Baden-Württemberg, **Germany**; on I. in Bodensee; tourist resort; p. (1986) 23,100.

Lindisfarne or **Holy I.**, off cst. of Northumberland, **Eng.**; connected to mainland by stretch of sand and causeway at low tide; abbey founded 635 A.D. as first establishment of Celtic Christianity in Eng.

Lindsey. See Lincolnshire.

Line Is., Pac. Oc., coral gr. admin. by U.K., except Palmyra, Kingman and Jarvis, which belong to USA; coconuts; airfields, meteorological stas.

Linköping, t., S.E. **Sweden**; aero-engin., pianos, furniture; cath.; p. (1992) 126,377.

Linlithgow, burgh, W. Lothian, **Scot.**; distilling, brewing, paper, shoes; birthplace of Mary Queen of Scots; p. (2002) 13,370.

Linnhe, Loch, Highland, Argyll and Bute, **Scot.**; 21 miles long; entrance to Caledonian Canal.

Linslade. See Leighton Buzzard.

Linz, c., cap. of Upper **Austria**; pt. on Danube; comm. and industl. ctr. with iron and steel wks.; cath.; p. (1991) 202,855.

Lipari Is. or **Aeolian Is.**, volcanic gr. between Sicily and toe of **Italy**; inc. Stromboli (927 m), Lipari, Vulcano, Salina; olives, grapes, cur-rants, pumice; p. (1981) 10,208.

Lipetsk, c., **Russia**; on Voronezh R.; ctr. of iron-ore mng. a.; engin., steel; p. (1989) 450,000.

Lippe, R., **Germany**; trib. of Rhine; paralleled by L. canal, forms N. bdy. of Ruhr industl. dist.; 176 km long.

Lippstadt, t., N. Rhine–Westphalia, **Germany**; on R. Lippe; metallurgy, textiles rly. ctr.; p. (2002) 67,231.

Liri, R., central **Italy**; rises in Alban Hills, flows S.E. to Cassino and then S.W. to G. of Gaeta; valley followed by main road from Rome to Naples; length 168 km.

Lisbon (**Lisboa**), c., cap of **Portugal**; on R. Tagus, 14 km from mouth; spt. with fine natural har-bour; cas., cath., univ.; admin., comm., and industl. ctr.; expanding inds., airpt.; attracts p. from rural areas; p. (2000) 3,826,000 (met. a.).

Lisburn, c., l. gov. dist., **N. Ireland**; on R. Lagan, 10 km S.W. of Belfast; p. (2001) 108,694 (dist.), 42,110 (c.). Created a city, 2002.

Lisieux, t., Calvados dep., **N. France**; historic t., severely damaged in second world war; cath.; Camembert cheese; p. (1999) 22,940.

Liskeard, mkt. t., Caradon, Cornwall, **Eng.**; on R. Looe at S. edge of Bodmin Moor; p. (1991) 7,044.

Litherland, t., Sefton, Merseyside, **Eng.**; N. sub. of Liverpool; p. (2001) 22,242.

Lithuania, former constituent rep., USSR; borders Baltic Sea; agr. development on reclaimed marsh-land; dairy farming, stockraising, fishing, timber inds., food-processing, ship bldg., textiles, machin.; EU member (2004); cap. Vilnius; a. 65,201 km²; p. (2004) 3,607,899.

Little Belt (Lille Bælt), strait, **Denmark**; separates Fyn I. from Jutland; too shallow for lge. ships; road/rly., motorway bridges cross narrow N. section nr. Frederidicia; 48 km long.

Little Bighorn, R., Wyo, Mont., **USA**; Custer's last battle on ridge overlooking R. (1876); 144 km long.

Littleborough, t., Gtr. Manchester, **Eng.**; textiles and textile finishing; p. (1991) 13,638.

Little Dunmow, v., 3 km E. of Great Dunmow; Uttlesford, Essex, **Eng.**; historic Dunmow Flitch (side of bacon); bacon factory closed (1983).

Littlehampton, t., Arun, West Sussex, **Eng.**; on S. cst. at mouth of R. Arun; holiday resort, sm. spt.; p. (2001) 55,716.

Little Lever, t., Gtr. Manchester, **Eng.**; 5 km S.E. of Bolton; residtl. and industl.; p. (1991) 11,589.

Little Rock, c., cap. of Ark., **USA**; N.E. of Hot Springs, on Ark. R. opposite N. Little Rock; comm. and mnf. ctr. in cotton and dairy farming a.; bauxite nearby; p (1990) 175,795 (c.), 513,117 (met. a. with N. Little Rock).

Littoria. See Latina.

Liuchow. See Liuzhou.

Liuzhou (**Liuchow**), c., Guangxi, S. **China**; on trib. of Xijiang; route ctr. and R. pt.; p. (1994) 707,200.

Liverpool, c., spt., met. dist., Merseyside, **Eng.**; on N. bank at entrance to Mersey estuary; deep-sea container berths at Seaforth; shipping and ship-repairing; elec. mnfs. and engin., flour milling, sugar refining, seed and rubber processing, cars; cath., univs.; second Mersey tunnel opened 1971; birthplace of The Beatles; European City of Culture, 2008; Tate Liverpool (art gallery); p. (2001) 439,473 (dist).

Liverpool, t., N.S.W., **Australia**; within met. a. of Sydney; major source of poultry, vegetables and dairy prods. for Sydney.

Livingston, new t. (1962), W. Lothian, **Scot.**; nick-named 'Silicon Glen'; p. (2002) 50,826.

Livingstone, t., **Zambia**; on Zambesi R. where rly. bridges R.; stands at c. 900 m; former cap.; sawmilling ctr.; p. (1989) 102,000.

Livorno (**Leghorn**), spt., cap. of L. prov., **Italy**; on Ligurian Sea; p. (1992) 166,394.

Lizard, The, C., Cornwall, **Eng.**; S. point of Eng.

Ljubljana, c., cap. of **Slovenia** (formerly Yugoslavia); on trib. of Sava R.; industl. ctr., local coal, hydroelectric power; route ctr.; airport; univ.; mediaeval fortress; ctr. of Slovene nat. movement in 19th cent.; p. (1997) 330,000.

Llanberis, pass, Gwynedd, N. **Wales**; between Snowdon and Glyder Fawr; road carries heavy tourist traffic; summit 356 m; nearby tourist resort of Llanberis; p. (1991) 1,859.

Llandeilo, mkt. t., Carmarthenshire, **Wales**; in Vale of Towy, E. of Carmarthen; cas.; p. (1991) 1,666.

Llandovery, t., Carmarthenshire, **Wales**; on R. Bran, ˌˌˌ ˌˌˌ ˌˌˌ ˌ ˌˌˌˌ ˌˌˌ ˌˌˌ ˌˌˌ ˌ ˌ p. (1991) 2,037.

Llandrindod Wells, t., Powys, **Wales**; medicinal waters; p. (1991) 4,362.

Llandudno, t., Conwy, **Wales**; between Gr. Ormes and Little Ormes headlands; resort; p. (1991) 14,576.

Llanelli, t., Carmarthenshire, **Wales**; pt. on Burry inlet, 18 km N.W. of Swansea; industl. and comm. ctr.; coal mng., steel and tinplate wks., mng. machin.; cas.; p. (1991) 44,953.

Llanfairfechan, t., Conwy, **Wales**; at foot of Penmaenmawr mtn.; seaside resort; granite quarrying; p. (1991) 3,338.

Llangefni, t., Isle of Anglesey, **Wales**; in ctr. of the I.; mkt. and agr. t.; p. (1991) 4,643.

Llangollen, t., Denbighshire, **Wales**; on R. Dee; Vale of L., tourist ctr.; annual International Eisteddfod; p. (1991) 3,267.

Llanidloes, t., Powys, **Wales**; on R. Severn; surrounded by hills; anc. mkt. house; p. (1991) 2,616.

Llanos, lowland region, **Venezuela** and **Colombia**, S. America; drained by R. Orinoco and tribs.; high temperatures throughout year, but rain chiefly in summer; dry. vegetation, coarse grass which withers during dry season (Dec. to May).

Llanrwst, mkt. t., Conwy, **Wales**; on R. Conwy; tourist ctr.; p. (1991) 3,012.

Llanstephan, v., Carmarthenshire, **Wales**; at mouth of R. Towy; ruins of Norman cas.

Llantrisant, new t., Rhondda, Cynon, Taff, S. **Wales**; iron-ore quarrying; Royal Mint; p. (1991) 9,136 (with Pontyclun).

Llantwit Major, t. Vale of Glamorgan, **Wales**; famous

centre of learning in Celtic times.

Lleyn, peninsula, Gwynedd, N. **Wales**; from Snowdonia to Bardsey I.; crystalline rocks form hills in E., otherwise low, undulating; pastoral farming, sheep, cattle; sm. seaside resorts; ch. t. Pwllheli.

Loanhead, burgh, Midlothian, **Scot.**; 8 km S.E. of Edinburgh; coal, engin.; p. (2002) 6,384.

Lobito, spt., **Angola**; on Atl. Oc.; 29 km N. of Benguela; fine natural deepwater harbour; rly. terminus; varied exps.; oil-refinery.

Locarno, t., **Switzerland**; on L. Maggiore; tourist ctr.; L. treaty 1925; p. (1986) 14,341.

Lochalsh. See Kyle of Lochalsh.

Lochgelly, burgh, Fife, **Scot.**; nr. Dunfermline; p. (2002), 6,749.

Lochgilphead, Argyll and Bute, **Scot.**; at head of Loch Gilp, 3 km N. of Ardrishaig; tourist ctr.; p. (2002) 2,326.

Lochmaben, burgh, Dumfries and Galloway, **Scot.**; in Annandale, 11 km N.E. of Dumfries; p. (2002) 1,952.

Lockerbie, burgh, Dumfries and Galloway, **Scot.**; in Annandale, 16 km E. of Dumfries; sheep mkt.; air disaster 1988, caused by terrorist bomb; p. (2002) 4,009.

Lockport, t., N.Y., **USA**; on N.Y. st. barge canal, 38 km N.E. of Buffalo; power from Niagara falls supplies paper, metal, and other inds.

Lodi, t., **Italy**; on R. Adda, S.E. of Milan; cath.; scene of Napoleon's victory over Austrians 1796; p. (1981) 42,873.

Lodore Falls, waterfalls, Cumbria, **Eng.**; in Watendlath beck at foot of Derwentwater.

Lódz, c. and prov., central **Poland**; second c. of rep. and ctr. of textile ind.; machin., elec. equipment, chemicals, metals; univ.; cultural ctr.; problems of water-supply; p. (1995) 825,615 (c.), 1,118,248 (prov.).

Lofoten Is., storm-swept chain of Is. off N.W. cst. **Norway** within Arctic Oc., stretching 240 km; rich cod and herring fisheries.

Loftus, t. Redcar and Cleveland, **Eng.**; on N.E.flank of Cleveland Hills; p. (1991) 5,931.

Logroño, t., N. **Spain**; on Ebro R.; in wine growing a.; industl. and agr. ctr.; p. (1998) 125,600.

Loire, R., **France**; longest in cty., flows from Cevennes mtns. to Atl. Oc. at St. Nazaire; vineyards and many castles in attractive valley; 1,000 km long.

Loire, dep., E. central **France**; in part of the former provs. of Beaujolais and Lyonnais; agr.; coal mng., cattle raising; cap. St. Etienne; a. 4,799 km²; p. (1999) 728,785.

Loire-Atlantique, dep., W. **France**; mainly agr., salt-marsh on cst.; inds. at cap. Nantes; a. 6,980 km²; p. (1999) 1,132,251

Loiret, dep., N. central **France**; agr., vineyards, distilling, mfg.; cap. ˌˌˌ ˌˌˌ ˌ ˌˌˌˌ ˌˌ ˌˌˌˌ ˌˌ ˌˌˌ ˌ ˌˌˌˌ ˌ ˌˌ ˌ ˌˌ ˌ ˌ ; p. (1999) 617,937.

Loir-et-Cher, dep., central **France**; contains fertile a. of Beauce; cap. Blois; a. 6,421 km²; p. (1999) 314,663.

Lolland or **Laaland**, Danish I. part of **Denmark** in Baltic Sea; a. 1,241 km²; agr. forests; ch. ts. Maribo, Nakshov; p. (1990) 73,191.

Lomami, R., central **Congo**; trib. of Congo R., rich coal-bearing strata at confluence; 1,812 km long.

Lombardy, Plain of, N. **Italy**; extensive low-land flanked by Alps, Apennines, Adriatic Sea; built up by alluvium from R. Po, its tribs. and R. Adige; intensively cultivated; rice, maize, flax, clover, lucerne, wheat, apples, dairy cattle; densely populated; many industl. ts., Milan, Novara, Pavia, etc.; p. of region (1992) 8,882,408

Lombok, one of the lesser Sunda Is., **Indonesia**; mtnous. volcanic terrain; Wallace's Line passes between Lombok and Bali; religious riots, January 2000; ch. t. Mataram; p. 1,300,000.

Lomé, spt., cap. of **Togo**, W. Africa; on G. of Guinea; deepwater pt.; p. (1999) 790,000.

Lomond, Loch, Stirling, lgst. loch in **Scot.**, studded with 38 Is., surrounded by hills with Ben Lomond on E. side. Centrepiece of Scotland's first National Park.

Lomza, t. and prov., **Poland**; on Narew R., metal inds., foodstuffs; p. (1995) 62,974 (t.), 353,721 (prov.).

London, cap. of U.K., **Eng.**; at head of Thames estuary; seat of govt., world ctr. of finance and communication; cultural and artistic ctr.; comprises the City, 12 inner and 20 outer bors.; Port of London; upstream docks now closed; main pt. downstream at Tilbury; losing p. and inds. to outer met. a.; univs. (London, Brunel, City *etc.*), caths., historic bldgs., theatres, museums, galleries, libraries, and parks; new GLA elected, May 2000; hosts 2012 Olympics; p. (2001) 7,185 (City of London), (2001) 2,766,114 (Inner London), (2001) 7,172,091 (Greater London).

London, t., Ont., **Canada**; on R. Thames, 104 km W. of Hamilton; industl. ctr.; univ.; p. (1991) 303,165 (c.), (1996) 398,616 (met a.).

Londonderry (Derry) c., Derry, **N. Ireland**; on R. Foyle, 6 km upstream from Lough Foyle; regional education hub and admin centre; training ctr. for ind.; tourism; p. (2001) 105,335.

Londrina, c., Parana, **Brazil**; industl. and agr. ctr., coffee, maize, cotton, livestock; p. (1996) 412,900.

Long Beach, c., Cal., **USA**; Pac. cst. resort and industl. suburb of Los Angeles met. a.; p. (2000) 461,522 (c.). *See* Los Angeles.

Long Eaton, t. Erewash, Derbys., **Eng.**; on R. Trent, 8 km S.W. of Nottingham; former ctr. for lace mftg., elec. cables, flexible tubing, hosiery; p. (2001) 46,490.

Longford, co., Leinster, **R.o.I.**; peat bogs; dairy farming; co. t. Longford; a. 1,090 km². p. (1986) 31,496.

Longford, co. t., Longford, **R.o.I.**; cas., cath.; mkt. t.; p. (1986) 6,457.

Long Forties Bank, submarine sandbank, N. Sea; 128 km E. of Aberdeen; valuable fishing-grounds; depth of water, from 45–75 m.

Long I., part of N.Y., **USA**; separated from mainland by East R.; contains Queens and Brooklyn bors. of N.Y. City; mkt. gardening, fisheries, oysters, holiday resorts; a. 4,356 km².

Longridge, t., Ribble Valley, Lancs., **Eng.**, 10 km N.E. of Preston; p. (1991) 7,351.

Longstanton, Cambs., **Eng.**; proposed site of new town between Cambridge and Huntingdon.

Longview, t. Texas, **USA**; oil, chemicals, plastics; p. (1996) 74,572.

Longwy, t., Meurthe-et-Moselle dep., N.E. **France**; on Belgian–Luxembourg frontier; upper part fortfd.; lower part industl with iron and steel ind.

Lons-le-Saunier, cap. of Jura dep., E. **France**; saline springs; agr. ctr.; p. (1999) 18,483.

Looe, t. Caradon, Cornwall, **Eng.**; on Looe estuary; holiday resort; p. (1991) 5,022.

Lop Nor, marsh, Xinjiang, W. **China**; in Tarim Basin at foot of Altun Shan; ctr. of inland drainage, receives water from R. Tarim; atomic testing grounds.

Lorain, t., Ohio, **USA**; on L. Erie; shipbldg., steelwks., fisheries; p. (1990) 71,245 (c.), 271,000 (met. a. with Elyria).

Lorca, t., Murcia, **Spain**; agr. prod., woollens, chemicals; bishop's palace; p. (1990) 67,300.

Lord Howe I., forested volcanic I., S. Pac. Oc., 698 km N.E. of Sydney; palm seed ind.; admin. by N.S.W. **Australia**; p. (1991) 320.

Lorient, spt., Morbihan dep., N.W. **France**; on Atl.; naval shipyard, fishing harbour; p. (1999) 59,075.

Lorraine, region and former prov., N.E. **France**; inc. deps. Moselle, Meurthe-et-Moselle, Meuse, and Vosges; ch. t. Nancy; rich iron-ore deposits, impt. but declining industl. a.; mkt. gardening, vineyards; with Alsace long disputed between Germany and France; p. (1999) 2,308,796.

Los Alamos, t., N.M., **USA**; site of research for first atomic bomb.

Los Angeles, c., S. Cal., **USA**; booming modern c. ("the city of angels"), busiest pt. in Cal.; fine harbour; riots 1992; many prosperous inds., inc. aircraft, missiles, chemicals, machin., electronic equipment, food-processing, oil refining; film ctr.; earthquake 1994; p. (2000) 3,694,820 (c.), 8,863,000 (met a. with Long Beach).

Los Lagos, reg. Chile; cap. Puerto Montt; a. 67,247 km²; p. (1992) 953,330.

Lossiemouth, burgh, Moray, **Scot.**; on Moray F., 8 km N. of Elgin; birthplace of Ramsay MacDonald; fishing; p. (2002) 6,803.

Lostwithiel, mkt. t. Cornwall, **Eng.**; on R. Fowey S.E. of Bodmin; anc. Stannary t.; p. (1991) 2,452.

Lot, dep., S.W. **France**; livestock, wine, cereals, coals, iron; a. 5,227 km²; cap. Cahors; p. (1990) 155,800.

Lot, R., S. **France**; trib. of Garonne R., 435 km long.

Lot-et-Garonne, dep., S.W. **France**; agr. (cereals, vines, fruit); cap. Agen; a. 5,385 km²; p. (1999) 305,368.

Lötschental, picturesque valley, Valais, **Switzer-land**; ch. v. Kippel.

Loughborough, t., Charnwood, Leics., **Eng.**; on R. Soar 16 km N. of Leicester; engin., elec. gds., chemicals, textiles; univ.; former hosiery t.; bell foundry; home of National Cricket Academy; p. (2001) 55,258.

Loughor. *See* Llwchwr.

Loughrea, sm. mkt. t., Galway, **R.o.I.**; cotton mill.

Louisiana, southern st., **USA**; Pelican St.; admitted to Union 1812; st. flower Magnolia, st. bird Eastern Brown Pelican; leading producer of rice, sugarcane, sweet potatoes, also cotton, maize, tobacco, oil, natural gas, lumber; cap. Baton Rouge; New Orleans major pt.; devastated by Hurricane Katrina, 2005; a. 125,675 km²; p. (2002) 4,482,646.

Louisville, c., Ky., **USA**; on Ohio R.; univ.; lgst. tobacco mkt. in world; chemicals, paints, cars, machin., elec. gds., synthetic rubber; p. (2000) 256,231 (c.), 953,000 (met. a.).

Lourdes, t., **France**; on R. Pau; Catholic pilgrim centre.; slate, marble.

Lourenço Marques. *See* Maputo.

Louth, t., East Lindsey, Lincs., **Eng.**; on E. edge of Lincoln Wolds; abbey ruins; cattle mkt., farm implements, plastic bags, corrugated board; p. (1991) 14,248.

Louth, maritime co., Leinster, **R.o.I.**; mtns., bog and barren land; salmon fishing; cap. Dundalk; a. 818 km²; p. (1986) 91,810.

Louvain (Leuven), c., Brabant prov., **Belgium**; on R. Dyle; univ. (Erasmus taught here); brewing ctr., bell foundries; p. (1993) 85,592.

Low Archipelago. *See* Tuamotu Is.

Low Countries, name for Belgium and the Neth.

Lowell, c., Mass., **USA**; at junc. of Merrimac and Concord Rs.; 48 km N. of Boston; textiles, machin., chemicals, carpets; birthplace of Whistler; p. (1990) 103,439 (c.), 273,000 (met. a.).

Lower California (Baja California), peninsula, N.W. **Mexico**; separating G. of Cal. and Pac. Oc.; isolated, arid; divided into 2 sts., Baja California (cap. Tijuana) p. (1990) 1,657,927, and Baja California, Territorio Sur (cap. La Paz) p. (1990) 317,326; a. 143,963 km².

Lower Hutt, c., N.I., **N.Z.**; rapid industl. devcl.; engin., plastics, textiles, vehicle assembly; p. (1991) 94,540.

Lower Saxony (Nieder Sachsen), *Land*, **Germany**; inc. Lüneburg heath and Harz mtns.; cap. Hanover; a. 47,205 km²; p. (2005) 7,980,000.

Lowestoft, old fish pt., Waveney, Suffolk, **Eng.**; on E. Anglian cst. 14 km S. of Gr. Yarmouth; holiday resort, nr. Broads; food processing plants; base for N. Sea gas; p. (2001) 68,340.

Lowther Hills, mtns., between S. Lanarkshire and Dumfries and Galloway **Scot.**; hgst. point 733 m.

Loyalty Is., S. Pac. Oc.; included in Fr. administration of New Caledonia; cupra; lgst. Is. Maré, Lifou, Uvéa; a. *c.* 2,100 km².

Lozère, dep., S.E. **France**; traversed by Cevennes mtns.; cap. Mende; a. 5,170 km²; p. (1990) 72,800.

Lualaba, R., **Congo**, central **Africa**; rises nr. Lubumbashi in Shaba prov., flows N. circa 800 km to Kikondja, where joined by R. Lufira to form R. Congo; name also applied to main stream of R. Congo as far downstream as Ponthierville.

Luanda, c. cap. of **Angola**; pt. on Atl. Oc.; exp. coffee, cotton, palm prod.; industl. ctr.; foodstuffs, tobacco, plastics; oil refining; hydro-electric power; p. (2000) 2,680,000.

Luang Prabang, c., N.W. **Laos**; at confluence of Mekong and Kahn Rs.; rubber, rice, teak; former royal cap.; p. (1985) 68,399.

Lubbock, c., N.W. Texas, **USA**; on Double Mountain fork of Brazos R.; ctr. of cotton-growing a.; p. (2000) 199,564.

Lübeck, c., pt. of Schleswig-Holstein, **Germany**; on Baltic Sea at mouth of Trave R.; cath.; shipbldg., machin., chemicals, textiles, iron, foodstuffs; birthplace of Thomas Mann; p. (2002) 213,496.

Lublin, c. and prov., E. **Poland**; motor vehicle and elec. engin.; agr. tr. and processing; cultural ctr., univ.; cas.; p. (1995) 353,300 (c.), 1,025,800 (prov.).

Lubumbashi (Elizabethville), t., Shaba, **Congo**; copper-mng. ctr.; p. (1991) 739,082.

Lucca, c., cap. of L. prov., Tuscany, Italy; cath., churches, palaces; noted for olive oil, pasta, wine; silk, cotton, jute, tobacco inds.; p. (1981) 91,246.

Lucerne (Luzern), can., **Switzerland;** agr., pastoral, vineyards; oil refinery projected at Schötz/Ettiswil; cap. Lucerne; a. 1,492 km²; p. (1990) 319,500.

Lucerne (Luzern), c., cap. of L. can., **Switzerland;** at N.W. end of L. Lucerne; aluminium gds., sewing machin.; tourist ctr.; p. (1990), 60,035 (c.), 161,000 (met. a.).

Lucerne, L., Switzerland; also known as L. of the Four Cantons; length 37 km; a. 70 km².

Luchon or **Bagnères-de-Luchon,** resort in Fr. Pyrenees, Haute-Garonne dep., S. **France;** warm sulphur springs; winter sports ctr.; p. (1991) 2,888.

Luchow. See **Zuzhou.**

Lucknow, c., cap. of Uttar Pradesh st., N. **India;** on R. Gumti (trib. of Ganges); educational and cultural ctr. with textile inds.; rly. ctr.; scene of 1857 mutiny; p. (1991) 1,619,000.

Lüda, special mun., S. Liaoning prov., **China;** comprising Port Arthur Naval Base District and the pts. of Port Arthur and Talien (Dairen); chemicals, machin., shipbldg., textiles; p. (1991) 1,723,000.

Lüdenscheid, t., N. Rhine–Westphalia, **Germany;** metal mngs., domestic hardware; supplied structures for first Zeppelins; p. (2002) 80,509.

Ludhiana, t., Punjab st., N.W. **India;** S. of Sutlej R.; industl. ctr.; hosiery, knitwear; p. (1991) 1,043,000.

Ludlow, t., South Shrops., **Eng.;** agr. mkt.; agr. engin.; cas.; p. (1991) 9,040.

Ludwigsburg, t. Baden-Württemberg, **Germany;** N. of Stuttgart; cas.; textiles, foodstuffs, machin., toys; p. (2002) 87,502.

Ludwigshafen, t., Rhine-Palatinate, **Germany;** on R. Rhine, opposite Mannheim; chemicals, marine diesel engines, metallurgy, glass; R. pt. and rly. junc.; oil pipeline from Rotterdam under construction; p. (2002) 162,458.

Lugano, t., Ticino can., **Switzerland;** on L. Lugano; tourist resort; p. (1980) 27,815.

Lugano, L., lies at S. foot of Alps between **Switzerland** and **Italy;** attractive scenery, tourism; a. 49 km².

Lugansk (Voroshilovgrad), industl. t., **Ukraine;** S. of R. Donets in Donbas Region; impt. rly. engin. factories; textiles; p. (1990) 501,100.

Lugo, c., cap. of L. prov., N.W. **Spain;** in Galicia, on Miño R.; in fertile agr. a.; cath.; p. (1990) 81,500, (t.), (1998) 367,800 (prov.).

Luleå, spt., N. **Sweden,** cap. of Norrbotten co.; on Lule R. at head of G. of Bothnia; iron ore; smelting plant, engin.; p. (1992) 68,924.

Luluabourg. See **Kananga.**

Lulworth Cove, sm. inlet, Dorset, **Eng.;** scenic cove; tourism.

Lund, t., S. **Sweden;** 16 km N.E. of Malmö; 11th cent. Romanesque cath.; univ.; publishing ctr.; p. (1992) 92,027.

Lundy I., Bristol Channel, N. Devon, **Eng.;** 19 km N.W. of Hartland Point; wildlife sanctuary; about 5 km long and 1 km wide.

Lune, R., Cumbria, **Eng.;** flows 72 km to Irish Sea; attractive valley.

Lüneburg, t., Lower Saxony, **Germany;** on Ilmenau R., S.E. of Hamburg; R. pt.; iron wks., chemicals; dates from 8th cent.; p. (2002) 68,234.

Lüneburg Heath, Lower Saxony, **Germany;** lies to S. of Lüneburg; glacial outwash plain of sands and gravels; heather, scrub; some agr. but infertile acid soils.

Lünen, t., N. Rhine–Westphalia, **Germany;** in Ruhr conurb.; coal, metallurgy, glass, wood; R. pt. and rly. ctr.; p. (2002) 92,005.

Lunéville, t., Meurthe-et-Moselle dep., N.E. **France;** in Lorraine, on R. Meurthe; 18th cent. château.

Lungi, t., Sierra Leone, W. **Africa;** nr. Freetown; only civil airport in st.

Luoyang (Loyang), c., Henan prov., **China;** industl.; ball bearing and mng. machin.; lge. car and tractor plant, oil refinery, textiles; p. (1994) 863,300.

Lurgan, t., Craigavon, **N. Ireland;** textiles, tobacco mfctg.; merging with Portadown to form new c. of Craigavon; p. (1991) 21,905.

Lusaka, c., cap. of **Zambia;** comm. and admin. ctr.; at junc. of routes to Tanzania and Malawi; motor assembly, footwear, metal prods., clothing; p. (2000) 1,640,000.

Lushun. See **Lüda.**

Lutherstadt-Wittenberg. See **Wittenburg.**

Luton, t., unit. auth. created in 1997, formerly part of Beds., **Eng.;** in Chiltern Hills nr. source of R. Lea; motor vehicles (closure announced, Dec. 2000); engin., hat mkg., aircraft, instruments; expanded t.; univ.; airport (now renamed London Luton Airport); car production ended (2002); p. (2001) 185,543 (unit. auth.).

Lutong, main oil pt. of Sarawak, E. **Malaysia;** oil refining.

Lutsk, c., **Ukraine;** pt. on Styr R.; one of oldest ts. in Volhynia; coal mng., machin.; architectural monuments; p. (1990) 204,100.

Lutterworth, t., Leics., **Eng.;** church with relics of John Wyclif, religious reformer; p. (1991) 7,380.

Luxembourg, prov., S.E. **Belgium;** on Fr. border; wooded and hilly; a. 2,784 km²; cap. Arlon; p. (1993) 236,850.

Luxembourg, grand duchy, W. **Europe;** lies between Belgium, Germany, and France; divided into 12 admin. cans.; official language French though German frequently used; well wooded, most of a. over 300 m; economic prosperity based upon iron and steel inds. and lge. deposits of iron-ore; agr. and cattle raising impt.; sm. size of home market makes L. keen member of EU and cap. of L. contains many European organisations; tourist ind. based upon scenery and cas. ts.; a. 2,587 km²; p. (2005) 465,000.

Luxembourg, c., cap. of grand duchy of **Luxembourg;** historic t., perched above valleys of Alzette and Petrusse Rs.; cath.; seat of European Court of Justice; p. (2000) 80,700.

Luxor, t., Upper Egypt; on E. bank of Nile; site of Thebes; tomb of Tutankhamun; p. (1986) 138,000.

Luzon, I., lgst. and most N. of **Philippines;** mtn. ranges; fertile Cagayan valley; rice, sugar cane, cotton, coffee, hemp, tobacco; mineral deposits; cap. Manila; a. 104,688 km²; p. (1990) 28,289,866.

Lviv (Lvov), c., **Ukraine;** founded 13th cent.; univ., caths.; major industl. ctr.; petroleum refining; natural gas nearby; p. (1990) 797,800.

Lvov. See **Lviv.**

Lyallpur. See **Faisalabad.**

Lydd, Shepway, Kent, **Eng.;** anc. t. on Romney marsh, at edge of Dungeness shingle; explosive lyddite mnf.; airport; p. (1991) 3,173.

Lydney, t., Gloucs., **Eng.;** in Forest of Dean; spt. on Severn estuary; new lt. inds.; p. (1991) 7,413.

Lyme Regis, spt., West Dorset, **Eng.;** on bdy. between Devon and Dorset; holiday resort; p. (1991) 3,851.

Lymington, t., Hants., **Eng.;** on the Solent; ferry to I. of Wight; abbey; p. (1991) 13,508.

Lymm, t., Cheshire, **Eng.;** 8 km W. of Altrincham; mainly residtl.; p. (1991) 9,721.

Lynchburg, c., Va., **USA;** on James R. in foothills of Appalachians; tobacco ctr.; p. (1996) 67,250.

Lyndhurst, v., Hants, **Eng.;** recognised as cap. of New Forest; tourisml; p. (1991) 2,381.

Lynn, industl. c., Mass., **USA;** on Mass. Bay; footwear, elec. appliances; Mary Baker Eddy lived here; p. (1996) 80,563.

Lynton, t., North Devon, **Eng.;** 27 km W. of Minehead on Bristol Channel; tourist ctr. for Exmoor; sm. harbour of Lynmouth 130 m below; devastating flood of R. Lyn 1952; p. (1981) 2,037.

Lyons, c., cap. of Rhône dep., **France;** at confluence of Rs. Saône and Rhône; silk, rayon, chemicals, engin., heavy lorries; oil refinery nearby; univ.; world ctr. for cancer research; p. (1990) 422,444 (c.), 1,262,223 (met.a.).

Lytham St. Annes, t., N. Lancs., **Eng.;** on N. cst. of Ribble estuary, 6 km S. of Blackpool holiday ctr.; p. (2001) 41,327.

Lyttelton, spt., S.I., **N.Z.,** on N. cst. of Banks peninsula; imp. pt.

M

Ma'an, t., S. **Jordan,** terminus of rly. through Amman to Beirut; Hijaz rail line to Medina; p. (1989) 108,300.

Maas, R., Dutch name for the R. Meuse after it has entered the Neth.

Maastricht, t., cap. of Limburg prov., **Neth.;**

on R. Maas; pottery, glass, textiles, brewing; univ.; p. (1994) 118,102 (c.) 164,153 (met. a.).

Mablethorpe, t., East Lindsey, Lincs., **Eng.**; holiday resort; p. (1991) 9,719.

Macao, former Portuguese col., S.E. **China**; finally returned to China in 1999; gambling, tourism, recreation for Hong Kong; new deep water port; rapid recent industl. growth (toys, textiles and transistors) with influx of capital; once the oldest European col. in Far East (1557); now Special Administrative Region; global gaming hub (as impt. as Las Vegas); a. 17 km²; p. (2004) 445,286.

Macapá, c., cap. of Amapá st., **Brazil**; at mouth of R. Amazon; rubber; p. (1996) 214,200.

Macclesfield, t., l. gov. dist., Cheshire, **Eng.**; at foot of Pennines, 16 km S. of Stockport; on R. Bollin; mkt., textiles, clothing, paper prods., engin.; expanded t.; old silk capital of England; p. (2001) 150,155 (dist.), (2001) 50,688 (t.).

Macdonnell Range, mtns., N.T., **Australia**; highest part of desert tableland, centrally situated within the continent; some gold and mica mines, but development hampered by aridity and isolation; highest alt. 1,500 m.

Macduff, spt., burgh, Aberdeenshire, **Scot.**; 3 km E. of Banff; fishing; p. (2002) 3,767.

Macedonia, region of Balkan peninsula, covering parts of Greece, Bulgaria and Macedonia itself.

Macedonia, dist., **Greece**; mtnous.; cereals, tobacco; chromium; cap. and pt. Salonika; a. 33,945 km²; p. (1991) 2,236,019.

Macedonia, rep., formerly Yugoslavia; agr., chromium; cap. Skopje; a. 27,436 km²; p. (2004) 2,071,210. Applying for EU membership.

Maceio, spt. cap. of Alagôas st., **Brazil**; cotton, sugar, tobacco, soap; p. (1991) 628,209.

Macerata, t., cap. of M. prov., **Italy**; cath., univ.; terracotta, glass, chemicals; p. (1981) 43,782.

Macgillicuddy's Reeks, mtns., Kerry, **R.o.I.**; highest peak, Carantuohil, 1,041 m.

Machala, t., Tibet, **China**; hgst. coalmine in world.

Machilipatnam (Bandar, Masulipatnam), spt., Andhra Pradesh, **India**; on Coromandel cst.; cotton mftg., rice; p. (1991) 159,007.

Machynlleth, t., Powys, **Wales**; on R. Dovey; alternative technology research; clothing; tourism; p. (1991) 2,033.

Macintyre, R., N.S.W., **Australia**; forms border between Queensland and N.S.W.; trib. of R. Darling; 645 km. long.

Mackay, spt., Queensland, **Australia**; sugar; artificial deep-water pt. for sugar exp.; p. (1991) 53,225 (met.a.)

Mackenzie, R., N.W. Terr., **Canada**; lgst. in N. America; rises in Rocky mtns. as Athabaska, flows into Athabaska L., leaves as Slave R., thence into Gr. Slave L., below which it is known as Mackenzie R., across arctic plains to Beaufort Sea; 4,000 km. long.

Mackenzie Mtns., N.W. Terr., **Canada**; range of Rockies; game preserve; max. alt. 2,760 m.

Mâcon, t., cap. of Saône-et-Loire dep., **France**; on R. Saône; Burgundy wines; p. (1999) 34,122.

Macon, c., Ga., **USA**; on Ocmulgee R.; industl. and shipping ctr. for agr. a., cotton, livestock; cotton mftg.; p. (1990) 106,612 (c.), 281,000 (met. a. with Warner Robins).

Macquarie, I., Australian I., **S. Pac.**; 1,440 km S.E. of Tasmania; rich in wildlife, Tasmanian st. reserve (1972).

Macquarie, R., N.S.W., **Australia**; trib. of R. Darling; 960 km long.

Madagascar (formerly Malagasy Rep.), I. off Mozambique; former Fr. col.; distinctive evolution of flora and fauna; p. engaged in agr.; rice staple food, coffee and cloves main exp.; inds. based on processing; offshore petroleum deposits; new refinery at ch. pt. of Toamasina; recent sapphire discoveries; major reserves of ilmenite; cap. Antananarivo; a. 587,041 km²; p. (2004) 17,501,871.

Madang, t., Papua New Guinea; entrepôt pt. on N. cst.; international airpt.; p. (1990) 27,057.

Madeira, R., Brazil; trib. of Amazon; with Mamoré R., c. 3,200 km long.

Madeira Is., volcanic archipelago, Atl. Oc., part of met. Portugal; partial autonomy by regional gov. (1977); wine, sugar, fruits; tourism; cap. Funchal on Madeira I., lgst. of gr.; a. 790 km²; p. (1986) 269,500.

Madhya Pradesh, st., **India**; absorbed sts. Bhopal, Vindhya Pradesh, Madhya Bharat, 1956; rice, jute, pulses, oilseeds, cotton; forests; manganese, coal, marble, limestone; cotton textile mftg.;

cap. Bhopal; a. 443,452 km²; p. (2001) 60,385,100.

Madinat ash Sha'b (Al Ittihad), t. **Yemen**; cap. of Democratic Rep. of Yemen; N.W. of Aden.

Madison, c., cap. of Wis., **USA**; educational and admin. ctr.; univ.; mnfs. agr. tools, footwear; p. (2000) 208,054 (c.), 367,085 (met. a.).

Madras. See Chennai.

Madras. See Tamil Nadu.

Madre de Dios, R., Bolivia; trib. of R. Madeira; rises in Peru; 960 km long.

Madrid, c., cap. of **Spain**; and of M. prov. on Manzanares R.; stands at 665 m (highest cap. in Europe) in vast open plains; although remote with relatively few inds. is ctr. of Spanish admin. and communications; univ., cath., Prado gallery; printing, publishing; p. (1998) 2,881,500 (c.), 5,091,300 (prov.).

Madura, I., Indonesia; off N.E. Java; dry climate, limestone soils; arable and pastoral agr.; salt; a. 4,584 km²; p. c. 2,000,000.

Madurai, t., Tamil Nadu, **India**; univ., impt. textile ctr.; p. (1991) 941,000.

Maebashi, c., central Honshu, **Japan**; N.W. Kanto plain; silk textile ctr.; p. (1990) 286,261.

Maelstrom, tidewater whirlpool, in Lofoten Is., Norway.

Maentwrog, v., Gwynedd, N. **Wales**; in Vale of Ffestiniog, 3 km E. of Ffestiniog; hydroelectric power sta. run by Nuclear Electric.

Maesteg, t., Bridgend, **Wales**; dormitory t. for steel wks. at Pt. Talbot; cosmetics; p. (1991) 20,576.

Mafikeng, (Mafeking) t., cap., North-West Prov., **S. Africa**; famous siege at outbreak of Boer War 1899–1900; p. (1991) 6,500.

Magadan, spt., **Russia**; on N. side of Sea of Okhotsk; marine engin.; fishing; former Soviet prison camp; p. (1999) 133,000.

Magallanes, reg. Chile; cap. Punta Arenas; a. 132,034 km²; p. (1992) 143,058.

Magdalena, R., Colombia; forms basis of inland navigation system, opening up interior; 1,600 km long.

Magdeburg, cap., Saxony - Anhalt Land, Germany; on R. Elbe; cath.; beet-sugar ctr., sugar-refineries; chemicals, steel, mng. machin., heavy engin.; route ctr. and lge. inland pt.; p. (2002) 229,755.

Magellan, strait, between Tierra del Fuego and Chile, separates Atl. and Pac. Ocs.

Maggiore, L., N. **Italy-Switzerland**; a. 212 km²; contains Borromean Is.; tourist resort.

Magherafelt, l. gov. dist., centred on t. of M., **N. Ireland**; agr. a. bordering L. Neagh; p. (2001) 39,780 (dist.), 6,682 (t.).

Maghreb, collective name given to Arabic-speaking countries bordering Mediterranean in N. Africa, inc. Algeria, Morocco and Tunisia.

Magnet Mtn., S. Urals, **Russia**; very rich deposit of magnetite iron ore, smelted at Magnitogorsk, and in Kuzbas region.

Magnitogorsk, c., **Russia**; new t. in S. Urals, on R. Ural; sited on magnetite deposits; metallurgical ctr.; oil pipeline from Shkapovo in Bashkira; p. (1989) 440,000.

Mahajanga (Majunga), t., Madagascar; second t. and pt.; meat conserves, sacks, cement; p. (1990) 121,967.

Mahalla El Kubra. See El Mahalla el Kubra.

Maharashtra, st., W. India; on Arabian Sea, ch. ts. Bombay (cap.), Poona, Nagpur; fertile lava soils; impt. cotton-growing dist. of Deccan; a. 307,477 km²; p. (2001) 96,752,200.

Mahé, former Fr. prov., S. India; united with India 1954; cap. Mahé part of Union Territory of Pondicherry; p. (1991) 33,425.

Mahon, spt., cap. of Minorca, Balearic Is., Spain; p. (1990) 24,000.

Maidenhead, t., Windsor and Maidenhead, Berks., Eng.; on R. Thames, 14 km above Windsor; residtl.; p. (2001) 58,848; See Windsor.

Maidens, The, gr. of dangerous rocks off Larne cst., N. Ireland.

Maidstone, co. t., l. gov. dist., Kent, Eng.; on R. Medway; regional ctr.; brewing, paper, agr. tools, confectionery, timber inds.; p. (2001) 138,948 (dist.), (2001) 89,684 (t.).

Maiduguri, t., Nigeria; cap. Bornu st.; on rly. from Bornu; mkt.; p. (1992) 289,100.

Maikop, c. cap. of Adygei aut. oblast, Krasnodar terr., Russia; oilfields nearby; oil-refineries, woodwkg., food-processing; p. (1989) 149,000.

Main, R., Germany; joins Rhine opposite Mainz; linked with Danube via Ludwig canal; and newer

Rhine-Main-Danube canal creating waterway from N. Sea to Black Sea of 3,500 km; 448 km long.

Maine, st., New England, **USA**; Pine tree St.; admitted to Union 1820; st. flower White Pine Tassel, st. bird Chickadee; mtnous., with much forest; potatoes, paper, pulp, metals, woollens, shoes, processed foods; cap. Augusta; ch. spt. Portland; a. 86,027 km²; p. (2002) 1,294,464.

Maine-et-Loire, dep., **France**; agr. vineyards; cap. Angers; a. 7,280 km²; p. (1999) 732,631.

Mainland, I., lgst. of Shetland Is., **Scot.**; p. (1991) 17,596.

Mainland, I., Orkney Is. *See* Pomona.

Mainz, c., cap of Rhineland-Palatinate, **Germany**; at confluence of Rs. Rhine and Main; R. pt.; cath., univ., cas.; cement, engin., optical glass, food-processing; p. (2002) 185,293.

Maisons-Alfort, t., **France**; S.E. sub. of Paris; p (1999) 51,022.

Maitland, t., N.S.W., **Australia**; on R. Hunter, nr. Newcastle; ctr. for fertile Hunter Valley; coal mng. decreasing; p. (1991) 45,200.

Majorca (Mallorca), lgst Balearic Is., **Spain**; major tourist ctr.; ch. t. and pt. Palma; a. 3,639 km².

Majunga. *See* Mahajanga.

Makalu, mtn., Nepal and Tibet, **China**; fifth hgst. mtn. in world; part of Himalayas; alt. 8,486 m.

Makasar. *See* Ujung Pandang.

Makassar, strait, **Indonesia**; separates Kalimantan from Sulawesi; 384 km wide.

Makeyevka, c., **Ukraine**; in Donets basin; metallurgical and coal-mng. ctr.; p. (1990) 426,700.

Makhachkala, c., cap. of Dagestan aut. rep., **Russia**; pt. on Caspian Sea; comm. and industl. ctr.; oil refineries linked by pipeline to Grozny fields; p. (1989) 317,000.

Makran, dist., **Pakistan** and **Iran**; coastal dist.; lowland route between India and Middle E.

Makwar, v., **Sudan**, N.E. Africa; on Blue Nile; site of Sennar Dam.

Malabar Coast, India; name applied to W. cst. of India from Goa to southern tip of peninsula at C. Comorin; sand dunes backed by lagoons; coastlands intensively cultivated, rice, spices, rubber, coconuts; ch. pt. Cochin.

Malabo (Santa Isabel), cap of **Equatorial Guinea**; on Marcias Nguema I.; ch. pt. for I., exp. cacao; comm. and financial ctr.; p. (1995) 30,000.

Malacca (Melaka), st., S.W. **W. Malaysia**; originally part of Brit. Straits Settlements (*q.v.*); cap. M.; a. 1,658 km²; p. (2005) 640,000.

Malacca (Melaka), strait, separates Sumatra, **Indonesia**, from **W. Malaysia**; 38 km wide at narrowest point; international routeway but attempts by Malaysia and Indonesia to claim it as territorial water.

Maladetta, with **Pic d'Anéto**, hgst. point in Pyrenees, **Spain**; alt. 3,408 m.

Malaga, c. cap. of Malaga prov., **Spain**; in Andalusia on Bay of M.; impt. spt.; olive oil, wine, fruit; oil pipeline from Puertollano; winter resort; cath., citadel; birthplace of Picasso; new Picasso Museum opened (2003); p. (1998) 528,000 (c.), 1,240,500 (prov.).

Malagasy Rep. *See* Madagascar.

Malang, t., Java, **Indonesia**; ctr. of fertile agr. basin; p. (1995) 763,000.

Mälar, L., S.E. **Sweden**; connected with Baltic by Södertelge canal; 1,260 Is.; length 128 km; a. 1,235 km².

Malatya, c., cap. of M. prov., central **Turkey**; at foot of Taurus mtns.; ctr. of rich agr. a.; fruit, opium; p. (1990) 304,760 (c.), 702,055 (prov.).

Malawi, land locked rep., Central Africa; L. Malawi to S. and E.; tropical climate modified by alt.; few natural resources; economy based on agr.; one of most fertile soils in Africa but only 50 per cent cultivated; exp. tobacco and tea; new cap at Lilongwe (old cap. Zomba); av. life expectancy, 38; a. 117,614 km²; p. (2004) 11,906,855.

Malawi, L., central **Africa**; southward extension of the Gr. Rift valley; c. 450 m a.s.l.; 560 km by 64 km; drains by R. Shire into R. Zambezi; petroleum under L. bed. Currently facing envir. catastrophe from choking water-weed.

Malaya. *See* Malaysia, West.

Malay Archipelago, lge. gr. of Is. extending 7,680 km from Nicobar Is. in Bay of Bengal to Solomon Is. in Pac.; inc. Sumatra, Java, Kalimantan, Sulawesi, Philippines, New Guinea, Bismarck archipelago.

Malaysia, East, part of **Fed. of Malaysia** inc. Sarawak and Sabah (formerly Brit. N. Borneo); less devel-

oped than W. Malaysia; p. concentrated on cst; hill tribes engaged in hunting in interior; diversification of Malaysian agr. has introduced cocoa as a major crop; oil major exp., exploration off cst.; separated from W. Malaysia by S. China Sea; a. 200,971 km²; p. (1980) 2,318,628.

Malaysia, Federation of, indep. federation (1963), S.E.Asia; member of Brit. Commonwealth; inc. W. Malaysia (Malaya) and E. Malaysia (Borneo sts. of Sarawak and Sabah); old cap. Kuala Lumpur; new cap. at Putrajaya; a. 329,293 km²; p. (2000) 23,253,000.

Malaysia, West (Malaya), part of **Federation of Malaysia**; consists of wide peninsula S. of Thailand; most developed in W.; world's leading producer of natural rubber; worlds leading exporter of tin; but decline in world prices of both these prod. has encouraged economic diversification; timber exports also declining due to efforts to conserve rainforest; palm oil, petrol, electrical and electronic machin. now impt. export; new gas discoveries, attempts to convert palm oil into diesel fuel; tree port at Pasir Gudang to divert exports from Singapore; 35 per cent of p. Chinese; a. 131,588 km²; p. (2004) 23,522,482.

Malbork (Marienburg), t., Elblag prov., **Poland**; R. pt. on Nogat R.; p. (1989) 39,016.

Malden, t., Mass., **USA**; mftg. sub. of Boston; rubber gds., hosiery, furniture; p. (1996) 52,749.

Maldive Is., indep. rep. (1968), former Brit. prot., Indian Oc.; chain of coral atolls c. 640 km S.W. of Sri Lanka; 1,190 Is., 193 inhabited; economy based on fishing (bonito and tuna); dried fish main exp.; modernisation of fishing with Japanese aid; coconuts, copra, coconut oil, coir, cowrie shells; future threatened by rising sea levels; cap. Male; former Brit. air base on Gan. I. (until 1976); riots and political unrest (2003); a. 298 km²; p. (2004) 339,330.

Maldon, t., l. gov. dist., Essex, **Eng.**; sm. pt. at head of Blackwater estuary; agr. machin., steel windowframes, flour-milling; p. (2001) 59,418 (dist.), (2001) 20,731 (t.).

Malegaon, t., Maharashtra, **India**; in Satmala Hills N.E. of Bombay; p. (1991) 342,000.

Malham Cove, North Yorks., **Eng.**; in Craven dist. of N. Pennines, 16 km N.W. of Skipton; semicircular amphitheatre limestone cliffs from base of which emerges R. Aire.

Mali, Rep. of, W. Africa; landlocked st.; former Fr. col. of Soudan; dry semi-desert climate in S.; extends into Sahara desert in N.; badly affected by Sahelian drought after 1971; few natural resources; nomadic pastoralist p. in N.; only 20 per cent of a. cultivable; livestock basis of inds. (hides, wool, etc.) and exps.; many minerals but not exploited; cap. Bamako; a. 1,204,350 km²; p. (2004) 11,956,788.

Malinda, t., **Kenya**; tourist resort on Indian Ocean cst.

Malin Head, Donegal, **R.o.I.**; most N. point.

Malines (Mechelen), t., **Belgium**; on R. Dyle; cath.; rly. ctr., textiles, furniture; once famous for lace; p. (1993) 75,740.

Malling, t., Kent, **Eng.**; 5 km W. of Maidstone; fruit, chemicals. *See* Tonbridge.

Mallow, mkt. t., Cork, **R.o.I.**; on R. Blackwater; agr. fishing, flour mills, tanneries, condensed milk, dehydrated foods; p. (1986) 6,488.

Malmesbury, t., North Wilts., **Eng.**; anc. hilltop t. in Cotswolds; mkt.; abbey; elec. engin.; birthplace of Thomas Hobbes; p. (1991) 4,439.

Malmö, c., spt., S. **Sweden**; on the Sound opposite Copenhagen; third lgst. c. in cty.; naval and comm. pt.; former ctr. for shipbldg., textiles, machin.; founded in 12th cent.; car and aerospace engin. plant developed; p. (1992) 236,684.

Malta, indep. st. within Brit. Commonwealth (1964), rep. (1974); I. in Mediterranean, 93 km S. of Sicily; strategic location; former British naval and military base; agr. ch. occupation with shiprepairing at dry- docks of Valletta; sm.-scale inds. growing; tourism exploits Mediterranean climate; major airport at Luqa; awarded George Cross for bravery in second world war; EU member (2004); cap. Valletta; a. 316 km²; p. (2004) 396,851.

Maltby, t., Rotherham, South Yorks., **Eng.**; mine still open 1994; p. (1991) 18,158.

Malton, mkt. t., North Yorks., **Eng.**; on R. Derwent, in S.W. of Vale of Pickering; brewing; p. (1991) 4,294.

Malvern, t., Worcs., **Eng.**; at E. foot of Malvern hills; spa; annual dramatic festival; Elgar lived here; p. (1991) 31,537.

Malvern Hills, narrow ridge forming bdy. between Worcs. and Hereford, **Eng.**; rises very abruptly from Severn valley to over 300 m between Malvern and Bromsberrow; moorland, woodland on lower slopes; forms l. gov. dist.; p. (2001) 72,172.

Mammoth Cave, Ky., **USA**; to S. of Green R. in hilly forested parkland; spectacular limestone formations (stalactites, stalagmites), lakes and rivers (e.g. Echo R., 110 m below surface) in avenues aggregating 240 km long; included in Nat. Park.

Mam Soul, mtn., Highland, **Scot.**; alt. 1,178 m.

Manacle Rocks, dangerous reef off cst. of Cornwall, **Eng.**; 12 km S. of Falmouth.

Manacor, t., Majorca, **Spain**; artificial pearls, wine, stalactite caves of Drach and Hams.

Managua, c., cap. of **Nicaragua**; on S. shore of L. Managua; industl. and comm. ctr.; oil refining, agr. processing, textiles, steel; univ.; 48 km from pt. Puerto Somoza; violent earthquake Dec. 1972; p. (1992) 974,000.

Managua, L., **Nicaragua**; second lgst. L. in Central America.

Manāmah, Al, cap. and ch. pt. **Bahrain**, Persian G.; free pt., comm. ctr.; declining pearl-fishing ind.; linked by causeway to internat. airpt.; p. (2000) 148,000.

Manáus (Manaos), c., cap. of Amazonas st., N.W. **Brazil**; on Rio Negro nr. confluence with Amazon; impt. R. pt., airport.; oil refinery; former rubber ctr.; in free zone (10,360 km²) recently set up to encourage development in Amazonas; new inds. include steel wks., oil refinery; boom now far exceeds 19th century rubber boom; tourism; internat. airpt.; p. (1996) 1,158,300.

Manche, dep., N.W. **France**; on English Channel; agr. and dairying; cap. Saint Lô; ch. pt. Cherbourg; a. 6,410 km²; p. (1999) 481,521.

Manchester, c., Gtr. Manchester, **Eng.**; on R. Irwell; terminus of Manchester Ship Canal; ctr. of cotton and man-made fibre textile inds.; heavy, lt., and elec. engin., machine tools, petrochemicals, dyestuffs, pharmaceutical prods.; univs; cultural and recreational cap. of N.W. Eng.; city centre rebuilt after IRA bomb, reopened 1999; Imperial War Museum (North), opened 2002; p. (2001) 439,549 (met. dist.)

Manchester, c., N.H., **USA**; at Amoskeag falls, on the Merrimac R.; textiles, footwear, machin.; p. (1996) 100,967.

Manchester Ship Canal, ship canal, Cheshire/Merseyside/Gtr. Manchester, **Eng.**; joins Manchester to Mersey estuary at Eastham; 57 km long.

Manchuria. See **North-East China**.

Mandalay, c., **Myanmar**; on R. Irrawaddy, 640 km N. of Rangoon; former cap.; lost importance with rise of Irrawaddy delta; many temples, palaces; p. (2001) 1 m. (est.).

Manfredonia, mkt. t., Foggia, **Italy**; fish. pt.; cath.; p. (1981) 52,674.

Mangalore, spt. Karnataka, **India**; exp. coffee, coconuts, rice, spices, fertiliser; p. (1991) 273,000.

Mangere, N.I., **N.Z.**; 21 km S of Auckland; international airport (opened 1965).

Mangla Dam, **Pakistan**; world's lgst. earth-filled dam, on Jhelum R., part of Indus Basin irrigation scheme.

Manhattan, I., N.Y., **U.S.A.**; at mouth of Hudson R.; a. 57 km²; forms major part of bor. of Manhattan of N.Y.; target of terrorist attack (2001); p. (1990) 1,487,536 (bor.).

Manila, c., S.W. Luzon, **Philippines**; cap. and ch. pt. of Is.; entrepôt tr.; modern skyscrapers; univ.; cath.; airpt.; p. (1995) 9,450,000.

Manipur, new st. (1972), E. **India**; borders Myanmar (Burma); former princely st.; cap. Imphal; a. 22,274 km²; p. (2001) 2,388,600.

Manisa, c., cap. of M. prov., W. **Turkey**; agr. ctr.; mineral deposits nearby; p. (1990) 158,426, 1,154,418 (prov.).

Manitoba, prov., **Canada**; wheat, rich mineral deposits, fisheries; diverse inds.; cap. Winnipeg; a. 650,090 km²; p. (1996) 1,113,898.

Manitowac, c., Wis., **USA**; on L. Mich.; shipbldg., aluminium wks., flour mills; p. (1980) 32,547.

Manizales, c., cap. of Caldas, **Colombia**; at 2,155 m in the Central Cordillera; in rich coffee a.; route ctr.; p. (1992) 327,115.

Mannar, G., with Palk Strait separates **India** from **Sri Lanka**.

Mannheim, c., Baden-Württemberg, **Germany**; major R. pt. at confluence of Rs. Neckar and Rhine, opposite Ludwigshafen; heavy and lt. inds., notably precision instruments, machin., vehicles; p. (2002) 308,385 (c.), 1,568,679 (met.a.).

Manresa, industl. t., N.E. **Spain**; in Catalonia; textiles; associated with Ignatius of Loyola; place of pilgrimage; p. (1990) 65,800.

Mansfield, t., l. gov. dist., Notts., **Eng.**; on E. flank of Pennines, 19 km N. of Nottingham; 2 remaining coal mines; sand-quarrying, textiles, footwear, metal boxes, machin.; p. (2001) 98,181 (dist.); (2001) 69,987 (t.).

Mansfield Woodhouse, t., Notts., **Eng.**; 3 km N. of Mansfield; stone quarries; Roman remains; p. (1991)18,204.

Manston, Kent, **Eng.**; former RAF base, now Kent International Airport.

Mansûra, c., Lower **Egypt**; pt. on Nile; cotton mftg.; univ. p. (1986) 316,870.

Mantua (Mantova), c., cap. of M. prov., N. **Italy**; on R. Mincio; old fortfd. c.; p. (1981) 60,866.

Manukau, c., N.I., **N.Z.**; new c. (1965) formed from amalgamation of suburban communities around Auckland; p. (1996) 254,603, now lgst. c. of N.Z.

Manych, R., **Russia**; trib. of R. Don; 480 km long; canal being built through R. to Caspian to provide through connection with Black Sea.

Manzala (Menzala), lagoon, Mediterranean cst., **Egypt**; extends E. from Damietta mouth of Nile to Pt. Said; fringed by salt marsh; a. 2,072 km².

Manzanillo, spt., S.E. **Cuba**; exp. sugar, rice, tobacco; p. (1990) 107,650.

Manzanillo, c. Colima, W. **Mexico**; ch. pt. on Pac. Oc.; exp. coffee, timber, minerals; p. (1990) 92,168.

Maputo (Lourenço Marques), spt., cap. of **Mozambique**; at head of Delagoa Bay; rly. terminus; oil refining, deposits of bentonite worked nearby; ore terminal, much transit tr.; second lgst. pt. in Africa; p. (2000) 3,025,000.

Maracaibo, spt. cap. of Zulia st., **Venezuela**, deepwater harbour; on W. of narrow entrance on L. Maracaibo; univ.; oilfields and refineries; exp. coffee, cocoa; p. (1990) 1,207,513.

Maracaibo, G., and L., Zulia st., **Venezuela**; brackish lake, 192 km long, 96 km wide; oilwells on fringes and drilled into lake floor.

Maracay, c., N. **Venezuela**; on L. Valencia, 112 km from Caracas; p. (1990) 354,428.

Marajó, I., at mouth of Rs. Amazon and Pará, **Brazil**; a. 38,850 km².

Maralinga, S. **Australia**; 320 km N.E. Eucla; joint U.K.-Australian atomic testing ground, first weapon exploded here 27 Sept. 1956.

Maranhão, st., N.E. **Brazil**; rice, cotton, sugar, tobacco, coffee, cattle, gold, copper; oil in the Barrierinhas a.; cap. São Luiz; a. 334,812 km²; p. (1996) 5,218,500.

Marañon, R. See **Amazon, R.**

Maras, t. and prov., S. central **Turkey**; tr. in Kurdish carpets; p. (1985) 210,371, (1990) 892,952 (prov.).

Marathon, v. and plain, **Greece**; 32 km N.E. of Athens; here the Athenians defeated the Persians 490 B.C.

Marburg on Lahn, t., Hesse, **Germany**; univ., cas.; noted for optical instruments; p. (2002) 77,550.

March, mkt. t., Fenland, Cambs., **Eng.**; on R. Nene in Fens; rly. junc.; farm tools; p. (1981) 14,475.

Marches, region, central **Italy**; extending from eastern slopes of Apennines to Adriatic cst.; embracing provs. of Macerata, Ascoli- Piceno, Ancona, and Pesaro e Urbino; a. 9,697 km²; p. (1992) 1,433,994.

Marcias Nguema. See **Biako**.

Mar del Plata, c., **Argentina**; on C. Corrientes; Atl. cst. resort; p. (1980) 407,024.

Maree, loch, Highland, **Scot.**; 21 km long, c. 3 km wide; rocky shores; studded with wooded islets.

Maremma, coastal region along Tyrrhenean Sea, S. Tuscany, **Italy**; once malarial, now drained with wide fertile areas.

Mareotis or **Birket-et-Mariut**, L., Lower **Egypt**; separated from Mediterranean by ridge of sand on which stands Alexandria; 80 km long, 32 km wide.

Margam, part of Pt. Talbot, Neath Pt. Talbot, S. **Wales**; on cst. of Swansea Bay; lge. new steel-wks.; lgst. steel-rolling mill in Europe.

Margarita, I., in Caribbean off N. **Venezuela**; tourism; formerly pearl-fishing ctr.; cap. Asunción; a. 1,166 km².

Margate, t., Kent, **Eng.**; W. of N. Foreland, in the Isle of Thanet; seaside resort; new Turner Centre; p. (1991) 56,734.

Margolan, t., E. **Uzbekistan**; in Ferghana Valley; noted for silk ind.; p. (1990) 124,900.

Mari, aut. rep., **Russia**; timber, paper inds.; p. (1986) 729,000.

Maribor, t., **Slovenia** (formerly Yugoslavia); on Drava R., nr. Austrian border; metallurgical inds.; ctr. of agr. a.; p. (1981) 185,699.

Mariinsk Canal. See **Volga Baltic Waterway.**

Maritime Provinces, group of provs. in **Canada**— Nova Scotia, New Brunswick, Prince Edward I.

Maritsa, R., **Bulgaria** and **Greece**; used for irrigation and hydroelectric power; 416 km long.

Mariupol, (Zhdanov), spt., S.E. **Ukraine**; on Sea of Azov; metallurgical ctr., chemicals; fishing and fish-processing; p. (1990) 519,900.

Market Drayton, t., North Shrops., **Eng.**; on R. Tern, 21 km S.W. of Newcastle-under-Lyme; dairy products; processed food; p. (1991) 9,482.

Market Harborough, t., Harborough, Leics., **Eng.**; on R. Welland, 13 km N.W. of Kettering; elec. engin.; footwear; industry; p. (2001) 20,127.

Market Rasen, t., West Lindsey, Lincs., **Eng.**; agr. ctr.; racecourse; p. (1991) 2,948.

Markinch, burgh, Fife, Scot., 13 km N. of Kirkcaldy; paper mftg., whisky blending and bottling factory closed 1983; p. (2002) 2,254.

Marl, t., N. Rhine–Westphalia, **Germany**; in Ruhr; coal inds.; chemicals; p. (2002) 92,628.

Marlborough, t., Wycombe, Wilts., **Eng.**; on R. Kennet in heart of Marlborough Downs; public school; p. (1991) 6,429.

Marlborough, dist., S.I., **N.Z.**; pastoral; a. 10,930 km²; cap. Blenheim; p. (1991) 36,765.

Marlborough Downs, hills, Wilts., **Eng.**; chalk; highest point, Milk Hill, 298 m.

Marlow, t., Bucks., **Eng.**; on R. Thames; mkt., tourist ctr.; home of Shelley; p. (2005) 17,000.

Marmara, Sea of, separates Europe from Asia; connected with Black Sea through the Bosporus, with Aegean Sea through Dardanelles; shores belong to **Turkey.**

Marne, dep., N.E. **France**; in Champagne; ctr. of champagne ind.; cap. Châlons-sur-Marne; a. 8,205 km²; p. (1999) 564,929.

Marne, R., central **France**; rises in Plateau de Langres, flows across Champagne Humide, Champagne Pouilleuse, and Beauce, joins R. Seine just above Paris; with Marne-Rhine and Marne-Saône canals forms impt. inland waterway linking Seine with Rhine and Rhône valleys; c. 520 km long.

Marple, t., Gtr. Manchester, **Eng.**; 5 km. E. of Stockport; engin., residtl.; p. (1991) 19,829.

Marquesas Is., volcanic gr. in central Pac. Oc., part of Fr. Polynesia; lgst. Nukuhiva and Hivaoa; mtnous., fertile; exp. copra, vanilla, tobacco, cotton; a. 1,274 km²; p. (1983) 6,548.

Marrakesh, c., **Morocco**; tourist ctr.; known as the 'Red City'; leather gds., carpets; p. (1994) 621,914.

Marsa el-Brega, new pt., G. of Sirte, **Libya**; oil pipeline from Zelten; gas liquefaction plant opened 1970; airport.

Marsala, pt., Sicily, **Italy**; on site of anc. Carthaginian settlement; wine ctr.; p. (1981) 79,093.

Marseille, c., spt., cap. of Bouche-du-Rhône dep., S. **France**; on Provence cst.; passenger and gds. traffic; pt. inds., marine engin., oil refining; oil pipeline to Karlsruhe; industl. expansion at G. of Fos; cath., univ., palace; founded as Massilia by Phocaean Greeks of Asia Minor 600 B.C.; p. (1990) 807,726 (c.), 1,087,376 (met.a.).

Marshall Is., Rep. of, gr. of coral Is., central Pac. Oc.; internal self-government (1978), comprising 34 atolls; exp. copra, sugar, coffee; admin. ctr. Jaluit I.; joined UN 1991; nuclear bomb tests; a. 181 km²; survival threatened by long-term global warming; p. (2004) 57,738.

Marske-by-the-Sea, t. Langbaurgh, Cleveland, **Eng.**; seaside resort; p. (1991) 8,936.

Martha's Vineyard, I., S.E. Mass., **USA**; state forest; summer resort; ch. ts., Vineyard Haven, Oak Bluffs, Edgartown.

Martigny, t., Valais, **Switzerland**; linked by road tunnel to Aosta, Italy; p. 6,572.

Martin, t. Slovakia, S. E. of Zilina; rly.; p. (1990) 66,000.

Martina Franca, t., S. **Italy**; in Puglia; wine, olive oil; summer resort.

Martinique, I., Fr. overseas dep., Windward Is., **W.I.**; dominated by volcanic peak Mt. Pelée which erupted 1902 destroying t. of St. Pierre; hurricanes, earthquakes; economy based on sugar-cane and fruit prod.; much emigration to France; cap. Fort de France; a. 1,088 km²; p. (2004) 429,510.

Martos, t., Jaén prov., Andalusia, **Spain**; castled hilltop t.; wines, sulphur springs; mftg.; p. (1990) 22,800.

Mary (Merv), c., **Turkmenistan**; in oasis in Kara-Kum desert; anc. c. founded 3rd cent. B.C.; textile ctr.; p. (1990) 93,800.

Maryborough. See **Port Laoighise, Ireland.**

Mary Kathleen, t., Queensland, **Australia**; new t., nr. uranium field in Cloncurry.

Maryland, one of original 13 sts. of **USA**; Old Line St.; admitted to Union 1788; st. flower Black eyed Susan, st. bird Baltimore Oriel; on shores of Chesapeake Bay; humid continental climate; mkt. gardening; sea-fishing; cap. Annapolis, lgst. c. Baltimore; a. 27,394 km²; p. (2002) 5,458,137.

Maryport, t., Allerdale, Cumbria, **Eng.**; former pt.; modern lt. inds. in industl. estate to S. of t.; p. (1991) 5,757.

Masbate, I., prov. **Philippines**; gold mng.; a. 3,269 km²; p. (1990) 599,915.

Mascarene Is., collective name of **Mauritius**, **Rodriguez** and **Réunion**, in **Indian Oc.**

Maseru, c., cap. **Lesotho**; nr. border with S. Africa on Caledon R.; two new industl. estates to encourage light inds.; tourists from S. Africa; p. (1999) 373,000.

Masham, t., North Yorks., **Eng.**; on R. Ure; mkt.

Mashhad, c., N.E. **Iran**; cap. of Khorassan prov.; linked by oil pipeline to Esfahan and rly. to Turkmenistan; p. (1994) 1,964,000.

Mashonaland, dist., **Zimbabwe**; a. inhabited by the Mashona tribe; ch. t. Salisbury; p. (1992) 857,318 (C.) 1,033,336 (E.).

Masjid-i-Sulamain, t., **Iran**; impt. oilfield and refinery; p. (1982) 117,000.

Mask, L., Mayo and Galway, **R.o.I.**; 19 km long 3–6 km wide.

Mason City, t., Iowa, **USA**; on Sheel Rock R.; tr. ctr. of lge. agr. a.; p. (1990) 29,040.

Mason–Dixon Line. See **Section L.**

Massachusetts, st., New England, **USA**; Bay St.; admitted to Union 1788; st. flower Mayflower, st. bird Chickadee; on Atl. cst.; humid continental climate; hilly interior severed by N.–S. Connecticut valley; major fishing ind.; replacement of traditional textile inds. by modern science-based inds., especially around M. Institute of Technology; impt. arable gr. a.; cap. Boston; a. 21,386 km²; p. (2002) 6,427,801.

Massa di Carrara. See **Carrara.**

Massawa. See **Mits'iwa.**

Massif Central, upland a., **France**; variable geology and scenery inc. volcanic Auvergne and limestone Causses; much rural depopulation, pastoral agr.; industl. ts. inc. St. Etienne based on sm. coalfields in N.E.; others ts. inc. Limoges and Clermont-Ferrand.

Masulipatnam. See **Machilipatnam.**

Masvingo. See **Fort Victoria.**

Matabeleland, dist., **Zimbabwe**; a. inhabited by Matabele tribe; ch. t. Bulawayo; p. (1992) 640,957 (N.), 591,747 (S.).

Matadi, spt., **Congo**; on R. Congo; main pt.; exp. forest prod.; proposed Inga power project nearby; p. (1990) 172,926.

Matagalpa, t., **Nicaragua**; ctr. of agr. a., food processing; second lgst. t. of Nicaragua; p. (1985) 37,000.

Matamoros, irrigated region, **Mexico**; around t. of M. on Rio Grande delta; Mexico's leading producer of cotton.

Matamoros, t., **Mexico**; on Rio Grande; livestock tr. ctr.; p. (1990) 303,392.

Matanzas, spt., cap. of M. prov., **Cuba**; exp. sugar, cigars; rayon plant; p. (1990) 113,724, 599,500 (prov.).

Mataró, spt., **Spain**; nr. Barcelona; fisheries, textiles, chemicals, paper; p. (1991) 101,172.

Matera, t., cap. of M. prov., S. **Italy**; stands on limestone ridge cleft by canyon; agr. ctr.; 13th cent. cath. and cas.; p. (1981) 50,712.

Mathura (**Muttra**), t., Uttar Pradesh, **India**; sacred t. on R. Jumna; Hindu pilgrimage ctr.; textiles; p. (1991) 226,691.

Matlock, t., Derbys. Dales, **Eng.**; on R. Derwent, 24 km N. of Derby; admin. ctr.; tourist ctr., limestone quarrying, lt. inds.; Peak District Mining Museum.

Mato Grosso, st., **Brazil**; cap. Cuiabá; a. 1,232,081 km²; p. (1996) 2,228,000.

Mato Grosso, plateau, Mato Grosso st., **Brazil**; average alt. 900 m, acts as divide between Amazon and Paraná-Paraguay R. systems; reserves of gold, diamonds, manganese but largely undeveloped; lge. areas of tropical rain forest.

Mato Grosso de Sul, st. Brazil; cap. Campo Grande; separated from Mato Grosso state in 1979; a. 350,548 km²; p. (1991) 1,778,494.

Matsumoto, c., central Honshu, **Japan**; machin., food-processing, paper; once impt. for silk; remains of 16th cent. cas.; p. (1990) 200,723.

Matsuyama, c., **Japan**; pt. based inds. of oil refining and petrochemicals; univ., feudal cas.; p. (1990) 443,317.

Matterhorn (Fr. **Mt. Corvin**. It. **Monte Cervino**); alt. 4,477 m; Pennine Alps, **Switzerland**.

Mauchline, mkt. t., E. Ayrshire, **Scot.**; associated with Robert Burns; p. (2002) 4,105.

Maule, reg. **Chile**; cap. Talca; a. 30,518 km²; p. (1992) 834,053.

Mauna Kea, volcano, **Hawaii**; alt. 4,208 m; dormant.

Mauna Loa, volcano, **Hawaii**; alt. 4,172 m; one of the world's lgst. volcanoes.

Mauritania, Islamic Rep. of, W. Africa; desert in N., S. more fertile; Senegal R. forms main artery of transport; mainly pastoral agr. (nomadic); severe effects of Sahelian drought after 1971 caused p. to become settled and move to ts.; urban p. 35% (1984); deposits of iron ore (Fort Gouraud) and copper (Bakel Akjoujt); new off-shore oil discoveries promise big yields; fishing; new pt. development at Nouadhibou; cap. Nouakchott; a. 1,085,210 km²; p. (2005) 3,110,000.

Mauritius, I., rep. within Brit. Commonwealth; Indian Oc.; volcanic I., surrounded by coral reefs, 800 km E. of Madagascar; subtropical climate, prone to cyclone; racially mixed; dependent on sugar for 95 per cent of exps.; attempts to deter this dependence by Export Processing Zone (tax-free industrial zone), and incr. tea output; dense p. and unemployment cause social tension; former residents of Chagos Arch. resettled on 2 of Agalega Is.; tourism incr. impt.; cap. Port Louis; a. (inc. Rodriguez and Agalega) 2,038 km²; p. (2004) 1,220,481.

Maybole, burgh, S. Ayrshire, **Scot.**; 13 km S. of Ayr; commuter centre for Ayr etc; cas.; p. (2002) 4,552.

Mayenne, dep., N.W. **France**; pastoral and agr.; cap. Laval; a. 5,146 km²; p. (1999) 285,337.

Mayfair, dist., City of Westminster, London, **Eng.**; fashionable residtl. and comm. a., to E. of Hyde Park; clubs and hotels.

Mayo, maritime co., Connacht, **R.o.I.**; broken cst., much barren mtn. land, many lge. lakes; agr.; co. t. Castlebar, a. 5,506 km²; p. (1986) 115,184.

Mayotte, I., Comoro Archipelago, Mozambique Channel; rejected indep. to remain Fr. terr. (1975); sugar-cane, vanilla, cacao; a. 363 km²; p. (2004) 186,026.

Mazandaran, prov., N.E. **Iran**; Caspian Sea; subtropical climate; agr.; cap. Sari; p. (1982) 2,375,994.

Mazar-i-Sharif, c., **Afghanistan**; chemical fertilisers from natural gas; textiles, bricks, flour-milling; noted mosque; p. (1990) 128,000.

Mazatlán, c., N.W. **Mexico**; major spt. on Pac. cst.; comm. and industl. ctr.; exp. metals, hides, fish prods., woods; oil refinery; fishing, tourism; p. (1990) 314,249.

Mbabane, cap. of **Swaziland**; stands at c. 1,160 m; admin. ctr.; tin mng.; p. (1999) 73,000.

McMurdo Sound, ice-locked channel, Antarctica; base for many expeditions.

Mead, L., Arizona/Nevada., **USA**; on R. Colorado behind Hoover Dam; one of world's lgst. reservoirs; stores water for irrigation in Imperial Valley and Yuma dist.; tourist attraction; 184 km long, 2-13 km wide.

Meath, maritime co., Leinster, **R.o.I.**; pastoral; co. t., Trim; a. 2,347 km²; p. (1986) 103,881.

Meaux, t., Seine-et-Marne dep., **France**; on R. Marne; cath.; comm. and industl. ctr.; p. (1982) 55,797 (met. a.).

Mecca, holy c. of Islam, cap. of **Saudi Arabia**; birthplace of Mohammed; pilgrimage ctr.; Gr. Mosque enclosing the Kaaba; univ. (with Jidda); p. (2000) 919,000.

Mechelen. See **Malines**.

Mecklenburg-West Pomerania, *Land*, **Germany**; part of N. European plain, bordering Baltic Sea; cap. Schwerin; a. 22,947 km²; pop. (2005) 1,750,000.

Medan, c., cap. of N. Sumatra prov., **Indonesia**; ctr. for rubber, tobacco, tea; printing; univ.; pt. is Belawan; p. (1995) 1,910,000.

Médéa, dep., t. 80 km S. of El Djezair, **Algeria**; projected industl. complex; p. (1983) 84,292 (t.), (1987) 650,623 (dep.).

Medellin, c., cap. of Antiquia prov., **Colombia**; at 1,533 m in Central Cordillera; second c. of rep.; univ.; ctr. of drug trade; coffee; textiles, steel, sugar refining, glass; coal, gold, silver mined nearby; hydroelec. power; p. (1992) 1,581,364.

Medicine Hat, t., Alberta, **Canada**; on S. Saskatchewan R.; rly. junc.; coal, natural gas, flour mills; p. (1996) 56,570.

Medina, c., Hejaz, **Saudi Arabia**; 352 km N. of Mecca; tomb of Mohammed; place of Moslem pilgrimage; univ.; harbour at Yanbu' on Red Sea; p. (1986) 500,000.

Mediterranean, gr. inland sea, almost tideless, dividing Europe from Africa; communicating with Atl. by Strait of Gibraltar and Black Sea by Dardanelles, Sea of Marmara and Bosporus, E. part touches Asia in the Levant; total length W. to E. 3,520 km; greatest width of sea proper c. 1,120 km; water a. 2,331,000 km²; greatest depth 4,482 m; ch. Is.; Corsica, Sardinia, Sicily, Crete, Cyprus, and the Balearic, Lipari, Maltese, Ionian grs., also Greek arch.

Médoc, region, Gironde, **France**; extending for about 77 km along Garonne R.; noted for wines.

Medway, unit. auth. and R., Kent, **Eng.**; flows N.E. past Tonbridge, Maidstone and Rochester (where it becomes estuarial) to mouth of Thames; 112 km long; Medway Bridge completed 1962. p. (2001) 249,488 (unit auth.).

Meekatharra, t., W. **Australia**; Flying Doctor and School of the Air ctr. p. (1991) 1,400.

Meerut, c., Uttar Pradesh, **India**; scene of outbreak of Indian mutiny 1857; p. (1991) 850,000.

Meghalaya ("Home of the Clouds"), new st. (1970), **India**; former Khasi-Jaintia Hills and Garo Hills dists. of Assam; cap. Shillong; a. 22,549 km²; p. (2001) 2,306,100.

Meiling Pass, on bdy. between Guandong, Jianxi, S. **China**; provides historic routeway across Nanling mtns., followed by old imperial highway from Nanjing to Guangzhou; alt. c. 300 m.

Meiningen, t., **Germany**; on R. Werra; cas.; machin., chemicals, timber inds.; drama ctr. in second half 19th cent.; p. (1999) 22,500.

Meissen, t., Saxony, **Germany**; on R. Elbe; cath.; famous porcelain popularly known as Dresden china; p. (1999) 30,500.

Meknès, c., **Morocco**; one of the caps. of M.; agr. ctr., olives; p. (1994) 293,525.

Mekong, R., S.E. **Asia**; rises in Tibet, flows through China, Laos, Cambodia and Vietnam, entering China Sea in extensive swampy delta; used for sm. boats but many rapids; 4,000 km long; new R. project for flood control, irrigation and hydroelectric power.

Melaka. See **Malacca**.

Melanesia, archipelago, S.W. Pac. Oc., inc. Admiralty, Solomon, Santa Cruz, Vanuatu, Loyalty, New Caledonian, and Fiji Is.; New Guinea is sometimes included; ethnic region.

Melbourne, c., cap. of Victoria, **Australia**; at mouth of Yarra R. and N. head of Port Phillip Bay; focal point of trade, transport and inds., produces 30 per cent of total factory output in Australia; varied inds. inc. car and aircraft assembly, petrochemicals, foodstuffs; internat. airport; 2 univs., 2 caths.; p. (1993) 3,189,200 (met. a.), 71 per cent of st. p.

Melilla, spt. and enclave in **Morocco**, on Mediterranean cst., belonging to Spain; exp. iron ore; p. (1981) 53,593.

Melitopol, t., **Ukraine**; on Molochnoy R.; ctr. of rich fruit-growing a.; heavy machin., food-processing; p. (1990) 175,800.

Melksham, t., West Wilts., **Eng.**; on R. Avon, 8 km N.E. of Bradford-on-Avon; rubber wks., engin., flour mills, creameries, rope and matting; p. (1991)13,074.

Melrose, burgh, Borders, **Scot.**; on R. Tweed; 6 km E. of Galashiels; ruined abbey; p. (2002) 1,656.

Melton Mowbray, t., Leics., **Eng.**; on Lincoln Heights, 24 km N.E. of Leicester; mkt., hunting dist.; famous pork pies; footwear, pet foods, Stilton cheese; with surrounding a. forms l. gov. dist. of **Melton**; p. (2001) 47,866 (dist.), (2001) 25,554 (t.).

Melun, t., cap. of Seine-et-Marne dep., N. **France**; on R. Seine; agr. tools and prod.; Romanesque church; p. (1999) 35,591.

Melville I., off N. cst., Arnhem Land, **Australia;** Aboriginal settlement; a. 4,350 km².

Melville I., N.W. Terr., Arctic **Canada;** natural gas; a. 41,958 km².

Memel. See **Klaipeda.**

Memphis, anc. c., **Egypt;** on R. Nile; 19 km S. of Cairo; nearby are Saqqara ruins.

Memphis, c., Tenn., **USA;** on R. Mississippi; rly. ctr., pt. of entry, lgst. c. in st., mkt. ctr. for cotton and hardwoods; cottonseed oil, textiles, farm machin.; natural gas and hydroelectric power; univ.; Martin Luther King assassinated (1968); p. (2000) 650,100 (c.), 981,747 (met. a.).

Menado, t., Sulawesi, **Indonesia;** second t. of I.; pt. for transit tr.; p. (1980) 217,159.

Menai Strait, separates Isle of Anglesey from mainland, **Wales;** crossed by Telford's suspension bridge (1825) and Britannia rly. bridge (1850).

Menam Chao Phraya, R., **Thailand;** main R. of cty.; dense p. in valley, lge. multi-purpose scheme for hydroelectric power and irrigation; 1,190 km long.

Mendip Hills, Somerset, **Eng.;** limestone range containing many karst features inc. Cheddar gorge and Wookey Hole; a. of outstanding natural beauty; quarrying; motor-way; hgst. point 325 m; forms l. gov. dist. **Mendip,** inc. Frome, Wells, Shepton Mallet, Glastonbury and Street; p. (2001) 103,869.

Mendoza, prov., W. **Argentina,** on Chilean border; Andean peaks Aconcagua and Tupungato; oilfields; alfalfa, vines, olives, fruit, peppermint; cap. M.; a. 148,783 km²; p. (1991) 1,412,481.

Mendoza, c., cap. of M. prov., W. **Argentina;** stands at c. 730 m in oasis known as "garden of the Andes"; starting point of Transandine rly.; univ.; petroleum, agr. processing; p. (1991) 121,696.

Mendoza, R., **Argentina;** enters L. Guanacache; used for hydroelectric power; 320 km long.

Menin (Meenen), t., **Belgium;** on R. Lys on Fr. border; mediaeval cloth ctr.; tobacco tr., textiles, rubber gds., soap; scene of fierce fighting in first world war; p. (1991) 32,650.

Menton, t., Alpes-Maritimes dep. S. **France;** Riviera resort; p. (1982) 25,449.

Mercedes, t., S.W. **Uruguay;** livestock ctr., E. of its pt. Fray Bentos; p. (1985) 37,110.

Mérida, c., cap. of Yucatan st., S.E. **Mexico;** sisal-hemp; Spanish colonial architecture; tourism; Mayan ruins; p. (1990) 557,340.

Mérida, c. Badajoz prov., S.W. **Spain;** on Guadiana R.; comm. ctr. of Estremadura; impt. Roman remains; p. (1991) 53,700.

Mérida, t. cap. of M. st., **Venezuela;** in Andes; univ.; cath.; tourist ctr.; world's highest cable rly. to Espejo peak (4,690 m); p. (1990) 167,922 (t.), 615,503 (st.).

Meridian, t., Miss., **USA;** mkt. ctr. in cotton, livestock, lumber a.; rly. and route ctr.; textiles, clothing; p. (1980) 46,577.

Merionethshire, historic co., N.W. **Wales,** now part of Gwynedd.

Merowe Dam, major new dam (to be completed 2008) on 4th cataract of R. Nile.

Mersea, I., at mouth of R. Colne, Essex, **Eng.;** oysters; holiday resort; 8 km long, 3 km wide.

Merseburg, c., Saxony - Anhalt, **Germany;** on R. Saale; ctr. of gr. lignite field; paper mills, chemical wks.; historic c.; p. (1981) 50,932.

Merse of Berwick, region, S.E. **Scot.;** lower valleys of Rs. Tweed and Teviot; glacial clays; arable agr. for barley, wheat; dairy cattle; ch. t. Berwick-on-Tweed.

Mersey, R., Cheshire/Gtr. Manchester/Merseyside, **Eng.;** enters Irish Sea by fine estuary at Liverpool; 109 km long.

Merseyside, former met. co., N.W. **Eng.;** a. around lower Mersey estuary inc. N. Wirral penin., pts. of Liverpool, Birkenhead and Bootle; many chem. and pt. processing inds.; p. (2001) 1,362,026.

Mersin, c., S. **Turkey;** freeport (1986), on Mediterranean cst.; oil refinery; dates from c. 3,600 B.C.; now known as Icel; p. (1980) 216,308.

Merthyr Tydfil, t., unit. auth. created in 1996 from former l. gov. dist., S. **Wales;** in narrow valley of R. Taff, 35 km N.W. of Cardiff; former coal mng. ctr.; hosiery, aircraft, bricks, elec. domestic prods.; p. (1991) 39,482 (t.), (2001) 55,981 (unit. auth.).

Merton, outer bor., Greater London, **Eng.;** inc. former bors. of Mitcham, Wimbledon, and Merton and Morden; p. (2001) 187,908.

Meru, mtn., Tanzania, E. Africa; extinct volcano overlooking E. arm of Gt. Rift valley; coffee plantations at alt. 1,500–1,800 m, some rubber below 1,200 m; alt. summit 4,560 m.

Merv. See **Mary.**

Mesa, t., Arizona, **USA;** in Salt River Valley, founded by Mormons 1878; agr. ctr., helicopter mftg.; p. (2000) 396,375.

Mesa Central, plateau, **Mexico;** part of Mexican plateau, major a. of comm. agr. (maize, wheat, agave); contains cap. Mexico City; dense p. and industl. comm. ctrs.

Mesa del Norte, plateau, **Mexico;** northern part of Mexican plateau.

Mesabi Range, hills, N.E. Minn., **USA;** vast iron ore deposits, now running out.

Mesa Verde National Park, S.W. Col., **USA;** Indian cliff dwellings.

Mesopotamia, anc. region, S.W. **Asia;** between Tigris and Euphrates Rs.; a. of early civilisation.

Messenia, anc. region, Peloponnesus, **Greece;** corresponding to present Messinia, densely p. agr. dep. cap. Kalamata; a. 3,400 km²; p. (1991) 166,904.

Messina, c., spt., Sicily, **Italy;** opposite Reggio; univ.; exp. fruit, wine, oil; p. (1992) 232,911.

Messina, strait, between Sicily and Italian mainland; heavily trafficked; length 35 km, minimum width 5 km.

Mesta, R., **Bulgaria, Greece;** rises in Rodopi mtns., flows S.E. into Aegean Sea 24 km E of Kavalla; valley famous for tobacco; known in Greece as Nestos; c. 280 km long.

Mestre, t., **Italy;** on lagoon at landward end of causeway linking Venice to mainland.

Meta, R., **Colombia** and **Venezuela;** navigable for 640 km; trib. of R. Orinoco; 1,200 km long.

Metz, c., cap of Moselle dep., N.E. **France;** on R. Moselle 40 km N. of Nancy; cultural and comm. ctr. of Lorraine; impt. iron mines; wines; mediaeval bldgs.; birthplace of Verlaine; p. (1990) 123,920(c.), 193,117 (met. a.).

Meudon, t., Hauts-de-Seine, **France;** S.W. sub. of Paris; observatory; glass, linen, ammunition; p. (1999) 43,636.

Meurthe, R., N.E. **France;** rises in Vosges and joins Moselle N. of Nancy.

Meurthe-et-Moselle, dep., N.E. **France;** borders on Belgium and Luxembourg; cap. Nancy; a. 5,276 km²; p. (1999) 712,832.

Meuse, dep., N.E. **France;** borders on Belgium; cap. Bar-le-Duc; a. 6,237 km²; p. (1990) 196,300.

Meuse (Maas), R., **France;** rises in Haute-Marne, flows past Verdun into Belgium past Namur, and Liège into the Neth. and joins the Waal, left arm of the Rhine; impt. routeway; 912 km long.

Mexborough, t., South Yorks., **Eng.;** on R. Don, 16 km above Doncaster; potteries; p. (1991) 15,282.

Mexicali, c., Baja Cal., **Mexico;** border resort; p. (1990) 602,390.

Mexican Plateau, central plateau, **Mexico;** between the branches of the Sierra Madre; highest point over 2,400 m; impt. landform and a. of human settlement.

Mexico, fed. rep., Central America; inc. 31 sts., and fed. dist. of Mexico City; mtnous.; Sierra Madre covers most of rep.; variety of climate according to alt.; W. mostly desert; one of world's fastest-growing p.; agr. requires irrigation; major world exporter of cotton, fruit, sulphur, silver, oil; 14 oil refineries, new petrochemical complex at Cosoleacaque; rapid industl. expansion for consumer gds.; attempts to decentralize inds. from Mexico City not very successful; tourism for Americans; severe drought, 1999; cap. Mexico City; a. 1,972,360 km²; p. (2004) 104,959,594.

Mexico, st., **Mexico;** encircles fed. dist. of Mexico City; cap. Toluca; a. 21,412 km²; p. (1990) 9,815,901.

Mexico City, c., cap. of **Mexico;** lgst. c. in Latin America; on plain at 2,275 m; altitude and basin site trap pollutants; many note-worthy bldgs., cath., univ.; admin., comm. and industl. ctr.; nuclear reactor nearby; lge. earthquake (1985) destroyed many parts of c.; surrounded by shanty ts.; p. (1995) 8,489,000.

Mexico, Gulf of, lge. inlet of Atl. Oc. (1,600 km E. to W. by 1,280 km N. to S.) lying S. of USA and E. of Mexico; communicates by Florida strait with Atl. and by Yucatan strait with Caribbean Sea; submarine oil drilling.

Mexico, Valley of, Meseta Central, **Mexico;** major industl. zone; over 60 per cent by value of Mexican mngs. produced; wide range of inds.;

major ctr. Mexico City; attempts to decentralise p. and economic activity throughout Mexico; once ctr. of Aztec p.

Meyrin, t., Switzerland: H.Q. of CERN (*Organisation Européene pour la Recherche Nucléaire*); nr. Geneva.

Mezzogiorno, lge. underdeveloped region, southern **Italy;** comprising Abruzzo and Molise, Campania, Basilicata, Apulia, Calabria and the Is. of Sicily and Sardinia; major govt. attempts to develop a.; agr. reforms and industl. growth, oil refining, iron and steel, petrochemicals; contains 35 per cent of p. of Italy, much emigration; much devastated by earthquake (1980); p. (1981) 20,053,334.

Miami, c., Fla., USA; on Biscayne Bay, at mouth of Miami R.; famous resort and recreational ctr.; varied inds.; international airport; world's 5th lgst. cargo airpt.; 3rd container pt. on U.S. East cst.; lge. freeport; M. beach across Biscayne Bay; ctr. of Cuban exiles; p. (2000) 362,470 (c.), 1,937,000 (met. a. with Hialeah).

Michigan, st., USA; Wolverine St.; admitted to Union 1837; st. flower Apple Blossom, st. bird Robin; in valley of Gr. Ls.; industl.; cars, iron and steel gds., petroleum, minerals; some agr.; cap. Lansing; a. 150,779 km²; p. (2002) 10,050,446.

Michigan Lake, 3rd lgst of Gr. Ls. and the only one wholly in **USA;** in basin of St. Lawrence R., enclosed by two peninsulas of the st. of Mich. and by Wis., Ill., and Ind.; a. 61,901 km²; discharges by Straits of Mackinac to L. Huron.

Michoacan, st., Mexico; on Pac. Oc.; mtnous., rich in minerals; cap. Morelia; a. 60,088 km²; p. (1990) 3,534,042.

Micronesia, Federated States of, ind. state, includes W. Pac. Is. of Yap, Truk, Ponape and Kosrae; p. (2004), 108,155.

Mid Bedfordshire, l. gov. dist., Beds., Eng.; S. of Luton and inc. Biggleswade, Sandy and Ampthill; p. (2001) 121,024.

Mid Devon, l. gov. dist., Devon, **Eng.;** based on Tiverton; p. (2001) 69,774.

Middleburg, t. cap. of Zeeland prov., **Neth.;** on Walcheren I. nr. Flushing; margarine, timber, optical instruments; cloth ctr. in mediaeval times; p. (1994) 40,118.

Middlesbrough, t., unit. auth. created in 1996, formerly part of Cleveland, **Eng.;** expanded t.; pt. on S. side of Tees estuary; impt. iron and steel ind., heavy engin., chemicals; p. (2001) 142,300 (unit. auth.).

Middlesex, historic co., S.E. **Eng.;** N. of R. Thames; largely absorbed in Greater London 1964.

Middleton, t., Gtr. Manchester, **Eng.;** in valley of R. Irk; p. (2001) 45,314.

Middletown, t., Ohio, **USA;** on Miami R. and canal; steel; paper; p. (1990) 46,022.

Middlewich, t., Cheshire, **Eng.;** on Rs. Dane, Wheelock and Croco, 8 km N. of Crewe; salt, chemicals, clothing; p. (1991) 10,100.

Midhurst, t., West Sussex, **Eng.;** on R. Rother; famous polo grounds; birthplace of Richard Cobden; p. (1991) 6,451.

Midi-Pyrénées, region, S.W. **France;** inc. deps. Ariège, Aveyron, Haute-Garonne, Gers, Lot, Hautes-Pyrénées, Tarn, Tarn-et-Garonne; mountainous region on Spanish border descending to agricultural lowlands north-eastwards; p. (1999) 2,550,983.

Midland, t., Texas, **USA;** oilfield ctr.; cotton ginning, natural gas; p. (1990) 89,443.

Midlands, region, Eng.; comprises cos. of Staffs., Derbys., Notts., Leics., Warwicks., Northants.; includes Birmingham conurbation; impt. a. for lt. engin.

Midlothian, E. Scot., unit. auth. created in 1996, incorporating part of historic co. which was divided between the Borders and Lothian in 1974 and is now divided between Borders, E. Lothian, Edinburgh, Midlothian and W. Lothian; p. (2002) 80,500.

Mid Suffolk, l. gov. dist., Suffolk, **Eng.;** rural a. inc. Eye and Stowmarket; p. (2001) 86,837.

Mid Sussex, l. gov. dist., West Sussex, **Eng.;** a. inc. Cuckfield and Burgess Hill; p. (2001) 127,378.

Midway Islands, I., Pac. Oc.; stop-over on air- routes betweeen San Francisco and Asia, midway between Asia and **USA** (to which it belongs); US Navy moved out, 1997. Now wildlife reserve.

Mikkeli, c., cap. of M. prov., **Finland;** L. pt. in Saimaa L. region; p. (1993) 32,394.

Milan, c., cap. of M. prov., N. **Italy;** route ctr. in Lombard plain; second lgst. c. in rep.; ctr. of commerce and ind.; textiles, chemicals, printing, publishing, machin., cars, aircraft, porcelain; cath., univ.; p. (1992) 1,358,627.

Mildenhall, t., Forest Heath, Suffolk, **Eng.;** on R. Lark; 13th cent. church; R.A.F. sta. nearby; expanded t.; p. (1991) 10,468.

Milford Haven, spt., Pembrokeshire, **Wales;** magnificent deepwater harbour; major tanker terminal (250,000 tonnes); 2 refineries; pipeline from Angle Bay to Llandarcy (nr. Swansea); major white fish pt.; trawlers built and repaired; net mkg.; p. (1991) 13,194.

Milford Sound, inlet, a. S. of S.I., **N.Z.;** tourist resort; noted for scenery and rare birds.

Millom, t., Copeland, Cumbria, **Eng.;** on N.W. cst. of Duddon estuary; ironwks. (closed 1968 after 100 years); hosiery; declining p.; p. (1991) 6,455.

Millport, burgh, N. Ayrshire, **Scot.;** on Gr. Cumbrae I., in F. of Clyde; resort; cath.; p. (2002) 1,253.

Milngavie, burgh, E. Dunbartonshire, **Scot.;** 8 km N.W. of Glasgow; textiles; p. (2002) 12,795.

Milo or **Melos,** I., Cyclades, **Greece;** cap. Plaka, nr. site of anc. c.; famous statue of Venus of Milo (now in Louvre) found here in 1820.

Milton Keynes, t., unit. auth. created in 1997, formerly part of Bucks., **Eng.;** new c. for London overspill comprising Bletchley, Wolverton and Stony Stratford; Open University; massive pop. increase (to 370,000) planned by 2024; p. (2001) 207,057 (unit. auth.).

Milwaukee, c., Wis., **USA;** lgst. c. and ch. pt. of st.; on L. Mich.; 112 km N. of Chicago; univ.; major mftg. ctr. with numerous inds., notably machin. and transport equipment, meat-canning, beer; p. (2000) 596,974 (c.), 1,432,149 (met. a.).

Min, R., Sichuan, W. **China;** flows S., diverted into irrigation channels; joins Chang Jiang at Yibin; length 800 km, navigable.

Mina Hassan Tani (Kenitra), spt., **Morocco;** exp. grain; p. (1981) 450,000.

Minas Gerais, st., Brazil; vast iron ore reserves; gold, diamonds, manganese, uranium, aluminium; cotton, coffee; hydroelec. power sta.; cap. Belo Horizonte; heavy inds.; a. 585,472 km²; p. (1996) 16,661,000.

Mina Sulman, free transit pt., **Bahrain;** deepwater pt., dry dock for OPEC super-tankers, entrepôt.

Minch, The, channel between the mainland of **Scot.** and the N. portion of Outer Hebrides. 38–64 km wide; very rapid current.

Minch, The Little, channel between I. of Skye, **Scot.,** and the middle portion of Outer Hebrides. 22–32 km wide.

Minchinhampton, t., Gloucs., **Eng.;** in Cotswolds. 6 km S.E. of Stroud; p. (1991) 3,201.

Mindanao, second lgst. I. of **Philippines;** forested mtns., volcano Mt. Apo; exp. pineapples, hemp, coconuts, coffee; iron, gold, copper mined; plywoods and veneer, paper, pulp; ch. ts. Zamboanga, Davao; a. of govt. sponsored immigration; lge. Moslem p.; greatest ocean depth Mindanao Deep, off Philippines, 11,524 m; a. 94,628 km²; p. (1990) 14,297,462.

Minden, c., N. Rhine–Westphalia, **Germany;** on R. Weser at crossing of Mittelland canal; pt., rly. junc.; cath. (12th–14th cent.) destroyed in second world war; p. (2002) 82,898.

Mindoro, I., Philippines, S. of Luzon; mtnous., thickly forested; rice, coconuts grown on cst., a. 9,376 km²; p. (1990) 832,642.

Minehead, t., West Somerset, **Eng.;** at N. foot of Exmoor, on Bristol Channel cst.; mkt., holiday resort; p. (1991) 9,158.

Minicoy Is., Arabian Sea; joined with Laccadive and Amindivi Is. to form union terr. of Lakshadweep, **India.**

Minneapolis, c., Minn., **USA;** on Mississippi R., at falls of St. Anthony; lgst. c. of st., pt. of entry, rly. terminus; wheat mkt., comm. and industl. ctr.; wide range of inds.; univ.; p. (2000) 382,618 (c.), 2,464,124 (met. a. inc. St. Paul which it faces).

Minnesota, st., USA; North Star St.; admitted to Union 1858; st. flower Lady's Slipper, st. bird Common Loon; W. of L. Superior; studded with Ls., many Rs.; iron ore; maize, wheat, livestock, dairying; cap. St. Paul; a. 217,736 km²; p. (2002) 5,019,720.

Minorca (Menorca), I. off **Spain;** 2nd lgst. of Balearic Is.; Mediterranean agr.; developing tourism; cap. Mahón; a. 733 km².

Minsk, c., cap. of **Belarus;** lge. rly. junc.; cultural and industl. ctr.; univ.; engin., computers; rebuilt since second world war; p. (2000) 1,772,000.

Minya, c. and prov., central **Egypt;** on Nile; cotton tr. ctr.; p. (1986) 179,136 (c.), (1991) 3,003,000 (prov.).

Minya Konka, mtn., S.W. Sichuan prov., **China;** in Himalayas; highest peak in China; 7,570 m.

Mirfield, t., West Yorks., **Eng.;** on R. Calder, 5 km S.W. of Dewsbury; woollens; p. (1991) 18,459.

Miri, t., Sarawak, E. **Malaysia;** impt. oil ctr.; p. (1989) 91,000.

Mirzapur, t. Uttar Pradesh, **India;** on R. Ganges; carpets, brassware; p. (1991) 169,336.

Misiones, prov., N.E. **Argentina;** densely forested subtropical region; sugar cane, tea, timber, sandstone and basalt mining; cap. Posadas; a. 29,801 km²; p. (1991) 788,915.

Miskolc, c., N.E. **Hungary;** impt. industl. ctr.; iron ore, lignite nearby; varied inds., inc. textiles, porcelain, engin., bricks, refrigeration planting; p. (1997) 178,000.

Mississauga, c., Ontario, **Canada;** lies to W. of Toronto; part of T. met. a.; p. (1991) 463,388.

Mississippi, st., 3. **USA;** Magnolia St.; admitted to Union 1817; st. flower Magnolia, st. bird Mockingbird; in lower M. valley; bounded on S. by G. of Mexico; cotton, sweet potatoes, pecan nuts, rice, sugar-cane, sorghum-cane, fruit, livestock raising; petroleum, natural gas; cotton textiles, chemicals, fish-processing; damaged by Hurricane Katrina, 2005; cap. Jackson; a. 123,584 km²; p. (2002) 2,871,782.

Mississippi, principal R. of **USA;** rises in N. Minn. nr. L. Itasca; drains c. 3,170,000 km²; enters G. of Mexico in lge. delta nr. New Orleans; navigable, flood control problems; length 3,760 km (Mississippi–Missouri–Red Rock 6,176 km).

Missolonghi, sm. t., **Greece;** pt. on inlet of G. of Patras; fish, tobacco; Byron died here 1824.

Missoula, t., Mont., **USA;** on Klark R.; univ.; rly. wks., agr., fruit, oil refinery; tourism; p. (1996) 51,204.

Missouri, st., central **USA;** Show-me St.; admitted to Union 1821; st. flower Hawthorn, st. bird Bluebird; dominated by Mississippi and Missouri Rs.; predominantly agr.; livestock, maize; coal, iron; transport equipment; cap. Jefferson City; ch. t. St. Louis; a. 180,456 km²; p. (2002) 5,672,579.

Missouri, longest R. of **USA;** 3,942 km; trib. of Mississippi R.; main headstream Jackson R.; flood, power and irrigation schemes.

Missouri Coteau, hill ridge, N. **America;** runs N.W. to S.E. across prairies of Saskatchewan (Canada), N. and S. Dakota (USA); rises abruptly from 480–600 m.

Misurata, t., Tripolitania, **Libya;** on cst. of Mediterranean, 176 km E. of Tripoli; mkt. for local agr. produce; p. (1984) 178,295.

Mitau. See Jelgava.

Mitidja, plain, **Algeria,** N. Africa; borders Mediterranean; ch. ts. Algiers, Blida.

Mito, c. Honshu, **Japan;** cas.; commun. ctr.; famous for lime trees; site of two nuclear power plants nearby; p. (1990) 234,970.

Mits'iwa (**Massawa**), spt., **Eritrea** on Red Sea; fine harbour; fishing; fish meal; p. (1989) 19,404.

Mittelland Canal, inland waterway system, **Germany;** system of canals and canalised Rs.; links Dortmund–Ems canal nr. Rheine through Minden, Hanover, Magdeburg, Berlin to R. Oder at Frankfurt-on-Oder; makes use of natural E.–W. troughs across the N. German plain.

Miyazaki, c., Kyushu, **Japan;** famous shrine; ctr. of sandy plain with lagoons; p. (1990) 287,367.

Mizoram ("Land of Highlanders"), union terr. (1972); new st. (1986); Assam, N.E. **India;** former Mizo Hills dist. of Assam; 80 per cent p. Christian; 44 per cent literate, higher proportion than any other a. except Kerala; new cap. Aizawl; a. 21,238 km²; p. (2001) 891,100.

Mjosa, lgst. L., **Norway;** 88 km long.

Mladá Boleslav (Jungbunzlau), t., Bohemia, **Czech Rep.;** vehicles, agr. machin., textiles; once ctr. of Bohemian Brethren (followers of John Hus); p. (1984) 47,686.

Mobutu Sese Seko, L., (L. Albert), **Congo, Uganda;** on floor of Gt. Rift Valley; crocodile farming; tourism; impt. pt. Kasenyi; 160 km long, 32 km wide; alt. 640 m; a. 5,346 km².

Mobile, c., spt., Ala., **USA;** on R. M.; shipbldg. pt. inds.; exp. cotton; p. (2000) 198,915 (c.), 476,923 (met. a.).

Moçambique. See Mozambique.

Moçambique Channel. See Mozambique Channel.

Moçambique Current. See Mozambique Current.

Moçâmedes. See Namibe.

Modane, t., S.E. Savoie, **France;** commands routes via Mont Cenis Pass and tunnel; electrometallurgy; p. (1999) 3,657.

Modena, t., cap. of M. prov. **Italy;** cath.; univ.; textiles, leather, engin.; p. (1992) 176,972.

Modesto, t., Cal., **USA;** fruit (especially peaches), vegetable-processing; p. (1990) 164,730 (t.), 371,000 (met. a.).

Modica, t., S.E. Sicily, **Italy;** agr. ctr.; limestone grottoes, cave dwellings; Cava d'Ispica; p. (1981) 45,769.

Moe. See Yallourn.

Moers, t. North Rhine-Westphalia, **Germany;** W of Duisburg in the Ruhr; ind. coal; p. (2002) 107,421.

Moffat, burgh, Dumfries and Galloway, **Scot.;** 24 km N.W. of Lockerbie; resort; p. (1991) 2,342.

Moffat Tunnel, Col., **USA;** carries trunk rly. from Chicago to San Francisco under Rocky mtns. between Denver and Salt Lake City; 10 km long; alt. 2,774 m.

Mogadishu, c., cap. of **Rep. of Somalia;** on Indian Oc.; modernised deep-sea pt., airpt.; p. (2000) 1,219,000.

Mogador. See Essaouira.

Mogi das Cruzes, t., São Paulo, **Brazil;** agr.; bauxite mng.; p. (1996) 314,950.

Mogilev, c., **Belarus;** on R. Dnieper; industl.; rly. and route junc.; p. (1990) 362,600.

Mohács, t., S. **Hungary;** on Danube; impt. R. pt.; strategic site; battle 1526; p. (1997) 20,000.

Mohammedia, t., Morocco, N. **Africa;** oil refining; p. (1994) 170,063.

Mohawk, R., N.Y., **USA;** trib. of Hudson R.; followed by impt. road, rly. and canal routes across Appalachian mtns.; 280 km long.

Mojave or **Mohave,** S. Cal., **USA;** desert region of mtns. and valleys; a. 38,850 km².

Moji, spt., Kyushu, **Japan;** exp. coal, cement, timber; linked by bridge to Honshu. See Kitakyushu.

Mol, t., N.E. **Belgium;** nuclear energy research ctr.; p. (1991) 30,800.

Mold, t., Flintshire, N. **Wales;** on R. Alyn; chemicals, roadstone; p. (1991) 8,745.

Moldau. See Vltava.

Moldova, CIS former constituent rep., **USSR;** fertile fruit growing a. especially for vines; inds. based on fruit; cap. Kishinev (now called Chisinau); a. 34,188 km²; p. (2004) 4,446,452.

Mole Valley, l. gov. dist., Surrey, **Eng.;** based on Mole R. ts. of Leatherhead and Dorking; p. (2001) 80,287.

Mole R., Surrey, **Eng.;** rises in central Weald; flows N. into R. Thames nr. Molesey; cuts impt. gap through N. Downs between Dorking and Leatherhead; 80 km long.

Molenbeek-Saint-Joan, t., **Belgium;** nr. Brussels; lge mftg. ctr.; p. (1991) 68,800.

Molfetta, spt., Apulia, **Italy;** olive oil, macaroni, wine, caths.; p. (1981) 65,951.

Moline, t., Ill., **USA;** on Mississippi R.; agr. implements, ironwks.; flour; p. (1980) 46,278.

Molise, region, central **Italy;** subsistence arable and pastoral farming; a. 4,437 km²; p. (1992) 331,494.

Mölndal, t., S.W. **Sweden;** paper, textiles; margarine; p. (1992) 52,423.

Moluccas or **Spice Is.,** prov. **Indonesia;** gr. of Is. between Sulawesi and W. Irian; mtnous., fertile; spices, sago, timber, pearls, rice, copra, ch. t. Ternate; attempts at independence by S. Moluccans; a. 496,454 km²; p. (1983) 1,534,300.

Mombasa, spt., **Kenya;** ch. harbour, Kilindini; rly. terminus; oil refinery; exp. tropical produce (hides, rubber, etc.); fertiliser plant, sheet glass, steel rolling mill; p. (1995) 465,000.

Monaco, principality on Mediterranean cst. between France and Italy, W. Europe; economy based on tourism; benefits from climate and amenities, inc. famous casino; tax laws attract p. and shortage of land causes M. to build out into sea; much revenue derived from transactional laws, sales of tobacco and postage stamps; monarch, Prince Albert II (since 2005); cap. Monaco Ville; a. 146 ha; p. (2004) 32,270.

Monadhliath Mtns., Highland, **Scot.;** between Spey R. and Loch Ness; hgst. peak Carn Mairg, 1,216 m.

Monadnock Mt., peak, 965 m high, N.H., **USA;** name used as a term for the geomorphological feature of an isolated hill which has successfully resisted erosion.

Monaghan, co., **R.o.I.;** mainly pastoral and agr.; a. 1,295 km²; p. (1986) 52,379.

Monaghan, co. t., Monaghan, **R.o.I.;** on the Ulster canal; cath.; p. (1986) 6,075.

Monastir. *See* **Bitola.**

Mönch, peak, Bernese Alps, **Switzerland**; 4,101 m.

Mönchengladbach, t., N. Rhine–Westphalia, **Germany**; 26 km W. of Düsseldorf; rly. ctr. textiles; p. (2002) 262,963.

Moncton, t., N.B., **Canada**; rly. ctr., textiles; oil nearby; p. (1996) 113,491.

Monfalcone, t., N.E. **Italy**; on Adriatic; modern industl. t.; shipbldg., oil refining; p. (1981) 30,277.

Monferrato, low hills, Piedmont, N. **Italy**; S. and S.E. of Turin between valleys of Po and Tanaro; celebrated vineyards, produce Asti Spumante wines; alt. never exceeds 460 m.

Mongolia, Inner. *See* **Inner Mongolia.**

Mongolia, Rep. of (Outer Mongolia), central Asia; landlocked, extensive plateau at 1,200 m bordering Gobi desert in S.; dry continental climate with extremely cold winters; pastoral agr. collectively organised for horses, sheep, camels, oxen, and goats; cap. Ulan Bator; incr. mechanisation; food processing, livestock prods.; new constitution, 1992, ended Communist monopoly of power; a. 1,564,360 km²; p. (2004) 2,751,314.

Monmouth, t., Monmouthshire, **Wales**; at confluence of Rs. Wye and Monnow; mkt. ctr.; timber, crushed limestone; p. (1991) 7,246.

Monmouthshire, S.E. **Wales,** unit. auth. created in 1996 from former l. gov. dist., reinstating part of historic co. split up in 1974; drained by the Usk and Wye Rs.; inc. ts. of Abergavenny, Chepstow and Monmouth; p. (2001) 84,885.

Monopoli, spt., Apulia, **Italy**; oil, wine, fruit, flour tr.; p. (1991) 46,700.

Monroe, t., La., **USA**; cotton ctr., natural gas, paper, printing ink; p. (1996) 54,588.

Monrovia, c., cap. of **Liberia,** W. Africa; free port and industl. free zone on Atl. at mouth of St. Paul R.; exp. rubber, palm oil; ship registration; p. (2000) 962,000.

Mons, c., cap. of Hainaut prov., W. **Belgium,** nr. Fr. border; cath.; inds. linked with Borinage coal-mng. dist.; varied mnfs.; scene of many battles; NATO (SHAPE) H.Q. nearby at Casteau; p. (1993) 92,533.

Montana, st., N.W. **USA**; Treasure St.; admitted to Union 1889; st. flower Bitterroot, st. bird Western Meadowlark; in Rocky mtns. region; cap. Helena; lgst. c. Great Falls; copper, silver, gold, zinc, lead, manganese; coal, petroleum, natural gas; pastoral agr.; Glacier Nat. Park, tourism; a. 377,456 km²; p. (2002) 909,453.

Montauban, t., Tarn-et-Garonne dep., **France**; on R. Tarn; cath.; agr. prod., wines; p. (1999) 51,855.

Montbéliard, t., Doubs dep., **France**; S. of Belfort; textiles, watches, typewriters, vehicles; p. (1990) 30,639(t.), 117,510 (met. a.).

Mont Blanc, mtn., Alps; on confines of **Italy** and **France**; alt. 4,814 m; major road tunnel (opened to traffic 1965) linking Courmayeur (Italy) and Chamonix (France), length 12 km.

Montceau-les-Mines, t., Saône-et-Loire dep., **France**; coal, textiles, metal-working; p. (1982) 51,290 (met. a.).

Mont Cenis Pass and Tunnel, W. Alps; on bdy. between **France** and **Italy**; approached from W. by Isère-Arc valleys, from E. by Dora Riparia; alt. 2,097 m; tunnel carries main rly. from Lyons to Turin under Col de Fréjus; opened 1871; 12 km long.

Mont-Dore, spa, Puy-de-Dôme dep., **France**; 48 km S.W. of Clermont-Ferrand; Puy de Sancy (1,887 m) hgst. peak of Mont-Dore mtn. gr.; p. (1999) 1,679.

Monte Bello Is., gr. off N.W. cst., **Australia**; about 136 km N. of pt. of Onslow; first Brit. atomic weapon exploded here 3 Oct. 1952.

Monte Carlo, t., **Monaco**; tourist resort, casino.

Monte Corno, mtn., **Italy**; in Central Apennines; alt. 2,923 m.

Monte Cristo, Italian I., 42 km S. of Elba, in Tyrrhenian Sea; famed by novel by Dumas.

Monte Gargano, peninsula, S. **Italy**; projects into Adriatic Sea nr. plain of Foggia; formed by limestone plateau, alt. over 900 m; pasture on upper slopes, woodland on lower; a. 1,030 km².

Montego Bay, spt., **Jamaica**; main ctr. for tourism; p. (1991) 83,446.

Montélimar, t., Drôme dep., **France**; bricks, tiles, nougat; hydroelectric barrage on R. Rhône; p. (1999) 31,235.

Montenegro, ind. rep. since 2006; agr., pastoral; cap. Podgorica; historic tension with Serbia; referendum vote for independence, May 2006; a. 13,812 km²; p. (2006) 670,000.

Monterey, t., Cal., **USA**; S. of San Francisco, resort of artists and writers; sardine ind., fruit and vegetable canneries.

Monteria, c., cap. of Cordoba prov., **Colombia**; tobacco, cacao, cotton, sugar; p. (1992) 265,754.

Monte Rosa, hgst. peak, 4,637 m, Pennine Alps, on border of **Italy** and **Switzerland**.

Monte Rotondo, hgst. mtn., Corsica, **France**; 2,767 m.

Monterrey, t., cap. of Nuevo León prov., **Mexico**; third lgst. c.; cath.; textiles, brewing, ironwks.; minerals; thermoelec. plant; sheet metal; p. (1990) 1,064,197.

Monte Sant'Angelo, hilltop t., **Italy**; on Gargano promontory; notable ctr. of pilgrimage; p. (1981) 16,500.

Montevideo, c., cap. **Uruguay**; major pt. on Rio de la Plata; dominates life of rep. as financial, comm. and industl. ctr.; fisheries, oil-refining, food-processing, tourism; cath., univ.; p. (2000) 1,236,000.

Montgomery, c., cap. of Ala., **USA**; at head of Alabama R.; cotton, livestock, timber, dairying, fertilisers; hydroelec. power; p. (2000) 201,568 (c.), 292,517 (met. a.).

Montgomery, t., Powys, central **Wales**; in upper Severn valley, 13 km N.E. of Newtown; agr. mkt.; cas.

Montgomeryshire, historic co., central Wales, now part of Powys.

Montluçon, t., Allier dep., **France**; on R. Cher; terminus of Berry canal, linking Commentry coalfields with Loire; iron foundries, glassmaking; cas.; p. (1999) 41,555.

Montmartre, dist., N. Paris, **France**; on Butte de M. (101 m), commands superb view S. over Paris; picturesque square, frequented by artists; basilica of Sacré Coeur.

Montparnasse, dist., Paris, **France**; on left bank of Seine R.; haunt of artists and writers.

Montpellier, t., cap. of Hérault dep., **France**; 8 km N. of Mediterranean cst. on coastal lowland route to S.W. France; comm. and cultural ctr.; univ.; wines, fruit tr.; silk, chemicals; many anc. bldgs. inc. cath.; p. (1999), 225,020.

Montreal, c., spt., Quebec, **Canada**; at confluence of Ottawa and St. Lawrence Rs.; caths., univs.; major industl., comm. and financial ctr.; extensive harbour installations, lge. grain exp.; diverse mnfs.; lgst. c. and spt. in Canada; p. mainly French-speaking; p. (1991) 1,017,666 (c.), (1996) 3,326,510 (met. a.).

Montreuil-sous-Bois, E. sub. Paris, **France**; hothouse flowers and fruit for Paris mkt.; peach growing; mnfs.; p. (1990) 95,038.

Montreux, t., **Switzerland**; on L. Geneva; tourist ctr.; Chillon cas.; p. (1980) 19,685.

Montrose, spt., burgh, Angus, **Scot.**; on E. cst. at mouth of S. Esk R.; chemicals, rope wks.; vegetable-canning, boat-bldg.; fishing; supply base for N. Sea oil; p. (2002) 10,845.

Mont-Saint-Michel, rocky granite I., in English Channel, off Normandy cst., **France**; tourist ctr. with Benedictine abbey; connected to mainland by causeway; surrounding marshland reclaimed for agr.; alt. 79 m.; p. (1999) 46.

Montserrat, volcanic I., Brit. crown col., Leeward Is., W.I.; chiefly agr.; exp. sea-island cotton, limes, sugar-cane and tomatoes; cap. Plymouth; a. 101 km²; p. (2004) 9,245. Devastated by major volcanic eruption, 1997.

Montserrat, mtn., Catalonia, **Spain**; Benedictine monastery, alt. 1,236 m.

Monument Valley, Utah and Arizona, **USA**; home of Navajo Indians.

Monza, c., Lombardy, N. **Italy**; 14 km from Milan; cath.; textiles, leather, hats; former royal residence; King Umberto I assassinated here, 1900; motor-racing circuit; p. (1992) 120,054.

Moose Jaw, c., Saskatchewan, **Canada**; rly. junc.; agr. ctr.; oil refining, p. (1991) 33,593.

Moradabad, c., Uttar Pradesh, N. **India**; rly. junc.; cotton mills, brassware; mosque; p. (1991) 444,000.

Morava, R., Slovakia and **Austria**; trib. of R. Danube; navigable in lower course; 339 km long.

Morava, R., Serbia; formed from W. Morava and S. Morava, flows N. into Danube 80 km below Belgrade to Istanbul; 560 km long.

Moravia, region, Czech Rep.; part of Bohemian plateau, drained by Morava R.; inc. fertile agr. a.; mineral resources and industl. ts.

Moray, E. Scot., unit. auth. created in 1996, incorporating historic co. of **Morayshire** which became part of Grampian in 1974; borders M. Firth; arable agr. benefiting from glacial soils; p. (2002) 86,740.

Moray Firth, arm of N. Sea; on Scottish E. cst., between Highland and; plans for lge.-scale industl. expansion; offshore oil platforms at Arderseir; valuable inshore oilfield.

Morbihan, dep., N.W. **France**; on Bay of Biscay; agr., fishing; cap. Vannes; a. 7,094 km²; p. (1999) 638,694.

Mordovia, aut. rep., **Russia**; forested steppe between Rs. Oka and Volga; pastoral agr., lumbering; food processing; a. 25,493 km²; p. (1989) 963,500.

Morea. See Peloponnesus.

Morecambe and Heysham, t., N. Lancs., **Eng.**; on S. shore of M. Bay; M. holiday resort; H., pt. for N Ireland and oil refinery; two advanced gas-cooled reactor nuclear power stas.; p. (2001) 49,569.

Morecambe Bay, between Lancs. and Cumbria, **Eng.**; isolates Furness dist. of Lancs.; many proposed barrages across Bay, now project increasingly probable as water shortage in N.W. Eng. grows; discoveries of nat. gas.

Morelia, c., cap. of Michoacán st., W. **Mexico**; on rocky hill, 1,891 m in fertile valley; cath.; textiles, pottery; p. (1990) 489,758.

Morelos, inland st., **Mexico**; mtns., forested; arable agr.; cap. Cuernavaca; a. 4,962 km²; p. (1990) 1,195,381.

Morgantown, c., W. Va., **USA**; univ.; coal, oil, gas fields; chemicals, heavy ind.; p. (1980) 27,605.

Morioka, c., N. Honshu, **Japan**; textiles, ironwks.; p. (1990) 235,440.

Morley, t., West Yorks., **Eng.**; 5 km S.W. of Leeds; woollens, stone quarrying; p. (2001) 54,051.

Morocco, kingdom, N.W. Africa; csts. on Atl. Oc. and Mediterranean Sea; rises to Atlas mtns. inland; leading world producer of phosphates; other minerals inc. iron-ore, lead and manganese; agr. main occupation, provides 30 per cent of exp.; fishing and tourism well developed; cap. Rabat; a. 466,200 km²; p. (2004) 32,209,101.

Moron, t., **Venezuela**; on cst. nr. Puerto Cabello; industl.; natural gas, oil refining.

Morón de la Frontera, t., S.W. **Spain**; agr. tr. ctr.; ruined Moorish cas.; p. (1990) 29,200.

Morpeth, t., Northumberland, **Eng.**; finely situated in valley of Wansbeck; coal mng., iron-founding; mkt.; Norman cas. remains; p. (1991) 14,393.

Mors, I., N. Jutland, **Denmark**; in Lim fjord; a. 357 km²; p. (1990) 23,774.

Morwell, t., Victoria, **Australia**; ctr. for brown coal extraction and briquettes; inds. attracted by cheap power; p. (1991) 15,423.

Moscow, c., cap. of **Russia**; leading cultural, political, comm., industl. and route ctr.; on Moskva R.; served by several airpts., R. and canal pts.; contains Kremlin in c. ctr. with Red Square; caths., univs., palaces, many theatres and art galleries; p. (2000) 9,321,000 (met. a.).

Moscow Sea (Ucha Reservoir), artificial L., **Russia**; created behind dam on R. Volga at Ivankovo; supplies water to Moscow, maintains level on Moscow–Volga canal, and supplies water to 8 hydroelec. power-stas.; a. 329 km².

Moscow–Volga Canal, Russia; links R. Volga at Ivankovo with Khimki sub. of Moscow; forms part of St. Petersburg–Moscow inland waterway; opened 1937; 128 km long.

Moselle, dep., N.E. **France**; iron-ore, coal mng.; metal inds.; cap. Metz; a. 6,224 km²; p. (1990) 1,011,300.

Moselle, R., **France** and **Germany**; trib. of R. Rhine; canalised between Thionville and Koblenz (269 km); lower valley forms famous wine dist.; 525 km long.

Moshi, t., N. **Tanzania**; on southern slope of Mt. Kilimanjaro; ctr. of coffee-growing dist.; airpt. at 854 m (S.W. of t.).

Mosi-oa-Toenja. See **Victoria Falls.** The local name means "Smoke of the Thunders."

Moskva, R., central **Russia**; trib. of R. Oka; Moscow stands on its banks; linked with upper Volga by Moscow–Volga canal (128 km long); 400 km long.

Mosquito Cst., lowland, E. cst. **Nicaragua**; 400 km N.–S., 192 km E.–W.; lumbering, bananas; ch. t. Bluefields; sparse p.

Mossamedes. See Moçâmedes.

Mossley, t., Tameside, Gtr. Manchester, **Eng.** 5 km

E. of Oldham; mkt. t., textiles; p. (1991) 10,569.

Most, t., Czech Rep.; lignite, chemicals; Druzhba crude oil pipeline extended to chemical wks.; p. (1990) 71,000.

Mostaganem, t., dep., N.W. **Algeria**; spt. on Mediterranean cst.; E. of Oran; exp. wine and fruits; gas pipeline from Hassi Massaoud; p. (1987) 114,037 (t.), 504,124 (dep.).

Mostar, t., Bosnia-Herzegovina, formerly Yugoslavia; on R. Naretva; bauxite, lignite; inds., wine, food processing, aluminium plant; devastated in civil war 1993; old bridge restored, 2005, p. (1981) 110,377.

Móstoles, t. Madrid prov. C. **Spain**; agr. ctr.; p. (1998) 195,300.

Mosul, t., N. **Iraq**; on R. Tigris; in region producing cereals, citrus fruit, cattle; impt. oilfields nearby; metal works; impt. during crusades; p. (1985) 570,926.

Motala, t., on L. Vättern, **Sweden**; radio sta.; engin., woollen gds.; p. (1992) 42,264.

Motherwell, burgh N Lanarkshire, **Scot.**; in Clyde valley, 24 km S.E. of Glasgow; iron, steel, machin., engin., textiles; p. (2002) 30,311.

Moulins, c., cap. of Allier dep., **France**; on Allier R.; leather gds., clothing; cath., ruined château, art treasures; p. (1999) 21,892.

Moulmein (Mawlamyine), spt., **Myanmar**; on R. Salween; exp. teak, rice; p. (1983) 219,991.

Mountain Ash, t., Rhondda, Cynon, Taff, **Wales**; in narrow valley 5 km S.E. of Aberdare; former coal mng. a.; p. (1991) 21,301.

Mount Adams, mtn., S. Wash. **USA**; beautiful volcanic scenery in Cascade Range; pine forests; alt. 3,803 m.

Mount Alberta, mtn., W. Alberta, **Canada**; in Canadian Rockies and Jasper Nat. Park; alt. 3,622 m.

Mount Assiniboine, mtn., Alberta, B.C., **Canada**; "Matterhorn" of Canadian Rockies; alt. 3,620 m.

Mount Carmel, mtn., N.W. **Israel**; rises to 554 m and extends 10 km as penin. into Mediterranean Sea, forming S. limit to Bay of Acre; ass. with prophets Elijah and Elisha.

Mount Cook. See under **Cook.**

Mount Gambier, t., S. **Australia**; at foot of extinct volcano; forestry, sawmilling of radiata pine; p. (1991) 21,156.

Mount Goldsworthy, t., W. **Australia**; new t. being developed in iron ore mng. a.

Mount Lofty Range, mtn. range, S. **Australia**; forms barrier to routes leaving Adelaide.

Mount Lyell, Tasmania, **Australia**; impt. copper mines, and refinery.

Mount McKinley, Alaska, **USA**; in Alaska Range and Nat. Park; highest point in N. America, c. 6,191 m.

Mount Newman, W. **Australia**; t. built 1967 to exploit nearby iron ore.

Mount of Olives, Jordan; ridge (817 m), E. of Jerusalem; Garden of Gethsemane on lower slopes.

Mount Pierre Elliott Trudeau. See Logan, Mount.

Mount's Bay, inlet, S. cst., Cornwall, **Eng.**; 32 km wide; fishery grounds.

Mount Tom Price, W. **Australia**; new t., being developed in iron ore mng. a.

Mount Vernon, c., N.Y., **USA**; on Bronx R.; sub. of N.Y.; residtl.; takes name from George Washington's house on Potomac, Va., 24 km S. of Washington D.C.; varied inds., notably electronic equipment; p. (1996) 67,112.

Mousehole, v., Cornwall, **Eng.**; nr. Penzance; former fishing pt.; now reliant on tourism.

Mouscron, sm. t., **Belgium**; textile ctr. nr. Fr. border.

Moyle, l. gov. dist., N. **Ireland**; borders N.E. cst.; inc. Rathlin I., Giants Causeway; main t. Ballycastle; p. (2001) 15,933.

Mozambique, former Portuguese prov., indep. st. (1975), E. Africa; wide cstl. plain rising inland to 2,100 m; crossed by Zambesi R.; few exp. inc. cashew nuts, cotton, sugar, tea; deposits of coal and bauxite; Beira and Maputo (cap.) serve as import pts. for transit tr.; 40% GNP from tourism and transport; Cabora Bassa Dam in Tete dist.; severely hit by flooding in 2000; civil war ended 1992; joined Brit. Commonwealth, 1995; a. 771,820 km²; p. (2004) 18,811,731.

Mozambique Channel, strait, Indian Oc.; separates Madagascar from mainland of Africa; 1,600 km long, 400–960 km wide.

Mozambique Current, ocean current, flows N. to S. along E. cst. of Mozambique and Natal, E. Africa; relatively warm water.

Mpumalanga, prov., **Rep. of S. Africa**, bordering Mozambique and Swaziland in the east; high plateau grasslands, mountains, escarpment, large freshwater lake and abundant aquatic birds; dairy products, coal, fruit, vegetables, cotton, tobacco, wheat, sugar, wool, gold, timber, paper, steel, vanadium; cap. Nelspruit; a. 79,490 km²; p. (1996) 2.8 m.

Mudanjiang (Mutankiang), c., Heilongjiang prov., **China**; pulp, paper, machin., flour milling; site of dam on Mudan R.; oil shale found locally; p. (1994) 602,700.

Mühlhausen, t., Erfurt, **Germany**; on R. Unstrut; textiles, machin., tobacco; p. (1981) 43,348.

Mukden. See Shenyang.

Mulhacen, mtn., Sierra Nevada range, **Spain**; 3,483 m (hgst. peak Europe, outside Alps).

Mülheim-an-der-Ruhr, t., N. Rhine–Westphalia, **Germany**; on R. Ruhr; cas.; coal mng., iron, steel., tobacco, engin., elec., oil refining; airpt.; p. (2002) 172,332.

Mulhouse, t., Haut-Rhin dep., **France**; impt. textile ctr.; potash deposits to N. supply chemical inds.; p. (1999) 110,287.

Mull, I., Argyll and Bute, **Scot.**; included in Hebrides; pastoral farming, fishing, tourism; ch. t. Tobermory; p. (1991) 2,708.

Mullet, The, peninsula, W. cst. Mayo, **R.o.I.**

Mullingar, c. t., Westmeath, **R.o.I.**; on Brosna R.; mkt., agr. ctr.; cath.; p. (1986) 8,077.

Multan, t., W. Punjab, **Pakistan**; on R. Chenab; carpets, silks, pottery, steel, thermal sta.; import gas pipeline to Lyallpur; nuclear fuel enrichment plant based on Pakistan's main uranium deposits nearby; p. (1981) 730,000.

Mumbai (Bombay), spt., cap. of Maharashtra st., India, harbour, docks, rly. ctr.; univ.; greatest cotton ctr. in republic; pt. handles nearly half of India's foreign tr.; oil refinery; film industry ("Bollywood"); univ., fine public bldgs.; new name Mumbai (1995); p. (2000) 18,070,000.

Muncie, t., Ind. **USA**; on White R.; iron, steel, glass and paper; p. (1996) 69,058.

Munich or **München**, c., cap. Bavaria, **Germany**; on R. Isar; cultural ctr. with univ., cath., many old bldgs.; inds. varied, notably scientific instruments, brewing, elec. engin., chemicals; famous film studios; annual beer festival; p. (2002) 1,227,958 (c.), 1,893,715 (met.a.).

Münster, c., N. Rhine–Westphalia, **Germany**; pt. on Dortmund-Ems canal; heavy machin., with varied mnfs.; cath., univ. and mediæval bldgs. damaged or destroyed in second world war; p. (2002) 267,197.

Munster, prov., S.W. **R.o.I.**; includes cos. Waterford, Kerry, Cork, Limerick, Clare, Tipperary; a. 24,540 km²; p. (1986) 1,020,577.

Murano, t., Venice, **Italy**; famous since Middle Ages for glass ind.

Murchison Falls. See Kabelega Falls.

Murchison, R., W. **Australia**; flows to Indian Oc., spectacular gorge, Nat. Park; length 1,280 km.

Murcia, prov. and former Moorish kingdom, S.E. **Spain**, on Mediterranean, irrigated agr., cereals and fruit; cap. Murcia; a. 8.467 km²; p. (1998) 1,115,000.

Murcia, c., cap. of Murcia prov., S.E. **Spain**; on R. Segura; cath., univ.; textiles and food inds.; p. (1998) 349,000.

Murmansk, spt., **Russia**; on Kola peninsula; ice-free throughout year; engin., elec. power; fishing, shipbldg.; submarine base; marine power sta. utilising tidal energy projected; p. (1989) 468,000.

Murom, t., **Russia**; pt. on Oka R.; anc. t.; textiles, engin.; p. (1989) 124,000.

Murray, R., separates N.S.W. and Victoria, **Australia**; major irrigation schemes support intensive agr.; hydro-electric power; 2,560 km long; length Murray-Darling system 3,696 km.; p. (1992) 109,600 (dist.).

Murrumbidgee, R., N.S.W., **Australia**; trib. of R. Murray; used extensively for irrigation; 2,160 km long; p. (1992) 148,300 (dist.).

Mururoa, coral Is., S. Pac.; used by France as nuclear testing site; p. (1985) 3,000.

Musa Jebel, mtn., **Egypt**; 2,249 m; identified with the biblical Sinai.

Muscat, t., cap. of Oman, Arabia; on S. cst. of G. of Oman; gd. harbour; dates, mother-of-pearl; terminal of oil pipeline; p. (2001) 770,000 (met. a.).

Muscat and Oman. See Oman.

Musgrave Range, mtns., on bdy. between S. Australia and N.T., **Australia**; isolated high-

land in ctr. of continent; arid; rise to 1,520 m.

Musselburgh, burgh, East Lothian, **Scot.**; on F. of Forth at mouth of R. Esk; wire, cables, nets, twine; paper mkg.; golf course; p. (2002) 22,112.

Mutankiang. See Mudanjiang.

Mutari. See Umtali.

Muttra. See Mathura.

Muzaffarnagar, t., Uttar Pradesh, **India**; N.E. of Delhi; p. (1991) 240,609.

Muzaffarpur, t., Bihar, **India**; in middle Ganges valley N. of Patna; p. (1991) 241,107.

Mwanza, t., N. **Tanzania**; pt. on L. Victoria; rly. term.; gold and diamonds mined; p. (1988) 233,013.

Mweru, L., between Congo and Zambia; a. 6,993 km² at c. 900 m.

Myanmar, Union of, until 1989 Burma; rep., S.E. Asia; Irrawaddy R. basin, developed by British in 19th cent., forms major cluster of p., routeways and source of rice of which M. is one of few exporters; surrounding mtns. relatively underdeveloped, although they are a source of teak and hardwood exps.; almost self-sufficient in petroleum from deposits in N.; natural gas prod. increasingly impt.; monsoon climate; p. mainly Buddhist; secessionist moves in Muslim Arakan st., ch. ts., Mandalay, cap. Rangoon; repressive govt., a. 676,580 km²; p. (2004) 42,720,196.

Mycenae, anc. c., N.E. Peloponnesus, **Greece**; excavations by Schliemann.

Myingyan, t., **Myanmar**; on R. Irrawaddy, S.W. of Mandalay; cotton spinning mill, zinc smelting, chemicals, fertilisers.

Myitkyina, t., **Myanmar**; on R. Irrawaddy; terminus of caravan route to China.

Mymensingh, t., **Bangladesh**; rice, jute; p. (1991) 185,517

Mysłowice, t., Katowice, **Poland**; ctr. of coal-mng. dist.; technical porcelain; p. (1995) 79,960.

Mysore. See Karnataka.

Mysore, t., Karnataka, **India**; univ.; new inds. based on hydroelec. power; p. (1991) 481,000.

N

Naantali, t., S.W. **Finland**; pt. for Turku, on Baltic Sea; oil-refining, chemicals; founded 15th cent.

Naas, co. t., Co. Kildare, **R.o.I.**; former cap. of Leinster prov.; p. (1986) 10,017.

Nabeul, governorate, **Tunisia**, N. Africa; p. (1984) 461,405.

Nablus, t., **Jordan**, N. of Jerusalem; nr. site of anc. Schechem and Jacob's Well.

Nadiad, t., Gujarat, **India**; S. of Ahmadabad; p. (1991) 167,051.

Nagaland, st., **India** formerly part of Assam, separate st. since 1963; many border disputes; incorporates Naga Hills and Tuengsang; tribal a., cap. Kohima; a. 16,488 km²; p. (2001) 1,988,600.

Nagano, c., central Honshu, **Japan**; on R. Sinanogawa, 160 km S.W. of Nigata; cultural ctr.; publishing, machin., food-processing; textiles; 1998 Winter Olympics; p. (1990) 347,036.

Nagaoka, t., N.W. Honshu, **Japan**; lge. oil production ctr.; p. (1990) 185,938.

Nagasaki, c., spt., Kyushu, **Japan**; on narrow peninsula; second c. destroyed by atomic bomb in second world war; impt. shipbldg. ctr. and associated engin.; p. (1990) 444,616.

Nagercoil, t., Tamil Nadu, **India**; extreme S. of Indian peninsula; coconut-processing; p. (1991) 190,084

Nagh Hamadi (Nag' Hammâdi), t., Upper **Egypt**; on R. Nile 256 km above Asyût; site of barrage (opened 1930) to regulate Nile flood and ensure irrigation of Girga prov.; barrage carries Cairo-Shellal rly. across Nile.

Nagorno-Karabakh, aut. oblast, S.W. **Azerbaijan**; on E. of Lesser Caucasus; forested mtns.; unrest 1990; cap. Stepanakert; a. 4,403 km²; p. (1990) 192,400.

Nagoya, third c. of **Japan**; on Ise Bay, central Honshu; major pt. and industl. ctr.; univ.; textile mills, ceramic ctr., oil-refining; 16th cent. fortress t.; p. (2000) 3,157,000 (met. a.) 8,852,000.

Nagpur, c., Maharashtra st., **India**; univ.; admin. ctr.; textiles; Hindu temples; p. (1991) 1,625,000.

Nagy Banya. See Baia-Mare.

Nagykanizsa, t., S.W. Hungary; industl. ctr.; heavy equipment, glasswks., beer; p. (1997) 52,000.

Nagymáros, t., Hungary; on Danube R. between Budapest and Austrian border; site of hydro-electr. dam built jointly with Austria.

Nailsworth, t., Gloucs., Eng.; in Cotswold Hills 6 km S. of Stroud; p. (1991) 5,242.

Nairn, royal burgh, Highland, N.E. Scot.; fishing ctr.; cas.; p. (2002) 8,418.

Nairnshire, historic co., E. Scot., now part of Highland.

Nairobi, c., cap. of Kenya; stands at c. 1,500 m on edge of Kenya highlands; c., 528 km from Mombasa; univ.; tourist ctr.; lt. inds.; steel rolling mill; inland ctr. for containers; wildlife game reserve; p. (2000) 2,310,000.

Najaf or Nejef, c., Iraq; in Euphrates valley; major Shiite Muslim pilgrimage ctr.; p. (2004) 600,000 (est.).

Nakhichevan, c. Azerbaijan, food and wine inds.; ctr. of Nakhichevan aut. region; p. (1000) 60,100.

Nakhicheva, aut. rep. Azerbaijan; borders Iran and Turkey; cotton, tobacco, rice, wheat in irrigated lowlands; salt and mineral deposits; a. 5,439 km²; p. (1990) 300,400.

Nakhodka, t., Russia; outpt. for Vladivostok on Sea of Japan; p. (1989) 160,000.

Nakhon Pathom, t., Thailand; in central plain, S.W. of Bangkok; mkt. t.; p. (1980) 45,242.

Nakhon Ratchasima, t., Thailand; on Mun R., in Korat plateau; rly. junc.; copper deposits nearby; p. (1991) 202,503.

Nakhon si Thammarat, t., Thailand; in S. of Isthmus of Kra, on G. of Thailand; anc. t.; mkt.

Nalchik, c., cap. of Kabardino-Balkar aut. rep., Russia; in foothills of N. Caucasus; food-processing; tourist resort; p. (1989) 235,000.

Namangan, c., Uzbekistan; on Syr Dar'ya R., in Ferghana Valley; textiles, leather; p. (2001) 340,000.

Namaqualand, region, S.W. cst. of Africa; divided by Orange R. into Gr. N. in Namibia, and Little N. in Cape Prov., Rep. of S. Africa; semi-arid; a. 259,000 km²; copper, diamonds.

Namhol. See Foshan.

Namib Desert, desert a. along S.W. coastal strip of Africa for 1,200 km; very dry a., and almost unused.

Namibia, indep. st. (1990); formerly mandated territory under S.Af. rule; became (1990) 50th member of Commonwealth; scanty rainfall; stock rearing; alluvial diamonds from Lüderitz on Orange R.; copper, lead, zinc mng. in Grootfontein dist.; coal and offshore natural gas discovered; minerals provide 60 per cent exp. earnings; ch. pt. Walvis Bay; cap. Windhoek; summer cap. Swakopmund; a. 824,296 km²; p. (2004) 1,954,033.

Namur, c., cap. of N. prov., Belgium; at confluence of Meuse and Sambre Rs.; agr. process-sing, cutlery, glass; p. (1993) 104,372 (c.), 429,536 (prov.).

Nanaimo, t., B.C., Canada; pt. on Vancouver I.; timber and allied inds.; fisheries; boating and yachting; tourism; p. (1996) 85,585.

Nanchong, c., Sichuan, China; on Kan R.; major transportation and industl. ctr.; textiles, machin., chemicals, paper; tractor wks.; dates from Sung dynasty (12th cent.); p. (1994) 330,000.

Nancheng. See Hanzhong.

Nancy, c., Meurthe-et-Moselle dep., France; industl. and admin. ctr.; univ., cath.; chemical ind. (based on local salt); anc. cap. of duchy of Lorraine; p. (1999) 102,603.

Nanda Devi, mtn., Uttar Pradesh, India; in Himalayas, 7,822 m; first scaled, 1936.

Nanded, t., Maharashtra, India; p. (1991) 275,000.

Nanga Parbat, mtn., N.W. Kashmir, India, in W. Himalayas; alt. 8,131 m.

Nanjing (Nanking), c., Jiangsu, China; on Chang Jiang; cap. of China during Kuomintang régime 1928–49; rape of Nanjing, massacre by Japanese troops in 1937 kills 300,000; famous seat of learning; tombs of founders of Ming dynasty; lge. motor vehicle plant, electronics, precision instruments, insecticides, cotton cloth, oil-refining; road-rail bridge over lowest reaches of Chang Jiang opened 1969; p. (1994) 2,225,000.

Nanning, c., cap. of Guangxi prov., China; on Yu R.; ch. mkt. on S. frontier; rice transplanter factory; p. (1994) 829,500.

Nan Shan, mtns., central China; branch range of Kunlun; rise to over 3,600 m.

Nanterre, N.W. sub. of Paris, France; cap. of Hauts-de-Seine dep.; aluminium mftg.; p. (1990) 86,627.

Nantes, spt., cap. of Loire-Atlantique dep., W. France; on R. Loire; ocean pt. St. Nazaire; impt.

industl. and shipping ctr.; univ., cath., cas.; p. (1999) 269,131.

Nantong (Nantung) c., Jiangsu, China; on N. bank of Chang Jiang estuary; cotton; p. (1994) 422,000.

Nantucket, I., Mass., USA; official W. end of trans-Atlantic sea-crossing; former whaling centre; summer resort; fishing; p. (1980) 3,229.

Nantung. See Nantong.

Nantwich, mkt. t., Crewe and N. Cheshire, Eng.; on R. Weaver, 5 km S.W. of Crewe; brine baths; clothing, food prods.; p. (1991) 11,695; see Crewe.

Nantyglo and Blaina, t., Blaenau Gwent, Wales; in narrow valley 3 km N. of Abertillery; footwear, rubber prods.; p. (1981) 9,862.

Napier, c., N.I., N.Z.; pt. and ch. c. of Hawke's Bay prov. dist.; exp. frozen meat; timber processing, fishing; p. (1991) 51,645.

Naples (Napoli), c., Campania, S. Italy; spt. on Bay of N., at foot of Vesuvius, opposite anc. Pompeii; exp. food prods.; impt. industl. ctr.; shipbldg., oil refining, food-processing; cultural and artistic ctr.; univ., cath.; tourism; earthquake, 1980; mudslide, 1998; p. (1992) 1,071,744.

Nara, c., S. Honshu, Japan; anc. religious ctr. and place of pilgrimage; colossal image of Buddha (16·3 m high); cap. of Japan A.D. 710–84; tourism; p. (1990) 349,356.

Nara Basin, Honshu, Japan; agr. dist. serving the Kinki plain; intensive rice cultivation.

Narayanganj, c., Bangladesh; S. of Dacca in middle Ganges delta; p. (1991) 268,952.

Narbonne, t., Aude dep., S. France; in Languedoc; nr. Mediterranean cst.; in wine-growing a.; impt. in Roman times; cath., palace (now town hall); p. (1982) 42,657.

Narew, R., Poland and Russia; flows to R. Vistula nr. Warsaw, c. 432 km long; ch. trib. W. Bug.

Narmada, R., central India; flows W. through Madhya Pradesh and Gujarat to G. of Cambay; 1,280 km long.

Narrabri, t., N.S.W., Australia; 570 km N.W. Sydney; observatory with stellar interferometer; p. (1991) 6,700.

Narva, t., N.E. Estonia; textiles, machin., sawmills; founded by Danes 1223; p. (1991) 87,900.

Narvik, pt., N.W. Norway; sheltered by Lofoten Is.; ice-free; linked by rly. to iron-ore fields in N. Sweden; scene of fierce sea-battles between British and Germans 1940; p. (1990) 13,873.

Naseby, v., Northants., Eng.; battle where parliamentarians under Fairfax and Cromwell beat royalists under Charles I and Prince Rupert 1645.

Nashville, c., st. cap. Tenn., USA; pt. on Cumberland R.; rly. ctr.; impt. shipping, industl. and educational ctr.; food and tobacco prods., cellophane, rayon; univs. and colleges; p. (2000) 569,891 (c.), 985,026 (met. a. with Davidson).

Nasik, t., Maharashtra, India; on R. Godavari; Hindu pilgrimage ctr.; p. (1991) 657,000.

Nassarawa, new st. (since 1996) in north of Nigeria. Created from Plateau. Headquarters at Lafia.

Nassau, spt., cap. Bahamas, W.I.; exp. forest, sea and agr. prods.; resort; p. (1999) 214,000.

Nassau, I., Cook Is., S. Pac. Oc.; N.Z. terr.; uninhabited; radio telegraph sta.

Nasser City, t., Egypt; rural development at Kom Ombo, N. of Aswan, for resettlement of 50,000 Nubians before formation of Lake Nasser behind the High Dam.

Natal, spt., cap. of Rio Grande do Norte st., Brazil; above mouth of Potengi R.; exp. sugar, cotton, salt, carnauba wax, hides; industl. expansion; textile mills; airport on main routes from Africa to S. America; p. (1991) 606,541.

Natanya or Nathania, t., Israel; resort on Mediterranean cst.; food-processing; p. (1992) 139,700.

Naucratis, anc. c., Egypt; between Cairo and Alexandria; excavated by Flinders Petrie and Gardiner.

Naumburg, t., Saxony - Anhalt, Germany; on R. Saale; cath.; textiles, leather, toys; p. (1989) 30,706.

Nauplia (Gr. Nauplion), pt. and comm. ctr., on E. cst. Peloponnesus, Greece; the anc. Argos; first cap. of indep. Greece 1830–4, when it was superseded by Athens; p. (1981) 10,611.

Nauru, I., indep. rep. (1967), central Pac. Oc.; formerly admin. by Australia; coral I., heavily dependent on phosphate-mng.; economy in decline now phosphate almost exhausted, 80% uninhabitable because of this; island threatened by rising sea levels; a. 21 km²; p. (2004) 12,809.

Navarre, prov., N. **Spain**; bounded by Pyrenees; thickly wooded; cap. Pamplona; sugar-beet, cereals, cattle, hardwoods, vineyards; former kingdom; p. Basque; p. (1998) 530,800.

Naver, R., Highland, **Scot.**; flows N. to Pentland Firth; valley once densely p., cleared early 19th cent. to make room for sheep.

Naxos, I., **Greece**; in Aegean Sea, lgst. of the Cyclades; famous for wine and fruit; a. 425 km²; p. 19,000.

Nayarit, st. W. **Mexico**; agr.; cap. Tepic; a. 26,979 km²; p. (1990) 816,112.

Nazareth, t., **Israel**; St. Acre; home of Jesus Christ. Pop. (mainly Muslim), 64,300 (1995).

Naze, The, headland in Essex, 5 m. s. of Harwich.

Nazilli, t., S.W. **Turkey**; on R. Menderes; agr., especially olives; p. (1985) 77,627.

N'djamena (founded by French as Fort Lamy), c., cap. of **Chad Rep.**; at confluence of Shari and Logone Rs.; isolated but ctr. of caravan tr.; airpt.; p. (2000) 1,043,000.

Ndola, t., **Zambia**; nr. bdy. with Congo, 176 km by rail N. of Kabwe; ctr. of rich copper-mng. a., less impt. lead- and zinc-mng.; minerals despatched by rail E. to Beira and W. to Lobito Bay; oil refining nearby; international airpt. being built; p. (1989) 467,000.

Neagh, Lough, L., **N. Ireland**; lgst. freshwater L. in Brit. Is.; a. 396 km²; drained by R. Bann.

Neath, t., Neath Pt. Talbot, **Wales**; 10 km up R. Neath from Swansea Bay; coal, aluminium inds., oil refining; cas., abbey; p. (1991) 45,965.

Neath Port Talbot, S. **Wales**, unit. auth. created in 1996 from former l. gov. dists. of Neath and Pt. Talbot; p. (2001) 134,468.

Nebraska, st., **USA**; Cornhusker St.; admitted to Union 1867; st. flower Golden rod, st. bird Western Meadowlark; mainly prairie; cap. Lincoln, farming, meat-packing, wheat, maize, hay, potatoes, sugar-beet, apples, wool, livestock, oil, cement; a. 200,147 km²; p. (2002) 1,729,180.

Neckar, R., **Germany**; rises between Swabian Jura and Black Forest; flows through Baden-Württemberg to Rhine at Mannheim; 384 km long.

Needles, chalk stacks in English Channel, off W. cst. of I. of Wight, **Eng.**

Negev, desert, region, S. **Israel**; new a. of irrigated agr.; oil and natural gas.

Negombo, t., S.W. **Sri Lanka**; at mouth of Negombo lagoon; ctr. of coconut belt; metalware, ceramics; p. (1981) 61,376.

Negril Beach, Jamaica; 40 km W. of Montego Bay; new resort designed to further Jamaica's tourist tr.

Negri Sembilan, st., W. **Malaysia**; on Strait of Malacca; tin and rubber; cap. Seremban; a. 6,682 km²; p. (2005) 860,000.

Negro Rio, R., **Argentina**; flows into G. of St. Mathias. Atl. Oc.; used for irrigation, partly navigable.

Negro Rio, R., **Brazil**; one of ch. tribs. of R. Amazon; rises in Colombia, joins Amazon nr. Manaus; c. 1,520 km long.

Negro Rio, R., **Uruguay**; flows from Brazil border to Uruguay R.; major multi-purpose project at Rincon del Bonete; 800 km long.

Negros, I., **Philippines**; S. of Mindanao; impt. sugar producing I.; copper deposits; a. 12,704 km²; p. (1990) 3,182,219.

Neisse or Nisa, two tribs. of R. Oder. (1) Western or Glatzer Neisse, frontier between Poland and E. Germany, 224 km long, (2) Eastern or Lausitzer Neisse, E. Silesia, Poland, 192 km long.

Neiva, t., **Colombia**; at head of navigation of R. Magdalena, tr. in cattle and coffee; panama hats; p. (1992) 232,610.

Nejd, C. prov.; with Hejaz, forms kingdom of **Saudi Arabia**; mainly desert; impt. oil wells, horses, camels, dates; cap. Riyadh; a. 1,087,800 km²; p. (1991) 316,000.

Nellore, t., Andhra Pradesh, **India**; admin. ctr.; p. (1991) 316,000.

Nelson, R., **Canada**; drains L. Winnipeg to Hudson Bay; length (with its gr. trib. the Saskatchewan) 2,320 km.

Nelson, t., Pendle, Lancs., **Eng.**; on N. flank of Rossendale 5 km N.E. of Burnley; cotton, iron and brick wks., lt. engin., paper; p. (2001) 28,998.

Neman (Pol. Nieman, Ger. Memel), R., **Lithuania** and **Belarus**; rises S.W. of Minsk and flows c. 920 km into Kurisches Haff (Courland Lagoon), Baltic Sea, forming sm. delta.

Nene, R., Northants., **Eng.**; rises nr. Naseby and flows 144 km to the Wash.

Nepal, indep. kingdom, S.E. Asia; on S. slopes of Himalayas and inc. Mt. Everest; isolated from India by malarial forested zone of Terai; N. mostly tropical forest and jungle; home of Gurkhas; poor infrastructure hinders development; oil exploration (2004); agr. in fertile valleys, rice, wheat, maize; forestry impt. but deforestation a problem; growing guerrilla revolt; massacre of royal family (June 2001); cap. Katmandu; a. 141,414 km²; p. (2004) 27,070,666.

Nerbudda. See **Narmada**.

Ness, Loch, Highland, **Scot.**; occupies N.E. end of Glen More; forms link in Caledonian Canal; very deep; 36·4 km long.

Neston, t., Cheshire, **Eng.**; on N. side of Dee estuary; residtl.; sea bed engin.; p. (1991) 15,585; See **Ellesmere Port**.

Nestos, R. See **Mesta**.

Netherlands, kingdom, N.W. Europe; bounded by North Sea, Belgium and by Germany; comprises 11 provs.; since second world war has taken advantage of location at mouth of Rhine, opposite Thames estuary, to develop lge.-scale coastal inds., inc. iron and steel at IJmuiden, oil refining, petrochemicals at major European pt. complex of Rotterdam–Europort; similarly major industl. growth in conurbation of Randstad Holland in steering economy far away from formerly predominant agr. basis; agr. still impt. and major sea-flood control schemes around IJsselmeer and Rhine estuary have created valuable land for intensive agr. in a densely populated cty.; important discoveries of natural gas in Groningen have turned cty. into major supplier of energy for European mkts.; practises advanced policy of social welfare; EU member; cap. Amsterdam; seat of govt. at The Hague; a. 36,175 km²; p. (2004) 16,318,199

Netherlands Antilles, 2 gr. of Is. in Caribbean Sea, part of Lesser Antilles; main gr. off Venezuela inc. Curaçao, Bonaire and formerly Aruba; 2nd gr. inc. volcanic Is. of St. Eustatius, Saba, and St. Maarten (S. part only); agr. of sm. importance as a result of low rainfall; benefits from Venezuelan oil ind.; oil refineries in Curaçao; petrochemical inds.; indep. planned; Aruba separated (1986) with full internal self- government; cap. Willemstad; a. 1,020 km²; p. (2004) 218,126.

Netze. See **Notec**.

Neubrandenburg, c., Brandenburg, N. **Germany**; fibreglass, machin., chemicals; p. (1982) 620,600 (dist.).

Neuchâtel, can., **Switzerland**; in Jura mtns.; forested with some pastures; cattle, cheese, wine; watches, cutlery, cottons, hosiery; asphalt from Val de Travers; a. 800 km²; p. (1990) 160,600.

Neuchâtel, cap. of Neuchâtel can., **Switzerland**; on N. slope of Lake Neuchâtel; cas.; univ.; watches, jewellery, condensed milk; p. (1990) 33,060.

Neuchâtel, L., **Switzerland**; at S.E. foot of Jura mtns.; drains N.E. to R. Aare; vineyards on S. facing slopes; remains of lake dwellings, anc. Celtic site of La Tène culture.

Neuilly-sur-Seine, sub., W. of Paris, Hauts-de-Seine, **France**; fine bridge and cas.; engin.; p. (1999) 58,571.

Neumünster, t., Schleswig-Holstein, **Germany**; rly. ctr.; leather, paper and textile inds., p. (2002) 79,646.

Neunkirchen, t., Saarland, **Germany**; iron and steel mngs.; coal ming.; p. (2002) 50,664.

Neuquén, prov., S. **Argentina**; natural gas reserves; pipeline planned; p. (1991) 388,833.

Neuquén, t., cap. of N. prov., **Argentina**; at confluence of Rs. Limay and Neuquén, in ctr. of fruit farming dist.; p. (1991) 243,803.

Neusalz. See **Nowa Sól**.

Neusandetz. See **Nowy Sacz**.

Neuss, c., N. Rhine–Westphalia, **Germany**; rly. junc., canal pt.; nr. Rhine, opposite Düsseldorf; metal gds., food-processing; p. (2002) 150,957.

Neustadt, t., Rhineland-Palatinate, **Germany**; on R. Haardt; agr. machinery; impt. wine tr.; p. (1990) 147,200.

Neustadt. See **Wiener-Neustadt**.

Neva, R., **Russia**, on which St. Petersburg stands; drains L. Ladoga to G. of Finland; navigable but liable to flooding; 74 km long.

Nevada, st., **USA**; Silver St.; admitted to Union 1864; st. flower Sagebrush, st. bird Mountain Bluebird; in Rocky mtns., continental climate; mng. basis of economy gold, silver, copper, tungsten, gypsum, iron, lead; livestock agr.; timber; tourism; ts. inc.

Las Vegas and cap. Carson City; a. 286,299 km²; p. (2002) 2,173,491.

Nevers, c., cap. of Nièvre dep., **France**; on R. Loire; anc. iron and steel ind.; porcelain and faience; cath., historic bldgs.; p. (1999) 40,928.

Nevis, I., **Lesser Antilles**, W.I.; cotton, sugar; ch. t. Charlestown; part of ind. country of St. Kitts-Nevis; separatist demands (1997); a. 130 km²; p. (1991) 8,794.

New Amsterdam, Dutch settlement, Manhattan I., **USA**; taken by English 1664, renamed New York.

Newark, mkt. t., part of l. gov. dist. of Newark and Sherwood, Notts., **Eng.**; on R. Trent 27 km N.E. of Nottingham; ball bearings, brewing and malting; cas.; coal mining at Bilsthorpe; p. (2001) 106,273 (dist.), (2001) 35,454 (t.).

Newark, c., N.J., **USA**; meat-packing, printing, elec. gds., paints, chemicals, cars aircraft, leather; airport; p. (2000) 273,546 (c.), 1,824,000 (met. a.).

New Bedford, c., spt., Mass., **USA**; on estuary of R. Acushnet; whale fishery ctr.; mnfs. cottons, cordage, glass, shoes; resort; p. (1996) 96,903.

Newbiggin-by-the-Sea, t., Wansbeck, Northumberland, **Eng.**; sm. seaside resort; p. (1991) 7,100.

New Brighton, t., Merseyside, **Eng.**; at entrance to Mersey estuary; residtl. dist. of Wallasey, resort.

New Britain, lgst. I., Bismarck Archipelago, **Papua New Guinea**; volcanic mtns.; exp. copra, cacao; a. (with adjacent Is.) 37,814 km²; p. (1990) 311,955.

New Britain, t., Conn., **USA**; iron and brass mnfs.

New Brunswick, maritime prov., **Canada**; forest-clad mtns.; impt. timber inds.; fishing and fish-processing; many minerals; road and rail link with Prince Edward I.; cap. Fredericton; a. 72,481 km²; p. (1991) 723,900.

New Brunswick, t., N.J., **USA**; on Raritan R.; chemicals, motor lorries, leather, hosiery and hardware; univ.; p. (1996) 738,795 (met. a.).

Newburgh, burgh, Fife, **Scot.**; on S. side of F. of Tay, 13 km E. of Perth; fish. ind.; former linoleum industry; p. (2002) 1,954.

Newburn, t., Tyne and Wear, **Eng.**; on R. Tyne 5 km W. of Newcastle; pure graphite for nuclear reactors; p. (2001) 41,294.

Newbury, t., l. gov. dist., Berks., **Eng.**; on R. Kennet, 27 km S.W. of Reading; engin., furniture, paper, cardboard box making; mkt.; race-course; controversial by-pass opened, 1998; p. (2001) 32,675 (t.).

New Caledonia, overseas terr. of **France**; volcanic I. in S. Pac. Oc.; nickel and chrome deposits; nickel processing; cap. Nouméa; independence movements to establish separate Melanesian reg. in S. Pacific and much unrest since 1984; referendum on full independence planned; a. 22,139 km² p. (2004) 213,679.

Newcastle, c., N.S.W., **Australia**; spt. at mouth of R. Hunter; second c. of st.; lgst. exporter of coal in Australia; iron and steel based on coal resources; new inds. on reclaimed land; mineral sand mng. (rutile, zircon); p. (1993) 454,800 (met. a.).

Newcastle, spt., on Dundrum Bay, Down, **N. Ireland**; resort; p. (1991) 7,214.

Newcastle-under-Lyme, t., l. gov. dist., Staffs., **Eng.**; 3 km W. of Stoke-on-Trent, on Lyme Brook; coal mng.; brick and tile mnfs.; p. (2001) 122,030 (dist.), (2001) 74,427 (t.).

Newcastle upon Tyne, c., met. dist., Tyne and Wear, **Eng.**; spt. on N. bank of Tyne R., 16 km from N. Sea; shipbldg., heavy engin., chemicals; connected by bridges across Tyne to Gateshead; univs., cath.; many fine public bldgs.; partially preserved in redevelopment of c. ctr.; airport; metro system; p. (2001) 259,536 (dist.), (2001) 189,863 (c.).

New Delhi. See Delhi.

New England, N.S.W., **Australia**; dist. of N. Tablelands; pastoral cty. for sheep and beef; ch. ts. Armidale, Glen Innes, and Tenterfield.

New England, the six N.E. Atl. sts. of **USA**; Me., N.H., Vt., Mass., R.I., Conn.; humid-continental climate, infertile soils, poor agr. conditions; fishing; recent industl. metamorphosis as traditional inds. are replaced by modern science-based, high-value inds.; tourism; ch. t. Boston; p. (1990) 13,206,943.

Newent, mkt. t., Gloucs., **Eng.**; 13 km S. of Ledbury.

New Forest, forest and heathland, Hants., **Eng.**; relic of Royal Forest; now partly owned by Forestry Commission; proposed as new National Park (1999); pasture, ponies, tourism, residtl.; oil reserves but no drilling yet as conflicts with conservation; ch. t. Lyndhurst; forms l. gov. dist.; p. (2001) 169,331.

Newfoundland and Labrador, prov., of **Canada**; E. of the G. of St. Lawrence; in E. low; in W. rugged mtns., many Ls.; coniferous forest; fishing, cod, salmon, halibut, lobster, seal; lumber, wood-pulp, paper; iron ore, lead, zinc, copper, asbestos; hydroelec. power; climate is severe; cap. St. John's; a. prov. 404,519 km² (I. 112,300 km², Labrador 292,219 km²); p. (1996) 551,792.

New Galloway, burgh, Dumfries and Galloway, **Scot.**; on R. Dee; nearby Clatteringshaws hydroelec. sta.

New Guinea, I., S.W. Pac. Oc.; N. of Australia; equatorial climate; dense forest; central mtn. chain; lge. a. of lowland in S.; divided politically between Irian Jaya in W. (Indonesia) and Papua New Guinea in E.; economically underdeveloped; a. 831,390 km². See Papua New Guinea, Irian Jaya.

Newham, inner bor., Greater London, **Eng.**; W. of R. Lea; contained Royal group of London docks (now all closed); p. and industl. decentralisation from a.; proposed Stratford City devel., one of largest in London; p. (2001) 243,891.

New Hampshire, st., New England, **USA**; borders on **Canada**; Granite St.; admitted to Union 1788; st. flower Purple Lilac, st. bird Purple Finch; forested mtns.; agr., fruit-growing; paper and forest prods.; textiles, shoes; granite; cap. Concord; ch. spt. Portsmouth; ch. mftg. ctr. Manchester; a. 24,097 km²; p. (2002) 1,275,056.

Newhaven, t., East Sussex, **Eng.**; on S. cst. at mouth of R. Ouse, 14 km E. of Brighton; passenger pt. for Dieppe; boat-bldg. and lt. indus.; p. (1991) 11,208.

New Haven, c., pt., Conn., **USA**; on inlet of Long I. Sound; Yale Univ.; firearms, clocks, hardware, radiators, rubber gds.; p. (1990) 130,374 (c.), 530,000. (met. a. with Meriden).

New Hebrides. See Vanuatu.

New Holland, v., N. Lincs., **Eng.**; rly. terminus, ferry pt. for crossing to Hull.

New Ireland, volcanic I., **Papua New Guinea**, in Bismarck archipelago; mtnous.; ch. pt. Kavieng; exp. copra; a. (with adjacent Is.) 9,842 km²; p. (1990) 87,194.

New Jersey, st., **USA**; Garden St.; admitted to Union 1787; st. flower Purple Violet. st. bird Eastern Gold Finch; on Atl. cst. plain, adjacent to N.Y. c.; intensive agr., mkt. gardening; heavily industrialised; oil refining, glass sand, zinc, iron ore, clay, chemicals, motor vehicles; cap. Trenton; ch. cs. Newark, Jersey City; a. 20,295 km²; p. (2002) 8,590,300.

Newmarket, t., Forest Heath, Suffolk, **Eng.**; at foot of E. Anglian Heights; horse racing centre; p. (1991) 16,199.

New Mexico, st., **USA**; popular name "Land of Enchantment"; admitted to Union 1912; st. flower Yucca, st. bird Road Runner; N. of Mexico, S. of Col. st.; traversed by Rocky mtns.; dry climate; agr. dependent upon irrigation; dry farming, arable crops, livestock; uranium, potash salts, pumice, beryllium, copper, petroleum; ch. ts., Albuquerque and cap. Santa Fé; a. 315,115 km²; p. (2002) 1,855,059.

New Mills, industl. t., High Peak, Derbys., **Eng.**; at W. foot of Pennines; textile printing, bleaching and dyeing; rayon, paper; p. (1991) 9,092.

Newmilns and Greenholm, burgh, E. Ayrshire, **Scot.**; on R. Irvine, 19 km E. of Kilmarnock; muslin and lace curtain mnf.; p. (2002) 3,057.

New Mirpir, t., **Pakistan**; new t. 3 km. from old Mirpur submerged by Mangla L. 1967.

New Orleans, c., spt., La., **USA**; on delta of Mississippi R.; the gr. cotton mart of America, busy comm., mftg. and cultural ctr., home of jazz; sugar refining, oil refining; devastation caused by Hurricane Katrina and massive flooding (2005); city evacuated.

New Plymouth, dist., N.I., **N.Z.**; on W. cst. at N. foot of Mt. Egmont; oil and natural gas deposits; dairy-farming; p. (1991) 67,951.

Newport-on-Tay, burgh, Fife, **Scot.**; on S. side of F. of Tay, opposite Dundee; p. (2002) 4,214.

Newport, cap. I. of Wight, **Eng.**; on R. Medina, in gap through central chalk ridge; mkt.; brewing, joinery, bait mnfs.; prison; p. (2001) 22,957.

Newport, mkt. t., The Wrekin, Shrops., **Eng.**; 13 km N.E. of Wellington; p. (1991) 10,964.

Newport, spt., **Vietnam**; on N. outskirts of Ho Chi-minh City; lge. pt. inaugurated 1967.

Newport, t., R.I., **USA**; on Narragansett Bay; fashionable seaside resort; precision instruments; p. (1996) 24,295.

Newport, c., unit. auth. created in 1996 from former l. gov. dist., S.E. **Wales**; on R. Usk, 8 km from its mouth; timber terminal and deep-water berth; engin., iron and steel, aluminium, paperboard, confectionery, chemicals, plastics; p. (1991) 115,522 (c.), (2001) 137,011 (unit. auth.). Created a city, 2002.

Newport News, c., spt., Va., **USA**; on N. shore of estuary of James R. on Hampton Roads; lge. harbour; shipbldg.; outlet for Virginian tobacco and Appalachian coal; p. (1990) 170,045 (c.), 1,396,000 (met. a. with Norfolk-Virginia Beach).

Newport Pagnell, mkt. t., Bucks., **Eng.**; on R. Ouse; mnfs. Aston Martin cars; p. (1991) 12,285.

New Quay, t., Ceredigion, **Wales**; on cst. of Cardigan Bay; fishing; resort; p. (1981) 766.

Newquay, t., Restormel, Cornwall, **Eng.**; on N. Cornish cst.; seaside resort; p. (1991) 17,390.

New Radnor, t., Powys, **Wales**; on slope of Radnor Forest, 10 km S.W. of Presteign.

New Romney, t., Shepway, Kent, **Eng.**; nr. S. cst. to E. of Dungeness; in rich agr. dist. of Romney Marsh; Cinque pt.; old harbour silted up by shingle, now a mile from sea; p. (1991) 8,340.

New Ross, mkt. t. Wexford, **R.o.I.**; brewing and malting; p. (1986) 5,343.

Newry, c., Newry and Mourne, **N. Ireland**; pt. at head of Carlingford Lough; machin., rope, brewing; p. (1991) 21,633. Created a city, 2002.

Newry and Mourne, l. gov. dist., **N. Ireland**; surrounds t. of N., borders R.o.I., Irish Sea; inc. Mtns. of Mourne; p. (2001) 87,058.

New South Wales, st., S.E. **Australia**; first col. established by Brit. in A.; much mineral wealth in tablelands and mtns.; climate equable and well suited to both arable and pastoral agr.; leading agr. st. in Australia; major irrigation schemes in drier E. plains of Murray, Murrumbidgee, and Lachlan Rs.; coal mng. and heavy inds. at Newcastle, Port Kembla, Wollongong; hydroelectric power from Snowy mtns. scheme; lge. concentration of p. in cap. c. of Sydney; major bush fires (2002); a. 801,431 km² (excluding Cap. Terr. of Canberra); p. (1996) 6,038,700.

Newton, t., Mass., **USA**; on R. Charles; in met. a. of Boston; lt. inds.; p. (1996) 80,238.

Newtownabbey, t., l. gov. dist., **N. Ireland**; sub. of Belfast, textiles, lt. inds.; p. (2001) 79,995 (dist.), 56,811 (t.).

Newton Abbot, mkt. t., Teignbridge, Devon, **Eng.**; at head of Teign estuary; rly. junc.; pottery, lt. engin.; agr. processing; p. (1991) 23,801.

Newton Aycliffe, t., Durham, **Eng.**; 10 km N.W. of Darlington; new t. (1947); engin., textiles, plastics, paint; p. (2001) 25,655.

Newton-le-Willows, t., Merseyside, **Eng.**; engin., printing, sugar-refining; p. (2001) 21,307.

Newton-Stewart, burgh, Dumfries and Galloway, **Scot.**; on R. Cree, 8 km N. of Wigtown; mkt.; wool, creameries and agr. inds.; p. (2002) 3,573.

Newtown and **Llanllwchaiarn**, mkt. t., Powys, **Wales**; on R. Severn 13 km S.W. of Montgomery; precision instruments, machine tools; p. (1991) 10,548.

Newtownards, spt., mkt., Ards, **N. Ireland**; 11 km E. of Belfast; textile and engin. inds.; p. (1991) 23,869.

Newtown St Boswells, burgh, Borders, **Scot.**; p. (2002) 1,100.

New Waterway. See Nieuwe Waterweg.

New Westminster, t., B.C., **Canada**; spt. on estuary of R. Fraser; exp. timber; agr. ctr., food-processing and canning; fishing; oil refining; forms part of Vancouver met. a.; p. (1986) 39,972.

New York, st., N.E. **USA**; popular name "Empire St."; admitted to Union 1788; st. flower Rose, st. bird Bluebird; one of 13 original sts., borders Canada on N., faces Atl. Oc. in S.; Adirondack mtns. in N., with lowland in E. alongside L. Ontario; Hudson valley impt. routeway; humid-continental climate; second lgst. st. in p. size and despite p. movement to W., remains major a. of urbanisation (megalopolis) with comm. and industl. activity; ch. ts. inc. Buffalo, Rochester, Syracuse; st. cap. Albany, metropolis New York city; decline of N. ts. offset by inds. from Quebec, leaving Canada because of separatist moves; dairy farming and intensive agr. serve urban mkts.; a. 128,402 km²; p. (2002) 19,157,532.

New York, c., spt., N.Y., **USA**; on N.Y. Bay at mouth of Hudson R.; lgst. c. in USA and one of lgst. in world; comprises 5 bors., Manhattan, Bronx, Queens, Brooklyn, Richmond; originally founded by Dutch settlers as New Amsterdam on Manhattan I.; gr. comm. ctr. and cultural cap.; univ.; fine parks, bridges, skyscrapers, and deepwater harbour; varied inds., inc. clothing, food-processing, printing and publishing, shipbldg.; despite p. and industl. decentralisation concentration of socially needy in c.; devastating terrorist bombing of Manhattan, 2001; 2 intern. airports; p. (2000) 8,008,278 (c.), 8,546.846 (met. a.).

New York State Barge Canal (Erie Canal), N.Y. st., **USA**; links Tonawanda on Niagara R. with Hudson R. via the Mohawk gap through Appalachian mtns.; provides through water route from N.Y. to Gr. Ls.; opened as Erie Canal 1825, improved 1918; length 542 km (with branches 840 km), depth 4 m.

New Zealand, indep. sov. st. within Brit. Commonwealth, S. Pac. Oc.; 1,920 km E. of Sydney, Australia; consists of two major Is., N.I. and S.I., separated by Cook Strait, and several smaller Is., inc. Stewart I. to S.; mtnous., glaciated, volcanic; landscapes with superb scenery; dependent upon pastoral prods., taking advantage of equable climate and excellent grass growing conditions, but mainly reliant on Brit. mkts.; economic diversification; expansion of lt. indus., inc. car assembly, pulp and paper, textiles; oil and natural gas discovered; advanced social services; cap. Wellington; ch. pt. Auckland; a. 268,676 km²; p. (2004) 3,993,817. The Maori name for New Zealand is Aotearoa.

Neyland, t., Pembrokeshire, **Wales**; on Milford Haven, rly. terminus and sm. pt.; p. (1991) 3,006.

Niagara, R., forms part of boundary between **Canada** and **USA**; flows from L. Erie to L. Ontario; rapids and famous falls utilised by gr. hydroelec. power sta. heavily polluted with toxic waste; 56 km long.

Niagara Falls, waterfall, Niagara R., on bdy. of **USA** and **Canada**; in two sections, American (51 m high) and Canadian (48 m high), separated by Goat I.; major tourist attraction and hydroelec. power sta.

Niagara Falls, t., Ontario, **Canada**; opposite the falls; hydroelectric power sta.; timber and agr., inds., tourism; p. (1986) 72,107.

Niagara Falls, c., N.Y., **USA**; extends along summit of cliff for 5 km; paper, flour, aluminium, chemicals, hydroelectric power stas.; univ.; p. (1990) 61,840 (c.), 221,000 (met. a.).

Niamey, t., cap of **Rep. of Niger**, W. Africa; one of the termini (the other is Zinder) of the trans-Sahara motor routes; agr. tr. ctr.; p. (1988) 398,265.

Nicaragua, rep., Central America; civil war (1970), lies across isthmus with Pac. Oc. to W., Caribbean Sea to E.; sparsely populated; central mtn. range, marshy E. cst.; tropical rain forest and climate; limited a. of fertile soils but 70 per cent. p. farmers, main exps. coffee, cotton; industl. growth was based on US investment, gold and silver mng.; food shortages caused by war and US trade embargo; declining coffee exports; devastated by 1998 hurricane; cap. Managua; a. 148,006 km²; p. (2004) 5,359,759.

Nicaragua, Lake, S.W. **Nicaragua**; lgst. L. in Central America; 24 km from Pac. Oc., but discharges into Caribbean via San Juan R.; fisheries; 160 km N.W. to S.E., 67 km S.W. to N.E.

Nice, c., spt., cap. of Alpes Maritimes dep., **France**; on Mediterranean cst., at foot of Alps; pleasant climate and surroundings; adjoins anc. t. of Cimiez; ceded to France 1860 by Sardinia; resort; fruit and flower exp., perfume mftg.; science-based inds.; major airport; p. (1999) 340,486.

Nicobar Is. See Andaman and Nicobar Is.

Nicosia, c., cap. of **Cyprus**; agr. tr. ctr.; textiles, cigarettes, leather, pottery mnfs.; remains of Venetian fortifications; mosques; airport; cap. of admin. dist. of Nicosia; tourism; new name Lefkosia (1995); p. (1997) 250,000.

Nidd, R., trib. of R. Ouse, North Yorks., **Eng.**; 80 km long.

Nidwalden. See Unterwalden.

Nieder Sachsen. See Lower Saxony.

Nièvre, dep., central **France**; traversed by Morvan mtns., forests, arable agr.; cap. Nevers; a. 6,887 km²; p. (1990) 233,300.

Niger, landlocked rep., W. Africa; 90 per cent p.

dependent upon agr. but only 3 per cent of land cultivated; livestock (cattle, sheep, goats), cotton; exp. of groundnuts main source of wealth; rainfall diminishes to N. giving way to Sahara Desert; discovery and exploitation of uranium (1967); fishing in L. Chad; game hunting; close economic ties with France; Muslims 80% of population; numerous military coups; humanitarian crisis (2005); cap. Niamey; a. 1,253,560 km²; p. (2004) 11,360,538.

Niger, R., W. **Africa**; rises nr. sea in outer mtn. zone of W. Africa as R. Tembi, sweeps round by Timbuktu to delta in G. of Guinea, on circuitous course of 4,160 km, receiving its gr. trib., the R. Benue about 400 km from the mouth; navigable for 1,600 km; Kainji (Nigeria) hydroelec. plant and dam opened 1969; now organised by international Niger Basin Authority.

Nigeria, fed rep., W. Africa; within Brit. Commonwealth, susp. 1995–9; federation of 36 sts. climate, wet, tropical in b., increasingly dry to N.; main economic development in S.; exp. agr. prods., especially cocoa; exp. hardwoods; economic growth based on cstal. oil deposits (sulphur free); fall in oil prices causing decline in production and exp.; 2nd oil producer in Africa; former cap. Lagos, lgst. c. Ibadan; cap. Abuja; religious violence, 2000; a. 923,773 km²; p. (2004) 137,253,133 (largest in Africa).

Niigata, c., Honshu, **Japan**; pt. on W. cst. exp. locally produced petroleum; chemical inds.; p. (1990) 486,097.

Nijmegen, c., E. **Neth.**; on R. Waal, nr. German bdr., 18 km S. of Arnhem; Hanse t. in Middle Ages; historic bldgs., univ.; p. (1994) 147,018 (c.), 247,822 (met. a.).

Nijni-Novgorod. *See* Gorki.

Nikko, t., Honshu, **Japan**; famous temples and shrines; tourist resort; p. (1990) 20,128.

Nikolayev, c., cap. of N. oblast, **Ukraine**; major spt. at head of Dnieper–Bug estuary on Black Sea; shipbldg., ctr.; exp. minerals, grains; founded 1784 as fortress; p. (1990) 507,900.

Nikolayevsk, R. pt., Khabarovsk terr., **Russia**; on R. Amur; shipyards; fishing, canning, lumbering, oil refining.

Nikopol, c., **Ukraine**; on Dnieper; manganese mng. ctr.; steel, machin.; pollution; p. (1990) 158,000.

Nikšić, t., **Montenegro**; N. of Cetinje; bauxite mng., growing industl. ctr.; p. (1981) 72,299.

Nile, longest R. in Africa (*see* **White Nile** (Bahr-el-Abiad) and **Blue Nile** (Bahr-el-Azrek);); flows through a longer stretch of basin (over 3,920 km in a direct line) than any other R., and along all its windings measures 6,670 km; on Upper Nile navigation is hindered by sudd (floating vegetation); R. rises April, overflows Sept.; formerly cultivation entirely dependent on annual floods, but now assisted by dams, at Asyût, Aswan, Sennar, for regulating flow and navigation; Aswan High Dam completed 1970, but complex problems of delta erosion and dam-lake silting. *See also* Egypt.

Nilgiri Hills, Tamil Nadu, S. **India**; tea-growing dist.; resort a.

Nîmes, c., cap. of Gard dep., S. **France**; in Cevennes; Roman antiquities, notably Maison Carrée; wines; tourism; p. (1999) 132,909.

Nineveh, celebrated anc. c., **Iraq**, stood on R. bank of upper R. Tigris, opposite modern Mosul.

Ningbo (Ningpo), c., spt., Zhejiang, **China**; 160 km from Shanghai; leading fish, pt., comm. and mnf. ctr.; exp. agr. and fish prods.; c. opened to foreign investment under new economic reforms; p. (1994) 612,000.

Ningxia Hui, aut. region, N.W. **China**; bounded on N. by Inner Mongolia; dry a. but modern irrigation projects allow growth of spring wheat and rice; coal reserves, salt; cap. Yingchuan; a. 66,408 km²; p. (1994) 5,030,000.

Niort, c., cap. of Deux-Sèvres dep., W. **France**; noted for mkt. gardens and leather gds. (gloves); birthplace of Mme de Maintenon; p. (1999) 56,809.

Nipigon, Lake, in Thunder Bay dist., Ont., **Canada**; 106 km long, 74 km wide; studded with Is.; discharges by Nipigon R. to L. Superior.

Nipissing, Lake, S. Ont., **Canada**; 855 km²; drained by French R. to Georgian Bay.

Niš, t., **Serbia**; on R. Nishava; route ctr.; rly. engin.; univ.; p. (1991) 175,555.

Nišava, R., **Serbia**; flows N.W. into R. Morava nr. Niš; valley used by trunk rly. from Belgrade to Istanbul; length over 160 km.

Nishapur, mkt. t., N.E. **Iran**; S.W. of Mashhad; in fertile a.; cotton, fruits; famous turquoise mines nearby; the birthplace of Omar Khayyám; impt. archaeological finds dating from 9th and 10th cent.

Nishinomiya, c., S. Honshu, **Japan**; produces famous liquor called saké; machin., chemicals; p. (1990) 426,919.

Niterói, t., cap. of Rio de Janeiro st., **Brazil**; shipbldg.; residtl. sub. of Rio de Janeiro c. to which it is linked by bridge; p. (1996) 450,100.

Nith, R., S.W. **Scot.**; flows to Solway F., S. of Dumfries; followed by main rly. from Carlisle to Kilmarnock and Glasgow; 114 km long.

Nitra, t. **Slovakia**, on R. Nitra N.E. of Bratislava; first Christian church in region there; agric. industries; p. (1990) 91,000.

Niue (Savage) I., Pac. Oc., one of Cook Is., overseas terr. of N.Z., self government 1974; ch. pt. Alofi; copra, passive uranium reserves, plaited basketware, sweet potatoes; a. 259 km²; p. (2004) 2,156.

Nizamabad, t., Andhra Pradesh, **India**; road and rly. ctr. N. of Hyderabad; p. (1991) 240,924.

Nizhneudinsk, t., W. Irkutsk, **Russia**; new mftg. t.

Nizhniy Novgorod, (Gorki), c., **Russia**; cap. of forested region, on Rs. Oka and Volga; univ., churches, 13th cent. kremlin; gr. industl. ctr. with heavy engin., steel, textiles, chemicals, oil refining, cars, glass, timber inds.; birthplace of Maxim Gorky; p. (2000) 1,458,000.

Nizhniy Tagil, t., **Russia**; in Ural mtns.; metallurgical ctr. using ore from Mt. Visokaya.

No, Lake, Bahr-el-Ghazal prov., **Sudan**; N.E. Africa; vast swamp a., 906 km S.W. of Khartoum; flow of water blocked by papyrus reed and floating weed (sudd)

Nobi Plain, S. Honshu, **Japan**; at head of Ise Bay; consists of low, badly drained alluvial plain on W. under intensive rice cultivation, with higher, drier, terraces on E. under mulberry, vegetables, pine-woods; very dense urban and rural p.; ch. textile and pottery mftg. a. in Japan; inc. cs. Nagoya, Gifu, Yokkaichi; a. 1,865 km².

Nocera Inferiore, t., **Italy**; nr. Naples; vegetable-canning, textile mnfs.; p. (1981) 47,698.

Nogales, Sonora, **Mexico**; mng. and agr. ctr.; p. (1990) 107,119.

Nola, c., **Italy**; at foot of Vesuvius, 19 km N.E. of Naples; ctr. of fertile arable agr. a. in Campania plain; anc. c., home of Giordano Bruno; p. (1981) 30,979.

Nome, c., W. Alaska, **USA**; on Seward peninsula; gold rush (1900).

Noord Brabant, prov., **Neth.**; s. of Gelderland; N. half former Duchy; cattle, grain, hops; cap. 's-Hertogenbosch; a. 4,973 km²; p. (1994) 2,259,779.

Noord Holland, prov. **Neth.**; a. 2,709 km²; Haarlem; natural gas in Schermer Polder nr. Alkmaar; p. (1994) 2,457,329.

Noordoostpolder, Overijssel, **Neth.**; land reclaimed from Zuider Zee, 1942; now used for intensive agr.; a. 479 km²; p. (1993) 39,053.

Nord, dep., N. **France**; borders on Belgium and N. Sea; flourishing agr., mng. iron and coal, textile and chemical mnfs.; cap. Lille; a. 5,773 km²; p. (1999) 2,550,784.

Norderney, one of the E. Frisian Is., **Germany**; low-lying sand-dunes; resort at Nordseebad.

Nordhorn, t., Lower Saxony, **Germany**; nr. Neth. frontier; textiles; p. (2002) 52,479.

Nordkyn, Cape, northernmost pt. of European mainland, Finnmark prov., N. **Norway**.

Nordland, co., N. **Norway**; fjord cst.; p. on cst. lowlands; fishing, livestock; iron-ore, electro-chemical and metallurgical inds. based on local hydroelec. power; spt. Narvik; a. 38,146 km²; p. (1990) 238,345.

Nord-Pas-de-Calais, region, N.E. **France**; inc. deps. Nord, Pas-de-Calais; north-eastern corner of France, bordering Belgium; inc. ports of Boulogne, Calais, Dunkirk and southern end of Channel Tunnel; p. (1999) 3,992,284.

Norfolk, non-met. co., E. **Eng.**; low-lying fens in W.; low sandy cst. suffers from erosion; intensive arable agr. on lge. farms; wheat, barley, root crops; inds. based on agr. processing and provision of agr. requisites; tourism on Norfolk Broads; co. t.. Norwich; p. (2001) 796,728.

Norfolk, c., Va., **USA**; naval base on Hampton Roads; fine deepwater harbour; exp. coal, industl. prods.; shipbldg., car assembly, food-processing, timber inds., fertilisers; p. (2000) 234,403 (c.),

1,396,107 (met. a. with Virginia Beach-Newport News).

Norfolk I., remote dependency of **Australia**; Pac. Oc.; volcanic I., 1,676 km N.E. of Sydney; unique ecology; fertile agr.; discovered by Cook 1774; penal settlement 1788-1853; tourism; tax haven; highest pt., Mt. Bates, 319m; a. 34 km²; p. (2004) 1,841.

Norilsk, t., Krasnoyarsk terr., **Russia**; in N. Siberia; northernmost t. in Russia; mng. of coal, uranium, nickel (largest in world), copper; natural gas pipeline from W. Siberia; p. (1989) 175,000.

Normandy, historic prov. of **France**; on English Channel; now divided into deps. Manche, Calvados, Eure, Seine-Maritime and part of Orne; Rouen was cap.; Channel Is. were part of the old duchy; conquered England 1066; allied invasion of Europe 1944.

Normanton, t., West Yorks., **Eng.**; 5 km N.E. of Wakefield; coal mng.; p. (1991) 18,775.

Norrbotten, prov., N. **Sweden**; rich iron deposits at Kiruna; ore exp. via ice-free Narvik on Norwegian cst.; many Ls. and Rs., highest peak in Sweden, Kebnekaise; cap. Pitea; a. 105,553 km²; p. (1992) 266,089.

Norris Dam, Tenn., **USA**; across R. Clinch at confluence with R. Tennessee, N.W. of Knoxville; lgst. dam Tenn. Valley Authority (TVA); built for flood control and hydroelectric power.

Norrköping, c., S.E. **Sweden**; nr. inlet of Baltic Sea; industl. and shipping ctr.; ocean-going shipping through Lindö canal; p. (1992) 120,798.

Northallerton, mkt. t., Hambleton, North Yorks., admin. ctr., **Eng.**; in broad gap between Cleveland hills and Pennines; in dairy farming and agr. dist.; p. (1991) 13,774.

North America, northern continent of W. hemisphere; comprises Greenland (on N. American continental shelf), Canada, USA, Mexico; high W. Cordilleras, inc. Rocky mtns., run N. to S. from Alaska to Mexico; lower range of Appalachian mtns. in E. with vast interior basin, inc. Gr. Ls., Saskatchewan, St. Lawrence, and Miss.-Mo. R. systems; gr. variation in climate and vegetation from subtropical in S. and Mediterranean in W. to Arctic in N. and continental in interior; enormous endowment of natural resources provide basis for vast economies of USA and Canada, but contemporary public concern for natural environment of continent; formerly inhabited by Indians, now mainly occupied by a white p. with lge. European minorities, and an African-based, black p.

Northampton, co. t., l. gov. dist., Northants., **Eng.**; on R. Nene; footwear, engin., leather prods.; new t. designation; univ.; p. (2001) 194,458 (dist.)

Northamptonshire, non-met. co., **Eng.**; E. Midlands; chiefly agr.; iron mng. and mftg.; footwear, engin., leather; p. (2001) 629,676.

North Atlantic Drift, drift of surface waters of Atl. Oc. N.E. from Gulf Stream towards Europe; relatively warm; supplies prevailing S.W. winds with warmth and moisture to modify climate of Brit. Is. and N.W. Europe.

North Ayrshire, unit. auth. created in 1996, formerly part of Strathclyde, W. **Scot.**, borders F. of Clyde and inc. I. of Arran; p. (2002) 135,650.

North Bay, t., Ont., **Canada**; on L. Nipissing; air base; tourism, route ctr.; p. (1996) 64,785.

North Berwick, royal burgh, E. Lothian, **Scot.**; on S of F. of Forth, 32 km E. of Edinburgh; seaside resort, golf course; fishing pt.; p. (2002) 6,223.

North Carolina, st., S.E. **USA**; Tarheel St.; admitted to Union 1789; st. flower Flowering Dogwood., st. bird Cardinal; bounded on E. by Atl. Oc.; one of 13 original sts.; sandy, indented cst., rising in W. to Appalachian mtns.; humid subtropical climate, modified by alt.; agr. impt., maize, cotton, tobacco; mica; textiles; ch. pt. Wilmington; cap. Raleigh; a. 136,524 km²; p. (2002) 8,320,146.

North Channel, gives access from Atl. Oc. to Irish Sea between S.W. Scotland (Dumfries and Galloway) and N.E. Ireland (Larne); length 96 km; narrowest width 24 km.

North China Plain, China; alluvial lowland of Huang-He basin; notorious floods but R. now controlled; wheat and millets; very dense population.

North Cornwall, l. gov. dist., **Eng.**; lge. a. on cst. stretching from Bodmin to Bude; p. (2001) 80,509.

North Crimean Canal, Ukraine; links R. Dnieper with Black Sea and Sea of Azov, crossing steppes

of S. Ukraine and Crimea, terminating at Kerch; first section (123 km long) opened 1963; when completed will be 352 km long, 200 km of which will be navigable.

North Dakota, st., N.W. **USA**; Flickertail St.; admitted to Union 1889; st. flower Wild Prairie Rose, st. bird Western Meadowlark; rolling prairie, rising from E.-W.; drained by Missouri R., controlled by multi-purpose Garrison Reservoir; arable agr., mainly grains, but eroded "Badlands" in S.; coal mng., petroleum; cap. Bismarck; a. 183,022 km²; p. (2002) 634,110.

North Devon, l. gov. dist., **Eng.**; inc. Exmoor and ts. of Barnstaple, Ilfracombe and Lynton; p. (2001) 87,508.

North Dorset, l. gov. dist., Dorset, **Eng.**; mainly rural but inc. ts. of Shaftesbury, Sturminster Newton and Blandford Forum; p. (2001) 61,905.

North Down, l. gov. dist., N. **Ireland**; borders Belfast Lough; main ts. Bangor, Holywood; p. (2001) 76,323.

North Downs, Surrey/Kent, **Eng.**; chalk escarpment running E. to W. across S.E. Eng.; form "white cliffs of Dover"; followed in part by Pilgrim's Way; Box Hill 233 m.

North-East China, formerly known as Manchuria, comprising provs.—Liaoning, Jilin, Heilongjiang; mtnous., N.W. and E.; drained to N. by Songhua Jiang and S. by Liao Rs.; forested; soya-beans, wheat, coal, iron; impt. a. for iron and steel; occupied by Japanese in 1931 and returned to China in 1947.

North East Derbyshire, l. gov. dist., Derbys., **Eng.**; industl. a. of Clay Cross and Dronfield; p. (2001) 96,940.

North-East Frontier Agency. See Arunachal Pradesh.

North East Lincolnshire, unit. auth. created in 1996, formerly part of Humberside, **Eng.**; inc. t. of Great Grimsby and Humberside resort of Cleethorpes; p. (2001) 157,979.

North East Passage, along N. cst. Europe and Asia between Atl. and Pac. See Section L.

Northern Cape, coastal prov., **Rep. of S. Africa**, arid plains, Karoo Bushland, Orange River; several national parks: sheep, dried fruit, wine, tourism, nature conservation, minerals, diamonds, iron ore, copper, asbestos, manganese, fluorspar, marble, fruit, wheat, peanuts, maize, cotton, pelts; cap. Kimberley; a. 361,830 km²; p. (1996) 840,000.

Northern Ireland, part of **UK.**; occupies N.E. a. of Ireland, consisting of 26 l. gov. dists.; mild, temperate climate, exploited by dairy farming using excellent grass; arable agr. inc. barley, potatoes; traditional inds. inc. linen, shipbldg., food-processing, tobacco; modern inds. encouraged by extensive government aid inc. artificial fibres, carpets, elec. and aero-engin.; heavily dependent upon Brit. mkt.; serious social disturbance after 1969, based upon longstanding religious differences between Roman Catholic and Protestant as a result of discrimination against minority; Catholics now (2001) 44 % of pop., Protestants 53 %; Stormont Parliament replaced by Assembly (suspended 29 May 1974 and direct rule resumed); new Assembly created (see Section D); returns 18 members to Westminster (17 prior to May 1997 general election); a. 14,121 km²; p. (2006) 1,700,000.

Northern Marianas, chain of Is., W. Pac.; former US Trust Terr. now a commonwealth in union with USA; a. 479 km²; p. (2004) 78,252.

Northern Province, prov., **Rep. of S. Africa**, bordering Botswana, Zimbabwe and Mozambique; savannah, bushveld, mountains, forests, Limpopo River, Kruger National Park; grapes, sunflowers, cotton, maize, nuts, tea, coffee, timber, fruits, cattle, ranching, hunting, copper, asbestos, coal, iron ore, platinum, chrome, diamonds, phosphates, tourism; cap. Pietersburg; a. 123,910 km²; p. (1996) 4·929 m. Current (2005) plans to rename province Limpopo.

Northern Territory, self governing st. (1978) N. **Australia**; variable rainfall decreasing inland from N. to S.; land rises generally N. to S. and reaches over 1,800 m in Macdonnell ranges; lge. semi-nomadic Aboriginal p.; livestock agr. dependent upon rail, road access to mkt.; mng.; newly opened uranium mines abuse aborigine terr.; ch. ts. Darwin on N. cst., Alice Springs; a. 1,356,176 km²; p. (1996) 195,100.

Northfleet, t., Kent, **Eng.**; on S. bank of R. Thames, adjoining Gravesend; cement, paper, rubber, tyres, cables; p. (2001) 23,457.

North Foreland, E. Kent, Eng.; chalk headland.

North Hertfordshire, l. gov. dist., Herts., Eng.; stretches from Baldock, Letchworth and Hitchin to Royston; p. (2001) 116,908.

North Island, I., **N.Z.;** one of the two major Is. of N.Z., separated from S.I. by Cook Strait, volcanic mtns., Waikato R. drains L. Taupo, cap. Wellington, spt. Auckland, oil deposits on E. and W. csts.; a. 114,688 km²; p. (1991) 2,553,413.

North Kesteven, l. gov. dist., Lincs., Eng.; rural a. based on Sleaford; p. (2001) 94,024.

North Korea. See **Korea.**

North Lanarkshire, unit. auth. created in 1996, formerly part of Strathclyde, central **Scot.;** lies immediately E. of Glasgow; p. (2002) 321,350.

Northleach, t., Cotswold, Gloucs., **Eng.;** once impt. woollen tr.

North Lincolnshire, unit. auth. created in 1996, formerly part of Humberside, **Eng.;** a. S. of the R. Humber inc. lowland a. ot l. of Axholme and ts. of Barton on Humber, Brigg, Goole and Scunthorpe; p. (2001) 152,849.

North Norfolk, l. gov. dist., Norfolk, **Eng.;** cstl. a. inc. Wells-next-the-Sea, Cromer, Sheringham, Walsingham and North Walsham; p. (2001) 98,302.

North Ossetia-Alana, aut. rep., **Russia** on N. slope of Gr. Caucasus; cap. Vladikavkaz; agr. in valleys; lead, silver, zinc, and oil deposits with metallurgical and food-processing inds.; many Russian military bases; a. 8,029 km²; p. (2005) 710,000.

North Platte, R., **USA;** rises N. Col., flows 1,088 km through Wyo., across W. Nebraska to join S. Platte at c. of North Platte; extensive power and irrigation developments.

North Rhine–Westphalia, *Land,* **Germany;** highly industrialised, coal mng., iron and steel, textiles; cap. Dusseldorf; a. 34,066 km²; p. (2005) 18,075,000.

North Sea, arm of the Atl., E. of Gr. Brit., W. of Norway, Sweden, and N. Germany, and N. of Holland, Belgium, and France; length 960 km, width 640 km; gd. fisheries; major natural gas, coal and oil deposits.

North Sea Canal, ship canal, N. Holland, **Neth.;** connects Amsterdam to N. Sea at Ijmuiden; depth 14 m, length 26 k.

North Shields, t., frm. Tyne and Wear, **Eng.;** Tyne pt.; fishing rt.; marine engines, chain cables, anchors, rope; mkt.; p. (2001) 39,042.

North Shropshire, l. gov. dist., Shrops., **Eng.;** a. N. of Shrewsbury and inc. Market Drayton; p. (2001) 57,108.

North Solomons, Rep. of, formed 1975 when Bougainville I. seceded from Papua New Guinea; p. (1981) 128,794.

North Somerset, unit. auth. created in 1996, formerly part of Avon, **Eng.;** inc. Severnside ts. of Clevedon and Weston-super-Mare; p. (2001) 188,564.

North Tyneside, met. bor., frm. Tyne and Wear, **Eng.;** a bridging point over Trent R.; lace hosiery, Wallsend; p. (2001) 191,659.

Northumberland, non-met. co., N. **Eng.;** on border of Scot. along Cheviots and R. Tweed; drained by Tyne, Blyth, Coquet Rs.; pastoral agr., especially sheep; coal mng. with former impt. exp. to London and S.E. Eng.; isolation and wild landscape attractive to tourists; p. (2001) 307,190.

Northumberland Straits, separate Prince Edward I. from Nova Scotia and New Brunswick, **Canada;** 14 km combined road and rail tunnel, bridge and causeway to link provs. projected.

Northumbria, Anglo-Saxon kingdom stretching from the Humber to the Forth; conquered by the Danes 9th cent.

North Walsham, mkt. t., North Norfolk, **Eng.;** 22 km N. of Norwich; former wool-weaving ctr.

North Warwickshire, l. gov. dist., Warwicks., **Eng.;** based on Atherstone; p. (2001) 61,860.

North West Leicestershire, l. gov. dist., Leics., **Eng.;** inc. Ashby de la Zouch, Ashby Woulds, Coalville and Castle Donington; p. (2001) 85,503.

North-West Passage, between Atl. and Pac. along Arctic cst. of **Canada;** potentially of gr. importance as a W. outlet for Alaskan oil; sovereignty claimed by Canada but disputed by USA, who claims it is an internat. strait. *See* **Section L.**

North-West Province, land-locked northern prov., **Rep. of S. Africa,** bordering with Botswana; bushveld, savannah, grassland; tourism, maize, sunflowers, groundnuts, cattle, tobacco, citrus, paprika, wheat, peppers, cotton, diamonds, gold, platinum, uranium, fluorospar, marble; cap. Mafikeng; a. 116,320 km²; p. (1996) 3.355 m.

Northwest Territories, N.W. region and terr. of **Canada;** N. of 60° Lat. N., between Yukon (W.) and Hudson Bay (E.); comprises 3 dists., Franklin, Mackenzie, Keewatin; varied physical geography, inc. vast areas of lowland with some of highest peaks in E.N. America; tree-line marks physical bdy. between N. and S.; drained in W. by Mackenzie R.; major inds. gold and silver mng. around cap. Yellowknife, zinc and lead in the High Arctic; petroleum, fur-trapping, fisheries; first diamond mine opened (1998); new Inuit self-governing territory of Nunavut came into being 1 April 1999; p. (1996) 64,402.

Northwich, t., Cheshire, **Eng.;** on R. Weaver; impt. chemical inds. based originally upon local salt deposits, now much subsidence in a. due to salt extraction; p. (2001) 39,568.

North Wiltshire, l. gov. dist., Wilts., **Eng.;** rural a. inc. ts. of Calne, Chippenham and Malmesbury; p. (2001) 125,372.

North York Moors, limestone plateau, North Yorks., **Eng.;** lies S. of estuary of R. Tees, heather moorland; some pastoral farming on lower slopes; alt. varies from 300–450 m; formerly impt. iron-ore quarrying along N. edge.

North Yorkshire, non-met. co., N. **Eng.;** inc. much of former N. Riding; stretches from Pennines (W.) to Vale of York (central), N. York Moors and Yorks. Wolds (E.); crossed by R. Ouse and tribs.; mainly rural, mixed agr.; ch. ts. cstl. resort of Scarborough and spa of Harrogate; p. (2001) 569,660.

Norton-Radstock, t., Bath and N.E. Somerset, **Eng.;** footwear, sm. coalfield; p. (1991) 19,032.

Norwalk, t., Conn., **USA;** gd. harbour on Long I. Sound; lt. inds., clothing; formerly impt. oyster ind. diminished by industl. pollution; p. (1996) 77,977.

Norway, kingdom, W. Scandinavia, N. Europe; long fjord cst. stretches from Arctic to N. Sea; mtnous.; cool damp climate, influenced by prevailing W. winds; excellent conditions for hydroelectric power and electro-inds.; sm. p. makes N. heavily dependent upon foreign tr., especially exp. of aluminium, wood-pulp, paper, fish; lge. deposits of petroleum in N. Sea; arable agr. limited to fjord lowlands and a. around cap. Oslo; a. 322,600 km²; p. (2004) 4,574,560.

Norwich, c., co. t., l. gov. dist., Norfolk, **Eng.;** on R. Wensum just above confluence with R. Yare; univ.; cath., cas.; cultural and agr. ctr.; food mnfs., footwear, printing; decentralization of office employment from London; new Forum opened (2001); p. (2001) 121,550 (dist.).

Notodden, t., S. **Norway;** nr. Tinnfoss falls which provide hydroelectric power; iron smelting, nitrates; p. (1990) 8,275.

Nottingham, c., co. t., unit. auth. l. gov. dist., Notts., **Eng.;** a bridging point over Trent R.; lace hosiery, tobacco, pharmaceutical; Raleigh cycles (production ended, 2002); univs., cas.; p. (2001) 266,988 (unit. auth.); (2001) 249,584 (c.).

Nottinghamshire, non-met. co., Midlands, **Eng.;** contains part of productive E. Midlands coalfield serving many power stas. along Trent R.; urban growth concentrated mainly on coalfield; engin., hosiery; wheat, barley, cattle, roses; brilliantly characterised in writings of D. H. Lawrence; p. (2001) 748,510.

Nouadhibou, pt., **Mauritania;** new pt. for bulk carriers to exp. iron ore; fish processing plants; pelletizing plant.

Nouakchott, t., cap. of **Mauritania,** W. Africa; comm. ctr. on caravan route; tr. in agr. prods.; planned industl. zone; rapid growth with mass migration of nomadic p. to shanty ts. as response to Sahelian drought; p. (1990) 881,000.

Nouméa (Port de France), t., cap. of Fr. **New Caledonia;** ch. pt. of Is.; p. (1983) 60,112.

Nouvelle Amsterdam, I., **Indian Oc.;** part of Fr. Southern and Antarctic Terrs.; volcanic; ctr. of meteorological research; a. 65 km².

Nova Iguaçú, t., Rio de Janeiro, **Brazil;** steel, tyres, chemicals; p. (1996) 801,200.

Nova Lisboa (Huambo), central **Angola,** Africa; E. of Benguela; rly. repair shops; agr. comm. ctr.; p. (1995) 400,000.

Novara, c., cap. of N. prov., N. **Italy;** agr. and mnf. ctr., textiles, chemicals, cheese; Romanesque church; p. (1992) 102,029.

Nova Scotia, maritime prov., **Canada;** mainly fertile upland and rich valleys with agr. aided by temperate maritime climate; fruit, livestock, dairying; forested uplands along cst. nr Bay of

Fundy give rise to impt. timber inds. with many pts. along indented cst.; fishing and fish-processing; local coal supplies, iron and steel ind.; cap. Halifax; a. 54,556 km²; p. (1996) 909,282.

Novaya Kakhovka, c., **Ukraine;** built (1951) on K. Sea nr. hydroelec. power sta. on Dnieper R.; tourism; p. (1990) 57,700.

Novaya Zemlya, archipelago, Arctic Oc. **Russia;** 2 main Is.; lofty and rugged, severe climate; nuclear testing a.; a. 90,750 km².

Novgorod, c., **Russia;** on Volkhov R. nr. exit from L. Ilmen; food and timber inds., engin.; in mediaeval times gr. comm. and cultural ctr., cap. of an indep. rep.; damaged by Germans in second world war; p. (1989) 229,000.

Novi Sad, c., **Serbia;** R. pt. on Danube R., formerly royal free c.; almost destroyed by Austrians 1849; tr. in fruit, wine, vegetables, corn; Danube bridges attacked by NATO, 1999; p. (1991) 178,896.

Novokuybyshevsk, t., **Russia;** S.W. of Kuybyshev; lge. oil processing plant; p. (1989) 113,000.

Novo Kuznetsk, c. **Russia;** grew up as iron and steel ctr. of Kuznetsk Basin; p. (1989) 600,000.

Novorossiisk, spt., **Russia;** on N.E. cst. of Black Sea; engin., textiles; lgst. cement producer in Russia; exp. industl. prods.; p. (1989) 186,000.

Novosibirsk, c., **Russia;** on Ob R. and Trans-Siberian rly.; lgst. industl. ctr. of Siberia, nr. Kuznetz Basin; hydroelec. power; varied inds., uranium nearby; univ.; p. (2000) 1,478,000.

Novovoronezh, Russia; on R. Don, S. of Voronezh; nuclear power sta.

Nowa Huta, t., **Poland;** 10 km S.E. Kraców on Vistula R.; heavily polluted Lenin metallurgical combine and modern residtl. a. within c. of Kraców; p. (1989) 224,386.

Nowy Sacz, t. and prov., S. **Poland;** on Dunajec R.; lignite nearby; rly. engin., mftg.; ctr. of a. renowned for beauty and tourist attractions; p. (1995) 82,070 (t.), 730,265 (prov.).

Nubia, anc. region, N.E. **Africa,** extending on both sides of Nile from first cataract at Aswan to Khartoum, Sudan; largely desert.

Nueva Esparta, st., **Venezuela;** consists of over 70 Is.; impt. fisheries; cap. La Asunción; a. 1,150 km²; p. (1990) 200,777.

Nueva San Salvador, t., **El Salvador;** agr. comm. ctr. in coffee-growing and livestock region; p. (1992) 116,575.

Nuevo Laredo, c., N.E. **Mexico;** entry point for American tourists driving to Mexico; tr. ctr. in pastoral and arable agr. a.; p. (1990) 217,912.

Nuevo Léon, st., N.E. **Mexico;** arable agr. needs irrigation in arid climate; impt. iron and steel inds.; cap. Monterrey; a. 65,097 km²; p. (1990) 3,086,466.

Nuku'alofa, cap. of Polynesian kingdom of **Tonga;** p. (1999) 37,000.

Nukus, c., cap. of Karakalpak aut. rep., **Uzbekistan;** on Amu Dar'ya R. in Khorezm oasis; clothing inds.; p. (1993) 185,000.

Nullarbor Plain, S. **Australia;** low, level, limestone plateau fringing Gr. Australian Bight; arid; treeless, salt-bush scrub; crossed by Trans-continental rly. between Naretha (W. Australia) and Ooldea; rly. is dead straight, dead level for 477 km.

Numazu, t., Honshu, **Japan;** nr. Tokyo; ctr. of industl. dist. with varied mnfs. inc. machin., p. (1990) 211,731.

Nunavut, self-gov. region, **Canada;** capital Iqaluit; estab. 1999 from N.W. Territories; area larger than Alaska.

Nuneaton, t., part of l. gov. dist. of Nuneaton and Bedworth, Warwicks., **Eng.;** on Anker R.; coal mng., textiles, lt. inds.; mkt.; birthplace of George Eliot; p. (2001) 119,132 (dist.), (2001) 70,721 (t.).

Nürnberg (Nuremberg), c., Bavaria, **Germany;** historic c. of architectural beauty; industl. ctr. with elec. mnfs., machin., heavy vehicles, precision instruments, chemicals, toys, pencils and crayons; rly. junc.; inland pt. on Rhine–Danube waterway; p. (2002) 491,307 (c.), 1,018,211 (met.a.).

Nusa Tenggara, Is., **Indonesia;** part of Lesser Sunda Is.; p. (1980) 5,461,830.

Nuuk. See Godthåb.

Nyasa, L. See Malawi L.

Nyasaland. See Malawi.

Nyíregyháza, t., N.E. **Hungary;** ctr. of reclaimed agr. a.; mkt. for tobacco, wine, fruits; domestic ware; p. (1997) 113,000.

Nyborg, t., **Denmark;** on Fyn I.; terminal of train-ferry across Gr. Belt; shipyards; textile ind.; p. (1990) 18,207.

Nyköbing, spt., Falster I., **Denmark;** admin. ctr. of Storstrøms prov.; p. (1990) 25,214.

Nyköping, spt., **Sweden;** at head of inlet on Baltic cst.; comm. and industl. ctr.; p. (1992) 68,093.

Nystad. See Uusikaupunki.

O

Oadby, t., Leics., **Eng.;** 5 km S.E. of Leicester; footwear; part of l. gov. dist. of Oadby and Wigston, S. of Leicester; p. (2001) 55,795 (dist.), (2001) 22,679 (t.).

Oahu, I., Hawaii, Pac. Oc.; sugar, pineapples; tourist tr.; cap. Honolulu; a. 1,564 km²; p. (1990) 838,500.

Oakengates, t., The Wrekin, Shrops., **Eng.;** 24 km N.W. of Wolverhampton; iron and steel, precast concrete, engin.; now part of new t. of Telford; p. (2001) 31,246.

Oakham, t., Rutland, **Eng.;** mkt.; hosiery, footwear; p. (1991) 8,691.

Oakland, c., Cal., **USA;** on San Francisco Bay; residtl. sub.; cars, shipbldg., fruit canning, elec. machin., clothing, tanneries, chemicals; p. (2000) 399,484 (c.), 2,083,000 (met. a.).

Oak Park Village, t., Ill., **USA;** now included in Chicago; birthplace of Ernest Hemingway; p. (1996) 51,585.

Oak Ridge, t., Tenn., **USA;** Atomic Energy Commission's major research ctr.; p. (1990) 27,310.

Oaxaca, st., Pac. cst., S. **Mexico;** mtnous., subsistence agr. in fertile valleys; comm. prod. of coffee, cotton, tobacco; stock-raising; mng. in mtns.; cap. Oaxaca; a. 94,201 km²; p. (1990) 3,021,513.

Oaxaca, c., cap. of O. st., S. **Mexico;** stands at c. 1,500 m; coffee; gold and silver mines; handicraft mkt.; table linen weaving, wool zarapes; tourist ctr.; p. (1990) 212,943.

Ob', R., W. Siberia, **Russia;** one of the world's lgst. Rs., flows from Altai mtns. to G. of Ob'; crossed by Turk-Sib. rly. at Barnaul and by Trans-Siberian rly. at Novosibirsk; ch. trib. Irtysh; hydroelec. power; navigable; oilfields in middle section; outlet of Ob basin Novy-Port (Gdansk); plans to divert waters to irrigate Kazakhstan by 2,500 km canal; 4,160 km long.

Oban, spt., burgh, Argyll and Bute, **Scot.;** on F. of Lorne; resort; ctr. for local shipping; woollens, tartans; p. (2002) 8,120.

Obeid, El, t., Kordofan, **Sudan;** economically dependent upon rly. link to Khartoum; agr. tr. ctr.; p. (1993) 228,000.

Oberammergau, v., Upper Bavaria, **Germany;** scene of decennial Passion Play; winter sports; p. (1989) 4,980.

Oberhausen, t., N. Rhine–Westphalia, **Germany;** industl. ctr. of Ruhr conurb.; rly. junc., canal pt.; p. (2002) 221,619.

Obihiro, t., Hokkaido, **Japan;** mkt.; sugar-beet refining, flax, dairy prods.; p. (1990) 167,389.

Obuasi, t. **Ghana,** W. Africa; ctr. of gold mng.; lge. deep-level mine, modernised 1984.

Obwalden, demi-canton, **Switzerland;** a. 492 km²; p. (1990) 28,800.

Ocean City, t., N.J., **USA;** seaside resort founded by the Methodists; p. (1980) 13,949.

Oceania, name given to the Is. of the Pacific; comprising Australasia, Polynesia, Melanesia, Micronesia; p. (2003) 32,000,000.

Ochil Hills, volcanic hill range, **Scot.;** stretching 40 km N.E. to S.W. from F. of Tay to nr. Stirling; loftiest Ben Cleugh, 721 m; beautiful glens and valleys.

Odense, spt., **Denmark;** admin. ctr. of Fyn prov.; varied inds.; exp. dairy prod.; birthplace of Hans Andersen; p. (1990) 176,133.

Odenwald, forested hills, Hesse and Baden-Württemberg, **Germany;** highest point Katzenbuckel 626 m.

Oder (Pol. Odra), R., central **Europe;** flows from Moravia to Baltic through Silesia and Pomerania, forming from junc. with Neisse R. frontier between Poland and Germany; ch. trib. Warta R.; impt. comm. waterway below Wroclaw; 896 km long.

Odessa, t., Texas, **USA;** impt. oil ctr., chemicals, foundry prod., livestock tr.; p. (1990) 89,699.

Odessa, spt., **Ukraine;** on Black Sea; cultural, industl. ctr.; cath., univ.; gr. grain exp.; engin., oil refining, chemicals; ice-bound for a few weeks in winter; p. (1990) 1,106,400.

Offaly, co., Leinster, **R.o.I.**; much marshy land (inc. Bog of Allen), barren uplands (inc. Slieve Bloom); pastoral agr., wheat; p. mainly rural; agr. processing inds. in ts.; co. t. Tullamore; a. 1,999 km²; p. (1986) 59,835.

Offa's Dyke, earthwork constructed by Offa, king of Mercia (757–96) as bdy. between the English and the Welsh; still forms part of border between the two countries; long-distance footpath along the Welsh marches, 269 km.

Offenbach, t., Hesse, **Germany**; on R. Main; cas., leather museum; machin., chemicals, leather gds., metals; p. (2002) 118,429.

Offenburg, t., Baden-Württemberg, **Germany**; on R. Kinzig; textiles, glass, rly. junc.; cas.; p. (2002) 58,280.

Ogaden, arid region, S.W. **Ethiopia**; on border of Rep. of Somalia. Territory still disputed by Somalia.

Ogaki, t., Honshu, **Japan**; route ctr. in lowland em payment, 10 km N.W. of Nagoya; p. (1000) 148,281.

Ogbomosho, t., S.W. **Nigeria**; ctr. of agr. dist.; cotton weaving; p. (1992) 660,600.

Ogden, c., Utah, **USA**; stands at 1,324 m., nr. Gr. Salt L.; rly. ctr.; beet-sugar, meat-packing, flour-milling, clothing, cement; p. (1996) 65,720.

Ogmore Vale, t., Bridgend, **Wales**; in narrow valley, 10 km N. of Bridgend; industl.; cas.; p. (1991) 6,693.

Ogooué, R., Gabon, **Congo**; site of Schweitzer's hospital at Lambaréné; 800 km long.

Ohau, Lake, S.I., **N.Z.**; in Mt. Cook dist.; fed by glaciers; 19 km by 35 km; hydroelectric power potential.

Ohio, R., trib. of Mississippi R., **USA**; formed in Penns., by junc. of Monongahela and Allegheny Rs. at Pittsburgh, thence navigable for 1,560 km to Cairo in Ky.; an impt. comm. waterway for industl. raw materials; flood protection schemes.

Ohio, st., N. **USA**; admitted to Union 1803; st. flower Scarlet Carnation, st. bird Cardinal; gr. agr. and industl. region; maize, wheat, cattle; major deposits of coal form basis of heavy inds., especially in major ts. of Cleveland, Cincinnati, Toledo, Akron, Dayton, Youngstown; petroleum; timber inds.; cap. Columbus; a. 106,508 km²; p. (2002) 11,421,267.

Ohre (Eger), R., Bohemia, **Czech Rep.**; rises in Fichtelgebirge, flows N.E. into Labe (Elbe) and through Karlovy Vary; 224 km long.

Ohrid or **Ochrida**, L., forms part of bdy. between **Albania** and **Macedonia**; alt. c. 850 m; deepest L. in Balkans; scenic tourist a.; monasteries on shores.

Ohrid or **Ochrida**, t., **Macedonia**; on N.E. shore of L.; airport and tourist ctr.; p. (1995) 167,403 (t.) 770,444 (prov.).

Oich, Loch, Gr. Glen, Highland, **Scot.**; forms part of Caledonian Canal.

Oise, dep., N. **France**; traversed by R. Oise; fertile, forested; cap. Beauvais; a. 5,884 km²; p. (1999) 765,731.

Oise, R., trib. of R. Seine, **France**; canalised navigable to Chauny; 298 km long.

Oita, c., spt., N.E. Kyushu, **Japan**; on Beppu Bay; wire, carbon, iron, and steel; oil refinery; p. (1990) 408,502.

Ojos del Salado, mtn., N.W. **Argentina**; alt. 6,908 m.

Okavango, R.; rises in Angola, flows to Ngami depression, **Botswana**, where it forms swampy delta; 1,600 km long.

Okayama, c., Honshu, **Japan**; textiles; lt. inds.; p. (1990) 593,730.

Okazaki, t., Honshu, **Japan**; nr. G. of Ovari; industl. ctr.; textiles, chemicals, machin.; p. (1990) 306,821.

Okeechobee, L., S. Fla., **USA**; drains to Atl. Oc. via Everglades; tourist attraction especially for fishing; also comm. fisheries.

Okefenokee, swamp, Ga./Fla., **USA**; forms O. Nat. Wildlife Refuge.

Okehampton, mt. t., West Devon, **Eng.**; on N. flank of Dartmoor; granite quarries; p. (1991) 4,841.

Okha, spt., E. cst. Sakhalin I., **Russia**; exp. petroleum; rly. refinery.

Okhotsk, Sea of, N.E. **Asia**; 1,600 km by 800 km; enclosed by the Siberian mainland, Kamchatka, the Kurils and Sakhalin I.

Okinawa, I., **Japan**, under U.S. control until 1972; lgst. and most impt. of Ryuku Is. US air bases at Kadena and cap. Naha; a. 1,500 km²; p. (1990) 1,222,398.

Oklahoma, st., **USA**; Sooner St.; admitted to Union 1907; st. flower Mistletoe, st. bird Scissor-tailed Fly-catcher; prairie, plains and mtns.; continental climate; cereals, cotton, stock-raising; petroleum, gas, zinc, coal, gypsum, lead; ch. ind. petroleum refining; cap. Oklahoma City; a. 181,090 km²; p. (2002) 3,493,714.

Oklahoma City, c., cap. of Okla. st., **USA**; univ.; livestock mkt.; tr. and processing ctr.; oil and byprods., field machin., flour mills, meat-packing; scene of horrific extremist bombing, April 1995; p. (2000) 506,132 (c.), 959,000 (met. a.).

Oktyabrsky, t., Bashkir aut. rep., **Russia**; on R. Ik; in new oil-mng. dist., the "New Baku"; p. (1989) 105,000.

Öland, I., Baltic Sea; off E. cst. **Sweden**; connected by Europe's longest bridge to mainland; agr., limestone quarries; ch. t. Borgholm; seaside resorts; a. 1,341 km²; p. (1083) 23,874.

Oldbury. *See* Warley.

Oldbury-on-Severn, S. Gloucs., **Eng.**; nuclear power sta.

Old Castile, historical div., **Spain**; now divided into Santander, Soria, Segovia, Logrono, Avila, Valladolid, Palencia, and Burgos provs.

Oldenburg, c., Lower Saxony, **Germany**; on R. Hunte nr. Hunte-Ems canal; rly. junc.; mkt. for horses and cattle; lt. inds.; natural gas nr. to cst.; p. (2002) 155,908.

Oldham, c., met. dist., Gtr. Manchester, **Eng.**; on R. Medlock, 11 km N.E. of Manchester; manmade fibre and cotton textiles, machin.; industl. diversification inc. electro- and aero-engin., leather, paints; p. (2001) 217,273 (dist.), (2001) 103,544 (c.).

Oldmeldrum, burgh, Aberdeenshire, **Scot.**; 6 km N.E. of Inverurie; p. (2002) 2,003.

Olenek, R., **Russia**; N. Siberia; flows W. of Lena R. into Laptev Sea, Arctic Oc.; abounds in fish; 2,160 km long, 960 km navigable.

Oléron, Ile d', I., Charente-Maritime dep., **France**; lies off estuary of Charente, Bay of Biscay; oysters, early vegetables; a. 176 km².

Olifant, R., **S. Africa**; trib. of Limpopo; irrigation for intensive agr. in valley.

Olinda, c., Pernambuco st., **Brazil**; seaside resort; phosphates; p. (1996) 341,400.

Oliva, t., Valencia, **Spain**; nr. Alicante; wine dist., ducal palace; p. (1990) 20,700.

Olmütz. *See* Olomouc.

Olney, t., Milton Keynes, **Eng.**; mkt., dairy produce; Shrove Tuesday pancake race; p. (1991) 4,484.

Olomouc (Olmütz), Czech Rep.; industl. ctr., steel wks., elec. equipment, textiles, food prod.; cath., univ.; formerly one of ch. fortresses of Austria; p. (1990) 107,000.

Olsztyn (Allenstein), t., and prov. N.W. **Poland**; on R. Alle, 160 km N. of Warsaw; cas.; machin.; p. (1995) 167,403 (t.) 770,444 (prov.).

Olympia, anc. c., Peloponnesus, S. **Greece**; at confluence of Alphaeus and Cladeus Rs.; site of gr. temple of Zeus and scene of Olympic games; modern v. of O. nearby; museum.

Olympia, cap. of Washington st., **USA**; spt. on Puget Sound; exp. timber; machin., agr.-processing inds.; p. (1984) 29,200 (c.), 138,300 (met. a.).

Olympus, Mt., highest mtn. in **Greece**; on border of Thessaly and Macedonia, nr. Aegean cst.; alt. 2,975 m; regarded by anc. Greeks as home of the Olympian gods.

Omagh, t., l. gov. dist., **N. Ireland**; on R.; Stule agr. mkt.; tourist ctr.; bomb killed 29 people, Aug. 1998; p. (2001) 47,952 (dist.), 17,280 (t.).

Omaha, c., Nebraska, **USA**; on Missouri R.; one of lgst. livestock and meat-packing ctrs. in US, gold and silver smelting and refining, steel fabrication, industl. alcohol prod.; univ.; p. (2000) 390,007 (c.), 618,000 (met. a.).

Oman (Muscat and Oman until 1970), sultanate, S.W. Asia; fertile coastal plain, interior desert plateau; irrigated agr., especially impt. for dates; fishing; oil discovered 1964, now main exp.; a. 212,380 km²; p. (2004) 2,903,165.

Oman, G. of, Arabian Sea; connected through strait of Kormuz to Persian G.; length 480 km, width 208 km.

Omaruru, t. and dist. **Namibia**; creamery; aerodrome; p. (1991) 7,446 (dist).

Omdurman, c., central **Sudan**, on Nile, opposite Khartoum; site of Mahdi's tomb; here Kitchener defeated the dervishes 1898; important mkts.; p. (1993) 229,000.

Omsk, c., W. Siberia, **Russia**; at confluence of

Irtysh and Om Rs.; major R. pt. on Trans-Siberian rly.; in agr. region; engin., chemicals, textiles, oil refining, food processing; cath.; founded as fortress 1716; p. (1989) 1,148,000.

Omuta, t., W. Kyushu, **Japan;** on Amakusa Sea; local coal at Miike giving rise to chemical inds.; pt. exp. coal; p. (1990) 150,461.

Onega, Lake, Russia; between L. Ladoga and White Sea; second lgst. L. in Europe (L. Ladoga is lgst.); a. 9,751 km²; ch. c. Petrozavodsk; Onega canal forms part of Volga-Baltic waterway.

Onega, R., **Russia;** flows to G. of Onega; 640 km long.

Onitsha, t., **Nigeria;** on R. Niger; agr. tr. ctr.; p. (1992) 336,600.

Ontario, prov., **Canada;** bounded on N. by Hudson Bay, on S. by Gr. Ls.; extreme continental climate in N., milder in S. peninsula; extensive coniferous forest in N.; temperate agr. in S.; leading mineral producer, nickel, uranium, copper, gold; well-developed inds. using plentiful hydroelectric power; agr.-processing, machin., engin.; cap. Toronto; contains fed. cap. of Ottawa; a. 1,068,587 km²; p. (1996) 10,753,573, concentrated in S.E.

Ontario, L., **N. America;** smallest of the Gr. Ls. of the St. Lawrence basin, separating the Canadian prov. of Ont. from N.Y., USA; navigable, carries industl. raw materials; polluted waters; a. 19,425 km²; depth 226 m.

Ontario, t., Cal., **USA;** aircraft components; fruit comm. ctr.; p. (1990) 133,179.

Ootacamund, t., Tamil Nadu, **India;** in Nilgiri hills, c. 2,100 m; summer H.Q. of st. govt.; sanatorium; p. (1991) 81,800.

Opatija (It. Abbazia), t., **Croatia** (formerly Yugoslavia); tourist resort, known as the Nice of the Adriatic; p. (1981) 29,274.

Opland or **Oppland,** co., central **Norway;** mtnous. N. inc. alpine region of Jotunheimen; forestry prods.; a. 24,885 km²; p. (1990) 182,593.

Opole (Oppeln), c. and prov., S. **Poland;** on R. Oder; R. pt., rly. junc.; cement, metals, furniture; 3 univ. schools; cap. Prussian prov. of Upper Silesia 1919-45; p. (1995) 130,570 (c.), 1,026,580 (prov.).

Oporto (Porto), c., spt., **Portugal;** second c. of rep., built high above Douro R.; ctr. of port wine tr.; cath., univ., historic bldgs.; sardine fisheries, cotton and wool textiles, sugar refining, distilling, oil refining; outer harbour at Leixões; p. (2000) 1,922,000.

Oradea t., **W. Romania,** on Crisul Repede R., nr. Hungarian border; cap. Bihor prov.; baroque architecture; p. (1992) 220,848.

Oran. See **Ouahran.**

Orange, t., N.S.W., **Australia;** in fertile fruit growing a., agr. processing; tourism; with Bathurst is planned growth ctr.; p. (1991) 29,600.

Orange, historic t., Vaucluse, **France;** title founded by Charlemagne passed to William the Silent of the house of Nassau; Roman amphitheatre; tourism; p. (1999) 27,989.

Orange, R., **S. Africa;** flows from Lesotho to Atl.; part forms S. bdy. between old Cape Prov. and Free State; Verwoerd dam (1972) for power, irrigation, flood control; Highlands Water Project (1986) to export water from Lesotho to S. Africa; 2,080 km long.

Orange Free State, former prov., **Rep. of S. Africa.**

Oranienburg, t., Potsdam, **Germany;** on R. Havel; industl.; chemicals, metals; p. (1989) 28,978.

Ord of Caithness, hill, headland, nr. Helmsdale, **Scot.;** alt. 366 m.

Ordos, desert region, Inner Mongolia, **China;** lies S. of Huang He; mean alt. 1,000 m; dry cropping, especially millets; pastoral farming.

Ord, R., W. **Australia;** in Kimberley dist.; since 1972 Ord Irrigation Project; hydroelectric power.

Ordu, spt. and prov., **Turkey;** on Black Sea; exp. manganese; p. (1985) 80,828 (t.), (1990) 850,105 (prov.).

Ordzhonikidze. See **Vladikavkaz.**

Örebro, c., cap. of Örebro prov., **Sweden;** on R. Svartå at entrance to Hjälmar L.; anc. t., cas.; footwear, biscuits; p. (1992) 123,188 (t.), 274,325 (prov.).

Oregon, st., N.W. **USA;** Beaver St.; admitted to Union 1859; st. flower Oregon Grape, st. bird Western Meadowlark; borders Pac. Oc.; ch. physical features, Coast ranges, Cascade mtn. region, Blue mtns., Columbia R. and tribs., Willamette valley; rainy cst., drier interior (agr. with irrigation); cereals, sugar-beet, fruit, cattle; gold, silver, copper, coal, uranium; fisheries, can-

ning, meat-packing, timber, milling; cap. Salem; a. 250,948 km²; p. (2002) 3,521,515.

Orekhovo-Zuyevo, t., **Russia;** E. of Moscow, on R. Klyazma; textile inds.; p. (1989) 137,000. Now called Oryakhovo.

Orel, c., **Russia;** on R. Oka; univ.; rly. junc.; engin., textile mills, food prods.; birthplace of Turgenev; p. (1989) 337,000.

Orenburg (Chkalov), c., cap. of Orenburg oblast, **Russia;** on Ural R.; rly. junc.; food processing, agr. machin.; oil and natural gas in region; p. (1989) 547,000.

Orense, t., cap. of Orense prov., **Spain;** on R. Minho; flour, leather, iron; p. (1991) 107,247, (1998) 344,170 (prov.).

Orford Ness, coastal sandspit, Suffolk, **Eng.;** cas. keep at Orford.

Oriente, terr., **Peru/Ecuador;** for long in dispute between the two ctys., partially settled by treaty (1942); lies E. of Andes, between Putumayo and Marañon Rs.; mainly dense forest, reputedly rich in minerals.

Orihuela, t., Alicante, **Spain;** on R. Segura; leather, textiles, wine; univ., cath.; p. (1990) 46,500.

Orinoco, R., **Venezuela;** rises in Parima mtns., flows to Atl., connected to Rio Negro and Amazon; impt. industl. development on lower O., based on hydroelec. power and iron ore; experimental scheme to reclaim delta for agr.; 2,368 km long.

Orissa, st., **India;** agr. with few ts.; Hirakud dam across Mahanadi R.; Paradeep being developed as pt.; rice; cap. Bhuvaneshwar; a. 155,825 km²; p. (2001) 36,706,900.

Orizaba, t., Veracruz, **Mexico;** textiles, paper mills, breweries; import. p. (1990) 113,516.

Orizaba, mtn., Veracruz, **Mexico;** volcanic; called Citlatepetl in Aztec times; alt. 5,704 m.

Orkney Islands, l. gov. auth., **Scot.;** gr. of 68 Is. in N. Sea, inc. Pomona, Sanday, Westray; 29 inhabited; antiquarian remains, stone circles (World Heritage Site); farming, fishing; North Sea oil; cap. Kirkwall; total a. c. 932 km²; p. (2002) 19,210.

Orlando, c., Fla., **USA;** winter resort; inds. based on citrus fruit and mkt. garden prods.; p. (1990) 164,693 (c.), 1,073,000 (met. a.).

Orléans, c., cap. of Loiret dep., **France;** on R. Loire; cath., univ.; regional tr. ctr.; wine, textiles, chemicals, farm implements; statue of Joan of Arc; p. (1999) 113,121.

Ormoc, c., W. Leyte, **Philippines;** pt. and agr. ctr.; exp. hemp, rice; p. (1990) 129,456.

Ormskirk, t., West Lancs., **Eng.;** 22 km N.E. of Liverpool, in mkt. gardening a., lt. engin.; clothing; p. (2001) 23,392.

Orne, dep., N. **France;** agr., dairying, stock-keeping, fruit-growing. Camembert cheese; cap. Alençon; a. 6,143 km²; p. (1999) 292,158.

Orpington. See **Bromley.**

Orsha, c., **Belarus;** impt. industl. and transport ctr. on R. Dnieper; textiles, food-processing; once a frontier fortress; p. (1990) 124,000.

Orsk, c., **Russia;** in Ural mtns. on Ural R.; inds. based on surrounding mng. a.; oil pipeline terminus; oil refining; hydroelectric power sta. nearby; p. (1989) 271,000.

Orta, L., **Italy;** W. of Lago Maggiore; a. 18 km².

Orthez, t., Pyrénées-Atlantique, **France;** scene of Wellington's victory over Soult (1814); Bayonne hams; p. (1999) 10,124.

Orumiyeh. See **Rezaiyeh.**

Oruro, c., **Bolivia;** cap. of O. prov. at alt. 3,700 m; once impt. ctr. for silver mng.; now other minerals impt.; tin smelter; p. (1992) 183,194 (t.), (1988) 388,300 (dep.).

Orvieto, t., Umbria, **Italy;** on R. Paglia; cath., Etruscan antiquities; wines, olive oil; pottery.

Oryakhovo. See **Orekhovo.**

Osaka, c., Honshu, **Japan;** ctr. of Kinki plain; built on delta in shallow O. Bay; comm. ctr.; banking, heavy industry, metals, machin., clothing; p. (2000) 2,599,000 (c.), 16,567,000 (met. a.).

Osasco, t., São Paulo st., **Brazil;** industl. satellite of São Paulo with traditional and new inds.; p. (1996) 622,380.

Osh, t., **Kirghizia;** textiles, food-processing; one of oldest ts. in central Asia; p. (1990) 217,500.

Oshawa, t., Ont., **Canada;** pt. on L. Ont.; motor vehicles; p. (1991) 129,344 (c.), (1996) 268,773 (met. a.).

Oshkosh, t., Wis., **USA;** on Fox R.; meat packing, flour, motors; p. (1990) 55,006 (c.), 315,000 (met. a. Appleton-Oshkosh-Neenah).

Oshogbo, t., **Nigeria**; comm. and educational ctr.; serves agr. dist.; cotton-ginning; new steel rolling mill; p. (1992) 441,600.

Osijek, t., **Croatia** (formerly Yugoslavia); on Drava R.; growing industl. ctr. for textiles and leather; p. (1991) 104,761.

Osinniki, t., **Russia**; W. Siberia; new ctr. of coal mng.; thermal power sta.

Osipenko. *See* **Berdyansk**.

Oslo (**Christiania**), c., cap. of **Norway**; at head of Oslo Fjord; ch. spt., comm., industl. and cultural ctr.; ice-free harbour, cath., univ.; new airport (Gardermoen) opened, 1998; p. (2000) 507,500.

Osnabrück, c., Lower Saxony, **Germany**; on R. Hase; stands on a branch of the Mittelland canal; inland pt. and industl. ctr.; iron and steel; mach., textile and paper mnfs.; p. (2002) 164,195

Usorno, t., **Chile**; agr. ctr.; in beautiful forested cty., Germanic influence; food-processing; tourism; p. (1992) 128,709

Ossett, t., West Yorks., **Eng.**; 5 km W. of Wakefield; p. (2001) 21,076.

Ostend, spt., **Belgium**; passenger route between Britain and continent of Europe; popular resort; casino, fisheries, shipbldg., textiles, tobacco; p. (1993) 69,148.

Östergötland, co., **Sweden**; on Baltic cst.; rises to uplands of Småland in S. where p. declining; lowland, a. crossed by Gota canal; cap. Linköping; a. 11,050 km²; p. (1992) 408,268.

Östfold, co., S.E. **Norway**; hilly a. crossed by R. Glomma; dairy prods. for Oslo; a. 4,178 km²; p. (1990) 238,345.

Ostia, anc. c., **Italy**; once pt. of Rome, at mouth of R. Tiber, founded 4th cent. B.C.; layout revealed by excavations; modern v. of O. nearby on plain reclaimed from salt marsh.

Ostrava, c., **Czech Rep.**; at junc. of Oder and Ostravice Rs.; industl. ctr. of Ostrava–Karvinna coalmng. region; iron and steel, machin., chemicals, oil refining; p. (1990) 331,000.

Ostroleka, t. and prov., N.E. central **Poland**; on R. Narew; cellulose, paper; p. (1995) 53,685 (t.), 407,663 (prov.).

Ostrow Wielkopolski, t., Kalisz prov., **Poland**; agr. machin., clothing; p. (1995) 74,712.

Ostrowiec Swietokrzyski (**Ostrovets**), t., Kielce, **Poland**; on R. Kamienna; ceramic and metallurgical inds. p. (1995) 79,179.

Oswaldtwistle, t., Hyndburn, Lancs., **Eng.**; at N. foot of Rossendale Fells; chemicals, textiles.

Oswestry, t., l. gov. dist., Shrops., **Eng.**; at foot of Welsh mtns.; cas.; engin.; p. (2001) 37,308 (dist.), (1991) 15,612 (t.).

Oswiecim (Ger. **Auschwitz**), t., Bielsko prov., **Poland**; at confluence of Rs. Iola and Vistula; lge. chemical wks.; German concentration camp (1940–44), now World Heritage Site; p. (1998) 44,385.

Otago, reg., S.I., **N.Z.**; forested mtns.; gold; farming, sheep, fruit; lge. deposit of jade found at head of L. Wakatipu; coalfields; cap. Dunedin; a. 65,320 km²; p. (1991) 186,067.

Otago Harbour, Otago dist., S.I., **N.Z.**; Dunedin and Port Chalmers are ports on this harbour.

Otaru, reg., Hokkaido, **Japan**; herring fisheries; coal mng., lumbering; p. (1990) 163,215.

Otley, t., West Yorks., **Eng.**; on R. Wharfe; printing, machin., wool, paper mkg., leather, furnishings; birthplace of Thomas Chippendale; p. (1991) 13,596.

Otranto, t. S. **Italy**; on Strait O.; once a flourishing c., fine mosaic pavement, cath., cas.; submarine cable sta.; bauxite exp., fishing; p. (1981) 4,811.

Otsu, t., Honshu, **Japan**; on L. Biwa; p. (1990) 260,004.

Ottawa, c. Ont. cap. of **Canada**; on R. Ottawa; univ., caths., parliament bldgs.; hydroelec. power, lumbering, sawmills, paper, flour, leather, matches, machin., ironware; p. (2000) 1,100,000 (met. a. with Hull).

Ottawa, R., **Canada**; trib. of St. Lawrence, forming bdy. between Ont. and Quebec; timber transport, hydroelec. power; 1,000 km long.

Ottery St. Mary, mkt. t., East Devon, **Eng.**; 16 km E. of Exeter; birthplace of Coleridge; p. (1991) 3,253.

Ötzal, valley, Austria; longest side valley of R. Inn; tourist dist.

Ouachita or **Washita**, R., Ark., **USA**; trib. of Red R.; 880 km long.

Ouachita National Forest, Ark., Okla., **USA**; part of forested O. highlands.

Ouagadougou, cap. of **Burkina Faso**; tex., soap, peanuts, comm.; p. (2000) 1,130,000.

Ouahran (**Oran**), spt., dep., N. **Algeria**; founded by Moors 10th cent.; occupied by French 1831–1962; handles wines, wool, cereals, meat, skins; fine roadstead at Mers-el-Kebir; former French naval and military sta.; p. (1987) 609,823 (t.), 916,578 (dep.).

Oudenaarde (**Audenarde**), t., **Belgium**, on R. Scheldt; textile ctr.; scene of Marlborough's victory over French 1708; p. (1991) 27,160.

Ouenza, dist., **Algeria**; 75 per cent of Algerian iron-ore produced in dist.

Oujda, t., N.E. **Morocco**; comm. ctr.; phosphate, lead and zinc-mng. dist.; p. (1994) 419,063.

Oulton Broad, L., Suffolk, **Eng.**; nr. Lowestoft. *See* **Broads**.

Oulu, spt., cap. of Oulu prov., N.W. **Finland**; oil ch. of Bothnia at mouth of R. Oulu, univ.; p. (1993) 104,346.

Oundle, mkt. t., East Northants., **Eng.**; on R. Nene; public school.

Ouro Prêto, old colonial t., **Brazil**; former cap. of Minas Gerais st.; as gold mng. ctr.; founded 1711; school of mines; p. (1996) 61,600.

Ouse or Great Ouse, R., **Eng.**; rises in S. Northamptonshire and flows N.E. via the Fens to the Wash; 250 km long.

Ouse, R., East Sussex, **Eng.**; flows to English Channel at Newhaven; 48 km long.

Ouse, R., York/North Yorks., **Eng.**; formed by R. Ure at Ouse Gill Beck, flows to Humber estuary; 208 km long.

Outer Hebrides. *See* **Hebrides**.

Overijssel, prov., **Neth.**; dairying, fishing; ch. ind. textiles; a. 3,364 km²; p. (1994) 1,044,648.

Oviedo, coastal prov., N. **Spain**; agr., fruit, sardine, and other fisheries; cap. O.; a. 10,888 km²; p. (1998) 1,081,800.

Oviedo, c., cap. of O. prov., **Spain**; on R. Nalón; cath., univ.; industl. and comm. ctr. for agr. and mng. dists. of Asturias; p. (1998) 199,500.

Owen Falls, **Uganda**; dam since 1954 to supply Uganda with hydroelectric power; also converts L. Victoria into reservoir for irrigation of Egypt.

Owensboro', t., Ky., **USA**; petroleum; ctr. for stock raising and tobacco growing a.; p. (1996) 54,350.

Owens, L., S. Cal., **USA**; on E. flank of Sierra Nevada, 32 km S.E. of Mt. Whitney; water taken by 360 km-long aqueduct to Los Angeles; a. 311 km².

Owen Sound, t., L. pt., Ont., **Canada**; on S.W. cst. of Georgian Bay, L. Huron; E. terminus of lgst. wheat-carrying L. steamers; linked by rly. to Toronto (200 km) and Montreal; p. (1981) 19,883.

Oxelösund, spt., E. **Sweden**; on Baltic cst., S. of Nyköping; iron and steel wks.; p. (1990) 14,080.

Oxford, c., l. gov. dist., Oxon., **Eng.**; between R. Thames and R. Cherwell; 13th cent. univ. and residtl. colleges; also Oxford Brookes Univ., printing, cars; p. (2001) 134,248 (dist.).

Oxfordshire, non-met. co., **Eng.**; formed by Chilterns and Cotswolds, drained by R. Thames and tribs.; mainly agr. with lge. arable farms; p. (2001) 605,488.

Oxnard, t., Cal., **USA**; citrus fruits, sugar beet, oil refining; p. (1990) 142,216 (t.), 669,000 (met. a. with Ventura).

Oxus, R. *See* **Amu Darya**.

Oyashio. *See* **Bering Current**.

Oyo, t., **Nigeria**; cotton weaving; mkt.; p. (1992) 237,040 (t.), (1991) 3,488,789 (state).

Ozark Mtns., Okla. and Ark., **USA**; lead, zinc; ch. t, Joplin; forested.

P

Paarl, t., Western Cape Prov., **S. Africa**; summer resort extending along Gt. Berg R.; wines, fruit, tobacco; flour, saw and textile mills; p. (1980) 108,860 (dist.).

Pabna, t., and dist., Bengal, **Bangladesh**; dist. is a fertile alluvial plain; t. serves as trading, industl. and admin. ctr. for a.; hosiery, carpets; p. (1991) 104,479 (t.), 4,305,000 (dist.).

Pachitea, R., **Peru**; rises in Andes, flows N. to R. Ucayali; sm. German immigrant colonies in upper valley; 512 km long.

Pachmarhi, Madhya Pradesh, **India;** summer cap., tourist ctr.

Pachuca, cap., Hidalgo st., **Mexico;** silver mnfs. and mng.; woollen and leather gds.; p. (1990) 179,440.

Pacific Islands, Trust Terr. of, external terr. of **USA** held under U.N. trusteeship; consists of Mariana Is. (except Guam), Caroline and Marshall Is., W. Pac. Oc.; inc. 2,141 Is., grouped into 6 admin. dists.; cap. (provisional) Saipan, **Mariana Is.**; total land a. c. 1,800 km²; p. (1985) 154,000.

Pacific Ocean, a. 176,120,000 km²; lgst. ocean in the world; extends from W. cst. of America to E. cst. of Asia and Australia and the S. Ocean in the S.; enters Arctic Oc. via Bering Strait; greatest length N. to S. 1,280 km; breadth. 16,000 km; mean depth 3,830 m, 11,524 m in the Mindanao trench; many coral and volcanic Is. in S.W.

Padang, spt., W. cst. Sumatra, **Indonesia;** exp. agr. prods., coffee, copra, rubber and coal; cement mnfs.; univ.; p. (1995) 721,000.

Paddington. See **Westminster, City of.**

Paderborn, c., N. Rhine–Westphalia, **Germany;** cath. and other historic bldgs. severely damaged in second world war; foodstuffs, textiles, metals; p. (2002) 140,869.

Padiham, t., Lancs., **Eng.;** at N. foot of Rossendale Fells, textiles, engin., p. (1991) 12,570.

Padstow, mkt. t. Camel estuary, Cornwall, **Eng.;** silting has caused pt. decline; lt. inds.; seaside resort; p. (1991) 2,460.

Padua (Padova), c., cap. of P. prov., N.E. **Italy;** cath., arcades, anc. bridges; univ. founded 1222 (Galileo taught here); flourished as artistic ctr.; birthplace of Livy; machin., chemicals, cloth, distilling; agr. ctr.; p. (1992) 213,656.

Paducah, c., Ky., **USA;** pt. on Ohio R.; saw-mills, tobacco, railway wks.; atomic energy plant; p. (1990) 27,256.

Paestum, anc. c., S. **Italy;** S.E. of Salerno; founded by the Greeks 600 B.C.; ruins of temples, Roman forum and amphitheatre.

Pagan, ruined c., central **Myanmar;** on Irrawaddy R.; founded circa 849, sacked 1299; in ctr. of a. covered with pagodas, place of Burmese pilgrimage; lacquer work.

Pago Pago, spt., cap. of American **Samoa,** S. Pac.; on Tutuila I., magnificent harbour; US naval and radio sta.; airport; p. (1990) 46,773.

Pahang, st., **Malaysia,** central Malaya; isolated from rest of Malaya, less economically developed; largely covered with forest; some rubber production, gold, tin mng.; cap. Kuala Lipis; a. 34,395 km²; p. (2005) 1,300,000.

Pahlevi. See **Bandar-e-Pahlevi.**

Paignton, t., S. Devon, **Eng.;** incorporated in Torbay; resort; p. (1991) 42,989.

Painted Desert, Arizona, **USA;** a. of bare multicoloured shale and sandstones; arid.

Paisley, burgh, Renfrewshire, **Scot.;** 8 km W. of Glasgow; anc. abbey; former inds. included shipbldg., chemicals, engin., preserves, car bodies, cotton thread; univ; p. (2002) 74,170.

Paita, pt., **Peru;** exp. cotton, wool, flax, panama hats; lge. whaling sta. to S.

Pakistan, Islamic Rep. of, forms part of Indian subcontinent, S. Asia; formerly split into two separate units, E. Pakistan (cap. Dacca) and W. Pakistan, (cap. Lahore), 1,600 km apart; politically separate since 1972; W. part now forms Pakistan; E. part indep. st. of Bangladesh; dry semi-desert, irrigated by Indus R. and tribs.; cash crops, sugar, wheat, cotton; natural gas fields; new cap. Islamabad; main spt. Karachi, military coup (1999), suspension from Commonwealth, 1999–2004; a. 803,944 km²; p. (2004) 159,196,336.

Paknampoh, t., **Thailand;** on R. Menam, at upper limit of navigation; terminus of private rly.; fish breeding in L. created from swamp.

Pakokku, t., Upper **Myanmar;** pt. on Irrawaddy R.; shipping ctr. for a. producing sugar, tobacco, teak, petroleum; Yenangyaung oilfields nearby.

Paktia, prov., **Afghanistan;** mtnous., forested; difficult to govern, inhabited by sm. indep. tribes, but sparse p.; livestock basis of agr.; timber exp; a. c. 12,950 km²; p. (1984) 525,000.

Palau, Rep. of, formerly Western Carolines; group of Is. 300 km. E. of Philippines; independent from 1994, formerly part of US Trust Terr. of Pacific Is.; p. (2004) 20,016.

Palawan I., prov. **Philippines;** elongated I., rising to 1,731 m; coffee, resin, timber; prov. a. 11,784 km²; p. (1990) 528,287.

Palembang, cap. of S. Sumatra prov., **Indonesia;** R. pt. of Musi R., 80 km from sea; terminus of S. Sumatran rly. systems; exp. coffee and petroleum prods. from nearby oilfields; inds. based on agr. processing and oil refining; p. (1995) 1,352,000.

Palencia, t., cap. of P. prov., N.W. **Spain;** industl. ctr.; rly. engin.; cath.; p. (1990) 77,500 (t.); (1998) 179,600 (prov.).

Palermo, spt.; cap., Sicily, **Italy;** cath., univ.; shiprepairing; processes agr. prod. from surrounding fertile Conca d'Oro; p. (1992) 696,735.

Palestine, historic reg. and state; ongoing conflict over land with Israel; split into West Bank (a. 5,879km² p. (1997) 1,500,000) and Gaza Strip (a. 378km² p. (1997) 800,000); 700,000 living in Israel; severe water shortage in Gaza; Palestine National Authority based in Jericho.

Palghat, t., Kerala, **India;** commands Palghat gap through W. Ghats; p. (1991) 180,000.

Palitana, t., Gujarat, **India;** t. of Jain temples inhabited by priests and their servants; mkt. ctr. for millet, cotton, wheat.

Palk Strait, separates **India** from Sri Lanka. Dredging underway to create ship canal.

Palma de Mallorca, spt., Mallorca I, **Spain;** cath., palaces, varied inds.; agr. exp.; well-known tourist resort; p. (1998) 319,200.

Palm Beach, t., Fla., **USA;** Atl. coastal resort; permanent p. (1980) 9,729.

Palmerston North, c., N.I., **N.Z.;** rly. junc. at ctr. of Manawatu R. lowlands; sheep and dairy prod.; univ.; p. (1991) 70,318. Moves to rename city Manawatu.

Palm Springs, Cal., **USA;** resort; p. (1980) 32,366.

Palmyra, anc. c. in Syrian desert, 192 km. N.E. of Damascus; extensive ruins.

Palmyra Is. See **Line Is.**

Palo Alto, t., sub. development 48 km S.E. San Francisco, Cal., **USA;** attractive wooded site of variable relief; on shore of San Francisco Bay peninsula; Stanford Univ.; science-based inds.; p. (1980) 55,225.

Palomar, Mount, peak, 1,868 m high, S. Cal., **USA;** observatory with 5,080 mm reflecting telescope.

Palos de la Frontera, t., Huelva, S.W. **Spain;** on Rio Tinto; starting point for Columbus in 1492; pt. now silted up; p. (1990) 6,700.

Palua, pt., **Venezuela;** pt. of shipment for iron mines at El Pao; nearby Caroni hydroelec. plant serves steel wks. and aluminium plant.

Pamir Mtns., high mtn. plateau ("roof of the world"), **Tajikistan, Central Asia;** Mt. Communism (now renamed Mt. Garmo) (7,495 m) climbed by Russo-British team 1962; name derives from high mtn. valleys known as pamirs.

Pampas, Argentina; vast plains stretching from the Rio Negro in the S. to the Gran Chaco in the N., and E. from the Andes to the Atl.; woodless, level country; rich pastures in E., supporting countless numbers of sheep and cattle, a major influence upon the Argentinian economy, source of livestock exps.; W. mostly barren.

Pamplona, c., cap. of Navarre, N. **Spain;** at foot of Pyrenees, anc. Baxque c.; cath., fortress, univ.; industl. ctr. with varied mnfs.; p. (1998) 171,100.

Panaji, cap. of Goa state, **India;** p. (1991) 43,300.

Panama, rep., **Central America;** narrow strip of terr. at S. end of isthmus separating N. and S. America; mtnous, and tropical, thickly forested; 9 prov. and 1 autonomous Indian reservation; Panama Canal returned by USA (1999) to Panamanian sovereignty; shipping registration and other services impt.; subsistence agr.; exp. bananas, shrimps, sugar, coffee; rich copper deposits found 1975; poor communications; Cap. Panama City; a. 74,009 km²; p. (2004) 3,000,463.

Panama Canal Area, Panama; strip of land 82 km long 16 km wide on either side of Canal; 1979 former Canal Zone transferred by US to Panamanian sovereignty; a. 1,675 km².

Panama City, c. spt., cap. of **Panama;** free pt. at S. entrance to Canal; cath.; oil refining, steel rolling mill, cement plant, lt. inds.; contains 25 per cent p. Panama rep.; p. (2000) 1,173,000 (met. a.).

Panama City, t., Fla., **USA;** pulp and paper mill; resort; p. (1984) 34,100 (t.), 108,500 (met. a.).

Pan American Highway, international road project, not yet fully complete, from Alaska to Chile, down W. csts. of continents; section between USA and Mexico is called Central American Inter-American Highway.

Panay, I., Philippines; between Negros I. and Mindoro I.; coconuts, maize grown in E., fertile lowland; ch. t. Iloilo; a. 11,515 km²; p. (1990) 8,031,271.

Pančevo, t., N.E. Serbia; agr. ctr. for grain growing a., flour-milling; developing industl. ctr., fertilizers, oil refining; p. (1991) 72,717.

Pangalanes Canal (Canal Des Pangalanes), Madagascar; follows E. cst from Farafangana to Tamatave, through series of lagoons; 480 km long.

Panipat, t., Haryana, N.W. India; on Jumna R.; on route from Afghanistan to central India; scene of battles; p. (1991) 101,212.

Panjim, cap. of Goa, India; pt.; old cap. (Velha Goa) in ruins; p. (1981) 43,165.

Panjsher Valley, Afghanistan; silver and mica mines.

Pantelleria, volcanic I., Mediterranean, **Italy;** midway between W. Sicily and Tunisia; figs, raisins, vines, capers, cereals; fishing; a. 150 km²; ch. t. P.; p. (1981) 7,917.

Paoki. See Baoji.

Paoting. See Baoding.

Paotow. See Baotou.

Papaloa, R., Mexico; agr. and industl. development; Papaloan project for flood control and electricity generation.

Papal States, Italy, areas ruled by the Pope until 1870; comprised Latium, Umbria, the Marches, and Emilia-Romagna.

Papatoetoe, c., N.I., N.Z.; residtl. ctr. close to Auckland; p. (1987) 21,900.

Papeete, t., pt., Tahiti I., Pac. Oc.; cap. Tahiti and of Fr. Settlements in Oceania; exp. copra, vanilla, phosphates and mother-of-pearl; p. (1983) 78,814.

Paphos (Pafos), admin. dist., W. cst **Cyprus;** anc. c.; Old P. dates from 3000 B.C., New P. impt. spt.; rich deposits of copper and iron pyrites, sulphur in Vretsia a.; scene of ambitious project (completed 1983) to grow tropical fruits (mango, avocado, papaya) with irrigation; p. (1992) 32,575 (c.).

Papua New Guinea, E. New Guinea, S.E. Asia; indep. st. (1975); mtnous., thickly forested; under-developed; copra, rubber and timber prods.; many valuable reserves of gold, oil and copper; cap. Pt. Moresby; a. 461,693 km²; p. (2005) 5,800,000.

Pará, st., Brazil; densely forested; rubber, fruits, cacao, Brazil nuts; massive iron ore deposits in Serra do Carajás with new road and rail ⊔⊔⊔⊔⊔⊔ ⊔⊔⊔⊔ ⎮⎮.⎮ 1,000,001 km²; p. (1996) 5,552,800.

Paracel Is., S. China Sea; claimed by China, Taiwan and Vietnam.

Paraguay, landlocked rep., S. America; undulating cty., swamps, forest; hot summers, warm winters, high but seasonal rainfall; sm. densely populated areas, lge. areas with no p.; most economically developed in E.; in and around cap. Asunción 25 per cent p.; economy based on agr., decline of meat and timber but agr. expansion in other prods.; cereals, livestock, fruit, cotton, oil-seeds, but food imported; aid from USA for rural development; few fuel resources (a few oilfields in the Chaco Borea) and low energy consumption; hydroelectric plant on Paraná (Itaipu dam), Paraguay Rs. and at Guaira Falls; electricity exp. to Brazil; new inds. with cheap power; first steel mill (1982); some agr. based inds.; a. 406,630 km²; p. (2004) 6,191,368.

Paraguay, R., S. America; rises in plateau of Mato Grosso, flows S. and joins R. Paraná nr. Corrientes; forms bdy. between Brazil and Bolivia, Brazil and Paraguay; impt. navigable waterway to Cáceres (Brazil); 1,920 km long.

Paraíba, st., N.E. Brazil; livestock, cotton, sugar cane; tin, scheelite; cap. João Pessoa; a. 56,462 km²; p. (1991) 3,200,620.

Paraíba do Sul, R., S. Brazil; rises in São Paulo st., and flows between Rio de Janeiro and Minas Gerais to Atl. N.E. of Rio de Janeiro; forms routeway between São Paulo and Rio de Janeiro; 1,040 km long.

Paramaribo, spt., cap. of **Suriname;** on Suriname R.; exp. bauxite, timber, rubber, rice, fruit; t.

built on grid pattern with canals and tree-lined streets; p. (1997) 289,000.

Paraná, c., cap. of Entre Rios prov., N.E. Argentina; pt. of P. R. for grain, cattle, sheep; road tunnel to Santa Fé; p. (1991) 277,338.

Paraná, R., S.W. Brazil; formed by junc. of Rs. Rio Grande and Paranaíba; flows W. between Paraguay and Argentina; flows into Rio de la Plata; navigable to Brazil frontier nr. Iguaçu Falls; forms part of international inland waterway system; hydroelec. power, Itaipú lgst. sta. in world; joint hydroelec. scheme between Paraguay, Brazil and Argentina; 3,280 km long; rapid rise in p. with indust. expansion from electricity.

Paraná, st., S. Brazil; between Paraná R. and Atl. Oc.; extensively forested; maté, timber, coffee; cap. Curitiba; a. 201,287 km²; p. (1996) 8,986,000.

Paranaguá, spt., Paraná st., **Brazil;** ch. pt. for Paraná, in lagoon harbour; coffee exported; modern highway links with Asunción (Paraguay).

Paricutín, Mt. Michoacán, Mexico, volcano formed between 1943 and 1952, 2,501 m high; of great interest to scientists.

Paris, c., cap. of France; dominates rep. politically, economically, and socially, partly as result of extreme centralisation of political power in cap.; on R. Seine, 176 km from mouth, in ctr. of Paris Basin; forms major ctr. of communications; planning of Haussmann gives spacious appearance, 12 boulevards radiate from Arc de Triomphe; many historic bldgs., especially on and around Ile de la Cité, an I. on R. Seine, site of cath. of Notre Dame; major cultural and tourist ctr.; univs.; comprises 20 admin. arrondissements; major ctr. of inds. with concentration of modern science-based inds. hindering planned attempts at decentralisation; p. (1999) 2,120,304.

Paris Basin, concentric limestone escarpments form saucer-shaped depression with Paris at ctr.; impt. agr. dist., wheat, dairy prod. and wines.

Parkersburg, t., W. Va., USA; on Ohio R.; iron- and steel-wks., oil and natural gas, coal, glassware, rayon, porcelain; p. (1996) 32,766.

Parkes, t., N.S.W., Australia; mkt.; rly. junc.; radio telescope; p. (1991) 8,800.

Parma, c., cap. of P. prov., Italy; between Apennines and Po R.; tr. ctr. rly. junc.; food-processing, wine, Parmesan cheese, precision instruments, agr. machin.; Roman remains, many historic bldgs., univ., cath.; p. (1992) 170,555.

Parnaiba, R., rises in Brazil; flows into N. Atl. Oc., forms bdy. between Maranhão and Piauí; 1,200 km long.

Parnassus, mtn. ridge, Greece; 133 km N.W. of Athens, nr. the anc. Delphi, the modern Liakhura; hgst. peak Licoreia 2,461 m.

Páros, I., Grecian Archipelago; W. of Naxos; source of Parian marble; cap. P.; a. 163 km².

Parramatta, c., N.S.W., Australia; pt. nr. head of Parramatta R. in inlet a. of Sydney, and Brit. settlement in Australia; p. (1991) 131,800.

Pasadena, c., Cal., USA; N. of Los Angeles; in fruit-growing region, base of San Gabriel mtns.; 5,080 mm telescope on Mt. Palomar; famous for its carnival; p. (1990) 131,591.

Pasco. See Cerro de Pasco.

Pas-de-Calais, dep., N. **France;** impt. heavy industl. a. based upon local extensive coal deposits; heavy inds. inc. iron and steel, but many ts. in decline as importance of coal diminishes; prosperous agr. based on arable farming; N. cst. faces English Channel and inc. pts. of Calais and Boulogne; severe devastation in both world wars; cap. Arras; a. 6,750 km²; p. (1999) 1,441,500.

Pasir Gudang, free port , **Malaysia;** across Jahore Str. from Singapore; opened (1984) to divert M.'s exports from Singapore.

Passau, c., Germany; at confluence of Rs. Danube, Inn and Ilz, nr. Austrian frontier; trans-shipment base, inds. inc. leather, porcelain, tobacco and brewing; cath., picturesque tourist ctr.; p. (2002) 50,669.

Passendale (Passchendaele), t., Belgium; strategic point in first world war; battle 31 July–6 Nov. 1917.

Passero I., Mediterranean Sea; off S.E. cst. of Sicily, **Italy.**

Passy, residtl. part of W. Paris, **France;** between Bois de Boulogne and right bank of Seine; residence of Balzac.

Pasto, t., cap. of Narino dep., Colombia; on flank of Pasto volcano; univ.; agr. comm. ctr.; gold nearby; p. (1992) 303,401.

Patagonia, extensive region, E. of Andes, **Argentina/Chile;** elevated plateau, arid, sterile; prin. Rs. Colorado, Río Negro, and Chubut; impt. source of oil at Commodoro Rivadavia; lge. tracts of grazing for livestock; much of p. Welsh descendants; plans to decentralise cap. of A. to small Ts. of Viedma and Carmen de Patagones.

Patan, c. **Nepal;** impt. ctr. of Buddhism; gold and silver gds.; p. (1991) 117,203.

Patani or **Pattani,** pt., S. **Thailand;** on E. cst. of Malay peninsula; spices, rubber, coconuts; tin mng.; former Malay sultanate.

Paterno, t., Sicily, **Italy;** N.W. of Catania; cath., cas.; mineral springs, wines; p. (1981) 45,144.

Paterson, c., N.J., **USA;** on Passaic R. whose falls provide hydroelectric power for gr. silk mnf. ind.; now inds. diversified; in addition to textiles and textile machin., aeroplane engines, metallurgical inds., electronic equipment; p. (1996) 150,270.

Patiala, t., Punjab, **India;** metal gds., flour; cement; p. (1991) 269,000.

Patino Mines. See Unicia.

Pátmos, I., one of the Dodecanese, **Greece;** in Aegean Sea; St. John wrote the Revelation here; a. 34 km²; p. 3,000.

Patna, c., cap. of Bihar, **India;** univ.; rly. junc.; agr. tr., rice, oilseeds, cotton; handicraft inds.; p. (1991) 917,000.

Patras (**Pátrai**), spt., cap. of Akhaia, **Greece;** citadel and cas.; exp. currants, raisins, figs, olive oil; inds. based on agr. processing; p. (1991) 152,570.

Pau, c., cap. of Pyrénées-Atlantique dep., **France;** on Gave-de-Pau; impt. mkt. and regional ctr.; summer and winter resort; linen, chocolate, hams, wine; natural gas nearby; p. (1999) 78,715.

Pauillac, t., Gironde dep., **France,** pt. on Gironde estuary; ships, wines, timber; oil refinery, natural gas; p. (1982) 6,359.

Paulo Affonso, falls, São Francisco R., **Brazil;** 79 m; Tres Marías dam and power sta. opened 1960; in Nat. Park.

Pavia, c., prov. cap., N. **Italy;** on R. Ticino; route ctr. and agr. mkt. in Po valley; olives, wine, Parmesan cheese; oil refining at Spineto; walled c.; battle 1525; birthplace of Lanfranc; p. (1981) 85,029.

Pavlodar, pt., **Kazakhstan;** on R. Irtysh; chemicals, sulphates, agr. machin., locomotives, aluminium, oil processing; food prod.; p. (1990) 336,800.

Pawtucket, c., R.I., **USA;** on Pawtucket R. at head of navigation; first water-power cotton spinning factory in USA 1790; textiles remain most impt. ind.; p. (1990) 329,000 (met. a. with Woonsocket–Attleboro).

Paysandú, dep., W **Uruguay;** rich pastoral a.; ranching, cattle, sheep; arable agr., cereals, mkt. gardening around c. of P.; a. 13,406 km²; p. (1985) 103,487.

Paysandú, cap. of P. dep., W. **Uruguay;** pt. on Uruguay R. with meat-packing, soap and footwear inds.; p. (1985) 74,014.

Pays de la Loire, region, W. **France;** inc. deps. Loire Atlantique, Maine-et-Loire, Mayenne, Sarthe, Vendée; region based upon lower reaches of R. Loire; ch. ts. Le Mans, Nantes; p. (1999) 3,220,200.

Peace, R., **Canada;** one of ch. headstreams of Mackenzie R.; rises in Rocky mtns., and flows generally N. to Gr. Slave R, nr. L. Athabaska; a. of very mild climate in lower course, fertile agr. valley; 1,680 km long.

Peak Dist., Pennine hill dist., mid-**Eng.;** extends from Chesterfield to Buxton, and Ashbourne to Glossop; composed of limestone with typical karst features; within P.D. Nat. Park, tourist and recreation a. for cities to E. (Sheffield) and W. (Manchester); limestone quarrying for cement.

Pearl Harbor, landlocked harbour, Oahu I., **Hawaii,** one of finest natural harbours in E. Pac.; US naval base; attacked by Japanese without warning 7 Dec. 1941 (7.55 a.m., local time), precipitating U.S. entry into Second World War.

Pearl Is., archipelago, G. of Panama; sea fishing, pearls.

Pearl R. See Chu-kiang.

Pechenga (**Petsamo**), spt., **Russia;** on inlet of Barents Sea; formerly Finnish, ceded to USSR Sept. 1944; ice-free throughout year; exp. nickel, timber, cobalt.

Pechora, dist., **Russia;** E. of Urals; coalfields; coking coal; ch. ts., Vorkuta and Inta.

Pechora, R., **Russia;** rises in Urals and flows N. into Arctic Oc.; 1,120 km navigable between June and Sept. for transport of timber from its basin; fishing; 1,792 km long.

Pecos, R., N.M. and Texas, **USA;** trib. of Rio Grande; water control schemes provide irrigation for lge. a.; 1,482 km long.

Pécs, c., S.W. **Hungary;** on Yugoslav border; one of oldest and most pleasantly situated ts. of Hungary; cath., univ., airport; in coal-mng. a.; coke, chemicals, majolica, leather gds., engin., brewing; p. (1997) 161,000.

Peebles, royal burgh, Borders, **Scot.;** on upper course of R. Tweed; woollen cloth, knitwear; mkt., tourist ctr.; p. (2002) 8,065.

Peeblesshire, historic co., S. **Scot.;** now part of Borders.

Peel, t., **Isle of Man;** resort, fishing pt. midway along W. cst.; cas., cath.; p. (1991) 3,829.

Peel Fell, mtn. Northumberland, Eng.; 1,964 ft.

Pegu (**Bago**), c., Pegu prov., S. **Myanmar;** R. pt., rly. junc.; many temples, notably Shwe May Daw Pagoda; once cap. of Burmese kingdom; came under Brit. rule 1852; p. (1983) 150,447.

Pegu Yoma, mtns., **Myanmar;** between valleys of Rs. Irrawaddy and Sittang; thickly forested with teak which is comm. exploited and forms impt. exp.

Peipus, Lake, Estonia; drained by Narva R. into G. of Finland; Pskov lies to S.; scene of Alexander Nevsky's victory over the Germans 1242; a. 3,626 km².

Pekalongan, t., N. cst. Java, **Indonesia;** exp. sugar, rubber; p. (1995) 449,000.

Peking. See Beijing.

Pelagi, gr. of Italian Is., inc. Lampedusa and Linosa, between Malta and Tunisian cst.

Pelée, mtn., **Martinique;** active volcano, devastated town of St. Pierre 1902; alt. 1,342 m.

Pella, dep. of Macedonia, **Greece;** mtnous.; cotton, wheat, tobacco; cap. Edessa; a. 2,802 km²; p. (1991) 138,761.

Peloponnesus (**Peloponnisos**), peninsula and reg., S. **Greece;** separated from mainland by G. of Corinth, but joined in N.E. by Isthmus of Corinth; mtnous.; livestock agr., drought-resistant sheep and goats; ch. ts., Kalamata, Tripolis; a. 21,642 km²; p. (1991) 1,086,935 (inc. region of Peloponnesus and district of Akhaia and Elia).

Pemba, I., part of **Tanzania;** cloves, copra, coconuts; exp. mangrove bark for tannin; a. 984 km²; p. (1988) 265,039.

Pembroke, mkt. t., Pembrokeshire, **Wales;** on S. side of Milford Haven, sm. pt., dock facilities; cas., ruins of Monkton priory; birth-place of Henry VII; p. (1991) 6,773.

Pembroke Dock, Pembrokeshire, **Wales;** site of government dockyard (1814) with consequent growth of a new t.; p. (1991) 8,651.

Pembrokeshire, S.W. **Wales,** unit. auth. created in 1996 from former l. gov. dists. of Preseli, Pembrokeshire and South Pembrokeshire, reinstating historic co. split up in 1974; p. (2001) 114,131.

Penang, t., st. W. **Malaysia;** cap. George Town, pt. for N. Malaya handling rubber and tin; paper mill; the first Brit. Straits Settlement (q.v.); linked by bridge (1985) to mainland; longest bridge (13 km.) in Asia; a. 1,036 km²; p. (2005) 1,300,000.

Penarth, t., Vale of Glamorgan, **Wales;** former sm. pt. on Severn estuary, 3 km S. of Cardiff; seaside resort; p. (1991) 23,434.

Pendle, l. gov. dist., Lancs., **Eng.;** ts. of Barrowford, Colne and Nelson; p. (2001) 89,248.

Pengpu. See Bengbu.

Penicuik, burgh, Midlothian, **Scot.;** on R. Esk; paper; p. (2002) 14,759.

Penistone, t., South Yorks., **Eng.;** on R. Don; steel; mkt.; p. (1991) 8,627.

Penki. See Benxi.

Penmaenmawr, t., Conwy, **Wales;** 6 km. S.W. of Conwy; resort.

Pennine Alps, Switzerland; div. of Alpine system; ch. peaks; Mont Blanc (4,814 m) Monte Rosa (4,637 m), Matterhorn (4,477 m); winter sports.

Pennine Range, mtn. range, "backbone of England," extends 224 km southwards from Cheviot hills to Derbyshire; limestone, mill-stone grit; moorland sheep, dairying in valleys, quarrying, tourism; inc. Peak Dist. Nat. Park and Pennine Way long distance route; water supply, forestry; Cross Fell, 895 m.

Pennsylvania, st., **USA**; "Keystone St."; admitted to Union 1787; st. flower Mountain Laurel, st. bird Ruffed Grouse; originally proprietary colony of Penn family, later one of the 13 original sts. in the Union; traversed N.E. to S.W. by Appalachians; ch. Rs.: Delaware, Susquehanna, Allegheny, and Monogahela; major industl. st.; iron and steel, coal (bituminous and anthracite), natural gas, petroleum; maize, wheat, oats, rye; textiles, machin., motor cars, tobacco; cap. Harrisburg; ch. ts.: Pittsburgh, Philadelphia; a. 117,412 km²; p. (2002) 12,335,091.

Penrith, mkt. t., Eden, Cumbria, **Eng.**; at N. foot of Shap Fell, 29 km S.E. of Carlisle; agr. mkt.; tourist ctr.; p. (1991) 12,049.

Penryn, t., Carrick, Cornwall, **Eng.**; on R. Fal estuary; sm. pt., boat repairs; once ctr. of granite quarrying; p. (1991) 7,027.

Pensacola, t., Fla., **USA**; on N. shore of P. Bay; originally a Spanish settlement, retaining much Spanish influence in squares, bldgs., street names; fishing, sea food inds.; univ.; naval air training school; p. (1984) 62,000 (t.), 318,700 (met. a.).

Pentonville, dist., London, **Eng.**; prison; birthplace of John Stuart Mill.

Pentland Firth, strait, between Orkney Is. and Highland, **Scot.**, connecting N. Sea and Atl. Oc.; dangerous tidal currents.

Pentland Hills, range, **Scot.**; extend from Lanark to Edinburgh; hgst. Scald Law, 878 m.

Penwith, l. gov. dist., Cornwall, **Eng.**; S.W. tip of Cornwall inc. Penzance, St. Just and St. Ives; p. (2001) 63,012.

Penza, c., cap. of P. oblast, **Russia**; on Sura R.; rly. junc.; agr. ctr., especially for grain tr. to Moscow; food-processing and wide range of mnfs.; oil pipeline from Mozyr'; p. (1989) 543,000.

Penzance, t., Penwith, Cornwall, **Eng.**; on Mount's Bay; tourist ctr.; ferry to Scilly Isles; engin.; birthplace of Sir Humphrey Davy; p. (1991) 19,709.

Peoria, t., Ill., **USA**; machin., domestic gds.; univ.; p. (1990) 113,504 (t.), 339,172 (met. a.).

Perak, st., **W. Malaysia**; tin-dredging a., in basin of Perak R.; rubber; cap. Taiping; a. 20,668 km²; p. (2005) 2,075,000.

Pereira, t., Caldas, **Colombia**; cath.; comm. ctr. for coffee; severe earthquake devastation (1999); p. (1992) 335,960.

Périgord, dist., S.W. **France**; limestone plateau crossed by Dordogne R.; famous for truffles.

Périgueux, t., cap. Dordogne, **France**; on R. Isle; cath.; famous for pâté de foie gras; engin., china; p. (1999) 30,193.

Perlis, st., **W. Malaysia**; agr. dist. for rice and coconuts; tin; a. 803 km²; p. (2005) 200,000.

Perm, oblast, **Russia**; major mng., timber, and (Kizel), hydroelectricity, and potash (Solikamsh); cap. Perm.

Perm (Molotov), c., cap. of P. oblast, **Russia**; on Kama R.; machin., chemicals, oil refineries; univ.; p. (1989) 1,091,000.

Pernambuco, st., N.E. **Brazil**; mtnous. interior, cst. fertile; cap. Recife; sugar, cotton, manioc, tobacco, fruits; a. 98,322 km²; p. (1991) 7,109,626.

Pernis, t., opposite Rotterdam, **Neth.**; lge. oil refinery; pipeline to Wesserling (nr. Cologne).

Perpignan, c., cap. of Pyrénées-Orientales dep., **France**; nr. Spanish border and Mediterranean; on Paris–Barcelona rly.; mkt. and comm. ctr. for wines and fruits; cath.; tourism; p. (1990) 108,049 (c.), 138,735 (met. a.).

Persepolis, anc. c., **Iran**; former cap. of Persian empire, now in ruins; tourism.

Pershore, t., Wychavon, Worcs., **Eng.**; on R. Avon; ctr. of fruit-growing a.; p. (1991) 7,087.

Persia. *See* Iran.

Persian Gulf, inlet from Indian Oc. through G. of Oman and Strait of Hormuz, between Iran and Arabia; oilfields in surrounding land and now in G. itself; ch. pts. Bandar-e-Büshehür, Abadan, Kuwait, Dubai; Bahrain, lgst. I. Sometimes called Arabian Gulf.

Perth, c., cap. of W. **Australia**; on R. Swan; well planned garden c.; univ., cath., airport; many employed in services; inds. moving to Fremantle (c.) or to Kwinana; p. (1993) 1,221,200 (met. a., 73 per cent of st. p.).

Perth, c., royal burgh, Perth and Kinross, **Scot.**; on R. Tay; rly. junction; cap. of Scot. until assass-

ination of James I, 1437; impt. cattle mkt.; cath; p. (2002) 43,450.

Perth and Kinross, unit. auth. created in 1996, formerly part of Tayside, E. **Scot.**; p. (2002) 135,160.

Perthshire, historic co., E. **Scot.**, now divided between Perth and Kinross and Stirling.

Peru, Andean rep., S. America; consists of 3 N.W.–S.E. regions; Costa (cst.) Sierra (Andes, rising to over 6,100 m) and Selva (interior *montaña* and R. basins); 40 per cent p. in Costa, 60 per cent total a.; ch. Rs. Ucayali, Marañon; L. Titicaca shared with Bolivia; El Misti volcano in S.; cap. Lima on Pac. cst. with 20 per cent p.; agr. diversified and being extended by irrigation schemes; fishing main single ind.; mng. impt. in Andes; major world producer of silver, phosphates, potash, copper, petroleum; social, economic and political problems provoking long-lasting guerrilla revolt; new highway to Brazil planned; a. 1,249,048 km², p. (2004) 27,544,305.

Peru Current (Humboldt), ocean current, S. Pac. Oc.; flows N. along cst. of N. Chile and Peru; causes clouds and fog.

Perugia, t., Umbria, **Italy**; on R. Tiber; univ., observatory; woollens, silks, lace; foodstuffs, furniture, pottery, chemicals, agr. machin.; p. (1992) 146,160.

Pesaro, c., central **Italy**; on Adriatic cst.; agr. ctr., seaside resort; birthplace of Rossini; p. (1981) 90,412 (inc. Urbino).

Pescara, c., cap. of P. prov., S. **Italy**; on estuary of R. Aterno; fish. pt., olive oil, soap, pasta, pottery; resort; birthplace of D'Annunzio; p. (1992) 121,424.

Peshawar, c., cap. of North-West Frontier Prov., **Pakistan**; 18 km E. of Khyber pass, commanding route to Afghanistan; military sta.; univ.; handicrafts, textiles, furniture; p. (1981) 555,000.

Petah Tikva, oldest modern Jewish settlement in **Israel** (1878); ctr. for oranges; mnfs. inc. textiles; p. (1992) 148,900.

Peterborough, t., Ont., **Canada**; flour-milling, elec. machin., trailers, agr. equipment, plastics, textiles, paper; p. (1996) 100,193.

Peterborough, c., unit. auth., Cambs., **Eng.**; on R. Nene on margin of Fens; cath.; rly ctr.; ctr. of brick ind. (Oxford clay around Fletton); diesel engines, agr. machin., gen. engin.; expanding t.; p. (2001) 156,061 (unit. auth.), (2001) 136,292 (c.).

Peterborough, Soke of. *See* **Cambridgeshire**.

Peterhead, spt., burgh, Aberdeenshire, **Scot.**; on E. cst., 43 km N.E. of Aberdeen; herring fisheries, leading EU white fish port (2000); fish-processing, granite quarrying; supply base for N. Sea oil; p. (2002) 17,947.

Peterlee, new t. (1948), Durham, **Eng.**; coal-mng. dist.; textiles, science-based inds.; p. (2001) 29,936.

Petersfield, t., East Hants., **Eng.**; on R. Rother, N.W. of Chichester; mkt.; p. (1991) 12,177.

Petra, anc. c., **Jordan**; temples, rock tombs and Roman ruins; called Sela in Bible (2 Kings 14. 7); rediscovered by Burckhardt 1812. Now threatened by erosion.

Petropavlovsk, t., **Kazakhstan**; on Ishim R.; rly. junc.; flour, leather, meat canneries, furs, engin.; p. (1990) 245,200.

Petropavlovsk-Kamchatsky, t., **Russia**; spt. on Pac. cst.; shipyard, timber mills, engin.; fishing and whaling fleet; p. (1989) 269,000.

Petrópolis, t., Rio de Janeiro, **Brazil**; health resort, c. 700 m a.s.l.; cath.; p. (1996) 267,700.

Petsamo. *See* Pechenga.

Petten, t., **Neth.**; 48 km N.W. of Amsterdam, on cst.; atomic research ctr.

Petworth, mkt. t., West Sussex, **Eng.**; in Rother valley, 19 km N.E. of Chichester; associated with Turner; p. (1991) 2,156.

Pevensey Levels, marshy a., East Sussex, **Eng.**; now largely drained, cattle pastures; a. 62 km².

Pforzheim, t., Baden-Württemberg, **Germany**; S.E. of Karlsruhe; gold, silver, metal wks., jewellery; p. (2002) 118,002.

Phetburi, t. and prov., **Thailand**; on Isthmus of Kra crossed by Phetburi R.; p. (1980) 366,612 (prov.).

Philadelphia, c., pt., Penns., **USA**; on Delaware

TIME ZONES 1

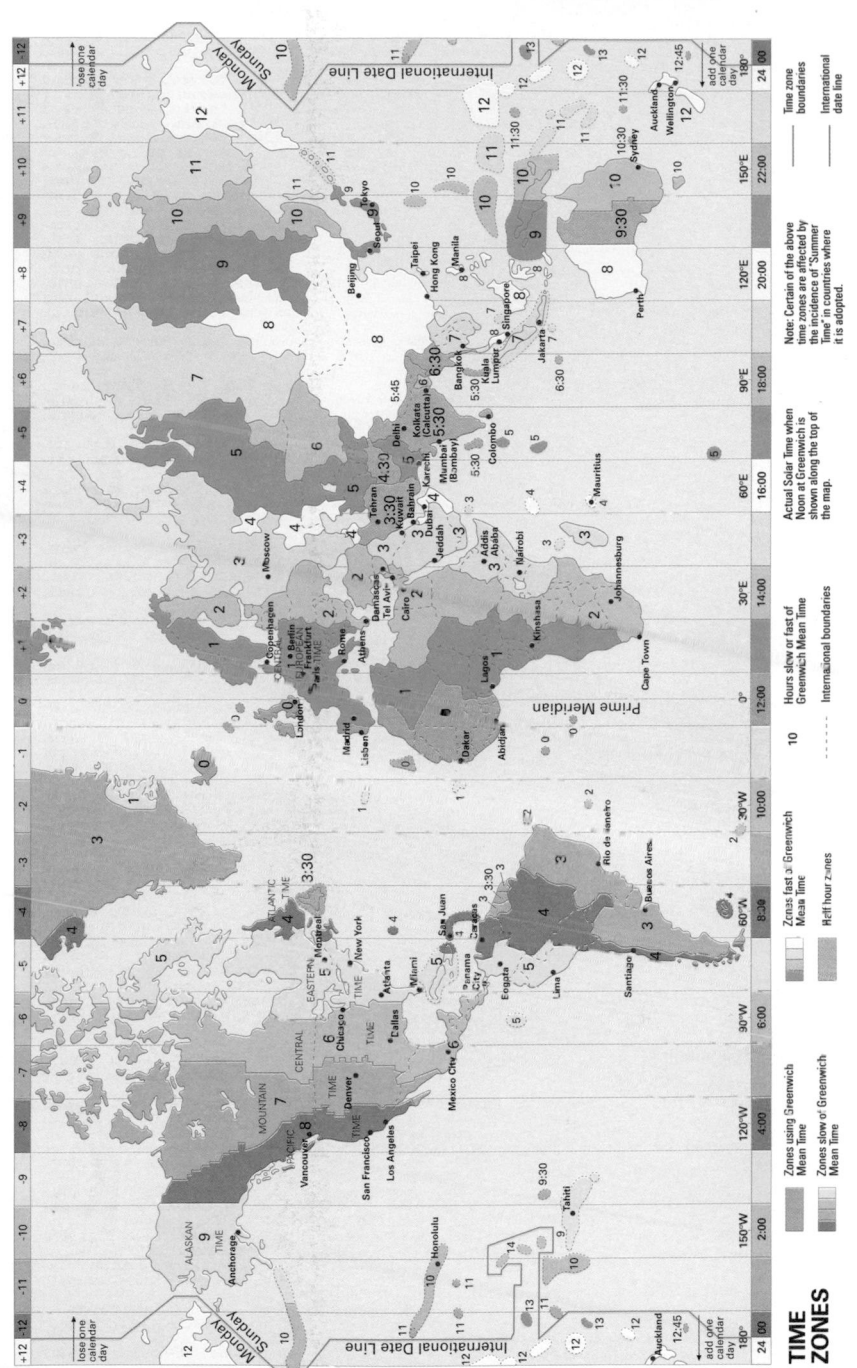

TIME ZONES

+12	-12	-11	-10	-9	-8	-7	-6	-5	-4	-3	-2	-1

lose one calendar day

add one calendar day

Zones using Greenwich Mean Time

Zones fast on Greenwich Mean Time

Time zone boundaries

Zones slow of Greenwich Mean Time

Half hour zones

International date line

Note: Certain of the above time zones are affected by the incidence of 'Summer Time' in countries where it is adopted.

Actual Solar time when Noon at Greenwich is shown along the top of the map.

Hours slow or fast of Greenwich Mean Time

Internarional boundaries

─────────────────────── **SETTLEMENTS** ───────────────────────

■ **PARIS**   ■ **Berne**   ◉ **Livorno**   ⊙ **Brugge**   ⊚ Algeciras   ○ *Frejus*   ○ *Oberammergau*   ○ *Thira*

Settlement symbols and type styles vary according to the scale of each map and indicate the importance
of towns on the map rather than specific population figures

─────────────────────── **ADMINISTRATION** ───────────────────────

────── International Boundaries   ─ ─ ─ International Boundaries
(Undefined or Disputed)   ⋯⋯⋯ Internal Boundaries

International boundaries show the *de facto* situation where there are rival claims to territory

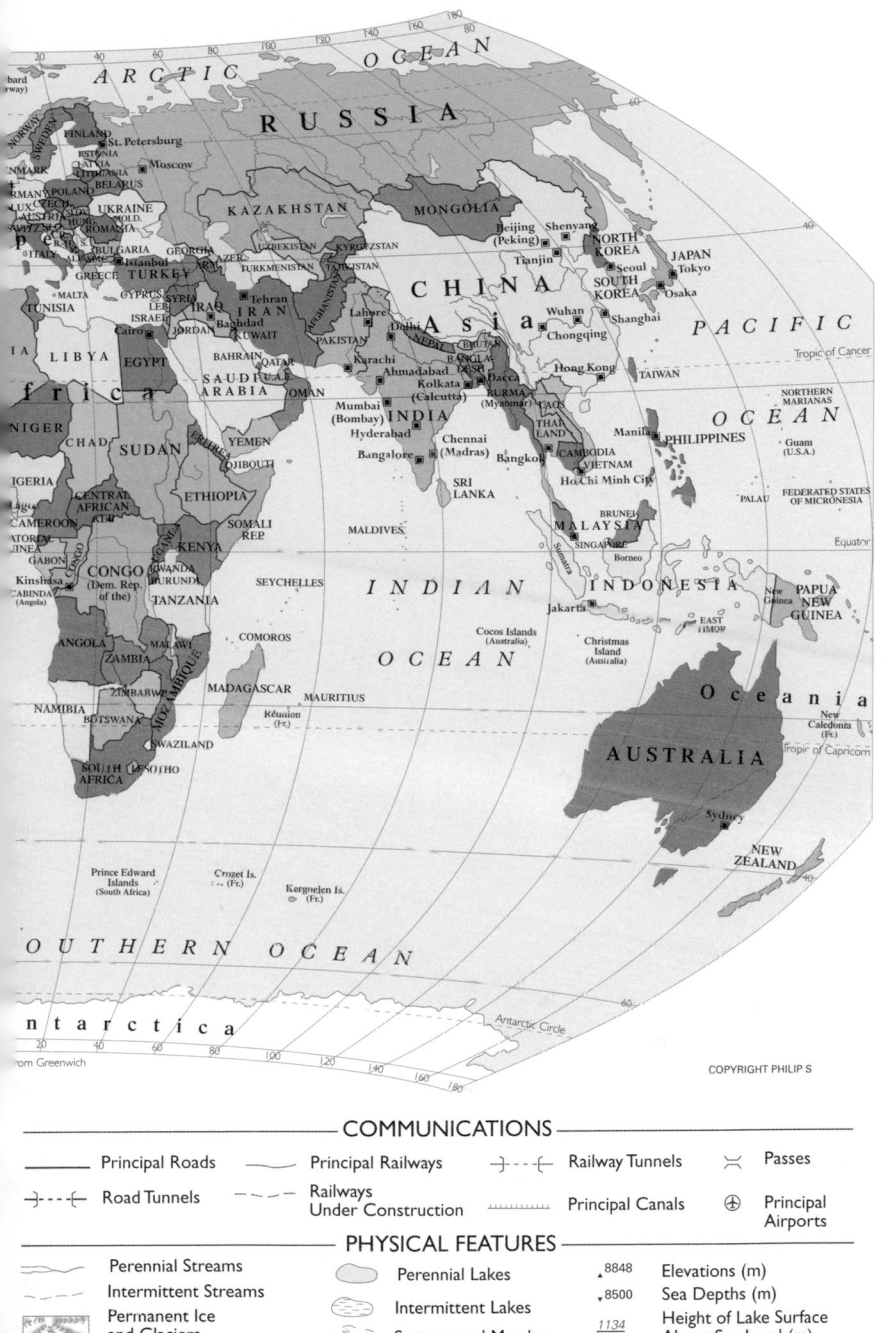

COMMUNICATIONS

Principal Roads	Principal Railways	Railway Tunnels	Passes
Road Tunnels	Railways Under Construction	Principal Canals	Principal Airports

PHYSICAL FEATURES

Perennial Streams

Intermittent Streams

Permanent Ice and Glaciers

Perennial Lakes

Intermittent Lakes

Swamps and Marshes

.8848   Elevations (m)

.8500   Sea Depths (m)

1134   Height of Lake Surface Above Sea Level (m)

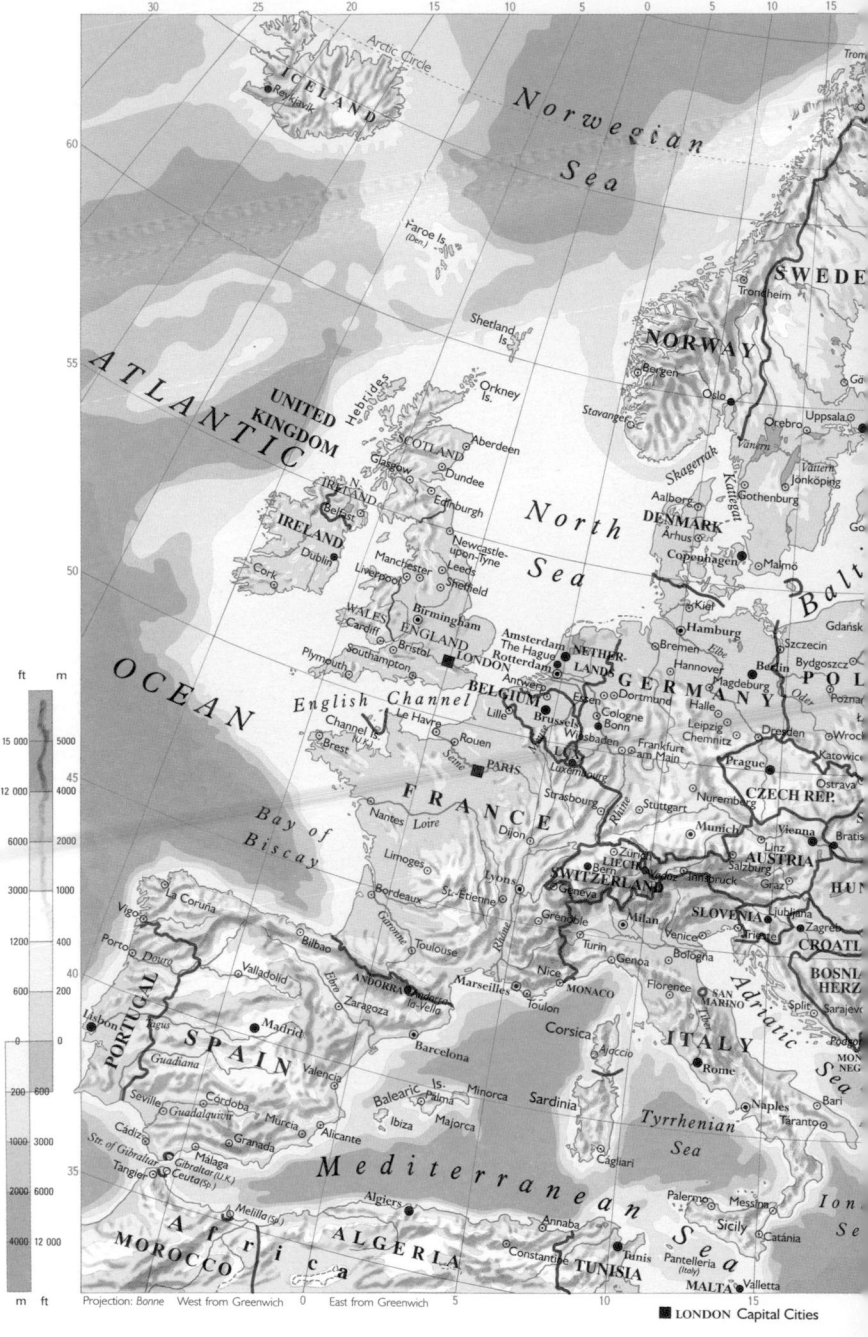

ICELAND
Reykjavik

Norwegian Sea

Faroe Is.
(Den.)

SWEDE

Trondheim

NORWAY

Bergen
Oslo
Ga
Stavanger
Orebro
Uppsala

Shetland Is.

Orkney Is.

UNITED
KINGDOM
Aberdeen

SCOTLAND
Glasgow
Dundee
Edinburgh

Vanern
Jönköping
Vattern
Go

ATLANTIC

Hebrides

North Sea

Aalborg
DENMARK
Arhus
Copenhagen
Malmö

Kattegat
Skagerrak

Go

Balt

N. IRELAND
Belfast

IRELAND
Dublin
Cork

Newcastle-
upon-Tyne
Leeds
Liverpool
Manchester
Sheffield

Kiel
Hamburg
Szczecin
Bydgoszcz
POL

OCEAN

WALES
Cardiff
ENGLAND
Birmingham
Bristol
LONDON
Southampton
Plymouth

Amsterdam
The Hague
Rotterdam
NETHER.
LAND
Antwerp
BELGIUM
Brussels

Bremen
Hannover
Dortmund
Essen
Cologne
Bonn
GERMANY
Magdeburg
Berlin

Halle
Leipzig
Frankfurt
am Main
Chemnitz
Dresden
Prague
CZECH REP.

Oder
Poznań
Wrocła
Katowice
Ostrava

English Channel
Channel Is.
(U.K.)
Brest
Le Havre
Lille
Rouen
Seine
PARIS
Luxembourg
LUX
Strasbourg
Wiesbaden
Stuttgart
Nuremberg
Munich

Vienna
Linz
AUSTRIA
Salzburg
Bratis
Graz
HU

Bay of
Biscay

Nantes
Loire
Limoges
FRANCE
Dijon
St-Étienne
Lyons
Grenoble
Bordeaux
Toulouse
Garonne
Rhône

LIECH
SWITZERLAND
Geneva
Zürich
Innsbruck
Milan
Turin
Venice
Genoa
Bologna
Trieste
SLOVENIA
Ljubljana
Zagreb
CROATI

Vigo
La Coruña
Porto
Douro
Bilbao
ANDORRA
la-Vella
Nice
MONACO
Marseilles
Toulon
Florence
SAN
MARINO
Split
Sarajevo
BOSNI
HERZ
Adriatic

PORTUGAL
Lisbon
Valladolid
Zaragoza
Ebro
Madrid
SPAIN
Barcelona
Valencia
Corsica
Ajaccio
ITALY
Rome
MON
NEG
Podg
Bari

Guadiana

Balearic Is.
Minorca
Palma
Majorca
Ibiza
Sardinia
Tyrrhenian
Sea
Naples
Taranto
Ion
Se

Tagus
Guadalquivir
Seville
Cádiz
Córdoba
Granada
Málaga
Murcia
Alicante

Str. of Gibraltar
Tangier
Gibraltar (U.K.)
Ceuta (Sp.)

Mediterranean Sea

Cagliari

Palermo
Messina
Sicily
Catánia

MOROCCO

A f r i c a

Melilla (Sp.)
Algiers
Annaba

ALGERIA
Constantine
Pantelleria
(Italy)
TUNISIA
Tunis
MALTA
Valletta

---

ft   m

15 000   5000

12 000   4000

6000   2000

3000   1000

1200   400

600   200

0   0

200   600

1000   3000

2000   6000

4000   12 000

m   ft

Projection: Bonne   West from Greenwich   0   East from Greenwich   5   10   15

■ LONDON Capital Cities

5

100 0 100 200 300 400 500 600 700 800 km
100 0 100 200 300 400 500 miles

35 40 45 50 55 60 65 70

Hammerfest

Murmansk

60

White Sea

Arkhangelsk

N. Dvina

una

Luleå

L. Onega

Kotlas

Perm

Nizhniy Tagil

FINLAND

Vaasa

Kirov

Yekaterinburg

Chelyabinsk

55

mpere

Vyborg L. Ladoga

Vologda

Ufa

Turku

Helsinki

ST.PETERSBURG

Rybinsk Res.

Yaroslavl

Kostroma

Kazan

Magnitogorsk

m

Tallinn

L. Chudskoye

Ivanovo

Nizhniy Novgorod

ESTONIA

R U S S I A

L A T V I A

Riga

MOSCOW

Simbirsk

Samara

Orenburg

W. Dvina

Tula

Penza

LITHUANIA

Kaunas

Vitebsk

Smolensk

Volga

Uralsk

Kaliningrad

Vilnius

Mogilev

Orel

Tambov

Saratov

K A Z A K H S T A N

B E L A R U S

Minsk

Kursk

Voronezh

Atyrau

Białystok

Brest

Gomel

Pripet

Volgograd

Warsaw

Chernigov

Don

D

Lublin

Zhitomir

Kiev

Dnieper

Kharkov

Astrakhan

45

REP

kov

Lvov

U K R A I N E

Dnepropetrovsk

Donetsk

Caspian Sea

iskóld

Dniester

Krivoy Rog

Zaporozhye

Taganrog

Bug

Rostov

Makhachkala

Debrecen

MOLDOVA

Nikolayev

Kherson

Stavropol

Cluj-Napoca

Kishinev

Odessa

R O M A N I A

Brasov

Galati

Crimea

Krasnodar

Mt.Elbrus 5642

GEORGIA

Tbilisi

AZERBAIJAN

40

Timisoara

Ploiesti

Sevastopol

GEORGIA

Baku

Igrade

Bucharest

Constanta

B l a c k S e a

ARMENIA

Yerevan

Niš

Danube

Varna

Samsun

Erzurum

Apras

Tabriz

BULGARIA

Sofia

Bosporus

I R A N

Skopje

Plovdiv

ISTANBUL

a

ACEDONIA

Thessaloníki

Bursa

T U R K E Y

Diyarbakir

REECE

Ankara

Kayseri

35

Izmir

Konya

A

Patrai

Athens

Adana

Aegean Sea

Antalya

S

I R A Q

Baghdad

Rhodes

CYPRUS

Nicosia

Aleppo

Euphrates

Tigris

Crete

SYRIA

45

30 35

COPYRIGHT PHILIP'S

50 0 100 200 300 400 km

50 0 50 100 150 200 250 miles

COPYRIGHT PHILIP'S

Projection: Conical with two standard parallels

20 East from Greenwich

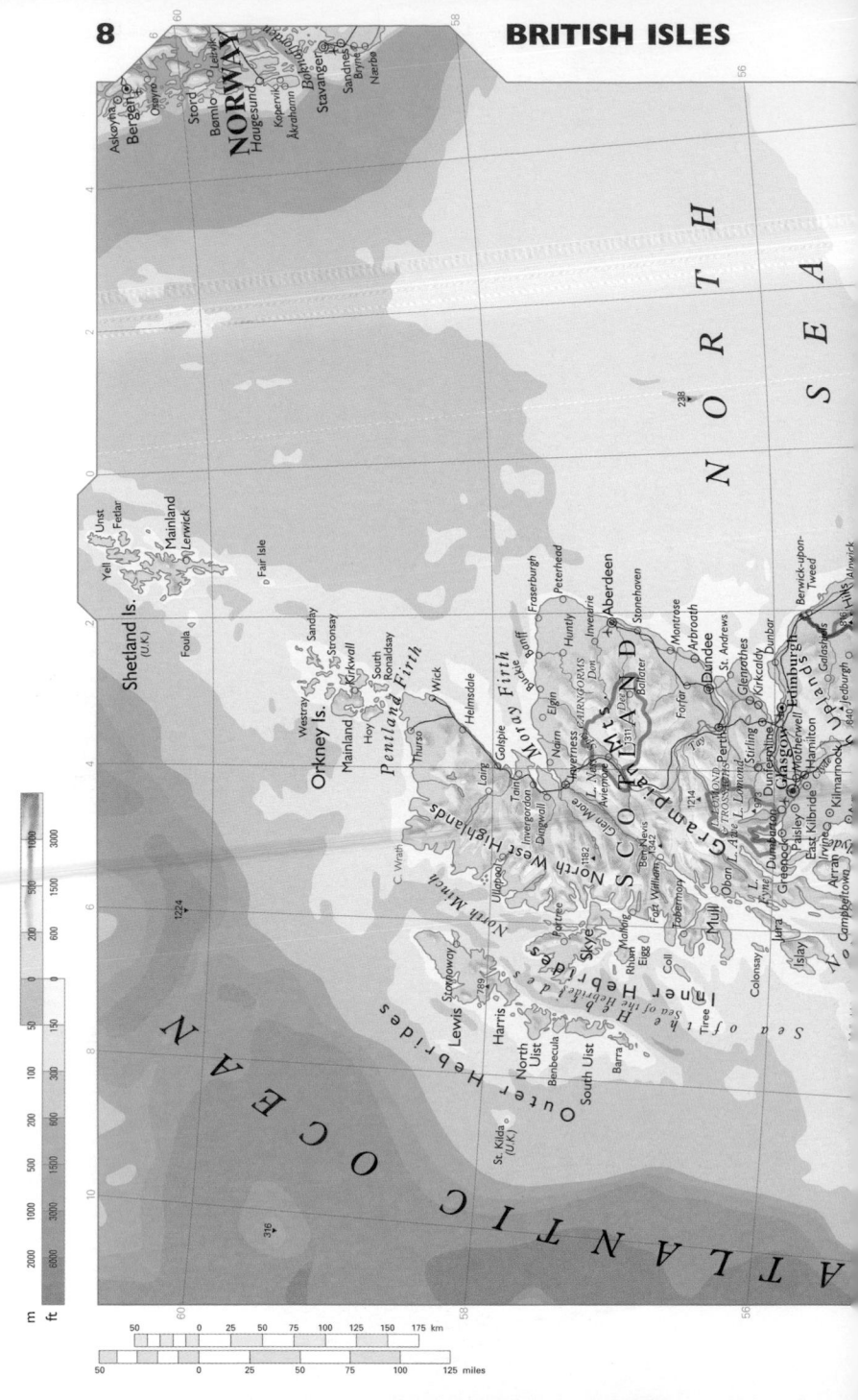

NORWAY

Askvoll
Bergen
Osøyrø
Fjell
Jølster
Stord
Bømlo
Kopervik
Haugesund
Åkrehamn
Sandnes
Bryne
Nærbø
Stavanger

NORTH SEA

238

Shetland Is.
(U.K.)

Yell
Unst
Fetlar
Mainland
Lerwick

Foula

Fair Isle

Orkney Is.
Westray
Sandoy
Stronsay
Kirkwall
Mainland
Hoy
South
Ronaldsay

Penland Firth

1224

Thurso
Wick
Helmsdale
Golspie
Dornoch
Tain
Lairg
Loch
Shin
Invergordon
Dingwall
Inverness
Nairn
Fraserburgh
Peterhead
Huntly
Elgin
Banff
Ballater
Aberdeen
Stonehaven
Montrose
Arbroath
Dundee
St. Andrews
Forfar
Glenrothes
Kirkcaldy
Dunbar

Moray Firth

CAIRNGORMS
1311
Ben
Macdui

Glen More

C. Wrath

North West Highlands

Ullapool

Loch
Maree

Ben Nevis
1342

Fort William

Tobermory

Mull

Oban
L. Awe
L. Linnhe
L. Lomond
Perth
Stirling
Dunfermline
Glasgow
Dumbarton
Greenock
Paisley
Motherwell
Hamilton
East Kilbride
Kilmarnock
Irvine
Ayr

SCOTLAND

GRAMPIAN

Tay

840
1214

Lammermuir
Hills
Edinburgh
Berwick-upon-Tweed
Galashiels
Jedburgh
St. Hills
Alnwick

Southern
Uplands

Loch
Ness

Loch

Dee

Skye
Raasay
Rhum
Eigg
Coll
Tiree
Colonsay

Inner Hebrides

Portree

Scalpay

789

Islay
Jura
Kintyre
Firth
Campbeltown
Arran

Sea of the Hebrides

North Minch

Lewis

Harris

Scalpay

Outer Hebrides

North
Uist
Benbecula
South Uist
Barra

St. Kilda
(U.K.)

376

ATLANTIC OCEAN

m
ft

1000   3000
500   1500
200   600
50   150
0   0
50   150
100   300
200   600
500   1500
1000   3000
2000   6000

50   0   25   50   75   100 125 150 175 km

50   0   25   50   75   100 125 miles

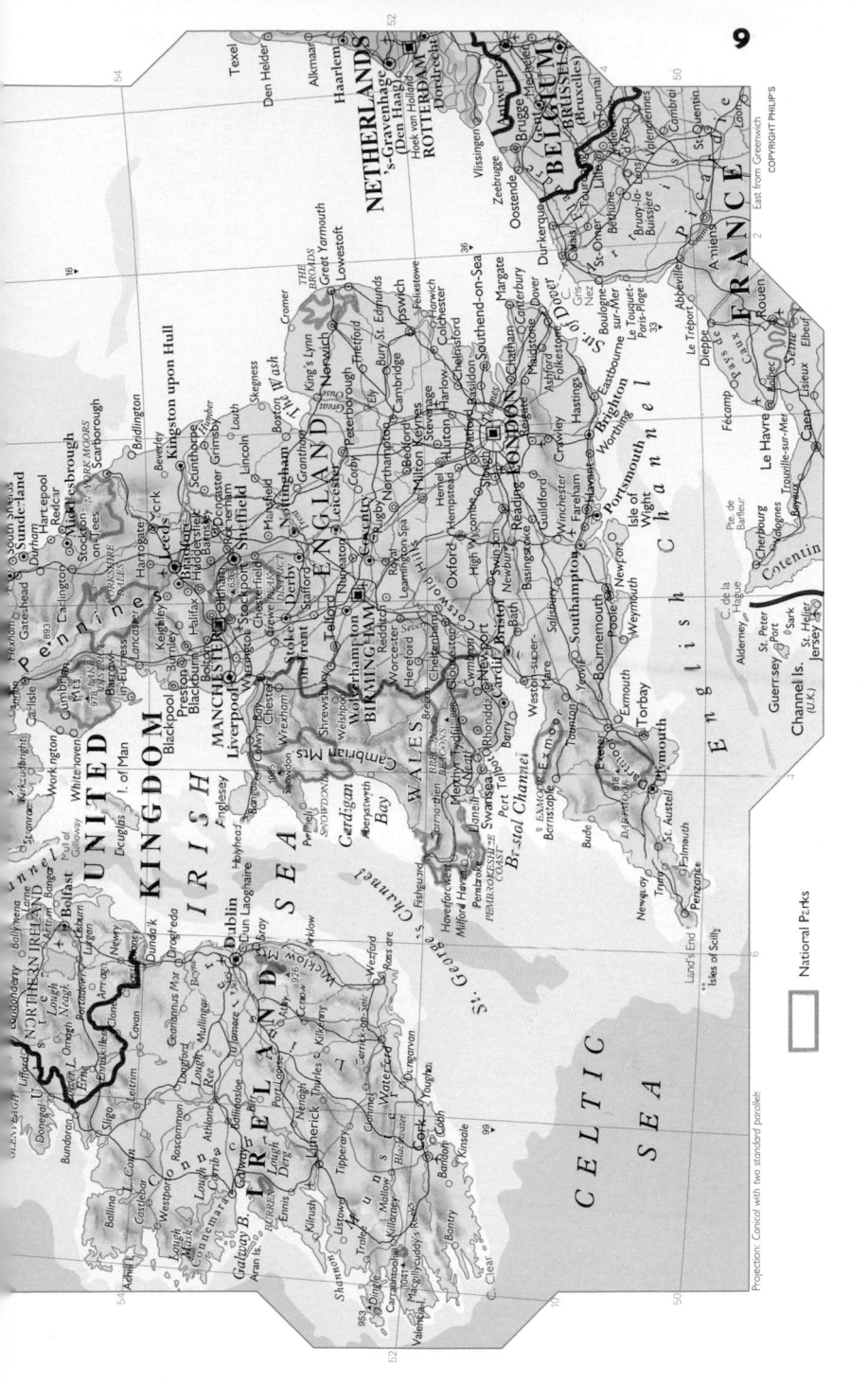

National Parks

Projection: Conical with two standard parallels

2   East from Greenwich   0   COPYRIGHT PHILIPS

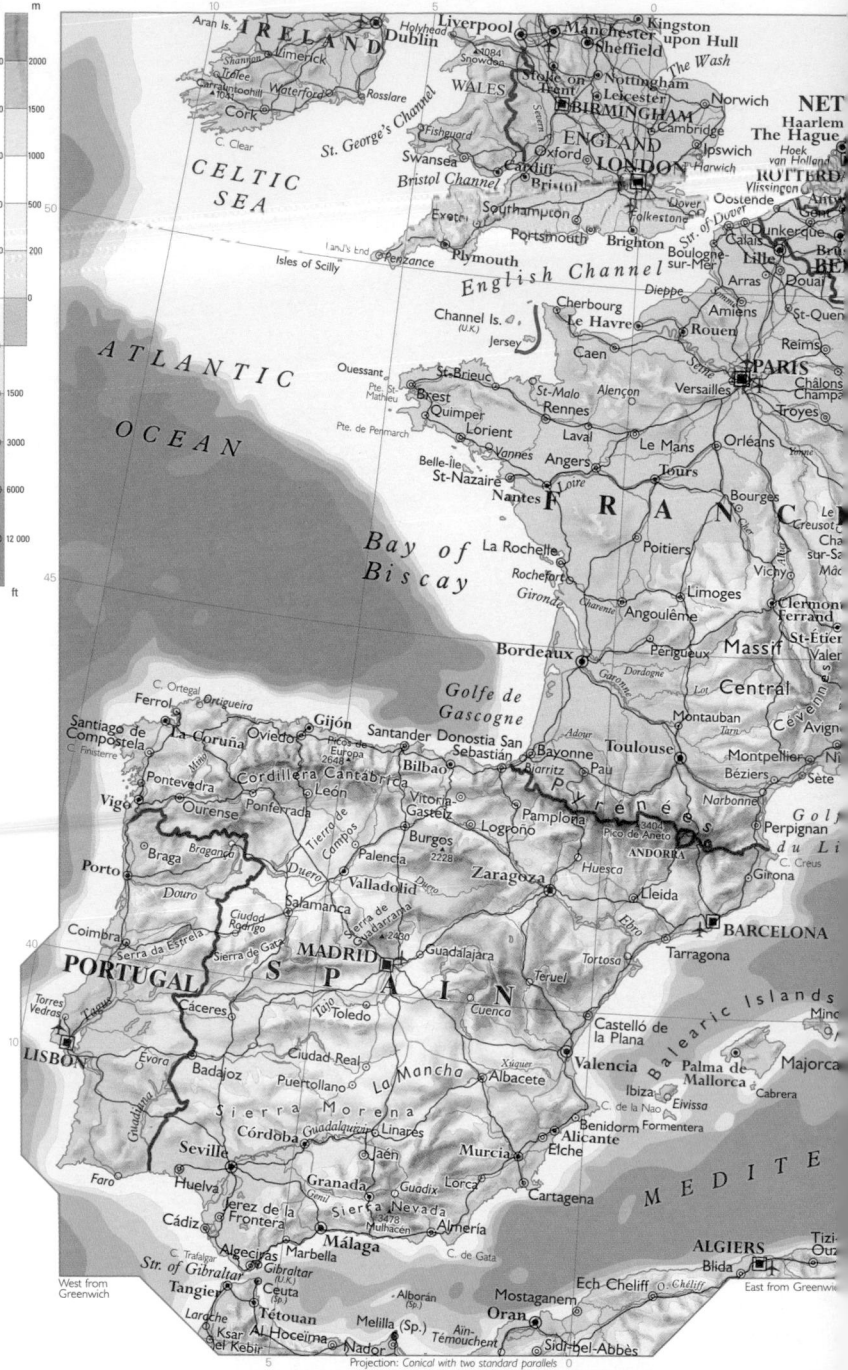

ft   m

6000   2000
4500   1500
3000   1000
1500   500
600   200
0   0
200
500   1500
1000   3000
2000   6000
4000   12 000

m   ft

Aran Is.   IRELAND   Dublin   Holyhead   Liverpool   Manchester   Kingston upon Hull   Sheffield
Shannon   Limerick   Snowdon   Stoke-on-Trent   Nottingham   The Wash
Tralee   Carrantoohill   Waterford   Rosslare   WALES   Leicester   Norwich   NET
1041   Cork   St. George's Channel   Fishguard   BIRMINGHAM   Cambridge   Haarlem   The Hague
C. Clear   Swansea   Cardiff   ENGLAND   Oxford   Ipswich   van Hollend   ROTTERD
CELTIC   Bristol Channel   Bristol   LONDON   Harwich   Vlissingen   BE
SEA   Southampton   Dover   Oostende   Bru
Exeter   Portsmouth   Brighton   Str. of Dover   Calais   Dunkerque   Lille   Douai
Land's End   Penzance   Plymouth   Folkestone   Boulogne-sur-Mer   Arras   St-Quen
Isles of Scilly   English Channel   Dieppe   Amiens   Reims
Cherbourg   Le Havre   Rouen   Châlons
ATLANTIC   Ouessant   St-Brieuc   Caen   Seine   PARIS   Champa
Pte. de Mathieu   Brest   St-Malo   Alençon   Versailles   Troyes
OCEAN   Quimper   Rennes   Laval   Le Mans   Orléans   Yonne
Pte. de Penmarch   Lorient   Vannes   Angers   Tours   Bourges   Le
Belle-île   St-Nazaire   Nantes   Loire   FRANC   Creusot   Cha sur-Sa
Bay of   La Rochelle   Poitiers   Vichy   Mâc
Biscay   Rochefort   Gironde   Charente   Angoulême   Limoges   Clermont-Ferrand   St-Étien
Bordeaux   Périgueux   Massif   Valer
Golfe de   Garonne   Dordogne   Lot   Central   Cévennes   Avig
Gascogne   Montauban   Tarn
C. Ortegal   Ortigueira   Gijón   Santander   Donostia San   Bayonne   Toulouse   Montpellier   Ni
Ferrol   Oviedo   Picos de   Sebastián   Biarritz   Pau   Béziers   Sete
Santiago de   La Coruña   Europa   Bilbao   Pyrénées   Narbonne   Gol
Compostela   C. Finisterre   Cordillera Cantábrica   Vitoria   Pico de Aneto   Perpignan   du Li
Pontevedra   León   Ponferrada   Gasteiz   Logroño   Pamplona   ANDORRA   C. Creus
Vigo   Ourense   Miño   Burgos   Huesca   Lleida   Girona
Braga   Bragança   Tierra de   Palencia   Duero   Zaragoza   BARCELONA
Porto   Campos   Valladolid   Ebro
Douro   Salamanca   Sierra de   Huesca   Tarragona
Coimbra   Ciudad   Guadarrama   MADRID   Guadalajara   Tortosa
Sierra da Estrela   Rodrigo   SPAIN   Teruel   Balearic Islands
PORTUGAL   Cáceres   Sierra de Gata   Toledo   Cuenca   Castelló de   Minc
Torres   Tajo   la Plana
Vedras   Évora   Ciudad Real   Xúquer   Valencia   Palma de   Majorca
LISBON   Badajoz   Puertollano   Albacete   Ibiza   Mallorca   Cabrera
Sierra Morena   La Mancha   Benidorm   Formentera
Sierra Morena   Córdoba   Guadalquivir   Linares   Alicante   C. de la Nao   Eivissa
Guadiana   Jaén   Murcia   Elche
Seville   Granada   Guadix   Lorca   Cartagena   MEDITE
Faro   Huelva   Genil   Sierra Nevada   Almería   C. de Gata
Cádiz   Jerez de la   Mulhacén   3478
Frontera   3478
C. Trafalgar   Algeciras   Marbella   C. de Gata   ALGIERS   Tizi
Str. of Gibraltar   Gibraltar   Málaga   Ouz
Tangier   Ceuta   (Sp.)   Alborán   Mostaganem   Ech Cheliff   Blida
Larache   Tétouan   Melilla (Sp.)   (Sp.)   Oran   East from Greenwi
Ksar   Al Hoceima   Aïn-   Sidi-bel-Abbès
el Kebir   Nador   Témouchent

West from Greenwich

Kolomyya
Kamyanets-Podilskyy
Mohyliv-Podilskyy
Uman
Kirovohrad
DNEPROPETRO
Dnyeprodzerzhinsk
Kremenchuk

Debrecen
Baia Mare
Chernovtsy
Bălți
Balta
Pervomaysk
Kriv
Rog
Nik

Satu Mare
Botoşani
MOLDOVA
Voznesensk
Inhulec
Vdskh.
Kakhovske

Oradea
Iaşi
Kishinev
Tiraspol
Nikolaev
Dniepet
Kherson

Cluj-Napoca
Bacău
Tighira
Kishinev
ODESSA
UKRA

ROMANIA
Focşani
Bilhorod-Dnistrovskyy
Karkinitska Zatoka
Mys Tarkhankut
Dzha

Sibiu
Braşov
Galaţi
Yevpatoriya
CRIM

BELGRADE
Transylvanian Alps
Buzău
Brăila
Izmayil
Simferopol

Timişoara
Râmnicu Vâlcea
Piteşti
Ploieşti
Sevastopol

SERBIA
Drobeta-Turnu Severin
BUCHAREST
Balaklava

Kragujevac
Vidin
Craiova
Danube
Silistra
Ruse
Constanţa

MONTENEGRO
Niš
Pleven
Veliko Túrnovo
Dobrich

Novi Pazar
Priština
Kosovo
SOFIA
Varna

ALBANIA
Skopje
MACEDONIA
BULGARIA
Sliven
Burgas

Tirana
Bitola
Plovdiv
Khaskovo

Vlorë
GREECE
Rhodope Mts.
Edirne

Thessaloníki
Kavala
İSTANBUL
Zonguldak
Karabük

Alexandroúpolis
Tekirdağ
Sea of Marmara
Ereğli
Sakarya

Lárisa
Limnos
Çanakkale
BURSA
Kocaeli
(İzmit)
Bolu

Vólos
Balıkesir
Kütahya
Eskişehir
ANKARA
Kırıkkale

ATHENS
Manisa
İZMIR
(Smyrna)
Uşak
KONYA

Peloponnese
Aydın
Denizli
Isparta
Antalya

Crete
Iráklion
Rhodes
(Greece)
Antalya Körfezi

Morphou
Nicosia
CYPRUS
Limassol

MEDITERRANEAN SEA

ISR
TEL AVIV-JAF

Darnah
Tubruq
ALEXANDRIA
Dumyât
Port Said
Jerus

LIBYA
Marsá Matrûh
EGYPT
El Mansûra
Suez

EL GIZA
CAIRO

Projection: Conical with two standard parallels

50 0 100 200 300 400 km

50 0 50 100 150 200 250 miles

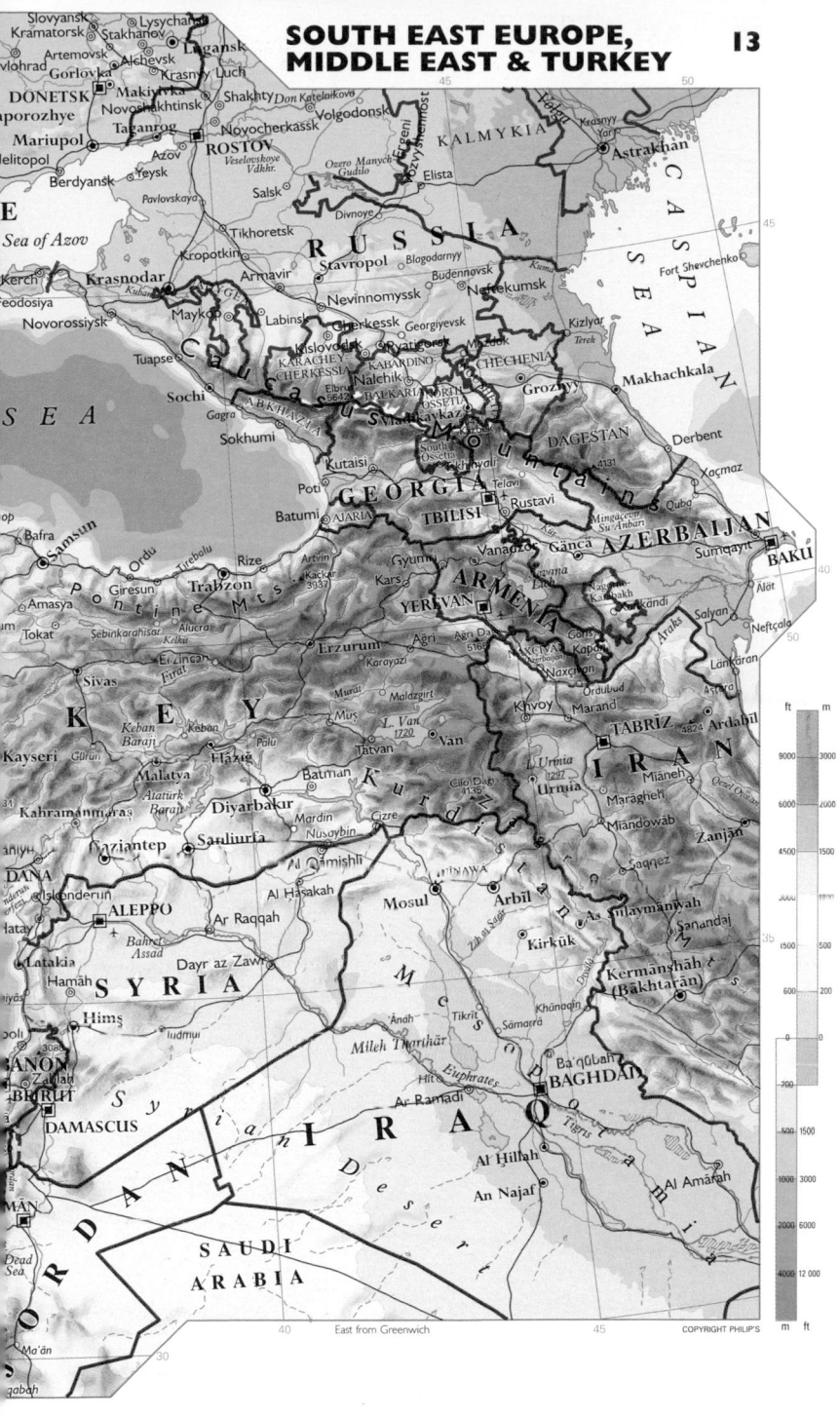

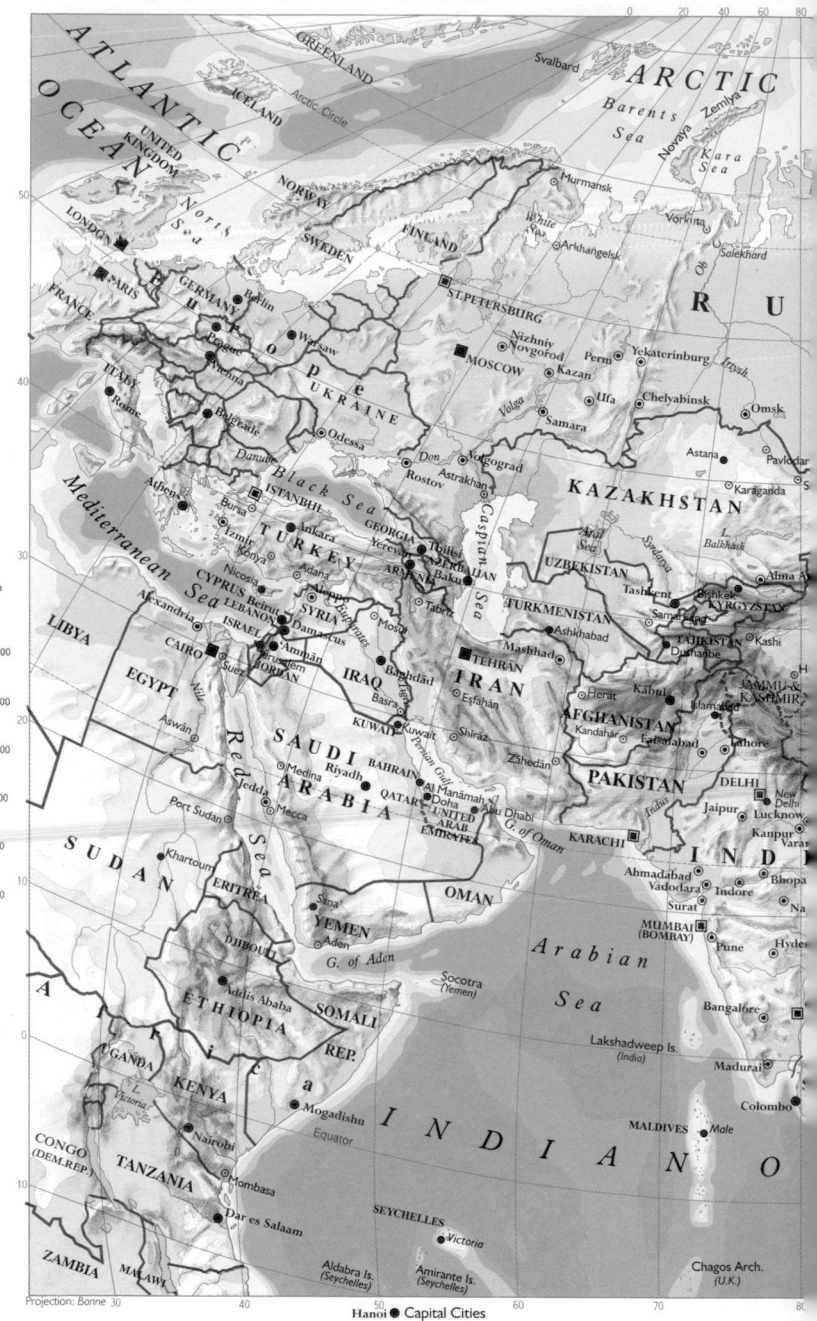

ATLANTIC
OCEAN

GREENLAND

ICELAND
Arctic Circle

Svalbard

ARCTIC

Barents
Sea

Novaya Zemlya

Kara
Sea

UNITED
KINGDOM

North Sea

NORWAY

SWEDEN

FINLAND

Murmansk

Vorkuta

R   U

LONDON

PARIS

FRANCE

GERMANY
Berlin

Prague

Vienna

Warsaw

Budapest

Belgrade

ITALY
Rome

UKRAINE

Danube

Odessa

Black Sea

ISTANBUL

Bursa
Izmir

TURKEY
Ankara

Konya
Adana

CYPRUS
LEBANON
Beirut
ISRAEL
Jerusalem
Amman
JORDAN
West Bank

Aleppo
SYRIA
Damascus

Nicosia

ST.PETERSBURG

Nizhniy
Novgorod

Perm

Yekaterinburg

Irtysh

MOSCOW

Volga

Kazan

Ufa

Chelyabinsk

Omsk

Rostov

Don

Volgograd

Astrakhan

Samara

Astana

Karaganda

Pavlodar

KAZAKHSTAN

Aral
Sea

Syr Darya

Balkhash

GEORGIA
Tbilisi
Yerevan
ARMENIA
AZERBAIJAN
Baku

Caspian Sea

UZBEKISTAN
Tashkent

Bishkek
KYRGYZSTAN
Alma Ata

Mosul

Tabriz

TURKMENISTAN

Ashkhabad

Samarkand

TAJIKISTAN
Dushanbe

Kashi

Athens

Mediterranean Sea

Alexandria

LIBYA

EGYPT

Cairo

Suez

Aswān

Nile

Red Sea

Port Sudan

Jedda

Mecca

Medina

SAUDI
ARABIA

Riyadh

Baghdad

IRAQ

Basra

KUWAIT
Kuwait

BAHRAIN
QATAR
Doha
Manamah
Abu Dhabi
UNITED
ARAB
EMIRATES

Euphrates

Mashhad

TEHRĀN

Eşfahān

Shiraz

IRAN

Herat

Zāhedan

Persian Gulf

G. of Oman

Kābul
Islamabad
AFGHANISTAN
Kandahar
Faisalabad

Mashhad

JAMMU &
KASHMIR

Lahore

PAKISTAN

KARACHI

DELHI
New
Delhi

Jaipur

Lucknow

Kanpur

Varanasi

Indus

SUDAN

Khartoum

ERITREA

Sana'
YEMEN
Aden

DJIBOUTI

OMAN

G. of Aden

Socotra
(Yemen)

Arabian
Sea

Ahmadabad
Vadodara
Indore

Bhopal

Na

MUMBAI
(BOMBAY)

Pune

Hyde

Bangalore

Lakshadweep Is.
(India)

Madurai

Colombo

I N D

Addis Ababa

ETHIOPIA

SOMALI
REP.

UGANDA

KENYA

Africa

Mogadishu

Equator

MALDIVES
Male

INDIAN O

CONGO
(DEM.REP.)

TANZANIA

Nairobi

Mombasa

ZAMBIA
MALAWI

Dar es Salaam

SEYCHELLES

Victoria

Aldabra Is.
(Seychelles)

Amirante Is.
(Seychelles)

Chagos Arch.
(U.K.)

ft   m

12 000   4000

9000   3000

6000   2000

3000   1000

1500   500

600   200

0   0

200   600

1000   3000

2000   6000

4000   12 000

6000   18 000

8000   24 000

m   ft

Projection: Bonne

Hanoi ● Capital Cities

500 0 250 500 750 1000 1250 1500 1750 km
500 0 250 500 750 1000 1250 miles

20   140   160   180

OCEAN
naya
nlya
Laptev Sea
New Siberian Is.
Wrangel I.
ALASKA (USA)
Bering Sea
Aleutian Is. (USA)
50

Khatanga
Verkhoyansk
Gizhiga
40

k
Lena
Okhotsk
Magadan
Sea of Okhotsk
Petropavlovsk-Kamchatskiy

S   I   A
Yakutsk
Komsomolsk
Sakhalin
Kuril Is.

Angara
Krasnoyarsk Bratsk L. Baikal Chita
Blagoveshchensk
Khabarovsk
Yuzhno-Sakhalinsk
Hokkaido
Sapporo
40

rsk
yokuznetsk
Irkutsk Ulan Ude
Hailar
Amur
Qiqihar
Harbin
Changchun
Jilin
Vladivostok
Honshū
TOKYO
Yokohama
30

Ürümqi Hami
Ulan Bator
MONGOLIA
SHENYANG
Jinzhou
Anshan
NORTH KOREA
PYONGYANG
Sea of Japan
Nagoya
Kyoto
JAPAN

Yumen
Bator
Bagtou
BEIJING TIANJIN
Dalian
SEOUL
SOUTH KOREA
Hiroshima
Osaka
Kitakyūshū
Bonin Is. (Japan)
20

Lanzhou
Taiyuan
Jinan
Huang-ho
Pusan
Ryukyu Is.
Volcano Is. (Japan)
Tropic of Cancer

CHINA
Xian
Nanjing
SHANGHAI
East China Sea
PACIFIC

Mt. Everest Lhasa
Chengdu
CHONGQING
Wuhan
HANGZHOU
Nanchang
Fuzhou

ET
8850
Brahmaputra
Changsha
GUANGZHOU
TAIWAN
Taipei
GUAM (USA)

Kunming
Si Kiang HONG KONG
Macau
10

ges
BANGLADESH
BURMA (MYANMAR)
Hanoi Haiphong
Hainan
Luzon
MANILA PHILIPPINES
FED. STATES OF MICRONESIA

DACCA (ITTA)
Chittagong
LAOS
VIETNAM
Cebu
PALAU

Bay of Bengal
Rangoon
THAILAND
BANGKOK
CAMBODIA
Phnom Penh
Ho Chi Minh City
Palawan
Sulu Sea
Mindanao
Davao
0

Andaman Is. (India)
G. of Thailand
Zamboanga

Nicobar Is. (India)
South China Sea
BRUNEI SABAH
Bandar Seri Begawan
Celebes Sea
Manado
Halmahera
Papua

A
PEN. MALAYSIA
Kuala Lumpur
SARAWAK
Celebes
Ceram
Ambon
Banda Sea
Arafura Sea

Medan
MALAYSIA
SINGAPORE
Borneo
INDONESIA
10

AN
Sumatra
Banjarmasin
Ujung Pandang
Palembang
Java Sea
Flores
Timor
EAST TIMOR
Timor Sea
AUSTRALIA

JAKARTA Bandung
Semarang
Surabaya
Java
Sumba

eenwich 90   100   110   130   140

COPYRIGHT PHILIP'S

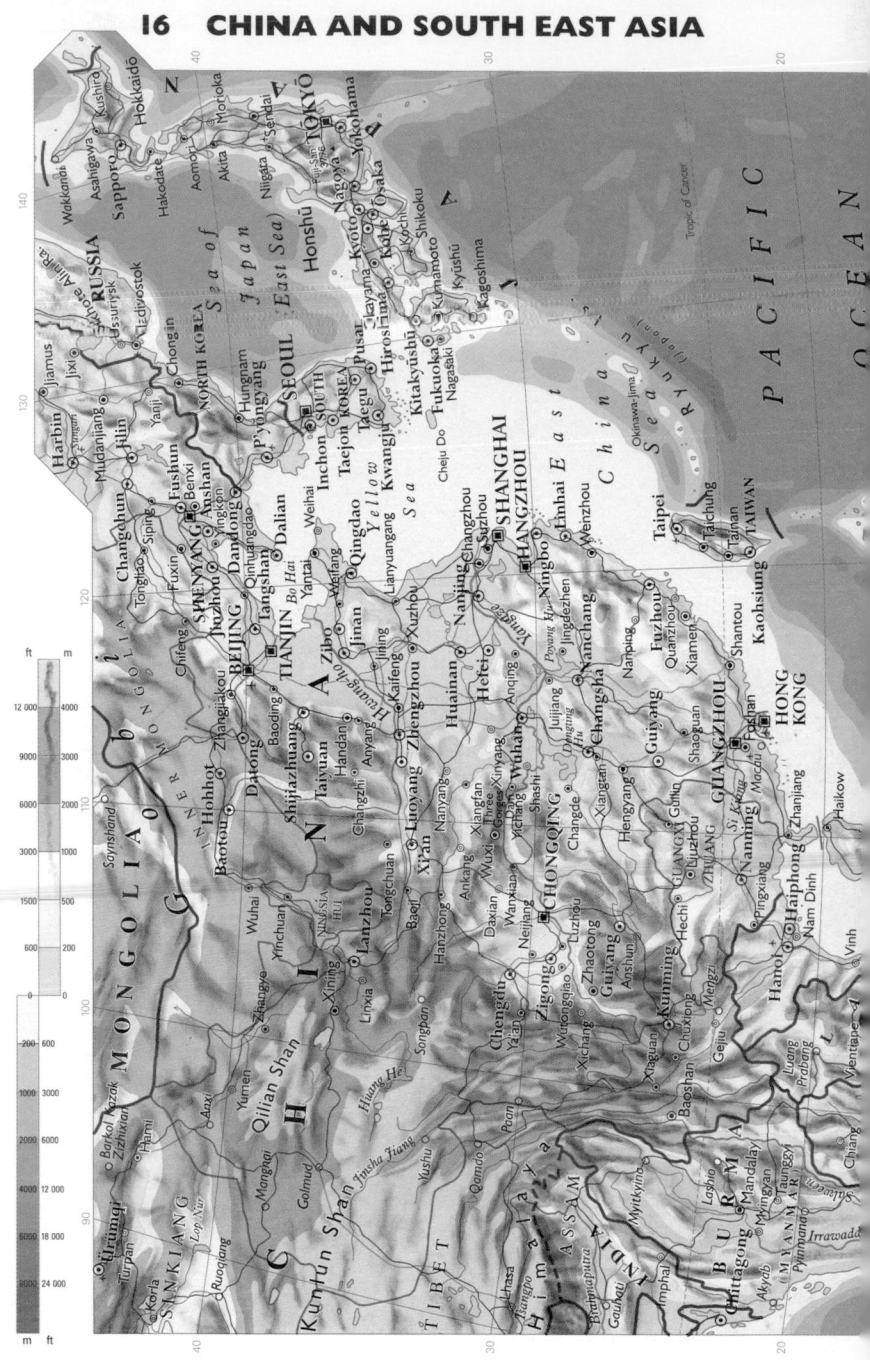

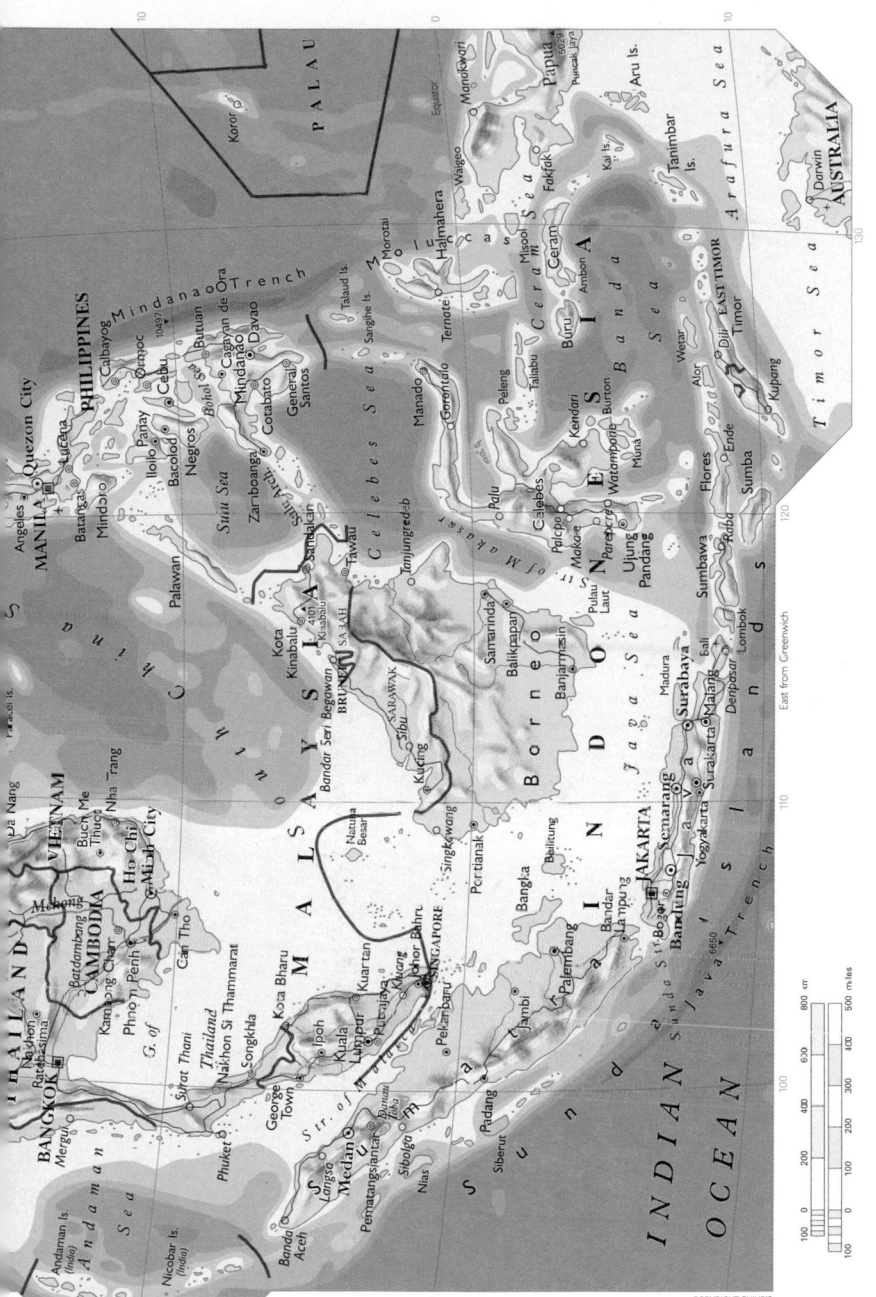

ft   m
18 000   6000
12 000   4000
9000   3000
6000   2000
3000   1000
1200   400
600   200
0   0
        200 600
        2000 6000
        4000 12 000
m ft

TURKEY
Malatya
Gaziantep
Diyarbakır
Erzurum
YEREVAN
ARMENIA
AZERBAIJAN
BAKU
KAZAKHSTAN
Nukus
Urgench
UZBEKISTAN
KAZ.
Türk.
Bukhara
Sama
ALEPPO (HALAB)
Hamāh
SYRIA
Hims
Mosul
Arbil
TABRIZ
Lankāran
Rasht
Zanjan
Caspian Sea
Garabogazköl Aylagy
Türkmenbashi
Kara
Kum
Chärjew
Qarshi
Kirkūk
Hamadān
Qazvin
TEHRĀN
Elburz Mountains
Bābol
Gorgān
Ashkhabad
Kopet Dag
Mary
Boyramaly
Kerki
Shibirghan
TURKMENISTAN
MASHHAD
Meymaneh
Herat
IRAQ
BAGHDĀD
Karbalā'
An Najaf
An Nāṣirīyah
Baṣra
Qom
Arāk
Kāshān
Dasht-e Kavir
Tabas
Birjand
Gonābād
AFGHANISTAN
Farāh
Gereshk
Kandahar
SYRIA
Desert
An Nafūd
Ḥā'il
ESFAHĀN
Yazd
Dasht-e Lūt
Dāryācheh-ye Seistan
Dasht-e Mārgow
Helmand
PAK
Nushki
Shik
KUWAIT
Al Kuwait
Shaṭṭ al 'Arab
Bandar-e Khomeynī
Shīrāz
Kāzerūn
Kermān
Zāhedān
Meresht
Dasht-i Tahlab
Central Makran Ra.
Nawa
SAUDI
Burayda
Medina
Rabigh
ARABIA
RIYADH
Ad Dammām
Al Mubarraz
Al Hufūf
BAHRAIN
Al Manāmah
QATAR
Doha
Bushehr
Jahrom
Bandar 'Abbās
Ra's al Khaymah
Dubai
Ash Shāriqah
Jāsk
Gābrik
Chāh Bahār
Gwādor
Pasni
Ormara
Baluchistan
Hydera
KARACHI
Mecca
Ta'if
Layla
As Sulayyil
Abū Dhabi
UNITED ARAB EMIRATES
Jabal Ghānim
Ṣuḥār
Masqaṭ
Tropic of Cancer
Ra's al Ḥadd
Abhā
Rub' al Khālī
Maṣīrah
Jazā'ir Farasān
OMAN
Zafār
Ra's al Madrakah
Al Hudaydah
San'ā'
Shibām
Hadramawt
Salālah
Mirbāt
J. Khuriyā Muriyā
YEMEN
Ta'iz
Al Mukhā
Shuqrā
Al Mukallā
Sayḥūt
Rās Fartak
Bāb el Mandeb
Aden
Madinat ash Sha'b
DJIBOUTI
Djibouti
Gulf of Aden
Socotra (Yemen)
Ras Asir (C. Guardafui)
Berbera
Erigavo
Bosaso
ARABIAN
SEA
Burao
Bender Beila
SOMALI REP.
Eil
Obbia
INDI

50 0 100 200 300 400 500 600 km
50 0 100 200 300 400 miles

Taraz
ymkent
Bishkek
KYRGYZSTAN
Namangan
Farghona
Ysyk-Köl
Pk Pobedy
7439
Aksu
Kashi
Shache
Hotan
TAJIKISTAN
Pamir
SINKIANG
Tarim Pendi
Taklamakan Shamo
Altun Shan
Bosten Hu
Korla
Kuruktag
Lop Nur
Yümen
Qilian Shan
6346
Qinghai Hu
Qaidam Pendi
Golmud
Goyang Hu
QINGHAI
Yushu
Qamdo
Kunlun Shan
Tanggula Shan
XIZANG ZIZHIQU (TIBET)
Nyainqentanglha Shan
Nam Co
Yarlung Zangbo
CHINA
KABUL
North West Frontier
hawar
Peshawar
Rawalpindi
Islamabad
Srinagar
JAMMU & KASHMIR
Gilgit
Chilas
K2
Karakoram
HIMACHAL PRADESH
Dehra Dun
Hardwar
Simla
Ambala
Chandigarh
Patiala
UTTARANCHAL
HIMALAYA
Mt Everest
8850
Dhaulagiri
8167
Pokhara
Kathmandu
NEPAL
Biratnagar
ARUNACHAL PRADESH
BHUTAN
Thimphu
Tezpur
FAISALABAD
LAHORE
Amritsar
Jullundur
PUNJAB
LUDHIANA
Multan
Sialkot
Gujranwala
Bahawalpur
Sahiwal
HARYANA
Meerut
Saharanpur
Moradabad
Rampur
Bareilly
DELHI
New Delhi
Aligarh
Mathura
Bikaner
Etawah
LUCKNOW
Gorakhpur
Chhapra
Darbhanga
MEGHALAYA
NAGALAND
ASSAM
Shillong
JAIPUR
RAJASTHAN
Jodhpur
Ajmer
Bewar
Agra
Gwalior
KANPUR
Allahabad
UTTAR PRADESH
Jaunpur
VARANASI
BIHAR
PATNA
Gaya
Bhagalpur
BANGLADESH
DACCA
Rajshahi
MANIPUR
MIZORAM
TRIPURA
BURMA
Thar Desert
Kota
Jhansi
Mirzapur
Son
JHARKHAND
Ranchi
Asansol
Dhanbad
WEST BENGAL
Khulna
Barisal
CHITTAGONG
Shwebo
AHMADABAD
Rajkot
INDORE
BHOPAL
MADHYA PRADESH
Jabalpur
Sagar
Bilaspur
CHHATTISGARH
Raurkela
KOLKATA (CALCUTTA)
Kharagpur
Akyab
Myingyan
Minbu
VADODARA
Bharuch
SURAT
Dhule
Amravati
NAGPUR
Raipur
ORISSA
Cuttack
Bhubaneswar
Puri
Ramree I.
Cheduba I.
G. of Khambhat
Nasik
Thane
MUMBAI (BOMBAY)
PUNE
MAHARASHTRA
Nanded
Jalna
Ahmadnagar
Nizamabad
Warangal
Kottagudem
Rajahmundry
Kakinada
Bay of Bengal
Godavari
Indravati
Jagdalpur
Brahmapur
Solapur
Gulbarga
Sangli
Bijapur
Bhima
Krishna
HYDERABAD
Vijayawada
Guntur
Eluru
Kolhapur
Belgaum
Dharwad
Gadag
Bellary
Davangere
Shimoga
GOA
Panaji
KARNATAKA
Adoni
Kurnool
ANDHRA PRADESH
Nellore
Mangalore
BANGALORE
Mysore
Kolar
Vellore
CHENNAI (MADRAS)
Puducherry
Coromandel Coast
Andaman Islands (India)
Port Blair
Malabar Coast
Calicut
COIMBATORE
Salem
Palghat
TAMIL NADU
Tiruchchirappalli
Kumbakonam
shadweep Is. (India)
Cochin
Mattancheri
MADURAI
Rameswaram
Palk Strait
Jaffna
Trincomalee
Quilon
Tuticorin
Tirunelveli
Mannar
SRI LANKA
Batticaloa
Trivandrum
Nagercoil
Kanyakumari (C. Comorin)
G. of Mannar
Puttalam
Kandy
Pidurutalagala
2524
COLOMBO
Galle
Dondra Head
MALDIVES
OCEAN

COPYRIGHT PHILIP'S

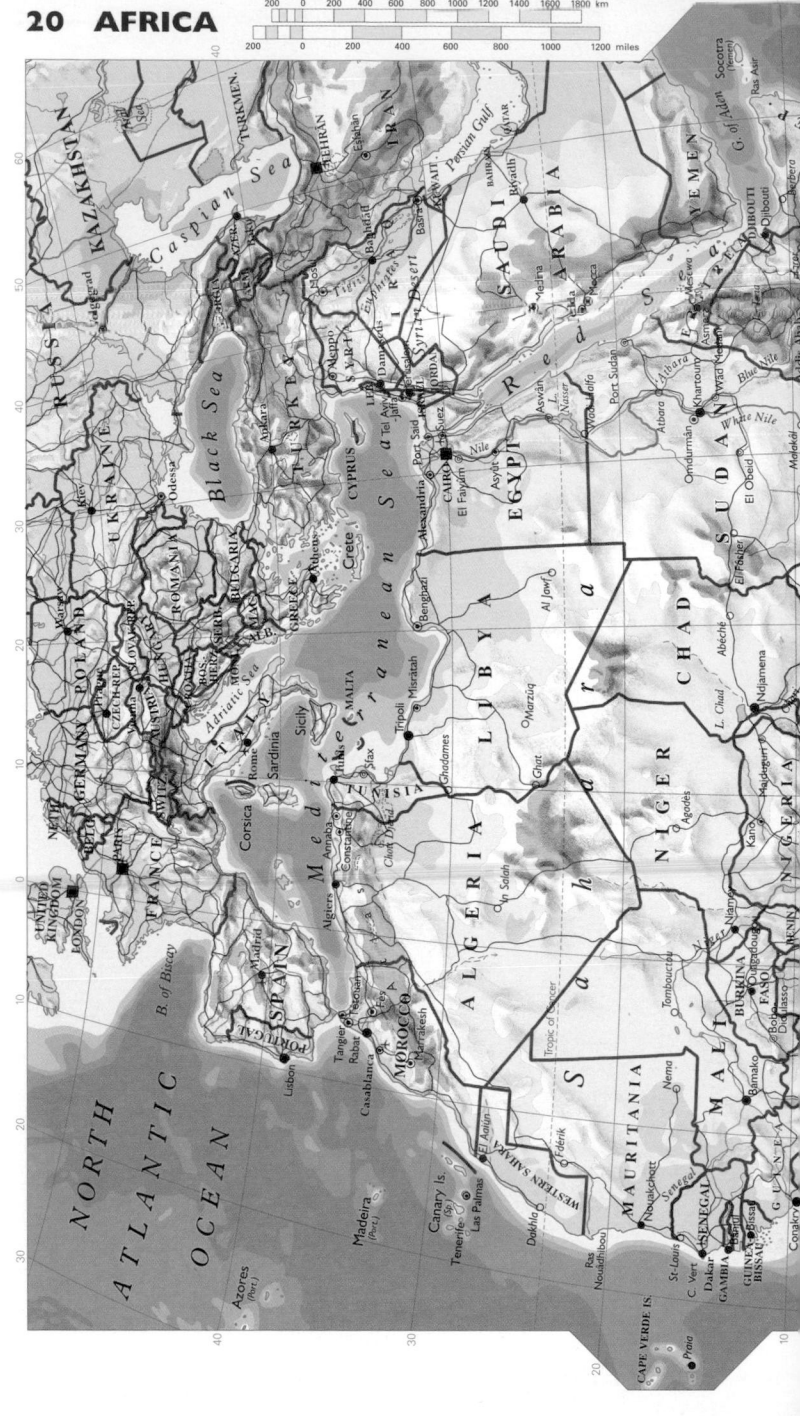

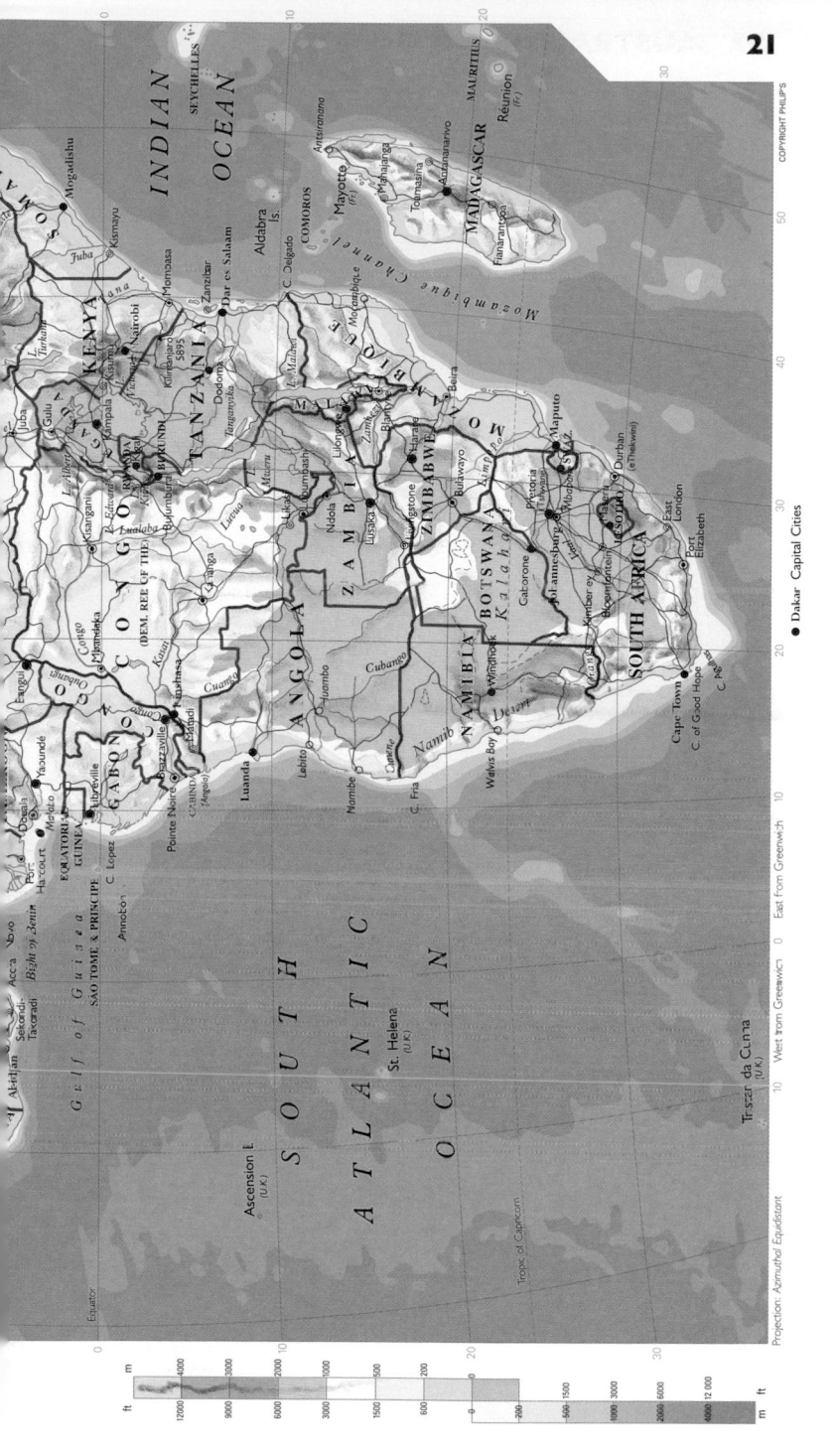

21

INDIAN

OCEAN

SEYCHELLES

MAURITIUS

Réunion (Fr.)

Mogadishu

SOMALIA

Kismayu

Juba

Mombasa

Zanzibar

Dar es Salaam

C. Delgado

COMOROS

Mayotte (Fr.)

Aldabra Is.

Antsiranana

Mahajanga

MADAGASCAR

Toamasina

ANTANANARIVO

Fianarantsoa

Mozambique Channel

KENYA

Nairobi

Kisumu

Kampala

L. Turkana

Gulu

Juba

Kilimanjaro 5895

Dodoma

TANZANIA

MALAWI

Lilongwe

Blantyre

MOZAMBIQUE

Nacala

Beira

Pemba

UGANDA

RWANDA

BURUNDI

Bujumbura

Kisangani

Mbandaka

CONGO (DEM. REP. OF THE)

L. Albert

L. Victoria

L. Tanganyika

L. Malawi

Zambezi

ZAMBIA

Lusaka

Ndola

Kitwe

Livingstone

Bulawayo

ZIMBABWE

Harare

Maputo

Mbabane

SWAZILAND

Durban (eThekwini)

Luanda

ANGOLA

Cabinda (Angola)

Congo

Brazzaville

Pointe Noire

Kinshasa

GABON

Libreville

EQUATORIAL GUINEA

Malabo

Yaoundé

CAMEROON

Port Harcourt

SÃO TOMÉ & PRÍNCIPE

Annobón

C. Lopez

Bight of Biafra

Gulf of Guinea

Accra

Lomé

Secondi
Takoradi

Abidjan

Bangui

Oubangi

Mbuji-Mayi

Kananga

Kananga

Luanda

Lobito

Benguela

Namibe

C. Fria

NAMIBIA

Windhoek

Walvis Bay

Namib Desert

Cubango

Cuanza

Cunene

Okavango

BOTSWANA

Gaborone

Kalahari

Desert

Orange

SOUTH AFRICA

Johannesburg

Pretoria

Bloemfontein

Kimberley

Cape Town

C. of Good Hope

Port Elizabeth

East London

C. Agulhas

ATLANTIC

SOUTH

OCEAN

Ascension I. (U.K.)

St. Helena (U.K.)

Tristan da Cunha

Equator

Tropic of Capricorn

Projection: Azimuthal Equidistant

West from Greenwich   East from Greenwich

● Dakar Capital Cities

COPYRIGHT PHILIP'S

m

ft

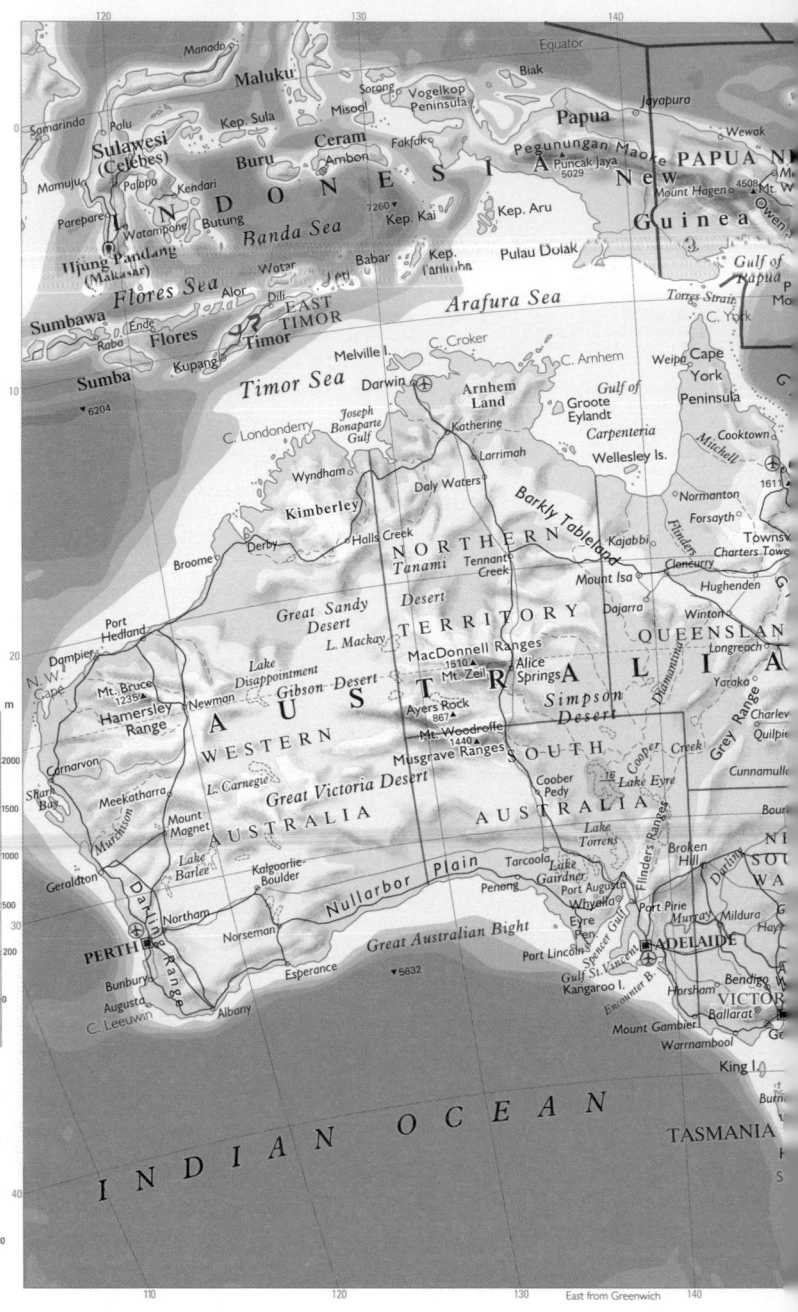

INDONESIA

Manado

Maluku

Sorong Vogelkop
Peninsula

Biak

Equator

Jayapura

Wewak

Samarinda

Palu

Sulawesi
(Celebes)

Misool

Papua

Pegunungan Maoke
Puncak Jaya
5029

PAPUA N

Mamuju

Palopo

Kep. Sula

Buru

Ceram

Fakfak

New

Mount Hagen

4508
Mt. W

Parepare

Kendari

Watampone Butung

Ambon

Kep. Kai

Guinea

Owen

Ujung Pandang
(Makasar)

Banda Sea

Kep. Aru

Pulau Dolak

Gulf of
Papua

Flores Sea

Babar

Kep.
Tanimbar

Torres Strait

P

Sumbawa

Alor

Weta

Arafura Sea

C. York

Mo

Raba Ende

Flores

Dili

EAST
TIMOR

Timor

Melville I.

C. Croker

C. Arnhem

Weipa

Cape
York

G

Sumba

Kupang

6204

Timor Sea

Darwin

Arnhem
Land

Gulf of
Carpentaria

Groote
Eyland

Peninsula

Cooktown

C. Londonderry

Joseph
Bonaparte
Gulf

Katherine

Larrimah

Wellesley Is.

Mitchell

161

Wyndham

Daly Waters

Normanton

Forsayth

Kimberley

Halls Creek

NORTHERN

Tanami

Tennant
Creek

Barkly Tableland

Kajabbi

Cloncurry

Townsv

Charters Tow

Broome

Derby

Desert

Mount Isa

Hughenden

Port
Hedland

Great Sandy
Desert

L. Mackay

TERRITORY

Dajarra

Winton

QUEENSLAN

Longreach

Dampier

N.W.
Cape

Mt. Bruce
1235

Hamersley
Range

Newman

Lake
Disappointment

Gibson Desert

MacDonnell Ranges
1510
Mt. Zeil

Alice
Springs

Simpson
Desert

Yaraka

Charlev

6000 2000

AUSTRALIA

WESTERN

Ayers Rock
867
Mt. Woodroffe
1440
Musgrave Ranges

SOUTH

Cooper Creek

Grey Range

Quilpie

Carnarvon

L. Carnegie

Great Victoria Desert

AUSTRALIA

Cunnamull

4500 1500

Shark
Bay

Meekatharra

Mount
Magnet

Lake
Barlee

Coober
Pedy

16

Lake Eyre

Bourk

3000 1000

Geraldton

Kalgoorlie-
Boulder

Lake
Torrens

Lake
Gairdner

Darling Range

Tarcoola

Broken
Hill

NI
SOU

1500 500

PERTH

Northam

Norseman

Nullarbor Plain

Penong

Port Augusta

Whyalla

Port Pirie

Murray

Mildura

Hay

30

Bunbury

Esperance

Great Australian Bight

Eyre
Pen.

Port Lincoln

Spencer Gulf

ADELAIDE

VICTOR

Bendigo

Augusta

Albany

5632

Gulf St. Vincent

Horsham

Ballarat

Ge

C. Leeuwin

Kangaroo I.

Encounter B.

Mount Gambier

Warrnambool

King I.

Butr

INDIAN OCEAN

TASMANIA

S

200

500 1500

1000 3000

40

2000 6000

4000 12 000

m ft

110

120

130

East from Greenwich

140

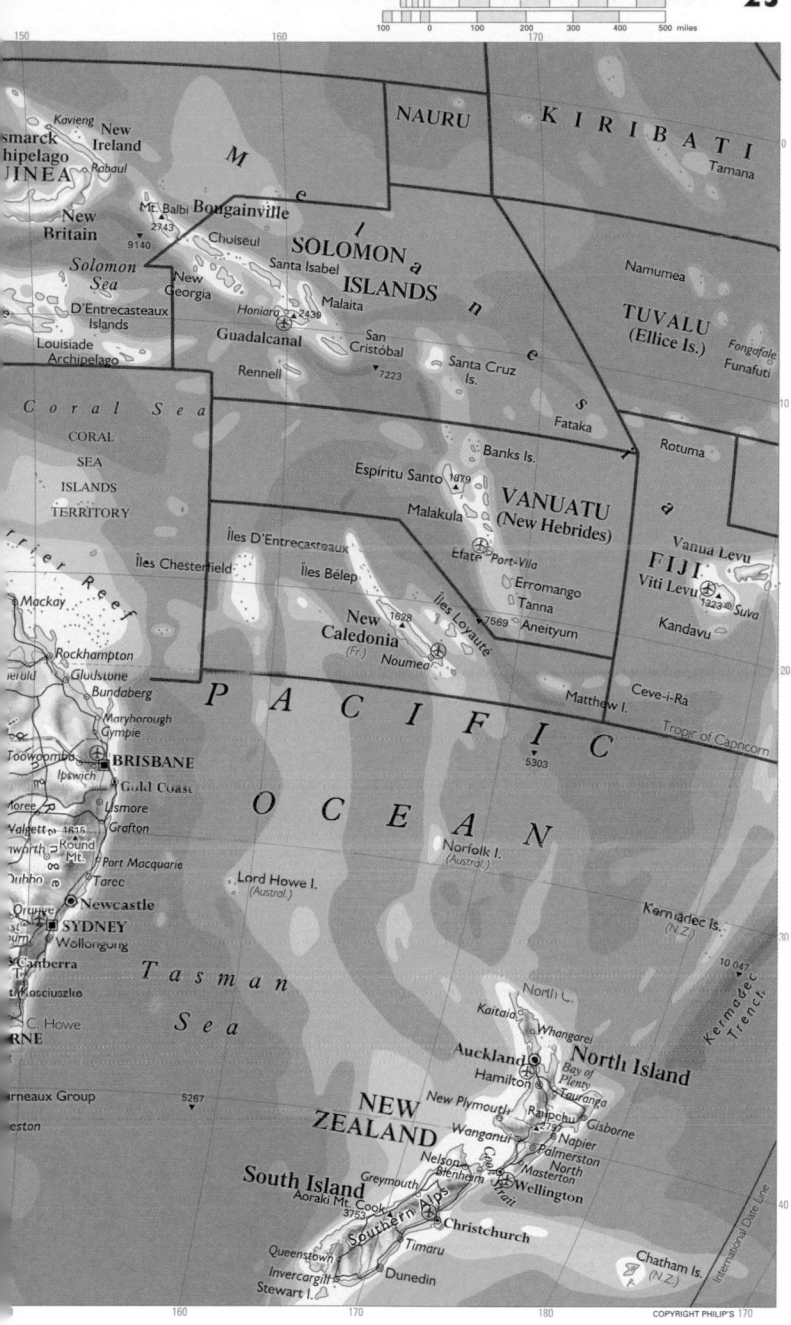

100 0 100 200 300 400 500 600 700 800 km
100 0 100 200 300 400 500 miles

150   160   170

NAURU

K I R I B A T I
Tamana

Kavieng   New
smarck   Ireland
hipelago   *Rabaul*
JINEA

M
e
l

Mt. Balbi **Bougainville**
2743
9140   Choiseul
New   Santa Isabel
Britain   New
Solomon   Georgia   Malaita
Sea   Honiara   2439
D'Entrecasteaux   **Guadalcanal**   San
Islands   Cristóbal
Louisiade   Rennell
Archipelago

SOLOMON
ISLANDS

a
n

Namumea

TUVALU
(Ellice Is.)   Fongafale
Funafuti

Santa Cruz
Is.
7223

e
s

Fataka

Rotuma

C o r a l   S e a

CORAL
SEA
ISLANDS
TERRITORY

Banks Is.

Espíritu Santo   1879
Malakula   **VANUATU**
(New Hebrides)

a

Vanua Levu

Íles D'Entrecasteaux

rrier Reef
Íles Chesterfield

Efate   Port-Vila
Íles Bélep

Erromango
Tanna
7569   Aneityum

FIJI
Viti Levu   1323   Suva

Kandavu

Mackay

New   1628   Íles Loyauté
Caledonia
(Fr.)   Noumea

Ceve-i-Ra

Rockhampton
Gladstone
Bundaberg

P A C I F I C

Matthew I.

Tropic of Capricorn

Maryborough
Gympie
Toowoomba   **BRISBANE**
Ipswich   Gold Coast
lsmore

O C E A N

5303

Grafton
Valgett   *Round*
Mt.
Port Macquarie
Taree

Norfolk I.
(Austral.)

Newcastle
SYDNEY
Wollongong

Lord Howe I.
(Austral.)

Kermadec Is.
(N.Z.)

Canberra
Kosciuszko
RNE

T a s m a n

North C.

10.047

S e a

Kaitaia

rneaux Group   5267
eston

Whangarei

Auckland   Bay of
Hamilton   Plenty
Tauranga
North Island
New Plymouth   Ruapehu   Gisborne
NEW   Wanganui   Napier
ZEALAND   Nelson   Palmerston
Blenheim   North
Greymouth   Masterton   Wellington
South Island   Hari
Aoraki Mt. Cook   *Southern Alps*
3753   **Christchurch**

Queenstown   Timaru
Invercargill   Dunedin
Stewart I.

Chatham Is.
(N.Z.)

Kermadec   *Trench*

International Date Line

160   170   180   COPYRIGHT PHILIP'S 170

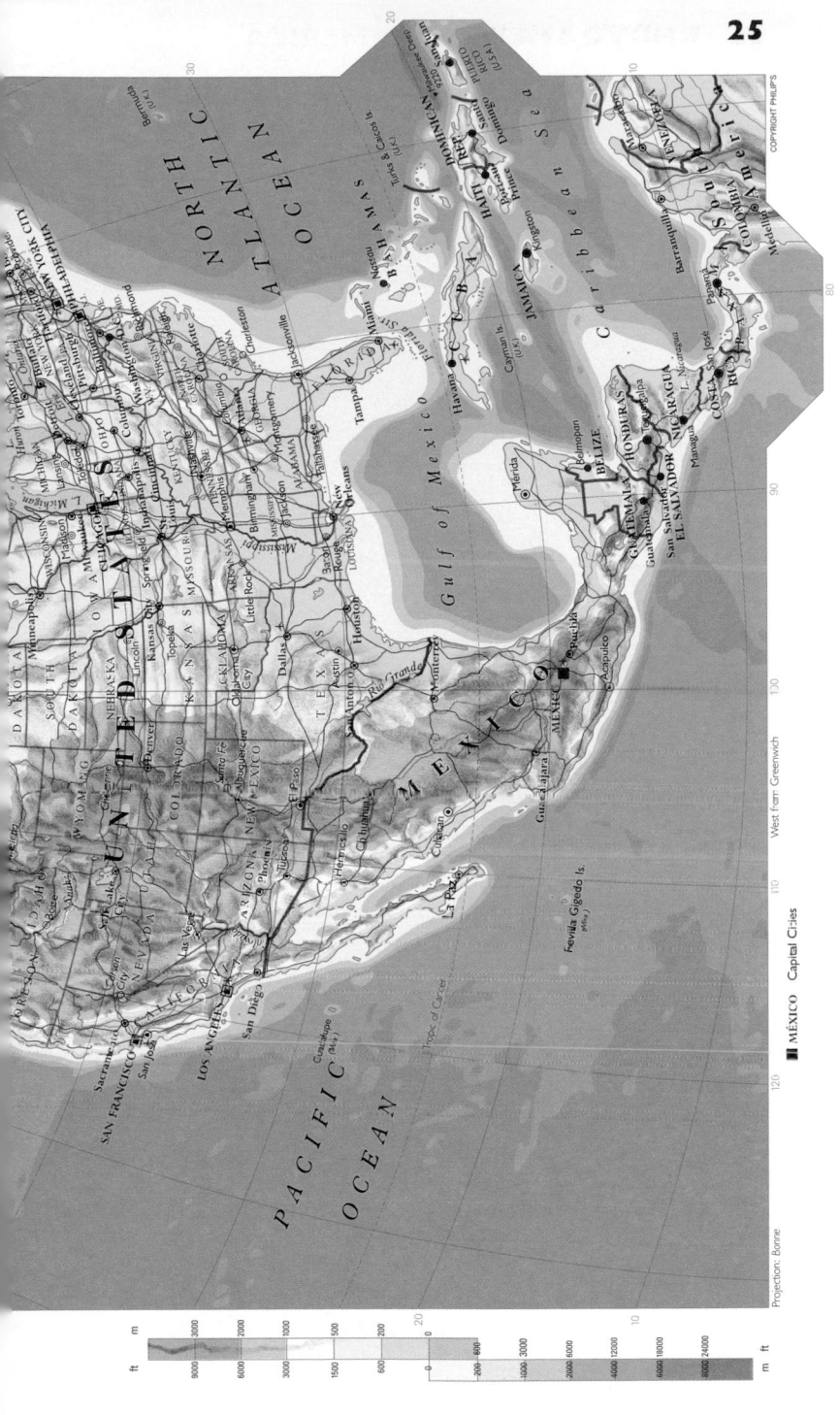

Projection: Bonne

West from Greenwich

■ MÉXICO Capital Cities

m

ft

ft

m

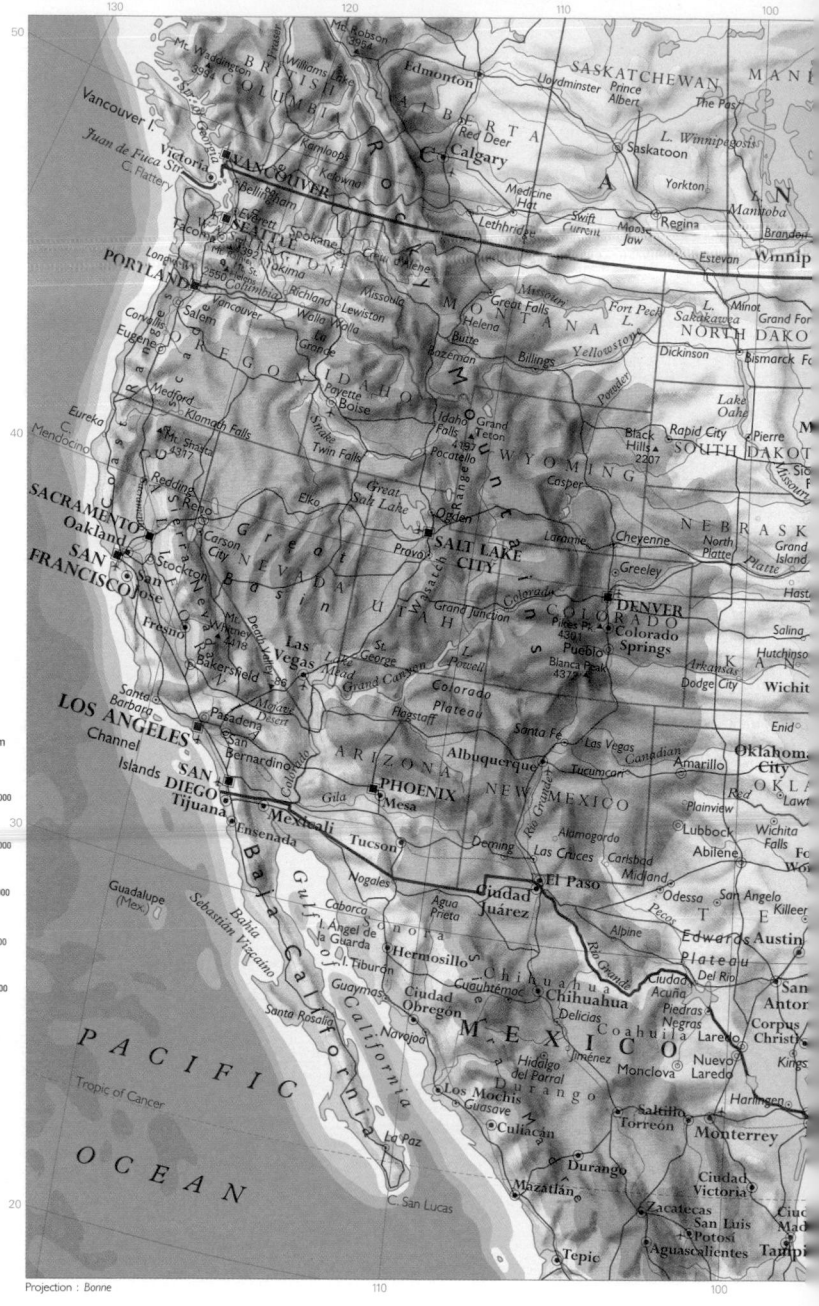

Projection : Bonne

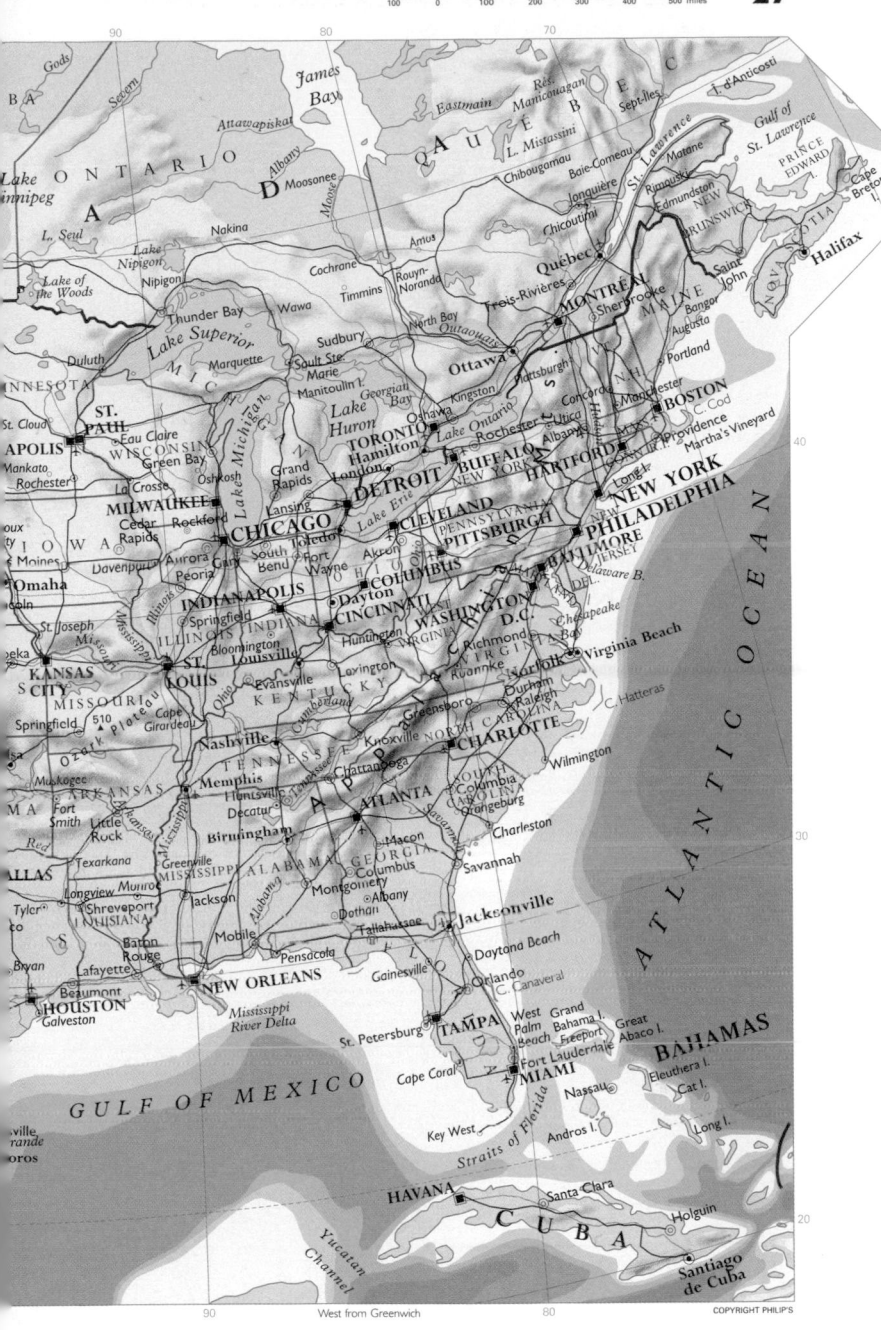

100 0 100 200 300 400 500 600 700 800 km
100 0 100 200 300 400 500 miles

West from Greenwich

COPYRIGHT PHILIP'S

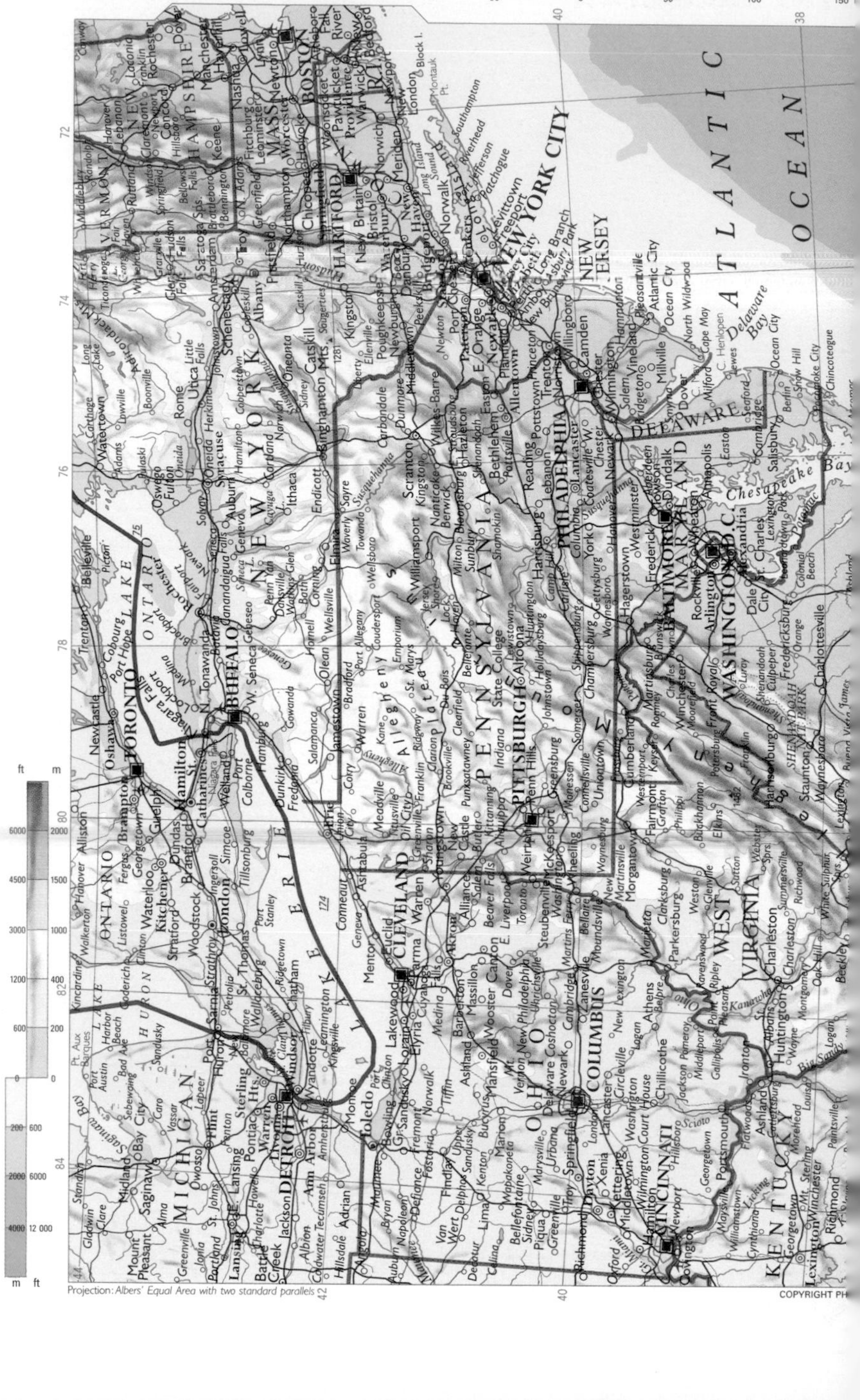

50 0 50 100 150 200 km

ft m

6000 2000
4500 1500
3000 1000
1200 400
600 200
0 0
200 600
2000 6000
4000 12 000

m ft

Projection: Albers' Equal Area with two standard parallels

COPYRIGHT PH

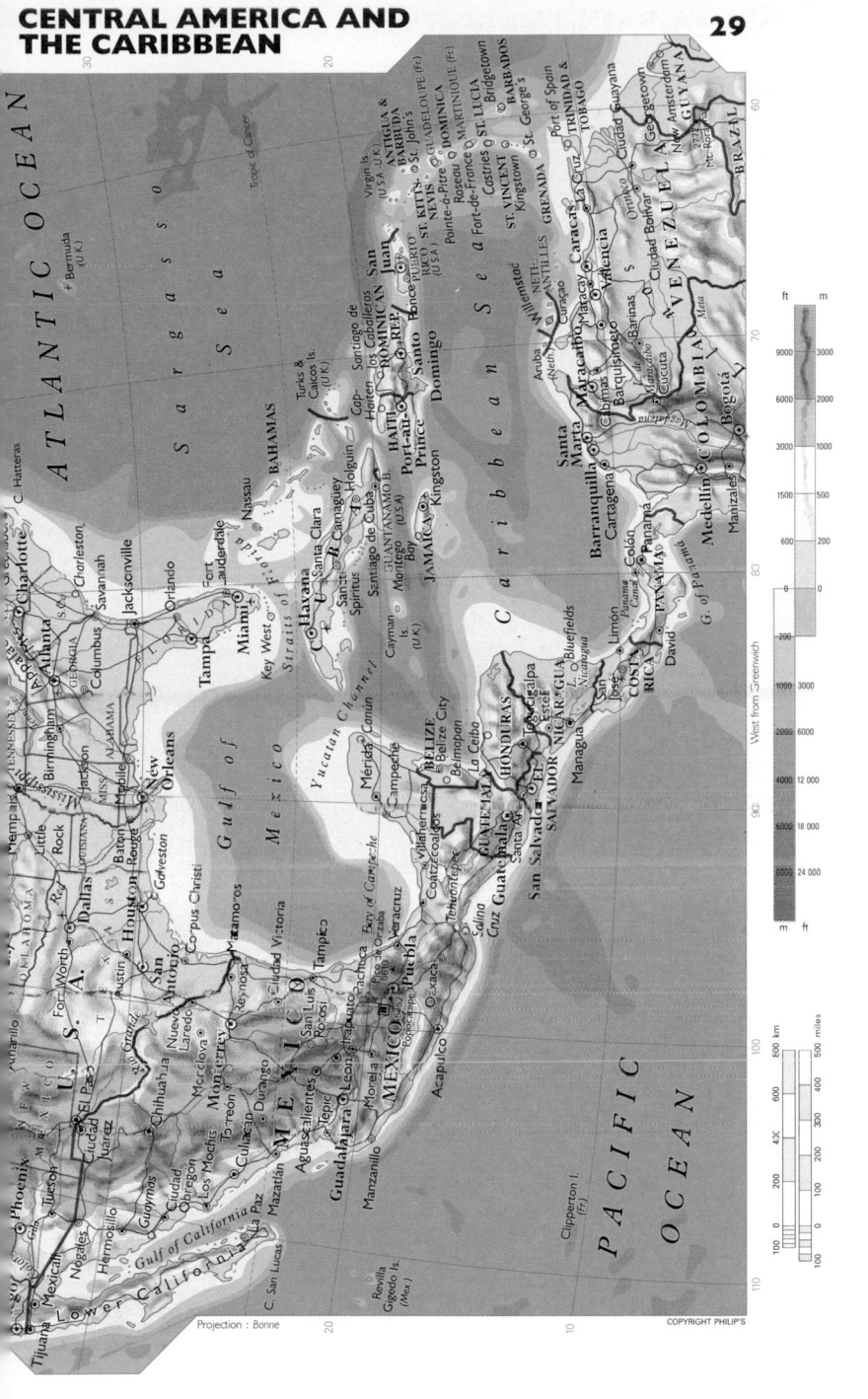

ATLANTIC OCEAN

Sargasso Sea

PACIFIC OCEAN

Gulf of Mexico

Caribbean Sea

MEXICO

U.S.A.

BAHAMAS

CUBA

JAMAICA

HAITI

DOMINICAN REP.

GUATEMALA

BELIZE

HONDURAS

EL SALVADOR

NICARAGUA

COSTA RICA

PANAMA

COLOMBIA

VENEZUELA

BRAZIL

GUYANA

Projection : Bonne

COPYRIGHT PHILIP'S

PACIFIC

OCEAN

Tropic of Capricorn

San Felix
(Chile)

San Ambrosio
(Chile)

Arch. de Juan Fernández
(Chile)

Projection: Lambert's Azimuthal Equal Area

MINAS GERAIS

Goiânia

Espírito
Santo

Vitória

Campos

Belo
Horizonte

Juiz
de Fora

RIO DE
JANEIRO

Niterói

Rio Preto O

SÃO PAULO

SÃO PAULO

Santos

Ribeirão
Preto O

MATO GROSSO

MS
DO SUL

PARANÁ

Curitiba

Ponta Grossa

PARAGUAY

Asunción

Pilcomayo

Paraguay

Corrientes

SANTA
CATARINA

RIO GRANDE
DO SUL

Porto Alegre

Pelotas

Uruguay

Resistencia

URUGUAY

Montevideo

Río de la Plata

Cuiabá

Cochabamba

Santa Cruz

Sucre

Salta

S. M. de
Tucumán

San Miguel de
Tucumán

Córdoba

San Juan

Mendoza

Santa Fe

Paraná

Rosario

BUENOS AIRES

La Plata

Salado

Bahía
Blanca

Mar del Plata

ARGENTINA

Iquique

Antofagasta
8050

M. Aconcagua
6960

Viña del Mar

Valparaíso

SANTIAGO

CHILE

Concepción

Valdivia

Puerto Montt

Colorado

Negro

Neuquén

Chubut

Bahía

Comodoro Rivadavia

Gulf of San Jorge

Gulf of Penas

Magellan's Str.

Punta Arenas

Tierra del Fuego

C. Horn

West Falkland

FALKLAND IS.
(U.K.)

Stanley

East Falkland

SOUTH

ATLANTIC

OCEAN

South Georgia
(U.K.)

60° West from Greenwich 50

COPYRIGHT PHILIP'S

■ LIMA   Capital Cities

m

ft

4000

3000

2000

1000

500

200

0

200

m   ft

12000
9000
6000
3000
1500
600
0

600
1200
6000
12000
18000
24000

m   ft

100 0 200 400 600 800 1000 1200 1400 km
100 0 200 400 600 800 1000 miles

COPYRIGHT PHILIP'S
Projection : Zenithal Equidistant

SOUTHERN OCEAN

West Ice Shelf
Drygalski I.
Davis Sea
Masson I.
Mill I.
Bowman I.
Shackleton Ice Shelf
C. Penzett
Casey (Aust.)
Totten Glacier
Dalton Iceberg Tongue
Porpoise Bay
Blizzard Iceberg Tongue
South Magnetic Pole
Commonwealth Bay
Dumont d'Urville (Fr.)
Terre Adélie
Clarie Coast
Banzare Coast
Sabrina Coast
Budd Coast
Denman Glacier
Scott Glacier

Wilhelm II Coast
Zhongshan (China)
Davis (Aust.)
Prydz Bay
Ingrid Christensen Coast
Mawson (Aust.)
Lars Christensen Coast
Stefansson B.
C. Darnley

Enderby Land
Kemp Land
Mawson Coast
MacRobertson Land
Prince Charles Mts.
Lambert Glacier
American Highland

Queen Mary Land
Wilkes Land

▲645
▲2243

3355
1840
3030 2570
3488 3700
▲4030 1040
2801 3491
2407 3087
2216 2798
2436 4776
▲3719

Larsen-halvøya
Holtinhella
Raufjell-Cooper
Konprins Olav Kyst
Mühlig-Hofmann
Prins Harald Kyst
Prinsesse Astrid Kyst
Prinsesse Ragnhild Kyst
Sør-Rondane
3630 Kyst

Ragnhild
Georg Forster (Germany)
Georg von Neumayer (Germany)

Queen Maud Land
East Antarctica
Antarctica

South Pole
Amundsen-Scott (U.S.A.)
SOUTH POLE

3556 2000
3318 2990
3212 3039
2311 1431
2773
2407 2407
3810
3057

Queen Maud Mountains
Horlick Mts.
Thiel Mts.
Pensacola Mts.

Transantarctic Mts.

Mt. Markham 4349
Mt. Kirkpatrick
Queen Alexandra Ra.
Shackleton Inlet
Scott (N.Z.) McMurdo (U.S.A.)
Mt. Erebus
Mt. Melbourne
Mt. Lister
Prince Albert Mts.
Victoria Land
George V Land
Mt. Murchison
Coulman I.
Franklin I.
Ross I.
Roosevelt I.
Bay of Whales
C. Colbeck
Ross Ice Shelf
Ross Sea
Possession I.
C. Adare

Vahsel Bay
Coats Land
Luitpold Coast
Filchner Ice Shelf
Berkner I.
Ronne Ice Shelf

West Antarctica

Marie Byrd Land
Edward VII Pen.
Sulzberger Ice Shelf
Rockefeller Plateau
Mt. Sidney
Executive Committee Ra.
Kohler Ra.
Walgreen Coast
Bakutis Coast
Hobbs Coast
Ruppert Coast
Saunders Coast

Ellsworth Mts.
Vinson Massif 4897
Sentinel Ra.

Palmer Land
Antarctic Pen.
Graham Land
Alexander I.
Charcot I.
Peter I Øy
Thurston I.
Abbot Ice Shelf

2896
2680
4191
375 158 1313
1797 4385
3022
668 2080
3181 3496
158

Weddell Sea
Bellingshausen Sea
Amundsen Sea
PACIFIC OCEAN

Halley (U.K.)

Antarctic Circle

South Orkney Is. (U.K.)
Orcadas (Arg.)
Signy I. (U.K.)
Coronation I.
Clarence I.
Elephant I.
King George I.
South Shetland Is.
Deception I.
Joinville I.
James Ross I.
Robertson I.
Esperanza (Arg.)
Marambio (Arg.)
O'Higgins (Chile)
Gen. Bernardo
Bellingshausen (Russia)
Biscoe Is.
Rothera (U.K.)
Adelaide I.
Stonington I.
San Martín (Arg.)
George VI Sound

Falkland Is. (U.K.)
Stanley
Tierra del Fuego
C. de Hornos
Drake Passage

ice cap
Permanent ice shelf
Maximum extent of sea ice
March (Summer) extent of sea ice
Surface elevation and depth of ice (in metres)
▲3488 3700

m 4000 2000
ft 12 000 6000
500 1500 3000 6000 9000 12 000 15 000

R.; comm., industl. and cultural ctr.; univ.,
R.C. cath., masonic temple, mint, academy of
fine arts; shipbldg., locomotives, machin.,
surgical instruments, carpets, woollens, cottons,
worsteds; sugar, and petroleum refining; ctr.
of War of Independence 1775–1783; founded
as Quaker col. by William Penn 1682; p. (2000)
1,517,550 (c.), 4,857,000 (met. a.).

Philippeville. See **Skikda**.

Philippines, Rep. of, S.E. Asia; chain of 7,100 Is. in
Pac. Oc., stretching over 1,760 km; ch. Is.
Luzon, Mindanao, Negros, Cebu, Mindoro, and
Palawar; lie in track of cyclones; tropical
climate; mtnous., agr. aided by intricate terrac-
ing system; most Is. underdeveloped except
Luzon where p. concentrated; subsistence agr.
rice and maize; 60 per cent of households live below the poverty line; coconuts major
export crop; sugar impt. once but falling world
prices have curtailed production; electronics and
garments also exported; income generated by
Filipinos working abroad sending wages home;
geothermal energy used; coconut shells burnt
for fuel; rise in terrorist acts by Muslim insurgents; cap. Manila; a. 299,681 km²; p. (2004)
86,241,697 (est.).

Phnom Penh, c., cap. of **Cambodia,** S.E. Asia; pt.
on Mekong R.; handles ships up to 2,500 tonnes;
linked to Kompong Som by modern highway;
multi-purpose dam to W.; univ., royal palace;
airport; p. (1999) 938,000.

Phoenix, c., Arizona, **USA;** on Salt R., ctr of
Salt River Valley irrigated region; electronics
research, steel, aircraft, clothing; fastest-growing
city in USA; p. (2000) 1,321,045.

Phoenix Group, Is., Pac. Oc.; part of Kiribati; a.
41 km²; US have some rights over Canton and
Enderbury; Canton used as international airport.

Phuket I., Thailand; off Kra Isthmus; main
alluvial tin-working region of Thailand; new
tourist developments; tsunami devastation, 2004;
ch. t. Phuket; a. 534 km².

Piacenza, c., cap. of P. prov., **Italy;** in Emilia-
Romagna, on R. Po; agr. and comm. ctr.;
cath., palaces, arsenal; cars, chemicals, cement;
p. (1992) 102,161.

Piauí, st., **Brazil;** semi-arid, underdeveloped dist.;
thorn scrub; livestock rearing; cap. Teresina;
a. 249,319 km²; p. (1991) 2,581,054.

Piave, R., N.E. **Italy;** flows to Adriatic, 200 km
long.

Picardy (Picardie), former prov. and region inc.
deps. Aisne, Oise, Somme, **France;** old battle
sites, Agincourt and Crécy; rich agr. a.; textiles; p.
(1999) 1,857,033.

Pichincha, prov., **Ecuador;** p. concentrated in
Andes; many resources inc. lime, gypsum, silver;
tropical hardwoods; cattle raising; cap. Quito; a.
16,105 km²; p. (1990) 1,756,228.

Pickering, mkt. t., Ryedale, North Yorks., **Eng.;**
on N. margin of Vale of P.; church with murals;
cas.; gas terminal; p. (1991) 5,914.

Pickering, Vale of, North Yorks., **Eng.,** wide, flat-
floored vale, once occupied by glacial lake;
bounded to N. by N. York Moors, to S. by York
Wolds; drained W. by R. Derwent, alluvial soils,
marshy in ctr.; crop farming along margins, cattle
grazing in damper meadows in ctr., ch. ts.
Pickering, Malton, Helmsley.

Picos de Europa, mtn. massif, N. **Spain;** hgst. massif in Cantabrian mtns., rising to 2,650 m;
partially inc. in Nat. Park.

Pictou, t., Nova Scotia, **Canada;** on Northumberland Strait; founded by Scottish settlers.

Pidurutalagala, mtn., **Sri Lanka;** alt. 2,530 m;
hgst. peak in rep.

Piedmont (Piemonte), region, N. **Italy;** rice, wheat,
vines, fruit; cottons, woollens; a. 25,416 km²; p.
(1992) 4,303,830.

Pietermaritzburg, c., cap., KwaZulu-Natal prov., **S.
Africa;** named after Piet Retief and Gerhardus
Maritz, two Boer leaders; lt. inds.; tanning; iron-
ore mng. in a.; part of univ. of Natal; 2 caths.;
p. (1991) 229,000.

Pietersburg, t., cap., Northern Province, **S. Africa;**
gold, asbestos, tin; comm. ctr. for cereals,
tobacco, cotton, citrus fruits.

Piła (Schneidemühl), t. and prov., N.W. **Poland**
(since 1945); formerly in Prussian prov. of
Pomerania; tr. ctr., lignite mines nearby; p. (1995)
75,737 (t.), 492,826 (prov.).

Pilar, sm. t., **Paraguay;** impt. R. pt.; sawmills;
textiles.

Pilsen. See **Plzeň**.

Pinar del Rio, c., prov. cap., **Cuba;** tobacco; p.
(1990) 121,774 (1989) 681,500 (prov.).

Pinatubo, volcano **Philippines;** erupted June 1991.

Pinawa, t., Manitoba, **Canada;** 88 km N.E. of
Winnipeg; nuclear research; p. (1986) 2,078.

Pindus, mtn. chain, between Thessaly and Albania,
Greece; hgst. peak 2,455 m.

Pingxiang, c., Jianxi, **China;** supplies coking
coal to Wuhan; p. (1994) 451,700.

Pinneberg, sm. t., Schleswig-Holstein, **Germany;** N.W.
of Hamburg; rose cultivation, metals, leather.

Pinsk, c., **Belarus;** in Pripet Marshes, pt. on Pina
R.; paper, wood-working inds., matches; Jewish
residents exterminated during German occupation
second world war; p. (1996) 130,000.

Piombino, t., **Italy;** mainland pt. for island of
Elba; steel wks.; p. (1981) 39,389.

Piotrkow Trybunalski, t. and prov., **Poland;** cas.;
timber and glass inds.; new textile combine; p.
(1995) 81,181 (t.), 644,105 (prov.).

Piqua, t., Ohio, **USA;** N. of Dayton; ironwks.,
woollens; nuclear reactor; p. (1980) 20,480.

Piracicaba, t., São Paulo, **Brazil;** ctr. of agr.
dist.; sugar-refining, brandy, flour; p. (1996)
302,600.

Piraeus, c., **Greece;** pt. of Athens and prin. pt.
of Greece; major industl. and comm. ctr.;
p. (1991) 182,671.

Pirmasens, t., Rhineland-Palatinate, **Germany;**
S.W. of Mannheim; footwear; p. (2002) 44,822.

Pirot, t., **Serbia;** nr. Bulgarian border; in economic
development a.; p. (1981) 69,653.

Pisa, c., **Italy;** at head of Arno delta, 19 km N.E.
of Livorno; famous leaning tower, cath., univ.;
textiles, chemicals, engin.; airport; tourism;
p. (1984) 103,894.

Pistoia, t., Tuscany, **Italy;** on Arno plain, N.W.
of Florence; iron and steel gds., macaroni;
p. (1981) 92,274.

Pit, R., Cal., **USA;** rises in Goose L.; cuts
spectacular gorges in the Cascades; used for
hydroelectric power.

Pitcairn I., E. Pac. Oc., Brit. col.; inc. atolls of Ducie
and Oeno and I. of Henderson; sweet potatoes,
bananas, oranges, coconuts; a. 5 km²; p. mostly
descendants of mutineers of the *Bounty;* p. (2004)
46.

Pitch lake, Trinidad, W.I.; S. of I., 16 km S.W.
of San Fernando; natural deposit of asphalt;
tourism; a. 86 ha.

Pitesti, t., **Romania;** on Arges R.; petroleum,
fruit, grain; lge. automobile plant; oil refinery;
p. (1992) 179,179.

Pitlochry, burgh, Perth and Kinross, **Scot.;** on R.
Tummel, 6 km S. of Pass of Killiecrankie; summer
resort; distilleries, hydros; p. (2002) 2,564.

Pittenweem, burgh, Fife, **Scot.;** at entrance to F. of
Forth; fisheries; p. (2002) 1,747.

Pittsburgh, c., Penns., **USA;** univ.; R.C. cath.; pt.
on Ohio R.; ctr. of richest American coal-field;
natural gas, petroleum, iron and steel, machin.,
metal gds. meat-packing, glass, aluminium,
chemicals, p. (2000) 334,563 (c.), 2,057,000 (met.
a.).

Piura, prov. and t., N. **Peru;** on Piura R.; oldest
Spanish t. in Peru; cotton mkt. and processing, p.
(1993) 1,388,264 (prov.), 277,964 (t.).

Plata, Rio de la (Plate R.), estuary between
Argentina and **Uruguay;** receives waters of
Rs. Paraná and Uruguay; est. provides sites for
lge. spts., Buenos Aires, La Plata, Montevideo.

Plateau, st., **Nigeria;** cap. Jos; a. 65,735 sq. km.;
p. 3,284,000 (1991). Over 50,000 killed in recent
Christian-Muslim clashes.

Platte, R., Nebraska, **USA;** formed by union of
N. Platte and S. Platte Rs.; total length 2,240
km; irrigation, hydroelec. power.

Plenty, Bay of, reg. and bay, N.I., **N.Z.;** on E.
cst.; 208 km wide; p. (1991) 208,163.

Plettenberg, t., N. Rhine–Westphalia, **Germany;** on
R. Lenne; iron wks.; p. (1986) 27,600.

Pleven, mkt. t., **Bulgaria;** many mosques; famous
siege 1877; textiles, wines; p. (1990) 138,323.

Plitvička Jezera, lakes, W. **Croatia** (formerly Yugoslavia); beautiful scenery; tourism; fishing. Now
World Heritage Site.

Ploče, new spt., **Croatia** (formerly Yugoslavia); on
Dalmatian cst.; industl. and rly. ctr.

Plock, t. and prov., **Poland;** on R. Vistula, nr.
Warsaw; agr.; oil refinery and petrochemical
plant; food processing; agr. machin.; p. (1995)
126,931 (t.), 531,704 (prov.).

Ploiesti, t., Prahova dist., **Romania**; petroleum, engin.; p. (1992) 252,073.

Plovdiv (Philippopolis), c., **Bulgaria**; on R. Maritsa; univ., Greek cath.; second c. of rep.; agr. processing, metals, engin.; p. (1990) 379,083.

Plymouth, c., spt., unit. auth., S. Devon, **Eng.**; on Plymouth Sound; comprises the "three towns" of Plymouth, Devonport, and Stonehouse; Brit. fleet faced Armada 1588; R.C. cath., guildhall, museum; Naval dockyard; seaside resort; fishing and fish-canning, lt. inds.; univ.; deposit of tungsten thought to be lgst. in W. Europe but lies within Dartmoor Nat. Park; p. (2001) 240,720 (unit. auth.), (1991) 245,295 (c.).

Plymouth, ch. t., **Montserrat** I., W.I.; p. (1985) 0,300. Volcanic destruction, 1997. Depopulated.

Plymouth, spt., Mass., **USA**; on Plymouth Bay, S.E. of Boston; here Pilgrim Fathers landed 1620 from *Mayflower* to form first English col.; Pilgrim Hall, Pilgrim Rock; textiles, cordage, machin.; tourism; p. (1980) 7,232.

Plynlimmon, mtn., Powys and Ceredigion, **Wales**; alt. 753 m; source of R. Severn.

Plzeň (Pilsen), c., W. Bohemia, **Czech Rep.**; ctr. of coal-mng. region; famous for beer and Lenin (former Skoda) armament wks.; p. (1990) 175,000.

Po, R., **Italy**; flows from Monte Viso, through Piedmont and Lombardy to the Adriatic; valley forms a major component of N. Italian lowland; natural gas deposits in valley; liable to flooding; 648 km long.

Pocklington, mkt. t., East Riding of Yorks., **Eng.**; foot of York Wolds, 19 km E. of York; ctr. of agr. dist.; 16th cent. grammar school; p. (1991) 5,908.

Podgorica, (Titograd) t., cap. of Montenegro, **Serbia and Montenegro**; nr. Albanian frontier; anc. t. but now mainly modern with growing industl. activity; agr. processing, aluminium smelting; airport; p. (1991) 118,059.

Podolsk, t., **Russia**; on main rly. from Moscow to S.; engin., tin-smelting, food-processing; p. (1989) 209,000.

Pohai. *See* Bo Hai.

Point-à-Pierre, **Trinidad**; oil refinery; natural gas pipeline from Forest Reserve field.

Point-à-Pitre, ch. t. and pt. **Guadeloupe**, Fr. W.I.; on Grande Terre I.; exp. agr. prods., bananas, sugar; p. (1982) 25,310.

Pointe-Noire, spt., **Congo Rep.**; airport, rly. to Brazzaville; agr. exp.; potash deposits nearby; linked to deepwater terminal for bulk carriers but mine closed due to flooding; petroleum refinery (1982); gas reserves; p. (1992) 576,206.

Poitiers, c., cap. of Vienne dep., **France**; many attractive bldgs., cath.; agr. tr.; mnfs. chemicals, hosiery; Black Prince defeated Fr. 1356; p. (1999) 82,957.

Poitou-Charentes, region, **France**; on western seaboard inc. deps. Charente, Charente-Maritime, Deux-Sèvres, Vienne; agr., vineyards; p. (1999) 1,639,733.

Pokrovsk, (Engels), c., **Russia**; on Volga; R. pt., mftg. and food-processing ctr.; engin., petroleum refining, textiles; p. (1989) 181,000.

Poland, rep., E. Europe; history of country dominated by constantly changing sovereignty between E. and W. powers; strong national identity, based esp. on Catholic church; mainly lowland; continental climate; economy retarded by history of political fluctuation; growth of export-based inds. almost halted in 1980s depression; major ctr. of mng. and heavy inds. in conurb. of Upper Silesia, agr. land remains largely in private ownership, but govt. attempts to rationalise farm structure, major pts. at Gdynia, Gdansk, and Szczecin, international airport at cap. Warsaw, 17 historic provs. replaced by 49 large dists.; border with Germany fixed along Oder-Neisse line; EU member (2004); a. 311,700 km²; p. (2004) 38,626,349.

Poltava, c., **Ukraine**; industl. and food-processing ctr. in rich agr. dist.; countryside described in Gogol's work; textiles, synthetic diamond plant; battle 1709 between Swedish and Russian armies; p. (1990) 317,000.

Polynesia, ethnic region, **Oceania**; I. grs. in Pac. Oc. within 30° N. and S. of equator; between longitude 135° E. and W.; p. (1984) 498,000.

Pomerania, former prov., N. Germany; in post-war redivision part E. of R. Oder to **Poland**; part W. of R. Oder incorporated in Mecklenburg, **E. Germany**; farming, shipbldg., fishing.

Pomona (Mainland), lgst of the Orkney Is., **Scot.**; Kirkwall (cap.) and Stromness on I.; p. (1991) 15,128.

Pomorze. *See* Bydgoszcz.

Pompeii, ruined c., **Italy**; stood 21 km S.E. of Naples, at foot of Vesuvius; destroyed A.D. 79 by volcanic eruption, site re-discovered 1748; many interesting excavations; also modern c. nearby; fine church with famous collection of silver and gold plate; p. (1981) 22,896.

Ponce, c., **Puerto Rico**; recently improved harbour on S. cst.; well connected with other ts. in rnt. area of fertile, irrigated sugar-cane a., industl. ctr.; p. (1990) 187,749.

Pondicherry, spt., Tamil Nadu st., **India**; on Coromandel cst.; cap. of P. Union Territory.; tr. ctr. for local prod.; p. (1991) 203,065 (c.), (2001) 973,800 (terr.).

Ponta Grossa, c., Paraná, **Brazil**; rly. junc.; comm. ctr.; maté, rice, timber, tobacco, bananas, cattle, jerked beef; p. (1996) 252,700.

Pontardawe, t., Neath Pt. Talbot, S. **Wales**; on R. Tawe, N.E. of Swansea; zinc smelting and refining; p. (1991) 18,479.

Pontchartrain, Lake, shallow L., lower Mississippi flood plain, **USA**; connected by canal to New Orleans 10 km to S., and by deltaic channels to G. of Mexico.

Pontefract, mkt. t., West Yorks., **Eng.**; 11 km E. of Wakefield; coal, furniture, confectionery, mkt. gardening; cas. ruins; p. (2001) 28,250.

Pontevedra, prov., **Spain**; on deeply indented Atl. cst.; transatlantic pt. Vigo; scenery and fiesta attractions for tourists; agr., livestock, timber, fisheries; cap. P.; a. 4,390 km²; p. (1998) 906,300.

Pontevedra, c., cap. of P. prov., N.W. **Spain**; fish. pt., handicrafts, agr. tr.; p. (1990) 70,400.

Pontiac, t., Mich., **USA**; on Clinton R.; fishing and shooting, motor cars, rubber gds., machin., varnish; p. (1996) 70,471.

Pontianak, t., cap. of Kalimantan, **Indonesia**; exp. rubber, copra; rubber processing; p. (1983) 355,000.

Pontine Is., off W. cst. of **Italy**; in Tyrrhenian Sea; a. 11·6 km²; p. 6,000.

Pontine Marshes, region, Latium, S. **Italy**; coastal zone S.E. of Rome extending from Velletri to Terracina; formerly highly malarial fens, largely drained and colonised 1930–35; 3,200 new farms, 4 new ts.; ch. t. Littoria; a. 647 km².

Pontresina, t., Grisons, **Switzerland**; E. of St. Moritz; tourist resort.

Pontypool, t., Torfaen, **Wales**; coal, steel, glass, bricks, tin galvanising, nylon at Manhilad; p. (1991) 35,564.

Pontypridd, t., Rhondda, Cynon, Taff, **Wales**; on R. Taff, 19 km N.W. of Cardiff; formerly coal, ironfounding; univ; p. (1991) 28,487.

Poole, t., unit. auth. created in 1997, formerly part of Dorset, **Eng.**; spt. on Poole Harbour, 6 km W. of Bournemouth; imports clay for local pottery inds; petroleum production began 1979; tourism, yachting, marine engin., chemicals; p. (2001) 138,288 (unit auth.), (1991) 138,479 (t.).

Poona. *See* Pune.

Poopó, salt L., Oruro dep., **Bolivia**; fed from L. Titicaca by R. Desaguadero, which flows over saline beds; no outlet; c. 3,600 m a.s.l.; a. 2,600 km².

Popayan, c., S.W. **Columbia**; 1,677 m above Cauca R.; cath., univ.; food processing, coffee, flour; mng. nearby; p. (1992) 203,722.

Poplar. *See* Tower Hamlets.

Popocatepetl, volcano, nr. Puebla, **Mexico**; alt. 5,456 m; dormant after 1702; renewed activity, 2000.

Porbandar, spt., Gujarat, **India**; exp. silk, cotton; imports coal, dates, timber, machin., petroleum; birthplace of Gandhi; p. (1991) 116,671.

Pori (Björneborg), spt., S. **Finland**; at mouth of R. Kokemäen; copper refinery, rolling mills, match, paper and pulp wks.; p. (1993) 76,422.

Porjus, t., Norrbotten, N. **Sweden**; on R. Lulea, hydroelectric plant supplies power to iron-ore mng. dists. of Gallivare and Kiruna, also to Narvik rly.

Port Adelaide, main pt., S. **Australia**; serves Adelaide; exp. agr. prods. from hinterland; imports bulk cargoes (petroleum, phosphate, limestone); p. (1991) 39,000.

Portadown, t., Craigavon, **N. Ireland**; on R. Bann, 40 km S.W. of Belfast; linen (no longer manufactured); food processing; merged with Lurgan to form new c. of Craigavon; p. (1991) 21,299.

Portaferry, spt., Ards, **N. Ireland**; shipping fisheries; p. (2002) 3,286.

Portage la Prairie, t., Manitoba, **Canada**; sm. pt. on Assiniboine R.; grain and potato tr.; p. (1991) 13,186.

Port Amelia. See Pemba.

Portarlington, mkt. t., Offaly, **R.o.I.**; farming; first place to have elec. power-sta. using local peat fuel; p. (1986) 3,295.

Port Arthur. (Canada) See Thunder Bay.

Port Arthur (China). See Lushun.

Port Arthur, t., Texas, **USA**; pt. on L. Sabine; exp. petroleum, chemicals, grain; p. (1996) 57,701.

Port Arzew, pt., **Algeria**; world's first plant to liquefy natural gas (1964); oil pipeline from Haoud el Hamra; oil refinery.

Port Augusta, t., spt., S. **Australia**; at head of Spencer G.; fine harbour; salt field; exp. wheat, fruit; impt. rly. junction; p. (1991) 14,966.

Port-au-Prince, c., cap. of **Haiti**; spt. on bay in G. of La Gonave; cultural and political ctr.; univ., cath.; food processing and exp.; oil refinery; p. (2000) 1,769,000.

Port Blair, spt., cap. of Andaman and Nicobar Is., **India**; p. (1991) 74,955.

Port Chalmers, t., bor., **S.I. N.Z.**; container pt., timber exp.

Port Colborne, t., Ont., **Canada**; pt. on L. Erie; iron smelting; nickel and copper refining; power from Niagara falls; p. (1986) 18,281.

Port Elizabeth, spt., Eastern Cape Prov., **S. Africa**; on Algoa Bay, bilingual univ.; exp. skins, wool, ostrich feathers, mohair; foundries, soap, chemicals, car assembly, food preservation, sawmills; p. (1991) 853,000.

Port Erin, v., Isle of **Man**; on S.E. cst.; seaside resort, fisheries.

Port Essington, N. point, of Coburg peninsula, N.T., **Australia**; pearl culture experiments.

Port Etienne, See Nouadhibou.

Port Franequi, See Ilebo.

Port Gentil, spt., **Gabon**, Eq. Africa; exp. palm-oil, mahogany, ebony; sawmills, fishing, centre of Gabon's main oil reserves, oil refining; p. (1993) 164,000.

Port Glasgow, burgh, spt., Inverclyde, **Scot.**; on S bank of R. Clyde, 27 km below Glasgow; shipbldg. and repairing, textiles, rope, canvas mftg.; p. (2002) 16,617.

Port Harcourt, spt., **Nigeria**; 48 km from sea on E. branch of Niger delta; terminus of E. Nigerian rly. system; tin, palm oil, groundnuts; bitumen plant, tyres; oil refining, p. (1992) 371,000.

Porthcawl, t., Bridgend, **Wales**; on cst. 16 km S.E. of Pt. Talbot; resort; p. (1991) 15,922.

Port Hedland, sm. spt., **W. Australia**; new t, being built 8 km inland to absorb impact of Mt. Newman ore project; twin ts. linked by industl. belt; exp. iron ore to Japan; p. (1991) 12,599.

Porthmadog (Portmadoc), t., Gwynedd, **Wales**; pt. on Tremadog Bay; terminus of Festiniog lt. rly.; p. (1991) 3,048.

Port Huron, t., Mich., **USA**; on L Huron; summer resort, dry docks, grain elevators; motor-car parts; p. (1980) 33,981.

Portici, spt., Campania, **S. Italy**; on Bay of Naples; dockland sub. of Naples; p. (1981) 79,259.

Portile de Fier. See Iron Gate.

Portishead, pt., N. Somerset, **Eng.**; on Severn estuary 5 km S.W. of Avonmouth; p. (1991) 14,721.

Port Jackson, N.S.W., **Australia**; deep natural harbour used by Sydney and crossed by Sydney bridge.

Port Kelang (Port **Swettenham**), major spt. of **Malaysia**; 48 km W. of Kuala Lumpur; exp. primary prods. inc. tin, rubber, fruit; imports mnfs.; p. 11,300.

Portknockie, burgh, Moray, **Scot.**; on N. Buchan cst., 8 km E. of Buckie; sm. fish. pt.; p. (2002) 1,217.

Portland, t., Weymouth and P., Dorset, **Eng.**; 6 km S. of Weymouth on sheltered N.E. side of I. of Portland; lge artificial harbour; former naval base, prison.

Portland, c., Ore., **USA**; gr. wheat and wool tr.; flour milling, shipbldg., fishing and canning, aluminium, lumber; p. (2000) 529,121 (c.), (1990) 1,240,000 (met. a.).

Portland Canal, fjord, N.W. cst of America, forming bdy. between Alaska and B.C.

Portland, I. of, Dorset, **Eng.**; limestone mass, linked to mainland by shingle spit, Chesil Bank, terminates S. in Portland Bill; former naval base, Borstal institution; limestone quarrying; masonry wks.

Port Louis, c., cap., of **Mauritius**; pt. on Indian Oc.; exp. sugar; contains 42% of Mauritius p. in met.a., port extension and bulk sugar terminal; p. (1999) 172,000.

Port Macquarie, t., N.S.W., **Australia**; former penal settlement on Hastings R.; resort; p. (1991) 26,800.

Port Moresby, t., cap. of **Papua New Guinea**, 2,880 km from Sydney; spt., airpt.; univ.; p. (1995) 193,242.

Port Nelson, spt., Manitoba, **Canada**; on cst. of Hudson Bay at mouth of R. Nelson; linked by rly. to trans-continental systems; exp. wheat, minerals; closed by ice 7 months each year.

Port Nolloth, spt., **S. Africa**; serves copper- and diamond-mng. dists.; now a declining crayfish pt.

Porto. See Oporto.

Pôrto Alegre, c., cap. of Rio Grande do Sul st., **Brazil**; exp. lard, preserved meats, rice, timber, tobacco; textiles, chemicals, furniture, brewing, metallurgy; oil refinery under construction; pipeline connects with Rio Grande; 2 univs.; p. (1991) 1,262,631.

Portobello, resort, **Scot.**; on F. of Forth, 5 km E. of Edinburgh.

Port of Spain, c., cap. of **Trinidad**; attractive c. with squares; 2 caths.; mosque; spt. exp. cocoa, sugar, asphalt, oil; natural gas pipeline from Penal; food processing; p. (1999) 53,000.

Porto Marghera, spt., Venezia, **N. Italy**; the modern pt. of Venice, reached by ship canal dredged through shallow lagoon; oil refineries; chemicals, metal refining.

Porto Novo, t., cap. of **Benin Rep.**; on coastal lagoon; spt.; fishing; many old colonial bldgs.; p. (1994) 200,000.

Pôrto Velho, c., cap of Rondônia st., **Brazil**; in a. producing maize, rice, rubber, tin; p. (1996) 287,500.

Portoviejo, t., **Ecuador**; mkt. and comm. ctr. for agr. dist.; p. (1990) 132,937.

Port Pirie, t., spt., **S. Australia**; major pt. on Spencer Gulf; refines zinc and lead from Broken Hill; exp. wheat; p. (1991) 14,398.

Port Radium, t., N.W. Terr., **Canada**; on Gr. Bear L.; pitchblende deposits.

Portree, spt., v., I. of Skye, Highland, **Scot.**; landlocked harbour on P. Bay, Sound of Raasay; fishing; tweed mill; p. (2002) 1,917.

Portrush, spt., Coleraine, **N. Ireland**; 8 km N. of Coleraine; tourism; p. (1991) 5,598.

Port Said, (Bur Sa'îd), spt. and prov., **Egypt**; at N. end of Suez Canal; free tr. a.; impt. fuelling sta.; entrepôt tr.; p. (2001) 449,000, (1990) 461,000 (prov.).

Portsdown Hill, chalk ridge, Hants., **Eng.**; extends E. to W. behind Portsmouth from Havant to Fareham.

Portsea I., artfd. I., between Portsmouth and Langston harbours, Portsmouth, Eng.

Portslade-by-Sea, t., Brighton and Hove, **Eng.**; W. of Hove; p. (1991) 17,762.

Portsmouth, c., naval pt., unit. auth. created in 1997, Hants., **Eng.**; opposite Isle of Wight; famous naval establishment; Portsmouth is the garrison t.; Portsea has the naval dockyards, Landport is residtl., and Southsea is a popular resort; naval dockyard for fleet maintenance and repair closed 1984; across the harbour is Gosport; shipbldg.; univ.; birthplace of Charles Dickens and I. K. Brunel; p. (2001) 186,701 (unit. auth.).

Portsmouth, t., N.H., **USA**; summer resort, naval dockyard, cotton; the 1905 Peace Treaty between Japan and Russia was negotiated here; p. (1996) 25,034.

Portsmouth, spt., Va., **USA**; naval dockyard; farm produce, cotton, rly. wks.; p. (1996) 101,308.

Portsoy, burgh, Aberdeenshire, **Scot.**; spt. 8 km W. of Banff; fisheries and meal milling; p. (2002) 1,734.

Port Sudan, spt., **Sudan**; 48 km N. of Suakin; linked by rail to Atbara and Khartoum; oil refining; p. (1993) 305,000.

Port Sunlight, Merseyside, **Eng.**; garden v. founded

1888 by Lord Leverhulme for the employees of the Port Sunlight factories. Soap production ended (2000).

Port Swettenham. See **Port Kelang.**

Port Talbot, t., Neath Port Talbot, S. **Wales;** on E. side of Swansea Bay; impt. iron and steel ind., copper, coal; new deep-water harbour serves as ore terminal; p. (1991) 37,647.

Portugal, rep., Iberia, W. Europe; member of EU (1986); mild temperate climate on cst., drier and hotter in interior; economy based on an inefficient agr. sector, located in wide fertile valleys and associated processing inds.; major exp. of cork, but few industl. raw materials; textiles; post-war growth of tourist inds.; cap. and airport Lisbon; worst drought on record (2005), a. 91,945 km²; p. (2004) 10,524,145.

Portuguesa, st., **Venezuela;** inc. llanos plains; livestock raising; cap. Guanare; a. 15,200 km²; p. (1990) 625,576.

Portuguese Guinea. See **Guinea-Bissau.**

Posadas, c., cap. of Misiones prov., N.E. **Argentina;** on upper Paraná R.; on border of Paraguay; yerba-maté, tobacco, cereals; connection for Iguaça falls; p. (1991) 210,755.

Posen. See Poznan.

Pössneck, t., Gera, **Germany;** S.E. of Weimar; porcelain, textiles, leather; p. (1989) 17,410.

Postojna (Adelsberg), t., **Slovenia** (formerly Yugoslavia); 32 km N.E. of Trieste; extensive grotto and stalactite cavern.

Potchefstroom, t., North West Province, **S. Africa;** on Mooi R.; univ.; agr.; malt, timber, engin.; p. (1980) 141,000 (dist.).

Potenza, t., cap. of P. prov., **Italy;** on hill 220 m above Basento R.; agr. and industl. ctr.; univ.; p. (1981) 64,358.

Poti, spt., **Georgia;** exp. manganese; fish processing, timber-milling, engin.; p. (1990) 137,300.

Potomac, R., **USA;** divides Va. from Md.; flows past Wash., to Chesapeake Bay; 464 km long.

Potosi, dep., **Bolivia;** famous for silver- and tin-mines; zinc ore; cap. Potosi; a. 116,630 km²; p. (1988) 667,800.

Potosi, c., **Bolivia;** on slope of Cerro Gordo de Potosi, 4,072 m a.s.l.; tin, silver, copper, lead mng.; p. (1992) 112,291.

Potsdam, c., cap. of Brandenburg Land, **Germany;** on R. Havel, 29 km S.W. of Berlin; beautiful parks and gardens, many palaces; scene of conference between Allies on bdy. questions, 1945; motor and locomotive wks., engin.; precision instruments; p. (2002) 130,435.

Potteries, The, dist., Stoke, **Eng.;** ctr. of earthenware ind., comprising ts. Burslem, Hanley, Fenton, Tunstall, Stoke and Longton.

Potters Bar, t., Hertsmere, Herts., **Eng.;** residtl.; in London commuter belt; p. (2001) 22,008.

Poulton-le-Fylde, t., Lancs., **Eng.;** ctr. of mkt. gardening, poultry rearing dist.; p. (1991) 18,939.

Powys, central **Wales,** unit. auth. created in 1996 from former l. gov. dists. of Brecknock, Montgomeryshire and Radnorshire; mtnous a. bordering Eng.; forestry, stockraising and water catchment for Eng.; crossed by Rs. Wye and Severn; sparse p.; p. (2001) 126,354.

Powys, Vale of, t., Powys, **Wales;** drained by R. Severn; cattle-rearing; ch. t. Welshpool.

Poyang Hu, lge. L., Jiangxi, **China;** on S. margin of Chang Jiang plain; surrounded by flat, intensively cultivated land, rice, sugar, mulberry; size varies greatly with season, max. a. (in late summer) 4,662 km².

Poznan, prov., W. **Poland;** drained by Warta and Notec Rs.; mainly agr.; stock-raising; mnfs. inc. locomotives; a. 26,705 km²; p. (1995) 1,352,057.

Poznan, c., cap. of P. prov., **Poland;** on Warta R.; route ctr., industl. and educational ctr.; cath. univ.; engin., iron-founding, chemicals; anc. c., once cap. of Poland; p. (1995) 581,772.

Pozzuoli, t., **Italy;** 3 km W. of Naples; anc. Puteoli; mineral baths, ordnance wks.; Roman ruins; p. (1981) 70,350.

Prague (Praha), c., cap. of Czech Rep.; picturesque, anc. c. on R. Vltava; comm. and cultural ctr.; univ. (founded 1348); outstanding architecture; extensive mnfs.; machin., sugar, chemicals; severe flooding, 2002; p. (2000) 1,226,000.

Prato, t., **Italy;** 13 km N.W. of Florence; cath., mediaeval cas. and fortifications; cottons, woollens, machin.; p. (1992) 166,108.

Predeal Pass, Romania; carries main road and rly. across Transylvanian Alps from Bucharest to Brasov; alt. over 1,200 m.

Pregel, R., **Poland;** flows to Frisches Haff, nr. Kaliningrad; 200 km long.

Prek Ihnot, Cambodia; power and irrigation development project on lower Mekong R.

Prescot, mftg. t., Knowsley, Merseyside, **Eng.;** 6 km. S.W. of St. Helens; mkt., elec. cable ind.; p. (2001) 36,695.

Prestatyn, t., Denbighshire **Wales;** on N. cst., 5 km E. of Rhyl; seaside resort.

Presteigne, mkt. t., Powys, **Wales;** on R. Lugg, 16 km N.W. of Leominster; p. (1991) 1,815.

Preston, c., l. gov. dist., Lancs., **Eng.;** pt. on R. Ribble; textiles, engin., aircraft wks.; p. (2001) 129,633 (dist.).

Prestonpans, burgh, E. Lothian, S.E. **Scot.;** on F. of Forth, 14 km E. of Edinburgh; scene of Jacobite victory 1745; p. (2002) 7,153.

Prestwich, t., Gtr. Manchester, **Eng.;** in valley of R. Irwell, 6 km N.W. of Manchester; cotton bleaching and dyeing, soap, furnishings; p. (2001) 31,693.

Prestwick, burgh, S. Ayrshire, **Scot.;** on F. of Clyde, 5 km N. of Ayr; golfing ctr. and trans- atlantic airpt. and freeport (1984); resort; p. (2002) 14,934.

Pretoria (Tshwane), c., Transvaal, admin. cap. of **Rep. of S. Africa;** univ., tr. ctr.; inds. inc. engin., chemicals, iron, and steel; p. (2000) 1,508,000. Now renamed Tshwane.

Pribilof Is., off S.W. Alaska, **USA;** a. 168 km².

Prijedor, t., **Bosnia-Herzegovina,** formerly Yugoslavia; on E. flank of Dinaric Alps, 104 km S.E. of Zagreb; rly. junc.; iron-ore mines.

Prilep, t., **Macedonia,** formerly Yugoslavia; mkt.; refractory materials, tobacco processing; p. (1981) 99,770.

Primorskiy Kray, terr., **Russia;** S.E. Siberia, on Sea of Japan; coal, iron ore, and various metals in vicinity; fisheries; millet and rice; slow economic development results from isolation; wants economic links with China; ch. cs., Vladivostok (cap.), Ussuriysk; a. 168,350 km²; p. (1989) 2,256,100.

Prince Albert, t., Saskatchewan, **Canada;** lumbering, furs; p. (1991) 34,181.

Prince Edward I., prov., **Canada;** sm. I. in G. of St. Lawrence; physically poorly endowed; rocky, with thin soils; pastoral agr., furfarming, fishing; cap. Charlottetown; a. 5,657 km²; p. (1996) 134,557.

Prince George, t., B.C., **Canada;** oil refining; lumbering, mng., fur tr.; p. (1996) 75,150.

Prince Rupert, t., B.C., **Canada;** Pac. pt. of Canadian National rly.; service ctr., fishing and fish-processing; p. (1986) 15,755.

Princeton, bor., N.J., **USA;** seat of Princeton Univ.

Principe. See São Tomé.

Pripet Marshes, Belarus; forested swampy region crossed by Pripet R. and its streams; greater part reclaimed; coal and petroleum; a. 46,620 km².

Pripet (Pripyat), R., **Belarus;** trib. of R. Dnieper; 560 km long.

Privas, t., cap. of **Ardèche** dep., **France;** p. (1999) 9,170.

Pristina, c., cap. of Kosovo aut. region, S.W. **Serbia;** on Sitnic R.; admin. ctr.; many mosques; devastated in 1999 war.

Prokopyevsk, t., S.W. Siberia, **Russia;** in Novosibirsk dist.; one of the main coalfields of Kuznetsk Basin; mng. machin., metallurgy; p. (1989) 274,000.

Prome, c. **Myanmar;** pt. on R. Irrawaddy; connected by rail and road to Rangoon; tr. in rice, cotton, tobacco; one of oldest cs. in Burma, founded 8th cent.

Proskurov. See Khmel'nitskiy.

Prostejov, t., N. Moravia, **Czech Rep.;** rly. junc.; agr. machin., textiles; historic bldgs.; p. (1984) 51,100.

Provence, former prov. now incorporated in **Provence-Alpes-Côte d'Azur, France;** inc. deps. Alpes-de-Haute-Provence, Hautes-Alpes, Alpes-Maritimes, Bouches-du-Rhône, Var, Vaucluse; mkt. gardening, tourism esp. along coast; ch. city Marseille; p. (1999) 4,495,168.

Providence, c., R.I. **USA;** at head of Narragansett Bay; univ.; jewellery, textiles, silverware, rubber gds., machin., oil, coal; p. (1990) 160,728 (c.), 655,000 (met. a.).

Provo, t., Utah, **USA;** at base of Wasatch mtns., nr. shore of Utah L.; univ.; flour, bricks, blast furnaces; p. (1990) 264,000 (met. a. with Orem).

Prudhoe, Northumberland, **Eng.;** former coal mng. t.; chemicals, paper; p. (1991) 11,204.

Prudhoe Bay, N.E. Alaska, **USA**; the jewel in Alaska's oil crown; arctic conditions make extraction and transport of oil difficult and ecologically dangerous but despite opposition from environmentalist groups 1,262 km pipeline to ice-free pt. of Valdez.

Prussia, former kingdom (1701–1806); former st. (1806–1945), **Germany**; consisted of 13 provs., cap. Berlin; formally abolished 1947; E. Prussia partitioned between USSR and Poland.

Prut, R., rises in **Ukraine** and then forms the boundary between **Romania** and **Moldova** as it flows from the Carpathian mtns. to the Danube R.; 576 km long.

Przemyśl, c. and prov., S.E. **Poland**; on San R. (trib. of Vistula) nr. bdy. between Poland and Ukraine; anc. fortress t.; sewing machin.; p. (1995) 68,866 (c.), 414,072 (prov.).

Pskov, c., **Russia**; on R. Velikaya, nr. entry to L. Peipus; rly. junc.; flax tr.; historic bldgs.; scene of abdication of Nicholas II, March 1917; p. (1989) 204,000.

Pudsey, t., West Yorks., **Eng.**; between Leeds and Bradford; woollens; p. (2001) 32,391.

Puebla, c., cap. of P. st., **Mexico**; one of oldest and most impt. cs. of rep.; fine cath., theatre, univ.; cotton mills, onyx quarries, glazed tiles; p. (1990) 1,054,921.

Puebla, st., **Mexico**; on interior plateau at 2,400 m; fertile valleys for coffee and sugar; mng. impt.; dense p.; a. 33,991 km²; p. (1989) 4,118,059.

Pueblo, c., Col., **USA**; on R. Arkansas, in foothills of Rockies; iron and steel ctr.; coal and various metals nearby; p. (1990) 98,640 (t.), 123,051 (met. a.).

Puerto Barrios, pt., **Guatemala**; rly. terminus; oil refining; p. (1989) 338,000.

Puerto Cabello, spt., N. **Venezuela**; on Caribbean nr. Valencia; excellent harbour; linked by rail and highway to Caracas; asbestos, vegetable oils, soap, candles, meat-packing; p. (1980) 94,000.

Puerto Cortés, spt., N.W. **Honduras**; on Caribbean; exp. bananas, hardwoods; p. (1988) 43,300.

Puerto de Santa Maria, El, spt., S.W. **Spain**; on Bay of Cadiz; exp. mainly sherry; p. (1990) 64,800.

Puerto la Cruz, t., **Venezuela**; 16 km from Barcelona; oil refining; p. with Barcelona (1981) 81,800.

Puerto Limón. See **Limón**.

Puerto Montt, spt., **Chile**; cap. Los Lagos region; in sheep-farming dist.; S. terminus of rlys.; devastated by earthquake 1960; p. (1992) 130,737.

Puerto Ordaz. See **Santo Tomé de la Guayana**.

Puerto Rico, I., terr. of **USA**, W.I.; since 1952 free commonwealth ass. with USA; democratic economic growth aided recently by falling birth-rate; mtnous., eroded soils, alt. modifies tropical climate; exp. mnfs., but agr. impt. internally; 80 per cent land under cultivation, sugar, tobacco, coffee; tourism; cap. San Juan; a. 8,866 km²; p. (2004) 3,897,960.

Puerto Saurez, R. pt., **Bolivia**; on R. Paraguay; collecting ctr. for rubber, coffee, Brazil nuts.

Puget Sound, Wash., **USA**; inlet of Pac. Oc.

Puglia, region, S.E. **Italy**; hilly, cstl., pastoral plain; grain, fruits, livestock; wine, olive oil; a. 19,347 km²; p. (1992) 4,049,972.

Puket. See **Phuket**.

Pula, spt., **Croatia**, (formerly Yugoslavia); on Adriatic; industl. ctr. with shipyards, docks, and various inds.; ch. naval base of Habsburg empire; tourism; Roman remains; p. (1981) 77,278.

Pulia. See **Puglia**.

Puna, cold, bleak, and barren plateau of Andes in **Peru** and **Bolivia**, 3,600–5,500 m.

Pune (Poona), c., Maharashtra, **India**; in W. Ghats; temperate pleasant climate; cultural, educational (univ.) and political ctr.; military base; agr. tr. ctr.; cotton gds., paper; p. (1991) 1,567,000.

Punjab, region N.W. Indus plains, Indian sub- continent; extensive irrigation from the "five rivers"—Jhelum, Chenab, Ravi, Bias, Sutlej; now divided politically between **India** and **Pakistan**; impt. cotton, wheat, and sugar dist.; coal deposits.

Punjab, st., **India**; formerly part of larger, linguistically divided, E. Punjab st.; a. 50,375 km²; p. (2001) 24,289,300. (see also **Haryana, Chandigarh**).

Punjab (West) prov., **Pakistan**; old prov. revived 1970; p. (1981) 47,292,441.

Punta Arenas, c., cp. of Magallanes prov., S. **Chile**; most S. c. in world; mutton, wool; coal nearby; natural gas pipeline from Kimiri-Aike; p. (1992) 113,661.

Puntarenas, spt., **Costa Rica**, on G. of Nicoya; fishing; fish-processing; resort; p. (1984) 37,390 (dist).

Purbeck, I. of, sm. penin., Dorset cst., **Eng.**; anc. v. of Corfe Castle in ctr.; limestone ("Purbeck marble") quarries; site of Britain's lgst. onshore oilfield; once a royal deer forest; forms 1. gov. dist. of **Purbeck**, inc. Wareham and Swanage; p. (2001) 44,416.

Puri, t., Orissa, **India**; long famous for its temple and festival of the god Vishnu and his monster car, Juggernaut; p. (1991) 125,199.

Purus, R., **Peru** and **Brazil**; rises in Andes, flows to Amazon R. through underdeveloped a.; 3,360 km long.

Pusan, main pt. of **S. Korea**; on Korean Strait at head of Naktong R. basin; textiles; steel mill at Pohang nearby; Korea's first nuclear power sta.; p. (1990) 3,797,566.

Pushkin, c., **Russia**; nr. St. Petersburg; summer palaces of Tsars; Pushkin museum; Pulkovo observatory nearby.

Putney, sub. of London, **Eng.**; Thamesside dist.

Putrajaya, Malaysia. Planned new capital of Malaysia, 25 km. from Kuala Lumpur.

Putrid Sea. See **Sivash**.

Putumayo, R., trib. of Amazon; rises in Colombia, forming bdy. with Ecuador and Peru; here in wild-rubber region, Roger Casement exposed cruel exploitation of native labour; 1,600 km long.

Puy-de-Dôme, extinct volcano, Massif Central, **France**; lgst peak of Auvergne mtns., 1,466 m.

Puy-de-Dôme, dep., **France**; in Auvergne; cap. Clermont-Ferrand, industl. ctr. Thiers; a. 8,003 km²; p. (1999) 603,038.

Puymorens Tunnel, Pyrenees, on bdy. between **France** and **Spain**; carries main rly. between Toulouse and Barcelona.

Pwllheli, t., Gwynedd, N. **Wales**; sm. pt. on S. cst. Lleyn Peninsula; seaside resort; in-shore fishing, boat-bldg.; p. (1991) 3,974.

Pyatigorsk, c., N. Caucasus, **Russia**; ctr. of Caucasian mineral water springs; Lermontov shot here in duel 1841; p. (1989) 129,000.

Pylos, pt., S.W. Peloponnesus, **Greece**; shipbldg.; sea-battles 1827 (Navarino), 425 B.C.

Pyongyang, c., cap. of **N. Korea**; stands high above Taedong R.; major industl. ctr. with coal and iron ore deposits nearby; univ.; many historic relics; p. (2000) 3·2 m.

Pyrenees, range of mtns., S.W. **Europe**; dividing France from Iberian peninsula; 432 km long; lgst peak Pic d'Anéto (Maladetta) 3,408 m.

Pyrénées-Atlantiques, dep., S.W. **France**; mainly agr., sheep and cattle raising; ch. ts. Pau (cap.), Bayonne, Biarritz; a. 7,713 km²; p. (1999) 599,858.

Pyrénées-Orientales, dep., S. **France**; on Mediterranean; wine, fruit, olives; cap. Perpignan; a. 4,141 km²; p. (1999) 392,640.

Q

Qacentina (Constantine), c., dep., N. E. **Algeria**; 650 m. alt. on gorge of R. Rhumel; textile and engin. wks.; lge tractor and diesel engine complex; p. (1987) 440,842 (c.), 662,330 (dep.).

Qandahar, c., former cap of **Afghanistan**; alt. 1,037 m.; fruit preserving and canning; airpt; former Taleban stronghold; textiles; p. (1990) 238,000.

Qatar, c., emirate, indep. st. (1971), Arabia; peninsula on Persian G.; economy based on oil; inland production declining, but increasing offshore drilling; political stability less certain after withdrawal of Brit. military protection (1971); cap. Doha; a. 10,360 km²; p. (2004) 840,290, includes many foreign workers.

Qattara Depression, N. **Egypt**; 134 m below sea level, salt marsh produced by seepage and evaporation of artesian water; marshes; few inhabitants; scheme to flood depression with sea water to generate electricity now under construction.

Qenâ, t. and prov., central **Egypt**; on R. Nile; water jars and bottles; agr. tr., cereals, dates; p. (1986) 119,794 (t.). (1991) 2,598,000 (prov.).

Qingdao (Tsingtao), c., Shandong prov., **China**; spt. with excellent harbour at head of bay; tourism impt.; mnfs. locomotives, cement, textiles, machin., chemicals; special development zone to attract high technology inds.; oil jetty for Shengli oil field; new container port planned; p. (1994) 1,584,000.

Qinghai (Tsinghai), prov., W. China; between Xinjiang and Xizang Zizhou (Tibet), inc. c. plateau; local coal and iron ore but exploitation hindered by isolation; two new iron and steel plants; new rly.; massive hydro-electricity plant; international airpt. link with Hong Kong; attempts to increase economic development; oil exploration; a. 721,004 km²; p. (1994) 4,510,000.

Qinghai Hu (Koko Nor), salt L., Qinghai prov., China; at over 3,000 m. in Tibetan highlands; a. 5,957 km²; no outlet.

Qinhuangdao (Chinwangtao), c., sub., former treaty pt., Hebei, N. China; on Yellow Sea cst. 240 km N.E. of Tianjin, only good natural harbour on N. China cst.; exp. coal from Gailan mines; machin., textiles, chemical inds.; designated a development zone to attract foreign investment; p. (1994) 412,500.

Qiqihar (Tsitsihar), c., Heilongjiang prov., N. China; on Vladivostok portion of Trans-Siberian rly.; food processing and tr., chemicals; potential oilfield; p. (1994) 1,104,000.

Qisil-Qum, desert region, Central Asia; covering dried-up a. of extended Pleistocene Aral Sea.

Qom (Qum), c., Iran; pilgrimage ctr., shrine of Fatima; rly. junction; p. (1994) 780,000.

Qornet es Sauda, mtn., Lebanon range, Levant, Lebanon; max. alt. 3,050 m.

Quantock Hills, Somerset, Eng.; S. of Bridgwater Bay; hgst. pt. 385 m.

Quauzhu. See Zhengzhou.

Queanbeyan, t., N.S.W., Australia; rapid growth as commuter ctr. as only 13 km from Canberra; pastoral, dairying dist.; mkt. and service ctr.

Quebec, c., cap. of Q. prov., Canada; spt. with fine harbour on St. Lawrence R. at mouth of St. Charles; cultural cap. of French Canada; inds. based on local raw materials of timber, agr. prods.; oil refining at St. Romauld; historic c. with many fine bldgs., univ., tourism; p. (1991) 167,517 (c.), (1996) 671,889 (met. a.).

Quebec, prov., Canada; mainly within Canadian Shield; continental climate; forests and timber inds.; agr. in S.; hydroelectric power and abundant minerals; p. mainly French-speaking; ch. cs., Quebec (cap.), Montreal; strong separatist movements causing decline in investment and movement of some inds. to USA; a. 1,540,687 km²; p. (1997) 7,400,000.

Quebec-Labrador Trough, Canada; geological formation extending through central Quebec prov. to Ungava Bay, Hudson Strait; immense reserves of iron-ore (locally "red-gold").

Quedlinburg, t., Saxony-Anhalt, Germany; at foot of Harz mtns.; cas., cath.; aniline dyes, metals, engin., horticultural mkt. t.; p. (1999) 25,200.

Queen Charlotte's Is., archipelago, N. of Vancouver I., off cst. B.C., Canada; halibut fishing, lumbering.

Queen Charlotte Sound, strait, separating Vancouver I. from B.C. mainland Canada; a continuation of Johnstone Strait.

Queen Elizabeth Is., Canada; I. gr. in Canadian Arctic; most N. land of N. America; a. 349,443 km².

Queen Maud Land, Norwegian sector of Antarctica; ice crystal mtns., 3,050 m high for 160 km along cst.

Queens, bor., N.Y. City, USA; residtl. dist. N. of Manhattan; lgst. bor. of N.Y. c.; p. 1,951,598.

Queensbury and Shelf, t., West Yorks., Eng.; textiles; p. (1991) 11,661.

Queensferry, royal burgh, Edinburgh, Scot.; at S. end of Forth road and rail bridges; p. (2002) 9,370.

Queensland, st., N.E. Australia; sub-tropical a. rising from cst. to Gt. Dividing Range and Western Plains (inc. Gt. Artesian Basin); Barrier Reef off cst.; p. concentrated on cst. where sugar cane and tropical fruits grown, popular all year tourist resorts and retirement ctrs.; all year mkt. gardening replaced by extensive cattle and sheep ranching in W.; coal, copper, uranium, bauxite; oil at Moonie; mftg.; cap. Brisbane; a. 1,727,200 km²; p. (1996) 3,368,900.

Queenstown. See Cobh.

Queenstown, S.I., N.Z., tourist ctr. on L. Wakatipu in S. Alps; p. (1991) 15,123.

Quelimane, pt., Mozambique; at head of estuary; rly. terminus; exp. copra, sisal, tea; notorious in 18th and 19th cent. as slave mkt.; p. (1980) 60,151.

Quelpart. See Cheju.

Quemoy, gr. of Is. off Chinese mainland nr. Amoy; heavily fortified.

Querétaro, t., cap. of Q. st., Mexico; site of pre-Aztec settlement at 1,881 m; cath., many colonial bldgs.; old cotton ind.; p. (1990) 454,049.

Querétaro, st., Mexico; in Central Plateau; arid with fertile valleys; variety of crops; mng. impt.; famous for opals; cap. Q.; a. 11,479 km²; p. (1990) 1,044,227.

Quetta, t., cap. of Baluchistan, Pakistan; at 5,000 ft., commands routes to Bolan Pass, ctr of irrigated agr. a.; military ctr.; coal mng. nearby; damaged by severe earthquake (1935); p. (1981) 285,000.

Quezaltonango (Xela), t., S.W. Guatemala; second c. of rep.; at 2,333 m at foot of Santa Maria volcano; univ.; comm. ctr. for rich agr. region; textiles, handicrafts; p. (1994) 90,800.

Quezon City, c., Philippines; new city within metropolitan Manila; univ.; p. (1995) 1,989,000.

Quillon, t., Kerala, India; on Malabar cst., ctr. of coconut tr. and processing; p. (1991) 140,000.

Quimes, t., Buenos Aires, Argentina; on Rio de la Plata estuary; English public school; resort; oil refining, textiles, glass; p. (1980) 441,780.

Quimper, t., cap. Finistère dep., France; tourist ctr. for S. Brittany; Breton pottery; Gothic cath.; p. (1999) 62,705.

Quincy, t., Ill., USA; at bridging point of R. Mississippi; agr. machin., clothing, footwear, food inds.; p. (1980) 42,554.

Quincy, t., Mass., USA; in Mass. B., 13 km S.E. of Boston; shipbldg. ctr.; p. (1996) 85,532.

Quindio, pass, Colombia; provides impt. routeway through Cordillera Central; 11,099 ft.

Qui Nhon, t., S. Vietnam; cst. tr.; tr. in coconut prods.; fishing; p. (1992) 163,000.

Quintana Roo, st., S.E. Mexico; on Caribbean; low-lying swamp, underdeveloped; cap. Chetumal; a. 50,344 km²; p. (1990) 493,605.

Quito, c., cap. of Ecuador; in Andes at 2,852 m, 24 km S. of equator; anc. Inca c., cath., univ., slower growth than coastal ts.; impt. textile ctr.; p. (2000) 1,754,000 (met. a.).

Quorndon (Quorn), sm. t., Leics., Eng.; on R. Soar, 5 km S. of Loughborough; former ctr. of foxhunting dist.; p. (1991) 4,614.

Qwaqwa, frmr. homeland, S. Africa.

R

Raasay, I., E. of Skye, Highland, Scot.; 21 km long, 5-6 km wide; p. (1991) 163.

Rab I., at head of Adriatic, off Croatia; tourism; a. 192 km².

Rabat, t., cap. of Morocco; spt. at mouth of Bu Regreg R. on Atl. cst.; cath., univ.; textiles, carpets, rugs; p. (2000) 1,496,000.

Rabaul, spt., New Britain, Papua New Guinea; ch. pt., exp. copra; damaged by volcanic eruption (1937) former cap. of New Guinea; p. (1990) 17,022.

Raciborz (Ratibor), t., Upper Silesia, Poland (since 1945); on R. Oder; textiles, metals, wood engin.; p. (1995) 65,116.

Racine, c., Wis., USA; sm. pt. on L. Mich., 16 km S. of Milwaukee; agr. machin., tractors, car parts; p. (1990) 84,298 (c.), 175,034 (met. a.).

Radcliffe, t., Gtr. Manchester, Eng.; N.W. of Manchester; paper, rubber, paint, engin.; p. (2001) 34,239.

Radium Hill, v., S. Australia; ctr. for radium mng. 1920-30 and uranium later; mines now closed (since 1961).

Radnorshire, historic co., central Wales, now part of Powys.

Radom, t. and prov., Poland; in Radomska Plain; route ctr.; metal and chemical inds.; lge. tobacco factory; p. (1995) 232,261 (t.), 763,027 (prov.).

Radomsko, t., Piotrków, Poland; on edge of Lodz Upland; metallurgical wks., food inds.; bentwood chairs for exp.; p. (1995) 50,996.

Ragusa. See Dubrovnik.

Ragusa, t., Sicily, Italy; oil and asphalt production; p. (1981) 64,492.

Raichur, t., Karnataka, India; comm. ctr.; agr. processing; p. (1991) 157,551.

Rainford, t., Merseyside, Eng.; nr. St. Helens; former coal-mng. a.; p. (1991) 6,382.

Rainier, mtn., Wash., USA; 4,432 m; forms Nat. Park.

Raipur, t., Madhya Pradesh, India; ctr. of fertile rice growing a.; p. (1991) 439,000.

Rajahmundry, t., Andhra Pradesh, India; on delta of Godivari R.; agr. tr.; p. (1991) 325,000 .

Rajasthan, st., India; dry a. inc. Thar desert; sparse p. where primitive irrigation; agr., millets, pulses, cotton; impt. gypsum deposits; impt. oil find (2004); cap. Jaipur; a. 342,274 km²; p. (2001) 56,473,100.

Rajkot, t., Gujarat, India; p. (1991) 559,000.

Rajshahi, t., Rajshahi dist., Bangladesh; on R. Ganges; univ.; silk inds.; p. (1991) 299,671.

Raki-Ura I. See Stewart I.

Raleigh, c., cap. of N.C., USA; educational ctr. univ.; printing, cotton tr. and processing; p. (2000) 276,093 (c.), 735,000 (met. a. with Durham).

Ramat Gan, t., Israel; in plain of Sharon; univ.; lt. inds.; p. (1992) 122,700.

Rambouillet, t., Yvelines, France; nr. Versailles; anc. château; p. (1982) 22,487.

Rameswaram, t., Tamil Nadu. India; on Rameswaram I., Palk Strait; contains Dravidian temple, Hindu holy place of pilgrimage.

Ramla, t., Israel; S. of Lydda; former cap. of Palestine; ass. with crusaders.

Rampur, t., Uttar Pradesh, India; N.W. of Bareilly, agr. tr.; sugar refining; chemicals; cap. of former princely st. of R.; p. (1991) 243,742.

Ramsbottom, t., Lancs., Eng.; on R. Irwell, 6 km N. of Bury; engin., paper, textiles; p. (1991) 17,318.

Ramsey, mkt. t., Cambs., Eng.; on edge of Fens, 11 km N. of St. Ives; engin.; abbey ruins; p. (1991) 7,577.

Ramsey, t., spt., I. of Man, Eng.; on N.E. cst.; holiday resort; p. (1991) 6,496.

Ramsgate, t., Kent, Eng.; on S. cst. of I. of Thanet; seaside resort; p. (1991) 37,895.

Rancagua, t., Libertador region, Chile; ctr. of fertile valley in Andean foothills; tractors, agr. processing; p. (1992) 184,134.

Rance, R., Brittany, France; world's first major tidal hydroelectric power sta. (opened 1966).

Ranchi, t., Jharkhand, India; hot season seat of govt. in Chota Nagpur plateau; univ.; heavy engin.; p. (1991) 599,000.

Rand. See Witwatersrand.

Randers, pt., Denmark; on Randers Fjord, inlet of Kattegat; machin., foundries; exp. dairy prod.; mediaeval monastery; p. (1990) 61,020.

Randfontein, t., Gauteng, S. Africa; gold-mng. ctr.; uranium plant; p. (1980) 91,460 (dist.).

Randstad, conurb., Neth.; Dutch "urban ring." inc. Rotterdam, The Hague, Leiden, Amsterdam and Utrecht, contained within radius of 16 km; a. of rapid industrialisation.

Rangoon (Yangon), c., cap. of Myanmar; on E. arm of Irrawaddy delta; 2 caths., many mosques, temples and pagodas; replaced Mandalay as cap.; ctr. of rice tr. and exp.; oil refining; teak collecting ctr.; p. (2000) 4,196,000.

Rangpur, t., Bangladesh; on R. Ghaghat; jute; p. (1991) 203,931.

Rannoch, Loch, Perth and Kinross, Scot.; 14 km long, 1·6 km wide; drained to R. Tay.

Raoul I. See Sunday I.

Rapallo, t., Liguria, N.W. Italy; on G. of Genoa, 35 km E. of Genoa; most celebrated resort on Italian Riviera di Levante; p. (1981) 28,318.

Rapa Nui. See Easter I.

Rapid City, t., S.D., USA; second t. of st.; comm. ctr. for agr. and mng. a.; p. (1996) 57,642.

Rarotonga, volcanic I., Pac. Oc.; lgst. of Cook Is.; fruit canning; ch. t. and pt. Avarua; p. (1981) 9,530.

Ra's al Khaimah, emirate, member of the United Arab Emirates; p. (1985) 116,470.

Rasht (Resht), c., Iran; cap. of Gilan prov., in a. producing rice, cotton, silk; carpets; nearby Pahlevi serves as pt.; p. (1994) 374,000.

Ras Tannura, spt., Nejd, Saudi Arabia; lge. oil refinery; oil exp.

Rathenow, t., Brandenburg, Germany; on R. Havel; optical and precision instruments; p. (1989) 30,935.

Ratibor. See Racibórz.

Ratingen, t., N. Rhine–Westphalia, Germany; N.E. of Düsseldorf; textiles, machin., glass; famous for Blue L.; p. (2002) 91,793.

Ratisbon. See Regensburg.

Ratlam, t., Madhya Pradesh, India; rly. junc. in Malwa Plateau; p. (1991) 195,776.

Ratnapura, t., Sri Lanka; former ctr. of gem mng.; p. (1981) 37,354.

Raunds, t., East Northants., Eng.; 8 km N.E. of

Wellingborough; p. (1991) 7,493.

Raurkela, t., Orissa, India; steel, tinplate, iron, fertilisers; p. (1991) 398,864.

Ravenglass, t., Cumbria, Eng.; nr. mouth of R. Esk; old pt.; Roman remains.

Ravenna, c., cap. of Ravenna prov., Emilia-Romagna, Italy; on reclaimed plain nr. Po delta; connected to Adriatic by canal; ctr. of fertile agr. dist., agr. processing; new inds. aided by discovery of methane N. of c.; oil refineries, chemicals, fertilisers; cath., mausoleum, famous mosaics; p. (1992) 136,009.

Ravenna, prov., Emilia-Romagna, Italy; N. Italian plain rising to Apennines; fertile agr. a.; cap. R.; a. 1,852 km²; p. (1981) 358,654.

Ravensburg, t., Baden–Württemberg, Germany; nr. Konstanz; engin., textiles; p. (2002) 47,974.

Ravi, R., Punjab, India; trib. of Chenab; used for irrigation; 720 km long.

Rawalpindi, c., Pakistan; seat of govt. until completion of Islamabad; admin., comm. and rly. ctr.; foundries, oil refining, industl. gases; p. (1981) 928,000.

Rawmarsh, t., South Yorks., Eng.; 3 km N.E. of Rotherham; engin.; p. (1991) 18,085.

Rawtenstall, t., Rossendale, Lancs., Eng.; on R. Irwell in ctr. of Rossendale Fells; felts; footwear, textiles; p. (2001) 21,797.

Rayleigh, t., Rochford, Essex, Eng.; 8 km N.W. of Southend; lt. inds.; dormitory for London; p. (2001) 30,629.

Ré, Ile de, I., W. cst. of Charente-Maritime dep. France; off La Rochelle; citadel (built 1681) at St. Martin de Ré is now a prison.

Reading, t., unit. auth., Berks., Eng.; at confluence of Rs. Thames and Kennet; univ.; biscuits, engin., electronics, mkt. gardening, tin- box mftg., printing; p. (2001) 143,096 (unit. auth.).

Reading, c., Penns., USA; on Schuylkill R.; steelwks. using local coal, optical gds.; p. (1996) 75,723.

Recife, spt., cap. of Pernambuco st., N.E. Brazil; fine natural harbour; univ.; processing and exp. of sugar from surrounding a.; "Venice of Brazil" because of I. and peninsula site; lge. petrochemical wks. nearby; recent industl. expansion and diversification; engin., chem., electrical and telecommunications equipment; integrated steel wks.; p. (1991) 1,290,149.

Recklinghausen, t., N. Rhine–Westphalia, Germany; nr. Dortmund; collieries, iron, machin., textiles, chemicals; p. (2002) 124,587.

Recôncavo, dist., Bahia st., N.E. Brazil; surrounds bay at mouth of R. Paraguassu; intensive cultivation of sugar-cane, cotton, tobacco, rice, by black farmers; oil production; ch. ts. São Salvador, Cachoeira.

Rodbridge, outer bor., E. London, Eng.; incorporates Ilford, Wanstead and Woodford, Chigwell (Hainault Estate), Dagenham (N. Chadwell Heath ward); mainly residtl.; p. (2001) 240,796.

Redcar, t., Redcar and Cleveland, Eng.; lge. iron and steel wks.; p. (2001) 36,443.

Redcar and Cleveland, unit. auth. created in 1996, formerly part of Cleveland, Eng.; inc. Cleveland Hills and ts. of Guisborough, Redcar and Skelton; p. (2001) 139,132.

Red Deer, t., Alberta, Canada; on Red Deer R.; mkt. t. in farming a.; lge. natural gas processing plant nearby; p. (1996) 60,075.

Redditch, t., l. gov. dist., Worcs., Eng.; 19 km S. of Birmingham; needles, fishing tackle, cycles, springs, aluminium alloys; new t. (1964); p. (2001) 76,700 (dist.).

Redhill. See Reigate.

Redlands, t., Cal., USA; univ.; citrus fruit packing and canning; p. (1996) 66,693.

Redonda, I., Leeward gr., Antigua and Barbuda; between Montserrat and Nevis; uninhabited.

Redondo Beach, t., Cal., USA; residtl.; tourism; p. (1996) 62,367.

Red R. (China and Vietnam). See Song-koi.

Red R., USA; southernmost of lge. tribs. of Mississippi R.; derives name and colour from red clay in upper course; dammed for flood control and hydroelec. power; 2,560 km long.

Red R. of the North, USA; rises in Minn., flows N. into Canada to empty into L. Winnipeg; 1,040 km long.

Redruth, t., Cornwall, Eng.; once major ctr. of tin mng.; p. (1991) 35,915 (inc. Camborne).

Red Sea, arm of sea separating Arabia from Africa; connects with Indian Oc. by Straits of Bab-el-

Mandeb; extension of Great African Rift Valley which further N. encloses the Dead Sea; 2,240 km long.

Redwood City, t., W. Cal., **USA**; timber tr.; electronics; p. (1996) 71,140.

Ree, Lough, L., **R.o.I.**; between Roscommon, Longford and Westmeath, an extension of R. Shannon; 27 km long.

Regensburg (Ratisbon), c., R. pt., Bavaria, **Germany**; N.E. of Munich on R. Danube; timber processing, chemicals; p. (2002) 127,198.

Reggio di Calabria, spt., Calabria, **Italy**; on Strait of Messina; cath.; fishing, ferry to Sicily; mkt. for citrus fruit; tourism; agr. processing; rebuilt after 1908 earthquake; p (1992) 179,012.

Reggio nell' Emilia, c., cap. of prov. of same name, in Emilia-Romagna, N. **Italy**; at foot of Apennines; Renaissance church of the Madonna della Ghiara; locomotives, aircraft, agr. engin.; birthplace of Ariosto; p. (1992) 133,191.

Regina, t., cap. of Saskatchewan, **Canada**; ctr. of wheat growing dist. of Prairies; connected by pipeline to Alberta oilfields; oil refining, chemicals, agr. machin.; p. (1991) 179,178 (c.), (1996) 193,652.

Rehovoth, Israel; t., in citrus fruit dist.; Weizmann Institute of Science.

Reichenbach, t., Saxony, **Germany**; at foot of Erzgebirge; p. (1989) 25,663.

Reichenberg. See Liberec.

Reigate, t., Surrey, **Eng.**; at foot of N. Downs, 8 km E. of Dorking; dormitory for London; part of l. gov. dist., **Reigate and Banstead**; p. (2001) 126,523 (dist.), (2001) 50,436 (t.) (with Redhill).

Reims, c., Marne dep., N.E. **France**; on R. Vesle; famous Gothic cath.; univ.; champagne ctr., textiles; p. (1999) 187,149.

Reindeer L., Saskatchewan, Manitoba, **Canada**; Indian settlement on shore; a. 6,475 km².

Rejang R., Sarawak; **Malaysia**; navigable for 72 km by ocean boats; main R. of Sarawak.

Remscheid, t., N. Rhine–Westphalia, **Germany**; nr. Düsseldorf; iron and steel ctr.; machin. tools; p. (2002) 118,753.

Renaix. See Ronse.

Rendsburg, t., Schleswig-Holstein, **Germany**; on Kiel Canal; shipbldg., elec. gds.; p. (2002) 29,251.

Renfrew, royal burgh, Renfrewshire, **Scot.**; nr. R. Clyde, 8 km W. of Glasgow; p. (2002) 20,251.

Renfrewshire, W. **Scot.**, unit. auth. created in 1996, incorporating part of historic co. which became part of Strathclyde in 1974 and is now divided between Inverclyde, E. Renfrewshire and Renfrewshire; lies immediately W. of Glasgow; p. (2001) 171,940.

Rennes, c., cap. of Ille-et-Vilaine dep., **France**; only major inland t. of Brittany, in fertile agr. basin; univ., comm. ctr.; cars, engin.; p. (1999) 205,875.

Reno, lgst. t. of Nevada, **USA**; univ.; st. agr. college; famous for easy divorce procedure and gambling; p. (1990) 133,850 (t.), 255,000 (met. a.).

Repton, t., South Derbyshire, **Eng.**; famous public school in priory; former Saxon cap. of Mercia; p. (1991) 2,012.

Resht. See Rasht.

Resina, t., S. **Italy**; on Bay of Naples at W. foot of Vesuvius; nr. site of anc. Herculaneum; resort.

Resistencia, t., cap. of Chaco prov., **Argentina**; served by R. pt. of Barranqueras on R. Paraná; tr. in cattle, timber, cotton; agr. processing; p. (1991) 292,350.

Restormel, l. gov. dist., Cornwall, **Eng.**; inc. N. and S. cst. and ts. of Newquay and St. Austell; p. (2001) 95,562.

Retalhuleu, dep., **Guatemala**; ctr. for coffee, sugar; a. 1858 km²; p. (1991) 238,857.

Réunion (Ile de Bourbon), I., overseas terr. of **France**; in Indian Oc., between Mauritius and Madagascar; volcanic I.; impt. sugar producer; cap. St. Denis; a. 2,512 km²; p. (2004) 766,153.

Reus, t., Tarragona, prov., **Spain**; textiles; agr. tr.; p. (1990) 86,400.

Reuss, R., **Switzerland**; flows N. from the St. Gotthard Pass through L. Lucerne, joining Aare R. nr. Brugg; 157 km long.

Reutlingen, t., Baden–Württemberg, **Germany**; S. of Stuttgart; textiles, metals, machin., leather; p. (2002) 111,338.

Reval. See Tallin.

Revelstoke, t., B.C., **Canada**; rly. junc.; in timber producing a.; ctr. for R. Nat. Park; p. (1986) 8,279.

Revillagigedo Islands, archipelago, Pac. Oc., off S.W. **Mexico**; ch. Is., Socorro, San Benedicto (volcano suddenly arose on I. 1952).

Reykjavik, c., cap. of Iceland; on S.W. cst.; impt. fish. pt.; fish exp. and processing; water piped from geysers; airport; univ.; 2 caths.; p. (2000) 110,000.

Rezayeh, (Orūmiyeh) c., **Iran**; cap. of W Azerbaijan prov.; comm. ctr. of agr. region; p. (1980) 304,823.

Rheidol, R., Ceredigion, **Wales**; flows from Plynlimmon in deeply incised valley (Devil's Bridge) to Aberystwyth; famous narrow-gauge rly; hydroelec. power; 38 km long.

Rheine, t., N. Rhine–Westphalia, **Germany**; on R. Ems; textiles, machin.; p. (2002) 75,925.

Rheingau, dist., **Germany**; famous wine a. on right bank of Rhine from Biebrich to Assmanshausen.

Rheinhausen, t., Rhine–Westphalia, **Germany**; on left bank of Rhine opposite Duisburg; coal mng., iron, textiles.

Rhin (Bas). See Bas Rhin.

Rhine, R., rises in Switzerland, can. Grisons, passes through L. Constance, skirts Baden, traverses Hesse, Rhineland, and the Neth., flowing to N. Sea by two arms, Oude Rijn and the Waal (the latter discharging finally by the Maas); famous for its beauty, especially between Bonn and Bingen; ch. falls at Schaff hausen; once a natural barrier between E. and W. Europe spanned by 30 rly. bridges; linked to Rhône by 1985 and Rhine-Main-Danube canal allows navigation from N. Sea to Black Sea for 3,500 km. (Trans European waterway); very polluted; 1,280 km long.

Rhine-Hern, canal, **Germany**; impt. Ruhr waterway, part of Mittelland Canal; 38 km long.

Rhineland Palatinate (Rheinland-Pfalz), Land, Germany; borders France, Luxembourg and Belgium; drained by Rhine and Moselle, inc. Hunsrück and Eifel mtns.; arable agr. in Rhine valley; vineyards; cap. Mainz; a. 19,852 km; p. (2005) 4,060,000.

Rhode Island, st., New England, **USA**; "Little Rhody"; admitted to Union 1790; st. flower violet, st. bird R.I. Red; washed by Atl. Oc., surrounded by Mass. and Conn.; divided by Narragansett Bay, with many Is. lgst. being that from which the st. takes its name; smallest and most densely populated st.; famous for poultry; major ind. textiles; cap. Providence; a. 3,144 km²; p. (2002) 1,069,725.

Rhodes (Rhodos), I., Dodecanese Is.; off S.W. cst., Anatolia, belonging to **Greece**; cap. R.; p. (1981) 87,831.

Rhodes, cap. of I. of Rhodes, **Greece**; on N.E. cst.; picturesque; p. (1981) 41,425.

Rhodesia. See Zimbabwe.

Rhodope Mtns. See Rodopi Mtns.

Rhondda, t., Rhondda, Cynon, Taff, **Wales**; in narrow R. valley; former coal mng. ctr.; lt. inds. introduced since 1930s depression; picturesque a. in upper R. valley; p. (1991) 59,947.

Rhondda, Cynon, Taff, S. Wales, unit. auth. created in 1996 from former l. gov. dists. of Cynon Valley, Rhondda and Taff-Ely; upland in N. dissected by deep R. valleys containing former coal mng. settlements; inc. ts. of Aberdare and Pontypridd; p. (2001) 231,946.

Rhône, dep., S.E. **France**; drained by R. Rhône, and its trib. Saône, which unite at Lyons; agr. grain, potatoes, wine; vine-growing, many mnfs., silks, textiles; cap. Lyons; a. 2,859 km²; p. (1999) 1,576,297.

Rhône, R., **Switzerland** and **France**; rises in Rhône glacier of St. Gotthard mtn. gr., and flows through L. of Geneva and E. France to G. of Lyons in Mediterranean; power stas. at Sion and Geneva; canals, dams, locks and power stas. from part of Fr. Rhône Valley project (1937–72); linked to Rhine by 1985; 811 km long.

Rhône-Alpes, region, S.E. **France**; inc.deps. Ain, Ardèche, Drôme, Isère, Loire, Rhône, Savoie, Haute-Savoie; based on the upper Rhône valley, inc. important industrial ctrs. of Lyon and Grenoble; p. (1999) 5,640,228.

Rhône-Saône Corridor, routeway, **France**; impt. transport artery using Rhône, Saône R. valleys as a means for linking Paris, Lorraine and Rhine rift valley with Mediterranean cst.; rlys., roads, with major pt. of Marseille serving the S. terminus.

Rhyl, t., Denbighshire, N. **Wales**; at entrance Vale of Clwyd; resort developed from sm. fishing v.; p. (1991) 24,909.

Rhymney, t., Caerphilly, **Wales**; on R. Rhymney, E. of Merthyr Tydfil; former colly. and iron founding ctr.; engin.; p. (1991) 7,991.

Ribble, R., North Yorks., Lancs., **Eng.**; rises in Pennines, flows W. to Irish Sea nr. pt. of Preston; 120 km long.

Ribble Valley, l. gov. dist., N. Lancs., **Eng.**; inc. Forest of Bowland and ts. of Clitheroe and Longridge; p. (2001) 53,960.

Ribe, mkt. t., Jutland, S. **Denmark**; admin. ctr. of R. prov.; impt. mediaeval c.; Romanesque cath.; many fine bldgs.; p. (1990) 17,872.

Ribeirão Prêto, t., São Paulo st., **Brazil**; mkt. in rich agr. a., coffee, cotton, sugar; p. (1996) 452,800.

Richard's Bay, **S. Africa**; new pt. to supplement congested Durban; on natural harbour; silting problem but designed for bulk carriers; plans to attract as. industl. development.

Richborough, pt., Kent, **Eng.**; at mouth of R. Stour; Caesar's ch. pt., major Roman remains; pt. has been privately redeveloped; chemicals.

Richmond, t., North Yorks., **Eng.**; at E. foot of Pennines on R. Swale; mkt. t., agr. tr.; 14th cent. grammar school; Norman cas.; forms l. gov. dist. of Richmondshire with surrounding a. of Aysgarth and Leyburn; p. (2001) 47,010 (dist.), (1991) 7,862 (t.).

Richmond, c., Cal., **USA**; deepwater pt.; oil refining; car assembly, chemicals, electronics; p. (1996) 91,018.

Richmond, c., cap. of Va., **USA**; on falls on R. James; pt. at head of navigation; financial, and tr. ctr.; tobacco inds., and mkt.; chemicals, iron and steel; p. (2000) 197,790 (c.), 866,000 (met. a. with Petersburg).

Richmond upon Thames, outer bor., Greater London, **Eng.**; inc. Barnes, Richmond and Twickenham; industl. and residtl.; park and Kew Gardens; p. (2001) 172,335.

Rickmansworth, t., Three Rivers, Herts., **Eng.**; residtl. sub of London; p. (1991) 10,767.

Ridder, (Leninogorsk), c., **Kazakhstan**; in Altai mtns.; lead, zinc, and silver mines; metallurgical plants; p. (1990) 69,200.

Rideau Canal, Ont., **Canada**; from Ottawa R. at Ottawa to Kingston on L. Ontario; 211 km long.

Riesa, t., Saxony, **Germany**; R. pt. on Elbe R. nr. Meissen; p. (2002) 38,567.

Riesengebirge, mtn. range, between Silesia (**Poland**) and Bohemia (**Czech Rep.**); highest peak Schneekoppe (Czech Snežka, Polish Sniezka), 1,604 m.

Rieti, Latium, **Italy**; an anc. Sabine c. with mediaeval townscape; in fertile Apennine basin; route ctr. and cap. of R. prov.; chemicals, sugar refinery, textiles; p. (1981) 43,079.

Riff or **Rif**, mtns., **Morocco**, N.W. Africa; extend along N. African cst. for 320 km from Straits of Gibraltar; inaccessible and economically unattractive, terr. of semi-nomadic tribes, rise to over 2,100 m in many places.

Riga, cap. of **Latvia**; Baltic pt.; exp. wheat, flax, hemp, dairy produce; industl. ctr., diesel rly. engin., furniture; univ.; local bathing beaches; p. (2000) 775,000.

Rigi, mtn., nr. L. Lucerne, **Switzerland**; viewpoint reached by rack and pinion rly.; 1,801 m.

Rijeka-Susak, c., **Croatia** (formerly Yugoslavia); formerly Fiume, ceded to Yugoslavia by Italy after second world war; rival pt. to Trieste on Adriatic Sea; oil refining, shipbldg., tobacco, chemicals; hydroelectric power; p. (1991) 167,364.

Rimini, c., Emilia-Romagna, **Italy**; on Adriatic cst. at junc. of Via Emilia and Via Flaminia; mkt. for fertile agr. a.; sm. inds.; bathing resort; p. (1992) 129,876.

Ringerike, t., Buskerud, **Norway**; new t., 40 km N.W. of Oslo and inc. former t. of Hönefoss; p. (1990) 27,433.

Riobamba, t., Chimborazo, **Ecuador**; on R. St. Juan; woollens, cotton gds., cement, ceramics; Inca palace ruins; p. (1990) 94,505.

Rio Branco, t., cap. of Acre st., **Brazil**; p. (1996) 228,900.

Rio de Janeiro, c., spt., S.E. **Brazil**; cap. of Guanabara st., on G. Bay, Alt. Oc.; former fed. cap.; beautiful natural harbour, many fine bldgs., Sugar Loaf mtn., Copacabana beach; flourishing tr. and inds.; mnfs. inc. textiles, foodstuffs, pharmaceutics, china, sheet glass; oil refining; p. (1991) 5,336,178 .

Rio de Janeiro, st., S.E. **Brazil**; on Atl. Oc.;

consolidated with Guanabara (1975); consists of cst. plain, central Sero do Mar escarpment, fertile Paraíba R. basin in W.; coffee, sugar, fruit; ctr. of heavy ind.; cement, textiles, sugar refineries at Campos, steel wks. at Volta Redonda; offshore oil finds in Campos basin; cap. Niterói; a. 42,735 km²; p. (1996) 13,316,500.

Rio Gallegos, cap. of Santa Cruz prov., S. **Argentina**; agr. ctr.; p. (1991) 64,640.

Rio Grande, headstream of R. Paraná., **Brazil**; Furnas dam, Estreito dam for hydroelec. power; 1,040 km long.

Rio Grande, R., flows from st. of Col. through N.M. to G. of Mexico; forms bdy. between Texas, **USA** and **Mexico**; Elephant Butte, Caballo, and Falcon multi-purpose dams; known also as Rio Grande do Norte and Rio Bravo; c. 3,016 km long.

Rio Grande do Norte, st., N.E. **Brazil**; cst. plain rising to S. plateau; climate semi-arid; cotton, sugar, salt, scheelite; cap. Natal; a. 53,038 km²; p. (1996) 2,415,600.

Rio Grande do Sul, st., S. **Brazil**; grassy plains, rolling plateaux; cool climate; stock-raising, meat-processing, wheat, wine, wool; lge. coal deposits at São Jeronimo; cap. Pôrto Alegre; a. 267,684 km²; p. (1996) 9,445,000.

Rioja, region and prov., N. **Spain**; upper Ebro valley; famous for wines and orange groves; ch. ctr. Logroño; p. (1998) 263,600.

Riom, t., Puy-de-Dôme dep., **France**; former cap. of Auvergne; old bldgs. built of lava; p. (1999) 18,585.

Rio Muni, terr., **Equatorial Guinea**; former Spanish terr. on cst. between Cameroon and Gabon, inc. offshore Is. of Corisco, Elobey Grande, Elobey Chico; with Biako forms Equatorial Guinea; equatorial forest; exp. tree prods. of cacao, coffee, hardwood; ch. t. Bata; a. 26,003 km²; p. (1983) 240,804.

Rion, R., **Georgia**; flows from Caucasus to Black Sea; lower half navigable, hydroelec. sta. at Kutaisi. (In Greek mythology the R. Phasis of the Argonauts.)

Rio Negro, prov., **Argentina**; in N. Patagonia; irrigated agr. in R. valley, fruits, grain crops; elsewhere stock-raising; cap. Viedma; a. 201,010 km²; p. (1991) 506,772.

Rio Negro, dep., **Uruguay**; livestock fattening from N. Uruguay; grain crops; ch. t. and cap. Fray Bentos; a. 8,466 km²; p. (1985) 48,241.

Rio Tinto, t., **Spain**; at W. end of Sierra Morena 64 km N.E. of Huelva; major world ctr. of copper production.

Riouw-Lingga Archipelago, I. gr., **Indonesia**; S. of Malaya; Bintan lgst. I. where bauxite mng.; pepper and rubber cultivation; a. 5,905 km².

Ripley, mkt. t., Amber Valley, Derbys., **Eng.**; 11 km N.E. of Derby; coal, iron, heavy engin., bricks, agr. implements; p. (1991) 18,310.

Ripon, c., North Yorks., **Eng.**; on R. Ure; cath.; old mkt. square; old custom of wakeman; tourism; p. (1991) 13,806.

Risca, t., Caerphilly, **Wales**; on R. Ebbw; former coal mng. dist.; limestone quarrying; bricks, plastics; p. (1991) 15,124.

Risdon, t., Tasmania, **Australia**; first white settlement in Tasmania, opposite Hobart; electrometallurgy.

Rivera, dep., **Uruguay**; on Brazilian border; noted for cattle and sheep ranches; cap. R.; a. 9,824 km²; p. (1985) 88,800

Rivera, t., cap. of R. dep., **Uruguay**; on Brazilian frontier opposite Santa Ana; agr. mkt.; p. (1985) 56,335.

Riverina, pastoral cty., N.S.W., **Australia**; between Lachlan-Murrumbidgee and Murray Rs.; merino sheep in W., good wheat yields in E.; gtr. crop variety with irrigation; a. 68,894 km²;.

River Rouge, t., Mich., **USA**; ctr. of Ford car mnf.; many heavy inds.; rapidly growing t.; p. (1980) 12,912.

Riverside, t., Cal., **USA**; ctr. for citrus fruit packing and tr.; resort; p. (2000) 255,168 (t.), 2,589,000 (met. a. with San Bernardino).

Riviera, the belt of cst. between the Alps and the Mediterranean from Spezia to Hyères, **France** and **Italy**; picturesque scenery, sheltered, mild climate; fashionable health resorts.

Riyadh, t., royal cap. of **Sandi Arabia**; 368 km inland from Persian G.; palace; univ.; route and tr. ctr., linked by rail with pt. of Zahran; new link to Jeddah proposed; p. (2000) 3,324,000.

Rizaiyeh (Urmia), c., cap. of Azerbaijan prov., **Iran**; nr. L. Urmia; comm. ctr.; birthplace of Zoroaster; p. (1983) 262,588.

Rizal, prov., central Luzon, **Philippines**; rapidly growing prov. in fertile Central Plain; new inds. developing; cap. Pasig; a. 2,049 km²; p. (1990) 980,194.

Rize, t. and prov., **Turkey**; nr. Trabzon, on Black Sea; ctr. of Turkish tea inds.; p. (1985) 50,221 (t.), (1990) 348,776 (prov.).

Road Town, spt., Tortola; cap. of the Brit. **Virgin Is.**; tr. in fish, poultry; p. (1991) 6,330.

Roanne, t., Loire dep., **France**, on R. Loire; château ruins; textiles; p. (1990) 42,848 (t.), 77,160 (met.a.).

Roanoke, R., Va., and N.C., **USA**; flows into Albemarle Sound; hydroelec. power; 656 km long.

Roanoke, c., S.W. Va., **USA**; between Blue Ridge and Allegheny mtns.; rly. junc.; engin. p. (1996) 95,548.

Roanoke I., off cst. N.C., **USA**; attempted settlement of colony by Raleigh.

Roaring Creek, Belize, Central America; site of new cap. 80 km inland, at junc. of W. highway with Hummingbird highway.

Robben I., at entrance of Table Bay, Western Cape Prov., **S. Africa**; penal settlement which housed Nelson Mandela; last prisoners left, Nov. 1996. Now called Siqithini (Xhosa for 'place of healing').

Robin Hood's Bay, v., North Yorks., **Eng.**; picturesque site in inlet; tourism, fishing.

Robinson Crusoe Is. *See* **Juan Fernandez Is.**

Robson, Mt., **Canada**; on B.C. and Alberta border; alt. 3,956 m; in Nat. Park.

Rocha, dep., **Uruguay**; borders Atl. Oc.; a. of cattle and sheep rearing; cap. R.; a. 11,850 km²; p. (1985) 66,440.

Rochdale, t., met. dist., Gtr. Manchester, **Eng.**; at S. foot of Rossendale Fells, on R. Roch; textiles, engin., asbestos; co-operative movement started (1844); p. (2001) 205,357 (dist.), (2001) 95,796 (t.).

Rochefort, t., Charente-Maritime dep., **France**; fishing pt.; former impt. naval base; p. (1982) 27,716.

Rochester, t., part of l. gov. dist. of **Rochester-upon-Medway**, Kent, **Eng.**; on R. Medway, adjoining Chatham; cath., cas.; many associations with Dickens; aeronautical, elec. and mechanical engin., paint, varnish, cement; p. (1995) 144,200 (dist.), (1991) 23,971 (t.).

Rochester, t., Minn., **USA**; famous for Mayo clinic, and Mayo medical research ctr.; p. (1996) 75,638.

Rochester, c., N.Y., **USA**; on Genesee R.; univ.; cameras, films, optical instruments, thermometers, electronic equipment; hydroelectric power; p. (2000) 219,773 (c.), 1,002,000 (met. a.).

Rochford, t. and l. gov. dist., Essex, **Eng.**; cstl. a. inc. Rochford and Rayleigh; p. (2001) 78,489 (dist.), (1991) 15,081 (t.).

Rock, R., Wis., Ill., **USA**; formerly home of native Indians; focus of white settlement since 1830; 456 km long.

Rockall, sm. I., Atl. Oc.; lies 320 km W. of Outer Hebrides; forms hgst. part of submarine bank which forms good fishing-ground; uninhabited; annexed by Britain 1955; formally incorporated into Inverness-shire (1972) to ensure control of oil and natural gas deposits; claimed also by Ireland and Iceland; rock samples aged 1,000 million years place it with some Canadian rocks.

Rockall Deep, submarine trench, N. Atl. Oc.; between N.W. Ireland and Rockall I.; suspected oil and natural gas reserves.

Rockford, c., Ill., **USA**; serves agr. dist.; agr. machin., machin. tools; p. (1990) 139,426 (c.), 283,719 (met. a.).

Rockhampton, t., pt., Queensland, **Australia**; on Tropic of Capricorn; outlet for vast pastoral and mng. a.; comm. cap. of central Queensland; meat-preserving; p. (1991) 63,598.

Rockingham, t., W. **Australia**; satellite of Perth; major pt. planned to serve Kwinana; p. (1991) 36,700.

Rock Island, c., Ill., **USA**; on R. Mississippi; former site of US arsenal; agr. machin., timber and agr. processing; p. (1980) 46,928.

Rocky Mtns., vast mtn. chain, N. America;

extend from Alaska, through Canada, USA to Mexico; made up of several parallel ranges separated by intermontane basins and plateaux; barrier to spread of settlers to W. cst. in 19th cent.; climatic barrier; extensive snow and glacier fields in N.; dry desert landscapes in S.; many Nat. Parks; sparse p.; hydroelectric power; hgst. peak Mt. Logan (6,054 m); length 5,120 km.

Rodez, t., cap. of Aveyron dep., **France**, on R. Aveyron; cath.; woollens; p. (1990) 23,707.

Rodosto. *See* **Tekirdag.**

Rodrigues, I., Brit. dependency of **Mauritius**, Indian Oc.; 560 km N.E. of Mauritius; mainly agr. and fishing; cap. Port Mathurin; a. 109 km²; p. (1993) 34,536.

Roeselare, (Roulers) t., W. Flanders, **Belgium**; on R. Lys, nr. Kortrijk, textile ctr.; p. (1993) 53,455.

Rohtak, t., Haryana, **India**; N.W. of Delhi; p. (1991) 216,096.

Roissy-en-France; 26 km N.E. of Paris, **France**; site of Charles de Gaulle airport; p. (1999) 2,367.

Roman, t., **Romania**; on R. Moldava; cath.; agr. processing; p. (1983) 67,962.

Romania, Rep. of, S.E. Europe; country bounded by Ukraine, Moldova, Hungary, Serbia, Bulgaria, and Black Sea; Carpathian mtns., Transylvanian Alps, wide Walachian plain, Moldavian plateau; drained by Danube and its tribs.; cold winters and hot summers; since second world war transformation of economy from agr. to industl. basis, although agr. still impt., contributing many exps., especially timber, wine, fruit; major pt. Constanta on Black Sea; oilfields at Ploiesti; cap. Bucharest; ch. tr. partners Russia and E. Europe; Danube used for navigation; Iron Gates power and navigation system being constructed; tourism from W. Europe and N. America encouraged; revolution 1989, popular uprising against Ceaussecu dictactorship; new constitution, 1991; awaiting EU membership; a. 237,428 km²; p. (2004) 22,355,551.

Rome (Roma), cap. of **Italy**, and of Latium and Rome prov.; on R. Tiber, 24 km from sea; in Roman legend founded by Romulus 753 B.C.; once cap. of anc. Roman empire; inc. Vatican c., ctr. of Roman Catholic Church; situated on original "seven hills," and along the R.; leading cultural ctr.; St. Peter's basilica, Colosseum, Pantheon; univ.; admin. ctr.; tourism; created cap. of United Italy 1871; p. (1999) 2,645,500.

Romford. *See* **Havering.**

Romney Marsh, coastal marsh, Shepway, Kent, **Eng.**; formed by blocking of R. Rother by shingle spit of Dungeness which extends from Rye to Hythe; largely drained; pastures for special Romney Marsh breed of sheep; a. 129 km².

Romsey, t., Test Valley, Hants., **Eng.**; on R. Test, 14 km N.W. of Southampton; mkt. ctr.; Norman abbey; p. (1991) 17,032.

Ronaldshay, North, most N. of Orkney Is. **Scot.**; p. (1991) 92.

Ronaldshay, South, most S. of Orkney Is. **Scot.**; p. (1991) 943.

Roncesvalles, mtn. pass in Pyrenees, Navarre, **Spain**; 32 km N.E. of Pamplona; defeat and death of Roland 778.

Ronda, t., Málaga, **Spain**; in Andalusia; anc. Moorish t., divided by deep gorge crossed by bridge; p. (1990) 34,100.

Rondônia, st., **Brazil**; on Bolivian border; forest covered; forest prods.; nomadic Indian tribes; cap. Pôrto Velho; a. 243,071 km²; p. (1996) 1,132,700.

Rønne, t., **Denmark**; cap. of Bornholm I.; fish. pt.; shipyards, ceramics; p. (1990) 15,187.

Roodepoort-Maraisburg, t., Gauteng, **S. Africa**; ctr. Witwatersrand goldfields; p. (1991) 163,000.

Roosendaal, t., S.W. of N. Brabant, Neth., sugar-refining; p. (1994) 62,784.

Roosevelt Dam (1903–11), Arizona, **USA**; on R. Salt in canyon E. of Phoenix on edge of Col. plateau; used for irrigation and hydroelectric power; part of Salt river project.

Roquefort-sur-Soulzon, t., S.E. Aveyron, **France**; caves in limestone cliffs used for ripening cheese; p. (1999) 679.

Roraima, mtn., at junc. of boundaries of **Brazil**, **Guyana**, and **Venezuela**; 2,852 m, hgst. point of Guiana Highlands.

Roraima (Rio Branco), fed. terr., **Brazil**; underdeveloped rain forest; devastation caused by forest fires (1998); cap. Boa Vista; a. 214,320 km²; p. (1996) 247,700.

Rosa Monte, Pennine Alps, Swiss-Italian border; alt. 4,637 m.

Rosario, t., Santa Fé prov., **Argentina**; second t. of rep.; R. pt. on Paraná R.; agr.-processing, iron and steel, lt. inds.; univ., cath.; p. (1991) 1,078,374.

Roscommon, co. t., Roscommon, **R.o.I.**; mkt.; cas., priory; p. (1986) 1,673.

Roscommon, inland co., Connaught, **R.o.I.**; extensive peat bog and Ls.; pastoral agr.; cap. R.; a. 2,458 km²; p. (1986) 54,592.

Roseau, t., cap. **Dominica**, W.I.; p. (1995) 21,000.

Rosetta (Rashid), t., Lower Egypt; nr. Rosetta mouth of Nile; Rosetta stone found nearby gave key to Egyptian hieroglyphics.

Roskilde, t., spt., Sjaelland, **Denmark**; former cap.; cath. contains tombs of kings; admin. ctr. of R. prov.; p. (1990) 49,081.

Ross and Cromarty, historic co., N.W. **Scot.**, now part of Highland.

Rossendale Fells (or Forest), upland, S.E. Lancs./ Gtr. Manchester, **Eng.**; extension of Pennines between Rs. Mersey and Ribble; millstone grit moorland used for reservoirs; alt. mainly above 360 m; forms l. gov. dist. Rossendale in Lancs., inc. ts. of Haslingden, Rawtenstall, Bacup and Whitworth; p. (2001) 65,652.

Ross Dependency, Antarctica; **N.Z.** sector; inlet of Ross Sea; a. 414,400 km²; no permanent p.

Rosslare, spt., Wexford, **R.o.I.**; on extreme S.E. of Ireland; connections to Fishguard; p. (1986) 704.

Ross-on-Wye, t., South Herefordshire, Hereford, **Eng.**; mkt., tourism; p. (1991) 9,606.

Ross Sea, area extending to 85° S. in **Antarctic**.

Rostock, c. Mecklenburg - West Pomerania, **Germany**; pt. nr. Baltic cst., outport of Warnemünde; shipbldg., fish-processing, chemicals; univ.; mediaeval t.; p. (2002) 198,964.

Rostov, c., **Russia**; pt. on R. Don, nr. Azov Sea (Black Sea); one of Russia's finest and oldest cs.; ctr. of agr. dist.; grain mkt.; agr.-processing; univ.; p. (1989) 1,019,000.

Rosyth, t., Fife, **Scot.**; naval dockyard (closed 1995); p. (2002) 12,428.

Rothamsted, v., Herts., **Eng.**; in Chiltern Hills, S. of Harpenden; famous agr. research sta.

Rother, l. gov. dist., East Sussex, **Eng.**; rural a. inc. Rye, Bexhill and Battle; p. (2001) 85,428.

Rother, R., Derbys. and South Yorks., **Eng.**; flows to R. Don at Rotherham; 34 km long.

Rother, R., East Sussex and Kent, **Eng.**; rises in the Weald, flows S.E. into English Channel at Rye; 50 km long.

Rotherham, t., met. dist., South Yorks., **Eng.**; on R. Don, 6 km N.E. of Sheffield; coal mining, iron, steel, wire, springs, glass; new Magna Science Centre; p. (2001) 248,175 (dist.), (2001) 117,262 (t.).

Rothes, burgh, Moray, **Scot.**; on R. Spey 19 km S.E. of Elgin; p. (2002) 1,156.

Rothesay, royal burgh, Argyll and Bute., **Scot.**; on E. cst. of I. of Bute in F. of Clyde; tourism; p. (2002) 5,017.

Rothwell, West Yorks., **Eng.**; on R. Aire, suburb of Leeds; coal-mng. ctr., engin.; p. (1991) 7,070.

Rotorua, c., leading spa of **N.Z.**; on volcanic plateau, Auckland, N.I.; hot springs; p. (1991) 65,096.

Rotterdam, c., spt. **Neth.**; Europe's lgst. spt., on Nieuwe Maas, part of Rhine-Maas Scheldt delta; linked to outport Europoort (q.v) by New Waterway; serves hinterland of Rhine valley and central Europe; freeport; processing of imports, especially oil refining and petrochemical inds.; badly damaged in second world war; p. (1994) 598,521 (c.), 1,074,387 (met. a.).

Roubaix, t., Nord dep., **France**; nr. Lille; on Roubaix canal close to Belgian frontier; major textile ctr., especially for woollens; p. (1999) 95,629.

Rouen, c., Seine-Maritime dep., **France**; gr. R. pt., 125 km up R. Seine; oil refining, textiles, chemicals; cath.; Joan of Arc burned here; birthplace of Corneille and Flaubert; badly damaged in second world war; p. (1999) 106,044.

Rousay, I., Orkney Is., **Scot.**; p. (1991) 291.

Roussillon, former prov., S. **France**; now part. of Pyrénées-Orientales; irrigated by many sm. streams; olives, wine, fruit; historical cap. Perpignan.

Rovaniemi, t., **Finland**; on Kemi R.; timber and saw mills; p. (1993) 34,438.

Rovigo, prov., Venetia, **Italy**; part of N. Italian plain extending to Adriatic; impt. agr. dist.; cap. R.; a. 218 km²; p. (1981) 253,508.

Rovigo, t., cap. of R. prov., **Italy**; on R. Adige. cath., cas. ruins, palace; p. (1981) 52,218.

Rovno, c., cap. of R., oblast, **Ukraine**; rly. junct.; industl. ctr.; ruins of mediaeval palace; p. (1990) 232,900.

Roxburghshire, historic co., S. **Scot.**; now part of Borders.

Royal Oak, t., Mich., **USA**; residtl.; Detroit zoological park here; p. (1996) 64,942.

Royston, mkt. t., North Herts., **Eng.**; at N. foot of E. Anglian Heights, 11 km N.E. of Baldock; p. (1991) 14,087.

Royton, t., Gtr. Manchester, **Eng.**; 13 km N.E of Manchester; textiles; p. (2001) 22,238.

Ruanda-Urundi. See **Rwanda** and **Burundi**.

Ruapehu, highest mtn., N.I., **N.Z.**; volcanic peak at S. extremity of central volcanic dist.; crater L. at summit; alt. 2,798 m; gives name to dist.; p. (1991) 18,104.

Rubicon, R., central **Italy**; flows to Adriatic; crossed by Julius Caesar and his armies 49 B.C.; has been identified with the Fiumicino or the Uso.

Ruda Slaska, t., Katowice, **Poland**; coal-mng. ctr.; iron and steel wks.; p. (1995) 166,337.

Rudnyy, t., **Kazakhstan**; t. 48 km S.W. of Kustanay; iron-ore mng. and dressing plant supplying Magnitogorsk; p. (1990) 126,200.

Rudolf, L., N.W. **Kenya**; in Great Rift Valley; a. 9,065 km²; ctr. of semi-arid region; renamed **Turkana**.

Rudolph I, N. of Franz Josef Land Arctic Oc.; **Russia** naval base; met. sta.

Rudolstadt, t., **Germany**; on R. Saale, in former st. of Thuringia; seat of counts of Schwarzburg-Rudolstadt (1584-1918); tourism; porcelain, p. (1999) 28,500.

Rueil-Malmaison, sub. of Paris, **France**; château; tomb of the empress Josephine; p. (1999) 73,469.

Rugby, mkt. t., l. gov. dist., Warwicks, **Eng.**; on R. Avon, 18 km E. of Coventry; famous public school; elec. and gen. engin., motor and aircraft patterns; p. (2001) 87,453 (dist.), (2001) 61,988 (t.).

Rugeley, mkt. t., Staffs, **Eng.**; on R. Trent, 14 km S.E. of Stafford; coal, iron, tanning; expanded t.; p. (2001) 22,724.

Rügen, I., **Germany**; in Baltic Sea, off Stralsund; ch. t. Bergen; pt. Sassnitz, terminus of train ferry; steamer services to Trelleborg, Sweden.

Ruhr, industl. dist., **Germany**; lies to E. of R. Rhine, on either side of R. Ruhr; rich coalfield; impt. iron and steel, heavy engin. inds. based on local coal and iron ore from Luxembourg, Spain, Sweden, water communications to N. Sea along R. Rhine and Dortmund-Ems Canal; ch. ts. Essen, Duisburg, Düsseldorf, Dortmund, Bochum.

Ruhr, R., **Germany**, trib. of Rhine; flows S. of Itum conurb.; 232 km long.

Rukwa, L., E. **Africa**; between L. Tanganyika and L. Malawi in the rift valley; 48 km by 19 km, a, increasing.

Rum, I., Inner Hebrides, Highland, **Scot.**; nature reserve, highland ecology.

Rumaila, **Iraq**; oilfield; pipeline links to the Zubair-Fao system.

Rum Jungle, N.T., **Australia**; 64 km S.E. of Darwin; site of Australia's first major uranium project; ceased operation in 1970.

Runcorn, t., Halton, Cheshire, **Eng.**; on S. side of Mersey estuary; new t. (1964); chemicals; pipeline carrying petrochemical feedstock from Teeside; p. (2001) 60,072.

Rungis, Paris, **France**; site of major new mkt. to replace Les Halles; nr. Orly airpt., Val de Marne dep.; p. (1999) 5,424.

Runnymede, site of signing of Magna Carta; l. gov. dist., Surrey, **Eng.**; comprises Egham and Chertsey; p. (2001) 78,033.

Ruse, t., **Bulgaria**; on R. Danube, opposite Giurgiu in Romania; univ.; Roman t.; agr. processing; p. (1990) 192,365.

Rushcliffe, l. gov. dist., Notts., **Eng.**; a. S.E. of Nottingham inc. West Bridgeford; p. (2001) 105,599.

Rushden, t., East Northants., **Eng.**; 5 km E. of Wellingborough; shoes; p. (2001) 25,331.

Rushmoor, l. gov. dist., Hants., **Eng.**; small a. of Farnborough and Aldershot; p. (2001) 90,987.

Rüsselsheim, t., **Germany**; impt. car factory; p. (2002) 59,550.

Russia, CIS; former constituent rep., USSR; lgst. rep. by a. and p.; economic development; inds. centred on St Petersburg and Moscow with new inds. being developed in Urals and Kuznetz basin; extends from Baltic to Pac. Oc. (8,000 km), from Arctic to Caspian Sea (4,000 km); part of N. European plain in W. and Siberian plain in E., separated by Ural mtns.; major Rs. Volga, Don, Ob, Yenisey, Lena, Amur; gr. variety in climate and p. density; major agr. region for wheat, sugarbeet, livestock; vast mineral deposits have aided economic growth; oil around Volga valley; metallic ores from Ural and Black Sea; hydroelectric power from Volga, Yenesey and Ob Rs.; cap. Moscow; a. 16,838,885 km²; p. (2004) 143,782,338.

Rutbah, t., **Iraq;** on oil pipeline from Iraq to Haifa; impt. ctr. on trans-desert routes.

Rutherglen, royal burgh, Glasgow, **Scot.;** on R. Clyde, S.E. of Glasgow; chemicals, tubes, paper.

Ruthin, t., Denbighshire, **Wales;** Vale of Clwyd, 13 km S.E. of Denbigh; p. (1991) 5,029.

Rutland, Eng., unit. auth. created in 1997, reinstating historic co. based on Oakham which became part of Leics. in 1974; p. (2001) 34,563.

Rutland Water, reservoir, Rutland, **Eng.** Largest man-made lake in western Europe.

Ruwenzori mtn. range, on **Uganda-Congo** border; overlooking W. arm of Gt. Rift Valley, midway between L. Mobutu Seso and L. Edward; hgst. peaks, Mt. Margherita (5,123 m), Mt. Alexandra (5,109 m); lower slopes covered in equatorial rain forest, coffee plantations on middle slopes above 1,500 m.

Rwanda, indep. rep., Central Africa; former kingdom of Ruanda, part of UN trust terr. of Ruanda-Urundi under Belgian admin. (until 1962); sm., landlocked st., S. of equator, consisting of upland plateau at 1,200 m; mainly subsistence agr. under gt. strain with rapid p. growth; coffee (ch. exp.), cotton, pyrethrum; cattle; tin, tungsten and natural gas discoveries; little ind.; bitter tribal warfare in 1990s; cap. Kigali; a. 26,338 km²; p. (2004) 7,954,013.

Ryazan, c., cap. of R. oblast, **Russia;** on Oka R.; food inds., agr. machin., footwear, chemicals; mediaeval architecture; p. (1989) 515,000.

Rybinsk. c., cap. of R. oblast, **Russia;** on Upper Volga; tr. and shipping ctr. since 16th cent.; site of hydroelectric power sta.; shipbldg., engin.; renamed Andropov 1984 to honour dead General Secretary; p. (1989) 251,000.

Rybinsk Sea (Rybinsk Reservoir), Russia; artificial L.; created behind dams on R. Volga and R. Sheksna at Rybinsk; part of scheme to regulate flow of R. Volga and to incorporate it in a vast inland waterway system; opened 1945; a. 3,885 km.

Rybnik, t., Katowice prov., S.W. **Poland;** ctr. of coal-mng. dist.; p. (1995) 144,311.

Rydal Water, L., nr. Ambleside, Cumbria, **Eng.;** adjacent v. contains Rydal Mount, home of Wordsworth.

Ryde, t., I. of Wight, **Eng.;** on N.E. cst.; yachting ctr. and seaside resort; boat and yacht bldg.; steamer connection across Spithead to Portsmouth; p. (2001) 22,806.

Rye, t., Rother, East Sussex, **Eng.;** at mouth of R. Rother to W. of Dungeness; Cinque pts.; Ypres cas.; tourist ctr.; p. (1991) 3,708.

Ryedale, l. gov. dist., North Yorks., **Eng.;** lge. a. inc. Malton, Pickering, Norton, Kirby Moorside and Helmsley; p. (2001) 50,872.

Ryton, t., Tyne and Wear, **Eng.;** on R. Tyne, W. of Newcastle; p. (1991) 15,952.

Ryukyu Is., archipelago, between Kyushu I., **Japan,** and Taiwan; ch. t. Naha on Okinawa I.; following second world war Is. S. of Lat. 30° N. occupied by USA; Amami and Tokara grs. returned to Japan 1953; American military installations on Okinawa withdrawn 1972; lge. Is. mtnous., volcanic; sweet potatoes, sugar-cane, pineapples; 3 lge. oil refineries; a. 2,196 km²; p. (1990) 1,222,398.

Rzeszów, c. and prov., S.E. **Poland;** at foot of Carpathian highlands; route ctr.; growing industl. t.; p. (1995) 160,342, (c.), 744,969 (prov.).

S

Saale, R., **Germany;** rises in Fichtelgebirge flows N. through Thuringia to Elbe; attractive, well wooded valley; irrigation; hydroelec. power; 360 km long.

Saalfeld, t., Gera, **Germany;** on R. Saale; famous cas., iron-mng.; chocolate; p. (2002) 182,858 (c.), 959,084 (met.a.).

Saarbrücken, c., cap. of Saarland, **Germany;** on R. Saar, nr. Fr. border; cas.; rich coalfield; iron and steel wks., textiles, leather, paper, oil refining at Klarenthal nearby; p. (2002) 182,858 (c.), 959,084 (met.a.).

Saarland, Land, **Germany;** heavy inds. based on lge. coalfields; drained by R. Saar; cap. Saarbrücken; admin. by League of Nations 1919–35, returned to Germany after plebiscite; economic attachment to France after second world war; reunited politically with W. Germany 1957; a. 2,567 km²; p. (2005) 1,065,000.

Saarlouis (Saarlautern), Saarland, **Germany;** on R. Saar; coal mng.; wood and metal inds.; founded by Louis XIV; birthplace of Marshal Ney; p. (1999) 38,600.

Sabadell, t., **Spain;** N.W. of Barcelona; textiles, fertilisers, paper; p. (1998) 184,800.

Sabah, E. Malaysia; attempted secession 1975; formerly N. Borneo; underdeveloped; tropical forest; forest prods., inc. rubber, the major exp.; main pt. Sandakan; cap. Kota Kinabalu; a. 76,112 km²; p. (1991) 1,736,902

Sabahiyah, t., **Kuwait;** new t. being built between Ahmadi and Fahahil.

Sabara, t., Minas Gerais, **Brazil;** historic c.; museum of gold; p. (1996) 100,600.

Sabine, R., Texas and La., **USA;** flows through S. Lake (an expansion of the R. 29 km long) to G. of Mexico; 936 km long.

Sable I., off S.E. cst. Nova Scotia, **Canada;** sandy I., scene of many shipwrecks.

Sacramento, c., st. cap. Cal., **USA;** on R. Sacramento; shipping and industl. ctr.; rly. wk.-shps., smelting, meat and fruit packing, flour, lumber, metal prods.; rocket and missiles ind.; p. (2000) 407,018 (c.), 1,481,102 (met. a.).

Sacramento, R., Cal., **USA;** forms N. section of Central Valley projected for irrigation, hydro-electric power and flood control; 624 km long.

Saddleback (Blencathara), mtn., Cumbria, **Eng.;** nr. Keswick; alt. 868 m.

Saddleworth, t., Gtr. Manchester, **Eng.;** in Pennines, 8 km N.E. of Oldham; woollens, paper mkg., engin.; p. (1981) 21,851.

Saffron Walden, mkt., t., Uttlesford, Essex, **Eng.;** on E. Anglian heights; cas., abbey ruins; saffron crocus once cultivated; p. (1991) 13,201.

Safi, spt., **Morocco;** on Atl. Oc.; linked by rail to phosphate deposits at Youssoufia; pottery, fish-processing; resort; p. (1994) 822,564.

Saga, c., cap. of S. pref., Kyushu, **Japan;** coal-mng. ctr., textiles, ceramics; p. (1990) 169,964.

Saginaw, c., Mich., **USA;** on R. Saginaw; former fur and lumbering region; coal; beans, sugarbeet; various mnfs.; p. (1990) 399,000 (met. a. with Bay City–Midland).

Saguenay, R., Quebec, **Canada;** trib. of St. Lawrence R.; outlet of L. St. John; used for hydroelec. power; tourism; length c. 176 km.

Sagunto, t., **Spain;** nr. Valencia; integrated steelwks. projected; anc. t., sieged by Hannibal; p. (1990) 58,100 (met. a.).

Sahara, the gr. N. African desert between the Sudan and the Mediterranean, extending from the Atl. to the Nile, inc. Tripoli and Fezzan; a. 16,835,000 km²; numerous oases with ts. and tr. ctrs.; oil pipelines to Algerian and Tunisian csts.; nomadic Arab and Berber tribes. The Sahara abounded with lakes and grassland until c. 6,000 years ago.

Saharan Arab Democratic Rep. See Western Sahara.

Saharan Atlas, S. range of Atlas mtns. in **Algeria;** ch. peaks., Jebel Aurès, 2,331 m. J. Aissa, 2,242 m, J. Ksel, 2,011 m.

Saharanpur, c., Uttar Pradesh, N.W. **India;** wood-carving, furniture, agr.-processing inds.; p. (1991) 375,000.

Sahel, region of **W. Africa,** inc. Chad, Mali, Mauritania, Niger, Senegal and Bourkina Faso; suffered severe famine and drought 1972–4 and 1984–5 caused by desertification.

Saïda (Sidon), t., **Lebanon;** on Mediterranean, S. of Beirut; terminus of oil pipeline from Saudi Arabia; refinery; p. (1988) 38,000.

Saigon. See Ho Chi-minh City.

Saimaa, L. system, **Finland;** gr. of water which forms basin of R. Vuoksi; canal connects with G. of Finland and runs partly through Russian terr.; a. 1,699 km².

St. Abb's Head, rocky promontory, lighthouse, Borders, **Scot.**

St. Albans, c., l. gov. dist., Herts., **Eng.**; on N. margin of Vale of St. Albans, 32 km N.W. of London; faces remains of Roman Verulamium across R. Ver; lt. inds., electronics, instrument mkg.; cath.; residtl.; p. (2001) 129,005 (dist.), (2001) 82,429 (c.).

St. Amand, t., Cher dep., **France**; on R. Cher; Roman remains; new recreational park; p. (1982) 12,801.

St. Andrews, royal burgh, Fife, **Scot.**; seaside resort; univ.; famous golf course; p. (2002) 14,209.

St. Anthony, waterfalls, on R. Mississippi; **USA**; predominant factor in site of Minneapolis.

St. Asaph, t., Denbighshire, N. **Wales**; on R. Clwyd; p. (1991) 3,399.

St. Austell, mkt. t., Restormel, Cornwall, **Eng.**; on S. flank of Hensbarrow; ctr. of Cornwall's china clay ind.; p. (1991) 21,622.

St. Barthélemy, Fr. I., **W.I.**; dependency of Guadeloupe.

St. Bees Head, promontory, 4 km N.W. of St. Bees, Cumbria, **Eng.**; freestone quarries, anhydrite.

St. Bernard Pass, Great, on Italian–Swiss bdy., W. Alps; carries main road from W. Switzerland to Plain of Lombardy; 2,477 m a.s.l.; road tunnel (5·6 km) constr. 1958–62 links Cantine de Proz (Valais can., Switzerland) and St. Rhémy (Italy); under tunnel will run projected 416 km pipeline from Genoa to Aigle.

St. Bernard Pass, Little, on French–Italian bdy. W. Alps; links Isère valley with Val d'Aosta; alt. 2,190 m.

St. Brides Bay, Pembrokeshire, **Wales.**

St. Brieuc, t., cap. of Côtes-du-Nord dep., N.W. **France**; sm. fish. pt.; iron and steel wks.; cath.; p. (1990) 47,340 (t.), 83,661 (met.a.).

St. Catharines, c., Ont., **Canada**; on Welland Ship Canal; mkt. for Niagara fruit-growing region; agr. implements, textile, paper and flour mills, vehicle components; resort; p. (1991) 129,300 (c.), (1996) 372,406 (met. a. with Niagara).

St. Chamond, t., Loire, **France**; nr. St. Etienne; ribbons, rayon; rly. wks.; coal mng.; p. (1990) 39,262 (t.), 81,795 (met. a.).

St. Clair, R., **N. America**, flows from L. Huron through L. of St. Clair into L. Erie; forms bdy. between Mich. (USA) and Ont. (Canada); impt. link in Gr. Ls. waterway; length 136 km, depth dredged to 8 m.

St. Cloud, W. sub. of Paris, **France**; fine park; porcelain; p. (1999) 28,156.

St. Cloud, t., Minn., **USA**, on R. Mississippi; granite quarries; st. college; p. (1990) 60,801.

St.-Cyr-l'Ecole, t., Yvelines, **France**; once famous for military school founded by Napoleon; bldgs. destroyed second world war; p. (1999) 14,566.

St. Davids, c., Pembrokeshire, **Wales**; 24 km S.W. of Fishguard; on site of anc. Minevia; cath., ruins of Bishop Gower's palace (1342); p. (1991) 1,627.

St. David's Head, promontory, Pembrokeshire, **Wales.**

St. Denis, t., N. sub., Paris, **France**; on R. Seine; abbey, burial place of Fr. kings; chemicals., machin.; p. (1999) 85,823.

St. Denis, spt., cap. of Ile de la Réunion (Fr.), Indian Oc.; p. (1990) 122,875.

St. Edmundsbury, l. gov. dist., Suffolk, **Eng.**; based on Bury St. Edmunds and inc. Haverhill; p. (2001) 98,193.

St. Elias, mtns., Alaska, **USA**; and Yukon, **Canada**; inc. Mt. McKinley (5,780 m); source of world's lgst. icefield outside polar regions.

Saintes, t., Charente-Maritime dep., **France**; cath.; Roman antiquities; suffered in Huguenot wars; agr. implements; earthenware; p. (1999) 25,596.

St. Etienne, t., cap. of Loire dep., **France**; nr. Lyons; in sm. coal basin on edge of Central Massif; famous for firearms; modern inds. inc. engin., dyes; p. (1999) 179,755.

St. Gall (St. Gallen), t., cap. of can. St. G., **Switzerland**; founded around Benedictine monastery (7th–8th cent.); embroidered cottons; p. (1990) 74,136.

St. Gall (St. Gallen), can., **Switzerland**; borders L. Constance, rising to S.; mainly industl.; ch. ind. textiles; cap. St. G.; a. 2,012 km²; p. (1990) 420,300.

St. George's Channel, part of Irish Sea, separating Wales from Ireland.

St. George's, t., cap. of **Grenada,** W.I.; ch. spt.; built around submerged volcanic crater forming

St. G. Bay; p. (1997) 35,750.

St. Germain-en-Laye, t., Yvelines, **France**; on R. Seine; outer sub. of Paris; residtl.; popular resort; birthplace of Debussy; p. (1999) 38,423.

Saint Gotthard, mtn. gr., Alps, S. central **Switzerland**; crossed by St. G. pass (2,115 m); rly. passes through St. G. tunnel (14·8 km, max. alt. 1,155 m); road tunnel (16·3 km) opened 1980; motorways link pass with Zürich, Basle, and Lugano.

St. Govan's Head, promontory, Pembrokeshire, **Wales.**

St. Helena, I., Brit., col., Atl. Oc.; 1,920 km from W. cst. Africa; spt. and only t. Jamestown; Napoleon imprisoned 1815–21, and Boer captives 1900; famous for its wirebird, species of plover peculiar to I.; first TV transmissions, 1995; a. 122 km²; p. (2004) 7,415.

St. Helens, t., met. dist., Merseyside, **Eng.**; 19 km E. of Liverpool; connected by canal with R. Mersey; coal, iron, alkali; copper smelting, glass, fibreglass, plastics; p. (2001) 176,843 (dist.), (2001) 102,629 (t.).

St. Helier, spt., **Jersey,** Channel Is.; resort; cas.; tr. in early vegetables.

Saint-Hyacinthe, t., spt., Quebec, **Canada**; on Yamaska R.; cath.; famous for organs; lt. inds.; p. (1996) 50,027.

St. Ives, t., Penwith, Cornwall, **Eng.**; at entrance to St. Ives Bay; fishing, holiday resort; Tate St Ives (art gallery); p. (1991) 10,092.

St. Ives, t., Camb., **Eng.**; on R. Ouse, 6 km E. of Huntingdon; borders the Fens; R. Ouse crossed by 16th cent. bridge containing a chapel; p. (1991) 16,510.

Saint John, c., spt., N.B., **Canada**; lgst. c. of N.B.; ice-free pt.; lge. dry docks; rly. terminus; impt. inds. inc. sugar- and oil-refining, paper, textiles; p. (1991) 90,457 (c.), (1996) 125,705 (met. a.).

St. John, R., Maine, N.B., **Canada, USA**; flows to B. of Fundy forming section of international boundary; 720 km long.

St. John's, t., cap. of **Antigua,** W.I.; pt., airpt.; cath.; ch. comm. ctr. of I.; p. (1999) 25,000.

St. John's, c. spt., cap. of Newfoundland and Labrador, **Canada**; on E. cst.; first English settlement in America early 16th cent.; gr. tr. in fish with allied inds.; univ., 2 caths.; p. (1986) 96,216 (c.), (1996) 174,051 (met. a.).

St. John's Wood, residtl. dist., Westminster London, **Eng.**; contains Lord's Cricket Ground, home of English cricket.

St. Just, t., Penwith, Cornwall, **Eng.**; nr. Lands End, 10 km W. of Penzance; former tin-mng. ctr.; p. (1991) 2,092.

St. Kilda, rocky I., most W. of the Hebrides, **Scot.**; 5 km long; bird sanctuary, famous for its wren.

St. Kitts-Nevis, Leeward gr. of Is., **W.I.**; aut. st. in association with Gt. Britain; indep. (1983); sugar, sea island cotton, molasses; a. 262 km²; cap. Basséterre; p. (2004) 38,836.

Saint-Laurent, t., Quebec, **Canada**; industl. t. on Montreal I., W. of Montreal; p. (1991) 72,402.

St. Lawrence, G. of, Canada; arm of Atl. Oc., partly enclosed by Newfoundland and Nova Scotia; impt. fisheries.

St. Lawrence I., Alaska, **USA**; in Bering Sea; 160 km long.

St. Lawrence, R., Canada; major outlet from Gr. Lakes; forms bdy. between USA and Canada; ch. tribs. Ottawa, Richelieu, St. Maurice, Saguenay Rs.; with St. L. Seaway forms a major waterway facing Europe; grain, timber, oil, iron-ore traffic; used for hydro-electric power; total length from source (St. Louis) 3,360 km.

St. Lawrence Seaway, N. America; joint Canada–USA project links head of the Gr. Lakes with Atl. Oc., providing channel for lge. ocean-going vessels to reach American continent; provides major source of hydroelectric power to industl. a.; opened 1959.

St. Lô, t. cap. of Manche dep., N.W. **France**; built on rocky hill overlooking R. Vire; cath.; p. (1999) 20,090.

Saint-Louis, t., Senegal, W. Africa; at mouth of R. Senegal; cath.; former cap.; comm. ctr.; impt. fish. pt.; p. (1992) 125,717.

St. Louis, c., Mo., **USA**; on R. Mississippi 16 km below confluence of Rs. Mississippi and Missouri; two univs.; impt. rly. and river junc.; mkt. for furs, livestock, grain, farm prod.; banking and fin. ctr.; varied mnfs.; machin., cars, aircraft, leather gds., beer, chemicals; p. (2000) 348,189 (c.), 2,444,099 (met. a.).

St. Lucia I., indep. st. (1979) within Commonwealth; Windward Is., W.I.; volcanic, forested, fertile valleys; exp. bananas and other tropical agr. prod.; airpt.; cap. Castries; a. 616 km²; hurricane disaster 1980; p. (2004) 164,213.

St. Malo, spt., Ile-et-Vilaine dep., N.W. France; on Normandy cst.; once fortfd.; shipping, fishing, and tourist inds.; p. (1999) 50,661.

St. Martin, I., Leeward Is., W.I.; N. part Fr. dependency of Guadeloupe, S. part belongs to Neth. Antilles; divided since 1648; ch. exp. salt; total p. (1981) 13,156.

St. Marylebone. See Westminster, City of.

St. Maur-des-Fossés, residtl. garden sub. of Paris, Val-de-Marne dep., France; p. (1999) 72,955.

St. Maurice, v., Valais, Switzerland; nr. Martigny; 6th-cent. abbey; once a leading Burgundian t.; p. c. 10,000.

St. Mawes, v., Cornwall, Eng.; on E. cst. of estuary of R. Fal; cas.; holiday resort, fishing.

St. Michael's Mt., castled rock, Cornwall, Eng.; the anc. Ictis; alt. 70 m.

St. Monans, burgh, Fife, Scot.; resort; p. (2002) 1,435.

St. Moritz, resort and winter sports ctr., Switzerland; in the Upper Engadine; alt. 1,857 m.

St. Nazaire, t., Loire-Atlantique dep., W. France; spt. at mouth of R. Loire, outport for Nantes; growing pt. and industl. ctr.; shipyds., iron and steel, fertilisers, aircraft, oil refining; p. (1999) 65,874 (t.), 131,511 (met.a.).

St. Neots, mkt. t., Cambs. Eng.; on R. Ouse, 16 km N.E. of Bedford; brewing, milling, paper-mkg.; expanded t.; p. (2001) 27,372.

St. Niklaas, mftg. t., E. Flanders, Belgium; nr. Antwerp; textile ctr., carpets; p. (1993) 68,472.

St. Omer, t., Pas-de-Calais dep., N. France; ctr. of mkt.-gardening a.; textiles, food inds.; cath., abbey ruins; p. (1982) 53,748 (met. a.).

St. Pancras. See Camden.

St. Patrick, t. Missouri, USA, the only town in America named after St. Patrick.

St. Paul, c., cap. of Minn., USA; faces Minneapolis across Mississippi; cath.; univ.; ctr. of agr. dist.; agr. mkt. and processing; car assembly, oil refining, electronics; p. (2000) 287,151 (c), 2,464,000 (met. a. with Minneapolis.)

St. Paul, I., Indian Oc.; bare volcanic islet rising to 493 m; part of Fr. Southern and Antarctic Terr.; uninhabited.

St. Peter Port, spt., cap. of Guernsey, exp. fruit, flowers, vegetables; resort.

St. Petersburg, c., formerly Leningrad, Russia; at mouth of Neva R.; cultural ctr. with many fine bldgs., inc. winter palace, Hermitage museum, cath., admiralty bldg.; former cap. of Russia; major pt. and industl. ctr.; exp. timber, furs, and raw materials; ice-bound December–March; founded (1703) by Peter the Great as St. Petersburg; p. (2000) 5,133,000 (met. a.).

St. Petersburg, c., Fla., USA; resort on Tampa Bay; birthplace of commercial aviation; p. (2000) 248,332.

St. Pierre, t., Martinique I., Fr. W.I.; utterly destroyed and all inhabitants save one by eruption of Mt. Pelée 1902; tourism.

St. Pierre, t., Réunion, French Territory, Indian Ocean; sm. artificial harbour.

St. Pierre and Miquelon, Fr. terr. consisting of 8 sm. Is. off S. cst. of Newfoundland; a. of St. Pierre gr. 26 km²; a. of Miquelon gr., 215 km²; ch. t. St. Pierre, fisheries; p. of St. P. and M. (2004) 6,995.

St. Pölten, cap. of Lower Austria; nr. Vienna; founded round an abbey; textiles, machin.; p. (1991) 49,805.

St. Quentin, t., Aisne dep., France; on R. Somme; impt. textile ctr.; p. (1999) 59,066.

St. Raphaël, t., Var dep., S.E. France; resort on Fr. Riviera, S.W. of Cannes; marina; p. (1982) 24,310.

St. Rémy, t., Bouches-du-Rhône dep., France; Roman antiquities; p. (1999) 9,806.

St. Thomas, I., Atl. Oc.; main economic ctr. of USA Virgin Is.; tourism; p. (1990) 48,166.

St. Thomas I. See São Tomé.

St. Trond, t., Limburg, Belgium; impt. fruit mkt.; p. (1991) 37,000.

St. Tropez, t., Var dep., S.E. France; on Fr. Riviera; popular, fashionable tourist resort; marina; p. (1999) 5,440.

St. Vincent, t., S.W. Portugal; Spanish fleet defeated by British 1797.

St. Vincent, Gulf of, lge. inlet, S. Australia; penetrates 160 km inland, max. width 65 km; Pt.

Adelaide is on E. side.

St. Vincent, I., part of St. Vincent and the Grenadines, ind. st. (1979) within Commonwealth; one of Windward gr., W.I.; volcanic; exp. bananas, arrowroot from alluvial soils in S.W. which has majority of p.; subsistence agr. on hill slopes; cap. Kingstown; a. 389 km² (inc. attached Grenadine Is.); p. (2004) 117,193.

Saitama, c., Honshu, Japan; near Tokyo; new c. formed in 2001 by uniting cities of Urawa, Omiya and Yonu; p. (2000) 1,004,000.

Sakai, mft. of Osaka, Honshu, Japan; industl. ctr., engin., chemicals, textiles, electricity generation; p. (1990) 807,859.

Sakhalin, I., off cst. of Siberia; with Kuriles forms Sakhalin oblast of Russia; herring fisheries, coal, naphtha, alluvial gold, oil, timber, natural gas; oil pipelines connected to Komsomolsk and Khabarovsk refineries; a. c. 63,610 km²; p. (1995) 673,100.

Sakashima Is. See Ryuku.

Sakura-jima, peninsula, S. Kyushu, Japan; former I. joined to mainland by lava flows; famed for fruit and vegetables.

Sala, t., Västmanland, Sweden; silver mine worked for over 400 years, now to limited extent; lime, bricks.

Salado, R., N.W. Argentina; impt. Andean trib. of Paraná R.; 800 km long.

Salamanca, t., Guanajuato st., Mexico; oil refining; ammonia plant; natural gas pipeline to Guadalajara; p. (1990) 206,275.

Salamanca, t., cap. of S. prov., Spain; on R. Tormes; old univ., 2 caths., many convents; p. (1998) 158,400 (c.), 349,500 (prov.).

Salamis, I., Greece; opposite harbour of Athens; spt. and ch. t. S.; famous naval battle 480 B.C.; p. (1981) 20,807.

Salavat, t., Russia; in Bashkiria, 144 km S. of Ufa; ctr. of oilfield; glass factory; became t. in 1954; p. (1989) 150,000.

Sala-y-Gomez, barren, uninhabited volcanic I., Pac. Oc.; belonging to Chile, 328 km E.N.E. of Easter I.

Salazar, Mexico; nr. Mexico City; alt. 2,897 m; nuclear reactor for radioisotopes for medical, industl. and agr. purposes.

Salcombe, t., South Hams, S. Devon, Eng.; mkt.; fishing; resort; p. (1991) 1,921.

Sale, t., Trafford, Gtr. Manchester, Eng.; residtl. sub. of Manchester; p. (2001) 55,234.

Sale or Salch, spt., Fez, Morocco; former pirate headquarters; fishing, fish-processing, carpets; p. (1994) 631,863.

Salem, t., Tamil Nadu, India; industl. ctr., rly. junc. in picturesque valley; local iron ore, manganese mng.; mineral processing, textiles; p. (1991) 367,000.

Salem, t., Mass., USA; 24 km from Boston; one of oldest New England ts.; many fine bldgs.; textiles, leather prods., machin., electronics; p. (1990) 264,000 (met. a. with Gloucester).

Salem, t., st. cap. Ore., USA; on Willamette R.; univ.; fruit packing, flour milling and canning; p. (1990) 107,786 (t.), 278,000 (met. a.).

Salemi, t., Sicily, Italy; the anc. Halicyæ; Norman cas., terracotta vases.

Salerno, c., cap. of Salerno prov., in Campania, S. Italy; on G. of S.; fishing pt. and comm. ctr.; machin., textiles, food processing; univ.; famous for Allied landing 1943; p. (1992) 147,564.

Salford, t., met. dist., Gtr. Manchester, Eng.; on R. Irwell, adjoining Manchester; inc. terminal docks of Manchester Ship Canal; univ.; varied inds.; p. and industl. decentralization; new Lowry Centre opened, Apr. 2000; p. (2001) 216,103 (dist.), (2001) 72,750 (c.).

Salinas, t., Cal., USA; comm., tr. and processing ctr. for fertile Salinas valley; birthplace of John Steinbeck; p. (1990) 108,777 (t.), 356,000 (met. a. with Seaside-Monterey).

Salinas, R., Cal., USA; rises in US Coast Range, flows N.W. into Bay of Monterey, Pac. Oc.; fertile valley floor irrigated to produce hard and stone fruits, mkt. garden produce (especially lettuce), alfalfa; 166 km long.

Salisbury, t., South Australia; part of Adelaide; research ctr. for long-range weapons.

Salisbury (New Sarum), cath. c., historic county town and l. gov. dist., Wilts., Eng.; on S. edge of Salisbury Plain at confluence of Rs. Avon, Ebble, Nadder, Wylye and Bourne; Old Sarum to N. was the Roman Sorbiodunum and present site represents a move (1220) to a more sheltered and better watered a. in valley; cath. pure Early English with tallest spire in Eng. (123 m); ctr. mediaeval woollen ind.; engin. ind.; p. (2001) 114,613 (dist.), (1991) 39,268 (c.).

Salisbury. Former name of **Harare** (*q.v.*).

Salisbury Plain, Wilts., **Eng.**; chalk upland, N. of Salisbury; Stonehenge; army training a.; a. 777 km².

Salonika. *See* Thessaloniki.

Salmon, R., Idaho, **USA**; canyon *c.* 1·6 km deep and 16 km wide in places; rapids navigable downstream only, thus its name of River of No Return; l. *c.* 680 km.

Salop. *See* Shropshire.

Salsette, I., **India**; connected by bridge and causeway with Mumbai; popular seaside resort at Juhu; a. 624 km².

Salt, R., Arizona, **USA**; rises in Colorado plateau, flows into Gila R. below Phoenix; rich, irrigated fruit growing valley in lower course; many multipurpose schemes in Salt River Valley project; length 384 km. *See also* **Roosevelt Dam.**

Salta, c., cap. of Salta prov., **Argentina**; on R. Salta; picturesque c. with colonial atmosphere, cath.; comm. ctr. for rich agr. a.; p. (1991) 370,904 (c.), 866,153 (prov.).

Saltash, mkt. t., Caradon, Cornwall, **Eng.**; on W. side of Tamar estuary; Brunel's rly. bridge (1859) and toll road bridge; p. (1991) 14,139.

Saltburn-by-the-Sea, t., Redcar and Cleveland, **Eng.**; seaside resort; 16 km E. of Middlesbrough; p. (1991) 6,145.

Saltcoats, burgh, N. Ayrshire, **Scot.**; on Firth of Clyde 3 km S. of Ardrossan; sm. harbour; hosiery; mainly residtl.; p. (2002) 11,260.

Saltillo, c., cap of Coahuila st., **Mexico**; comm., industl., and mng. ctr., p. (1990) 440,845.

Salt Lake City, c., cap. of Utah, **USA**; nr. Gr. Salt L., H.Q. of Mormonism; temple and univ.; agr. comm. ctr. for irrigated a.; meat packing; p. (1990) 159,936 (c.), 1,072,227 (met. a. with Ogden).

Salto, c., cap. of S. dep., **Uruguay**; on Uruguay R., nr. Concordia (Argentina); rly. and tr. ctr. for agr. a.; citrus fruit grapes, wine; p. (1985) 80,787.

Salton Sea, l., S. Cal., **USA**; 80 m below sealevel in depression which extends N.W. from head of G. of Cal.; ctr. of inland drainage; a. 699 km². *See also* **Imperial Valley.**

Salvador, spt., cap. of Bahia, **Brazil**; Brazil's first cap.; many years of economic stagnation now replaced by rapid growth; Brazil's first oil strike here in 1939; refining less impt. than petrochemicals at Camaçari complex (started 1972); new pt., naval base; hydro-elect. from Paulo Afonso encouraging many new light inds.; cement, aluminium, laminated timber, special alloys; p. (1991) 2,056,013 .

Salween, R., S.E. Asia; rises in E. Tibet, crosses Yunnan, descending into Burma to empty in G. of Martaban; many rapids; navigable to Moulmein; hydroelec. scheme; 2,880 km long.

Salzburg, c., cap. of Salzburg prov., **Austria**; on R. Salzach; cath., cas.; birthplace of Mozart; annual music festival; p. (1991) 143,971.

Salzburg, prov., **Austria**; adjoins Bavaria and the Tyrol, on N. slope of E. Alps; pastoral agr.; timber and some mineral wealth; hydroelectric power; cap. Salzburg; a. 7,154 km²; p. (1991) 483,880.

Salzgitter, t., Lower Saxony, **Germany**; S.W. of Brunswick; steel, engin., wagon bldg., fertilisers; p. (2002) 111,696.

Salzkammergut, lake dist., Upper **Austria**; saline baths at Aussee and Ischl; tourist region; stock-raising forestry.

Samar, I., **Philippines**; separated from Leyte by narrow strait; mainly forested mtns.; hemp, rice in lowlands; cap. Catbalogan; typhoons; a. 13,080 km²; p. (1990) 1,246,722.

Samara, (Kuybyshev), c., cap. of S. oblast, **Russia**; on R. Volga; major R. pt., rly. junc. on Moscow–Siberian line, airport; hydroelectric power sta.; comm. ctr. with varied mnfs., inc. cars, aircraft, textiles, synthetic rubber; oil refining; grain and livestock exp.; p. (1989) 1,254,000.

Samarqand (Samarkand), c., **Uzbekistan**; one of oldest cs. in world, sited in productive oasis on Zeravshan

R.; many historical associations and anc. bldgs; agr. tr. ctr.; cotton, silk; univ.; p. (2000) 369,000.

Samarra, t., **Iraq**; on Tigris R., N. of Baghdad; holy c. of Shiite sect.

Sambhar, salt lake, Rajasthan, **India**; exploited on lge. scale; a. 233 km².

Sambre, R., trib. of R. Meuse at Namur; crosses Franco-Belgian coal basin; part of N. Fr.– S. Belgian waterway system; 176 km long.

Samoa, archipelago, S. Pac. Oc.; volcanic mtns., tropical climate; agr., fishing; divided into two parts. *See* **Samoa** (below) and **American Samoa.**

Samoa, indep. sov. st., S. Pac. Oc.; member of Commonwealth (1970); gained independence from N.Z. 1962; consists of 2 lge Is. (Savai'i, Upolu) and 7 sm. Is.; 70 per cent p. in agr.; c. 30 per cent a. devoted to bananas; exp. bananas, copra, cacao beans; ch. spt. Apia on Upolu I.; a. 2,841 km²; p. (2004) 177,714. Formerly known as Western Samoa.

Sámos, I., Aegean Sea, off W. cst. Anatolia. belonging to **Greece**; mtnous., fine climate, fertile soils; wine, tobacco, dried fruit; ch. t. Vathy; a. 466 km²; p. (1991) 41,965.

Samothrace, I., Aegean Sea, **Greece**; barren, mtnous.; sparse p.; goats, grain, olives, sponge fishing; a. 184 km²; p. c. 4,000.

Samsun, spt., Trabzon, **Turkey**; on Black Sea cst.; exp. tobacco, grain, timber, wax, wool, skins, copper gds., antimony, chemical complex; p. (1990) 277,222 (t.), 1,158,400 (prov.).

Sana'a, c., cap. of **Yemen**; walled c. at 2,217 m; tr. in silk, cottons, hides, grapes; handicraft inds.; Islamic cultural and educational ctr.; p. (2000) 1,303,000 (met. a.).

San Andreas Fault, Cal., **USA**; shearing plate bdy. which extends from G. of Cal. to San Francisco; stress liable to cause sudden sharp earthquakes.

San Antonio, c., cap. of Bexar co., Texas, **USA**; in fertile San Antonio valley; serves farming and livestock a.; oil refining, food processing, meat packing; military installations in a.; warm climate attracts winter tourist tr.; Mexican atmosphere, siege of Alamo (1836); p. (2000) 1,144,646 (c.), 1,302,099 (met. a.).

San Bernardino, c., Cal., **USA**; founded and planned by Mormons (1852) rly. ctr.; citrus fruit packing and tr.; p. (1990) 164,164.

San Cristóbal, c., cap. of Táchira st., **Venezuela**; at 830 m nr. Colombian bdy., mng. and comm. ctr.; coffee, cacao, sugar; food-processing, cement; cath.; p. (1990) 220,697.

Sancti Spíritus, t., Las Villas, **Cuba**; comm. ctr. in grazing dist.; tr. in sugar tobacco; agr. processing; p. (1986) 75,600.

Sandakan, t., Sabah, **Malaysia**; fine natural harbour on N.E. cst.; exp. agr. prods., timber, rubber, fishing; p. (1990) 223,432.

Sanday, I., Barra Is., Orkney Is., **Scot.**; flat, many shipwrecks; agr., fishing.

Sandbach, mkt. t., Cheshire, **Eng.**; 8 km N.E of Crewe; salt, chemicals, comm. vehicles; p. (1991) 15,839.

Sandhurst, v., Berkshire, **Eng.**; 16 km S.E. of Reading; Royal Military Academy, National Army Museum; p. (1991) 19,153.

Sandia, t., N.M., **USA**; atomic research ctr.

San Diego, c., Cal., **USA**; first Spanish settlement in Cal. 1542; on Pac. cst., 16 km N. of Mexican border; fine natural harbour, naval base; fish-canning, aircraft; comm. ctr. for fruit- and vegetable-growing dist.; p. (2000) 1,223,400 (c.), 2,498,016 (met. a.).

Sandlings, The, S.E. Suffolk, **Eng.**; a. of glacial sands, forming heathland; difficult agriculture.

Sandown-Shanklin, t., I. of Wight, **Eng.**; on Sandown Bay; resort; p. (1991) 17,305.

Sandringham, v., Norfolk, **Eng.**; Royal residence since 1861.

Sandviken, t., Gävleborg, **Sweden**; impt. steel inds.; p. (1986) 40,000.

Sandwell, met. dist., West Midlands, **Eng.**; comprises Warley and West Bromwich; p. (2001) 282,904.

Sandwich, t., Kent, **Eng.**; Cinque pt. at mouth of Stour R.; harbour silted up 16th cent.; mkt. lt. inds.; p. (1991) 4,164.

Sandy, t., Mid Beds., **Eng.**; 5 km N.W. of Biggleswade; mkt. gardening; p. (1991) 8,554.

Sandy Hook, peninsula, N.J., **USA**; projects into lower bay of N.Y.; government reservation.

San Felipe, cap. of Yaracuy st., **Venezuela**; ctr. of

agr. dist. producing coffee, sugar and other tropical prods.; p. (1980) 57,526.

San Fernando, t., Bay of Cadiz, S. **Spain**; pt. has naval arsenal; salt mftg.; much of surrounding marshland now reclaimed; p. (1990) 83,900.

San Fernando, spt., **Trinidad**, W.I.; on W. cst. 40 km S. of Port of Spain; exp. sugar, asphalt, petrol; p. (1990) 30,100.

San Francisco, c., Cal., **USA**; spt. on S. F. Bay; entrance spanned by Golden Gate Bridge; attractive hilly site; cosmopolitan c. with several immigrant quarters; comm. and financial ctr. with many varied inds univ.; sudden earthquake (1906) destroyed much of c.; p. (2000) 776,000 (c.), 1,604,000 (met. a.).

Sangihe Is., Indonesia; volcanic archipelago between Kalimantan and Philippines; sago, nutmeg, copra; ch. t. and spt. Tahuna; a. 813 km²; p. c. 90,000.

San Gimignano, hill t., Tuscany, **Italy**; overlooks Val d'Elsa; 13th cent. mediaeval t., preserved as national monument; tourist ctr.; p. (1981) 7,377.

San Giovanni in Fiore, t., Calabria, **Italy**; agr. ctr. at 1,006 m nr. confluence of Neto and Arvo Rs.; p. (1981) 20,154.

Sangli, t., Maharastra, **India**; nr. Miraj on Karnataka border; p. (1991) 193,197.

Sangre de Cristo Mtns., part of Rocky mtns. **USA**; name (Span.—Blood of Christ) derives from reddish hue seen at sunset; highest summit Blanca Peak 4,367 m.

San Joaquin, R., Cal., **USA**; forms part of Central Valley project for irrigation of farmlands of R. valley; 512 km long.

San José, prov., **Costa Rica**; bauxite mng. nr. San Isidro del General projected with road to Punta Uvita where sm. will be built; cap. San José; a. 4960 km²; p. (1984) 1,105,844.

San José, c., cap. of **Costa Rica**; sited at c. 1,160 m in S. J. basin; cath., univ., observatory, theatre, park; ch. industl. and comm. ctr. of rep.; oil refining, agr. processing; major route ctr., international airport; p. (1984) 296,625.

San José, t., cap. of San José prov., **Uruguay**; impt. mkt.; flour-milling; p. (1985) 31,732.

San José, c., Cal., **USA**; in fertile Santa Clara valley; fruit and vegetable canning and processing, chemicals, paper, electronics; p. (2000) 894,943 (met. a.).

San Juan, prov., **Argentina**; at foot of Andes; gold, copper mng.; cap. S. J.; a. 89,179 km²; p. (1991) 528,715.

San Juan, c., cap. of San Juan prov., **Argentina**; comm. ctr. of agr. a., tr. in wine, fruit, cattle; p. (1991) 352,691.

San Juan, c., cap of **Puerto Rico**; built in part on I.; major spt. on N.E. cst.; exp. agr. prod. to USA; agr. processing; modern inds. inc. oil refining, cement, metallurgy, pharmaceuticals; cath., univ.; p. (1990) 437,745.

San Juan, R., **Central America**; divides Nicaragua and Costa Rica; plans made for its canalisation, which would give both countries a clear waterway from Caribbean to Pac.; 144 km long.

San Juan, R., Col., N.M., and Utah., **USA**; flows in goose-neck incised meanders; Navajo Dam part of Colorado River storage project, bringing irrigation to Navajo Indian reservation; 640 km long.

Sankt Ingbert, t., Saarland, **Germany**; N.E. of Saarbrücken; coal mng.; iron, glass, machin., textiles, leather; p. (1986) 40,500.

San Leandro, t., Cal., **USA**; food processing; Portuguese residents have annual religious festival; p. (1995) 69,976.

San Lorenzo, t., **Argentina**; 22 km N. Rosario; lge. chemical wks., oil refining.

Sanlúcar de Barrameda, pt., Cadiz prov., **Spain**; nr. mouth of R. Guadalquivir; wines and agr. prod.; mediaeval cas.; bathing resort; p. (1990) 56,400.

San Luis, c., cap. of S. L. prov., **Argentina**; ctr. of cattle, grain, wine producing dist.; rich mineral deposits in surrounding a.; hydro-electric power sta. and irrigation dam nearby; p. (1991) 110,136 (c.), 286,458 (prov.).

San Luis Potosí, st., **Mexico**; leading mng. st.; metals melting; cap. San Luis Potosí; a. 63,235 km²; p. (1990) 2,001,966.

San Luis Potosí, t., cap. of San Luis Potosí st., **Mexico**; industl. and comm. ctr.; metallurgy textiles; cath.; palace; p. (1990) 525,819.

San Marino, sm. indep. rep., **Italy**; in Apennines nr. Rimini; has kept its independence since 4th cent. A.D.; exp. wine, textiles, building stone; cap. San Marino; a. 62 km²; p. (2004) 28,503.

San Marino, t., cap. of **San Marino**; on slope of Mt. Titano, 19 km. S.W. of Rimini; tourism; p. (1999) 4,464.

San Miguel, c., **El Salvador**, at foot of San Miguel volcano; sisal-fibre, coffee, cattle, cotton, indigo; cath.; p. (1992) 182,817.

San Miguel Allende, t. (Guanajuato) st., **Mexico**; picturesque hill, site; famous art institute; p. (1990) 110,057.

San Miguel de Tucumán, c., cap. Tucumán prov., **Argentina**; on R. Sali; univ.; breweries, sawmills, flour, sugar; p. (1991) 622,324 (c.), 1,142,105 (prov.).

San Millán de la Cogolla, Spain; oldest (6th cent.) monastic foundation in Spain; in Cárdenas valley (Logrono prov.); p. (1990) 306.

Sanniya Hor, shallow l., **Iraq**; linked to R. Tigris; acts as flood control reservoir.

San-Pedro, spt., **Côte d'Ivoire**; pt. linked with development of timber production in hinterland and to Bangolo iron ore deposits; iron pelletizing plant; p. (1980) 50,000.

San Pedro, spt., a. of Los Angeles, Cal., **USA**; shipyds., oil refining, fruit canning.

San Pedro Sula, t., **Honduras**; ctr. for banana and sugar inds.; food processing; p. (1991) 325,900.

Sanquhar, burgh, Dumfries and Galloway, **Scot.**; coal mng., brick mkg.; p. (2002) 2,028.

San Remo, sm. pt., **Italy**; winter resort on Italian Riviera; flower mkt., olive oil, lemons, wine; 12th cent. church; p. (1981) 60,787.

San Salvador (Watling's I.), Bahama Is., **W.I.**; discovered by Columbus 1492, his first sight of the New World; a. 155 km²; p. (1990) 539.

San Salvador, c., cap. of **El Salvador**; stands c. 600 m a.s.l.; ch. comm. and industl. ctr.; food processing, textile and tobacco inds.; univ., observatory; oil refining; liable to earthquakes; p. (2000) 1,408,000 (met. a.).

San Salvador de Juyjuy, cap. of Juyjuy prov., N. **Argentina**; tourist resort, cath., agr. and tr. centre; p. (1991) 180,102.

Sansanding, t., **Mali**, W. Africa; lge. barrage across R. Niger.

San Sebastian, c., cap. of Guipúzcoa prov., N. **Spain**; spt. on Bay of Biscay, at foot of Mt. Urgull; seaside resort; fishing, textiles, paper, glass; captured by Wellington 1813; p. (1998) 178,200.

San Severo, mkt. t., S. **Italy**; hilltop site, 24 km N.W. of Foggia, Apulia; cath.; wine ctr., cream of tartar, bricks; p. (1981) 54,273.

Santa Ana, c., W. **El Salvador**; second lgst. c. of rep.; coffee, sugar, cattle; Santa Ana volcano nearby; p. (1992) 202,337.

Santa Ana, c., Cal., **USA**; S.E. of Los Angeles; in fruit farming a.; fruit pkg., walnuts, oranges; p. (2000) 337,977.

Santa Barbara, c., Cal., **USA**; resort on Pac. cst., picturesque setting, mild climate; p. (1990) 370,000 (met. a. with Santa Maria–Lompoc).

Santa Barbara Is., Cal., **USA**; along S. cst. of Cal.; inc. Santa Catalina I., a favourite resort.

Santa Catarina, st., **Brazil**; between Atl. and Argentina; tobacco, manioc, fruit, hogs; impt. coal producer; cap. Florianópolis; a. 95,830 km²; p. (1996) 4,865,100.

Santa Clara, c., **Cuba**; attractive site at over 360 m; agr. and comm. ctr. for sugar and tobacco; decisive victory for guerrilla army of Fidel Castro 1959; remains of Che Guevara interred here (1997); p. (1990) 194,354.

Santa Clara, c., W. Cal., **USA**; citrus fruit pkg.; electronics, plastics, chemicals; univ.; p. (1996) 98,726.

Santa Clara Valley, Cal., **USA**; extends S. from San Francisco Bay; intensive fruit-growing under irrigation, prunes; ch. t. San José.

Santa Cruz, prov., S. **Argentina**, cap. Rio Gallegos; a. 243,943 km²; p. (1991) 159,839.

Santa Cruz, c., cap. of S.C. dep., **Bolivia**; alt. 457 m; agr. mkt. for sugar, coffee, rice, cattle; oil refining; gas pipeline planned; international airport; impt. reserves iron ore; univ.; p. (1992), 694,616 (c.), (1988) 1,110,100 (dep.).

Santa Cruz de Tenerife, pt. on Tenerife I., **Canary Is.**; cap. of S.C. de T. prov., **Spain**; gd. harbour, oil refinery; exp. agr. prods.; developing resort in attractive a. with mild climate; p. (1998) 211,900 (c.), 780,200 (prov.).

Santa Fé, c., cap. of S.F. prov., **Argentina**; impt. R. pt. on I. in Salado R.; comm. ctr. for surrounding grain and livestock a.; food processing; univ., cath.; p. (1991) 406,388 (c.), 2,798,422 (prov.).

Santa Fé, t., N.M., **USA**; at base of Sangre de Cristo range; oldest capital in US; originally founded by Spaniards 1610; tourist and comm. ctr.; p. (1996) 66,522.

Santa Isabel. *See* Malabo.

Santa Maria, t., Rio Grande do Sul, **Brazil**; rly. junc., rly. engin., agr. tr. and processing; p. (1991) 217,600.

Santa Maria de Garoña, **Spain**; nr. Burgos; nuclear power plant being built.

Santa Marta, spt., cap of Magdalena dep., **Colombia**; banana pt. on deep bay at mouth of Manzanares R., serving local plantations; p. (1992) 286,471.

Santa Monica, c., Cal., **USA**; W. of Los Angeles; attractive site on Santa Monica Bay; aircraft, plastics, cosmetics; p. (1996) 88,471.

Santander, c., cap. of Santander prov., N. **Spain**; spt. and seaside resort on Bay of Biscay; exp. iron and zinc ore, agr. prods.; heavy inds., shipbldg., oil refining, chemicals; former summer resort of Spanish court; cath.; p. (1998) 184,200 (c.), 527,100 (prov.).

Santarém, t., Pará, **Brazil**; rubber, cacao, Brazil nuts, sugar; p. (1985) 227,400

Santarém, t., cap. of Ribatejo prov., **Portugal**; on slope of hill overlooking Tagus R.; Moorish cas.; mkt. for agr. prod.; p. (1996) 242,800.

Santa Rosa, t., cap. of La Pampa prov., **Argentina**; p. (1991) 80,592.

Santa Rosa, t., Cal., **USA**; tr. and industl. ctr. for Somona Valley fruit-growing a.; p. (1990) 113,000 (t.), 388,000 (met. a. with Petaluma).

Santiago, c., cap of Chile and Metropolitan reg.; planned t. ctr. in broad valley of Mapoche R., one of lgst. and most attractive cs. in S. America; cultural, comm., political and financial ctr.; focus of routes; univ.; textiles, chemicals, paper, iron and steel; rapidly growing p.; p. (2000) 5,538,000 (met. a.).

Santiago de Compostela, c., La Coruña, **Spain**; on R. Sar, surrounded by hills; univ., palace, cath. (with tomb of St. James); famous place of pilgrimage; agr. tr., food processing, tourism; p. (1991) 105,527.

Santiago de Cuba, c., **Cuba**; spt. on S. cst., exp. minerals, agr. prods., sugar, tobacco; oil refining, cigars, soap; cath., univ.; p. (1990) 405,354.

Santiago del Estero, c., cap. of S. del E. prov., **Argentina**; transportation ctr. of Argentine Chaco; agr. tr., cattle, food processing; p. (1991) 263,471 (c.), 671,988 (prov.).

Santiago de los Caballeros, t., **Dominican Rep.**; comm. agr. ctr. in fertile a.; food processing, coffee, rice, tobacco; cigars, cigarettes; p. (1991) 375,000.

Santis, mtn., on border cans. St. Gallen and Appenzell, **Switzerland**; alt. 2,500 m. Europe's hgst. television transmitter on summit.

Santo Andre, c., **Brazil**; part of industl. complex built to S.E. of São Paulo to relieve congestion; specialises in metalware and chems., p. (1996) 625,300.

Santo Domingo, cap. Dominican Rep.; pt. on S. cst. exp. agr. prods.; reputed burial place of Columbus; univ.; p. (2000) 3,599,000 (met. a.).

Santorine. *See* Thira.

Santos, c., spt., São Paulo, **Brazil**; world's ch. coffee pt.; also exp. oranges, bananas, cotton, and industl. prod. from modern harbour; p. (1996) 412,300.

Santo Tomé de la Guayana (Puerto Ordaz) c., S.E. **Venezuela**; new industl. c. nr. confluence of Orinoco and Caroní Rs.; iron mines, steel, hydroelec. power and aluminium plants in a.; industl. complex.

San Vicente, t., cap. of S.V. dep., **El Salvador**; ctr. for coffee, sugar, tobacco; mnfs. leather gds., shawls, hats; p. (1992) 45,842.

São Bernardo do Campo, c., **Brazil**; part of industl. complex built to relieve congestion in São Paulo which lies to N.W.; p. (1996) 658,800.

São Caetano, c., **Brazil**; ctr. for metalwk. built to S.E. of São Paulo to relieve congestion; p. (1996) 140,800.

São Carlos, t., São Paulo st., **Brazil**; 192 km N.W. of São Paulo; ctr. of coffee-growing a.; textiles, refrigerators, furniture; p. (1996) 175,300.

São Francisco, R., **Brazil**; flows from Minas Gerais prov. to Alt.; navigable for 1,440 km of middle course; used for hydroelectric power at Paulo Afonso falls and Três Marias dam; 2,560 km long.

São Goncalo, c., Rio de Janeiro, **Brazil**; fast-growing c.; p. (1991) 747,891.

São João do Meriti, c., Rio de Janeiro, **Brazil**; industl. and comm. ctr.; p. (1991) 425,038.

São José dos Campos, c., São Paulo, **Brazil**; ctr. of Brazil's aircraft ind.; synthetic fibres, telecommunication equipment, chems., motor vehicle components; p. (1996) 485,800.

São Luis, pt., cap. of Maranhão st., **Brazil**; on São Luis I.; noted cultural ctr. in 19th cent.; aluminium plant; p. (1996) 781,100.

São Miguel, I., **Azores**; lgst. and most productive I. of archipelago; ch. t. and spt. Ponta Delgada, exp. agr. prods., pineapples; volcanic landscape a tourist attraction; p. (1981) 131,908.

Saône, R., **France**; rises in Vosges and flows to R. Rhône at Lyons; navigable, canalised; 451 km long.

Saone-et-Loire, dep., **France**; mtnous.; noted vineyards; cap. Mâcon; a. 8,627 km²; p. (1990) 559,400.

São Paulo, st., **Brazil**; on Atl. cst.; major industl. a. of S. America; coffee, cotton, sugar, rice, maize; vehicles, elec. gds., chemicals, textiles, telecomm. equipment, metal-wkg. plants; cap. São Paulo; Santos lgst pt. in Brazil; a. 247,226 km²; p. (1996) 34,055,700.

São Paulo, c., cap. of São Paulo st., **Brazil**; fast-growing c., comm. and industl. ctr. of rep. and leading c. of S. America; vehicles, machin., elec. gds., textiles, pharmaceuticals; aluminium refinery; nearby pt. Santos ships rich agr. prod. from hinterland; univs., cath.; p. (1999) 9,928,000.

São Tomé, cap. São Tomé and Principe; p. (1991) 43,420.

São Tomé and Principe, former Portuguese col., W. Africa; volcanic Is. in G. of Guinea; cocoa, coffee; cap. São Tomé; a. 963 km²; airpt. extended to encourage tourism; indep. achieved as democratic rep. 1975; coup, 2003; vast undersea oil reserves; p. (2004) 181,565.

São Vicente, c., S.E. São Paulo, **Brazil**; first Portuguese settlement in Brazil (1532), on I. off mainland, sub. of Santos; fashionable beach resort; p. (1996) 279,600.

Sapporo, c., Hokkaido, **Japan**; main t. of Hokkaido; planned t.; univ.; brewing, dairy processing, sawmills; p. (2000) 1,984,000.

Saqqara, v., **Egypt**; necropolis of anc. Memphis; step pyramids.

Sarajevo, c., cap. of Bosnia-Herzegovina, formerly **Yugoslavia**; major route ctr., airport, ctr. of Yugoslav Muslims; mosques, caths.; diversified mnfs., metallurgy, elec. prods., textiles, tobacco, pottery; assassination 28 June 1914 of Archduke Francis Ferdinand precipitated First World War; under siege in civil war, 1992; p. (1999) 415,600.

Saransk, c., Mordovian aut. rep., **Russia**; 232 km S.E. of Gorki; univ.; elec. equipment, engin., agr. processing; p. (1989) 312,000.

Sarasota, Fla., **USA**; exp. fruit, veg.; resort; p. (1990) 278,000 (met. a.).

Saratoga Springs, N.Y., **USA**; summer resort at foot of Adirondack mtns., mineral springs; horse-racing; casino; p. (1980) 23,906.

Saratov, c., **Russia**; pt. on R. Volga; regional ctr. for agr. prod. of lower Volga valley and oil from Baku; univ.; engin., ball-bearings; textiles, oil refining, sawmilling; p. (1989) 905,000.

Sarawak, st., E. **Malaysia**; mtnous. inland with sparse p.; rubber, sago, pepper grown along coast.; oil; cap. Kuching; a. 121,914 km²; p. (1992) 1,583,000.

Sardinia (Sardegna), I., aut. region, **Italy**; mtnous., dry climate; fertile Campidano plain with fruit, wines, sheep; zinc and lead mng.; tourism; fishing; major petrochemical complex at Ottana; part of former kingdom of Sardinia belonging to house of Savoy; a. 24,002 km²; p. (1992) 1,651,902.

Sargasso Sea, zone S.W. of N. Atl. Oc.; relatively still sea within swirl of warm ocean currents; noted for abundance of gulf-weed on its surface, rich in marine life; named by Columbus.

Sari, c., cap. of Mazandaran prov., **Iran**; p. (1994) 186,000.

Sark, I., dependency of **Guernsey**, Channel Is.; 10 km E. of Guernsey; picturesque scenery; tourist ctr.; farming; a. 516 ha; p. (1986) 550.

Sark, R., forms extreme W. bdy. between **Scot.** and **Eng.**

Sarno, t., Campania, **Italy**; spa at foot of mtns. on E. edge of fertile Sarno plain; agr. mkt., textile ctr.; cas.; p. (1981) 30,583.

Sar-Planina, mt. range on border of Macedonia and Serbia; impt. chrome deposits; ctr. of mtn. tourism.

Sarreguemines, t., Moselle dep., **France**; in Lorraine; potteries based on local clay; coal mng.; p. (1982) 25,178.

Sarthe, dep., N.W. **France**; undulating surface; farming; coal, linen, potteries; cap. Le Mans; a. 6,247 km²; p. (1999) 529,846

Sarthe, R., France (r'b. of R. Loire; 265 km long.

Sasebo, spt., Kyushu, **Japan**; ctr. of coalfield; engin., shipbldg.; p. (1990) 244,603.

Saskatchewan, prov., **Canada**; coniferous forests and plains; Rs. Saskatchewan and Churchill; many lge. Ls.; extreme climate; hydroelec. power; gr. wheat prov.; livestock, dairying; oil, copper, uranium, helium plants, furs, fisheries; cap. Regina; a. 651,903 km²; p. (1996) 990,237.

Saskatchewan, R., **Canada**; flows from Rocky mtns. through L. Winnipeg and thence by R. Nelson to Hudson Bay; 2,320 km long.

Saskatoon, c., Saskatchewan, **Canada**; grew rapidly after arrival of rly. (1890); comm. ctr. for grain producing a.; meat packing and tr.; varied inds., cement, oil refining; univ.; p. (1991) 186,058 (c.), (1986) 200,665 (met. a.).

Sassari, t., Sardinia, **Italy**; nr. G. of Asinara; cath., univ., palaces; tobacco and macaroni wks., cheese; p. (1992) 121,961.

Sattahip, pt., **Thailand**; new pt. inaugurated 1967.

Satu Mare, t., N.W. **Romania**; agr. machin., handicraft inds. based on local prods., food-processing; cath.; p. (1992) 131,859.

Saudi Arabia, kingdom, Arabian peninsula, S.W. Asia; mainly desert, agr. in oases and S.W. upland region of Asir; lgst. producer of oil in Middle East; oil sales account for 85 per cent govt. revenue; steel inds. and oil refinery at Jiddah, petrochemicals at Dammam; Muslim holy cs. Mecca and Medina; cap. Riyadh (royal), Mecca (religious), Jiddah (admin.); main pt. King Faisal Port.; growing Islamic fundamentalism threatens stability; new rly. links planned to link Jeddah, Riyadh, Dammam etc.; a. 2,400,930 km²; p. (2004) 25,795,938 (includes thousands of foreign workers).

Sauerland, dist., N. Rhine–Westphalia, **Germany**; plateau, alt. from 150–450 m E. of Rhine; agriculturally poor, largely forested; crossed by R. Wupper, with which are associated industl. ts. Wuppertal (textiles), Solingen and Remscheid (cutlery and special steel); supplies hydroelectric power to Ruhr.

Sault Ste. Marie, t., Ont., **Canada**; on St. Mary's R., opposite Sault Ste. Marie, Mich., to which it is connected by bridge; pulp, paper, iron and steel; tourist ctr. for L. and forest region; p. (1996) 83,619.

Sault Ste. Marie, t., Mich., **USA**; pt. on St. Mary's R.; opposite Sault Ste. Marie, Ont.; calcium carbide; tourist ctr. for fishing, hunting a.

Sault Ste. Marie Canals (Soo), **Canada** and **USA**; twin canals on Canadian and American side of shallow channel linking L. Superior and L. Huron; traversed by all wheat and iron-ore traffic from L. Superior pts.; length (Canadian) 2 km; depth 5 m.

Saumur, t., Maine-et-Loire dep., **France**; on R. Loire, 48 km S.W. of Tours; sparkling wines, brandy; vegetable mkt.; cas.; p. (1982) 33,953.

Sauternes, v., Gironde, **France**; name applied to white wines of dist.; p. (1999) 584.

Sava, R., Slovenia, joins Danube at Belgrade; used for hydroelectric power; agr. in valleys; transport axis; 928 km long.

Savage I. See Niue.

Savai'i I., lgst. is. of Samoa, Pac. Oc.; volcanic, mtnous., fertile; exp. bananas, copra, cocoa; a. 1,821 km².

Savannah, c., Ga., **USA**; spt. nr. mouth of Savannah R.; rly., fishing and comm. ctr. for Sea Is., Savannah valley and surrounding plantations; mkt. for naval stores; sugar refining, paper, oil refining, diverse mnfs.; tourist ind. stimulated by mild climate; p. (1996) 136,262.

Savannah, R., **USA**; flows between Ga. and S.C., to Atl. Oc.; used for hydroelectric power.

Saverne, Col de, low pass, N.E. **France**; carries

trunk rly. from Paris to Strasbourg and the East between Vosges and Hardt mtns.; gradual approach from W., steep descent to E. into Rhine valley.

Savoie (Savoy), dep., **France**; borders Italy in Savoy Alps; part of former duchy; dairying and vineyards; hydroelectricity forms basis of metallurgical inds.; first Fr. National Park (Vanoise Park); cap. Chambéry; a. 6,188 km²; p. (1999) 373,252.

Savona, spt., Genoa, **Italy**; cath.; iron, shipbldg., glass and tinplate wks, wp., preserved fruits and tomatoes, imports coal, oil, iron-ore; p. (1981) 75,353.

Sawankalok, t., **Thailand**; impt. teak collecting ctr.

Sawbridgeworth, t., East Herts., **Eng.**; on R. Stort, 6 km S. of Bishops Stortford; malting, fruit preserving; p. (1991) 9,432.

Saxham, t., Suffolk, **Eng.**; agr. machin.

Saxmundham, mkt. t., Suffolk Coastal, Suffolk, **Eng.**; 29 km N.E. of Ipswich; p. (1991) 2,529.

Saxony, Land, **Germany**; turbulent political and territorial history, now comprises admin. dists. of Leipzig, Dresden, Chemnitz inc. Erzgebirge; kaolin deposits basis for porcelain ind. at Meissen; industrialised in 19th and 20th cent. with notable textile ind.; coal mng. nr. Zwickau; inds. concentrated around Chemnitz; cap. Dresden; comm. ctr. at Leipzig; a. 16,996 km²; pop. (2005) 4,350,000.

Saxony-Anhalt, Land, **Germany**; inc. Halle and Magdeburg; cap. Magdeburg; pop. (2005) 2,550,000.

Sayan Mtns., range of mtns.; between Rs. Yenisey and Angra, **Russia**; form part of Sino-Russian border; mineral resources.

Scafell Pike, mtn., Cumbria, **Eng.**; in Cumbrian Mtns, Lake Dist.; highest in Eng.; alt. 979 m.

Scalby, t., North Yorks., **Eng.**; 5 km N.W. of Scarborough; p. (1991) 9,019.

Scalloway, Shetland Is., **Scot.**; on W. cst. of Mainland; the anc. cap.; ruined cas.; fish. pt.; p. (2002) 812.

Scalpay, I., off E. cst. of Skye, Highland, **Scot.**

Scalpay, I., Harris, Outer Hebrides, Western Isles, **Scot.**; p. (1991) 382.

Scandinavia, name given to lge. peninsula in N.W. Europe; comprises kingdoms of Sweden and Norway; sometimes inc. Denmark, Finland and Iceland; rugged a. of anc. peneplained rocks; climate varies from arctic (N.) to humid maritime (S.W.); rich in timber and mineral ores. esp. iron and copper; W. cst. waters valuable fishing grounds.

Scapa Flow, strait, N. **Scot.**; between Pomona and Hoy, Orkney Is.; surrendered German fleet scuttled 1919; Brit. battleship Royal Oak sunk at anchor 1939.

Scarba, I., Argyll and Bute, **Scot.**; off N. end of Jura, red deer in woods and moorlands; p. (1991) 547.

Scarborough, c., Ontario, **Canada**; part of Toronto met. a.; p. (1991) 524,568.

Scarborough, t., l. gov. dist., North Yorks., **Eng.**; on E. cst., seaside resort; cas.; former spa; p. (2001) 106,243 (dist.), (2001) 38,364 (t.).

Scarpanto. See Karpathos.

Schaffhausen, most. N. can., **Switzerland**; on R. Rhine; pastoral, forested; cereals, fruit, vegetables, wine; hydroelectric power from S. falls on Rhine; cap. S.; a. 298 km²; p. (1990) 71,700.

Schaffhausen, c., cap. of S. can., **Switzerland**; on Rhine below L. Constance; falls to S.W. of c.; hydroelectricity supplies power for electro-chemical ind. and aluminium wks.; p. (1990) 34,324.

Schefferville, t., **Canada**; 576 km N. of St. Lawrence estuary and connected to it (at Seven Islands) by rly.; ctr. of iron-ore mines in Quebec–Labrador trough; p. (1986) 322.

Scheldt (Dutch Schelde, French Escaut), R., **France**, **Belgium**, **Neth.**; rises in Aisne, France, flows to N. Sea forming extensive delta with Rhine (Rijn) and Meuss (Maas) in Netherlands; navigable; 432 km long; network of canals.

Schenectady, c., N.Y., **USA**; on Mohawk R., N.W. of Albany; electrical plants, locomotive wks.; p. (1996) 62,893.

Scheveningen, seaside resort, **Neth.**; 3 km N.W. of The Hague; fish. pt.

Schiedam, t., **Neth.**, on Nieuwe Maas, 4 km downstream from Rotterdam; forms part of Rotterdam–Europoort; diverse pt.-based inds.; gin; p. (1994) 72,515.

Schiehallion, mtn., Perth and Kinross, **Scot.**; alt. 1,082 m.

Schio, t., Veneto, **Italy**; at foot of Alps on Leogra R.

Schleswig, t., Schleswig-Holstein, **Germany**; fish. pt. on Schlei inlet; lt. inds.; p. (1986) 23,300.

Schleswig-Holstein, *Land*, **Germany**; occupies S. part of Jutland peninsula; a. disputed between Denmark and Prussia in 19th cent.; mainly agr.; many sm. pts.; crossed by Kiel Canal; cap. Kiel; a. 15,664 km²; p. (2005) 2,815,000.

Schneidemühl. *See* Pila.

Schönebeck, t., Saxony—Anhalt, **Germany**; pt. on R. Elbe; metals, chemicals; p. (1989) 44,660.

Schoonebeek, v., Drenthe, **Neth.**; S. of Emmen; lge. oilfield.

Schouwen-Duiveland, I., Zeeland prov., **Neth.**; cap. Zierikee; formerly 2 separate Is.

Schwäbisch-Gmünd, t., Baden–Württemberg, **Germany**; at foot of Swabian Jura, E. of Stuttgart; clocks, glass, optical, precious metal and jewellery inds.; mediaeval and baroque bldgs.; p. (2002) 61,873.

Schwarzwald (Black Forest), forested mtn. range, Baden–Württemberg, **Germany**; highest peak Feldberg 1,496 m; tourism; famous for clock and toy inds.

Schwedt, t., Brandenburg, **Germany**; on R. Oder; lge. oil refinery; pipeline from Mozyr' (USSR); paper, fertilisers; p. (2002) 39,046.

Schweinfurt, t., Bavaria, **Germany**; on R. Main, N.E. of Würzburg; metals, machin., ball bearings, dyes, brewing; p. (2002) 54,568

Schwenningen, t., Baden–Württemberg, **Germany**; clocks, precision instruments, optical apparatus; p. with Villingen (1986) 76,200.

Schwerin, c., cap. of Mecklenburg-West Pomerania, *Land*, **Germany**; on Schwerin L., surrounded by smaller Ls.; comm. and industl. ctr. of agr. dist.; food processing, engin., furniture; cath., cas.; p. (2002) 99,978.

Schwyz, can., **Switzerland**; mtnous. in S.; forested; dairying impt.; original member of confederation; cap. S.; a. 907 km²; p. (1990) 110,500.

Schwyz, c., of Schwyz can., **Switzerland**; tourist ctr. nr. Lucerne; p. (1980) 12,100.

Sciacca, sm. pt., Sicily, **Italy**; nr. Agrigento; mineral springs; p. (1981) 34,294.

Scilly Is., *See* Isles of Scilly.

Scone, par., Perth and Kinross, **Scot.**; place of residence and also of coronation of early Scottish kings; from here Edward I removed Stone of Destiny to Westminster Abbey 1297; tourism.

Scoresbysund, E. **Greenland**; lgst. fjord system in the world; length 304 m; fishing and hunting; onshore oil drilling.

Scotland, Brit. Is., N. part of **Gt. Britain**, 32 unit. auths. created in 1996; devolution referendum in 1997 voted for new Scottish Parliament. Physically divided into 3 parts; (1) the Highlands and Is., an upland a. suffering from depopulation, economically reliant on stock-rearing, tourism, hydroelec. power, whisky and fishing; intrusive impact of N. Sea oil on N.E. cst.; (2) the Central Lowlands, containing most p., based in industl. ts. on sm. coalfields, inc. lgst. c. Glasgow and cap. Edinburgh; (3) the S. Uplands, a stock-rearing a. bordering Eng.; p. (2006) 5,100,000.

Scott Base, main base Ross Dependency, Antartica.

Scrabster, pt. nr. Thurso, Highland, **Scot.**; main ferry terminal for Orkneys.

Scranton, c., Penns., **USA**; on Lackawanna R.; anthracite ctr.; chemicals, shoes, textiles; univ.; p. (1990) 734,000 (met. a. with Wilkes-Barre).

Scunthorpe, t., N. Lincs., **Eng.**; on Lincoln Edge, 10 km S. of Humber; iron, limestone mng. and major iron and steel ind.; p. (2001) 72,660 (t.).

Scutari (Albania). *See* Shkodër.

Scutari (Turkey). *See* Usküdar.

Seaford, t., East Sussex, **Eng.**; 5 km E. of Newhaven; seaside resort; declined as a pt. with shift of Ouse R. channel to Newhaven; p. (2001) 21,851.

Seaforth, Loch, Lewis, Outer Hebrides, **Scot.**; 22 km long.

Seaham, spt., Durham, **Eng.**; Seaham Harbour on E. cst. 6 km S. of Sunderland; colly. workings extend under sea, closed 1993; p. (2001) 21,153.

Sea Islands, **USA**; chain of Is. off Atl. cst. of S.C., Ga. and Fla.; formerly impt. for sea-island cotton, since 1919 the islands infested with boll weevil.

Seathwaite, v., Cumbria, **Eng.**; 11 km from Keswick, close to Styhead (436 m); exceptionally heavy annual rainfall (above 3,800 mm).

Seaton, t., East Devon, **Eng.**; on Lyme Bay at mouth of R. Axe, seaside resort; freestone quarries; p. (1991) 7,579.

Seaton Delaval, t., Blyth Valley, Northumberland, **Eng.**; former coal mng.; p. (1991) 7,333.

Seattle, c., Wash., **USA**; spt. between Puget Sound and L. Wash.; S.E. is Mt. Rainier, N.E. Mt. Baker; tr. with Far East and Alaska from wooded, agr. hinterland; fishing and fish exp.; lgst. c. of Wash., a major industl. and comm. ctr.; aircraft (home of Boeing), shipbld., food processing; univs., cath.; p. (2000) 563,374 (c.), 1,973,000 (met. a.).

Secunderabad, t., Andhra Pradesh, **India**; now incorporated within Hyderabad; comm. ctr., rly. junc.; p. (1991) 136,000.

Sedan, t., Ardennes dep., **France**; on R. Meuse; machin., metal ware, woollens, flour; Napoleon III surrendered to Prussians 1870; p. (1999) 20,548.

Sedbergh, mkt. t., South Lakeland, Cumbria, **Eng.**; woollen ind., public school; p. (1991) 1,670.

Sedgefield, t., l. gov. dist., S.E. Durham, **Eng.**; in fertile agr. a.; cattle mkt.; racecourse; p. (2001) 87,206 (dist.), (1991) 4,424.

Sedgemoor, l. gov. dist., Somerset, **Eng.**; based on Bridgwater, Burnham and surrounding a.; p. (2001) 105,881.

Sefton, met. dist., Merseyside, **Eng.**; comprises Crosby, Bootle and Litherland; p. (2001) 282,958.

Ségou, t., R. pt., **Mali**; W. Africa; on R. Niger; ctr. of irrigation scheme; cotton, hides, cattle; cap. of former kingdom; p. (1984) 99,000.

Ségou Canal, Mali, W. Africa; leaves R. Niger 6 km below Bamako, extends 208 km N.E. to Segou; irrigates 7,770 km² on right bank of Niger and assists navigation.

Segovia, c., cap. of S. prov., Old Castile, **Spain**; on hill above Eresma R.; Roman aqueduct, cath.; p. (1991) 55,000, (1998) 146,800 (prov.).

Segovia, R., rises in N.W. Nicaragua, flows N.E. to Caribbean; forms part of S. limit of Mosquito cst., and bdy. between **Honduras** and **Nicaragua**; 480 km long.

Segre, R., Lérida, N.E. **Spain**; rises in E. Pyrenees flows S.W. into R. Ebro; water irrigates the a. around Lérida, the lgst. block of irrigated land in Spain; c. 272 km long.

Segura, R., **Spain**; flows to Mediterranean at Guardamar; 288 km long.

Seikan Tunnel, **Japan**; links Honshu with Hokkaido under Tsugaru strait, 67 km long

Seine, R., **France**; rises in Côte d'Or dep. and flows past Paris and Rouen to English Channel at Havre; navigable, part of French waterway network; 757 km long.

Seine-et-Marne, dep., N. **France**; agr., stockraising, dairying; impt. source of food for Paris mkts.; Brie cheese; cap. Melun; a. 5,892 km²; p. (1999) 1,193,392.

Seine-Maritime, dep., N. **France**; undulating a.; fertile; grain, dairying; heavy inds. at major Rouen; oil refineries; beach resorts; p. (1999) 1,238,115.

Seine-Saint Denis, dep., N.E. Paris, France; mkt. gardens; cap. Bobigny; p. (1999) 1,382,520.

Seistan and Baluchistan, twin prov., Iran; co. ts. Zabol, Zahedan; rly. terminus Pakistan rly. from Quetta through Mirjaveh.

Sekondi-Takoradi, t., S.W. **Ghana**; spt. on G. of Guinea; developed after construction of rly. (1903) to tap wealth of hinterland; deepwater harbour at Takoradi constructed 1928; fisheries, saw milling; p. (1996) 120,000.

Selangor, st., central Malaya, **W. Malaysia**; former sultanate; economically well developed; chemicals, rubber, tin, coal, pineapples; ch. pt., Port Kelang; fisheries; new st. cap. designated to relieve congestion of Kuala Lumpur; p. (2005) 4,190,000.

Selby, mkt. t., l. gov. dist., North Yorks., **Eng.**; on R. Ouse, 20 km. S. of York; anc. abbey church; flour milling, flax, oil-cake; development of major coalfield after 1983 linked to bldg. of power sta. in Aire Valley, but closure of Selby mine announced for 2004; p. (2001) 76,468 (dist.), (1991) 15,292 (t.).

Sele, R., S. **Italy**; rises in S. Apennines, flows W. into G. of Salerno; headwater carried E.

through gr. Apennine tunnel (11 km) to irrigate plateau of Apulia in S.E. Italy.

Selenga, Asiatic R., rises in **Mongolia**, enters **Russia** nr. Kiachta from where it is navigable to its delta in L. Baykal; c. 1,100 km long.

Selkirk, royal burgh, Borders, **Scot.**; on Etterick Water; 6 km S. of Galashiels; mkt. t.; tartans, tweeds; p. (2002) 5,742.

Selkirk Mtns., B.C. **Canada**; run N.W. to S.E. parallel with Rocky mtns.; anc. rocks, highly mineralised; rise to over 2,700 m.

Selkirkshire, historic co., S. **Scot.**; now part of Borders.

Sellafield, nuclear power plant, Cumbria, **Eng.**; formerly Windscale; reprocesses nuclear waste.

Selwyn Range, mtns., Queensland, **Australia**, extend 560 km W. from Gr. Dividing Range.

Semarang, spt., Java, **Indonesia**, exp. sugar, tobacco, tapioca, kapok; shipbldg., rly. repairs; univ.; p. (1995) 1,366,000.

Semipalatinsk (Semey), t., **Kazakhstan**; on R. Irtysh; lge. meat-packing plant; textiles, engin.; rich gold deposit found in a. 1965; p. (1990) 338,800.

Semmering Pass, low pass, **Austria**; provides route across E. Alps for rly. from Vienna to Venice; scenic resort; alt. below 915 m.

Semnan, t., Central Prov., **Iran**; comm. ctr. for tobacco growing region; p. (1986) 418,152.

Sendai, t., Honshu, **Japan**; cas.; univ.; metallurgy, food processing, lacquer ware; p. (2000) 1,008,000.

Senegal, rep., W. cst. Africa; union with Gambia (1982), dissolved 1989; flat savannah; tropical climate with long dry season; agr. main occupation, groundnuts accounting for 72 per cent exp.; production hit by severe drought (1982–3); groundnut and agr. processing provide industl. basis; bauxite, phosphate, titanium, zirconium mng.; oil refinery at cap. Dakar; a. 197,109 km²; p. (2004) 10,852,147.

Senegal, R., W. Africa; flows from Kong mtns. W. and N.W. to Atl. at St. Louis, above Cape Verde; lower valley forms fertile agr. land; partially navigable; plans for economic development of valley; joint water scheme with 3 dams to relieve water shortages, improve navigation and provide hydro-electric power for Mali, Senegambia and Mauritania, 1,600 km long.

Senegambia, former rep., W. cst Africa; formed (1982) from unification of Senegal and Gambia following attempted coup (1981); union dissolved, 1989. *See* Senegal and Gambia.

Senigallia, t., **Italy**; resort and spt. on Adriatic; fishing and agr. ctr.; food processing, agr. machin.; p. (1981) 40,108.

Senlis, t., Oise dep., **France**; Gallo-Roman wall; tourist ctr. in forested region, 43 km N.E. of Paris; mkt. t., furniture, rubber gds.; p. (1999) 16,351.

Sens, t., Yonne dep., **France**; on R. Yonne; known to Romans as Agedincum; Gothic cath.; agr. tr., food processing, farm implements, boots, chemicals, cutlery; p. (1999) 26,903.

Senta, t., **Serbia**; pt. on Tisa R.; agr. ctr.; food processing, agr. machin.

Seoul, c., cap. of **S. Korea**; in Han R. valley; food processing, textiles, rly. engin.; univs., anc. walls; international airport, connected by rly. to outport of Inchon; new cap. planned for Yongi-Kongju,100 miles south; p. (2000) 9,888,000.

Sepik, R., N. **Papua New Guinea**; flows E. to Bismarck Sea; drains vast mtn. a.; very fast flow; navigable by shallow craft; 800 km long.

Sept-Îles (Seven Islands), pt., on St. Lawrence, Quebec, **Canada**; iron brought by rail from Schefferville; airline service but no highway; p. (1986) 25,637.

Sequoia National Park, Cal., **USA**; sequoia trees.

Seraing, t., Liège, **Belgium**; on R. Meuse; coal mng.; iron and steel heavy inds.; seat of famous Cockerill iron wks. (1817) and glass wks. (1825); p. (1993) 61,225.

Seram (Ceram), I., Moluccas, **Indonesia**; W.-E. mtn. range rising to 3,357 m; a. 17,143 km².

Serampore, t., W. Bengal, **India**; former Danish settlement; cotton and silk weaving, pottery, jute and paper mills; p. (1991) 137,028.

Serbia, Rep. in S.E. Europe; also comprises aut. regions of Kosovo and Vojvodina; former Yugoslav constituent reps. of Croatia and Slovenia recognised as independent by EU 1991; Bosnia-Herzegovina and Macedonia have achieved independence; Kosovo now under UN administration; Montenegro voted in referendum for indepen-

dence, 2006; Serbia and Montenegro became separate republics, 2006; climate continental in interior; distinctive political development after second world war; refused to accept Soviet hegemony; well-developed links with W.; with major attempts to industrialise, based on energy, heavy and consumer inds. less p. engaged in agr.; economic decision-making increasingly freed from central control; cap. Belgrade; a. 241,886 km²; p. (2006) 10,250,000. In 2003 Yugoslavia formally adopted a new name, the Union of Serbia and Montenegro.

Serbia and Montenegro, the name adopted in 2003 by the two former constit. republics of Yugoslavia. Montenegro voted for indep. in May 2006 and the two reps. separated. *See* Serbia and Montenegro.

Seremban, t., cap. of Negri Sembilan st., **W. Malaysia**; on Linggi R.; linked by rly. to Pt. Dickson; comm. ctr. for rubber and tin a.; p. (1980) 136,625.

Sergipe, cst. st., **Brazil**; sandy cst. rising to undulating plateau in interior; well wooded and cropped for sugar, cotton; drier interior devoted mainly to stock-raising; oil deposits; a. 21,054 km²; p. (1996) 1,617,400.

Sergiyev Posad, (Zagorsk) c., **Russia**; 70 km N.E. of Moscow; woodcarving, toy mkg.; site of famous Troitse-Sergiyeva Lavra monastery, converted into museum 1920; p. (1989) 115,000.

Sergo. *See* Kadiyevka.

Seria, t., **Brunei**; coastal t., protected from sea by 8 km dyke; oil ctr., linked by pipeline with Lutong; p. (1988) 23,415.

Serov, t., **Russia**; in Urals; iron and steel; natural gas pipeline from Ingrim; p. (1989) 104,000.

Serowe, t., **Botswana**, Southern Africa; seat of Bamanguato tribe; mkt. ctr.; lge coal reserves widening economic base of Botswana and reducing dependence on S. Africa; p. (1989) 95,041.

Serpukhov, t., R. pt., **Russia**; on R. Oka, planned canal link to Moscow; p. (1989) 144,000.

Serra da Mantiqueira, mtn. range, hgst. in Brazil.

Serra do Mar, mtns., **Brazil**; form steep E. edge of Brazilian Plateau S. from Rio de Janeiro.

Serrai (Seres), dep., Macedonia, N. **Greece**; N. mtns. form frontier with Bulgaria in gorge of Struma R. valley; lower Struma R. basin fertile agr. a., producing cotton, tobacco; mkt. ctr. at cap. Serrai; a. 4,053 km²; p. (1981) 46,317 (t.).

Sesto San Giovanni, sub., Milan, **Italy**; machin., glass, chemicals, plastics.

Sète, spt., Hérault dep., **France**; on Med. cst.; chemicals, fisheries; exp. oysters, brandy, wine; oil pipeline under sea to Frontignan; importance originally based upon canal network, now supplanted by rlys.; tourism of growing importance; p. (1990) 41,510.

Setesdal (Saetersdal), Aust-Agder, S. **Norway**; remote valley retaining traditional social customs; arable pastoral agr.

Sétif. *See* Stif.

Seto, t., central Honshu, **Japan**; porcelain ctr. (since 13th cent.); p. (1990) 126,343.

Setté Cama, spt., **Gabon**, Equatorial Africa; open roadstead, landing difficult owing to swell; exp. timber; oil nearby.

Settle, mkt. t., Craven, North Yorks., **Eng.**; on R. Ribble in heart of Craven dist.; tourist ctr. for limestone ctr. of N. Pennines; p. (1991) 3,082.

Settsu Plain, S. Honshu, **Japan**; at head of Osaka Bay at E. end of Inland Sea; intensively cultivated alluvial lowlands, ch. crops, rice, vegetables, oranges; gr. industl. belt extends along cst. through Kobe, Osaka, Kishiwada; engin., chemicals, textiles; a. 1,295 km².

Setubal, t., Estremadura, S. **Portugal**; impt. pt. on Sado R., estuary; exp. cork, wine, oranges; fishing, fish processing, shipyds.; p. (1987) 77,885.

Sevan (Gokcha), lge. L., **Armenia**; alt. 1,934 m; never freezes; surrounded by high barren mtns.; drained by Razdan R.; hydroelectric power stas.

Sevastopol, spt., **Ukraine**; built on ruins left after famous siege 1855; Black Sea resort; rebuilt after second world war; one of most beautiful Crimean cs.; p. (1990) 361,400.

Sevenoaks, mkt. t., l. gov. dist., Kent, **Eng.**; in Vale of Holmesdale; residtl.; agr., lt. inds.; Knole Park; public school founded in 1432; p. (2001) 109,305 (dist.), (2001) 26,699 (t.).

Severn, R., Ont., **Canada**; flows to Hudson Bay; tr. post at mouth; 560 km long.

Severn, R., W. of Eng. and N. **Wales**; rises in Powys and flows to Bristol Channel; suspension bridge at estuary opened 1966; several proposals for major economic development around shores of estuary; 344 km long.

Severn Tunnel, Eng.; under estuary of R. Severn between Pilning (S. Gloucs.) and Severn Tunnel Junction (Monmouthshire); carries main rly. from London to S. **Wales**; longest main-line rly. tunnel in Brit. Is ; 7 km long.

Severodvinsk, t., Russia; on Dvina Bay, White Sea; metals, bldg. materials; p. (1989) 249,000.

Seville, c., cap. of Seville prov. and of Andalusia, **Spain**; spt. on Guadalquivir R., canal link with Atl. Oc.; exp. agr. prod., imports industl. raw materials; major industl., comm. and cultural ctr.; diverse mnfs.; beautiful c. with Moorish influence, prominent in narrow streets of ctr. a.; Alcázar palace; Gothic cath.; bullfighting, tourist ctr.; p. (1998) 701,900 (c.), 1,714,800 (prov.)

Sèvres, t., Hauts-de-Seine, dep., N. **France**; S.W. sub. of Paris on Seine R.; celebrated porcelain mnfs.; headquarters of International Bureau of Weights and Measures; p. (1999) 22,534.

Seward, t., S. Alaska, **USA**; rly. terminal, airfield and ice-free harbour make it an impt. supply ctr. for interior Alaska; p. (1980) 1,843.

Seychelles Is., indep. rep. (1976) within Commonwealth, Indian Oc.; consists of 86 Is. (37 granitic, 49 coralline), among most beautiful in world; lgst. I. Mahé; cap. Victoria; fishing, heavy dependence on tourism pays for dependence on imported food; petroleum exploration; exp. copra, cinnamon bark; famous for species of nut; total a. 404 km²; p. (2004) 80,832.

Seyne, or La Seyne-sur-Mer, t., Var dep., **France**; nr. Toulon; shipbld.; p. (1999) 59,322.

Sfax, spt., Tunisia; admin. ctr.; exp. phosphate, olive oil, salt, esparto grass, cereals, dates, hides; imports food, coal, textiles, soap; sponges; fishing; natural gas found in a.; surrounded by irrigated gardens and olive groves; p. (1984) 231,911.

Sgurr Mor, mtn., Highland, **Scot.**; alt. 1,109 m.

Shaanxi (Shensi), prov., N. **China**; Great Wall runs nr. N. border with Inner Mongolia; from N.-S. four main regions: (1) dry, fertile loess plateau, notorious famine region, but increasingly irrigated; (2) fertile Wei R. valley, ctr. of p. and agr.; (3) Hua Shan (4) agr. a. of upper Han R.; grain, livestock; coal, petroleum; developing transportation network aiding economic development; cap. Xi'an; a. 188,860 km², p. (1994) 34,010,000.

Shaba (Katanga), prov., **Congo**; many varied mineral deposits inc. copper, tin, iron-ore, cobalt, radium; cap. Lubumbashi; a. 466,200 km²; (1991) 5,207,000.

Shache (Yarkand), c., Xinjiang prov., **China**; tr. ctr. in S. oasis; tr. in wheat, rice, beans, fruit, carpets, textiles.

Shache (Yarkand), R., Xinjiang prov., **China**; trib. of Gan R.; 800 km long.

Shaftesbury, mkt. t., North Dorset, **Eng.**; Saxon hilltop t., abbey ruins; ctr. for agr. a.; p. (1991) 6,203.

Shahjahanpur, t., Uttar Pradesh, **India**; on Deoha R.; agr. mkt. t. and rly junc.; grain, sugar tr. and processing; p. (1991) 237,717.

Shakhty (Alexandrovsk Grushevski), t., Russia; anthracite mng. in Donets Basin; leather, textiles, metal wkg., food inds.; p. (1989) 226,000.

Shandaken Tunnel, N.Y. st., **USA**; carries water under Catskill mtns. to augment water supply of c. of N.Y.; 29 km long.

Shandong (Shantung), coastal prov., N. **China**; S. of fertile plain of Huang He; dense p. but agr. potential limited by dry climate; wheat, millet, maize, soyabeans, cotton, hemp, fruits; E. mtns. contain coal, iron, bauxite, kaolin; iron and steel inds. and cotton mills at main industl. ts. of Jinan and Qingdao; special economic zones to encourage foreign investment; birthplace of Confucius at foot of sacred peak Tai; cap. Jinan; a. 146,198 km²; p. (1994) 86,520,000.

Shanghai, c. and mun., **China**; major spt. on left bank of Huangbu; its strategic location developed, largely by Brit. businessmen, as ctr. for imperialist trading; rich agr. region; handles major share of Chinese shipping but dredging required; machin., chemicals, electronics, cars,

steel, shipbldg., are main inds.; major educational and research ctr.; open to foreign investment, esp. for high technology inds.; new business district (Pudong); Maglev train link to Pudong Intl. airport; fast-growing c.; a. 6,186 km²; (2000) 12,900,000.

Shannon Airport, Clare, **R.o.I.**; N.W. of Limerick; on main transatlantic air route; ctr. of customsfree industl. estate built (1958) to compensate for decline in air traffic with larger planes; p. (1981) 7,998 (t.).

Shannon, R., Ireland; separates Connaught from provs. of Leinster and Munster, flows to Atl. at Loop Head; hydroelectric power sta. at Ardnacrusha; 358 km long.

Shan State, div., **Myanmar**; elevated plateau through which flows Salween R.; impt. mng. dist., lead, zinc, silver at Bawdwin, smelters at Namtu; also tungsten, tin, antimony, manganese; home of Shan people; former Shan and Wa sts.; cap. Taunggyi; a. 155,801 km²; p. (1983) 3,718,706.

Shantou (Swatow), c., spt., S.E. Guandong, **China**; at mouth of Han R.; mftg. and exp. tr.; univ.; special economic zone to attract foreign inds. and new dock also being built; p. (1994) 718,800.

Shanxi (Shansi), prov., N. **China**; bounded W. and S. by Huang He; mainly high plateaux; fertile loess deposits, but drought conditions limit agr. potential; dry crops and livestock; coal, iron-ore, petroleum; cap. Taiyuan; a. 156,420 km²; p. (1994) 29,910,000.

Shaoxing (Shaohing), c., N. Zhejiang prov., S.E. **China**; agr. ctr. on Hangzhou Bay; rice, wheat, cotton; p. (1994) 205,300.

Shaoyang, c., Hunan prov., **China**; coal and iron mng.; timber; p. (1994) 277,300.

Shap, mkt. t., Cumbria, **Eng.**; nearby in Shap Fell 279 m, an impt. pass traversed by rly. and by a main road; granite quarries.

Shapinsay, I., Orkney Is., **Scot.**; p. (1991) 322.

Sharjah, emirate, member of the United Arab **Emirates** (1971), Persian Gulf; international airport at cap. Shārjah (p. 25,000); natural harbour at Khawr Fakhan; oil exploration, fishing; p. (1985) 268,722.

Sharon, plain, **Israel**; citrus fruits, vines, poultry.

Shashi, t., S. Hubei prov., **China**; agr. mkt. ctr. and canalised R. pt.; tr. in cotton, grain; flour milling, textiles; now known as Jinsha; p. (1994) 683,000.

Shasta Dam, Cal., **USA**; dams water of Rs. Pit, McCloud, Sacramento for hydroelectric power; irrigation, flood control and reclamation of lower Sacramento valley.

Shatt-al-Arab, R., Iraq; formed by union of Tigris and Euphrates, flows thence to head of Persian G.; swampy delta in rich agr. a.; deepest-water line of R.'s estuary defined (1975) as new Iraq/Iran bdy.; 192 km long.

Shawnee, c., Okla., **USA**; rly. and tr. ctr. for rich agr. a.; electronics, aircraft components; p. (1980) 26,506

Sheaf, R., South Yorks., **Eng.**; rises in S.E. Pennines, flows N.E. to join R. Don at Sheffield; 18 km long.

Sheboygan, t., Wis., **USA**; on L. Michigan; ctr. for dairy farming and resort a.; cheese, leather gds., hardware; p. (1990) 49,676.

Sheerness, Kent, **Eng.**; on I. of Sheppey at entrance to estuary of R. Medway; former royal dockyard and garrison; deepwater comm. pt.; electronics, furniture, coach bldg.; p. (1991) 11,653

Sheffield, c., met. dist., South Yorks., **Eng.**; on cramped site at confluence of Rs. Sheaf and Don; univs.; heavy engin. ctr., famous for high quality steels, cutlery, tools; major post-war redevelopment of c. (1991) 513,234 (dist.), (2001) 439,866 (c.).

Shellhaven, oil refineries, Essex, **Eng.**; on N. side of Thames estuary, nr. Standord-le-Hope.

Shenandoah National Park, Va., **USA**; extends along forested Blue Ridge mtns.; views of Shenandoah valley and Allegheny mtns.

Shenandoah, R., Va., **USA**; trib. of Potomac R.; picturesque valley noted for rich apple orchards and pastures; scene of several campaigns in Civil War; 272 km long.

Shensi. See Shaanxi.

Shen-yang (Mukden), c., cap. of Liaoning prov., N.E. **China**; on Hun R. in narrowest part of lowland with hilly country on both sides; impt. rly. junc. with main routes N. to Harbin and Trans-Siberian rly., S. to Beijing, Luta and into Korea; comm. and educational ctr.; impt. textile ctr., heavy inds., univ.; p. (1994) 3,762,000.

Shenzhen, special economic zone, Guandong, **China**; a. selected (1980) to encourage foreign investment; close to Hong Kong; soft drinks, cement, electronic equipment, petrochems. relocated from Hong Kong; spt.; univ.; planned nuclear power plant to supply Hong Kong; p. (1994) 695,600 (many temporary workers).

Sheppey, I. of, Kent, Swale, **Eng.**; in Thames estuary E. of mouth of R. Medway; sheep-rearing, steel wks.; ch. t. Sheerness, a. 117 km².

Shepshed, t., Charnwood, Leics., **Eng.**, 5 km W of Loughborough; hosiery; p. (1991) 12,061.

Shepton Mallet, mkt. t., Mendip, Somerset, **Eng.**; at foot of Mendip Hills, 8 km S.E of Wells; old woollen ctr.; bacon curing, brewing; p. (1991) 7,581.

Shepway, l. gov. dist., S.E. Kent, **Eng.**; cstl. a. of Folkestone, Hythe, New Romney and Lydd; p. (2001) 96,238.

Sherborne, mkt. t., West Dorset, **Eng.**; 6 km E. of Yeovil; famous abbey and school; Norman cas. ruins; glass fibre; p. (1991) 7,606.

Sherbrook, t., S.E. Quebec, **Canada**; comm. and mkt. ctr. for surrounding agr. region; inds. based on local sources of hydroelectric power from Magog R.; textiles, paper mills, machin., flour milling; deposits of asbestos nearby; p. (1991) 76,429 (c.), (1996) 147,384 (met. a.).

Sheringham, t., North Norfolk, **Eng.**; on cst. 6 km W. of Cromer; resort; fishing; p. (1991) 7,620.

Sherwood Forest, anc. royal woodland, Notts., **Eng.**; now restricted to infertile Bunter Sandstone cty.; inc. several estates and parks, notably the Dukeries; created a National Nature Reserve (2002).

Shetland Is., l. gov. auth., **Scot.**; 80 km N.E. of the Orkneys; about 100 in gr., ch. I., Mainland; lge. number of rainy days, but climate mild and tourists attracted by isolation, scenery and wildlife; Fair Isle famous for knitted clothes; fishing, livestock, agr., potatoes; rapid growth with oil drilling in N. Sea: lge. oil terminal of Sullum Voe; wreck of oil tanker *Braer*, Jan 1992; ch. t. Lerwick; p. (2002) 21,940.

Shigatze. *See* Zigaze.

Shijiazhuang (Shihkiachwang) c., Hebei prov., **China**; cotton milling, glass mftg.; grew rapidly with coming of rly.; p. (1994) 1,160,000.

Shikarpur, t., N. Sind, **Pakistan**; tr. ctr. for grain, precious stones; engin., food processing; p. (1981) 88,000.

Shikoku, I., Japan; S. of Honshu; smallest of Japan's 4 main Is.; sparsely populated, mtnous. interior, heavily forested; arable agr. in lowlands; ch. cs., Matsuyama, Kochi, Tokushima; a. 18,772 km²; p. (1990) 4,195,000.

Shillelagh, v., Wicklow, **R.o.I.**; oak forest, gave its name to oak or blackthorn cudgel; p. (1986) 334.

Shillong, c., cap. Meghalaya, former cap. of Assam, **India**; at alt. 1,372 m in Khasi hills; ctr. of impt. tea-growing dist.; pleasant climate attracts summer tourists; p. (1991) 223,400.

Shimla (Simla), t., Himachal Pradesh, **India**; famous hill-station c. 2,158 m high on forested ridge of Himalayas, 280 km N. of Delhi.

Shimoga, t., Karnataka, **India**; on Tunga R.; cottonginning, rice-milling; p. (1991) 178,882.

Shimonoseki, spt., Honshu I., **Japan**; at extreme S.W. of I.; tunnel and bridge links island of Kyushu; rly. ctr.; engin., chemicals based on local coal; fishing; p. (1990) 262,635.

Shin, Loch, Highland, **Scot.**; 26 km long; drained by R. Shin to R. Oykell.

Shipley, t., West Yorks., **Eng.**; on R. Aire, 13 km N.W. of Leeds; worsted mnfs.; inc. model v. of Saltaire, built by Titus Salt (1851) to house his alpaca mill workers; p. (2001) 28,162.

Shiraz, c., cap. of Fars prov., **Iran**; beautifully sited in vine-growing dist.; textiles, rugs, metal wks., lt. elec ind., tourist ctr.; tombs of mediaeval poets Saadi and Hafez; known as "city of roses and nightingales"; pleasant winter climate; univ., airpt.; oil refinery; p. (1994) 1,043,000.

Shizuoka, c., cap. of S. pref., Honshu, **Japan**; pt. on Suruga Bay; impt. ctr. for tea and oranges; lacquerware, textiles; p. (1990) 472,199.

Shkodër (Scutari), c., N. **Albania**; stands at foot of L. Scutari, 26 km from Adriatic; mkt. ctr.,

tobacco, cement, textiles; enjoyed greatest comm. prosperity after Ottoman conquest; several mosques; rail link to Podgorica, Albania's first external rail link, used mainly for metal ore export; p. (1991) 83,700.

Shkodër (Scutari), L., on borders of **Montenegro** and **Albania**; outlet via R. Boyana into Adriatic, 46 km long.

Sholapur, c., Maharashtra, **India**; between Hyderabad and Poona; rly. junc., impt. textile ctr.; p. (1991) 604,000.

Shoreham-by-Sea, t., Adur, West Sussex, **Eng.**; at mouth of R. Adur, 8 km E. of Worthing; spt. and mkt. t.; oil jetty; boat bldg., chemicals, soap, preserves; p. (1991) 17,932.

Shoshone Falls, on Snake R., Idaho, **USA**; height 61 m, used for irrigation projects.

Shott el Jerid, Algeria and Tunisia; deep depression in the desert.

Shreveport, c., La., **USA**; industl. ctr. in cottongrowing dist.; petroleum; p. (2000) 200,145 (c.), 334,000 (met. a.).

Shrewsbury, co. t., Shrops., **Eng.**; on R. Severn 19 km above Ironbridge gorge between the Wrekin and Wenlock Edge; agr. and dairy equipment, machin., elec. prods.; cattle and sheep mkt.; public school; part of l. gov. dist. of Shrewsbury and Atcham; p. (2001) 95,850 (dist.), (2001) 67,125 (t.).

Shropshire (Salop), non-met co., **Eng.**; on Welsh border, crossed by R. Severn; fine pastoral cty.; with hills and woodland, agr. and dairying; industl. activity at co. t. Shrewsbury; p. (2001) 283,173.

Shumen, c., cap. of S. prov., N. E. **Bulgaria**; agr. tr.; Moslem architecture; p. (1990) 111,754.

Shusha, t., Azerbaijan; health resort; silk spinning, rug making; Armenian p. massacred by Tartars 1926; p. c. 6,000.

Shustar, t., **Iran**; carpets, woollens, pottery; shallow-draught boats can reach Shallili, nr. S. by R. Karun.

Shymkent. *See* Chimkent.

Sialkot, t., **Pakistan**; N.E. of Lahore; sports gds., musical and surgical instruments, paper; agr. tr. and processing ctr.; p. (1981) 296,000.

Siam. *See* Thailand.

Sian. *See* Xi'an.

Siangtan. *See* Xiangtan.

Siauliai, t., **Lithuania**; 184 km N.W. of Vilna; rly. junc.; food and leather inds.; p. (1990) 147,600.

Siberia, terr., **Russia**; extends from Urals to Sea of Okhotsk and Bering Strait, bounded by Arctic on N. and by Mongolia and Turkestan on S.; climate mostly severe; ch. ts., Novosibirsk (cap. W. S.) and Irkutsk (cap. E. S.); rich in coal, iron, minerals; oil and gas in W. Siberian lowland; liquified coal pipeline under construction to Moscow; p. and economic activity clustered around rlys., esp. Trans-Siberian rly.; affected by global warming, 1990s; a. c. 12,950,000 km²; p. (1983) 29,587,000.

Sibiu, t., central **Romania**; picturesque site at foot of Transylvanian Alps; retains mediaeval character despite being an impt. industl. ctr.; lge. German minority p.; caths.; p. (1992) 169,696.

Sichuan (Szechwan), prov., S.W. **China**; mostly occupied by Chang Jiang; known as Red Basin because of colour of its sandstone; fertile a. with mild climate; rice, tea, citrus fruits, tobacco, sugar-cane; lge coal reserves; exp. tung oil; silk producing a.; most populous prov.; cap. Chengdu; a. 568,977 km²; p. (1994) 110,850,000.

Sicily, lgst. I., Mediterranean Sea; former kingdom and now aut. region of **Italy**; pleasant climate, mtnous.; fertile lowlands, especially plain of Catania; lge. range of Mediterranean crops; fishing; sulphur; petroleum reserves, refining and petrochemical inds.; volcanic Mt. Etna erupted in 1971; a. 25,708 km²; cap., Palermo; p. (1992) 4,997,705.

Sidi-bel-Abbès, t., dep., W. **Algeria**; old fortress t., became HQ of Fr. Foreign Legion; agr. mkt. ctr. for region producing grain, grapes, olives, livestock; p. (1987) 152,778 (t.), 444,047 (dep.).

Sidlaw Hills, low mtn. range, Angus, **Scot.**; max. alt. 455 m.

Sidmouth, mkt. t., East Devon, **Eng.**; on S. cst., 24 km S.E. of Exeter; seaside resort; retirement ctr.; p. (1991) 10,767.

Sidon. *See* Saïda.

Siebengebirge, sm. wooded range of seven hills, **Germany**; of volcanic origin rising to 457 m on right bank of Rhine; famous for Drachenfels association with the Siegfried saga.

Siedlce, t. and prov., Poland; E. of Warsaw; rly. junc.; agr. inds.; p. (1995) 74,130 (t.), 661,590 (prov.).

Siegburg, t., N. Rhine–Westphalia, Germany; on R. Sieg; Benedictine abbey; dyes, iron, ceramics; p. (1986) 34,100.

Siegen, t., N. Rhine–Westphalia, Germany; on R. Sieg; 2 cas.; iron mng. and smelting, machin., leather; p. (2002) 108,397.

Siemianowice Slaskie, t., Poland; nr. Katowice; ctr. of mng., industl. region; iron and steel, machin.; cas.; p. (1995) 78,099.

Siena, hill-town, Tuscany, Italy; 51 km S. of Florence; spreads over three hilltops with Piazza del Campo in between where celebrated Palio festival (horse-races) are held; 13th- and 14th-cent. arch., cath.; agr. mkt., tanning, glass, textiles, bricks; *panforte* confectionery; tourist ctr.; p. (1981) 61,989.

Sieradz, t. and prov., central Poland; R. Warta; old medieval t.; tourism; p. (1995) 44,724 (t.), 412,320 (prov.).

Sierra Leone, rep., W. cst. Africa; mangrove swamps on cst., high plateau, with peaks over 1,800 m in interior; climate hot, humid; economy based on subsistence agr. with rice, coffee and cocoa for exp.; iron ore mng. at Marampa; main exp. diamonds; fishing along cst.; renewed fighting in civil war, May 2000; cap. Freetown; a. 72,326 km²; p. (2004) 5,883,889.

Sierra Madre Occidental, mtn. range, Mexico; volcanic, forms W. edge of Mexican plateau; average alt. 2,100 m.

Sierra Madre Oriental, mtn. range, Mexico; limestone, forms E. edge of Mexican plateau; average alt. 2,400 m.

Sierra Maestra, mtn. range, Oriente prov., S.E. Cuba; rises abruptly from cst.; rich in minerals.

Sierra Morena, mtn. range, Spain; between Guadalquivir and Guadiana basins, highest point 1,677 m; rich in minerals.

Sierra Nevada, mtn. range, Granada, Spain; highest summit Mulhacén 3,483 m.

Sierra Nevada, mtn. chain, Cal., USA; highest peak Mt. Whitney 4,544 m; nat. parks.

Sierra Nevada de Mérida, mtn. range, W. Venezuela; extends N.E. from San Cristóbal to Barquisimeto; extension of E. range of Andes, alt. over 4,880 m; impt. coffee plantations from 900–1,800 m on slopes.

Sierra Pacaraima, mtn. range, Brazil, Venezuela; forms part of international bdy. and watershed between Amazon and Orinoco basins.

Sigtuna, t., Stockholm, Sweden; on Mälaren L.; first cap. of Sweden, educational ctr., tourist resort; p. (1983) 28,681.

Sihanoukville. See Kompong Som.

Sikhote-Alin, mtn. range, S.E. Asiatic Russia; rises to 1,800 m and extends for 1,200 km parallel to Pac. cst.; hinders access to W. bashis, forestry, minerals.

Si-Kiang. See Xi Jiang.

Sikkim, st., India; on S. slopes of Himalayas; incorporated as 22nd st. 1975; forest covered; economically underdeveloped; scene of rivalry between India and China; cap. Gangtok, a. 7,110 km²; p. (1991) 406,457.

Sila, La, massif, Calabria, S. Italy; granite mass occupying full width of peninsula; alt. over 1,060 m, max. 1,930 m.

Silchester, par., Hants., Eng.; ruins of Roman t., Calleva Atrebatum; impt. ctr. of Roman communications network.

Silesia (Polish Slask, Czech Slezsko, German Schlesien), geographical region, Central Europe; since 1945 divided between Poland, Czech Republic and Germany; extends along both banks of Oder R.; bounded in S. by Sudeten mtns.; forested mtns., fertile arable agr. in lowlands; major concentration of economic activity based on coalfield of Upper Silesia (ceded to Poland 1922); complex territorial history; now forms highly urbanised industl. conurb. mainly in Poland, admin. by Katowice, Opole, Wroclaw, Wroclaw (c.), and part of Zielona Gora; Czech Republic portion forms part of N. Moravia; Germany retains sm. part of Lower Silesia W. of Neisse R.; total a. 46,600 km².

Silkeborg, t., Jutland, Denmark; tourist resort in beautiful forest and lake region; p. (1990) 48,280.

Silsden, t., West Yorks., Eng.; wool textiles.

Silver Spring, t., Md., USA; sub. N. of Washington, D.C.; science-based inds. and research laboratories; p. (1990) 76,046.

Simbirsk, (Ulyanovsk), c., cap. of S. oblast, Russia; industl. ctr. of middle Volga region; birthplace of Lenin whose real name was Ulyanov; p. (1989) 625,000.

Simcoe, L., S. Ont., Canada; several resorts; boating, fishing; 48 km by 42 km.

Simeulue, I., S.W. of Sumatra, Indonesia; indigenous islanders; fishing and shifting cultivation.

Simferopol, t., Ukraine; on R. Salghir nr. Sevastopol; industl. ctr. in rich agr. a., fruit-canning, tobacco, machin.; p. (1990) 348,900.

Simla. See Shimla.

Simplon, mtn., Switzerland; alt. 3,567 m; the pass over the Simplon (alt. 2,011 m) from Domodossola, Italy, to Brig in the Rhône valley, Switzerland, was originally made by Napoleon I. The Simplon rly. tunnel leads from Brig on the Swiss side to Iselle in the Val di Vedro on the Italian and is the longest in the world, 19.7 km.

Simpson Desert, Central Australia; uninhabited arid a. covered in ridge dunes and spinifex; a. 77,000 km².

Sinai, peninsula, easternmost part of Egypt; between Gs. of Aqaba and Suez, at head of Red Sea; mainly desert in N., granitic ridges in S. rising to 2,592 m at Jebel Katrun; Jebel Musa or Mt. Sinai (2,244 m) is one of numerous peaks; mineral resources; coal mine at Maghâra; occupied by Israeli troops, Nov. 1956–March 1957, and since June 1967; phased Israeli withdrawal began 1979, completed 1982; prov. N. Sinai and S. Sinai; a. 28,632 km²; p. (1991) 223,000 (N.), 41,000 (S.).

Sinaia, t., S. Romania; health and winter sports resort in Transylvanian Alps; until 1947 summer residence of Romanian kings; palaces.

Sinaloa, st., Mexico; on G. of Cal.; agr. and mng., rich in gold, silver, copper, iron and lead, cereals on uplands; sugar, cotton on lowlands; cap. Culiacán; a. 48,482 km²; p. (1990) 2,210,766.

Sind, prov. (revived 1970), Pakistan; lower Indus valley; dry climate; E. part reaches edge of Thar desert; agr. depends on irrigation; irrigated by Sukkur and Kotri systems; wheat, rice, cotton, oilseeds, sugar-cane, fruits; handicraft inds. in ts.; ch. ts., Karachi, Hyderabad, Sukkur, Shikarpur; a. 129,500 km² p. (1981) 19,028,666.

Singapore, rep., S.E. Asia; I. separated from Malaysian mainland by Johore Strait and linked by causeway; equatorial climate; cap. Singapore on S. cst. has fine well-developed natural harbour; currently world's biggest port; world ctr. of rubber and tin mkts.; tr. in machinery, petrol prods., mnfs., with Japan, Malaysia and USA; increasingly impt. as regional financial centre; oil refining, shipbldg., but industl. development slowing down since 1985; only 20 per cent of land cultivated; fruit, mkt. gardening; second hst. standard of living in Asia; a. 620 km²; p. (2004) 4,353,893.

Singhbhum, former dist., Bihar, India; iron and steel wks. based on local iron mng.; now Purba (E.) Singhbhum and Paschim (W.) Singhbhum.

Sinhailion. See Lianyungang.

Sining. See Xining.

Sinkiang-Uighur. See Xinjiang Uygur.

Sinop, cap. of S. prov., Turkey; sm. pt. with gd. harbour on Black Sea but poor communications with hinterland; p. (1985) 23,148 (t.), (1990) 265,153 (prov.).

Sintra (Cintra), t., Portugal; summer resort, 29 km from Lisbon; Moorish castle, royal palace; p. (1981) 126,010 (met. a.).

Sinuiju, c., W. N. Korea; spt. at mouth of Yalu R. on Yellow Sea; linked by bridge to Antung (China); industl. ctr.; chemicals, aluminium inds., using power from Supung Dam; selected as new capitalist zone (2002); p. (1984) 500,000.

Sinyang. See Xinyang.

Sion, t., cap. of Valais can., Switzerland; on R. Rhône; built on two castled hills; cath.; horticultural mkt. ctr.; hydroelectric power stas. and coal mines nearby; p. (1980) 22,877.

Sioux City, Iowa, USA; on R. Missouri; meatpacking, foundries; p. (1996) 83,791.

Sioux Falls, t., S.D., USA; on Big Sioux R.; in rich wheat region; machin., cars, farming implements; nuclear reactor; p. (1996) 113,223.

Siracusa (Syracuse), c., S.E. Sicily, Italy; old t. on Ortygia I., off E. cst., modern t. on mainland, connected by bridge; founded c. 734 B.C.; ctr. of anc. Greek culture; exp. olive oil, oranges, lemons, wine; chemicals at Priolo; many Greek and Roman remains; p. (1992) 126,800.

Siret, R., Romania, Ukraine; flows S. from Carpathians to Danube; steep forested left bank, fertile terraced right bank; hydroelectric power and irrigation schemes; 448 km long.

Sistan and Baluchistan, twin prov., **Iran**; bounded by Afghanistan and Pakistan; cap. Zahedan; much desert land; arid, very hot; p. (1982) 664,292.

Sitra, I., Persian G.; forms part of st. of **Bahrain**, 5 km long and 1·6 km wide; oil pipeline and causeway carrying road extends out to sea for 5 km to deep-water anchorage; oil refinery; power sta. and desalinisation plant.

Sittang, R., Myanmar; rises in Pegu Yoma, flows S. to. G. of Martaban through delta; valley intensively cultivated, delta forested; irrigation project; 976 km long.

Sittard, mkt. t., Limburg, **Neth.**; tanning; p. (1993) 46,578, 184,097 (met. a. with Geleen)

Sittingbourne and Milton, mkt. t., Swale, Kent, Eng.; on Milton Creek, 14 km E. of Chatham; paper mills, brick wks.; cement; insecticides; ctr. of fruit-growing dist.; p. (2001) 39,974.

Sivas, c., cap. of S. prov., **Turkey**; impt. tr. and agr. ctr. in Kizil Irmak valley; cement, rugs; copper mng. nearby; foundations of modern Turkey laid here by Atatürk 1919; p. (1990) 219,949 (c.), 767,481 (prov.).

Sivash Sea or **Putrid Sea**, lagoon on N.E. cst. of Crimea, **Ukraine**; 20 per cent salt; a. 2,590 km².

Siwa, oasis, **Egypt**; in Libyan Desert, c. 480 km S.W. of Alexandria; dates, olives; remains of temple of Zeus Ammon (visited by Alexander the Great); 32 km long, 1·6 km wide.

Sizewell, Suffolk, **Eng.**; Magnox nuclear power sta.; Britain's 1st pressurised water nuclear reactor sta. under construction.

Sjaelland, I., **Denmark**; lgst. I., separated from Fyn I. by the Gr. Belt; fertile glacial clays but rapidly spreading ts.; ch. c. Copenhagen; a. 7,356 km²; p. (1990) 1,972,711.

Skagerrak, arm of N. Sea, giving access to the Kattegat, between Norway and Denmark, 112–144 km wide.

Skagway, sm. spt., Alaska, **USA**; at head of Lynn Canal inlet, 640 km N.W. of Prince Rupert; linked by rly. to Whitehorse on upper R. Yukon; boomed in gold rush (1898); p. (1990) 4,385 (inc. Yakutat and Angoon).

Skåne (**Scania**), old prov. and peninsula, extreme S. of **Sweden**; corresponds approx. to cos. Malmöhus, Kristianstad; most favoured part of Sweden in relief, soil, climate; intensive farming, wheat, barley, sugar-beet, fodder crops, dairy cattle; ch. ts. Malmö, Lund, Hälsingborg; a. 10,939 km².

Skaraborg, co., **Sweden**; between Ls. Vänern and Vättern; a. 8,467 km²; p. (1992) 278,860.

Skara Brae, prehistoric v., Mainland, Orkney Is., **Scot.**; v. excavated from under sand dunes.

Skaw The (**Grenen**), C., at extreme N. of **Denmark**.

Skeena, R., B.C., **Canada**; rises in N. Rocky mtns., flows S.W. to Pac. Oc. at Prince Rupert; lower valley used by Canadian National Rly.; 640 km long.

Skegness, t., East Lindsey, Lincs., **Eng.**; on E. cst.; resort; lt. engin.; p. (2001) 20,694.

Skellefteå, t., N. **Sweden**; on Bothnia G.; growing since discovery of Boliden ores nearby; iron and copper ore smelting; p. (1992) 73,734.

Skelmersdale, t., West Lancs., **Eng.**; coal, bricks, drainpipes; new t. (1961); p. (2001) 39,279.

Skelton, t., Redcar and Cleveland, **Eng.**; at N. foot of Cleveland Hills, 16 km E. of Middlesbrough; steel flooring; p. (1991) 10,088.

Skiddaw, mtn., Cumbria, **Eng.**; E. of Bassenthwaite L.; alt. 931 m.

Skien, spt., Bratsberg, **Norway**; on R. Skien; saw-mills, timber tr.; birthplace of Ibsen; p. (1990) 29,328.

Skierniewice, t. and prov. central **Poland**; fruit and vegetables, elec. engin; p. (1995) 47,910 (t.), 423,616 (prov.).

Skikda (**Philippeville**), t., spt., dep., N.E. **Algeria**; exp. prods. from Saharan oases; oil pipeline to Mesdar; vast petrochemical plant; p. (1987) 128,747 (t.), 619,094 (dep.).

Skipton, t., Craven, North Yorks., **Eng.**; on R. Aire; cotton and rayon inds.; cas.; p. (1991) 13,583.

Skopje, t., cap. of **Macedonia**, formerly Yugoslavia; anc. Scupi, one of oldest ts. in Balkans; oriental appearance; destroyed by massive earthquake (1963); food processing, iron and steel wks.; new oil refinery; airpt., route ctr.; p. (1994) 430,000.

Skövde, t., **Sweden**; between Ls. Vänern and Vättern; garrison t.; p. (1992) 48,460.

Skye, I., lgst. of Inner Hebrides, Highland, **Scot.**; connected by bridge to mainland 1995; mtnous.; sheep-farming and fisheries; tourism; only t. Portree; a. 1,417 km²; p. (1991) 8,868.

Skyros, I., Sporades, **Greece**; in Aegean Sea; mainly agr.; a. 199 km².

Slagelse, t., Sjaelland, **Denmark**; food inds.; iron wks.; 11th cent. church; p. (1990) 34,279.

Slave Coast, name given to the Guinea cst. of W. Africa between the Volta and Niger deltas where large numbers of slaves were shipped from 16th to 19th cent.

Slave, R., N.W. Terr., Canada; flows into Gr. Slave L.; length 410 km

Slavonia, historic region, **Croatia** (formerly Yugoslavia), between Drava R. (N.) and Sava R. (S.); ch. t. Osijek.

Sleaford, mkt. t., North Kesteven, Lincs., **Eng.**; 19 km N.E. of Grantham; agr. and agr. implements; p. (1991) 10,388.

Sleat, Sound of, Highland, **Scot.**; separates I. of Skye from the mainland; 11 km wide.

Slezsko. *See* Silesia.

Sliema, t., **Malta**; E. of Valletta; resort.

Slieve Bloom, hill range, Offaly and Laoghis cos., **R.o.I.**; highest point 529 m.

Slieve Donard, mtn., **N. Ireland**; highest of the Mourne mtns.; alt. 835 m.

Sligo, co., Connacht, **R.o.I.**; borders Atl. Oc.; rises to Ox Mtns. over 600 m; pastoral agr.; fishing; co. t. S.; a. 1,909 km²; p. (1986) 56,046.

Sligo, co. t., Sligo, **R.o.I.**; on S. Bay; pt., exp. agr. prods.; abbey ruins; cath.; p. (1986) 17,259.

Sliven, t., **Bulgaria**; in Balkan mtns.; impt. woollen mnf. ctr.; carpets; p. (1990) 112,220.

Slough, t., l. gov. dist., Berks., **Eng.**; on river terrace N. of R. Thames, 37 km W. of London; many lt. inds.; p. (2001) 119,067 (dist.).

Slovakia, formerly eastern part of Czechoslovakia, cap. Bratislava; extends from Carpathians to Danube valley; mainly agricultural, depressed industry; EU member (2004); a. 49,035 km²; p. (2004) 5,423,567.

Slovenia, former constituent rep., Yugoslavia; independence recognised by EU, 1991; mtnous., but many minerals inc. coal; highly developed region; EU member (2004); cap. Ljubljana; a. 16,229 km²; p. (2004) 2,011,473.

Slupsk (**Stolp**), t. and prov., N.W. **Poland** (since 1945); formerly in Pomerania; on R. Stupia, nr. Baltic Sea; cas.; wood, metal, food processing; p. (1995) 102,727 (t.), 425,403 (prov.).

Småland, historic prov., S. **Sweden**; barren upland a. S. of L. Vättern; moorland, deciduous forest; contrasts greatly with remainder of S. Sweden; a. 29,322 km².

Smederevo, t., **Serbia**; nr. Belgrade; pt. on R. Danube; walled t.; steel wks.; p. (1991) 64,257.

Smethwick. *See* Warley.

Smolensk, c., cap. of S. oblast, **Russia**; on upper Dnieper; anc. c. damaged in many wars; route ctr.; vehicles, machin., food processing; p. (1989) 344,000.

Smyrna. *See* Izmir.

Snaefell, highest mtn., **Isle of Man**; alt. 620 m.

Snake R., or **Lewis Fork**, trib. of Columbia R., flows from Wyo. to Wash., **USA**; gorges; hydroelectric power; 1,680 km long.

Snowdon, mtn., Gwynedd, **Wales**; highest in Eng. and Wales, alt. 1,086 m; forms part of Snowdonia Nat. Park.

Snowy Mtns., N.S.W., **Australia**; part of Australian Alps inc. Australia's hgst. peak (Mount Kosciusko); rise to over 2,000 m; S.M. scheme (1950) diverts water from headstreams in tunnels through mtns. to provide water for irrigation and hydroelectric power; completed 1972.

Snowy, R., N.S.W. and Victoria, **Australia**; rises in Mt. Kosciusko, flows S. into Bass strait 128 km W. of C. Howe; part of Snowy Mtn. scheme; 432 km long.

Soar, R., Leics., Notts., **Eng.**; rises S. of Leics., flows N.W. to join R. Trent; 69 km long.

Sobat, R., **Sudan** and **Ethiopia**; made up of several sm. Rs.; trib. of White Nile; 800 km long.

Soche. *See* Yarkand.

Sochi, t., **Russia**; on Black Sea at foot of main Caucasian range; health resort with subtropical climate and sulphur springs; developed since 1933; p. (1989) 337,000.

Society Is., Fr. Polynesia, S. Pac. Oc.; comprise Windward Is. (Tahiti, Moorea, Mehetia, *etc.*) and Leeward Is. (Huahune, Raiatea, *etc.*); visited by Captain Cook; main prods. phosphate and copper; cap. Papeete; a. 1,647 km²; p. (1983) 142,129.

Socotra, I., G. of Aden, Indian Oc.; since 1967 part of **Yemen;** under Brit. protection 1886–1967; lofty tableland; myrrh, frankincense, aloes; cap. Tamrida; a. 3,626 km².

Södermanland, co., **Sweden;** between Baltic cst. and L. Mälar; cattle-rearing; mng.; a. 6,822 km²; p. (1992) 257,858.

Södertälje, t., **Sweden;** on S. canal linking L. Mälar with Baltic cst.; vehicles, chemicals, tobacco; p. (1992) 81,770.

Soest, c., N. Rhine–Westphalia, **Germany;** one of oldest ts.; member of Hanseatic league; suffered heavily in second world war; soap, textile machin., engin.; p. (1999) 48,400.

Sofia, c., cap. of **Bulgaria;** Roman Serdica, and Triaditsa of Byzantine Greeks; nr. Yugoslav border; impt. route ctr. and ch. industl. ctr. of rep.; machin., textiles, chemicals, elec. engin.; cath., univ., and many historic bldgs.; p. (1999) 1,192,000.

Sogne Fjord, Norway; longest fjord in Norway; length 176 km; tourism.

Sogn og Fjordane, co., W. **Norway;** borders Atl. Oc., indented by Sogne Fjord; lge. hydroelectric power resources; tourism; a. 18,480 km²; p. (1990) 106,614.

Sohag, t. and prov., **Egypt;** on R. Nile; cotton processing; p. (1986) 132,965 (t.), (1991) 2,763,000 (prov.).

Soho, dist., London, **Eng.;** settled by Fr. Huguenots 16th cent.; high proportion of foreign residents, known as London's "Latin quarter"; night-clubs, theatres, film-company offices.

Soissons, t., Aisne dep., **France;** anc. Augusta Suessionum; commands N.E. approaches to Paris; cath.; agr. tr.; p. (1999) 29,452.

Sokoto, t., **Nigeria,** W. Africa, founded 1809 as cap. of native st. of S., p. mainly Hausa and Fulani; tr. ctr.; p. (est. 1983) 148,000, (1991) 4,392,391 (state).

Solent, The, strait separating I. of Wight from Hampshire mainland, **Eng.;**

Solihull, t., met. dist., West Midlands, **Eng.;** 8 km S.W. of Birmingham; residtl.; motor vehicles; p. (2001) 199,517 (dist.), (2001) 94,753 (t.).

Solikamsk, t., **Russia;** on R. Kama; chemicals from local potash; rapidly growing t.; p. (1989) 110,000.

Solingen, t., N. Rhine Westphalia, **Germany;** 24 km E. of Dusseldorf; p. (2002) 165,032.

Solnechny. *See* Gornyy Snezhnogorsk.

Solomon Is., S. Pac. Oc.; internal self-gov. (1976); full independence (July 1978); archipelago of volcanic Is.; N. Is. form part of Papua New Guinea; remainder were Brit.; dependent on exp. of copra, timber, fish; threatened by insect pests; *coup* and unrest (2000); a. 29,785 km²; p. (2004) 523,617 (mostly Melanesian).

Solothurn (Soleure), can., N.W. **Switzerland,** crossed by Jura mtns., and R. Aare; 07 per cent cultivated; dairying; many industl. ts.; cap. S.; a. 793 km²; p. (1990) 226,700.

Solothurn (Soleure), t., cap. of S. can., **Switzerland;** on R. Aare; anc. t., cath.; watches, motor mnf.; p. (1980) 15,778.

Solway Firth, arm of **Irish Sea,** Dumfries and Galloway, Scot., and Cumbria, Eng.; 6 km long.

Somalia (Somali Democratic Rep.), E. cst. Africa; narrow cst. plain in N., widens in S., interior plateau reaching c. 2,400 m; dry, hot climate; 75 per cent. p. nomadic; livestock herding; permanent agr. in irrigated R. valleys; sugar, banana plantations in Webi Shebeli and Juba Rs. in S.; potential for mineral exploitation; cap. Mogadishu; a. 637,658 km²; p. (2004) 8,304,601.

Somaliland, French. *See* Djibouti.

Somersby, v., Lincs., **Eng.;** the birthplace of Tennyson.

Somerset, non-met. co., S.W. **Eng.;** inc. part of Exmoor, Mendips, Quantocks and Blackdown Hills; to N. is drained marshland of Somerset levels; dairying; coastal resorts; co. t. Taunton; p. (2001) 498,093.

Somme, dep., N. **France;** borders Eng. Channel; crossed by R. Somme; low-lying agr. a.; textile inds.; cap. Amiens; a. 6,327 km²; p. (1999) 555,497.

Somme, R., France; flows in deps. Aisne and Somme

to English Channel; scene of battles 1916; linked to Rs. Oise and Scheldt by canal 186 km long.

Somport Tunnel, on bdy. **France–Spain;** carries main rly. from Pau to Zaragoza under Pyrénées; 8 km long.

Sönderborg, spt., S. Jutland, **Denmark;** older part of c. on Als I.; palace; p. (1990) 28,291.

Sondrio, t., cap. of S. prov., **Italy;** commands the Adda valley, impt. routeway through Alps; agr. mkt.; textiles; p. (1981) 22,747.

Songhua R., (Sungari R.), N.E. **China;** trib. of R. Amur; length 1,840 km.; hydroelectric power.

Songkhla, t., **Thailand;** most S. t.; ctr. of rubber growing dist.; third t. of cty.; p. (1980) 172,604.

Song-koi (Red R.), R., rises in Yunnan plateau, S.W. **China,** flows S.E. through N. **Vietnam,** enters G. of Tongking; Hanoi is nr. head of delta; Haiphong nr. one of R. mouths; lower valley densely populated and intensively cultivated; c. 1,280 km long.

Sonora, st., **Mexico;** on G. of Cal.; crossed by Sierra Madre Occidental; irrigated agr.; ch. producer of wheat, cattle; fish exp.; cap. Hermosillo; a. 182,535 km²; p. (1990) 1,822,247.

Sonoran Desert, Arizona, **USA;** alt. 900 m; enclosed basins and salt marshes.

Sonsonate, t., **El Salvador;** old t. with cath.; comm. ctr. of richest agr. region of rep., famed for coffee and dairy prod.; nr. Isalco volcano; p. (1992) 76,200.

Soo Canals. *See* Sault Ste. Marie Canals.

Soochow. *See* Suzhou.

Sorau. *See* Zary.

Soria, t., cap. of prov. of Soria, **Spain;** on R. Duero at c. 900 m; agr.-processing; retains mediaeval appearance; p. (1990) 32,600 (t.); (1998) 91,600 (prov.).

Sorocaba, t., São Paulo st., **Brazil;** textiles, food processing; p. (1996) 431,400.

Sorrento, cst., S. **Italy;** nr. S. extremity G. of Naples; popular resort, celebrated for its wines in anc. times; p. (1981) 17,301.

Sosnowiec, t., Katowice prov., **Poland;** coal-mng. ctr., iron wks.; metal and textile inds.; cas.; p. (1995) 248,980.

Sound, The, channel between Kattegat and Baltic, 5 km across at narrowest part; proposed tunnel between Denmark and Sweden.

Sousse (Susa), spt., **Tunisia;** exp. olive oil, phosphates; resort; p. (1984) 83,509.

South Africa, Republic of, lies in most S. part of Africa between Atl. and Indian Ocs. Comprises nine provinces, Eastern Cape, Free State, Gauteng, KwaZulu-Natal, Mpumalanga, Northern Cape, Limpopo (old Northern Province), North-West Province and Western Cape. Narrow cst. plain, several interior plateaux (600–1,800 m) with upland grasslands (Veld) and fringed by escarpments; climate warm and sunny; most highly developed cty. in Africa, based on mineral resources of gold and diamonds, and successful economic diversification; coal in Witbank and Vryheid dists. serves Iron and steel ind. at Pretoria (Tshwane); growing textile, food-processing inds. at pts. Cape Town, Durban and rubber at Pt. Elizabeth; agr. dependent upon water supply; rich fruit growing a. around Cape Town, extensive grain growing and pastoral areas extended by irrigation; badly affected by AIDS epidemic; cap. Tshwane (formerly Pretoria). p. (2004) 42,718,530.

Southall. *See* Ealing.

South America, S. continent of Western Hemisphere; inc. all ctys. S. of Panama. *See* **Latin America.**

Southampton, c., spt., unit. auth. created in 1997, part of Hants., **Eng.;** at head of Southampton Water on peninsula between estuaries of Rs. Test and Itchen; univs.; decline of passenger liners, now one of Britain's biggest container pts.; ship repairing, oil refining, cable mkg., electronics, synthetic rubber; free-port (1984); p. (2001) 217,445 (unit. auth.).

Southampton Water, inlet, Hants., **Eng.;** comprises drowned estuaries of Rs. Itchen and Test; gives access from Solent and Spithead to spt. of Southampton; 14 km by 1·6–2·4 km.

South Australia, st. of the **Australian Commonwealth;** the "desert state"; barren undulating interior forms part of central plateau of continent but inc. mtns. in S. and S.E. and L. Eyre basin 12 m below sea level; Nullarbor Plain in S.W.; sheep in S.E., intensive agr. in Murray R. valley; some interior mng. inds. but st. cap. of Adelaide contains most inds. and 69 per cent of p.; a. 984,381 km²; p. (1996) 1,427,900.

South Ayrshire, unit. auth. created in 1996, formerly part of Strathclyde, S.W. **Scot.**; borders F. of Clyde; ch. t. Ayr; p. (2002) 111,670.

South Bedfordshire, l. gov. dist., Beds., **Eng.**; close to Luton and inc. Dunstable and Leighton-Linslade; p. (2001) 112,637.

South Bend, c., Ind., **USA**; on St. Joseph R.; ctr. of fruit and dairy region; motorcars, aircraft, agr. machin.; p. (1996) 102,100.

South Buckinghamshire, l. gov. dist., Bucks., **Eng.**; based on Beaconsfield; p. (2001) 61,945.

South Cambridgeshire, l. gov. dist., Cambs., **Eng.**; rural a. surrounding Cambridge; p. (2001) 130,108.

South Carolina, st., **USA**; "Palmetto St."; admitted to Union 1788, st. flower Carolina Jessamine, st. bird Carolina Wren; level in E., mtns. in W.; subtropical climate; part of cotton belt; pigs and maize also impt.; cotton textiles; cap. Columbia; a. 80,432 km²; p. (2002) 4,107,183.

South Dakota, st., **USA**; "Cayote St."; admitted to Union 1889; st. flower Pasque flower, st. bird Ring Necked Pheasant; lies in Gt. Plains; crossed by R. Missouri; irrigated agr.; part of spring wheat belt, but now more diversified crops; agr. processing; cap. Pierre; a. 199,552 km²; p. (2002) 761,063 (inc. 50,000 Indians).

South Derbyshire, l. gov. dist., Derbys., **Eng.**; a. S. of Derby and inc. Repton and Swadlingcote; p. (2001) 81,562.

South Downs, chalk escarpment, East and West Sussex and Hants., **Eng.**; stretch from Chichester to Eastbourne; rise to over 240 m.; proposed as new National Park (1999).

Southend-on-Sea, t., unit. auth., Essex, **Eng.**; on N. side of Thames estuary; varied lt. inds.; air ferry terminal; resort; dormitory for London; famous pier badly damaged (2005); p. (2001) 160,257 (unit auth.).

Southern Alps, mtns., S.I., **N.Z.**; alt. 3,000 m.

Southern Ocean, surrounds **Antarctica**; pack ice.

Southern Uplands, region, S. **Scot.**; broad belt of hilly cty., N. part bleak moorland, S. part deeply cut by glens; sheep-rearing; dairying in valleys.

South Georgia, Brit. I., S. Atl. Oc.; former whaling ctr; new permanent research base, established 2001; a. 4,144 km².

South Gloucestershire, unit. auth. created in 1996, formerly part of Avon, **Eng.**; inc. ts. of Chipping Sodbury and Kingswood; p. (2001) 245,641.

South Hams, l. gov. dist., S. Devon, **Eng.**; a. between Torquay and Plymouth inc. Totnes, Kingsbridge and Salcombe; p. (2001) 81,849.

South Herefordshire, l. gov. dist., Hereford., **Eng.**; lge rural a. which inc. Ross-on-Wye.

South Holland, l. gov. dist., Lincs., **Eng.**; fenland a. around Spalding; p. (2001) 76,522.

South I., lge. I., **N.Z.**; inc. S. Alps (highest Mt. Cook, 3,764 m.), Canterbury Plains, impt. sheep-rearing dist.; cool climate; considerable hydroelectric power resources; tourism; a. 150,461 km²; p. (1991) 881,537.

South Kensington, dist., W. London, **Eng.**; contains Victoria and Albert Museum, Geological and Science Museums, British Museum of Natural History, Commonwealth Institute, Albert Hall.

South Kesteven, l. gov. dist., Lincs., **Eng.**; rural a. and ts. of Grantham and Bourne; p. (2001) 124,792.

South Korea. See **Korea.**

South Lakeland, l. gov. dist., Cumbria, **Eng.**; lge. a. around Morecambe Bay and inc. Ulverston, Grange, Kendal and Sedbergh; p. (2001) 102,301.

South Lanarkshire, unit. auth. created in 1996, formerly part of Strathclyde, S. **Scot.**; lies S. of central Clydeside conurb.; p. (2002) 302,110.

South Norfolk, l. gov. dist., Norfolk, **Eng.**; lge. a. inc. Diss and Wymondham; p. (2001) 110,710.

South Northamptonshire, l. gov. dist., Northants., **Eng.**; inc. Brackley and Towcester; p. (2001) 79,293.

South Orkney Is., Antarctica; S.W. of S. Georgia; part of Brit. **Antarctic Terr.** (1962); meteorological sta.

South Ossetia, aut. oblast, **Georgia**; in Caucasus mtns.; goat and sheep rearing dist.; a. 3,898 km²; p. (2005) 71,000.

South Oxfordshire, l. gov. dist., Oxon., **Eng.**; Wallingford, Thame and Henley-on-Thames; p.

(2001) 128,188.

Southport, t., Sefton, Merseyside, **Eng.**; on S. side of Ribble estuary; 29 km N. of Liverpool; leisure centre; residtl.; p. (2001) 91,404.

South Ribble, l. gov. dist., Lancs., **Eng.**; a. S. of Preston and inc. Walton-le-Dale; p. (2001) 103,867.

South Sandwich Is., Brit. dependency, Antarctica; sm. volcanic Is.; a. 337 km²; no permanent p.

South Shetland, archipelago, S. Atl. Oc.; 640 km S. of C. Horn; part of Brit. **Antarctic Terr.** (1962).

South Shields, t., frm. Tyne and Wear, **Eng.**; pt. on S. bank at mouth of R. Tyne; holiday resort; marine engin., new lt. inds.; p. (2001) 82,854.

South Shropshire, l. gov. dist., Shrops., **Eng.**; of Shrewsbury and inc. Ludlow; p. (2001) 40,410.

South Somerset, l. gov. dist. inc. Yeovil; p. (2001) 150,969.

South Staffordshire, l. gov. dist., Staffs., **Eng.**; a. borders W. Midlands conurb.; p. (2001) 105,896.

South Tyneside, met. bor., frm. Tyne and Wear, **Eng.**; comprises Jarrow, Hebburn and South Shields; p. (2001) 152,785.

Southwark, inner bor., London, **Eng.**; S. of R. Thames, incorporating former bors. of Bermondsey and Camberwell; cath.; site of former Globe theatre; p. (2001) 244,866.

South West Africa. See **Namibia.**

Southwick, t., Adur, West Sussex, **Eng.**; on S. cst. 6 km W. of Brighton; p. (1991) 11,067.

Southwold, spt., Waveney, Suffolk, **Eng.**; on E. cst. 13 km S. of Lowestoft; fishing; resort; new pier opened (2001).

South Yorkshire, met. co., **Eng.**; mainly industl. a. E. of Pennines; inc. productive coalfield nr. Barnsley and Doncaster and steel producing ts. of Sheffield and Rotherham; p. (2001) 1,266,338.

Sovetsk (Tilsit), t., **Russia** (since 1945); on R. Niemen, formerly in E. Prussia; timber and paper inds.; famous for Treaty of Tilsit between Napoleon and Russia 1807.

Sowerby Bridge, t., Calderdale, West Yorks., **Eng.**; on R. Calder, 5 km W. of Halifax; woollens.

Spa, t., Liège, **Belgium**; mineral springs, resort; gave name to "spas"; p. (1991) 10,100.

Spain, indep. sov. st., Iberia, S.W. Europe; member of EU (1986); lge. land a. takes up 80 per cent of Iberian peninsula and helps to make climate continental; mtnous. interior and narrow coastal strip encourages regional isolation and development of regional culture; civil war 1936-9 hindered modern economic growth; economy based on agr., but much of land is arid and although industl. raw materials in N. Spain and an oil refinery recently constructed at Bilbao; spectacular growth of tourism; Europe's biggest car exporter; inds. attracted by labour costs; monarchy revived 1975; cap. Madrid; a. 504,747 km²; p. (2004) 40,280,780.

Spalding, mkt. t., South Holland, Lincs., **Eng.**; in Fens, 16 km up R. Welland from Wash; agr., bulb mkt., agr. machin., sugar-beet, fruit canning; p. (2001) 22,081.

Spandau, t., Potsdam, **Germany**; previously gr. military ctr.; at confluence of Rs. Havel and Spree; now part of Berlin.

Spanish Guinea. See **Equatorial Guinea.**

Spanish Sahara. See **Western Sahara.**

Sparta (Spárti), famous anc. c., **Greece**; on R. Eurotas, in Peloponnesus; passed under Roman rule 146 B.C.; modern c. dates from 1834; p. (1981) 14,388.

Spelthorne, l. gov. dist., Surrey, **Eng.**; close to Gtr. London; inc. Staines and Sunbury-on-Thames; p. (2001) 90,390.

Spencer Gulf, lge. inlet, S. **Australia**; penetrates 384 km inland, many impt. pts. along cst. (Whyalla, Pt. Pirie, Pt. Augusta).

Spennymoor, t., Durham, **Eng.**; growing industl. t. S. of Durham; p. (1991) 17,381.

Sperrin Mtns., Strabane, **N. Ireland**; peat-covered schists; Sawell, 683 m.

Spey, R., Moray, Highland, the most rapid in **Scot.**; flows N.E. to Moray Firth; used for hydroelec. power; 171·2 km long.

Speyer, t., Rhineland–Palatinate, **Germany**; Roman origin; Romanesque cath.; famous Diet 1529 condemning Reformation gave rise to the term "Protestant"; cas; publishing.; p. (1999) 49,700.

Spitalfields, par., E. London, **Eng.**; formerly noted for silk weaving, introduced by Huguenots 17th cent.; name derives from spital or hospital of St. Mary, founded 12th cent.

Spithead, roadstead, between Portsmouth and I. of Wight, **Eng.**; used by ships of Royal Navy.

Spitsbergen (Svalbard), I. gr. belonging to **Norway**; within Arctic; mtnous.; sealing and whaling; coal mng.; asbestos, copper, gypsum; a. 62,921 km²; p. (2004) 2,765.

Split (Spalato), t., **Croatia** (formerly Yugoslavia); spt. on Adriatic; airport; food processing; now UNESCO World Heritage Site; p. (1991) 189,388.

Spokane, c., Wash., **USA**; on R. Spokane at falls used for hydroelec. power; timber tr. impt.; flour and saw mills, elec. gds.; lge. aluminium wks.; p. (2000) 195,629 (c.), 361,000 (met. a.).

Spoleto, c., Umbria, central **Italy**; cath., many Roman remains; textiles; p. (1981) 36,839.

Sporades, scattered Is. belonging to **Greece** in Aegean Sea, inc. Skyros, Skiathos and Skopelos.

Spratley Is., **S. China Sea**; cluster of about 50 reefs and sand bars, thought to contain petroleum; ownership disputed by China, Taiwan, Philippines, and Vietnam.

Spree, R., **Germany**; flows W. past Berlin to the Havel at Spandau; 363 km long.

Spremberg, t., Brandenburg, **Germany**; on R. Spree; cas., older part of t. on I.; glass; p. (1989) 24,547.

Springfield, c., cap. of Ill., **USA**; in rich agr. and coal mng. a.; farming and elec. machin., food processing; home of Abraham Lincoln; new Lincoln Library opened, 2002; p. (1990) 105,227 (c.), 189,550 (met. a.).

Springfield, c., Mass., **USA**; varied mnfs.; US armoury establ. 1794; p. (1990) 156,983 (c.), 530,000 (met. a.).

Springfield, c., Mo., **USA**; agr. ctr.; flour milling, engin.; p. (1996) 143,407.

Springs, t., Gauteng, **S. Africa**; E. of Johannesburg; gold mng., engin., cars, elec. gds.; uranium plant; p. (1980) 170,180 (dist.).

Spurn Head, E. Riding of Yorks., **Eng.**; sand spit at mouth of Humber estuary.

Sri Lanka (Ceylon), indep. rep. (1972) within Brit. Commonwealth (1948); in Indian Oc.; S.E. of India; fertile plains with cash crops of coconuts and rubber (S.W.) but dry in N.; mtnous. interior ameliorates climate where tea cultivation; varied p. composition inc. Sinhalese (70 per cent of p.), Tamils, Burghers (Portuguese and Dutch); agitation for Tamil independence; peace deal brokered (2003); dependent on exp. of primary produce; inds. growing; cap. and ch. spt. Colombo; tsunami devastation, 2004; a. 65,610 km²; p. (2004) 19,905,165.

Srinagar, t., cap. of Kashmir, **India**; in vale at c. 1,600 m. on Jhelum R. in W. Himalayas; beautiful surrounding cty.; summer resorts; mnfs. silks, tourism; p. (1991) 595,000.

Srirangam, t., Tamil Nadu, **India**; on R. Cauvery; temple dedicated to Vishnu; pilgrimage ctr.; p. (1991) 70,100.

Staffa, I. on Inner Hebrides, W. **Scot.**; 10 km N. of Iona, off W. cst. Mull; grand basaltic caverns, inc. Fingal's Cave, 69 m long, 13 m wide, 20 m high.

Stafford, co. t., l. gov. dist., Staffs., **Eng.**; on R. Sow, 24 km N. of Wolverhampton; heavy elec. and other engin.; expanded t., p. (2001) 120,670 (dist.), (2001) 63,681 (t.).

Staffordshire, non-met. co., W. Midlands, **Eng.**; plain drained by R. Trent and tribs.; p. (2001) 806,744.

Staffordshire Moorlands, l. gov. dist., Staffs., **Eng.**; borders S. Pennines and inc. Leek, Biddulph and Cheadle; p. (2001) 94,489.

Staines, mkt. t., Spelthorne, Surrey, **Eng.**; on R. Thames, 6 km S.E. of Windsor; nr. birthplace of Matthew Arnold; p. (2001) 50,538.

Stainmore, pass, North Yorks./Durham, **Eng.**; crosses N. Pennines from Greta valley into upper Eden valley; used by main road; alt. 418 m.

Staithes, v., North Yorks., **Eng.**; potash mng.

Stalino. See Donetsk.

Stalybridge, t., Gtr. Manchester, **Eng.**; on R. Tame, 13 km E. of Manchester; cotton and wool engin., plastics, rubber, gds., elec. cables; p. (2001) 22,568.

Stamboul. See Istanbul.

Stamford, mkt. t., Lincs., **Eng.**; old bldgs., one of 5 Danelaw ts.; agr. inds., elec. gds., plastics; p. (1991) 17,492.

Stamford, c., Conn., **USA**; on shore of Long I. Sound; p. (1990) 108,056 (c.), 203,000 (met. a.).

Stanislav. See Ivano-Frankovsk.

Stanley, t., Derwentside, Durham, **Eng.**; former colly. dist.; p. (2001) 29,202.

Stanley, spt., cap of **Falkland Is.**; former whaling port., contains over half p. of Falklands; p.

(1991) 1,557.

Stanley Falls. See Boyoma Falls.

Stanley Pool. See Pool Malebo.

Stanleyville. See Kisangani.

Stanlow, Cheshire, **Eng.**; petrol refinery, oil storage, docks, chemicals, linked to Anglesey by pipeline.

Stansted, site of London's third airport; 55 km N.E. of London. Current capacity, 8m passengers.

Stara Zagora, t., central **Bulgaria**; textiles, agr. processing; educational ctr.; p. (1990) 164,553.

Stargard Szczecinski, t., N.W. **Poland** (since 1945); formerly in Pomerania; rly. junc.; devastated in second world war; p. (1995) 72,908.

Start Point, C., nr. Dartmouth, Devon, **Eng.**

Stassfurt, t., Saxony - Anhalt, **Germany**; in gr. potash mng. region; chemicals, metals; p. (1989) 26,466.

Staten I., the most S. point N.Y. st. **USA**; shipyds.; linked with Brooklyn by Verrazano-Narrows bridge (opened 1964); residtl; p. (1990) 378,977.

Stavanger, spt., cap. of Rogaland co., S.W. **Norway**; comm. and industl. ctr.; oil refinery at Sola; cath., airport; most int. city in Norway; p. (1990) 97,328.

Staveley, t., Derbys., **Eng.**; 5 km N.E. of Chesterfield; iron, chemicals, concrete and iron pipes; p. (2001) 25,763.

Stellenbosch, t., Western Cape Prov., **S. Africa**; 40 km. E. of Cape Town; univ.; wines, saw milling, brick and tile mkg.; p. (1980) 64,100 (dist.).

Stelvio Pass, between **Italy** and **Switzerland**; road pass, alt. 2,762 m.

Stendal, c., Saxony - Anhalt, **Germany**; impt. rly. junct.; sugar, metal and food inds.; cath.; Stendhal (Henri Beyle) took his name from the c.; p. (1999) 42,200.

Stepney. See Tower Hamlets.

Sterlitamak, t., Bashkir aut. rep., **Russia**; on S.W. flank of Ural mtns.; impt. oil refineries on "second Baku" oilfield; linked by pipeline to Togliatti.

Stettin. See Szczecin.

Stevenage, t., l. gov. dist., Herts., **Eng.**; 6 km S.E. of Hitchin; first new t. to be designated under the New Towns Act 1946; old t. known in Domesday as Stevenach; agr., lt. engin., elec. goods, chemicals, aircraft parts; p. (2001) 79,715 (dist.), (1991) 76,064 (t.).

Stevenston, burgh, N. Ayrshire, **Scot.**; p. (2002) 9,129.

Steventon, v., Hants., **Eng.**; birthplace of Jane Austen.

Stewart I., S. of S.I., **N.Z.**; a. 1,735 km²; rises to over 900 m; famous for oysters.

Stewarton, burgh, E. Ayrshire, **Scot.**; woollens, carpets; p. (2002) 6,582.

Steyning, v., West Sussex, **Eng.**; on R. Adur, 6 km N. of Shoreham at entrance to gap through S. Downs; residtl.; p. (1991), 8,962 (with Upper Beading).

Steyr, t., **Austria**; at confluence of Rs. Enns and Steyr; industl. ctr.; historic bldgs.; p. (1991) 39,542.

Stif (Sétif), t., dep., N.E. **Algeria**; agr. ctr. for surrounding plateaux; grain, livestock; phosphates in a.; p. (1987) 170,182 (t.), 997,482 (dep.).

Stilton, v., Cambs., **Eng.**; 10 km S.W. of Peterborough; famous for cheese; p. (1991) 2,219.

Stirling, royal burgh, unit. auth. created in 1996, formerly part of Central Region, **Scot.**; stretches from Grampian mtns. to Central Lowlands; c. lies on R. Forth in gap between Campsie Fells and Ochil Hills; cas., univ.; coal mng., engin., concrete, wool, rubber prods.; p. (2002) 32,673 (c.), (2002) 86,150 (unit. auth.). Created a city, 2002.

Stirlingshire, historic co., central **Scot.**, now divided between E. Dunbartonshire, Falkirk, N. Lanarkshire and Stirling.

Stockholm, c., cap. of **Sweden**; freeport; on I. at outlet of L. Malar; called the "Queen of the Baltic" for the beauty of its surroundings; comm. ctr.; machin., textiles, leather, sugar, chemicals; univ. and many academic institutions; chosen Cultural Capital of Europe, 1998; p. (2000) 1,583,000.

Stockport, t., met. dist., Gtr. Manchester, **Eng.**; on R. Mersey, S.E. of Manchester; cotton manmade fibres, engin.; p. (2001) 284,528 (dist.), (2001) 136,082 (t.).

Stocksbridge, t., South Yorks., **Eng.**; iron and steel; p. (1991) 13,182.

Stockton, t., Cal., **USA**; R. pt. on San Joaquin R.; agr. processing, farm implements; p. (2000) 243,771 (t.), 481,000 (met. a.).

Stockton-on-Tees, mkt. t. 6 km W. of Middlesbrough, **Eng.**; unit. auth. created in 1996, formerly part of Cleveland; inc. t. of Billingham; impt. iron and steel inds., plywood; first rly. for passenger traffic opened 1825 between Stockton and Darlington; 18th cent. town hall; racecourse; p. (2001) 178,408 (unit. auth.), (2001) 80,060 (t.).

Stoke Newington. *See* **Hackney.**

Stoke-on-Trent, c., unit. auth. of **Stoke** created in 1997, formerly part of Staffs., **Eng.**; at S.W. foot of the Pennines; formed in 1910 by union of the five towns of Arnold Bennett's novels, Hanley, Burslem, Tunstall, Longton, and Fenton (with Stoke-on-Trent); ceramics, iron and steel, engin., brick and tile works, rubber prods.; univ.; p. (2001) 240,636 (unit. auth.).

Stolberg, t., N. Rhine–Westphalia, **Germany**; E. of Aachen; metals, glass, wood, chemicals, p. (2002) 58,718.

Stolp. *See* **Slupsk.**

Stone, mkt. t., Staffs., **Eng.**; on R. Trent, 11 km S. of Stoke-on-Trent; footwear, tiles, porcelain, scientific glassware; p. (1991) 12,305.

Stonehaven, t., burgh, Aberdeenshire, **Scot.**; fish. pt. on E. cst., 22 km S. of Aberdeen, distilling, net mftg.; p. (2002) 9,577.

Stonehenge, prehistoric gr. of monumental stones, on Salisbury Plain, Wilts., **Eng.**; date of erection est. between 2100–1600 B.C.; now UNESCO World Heritage Site.

Stornoway, spt., burgh, Western Isles, **Scot.**; on E. cst. of I. of Lewis, Outer Hebrides; ctr. Harris Tweed ind.; fishing ctr.; p. (1991) 5,975.

Stour, R., Kent, **Eng.**; flows past Canterbury to Pegwell Bay; 64 km long.

Stour, R., Somerset, Dorset, **Eng.**; trib. of R. Avon.

Stour, R., Suffolk and Essex, **Eng.**; flows E. to sea at Harwich; 67 km long.

Stour, R., Hereford and Worcs./West Midlands, **Eng.**; trib. of R. Severn; 32 km long.

Stourbridge, t., West Midlands, **Eng.**; on R. Stour; 14 km W. of Birmingham; brick and glass wks.; p. (2001) 55,480.

Stourport-on-Severn, mkt. t., Worcs., **Eng.**; at confluence of Rs. Stour and Severn; carpets, iron and steel gds., porcelain, ceramics; old canal and R. pt.; p. (1991) 18,283.

Stowmarket, t., Mid Suffolk, **Eng.**; on R. Gipping, 18 km N.W. of Ipswich; I.C.I. paint factory; p. (1991) 13,229.

Strabane, t., l. gov. dist., N. Ireland; agr. ctr., shirt mkg.; p. (2001) 38,248 (dist.), 11,670 (t.).

Stralsund, spt., Mecklenburg - West Pomerania, **Germany**; opposite Rügen I.; grain tr., machin., metals, fish smoking, shipbldg.; p. (2002) 59,970.

Strangford Lough, arm of sea, Down and Ards, N. Ireland; 29 km long, 10 km wide at entrance.

Stranraer, royal burgh, Dumfries and Galloway, **Scot.**; at head of Loch Ryan; steamer service to Larne, N. Ireland; creameries, brewing, knitwear; cas.; mkt.; p. (2002) 10,851.

Strasbourg, c., cap. of Bas-Rhin dep., E. **France**; impt. pt. in Rhine valley on Ill R., 16 km S. of confluence with Rhine; terminus of Marne-Rhine and Rhône-Rhine canals; industl. comm. and cultural ctr. of economically impt. Alsace region; food processing and varied mnfs.; historic c., with many fine bldgs., inc. cath., univ., imperial palace; surrendered to Germany 1871, recovered 1919; meeting-place of European Parliament; p. (1999) 264,243.

Stratford. *See* **Newham.**

Stratford-on-Avon, t., l. gov. dist., Warwicks., **Eng.**; on R. Avon; birthplace of Shakespeare; memorial theatre, library; many bldgs. ass. with Shakespeare; tourist ctr.; lt. inds.; p. (2001) 111,484 (dist.), (2001) 22,187 (t.).

Strathmore, lowland belt, central **Scot.**; flanked to N. by Grampians, to S. by Sidlaw and Ochil Hills; drained by Rs. Earn, Tay, Isla, S. Esk; famous for cereals and small fruits; length 96 km, width 11–16 km.

Strathspey, valley of the Spey, **Scot.**; 112 km long.

Stratton and Bude, North Cornwall, **Eng.**; 19 km S. of Hartland Point; resort; p. (1991) 5,979.

Strawberry, R., Utah, **USA**; on E. slopes of Wasatch mtns. 128 km S.E. of Salt Lake City; dammed to supply irrigation water led through tunnel under Wasatch mtns. to 259 km² cultivable land round L. Utah.

Street, v., Mendip, Somerset, **Eng.**; at foot of Polden Hills, 11 km S.W. of Wells; footwear, leather; p. (1991) 10,539.

Stretford, t., Gtr. Manchester, **Eng.**; borders Manchester Ship Canal; inc. Trafford Park

industl. estate; residtl.; Lancashire co. cricket ground, Manchester United football ground at Old Trafford; p. (2001) 42,103.

Stromboli, I., Lipari Is., Tyrrhenian Sea, N. of Sicily, **Italy**; active volcano, alt. 927 m.

Stromness, burgh, Mainland, Orkney Is., **Scot.**; 21 km W. of Kirkwall; mkt., fish. pt.; p. (2002) 1,609.

Stronsay, I., Orkney Is., **Scot.**; p. (1991) 382

Stroud, mkt. t., l. gov. dist., Gloucs., **Eng.**; on R. Frome, in Cotswolds; former ctr. of impt. cloth ind. in W. Eng.; woollens, dyes, plastics, engin.; p. (2001) 107,898 (dist.), (1991) 38,835 (t.).

Sturminster Newton, t., North Dorset, **Eng.**; impt. cattle mkt. on Stour R.; creameries; p. (1991) 2,155.

Sturts Stony Desert, a N.W. of S. **Australia**; named after Charles Sturt, explorer.

Stuttgart, c., cap. of Baden-Württemberg, **Germany**; on Neckar R.; cas., cath., rly. junc.; industl. and comm. ctr.; publishing, science-based inds.; oil refinery nearby; p. (2002) 587,152.

Styria, prov., **Austria**; borders Slovenia on S.; mtnous. with forests and pastures; lignite and iron mng., inds. around cap. Graz; grain, wine, fruit, stock-rearing; tourism; p. (1991) 1,184,593

Subotica, t., **Serbia**; univ.; agr. ctr. with Hungarian culture; agr. processing; expanding industl. ctr.; p. (1991) 100,219.

Suceava, t., S. Bukovina, N.E. **Romania**; mkt. t. on Suceava R.; once the residence of Moldavian princes; p. (1992) 114,355.

Suchow. *See* **Zuzhou.**

Sucre, c., cap. of Chuquisaca dep. and *de jura* cap. of **Bolivia** (La Paz is *de facto* cap.); in valley of Andes at 2,600 m; agr. ctr., oil refining; p. (1992) 130,952.

Sucre, st., **Venezuela**; on Caribbean cst.; coffee and cacao; fishing impt.; fish canning at cap. Cumaná; a. 11,800 km²; p (1991) 722,707.

Sudan, The, rep., N.E. Africa; climatic transition from N. desert to rainy equatorial S.; mainly plateaux, dissected by Nile R. system; prolonged conflict between N. and S., 1956–72, 1983 to date; 3 southern provs. now form an autonomous reg.; long staple cotton, grown in irrigated areas, provides most valuable exp.; gum arabic from lge. forest areas; food processing; dams constructed on Atbara and Blue Nile Rs.; periodic severe famines; conflict in Darfur; growing oil production; cap. Khartoum; a. 2,530,430 km²; p. (2004) 39,148,162.

Sudbury, t., Ont., **Canada**; nickel, copper mng.; refining; univ.; p. (1991) 92,727 (c.), (1996) 160,488 (met. a.).

Sudbury, t., Babergh, Suffolk, **Eng.**; on R. Stour, 19 km N.W. of Colchester; p. (2001) 20,188.

Sudetenland, region of Czech Rep. bordering Germany, until 1945 German-speaking; annexed by Hitler 1938, recovered by Czechoslavakia 1945; named after Sudeten mtns.

Sudeten Mtns. or **Sudetes,** mtn. range along borders of Czech Rep. and Poland; separating Bohemia and Moravia from Silesia; minerals.

Suez (Es-Suweis), spt. and prov., **Egypt**; the anc. Arsinoë; at head of G. of Suez (arm of Red Sea) and S. entrance of Suez canal, which crosses the isthmus of Suez to the Mediterranean at Port Said; Port Tewfiq adjoining has quay and docks; declined during closure of canal 1967–75; oil refining, fertilisers; p. (1990) 392,000 (c.), (1991) 376,000 (prov.).

Suez Canal, ship canal, **Egypt**; connects Mediterranean Sea (Pt. Said) with Red Sea (Suez) through Ls. Manzala, Timsah, and Bitter; length 162 km; closed after Arab-Israeli war of June 1967; reopened 1975; tunnel links Egypt and Israel (1980); widening and deepening of canal to accommodate larger oil tankers, complete (1980).

Suez, G., Red Sea; N.W. arm of Red Sea between Arabian desert and Sinai peninsula, **Egypt**; southern approach to Suez canal; length 304 km., width varies from 19–40 km.

Suffolk, non-met. co., E. Anglia, **Eng.**; bounded on E. by N. Sea, drowned coastline; rises to 90 m in E. Anglian Heights in W.; impt. agr. a., lge. farms, mixed farming; inds. based on agr.; many expanded ts. in S.; co. t. Ipswich; p. (2001) 668,553.

Suffolk Coastal, l. gov. dist., E. Suffolk, **Eng.**; lge. rural a. inc. ts. of Leiston-cum-Sizewell, Saxmundham, Aldeburgh, Woodbridge and Felixstowe; p. (2001) 115,141.

Sukkur, t., **Pakistan;** major bridging point of R. Indus; 368 km N.E. of Karachi; dam for irrigation; thermal sta.; p. (1981) 193,000.

Sula Is., I. gr. in Molucca Sea, E. of Sulawesi, **Indonesia;** little developed.

Sulawesi (Celebes), I., **Indonesia;** mtnous., lge. forests; copra, coffee, gold, nickel, copper, asphalt; ch. pts. Menado, Makasar; a. 189,484 km²; p. (1983) 11,112,200.

Sulaymāniyah, t., **Iraq;** in hill dist. nr. Iran border; p. (1985) 279,424.

Sullom Voe, Shetland Is., **Scot.;** oil terminal and receiving ctr. for N. Sea oil.

Sultanabad. See Arak.

Sulu Is., prov. **Philippines;** archipelago between Borneo and the Philippines; inc. over 400 volcanic Is. and coral islets; a. 2,461 km²; under US control 1899–1940; p. (1990) 469,971.

Sumatra, I., **Indonesia;** relatively under-developed; growing p.; main development in Cultuurgebied, rubber, oil palm, sisal, tobacco; impt. oil deposits and new oil refineries; much resettlement in 1990s from other islands; devastated by 2004 tsunami; a. 473,607 km²; p. (1998) 42,500,000.

Sumba or **Sandalwood I.,** S. of Flores, **Indonesia;** horse-breeding; rice, maize, tobacco, timber, cinnamon; cap. Waingapu; a. 11,150 km².

Sumbawa, I., **Indonesia;** between Flores and Lombok; wet climate, sparse p.; a. (inc. nearby Is.) 13,572 km²; p. (1980) 320,000.

Sumgait, t., **Azerbaijan;** on Caspian Sea; 40 km N.W. of Baku; metallurgical ind.; chemicals; p. (1990) 234,600.

Sunbury-on-Thames, t., Spelthorne, Surrey, **Eng.;** W. of London; residtl., water wks., gravel pits; petrol research establishment; p. (2001) 27,415.

Sunda Is., Indonesia; between S. China Sea and Indian Oc.; form two grs., Greater Sunda Is., inc. Java, Sumatra, Borneo, Sulawesi, Banka, and the Lesser Sunda Is. (renamed Nusa Tenggara 1954) inc. Bali, Lombok, Sumbawa, Timor.

Sundarbans, The, tract of forest and swamps, fringing the delta of the Ganges, **India/Bangladesh;** 130 km wide; rice grown in N.; tigers and crocodiles found in S.

Sunda Strait, between Java and Sumatra, **Indonesia;** 21 km wide, contains the volcanic I of Krakatao.

Sunday I. or **Raoul I.,** lgst. and only inhabited of Kermadec Is., **N.Z.;** 32 km in circuit; meteorological and radio sta.

Sunderland, c. (1992), spt., met. dist., frmr Tyne and Wear, **Eng.;** at mouth of R. Wear; precision and aero-engin., univ., shipbldg., Nissan car plant; p. (2001) 280,807 (dist.), (2001) 177,739 (c.).

Sundsvall, spt., Västernorrland, **Sweden;** on a wide bay of the Baltic nr. Hernösand; timber and wood-pulp inds.; p. (1992) 94,329.

Sungari. See Songhua R.

Sunnyvale, t., Cal., **USA;** ctr. of fruit-growing a.; lt. inds.; p. (1990) 117,229.

Superior, t., Wis., **USA;** at head of L. Superior; tr. in grain, timber, coal; shipbldg. and flour mills; oil refining; p. (1980) 29,571.

Superior, L., N. America; lgst. sheet of fresh water in the world; lies between **Canada** and **USA;** one of chain of gr. Ls. in St. Lawrence system, outlet to L. Huron by St. Mary's R.; receives waters of St. Louis, Pigeon and Nipigon; impt. waterway; a. 82,880 km².

Surabaya, spt., Java, **Indonesia;** ch. naval base; handles nearly half Indonesia's tr.; shipbldg., oil refining, food processing; p. (1995) 2,701,000.

Surakarta (Solo), Java, **Indonesia;** on Solo R.; tr. ctr. for agr. region; former sultan's palace; p. (1995) 516,000.

Surat, c., Gujarat, **India;** on R. Tapti; gold and textile ctr.; notable as first English trading post 1612; plague (1994); p. (1991) 1,499,000.

Surbiton, Gtr. London, **Eng.;** on R. Thames, inc. in Royal Borough of Kingston-upon-Thames; residtl.; lt. engin., elec. components.

Suriname (Dutch Guiana), former self-gov. terr. of Neth.; indep. 1975; S. America; sub-tropical climate; p. concentrated on cst. where rice, sugar, and citrus fruits grown; great agr. potential; main exp. bauxite (80 per cent of total exp. though recently declining); iron ore, timber, hydro-electr. oil; cap. Paramaribo; a. 163,265 sq. km; p.

(2004) 436,935.

Surinumu Dam, 48 km from Port Moresby, **Papua New Guinea;** part of hydroelectric scheme; opened 1963.

Surrey, non-met. co., S. **Eng.;** S. of R. Thames inc. part of N. Downs; serves as dormitory a. and recreational dist. for London; mkt. gardening, dairying; co. t. Guildford; p. (2001) 1,059,015.

Surrey Heath, l. gov. dist., Surrey, **Eng.;** based on Bagshot, Frimley and Camberley; p. (2001) 80,314.

Susa. See Sousse.

Susquehanna, R., N.Y., Penns., and Md., **USA;** flows to Chesapeake Bay through highly industl. a.; routeway W. from Philadelphia and Baltimore across Appalachian mtns.; not navigable; hydroelectric power; 675 km long.

Sussex. See East Sussex, and West Sussex.

Susten Pass, alpine road, alt. 2,225 m between Hasli Tal and Reuss valley, links Bernese Oberland with Gotthard road, **Switzerland.**

Sutherland, historic co., N.W. Scot., now part of Highland.

Sutlej, R., **Pakistan;** rises in the Himalayas and flows to the R. Indus; used for lge. scale irrigation; 1,600 km long.

Sutton, outer bor., Greater London, **Eng.;** inc. former bors. of Beddington and Wallington, Sutton and Cheam, and Carshalton; residtl.; p. (2001) 179,768.

Sutton Coldfield, t., West Midlands, **Eng.;** 10 km N.E. of Birmingham; residtl.; hardware, plastics; p. (2001) 105,452.

Sutton-in-Ashfield, t., Ashfield, Notts., **Eng.;** 5 km S.W. of Mansfield; lt. engin.; hosiery; former coalmng. dist.; p. (2001) 41,951.

Suva, c., cap. of **Fiji Is.;** on Viti Levu I.; fine harbour; exp. coconut prods., sugar; international airport; p. (1999) 196,000.

Suwalki, t. and prov., N.E. **Poland;** nr. Lithuanian bdy.; timber, grain, woollens; p. (1995) 66,198 (t.), 485,175 (prov.).

Suwannee, R., Fla., and Ga., **USA;** flows to G. of Mexico; known as Swanee River, 400 km long.

Suzhou (Soochow), c., Jiangsu, **China;** nr. Shanghai; former treaty pt.; p. (1994) 710,900.

Svalbard. See Spitsbergen.

Sverdlovsk See Yekaterinburg.

Swabia, historic region, mediaeval duchy, **Germany;** now forms part of Baden–Württemberg and Bavaria; contains Black Forest.

Swabian Alps, mtns., Baden–Württemberg, **Germany;** inc. the Swabian Jura range between valleys of Neckar and Danube.

Swadlincote, t., South Derbys., **Eng.;** 5 km E. of Burton-on-Trent; potteries; p. (2001) 39,322.

Swaffham, mkt. t., Breckland Norfolk, **Eng.;** fruit canning; p. (1991) 5,332.

Swale, R., North Yorks., **Eng.;** joins R. Ure; 96 km long.

Swale, l. gov. dist., mid Kent, **Eng.;** nr. Thames estuary inc. Sittingbourne, Faversham and I. of Sheppey; p. (2001) 122,801.

Swanage, mkt. t., Dorset, **Eng.;** on bay, E. cst. I. of Purbeck; seaside resort; p. (1991) 9,947.

Swansea, c., spt., **Wales;** on Swansea Bay; univ.; grew with exp. of coal; now imports minerals; copper and zinc refining; steel, aluminium, wire, plastics; unit. auth. created in 1996 from former l. gov. dists. of Lliw Valley and Swansea; inc. Gower Penin.; p. (1991) 171,083 (c.), (2001) 233,301 (unit. auth.).

Swatow. See Shantou.

Swaziland, indep. kingdom, S. Africa; within Brit. Commonwealth (1968), govt. based on tribal communities; bordered by S. Africa on S., W., and N. and by Mozambique on E.; four north-south regions; high, middle, low veld and Lebombo escarpment; rainfall increases with alt.; agr. basis of economy and sugar impt. exp., but iron-ore major exp.; asbestos mng., food processing inds.; cattle raising main internal activity; world's highest AIDS infection (39 % of population); cap. Mbabane; a. 17,363 km²; p. (2004) 1,169,241.

Sweden, kingdom, Scandinavia, N.W. Europe; divided for admin. purposes into 24 cos.; cap. c. Stockholm; mtnous. in N. and S. with central lowland belt containing major agr. a. and lge. proportion of p.; sm. home mkt. makes for dependency on exps., especially of mftg. products and minerals; inc. high-grade iron-ore from Kiruna and Malmberget, N. of Arctic circle; development of high-value science-based inds.;

furniture, porcelain and glass mnfs. have international reputation; social democratic st. since 1932; remained neutral in second world war; highly advanced system of social security; joined EU 1995; a. 449,792 km²; p. (2004) 8,986,400.

Swidnica (Schweidnitz), t., Walbrzych, **Poland** (since 1945); formerly in Lower Silesia; metals, elec. machin., leather, textiles; p. (1989) 62,424.

Swilly, Lough, N.E. Donegal, **R.o.I.**; arm of Atl. Oc. between Fanad Point and Dunaff Head; extends 40 km inland.

Swindon, t., unit. auth. created in 1997, formerly part of Wilts., **Eng.**; in upper Thames Valley (Vale of White Horse), 43 km S.W. of Oxford; impt. rly. junc.; rly. workshops closed (1986); Railway Heritage Control mint. for local dist., heavy engin., textiles, tobacco; expanded, fast growing t.; one of largest housing projects in Europe; ctr. for micro-electronics inds.; p. (2001) 180,051.

Swinoujscie (Swinemünde), spt., N.W. **Poland** (since 1945); formerly in Pomerania; on I. of Usedom (Uznam), Baltic Sea; spt. for Szczecin; spa and summer resort; fishing; p. (1995) 43,175.

Swinton and Pendlebury, ts., Gtr. Manchester, **Eng.**; 8 km W. of Manchester; cotton spinning, engin.; p. (2001) 41,347.

Switzerland, confederation, central Europe; landlocked mtnous. st. with major physical features dominated by Alpine mtn. system; divided into 26 cantons and half-cantons for purposes of govt.; 3 official languages; German (72 per cent), French (20 per cent), Italian (6 per cent) in addition to Romansch; like Norway, major natural resource is water power; industl. specialisation on precision engin., especially watch and clock mnfs.; agr. in valleys with impt. output of dairy prod., transhumance between mtn. pastures and valley bottoms; tourism provides valuable source of income; neutral; became 190th member of the UN (2002); cap. Berne; a. 41,310 km²; p. (2004) 7,850,467 (1·3m foreign residents).

Sydney, c., cap. of N.S.W., **Australia**; pt. and c. built around natural harbour of Pt. Jackson, crossed by S. Harbour Bridge and bordered bymany impt. bldgs. and parks (Opera House, Government bldgs.); one of best harbours on E. cst., pt. developed with improved transport; site of first European settlement; contains 61 per cent of state p., 22 per cent of Australia's p.; covers vast a. as suburbs grow rapidly; caths., 3 univs., airpt. on Botany Bay where heavy inds. developing; services most impt. employment; hosted 2000 Olympics; p. (1993) 3,713,500 (met. a.).

Syktyvkar, c., Komi, aut. rep., **Russia**; R. pt. on Vychegda R.; shipyds., sawmilling, engin.; cultural ctr. of Komi people; p. (1989) 232,000.

Sylhet, t., **Bangladesh**; on Surma R. in tea growing dist.; fertilisers; p. (1991) 169,000.

Syracuse. *See* Siracusa.

Syracuse, c., N.Y., **USA**; on Erie Barge canal; impt. industl. ctr. for chemicals, electronics, machin.; formerly salt-producing ctr.; univ.; p. (1990) 163,860 (c.), 660,000 (met. a.).

Syr Darya, one of main Rs. of central Asia; formed in Ferghana Valley in **Uzbekistan**; flows through **Tajikistan** and **Kazakhstan** to Aral Sea; not navigable but used for irrigation and hydroelectric power; 2,400 km long.

Syria (Syrian Arab Rep.), S.W. Asia; on E. cst. Mediterranean; much of a. mtnous. and semidesert; climate hot, but cold winters in highland interior; 32 per cent p. engaged in agr. which provides 20 per cent nat. income; mainly pastoral, but grains, fruit and cotton grown in well watered Euphrates R. valley and along cst.; oil exp. since 1968; phosphate mines in Palmyra a.; textiles, food processing in Aleppo and cap. Damascus; a. 187,086 km²; p. (2004) 18,016,874.

Syros or **Syra**, I., one of Cyclades, Aegean Sea, S. **Greece**; heath-covered; most populous of Cyclades; ch. t. Hermoupolis.

Syzran, c., **Russia**; impt. R. pt. on Volga nr. confluence with Syzran R.; rly. ctr.; engin., oil refining; p. (1990) 174,000.

Szczecin (Stettin), c., N.W. **Poland** (since 1945); formerly cap. of Prussian prov. of Pomerania; impt. spt. at mouth of R. Oder; deep-sea fishing base; shipbldg., metallurgy, engin., chemicals, technical univ.; p. (1995) 419,272.

Szczecin, prov., **Poland**; borders Baltic Sea; drained by R. Oder; mainly agr.; a. 31,339 km²; p. (1995) 989,674.

Szechwan. *See* Sichuan.

Szeged, t., **Hungary**; nr. confluence of Rs. Tisza and Maros; anc. R. pt. destroyed by floods 1879, since rebuilt; p. (1997) 166,000.

Szekesfehérvár, t., **Hungary**; nr. Budapest; mkt. t., with aluminium and metal inds., food processing; known since Roman times; once cap. of Hungarian kings; p. (1997) 106,000.

Szeping. *See* Siping.

Szombathely, t., W. **Hungary**; rly. ctr.; agr. machin., textiles, shoes; birthplace of St. Martin of Tours (c. A.D. 316); p. (1997) 84,000.

T

Tabasco, coastal st., **Mexico**; on Bay of Campeche, low-lying; rapid development with drainage of swamps; cash crops of cacao, coffee, sugar, tobacco; major petroleum deposits aiding industl. development; cap. Villa Hermosa; a. 25,335 km²; p. (1990) 1,501,183.

Table Bay, inlet of Atl., cst. of C. of Good Hope, **S. Africa**; site of Cape Town.

Table Mountain, Western Cape Prov., **S. Africa**; nr. Cape Town; alt. 1,082 m.

Tabor, t., **Czech Rep.**; S. of Prague, on R. Luznice; rly. junc.; textiles, tobacco; p. (1984) 33,757.

Tabora, t., central **Tanzania**, E. Africa; at junc. of rlys. from Dar es Salaam and L. Victoria; p. (1985) 134,000.

Tabriz, c., **Iran**; cap. of Azerbaijan; metal inds., carpets, leather, soap; famous blue mosque; univ.; impt. oil refining ctr.; p. (1994) 1,166,000.

Tachira, st., **Venezuela**; mtnous. inland st. bordering Colombia; coffee; cap. San Cristobal; a. 11,100 km²; p. (1990) 859,861.

Tacna, t., cap. of Tacna prov., **Peru**; in fertile valley of mtnous. region; agr. t.; p. (1990) 150,200.

Tacna, prov. and t., **Peru**; mtnous. and arid, some irrigated valleys; transferred from Chile by treaty 1929; subject to earthquakes; a. 12,769 km²; p. (1993), 218,353 (prov), 174,335 (t.).

Tacoma, spt., Wash., **USA**; on Puget Sound; shipping, fishing; grew with Alaskan and Pac. tr.; port inds. and agr. processing; p. (2000) 193,556 (c.), 586,000 (met. a.).

Tadoussac, v., Quebec, **Canada**; on R. Saguenay, where it enters St. Lawrence R.; tourist ctr.; settlement dates from 1599; p. (1986) 838.

Taegu, c., **S. Korea**; textiles; p. (1990) 2,228,834.

Taejon, t., **S. Korea**; S. of Seoul; fish, petroleum; p. (1990) 1,062,084

Taff, R., S.Wales; rises in Brecon Beacons, flows S.E. across coalfield to Bristol Channel at Cardiff; 64 km long.

Taganrog, c., **Russia**; spt. on Sea of Azov; iron and steel, engin.; site of fortress founded by Peter the Great 1698; birthplace of Chekhov; p. (1989) 292,000.

Tagliamento, R., N.E. **Italy**; rises in Carnic Alps, flows W. into Adriatic; 160 km long.

Tagus, R., **Spain** and **Portugal**; rises in E. Spain and flows across the Meseta to Atl. Oc. at Lisbon where there is a magnificent bridge; its estuary forms one of the finest harbours in Europe.

Tahiti, ch. I., Society Is., **Fr. Polynesia**; contains Papeete, main admin. ctr. of Fr. Oceania; fertile alluvial belt; exp. copra, phosphates, vanilla; tourism; a. 1,041 km²; p. (1983) 115,820.

Taichow. *See* Taizhou.

Taichung, t., co., **Taiwan**; agr. mkt.; food processing; p. (1995) 655,196 (c.), 849,549 (co.).

Tai Hu, L., Jiangsu, **China**; focus of intensive system of small canals and waterways, 96 km N. of Shanghai; a. c. 260 km².

Taimyr Peninsula, N. cst., Siberia, **Russia**; terminates with C. Chelyuskin; occupies most of Taimyr National Area, inhabited by nomadic Samoyeds; p. (1986) 54,000.

Tainan, t., co., S.W. cst. of **Taiwan**; former cap.; univ.; p. (1995) 705,940 (c.), 705,940 (co.).

Taipei, c., co., cap. of **Taiwan**; on cst. plain in N. Taiwan, nucleus of major industl. a.; major transport ctr.; international airpt.; univ.; p. (1995) 2,639,283 (c.), 3,297,579 (co.).

Taiwan (Formosa), I., off cst. of S.E. China; beautiful I. with intensive agr. on W. cst.; most densely populated cty. in the world; part of Japan 1895–1945; returned to China 1945;

occupied by Nationalist government after 1949; growing political isolation; USA aid has built growth economy, textiles, plastics, electronics exp. to USA esp.; earthquake devastation, 1999; cap. Taipei; a. 35,975 km²; p. (2004) 22,749,838.

Taiyüan, c., cap. of Shanxi prov., N. **China;** on Fen R.; walled c.; univ.; ctr. of rapid industl. development; integrated iron and steel plant; chemicals, machin., paper, textiles; p. (1994) 1,642,000.

Tajikistan, CIS, former constituent rep., USSR; borders China and Afghanistan; mainly mtnous., inc. Pamirs and Turkestan and part of highly cultivated Ferghana Valley; cattle breeding; cotton main cash crop; impt. oil and hydroelec. power resources; armed Islamic insurgency since 1993; cap. Dushanbe; a. 144,263 km²; p. (2004) 7,011,556.

Takamatsu, t., **Japan;** N. cst. Shikoku; ferry terminal; univ.; tourism; p. (1990) 329,684.

Takasaki, t., Honshu, **Japan;** radiation chemistry research ctr.; textiles; p. (1990) 236,463.

Taklimakan Shamo, desert, W. **China;** basin of inland drainage; home of the Turko people; surrounded by a ring of oases.

Takoradi. See **Sekondi-Takoradi.**

Talavera de la Reina, t., Toledo prov., central **Spain;** on Tagus R.; ceramics; scene of battle 1809; p. (1990) 69,200.

Talca, t., cap. of Maule region., **Chile;** S. of Santiago; lge. mftg. ctr.; matches, footwear, paper, and flour mills, foundries; p. (1992) 171,467.

Talcahuano, spt., **Chile,** nr. Concepción; naval sta.; steel plant at Huachipato; fish processing, oil refining; p. (1992) 246,566.

Talien. See **Lushun.**

Tallahassee, t., Fla., **USA;** univ.; timber-based inds.; p. (1996) 136,812.

Tallinn, spt., cap. of **Estonia;** on G. of Finland; diverse inds. inc. radio equipment; mediaeval architecture; p. (2000) 408,300. Formerly known as Revel.

Tamale, t., cap. of Kaduna st., **Ghana,** W. Africa; admin. ctr., cotton milling, peanut processing; p. (1984) 83,653.

Tamar, R., Devon and Cornwall, **Eng.;** flows S. to Plymouth Sound; 72 km long.

Tamatave, See **Toamasina.**

Tamaulipas, st., **Mexico;** on G. of Mexico, S. of Texas; petroleum is main resource; fishing along lagoon cst.; cotton, livestock; cap. Ciudad Victoria; a. 79,593 km²; p. (1990) 2,244,208.

Tambov, c., cap. of Tambov oblast, **Russia;** on Tsna R.; regional ctr. serving agr. dist.; engin.; p. (1989) 305,000.

Tameside, met. dist., Gtr. Manchester, **Eng.;** comprises Dukinfield, Ashton-under-Lyne, Hyde and Mossley; p. (2001) 213,043.

Tamil Nadu (formerly **Madras**), st., **India;** on S.E. cst. of peninsula; home of Tamils; crossed by R. Cauvery; dry crops; acute water shortages relieved by water and sewerage development plan; ch. ts. Madras (Chennai), Madura; a. 130,357 km²; p. (2001) 62,110,800.

Tampa, c., Fla., **USA;** popular winter resort, cigar factories, phosphates, electronics; fruit growing and canning; p. (2000) 303,447 (c.), 2,067,959 (met. a. with St. Petersburg-Clearwater).

Tampere (**Tammerfors**), t., S. **Finland;** on rly. between Helsinki and Vaasa; textiles, leather, paper, based on local hydroelec. power; cath.; airport; p. (1993) 176,149.

Tampico, spt., **Mexico;** on R. Panuco, 14 km from G. of Mexico; exp. petroleum; oil refining, fish processing, chemicals; tourism; p. (1990) 271,636.

Tamworth, t., N.S.W., **Australia;** impt. service and shopping ctr. for N. Tablelands; p. (1991) 31,700.

Tamworth, t., l. gov. dist., Staffs., **Eng.;** on R. Tame, 8 km S.E. of Lichfield; Anc. cas.; lt. engin.; expanded t.; p. (2001) 80,000 (dist.).

Tana, lge. freshwater L., N.W. **Ethiopia,** nr. Gondar; source of Blue Nile, surrounded by marsh, papyrus swamp.

Tana, R., **Kenya;** rises nr. Mt. Kenya and flows to Indian Oc.; impt. elephant habitat in valley; 5 major hydro-elect. sta.; 800 km long.

Tananarive. See **Antananarivo.**

Tandridge, l. gov. dist., Surrey, **Eng.;** S. of Gtr. London, inc. Caterham and Godstone; p. (2001) 79,267.

Tanga, spt., **Tanzania,** E. Africa; on plateau overlooking Tanga Bay; rly. terminus; new plywood plant; p. (1988) 187,634.

Tanganyika, gr. L., E. **Central Africa;** lies in Gt. Rift Valley; c. 672 km long, 24–32 km wide; second lgst. L. in Africa and except for L. Baykal deepest L. in world; c. 823 m a.s.l.; discovered by Burton and Speke 1858, explored by Livingstone and Stanley 1871.

Tangier, free pt., **Morocco,** N. Africa; on Strait of Gibraltar; no longer internationalised zone but integral part of kingdom of Morocco; summer cap.; shipyard; cigarettes, fishing; p. (1994) 627,963.

Tangshan, c., Hebei prov., **China;** impt. industl. ctr.; steel, machin.; textiles, cement, oil refining; devastated by a series of earthquakes (1976); p. (1994) 1,110,000.

Tanta, t., Lower **Egypt;** 88 km N. of Cairo; impt. rly. junc.; religious fairs; cotton processing; univ. proposed; p. (1986) 334,505.

Tanzania, rep., E. cst. Africa; inc. Is. of Zanzibar and Pemba, united since 1964; narrow coastal plain rises to inland plateau (Mt. Kilimanjaro, 5,895 m, hgst. peak in Africa); climate varies with alt., tropical in Zanzibar, temperate inland; predominantly subsistence agr., maize, millet, groundnuts, livestock; comm. crops inc. sisal, sugar, cotton, coffee; cloves on Is., especially Pemba; food processing, textile inds.; 5-year planning system to assist economic development; 12 National Parks (inc. Serengeti); old cap. Dar es Salaam; new cap. Dodoma (since 1974); a. 939,706 km²; p. (2004) 36,588,225.

Taormina, resort, E. Sicily, **Italy;** 230 m above sea at foot of Mt. Etna; magnificent scenery and anc. ruins.

Tapachula, c., Chiapas st., S. **Mexico;** on Pac. cst. lowlands; comm. ctr. for agr. dist.; p. (1990) 222,282.

Taranaki, reg., N.I., **N.Z.;** impt. stock rearing and dairying a.; offshore oil and gas fields; a. 9,713 km²; p. (1991) 107,222.

Taranto, t., Lecce, **Italy;** on G. of Taranto, inlet of Ionian Sea; maritime arsenal with gr. comm. and industl. interests; strong cas.; steel wks.; cement; oil refinery; famous for its oyster and mussel fisheries; p. (1992) 230,207.

Tarapacá, region, N. **Chile;** cap. Iquique; hot, arid desert; nitrate deposits; a. 55,270 km²; p. (1992) 341,112.

Tarascon, t., Bouches-du-Rhône dep., **France;** connected by bridges with Beaucaire on opposite bank of R. Rhône; old cas., famous festival; p. (1999) 12,640.

Tarawera Mtn., volcanic peak, N.I., **N.Z.;** 305 m; in Hot Springs dist.; eruption 1886 destroyed L. Rotomahana (water later returned to form bigger and deeper L.).

Tarbes, t., cap. of Hautes-Pyrénées dep., **France;** on R. Adour; cath.; p. (1999) 46,275.

Tarifa, sm. t., **Spain;** on Gibraltar Strait; most S. point of mainland of Europe; fish tr., cereals, oranges, wines.

Tarija, dep. **Bolivia;** part of Gran Chaco rising to W.; extensive agr. and forests; cap. T.; a. 64,196 km²; p. (1988) 246,000.

Tarija, t., cap. of T. prov., **Bolivia;** alt. 1,906 m; cath., univ.; mkt. t.; p. (1992) 90,000.

Tarim Basin, depression, Xinjiang, **China;** desert with oases; crossed by Silk Road; anc. civilisation; state farms for wheat, millet, maize, cotton; major discovery of gas (2003).

Tarn, dep., S. **France;** watered by Tarn and its tribs.; between Central Massif and basin of Aquitaine; mainly agr.; cap. Albi; a. 5,781 km²; p. (1999) 342,650.

Tarn, R., **France;** trib. of R. Garonne; rocky gorge 50 km long in its upper course; 376 km long.

Tarn-et-Garonne, dep., W. **France;** alluvial plain formed by Rs. Tarn, Garonne and Aveyron; mainly agr.; cap. Montauban; a. 3,730 km²; p. (1995) 206,005.

Tarnobrzeg, t. and prov., S.E. **Poland;** sulphur mng. and processing; p. (1995) 50,656 (t.), 609,097 (prov.).

Tarnow, t. and prov., **Poland;** E. of Kraków; industl. ctr.; lge. nitrogen factory; synthetic fibres, metallurgy; cath.; p. (1995) 121,521 (t.), 691,648 (prov.).

Tarpon Springs, t., Fla., **USA;** pt.; main source of sponges in USA.

Tarragona, prov., **Spain;** on Mediterranean,

vineyards and agr.; cap. Tarragona; a. 6,283 km²; p. (1998) 580,200.

Tarragona, spt., cap. of T. prov., **Spain**; at mouth of R. Francoli; exp. agr. prod. of Ebro valley; cath.; many Roman remains, inc. aqueduct; liqueur; p. (1998) 112,800.

Tarsus, anc. c., S. **Turkey**; nr. Adana; orange and citrus groves; ruined Roman temple; birthplace of St. Paul; p. (1990) 168,654.

Tartu c., **Estonia**; pt. on Emayygi R.; rly. junc.; famous univ. founded 1632; agr. machin., tobacco ind.; p. (1991) 115,300.

Tashkent, c., cap. of **Uzbekistan**; cultural, industl. and scientific ctr. of central Asia; on Trans-Caspian rly. in fertile Ferghana valley; univ., diverse inds.; terminus of gas pipeline; p. (2001) 2,160,000.

Tasman Bay, lge inlet, S I N Z.; penetrates N. cst., between Separation Point and D'Urville I.; enclosed by mtns., sheltered, fertile, coastal fringe; ch. ts. Nelson, Motueka; gives name to dist.; p. (1991) 36,416.

Tasman Glacier, S.I., **N.Z.**; one of lgst. in the world.

Tasmania (formerly **Van Diemen's Land**), I., st., **Australia**; smallest and least populous st. of Australia, second to be colonised (in 1803); mountainous with rugged cst.; temperate climate aids hydro-electric development and consequent rapid industl. ex-pansion; plans for hydro-electric sta. on Franklin R. to help relieve high unemployment but fiercely opposed because of region's rare and striking natural beauty; 9 Nat. Parks; mng.; pastoral agr.; for-estry; cap. Hobart; a. 67,897 km²; p. (1996) 459,700.

Tasman Sea, Australia; part of Pac. Oc. between Australia and New Zealand.

Tatar, aut. rep., **Russia**; in middle Volga valley; wooded steppeland; extensive oil deposits and natural gas fields; cap. Kazan; now asserting independence; a. 67,988 km²; p. (1999) 4,000,000.

Tatra Mtns., highest mtn. gr. of W. Carpathians, on border of **Slovakia** and **Poland**; highest peak Gerlach in Slovakia, 2,664 m; mountaineering and winter sports.

Tatung. See Datong.

Taunton, co. t., Somerset, **Eng.**; on R. Tone at W. end of Vale of Taunton; old cas.; with Wellington forms l. gov. dist. of **Taunton Deane**; p. (2001) 102,299 (dist.), (1991) 55,856 (t.).

Taunton, t., Mass., **USA**; cotton, iron foundries, machin., plastics; p. (1980) 45,001.

Taunus, mtn. range, Hesse, **Germany**; between Rs. Lahn and Rhine and Main; vineyards and spas.

Taupo, L., N.I., **N.Z.**; lgst. L. in N.Z.; geysers, hot springs in vicinity; 40 km by 27 km; gives name to dist.; p. (1991) 30,721.

Taurus Mtns., range, S. **Turkey**; rise to 3,660 m.

Tavastehus. See Hämeenlinna.

Tavistock, mkt. t., West Devon, **Eng.**; on R. Tavy; anc. stannary t.; Drake born nearby; p. (1991) 10,222.

Taw, R., Devon, **Eng.**; flows from Dartmoor to Barnstaple Bay; 80 km long.

Tawe, R., S. **Wales**; flows into Swansea Bay; 104 km long.

Taxco, t., **Mexico**; alt. 1,700 m; gold- and silver-mng.; tourist ctr.; anc. Aztec t.; p. (1990) 86,811.

Taxila, ruined c., **Pakistan**; nr. Rawalpindi; anc. seat of learning; ruins of Buddhist univ.

Tay, R., Scot.; flows S.E. from Loch Tay in Perth and Kinross, to Firth of Tay; longest R. in Scot., 188 km; salmon fisheries.

Tay, Firth of, lge. inlet, E. cst. Scot.; extends inland almost to Perth.

Tayport, burgh, Fife, Scot.; at entrance to Firth of Tay; opposite Broughty Ferry; linen, jute; p. (2002) 3,847.

Tbilisi (Tiflis), c., **Georgia**; route ctr. on Kura R.; major admin., economic and cultural ctr. of Transcaucasia; machin., textiles, tanneries, furniture, food processing; power from hydroelectric power stas.; anc. tr. ctr.; some mediaeval fragments in c. ctr.; p. (2000) 1,310,000 (met. a.).

Team Valley, Tyne and Wear, **Eng.**; impt. trading estate.

Tebessa, t., dep., N.E. **Algeria**; in Atlas mtns., at 851 m; mkt.; carpets; phosphate deposits nearby; p. (1987) 107,559 (t.), 409,317 (dep.).

Tees, R., N. **Eng.**; rises on Cross Fell, Cumbria, flows E. to N. Sea between Hartlepool and Redcar; heavy inds. in lower section; 112 km long.

Teesdale, l. gov. dist., Durham, **Eng.**; Pennine a.

inc. Barnard Castle; p. (2001) 24,457.

Teesport, oil refinery, between Redcar and Middlesbrough, Redcar and Cleveland, **Eng.**

Teesside, former admin. dist., N.E. **Eng.**; inc. Middlesbrough, Redcar, Thornaby-on-Tees, Stockton-on-Tees, Billingham, and Eston.

Tegal, spt., Java, **Indonesia**; textiles, sugar refining; lge. dam nearby; p. (1995) 313,000.

Tegucigalpa, c., cap. of **Honduras**; on R. Choluteca at 976 m; inter-ocean highway connects with Caribbean and Pac. Oc.; former ctr. of silver mng.; inc. Comayagüela, the modern part of c., where the nat. univ. is situated; p. (2000) 950,000.

Tehran (Tehran), c., cap. of **Iran** 112 km S. of Caspian Sea; mftg. and comm. ctr.; modern bldgs.; gas pipeline to north; international airpt.; univ.; car assembly, textiles, chemicals, glass; new oil refinery; ctr. for more than 90 per cent of all industl. firms in Iran; p. (2000) 7,225,000.

Tehuantepec, Isthmus of, separates G. of Mexico from Pac. Oc. at narrowest point of **Mexico**; width 200 km.

Teifi, R., S. **Wales**; rises in Cambrian mtns., flows S.W. to Cardigan Bay; 150 km long.

Teign, R., Devon, **Eng.**; flows to sea at pt. of Teignmouth from Dartmoor; picturesque estuary; 48 km long.

Teignbridge, l. gov. dist., S. Devon, **Eng.**; lower T. valley and ts. of Dawlish, Teignmouth, Newton Abbot and Ashburton; p. (2001) 120,958.

Teignmouth, t., Teignbridge, Devon, **Eng.**; at mouth of R. Teign, 21 km S. of Exeter; resort; revival of pt. with ball clay exp.; p. (1991) 13,528.

Tekirdag, t. and prov., **Turkey**; on Sea of Marmara, W. of Istanbul; former Greek settlement; p. (1985) 63,215 (t.), (1990) 468,842 (prov.).

Tel Aviv-Jaffa, c., **Israel**; on Mediterranean; lgst. c. of cty.; financial and cultural ctr.; univ.; founded by Zionists 1909; p. (1992) 353,200.

Telemark, co., **Norway**; borders Skagerrak; mtnous., lake-covered, much forested; hydroelectric power forms basis for electrochemical inds.; a. 15,118 km²; p. (1990) 162,869.

Telford, new t. (1963), Shropshire, **Eng.**; 32 km W. of Wolverhampton; part of **Telford and Wrekin**, unit. auth. p. (2001) 158,325 (unit. auth.); (2001) 40,437 (c.).

Tellicherry (**Thalassery**), t., spt., Kerala, **India**; exp. pepper; lge. college; furniture; p. (1991) 103,600.

Tema, pt. (opened 1962), nr. Accra, **Ghana**; deepwater harbour, oil refinery, aluminium smelter; impt. industl. development; p. (1996) 200,000.

Teme, R., on border of Wales and Hereford and Worcs., **Eng.**; trib. of R. Severn; 112 km long.

Temir-Tau, c., **Kazakhstan**; on Nura R.; industl. ctr.; iron, steel, synthetic rubber, soda; lge. thermal power sta.; p. (1990) 213,100.

Temuco, c., cap. of Araucania region., **Chile**; cath.; tr. in cereals, apples, timber; Araucanian Indian mkt.; p. (1992) 240,880.

Tenasserim, div., lower **Myanmar**; on Thailand border; extends along Isthmus of Kra; tin and rubber; a. 92,945 km². p. (1983) 917,628.

Tenby, mkt. t., Pembrokeshire, **Wales**; on W. side of Carmarthen Bay, Bristol Channel; seaside resort; walled cas. t.; p. (1991) 5,619.

Tendring, l. gov. dist., E. Essex, **Eng.**; inc. cstl. ts. of Harwich, Frinton, Clacton and Brightlingsea; p. (2001) 138,539.

Tenerife, I., Canary Is.; volcanic landscapes and mild climate attracts tourists; cap. Santa Cruz; a. 2,025 km².

Tennessee, R., Tenn., Ky., **USA**; lgst. and most impt. branch of Ohio R.; valley once liable to flooding, now controlled by dams, and improved by the Tenn. Valley Authority; 1,251 km long.

Tennessee, st., **USA**; "Volunteer State."; admitted to Union 1796; st. flower Iris, st. bird Mockingbird; rises to Appalachians in E., crossed by Tennessee R. and tribs.; a. of heavy rainfall and severe soil erosion necessitated the public Tenn. Valley Authority scheme of conservation, dam bldg., and afforestation; cap. Nashville; a. 109,412 km²; p. (2002) 5,797,289.

Tenterden, mkt. t., Kent, **Eng.**; 13 km N. of Rye; grew with wool tr., church with famous tower; p. (1991) 6,803.

Tepic, c., cap. of Nayarit st., **Mexico,** comm. ctr. for agr. dist.; nr. Sanguaney volcano; p. (1990) 238,101.

Teramo, c., cap. of T. prov., **Italy;** 24 km from Adriatic; route and agr. ctr.; cath.; textiles; the anc. Interamnium; p. (1981) 51,092.

Teresina, t., cap. of Piauí st., **Brazil;** comm. ctr.; lt. inds.; p. (1991) 598,449.

Teresópolis, t., Rio de Janeiro, **Brazil;** health resort; textiles; p. (1996) 122,600.

Terni, t., Perugia, **Italy;** among the Apennines; iron and steel wks., arms factory; cath.; p. (1992) 108,150.

Ternopol (Tarnopol), t., **Ukraine;** E. of Lvov; rly. junc., mkt.; agr. machin., food inds.; p. (1990) 211,600.

Terrassa, t., Barcelona, **Spain;** p. (1998) 165,600.

Terre Adélie, part of Fr. Antarctic terr., S. **Indian Oc.;** research stn.; est. a. 424,400 km².

Terre Haute, t., Ind., **USA;** coal, natural gas, flour, paper, glass, foundries; p. (1996) 54,585.

Teruel, t., cap. of Teruel prov., **Spain;** on R. Turia; walled t., cath.; p. (1990) 28,500 (t.), (1998) 136,800 (prov.).

Test Valley, l. gov. dist., W. Hants., **Eng.;** stretches from Andover to Romsey; p. (2001) 109,801.

Tetovo, t., **Macedonia,** formerly Yugoslavia; chemicals, electro-metallurgy, textiles; p. (2000) 200,000 (30 % Albanian).

Tetuan, ch. spt., **Morocco,** N. Africa; walled t. p. (1994) 537,290.

Teviot, R., Borders, **Scot.;** trib. of R. Tweed; 59 km long.

Tewkesbury, mkt. t., l. gov. dist., Gloucs., **Eng.;** on R. Avon, close to confluence with R. Severn; Norman abbey; p. (2001) 76,405 (dist.), (1991) 9,488 (t.).

Texarkana, t., Texas and Ark., **USA;** bdy. passes down middle of main street; timber and cotton; total p. (1984) 32,900 (t.), 118,500 (met. a.).

Texas, st., S.W. **USA;** "Lone Star St."; admitted to Union 1845; st. flower Bluebonnet, st. bird Mocking bird; second lgst. st. by a.; borders Mexico; dry plains in W., humid cst. in E.; problems of soil erosion yet leading agr. st.; leading producer of petroleum and natural gas; cap. Austin; a. 692,408 km²; p. (2002) 21,779,893.

Texel, one of the W. Frisian Is., **Neth.;** scene of several naval battles; p. (1991) 12,726.

Thailand (Siam), kingdom, S.E. Asia; 4 main regions; parallel N.–S. hill ranges (2,400 m) and valleys in N. producing teak; rice growing, fertile plain of Chao Phraya R. in ctr.; thinly populated E. plateau, drained by Mekong; S. coastal strip on G. of Siam; monsoon climate; predominantly agr., accounting for 60 per cent of p. and 60 per cent of exports; fifth lgst. exporter of foodstuffs in the world, mainly rice, tapioca, rubber and maize to USA, Japan & Singapore esp.; desire to conserve rainforest now resulting in the intensification of agr.; recent offshore gas discoveries; mnfg. development centres on cap. Bangkok; tourism and fishery increasingly impt.; a. 519,083 km²; p. (2004) 64,865,523.

Thailand, G. of, lge. inlet, S. China Sea; sheltered with shallow water; length 616 km N.W. to S.E.

Thame, mkt. t., South Oxford, **Eng.;** on R. Thame, 11 km S.W. of Aylesbury; p. (1991) 10,866.

Thames, R., **Eng.;** rises in Cotswold hills and flows past Oxford, Reading, Windsor, and London to the N. Sea; tribs. inc. Windrush, Cherwell, Thame, Kennet, Colne, Lea, and Roding; estuary impt. industl. a. with many oil refineries; flood barrier at Silvertown in Woolwich (1983), 336 km long; major regeneration of Thames Gateway area now proposed.

Thameshaven, lge. oil refinery, Essex, **Eng.;** on N. cst. of Thames estuary 13 km below Tilbury.

Thane (Thana), t., Maharashtra, **India;** textiles, chemicals; p. (1991) 803,000.

Thanet, I. of, lge. promontory, N.E. extremity of Kent, **Eng.;** formed by bifurcation of R. Stour; also forms l. gov. dist. of **Thanet,** inc. Margate, Ramsgate, and Broadstairs; p. (2001) 126,702.

Thanjavur, t., Tamil Nadu, **India;** silks, carpets, jewellery, inlaid metals; impt. Brahman ctr.; p. (1991) 202,013.

Thar Desert, on bdy. of **India** and **Pakistan;** covers slopes between N.W. Deccan and R. Indus; barren, lack of Rs. or level land prevents irrigation; crossed by caravan routes.

Thebes, c., of Boeotia, in anc. **Greece;** Mycenaean

site; destroyed by Alexander the Great 335 B.C.; modern c. of Thivai on site; p. (1981) 18,712.

Thebes, c. of anc. **Egypt;** on banks of Nile; site now partly occupied by vs. Karnak and Luxor; archeological discoveries in Valley of the Kings 1922, inc. tomb of Tutankhamun.

Thermopylae, celebrated pass between Mt. Oeta and the sea, N.E. **Greece;** heroic battle between Spartans and Persians 480 B.C.

Thessaloniki, c., **Greece;** spt. at head of G. of T.; with fiscal free zone; second c. of Greece; impt. route and industl. ctr.; univ.; p. (1991) 383,967.

Thessaly, prov., central **Greece;** fertile plain drained by R. Piniós; mainly agr.; a. 13,489 km²; p. (1991) 734,846.

Thetford, t., Breckland, Norfolk, **Eng.;** on Little Ouse; industl. estate for London overspill; fruit and vegetable canning, pulp mftg., engin.; p. (2001) 21,760.

Thienen (Tirlemont), t., Brabant prov., **Belgium;** ctr. of Belgian beet-sugar refining; captured by Marlborough 1705; p. (1991) 32,600.

Thimphu, t., cap. **Bhutan;** hydroelectric plant; 176 km road link to Phuntsholing (Sikkim) 1968; p. (1995) 22,000.

Thionville, t., Moselle dep., N. **France;** in Lorraine ironfield conurb.; metallurgical and chemical inds.; p. (1990) 40,835 (t.), 132,413 (met.).

Thira (Santorine), volcanic I., Cyclades, **Greece;** wine prods.; max. alt. 567 m; a. 75 km².

Thirlmere, L., Cumbria, **Eng.;** 5 km long; furnishes part of water supply of Manchester.

Thirsk, mkt. t., Hambleton, North Yorks., **Eng.;** in wide gap between Pennines and Cleveland Hills, 11 km S.E. of Northallerton; racecourse; p. (1991) 6,860.

Thompson, R., B.C., **Canada;** trib. of R. Fraser; forms impt. routeway through Rocky mtns.; 448 km long.

Thon Buri, c., **Thailand;** on R. Menam opposite Bangkok; second c. of T.; former cap., "Temple of Dawn"; p. (1991) 264,201.

Thornaby-on-Tees. See Teesside.

Thornbury, mkt. t., S. Gloucs., **Eng.;** 16 km N. of Bristol; aircraft mftg.; expanded t.; Oldbury Magnox nuclear power sta.; p. (1991) 12,108.

Thornton Cleveleys, t., Wyre, Lancs., **Eng.;** 6 km N.E. of Blackpool; resort; p. (2001) 31,157.

Thórshavn, c., on Stromo I.; cap. of **Faroe Is.;** anc. fortress; lighthouse; p. (1986) 15,287.

Thousand Isles, gr. of over 1,500 Is. in St. Lawrence R. which extend up-river for c. 48 km from Brockville to Gananoque, at junc. of L. Ont. and St. Lawrence R.; partly in N.Y. st. and partly in Canada.

Thrace, anc. name of terr. in S.E. Europe, part of which has been added to **Greece;** successively under Macedonian, Roman, Byzantine, and Turkish rule, before passing to Greece; consists of districts of Euros, Rhodope, Xanthi, tobacco, a. 8,586 km²; p. of dep. (1991) 338,005.

Three Gorges Dam (China). On Yangtze R., the largest planned dam in the world (1·3 miles long, 610 feet high). It will hold 39·3 billion cubic metres of water. Completion due, 2009; electricity production began, 2003. Many environmentalists have expressed major concerns.

Three Rivers, l. gov. dist., S.W. Herts., **Eng.;** close to London and inc. Rickmansworth and Chorleywood; p. (2001) 82,848.

Thule (Qaanaaq), N.W. **Greenland;** 1,600 km from N. Pole; American air base and site of ballistic missile early warning sta.; spt. open 2–3 months per annum; p. (1990) 846.

Thumba, Kerala, **India;** space science and technological ctr.

Thun, L., Berne can., **Switzerland;** occupies valleys of R. Aare where it leaves Alpine region; separated from L. Brienz by deltaic neck of land on which is Interlaken; a. 48 km².

Thun, t., Berne, **Switzerland;** on N.W. end of L. Thun; cas. on hill above t.; p. (1990) 38,124.

Thunder Bay, t., Ontario **Canada;** formed from Port Arthur and Port William; pt. on N.W. cst. of L. Superior; grain exp. ctr.; p. (1991) 113,746 (c.), (1996) 125,562 (met. a.).

Thurgau, can., N.E. **Switzerland;** on L. Constance, bordered by R. Rhine; prosperous agr. a.; inds. ass. with textiles; cap. Frauenfeld; a. 1,005 km²; p. (1990) 205,900.

Thuringia, Land, **Germany;** bordered by Bavaria, Saxony-Anhalt, Lower Saxony, and Hesse; drained by Rs. Saale and Werra; crossed by Thüringer Wald and extending to Harz mtns.; fertile arable agr. a.; cap. Erfurt; pop. (2005) 2,390,000.

Thuringian Forest or **Thüringer Wald**, forested range of hills **Germany**; rising to 982 m in Beerberg; famous for romantic scenery and legends; resorts.

Thurles, mkt. t., Tipperary, **R.o.I.**; on R. Suir; agr. processing; cath., cas.; p. (1986) 7,049.

Thurrock, t., unit. auth. Essex, **Eng.**; on Thames, nr. Tilbury; oil refining, metal refining, cement, paper board; new container port planned; p. (2001) 143,128 (unit. auth.).

Thurso, burgh, Highland, **Scot.**; nr. Dounreay; anc. stronghold of Vikings; p. (2002) 7,737.

Tianjing (Tientsin) c. and mun., **China** 112 km S.E. of Beijing; impt. pt. using poor harbour on Hai R.; industl. ctr., oil refining, textiles, elec. instruments, steel rolling mills, machine tools, chemicals, tobacco, food processing, univ., p. (1994) 4,721,000 (c.), 5,922,000 (met. a.).

Tiaret, t., dep., W. **Algeria**; N. Africa; in strategic pass; walled; agr. mkt.; cereals, wool, cattle; p. (1994) 4,721,000 (c.), 5,922,000 (met. a.).

Tiber, R., **Italy**; flows from Apennines to Mediterranean, through Rome; 352 km long.

Tiberias, t., **Israel**; on Sea of Galilee (L. Tiberias); agr. ctr.; health resort with medicinal springs.

Tibet (Xizang Zizhiqu), aut. region, **China**; lofty plateau called "the roof of the world" its lowest plains being 3,660 m a.s.l.; semi-desert; network of roads inc. one across Himalayas to Katmandu; pastoral agr. sheep; arable agr. in R. valleys, especially Zangbo valley, wheat, barley, fruit, vegetables; tr. of wool, musk, gold, skins, drugs traditionally carried by yaks which can stand intense cold; salt, alluvial gold, radioactive ores; new rly. opened (Oct. 2005) (highest in world); cap. Lhasa; a. 1,217,308 km²; p. (2001) 2,600,000 (est.).

Ticino, R. **Switzerland** and **Italy**; trib. of Po; forms S. approach to St. Gotthard Pass; irrigation in lower course; length 240 km.

Ticino, can., **Switzerland**; on S. slopes of central Alps, bordering Italy; contains parts of Ls. Maggiore and Lugano; mainly pastoral agr., but wine, corn, tobacco in valleys; industl. a., in S. based on hydroelectric power, chemicals, metallurgy; many tourist resorts inc. Locarno, Lugano; cap. Bellinzona; a. 2,813 km²; p. (1990) 286,700.

Ticonderoga, V., N.E., N.Y., **USA**; resort between Ls. George and Champlain; L. George falls provide hydroelectric power for paper mill; local graphite used in pencil ind.; p. (1980) 2,938.

Tideswell, t., Derbys., **Eng.**; tourist ctr.; limestone quarrying in a.; lge. 14th cent. church known as "cath. of the Peak." p. (1991) 1,717.

Tien Shan (Celestial Mtns.) mtn. chain, central Asia, along **China-Russia** border; highest peak 7,320 m; source of Syr-Dar'ya, Chu, Ili and many other Rs.

Tierra del Fuego, archipelago, southernmost part of S. America; separated from Patagonia by Strait of Magellan; W. **Chile** and E. prov. of **Argentina**; timber, pastoral agr., sheep; oilfield at Rio Grande; mng.; a. of Argentinian prov. 21,571 km²; p. (1991) 69,369.

Tigre, st., **Ethiopia**; formerly an independent kingdom; cap. Adua; severe drought 1982–3.

Tigris, R., S.W. **Asia**; rises in Taurus mtns. S. Turkey, flows through Iraq where it is joined by the Euphrates and proceeds to Persian G.; comm. routeway; dams for flood control and irrigation; many of the earliest cs. located in valley; 1,840 km long.

Tijuana, t., Baja Cal. st., **Mexico**; resort catering for Americans; casinos, race-tracks, bull-fights; p. (1990) 742,686.

Tilburg, c., N. Brabant, **Neth.**; nr. Breda; woollens, textiles, tobacco, leather; p. (1994) 163,383 (c.), 236,838 (met. a.).

Tilbury, pt., Essex, **Eng.**; on N. Bank of R. Thames 32 km E. of London; within Port of London; major container terminal; p. (1991) 11,658.

Tilimsen (Tlemcen), t., dep., N. W. **Algeria**; picturesque medieval t.; agr. ctr. in fertile region; textiles, furniture, handicrafts; p. (1987) 107,632 (t.), 707,453 (dep.).

Tillicoultry, burgh, Clackmannan, **Scot.**; on Devon R.; woollen and worsted fabrics, paper; p. (2002) 5,400.

Tilsit. *See* **Sovetsk.**

Timaru, c. and dist., S.I., **N.Z.**; E. cst. spt., exp. frozen foods; fishing; regional ctr. for S. Canterbury; p. (1991) 34,208 (dist.).

Timbuktu. *See* **Tombouctou.**

Timisoara, c., W. **Romania**; comm., industl. and educational ctr.; univ., 2 caths., cas.; once a frontier fortress; p. (1999) 328,000.

Timmins, t., Ont., **Canada**; gold mng. declining; vast deposits of copper, zinc, silver, discovered 1964; timber inds., brewing; p. (1986) 46,657.

Timor, lgst. of Lesser Sunda Is., **E. Indies**; divided politically until 1975 into W. Timor, part of Indonesia, and East Timor. From 1975 to 1999 East Timor was forcibly incorporated into Indonesia.

Timor Sea, that part of the Indian Oc. N.W. of W. Australia, and S. of Timor I.

Tintagel, v. Cornwall, **Eng.**; ruined Norman cas · reputed birthplace of King Arthur; tourism.

Tintern, v., Monmouthshire, **Wales**; Cistercian abbey.

Tinto, R., Huelva prov., S.W. **Spain**; in Andalusia; flows W. to Alt. Oc.; gives its name to Rio Tinto copper mng. region which it crosses; 104 km long.

Tipperary, inland co., Munster, **R.o.I.**; drained by Rs. Suir and Shannon; mtnous., Knockmealdown and Galty mtns.; fertile Golden Vale in S.W.; dairying, sugar-beet; divided into N. and S. Ridings; co. t. Clonmel; p. (1986) 59,522 (N.R.), 77,097 (S.R.).

Tipperary, t., Tipperary, **R.o.I.**; 46 km S.E. Limerick; dairy processing; p. (1986) 5,033.

Tirana, t., cap. of **Albania**; agr. processing, engin., clothing, glass; univ.; airport; p. (1999) 279,000.

Tiraspol, c., S.E. **Moldova**; on R. Dniester; agr. processing ctr.; heat and power sta. recently constructed; p. (1990) 183,700.

Tiree, I., Inner Hebrides, Argyll and Bute, **Scot.**; off cst. of Mull; 22 km long, up to 10 km wide; sm. freshwater lochs and prehistoric forts; p. (1991) 768.

Tirgu Mures, c., **Romania**; on R. Mures; ch. t. of Magyar aut. region in Transylvania; old fort, Gothic Calvinist cath.; agr. tr. and processing; p. (1992) 163,625

Tiruchirapalli (Trichinopoly), c., Tamil Nadu, S.E. **India**; on R. Cauvery; rly. ctr.; textiles, cigars, goldsmithery; p. (1991) 387,000.

Tirupur, t., Tamil Nadu, **India**; nr. Coimbatore; textile capital of India (known locally as T-shirt city); p. (1991) 235,661.

Tisa (Tisza), R., **E. Europe**; rises in E. Carpathians, W. Ukraine, flows across Hungary into Serbia where it joins the Danube 72 km below Novi Sad; ch. tribs. Koros and Mures; length c. 960 km; navigable in part. Heavily polluted, February 2000.

Titicaca, L., **S. America**; between two ranges of Andes, on borders of Bolivia and Peru; 3,812 m a.s.l.; highest lge. L. in world; max. depth 300 m; crossed by steamers; fishing; a. c. 8,300 km².

Titograd, *See* **Podgorica.**

Titov Veles, t., central Macedonia, formerly Yugoslavia; on R. Vardar, and main rly. to Belgrade; recent industl. growth; p. (1981) 64,799.

Tiverton, mkt. t., Mid Devon, **Eng.**; 22 km N. Exeter; once famous for lace; textiles, engin.; p. (1991) 14,805.

Tivoli, the anc. Tibur, nr. Rome, **Italy**; on Aniene R., magnificent situations; hydroelec. power; resort; remains of Hadrian's villa.

Tlaxcala, smallest st., **Mexico**; on Mesa Central; dense p.; mainly agr.; cap. T.; a. 4,027 km²; p. (1990) 763,683.

Tlemcen *See* **Tilimsen.**

Toamasina (Tamatave), t., **Madagascar**; lge seapt. on Indian Oc., handles 70 per cent of M. tr.; industl. complex, car assembly, oil refinery; p. (1994) 128,000.

Tobago, southernmost I., Windward Is., **W.I.**; volcanic, forested, picturesque, irregular topography; resorts utilising pleasant climate; exp. coconuts, copra, cacao, limes; ch. t. Scarborough; seeks internal self-gov.; a. 300 km²; p. (1990) 46,400. *See* **Trinidad and Tobago.**

Tobata. *See* **Kitakyushu.**

Tobermory, burgh, Argyll and Bute, **Scot.**; on I. of Mull at N. entrance to Sound of Mull; fish. pt., resort; p. (2002) 980.

Tobruk, spt., **Libya**, N. Africa; on cst. 352 km

E. of Benghazi; exp. oil, served by pipeline from Libyan oilfields; p. (1984) 94,006.

Tocantins, R., central **Brazil**; rises in Goias prov., flows N. across plateau of Brazil through Pará estuary to Atl. Oc.; navigation interrupted by rapids 320 km above Pará; ch. trib. Araguaya R.; 2,560 km long.

Toce, R., N. Italy; rises in Lepontine Alps, flows S. and S.E. into L. Maggiore; valley used by trunk rly. from Milan to Berne as S. approach to Simplon Tunnel; 86 km long.

Todmorden, mkt. t., Calderdale, West Yorks., **Eng.;** nr. source of R. Calder, 10 km N.E. of Rochdale; cottons, machin.; p. (1991) 11,969.

Togo, Rep. of, W. Africa; narrow strip between Ghana (W.) and Benin (E.); N. and S. lowlands separated by mtns. (1,000 m); climate hot and humid, but drier savannah conditions in N.; coffee on slopes of central mtns., cacao, copra in S., maize in N.; phosphate mng.; major iron ore deposits in N. now form ch. exp.; developing food-processing inds.; cap. Lomé; a. 54,960 km²; p. (2004) 5,556,812.

Tokaido, Japan, one of gr. feudal highways, along S. cst. Honshu, now forms main line of modern communications network.

Tokaj, t., **Hungary;** at confluence of Bodrog and Tisa Rs.; nearby slopes of Hegyalia produce Tokay wine.

Tokat, t., cap. of T. prov., **Turkey;** copper refining, leather mnfs.; p. (1985) 73,008 (t.), (1990) 719,251 (prov.).

Tokelau (Union Isles), gr. of 3 coral atolls, S. Pac., N. of W. Samoa; belonging to **N.Z.;** Fakaofo, Nukunono and Atafu; natives are Polynesians; no airstrips (access only by boat from Samoa); p. (2004) 1,400.

Tokushima, t., Shikoku, **Japan;** spt. on E. cst.; mkt. ctr., cotton mnfs.; p. (1990) 263,356.

Tokyo, c., cap. of **Japan;** spt. with deepened harbour handling mainly S. coastal tr.; major industl. ctr. with diverse mnfs. and major problems of pollution; built on marshy site with much expensive reclamation from sea; planned decentralisation of p. and economic activity in progress; with Osaka–Kobe–Kyoto conurbs. (480 km long ribbon development) spoken of as Tokaido (*q.v.*) megalopolis; major educational ctr. with many univs.; p. (2000) 8,135,000 (c.), 30,724,000 (met. a.).

Tolbukhin, *See* Dobrich.

Toledo, prov., **Spain;** mtnous.; agr., vineyards, stock-raising; a. 15,346 km²; p. (1998) 519,700.

Toledo, anc. c., cap. of T. prov., **Spain;** in New Castile; on hill above Tagus R.; Gothic, Moorish, and Castillian architecture; picturesque narrow streets; Alcázar citadel; associated with El Greco; sword mkg. still flourishes; sm. arms; tourism; p. (1990) 60,700.

Toledo, c., Ohio, **USA;** rly. ctr. and L. pt. with natural harbour on Maumee R.; exp. mnfs., oil, coal, agr. prod.; imports iron-ore, glass mkg., shipbldg., car components and many varied mnfs.; p. (2000) 313,619 (c.), 614,128 (met. a.).

Tolentino, t., in the Marches, central **Italy;** on R. Chienti; mediaeval walls and houses; cath.; sm. handicraft inds.; spa and tourist ctr.; p. (1981) 17,984.

Toliary, spt. S.W. **Madagascar;** cap. T. prov.; p. (1990) 61,460.

Tolosa, t., Guipúzcoa prov., **Spain;** in the Basque cty.; mediaeval bldgs., and armour; paper mills; p. (1990) 18,200.

Tolpuddle, v., Dorset, **Eng.;** 11 km N.E. of Dorchester; famous for Tolpuddle martyrs, agr. labourers condemned to transportation for trying to form a trade union (1834).

Toluca, c., cap. of Mexico st., central **Mexico**; stands at 2,672 m; brewing, flour, cottons, pottery; especially noted for basket weaving; p. (1990) 487,630.

Tol'yatti, c., **Russia;** on R. Volga 56 km W.N.W. of Kuybyshev; named after Italian Communist Palmiro Togliatti; engin., motor wks., natural gas pipeline to Moscow; chemicals; p. (1989) 631,000.

Tombigbee, R., Miss., **USA;** flows S. to join Alabama R. to form Mobile and Tensaw Rs.; navigable, partially canalised; length 654 km.

Tombouctou, formerly Timbuktu, **Mali,** W. **Africa;** nr. Niger R. on border of Sahara; salt tr., handicraft inds.; flourished as comm. mart and Moslem ctr. 14th–16th cent.; p. (1987) 453,032 (reg.).

Tomsk, c., cap. of marshy T. oblast, **Russia;** one of few lge. ts. in N. Siberia; major pt. on R.

Tom; rly. junc. on Trans-Siberian rly.; educational ctr.; univ., cath.; engin., chemicals; p. (1989) 502,000.

Tonawanda, t., N.Y. st., **USA;** on Niagara R. at terminus of Erie Barge Canal; steel, plastics, chemicals; power from Niagara Falls, adjacent to N. Tonawanda; p. (1980) 18,693.

Tonbridge, t., Kent, **Eng.;** on R. Medway; food processing; lt. inds., inc. cricket balls; Norman cas. gatehouse; public school; part of 1. gov. dist. of Tonbridge and Malling; p. (2001) 107,561 (dist.), (1991) 34,260 (t.).

Tone, R., Honshu, **Japan;** flows E. across Kanto Plain to Pac. Oc., N. of Tokyo; longest R. in Japan.

Tonga, I. gr., S. Pac. Oc.; Polynesian kingdom, gained independence 1970; 158 coral and volcanic Is.; 50 per cent. p. on Tongatabu I.; exp. copra, bananas; fishing; oil discovered 1969; airport; cap. Nuku'alofa; a. 699 km²; p. (2004) 110,237.

Tongariro, volcanic peak, N.I., **N.Z.;** nat. park in ctr. of volcanic dist.; alt. 1,970 m.

Tonghua (Tunghwa), c., S.W. Jilin, **China;** rly junc.; soya bean processing; local iron and coal reserves; p. (1994) 349,500.

Tonkin, region, N. **Vietnam;** mtns. in N. and W., alluvial plain in E. around delta of Red R., containing most p. and lge. cs.; fertile agr.; ch. t. Hanoi; pt. Haiphong; a. 104,973 km².

Tönsberg, c., Vestfold prov., S.E. **Norway;** one of oldest Norwegian cs., on Skagerrak at entrance to Oslo fjord; p. (1990) 38,333.

Toowoomba, t., S.E. Queensland, **Australia;** regional ctr. for Darling Downs, a rich wool and beef a; planned with parks and gardens; agr. based inds., engin.; p. (1991) 82,138.

Topeka, c., cap. of Kansas st., **USA;** on Kansas R.; impt. tr. ctr. in rich agr. region; food processing, rly. ctr. and engin.; p. (1996) 119,658.

Torbay, unit. auth., S. Devon, **Eng.;** formed by amalgamation of Torquay, Paignton and Brixham; located around Tor Bay; tourism; p. (2001) 129,706 (unit. auth.).

Torcello, i., with anc. Byzantine cath., on lagoon nr. Venice, **Italy.**

Torfaen, S.E. **Wales,** unit. auth. created in 1996 from former l. gov. dist.; inc. ts. of Cwmbran and Pontypool; p. (2001) 90,949.

Torgau, t., **Germany;** R. pt. on Elbe; industl. ctr.; American and Soviet armies met here 1945; p. (1999) 21,300.

Torne, R., N. **Europe;** rises in Sweden, drains L. Tornetrask and flows S.W. to G. of Bothnia, forming Finno–Swedish bdy.; rich in salmon; 512 km long.

Torness, East Lothian, **Scot.;** site of advanced gas cooled nuclear power sta.

Toronto, c., cap. of Ont. prov., **Canada;** major Gt. Ls. pt., on L. Ont.; spacious harbour; exp. lge. quantities of wheat; comm., financial, industl and educational ctr.; many varied mnfs., univ., notable bldgs., parks; a. 622 km²; p. (1991) 635,395 (c.), (1996) 4,263,757 (met. a.); lgst. c. of C.

Torpoint, t., Cornwall, **Eng.;** on Plymouth Sound.

Torquay, t., S. Devon, **Eng.;** incorporated in Torbay; on N. side of Tor Bay; seaside resort with all-year season; p. (1991) 59,587.

Torre Annunziata, Campania, **Italy;** at foot of Vesuvius; spt., spa, bathing resort on Bay of Naples; arms factory, pasta mnf.; p. (1981) 57,097.

Torre del Greco, t., Campania, **Italy;** spt. and resort on Bay of Naples at foot of Vesuvius; coral fishing; pasta mnf.; p. (1992) 100,688.

Torremolinos, cst. resort, **Spain;** S. of Malaga; impt. tourist centre.

Torrens, L., S. **Australia;** 2nd lgst. salt L. in A.; varies from brackish lake to salt marsh.

Torreon, c., Coahuila, N. **Mexico;** cotton in surrounding Laguna dist.; cotton mills, rubber, smelting, food processing; rly. connection with ts. in S. Mexico; p. (1990) 459,809.

Torres Strait, between C. York, Queensland, **Australia,** and **New Guinea;** 144 km wide, strong tidal currents endanger navigation; contains volcanic and coral Torres Strait Is., part of Vanuatu; p. (1986) 4,837.

Torridge, R., Devon, **Eng.;** flows from Hartland dist. to a confluence with the Taw at Bideford Bay; 85 km long.

Torridge, l. gov. dist., N.W. Devon, **Eng.;** inc. N. cst. ts. of Northam and Bideford and stretches inland to Great Torrington; p. (2001) 58,965.

Tortona, t., Piedmont, N. **Italy;** on Scrivia R.;

textiles, metallurgy, engin., wines; cath.; the Roman Dertona; p. (1981) 28,806.

Tortosa, c., Tarragona prov., N.E. **Spain**; pt. on Ebro R., 35 km from mouth; food processing, soap, pottery; cath.; impt. Moorish t.; p. (1990) 30,000.

Tororo, t., **Uganda**; lge. chemical wks., cement, fertilisers.

Tortuga or **Ile de la Tortue,** I., Caribbean Sea; off N. cst. **Haiti**; provides shelter from N.E. tr. winds for Port-de-Paix; private development to convert I. into free pt. with tax incentives for inds.; scenic attractions being tapped to develop tourist tr.; airport under construction; subsistence agr. fishing; a. c. 65 km².

Torun (Ger. **Thorn**), c. and prov., **Poland**; rly. junc., pt. on Vistula, industl. ctr.; chemicals, elec. gds., clothing, metallurgy, engin., food processing; univ. bears name of Copernicus who was born here; p. (1995) 204,348 (c.), 670,310 (prov.).

Totnes, t., South Hams, Devon, **Eng.**; on R. Dart 10 km N.W. of Dartmouth; mediaeval t.; agr. mkt., food processing; p. (1991) 6,929.

Tottenham. *See* **Haringey.**

Toulon, c., Var dep., S.W. **France**; reinstated as cap. of Var dep. (1974); on Mediterranean cst.; base of Fr. navy; fine natural harbour; comm. pt. and industl. ctr.; many fine bldgs.; Port-Cros Nat. Park nearby; p. (1999) 160,406.

Toulouse, c., cap. of Haute-Garonne dep., S. **France**; in Languedoc on Garonne R. and Canal du Midi, commanding route through Gate of Carcassonne; industl. and agr. tr. ctr.; food processing, varied mnfs.; aircraft (home of Airbus Industries); many fine bldgs., notably mediaeval univ., basilica, Gothic cath.; p. (1999) 390,775.

Touraine, former prov. of **France**, of which Tours was the cap.; now occupied by Indre-et-Loire dep. and part of Vienne dep.; known as the "garden of France."

Tourcoing, c., Nord dep., N. **France**; 16 km N.E. of Lille; with twin t. of Roubaix forms major wool textile ctr.; p. (1999) 93,532.

Tournai, c., Hainaut prov., W. **Belgium**; on R. Scheldt, nr. Mons; historic c.; cath.; textiles, carpet mftg., cement ind.; p. (1993) 67,875.

Tours, c., cap. of Indre-et-Loire dep., **France**; in Touraine, on R. Loire; tourist ctr. for the châteaux of the Loire; route ctr.; agr. inds.; printing, engin.; Gothic cath.; p. (1999) 133,242.

Towcester, mkt. t., South Northants., **Eng.**; 14 km S.W. of Northampton; "Eatanswill" of *Pickwick Papers*; p. (1991) 7,006.

Tower Hamlets, inner bor., E. London, **Eng.**; inc. former bors. of Bethnal Green, Stepney and Poplar; undergoing rapid economic and social change as p. and inds. are decentralised; site of lge. a. of London Docks now all closed but largely redeveloped; clothing, brewing; p. (2001) 196,106.

Townsville, spt., Queensland, **Australia**; coastal outlet for rich dairying, pastoral and mng. a. along Great Northern Rly; artificial harbour; univ.; copper refining; p. (1993) 121,700.

Towton, v., North Yorks., **Eng.**; nearby Towton field, scene of bloodiest battle of Wars of the Roses 1461; Lancastrians under Henry VI defeated by Yorkists under Edward IV.

Toyama, c., Honshu, **Japan**; on Etchu plain to E. of Noto peninsula; regional admin. and comm. ctr.; patent medicines, aluminium smelting, machin.; p. (1990) 321,254.

Toyohashi, t., Honshu, **Japan**; food processing, textiles; p. (1990) 337,988.

Trabzon or **Trebizond,** spt., **Turkey**; on Black Sea; exp. tobacco, food prods., carpets; once a gr. tr. ctr. on caravan route between Persia and Europe; founded 8th cent. B.C. by Greek colonists; p. (1990) 173,354 (t.), 795,849 (prov.).

Trafalgar, C., S.W. cst., Cadiz, **Spain**; Nelson's famous victory 1805.

Trafford, met. dist., Gtr. Manchester **Eng.**; comprises Sale, Hale, Altrincham, Urmston and Stretford; p. (2001) 210,145.

Tralee, mkt. t., spt., Kerry, **R.o.I.**; on R. Lee; exp. grain, butter; p. (1986) 17,109.

Trani, spt., N. Apulia, **Italy**; on Adriatic; mkt. t. for fertile coastal a.; fishing, food processing; cath., cas.; p. (1981) 44,235.

Transbaykal, region, Siberia, **Russia**; E. of L. Baykal; mineral wealth; ch. t., Chita.

Transcaucasia, region between the Black Sea and the Caspian Sea; comprising the constituent reps. of Georgia, Armenia, and Azerbaijan; ch. t. Tbilisi.

Transvaal, former prov., **Rep. of S. Africa**.

Transylvania, historic region and prov., central **Romania**; high plateau surrounded by Carpathians; forested; mineral wealth not yet fully realised; arable agr. in valleys; ch. ts. Cluj, Brasov.

Transylvanian Alps, range of mtns., **Romania**.

Trapani, t., cap. of T. prov. W. Sicily, **Italy**; spt. on promontory, sheltering natural harbour; exp. wine, pasta, tuna fish caught locally; p. (1981) 71,927.

Trasimeno, L., Umbria, central **Italy**; occupies lge. extinct volcanic crater; drained S. to R. Tiber; a. c. 155 km².

Tras-os-Montes e Alto-Douro, prov., N **Portugal**; high, bleak plateau, cultivated valleys; climate cold except in S.; port wine cty. of Douro R.; remote, sparsely populated, a. 11,834 km²

Trebizond. *See* **Trabzon.**

Tredegar, t., Blaenau Gwent, **Wales**; in narrow valley 5 km W. of Ebbw Vale; engin.; home of Aneurin Bevan; p. (1991) 15,390.

Treforest, t., Rhondda, Cynon, Taff, **Wales**; on R. Taff; lge. trading estate established in 1930s to alleviate unemployment in primary inds. of S. Wales; aircraft accessories, electronics, chemical, pharmaceutical, rayon, metal wks.

Trelleborg, spt., S. **Sweden**; on Baltic Sea; most impt. rubber factory in cty.; p. (1983) 34,146.

Trengganu, st., **Malaysia**; N.E. Malaya; rice, rubber, coconuts; tin, iron; cap. Kuala Trengganu; a. 13,080 km²; p. (1980) 540,627.

Trent, R., **Eng.**; rises in N. Staffs, flows round S. Pennines and joins the Ouse to form estuary of the Humber; many power stas. along its banks; polluted waterway, especially between Humber and Nottingham; 240 km long.

Trentino-Alto Adige, aut. region, N.E. **Italy**, between Austrian and Swiss Frontiers and L. Garda; embraces provs. Trento and Bolzano; cap. Trento; formerly called Venezia Tridentina; a. 13,598 km²; p. (1992) 896,722.

Trento, t., cap. of Trento prov. and ch. t. of Trentino-Alto Adige, N. **Italy**; on R. Adige and route to Brenner Pass; chemicals, cement, elec. engin.; picturesque t.; cath.; p. (1981) 99,179.

Trenton, c., cap. N.J. st., **USA**; on Delaware R.; transport and industl. ctr.; noted for its wirerope and pottery inds., established mid-19th cent.; crockery, machin., metal and rubber gds.; p. (1990) 88,675 (c.), 326,000 (met. a.).

Trèves. *See* **Trier.**

Treviso, c., cap. of T. prov., Venetia, N.E. **Italy**; on R. Sile; agr. ctr. on fertile Venetian plain; silk mills, paper, furniture, fertilisers, pottery; p. (1981) 87,696.

Trichinopoly. *See* **Tiruchirapalli.**

Trichur, t., Kerala, **India**; comm. and educational ctr.; p. (1991) 275,000.

Trier (**Trèves**), c., Rhineland-Palatinate, **Germany**; on R. Moselle; Roman origin. (Augusta Trevorum, the Rome of the North), cath.; Porta Nigra; ctr. of Moselle wine reg.; textiles, leather goods; birthplace of Marx; p. (2002) 100,024.

Trieste, spt., cap. of T. prov., Friuli-Venezia Giulia, N.E. **Italy**; shipbldg., fishing, oil refining; pipeline to Schwechat, nr. Vienna; cath., cas., Roman antiquities; univ.; p. (1992) 228,398.

Trieste Free Territory, former free terr. on the Adriatic; constituted by Peace Treaty with Italy, 1947, as compromise between conflicting Yugoslav and Italian claims; a. 743 km²; Zone A handed over to Italy, Zone B to Yugoslavia 1954. Yugoslav/Italian agreement 1975 settled border dispute and established free industl. zone on both sides of border in region of Sezana-Fernetti.

Trikkala, t., cap. of T. dep., W. Thessaly, N. **Greece**; mkt. t. for pastoral prods.; damaged by earthquake 1954; p. (1981) 45,160, (1991) 137,819 (dep.).

Trim, co. t., Meath, **R.o.I.**; mkt. t. on R. Boyne; anc. seat of Irish Parliament; p. (1986) 1,967.

Trincomalee, t., N.E. cst. **Sri Lanka**; excellent natural harbour; formerly a British naval base.

Tring, mkt. t., Dacorum, Herts., **Eng.**; in gap through Chiltern hills, 14 km N.W. of Hemel Hempstead; p. (1991) 11,455.

Trinidad, I., **W.I.**; N. of Venezuela; climate warm and humid; oil, natural gas, asphalt, sugar, rum, coconut oil, molasses, citrus fruits; tourism; cap.

Port of Spain; a. 4,828 km². *See* Trinidad and Tobago.

Trinidad, t., central **Cuba**; picturesque old t. of colonial period declared a national monument.

Trinidad and Tobago, indep. st. within Commonwealth (1962), rep. (1976), W.I.; main exps. crude oil and petroleum prods. which with natural asphalt represent over 20 per cent national income; lge. offshore gas deposits with rising production; oil refining; tropical crops and food processing; sugar, molasses, rum, fruits, textiles; cap. and major spt. Port of Spain; internal self-gov. sought by Tobago; a. 5,128 km²; p. (2004) 1,096,585.

Trinity, R., Texas, **USA**; flows S.E. to Galveston Bay; used for reservoirs; valley contains lge. p. and much economic activity; 800 km long.

Trino, Piedmont, N. **Italy**; 18 km S.S.W. of Vercelli; nuclear power sta.

Tripoli, c., **Lebanon**; spt. on Mediterranean; admin. ctr. for N. Lebanon; terminus of oil pipeline from Iraq; oil refining; exp. agr. prods.; p. (2000) 1,822,000 (met. a.).

Tripoli, t., cap. of **Libya** on Mediterranean; stands on edge of palm-oasis, site of anc. Oea; tourist, comm. and mnf. ctr.; gd. harbour; p. (1984) 990,687.

Tripura, st. **India**; N.E. Ganges delta, bordering Assam and Bangladesh; cap. Agartala; rice, jute, cotton, sugar-cane; a. 10,360 km²; p. (2001) 3,191,200.

Tristan da Cunha, sm. gr. of Is., S. Atl. Oc.; dependency of Brit. col. **St. Helena**; ch. I. Tristan; evacuated 1961 (volcanic eruption) but resettled 1963; weather sta. (Gough I.); major hurricane (2001); remotest inhabited island in the world; all residents live in settlement of Edinburgh; a. 117 km²; p. (2006) 300.

Trivandrum, c., cap. of Kerala st., S.W. **India**; pt. on Arabian Sea; textiles coconut processing; univ.; p. (1991) 826,000.

Trnava, c., W. **Slovakia**; mkt. t. in fertile agr. region on Váh R.; food processing, steel wks.; cath., monasteries, called "little Rome"; p. (1990) 73,000.

Trnovo or **Tirnovo,** c., **Bulgaria**; on Jantra R.; anc. cap. of Bulgaria.

Trogir, t., **Croatia** (formerly Yugoslavia); sm. pt. and seaside resort, partly sited on I. of Ciovo; mediaeval bldgs., inc. cath., palaces; p. c. 20,000.

Trois Rivières, t., Quebec, **Canada**; industl. ctr. on St. Lawrence R.; noted for newsprint; hydroelectric power from St. Maurice R.; p. (1986) 50,122 (c.), (1996) 139,956 (met. a.).

Trojmiasto (Tri-City), Poland; name given to the three municipalities of Gdansk, Gdynia, and Sopot, a loosely-knit conurb.

Trollhättan, t., S.W. **Sweden**; on Göta R., nr. T.; falls which generate power for metallurgical and chemical inds.; car and aircraft components; p. (1992) 51,073.

Trombay, I., off Bombay, **India**; oil refining; atomic reactor; uranium processing and nuclear waste reprocessing plant; zirconium metal produced; fertilisers.

Troms, co., N. **Norway**; deep fjords, offshore Is., fishing, livestock, boat-bldg.; cap. Tromsö; a. 25,916 km²; p. (1990) 146,816.

Tromsö, t., cap. of Troms prov., N. **Norway**; spt. on sm. I. of T. in Norwegian Sea; arctic fishing; fish processing; univ.; p. (1990) 41,651.

Trondheim, c., spt., **Norway**; on W. cst. on S. side of T. fjord; shipbldg., engin.; exp. timber and wood-pulp, fish, copper; anc. cath., burial place of early Norwegian kings and place of coronation of recent sovereigns; univ.; p. (1990) 130,522.

Troon, burgh, S. Ayrshire, **Scot.**; on F. of Clyde, 10 km N. of Ayr; good harbour and graving docks; shipbldg., hosiery; seawater distillation research ctr. project; resort; p. (2002) 14,766.

Troppau. *See* Opava.

Trossachs, Stirling, **Scot.**; picturesque wooded glen; tourist resort.

Trowbridge, mkt. t. and county admin. ctr., West Wilts., **Eng.**; cloth wks., bacon curing, dairying, engin.; p. (1991) 29,334.

Troy, c., N.Y., **USA**; at confluence of Rs. Hudson and Mohawk; gr. shirt-mftg. ctr.; p. (1990) 54,269.

Troyes, c., cap. of Aube dep., N.E. **France**; on R. Seine; once cap. of Champagne; hosiery, textile machin., food processing; cath.; site of mediaeval fairs which standardised Troy weight; p. (1990) 60,755 (c.), 122,763 (met.a.).

Trucial States. *See* United Arab Emirates.

Trujillo, c., N.W. **Peru**; comm. and mkt. ctr. for irrigated agr. region, on Moche R., in foothills of Andes; sugar, cocaine; univ., cath.; p. (1993) 509,312.

Trujillo, t., cap. of T. st., W. **Venezuela**; on Transandean highway at 805 m; agr. mkt. for region producing coffee, cacao, tobacco, maize; p. (1980) 31,774 (t.), (1990) 520,292 (st.).

Truro, t., Nova Scotia, **Canada**; on Salmon R.; hosiery, lumber mills, printing, metallurgy, machin.; p. (1991) 11,683.

Truro, c., Carrick, Cornwall, **Eng.**; at confluence of Rs. Kenwyn and Allen; mkt. t.; admin. ctr. of Cornwall; cath.; p. (1991) 18,966.

Tsavo, major National Park in **Kenya**.

Tselinograd (Aqmola), c., **Kazakhstan**; cap. Virgin Lands terr.; on Ishim R.; p. (1990) 281,400.

Tshwane. *See* Pretoria.

Tsugaru Strait, Japan; separates Is. Hokkaido and Honshu; links Sea of Japan with Pac. Oc.; 72 km long, 24–32 km wide.

Tsuruga, spt., **Japan**; on W. cst. Honshu; rayon textiles, cotton, atomic power plant; p. (1990) 68,041.

Tuapse, c., S. Krasnodar terr., **Russia**; at foot of Caucasus on Black Sea; major petroleum pt. at W. end of pipeline from Baku and Makhachkala; oil refineries.

Tübingen, t., Baden-Württemberg, **Germany**; on R. Neckar; 15th cent. univ., cas.; mediaeval c.ctr.; birthplace of Hölderlin; p. (2002) 82,444.

Tubruq. *See* Tobruk.

Tucson, c., S.E. Arizona, **USA**; mkt. and distribution ctr. on Santa Cruz R.; cultural ctr. and winter resort based on Spanish heritage and warm dry climate; food processing, missile components; p. (2000) 486,699 (c.), 667,000 (met. a.).

Tucumán. *See* San Miguel de Tucumán.

Tudela, t., Navarre, N. **Spain**; mkt. ctr. for fertile fruit-growing dist. and I. of La Majana in Ebro R.; fine cath., Roman bridge; p. (1990) 27,100.

Tuggurt. *See* Touggourt.

Tula, c., cap. of T. oblast, **Russia**; mnf. ctr. in Moscow industl. region; local iron and lignite mng.; Yasnaya Polyana, home of Tolstoy, nearby; p. (1989) 540,000.

Tulare, L., S. Cal., **USA**; ctr. of inland drainage 64 km S. of Fresno; streams feeding it used for irrigation; in drought years L. dries up completely; a. 233 km².

Tullamore, mkt. t., Offaly, **R.o.I.**; on Grand Canal; farming, distilling, brewing; p. (1986) 8,484.

Tulle-sur-Mer, t., cap. of Corrèze dep., **France**.

Tulsa, c., Okla., **USA**; impt. oil ctr., based on lge. local deposits, machin., aeroplanes; well laid out with many parks; p. (2000) 393,049 (c.) 709,000 (met. a.).

Tummel, R., Perth and Kinross, **Scot.**; trib. of R. Tay; used by Pitch to Inverness rly. as S approach to Drumochter Pass; hydroelec. scheme nr. Pitlochry; 88 km long.

Tunbridge Wells (officially **Royal Tunbridge Wells**), t., l. gov. dist., Kent, **Eng.**; on border of East Sussex; chalybeate waters; attractive 17th cent. promenade known as "The Pantiles"; p. (2001) 104,030 (dist.), (2001) 60,095 (t.).

Tunghwa. *See* Tonghua.

Tung Ting Hu. *See* Dong Ting.

Tunguska, Upper, Stony and Lower, Rs., Siberia, **Russia**; all rise in Sayan mtns. nr. L. Baykal.

Tunguska Basin, coalfield between Yenisey and Lena Rs., **Russia**; main ts. Norilsk, Igarka, Yeniseysk.

Tunis, c., cap. of **Tunisia**, N. Africa; spt. on inlet of Mediterranean; exp. raw materials; base for fishing fleets; univ., notable mosques; tourist ctr.; ruins of anc. Carthage to N.E.; p. (2000) 1,897,000 (met. a.).

Tunisia, indep. st., N. Africa; bounded by Algeria on W., by Libya on E., indented Mediterranean cst., Atlas mtns. penetrate into N.; temperate cst. climate, hot and dry in S. desert; agr. and mng. basis of economy; wheat, olive oil, wine, fruits, limited to wetter coastal areas and irrigated valleys; phosphates around Ghafsa; iron ore and lead in N.W.; steelwks. at Menzel Bourguiba; chemical and paper inds. based on local phosphates; cap. Tunis; a. 164,108 km²; p. (2004) 9,974,722.

Tunja, c., cap. of Boyacá dep., **Colombia**; route and agr. ctr.; p. (1992) 112,360.

Turda, t., Transylvania, **Romania**; local salt mines and quarrying aid chemical and ceramic inds.; p. (1983) 59,695.

Turfan, depression, E. Xinjiang prov., **China;** on S. slopes of Tien Shan mtns.; desert a. irrigated by wells and canals for animal husbandry, fruit, cotton, grain; 275 m below sea level; ch. t. Turfan; archaeological finds.

Turgutlu (Kassaba), t., Manisa prov., **Turkey;** 48 km E.N.E. of Izmir; lignite, cotton, melons.

Turin or **Torino,** c., cap. of T. prov., N. **Italy;** on R. Po at confluence with the Dora Riparia; former cap. of Piedmont and kingdom of Sardinia; univ., cath., many historic monuments; headquarters of Italian motor ind.; clothing, machin., furniture, chemicals; oil refinery nearby; p. (1992) 952,736.

Turkana, L. See **Rudolf, L.**

Turkestan E., terr. included in Xinjiang China; separated from W. or former Russian Turkestan by Pamir plateau; mainly desert.

Turkestan W., terr. inc. **Turkmenistan, Uzbekistan, Tajikistan, Kirghizia,** and part of **Kazakhstan.**

Turkey, rep., S.W. Asia and E. Europe; occupies mtnous. Anatolian penin.; equable climate on coastal margins, continental severity in interior; economy predominantly agr. but hampered by poor land resources; grain grown on Anatolian plateau and a Mediterranean variety of crops around cst.; noted for tobacco; industl. development based on mng. resources and oil in S.E.; lge cities in W. act as magnet for the poorer areas of E.; 30 percent of p. in 5 cities; many migrate to Europe & Middle East as migrant workers; violence by Kurdish separatists; econ. crisis and devaluation, 2001; seeking EU membership; cap. Ankara; a. 814,578 km²; p. (2004) 68,893,918.

Türkmenbashi. See **Krasnovodsk.**

Turkmenistan, CIS, former constituent rep., USSR; borders on Afghanistan, Iran, and the Caspian Sea; much of a. in Kara-Kum desert; agr. based on irrigation; fruit, cotton, wool; sulphates, petroleum; p. concentrated in oases and industl. ctrs. of cap. Ashgabat, Mary-Chadzhou, along Trans-Caspian rly.; a. 491,072 km²; p. (2004) 4,863,169.

Turks and Caicos, Is., Caribbean Sea, W.I.; about 30 sm. Is., geographically S.E. continuation of Bahamas; dry climate, poor limestone soil; exp. salt, crawfish; cap. Grand Turk; a. 430 km²; p. (2004) 19,956.

Turku (Abo), spt., S.W. **Finland;** on Baltic Sea; ctr. of fertile agr. a.; exp. agr. prods.; industl. ctr.; shipbldg., steel, machin., textiles; Finnish and Swedish univs.; p. (1993) 160,390.

Tuscaloosa, c., Ala., **USA;** on Black Warrior R.; rly. and industl. ctr. based on local coal, iron, cotton, timber; univ.; p. (1990) 77,759 (c.), 150,522 (met. a.).

Tuscany, region, central **Italy;** inc. provs. Arezzo, Firenze, Livorno, Siena, Grosseto, Lucca, Pisa, Massa and Carrara, Pistoia; mainly mtnous., drained by Arno R. system; wines, olive oil, cereals; iron ore from Elba, marble from Apuan Alps around Carrara; pt. at Livorno (Leghorn); cap. Firenze (Florence); a. 22,989 km²; p. (1992) 3,528,735.

Tuva aut. rep., **Russia;** bounded by Siberia and Mongolia; mtn. basin, forested; timber inds., coal mng., asbestos, pastoral agr.; cap. Kyzyl; a. c. 165,800 km²; p. (1989) 308,600.

Tuvalu, formerly Ellice Is., until 1975 part of Gilbert and Ellice Is., W. Pac. Oc.; indep. (1978); p. mainly Polynesian; cap. Funafuti; coconut cultivation in high temps on poor coral soils; exp. copra; joined UN, 2000; future threatened by rising sea levels due to global warming; evacuation plans prepared; a. 25 km²; p. (2004) 11,468.

Tuxtla Gutiérrez, c., cap. of Chiapas st., **Mexico;** in fertile valley at 450 m; ctr. for sisal, tobacco, coffee, cattle; on Inter-American Highway; Mayan ruins nearby; p. (1990) 295,615.

Tuzla, t., **Bosnia-Herzegovina,** formerly Yugoslavia; salt, lignite, coal; hydroelectric power in a.; agr. mkt. ctr.; textiles; civil war 1992 onwards; p. (1981) 121,717.

Tver, (Kalinin), c., **Russia;** on upper Volga; inds.; 17th cent. cath. and cas.; p. (1989) 451,000.

Tweed, R., S.E. **Scot.;** rises in Tweeddale, and reaches sea at Berwick; salmon fisheries; length 155 km.

Twickenham. See **Richmond-upon-Thames.**

Tyler, c., Texas, **USA;** oil ctr. on E. Texan field; agr. ctr. for local mkt. gardening; famous for rose growing; p. (1990) 75,450.

Tyne, R., frmer Tyne and Wear, Durham and Northumberland, **Eng.;** formed by confluence of N. Tyne and S. Tyne at Hexham; flows E. to sea at Tyne-mouth and S. Shields; valley gives easy route across mtns. from Newcastle to Carlisle; lower course forms harbour (with shipbldg. and other wks.) from Newcastle to Tynemouth; road tunnel between Wallsend and Jarrow; 128 km long.

Tynedale, l. gov. dist., W. Northumberland, **Eng.;** lge. inland a. inc. Haltwhistle, Hexham and Prudoe; p. (2001) 58,808.

Tynemouth, t., North Tyneside, frmly Tyne and Wear, **Eng.;** pt. on N. bank of Tyne R.; ruined priory and cas.; residtl., resort; p. (1991) 17,422.

Tyne and Wear, former met. co., N.E. **Eng.;** mainly industl. a. around lower T. and W. R.; inc. Newcastle-upon-Tyne, Tynemouth, Gateshead, South Shields and Sunderland; traditionally ass. with shipbldg. and coal mng., but inds. increasingly diversified; p. (2001) 1,075,938.

Tyre (Sur), Lebanon; former Phoenician c. and spt.; founded c. 15th cent. B.C.; now sm. comm. t., tr. in cotton, tobacco; p. (1988) 14,000.

Tyrol, Alpine region, **Europe;** falls within Austria and Italy, linked by Brenner Pass; embraces highest peaks of Austrian Alps, culminating in Ortler Spitz; two-fifths forest, timber inds.; mtn. pasture; tourism; Austrian prov. of Tyrol; cap. Innsbruck; a. 12,650 km²; p. (1991) 630,358.

Tyrone, former co., **N. Ireland;** now replaced by Strabane, Omagh, Dungannon and Cookstown l. gov. dists.

Tyrrhenian Sea, part of Mediterranean between Italy and Corsica, Sardinia and Sicily.

Tyumen, c., **Russia;** one of oldest Siberian ts., rly. ctr. on Trans-Siberian rly., R. pt. on Tura R.; many heavy inds.; ctr. of oil and natural gas region; p. (1989) 477,000.

Tywyn, mkt. t., Gwynedd, **Wales;** on cst. of Cardigan Bay, 5 km N.W. of Aberdyfi; p. (1991) 2,864.

Tzekung. See **Zigong.**

Tzepo. See **Zibo.**

U

Ubangi, major R., **Central Africa;** trib. of R. Congo, rises on bdr. of Central Africa Emp. and Congo flows W. and S. to join Congo R. at Irebu; partially navigable; 2,240 km long.

Uberaba, t., Minas Gerais, **Brazil;** ctr. of cattle rearing and arable agr. region; sugar milling, mnfs. lime; p. (1996) 232,130.

Uberlandia, t., Minas Gerais st., **Brazil;** rail junc., agr. processing; p. (1996) 437,100.

Ucayali, R., **Peru;** headstream of R. Amazon; over 2,240 km long, navigable for 1,600 km; gives name to prov.; p. (1993) 314,810.

Uckfield, mkt. t., East Sussex, **Eng.;** 13 km N.E. of Lewes; a. ctr. of former Sussex iron ind.; p. (1991) 13,531.

Udaipur, c., Rajasthan, N.W. **India;** in picturesque valley at 760 m a.s.l.; cap. of former princely st. of U.; maharajah's palace; p. (1991) 309,000.

Uddevalla, spt., S. **Sweden;** N. Göteborg; former shipyds., prefab. houses, timber, granite quarrying, textiles; p. (1992) 48,178.

Udi, t., S. **Nigeria,** W. Africa; 160 km N. of Pt. Harcourt; impt. mng. ctr. on Enugu coalfield; linked by rail to Kaduna and Pt. Harcourt.

Udine, c., cap. of U. prov., Friuli-Venezia Giulia, N.E. **Italy;** between Alps and G. of Venice; route and industl. ctr. in agr. region; textiles, chemicals, engin., leather, woodwork; cath.; many attractive bldgs., piazzas; severe earthquakes (1976); p. (1984) 101,179.

Udmurt aut. rep. **Russia;** part of Urals industl. a.; two-fifths forested, timber inds.; arable agr., flax; steel inds. at cap. Izhevsk, Votkinsk, Sarapul; p. (1989) 1,605,700.

Udokan Khrebet, mtns., **Russia;** world's lgst. reserve of copper.

Ufa, c., cap. of Bashkir aut. rep. **Russia;** in Urals industl. a., at confluence of Rs. Belaya and Ufa; p. (1989) 1,082,000.

Uganda, rep., E. Africa; dictatorship overthrown (1979); 4 regs. established for economic devel.; equatorial cty., climate modified by alt.; forms part of E. African plateau (1,200 m); well-developed economy; coffee, tea, tobacco, cotton for exp.;

developing pastoral economy, fishing on L. Victoria; copper at Kilembe, tin; hydroelectric power from Owen Falls, second project at Kabelega Falls; electricity exp. to Kenya; savannah areas contain abundant wildlife in Nat. Parks and Game Reserves; cap. Kampala; a. 235,887 km²; p. (2004) 26,404,543.

Uist, N. and S., Is., Outer Hebrides, Western Isles, **Scot.**; indented csts.; N. Uist boggy in E., hilly in W.; S. Uist smaller but mtnous.; crofting, fishing; p. (1991) 1,404 (N.), 2,106 (S.).

Ujiji, t., in sm. terr. same name (a. 2,383 km²) on E. shore L. Tanganyika, **Tanzania**; where Stanley found Livingstone 1871.

Ujiyamada. See Ise.

Ujjain, t., Madhya Pradesh, **India**; sacred c. and formerly cap. of Malwa; univ.; p. (1991) 362,000.

Ujung Pandang (Makasar), c., Sulawesi, **Indonesia**; in dist. of rich volcanic soils; major spt. and airpt., entrepot tr.; p. (1995) 1,092,000.

Ukraine, CIS former constituent rep., USSR; in Eastern Europe; drained by Rs. Dnieper, Dniester, S. Bug, Donets; Pripet Marshes in N., wooded steppes in ctr., fertile black-earth a. in S.; major wheat-growing a. of Europe; highly mineralised, many industl. raw materials and ctrs. of metallurgical and heavy inds.; political crisis ('Orange Revolution'), December 2004; rapidly growing AIDS problem; divisions between west Ukraine (ethnic Ukrainian) and east Ukraine (many ethnic Russians); cap. Kiev; a. 582,750 km²; p. (2004) 47,732,079.

Ulan Bator (Ulanbataar), c., cap. of **Mongolian Rep.**; in stock-raising region; industl. ctr. of cty.; woollen gds., saddles, knitwear; new indust. ctr at Darkhan nearby; rly. link to China and Russia; contains one-quarter of p. of rep.; p. (1999) 744,000.

Ullapool, v., Highland, **Scot.**; fish. pt. (herring landings), on L. Broom, 72 km N.W. of Inverness; landed more fish in 1981 than any other British pt.; attractive mtn. and cst. scenery in a.; p. (2002) 1,308.

Ullswater, L., Cumbria, **Eng.**; 13 km long; supplies water to Manchester; attractive tourist a.

Ulm, c., Baden-Württemberg, **Germany**; route ctr. at limit of barge navigation on Danube, although navigable limits being extended by canalisation; food-processing, metal gds., textiles; cement; p. (2002) 118,347.

Ulsan, t., **South Korea**; oil refining, fertilisers; nuclear power sta. (1983) built to reduce oil imports; p. (1990) 682,978.

Ulster. anc. prov of **Ireland.** consisting of counties of Cavan, Donegal, Monaghan and the six counties now **N. Ireland.** The six counties of Northern Ireland (q.v.) are Antrim, Armagh, Down, Fermanagh, Londonderry and Tyrone.

Uluru (Ayers Rock) N.T., **Australia**; giant terra-cotta monolith, rising abruptly to 335 m; sacred to Aborigines; major tourist attraction. Formerly called Ayers Rock.

Ulva, I., Argyll and Bute, **Scot.**; off W. cst. of Mull; 8 km long.

Ulverston, mkt. t., South Lakeland, Cumbria, **Eng.**; nr. Morecambe Bay; antibiotics, elec. gds., tanning; p. (1991) 11,866.

Ulyanovsk. See Simbirsk.

Uman, c., **Ukraine**; at confluence of Kamenka and Umanka Rs.; rly. junc.; p. (1990) 91,300.

Umanak, t., W. **Greenland**; hunting and fishing base on arm of Baffin Sea; marble mng.

Umbria, region, central **Italy**, comprising provs. of Perugia and Terni, crossed by Apennines and upper Tiber; agr. mainstay of economy; inds. based on hydroelectric power at Terni; chemicals; tourist tr.; cap. Perugia; a. 8,472 km²; p. (1992) 814,796.

Umeå, c., cap. of Västerbotten prov., N.E. **Sweden**; on G. of Bothnia at mouth of Ume R.; cultural ctr.; woodpulp; p. (1992) 94,912.

Umm-al-Quaywayn, emirate, member of **United Arab Emirates**; p. (1985) 29,229.

Umm Qasr, t., **Kuwait**; on Iraq border; new deepwater port planned.

Umtali (Mutare), t., **Zimbabwe**; comm. ctr. for rich agr. a.; oil refinery at Feruka; pipeline to Beira; paper milling, food processing, vehicle assembly; p. (1982) 69,600.

Umtata, t., Eastern Cape Prov., **S. Africa**; cath.; p. (1980) 25,000.

Uncia, t., Oruro dep., **Bolivia**; alt. 3,900 m in

E. Cordillera of Andes, 96 km S.E. of Oruro; site of impt. Patino tin mines.

Ungava Bay, arm of Hudson Strait, projecting into Labrador, N.E. **Canada**; minerals abundant.

Union Isles. See Tokelau.

Union of South Africa. See South Africa, Rep. of.

Union of Soviet Socialist Republics. See Russia.

United Arab Emirates (Trucial Sts.), indep. sov. st. on Persian G., S.W. Asia; formed (1971) from Trucial Sts. (Abū Dhabi, Ajmān, Dubai, Al Fujayrah, Ra's al Khaimah, Shārjah, Umm-al-Quaywayn) after withdrawal of Brit. forces and termination of special defence treaty (1820–1971); continued immigration from Middle and Far East as oil-based economic growth proceeds, esp. in Abu Dhabi; a. 82,880 km²; p. (2004) 2,523,915.

United Kingdom, cty., N.W. Europe; separated from continent of Europe by English Channel; consists of Gr. Britain (Eng., Wales, Scot.) and N. Ireland; member of EU; a. 244,022 km²; p. (2001) 58,789,194.

United States of America, fed. rep., N. America; world's major economic power; variety of climatic and physical conditions (see **N. America**); economically self-supporting, but imports petroleum, coffee, machin., textiles; extremely diversified mnfs.; exp. capital goods, industl. supplies, vehicles and food; consists of 50 sts. and Dist. of Columbia, co-extensive with cap. of Washington; outlying dependencies inc. Puerto Rico, U.S. Virgin Is., Guam, American Samoa, Trust Terr. of the Pac. Is.; assertive foreign policy; proclaimed 'war on terrorism' following September 2001 atrocities, with involvement in Afghanistan and campaign against Iraq; a. 9,363,160 km²; p. (2006) 300 million.

Unst, I., Shetland Is., **Scot.**; most N. of gr.; length 20 km; p. (1991) 1,055.

Unterwalden, can., **Switzerland**; divided into Obwalden and Nidwalden; dairying, fruit and livestock; cap. Stans; a. 767 km²; p. (1986) 58,000.

Upernavik, t., W. **Greenland**; on sm. I. in Baffin Bay; sealing and whaling base.

Upper Austria, prov., **Austria**; borders on W. Germany and Slovakia; hilly and forested; drained by Danube R. system; inc. Salzkammergut resort a.; agr, forestry; inds. centred on Linz (cap.), Steyr and Wels; a. 11,979 km²; p. (1991) 1,340,076.

Upper Volta. See Burkina Faso.

Uppingham, mkt. t., Rutland, **Eng.**; 16th cent. school; p. (1991) 3,140.

Uppsala, c., cap. of U. prov., **Sweden**; on R. Sala, 72 km from Stockholm; historic ctr. of anc. Sweden; cultural ctr., famous univ. (Linnaeus taught there); cath.; lt. inds.; p. (1992) 174,554 (t.), 278,610 (prov.).

Ur, anc. Chaldean c., **Iraq**; 208 km W.N.W. of Basra; ruins; flourished about 3,000 B.C.

Ural, R., **Russia**; flows S.W. and S. to Caspian Sea; used for domestic and industl. water supply; navigable; 2,400 km long.

Ural Mts., **Russia**; mtn. system, forms bdy. between Europe and Asia and separates Russian plain from W. Siberian lowlands; extends N.-S. for 2,400 km; highest peaks Narodnaya and Telpos-Iz; rich mineral resources have given rise to huge ctrs. of heavy ind., inc. Sverdlovsk, Chelyabinsk, Magnitogorsk.

Uralsk, N.W., **Kazakhstan**; on R. Ural; grain-trading and cattle-mart ctr.; flour, leather, woollens, iron-ware; p. (1990) 206,700.

Uranium City, N Saskatchewan, **Canada**; nr. N. shore of L. Athabasca, ctr. of Beaverlodge uranium-mng. a.; founded 1951.

Urawa. See Saitama.

Urbino, t., in the Marches, central **Italy**; agr. mkt. and route ctr.; picturesque tourist ctr.; cath., univ., palace; p. with Pesaro (1981) 15,918.

Ure, R., North Yorks., **Eng.**; flows E. and S.E. to join the Swale, then forms the Ouse at Ouse Gill Beck; upper part of valley known as Wensleydale; 80 km long.

Urengoy, dist., Siberia, **Russia**; lge. natural gas field with 5,400 km. pipeline to W. Europe.

Urfa, prov. S.E. **Turkey**; a. 18,584 km²; p. (1990) 1,001,455.

Urgench, t., cap. of Khorezm oblast, **Uzbekistan**; pt. on Amu Dar'ya R. in Khiva oasis; cotton, food-processing; p. (1990) 128,900.

Uri, can., **Switzerland**; S. of L. of Lucerne;

forest and mtns.; traversed by St. Gotthard rly. and R. Reuss; sparse p., German speaking; cap. Altdorf; a. 1,075 km²; p. (1990) 33,700.

Urmston, Trafford, Gtr. Manchester, **Eng.**; residtl. sub. of Manchester; inc. part of Trafford Park industl. estate; p. (2001) 40,964.

Uruapan, t., Michoacán, W. **Mexico**; mkt. ctr. for semi-tropical mtnous. a.; famous handicrafts; parks, gardens; p. (1990) 217,142.

Urubamba, R., **Peru**; rises in E. Cordillera of Andes; forms one of headstreams of R. Amazon; length 560 km.

Urubupunga, t., **Brazil**; new. t., at site of hydroelectric power sta. on U. Paraná R.

Uruguay, rep., S. America; smallest of S. American reps.; situated on N. bank of Rio de la Plata estuary; low hills in N.; temperate climate; 60 per cent land a. devoted to livestock rearing, especially cattle, sheep, based on extensive natural grasslands; arable land in S., grains; ch. t. Montevideo, cap. and main ctr. of inds.; food processing, leather, metallurgy, textiles, rubber; a. 186,925 km²; p. (2004) 3,399,237.

Uruguay, R., **S. America**; rises in S. Brazil, flows 1,360 km to Rio de la Plata; forms bdy. between Argentina and Uruguay and part of bdy. between Argentina and Brazil.

Ürümqi (Wulumuchi), c., cap. of Xinjiang Aut. Reg., N.W. **China**; admin., comm. and industl. ctr.; iron and steel, cement, textiles, nitrogenous fertilisers, agr. machin.; local coal, tin, silver mng.; p. (1994) 1,130,000.

Usak, t. and prov., **Turkey**; connected by rail with Izmir; noted for pile carpet-weaving; p. (1985) 88,267 (t.), (1990) 290,283 (prov).

Usambara, mtns., N.E. **Tanzania**; scene of early European settlement (1902); lumber, tea, coffee produced on slopes; max. alt. 2,560 m.

Usedom (Uznam), I., Baltic Sea; off mouth of R. Oder; since 1945 E. part belongs to **Poland,** W. (the larger part) to Germany; a. 445 km²; p. 45,000.

Ushant, I., off cst. of Finistère, **France**; at entrance to English Channel; it was off Ushant that Lord Howe gained his gr. naval victory on the "glorious first of June" 1794; lighthouse, fishing; p. 2,000.

Ushuaia, t., cap. Tierra del Fuego prov., **Argentina**; most S. t. in world; sheep farming, timber, furs; freezing plant; p. (1991) 29,166.

Usk, mkt. t., Monmouthshire, **Wales**; 13th cent. cas.

Usk, R., Gwent, S. **Wales**; flows S. through Monmouthshire and Newport to Bristol Channel; picturesque, good fishing; 91 km long.

Usküdar (Scutari), t., **Turkey**; on Bosporus, opposite Istanbul; mkt. ctr.; new bridge to European side of Bosporus; Crimean memorial cemetery for Brit. troops; Muslim cemeteries.

Uspallata Pass, 3,800 m high over Andes between Mendoza, **Argentina,** and Santiago, **Chile**; monument "Christ of the Andes" marks international bdy. settlement; used by Mendoza–Valparaiso rly.

Ussuri, R., rises in Maritime prov. of Russia, flows c. 800 km to R. Amur; final 480 km forms Sino-Russian bdy.

Ussuriysk (Voroshilov), t., **Russia**; 112 km N. of Vladivostok; rly. junc. of Trans-Siberian and Chinese Eastern rlys.; engin.; p. (1989) 158,000.

Ustica, I., Palermo, **Italy**; basalt; agr., fishing, handicrafts; a. 8 km².

Ustinov. See **Izhevsk.**

Ust Kamenogorsk, c., **Kazakhstan**; on Irtysh R.; mng. ctr.; food processing, clothing; hydroelectric power sta. nearby; p. (1990) 329,900.

Usumbura. See **Bujumbura.**

Utah, st., **USA**; "Beehive St.'; admitted to Union 1896; st. flower Sego Lily, st. bird Sea Gull; Rocky mtns. in E.; forms part of Gr. Basin in W.; Gr. Salt L. in N.W.; dry continental climate; poor agr. conditions, soil erosion; copper, gold; tourism; Nat. Parks; cap. Salt L. City; a. 219,932 km²; p. (2002) 2,316,256.

Utica, c., N.Y., **USA**; on Mohawk R. and Barge Canal; in rich dairying region; textiles, electronics, tools, firearms; p. (1990) 68,637 (c.), 317,000 (met. a. with Rome).

Utrecht, c., **Neth.**; on Old Rhine (Oude Rijn); univ., cath.; chemical and cigar factories; printing, machin., woollens, silks, velvets; major transport and financial ctr.; picturesque; p. (1994) 234,108 (c.), 545,796 (met. a.).

Utrecht, prov., **Neth.**; between Gelderland and N.

and S. Holland; fertile agr., cattle rearing, horticulture; a. 1,362 km²; p. (1994) 1,851,402.

Utsunomiya, t., Honshu, **Japan**; ctr. for Nikko Nat. Park; p. (1990) 426,809.

Uttaranchal, st., **India,** new st. created 1997 from N. W. sect. of Uttar Pradesh, p. (2000) 8,479,600.

Uttar Pradesh, st., **India**; Himalayas on N. bdy., drained by Ganges and Jumna; irrigation; wheat, rice, millet, barley, maize, cotton, sugar, oil-seeds; ch. ts. Allahabad, Lucknow (cap.), Varanasi, Kanpur, Agra, Meerut; a. 293,732 km²; p. (2001) 166,052,900.

Uttlesford, l. gov. dist., Essex, **Eng.**; inc. Saffron Walden and Dunmow; p. (2001) 68,946.

Uttoxeter, t., East Staffs., **Eng.**; on R. Dove; machin., biscuit mftg.; expanded t.; p (1991) 10,329.

Uzbekistan, CIS former constituent rep., USSR; crossed by Rs. Amu Darya and Syr Darya; contains part of fertile Ferghana Valley; intensive farming based on irrigation; rice, cotton, fruits, silk, cattle, sheep; ch. cs. Tashkent (cap.), Samarkand; major alluvial gold deposits and bauxite in Kizil- Kum desert; impt. US air bases; anti-government uprising, May 2005 against repressive regime; a. 412,250 km²; p. (2004) 26,410,416.

Uzhgorod, c., **Ukraine**; economic and cultural ctr.; pipeline from Kuybyshev; univ.; p. (1990) 119,600.

V

Vaal, R., **S. Africa**; rises in Drakensberg mtns., flows W.S.W. to join the Orange R. nr. Kimberley. Vaal dam irrigates lge. a. of Witwatersrand; 896 km long.

Vaasa, c., cap. of Vaasa prov., W. **Finland**; pt. on G. of Bothnia; exp. timber and timber prods.; agr. ctr.; food processing, textiles, timber inds.; p. (1993) 54,713.

Vác, t., **Hungary**; on R. Danube; comm. ctr.; summer resort for Budapest; cath.; p. (1997) 34,000.

Vadso, cap. of Finnmark prov., N.E. **Norway**; ice-free Arctic pt. on N. side of Varangar fjord.

Vaduz, mkt. t., cap. of **Liechtenstein**; nr. Rhine; sm. tourist resort; p. (1997) 5,000.

Valais, can., **Switzerland**; in upper valley of R. Rhône; surrounded by mtns., forested on slopes; vines and cereals in valleys; ch. resort Zermatt, cap. Sion; a. 5,234 km²; p. (1990) 248,300.

Valdai Hills, morainic ridges between Leningrad and Moscow, **Russia**; rise to c. 348 m and form ch. watershed of rivers, Vlga, Dvina and Dniester.

Val-de-Marne, dep., S.E. of Paris, **France**; cap. Créteil; a. 243 km²; p. (1990) 1,215,500.

Valdez, t., Alaska, **USA**; ice-free pt., fishing; terminal of oil pipeline from North Slope.

Valdivia, c., S. **Chile**; on R. Callecalle nr. the sea (pt. Corral); damaged by earthquake and tidal wave 1960; univ.; metal, wood and leather gds.; paper, flour, brewing; p. (1992) 122,436.

Val d'Oise, dep., N.W. of Paris, **France**; cap. Pontoise; a. 1,248 km²; p. (1999) 1,104,162.

Valdosta, t., Ga., **USA**; rly. and tr. ctr. for region producing tobacco, cotton, timber; p. (1996) 41,816.

Valence, t., cap. of Drôme dep., S.E. **France**; on R. Rhône; silks., hosiery, vineyards; agr. mkt.; p. (1999) 63,332.

Valencia, region, E. **Spain**; on Mediterranean; comprises provs. of Alicante, Castellón de la Plana and Valencia; mtnous., with densely populated, fertile coastal plain; irrigation makes a. a major producer of Mediterranean fruit and crops; a. 23,305 km² p. (1998) 2,172,800.

Valencia, c., cap. of V. prov., E. **Spain**; pt. on Mediterranean at mouth of R. Turia; one of most impt. agr. ts. of cty., and active industl. and comm. ctr.; univ., cath.; resort; p. (1998) 739,400.

Valencia, c., N. **Venezuela**; nr. L. Valencia; ctr. of agr. a., sugar-cane, cotton; leading industl. t.; cattle mart; cotton mills, meat packing; cath.; p. (1990) 903,076.

Valenciennes, c., Nord dep., N. **France**; in Hainaut cty. on R. Escaut (Scheldt); metallurgical and chemical inds.; once famous for hand-made lace; birthplace of Froissart and Watteau; chosen (1997) as site for new Toyota car factory; p. (1999) 41,245.

Valentia, I., S.W. Kerry, **R.o.I.**; in Dingle Bay.

Vale of Glamorgan, The, S. **Wales**, unit. auth. created in 1996 from former l. gov. dist; lowland bordering Bristol Channel; inc. cstl. ts. of Barry and Penarth; p. (2001) 119,292.

Vale of White Horse, l. gov. dist., Oxon., **Eng.**; based on Abingdon, Faringdon and Wantage; p. (2001) 115,627.

Vale Royal, l. gov. dist., Cheshire, **Eng.**; a. in ctr. of co. and inc. saltfield ts. of Northwich and Winsford; p. (2001) 122,089.

Valladolid, c., cap. of V. prov., **Spain**; on R. Pisuerga (trib. of Douro); grain tr.; route, industl. and comm. ctr.; food processing, textiles; cath., univ.; p. (1998) 319,900 (c.), 492,000 (prov.).

Valle d'Aosta, aut. region, N.W. **Italy**; high Alpine cty., borders France and Switzerland; cap. Aosta; agr., hydroelectric power; winter resorts; a. 3,263 km²; p. (1992) 117,204.

Valle del General, upland, S.W. **Costa Rica**; pioneer subsistence agr., maize, tropical fruit, cattle; improving transport.

Vallejo, t., Cal., **USA**; at mouth of Napa R. on San Pablo Bay; pt. and processing ctr. for farm prod.; naval shipyard; p. (1990) 109,199 (t.), 451,000 (met. a. with Fairfield-Napa).

Valletta, c., cap. of **Malta**; ch. spt. on rocky penin. of Mt. Scebarras, E. cst.; formerly naval base; cath., univ.; UNESCO World Heritage Site; p. (1999) 7,073.

Valli di Comacchio, lagoon a., N.E. **Italy**; ctr. of an impt. eel industry; a. 259 km².

Valparaiso, c., central **Chile**; leading pt. on Pac. cst. of S. America; attractive c. with backdrop of steep hills; mftg., comm. and industl. ctr. of rep. with textile mills, sugar refineries, paint, shoe and chemical factories; univ.; p. (1992) 276,736, (1992) 1,373,967 (region).

Valtellina, fertile valley, **Italy**; in Lombard Alps above L. Como; impt. for vine cultivation; hydroelectric power resources; tourism.

Van, c., cap. of Van prov., S.E. **Turkey**; stands at 1,726 m on shore of salty L. Van; tr. ctr. of wheat-growing a.; new Turkish-Iranian rail link; p. (1990) 126,010 (t.), 637,433 (prov.).

Vancouver, c., B.C., **Canada**; Pac. cst. spt. with excellent natural harbour; international airport and terminus of transcontinental rly.; timber inds., shipbldg., fishing, oil and sugar refining; exp. prod. from these inds.; protection by mountains and mild climate make c. a major tourist ctr.; fastest-growing city in Canada; second lgst. Chinese community outside China; econ. links w. N.W. USA; univ.; p. (1986) 431,147 (c.), (1996) 1,831,665 (met. a.).

Vancouver, I., B.C., **Canada**; off W. cst.; mtnous., forested; woodpulp, paper; indented cst. provides many natural harbours; fishing; cap. Victoria; a. 33,797 km².

Vancouver, t., Wash., **USA**; spt. on Columbia R. opposite Portland (Ore.); exp. grain, timber; food processing; p. (1996) 59,982.

Vanderbijlpark, t., **S. Africa**; on Vaal R.; ctr. for steel wks.; p. (1991) 774,000 (dist.).

Vänern, lge. L., **Sweden**; W.N.W. of L. Vättern, with which it is connected by canal (and thence with the Baltic); a. 5,566 km².

Vannes, t., cap. of Morbihan dep., N.W. **France**; sm. pt. on S. cst. Brittany; cath.; dates from Roman times; p. (1999) 51,537.

Vanuatu, (**New Hebrides**), former Anglo-French condominium, S. Pac. Oc.; between New Caledonia and Fiji Is.; indep. st. 1980; strong separist moves in Santo I.; mostly subsistence agr.; few cash crops; ch. crop coconuts; no worked minerals; thickly forested; cap. Vila; a. 14,763 km²; p. (2004) 202,609.

Var, dep., S.E. **France**; in Provence, on Mediterranean; mainly agr. with some inds. at Draguignan and Toulon (cap. since 1974); bauxite at Brignoles; rapid growth of p.; inc. many coastal resorts; a. 6,042 km²; p. (1999) 896,454.

Varanasi (Benares), c., Uttar Pradesh, **India**; famous holy c. on Ganges, 640 km N.W. of Kolkata (Calcutta); place of annual pilgrimage; univ.; handicrafts, brasses, brocades, embroideries; p. (1991) 932,000.

Varanger Fjord, inlet of Arctic Oc. into Finnmark, **Norway**; iron mng. on S. shore.

Vardö, t., Finnmark prov., N.E. **Norway**; sm. ice-free pt. on Vardoy I. with fish and oil interests; p. (1990) 3,008.

Varese, t., Lombardy, **Italy**; in Alpine foothills; resort and industl. ctr.; engin., furniture, paper, textiles, wines; p. (1981) 90,527.

Värmland, prov., **Sweden**; agr., iron mng. and processing, timber inds.; cap. Karlstad; a. 19,236 km²; p. (1992) 284,691.

Varna, t., **Bulgaria**; spt. on Black Sea; industl. ctr. of heavy inds.; summer resorts on cst. nearby; p. (1990) 314,913.

Varnsdorf, t., **Czech Rep.**; rly. junc. on German bdr.; impt. textile ctr.

Västerås, c., cap. of Västmanland prov., **Sweden**; on L. Mälar; impt. elec. and metallurgical inds.; power sta.; impt. mediaeval c., cath., cas.; p. (1992) 120,889.

Västerbotten, prov., **Sweden**; forested; timber inds.; cap. Umeå; a. 59,153 km²; p. (1992) 255,987.

Västernorrland, prov., **Sweden**; forests and timber inds.; cap. Harnosand; a. 25,706 km²; p. (1992) 260,829.

Vastervik, t., Kalmar prov., **Sweden**; on Baltic cst. engin., chemicals, paper; p. (1992) 39,731.

Västmanland, prov., **Sweden**; N. of L. Mälar; mkt. gardening in S.; iron and silver mng. in N.; iron and steel inds.; cap. Västerås; a. 8,363 km²; p. (1992) 260,096.

Vasto, t., Abruzzi e Molise, **Italy**; agr. ctr. on steep-sided, vine-producing plateau; sm. Adriatic fishing pt.; p. (1981) 30,036.

Vatican City, indep. sov. Papal st., **Italy**; forms an enclave in Rome; inc. Papal residence, St. Peter's cath.; the world's smallest state; a. 44 ha; p. (2004) 921.

Vatna Jökull, mtn., **Iceland**; elevated snowfield; active volcano; alt. 2,120 m.

Vaucluse, dep. S.E. **France**; in Provence; cap. Avignon; a. 3,577 km²; p. (1999) 500,358.

Vaud, can., W. **Switzerland**; N. of L. Geneva; forests and vineyards; cap. Lausanne; a. 3,209 km²; p. (1990) 583,600.

Växjö, t., S. **Sweden**; engin., timber wks., hosiery; p. (1992) 70,074.

Vejle, spt., Jutland, **Denmark**; admin. ctr. V. prov.; industl.; p. (1990) 51,263.

Velbert, t., N. Rhine-Westphalia, **Germany**; N.W. of Wuppertal; metal ind., locks and keys; p. (2002) 89,823.

Vélez-Málaga, t., Málaga prov., S. **Spain**; famous for wine, raisins, sugar, olive oil; Moorish cas.; p. (1990) 54,200.

Velletri, t., central **Italy**; at foot of Alban hills overlooking Pontine marshes; wine; Garibaldi routed Neapolitans here 1849; p. (1981) 41,114.

Vellore, t., Tamil Nadu, **India**; agr. mkt. t.; scene of Sepoy mutiny 1806; p. (1991) 175,061.

Velsen, t., N. Holland prov., **Neth.**; nr. entrance to N. Sea Canal, inc. IJmuiden iron and steel wks.; lge. paper mill; met. a. with Beverwijk; p. (1994) 63,617 (c), 133,704 (met. a.).

Veluwe, dist., Gelderland, **Neth.**; between Arnhem and IJselmeer; low hills of glacial sands and sand-dunes; heathland and pinewoods; relatively low p. density.

Vendée, dep., W. **France**; on Bay of Biscay; fish. pts., beach resorts, agr. pasturage, vineyards; cap. La Roche-sur-Yon; a. 6,972 km²; p. (1999) 539,353.

Venetia (Veneto), region, N.E. **Italy**; between the Alps and the Adriatic; embraces provs. Vicenza, Verona, Venice, Udine, Treviso, Padua, Belluno, and Rovigo; mtnous. in N., inc. Dolomite Alps; fertile plain of Po R. in S.; intensive arable agr.; ch. c. Venice; a. 18,384 km², p. (1992) 4,395,263.

Venezia Giulia. *See* Friuli-Venezia Giulia.

Venezuela, fed. rep., N. cst. S. America; wealth derived from long-established oil ind. (90 per cent of exp. are oil); tropical climate, with temperate uplands, tropical forests and tall grass savannah lands (llanos); most economically advanced a. around cap. Carácas and oilfield a. of L. Maracaibo; counter pole of development based on hydroelectric power resources and iron ore in Caroní R. region; growing steel inds., government investment in lge. agr. areas, esp. maize and cereals; coffee from highlands exported; disastrous floods (1999); large foreign debt; a. 912,050 km²; p. (2004) 25,017,387. Widespread protests and political instability early in 2003 disrupted oil production with serious economic consequences.

Venice (Venezia), c., cap. of V. prov. and ch. c. of Venetia, N.E. **Italy**; built on gr. of islets within lagoon in G. of V., at head of Adriatic; splendid architecture, rich in art treasures and historic associations; extensive canal network, inc. Grand Canal, intensive use leading to erosion of bldgs.; gradually sinking into Adriatic, lge.-scale projects to preserve c.; new scheme of dams to protect from high tide; industl. zone on landward side in subs. of Porto Marghera and Mestre; craft and heavy inds.; p. (1992) 305,617.

Venlo, t., **Neth.**; on R. Maas; agr. mkt. and rly. junc.; chemicals, optical instruments, electric lamps; p. (1994) 65,367.

Ventimiglia, t., Liguria, N.W. **Italy**; on Mediterranean cst. on Fr. border; cath.; flower mkt.; tourism; p. (1981) 26,373.

Ventnor, t., I. of Wight, **Eng.**; on S. cst. 18 km S. of Ryde; mild climate, tourist and health resort; p. (1991) 5,710.

Veracruz, st., E. **Mexico**; narrow coastal plain rising to Sierra Madre Oriental; contains volcano Orizaba; recent agr. improvements; growth of petroleum inds.; cap. Jalapa; a. 71,836 km²; p. (1990) 6,215,142.

Veracruz, c., V. st., E. **Mexico**; spt. on G. of Mexico; comm. and industl. ctr. of oil region; nearby Laguna Grande, Mexico's first nuclear power sta. (1984); nr. site where Cortés landed 1519; p. (1990) 327,522.

Vercelli, c., cap. of V. prov., N. **Italy**; in Piedmont, on Sesia R.; rice mkt. for lge. irrigated plain textiles, machin., aircraft parts; p. (1981) 52,488.

Verdun, c., Meuse dep., N.E. **France**; in Lorraine, on R. Meuse; strategic ctr. with varied mnfs.; 12th cent. cath.; famous battle 1916; p. (1999) 19,643.

Vereeniging, c., Gauteng prov., **S. Africa**; on Vaal R.; coal, iron and steel, bricks; Treaty of Vereeniging 1902 ended Boer War; p. (1985) 177,220 (dist.).

Verkhneudinsk. See Ulan-Ude.

Verkhoyansk, t., Yakutsk, aut. rep., **Russia**; in N.E. Siberia; coldest permanently inhabited place in world; mean Jan. temp. of −59° F.

Vermont, st., New England, **USA**; "Green Mtn. St."; admitted to Union 1791; st. flower Red Clover, st. bird Hermitt Thrush; traversed by the Green mtns.; farming, dairying, stock-raising, lumbering, quarrying, machine tool and textile mftg.; traditional inds. revitalised by new inds. coming from neighbouring Quebec; cap. Montpelier; famous for autumn colours; a. 24,887 km²; p. (2002) 616,592.

Verona, c., cap. of V. prov., N.E. **Italy**; on R. Adige; commands route from central Europe to Brenner pass and from Venice to Milan; cath. and notable monuments; active agr. tr. and inds., printing; p. (1992) 255,492.

Versailles, c., cap. of Yvelines dep., N. **France**; S.W. sub. of Paris; famous royal palace; mkt. gardening, distilleries; Treaty of Versailles 1919; p. (1999) 85,726.

Vesoul, t., cap. Haute-Saône dep., **France**; p. (1990) 19,404.

Vestmannaeyjar or **Westman Is.**, archipelago, S. W. **Iceland**; impt. cod fishing ind. based on Heimaey I; p. (1993) 4,886.

Vesuvius, famous active volcano, S. **Italy**; on shore of Bay of Naples; alt. c. 1,186 m; its eruption in A.D. 79 destroyed Pompeii and Herculaneum, and frequent eruptions have since been recorded; observatory founded 1844; funicular rly. from base of mtn. to rim of crater existed from 1880 to 1944 (destroyed by eruption).

Veszprem, c., **Hungary**; in fruit-growing dist., 96 km S. of Budapest; cath., univ. for chemical ind.; p. (1997) 64,000.

Vevey, t., Vaud can., **Switzerland**; on N. shore of L. Geneva; beautiful situation; chocolate, watches; resort; p. (1986) 15,149.

Viareggio, beach resort, Tuscany, **Italy**; on Tyrrhenian Sea, nr. Pisa; monument to Shelley; p. (1981) 58,136.

Viborg, t., Jutland, **Denmark**; admin. ctr. V. prov.; comm. and route ctr.; anc. cath.; textiles, machin., food processing; p. (1990) 39,395.

Vicenza, c. cap. of V. prov., N.E. **Italy**; in Venetia; mkt. ctr. for surrounding fertile agr. plain; textiles, iron and steel; many examples of Palladian architecture; p. (1992) 107,481.

Vichy, t., Allier dep., **France**; on Allier R.; famous spa; hot mineral springs; lge. exp. of V. water; seat of Pétain govt. during German occupation 1940–3; p. (1999) 26,527.

Vicksburg, t., Miss., **USA**; R. pt., on bluffs of Mississippi at junc. of Yazoo canal; shipping and mftg. ctr. in cotton and timber region; prominent in American Civil War; Confederate surrender 1863; p. (1996) 27,056.

Victoria, st., **Australia**; settled rapidly in 19th

century with gold rush; now most densely populated yet smallest mainland st.; Latrobe brown coal, offshore natural gas, hydroelectric power encourage rapid industrialisation; dominated by cap. Melbourne; rural a. of Great Dividing Range produces wheat, sheep and dairy prods.; a. 227,516 km²; p. (1996) 4,373,500.

Victoria, c., cap. of B.C., **Canada**; spt. on Vancouver I.; fishing and fish-processing; sawmills, chemicals, cement; beautiful scenery; tourist ctr.; p. (1986) 66,303 (c.), (1996) 304,287 (met. a.).

Victoria, main pt. and harbour between Hong Kong I. and Kowloon, **China**; built on reclaimed land; admin. ctr. of Hong Kong.

Victoria, t., cap. of Labuan I., Sabah, **Malaysia**; fine harbour; p. 3,213.

Victoria, c., cap. of Seychelles, Ind. Oc.; harbour on lgst. and most impt. I. of Mahé p. (1999) 28,000

Victoria Falls (Mosi-oa-Toenja), on R. Zambesi, **Zambia**; discovered by Livingstone 1855; falls are 1,674 m wide and broken by islands and rocks.

Victoria, Lake, lgst. L. of **Africa**; bordered by Kenya, Uganda, Tanzania; in depression of Gt. Rift Valley, at alt. 999 m. a. c. 67,340 km²; discharges into Victoria Nile; impt. fisheries; discovered by Speke 1858.

Victoria Land, region, **Antarctica**; discovered by Ross in 1841.

Victoria Nile, R., **Uganda**; E. Africa; name of R. Nile from its source at L. Victoria until it enters L. Mobuto Seso.

Viedma, cap. of Rio Negro prov., S. central **Argentina**; agr. centre; p. (1991) 57,473.

Vienna (Wien), c., cap. of **Austria**; R. pt. on branch of Danube; surrounded by Wiener Wald (Vienna forest) and Carpathian foothills; major industl., comm. and transport ctr.; many fine bldgs., inc. univ., cath., parliament bldgs.; magnificent Prater park; influential ctr. of music, cultural and scientific ctr.; home of Haydn, Mozart, Beethoven, Schubert, Mahler, Brahms, and Freud; p. (2000) 2,070,000 (met. a.).

Vienne, dep., W. **France**; drained by R. Vienne; mainly agr. dist.; cap. Poitiers; a. 7,021 km²; p. (1999) 398,393.

Vienne, t., Isère, **France**; nr. Grenoble, on R. Rhône; textiles, metallurgical inds.; Roman remains; overshadowed by Lyons 27 km to N.; p. (1999) 29,972.

Vientiane, admin. cap., **Laos**; pt. and comm. ctr. on Mekong R.; p. (1999) 640,000.

Vietnam, Socialist Rep. of, S.E. Asia; comprises regions of Cochinchina and Tonkin in former French Indo-China; from 1954–76 two separate countries, N. and S. Vietnam, based on two rivers, Song-koi and Mekong respectively, and separated by the high Annamite chain of mtns.; long period of civil war resulted in reunification; intensive agr. based on rice cultivation now largely collectivised; monsoon climate and river irrigation aid high yields; coffee, tea, rubber, sugar, main comm. crops but much devastation as result of war; minerals mainly concentrated in the N. with impt. anthracite deposit at Quang-Yen; industl. devel. also mainly in N. around Hanoi and ch. pt. Haiphong; hill tribes practising subsistence agr. inhabit the intervening Annamite mtns.; since reunification ts. expanding rapidly; a. 335,724 km²; p. (2004) 82,689,518.

Viet-Tri, t., N. **Vietnam**; 122 km N.W. of Hanoi; chemicals, paper mill, sugar refining; p. (1992) 116,000.

Vigevano, t., Lombardy, **Italy**; on R. Ticino; impt. agr. and industl. ctr.; footwear, plastics, textiles; cath.; p. (1981) 65,228.

Vigo, spt., **Spain**; transatlantic pt. on V. Bay; processing of imports; oil refining; p. (1998) 283,100.

Vijayanagar, ruined c., S.E. **India**; once cap. c. of Hindu empire in S. Deccan; 26 km in circumference; destroyed by Moslem forces at battle of Talikota 1565.

Vijayavada, t., Andhra Pradesh, **India**; rly. junc.; comm. ctr.; irrigation dam, Kistna R.; p. (1991) 702,000.

Vila, t. cap. of **Vanuatu**, on S.W. coast of Efate I; p. (1989) 19,400.

Villach, t., Carinthia, S. **Austria**; at junc. of Gail and Drava Rs.; impt. route ctr.; tourism; p. (1991) 55,165.

Villahermosa, c., cap. of Tabasco, S.E. **Mexico**; agr. mkt., sugar processing; rich local petroleum deposits; p. (1990) 390,161.

Villa Maria, t., **Argentina**; rly. junc.; ctr. of grain, timber, dairying dist.; p. (1980) 67,490.

Villavicencio, t., E. **Colombia**; in foothills of Andes; comm. ctr. for the *llanos*; cattle tr.; p. (1992) 233,026.

Villaviciosa, t., Oviedo prov., N.W. **Spain**; major fishing pt. on Bay of Biscay; p. (1990) 15,400.

Vilnius, (Pol. **Wilno**), c., cap. of **Lithuania** on Vilija R. (trib. of Niemen); cultural ctr., cath., univ., historic bldgs.; held by Poland 1920–39; lt. inds., food processing; p. (2000) 578,000.

Vilyui, R., Yakut aut. rep., **Russia**; flows E. from Siberian uplands into Lena R.; R. basin impt. agr. and mng. a.; fishing; 2,400 km long.

Vimy, t., Pas-de-Calais dep., N. **France**; nearby Vimy Ridge, site of Allied victory led by Canadians 1915; p. (1999) 4,677.

Viña del Mar, seaside t., central **Chile**, nr. Valparaiso; fashionable S. American resort; oil and sugar refining, textiles; p. (1992) 302,765.

Vincennes, t., Val-de-Marne dep., **France**; sub. of Paris; famous cas. and Bois; industl. and residtl.; p. (1999) 43,588.

Vindhya Hills, mtn. range, central **India**; separating the Deccan from the Ganges basin; *c.* 640 km long.

Vinnitsa, t., **Ukraine**; on R. Bug 192 km S.W. of Kiev; agr. mkt. t.; engin. chemicals, textiles; p. (1990) 378,800.

Virginia, st., **USA**; one of original 13 sts.; "Old Dominion" St.; admitted to Union 1788; st. flower Dogwood, st. bird Cardinal; wide Atl. coastal plain rising inland to Blue Ridge; famous for high quality "Virginia Leaf" tobacco; industl. ts. of Norfolk, Richmond, Portsmouth and Newport News; cap. Richmond; a. 105,711 km²; p. (2002) 7,293,542.

Virgin Is. (Brit.), W.I.; gr. of Is. E. of Greater Antilles; most impt. Tortola, Virgin Gorda, Anegada; water scarcity, semi-subsistence agr. economy; livestock, fish, fruit, vegetables; a. 153 km²; p. (2004) 22,187.

Virgin Is. (USA), W.I., external terr. of USA E. of Greater Antilles, 64 km E. of Puerto Rico; 3 main Is., St. Thomas, St. John, St. Croix; bought from Denmark 1917; favourite tourist a. in Caribbean; cap. Charlotte Amalie on St. Thomas; livestock, sugar; rum distilling; a. 344 km²; p. (1998) 118,211.

Vis (**Lissa**), I., off **Croatia**, Adriatic; fish-canning ctr.; a. 91 km²; anc. remains; resort; sea battle 1866 between Italian and Austrian ironclads; p. 3,000.

Visby, old spt., **Sweden**; on Gotland I. in Baltic Sea; rich in historic interest; resort; p. (1984) 20,000.

Vishakhapatnam, spt., Andhra Pradesh, **India**; deepwater harbour on Bay of Bengal; exp. manganese and oilseeds from Madhya Pradesh; shipbldg.; p. (1001) 752,000.

Vistula, R., **Poland**; rises in Beskids range of Carpathians, flows through Poland past Kraków to Baltic Sea nr. Gdansk; forms major link in E. European waterway system; coal and timber transport; 1,056 km long.

Vitebsk, c., **Belarus**; R. pt. on W. Dvina and impt. rly. junc., in agr. region; textiles, machine tools, food processing; p. (1996) 335,000.

Viterbo, c., cap. of V. prov., **Italy**; N. of Rome; agr. ctr., food-processing; 12th cent. cath. and historic bldgs.; p. (1981) 57,632.

Vitória, spt., Espirito Santo, **Brazil**; new ocean terminal capturing tr. from Rio de Janeiro; exp. coffee, cocoa, fruit, iron ore; sugar refining, shoes, textiles, cement; p. (1996) 263,700.

Vitoria, c., cap. of Alava prov., **Spain**; in Basque ctry.; stands on hill at 534 m; furniture mnf.; defeat of Fr. by Wellington 1813; p. (1998) 216,500.

Vitry-sur-Seine, S.E. sub., Paris, **France**; flower growing on sand and gravel terraces of Seine R., acreage being reduced by competition from housing and inds.; p. (1999) 78,613.

Vittoria, t., Sicily, **Italy**; mkt. for wine; p. (1981) 50,220.

Vittorio Veneto, t., **Italy**; N. of Venice; resort; textiles; p. (1981) 30,028.

Vizcaya, Basque prov., N. **Spain**; on Bay of Biscay; iron mng.; iron and steel inds.; dense p.; cap. Bilbao; a. 2,165 km²; p. (1998) 1,137,600.

Vlaardingen, t., S. Holland prov., **Neth.**; 8 km W. of Rotterdam, on Nieuwe Maas; leading fish. pt.; p. (1994) 73,820.

Vladikavkaz (**Ordzhonikidze**), c., cap. of N. Ossetian aut. rep., **Russia**; on R. Terek at foot of Caucasus, ind. ctr., metallurgical inds.; natural gas pipe-line to Tbilisi; hydroelec. power sta.; p. (1989) 300,000.

Vladimir, c., cap. of V. oblast, **Russia**; between Gorki and Moscow, on trib. of Oka R.; founded 12th cent.; caths., historic bldgs.; machine tools, agr. machin., textiles; p. (1989) 350,000.

Vladimir-Volynski, c., N.W. **Ukraine**; one of oldest Ukrainian settlements, founded 9th cent.; agr. mkt. ctr.; p. (1990) 38,400.

Vladivostok, c., spt., **Russia**; ch. pt. and naval base on Pac.; terminus of Trans-Siberian rly. and airline from Moscow; ch. cultural ctr. of Far East; shipyards, fisheries, oil refining, engin., chemicals; economic development in hinterland hindered by distance from major ctrs. of p. and ind.; p. (1989) 634,000.

Vlissingen or **Flushing**, spt., Zeeland prov., S.W. **Neth.**; on Walcheren I.; shipyards, oil refining, fishing; resort; birthplace of Admiral de Ruyter; p. (1993) 44,147.

Vlorë, spt., S.W. **Albania**; on Strait of Otranto, Adriatic Sea; salt; oil pipeline connects from Kucovë nr. Berat; p. (1991) 76,000.

Vltava or **Moldau**, R., Bohemia, **Czech Rep.**; rises in Sumava mtns. (Bohemian Forest) and flows to R. Elbe below Prague; used for hydro-electric power; *c.* 416 km long.

Voghera, t., Lombardy, **Italy**; rly. junc. and agr. mkt.; textiles, machin. engin.; cas., cath.; p. (1981) 42,639.

Voi, t., **Kenya**, E. Africa; 144 km N.W. of Mombasa on rly. to Nairobi; branch connection with Tanzania rly. system allows agr. prod. from Arusha and Moshi dists. to pass through Mombasa as alternative to Tanga; shoe factory.

Vojvodina, aut. prov., N. **Serbia**; impt. and fertile agr. dist. crossed by Danube R.; intensive agr., prosperous and dense p.; fruit, vegetables, livestock, food processing; ch. c. Novi Sad; a. 22,489 km²; p. (1981) 2,034,772.

Volcano Is., **Japan**; 3 volcanic Is. in Pac. Oc. S. of Japan, admin. by USA until 1968, now Japanese.

Volga, R., **Russia**; rises in Valdai hills, flows in serpentine course to Caspian at Astrakhan in wide delta; ch. tribs., Oka, Sura, Vetluga, Kama, Samara; major waterway linked to Baltic Sea, Azov, and Black Seas, and to Moscow; hydroelectric developments reducing sturgeon in Caspian Sea and caviar prod. declining; longest R. in Europe, 3,720 km.

Volga Baltic Waterway (**Mariinsk Waterway**), **Russia**; inland deepwater navigation network linking Black Sea and Caspian Sea in S. with Baltic Sea and White Sea in N.

Volgograd (**Stalingrad**), c., **Russia**; R. pt. on Volga and major rly. ctr.; exp. raw materials, fish; industl. ctr. for steel, engin., chemicals, oil refining; hydroelectric power sta.; fierce siege and successful defence 1942 turning point of second world war; p. (1989) 999,000.

Volhynia, historic region, **Ukraine**; on Polish frontier; rich agr. lowland; coal mng. at Novovodinsk; cap. Lutsk.

Volkhov, R., **Russia**; flows from L. Ilmen to L. Ladoga; navigable; hydroelectric power sta. and aluminium smelting plant at Volkhov (St. Petersburg oblast); 208 km long.

Vologda, c., **Russia**; R. and rly. junc. on upper Sukhona R.; in dairying a.; engin., textiles, sawmilling, paper, dairy inds.; cath.; historic bldgs.; p. (1989) 283,000.

Volos, spt., **Greece**; at head of G. of V.; impt. transport, industl., comm. ctr.; exp. agr. prods.; car mnfs.; p. (1981) 71,378.

Volta (**White Volta**), major R., **W. Africa**; drains extensive terr. in Niger bend, flows S. through Ghana to delta on Guinea cst., 112 km E. of Accra; main means of communication but rapids make through navigation impossible; Volta R. project for industrialisation of Ghana; dam and power plant at Akosombo, aluminium smelter at Tema; power decr. with decline in reservoir size from drought in Sahel; 1,520 km long. *See also* Black Volta.

Volta Redonda, t., Rio de Janeiro, **Brazil**; state-owned steel plant; p. (1996) 229,000.

Volterra, hill t., Tuscany, **Italy**; Etruscan and mediaeval walls; alabaster, salt; p. (1981) 14,080.

Volzhsky, t., **Russia**; industl. t. on Volga R.; aluminium smelting, chemicals; p. (1989) 269,000.

Vorarlberg, prov., **Austria**; forestry, dairying,

tourism; inds. based on hydroelectric power; textiles; cap. Bregenz; a. 2,600 km²; p. (1991) 333,128.

Vorkuta, ctr. of Pechora coal basin, **Russia**; beyond Arctic circle, which supplies entire European N. Russia; p. (1989) 116,000.

Voronezh, c., **Russia**; R. pt. on Voronezh R. nr. junc. with Don; impt. comm. ctr. in fertile agr. dist.; machin., rubber, oil refining, food processing; nuclear power sta.; univ., cath.; p. (1989) 887,000.

Voroshilovgrad, *See* Lugansk.

Voroshilovsk. *See* Kommunarsk.

Vosges, dep., E. **France**; on Franco–German frontier; dairying, vineyards, stone quarrying, textiles; cap. Épinal; a. 5,970 km²; p. (1999) 380,651.

Vosges, highlands, E. **France**; structurally similar to Black Forest, from which they are separated by Rhine rift valley; forested slopes, vineyards; source of Meurthe, Moselle, Sarve, Ill, and Saône Rs.; highest summit Ballon de Guebwiller, 1,425 m.

Votkinsk, t., **Russia**; 61 km N.E. of Izhevsk; lge. engin. plant; hydroelectric power sta.; birthplace of Tchaikovsky; p. (1989) 104,000.

Vulcano, I., Lipari gr., **Italy**; off N.E. cst. Sicily; active volcano; gave its name as generic title for this type of mtn.

Vyatka, (**Kirov**), c., **Russia**; pt. on Vyatka R.; rly. junc.; engin., saw milling, chemicals, leather inds.; cath.; p. (1989) 478,000.

Vyatka, R., **Russia**; rises in foothills of Urals, flows past Vyotka into Kama R.; timber transport, fishing; *c.* 1,360 km long.

Vyborg (**Viipuri**), c., **Russia**; spt. on G. of Finland, occupies strategic site on Karelian Isthmus, N.W. of St. Petersburg; Finnish until 1945; exp. timber; shipyards, engin., food processing.

Vyrnwy, L., reservoir, Powys, **Wales**; with dam 360 m long supplies water for Liverpool; a. 454 ha.

W

Waco, c., Texas, **USA**; in Brazos valley; route ctr., airport; regional cultural ctr.; univ.; textiles, leather; scene of Branch Davidian cult suicides, 1993; p. (1990) 103,590.

Waddenzee, stretch of shallow water between W. Frisian Is. and **Neth.** mainland.

Wadebridge, spt., Cornwall, **Eng.**; at head of Camel estuary, 10 km N.W. of Bodmin; agr. mkt.; p. (1991) 5,291.

Wadi Halfa, t., **Sudan**; on R. Nile at second cataract; rly. terminus of Sudan rlys.; inundated by Aswan L.; new t. Khashm el Girba for inhabitants.

Wadi Medani, t., cap. of Blue Nile prov., **Sudan**; ctr. of cotton growing dist.; p. (1983) 141,065.

Wagadugu. *See* Ouagadougou.

Wagga Wagga, t., N.S.W., **Australia**; on R. Murrumbidgee; ctr. of agr. and pastoral dist.; p. (1991) 40,900.

Waikato, R., N.I., **N.Z.**; rises in L. Taupo and flows N.W. into Tasman Sea; coalfields, hydroelec. power stas.; longest R. of N.Z.; 422 km long; gives name to dist. and region; p. (1991) 37,556 (dist.), 338,959 (region).

Wairakei, N.I., **N.Z.**; on L. Taupo; health resort; geothermal power sta.

Waitemata, c., N.I., **N.Z.**; part of Auckland on picturesque inlet; p. (1987) 98,500.

Wakamatsu. *See* Kitakyushu.

Wakatipu, L., Otago, S.I., **N.Z.**; 83 km long, 5 km wide, 360 m deep, 320 m a.s.l.

Wakayama, spt., Honshu, **Japan**; textiles; new iron and steel plant; p. (1990) 396,553.

Wakefield, c., met. dist., West Yorks., **Eng.**; on R. Calder; 13 km S. of Leeds; cath.; former ctr. of coal mng. a.; woollen and worsted prods., chemicals, engin.; p. (2001) 315,172 (dist.), (2001) 76,886 (c.).

Wakefield, t., Va., **USA**; on Potomac R., nr. Fredericksburg; birthplace of George Washington.

Wake I., coral atoll, **Pac. Oc.**; between Marianas and Hawaii; comm. and naval base on route to Far East, belonging to **USA**; p. (1995) 302.

Walachia, region, S. **Romania**; wide plain bounded by Transylvanian Alps and separated from Serbia by the river Danube; rich agr. a., "the

bread-basket of Romania"; Ploiesti oilfields; inds. nr. ch. c. Bucharest; a. 76,563 km².

Walbrzych (**Waldenburg**), c. and prov., S.W. **Poland** (since 1945); formerly in Lower Silesia; industl. and mng. ctr. at 427 m; porcelain, machin., engin.; p. (1995) 139,622 (c.), 740,072 (prov.).

Walchensee, Lake, Bavaria, **Germany**; a. 16 km²; hydroelectric power sta.

Walcheren, I., Zeeland prov., S.W. **Neth.**; in N. Sea at entrance to Scheldt estuary; mainly agr.; ch. ts., Vlissingen, Middelburg; flooded 1944 to stop German advance; tourism.

Waldenburg. *See* **Walbrzych**.

Wales, principality, **Great Britain**; mostly mtnous.; Cambrian mtns. rise to 1,085 m at Snowdon; contrast between N. and Central Wales (pastoral farming, forestry, water supply, tourism, rural depopulation) and S. Wales (former coalfield, metal-based inds., lge. ts.); referendum (1997) paved way for new Welsh Assembly; cap. Cardiff; p. (2006) 2,903,085.

Wallasey, t., Wirral, adjoining Birkenhead, Merseyside, **Eng.**; residtl., seaside resort (New Brighton); p. (2001) 58,710.

Wallingford, t., South Oxon., **Eng.**; on R. Thames, to N. of its gap between Chilterns and Lambourn Downs; p. (1991) 9,315.

Wallis and Futuna Is., gr. of coral Is., S. Pac. Oc.; overseas terr. of **France**; copra; a. 275 km²; p. (2004) 15,880 (mostly Polynesians).

Wallsend, t., frmly. Tyne and Wear, **Eng.**; on N. bank of Tyne, 6 km below Newcastle; Tyne tunnel links with Jarrow; shipbldg., engin., iron, plywood; at end of Hadrian's Wall; p. (2001) 42,842.

Walmer, t., Kent, **Eng.**; 3 km S. of Deal; holiday resort; cas., residence of Warden of Cinque Ports.

Walney, I., off cst. of Cumbria, **Eng.**; opposite Barrow.

Walsall, t., met. dist., West Midlands, **Eng.**; 8 km E. of Wolverhampton; leather and iron prods., engin., steel tubes; p. (2001) 253,499 (dist.), (2001) 170,994 (t.).

Walsingham, v., North Norfolk, **Eng.**; many old bldgs., priory ruins, abbey; pilgrimage ctr.

Walsum, t., N. Rhine–Westphalia, **Germany**; at confluence of Rhine and Emscher canal; R. pt. for Oberhausen steelwks.

Waltham, c., Mass., **USA**; nr. Boston; science-based inds.; univ.; p. (1996) 57,214.

Waltham Abbey, t., Epping Forest, Essex, **Eng.**; 21 km N.E. London, on edge of Epping Forest; tomatoes; Norman nave of abbey part of parish church; p. (1991) 15,629.

Waltham Forest, outer bor., E. London, **Eng.**; incorporating former bors. of Chingford, Leyton, Walthamstow; industl. and residtl.; p. (2001) 218,341.

Walthamstow. *See* **Waltham Forest**.

Walton and Weybridge, ts., Elmbridge, Surrey, **Eng.**; on R. Thames, 27 km S.W. of London; eng., aircraft; p. (2001) 52,890.

Walvis Bay, spt., **Namibia**, ceded by S. Africa in 1994; Atl. Oc.; fishing, fish processing; p. (1980) 20,740 (dist.).

Wandsworth, inner bor., S.W. London, **Eng.**; inc. Battersea; on R. Wandle at influx into Thames; oil mills, metal wks.; paper, brewing; p. (2001) 260,380.

Wanganui, c. and dist., N.I., **N.Z.**; pt. on R. Wanganui; tr. ctr. for wool, grain, meat, dairy prod.; agr. processing, steel-pipes, fertilisers; iron ore deposits; p. (1991) 45,082.

Wanganui, R., N.I., **N.Z.**; famous for its beauty; 265 km long.

Wankie, t., **Zimbabwe**; site of coal-mng. ind.; 344 km N.W. of Bulawayo; modern coal fired power sta.; p. (1982) 39,200.

Wanne-Eickel, t., N. Rhine–Westphalia, **Germany**; pt. on Rhine-Herne canal; coal-mng. ctr. of Ruhr.

Wansbeck, R., Northumberland, **Eng.**; flows E. from Pennines into N. Sea 5 km N. of Blyth.

Wansbeck, l. gov. dist., Northumberland, **Eng.**; inc. Newbiggin, Ashington and Bedlington; p. (2001) 61,138.

Wantage, mkt. t., Oxon., **Eng.**; in Vale of the White Horse; birthplace of King Alfred; p. (1991) 9,452.

Wapping, Thames-side dist., London, **Eng.**

Warangal, t., Andhra Pradesh, **India**; textiles, carpets; p. (1991) 448,000.

Ware, mkt. t., East Herts., **Eng.**; on R. Lea; 3 km N.E. of Hertford; p. (1991) 17,000.

Wareham, mkt. t., Purbeck, Dorset, Eng.; on R. Frome, on N. of I. of Purbeck, 13 km S.W. of Poole; p. (1991) 6,500 (est.).

Warminster, t., West Wilts., Eng.; on Wylye watershed at edge of Salisbury Plain; agr. mkt., gloves; p. (1991) 16,379.

Warnemünde, spt., Germany; ferry pt. for rail traffic between Berlin and Copenhagen; shipbldg.; outport for Rostock; resort.

Warren, t., Ohio, USA; on Mahoning R.; iron and steel mftg.; p. (1990) 50,793.

Warrenpoint, spt., Newry and Mourne, N. Ireland; at head of Carlingford Lough; p. (1991) 5,408.

Warrington, t., unit. auth., Cheshire, Eng.; on R. Mersey and Manchester Ship Canal; metal inds. (wire-drawing), chemicals, brewing, paper; expanded as new c. (to take people from Manchester); attracting high technology inds.; p. (2001) 191,080 (unit. auth.), (2001) 80,661 (t.).

Warsaw (Warszawa), c., cap. of Poland; on R. Vistula; devastated 1939–45; facsimile rebuilding based on Canaletto's paintings; cath., univ.; rly. ctr.; iron, steel, engin., textiles, chemicals; p. (1995) 1,638,227 (c.), 2,415,514 (prov.).

Warsop, t., Notts., Eng.; 6 km N.E. of Mansfield; limestone, gravel; p. (1991) 10,083.

Warta, R., Poland; trib. of R. Oder; connected to R. Vistula by canal; 720 km long.

Warwick, t., Queensland, Australia; sawmilling, agr. processing; p. (1992) 9,540.

Warwick, co. t., l. gov. dist., Warwicks., Eng.; on R. Avon, 13 km S.W. of Coventry; cas.; agr. implements, brewing, malting; p. (2001) 125,931 (dist.); (2001) 23,350 (t.).

Warwick, c., R.I., USA; on Narragansett Bay; textile ctr.; p. (1996) 84,514.

Warwickshire, non-met. co., W. Midlands, Eng.; undulating, drained by tribs. of Rs. Severn and Trent, crossed by Cotswolds to S.; sm. coalfield to N.; potential new coalfield in S.; p. (2001) 505,860.

Wash, The, bay, N. Sea between Lincs. and Norfolk, Eng.; 35 km long, 24 km wide; partly reclaimed to form the Fens; proposed barrage to aid further reclamation and water storage.

Washington, t., Tyne and Wear, Eng.; 8 km S.E. of Gateshead; coal, iron and steel, stone quarrying, chemicals; new t. 1964; p. (2001) 53,388.

Washington, c., cap. of USA; in Dist. of Columbia on Potomac R.; c. planned as national seat of Government; White House, Capitol, Pentagon (attacked by terrorists, Sept. 2001); univs.; p. (dist.) (2002) 570,898.

Washington, st., USA; "Evergreen St.' admitted to Union 1889; st. flower Western Rhododendron, st bird Willow Goldfinch; in extreme N.W., stretching from Pac. Oc. into Rocky mtns.; over half a. forested; Colombia R. and tribs. provide hydroelectric power; timber, fishing, tourism; cap. Olympia; a. 176,617 km², p. (2002) 6,068,996.

Wassatch Mtns., range of Rocky mtns., Utah and Idaho, USA, alt. 3,600 m.

Wast Water, L. Dist., deepest L. in Eng.; 5 km long, 79 m deep.

Watchet, t., West Somerset, Eng.; sm. pt. on cst. of Bristol Channel; p. (1991) 3,147.

Watenstedt-Salzgitter. *See* Salzgitter.

Waterbury, c., Conn., USA; on Naugatuck R.; ctr. of brass ind. and metal gds.; p. (1996) 106,412.

Waterford, co., Munster, R.o.I.; mtnous. co. in S.E.; mainly agr., dairying, pigs; fishing; co. t. Waterford; a. 1,867 km²; p. (1986) 91,151.

Waterford, co. t., spt., Waterford, R.o.I.; on R. Suir; cath.; brewing, fishing, glass mnfs.; p. (1986) 39,529 (t.).

Waterloo, t., Brabant prov., Belgium, nr. Brussels; battle nearby 1815; p. (1991) 27,900.

Waterloo, c., Ont., Canada; known as "the insurance capital of Canada"; two major universities; a city since 1948; p. (1995) 89,663.

Waters of Merom (L. Hula), Upper Galilee, Israel; extensive drainage completed 1957; a. 14 km².

Waterton Glacier International Peace Park, Albert and Mont., Canada and USA; glacial and lake scenery; a. 596 km².

Watertown, t., Mass., USA; on Charles R.; textiles, clothing; p. (1980) 34,384.

Watford, t., l. gov. dist., Herts., Eng.; on R. Colne, 26 km N.W. of London; mkt.; varied inds.; paper, printing; home of Camelot (lottery operator) and Leavesden film studio; p. (2001) 79,726 (dist.).

Wattenscheid, t., N. Rhine-Westphalia, Germany; E. of Essen; coal, metals, footwear; p. (1980) 67,653.

Waukegan, c., Ill., USA; on L. Michigan; summer resort; steel, brass, motors, sugar refining; p. (1996) 74,166.

Waveney, R., Norfolk and Suffolk, Eng.; 80 km long.

Waveney, l. gov. dist., Suffolk, Eng.; based on Lowestoft, Beccles and Bungay; p. (2001) 112,342.

Waverley, l. gov. dist., Surrey, Eng.; inc. Farnham, Godalming and Haslemere; p. (2001) 115,665.

Wayatinah, hydroelectric commission v., Tasmania, Australia; dam, lagoon and power sta. at confluence of Rs. Nive and Derwent.

Wazirabad (Balkh), t., Afghanistan; anc. Bactra, cap. of Bactria, called the "mother of cities", destroyed by Genghiz Khan 1221.

Weald, The, wooded and pastoral tracts S.E. Eng.; extending from Folkestone, Kent, through Surrey, Hants., and Sussex to the sea at Beachy Head; former a. of iron working; name derived from German *Wald* = forest.

Wealden, l. gov. dist., East Sussex, Eng.; stretches from Uckfield to S. cst.; p. (2001) 140,023.

Wear, R., Durham/Tyne and Wear, Eng.; rises in Pennines, flows through Durham to N. Sea at Sunderland; 96 km long.

Wear Valley, l. gov. dist., Durham, Eng.; Pennine a. inc. Bishop Auckland, Crook and Willington; p. (2001) 61,339.

Weaver, R., Cheshire, Eng.; industl. trib. of R. Mersey; 72 km long.

Weddell Sea, arm of S. Atl. Oc., Antarctica; whaling and sealing.

Wednesbury, t., West Midlands, Eng.; former metal wkg. t.

Wednesfield, t., West Midlands, Eng.; metal tubes, materials handling engin.; expanded t.

Wei, R., Shaanxi prov., W. China; rises in highlands of Kansu, flows E. between highlands of Shaanxi and Hua Shan to join Yellow R; valley contains very fertile loess soils; formed cradle of Chinese civilisation; c. 800 km long.

Weifang, c., Shandong prov., China; coal-mng. ctr.; tobacco processing; p. (1994) 564,600.

Weimar, t., Erfurt, Germany; on R. Ilm; ctr. of music and culture in 19th cent., associated with Goethe, Schiller, Nietzsche, Liszt, Herder; scene of establishment of German rep. 1919; elec. and metal inds., musical instruments, glass; European City of Culture (1999); p. (2002) 63,522.

Weipa, Queensland, Australia; Aboriginal community t., since 1965 taken over by Queensland to overcome opposition to bldg. of new t., pt., and alumina plant; bauxite nearby at Aurukin.

Weisshorn, mtn. peak, Switzerland; alt. 4,505 m.

Wejherowo, t., Gdansk, Poland; on R. Reda; mediaeval stronghold; palace; p. (1995) 47,302.

Welkom, t., Free State, S. Africa; ctr. of goldfields. p. (1980) 187,660 (dist.).

Welland Ship Canal, Ont., Canada; connects Ls. Erie and Ont.; 43 km long; 2-lane waterway.

Wellingborough, t., l. gov. dist., Northants., Eng.; on R. Nene, 14 km N.E. of Northampton; mkt.; footwear; expanded t.; p. (2001) 72,519 (dist.), (2001) 46,959 (t.).

Wellington, mkt. t., The Wrekin, Shrops., Eng.; brewing, sugar refining, timber, toys; name derived from "Watling Town" (stood on Watling Street); with Dawley and Oakengates forms new t. of Telford; p. (2001) 22,319.

Wellington, mkt. t., Somerset, Eng.; 10 km S.W. Taunton, anc. woollen ind. still survives; dairy prod.; p. (1991) 9,621.

Wellington, c., spt., N.I., cap. of N.Z.; univ.; impt. exp. ctr. for dairy prod., wool, meat; new inds. developing in Hutt valley with vehicle assembly, rubber, oil refineries; p. (1991) 150,301, 356,682 (urban a.).

Wellington, prov., N.I., N.Z.; mtnous., pastoral and dairy farming; a. 28,153 km²; p. (1985) 587,700.

Wells, cath. t., Mendip, Somerset, Eng.; on S. flank of Mendip hills; cath., bishop's palace; paper mftg.; tourism; p. (1991) 9,763.

Welshpool, mkt. t., Powys, Wales; on R. Severn; nearby is Powys cas.; p. (1991) 5,724.

Welwyn Garden City, t., Welwyn-Hatfield, Herts., Eng.; 34 km N. of London; founded by Sir Ebenezer Howard (1920) as first satellite t. of London; new t. 1948; pharmaceuticals, plastics, radio, and electronics, lt. inds.; p. (1991) 42,087.

Welwyn Hatfield, l. gov. dist., Herts., **Eng.**; comprises Welwyn Garden City and Hatfield; p. (2001) 97,553.

Wembley, former M.B., Middx., **Eng.**; now inc. in Brent outer bor. Greater London; lt. inds.; home of Wembley Stadium (now redeveloped as 90,000 seat stadium); British Empire Exhibition 1924–5.

Wenlock Edge, narrow ridge, Shrops., **Eng.**; extends 29 km S.W. from Much Wenlock to Craven Arms; limestone; moorland, mainly above 290 m.

Wensleydale, North Yorks., **Eng.**; valley in N. Pennines drained E. by R. Ure; cattle reared for fattening on lowland farms; some dairying (cheese); length 56 km.

Wenzhou (Wenchow), c., spt., Zhejiang prov., **China**; pt. on estuary of Wu R., E. China Sea; fishing, coastal tr., exp. wood, tea, agr. prod.; univ.; textile, leather and medicine inds.; designated an economic development zone, communications being improved; p. (1994) 449,700.

Wesel, t., N. Rhine–Westphalia, **Germany**; R. pt. at confluence of Rs. Lippe and Rhine, Ruhr conurb.

Weser, R., **Germany**; formed by confluence of Fulda and Werra Rs. at München; flows N. to N. Sea at Bremerhaven; linked by Mittelland canal to Rhine, Ems, and Elbe; navigable for entire length of 330 m.

Wesermünde. See **Bremerhaven.**

Wessex, anc. kingdom, S. **Eng.**; inc. Berks., Hants., Wilts., Dorset, Somerset and Devon.

West Bengal, st., N.E. **India**; W., mainly Hindu section of former presidency of B. (Muslim E.B. now Bangladesh); on Ganges delta and flood plain; humid sub-tropical climate; very dense p.; rice, jute; ch. c. Kolkata (Calcutta); a. 87,617 km²; p. (2001) 80,221,200.

West Berkshire, unit. auth., Berks, **Eng.** p. (2001) 144,483.

West Bridgford, t., Rushcliffe, Notts., **Eng.**; at junc. of Grantham canal with R. Trent; residtl. sub. of Nottingham; p. (2001) 43,395.

West Bromwich, t., Sandwell, West Midlands, **Eng.**; on R. Thame, 8 km N.W. of Birmingham; heavy engin. and allied inds., chemicals, springs, oil refining; p. (2001) 136,940.

West Derbyshire. See **Derbyshire Dales.**

West Devon, l. gov. dist., Devon, **Eng.**; rural W. of Dartmoor and ts. of Tavistock and Okehampton; p. (2001) 48,843.

West Dorset, l. gov. dist., Dorset, **Eng.**; inc. Lyme Regis, Bridport, Sherborne and Dorchester; p. (2001) 92,360.

West Dunbartonshire, unit. auth. created in 1996, formerly part of Strathclyde, W. **Scot.**; bordered S. by R. Clyde and N. by Loch Lomond; p. (2002) 92,830.

Western Australia, st. of the **Australian Commonwealth**; cut off from the rest of A. by desert; lgst. st., nearly a third of continent with only 9 per cent of p. concentrated in S.W. around st. cap. of Perth in fertile Mediterranean-like a.; diversity of relief, Hammersley range in N.W., Kimberley range in N.E., Gibson desert in interior; rich but irregularly distributed mineral deposits; intensive agr. in S.W., wheat and sheep in interior; a. 2,525,500 km²; p. (1993) 1,687,300.

Western Cape, coastal prov., **Rep. of S. Africa**, mountains, forests; fisheries, timber, tourism, agriculture, fruit, wine, leather, wheat, ostrich meat and feathers, wool, meat, textiles, publishing; cap. Cape Town; a. 129,370 km²; p. (1996) 3.96 m.

Western Desert, Egypt; part of Libyan Desert; inc. Qattara depression; coastal road from Cairo to Tripoli; fighting in second world war.

Western Isles, l. gov. auth., **Scot.**; remote a. of Outer Hebrides where pastoral farming and fishing are the traditional livelihood; p. (2002) 26,200.

Western Pacific High Commission Territories, inc. Solomon Is. and Kiribati and Tuvalu Is.

Western Sahara (Spanish Sahara), N.W. African cst.; comprising Rio de Oro and Saguí el Hamra; desert; rich phosphate mines at Bou Craa connected to El Aaiun pt. by rly.; upon decolonisation terr. split between Morocco and Mauritania (1976) but declared Saharan Arab Democratic Rep. by Algerians (Polisario) and still disputed; referendum planned; a. 265,993 km², p. largely nomadic (2004) 267,405.

Western Samoa. See **Samoa.**

Westerwald, plateau of old volcanic rocks,

Germany; ending in steep slope E. of R. Rhine; fertile soil; pastureland or deciduous woodland.

West Ham, former C.B., Essex, **Eng.**; sub. to E. of London; bordered by Rs. Thames and Lea; now inc. in Newham bor., Greater London.

West Hartford, t., Conn., **USA**; residtl. sub. of Hartford; metal gds., ctr. for dairying, tobacco-growing dist.; p. (1980) 61,301.

West Indies or **Antilles**, I. grs., **Atl. Oc.**; extend between csts. of Fla. and Venezuela, separating Caribbean Sea and G. of Mexico from Atl.; inc. Cuba, Haiti, Dominican Rep., Bahamas, Barbados, Jamaica, Leeward Is., Trinidad and Tobago, Windward Is., Guadeloupe, Martinique, Curaçao, Puerto Rico, Virgin Is.; mostly volcanic and coral Is., former colonial terr. developed for plantation agr worked by W. African slaves; most of indigenous Indians killed.

West Irian. See **Irian Jaya.**

West Lancashire, l. gov. dist., Lancs., **Eng.**; N. of Merseyside, inc. Skelmersdale and Ormskirk; p. (2001) 108,378.

West Lindsey, l. gov. dist., Lincs., **Eng.**; lge. a. N. of Lincoln and inc. Market Rasen and Gainsborough; p. (2001) 79,515.

West Lothian, central Scot.; unit. auth. created in 1996, incorporating most of historic co. which became part of Lothian in 1974 and is now divided between Edinburgh, Falkirk, and W. Lothian; industl. dist. in Central Lowlands close to Edinburgh; p. (2002) 159,960.

Westmeath, co., Leinster, **R.o.I.**; low-lying, drained by R. Shannon, many Ls.; dairying; co. to Mullingar; ch. t. Athlone; a. 1,834 km²; p. (1986) 63,379.

West Mersea, t., Essex, **Eng.**; on Mersea I.; p. (1991) 6,602.

West Midlands, former met. co., **Eng.**; mainly industl. a. centred around Birmingham and the S. Staffs. coalfield (Black Country) and Coventry; many forms of engin. and light inds. inc. vehicle mftg.; p. (2001) 2,555,592.

Westminster, City of, inner bor., London, **Eng.**; on N. bank of R. Thames; W. of City of London; incorporates former bors. of Paddington and St. Marylebone; contains Houses of Parliament, Westminster Abbey, Government offices, Royal Palaces (Buckingham Palace and St. James's); p. (2001) 181,286.

Westmorland, historic co., **Eng.**; now part of Cumbria non-met. co.

Weston-super-Mare, t., N. Somerset, **Eng.**; on Bristol Channel, 32 km S.W. of Bristol; holiday resort; expanded t.; p. (1991) 69,372.

West Orange, t., N.J., **USA**; elec. equipment; home of T. A. Edison; p. (1980) 39,510.

West Oxfordshire, l. gov. dist., Oxon., **Eng.**; inc. Cotswolds and ts. of Chipping Norton, Witney and Woodstock; p. (2001) 95,640.

West Pakistan. See **Pakistan.**

West Palm Beach, Fla., **USA**; domestic hardware; spt.; tourism; p. (1990) 864,000 (met. a. with Boca Raton-Delray Beach).

Westphalia. See **North Rhine-Westphalia.**

West Point, military sta., N.Y., **USA**; on Hudson R.; military academy.

Westport, spt., Mayo, **R.o.I.**; on Clew Bay; fishing; mkt.; p. (1986) 3,456.

Westray, I., Orkney Is., **Scot.**; 16 km long; p. (1991) 704.

West Somerset, l. gov. dist., Somerset, **Eng.**; inc. Exmoor and cstl. ts. of Watchet and Minehead; p. (2001) 35,075.

West Sussex, non-met. co., S.E. **Eng.**; crossed by E.–W. chalk ridge of S. Downs and forested Weald; diverse agr.; dormitory, retirement and tourist ts. on cst. inc. Bognor Regis and Worthing; Crawley new t. in N.; p. (2001) 753,614.

West Virginia, st., **USA**; "Mountain St.' admitted to Union 1863; st. flower Big Rhododendron, st. bird Cardinal; inc. Allegheny plateau; impt. mng. st. for coal; fruit farming; many industl. ts.; cap. Charleston; a. 62,629 km²; p. (2002) 1,801,873.

Westward Ho!, v., N. Devon, **Eng.**; named after Kingsley's novel.

West Wiltshire, l. gov. dist., Wilts., **Eng.**; stretches from Melksham, Bradford-on-Avon and Trowbridge to Warminster; p. (2001) 118,150.

West Yorkshire, met. co., **Eng.**; industl. and mainly built-up a. E. of Pennines; traditionally ass. with woollen textile mftg.; inc. major ctrs. of Bradford and Leeds; p. (2001) 2,079,211.

Wetar I., Indonesia; N. of Timor I.; mtns.; underdeveloped; sparse p.; a. 31,080 km².

Wetherby, sm. t., West Yorks., Eng.; on R. Wharfe; mkt., t.; racecourse.

Wethersfield, t. Conn., **USA;** oldest settlement (1634) in st.; aircraft parts, agr. implements.

Wexford, coastal co., Leinster, S.E. R.o.I.; mixed farming, fishing; cap. Wexford; a. 2,334 km²; p. (1986) 102,552.

Wexford, t., cap. of Wexford; Leinster, S.E. **R.o.I.;** on R. Slaney; agr. processing; outport at Rosslare; p. (1986) 10,336.

Wey, R., Hants., Surrey, Eng.; rises in W. Weald, flows N. into R. Thames nr. Weybridge; cuts impt. gap through N. Downs at Guildford; length 56 km.

Weybridge. See **Walton and Weybridge.**

Weymouth, t., part of l. gov. dist. of Weymouth and Portland, Dorset, **Eng.;** on Weymouth Bay, 13 km S. of Dorchester; torpedo and boatbldg., bricks, tiles, engin.; holiday resort; p. (2001) 63,648 (dist.), (1991) 46,065 (t.).

Whaley Bridge, t., High Peak, Derbys., Eng.; textile bleaching and finishing; p. (1991) 4,530.

Whangarei, c. and dist., N.I., N.Z.; deep harbour; oil refining; natural gas pipelines from Kapuni; fertilisers, sheet glass; p. (1996) 67,202.

Wharfe, R., West and North Yorks., Eng.; trib. of R. Ouse; 96 km long.

Wheeling, c., W. Va., USA; pt. on Ohio R.; comm. and mftg. ctr. in coal and natural gas a.; iron, steel, and metal plants; p. (1996) 33,311.

Whickham, t., Tyne and Wear, Eng.; nr. Gateshead; chemicals, paper; p. (1991) 17,428.

Whitburn, burgh, W. Lothian, Scot.; 32 km S.W. of Edinburgh; coal, limestone; p. (2002) 10,391.

Whitby, t., North Yorks., Eng.; at mouth of R. Esk, 27 km N.W. of Scarborough; anc. spt. and fishing t.; residtl. and coastal resort; abbey; famous for jet ornaments; potash to be mined nearby, p. (1991) 13,640.

Whitchurch, t., Shrops., Eng.; 21 km S.W. of Crewe; dairy prods; p. (1991) 7,868.

White, R., Ark. and Mo., USA; trib. of Mississippi; hydroelectric power; 1,104 km long.

Whiteadder, R., Borders, Scot.; trib. of R. Tweed; 54 km long.

Whitehaven, spt., Copeland, Cumbria, Eng.; on Solway F. 5 km N. of St. Bees Head; coal, methane gas, cement, chemicals; p. (2001) 24,978.

Whitehead, t., Carrickfergus, N. Ireland; at entrance to Belfast Lough; seaside resort; p. (1991) 3,761.

Whitehorse, t., cap. of Yukon terr., **Canada;** ctr. coal and copper mng., hunting and fur trapping; once a gold "boom town", H.Q. Royal Canadian Mounted Police; end of Alaska highway linking Edmonton, Alberta; p. (1996) 21,808.

White Mtns., part. of Appalachian system, N.H., **USA;** highest summit Mt. Washington, 1,918 m.

White Nile (Bahr-el-Abiad), R., Sudan; N.E. Africa, strictly, name applied to stretch of R. Nile between L. No and Khartoum; 800 km long.

White Plains, t., N.Y., USA; on Bronx R.; residtl.; battle 1776; p. (1990) 48,718.

White Russia. See Belorussia.

White Sea or G. of Arkangelsk, inlet of Barents Sea, **Russia;** frozen for 6 months of year; connected to Baltic Sea by deep-water canal; impt. fisheries.

Whitley Bay, t., North Tyneside, Eng.; 5 km N of Tynemouth; seaside resort; plastics; p. (2001) 36,544.

Whitstable, spt., Kent, Eng.; on Thames estuary 10 km N. of Canterbury; holiday resort, oysters; p. (1991) 28,907.

Whittlesey, t., Fenland, Cambs., Eng.; in the Fens, 13 km W. of March; bricks, mkt. gardening; p. (1991) 10,275.

Wichita, c., Kan., USA; in Arkansas valley; rly. wks., oil refineries and equipment, meatpacking ctr. in agr. and stock-raising region; univ.; p. (2000) 344,284 (c.), 485,000 (met. a.).

Wichita Falls, c., Texas, USA; oil refining, ctr. in agr. and ranching a.; p. (1990) 92,259.

Wick, spt., sm. burgh, Highland, Scot.; on E. cst., 22 km S. of John O'Groats; airport to Orkneys and Shetlands; herring fishing ctr.; p. (2002) 7,333.

Wicklow, coastal co., Leinster, R.o.I.; crossed by

Wicklow mtns.; pastoral agr. and tourism; cap. Wicklow; a. 2,033 km²; p. (1986) 94,542.

Wicklow, t., cap. of Wicklow, Leinster, **R.o.I.;** on S.E. cst., 56 km S. of Dublin; mkt.; sm. seaside resort; p. (1986) 5,304.

Wicklow, mtns., Wicklow, R.o.I.; highest summit Lugnaquillia, 927 m.

Widecombe, v., Devon, Eng.; Dartmoor tourist ctr.; famous through ballad "Widecombe Fair."

Widnes, t., Halton, Cheshire, Eng.; on R. Mersey 19 km E. of Liverpool; impt. chemical inds.; expanded t.; p. (2001) 55,686.

Wiener Neustadt, t., Lower Austria; rly. and industl. ctr.; heavy machin.; founded 1192; anc. bldgs., cas., cath.; education ctr.; p. (1991) 35,268.

Wieringermeer Polder, reclaimed a., N. Holland, **Neth.;** N.W. of IJsselmeer; a. 202 km².

Wiesbaden, c., cap. of Hesse, **Germany;** on Rhine, at S. foot of the Taunus; famous spa.; cas.; ctr. for Rhine wines; chemicals, metal gds.; p. (2002) 271,076 (c.), 780,190 (met.a.).

Wigan, t., met. dist., Gtr. Manchester, Eng.; 26 km N.E. of Liverpool; engin., chemicals, cement, food processing, paper; former coal mng. ctr.; p. (2001) 301,415 (dist.), (2001) 81,203 (t.).

Wigston, t., Leics., Eng.; 6 km S. of Leicester; engin., hosiery; p. (2001) 33,116. See **Oadby.**

Wigtown, sm. burgh, Dumfries and Galloway, Scot.; on W. Bay, Solway F.; located in historic co. of **Wigtownshire,** now part of Dumfries and Galloway; p. (2002) 987.

Wilhelmshaven, c., Lower Saxony, Germany; on inlet of N. Sea, 64 km N.W. of Bremen; ch. German naval base until 1945; industl. ctr. with heavy machin., elec. equipment, textiles, furniture; oil pipeline; p. (2002) 84,994.

Wilkes-Barre, c., Penns., USA; on Susquehanna R.; industl. ctr. in anthracite mng. a.; p. (1990) 47,500.

Wilkes Land, Antarctica; featureless plateau, alt. 2,900 m; immense glaciers; U.S. base taken over by Australia 1959.

Willamette, R., Ore., USA; rises in Cascade mtns., flows N. into Columbia R. below Portland; valley gives rich agr. land, wheat, rootcrops, dairy prod., hard and soft fruits; ch. ts. Eugene, Salem, Oregon City, Portland; used for hydroelectric power; 480 km long.

Willemstad, pt., cap. of **Neth. Antilles;** on Curaçao I.; oil refining; tourism; p. (1983) 50,000.

Willenhall, t., West Midlands, Eng.; locks and keys, drop forgings.

Willesden, former M.B., Middx., Eng.; now inc. in Brent outer London borough; Greater London impt. rly. junc.; residtl. and industl.

Williamsburg, c., Va., USA; between James and York Rs.; historic t.; settled 1632, rebuilt in 1920s to original plan; in Colonial Nat. Historical Park; p. (1980) 9,870.

Williamsport, t., Penns., USA; on Susquehanna R.; rly. ctr., timber, machin.; summer resort; p. (1984) 32,300 (t.), 117,100 (met. a.).

Willow South, was to be new cap. (1977), Alaska, **USA;** replacing Juneau; closer to ctr. of p.; lack of finance halted construction.

Wilmington, t., spt., Del., USA; on Delaware R.; shipbldg., machin., iron and steel wks.; chemicals; leather, cotton, rubber gds.; p. (1990) 71,592 (t.), 579,000 (met. a.).

Wilmington, t., N.C., USA; exp. cotton, tobacco, timber, fertilizers, shipbldg., textiles, chemicals; p. (1996) 62,192.

Wilmslow, t., Cheshire, Eng.; on R. Bollen, 10 km S.W. of Stockport; residtl.; pharmaceuticals; p. (2001) 34,087.

Wilton, t., Wilts., Eng.; on R. Wylye, 5 km W. of Salisbury; agr. mkt., carpets, felt; anc. cap. of Wessex; many old bldgs.; p. (1991) 3,717.

Wilton, industl. estate, Redcar and Cleveland, Eng.; on S. side of Tees estuary; heavy organic- and petro-chemicals; nylon polymer plant.

Wiltshire, non-met. co., Eng.; crossed by chalk downland and Salisbury Plain; barley, wheat, dairying, pigs; co. t. Salisbury; p. (2001) 432,973.

Wimbledon, dist., London, Eng.; lge. open common; site of international tennis tournament; part of London Bor. of Merton. Major redevelopment of town centre. New tramlink to Croydon (2000).

Wimborne Minster, mkt. t., Dorset, Eng.; on R. Stour; Roman settlement and home of early Saxon kings; Badbury Rings earthworks nearby; p. (1991) 15,274.

Winchcombe, t., Gloucs., **Eng.;** nr. Cheltenham; old mills; pottery, paper; nearby cas.; p. (1991) 4,243.

Winchelsea, anc. t., East Sussex, **Eng.;** 3 km S.W. of Rye; once impt. walled spt. and Cinque port, now 3 km inland.

Winchester, cath. c., l. gov. dist., Hants., **Eng.;** on R. Itchen, 19 km N. of Southampton; anc. Anglo-Saxon cap.; meeting place of parliaments until time of Henry VII; magnificent cath., famous public school; p. (2001) 107,222 (dist.), (1991) 36,121 (t.).

Windermere, t. Cumbria, **Eng.** and lgst. English L.; outlet to Morecambe Bay; supplies water to Manchester; 16 km long, 1·6 km wide; p. (1991) 6,847.

Windhoek, t., cap. of Namibia; in hills at 1,700 m; comm. ctr., agr. processing; tr. in karakul (Persian lamb); p. (1999) 202,000.

Windrush, R., Oxford, Gloucs., **Eng.,** trib. of R. Thames.

Windscale. See Sellafield.

Windsor, c., pt., Ont., **Canada;** on Detroit R., linked to Detroit, USA, by tunnel, bridge and ferry; ctr. for car mftg., salt wks., chemicals, paints; univ.; p. (1991) 191,435 (c.), (1996) 278,685 (met. a.).

Windsor, t., part of unit. auth. of **Windsor and Maidenhead,** Berks., **Eng.,** on R. Thames, 32 km W. of London; Windsor has famous royal cas. (founded by William the Conqueror) and park, St. George's Chapel and the Royal Mausoleum; p. (2001) 133,628 (unit. auth.), (1991) 30,135 (t.) (with Eton).

Windward Is., W.I., extend S. from Leeward Is.; consist of Fr. Martinique and former Brit. cols. of Grenada, St. Vincent, St. Lucia and Dominica with their dependencies (the Grenadines divided between Grenada and St. Vincent) which attained associated statehood 1967; sm. limited resources, economically depressed; volcanic; p. (1984) 419,000.

Winnebago, L., Wis., **USA;** 43 km long; lgst. L. in Wis.

Winnipeg, c., cap. of Manitoba, **Canada;** at jctn. of Red and Assiniboine Rs.; cath., univ.; rly. ctr.; ch. world wheat mkt.; meat packing and food processing; lgst. garment mnf. ctr. in cty.; oil refining; p. (1986) 594,551 (c.), (1996) 667,209 (met. a.).

Winnipeg, L., Manitoba, **Canada;** 64 km N. of Winnipeg; 416 km long, 49–96 km wide; contains several lge. Is. (Reindeer, 181 km²; Big I., 155 km²); used for hydroelectric power.

Winnipegosis, L., Manitoba and Saskatchewan, **Canada;** a. (exclusive of Is.) 5,180 km²; 80 km W. of L. Winnipeg, into which it drains.

Winsford, t., Cheshire, **Eng.;** on R. Weaver; 6 km S. of Northwich; ctr. of salt inds., chemicals; expanded t.; computer peripherals; p. (2001) 29,440.

Winterthur, t., Zurich, **Switzerland;** on Eulach R.; rly. ctr., locomotives, machines, cottons; p. (1990) 86,143.

Wirksworth, t., West Derbys., **Eng.;** in Pennines, 8 km S.W. of Matlock; limestone, fluorspar wks.; ctr. of Derbys. former lead mng.; p. (1991) 4,235.

Wirral, penin., met. dist., Merseyside, **Eng.;** between estuaries of Dee and Mersey; residtl.; comprises Wallasey, Birkenhead, Bebington and Hoylake; p. (2001) 312,293.

Wisbech, t., Fenland, Cambs., **Eng.;** on R. Nene, 18 km from its mouth in the Wash; mkt. gardening, fruit growing and canning, agr. implements; p. (2001) 26,536.

Wisconsin, st., **USA;** "Badger St."; admitted to Union 1848; st. flower Wood Violet, st. bird Robin; bounded by Gr. Ls.; low lying; leading dairying st.; industl. ts. around Gt. Ls.; cap. Madison; ch. t. Milwaukee; a. 145,439 km²; p. (2002) 5,441,196.

Wisconsin, R., Wis., **USA;** trib. of R. Mississippi; used for hydroelectric power; 960 km long.

Wismar, spt., Mecklenburg West Pomerania, **Germany;** on Baltic Sea, N. of Schwerin; oil pt. and industl. ctr. with shipyards and food processing inds.; p. (2002) 46,544.

Witham, t., Essex, **Eng.;** 14 km N.E. of Chelmsford; ctr. of mkt. gardening a.; expanded t.; p. (1991) 22,684.

Witham, R., Leics. and Lincs., **Eng.;** flows into the Wash; cuts impressive gap through Lincoln.

Witney, t., Oxford, **Eng.;** on R. Windrush, 16 km W. of Oxford; woollens, blankets, gloves; p. (1991) 20,377.

Witten, t., N. Rhine-Westphalia, **Germany;** on R. Ruhr; glass, machin., metals, chemicals, optical inds.; p. (2002) 103,158.

Wittenberg, t., Saxony - Anhalt, **Germany;** on R. Elbe; ctr. of Reformation and burial place of Luther (Schlosskirche); cas.; machin., textiles; p. (2002) 47,860. Now called Lutherstadt-Wittenberg.

Witwatersrand, dist., Gauteng, **S. Africa;** gold-mng. dist. producing over 25 % of world's gold.

Wivenhoe, t., Essex, **Eng.;** on R. Colne; boat-bldg., oysters, lt. inds.; p. (1991) 7,073.

Wloclawek, t. and prov., river pt., N. **Poland;** on R. Vistula; impt. paper mnfs., ceramics; p. (1995) 123,143 (t.), 434,743 (prov.).

Woburn, t., Beds., **Eng.;** 8 km N.E. of Leighton Buzzard; Woburn Abbey (seat of Dukes of Bedford).

Woking, t., l. gov. dist., Surrey, **Eng.;** 6 km N. of Guildford; residtl.; p. (2001) 80,840 (dist.).

Wokingham, mkt. t., unit auth., Berks., **Eng.;** 8 km S.E. of Reading; agr. tr. and machin.; p. (2001) 150,229 (unit. auth.), (2001) 39,544 (t.).

Wolfenbüttel, t., Lower Saxony, **Germany;** on R. Oker, 11 km S. of Brunswick; noted for ducal library, founded 17th cent., of which Leibnitz and Lessing were librarians; p. (2002) 54,517.

Wolf Rock, isolated rock with lighthouse, at approach to English Channel from Bay of Biscay; 14 km S.W. of Lands End, Cornwall.

Wolfsburg, t., Lower Saxony, **Germany;** on R. Aller, N.E. of Brunswick; Volkswagen wks.; p. (2002) 121,887.

Wollongong, t., N.S.W., **Australia;** 7th. c. of A.; heavy inds. attracted by local coal especially at Pt. Kembla; iron, steel, chems.; Australia's only tinplate plant; p. (1993) 249,500.

Wolsingham, t., Durham, **Eng.;** on R. Wear; impt. steel wks.; p. (1991) 1,286.

Wolverhampton, c., met. dist., West Midlands, **Eng.;** heavy and lt. engin., boilers, rayon, elec. engin. and apparatus, iron wks., aircraft and motor components, hollow-ware, tools, etc.; p. (2001) 236,582 (dist.). Created a Millennium City, 2000.

Wolverton, t., Milton Keynes, **Eng.;** on R. Ouse, 24 km S.W. of Bedford; p. (2001) 60,359.

Wombwell, t., South Yorks., **Eng.;** at E. foot of Pennines, 11 km N. of Sheffield; coal mng.; bricks; p. (1991) 15,462.

Wonsan, spt., **N. Korea;** on Sea of Japan; major pt. and rly. ctr.; Japanese naval base in second world war; oil refining; p. (1984) 350,000.

Woodbridge, t., Suffolk Coastal, Suffolk, **Eng.;** on R. Deben; boat-building, tourism; p. (1991) 10,950.

Wood Green, former M.B., Middx., **Eng.;** now inc. in Haringey outer bor., Greater London.

Woodhall Spa, t., East Lindsey, Lincs., **Eng.;** 6 km S.W. of Horncastle; former spa, bromo-iodine springs; resort.

Woodstock, t., Oxford, **Eng.;** on Glyme R., 11 km N.W. of Oxford; glove mnfs.; Blenheim Palace.

Wookey Hole, cave, Mendip Hills, Somerset, **Eng.;** at foot of limestone hills, 3 km N.W. of Wells; R. Axe emerges from the cave.

Woolwich, dist. former met. bor., London, **Eng.;** on either side of R. Thames; impt. Tudor dockyard, now closed; now part of Greenwich and Newham bors.

Woomera-Maralinga, S. Australia; c., 432 km N.W. of Adelaide; base for joint U.K.-Australian guided-weapon testing range extending N.W. across the continent; established 1947; p. (1991) 1,600.

Wootton Bassett, mkt. t., N. Wilts., **Eng.;** expanded since the 1960s to provide housing for people wkg. in Swindon; p. (1991) 10,524.

Worcester, c. and l. gov. dist., Worcs., **Eng.;** on R. Severn, 38 km N. of Gloucester; cath.; machin., porcelain, glove mkg.; birthplace of Elgar; p. (2001) 93,353 (dist.).

Worcester, t., Western Cape Prov., **S. Africa;** viticultural and industl. ctr.; Goudini spa nearby; p. (1980) 95,100 (dist.).

Worcester, c., Mass., **USA;** univ.; cultural ctr.; machine tools, elec. engin.; p. (1990) 169,759 (c.), 437,000 (met. a.).

Worcestershire, historic Midland co., **Eng.;** part of Hereford and Worcs. until 1998; now recreated separate county; p. (2001) 542,107.

Workington, t., Allerdale, Cumbria, **Eng.;** sm. spt. on Solway F. at mouth of Derwent R., first Bessemer steel plant, closed (1981), engin.; industl. diversification on nearby industl. estates, inc. bus wks.; p. (2001) 21,514.

Worksop, t., Bassetlaw, Notts., **Eng.**; 24 km S.E. of Sheffield; coal-mng. dist.; brewing, knit-wear, glass, flour; p. (2001) 39,072.

Worms, t., Rhineland-Palatinate, **Germany**; on left bank of Rhine; historic ctr.; famous imperial diet 1521 when Luther refused to retract; scene of *Nibelungenlied*; ctr. for Liebfraumilch wines; chemical, textile, leather and metal inds.; p. (2002) 80,625.

Worms Head, promontory at W. end of Gower Peninsula, S. **Wales**.

Worthing, t., l. gov. dist., West Sussex, **Eng.**; on S. cst., 16 km W. of Brighton; holiday resort, popular as retirement ctr. in mkt. gardening dist.; p. (2001) 97,568 (dist.).

Woy Woy, t., N.S.W., **Australia**; resort and commuter t. for Sydney; clothing; p. inc. in Gosford.

Wrangel I., Arctic Oc., off Khabarovsk terr., **Russia**; weather sta.

Wrath, C., N.W. Scot.

Wrekin, The, l. gov. dist., Shrops., **Eng.**; inc. Newport, Wellington, Oakengates and Dawley; p. (1995) 144,600.

Wrexham, t. 18 km S.W. of Chester, N.E. **Wales**, unit. auth. created in 1996 from former l. gov. dists. of Wrexham Maelor and Glyndŵr; p. (1991) 40,614 (t.), (2001) 128,476 (unit. auth.).

Wrocław (Breslau), c., Silesia, **Poland**; on R. Oder; impt. route ctr. and R. pt.; univ., cath.; rapid industl. development; ctr. of electronics inds.; p. (1995) 642,671.

Wrocław (Breslau), prov., Lower Silesia, **Poland**; until 1945 part of Germany; heavy inds. based on local minerals; cap. Wrocław; a. 24,740 km²; p. (1995) 1,137,260.

Wroxeter, v., Shrops., **Eng.**; on R. Severn, 8 km S.E. Shrewsbury; Roman sta. Uriconium; lost Roman harbour uncovered (2000).

Wuchow. *See* **Wuzhou.**

Wuhan, c., Hubei prov., **China**; formed by union of Hankan, Hanyang and Zhifang; major metropolis on Chang Jiang; integrated iron and steel wks., machine tools, tractors, textiles, ship-bldg.; univ.; p. (1994) 3,519,600.

Wuhu, c., Anhui prov., **China**; former treaty pt. on Chang Jiang; textiles; p. (1994) 457,900.

Wuppertal, t., N. Rhine–Westphalia, **Germany**; formed by amalgamation of Barmen and Elberfeld; textiles, rubber gds., paper, metals, pharmaceuticals; p. (2002) 364,784 (c.), 846,815 (met.a.).

Würzburg, t., Bavaria, **Germany**; on R. Main; univ., cath.; historic bldgs., engin., chemicals, printing; p. (2002) 129,915.

Wychavon, l. gov. dist., Worcs. **Eng** inc. Vale of Evesham and Pershore in S. and Droitwich in N.; p. (2001) 112,957.

Wycombe, l. gov. dist., Bucks., **Eng.**; close to Oxon. and inc. High Wycombe and Marlow; p. (2001) 162,105.

Wye, R., Bucks., **Eng.**; rises in Chiltern hills, flows S.E. to R. Thames at Cookham.

Wye, R., **Eng.** and **Wales**; rises in Plynlimmon, flows S.E. into R. Severn at Chepstow; forms deeply incised valley at Symond's Yat; 208 km long.

Wye, t., Kent, **Eng.**; nr. Ashford; impt. agr. college (Univ. of London).

Wylfa Head, Anglesey, Isle of, N. **Wales**; Magnox nuclear power sta.

Wymondham, t., South Norfolk, **Eng.**; 14 km S.W. of Norwich; mkt.; Benedictine abbey founded 1107; p. (1991) 10,150.

Wyoming, st., **USA**; "Equality St.'; admitted to Union 1890; st. flower Indian Paintbrush, st. bird Meadowlark; inc. areas of Rocky mtns. and great plains; Yellowstone Nat. Park; scant rainfall; irrigation; cattle and sheep ranching; petroleum; sparse p.; cap. Cheyenne; a. 253,597 km²; p. (2002) 498,703.

Wyre, l. gov. dist., Lancs., **Eng.**; inc. Preesall, Fleetwood and Thornton Cleveleys; p. (2001) 105,618.

Wyre Forest, l. gov. dist., Worcs., **Eng.**; inc. Bewdley, Kidderminster and Stourport; p. (2001) 96,981.

X

Xalapa, c., cap. of Veracruz st., **Mexico**; c. 1,370 m. a.s.l.; luxuriant vegetation; agr. ctr.; tourism; p. (1990) 288,331.

Xanthi, t. and dep. Thrace, **Greece**; on R. Mesta; ctr. of tobacco-growing a.; p. (1991) 91,063 (dep.).

Xanthus, ruined c., **Turkey**; on R. Xanthus; destroyed 43 B.C.; tourism.

Xauen, t., Morocco, N. Africa; holy t. founded 15th cent.

Xiamen (Amoy), c., Fujian, **China**; rail link to Jianxi; tea, fruit, machin., chemicals, textiles, electronics, tourism; univ.; formerly treaty pt.; in special Economic Zone to encourage foreign investment; p. (1994) 458,000.

Xi'an (Sian), cap. of Shaanxi prov., **China**; impt. route and industl ctr.; machin.; tourism; iron and steel, chemicals; p. (1994) 2,114,900.

Xiangtan (Siangtan), c., Hunan prov., **China**; on navigable Xijiang; regional tr. ctr., tea, cotton, electrical goods, machin., textiles; Mao Tse Tung born nearby; p. (1994) 490,100.

Xi Jiang (Si Kiang), ch. R., S. **China**; headstreams rise in Yunnan plateau, R. then flows E. enters S. China Sea through lge delta nr. Hong Kong; lower valley intensively cultivated, rice, sugar cane, tea; tropical climate permits continuous cultivation of most crops through year; valley densely populated; c. 2,000 km. long.

Xingu, R., **Brazil**; trib. of Amazon; navigable in its lower course; Nat. Park and Indian reserve threatened by new cattle ranches; 1,920 km long.

Xinhailion. *See* **Lianyungang.**

Xining (Sining), cap. of Qinghai prov., **China**; ctr. of spring wheat a.; woollen mills, iron and steel; new rly. completed to help reduce isolation; p. (1994) 569,800.

Xinjiang Uygur (Sinkiang-Uighur), aut. region, N W China; very dry climate; remote until new roads and rlys. penetrated a.; ethnic minority p. of Turkish background and Islamic faith; many attempts to develop natural resources and industry by Chinese government; pastoral agr.; sheep, goats; new st. arable farms, wheat, maize, millet; lge. oil reserves; cap. Ürümqi; a. 1,646,800 km²; p. (1994) 16,050,000.

Xizang Zizhqu. *See* **Tibet.**

Y

Yaila Mtns., Ukraine; form S.E. margin of Crimea penin., extend from Sevastopol to Kerch; form marked climate barrier between Black Sea littoral and N. part.

Yakut, aut. rep., **Russia**; borders Arctic Oc.; home of Yakuts; tundra and forest region, isolated, fur trapping, diamond and gold mng., state farms; a. 3,963,355 km²; p. (1989) 1,094,100.

Yakutsk, t., cap. of Yakut. aut. rep., **Russia**, pt. on Lena R.; univ.; airport; p. (1989) 187,000.

Yallahs Valley, Jamaica; severe soil erosion; govt. improvement scheme of afforestation and new crops; a. 181 km².

Yalta, spt., **Ukraine**; sub-tropical resort on Black Sea, sheltered by Yaila mtns.; conference between Churchill, Roosevelt, and Stalin 1945; p. (1990) 88,800.

Yalu, R., forms bdy. between N.E. **China**, and N. **Korea**; flows into Yellow Sea.

Yamagata, t., Honshu, **Japan**; ctr. of rice-growing a.; cas.; p. (1990) 249,487.

Yamaguchi, t., cap. of Y. prov., S.W. Honshu, **Japan**; cas.; comm. ctr., chemicals; p. (1990) 129,461.

Yamal-Nenets National Okrug, **Russia**; inc. Yamal penin.; permafrost; hunting, fishing; cap. Salekhard; lge. natural gas finds; a. 670,810 km²; p. (1989) 494,800.

Yambol, t., **Bulgaria**; on R. Tunja; ruined mosque; agr. ctr.; recent inds. inc. canning, farm machin., textiles, ceramics; p. (1990) 99,225.

Yamoussoukro, t., Côte d'Ivoire; cap. replaced Abidjan (1983); p. (1990) 120,000.

Yangchow. *See* **Yangzhou.**

Yangchuan. *See* **Yanqan.**

Yangi-yer, t., **Uzbekistan**; founded 1957 as ctr. for new irrigated cotton lands of E. Uzbekistan.

Yangon. *See* **Rangoon.**

Yangtze River. *See* **Chang Jiang.**

Yangzhou, c., Jiangsu, **China**; in valley of Chang Jiang, N.W. of Shanghai; mkt. for local agr. prods.; p. (1994) 355,500.

Yantai, spt., Shandong prov., **China**; anc. c.; food processing, light ind., textiles, cement, steel; exp. foodstuffs esp. prawns & wines; pt. being enlarged as c. declared an economic development zone to attract foreign investment, esp. high technology; p. (1994) 791,000.

Yaoundé, t., cap. of **Cameroon Rep.,** W. **Africa;** lt. inds. inc. beer, cigarettes, textiles; p. (2000) 1,444,000.

Yapura, R., **Brazil** and **Colombia,** S. America; trib. of R. Amazon; length 2,400 km.

Yaracuy, st., **Venezuela;** crossed by Y. valley impt. agr. a. for bananas, coffee, sugar, tobacco; crossed by Pan-American Highway; cap. San Felipe; a. 7,099 km²; p. (1990) 411,980.

Yare, R., Norfolk, **Eng.;** flows E. to N. Sea at Gorleston; forms part of Norfolk Broads navigable waterways; 80 km long.

Yarkand. See Shache.

Yarmouth. See Great Yarmouth.

Yaroslavl, c., cap. of Y. oblast, **Russia,** on upper Volga in Moscow industl. region; founded 1010; comm. and industl. ctr.; mnfs. inc. textiles, motor vehicles, synthetic rubber, agr. machin.; Volkov theatre, 12th cent. monastery, churches; p. (1989) 633,000.

Yazd, c., Isfahan prov., **Iran;** in desert a. at 1,190 m; fine silks, carpets; p. (1994) 306,000.

Yazoo, dist., Miss., **USA;** flood plain of R. Mississippi and R. Yazoo; very fertile alluvial soil, but subject to disastrous floods; one of ch. cotton-growing dists. in USA.

Yekaterinburg, (Sverdlovsk), c., cap. of Y. oblast, **Russia;** on R. Iset in Ural mtns.; on Trans-Siberian rly.; industl. expansion during second world war; heavy machin., metallurgical and chemical plants; univ.; p. (1989) 1,365,000.

Yelizavetgrad. See Kirovograd.

Yellowhead Pass, B.C., Alberta, **Canada;** most N. and lowest of main passes across Rocky mtns.; carries Canadian Nat. rly. on route from Edmonton to Vancouver and Prince Rupert; summit alt. 1,130 m.

Yellowknife, t., N.W. Terr., **Canada;** on N. shore of Gr. Slave L.; ctr. of impt. gold-mng. dist.; linked by air to Edmonton, Alberta; p. (1991) 15,179.

Yellow R. See Huang He.

Yellow Sea. See Huang Hai.

Yellowstone, L., Wyo., **USA;** 32 km long, 24 km wide; alt. 2,360 m; in Y. Nat. Park.

Yellowstone National Park, N.W. Wyo., **USA;** volcanic scenery, geysers; a. 8,956 km².

Yemen, Rep. of, S.W. Arabian peninsula; cap. Sana'a, economic and commercial cap. Aden; divided after 1967 into Yemen Arab Republic (N. Yemen) and People's Democratic Rep. of Yemen (S. Yemen); reunification May 1990; climate hot and humid coastal strip, summer rainfall on high plateau and desert interior; agr. millet, maize, sorghum, oats (fruit, Mocha coffee; oil (1984); rich fishing grounds; British withdrawal and closure of Suez canal led to ec. decline in south; a. 540,000 km²; p. (2004) 20,024,867.

Yenangyaung, t., R. pt., **Myanmar;** on left bank of R. Irrawaddy, 448 km N. of Rangoon; ctr. of Burma oilfields.

Yenisey, R., Siberia, **Russia;** rises in Sayan mtns., flows N. into Arctic Oc.; ch. tribs., Angara, Stony Tunguska, Lower Tunguska; hydroelectric power sta. at Krasnoyarsk; linked to Ob R. by canal; middle course navigable; 5,280 km long.

Yeo or **Ivel,** R., Dorset, Somerset, **Eng.;** trib. of R. Parrett; 38 km long.

Yeovil, mkt. t., Somerset, **Eng.;** on R. Yeo; glove mnf., aero-engin., agr. machin., dairy processing; p. (1991) 38,805.

Yerevan or **Erivan,** c., cap. of **Armenia;** on Zanga R. in deep valley of Caucasus mtns.; earthquake 1988; major science-based, industl. ctr.; p. (2000) 1,284,000.

Yevpatoriya or **Eupatoria,** spt., Crimea, on Black Sea, **Ukraine;** popular resort; children's sanatoria; chemicals, leather, locks, dried fish; new pt. being built; p. (1990) 108,900.

Yezd. See Yazd.

Yichang (**Ichang**), c., S.W. Hubei, **China;** on Chang Jiang; site of famous gorges.

Yingchuan, t., cap. of Ningxian, aut. region, **China;** on Huang He; ctr. of fertile agr. a.; new lt. inds.; p. (1994) 412,900.

Ynys Môn. See Isle of Anglesey.

Yokkaichi, c., spt., S. Honshu, **Japan;** on Ise Bay, 37 km S. of Nagoya; textiles, petrochemicals, synthetic rubber, porcelain; p. (1990) 274,184.

Yokohama, leading spt., Honshu, **Japan;** on W. shore of Tokyo Bay; steel, chemicals, cars, oil refining, shipyards; univs.; with Tokyo and Kawasaki forms conurb. of Keihin; p. (2000) 3,427,000.

Yokosuka, spt., Honshu, **Japan;** S. of Tokyo; holiday

resort; thermal power sta.; p. (1990) 433,358.

Yonkers, c., N.Y., **USA;** on E. bank of Hudson R.; residtl.; lt. inds., textiles; p. (2000) 196,086.

Yonne, dep., **France;** in S.E. of Paris basin, inc. Champagne, Burgundy, Orléanais; drained by R. Yonne; cap. Auxerre; agr., Chablis wines; a. 7,495 km²; p. (1999) 333,169.

Yonne, R., **France;** major trib. of R. Seine; 288 km long.

York, c., unit. auth. created in 1996, formerly part of North Yorks. **Eng.;** on R. Ouse; in central position in Vale of York; anc. part of c. enclosed by walls; minster, cas., univ.; chocolate, confectionery, rly. wkshps.; p. (2001) 181,094 (unit. auth.), (2001) 137,505 (c.).

York, a., Penn., **USA;** ctr. of fertile agr. region; varied inds., inc. agr. tools, machin., textiles, metal gds.; p. (1990) 437,000 (met. a.).

York, C., Queensland, **Australia;** most N. point on mainland of Australia.

York, Vale of, broad lowland, North Yorks/York, **Eng.;** between Pennines and N. Yorks. Moors and Yorks. Wolds; drained to Humber by R. Ouse and tribs.; glacial and alluvial soils have required draining; crop farming, wheat, barley, root-crops, associated with fattening of beef cattle; settlement mainly marginal; ch. t. York; length 96 km, width from 16 km in N. to 48 km in S.

Yorkshire, historic co., N. **Eng.;** formerly divided into 3 separate admin. parts (Ridings), N., E., and W.; now split into the non-met. co. of N. Yorks., the met. cos. of W. Yorks. and S. Yorks., and 8 unit. auths. inc. Kingston upon Hull, Middlesbrough and York.

Yorkshire Moors, hills, North Yorks. and Redcar and Cleveland, **Eng.;** inc. N. Yorks. Moors, Cleveland Hills and Hambleton Hills; bounded to N. by Tees valley, S. by Vale of Pickering, W. by Swale valley, E. by sea; composed of oolitic limestone; good sheep pastures; impt. iron-ore deposits worked in Cleveland Hills; max. alt. 454 m.

Yorkshire Wolds, hills, E. Riding of Yorks., **Eng.;** extend N.E. from Humber and terminate in Flamborough Head; chalk; good sheep pasture; average alt. 180 m.

Yorktown, v., Va., **USA;** scene of surrender by Lord Cornwallis to Washington 1781.

Yosemite National Park, Cal., **USA;** in Sierra Nevada; contains Yosemite creek and canyon with three famous cataracts.

Youngstown, c., Ohio, **USA;** on Mahoning R.; 91 km N.W. of Pittsburgh; ctr. of one of most impt. iron and steel dists. in USA; heavy engin.; univ.; p. (1990) 95,732 (c.), 492,619 (met. a. with Warren).

Yoyang. See Yueyang.

Ypres (**Ieper**), t., W. Flanders prov., N.W. **Belgium;** textiles and textile machin.; ctr. of cloth ind. in middle ages; scene of battles 1914–17; p. (1991) 35,200.

Ystwyth, R., Ceredigion, **Wales;** flows 40 km to join R. Rheidol at Aberystwyth.

Yucatán, st., S.E. **Mexico;** limestone lowlands poor soils; henequen (sisal hemp), chicle (resin from which chewing gum is made); cap. Mérida; a. 61,968 km²; p. (1990) 1,363,540.

Yueyang (**Yoyang**), t., Hunan, **China;** at outlet of Dongting Hu and Chang Jiang; p. (1994) 337,500.

Yugoslavia. See Serbia.

Yukon, R., **Canada** and Alaska, **USA;** flows N.W. and W. into Bering Strait; navigable for 1,920 km; 3,200 km long.

Yukon Territory, prov., N.W. **Canada;** mtnous. (Mt. Logan 6,050 m); gold, silver, lead, zinc; Alaska Highway links with B.C. and Alberta; ch. ts. Dawson, and Whitehorse (cap.); incr. indep. since 1983; a. 536,327 km²; p. (1996) 30,786.

Yumen, c., N.W. Gansu prov., **China;** leading petroleum ctr.; precision instruments; on Old Silk Road to Xinjiang; p. (1994) 126,700.

Yunnan, prov., S. **China;** adjoins Burma; mtnous. a. of minority groups; rice, tobacco, tea, cotton; copper, tin; cap. Kunming; a. 420,466 km²; p. (1994) 38,390,000.

Yvelines, dep., **France;** W. of Paris; cap. Versailles; a. 2,271 km²; p. (1990) 1,307,200.

Z

Zaanstadt, t., N. Holland **Neth.;** industl. dist.; food processing p. (1994) 132,508.

Zabrze, t., Upper Silesia, Katowice, **Poland**; impt. coal-mng. ctr. with associated heavy inds.; cultural ctr.; p. (1995) 201,581.

Zacapa, t., cap. of Z. prov., **Guatemala**; mkt. t. at rly. junc.; tobacco tr. and processing; sulphur springs; p. (1989) 35,769.

Zacatecas, st., **Mexico**; on central plateau at 2,100 m; dry, agr. dist.; sm. mng. ctrs.; a. 72,836 km²; p. (1990) 1,278,279.

Zacatecas, t., cap. of Z. st., **Mexico**; cath.; ctr. of silver mng., pottery, clothing; p. (1990) 108,528.

Zadar (Zara), t., **Croatia** (formerly Yugoslavia); spt. on cst. of Adriatic Sea; formerly Italian (1920–47); Roman remains; cath.; car ferry to Pesaro (Italy); tourism; p. (1981) 116,174.

Zagazig, t., **Egypt**; on Nile Delta; tr. ctr. of fertile agr. a. producing cotton, grains; cotton mills; p. (1986) 255,000.

Zagorsk. *See* **Sergiyev Posad**.

Zagreb, c., cap. of **Croatia** (formerly Yugoslavia); on Sava R.; cath., univ.; tr. fair; many inds., notably petrochemicals based on local petroleum reserves, elec. engin.; airport; second c. of rep.; p. (2000) 1,060,000 (met. a.).

Zagros, mtns., **Iran**; inc. Iran's major oilfield; highest peak Zardesh Kuh, 4,551 m.

Zahedan, c., **Iran**; cap. of Sistan and Baluchistan prov.; airport; terminus of rly. from Pakistan.

Zaïre. *See* **Congo, Dem. Rep. of**.

Zaïre, R. *See under* **Congo**.

Zakinthos (Zante), Ionian I., **Greece**; cap. Zakinthos (Zante); devastated by earthquake 1953; a. 717 km²; p. (1981) 30,014.

Zakinthos (Zante), t., Zakinthos I., **Greece**; spt. on E. cst.; agr. tr. and processing; p. (1981) 9,764.

Zakopane, t., Nowy Sacz prov., **Poland**; in high Tatra mtns.; base for mountaineering and winter sports; health resort; tourism; p. (1995) 29,956.

Zambesi, R., S.E. **Africa**; flows E. to Moçambique Channel, Indian Oc.; forms frontier between Zambia and Zimbabwe; inc. Victoria Falls and Kariba and Cabora Bassa dams; navigable but impeded by rapids; 3,520 km long.

Zambia, rep., Central **Africa**; member of Commonwealth; tropical climate, modified by alt.; plateau (1,200 m); subsistence agr.; livestock on uplands free from tsetse fly; mng. basis of economy, especially in copperbelt; world's 4th lgst copper producer; exp. disrupted by Rhodesian UDI (1965); falling copper output as mines near exhaustion; need to develop alternative routes to cst.; pipeline from Ndola to Dar-es-Salaam; construction of Tan-Zam rly. financed by Chinese aid; cap. Lusaka; a. 752,618 km²; p. (2004) 10,462,436.

Zamboanga, c., Mindanao, **Philippines**; spt. on Basilian Strait, exp. prod. timber; p. (1995) 511,000.

Zamfara, new st. (since 1996) in north of **Nigeria**. Created from Sokoto. Headquarters at Gusau.

Zamora, prov., **Spain**; borders Portugal; drained by R. Duero; cereals, wine, merino sheep; cap. Zamora; a. 10,559 km²; p. (1998) 205,200.

Zamora, t., cap. of Zamora prov., **Spain**; on R. Duero; cath.; agr. tr. and processing ctr.; developing mnfs.; p. (1990) 63,400.

Zamosc, t. and prov., Lublin, **Poland**; Renaissance planned t. in valley of Lubianka R.; industl., comm. and cultural ctr.; p. (1995) 66,253 (t.) 493,506 (prov.).

Zangbo (Tsangpo), R., Tibet, **China**; one of head-streams of R. Brahmaputra; 1,350 km. long.

Zanjan, c., **Iran**; cap. of Gilan prov.; cotton, woollen gds.; p. (1994) 281,000.

Zanzibar, terr., E. **Africa**; comprises Is. of Z. and Pemba; joined Tanganyika to form **Tanzania** (1964); major world source of cloves; coconut and coconut prod. major exp. and basis of processing inds.; cap. Zanzibar; a. 2,642 km²; p. (1988) 640,578.

Zanzibar, spt., Zanzibar I., **Tanzania**; on W. cst. 35 km from E. Africa; outlet for clove exp., entrepot tr.; former slave mkt.; p. (1988) 157,634.

Zaporozh'ye, t., **Ukraine**; on R. Dnieper, nr. dam and hydroelec. power sta.; p. (1990) 891,000.

Zaragoza, prov., **Spain**; largely barren plain suffering from climatic extremes; a. 17,122 km²; cap. Z.; p. (1998) 841,400.

Zaragoza, cap. Z. prov., **Spain**; on R. Ebro; 2 caths.; univ.; former cap. of Aragon; rly. junc.; comm. ctr.; p. (1998) 603,400.

Zarga, t. Jordan; ind. ctr., phosphates.

Zaria, c., N. **Nigeria**; founded 15th cent., old part surrounded by walls; univ., cotton ctr.; rly. ctr., p. (1992) 345,200.

Zealand. *See* **Sjaelland**.

Zeebrugge, spt., **Belgium**; 14 km N. of Bruges; exp. coal, chemicals; oil refining; linked by canal to Bruges.

Zeeland, prov., **Neth.**; a. covering part of Scheldt estuary and Is.; low-lying; dairying; cap. Middelburg; a. 1,787 km²; p. (1994) 363,867.

Zeist, t., Utrecht, **Neth.**; chemicals, toys; p. (1994) 59,258.

Zeitz, t., Saxony - Anhalt, **Germany**; textiles, chemicals; p. (1991) 59,357.

Zelten, Libya, N. Africa; oilfield; 320 km S. of Benghazi; pipeline to Mersa al-Brega.

Zenica, t., **Bosnia-Herzegovina**, formerly Yugoslavia; lge. iron and steel wks.; ctr. of Z. basin; rly. junc.; p. (1981) 132,733.

Zeravshan, R., **Tajikistan** and **Uzbekistan**; flows for 736 km before evaporating in desert region N. of Chardzhou.

Zetland. *See* **Shetland**.

Zeugma, anc. city, **Turkey**. Old settlement on Euphrates River. Its Greco-Roman remains submerged by waters of new dam. The Turkish Pompeii'.

Zhangjiakou (Kalgan), c., Hebei, **China**; nr. Great Wall, 160 km N.W. of Beijing; a main route to Mongolia; lge wool, hides; p. (1994) 615,300.

Zhangzhou (Chuangchow), c., Fujian prov., **China**; former pt. now silted up; p. (1994) 199,600.

Zhanjiang (Tsamkong), c., Guandong prov., **China**; spt. on Liuzhou peninsula; machin., chemicals, elec. inds.; designated economic development zone; cotton, milling, leather mnfs.; p. (1994) 491,800.

Zhdanov. *See* **Mariupol**.

Zhejiang (Chinkiang), c., Jiangsu, **China**; former treaty pt. on Chang Jiang, 77 km. below Nanjing; tr. ctr.; p. (1994) 405,700.

Zhengzhou (Quauzhu), c., cap. Henan prov., **China**; 24 km. S of Huang He where it emerges on to N. China Plain; impt. route ctr. and rly. junc.; p. (1994) 1,323,700.

Zhijiang (Chekiang), coastal prov., S.E. **China**; cap. Hangzhou; impt. rice growing a.; major natural gas field; a. 102,269 km²; p. (1994) 43,410,000.

Zhitomir, t., **Ukraine**; engin., clothing; route ctr.; p. (1990) 295,900.

Zhuhai, special economic zone, **China**, N. of Macau; selected (1983) to attract foreign investment; new pt.; p. (1994) 308,600.

Zhujiang (Chukiang or Pearl R.), Guandong, S. **China**; one of most impt. waterways of China; 176 km. long from Guangzhou to Hong Kong; fertile delta known as "land of fish, rice and fruit"; around Guangzhou network of elec., drainage and irrigation stas; built since 1959; estuary now silting.

Zibo (Tzepo), c., Shandong, **China**; formed by merging of several coal mng. ts. in the 1950s; p. (1994) 1,346,300.

Zielona Gora, prov., **Poland**; borders E. Germany; glacial sands, wooded; brown coal deposits; cap. Z.G.; a. 14,514 km²; p. (1995) 673,110.

Zigong (Tzekung), c., Sichuan, **China**; petroleum, natural gas, salt wks.; p. (1994) 430,500.

Zilina, t., **Slovakia**; on R. Vah; paper, fertilisers; p. (1990) 97,000.

Zimbabwe, Central Africa; former Brit. col. (Rhodesia); indep rep. 1980; landlocked st.; much of land high veld above 900 m covered in savannah; impressive economic growth with removal of sanctions and end of warfare; manuf. limited by lack of skilled labour; still heavy dependence on agr., maize and tobacco, mng. also impt.; Wankie coal mine lgst. in world; also asbestos, chrome and copper; power from Kariba dam encourages lt. inds.; growing econ. and social unrest under rule of Mugabe; elections in 2002 marred by violence; withdrew from Commonwealth, 2003; cap. Harare; a. 389,329 km²; p. (2004) 12,671,860.

Zimbabwe National Park; site nr. Victoria, Mashonaland, of ruined t. built c. 15th cent. A.D. by a Bantu people; discovered 1868.

Zinder, t., Niger, W. **Africa**; terminus of trans-Saharan motor route; tr. ctr.; former cap.; second t. of Niger; p. (1988) 119,838.

Zion National Park, Utah, **USA**; contains Z. canyon; a. 596 km².

Zittau, t., Saxony, **Germany**; on R. Mandau; woollens, linens, machin., cars, chemicals; p. (1989) 36,246.

Zlatoust, t., S.W. **Russia**; in Ural mtns.; metallurgical ctr.; steel, chemicals, sawmilling; p. (1989) 208,000.

Zlin (Gottwaldov), t., Czech Rep.; 64 km E. of Brno; footwear, leather and domestic woodware inds.; home of Bata footwear; p. (1990) 87,000.

Znojmo or Znaim, t., Czech Rep.; anc. t., cas.; ctr. of fertile agr. dist.; p. (1984) 38,321.

Zomba, t., former cap. of Malawi, 884 m a.s.l. on slopes of Zomba mtn., 67 km N.E. Blantyre; Malawi's univ. t.; p. (1983) 46,000.

Zonguldak, t. and prov., Turkey; spt. on Black Sea; p. (1990) 124,862 (t.), 1,073,560 (prov.).

Zrenjanin, t., Vojvodina, Serbia; pt. on R. Begej; ctr. of agr. dist.; agr. processing; p. (1991) 81,328.

Zuetina, oil pt. (1968), Libya; pipeline links shore storage sta. with offshore berths.

Zug, smallest can., Switzerland; drained by R. Reuss; contains part of L. Z., dairying, fruit, cap. Z.; a. 241 km², p. (1990) 84,900.

Zug, t., cap. of Zug can, Switzerland; on L. Z.; elec. engin., printing; p. (1980) 21,609.

Zugspitze, mtn., Bavarian Alps, on Bavarian-Austrian bdr.; highest peak in Germany, 2,965 m; connected by rack-and-pinion to Garmisch-Partenkirchen at foot.

Zuider Zee. See IJsselmeer.

Zuid Holland, prov. Neth; crossed by R. Rhine; mkt gardening; a. 2,927 km²; p. (1994) 3,313,193.

Zulia, st., Venezuela; centred on L. Maracaibo, producing 70 per cent of Venezuelan oil; timber reserves; cap. Maracaibo; a. 63,902 km²; p. (1990) 2,387,208.

Zürich, c., cap. of Z. can., Switzerland; on L. Z. and R. Limmat; cath., univ.; leading world banking ctr.; inds. inc. textiles, paper; p. (1990), 341,300 (c.), 840,000 (met. a.).

Zürich, can., Switzerland; forested and agr. a.stretching N. from L. Z.; inds. at cap. Z. and Winterthur; a. 1,728 km²; p. (1990) 1,150,500.

Zürich, L. Z., Switzerland; drained by R. Limmat; length 40 km.

Zutphen, t., Gelderland, Neth.; on R. Ijssel; textiles, paper; Sir Philip Sidney died here 1586; p. (1993) 31,117.

Zunhou (Uushew), c., Jiangsu, China; at junct. of N. China plain and Chang Jiang basin; rly. junct.

Zuzhou (Luchow), c., Sichuan, China; coal, iron, kaolin; synthetic ammonia plant.

Zweibrücken, t., Rhineland-Palatinate, Germany; nr. Saarbrücken; cas.; machin., footwear, textiles; p. (1986) 32,700.

Zwickau, c., Saxony, Germany; on R. Mulde; cas.; coal, motors, machin., textiles; birthplace of Schumann; p. (2002) 101,726.

Zwolle, t., Overijssel, Neth.; canal ctr.; cattle mkt.; p. (1994) 99,139.

CENSUS 2001

The UK Census 2001

The most recent Census of the United Kingdom took place on 29 April 2001. The Census is a count of all people and households in the UK and is normally taken every ten years. No census can ever cover 100 per cent of the population, and therefore an independent survey of 330,000 households was used to cross-check the return of forms and to enable corrections to be made for non-response. The Census provides essential statistical information, enabling the planning and monitoring of public services including schools, health services, roads and libraries. Results are also available for research and education purposes, and information is available from the UK level down to small geographical areas. One innovation in the 2001 Census is the publishing of a large amount of the data on the Internet, which enables much wider dissemination of the results than was previously the case.

Population Size and Growth

The first results from the 2001 Census, showing the population on Census Day by age and sex, were published on 30 September 2002. The total population of the United Kingdom on Census Day was 58,789,194. England had a population of 49,138,831 (83·6 per cent of the total), Scotland 5,062,011 (8·6 per cent), Wales 2,903,085 (4·9 per cent), and Northern Ireland 1,685,267 (2·9 per cent).

The UK population has increased by 17 per cent since 1951 and is continuing to grow, adding approximately 1·5 million people in the last decade. However, overall growth in the past 50 years is substantially lower than in many other developed countries, as shown by the EU average of 23 per cent and the USA figure of 80 per cent. The cause of this population increase has changed since the late 1990s, when migration overtook natural change as the main source of growth.

Compared with estimates, the 2001 Census showed that the total population was around one million smaller than had been predicted. This inaccuracy was probably due to the great difficulty of calculating migration, especially the number of people leaving the country. Most of the over-prediction was for men aged 25 to 39, although there was also a small over-estimation for women in the same age group. It is thought that an unusually large number of young people have gone abroad for longer periods than previously, either on extended breaks from higher education or to participate in new forms of youth activity in the Mediterranean and East Asia.

Population Distribution

Most of the population growth is accounted for in the south of the UK. The population of England has grown by 5 per cent since 1981, although the North East and North West of England have seen a decline in population during this time. In contrast, the South West, East and South East have all seen population growth of 10 per cent or more. The fastest growing area in England is Milton Keynes, which has experienced a population increase of 65 per cent. In the last 20 years, the Welsh population has grown by 3 per cent and the Northern Irish population by 9 per cent, although Scotland shows a 2 per cent decrease in population over this time period.

The five largest local authorities are Birmingham (with a population of 977,091), Leeds (715,404), Glasgow City (577,869), Sheffield (513,234) and Bradford (467,668). This does not necessarily mean that these are the largest cities, as some large cities are composed of more than one local authority. London is made up of 33 local authority areas with a total population of 7,172,036 and Greater Manchester is composed of 10 local authority areas with a total population of 2,482,352.

The spatial distribution of the British population is also uneven, with local authority population densities varying from 8 persons per square kilometre to more than 13,000 persons per square kilometre (as shown in the table).

All ten of the most densely populated local authorities are located within Greater London, whereas eight of the ten least densely populated areas are located in Scotland.

Most densely populated local authority areas
(persons per square km)

Kensington & Chelsea	13,244
Islington	11,719
Hammersmith & Fulham	10,328
Hackney	10,141
Lambeth	9,858

Least densely populated local authority areas
(persons per square km)

Highland	8
Western Isles	9
Argyll & Bute	13
Shetland Islands	15
Orkney Islands	19

A Changing Population Structure

In the past 50 years the population of the UK has aged considerably. The under-16 population has decreased from 24 per cent to 20 per cent of the total population, whereas the proportion aged over-60 has increased from 16 per cent to 21 per cent. This is the first census which has shown people 60 and over forming a larger part of the population than children under 16. There has also been a large increase in the number of people aged 85 and over — an increase from 0·2 million (0.4 per cent of the population) in 1951 to 1·1 million.

This ageing of the population reflects longer life expectancy due to improvements in living standards and health care. It also reflects the fact that there have not been any events with a corresponding effect on life expectancy like that of the first and second world wars. However, it also has important economic implications, particularly with regards to the increased need for health care for elderly people, and the reduced proportion of the population which is active in the work force.

The local authorities with the highest proportion of persons aged under 1 and over 85 are shown in the table below.

Highest proportion of persons aged under 1

Newham	1·73 %
Hackney	1·68 %
Tower Hamlets	1·55 %
Strabane	1·51 %
Omagh	1·48 %

Highest proportion of persons aged over 85

Worthing	4·6 %
Rother	4·6 %
Eastbourne	4·4 %
Arun	4·2 %
East Devon	4·1 %

The population consists of 28,581,233 males and 30,207,961 females, with females outnumbering males in all age groups over 21. However, this age is lower than in the past — twenty years ago, males outnumbered females until the late forties. The local authorities with the highest number of males per female and the highest number of females per male are shown in the table below. As women tend to live longer than men, the areas with the highest ratio of females per male also tend to be areas with a relatively elderly population.

Highest number of males per female
(men per 100 women)

Richmondshire	107
Rutland UA	106
Limavady	104
Bridgnorth	103
Rushmoor	102

Highest number of females per male
(men per 100 women)

Eastbourne	87
Rother	88
Belfast	88
Worthing	88
Arun	89

GLOSSARY OF GEOGRAPHICAL TERMS

The following glossary of geographical terms is designed to display the variety of interests which are now encompassed within the discipline. Although geography is often divided into 'human' and 'physical' geography, there are many ideas and concepts which draw extensively on both of these areas. This glossary does not include terms which are in common usage (many of which readers will find in **Section L, General Information**). However, it does identify some words which have specialised geographical meanings, and it attempts to outline some of the important concepts informing much modern geographical thought and research. Readers may also wish to refer to **Section Y** for further discussion of environmental issues.

Accretion, an increase in the area of land as a result of sedimentation.

Acid precipitation, rain and snow with a pH of less than 5·6, usually caused by industrial pollution.

Aid, a limited (and often conditional) flow of resources from developed to underdeveloped countries. *See* **Section F.**

Alluvial fan, collection of deposited material, formed where the sediment carrying capacity of a stream is reduced due to a decrease in depth or velocity.

Anabatic flows, upslope winds usually produced by local heating of the ground during the day.

Aquifuge, an impermeable rock which blocks the flow of water.

Assimilation, the process by which nations or communities and the sub-nations or minorities within them intermix and become more similar.

Atmosphere, the gaseous envelope of air surrounding the earth and bound to it by gravitational attraction. *See* **Section L.**

Badlands, intensely dissected natural landscapes where vegetation is sparse or absent.

Barrio, squatter settlement, particularly in Latin America.

Base flow, the usual amount of river flow from a drainage basin.

Bedrock, the consolidated unweathered rock exposed at the land surface or underlying the soil and loose surface rocks.

Berm, a ridge of sand parallel to the coastline, commonly found on the landward side of steeply sloping beaches.

Bid-rent curve, a plot of the rent which people are prepared to pay against distance from some point, usually the city centre.

Biodiversity. *See* **Section Y.**

Biogeochemical cycling of minerals and compounds (especially carbon and nitrogen) through ecosystems.

Biome, a mixed community of plants and animals (a biotic community) occupying a major geographical area.

Bodden, an irregularly shaped coastal inlet caused when the sea enters an area of gently undulating terrain.

Carrying capacity, the maximum number of users (humans or animals) that can be sustained by a given set of land resources.

Central business district (CBD), the nucleus of an urban area, containing the main concentration of commercial land uses (shops, offices and warehouses).

Central place theory, a theoretical account of the size and distribution of settlements based on the assumption that markets are the chief urban function.

Channelization, the modification of river channels for the purposes of flood control, land drainage, navigation, and the reduction or prevention of erosion.

Cirque or **Corrie (Cwm,** Welsh), deep rounded hollow on mountain side, characteristic of regions that have been glaciated.

Civil society, that segment of the practices within a capitalist society which lies outside the sphere of production and the state.

Clast, a coarse sediment particle, usually larger than 4mm in diameter.

Clay, any material made up of particles less than about 0.002mm in diameter.

Colonialism, the establishment and maintenance of rule, for an extended period of time, by a sovereign power over a foreign country.

Comparative advantage, the principle whereby individuals (or territories) produce those goods or services for which they have the greatest cost or efficiency advantage over others, or for which they have the least disadvantage. The outcome tends to be specialization.

Conflict, a situation involving struggle, which affects many of the patterns that geographers analyse. The outcomes of conflict often themselves provide the context for further conflicts.

Conservation, in some contexts, the efficient and non-wasteful use of natural resources; in others, any form of environmental protection. *See* **Section Y.**

Continental shelf, the area of submerged continental rock forming the continental margin lying closest to the shore. The political significance of the continental shelf increased rapidly during the second half of the twentieth-century, as the exploitation of underwater resources, in addition to fisheries, has become a realistic process.

Conurbation, a built-up area created by the coalescence of once-separate urban settlements.

Core, the intensely hot inner part of the earth, beginning around 2900km under the surface.

Counterurbanization, a process of population deconcentration away from the large urban settlements.

Crater, a depression at the crest or on the flanks of a volcanic cone where a pipe or vent carrying gases and lava reaches the surface.

Crust, the outer shell of the earth, between 6km and 48km in thickness, which includes the continents and the ocean floor.

Deflation, the process whereby the wind removes fine material from the surface, e.g. a beach or a desert.

Deforestation, the removal of trees from a locality. This removal may be either temporary or permanent, leading to partial or complete eradication of the tree cover.

Demographic transition, a general model describing changes in levels of fertility and mortality over time.

Denudation, the laying bare of underlying rocks or strata by the removal of overlying material.

Dependency ratio, the number of children (aged 0–14) and elderly people (aged 65 or over) in a population as a ratio of the number of adults (aged 15–64).

Desert, an area in which the vegetation cover is sparse or absent and where the ground surface is thus exposed to the atmosphere and the associated physical forces. Generally deserts are areas where precipitation is small in amount and of infrequent and irregular occurrence.

Desertification, the process whereby an area of land becomes a desert. This normally involves the impoverishment of the ecosystem, through either climatic change or human impact (or a combination of the two), so that the land develops the characteristics of a desert area.

Distance decay, the reduction in occurrence of a pattern or process with distance from a central place.

Drought, the condition of dryness because of lack of precipitation. An absolute drought is defined as a period of at least 15 consecutive days during which no day reports more than 0.2mm of rain.

Dry farming, a farming technique for crop cultivation without irrigation in areas of low and variable rainfall.

Ecological fallacy, the problem of inferring characteristics of individuals from aggregate data referring to a population.

Ecosystem, a community of plants and animals within a particular physical environment.

Environmental audit, an inventory of the pollutants generated by a firm, corporation, or individual.

Environmental determinism, the doctrine that human activities are controlled by the environment.

Environmental hazard, a term generally used to refer to short-or long-term geophysical events that pose economic and physical threats to people.

Environmentalism, a wide range of ideas and practices evincing a concern for nature-society or human-environment relations.

Epicentre, the point on the earth's surface which lies directly above the focus of an earthquake.

Erosion, the group of processes whereby debris or rock material is loosened or dissolved and removed from any part of the earth's surface.

Ethnicity, in contemporary usage, is seen as both a way in which individuals define their personal identity and also a type of social stratification that emerges when people form groups based on their real or perceived common origins.

Famine, a relatively sudden event involving mass mortalities from starvation within a short period.

Fault, a break or crack in the earth's crust.

Fieldwork, a traditional means of data collection within geography, based on the assumption that reality is present in appearance, and can therefore be directly understood through observation.

Fold, a bend in a formerly flat rock structure resulting from movement of the crustal rocks.

Frontier, a zone of varying width that refers either to the political division between two countries or to the division between the settled and uninhabited parts of a country.

Garden city, a planned and relatively self-contained settlement, developed to a plan stressing spaciousness, environmental quality and 'greenness'.

Generational succession, a term borrowed from ecology to describe the tendency for subsequent generations of immigrants to disperse, thus leading to desegregation.

Gentrification, a process of neighbourhood regeneration by relatively affluent incomers, who displace lower-income groups and invest substantially in improvements to homes.

Geo, a deep, narrow cleft or ravine along a rocky sea coast which is flooded by the sea.

Ghetto, an urban residential district which is almost exclusively the preserve of one ethnic or cultural group.

Habitat, the overall environment, but more often specifically the physical environment in which organisms live. *See* **Section Y**.

Hinterland, the tributary area of a port, from which it collects material to be exported and through which it distributes imports.

Iconography, the description and interpretation of visual images in order to disclose their symbolic meanings.

Igneous rock, rock formed when molten material, magma, solidifies, either within the earth's crust or at the surface.

Imperialism, a relationship between states based on domination and subordination. This does not necessarily imply colonialism, as influence of economic and political activities can occur without military intervention or a colonial regime.

Informal sector, that part of an economy beyond official recognition and record which performs productive, useful and necessary labour without formal systems of control and remuneration.

Inner city, an ill-defined area close to the central business district, usually associated with dilapidation, poor housing and economic and social deprivation.

Invasion and succession, a term adopted from ecology to describe a process of neighbourhood change whereby one social group succeeds another in a residential area.

Isolines, lines on a map connecting points of equal data value. **Isobars** connect points of the same mean barometric pressure; **Isobaths** refer to depth below the sea surface; **Isohyets** link areas with the same mean rainfall; **Isotherms** connect places with the same mean temperature.

Katabatic flows, downslope winds, often influenced by the cooling of the ground at night.

Kettle (or **kettle hole**), an enclosed depression resulting from the melting of buried ice.

Landscape, an area of the earth's surface with a distinctive appearance, whether due to natural or human processes.

Leaching, the downward movement of water through the soil zone which results in the removal of water-soluble minerals from the upper horizons and their accumulation in the lower soil zone or groundwater.

Levee, natural or artificial embankments along the side of a river.

Location theory, a body of theories which seek to account for the location of economic activities.

Longshore drift, the transport of beach material along the coast by wave action.

Mantle, the zone within the earth's interior extending from 25 to 70km below the surface to a depth of 2900km and lying between the partially molten core and the thin surface crust.

Meandering, the sinuous winding of a river.

Meridian, a line of longitude circling the earth.

Metamorphic rock, rock changed by heat or by pressure beneath the surface of the earth.

Migrant labour, workers who move between regions or countries in order to find employment.

Migration, permanent or semi-permanent change of residence of an individual or group of people.

Mobility, a general term which includes all types of territorial movements, including migration.

Modernism, a way of representing and understanding the world strongly influenced by twentieth-century movements in the arts.

Modernity, the entire construct of power, knowledge and social practicies, developed from 16th and 17th century European philosophy. Modernity now forms the base of much of the dominant social order throughout the world.

Modernization, the process by which societies seek to adopt the characteristics of wealthier and apparently more advanced societies.

Moraine, a distinct landform fashioned by the direct action of a glacier.

Multiculturalism, a policy that endorses the right of different cultural or ethnic groups to remain distinct rather than assimilating to a dominant society's cultural 'mainstream'.

Nation, a community of people whose members are bound together by a sense of solidarity rooted in an historic attachment to territory and a common culture, and by a consciousness of being different from other nations.

Nation-state, a complex array of modern institutions involved in governance over a spatially bounded territory which enjoys monopolistic control over the means of violence.

Natural resources, properties of the physical environment that are considered useful for satisfying human wants.

Nature, often used to refer to areas unaltered by human action; but can also refer to the entire physical world (including humans).

Neocolonialism, a means of economic and political control articulated through the powerful states of developed economics (notably the USA, the former USSR, Japan and, collectively, the member states of the EU) over the economies and societies of the underdeveloped world.

Orogeny, the event, or mechanism, of the construction of mountain chains formed on continents.

Overpopulation, an excess of population in an area in relation to resources or to other broader economic or social goals.

Ozone layer, atmospheric layer 15-50km above the earth's surface, which absorbs most of the harmful ultraviolet radiation from the sun.

Parabolic dunes, crescentic sand accumulations in which the horns point away from the direction of dune movement.

Pediment, an area with a relatively smooth surface formed by erosion, typically sloping down from the foot of a highland area.

Permafrost, areas of soil and rock in which freezing temperatures persist throughout the year.

Permeability, a measure of the capacity of a rock or soil to transmit fluids.

Pingo, an ice-cored hill which is typically conical in shape and can only grow and persist in permafrost.

Place, a portion of geographical space occupied by a person or a thing.

Playa, a closed depression in an arid or semi-arid region that is periodically inundated by surface runoff, or the salt flat within such a closed basin.

Pollution, the release of substances in the environment in the wrong place or the wrong quantity—wrong because they degrade or damage the environment, as defined by some chosen criteria. *See* **Section Y**.

Population density, the number of people in relation to the space that they occupy.

Population pyramid, a diagrammatic representation of the age and sex structure of a population. Generally, the vertical axis represents age groups and the horizontal axis indicates the numerical or percentage distribution by sex.

Porosity, a property of a rock or soil concerned with the extent to which it contains pores through which a liquid can pass through.

Postcolonialism, a movement among artists and intellectuals that challenges the impact of imperialism on non-Western cultures, often aiming to 'decolonize the mind'.

Power, the ability to achieve certain aims, frequently used to characterize interpersonal and inter-group relationships, including those between states, but may also refer to the relationship between an individual or group and the natural world.

Quaternary, the period of time between 10,000 years ago and 1.8 million years ago during which much of Britain's glacial and periglacial scenery evolved.

Recycling, the re-use of resources, typically material or energy. *See* **Section L**.

Reef, a rocky construction found at or near sea-level, mainly composed of carbonate deposits created by minute organisms.

Reg, a stony desert or any desert region where the surface consists of sheets of gravel.

Remote sensing, the acquisition of information about an object by a sensor that is not in direct physical contact with the object.

Resource, a concept employed to denote sources of human satisfaction, wealth or strength.

Rural, areas which are dominated (either currently or recently) by extensive land uses such as agriculture or forestry, or by large open spaces of undeveloped land, which contain small, lower-order settlements demonstrating a strong relationship between buildings and surrounding extensive landscape, and which are perceived as rural by most residents.

Sedimentary rock, rock composed of the fragments and particles of older rocks which have been eroded and the debris deposited by wind or water, often exhibiting clear layers.

Siltation, the accumulation of fine sediment in a body of water.

Skid row, a run-down section of an urban area, usually close to the city centre, which houses a concentration of its transient population, notably those on the margins of economic survival.

Slum, an area of overcrowded and dilapidated, usually old, housing, occupied by people who can afford only the cheapest dwellings available in the urban area, generally in or close to the inner city.

Solifluction, the slow gravitational downslope movement of water saturated, seasonally thawed materials.

Space, the extent of an area in which geographical processes take place.

Squatter settlement, an urban development, usually predominantly residential, on land neither owned nor rented by its occupants.

Suburb, an outer district lying within the commuting zone of an urban area, often as a separate political jurisdiction.

Sustainable development, according to the World Commission on Environment and Development, is "development that meets the needs of the present without compromising the ability of future generations to meet their own needs".

Territorial sea, the areas of sea over which a state claims exclusive jurisdiction, internationally accepted as being up to 12 nautical miles from the coast.

Thermal pollution, an increase in water temperature caused by industrial processes, often damaging wildlife inhabiting streams and rivers.

Tropical cyclone, a collective term which refers to the intense cyclonic vortices that are observed principally across tropical oceans. They are known locally as **cyclones** in the Indian Ocean, **hurricanes** in the Caribbean, and **typhoons** in the north west Pacific.

Upwelling, the vertical movement of deeper water towards the sea surface.

Urbanism, a way of life associated with residence in an urban area.

Urbanization, the process of becoming urban, generally referring to the relative concentration of a territory's population in towns and cities.

Water table, the level of water in rocks and soils beneath the land surface.

Wetlands, usually flat areas which are covered either periodically, regularly or permanently by shallow water up to a depth of around 6m.

Wilderness, the United States Wilderness Act of 1964 defines wilderness as a landscape that "generally appears to have been affected primarily by the forces of nature, with the imprint of man's [*sic*] works substantially unnoticeable".

Zoning, the general process of sub-dividing geographical space for some purpose, especially for implementing public space-use policy.

GENERAL
INFORMATION

This section contains over 2,500 entries, all arranged alphabetically. Entries range across a wide spectrum of human knowledge, from the animal kingdom and geographical features to such popular topics as space exploration and the world of nature. There are also entries for many scientific terms, from astrophysics to zodiacal light. Readers may wish to refer to Section A for historical terms, Section B for the Nobel Prizes and Section N for art. Cross references direct the reader to fuller information elsewhere in the book. A Special Topic at the end of the section commemorates the 200th anniversary of the abolition of the slave trade.

MEASUREMENTS ARE GIVEN IN METRIC UNITS

Abbreviations

mm	= millimetre	m^2	= square metre
cm	= centimetre	km^2	= square kilometre
m	= metre	ha	= hectare
km	= kilometre	m^3	= cubic metre
km/h	= kilometres per hour	s	= second
g	= gram	min	= minute
kg	= kilogram	h	= hour
tonne	= metric ton		

Equivalents

Length

		Reciprocal
1 cm	= 0·394 in	2·540
1 m	= 1·094 yd	0·914
1 km	= 0·621 mile	1·609

Area

1 m^2	= 1·196 yd^2	0·836
1 km^2	= 0·386 $mile^2$	2·590
1 hectare	= 2·471 acres	0·405

Volume

1 m^3	= 1·308 yd^3	0·765
1 litre	= 0·220 gallon	4·546

Mass

1 kg	= 2·205 lb	0·454
1 tonne	= 0·984 ton	1·016

Temperature

$$C = (F - 32) \div 1·8$$
$$F = (1·8 \times C) + 32$$

See also **Metric Equivalents, T58–62**

GENERAL INFORMATION

A

Aard-vark (Dutch *aarde* = earth + *vark* = pig), a large nocturnal mammal found only in Africa. It feeds on termites and ants.

Abacus, a device for making arithmetical calculations, consisting of parallel bars on which are strung movable coloured beads. The earliest form of this instrument was used in Mesopotamia about 3000 B.C., and its use spread westwards throughout the Graeco-Roman world and eastwards to China. An efficient form of the abacus is still used in parts of Asia.

Abalone, shellfish regarded in the Far East as an aphrodisiac. The colourful pearly interior of the shell is used for beads and ornaments.

Aberration, in astronomy, is the apparent displacement of a star due to the speed of the observer with the earth (*see* **Parallax**). In optics (i) spherical aberration is when there is blurring of the image and fringes of colour at its edges, due to failure of lens to bring light to a single focus; (ii) chromatic aberration is due to the refractive index of glass being different for light of different colours. For instance, violet light is bent more than red.

Abiogenesis, or spontaneous generation; the origination of living from non-living matter. The term is applied to such discredited ideas as that frogs could be generated spontaneously by the action of sunlight on mud, or maggots arise spontaneously in dead meat without any eggs from which the maggots hatch being present. Spallanzani (1729–99) upset the hypothesis of spontaneous generation; Pasteur dealt it a death-blow.

Abominable Snowman. *See* **Yeti.**

Aborigines, a term for the original inhabitants of a country, in particular the aboriginal tribes of Australia. In contrast to their highly complex social and religious customs, the material culture of Australian aboriginals is very low and ill adapted to stand up to contact with European civilisation. The 1988 Australian bicentenary focused attention on their lack of legal right to ancient tribal lands and their welfare problems. The passage of the Native Rights Act in 1993 has generated heated debate and led to the controversial Native Title Amendment Bill. In 1999 the Australian parliament formally apologised to them for the "hurt and trauma" caused by white settlement. Recent years have seen a new respect for aborigine painting. Alcohol abuse and poor diet still contribute to low life expectancy.

Absolute Temperature, Absolute Zero. This is a refined notion requiring some study of thermodynamics for its full understanding. For setting up an absolute temperature scale one must first assign a numerical value to one fixed temperature. For this, the triple point of water has been chosen, *i.e.*, the temperature at which solid, liquid, and gaseous water are all in equilibrium. The triple point is defined to be 273·16 K where K is read for kelvin (after Lord Kelvin). This temperature is 0·01°C on the Celsius scale (*q.v.*) and is thus very close to the melting point of ice. Suppose the pressure and volume of a mass of gas are measured (i) at the triple point of water, giving (pV)tr as the product of the pressure and volume; and (ii) at any unknown temperature T K, giving (pV) as the product. Then the absolute temperature, T K, is defined by

$$T \text{ K} = 273 \cdot 16 \frac{(pV)}{(pV)\text{tr}}$$

It is to be understood that the gas pressure is very low. The nature of the gas is immaterial. More subtly, it can be shown that the temperature so defined is identical with that derived in a rather abstract way in the science of thermodynamics. The absolute scale is therefore also called the thermodynamic scale. Absolute temperatures can be obtained from Celsius temperatures by adding 273·15; thus the absolute temperature of melting ice is 273·15 K. Conversely, absolute zero is a temperature 273·15 K below the temperature of melting ice, *i.e.*, −273·15°C. Theory shows that absolute zero is unattainable, but it has been approached to within about 1 millionth of a degree. Within ten or so degrees of absolute zero, matter develops some remarkable properties. *See* **Kelvin, Cryogenics, Superconductor, Helium.**

Acadians. *See* **Cajuns.**

Acetic Acid, an organic acid produced when ordinary (ethyl) alcohol is fermented by the organism called *Acetobacter aceti*. The same oxidation process yields vinegar: this is a weak and crude solution of acetic acid obtained by trickling dilute alcoholic liquor over beechwood shavings at 35°C. The souring of wine is due to the same process. Acetic acid is used as a food preservative and flavouring material, and in the manufacture of cellulose acetate and white lead.

Acetylene (also called ethyne), a compound of carbon and hydrogen prepared from calcium carbide and water. A very reactive gas, it is used industrially on a large scale to prepare acetaldehyde, chlorohydrocarbon solvents, and many intermediates for plastics manufacture. Burns in air with a highly luminous flame, formerly used for lighting purposes, but is now widely used, with oxygen, in welding. For safe storage and transportation it is dissolved in acetone.

Acid Rain is the name given to rain, snow or sleet contaminated with acid substances so that its acidity is greater than the limit expected by normal concentrations of carbon dioxide dissolving in the rain to give carbonic acid (pH 5·5–5·6). The pH (*q.v.*) of acid rain therefore is less than about 5·5. The increased acidity is caused by larger concentrations of a number of contaminants, principally the strong acids, nitric and sulphuric, which arise from industrial effluents containing oxides of nitrogen and sulphur. The European emission of sulphur dioxide doubled between 1940 and 1980. In some European and North American areas such contamination can give a rain pH as low as 3 (which is 100 times more acid than pH 5). The acid rain can mark fruit and leaves, and adversely affect soil but its main effect is on the aquatic ecosystems especially in regions which cannot naturally buffer acidic inputs such as those with thin soils and granite rocks.

Acids, substances having a tendency to lose a positive ion (a proton). This general definition overcomes difficulties of earlier views which merely described their properties and asserted that they are chemically opposite to bases. As a whole acids contain ionisable hydrogen, replaceable by a metal, to form a salt. Inorganic acids are compounds of non-metals or metalloids, *e.g.*, sulphuric, phosphoric acid. Carboxylic acids contain the group –COOH.

Act of Settlement. *See* **Settlement, Act of, A47.**

Act of Union. *See* **Union, Treaty of, A48.**

Actinaria. *See* **Sea Anemones.**

Actinides, the fourteen metallic elements from thorium (no. 90) to lawrencium (no. 103). All known isotopes of these elements are radioactive and those with atomic number greater than 92 (uranium) have been produced only in significant quantities artificially. Plutonium (no. 94) is obtained from uranium during the course of nuclear reactor operation and the higher transuranic elements can be made from it by the successive capture of neutrons or nuclei of light atoms. The availability of only minute quantities of short-lived isotopes makes the determination of the physical and chemical properties of the higher actinides very difficult. Claims for the discovery of new elements can therefore be controversial and since the discoverers can name the elements their naming is also controversial. There were three different reports for Nobelium (no. 102). Lawrencium (no. 103) is called Jolistium by Russian authors. Element no. 104 was reported in 1964 by a Russian group and called Kurchatovium but is called Rutherfordium (Rf) in the West. Element no. 105 is called Hahnium (Hn).

Advent, the period including four Sundays devoted to religious preparation for the coming celebration of the Nativity (Christmas).

Advocatus Diaboli ("the devil's advocate"), a Roman Catholic functionary who presents opposing evidence in regard to the life of any deceased person it may be proposed to canonise.

Aerodynamics, the science of gases (especially air) in motion, particularly in relation to aircraft (aeronautics). The idea of imitating the birds by the use of wings is of ancient origin. Leonardo da Vinci first carried out experiments in a scientific manner. The invention of the balloon in 1783 and the researches of scientists and engineers in the 19th cent. ultimately led to the development of the aeroplane.

Aerolites, the name given to the class of meteorites composed chiefly of heavy silicates. The other two main classes are *siderolites* (nickel-iron and silicates) and *siderites* (nickel-iron).

Aerosol, a suspension of a liquid in a gas; for example, a fog is very small drops of water suspended in air. Formed by spraying the liquid in air, aerosols are used to disperse liquid over a wide area in crop spraying, air freshening and pest control. *See also* **Fluorocarbons.**

Afrikander, type of cattle bred in South Africa.

Afrikaner, an Afrikaans-speaking South African, usually of Dutch descent.

After-damp occurs in a mine after an explosion, causing suffocation. It is composed mainly of carbon dioxide and nitrogen and contains water vapour and carbon monoxide (produced by the burning, in a restricted supply of air, of fine coal dust).

Agaric, large fungi of the family *Agaricaceae,* which includes the mushroom and what are popularly called "toadstools", though the idea that these two lay terms sharply differentiate between edible and poisonous fungi is an incorrect one. Characteristic of the agarics is the presence of a cap or *pileus* (bearing underneath the spore-shedding gills) and a stalk or *stipe.*

Agave, the American aloe or Century Plant which sometimes does not attain to flowering maturity under sixty or seventy years, and then dies. The flower spray may reach a height of 6 m and in its development the rush of sap is so great that the Mexicans collect for brewing the strong spirit called mescal. 1,000 litres of sap can be obtained from a single plant. Some species of agave yield sisal (for making cord and rope).

Aggression is the use of armed force by a state against the sovereignty, territorial integrity, or political independence of another state or in any other manner inconsistent with the Charter of the UN. Iraq's invasion of Kuwait in 1990 was one recent example.

Air, a mixture of gases in the earth's atmosphere, the main constituents being nitrogen, oxygen and argon. Dry air contains these gases in the following proportions by volume: nitrogen 78·06%, oxygen 21%, argon 0·94%. Other gases are also present in small amounts. Of particular importance are water vapour and carbon dioxide. Water vapour is not only critical for life forms on land but also a major factor in the behaviour of the atmosphere—weather and climate. Carbon dioxide is utilised by green plants in photosynthesis.
  Air also contains traces of ammonia, nitrogen oxides, hydrogen, sulphur dioxide, ozone, and of the rare gases, helium, krypton, neon and xenon. Near cities and industrial areas there are also large quantities of dust and smoke particles (up to 100,000 particles per cc), and traces of other gases from industrial processes. A litre of air at 0°C and 760 mm pressure weighs 1·2932 g. *See also* **Atmosphere, Pollution.**

Air Glow is the general name given to a large number of relatively weak optical emissions from the earth's upper atmosphere in the height range 70 to 400 km (approx.). It is distinct from the aurora polaris (*q.v.*) which is usually much brighter and normally only observable at high latitudes. Air glow is produced by a combination of photochemical reactions in the upper atmosphere, excitation by photoelectrons, or by solar ultra-violet light. In the latter case it is more correctly called "dayglow." These

emissions occur in the ultra-violet and infra-red spectral regions as well as in visible light.

Alabaster, a soft crystalline form of sulphate of lime, or granulated gypsum, easily worked for statuary and other ornamental articles, and capable of being highly polished. Volterra, in Tuscany, yields the finest; that in highest ancient repute came from Alabastron in Egypt, near to the modern Antinoë.

Alb, white vestment reaching to the feet, worn by priests in religious ceremonies.

Albatross, a large sea-bird of almost pure white, black and white, or brown plumage. It nests in colonies on remote islands, but at other times rarely approaches land. Of the thirteen species, nine are found in the southern oceans, one in the tropics, three others in the North Pacific. Modern fishing methods are threatening the albatross with extinction (16 species are threatened).
  It is estimated that around 100,000 of the birds are hooked and then drowned each year by long-line fishing.
  Contrary to popular belief, it has now been discovered that the albatross does *not* wander aimlessly but for purposes of breeding and foraging. One recent survey found that some albatrosses make astonishing round-the-world journeys in as little as 46 days.

Albert Memorial, a large Gothic monument designed by Sir George Gilbert Scott, and embellished with sculptures by eminent artists. Erected in memory of Prince Albert in Kensington Gardens.

Alcázar the palace at Seville, famed for the beauty of its halls and gardens, formerly the residence of the Moorish kings.

Alchemy. *See* **Section J.**

Alcoholics Anonymous, organisation first formed to help alcoholics in the USA in 1935. The first group was formed in Britain in 1948 in London.

Alcohols. A class of organic compounds of general formula R–OH, where R is an aliphatic radical. "Alcohol" is the name used for ethyl alcohol (ethanol); this is produced by distilling fermented liquors, and synthetically from ethylene, a product of petroleum cracking. Industrially ethyl alcohol is used in the manufacture of chloroform, ether, perfumes, *etc.* Diluted with wood alcohol or other denaturants ethyl alcohol is called "methylated spirits"; the denaturants are varied according to the industrial purposes for which it is required, the methylated spirits then being largely exempt from duty. Wood alcohol (methyl alcohol or methanol) can be obtained by distilling wood or synthetically from water gas.

Alcoholic Strength. In 1980 Great Britain adopted the OIML (International Organisation of Legal Metrology) system of spirit strength measurement in metric units as required by EEC directive. The alcoholic strength of wine is expressed in percentage volume ("% vol") terms, *i.e.,* the number of volumes of pure alcohol in 100 volumes of the product at 20°C. For spirits the quantity for duty is the litre of alcohol at 20°C. For example, a case of 12 bottles of 75 cl each = 9 litres; at 40% volume 9 litres = 9 × 40% = 3.60 litres of alcohol. The alcoholic strength of spirits and liqueurs appearing on bottle labels is increasingly shown in % vol. terms (*e.g.,* "40.5% vol"). The USA continues to use the US proof gallon (1.37 US proof gallons = 1 British proof gallon).

Aldehyde, the generic term for a class of chemical compounds of general formula R–CHO, where R is an organic radical. Except for formaldehyde, which is a gas, aldehydes are volatile liquids. They are produced by oxidation of primary alcohols. Most important aldehyde is formaldehyde (methanal) used in making the plastics described as formaldehyde resins. Formalin (formaldehyde solution in water) is much used for preserving zoological specimens.

Alder, a river-side tree of the genus *Alnus,* including some 30 species and found in north temperate regions and the Andes. The only species native to Britain is *A. glutinosa,* which has been described as "guardian of river-banks" because of the way its roots bind together the sand and stones, and so slow down erosion. The wood is used for furniture and charcoal.

Aldine Editions are the beautiful books printed in Venice by the Renaissance printer Aldo Pio

Manuzio and his family between 1490 and 1597. Italics were first introduced in these books.

Algae, flowerless plants living mostly in water. Seaweeds and the green pond scums are the best known algae. The green powder found on trees is a microscopic alga (*Protoccus*).

Algebra, a branch of mathematics in which symbols are used in place of numbers. Sir Isaac Newton styled it the "universal arithmetic". The Chinese were able to solve the quadratic equation before the Christian era but it was Al-Khowarizmi, an Arab mathematician of the early 9th cent., who introduced algebra to Europe.

Alhambra, the ancient palace of the Moorish kings at Granada in Spain, built in the 13th and 14th cent. Though part of the castle was turned into a modern palace under Charles V, the most beautiful parts of the interior are still preserved—the graceful halls and dwelling-rooms grouped round the Court of Alberca and the Court of Lions, with their fountains, arcades, and lovely gardens.

Aliphatic describes derivatives of hydrocarbons having chains of carbon atoms, as distinct from rings of carbon atoms as in benzene (*see* **Aromatic**). The gas butane is aliphatic.

Alkali, the general name given to a number of chemicals which are bases (*q.v.*). The term should be limited to the hydroxides of metals in the first and second group of the periodic table and of ammonia, *e.g.*, NaOH, KOH. They are used commercially in the manufacture of paper, glass, soap, and artificial silk. The word comes from the Arabic *al-kali* meaning calcined wood ashes. Alkalis are extremely soluble in water and neutralise acids to form salts and water.

Alkaloids, a large group of natural products which contain nitrogen; they are usually basic. Isolated from plants and animals, they include some hormones, vitamins, and drugs. Examples are nicotine, adrenalin, and cocaine. Many alkaloids are made synthetically for medicinal use, *e.g.*, morphine, quinine. Their function in plants is not well understood. *See* **Belladonna**.

Alligator, the crocodile of America, found in the lower Mississippi and adjacent lakes *etc*. There is also a Chinese species. Alligators have broader snouts than other crocodiles.

Allotropy. Depending on the temperature, pressure or method of preparation, an element may exist in one of several forms, each having different physical properties (crystal structure, electrical conductivity, melting point, *etc.*). This is known as allotropy and the different forms of the element are called allotropes. Many elements exhibit allotropy, *e.g.*, sulphur, phosphorus, oxygen, tin and carbon, the most well-known allotropes of carbon being diamond and graphite.

Alloys are combinations of metals made for their valuable special properties, *e.g.*, durability, strength, lightness, magnetism, rust resistance, *etc*. Some well-known ones are brass (zinc + copper), coinage bronze (copper + zinc + tin), steels (iron + carbon + various other materials), soft solder (tin + lead), dental fillings (mercury + various ingredients).

All Saints' Day (1 Nov) is common to both the Anglican and Roman Catholic Churches, and is in commemoration of the saints generally, or such as have no special day set apart for them. Instituted by Pope Boniface IV, early in the 7th cent., this ecclesiastical festival was formerly called "All Hallows".

All Souls' Day (2 Nov) is a festival of the Roman Church, intended for the mitigation by prayer of the sufferings of souls in purgatory. The commemoration was enjoined by Abbot Odilo of Cluny during the 11th cent. upon the monastic order over which he presided, and was afterwards adopted generally throughout the Roman Communion.

Allspice, a flavouring obtained from a West Indian tree of the myrtle family, *Pimenta officinalis*, likened to the flavour of cinnamon, nutmeg and cloves combined. The berries resemble peppercorns and are used as a spice in mincemeat, etc.

Alluvium, river transported deposits of sand, mud and gravel which accumulate to form distinctive features such as levées, flood plains and deltas. The frequent renewal of alluvium by flooding

causes riverine lands to be some of the most fertile. In Asia alluvial lands support high densities of population, *e.g.*, The Hwang-ho plains and the Ganges delta.

Almond, the fruit of the *Amygdalus communis*, originally indigenous to Persia, Asia Minor and N. Africa; now cultivated in Italy, Spain, France, the USA and Australia. It yields both bitter and sweet oil. Bitter almond oil is obtained by macerating and distilling the ripe seeds; it is used for flavouring and scenting purposes, its fragrant odour being due to the presence of benzaldehyde and hydrogen cyanide. When the seeds are pressed sweet almond oil results: this is used in perfumery, and also as a lubricant for very delicate machinery.

Almuce, a fur stole worn by certain canons.

Aloe, large plants of the lily family, with about 180 species found mainly in the S. African veldt and karroo. The bitter purgative drug (aloes) is prepared by evaporating the plant's sap. *See* **Agave**.

Alpaca, a South American ruminant related to the llama whose long, fine wool is woven into a soft dress fabric known by the same name. Sir Titus Salt first manufactured alpaca cloth (1836). Saltaire, near Bradford, remains to evidence the success which for many years attended the enterprise.

Alpha Particle, or Alpha-ray, fast-moving helium nucleus ejected by some radioactive atoms, *e.g.*, polonium. It is a combination of 2 neutrons and 2 protons.

Alphabet (so called from the first two letters of the Greek alphabet—alpha, beta) is the term applied to the collection of letters from which the words of a language are made up. It grew out of the knowledge that all words can be expressed by a limited number of sounds arranged in various combinations. The Phoenicians were the first to make use of an alphabetic script derived from an earlier Semitic alphabet (earliest known inscriptions *c.* 1500–950 B.C.) from which all other alphabets have sprung. The stages in the development of the alphabet were mnemonic (memory aids), pictorial (actual pictures), ideographic (symbols), and lastly phonetic. All the ideographic systems died out, with the exception of that of the Chinese.

Altimeter, an instrument used in aircraft to estimate altitude; its usual essential feature is an aneroid barometer which registers the decrease of pressure with height. Roughly 1 millibar corresponds to 9 m. To read an aircraft altimeter correct for its destination, the zero setting must be adjusted for difference of ground height and difference of surface pressure, especially when pressure is falling or when flying towards low pressure.

Altitude, an astronomical term used to signify the angular elevation of a heavenly body; this is measured with a quadrant or sextant. In aeronautics it is the height above sea-level.

Alto-Relievo. *See* **Section N**.

Alum is a compound salt used in various industrial processes, especially dyeing, its constituents being the sulphate of one univalent metal or radical (*e.g.*, potassium, sodium, ammonium, rubidium, caesium, silver, thallium) and the sulphate of a tervalent metal (*e.g.*, aluminium, iron, chromium, manganese), and water of crystallisation.

Alumina is the oxide of aluminium. Very valuable as a refractory material. The ruby is almost 100 per cent. alumina; so also are the emerald, oriental amethyst, etc. An hydrated aluminium oxide is bauxite, chief ore of aluminium from which the metal is extracted electrolytically.

Aluminium, element no. 13, symbol Al, is a light metal which conducts electricity well. Its specific gravity at 20°C is 2·705. Melting point of aluminium is 660·2°C. It is made commercially by electrolysing bauxite dissolved in cryolite (double fluoride of aluminium and sodium). Aluminium alloys are being increasingly used for construction purposes.

Amadavat, a popular cage bird of the weaver family, mainly crimson with spots, so named because the first specimens came from Ahmadabad in India about 1700.

Amalgam is the term applied to any alloy of which mercury forms a part.

Amber, a brittle resinous substance; in origin, fossilised resin. Obtained mostly from the Baltic coasts, and used for ornaments *etc.*

Ambergris is a waxy substance produced in the intestines of the sperm whale, and generally found floating on the sea. It is a valuable perfumery material.

Amblyopsis, a species of fish, practically sightless, and with inoperative organs of hearing and feeling, that inhabit the Mammoth Cave of Kentucky. A remarkable illustration of the failure of senses not brought into use.

America's Cup. *See* **S24.**

Amethyst, the violet variety of quartz, used as a precious stone, containing traces of manganese, titanium and iron. The finest coloured specimens come from Brazil and the Urals.

Amice, a white linen vestment worn by Roman Catholic and many Anglican priests when officiating at Mass or Holy Eucharist.

Amines, organic chemicals composed of carbon, hydrogen and nitrogen. They are derived from ammonia, which they resemble in smell and chemical characteristics. The smell of bad fish is due to the presence of amines. Important industrially as intermediates in a wide variety of products, for example, the synthesis of dye-stuffs and man-made fibres such as nylon.

Amino acids, organic compounds containing an amine group and a carboxylic acid group. They are the "building bricks" of proteins (*q.v.*).

Ammeter, an instrument for measuring the current flowing in an electric circuit. A contraction of ampere-meter. *See* **Ampere.**

Ammonia, a colourless gaseous compound comprising three atoms of hydrogen to one of nitrogen. Formerly it was made by heating the horns and hoofs of deer, acquiring the name of spirits of hartshorn. The ammonia of commerce is now procured by coal decomposition in the course of gas-making and by direct synthesis. In the very important Haber process of ammonia production by fixation of atmospheric nitrogen, the nitrogen is made to combine with hydrogen and the ammonia so prepared is converted into nitric acid, ammonium nitrate or ammonium sulphate. The Haber process made Germany self-sufficient in nitrates in the first world war.

Ammonites, extinct animals related to the Nautilus. The chambered shell is coiled, usually in a plane spiral. They are confined to Mesozoic rocks.

Ammonium, the basic radical of ammonium salts, Composed of one atom of nitrogen and four of hydrogen, it behaves chemically like an ion of a monovalent alkali metal. Ammonium chloride is known as "sal ammoniac". "Sal volatile" is ammonium carbonate.

Amnesty, an act of grace by which a ruler or governing power pardons political offenders.

Amnesty International is the world's largest human rights organisation. It seeks to secure the release of prisoners of conscience, works for fair and prompt trials for all political prisoners, and campaigns against torture and the death penalty.

Since 1961, Amnesty has taken on over 43,500 cases. There are now (2006) around 2 million members in 4,000 local groups spread across 160 countries.

Amorphous, a term used to indicate the absence of crystalline form in any body or substance.

Ampere, unit of electric current in the SI system of units; named after André Marie Ampère, who in the 1820s helped to lay the foundations of modern electromagnetism. Defined as that constant current which, if maintained in two parallel rectilinear conductors of infinite length, of negligible circular cross section, and placed at a distance of one metre apart in a vacuum, would produce between these conductors a force which is equal to 2×10^{-7} newton per metre.

Amphioxus *or* **Lancelet,** a primitive chordate (*q.v.*), occurring in sand-banks.

Anabolism. *See* **Catabolism.**

Analysis is one of the major branches of modern pure mathematics and includes the theories of differentiation, integration, differential equations and analytic functions.

Anchor, an instrument used for keeping ships stationary. Great improvements have been introduced in recent years, stockless anchors being now chiefly used, consisting of a shank and a loose fluke. Lloyd's rules prescribe the number and weight of anchors which must be carried by merchant ships.

Anchorite is a religious person who retires into solitude to employ himself with holy thoughts. Among the early Christians, anchorites were numerous, but in the Western Church they have been few. Their reputation for wisdom and prescience was high, and kings and rulers in olden days would visit their cells for counsel. An anchorite or "ankret" was in mediaeval times a source of fame and often much profit to the monastic house within which he was voluntarily immured.

Anchovy, a fish of the herring family, distinguished by its large mouth and projecting snout, plentiful in the Mediterranean.

Ancient Lights are rights of light enjoyed by a property owner over adjoining land. Such a right is obtained either by uninterrupted enjoyment for twenty years, or by written authority, and once legally established cannot be upset, no building being permissible that would seriously interfere with the privilege.

Anemometer, an instrument for measuring the strength of the wind. In the most widely used pattern the rotation, about a vertical axis, of a group of hemispherical or conical cups gives a measure of the total flow of air past the cups, various registering devices being employed. The Dines anemograph provides a continuous record of the variation in both velocity and direction; changes of pressure produced in a horizontal tube, kept pointing into the wind by a vane, cause a float, to which a pen is attached, to rise and fall in sympathy with the gusts and lulls. The hot-wire anemometer, depending upon the change of electrical resistance experienced by a heated wire when cooled, enables very gentle air currents to be investigated.

Aneroid is the kind of barometer which does not depend upon atmospheric support of a mercury (or other liquid) column. It consists of a metallic box, partially exhausted of air, with a corrugated lid which moves with atmospheric changes. A lever system magnifies the lid movements about 200 times and atmospheric pressure is read from a dial. The construction of the vacuum chamber provides automatic compensation for temperature changes. An aneroid barometer is the basic component of an altimeter.

Angelica, an aromatic plant of the Umbelliferae order, *Angelica officinalis*, valuable as a flavouring and possessing medical properties. Once supposed to protect against poison.

Angelus, a church bell rung in Roman Catholic countries, at morn, noon, and sunset, to remind the faithful to say their Angelic Salutation.

Angles, a northern tribe originally settled in Schleswig, who with the Saxons and Jutes invaded Britain in the 5th cent.

Ångström, a unit of length equal to 10^{-10} metres. It is mainly used by astronomers to specify the wavelength of light and ultraviolet radiation. Named after the Swedish physicist A. J. Ångström (1814–74).

Aniline, a simple aromatic compound ($C_6H_5NH_2$) related to benzene and ammonia. It is obtained from coal-tar. The name recalls the fact that it was first prepared by distilling indigo (*anil* is Portuguese for indigo). In 1856 W. H. Perkin (1838–1907) discovered the first aniline or coal-tar dye, mauve, and thus founded the modern dyestuff industry.

Animal Kingdom. *See* **Section T.**

Anise, an umbelliferous plant (*Pimpinella anisum*) found in Egypt and the Levant, and valued for its fruit, aniseed, possessing certain medicinal properties and yielding an aromatic, volatile oil, Also used in cooking. The anise of the Bible is *Anethum graveolens*, *i.e.*, dill.

Annates. *See* **A40.**

Annunciation, Feast of the (25 March), is a Church festival commemorating the message of the incarnation of Christ brought by the angel Gabriel to the Virgin Mary, hence the title Lady Day.

Anointing is the pouring of consecrated oil upon the body as a mark of supreme honour. In England it is restricted chiefly to the ceremony of the monarch's coronation, and the spoon with which the oil is applied forms part of the English regalia. In the Roman Catholic Church anointing represents the sacrament of extreme unction.

Anschluss, German term for the union of Austria

and Germany achieved in March 1938. Pressure for the union of the two war allies, building up since the collapse of the Habsburg monarchy in 1918, increased when Adolf Hitler, an ardent advocate of union, became German Chancellor in 1933.

By threatening military action, Hitler secured the resignation of the Austrian Chancellor, Schushnigg. The pro-Nazi Seyss-Inquart was installed in his place and subsequently invited Germany to occupy Austria.

Ant. There are about 6,000 species of ants, which belong to the same order (Hymenoptera) as the bees, wasps and ichneumon flies. They are social in habit, living in communities of varying size and development. There are three basic castes in ants—the females or *queens*, the *males*, and the *workers* (the last-named being neuter), although specialised forms of workers are sometimes found, *e.g.*, the *soldiers* of the harvesting ants. In the communities of those species of ants which evolved most recently there is a highly complex social life and well-developed division of labour. Some species of these ants make slaves of other species, stealing the cocoons before the adult forms emerge.

Many ants "milk" green-flies, which they protect for their honey-like secretion, and most ants' nests contain many "guests", such as beetles and silver fish. Some ants harvest grains of corn, and others, from S. America, live on fungi which they cultivate in underground "mushroom beds".

Ants have lived on the Earth for more than 100 million years. They can drag an object 25 times their own body weight.

Antarctic Exploration. In earlier centuries it was thought that a great continent must exist in the southern hemisphere, around the South Pole, to balance the known land masses in the north. Its supposed extent was greatly reduced in the 18th cent., particularly when Capt. Cook sailed for the first time south of the Antarctic Circle and reached the edge of the ice-pack. A portion of the ice-covered continent—the coast of Graham Land—was first sighted by Lieut. Edward Bransfield in 1820. The first extensive exploration was made by Capt. James Clarke Ross, who with the *Erebus* and *Terror* penetrated into the Ross Sea in 1841, and discovered the Ross Ice Barrier in 78° South lat.

Interest in the Antarctic did not revive until after 1890, when an international scheme of research was drawn up. A Norwegian, C. E. Borchgrevink, in 1898–1900, was the first to winter in the Antarctic and to travel on the ice barrier. The British share in this work was carried out by Capt. R. F. Scott's expedition in the *Discovery*, 1901–4. Scott's party sledged across the barrier to 82° 17' South, then a record "farthest south". A little later, Ernest Shackleton beat this by travelling to within 160 km of the South Pole. The Scottish polar explorer William Spiers Bruce led the Scottish national Antarctic Expedition of 1902 in the *Scotia* and discovered Coats Land and founded a meteorological observatory on the South Orkneys.

In 1910 Captain Scott organised his second expedition in *Terra Nova*, and became engaged against his will in a "race for the Pole" when, after his departure, the Norwegian Arctic explorer, Roald Amundsen, suddenly announced that he was sailing for the Antarctic. Amundsen set up his base at the eastern end of the Barrier, and, relying on dog teams for hauling his sledges, reached the Pole on 14 December 1911. Meanwhile Scott and his party, their start delayed by adverse weather, were marching southwards, man-hauling their sledges, for Scott was against the use of dogs. After an arduous journey they reached the Pole one month after Amundsen. The return was a struggle against the weather and increasing weakness, until at last they perished within a few kilometres of their base.

After the first world war the development of the whaling industry greatly stimulated further exploration. Outstanding expeditions included that of Admiral R. E. Byrd, 1929, when he flew over the South Pole; the British Graham Land expedition, 1934, which carried out the first extensive mapping of any part of the

Antarctic continent; and the US Navy's Antarctic Expedition of 1940, when the whole continent was circumnavigated and great areas photographed from the air.

Some years later, the Antarctic was the scene of much activity during the International Geophysical Year (1957–58), when scientists from many countries participated in the explorations. The Commonwealth Trans-Antarctic Expedition set out from opposite sides of the continent and met at the South Pole, the UK party, led by Sir Vivian Fuchs, from the Falklands, and Sir Edmund Hillary and his party from New Zealand. The UK party accomplished the first crossing of the White Continent in 99 days. In 1993, the explorers Sir Ranulph Fiennes and Dr Michael Stroud completed the first unsupported crossing of the Antarctic land mass and the longest unsupported polar journey—both world records. In December 1994, Liv Arnesen (Norway) became the first woman to reach the South Pole alone.

Scientists now working in Antarctica have discovered that around 190,000,000 years ago the frozen waste was once a huge forest roamed by plant-eating dinosaurs. Meanwhile climate warming has led to the loss of 25 per cent of its sea ice over the last 100 years. The ozone hole over Antarctica is now (2006) larger than ever. In 1998 scientists made plans to explore a huge lake, two miles below the Antarctic ice-cap, insulated by ice for millions of years.

Thriving eco-systems of clams and bacteria have now been discovered deep below the surface. Since light does not penetrate the organisms do not photosynthesise but use methane to make energy.

The temperature on the polar plateau is −60°C for half the year. The lowest recorded temperature is −89.5°C.

Scientists estimate that its vast ice sheets contain *c.* 90% of the world's known fresh water.

Fascination with the wilderness of Antarctica—the last wilderness on the planet—is resulting in a growth of tourism, but warmer seas will threaten the food chain of its unique ecosystem.

Anteaters, a small family (the Myrmecophagidae) of mammals from Central and South America. They feed on ants, termites and other insects which they gather with a long tongue covered with sticky saliva. The anteater is the only mammal without teeth.

Antelope, a variety of hoofed mammal, including gazelles, pronghorns *etc.* They are mainly to be found in Africa. The rare Saiga antelope, found in Mongolia and Russia, is critically endangered.

Antennae, paired feelers of insects and crustaceans. In radio, the term "antenna" is equivalent to "aerial".

Anthem, A musical setting of a religious text (biblical or otherwise) in English, for choir with or without instrumental accompaniment. A "full" anthem is choral throughout: a "verse" anthem includes solo voice(s) The genre flourished in the Reformation and early Stuart periods (Tallis, Byrd, Tomkins) and after the Restoration (Locke, Humfrey, Purcell). Later composers of anthems include S.S. Wesley, Stainer, Stanford, Howells and Leighton.

Anthracite is a black coal with a brilliant lustre. It contains 92 per cent. and over of carbon and burns slowly, without smoke or flame. *See* **Coal.**

Anthropoid, meaning "resembling man", a sub-order of the primate mammals including man and also the gibbon, chimpanzee, orang-utan, and gorilla.

Antibiotics. *See* **Z65.**

Anticyclone, a region where barometric pressure is greater than that of its surroundings. Such a system is distinguished on weather charts by a pattern of isobars, usually circular or oval-shaped, enclosing the centre of high pressure where the air is calm. In the remaining areas light or moderately strong winds blow spirally outwards in a clockwise direction in the Northern Hemisphere (and in the reverse direction in the Southern Hemisphere), in accordance with Buys Ballot's law (an observer with back to wind in Northern Hemisphere has lower pressure to left; in Southern to right). Over the British Isles anticyclonic weather is generally quiet and settled, being fair, warm, and sunny in summer and either very cold and often foggy or overcast and gloomy in winter. These systems move slowly and sometimes remain practically stationary for days at a time, that over Siberia being particularly well defined.

Extensive belts of almost permanent anti-cyclones occur in latitudes 30° N and 30° S. Persistent anticyclonic weather with easterly winds during the months December 1962 to March 1963, brought the coldest and hardest winter to Britain since 1740.

Antimony. Metal element, no. 51, symbol Sb. In group 5 of the periodic table. Exists in various forms, the stable form being a grey metal with a layer structure. The other forms are non-conductors. On being burned, it gives off dense fumes of oxide of antimony. By itself it is not of special utility; but as an alloy for hardening other metals, it is much used. As an alloy with lead for type-metal, and with tin and copper or zinc for Britannia-metal, it is of great value. Most important antimony ore is stibnite (antimony sulphide).

Anti-Pope, one elected in opposition to one held to be canonically chosen; applied to the popes Clement VII and Benedict XIII, who resided at Avignon during the Great Schism (1378–1417).

Anti-Proton, the "negative proton", an atomic particle created in high energy collisions of nuclear particles. Its existence was confirmed in Oct. 1955. *See* **Section T.**

Antlers are the branched horns of deer, the branches being called tines. Antlers originate as outgrowths of the frontal bone, and are usually shed once a year. Except in the rein-deer and caribou they are restricted to the male.

Aotearoa, meaning "Long White Cloud", the Maori name for New Zealand.

Ape, a term applied to the gorilla, chimpanzee, orang-utan and gibbon—the anthropoid apes.

Aphelion, the point in the orbit of a planet farthest from the sun; the opposite of perihelion. At aphelion the earth is 1.52×10^8 km from the sun.

Aphids, green-flies or plant lice, a numerous species of destructive insects living on young shoots and foliage, some on roots. Reproduction is by parthenogenesis (virgin birth).

Apis, the sacred bull worshipped by the ancient Egyptians; also the scientific name for the bee.

Apocalyptic writings are those which deal with revelation and prophecy, more especially the Revelation of St. John.

Apocrypha. *See* **H3.**

Apogee, that point in the orbit of a heavenly body which is farthest from the earth; used in rela-tion to the sun, moon and artificial satellites. The sun's apogee corresponds to the earth's aphelion. *See* **Perigee.**

Apostasy is a revolt, by an individual or party, from one form of opinions or doctrinate to another. Julian, the Roman Emperor (331–63), brought up as a Christian, became converted to paganism and on coming to the throne (361), proclaimed religious toleration. Hence his name, Julian the Apostate.

Apostles. *See* **Section H.**

Apostles' Creed, the name of the most ancient of the Church's statements of its belief: "I believe in God the Father Almighty; and in Jesus Christ his only Son our Lord, who was born of the Holy Ghost and the Virgin Mary. . . ." A later version is used in the Church of England at morning and evening prayer.

Apostolic Fathers. *See* **Section H.**

Appian Way, the oldest and finest of the Roman roads originally laid by Appius Claudius (312 B.C.) from Rome to Capua and thence to Brundisium (Brindisi).

Approved Schools were residential schools, subject to Home Office inspection, for the training of young persons under 17 who were guilty of offences or in need of care and protection and had been sent to them by magistrates from juvenile or other courts. The approved school order was abol-ished by the Children and Young Persons Act 1969. For recent developments, *see* **Young Offenders' Institutions.**

April, the fourth month of the year, from the Roman *Aprilis* derived from *aperire* "to open" —the period when the buds begin to open.

Apse is a semicircular recess, arched or dome-roofed, at the end of the choir, aisles, or nave of a church.

Aquaculture, or fish-farming, is the fastest-growing sector (11% per annum) of the world food economy (production reached 31m. tonnes in 1998).

Aqueducts are conduits in which water flows or is conveyed from its source to the place where it is to be used. Most famous builders were the Romans and the oldest Roman aqueduct was the Aqua Appia, which dates from about 310 B.C. Among modern aqueducts may be mentioned that of Glasgow, which brings water to that city from Loch Katrine; that of Manchester, which taps Thirlmere; that of Liverpool, with Lake Vyrnwy in North Wales as its source, and the Fron Aqueduct, Powys, which carries water to the Birmingham area.

Arabian Nights Entertainment or **Book of a Thousand and One Nights,** a collection of fascin-ating tales of the Orient, of mixed Indian, Persian, Arabic, and Egyptian origination, and first made known in Europe by Antoine Galland's French translation (1704–17) from Arabian texts. The "master" tale tells how the princess Shahrazad so beguiles the king by telling of the tales over one thousand and one nights that her life was spared. English transla-tors include E. W. Lane (1840), Sir Richard Burton (1885–8), and John Payne (1882–4).

Arabic Numerals. The modern system of numbering, 0, 1, 2, 3, 4, 5, 6, 7, 8, 9, in which the digits depend on their position for their value is called the Arabic numerical notation. The method is, in fact, of Indian origin. By the 9th cent. Hindu sci-ence was available in Arabic, and the Persian mathematician Al-Kwarizimi (*c.* 830) in his *Arithmetic* used the so-called "Arabic" system of numbering. Gradually the method spread to Europe, taking the place of the Roman system which was useless for calculation.

The West is indebted to the Arabs for the zero symbol. It made the invention of decimal frac-tions possible.

Aragonite, the unstable form of calcium carbonate found as a mineral in some young deposits. It crystallises in the orthorhombic system but tends to revert to calcite.

Aramaic Languages, the Semitic dialects current in Mesopotamia and the regions extending south-west from the Euphrates to Palestine from about the 12th cent. B.C. until after the rise of Islam, when Aramaic was superseded by Arabic. Both Aramaic and Greek were spoken in Pales-tine during the time of Christ.

Archaeopteryx, a fossil bird providing a connecting link between reptiles and birds. It had feathers, jaws with teeth, no bill, reptilian bones and skull, a long tail, and it probably used its fore-limbs for gliding flight. The first specimen, found in 1861, in the Solenhofen limestone of Bavaria, is in London's Natural History Museum. It is *c.* 147 million years old.

Archbishop, the chief of the bishops of an ecclesi-astical province in the Greek, Roman, and Anglican churches. In the Church of England there are two Archbishops, the Archbishop of Canterbury, called the Primate of *all* England, and the Archbishop of York, styled the Primate of England. *See also* **A52.**

Archimedes' Principle. When a body is weighed in air and then in any fluid, the apparent loss in weight is equal to the weight of fluid displaced. This scientific fact was noted by the Syracusan philosopher Archimedes (287–212 B.C.) and is used as a basis for density measurements.

Architecture. *See* **Section N.**

Arctic Exploration. Modern exploration of the Arctic began in the 16th cent. when men sought to reach the East Indies by sailing through the Arctic to the Pacific Ocean.

The North-east Passage, via the shores of northern Asia, was the first attempted. In 1553 and 1554 the English navigators Sir Richard Chancellor and Stephen Burrough sailed into the White Sea, but were prevented by storms and ice from advancing farther eastwards. The project was later revived by the Dutch; Bar-endts in 1594 discovered Spitsbergen, but also failed to get beyond Novaya Zemlya. It was not, in fact, until 1879 that the Swede, A. E. Nordenskjöld, in the *Vega*, succeeded in reaching the Pacific.

The attempts to find a North-west Passage were more numerous and determined. In 1585 John Davis penetrated Davis Strait and coasted

L9

along Baffin Island. Hopes ran high when Henry Hudson discovered Hudson Bay in 1610, but a practicable passage continued to elude explorers. The problem was to find a navigable route through the maze of channels in the short summer season, and to avoid being frozen in with supplies exhausted. After the Napoleonic Wars the Admiralty sent out many naval expeditions which culminated in Sir John Franklin's expedition with the *Erebus* and *Terror* in 1845. The ships were beset by ice in Victoria Channel and, after Franklin's death, were abandoned by their crews, who perished from scurvy and starvation on their march southwards. To ascertain their fate, several further expeditions were despatched, and the crew of the *Investigator*, commanded by R. J. M'Clure, sailing eastwards from Bering Strait, were the first to make the Passage, though in doing so they were obliged to abandon their ship.

It was to be thirty years before the Norwegian, Roald Amundsen, succeeded in sailing the *Gjoa* from the east to west. In the meantime, the North Pole had become the goal of explorers. Nansen, in 1893, put the *Fram* into the ice-pack to drift across the Polar basin, and himself made an unsuccessful attempt on the Pole across the pack. This was eventually achieved by the American explorer Robert E. Peary, who after several expeditions in the North Greenland region, sledged to the Pole with Eskimo companions in 1909.

The next phase was the employment of airships. In 1926 Admiral Byrd made the first flight over the Pole, and in the same year Amundsen and Lincoln Ellsworth flew the airship *Norge* from Spitsbergern to Point Barrow Alaska. Two years later, the *Italia*, commanded by the Italian, Nobile, was wrecked on a return flight from the Pole, and Amundsen lost his life in an attempt to rescue the survivors. Wally Herbert, the explorer who completed the first surface crossing of the Arctic Ocean in 1969 was knighted in 2000. The first voyage under the North Pole was made in 1958 by the American nuclear-powered submarine *Nautilus*.

Scientists are now (2006) reporting that the North Pole icecap itself is today melting faster than previously thought, thus threatening many Arctic species. In time this will allow the economic exploitation of a region now almost totally unexplored.

The Arctic Census of Marine Life was launched in 2004. In 2005 it reported that it had already found many new species of jellyfish, sea cucumbers *etc*.

Environmentalists are striving to prevent oil drilling in the Arctic National Wildlife Refuge. They maintain that drilling, even with new technology, will do great damage to caribou, polar bears, musk oxen *etc*.

Global warming may even cause the Arctic to vanish by *c*. 2080, with summers seeing the melting of the Arctic ice-cap. The Ward Hunt Ice shelf (the largest in the Arctic) is now already breaking up.

Arenaceous Rocks, the rocks composed of grains of sand, chiefly sandstones; quartz is the most abundant mineral in these rocks.

Argillaceous Rocks are a sedimentary group, including the shales and clays.

Argon, chemical element no. 18, symbol A. This was the first of the inert gases (*q.v.*) to be isolated from air by Rayleigh and Ramsay in 1894. Argon is used for filling gas-filled metal filament electric lamps. In gas discharge tube it gives a blue glow. *See also* **Rare Gases.**

Arithmetic, the branch of mathematics that deals with numerical calculations as in counting, measuring, weighing. The early civilisations used simple arithmetic for commercial purposes, employing symbols and later letters of the alphabet as numerals.

When Hindu-Arabic numerals replaced Roman numerals in the Middle Ages it meant a great step forward and led to rapid developments—the invention of logarithms, slide-rule, calculating machines.

Arithmetic Progression, a sequence of numbers in which the successor of each number is obtained by adding or subtracting a fixed number, for example 2, 5, 8, 11, . . . or 100, 95, 90, 85. . . . .

Armadillo, a genus of animals related to the sloths

and anteaters, belonging to South America, and carrying a hard bony covering over the back, under which one species (*Tolypeutes*) can completely conceal itself when attacked, rolling itself up like a hedgehog.

Armageddon, according to the Revelation of St. John, the great battle in which the last conflict between good and evil is to be fought.

Armillary Sphere, an early form of astronomical apparatus with a number of circles representing equator, meridian, ecliptic, *etc*. Used by Hipparchus and Ptolemy and up to the time of Tycho Brahe for determining the position of the stars.

Armistice Day, the day (11 Nov 1918) when the First World War ended is now commemorated each year with a 2-minute silence on Remembrance Sunday.

Aromatic. A term used by chemists, originally to describe compounds like benzene, having a characteristic smell. It is a term which implies a collection of chemical characteristics, the salient features being a flat ring structure and a general similarity to benzene.

Arsenic, a metalloid element, no. 33, symbol As in group 5 of the periodic table usually met with as a constituent of other minerals, sometimes by itself. Its compounds are very poisonous. Lead arsenate is a powerful insecticide used for spraying fruit trees. The more stable allotropic form (grey) has a layer structure, and conducts electricity.

Artesian Wells take their name from Artois in France, where the first wells of this kind were constructed in 1126. They are to be found only when a water-bearing bed is sandwiched between two impervious beds. When a boring is made to the lower part of the bed, the pressure of water is sufficient to cause the water to overflow at the surface. Artesian wells were known to ancient Egypt and China, and have existed in the Sahara since the earliest times. The fountains in Trafalgar Square were once fed by artesian wells sunk through the London clay into the chalk about 250 m.

Articles. The *Six Articles* are those contained in an Act of Henry VIII, and were of Roman Catholic origin. The *Thirty-nine Articles* were drawn up for the English church at the Reformation. They are printed at the back of the Prayer Book. Candidates for holy orders in the Church of England are required to subscribe to them.

Arum, a genus of plants of the *Araceae* family of which there is but one British species, the wakerobin or cuckoo-pint, sometimes also styled "Lords and Ladies".

Arundel Marbles, a collection of ancient Greek sculptures formed by Thomas Howard, Earl of Arundel in the 17th cent. and presented to Oxford University by his grandson, Henry Howard, who became Duke of Norfolk.

Aryans, nomadic peoples who made their way in successive waves from the Eurasian steppes to the Indus and the Nile during the first half of the 2nd millennium B.C. They crossed the Hindu Kush into N.W. India and settled in the valleys of the Indus and Ganges, where an earlier Indus civilisation had flourished, c. 3240–2750 B.C. Their religious ideas are reflected in the Veda (oldest Hindu scriptures, written down many centuries later in Vedic, parent language of Sanskrit). Those who made their way to Syria and Egypt founded the Hyksos empire (c. 1720–1550 B.C.).

The Aryans introduced the horse-drawn chariot and spoke a language from which the great Indo-European family of languages is derived, with one group in India and Iran, and another in Europe. Because of the misuse of the term by the Nazis, Aryan is now referred to as proto-Indo-European.

Asafoetida, an acrid, strong-smelling gum resin exuded from the stem of umbelliferous plant, *Ferula foetida*, found in Iran and Afghanistan. Formerly used medicinally to treat hysteria; still used in cooking in such countries as India, Iran and France.

Ascension Day, or Holy Thursday, is the 40th day after Easter.

Ascot Races are an annual fashionable function dating from 1711 and taking place on Ascot Heath, only 10 km from Windsor, in June. These races have always had royal patronage. The course is *c.* 3 km long.

Ash, a familiar deciduous tree of the genus *Fraxinus*, of over 60 species, native to North temperate regions. The ash held an important place in Norse mythology, as it was supposed to support the heavens with its roots in Hell. The species native to Britain, and to Europe, is *F. excelsior*, a tall tree with compound leaves, greenish flowers, winged seeds, and black buds in winter. It is a valuable timber tree, tough and elastic, and much used for wheels and handles.

The rowan, or mountain ash, *Sorbus aucuparia*, with similar leaves and orange berries belongs to a different family.

F. pendula or weeping ash is a strain which makes an ideal natural summer house,

Ashes, The, the symbol which distinguishes the winning cricket team in the Australian Test Matches. In 1882 the Australians won at the Oval by 7 runs. After the match the following epitaph appeared in the *Sporting Times*: "In affectionate remembrance of English Cricket which died at the Oval on 29 Aug. 1882, deeply lamented by a large circle of sorrowing friends and acquaintances. R.I.P. NB. The body will be cremated and the ashes taken to Australia." When the English Eleven went to Australia the same winter it was said that they had come to recover the "ashes". England won two out of three matches, and after the third match the ashes of what was believed to have been a bail were presented in an urn to Ivo Bligh, later Lord Darnley. He bequeathed the urn to the MCC. It is now in the Memorial Gallery at Lord's. Recently, several historians have doubted the truth of this story. In 2005 the Ashes returned to England after one of the most exciting series ever.

Ashmolean Museum, the oldest public museum in Britain. Located in Oxford, it was founded in 1683 by Elias Ashmole (1617–92). It houses a variety of treasures.

Ash Wednesday, first day of Lent, the seventh Wednesday before Easter.

Asteroids or the minor planets are relatively small objects which move in orbits mainly between those of Mars and Jupiter. The first to be discovered (by Piazzi in 1801) was Ceres. Many thousands more have since been discovered, of which nearly 2,000 now have well-determined orbits and have been named. Among the largest are Ceres (800 km), Pallas (500 km), Vesta (530 km) and Juno (240 km). Few others have diameters of more than 80 km, while those of the majority are less than 5 or 10 km. Of particular interest are the Trojan group, located at the two stable "Lagrangian" points in Jupiter's orbit round the sun, where their locations make isosceles triangles with the sun and Jupiter. Also, a number of asteroids have orbits like that of Icarus which at perigee (*q.v.*) comes close to the sun.

The first probe designed to study asteroids (NEAR, Near Asteroid Rendezvous), launched in 1996, landed on the Eros 433 asteroid in 2001. This is one of the largest near-Earth asteroids. In 2002 an asteroid the size of a football pitch missed the Earth by only 75,000 miles.

Astrobiology, a new discipline bringing together those searching the universe for extra-terrestrial life in space.

Astrolabe, a mediaeval scientific instrument for taking altitudes, observing the sun by day and the stars by night, and used for telling the time and finding the latitude. Used by the ancient Greeks, later by the Arabs and Persians, and introduced into Europe by way of Spain in the 14th cent.

Astronomer Royal. *See* **Astronomy** (*below*).

Astronomical Unit, the mean distance between the centres of the sun and earth, or the semi-major axis of the earth's orbit, has a value of about 1.495979×10^8 km (149,597,900 km). This value has been constantly improved over the past 300 years, first using observations of the planets, later transits of Venus across the sun's disc, then observations of minor planets such as Eros as they came near the earth, and now by the transit time of a radar beam bounced off the planet Venus. The astronomical unit is fundamental for astronomers. *See* **Parsec.**

Astronomy. The Pythagoreans believed the stars and planets moved with uniform circular velocity in crystalline spheres, centred round the earth (the "harmony of the spheres"). Hipparchus (190–120 B.C.) made the first star catalogue, discovered the precession of the equinoxes and introduced the idea of epicyclic motion. His planetary system, in the form it was presented by Ptolemy 200 years later, held until the Renaissance when Copernicus revived the heretical view first put forward by Aristarchus of Samos (310–230 B.C.) that the sun and not the earth was at the centre. Galileo, accurate observer and experimenter, went beyond Copernicus; helped by the contributions of Tycho Brahe, Giordano Bruno, Kepler and others, he was able to overthrow the Ptolemaic system of the heavenly spheres and Aristotelian philosophy and pave the way for Newton and modern astronomy. To Galileo we owe the conception of acceleration; to Newton the theory of universal gravitation; they showed that the same laws govern both celestial and terrestrial physics. Three landmarks in more recent times were the discovery of Uranus by Herschel in 1781 which extended the solar system as then recognised; the estimation by Hubble in 1924 of the distance of Andromeda, which showed that our Galaxy was just one of many; and Einstein's theory of relativity which improved on Newton's theory of the solar system by bringing gravitation into the domain of space-time. Today optical, radio, sub-mm, ultra-violet, gamma ray and X-ray telescopes on the Earth and in space are revolutionising our understanding of astronomy.

The following have held the post of **Astronomer Royal** (period of office in brackets): John Flamsteed (1675–1719), Edmund Halley (1719–42), James Bradley (1742–62), Nathaniel Bliss (1762–65), Nevil Maskelyne (1765–1811), John Pond (1811–35), Sir George Airy (1835–81), Sir William Christie (1881–1910), Sir Frank Dyson (1910–33), Sir Harold Spencer Jones (1933–55), Sir Richard Woolley (1956–72), Sir Martin Ryle (1972–82), Sir Francis Graham Smith (1982–90), Sir Arnold Wolfendale (1991–95) and Sir (now Lord) Martin Rees (1995–). *See also* **Radio Astronomy.**

Astrophysics, the study of the properties, evolution and constitution of objects in the universe. It is concerned with the production and expenditure of energy in such systems as the stars and galaxies and their evolution. It was developed in the 19th century with the application of spectroscopy to the universe at large. Modern advances in particle physics, cosmology, X-ray, gamma-ray, infra-red, ultraviolet and radio astronomy have advanced this subject in recent years and are now usually considered subsections of astrophysics. *See* **Astronomy, Cosmology.**

Athanasian Creed, one of the three ancient creeds of the Christian Church, often referred to as the *Quicunque Vult*, is a statement of the doctrine of the Trinity and the Incarnation, and though named after St. Athanasius, it is thought to be the work of St. Ambrose (339–97).

Atmosphere is the gaseous envelope of the earth, and consists of a mixture of gases (*see* **Air**) and water vapour, the variability of the latter being of great importance meteorologically. The ozone layer, which absorbs solar ultra-violet radiation which would be lethal to plant life if it reached the ground lies between 12 to 50 km above the earth. The lower level of the atmosphere up to a height of about 12 km (10 km at the Poles and 16 km at the Equator) is known as the *troposphere*, and it is in this region that nearly all weather phenomena occur.

This is the region of most interest to the forecaster studying temperature, humidity, wind-speed, and the movement of air masses. Temperature falls with height by about 1°C per 152 m in this layer. The *tropopause* is the boundary between the troposphere and the *stratosphere*. Temperature varies little in the lower levels of this region: it is mainly cloudless, and has no vertical currents. Strangely enough, the lowest temperatures of the atmosphere are to be found not at the Poles, but at about 18 km above the Equator, where a temperature as low as −80°C has been recorded!

Temperatures begin to rise about 32 km from the earth's surface at about the same rate as they fall in the troposphere owing to the absorption of solar radiation by the concentration of ozone. The stratospheric air is extremely dry. Near the 100 km level a number of important atmospheric phenomena occur. Above this level the oxygen becomes predominantly monatomic in contrast to the normal diatomic form at lower altitudes. This is the *ionosphere* (q.v.). This layer acts as an electrical radio mirror which makes long-distance radio transmission possible. The region of the Van Allen belts (q.v.) above the earth is called the magnetosphere (q.v.).

The auroras are most frequently observed at altitudes between about 100 and 400 km but do extend at times far higher.

Many aspects of the upper air can still only be studied through space-research techniques. These include the composition and temperature of the charged particles in the ionosphere, the location of the electric currents in the ionosphere which produce the regular variations of the compass needle, as well as those which circulate during magnetic storms, the variation of the intensity of different radiation in the air-glow (q.v.) with height, the composition of the air at heights above 32 km, and so on. In addition, the pressures, density, temperatures, and wind distribution of the neutral atmosphere can be studied more directly, in much greater detail, and up to much greater altitudes than is possible if one is confined to the use of equipment on the ground. Instruments outside the atmosphere can make systematic observations on a world-wide basis of the atmospheric circulation, through observation of cloud cover and of the thermal radiation into space from the atmosphere. Such observations are of great importance for meteorology.

The atmospheres of other planets are vastly different to our own. For example, the Venusian atmosphere is considerably denser than the Earth's and is composed primarily of carbon dioxide. Carbon dioxide is also the main constituent of the Martian atmosphere, although this is much thinner than that of the Earth. Titan, the largest satellite of Saturn, has a nitrogen-rich atmosphere. *See also* **Ionosphere.**

Atmospherics are electrical impulses which are believed to originate in atmospheric electrical discharges such as lightning. They give rise to crashing background noises in the loudspeakers of radio sets, interfering with reception at distances of up to 6,400 km from the centre of the disturbance. The location of atmospherics with the aid of radio direction-finding methods gives warning of thunderstorms.

Atom. *See* **Section T.**

Atomic Pile, an apparatus containing a fissionable element and a moderator, such as heavy water or graphite, in which a self-sustaining fission process proceeds at a controllable rate. The first atomic pile, constructed on a squash court at Chicago, was operated for the first time on 2 December 1942, under the direction of Enrico Fermi. The pile contained 12,400 lb (5,580 kg) of uranium. *See* **Nuclear Reactors.**

Augsburg Confession, name given to the doctrine of faith of the Lutheran churches, drawn up by Melanchthon and endorsed by Luther for the Diet of Augsburg (1530).

August, named after the Emperor Augustus, because it was his "lucky" month.

Auks, duck-like sea-birds, black and white, with short, narrow wings, compact bodies and legs set well back. Breed in colonies on rocky coasts of N. Europe (incl. British Isles) and spend most time in coastal waters. Migrate south in winter. The Auk family includes the Razorbill, Little Auk, Guillemot and Puffin.

The Great Auk became extinct in the 19th cent. after ruthless hunting for its feathers.

Aurora Polaris. This wonderful phenomenon of the night sky is a common sight at high northern and southern latitudes, where it is called the aurora borealis and the aurora australis respectively. It is visible less often at temperate latitudes, and only rarely in the tropics. The auroral ovals, or zones of maximum frequency of aurora, surround both of the earth's geomagnetic poles, and the northern auroral oval includes the northern parts of Scandinavia, Canada and Alaska. The aurora is the visible manifestation of complex plasma processes occurring within the earth's magnetosphere (q.v.), whereby streams of high-energy electrons and protons (mainly) are accelerated and dumped via the earth's magnetic field lines into the upper atmosphere. This mechanism produces the light emission of the aurora. The brightest aurora, which may also extend to lower latitudes, occurs during geomagnetic storms, which are complex and large-scale plasma instabilities within the magnetosphere triggered by fluctuations in the solar wind (q.v.) —usually ascribed to "M" regions on the sun associated with coronal holes, flares and active sunspot groups. Auroral displays may take several forms—a faint glow, a diffuse ribbon of light crossing the heavens, great folded waving curtains or draperies, or the entire sky may be flooded with a rapidly varying brilliant panoply of light.

The aurora is a kind of light essentially different from that of the rainbow which is a partly subjective phenomenon. Each beholder sees his own rainbow, whose light is sunlight refracted and reflected by many raindrops. The raindrops that produce his rainbow depend on his position as well as on the direction of the sun. The aurora, on the contrary, is a light as objective as that of a candle, though produced differently. It is a self-luminescence of the air in regions of the atmosphere that lie far above the clouds.

Recent images from NASA's Polar spacecraft have confirmed the theory that auroras in the northern and southern hemispheres are nearly mirror images of each other.

Auto-da-Fé, or Act of Faith, was the ceremony connected with the sentencing of heretics under the Inquisition of Spain and Portugal, the persons found guilty being imprisoned or burned alive. The ceremony took place in some public square, often in the presence of the king and court.

Automation is a technical word used to designate the adoption of methods of automatic control either of manufacturing processes or of any business process involving a large mass of routine work. The word is used in broader and narrower senses. In its broadest sense it covers any form of mechanisation which largely replaces human labour by the work of automatic or semi-automatic machines, such as has been in progress continuously since the Industrial Revolution; but it it better kept to a narrower meaning, in which it is confined to the recent development of electronic or similar devices, involving feedback (automatic detection and correction of malfunction). Human labour is eliminated save for that needed for watching and maintaining the elaborate machines used.

Autumn, the third season of the year, begins with the autumnal equinox, and ends with the winter solstice, but the term is generally understood as covering the period from mid-August to mid-November.

Auxins, "plant hormones", organic substances produced by plants to regulate growth. Synthetic auxins are now widely used, e.g., for promotion of root formation in cuttings, differential weed control, prevention of premature dropping of fruit, in storage of potatoes etc., and to overcome frost damage to fruit buds.

Avalanches occur when layers of snow become unstable. Each of these 'white deaths' can send more than 1 million tons of ice, rock and snow thundering down mountain-sides.

Average is a single number designed to give a typical example of a set of numbers, e.g., a cricketer's batting average for a season gives an idea of his typical score. There are several kinds of average and their uses are studied in the science of statistics (q.v.). A statement that "so and so is the average value" can be misleading if one does not know which average is meant. Three common averages are: the arithmetic average (or mean), the mode, and the median. The arithmetic average of n numbers is found by adding them together and dividing by n; this is a very common method of averaging. The mode of n numbers is the most frequently occurring number. The median is the middle number, i.e., the number which is smaller than just as many of the other numbers as it exceeds. Of the numbers 1, 2, 2, 2, 3, 4, 5, 6, 8, 9, the arithmetic means is 4, the mode is 2, the median is 3.

Avocet, a graceful wading bird related to the stilts, of black-and-white plumage, bluish legs, and slender upturned bill. There are four species. Avocets nest in colonies. The return of the avocet as a breeding bird since the last war has been a success story for the RSPB.

Avogadro's Hypothesis. This is a fundamental concept of chemistry. Equal volumes of all gases under the same conditions of temperature and pressure contain the same number of molecules. This law was instrumental in assigning the formulae of molecules. The hypothesis was put forward in 1811, but not accepted until 1860.

Aztecs, the name of a powerful people found in Mexico when the Spaniards first discovered that country. At the height of Aztec power, *c.* 1325, their empire controlled a huge area of central America. There was an intricate system of tributes and blood sacrifice, The Spanish conquest obliterated much of their history and tradition. Centred on the capital Tenochtitlan, the empire stretched as far as Guatemala, Belize and El Salvador.

B

Babiroussa, a ferocious, long-legged wild pig, native of Sulawesi, sometimes called the horned-hog, because of the long upper tusks in the male, which are developments of the canine teeth.

Baboon, monkeys belonging to the African genus *Papio.* They are considered the lowest of the Old World (Catarrhine) monkeys, and walk on all fours. In the main terrestrial, but take to trees after food. The mandrill is closely related.

Babylonian Captivity, the period spent by the Jews in Babylon after Jerusalem was captured by Nebuchadnezzar, the Babylonian emperor, in 586 B.C. Traditionally the captivity lasted 70 years, but when Babylon was in turn taken by Cyrus in 538 B.C., the exiles were permitted to return to Jerusalem. The term is also applied in church history to the period 1309–78 when the papacy moved to Avignon.

Baccalaureate, a broadly-based academic award widely-used in Europe which it is planned will eventually replace 'A' levels in Britain.

Bacteriophage (Phage), literally "bacteria eater", *i.e.,* a virus which specifically infects bacteria. In common with viruses which attack animal or plant cells, isolated phages are inert, and can only reproduce by making use of the chemical apparatus of a more sophisticated host cell (in this case a bacterium). However phages may be of two types, virulent or temperate. Virulent phages completely disrupt the normal functioning of the infected bacterium and adapt its reproductive mechanism to produce more phage. This eventually kills the bacterium and the newly assembled phages are released. Temperate phages on the other hand may enter into a remarkable symbiotic relationship with the bacterium, known as lysogeny. The phage genetic material is incorporated into that of the bacterium and is reproduced each time the still functioning bacterium subsequently divides. Furthermore the bacterium is immune from attack by potentially virulent phages of the same type. When such lysogenic bacteria die, phage particles may again be released. Phages carried in lysogenic bacteria are in a state known as prophage and it is often difficult to obtain pure, prophage-free strains of bacteria. Phages have been extensively used in research on genetics and molecular biology.

Badger, a carnivorous mammal related to the weasel, of nocturnal and burrowing habits, inoffensive, subsisting chiefly on roots and insects, though sometimes mice, young rabbits and eggs form part of its diet. The badger does little harm and quite a lot of good. In Britain the badger is partly protected, but Ministry officials may destroy the animal in areas where bovine TB exists. There are increasing demands by farmers for a mass cull. The 1992 Badger Protection Act led to greatly increased numbers (now estimated at around 250,000 in the UK).

Bagpipe. Once popular all over Europe, this instrument is still played in Scotland, Ireland, Brittany and elsewhere. The bag acts as a reservoir of air and, when squeezed by the player's arm, forces air through the pipes. One of these, the Chanter pipe, provides the tune and is played by the fingers as in a flageolet. The remainder, the Drone pipes, give a continuous, unvarying note.

Bailey Bridge, invented by Sir Donald Bailey and first used in the N. African campaign 1942–3. Built up of prefabricated girders, it can be easily transported and erected.

Bailiwick, a feudal term denoting the limits of a bailiff 's jurisdiction. The term has survived in the Channel Islands (e.g. Jersey and Guernsey).

Baldachin (It. *Baldachino*), a canopy usually supported by four pillars over throne, altar *etc.*

Balearic Crane, the crowned crane of the Balearic Islands and the North African mainland, distinguished by its yellowish, black-tipped occipital tuft and by its trumpet note.

Baleen *or* "whalebone" the name given to a series of horny plates growing from the roof of the mouth in those whales classified as Whale-bone or Baleen Whales (*Mysticeti*). There are 300–400 or so plates on each side, and their inner edges are frayed, the whole system constituting a filter for collecting minute organisms used for food. The Baleen Whales include the Right-Whales, the Pacific Grey-Whale and the Rorquals. *See* **Whales.**

Ballet is a combination of four arts; dancing, music, painting, and drama, each of which is ideally of equal importance. The movement of the individual dancers and the "orchestration" of the whole group is in the hands of the choreographer. The dancer's training follows certain basic rules but save in classical ballet there is considerable freedom of movement.

Ballet today developed professionally at the Court of King Louis XIV of France, though it owes its origins to Italy and in the earliest times to Greece and Rome. Its movements were made up from the dances of courtiers, country folk and tumblers. Technique grew more complex as costume became modified, the body gaining complete freedom with the invention of tights. A succession of great dancers—French, Italian and latterly Russian left their imprint on the art. Contemporary ballet reflects the aesthetics of the Russian, Sergei Diaghilev. In England Dame Ninette de Valois laid the foundation of a national ballet, at Sadler's Wells and Covent Garden. A Royal Charter was granted in 1957 setting up the Royal Ballet to co-ordinate the activities of the Sadler's Wells group.

Ballistics, the science dealing with the motion of projectiles, especially shells, bombs and rockets. Great advances have been made in this science.

Balloon, the modern balloon consists of a bag of plastic material inflated with a gas lighter than air. The first ascent by man in a hot-air balloon was made on 21 November 1783, and in a hydrogen balloon on 1 December 1783. The most famous of the early scientific flights by manned balloons were those of the Englishmen Coxwell and Glaisher, in 1862, when a height of 11 km was reached. The first aerial crossing of the English Channel by Blanchard and Jeffries was made on 7 January 1785. Piccard's ascent to 16 km, in 1931, marked the conquest of the stratosphere. Four years later the American balloon *Explorer II,* inflated with nearly 112,000 m³ of helium, carried a team of scientists with their floating laboratory to an altitude of 23 km. Meteorologists send their instruments up in balloons to collect data about the upper atmosphere. In 2002 the American Steve Fossett became the first solo balloonist to circle the globe non-stop.

Balsam, a big genus (140 species) of flowering plants. Many species are cultivated for their showy flowers, *e.g., Impatiens noli-me-tangere,* the yellow balsam or "touch-me-not", so called because the fruit explodes when touched, slinging out the seeds. Balsam fir is a conifer (*Abies balsamea*) from which Canada balsam gum is obtained.

Bamboo, a genus of strong grasses, some species growing to over 36 m in height; much used in Asia for all kinds of purposes. Half the world's woody bamboo species is under threat of extinction as a result of forest destruction.

Banana (family *Musaceae*), a large herbaceous plant cultivated in moist regions of the tropics, and one of the most productive plants known. The main areas of commercial cultivation are in tropical America, the Canary Islands and West Africa. Bananas have overtaken the apple to become the favourite fruit in Britain, but long-term they are threatened with disease.

Bandicoots, Australasian marsupial mammals, of the size of a large rat or rabbit. They are burrowing animals living largely on insects. The rabbit-eared bandicoot, restricted to Australia, has shrew-like snout, long ears like a rabbit, long crested tail, and a silky coat. The long-nosed bandicoot has a spiny coat and comes from E. Australia. The pig-footed bandicoot has two functional toes on the foot, like a pig.

Bank of England. Founded by Royal Charter on 27 July 1694. Known as "The Old Lady of Threadneedle Street". The Labour Government elected in 1997 restored independence to the Bank in determining interest rates.

Bank Holidays. Public holidays in England and Wales comprise at present six bank holidays (New Year's Day, Easter Monday, May Day, Spring and Late Summer Holidays at the end of May and August respectively, and Boxing Day), with also two common law holidays (Good Friday and Christmas Day); in Scotland (beginning in 1996) seven bank holidays (New Year's Day, Good Friday, Easter Monday, May Day, Spring and Late Summer Holidays at the end of May and August respectively, and Christmas Day); and in Northern Ireland seven bank holidays (New Year's Day, St. Patrick's Day, Easter Monday, May Day, the Spring Late Summer Holidays at the end of May and August respectively, and Boxing Day) plus two other public holidays (Easter Tuesday and the anniversary of the Battle of the Boyne).

There are holidays in lieu of those public holidays which fall at weekends. In Scotland and Northern Ireland a general holiday is not necessarily observed on the same day as a bank holiday.

Bantu (native word = people), term loosely used for large family of black races of Southern Africa.

Baobab, a tropical African tree. The species *Adansonia digitata* is one of the largest trees known, though not the tallest; the trunk can reach 9 m in thickness. The fruit is woody, but its juice provides a cooling beverage. The bark yields a fibre used for making rope and cloth.

Barbary Ape, a large monkey belonging to the genus *Macaca*. It is the only monkey living in relative freedom in Europe, a small colony existing on the Rock of Gibraltar. It has no tail.

Barberry, a genus of berry producing shrubs containing a hundred species. Several species are cultivated for their flowers and bright berries. Has an interesting pollination mechanism; the base of each stamen is sensitive to touch, and insects probing for nectar cause top of stamen to spring inwards, so dusting visitor's head with pollen which can then be carried to the next flower visited. The common barberry (*Berberis communis*) harbours one stage of the fungus that causes rust of wheat.

Barbican, a fortified entrance to a castle or city, with projecting towers. In the London area called Barbican there was formerly a barbican in front of the city gates.

Barbiturates. A group of drugs derived from a parent compound called barbituric acid: phenobarbitone is the best-known example. They induce sleep and are used in the manufacture of sleeping pills, but they can be habit forming.

Barcarolle, a Venetian gondolier's song applied to instrumental as well as vocal compositions.

Bard, among the ancient Celts a poet or minstrel whose mission was to sing of heroic deeds. He was supposed to have the gift of prophecy, and was exempt from taxes and military service.

Barilla, soda carbonate or soda ash obtained by burning certain salt-marsh plants (*e.g.,* the saltwort, *Salsola kali*). It used to be in great demand, until the product of the Leblanc and then the Solvay ammonia-soda process was made available by the chemical industry.

Barium, metal element, no. 56, symbol Ba. In group 2 of the periodic table. The metal is soft and easily cut. It occurs as the sulphate and carbonate in nature. It was first prepared by Sir Humphry Davy in 1808, as an amalgam, by electrolysis of barium chloride. The pure metal was not isolated until 1901.

Barnacles constitute a sub-class (*Cirripedia*) of the Crustacea. The barnacle fouling the bottom of ships is the Goose Barnacle, which has a long muscular stalk and a shell composed of five plates. The Acorn Barnacles, which cover rocks, breakwaters, etc., just below high-water mark are similarly constructed, but have no stalk. The manner of feeding of barnacles was vividly described by T. H. Huxley, who said the barnacle is "a crustacean fixed by its head kicking the food into its mouth with its legs". It was a naval surgeon, J. Vaughan Thompson, who discovered in 1830 that barnacles have a free-swimming larva (or nauplius). In the Middle Ages a curious myth grew up to the effect that the Barnacle changed into a sea-bird called, for that reason, the Barnacle Goose.

Barnard's Star. A star discovered by the American astronomer Edward Emerson Barnard in 1916 and which has the largest stellarproper motion known. Barnard's Star is one of the closest stars to us and also one of the intrinsically faintest stars known.

Barometer is an instrument for measuring atmospheric pressure, invented at Florence by Torricelli, pupil of Galileo, in 1644. The standard method consists of balancing the air column against a column of mercury, used on account of its high density. The mercury is contained in a long glass tube, closed at one end, and inverted in a cistern also containing mercury. The height of the mercury column, supporting the air column, is taken as the pressure at the time, and can be read off very accurately by means of a vernier scale. Present-day tendency is to express the readings in units of pressure instead of length, the millibar being adopted (1 mb = 1,000 dynes per sq. cm.; 1,000 mb $\equiv$ 75 cm of mercury approx.). The standard instrument is correct for pressures at 0°C in Lat. 45°, so that corrections have to be applied for temperatures and latitudes other than these. Also a correction has to be made for reducing the pressure to mean sea level. *See* **Aneroid.**

Baron, title given in feudal England to a man who held his land directly from the king by military or other honourable service. The first baron created by letters patent was John Beauchamp de Holt, Baron of Kidderminster, in 1387. A baron is a member of the fifth and last grade of the peerage of the United Kingdom and is addressed as "Lord". Life peers and life peeresses rank with hereditary barons and baronesses according to the date of their creation. In Scotland the term baron is used of the possessor of a feudal fief, or the representative by descent of such a fief. The equivalent of the English baron, as a rank of the Scottish peerage, is Lord of Parliament.

Baronet, the lowest hereditary title, instituted by James I to provide funds for the colonisation of Ulster. The first baronet was Sir Nicholas Bacon. Between 1964 and 1983 no recommendations for hereditary honours were made. In 1990 the Queen bestowed the title on Denis Thatcher.

Barque, a small sailing vessel with three or four masts. A three-masted barque has fore- and mainmasts square-rigged, the mizzenmast fore-and aft-rigged.

Barrow is an ancient artificial mound of earth or stone raised over the site of a burial. In Britain barrows were built from 2500 B.C. until the late Saxon period, but the Egyptian are the earliest barrows known, the great pyramids being a spectacular development of the custom of ceremonial burial. Silbury Hill, south of Avebury, is the biggest artificial mound in Europe, 512 m in circuit at the base, 96 m at top, and 41 m high.

Baryons, the group of heavier subatomic particles which includes the proton, neutron, lambda and omega-minus particles (and their corresponding anti-particles, called anti-baryons). Baryons interact by means of all the known forces of nature (strong, weak, electromagnetic and gravitational). However, in any closed system the total baryon number (*i.e.,* the number of baryons minus the number of anti-baryons) is constant. This means that the proton, being the lightest known baryon, must be stable against spontaneous decay. Unlike the lighter leptons (*q.v.*), baryons are now thought to have internal structure reflecting the fact that they are composed of quarks (*q.v.*) *See also* **Section T.**

Basalt Rocks are fine-grained, dark coloured, of igneous origin and occur either as lava flows as in Mull and Staffa, or as intrusive sheets, like the Edinburgh Castle Rock and Salisbury Crags. One of the best examples of columnar basalt is the Giant's Causeway in Ireland.

Basanite (Lydian Stone), a smooth black siliceous mineral, or flinty jasper; a crypto-crystalline quartz used as a touchstone for testing the purity of gold, *etc.*, by means of the mark left after rubbing the metal with it.

Base, a substance having a tendency to accept a proton (H-). This is a wide definition and covers unconventional types of compounds. In aqueous solution bases dissolve with formation of hydroxyl ions, and will neutralise an acid to form a salt. In non-aqueous solvents, like liquid ammonia or hydrogen fluoride, compounds classically regarded as salts can be bases, *e g*, sodium fluoride is a base in hydrogen fluoride solution.

Basilisk, is a lizard of aquatic habits, with an elevated crest (which it can erect or depress at will) down the centre of its back.

Basques, people of N. Spain and S.W. France, oldest surviving racial group in Europe, who have preserved their unique ancient language.

Bastille, a castle or fortress in Paris, built in the 14th cent., and used as a state prison, especially for political offenders. Its bad repute as an instrument of despotism excited the hatred of the populace, who stormed and demolished it on 14 July 1789, at the start of the French Revolution.

Bastinado, an oriental punishment, by beating with a pliable cane on the soles of the feet.

Bats. These mammals fly by means of a membrane stretched between each of the long fingers of the hand and between the fifth finger and the body. Another membrane stretches between the legs and the tail. Most British bats, including the pipistrelle, long-eared bats, noctules, belong to the family Vespertilionidae (with the exception of the horseshoe bats which belong to the family Rhinolophidae). These all feed on insects which they catch on the wing. Vampire bats (of which there are 3 species) are found across Latin America.

The problem of how bats can detect their insect prey and avoid obstacles when flying in total darkness has interested zoologists for a very long time. The problem was solved with the advent of sensitive ultrasonic recording devices.

Scientists now know that bats can distinguish between two objects the width of a pencil line apart by using their sonar echo. Blindness does not affect this ability but deafness leaves bats comparatively helpless. One of the most interest... ... the fishing bat (*Noctilio*) found in central America, which can detect fish by being able to receive echoes from the ripples they make on the water surface. New European legislation to protect bats came into force in 1994. There are 16 species of bat in Britain, but their numbers are declining. See **Ultrasonics.**

Bath, Order of the, Britain's second oldest order of knighthood. Exclusive to men since its institution by Henry IV in 1399, women became eligible for admission to the order in 1971. The order has three grades: Knight Grand Cross (GCB), Knight Commander (KCB), and Companion (CB). Women members of the order are known as Dame Grand Cross, Dame Commander and Companion.

Battery, Electric, the common term for an electric cell but really meaning a combination of two or more cells. A cell is a device for converting stored chemical energy into electricity which can then be used for heat, light, traction, or any desired purpose. A *primary* cell will do this until the chemical action is completed and the cell is then useless. In a *secondary* cell, the chemical actions are reversible and the cell can be returned to its initial condition and used again. This is done by passing an electric current through—a process called recharging.

A common primary cell is the Leclanché dry cell; used in torches. This works by the action of sal-ammoniac on electrodes made of zinc and carbon. About a century after it came into common use it is still the chief source of power for portable equipment in armed forces. A common secondary cell is the lead and sulphuric acid accumulator used in cars. Many other types of cell are known and some are under development because the demands of space travel, medicine, warfare, *etc.*, call for batteries

of lighter weight, greater reliability, or special properties. See **Fuel Cell, Energy Conversion.**

Bauxite, the chief ore of aluminium. Chemically it is aluminium oxide. Aluminium metal is made industrially by electrolysing purified bauxite dissolved in fused cryolite.

Bayeux Tapestry, a famous tapestry representing the conquest of England by William the Conqueror. It is embroidered on a band of linen 70 m long and 51 cm wide in blue, green, red and yellow, divided into 72 scenes ranging over the whole story of the conquest. The accepted view is that the tapestry was commissioned for Bayeux Cathedral, but a new interpretation is that it is an Anglo-Norman secular work of art, much influenced by the contemporary *chansons de geste* (songs of deeds), executed by English embroiderers for a Norman patron. A representation can be seen in the V&A Museum.

Beagle, a small hound that tracks by scent, and extensively used for hare hunting.

Bears belong to the Ursidae family of the Carnivora. They are plantigrade mammals, walking (like man) on the soles of their feet. Found in most parts of the world except Australia. The common Brown Bear was once spread over the whole of Europe; it became extinct in England about the 11th cent.; 2–2·5 m in length, and stands 1 m or more at the shoulder.

The Grizzly Bear of N. America is larger, and the coat is shorter and greyer. The Polar Bear is remarkable in having a white coat all the year round; it spends much time in water, and unlike other bears is entirely carnivorous. Bearbaiting was made illegal in England in 1835. The last brown bears of Europe are suffering severely from poachers. It is now known that polar bears are cannibals. Climate warming threatens the future of the Arctic polar bear (there are around 20–30,000 polar bears in the wild, from Russia to Alaska and from Canada to Greenland and Norway's Svalbard archipelago).

Beaufort Scale of wind force is used to specify numerically the strength of the wind. Since the introduction of anemometers to measure the actual velocity, equivalent values of the ranges in miles per hour at a standard height have been agreed. See also **Wind.**

Beaver, a genus of mammals of the Rodentia order, with short, scaly ears, webbed hind feet, and a long broad scaly tail. They grow up to 1·2 m long, and live in communities, constructing complex dams and lodges where they breed. A campaign is now being launched to bring back beavers to Britain. The beaver, Europe's largest rodent, were nearly ... hunted for its pelts.

Bedlam (a corruption of Bethlehem) was a priory in Bishopsgate, afterwards converted into a hospital for lunatics. The asylum was transferred to St. George's Field, Lambeth, in 1815. The term "bedlamite" came to be applied to any person behaving like a madman.

Beech, a deciduous tree belonging to the genus *Fagus* of some eight or nine species found in north temperate regions. The common beech, *F. sylvatica,* is believed to be native to Britain and is one of our finest trees, with massive trunk, long, pointed winter buds, and smooth, grey bark. There is little undergrowth under its dense shade. It is shorter-lived than the oak taking about 200 years to reach full size and then declining. The timber of beech has a variety of uses, *e.g.*, spoons, handles, chairs, *etc.*

Bee-eater, name of a family of brilliantly coloured birds closely related to the rollers and kingfishers inhabiting the tropical and sub-tropical parts of Africa, Asia and Europe. The European species successfully nested in Britain for the first time in 1955 and a pair nested in Alderney in 1956. With their long curved beaks they catch insects on the wing, especially bees and butterflies, and lay their eggs in dark tunnels.

Beefeater, See **Yeomen of the Guard.**

Beeswax, the secretion of the bee, used for the formation of the cells or honey-comb of the hive; when melted it is what is commercially known as yellow wax, white wax being made by bleaching. Being impervious to water, it acts as a good resistant and is an article of much utility.

Beetles (Coleoptera) constitute one of the biggest orders of insects, numbering over 200,000 species. There are two pairs of wings; the hind pair are used for flight, while the front pair are hardened to form a pair of protective covers (elytra). Some beetles have lost the power of flight and then the elytra are joined together.

Bell, a hollow body of metal used for making sounds. Bells are usually made from bell-metal, an alloy of copper and tin. Small bells used for interior functions are often made of silver, gold or brass. Ordinary hand-bells are of brass. From the 7th cent. large bells have been used in England in cathedrals, churches and monasteries. The greatest bell in the world is the "King of Bells" in the Kremlin at Moscow which weighs about 198 tonnes, is 627 cm high and 691 cm in diameter. It was cast in 1733 but cracked in the furnace (the broken part weighed 11 tonnes) and is now preserved as a national treasure. Other large bells in Russia include the 171 tonne one at Krasnogvardersk, near St Petersburg, and the one of 110 tonnes at Moscow. The Great Bell (Great Paul) at St. Paul's, cast in 1881, weighs nearly 17 tonnes and is the largest in the UK.

Other huge bells are the Great Bell at Beijing (53 tonnes); Nanjing (22 tonnes); Cologne Cathedral (25 tonnes); Big Ben, Westminster (over 13 tonnes); Great Peter, York Minster (10 tonnes). The Curfew Bell is rung in some parts of England to this day, notably at Ripon.

The number of changes that can be rung on a peal of bells is the *factorial* of the number of bells. Thus four bells allow 24 and eight bells 40,320.

There are more than 400,000 bell ringers in the UK and more than 5,000 church towers where bells are rung.

Belladonna or **Deadly Nightshade** (*Atropa bella-donna*), a well-known poisonous wild plant found in Southern Europe and Western Asia. The alkaloid atropine it contains is valuable in medicine, although a large dose is poisonous.

Bell, Book and Candle. To curse by "bell book, and candle" was a form of excommunication in the Roman Church, ending "Close the book, quench the candle, ring the bell".

Benedicite, the canticle in the Book of Common Prayer, known also as "The Song of the Three Holy Children".

Benedictines are monks and nuns of the Benedictine Order who live under the rule of St. Benedict—the monastic code whose influence on the religious and cultural life of the West has been so powerful. The rule is marked by an absence of extravagant asceticism. The greatest of the early Benedictines was Pope Gregory I (590–604) who sent St. Augustine of Canterbury to Anglo-Saxon England. Gregorian plainsong is named after him. Benedictine (probably the oldest liqueur in the world) was first made by a Benedictine monk.

Benin Bronzes, 16th cent. objects of Yoruba art, seized by British troops from Nigeria in 1897. Nigerians see the technological sophistication of the Bronzes as symbolic of African heritage and want to see them repatriated.

Benzene. An aromatic hydrocarbon obtained from coal tar and some petroleum fractions. It is a volatile inflammable liquid with a characteristic smell. The molecule consists of a flat ring of six carbon atoms, each bound to one hydrogen atom. Benzene is the parent member of many aromatic organic compounds and is widely used in industry to synthesise inter-mediates for fibres, dyestuffs, explosives etc.

Beryl, a mineral, of which the emerald is a grass-green variety. Composed of beryllium and aluminium silicates. The pure mineral is colourless; the colour of most beryl comes from traces of impurities, notably iron and chromium. Otherwise it is yellowish, greenish-yellow, or blue, and is found in veins which traverse granite or gneiss, or embedded in granite, and sometimes in alluvial soil formed from such rocks.

Beryllium. Metallic element, no. 4, symbol Be. Very similar to aluminium, it is stronger than steel and only one-quarter its weight. It is not very abundant, its main source is the mineral, beryl. Copper containing 2 per cent. beryllium is used for making springs. Because of its special properties the metal is used as a component in spacecraft, missiles and nuclear reactors. This accounts for its recent development on a tech-nical scale. The metal powder is toxic.

Bessemer Process for making steel depends on the forcing of atmospheric air into molten pig iron to burn out the impurities. Ousted by the oxygen converter. *See* Steel.

Betel, the leaf of an Indian climbing plant, of pungent, narcotic properties. It is destructive to the teeth, and reddens the gums and lips.

Bhang, the Indian name for the hemp plant *Cannabis sativa*, the leaves and seed-capsules of which are chewed or smoked. The drug which comes from flowers of the female plant is called hashish in Arabia and marihuana in the USA.

Bible. *See* H3.

Big Bang Theory, a cosmological model in which all the radiation and matter in the universe originated in an explosion at a finite time in the past. It is thought the universe came into existence between 10 and 15 thousand million years ago. The big bang theory has been very successful in explaining the expansion of the universe, the cosmic microwave background radiation and the cosmic abundance of helium.

Billion, formerly in English usage a million million; now a thousand million or 10^9.

Binary Notation, for numbers, is a way of representing numbers using only two digits, 0 and 1. Electronic digital computers handle numbers in this form (*see* **Section V**). The ordinary, or decimal numbers, 0, 1, 2, 3, 4, 5, 6, 7, 8, 9, 10 are written in binary notation as follows: 0, 1, 10, 11, 100, 101, 110, 111, 1000, 1001, 1010. The reader might divine the rules from this. The point is you "carry 1", *i.e.*, move the digit 1 a place to the left, when you reach 2. In decimal notation you move 1 a place left when you reach 10. In other words, instead of columns for units, tens, hundreds, thousands, etc., the columns are for units, twos, fours, eights, etc. In binary notation: "1 + 1 = 0 with 1 to carry". Since every digit in binary notation is either 0 or 1 it requires one bit of information to specify a binary digit.

Bioethanol, a derivative of ethanol in the form of ethyl tertio-butyl-ether (ETBE), used as fuel and processed from agricultural crops (*e.g.* rape).

Bioglass. *See* T73.

Biological Clock. All living organisms undergo cyclical changes in activity of some sort. These are linked to the changes in their environment which are produced by the alternation of night and day, the phases of the moon and the tides, and the cycle of the seasons. These cycles of activity frequently persist if the organism is put into a constant environment in which there appear to be no external clues as to what time or what season it is. A squirrel, for example, wakes up at about the same time each evening even when it is put into constant darkness. It is usual to refer to these activity patterns as being driven by a biological clock inside the organism. But very little is known about how these biological clocks work.

Biological Warfare is the use for warlike purposes of bacteria, viruses, fungi, or other biological agents.

Biometrics, detailed measurements of human characteristics, such as the iris or fingerprints, now used in high-tech security systems.

Biosensors, micro-electronic or optoelectronic devices used to sense the presence of chemicals. This new technique for diagnosis and analysis has a host of applications in medicine, industry etc.

Biosphere, that part of the earth in which life exists—a very thin layer near the surface bounded by regions too hostile for life processes to occur. The upper limit is at about 9,000 m above sea level and the lower limit at about 10,000 m in the deep oceans. Ample supplies of solar energy, liquid water and places where liquid, solid and gas all meet seem to be requirements for a biosphere to exist and for all the biological cycles of water, oxygen, mineral, nitrogen, *etc.*, to function.

Birch, a genus of deciduous trees including about 40 species and found only in northern regions. Birches native to Britain, and to Europe generally, are of two species—the silver birch, *Betula pendula*, with its graceful, drooping branches and triangular leaves, and the white birch, *Betula pubescens*, which has erect branches and soft oval leaves. Birch timber is an important plywood timber, the bark is used for tanning leather, and wintergreen oil comes from the bark of black birch, *Betula lenta*, a North American species. The birch is not long-lived.

Birds, or Aves, are, next to mammals, the highest class of animal life. There are two kinds of modern birds—*Carinatae*, possessing keeled breast-bones and having power of flight; *Ratitae*, having raft-like breast-bones, and incapable of flight; and a sub-class of fossil birds, Archaeornithes, including *Archaeopteryx*.

Estimates of the number of birds breeding in Britain vary, but there are 229 breeding species. The commonest are wrens, house sparrows, blackbirds, chaffinches, robins and starlings. Many bird species are still (2006) declining (in the UK the skylark, song thrush and the linnet are under great pressure).

The wheatear is usually the first of the migratory birds to return, often reaching Britain at the end of February and always before the middle of March; the sand martin is the first of the "early swallows" to return, followed by the house martin. The first cuckoo arrives about the middle of April, and the whinchat, garden warbler, and sedge warbler during the last week in April. The nightjar, spotted flycatcher, and red-backed shrike are not seen until the first week in May. The swift is among the last to return from Africa and the earliest to depart.

Bird-nesting is illegal in Britain. With the passing of the Wildlife and Countryside Act in 1980 the trapping and caging of robins, nightingales, larks, kingfishers, cuckoos, owls, martins, fieldfares, flycatchers, ravens and other birds was made illegal in Britain.

Some scientists think birds did not evolve from feathered dinosaurs but rather from prehistoric lizards (*archosaurs*).

Recent research has shown that birds rival dolphins and chimpanzees in intelligence. Birds can understand each other's intentions and can use tools more efficiently than chimpanzees. Even though some birds only have pea-sized brains, their mental capacities can surpass those of chimps. *See also* **Section T**.

Birds of Paradise, over 40 species of tropical birds inhabiting the dense forests of New Guinea and neighbouring islands. The male birds are remarkable for their brilliant plumage, long tail feathers, and ruffs on wings and neck, which are displayed to advantage during courtship. Related to the Bower Birds of Australia.

Biretta, a four-cornered head-covering worn by ecclesiastics of the Roman Church and varying in colour according to rank. A cardinal's biretta is red, a bishop's purple, a priest's black.

Bise, a keen dry north wind prevalent in Switzerland and South France.

Bisextile. *See* **Leap Year.**

Bishop is a Christian ecclesiastic, a person consecrated for the spiritual government of an area, a diocese or province, to the spiritual oversight of which he has been appointed (diocesan bishops), or to aid a bishop so appointed (suffragan bishops). In the Church of England there are forty-three diocesan bishops, all nominated by the Crown. Two, Canterbury and York, are archbishops having primacy in the respective provinces. The archbishops of Canterbury and York and the bishops of London, Durham and Winchester and 21 other diocesan bishops in order of seniority are spiritual peers, and sit in the House of Lords.

The (Disestablished) Church of Ireland has two archbishops and twelve bishops; the (Disestablished) Church of Wales an archbishop and five bishops and the Episcopal Church in Scotland seven bishops. *See also* **Cardinal.**

Bismuth, metallic element, no. 83, symbol Bi, in group 5 of the periodic table. Like antimony, the stable form is a grey, brittle, layer structure; electrical conductor. It is readily fusible, melting at 264°C and boiling at about 1420°C. Wood's metal, an alloy with one of the lowest melting points (under 65°C, so that a spoon made of it will melt when placed in a cup of hot tea), contains four parts bismuth, two parts lead, one part tin, one part cadmium.

Bison, a genus of wild cattle, distinguished from the ox by its shorter, wider skull, beard under the chin, high forequarters, and, in winter, a great mane of woolly hair covering head and forequarters. There are two species, the European and the American bison. The European bison, which tends to browse (or munch trees and leaves rather than graze) is now poised to return.

Bit, formerly the word often referred to the metal piece in the mouth of a bridled horse, now more likely to be a technical expression in the mouth of a computer expert. A bit is a unit of information; it is the information that can be conveyed by indicating which of two possibilities obtains. Any object that can be either of two states can therefore store one bit of information. In a technical device, the two states could be the presence or the absence of a magnetic field, or of an electric voltage. Since all numbers can be represented in the binary system (*see* **Binary Notation**) by a row of digits which are *either* 0 *or* 1, it takes one bit of information to specify a binary digit. Bit is short for binary digit.

Bittern, a bird of the heron genus, with long, loose plumage on the front and sides of the neck. It is a solitary bird inhabiting marshes, but rare in Britain where its numbers fell to *c.* 15 breeding pairs in Norfolk, Suffolk and Lancashire. An ambitious scheme was launched in 1995 to save it from extinction and a recovery is now underway.

Bivalves, shell-fish whose shell consists of two hinged valves, lying one on each side of the body, such as mussels, oysters and cockles.

Blackbird, or Merle, a member of the Thrush family, a familiar song bird in Britain. Male is all-black with orange bill; female is mottled brown with brown bill; the young are spotted brown.

Blackcock and Greyhen (as the female is called) are closely related to the Capercaillies but smaller. They nest on the ground and prefer wooded country to open moors. Found in northern half of northern hemisphere. Polygamous, they perform excited courtship dances; the male is a handsome blue-black bird with white undertail, the female dark brown mottled.

Black Holes. *See* **Astronomy, Section T, Part I.**

Black-letter, the Old English or Gothic type first used in printing blocks.

Black Woodpecker (*Dryocopus martius*), a black bird about the size of a rook, with slightly crested scarlet crown, found in parts of Europe.

Blenny, a group of marine fishes with spiny rays part of the fin running along the back. Several species are found around the British coast.

Bluebird, a migratory bird of North America, deriving its name from its deep blue plumage, it has a pleasant warbling song and is a familiar sight in the woods from early spring to November. In India and Malaya there is the Fairy Blue-bird; the male is black with shiny blue upper parts. Used as the symbol of happiness by Maeterlinck in his play *The Blue Bird.*

Blue Marlin, the world's ultimate game fish, now increasingly threatened with extinction by over-fishing.

Blue Peter, a blue flag with a white square in the centre, is hoisted 24 hours before a ship leaves harbour (the letter P in the alphabet of the International Code of Signals).

Blue Ribbon, a term in general use to denote the highest honour or prize attainable in any field or competition. Thus the Derby is the blue ribbon of the turf. The expression is derived from the highest Order of Knighthood in the gift of the British Crown, the insignia of which is a garter of blue velvet.

Blue Stocking, an archaic term used to describe a learned or literary woman, particularly if pedantic and undomesticated. The term possibly derives from the Bas-Bleu club of Paris, which was attended by the literary savantes of the 17th cent. In England a similar literary club was formed about 1780, whose members were distinguished by their blue stockings.

"Blue" Sun, Moon, etc., a phenomenon caused by the scattering of sunlight by transparent particles suspended in the atmosphere, the effect being that blue light is transmitted, and red light extinguished to direct vision. The dust from the Krakatoa eruption in 1883 and the drifting layer of smoke from the forest fires in Alberta, Canada, in 1950 gave rise to "blue" moons and suns, phenomena sufficiently rare to be described as occurring "once in a blue moon".

Boa, a term applied to a family of snakes of large size, some attaining a length of 9 m. They are not poisonous, but kill their prey by crushing —constriction—hence the name "boa constrictor". They occur both in the Old World and the New, but are more abundant in the latter. Most Boas retain the eggs within the body until young are fully developed, whereas the Pythons almost all lay leather-shelled eggs.

Boar, or Wild Hog, an animal largely distributed over the forest regions of Europe, Asia, Africa and South America. It has a longer snout and shorter ears than its descendant the domestic hog, and is provided with tusks. Having to forage for itself, it is a more active and intelligent animal than the pig of the sty.

Boat, an open vessel, propelled by oars or sails, or both. The boats of a ship of war are the launch, barge, pinnace, yawl, cutters, jolly boat and gig; of a merchant vessel, the launch, skiff, jolly boat or yawl, stern boat, quarter-boat and captain's gig. Every ship is compelled to carry fully provisioned and equipped lifeboats.

Bode's Law, a numerical relationship formulated by Bode in 1772 (though pointed out earlier by J. D. Titius of Wittenberg), which states that the relative mean distances of the planets from the sun are found by adding 4 to each of the terms 0, 3, 6, 12, 24, 48, 96, and dividing each number by 10. The gap between Mars and Jupiter caused Bode to predict the existence of a planet there, later confirmed by the discovery of Ceres and other minor planets. The law breaks down for Neptune and Pluto.

Boers, name given to Dutch settlers, largely farmers, in South Africa after the 17th century. Discontented with British rule in the Cape after 1820, they emigrated northwards in 1835–37; after much fighting with the local people, they founded the Orange Free State (1836) and the Transvaal Republic (1848). The Transvaal declared itself independent in 1852. In 1877, after war with the Zulus, it was annexed to the British dominions; in 1879 it was declared a Crown Colony. For the **Boer War,** *see* **A40.**

Boiling-point is the temperature at which a liquid boils. At that point the pressure of the vapour is equal to the pressure of the atmosphere. Under increased pressure, the b.p. rises and under less pressure, as on the top of a mountain, it is lower. At standard atmospheric pressure (760 mm of mercury) the b.p. of water is 100°C; alcohol 78·4°C; ether 35·6°C.

Bonobo, or pygmy chimpanzee, is man's closest relative (sharing 98% of DNA). It lives in forests south of the Congo river.

Book of Hours, the most widespread devotional work of the Middle Ages. Most surviving copies are 15th century, but the earliest (the de Brailes Hours) dates from *c.* 1240.

Books, Classification of. All libraries are classified to facilitate reference, but the favourite system is the Dewey Decimal System, which divides the whole field of knowledge into ten Main Classes. Each of these Main Classes is again subdivided into ten main divisions. As an example: the main class of Sociology receives the number 300. This range 300 to 400 (the next main class) is graduated into tens, and Economics is 330. The range 330 to 340 is again graduated, and the subject of Labour and Capital is 331. This process is carried on by decimals so that 331·2 deals with Remuneration for Work, 331·22 with Wage Scales, and 331·225 with Extra Pay.

Borax (Sodium Pyroborate) is a white, soluble, crystalline salt. It is widely and diversely used, *e.g.,* as a mild antiseptic, in glazing pottery, in soldering, in the making of pyrex glass, as a cleansing agent and sometimes as a food preservative. Borax occurs naturally in the salt lakes of Tibet, where it is called tincal.

Bore. In physical geography, an almost vertical wall of water which passes upstream along certain estuaries. Its formation requires special conditions of river flow, incoming high tide, and shape of river channel. It can be spectacular and dangerous on some rivers. In Britain the best known is the Severn bore which can be over a metre high and move at 16–19 km/h. In parts of Britain the bore is called an eagre.

Boron. A metalloid element, no. 5, symbol B. There are two forms, one crystalline, the other amorphous. It is not very abundant in nature but occurs in concentrated deposits. It is best known in boric acid, which is used as a mild antiseptic (called boracic acid) and borax (*q.v.*). Boron compounds are essential to some plants, *e.g.,* beans. Used in the preparation of various special-purpose alloys, such as impact resistant steel. Compounds of boron and hydro-

gen are used as rocket fuels.

Borstal, an institution where young offenders under 21 on conviction were sent for detention and reform. Emphasis was placed on vocational training in skilled trades. The first was opened in 1902 at Borstal, near Rochester in Kent. Borstals were abolished by the 1982 Criminal Justice Act. Young offenders' are now referred to the Young Offenders' Institution (*q.v.*).

Bourgeoisie, a term used by Marxists to indicate those who do not, like the proletariat, live by the sale of their labour. They include, on the one hand, industrialists and financiers or members of the liberal professions and, on the other, small artisans and shop-keepers who, although their standard of living may not be appreciably higher (and today is often lower) than that of the proletariat, are described as the "petty bourgeoisie". According to the Marxist view, the bourgeoisie arose with modern industrialism after it had overthrown the old feudal aristocracy and thus replaced it as the ruling class.

Bovine Spongiform Encephalopathy (BSE). *See* **Mad Cow Disease.**

Bow, an instrument for propelling arrows, and, in the days when it was a weapon of war, was usually made of yew or ash, and was about 2 m long, with an arrow *c.* 1 m long. It was the weapon with which Crécy, Poitiers and Agincourt were won. The cross-bow was Italian and was adopted in France, but did not become popular in Britain.

Bow Bells is the peal of the London church of St. Mary-le-Bow, Cheapside, within sound of which one must be born to be entitled to be called a "cockney". Bow Bells had not been heard since 1939, but they once again rang out over the City of London on 20 December 1961.

Bowdlerise, to expurgate a book. Derived from Thomas Bowdler (1754–1825), the editor of the Family Shakespeare, in which "those words and expressions are omitted which cannot with propriety be read aloud in a family". Such prudery met with ridicule and hence the words "bowdlerism" "bowdlerist", *etc.*

Bower Bird, native to Australia and New Guinea and related to the Bird of Paradise, though often less striking in appearance. In the mating season the male builds a "bower" of sticks and grasses for elaborate courtship displays.

The Gardener Bower Bird of Papua makes a lawn in front of his bower and adorns it with bright coloured pebbles and flowers which are replaced as they wither. The female builds her nest away from the bower. So far, 18 species of bower bird have been identified.

Boxgrove. Site near Halnaker, West Sussex. In 1993 archaeologists discovered the 500,000 year old left shin bone of "Boxgrove Man", making it the site of the oldest human inhabitant in England.

Boycott, a term used in connection with a person that the general body of people, or a party or society, refuse to have dealings with. Originally used when Captain Boycott (1832–97) was made the victim of a conspiracy by the Irish Land League which prevented him making any purchases or holding any social intercourse in his district. He had incurred the League's hostility by a number of evictions.

Brass, an exceedingly useful alloy of copper and zinc. Much brass is about two-thirds copper but different proportions give different properties. It is harder than copper and easily worked. Brass in the Bible (Matt. x, 9) probably refers to bronze.

Breadfruit Tree (*Artocarpus altilis*), a native of the South Sea Islands; the fruits are a brownish green, about the size of a melon, and contain a white pulpy substance which is roasted before being eaten. The tree grows 12 m or more. Captain Bligh's ship *Bounty* was on a voyage to Jamaica carrying a cargo of 1,000 breadfruit trees when the mutiny occurred.

Breeder Reactor, a kind of nuclear reactor (*q.v.*) which besides producing energy by the fission process also produces ("breeds") more nuclear fuel at the same time. A typical reaction is: a neutron induces fission of a U-235 nucleus which breaks up into two medium-sized nuclei and some neutrons; one of the latter then enters a U-238 nucleus turning it into U-239 which then decays radioactively *via* neptunium into plutonium which is useful fuel. There are technical problems in breeder reactors which have delayed their practical use.

Breviary (Lat. *breviarium* = abridgment), the short prayer-book of the Roman Catholic Church which gives the Divine Office, *i.e.*, the services to be said daily. The directions for Mass are in the Missal. The current Roman breviary is a simplified version of the one decreed by the Council of Trent, 1568. *See also* **Matins**.

Bridges are structures for continuing a road, railway, or canal across a river, valley, ravine, or a road or railway at a lower level. From early times bridges were made of timber, stone, or brick, and it was not until the 19th cent. that wrought- and cast-iron were used. Today the materials mostly used are steel and reinforced concrete. Among the most famous of ancient bridges is that of S. Angelo at Rome, built by Hadrian as the Pons Aelius, A.D. 134. The Rialto bridge at Venice dates from 1588. The Ponte Santa Trinita at Florence, one of the finest Renaissance bridges and deemed the most beautiful in the world, was destroyed by German mines in 1944 but has now been reconstructed just as it was before. The first stone bridge across the Thames was begun in 1176. It had 19 arches and was lined with houses and stood until 1831 when it was replaced by the granite bridge designed by Sir John Rennie which stood until 1972. This has been replaced by a three-span concrete bridge with a six-lane carriageway and two footways.

The first cast-iron bridge was built by Abraham Darby at Coalbrookdale, Shropshire, in 1779. Telford's Menai suspension bridge (1825) has since been enlarged, the original design maintained. Robert Stephenson's tubular bridge across the Menai Straits (1850) was the prototype of all modern plate girder railway bridges.

Other bridges are the Niagara (suspension), Forth railway bridge (cantilever), London Tower bridge (suspension), Tay railway bridge, Victoria Jubilee bridge across the St. Lawrence at Montreal (an open steel structure), Sydney Harbour bridge, Lower Zambesi bridge, Storstrom bridge in Denmark, Auckland Harbour bridge, and Verrazano- Narrows bridge spanning New York's harbour from Brooklyn to Staten I., exceeding by 18 m the centre span of San Francisco's Golden Gate bridge.

Work on a suspension bridge 2-miles long, linking Italy and Sicily, could begin in the near future. Europe's longest road and rail bridge (opened in July 2000), is the Øresund bridge which links middle Denmark and southern Sweden. The longest suspension bridge in the world will link Hong Kong to its new airport. Europe's longest suspension bridge (opened in 1998) links the Danish island of Sjaelland (on which Copenhagen stands) to Funen. In 2001 the Italian government approved plans for a suspension bridge to link Sicily to the Italian mainland.

British bridges include the road suspension bridge across the Firth of Forth, completed 1964, the Severn suspension bridge (from which the design principles for the new bridge across the Bosporus were taken) and the Tay road bridge, both completed 1966, and the Humber suspension bridge, linking Hull and Grimsby, opened in 1981. When completed, it was the longest single- span suspension bridge in the world (1,410 m). The M25 "Dartford" bridge (opened 1991) is the largest cable-stayed bridge in Europe. The second Severn bridge, which opened in June 1996 is the longest in Britain. The proposed Thames Gateway Bridge (east of Woolwich) will link Beckton and Thamesmead in a major new crossing.

With the onset of the new century, a race is now on around the world to design a new generation of bridges. The Millennium Bridge, London's first new Thames crossing for 100 years, was opened in June 2000.

The world's highest road bridge (the Millau viaduct over the River Tarn in the Massif Central in France) was completed in 2004. It is 343m (1,125ft) tall and 2·4km (1·5 miles) long. *See also* **Bailey Bridge**.

Bridleway. In English law (sec. 27(6) of the National Parks and Access to the Countryside Act 1949) a highway over which the public have the following, but no other, rights of way: that is to say, a right of way on foot and a right of way on horseback or leading a horse, with or without a right to drive animals of any description along the highway.

Britannia Metal, an alloy of tin, antimony and copper, harder than pure tin, corrosion-resistant, used for teapots, jugs (often electro-plated).

British Association for the Advancement of Science, The, was founded in 1831 by a group of British scientists under Charles Babbage (1792–1871) to stimulate scientific inquiry.

British Commonwealth. The Commonwealth is a free association of independent member nations and their dependencies. The political status of the member nations is clarified and given legal substance in the *Statute of Westminster* drawn up in 1931, before the Commonwealth was founded, by the United Kingdom and the Dominions. The original Dominions were Australia, Canada, Irish Free State, Newfoundland, New Zealand and South Africa. On 1 June 1994, South Africa rejoined the Commonwealth, having left in 1961. In 1995 Cameroon and Mozambique joined the Commonwealth.

There are currently (June 2006) 53 members (*see* **A54** for full list of members). The Secretary-General (since April 2000) is Don McKinnon (New Zealand).

British Legion. *See* **Royal British Legion.**

British Museum, was created by an Act of Parliament in 1753, when the Sir Hans Sloane collection, which the British Government had acquired for £20,000, was added to the Cottonian Library and the Harleian Manuscripts. It was opened to the public in 1759 at Montague House Bloomsbury. The acquisition of the library of George III (known as the King's Library) in 1823 led to the construction of the present building with the new wing (1829), quadrangle (1852), domed reading room (1857), and later additions. The books and the reading room are now part of the British Library (*see also under* **Libraries**). The Natural History Department was transferred to South Kensington in the 1880s. As a museum it is perhaps the most famous in the world with its priceless collections. Its treasures include the Elgin Marbles (*q.v.*), the Rosetta Stone (*q.v.*) and the Portland Vase (*q.v.*). The famous domed Reading Room closed in 1997.

British Rail. *See* **Railways.**

British Standard Time, The British Standard Time Act of 1968 put Britain an hour ahead of Greenwich Mean Time (GMT) throughout the year for an experimental 3 years. This brought Britain into line with countries in Western Europe where Central European Time is observed. In 1970 Parliament called for the restoration of the previous position—BST in the summer months and GMT in the winter months—as from 31 October 1971. Attempts to change the law once again to give lighter evenings (but darker mornings) have gained much public support in recent years.

British Standards Institution (BSI). *See* **T58.**

Brocken-spectre or Glory. The series of coloured rings which an observer sees around the shadow of his own head (or an aeroplane in which he is travelling) as cast upon a bank of mist or thin cloud. This effect is produced by reflection and refraction of sunlight in minute water-droplets in the air just as in a rainbow.

Bromine. A non-metal element, no. 35, symbol Br, member of the halogen family (*q.v.*). It is a red, evil-smelling liquid (Greek *bromos*, a stink). It is an abundant element. In the USA bromine is extracted from sea-water on a large scale. It unites readily with many other elements, the products being termed bromides. Its derivatives with organic compounds are used in synthetic chemistry. Bromoform is a liquid resembling chloroform. Bromides were formerly used in medicine to calm excitement.

Bronze is primarily an alloy of copper and tin, and was one of the earliest alloys known. The Bronze Age (began c. 4,000 B.C. in Middle East) in the evolution of tool-using man came before the Iron Age (c. 2,000 B.C.) Some modern bronzes contain zinc or lead also, and a trace of phosphorus is present in "Phosphor-bronze". Important Bronze Age (2,700–700 B.C.) sites in Britain are Stonehenge (*q.v.*) and the Avebury Stone Circle (both in Wiltshire).

BSE. *See* **Mad Cow Disease.**

Bubble Chamber. An instrument used by physicists to reveal the tracks of fast fundamental particles (*e.g.*, those produced in large accelerating machines) in a form suitable for photography; closely related to the Wilson cloud chamber (*q.v.*), but the particles leave trails of small bubbles in a superheated liquid (often liquid hydrogen) instead of droplets of liquid in a supersaturated gas.

Buckingham Palace, London residence of British sovereigns since 1837. Originally built for the Duke of Buckingham (1703); bought by George III in 1762 and remodelled by Nash 1825–36.

Buntings, name of a group of finches, seed-eating birds, usually found in open country. The Yellowhammer, Reed Bunting, Corn Bunting and Cirl Bunting are resident in Britain; the Snow Bunting (which breeds in small numbers in Scotland) and Lapland Bunting are regular winter visitors. The Ortolan is a rare visitor.

Bustard, type of bird, related to the crane. The great bustard is being reintroduced into Britain after an absence of 200 years.

Butane, a colourless inflammable gas made of carbon and hydrogen; formula C_4H_{10}. Found in natural gas and made as a by-product of oil refining.

Butane, like propane (*q.v.*), can easily be liquefied and moved safely in cans and tanks. It is thus useful as a "portable gas supply"; also used in internal combustion fuels.

Butterflies, like moths belong to the order *Lepidoptera.* There are *c.* 20,000 species (though many are in decline). There are four stages in the evolution of a butterfly: *egg, caterpillar, pupa* and *adult butterfly.*

Buzzard, magnificent dark brown birds, three feet long, with an eye as large as a human eye. They need woods to nest in and land to forage over. Their numbers are now (2006) soaring.

C

Cacao, *Theobroma cacao*, is an evergreen tree, from 4–6 m high, growing abundantly in tropical America, West Africa, the West Indies, Sri Lanka, *etc.*, yielding seeds, called cocoa beans from which cocoa and chocolate are manufactured. The fruit is 17–25 cm long, hard and ridged; inside are the beans, covered with a reddish-brown skin, which are first fermented, then dried. The trees mature at five to eight years and produce two crops a year. The eating chocolate of today dates from Victorian times, but centuries earlier the Mayas of central America worshipped *cacao*.

Cacao production is threatened by plant disease in S. America and political instability in such countries as Ivory Coast.

Cactus, a family of flowering plants numbering about a thousand species adapted to living in very dry situations. The stem is usually fleshy, being composed of succulent tissue, remarkably retentive of water; commonly equipped with sharp thorns which deter animals from eating them. The roots are generally very long, tapping soil water over a large area; a "prickly pear" cactus may have roots covering a circular area 7 m or more in diameter. The leaves are commonly insignificant or absent, and the stem takes over the photosynthetic leaf function and becomes accordingly flattened to expose greater area to sunlight and air. In some kinds of cactus (*e.g.*, *Echinocactus*) the stem is shaped almost like a sea-urchin.

Cadmium. A metallic element, no. 48, symbol Cd, chemically similar to zinc and mercury. Used in alloys to lower the melting point, as in Wood's metal with bismuth and tin. Alloyed with copper to make electric cables. Like zinc, it is a protective metal and is used in electroplating. The cadmium-vapour lamp gives a characteristic frequency used in measuring wavelength.

Caesium, also spelt **Cesium,** is an alkali metal element, no. 55, symbol Cs, in first group of the periodic table. It resembles rubidium and potassium and was discovered by Bunsen and Kirchoff in 1860. It was the first element whose existence was discovered spectro-

scopically. The caesium atom consists of a heavy nucleus surrounded by 55 electrons, 54 of which are arranged in stable orbits, and one of which, known as the valency electron, is in a less stable orbit surrounding them. Used in the construction of photo-electric cells and as an accurate time standard (atomic clock).

Cajuns, corruption of Acadians. French-speaking inhabitants of Louisiana, descended from French Canadians who emigrated from Nova Scotia.

Calcium, a silvery-white metallic element, no. 20, symbol Ca. It melts at 810°C and is very reactive. It was discovered by Sir Humphry Davy in 1808, but not until 1898 was it obtained pure, by Moissan. Does not occur as metal in nature, but calcium compounds make up a large part of the earth's crust. Most important calcium sources are marble, limestone, chalk (all three are, chemically, calcium carbonate); dolomite, which is the double carbonate of calcium and magnesium; gypsum, a hydrated calcium sulphate; calcium phosphate and calcium fluoride. Igneous rocks contain much calcium silicate.

Calcium compounds are essential to plants and are used in fertilisers. Animals require calcium and phosphorus for bone and teeth formation; deficiency is treated by administration of calcium phosphate. Strontium is chemically similar to calcium, and the radioactive strontium 90 from atomic "fall-out" is easily assimilated by the body.

Calendar, a collection of tables showing the days and months of the year, astronomical recurrences, chronological references, etc. The Julian Calendar, with its leap year, introduced by Julius Caesar, fixed the average length of the year at 365¼ days, which was about 11 minutes too long (the earth completes its orbit in 365 days 5 hours 48 minutes 46 seconds of mean solar time). The cumulative error was rectified by the Gregorian Calendar, introduced in Italy in 1582, whereby century years do not count as leap years unless divisible by 400. This is the the rule we now follow. England did not adopt the reformed calendar until 1752, when she found herself 11 days behind the Continent. Until then, New Year's Day in England was on 25 March. Hence, in 1752, after the 11 days had been rectified, the new financial year began on 6 April—as it still does!

The Gregorian Calendar did not come into use in Russia until 1918. Old Style and New Style dates are classed as "O.S.", "N.S.".

Calends, the first day of the month in Roman times.

Callisto. A moon of Jupiter (*q.v.*). It has a subsurface ocean.

Calorie. Unit of quantity of heat. The "small" or fundamental calorie is the amount of heat required to raise the temperature of 1 gram of water from 14.5° to 15.5°C and is equal to 4·185 joules. This is the gram-calorie used in physics and chemistry. The large Calorie (written with a capital C), commonly used in nutritional connotations, is equal to 1000 small calories and is called the kilogram-calorie.

Calypso, West Indian song in the form of a doggerel lampoon composed spontaneously and sung to a guitar.

Cambridge University had a sufficiently good teaching reputation to attract Oxford students in 1209, when lectures at their own university were suspended. In 1226 it had a Chancellor who was recognised by King and Pope. The first college to be founded was Peterhouse in 1284.

The university was reorganised and granted a Charter of Incorporation by an act of Elizabeth in 1571. The colleges with their dates of foundation are Christ's (1505), Churchill (1960), Clare (1326), Clare Hall (1966), Corpus Christi (1352), Darwin (1964), Downing (1800), Emmanuel (1584), Fitzwilliam (1966), Gonville and Caius (1348), Jesus (1496), King's (1441), Magdalene (1542), Pembroke (1347), Peterhouse (1284), Queens' (1448), Robinson (1977) St. Catharine's (1473), St. Edmund's (1896), St. John's (1511), Selwyn (1882), Sidney Sussex (1596), Trinity (1546), Trinity Hall (1350) and Wolfson (1965).

The women's colleges to emerge were: Girton (1869), Newnham (1871), New Hall (1954) and Hughes Hall (formerly Cambridge T. C.) (1885). Lucy Cavendish College (1965) (for women research students and other graduates) received full college status in 1997. Homerton (f. 1824) now admits students for subjects besides Education.

Women were admitted to degrees (though not allowed to sit for examination) in 1920, and to full membership of the University in 1948. Newnham and New Hall still remain as all-women colleges.

In 2009 the University will celebrate its 800th anniversary.

Camel, a large ruminant quadruped, inhabiting Asia and Africa, where it is largely used as a beast of burden. There are two species—the Arabian camel or dromedary, with only one hump; and the Bactrian, or double-humped camel. There are no wild dromedaries, and the only wild bactrians occur in the Gobi Desert. The camel is able to go for long periods without water, not, as formerly believed, because it stored water in its hump, but because of the unique mechanism of its physiology which enables it to conserve water at the expense of not sweating until 40°C is reached. The last wild camels are found in Mongolia and China. (A new species of wild camel was found here in 2001.)

Campanile, or bell-tower, is separate from but usually adjoining its parent church. The most famous are in Italy. Giotto's tower at Florence, adjoining the cathedral of Santa Maria del Fiore, is architecturally the finest in the world. Others are at Cremona, the loftiest in Italy (110 m) and Pisa (the leaning tower). The magnificent pointed campanile of St. Mark's, Venice, which collapsed in 1902 (and since rebuilt in its original form), was begun in 902.

Canal, an artificial watercourse used for navigation which changes its level by means of locks. The completion of the Bridgewater Canal in 1761 to take coal from Worsley to Manchester marked the beginning of canal building in industrial Britain. There are over 4,000 km of navigable inland waterways in Great Britain today, c. 3,200 km of which are under the control of British Waterways The English network is based on the four great estuaries, Mersey, Humber, Severn and Thames. Many canals are now being developed for boating, fishing and other leisure pursuits. Many canals found a new use in the 1990s with the laying of optical fibre networks along their banks. The Rochdale canal, the "Everest of Canals" was reopened in 2003.

Candela unit of luminous intensity, symbol cd. An idea of the value which this unit represents may be gained from the fact that light obtained from a 40 W filament-type electric lamp or bulb is approximately the same as would be emitted by a point source of luminous intensity 30 cd. See **SI units, Section T.**

Candlemas, an Anglican and Roman Church festival in celebration of the Purification of the Virgin Mary. The date is 2 February.

Cannabis, a bushy plant found wild in many parts of the world. Cannabis was reclassified from a Class B to a Class C drug in January 2004. Possession remains illegal but is not an arrestable offence.

Canon, a term applied to signify a recognised rule for the guide of conduct in matters legal, ecclesiastical and artistic, or an authoritative ordinance: thus we have Canonical Scriptures, Canon Law, etc. Also a dignitary of the Church.

Canonical Hours were seven in number in the Western Church; Matins and Lauds, before dawn; Prime, early morning service; Terce, 9 a.m.; Sext, noon; Nones, 3 p.m.; Vespers, 4 p.m.; Compline, bed-time.

Canonisation, the entering of one of the faithful departed on the list of saints of the Roman Catholic Church. The rules governing canonisation were simplified by papal decree in 1969. The forty English martyrs, of whom Edmund Campion was one, executed between 1535 and 1679, were canonised in 1970. Beatification, by which a person is called blessed, is usually followed by canonisation.

Canticles, the name given to the scriptural passages from the Bible sung by the congregation in the various Christian liturgies. They are the Benedicite, Benedictus, Magnificat, Nunc Dimittis.

Capercaillie, the largest of the grouse family, found in the Scottish highlands and the pine forests and mountainous regions of Northern and Central Europe and Asia. The bird was reintroduced to Scotland by Sir Thomas Buxton in 1830.

Capuchins are members of a mendicant order of Franciscans, founded in the 16th cent. with the aim of restoring the primitive and stricter observance of the rule of St. Francis, so called from the capuce (pointed cowl) worn by them.

Caracals, the largest of the African small cats. They are very agile.

Carat, a term used in assessing the value of gold and precious stones. In connection with gold, it represents the proportion of pure gold contained in any gold alloy, and for this purpose the metal is divided into 24 parts. Thus 24-carat indicates pure gold, and any lesser number of carats shows the proportion of gold contained in the alloy. The carat as a measure of weight is now obsolete, having been replaced by the metric carat at 0.2 grms.

Caravan, a band of travellers or traders journeying together for safety across the Eastern deserts, sometimes numbering many hundreds. There are several allusions to caravans in the Old Testament. The great caravan routes of this period from Egypt to Babylon and from Palestine to Yemen linked up with the Syrian ports and so with Western sea commerce.

Carbohydrates. See Diet, Section Z.

Carbon, a non-metallic chemical element no. 6, symbol C, which occurs in crystalline form as diamonds and graphite; amorphous forms of carbon include charcoal and soot, while coke consists mainly of elementary carbon. The biochemistry of plants and animals largely hinges upon carbon compounds. The study of carbon compounds is called Organic Chemistry.

Carbon 14. A radioactive isotope of carbon, with a half-life c. 6,000 years, used in following the path of compounds and their assimilation in the body. Also used in determination of the age of carbon-containing materials such as trees.

Carbon Dioxide. Commonest of the oxides of carbon. It is formed when carbon and its compounds are burnt with abundant supply of air, and when carbon compounds are oxidised in the respiration process of animals. The atmosphere contains carbon dioxide to the extent of about 325 ppm and is increasing by about 1 ppm per year, principally because of the burning of fossil fuels and possibly because of deforestation which not only leaves more oxidisible material but lowers the amount of carbon dioxide removed by photosynthesis.

Carbon Monoxide is a colourless gas with no taste or smell. It is formed when coal and coke are burnt with a restricted supply of air; the blue flame to be seen in a coke brazier, for instance, is the flame of carbon monoxide. This gas is slightly poisonous, forming with the haemoglobin of the blood a compound which is useless for respiration and cherry red in colour, which gives a visible sympton of poisoning by carbon monoxide. With nickel it forms a volatile compound, called nickel carbonyl, and this reaction is the basis of the Mond process for extracting nickel.

Cardinal, one of the chief dignitaries of the Roman Catholic Church who constitute the Pope's council, or Sacred College, and when the papal chair is vacant elect by secret ballot a Pope from among themselves. There are three orders: cardinal bishops, members of the Roman Curia (the central administration of the Catholic Church) and bishops of sees near Rome; cardinal deacons, also members of the Curia, holding titular bishoprics; and cardinal priests who exercise pastoral duties over sees removed from Rome, though some are members of the Curia.

Pope John Paul I, who had been elected in Aug. 1978 to succeed Pope Paul VI, died suddenly after only 33 days. He was succeeded by Pope John Paul II (Cardinal Karol Wojtyla, Archbishop of Cracow). On his death in April 2005, the College of Cardinals comprised 117 members (under 80) eligible to elect the new pope. Papal insignia were trimmed of embellishment by papal decree in 1969 with the abolition, subsequently revoked, of the famous red hat (the galero) and the shoes with buckles. Cardinals aged 80 and over may not enter a conclave to elect a pope. Pope Benedict XVI named 15 new cardinals in 2006.

Cardinal Virtues, according to Plato these were justice, prudence, temperance, fortitude—natural virtues as distinct from the theological virtues of the Roman Catholic Church, faith, hope, charity. The phrase "seven cardinal virtues", combining the two, figures in mediaeval literature. *See* **Sins, Seven Deadly.**

Caribou, reindeer (*q.v.*) of N. America.

Carmelites, a body of mendicant friars taking their name from Mount Carmel, where the order was first established in the 12th cent. The original rule of the order required absolute poverty, abstinence from meat and a hermit life. The rigidity of the rule of the order was mitigated by Innocent IV. They wear a brown habit with white mantle, hence their name of White Friars. The order of Carmelite nuns was instituted in the 15th cent.

Carmine. *See* **Cochineal.**

Carp, a well-known fresh-water fish, found in plenty in most European and Asiatic still waters; reaches a length of about 60 cm and under favourable conditions lives for about 40 years. Familiar British members of the family are the roach, rudd, dace, chub, gudgeon, tench, minnow, barbel, bream and bleak.

The goldfish, popular in ornamental ponds, is the domesticated variety of Asian origin.

Carthusians, an order of monks founded in 1084 by St. Bruno at the Grande Chartreuse near Grenoble, and introduced into England about a century later. They built the Charterhouse (corruption of Chartreuse) in London in 1371. The chief characteristics of the order are a separate dwelling-house in the precincts of the charterhouse for each monk, and the general assembly in the Church twice in the day and once at night. They wear a white habit, with white scapular and hood. The liqueur *Chartreuse* was invented by the order and is still their valuable secret. The order of Carthusian nuns dates from the 12th cent.

Casein, the chief protein in milk and cheese. It is coagulated by the action of rennet or acid. An important class of plastics ("casein plastics") are produced from it, and these plastics are converted into buttons, kitting-needles, *etc.* 36,000 litres of milk yield about 1 tonne of casein.

Cassowary, a genus of ostrich-like birds which, together with the emu, forms a separate order found only in Australasia. All species are black, with brightly coloured necks, and with a horny crest on the head. Noted for fleetness.

Castor-oil Plant (*Ricinus communis*), an African shrub now cultivated in most tropical countries. It has broad palmate leaves and bears a spiny fruit containing seeds which when pressed yield the well-known oil.

Cat, the general name for all members of the class *Felidae* of the carnivorous order, from the lion down to the domestic cat. The latter is believed to be descended from the European and African wild cats. Egypt first domesticated the cat. Members of the cat family include tigers, lions, cheetahs, jaguars, pumas *etc.*

Catabolism, Anabolism, are the terms used to describe the two types of metabolic pathway. Catabolic pathways are routes by which large organic molecules are broken up by enzymes into their simpler constituents *e.g.,* starch into glucose. The anabolic pathways are the routes by which complex molecules are synthesised from simple sub-units, *e.g.,* proteins from amino acids.

Catalyst. A substance which alters the rate of reaction without itself being chemically changed. Various aluminium and titanium compounds are catalysts in the formation of polythene from ethylene. Palladium catalyses the reaction of hydrogen with oxygen (hence its use in gas lighters). Enzymes in the body hasten the breakdown of carbohydrates and proteins by catalytic action. *See also* **Section T.**

Cataracts are gigantic waterfalls. The most famous are those of Niagara in North America, the Orinoco in South America, the Victoria Falls on the Zambesi in Africa, and the Falls of the Rhine at Schaffhausen.

Cat-Bear. *See* **Panda.**

Catechism, an elementary book of principles in any science or art, but more particularly in religion, in the form of questions and answers. There is a great variety of these, including the Lutheran, prepared by Luther in 1529, Calvin's Geneva (in 1536), and the Anglican.

Caterpillar, the larva of a butterfly or moth, worm-like in its segmented body, with 3 pairs of jointed true legs, often curiously marked and coloured, and frequently more or less hairy.

Cathedral, the chief church of a diocese, so called from its containing a Bishop's seat, or episcopal chair. The town in which it is situated is a cathedral city. Some celebrated cathedrals are St. John Lateran of Rome, Notre Dame of Paris, the cathedrals of Cologne and Milan, St. Paul's in London, Canterbury, York Minster, and the cathedrals of Durham, Liverpool, and Coventry (destroyed by bombs, now rebuilt).

Cat's eye, a kind of quartz, much valued as a gem, opalescent, and of various shades. For long used in roads to mark guidelines for motorists.

Caves, natural hollow places in the earth, frequently found in Carboniferous limestone areas. The underground caves are formed by the action of rainwater carrying carbon dioxide, a dilute acid which slowly attacks the limestone rocks.

The main caves in the British Isles are in the Mendips, Derbyshire, Yorkshire, S. Wales and in County Clare. Many British inland caves are thought to have been formed at the end of the Ice Age when the water table rose. The scientific study of caves is known as spelaeology.

Caviar. *See under* **Sturgeon.**

Cedar, a dark-leaved, cone-bearing, horizontal-branched evergreen tree that grows to a considerable height and girth, the best known species in Britain being the Cedar of Lebanon, which was introduced in the 17th cent. The Egyptians used the resin of the Lebanese cedar to mummify their dead, whilst the Phoenicians built their ships from its timber.

Ceilidh, a Celtic evening of song, dance *etc.*

Celestial Sphere. The sky considered as an imaginary sphere that surrounds the earth. A fundamental tool in positional astronomy, it provides a surface on which to draw and study the directions and motions of the heavenly bodies.

Celluloid, one of the first synthetic thermoplastic materials, discovered by Alexander Parkes in 1865 when he was attempting to produce synthetic horn. It is made by treating cellulose nitrate with camphor and alcohol.

Photographic film is made of a similar, but less-inflammable material, formed by the use of cellulose acetate instead of the nitrate.

Cellulose, a carbohydrate, and a constituent of nearly all plants. Cellulose occurs in an almost pure state in the fibres of linen (flax), absorbent cotton, jute, and filter-paper.

Celsius was the 18th cent. Swedish scientist after whom the modern Celsius temperature scale is named. Since 1954, °C stands for "degree Celsius" instead of "degree Centigrade" but this is only a change in name. Both symbols refer to the temperature scale which calls the melting point of ice 0°C and the boiling point of water at one atmosphere pressure 100°C. *See* **Absolute Temperature.**

Celts, an ancient race found late in the third millennium B.C. in S.W. Germany, united by a common language and culture, who spread westward into Spain, northward into Britain, eastward to the Black Sea, reaching Galatia in Asia Minor. The "La Tène" iron-age Celts invaded Britain c. 250 B.C. After Britain was conquered by the Romans and invaded by the Angles and Saxons there remained as areas of Celtic speech only Wales (Brythonic speakers), Ireland, Scotland, the Isle of Man (Gaelic speakers), and in Cornwall. The late Celtic period in Britain produced a distinctive Christian art (*e.g.,* the Lindisfarne Gospel c. 700, and the Irish Book of Kells, dating from about the same time).

Surviving Celtic languages are Welsh, Irish, Breton, Scots Gaelic and a tiny Cornish tradition. Manx Gaelic is on the point of extinction.

Centrifuge, a machine which produces large accelerations by utilising the radial force caused by rotating a body about a fixed centre. Centrifuges have found extensive application in modern science. They can be used for the separation of one size of particle from another in biochemistry or in the training of astronauts where the accelerations occurring during rocket lift off can be simulated in a centrifuge on the ground.

Ceramics, are substances in which a combination of one or more metals with oxygen confers special and valuable properties. These include hardness, and resistance to heat and chemicals. Ceramic comes from the Greeek word for pottery, and pottery materials of mud and clay were probably the first man-made ceramics. Nowadays the range is enormous and growing; apart from all the pottery materials, there are firebricks, gems, glasses, concretes, nuclear reactor fuel elements, special materials for electronic devices, coloured pigments, electrical insulators, abrasives, and many other things. The scientific study of ceramics is part of materials science (*see* **Materials Science**). The need to design ceramic objects has inspired great art, and the production of ceramics has become a major industry.

Cerium, a scarce metallic element, no. 58, symbol Ce, discovered by Berzelius in 1803. A mixture of cerium and thorium nitrates is used in the manufacture of gas mantles, which owe their incandescent property to the deposit of cerium and thorium oxide with which they are coated.

CERN, French acronym for the European Laboratory for Particle Physics in Geneva. In 1989, the Large Electron Positron collider (LEP) was opened there. It recreates the swirl of matter just after the "Big Bang" created the universe.

Chalcedony, a mixture of crystalline silica and amorphous hydrated silica, *i.e.*, of quartz and opal. It has a waxy lustre, and is much used by jewellers for necklaces, bracelets, *etc*. Commonly it is white or creamy. Its bright orange-red variety is called carnelian; its brown variety, sard. Chrysoprase, plasma, bloodstone are varieties which are respectively pale apple-green, dark leek-green, green with red spots.

Chalk, a white limestone, calcium carbonate, found in the Upper Cretaceous deposits (formed from the shells of minute marine organisms). As chalk is porous, few streams form on its surface and consequently it is eroded slowly, although generally speaking it is a soft rock. Its juxtaposition with soft impervious clay in some areas results in its forming steep ridges known as escarpments, *e.g.*, N. and S. Downs and Chilterns. In contrast to the dry upland surfaces of chalk, lower levels are frequently saturated with water which emerges as springs.

Chamberlain, Lord, the senior officer of The Royal Household who is responsible for all ceremonial within the palace (levées, courts, garden parties, entertainment of foreign royalties and heads of state) but not the coronation or state opening of parliament. He is also in charge of appointments to The Royal Household. His office as censor of plays was abolished in 1968.

Chamberlain, Lord Great, one of the great officers of state whose duties are now mainly ceremonial. He attends the monarch at the state opening of parliament and at the coronation and is custodian of the Palace of Westminster (Houses of Parliament). The office is hereditary, dating from Norman times, and is held for one reign in turn by the descendants of the De Veres, Earls of Oxford.

Chameleon, a family of lizards with numerous species. Their ability to change colour is well known, but exaggerated, and is due to the movement of pigment cells beneath the skin. They are slow in movement, arboreal, and mainly insectivorous. Found in Africa, India, Sri Lanka, Madagascar and Arabia.

Chamois, a species of antelope, native of Western Europe and Asia. About the size of a goat, it lives in mountainous regions, and possesses wonderful leaping power, so that it is very difficult to capture. Its flesh is much esteemed, and from its skin chamois leather is made, although today sheep and goat skins are usually substituted. The mating season is October–November and the fawns are born in May or June. Live to be 20–25 years old.

Champagne is made from one of three grape varieties – *pinot noir*, *pinot meunier* and *chardonnay*. The fizz comes from adding sugar and yeast to the wine. It comes from the Champagne district of France.

Chancellor, Lord, the highest judicial functionary in Britain who also acted until 2006 as Speaker of the House of Lords (There is now a Lord Speaker). The Chancellor is a privy councillor and cabinet minister by virtue of office and a peer of the realm. The early Lord Chancellors were usually ecclesiastics and custodians of the Great Seal. Plans to reform the post have not yet become law.

Channel Tunnel, a scheme to bore a tunnel through 32–48 km of chalk under the sea between Dover and Calais has been a subject for discussion ever since Albert Mathieu first conceived the idea as a practical possibility in 1802. In the 1830s proposals for a bridge were made. In 1986 plans for a cross-channel fixed link were announced.

The tunnel (which is the longest underwater tunnel in the world) was officially opened on 6 May 1994, but fare paying passenger services did not start until 14 November 1994.

Chapel Royal, the church dedicated to the use of the Sovereign and Court. They include St. James's Palace, Buckingham Palace, Windsor, Hampton Court, the Tower, and Holyrood.

Charcoal, a term applied to wood that has been subjected to a process of slow smothered combustion. More generally it refers to the carbonaceous remains of vegetable, animal, or combustible mineral substances submitted to a similar process. Charcoal from special woods (in particular buckthorn) is used in making gunpowder. Bone charcoal finds use in sugar refining, as it removes dark colouring matter present in the crude syrup.

Charge-Coupled Device (CCD), a light-sensitive electronic detector, invented in 1970 and now widely used in cameras, hand-held video recorders and in astronomy. CCDs revolutionized astronomy, replacing the photographic plate. They are much more efficient than photographic plates and are thus well suited to imaging faint objects.

Charter 88, pressure group working for major constitutional reform, including a Bill of Rights, fair electoral system, democratic Upper House *etc*.

Chasuble, a sleeveless vestment worn by ecclesiastics over the alb during the celebration of Mass (to symbolise the seamless coat of Christ).

Cheese, an article of food made from the curd of milk, which is separated from the whey and pressed in moulds and gradually dried. There are about 500 varieties differing with method of preparation and quality of milk. They used to be made in the regions after which they are named but nowadays many of them are mass produced, *e.g.*, Cheddar is made not only in all parts of Britain but in Canada, New Zealand, Australia, Holland and the USA.

Cheeses may be divided into 3 main classes: (1) soft, *e.g.*, Camembert, Cambridge, l'Evêque; (2) blue-veined, *e.g.*, Stilton, Gorgonzola, Roquefort (made from ewe's milk), (3) hard-pressed, *e.g.*, Cheddar, Cheshire, Gruyère, Parmesan, Gouda.

Cheetah or "hunting leopard", the large spotted cat of Africa and Southern Asia, the swiftest four-footed animal alive.

Chelsea Pensioners, the former soldiers (around 440 in all) who live in the Royal Hospital in Chelsea. They wear distinctive red tunics. Women became pensioners for the first time in 2005.

Chemical Warfare. This term is usually restricted to mean the use in war of anti-personnel gases, aerosols and smokes, although explosives, napalm, herbicides and defoliants are also chemical agents that are used in war. Poison gas was first used on a large scale in the first world war; over 100,000 fatalities resulted from the use of principally chlorine, phosgene and mustard gas.

Worldwide revulsion at the hideous effects of chemical weapons and their potential as weapons of mass destruction resulted in the Geneva Protocol of 1925 which prohibited the use of both chemical and bacteriological weapons.

It has now been ratified by many nations including all the major powers (although Japan and America were quite late signatories). The Protocol has been generally well observed although notable violations have been by the Italians in Abyssinia (1935-6), the Japanese in China during the second world war (when over 100,000 were killed in Zhejiang Province), the Americans in S.E. Asia in the 1960s and Iraq (against the Kurds in the 1980s). Under the 1993 Chemical Weapons Convention (in force since 1997) signatories are obliged to remove chemical weapons left in other countries.

Chemistry. *See* **Section T**.

Chernobyl Disaster Site in the Ukraine of 1986 Soviet nuclear disaster, which caused major radioactive fallout across many countries. The scale of the disaster was kept from the Russian people.

Chestnut, the fruit of trees of the genus *Castanea*, members of the family *Fagaceae*. C. *sativa* is the sweet or Spanish chestnut, C. *dentata* the American chestnut and C. *crenata* the Japanese chestnut. The nut is edible. The wood is used in carpentry and fencing. *See also* **Horse Chestnut**.

Chiltern Hundreds, three hundreds—Stoke, Burnham and Desborough—the stewardship of which is now a nominal office under the Chancellor of the Exchequer. Since about 1750 the nomination to it has been used as a method of enabling a member of Parliament to resign his seat on the plea that he holds an office of honour and profit under the crown.

An alternate symbolic post for an MP giving up his seat is the stewardship of the Manor of Northstead in Yorkshire.

Chimpanzee, a large anthropoid ape, a native of tropical Africa, of a dark brown colour, with arms reaching to the knee, and capable of walking upright. Its brain is about a third of the weight of the human brain, but is anatomically similar. The animal has considerable intelligence and powers of learning. Chimpanzees have cultures as distinct as those found in human societies. It is now believed that they pass on new customs and technologies socially rather than genetically The AIDS virus is believed to have come from chimpanzees. There is a 98·5% match between the DNA of chimpanzees and humans. *See also* **Bonobo.**

China Clay. *See* **Kaolin.**

Chinchilla, a South American burrowing rodent. Grey in colour, and white underneath.

Chippendale Furniture was introduced in the reign of George I by Thomas Chippendale, a cabinetmaker from Yorkshire who migrated to London and set up for himself in St. Martin's Lane, Charing Cross. He was fonder of inventing designs for furniture than of making it, and in 1752 published a book of patterns; the London furniture-makers of the day soon began to model their work upon it.

Chivalry an international brotherhood of knights formed primarily during the 13th cent. to fight against the Muslims in the Crusades (**A41**). For the French the major battle was against the Muslims in the Holy Land and North Africa, the Spaniards fought the same enemy in their own country, and the Germans were concerned with the heathen of Baltic lands, but Chaucer's "very perfect gentle knight" had fought in all these areas. One did not easily become a knight who had to be of noble birth and then pass through a period of probation, beginning as a boy page in the castle of some great lord, serving his elders while he was taught manners, singing, playing musical instruments *etc.*

Probably he learned Latin, but he certainly learned French, which was the international language of knights as Latin was of scholars. At fourteen he became a squire and learned to fight with sword, battle-axe and lance, and to endure conditions of hard living while carrying out his duties of waiting on his lord, looking after his horses, and in time accompanying him in battle. Only if he showed himself suitable was he finally knighted by a stroke of the hand or sword on the shoulder from the king or lord. Knighthood was an international order and had its special code of behaviour; to honour one's sworn word, to protect the weak, to respect women, and defend the Faith.

Chlorine, a gaseous element, no. 17, symbol Cl, of the halogen family, first isolated in 1774 by Scheele by the action of manganese dioxide in hydrochloric acid. It unites easily with many other elements, the compounds resulting being termed chlorides. The gaseous element is greenish-yellow, with a pungent odour. It is a suffocating gas, injuring the lungs at a concentration as low as 1 part in 50,000, and was used during the first world war as a poison gas. It has a powerful bleaching action, usually being used in form of bleaching powder, made by combining lime and chlorine.

Chloroform, a volatile colourless liquid, compounded of carbon, hydrogen, and chlorine. It is a powerful solvent, not naturally occurring but synthesised on a large scale. When the vapour is inhaled it produces unconsciousness and insensibility to pain. It owes its discovery to Liebig, and its first application for medical purposes to Sir James Young Simpson.

Chlorophyll, the green pigment contained in the leaves of plants, first discovered by P. J. Pelletier (1788–1829) and J. B. Caventou (1795–1877) in 1818. Enables the plant to absorb sunlight and so to build up sugar. The total synthesis of chlorophyll was reported in 1960. *See* **Photosynthesis, Section T.**

Chocolate. *See* **Cacao.**

Chough, a member of the crow family, of glossy blue-green-black plumage, whose long curved bill and legs are coral red. It used to be abundant on the cliffs of Cornwall, but its haunts are now restricted to the rocky outcrops of the western coasts and in the mountains near by. It nests in cleft rocks and caves. The Alpine chough with yellow bill inhabits the mountainous districts of Europe and Asia. The chough is the emblem of Cornwall and appears on the county's coat of arms.

Christmas means "mass of Christ" from the old English *Cristes maesse,* which is celebrated by the Western church on 25 December. The actual day on which Christ was born is not known and there is some uncertainty about the year. 25 December as the day of Nativity was not generally observed until the 5th cent. A.D., though, as the winter solstice, it had long been observed as a pagan festival of *sol invictus* (unconquered sun). The first Christmas card dates from about 1843 and the Christmas tree, of pagan origin, was introduced into England from Germany. Santa Claus is a corruption of Santa Nikolaus (St. Nicholas) patron saint of children, whose feast day is on 6 December.

Chromium, a very hard, bluish-white metal element, no. 24, symbol Cr, melting at very high temperature (above 1,900°C). Its chief ore is chromite or chrome iron-ore (ferrous chromite). "Ferro-chrome" is produced by heating chromite and anthracite in an electric furnace, and chrome steels are prepared by adding the pre-calculated amount of ferro-chrome to melted steel. Best known chrome steel is stainless steel first made by Brearley in 1912 and since then developed greatly at Sheffield. A typical formula is 18 per cent. chromium, 8 per cent. nickel, 74 per cent. iron.

Equally important are Stellite alloys, containing chromium, cobalt, tungsten (or molybdenum), which have made possible modern high-speed cutting tools. Dies used in manufacture of plastics are commonly of chrome steel. The elementary metal finds little use alone except in chromium-plating for motor cars, *etc.*

Chromosomes, the structures contained within the nucleus of every animal and plant cell by which genetic information is transmitted. The chromosome number in somatic (body) cells is constant for each species of plant and animal, *e.g.,* man (46), cat (38), mouse (40) honey bee (16), fruit fly *Drosophila* (8), potato (48).

Chromosomes are long molecules composed of deoxyribonucleoproteins (*i.e.,* proteins and DNA). Human chromosomes have been the subject of much recent research since it has been found that certain disorders are associated with chromosomal aberration, *e.g.,* in Mongolism an extra chromosome is present. In 1997 US scientists created the first artificial human chromosomes *See also* **Section T.**

Church Commissioners. The Church Commissioners were established in 1948 by the amalgamation of Queen Anne's Bounty (established 1704) and the Ecclesiastical Commissioners (established 1836) to administer Church revenues and to manage Church property.

Cid, El, a famous Spanish hero of the 11th cent., Don Rodrigo Diaz de Vivar, also called Cid Campeador, whose exploits, against Christians and Moors alike, are widely celebrated.

Cilia, minute hair-like projections on the surface of some cells, which beat together in wavelike movements like the wind over a corn-field. These movements can be used as a means of locomotion as in the aquatic organism paramecium. Cilia are also found on the outer layers of the human trachea where they waft particles upwards to the throat, thus protecting the lungs. *See also* **Flagella.**

Cinque Ports, a number of seaport towns on the coast of Kent and Sussex, originally five; Hastings, New Romney, Hythe, Dover and Sandwich. Winchelsea and Rye were added later. These ports were required to furnish a certain number of ships, ready for service, and in return they were granted many privileges. The official residence of the Lord Warden is Walmer Castle, near Dover. The first-ever woman to hold the office was the Queen Mother (from 1979 to 2002).

Cistercians, an order of monks and nuns taking their names from Citeaux, near Dijon, where their first monastery was established in 1098. The order was noted for the severity of its rule. They were famous agriculturists. The habit is white, with a black cowl or hood.

Civets, creatures with cat-like bodies, but not cats at all. They are related to the mongoose.

Civil List is the estimate of the expenses to be incurred by the Sovereign in conducting her official business and engagements and those of the members of her family during each year. The amount is granted by Parliament upon the recommendation of a Select Committee and has to be settled afresh in the first six months of a new reign. The Civil List of Queen Victoria was £385,000, Edward VII and George V, £470,000; Edward VIII and George VI, £410,000; Elizabeth II £475,000. In 1990, a fixed 10-year Civil List arrangement was agreed for all the Royal Family. This was changed in 1992. Now (2006) only the Queen and Prince Philip receive Civil List payments.

The Prince of Wales does not receive a Civil List payment but derives his revenue from the Duchy of Cornwall. Other resources available to the Queen include (1) the sums which Parliament votes to government departments each year, e.g., upkeep of palaces (Department of the Environment); (2) privy purse (revenues of the Duchy of Lancaster); (3) personal fortune, the size of which is not disclosed. In 1992 the Queen agreed to pay tax on her private income and meet the working expenses of most junior members of the Royal Family. The system under which annual payments are made by the Government to the Queen was changed by the Civil List Act 1975; payments are now included in the annual estimates in the same way as the expenditure of a government department. In July 2000 the Civil List was frozen for ten years (until 2011).

Cleopatra's Needle on the Thames Embankment is from the time of Tuthmosis III (1500–1450 B.C.). The monolith had nothing to do with Cleopatra, as it only came to Alexandria after her death. It was first erected at the Biblical On (Greek Heliopolis), sacred City of the Sun. It was presented to the British Government by Mehemet Ali in 1819, but not brought to this country until 1878. Weight c. 183 tonnes; height, 20·8 m. Pollution has now changed its former rose-red granite to a grubby grey.

Climate has been defined by Professor H. H. Lamb as the total experience of the weather at any place over some specific period of time. Not only averages but extremes of temperature, variation of humidity, duration of sunshine and cloud cover, amount of rainfall and frequency of snow, frost, gales, etc., are amongst the data normally investigated. The interiors of great land masses are characterised by large ranges of temperature and low rainfall (continental climate), while proximity to oceans has an ameliorating effect with increase in rainfall (oceanic climate).

Presence of mountain ranges and lakes and configuration generally produce local modifications of climate, also apparent between the centre and the outlying suburbs of a city. Latitude introduces zones of climate, e.g., tropical rain, subtropical steppe and desert, temperate rain and polar. The climate is always changing in greater or less degree. Every decade, every century brings a somewhat different experience. The tendency in the 20th century was for much of the world to become warmer. See **Section Y.**

Clock, a device for measuring the passage of time. The earliest timekeeper was the shadow-clock, a primitive form of sundial, used in Ancient Egypt about 1500 B.C. To find the time at night the water clock or clepsydra was used. The sand-glass dates from the 15th cent. No one knows when the first mechanical clocks were invented, but it is known that a complicated mechanical clock driven by water and controlled by a weighbridge escarpment was built in Peking in 1090. The Dover Clock in the Science Museum is not the earliest surviving clock in England, as was once believed, but early 17th cent. The Salisbury Cathedral clock dates from 1386 and that of Wells Cathedral from 1392. The pendulum clock was invented by the Dutch scientist Christiaan Huygens (1625–95). The first watches were made in

Nuremberg shortly after 1500. The marine chronometer is a high-precision timepiece used at sea for giving Greenwich mean time. The quartz-crystal clocks are accurate to one thousandth of a second a day, and the improved atomic clock, developed at the British National Physical Laboratory, which makes use of the natural vibrations of the caesium atom, is an almost absolute measure of time. Its accuracy of 1 sec. in 300 years has been improved to 1 sec. in 1,000 years.

Cloud Chamber, an apparatus invented by C. T. R. Wilson in which the tracks of atomic particles can be made visible. Just as the vapour trails tell of the track of an invisible aircraft high up in the air, so the vapour trails of an invisibly particle can tell of its behaviour. The rays under investigation pass through a chamber containing a gas, e.g., air thoroughly cleansed of dust, supersaturated with water, or alcohol- vapour. As the particle passes through it forms a track of tiny water droplets which can be photographed. After a long and honourable history this wonderful instrument is now vir-tually obsolete. A later ingenious device for tracking fast fundamental particles is the Bubble chamber (q.v.).

Clouds are formed by the cooling of moist air, the type depending on the way the air cools and the height at which condensation occurs.

There are three main classes: (1) high cloud (about 6,100 m)—cirrus (delicate and fibrous), cirrostratus (thin white veil), and cirrocumulus (delicately rippled) consisting of ice crystals; (2) medium cloud (above 2,100 m)—altostratus (dense, greyish veil) and altocumulus (broken flattened cloudlets)—chiefly water particles, often supercooled; (3) low cloud (from near ground to 2,100 m)—cumulus (fair weather, broken, dome-topped), cumulonimbus (heavy, towering to great heights), stratocumulus (layer of globular masses or rolls), stratus (like fog but off the ground), nimbostratus (low, rainy cloud).

The highest clouds of all, and the rarest, are the noctilucent, seen only on summer nights in high latitudes. They form at about 80 km above the earth and consist of ice-coated dust from meteors. The spread of these noctilucent clouds may be due to global warming.

Clouds were first classified by the Quaker, Luke Howard, in 1804.

Clover, plants of the *Trifolium* genus, family *Leguminosae,* with about 250 species. These are "nitrogen fixing" plants and include red clover, white clover, alsike clover and crimson clover. They are of great importance in agriculture because in a good pasture they supply directly or indirectly most of the protein available to the animals. Seed of "wild white" clover has been accepted since about 1939 as the indispensable plant of good United Kingdom grassland, largely through the efforts of pioneers like D. A. Gilchrist (1859–1927).

Coal. Until recently the most important single fuel has been coal. It is a mineral of organic origin, formed from the remains of vegetation which over millions of years has changed to coal by the effects of heat and pressure from overlying rock or water. All coal contains moisture, inflammable volatiles, mineral impurities (some of which remain as coal ash after the coal is burnt), and fixed carbon (the coke that is left after the volatiles have been driven off). The relative proportions vary—from Anthracite, a hard coal containing the highest proportion of fixed carbon, to Lignite or brown coal which is little more than a hard peat. World reserves of bituminous coal have been estimated at 7·5 × 10^{12} tonnes. If one adds the reserves of brown coal and lignite, this figure is increased by about 15 per cent. The proportion of the reserves that could be economically recovered varies from country to country and estimates vary from 50 to 100 per cent of the reserves. The reserves are highly localised—over half being located in the former Soviet Union.

In the UK, coal long formed the basis of past industrial prosperity. Peak output occurred in 1913 when 290 million tonnes were mined, one third of which was exported. At the end of the second world war production had fallen to 186 million tonnes and was far below demand.

In 1947 the British coal industry was brought under public ownership and all its assets were vested in the National Coal Board. During the next ten years great efforts were made to increase coal output but, quite suddenly in 1956, demand for coal fell as oil became a popular fuel. The fall in demand was accompanied by increasing productivity, both mines and miners having been cut in their numbers by over half. Then as a result of the high cost of oil in 1973 came expansion of the industry. From 1984 the coal industry faced a bitter strike over plans to make large-scale pit closures. The defeat of the miners weakened the NUM and its leader, Arthur Scargill. The Government decision (in 1992) to close many of the remaining collieries and to privatise the industry created a bitter political controversy. By the beginning of 1995 the last pits had been privatised and the workforce now numbers below 10,000. Reduced demand for coal has threatened further job losses. The last coal mine in France closed in 2004.

Coat of Arms, in heraldry, a device containing a family's armorial bearings. In mediaeval times the coat upon which such device was embroidered; knights wore it over their armour.

Coati, a fox-sized creature belonging to the racoon family. Usually found in South America.

Cobalt, element no. 27, symbol Co, a white metal melting at 1490°C. Two main ores are *cobalt glance* (in which the element is combined with arsenic and sulphur) and *smaltite* (cobalt arsenide). The principal sources are Ontario and Zaïre. Various cobalt alloys are important, *e.g.*, stellite, ferrocobalt and carboloy. Its monoxide is an important colouring medium, and is used for colouring glass and porcelain blue.

Cobra, hooded and very venomous snakes. The best known species are the Indian Cobra, the Egyptian Cobra, and the Black-necked Cobra. Their food consists chiefly of small rodents, The King Cobra is almost exclusively a snake-eater. The "Spitting" Cobras (or Ringhals) of S. Africa are a related genus, capable of spitting their venom several yards. The King Cobra possesses enough venom to kill 100 people.

Coca, a S. American shrub, *Erythroxylon coca*, also cultivated in Java. The leaves yield cocaine, classified as a dangerous drug. When the local people chew the leaves they are enabled to withstand hunger and fatigue, as cocaine acts both as a mental stimulant and as an anaesthetic on the mucous lining of the stomach.

Cochineal or Carmine, a dyestuff consisting of the dried bodies of the female scale insect (*Dactylopius coccus*) which feeds on cacti. Of ancient origin, the dye was well known to the Aztecs, and was used widely in the Middle Ages. The scarlet tunics worn by the English during the Napoleonic wars owed their colour to carmine.

Cookatoo, a member of the parrot family, bearing a crest of feathers on the head, native to Australia and adjacent regions. Predominant colour is white tinged with yellow or scarlet while some species have dark plumage. The cockatoo of New Guinea is slaty black with pale red cheeks and can crack Kanary nuts which require a hammer to break them open. Its survival is threatened by the pet trade.

Cockchafer (*Melolontha*), one of the most destructive of beetles, the larvae feeding on roots. It is about 2·5 cm in length, of a brownish colour, and emits a loud whirring sound when flying.

Cockle, the popular name of the bi-valve shellfish of the genus *Cardium*, found in sandy bays.

Cockroach, inaccurately called the "black beetle"; a pest of bakeries and kitchens. In Britain two species are commonly found; the Common Cockroach (*Blatta orientalis*), about 2·5 cm long, with the wing covers long in the male and short in the female; and the German Cockroach (*Blatta germanica*), now the most common, half the size, dark yellow, with both sexes fully winged. All species have long antennae and flattened, leathery, shiny bodies. They are nocturnal and omnivorous. Cockroaches are the nimblest creatures on Earth until, like humans, old age reduces their agility.

Cocoa. *See* Cacao.

Coconut Palm (*Cocos nucifera*), a tropical tree, growing to a height of 30 m, with a slender trunk surmounted by giant feather-like leaves. One of the most important sources of food and raw material for people living in the tropics. The juice of the fruit, or coconut, is drunk; the kernel is eaten fresh or dried to form

copra, which yields animal feeding stuffs and oil, used in the manufacture of soap, margarine, cosmetics, synthetic rubber, *etc.*; leaves are used for thatching; leaf stalks for canes, fence posts, needles, *etc.*, and the trunk for houses and bridges. Main producing areas: Indonesia, Philippines, Malaysia, Sri Lanka and S. India.

Codes, a term used to designate a system of laws properly classified. The Code of Hammurabi, king of Babylon, *c.* 1751 B.C., had extensive influence over a long period. The Romans formulated several codes of historic importance including the Theodosian Code which summarised the Roman laws from the time of Constantine to 438 A.D. The final codification was made under order of the Emperor Justinian by his chief minister Tribonian and published in 529 with a new edition in 534. The most important of modern codes is the *Code Napoléon*, compiled between 1803 and 1810, and still in force. It has been used as an example for the codification of the laws of a number of countries from America to Japan. Under Frederick the Great the law of Prussia was codified. English law has never been codified, although the law on some subjects has been gathered up into a single statute. The Law Commission Act, 1965, sought to consolidate and codify the law.

Codex, a collection of written pages, stitched and bound together. The oldest extant codex is the Sinaiaticus of the 4th cent (*see below*). The Vatican codex of the same period and the Alexandrine codex of the 5th cent. are other examples.

Codex Sinaiticus. The British Museum, in 1933, purchased the *Codex Sinaiticus* from the Soviet Government for £100,000. The Sinaiaticus was written on 347 vellum leaves some fifteen to sixteen hundred years ago and the binding into 2 volumes was completed by Douglas Cockerill and his son in 1936. It was sold in 1981 for $5·2 million. It is one of the world's most important Christian manuscripts. Written in Greek at around the time of Constantine the Great, it once contained the entire Old and New Testaments and the Aprocrypha, but the Old Testament has been lost.

Coelacanth, a primitive fish living off the Comoros Islands (and also off Indonesia). The coelacanth represents the period in history when fish began slowly to evolve into four-legged animals.

Coffee, a shrub found originally in Arabia and Ethiopia, but now extensively grown in Brazil, Colombia, Ivory Coast, Uganda, Angola and Central America. It yields a seed or berry which after undergoing the necessary preparation, is ground and used in most countries as a breakfast beverage. The best coffee is the Mocha, an Arabian variety. The stimulating effect of coffee is due to the caffeine, which is also present in tea. The beverage was introduced into Europe in the 17th cent., and the first London coffee shop was opened in 1652.

A glut of low-quality coffee beans is currently (2006) driving millions of coffee growers into poverty.

Coinage. *See* Currency.

Coke is the solid residue remaining when coal is carbonised and nearly all the volatile constituents have been driven off. Used as fuel, and as an agent for reducing metallic oxides to metals.

Coleoptera. *See* Beetles.

College of Arms. *See* Heralds, College of.

Colorado Beetle, a serious pest of potato crops. Both adults and larvae feed on the foliage where the orange eggs are laid. The grub is reddish, with two rows of small black spots on each side. The adults are about 1·2 cm long with yellow and black striped wing cases. The beetle is avoided by birds because of its nasty taste, and is controlled by arsenical sprays.

Colosseum, the name of the Flavian amphitheatre at Rome, begun by Vespasian and finished by Titus A.D. 80. In general outline it still remains one of the most magnificent ruins in the world. In the arena the famous gladiatorial displays and mimic naval battles used to be given, and about 50,000 spectators could be accommodated.

Colossus is the name which the ancients gave to any statue of gigantic size. The Colossus at Rhodes, which was a bronze statue of the sun god, Helios, was the most famous, and reckoned among the seven wonders of the world. It stood over 30 m high at the mouth of the harbour. There is no truth in the legend that ships could pass between its legs. It fell in an earthquake in 224 B.C.

Colugo, also known as "flying lemur", caguan or kubuk, a remarkable mammal which may be regarded as an aberrant insectivore or an aberrant form of the earliest ancestor of the bats. It has nothing to do with lemurs. There are two genera, one inhabiting the Philippines and one inhabiting Malaysia. They have a parachute-like membrane which covers them from the neck to the tip of the tail, by means of which they can glide from treetop to ground.

Comets are celestial bodies which generally move about the solar system in elongated elliptical or nearly parabolic orbits. Most comets are in the latter category, having extremely long orbital periods, up to millions of years, and have therefore only been seen once in recorded history. They spend most of their lifetimes at extremely large distances from the sun, far outside Pluto's orbit. Those in elliptical orbits appear periodically and a few have been observed regularly.

Halley's comet, named after Edmund Halley, who first correctly predicted that this comet would reappear in 1758, was first observed in Roman times and is one of the brightest of the periodic comets. The nucleus of a comet, which appears as a faint star when the comet is very far from the sun, is no longer believed to be a frozen mixture of dust and materials called "ices". The core is now believed to be composed of hard material, not dust. Approaching the sun, the comet is heated by sunlight and the surface material is first vaporised and later photo-dissociated and ionised by sunlight. The gases and ions produce the fuzzy appearance of the coma of the comet.

Under the influence of sunlight acting on dust, and the solar wind and interplanetary field acting on the ions, the cometary tail (often multiple) is produced. This may stretch up to 200 million km, pointing away from the sun.

Donati's comet (1858) was possibly the most spectacular of all and was visible even in daylight. Kohoutek's comet (1975) was the first to be observed from space by the American Skylab and Russian Soyuz. Images from the Hubble telescope suggest there are c. 200 million comets orbiting the Sun in a belt that lies beyond the orbit of Neptune and engulfs that of Pluto.

A spectacular comet appearance in 1997 was Hale-Bopp (which was last visible from Earth c. 2600 B.C. The Rosetta space mission (launched in 2004) is planned to land on the comet Churyumov-Gerasimenko in 2014 after a 2.6 billion mile journey. The Stardust space probe, launched in 1999, has flown through the tail of the comet Wild-2, providing detailed pictures. In 2005 the Deep Impact probe collided with Tempel 1 to collect data. The longest comet tail ever recorded (350 million miles) was observed in 2000 (a trail left by the comet Hyakutake).

Commons are the remnants of the mediaeval open fields round villages in which the villagers had rights in common, e.g., (i) estover—the right of taking wood for house building or firewood; (ii) **pasture**—the right of grazing beasts; (iii) **turbary**—the right of digging turf; (iv) **piscary**—the right to fish. Many of these common lands were enclosed during the agrarian revolution which went on steadily in England from the 15th cent. onwards, and with their enclosure common rights vanished. A Royal Commission on Common Land described the commons in 1965 as the "last reservoir of uncommitted land" which provide, as far as the public is concerned, by far the largest part of the accessible open spaces of the country.

Under the Commons Registration Act, 1965, it was the duty of the relevant local council to make a register of all common land and all town and village greens in their areas.

Today (2006) there are 1·3 million acres of common land in England and Wales, held by a variety of bodies such as parish councils, the National Trust, the Ministry of Defence (and private individuals who may allow people particular rights). There are c. 10,000 village greens.

Commons, House of. See **Section D.**
Community Charge. See **Poll Tax.**
Compass or **Mariner's Compass.** It has been known since very early times that an iron needle, suspended freely to hang horizontally when not magnetised, comes to rest roughly along the geographical north–south line when magnetised. Further, it generally does not hang horizontally. This is the essential behaviour of the *compass*, a navigational instrument whose invention is obscure but which seems to have been known to the Chinese 4,500 years ago. That the behaviour of the compass shows the existence of a *magnetic field* associated with the Earth was first fully recognised by William Gilbert in 1600. Aircraft and ships now largely employ gyrostatic compasses which are not affected by electrical and magnetic disturbances. Sperry, Brown and Anschutz are three important types of gyroscopic compass.

Composite Materials, or more simply composites, are materials which derive useful properties by combining the virtues of two or more components. Combining clay with straw to make tougher bricks is an ancient example in which fibres (straw) are embedded in a matrix or body (the clay). A modern example is fibreglass in which glass fibres are embedded in a plastic matrix. Nature also uses composites as in bamboo in which a lignin matrix binds together the fibres of cellulose having a light strong structure. Composites may contain flakes or particles embedded in the matrix instead of fibres—it depends on the application. Although the idea is not new composite technology has made rapid strides in the last few decades guided by scientific insight into the nature of solids and the origin of their stengths and weaknesses.

The motivation had been that scientifically designed composites offer materials with exceptional strength/weight ratio, desirable magnetic properties and other technological advantages which meet the extreme demands of a variety of industries. For example, composite aluminium containing boron fibres or resin containing graphite fibres can have strength/ weight ratios over twice that of highstrength solid aluminium. Composites of many kinds are now widespread in industrial use.

Conclave, an assembly of Roman Catholic cardinals met together to elect a pope. The last Conclave was held in the Vatican in April 2005, when Cardinal Joseph Ratzinger of Germany was elected. He took the title Benedict XVI.

Concorde, supersonic airliner whose first flight was from Toulouse on 2 March 1969 and the first British flight from Felton in Bristol on 9 April 1969. More than 2½ million passengers travelled on Concorde between 1976 and its withdrawal from service in 2004. The plane could cruise at 1,350 mph at altitudes up to 60,000 ft. In February 1996 it flew from New York to London in 2 hrs 52 mins.

Condor, a large eagle of brilliant black plumage with a circlet of white feathers round its neck. It is a native of the Andes. There are two types of New World condor, the Andean and the Californian. Both are black, but the Andean condor has a pink head, the Californian a yellow head and red neck. They are among the rarest birds in the world. In a sense, the condor is the vulture of the Andes.

Coniferae are cone-bearing trees, including firs, pines, cedars, cypresses, junipers, yews, *etc.*, and are widely distributed in temperate regions.

Constellation, a grouping of stars that forms a pattern when seen from Earth. There are a total of 88 constellations in use on modern star charts, some of which are much larger than others. The stars within a particular constellation are not necessarily close to each other in space. In most cases they only appear close together due to their lying in more or less the same line of sight as seen from Earth.

Constitution, the fundamental organic law or principles of government of a nation, state, society, or other organisation, embodied in written documents, or implied in the institutions and customs of the country or society.

The government of the USA, unlike Great Britain, works upon a written Constitution. It was framed when the USA came into existence as a sovereign body, when the Constitution built a republic out of a federation of thirteen states, based on representative government. The constitution was adopted in 1789.

Continent, a word used in physical geography to denote the larger continuous land masses in contrast to the great oceans of the earth. They are: Eurasia (conventionally regarded as 2 continents, Europe and Asia), Africa, North America, South America, Australia and Antarctica. (Australasia is Australia, New Zealand and adjacent islands. Oceania is Australasia and the many islands of the S.W. Pacific.)

Continental Drift. The hypothesis of drifting continents is due to F. B. Taylor, an American geologist who published his theory in 1908, and to the Austrian meteorologist Alfred Wegener. The latter was impressed by the matching coasts of South America and Africa, which seemed to him to fit together like the pieces of a jigsaw puzzle. Since then other people have taken up and developed the idea. For a discussion of this topic, see **Plate Tectonics, T47–8.**

Conurbation, a term used in reference to an extensive and continuous area of urban land-use. Conurbations are frequently formed by the physical coalescence of several formerly freestanding towns. They may themselves coalesce to form an even higher order (a megalopolis).

Convention is an assembly of delegates, representatives, members of a party met to accomplish some specific civil, social, political object etc.

Convocation, an assembly called together to deliberate ecclesiastical affairs. In the Church of England the provinces of Canterbury and York each have their convocation. The term is also applied to assemblies of the graduates of certain universities.

Coot. A very widely distributed bird of the rail family and a common resident of the British Isles. The adult is black with a conspicuous white bald shield on the forehead and a white bill. The juvenile is brownish grey with whitish breast and throat. The coot flies heavily, but swims well. It dives frequently and can remain submerged for a considerable time. It is pugnacious and in winter gregarious. The food is chiefly vegetable. The large nest is usually built among aquatic vegetation and the young are fed by both parents. Another species, the Crested Coot, occurs in S. Europe.

Copper, one of the most familiar of metals, element no. 29, symbol Cu, used in ancient times as an alloy with tin in producing bronze, and preceding iron as an industrial material. Copper ores are most abundant in the USA, Chile, Canada, Zambia and Congo. All copper compounds are poisonous.

Copyright. Under the old Copyright Act, 1956, copyright subsists in every original literary, dramatic musical, and artistic work if the author is a British subject or a citizen of the Republic of Ireland or resident in the United Kingdom, or if the work is first published in the UK.

The Act provided that, except in certain special cases, the author of the work shall be the first owner of the copyright, and there are no formalities, such as registration or payment of fees, to be accomplished. Copyright includes the right to reproduce the work in any material form, to perform the work in public, or, if the work is unpublished, to publish the work.

The Act also protected sound recordings, films and television and sound broadcasts. Literary, dramatic, musical and artistic works which enjoy the protection of the Act are automatically protected in those countries which are parties to the Berne Copyright Convention or the Universal Copyright Convention.

In general, copyright in literary, dramatic, musical and artistic works is vested in the author for the period of his or her lifetime and 50 years following after which it passes into the public domain and becomes freely available to any who wish to make use of it. The Copyright Libraries, entitled to receive copies of books published in the United Kingdom are given under **Libraries.** The Berne Copyright Convention and the Universal Copyright Convention were revised at a diplomatic conference held in Paris in 1971. The effect of the revisions allows any national of a developing country to obtain, under certain conditions, a compulsory licence to translate and publish a copyright work for the purpose of teaching, scholarship and research, upon payment of compensation to the copyright owner of the original work.

The Copyright Designs and Patents Act, 1988, updated the old law on copyright (and has itself been amended in the light of recent EU regulations). In the USA, the 1998 Digital Millennium Copyright Act was enacted to combat Internet piracy (but that was almost immediately obsolete).

Coral, an order of small marine animals closely related to the sea-anemone, but differing from it in their ability to develop a limy skeleton. They multiply sexually and by budding. The structure of the coral secretions assumes a variety of forms, fan-like, tree-like, mushroom shape, and so forth. Red coral (the skeleton of *Corallium rubrum*) is mainly obtained from the Mediterranean. The coral reefs of the Pacific and Indian Oceans are often many miles in extent. Living corals occur only in warm seas at about 23°C. Scientists have predicted that most coral reefs will have been destroyed within 30 years by rising sea temperatures caused by global warming. They are also threatened by deep-sea trawling. Climate change is now (2006) damaging coral reefs in the Caribbean (as well as in the Indian and Pacific oceans). The amount of hard coral in the Caribbean has declined by 80% in the last 30 years.

Cordite, a smokeless explosive adopted for small arms and heavy artillery by the British Government in the naval and military services in 1889, and composed of 58 parts of nitro-glycerine, 37 of gun-cotton, and 5 of vaseline. It is a jelly or plastic dough, and used in the form of sticks. Invented by Sir Frederick Abel and Sir James Dewar in 1889.

Cork, the bark of a species of oak, *Quercus suber*, grown largely in the South of Europe and North America. The cork tree is said to yield bark every six to ten years for 150 years, and grows to a height of from 6–12 m. Its lightness, impermeability, and elasticity enable it to be used for a variety of commercial purposes, especially for stoppers of bottles.

Cormorant, a large, long-billed water bird which captures fish by diving. The common cormorant has bronze-black plumage with white cheeks and sides and is found round the sea coasts of most parts of the world, including the British Isles. It nests in colonies on sea cliffs and rocky ledges. The Shag or Green Cormorant is a smaller bird with green-black plumage and a crest.

Corncrake. Once a regular summer visitor to Britain. The harsh and piercing note of this bird was a familiar sound in cornfields. After nearly becoming extinct, its numbers are reviving.

Corona or **Solar Corona,** the outer atmosphere of the sun. This glows by virtue of light emitted by the sun and scattered by electrons and dust particles at various heights in the sun's atmosphere and also by light emitted from ionised atoms in the corona itself. Corona light is much fainter than the bright disc of the sun and is invisible against the normal blue of the sky. During total solar eclipses, the corona can be seen by the human eye as a faint glow extending irregularly outwards a few solar diameters from the sun. The sun's atmosphere extends much further than this but is invisible to the eye at large distances from the sun. The corona gases are thought to be very hot (millions of degrees) and in complex violent motion; the gross structure of the corona is connected with the sunspot cycle.

Corporal Punishment in Britain has seen much recent legislation. Caning in state schools was made illegal in 1986 (in public schools in 1999). Birching as a judicial punishment was abolished in 1948. Flogging was stopped in the Royal Navy in 1957 and in prisons and borstals in 1967. The 'reasonable chastisement' of children allowed under the 1933 Children and Young Persons Act was challenged (e.g. in 1998 in the European Court). An attempt to ban any form of smacking was defeated in November 2004. The first country to ban smacking was Sweden in 1979.

Cortes, the Parliaments of Spain and Portugal.

Cosmic Rays are a form of radiation coming from outer space, of deep penetrating power and of great scientific interest. The rays consist of extremely energetic atomic particles—protons, electrons and some heavier nucleons—travelling at speeds very close to that of light. A complex series of events result from their collision with the atmosphere, giving rise to showers of secondary high-energy particles containing many of those listed in **Section T.**

Low energy cosmic rays can be studied from space satellites and space probes. Intermediate energy cosmic rays are investigated using sensitive detector arrays on mountain tops or space-satellites. High-energy cosmic rays can only be studied indirectly at ground level. The great interest is because we now believe their origin to be in, or associated with, some of the most interesting objects in the universe—supernovae, neutron stars, pulsars and perhaps some gigantic galactic nuclei. *See* **Section T, Part I.**

Cosmology is the science which studies the whole universe, its origin, its nature, its size, age and evolution. It is presently a very active science because of many new discoveries The observations of celestial objects throughout the universe form the observational basis for cosmological models that provide possible representations of the universe in simple terms. Most standard cosmological models of the universe are mathematical and are based on the work of Aleksandr Friedmann in 1922. The so-called Friedmann universes assume homogeneity and isotropy of an expanding or contracting universe in which the only force in play is that of gravitation.

Cosmologists have to decide if the universe will expand for ever or eventually contract into a big-crunch. Recently observations of distant supernovae have motivated many cosmologists to invoke a cosmological constant in their models. *See* **Astronomy, Astrophysics and Supernova.**

Cosmonaut, the Russian term for a space traveller.

Cotton, the name of a plant of several species bearing large yellow flowers with purple centres. These centres expand into pods, which at maturity burst and yield the white fibrous substances known as cotton. The raw cotton contains a large proportion of seeds which are removed by "ginning". Long before the Christian era, cotton had been grown and used with great skill in India to make fabrics. The industry was not introduced into England until the middle of the 17th cent. when Protestant refugees from Flanders came to settle in the wool textile districts of East Anglia and Lancashire. With improvements in machinery and expansion of overseas trade in the 18th and 19th cent., Lancashire became the centre of the world's cotton industry but now man-made fibres have taken the place of cotton. The largest cotton producers in the world are the United States, China and Uzbekistan.

Cotton Gin, invented in 1793 by the American Eli Whitney. By automating the production of cotton fibre from seed pods, it revolutionised cotton-growing.

Coulomb, a unit of electric charge, named after the French naval engineer, Charles Augustin de Coulomb (1736–1806), equal to the quantity of electricity transferred in one second by a current of one ampere.

Council of Trent. *See* **Trent, Council of.**

Council Tax. *See* **Section E.**

County. After the 1972 reorganisation of local government in the UK the distinction between *administrative* counties and *geographical* counties no longer existed. Certain geographical counties disappeared (*e.g.,* Rutland and Pembroke), new counties appeared (*e.g.,* Avon and Gwynedd), while former counties were modified (*e.g.* Glamorgan and Yorkshire). *See* **Section D** for recent developments.

Court Leet, a court of record held annually before the steward of any particular manor or lordship; originally there was only one court for a manor, but in the time of Edward I it branched into two, the court baron and the court leet.

Courts. *See* **Magistrates.**

Coyote, an animal belonging to the dog family. Native to North and Central America, it displays an exceptional capacity for survival.

Coypu or **Nutria Rat,** a large beaver-like rodent found naturally in S. America.

Crane, a large, graceful wading-bird with elegant long legs and neck, greyish plumage, superficially resembling the heron and related to the bustard. They migrate in V or W formation and have trumpet-like voices. There are fourteen species, found in all continents except S. America, including the Crowned Crane with golden coronet and the Demoiselle with tuft-like crest of white feathers. The Common Crane nested in East Anglia in mediaeval times.

Creed (Latin *credo* = I believe), a formal statement of belief. The three orthodox Christian creeds are the Apostles' Creed (a summary of their teaching), the Nicene Creed (drawn up by the Church Council at Nicaea in A.D. 325 to define its theological doctrines), and the Athanasian Creed (on the nature and divinity of Christ).

Cremation, the ancient custom, revived in modern times, of burning the dead. Cremation was first legalised in Great Britain in 1884 and the first crematorium opened at Woking in that year. Application for cremation must be accompanied by two medical certificates. Orthodox Jews and Muslims forbid cremation. About 70% of Britons now choose cremation and there are over 250 crematoria.

Creutzfeldt-Jakob Disease, *See* **Mad Cow Disease.**

Cricket, a genus of insects of the grasshopper order which move by leaps. The male produces a chirping noise by rubbing its wing-covers together. Just as the males inherit the nerve machinery for emitting the song of the species, so the females receive and respond to that song and to no other.

Criminal Justice Act (1994). A controversial measure whose main proposals limit a defendant's right to silence, give powers to the police to establish a DNA database, extend offences for which 10-13 year olds can be given custodial offences *etc*.

Crinoids. *See* **Sea Lily.**

Crocodiles and their allies (alligators, caimans and gavials) are the largest of modern reptiles. They are well equipped for a predatory life in shallow waters, having powerful tails and strong jaws. Their eggs are laid on land, in sand or decomposing vegetation. Their wounds never become infected because of a bacteria-destroying protein in their blood. There are 23 species.

Crow, a family of birds including many well-known species such as the rook, raven, jackdaw, carrion crow, hooded crow, magpie, nutcracker, jaw and chough.

Crusades. *See* **A41.**

Crux. *See under* **Southern Cross.**

Cryogenics (Greek roots: productive of cold) is the science dealing with the production of very low temperatures and the study of their physical and technological consequences. "Very low" is often taken to mean below about −150°C.

The growth of cryogenics (essentially a 20th-cent. science) is connected with the discovery of how to liquefy all gases including even helium which resisted liquefaction until 1908. Scientifically, cryogenics is important partly because special phenomena (*e.g.,* superconductivity (*q.v.*)) appear at lower temperatures and partly because more can be learned about ordinary properties by studying them in the absence of heat. Technologically, cryogenics is becoming more and more significant, for example, liquefied gases are rocket propellants, superconductors make valuable magnets, tissue-freezing techniques (using very cold liquids) have been introduced into surgery. *See* **Absolute Temperature.**

Crystal, in everyday usage, a solid chemical substance bounded by plane surfaces which show a regular geometrical arrangement as, *e.g.,* quartz crystals, rock salt, snow flakes. In physics the term means any substances whose atoms are arranged in a regular three-dimensional array. This includes most solids, even those not particularly crystalline in appearance, *e.g.,* a lump of lead. *See* **Glass** and **Liquid Crystals.**

Cuckoo, a well-known migratory bird which is found in Great Britain from April to July, hawk-like in shape, with a very characteristic note, uttered during the mating season only by the male. The hen has a soft bubbling call. It lays its eggs in the nests of other birds, *e.g.,* the meadow pipit and hedge sparrow, but only one egg in each nest. Feeds mainly on insects, particularly hairy caterpillars. For 30 years, its numbers have been in decline.

Cucurbitaceae. *See* **Gourd Family.**

Cuneiform, (Latin = *wedge-shaped*), an ancient method of writing by impressing wedge-like strokes into tablets of damp clay which when dried and hardened formed a permanent script, Cuneiform writing developed from its original pictographic form into a phonetic writing and can be traced back to the non-Semitic Sumerians of ancient Mesopotamia, the earliest civilisation known to us. It passed to the Semitic Accadians of Babylonia in the 3rd millennium B.C. who adapted it to their own language. Decipherment by Sir Henry Rawlinson, 1835.

Curfew (Old F. *covre-feu* = cover fire), a regulation common throughout Europe in mediaeval times by which, at a fixed hour in the evening, the church bell was rung as a signal that fires were to be put out and the people were to go to bed. The custom originated in the fear of fire when buildings were built of timber. Nowadays a curfew is imposed by the military in areas where riots or disturbances are expected.

Curia, the central government of the Roman Catholic Church. By the reform which came into force in 1968, its twelve Sacred Congregations or "ministries" were reduced to nine.

Curie, a measure of the rate at which radioactive material emits radiation. One curie is a disintegration rate of 3.7×10^{10} disintegrations per second.

Curlew, a wading-bird of which there are several species. It frequents marshy places, feeds on worms, insects, molluscs and berries and possesses a very long, down-curved bill.

Currency is the name given to the types of cash money—metal or paper—in use in an area (*e.g.* pound, sterling, dollar, Euro). It also designates the actual coins or notes issued. Its amount is usually subject to regulation by the Government, or by a Central Bank acting on the Government's behalf. Britain changed over to a £-based decimal currency in February 1971. On 1 January 1985, ½p coins ceased to be legal tender. The old "halfpenny" first appeared in 1280. The Royal Mint has now produced a smaller and lighter 50p coin. The old 50p ceased to be legal tender on 28 February 1998. The first two-colour coin (the £2 coin) entered circulation in June 1998. The new design £20 banknote became legal tender in June 1999. It featured new devices to protect against counterfeiting. The new £5 note (issued in 2002) features a portrait of Elizabeth Fry.

The first pound coin was minted in 1489 by Henry VII. It was made of gold and became known as the sovereign.

Cybernetics, the science concerned with the automatic control and communication processes in both animals and machines. Thus it is concerned with brain function, information theory, electronic computers, and automation.

Cyclone, a term usually applied to a tropical revolving storm. Cyclones often occur towards the end of the hot seasons and are mainly confined to tracks in the western areas of the oceans, being known as hurricanes (Caribbean and Pacific), cyclones (Indian Ocean) and typhoons (China Seas). The circulation of air in a cyclone is similar to that in the *depression* of temperate latitudes, but the region of low pressure is much more localised and the pressure gradients steeper. Winds of hurricane strength and torrential rain occur generally, although at the centre of the storm there is a small area, known as the "eye", where fair, calm weather prevails. Hurricane Andrew, which hit Florida in August 1992, left 250,000 people homeless. The 1998 Atlantic hurricane season was the worst for 200 years. Hurricane Mitch devastated Honduras and Nicaragua. Since 1881, in the United States alone over 20,000 people have been killed by hurricanes. Hurricanes are graded in five classes.

Many scientists are now predicting that the global warming of the past decade will lead to more—and more powerful—hurricanes. It seems this is now beginning to happen (as in Orissa in India in 1999).

Cyclotron, a machine for accelerating charged particles such as protons to very high energies. Devised by E. O. Lawrence in California in 1930, it uses a magnetic field to make the particles traverse nearly circular paths and an electric field to give them an additional pulse of energy each time round. The accelerated particles impinge on targets, and the resulting events are a basic source of information for nuclear physicists. The cyclotron is obsolescent and has led to the development of other machines, *e.g.*, betatrons, synchrotrons. Britain has two major national high-energy machines: a 7 GeV proton synchrotron (to be closed and replaced by a "spallation neutron source"), and a 5 GeV electron synchrotron.

The European Organisation for Nuclear Research (CERN) (*q.v.*), carries out research at higher energies.

D

Dactylopterus, a fish of the gurnard family, with wing-like pectoral fins; sometimes known as the flying fish, though that appellation is more generally given to *Exocaetus exiliens*.

Dadaism. *See* Section N.

Daddy Longlegs, or **Crane-fly,** a slender long-legged fly of the family Tipulidae. The larvae which do damage to lawns and plants are called leather-jackets. The Americans call Harvestmen (*q.v.*) daddy longlegs.

Daguerreotype, the first practical photographic process, invented in Paris by M. Daguerre during the years 1824–39. The light-sensitive plate was prepared by bringing iodine in contact with a plate of silver. After exposure a positive image came by development of the plate in mercury vapour. Even for openair scenes the first daguerreotypes involved exposure of 5–10 minutes. The picture came in one copy and the process was therefore of limited use. The wet collodion process (1851) rendered the technique obsolete.

Dail Eireann, the name of the national parliament of the Irish Republic.

Dalai Lama, the temporal and religious leader of Tibet. The present Dalai Lama, Tenzin Gyabo (b. 1935), the 14th reincarnation, fled to India in 1959. Awarded the 1989 Nobel Peace Prize. Lamas (meaning 'superior ones') are Tibetan Buddhist monks. The Panchen Lama is held to be the reincarnation of the Buddha of Light.

Darter 1 Snakebirds, a genus of the pelican family, with long, pointed bill and serpent-like neck and resembling cormorants in appearance. There are 5 species. 2. Numerous species of small freshwater fish belonging to the perch family, found in N. America.

Date Palm. *Phoenix dactylifera*, one of the oldest known food plants widely cultivated in N. Africa and W. Asia. It grows to 30 m and continues to bear fruit for 2 or 3 centuries, its fruit being of great value as a food. From the leaves the Africans make roofs for their huts; ropes are made from the fibrous parts of the stalks; and the sap furnishes a stimulating beverage.

Day is the most natural unit of time and may be defined as the period of rotation of the earth relative to any selected heavenly body. Relative to the sun it is called the *solar day*. Relative to a fixed star it is called the *sidereal day*. Owing to irregularities in the earth's movements, the time taken for the earth to rotate through 360° relative to the sun is variable, and so the *mean solar day* of 24 hours has been introduced, which is the average throughout the year. The *mean solar day* is our standard, used for purposes of the calendar, and astronomers use *sidereal* clocks to check mean solar time. In practice, for convenience, the sidereal day is determined by the earth's rotation relative to the vernal equinox or first point of Aries, and is equal to 23 hours 56 minutes and 4·091 seconds of mean solar time (*i.e.*, about 4 minutes shorter than a solar day).

The lengths of day on other planets can differ greatly to that of the Earth. Jupiter spins once every 10 hours or so while the length of a day on Venus is equal to 243·01 Earth days, longer than its year of 224·7 days. *See* **Time.**

D-Day. *See* **A41.**

DDT (dichloro-dephenyl-trichloroethane). A very powerful insecticide which has had wide success in the control of diseases, such as malaria and typhus which are carried by insects. Mosquito swamps are sprayed with DDT to kill the carriers. Because this toxic chemical breaks down very slowly it builds up in birds and animals and its use is now banned in Britain. Its detection in Antarctic wild life confirmed that DDT pollution was virtually worldwide.

Deacon, an ecclesiastical official, who assists in some of the smaller ministerial duties in church or chapel.

Dead Languages are such as the ancient Greek and

Roman tongues, which are no longer spoken but are preserved in literature.

Dead Sea Scrolls. *See* **Scrolls, H24.**

Deadly Nightshade. *See* **Belladonna.**

Dean, a Church of England dignitary, ranking below a bishop, and the head of the chapter of a cathedral. A Rural Dean supervises a *deanery* or group of parishes. There are also Deans of Faculties in some universities, and at Oxford and Cambridge the Dean is in charge of chapel services and disciplinary arrangements.

Death Watch Beetle (*Xestobium rufovillosum*), a wood-boring beetle, larger than the common furniture beetle, found chiefly in the old oak beams of churches and other historic buildings. The grub bores from 1 12 years. The name "death watch" comes from the superstition that the ticking sound, made by the beetle striking its head against the wood, is a sign of approaching death. The death watch beetle found in the roof of Westminster Hall was smoked out by means of an insecticide called gamma benzine hexachloride. *See also* **Furniture Beetle, Woodworm.**

December, the last month of the year in our calendar, and the tenth in the old Roman.

Deciduous Trees are such as shed their leaves at certain seasons as distinguished from evergreens or permanent foliaged trees or shrubs.

Declaration of Independence. *See* **Section A.**

Defender of the Faith (*Defensor Fidei*), the title conferred upon Henry VIII by Pope Leo X in 1521 for entering the debate against Luther with his pamphlet in defence of the Seven Sacraments. After Henry assumed headship of the Church of England the Pope withdrew the title but it was confirmed to him by Parliament in 1544 and has been used ever since by English monarchs.

Dehydrate, to eliminate the water from a substance. The process of dehydration is now widely used in the food industry in making such things as dried egg and packet soups. Most vegetables contain over 90 per cent of water, and much of this can be removed under vacuum at low temperatures without impairing the flavour.

Deliquescence, the process of dissolving by the absorption of moisture from the atmosphere. For instance, chromic acid crystals on exposure to the air quickly deliquesce.

Democratic Party, one of the two great American political parties, originated about 1787, advocating restrictions on the federal governments and in opposition to the federalists. It was in 1825 that a group who were in favour of high tariffs seceded, later to become the Republican Party. The Democratic Party was split again over slavery before the Civil War (1861–65), and in the main the southern states have been supporters of the Democrats. The economic depression helped the Democrats to power in 1932 (*see* **New Deal**) and they held office until 1953 when Eisenhower became President. In 1960 Kennedy narrowly won the Presidency and in 1964 Lyndon Johnson swept in with a landslide victory over the Republican candidate. In 1968 and 1972 the Democratic candidates were beaten by Nixon. In 1976 Jimmy Carter won an easy victory, but after that the Democrats lost three successive presidential elections (1980, 1984, 1988) before winning a narrow but convincing victory under Bill Clinton in the 1992 election. It won again in 1996. The bitterly-divided 2000 presidential election resulted in a narrow Republican victory. A further defeat in the 2004 presidential election (when Senator Kerry was their candidate), as well as setbacks in Congressional elections, have left the party badly demoralised.

The symbol of the party is a donkey, invented, like the Republican's elephant, by the cartoonist Thomas Nast.

Dendrochronology. The science of establishing the age of trees. *See* **Tree Rings.**

Dendrite, a stone or mineral on or in which tree-like tracery appears, the result of the action of the hydrous oxide of manganese.

Density, a measure of the mass per unit volume of a material, usually expressed in grams per cubic centimetre. *Specific gravity* is the ratio of the density of a material at the termperature under consideration to that of water at the temperature of its maximum density (4°C). In grams per cubic centimetre the density of gold is 19·3, silver 10·5, lead 11·3, water 0·99997, air 0·00129.

Depreciation of a currency is a fall in its value in terms of gold or of other currencies.

Depression, a region where barometric pressure is lower than that of its surroundings. These areas of low pressure are usually less extensive than anticyclones (*q.v.*) and may vary from hundreds to thousands of kilometres in diameter. The winds, often of gale force where the depression is deep, blow round the system in an anticlockwise direction in the Northern Hemisphere (in the reverse direction in the Southern Hemisphere). Well above the earth's surface the winds blow along rather than down the pressure gradient but near the surface, friction causes the winds to blow slightly (c. 15°) across the isobars. The depression exists only as long as more air diverges out of its upper parts than converges into its lower parts.

Most depressions which cross the British Isles travel from the Atlantic, sometimes in series or families at rates from a few kilometres to a thousand kilometres a day, bringing their generally unsettled weather with them.

Derby, The, the most famous flat race for 3-year-old colts. First run at Epsom in 1780. The most successful Derby jockey is Lester Piggott (9 wins). The largest Derby field was 34 in 1862 (a maximum field of 20 was imposed in 2003). In June 1996 Alex Greaves, riding *Portuguese Lil*, became the first woman jockey to ride in the Derby. *See also* **Section S** (for winners).

Desalinisation, the process of removing minerals, chiefly salt, from sea or brackish water to provide pure water for drinking or industry. Small-scale desalinisation by distillation has been practised for many years on ships and small islands. By the 1960s, many large-scale distillation plants were in operation, many of them in hot dry countries as in the Middle East. Kuwait, for example, used oil revenues to buy desalination plant and powers the plant with natural gas. As water for large population centres becomes more precious and desalinisation techniques more efficient, the process may be more and more used though it is expensive in capital outlay and in the cost of heating required to distil the water. Methods other than distillation are under investigation.

Deserts, vast, barren, stone or sandy wastes where there is almost no rainfall and little or no vegetation. These regions are found in the interior of the continents Africa, Asia and America between 20° and 30° north and south of the equator. Europe is the only continent without deserts. The most famous are the Sahara, the largest in the world, the Gobi desert of central Asia, the Kalahari desert of southwest Africa and the great Australian desert.

The growing extension of deserts (desertification) is a topic of considerable contemporary debate. The increasing size of deserts is thought to result from both climatic change and also man's interference.

Détente. Diplomatic term signifying the relaxation of strained relations between states. The term is usually applied to the improved relations, beginning November 1969, between the Warsaw Pact countries (led by the USSR), and the West (headed by the USA), which were inaugurated by SALT (the Strategic Arms Limitation Talks). These ended in agreement on arms reductions in May 1973. The continued build-up of Soviet arms and the invasion by the USSR of Afghanistan in December 1979 called into question the validity of détente. The tension was finally eased with the fall of Communism.

Detention Centres in Britain were for young people (boys and girls) over 14 but under 21 who had been found guilty of an offence for which an adult could be sent to prison. They have now been replaced by Young Offenders' Institutions.

Deuterium or "heavy hydrogen". The second isotope of hydrogen; the third is called tritium. Deuterium atoms have in their nuclei a neutron as well as a proton; tritium nuclei have two neutrons and one proton. In ordinary hydrogen gas about one out of every 5,000 atoms is a deuterium atom. Deuterium was discovered in 1932 by Professor Harold Urey. The oxide of deuterium corresponding to water is called "heavy water". The nucleus of the deuterium atom is called a deuteron. An anti-deuteron consisting of anti-proton and anti-neutron was produced at Brookhaven in 1965, the first compound anti-nucleus ever to be produced.

Devonian System in geology refers to the strata between the Silurian and the Carboniferous formations. It includes the Old Red Sandstone formation. The fauna of the Devonian include the group of fishes known as the Rhipidistra (on the evolutionary route towards the amphibians), Actinistia (coelacanth), and the Dipnoi or lung fishes.

Dew, moisture deposited by condensation of water vapour on exposed objects especially during calm, cloudless nights. The loss of heat from the ground after sunset, by radiation, causes the layer of atmosphere close to the surface to be chilled below the temperature (the dew-point) at which the air is saturated with vapour. Part of the vapour condensed may be transpired from blades of grass and foliage of plants.

Dew Pond is a shallow artificial pond which is on high ground and rarely dries up, even during prolonged droughts, despite being used by cattle and sheep as a drinking source. The name arose from the belief that dew deposits at night provided the moisture for replenishment. Drainage of rain-water and mist condensed on neighbouring trees and shrubs are probably more important factors.

Diamond, a mineral, one of the two crystalline forms of the element carbon (the other is graphite), the hardest known substance, used as a gem and in industry. India was the first country to mine diamonds (the Koh-i-noor, which means "mountain of light", known since 1304, came from Golconda near Hyderabad and came into British possession when the Punjab was annexed in 1849). The celebrated diamond mines of South Africa were discovered in the 1870s. Other important diamond producing countries today are Russia, Congo, Ghana, Sierra Leone, Namibia, Angola and Tanzania. The world's biggest diamond used to be the Cullinan I (or Great Star of Africa) discovered near Pretoria, South Africa, in 1905. Since 1990 it has been the Golden Jubilee (now set in the King of Thailand's sceptre). Diamonds can be made artificially by subjecting carbon to very high temperatures and pressures; many industrial diamonds are made this way.

Antwerp is the main diamond centre of the world, London the main marketing centre, Amsterdam the main diamond cutting centre. Scientists believe diamonds may exist in large quantities on Neptune and Uranus.

Diatoms. One-celled algae, common in fresh and salt water. Distinctive feature is the siliceous wall which is in two halves, one fitting over the other like the lid of a box. These walls are often very finely and beautifully sculptured. The diatoms constitute a class of the plant kingdom known as the Bacillariophyta. *Diatom ooze* is a deep-sea deposit made up of diatom shells. *Diatomite* or *diatomaceous earth* is the mineral form that such diatom oozes assume (sometimes known as kieselguhr which mixed with nitroglycerine yields dynamite).

Diesel Engine, an engine in which the liquid fuel is introduced into a compressed or partially compressed charge of air, and which does not need an extraneous source of ignition. The modern oil engine has been evolved mainly from the principles enunciated by Herbert Akroyd-Stuart in his patent of 1890 and, like the steam and other inventions, represents the improvements achieved by many men, including those by Rudolf Diesel of Germany, in respect of high compression pressures and greater fuel economy.

Diffusion is the process of mixing which occurs when two liquids or gases are in contact. It is most rapid between gases, and, as laid down by Graham's law, "the rates of diffusion of different gases are in the inverse proportion to the square roots of their relative densities". Diffusion arises through the continual movement of molecules. Even in solids diffusion can occur. If a block of gold and a block of silver are welded together, after some time particles of gold are found in the silver, and *vice versa*.

Digital Television. *See* **Television.**

Dimensions in common speech are the magnitudes of length, breadth and thickness giving, the size of an object, thus a line has only one

dimension: length; a plane surface two: length and breadth; and a solid three: length breadth and thickness.

In mathematics, hypothetical objects with any number of dimensions are considered. In physics and mechanics, dimensions are numbers which relate the units in which any quantity is measured to the so-called fundamental units. The latter are usually but not necessarily those of length, mass and time.

Dimorphism, the quality of assuming two distinct forms. For instance, carbon, which is graphite in one form, is the diamond in another.

Dingoes, often considered the native dog of Australia, are in fact descendants of the Asian wolf. Their future is in doubt because so many are kept as pets and mate with other breeds.

Dinosaur, the name given to a group of extinct reptiles of the Mesozoic period, some of which were of immense size. Recent research suggests that massive volcanic activity, rather than the impact of meteorites, may have ended their 160 million year reign, but some scientists do not endorse this. The oldest dinosaurs ever found (in Madagascar in 1999) date back 230 million years. *See* **Diplodocus.**

Dip Needle. Instrument for measuring the *dip* or inclination of the earth's magnetic field.

Diplodocus, one of the best known of the extinct mammoth dinosaurs. Fossil remains have been discovered in the Jurassic rocks of the United States. Some reached a length of over 24 m.

Dipnoi *or* **Lung Fishes.** These have the air bladder adapted to function as a lung, and they can remain alive when the stream or marsh in which they live dries up. Species of lung fish occur in Australia, Africa and S. America.

Diptera, an order of insects. Their main characteristic is that they are two-winged, and the common house-fly is the best-known example. There are at least 50,000 species of these insects, including gnats, blow-flies, mosquitoes and tsetses.

Diptych was a folding two-leaved tablet of wood, ivory, or metal, with polished inner surfaces, utilised for writing with the style by the ancient Greeks and Romans. The same term was applied to the tablets on which the names of the persons to be commemorated were inscribed in the early Church. In art any pair of pictures hinged together is styled a diptych (*see* **N5**), a set of three, a triptych.

Discus, a circular piece of metal or stone about 30 cm in diameter, used in athletic contests by the ancient Greeks and Romans. Throwing the discus was a very favourite game, which was deemed worthy of celebration in Myron's famous *Discobolus* (c. 460 B.C.–450 B.C.), the best copy of which is in Rome.

Disk, an astronomical term for the seemingly flat surface of celestial bodies as seen by the eye.

Distillation, a process used to separate liquids of different boiling points. This is effected by placing the mixture in a distillation apparatus and heating. The liquid with the lower boiling point distils over first, the vapour being condensed and collected, forming the first *fraction*. With continued heating the second liquid reaches its boiling point, distils over and the mixture is said to be *fractionated*. Mixtures of liquids with close very high boiling points require more elaborate apparatus. Fractional distillation is a common process in the chemical industry, particularly in the refining of petroleum.

DNA (Deoxyribonucleic Acid), a polymer molecule in the form of a double-strand helix containing many thousands of sub-units. Contains the genetic information coded in sequences of sub units called bases. The Nobel Prize for medicine was awarded in 1962 for the discovery of the structure of DNA. *See* **Human Genome Project, Nucleic Acids.** and **Special Topic, end Section T.**

DNA Database. The world's first police DNA database was established at the Forensic Science Laboratory, Birmingham in April 1995. The database, which will eventually hold up to 5 million samples, will allow police to compare genetic material from crime scenes with DNA profiles of convicted criminals. DNA profiling has been developed from genetic fingerprinting, an earlier technique created in the mid 1980s by Sir Alec Jeffreys of Leicester University.

Docks are enclosed water spaces where ships rest while being loaded or unloaded, repaired, or waiting for cargo. There are three main types: the wet dock in which water is maintained at the level of high tide so that vessels remain afloat while loading and unloading; the tidal dock, with open entrance to permit free ebb and flow of tide (*e.g.*, Glasgow, Southampton (which has double tides)); and the dry dock, or graving dock, for overhauling and repairing vessels, so constructed that, after a ship has been docked, the water can be drawn off (*e.g.*, Southampton, Tilbury). The floating dock is a type of dry dock. Technological advances in the handling of cargo, *e.g.*, containers, have led to modernisation of the docks. Under the 1991 Ports Act many ports were privatised.

Dodo, an extinct bird, giant and flightless, which lived on the island of Mauritius up until 250 years ago. Another species, the white dodo, lived on Réunion. Some reached exceptional sizes. By the end of the 17th cent. Mauritius, Rodriguez, and Réunion had all been colonised, and the dodo along with many other birds vanished forever because of their inability to stand up to man and the animals imported by him. DNA scientists have established that the Nicobar pigeon of SE Asia is its nearest relative.

Dog-days, a period of 40 days (3 July–11 August) when Sirius rises and sets with the sun. The ancient superstition found in Greek literature, was that this star affected the canine race.

Doge. *See* A41.

Dogfish, a large family of small sharks, seldom more than 1 m in length. The flesh is sold as "rock salmon". The eggs are contained in horny cases called "mermaid's purses". The commonest of the British dogfishes are the spurdogs.

Doldrums, a nautical term applied to those areas of the Atlantic and Pacific within a few degrees of the Equator towards which the trade winds blow and where the weather is calm, hot and sultry. Pressure is low and the air often rises to produce heavy tropical rainfall and squalls, rendering navigation difficult.

Dolomite, a name applied to a limestone containing appreciable magnesium; also the mineral dolomite, a double carbonate of magnesium and calcium.

Dolphin, a mammal of the whale order, from 2–2·4 m long, with a long, sharp snout, and of an active disposition. They abound in most seas and swim in shoals. A few species live in great rivers (Ganges and Amazon). They can cruise for long periods at around 15 knots and produce bursts of speed in the region of 20 knots, the water apparently flowing smoothly past their bodies. Dolphins are some of the most intelligent of mammals and are the subject of scientific experiments in language and communication. They are masters of teamwork when searching for food. Dolphins use echoes (the skill known as echolocation) to locate food or detect other creatures. Scientists now know that dolphins stun their prey by blasting them with sound.

Domesday Book. *See* A41.

Dominicans, an order of mendicant preaching friars founded by St. Dominic in Languedoc in 1215 and confirmed by the Pope in 1216. The rule of the order was rigorous. The dress was a white habit and scapular with a long black mantle. This gave them the name of Black Friars. Their official name is Friars Preachers.

Donjon, the keep, or inner tower of a castle, and the strongest and most secure portion of the structure. This was the last refuge of the garrison, and there was usually a prison on the lower floor, hence the name *dungeon*.

Don Juan, the legendary hero of many famous works, supposedly based on the life and character of the unscrupulous gallant Don Juan Tenorio of 14th-cent. Seville. The first dramatisation of the legend and the most famous is Tirso de Molina's *El Burlador de Sevilla*. Don Juan was also the subject of Molière's *Le Festin de Pierre*, Mozart's *Don Giovanni*, Byron's *Don Juan*, and José Zorilla's *Don Juan Tenorio*. The latter is played on All Saints' Day throughout Spanish-speaking countries.

Don Quixote, the "knight of the doleful countenance", the hero and title of Cervantes' classic novel of 16th-cent. Spain. Don Quijote de la Mancha, a gentle country gentleman of lofty but unpractical ideals, having read many chivalric romances, believes he is called upon to redress the wrongs of the world. Mounted on his nag Rosinante and accompanied by his companion Sancho Panza, a hard-headed and practical peasant, he sets out on his journeys of knight-errantry.

Dormouse, a family of small, squirrel-like rodents widely distributed throughout Europe and Asia, and living mainly on fruit and nuts. It is of nocturnal habits and sleeps through the winter. One of nature's most secretive creatures, it is now again threatened with extinction in parts of Britain.

Dotterel, a handsome bird of the plover family found in northern Europe and Siberia.

Downing St, one of the most famous streets of London, off the west side of Whitehall. The official residence of the Prime Minister is at no. 10; that of the Chancellor of the Exchequer at no. 11. The public is now excluded from the street, named after an MP, George Downing (*c.* 1623–84).

Drachm (or **Drachma**), an ancient Greek silver coin and weight. One drachma was equivalent to six obols. The word has survived as the name of a weight: Avoirdupois, one-sixteenth part of an ounce; Apothecaries' Weight, one-eighth part of an ounce.

Drag. Term used in mechanics for resistance offered by a fluid to the passage of a body moving through it. When speed of sound is reached drag increases abruptly. The lift/drag ratio gives the aeroplane designer his measure of aerodynamic efficiency.

Dragon, a fabulous monster common to folk-lore in most countries; generally represented as a winged reptile with fiery eyes and breath of flame. A dragon guarded the garden of the Hesperides; St. George, England's patron saint, is supposed to have overcome the dragon; in heraldry the dragon has also a conspicuous place; and in China it was the imperial emblem.

Dragonet, the name of the fish of the *Callionymus* genus, beautifully coloured, and about 30 cm in length. They are common on the British coast and in the Mediterranean.

Dragon Fly, the common name of a well-known order of insects having two pairs of membraneous wings, and often of very brilliant colours. They are swift of flight and may be seen hovering over sheets of water in the sunshine all through the summer. Their chief food is mosquitoes.

Dragon's Blood, a dark-red resinous substance obtained from the fruit of a Malay palm, and possessing medicinal virtues. In a special technique used for making line blocks in printing, dragon's blood is used.

Drawbridge, a bridge that can be lifted up so that no passage can be made across it. It was a usual feature of a fortified castle in the Middle Ages, and was raised or lowered by chains and levers. It spanned the fosse, and on the approach of an attacking party was raised and formed a special barricade to the gate. Modern drawbridges are such as are raised to allow of the passage of boats up and down a river or estuary. The Tower Bridge is a famous London bridge of this type.

Driving Standards Agency, the national body responsible for driving tests for cars, lorries, buses *etc.* It also supervises approved driving instructors and training bodies.

Driving Test. The cost of a driving test rose to £42 in November 2004. The charge for motorcycle tests is £51. The driving test for car drivers now takes around 40 minutes.

Drongo. The King Crow or Indian Black Drongo is frequently seen in India perched on branches or telegraph wires, darting suddenly to catch insects and to attack crows and hawks. Other members of the family are found in Asia, Africa and Australia. Its plumage is black with steel-blue gloss.

Drosophila or **Fruit Fly.** More has been learnt by geneticists from breeding experiments with this insect than with any other.

Dross, the name applied to the refuse of molten metal, composed of slag, scales and cinders.

Drought occurs when there has been an absence of rain for a long period or a marked deficiency of precipitation over a much longer period in a climatic zone where precipitation is ordinarily adequate for vegetation or agriculture, river flow and water supplies. It is different from *aridity* which refers to the extreme dryness of desert or arid regions where rainless periods characterise the climate. Hitherto in the British Isles "an absolute drought" was defined as "a period of at least 15 consecutive days without measurable rainfall".

In the British Isles droughts occur from time to time but very long rainless spells at a place are rather rare. The longest recorded spell in the British Isles with no measurable daily rainfall lasted 61 days at Liss (Hants) from 16 March to 15 May 1893. Over the country as a whole the 12-month period beginning 1 May 1975 was the driest such period since records began. The South of England faced water restrictions in 2006 after 2005 was the third driest year on record since 1897. In many places the summer of 1995 was the driest since records began in 1727.

As the world gets hotter, drier and thirstier, the areas of our planet affected by drought have doubled in the last 30 years. (*See also* **Section Y**).

Drupe is the scientific term for stone fruit. The stone forms the inner part (endocarp) of the fruit, and encloses a seed or kernel which is liberated after the flesh part (pericarp) rots.

Dry-rot, the term was first used about 1775 to describe the fungal decay of timber in buildings. Creosote distilled from coal tar is the standard material for preservation of timber, and pentachlorophenol and copper naphthenate are two compounds now extensively used. Dry wood always escapes dry-rot. Chief fungi causing dry-rot are *Merulius* and *Poria*.

Duck, water bird smaller than the related goose and swan, which together form the family Antidae. Duck refers to the female, drake to the male. The duck family falls into two separate groups: the river or freshwater (surface feeding) ducks, such as the mallard, pintail, wigeon, shoveler, mandarin, teal, garganey; and the sea (diving) ducks, such as the goldeneye, pochard, scoter, eider, and the fish-eating mergansers or "sawbills". The ancestor of all domestic breeds, with the exception of the muscovy, is the mallard (now in serious decline in Britain).

Duckbill, *Ornithorhynchus anatinus*, also duck-billed platypus, a fur-covered, egg-laying, nest-building mammal inhabiting Australia and Tasmania. It has webbed feet and a muzzle like a duck's bill and is about 50 cm long. Adopted as the mascot for the 2000 Olympic Games in Sydney, but its numbers are declining.

Ductility is a property possessed by most metals which renders them capable of being stretched without breaking. Gold is the most, and lead the least ductile of metals, the order being gold, silver, platinum, iron, copper, palladium, aluminium, zinc, tin, lead. In animated nature the spider and the silkworm produce secretions of notable ductility.

Dugong. A marine mammal, belonging to the order Sirenia (sea-cows). Inhabits Red Sea and Indian Ocean; also found as far East as the Philippines and Australia. Lives on sea-weed. Related to the Manatee.

Duke, the highest rank in the British peerage. Edward, the Black Prince, eldest son of Edward III, who died before his father, was the first English duke, being created Duke of Cornwall in 1337.

Since then all Princes of Wales have held that title.

Dukeries, a stretch of English woodland and park country, mainly in Nottinghamshire, comprising the adjacent demesnes of several English dukes and nobles. The Dukeries include Sherwood Forest and the estates of Welbeck Abbey, Clumber Park, Worksop Manor and Thoresby Hall.

Dunes. Sand dunes are elliptical or crescent-shaped mounds of loose sand produced by wind action. The dune has a gentle slope on windward side; a steep slope on the leeward side.

Dunlin, very common small wading-bird of the Sandpiper family nesting in Britain. Its range extends to other areas where it also breeds.

Dunmow Flitch, a custom which originated in the parish of Little Dunmow, Essex, in the reign of Henry III, which was that the husband who was prepared to swear before the prior, convent,

and townsfolk of Dunmow that he had not repented of marriage or quarrelled with his wife for a year and a day, should be rewarded with the gift of a flitch of bacon.

Dunnock (*Prunella modularis*), a small bird of rich brown and dark grey plumage common in gardens and hedgerows. Sings a cheerful song all the year round. Called hedge-sparrow in southern England. Another member of the same family, the larger Alpine Accentor (*Prunella collaris*), is found on rocky mountain slopes of Europe and Asia.

Duodecimo, a sheet of paper folded into twelve leaves, written "12mo".

Dust, solid particles of matter floating in the atmosphere, produced chiefly by volcanic eruptions, sand-storms in desert regions, and industrial and domestic smoke. When the island of Krakatoa erupted in 1883, more than 4 km^2 of dust was thrown into the air and carried three times round the earth by the explosive wave. The particles in dust-storms are much finer than those in sand-storms and are swept up to far greater heights. The local whirlwinds which form over loose dry soils are termed dust-devils.

Dutch Elm Disease. *See under* **Elm.**

Dyke. A wall-like intrusion of igneous rock which cuts across the bedding or other layered structure of the country rock; the word also signifies in alternative usage, a sea-wall and an open drain.

Dynamite, a powerful explosive whose chief element is nitro-glycerine. It was discovered by Nobel in 1867, who absorbed nitro-glycerine in kieselguhr; has a disruptive force of about eight times that of gunpowder.

Dynamo. Machine for transforming mechanical energy into electrical energy. Depends on principle of electromagnetic induction whereby a current is produced in a conductor (*e.g.*, copper wire) traversing a magnetic field. The two essential parts of a dynamo are the conductors or *armature* and the *field magnets*.

E

Eagle, large bird of prey with huge hooked bill, related to the buzzard, kite, hawk, harrier, falcon and vulture, together forming the family *Falconidae*. There are many species to be found throughout the world, the Golden, Imperial, Tawny, Spotted and Lesser Spotted being found in Europe. The Golden Eagle, a magnificent-looking bird, nests in the Scottish Highlands, and the White-tailed Sea Eagle, which used to breed in Britain, is now only an occasional visitor.

The eagle has been the symbol of royal power for over 5,000 years, and the American or Bald Eagle is the emblem of the United States. The Bald Eagle has now been removed from the list of endangered species.

Earl, a British title of nobility of the third rank, duke and marquis coming first and second. The title dates from Saxon times, and until 1337 ranked highest in our peerage.

Earl-Marshal, in England ranks as the eighth of the great officers of state, is head of the College of Arms, attends the sovereign in opening and closing the session of Parliament, arranges state processions (especially coronations) and assists in introducing newly created peers in the House of Lords.

The office is hereditary in the family of the Dukes of Norfolk.

Earth, our habitable globe, is the third of the planets of the solar system in order from the sun and on an average throughout the year takes 24 hours to turn completely round relative to the sun, the whole earth revolving round the sun in a slightly elliptical orbit once in a year of 365·2564 days. The mean distance of the earth from the sun is 149,597,900 km.

Recent earth satellite studies have shown that small variations of the surface gravity field (or geoid) occur which are believed to be related more to the structures deep within the earth's mantle than to the location and dimension of crustal features, such as oceans, continents and mountain ranges.

The crust of the earth consists of a skin, 30 km thick under the continents, but only about 6–8 km thick under the ocean bed, comprised of rocks and sediments or soil. At the base of the crust is a sharp discontinuity (the Mohorovičić Discontinuity) to denser rocks of the mantle. This region, nearly 3,000 km thick, is in a process of slow but inexorable change, one of convection responding to heat sources (due mainly to radioactivity of the materials within the earth). This slow convection is responsible for many changes in the surface of the earth continental drift (q.v.), earthquakes and volcanic activity. The core is a region of very high density and temperature, comprised of heavy elements such as iron and nickel. The crustal rocks are mainly comprised of oxygen, silicon, aluminium, sodium, potassium, iron, calcium and magnesium, with traces of many other elements. The mass of the earth is c. 6,000 million million million tonnes, and it was formed c. 4,600 million years ago. The earth has one natural satellite, the moon. See **Section T.**

Earthquake, a sudden violent disturbance of the earth's crust; the region of the surface immediately above the "focus", or source where the earthquake originates, is termed the "epicentre". On account of their destructive power earthquakes have attracted attention from the earliest times, but accurate study dates only from the last century and the development of a world-wide network of recording stations from the present one. The majority of severe earthquakes result from fractures, usually along existing faults, in underlying rock strata subjected to great strains, the shearing movement sometimes extending to the surface. These dislocations set up vibrations which are propagated as waves throughout the bulk of the earth or round the crust. Frequently the main shock is followed by a series of smaller aftershocks.

Minor local earthquakes may be attributed to the effects of volcanic activity, but most of the larger ones originate in nonvolcanic regions along well-marked lines of weakness in the earth's crust. Generally the ground is felt to tremble, undergoing oscillations which may gradually or suddenly increase to a maximum and accompanied by sounds.

When there is movement of the sea-bed a tsunami (q.v.) may result. One of the most devastating of modern times (9·3 on the Richter scale) took place on 26 December 2004 under the Indian Ocean. Its epicentre was near northern Sumatra. Over 220,000 people died (and unknown thousands went missing) in the devastated countries around the Indian Ocean.

Among the notable shocks of the twentieth century were those of San Francisco (1906), Messina, Italy (1908), China (1920), Japan (1923), Napier, New Zealand (1931), Ionian Is. (1953), Chile (1960), Iran (1962), Yugoslavia (1963), China (1976), Mexico (1985) Armenia (1988), N.W. Iran (1990), Los Angeles (1994), Kobe (Japan), 1995 and Turkey and Taiwan (1999). The most devastating earthquake in recorded history hit Shanxi (China) in 1556, killing 830,000 people. Recent research has suggested that the collapse of the walls of Jericho in biblical times was due to an earthquake. In 1999 earthquakes in Turkey and Taiwan caused massive loss of life and destruction of property, making 1999 the "year of earthquakes". In 2005 a major earthquake devastated parts of Kashmir, with very heavy loss of life. Over 2 million people have died in earthquakes since 1900. See **Richter Scale.**

Earthworm, of which there are several species, has a cylindrical body, tapering at both ends and segmented into rings. It moves by contraction of its rings, aided by retractive bristles; is eyeless, but has a mouth, gullet and stomach. Earthworms exist in immense numbers, and perform an important part in the scheme of nature by loosening the soil and rendering it more amenable to tillage. They also form a valuable food for birds and many mammals, and are unequalled as bait for certain kinds of fish. The New Zealand flatworm (now spreading in Britain) is devouring native earthworms.

Earwig, a genus of insects possessing two pairs of wings and anal forceps. It is nocturnal, lives on vegetable matter, and hides by day under stones or in flowers, e.g., dahlias.

Easter, the annual Christian festival in commemoration of the resurrection of Christ, the English name being derived from Eostre, goddess of Spring. The date cannot fall earlier than 22 March nor later than 25 April. Many disputes arose among the early Christians as to the proper time to celebrate this day which governs all other movable feasts. It was eventually ruled at the Council of Nicaea in 325 that Easter Day should be the first Sunday after the full moon following the vernal equinox. If this happens to be a Sunday, then Easter Day is the Sunday after.

Eau-de-Cologne, a popular distilled perfume first manufactured at Cologne in the 18th cent. by Johann Maria Farina, an Italian.

Ebony, a name applied to various hard black woods, the best of which are grown in Mauritius and Sri Lanka. There are also Indian and American varieties. Only the inner portions, the heartwood, of the trees are of the necessary hardness and blackness. Ebony is largely used in ornamental cabinet work, for piano keys, etc.

Ecce Homo ("Behold the Man!"), used in reference to the pictures and sculptures representing Christ crowned with thorns.

Ecclesiastical Courts, courts for administering ecclesiastical law and maintaining the discipline of the Church of England. Introduced by the Normans.

Echidna, the spiny anteater, a native of the Australian outback.

Eclipse, the partial or complete obscuring of one heavenly body by another. An eclipse of the sun occurs when the moon, which is 1/400th of the diameter of the sun and about 1/390th as far away, obscures some portion of the sun as seen by an observer on the earth. A total eclipse occurs when the whole of the sun's disc is covered by the moon. Astronomers travel many thousands of miles to observe the outer layers of the sun and its corona, which is only possible when the light from the sun is totally obscured by the moon during the few minutes of an eclipse. The solar eclipse of 11 August 1999 attracted great attention (being Britain's first total solar eclipse for 70 years). Previous total solar eclipses occurred over parts of the British Isles in the years 1424, 1433, 1598, 1652, 1715, 1724, 1927, 1954 (visible from the Shetland Is.).

The next total eclipse visible from the UK will not occur until 23 September 2090. An eclipse of the Moon occurs when the Moon moves into the Earth's shadow. When this happens, the sunlight is cut off and the lunar surface becomes quite dark until it emerges from the shadow again. Lunar eclipses can be either partial or total, depending on whether all or part of the Moon moves into the Earth's shadow. They are more common than solar eclipses. A date to remember is 6 June 2012 which will mark a Transit of Venus (when Earth, Venus and the Sun all line up and the planet's disc travels across the face of our star.)

Ecliptic is the sun's apparent path in the sky: the great circle described by the sun from west to east in the course of a year. The sun is exactly on the equator on approx. 21 March, and 23 September, and the points where the celestial equator and ecliptic intersect on these days are called the *equinoctial points.* On approx. 21 June and 22 December the sun reaches its greatest and least midday elevation and its greatest distance north and south of the equator. The points on the ecliptic on these days are called the *solstices.*

These four points are equidistant from each other by 90°. The angle of the ecliptic to the earth's equator is called the obliquity of the ecliptic. Due to the gravitational perturbations of the other planets, both the equinoctial point and the obliquity of the ecliptic change with time. The value of the obliquity is c. 23·5.

Ecology, a term first described by the German biologist Haeckel in the 19th cent., is the study of the inter-relationships between living organisms and their environment. **Autecology** is the study of the environmental relationships of *individual* plants and species. **Synecology** is the study of plant and animal *communities* living together as groups. *See* **Section Y.**

Ecumenical Council, a general council of the Christian Church summoned when important questions of Church doctrine and policy are to be decided. The early councils were predominantly Greek and convoked by the emperor. Those summoned by the pope when they meet at the Lateran Palace in Rome are called Lateran Councils; others have met at Constance, Florence, Trent and the Vatican. Their decisions are not binding on the rest of Christendom. Only 21 Ecumenical Councils have been held in the history of Christendom. The first was held at Nicaea in 325 when the mystery of the Trinity was defined. The 21st (known as the 2nd Vatican Council), convened by Pope John, opened in October 1962 in St. Peter's, Rome, and ended in December 1965. Two of the principal themes were the reunion of all Christians with the Church of Rome and the Church's place in the modern world.

Edda, the name given to two important collections of early Icelandic literature—*the Elder or Poetic Edda*, poems handed down from the 9th and 10th cent., probably Norwegian in origin, and the *Younger* or *Prose Edda* of Snorri Sturluson compiled about 1230. They treat of legends of an early Scandinavian civilisation.

Eddystone Lighthouse, 21 km south of Plymouth, is one of the most isolated in the world. The tower is 51 m high, and its light can be seen for 28 km. The present structure is the fourth that has occupied this dangerous position. The first was of wood, completed by Winstanley in 1698, but it was destroyed by storm in 1703. In 1708 a second and stronger lighthouse was built by Rudyerd. This lasted until 1755, when it was destroyed by fire. Smeaton built the third lighthouse of granite and this withstood storm and tempest for over a hundred years, 1759–1881. The present lighthouse, also of granite, was built 1879–81 on a nearby rock by Sir James Douglass.

Eden Project, a giant greenhouse in Cornwall. Opened 2001, it recreates climates for over 10,000 species. A third biome, dedicated to the deserts of the world, is now planned.

Eels, edible fishes of the order Apodes, with snakelike body covered with minute scales embedded in the skin. The common or fresh-water eel *Anguilla anguilla* is found in the Atlantic coastal areas of N. America and Europe and in the Mediterranean, and breeds S.E. of Bermuda. The electric eel of S. America is able to cause electric shocks. Commercial sand eel fishing in the North Sea and elsewhere is depriving many birds, fish and marine mammals of their food.
Eel numbers are now declining due to loss of habitats, pollution and changes to ocean currents caused by global warming.

Egret, a slender, graceful bird of the heron family, of pure white plumage, famed for its beautiful silky plumes (aigrettes), which appear in the breeding season, and for which it was ruthlessly hunted and would have been exterminated had not international action been taken to protect it. The Little Egret with black bill, black legs, and yellow feet breeds in Mediterranean lands.

Eider, a large diving duck, found along the rocky coasts of northern latitudes, well known for the beautifully warm soft down, called "eider down", which the female bird plucks from her breast to line her nest. In Norway and Iceland the haunts of the eider are preserved and the birds protected by law on account of the much prized "eider down", which is collected from the nests just before the breeding season. "Eider down" is so elastic that a kilogram of it will fill an ordinary bed covering.

Eiffel Tower, built by the French engineer Alexandre Gustave Eiffel (1832–1923) for the Paris Exhibition of 1889. The tower which is made of iron is 300 m high and weighs about 7,000 tonnes. It is France's most popular tourist site.

Eisteddfod (a sitting) was originally a congress of Welsh bards and minstrels, and dates from before the 12th cent. These assemblies, discontinued for a long period, were resumed in 1819, and have been held yearly since, each lasting three or four days. Their object is to foster the Welsh patriotic spirit; they are devoted to orations and competitions in poetry, singing and harp-playing. Prizes are awarded.

Eland, largest species of antelope, native of Africa; large pointed horns, stands 1·5 m high at the withers, and weighs several hundred kg.

Elder, small trees of the *Sambucus* genus, with pinnate leaves, and clusters of white flowers and, later, small purplish-black berries. The black elder, the best known, thrives in Britain. A wine is made from its berries.

El Dorado, a "golden land", was an idea much favoured in the days of the early Spanish explorers. It was believed that somewhere on the South American continent there was a country abounding in gold and precious stones. Many expeditions were fitted out to discover it. Sir Walter Raleigh also embarked on this quest.

Electret, a piece of solid matter which retains a permanent electric polarisation analogous to the magnetic polarisation of a permanent magnet. There are various recipes for making them; carnauba wax is a common constituent.

Electricity. *See* **Section T** and **Energy Conversion.**

Electric Telegraph may be said to date from 1836, when Sir Charles Wheatstone and his co-inventor Cooke introduced their Single-Needle instrument, which was soon followed by the Double-Needle apparatus, Morse, in 1837, invented his famous recording instrument. The first electric cable was between Dover and France, and was laid in 1850. The first Atlantic cable was laid in 1858, and the second in 1866. It was in 1899 that the very first Marconi wireless telegraph messages were sent between England and France.

Electroencephalograph, an instrument which records the minute voltages produced by the electrical activity of the brain by means of electrodes taped to the scalp. The record of brain waves, known as EEG, shows that there is a general cycle of activity in the brain that underlies both sleep and wakefulness.

Electrolysis is the condition established when an electric current passes through a conducting substance, between electrodes, resulting in dc composition and separation into constituents. Water thus becomes decomposed into hydrogen and oxygen.

Electromagnetic Radiation. Radiation consisting of oscillating electronic and magnetic fields travelling together through space. Including visible light, the speed of travel is around 300,000 kms per second. Together with visible light, many different types exist including gamma rays, X-rays, ultraviolet and infrared radiation, microwaves and radio waves.

Electromagnetic waves. *See* **Section T.**

Electron. *See* **Section T.**

Electronic News Gathering (ENG), also known in the United States as Electronic Journalism (EJ) or Electronic Camera Coverage (ECC), is a system for obtaining fast TV pictures by means of very lightweight, portable electronic cameras. It is usually operated by a crew of two—cameraman and engineer—who are also equipped with a van or field car serving as a mobile base. Pictures from the unit can be used in three ways: they can be transmitted "live", beamed back by radio link to the studio, or recorded on to a videotape cassette on site and taken back to headquarters for editing and transmission.

Electronics. The science which deals with the behaviour and control of free electrons. It started with the discovery of the electron by Sir J. J. Thomson in 1897. The practical applications, constituting electronic engineering, have given us radio, radar, photo-electric cells, cathode-ray oscillographs, electronic microscopes, television. Nowadays electronics uses devices like transistors such that the electrons move inside solid matter instead of *in vacuo*. This is sometimes referred to as "solid state electronics". *See also* **Microelectronics.**

Electron Microscope. A microscope in which beams of electrons are focused by magnetic lenses in a manner analogous to the focusing of light beams in the ordinary optical microscope. Modern electron microscopes have very high resolving power and can magnify up to 1,500,000 times, making it possible to explore the cell and the virus. A development of the electron microscope is the scanning electron microscope (stereoscan), developed at Cambridge, which can examine an essentially thick object, giving a very large depth of focus.

Electronvolt, unit of energy used in nuclear physics. It is the amount of energy required to move one electronic charge through a potential difference of one volt. It is very small—$1\cdot6 \times 10^{19}$ joules—and therefore suited to atomic physics. 1 MeV = a million electronvolts; 1 GeV = a thousand million electronvolts; these larger units are used in high energy physics.

Elementary Particle, one of the basic constituents of the material universe. The idea that matter consists of tiny particles goes back to classical times but the modern concept of the atom grew out of the chemistry and physics of the 19th cent. With the discovery of the electron in 1897 and the rise of nuclear physics in the 20th cent., the chemical atom was understood to be a structure built of even more fundamental particles—the electron, the proton and the neutron. In the last few decades, many more particles have been discovered, especially in the study of cosmic rays and by the use of large accelerating machines like those at CERN (Geneva) and Brookhaven National Laboratory (Long Island, New York). Among the later discoveries are the neutrino, the positron, the antiproton, the muon, the pion. These differ in electric charge and mass and other intrinsic properties and many have only a very short lifetime before they change into something else. Whether there is a small number of really elementary particles out of which all the others can be constructed is an unanswered question of contemporary physics. *See* **Section T.**

Elements. In chemistry, substances which cannot be separated into two or more simpler chemical substances. 91 elements are found naturally on the earth, some are observed spectroscopically in the stars and planets, and a further fourteen have been made artificially. Between them these elements can appear in some 1,200 different isotopes, of which 317 occur in Nature. (There are 274 stable isotopes among 81 stable elements.) *See* **Table of Elements, T56.**

Elephant, a proboscidian mammal of which only two species survive—the Asiatic, in India, and the African elephant. No other animals possess a trunk. Both males and females have large ivory tusks, of considerable commercial value.

The Indian elephant is usually *c.* 2·7 m high and weighs about 3 tonnes; African elephants are larger, weighing about 6 tonnes, and are usually much fiercer. Several fossil elephants of still larger bulk have been discovered, including the mammoth and the mastodon. The Indian elephant is domesticated and used as a beast of burden, and may live 70 years. The ivory trade (banned in 1989) was responsible for the mass slaughter of perhaps 700,000 elephants. This evil trade still continues clandestinely. Today (2006) less than 50,000 Asian elephants still survive, with perhaps *c* 600,000 African elephants. One hundred years ago there were around 5 million African elephants. Elephants are famed for their memory (they never forget) but they are the only mammal that cannot jump.

Elephant Seal. *See* **Sea Elephant.**

Eleusinian Mysteries, festivals common throughout ancient Greece, agricultural in their symbolism.

Elgin Marbles, a collection of ancient Greek sculptures and architectural fragments got together by the 7th Earl of Elgin and brought to England between 1802 and 1812. These celebrated treasures had originally formed part of the Parthenon at Athens, and were probably carved by pupils of the sculptor Phidias. Lord Elgin expended over £70,000 upon them, and they were purchased for £35,000 for the British Museum.

In 1997 the Labour Government ruled out their return to Greece. However, a new Acropolis Museum has been built in Greece ready to house them if they are returned.

Elk, the largest animal of the deer family, with enormous antlers, and standing, when mature, about 2 m high. The American moose is of the same family.

Elm, a stately, wide-spreading tree having some 20 species spread over north-temperate regions, several of which are native and peculiar to Britain. The grandest of the field elms is the English elm, *Ulmus procera*, which may reach a height of *c.* 42 m and a girth of 8 m. The wych elm, *U. glabra*, or Scots elm, is a valuable hardwood and used in boat-building. The fungus that causes Dutch elm disease is carried from tree to tree by a bark beetle. The fungus came from infected veneer logs from central Europe. Ironically the disease was named after the Dutch workers who discovered its cause! Since re-entering Britain in 1963, Dutch elm disease has caused the death of many million trees. Genetically-modified elms, resistant to the disease, are now being developed.

Elzevir, the name of a celebrated family of Dutch printers, who produced editions of Latin, French and German classics, which were highly valued for their beauty of type and accuracy of printing. They flourished in the 17th cent.

Ember-days are set apart for fasting and prayer in the Western Church, at the periods appointed for ordination, viz., the Wednesday, Friday and Saturday after the first Sunday in Lent, Whit-Sunday, 14 September (Holy Cross Day), and 13 December (St. Lucia's Day); of very ancient origin.

Emerald. The rich green variety of beryl (beryllium aluminium silicate). The colour is due to the presence of chromium oxide.

Emu, a towering, flightless bird. A protected species which appears on the Australian national coat of arms alongside the kangaroo.

Encaenia, a festival commemorating a dedication; at Oxford University the annual commemoration of benefactors, accompanied by the conferring of honorary degrees, is held in June.

Encryption, the sending of messages written in code. The term is now used in computing.

Encyclical Letters, a term used in reference to letters addressed by the Pope to his bishops upon matters of doctrine or discipline.

Encyclopaedists, a term first applied to the eminent writers who collaborated in the French *Encyclopédie* (1751–65). They included Diderot, D'Alembert, Voltaire, Helvetius; their writings had great influence in popularising the social ideas which resulted in the French Revolution.

Energy. One of the most fundamental concepts of science. A body in motion possesses *kinetic energy* as a result of the *work* done by the forces creating the motion. But a force which does work to stretch a spring does not create motion. Instead, the work is stored up in the spring and is one example of *potential energy*. A raised body also possesses potential energy which turns into kinetic when the body falls. The *heat energy* contained in a body is the sum of the kinetic and potential energy of the constituent atoms which are vibrating all the time. Heat and motion are obtainable from electrical, magnetic, chemical, atomic, and other sources, and physicists therefore define corresponding forms of energy. The vital point is that all forms of energy are transferable into one another *without loss or gain.* This is the Law of Conservation of Energy. It is one of the most fundamental laws of science, and its general validity is the reason why energy is an important idea. Since Einstein, it has been recognised that mass also is interchangeable with energy. *See also* **Nuclear Energy.**

Energy Conversion. For practical purposes it is frequently necessary to change energy from one into another of its many forms; indeed almost every activity does this in one way or another. The primary sources of energy are the sun, uranium and other elements from which nuclear energy can be drawn, and the tides. The sun is not much used *directly* because its heat is intermittent and not very intense, but solar cookers and refrigerators have been invented and solar batteries (*q.v.*) are used in spacecraft. The sun can be used *indirectly* because it has produced, *via* living processes, fossil fuels like coal and oil and still continues to generate winds, rain and rivers and hence hydroelectric and wind power. Commonly both fossil fuels and the energy of river or tidal waters are converted into electricity. Windmill type electricity generators are also quite common. The bulk of electricity production is a two-stage process: first fossil or nuclear fuel is used to create heat (*see* **Nuclear Reactors**); then the heat is used to raise steam and drive generators. Efforts are being made to convert heat into electricity more directly, *e.g.*, by using thermoelectric or thermionic effects (*q.v.*), but these have not been used for large-scale production. Once electrical energy is available, factories can make chemical batteries in great numbers and these can then be used as portable energy sources, as can petrol and other refined forms of fossil fuel. *See* **Battery, Fuel Cell, Solar Battery.**

Enthalpy, another name for the heat content (H) of a system in thermodynamics. If a system generates heat it is presumed that the heat comes from the enthalpy of the system which by the 1st law of thermodynamics thus falls. It can be combined with the entropy (S) in an equation which defines the important thermodynamic quantity called the Gibbs Free Energy: $G = H - TS$ where T is the thermodynamic temperature. G is important in the prediction of chemical change.

Entropy, one of the most important quantities in thermodynamics, symbol S. According to Clausius' statement of the Second Law the entropy of an isolated system cannot decrease. Although introduced by Clausius it arose from a consideration of Carnot's studies of the limitation of the convertibility of heat into work. It is most easily viewed as disorder in the statistical approach introduced by Boltzmann. This may be illustrated by considering the separate sets of coloured balls in a box. This is an ordered arrangement (of low entropy). The natural tendency is for the balls to mix and for the colours to become disordered (of higher entropy). We do not expect the opposite process for the balls to spontaneously separate, *i.e.*, we do not expect the entropy to decrease. In the context of energy changes, say in heat engines, the entropy change is equal to the heat change divided by the (thermodynamic) temperature.

Enzymes. Organic catalysts which accelerate chemical processes occurring in living organisms. There are a large number present in the cell, and most have a high degree of specificity. Enzyme mechanisms are the key to basic biological processes. *See* **Section T.**

Ephemeroptera or **May-flies,** an order of insects. In the larval condition they exist from two to three years aquatically, but no sooner do they arrive at maturity than their lives are hurried to a close. They rise up in pyramids on warm summer nights, take no food, propagate and perish. The Latin name expresses the fact that the adults have an ephemeral existence.

Epiphany. *See* **H9.**

Equator, the imaginary great circle of the earth, every point of which is 90 degrees from the earth's poles, and dividing the northern from the southern hemisphere. It is from this circle that the latitude of places north and south is reckoned. The celestial equator is the circle in which the plane of the earth's equator meets the celestial sphere of the imaginary sphere, in which the observer is at the centre, used for representing the apparent positions of the heavenly bodies).

Equinox, the time when the sun crosses the plane of the earth's equator, making day and night of equal length. These occur on about 21 March and 23 Sept. *See* **Ecliptic.**

Eras are distinctive periods of time associated with some remarkable historical event or personage. *The Christian era* is computed according to a 6th-cent. reckoning to begin with Jesus's birth, A.D. 1. The date is placed some years too late. Scholars now believe that Jesus was born *c.* 4 B.C. The *Jewish era* dates from 3761 B.C.; the *Julian era* from the alteration of the calendar by Julius Caesar 45 B.C. The *Muslim era* dates from the *Hejira*, or the flight of Mohammed from Mecca to Medina, which is A.D. 622, 16 July, in the Julian Calendar.

Erbium, a rare-earth metal, discovered by Mosander in 1842. Element no. 68, symbol Er.

Erg, the unit of work and energy in the centimetre-gram-second system; the energy involved when a force of 1 dyne moves its point of application through a distance of 1 cm.

Ernie, the name given to the "electronic random number indicator equipment", the electronic machine which selected the prizewinning numbers in the first Premium Bond draw, June 1957. A record 18 billion Premium Bonds entered the January 2003 draw. A record £1·1 billion was invested in Premium Bonds in May 2003 (the month the limit on an individual's holding was raised to £30,000). The lowest value Bond to win £1 million was a £3 Bond bought in February 1959 which won the prize in July 2004. Around 23 million people own Premium Bonds.

Eros. This asteroid is 24–32 km in diameter.

It comes closer to the earth than any other member of the solar system with the exception of the moon and several very small asteroids. Determination of solar parallax based on observations of Eros in 1930–31 yielded until then the most accurate estimate of the distance of the sun from the earth. *See* **Astronomical Unit.**

Erse, a term used by Lowland Scottish, and English writers for the Gaelic language spoken in the Highlands of Scotland. Sometimes erroneously applied to Irish, the Gaelic language as spoken in Ireland and revived as an official language in recent times. Dr. Johnson, Sir Walter Scott, and other writers used "Erse" to signify Scottish Gaelic. The language of the Scottish Lowlands (that used by Robert Burns) is related to the English language and not to Gaelic and is variously termed Scots, Braid Scots, Doric, Scottish vernacular, and Lallans.

Escurial or **Escorial,** Spanish monastery built in the mountains near Madrid by Philip II to commemorate the victory over the French at Saint-Quentin (1557). A palace was added later and it also includes a church, library and royal mausoleum. Built in granite in sombre style, it is one of the finest buildings in Europe.

Eskimo. Popular name for the Inuit peoples of the Arctic, living in Canada, Greenland, Alaska and the northern territories of Russia. Canada has granted self-government to an Arctic Eskimo territory (Nunavut) (effective from 1999). Their lifestyle is now threatened by global warming.

Esperanto, an artificial international language created by Ludwig Zamenhof of Warsaw and first published in 1887. It does not seek to replace national languages but to serve as a second language for international communication. It is based on the internationality of many words in the principal modern languages, and is entirely phonetic in spelling and pronunciation. Other artificial languages are Volapuk, Ido and Glosa, a grammar-free international language based on Latin and Greek.

Estates of the Realm in Britain are the Lords Spiritual, the Lords Temporal and the Commons.

Esters. Organic chemicals formed by combining an alcohol with an acid. They have a pleasant smell, and occur naturally in plants as the scent of flowers. Manufactured for use in the perfumery industry, and as flavourings in food. Some esters are used as solvents, notably amylacetate ("pear drops") in quick-drying paints. The polymeric fibre "Terylene" consists of chains of molecules containing many ester groups, formed by reacting an alcohol having two alcoholic (OH) groups with an acid having two acid (COOH) groups.

Etching. *See* **Section N.**

Ether, in chemistry, is a volatile inflammable liquid composed of carbon, hydrogen and oxygen. It is a valuable anaesthetic obtained by heating alcohol with sulphuric acid. In physics, in the 19th cent., all space was supposed to be filled with a substance called ether, the chief property of which was to carry light waves, *i.e.*, light was supposed to be waves in this all-pervading medium known as the ether. Speculation and experiment concerned with the ether were very fruitful in advancing physics. Ultimately the attempts by Michelson and Morley to detect the motion of the earth through the ether were unsuccessful in this respect but profoundly successful in stimulating the theory of relativity. The ether concept has now been abandoned.

Ethylene (also called ethene). A gas compounded of carbon and hydrogen, it is related to acetylene and ethane. Industrially it is obtained as a by-product in petroleum refining. It has wide uses as a starting material in the industrial manufacture of intermediates, especially alcohol. Its most important application is in the production of polythene (poly-ethylene). *See* **Catalyst.**

Etruscans, people believed to have come from Asia Minor who colonised Italy about 900 B.C., settled in what is now Tuscany and part of Umbria, reached the height of their civilisation about 500 B.C., and were ultimately absorbed by the Romans. They were skilled technicians in bronze, silver and goldwork. Evidence of their advanced civilisation was unearthed in 1998 beneath the ruins of Pompeii. The language of the Etruscans remains a mystery (though the discovery of a 2,300 year-old bronze tablet in 1999 may reveal its secrets).

Etymology, the origin and history of words.

Euro, the name for the single European currency launched on 1 January 1999. Greece became the 12th member on 1 January 2001. From 1 January 2002 the new notes and coins replaced old currencies in the 'eurozone'. *See* **Section G.**

Euro-dollar Market. An international financial market, located mainly in Britain and Europe, for lending and borrowing dollars, *i.e.*, titles to dollar deposits in United States banks.

Europa, fourth largest moon of the planet Jupiter, (*q.v.*) on which scientists believe the preconditions for life could exist. NASA is planning further missions to Europa. Instead of a solid surface, Europa is covered in a 10-mile thick layer of brittle ice, below which liquid salty oceans may exist. Surface temperature is 145°C.

European Space Agency was created in 1975 with headquarters in Paris. Examples of space research which it has undertaken include the Giotto probe to Halley's Comet, involvement with the Cassini mission to Saturn and the space station Spacelab. It has recently launched a number of satellites including X-ray multi-mirror telescope (XMM) and Cluster II satellites. ESA is due to launch a number of satellites in its four 'cornerstone' missions, including solar astronomy (STEP), Far Infrared Space Telescope (FIRST) the Rosetta cometary mission and XMM.

Europium, element no. 63, symbol Eu, discovered by Demarcay in 1906. A rare-earth metal.

Evaporation is the process by which a solid or liquid is resolved into vapour by heat. The opposite process is condensation. Wherever a liquid or solid surface is exposed, evaporation takes place into the space above. If the vapour is continually removed the solid or liquid vanishes into vapour; the higher the temperature the quicker the process. If the vapour is confined, then it collects, getting more concentrated until as many atoms of vapour are condensing as are evaporating. The vapour is then said to be saturated. Evaporation of water from sea, soil, plants, skin, *etc.*, is continuously in progress.

Event Horizon. The boundary of a black hole which marks the critical limit where the escape velocity of a collapsing body becomes as large as the speed of light and so no information can reach an external observer. *See* **Black Hole, Supernova.**

Everest Expeditions. For many years after Mt. Everest had been shown to be the highest mountain in the world, political conditions in Nepal, lying south of the summit, and in Tibet, to the north, prevented mountaineers from attempting an ascent. At last in 1921 the Tibetan authorities gave permission, and the first expedition, organised by a joint committee of the Royal Geographical Society and the Alpine Club, was sent out. This was primarily a reconnaissance; besides mapping the northern flanks, it found a practicable route up the mountain.

By 1939, six further expeditions had climbed on the northern face. Some were baulked by bad weather, others by problems previously little known, such as the effect of high altitudes on the human body and spirit.

Nevertheless, important climbs were accomplished. In 1924, for example, Col. E. F. Norton reached 8,589 m, and it was on this expedition that George Mallory and Andrew Irvine were seen going well at about the same height. They never returned, however. The body of Mallory was eventually found in 1999.

When the 1953 Expedition led by Col. John Hunt (later Lord Hunt), was being organised, stress was laid on three main points; proper acclimatisation of the climbers; use of oxygen for the final stages; and the establishment of very high altitude camps, so that the final assault parties would set out fresh and unencumbered. Great attention was also paid to recent developments in diet, clothing and equipment. In all these matters the 1953 expedition was able to draw on the accumulated experience of its predecessors. By the end of April, a base camp had been established below the ice-fall, and with the aid of thirty-four Sherpa porters supplies had been carried up into the Western Cwm.

The next critical stage was the ascent of the steep head of the cwm, the Lhotse face, with the threat of avalanches always present. By most strenuous efforts, a camp was established on the South Col (7,869 m) on 21 May. From this camp on 26 May, T. D. Bourdillon and R. C. Evans climbed the South Peak of Everest (8,760 m), then the highest altitude ever attained. On 28 May Edmund Hillary and the Sherpa leader, Tenzing Norgay, spent the night at the highest camp (8,510 m) and on the following day, 29 May, climbed to the South Summit, negotiated the difficult final ridge, and reached the summit of Everest. On 17 May 1993 (exactly 40 years later) Rebecca Stephens became the first British woman to conquer Everest (the first-ever woman to climb Everest was the Japanese Junko Tabei on 16 May 1975) Everest has been conquered by over 1,300 climbers since 1953—but at a cost of 175 lives.

In 2004 a Sherpa, Pemba Dorji, set a new record for climbing Everest—in just 8hrs 10mins.

The Chinese (whose official name for Everest is Qomolangma) claim they first mapped the peak in 1717.

Evolution, The theory, as laid down by Darwin, is that all existing species, genera and classes of animals and plants have developed from a few simple forms by processes of change and selection. Up to the time of Darwin a large part of the western world believed that life had been created suddenly at the beginning of the world which God had created, according to Archbishop Usher, on 22 October 4004 B.C. The evidence of the rocks, however, has given a more convincing theory of creation, and by studying the fossils preserved in the various layers of the earth's crust the past history of the earth has been pieced together. Darwin has been called the Newton of biology. *See* **Section T.**

Exchequer, which derives its name from the checkered tablecloth on which accounts were calculated in early Norman times, is a term connected with the revenues of the Crown. In former times it had jurisdiction in all revenue matters. The term Exchequer is now applied to the Governmental department which deals with the public revenues.

Exploration. Modern exploration began in the second half of the 15th cent. with the voyages of the great Portuguese and Spanish discoverers. They were followed by sailors of other European nations, who profited from their developments in navigation and from their charts, and in less than one hundred years the coastlines of much of the Americas, Africa and South-west Asia had been revealed and the globe circumnavigated.

The motives of these early explorers were mixed: they were seeking adventure, trade, plunder, national power and conversion of the local people. Few if any were directly interested in advancing scientific knowledge. But from the reports of their voyages, scholars at home compiled descriptions of the new worlds.

One of the earliest English expeditions to be despatched for scientific research was that of William Dampier on the *Roebuck*, which was sent out by the Admiralty in 1699 to examine the coasts of North-west Australia. In the 18th cent. British explorers were at work mainly in the Pacific Ocean, with the object of breaking the Spanish monopoly of trade. Capt. James Cook sailed thither in 1769 to observe first the transit of Venus at Tahiti, and then to search for the alleged great southern continent. On this voyage he discovered and charted much of the coasts of New Zealand and the east coast of Australia. On his second voyage he was the first to sail across the Antarctic Circle, and he showed that the southern continent was much smaller than had been supposed.

By 1800 the outlines of the continents, except for Antarctica were known, and explorers in the 19th cent. were largely engaged in opening up the interiors. In Africa British explorers solved two problems which had puzzled men for centuries: Mungo Park and Richard Lander established the true course of the River Niger, and Sir Richard Burton, J. H. Speke, Sir Samuel Baker and others revealed the true sources of the Nile. The greatest African explorer of that age was undoubtedly David Livingstone, the missionary, who in three great journeys explored the Zambesi and the region of the Great Lakes, spreading the Gospel, fighting the slave trade, and opening up the interior to settlement and trade.

In North America Alexander Mackenzie was the first to cross the main breadth of the continent from sea to sea. In Asia famous explorers included men like Charles Doughty, who explored in Arabia, and Sir Francis Younghusband, who journeyed from China to India across the Gobi and the Himalayas.

Explosives, substances which burn violently to produce gases in such volume that an explosion is induced. Gunpowder was the first explosive to be used; Roger Bacon's powder, consisting of charcoal, sulphur and saltpetre, was the only effective explosive until the 19th cent., but it was difficult to control. Nitroglycerine (glyceryl trinitrate) was first compounded in 1847 by adding glycerine to a mixture of sulphuric acid and nitric acid. In 1866 Alfred Nobel discovered how to make dynamite by absorbing nitroglycerine in the fine sand kieselguhr. Cordite was the joint invention of Sir Frederick Abel and Sir James Dewar (1889).

It came into general use as a propellant. High explosives, providing bursting charge for shells and bombs, include TNT (trinitrotoluene), picric acid, cyclonite (RDX) and many others. Slurry explosives can be pumped on to the site and therefore offer advantages in transportation and safety; they are also waterproof.

Chemical explosives have now been eclipsed by nuclear explosives.

Expressionism. See Section N.

F

Fables are fictitious narratives intended to enforce some moral precept, and may be either in prose or verse, and deal with personified animals and objects or with human beings. Aesop in ancient times and Hans Christian Andersen and the Brothers Grimm (in many of their stories) in later days, have given fables. Mention must also be made of La Fontaine and Krylov.

Fairs were established in mediaeval times as a means of bringing traders and customers together at stated periods, and formed the chief means of distribution. The great English fairs of early times were those of Winchester and Stourbridge near Cambridge. Traders from the Netherlands and the Baltic gathered there with the great merchants of London, and goods of every kind, wholesale and retail, were sold. One of the biggest trade fairs was at Nijni-Novgorod, founded in the 17th cent.; other big continental fairs were those of Leipzig (founded in the 12th cent.), Lyons and Prague. Expositions of advanced industrial products are still popular today.

Fairy Rings are the circles caused in grassland by certain fungi. The circles expand outwards as the fungus spreads, the fruiting bodies being at the periphery. Further inward where the fungi are decaying the grass grows more strongly, fertilised by the nitrogen released from the rotting fungi. Once these rings were held to be the scene of fairy dances.

Falcon, name given to diurnal birds of prey which belong to the same family, *Falconidae*, as the hawk, eagle, buzzard, kite and harrier. They are swift of wing and feed on birds and small mammals. These birds have long, pointed wings, strong, hooked and notched bill, long, curved claws and an eye of great power. They are found all over the world. Those that breed in Britain are the Kestrel (the most common), Hobby (one of the swiftest of European birds), Merlin and Peregrine, a swift and magnificent bird with slate-grey back, blackish crown, black "moustache" and whitish breast. The peregrine is now in decline because of pesticides getting into its food supply.

Other members of the family are the Gyr Falcon from northern latitudes, Iceland and Greenland, which is a winter visitor to Britain, the Lanner, Saker, Eleonora's falcon, Red-footed falcon and the Lesser Kestrel. The Gyr Falcon and the Peregrine were used in the sport

of falconry in olden times. Because of its fearlessness and larger size, the female bird was used. When the quarry was sighted, the bird was unhooded, set free, and after mounting high into the air would dart swiftly down to strike the prey. The heron was the usual victim.

Research has proved that diving peregrine falcons are the fastest birds in the world.

Fall-out. Radioactive material produced by nuclear explosions which may cause bodily and genetic damage. (1) *Local fall-out,* due to the return to earth of larger particles, occurs locally, and within a few hours after the explosion; (2) *Tropospheric fall-out,* due to particles which remain in the troposphere and come down within a month or so, possibly all over the world, but within the altitude in which the explosion occurred; (3) *Stratospheric fall-out,* which comes from fragments taken up into the stratosphere and then deposited, in the course of many years, uniformly all over the globe.

The two radioactive materials which have given rise to the greatest concern for the health of the individual are strontium-90 and iodine-131. Both these materials are liable to become concentrated in certain parts of the human body, strontium-90 in bone and iodine-131 in the thyroid gland. Radiation exposure may produce genetic effects, that is effects which may show up in succeeding generations. An extensive survey was carried out by scientists of the US Atomic Energy Commission on the islands of Bikini atoll, site of some 23 nuclear tests, 1946–58. Their records, published in 1969, revealed that the intensity of radioactivity underneath the point of explosion was still exceedingly high. Most of the radiation remaining was due to the radioactive isotope caesium-137.

Fantail, a variety of the domestic pigeon; also a genus of Australian birds of the *Muscicapidae* family. A small New Zealand bird is called a fantail.

Fan Tracery. See Section N.

Fascism. See Section J.

Fata Morgana, the name given to a curious mirage often observed over the Straits of Messina, attributed to the magic of the fairy Morgana, half-sister of King Arthur, who was fabled to live in Calabria.

Fathers of the Church were early writers who laid the foundations of Christian ritual and doctrine. The earliest were the Apostolic Fathers (*q.v.*). The Four Fathers of the Latin Church were St. Ambrose, St. Jerome, St. Augustine and St. Gregory the Great. The Four Fathers of the Greek Church were St. Basil, St. Gregory Nazianzen, St. John Chrysostom and St. Athanasius.

Fathom, a nautical measure, the six-foot stretch (1·8 m) of a man's arms. Replaced by the metre on British Admiralty charts but continued on yachtsmen's coastal charts.

Fatigue, a condition leading to breakage when a solid component, *e.g.,* an axle, is subjected to a large number of fluctuating repetitive stresses. Fatigue is the cause of most failures in service of metal engineering components though fatigue is not confined to metallic materials alone.

Fatigue failures result from the *repetition,* not simply from the *size* of the stresses; indeed, fatigue breakage can result from stresses much lower than the material could stand if the load were applied steadily. Fatigue causes minute cracks, usually at the surface, which grow and spread. Early detection is difficult and fatigue, discovered by the railway engineers of the 19th cent., remains a severe engineering problem.

Fats are important foodstuffs. In physiology they constitute a valuable form of reserve food. They contain carbon, hydrogen and oxygen; chemically they are described as esters of glycerol (glycerine). Commonest fats are stearin, palmitin and olein, esters formed by the combination of glycerol with stearic, palmitic and oleic acid respectively. Fats are converted into soap by alkali; this process (saponification) also releases glycerol.

Fatwa, an edict issued by a Muslim religious leader (*e.g.* the death threat to Salman Rushdie issued in 1989 by Ayatollah Khomeini).

Fault, a term designating a breakage coupled with

displacement of geological strata.

Fauvism. See **Section N**.

February, the second month of the year, contains in ordinary years 28 days, but in leap years 29 days. When first introduced into the Roman calendar by Numa, c. 700 B.C. it was made the last month of the year, preceding January, but in 452 B.C. the position of the two months was changed, February following January.

Federation. See **Confederation**.

Félibrige, a movement founded in 1854 to revive the ancient glories of Provence, initiated by the French poet Frédéric Mistral.

Felspar, the name given to a group of minerals, silicates of aluminium with some calcium and sodium, or potassium, which make up probably more than half of the earth's crust. It is formed in granite and other rocks, both igneous and metamorphic. See also **Special Topic, T71**.

Fenestella, the niche set apart on the south side of the altar for the piscina in Roman Catholic churches.

Fermentation, the action of chemical ferments or *enzymes* in bringing about chemical changes in the materials of living animals and plants, e.g., the breaking-down of sugar by yeast into alcohol.

Ferret, a domesticated polecat. It is about half the size of a cat and is bred in captivity to hunt rats and rabbits. It has a long sinuous body and short legs which enable it to enter rabbit and rat holes and chase the quarry out to guns or into nets.

Ferrites are compounds containing iron, oxygen, and one or two of a certain range of other possible metallic elements. Ferrites have recently become very important technically, because, unlike ordinary magnetic materials, they combine strong magnetism with electrical insulating properties. Ferrite-rod aerials are now common in portable radios, and ferrite devices are used in radar.

Fieldfare, the largest member of the thrush family, a regular winter visitor to Britain from Scandinavia. It is brown in colour with a lighter spotted breast and a grey head.

Field-Marshal, the highest ranking title in the British army, and only bestowed on royal personages and generals who have attained great distinction. The first British Field-Marshal was created in 1736, when John, Duke of Argyll, had the title conferred upon him.

Fifth Column. See **A42**.

Fighting-Fish, small pugnacious Thai fish with long caudal and ventral fins. They are kept in glass globes in Thailand, and when brought into contact will fight to the death, these encounters being the occasion of much gambling.

Filibuster, a name first given to pirates and buccaneers in the 17th cent. who took possession of small islands or lonely coast lands, and there maintained themselves apart from any governing authority. In later times the term was used to specify men taking part in expeditions whose object was to appropriate tracts of country, and settle upon them in disregard of international law. The most notable expeditions of this kind in modern times were those of Narciso Lopez against Cuba in 1850–51, and of William Walker against Nicaragua, between 1855 and 1860. Both leaders were captured and executed. The term is also used to express the right of a minority in the US Senate for unlimited debate, which is used on occasions to delay legislation.

Finches, a large family of small birds belonging to the Passerine or perching order of birds. There are about 200 species, including greenfinch, hawfinch, chaffinch, goldfinch, siskin, bullfinch, crossbill, linnet, twite and bunting.

Fir, a cone-bearing tree with small evergreen leaves and of considerable use as timber. There are two types: the Silver Firs and the Douglas Firs numbering about 25 species. All these firs attain to a considerable height, and all yield turpentine or other resinous material.

Fire-damp. See **Methane**.

Fire-Fly, a small winged insect of the *Eleteridae* family, is able to throw out a strong phosphorescent light in the dark. There are some remarkable specimens in tropical countries.

Fire of London. See **A42**.

Fireworks. See **Explosives**.

Firkin, a former measure of capacity, the fourth part of a barrel, now only used in reference to a small cask or tub for butter, lard, etc.

Fischer-Tropsch Process. A process for making synthetic petrol from carbon monoxide and hydrogen. The synthesis is accelerated by cobalt-thoria and nickel-thoria catalysts.

Fish Louse. Parasitic crustacea found on marine and fresh-water fishes and whales.

Fission, Nuclear. A nuclear reaction in which the nucleus of an atom (e.g., uranium 235, plutonium) captures a neutron, and the unstable nucleus so produced breaks into two nearly equal fragments and throws out several neutrons as well. In biology the term fission is applied to reproduction by fragmentation of a single-cell organism, as in amoeba.

Flagella, single hair-like projections found on many micro-organisms. Their sole function is, by complicated motion, to move the organism about. They are longer and less versatile than cilia (q.v.).

Flag Officer, a British naval officer who enjoys the right of carrying a flag at the mast-head of his ship, and is of the rank of Admiral of the Fleet, Admiral, Vice-Admiral or Rear-Admiral.

Flagship, the ship that flies the Admiral's flag, and from which orders proceed.

Flamingo, a strangely beautiful, extremely slender wading bird of white and rose-pink plumage with long, slender legs and neck and a long, down-curved bill with which it rakes the mud and obtains its food of worms and molluscs. The wings are bright crimson, bordered with black, and a flock in flight is a picture of singular beauty. There is a large and famous colony in the Camargue, S.E. France.

Flash-Point. This is found by heating an oil in a special cup and taking the temperature at which sufficient vapour is produced to ignite when a small flame is applied. It is an index of the inflammability of oils.

Fleas. Fleas are small parasitic insects belonging to the order *Aphaniptera* (so called because these creatures have no wings). They obtain their food by sucking blood from their host. They are laterally compressed, which immediately distinguishes them from lice. The human flea (*Pulex irritans*) is able to jump vertically a distance of over 18 cm.

Fleet Prison, a noted debtors' prison that stood on the east side of Farringdon Street, London. It was notorious for the cruelties inflicted on prisoners, particularly under the wardenship of Thomas Bainbridge who took charge in 1728. It was pulled down in 1846.

Fleet Street, a famous thoroughfare in London, until 1990 the centre of journalism and the press, though it was long celebrated for its taverns. It takes its name from the Fleet stream which used to run from Hampstead through Holborn to the Thames at Blackfriars.

Flemings, the Dutch-speaking people of Flanders, whose medieval ancestors excelled in the textile arts: England owes its early eminence as a manufacturing nation to the migration of numbers of Flemings to this country in the 16th and 17th cent. See also **Walloons**.

Fleur de Lis, the former national emblem of France, the flower of the lily. It was superseded by the Tricolour in 1789, but is still adhered to by the supporters of the old French monarchy.

Flint, consists of granular chalcedony with some opaline silica, and occurs as nodules and bands in the Chalk. It is hard and has a conchoidal fracture, so enabling it to be used in making cutting implements in prehistoric times. Before the invention of lucifer matches, it was used along with steel for striking lights.

Flint implements are objects found in the younger geological strata, and constituting evidence of the condition and life of the period. They include knives, clubs, arrow-heads, scrapers, etc., used as weapons, tools and possibly as surgical instruments and in religious ceremonies. Similar to prehistoric specimens are the flint and obsidian implements of some of the primitive peoples of today. Ritual weapons and sacrificial knives continued to be made of stone long after the introduction of metals for practical purposes.

Flounder, one of the most familiar of the smaller

flat fishes common round the British coasts, and seldom attaining a weight of over 1·3 kg.

Fluoridation, the process of adding the element fluorine, in the form of suitable compounds, to something deficient in it. Commonly met with as a proposal to add fluorides (fluorine compounds) to drinking water to combat dental decay, especially in children. Some toothpastes are fluoridated and fluoride can also be taken as tablets and in other ways. In 1976 a working party of the Royal College of Physicians recommended that water supplies should be fluoridated when the natural fluoride level is below 1 mg/litre. This recommendation drew on many investigations throughout the world giving evidence for the effectiveness of fluoride in the prevention of decay without harmful side-effects. There is, however, a body of opinion unconvinced by this and opposed to adding fluoride to drinking water, one argument being that to take or not to take fluoride should be a personal decision.

Fluorine, chemical element, no. 9, member of the halogen family, symbol F, it is found in combination with calcium in fluorspar, and occurs in minute quantities in certain other minerals. Discovered by Scheele in 1771, it was first obtained by Moissan in 1886. A pale yellow gas, it is very reactive and combines with most elements except oxygen. Its acid, hydrogen fluoride, etches glass, the fluorine combining with the silicon to form volatile silicon fluoride. Organic fluorine compounds have found use as very stable polymers which resist a wide variety of chemical actions.

Fluorescent Lamp. *See under* **Electric Light and Ultra-Violet Rays.**

Fluorocarbons are hydrocarbons in which some or all of the hydrogen atoms have been replaced by atoms of chlorine or fluorine. They are nontoxic, non-flammable and chemically inert gases or low boiling point liquids. These properties make them very suitable for use as refrigerants, and propellants in fire-extinguishers and aerosols. The most widely used fluorocarbons are the chlorofluoromethanes (CCl_2F_2, CCl_3F and $CHClF_2$). In 1974 it was first suggested that the vast release of fluorocarbons into the atmosphere due to the greatly increased use of aerosols could cause a significant depletion of the protective ozone (*q.v.*) layer in the upper atmosphere. The mechanism for this involves the decomposition of fluorocarbons at high altitudes as a result of intense solar irradiation. The chlorine atoms so released can then catalyse the conversion of ozone into ordinary molecular oxygen. The degree of ozone depletion that will result is a matter of current controversy. Similarly, opinions differ as to the detrimental effect ozone depletion might have on the incidence of skin cancer and on the climate.

Fluorspar, a mineral; chemically calcium fluoride. Can be colourless, green or yellow, but is most commonly purple. Blue fluorspar under the name of Derbyshire "blue John" has been used for ornamental purposes.

Fly, the popular name for a large number of insects with one pair of wings and a proboscis terminating in a sucker through which fluid substances can be drawn up. The best-known species are the common house-fly, the bluebottle and the blow-fly. In the larval form flies are maggots, and feed upon decaying substances, animal flesh, *etc.* Flies are able to walk upon ceilings or upright surfaces by having suckers at the soles of their feet. *See* **Diptera.**

Flycatcher, name of a large family of small birds, the Muscicapidae. They are insect feeders, catch their food in the air, and are distributed over most countries of the world. The spotted and the pied nest in Britain, which they visit from April to September.

Flying Fish are frequently to be seen in southern waters, and are capable of gliding considerable distances without touching the water. To build up speed for its "take-off " the fish swims rapidly, to break the surface at 24–32 km/h. Maximum air speed is about 64 km/h.

Flying Fox, a member of the bat family, but of much larger size, and confined to the tropical and sub-tropical Old World. Like the bats, it is nocturnal, but it feeds entirely on fruits.

Flying Lemur. *See* **Colugo.**

Flying Lizard, or *Draco*, an Asiatic lizard, possessing wing-like projections from each side which enable it to make flying leaps through the air, though not sufficient for continuous flight.

Flying Squirrel, rodents of which there are several species in Europe, Asia and America. It possesses a parachute-like fold of skin by means of which it projects itself through the air. In appearance they are much like ordinary squirrels, to which they are related. African flying squirrels belong to a different family.

Fog is caused by the presence of particles of condensed water vapour or smoke in the surface layers of the atmosphere, the term being applied meteorologically when the resulting obscurity is such as to render objects invisible at distances of up to 1 km. Fogs are frequently formed when the air near the ground is cooled below its dew-point temperature by radiation on a still, cloudless night; by flowing over a relatively cold land or water mass; or by mixing with a colder air stream. An accumulation of smoke over a large city may cause a high fog cutting off the daylight and producing gloom. *See* **Pollution, Aerosol.**

Foliation, a geological term for rocks whose component minerals are arranged in parallel layers as the result of strong metamorphic action.

Folio, a printing term for a sheet of paper folded once, a half sheet constituting a leaf.

Folklore concerns itself with the traditional beliefs, customs, institutions and sayings that have been handed down from generation to generation by word of mouth and with the observation, recording and interpretation of such traditions. (The word *folklore* itself was first suggested and used—as two words *Folk Lore*—by W. J. Thoms in the *Athenaeum* of 22 August 1846, and was at once absorbed into the English language.) Traditional lore of the kind included in the term folklore takes many forms and ranges from omens of good and bad luck (spilling the salt, breaking a mirror, dropping an umbrella, *etc.*) and the wearing of amulets or the possession of talismans (such as the horseshoe) as protection against misfortune, to elaborate ceremonial dances such as the Abbots Bromley Horn Dance, the Hobby horses of Padstow and Minehead the Northern sworddances and the Christmas mummers' plays. Especially important are the beliefs and customs associated with birth, babyhood, marriage and death, such being occasions when the individuals concerned require special protection or when unusual happenings can be used for foretelling their future.

Another very large section of the subject of folklore deals with the traditional sayings and practices associated with particular days and seasons of the year—calendar customs, as they are called. The eating of pancakes on Shrove Tuesday; Mother Sunday customs and the simnel cake; Good Friday as the right day for planting potatoes, but emphatically the wrong day for washing clothes or cutting one's finger-nails; the necessity of wearing something new on Easter Sunday; the children's maypole dances and May garlands; midsummer fires; All Hallowe'en as the most favourable occasion for divining the future—especially in respect of marriage—and for games and sports such as apple-bobbing; the numerous practices accompanying the harvest. All these are examples of calendar customs; their full story would occupy several volumes.

Folklorists are interested in such oral tradition because they think that to a large extent it represents what folk have mentally stored up from the past and transmitted to their descendants throughout the centuries, and because therefore it is able to assist other historic methods—ethnographical, linguistic, archaeological, *etc.*—in the elucidation of the early story of man.

The Folk-Lore Society was founded in 1878, and that part of the subject represented by song and dance has now its own English Folk Dance and Song Society.

Food Standards Agency, an independent watchdog set up by the Government to restore consumer confidence in food safety. It began work in April 2000.

Foot-and-Mouth Disease, a highly contagious infection among cloven-hoofed animals with a devastating impact on farming. The 2001 outbreak devastated such areas as Cumbria. The outbreak was declared over in January 2002.

Footpath. In English law a highway over which the public have a right of way on foot only, other than such a highway at the side of a public road. *See also* **Long-Distance Walks.**

Force, as a term in physics, signifies an influence or exertion which, when made to act upon a body, tends to move it if at rest, or to affect or stop its progress if it be already in motion. In the c.g.s. system, the unit of force is the dyne; in the foot-pound-second system, the poundal; in the SI system, the newton.

Formaldehyde. Chemically it lies between methyl alcohol and formic acid; oxidation of methyl alcohol yields formaldehyde, and oxidation of formaldehyde produces formic acid. It is used as a disinfectant, in silvering mirrors, and in the manufacture of phenol-formaldehyde plastics (of which bakelite is the best-known example). Solutions of formaldehyde in water, formalin, are used to preserve biological specimens.

Forme, a body of letterpress type, composed and secured for printing from; or a stereotype or electrotype. The former is used more for newspaper formes and the latter in book work.

Formic Acid can be obtained from a colourless fluid secreted by ants and other insects and plants. It is a strong irritant. Commercially it is obtained from sodium formate, which is synthesised by the absorption of carbon monoxide in caustic soda. It is used in the electroplating, tanning and textile industries.

Fossils. Remains of animals and plants, or direct evidence of their presence, preserved in rocks. They include petrified skeletons and shells, leaf imprints, footprints, *etc.*

Foundation Hospitals, new concept of non-profit, public-interest companies running hospitals independent of Whitehall control. Critics see them as a move towards NHS privatisation.

Fox, carnivorous animal of the canine family, found in considerable numbers in most parts of the world. The common fox *Vulpes vulpes* of Europe is a burrowing animal of nocturnal habits, living upon birds, rabbits and domestic poultry, in the capture of which it displays much cunning.

Among other species are the Arctic fox and the red fox of North America, of which the valuable silver fox, coveted for its fur, is a variety. An estimated 15% of foxes are now to be found in the suburbs, scavenging the streets at night for leftover food.

The hunting of foxes with dogs in England and Wales became a criminal offence in February 2005, following successive votes to ban foxhunting by the House of Commons (and the eventual use of the Parliament Act to force legislation through). In Scotland, hunting with hounds became illegal in 2002.

Fox-Shark *or* **Thresher Shark,** a large species of shark common in the Atlantic and in the Mediterranean. It is very destructive to small fish, but although it attains a length of 4·5 m it is not dangerous to man.

Franciscans. *See* **Friars.**

Frankincense is of two kinds, one being used as incense in certain religious services and obtained from olibanum, an Eastern shrub, the other is a resinous exudation derived from firs and pines, and largely used in pharmacy.

Freedom of Information Act. *See* **D21.**

Freeport, a port exempt from customs duties and regulations. The north German towns of the Hanseatic League were among the earliest and most famous freeports.

Freira, small grey and white sea bird. Extremely rare, it nests on the island of Madeira. Likely to become the first European species to face extinction since the Great Auk in 1844.

French Horn. *See* **Horn.**

Friars, members of certain mendicant orders of the Roman Catholic Church. The four chief orders are the Franciscans or Grey Friars, the Dominicans or Black Friars, the Carmelites or White Friars and the Augustinians (Austin Friars).

Friday, the 6th day of the week, named after Frigga, the wife of Odin. It is the Muslim Sabbath, a general abstinence day of the Roman Catholic Church, and according to popular superstition, an unlucky day.

Frigate-Bird, a web-footed bird widely distributed over tropical latitudes, and deriving its name from its great expanse of wing and forked tail, resembling the shape of a swift vessel. It feeds on flying fish mostly, being unable to dive and also steals from other birds. A frigate-bird was found dying on the Hebridean island of Tiree in July 1953; only twice previously had one been recorded in Europe—on the German coast in 1792, and on the coast of France in 1902.

Frog, a familiar amphibian, breathing through gills in the earlier (tadpole) part of its existence and through lungs later. It remains three months in the tadpole stage. The frog hibernates underwater in the mud during the winter.

Britain now has only one species of native frog, the common frog (*Rana temporaria*). Frogs are now threatened by a deadly virus (known as red leg) sweeping the country.

Frost occurs when the temperature falls to, or below, 0°C, which is freezing point. Hoar frost is applied to the needles or feather-like crystals of the ice deposited on the ground, in the same manner as dew. Glazed frost is the clear icy coating which may be formed as a result of rain falling on objects whose temperatures are below the freezing point. These layers of ice, often rendering roads impassable for traffic, damaging overhead power and communication systems and endangering aircraft, can also be caused by condensation from warm, damp winds coming into contact with very cold air and freezing surfaces.

Froth-Hopper *or* **Frog-Hopper.** A family of bugs (belonging to the insect order *Hemiptera*) which in the larval stage surround themselves with a protective mass of froth ("cuckoo spit"). These insects, which suck the sap of plants, bear a faint resemblance to frogs, and the adults possess great leaping powers.

Fruit Fly. *See* **Drosophila.**

Fuel Cells were first demonstrated in action when in 1959 Bacon of Cambridge University used his fuel cell to drive a fork-lift truck and a welding machine. The Bacon fuel cell consists of two electrodes of porous nickel dipping into a solution of caustic potash in water. One electrode is supplied with hydrogen gas from an outside cylinder and the other with oxygen. These gases, forming layers on the nickel, are the active chemicals. The oxygen combines with water to make two negatively charged ions, each consisting of an oxygen and a hydrogen atom joined together (a hydroxyl ion). The hydroxyl ions travel through the solution to the hydrogen electrode, where they combine with hydrogen to form neutral water. Their negative charge (one electron per ion involved) has now arrived at the hydrogen electrode and is ready to flow back to the other electrode through any outside circuit that is provided. This flow constitutes the useful electric current, and it has been provided at the expense of creating water out of the original hydrogen and oxygen. The water can be removed in the form of steam.

What is the advantage of all this? In the first place the fuel gases are easy to make and to store in cylinders. Supplying a new gas cylinder is easier and quicker than recharging an ordinary accumulator. Furthermore, a fuel cell is lighter for a given power than an accumulator; satellite designers have found them useful. The fuel cell is not damaged by heavy overloading, and this is valuable for application to vehicle driving. Fuel-cell-driven buses could combine the advantage of diesel buses and trolleybuses. Fuel cells are still in the development stage.

Fulani, a people of Hamitic stock widely distributed in N.W. Africa, chiefly in Nigeria. There are two main branches: the dark-skinned Fulani, settled farmers and city dwellers, Muslim in religion; and the lightcoloured Bororo'en who are semi-nomadic herdsmen. The Fulani are different from any tribe in W. Africa though they resemble in some ways the Masai of E. Africa. The Fulani conquered the Hausa states at the beginning of the 19th cent. which passed under British suzerainty after 1903. Sokoto, built in 1810, was capital of the Fulani empire.

Fuller's Earth, a special kind of clay or marl possessing highly absorbent qualities, originally used in the "fulling"—that is, cleansing and clarifying—of cloth. Now used in clarifying oils. Deposits in America and also in the south of England.

Function. In mathematics, one quantity y is said to be a function of another quantity x, written $y = f(x)$, if a change in x results in some corresponding change in y. Thus $\sin x$ or $\log x$ are functions of x. If y depends not only on x but on several other quantities as well, y is called a function of many variables.

Fungi, a class of simple plants, which reproduce from spores and lack the green colouring matter *chlorophyll*. It includes moulds, rusts, mildews, smuts, mushrooms, etc. Potato blight is a fungus disease which caused the failure of the potato crop in Ireland in 1846. 50,000 different fungi are known. *See also* **Section T.**

Furniture Beetle (*Anobium punctatum*). The common furniture beetle is responsible for 80 per cent of all woodworm damage and is the great pest of the comparatively modern house, causing damage in the main to softwood roofing and flooring timbers. Adults are 3 mm long. The grub tunnels for about 33 months. *See also* **Woodworm, Death Watch Beetle.**

G

Gabardine, a long, loose, coarse, over-garment, worn by the poor in the Middle Ages, and prescribed by law as the distinctive garment of the Jews. The name is now given to a closely woven cloth of wool and cotton used to make raincoats.

Gabbro, a kind of igneous rock, often very coarse-grained, containing a good deal of plagioclase felspar, and monoclinic pyroxene; it may occasionally also include biotite, magnetite, ilmenite and hornblende. A gabbro containing nickel at Sudbury in Canada is one of the richest sources known of that metal.

Gadfly, a widely distributed family of flies with only one pair of wings, including the horse fly. The females are very voracious, being able to bite through the skin and suck the blood of animals. The males are harmless.

Gadolinium. An element, no. 64, symbol Gd, belonging to the rare-earths metals discovered in 1886 by Marignac. It is strongly magnetic.

Gaelic, relating to the Gaels and their language, a term now applied only to the Celtic people inhabiting the Highlands of Scotland, but formerly also to the Celts of Ireland and the Isle of Man. A century ago, 200,000 people spoke Scottish Gaelic. Now only 60,000 do (2001 census) and the language could soon face extinction.

Gaitskellites. Members of the Labour Party who supported the moderate and reformist policies of Hugh Gaitskell (1906–63) in the late 1950s and early 1960s. In 1955 Gaitskell was elected party leader, defeating Bevan. His supporters, many of whom came from the trade unions and their sponsored MPs, represented the social democratic tradition and found themselves in conflict with the more left-wing Bevanites.

Galago, "Bush Babies", related to the lemur, native to Africa, large-eyed, in keeping with its nocturnal characteristics.

Galaxy (or Milky Way Galaxy), the giant star system to which the Sun belongs. On a clear moon-less night a swathe of light can be seen stretching across the sky from horizon to horizon. This dramatic sight led the ancient Greeks to describe it as a river of milk flowing from the breast of Hera, wife of Zeus—the word "galaxy" comes from the Greek word for milk. The Romans saw this as Via Lactea, or Milky Way.

The Galaxy contains 100 billion stars and has a spiral structure that is highly flattened. The stars are organised into a thin disc with an ellipsoidal bulge, or nucleus, at its centre. The system is embedded in a roughly spherical halo of stars and globular clusters. The entire Galaxy is rotating about the centre. The Sun is situated near the inner edge of one of the spiral arms. At the Sun's distance from the centre, the rotation of the disc stars are 220 km per second. It takes the Sun 250 million years to travel once around the Galaxy.

The halo of the Galaxy is much less populated than the disc and its full extent is still uncertain. Many astronomers now believe there is a dark halo of unseen matter stretching out to a radius of about 100 thousand parsecs. The presence of such a halo is inferred from the manner in which the Galaxy rotates and the gravitational effect on the more distant globular clusters in the halo and on nearby dwarf galaxies.

In 2004 astronomers reported the most distant galaxies yet discovered, 12,600 million light years from Earth.

Gale, a high wind now technically defined as one of at least Beaufort force 8. Between thirty and forty gales a year occur on the north and west coasts of the British Isles and only about half of this number in the south-east. At St. Ann's Head, Dyfed, the anemometer registered a gust of 113 mile/h (182 km/h) on 18 Jan. 1945, which is a record for these islands. Gusts exceeding 113 km/h are rarely experienced in London. Gale warnings are issued by the Meteorological Office.

Galileo Space Mission. *See under* **Jupiter.**

Gall, abnormal vegetable growths caused by insects, mites, bacteria, or fungi, found on all parts of the plant. Oak-apples, Robin's pin-cushion (on wild rose), "witches' brooms" (on trees) are examples. Some are useful commercially, *e.g.*, oak apples yield tannic acid and the black oak gall is used in America as animal food.

Galleon, the name given to the old three-decked Spanish treasure vessels employed in conveying the precious minerals from the American colonies to Spain. The term is often applied to any large, especially stately, sailing vessel.

Galley, an oar-propelled sea-boat used by the ancient Greeks and Romans for transport purposes, manned by slaves. They were also used as warships from classical to relatively modern times, *e.g.*, Lepanto 1571. When so used the sides were raised to protect the rowers.

Gallic Acid, obtained from gall nuts, sumach, tea, coffee, and the seeds of the mango, is used in the manufacture of inks and as an astringent in medicine. It was discovered by C. W. Scheele (1742–86), a Swedish chemist.

Gallium, metallic element, no. 31, symbol Ga, related to aluminium, but which can be cut with a knife. It was discovered spectroscopically by L. de Boisbaudran in 1875. Long before Mendeleyev had predicted that an element with its properties would be found to fill the then existing gap in the Periodic Table; this gap came immediately below aluminium, so he suggested the name "eka aluminium" for it.

Gallup Poll, a system, introduced by Dr. Gallup in the United States, for testing public opinion on topical subjects by taking a test poll on questions framed to elicit opinions.

Galvanised Iron is iron coated with zinc. The name comes from the fact that such a coat protective against rust could be deposited electrolytically. Electrodeposition may be used, but the cheaper and more common process depends on dipping the iron in a bath of molten zinc.

Gamboge, a resinous gum obtained from the sap of *Garcinia morella*, a tree native to Thailand, Cambodia and Sri Lanka, and used as a yellow pigment in paints and also as a purgative.

Game is the term applied to wild animals which are protected from indiscriminate slaughter by Game Laws. In the UK game comprehends deer, hares, pheasants, partridges, grouse, black game, moor game, woodcocks, bustards and certain other birds and animals of the chase.

Game can only be killed (with few exceptions) by persons holding game licences. Occupiers of land and one other person authorised by them in each case are allowed to kill hares and rabbits on their land without licence.

Game cannot be sold except by a person holding a proper licence. There is a "close time" prescribed for the different classes of game; for instance, the selling or exposing for sale of any hare or leveret during March, April, May, June or July is prohibited by law. Grouse cannot be shot between 11 December and 11 August; partridges between 2 February and 31 August; pheasants between 2 February and 30 September; and black game between 11 December and 10 August. The government is currently reviewing the antiquated 1831 Game Act and the 1860 Game Licences Act which limit the sale of wild game.

Game reserves are legally protected areas where natural vegetation and wild life are allowed to remain unmolested.

Gaming, *or* **Gambling**—*i.e.*, staking money on the chances of a game—differs from betting in that it depends upon the result of a trial of skill or a turn of chance. The 1959 Betting and Gaming Act replaced all the old laws on gaming, which went back to an Act of 1541 entitled "An Acte for Mayntenance of Artyllarie and debarringe of unlauful games", under which some games were unlawful if played for money in any circumstances. Roulette and any game of dice were among such games. Under the 1959 Act any game was lawful, subject to certain conditions. Since then the Betting, Gaming and Lotteries Act, 1963, and the Gaming Act, 1968, have been passed, to deal with unlawful gaming and to prevent the exploitation of gaming by commercial interests. The playing of bingo is now restricted to clubs licensed for bingo only. Sunday betting on dogs and horses became legal in 1995. Playing of fruit machines in betting shops is now legal.

The controversial 2005 Gambling Bill proposed a major expansion of regional casinos (with unlimited jackpots). A new Gambling Commission was also proposed. Casinos would be open to the public, not operating as 24-hour membership clubs as they do now. See also **National Lottery.**

Gamma Ray. See **Section T.**

Gamma Ray Bursts, intense flashes of gamma rays, detected at energies up to one million electronvolts. Measurements have revealed that the distribution of the bursts is uniformly distributed across the sky and they are thought to originate outside our Galaxy. The physical origin still remains a mystery but is thought to involve neutron stars, black holes or a mixture of both. See **Black hole, Neutron star.**

Gammexane, a powerful insecticide, used particularly to kill the tsetse fly and mosquito.

Gannet, a fish-eating bird which dives on its prey from a great height, swallowing it under water, is found in large numbers off the coast of Scotland, and has breeding stations in the Hebrides, St. Kilda, Ailsa Craig, the Bass Rock, Grassholme Island and on Ortac and Les Etacs (rocks off Alderney). It is a bird of white plumage, black tips to long narrow wings and wedge-shaped tail, and weighs about 3 kg. The gannet breeds in colonies on ledges of steep, rocky, island cliffs. Related to the cormorants, pelicans and frigate-birds.

Ganymede, a moon of Jupiter. It is the first moon we know which possesses an independent magnetic field. It has a thin atmospheric layer.

Garden Cities in England were founded by Ebenezer Howard (1850–1928), and his ideas were put forward in his book *Tomorrow—A Peaceful Path to Real Reform* (later re-issued as *Garden Cities of Tomorrow*). New towns should be so placed and planned as to get the best of town and country life, an adaptation of the model villages of certain industrial philanthropists such as Salt, Richardson, Cadbury, Leverhulme and others. The Garden City Association (later the Town and Country Planning Association) was formed in 1899, and the first garden city was begun at Letchworth in 1903 and successfully established. Welwyn Garden City (1919) was Howard's foundation.

Gardener-Bird, a bird possessing many of the characteristics of the bower bird, found only in Papua–New Guinea. See also **Bower Bird.**

Gargantua, the giant hero of Rabelais' satire, of immense eating and drinking capacity, symbolical of the greed of the Church.

Gargoyle, a projecting spout for carrying off water from the roof gutter of a building. Gargoyles are only found in old structures, modern waterpipe systems having rendered them unnecessary. In Gothic architecture they were turned to architectural account and made to take all kinds of grotesque forms—grinning goblins, hideous monsters, dragons and so forth.

Garlic, a bulbous plant of the same genus as the onion and the leek, and a favourite condiment among the people of Southern Europe. It has a very strong odour and pungent taste.

Garnet, a group of minerals; chemically they are orthosilicates of the metals calcium, magnesium, titanium, iron, aluminium. Garnets can be coloured yellow, brown, black, green or red; the blood-red garnet is an important gemstone.

Garrotte, a method of strangulation used as capital punishment in Spain, and consisting of a collar which is compressed by a screw that causes death by piercing the spinal marrow. Garrotting was also applied to a system of highway

robbery common in England in 1862–63, the assailants seizing their victims from behind, and by a sudden compression of the windpipe disabling them until the robbery was completed.

Garter. The Most Noble Order of the Garter was founded (c. 1348) by King Edward III, and is the premier order of knighthood in Great Britain. The traditional story associating the garter and the motto with the Countess of Salisbury, who it was said dropped her garter while dancing with the King, who said "honi soit qui mal y pense" cannot be accepted.

The Order was originally limited to the Sovereign and 25 knights, but the number has been extended, and it may now be bestowed on royal personages and leading representatives of the British peerage. The insignia of the order are the garter of dark-blue velvet with the motto in letters of gold, the mantle of dark-blue velvet lined with white silk, the surcoat and hood, and the gold-and-enamel collar. The garter is worn on the left leg below the knee and by women as a sash over the left shoulder.

Recent recipients have been James Callaghan (1987), Sir Edward Heath (1992), the Princess Royal (1994), Sir Edmund Hillary, Baroness Thatcher (1995) and John Major (2005). See **Knighthood.**

Gas is an elastic fluid substance, the molecules of which are in constant rapid motion, and exerting pressure. The technique whereby gases are liquefied depends on increasing pressure and diminishing temperature. Each gas has a critical point; unless the temperature is brought down to this point no amount of pressure will bring about liquefaction. Last gas to be liquefied was helium (1908).

Gas from coal was first used as an illuminating agent by William Murdoch towards the end of the 18th cent. in Birmingham, and about 1807 was introduced in London, one side of Pall Mall being lighted with it. It became widely used as an illuminant, and for space heating and cooking. In the UK increasing attention has been paid to the use of a primary fuel—natural gas—instead of producing gas from coal or oil. The largest gas producer in the world is Russia.

Gas, Natural, natural mixture of gases often present with deposits of petroleum, found issuing from the ground in many parts of the world—in the oilfields of Venezuela and the Caucasus, in China, Saudi Arabia, but chiefly in North America. Its chief component is methane. Large industrial centres have made use of this gas since the latter part of the 19th cent., but much of this valuable fuel still goes to waste. Pipelines have been constructed to deliver the gas to where it is wanted. Britain began to ship liquid methane from the Saharan oilfield in 1964. Some of the world's largest natural gas fields have been discovered in the North Sea and are being actively exploited.

Domestic gas appliances have to be modified if the natural product is substituted for ordinary town gas because the burning characteristics are different. Oil production from the North Sea fields began in 1975 and the main single source of gas in the UK is now natural gas.

Gas Turbine. In this kind of engine mechanical movement is produced by a jet of gas impinging on a turbine wheel; used in aeroplanes, locomotives and ships. These engines are mechanically simple compared with internal combustion engines, and require less maintenance.

Gauge, a standard dimension or measurement, applied in various branches of construction. Thus the standard railway gauge is 4 ft 8½ in (143·5 cm) in the UK, USA and most European countries. Russia uses the broader gauge of 5 ft (152 cm). Narrow railway gauges of different standards are in use on very steep inclines in various countries. Other standard gauges are fixed in building and gun-boring.

Gauls were inhabitants of ancient Gaul, the country which comprised what is now France, Belgium and parts of the Netherlands, Switzerland and Germany.

Gault, a stratum of blue clay between the Lower Greensand and the Chalk. A typical section of the Gault can be seen at Folkestone.

Gauss, a unit of magnetic induction in the cgs system, named after the great German mathematician and astronomer, K. F. Gauss.

Gazelles, a group of small, graceful antelopes which live in the drier regions of Africa and Asia. They can run very fast at speeds of over 64 km/h.

GCSE, (General Certificate of Secondary Education), the school-leaving examination, introduced in 1988, which replaced the existing GCE and CSE examinations.

Geckos are nocturnal lizards. The secret of their ability to scuttle along ceilings lies in the millions of microscopic hairs on their feet which harness intermolecular forces to adhere to surfaces. They are the only lizards with a voice.

Gegenschein. A faint oval-shaped glow situated at the point in the sky directly opposite the Sun and caused by the reflection of sunlight from tiny interplanetary dust particles.

Geiger Counter, an electrical device, invented by Geiger, which can detect individual atomic particles, *e.g.*, electrons, protons, *etc.* It often consists of a tube of gas at a few cm Hg pressure, fitted with two electrodes—a cylinder and an axial wire. A high voltage is kept across the electrodes, and the passage of a charged particle through the gas releases ions which permit a momentary discharge between the electrodes.

Electronic circuits register this discharge as a "count". Geiger counters are used to detect and measure radioactivity and cosmic rays both for technical and research purposes.

Gelatine, a transparent, tasteless, organic substance obtained from animal membranes, bones, tendons, etc., by boiling in water. It is of various kinds, according to the substance used in making it. Isinglass, the purest form of it, is made from air-bladders and other membranes of fish, while the coarser kind—glue—is made from hoofs, skin, hides, *etc.* Its constituents are carbon, hydrogen, oxygen and nitrogen.

Gelatine is applied to an immense variety of purposes, from the making of food jellies to photographic materials.

Gemsbok, a large South African antelope of the open dry plains, sandy coloured with black and white markings on its face, and with long straight horns.

Generation, a time-measure reckoned at about 30 years when children are ready to replace parents; also the body of persons existing at the same time or period.

Generation, Spontaneous. *See* **Abiogenesis.**

Genes, the elementary units of heredity. They exist as highly differentiated regions arranged along the length of the chromosomes which the nuclei of cells carry. A chromosome may carry hundreds or even thousands of genes, each with its own particular structure and specific properties. The position of a particular gene on a chromosome is called its locus. The material of the gene is DNA (*q.v.*). *See* **T33 and end Section T.**

Genesis Mission, space probe launched in 2001. Its 3 year mission is to capture and return to Earth *c.* 10–20 micrograms of solar wind, the electrically-charged particles that stream away from the Sun, thereby shedding light on the origins of the solar system.

Genetic Code. The elucidation of the structure of DNA (*q.v.*) for which Crick, Wilkins and Watson were jointly awarded the 1962 Nobel Prize for medicine, revealed the code or chemical dictionary out of which messages serving as blueprints for living structures can be made. *See* **Human Genome Project** and **T62–8.**

Genetic Engineering is the name given to the introduction of human choice and design criteria into the construction and combination of genes. This refers not to breeding by selection, a traditional process, but to the biochemical alteration of the actual DNA in cells (*see* **Section T, Part IV**) so as to produce novel self-reproducing organisms. Such manipulations became possible when techniques were recently discovered for severing and rejoining DNA molecules and inserting sections into them. Many people regard this development as fraught with enormous significance.

As a result, when biologists realised they could create new lifeforms, *e.g.*, bacteria, with novel genes, they appreciated that, as well as medically beneficial strains, new virulent forms might by accident be produced and escape into the world. Ultimately, human beings may be able to design the genes of higher animals and even of humans themselves and thus consciously influ-

ence biological evolution. *See* **T62–8.**

Genetic Fingerprinting. *See* **DNA Database.**

Genetically-Modified Crops. *See* **Section Y.**

Genetics. *See* **T30(2)** and **T62–8.**

Genocide is an international crime, defined by the General Assembly of the United Nations in 1948 as "acts committed with intent to destroy, in whole or in part a national, ethnic, racial or religious group as such". The UN Convention came into force in 1951. Some recent conflicts (as in Rwanda) have seen acts of genocide, but the most notorious example is the Holocaust.

Genomes. *See* **T62–8.**

Genus, a term applied in biology to designate a group of similar species. A group of similar genera is called a family.

Geodesy, the science of calculating the configuration and extent of the earth's surface, and determining exact geographical positions and directions, with variations of gravity *etc.* Land-surveying is a branch of geodesy.

Geography, science concerned with the spatial organisation of natural features and life and man-made artifacts upon and immediately above the surface of the earth. It is increasingly concerned with the processes by which such patterns are generated and this concern is leading to both a greater degree of specialisation within the subject and the merging of its constituent parts with related disciplines of economics, sociology, political science, geology, biology and meteorology.

Geology, the science which deals with the condition and structure of the earth, and the evidence afforded of ancient forms of life. The geological strata are classified in the following categories: *Primary* or *Palaeozoic* (the oldest fossil-bearing rocks including the Cambrian, Ordovician, Silurian, Devonian, Carboniferous, Permian); *Secondary* or *Mesozoic* (Triassic, Jurassic, Cretaceous); *Tertiary* or *Cainozoic* (Eocene, Oligocene, Miocene, Pliocene, Pleistocene); *Post tertiary* (recent rocks). *See* **Section T.**

Geometrical Progression, term used to indicate a succession of numbers which increase or decrease at an equal ratio—as 3, 9, 27; or 64, 16, 4.

Geometry is the branch of mathematics which demonstrates the properties of figures, and the distances of points of space from each other by means of deductions. It is a science of reason from fundamental axioms, and was perfected by Euclid about 300 B.C. The books of Euclid contain a full elucidation of the science, though supplemented in modern times by Descartes, Newton and Carnot. In recent years non-Euclidean geometry has been developed.

Geophysics, the branches of physics which are concerned with the earth and its atmosphere. Meteorology, geomagnetism, aurora and air glow, ionosphere, solar activity, cosmic rays, glaciology, oceanography, seismology, rockets and satellites—all these are geophysical subjects.

Geothermal Energy. Some of the heavy elements within the earth's crust are radioactive and this gives rise to a temperature rise towards the centre of the earth. The practical exploitation of this geothermal energy comes about when there are hot springs or geysers. It is believed that these are caused by rainwater slowly percolating down to the hot rocks and blowing out as steam. The homes of people living in Reykjavik are heated by geothermal steam and there are a number of small power stations in various parts of the world. Although the costs in the few cases where geothermal power has actually been exploited are remarkably low, the expense of drilling, *etc.*, required when attempting to exploit the heat in the rocks where surface manifestations do not occur, is likely to limit the use of this source of power.

Geothermal Heating. The earth's interior is hot and in certain localities, often adjacent to volcanic or earthquake-prone regions, reservoirs of hot water or steam exist at accessible depths. Natural hot geysers occur in many such places and people, *e.g.*, the ancient Romans and present-day Japanese, use natural hot water for bathing, cooking and laundry. Occasionally the subterranean reserves permit large-scale power generation by drilling for hot steam and passing it into turbines to produce electricity. Pioneering work on this was done at Lardarello in Italy which can produce hundreds of megawatts. Other sites are in New Zealand, California, Japan and Iceland.

Germanium. A grey, hard, brittle chemical element, no. 32, symbol Ge, chemically related to silicon and tin. Discovered by Winkler in 1886. Its richest ore is germanite containing 6% of the metal. Coal is also a relatively rich source. Since 1948 it has assumed great importance as a semi-conducting material for making transsistors (*q.v.*). Because of this it has been so intensively studied that more is known about its physical properties than about those of any other element.

Gesta Romanorum (Latin = deeds of the Romans), a mediaeval collection of Latin stories of unknown authorship which circulated widely in Europe during the Middle Ages. First printed in the 15th cent. The stories were used by Chaucer, Shakespeare and others who used their many romantic incidents and legends.

Gestation, the carrying of young in animals during pregnancy, varies considerably in its length. In the case of an elephant, the period is 21 months; a camel, 12 months; a cow, 9 months; a cat, 8 weeks; a horse, 48 weeks; a dog, 9 weeks; and a pig, 16 weeks. Hens "sit" for 21 days; geese, 30; swans, 42; turkeys, 28; pigeons, 18.

Geysers, hot springs of volcanic origination and action, are remarkable for the fact that they throw out huge streams of boiling water instead of lava as in the case of a volcano. The most famous geysers are those of Iceland, which number over a hundred, the principal one having an opening of 21 m in diameter and discharging a column of water to a height of 61 m. There are also geysers in the Yellowstone Park (USA) and some in New Zealand.

Ghost-Moth or **Ghost Swift,** an interesting nocturnal insect (*Hepialus humuli*) common in England, possessing in the male a white collar and known for its habit of hovering with a pendulum-like action in the twilight over a particular spot where the female is concealed.

Gibbon, the name of a long-armed ape mainly inhabiting S.E. Asia. It is without tail, and possesses the power of very rapid movement among the trees of the forests.

Gin, a popular spirit distilled from malt or barley and flavoured with the juniper berry. The main varieties are the English and American, known as "Gin" or "Dry Gin", and the Dutch, referred to as "jenever" or "Hollandse jenever". In Germany and Austria it is called "Schnapps". The word "Gin" is an abbreviation of "Geneva", both being primarily derived from the French *genièvre* (juniper). The 'gin craze' in Britain refers to the period *c.* 1710–50.

Ginkgo. See **Maidenhair Tree.**

Giraffe, the tallest of existing animals, reaching a height of from 5–6 m when full grown. Its sloping back and elongated neck seem to be the natural evolution of an animal that has to feed on the branches of trees. It is a native of Africa, is of a light fawn colour marked with darker spots and has a prehensile tongue. Its remarkable eyesight can spot a predator two miles away.

Glaciers form in higher mountain ranges, and are immense consolidated masses of snow, which are gradually impelled by their force down the mountain-sides until they reach a point where the temperature causes them to melt, and they run off in streams. From Alpine glaciers five great rivers, the Rhine, the Po, the Rhône, the Inn and the Adige, have their source. The longest of the Swiss glaciers is the Gross Aletsch, which sometimes extends over 16 km.

Some of the glaciers of the Himalayas are four times as long. The Muir in Alaska is of enormous magnitude, and that of Justeldals Brae in Norway is the largest in Europe. Recent high levels of glacial retreat no doubt reflect global warming but could have disastrous consequences for irrigation, hydroelectric schemes *etc.* They could dilute the Gulf Stream and greatly affect the climate of the UK.

Gladiators were professional athletes and combatants in ancient Rome, contesting with each other or with wild beasts. At first they were drawn from the slave and prisoner classes exclusively, but so much were the successful gladiators held in esteem that men came to make a profession of athletics, and gladiatorial training schools were established. When a gladiator was vanquished without being killed in combat, it was left with the spectators to decide his fate, death being voted by holding the hands out with the thumb turned inward, and life by putting forth the hands with the thumb extended. Gladiatorial shows were the chief public displays in Rome from the 3rd to the 4th cent. A.D.

Glass is an amorphous, man-made substance, fluid when hot, solid, though fragile, when cooled. It is made of sand mixed with an alkaline flux, usually soda or potash. While hot, glass can be formed into almost any shape by moulding, blowing or, since the early 19th cent., by machine pressing. Unrefined glass normally has a greenish tinge, due to the iron content of most sands, but it is transparent or at least translucent. To make truly colourless glass is a difficult and expensive process, and such glass resembling the natural mineral, rock crystal, is given the name crystal. Glass can be tinted by the addition of various metallic oxides, cobalt producing blue, manganese mauve, *etc.* Because it is at once solid and transparent, glass is the perfect material for windows for which it has been used since Roman times. And since it can be made cheaply and is easy to clean, it has been used for containers in homes, shops and pharmacies, again since Roman days. Glass can also be made into things of beauty, by the use of coloured glass and by cutting, engraving, painting and gilding. The earliest vessels of glass so far found come from Egypt and date back to *c.* 1500 B.C. With the invention of glass-blowing in the 1st cent. A.D., the use of glass spread throughout the Roman empire. Many varieties were made, including superb art glass like the Portland vase (*q.v.*). The Arabs were great glassmakers after the 7th cent.

During the Renaissance era the Venetians created luxurious art glass, rich in colour and often manipulated into fantastic forms, Bohemia's 17th-cent. glass is wonderfully engraved with pictures and cut into glittering facets. During the 1670s in England George Ravenscroft invented a new, heavy, water-clear crystal, with an addition of lead as the magic ingredient, and English lead glass is still the basis for all modern crystals.

Glass-Snake, genus, *Ophisaurus*, of legless lizards with long fragile tails capable of re-generation when broken. Six species are known; in S.E. Europe, S.W. Asia, S.E. Asia and N. America. Attains a length of about 40 cm; main colouring, green, with black and yellow markings.

Glauconite. A green mineral, chemically a hydrated silicate of potassium and iron. Often found in marine sands (hence these rocks are known as "greensands") and sandstones.

Glaucus is a curious genus of sea slugs often called the Sea Lizard belonging to the molluscs. It is without shell and has a soft body, with horny mouth and four tentacles. It is a native of the Atlantic, and is not more than 30 cm in length.

Glee, an unaccompanied piece for three or more voices. Glee-singing was popular in England during the 18th and early 19th cent. and glee-clubs are still in existence.

Global Warming. See **Section Y.**

Globe Theatre. The original Globe Theatre was built on Bankside, London in 1599 and pulled down in 1644. Its foundations were excavated in 1989. Sam Wanamaker (1919–93), the actor, and Theo Crosby (1925–94), the architect had already conceived and designed a near-replica, which was built near the site of the Elizabethan theatre using traditional materials.

Globigerina, an oceanic unicellular animalcule with a perforated shell, and occurring in certain parts of the Atlantic in such vast numbers as to form a bed of chalk ooze with their empty shells.

Glockenspiel, an instrument composed of metal bars each of which is tuned to a note. The bars are struck by hand-hammers and give forth chiming sounds.

Glow-worm, a beetle, possessing the power (much stronger in the female than the male) of emitting phosphorescent light from the hind end of the body. The female is wingless.

Glucinium. See **Beryllium.**

Glucose, Dextrose or **Grape Sugar** is a carbohydrate (*q.v.*). It is produced by hydrolysis from cane sugar, dextrine, starch, cellulose, *etc.*, by the action of reagents. It also occurs in many plants, fruits and honey. For brewing purposes glucose is prepared by the conversion of starch by sulphuric acid. Malt also converts starch into glucose.

Glutton *or* **Wolverine,** the biggest animal of the weasel family, inhabits the northernmost parts of Europe and America. In build it resembles the bear, and is rather larger than a badger. Its fur is of a brown-black hue, but coarse.

Glycerine *or* **Glycerol,** occurs in natural fats combined with fatty acids, and is obtained by decomposing those substances with alkalis or by superheated steam. It is colourless and oily and sweet, and is put to many uses, being widely utilised for medicaments, for lubricating purposes, and in the manufacture of nitro-glycerine.

Glycols. Organic compounds containing two alcohol groups. Ethylene glycol is the most widely known example; it is used as an antifreeze in motor-car radiators on account of its property of greatly reducing the freezing point of water. Also used in the manufacture of "Terylene". *See* **Esters.**

Glyptodon, an extinct species of gigantic armadillo, fossil remains of which have been discovered in S. America. It was some 2·7 m long, carried a huge tortoise-like shell and had fluted teeth.

Gneiss, a metamorphic rock usually containing quartz, felspar and mica. It is banded, the light-coloured minerals being concentrated apart from the dark minerals.

Gnu *or* **Wildebeest,** a large antelope from Africa south of the Sahara, distinguished by its excessively short thick neck and large head with a pronounced roman nose. There are two species; the white-tailed gnu is almost extinct, the brindled gnu is still common and migrates in large herds.

Goat-Moth (*Cossus cossus*), a large moth of the *Cossidae* family, common in Britain, evilsmelling and very destructive in the larval stage to trees of the poplar and willow genus, into the wood of which the caterpillar bores during its three years' period of development.

Goats are horned ruminant quadrupeds, indigenous to the Eastern Hemisphere, but now domesticated in all parts of the world. Though related to the sheep, they are a much hardier and more active animal. The male has a tuft of hair under the chin. Many species, including those of Cashmere and Angora, are valuable for their hair, which is used for fine textile fabrics.

Goat milk is nutritive, and goat-skins are in demand for leather for gloves, shoes, *etc.* Recent research has shown that the goat pre-dates any other animal as the first to be domesticated by humans.

Gog and **Magog,** two legendary City of London giants who were brought captive to London and made to serve as prisoners at the Palace of Brute, which stood on the site of Guildhall. Effigies of the giants have stood in Guildhall since the time of Henry V. They were destroyed in the Great Fire of 1666, replaced in 1672 and used to be carried through the streets of London in the Lord Mayor's Show. The present figures replaced those carved in 1708 by Richard Saunders, which were destroyed in an air raid during the second world war. In the Bible, Ezekiel also makes reference to Gog and Magog.

Gold. Metallic element, no. 79, symbol Au (Latin *Aurum*) related to silver and copper, the coinage metals. The greatest amount of gold is obtained by treating gold-bearing quartz by the cyanide process. The gold is dissolved out by cyanide solution, which is then run into long boxes filled with zinc shavings when the gold is precipitated as a black slime. This is melted with an oxidising agent to remove the zinc. South Africa is the world's largest gold producer. India is the biggest market for gold jewellery.

Gold-Beaters' Skin is the outside membrane of the large intestine of the ox, specially prepared and used by gold-beaters for placing between the leaves of gold while they beat them. Thin membrane is of great tenacity, and gets beaten to such extreme thinness that it is used to put on cuts and bruises.

Gold Standard. Under the gold-standard system which was widely prevalent up to 1941, each gold-standard country fixed the value of its

currency in terms of a weight of gold of a certain fineness and was, broadly speaking, ready to exchange its currency freely for gold, which could then be exported without restriction. This involved keeping a gold reserve big enough to meet all likely demands and also to serve as a backing for the issue of notes. The gold standard had to be given up during the first world war; and though it was in substance restored in Great Britain in 1925 (when Churchill was Chancellor), the restoration was never complete. Sterling had to be devalued in the financial crisis of 1931 (which caused the fall of the Labour Government) and Great Britain was forced off the gold standard. *See also* **Section F.**

Golden Eagle. *See* **Eagle.**

Goldeneye, a species of wild duck, widely distributed over Arctic regions. It is a passagemigrant and winter-visitor to the UK. Has nested in Cheshire. Distinguished by a large white spot in front of each eye on a dark ground.

Golden Number, the number of any year in the metonic cycle of 19 years, deriving its name from the fact that in the old calendars it was always printed in gold. It is found by adding 1 to the number of the year A.D. and dividing by 19, the remainder being the Golden Number; or, if no remainder, the Golden Number is 19.

Goldfish, or *Carassius auratus* were introduced to Britain in the 18th century. Numbering 125 breeds, their sense of smell is even better than a bloodhound. First recorded in China, A.D. 400.

Goldsmiths Company, one of the richest London City Companies; the official assayers of gold and silver, invested with the power of "hallmarking" the quality of objects made from these metals. First charter granted in 1327.

Gondola, the old regulation black boats so common on the canals of Venice, propelled by a gondolier with one oar who stands at the stern.

Gondwana, the name of the ancient southern land mass linking Antarctica, Australia, India *etc.*

Gonfalon, the pennon affixed to a lance, spear or standard, consisting usually of two or three streamers and made to turn like a weather-cock.

Gonzo Journalism, a highly subjective and personal style of writing in which the writer is an essential part of the story. The leading exponent was Hunter S. Thompson.

Gophers. Rodent mammals. The pocket gophers are stout-bodied burrowers common in the USA. The slender burrowing gophers, also called "ground squirrels", occur in central and western USA. The sisel or suslik is a related European species. They are a great pest.

Gorilla, the largest of the anthropoid apes, found in the forests of Equatorial Africa, and at maturity standing from 1·2–1·5 m high. Mountain gorillas are one of the most endangered species in the world. Now (2006) less than 700 survive in the Congo, Rwanda and Uganda.

Goshawk (*Accipiter gentilis*), a diurnal bird of prey, fearless and extremely agile; loves wooded country and is very destructive of poultry and game-birds. It resembles the peregrine falcon in appearance, but has shorter, rounded wings. This bird was a great favourite of falconers in mediaeval times. A few have now been reintroduced from Scandinavia but are believed to be causing decline to the kestrel.

Goths. A Teutonic people who originally came from southern Sweden (Gotland) and by the 3rd cent. were settled in the region north of the Black Sea. They began to encroach on the Roman Empire and early in the 4th cent. split into two divisions: the "wise" Goths or Visigoths between the Danube and the Dniester (referred to as the West Goths), and the "bright" Goths or Ostrogoths in southern Russia on the Dnieper (referred to as East Goths).

The Ostrogoths were later conquered by the Huns *c.* 370, while the Visigoths under Alaric devastated Greece and sacked Rome in 410. Eventually the Visigoths spread to France and Spain and their last king Roderick fell in battle against the Moors in 711. The Ostrogoths regained their independence on the death of Attila in 453 and under king Theodoric the Great conquered Italy in 493. They lost their identity after Justinian regained Italy, 525–552.

Gourd Family *or* **Cucurbitaceae.** This family of

about 650 species of flowering plants includes the gourds, pumpkins, cantaloupes, cucumber, gherkin, water-melon and squashes. Most abundant in the tropics, the cucurbits are mainly climbing annuals with very rapid growth. The bathroom loofah is the skeleton of one cucurbit fruit, *Luffa cylindrica*. The squirting cucumber is another member of the family.

Governor. A device attached to an engine, turbine, compressor, *etc.*, which automatically controls the engine's speed in accordance with power demand. Most governors depend upon the centrifugal action of two or more balls which are thrown outwards as their speed of rotation increases and actuate a throttle valve or cut off. The centrifugal governor was invented by Thomas Mead, patented by him in 1787. Watt adapted it to the steam engine.

Grail, Legend of the Holy, a tale of Celtic origin which became part of Arthurian legend. According to the Christian version the grail was the cup which Christ used at the Last Supper, brought to England by St. Joseph of Arimathea.

Grand Prix, the "French Derby" was established by Napoleon III, in 1863. It is the chief French race and is for three-year-olds. The term is now also widely used in motor racing.

Granite is a coarsely crystalline igneous rock consisting of quartz and alkali felspars plus mica or hornblende. It is a much used ornamental and building stone; it forms the high ground of Dartmoor and Bodmin Moor.

Graphite *or* **Plumbago,** commonly called blacklead, is a form of carbon occurring in foliated masses in marble, schist, *etc.* It is soft, will make black marks on paper or other plain surfaces, and is mainly used for lead pencils. It is also a valuable lubricant. Pure graphite has found a new use with the construction of atomic piles. Important deposits occur in Siberia, Sri Lanka, Malagasy, Canada and USA.

Graphology, the science which interprets and analyses the way letters are formed and shaped.

Graptolites, fossil animals confined to Cambrian, Ordovician and Silurian strata.

Grasshopper. There are many species of these leaping insects which are related to the locusts and crickets. Most are vegetarians; some eat flies and caterpillars also. The chirping sound they make is made by scraping the hind legs against the wings; in some species a noise is produced by rubbing the wings together.

Gravitation. One of the four types of force known to physics. The others are electromagnetic, the weak nuclear and the strong nuclear forces. Gravitational forces are an attraction that one piece of matter has for another; they dominate astronomical phenomena, but inside the atom they are negligible compared with the other types of force. Einstein's General Theory of Relativity is the only theory which attempts to interpret gravitational forces in terms of more fundamental concepts. Scientists have now proved that gravity does indeed travel at the speed of light.

Graylag, the ordinary wild grey goose of Europe, the species from which domestic geese are derived; frequents fens and marshes; breeds in Iceland, Scandinavia and Scotland; distinguished by pinkish legs and feet and lack of black markings on bill.

Great Auk. *See under* **Auks.**

Great Fire of London. *See* **Fire of London, A42.**

Great Wall of China, the enormous wall (1,500 miles in length) built to protect China's northern frontier. Completed 204 B.C.

Grebe, a diving bird of beautiful plumage found over a great part of the world on lakes and oceans. The two species familiar in Great Britain are the Dabchick or Little Grebe and the large and handsome Great Crested Grebe, which has a feathery tuft, lost in the autumn, on each side of the head. Grebes have remarkable courtship displays. The breast feathers are of a downy softness and silver lustre, for which they were formerly much hunted.

Greek Alphabet. This is made up as follows:

A	α	alpha	N	ν	nu
B	β	beta	Ξ	ξ	xi
Γ	γ	gamma	O	ο	omicron
Δ	δ	delta	Π	π	pi
E	ε	epsilon	P	ρ	rho
Z	ζ	zeta	Σ	σ	sigma
H	η	eta	T	τ	tau
Θ	θ	theta	Y	υ	upsilon
I	ι	iota	Φ	φ	phi
K	κ	kappa	X	χ	chi
Λ	λ	lambda	Ψ	ψ	psi
M	μ	mu	Ω	ω	omega

Greek Fire, a combustible supposed to have been composed of sulphur, nitre, naphtha and asphalt, used with destructive effect by the Greeks of the Eastern Empire in their wars.

Greek Mysteries. *See* **Mysteries, Greek.**

Green Plover. *See* **Lapwing.**

Greenwich Mean Time. The first Nautical Almanac, for the use of navigators and astronomers, was published by the Astronomer Royal in 1767. It was based on the meridian at Greenwich, with longitude measured east and west of 0°. A master clock, which still exists, was built at Greenwich Observatory in 1852 to control the railway station clocks and Greenwich Mean Time, or Railway Time as it was sometimes called, prevailed. In 1884 Greenwich was chosen as the prime meridian of the world and GMT became known as Universal Time. The time-keeping role is now done by the International Bureau of Weights and Measures. GMT has become CUT (Coordinated Universal Time). Recently, the Daylight Extra Now group has campaigned to abolish GMT and have an extra hour of daylight in the evening. *See also* **British Standard Time** and **T60.**

Gregorian Calendar. *See* **Calendar.**

Gresham's Law states that if money, *i.e.*, money with the higher intrinsic value, and bad money are in circulation together, the bad money will tend to drive out the good money from circulation. For instance, the good money is more likely to be melted down or demanded in payment by foreign creditors.

Gretna Green, a celebrated village in Annandale and Eskdale, just over the border from England, where runaway marriages were performed from 1754 to 1856, though only completely stopped during present century.

Griffin, in ancient mythology, a winged creature with an eagle's head and the body of a lion, found in ancient sculptures of Persia and Assyria. Its origin is traced to the Hittites.

Grilse, a young salmon that has only been once to the sea.

Grimm's Law, formulated by Jacob Grimm, an eminent German philologist, lays down a principle of consonantal change in the Germanic languages. For instance, Lat. *pater,* Eng. *father,* Ger. *Vater;* Lat. *frater,* Eng. *brother,* Ger. *Bruder;* Lat. *decem,* Eng. *ten,* Ger. *zehn.*

Grogram (French = *gros grain*), a kind of rough fabric made of wool and some other fibre, such as silk, mohair or cotton.

Grotto, a natural or artificial cave. Among the most famous are the blue grotto of Capri and the grotto of Antiparos (Cyclades, Aegean).

Ground Wave, that part of the energy emitted by a radio transmitter which travels along the ground; as opposed to the sky wave which is reflected back to earth by the ionosphere.

With the lower radio-frequencies, the ground wave can be picked up over several thousand miles; in the broadcasting band, over a hundred or so miles; it is virtually useless at high frequencies.

Groundnut. *See* **Peanut.**

Grouse, game bird of the northern latitudes where some 20 species occur. They are stout, compact, ground-dwelling birds, protectively plumaged (the willow grouse turns white in winter), the male usually being larger and more brightly coloured than the female. The red grouse of the British moorlands has been introduced into Belgium and Germany. Of the same family are the blackcock, ptarmigan, capercaillie, American prairie-hen and the partridge. Grouse shooting begins in Britain on 12 Aug. The black grouse in Britain is in rapid decline.

Guanaco, a large species of llama, common to South America. Utilised as a beast of burden.

Guano, the excrement of sea-birds, found in large quantities on the rocky islands of the western coasts of South America and Nauru Is. It forms a useful fertilising agent, being rich in phosphate and ammonia, and first came into use in 1841, since which time Peruvian guano has been a recognised article of commerce. Beds of guano from 15–18 m in thickness are not uncommon. Fish guano and bat guano from caves in South America and the Bahamas are also used as fertilisers.

Gudgeon, a small fresh-water fish of the carp family with 2 small barbels on the upper lip.

Guildhall, the place of assembly of the members of a guild, and at one time, when guilds were in full strength, was practically the Town Hall. The London Guildhall is today the hall of meeting for the City of London Corporation.

Guilds for the fostering and protection of various trades have existed in England since Anglo- Saxon times and from the 12th to the 16th cent. exercised great influence and enjoyed many privileges. There were trades' guilds and craftsmen's guilds, and in all large cities and towns there was a guild hall. Their successes in the Middle Ages led to many mono-polistic abuses, and in the end it became neces-sary to free the country from their restrictive power. The City Guilds (Livery Companies of the City of London) derive their name from the 14th cent. dress assumed by their members.

Guillemot, a genus of sea-birds of the auk family, common in Northern Europe, two species—the Common Guillemot and the Black Guillemot—being natives of our own sea coasts, nesting on the cliffs. Brünnich's Guillemot, an Arctic species, is a rare straggler in Britain.

Guillotine, the famous French method of execution during the French Revolution. Devised by Joseph Guillotin (1738–1814). Last used in France in 1977.

Guinea, an English gold coin of the value of twenty-one shillings, current from 1663–1817, and deriving its name from the first guinea coin-age having been struck from gold obtained on the coast of Guinea.

Guinea-Pig, a rodent of the cavy family about 25 cm in length and with a tail so short that it does not project outside the body. It makes an excellent pet, though easily frightened. Its ancestors were species of the wild cavy of S. America domesticated by the Incas of Peru.

Gules, a heraldic term, denoting a rose of red tincture, indicated by vertical lines drawn or engraved without colour.

Gulf Stream is confined entirely to the western side of the N. Atlantic and is the warm-water current flowing through the Straits of Florida from the Gulf of Mexico parallel to the American coast up as far as Cape Hatteras. From there it continues north-eastwards as a slower, broader, cooler (yet even so, relatively warm) drift of water, merging with the North Atlantic Drift and losing its identity about 40° N. Lat., 60° W. Long. It is a common error to attribute the warmth of the British Isles and Western Europe generally to the Gulf Stream but this has no influence whatever except in so far as it feeds the North Atlantic Drift. Both the Gulf Stream and the North Atlantic Drift owe their movement to the direction of the prevailing winds, and it is the south-westerly airstream coming from warmer regions and passing over the surface waters of the Atlantic Drift that brings the warmth inland to influence the climate of Western Europe.

Gull. An extremely well-known, long-winged sea-bird with rather short legs and webbed feet. In almost all adults the body and tail are white whilst the back and most of the wings are grey or black. In the majority of cases the plumage of juveniles is partly or entirely dusky. Gulls are omnivorous, and are very useful as scavengers. They follow ships and quickly seize upon any refuse which may be thrown overboard. There are 44 species, which vary in size from moderately small to large. With certain exceptions, such as the Kittiwake in the North Atlantic, they are not found very far from land.

They are sociable and mostly breed in colonies on cliff-ledges, on islands, beaches and sandhills and among vegetation in swamps, sometimes a long way from the sea. The nest is usually substantial, and the eggs generally number from two to three. Of the 29 species breeding in the northern hemisphere, 14 occur in the British Isles. The pure white Ivory Gull is the most northerly of birds. Sabine's and the Swallow-tailed Gull have forked tails. Ross's Gull has

a black ring round the neck and one species, Franklin's Gull, migrates from the North, where it breeds, to pass the winter in the Southern hemisphere.

Gums are glutinous compounds obtained from vegetable sources, soluble in cold or hot water, but not in alcohol. There are innumerable varieties. Gum Arabic is exuded from a species of acacia grown in Senegal, the Sudan, Arabia, India etc., and is a valuable commercial product, used in dyeing, ink-making, as a mucilage, and in medicine. Indiarubber is an elastic gum. Gums are also made from starch, potatoes, wheat, etc., from seeds, bark, roots and weeds. Many so-called gums are resins.

Gun-Cotton, a powerful explosive manufactured by subjecting a prepared cotton to the pro-longed action of a mixture of three parts sul-phuric acid and one part of nitric acid. It burns without explosion on ignition, but by percussion explodes with a force five times greater than gunpowder does.

Gunpowder, also called "black powder", the oldest of explosive mixtures, consists of salt-petre, sulphur and charcoal, intimately mixed.

Gunpowder Plot. See A42.

Gurnard, a sea-fish, with large, bony head and diminutive body, of which there are some forty species. They are plentiful in British waters.

Gymnasium, originally the name given in ancient Greece to the public places where Greek youth used to exercise and receive instruction. Plato, Aristotle and other great teachers lec-tured there. The Greek institution was never very popular with the Romans, and it was not until the 18th and 19th cent. that the cult of combining physical with intellectual activity again found a place in educational systems. In Germany the name was applied to the classical grammar school.

Gypsies, a nomadic race, believed to be of Indian origin; their language, Romany, is related to the languages of N.W. India. The Roma are spread over many parts of the world, but are most common in Europe where they appeared towards the end of the Middle Ages. The English name *gypsy* comes from the Spanish *gitano* = Egyptian; other European names are *Zigeuner* (Ger.), *zingaro* (It.), *fzigany* (Magyar), all resembling the Persian *singar* = a saddler. Their history has been one of persecution. Hitler treated them like the Jews.

In Britain since 1945 they have been kept increasingly on the move, but in 1968 Parliament passed a Bill to make the provision of sites a duty of local authorities. However, the 1994 Criminal Justice and Public Order Act made it much easier to move on unwelcome gypsies. Economic pres-sure has largely removed their traditional crafts of tinkering, basket-making and peg-making. The majority now deal in scrap-iron. Today (2006) there are over 12 million European Gypsies and in some parts (such as Bulgaria and the Czech Republic) they are again subject to systematic ill-treatment. The first Gypsy member of the European Parliament was elected in 2004.

Gypsum, a whitish mineral consisting of hydrated sulphate of calcium. The finest gypsum is alabaster. When heated gypsum is converted into the powder called Plaster of Paris; the water it loses can be taken up when the plaster is wetted, and the reconversion of Plaster of Paris into gypsum accounts for the way in which the former sets hard. The name "Plaster of Paris" came from the location of important gypsum quarries in the Montmartre district of Paris. It was found after the flood disasters of January 1953 that gypsum could undo the effect of sea-water. By spreading it for the rain to wash into the soil, thousands of acres of farmland in Holland and Britain were made productive again.

Gyroscope is a symmetrical rapidly rotating ob-ject, typically wheel-like, which because of its mass and rotation possesses a lot of the dynam-ical property known as angular momentum. Basic dynamical laws tell us that angular momentum is conserved and a consequence of this is that the axis of rotation tends to stay pointing in the same direction. Disturbing in-fluences make a gyroscope's motion complicated but the general effect of the presence of a gyro-scope attached to any body is to help to stabilise the body's motion. This is made use of in reducing the rocking of ships and in compasses and control systems in aircraft, torpedoes *etc.*

H

Habeas Corpus, the name given to a writ ordering the body of a person under restraint or imprisonment to be brought into court for full inquiry into the legality of the restraint to be made.

The first Habeas Corpus Act was passed in 1679, though nominally such a right had existed from Magna Carta, but some of the more despotic kings had disregarded it. In times of public peril the privilege of *habeas corpus* is sometimes temporarily suspended.

Haber–Ostveldt Process, the important industrial process for synthesising ammonia from atmospheric nitrogen. Nitrogen and hydrogen are combined at high pressure (*c.* 350 atmospheres) and moderately high temperature (500°C) using a catalyst (made largely of iron). A yield of 30 % is obtained. The majority of the world's ammonia is produced in this way or from methods derived from it.

Habsburg (Hapsburg). *See* **A43.**

Haddock, one of the best-known fishes abounding in northern seas and averaging about 1·8 kg in weight. Related to the cod. Largely used for curing, and sold as "finnan haddies". Its spawning grounds are off Norway, Iceland and the Faroe Islands.

Hade of veins, a mining term indicating the particular inclination that any vein, seam or strata may have from the perpendicular; thus, in Weardale the veins mainly "hade" to the north.

Hadrian's Wall. *See* **Roman Walls.**

Haematite, ferric oxide, one of the principal iron ores, containing about 70 % of the metal. It is usually found in kidney-shaped masses, and is specular, red or brown, in thin fragments but greyish in bulk.

Haemocyanin, the respiratory pigment of crustaceans and molluscs. It functions like haemoglobin, from which it differs in containing copper instead of iron and being blue when oxidised instead of red.

Haemoglobin, the pigment containing iron which gives red blood corpuscles their colour. It is a respiratory pigment, having the property of picking up oxygen when the blood passes through the lungs to produce the compound known as oxyhaemoglobin. In other parts of the body the oxyhaemoglobin breaks down, liberating oxygen, which is used in the oxidation process (respiration) that the body tissues carry on.

Hafiz, a title conferred upon any Muslim who has committed the whole of the Koran to memory.

Hafnium, a metallic element, no. 72, symbol Hf, discovered by Coster and Hevesy in 1922 and important in the atomic-energy field. It occurs in most zirconium minerals to the extent of *c.* 5 %.

Hagiology, a branch of literature that is wholly given up to the history of the saints, and the setting out of their stories and legends.

Hail, hard, roughly spherical balls of ice, consisting of white cores covered by layers of both transparent and opaque ice, frequently falling during thunderstorms. They usually do not exceed 2·5 cm in size, but hailstones as large as tennis balls have been observed. The general theory of a hailstone is that near the top of a cumulonimbus cloud a raindrop becomes frozen, grows in size by condensation and through collisions with snow particles, and eventually becomes so weighty as to overcome the ascending air currents in the cloud. Falling, it first encounters supercooled water drops, immediately freezing on it, increasing the white core, and then at lower levels ordinary water drops, freezing more slowly, producing a layer of clear ice.

Before the hailstone arrives at the ground gusts and lulls may transport it several times up and down both regions, adding alternate coatings of soft white and hard clear ice.

Halcyon, a term associated in olden times with the kingfisher and days of soothing calm, "halcyon days" being a frequently used expression. The legend was that the kingfisher laid its eggs on the surface of the sea at the time of the winter solstice when the sea was unruffled. (Halcyon is the Greek for kingfisher.)

Halibut, one of the largest of the flat fishes, averaging when full grown from 1·2–1·8 m in length, and highly esteemed for the table. Specimens of still larger size occasionally occur. It is plentifully distributed. Its two eyes are on the right side of the head.

Hallmark. A mark or group of marks, impressed by an assay office on gold or silver articles (and on platinum since 1974) guaranteeing the standard of fineness of the precious metal used in them. These marks, which have been applied to silver made in London since the beginning of the 14th cent. and perhaps earlier, make it possible to establish the year and place of assay and also the name of the maker. English pieces of silver usually have not less than four marks, viz., (1) town mark; (2) maker's mark; (3) date letter; (4) sterling mark.

The town mark is rarely changed; in London a crowned leopard's head was used from the earliest days until 1820 with only minor modifications, except for the period 1697–1720 when a lion's head erased was substituted; since 1820 the crown has been omitted.

Until the late 17th cent. a symbol was often used as a maker's mark, from 1696–1720 the first two letters of the maker's surname, and subsequently the maker's initials. Owing to the destruction of the earlier mark plates at Goldsmiths' Hall no maker's name prior to the late 17th cent. can be identified with certainty.

The London date letter is changed at the end of May each year, so each letter covers seven months of one year and five months of the following. The London date cycle has usually consisted of twenty letters: the alphabet of each cycle is of different style, and the letters are enclosed in shields of different shape.

The sterling mark, the lion passant, was introduced in 1544 and continued in use until 1697, when the higher Britannia standard was introduced in order to discourage the practice current amongst goldsmiths of melting down coin of the realm to make plate. The leopard's head crowned and the lion passant were then replaced by a figure of Britannia and a lion's head erased. Though the regulation imposing a higher standard was withdrawn in 1720, a small amount of Britannia standard silver continued to be made and still is made.

From 1784 until 1890 a plate tax was levied on all silver assayed in Great Britain and an additional duty mark, the sovereign's head, was used during this period. A Jubilee mark bearing the head of George V and of Queen Mary was used between the years 1933 and 1935, and in 1953 a coronation mark with the head of Queen Elizabeth was introduced. A special Millennium hallmark was available in 1999 and 2000.

Under the Hallmarking Act 1973 the hallmarking of platinum is now compulsory; the hallmark symbol is an orb surmounted by a cross and encompassed by a pentagon. There are now assay offices in London, Birmingham, Sheffield and Edinburgh.

Halloween (31 October), the eve of All Saints' Day, a time associated, especially in Scotland, with certain old traditions. It is the night when young men and women are supposed, by observing certain rites, to have their future wives and husbands disclosed to them.

Halo, a luminous circle usually of 22° radius, surrounding sun or moon, produced by the refraction and reflection of light by ice crystals of high cirrus cloud. It is a very common occurrence, in the British Isles almost one day in three. The inner side is red and the outer a whitish-yellow colour. "Mock suns," *i.e.*, patches of light at the same elevation as the sun are much rarer occurrences, sometimes being of great beauty and brilliance. Halo is the Greek for threshing-floor. *See* **Corona.**

Halogens, the group name for the five non-metallic elements fluorine, chlorine, bromine, iodine and astatine. The term "halogen" means "salt-producer".

Halteres, the modified hind-wings of the two-winged flies or *Diptera* (*e.g.*, the house-fly). The equilibrium in flight of these insects depends on the halteres, which are commonly called "balancers".

Hand, a measure of 4 in (10 cm), the average size of the palm; used in reckoning height of horses.

Handfasting, an informal marriage custom once prevalent in Scotland, whereby a man and woman bound themselves to cohabit for a year and a day, and at the end of that period either confirmed their contract by a regular marriage or separated.

Hanoverians. See **A43.**

Hansard, the title given to the official reports of Parliamentary debates, so named after Luke Hansard who in 1774 became partner in a firm of printers to the House of Commons. His son T. C. Hansard was first the printer and then the publisher of an unofficial series of parliamentary debates inaugurated by William Cobbett in 1803. In 1909 production was taken over by H.M. Stationery Office and today's volumes contain full, substantially verbatim, reports of what is said in both Houses of Parliament.

Hara-kiri, the custom of suicide, as formerly practised in Japan, when in disgrace.

Hare, a rabbit-like animal with longer ears and legs. There are many kinds of hare distributed over the northern hemisphere and in Africa south to the Cape. They do not burrow as do rabbits but rely on camouflage, speed and mobility for safety. Sightings of hares across Britain have declined sharply since the 1960s. Hare-coursing was banned in February 2005. See **Game.**

Harleian MSS. comprise some thousands of volumes of MSS. and documents, collected by the first Earl of Oxford (1661–1724) and his son Edward. After the death of the latter, his widow handed the MSS. over to the nation for £10,000, and they are deposited in the British Museum.

Harlequin, the buffoon of ancient Italian comedy. As adapted to the British stage, however, harlequin is a pantomime character only, in love with Columbine, appearing in parti-coloured garments and carrying a wand, by which he exercises a magic influence in thwarting the fantastic tricks of the clown and pantaloon.

Harmattan, a dry wind which may blow between January and May across the Sahara to the Gulf of Guinea. Although affording relief from the tropical heat, vegetation withers because of its extreme dryness and much irritation is caused by the clouds of fine dust which it carries.

Harmonic Motion, regular periodic motion of the kind exemplified by a ball bobbing up and down at the end of a spring, and by the piston in a steam engine. It may be simple (simple harmonic motion) or composed of two or more simple harmonic motions. In simple harmonic motion the acceleration is proportional to the distance of the moving body from its original rest position.

Harp-seal, the ordinary Greenland seal, with a dark harp-shaped marking on its back, hence its name. It abounds in Newfoundland waters and further northward towards the Arctic.

Harpy Eagle, a large bird of prey named from the winged monsters of Greek mythology, inhabiting the forest regions of Central and South America. There are eight species, one with handsome grey plumage and large crest which attacks and kills animals much larger than itself, and was called by the Aztecs "winged wolf".

Harrier, a bird of prey of the falcon family; of the various species distributed over the world, three breed in Britain: the moorland hen harrier, the Marsh harrier and Montagu's harrier. They are large birds with long tails, long legs, long wings and gliding flight. They nest on the ground and eat small mammals, frogs, lizards and small birds.

Hartebeest, common African antelope of a grey-brown colour, with ringed and knotted horns bending backward and tapering to sharp points; gregarious, of large size. There are several species.

Harvest Bug, a very small insect, of a dark red colour, which appears in large numbers in the fields in autumn, and is peculiarly irritating to animals and man by the tenacity with which it attaches itself to the skin and burrows underneath. Probably the larvae of spinning mites (Trombidoids). In the USA they are called "chiggers".

Harvest Moon, the full moon that occurs nearest to the autumn equinox, in September. It rises for several nights running about the same time, and yields an unusually brilliant series of moonlight nights.

Harvestmen are, like spiders, members of the arachnid class but belong to the distinctly different order of Phalangida. They are common in the countryside in autumn and have small oval bodies and eight long slender legs which besides being mere organs of locomotion also act as sense organs. Known as "daddy longlegs" in America and Britain.

Hashish, an Arabic word for the narcotic substance prepared from the hemp plant (*Cannabis sativa*). It is known by a variety of names, *e.g.*, bhang in India and marijuana in America.

Hatchment, in heraldry, is a square board, in vertical diagonal position, placed outside a house or on the tomb at the death of a member of a family and so arranged that it indicates the sex and condition of the deceased.

Hawaiian Goose. See **Néné.**

Hawfinch, a well-known European bird of the finch family, having a variegated plumage, a sturdy bill and black-and-white tail. In England it is found in the Midland and Eastern counties, and locally in Scotland. Its numbers are now in sharp decline.

Hawk. This name is applied to almost any diurnal bird of prey other than eagle, falcon or vulture, but in its strict sense applies only to the *Accipiter* genus—the small Sparrow Hawk and the larger Goshawk, round-winged, long-tailed birds with barred under-parts. They prey upon small birds captured in flight and small mammals.

Hawk-moths, large species of moths, thick of body and strong of wing, which fly with rapid swooping motion, hence the name. There are numerous handsome species in Britain.

Heat, after prolonged controversy over whether or not heat is a "substance" (formerly called "caloric"), it was established in the 19th cent. that heat is a form of energy; it is in fact the combined kinetic and potential energy of the atoms of which a body is composed. Heat can be turned into other forms of energy, *e.g.*, a red hot body loses heat by radiating it in the form of electromagnetic waves ("radiant heat"—chiefly infra-red rays). Heat may also be transferred from one place to another by conduction and, in fluids, by convection. All three processes occur when a glowing fire heats a room.

A unit quantity of heat is the calorie, which is the amount of heat sufficient to raise the temperature of 1 g of water by 1°C. In general, adding heat to a body raises its temperature. The number of calories required per gram of material to raise the temperature 1°C is called the *specific heat* of the material. However, adding heat may not raise the temperature—but may instead cause a change of state, *e.g.*, from solid to liquid (melting) or liquid to gas (evaporation). The amount of heat required to melt 1 gram of a solid is called the latent heat of melting. Similarly, there is a latent heat of evaporation. Strictly speaking, the specific and latent heats of a substance depend on how much its pressure and volume are allowed to vary during the measurements. Water has a high specific heat, and this makes the oceans a vast heat reservoir, a factor of great meteorological significance. The science of heat is called thermodynamics.

Heat Pump, essentially a refrigerator working in reverse, *i.e.*, a device which warms up one place, say, a house by releasing into it heat transferred from another place, say, the air or earth outside the house. The idea is attributed to Lord Kelvin (1852) and later Haldane used a heat pump to heat his house in Scotland. In Summer, a house could be cooled by operating the device in reverse. As in a domestic refrigerator, the heat is transferred by a suitable fluid whose circulation has to be driven by an external supply of energy, *e.g.*, by running a mechanical compressor. With good design and favourable conditions, the energy required to run the heat pump is considerably less than would be required to produce the same warming effect directly. Since the 1930s heat pumps have been produced commercially for domestic and industrial use but, as always, careful consideration is needed to decide whether in a particular application they are cheaper to run than alternative methods of heating.

Heath, flowering plants of the *Ericaceae* family. Heaths are widely distributed over uncultivated spaces of Europe and Africa. In Britain they are represented by heather (of which there are several species) and ling (*Calluna vulgaris*), which cover thousands of acres of moorland. Some of the African or Cape heaths are very beautiful and much prized by florists. One species of heath (*Erica urbrum*) which grows in S. Europe and N. Africa has close-grained woody rootstock used for making briar pipes.

In N. Europe acid heathlands, dominated by heather and ling, form one of the most widespread vegetation areas created by man through the widespread destruction of forests, grazing *etc*.

Heathrow Airport, originally called London Airport (Heathrow) and named after a village where Terminal 3 now stands. It opened on 1 January 1946. The airport handles more than 90 airlines from 85 countries and offers direct flights to more than 170 destinations. In 2005 the airport handled 61,000,000 international passengers.

Terminal 5 was finally given approval in 2001 after a 525-day public enquiry costing £80 million (the UK's longest-ever planning inquiry). It will not open before 2008 and will cost £2·5 billion. It is currently Europe's largest construction project.

Restrictions on new night-time flights have failed to appease local residents. A new terminal, dubbed Heathrow East, is planned to open in 2012. Estimates suggest Heathrow will handle 90 million passengers a year by 2008 (when Terminal 2 closes as Terminal 5 opens).

Hegira, an Arab term signifying departure or flight, used in reference to Mohammed's departure from Mecca, A.D. 622, from which date the Muslim era is reckoned.

Helicopter, heavier-than-air aircraft which obtains its lift from blades rotating above the fuselage in windmill-fashion. The first successful helicopters were the Focke-Wulf 61, a German machine (1936), and the VS-300, designed by Igor Sikorsky, flown in 1937. Helicopters can hover, and rise and descend vertically, in addition to being capable of horizontal flight.

Heliosphere, the huge region surrounding the Sun that is permeated by the solar wind. The heliosphere is bounded by the heliopause, which is estimated to be 9,300 million miles from the Sun (see Voyagers 1 and 2.

Heliotrope, a favourite sweet-scented flowering plant, common in tropical and sub-tropical countries; the Peruvian heliotrope is the "cherry pie" of our summer garden borders.

Helium, a gaseous element, no. 2, symbol He, first discovered by means of the spectroscope in the sun's atmosphere. This discovery, made in 1868 by the astronomer Sir Norman Lockyer, was followed in 1895 by Sir William Ramsay's proof that the element existed on earth. He found it in the uranium ore, clevite. Later it was established that helium is formed by the radioactive decay of many elements which emit α-particles (nuclei of helium atoms) and is contained in all radioactive minerals. The largest source of helium is natural gas, the richest in helium being the gas from certain wells in Utah, USA. Next to hydrogen, helium is the lightest gas known, has a lifting power equal to 92 % of hydrogen and the advantage that it is inert and non-inflammable. It is used for inflating airships. Ordinary air contains 1 part in 200,000 of helium. It was the last gaseous element to be liquefied, this being achieved by Onnes in 1908 in Leyden. Scientists are currently concerned that the world's supplies of helium are becoming exhausted.

Liquid helium has many remarkable properties only imperfectly understood. It is indispensable in cryogenics (*q.v.*) as a medium for cooling other substances to temperatures near absolute zero. Hydrogen fusion in the "H bomb" produces helium.

Hellebore, a plant of the *Ranunculaceae* (buttercup) family. The best-known British examples are the green and stinking varieties. There is also a garden kind which flowers in December called the Christmas Rose. Hellebore yields a bitter substance once much used as a purgative.

Hemiptera, the order of insects to which belong the true bugs. Their wing structure is in most species incomplete, hence the term hemiptera (half-wing). This order includes the familiar water insects, the water boatman and water skater, also the aphids, cicadas, leaf hoppers, scale insects.

Hemlock, a plant of the *Umbelliferae* family, growing in all parts of Britain, and containing a strong alkaloid poison. Used medicinally, this alkaline substance is of considerable service, being a powerful sedative. According to Pliny, hemlock was the poison used by the Athenians in putting criminals to death.

Hemp (*Cannabis sativa*), name of a plant native to Asia, now cultivated widely for the valuable fibre contained in the stalk or in some species in the leaves. Hemp fibre has been replaced by cotton for textiles and by jute for sacks and is now chiefly used for cordage and twine. It contains a resinous substance from which the narcotic hashish is made. The seed yields a valuable oil. The term hemp is also used for other fibre plants, *e.g.* manila hemp from the Philippines, sunn hemp from India, sisal from W. and E. Africa and phormium from New Zealand.

Henbane, a plant found in Britain and other parts of Europe and Northern Asia. It belongs to the potato family *Solanaceae*, grows mostly on waste ground and bears yellow-brown flowers veined with purple. The leaves yield a poisonous alkaloid substance which is of great use in medicine. Tincture of henbane is often preferred to laudanum.

Hepatics. *See* Liverworts.

Heracleum, a plant of the *Umbelliferae* family, common in southern and central Europe, though only one species, the cow parsnip, grows in England. It has a bitter root, and from the juice of the stem an intoxicating liquor is occasionally prepared.

Herald, an officer of state empowered to make formal proclamations and deliver messages from the sovereign or other high personage whom he serves. In the developments which took place in armorial bearings, the herald was charged with the duty of their proper depiction.

Heraldry, the knowledge of armorial bearings, was mainly the outcome of the love of outward distinction which prevailed in mediaeval times. "Heraldry," says Stubbs, "became a handmaid of chivalry, and the marshalling of badges, crests, coat-armour, pennons, helmets and other devices of distinction grew into an important branch of knowledge. The shield, or escutcheon, is the ground upon which armorial signs are traced, the colour of the shield being called the *tincture*, the signs recorded the *charges*.

There are seven *tinctures*—*or* (gold), *argent* (silver), *gules* (red), *azure* (blue), *vert* (green), *purpure* (purple) and *sable* (black). The *charges* are classed as "Honourable" and "Subordinate" ordinaries, comprising lines and geometrical forms; and "Common" ordinaries, which latter includes all representations of natural objects. There is also a system of external signs, such as crowns, coronets, mitres *etc.*, each having its distinctive significance. *See* Hatchment, Quartering, Rampant.

Heralds' College or College of Arms, was incorporated by Richard III in 1483. Its head is the Earl Marshal (an office hereditary in the family of the Dukes of Norfolk), and there are three Kings of Arms, six Heralds and four Pursuivants. The business transacted is wholly connected with the tracing of genealogies and the granting of armorial bearings. In Scotland the Heraldic functions are performed by the Lord Lyon King of Arms.

Herbarium, a systematically classified collection of preserved plants. One of the largest in the world is at the Royal Botanic Gardens at Kew.

Heredity is the study of the transmission of physical and mental characteristics from one generation to another. Gregor Mendel (1822–84), a great experimenter in the field of inheritance, established the principle embodied in Mendel's law in his work published in 1866. The ideas which he put forward were forgotten until the early years of the 20th century, but today they form the basis of the modern study of genetics. Genes are the units of heredity; they are contained in the chromosomes of the cell nucleus. In human cells there are 46 chromosomes—22 pairs of characteristic shape, and a 23rd (the sex chromosomes) similar in women and dissimilar in men, which unite in the process of fertilisation. An individual can only develop, even under the most favourable surroundings, as far as his inherited characteristics, *i.e.*, his genes will allow him to do. It is in the development of personality that the interplay between heredity and environment becomes most apparent.

Hermaphrodite, animals or plants possessing both male and female reproductive organs, *e.g.*, snails, earthworms, most flowering plants.

Hermit Crab, a decapod, with a soft asymmetrical body which it protects by thrusting it into an empty gastropod shell, *e.g.*, whelk, which it carries about, only abandoning it when necessary for a larger one. Found in all seas, many live in commensal relationship with sea anemones *etc*.

Heroin. *See* **Opium.**

Heron, a large wading bird with long curved neck and pointed bill, is a member of the *Ardeidae* family, of which there are many species. Egrets and bitterns are included as herons. Herons are to be met with in marsh lands and near rivers and lakes, where they feed on fish and frogs. They nest in trees in large numbers, these colonies being called heronries. The common heron is native to England, and other species from the Continent are also visitors.

Herring (*Clupes harengus*), an important food-fish inhabiting the North Sea which has been subjected to much overfishing. In Britain the herring industry is based on the Shetlands and the coastal ports of E. Scotland and N.E. England. Marine biologists have recently reported on its unique structure for hearing which makes it receptive to sound frequencies over a very wide range and able to determine distance, direction and source of sound.

Hibernation, the dormant condition in which numerous mammals, reptiles, amphibians, insects, plants, *etc.*, pass the winter. The rate of metabolism slows down, and the body temperature drops to that of the surroundings. Work on these low temperatures and their physiological effect has led to improved surgical techniques. Animals of the torrid regions pass through an analogous period (aestivation) during the hot season, when the sources of food are dried up.

Hickory, several species of American tree of the walnut family, remarkable for its very hard, solid, heavy white wood, and bearing an edible, four-lobed nut.

Hieroglyphics are the earliest form of pictured symbolic expression, and are supposed to have been introduced by the ancient Egyptians. They consist of varied depletions of animals, plants, signs and objects, and in their later examples express, in abridged form, ideas and records from which significant historical information has been gleaned. The deciphering of Egyptian hieroglyphics long proved elusive, but gradually the key to the riddle was discovered, and most of the ancient records can now be understood. Besides the Egyptian there are also Hittite, Minoan and Mayan hieroglyphic scripts. *See* **Rosetta Stone.**

Hi-Fi (High Fidelity). A term used since the late 1940s to describe domestic sound reproducing equipment and originally implying superlative performance and particularly stereo capability as opposed to mere mono. In this usage it is now somewhat dated. The criteria for hi-fidelity performance were originally difficult to achieve in practise and therefore the appellation was of some consequence, but recent advances in technology, design, component standards and quality assurance procedures have ensured that the criteria can be met by almost every product on the market. Recent usage does not necessarily imply a qualitative judgment but simply describes equipment for home use. A Hi Fi system will probably include a number of sources such as a turntable and a tonearm combination for replaying vinyl discs, a tuner for receiving radio broadcasts or a compact disc (CD) player, in combination with a pre-amplifier/amplifier and loudspeakers or headphones. Quite frequently some sort of recording device such as a cassette deck will also be present.

From the early 1980s the compact disc became the primary distribution medium for prerecorded music, almost completely replacing vinyl discs. It was not until the late 1980s that digital recording systems such as RDAT (Rotary-head Digital Audio Tape) became available, but these have still not made a very substantial impact on the domestic market. With the more recent developments of DCC (Digital Compact Cassette) and MD (Mini Disc), consumers now have a choice of three digital recording systems and this has probably left many wondering which to choose.

Hindi, the official language of India.

Hindustani, the spoken form of Hindi (written in Devanagari script) and Urdu (written in Arabic characters).

Hippogriff, a fabulous animal like a horse in body, but with the head, wings and front legs and claws of an eagle. The monster frequently appears in the romances of the Middle Ages.

Hippopotamus or "river-horse" the largest living representative of the hippopotamidae family, widely distributed over Africa, where it lives in herds. It is of immense bulk, attaining a length of 3·6 m and a weight of 4 tonnes and stands about 1·5 m high. Its skin is hairless and about 5 cm thick, and it has a pair of tusks often weighing as much as 2·7 kg. It leads an amphibious way of life, and lives entirely on vegetation, both aquatic and terrestrial. The pigmy hippopotamus, which occurs in forests and swamps in W. Africa, is only half the size. Hippos are now known to be related to dolphins and whales.

Histology is the study of the structure of plant and animal tissues. These mainly consist of groups of cells with similar functions, *e.g.* brain tissue.

Hobby, a bird of the falcon family, 30–35 cm long. Local breeding visitor to England and Wales, April–September; irregular visitor to Scotland and Ireland. They winter in Africa.

Hog, the common name of animals of the Suidae family, including the wild boar, pig and sow. The wild boar, *Sus scrofa*, is the common ancestor. The skin of the hog is covered with bristles, the snout truncated and each foot has four hoofed toes. Hogs are omnivorous feeders and eat almost anything that is given them.

Hogmanay, the Scottish New Year's Eve festival and a national holiday of the country. The custom of demanding Hogmanay bread is still upheld in many parts of Scotland.

Hogshead, a cask of varying capacity, also a specific measure. In the old English measure a hogshead was 63 old gallons of wine (=52½ imperial gallons = 238·6 litres). Of beer 54 old gallons make a hogshead.

Holly, a hardy evergreen shrub, largely grown in England. Its bright dark green prickly curved leaves and clusters of red berries are familiar in all parts of the country, and used as house decoration between Christmas Eve and Twelfth Night, probably a relic from ancient customs. Its wood is white and hard, valued for carved work, while its bark yields a gummy substance which is converted into birdlime.

Holocaust Memorial Day, first marked in Britain on 27 January 2001 (the anniversary of the liberation of Auschwitz-Birkenau in 1945).

Hologram, a photographic record, taken under special optical conditions, of light reflected from a scene or object. The hologram is typically a piece of film. However it is nothing like a photographic negative of the ordinary kind; for one thing it will show an unintelligible pattern of light and dark patches. Nevertheless if it is illuminated (again under special optical conditions) the light coming through it will form a *three dimensional* image of the original object. Another radical difference between a hologram and an ordinary film is that if the hologram is cut up, each fragment can be used to construct the entire image.

Holography, as a method of recording and reproducing photographic information, was conceived by Gabor in 1947 but was only fully realised in practice after the invention of the laser (*q.v.*), which made available powerful sources of coherent light. The use of laser light is one of the "special conditions" referred to above. *See also* **T72.**

Holothurians. *See* **Sea Cucumbers.**

Holy Coat of Trèves, a garment preserved in the Cathedral of Trèves, said to have been worn by Christ. It was brought from Jerusalem by the Empress Helena in the 4th century.

Holy Grail. *See* **Grail.**

Holy Roman Empire. *See* **A43.**

Holy Rood, an annual Roman Catholic festival held on 14 September to celebrate the Elevation of the Cross in commemoration of its re-erection in Jerusalem by the Emperor Heraclius in 628 after retaking it from the Persians. Also included in the Church of England calendar.

Holyrood. *See* **A60.**

Holy Water, water blessed by a priest and kept in small fonts at the entrance to Roman Catholic and some Anglican churches.

Holy Week is the week preceding Easter Sunday, and embraces the days of the Sufferings of Christ. It includes Good Friday and Holy Saturday.

Honey, the sweet syrup formed by bees from the nectar of flower , the sucrose in the nectar being converted into a mixture of the simple sugars, glucose and fructose. Hybla, an ancient town of Sicily, on the southern slope of Mt. Etna, was famous for its honey.

Honey-eater, an Australian bird (of which there are many species) provided with a long curved bill and tufted tongue. It lives by sucking the nectar from the flowers which abound in rural parts of Australia and New Zealand.

Hookah, an Oriental pipe for tobacco smoking, the smoke being drawn through the water of a goblet (commonly a coconut shell) by means of a long flexible tube.

Hoopoe, a remarkably handsome bird with vivid black and white-barred wings and tail and black-tipped crest which opens like a fan. Ranges over Europe, Asia and Africa. It has bred in England and Wales and occurs in the UK in small numbers at all seasons. Other species are confined to Africa, Madagascar and India.

Hops, the female "cones" of the hop plant used in brewing; their essential oils give beer an aromatic flavour, and their tannin and resin act as a preservative as well as accounting for the bitter taste desired. The hop is a perennial climber belonging to the mulberry family. The male and female organs are on separate plants; as only the female flower-heads are commercially useful, female plants predominate in a hop garden, only a very few male plants being grown so that the female flowers can be fertilised.

Horizon, the limit of vision, the apparent line where sea and sky, or land and sky meet. This is termed the visible horizon. An ordinary person at the height of 1·5 m can see for 4·8 km, at 6 m 9·6 km, at 15 m 14·8 km and at 305 m 67·5 km. The figures are approximate.

Hormone, a chemical substance which is released by one part of the body and produces a response in other parts after having been carried there by the bloodstream or some other transport system. Prolactin, for example, is a hormone produced by the pituitary gland of nursing mothers and serves to stimulate and maintain the milk supply.

Horn or **French Horn,** a brass instrument of the trumpet family (*i.e.*, played by three valves) whose tube is very thin and long (Horn in F = 12 ft). In consequence the tube is curled in a complicated manner. Owing to the sweet tone it is capable of producing, the Horn sometimes plays as part of the wood-wind.

Hornbill, large bird found in Africa and oriental regions. Some species have a casque or a horny growth above the very powerful beak. It feeds on fruits. When the female has laid her eggs in the hollow of a tree, the male bird stops up the entrance, and keeps her imprisoned until the hatching is completed and the young ones are able to fly. There are about 45 species.

Hornblende, the commonest member of the amphibole group of minerals, a silicate of calcium, magnesium, iron and aluminium, of a dark green colour. It is a constituent of numerous rocks, including diorite, syenite and hornblende schist.

Horned Viper, any of a number of species of African viper which have scales over each eye resembling horns. Their bite is usually very poisonous. The significance of the horns is not known.

Hornet, a general name for many of the bigger wasps. It usually nests in hollow trees, and despite its rather fiercesome appearance does not sting unless unduly provoked.

Horology, the science of time-measurement, including the construction and management of clocks, watches, *etc.* Instruments of this kind are not known to have existed before the 12th cent. and until the introduction of the pendulum in the 17th cent., clocks were ill-regulated and inaccurate. The time-recording mechanisms of the present day include (*a*) the *clock*, which shows the hours and minutes by hands, and strikes the hours, and sometimes quarters; (*b*) the *timepiece*, which is not generally a fixture and shows the time, but does not strike; (*c*) the *watch*, which is a pocket time-keeper; (*d*) the *chronometer*, which indicates the minutest portions of times; (*e*) electric timepieces, mains electric clocks; (*f*) the highly accurate quartz-crystal and atomic clocks used for astronomical purposes. *See* **Clock.**

Horse Chestnut, one of the large forest trees, with ample branches, and full foliage, and much esteemed for parks and ornamental grounds. The flowers, which appear in May, are white tinged with red and yellow. The tree is native to the mountainous regions of northern Greece. *See also* **Chestnut.**

Horse Guards, the building in Whitehall which until 1872 was the headquarters of the Commander-in-Chief of the British Army. The archway is still sentinelled by mounted guards.

Horse Latitudes, the latitudes of the sub-tropical high pressure systems, between the trade winds and the prevailing westerlies, characterised by light variable winds and low humidity.

Hospitallers, Knights. *See* **A43.**

Hottentots, name given to certain African people by Dutch settlers in the 17th cent. They used to occupy much of Cape Colony and though driven out a number still survive in Namibia.

Hounds are dogs that were originally bred and trained for hunting, such as the greyhound, foxhound, bloodhound, wolf hound, deerhound, beagle, harrier, *etc.*, but now often kept also as domestic dogs. The greyhound, deerhound and wolf hound hunt by sight, the others, with the bloodhound first in order, track by scent.

House Flies are world-wide and prolific. Their eggs are hatched within 24 hours of being laid, and full maturity is attained in a month. They feed on decayed animals and vegetable matter.

Hovercraft, or air cushion vehicle, is a craft which is lifted on a pad of air underneath it. This pad or cushion must be at a pressure higher than that of the atmosphere and it is made by sucking in air above the craft and ejecting it in a downward stream all round the lower edge. Hovercraft were devised by Cockerell in the 1950s and a full-scale example appeared in June 1959.

The air pad support means that hovercraft can move over land, water or marsh. Cross-Channel hovercraft were introduced in 1966. The last cross-Channel service was withdrawn in 2000.

Howler Monkey, a genus of South American monkey noted for a laryngeal conformation which enables it to emit a loud reverberant noise something between a yell and a howl.

Huanuco-bark, a medicinal bark, brought from the Peruvian town of that name, and derived from the *Cinchona micrantha* tree.

Hubble Telescope. *See* **Telescope.**

Hubble's Law, the law, first proposed by Edwin Hubble in 1929 stating that the velocity of a distant galaxy is directly proportional to its distance. This means that the most distant galaxies are moving fastest away from us.

Huguenots. *See* **A43.**

Human Genome Project, the global scientific effort launched in the 1990s to unravel the human genetic blueprint. The tiny nematode worm became the first creature to have its entire genetic blueprint decoded. In 1999, for the first time, the complete genetic code of a human chromosome (chromosome 22) was deciphered. It revealed the existence of hundreds of genes, previously unknown in humans, but playing a vital role in disease. Scientists finished a preliminary draft of the human genome code in 2000. Scientists finished a complete sequence in April 2003. *See also* **T65.**

Humble-bee or **Bumble-bee,** the common name of the insects of the genus *bombus,* of the Hymenoptera order. They live in small communities comprising males, females and drones, their habitations being underground. They do not have one queen bee only like the hive bee, but several females occupy the same nest, and these alone live through the winter, breeding and forming new colonies in the spring. Their sting does not have a barb like the honey bee's.

Humidity, the state of the atmosphere with respect to the water-vapour it contains. "Absolute humidity" is defined as the density of the vapour present, while "relative humidity", more frequently employed indicates the degree of saturation, *i.e.*, the ratio of the actual vapour pressure to the saturation vapour pressure at the particular temperature, expressed as a percentage.

Humming Birds are so called because of the humming noise made by the vibration of their wings in flying (they flap their wings 50 times a second). They are of radiant plumage, and are among the smallest birds. The smallest bird in the world is the Fairy or Princess Helen's humming bird of Cuba, whose body is only 5·7 cm long. There are from four to five hundred species, and they are confined wholly to North and South America, being most numerous in the tropical latitudes. They have long, slender bills and tubular tongues which reach down into flowers to suck up the nectar on which they feed.

Hummum, the original name for what is now called the Turkish Bath in this country. One of the first of these baths was the Hummum in Covent Garden, London.

Huns. *See* **A43**.

Hurdy-Gurdy, a rustic musical stringed instrument of the lute order, the sounds of which are produced by the action of a rosined wheel turned by the right hand, the notes being made by the fingering of the left hand. It dates from at least the 12th century.

Hurricane. *See* **Cyclone, Wind.**

Hydra, an aquatic animal of simple structure, whose body is in the form of a cylindrical tube, with a disc-shaped base by which it attaches itself to any shifting substance. Its mouth is surrounded by tentacles by which it catches its food. The Hydra can reproduce lost parts.

Hydrates are compounds containing water of crystallisation.

Hydraulic Ram, a form of automatic pump, used to raise water to a height by the action of its own falling velocity.

Hydraulics, the science of applied hydrodynamics, or water-machine engineering, ranging from pumps to marine engines.

Hydrocarbons are compounds of carbon and hydrogen. They include the *paraffins*, which are saturated compounds (*e.g.*, methane), the ethylene, acetylene and other series which are unsaturated; compounds with ring structures, *e.g.*, benzene, naphthalene and anthracene. Petroleum is composed almost entirely of hydrocarbons.

Hydrochloric Acid, a solution of hydrogen chloride gas in water, and resulting in considerable quantities as a by-product of the soda-ash or salt-cake manufacture. Its solution forms the common hydrochloric or muriatic acid of commerce. It is present to the extent of nearly half a per cent, in the digestive juice secreted by the stomach.

Hydrocyanic Acid, cyanide of hydrogen or prussic acid; very poisonous, and of the odour of bitter almonds. It is formed by the action of acids on sodium or potassium cyanide. Used to kill wasps (and in the gas chamber in the USA). It is a very important chemical on account of the reactions of its derivatives in many synthetic fields. Discovered by Scheele in 1782.

Hydroelectric Schemes. The sun's energy has been indirectly exploited in the past by harnessing the energy of the winds and rain. The climate is due, essentially, to differential heating of the earth. The resulting convection currents in the air (the motion of which is complicated by the rotation of the earth) give rise to winds. Moisture is collected from the sea and deposited high up on mountains as rain. Some of the gravitational energy may be collected as hydropower. Simple windmills or waterwheels are so undependable that they have not been used to any extent since the beginning of the Industrial Revolution.

The modern form of the waterwheel—the hydroelectric generation plant —is extensively used in mountainous countries and about a third

of the world's electricity is produced by this means. The essential requirements for a modern hydroelectric scheme are a river with a sufficient flow of water to provide the required power, a large "head" of water so that a cheap, compact turbine can be used and a dam so that water can be stored until it is required. In some cases a hydroelectric scheme is made economic by being associated with an irrigation or drainage scheme. Such multi-purpose schemes are especially important in India and Pakistan, where most hydro projects are of this type.

Other well-known examples include the Snowy Mountains scheme in Australia and the Aswan High Dam in Egypt.

Although over 90 per cent of the electricity in certain individual countries, notably Norway, Sweden, Portugal, Switzerland and Uganda is now produced from hydroelectric schemes, only a relatively small fraction of the total potential has been exploited. This fraction varies from about a third in Western Europe to a quarter in the United States to a very small fraction in Canada, Africa or Asia.

Hydrofluoric Acid is obtained by distillation of fluorspar with sulphuric acid, and is a compound of fluorine and hydrogen. Its action is highly corrosive; a valuable agent in etching on glass, and a rapid decomposer of animal matter.

Hydrogen, symbol H, the simplest element, with an atomic number of 1, colourless, and the lightest of all substances. Cavendish in 1766 was the first to recognise that it was an element. It is 14·4 times as light as air, and is found in a free state in volcanic regions. It can be obtained by the action of metals on acids, and forms an explosive mixture with air, burning with oxygen to form water. Commercially it is used to produce the very hot flame of the oxy-hydrogen blowpipe for cutting metals, to fill balloons and airships; to harden certain oils and render them suitable for margarine- and soap-production. The gas can be liquefied, and the presence of the isotope deuterium was detected by Urey in 1931 in the residue of the evaporated liquid. The third isotope, tritium, is very rare. Vast quantities of hydrogen gas are thought to exist in the Earth's crust. *See also* **Deuterium, Tritium.**

Hydrography, the science of water measurement, as applied to seas, rivers, lakes, currents, rocks, reefs, *etc.*, and embracing the whole art of navigation.

Hydrometer, an instrument for measuring the specific gravity of liquids, especially for ascertaining the strength of spirituous liquors and solutions. It is usually in the form of a glass bulb, to the lower end of which a smaller bulb, containing mercury, is attached which forces the instrument to sink into the liquid which it is to test. The larger bulb has a scale fixed to it, and the indication on this scale of the sinking point shows the specific gravity. There are many varieties: Twaddell's—a pear-shaped bulb containing mercury: Beaumé's, of similar construction, but applicable to liquids both heavier and lighter than water: Sykes', largely employed for determinining the strength of alcohol: and Nicholson's, used for taking the specific gravities of solids.

Hydropathy, the method of treating disease with water, either by bathing or drinking. Natural springs of special chemical and therapeutic properties, such as sulphur springs, and other mineral sources, have been used since prehistoric times for this purpose. It is probably one of the most ancient methods of cure. Recently the beneficial effects of pure water treatment have been advocated. Hydropathic establishments have been set up in many health resorts.

Hydropolitics, term for the political struggle for water resources. *See* **Section Y.**

Hydroponics, or soilless growth, is the craft and science of growing plants in liquid nutrients instead of soil. Originally a laboratory technique, hydroponics has become since the 1930s a practical method of vegetable, fruit and flower production on both small and large scale. Basically, the growing plants have their roots in troughs of nutrient solution, either in or out of doors. Advantages include: much higher crop yields; the close control of weeds and diseases; quicker growth; and, very important, the possibilities of growing food in places where ordinary agriculture would be impracticable, e.g., deserts and stony land, city roofs, in houses and in remote situations like Antarctic stations. Hydroponics is widely practised and contributes usefully to agriculture and horticulture in many countries, including the USA, Britain, India and France. Its value in spaceships and planetary colonies has often been pointed out by technological prophets.

Hydrostatics, the science of the pressure and equilibrium of liquids that are non-elastic.

Hydrozoa are a class of water animals of the *Coelenterata* phylum to which hydra (*q.v.*) belongs. In one order of the hydrozoa, free-swimming colonies showing marked division of labour between the individual units occur; this order includes the Portuguese man-of-war.

Hyena, a nocturnal carnivore with powerful jaws. The striped hyenas inhabit N. Africa and S.W. India. The brown hyenas with long shaggy hair are natives of S. Africa. The spotted, or laughing hyena, noted for the peculiar cry from which its name is derived, is also confined to Africa.

Hygrometer, an instrument for measuring the amount of water vapour in the atmosphere. A simple form of hygrometer, known as the wet-and-dry bulb, consists of two vertical thermometers affixed to a frame. One bulb is exposed to the air, and the other is covered with muslin which dips into a water-bath to keep it moist. If the air is saturated, it takes up no moisture from the wet bulb and the two thermometers read the same. If the air is not saturated, evaporation takes place from the wet bulb, latent heat is absorbed from the air and the temperature of the wet bulb is lower than that of the dry bulb. Relative humidity and dew-point of the air can then be derived from suitable tables. Hygrometers depending upon the expansion of human hair and goldbeater's skin and the deposition of dew on a polished surface, when cooled sufficiently, are also in general use. *See* **Humidity.**

Hymenoptera, the order of insects to which bees, wasps, hornets, ants and sawflies belong. They have a well-defined waist, two pairs of membranous wings coupled together, mouth parts modified for biting or sucking; the females possess an ovipositor used for depositing eggs and is sometimes modified for stinging. There are about 70,000 species in this order and many live in highly organised communities. *See also* **Ichneumon Fly.**

Hyperbola. A curve described by certain comets that go round the sun and never return.

Hypsometer, an instrument formerly used by mountaineers to find the height above sea-level by indirectly measuring the atmospheric pressure by determining the boiling point of water at the particular height. Based on the fact that as pressure decreases with height so the boiling point is lowered. Superseded by the aneroid barometer.

I

Ibex, wild goats of several species found in the mountain regions of Europe, Asia and Africa. The male has exceedingly large curved ridged horns. The species that lives in the Alps is called the Steinbock or bouquetin.

Ibis, belongs to a family of birds related to the stork. The sacred ibis of ancient Egypt is now extinct in Egypt but is found in the lakes and swamps of the Sudan near the Upper Nile. It has white and black plumage and a long curved beak. Other species are found elsewhere, the Glossy Ibis (black plumage glossed with purple and green) occasionally visiting England. There are now less than 220 Bald Ibis in the world (all in Morocco).

Ibo (Igbo), a numerous people of S.E. Nigeria. After the end of British rule they were active in their struggle for national independence and under their leader, Ojukwu, embarked upon the secessionist state of Biafra and the unsuccessful civil war against Federal forces. Today there are over 20 million Ibo speakers. The Hausa and the Yoruba are the other main Nigerian groups.

Ice is frozen water. It is a colourless, crystalline and brittle solid. Being only 92% as dense as water, it floats on the latter; the expansion which occurs as water changes into ice causes the fracture of water-pipes, though the fracture only becomes obvious when the ice melts and leaks out through the crack. The temperature at which ice forms is 0°C, 32°F. Ice can be melted by pressure, and the ease and smooth ness with which one is able to skate on ice depends on this phenomenon.

Ice Ages. Periods during which the continents were partly or largely covered by ice-sheets and glaciers. The present-day ice-sheets of Greenland and Antarctica are relics of the most recent ice age (one of the eight major ones during the past 700,000 years), which began in the Pleistocene and ended about 10,000 years ago. During this last great glaciation ice sheets covered the northern part of Europe, Asia and North America. There is strong evidence that periodic changes in the earth's orbit around the sun caused the ice ages. The earth is now in one of its warm periods.
During the last Ice Age Britain was home to woolly rhinoceroses, mammoths, reindeer and Arctic lemmings.
A "Little Ice Age" gripped Europe from the mid-1400s until the mid-1800s, and was at its coldest from 1645 to 1715.

Icebergs are detached masses of glacier which subside into the sea and float as wind or current may take them. About one-ninth of an iceberg is above sea-level. The North Atlantic is the chief home of icebergs, which reach the ocean from the ice-clad plateaux of Greenland. Some of these floating masses of ice are of enormous proportions, and constitute in the spring and early summer seasons a great menace to the safety of ships, as was disastrously shown in the *Titanic* catastrophe of 1912. The increasing numbers of icebergs provide evidence of global warming. The largest iceberg ever recorded (half the size of Wales) broke away from the Ross Ice Shelf in Antarctica early in 2000.

Ice-breaker, a special heavy bow-plated ship for forcing a way through ice and used especially at ports of the Baltic Sea and the Great Lakes region of Canada which freeze during the winter.

Icelandic Literature, the old Norse literature, centred about Iceland, which includes numerous works of poetry, mythology and history of interest and importance. Much of this literature is in the saga form. *See also* **Edda.**

Iceland Moss, a kind of lichen (*Cetraria islandica*) which grows in great quantities in the mountain regions of Iceland and other Northern countries. It possesses certain nutritive qualities and is of some value in medicine.

Iceland Spar, a colourless form of calcite (calcium carbonate), frequently found in association with metallic ores; it has the power to produce strong double refraction of light so that two images are seen of an object viewed through a piece of Iceland spar. Once used in optical apparatus for producing polarised light.

Iceni, an ancient British race who in early times lived in Norfolk and other parts of Eastern England. Their most famous ruler was Queen Boadicea, who led her people against the Romans in A.D. 61.

Ice Man, name given to the frozen corpse of a middle-aged man, 5,300 years old, found in 1991 on a glacier in the Ötztal Alps. It is now thought he was murdered by someone from his own tribe.

Ice Plant, also called "dew plant" and "diamond plant". A South African mesembryanthemum commonly grown in British gardens. Introduced in 1690.

Ice Saints, St. Mamertus, St. Pancras and St. Servatius, so called because of the legendary cold on these Saints' Days, namely, 11–13 May.

Ichneumon, the Egyptian mongoose, popularly known as "Pharaoh's Rat". It is of great use in checking the multiplication of reptiles. It is frequently domesticated.

Ichneumon Fly, a numerous group of parasitic

hymenopterous insects abounding in many lands, and all having the peculiarity of depositing their eggs in the bodies of other insects. It destroys swarms of caterpillars, which become the unwilling hosts of its progeny.

Ichthyology, the natural history of fishes.

Ichthyosaurus was a gigantic marine reptile of the Mesozoic age. The fossils are mostly found in the lias formation. Some were over 9 m.

Icon, an image of a sacred personage used in the home or in churches for devotional purposes by Christians of the Eastern Orthodox churches. Icons can be painted on wood, perhaps with the figures picked out against a golden background, or they can be cast in bronze, in the form of a crucifix, diptych (*q.v.*) or triptych with details in coloured enamels. Subjects are taken from the life of Christ or of the Saints. In churches several icons are sometimes placed together on a screen (the iconostasis, which divides the altar and sanctuary from the main body of the church). The earliest preserved icons date from the 12th cent.

Icons are much venerated in Russia and remain, still in their archaic stylised form of mediaeval origin, a characteristic feature of the Greek and Russian Orthodox Churches.

ID Cards. Today *c.* 100 countries have compulsory ID cards, including Germany, Belgium and Spain. The ID cards introduced in Britain during the Second World War were abolished in 1952. Many oppose ID cards on civil liberties grounds, but the present government is moving towards their introduction.

Under current (2006) plans ID cards will be gradually introduced. From 2008 people applying for passports will have to accept an ID card (an opt-out until 2010 from compulsory ID cards was agreed in 2006). They will be credit-card size plastic strips with the holder's name, photo, reference no. *etc. See* **D21–2.**

Ides, in the ancient Roman Calendar, the 15th of March, May, July, October, and the 13th of all other months; always the eighth day after the Nones.

Idiom, an expression characteristic of a country, district, dialect or language, which usually gives strength and force to a phrase or sentence. The idioms of a language are its distinctive marks, and the best writers are the most idiomatic.

Idris, a famous giant belonging to the myths of Wales, commemorated by a chair of rock on the top of the Cader Idris mountain in Gwynedd.

Igneous Rocks are such as have been molten under conditions of great heat at some stage in their history: *e.g.*, granite, basalt.

Ignis Fatuus *or* **"Will-o'-the-wisp"**, a phosphorescent light which may often be seen on summer and autumn evenings hovering over marshy ground or graveyards. Its nature is hardly understood, though it is generally believed to be the result of the spontaneous combustion of the gases from decaying organic matter.

In ancient times when marshy grounds were more common than now, this "dancing light" was very frequently visible and was regarded with superstition.

Iguana, large South American lizard, with a long tail, a scaly back and head, a thick fleshy tongue and a prominent dew-lap in the throat. Specimens of the different species average 1·2–1·5 m in length, and they live mostly in trees, though they are equally at home on land or in the water. The flesh of some species is sometimes eaten, as are also the eggs. The tails of iguanas may sometimes be twice as long as their bodies.

Iguanodon, a genus of extinct dinosaurs, whose fossils are found in the Jurassic and Cretaceous rocks. Iguanodons were 4·5–7·6 m long, and walked on their hind legs, the front legs being small and adapted for grasping the branches of trees on the leaves of which they fed.

Ilex, mentioned by classical authors, the holm- or holly-oak, which flourishes round the Mediterranean. To botanists Ilex is the genus to which the holly and maté plant belong.

Iliad, the great epic poem of ancient Greece attributed to Homer (*c.* 700 B.C.). It consists of ancient folk tale and saga, welded into an artistic unity, having as plot the carrying off of Helen by Paris to Troy and the subsequent siege of Troy.

Illuminated MSS *See* **Section N.**

Ilmenite, a mineral widespread in igneous rocks: chemically it is an oxide of iron and titanium. Rich deposits have recently been found in the Allard Lake area of Quebec; the Travancore sands are also a source of ilmenite.

Immortelles are wreaths, crosses or other designs made from what are called everlasting flowers, which are obtained from certain plants of the Composite order, and retain their colours and compactness for a long time. Immortelles are largely used as mementoes for decorating graves, especially in France.

Impeachment. *See* **A43.**

Imprimatur, originally an official licence to print and an important formula in the early days of printing. The term is now used in the wider significance of authority, or endorsement.

Incas, an Indian people who inhabited ancient Peru, founded a great empire and civilisation; overthrown by the Spaniards in 1533.

Incense, an aromatic resinous substance which, under combustion, exhales a pungent odour, and is used, mixed with certain fragment perfumes, in the celebration of Mass in Roman Catholic churches. Olibanum or frankincense is ordinarily the leading ingredient.

Incisors, the sharp-edged cutting teeth at the front of mammalian jaws. Rodents have long, sharp incisor teeth. Elephant tusks are modified incisors.

Independence Day, commemorates the adoption of the Declaration of Independence on 4 July 1776. 4 July is celebrated as a holiday in the USA.

Independent Schools. *See under* **Public Schools.**

Index. The name given to a list of books, prepared by papal authority, which are declared to be dangerous to faith and morals, and therefore forbidden to Roman Catholics, called the *Index librorum prohibitorum.* One of the reforms of the Vatican Council was the closing in 1966 of the Curia office which judged writings for the Church's Index of forbidden books, though the Index itself still remains. The Pope ordered that nothing should be placed on the Index until the author had been given a chance of explaining his views. The first Index was issued by Pope Pius IV, in 1559.

Indian Summer, a period of dry, sunny weather extending deep into autumn. The term comes, not from the Indian sub-continent, but from early settlers in North America.

Indicators, substances which by a marked change in colour are used to indicate the course of a chemical reaction. Litmus paper, for instance, is red with acids and blue with alkalis. In biological work some radioactive substances are used as tracer elements.

Indigo, the substance obtained from the plant *Indigofera tinctoria*, a native of S. Asia, India being the chief producing country. The colouring matter is the result of the decomposition and fermentation of a glucoside contained in the plant. This is afterwards dried and becomes the caked indigo of commerce. Natural indigo has been eclipsed by artificial indigo, a coal-tar dye which came into commercial production at the end of the last century, and which is cheaper and more uniform in quality.

Indium, a scarce lead-coloured metallic element, no. 49, symbol In, found in zinc blende in Saxony and certain other ores. Discovered in 1863 by Reich and Richter. It is an important material in the manufacture of transistors.

Indulgence. In the Roman Catholic Church the remission granted by ecclesiastical authority to a repentant sinner of the temporal punishment still due after the guilt of sin has been forgiven by God.

The indiscriminate sale of Indulgences by Tetzel and other Papal agents in the 16th cent. was one of the grievances which led to the Reformation. The Council of Trent made such traffic unlawful. They were associated with some of the worst examples of corruption in the history of the Church.

Industrialisation is simply a name for industrial development. It is customarily used in particular to designate the course of events in a hitherto underdeveloped country which is seeking to increase its wealth and productivity by the introduction of more advanced techniques and by the establishment of industries previously not carried on within it. The word usually covers not only the development of modern industrial production but also the provision of electric power-stations, irrigation works and transport and other developments designed to improve production in any field by methods involving large capital investments. One often-quoted example by historians of rapid industrialisation was the former Soviet Union, which, unable to get the capital from abroad, had to carry it through by ruthless restriction of the people's consuming power.

Industrialisation has usually meant a high concentration on the expansion of the basic heavy industries and of power supply, coupled with much slower development of the industries supplying consumer goods and of agricultural production; but there is no reason why this should always be the case.

Inert Gases. See **Rare Gases**.

Inertia, a term used in mechanics for the property of matter by which it offers resistance to a change in its state of rest or in its state or direction of motion.

Inertial Navigation, an automatic method of dead-reckoning which at present finds its chief application in guided missiles, submarines and aircraft. Navigation by this means is carried out with reference to inertial space (i.e., space which is stationary with respect to the fixed stars) and not to the surface of the earth as in normal navigation (latitude and longitude). This is done by means of high-accuracy gyro-scopes combined with highly sensitive accelero-meters in an apparatus known as the Ship's Inertial Navigation System. The American nuclear-powered submarine *Nautilus* pioneered the new north-west passage under the polar ice by this method of dead-reckoning in 1958.

Inflorescence, a flowering shoot. Many arrangements of the flowers are possible and there are many kinds of inflorescence; e.g., the spike, catkin, umbel, capitulum (in composites).

Infra-red Radiation, electromagnetic radiation lying between the radio and visible bands of the electromagnetic spectrum. The wavelengths involved are from 0·8 micrometres (0.8×10^{-6}) to 1000 micrometres. Astronomers sub-divide this waveband into near, mid and far infra-red. Radiation above 300 micrometres is now called submillimetre radiation. Infra-red photography uses materials specially sensitized to infra-red radiation; applications include night time photography, haze-penetration and camouflage and forgery detection.

Infra-red Space Observatory (ISO), an orbiting tele-scope launched in 1995. By peering into the clouds of gas and dust in deep space it astonished astronomers by discovering vast quantities of water in the deserts of space. It ceased functioning in 1998. The Space Infra-Red Telescope Facility, the largest, most sensitive telescope of its type to be sent into space, was launched in 2003.

Infula, a sacred fillet, of woollen material, worn on the forehead by priests, magistrates and rulers in Roman times, also by persons fleeing for protection to sanctuary. Later, each of the two lappets of a bishop's mitre.

Ingoldsby Legends, a series of whimsical metrical tales written by the Rev. R. H. Barham, and first published in *Bentley's Miscellany* in 1837. The best known is the *Jackdaw of Rheims*.

Ink, a liquid pigment ordinarily made from an infusion of nut-galls, copperas and gum arabic. Shumac is substituted for nut-galls for inferior inks. An acid is sometimes added to prevent oxidation, and for the blue-black inks a small quantity of solution of indigo serves for colouring. Copying ink contains glycerine or sugar, which keeps the ink moist. Lampblack used to be the leading ingredient in printer's ink but now new methods of manufacturing have been developed. Marking ink is composed of a solution of nitrate of silver, gum, ammonia and carbonate of soda. For red, blue and other coloured inks, colouring solutions are used, e.g. Prussian blue. The earliest examples of ink writing (on wooden tablets) ever found in Britain were recovered from the well of a Roman villa (3rd cent. A.D.) at Chew Stoke, Somerset in 1954.

Ink Sac, a glandular organ found in squids and other cephalopods which contains an inky solution. When roused the animal discharges the contents of the ink sac into the water, to make a cloud through which its enemies cannot see. The pigment, sepia, comes from the ink sac of the cuttlefish.

Inns of Court, the four bodies in London which enjoy the privilege of calling candidates to the bar after they have studied for a certain number of terms and passed certain examinations. The Inns are: the Inner Temple, the Middle Temple, Lincoln's Inn and Gray's Inn.

Inquisition, a Roman Catholic ecclesiastical court which became a formidable weapon of the Church in the 13th cent. under Pope Innocent III in dealing with charges of heresy. It was effectively set up in the various Catholic countries of the Continent, obtaining its fullest and most sweeping organisation in Spain in the days of Ferdinand and Isabella, when Torquemada was made Grand Inquisitor, and used its powers with terrible severity. (See **Auto-da-fé**.) In the 18th century its influence began to wane, and the jurisdiction of the Congregation of the Holy Office at Rome was limited to the suppression of heretical literature (see **Index**). The attitude of the Catholic Church to the Inquisition is now being debated.

For recent studies, see Henry Kamen, *The Spanish Inquisition* (1997) and Michael Baigent and Richard Leigh, *The Inquisition* (1999).

Insectivorous Plants, plants which trap insects with special mechanisms. Plant enzymes or bacteria digest the prey, providing the plants with nitrogen usually scarce in the soil in which they grow. The most common British species are the Sun-dew and the Bladderwort.

Insects. This huge class of invertebrate animals (see **Arthropods, Section T**) includes c. 100,000 species. Insects are ubiquitous except in the sea, only a very few species being adapted to marine existence. Characteristic features are: the body is divided into three parts, head, thorax and abdomen: the head carries a pair of antennae, the thorax three pairs of legs and usually two pairs of wings. The most primitive insects constituting the sub-class *Apterygota* are wingless.

The other important sub-class, *Pterygota*, is divided into the *Exopterygota* (*Hemimetabola*), which have a simple metamorphosis, e.g. cockroach, and the *Endopterygota* (*Holometabola*), with a complex metamorphosis, e.g. butterfly, bee. Although many are parasitic on man, animals and plants, innumerable animals and some plants use them as food, and many flowering plants are dependent on a variety of insects for pollination. The disappearance of insect species in Britain is now of major concern (there are currently 22,000 insect species recorded in Britain).

Insignia, marks or badges of office or honour, such as stars, ribbons, etc.

Institut de France was formed in 1795, and after various modifications was in 1832 organised on its present basis. Its five academies are—the Académie Française, Académie des Inscriptions et Belles-Lettres, Académie des Sciences, Académie des Beaux-Arts, and the Académie des Sciences morales et politiques. It is restricted to 40 members.

Instruments, Musical. Musical instruments may be classified in a number of ways, but in general they fall into one of the three main classes, String, Wind and Percussion, according to how the sound in produced.

Stringed Instruments are those which produce the sound by the vibration of a string: (a) by plucking, as in Harp, Lyre, Psaltery, Zither, Lute, Guitar, Balalaika, Ukelele, Harpsichord; (b) by friction (bowed), as in Crwth, Rebec, Viol, Violin, Marine Trumpet, Hurdy-Gurdy; (c) by striking (hammered), as in Dulcimer, Pianoforte, Clavichord; (d) by wind (blown), as in the Aeolian Harp.

Wind Instruments are those in which the air in the instruments is set in vibration: (a) by blowing into a tube (flue-voiced), as in Recorder, Pandean Pipe, Flute, Organ; (b) by means of reeds (reed-voiced), as in Oboe, Clarinet, Saxophone, Bagpipe, Cor Anglais, Bassoon, Organ reed-stops; (c) those in which the sound is produced by the vibration of the player's lips against the mouth-piece (lip-voiced), as in Bugle, Horn, Trumpet, Tuba, Trombone, Saxhorn, Flügelhorn, Cornet. In the modern orchestra the *Brass:* the flute, oboe and clarinet families are the *Woodwinds.*

Percussion Instruments include the Drums, Cymbals, Tambourines, Castenets.

Insulator, a substance that will not conduct electric current. Many solids, liquids and gases are important insulators—rubber, cotton, silk, plastics, porcelain, glass, air, oil. If the applied voltage is too high, all insulators will "break down", *i.e.*, conduct electricity perhaps with resulting breakage, puncture or charring. Thermal insulators will not conduct heat; they are usually the same kinds of substance as electrical insulators.

Intelligence. Intelligence has been variously defined as the innate potential of a person to learn and understand; to make appropriate judgments; to see the relationships between things; to profit from experience; or to meet adequately new problems and conditions in life. There are many lines of evidence to show that intellectual capacity is closely related to heredity and influenced by environmental factors. The idea of intelligence testing was first devised by the French psychologist Binet at the start of the 20th century. He was asked by the French government to invent a test which would weed out backward children in state schools, and thus save public money and avoid holding back the work of the class by teaching children who were incapable of learning at a given standard.

Briefly, a series of problems are given to a large number of children and it is thus found out which series can be solved by the average child of a given age-group; if a child of 7 can only pass the tests suitable to the average child of 6, then his mental age is 6. The intelligence quotient or IQ is discovered by dividing his mental age by his chronological age and multiplying by 100. A gifted child can usually be spotted at an early age. Although IQ tests are the standard method of estimating intelligence, they are not universally accepted as a criterion; a teacher's general judgment may be the best assessment. High intelligence may be inherited, but fail to develop to the full because facilities for education are not available.

Recent research suggests that the growth of the brain may be permanently affected by undernutrition at the time of its fastest growth (the last weeks before birth, and, to a lesser extent, the first weeks after birth). At this vulnerable period even minor deprivation can affect the rate and final extent of growth of the brain.

Interest is the payment made for the use of borrowed money over time. The rate of interest is the rate per cent per annum charged for such loans. There are many such rates, varying with the length of time for which the loans are made, and with the degree of risk, if any, that the loans will not be duly repaid. Short-term loans are usually cheaper than longterm: the lowest rates are usually for "call money" repayable immediately on demand.

Bank loans, though usually made for fairly short terms, command higher rates. Long-term loans are made chiefly to public authorities, or as bonds or debentures to business concerns.

International Criminal Court (ICC) is the first-ever permanent, treaty-based criminal court. It was established by the UN to prosecute and punish war crimes, genocide and "crimes against humanity". It was established in 2002 at The Hague.

International Date Line, a line along the 180° meridian marking the difference in time between E. and W. For the westward-bound traveller crossing the line the date would be put forward one day, for the eastward-bound, back one day. To avoid difference of date in adjacent land areas, the line deviates from the 180° meridian where this crosses land.

International Standard Book Numbers (ISBNs), the system used to identify uniquely a title or edition of a book. The present 10-digit figure will increase to 13 in January 2007.

Introit, the psalm sung by the choir as the priest approaches the altar to celebrate the Eucharist.

Inuit. *See under* Eskimo.

Invention of the Cross, a Roman Catholic festival held on 3 May, to celebrate the finding of the alleged True Cross at Calvary by the Empress St. Helena in 326. Also included in the Church of England calendar. *See* Holy Rood.

Io, satellite of Jupiter (*q.v.*). It was discovered by Galileo in 1610. It is the most volcanically active object in our solar system. Temperatures of 1700°C have been recorded and there are *c.* 300–500 active volcanoes. Scientists have observed new forms of mountain-building not seen anywhere else. In 2001, scientists discovered a giant 47-mile wide crater (called Tupan Patera) on the surface of Io.

Iodine, a non-metal element, no. 53, symbol I, member of the halogen family (*q.v.*), a substance formerly exclusively obtained from the ribbon-wrack seaweeds. These were burnt and the ashes (kelp) extracted with water. After concentrating the iodides, these were distilled with manganese dioxide and sulphuric acid to yield iodine vapour which was condensed in stoneware bottles. Nearly all iodine now in use is derived from the iodine salt present in Chile saltpetre (natural sodium nitrate). Iodine is used in photography, as an antiseptic solution in alcohol or potassium iodide (tincture of iodine), and in medicine. Discovered by Courtois in 1812.

Ionosphere. Although a certain degree of ionisation occurs at all levels of the atmosphere due to cosmic rays and the radioactivity of rocks, *etc.*, the ionosphere is normally denoted as the region above about 70 km where the ultra-violet component of sunlight is able to ionise a significant fraction of the atoms and molecules present. This ionisation causes the reflection of radio waves by which the ionosphere was initially discovered and for many years, explored.

The nomenclature of the ionospheric layers— "D" region up to about 95 km, "E" region 95 km to about 180 km, and "F" region above 180 km—is due to the historical observations of radio wave reflections from "layers". Satellite and rocket observations have shown that the structure is in fact more continuous.

Solar flares and aurora cause enhancements of the electron density in the ionosphere, which may result in the disturbance of radio communications over very large distances (radio blackouts). *See also under* Atmosphere, Aurora, **Magnetosphere.**

Ions, electrically charged atoms, or groups of atoms. Atoms of the metals lose electrons to become positively charged ions, *e.g.*, the sodium ion (Na^+) has one electron less than the atom. The non-metal ions are negatively charged, *e.g.*, the chloride ion (Cl^-) has one electron more than the atom. Similarly, a group like the sulphate ion ($SO_4{}^{2-}$) has more electrons than the constituent atoms. Thus, the hydrogen atom without its electron is a hydrogen ion or *proton* and the helium atom without its two electrons is a helium ion or *alpha-particle.*

When an electric force is applied to certain solutions, the ions into which molecules of the dissolved substance are broken up are attracted to the oppositely charged electrodes, their movements constituting an electric current through the solution. In the same way gases, including air, conduct electricity by virtue of free ions. Combustion, radio-activity and ultra-violet and cosmic radiations produce ionisation.

Iridium, a white and very hard metallic element, no. 77, symbol Ir, discovered by Tennant in 1804. It occurs naturally as an alloy with platinum or osmium; tips for fountain-pen nibs have been made from the former native alloy. The former standard metre was composed of platinum–iridium alloy (*see* **Metre**) as are parts of scientific apparatus and surgical tools that must be non-corrodible.

Iris, the typical genus of the botanical order *Iridacae*, with tuberous rhizomes and swordshaped leaves, many of the family having beautiful flowers. About 100 species of Iris are recorded from the northern temperate zone, the most common species wild in Britain being the yellow flag. Orris root, used in perfumery, comes from another iris species.

Iron is a metallic element, no. 26, symbol Fe (Latin *ferrum*), occurring widely in nature in such ores as haematite, loadstone (magnetic iron oxide), spathic ore and iron pyrites. It is extracted by a process known as smelting, with coke and limestone in a furnace. Its many uses are familiar, the most important being in the manufacture of cast- and wrought-iron products and of steels, which are alloys mainly of iron with added carbon and various metals. Iron rust is formed by the action of oxygen and water, and is a coating of iron oxide. *See* **Smelting.**

Ironclads, ships of war cased in iron or steel plates

of sufficient thickness to resist projectiles. They were first introduced (1858) in the French Navy, and in 1860 the first British ironclad, the *Warrior*, was launched.

Iron Curtain. *See* A44.

Irrational Number, a number such as the square root of two, or pi, which cannot be expressed as the ratio of two whole numbers. *See* **Rational Number,** and *Pi*.

Irrigation, an artificial method of providing water for the growth of plants on lands where the natural supply of water is deficient. For many hundreds of years techniques of irrigation have been slow and primitive (*e.g.*, tanks, inundation canals and the Archimedes screw) and consequent inefficiencies include large water losses by evaporation and seepage, and the watering of only a small area. New developments in perennial irrigation, using barrages, large reservoirs and pumping stations, permit vast tracts of land to be irrigated. Yet these are not without their problems as witnessed after the construction of the Aswan High Dam on the Nile where complex problems of delta erosion and dam lake silting ensued. Irrigation also serves the purpose of supplying *warmth* in winter; *e.g.*, in the English water-meadows, and in the more highly developed Italian *marcite* and winter-meadows, where the water is mostly applied in winter when there is plenty of rain. There are several other functions of irrigation; *e.g.*, washing out of excess salts and the renewing of fertility by the addition of alluvium.

Isobars are the lines drawn on charts linking together points of equal barometric pressure.

Isochasms, lines connecting places at which there is an equal probability of seeing an aurora, taking the average over a number of years, based on the auroral catalogue of Fritz.

Isomers are chemical compounds having the same composition but different structural arrangements, and consequently different physical and chemical properties. For example, ethyl alcohol and methyl ether are isomers, since the molecules of both are built up of two atoms of carbon, six of hydrogen and one of oxygen, *viz.*, C_2H_6O; ethyl alcohol, C_2H_5OH; and methyl ether, CH_3OCH_3.

Isotherms are lines drawn on charts through points of equal temperature.

Isotopes. When one talks of an element, say, uranium or lead, the name of the element is a generic name for a collection of uranium species and lead species. The different species are called isotopes. For any particular element, the number and arrangement of electrons around atomic nuclei are the same in all the isotopes, so all the isotopes have the same chemical properties. Soddy has described isotopes as "elements, the atoms of which have similar outsides but different insides". For example, in the nucleus of the uranium isotopes, U 235, U 238 and U 239, there are respectively 143, 146 and 147 neutrons, but all have 92 protons. The isotopes have different atomic weights, in this instance respectively 235, 238 and 239. But all have the same chemical properties.

Ivory, the dentine substance of which the tusks of the elephant, hippopotamus, walrus, *etc.*, are composed. The tusks of the African elephant sometimes weigh as much as 45 kg, and reach a length of 2·4–2·7 m. A world-wide ban on trading in ivory was imposed in 1989, but pressure has grown for a partial lifting of this ban.

Ivory Gull, a small, beautifully shaped sea-bird with striking all-white plumage and black legs which breeds on the rocky shores of the Arctic, being found farther north than any other bird; it occasionally wanders south in the winter.

J

Jabiru, the Brazilian name for the giant stork of South America.

Jacamar, from *Jacameri*, the Brazilian name for a smallish bird with long, sharply pointed bill and brilliant plumage which inhabits the tropical regions of South America east of the Andes.

These birds are seen sitting motionless on trees, darting off at intervals, like flycatchers, to catch insects on the wing.

Jacanas, small water birds with immensely long toes which enable them to walk on water lily leaves. They are sometimes called "lily-trotters" and are found in tropical Africa and America. They live in swamps and feed on seeds and insects. Sometimes brilliantly coloured.

Jack, a small schooner-rigged vessel, used in the Newfoundland fisheries; a pike; an oscillating lever; a device used in roasting meat.

Jackal, *Canis aureus*, a small wild dog related to the wolf and resembling a fox. The Common Jackal is found in S.E. Europe, India and Sri Lanka; other species inhabit Africa and Egypt. The jackal is a well-known scavenger. It hunts singly or in pairs, unlike the wolf.

Jackdaw, one of the smaller members of the Crow family. This European bird is typically black with grey collar. It is easily tamed, makes an amusing pet and delights in making off with and taking to its nest bright objects, such as silverware.

Jacobins. *See* A44.

Jacobites. *See* A44.

Jade, an exquisite kind of hardstone, ranging in colour from a whitish green to a deep mauvish brown. It can be translucent or opaque and sometimes it is veined. Jade is the common name for two minerals—the rarer *jadeite* (found in Burma, Tibet and China), a sodium-aluminium-silicate, and *nephrite* (found in New Zealand, China, Turkestan and Siberia), a calcium-magnesium silicate. The presence of small quantities of other chemicals accounts for the wide range of shades. In China jade has for centuries been looked upon with great veneration, magical powers have been ascribed to it, and it has been fashioned into ritual objects, also into miniature sculptures of animals or even whole landscapes, charming to look at and incredibly skilfully made. The Chinese word for jade is *yü*, used as a symbol for all that is noble, beautiful and pure.

Jaguar, a South American carnivorous animal resembling the leopard, but larger and more powerful. It preys on other animals but rarely attacks man.

Janissaries. *See* A44.

January, the first month of the year, named after Janus, the two-faced god of the Romans. It was the *Wolf monath* and *Aefter Yule* of the

Jasmine, a graceful climber belonging to the olive family with odoriferous blossom, originally a Persian plant, but now acclimatised in many varieties in almost all parts of the world. Two species of jasmine (the common jasmine and the Spanish jasmine) yield oils used in perfumery.

Jasper, a precious stone of the chalcedony variety, opaque, and coloured red, brown, yellow and sometimes green. It was greatly esteemed in classical times, the Bible having numerous allusions to it.

Jay, a gaily-coloured bird of the Crow family, of many species—the Blue jay of N. America, the Canada jay, sometimes called "whisky jack", the Siberian jay and the British jay, fawn-coloured with black and whitish crest and bright blue feathers in the wings. It lives in woods and like the magpie, takes the eggs and young of small nesting birds.

Jazz, a rhythmical syncopated music characterised by a strong element of improvisation in the performance, probably originating among the black population of the Southern States of the USA. *See* Section P.

Jean, a stout kind of twilled cotton cloth, resembling fustian. Blue jeans, adopted by American city youngsters from farmworkers, became the fashion elsewhere and were worn not only as overalls by workmen but by both sexes in leisure time.

Jellyfish. The jellyfishes, which have gelatinous, translucent bodies fringed at the margin with delicate tentacles, constitute the coelenterate order *Scyphozoa*. The mouth, with a squarish opening, is seen on the underside, and there are four horseshoe-shaped sex organs. There are over 200 species. They are 95 per cent water.

Jerboa, small jumping mammals of the Rodent order. These mice-like animals have long tufted tails and very long hind legs, the front legs not being used for locomotion.

Jerusalem Chamber, a room in Westminster Abbey, deriving its name from the circumstance of its having originally been decorated with a view of Jerusalem. Henry IV died in this chamber, and the Committee for the Revision of the Bible met there in 1870 and later.

Jesuits, members of the Roman Catholic religious order founded by Ignatius Loyola in 1540. A long and vigorous course of study is prescribed before they are admitted into the privileges of full membership. They are required to take the vows of voluntary poverty, perfect chastity, perfect obedience and complete submission to the Pope with regard to the Mission of the Order. Pope Paul VI gave them the particular mission of initiating a dialogue with atheists.

Jet, a deep black fossil substance admitting of a high polish and much used for jewellery, ornaments and trimming. It is a form of lignite, the most important British deposit being found near Whitby, where jet manufacture has been an established industry for a long period.

Jet Engine, an aeroplane engine which derives its thrust from the high velocity of the gases it ejects. The essential units in a jet engine are a rotary compressor and a gas turbine, the latter driving the compressor. The first reliable, high-performance jet propulsion engine for aircraft was invented by Sir Frank Whittle.

Jet Stream, a meteorological term coined in 1946 to describe the relatively narrow belt of strong winds (160–320 km/h) at levels in the atmosphere from 5–11 km. These winds are important in forecasting weather, and can be a valuable aid to aircraft. From the ground, where there may be little wind, the jet stream can sometimes be seen as high cirrus cloud moving across the sky at high speed.

Jew's Harp. The name is believed to be a corruption of "jaws harp". This instrument consists of a metal frame with a central tongue of spring steel. The frame is pressed against the teeth, and the tongue of the harp is twanged with the finger, the mouth acting as a resonating chamber. By altering the shape of the mouth the resonant frequency and therefore the note can be varied.

Jockey Club, the governing body that, although possessing no legal status, frames rules and laws by which horse-racing and turf matters are regulated. The club-house is at Newmarket.

John Bull, the typical figure of an Englishman, bluff, big and burly. Arbuthnot's *History of John Bull* is supposed to have originated the character.

John Dory, a fish found in most temperate seas and common in British waters. It is of a golden-yellow colour (*jaune doré*), has a high dorsal fin with long filaments projecting from the spines, very protractile jaws and is much valued as a table fish. According to legend the dark spot on each side of its body is the thumbprint of St. Peter who took a coin from the fish's mouth.

John o' Groat's House, W. of Duncansby Head, Caithness, popularly named as the northernmost point of Scotland. According to legend the house, which has now disappeared, was built in octagonal form by a Dutchman Jan de Groot who came to live there in the 16th cent. The site is marked and an inn erected near it in 1876.

Jongleurs were minstrels and jesters who wandered from town to town singing songs, playing musical instruments, dancing and giving entertainments in mediaeval France and Norman England. Jongleurs were low-born in contrast to the Troubadours, who were often of the nobility.

Joule, a unit of energy in the SI system of units, defined as the work done when the point of application of a force of one newton is displaced through a distance of one metre in the direction of the force. Named after J. P. Joule (1818–89). The relationship between mechanical energy and heat energy is called the mechanical equivalent of heat. One British Thermal Unit (Btu) is equivalent to 778 ft.lb or 252 calories or $1 \cdot 054 \times 10^{10}$ ergs or, in SI units, $1054 \cdot 35$ joules. *See* **Section T.**

Julian Calendar, named after Julius Caesar, who in 45 B.C., finding the Roman year 90 days in advance of the real time, was the first to adopt the calculation of time by the solar year, the average length being fixed at $365\frac{1}{4}$ days. There was still an overplus of a few minutes every year, and this was rectified by the Gregorian Calendar, introduced in Italy in 1582 and adopted in England in 1752, from which date what is called the "New Style" begins.

July, the seventh month of the year, named after Julius Caesar. It was the *Maed monath* (Meadmonth) of the Saxons.

June, the sixth month of the year, containing 30 days and deriving its name from Juno. It was the *Sear* (Dry) *monath* of the Saxons.

Juniper, one of only three native English conifers. A distinctive, sprawling evergreen only to be found on rocky soils in remote upland areas. Its berries are a main flavouring ingredient of gin. (*q.v.*)

Jupiter is the largest of the planets, 11 times the diameter of the earth, 318 times its mass but only one fourth its density. It is the fifth farthest from the sun and is the second brightest. Our knowledge of Jupiter, with its 61 moons, its ring and its magnetosphere was enormously increased in 1979 by data from the Voyager 1 and 2 space-probes which passed the planet at distances of 349,000 km and 722,000 km on March 5 and July 9 respectively. Jupiter is a gaseous planet composed mainly of hydrogen and helium like the sun, possibly with a small molten core of silicates. The centre is presumed to be at a very high temperature (30,000°C) and enormous pressures—a hundred million earth atmospheres—which make hydrogen not only liquid but metallic. This metallic flux leads to intense magnetic fields. Jupiter's large magnetosphere is distorted by the solar wind and contains trapped high energy particles in radiation belts which would be lethal to man. Its existence was first inferred from its radio emissions and was confirmed by Pioneer 11 in 1974.

Jupiter's outer gaseous surface is very cold (−120°C) and consists of three layers of crystal clouds (ice ammonium hydrogensulphide and ammonia) interspersed with gaseous hydrogen and helium. It shows massive persistent features like the swirling high pressure Red Spot (larger when first seen in 1664 but which could hold two earths) and the neighbouring white oval formations. All these features are in relative motion, some moving east and others west which account for Jupiter's banded appearance. The persistence of the features arises because Jupiter has no terrain to break them up and because the surface temperature is low. Lightning continuously flashes over the Jovian surface and at the poles there are large auroras caused by an electric current of five million amperes which flows from the poles out to Io, one of the four moons discovered in 1610 by Galileo. The others were Europa, Ganymede and Callisto.

The fourteenth moon was found in 1979 by Voyager 2 at the outer edge of the thin ring of particles discovered by Voyager 1, which also discovered high plumes due to volcanic activity on Io, the first seen beyond earth (although a recent suggestion is that the plumes are caused by the electric current). Io's sulphurous surface shows no meteoric craters and Europa's smooth ice surface shows only a few impacts and is probably young, unlike the older Ganymede and Callisto whose ice-crust surfaces have many. Ganymede's crust has been reworked, however, by extensive tectonic movements. Ganymede is now known to be the largest moon in the solar system, larger than the planet Mercury. A total of 61 moons around Jupiter has now been discovered. In 1994, Jupiter was struck by the Shoemaker-Levy-9 comet whose impact sent seismic waves across the planet.

In 1995, the Hubble telescope found oxygen on Europa, one of Jupiter's moons. More recently salt has been discovered. Late in 1995 the Galileo spacecraft successfully entered the atmosphere of Jupiter. First data from Galileo suggested Jupiter's atmosphere was hotter and drier than expected with hurricane winds of 330 mph. Images from Galileo in 1997 appeared to show ice-berg-like structures on Europa. The origin of Jupiter's swirling rings was discovered in 1998 to be the detritus thrown up by meteoroids crashing into the moons Amalthea, Thebe *etc*. Colour images of Io taken in January 2001 show great volcanic activity. The first pictures of Callisto (2001) showed jagged hills of ice and rock. The 14-year mission of Galileo ended in September 2003 when it crashed onto the surface of Jupiter. It had found volcanic activity on Io perhaps 100 times greater than on Earth.

Jurassic Formation, a series of rocks (the evidences of which are most marked in the Jura Mountains) coming between the Cretaceous and Triassic groups and including the Oolite and the Lias. It is a formation rich in fauna, abounding in echinoids, lamellibranchs, ammonites and belemnites; large reptiles, marine and land, are common, as are the plants called cyads. In Britain the Jurassic outcrop extends from the Dorset coast to the Yorkshire moors.

Jury, a body of private citizens chosen and sworn to hear and pass verdict upon evidence brought forward at a trial, inquest or inquiry. The origin of the English jury is obscure but it is thought to have been introduced by the Normans. The jurors are the sole judges of the true facts upon the evidence laid before them.

Under the Criminal Justice Act of 1967 their verdicts in criminal courts in England and Wales no longer had to be unanimous but may be by a majority of 10 to 2. The age limit has been reduced from 21 to 18 and raised from 60 to 65. In Scotland 45 jurors are summoned in criminal cases, of whom 15 are chosen by ballot, and majority verdicts are accepted: not guilty, not proven and guilty. Proposals to limit the right to trial by jury (and scrap the double jeopardy rule) have attracted much criticism. There is more support to scrap juries in very complex and lengthy fraud trials.

Justices of the Peace. *See* **Magistrates.**

Jute, the name given to the fibre of a plant grown largely in Bangladesh in the Ganges delta and used for the manufacture of coarse cloths, cordage and sacks. Kolkata (Calcutta) is the biggest jute-manufacturing centre of the world, as Dundee was in the 19th cent.

Jutes, a Low German race who in the 5th cent. invaded the south-eastern part of England, establishing themselves in Kent and making Canterbury their capital.

K

Kangaroo, pouched (marsupial) mammals of Australia and adjacent islands. There are over 50 species, the smaller ones being known as "wallabies". Kangaroos leap in a succession of springy bounds 3–6 m long, the forefeet not touching the ground. They can reach a height of over 2 m and a weight of 90 kg. First seen by white men when Capt. Cook's expedition visited Australia in 1770. Related genera include the tree kangaroos, rat kangaroos and the Tasmanian Jerboa kangaroo. There are an estimated 20 million Kangaroos in Australia. Remains found in 2002 were those of a prehistoric kangaroo 9ft tall.

Kaolin or China Clay is an essential ingredient in hard-paste porcelain (*q.v.*). It results from the decomposition of felspar, and is widely found in China, Japan and the USA. The richest deposits in Europe are in Cornwall, near Limoges in France, and in the Czech and Slovak Republics.

Kea, the Alpine parrot of New Zealand.

Kelvin. Lord Kelvin, an important 19th-cent. physicist, gave his name to the kelvin, symbol K, a measure of temperature on the absolute scale. The Kelvin scale is a development of the scale invented by Celsius (*q.v.*) for everyday use, long known as the "centigrade" scale; the degree interval on both scales is the same. The conversion formula for the or Kelvin scale is K = C +273·15. *See* **Absolute Temperature.**

Kerguelen, the lost continent formed 110 million years ago which sank back beneath the present Indian Ocean 20 million years ago.

Kernewek. The native language of Cornwall which almost died out *c.* 1770 but is now being revived. Cornish has now been granted protection under the EU charter on "minority languages".

Kestrel, the most common British falcon, well known for its habit of hovering for minutes at a time with vibrating wings and then swooping down to attack mice and insects. The male has spotted chestnut-brown back, greyish head and tail, with a broad black band near tip. Kestrel numbers are now rapidly declining.

Ketones. A class of organic compounds, related to aldehydes, of general formula R_2CO (where R is an organic radical). The simpler ketones, especially acetone, are widely used as solvents for lacquers, synthetic rubber and polymers, such as cellulose acetate and perspex. More complex ketones occur in nature, and some are used in the perfumery industry, muscone (from the musk deer (*q.v.*)) is an example.

Kew Gardens, officially known as the Royal Botanic Gardens, are among the most celebrated gardens in the world. They were started in 1759 by Princess Augusta of Saxe-Gotha, widow of Frederick, Prince of Wales, and mother of George III. They remained private property until 1841, when control passed to the Commissioners of Woods and Forests. They now cover 121 hectares and are administered by an independent body under the 1983 National Heritage Act. Since 1841 the gardens have been open to the public. They suffered severe damage in 1987. Kew is a World Heritage Site.

Keys, House of, is the Manx representative assembly. *See* **Tynwald.**

Keystone, the stone which occupies the centre and highest point of an arch and is usually the last to be inserted.

Khaki, a clay-coloured cloth adopted for uniforms in the British Army in the time of the war with the Boers, and used in the first and second world wars. First used by Indian regiments.

Kibbutz (Hebrew, gathering). An Israeli collective farm. The place and function of the kibbutzim has played a large part in independent Israel.

Kilderkin, once a common liquid measure in England, representing 18 gallons or 82 litres.

Kilogram, unit of mass, defined as the mass of the international prototype kilogram of platinum-iridium kept at the International Bureau of Weights and Measures at Sèvres. A remeasurement of Avogadro's Number (**T24**) may lead to an atomic standard of mass (the second and the metre are already defined in atomic terms), but this will depend on the precision with which atoms can be counted.

Kilowatt. Unit of power, equal to one thousand watts. *See* **Watt.**

Kinetic Energy, the energy (*q.v.*) possessed by a particle or body in virtue of its motion. If the motion is destroyed, *e.g.*, by the impact of the body with an obstacle, the kinetic energy vanishes, being turned into other forms of energy such as heat and sound. If the body has mass m and speed v its kinetic energy (leaving out corrections due to relativity) is $\frac{1}{2}mv^2$.

King Crab, remarkable arthropods now classified separately known both Arachnids and Crustacea which they resemble, inhabiting the sea coasts of America, Japan, India and Malay Peninsula, carrying a shield-shaped shell, and having a long pointed spine projecting from the posterior. The body comprises three separate sections articulated together. These crabs—in America known commonly as the horseshoe crab because of their shape—are from 45–60 cm in length. Fossil king crabs are found as far back as the Silurian. There are about six living species.

Kingfisher, a well-known family of brilliant-plumaged birds, found in all continents, comprising some 250 species and sub-species. The British kingfisher, *Aceldo atthis*, haunts the rivers and streams, and is one of the most beautiful of native birds, having iridescent blue-green, white and rich chestnut in its plumage and bright-red feet. All kingfishers have long, dagger-shaped bills. In the Malayan region, New Guinea, the Moluccas and Australia, the varieties are very numerous. The quaint *Laughing Jackass* of Australia is among the largest of the kingfisher family. The European kingfisher is the bird of the Greek legend of the Halcyon. Cleaner rivers and more sensible management of river banks are encouraging the kingfisher to return.

King-of-Arms, the name of the chief officials of the Heralds' College. There are several in England —the principal are the Garter, Norroy and Ulster, Clarenceux. *See* **Heralds' College.**

Kirimon (*Kiri no go Mon*) and **Kikumon** (*Kiki no go Mon*), the two Japanese imperial crests, the first a design of leaves, stems and flowers of the Paulownia plant, and the other representing the sixteen-petalled chrysanthemum.

Kite, name of several birds of prey, widely distributed, related to the hawks and eagles, graceful in flight, and distinguished by their long wings and deeply forked tails. The red kite, light chestnut brown, once the most familiar bird of prey in Britain, seen scavenging the streets of London, is now the rarest, and found only in Wales. The Egyptian kite and the pariah kite of India, notorious for their daring thefts, are closely related to the black kite, a smaller European species, with less forked tail and blackish-brown plumage.

Kittiwake, a beautiful white and pearl-grey gull with black legs, dark eyes and greenish-yellow bill. Its range is wide, and includes the British Isles, where it is a local resident. The flight of this only truly oceanic gull, which except in the breeding-season is generally found offshore, is graceful, swift and buoyant. A triangular black patch, noticeable on the ends of the wings when open, is characteristic of the species, as is the call kitti-wake, from which the bird derives its name. It nests in colonies on the ledges of caves and steep cliffs.

Kiwi, flightless, stoutly-built birds of New Zealand now very rare and carefully protected by the Government. They are little larger than a domestic hen, and lay astonishingly large eggs for their size. Incubation and care of chicks fall to the male bird. They have rudimentary wings concealed by the plumage, and the feathers are hair-like. They are nocturnal.

Knighthood In Britain the main orders of knighthood are those of the Garter, the Bath, the Thistle and St. Patrick; in addition to which there are several other orders, *e.g.* the Order of St. Michael and St. George, the Star of India. There are also Knights Bachelors not associated with any special order. The title is not hereditary, and ranks below that of a baronet, though both are entitled to the prefix "Sir".

Knights of Malta. *See* **Hospitallers, Knights.**

Knot, a nautical measure of speed (1 sea mile per hour), and formerly measured by a log-line, divided by knots at equal distances $\frac{1}{120}$ of a geographical mile. The number of knots travelled by the ship in a half a minute corresponded to the numbers of sea miles it travelled per hour. A sea mile is equal to about 1¼ of a statute mile or 1·9 km. Also, a grey and white wading bird, usually a winter visitor to Britain found in flocks on the coast.

Knout, a whip of many thongs, often fatal in its effects, formerly used in Russia for flogging.

Koala, the Australian arboreal marsupial mammal that looks like a tiny teddy-bear, with ashy grey fur, bushy ears and rudimentary tail. It feeds on the leaves and shoots of certain eucalyptus trees, and is not more than 60 cm in length. Today fewer than 100,000 remain and their habitat is threatened.

Kohl, a powder prepared from antimony or burnt almond shells, and in common use by the women of the East for darkening the eyelids.

Komodo Dragon. *See under* **Monitor.**

Koto, a musical instrument In general use in Japan consisting of a series of 13 silken strings stretched across a curved wooden surface, and played with the fingers. Each string is 1·5 m long, and has a separate bridge so fixed as to give the vibration necessary for the note it has to produce. It is a sort of horizontal harp, and in the hands of an expert player is capable of giving forth excellent music.

Kremlin, the citadel or walled area within a Russian city which during the Middle Ages served as an administrative and religious centre and offered protection. That of Moscow, now the headquarters of the Russian government, contains the cathedral where the Tsars were crowned, an imperial palace and the "King of Bells" (*see* **Bells**). Its walls which are topped with towers were built in the 15th cent.

Krill, shrimp-like crustaceans at the heart of the food chain in the oceans. Their decline around Antarctica because of rising temperatures is threatening the penguins, seals and whales.

Krypton, one of the rare gas elements, no. 36, symbol Kr, occurring in the air to the extent of 1 part in 20 million. It was discovered in 1898 by Ramsay and Travers. It is used in gas-filled electric lamps.

Kuiper Belt. A disc of many millions of comets that is formed on the plane of the solar system and lies between 35 and 1000 Astronomical units from the sun.

Kumara. *See* **Sweet Potato.**

Kurds, an Indo-European people who have faced repeated oppression in Iraq and Turkey (and to a lesser extent in Iran and Syria). Kurdistan, the mountainous 'land of the Kurds', which has been their homeland for thousands of years, straddles the four countries just mentioned. Their religion is Sunni Muslim. Iraq's northern Kurdish region has been autonomous since 1991.

Kusti, the sacred cord or girdle of the Parsees, consisting of 72 threads—the number of the chapters of the *Yasna*—and two branches, each branch containing six knots, together standing for the 12 months of the year.

Kyrie Eleison ("Lord, have mercy"), the name of a common form of prayer in the Anglican, Roman Catholic and Greek Churches; also applied to the English Church responses after the recital of the commandments.

Kyrle Society, named after Pope's "Man of Ross", John Kyrle, founded by Miss Miranda and Miss Octavia Hill in 1875, and having among its objects the promotion among the poor of a taste for literature, music and outdoor recreation.

L

Labradorite, a felspar rich in calcium and of a pearly lustre on cleavage, found in masses in igneous rocks, the best samples of which come from Labrador.

Labyrinth, or **Maze,** a combination of roads and passages so constructed as to render it difficult for anyone ignorant of the clue to trace the way to the central part. The Egyptian labyrinth near Lake Moeris had 3,000 rooms, half of them subterranean and the remainder above ground.

The labyrinth in Crete, according to Greek myth, was built by Daedalus to house the Minotaur. There was one at Lemnos, renowned for its stalactite columns; and another at Clusium constructed by Porsenna, King of Etruria, about 520 B.C. The labyrinth in which Fair Rosamond was concealed was at Woodstock. Hampton Court maze dates from the 16th cent.

Labyrinthodonts, gigantic fossil amphibians which get their name from the curious labyrinthine structure of their teeth, probably an evolutionary link between fishes and reptiles. They occur in the Carboniferous, Permian and Triassic formations, and remains have been found in Britain and other parts of Europe.

Their heads were long, and their footprints, by which they were discovered, closely resemble the prints of the human hand.

Lac, a resinous matter deposited on the branches of a number of tropical trees by the females of the lac insect, the exudation including eggs and a viscous covering. At the gathering time the twigs are broken off and dried in the sun, when the insects die, and the lac that remains is termed *stick-lac.* From this, by the removal of extraneous accretions and dissolving, *seed-lac* is produced. *Shell-lac* is seed-lac after it has been melted and otherwise prepared, and this is the best known of the lacs, used in printing and the manufacture of varnishes and sealing-wax, and for other commercial purposes.

Lace, a delicate fabric of linen, silk or cotton threads, made by hand or machinery, and worked in various ornamental designs. The kinds of lace are many, deriving their distinctive names either from the method employed in production or from the place where any special variety was originally made. The best-known makes are pillow or bobbin-lace, woven and plaited by hand; needle-point lace, worked by the needle over a traced design; and machine lace, which practically dates from Heathcote's invention of the early part of the 19th century.

Some of the most famed laces are the following: *Alençon,* a needle-point lace; *Brussels,* a very fine kind, with needle-point sprigs and flowers;

Chantilly, a silk variety with flowers and open-work; *Cluny*, a netlace with darned stitch; *Honiton*, a delicate kind with dainty sprigs and figures; *Mechlin*, generally made in one piece and very varied in design; and *Valenciennes*, or bobbin lace, of great durability, the pattern and ground of which are made at the same time, being one of the best and most costly of laces, now manufactured mainly in Belgium. Nottingham was famous for its lace.

Lace-Wings, insects with frail, transparent and much-veined wings whose grubs eat large numbers of insect pests such as aphids. The eggs are borne at the ends of threads attached to plants.

Ladybird, the common name of a large family of beetles—the *Coccinellidae*. The insect is usually of a red or yellow colour with small black or coloured spots. Ladybirds are of good service to the gardener because their larvae feed on aphids. There are about 2,000 species (46 native to Britain). They are currently under threat in Britain from a foreign invader, the harlequin ladybird.

Lady-Day, the day of the festival of the Annunciation of the Virgin Mary, 25 March. One of the four English quarter days.

Lake Dwelling, the name given to certain prehistoric habitations which were thought to have stood on platforms over lakes, like villages in certain Pacific islands. Major excavations at the Lake of Burgäschi in Switzerland show that the prehistoric Swiss pile dwellings probably stood on the shores of lakes, not on platforms over the water.

Lakes are bodies of water collected in depressions of the earth's surface. The most notable lakes are the Great Lake series of North America, including Superior, Michigan, Huron, Erie and Ontario, all discharging into the St. Lawrence River. Africa has an enormous area of lakes, including Mobutu Sese Soko and Victoria, forming the sources of the White Nile. Smaller lakes are numerous in other countries—Switzerland, Finland, Italy, England, Ireland, Scotland, all having their lake regions, where the scenery is invariably beautiful and romantic. The Kariba Dam (Zimbabwe-Zambia border) and the Nasser (Egypt) are the largest man-made lakes in the world.

Many of the world's lakes are now diminishing because of global demand for water, but global warming could cause lakes in the Himalayas to burst their banks. Among lakes now in major decline are Lake Chad in Africa, and others in central Asia and the Aral Sea.

Lake School, the name given, at first in ridicule, to a distinguished trio of poets—Wordsworth, Coleridge and Southey—who made their homes in the English Lake District.

Lamellibranchs (Pelecypods), the class of aquatic, bi-valve molluscs to which the oysters, cockles, mussels, clams and scallops belong. In these animals the body, which is compressed laterally, is enclosed in two hinged shells held together by muscular action. The gills are thin plates hence the name "lamellibranchs".

Lamination, stratification on a very fine scale, as in shales.

Lammas Day is one of the oldest of the Church festivals, probably derived from the loaf-mass (*hlafmaesse*) of the Anglo-Saxons. It occurs on 1 August. It was formerly the day when loaves were given in place of first-fruit offerings.

Lammergeyer, the bearded vulture of alpine regions, resembling an eagle in appearance. It has a white head with black tufts at base of the bill, and its general plumage is dark brown, nearly black. It is found in the remote mountain ranges from southern Spain and parts of Africa to China, and is becoming scarce.

Lampblack, a carboniferous pigment obtained from flame-smoke, and now produced in specially constructed furnaces in which bodies rich in carbon, such as tar, resin, petroleum, *etc.*, are burned. The smoke or soot resulting is collected from the sides of the furnace, and forms lampblack. It finds use in making printer's ink, black paint, *etc.* and in making dynamo brushes and arc-lamp carbons.

Lamprey. Eel-like fish having no scales, bones, paired fins or jaws. They attach themselves by their mouths to fish whose blood they suck.

Together with the hagfishes, the lampreys are placed in a special class—the Cyclostomes. There are three British lampreys.

Lancelet. See **Amphioxus**.

Land Crab, a family of crabs (*Gecarcinidae*) which live mainly on land, though migrating to the seas to deposit their eggs.

Landrail, old word for Corncrake (*q.v.*).

Landslip, a sudden downward sliding under gravity of large masses of rock, soil, *etc.*; often set off by earthquake shock or saturation of a particular stratum with water. Many serious landslides have occurred from time to time. In 1618, an earthfall happened at Plurs, on Lake Como, involving the destruction of many buildings and the loss of numerous lives. In 1806 a portion of Rossberg mountain in Switzerland slipped from its position, and falling into the valley below buried many villages and hamlets and over 800 people. A chalk cliff 30–45 m high and 1·2 km long fell at Lyme Regis, in Dorset, in 1839, doing great damage. Over 200 people were killed by a landslip in Naini Tal, in India, in 1880; and at Quebec, in 1889, a rocky eminence called Cape Diamond gave way, buildings being destroyed and lives lost.

Notable landslips have occurred at Amalfi (Italy) in 1924, at Murchiston (New Zealand) in 1929, at Aberfan (Wales) in 1966, near St. Gervais (France) in 1970 and at Guinsaugon in the southern Philippines in 2006. Submarine landslips (*i.e.* landslips under the oceans) may give rise to tsunamis.

Languages. See *under* **Sanskrit**, **Aryan** *etc.*

Langue d'oc and Langue d'oïl, the two principal mediaeval French dialects, *oc* and *oïl* being their respective words for the affirmative particle (modern French *oui*). *Langue d'oc*, spoken south of the Loire, was the language of the troubadours. Provençal, one of its dialects had a literary revival in the 19th cent. under the influence of the poet Frédéric Mistral. *Langue d'oïl* was spoken in northern France, and it was the dialect of the Paris region, developing into modern French.

Lantern Fly, bugs belonging to the family *Fulgoridae* in which the head is drawn out to form a lantern-like structure. In no instance is the "lantern" luminous as once thought.

Lanthanides, the fourteen metallic elements following lanthanum in the Periodic Table, *i.e.*, the elements cerium (no. 58) to lutetium (no. 71). They are also known as the rare-earth metals, though they are in fact all more terrestrially abundant than, for instance, mercury or arsenic (with the exception of the unstable radioactive element promethium, no. 61).

The lanthanides are distinguished by having an incomplete inner electron sub-shell (the 4f level), this feature giving them interesting magnetic properties. For instance, gadolinium, holmium and dysprosium are ferromagnetic at low temperatures. Chemically, the lanthanides behave similarly, being highly reactive metals usually forming trivalent salts. See **Periodic Table**, **T57.**

Lapis Lazuli, an azure-blue mineral, being a silicate of aluminium and sodium. The pigment ultramarine is made by grinding it, though artificial ultramarine has largely superseded it. The mineral (also called *lazurite*) has been used as a gemstone from antiquity.

Lapwing *or* **Green Plover**, familiar British bird on moors and marshlands with iridescent greenish-black plumage, white underparts and black crest. Often called "peewit" from its cry. Protected under Protection of Birds Act, 1967. It is nevertheless in serious decline in Britain.

Larboard is the old nautical term indicating the left-hand side of a ship, and changed by Admiralty order to "port" in 1844. Starboard is the right-hand side.

Larch, a familiar coniferous tree in the mountain regions of northern Europe, and though not native to Britain, the Common Larch is successfully cultivated in various parts of the kingdom. It is one of the best of all turpentine-yielding trees, and the bark is valued for tanning. The larch is an unusual conifer in being deciduous.

Lark, a family of song birds (*Alaudidae*) of many species, some of which—notably the skylark—are famed for their habit of soaring into the air, singing all the while. They build their nests on the ground in the open country and, except for the black lark of Russia, have streaked brown plumage. The skylark and woodlark are the best known British species, while the crested lark and shore lark are among the occasional visitors. Africa has the greatest number of larks; America has only one species, the horned lark. In Britain lark numbers are declining due to the switch to autumn-sown cereals.

Larkspur, the common name of the genus *Delphinium,* a favourite flower introduced into British gardens from Switzerland in 1573. The common larkspur is *D. consolida.*

Larva, the undeveloped form of any animal which before maturity undergoes metamorphosis, usually differ from the adult in structure and habits.

Laser. A remarkable kind of light source that was discovered in 1960. With the laser it is possible to probe the behaviour of matter under the influence of enormous energy densities, range and survey vast distances to microscopic accuracy and send millions of telephone and television messages between any two points that can see each other with telescopes. Laser light, in contrast to natural light, is coherent and can be expressed as a regular progression of waves carrying energy along a particular path. Thus the essential difference is that laser light is an orderly sort of wave motion in contrast to ordinary light which is inherently unsteady and thus an inefficient carrier of information in time.

The name *maser,* which is the microwave parent of the laser, derives from the expression "*microwave amplification by the stimulated emission of radiation*". Upon application to light wavelengths the microwave part of the name lost its meaning and the term maser became generally descriptive of any device in which stimulated emission dominates.

Laser Fusion is a method by which it has been proposed that thermonuclear reactions may be controlled and exploited as a source of energy (*see* **Nuclear Fusion**) The idea is to irradiate a millimetre-sized pellet of a mixture of frozen deuterium and tritium with a short (~10^{-9} s) but very intense pulse of energy in the form of laser light. This has the effect of both compressing the pellet by a factor of at least a thousand and heating it to about 10^8 °C. Under these conditions, thermonuclear reactions (principally $^2D + ^3T \rightarrow ^4He + ^1n$) proceed sufficiently fast that a net output of energy is obtained before the pellet explosively separates.

Formidable technical problems need solving before laser fusion can become a practical proposition. These include the development of efficient high-powered lasers and the design of a suitable reactor that can withstand up to 100 micro-hydrogen bomb explosions per second. It is still not clear whether this method of controlling nuclear fusion is more practical than the more conventional approach involving the magnetic confinement of plasmas.

Latent Heat is the quantity of heat required to convert 1 gram of a substance from one form into another. For example, when a solid changes into a liquid or a liquid into a gas, the addition of heat to bring about the change produces no rise in temperature, the energy being absorbed in the form of latent heat. An equal amount is released when the process is reversed. The latent heat of fusion of ice is about 79·6 calories per gram, that of the vaporisation of water about 539 calories per gram.

Lateran Councils were the religious conventions held in the Lateran basilica at Rome for deciding important questions of Church doctrine. The most brilliant was that of 1215 which pronounced in favour of a Crusade.

Lateran Treaty, 1929, between Italy and the Papacy established the Vatican City as an independent sovereign state.

Laterite refers to any tropical soil or soil horizon rich in hydrated ferric and aluminium oxides which harden when exposed to the atmosphere. It is difficult to cultivate and is commonly used for bricks and road metal. Laterite buildings have been known to withstand the weathering for many centuries and a number of fine examples are found in India and S.E. Asia.

Latitude of a point on the earth's surface is its angular distance from the equator, measured on the surface of the earth in degrees, minutes and seconds. Thus the equator is 0° Lat. and

the poles 90° Lat. (N. or S.). First determined by Hipparchus of Nicaea about 160 B.C. Latitude introduces zones of climate, *e.g.,* tropical rain, subtropical steppe, temperate rain *etc.*

Laughing Gas. *See* **Nitrous Oxide.**

Launce *or* **Sand Eel,** a family of eel-like sea fishes found in large numbers on the coasts of North America and Europe. There are two species common to British waters. These fishes are of a bright silvery hue, and live much in the sand underneath the water. They are prized as food.

Laurentian Shield refers to the Pre-Cambrian rocks in the region of the Upper Lakes of Canada, nearly 5 million sq km in extent. Of enormous importance to Canada on account of the mineral wealth, forests yielding valuable timber and wood-pulp, and water-power.

Lava, the molten rock which is erupted from a volcanic vent or fissure. Also the same material which has cooled and solidified.

Lawn, very fine sun-bleached linen it used to be called "cloth of Rheims".

Lead, a soft malleable metallic element, no. 82, symbol Pb (Latin *plumbum*), occurring in numerous ores, which are easily smelted. Its most important source is the mineral galena which consists chiefly of lead sulphide; rarely is it found free. Lead is largely used in plumbing on account of its pliability, and in nuclear reactors as a shield against radiation because of its high density.

As an alloy element it combines in the formation of type metal, stereo metal, shot metal, pewter and many other compounds. Oxides of lead are used in some types of glass and in the manufacture of paints (red lead). All lead compounds are poisonous. Leading producers of lead are the United States (Missouri), Australia (Broken Hill) and Russia.

Leaf Miners, insect larvae which tunnel between the upper and lower skins of leaves. Most leaf miners are caterpillars of tiny moths; some sawfly larvae have the same habit.

Leap Year *or* **Bissextile,** was fixed by Julius Caesar, 45 B.C., the addition of one day in every four years bringing the measure of the calendar year even with the astronomical year with three minutes per year over. The Gregorian Calendar corrected this by dropping leap year at the centuries not divisible by 400. For instance, 1700, 1800 and 1900 were not leap years, but 2000 was.

Leather was made in ancient Egypt, Greece and Rome, and has through succeeding centuries played an important part in the service of man. It consists of the dressed hides or skins of animals after the process of tanning has been gone through. Untanned skins are known as pelts. Leather is classed either according to the skins from which it is made or the system of preparation employed. The best-known kinds are morocco, kid, Russian, chamois, Cordovan, grained, patent, russet, tan, calf, Hungarian.

Leech, an aquatic blood-sucking worm, mostly found in fresh-water ponds. Each end of the body is provided with a sucker, but that at the head end has jaws and teeth. There are 650 different species. The medicinal leech has three jaws. Used medicinally since the 6th cent. B.C.

Leeward, a nautical term, meaning the sheltered side of a vessel—that is, the opposite side to that from which the wind is blowing.

Legion (Roman). *See* **A44.**

Legion of Honour, the French order for distinguished services, military or civil, was instituted by Napoleon I in 1802, and confirmed and modified under later rules. There are five grades—Grands Croix, Grands Officiers, Commandeurs, Officiers and Chevaliers.

Legume, the fruit typical of the pea, bean family, or *Leguminosae.*

Lemming, small light-brown rodents with dark spots, abounding in Scandinavian countries and in Siberia, about 12 cm long, with a short stump of a tail. The migrations of the lemming are famous, probably caused by overbreeding when food is plentiful. So insistent is the urge to keep moving that these animals will march on into the sea in their thousands and be drowned.

Lemur, almost the most primitive member of the primate order of mammals (to which man, apes and monkeys also belong). They are noted for having strong pliant toes enabling them to use their feet as hands, and also well-developed thumbs on the hands. They have long squirrel-like tails, fox-shaped heads and large staring eyes. True lemurs are confined to the Malagasy Rep.; closely related are the "bush-babies" of southern Africa.

Lenses, pieces of transparent material designed to focus an image of an illuminated object. Usually of glass, but plastic lenses are common, and quartz, *etc.* are used for special purposes. The surfaces of the simplest lenses are parts of spheres. Lenses which are thickest, or thinnest, at the centre are called convex and concave respectively. Lenses of complex shape are often used in microscopes, *etc.* Electron lenses are arrangements of electric or magnetic fields which focus beams of electrons, *e.g.*, on to TV screens.

Lent, the forty days' period of fasting that precedes Easter.

Lepidoptera, the order of insects with scaly wings and bodies, to which the 90,000 butterflies and moths belong.

Leptons. A group of particles which include electrons, neutrinos and muons. All are much lighter than protons or any baryons (*q.v.*).

Lepus, the constellation of the Hare, situated under the Orion group, and one of the constellations with which the ancients were familiar.

Lewis, a contrivance for stone-lifting, the principle of which was known to the ancient Romans; it consists of two dovetail tenons of iron or other metal, expanded by an intervening key in a dovetail-shaped mortice in the stone, and shackled by a ringed bolt to the hoisting chain.

Leyden Jar, the earliest form of electrical condenser. Its invention is usually credited to Muschenbroeck of Leyden (1745). It consisted of a jar coated inside and out with tinfoil for about two-thirds of its height and having its inner coating connected with the top by a brass knob and chain. The jar was charged by connecting it to an electrostatic machine.

Lias, a geological term referring to the lower section of the Jurassic group, and mainly comprising shales and limestones.

Libraries, before the invention of printing, were few, and collected together at enormous cost. At Nineveh remains of libraries, consisting of tablets of baked clay, have been discovered. There were two libraries at Alexandria containing a vast collection of rolls or volumes, founded by Ptolemy I Soter (367–382 B.C.) and established by Ptolemy II Philadelphus (309–246 B.C.).

The great libraries of later times included the Vatican Library at Rome, moved to its present premises in 1588; the Royal Library in Paris which later became the Bibliothèque Nationale; The Astor Library, New York; and in England, the Bodleian Library, Oxford, and the British Library (*see below*). Since 1850 public libraries have been established in all the chief cities and towns of the kingdom. The first lending library was opened in Edinburgh in 1726.

The British Library in London, the National Library of Scotland, in Edinburgh, that of Wales in Aberystwyth, the Bodleian Library of Oxford, Cambridge University Library and Trinity College Dublin comprise the "copyright" libraries, entitled to receive a copy of each new book and journal published in Britain. The British Library Act 1972 brought together into a single organisation (a) the former British Museum Library (the books remaining in the Museum) and the Science Reference Library in Holborn and Bayswater, the whole now being known as the British Library, Reference Division; (b) the former National Lending Library for Science and Technology and its arts and humanities counterpart, the National Central Library, together now known as the British Library, Lending Division and located at Boston Spa, Yorkshire. The new Reference Division, near Euston Station, was officially opened on 25 June 1998. Lending Division remains in Yorkshire.

Great emphasis is now being placed on new developments in IT to transform libraries into a fully electronic network. Book borrowing is declining but Internet use of libraries is now (2006) rising rapidly.

Libretto (It. booklet), the literary text of an opera or oratorio. Usually the composer and the librettist collaborate in the writing of an opera, but several composers (*e.g.*, Wagner) wrote their own librettos. Boito, librettist to Verdi for *Otello* and *Falstaff*, himself composed two

operas *Mefistofele* and *Nerone*. Most famous of Italian opera librettists was the poet and dramatist Metastasio (1698–1782). His librettos were set to music by many composers, including Gluck, Handel, Mozart, Rossini.

Licence is a permission given to do some act, which without such permission, it would be unlawful to do. Licences are required for operating TVs, for driving a motor vehicle, for killing game, for setting up as a bookmaker, for selling beer, wines and spirits, tobacco, *etc.* and for importing certain items such as arms, ammunition, radioactive materials, animals, plants, drugs and explosives. The dog licence was abolished in 1988. The 2003 Licensing Act for pubs took effect on 24 November 2005.

Lichens. In every lichen, two plants are associated, one being an alga and the other a fungus. The fungus derives its food from the alga; probably the alga gains too from the association, being protected against desiccation by the fungus (an example of symbiosis). Lichens are the first plants to colonise bare rocks.

Lifeboats were invented by three men, Lionel Lukin who converted a coble into a boat for saving life in 1785; William Wouldhave, who discovered how to make a boat right herself if she capsized; and Henry Greathead, who built a lifeboat, partly from Wouldhave's model, in 1789. This boat was stationed at South Shields, although the earliest recorded reference to a lifeboat station was in 1770 at Formby, Lancs. It was not until 1851 that the first lifeboat able to self-right was built, and a motor was first installed in a life-boat in 1904. Mersey class lifeboats, introduced in 1988, have twin turbo-charged diesel engines with maximum speed of 17·5 knots. Most coastal life-boats in this country are maintained by the Royal National Lifeboat Institution founded by Sir William Hillary on 4 March 1824. It is supported entirely by voluntary contributions, and has saved over 136,000 people. Its headquarters are in Poole, Dorset. In 2006, its annual operating cost was over £90,000,000. There are 233 lifeboat stations around the UK and Ireland. UK lifeboats were launched a record 8,273 times in 2005.

Light, a particular kind of electromagnetic disturbance capable of travelling through space, and some kinds of matter, and of affecting our eyes to cause vision. Its finite speed was first demonstrated by O. Römer, using observations of the eclipses of Jupiter's satellites in 1675. In 1860 Maxwell showed that light waves are electromagnetic. Since Einstein's theory of relativity (1905) it has been generally realised that the speed of light is a fundamental natural constant. Visible light with wavelengths between about 4 and 7×10^{-5} cm is only a small part of the electromagnetic spectrum. The speed of light in vacuum is c. $2 \cdot 997925 \times 10^8$ m/s. Scientists have now succeeded in "freezing" light (for a few hundredths of a millisecond) in an experiment that could help develop super-computers.

Light Year, a measure of astronomical distance, equal to the distance light travels in a period of one year. A light year is $9 \cdot 463 \times 10^{12}$ km but the unit parsec is now preferred. (1 pc = $3 \cdot 2616$ l.y.).

Lighthouses, to warn ships of dangerous places and indicate coasts, points, harbours, *etc.*, have existed since the building of the Pharos, a tower of white marble 183 m high, built by Ptolemy II Philadelphus at Alexandria about 283 B.C. In early lighthouses the lights were simple fires. The most famous and one of the earliest UK lighthouses is the Eddystone (*q.v.*).

Dungeness lighthouse, opened in 1960, was very modern in design, capable of automatic operation and the first of its kind to incorporate the xenon electric arc lamp as a source of illumination. The electric fog signal consists of sixty loud-speaker units built into the tower just below the lantern, giving a honeycomb effect.

The lighthouses of England and Wales, the Channel Islands and Gibraltar are under the control of Trinity House; Commissioners of Northern Lighthouses control those of Scotland; the Commissioners of Irish Lights control the coasts of Ireland. Particulars of lights in all parts of the world are published for the guidance of navigation in the *Admiralty Lists of Lights*. Under the 1987 Pilotage Act, responsibility for pilotage now rests with harbour authorities. All lighthouses are now automatic, the last manned lighthouse in Britain went over to computer control in 1998. Trinity House built its first lighthouse at Lowestoft in 1609. *See also* **Eddystone Lighthouse**.

Lightning, the flash of a discharge of electricity between two clouds, or between a cloud and the earth, when the strength of the electric fields becomes so great as to break down the resistance of the intervening air. With "forked" lightning the actual path, often branched, is visible, while with "sheet" lightning the flash is hidden by the clouds which themselves are illuminated. "Ball" lightning or fireballs is the name given to the luminous balls which have been seen floating in the air during a thunderstorm. The Boys camera has provided much information regarding the sequence of events in a lightning discharge.

A flash consists of a number of separate strokes, usually four or five, and the discharge of electricity to earth begins with a faintly luminous "leader" moving downwards and branching at intervals. As the ground is approached a much brighter luminosity travels back along the conducting channels, lighting up with several branches. The multiple strokes which follow in fractions of a second have the same "return" nature and are rarely branched.

Lightning flashes to earth damage structures, cause loss of life and endanger overhead power systems, often interrupting electricity supply. Such storms generally affect radio transmissions and present hazards to aircraft. Thunderclouds may develop energy far exceeding that of our largest power generating stations.

Megalightning is the form of lightning that strikes from the clouds up into space and is thousands of times more powerful than conventional lightning.

Scientists are now looking at the link between lightning and cosmic rays.

Lightning Conductor, a metal rod, the upper part of which is of copper with a conical point, the lower portion being iron, which extends into the earth. Its effect is to gather to itself the surrounding electricity and discharge it into the earth, thus preventing its falling upon the protected building. In ships, lightning conductors are fixed to the masts and carried down through the ship's keel-sheathing. Benjamin Franklin was the first to realise the possibilities of lightning protection and, in 1752, carried out his famous experiment of drawing electricity from thunder-clouds, with the aid of a sharp-pointed conductor fixed to a kite.

Lillibulero, an old marching song arranged by Purcell. With words by Wharton, it is said to have "sung James II out of three kingdoms". Used by the wartime BBC as a station identification signal preceding news bulletins.

Lily Family (Liliaceae), one of the largest families of flowering plants, with 200 genera and 2,500 species. It includes the true lilies (*Lilium*), tulips and hyacinths. Vegetables belonging to the family are the onion and asparagus.

Limes, trees of the genus *Tilia*, including some 30 species spread over north temperate regions. The word is a corruption of "linden". Limes native to Britain are the small-leaved *T. cordata* and the broad-leaved *T. platyphyllos*. The hybrid *T. vulgaris* was introduced into Britain from the Continent during the 17th cent. and is frequently seen in streets and parks. Lime-wood was used by Grinling Gibbons for his fruit, flower and bird decorations.

Limestones, sedimentary rocks composed wholly or largely of calcium carbonate and formed by two main processes, (1) organic (skeletal remains of organisms), *e.g.*, chalk (*q.v.*) and (2) chemical (precipitation of calcium carbonate), *e.g.*, oolite (*q.v.*). Marble is limestone that will polish after cutting.

Lindisfarne Gospels. *See under* **Illuminated MSS**.

Linen, a textile fabric manufactured from flax fibre, known to the ancient Egyptians, and first manufactured in England under Henry III by Flemish weavers. The greatest linen-manufacturing region in the world is Northern Ireland (largely yarns and the lighter types of fabrics); Scotland produces coarse linens and canvas as well as household linens.

Ling, a sea-fish common on the coasts of Britain,

and abounding in more northern waters. It averages about 1 m in length, and is a voracious feeder, living chiefly on small fish. Ling is also the name applied to *Calluna vulgaris*, the plant commonly called "heather".

Linseed, the seed of the flax plant, containing, apart from its fibrous substance, certain oily and nitrogenous matter of considerable commercial value. This yields linseed oil. Some of the residue is used to make cattle food.

Lion, the most impressive of the Cat family. It is chiefly found in open bush country in Africa, being comparatively rare in Asia. Its large square head, its flowing mane (in the males only) and its tufted tail distinguish it. Tip to tip it can reach a length of 3m; a weight of 225 kg. African lion numbers in 2006 had fallen to 15,000—down from 200,000 in two decades. Many are dying from Lentivirus, the lion form of AIDS.

Lion and Unicorn, the supporting figures of the royal arms of Great Britain, date from the union of Scotland with England (1603) at the accession of James I (James VI of Scotland), the lion representing England and the unicorn Scotland.

Liqueurs are essences combined with alcoholic liquid, and are of many kinds, named according to their flavouring or place of production, and include Cointreau, Chartreuse, Curaçao, Benedictine, Tia Maria, Drambuie *etc*.

Liquid, the name given to matter in such state that it takes its shape from the containing vessel. The volume it occupies is independent of the container, however.

Liquid Crystals form a special class of substance and are true liquids in that they flow easily and can be poured. However, unlike ordinary liquids, liquid crystals have their molecules arranged with geometrical regularity in one or two dimensions, so that they have a certain internal structure similar to that of solid crystals. They are fairly complicated chemicals with somewhat elongated molecules. Liquid crystals are of interest to biologists as well as to chemists and physicists, and not just because they account for the iridescence of beetles. Some body fluids are in fact liquid crystals. There are also technological applications because of their unique electrical and optical properties.

Litanies were first used in church processions in the 5th cent. The first English litany was commanded to be recited in the Reformed churches by Henry VIII in 1544.

Lithium, a soft metallic element, no. 3, symbol Li, similar to sodium. It is very reactive and is stored under paraffin oil. It is the lightest metal element.

Litre, a metric measure, was abolished in 1964 as a scientific unit of volume, but remains as a special name for the cubic decimetre and as an everyday unit, *e.g.*, a litre of petrol.

Liturgy, the name given to the Church ritual, though strictly applying only to the portion used in the celebration of the Eucharist or Lord's Supper. The Anglican liturgy is laid down in the Book of Common Prayer (1662).

Temporary powers granted by Parliament in 1965 to the Church to make changes in the form of worship were made permanent in 1974. The Alternative Service Book dates from 1980. The new book of prayer, *Common Worship*, was introduced on 3 December 2000.

Liverworts (Hepatics), a class of simple green plants related to the mosses. Liverworts are most common in damp situations, such as the banks of ditches. The majority of British species are leafy, only some are thalloid.

Lizard, the name given to a diversified order of reptiles, of which there are *c*. 1,600 species. They include the geckos, chameleons, glass snakes *etc*.

Llama, mammals related to the camels, from which they differ in small size, absence of the humps, and more woolly coat. The domestic llama of S. America is used as a beast of burden, also providing wool, meat and milk. *See also* **Alpaca, Guanaco**.

Loadstone *or* **Lodestone**, an oxide of iron, found chiefly in Sweden and Norway. Its scientific name is magnetite. It has the power of attracting pieces of iron and served as the first magnets used in compasses. One of the class of nonmetallic magnetic materials nowadays known as "ferrites" (*q.v.*).

Lobsters are marine crustacean animals existing in

large numbers in the northern seas of Europe and America and in fair proportion on some British coasts (*e.g.* the Channel Islands).

Locust, insects of the grasshopper family, but much more powerful. They are inhabitants of hot countries, and often make their appearance in untold millions, like locusts, devastating all the vegetation that comes within their course.

The locust-tree (*Ceratonia siliqua*) is supposed to have furnished food to St. John the Baptist in the wilderness, and its "beans" have accordingly been styled "St. John's Bread".

Loess, a deposit of silt or marl laid down by wind action. The biggest loess deposits are in Asia, the source of the dust of which they are composed probably being the deserts of Central Asia. Large deposits in Europe originated from the edge of ice sheets during the Ice Age.

Logarithms, a system of calculation invented by John Napier in 1614, and developed by Henry Briggs a few years later. Thus if a number is expressed as the power of another number, *i.e.*, if $a = b^n$, then n is said to be the logarithm of a to base b, written $\log_b a$. Common logs are to base 10 and Napierian to base $2{\cdot}7182818 \ldots$, expressed as e.

Lombards, a German people, originating on the Elber, who settled in Italy in the 6th cent., occupying northern and central regions, and establishing a kingdom with Pavia as capital. They were conquered by Charlemagne in 774, but left their name to the region of Lombardy. Lombard Street, London, takes its name from the Lombard merchants and bankers who came to settle there in the 12th cent.

London Clay, geological stratum which occupies much of the London Basin and part of the Hampshire Basin. It represents the lower stratum of the Eocene. Outside the metropolis, brickfields utilise the clay for brickmaking. Water held down in the Chalk by this impervious stratum is tapped by a number of artesian wells in London. The tunnels of the underground run through the London Clay.

London Eye, the "big wheel" by the Thames, nearly three times as high as Tower Bridge. The wheel can carry 15,000 visitors a day.

London University. Originated in the foundation of a non-sectarian college in Gower Street in 1828. Among the chief colleges are: UCL (University College London), King's College, (inc. former Chelsea College and Queen Elizabeth), Imperial College of Science and Technology, London School of Economics, O.L. of O.L. and the African Studies, Queen Mary and Westfield, Birkbeck (founded in 1823 and specialising in part-time evening study), together with Royal Holloway and Bedford New College. London University was the first to open all degrees to women (as from 1878). The London Institute became the University of the Arts in May 2004. Some colleges now (2006) are planning to leave and become independent.

Long Distance Walks. The National Parks and Access to the Countryside Act 1949 provided for the establishment in England and Wales of Long Distance Footpaths and Bridleways. Among walks which have opened are: Pennine Way (the first long-distance footpath, a magnificent hill walk of 270 miles from Edale in Derbyshire along the Pennines over the Cheviots and the Scottish border); Pembrokeshire Coast Path (from St. Dogmael's to Amroth, 180 miles); Offa's Dyke Path (176 miles along the marches of Wales); South-West Peninsula Coast path (Minehead to Poole Harbour, 520 miles); Coast to Coast Path from Robin Hood's Bay to St. Bee's (190 miles); Ridgeway (Avebury to Ivinghoe Beacon, 90 miles); Pilgrim's Way (Winchester to Canterbury, 116 miles); Cotswold Way (Bath to Chipping Campden, 95 miles); West Highland Way (Glasgow to Fort William, 95 miles).

Some paths opened in the 1990s include the 147-mile Grand Union Canal walk (1993), the 88-mile Jurassic Way from Banbury to Stamford (1994) and the 225-mile Midshires Way (which will link with the Pennine Bridleway). The 180-mile Thames Path, inaugurated in 1996, is one of the Countryside Commission's national trails (running from Kemble, Gloucs., to the Thames Barrier).

The 150-mile London Outer Orbital Path has now opened. Britain's longest riverside walk, the 220-mile Severn Way, was opened in 1998. It runs from the Plynlimon plateau in Powys to the Bristol Channel. The E8 (Trans Pennine Trail) was the first path in Britain to connect to the hiking trails which criss-cross Europe. The E9 path will connect Dover to Plymouth. *See* **National Parks.**

Longitude of a point on the earth's surface is the angle which the meridian through the poles and that point makes with some standard meridian. The meridian through Greenwich is usually accepted as the standard meridian and the longitude is measured east or west of that line. As the earth revolves through 360° in 24 h, 15° longitude represent 1 hour's difference in apparent time.

Lord Chamberlain. *See* **Chamberlain, Lord.**

Lord Chancellor. *See* **Chancellor, Lord.**

Lord Lieutenant is the Queen's representative in the county, and his office is now largely ceremonial. On his recommendation the magistrates or JPs are appointed by the Lord Chancellor. The office was created in 1549.

Louse, parasitic insect found on the skin of birds and mammals. The two sub-species that parasitise man are the body louse and the head louse. Typhus can be transmitted by lice.

Louvre, one of the old royal palaces of Paris, was built in its present form partly by Francis I and added to by later monarchs, Louis XIV completing the edifice. Napoleon I turned it into a museum and enriched it with the plunder of many foreign art galleries.

The great extension to the Louvre building begun by Napoleon I was completed under Napoleon III in 1857. Much injury was done to the building during the Commune of 1871. Amongst other famous treasures it houses the Venus de Milo and Leonardo da Vinci's masterpiece, *La Gioconda.*

Lung Fishes. *See* **Dipnoi.**

Lutecium, element (no. 71) of the rare-earth metal group discovered in 1907 by Urbain. Symbol Lu.

Lynx, cats of sturdy build, with tufted ears and spotted fur, inhabiting many parts of the world, including Northern and Central Europe. They commit serious ravages among sheep and goats.

Lyon King of Arms, the President of the Scottish Lyon Court, and head of the heraldic organisation for Scotland.

Lyre-Bird, a remarkable family of Australian birds, the males of which possess a beautiful lyre-shaped tail. The bird is not more than 38 cm long, but its tail, displayed during its remarkable courtship dances, is 60 cm in length. There are two species: the Superb and Albert's.

M

Macaque. A family of monkeys which includes the Barbary ape (specimens of which live on Gibraltar), the Rhesus macaque (the organ grinder's monkey and the one used for experimental work in the investigation of disease), the Bonnet monkey of southern India and Sri Lanka, the Crab-eating and the Pig-tailed monkeys of south-eastern Asia.

Macaw, a genus of large parrots with brilliant scarlet and sky-blue plumage, with interminglings of green. Native to South and Central America. Many species currently face extinction.

McCarthyism. *See* A45.

Mace, originally a weapon of offence, now an ensign of authority borne before officers of state and other dignitaries. In the House of Commons the mace is handed to an official of the Crown by the Sergeant-at-Arms at the close of a session.

Mach Number. Unit of flight speed. The ratio of speed of flight to speed of sound under same conditions of pressure and density. Speed of sound at sea-level is 762 mile/h (1,226 km/h), so flight speed of 381 mile/h (613 km/h) is equivalent to a Mach Number of ½. At supersonic speeds the Mach Number is greater than 1; subsonic speeds, less than 1.

Machu Picchu, the lost city of the Incas. Discovered in the Peruvian Andes by Spaniards (1532). Rediscovered, 1911, by Professor Hiram Bingham.

Mackerel, a sea-fish existing in large numbers in

the northern Atlantic off America and Europe. They are beautiful fish with a streamlined body and among the fastest fish in the sea.

Macromolecules are very large molecules about 10,000 times or more as heavy as ordinary small molecules like hydrogen. Most are built up from a large number of simple sub-units, *i.e.*, are polymers (*q.v.*). The term macromolecule is often used in biology, *e.g.*, starch and cellulose are biological macromolecules, both built from glucose sub-units. Other important ones are proteins and nucleic acids. The properties of macromolecules depend on the sub-units of which they are composed.

Mad Cow Disease, the common name for Bovine Spongiform Encephalopathy (BSE), a fatal brain disease in cattle. Concern resurfaced in 1996 over possible links with the brain disorder variant Creutzfeldt-Jakob disease (vCJD) which had begun to claim human lives. The Government admitted that it was possible that mad cow disease might be passed to humans by eating beef. Selective culling of cattle born between 1988 and 1993 was begun.

The number of cases of BSE in Britain has declined from a peak of 36,000 in 1992. However, renewed concerns about long-term health risks to humans led the government to impose a ban on the sale of all cuts of beef off the bone in 1997.

The EU ban on British beef exports was lifted in 2006.

Madder, one of the most important of dye-stuffs, largely used in producing Turkey-red dye, but now superseded by synthetic alizarin. Natural madder is the root of the *Rubia tinctorum*.

Maelstrom, a great whirlpool. The most famous is that off the coast of Norway, between the islands of Moskenës and Mosken, of the Lofoten group.

Mafia. A term which is connected with Italo-American organised crime. Historically, remoteness from the central government of Italy encouraged the growth in Sicily in the 19th cent. of *mafiosi*, key-men who gained power through fear and violence. Emigration of vast numbers of southern Italians to the United States led to a new type of urban *mafioso* who became connected with gangsterism and vice. Sometimes called the *Cosa Nostra*, the organisation has infiltrated city governments and is reputed to be in control of drug smuggling and other illegal operations. Organisations of gangsters similar to the Mafia are thriving in post-communist Russia and eastern Europe.

Magellanic Clouds, two small irregular galaxies that are close neighbours to our own Galaxy, first recorded in 1519 by Ferdinand Magellan. Both clouds are visible, with the naked eye, from the southern hemisphere. The Large Magellanic Cloud is 163,000 light years away and the Small Magellanic Cloud is 195,000 light years. They are receiving much attention from astronomers.

Magenta, a blue-red aniline dye discovered in 1859 by Sir W. H. Perkin, and named after the battle of that year between the French and Austrians.

Magic. *See* Section J.

Magic Circle, the world's most famous magical society. Its motto is *Indocilis Privata Loqui* which means "not apt to disclose secrets". This prestigious institution was established in 1905. With 1400 members, its current headquarters is at 12 Stephenson Way London NW1 2HD.

Magistrates *or* **Justices of the Peace** preside over petty sessional and Youth Courts *etc.* and are appointed by the Lord Chancellor on the recommendation of the Lord Lieutenant of the County. Most JPs are laymen and are unpaid. In certain big towns a legally- qualified, paid, full-time magistrate is appointed, known as a stipendiary magistrate. In London stipendiaries are known as Metropolitan Stipendiary Magistrates. JPs are no longer appointed over the age of 60 and they must retire when they reach 70. It is proposed to lower the age for eligibility to 18 from 21. The judicial office of JP derives from a statute of 1361.

Magistrates, though mostly laymen and unpaid, are now subject to compulsory training. Renewed attempts are now being made to ensure magistrates reflect the social mix of the country more fairly. Of the 3,636 senior judges in Britain in 2004, only 93 were black or Asian, only 544 were women and only 87 under 40.

Magma, molten rock material rich in volatile constituents prior to its eruption at the surface. With the loss of volatiles it becomes lava.

Magnesium, a metallic element, no. 12, symbol Mg, first isolated in 1808 by Sir Humphry Davy, who prepared it by electrolysing the chloride. Its chief ores are magnesite and dolomite. Industrially it is obtained by electrolysis. Many important light alloys contain magnesium. The metal burns with a very bright light, and for this reason it is used in photographers' flash bulbs and also in firework manufacture.

Magnetic Storms. These are the effects of magnetospheric storms observed world-wide at ground level as fluctuations of as much as 5 % in the earth's magnetic field. These are especially prevalent during sunspot maximums – a time when the sun is more active. The largest effects are observed at high latitudes, in the auroral ovals, and are due to electric currents flowing in the ionosphere and between the ionosphere and the magnetosphere. There may be concurrent disruption of radio communications. *See* **Magnetosphere** and **Aurora Polaris**.

Magnetism, originally the name given to the quality of attraction for iron possessed by lodestone (*q.v.*). Now known to be a phenomenon inseparably connected with electricity. Strong magnetic attraction is possessed by a comparatively small class of substances; iron, nickel and cobalt are the most common elements, but there are several less well known, *e.g.*, gadolinium. Many alloys have valuable magnetic properties which make possible numberless technical devices. New magnetic substances are being developed (*see* **Ferrites**).

The earth itself acts like a huge magnet with its axis inclined at about 11° to the axis of rotation, the magnetic poles being on the Boothia Peninsula (North Canada) and South Victoria Land (Antarctica). The magnetic field at the surface consists of the regular field of a magnetised sphere with an irregular field superimposed upon it. Variation in the magnetic forces occurs from place to place and from time to time, and maps showing the distribution over the globe of points of the same declination (*i.e.*, the angle which the magnetic meridian makes with the geographical one) are of the utmost importance in navigation. Little is known regarding the origin of the main (regular) field of the earth, but it is believed that the irregularities are due to the presence of intense electric currents in the upper atmosphere and local magnetisation of rock strata. In 1967 the discovery was made of isolated magnetic poles, *i.e.*, north and south magnetic poles existing separately, just as positive and negative electrical charges exist separately.

This discovery ranked as one of the great experimental results of the 20th cent., because of its significance for the theory of electromagnetism and fundamental particles. Magnetic field strengths are measured in gauss (cgs) or tesla (SI) units.

Scientists have now discovered that the magnetic field surrounding the Earth (protecting us from harmful radiation) is fast disappearing.

Magnetohydro-dynamics. A current-carrying wire always experiences a force if it is in a magnetic field. This is the well-known electrodynamic force, and electric motors work because of it. If the current is carried in a fluid, *e.g.*, a liquid metal or a plasma, these forces cause bodily movements to the fluid, which are in general very difficult to calculate. The forces are then called *magnetohydro-dynamic forces*. Now magnetic fields are themselves produced by electric currents; so a current flowing in a fluid produces a magnetic field, which then reacts on the fluid itself by means of the magnetohydro-dynamic forces. In the Harwell machine Zeta, which was used to study technical problems of thermonuclear reactions, this effect acted so as to constrict the electric discharge on to the axis of the tube and thus keeps it away from the walls. This action was assisted by an extra magnetic field produced by a separate current flowing in metallic conductors outside the tube. Thus the hot plasma was contained by magnetohydro-dynamic forces and not at all by the material tube wall. In practical devices of the future magnetic forces may have to sustain plasma pressure of 60 atmospheres—a pressure for which a thick steel wall would normally be used! *See also* **Plasma Physics**.

Magnetosphere. The magnetic field of the earth prevents the plasma of the solar wind from directly impinging on the earth's upper atmosphere and ionosphere. The cavity thus maintained within the solar wind is known as the magnetosphere. The tenuous plasma within this cavity is partly of solar and partly of terrestrial origin, from the solar wind and the ionosphere respectively. These plasmas are subject to large perturbations, known as magnetospheric storms, triggered by fluctuations within the solar wind. These storms generate intense auroral displays, magnetic field fluctuations at ground level, and often major disturbances of the upper atmosphere and ionosphere which may result in disruption of radio communications. The inner parts of the magnetosphere contain the Van Allen radiation belts (q.v.). On the sunward side the magnetosphere extends to between 12 and 20 earth radii. However, on the side of the earth away from the sun it extends, like a comet tail, for many millions of km. Jupiter's large magnetic field produces a large magnetosphere, one of the largest features in our planetary system being as large as the Sun itself. The earth's magnetosphere is currently being examined by the Cluster II satellites launched in 2000.

Magnitude in astronomy is a measure of the apparent brightness of a star, which is inversely proportional to the square of its distance. A low number indicates a bright star, and a high one a faint star. The *absolute magnitude* is a measure of *real* brightness, i.e., the brightness a star would have at a standard distance away of 10 parsecs (32·6 light years). The distance can be calculated if the apparent and absolute magnitudes are known. Another magnitude system used by astronomers is bolometric magnitude, which is a measure of the total radiation emitted by a star at all wavelengths. See **Light Year** and **Parsec**.

Magpie, a well-known bird of the crow family, of glossy black and white plumage, famed for its intelligence and mischievous propensities.

Magyars, the Hungarian race who came to eastern Europe from S.W. Asia and settled in Hungary in the 10th cent. Their language belongs to the Finno-Ugrian group.

Maidenhair Tree or **Ginkgo**. This tree takes its name from the shape of its leaves, which resemble those of the maidenhair fern. Widely cultivated in China and Japan. It is the only survivor of an order of gymnosperms which flourished in Mesozoic times. Botanically interesting because the male gametes are motile.

Maillardson, Château at Rueil-Malmaison, a western suburb of Paris. It derives its name from having been inhabited in the 11th cent. by the Norman brigand Odon, and afterwards, according to the tradition, by evil spirits, exorcised by the monks of St. Denis. It was the residence of Napoleon and of the Empress Josephine after her divorce. She died there in 1814. In 1900 it was given to the nation.

Mamluks. See **A45**.

Mammoth, extinct elephants of gigantic size. In 1799 the first perfectly preserved specimen was found in Siberia in a block of ice. It was in prehistoric times found in Britain and other parts of Europe, as well as in Asia and America. Scientists are planning to extract DNA from the 23,000 year-old "Zharkov mammoth" discovered intact in 1999 in the Siberian permafrost.

Mammoth Cave of Kentucky, one of the largest known limestone caverns in the world, with subterranean passages at different levels, lakes and rivers (the Echo R. flows 110 m below the surface); stalactites and stalagmites abound.

Manatee, an aquatic mammal of the sea cow (Sirenia) order of mammals, averaging when full grown from 3–3·6 m in length, with shovelshaped tail, and forelimbs and nails which almost give the appearance of arms and hands. Gentle and trusting they are under threat from man. Protected in Florida. In spite of their ungainly aspect, they are believed to have given rise to the legend of mermaids. They now number only an estimated 2,600.

Manchus, originally nomads inhabiting northern Manchuria who invaded China early in the 17th cent. A Manchu dynasty occupied the imperial throne of China from 1644 to 1911.

Mandarin, the name given to a powerful Chinese official, civil or military, under the old régime, whose rank was shown by the wearing of a button on the cap. Mandarin is the major language of N. China.

Manganese, a metallic element, no. 25, symbol Mn, discovered by Scheele, 1774. It is white-grey, not very hard (it forms a hard alloy with carbon), brittle, and tarnishes when exposed to air. Its chief ore is pyrolusite (manganese dioxide). Steels containing manganese are very tough. Manganese added to glass makes it clear or violet-coloured.

Maniple, eucharistic vestment worn over left arm.

Manna, a tree of the ash genus, *Fraxinus ornus*, growing in the South of Europe and in the East and exuding a sweet substance which is gathered, boiled and eaten.

Manometer, instrument used to measure gas pressure. Usually a 7-tube containing water or mercury, one end open to the atmosphere, the other to the gas whose pressure is to be measured. More sensitive for small pressures than the Bourdon gauge.

Mansion House, the official residence of the Lord Mayor of London, stands opposite to the Bank of England, and was erected in 1739–53 from the designs of George Dance.

Mantis. Large insects belonging to the same order as the locusts and grasshoppers. The manner in which the forelegs are held, as though in suppliance, has gained for these insects the common name of "praying mantis". They are distributed throughout the warmer countries.

Manx, the Celtic dialect (Manx Gaelic) of the Isle of Man, extinct since the 1970s.

Maoris, the race living in New Zealand at the time it was first visited by Captain Cook in 1769. They are believed to have migrated from Polynesia about 1350. Up to 1871 they were frequently in arms against the European settlers but their high intelligence and stamina enabled them to adapt themselves and the New Zealand laws have encouraged equal citizenship. They number c. 520,000 (2002). In 1994 Maoris in the upper North Island were offered land and money in compensation for land seized in the 19th century.

Maple, trees native to the northern hemisphere. There are over 100 species. The sycamore is the best-known species growing in Britain. The sugar maple abounds in Canada and the eastern parts of the United States. The sugar is tapped by boring holes in the tree in February and March, and the juice that escapes is collected and evaporated. The maple-leaf is the Canadian national emblem.

Mappa Mundi, the world-famous medieval map of the world in Hereford Cathedral.

Marathon, first run by Pheidippides from Marathon to Athens in 490 B.C. to announce the Greek victory over the Persians. The modern marathon is 26 miles 385 yards.

Marble is limestone in its hardest and most crystalline form. There are many varieties—33 were used in the building of the Paris Opera House—but white is the purest and rarest. White marble was used by the ancient Greeks for their temples and statues. Among the famous marbles of Italy are the Carrara and Siena marbles. Devonshire and Derbyshire yield some beautiful marbles and Connemara furnishes a serpentine-marble.

March, the third month of the year, and the first of the old Roman Calendar. It was named after the god Mars, and was the *Hlyd* (storm) *monath* of the Anglo-Saxons.

Mardi Gras, the last day of the Carnival in Trinidad, New Orleans, Rio etc, (Shrove Tuesday).

Mariner's Compass. See **Compass**.

Marionettes are puppets moved by strings. They originated in the *Fantoccini* of the 15th cent. which had such a vogue in Italy and elsewhere on the Continent. The English *Punch and Judy* is a version of Punchinello.

Marmoset, small monkeys confined to the New World. Very squirrel-like in appearance, with long bushy tails, and thick woolly fur, they are pretty little animals and the smallest of all monkeys. There are claws, not nails, on their digits, the big toe excepted.

Maronite, Christian sect living mainly in Lebanon and Syria. Now part of the Catholic Church.

Marquess or **Marquis**, the title next in precedent to that of duke. The first English marquess was Rovery de Vere, Earl of Oxford, who was honoured by Richard II, in 1385.

Mars, the fourth nearest planet to the sun. The

enormous amount of new information from the pioneer visits to Mars, primarily by the US *Mariner* and *Viking* spacecraft, in 1971 and 1976 respectively, has revolutionised our understanding of the planet. These missions showed that the planet's surface displayed many contrasts—the ancient crated terrains glimpsed previously, enormous volcanos, far larger than any on earth, vast wastelands, particularly near the polar regions, scoured by wind-blown dust over many aeons, and most tantalising, in many regions water had set unmistakable marks.

We see the plains which have been subject to great deluges of rain in, probably, a number of different episodes over hundreds of millions of years. Other regions, extending over hundreds of km, show great gorges and canyons cut by catastrophic floods, when some natural dam has burst, releasing the pent-up waters of a gigantic lake or sea. This pictorial evidence, and more detailed information of the atmosphere and surface obtained from the *Viking* spacecraft tell us that its climate was once quite different from that observed today. The atmosphere, if only for brief interludes, must have been much denser, and warmer, and rain must have been able to fall.

Mars is today too cold and dry for water but there are polar ice caps, and the nature of the meteoric craters suggests that the surface is rock over ice and solid carbon dioxide. Evidence continues to mount of vast quantities of ice below the surface. The search for life carried out by *Viking* produced much new information, but no traces of organic compounds as evidence, or precursors, of life.

Mars has two small moons, Phobos and Deimos. Early findings from the Mars *Pathfinder* mission (which landed on Mars in 1997) suggest there was abundant water in the past and also that Mars may be much more like Earth than previously thought. In 2001 the *Odyssey* probe entered into Martian orbit after a 285-million mile journey from Earth. Its mission was to scour the planet for signs of life. Its evidence of underground ice reservoirs at the South Pole was subsequently confirmed by Europe's *Mars Express*.

In March 2006 the *Mars Reconnaissance Orbiter* (MRO) successfully slipped into orbit around Mars.

Despite setbacks suffered by unmanned Mars probes, in January 2004 President Bush reiterated that America planned a £540 billion manned mission to Mars.

Marseillaise, the French national hymn, written and composed by Rouget de L'Isle, a French engineer officer, who was inspired to write it in 1792 to encourage the Strasburg conscripts. It immediately became popular, and received its name because it was sung by the Marseillaise troops while marching into Paris.

Marshalsea, a former prison in Southwark, London, closed 1849. It existed as early as Edward III's time and was used as a jail for royal servants convicted of offences. In its later days it became a debtors' prison. Dickens described it in *Little Dorrit.*

Marsupials, members of the order of pouched mammals. Except for the opossums of America, all marsupials occur in Australasia, and include kangaroos, wallabies and wombats. Scientists now believe they may have first originated in China.

Marten, carnivorous animals of the weasel family; one species (the Pine Marten) was once common in Britain. Now it is only found in remoter areas. Most famous for their fur are the Siberian Sable and the American Marten.

Martin, a well-known bird-visitor to Britain. It belongs to the swallow family, and the two species that spend their summers here are the house-martin, which makes its nest of mud under the eaves of houses, and the sand martin, which builds in sandy banks.

Martinmas *or* **St. Martin's Day,** falls on 11 November, and is one of the Scottish quarter days. St. Martin was a very popular Saint with our ancestors and Martinmas was a busy time for the mediaeval housewife. It was the important date when "Martlemas Beef" was dried in the chimney, and enough bacon and mutton cured to last until the spring. This diet of dried meat without vegetables caused scurvy. The late spell of fine weather

sometimes occurring at Martinmas is called St. Martin's Summer.

Martyrs. People who suffer death in testimony to their faith. Stephen (Acts 6; 7) was the first Christian martyr in 39. The first English martyr was St. Alban, 286, and in Tudor times many eminent churchmen went to the stake. The Smithfield martyrs' memorial church used to be St. Peter's, St. John Street, Clerkenwell. After its demolition the memorial moved to the Church of St. James, Clerkenwell Green.

Mason-Dixon Line, the boundary line between Pennsylvania and Maryland, for long a source of dispute, drawn up by two English surveyors, Charles Mason and Jeremiah Dixon, between 1763 and 1767. It came to designate the boundary dividing the slave states from the free states of America, and is still used in distinguishing the "North" from the "South".

Masques were light dramatic compositions set to music and performed on special occasions. One famous example is Milton's "Comus", which was given at Ludlow Castle in 1634.

Mass, the service in the Roman Catholic Church defined as the Propitiary Sacrifice of Calvary, reoffered by the Priest acting *in persona Christi.* It was first celebrated in Latin in the 4th cent., and was introduced into England in the 7th cent. The use of a vernacular language was sanctioned by the 2nd Vatican Council (1965).

Mass Spectrograph, an instrument for separating isotopes. It works by sorting electrified particles according to their masses; the particles stream through a magnetic and possibly an electric field, and the lightest particles undergo the greatest deflection. *See* **Spectrograph.**

Massorah. *See* **Section H.**

Mast, a long round piece of timber or tubular steel or iron, standing upright in a vessel, and supporting the yards, sails and rigging in general. The earliest ships had only one mast, carrying a simple sail. The number increased until there were 4 or 5, or even more. Above the lower mast of a sailing-ship comes the topmast, and above that, the topgallantmast and royalmast. The position of each mast is indicated by a prefix, as foremast, foretopmast, foreroyalmast, mainmast, maintopmast, *etc.*

The foremast is in the fore of the ship, the mainmast in the centre and the mizzen nearest the stern. In large vessels nowadays the mast does not extend to the keel, as it formerly did, but is usually stopped at the second deck.

Master of the Revels a former Court official upon whom devolved the arrangement of Court festivities. The office is at least as old as the time of Edward III. By 1737 it seems to have died.

Master of the Rolls, one of the senior English judges, since 1881 a Judge of the Court of Appeal only. He has charge of the rolls or records of Chancery and ranks next to the Lord Chancellor and Lord Chief Justice.

Mastodon, an extinct order of quadruped closely resembling the elephant, but larger.

Materials Science is a blend of science and technology; it is the use of scientific research methods to study and improve materials for practical use. The deeper understanding so obtained enables scientists to design new substances with hitherto unknown combinations of properties that are useful in engineering, aircraft, nuclear power, surgery, *etc.*

Mathematics is a body of knowledge expressed in a language of symbols. *Pure* mathematics studies the propositions that can be deduced in this language by applying definite rules of reasoning to sets of axioms. In *Applied* mathematics, the mathematical language is used, often with great effect, to discuss problems of the real world, such as mechanics, statistics and science generally. In range, subtlety, complexity and depth mathematics is unsurpassed among the intellectual disciplines.

Matins, the first of the canonical hours or services of the day in the Roman Catholic Church and Morning Prayer in the Anglican Church. The daily service in the Roman breviary *(q.v.)* used to consist of eight offices or "hours", fixed by canon, for prayer and devotion but since the second Vatican Council the structure has been simplified. Formerly, Matins was recited or sung at midnight, Lauds at sunrise, Prime at 6 a.m., Terce at 9 a.m., Sext at midday, Nones at 3.

p.m., Vespers at sunset and Compline before retiring for the night. Lauds are now commonly
joined to Matins.

Matrix, a rectangular array of numbers considered
as a single mathematical object. There are
special rules for multiplying and adding matrices
and they are often used in mathematics, physics
and elsewhere to simplify calculations and as a
notational device.

Maundy Thursday, the day before Good Friday,
commemorates the Last Supper. "Maundy"
derives from Christ's command (mandatum) to
his disciples on that day to love one another.
For many centuries the sovereigns of England,
through their almoners, have distributed money,
food and clothing to "as many old men and as
many old women as the Sovereign is years of
age". The Royal Maundy ceremony is still observed, maundy coins being struck from standard
silver.

Mausoleum, a special place of sepulture, generally
for the reception of the remains of members of
a royal or other family of distinction. The
name is derived from the tomb of King Mausolus
at Halicarnassus, erected 352 B.C., and forming
one of the seven wonders of the ancient world.
Another mausoleum of antiquity is that of
Hadrian in Rome.

Mauve, a colouring matter produced from lichens
by Dr. Stenhouse in 1848, but in 1856 obtained
from aniline by William Perkin (1838–1907),
who gave it the name Mauveen. This was the first
synthetic organic dyestuff ever to be produced,
which led to the building up of the great synthetic
dyestuffs industry (which Germany dominated
before the first world war).

May, the fifth month of the year, but the third of
the ancient Roman calendar. Supposed to be
named after Maia, the mother of Mercury, to
whom sacrifices were offered on the first day of
this month. In England in former days May
Day was made the occasion of many festivities,
including the crowning of the May Queen,
dancing round the Maypole, *etc.*

Maya, a civilisation centred on Guatemala, Belize,
Honduras *etc.* which peaked *c.* A.D. 300–900.

May Fly. *See* Ephemeptera.

Mazarin Bible, an edition of the Latin Vulgate,
acknowledged as the masterpiece of the Gutenberg press (1456). It was the first book completely printed from movable types. It is
called the Mazarin Bible because the first copy
to capture the attention of scholars was found
in the library of Cardinal Mazarin, in Paris.
Also called the Gutenberg or the 42-line Bible.

Maze. *See* Labyrinth.

Mean. In statistics and mathematics generally
understood to be the arithmetic mean. The
geometric mean between two quantities is the
square root of their product. *See* Average.

Mechanical Equivalent of Heat. *See* Joule.

Medals, as decorations for military service, were
first issued in this country by Charles I, who
ordered medals for gallantry to be distributed
to certain soldiers in 1643. Medals were also
issued to officers and men who were victorious
against the Dutch fleet in 1653. After Lord
Howe's victory in 1794 a naval medal was
instituted. Medals were also struck for the
victory of Waterloo, and since that time special
medals have been issued in connection with all
our wars. The Victoria Cross, a special reward
for personal gallantry, was instituted in 1856. The
George Cross for gallantry instituted in 1940 ranks
next to the Victoria Cross. The Military Cross was
instituted in 1914.

Megalith, a prehistoric monument, consisting of a
large single stone or a group of such stones, in a
circle as at Stonehenge or in burial chambers
as at New Grange, Ireland. Megalithic monuments have been constructed by different
peoples in different parts of the world since the
third millennium B.C.

Meiosis, special type of cell division by which the
gametes or sex cells are generated, resulting in
the sperm or ovum receiving only half the
number of chromosomes found in a somatic
cell. *See* Mitosis.

Mela, the Sanskrit term for a gathering or community festival.

Mendelian Law. *See* **Section T.**

Mendicant Friars, certain religious orders which
spread over Europe in the 13th cent., and

comprised the Franciscans, Dominicans, Augus-
tines and Carmelites. Originally they depended entirely on alms.

Mercator's Projection, a method of indicating
meridians and parallels of latitudes on maps,
introduced by Mercator in the 16th cent., and
still universally used in navigators' charts.

Mercury, the second smallest of the planets (*c.*
one-twentieth of the earth's mass) is the closest to the sun at little more than one-third of
the earth's average distance. It appears to
resemble the earth in its interior and has
about the same density but its surface resembles the moon and is heavily cratered.
    Mercury was visited by Mariner 10 which
passed within a few hundred kilometres in March
1974 and which relayed pictures on the two
following passes in September 1974 and March
1975 before control of its altitude was lost. It
nevertheless continues to revisit Mercury every
176 days (two mercurian years). Mariner 10
was guided to Mercury by the gravitational
field of Venus before it became a satellite of
the smallest planet. The relayed pictures
showed that the planet has an approximately
59-day rotation period exactly two thirds of
its orbital period of 88 days. This relationship
means that unlike on earth the seasonal variations are with longitude not latitude. Surface
temperatures vary from 400°C to −200°C and
there is virtually no atmosphere except a thin
envelope of helium gas.
    Mariner 10 measured a small magnetic field at
the surface about 1% of the earth's but much
stronger than for Venus or Mars.
    The *Messenger* spacecraft, launched in 2004, is
designed to orbit Mercury when it arrives in 2011.

Mercury or **Quicksilver,** element no. 80, symbol
Hg (Latin *hydrargyrum*) is one of the oldest-
known metals, whose chief ore is the sulphide,
cinnabar, found in certain parts of Spain, China,
Japan and South America. It is liquid at
ordinary temperature and is used in the construction of barometers and thermometers.
Alloys of mercury are called amalgams. It is
also of great value in medicine. The metal is
used in the mercury-vapour (or "sunlight")
lamp, since the vapour gives a bright yellow-
white glow in an electric discharge.

Meridian, an imaginary circle extending through
the North and South Poles and any given place.
When the sun is at its midday height at any
place it is "on the meridian"; hence the
terms ante-meridian (a.m.) and post-meridian
(p.m.). *See also* Greenwich Mean Time.

Merino Sheep were imported into England from
Spain in 1788 and had great influence in improving native breeds regarding wool.

Merit, Order of, founded by King Edward VII in
1902 as a special distinction for eminent men
and women without conferring a knighthood
upon them. The Order has twenty-four British
companions in addition to foreign honorary
members limited in number, as the choice of
members is, by the Sovereign's pleasure. Lord
Kelvin was the founder companion. Florence
Nightingale (1907), Professor Dorothy Hodgkin
(1965), Dame Veronica Wedgwood (1969),
Mother Theresa of Calcutta (honorary member,
1983), Margaret Thatcher (1990) and Betty
Boothroyd (2005) are the only women to have
received this decoration. Nelson Mandela was
made an honorary member in 1995.

Mesons (from Greek *meso* = middle). One of the four
groups of sub-atomic particle given by the
Standard Model: gauge bosons (the most famous
of which is the photon), the leptons (very light
particles, including the electron), the mesons and
the baryons. The latter two groups (together
termed hadrons) are not truly fundamental, being
made up of different combinations of quarks
(three quarks forming a baryon, two a meson).
The mesons are characterised by their instability;
their life expectancy does not exceed 5×10^{-8}
seconds. Examples of the meson group are the
pions, the kaons, the charmed D's, the upsilon
particle and the bottom B's.

Mesozoic. The geological era, including the Triassic,
Jurassic and Cretaceous rocks.

Metamorphic Rocks are such geological deposits as
have undergone alterations of structure and
mineral reorganisation. The most active agents
in producing these metamorphic changes are

heat, water and pressure.

Metamorphosis, period of development from egg to adult, during which the animals have different forms, as found, *e.g.*, in the life histories of frog and butterfly.

Meteorites are small bodies, asteroids, or fragments of asteroids, which survive their fiery passage through the earth's atmosphere and hit the ground. The present surfaces of the moon, Mars and Mercury tell us that all the planets have been subjected since their formation to bombardment by meteorites. Though some large craters are still to be found on the earth, most have disappeared due to extensive weathering over thousands of millions of years. In some meteorites iron and nickel are the chief metals (siderites), others are like rock (aerolites). The iron meteorites are more common amongst those which have been preserved, but falls of rock-like meteorites occur more frequently. At L'Aigle in France in 1803 from 2000 to 3000 meteorite stones fell; this fall is famous because it convinced scientists that meteorites really came from outside our atmosphere.

The largest meteorite stone actually known to have fallen to earth is one which descended in Emmott County, Iowa, in 1870, weighing 197 kg. A meteorite weighing no less than 37 tonnes found in Greenland is now in New York.

On 30 June 1908, an enormous object fell in Siberia in a sparsely-inhabited region. A hot blast destoyed all trees within a radius of about 8–16 km. There is still controversy about the Siberian meteorite, whether it was an asteroid or the nucleus of a small comet. *See* **Asteroid**.

Meteoroid, the collective term for meteoritic material found in the solar system. Meteoroids are normally produced by the decay of short-period comets and the collisional fragmentation of asteroids. When meteoroids fall into the Earth's atmosphere they burn up producing a meteor. *See* **Asteroid**.

Meteorology, the science of the atmosphere considered as a heat engine. Deals with weather, climate, optical phenomena, atmospheric electricity, physical processes such as radiation and precipitation, the dynamics and structure of cyclones, anticyclones, *etc.* Wide application to problems of aviation, agriculture, commerce and shipping. Meteorological observing stations are in operation all over the world, and on the simultaneous or synoptic reports of their instrument readings and estimates of pressure, temperature, humidity, speed and direction of wind, rain, character and amount of cloud, visibility, *etc.*, forecasts and warnings are based.

Instruments now carried by earth satellites (*e.g.*, *Tiros*, *Nimbus*) outside the atmosphere can make systematic observations on a worldwide basis of the atmospheric circulation, through observation of cloud cover and of the thermal radiation into space from the atmosphere.

A new generation of weather satellites (Meteosat Second Generation, MSG) was launched in 2002.

Such observations together with the use of computers are of great importance for weather analysis and forecasting. The main communications centre for the UK is at the headquarters of the Meteorological Office, where the collection, editing and re-transmission of weather messages continue day and night throughout the year.

Meteors or more commonly, "shooting stars", are small objects which enter the upper atmosphere to burn up in a bright streak of light. Their origin is mainly in the dust particles ejected in large quantities from comets. Some, particularly the larger and more brilliant ones, called fireballs, are debris of asteroids. Those which reach the earth's surface are called meteorites (*q.v.*).

Methane. The simplest hydrocarbon, compounded of one carbon atom and four hydrogen atoms. This gas occurs over marshes and swamps, where it is liberated in the decay of vegetable matter. It is the main constituent of natural gas, and also occurs in coal-mines, where it is called "fire-damp" because of the explosive character of its mixture with air.

Formerly this natural gas was removed from the coal seams and ran to waste; now in many countries (including Britain) it is being used for commercial purposes.

Methylated Spirit, a mixture of 90 parts by volume ethyl alcohol, 9½ parts wood naphtha (methyl alcohol), ½ part crude pyridine, together with small amounts of petroleum oil and methyl violet dye. Industrial methylated spirit consists of a mixture of 95 parts by volume ethyl alcohol and 5 parts wood naphtha. It is used as a solvent and a fuel.

Metre (1), the rhythmical pattern of Verse. (2), unit of length in the metric system; since 1983 has been redefined as "the length of the path travelled by light in vacuum during a time interval of 1/299 792 458 of a second". This definition replaces that adopted in 1960 which used the wavelength of the orange-red line of krypton-86. Before that the "international prototype metre" was the distance between marks on the platinum-iridium bar placed at Sèvres in 1889.

Metric System, the system of weights and measures based on the gram and the metre, smaller and larger units being decimals and multiples of the primary units respectively. A decimal currency was adopted in France in 1795 and the metric system of weights and measures in 1799. (In that year the quadrant of the earth was surveyed and the standard metre adopted.) Since then the metric system has been adopted in most of the continental countries and is used universally in scientific work.

In Britain, it was not until 1965 that the Government encouraged the adoption of the metric system of weights and measures. The changeover to decimal coinage was made in 1971; the system of weights and measures in industry is now mainly metric and "Metrication Day" for the ordinary shopper came on 1 October 1995. The final changeover to the metric system comes on 31 December 2009. *See* **T58–61** for **SI** units.

Mica. The mica of commerce is a nearly transparent mineral, which has great heat-resisting power, and can be split into thin plates. The most important micas are muscovite (potassium mica), the commoner variety, phlogopite (magnesium mica) and biotite (the magnesium and iron mica). *See* **T71**.

Michael, St., and George, St., an order of knighthood originally founded for the Ionian Isles and Malta in 1818, and reorganised in 1869 to admit Crown servants connected with the Colonies.

Michaelmas Day, the festival day of St. Michael and All Angels, 29 September, one of the English quarter days.

Microbe, a term proposed by Sédillot in 1878 to denote any microscopic organism, vegetable or animal, or found on the borderland between the two great natural kingdoms. The term is commonly used, but not by scientists.

Microelectronics, a rapidly developing technology of the 1960s which reduces entire electronic circuits to minute size and embeds them in tiny chips of solid material. These are then called integrated circuits. A circuit consisting of, say, a dozen transistors and fifty resistors can be built into a small piece of semiconductor (*q.v.*) measuring not more than a couple of millimetres in any direction. Hundreds of these circuits can be made simultaneously in penny-size wafers of silicon about one-hundredth of an inch thick. There are great advantages in cheapness, reliability, robustness and speed of electronic performance. The small size is in itself an advantage in space vehicles and medical instruments.

Applications to computers and communications equipment are no doubt only the first fruits of this new technological revolution.

Micrometer, an instrument for measuring minute distances; usually attached to the eye-pieces of a microscope or telescope, and consisting of two very fine hairs or wires stretched across the field of view, one fixed, the other movable. It was invented by William Gascoigne in the 17th cent. and improved by later inventors. Sir Joseph Whitworth made one in 1858 designed to measure the millionth part of an inch.

Micro-organisms, the collective term applied to several types of organism, the most important of which are fungi, viruses, bacteria and protozoa. It is a classification of convenience in biological studies. These organisms are generally simple in their environmental requirements (*e.g.*, have simple nutritional needs) and in cellular organisation. This makes them very suitable for modern biological research. Much of the information on the nature of the genetic code was obtained from these organisms.

Microphone, device for converting the acoustic

energy of sound waves into waves of electrical energy, used in sound amplifying systems. Developed independently by Edison (1877) and Hughes (1878).

Microscope, invented about 1590 by Janssen, and improved by Galileo, Fontana and others, is an instrument which by a lens system magnifies minute objects. Microscopes are simple, compound and binocular. *See also* **Electron Microscope**.

Middle Ages. *See* **A45**.

Midrash, name given to the homiletical interpretation of some of the Hebrew Scriptures in which allegory and legendary illustration were freely used. Compiled by Jewish rabbis from *c.* A.D. 200.

Milky Way. *See* **Galaxy**.

Millennium, a period of a thousand years. The term is specifically used of the period of a thousand years during which, according to Rev. xx. 1–5, Christ will reign in person on earth. The Millenarians are a sect that interprets the "Millennium" as beginning with the commencement of the 6001st year from the Creation, which, according to Archbishop Ussher (1581–1650), was in 4004 B.C. A Millennium Commission was established in February 1994 to distribute 20% of money allocated to good causes by the National Lottery for projects associated with the millennium. In 1996 Greenwich was chosen as the site for the Millennium Exhibition.

Millipede. Arthropods (**Section T**) allied to the centipedes, from which they differ in having two pairs of legs to each body segment (except the first three) instead of one pair. Worm-like in shape but with a pair of antennae on the head, they can do much harm to garden plants, unlike centipedes which are beneficial. A 420 million-year-old millipede fossil found in Scotland provides evidence it was the earliest creature known to have lived on dry land.

Millstone-Grit, a series of grits and sandstones of deltaic origin underlying the coal measures of the Carboniferous system and attaining in England a thickness in parts of 1,525 m. It is from this rock that millstones were made.

Mimicry, protective similarity of an animal to another animal or to inanimate objects. Examples of the former are the hover flies, which mimic wasps and bees; of the latter, leaf insects, stick insects and caterpillars that look like dead twigs.

Minerals. *See* Special Topic, **T70–71**.

Ming. *See* **A45**.

Minimum Wage. *See* **National Minimum Wage**.

Mink. Semi-aquatic mammals closely related to polecats. There is one American species and one European. The fur, which varies light to dark brown, is soft and thick, and is among the most valuable of commercial furs. They are now well-established in the wild in the UK. An estimated 60,000 mink are housed on 15 fur farms. Mink usually produce a litter of up to 10 kits.

Minnesingers were minstrel poets of Germany who, during the 12th and 13th cent., composed and sang verses of heroism and love. They were of knightly rank, like the French troubadours.

Minnow, a small fresh-water fish of the carp family, abounding in all the waters of Europe; it has a mottled back and silvery belly, and forms a popular bait for trout.

Minor Planets. *See* **Asteroids**.

Minstrels were originally specially appointed instrumentalists and singers—pipers, harpers and gleemen—engaged by barons and manorial lords to amuse their tenants. Later, minstrels assumed nomadic habits, made their way into the houses of the great and were generally welcome. By Elizabeth's time, however, they were too numerous, and classed as vegabonds.

Miracle Plays, mediaeval verse plays, popular in England in the 15th cent., usually religious.

Mirage, an optical illusion caused by unequal temperatures in different layers of the atmosphere near the earth's surface. These temperature variations alter the refracting power of the air and cause light rays to be curved, making the air act as a huge distorting lens. This can happen at sea, in deserts and elsewhere and various types of mirage are known. A common kind in deserts curves light from the sky so that it appears to come from the ground, deceiving the observer into thinking that the sky is reflected in a lake of water.

Mishna, the first part of the Talmud, setting forth the "Oral Law" of the Jews.

Missal, the name of the mass-book of the Roman Church compiled 492–96 by Pope Gelasius I. The missal used until modern times was sanctioned by the Council of Trent, 1546–63, but the current missal was authorised by Pope Paul VI in 1969 after the Second Vatican Council. In the Anglican Communion the Book of Common Prayer superseded the Missal in 1549.

Mistle Thrush receives its name from its partiality to the mistletoe-berry. Larger than the song-thrush, with spotted breast rather than speckled.

Mistletoe, a parasitic evergreen with white berries used as a decoration at Christmas-time. The familiar mistletoe of Europe is the *Viscum album*, which grows on the boughs of lime, willow, apple, poplar, maple, ash, hawthorn but seldom on oak-trees. It was sacred to the Druids, and in Norse mythology it was a mistletoe dart that killed the god Baldur.

Mistral, a cold, dry, northerly wind peculiar to the French coast of the Mediterranean.

Mitosis, cell division whereby each daughter cell receives the same number of chromosomes as the parent cell. When the gametes (sex cells) are formed a special type of division occurs (meiosis) in which the number of chromosomes is halved.

Mitre, the twofold pointed head-dress of bishops and certain abbots of the Western Church and occasionally of other ecclesiastics.

Moa, the name for several species of ostrich-like extinct birds related to the New Zealand kiwi. The largest species, *Diornis maximus*, stood 2·6 m high, the smallest, *Anomalopteryx parea*, was nearer the size of a turkey. This wingless bird became extinct because of hunting by the Maoris from whom the name comes.

Moabite Stone. *See* **H19**.

Moderator, a material used to slow down neutrons in an atomic pile. Examples are pure graphite and heavy water. *See* **Nuclear Reactors**.

Mohole Project, a scheme to bore through the earth's crust to take samples of the mantle rocks beneath. Drilling trials, led by an American team of geophysicists, began in 1961 near the island of Guadalupe off the Mexican coast in the Pacific. The project, however, was cancelled in 1966 on account of the escalating cost.

The boundary between the earth's crustal and mantle rocks is known as the Mohorovičić Discontinuity, or, more simply, as the Moho. The technology of deep sea drilling came from this project.

Molasses, sugar-cane juice in its uncrystallised form after boiling. The crystallised part is the raw sugar. Used to make rum.

Mole, a small burrowing animal with long, sensitive nose, about the size of a small rat, with short legs and forefeet armed with strong claws for digging in the earth. Their subterranean dwellings are of curiously ingenious construction, and they do not often leave them except to make raids on mice, frogs, snails, *etc.* The earth-worm, however, is the mole's chief item of food. Not to be confused with the vole which has a blunt nose.

Mole, or gram molecular weight.

Molecular Anthropology, the relatively new science of the study of the DNA of indigenous peoples to throw new light on human evolution.

Molecular Biology, a rapidly expanding branch of science mainly concerned with cell structure and function at a molecular level, in particular with genes and enzymes and the interaction between the two. Research work in Britain led to the unravelling of the structure of DNA, the hereditary substance of the genes, and played a major part in uncovering the molecular mechanism of the transfer of hereditary information and the nature of the genetic code. *See* **Section T**.

Molecule. A group of atoms held together by chemical forces. See **Section T**, *also* **Macro-molecule**.

Molybdenum, element no. 42, symbol Mo, a fairly hard white metal with properties resembling those of chromium. Its commonest ore is the sulphide, molybdenite. The chief use of the metals is in the manufacture of alloy steels.

Monazite, a cerium mineral containing some thorium. Occurs as grains, often as sand ("monazite sands"), derived from granites.

Monday, the second day of the week, called by

the Anglo-Saxons *Monandaeg* (moon-day).

Mongoose, species of mammals related to the civets, feeding on vermin and reptiles. These animals, which have long tails and short legs, occur in Africa and Asia (especially India). The biggest mongoose is the Egyptian ichneumon, introduced into the W. Indies because of its ability to kill large poisonous snakes.

Monitor, family of lizards resembling dragons. There are c. 30 species widely distributed over the tropics. The largest is the komodo dragon.

Monkey Nut. *See* **Peanut.**

Monsoons, regular persistent winds which blow at certain seasons in middle latitudes, mainly in South and East Asia. Their occurrence is related to the great changes of pressure which take place between summer and winter over the land mass. In India the south-west monsoon (June-October) is moisture-laden from its long passage over the sea and in the higher regions, especially, there is heavy rainfall. Sudden reversal of the wind results in the cold north-east monsoon (October-March) which is dry on account of the shelter afforded by the mountain ranges to the north. Frequently the term "monsoon" is applied to denote the associated rainfall, not the actual winds.

Monstrance, an ornamental transparent receptacle in which the Sacred Host is carried in procession or exposed for adoration.

Month, the 12th part of the calendar year. A lunar month is the interval of new moon to new moon or full moon to full moon; mean length, 29 days, 12 hours, 44 minutes, 2·87 seconds. A sidereal month represents the time of the moon's revolution from a given star back to the same again, 27 days, 7 hours, 43 minutes, 11·5 seconds. In English law, since 1926, a month means a calendar month.

Monument of London, a 202 ft (61·6 m) column, overlooking Billingsgate, designed by Wren and erected (1671-77) to mark the starting-point of the Great Fire of London (1666). The original inscription on it ascribed the fire to "the treachery and malice of the popish faction", which stood until 1831, when the words were erased as objectionable. The black marble staircase has 345 steps (311 to the balcony).

Moon, the earth's satellite, 3,475 km in diameter and 384,400 km distant from the earth. It rotates in the same time as it revolves round the earth (27 days 7 hours 43 minutes), so that the same face is always presented to the earth. The lunar surface is pockmarked by innumerable collisions with solid particles of all sizes.

Unlike the earth, it is unprotected by any atmosphere and for aeons of time it has been exposed to every kind of cosmic influence, including the parching effect of solar radiation. All moonlight derives from the sun but on the whole it is a pretty poor reflector. The exploration of the moon by means of rockets began in 1959 when the Russian *Luna 2* crashlanded on the plains of the *Mare Imbrium.* 1969 will be remembered as the year of the U.S. *Apollo* triumphs when man first set foot on the moon.

The samples of lunar rock and dust brought back to earth were closely studied by lunar scientists. Samples date back further than any found on Earth as yet. The most famous, known as the Genesis Rock, is 4,100 million years old. Scientists believe ice may exist in a deep crater near the lunar south pole. The existence of water was confirmed by the *Lunar Prospector* probe in 1998, the first moonshot for 25 years.

Moorhen, a widely distributed bird of the rail family, a common resident in the British Isles. The adult is blackish with white under tail coverts, a white line on the flanks and a yellow-tipped bill. The frontal shield and the base of the bill are vermilion. It bobs its head, flirts its tail and dives well. The nest is usually placed close to the water's edge or on an overhanging branch. In feeding the young the parents are sometimes helped by their offspring of a previous brood of the season. In N. America it is known as the Florida Gallinule.

Moors, the name given to the Muslims who live in N.W. Africa and to those who once lived in Spain. In 711 Moorish Arabs invaded Spain and spread beyond the Pyrenees into France, where they were driven back by the end of the century. Spain, however, remained virtually under Moorish domination until the 11th cent. and during that period was the most civilised and prosperous part of Western Europe.

In the arts and sciences the impact of Moorish culture was profound and lasting. Examples of the brilliant splendour of Moorish architecture are still to be seen in Toledo, Córdoba, Seville and Granada. During the long struggle for the Christian reconquest thousands were killed and expelled, and in 1492 Granada, their last remaining kingdom, was forced to surrender. They were virtually exterminated by the Inquisition, and the last were expelled in 1609.

Moose, the largest members of the deer family. The N. American Moose stands up to 2·4 m high, and has huge palmate antlers. There is another New World species, occurring in Alaska. The European species is known as the elk.

Morse Alphabet, a system of dots and dashes intended to be used in combination with the indicator in telegraphy; but usually read by sound, the receiving operator writing down the words in the system as transmitted. This system of signals was invented by the American inventor and artist Samuel Finley Breese Morse (1791-1872) of Charlestown, Massachusetts. The Morse Code was replaced on 31 December 1997 by more advanced technology.

Mosaic. *See* **Section N.**

Mosque, a house or any open space of prayer for Muslims. The mosque has many functions—social and educational as well as religious. Britain has around 1,200 mosques and over 2,000 imams .

Mosquito, small two-winged flies with long legs and slender body. Their larvae are aquatic. The females of some species are blood-suckers, and thus come to transmit the blood parasites which cause malaria and dengue fever, for example. *See* **DDT** *and* **Gammexane.**

Mosses. With liverworts, mosses comprise an important group of relatively simple non-vascular land plants, the bryophytes (**Section T**). They are usually small plants, the largest between 30-70 cm high, having been recorded in the Southern Hemisphere. Mosses rarely occur singly, but usually form cushions or small colonies on moist soil, bark, wood, rock or walls. The genus *sphagnum* known as "peat" or "bog moss" is of commercial value in horticulture. In Lancashire and Cheshire lowland moors in which sphagnum is common are known as "mosses". Reindeer moss is a lichen and Spanish moss a seed plant.

Moths, of the insect order, *Lepidoptera*, differing from butterflies which have clubbed antennae, in having feathery, sometimes thin, pointed antennae, rarely clubbed. Most are nocturnal, and the pupae are usually brown and enclosed in a cocoon unlike those of the butterfly, which are usually naked. *See also* **Lepidoptera.**

Motion, Laws of. According to Newton: (1) A body continues in its state of rest or uniform motion in a straight line except in so far as it is compelled by external forces to change that state. (2) Rate of change of momentum is proportional to the applied force, and takes place in the direction in which the force acts. (3) To every action there is an equal and opposite reaction. These laws are the basis of almost all engineering and everyday mechanics. Corrections to them have been made by relativity and the quantum theory. *See* **Section T.**

Mountains. *See under* individual names in **Section K.** *See also* **Everest Expeditions, L38.**

Mule, a cross between a male ass and a horse mare; a hinny is a cross between an ass mare and a horse stallion. Also the name of the spinning machine invented by Crompton in 1779 which combined the principle of Hargreaves' spinning jenny with the machine invented by Arkwright.

Mullions. *See* **Section N.**

Musk Deer, a small deer of the Himalayas, standing about 51 cm high. It is grey in colour, slightly brindled, and carries a small pouch in the abdominal region, containing what is commercially known as musk. The active constituent of musk, muscone, is now made synthetically.

Mutton Bird, an Australian name of controversial origin for a shearwater or petrel, *e.g.*, the Short-tailed and Sooty Shearwaters and the Great-winged, Kermadec, and White-headed Petrels. The young are taken by hand for human food.

Myrrh, a resinous substance obtained from a tree of the natural order *Amyridaceae*, growing plentifully in Ethiopia and Arabia. Its use for embalming, medical and aromatic purposes may be traced back to the most remote times.

Mysteries, Greek, secret mystic ceremonies of the ancient Greeks, religious drama accompanied by dancing, the most well known being the Eleusinian and Orphic ceremonies.

Mystery Plays were mediaeval religious dramas performed at great ecclesiastical festivals, particularly in France and Bavaria, staging the Nativity, Passion and Resurrection stories.

N

Nadir, one of the two poles of the horizon, the other being the zenith. The nadir is the pole vertically below the observer's feet.

Nanotechnology. The science of working with tiny things—*e.g.* atoms and molecules. It has the potential to revolutionise electronics, medicine *etc.*

Naphtha, a liquid combustible believed to have been one of the ingredients of "Greek fire". Naphtha is a light, highly inflammable oil obtained by distilling petroleum, shale oil, or coal tar. The petroleum naphtha consists of a mixture of paraffins; that from shale contains olefines as well as paraffins. Coal-tar naphtha contains xylol.

Naphthalene is an aromatic hydrocarbon; it is obtained from coal tar, and its derivatives are much used in the manufactures of colours for dyers and printers. "Moth balls" are made of naphthalene.

Narcotics. *See* **Z66.**

Nardus, a genus of coarse grasses, growing on bleak upland heaths and hill slopes. *Nardus stricta,* known as "mat-weed", is a British species.

Narghile, an oriental tobacco pipe so constructed that smoke passes through water and up a long flexible tube before reaching lips of the smoker.

NASA, the United States government agency which carries out research into spaceflight and aeronautics. NASA was founded in 1958.

National Aeronautics and Space Administration. *See under* **NASA.**

National Anthem. The national anthem of the United Kingdom, "God save the King (Queen)", probably dates from the late-17th cent, to mid-18th cent. It was sung in 1745, the year of the landing of the Young Pretender. It had no one composer and was probably a recasting of folk-tunes and plainsong. Resemblances can be traced in pieces by Purcell and John Bull.

National Archives, formerly the Public Record Office and previously in Chancery Lane, London. The National Archives are where the Public Records of England are preserved, including Domesday Book. These records have now been moved to Kew and Chancery Lane was closed in 1996. Modern records are subject to at least a 30-year restriction on access. Some records may be closed for 100 years.

National Assembly. *See* **A45.**

National Covenant. *See* **A45.**

National Curriculum. The Education Reform Act (1988) originally provided for a national curriculum in state schools in England and Wales with three *core subjects* – maths, English and science – and also seven *foundation subjects* – history, geography, technology, music, art, physical education, and a modern language.

In 1995 the compulsory curriculum was reduced (history and geography were no longer compulsory after 14) and attempts to reduce teachers' workloads were made. Now, each summer, although all children aged 7, 11 and 14 take national tests in English and maths, and 11- and 14-year-olds take tests in science as well, the compulsory national curriculum has effectively been abandoned. A 2002 Green Paper proposed a more flexible curriculum for 14–19 year olds.

National Cycle Network, an ambitious project to build traffic-free cycle routes. When completed it will put 20 million people within a 10-minute cycle ride of their nearest route.

National Forest, a new forest given approval by the government in 1994. It covers 194 sq. miles in Derbyshire, Leicestershire and Staffordshire.

National Gallery, established in 1824 at Pall Mall, London, with the Angerstein Collection of 38 pictures, purchased for £60,000, as a nucleus. The existing building which was opened in 1838 has been enlarged several times. The National Gallery at Millbank, the Tate Gallery, was given to the nation by Sir Henry Tate in 1897. *See* **Tate Britain.**

Nationalisation is the taking over by the State of the ownership and operation of an industry or service *e.g.,* coal mining, railways, transport, gas and electricity.

National Lottery, proposed in 1992 Budget. The first National Lottory draw was on 19 November 1994. The last previous national lottery in Britain was in 1826. Oflot is the Office of the National Lottery. The mid-week lottery draw began in February 1997. In 2002 the National Lottery was revamped—with a new name, Lotto—but sales have continued to decline.

National Minimum Wage. This became law on 1 April 1999. Workers aged 22 or more had to be paid a minimum £3.60 per hour (18–21 year olds at least £3.00). This rate has gradually been increased. The adult rate rose to £4.50 per hour from October 2003 (and the lower rate to £3.80). From October 2004 the respective rates were set at £4.85 and £4.10. From October 2005 the rates became £5.05 (rising to £5.35 in October 2006) and £4.25. In January 2004 it was proposed that a minimum wage (at a lower rate) for 16 and 17 year olds should be introduced.

National Nature Reserves (NNRs), reserves to safeguard flora, fauna and physical features, managed by English Nature, the Countryside Council for Wales and Scottish Natural Heritage.

National Parks. Under the National Parks Act 1949 a National Parks Commission was set up to create National Parks in England and Wales. Ten have been established: Peak District, Lake District, Snowdonia, Yorkshire Dales, Exmoor, Brecon Beacons, Dartmoor, Pembrokeshire Coast (the only coastal national park), North York Moors and Northumberland. They cover an area of some 13,618 km², or 9 per cent of the total area of England and Wales. It is not intended to change the character of these territories but to control their development so as to harmonise with the two dominant principles: (*a*) that the characteristic beauty of the landscape within the Park area shall be preserved and (*b*) that the visiting public shall have ample access and facilities for recreation and enjoyment.

The Commission also has power to designate areas in England and Wales outside the national parks as "areas of outstanding natural beauty".

In 1968, the National Parks Commission was reconstituted as the Countryside Commission. In 1988, a special authority was established to manage the waterways constituting the Norfolk Broads and in 1991 national park status was granted to the New Forest. It formally came into existence (as England's smallest by area) on 1 March 2005.

Scotland's first national park (covering Loch Lomond and the Trossachs) was opened in 2002. A second park (the biggest in Britain) was opened in the Cairngorms in 2003. In June 2004 it was announced that a national park was to be created in the New Forest. In 2000, the Scottish Parliament passed its own National Parks Act. *See also* **Long Distance Walks** and **Marine Nature Reserves.**

National Physical Laboratory, situated at Teddington, is one of the world's largest and best-equipped laboratories. It conducts research in its three main groups: Measurement, Materials and Engineering Sciences, and maintains British primary standards and physical units. First established in 1900 and managed by the Royal Society. Under privatisation it became an Executive Agency in 1990.

National Portrait Gallery, established in 1856, and now located in a building adjoining the National Gallery. Contains portraits of eminent people in British history as well as a valuable collection of medals and autographs.

National Trust, founded in 1895. "A non-profit-making organisation incorporated by Act of Parliament for the purposes of promoting the permanent preservation of lands and buildings of historic interest or natural beauty for the benefit and access of the people." As a consequence of gifts and public-spirited individuals the Trust, now Britain's largest conservation charity, protects 612,000 acres of countryside, 700 miles of coastline and 630 properties (including 300 country houses).

Since 1946 lands and houses may be given to the National Trust in lieu of death duties.

Nativity. *See* **Section H.**

NATO, the North Atlantic Treaty Organisation, established 4 April 1949. A defence grouping of Western European states, America and Canada. Britain is a member. The Russian equivalent was the Warsaw Pact (signed 1955, disbanded, 1991). In March 1999 NATO was extended to include Hungary, Poland and the Czech Republic. Seven additional nations were invited to join NATO at the 2002 Prague Summit. These were Latvia, Estonia, Lithuania, Bulgaria, Romania, Slovakia and Slovenia. After the 2001 terrorist attack, NATO invoked Article 5 of its treaty (commiting signatories to come to the aid of another member) for the first time in its history. In early 2003 NATO was faced with an internal crisis over war in Iraq. The biggest expansion in NATO's history was in 2004 as 7 former communist countries joined.

Natterjack, a curious warty, prominent-eyed, brown toad (*Bufo calamita*), having a bright yellow line down the middle of its back. It utters a muttering sort of croak, hence its name.

Natural Gas. *See* **Gas.**

Natural Numbers, the counting numbers 1, 2, 3, 4, 5, ...

"Nautical Almanac", published under the authority of the Admiralty, contains information specially prepared for the use of navigators and astronomers. It first appeared in 1767.

Nautilus, a term now applied only to the pearly-shelled nautilus, the sole surviving example of the four-gilled section of the *Cephalopoda*. Its fossil relatives are called Ammonites. The spiral shell is divided into a number of compartments, the animal living in the last and largest chamber. There are three or four species, all living in tropical seas. The Paper Nautilus is not related to the Pearly Nautilus, belonging to the same order as the octopus.

Nave is the body or main open portion of a cathedral or church, and extends from the chief entrance to the choir, or chancel, and is usually flanked by aisles.

Neanderthal, the name of the valley lying between Düsseldorf and Wuppertal, where in a limestone cave a skull of a very early species of prehistoric man was discovered in 1856.

Nebula, a cloud of gas and dust in space. There are three basic types; emission nebulae create their own light, shining through the effects of very hot stars embedded within them; dust particles within reflection nebulae simply reflect the light from accompanying stars; dark nebulae contain no stars and appear as dark patches against a brighter background.

Negus, title of the kings of Abyssinia or Ethiopia. The last emperor of Ethiopia, Haile Selassie, was deposed by a military *coup d'état* in 1974.

Nekton, term used to differentiate actively swimming aquatic organisms (*e.g.*, fishes) from the "drifters" or plankton.

Nelson Column, in Trafalgar Square, London, designed by Mr. William Railton, was chosen from among a number of designs—temples, obelisks and various sculptural groups—sent in as a result of a competition held in 1839. The erection of the column was begun in 1840. Twenty-six years later the lions designed by Landseer were set up at the foot of the completed column. The statue of Nelson himself was made by E. H. Bailey and the bronze reliefs at the base executed by Carew, Woodington, Ternouth and Watson, representing the Battles of the Nile, St. Vincent, Copenhagen and Trafalgar. Height 52 m, executed in Dartmoor granite from Foggin Tor quarries.

Néné *or* **Hawaiian Goose.** This rare bird was famously saved from extinction at the Severn Wildfowl Trust at Slimbridge by Sir Peter Scott (1909–89).

Neo-Classical Style. *See* **Section N.**

Neodymium, element no. 60, symbol Nd, belonging to the rare earth metals. Discovered 1885. Named after the Greek word for "new twin", from twin lines in its spectrum.

Neo-Impressionism. *See* **Section N.**

Neon, inert gas present in air to the extent of about 1 part in 65,000. The crimson glow produced when an electric discharge passes through the gas is familiar in advertising signs. Element no. 10, symbol Ne.

Nepotism, the bestowal of patronage by reason of relationship rather than of merit.

Neptune. Apart from Pluto this is the most distant of the planets, estimated to be about $4,497 \times 10^6$ km from the sun, and taking about 165 years to revolve around it. Discovered by the German astronomers Galle and D'Arrest in Sept. 1846, after its existence had been predicted by Leverrier and Adams. The planet was visited by Voyager 2 in 1989, its last planetary stop. This revealed Neptune had eight moons (not just Triton and Nereid as previously thought) and a ring system. By 2003 the number of Neptune's known moons had risen to 11. Its diameter is 49,528 km. A huge Earth-sized storm has been observed, which has been named the "Great Dark Spot'. Winds blow at nearly 900 mph around Neptune's equator, making it the windiest corner of the solar system. The planet is now known to be surrounded by ring arcs. It has an average temperature of -218°C and 900 times less sunlight than reaches Earth. It has a winter lasting 41 years.

Neptunium, element no. 93, symbol Np, one of the four new elements discovered during the progress of the atomic bomb project in the second world war, Neptunium is formed when a neutron enters nucleus of Uranium 238, and it decays radio-actively to yield plutonium.

Network Rail. *See* **Railways.**

Neutrino, a neutral particle which carries energy and spin and although possessing little or no mass plays an important part in the interaction of other fundamental particles. The discovery that there are in fact two distinct neutrinos, each with its counterpart, was discovered in 1962 as a result of an experiment made with the 30,000 million-electronvolt proton accelerator at Brookhaven. The neutrino was 'weighed' for the first time in 2002. *See* **Section T.**

Neutron, a neutral particle present in all atomic nuclei except the hydrogen nucleus which is a single proton. In the development of nuclear science and technology the neutron has played a most important role and neutrons produce the radioisotopes now widely used in medicine, agriculture and industry. Neutrons and protons are termed nucleons. *See* **Section T.**

Neutron Bomb, a thermonuclear fusion weapon which produces increased lethal radiation while the destructive blast and fallout are significantly less than for a fission weapon of equivalent yield; it kills organic life while sparing property, except within a small radius.

Neutron Star. An extremely dense compact star that has undergone huge gravitational collapse so that most of its material has been compressed into neutrons. They are the remaining core after a star has undergone a supernova explosion. A typical neutron star may be only about 15km across and has an intense magnetic field.

New Commonwealth, term used to describe the former British colonies which became members of the Commonwealth following their post-World War II independence. The New Commonwealth, mainly black and Asian, was contrasted with the 'old' white Commonwealth dominions.

Newgate Prison was situated at the western end of Newgate Street, opposite the Old Bailey at the site of one of the old London city gates. There is a record of a prison upon this spot in the 13th cent. Later a new one was built by the executors of Richard Whittington, but this was destroyed by the Great Fire in 1666. Still another new prison on this site was erected between 1778 and 1780. In the Gordon Riots it was destroyed by fire and re-erected. It was not used as a prison after 1880.

Newspapers. The first news-books to be published at regular intervals in Britain appeared in 1662 with news of what was going on abroad translated from German and Italian news-sheets. Licence to print was obtained from the Star Chamber, which until its abolition in 1641 allowed only the printing of foreign news. With the lifting of the ban on domestic news the Press became free.

In the reign of Queen Anne newspapers employed writers of great intellectual power and versatility. Despite the newspaper tax introduced in 1712, the number of newspapers published in London in 1776 had increased to 53, though the standard of writing was below that of earlier times. The development of the Press was greatly assisted in the 19th cent. by the abolition of the "taxes on knowledge", by the introduction of the cheap postal system and by improvements in printing, distribution, collection of news and advertising.

The *London Gazette*, founded in 1665 (and still appearing twice weekly as the official organ of the Government), is the oldest newspaper living. *The Times*, known throughout the world, began as the *Daily Universal Register* in 1785, and adopted its present title in 1700.

The *Manchester Guardian* (renamed *Guardian* in 1959), began life as a weekly in 1821, and became a daily in 1855. The *Scotsman*, founded as a weekly in 1817 and established as a daily in 1855, and the *Glasgow Herald*, which began as the *Glasgow Advertiser* in 1783, are the leading Scottish newspapers. The first evening newspaper, the *Star and Evening Advertiser* was published in London in 1788. During 1989, the last national newspapers left Fleet St. In 1993 *The Guardian* acquired *The Observer*. In November 2003 a "compact" version of *The Times* was published (for the first time in 218 years). From November 2004 only the compact edition has been published.

The new format "Berliner" *Guardian* was launched on 12 September 2005. *The Observer* followed on 8 January 2006.

Newt, amphibian of lizard shape and mottled markings. There are three British species, the largest being the Great-Crested Newt (*Triturus cristatus*), which attains a length of 15 cm.

Newton, the unit of force in the SI system of units. Under its influence a body with a mass of 1 kilogram will accelerate at a rate of 1 metre per second each second.

Newton's Rings. Concentric circular rings, due to the phenomenon of interference, which are seen around the point of contact of a slightly convex lens with a flat plate of glass.

New Towns. Under the New Town Act 1946 and subsequent Acts some 33 new towns were designated in Britain; 23 are in England and Wales, five in Scotland and four in Northern Ireland. They were: Basildon, Bracknell, Crawley, Harlow, Hatfield, Hemel Hempstead, Milton Keynes, Northampton, Peterborough, Stevenage and Welwyn (to relieve housing problems in Greater London); Newton Aycliffe, Corby, Cwmbran, Peterlee and Washington (to serve the special needs of their areas); Newtown (to help stem rural depopulation in mid-Wales); Runcorn and Skelmersdale (to meet the over-spill needs of Liverpool and north Merseyside); Telford and Redditch (to take population from Birmingham); Warrington (expanded to take people from Liverpool and Manchester); Central Lancashire New Town (based on existing towns of Preston, Leyland and Chorley).

The five Scottish new towns comprise Cumbernauld, East Kilbride, Glenrothes, Irvine and Livingston. In Northern Ireland Craigavon was developed as a new city; Antrim and Ballymena were to become centres of economic growth; Londonderry and the surrounding district were designated as an area of special development.

New Year's Day, 1 January. The first New Year's festival of which we know is that constituted by Numa 713 B.C., and dedicated to Janus.

Nibelungenlied, the German epic of the early 13th cent. comprising numerous mythical poems or sagas. Wagner's *The Ring of the Nibelungs* was based on Norse legends and the Nibelungenlied.

Nicene Creed, a summary of the principles of Christian faith, first issued in 325 by the Council of Nicaea (summoned by the emperor Constantine the Great) for the purpose of thwarting the Arian heresy and asserting the godhead of Christ. Date of Easter fixed at Council of Nicaea.

Nickel, silver-coloured metallic element, no. 28, symbol Ni, fairly soft though harder than iron. Chief source of the metal is the nickel sulphide in iron-copper pyrites deposits in Ontario. Chief uses are: in electroplating, in coins, as an element in alloy steels. A novel method of making pure nickel (by treating the metal with carbon monoxide and heating the resulting liquid, nickel carbonyl) was devel-

oped in 1890 by Mond. This discovery led to many technical advances in industrial chemistry, one of which is the production of catalysts. Discovered by Crondstedt in 1751 as an impurity in copper ore. Substituted for silver in French coinage in about 1882.

Night Heron, a stocky, short-legged heron of black and white plumage, red eyes and yellowish legs, crepuscular except in breeding season, and an occasional visitor to Britain.

Nightingale, a familiar singing bird which visits the southern counties of England every summer, and is sometimes found as far north as Yorkshire. It is a shy, brown bird, not often seen, but the song of the male usually heard in the late evening or at early morn, is of remarkable sweetness and variety. After its wooing period is over its song ceases.

Nightjar, nocturnal, insectivorous bird, owl-like in appearance, with mottled brown plumage of "dead leaf " pattern, and a churring song. It is a common breeding visitor to the British Isles, April to September, laying its eggs on bare ground. Nightjar numbers have doubled since 1981 as their heathland habitat has been restored.

Niobium is a metal element, no. 41, symbol Nb, related to vanadium. Technical development has been slow because of its rare occurrence, although niobium is now used in ferrous alloys to increase resistance to corrosion and produce steel which can be used at high temperatures.

Nitre or **Saltpetre,** is now mostly manufactured by the double decomposition of sodium nitrate and potassium chloride. Its chief use is the manufacture of gunpowder and fireworks. It has been manufactured in England since 1625.

Nitrogen, a non-combustible gaseous element, no. 7, symbol N, devoid of taste or smell, and constituting nearly four-fifths of the atmospheric air. Nitrogen compounds are essential to plants and animals, and are used in fertilisers.

Nitro-Glycerine, an explosive yellow fluid produced by mixing small quantities of glycerine with a combination of one part of nitric acid and two parts of sulphuric acid. By itself it is a dangerously explosive substance to handle. In 1867, Nobel produced dynamite, a safe explosive made by absorbing nitro-glycerine in kieselguhr.

Nitrous Oxide, a compound of nitrogen and oxygen possessing mild anaesthetic power. Termed "laughing gas" on account of its exhilarating effect. It is still used in dentistry, and for minor operations and has proved useful in a new technique for finding leaks in water mains.

Nobel Prizes. The Nobel Foundation was established to give effect to the wishes expressed by Alfred Nobel (*see* **Section B**) in his Will. By the terms of the Will the judges are the Swedish Academy of Science, the Caroline Medico-Surgical Institute, the Swedish Academy and five members of the Norwegian Storting. The award of a Nobel Prize is the highest form of international recognition in the field in which it is given: physics, chemistry, medicine, literature, peace and, since 1969, economics. *See* **B67–70** for winners.

Nones were dates of the Roman calendar which fell on the 5th of each month, excepting March, May, July and October, when they fell on the 7th.

North-East Passage, from the North Atlantic to Bering Strait was rapidly developed by the former USSR as a northern sea route to render accessible vast areas of northern Siberia. Attempts to find a North-East passage were made by Englishmen and Dutchmen in the 16th cent. but they were always defeated by the ice, for the sea is completely frozen for some 4,800 km for 9 months of the year. A Swede succeeded in sailing from Europe to Japan via the Arctic in the late 19th cent. *See also* **Arctic Exploration.**

North-West Passage, from the Atlantic to the Pacific through the Arctic Seas, has been the dream of navigators for centuries. Attempts to find it were made in the 16th and early 17th cent. by John and Sebastian Cabot, Frobisher, Gilbert, Davis, Hudson and Baffin. Two centuries later Ross, Parry, Franklin and others made the attempt; but it was not until 1903–5 that Amundsen, discoverer of the South Pole, made the complete voyage in the *Gjoa*. The Canadian icebreaker *Labrador* was the first deep-draft vessel to traverse the North-West Passage (1954) and the US tanker *Manhattan* was the first commercial vessel to do so (1969). Continued global warming may now open up the possibility of commercial shipping.

Notornis. *See* **Takahe.**

Notre Dame, the famous Paris cathedral, was founded in 1163. Famous Gothic architecture.

November, the 9th month of the year originally, but from *c.* 700 B.C., when Numa added January and February, it became the 11th month.

Nuclear Energy. Atomic nuclei consist of protons and neutrons joined in various proportions **(T11)**. The heaviest naturally occurring nucleus contains 238 particles (92 protons, 146 neutrons) and is uranium 238 (U^{238}); the lightest is hydrogen, which consists of 1 proton. Neutrons and protons attract one another by very strong forces which are not at all well understood; they are called *nuclear forces*. Consequently it requires energy to be supplied if a nucleus is to be pulled apart into its constituent particles. The energy is required to overcome the attractions of the nuclear forces. Conversely, when the particles rush together to form a nucleus energy is released as heat or radiation.

The energy released when protons and neutrons coalesce to form a nucleus is called *Binding Energy*. The binding energy of a nucleus divided by the number of particles involved is called the binding energy per particle, which we will call B. It is very difficult to overestimate the importance of B to the human race. B varies from nucleus to nucleus, and the exact form of its variation is only roughly understood at the present time. But the most significant thing is that B is greatest for elements of medium atomic weight and lowest at the heavy (uranium) and light (hydrogen) ends of the periodic table. This means that if middleweight nuclei can be formed either from heavy ones or from light ones, B increases and energy is released in either case.

Nuclear Fission. *See under* **Fission.**

Nuclear Fusion. If light nuclei are hurled at high speeds into intimate contact they sometimes coalesce and release binding energy (*see* **Nuclear Energy**). This has been studied in laboratories where powerful and energy-consuming machines accelerate small numbers of particles for purely experimental purposes. If useful amounts of energy are to be gained these fusion reactions will have to occur on a bigger scale in an apparatus from which the resulting heat can be extracted in a controlled way.

The one "useful" fusion device so far made is the thermonuclear bomb ("H-bomb"). Thermonuclear is the important word. If a suitable gas can be raised to a very high temperature the nuclei are stripped of their electrons and all particles move with very high speeds. The gas is then called a plasma. High enough temperatures will make speeds great enough for fusion reactions to occur and nuclear energy to be released. This is a thermonuclear reaction. For example, in deuterium gas, at temperatures over a million degrees Centigrade, the deuterium nuclei (*i.e.*, heavy hydrogen nuclei consisting of 1 proton joined to 1 neutron) interact to produce helium nuclei. To obtain a net gain in energy from this process, the temperature must be raised to about 100 million degrees C and maintained long enough; otherwise the energy released is less than that required to heat the fuel and to make up for heat losses.

New attempts to study the staggering technical problems are being made, and fusion research is very active in Britain, the USA, Japan and the Russian Federation. The joint European Torus (JET) fusion research project sited at Culham near Oxford aims to develop a new source of energy for the generation of electricity for the 21st cent. In 1991, the JET project achieved a two minute successful nuclear fusion, bringing nearer the prospect of new energy sources. A new way to use lasers to make atoms fuse together to release vast amounts of fusion energy was reported in 2001. The new technique is known as "fast ignition".

Nuclear Power Stations. In 2006 Britain generated around 23% of her electricity in nuclear power stations. The numerous older nuclear power stations all developed from the classic Calder Hall type, burning natural uranium inserted in a graphite moderator and cooled by carbon dioxide gas.

They are called Magnox stations because the fuel elements of natural uranium rods are encased in magnesium alloy cans. A second nuclear power programme based on the advanced gas cooled reactor (AGR) at Windscale included the reactors at Dungeness "B", (1983) and those at Hinkley Point "B", Hunterston "B", Hartlepool (Cleveland) and Heysham (Lancashire). In 1987, after the Layfield Report, the Government gave approval for the Sizewell B project to become Britain's first pressurised water reactor.

In 1994 the Government gave the go-ahead for the controversial Thorp nuclear reprocessing plant at Sellafield. The Sizewell B PWR became the latest (and possibly last) nuclear power station in February 1995. After the Government's 1995 Nuclear Review, the industry was substantially restructured in preparation for privatisation in July 1996. The future of nuclear power in Britain became more uncertain in 1995 when plans to build two new nuclear reactors, Sizewell C in Suffolk and Hinkley C in Somerset, were abandoned.

Under a 15-nation agreement signed in 1998, eight old Magnox stations will have to be closed and discharges from Sellafield massively reduced by 2020. In 2001, a Mixed Oxide Fuel (MOX) plant at Sellafield was given the go-ahead. The current major debate on the future of nuclear energy is discussed on **Y17**.

Nuclear Reactors are pieces of apparatus designed to permit nuclear chain reactions to occur under controlled conditions. (Uncontrolled chain reactions are dangerous, *e.g.* atomic bombs.) The success of a reactor depends on the neutrons reaching the U^{235} nuclei to produce more fissions and not being wasted in irrelevant processes or simply escaping through the wall of the apparatus (neutrons are quite difficult to contain). The neutrons leaving the scene of fission are rapidly moving, and they stand more chance of causing another fission if they are slowed down. Consequently a material other than the uranium has to be present to facilitate this, and it is called a moderator. A useful moderator is pure graphite.

Thus a reactor may consist of alternate blocks of uranium and graphite. If the reactor is too small so many neutrons escape that there are not enough to keep the chain reaction going. The reactor must therefore be greater than a certain *critical size*. In order to intensify or damp down the chain reaction it is arranged for pieces of neutron-absorbing material, such as cadmium, to be inserted or withdrawn as required. While the chain reaction is proceeding countless numbers of fissions are occurring, each one liberating energy which turns into heat. The temperature therefore increases, and to prevent a catastrophic rise, cooling has to be provided.

Hence the reactor has cooling pipes through which a fluid coolant is pumped. The coolant carries the heat away and, in a reactor designed to produce electrical power, the heat is taken to steam- raising boilers and the high-pressure steam is led to turbines which drive the electric generators.

What has been briefly described is the type of reactor first used for serious power production at Calder Hall (1956). This was a graphite-moderated, gas-cooled reactor using as fuel natural uranium (*i.e.*, fissile U^{235} greatly diluted with U^{238}). Other thermal types of nuclear reactor are the advanced gas-cooled reactor (AGR), the high temperature reactor (HTR), the steam-generating heavy-water (SGHWR) and the light-water reactor (LWR). It is also possible to make reactors work without slowing the neutrons with a moderator; these are called *fast reactors*. The design of the prototype fast reactor (PFR) at Dounreay was based on experience gained with the Dounreay experimental fast breeder reactor (closed 1977 after 17 years' safe operation) which was the first to produce electricity on a commercial scale (1962) and achieved the highest power output of any of its type in the world. These fast reactors can produce new nuclear fuel in the course of their operation and therefore offer great economies; but they are more difficult to develop than thermal reactors. The fuel is made from the mixed oxides of plutonium and uranium and the coolant is liquid sodium metal.

Environmental considerations have become

of increasing concern. Most of the products of the fission process are of necessity radioactive isotopes: they could be gaseous, like krypton, xenon and tritium or solid like strontium, caesium, zirconium and ruthenium. There are also present the new radioactive elements plutonium, curium, actinium, etc. Further, in both the nuclear reactor and in the plant which is used to chemically treat and reprocess the nuclear fuel, radioactivity will be induced in associated structural materials, to varying degrees. In this latter case, unlike the former, the radioactive waste with which one is left can to a great extent be selected and is largely overshadowed in importance by the waste arising from the fission and breeding processes. Even if the whole of the UK electrical power was produced by nuclear means, the volumes of such wastes would be relatively small and need in principle tens of acres of storage area. Much of the activity would decay in a decade, a great deal more in a century, but that associated with the elements bred from uranium, would be present for thousands of years: Pu^{239} has a half-life of 25,000 years.

Segregation of the various types of activity is feasible; their incorporation into physically and chemically stable form has received a great deal of study so that storage, readily monitored even for many generations, seems entirely possible. The radioactive properties of these wastes can only be changed by nuclear reactions. Bombardment with neutrons or other highly energetic particles can bring about such reactions so that forms of "nuclear incineration" are feasible but are not yet fully explored.

Nucleic Acids. Living matter is built up of cells each of which has a nucleus surrounded by cytoplasm. Cell nuclei are composed chiefly of substances called nucleoproteins, which consist of a protein attached to a nucleic acid (this original name is still used, although nucleic acids are found in the cytoplasm as well as the nucleus). Nucleic acids are complex organic structures made up of chains of compounds called nucleotides.

Nucleotide molecules have a sugar group attached to a nitrogenous base and a phosphate group. Only two sugar groups are found in the nucleotides, ribose, giving rise to ribonucleic acids (RNAs, found mainly in the cytoplasm) and deoxyribose, which forms deoxyribonucleic acids (DNAs, found mainly in cell nuclei). Seven different nitrogenous bases have been isolated, so that a number of different nucleotides are possible. A repeating regular pattern of nucleotides is linked by the phosphate groups, forming nucleic acids.

The functions of nucleic acids are of fundamental importance. They are concerned in the process of transmission of inherited qualities in reproduction and in building up body proteins.

Nucleosynthesis, the creation of the elements in the universe. This occurred approximately 100 seconds after the big bang, ceasing c. 900 seconds later.

Nuthatch, name of a number of tree-creeping birds, plump, with a short tail, bluish-grey plumage and black stripe under eye. Nest in holes and wedge nuts in bark of trees, hammering them to get a kernel. There are three European species, one, *Sitta europaea*, thriving in England.

Nutria Rat. *See* **Coypu.**

Nylon, a generic term for any long-chain synthetic polymeric amide which has recurring amide groups as an integral part of the main polymer chain, and which is capable of being formed into a filament in which the structural elements are orientated in the direction of the axis. The first nylon of commercial interest was made in 1935, and the world's first nylon factory—in the United States—began production in 1940.

O

Oak, a tree of the genus *Quercus,* including some 300 species distributed over the northern hemisphere and into the tropics. Two species are native to Britain, where the oak is the commonest tree (1 in 3)—*Q. petraea,* more common in the west and north on shallower, lighter soils, and *Q. robur,* more common in the south on deeper, heavier soils. Oak timber is much prized for its strength and durability, and from the time of the Spanish

Armada to Nelson's day was in great demand for naval construction. It has always been used for building, flooring, furniture and cabinet work. The oak is attacked by many insects, the round nut-like oak galls, or oak-apples, being produced by the sting of certain minute gall wasps.

Recently a new disease (sudden oak death) has been confirmed in England. The disease is similar to the blight that caused the Irish famine.

"Oaks", a famous race for three-year-old fillies run at Epsom one day after the "Derby".

Oarfish. *See* **Ribbon Fish.**

Obelisk, a tapering monolithic column, square at the base and pyramidal at the top, regarded by the ancient Egyptians as a sacred stone and usually found at the entrance to the sun temples. Many were transported from Egypt and set up at various times: there is one in the Place de la Concorde in Paris, and one on the Embankment in London—Cleopatra's Needle—originally erected at Heliopolis, centre of the sun-cult, by Tuthmosis III c. 1500 B.C.

Observatories. *See* **Astronomy** *and* **Telescope.**

Obsidian, a black volcanic glass-like rock.

Occultation, the passage of one celestial object in front of another, where the closer object has a larger apparent diameter than the more distant one and which, therefore, temporarily hides it from view. An example is the passage of the Moon across the Sun during a total solar eclipse.

Ocean, comprises the great body of water which covers seven-tenths of the surface of the earth, and has an average depth of 3·2 km. The principal oceans are the Pacific, Atlantic, Indian and Arctic. The greatest ocean depth is in the Pacific, in the Mindanao Deep, 37,782 ft (11,524 m).

The current Neptune Project is creating a massive submarine laboratory to examine the almost unknown world at the bottom of the oceans.

Ocean Currents are well-defined streams running over certain portions of the ocean and caused mainly by wind-friction, slope of the sea surface and differences in density of the water, all movements being influenced by the deflective forces due to the earth's rotation. The climatic importance of the great ocean currents is that they constitute one means whereby heat is transferred from lower to higher latitudes.

Oceanography is the scientific study of the world ocean, *i.e.,* the single connected body of water that covers 70·8 per cent of the earth's surface. Modern oceanography dates from the voyage of HMS *Challenger* (1872–6) during which wide-ranging observations of the ocean were made for the first time going well beyond what was directly required to assist shipping.

Oceanography has now matured into a highly technical and interdisciplinary science which may be divided into: biological oceanography (the study of marine organisms and marine ecology); chemical oceanography (concerned with the composition of sea-water); physical oceanography (the study of ocean currents, tides and waves and the role played by the oceans in climate and weather); and geological oceanography (concerned with the formation, composition and evolution of the ocean basins).

Ocelot, the most common wild cat of S. America. It is about 1·2 m in length, including tail, and of a grey or tawny colour and spotted. Closely related to the Leopard cats.

Octane Number, the index of the knock-rating of petrol. It is based on the arbitrary scale in which iso-octane (which does not cause "knocking") has a value of 100, and normal heptane (which is prone to "knocking") has a value of 0. A good fuel for modern cars must have an octane number greater than 80.

October, the 10th month, but the 8th in the old Roman calendar. It was held sacred to Mars.

Octopus, a genus of marine molluscs with eight tentacles that bear suckers.

Odin, the chief god of Scandinavian mythology.

Odyssey, Homer's epic setting forth the incidents of the wanderings of Odysseus on his way back to Ithaca after the siege of Troy.

Oersted, a unit of magnetic-field intensity in the cgs system.

Ohm's Law, propounded by G. S. Ohm in 1826, is expressed in the equation: electromotive force (in volts) = current (in amperes) × resistance (in ohms). The ohm is the unit of electrical resistance in the metre-kilogram-second system.

Oil. The great expansion in energy demand over recent years has been met to a large extent by petroleum oil. This contains a wide range of hydrocarbon molecules of varying complexity. The various components are separated from each other by making use of their different boiling points. Crude oil is heated in the base of a fractionating tower; the various components condense at different temperatures in trays at different levels of the tower. The fraction of a given composition can be increased by "cracking" or breaking down the heavier hydrocarbons into lighter ones. The total world reserves of petroleum oil are still uncertain since large parts of the world are still not fully prospected. The cutback and the rise in the price of Middle Eastern oil following the 1973 Arab-Israeli war was succeeded for 25 years by a glut of oil and falling prices. Fears over world oil supplies caused the price to rise sharply in 2004.

Development began in 1996 of oil production in the Atlantic (there are huge reserves in the Foinaven field west of the Shetland Islands). This area is known as the "new North Sea". The first British North Sea field (the Argyll) dried up in 1992 having produced 97m barrels. Britain's largest on-shore oilfield is at Wytch Farm (Dorset).

In 2000, output of crude oil and natural gas liquids in the UK averaged 2·7 million barrels a day (making the UK the world's tenth largest producer). UK oil production peaked in 2002. Major new oilfields were discovered around the world in the early 1990s. Some leading oil producers are (in rank order) (with 2003 figures for millions of barrels per day):

Saudi Arabia	9,817
Russian Federation	8,543
USA	7,454
Iran	3,852
Mexico	3,789
Norway	3,260
Venezuela	2,987
Canada	2,986
United Arab Emirates	2,520
UK	2,245

Okapi, nocturnal ruminant mammal, smaller than the giraffe, chestnut brown in colour with zebra-striped legs, native to the Congo.

Olbers' Comet was discovered in 1815 by Olbers the German astronomer. Olbers also discovered the asteroids Pallas and Vesta (1802–07).

Old Red Sandstone, the continental rocks formed during the Devonian period. See also Geology.

Olefines, a series of hydrocarbons, in which the hydrogen atoms are double the number of carbon. The first member of the series is ethylene.

Olive. This small tree, whose fruit yields olive oil, is a native of the eastern Mediterranean countries, but has been introduced into cultivation elsewhere. The green unripe fruit is pickled in brine for table olives.

Olmec, ancient civilisation of Mesoamerica (Central America), now seen as the "mother culture" of the Maya and Aztec. They developed urban ritual and political centres and may have been the first to formalise writing.

Olympiads were periods of four years which elapsed between each celebration of the Olympic games, held at Olympia in honour of Zeus. These festivals included competitions in literature, art, drama, rhetoric, music and gymnastics, and they were continued, with intervals, from 776 B.C. to A.D. 394. Modern Olympics have taken place at Athens 1896, Paris 1900, St. Louis 1904, London 1908, Stockholm 1912, Antwerp 1920, Paris 1924, Amsterdam 1928, Los Angeles 1932, Berlin 1936, London 1948, Helsinki 1952, Melbourne 1956, Rome 1960, Tokyo 1964, Mexico City 1968, Munich 1972, Montreal 1976, Moscow 1980, Los Angeles 1984, Seoul 1988, Barcelona in 1992, Atlanta, Georgia, 1996 (the Centennial Olympics), Sydney, 2000 and Athens, 2004. The first Winter Olympics were held at Chamonix in 1924. The last were in Turin in 2006. The next will be in Vancouver in 2010. The 2008 Olympics are in Beijing. In July 2005 London won its bid to host the 2012 Olympics. The current (2006) President of the International Olympic Committee is Jacques Rogge (from Belgium).

A record 85 nations took part in the 2006 Winter Olympics with contestants taking part in 15 disciplines.

Onomasticians are scientists who study the fascinating subject of names—names of places and names of people—to find out their origins. They tell us, for example, that Cambridge is an Anglo-Norman corruption of *Grantabrycg* =bridge over the Granta; that Harrow-on-the-Hill was an early Anglo-Saxon settlement—"heathen temple on the hill"; that we owe the ridings of Yorkshire to the Vikings (Old Norse *thrithungr* = third part); that in Scotland *-ton* and *-toun* indicate not a town but a hamlet or village. Onomasticians desire international standardisation of place names.

Onyx or **Sardonyx,** a variety of chalcedony built up of different-coloured layers, which are parallel and straight (not curved as in agate).

Oolite, a geological term for the Jurassic oolitic limestones existing through a long stretch of country extending from Yorkshire to Dorset. It abounds in fossils of molluscs and reptiles. The term "oolite" derives from the fact that these rocks are made of egg-shaped particles of calcium carbonate.

Opal, a mineral consisting of hydrous silica, occurring in numerous varieties and colours. Opals have been prized as gems since at least 400 B.C. Their unique internal "fire" or opalescence is a result of the diffraction of light by a regular array of tiny silica spheres, about 100 nm in diameter, of which gem opals are now known to be composed. Opal miners are called gougers. Chief source—the Andanooka and Coober Pedy fields of South Australia.

Open University. See Universities.

Opium. See Z66.

Opossum, marsupial mammals found in the more southerly of the United States, South America and Australasia. They are arboreal except for the water-opossum, which eats fish.

Optics, the branch of physics which investigates the nature and properties of light and the phenomena of colour. Burning lenses were known to the ancient Greeks and Ptolemy wrote a treatise on optics A.D. 150. Lenses as visual aids were known in ancient China but eyeglasses were not in use until the 13th cent. Spectacles were in more general use after the invention of printing in the 15th cent. The camera obscura was invented in the 16th cent. and the telescope and microscope early in the 17th cent.

Oracles were in ancient times supposed to be words spoken by the gods, and it was the custom on important occasions to consult them about the future. The Greeks had the Oracles of Zeus at Dodona, and Apollo at Delphi, while the Romans consulted the Oracles of Mars, Fortune and others.

Orange, a fruit growing in most sub-tropical climates and in universal demand. It is grown on an evergreen tree that attains a height of about 6 m at maturity.

Orang-utan, one of the largest of the anthropoid apes, found only in the swampy forests of Borneo and Sumatra. When full-grown it stands over 1·2 m in height and weighs c. 67 kg. Fruit is the mainstay of their diet. The male may live up to 45 years. All of the great apes face an uncertain future from deforestation and demands for food ("bushmeat").

Orbit, is the path of one celestial object around another. For example, the path of the Earth around the Sun. Also applied to the path of an artificial satellite around the Earth.

Orchestra, a group of instruments and instrumentalists whose playing is under the direction of a conductor. The composition of a typical symphony orchestra is as follows: STRINGS: 1st Violin (16), 2nd Violin (16), Viola (12), Violoncello (12), Double Bass (8). WOODWIND: Flute (3–4), Piccolo (1), Oboe (3), Cor Anglais (1), Bass Oboe (1), Clarinet (3), Bass Clarinet (1), Bassoon (3), Contra-bassoon (1). BRASS: Horn (6), Trumpet (5), Trombone (3–4), Tuba (2). PERCUSSION: Timpani (3–6), Side Drum (1), Bass Drum (1), Cymbals (1), Harp (2).

Order of Merit. See Merit, Order of.

Ordination, the ceremony of installing ministers or clergymen in clerical offices, has existed from the earliest times. In the Anglican and Roman Catholic Churches the rites of Ordination are performed by bishops; among Nonconformists it is done by the governing bodies. The first women were ordained Anglican priests in Bristol Cathedral in March 1994.

Ordnance Survey. Founded initially in 1791 as the Trigonometrical Survey, the Ordnance Survey was established by the 1841 Ordnance Survey Act. The famous maps were first produced on a scale of 1 inch to the mile (but are now available on various scales and constantly revised).

Organ. See P31.

Organic Farming, means the production of food or other farm produce without artificial fertilisers or chemical pesticides.

Original Sin, according to Christian doctrine the corruption that is born with us, as a result of Adam's fall.

Orimulsion, an emulsified bitumen fuel which comes from Venezuela.

Orioles, brilliantly coloured birds, members of the passerine family *Oriolidae*, found in the tropical regions of Asia, Africa and Australia. The golden oriole, perhaps the most beautiful of them all, with brilliant yellow plumage, black wings and tail, winters in Africa, visits England and is known to have nested here.

Orion, a famous constellation of the heavens, comprising nearly a hundred stars, all visible to the naked eye. It contains three stars of the second magnitude in a line, called "Orion's Belt".

Ormer, a shellfish (*Haliotis tuberculata*) which occurs in the Channel Islands and on parts of the French coast. It is a great delicacy.

Ornithology, the scientific study of birds.

Ornithorhynchus. See Duckbill.

Orogeny, large-scale earth movements, including faulting and folding and sometimes igneous activity, which produce a linear belt of mountains, e.g., the Alpine orogeny in Europe which produced the Alps.

Orphrey, the name of an ornamental strip richly embroidered on ecclesiastical vestments.

Orrery, an instrument used in the 18th and early 19th cent. which showed the motions of the planets round the sun and the satellites round their primaries. The first orrery made was named after Charles Boyle, Earl of Orrery.

Osborne House, near Cowes, in the Isle of Wight. Queen Victoria's favourite winter-residence, and where she died.

Osier, a species of willow growing in damp soils and yielding branches utilised in basket-making.

Osmium, a very hard, bluish-white metallic element, no. 76, symbol Os, of the platinum group and one of the heaviest of known metals. It is obtained from certain sands of S. America, California, Australia and Russia. The alloy of osmium and iridium (osmiridium) provides tips for gold fountain-pen nibs. Discovered by Tennant in 1803.

Osmosis, the process by which absorption of liquids through semi-permeable membranes takes place. A solution exerts osmotic pressure (O.P.) or suction in proportion to concentration but also depending on kind of dissolved substance. The roots of the higher plants are covered with fine root-hairs, within the cell-walls of which the sap is normally of a higher concentration than the dissolved matter in the surrounding soil. The root-hairs, therefore, draw into themselves these weaker salt-solutions. (The explanation of water and salt exchanges is complicated by the selective ability of some cells (e.g., roots) to accept or reject particular dissolved substances along with the water. The absorption of salts by a plant is selective, each plant selecting through the semi-permeable membranes of its root-hairs those substances which are most suited to it.)

Osprey (*Pandion haliaëtus*), a large and magnificent bird of prey, dark brown above and nearly white below. The head is whitish with a dark band from eye to nape. To the British Isles it is a rare passage migrant. Back in 1955, thanks to the energy of the Royal Society for the Protection of Birds, a pair nested in a Scots pine in Inverness-shire and reared three young. Since then more young ospreys have been safely fledged.

The food consists almost entirely of fish, which the bird seizes with its talons. The so-called osprey plumes in fact come from the egret.

Ostrich, the largest living bird, related to the rhea, emu and extinct moa, now found only on the sandy plains of Africa and parts of S.W. Asia. The male has beautiful white plumes on wings and tail. The wings are useless in flight, but the birds have a speed exceeding that of the swiftest horse. An ostrich's egg weighs 1·3 kg.

Otary, any seal which has external ears (as opposed to the *true seals* which lack them). The eared seals make up the family *Otariidae*, which includes the Sea-lion and the Fur-seal.

Otter, an aquatic carnivorous mammal widely distributed over Europe, and until the 1950s very common in England and Wales. The otter averages about 60 cm in length, exclusive of tail, has web-feet and is a very expert swimmer. Otters are harmless and their hunting is a cruel and senseless blood sport. Having almost disappeared by 1980, the otter is now protected by the 1981 Wildlife and Countryside Act. In 1995 the otter was officially declared "saved" in England and Wales. Indeed it is now more numerous than at any time since the Second World War. The Otter Trust is based at Earsham near Bungay, Suffolk. Otters have the densest fur in the animal world. There are 13 species of otter, but only the Eurasian *Lutra lutra* is native to Britain.

Ounce or **Snow Leopard,** a very beautiful pale spotted cat from the Himalayas the size of a labrador retriever but with a long furry tail. They are hunted for their pelts. Only around 3,500 are now left across all of central Asia.

Outcrop. Where a bed of rock appears at the surface of the ground, there is an outcrop of the particular rock. The mining of outcrop coal is called open-cast mining.

Oviparous, a term referring to animals which lay eggs to be hatched outside the body of the parent.

Ovipositor, the organ by means of which female insects lay their eggs.

Owls, nocturnal birds of prey, distributed over the greater part of the world. Their forward-looking eyes, embedded in rings of feathers, give them a characteristic "owl-like" appearance, and their plumage, usually a mottled blend of browns and greys, is so soft that their flight is almost noiseless. Owls live on small mammals, reptiles, birds, insects and fish, and are very valuable birds to the farmer. British owls include the barn owl (screech owl), short-eared owl, long-eared owl, tawny owl and little owl. The decline in Britain's five native owl species is causing widespread alarm.

Ox, the popular name of the mammals included in the genus *Bos*. They are hollow-horned ruminants and hoofed quadrupeds, and include the various classes of domestic cattle as well as the different wild species. The adult male is called a bull, the female a cow and the young a calf. The best-known breeds of domesticated cattle are the Durham or Shorthorn, the Angus, the Jersey, Ayrshire, Suffolk and Hereford.

Oxalic Acid, an organic acid obtained from numerous plants, such as sorrel and rhubarb, and produced artificially for commercial purposes from sawdust, treated with caustic potash or caustic soda. It combines with metals to form oxalates; used in the manufacture of ink.

Oxford Clay, a geological formation consisting of a bed of blue clay c. 200 m thick, and forming the lower portion of the Upper Jurassic. It makes good bricks.

Oxford University. The early history of the university is obscure. There was a school at Oxford as early as 1115 and it is known that Robert Pullen, a theologian from Paris, lectured there in 1133. Allusions to Oxford as the most celebrated centre of learning in England occurred in a work of Gerald of Wales in 1184–5.

The earliest colleges to be founded were University College (1249), Balliol (about 1263), Merton (1264). In 1571 the university was reorganised and granted a Charter of Incorporation by an Act of Elizabeth.

Other colleges with their dates of foundation incude: All Souls (1438), Brasenose (1509), Christ Church (1546), Corpus Christi (1517), Exeter (1314), Hertford (1874), Jesus (1571), Keble (1868), Linacre (1962), Lincoln (1427), Magdalen (1458), New College (1379), Nuffield (1937), Oriel (1326), Pembroke (1624), Queen's (1340), St. Anthony's (1950), St. Catherine's (1962), St. Cross (1965), St. Edmund Hall (1270), St. John's (1555), St. Peter's (1929), Trinity (1554), Wadham (1612), Wolfson (1965), Worcester (1714), Campion Hall (1962), St. Benet's Hall (1964), Mansfield (1886), Regent's Park (1958), Greyfriar's Hall (1953), Templeton (1984), Harris Manchester College

(1990) and Kellogg College (1990, formerly Rewley House). The most recent foundation is the postgraduate Green College.

The original women's colleges were:— Lady Margaret Hall (1878), Somerville (1879), St. Hugh's (1886), St. Hilda's (1893) and St. Anne's (1952). Women were not admitted to degrees (though allowed to sit for examination) till 1920. The last college to admit only women was St Hilda's (which finally agreed to admit men in June 2006).

Currently, the University is divided over the transfer of powers from the individual colleges to a single university academic council and an independent board of trustees.

Oxygen is the most abundant of all terrestrial elements, no. 8, symbol O. In combination, this gaseous element forms about 46% of the earth's crust; one-fifth of the atmosphere; eight-ninths by weight of all water. Discovered independently by Scheele (c. 1773) and Priestley (1774). It is colourless, tasteless and odourless, and forms the chief life-supporting element of our world.

Oxyrhynchus Papyri, the famous hoard of 400,000 documentary fragments unearthed over 100 years ago in central Egypt. Many contain writings from famous authors such as Sophocles, Euripides, Hesiod etc., lost for millennia. There are probably very early lost Christian gospels, now awaiting decipherment by new multi-spectral imaging techniques which mean they can be read for the first time.

Oyster, a bivalve mollusc, of the genus *Ostrea*, having very numerous species and abounding in nearly all seas. The shell is rough and irregular. Oysters are exceedingly prolific, spawning in May and June. In England and Scotland deep-sea oysters are not allowed to be sold between 15 June and 4 August, and other kinds between 14 May and 4 August.

In Ireland, no oysters may be taken between 1 May and 1 September, except in certain waters. The Whitstable oyster beds have existed since pre-Roman times.

Oystercatcher, a wading bird with black and white plumage and long, orange bill, inhabiting estuaries and sea-shores. Feeds on mussels, shell fish, etc., but not oysters.

Ozone, a modified form of oxygen, containing three atoms of oxygen per molecule instead of two. It is prepared by passing oxygen through a silent electric discharge. When present in air to the extent of 1 part in 4 million parts of air it kills bacteria, and has been used for this purpose in ventilating systems, e.g., that of underground railways. It is present in extremely small quantities in the lower atmosphere (q.v.) but is comparatively plentiful at heights between 12 and 50 km.

As ozone absorbs ultraviolet light of certain wavelengths spectroscopic methods, involving the analysis of sunlight, are chiefly used in ozone determination.

P

Paca, a genus of large rodents found in Central and South America, and resembling the guinea-pig. It is of nocturnal habits, has streaked and spotted fur and lives on fruits and plants.

Pacific Ocean. The first European to recognise the Pacific as distinct from the Atlantic was the Spanish explorer, Vasco Nuñez de Balboa, who discovered its eastern shore from a peak in Panama in 1513. The first European to sail upon it was Magellan, who entered it by the strait that bears his name in 1520. Sir Francis Drake was the first Englishman to sail upon it in 1577.

The world's greatest known ocean depth is in the Mindanao Trench, off the Philippines, 37,782 ft (11,524 m).

Pagan, a person who does not worship God; a heathen. The word is derived from the Latin *paganus* (a countryman or uncultivated person). In the Middle Ages the term was used largely to describe Muslims. See **Paganism, Section J.**

Pagoda, the name given in China, India etc. to a high pyramidal tower, usually, but not necessarily, connected with a temple.

Palaeontology, the science which is devoted to the investigation of fossils: animal (palaeozoology) and plants (palaeobotany). By studying the markings and fossils of living things in the stratified rocks, palaeontologists have been able to establish with astonishing accuracy a record of the evolution of life through geological time. The geologist at the same time with the evidence of the fossils has been able to work out the order and the age of the rocks. See also **Section T.**

Palimpsests are ancient MSS. or parchments which have been partly effaced and used for fresh writings. Many valuable MSS. were thus lost, but sometimes the second writing has been washed out, enabling the original writings to be deciphered. Among such restorations are a dialogue of Cicero's, a part of a book of Livy.

Palladium, a scarce metallic element, no. 46, symbol Pd, similar to platinum, with which it is usually found. It is an expensive metal, with desirable properties as a catalyst in reactions involving hydrogen, since it has a remarkable capacity for absorbing this gas; for example, coal gas and air will inflame in the presence of palladium at room temperature. It forms a silver-white alloy with gold, and this is used in some kinds of jewellery. It is used in expensive watches to make non-magnetic springs.

Pallium, a vestmental ornamentation of white wool presented by the Pope to archbishops on their appointment.

Palm, a large straight-trunked plant or tree common to tropical countries, and usually fruit yielding, such as dates, coconuts, etc. Many commodities useful to man are obtained from plants of the Palm family (*Palmaceae*).

Palm Sunday, the Sunday before Easter, upon which occasion it is customary to carry palms to the churches in some countries, in commemoration of Christ's entry into Jerusalem for the Feast of the Passover, when the people went to greet Him with palm branches.

Panama Canal. In 1903 the United States signed a treaty with Panama (which had previously seceded from Columbia) which gave the United States rights in perpetuity over a 16 km-wide strip of land extending across the isthmus for the purposes of building and running the canal.

The canal connects the Atlantic and Pacific Oceans, is just over 80 kilometres long (with sea approaches) and the depth varies from 12 to 26 m. It is constructed above sea-level, with locks, and has been available for commercial shipping since 3 August 1914. Under the agreement reached in 1978 the USA formally returned the canal to Panama in December 1999.

Panda, or **Cat-Bear,** is related to the Raccoon. There are two kinds, the Red or True Panda, resembling a large domestic cat, which lives in the eastern Himalayas and S.W. China, and the Giant Panda, which is more like a bear in appearance and inhabits the mountains of western China. Both frequent the dense bamboo forests of these regions. Today about 2,000 giant pandas survive in the wild in China.

Pangolin, the scientific name of the "scaly anteater", a toothless mammal, found in W. Africa and S.E. Asia. It has a long extensible tongue which it uses in catching ants and termites, its chief food. When attacked the pangolin rolls itself into a ball, and its scales assume the form of sharp spikes.

Pangolins have an Order of their own—the *Pholidota*, the scale-bearers. The animal is now threatened with extinction.

Pantagruel, the leading character in one of the satires of Rabelais.

Pantheon, the famous temple in Rome, originally consecrated to the gods, built by Agrippa in 27 B.C. and rebuilt in the 2nd cent. by Hadrian. Its splendid dome and portico make it one of the most interesting architectural monuments of ancient days. Since the 7th cent. it has been used as a Christian church.

Panther, another name for the leopard, *Panthera pardus*, related to the lion, carnivorous, active climber, found in India, and other parts of Asia, also in Africa.

Paper has been known in one form or another from very early times. As early as 3,500 B.C., the papyrus reeds of the Nile swamps served the ancient Egyptians for sheets upon which to inscribe their records. Almost all surviving Greek and Roman literature is written on this. The

Chinese and Japanese, centuries later, were using something more akin to modern paper in substance, an Asiatic paper-mulberry, yielding a smooth fibrous material, being utilised.

With the spread of learning in Western Europe the necessity of a readier medium made itself felt and paper began to be manufactured from pulped rags and other substances. The first known English paper-mill was Sele mill near Stevenage, built about 1490, which produced the paper for an edition of Chaucer in 1498. Other mills were set up under Elizabeth, using linen and cotton as raw material. Other papermaking staples were later introduced, such as straw, wood-pulp &c. Bleaching of paper with chlorine was invented in 1774. The chief raw material in the paper industry is wood pulp, the main exporters being the timber growing countries of Canada, Sweden and Finland. Canada is the world's chief producer of newsprint.

Papyrus, the earliest known paper made in Egypt at a very remote period from a large species of reed, *Cyperus papyrus.* This plant is to be found all over tropical Africa, especially in the "sudd" region of the White Nile.

Parachute, the umbrella-shaped safety device used in emergency by the crew and passengers of aircraft. The first parachute descent from a great height was made in 1797 by André Garnerin who dropped 915 m from a balloon. Rate of descent for a parachute jump is *c.* 5 m/s.

Paradise, a Persian word used by the translators of the Old Testament to designate the Garden of Eden, and since meaning any place of happiness.

Paraffin, a mixture of hydrocarbons of higher boiling point than petrol. Paraffin was first obtained by distillation of coal, the process being discovered about 1830. About 1848, James Young procured it from mineral oil, and Irish peat also yielded it. The main source of paraffin supply today is crude petroleum. Used in the manufacture of candles, for waterproofing and numerous other purposes.

Parakeets, various small parrots of vivid plumage native to Australia, Polynesia, Asia and Africa. One of the loveliest of the parakeets is the budgerigar of Australia. They tend to travel in large flocks in the wild. Their diet consists of fruit, nuts and berries. They were introduced to England in 1840.

Parallax, the change in direction of a body caused by a change in position of the observer. If the parallax is measured (in degrees of angle) and the distance between the two observation points is known the distance of the observed body can be calculated. The distance of heavenly bodies has been found this way. The first stellar distances were so obtained in 1838 by Henderson, Struve and Bessel. Stellar distances are so great that even when the two observations are made at opposite points of the earth's orbit round the sun, the parallax is always less than 1·0″ of arc. See **Aberration.**

Parameter, a number which is fixed for the application of a theory to one particular situation but may be different for other situations. For example, in a theory of motion near the surface of a planet the acceleration due to gravity may be regarded as a parameter constant for a particular planet but differing from planet to planet. The word is often used in a similar way in discussions of economic affairs.

Parchment, made chiefly from the skins of animals, usually of goats and sheep, was employed in olden times before printing was invented and superseded papyrus as writing material. Vegetable parchment, invented by W. E. Gaine in 1853, though not equal in strength and durability to skin parchment, is about five times stronger than ordinary paper. Vellum is parchment made from the skins of young calves or lambs.

Parliament. See **Section D.**

Parquetry, the name of a style of flooring consisting of small rectangular wooden blocks laid down according to geometrical pattern.

Parrot, the popular name of a widely distributed family of tropical birds, including the African grey parrot, the green parrot of South America —both familiar cage pets in this country—and the various parakeets, cockatoos, macaws, *etc.*

Many of these birds possess a remarkable gift of imitating sound, especially human voices. Of the 330 remaining parrot species in the world,

conservationists warned in 1999 that 89 could disappear, through habitat destruction, hunting for food and the demands of the pet trade.

Parsec, modern unit of astronomical distance, particularly for distances beyond the solar system. One parsec equals 206,265 Astronomical Units (AU), and 3·26 light-years. See **Astronomical Unit, Light-year.**

Parthenogenesis. The development of animals from unfertilised eggs. The drones of the honey bee are parthenogenetic, and the phenomenon is also common among aphids.

Parthenon, the famous Temple of Athena on the Acropolis at Athens, was built under the rule of Pericles between 447 B.C. and 432 B.C. It was made wholly of marble without mortar. The famous sculptured friezes, known as the Elgin Marbles, are now in the British Museum.

Particulates, microscopic specks of acids and chemicals in the atmosphere. When inhaled into the lungs (*e.g.* from vehicle emissions) they can cause serious health problems. *See also* **Y27.**

Partisans. Term originating with the Russians who raided French supply lines on Napoleon's 1812 Moscow campaign; now used generally to refer to armed bands offering resistance behind enemy lines. In World War II it took on a specifically left-wing connotation when Stalin urged partisan activities in German-occupied Russian territory in 1941–42. At the same time communist-led partisan bands were formed in Albania, Slovakia and Greece. In Yugoslavia the communists led by Tito styled themselves 'partisans' in July 1941.

Partridge, a well-known British game-bird. Close time: 2 February to 31 August. Two species are common in Britain.

Passport is an official document issued to a person by his own government, certifying to his citizenship and permitting him to travel abroad. Passports to British subjects issued by the United Kingdom Passport Agency (an Executive Agency of the Home Office) authorise bearer to leave the country and guarantee him the state's protection. Renewal passports now (2006) cost £42—and are issued for a period of 10 years. Children over 16 already require separate passports (costing £25.00 in 2006). For those making frequent visits abroad a 94-page passport, first issued in 1973, can be obtained. First-time passports may cost more (around £49).

Free passports for those born on or before 2 September 1929 were introduced in 2004.

From 1988, British citizens began using a common wine-coloured EU passport. Existing blue passports remained valid until 1999. The old one-year British visitor's passport and the British Excursion Document (used by short-stay visitors to France) were abolished from early 1996. To facilitate obtaining a 10-year passport, an application can now be handed in at any post office (for a small extra charge).

The main passport office is at Globe House, Ecclestone Square, London SW1V 1PN.

Reform of the quarantine laws led in 1998 to proposals for 'pet passports' with animals fitted with electronic tagging devices. Trials of the first Pet Travel Scheme (PETS) for dogs and cats began in 2000.

Passports in future will have biometric (*q.v.*) details added and be linked to the ID card. A combined passport/ID card may cost around £93. Since 2006 adults applying for a passport for the first time have to do so in person.

Paul's Cathedral, St. See **L96.**

pC Value, introduced by Dr. C. L. Whittles in 1935 as a measure of salinity of aqueous solutions (soil extract, irrigation water, *etc.*); defined as the negative logarithm of specific electrical conductivity in reciprocal ohms. Alone or joined with *pH* (*q.v.*) is useful as an index of osmotic pressure (*see* **Osmosis**) and related hindrance to plant growth resulting from excess of fertiliser or soil salts. If manuring is balanced, growth is best about *pC* 3.3.

Peacock, a bird of large size and beautiful plumage, its characteristic feature being a tail of brilliant "eyed" feathers, which it can erect and spread out, the males possessing resplendent feathering to a much greater extent than the females. It is related to the pheasant; one species is found wild in the forests of India, and another inhabits Burma and the Malaysian regions. In Africa there is the Congo Peacock.

Peanut, Groundnut *or* **Monkey Nut.** A member of the pea family native to S. America, but now cultivated in many parts of the world. After pollination, the flower stalk bends down and buries the pod containing the peas ("nuts") in the ground. The oil from these "nuts" can be used for margarine manufacture.

Pearl is produced by certain shelled molluscs, chiefly the oyster. The inner surface of the shells of the pearl oyster yield "mother-ofpearl", and distinct pearls are believed to be morbid secretions, caused by some external irritation. Many fine pearls are found in the actual body of the oyster. The Persian Gulf, Sri Lanka, the northwest coast of Western Australia, many Pacific islands and the Gulf of Mexico are among the most productive pearlfishing grounds. In ancient times Britain was renowned for its pearl fisheries, the pearls being obtained from a species of freshwater mussel. Western Australia has produced a 40-grain pearl, the finest the world has seen. The largest pearl ever found was the "Beresford-Hope Pearl", which weighed 1,800 grains, over six times as much as the oyster that produced it.

Peat, decayed vegetable matter found mostly in marshy positions, and common in Ireland and Scotland. Peat is coal in its first stage of development; burnt for fuel in many cottages.

Peccary, a pig-like animal native to the Americas. There are two species: the collared peccary and the white-lipped peccary, the latter being a vicious and dangerous animal.

Pelican, a genus of bird with long depressed bill pouched underneath, thus able to hold fish in reserve. It has immense wings and webbed feet. There are eight species.

Pemmican, venison or other meat, sliced, dried, pounded and made into cakes, used by explorers and others when out of reach of fresh meat.

Penguin, a genus of flightless, fish-eating sea-birds of the southern hemisphere. They are stoutbodied, short-necked and of small, moderate or large size. The Emperor and King Penguins make no nest but protect and incubate the single egg by carrying it in the down feathers between the feet and the body. Other species brood in the usual way and may lay up to three eggs. Penguins use their flippers for swimming under water. All 17 species are bluish-grey or blackish above and white below. They are very sociable and breed in colonies. They have more feathers than any other bird. The emperor penguins use a unique vocal 'identity code' to pick out their families in dense colonies.

Peninsular War lasted from 1808 to 1814. Fought in Spain and Portugal by the British, Spanish and Portuguese forces, chiefly under Wellington, against the French. The latter were defeated.

Penny Black, the most famous British postage stamp ever. In use, 6 May 1840 until Jan. 1841.

Pentagon, government office in Washington, housing the US Defence Department.

Penumbra, the half shadow of the Earth or Moon during an eclipse. The term is also used to describe the lighter, outer part of a sunspot.

Pepys Diary, by Samuel Pepys, was first published in 1825. It gives a picture of the social life of the period 1 January 1660 to 31 May 1669. He bequeathed the manuscript, together with his library, to Magdalene College, Cambridge

Perch, a well-known family of fresh-water fish, with dark striped sides. The common perch of British rivers and lakes falls an easy prey to the angler because of its voracity.

Peregrine. *See under* Falcon.

Perfumes are essences or odours obtained from floral and other substances. The chief flower perfumes are those obtained from rose, jasmine, orange flower, violet and acacia. Heliotrope perfume is largely obtained from vanilla and almonds. Among the aromatic herbs which yield attractive perfumes are the rosemary, thyme, geranium, lavender, *etc.*, while orange peel, citron peel, musk, sandalwood, patchouli and other vegetable products are largely drawn upon. Many of the popular perfumes of today are chemically prepared *See* Musk Deer.

Perigee, the closest point of the orbit of an object such as a satellite to the earth. The opposite of apogee (*q.v.*).

Perihelion. That point in a planet's orbit when it is nearest to the sun; opposite of aphelion. The earth is at perihelion (1·47 × 10⁸ km) in mid-winter, about 3 January.

Peripatus, an animal which stands as a link between the annelid worms and the arthropods. Wormlike with short unjointed legs it breathes by a system of air tubes like those in insects. Certain other points of internal structure point to a relationship with annelid worms. There are some fifty species, the best known being the S. African *Peripatus capensis*.

Perjury, the offence of giving false evidence. The ancient Romans threw the perjurer from the Tarpeian Rock, and after the Empire was Christianised, those who swore falsely upon the Gospel had their tongues cut out. The usual punishment in England from the 16th to 19th cent. was the pillory, fine and prison.

Permian Formation, a group of rocks lying between the Trias and the Carboniferous strata. It has three subdivisions, Upper, Middle and Lower Permian.

Per Procurationem signature means that the subject of the correspondence has been put into the writer's care by his principal for him to use his personal judgment in the matter, and that he is authorised to sign on behalf of his principal. Normally contracted to *per pro* or *p.p.*

Persids, a major meteorite shower, maximizing on 12 Aug. The shower has been regularly observed for the last 100 years. First recorded in A.D. 36.

Peruke, the name given to the wigs worn by men in the latter half of the 18th cent. Wigs are still worn by the Speaker of the House of Commons, judges and barristers (although plans to modernise court dress were put forward in 2003).

Pet Passports. *See* Passports.

Petrel, the name given to a member of a large, widely-distributed family of sea-birds of great diversity of size and colouring and distinguished by tube-like external nostrils. They usually skim low over the waves, and some, for this reason, are known as shearwaters. The storm petrel or Mother Carey's chicken occasionally patters along the surface, and is often called Little Peter—a reference to St. Peter walking on the water. Except when breeding, petrels are always at sea. They mostly nest in holes and crevices on islands and lay one egg, which is invariably white. The storm petrel, Leach's petrel, Manx shearwater and the fulmar petrel are resident in the UK. *See also* Mutton Bird.

Petroleum. *See* Oil.

Pewter, alloy of tin and lead formerly used for making household utensils and ornaments.

*p*H **Value.** Introduced in 1909 by the Danish chemist Sørensen to indicate hydrogen-ion concentration on the basis of electrical conductivity and a view of ionisation since discarded; is now taken as a logarithmic scale of acidity or alkalinity of aqueous solutions: acidity 0–7, neutrality at 7·0, alkalinity 7–14. The *p*H of blood is about 7·6 (faintly alkaline).

Phalanger, pouched marsupial mammals. They are arboreal and superficially resemble squirrels. There are two genera of flying phalangers or flying squirrels, which have a remarkable membrane along each side of the body enabling the animals to glide through the air. The members of the phalanger family are confined to the Australasian and oriental regions.

Phalangid, a member of the arachnid family Phalangida: popularly known as "harvesters".

Phalanx, a name applied by the ancient Greeks to a body of pike-men drawn up in close array, with overlapping shields, and eight, ten or more rows deep. The Macedonians stood 16 rows deep. As many as 500 men could be in the front row.

Pharaoh. *See* Section H.

Pharos, the name of the first lighthouse, built by Ptolemy II about 280 B.C., on the Isle of Pharos, at the entrance to the harbour of Alexandria. It was said to be 180 m high but this is doubtful. One of the "seven wonders" of the ancient world.

Pheasant, game birds related to the partridges, quails, peacocks, chickens and turkeys, males distinguished by their brilliant plumage and long tapering tail. First found by the Greeks in Georgia where the River Phasis flows through to the Black Sea. Close time: 2 Feb to 30 Sept. It has remarkably powerful muscles for take-off, but its flight is cumbersome.

Phillippics, the oration delivered by Demosthenes, 352–341 B.C., against Philip of Macedon—remarkable for their bitter invective. The word was also used for Cicero's speeches against Antony. In modern use, any impassioned invective.

Phoebe, the outermost moon of Saturn, thought to have begun life as an icy comet.

Phoenicians. *See* **Phoenicia, Section H.**

Phosphorus is a non-metal element, no. 15, symbol P. Most familiar as a waxy, yellow solid which is spontaneously inflammable in air. It has chemical similarities to arsenic, like which it is very poisonous. It was discovered by Brandt in urine in 1669. It is found in most animal and vegetable tissues. It is an essential element of all plants and of the bones of animals. In combination with various metals it forms different phosphates, which are largely utilised as manures. The chief commercial use of phosphorus is in the preparation of matches.

Photoelectric Cell, a device which gives a useful electrical response to light falling on it. There are several kinds depending on the different effects which light may have on a suitably chosen solid (usually a semiconductor), *viz.,* the emission of electrons from the surface ("photoemissive cell"); change in electrical resistance ("photoconducting cell"); generation of electric current from a specially designed sensitive structure ("barrier layer" or "photovoltaic cell", "solar battery"). Different cells respond differently to lights of various wavelength and must be chosen for each application. *See also* **Solar Battery.**

Photogrammetry, the science of measurement from photographs taken from an aircraft. Aerial photography has many uses and is of great value to military intelligence and for mapmaking.

Photon. When light behaves like a stream of discrete particles and not like waves, the particles are called photons. *See* **Section T.**

Photosynthesis. *See* **Section T.**

Phylloxera, a genus of plant-lice related to the aphids, which attacks the grape vine. Many vineyards of France, in common with the rest of Europe, were replanted with native vines grafted on immune stocks from California in 1879 after being ravaged by the insect (which came from America). Curiously enough, the remedy also came from America, the vine stocks there being immune to *phylloxera.*

Pi is the unique number denoted by the Greek letter π and obtained by dividing the length of the circumference of any circle by its diameter. Its value is approximately 3·14159.

Picts, inhabitants of Scotland in pre-Roman times, are held by some historians to be a branch of the old Celtic race, by others to have been of Scythian origin. They occupied the north-eastern portion of Scotland, and were subdued by the Scots in Argyll in the 9th cent., Kenneth MacAlpin becoming king of a united kingdom of the Picts and Scots—the kingdom of Alban.

Pike, a familiar fresh-water fish abundant in the temperate regions of both hemispheres. It forms good sport for the angler in rivers and lakes, and sometimes attains a weight of from 9–13 kg. It is extremely voracious, is covered with small scales and has a ferocious-looking head.

Pilchard, a fish of the herring family, but with smaller scales and more rounded body. It used to appear off the Cornish coasts in vast shoals, but over-fishing has led to a decline.

Pilgrimage. The undertaking of a journey to a religious place or shrine. The first recorded pilgrimage is that of the Empress Helena to Jerusalem in 326. In the Middle Ages pilgrimages became common, and were undertaken by monarchs and people of rank in all Christian countries. Muslims have been making pilgrimages to Mecca (the *Haj*) since the death of the Prophet, such duty being enjoined by the Koran.

Among the great centres of Christian pilgrimages are Jerusalem, Rome, the tomb of Becket at Canterbury and Lourdes in France.

Pillory, a wooden instrument of punishment in use in England until 1837. It consisted of a pair of movable boards with holes through which the culprit's head and hands were put, and was usually erected on a scaffold. While a person was undergoing this punishment the mob generally pelted him with stones and rubbish, sometimes to his serious injury. People convicted of forgery, perjury or libel were often condemned to the pillory, but from 1816–1837 the only offence for which it could be inflicted was perjury.

Pine, a conifer of the genus *Pinus,* which flourishes all over the northern hemisphere and includes 80–90 species, which afford valuable timber and yield turpentine and tar. The Scots Pine, *Pinus silvestris,* with its blue-green, short needles, set in pairs, and its rosy-orange branches, is native to Britain, as it is to the whole of Europe. It provides the red and yellow deal in everyday use.

Pine Marten. *See under* **Marten.**

Pitcairn Islanders were originally the mutineers of the *Bounty.* They took possession of the island in 1790, and it was not until 1814 that their whereabouts was ascertained, accidentally, by a passing ship. The mutineers, under their leader, Adams, had settled down to a communal existence, married Tahitian women and increased so in numbers that they were too many for the island to support, and in 1856 they were removed to Norfolk Island. A small number returned to Pitcairn.

Pitchblende *or* **Uraninite,** a relatively scarce mineral. It is nearly all uranium oxide, but lead, thorium, *etc.,* are also present. Pitchblende was the material in which radium was discovered by the Curies. Sources include the Great Lakes region of Canada and the Congo.

Pitohui, a song-bird found in Papua New Guinea which produces a powerful nerve toxin.

Plainsong, a style of musical composition sung in unison (all voices singing the same tune without harmony). *See* **P3.**

Planetarium, a complex optical system which projects into the interior of a dome a replica of all the phenomena of the sky that can be seen by the naked eye, *e.g.,* sun, moon, planets, *etc.*

Planets, the name given to such celestial bodies as revolve round the sun in elliptical orbits. The name was first used by the Greeks to indicate their difference from the fixed stars. There are nine major planets, Mercury, Venus, Earth, Mars, Jupiter, Saturn, Uranus, Neptune and Pluto (though the status of Pluto is debated).

There are also a large number of minor planets or asteroids. Saturn, Uranus and Jupiter are ringed. Many important questions can be answered by means of probes sent to the neighbourhood of the planets. These include the measurement of the magnetic field, if any, of the planets, the study of their atmospheres, much of which can be done without actually penetrating to the surface. With instruments landed gently on the surface it is possible to investigate surface conditions and composition by many methods. Even without a soft-landing information can be obtained by photography and subsequent transmission of the picture back to earth.

The US Mars probe *Mariner IV* pictures of the Martian surface in 1965, the Russian *Venus IV* in 1967 made a soft-landing on Venus, and the US *Pioneer 11* came within 43,000 km of Jupiter in December 1974. Two US *Voyager* spacecraft were launched in 1977 flying by Jupiter (1979), Saturn (1980, 1981) Uranus (1986) and Neptune (1989), sending back important new data. Exciting pictures were received in 1998 from the Hubble telescope of a planet outside our own solar system. By 2006 over 170 extra-solar planets had been detected by astronomers (some very similar to Earth).

Currently (2006), there are numerous exciting space missions, mainly to Mars (NASA's Mars Surveyor missions) and also Saturn (Cassini). The Cassini spacecraft is the biggest interplanetary spacecraft ever launched by NASA. In 2004 it arrived at Saturn and began conducting the most extensive survey to date of any planetary system. Cassini has released the Huygens probe into the atmosphere of Saturn's largest moon, Titan.

A gas-giant planet 3 times older than Earth and 800 times larger (near 37 Gem) was discovered in 2003. The first photograph of a planet (2M1207b) beyond our solar system was made in 2004.

Scientists are currently debating whether to classify the distant rocky objects such as Pluto, Xena and Sedna as trans-Neptunian planets (or even ice-dwarfs).

Plankton, a word which first came into biological use in 1886 to describe the usually microscopic plants and animals floating, swimming and drifting in the surface waters of the sea. To be distinguished from *nekton* (swimming animals like fishes and squids) and *benthos* (plants and animals living on the sea bottom, like fixed algae, sponges, etc.). Of great economic importance, providing food for fish and whales.

Plants. *See* **Section T.**

Plasma Physics is the physics of wholly ionised gases, i.e., gases in which the atoms initially present have lost practically the whole of the electrons that usually surround their nuclei, so that the gas consists of a mixture of two components, positively charged ions and negatively charged electrons. The physical properties of a *plasma* are very different from those of an unionised gas. In particular, a plasma has a high electrical conductivity and can carry large currents. *See also* **Nuclear Fusion.**

Plastics, a broad term covering those substances which become plastic when subjected to increased temperatures or pressures. The Plastics Industry is based on synthetic organic examples of this group. There are two classes of plastics: the *thermoplastic*, which become plastic every time they are heated (e.g. cellulosic plastics) and *thermosetting*, which undergo chemical change when heated, so that once set they cannot be rendered plastic again (e.g., Bakelite). Plastics are composed of long-chained molecules, e.g., polyethylene.

Plate Tectonics. *See* **Section T.**

Platinum, a metallic element, no. 78, symbol Pt. It is a scarce white metal generally allied with iridium, osmium, ruthenium and palladium. It can only be melted in an oxyhydrogen or electric furnace, but can be rolled out into a film-like sheet, or drawn out to the finest wire; being resistant to acids it is termed a noble metal. Named after the Spanish for "silver-coloured" -platina. First found in the sands of the River Pinto in S. America.

Platonic Solids, five regular solid figures known to the ancient world. They are the tetrahedron (4 triangular faces), cube (6 square faces), octahedron (8 triangular faces), dodecahedron (12 five-sided faces), icosahedron (20 triangular faces). All the faces and angles of each solid are identical.

Platypus. *See under* **Duckbill.**

Pleiades, famous cluster of stars in the constellation of Taurus. Of the seven principal stars in the group, one is rather faint, and many myths have sprung up about this "lost Pleiad".

Pleistocene, the geological period that succeeded the Pliocene. During the Pleistocene, also known as the *Great Ice Age*, there were four cold periods, when the ice sheets covered northern Europe and N. America, separated by warm periods when the glaciers drew back into the mountains. From recent studies based on rock magnetic measurements the transition to Pleistocene took place c. 1,850,000 years ago.

Pliocene, the geological period preceding the Pleistocene, and the last major division of the Tertiary strata. It began fifteen million years ago.

Plough Monday, the first Monday after Epiphany.

Plover, wading birds, widely distributed over marshy places of Europe. Several species occur in Britain, including the Golden-plover, the Ringed plover, Kentish plover and Dotterel.

Plumbago. *See* **Graphite.**

Pluto, the last planet to be discovered was searched for following the 1914 predictions of P. Lowell and discovered by C. W. Tombaugh at the Flagstaff Observatory in Arizona in January 1930. Generally the most distant of the planets its orbit is much more elliptical than the other planetary orbits and so it sometimes approaches the sun closer than Neptune. It was thought to be different from the other outer Jovian planets which are gaseous and to consist of rock covered in frozen methane gas. Recently the size of Pluto has been revised downwards by interferometric measurement of its diameter. The diameter of Pluto is estimated to be 2320 km.

It is the only planet in the solar system not yet visited by spacecraft (although the New Horizons spacecraft began its journey there in 2006, with July 2015 its scheduled arrival time).

Pluto's own moon, Charon, was also detected by earth-based telescopes using special photometric measurements. It is composed almost entirely of ice. Images of the surface of Pluto reveal ragged icy polar caps and clusters of bright and dark features. Its atmosphere freezes in winters that last for 100 years.

Pluto has been considered the outermost planet of the solar system, but a new planet, Sedna, was discovered in 2004 at three times further from the earth. It was named Sedna after the Eskimo goddess of the seas. A number of astronomers believe neither Sedna nor Pluto should be classed as proper planets, but called ice-dwarfs. *See* **Section T. Part I.**

Plutonium, a chemical element, no. 94, symbol Pu, capable of nuclear fission in the same way as Uranium 235. Not until after it had been synthesised in atomic piles during the second world war was it shown to occur in infinitesimally small traces in nature. Its synthesis in the atomic pile depends on the capture by Uranium 238 nuclei of neutrons; immediate product of this reaction is the element neptunium, but this undergoes rapid radioactive disintegration to plutonium.

Poet Laureate is the poet attached to the royal household, an office officially established in 1668, though its origins go back to the early Middle Ages, when minstrels were employed at the courts of English kings. Chaucer, Skelton and Spenser, though not court poets, were all unofficial poets laureate. Ben Jonson has been called the first "official laureate" (1616), but the office was not officially recognised until 1668, when Dryden was formally granted the office. It is customary for the poet laureate to write verse in celebration of events of national importance. The current Poet Laureate is Andrew Motion (*see* **Section B**).

Some famous holders have been John Dryden 1668- 1689, Thomas Shadwell 1689–1692. Robert Southey 1813–1843, William Wordsworth 1813–1850, Alfred Tennyson 1850–1892, Alfred Austin 1896– 1913, Robert Bridges 1913–1930, John Masefield 1930–1967, Cecil Day-Lewis 1968–1972, John Betjeman 1972–1984 and Ted Hughes 1984–98.

Scotland now has its own poet laureate, Edwin Morgan, "the Scots Makar".

Polar Bear. *See* **Bear.**

Polecat, an animal of a dark-brown colour, about 46 cm in length, exclusive of tail; the ears and face-markings are white or light brown. It is carnivorous and belongs to the weasel family. Its numbers are recovering in England.

Pole-Star is of the second magnitude, and the last in the tail of the Little Bear constellation. Being near the North pole of the heavens—never more than about one degree from due north— it always remains visible in the Northern hemisphere; hence its use as a guide to seamen.

Police, a regular force established for the preservation of law and order and the prevention and detection of crime. The powers they have vary from country to country and with the type of government; the more civilised and democratic the state, the less police intervention. England, compared with countries abroad, was slow to develop a police force, and it was not until 1829 that Sir Robert Peel's Metropolitan Police Act established a regular force for the metropolis, later legislation establishing county and borough forces maintained by local police authorities throughout England and Wales. Up to that time police duties were discharged by individual constables and watchmen appointed by local areas in England and Wales. The police service in Great Britain today faces radical change with many smaller county forces to be abolished and c. 24 larger regional 'strategic' forces created.

The current structure is:

1. County forces (43 in 2006) under a police committee of local councillors and magistrates.

2. Combined forces, covering more than one county, also under a police committee consisting of local councillors and magistrates and representatives from constituent areas.

3. The Metropolitan Police Authority (MPA), covering an area within a 15-mile (24-km) radius of Charing Cross, but excluding the City of London (since 2000 under the GLA).

4. The City of London Force under the Court of Common Council.

In Scotland the police authorities, (since April 1996), are four joint police boards made up of local councillors. Police ranks are: chief constable, assistant chief constable, chief superintendent, superintendent, chief inspector, inspector, sergeant and constable. In the Metropolitan Police area the chief officer is the Commissioner of Police of the Metropolis. Central authority rests with the Home Secretary in England.

Great opposition faced the Sheehy Report

when it proposed fixed-term contracts and also performance-related pay. The 1994 Police and Magistrates Court Act changed the relationship between central government, police authorities and chief constables. The new National Crime Squad (NCS) to tackle organised crime was launched in April 1998. In 1997 Britain ratified the treaty creating Europol (the first EU country to do so).

The problem of racism in the police force is currently of particular concern. Recruitment for the police among ethnic minorities is also now a priority to achieve a balanced force. The police are also to be brought within the provisions of the Race Relations Act and civilians will head police complaint inquiries. Britain's first black chief constable was appointed in 2003 (to head the Kent force). There are now 155,000 Neighbourhood Watch Schemes in England and Wales.

In Northern Ireland, the Royal Ulster Constabulary (RUC) became the Police Service of Northern Ireland in 2001.

In 2005 it was announced that Special Branch was to merge with the Anti-Terrorism Branch to form a new counter-terrorism division.

A new FBI-style Serious Organised Crime Agency (SOCA) began working in 2006 to combat the menace of serious crime.

Poll Tax, common name for the Community Charge, which replaced the rates. It was itself replaced by the Council Tax from 1993. *See* **Section E.**

Polonium, a radioactive element, no. 84, symbol Po, discovered by Madame Curie in 1898, and named after her native land of Poland.

Polymerisation is the linking together of small molecules to make a large long-chain molecule. The general name for polymers of ethylene is Polythene, a wax-like plastic solid.

Pomology, the science of fruit-growing.

Pope, The, the head of the Roman Catholic Church, recognised by that Church as the lawful successor of St. Peter. He is elected by the body of Cardinals. Since 1870, when the King of Italy deposed the holder from temporal power, no Pope had left the Vatican between appointment and death until 1929, when peace was made between the Church and State in Italy. *See also* **A53.**

Population. *See* **World Population, L117.**

Porcelain. The word is thought to be derived from the Italian *porcellana*, indicating the texture of a piglet. The majority of porcelain made on the continent was of "hard-paste", or true porcelain, similar to that discovered by the Chinese as early as the T'ang Dynasty (A.D. 618–907). It was composed of *kaolin* (china-clay) and *petuntse* (china-stone) which when fired in a kiln at a temperature of *c*. 1300°C became an extremely hard and translucent material. The recipe of "hard-paste" porcelain remained a secret of the Chinese until 1709, when it was re-discovered in Europe by Johann Böttger of the Meissen factory (popularly known as Dresden). Aided by disloyal Meissen workmen, factories were later established at Vienna, Venice and in many parts of Germany. Plymouth and Bristol were the only English factories to produce this type of porcelain, from 1768 to 1781. Elsewhere, both in England and France, the material manufactured was known as "soft-paste" or artificial porcelain which was made by blending varying white-firing clays with the ingredients of glass. The French factory of Sèvres began to make some hard-paste porcelain by 1768 and by the 19th cent. such porcelain was the only type being made throughout the whole of the continent. In England Josiah Spode is credited with the introduction of "bone-china" about 1794. This hybrid-paste was quickly adopted by many factories and remains popular.

Porphyry, a form of crystalline rock of many varieties that in ancient Egypt was quarried and used for the decorative portions of buildings and vessels. The term is applied generally to the eruptive rocks in which large well-formed crystals of one mineral are set in a matrix of other minerals.

Porpoise, a highly intelligent marine mammal of the dolphin and whale family, and a common inhabitant of northern seas. Porpoises travel in shoals, their progression being marked by constant leapings and plungings. Their average length is from 1·2–1·5 m. There are several species, nearly all confined to northern oceans.

Port, a special kind of red Portuguese wine, taking its name from Oporto.

Portland Vase. *See* **Section N.**

Portreeve was an official appointed to superintend a port or harbour, and before the name of mayor was used for the chief magistrate of London.

Positron, the "positive electron", an atomic particle having the same mass but an electric charge equal but opposite to that of an electron. It was discovered in 1932. *See also* **Section T.**

Post Office, The. This is now a State owned Limited Company. Its corporate name was briefly changed to Consignia before becoming Royal Mail. In 2002 it announced over 15,000 job cuts amid a growing financial crisis. Meanwhile, the Post Office lost its monopoly of mail delivery on 1 January 2006. Closure of post offices is an area of current public concern (their numbers have declined from 19,000 in 1999 to only 15,000 in 2005).

Potassium, a metal, no. 19, symbol K (German *Kalium*). It is similar to sodium, reacting violently with water. It was discovered by Sir Humphry Davy in 1807, and is now generally obtained by the electrolysis of fused potassium hydroxide or chloride/fluoride mixture. Its principal minerals are carnallite and kainite, and it is relatively common in rocks, accounting for about 2½% of the earth's crust. An essential element for healthy plant growth; the ashes of plants are relatively rich in potassium.

Potato Famine. *See* **A46.**

Prado Gallery, the great public picture collection of Madrid, containing a superb collection of paintings by Velasquez, Murillo, Raphael, Titian, Dürer, Van Dyck, Rubens and Goya.

Prefect, chief magistrates in ancient Rome. The title is now applied to the chiefs of administration of the departments of France.

Prescription Charges. *See* **Z6.**

Press-Gang. *See* **A46.**

Printing by movable types was first used in Europe in 1454 by Johann Gutenberg, a citizen of Mainz (typeset books had been produced in China and Korea very much earlier). The invention is also claimed for Laurens Koster of Haarlem. It was introduced into England by Caxton, who set up a printing press in Westminster in 1476. Gothic characters were first used, being superseded by Roman letters in 1518. In 1798 Earl Stanhope replaced the wood printing press by one of iron.

In 1814 Friedrich Koenig applied the principle of steam power to the press. Mr. John Walter, of *The Times* newspaper, was the first to use the steam press. Improvements were introduced by Applegarth and Cowper in 1828 and great strides were made in 1858 when the Hoe machine was put on the market. Then came the Walter press in 1866 which printed on continuous rolls of paper from curved stereotyped plates. The Monotype machine casts single letters and the Linotype whole lines. The term letterpress is used for all printing methods using plates where the characters stand in *relief*. The other main printing methods are *intaglio* and *planographic*. The development of computer technology using electronic methods has introduced a new era in printing.

Prion, a tiny micro-organism, one hundred times smaller than a virus.

Privatisation, selling of state-owned industries to private businesses and individuals, encouraged by the government after 1979 as part of its free market policies. Among the industries partly or wholly sold off were British Aerospace and Britoil (1983), British Telecom (1984) and British Gas (1986). Others included British Airways, British Coal and later British Rail. A further aspect of privatisation was the requirement of local authorities to contract out activities to private companies and the introduction of "internal markets" in the NHS. Labour in power has not reversed the privatisation process.

Privy Council, The is the Sovereign's own council, consisting of about 300 persons who have reached eminence in some branch of public affairs (Cabinet ministers must be Privy Counsellors), on whose advice and through which the Sovereign exercises his or her statutory and a number of prerogative powers. From it have sprung many organs of the constitution and many of our government departments have grown from committees of the Privy Council.

Thus the Judiciary or courts of justice have grown from the Sovereign's Council sitting as a Court of Justice, and today the Judicial Committee of the Privy Council is a body of distinguished lawyers acting as a Court of Appeal from courts of the Commonwealth.

Probation Officers are attached to particular Courts, sometimes a Magistrates' or a higher court. Sometimes an offender is not sentenced to punishment, but is released "on probation", that is on the condition that he behaves well and follows directions given by the Court or by a probation officer. Such an officer is a trained man (or woman) who advises, assists and befriends people who are placed under his supervision by a court of law. The probation officer, by his assessment of the social background of the offender, can advise the court upon the wisdom of putting the offender on probation. The probation officer by his understanding can so befriend an offender as to provide a basis for his rehabilitation. He undertakes the "after care" of those released from prison or Young Offenders' Institutions.

A merger of the probation and prison services has been mooted.

Productivity. Physical productivity is the output of products during a time unit, e.g., so many products per man hour, or day, or year. Total productivity is the sum of all the units of product created during the given time.

Labour productivity is the part of the total that is attributed to labour as a factor of production. Productivity of capital is the element attributed to capital as a factor. Productivity of land is the element attributed to the natural powers of the soil, as distinct from what is contributed by the application to it of capital or labour.

Propane, a colourless inflammable gas made of carbon and hydrogen; formula C_3H_8. It is easily liquefied and transported liquid in cylinders and tanks. In this form it is familiar as a "portable gas supply" for domestic and industrial uses. It is sometimes mixed with butane (q.v.) for this purpose. Propane occurs in natural gas and is a by-product of oil refining.

Proteins are the main chemical substances of living matter: they are a part of every living cell and are found in all animals and plants. All proteins are basically constructed of carbon hydrogen, oxygen and nitrogen, and some contain sulphur, phosphorus (nucleoproteins) and iron (haemoglobin). Proteins are built up of very long chains of amino-acids connected by amide linkages (like the synthetic polymers such as "nylon" and casein plastics (from milk) are built up of the same linkages). The structure of protein molecules allows a variety of function. Enzymes, which bring about chemical reactions in living cells, are proteins having specific properties. See also **Section T.**

Proton, a basic constituent of the atomic nucleus, positively charged, having a mass about 1836 times that of the electron. It is a positive hydrogen ion.

Prout's Hypothesis. The English chemist William Prout (1785–1850) advanced the idea that all atoms are made of hydrogen, and their weights are exact multiples of the weight of a hydrogen atom.

With the modification that neutrons as well as protons occur in the nucleus, Prout's belief has been substantially vindicated.

Provost, a Scottish official similar in rank to an English mayor. The Provosts of Edinburgh, Glasgow, Aberdeen, Perth and Dundee are styled Lords Provost. The title of provost is also given to the heads of certain colleges.

Ptarmigan, birds of the grouse family, one species of which inhabits the Scottish Highlands. In the winter the bird assumes a white plumage.

Ptomaines, amino acids produced during the putrefaction of proteins of animal origin. Not a cause of food poisoning, as was once generally supposed, which is almost invariably due to certain specific bacteria.

Publicans, under the Roman Empire, were people who farmed the public taxes. It is this class of officials that is alluded to in the "publicans and sinners" phrase in the New Testament.

Public Corporations, statutory bodies which operated major industries and services in the public interest, e.g., UK Atomic Energy Authority, Bank of England, BBC, Electricity Authorities, Gas Council, British Coal Corporation, British Steel Corporation, British Railways Board, the Post Office, British National Oil Corporation, British Nuclear Fuels, British Airports Authority. They were accountable to Parliament but their staffs were not civil servants.

Conservative Governments from 1979 to 1997 pursued a policy of privatisation of most of these bodies, and many (e.g. British Gas) became public companies.

Public Lending Right, a scheme established by Act of Parliament in 1979 which gives authors the legal right to receive remuneration from the government for the use by the public of their work through the public library system. Payments (c. £7 million each year) are now made to c. 30,000 authors, illustrators and other contributors.

Public Record Office. See **National Archives.**

Public Schools. The Public Schools Act of 1864 named nine "public" schools: Eton, Harrow, Rugby, Winchester, Westminster, Shrewsbury, Charterhouse, St. Paul's and Merchant Taylors'. Today the term embraces many more, and can be applied to all those schools which are financed by bodies other than the State and whose headmasters belong to the Headmasters' Conference as distinct from the Headmasters' Association.

There are very many such schools in Britain, including such famous examples as Eton College (founded 1440), Harrow (1571), Uppingham (1584), Rugby (1567) and Sevenoaks (1418).

Public schools for girls include: Cheltenham Ladies' College (founded by Miss Beale in 1853), North London Collegiate School (founded by Miss Buss in 1850), Roedean (1885), Wycombe Abbey (1896).

Many public schools have become coeducational. Public Schools are now known as Independent Schools.

In July 2000 a national code of boarding standards was set out, outlawing old-fashioned punishments and ceremonies.

Puffin, bird of the auk (q.v.) family. It has a large deep bill and is found in the N.E. Atlantic. In Britain, the largest colony is found on the archipelago of St Kilda, off the west coast of Scotland.

Pulsars. A regular pulsing of radiation which almost certainly comes from a swiftly rotating neutron star. The pulse of radiation ranges from around 1·6 milliseconds to 4 seconds. The radiation sweeps past the Earth in an identical manner to the flashes produced by a lighthouse lamp. Originally discovered at radio wavelengths, a few have been discovered in other wavelengths.

Over 500 pulsars are now known and the total number of pulsars in the Galaxy is estimated to be c. 100,000.

Puma, mountain-lion or cougar, a large wild cat found throughout the Americas. It looks like a lean greyish lioness. It is known as the "lion of the Andes".

Putsch. A conspiracy to overthrow a regime by force. The term is often used of the abortive Kapp putsch of March 1920 in Germany.

Pyramids of Egypt, on the west bank of the Nile, are vast stone or brick-built structures with inner chambers and subterranean entrances, built by the Pharaohs as royal tombs and dating from about 2700 B.C. The most celebrated are at Gizeh built during the 4th dynasty. The largest, originally 147 m high, is called the Great Pyramid, one of the seven wonders of the world, built by the Pharaoh Khufu, better known as Cheops, and there he was buried, 100,000 men, according to Herodotus, being employed for 20 years upon it. Chephren, successor of Cheops, erected the second pyramid, and the third was built by Mycerinus, a son of Cheops.

The pyramid at Meidum built by King Snefru, founder of the 4th dynasty, is the most imposing of all. Historians now doubt that slave labour was used in pyramid construction.

Pythons, large snakes, non-poisonous and destroying their prey by crushing it. Some species may reach 9 m in length, and prey upon deer and other small mammals. Found in Asia, Africa and Australia. They lay eggs.

Q

Quadrant, an astronomical instrument for measuring altitudes, superseded for navigational purposes in modern times by the sextant. It consists of a graduated arc of 90° with a movable radius for measuring angles on it.

Quagga, an extinct African animal, resembling a zebra from the front and a horse from the back.

Quai d'Orsay. An embankment in Paris where the French Foreign Office is situated.

Quail, an edible bird of the partridge family, of which only one species, the Common Quail, is found in England. It is not more than 20 cm long. It is found in most of the warmer regions of the world. In England and Wales the Quail is covered by the Wild Bird Protection Acts.

Quantum Theory. The rapid development of quantum theory has been almost entirely due to the experimental and theoretical study of the interactions between electromagnetic radiation and matter. One of the first steps was taken when it was discovered that the electrons emitted from metals due to the action of ultraviolet radiation have an energy which is not related to the intensity of the incident radiation, but is dependent on its wavelength. Einstein showed in 1905 that this could only be explained on the basis that energy is transferred between radiation and matter in finite amounts, or *quanta*, which are inversely proportional to wavelength. *See also* **Section T.**

Quaoar. *See* **Pluto.**

Quarantine, the strict control of animals *etc.* to prevent rabies and other diseases entering the country. Dogs, cats and rabbits are eligible to enter under the Pet Travel Scheme from rabies-free countries.

Quarks are hypothetical subnuclear particles which were postulated by theoretical physicists concerned with the so-called elementary particles. There are believed to be six kinds of quarks. Quarks carry electrical charges which are fractions of those carried by familiar particles like electrons and protons. This and other special properties of quarks make them suitable for explaining the existence of the large number of other particles referred to in **Section T.** Now the existence of the sixth and final quark has been demonstrated by experiment.

Quartering, in heraldry, is the disposition of various escutcheons or coats of arms in their proper quarters of the family shield, in such order as indicates the alliances with other families.

Quartermaster, a military officer charged with the provisioning and superintendence of soldiers in camp or barracks, and holding the equivalent rank to a lieutenant. The Quartermaster-General is an officer who presides over the provisioning department of the whole army.

A Quartermaster in the Navy is a petty officer responsible to the Officer of the Watch; at sea for the correct steering of the ship and in harbour for the running of the ship's routine.

Quarto, a sheet of paper folded twice to make four leaves, or eight pages; abbreviated to "4to".

Quartz is a common and usually colourless mineral, occurring both crystallised and massive. In the first form it is in hexagonal prisms, terminating in pyramids. When pure its specific gravity is 2·66. It is one of the constituents of granite, gneiss, *etc.* Among the quartz varieties are *rock crystal* (colourless), *smoky quartz* (yellow or brown), *amethyst* (purple), *rose quartz* (pink) and *milky quartz* (white). Quartz veins in metamorphic rocks may yield rich deposits of gold. Mining for gold in the rock is termed quartz-mining.

Quasars, or in preferred terminology, quasi-stellar radio-sources, form a new class of astronomical objects, first identified in the period 1960 to 1962. They have enormous energy output, and are at vast distances. Many are strong sources of radio waves and fluctuate in intensity. There is still controversy over the nature of these objects.

Scientists presently consider that the intense emission comes from a relatively small region at the centre of peculiar galaxies. While a plausible explanation would be the existence of a gigantic black hole formed by the gravitational collapse of the nucleus of the galaxy, dragging in surrounding material, including entire star systems, our

information is not yet conclusive, and has been further questioned by the findings of the Hubble telescope.

Queen Anne's Bounty, established by Queen Anne in 1704 for the augmentation of the maintenance of the poor clergy. After 1 April 1948 Queen Anne's Bounty and the Ecclesiastical Commissioners ceased to exist and became embodied in the Church Commissioners for England.

Queen's (or King's) Speech is the speech prepared by the Government in consultation with the Queen and delivered in person or by her deputy, at the opening of a Parliamentary session.

Quetzal, a green bird with iridescent plumage, once revered as a god by the Aztecs.

Quicksilver. *See* **Mercury.**

Quirinal, one of the seven hills of Rome.

Quisling. *See* **A46.**

Quorum, the number of members of any body or company necessary to be present at any meeting or commission before business can be done.

R

Rabbi, a Jewish term applied to specially ordained officials who pronounce upon questions of legal form and ritual, and also generally accorded to any Jewish scholar of eminence.

Rabbits, herbivorous burrowing mammals. In their wild state they have brownish fur and erect ears. They breed rapidly, having several litters a year. Decimated by the disease myxomatosis, they have been threatened by a deadly new disease RVHD (Rabbit Viral Haemorrhagic Disease), first reported in China in 1984. Rabbits can eat up to one-third of their body weight in a single evening. The 37 million rabbits in Britain are now threatened with a return of myxomatosis.

Rabies, a virus infection affecting animals (*e.g.* dogs, foxes). Since strict quarantine laws in 1901, Britain has been free of rabies. Proposals for reviewing Britain's anti-rabies laws have recently been put forward.

Raccoon, plantigrade carnivorous mammals common to the American continent. There are several species. The common Raccoon (*Procyon lotor*) is about 60 cm long with a long ringed tail. Its fur is thick about. Its skin is valuable.

Race. Traditionally anthropologists have been concerned with the differences between the races of Man. Those who study Man from this point of view further subdivide each group into others. Thus White Man may be divided into Nordic, Alpine and Mediterranean; Black Man into Hamitic, Bushman and so on. Each of these groups tends to have physical traits which its members hold in common, although, of course, there are no *pure* racial types. All existing races have been fairly well mixed. Anthropology dismisses all theories of a superior race as unscientific: there is not the slightest evidence that one race differs in any way from another in its psychological potentialities; Jews, Irish, Scots, Italians do differ: but their differences are due to their situation and not to anything inborn. *See* **Racism, Section J.**

Raceme, an inflorescence in which the main stem bears stalked flowers, *e.g.*, lupin, foxglove. The youngest flowers at the tip of this axis.

Radar. The basic principle of radar is very similar to that of sight. We switch on a light in the dark, and we *see* an object because the light waves are reflected from it and return to our eye, which is able to detect them. Similarly, the radar station *sees* an object because the invisible radio waves sent out from the transmitter are reflected from it and return to the receiver, which is able to detect them. Thus radar is the use of radio signals that man broadcasts.

The utilisation of radio waves for the detection of reflecting surfaces began with the classical experiment of the late Sir Edward Appleton in 1925, which he conducted in order to demonstrate the existence of the Heaviside layer in the upper atmosphere. During the course of the last war developments took place which tremendously improved the methods and instruments used. As in the case of so many of the inventions primarily developed for the purpose of waging war, many useful applications have been found for radar in times of peace, and, in particular, it has proved of great service as an aid to aerial and marine navigation, and in meteorology and astronomy. Radar astronomy investigates the solar system with the echoes of signals sent out from the Earth.

Radiation, energy emitted in the form of a beam of rays or waves, *e.g.,* acoustic (sound) radiation from a loudspeaker, radiant heat from a fire, β-radiation from a radioactive substance. The radiation of electromagnetic waves from a body depends on its temperature, the amount of energy radiated per second being proportional to the fourth power of the absolute temperature. The hotter the body, the shorter the wavelengths of the radiation; thus the colour of a glowing body depends on its temperature.

Of paramount importance to us is radiation from the sun. Amongst other radiations, the sun sends ultra-violet, visible and infra-red (heat) waves. The principal gases of the atmosphere are transparent to practically all of the solar and sky radiation and also that which the earth re-transmits to space. Carbon dioxide and water vapour, however, strongly absorb certain types, the latter, as clouds, playing an important rôle in regulating the temperature of the globe. The cooling of the ground on a clear night is a result of the outgoing long-wave radiation exceeding that coming down from the sky; at sunrise cooling ceases as the incoming radiation becomes sufficient to compensate for the loss of heat.

Radiation, Cosmic. *See* **Section T, Part I.**

Radio. The theory of electromagnetic waves—of which the radio wave is one—was originated by the British physicist James Clerk Maxwell. He was able to show that both electrical and optical phenomena in space are essentially similar in character, and that the waves if short in wavelength are those of light, and if of longer wavelength those of radio waves. Heinrich Hertz made many useful discoveries about the waves themselves, and about their behaviour under differing conditions, and also about the apparatus for producing them. Marconi developed the practical use of radio waves.

Radio methods are vital for the transmission of observed data from space vehicles back to earth, a process known as "telemetering". This is done by converting the observations into electrical pulses which actuate a suitable radio transmitter so that it radiates a signal, in coded form, which can be received at a ground station and decoded. The transmission of such a signal can also be remotely controlled by means of signals from the earth. Photographic and television techniques may also be employed for obtaining the desired information and sending it back to earth, as in the case of the Russian picture of the reverse side of the moon and the American pictures of the lunar surface.

Data may be stored within the spacecraft for a time, and then, upon receipt of a particular radio signal from the earth transmitted by the spacecraft at a time convenient for its reception. Soviet scientists, by a special technique, were able in the case of their *Venus IV* probe (October 1967) to parachute an instrumented canister from the spacecraft so that it could descend slowly to the surface of the planet. Another breathtaking achievement was the transformation of the faintest of signals from a billion miles away into superb pictures of the planet Saturn and its rings (*see* **Voyagers 1 and 2**). *See also* **Radio Astronomy, Telemetry.**

Radioactivity is the spontaneous transformation of atomic nuclei, accompanied by the emission of ionising radiations. It was discovered in 1896 by Becquerel, who noticed that salts containing uranium sent off radiations which, like X-rays, can blacken a photographic plate.

Two years later Marie and Pierre Curie discovered several new chemical elements which possessed the same property, but many times more intense than uranium; the most important of these was radium. Shortly afterwards it was established, mainly by Rutherford, that three types of radiations called α-, β- and γ- rays, are emitted from radioactive substances.

It was also Rutherford who, jointly with Soddy, deduced that the emission of the radia-

tions is associated with the spontaneous disintegration of atoms which result in the transformation of one radioactive substance into another. A series of such transformations ends when a stable element is produced. All of the heavy radioactive elements can be arranged in three radioactive series, called, the uranium, thorium and actinium series. Initially, radioactivity was thought to be a property confined only to a few elements occurring in nature.

In 1934, however, Irene and Frederick Joliot-Curie discovered that ordinary elements can be transformed into radioactive forms by subjecting them to bombardment with α-particles. Following this, it was found that beams of other fast particles produced in accelerators can also render ordinary substances radioactive. Nowadays it is known that radioactivity is a general property of matter; any chemical element can be produced in one or more radioactive forms, or isotopes. *See* **Section T.**

Radio Astronomy. The science of radio astronomy makes use of radio apparatus and techniques for the observation of events occurring in far distant parts of the universe, and, in so doing, is able to enlarge upon the observational field of optical astronomy in a remarkable way. By means of radio telescopes it is possible to observe parts of the universe so far distant that the radio waves received have taken thousands of millions of years to travel from their source to the earth, and thus to observe happenings which may have occurred near the beginning of the history of the universe. Thus radio astronomy works with signals broadcast by objects in space.

There are two main types of radio telescope. The first, known as the interferometer, uses aerials spaced at large distances to obtain very high angular resolution. Indeed, the so-called very long baseline interferometers (VLBI) use receivers with separations of many thousands of km to obtain higher resolution than any optical telescope. The second, and "steerable", type, is that of the radio telescope at Jodrell Bank, Cheshire, which consists of an enormous concave metal bowl, with the radio aerials at its centre. This, though it has a lower "resolution", can be directed or "steered" on to any part of the sky which is above the horizon. The interferometers, particularly the VLBI, have been used to examine the fine structure of many objects, including the nuclei of large and unusual galaxies. The jet-like structures recently found in several galaxies are of particular interest.

As well as exploring the structure of gas clouds and clusters in our galaxy and in more distant ones, several of the large steerable telescopes have been used as radar antennae, for example to explore the surface of the cloud-covered Venus, and to locate suitable landing sites for the *Viking* spacecraft exploring Mars.

Increasingly the radio telescope is used as one of an armoury of instruments available to explore objects of astronomical interest.

Radiocarbon Dating is a method of dating the origin of organic materials or objects by observing their radioactivity. It is of great importance to archaeology because it enables prehistoric dates back to about 50,000 B.C. to be established for animal and vegetable remains. It works because cosmic rays (*q.v.*) entering the atmosphere create neutrons which convert nitrogen in the air to radioactive carbon. This forms radioactive carbon dioxide and gets incorporated into animals and vegetables throughout the world along with ordinary carbon dioxide in a definite ratio, approximately 1 radio carbon atom to 0.8×10^{13} ordinary carbon atoms.

When the tissue dies it stops inter-changing its carbon with the atmosphere, *e.g.,* by breathing, and the radioactive carbon in it gradually turns into nitrogen emitting a β-particle (**Section T**). The radiocarbon content decreases by about 1% in 88 years. By measuring the proportion of radioactive carbon left in, say, dead wood, and comparing it with living wood, the age of the dead sample can be calculated. This needs careful laboratory experiments.

It is now believed by scientists that the proportion of radioactive carbon in the atmosphere varied from time to time in the past because changes in the earth's magnetic field affected the cosmic rays. This has to be allowed for in calculating the radiocarbon date. One use of radiocarbon dating has been to trace the spread of agriculture through the world from its origin in the Near East c. 7000 B.C. See **Tree Rings.**

Radiosonde, a weather station in miniature carried aloft by a free balloon to heights normally in the neighbourhood of 16 km. Signals representative of values of atmospheric pressure, temperature and humidity are transmitted simultaneously by radio to ground receiving apparatus. The position of the balloon at any instant can be determined by radar, enabling the speed and direction of the upper winds to be deduced.

Radium, a radioactive metallic element, no. 88, symbol Ra, discovered by Marie and Pierre Curie in 1898. Atomic weight 226. Radiotherapy (use of X-rays from radium) is used to treat cancer.

Radon, a radioactive gaseous element, no. 86, symbol Rn, formed by radioactive decay of radium. Its discovery completed the series of elements known as the inert (or rare) gases. Radon has increasingly been linked to lung cancer.

Railways. In 1948 the railways of Britain were unified as British Railways (British Rail). Under the Transport Act 1962 the British Railways Board was set up to manage railway affairs. The most far-reaching change since 1955 has been the replacement of steam traction by electric and diesel locomotives. Under Beeching the British Railways Board planned a viable railway system by closing uneconomic branch lines, and by utilising a more limited trunk route system.

Under the Transport Act 1968 some railway passenger services became eligible for grants on social grounds, including urban railways and unprofitable rural services. High-speed inter-city passenger services came into operation in 1976 and in 1985 it was announced that the Advanced Passenger Train (the Electra) would go into production.

Following the 1993 Railways Act, the privatisation of British Rail began on 1 April 1994 when a new company, Railtrack, took over the management of the track, signalling and other infrastructure. In 1994, the government announced its intention to privatise Railtrack, which owned 2,500 stations and 11,000 miles of track. This took place in 1996. The first privatised rail services' since 1948 began in February 1996. Fears over track safety after the Hatfield crash of October 2000 brought major disruption to the rail network. A year later, Railtrack collapsed, to be replaced in 2002 by Network Rail. In 2003, following widespread safety concerns, Network Rail took over maintenance work from private contractors. A new 208 mph UK speed record was established by Eurostar in Kent in July 2003.

Rail journeys are now (2006) at their highest level since 1961.

Rain. When moist air rises into lower temperatures and becomes saturated, condensation takes place on the numerous hygroscopic particles present in the atmosphere. If the temperature is above freezing a cloud of small droplets is formed. These droplets may then grow larger by coalescing with each other as they pass through the cloud until their weight is great enough to make them fall to the earth as rain. In clouds which extend above freezing level, snow and rain both form from the prefer-ential growth of ice crystals at the expense of liquid water droplets. If the resultant ice particle melts as it falls to earth, it gives rain: if not it gives snow. See also **Acid Rain.**

Rainbow, a beautiful colour effect visible to an observer with back to the sun and facing a rain shower, caused by the refraction and reflection of sunlight in minute water-droplets in the air. From high in the air it would be possible to see a rainbow as a complete circle, but from the ground the most that can be seen is a semicircle when the sun is just on the horizon; the higher the sun is, the smaller the arc of the rainbow. When conditions are suitable two bows are seen, the secondary with the colours of the spectrum reversed. The colours of the rainbow are seven; red, orange, yellow, green, blue, indigo and violet—the colours of the spectrum. See also **Aurora.**

Raingauge, an instrument consisting of a deep metal funnel whose stem dips into a graduated glass jar from which the depth of the rain water collected can be read. Continuous records of rainfall are provided by self-registering instruments.

Ramblers' Association, an organisation formed with 1,200 members in 1935 and which now numbers c. 100,000. It has played a decisive influence on the creation of new long-distance paths (q.v.). It supports the "Right to Roam" across all un-cultivated land and in 1998 launched the 'Free Your Paths' campaign. The new Countryside and Rights of Way Act came into force on 19 September 2004, opening up 4,000 sq. miles of mountain, moor, heath and down land.

For the most up-to-date information and maps showing where you can go and what you can do on access land, including details of any local restrictions and closures, visit the open access pages in "Places to Go" on the website: www.countrysideaccess.gov.uk.

Rambouillet, a royal French château (14th cent., rebuilt 18th cent.), near Paris, and the official summer residence of the President of the French Republic. Also the name of the literary salon of the Marquise de Rambouillet (1588–1665).

Rampant, in heraldry, is a term applied to the figure of an animal with forelegs elevated, the dexter uppermost. When the animal is shown side-faced it is *rampant displayed*, when full-face, *rampant guardant*; when looking back *rampant reguardant*; and when in sitting position *rampant sejant*.

Rape, a cruciferous plant yielding coleseed or rapeseed, extensively grown in all parts of Europe and India. Rape oil is made from the seeds and as oilcake is a valuable animal feeding-stuff.

Rare Gases (also called **Inert Gases**). These are a group of elements which are chemically inert, comprising helium, neon, argon, krypton, xenon and radon. Cavendish in 1785 noticed that there was in air some gas which was not oxygen, nitrogen or carbon dioxide, but it was not until 1894 that the first of the rare gases was found by Rayleigh and Ramsay. This they called argon (inert). After the discovery of helium in 1895 Kayser, Rayleigh and Travers soon isolated the other gases except radon, which was later detected as a radioactive decay product of radium. Some of these inert gases are used to fill electric-light bulbs, and helium is used in balloons, since it is very light and non-imflammable.

Rat, a well-known group of rodent embracing many species. The *brown rat* appeared in Europe early in the 18th cent., coming from the East and entering by way of Russia; now it is widespread and met with in Britain and all parts of the Continent. The *black rat*, which was the common rat before the arrival of the brown species, is a smaller animal and now comparatively scarce. There are numerous other kinds.

Rational Number, a number which can be expressed as a ratio of two whole numbers. Examples are 2, $\frac{1}{4}$, 0·3, −8. See **Irrational Number.**

Rattlesnake, venomous snakes which obtain their name from the possession of a rattle in the end of their tail, consisting of horny pieces so arranged that when vibrated they make a rattling sound. They are only found in N. and S. America.

Raven, a black-plumaged bird of the crow family, with raucous voice and massive bill. Occurs in many parts of Europe, Asia and America. Ravens were once a symbol of death and foreboding. Dickens had one, described in *Barnaby Rudge*.

Ray, fish with a very flat body and broad and fleshy pectoral fins, related to the sharks. There are c. 500 species. Also known as *skate*.

Razorbill, a sea-bird of the auk family, having a high, furrowed bill and black-and-white plumage. It inhabits rocky cliffs during the breeding season, and at other times is mostly out on the open sea.

Rectifier, an electrical device which will allow electric current to flow in one direction only and can therefore be used for turning alternating current into direct current. Since electricity is usually supplied in alternating form and frequently needed in direct form, rectifiers are of very common use in both industry and the home, for example in radio and television and for battery chargers. Rectifying properties are possessed by a number of different devices, one of which is a thermionic diode (see **Valve**).

Very large valves filled with mercury vapour are often used for rectifying heavy currents for industrial purposes. Many other rectifiers use semiconductors in close contact with metals or with other semiconductors because such junctions have the property of passing electric current easily only in one direction.

Recusants, people who refused to attend the Anglican Church or to accept the ecclesiastical supremacy of the Crown in the 16th and 17th cent.

Recycling, the process of sorting and re-using waste products. Britain now dumps over 65m tons of waste annually from households, commerce and industry.

Red Rum, the most famouse racehorse of modern times. Winner of three Grand Nationals (1973, 1974, 1977).

Redbreast. See Robin.

Redstart, a small bird of the Thrush family of handsome plumage and striking song. Two species visit Great Britain: the Common Redstart, with bright chestnut rump and tail, white forehead and black cheeks, favours wooded country, and the Black Redstart, with black breast and throat, chestnut tail and white wing bars, prefers rocky ground or ruins, and breeds in S. England.

Redwing, a bird of the Thrush family which finds its way to this country for the winter. Resembles the song thrush, but distinguished by smaller size, buffish-white eye-stripe, chestnut flanks and underwings. It has bred in Scotland and on Fair Isle.

Redwood or **Sequoia.** This genus of coniferous tree comprises two species of Redwoods occuring in N.W. America. Specimens of one species, the Giant Redwood, reach a height of over 90 m and a thickness of 11 m. The age of the largest, the General Sherman tree, is put at over 3,500 years.

Referendum and Initiative, two methods by which the wishes of electors may be expressed with regard to proposed legislation. It is developed to the highest extent in Switzerland. In a *Referendum* some specific matter is referred to the electors. The *Initiative* is the means by which electors can compel their representatives to consider a specific issue. The British Labour Government held a referendum in June 1975, asking voters whether they wanted to remain in or withdraw from the European Economic Community. An Act of Parliament was required to authorise the referendum (which was something new in British constitutional history). The result was for continued membership.

More recently referenda have been held in Scotland and Wales over devolution of power to elected assemblies. In May 1998 Londoners voted in favour of an elected Assembly and Mayor. In 1999 Australia voted against becoming a republic in a referendum. In 2002 Switzerland voted to join the UN. In 2005 both France and the Netherlands rejected the proposed new EU constitution. In 2006 Montenegro voted for independence from Serbia.

Reform Acts. See A46.

Refraction. The change of direction which light rays undergo when passing from one medium to another. The phenomenon is due to the fact that in different media light (and other forms of radiation) has different speeds.

Refractory, a substance capable of standing high temperatures and therefore useful for making furnaces and allied apparatus. Some insulating refractories are fire-clay, alumina, porcelain, carborundum, graphite and silica. Some refractory metals are platinum, molybdenum, tungsten and also the alloys nichrome, chromel and alumel.

Refuge, charity supporting women experiencing domestic violence. Its national crisis line (0990 995 443) is available 24 hours a day.

Reindeer, a genus of deer horned in both sexes, occurring only in northerly regions. It has an average height of 1·3 m, is very fleet of foot and the Laplanders utilise it for draught purposes and for food. All reindeer antlers are a unique shape.

Relativity. The laws of relativity have been substantially proved and have revolutionised our ideas as to the nature of space, time, matter and energy and forced us to think along new lines. In 1949 a new theory by Einstein was announced which sets forth in a series of equations the laws governing both gravitation and electromagnetism, which is said to bridge the gap that separates the universe of the stars and galaxies and the universe of the atom. At pre-

sent the one is explained by relativity, the other rests on the quantum theory **Section T.**

Remembrance Sunday. See Armistice Day, L9.

Republican Party of the United States was born by the fusion in 1854 of the group who called themselves National Republicans, having split from the Democrats over tariffs in 1825, and the northern Democrats, both of them being opposed to slavery. It came to power when Abraham Lincoln was elected President in 1860 and won 14 of the 18 presidential elections held between 1860 and 1932. It was defeated in 1932 largely as a result of the economic depression and reached its lowest ebb in the years of Roosevelt's New Deal (*q.v.*) The Party went on being defeated every four years until Eisenhower's victory in 1952. Nixon narrowly failed to defeat Kennedy in 1960 and Goldwater was decisively beaten by Lyndon Johnson in 1964. In 1968 and again in 1972 Nixon was successful in winning the Presidency. His fall from power in the aftermath of Watergate made 1974 a bad year for the Republican Party. In 1980 and in 1984, Ronald Reagan won landslide victories. George Bush completed a trio of Republican victories in 1988.

George Bush was himself defeated by Bill Clinton in 1992. The party was again defeated in the 1996 presidential election but narrowly secured the election of George W. Bush in 2000. In November 2004 Bush secured a more decisive victory for the Republicans. The symbol of the Party is an elephant, the invention of Thomas Nast, a cartoonist, in 1874.

Requiem. Properly a mass for the dead, the term is extended to cover musical settings by Palestrina, Mozart, Verdi and others.

Reredos, the ornamental screen at the back of the altar or communion table. It is often of a highly decorative character and is an architectural feature in many churches in Spain. Other examples are to be found in the following cathedrals in England: Southwark, St. Albans, Winchester, Durham and Liverpool.

Resins, natural resins are vegetable compounds largely employed in the industrial arts. They comprise india-rubber, amber, mastic, copal, *etc.* "Synthetic resins" is a term sometimes used as a synonym for "plastics".

Retrovirus. See **T68.**

Reuter, an international news agency, founded by Baron J. de Reuter in 1849. Now a public company, it left Fleet St. in 2005.

Rhea, a large flightless bird, the "ostrich" of S. America, distinguished from the ostrich proper by smaller size, longer beak, larger wings, no tail and 3 toes instead of 2. There are 2 species.

Rheology, science of flow.

Rhinoceros, a large almost hairless animal related to the horse. Two kinds in Africa and several others in Asia. They have a horn, sometimes two, over the snout composed of modified hair. Most are leaf eaters but the largest species, the white rhino of South Africa, is a grazer. They have been much hunted for their horns. The numbers of rhinos, which fell sharply in the last two decades, are now reviving. However, the Sumatran rhino now (2006) faces extinction.

Rhodium, a metallic element, no. 45, symbol Rh, discovered by Wollaston in 1804. It is found in platinum ores in small amounts, generally less than 2 per cent. With platinum it gives a hard and durable alloy. It is also used, instead of silver, in putting the reflecting layer on a mirror.

Ribbon Fish or **Oarfish,** a deep-sea fish, deriving its name from its ribbon-like shape. Though fairly long, it is only a few centimetres thick. The ribbon fish is rarely met with because of its habitat, and most of what is known about it was first learnt from specimens cast ashore.

Rice, a grain-yielding grass, of which thousands of strains are known today, extensively cultivated in China, India, S.E. Asia and certain parts of America, and forming the main food of the peoples of China, Japan, India and S.E. Asia. Some 95 per cent. of the world's rice is produced and consumed in the Orient. The grain with the husk is known as "paddy". Arrack, an alcoholic liquor, is made from fermented rice seeds. There are over 120,000 varieties of rice with a range of exotic names, *e.g.* Basmati, Jasmine, Texmati, Valencia *etc.* The genetic code of rice has now been completely mapped.

Richter Scale, a series of numbers used to record the relative magnitude of earthquakes. Devised by F. Richter of the California Institute of Technology. An earthquake is given a number on the scale by measuring the amplitude of earth movements, *i.e.*, the size of the to and fro motion in an earthquake wave, with a special instrument called a seismometer. The reading is corrected by calculation to allow for the distance of the instrument from the earthquake and the corrected results by observers at different places agree quite well. The scale is logarithmic, *i.e.*, earthquakes differing by one unit on the Richter scale are a factor 10 different in amplitude. An earthquake allotted zero on the scale would give a reading of 10⁻⁶ m on a standard seismometer 100 km from the centre of the earthquake. Smaller disturbances would have negative values on the scale. The largest earthquakes had Richter values between +8 and +9, *i.e.*, they had 10^{+8} to 10^{+9} bigger amplitudes than earthquakes of magnitude zero.

It is a widespread misconception that the scale has an upper limit of 10; there are no upper or lower limits to the scale.

Rime, a crystalline deposit of ice formed on objects exposed to wet fog at the same time as frost.

Rinderpest *or* **Cattle Plague,** is a highly contagious disease affecting cattle, sheep and other ruminants. In Europe the disease has been eradicated, but it was formerly very widespread and caused great loss of life among cattle. The disease is caused by a filtrable virus, and is attended by fever and congestion of the mucous membranes.

Ring Dove *or* **Wood Pigeon,** a blue-grey bird, distinguished from other pigeons by larger size (41 cm), white wing-bar, glossy green-and-purple neck and white half-collar. It is very common in Britain.

Rituale, the book of rites used in the Roman Catholic Church for the administration of certain sacraments and ceremonies.

RNA (Ribonucleic Acid). *See* **Nucleic Acids.**

Roaring Forties, name applied to the prevailing westerly winds over the oceans in the temperate latitudes of the Southern Hemisphere. Because unimpeded by large land areas the winds are more regular and stronger than the westerlies in the Northern Hemisphere.

Robin (or Redbreast). A small bird with olive-brown upper parts and orange and shand, throat and breast, both sexes look alike. The young are speckled, lacking the red breast. Its wide European distribution includes the British Isles, where it is the national bird. It also occurs in N. Africa and W. Asia. The nest is placed in a great variety of situations including holes in banks, trees and walls; in sheds, amongst ivy and sometimes in old tins. Nesting-boxes are readily adopted, but care should be taken to ensure that the entrance-hole is small enough to exclude starlings. Robins are pugnacious and defend their territories with vigour.

Their very attractive appearance, trustful disposition, engaging ways and sweet song make them extremely popular. Robin numbers which were declining because of cold and rain, habitat loss and pollution revived in the late 1990s. They are now (2006) declining again.

The name robin is also applied to a number of very different birds, one of which, the American Robin, occasionally wanders to Europe.

Robotics. *See* **T73.**

Rock Dove, the grey pigeon *Columbia livia* of Europe and Asia, ancestor of the domestic pigeons as Darwin was the first to show.

Rockets were invented by the Chinese as long ago as the 11th cent. The Germans devised the huge V2 rocket, carrying a ton of explosive, which was used near the end of the war to bombard London. Rockets are propelled by the burning of fuel (*e.g.*, hydrogen), the exhaust, being ejected at high velocity, thrusts the rocket forward. For the study of the properties of the atmosphere vertical sounding rockets are used.

The provision of enough launching velocity involves the use of rocket motors with adequate thrust. To launch a satellite into an orbit circulating within a few hundred kilometres of the surface a velocity of 29,000 km/h must

be imparted. This may be done by using a multi-stage launching system. When the first-stage motor has burned out it drops off, so that, when the second-stage motor ignites, it does not have to support the weight of the first-stage, and so on. If the launching velocity is increased to 40,000 km/h the vehicle will not return to the neighbourhood of the earth but pass out of the range of the earth's gravitational pull completely.

Unless the launching velocity reaches 144,000 km/h it will not escape from the sun and will become an artificial planet.

Rock Magnetism. The study of natural occurring magnetism in rocks is a subject which has gained considerable importance in recent years. There are two principal reasons for this. One is that this so-called "fossillised magnetism" may be able to tell us more about the past history of the earth's magnetic field. The other is that after many years of heated dispute between geologists rock magnetism promises to settle once and for all the controversy as to whether or not the continents have changed their relative positions in past times (continental drift theory (*q.v.*)). This branch of geophysical research, in addition to its academic interest, may well have important economic consequences.

Thus, it might, for instance, become possible to locate mineral deposits once accumulated under special conditions at certain latitudes but now drifted to other places. Salt and similar deposits formed by the continuous evaporation of solutions in hot countries are one example; oil may well be another. There has been a *steady* change in rock magnetisation direction with geological time. It is known with some accuracy that the most recent reversal took place 700,000 years ago. It has been found that the older the rock, the farther removed is its fossil magnetisation from the present field.

Roe, popular name given to organs in fish which produce eggs and sperms. "Hard roe" is that of the female and consists of eggs; that of the male is the soft roe or milt.

Roe Deer (*Capreolus capreolus*) deer native to Europe and found in England and Scotland but not Ireland. "Roebuck" is the name of the male adult.

Roller, a tropical Old World bird of the Coraciidae family, related to the hoopoe, kingfisher and woodpecker, of strikingly brilliant blue, chestnut, greenish-blue plumage. There are fifteen species, one of which breeds in the far north and visits the British Isles on its migrations to and from its winter quarters in Africa.

Roman Numerals. The following table gives the modern equivalent of some Roman numerals.

I	.	.	.	1	LX	.	.	60
II	.	.	.	2	LXX	.	.	70
III	.	.	.	3	LXXX	.	.	80
IV	.	.	.	4	LXXXVIII	.	88
V	.	.	.	5	XC	.	.	90
VI	.	.	.	6	C	.	.	100
VII	.	.	.	7	CX	.	.	110
VIII	.	.	.	8	CXI	.	.	111
IX	.	.	.	9	CXX	.	.	120
X	.	.	.	10	CC	.	.	200
XI	.	.	.	11	CCX X	.	220
XII	.	.	.	12	CCC	.	.	300
XIII	.	.	.	13	CCCXX	.	320
XIV	.	.	.	14	CD	.	.	400
XV	.	.	.	15	D	.	.	500
XVI	.	.	.	16	DC	.	.	600
XVII	.	.	.	17	DCC	.	.	700
XVIII	.	.	.	18	DCCC	.	800
XIX	.	.	.	19	CM	.	.	900
XX	.	.	.	20	XM	.	.	990
XXX	.	.	.	30	M.	.	.	1000
XL	.	.	.	40	MD	.	.	1500
L	.	.	.	50	MDCCC	.	1800
LV	.	.	.	55	MM	.	.	2000

Roman Roads, long-lasting highways constructed by the Romans. The best known British roads were *Ermine Street* (London, Lincoln, York), *Fosse Way* (Lincoln through Leicester, Cirencester, Bath, Exeter) and *Watling Street* (Channel Ports, London to Shropshire).

Roman Towns, among Roman towns were Aquae Sulis (Bath), Durovernum (Canterbury), Eboracum (York), Londinium (London), Ratae Coritan-norum (Leicester), Venta Belgarum (Winchester) and Verulamium (St. Albans). *See also* **A52**.

Roman Walls were built as frontier barriers under the Emperors Hadrian (76–138) and Antoninus Pius (86–161). Hadrian's works, linking Wall-send-on-Tyne with Bowness-on-Solway, comprised a twenty-foot stone wall, ditches, turrets, "milecastles", fortresses and a double earthen mound, or "Vallum". Impressive ruins are still visible at Chesters and Housesteads.

Antoninus Pius, Hadrian's successor, made a further advance, but the turf wall which he built between Forth and Clyde was soon abandoned. Septimius Severus (146–211) restored Hadrian's wall after the assassination of Commodus and the subsequent civil wars. It was finally abandoned between 380 and 390. It is now a UNESCO World Heritage Site.

Romany. *See* **Gypsies**.

Rood Screen, an ornamental partition, separating the choir from the nave in a church, and supporting a crucifix or rood.

Rook, a member of the crow family, abounding in most parts of the British Isles and found in Europe, Asia and N. Africa. It has been introduced into New Zealand. Rooks usually nest in colonies in tall trees. They are highly intelligent birds.

Rosary, a circular chain of beads, used by Catholics when reciting a particular form of prayer. Each bead represents an entire prayer, and the combined prayers constitute the Rosary.

Roses, Wars of the. *See* **A46**.

Rosetta Stone, discovered in 1799 by the French at Rosetta in Egypt, and deposited in the British Museum. It is a piece of black basalt about 91 cm long, and contains a decree of the Egyptian priests of Ptolemy V Epiphanes (205–181 B.C.) in (1) hieroglyphics, (2) demotic and (3) Greek characters. It was the three different inscriptions on the same stone that enabled hieroglyphic writing to be deciphered. In 1996 Egypt asked for the return of the Rosetta Stone to Cairo.

Rotary Engine. *See* **Wankel Engine**.

Rotten Row, a corruption of *route de roi* (king's drive), the riding resort in Hyde Park.

Roulette, a gambling game played on a table carrying a revolving wheel divided into 37 compartments. Each compartment bears a number, 0 (zero) and 1 to 36. The numbers are mixed and do not follow any particular order, Of these 37 numbers 18 are black and 18 are red, whereas zero is green. The players stake their money on any compartment, colour or combination of numbers they please. The wheel is whirled round and a ball is set rolling in the opposite direction, dropping finally into one of the compartments, thus deciding the winning number and colour.

Roundhead. *See* **A46–7**.

Royal Academy of Arts was founded in London in 1768, under the patronage of George III. The early exhibitions of the Academy were held first in Pall Mall, and later in Somerset House where the exhibitions continued to be held until 1836, when the National Gallery being built, the Academy moved its quarters to that building. In 1869 the present Royal Academy at Burlington House was opened. List of presidents: Sir Joshua Reynolds (1768), Benjamin West (1792), James Wyatt (1805), B. West (1806), Sir Thomas Lawrence (1820), Sir M. A. Shee (1830), Sir C. Eastlake (1850), Sir F. Grant (1866), Lord Leighton, (1878), Sir J. E. Millais (1896), Sir E. J. Poynter (1896), Sir Aston Webb (1919), Sir F. Dicksee (1924), Sir William Llewellyn (1928), Sir E. Lutyens (1938), Sir A. J. Munnings (1944), Sir Gerald F. Kelly (1949), Sir A. E. Richardson (1954), Sir Charles Wheeler (1956), Sir Thomas Monnington (1966), Sir Hugh Casson (1976), Sir Roger de Grey (1984), Sir Philip Dowson (1993), Professor Sir Philip King (1999) and Sir Nicholas Grimshaw (2004).

The Royal Academy of Arts holds an exhibition of pictures, designs *etc.* every summer.

Royal Botanic Gardens. *See* **Kew Gardens**.

Royal British Legion, the ex-servicemen's welfare organization founded by Earl Haig in 1921. A non-political organization, it organizes the sale of poppies on Remembrance Day.

Royal Hospital, Chelsea, built by Wren, opened in 1694 as an institution for invalid soldiers.

Royal Institution, established 1799, and incorporated by Royal Charter in 1800 for "the promotion, extension and diffusion of Science and of Useful Knowledge". It was in the building of the Institution that Faraday conducted his experiments. Today it has extensive research laboratories. It is now also famous for its Christmas lectures for young people.

Royal Mail. *See* **Post Office**.

Royal Society was founded in 1660 and incorporated by Royal Charter in 1662. Viscount Brouncker being named the first president. Its *Philosophical Transactions* date from 1665.

Among those who served as president of the Royal Society are Sir Christopher Wren, Pepys, Sir Isaac Newton, Sir Joseph Banks, Sir Humphry Davy, Prof. T. H. Huxley, Lord Rayleigh, Sir Archibald Geikie, Sir J. J. Thomson, Lord Rutherford, Sir William Henry Bragg, Sir Henry Dale, Sir Robert Robinson, Lord Adrian, Sir Cyril Hinshelwood, Lord Florey, Lord Blackett, Sir Alan Hodgkin, Lord Todd, Sir Andrew Huxley, Lord Porter and Lord May. The current (2006) President is Lord Rees.

Royal Society for the Protection of Birds (RSPB), one of the foremost conservation societies. With over 1 million members it is the largest wildlife organisation in Western Europe.

Rubber, substance obtained from the milky juice (latex) exuded by certain tropical trees and shrubs after tapping. Demand spread so rapidly in the 19th cent. that plantations were established wherever the tree would grow. Seeds of the Para rubber tree (*Hevea brasiliensis*) native to the Amazon basin were obtained by Kew, the young plants shipped to Ceylon and it was from these cultivated trees that the vast plantations of Malaysia and Indonesia developed. Recent years have seen great advances in the production of synthetic rubber.

Rubicon, a small river falling into the Adriatic, and forming one of the Italian boundaries, the crossing of which anciently involved decisive action and constituted a declaration of war. Thus the phrase "crossing the Rubicon", denoting an act from which there is no withdrawal.

Rubidium, a metallic element, no. 37, symbol Rb, most closely resembling potassium. It is silver-white and very soft, and was discovered in 1861 by Bunsen and Kirchhoff, using the spectroscope. It is rare, occurring in small amounts in the mica called lepidolite and in potash salts of the Stassfurt deposits in Germany.

Rubrics are instructions in regard to the ceremonies of the Church, appearing in red in the Prayer Book.

Ruby is a deep red variety of Corundum (aluminium oxide); one of the most valued of precious stones. Myanmar (Burma) yields some of the finest, and rubies of inferior colour are found in Thailand, Sri Lanka, South Africa and Brazil.

Rudd, a fresh-water fish of wide distribution, plentiful in the rivers of Britain. It is of a reddish-gold colour, with a greenish-blue beard.

Ruff, a bird related to the common sandpiper, once common in the Fen districts. The males have a ruff of feathers round the neck in the breeding season. The female is the Reeve.

Ruffe *or* **Pope,** a small fresh-water fish common in most parts of central Europe, and similar in appearance to the ordinary perch. It is found in British rivers.

"Rule, Britannia!" the national sea-song of England, was written by James Thomson (1700–48), the author of the "Seasons", and set to music by Dr. Arne about 1740. The poet's words were "Britannia, rule the waves!" but it is usually rendered "Britannia rules the waves."

Rum, a ardent spirit distilled from molasses, and containing from 40 to 50 per cent. of alcohol. It is chiefly manufactured in the West Indies, and derives its special flavour from a volatile oil.

Ruminants, animals that chew the cud, being provided with a compartmented stomach, enabling them to swallow food, and later to bring it back to the mouth for mastication; *e.g.,* sheep, goats, oxen, *etc.* While in the rumen some digestion of food, especially cellulose, takes place by bacterial action.

Runcible Spoon, a kind of fork used for pickles having three broad prongs. The word was used by Edward Lear about 1870 as a nonsense word and may be derived from *Rouncival* meaning large or huge from the bones said to have been dug up at *Roncesvalles* where Roland fell. Rouncival peas are the large peas called "marrowfats".

Runes, certain characters of an alphabet found in inscriptions in the Germanic languages, found cut into buildings and implements of stone or wood in many parts of northern Europe, including Britain. The runic alphabet originally had 24 letters. Scholars agree that some runes derive from Greek, others from Latin.

Ruskin College, the first residential college for working people, founded at Oxford in 1899 by the American Walter Vrooman.

Rusts, parasitic fungi, some common species of which have reddish spores which in a mass have a rusty appearance. A well-known species is the Wheat Rust (*Puccinia graminis*), which has an alternative host in the barberry.

Ruthenium, a greyish-white metallic element, no. 44, symbol Ru, discovered by Claus in 1845. It is harder and more brittle than platinum, in whose ores it occurs.

Rutile, mineral titanium dioxide. It is found in many igneous rocks, and in gneisses and schists, Its commonest colour is reddish-brown.

S

Sabbath and Sunday. Sunday, or the Lord's Day, is the first day of the week in the Christian year. It was substituted for the Jewish Sabbath in the 1st cent. A.D. as the Christian day of worship in commemoration of the Resurrection. *See also* **Sabbatarianism, Section J**.

Sabbatical Year was instituted by the Jews in ancient times for the purpose of giving the soil a rest from cultivation. This was every seventh year. In universities a sabbatical year is a year of absence from duty for the purpose of study and travel, granted to senior staff at certain intervals.

Sable, a furred mammal of the weasel family mainly inhabiting Siberia. It is bright brown in colour, and has a long, bushy tail. American sable is a marten.

Saccharin, a white crystalline solid manufactured from toluene, 550 times as sweet as cane sugar. It is used as a sweetening agent; as a substitute for sugar when sugar is forbidden, as in certain diseases, or when there is a shortage.

Safety Lamp, as used in coal-mines, was invented by Sir Humphry Davy in 1816. The flame is enclosed in a cage of fine-meshed wire which allows air to enter and promote burning, but conducts away the heat generated in combustion so that no product of combustion escapes at a temperature high enough to ignite explosive gases in the mine.

Saffron, a plant similar to a purple crocus. It is used for orange flavouring and colouring.

Sainfoin, a widely cultivated forage plant, especially adapted for sheep. It is of strong, leafy growth and bears bright red flowers. It belongs to the same family of plants as peas and beans.

St. Elmo's Fire, a glowing brush-like discharge of electricity which takes place from sharp-pointed objects on mountains or the masts of ships exposed to the intense electric fields of thunder-clouds.

St. John's Wort, a shrublike wild plant with bright yellow flowers. It yields hypericum and is used in herbal medicine.

St. Paul's Cathedral is the third cathedral church to be built on the site. It was preceded by a Norman building which was practically destroyed by the Great Fire in 1666. This followed a Saxon church which was burnt in 1086. The present building was designed by Sir Christopher Wren. The foundation stone was laid in 1675 and the structure was completed in 1710. It cost a little under £748,000. Its central feature is the dome, crowned by its cupola and lantern with the golden ball and cross. It escaped serious damage during the air raids of the blitz.

Saints' Days. In the liturgy of the Roman Catholic church a saint is commemorated and his intercession sought on a special day (saint's day), usually the anniversary of his death.

Pope Paul decreed that from 1 January 1970 many saints were to be dropped from the calendar and others demoted. There are now only 153 saints' days in addition to those in honour of the Apostles, Saint Joseph and the Virgin Mary. The festival of All Saints is on 1 November.

Salamanders are amphibia superficially resembling lizards, from which they differ in having a moist skin and no scales. *See* **Law.** *See* **A47**.

Salmon, a fish notable for its habit of returning from the sea to spawn in the river where it was itself hatched. Their origin can be inferred from the chemical composition of certain blood proteins. Salmon from the two sides of the Atlantic migrate to communal feeding grounds off Greenland. The decline of wild salmon in Scottish rivers is now alarming conservationists. Scotland currently has the world's third largest salmon farming industry.

Saltpetre. *See* **Nitre**.

Salvarsan, the organic arsenical compound asphenamine, which Ehrlich discovered was able to kill inside the human body the spirochaete germ that causes syphilis. Also known as "606". It was superseded first by neosalvarsan and now by penicillin.

Salvation Army. *See* **Section J**.

Samarium, metallic element, no. 62, symbol Sm, one of the lanthanides (*q.v.*). Discovered in 1879 by Boisbaudran.

Sami (Laplanders). The bedouin of the far north, last nomadic tribes of Europe. Their way of life is intimately bound up with the reindeer. The reindeer herds feed, clothe and shelter the Sami of Finland, Norway and Sweden.

San Andreas Fault, is the dividing line between the North American plate and the North Pacific Ocean plate where "plate" means one of the rigid sections of the earth's crust as conceived in the theory of plate tectonics (*q.v.*). The fault runs roughly north-west-south-east in California passing near San Francisco. The Pacific Ocean bed and the North American continent are sliding past each other along this fault at about 5 cm per year. As at all plate-to-plate boundaries—another is the Western Pacific coast—the San Andreas fault is the scene of great earthquake activity. Between 1934 and 1970 there were over 7,000 earthquakes severer than magnitude 4 on Richter scale (*q.v.*) in and near southern California.

Because of large population centres, the activity of San Andreas region is studied with great care and some apprehension about a repeat of the San Francisco earthquake of 1906 which caused displacements of up to 6·4 m along the San Andreas Fault.

Sand Eel. *See* **Launce**.

Sanderling, small wading bird of sandpiper family; breeds in tundra regions of far north, and is seen on sandy beaches of Britain as a winter visitor, Conspicuous white wing stripe and, like Curlew, Sandpiper, Knot, Dunlin and other members of sandpiper family, has marked change of plumage between winter and summer.

Sandpiper, small- to medium-sized wading birds of several species whose migratory powers are so great that they are found in most parts of the world. They include the Common Sandpiper, a bird about 18 cm long, greenish-brown head and back, white under-parts, beak long and slender; Purple, Wood and Curlew-Sandpipers.

Sanskrit is the language of ancient India, spoken by the Brahmins, and existing in early Oriental literature. It was the language of literature and government until *c.* A.D. 1100. It is now confined to temples and places of learning. It is an Indo-European language, related to Latin and Greek.

Saponin. The term is a generic one applied to a range of organic compounds which produce frothy, soapy solutions. Saponins are extracted from the soapwort root, horse chestnut seeds, *etc.* Saponin is the basis of the "foam" used for fire fighting; it can be used like soap to make insecticides and fungicides adhere to the leaves of plants. Also used as detergents.

Sapphic Verse, a form of verse said to have been invented by Sappho, the lyric poetess of Lesbos.

Sapphire, a valuable deep blue variety of Corundum (aluminium oxide) found mostly in India,

Sri Lanka and Northern Italy. Synthetic sapphire is often used for gramophone styli.

Saracen, the name given in classic times to the Arab tribes of Syria and adjacent territories. In the Middle Ages the common designation among Christians for their Muslim enemies.

Sarcophagus, the name given to a stone coffin, such as was used by the ancient Egyptians, Greeks, and Romans, for receiving the remains of their famous dead. These sarcophagi were often decorated with carvings and sculptures.

Sardonyx. See **Onyx.**

Satellite Communication, the system for transmitting telephone and television signals over long distances. The global satellite system Intelsat (International Telecommunications Satellite Organisation) was founded in 1964 to establish a worldwide system on a commercial basis. The first generation of Intelsat satellites to be launched was *Early Bird* in June 1965.

Today, satellites have a vast range of functions. Some astronomical earth satellites study the radiations from space that cannot penetrate the atmosphere: X-ray, gamma-ray, ultraviolet and infra-red astronomy have been revolutionised by recent satellites. Satellites are crucial for communications, weather forecasting and as navigational aids.

Satrap, the name given to the governor of a province (satrapy) in the ancient Persian monarchy.

Saturday, the seventh day of the week (the Jewish Sabbath), derived name from planet Saturn.

Saturn, the sixth planet in order from the sun, from which it is distant 1427×10^6 km and around which it makes a revolution in 29.46 years. It is 120,200 km in diameter or 9.42 times as large as the Earth and rotates on its axis in 10h 14 min. Saturn is noted for its magnificent ring system which is composed of myriads of ice-covered particles. Among the planet's 33 moons are Mimas, Enceladus, Tethys, Dione, Titan, Rhea, Hyperion, Iapetus and Phoebe. Titan is the largest (radius 2,575 km), being the second largest satellite in the solar system, about the size of the planet Mercury. Galileo was the first to observe that Saturn was ringed; Christiaan Huygens the first to study the nature of the rings; and Jacques Cassini the first to suggest that they were composed of myriads of particles.

Our knowledge of the planet and its moons and rings has been greatly increased by the spacecrafts Pioneer 11 (flyby Sept 1979), Voyager 1 (flyby autumn 1980) and Voyager 2 (flyby Aug 1981). The Cassini-Huygens space probe, launched in 1997, captured spectacular images of Saturn and its rings in 2004. It has sent back images of Saturn's tiny moon Enceladus which acts like a pressure cooker, shooting jets of ice and water vapour from its south pole. See also **Voyager 1 and 2.**

Saturnalia, festivals held in ancient Rome in honour of the god Saturnus.

Sawfly. These insects are considered to be the most primitive members of the order (*Hymenoptera*) to which the bees and wasps belong. In appearance they resemble somewhat the latter, but there is no waist separating thorax and abdomen. The ovipositor is never used as a sting: usually it is saw-like so that the female can use it to make incisions into tissues of plants where the eggs are laid. The larvae look like caterpillars of butterflies and moths.

Saxons, a Teutonic race originally inhabiting what is now Holstein. By the 7th cent. they had, with the Angles and Jutes, conquered and colonised most of England. The three main Anglo-Saxon kingdoms were Northumbria, Mercia and Wessex. The Saxons first arrived *c.* 449 A.D.

Scallop, marine bivalve molluscs of the genus *Pecten,* which is widely distributed. The scalloped edge to the shell results from a pattern of radiating groves. Related to the oyster.

Scandium, a metallic element, no. 21, symbol Sc. It was discovered in 1879 by Nilson, and occurs in small quantities in certain rarer minerals.

Scarabaeidae, a family of beetles (Scarabs) widely distributed through Africa and Asia and the inner parts of Europe. It is to this genus that the "Sacred Beetle" of the Egyptians belongs, and numerous representations of it are found on ancient monuments.

Sceptre, the staff or rod used since ancient times to symbolise supreme authority. The sceptre

used for the coronation of Queen Elizabeth II is the one made for Charles II. It is about 90 cm long and tipped with a jewelled cross.

Schism, an ecclesiastical term for division in a church. The East–West Schism was the separation of the Greek Church from the Latin, finally established in 1054. The Great Schism was the division in the Roman Catholic Church from 1378 to 1415, when there were two lines of popes, one at Rome and one at Avignon.

Schist, the geological name of certain metamorphic rocks composed for the most part of mineral with thin plate-like crystals (*e.g.,* mica) so that the layers of a schist are closely parallel. Quartz occurs in schists, and where it preponderates the term "quartz schist" is applied.

Schoolmen. See **J47.**

Scientific Units. The International Bureau of Weights and Measures at Sèvres near Paris, is the custodian of accurate scientific measurement in terms of internationally agreed units.

Methods of measurement are continually being improved and measurements of new kinds coming into use. In defining units certain principles have evolved which can be expressed as a statement of priorities:

(i) units should be so defined that measurements made in one laboratory should be reproducible in another with as much consistency as possible;

(ii) units of all kinds should, so far as practical, form an interrelated system based on as few fundamental units as possible;

(iii) the fundamental units adopted should have a natural basis, independent of particular man-made objects such as metal bars or weights. An invariable universal natural standard was achieved for the metre in 1958 when it was defined in terms of the wavelength of a line in the spectrum of krypton-86. This was changed in 1983. See **Metre and SI Units.**

Scone, Stone of, the ancient symbol of Scottish sovereignty. Known as the 'Stone of Destiny' it was placed in Edinburgh Castle in November 1996 (having been taken from Scotland in 1296 by Edward I, the 'Hammer of the Scots').

Scorpion. The scorpions constitute an order of the arthropods. Distinctive features are the pair of powerful claws at the head and a "sting" at the tail, which curves over the back in attack or defence so that it points forwards. The poison injected by the sting is potent, causing instant death in spiders, centipedes, *etc.,* and acute discomfort to humans. A cornered scorpion cannot sting itself to death; scorpions are immune to their own poison.

Scorpion Fly. The scorpion fly, of which there are less than 500 species, constitute a separate order of insects, the *Mecoptera.* They have 2 pairs of membranous wings, and gain their popular name because in some species the end of the abdomen is turned up, though it does not function as a sting.

Scree or **Talus,** the mass of loose, angular rock fragments which accumulate towards the bottom of hill-sides and mountain-sides. These fragments have been detached by weathering processes, in particular frost action.

Scythians, nomadic conquerors and skilled horsemen (9th—3rd cent. B.C.) who inhabited much of Southern Europe and Asiatic Russia.

Sea Anemones or **Actinaria,** an order of marine animals of the coelenterate class *Antozia.* They form a large and varied group of about 1,100 species and occur in many beautiful colours, flower-like in form.

Seaborgium, 106th element in the periodic table, named in 1994 after Glenn T. Seaborg (1912–99).

Sea Butterfly, marine molluscs which propel themselves by two "wings", or side expansions of the foot. They constitute the order *Pteropoda.*

Sea Cow. See **Manatee** and **Dugong.**

Sea Cucumbers or **Holothurians.** These animals constitute the class of echinoderms called *Holothuroidea.* They are elongated and worm-like, with a ring of about twenty tentacles round the mouth. There are about 500 species.

Sea Eagle, a genus of flesh-eating birds related to the true eagles, kites and other birds of prey. Examples are the Bald Eagle, emblem of the USA, White-tailed Eagle (Grey Sea Eagle), and Steller's Sea Eagle of the Pacific coast of Asia. Last known in Britain in 1911, but successfully reintroduced from Norway in 1976 to the coast of Scotland and now breeding well.

Sea Elephant or **Elephant Seal**, a curious genus of seal, the males of which possess a proboscis of *c.* 30 cm in length that suggests an elephant's trunk. They are found on the coast of California and in parts of the Southern Ocean. Antarctic elephant seals can dive to 6,000 ft. and stay submerged for up to two hours—a world record for lung power.

Sea Gravimeter, an instrument to determine the density of the earth's crust beneath the oceans. Designed by Dr. A. Graf of Munich and Dr. J. Lamar Worzel of Columbia University, it can detect changes of one-millionth of the value of gravity at the earth's surface.

Sea Hare, a genus of molluscs (*Aplysia*), so-called because of resemblance to a crouching hare. The shell is thin curved plate largely sunk in the animal's body. They have four tentacles, occur in Britain in the laminaria or ribbon wrack zone, and discharge a purple fluid when molested.

Sea Horse, sea-fish (*Hippocampus*), very numerous in the tropics and comprising some twenty species. Their bodies are ringed and they have prehensile tails. Their heads are horse-shaped, and they swim in a vertical position. The seahorse is unique in that males become pregnant. Seahorses are no longer thought to be monogamous.

Seal, a marine mammal of the *Phocidae* family. They are found in the cold seas of the world, including the waters around Britain. The phocine distemper virus (PDV) has returned to threaten their numbers.

Sea Lily. A class of echinoderms, the sea lilies may be roughly described as "stalked starfishes". There are about 400 living species and several thousand extinct species are known. Otherwise called Crinoids.

Sea Lizard. *See* **Glaucus**.

Sea Mouse, a genus of marine worms called *Aphrodite*, oval in shape, 20–23 cm long, iridescent, covered with fine bristles.

Seasons comprise the four natural divisions of the year, and are due to the inclinations of the earth's axis to the plane of the ecliptic (*q.v.*).

Sea Squirts or **Tunicates**. These animals are placed in the sub-phylum called *Urochorda*; found growing in rounded, jelly-like masses on rocks near low-water level. They get their name through the water jets they discharge.

Sea Urchin, species forming the class *Echinoidae*. The body is globular and covered with spines which may be used for both defence and locomotion. The main organs of locomotion are, however, the tube feet, as in starfishes.

Secondary Sexual Characters, characters of animals which are distinctive of sex, but have no direct connection with the reproductive process. Examples are: the mane of the lion and the antlers of some deer.

Secretary Bird, so called because of the quill-like plumes about its ears, is a bird of prey related to the eagles and vultures; common in Africa, and of considerable service as an exterminator of snakes. It is a large bird about 1·2 m in height.

Sedimentary Rocks. *See* **Section T, Part I.**

Sedna. *See* **Pluto**.

Seismology, the branch of geophysics devoted to the study of earthquakes and other earth movements. The instruments used for the registration of earth tremors are termed seismographs and consist in principle of a pendulum system, the supporting framework following the ground movement and the bob remaining at rest, thus setting up a relative movement between two parts. In order to record the displacements completely, at one station, three seismographs are necessary to show the two horizontal and the vertical components of the motion. *See also* **Richter Scale**.

Selenium, a non-metallic element, no. 34, symbol Se; related to sulphur it is a dark red colour, and solid, found associated with sulphur, iron, pyrites, *etc.*, though only in small quantities.

It is a semiconductor (*q.v.*) and its special electrical properties have led to its use in photoelectric cells and rectifiers. Selenium is widely used in the chemical industry as a catalyst (*q.v.*) in producing aromatic hydrocarbons from less useful hydrocarbons. Also used in making some types of glass.

Recently, selenium has been seen to be helpful in reducing the risk of prostate cancer.

Selfish Genes. Genes are understood to be relatively small sequences of DNA, which are likely to last for many generations. Selfish Gene Theory proposes that the primary function of genes is self replication. The purpose of the organism in which the genes are carried is to ensure that the genes survive and reproduce whether they are advantageous to the organism or not. The concept was popularized by Richard Dawkins in his book *The Selfish Gene* (1976).

Semiconductors, substances with numerous special and useful electrical properties. These include:

(i) they conduct electricity much better than do insulators, but much less well than metals (hence their name);

(ii) their power to conduct depends strongly on their temperatures—which makes them useful for temperature sensitive devices;

(iii) they are sensitive to light—hence their use in photoelectric cells and solar batteries;

(iv) when in contact with metals, or with other suitable semiconductors, they form a boundary layer which conducts electricity much better one way than the other—this is the basis of many rectifiers some of which, called crystal diodes, are an important component in radios and electronic devices;

(v) their electrical properties can be greatly influenced by putting in minute amounts of impurity, this enables semiconductor devices, especially transistors, to be made with carefully selected properties.

Semiconductors were known to Faraday, but the semiconductor age really arrived with the invention of the transistor (*q.v.*) in 1947. The ubiquitous transistor is only one of very many semiconductor devices which perform a variety of functions in technical apparatus of all kinds. Semiconductors used in technology are usually small crystals, frequently of germanium or silicon, and their robustness and small power consumption often make them superior to other devices, such as thermionic valves, which they often replace. Other semiconducting materials are cadmium sulphide, cadmium lead telluride, indium antimonide.

Senate, the higher governing Assembly of a Legislature. The word, applied primarily to the Roman council, is also used to denote the upper chamber in the legislatures of France, the United States, *etc.*

Sensitive Plant. A species of Mimosa (*Mimosa pudica*), whose leaves are extremely sensitive to touch, shaking and burning.

Sepia, the "ink" of the cuttlefish. *See* **Ink Sac**.

September, the ninth month of the year, and the seventh of the old Roman calendar; hence the name, from Septimus. The designation was several times changed by the Emperors, but none of the new names survived for long.

Septuagesima Sunday, the 3rd Sunday before Lent.

Septuagint, the Greek translation of the Old Testament made by Alexandrian Jews between 250 B.C. and 100 B.C. from Hebrew texts now lost. There are many differences between the Septuagint and the Massoretic version (A.D. 900), and therefore it is of great value for textual criticism. The symbol for the Septuagint is LXX.

Sequoia. *See under* **Redwood**.

Serpentine, a mineral: chemically a hydrous silicate of magnesium. Green serpentine is used as an ornament stone. Fibrous serpentine is called asbestos.

Serval, a collie-dog-sized cat, long-limbed and spotted, from Africa. Preys on a variety of animals, from lizards to small antelope. Black servals occur mainly in mountainous regions.

Set, both in everyday speech (as in tea set, chess set) and in mathematics, a set is a collection of things. The members of the set can be specified by listing them or by describing the properties necessary for membership of the set, *e.g.*, the set of ginger-haired boxers. Set theory is a very important branch of mathematics founded by a great mathematician, Georg Cantor (1845–1918). Its development has influenced many other branches of mathematics.

Seven Champions of Christendom. *See* **H24**.

Seven Churches of Asia. *See* **H24.**

Seven Deadly Sins. *See* **Sins.**

Seven Wonders of the World were: 1. The Pyramids of Egypt; 2. the Tomb of Mausolus, King of Caria (hence the word mausoleum); 3. the Temple of Diana at Ephesus; 4. the Walls and Hanging Gardens of Babylon; 5. the Colossus at Rhodes; 6. the Ivory and Gold Statue of Jupiter Olympus; and 7. the Pharos, or Watch Tower, built at Alexandria by Ptolemy Philadelphus, King of Egypt (the foundations of this were discovered in 2005 by French archaeologists). Some people class the Terracotta Army (*q.v.*), found in China, as an eighth wonder of the world.

Sexagesima Sunday, the 2nd Sunday before Lent.

Sextant, a reflecting instrument for measuring the angular distances of objects. It is of special importance in navigation and surveying, and contains 60 degrees described on a graduated arc. A small telescope is attached and there are also a couple of mirrors which reflect the distant objects so as to enable them to be accurately observed. The invention is attributed to John Hadley, and to Thomas Godfrey independently, about 1780. The principle had been foreseen, and its application described, at earlier dates by Newton, Halley and Hooke.

Shad, a marine fish belonging to the same genus as the herring. It is found along the Atlantic Coast of the USA, and ascends rivers to spawn.

Shagreen, shark's skin; also untanned leather of peculiar grain made from skins of wild asses, camels and horses.

Shalloon, a kind of cloth manufactured from wool and worsted, and used chiefly for women's dresses and coat linings. It gets its name from the fact that it was originally made at Châlons-sur-Marne. It was called "chalouns" by Chaucer and "shalloons" by Swift.

Shamrock, the three-leaved clover like plant native to Ireland and its national emblem.

Shark, a large and powerful ocean fish, comprising *c.* 300 species, very widely distributed, but most numerous in tropical seas. They have formidable teeth and are the most carnivorous of all fishes. They usually attain a large size, the whale-shark being often of a length of 15 m. Commercially the shark yields shagreen from its skin, the fins are made into gelatine, and an oil is obtained from the liver. Some shark species are now (2006) threatened with extinction as a result of over-fishing by man (*e.g.* in the NW Atlantic). A 409 million-year-old shark fossil was discovered in Canada in 2003.

Sheep, a well-known family of ruminants of great utility as wool-producers, and for food. From the earliest times sheep have been a source of wealth to England. So much were they valued in the 15th and 16th cent., that their exportation was frequently prohibited.

Sheep are classified as (1) longwools; (2) short-wools; and (3) mountain breeds. Most of the longwools carry Leicester blood in their ancestry and the shortwooled Down breeds carry the blood of the Southdown. The Southdown produced the present Suffolk, one of the most popular breeds. Cheviot is an important mountain breed. Of the foreign breeds the most valued are the Merino sheep of Spain, which yield a fine long wool. Australia. The first successful cloning of an adult sheep (Dolly) was achieved in 1997. *See also* **Wool.**

Shelduck, a handsome genus of surface-feeding ducks, one of which, the common shelduck, is an inhabitant of Great Britain. It is a beautiful white-and-chestnut plumaged bird with dark-green head and neck and red bill. The ruddy shelduck appears in Britain occasionally.

Shellac. This resin is the secretion of the lac insect (*Coccus lacca*), which occurs in forests of Assam and Thailand. It is used for making varnish *See also* **Lac.**

Shelter, the charity for the homeless, founded 1966.

Sherardizing. Process for coating steel or iron parts with zinc to prevent corrosion; this is done by heating the parts in a closed rotating drum containing zinc dust.

Shilling has been an English coin from Saxon times, but it was not of the value of 12 pence until after the Conquest. It is interchangeable with the 5 new pence decimal piece which came into circulation in 1968. A new, smaller 5p coin was introduced after 1991.

Ships have existed from prehistoric times. There is mention of one that sailed from Egypt to Greece in 1485 B.C., and in 786 B.C. the Tyrians built a double-decked vessel. No double-decked ship was known in England, however, before the *Royal Harry* was built by Henry VII, and it was not until the 17th cent. that shipbuilding was carried on in Great Britain as a prominent industry.

Shoddy, the name given to a kind of cloth mainly composed of woollen or worsted rags, torn up and re-fabricated by powerful machinery. It was first made at Batley in Yorkshire *c.* 1813, and became a very important local industry.

Shooting Star, the popular name for a meteor.

Shot, the name given to solid projectiles fired from guns. In the time of Henry V stone shot was used, later leaden shot, then iron, and finally steel, introduced by Sir Joseph Whitworth.

Shrike, a large and varied family of birds of hawk-like behaviour found in all continents except S. America. The Red-backed Shrike, which winters in Africa, is a breeding visitor to England and Wales. It is commonly called the "Butcher Bird" from the way it impales its prey (small birds and insects) on thorn-twigs. The other species on the British list are the Great Grey Shrike, the Lesser Grey Shrike, the Woodchat Shrike, and the Masked Shrike.

Shrove Tuesday, the day before the first day of Lent, receiving its name from the old custom of shriving, or making confession, on that day. In England the day has always been associated with the making of pancakes.

Sicilian Vespers. *See* **A47.**

Silence, Tower of, or *dakhma*, a tower about 8 m high, built by the Parsees for their dead.

Silicon, an important non-metallic element, no. 14, symbol Si, it is related to carbon. Next to oxygen, it is the most abundant constituent of the earth's crust (27 % by weight). It occurs in many rocks, and its oxide occurs in many forms (*e.g.* quartz, sand, flint, agate, chalcedony, opal, *etc.*). Principally used as a semi-conducting material for making transistors and similar devices. The circuitry of the computer is etched on a chip of silicon.

Silicones are synthetic organic derivatives of silicon which because of their high resistance to heat and moisture have special uses, *e.g.*, lubricants, heat-resistant resins and lacquers, and water-repellent finishes. Silicones are compounds in which the molecules consist of chains of atoms of silicon and oxygen alternately. Silicones were developed in the United States from discoveries first made by Prof. F. S. Kipping at Nottingham University. Manufacture began in Britain in 1950, and in the form of fluids, resins, rubbers and greases they find wide use in industry.

Silk, the name given to a soft glossy fabric manufactured from the fine thread produced by the silkworm. It was known to, and highly prized in antiquity, being at one time paid for, weight for weight, with gold. The manufacture of silk was carried on in Sicily in the 12th cent., later spreading to Italy, Spain and France, where Lyons has been the great centre of production from 1450 to this day. It was not manufactured in England before 1604; but when certain French refugees established themselves at Spitalfields in 1688, the industry was developed and became of importance. In the 18th cent. the Lombes of Derby achieved great success in this industry. Japan, China, Italy, and Korea are the chief silk-producing countries. Silk was first produced in ancient China *c.* 2640 B.C.

Silk Road. A network of great trading routes which linked China in the East with the commercial centres of the Mediterranean.

Silkworm, the larva of a species of moth, *Bombyx mori*. It is native to China, and has been cultivated with success in India, Iran, Turkey and Italy. The silkworm of commerce feeds on mulberry leaves and produces a cocoon of silk varying in colour from white to orange. The cocoon is the silken habitation constructed by the worm for its entrance upon the pupal condition, and to obtain the silk the pupa is killed by immersing it in hot water.

Sill, a sheet-like mass of igneous rock which has been intruded parallel with the stratification of the country rock, *cf.* a dyke.

Silurian. This geological period is one of the major subdivisions of the Palaeozoic era. Its beginning is estimated at 440 million years ago, and the period lasted about 40 million years. Maximum thickness of the Silurian strata in Britain measures 4,575 m.

Silver, a white precious metallic element, no. 47, symbol Ag (Latin *argentum*) found in a free state, also in certain combinations, and in a variety of ores. The chief silver-producing regions are the Andes and Cordilleras. Peru, Bolivia and Mexico have yielded vast supplies of the metal since the 16th century, and Colorado and Nevada in the United States have also been very prolific.

In England standard silver (that used for coinage) formerly contained 92½ per cent. fine silver and 7½ per cent. alloy, but when the price rose to 89½d. per oz and the coins became worth more than the face value, the Coinage Act of 1920 was passed, reducing the fineness to half.

To provide silver bullion for industry and for a fund towards the redemption of our silver debt to America, it was decided in 1946 to replace the United Kingdom silver coinage by one made of cupro-nickel (75 per cent. copper, 25 per cent. nickel). Maundy money, however, is of the original silver standard. Silver chloride and bromide are light-sensitive compounds and are used in photography.

Simony, the offence of trading in church offices, has been contrary to English law since the time of Edward VI. Elizabeth also promulgated laws against simony. Strict laws against simony are now in existence.

Sinn Fein (*Irish* = ourselves alone), Irish nationalistic movement founded in 1905 which developed into a mass republican party and triumphed in the establishment of the Irish Free State.

A continuing group has survived which represents politically the outlawed I.R.A. In Northern Ireland Sinn Fein was legalized in 1974.

Sins, The Seven Deadly or Capital Sins are pride, avarice, lust, anger, gluttony, envy and sloth.

Sirius, the dog-star, so called because of its situation in the mouth of the Dog (Canis Major): it is the brightest star in the sky, and is also one of the nearest to us.

Sirocco, a warm, southerly, often dust-laden, wind blowing across Mediterranean lands from the Sahara, in advance of an eastward-moving depression over the Mediterranean.

Siskin, a small bird of the finch family, common in Northern regions, nesting in Britain. The common Siskin has a yellow-green colour and is a lively, swift-flying bird with a stout bill.

Sistine Chapel, the chapel of the Pope in the Vatican, renowned for its frescoes by Michelangelo.

SI Units (*Système International d'Unités*) form an internationally recognised system of metric units for scientific and technical quantities. The basic units of length, time, mass, electric current, temperature, amount of substance, and luminous intensity are, respectively the metre, second, kilogram, ampere, kelvin (*see* **Absolute Temperature**), mole (*see* **T24**) and candela.

The SI was agreed for general adoption by a number of international organisations such as the General Conference on Weights and Measures (1960). Many countries have made or are making the SI the only legally recognised set of Units. Gt. Britain's decision to "go metric" has brought general use of SI units in its train. *See also* **T58–61**.

Skate. *See* **Ray**.

Skink. The skinks constitute a large family of lizards with large smooth scales, under each of which is a bony plate. The largest species, found in Australia, is about 61 cm long. Some skinks have adopted a burrowing habit and degeneration of the limbs is associated with this. The Common Skink is a small species *c.* 12 cm long, living in deserts of N. Africa.

Skua, falcon-like marine birds related to the gulls found throughout the world. Known as "Robber Birds" because they steal not only the young and eggs of other birds (including penguins) but also their food, which they force them to disgorge in mid-air. The Arctic Skua breeds as far south as Scotland. The Great Skua breeds in both Antarctica and Arctica. Other species are the Pomarine, the Long-tailed, and McCormick's Skua.

Skunk, a North American mammal of the weasel family, with short legs and long bushy tail. All fifteen species are black and white, some being striped and the rest spotted. It secretes and ejects at will a foul-smelling fluid.

Sky. The blue colour of the sky on a summer's day is the result of the scattering of light waves by particles of dust and vapour in the earth's atmosphere. Blue light having almost the smallest wavelength in the visible spectrum (0·00004 cm) is scattered laterally about 10 times as much as the red (0·00007 cm).

Skylark. *See* **Lark**.

Skyscraper. Owing to lack of ground space, increasing cost of land, and growth of modern cities, buildings are being made higher than broader; hence the name. The structures are constructed of steel framework usually clothed in concrete or reinforced concrete.

The first modern skyscraper was the Home Insurance Building in Chicago, designed (1883) by William Le Baron. The New York skyscrapers include the Empire State building (102 stories), Chrysler (77 stories), Rockefeller Center (70 stories), and 60 Wall Tower (67 stories). The World Trade Center building (110 stories) was destroyed in the September 2001 terrorist attack. It is planned to replace it with the Freedom Tower.

Even taller than any New York skyscraper is the Sears Tower, Chicago (447m). The Petronas Towers in Kuala Lumpur (opened in 1996) reach 450 m (1477ft). Even taller will be the Daewoo Centre in Shanghai, China. The Sumida Tower in Tokyo is planned to be the world's tallest tower.

The tallest building in the UK is the 50-storey Canary Wharf tower (243·7m), visible from 20 miles away in Kent. It has now overtaken Tower 42 (formerly the NatWest Bank tower) (183m) and the BT radio tower (177m). It may itself be overtaken by the proposed London Bridge Tower (the 'Shard of Glass') and also the 1,008ft Bishopsgate Tower. The tallest *structure* in Britain is the IBA mast at Belmont, Lincs.

The tallest *residential* building in the world is the Trump World Tower in New York.

The tallest public viewing tower in the UK is the Spinnaker Tower (360ft) in Portsmouth, opened in 2005.

Slate, fine-grained clayey rocks which have undergone metamorphism. They cleave easily, and it is this property of cleavage which makes them a valuable source of roofing material. Important quarries producing mainly green slate are in the Coniston–Ambleside area of the Lake District.

Slavery. In its earlier forms, as in the times of ancient Greece and Rome, in the feudal ages, when vassalage and villeinage existed, and in the serfdom of Russia and other northern nations, slavery was attended by many inhumanities and evils; but perhaps in the slavery system which prevailed in the British colonies for upwards of 200 years and in certain parts of the USA up to 1865, it attained its highest point of inhumanity. In 1833 the Act of Emancipation was passed, emancipating all slaves in British territories, though slavery continued to be tolerated in parts of Africa long after that date.

There are still today (2006) many million people living in servitude in some areas of the world. *See* **Special Topic, L119–120**.

Slide Rule, an instrument which consists of two logarithmic scales sliding alongside each other. By its use multiplication, division, extraction of roots, *etc.*, are speedily carried out.

Sloth, a curious family of mammals, only found in Central and South America. They dwell almost entirely in the trees, proceeding from branch to branch with their bodies hanging downwards, their weight being supported by their large hook-like claws. They eat foliage.

Slow-Worm, a species of lizard found in Britain which lacks legs. Silver with longitudinal brown stripes, it lives almost entirely on slugs.

Smacking. *See* **Corporal Punishment**.

Smelting. The process of heating an ore with a reducing agent to convert ore into metal, and with a flux to convert rocky impurities into a slag that will float on top of the molten metal. Slag and metal can then be tapped separately. An example is iron smelting; the reducing agent is coke, and limestone is added as the flux; the smelting is carried out in a blast furnace.

Smoking. *See* **Tobacco**.

Snake. The snakes constitute the important reptilian order *Ophidia.* Snakes have a scaly, cylindrical, limbless body, lidless eyes, forked tongue, and the upper and lower jaws joined at the chin by an elastic ligament. Most (but not all) snakes have teeth used for seizing prey, and the poisonous varieties are furnished with poison fangs in the upper jaw.
Over 2,500 species of snakes are known, divided into 13 families. There are 3 British species—the grass-snake, smooth-snake, and adder.

Snipe, a wading bird, long-legged, with long, slender, straight bill, brown plumage, and zig-zag flight. The Common Snipe breeds locally throughout Britain; the Great Snipe and small Jack Snipe are occasional visitors. The close season is 1 February to 11 August.

Snow. When water vapour condenses at high levels at a temperature below freezing (sub-limation), a cloud of ice particles is formed. If these frozen droplets are small, they fall slowly and gradually assume a feathery crystalline structure, reaching the earth as snowflakes if the temperature remains below freezing.

Snow Leopard. *See* **Ounce.**

Soda, carbonate of sodium, is now mainly obtained by certain processes of manufacture from common salt. It was formerly obtained from the ashes of plants. Bicarbonate of sodium is the primary product in the Solvay or Ammoniasoda method for commercial manufacture of soda; it is also formed when carbon dioxide is passed into strong soda solution. The bicarbonate is used in medicine and in the preparation of baking powder.

Sodium, a metallic element, no. 11, symbol Na (Latin *Natrium*), first obtained by Sir Humphry Davy in 1807 from caustic soda by means of the electric battery. Its chloride is *common salt;* the deposits of salt (*e.g.,* in Cheshire and at Stassfurt) have come into existence through the drying up of inland seas. Salt occurs in sea-water to the extent of about 3 per cent.; the Dead Sea contains about 22 per cent. The blood of animals is maintained at a level of about 0·6% sodium chloride. That there is sodium in the sun's atmosphere was confirmed in 1859 by Kirchhoff from his spectroscopic observations. Liquid sodium metal has properties which make it suitable as a coolant in some nuclear reactors, a technique of handling this very reactive liquid has had to be developed.

Soil Erosion occurs when the soil is removed from an area at a faster rate than soil formation. This situation usually occurs as a result of man's interference with the natural balance of the environment by the removal of natural vegetation, overgrazing or by poor farming techniques. Soil thus exposed is then removed by the wind (as in the Dust Bowl in the 1930s) or by rain in the form of gully or sheet erosion (as in the Tennessee Valley, USA). Methods introduced to stop soil erosion include contour ploughing, afforestation and dry farming techniques.

Solar Battery, one of the innumerable devices made possible by the development of semi-conducting materials, notably germanium and silicon. This device creates an electric current from light falling on it. The current can be put to use or stored in storage batteries. The energy of the current is derived from the sunlight.
The solar battery is thus an *energy converting* apparatus. Solar batteries have provided power for the instruments in satellites.

Solar Corona. *See* **Corona.**

Solar Eclipse. *See* **Eclipse.**

Solar System, the system dominated by the Sun, containing the nine major planets and their satellites, the asteroids, comets, meteoroids and interplanetary gas and dust. In 1999 scientists discovered the first known solar system beyond our own Sun (Upsilon Andromeda). The first to resemble our own was discovered in 2001. *See also* **Section T.**

Solar Wind, a continuous stream of electrically charged particles blowing outwards from the sun, supplemented from time to time by intense outbursts from regions of the sun's surface. These streams of protons and electrons on encountering the earth's magnetic field distort it and cause magnetic storms (*q.v.*) and aurorae.

Soldering is a means of joining together two pieces of material, usually metals, by melting a third metal (the solder) into the joint. The solder solidifies in the pores of the other metals and holds them together. The materials to be joined are not themselves melted so the technique requires less heat than welding. Solders are alloys; there are many kinds depending on the materials to be joined and the strength of joint desired. *See* **Welding.**

Solstice, an astronomical term indicating the point at which the sun is most distant from the equator.

Solvents. The abuse of solvents such as glue, paints, nail-varnish removers *etc.* has grown recently among teenagers. Solvent abuse can lead to brain damage and dependence.

Soundings at sea, to determine depth at any point, have been taken in all seas, and with considerable accuracy. A deep reading was that of the *Challenger* expedition in 1873, near St. Thomas's in the North Atlantic, when 3,875 fathoms (7,091 m) were sounded. In 1851 H.M.S. *Challenger* recorded the then maximum ocean depth in the Marianas Trench (W. Pacific) by echo-sounding as between 5,882 and 5,950 fathoms (10,764 and 10,800 m). Another deep was located in the S. Pacific in 1952–53 of 5,814 fathoms (10,640 m) in the Tonga Trench, 290 km S. of Tonga Tabu. Since then greater depths have been recorded, in the Marianas Trench and the Mindanao Deep. *See* **Pacific Ocean.**

Southern Cross, popular name of *Crux,* is the smallest constellation in the entire sky and can be observed from latitudes below 30°. Its four brightest stars form a conspicuous Latin cross. The constellation is a vital guide to seafarers.

Soviet Union. *See* **Union of Soviet Socialist Republics.**

Space Flight. The Soviet Union was the first country to launch a man into space and bring him safely back to earth. This epoch-making event took place on 12 April 1961, when Yuri Gagarin, tragically killed in an air crash in 1968, circled the earth in a spaceship weighing about 4,826 kg. It was launched by rocket in an elliptical orbit with greatest height 300 km and least 175 km. The inclination of the orbit to the equator was 65° 4', and the period of revolution was 89 min. 6s.
Since then, the *Vostok* cosmonauts Titov (17 orbits), Nikolayev (64 orbits), Popovich (48 orbits), Bykovsky (81 orbits), Tereshkova, the first woman space traveller (48 orbits), the *Voskhod* cosmonauts Komarov, Feoktistov and Yegorov (16 orbits), Belyaev and Leonov (17 orbits), the American *Mercury* astronauts Glenn (3 orbits), Carpenter (3 orbits), Schirra (6 orbits), Cooper (22 orbits), the *Gemini* astronauts Grissom and Young (3 orbits), McDivitt and White (62 orbits), Cooper and Conrad (120 orbits), Borman and Lovell (206 orbits), Schirra and Stafford (15 orbits), Armstrong and Scott (6·6 orbits), Stafford and Cernan (44 orbits), Young and Collins (43 orbits), Conrad and Gordon (44 orbits), Lovell and Aldrin (60 orbits) were among the first to complete successful missions in space. Leonov was the first to perform an extra-vehicular (EVA) experiment (1965).
Russia was the first to achieve an automatic docking (link-up) between two unmanned spacecraft in orbital flight (October 1967), and of two unmanned spacecraft (January 1969). The American *Apollo* mission was accomplished when Armstrong and Aldrin became the first men to set foot on the moon (July 1969). A joint Soviet-American project culminated in a *Soyuz-Apollo* link-up 225 km up on 17 July 1975. On 11 January 1978 two Soviet spacecraft docked with an orbiting laboratory, the first triple link-up in space. The longest endurance record is held by Valentin Lebedev and Anatoly Berezevoy (211 days in space aboard *Salyut 7* in 1982). The first free walk in space was made by two American astronauts on 7 February 1984 from the space shuttle *Challenger.*
The *Challenger* disaster in 1986 disrupted America's space programme. *Challenger* has been succeeded by *Endeavour,* the most technologically advanced shuttle yet developed. Details emerged in 1996 of the next generation of U.S. spacecraft. These re-usable delta-shaped craft (the X-33) are planned to be in service by 2007.
In 1991, Helen Sharman became the first Briton in space, whilst in 1995, Michael Foale became the first Briton to walk in space. In 1995, the Russian cosmonaut Valeri Poliakov broke the record for the longest time spent in space when he

completed 438 days aboard the Mir space station. The US astronaut Shannon Lucid spent 188 days and 5 hours in space in 1996, a record for a woman. The loss of the US space shuttle *Columbia* in February 2003 was a very serious setback. In October 2003 China became the third nation to send a man into space.

Since the Space Age began in 1957 over 8,000 satellites and spacecraft have been launched from 30 countries.

Space Research. By space research we mean scientific research work which can only be carried to otherwise inaccessible observing locations by rocket propulsion. Such propulsion does not rely on the presence of an atmosphere to provide oxygen so that it is capable in principle of conveying objects to unlimited distances.

Space research is not a single discipline, but can provide data of great importance for many, such as the physics of the earth, the sun, moon and other bodies of the solar system, astronomy, geodesy and the study of gravitation. The prospect of investigating the biological conditions on different planets such as Mars and Venus is also opened, as well as that of experimental biological studies under conditions of zero gravity.

During recent years both the American and Russian space programmes have developed the concept of space stations for providing facilities for continuous manned observatories and laboratories in the future. There have now been successful soft landings on Mars and Venus, and "fly by" visits to Jupiter and Saturn. Voyager 2 (*q.v.*) left Saturn in 1981 visiting the planets Uranus (1986) and Neptune (1989) and continuing beyond.

The launching of the Galileo probe into the atmosphere around Jupiter late in 1995 greatly increased our knowledge of that planet. The Cassini Mission to Saturn was launched in 1997.

Work is now well-advanced on the projected 400-ton Russian-American International Space Station (named Alpha). NASA probes to search for evidence of past life on Mars successfully landed in January 2004.

A host of deep space missions have been recently launched to investigate the nature of our universe including X-ray, UV and Gamma-ray space telescopes (*see* European Space Agency) as well as the planned microwave telescopes being launched by NASA (MAP) and ESA (PLANCK) between 2000 and 2007 respectively.

Space Shuttle. The first reusable manned space vehicle, *Columbia*, was launched on 12 April 1981 from Cape Canaveral, Florida. It orbited the earth 36 times and returned on 14 April landing in California after a flight of 34 h 22 min. *See also* Space Flight.

Spacetime, the single physical entity into which the concepts of space and time are unified such that any event can be specified by four coordinates, three giving the position of space and one the time. The concept was used by Einstein in both the special and general theories of relativity.

Sparrow, name given to finch-like birds found in most parts of the world, of which the House Sparrow *Passer domesticus*, is the most familiar of British birds. Also native to Britain is the rural Tree Sparrow, distinguished from the male House Sparrow by its chestnut crown. Other European species are the Italian, Spanish and Rock Sparrows. Tree sparrows are now in serious decline in Britain.

Specific Gravity, the ratio of the mass of a particular volume of a substance to the mass of an equal volume of water at 4°C. *See* Hydrometer.

Spectral Classification, the different groups into which all stars such as our Sun may be classified. The majority of stars can be divided into seven spectral types O, B, A, F, G, K, M. O type stars are the hottest and M the coolest. The stellar types are subdivided into 10 subclasses denoted by the digits 0 to 9. Our Sun is a G2 star.

Spectrograph. An instrument used to separate and record spectral components of light or other radiation. They are a crucial astronomical tool for analysing the physical processes and composition of stars and other celestial objects. *See* Spectroscopy (*below*).

Spectroscopy. Newton's arrangement with the prism was the first spectroscope; its function was to separate out the colour components of a source of light. Two hundred years elapsed before this apparatus was developed into a precise scientific instrument, capable of measuring both the wavelength and intensity of each colour component. In this form it is called a spectrometer. All atoms and molecules have well defined characteristic spectra which can be used to recognise them. In order to produce emission spectra it is necessary to energise the material under investigation by some means, such as by heating in a flame. The resulting radiation then consists largely of sharp bright lines, characteristic of the material. Absorption spectra are produced by interposing the experimental material between a white light source and the spectrometer. Then dark lines are seen, corresponding to absorptions of energy, in exactly the same places as the bright lines are observed in the emission spectra.

Spectroscopic techniques have now been developed to such an extent that accurate measurements of wavelength and intensity are possible not only in the visible region, but over almost the whole of the electromagnetic spectrum. Two of the most useful types for the chemist are infrared spectroscopy which reveals absorption characteristic of the type of chemical bonds because of their different bond vibration frequencies and nuclear magnetic resonance spectroscopy which operates in the radiofrequency region. It reveals the structure environments of atoms containing particular nuclei.

Not only does spectroscopy play an important rôle in probing the structure of matter, but it can be applied in the field of astronomy. The use of radio wave spectroscopy has led to the discovery of several new types of stellar object.

Spelaeology. *See* Caves.

Sphenodon. *See* Tuatara.

Spiders. *See* **T36**(1) under arthropods.

Spirituals, Afro-American melodies with religious inspiration and which are still spontaneously created, but have also passed into art-music.

Sponge. *See* Porifera, Section T.

Spoonbill, a long-legged, marsh bird, closely related to the ibis and stork, remarkable for its snow-white plumage and broad, flat, spoon-shaped bill. The European species has not bred in England since the beginning of the 17th cent., but is still a regular summer visitor from the Netherlands, where it nests in colonies in reed beds and islets (*e.g.* Texel).

Sputniks, the name of the Russian earth satellites first launched in 1957. *Sputnik I*, launched 4 October 1957, became the first man-made earth satellite. *Sputnik II*, launched a month later carried a dog as passenger. *Sputnik III*, launched in May 1958, was the first space laboratory.

Stalactites are deposits of calcium carbonate formed on the roofs and sides of limestone caves, and in tunnels, under bridges, and other places where the carbonic acid of rain-water percolates through and partly dissolves the limestone, resulting in the growth of icicle-like forms that often assume groupings. The water that drops from these may deposit further calcium carbonate, which accumulates and hardens into sharp mounds or hillocks called stalagmites.

Standard Deviation. In statistics it is often desirable to compare the variability or "spread" of different sets of data. For example, two kinds of light bulb could have the same average life but one kind could be more uniform or consistent than the other. The standard deviation is one of the commonest measures of spread.

It is found as follows. If x is one of the data and x̄ is the mean of all the x's, then x − x̄ is called the deviation. Every deviation is now squared and the average squared deviation calculated. The standard deviation is then the square root of the average squared deviation. The lifetimes of the more uniform kind of light bulb would have a smaller standard deviation than those of the more erratic one.

Star, a luminous ball of hot gas which produces its own light and energy. *See* Section T.

Starboard. The right-hand side of a ship.

Starling (*Sturnus vulgaris*), a well-known European bird now common in many parts of the world. It has handsome iridescent blackish plumage and nests in holes and crevices. Flocks of starlings are often seen wheeling in the air; thousands roost on buildings in the heart of London.

Other European species are the Spotless and Rose-coloured starlings. The latter sometimes wanders to the British Isles.

Statue of Liberty, presented to the USA by Frenchman Ferdinand de Lesseps in 1884.

Steam Engine, a machine whereby steam becomes the active agent of the working of machinery, and of very wide application. The leading types of steam engine are: (a) condensing, or low-pressure engines, where the steam is generated by a boiler; (b) non-condensing, in which the cylinder exhausts its steam into the open air. Engines of the latter type are used where portable engines are required.

Steam-Hammer, invented (1839) by the Scottish engineer James Nasmyth. Consists basically of a vertical steam cylinder atop two legs with piston-rod passing through cylinder base and attached to a tup (hammer) of from 100 kg to 15 tonnes which rests on an anvil. The tup slides in V grooves on inside of legs. Length of stroke and therefore weight of blow can be accurately controlled from a light tap to a massive punch.

It made possible the forging in one piece of multi-throw crankshafts for marine engines, etc. and the mass production of high-class axles and wheels, con rods and buffers, etc. for locomotives and rolling stock.

Stearin is the portion of fatty matters and oils which remains solid at an ordinary temperature, and is a compound of stearic acid with glycerine. It is largely used in the manufacture of candles. With caustic soda stearin forms a soap (sodium stearate), which is present in most commercial soaps which contain sodium palmitate and oleate in addition.

Steel, an alloy of iron and carbon, with varying proportions of other minerals. The famous blades of Damascus and steels of Toledo were made by the cementation and crucible method. The metal produced by the "Bessemer process" (q.v.) is of the highest value for structural purposes, rails, etc.

The technique known as continuous casting bypasses some major steps in the conventional process of steel-making.

Stereophonic Broadcasting. A person having normal hearing is able to determine the direction from which a sound reaches him by virtue of the fact that he has two ears, and, therefore, the sound will reach one of them a fraction of a second before it reaches the other. This difference in arrival time allows the brain to calculate direction.

The aim of stereophonic broadcasting, or sound reproduction therefore, is to restore the listener's ability to locate the position in space of the various sources of sound and to follow movement (just as if he or she were in a concert hall).

To do this it is necessary to use two microphones in the studio—to simulate the two human ears—and to transmit their outputs, through two similar, but separate, chains of equipment, to two radio receivers and their two loudspeakers, which must be placed some distance apart, in the listener's home.

The main work on two-channel stereophony was done by A. D. Blumlein (1903–42), his original patent being dated 1931.

Stereotype, a metal cast taken from movable type which has been set up in the ordinary way. The first to introduce the process in practical form in this country was William Ged of Edinburgh in 1730. An impression of the type matter is first taken by means of a mould of prepared plaster of Paris or moistened sheets of specially prepared paper and when molten stereo metal is poured upon the mould and allowed to cool and harden, the stereo plate is formed, and can be printed from as a solid block for some time.

Steroids. A class of structurally related compounds, based on a system of condensed rings of carbon and hydrogen, which are widely distributed in animals and plants. Included in the steroid family are sterols, found in all animal cells, vitamin D, sex hormones, bile acids and cortisone.

Stickleback, a family of small spiny-finned fish widely distributed in both fresh and salt water. Male constructs roofed nest held together by sticky secretion from glands near kidneys. Several females deposit eggs therein which he guards until after young are hatched.

Stirrup, a loop of metal 7-shaped strap suspended from the sides of the saddle, used for mounting and to support the horseman's foot. Some authorities allege their use as far back as the early Iron Age, and it is generally believed that they were used in battle in A.D. 378, when the Gothic cavalry defeated the legionaries of the Emperor Valens at Adrianople. Stirrups relieved the tension of the rider's knees and so enabled him to be armed from top to toe.

Stoat, a slender, carnivorous mammal with short legs, related to the weasels. The stoat is distinguished from the latter by its longer tail, which has a black tip. The black tip is retained even in the winter when the animal turns white, the fur then being known as "ermine". It is found in northern latitudes, and is abundant in Arctic America.

Stoma (pl. **Stomata**), microscopic pores on the surfaces of leaves through which gaseous exchanges take place and water is lost. It is estimated that a single maize plant bears 200 million stomata, usually closed at night.

Stone of Scone. See under **Scone.**

Stone-Flies, comprise the order of insects called Plecoptera, which includes some 700 species, of which about thirty occur in Britain. The wings are membranous, and two long, thread-like feelers protrude at the tail end. The larvae are aquatic.

Stonehenge, a remarkable collection of Bronze Age monuments on Salisbury Plain. The site which contains ditches, earthwork-banks and megaliths (large stones) has long been recognised for its architectural innovations (the trilithon or free-standing arch and the circle of dressed and lintelled stone blocks) and for its astronomical, numerical and geometrical properties. The building and rebuilding, according to modern archaeological research, lasted from about 2100 to 1600 B.C. It became a World Heritage Site in 1986.

It is still not known who built Stonehenge or what its true purpose was.

Stork, a family of heron-like birds with long bills, freely distributed over Europe, Asia, Africa and S. America. The White Stork is an occasional visitor to England, and, more rarely, the Black Stork; these are the only two European storks.

Stratosphere, a layer of the earth's atmosphere which lies between the tropopause (c. 12 km above the earth) and the stratopause (c. 50 km). The ozone layer lies within the stratosphere and is responsible for the relatively high temperature there. The region is less turbulent than the troposphere, and is usually clear of clouds etc., making it attractive for air transport.

Stratum (pl. **Strata**), a bed or layer of rock.

Strontium. This silver-white metallic element, no. 38, was discovered by Hope and Klaproth in 1793, and isolated by Sir Humphry Davy in 1808. The chief strontium minerals are celestite (sulphate) and strontianite (carbonate). Compounds of strontium give a brilliant colour to fireworks and signal flares. Radioactive isotopes of strontium (strontium-90) are formed as fission products in nuclear explosions and tend to collect in bone on account of the chemical similarity of strontium and calcium (q.v.). This hazard is a cause of great alarm. See **Fall-out.**

Sturgeon, a large fish found in northern seas and rivers with five rows of bony plates along the back and sides and pointed mouth with four barbels. Caviar is prepared from sturgeon ova. The Caspian sturgeon is now a fast-disappearing species (because of over-farming). In January 2006 a ban was announced on the international trade in caviar.

Sublimation, when a solid substance is heated and turns into vapour without passing through the liquid stage and then condenses as a solid on a cold surface, it is said to "sublime" and the process is called "sublimation". Iodine behaves in this way, and sublimation is used as a method of purifying it.

Submarine, the first submarine, the Nautilus, was designed by Robert Fulton and tried out in the river Seine and in the sea off Brest in 1801. The idea was too revolutionary to find acceptance and it was not until electricity for under-water propulsion became available that the submarine underwent extensive development. Britain became interested around 1901 and the Germans developed it and made it into an instrument of warfare. The first voyage under the North Pole was made in 1958 by the American nuclear-powered submarine Nautilus. The Government in March 1982 decided to replace the Polaris force with a new fleet of Trident II submarines at a cost of £7,500m. The first Trident submarine, HMS *Vanguard*, was launched in 1992. The fourth (and final) Trident submarine was launched in September 1998. The last Polaris submarine was withdrawn in 1996.

Submillimetre Astronomy, a new branch of astronomy that deals with the wavelength range 0·3 to 1 millimetre. It is the highest frequency range in which radio astronomy can be carried out and is particularly important because of the large number of molecular emission lines found in this range. There are a number of new telescopes on land and in space that probe this waveband including the 15m James Clerk Maxwell Telescope on Mauna Kea, Hawaii. The Far Infrared Submillimetre Telescope (FIRST) will be launched in 2007.

Sudoku first appeared in its modern form in an American magazine around 25 years ago. It was taken up by a Japanese publisher in the 1980s. The original puzzle format derives from the "Latin Squares" idea of the famous Swiss mathematician Leonard Euler (1707–83).

Suez Canal, connecting the Mediterranean and the Red Sea, was built by the French engineer Ferdinand de Lesseps and opened in 1869. An Egyptian company, *Canal Maritime de Suez*, was formed in 1866 with a capital of 200 million francs. The British Government acquired 176,602 shares out of a total of 400,000 for £4 million. Under the Convention of 1888 all nations were granted freedom of navigation without discrimination in peace or war. The right was recognised by Egypt in the Anglo-Egyptian Agreement of 1954, under which Britain agreed to give up the Suez base. The Suez Canal Company was nationalised by the Egyptian Government without warning in 1956, since when it has been widened and deepened and the average time of transit reduced.

Sugar, to the chemist the term is a generic one covering a group of carbohydrates, including cane sugar (sucrose), glucose, fructose, and maltose. In ordinary parlance sugar means sucrose, which is obtained from the sugar cane, sugar beet or sugar maple. Natural unrefined cane sugar—sometimes called *muscovado*, the Portuguese word for unrefined—is brown.

Sulphur, element no. 16, is a brittle, crystalline solid, symbol S, abounding in the vicinity of volcanoes. It is yellow in colour. It occurs in combination with other elements, as sulphates and sulphides, and allied with oxygen, hydrogen, chlorine, *etc.*, is of great commercial utility. Used in its pure state it constitutes the inflammable element in gunpowder; it is also used for matches and for making sulphuric acid.

Sulphuric Acid, a compound of great commercial importance, used in many manufactures, and composed of sulphur, oxygen and hydrogen. Extremely corrosive, and is present in acid rain (*q.v.*).

Sun, the centre of our solar system, is only one of millions of stars in our galaxy. The earth orbits the sun, which has a diameter of 1·39 million km, at a distance of 149·6 million km. The sun thus has a volume a million times that of the earth. At the surface, the gravitational field is 28 times that at the earth's surface. It rotates on its axis from east to west, though not as a solid, the solar equator turning once in about 25½ days and the poles in about 34 days.

Large spots are observed on the sun which form and disappear at irregular intervals. The area of the disc covered by the spots, however, reaches a maximum roughly every 11 years, when the sun's heat seems rather greater than usual and magnetic storms more frequent (sunspot cycle). Spectrum analysis shows that the sun is composed of many elements found in the earth. Its surface temperature is *c.* 6,000°C.

The earth is in the outer atmosphere of the sun and subject to its winds and storms. The apparently inexhaustible heat of the sun, which has maintained life on the earth for millions of years, is derived from the destruction of matter, involved in the transmutation of hydrogen nuclei into helium nuclei, in which process about four million tonnes of matter are destroyed every second. At this rate of conversion the sun will go on radiating for 30,000 million years. The Soviet space rocket *Lunik 1*, fired on 2 January 1959, became the Sun's first artificial planet. Modern research has shown that the Sun blows

out bubbles—known as coronal mass ejections (CMEs)—every few days at a speed of 90,000 miles an hour. These can wipe out satellite communications and bring down power systems on Earth. The interior of the Sun is also more strange than suspected. Astronomers have found that, while the Sun's surface is resonating, regions below the surface appear to be smooth and flat. Eventually, in 6 billion years time, the Sun will expand into a red giant and burn the Earth to a cinder. Our knowledge of the Sun has been transformed by the Solar Heliospheric Observatory (SOHO) and Ulysses satellites launched in 1995 and 1990 respectively. SOHO has been studying the Sun's internal structure and processes which form and heat the solar corona that give rise to the solar wind. Ulysses has been examining the solar wind especially over the polar regions. *See also* **Section T, Part I.**

Sunday. *See* **Sabbath.**

Superconductor, a metal in a state in which its electrical resistance has entirely vanished so that electric currents can flow indefinitely without generating heat or decreasing in strength.

The superconducting state of metals was first discovered in mercury by Onnes in Leiden in 1911. There are many magnetic and thermal properties associated with superconductivity and the phenomenon as a whole has proved to be of great scientific interest.

Many metals and alloys were found to show the property but only at very low temperatures—below *c.* −260°C. There is a growing number of practical applications, *e.g.*, coils of superconducting wire (kept very cold by liquid helium) can be made to carry enough electric current to produce strong magnetic fields. Such fields are very constant and do not require the large supply of electrical power that ordinary electromagnets need. By the 1990s, scientists seemed on the point of developing a revolutionary material that would superconduct (*i.e.* lose all electrical resistance) at *room temperature*. Such a development would revolutionise computers, power transmission and medicine. *See* **T74.**

Supernova. A large old star that has exploded violently and is observed to brighten dramatically over a short period of time. This explosion blows off most or all of the star's outer regions and is the result of an uncontrolled nuclear reaction in the core. The core of the supernova may go on to form a neutron star or black hole.

Observationally, supernova have been divided into two groups, based on the absence (type I) or presence (type II) of hydrogen. Recent observations have revealed a rich diversity of types and so sub-classifications have occurred. Supernova 1987A was the first naked-eye supernova since 1604 and the remnants of the explosion are still being studied. *See* **Neutron Star, Black Hole.**

Supersonic Speed, a speed greater than the speed of sound (in air at sea-level sound waves travel at about 1223 km/h). When a body travels at a speed which is greater than the speed at which disturbances themselves can travel, a mechanism exists for the generation of waves of enhanced intensity. Thus aircraft travelling at supersonic speeds produce shock waves in the air somewhat analogous to the bow waves of fast-moving ships. These shock waves are regions of intensely disturbed air which produce the sonic boom effect so distressing to people living near supersonic routes. *Supersonic* is not to be confused with *ultrasonic (q.v.).*

Surface Tension. The surfaces of fluids behave in some respects as though they were covered by a stretched elastic membrane. This property is called "surface tension". The action of detergents may be attributed in part to a reduction in the surface tension of water, allowing it to wet the surface of dirty articles.

Swans, large, graceful birds which together with the ducks and geese form the family Anatidae. There are three European species with white plumage; the Mute Swan distinguished by its orange bill with black knob (less prominent in female), a familiar sight on the rivers and ornamental lakes of Great Britain. Two wild swans are winter visitors here, the Whooper and Bewick's Swan. The "pen" (female) and "cob" (male) mate for life and the young swans are called "cygnets".

Swan-upping. The annual census of the Thames

swans which takes place during the third week of July. This ancient ceremony dates back to the 12th cent. when all the Thames swans were declared to be Royal birds owned by the Crown.

Two city guilds—the Vintners' and Dyers' Companies—own about a third of the 200 swans now on the Thames. This privilege was granted to them by King Edward IV in return for money. The swans are now under threat from wild mink.

Sweet Potato. This plant (*Ipomoea batatas*), which is a climbing perennial belonging to the convolvulus family, has thick roots that are rich in starch, and are eaten like potatoes. A native of the W. Indies and Central America, new varieties of sweet potato have been bred which stand cooler climates and can be grown as far north as Cape Cod. The sweet potato of New Zealand is called the Kumara.

Swift, a bird so-called from the extreme speed of its flight, resembling a swallow but related to the humming-bird. It has long, scythe-like wings, sooty-black plumage and greyish-white chin. There are several species inhabiting most parts of the world, particularly the tropics. The British breeding bird is among the latest to return from Africa and the earliest to go. Swifts are the only birds to use saliva for their nests. One oriental species builds its nest entirely from saliva. Swifts are known to fly as high as 10,000ft at night-time.

Sword, hand weapon of metal used in open combat, characterised by a longish blade. During the Middle Ages the most famous blades were those made by the Arabs at Damascus and in Toledo.

Symbiosis. When two organisms live together and both derive mutual benefit from the association, the partnership is known as symbiosis. An example is the symbiosis of an alga and a fungus in lichens; another is the ordinary pea plant and the bacteria which live in the nodules on the pea's roots.

Synapse is the point of association between one nerve cell and another. The nervous impulse travelling along one nerve has to be transmitted to the next across a minute gap. This is the synaptic gap. The mode of transmission is chemical though it was at first thought to be electrical. The impulse arriving at the synapse releases a chemical transmitter which diffuses across the gap and stimulates an impulse in the adjacent nerve cell.

Synod, an assembly of the clergy of a particular church, state, province, or diocese. The Synod of Whitby (664) settled the dispute between the Celtic and the Roman churches over Easter in favour of the Roman system of reckoning.

Synoptic Charts. These are meteorological charts used in forecasting on which weather conditions at a network of stations are recorded.

Synoptists. *See* Section H.

T

Taius. *See* Scree.

Taj Mahal, the white marble mausoleum built at Agra by Shah Jehan in memory of his favourite wife who died 1629. Over 20,000 men were occupied for over 20 years in its erection.

Takahe or Notornis, large New Zealand bird of the rail family which for many years was believed to be extinct. The bird is strictly protected.

Talus. *See* Scree.

Tantalum, a scarce bluish metallic element, no. 73, symbol Ta, discovered by Ekeburg in 1802. Chemically related to vanadium and niobium, it is usually associated with the latter in nature. For several purposes it can be used in place of platinum, and it finds application in the making of surgical instruments. Tantalum is very hard, and resistant to acids (other than hydrofluoric acid); it is used in alloys. Tantalum is a component of every mobile phone.

Taoiseach, the name for the Irish Prime Minister.

Tapirs. The tapirs constitute a family close to the horse family and the rhinoceros in the Ungulate order. They have four toes on the front feet and three on the hind. The snout is drawn out into a short trunk. The largest tapir is the Malayan tapir, which stands 1 m at the shoulder. Four species occur in C. and S. America.

Tar is a dark viscid product obtained from the destructive distillation of wood, coal, peat, *etc.* Wood tar is acid owing to the presence of

acetic acid ("pyroligneous acid"). The highest proportion of coal tar goes into road making. Distillation of coal tar yields many valuable compounds, including benzene, phenol (carbolic acid), naphthalene and creosote; the final residue after distillation is pitch. Based on the chemical manipulation of compounds from coal tar is the preparation of many perfumes, food essences, drugs, antiseptics and plastics.

Tarpeian Rock at Rome received its name from the tradition that Tarpeia, the daughter of the Governor of the Citadel who betrayed the fortress of the Sabines, was crushed to death by their shields and buried beneath the rock. From this height persons guilty of treason were hurled to death.

Tate Britain, named after its founder, Sir Henry Tate, at Millbank, London, was opened in 1897; Sir Henry Tate bore the cost of the building (£80,000) and also gave the nucleus of the present collection. "The Turner Wing", the gift of Sir Joseph Duveen, was added in 1910. The Tate Gallery was renamed Tate Britain in March 2000.

Tate Modern, which is along the Thames at Bankside, houses contemporary international art works. It was opened on 12 May 2000.

Tay Bridge spans the Tay at Dundee, opened for rail traffic on 20 June 1887. A previous bridge, completed in 1877, was blown down on 28 December 1879, as a train was passing over it. A new bridge was opened on 18 August 1966 for road traffic, 2,244 m in length, the longest road bridge in Britain when it was first opened.

Tea was introduced into England about the middle of the 17th cent., when it was a great luxury, and fetched from £6 to £10 a pound. It is an Asiatic plant, native properly to China, Japan and India. Up to *c.* 1885 most of the tea imported into this country came from China. The bulk now comes from India and Sri Lanka. Darjeeling is sometimes called the champagne of teas.

Iced tea was first created in 1908. The teabag was invented by Thomas Sullivan of New York.

Teal, the smallest of the European ducks and next to the Mallard the commonest British species. It is a handsome swift flier, but not as swift as the Garganey or Summer Teal.

Telecommunications. The sending of messages over a distance. The term is generally applied to the sending of messages by telegraph, telephone, radio, television or radar. The first submarine telegraph cable between England and France was laid in 1850 and, following Hertz's investigations into electric waves, Marconi's invention led to Britain being linked with Europe by wireless telegraphy in 1899. The first permanently successful telegraph cable across the Atlantic was laid in 1866. The first telephone service between London and Paris was opened in 1891. The electromagnetic telephone was invented by Alexander Graham Bell, a Scottish-born American, in 1876.

The first submarine telephone cable to span the Atlantic was laid in 1956 connecting Britain with Canada and the United States, and many submarine telephone cables have since been laid.

The spectacular advances in space research depended on the new tools of work provided by parallel developments in telecommunications, *e.g.,* long-range radio and television transmission, electronic computer control. *See* **Satellite Communication, Radar, Radio, Television.**

Telemetry, measurement at remote distances by means of a radio-link from the object (missile or satellite) to the ground. The third Russian sputnik, for instance, carried apparatus for measuring, among other things, the pressure and composition of the atmosphere, and the intensity of different kinds of radiation from the sun. Its radio transmitter, powered by solar-energy batteries, sent out the information in coded form by means of uninterrupted signals at 20·005 megacycles with a duration of 150–300 milli-seconds. Radio telemetry from inside the body is increasingly used in medical and biological research; miniature radio transmitters can be swallowed or implanted in man or animal to detect physiological conditions.

Teleprinter, a telegraph transmitter with a typewriter keyboard, by which characters of a message are transmitted electrically in combinations of 5 units, being recorded similarly by the receiving instrument, which then translates the matter mechanically into printed characters.

Telescope, an optical instrument for viewing objects at a distance, "the astronomer's intelligencer". Lippershey is credited with construction of the first in 1608; Galileo constructed several from 1609 and Newton was the first to construct a reflecting telescope. The ordinary telescope consists of an object-glass and an eye-lens, with two intermediates to bring the object into an erect position. A lens brings it near to us, and the magnifier enlarges it for inspection. A refracting telescope gathers the rays together near the eye-piece and is necessarily limited as to size, but the reflecting telescope collects the rays on a larger mirror, and these are thrown back to the eye-piece.

The world's largest optical reflecting telescopes are the 10m Keck telescope at Mauna Kea in Hawaii (USA), the Very Large Telescope (VLT) located at the European Southern Observatory sited on Cerro Paranal in Chile, consisting of four 8m telescopes and the 8m Gemini telescopes on Mauna Kea and Chile. UK Infrared Telescope (UKIRT) is the world's largest infrared telescope. The mirror is 3·8 metres in diameter. The *Hale* 200 in telescope at Mount Palomar revealed objects never before photographed; it is able to probe space and photograph remote galaxies out to a limiting distance of 2,000 million light years. The *Schmidt* telescope at Mount Palomar has been used to make a huge map of the universe.

Today the largest single radio dish in the world is the non-steerable 300 m instrument at Arecibo in Puerto Rico. Another instrument of radio astronomy is the interferometer which consists of spaced aerials. The biggest of these is in New Mexico. In 1990, the project to put the Hubble Space Telescope into space became reality. The Hubble used gravity to magnify distant galaxies and its findings gave scientists new evidence of the age of the universe. It has peered into space to capture light generated 13 billion years ago. A new type of telescope named COAST (Cambridge Optical Aperture Synthesis Telescope) has been perfected that can take even sharper pictures than the Hubble. The world's biggest radio telescope, the Very Long Baseline Interferometer, (VLBI), a series of linked instruments stretching from the Caribbean to Hawaii, is now operational. This huge array of detectors is capable of seeing detail equivalent to a postage stamp 7,500 miles away. Astronomers will gain unprecedented insights into such mysteries as the birth of galaxies. The upgrading of the e-Merlin radio telescope network (to become the most powerful in the world) should be completed in 2007. *See* **Astronomy, Radio Astronomy, Infra-Red Space Observatory, Space Research** *etc.*

Teletext, the system of displaying printed information and simple diagrams on domestic TV.

Television, or the transmission of images of moving objects by radio or via the cable and satellite systems. To understand the problems of television it is necessary to consider the action of the human eye. Basically the eye consists of a lens which projects an image of the scene before it upon the retina, a light-sensitive screen at the back of the eye. The retina is made up of several millions of tiny light sensitive elements, each quite separate and distinct from its neighbours, and each separately connected to the brain by an individual fibre in the optic nerve. Thus the eye is a very complex organ, and it is able to pick out numbers of tiny details from a scene and convey each detail separately and simultaneously to the brain. It does not send a blend of different points of light and shade in the same way that the ear sends a blend of different sounds; if it did the brain would receive a completely unintelligible blur.

From this it is clear that a TV system which transmitted a mixture of detail would be useless; it must transmit all the details in a scene separately, yet almost simultaneously, and reassemble them at such a speed that the eye cannot observe the building-up process.

A means of doing this was provided by Nipkow in 1884, when he invented his famous scanning disc, and later Weiller invented the mirror drum for the same purpose. Such mechanical devices as these held the field for many years and in 1923 Baird in this country and Jenkins in America were both using them for the experiments which, in 1925, led to the successful transmission of shadows and simple outlines. It was not until 1926, however, that the first practical demonstration of television took place when Baird transmitted by radio moving pictures of living human faces over a short distance. The BBC began televised broadcasts in 1930; the ITA in 1955. The first television exchange across the Atlantic was made in 1962 by way of the *Telstar* satellite.

A major development underway in the 1990s was the advent of digital television. For the past 75 years, television broadcasting had used the same analogue technology. Over the next few years the change to digital systems will dramatically increase the number of channels available for broadcast. In 1996 the British government legislated to allow licensing for six groups of digital channels, or multiplexes. The BBC, for example, has been granted its own multiplex and a financing deal designed to help with the transition to digital formats. It is hoped that one day the new technology will allow not only vastly more audio and visual services, but also a degree of interaction; the use of a television will blur with that of a telephone or a computer. For the time being, both industry and consumers face a bewildering array of unstandardised technologies. In 1998 the BBC began transmissions of BBC1 and BBC2 in digital widescreen format and BSkyB began a 200-channel digital service.

BBC Choice was BBC's first new general television channel for 34 years. In September 2001, the Government approved eight BBC digital services (including BBC4, two TV channels for children and five digital radio stations). The collapse of ITV Digital in 2002 led eventually to the launch of BBC Freeview. The new BBC3 digital service (aimed at 18–35 year olds) was launched in 2003.

TV manufacturers are now competing for the heavy demand for liquid crystal (LCD) televisions. In 2005 the government confirmed that the UK is switching to digital TV by 2012. The Borders starts the switch in 2008.

High definition (HD)TV will be the biggest change in TV picture quality in decades, with up to 4 times more picture detail than current conventional TV signals.

Television Licence. The cost of a current colour TV licence rose from £126·50 to £131·50 from April 2006. Free TV licences for all those aged 75 or over (or households with someone of this age) were introduced from October 2000. If you are 74 (and will turn 75 during your licence year) you qualify for a reduced fee Short Term Licence. The current (2006) black and white fee is £44.

Tellurium, a relatively scarce element, no. 52, symbol Te, discovered in 1782 by von Reichenstein. Chemically it behaves rather like sulphur; its salts are known as tellurides. It occurs chiefly combined with metals in ores of gold, silver, copper and lead. It is a semiconductor, and some of its compounds (also semiconductors) are coming into use in technical devices.

Temperature. *See* **T58.**

Templars were soldier knights organised in the 12th cent. for the purpose of protecting pilgrims in their journeyings to and from Jerusalem, and obtained their name from having had granted to them by Baldwin II a temple for their accommodation. At first they were non-military, and wore neither crests nor helmets, but a long wide mantle and a red cross on the left shoulder. They were established in England about 1180. During the crusades they played a very important role.

In the 12th century they founded numerous religious houses in various parts of Europe and became possessed of considerable wealth. It was this that caused their downfall. Kings and Popes alike grew jealous of their influence, and they were subjected to much persecution, and Pope Clement V abolished the Order in 1312. Edward II in 1308 seized all the property of the English Templars. The English possessions of the Order were transferred to the Hospitallers of St. John, afterwards called the Knights of Malta. *See also* **Hospitallers, Knights, Teutonic Order.**

Temple, of the temples built by the ancient Greeks, Olympia, Athens and Delphi were the most famous. The Temple of Diana at Ephesus was another. The Temple of Solomon at Jerusalem was destroyed and rebuilt several times; Herod's Temple was destroyed by the Romans in A.D. 70.

Temple Bar, an historic gateway (designed by Sir Christopher Wren in 1672) that until 1877 stood at the junction of the Strand and Fleet Street, London, dividing the City from Westminster. It was re-erected at the entrance to Theobald's Park, near Cheshunt, Herts., in 1888.

Terbium, an element, no. 65, symbol Tb, discovered in 1842 by Mosander, belonging to the group of rare-earth metals.

Teredo, the scientific name of the ship-worm, a peculiar bivalve mollusc, which lodges itself when young on the bottoms of wooden ships and bores its way inwards, causing much injury.

Termites, also known as *White Ants,* though they are not related to the true ants and are placed in an entirely different insect order (*Isoptera*). They abound in the tropics and also occur in temperate countries, though only two species are common in Europe. There is no British species. They live in colonies and their nests take the form of mounds of earth and wood, cemented together with saliva, and up to 6 m in height. Five separate castes are recognised, three of them being capable of reproduction, and the other two are sterile.

Tern. This slender, gull-like bird has long pointed wings, a deeply-forked tail, pale grey and white plumage, black cap, and is a very graceful flier. There are several species, some of which are summer migrants to Britain. The Arctic tern winters in the Antarctic, returning to find a nesting place in the spring. In 1997 a common tern set a world record for the longest known flight by a bird, 16,000 miles from Finland to Victoria (Australia).

Terracotta Army, the thousands of life-sized figures in fired clay of soldiers who were to guard China's Emperor Qiu Shihuangdi after his death in the 3rd century B.C. Discovered at Xian in 1974. So far 8,000 figures have been unearthed.

Terrapin, a kind of fresh-water tortoise. They are native to tropical areas of Asia and Central America.

Tertiary Rocks, in geology the rocks formed during the Caenozoic era comprising the Eocene, Oligocene, Miocene and Pliocene periods.

Teutonic Order, of German military knights, was founded in the Holy Land at the end of the 12th cent. for succouring the wounded of the Christian army before Acre. They were dispersed in the 15th cent. but the Order continued to exist until 1809, when Napoleon I confiscated its properties. In 1840 the order was resuscitated in Austria as a semi-religious knighthood. *See also* **Hospitallers, Knights, Templars.**

Textured Vegetable Protein, often referred to as TVP, is an edible protein material given a fibrous texture in the course of its manufacture from agricultural products. Nutritionally the material resembles meat and the extent to which it also resembles meat in succulence, flavour, feel in the mouth, suitability for chewing, *etc.* depends on the sophistication of the manufacturing technique and on the skill of the cook. The common starting material is the soya bean which is rich in protein and oil. The latter is removed, also for use in the food industry, and the residue is further processed to concentrate the protein and to remove unwanted flavours. A paste of suitable consistency is then forced under pressure through small holes and solidified as fibres. Bound together with a suitable binder and appropriately flavoured, these fibres form a lump of protein substance like meat.

Thallium, a blue-grey metallic element, no. 81, symbol Tl, discovered by Crookes in 1861. It is obtained from the flue dust resulting from the burning of pyrites for making sulphuric acid.

Thanksgiving Day, a national holiday in the United States, observed on the fourth Thursday in November: instituted in 1621 to celebrate the occasion of their first successful harvest.

Theodolite. The instrument used by surveyors for measuring angles in the horizontal and vertical planes; also used in meteorology for following balloons to measure windspeed *etc.*

Therm. The charges for gas for lighting and heating (formerly reckoned at per cubic foot) are now based on the calorific, or heat, value of the gas, and the unit used is termed a therm. The therm is 100,000 British thermal units.

Thermionic Emission is the departure of charged particles from matter under the influence of

heat. The higher the temperature the greater the flow of escaping particles. The most common example is the emission of electrons from red-hot electrodes—this is the basic phenomenon made use of in thermionic valves (*see* **Valve**). If the hot electrode (the cathode) is enclosed in an evacuated or gas-filled bulb, the emitted electrons can be collected at another electrode (the anode) and will flow through an external circuit back to the emitter. Thus an electric current has been generated by heat.

Thermodynamics, a term first applied by Joule to designate that branch of physical science which treats of the relations of heat to work. What is called the first law of thermodynamics is thus stated by Clerk Maxwell: "When work is transformed into heat, or heat into work, the quantity of work is mechanically equivalent to the quantity of heat." In one of its many formulations, the second law asserts that "the heat tends to flow from a body of hotter temperature to one that is colder, and will not naturally flow in any other way".

Thermo-electric Devices. If two wires of different materials are formed into a loop and if the two joins are kept at different temperatures a current flows in the loop. This was discovered by Seebeck in 1822, and the device is called a thermocouple. The electric current could in principle be made to drive some useful machine, and the energy comes from the heat that is absorbed by the thermocouple –if one part of the thermocouple is not hotter than the others it will not work. It has long been realised that this is a device that converts heat directly into electricity without raising steam and driving dynamos as in a power-station. However, until recently nobody has used thermocouples for much besides temperature measurement, for which they are exceedingly useful. The new development is the manufacture of semiconductors (*q.v.*); for the thermo-electric effects of these new materials are much greater than those of metals. A material much studied in this connection is a compound of bismuth and tellurium, bismuth telluride. It now seems practicable to generate useful electricity from suitably designed thermocouples. For example, Russia produces a thermo-electric device which uses the heat from the chimney of a domestic oil-lamp to produce enough electricity to work a radio. Presumably this is very useful in remote parts with no electricity supply. But the possibilities do not stop there. Indeed, an eminent Russian authority has stated that thermocouples could produce electricity direct from the warmth of sunlight on a scale and at a cost comparable with conventional fuel-burning power-stations. Even if solar energy cannot be so used, it might be possible to use the heat of nuclear reactors, but this means that the thermo-electric devices would have to withstand very heavy radioactivity and still work.

Thermometer, an instrument by which the temperature of bodies is ascertained. The most familiar kind of thermometer consists of a glass tube with a very small bore, containing, in general, mercury or alcohol. This expands or contracts with variation in the temperature, and the length of the thread of mercury or alcohol gives the temperature reading on a scale graduated in degrees. *See also* **T58–61.**

Thermonuclear Reactions. *See* **Nuclear Fusion.**

Thirty-nine Articles. *See* **Articles.**

Thistle, Order of. *See* **Knighthood.**

Thorium, a scarce, dark grey, metal element, no. 90, symbol Th, discovered by Berzelius in 1828. All substances containing thorium are radioactive. Chief source of thorium is monazite sand, big deposits of which occur in Travancore (India), Brazil and the USA. Important as a potential source of atomic energy since the discovery that it can be transmuted into U^{233}, which is capable of fission like U^{235}.

Thrush, a large family of song-birds of the *Passeriform* order, distributed all over the world. The British species include the robin, redstart, nightingale, song-thrush (or mavis), blackbird, mistle-thrush, ring-ouzel of the mountains and large numbers of migrant fieldfares and redwings from northern Europe are winter visitors. The song-thrush is one of Britain's most familiar but rapidly declining birds.

Thunder, the sound heard after the occurrence of a lightning flash. It is due to vibrations of the air along the path of the flash, which are set up by the sudden heating (and expansion) followed by the rapid cooling (and contraction) to which the air is subjected. It is unusual for thunder to be heard more than 16 km away, the distance being estimated roughly by allowing 1 km for every 3 seconds which elapse between seeing the flash and hearing the thunder. Continued rolling of thunder results from the zig-zag nature of the flash and the multiple strokes of which it is composed, variations in the energy developed along the path, and echo effects. Thunderstorms are caused by powerful rising currents of air within towering cumulonimbus clouds.

Thursday, the 5th day of the week, named after Thor, the Scandinavian deity. To the Romans Thursday was *dies Jovis,* or Jupiter's day.

Tidal Power. The principle of exploiting the energy of the tides is similar to hydro-power since it involves the harnessing of falling water. A barrage across a bay or estuary is filled during flow tide and closed during ebb tide creating a difference in level. When the water is allowed to fall towards the lower side of the barrage it operates a turbine which drives a generator. More sophisticated schemes would incorporate pumped storage facilities. An essential requirement is a large tidal range in order to get a sufficient head of water. Britain's first commercial wave-power station is planned for Islay in Scotland. *See also* **Hydroelectric Schemes.**

Tides, the periodical rise and fall of the waters of the ocean and its arms, are due to the gravitational effect of the moon and sun. Newton was the first to give a general explanation of the phenomenon of the tides. He supposed the ocean to cover the whole earth and to assume at each instant a figure of equilibrium, under the combined gravitational influence of earth, sun and moon, thus making and controlling the tides. At most places there are two tides a day, and the times of high- and low-water vary according to the positions of the sun and moon relative to the earth.

When earth, moon and sun are in line (at full moon and new moon) the gravitational pull is greatest and we get "spring" tides. When sun and moon are at right angles (first and third quarters of the moon's phases) we get the smaller "neap" tides.

Tiger, a powerful carnivorous animal of the cat family, which occurs in India and certain other parts of Asia. Its skin is of a tawny yellow, relieved by black stripings of great beauty of formation. Some tigers attain a length of from 3 to 3·6 m. There are currently only an estimated 10,000 tigers in the wild, whereas in 1900 there were 40,000 tigers in India alone. The tiger is proving remarkably resilient but fears that it will face extinction still remain, particularly in India. The Siberian tiger is the world's largest cat. The tiger was listed as an endangered species in 1972.

Time. The measurement of time has become of increasing importance to man with the advance of civilisation. It was at first almost inevitably based on the succession of night and day, the waxing and the waning of the moon, and on the changing seasons of the year, and the astronomical observation of these three periodic effects has served as the basis of time measurement until recent years. The precision of the observations has continually increased, and clocks have been developed for dividing the day into smaller units. The clocks were adjusted so as to keep in step with the rotation of the earth on its axis, but now an atomic standard of time has been developed, and clocks are adjusted so as to keep in step with the natural period of an atomic vibration. *See* **Clock, Greenwich Mean Time, British Standard Time.**

Tin is a white, metal element, no. 50, symbol Sn (Latin *Stannum*), whose commonest ore is cassiterite (tin oxide), which occurs in Malaya, Indonesia, Bolivia, Congo, Nigeria and Cornwall. It protects iron from rusting, and the tin coating on tinplate is applied by dipping the thin steel sheet in molten tin or by electrolysis. Tin alloys of importance include solder, bronze, pewter and Britannia metal. South Crofty, the last tin mine in Europe, was closed in March 1998.

Tincal. *See* **Borax.**

Tit *or* **Titmouse,** a small insectivorous bird of the woodlands and forests, bright of plumage and very active and agile, often seen hanging upside down searching for food. There are over fifty species, eight of which occur in Britain: the Great and Blue Tits, familiar in gardens and countryside, the Cole Tit, Marsh Tit, Willow Tit, Bearded Tit, Long-tailed or "Bottle" Tit and the Scottish Crested Tit. The Willow Tit is in serious decline in Britain.

Titan, the largest moon of Saturn (*q.v.*). Currently receiving much attention from planetary scientists. It is the only moon in the solar system with a thick atmosphere. The Cassini Mission beamed back the first images of Titan in October 2004. Its Huygens probe confirmed that Titan contains water and vital organic chemicals.

Titanium, a scarce metallic element, no. 22, symbol Ti, difficult to extract from ores, found in association with oxygen in rutile, anatase and brookite, as well as with certain magnetic iron ores. It combines with nitrogen at a high temperature. Discovered by the Rev. William Gregor in 1791.

Titanium alloys, being very resistant to stress and corrosion, and combining strength with lightness, find wide application not only in marine and chemical engineering but in the building of aircraft, rockets, and the nuclearenergy field. Titanium dioxide is now used in making paints.

Tithes, an ecclesiastical tax consisting of a tenth part of the annual produce known to the ancient Jews, and first imposed by Christian authorities in the 4th cent., although not compulsory in England before the 9th cent. After the Tithes' Commutation Act of 1836, tithes were gradually converted into rent charges.

Titmouse. *See* **Tit.**

TNT (**Trinitrotoluene**). A high explosive formed by the action of a mixture of nitric and sulphuric acids on toluene. Not highly sensitive to shock, it can be used in shells without danger, and is exploded by a time, or detonator, fuse. Apart from wartime applications, it is used in blasting in quarries and mines.

Toad, an amphibian, differing from the frog in having a dry, warty skin, a heavier, squat build and shorter limbs. It has a similar metamorphosis, is largely nocturnal, and will wander far from water after the breeding season. Two toads occur in Britain, the Common Toad and the Natterjack. The latter have a narrow light stripe running down the middle of the back.

Tobacco is made from the leaves of various narcotic plants of the *Nicotiana* family, which contain a volatile oil and an alkaloid called nicotine. Tobacco is grown in countries with a warm climate. The leaves undergo various processes of preparation. The leaves are first dried, then cut into small pieces, moistened and compressed, and in this form it is known as cut or "shag" tobacco; when moistened with syrup or treacle and pressed into cakes, it is Cavendish; when twisted into string form, it is "twist" or "pig-tail." For cigars the midribs of the dry leaves are removed, and what is left is moistened and rolled into cylindrical shape. For snuff, the tobacco leaves are moistened and allowed to ferment, then dried, powdered and scented. The world's largest producers of tobacco are China, the USA and India.

In 1997, the EU agreed to ban tobacco advertising, the ban to be phased in over an 8-year period. The advertising of tobacco on billboards and in newspapers became illegal in 2003.

Smoking in public places was outlawed in Scotland from March 2006 (it is also banned in Ireland, New Zealand and in Norway). In 2004 the Health Secretary, John Reid announced plans for an almost complete ban on smoking in public places from 2008, but this proposal has been diluted. A proposal to raise the minimum smoking age to 18 has been mooted.

In 2000, 5,500 *billion* cigarettes were consumed world-wide, compared with 600 billion in 1930.

Tolls. Payments for privileges of passage were first exacted in respect of ships passing up rivers, tolls being demanded on the Elbe in 1109. Tolls for land passage are said to have originated in England in 1269, toll-bars being erected at certain distances on the high-roads in the 17th cent., where toll had to be paid for all vehicles passing to and fro. After about 1825 they began to disappear, but still linger on some country roads and bridges. Tolls on London river bridges ceased in 1878-79. Today, tolls are a feature of motorways and major bridges.

Tonic Sol-Fa, a system of musical notation in which monosyllables are substituted for notes. Thus the major diatonic scale is represented by Doh, Ray, Me, Fah, Soh, La, Te, Doh.

The system was invented by Miss Glover of Norwich in about 1840 and has proved of great assistance in the teaching of music in schools.

Tonsure, the shaven part of the head of a Roman Catholic ecclesiastic, dates from 5th or 6th cent.

Topaz, a transparent mineral gem, being a silicate and fluoride of aluminium and generally found in granite rocks. Its colour is yellow, but it also occurs in pink and blue shades. The best kinds come from Brazil.

Topiary, the art of clipping and trimming trees, shrubs, etc., into ornamental shapes. In Britain this art goes back before Elizabethan times when gardens were formal and the shapes simple and symmetrical. By the end of Queen Anne's reign topiary had become much more elaborate, and all kinds of fanciful shapes were produced. Pliny in his *Letters* tells how box hedges were clipped even in Roman times.

Topology is a branch of mathematics which studies geometrical objects from the point of view of their general shape rather than their precise measurements. For example, from the point of view of topology a ring doughnut and a picture frame have the same shape because they both have one single hole through them.

Topology is used to deduce geometrical facts about an irregularly shaped object such as the Earth from the geometry of a regular object such as a perfect sphere of the same general shape.

Tornado, a violent whirlwind, characterised by a black, funnel-shaped cloud hanging from heavy cumulonimbus and travelling at speeds up to 60 km/h. Tornadoes vary in diameter from less than a metre to a kilometre and occur frequently in the Mid-West region of the USA (known as tornado alley), where it has been estimated that the circling winds of the vortex may reach a velocity of 600 km/h. Tornadoes are measured on a scale of 1 to 5. In West Africa the term is applied to thundery squalls.

Tortoises and Turtles, are cold-blooded reptiles, four-footed and encased in a strong shell protection, the shells of some species being of beautifully horny substance and design, once in much demand for combs, spectacle frames and ornamental work. It is the custom to designate the land species as tortoises and the aquatic kinds as turtles. The green turtle, so called because its fat has a green tinge, is in great demand for soup. Together the tortoises and turtles make up the reptilian order called *Chelonia,* the biggest representatives of which are the giant land tortoises of the Galapagos Islands, reaching a weight of 225 kg and living a century. Some of these giant tortoises are said to have lived 200 or 300 years.

The market for food and medicines is driving tortoises and turtles towards extinction. Rising temperatures now threaten male green turtles.

Toucan, a South and Central American family of brilliantly coloured birds, noted for their huge bills. Toucans live on fruit, are of arboreal habits, and nest in holes. There are c. 37 species.

Touchstone, a kind of jasper called by the ancients "Lydian stone", of economic value in testing the quality of metal alloys, especially gold alloys. The testing process is very simple. The alloy is drawn across the broken surface of the Touchstone, and from the nature of the mark or streak it makes the quality of the alloy can be ascertained.

Tourmaline, a mineral occurring in different colours in prismatic crystals. It is a well-known example of a pyro-electric crystal, *i.e.,* one that has a permanent electric polarisation. A double silicate of aluminium and boron, it occurs in S.W. England, S. America and Asia.

Tournaments were equestrian contests between military knights and others armed with lances. The Normans introduced them to England.

Tower of London was built as a fortress by William the Conqueror. It was a royal palace in the Middle Ages and later used as a garrison and prison. Many distinguished prisoners were executed there, or on the neighbouring Tower Hill, including Anne Boleyn, Catherine Howard,

Lady Jane Grey, the 2nd Earl of Essex, and the Duke of Monmouth. The Chapel Royal of St. Peter ad Vincula in the Tower was built in 1105 and took its present shape in the reign of Henry VII.

The Crown Jewels are kept at the Tower, and in the Armoury a fine collection of armour is preserved. The staff (in Tudor dress) are called Yeomen Warders of the Tower.

Trademark, a mark used in relation to goods for the purpose of indicating a connection in the course of trade between the goods and some person having the right, either as a proprietor or registered user, to use the mark. Trade marks can be registered, the registration holding good for 7 years and being renewable thereafter indefinitely for periods of 14 years. Infringement of a registered trademark renders the infringer liable to damages. In 1994, a new law was brought in to harmonise British trademark law with the EU. Owners of registered trademarks will now also be able to have their sign protected in international law.

Trade Winds form part of the circulation of air round the great permanent anticyclones of the tropics and blow inwards from north-east (Northern Hemisphere) and south-east (Southern Hemisphere) towards the equatorial region of low pressure. Atlantic trades are more regular than those of the Pacific. The belts may extend over 2,400 km of latitude and, together with the Doldrums, move north and south in sympathy with the seasonal changes in the sun's declination, the average annual range being about 5 degrees of latitude.

Trafalgar Square. The site has often been referred to as the finest in Europe. It was conceived originally as a square by John Nash (1752-1835) when the project was considered of linking Whitehall with Bloomsbury and the British Museum. It was to be named after the new monarch as King William the Fourth's Square but on the suggestion of George Ledwell Taylor (a property owner near the site) alteration to the more popular name Trafalgar Square was agreed to by the King. On the north side the National Gallery was planned by Nash and erected by William Wilkins on the place of the Royal Mews—a work of William Kent a century before. The layout was the idea of Charles Barry but he did not approve the erection of the Nelson column (which see). His idea was for the square to have a grand flight of steps from the north side with sculptural figures of Wellington and Nelson but the Commons decided otherwise and the column as designed by William Railton was begun in 1840. Now the newly-reconstructed Trafalgar Square much more closely resembles the original grand Piazza plan.

The two fountains by Barry were supplanted in 1948 by ones designed (1938) by Sir Edwin Lutyens. Executed in Portland stone they are flanked by some bronze sculptures. In the same year memorial busts of Lords Jellicoe and Beatty were placed by the north wall.

Transept. The cross aisles of a church, projecting at right angles from the nave or choir.

Transistor. An electronic device consisting of a small piece of semiconducting solid (usually germanium or silicon) to which contact is made at appropriate places by three wires. The three parts resemble in function (not construction or behaviour) the cathode, anode, and grid of a thermionic valve, and transistors can perform many of the operations that valves had originally been used for in radio, television, etc. They possess several advantages over valves since there is no need for evacuated glass bulbs nor for a heated emitter to give off electrons. This lead to much greater compactness and economy as well as to a much longer life. Just as the valve was superseded by the transistor, the transistor has now been replaced with the integrated circuit. The transistor was invented by the Americans Bardeen, Brattain and Shockley in 1948.

Treasure-Trove, a legal term applying to treasure (coin, bullion, gold or silver articles) found hidden in the earth or other place, for which no owner can be discovered. The treasure legally belongs to the Crown, but it is the practice to return to the finder all articles not required for national museums and to reward him with the full market value of such as may be retained. It is the duty of the finder to report to the Coroner for the district in which the find is made. The old treasure-trove inquest with a jury has now been abolished. People are obliged to report items more than 300 years old under the 1996 Treasure Act.

Tree Frog, occurs most commonly in America and Australasia. The common European tree frog is a brilliant green animal, the adhesive discs at the tips of its fingers and toes enabling it to cling to trees, *etc.*, with ease.

Tree Rings as Natural Calendar. The approximate relationship between radiocarbon dating (q.v.) and true calendar age for the past 7,000 years has been established from measurements on tree-rings. Because one tree-ring is formed annually and its thickness is characteristic of the climatic conditions during its growth, it is possible, by comparing distinctive groups of rings, to date a series of trees. By using the long-lived Bristle Cone pines, tree-rings dating back to 500 B.C. have been obtained. It has been found that the radiocarbon age around, say, 3000 B.C. is too young by *c.* 600 years and because of short-term fluctuations near, say, 2000 B.C., a particular radiocarbon age can correspond to more than one true calendar age. These corrections are far less than those proved necessary after the publication of the first radiocarbon dates. Tree-rings (based on the measurement of deuterium in wood) can also show the pattern of temperature fluctuations and thus make it possible to trace climatic changes before written records began. The term for tree-ring dating is dendrochronology.

Tree Shrew, an arboreal insectivorous mammal of Asia belonging to the family *Tupaiidae.* Tree shrews are related to the shrews, though in appearance they resemble squirrels except for their sharply pointed snout. They occur in Borneo, Thailand, China and Malaya.

Trees. *See under* Ash, Elm, Oak *etc.*

Trent, Council of, the longest and one of the most important in the history of the Roman Catholic Church, was convened to combat the doctrines of Martin Luther. It first sat in 1545, the last sitting being in 1563. At this Council the general policy, principles and dogmas of the Roman Catholic Church were settled.

Triassic *or* **Trias,** the earliest geological period in the Mesozoic era, which began some 225 million years ago. Triassic formations 7,600 m thick occur in the Alps. Modern insects were appearing, and also small reptile-like mammals. Other important Triassic animals were: dinosaurs, ichthyosaurs (marine reptiles), and pterosaurs (flying reptiles). *See* **Section T.**

Tribunes, name assigned to officers of different descriptions in ancient Rome. The original tribunes were the commanders of contingents of cavalry and infantry. The most important tribunes were the tribunes of the plebs, first elected in 494 B.C. as the outcome of the struggle between the patrician and the plebeian orders. They held the power of veto and their persons were sacred.

Trichoptera. This is the insect order comprising the Caddis-flies. These are moth-like insects having hairs on the wings. They are usually found fluttering weakly near water. The larvae are aquatic and are remarkable for the cases (caddis cases) which they build out of sticks, small stones, sand grains, and shells.

Tricolour, the flag of the French Republic since 1789, consisting of three nearly equal vertical bands of blue, white and red (ratio 90 : 99 : 111).

Trilobites, extinct marine arthropods, most abundant in the Cambrian and Ordovician systems. Their appearance may be roughly described as resembling that of a woodlouse, and like that animal the trilobites were capable of rolling their bodies up into a ball.

Trinity. *See* **Section J.**

Trinity House, on Tower Hill, London, was incorporated in 1514 as an association for piloting ships, and has ever since been entrusted with various matters connected with the regulation of British navigation. Since 1854 the lighthouses of the country have been under its supervision. The acting Elder Brethren act as Nautical Assessors in Marine cases which are tried by the High Court of Justice. Under the 1987 Pilotage Act, Trinity House lost its responsibility as the principal pilotage authority to local harbour authorities.

Trireme, an ancient vessel with three rows of oars of great effectuality in early naval warfare.

Mentioned by Thucydides. It was a long, narrow vessel propelled by 170 rowers. The Romans copied it from the Greeks.

Tritium, a radioactive isotope of hydrogen which has three times the weight of the ordinary hydrogen atom. It is produced by bombarding an isotope of lithium with neutrons and has a half-life of 12½ years, decaying with the emission of β-particles (electrons).

Triumvirate a term used to denote a coalition of three persons in the exercise of supreme authority. The first Roman triumvirate was that of Pompey, Julius Caesar, and Crassus, 60 B.C.: the second was that of Mark Antony, Octavus and Lepidus, 43 B.C.

Tropic-Bird, a long-tailed sea bird, of which there are 3 species (the Red-billed, the White-tailed, and the Red-tailed), frequenting the tropical regions of the Atlantic, Pacific and Indian oceans. They are often called Bo'sun Birds.

Troposphere. The atmospheric layer which extends from the earth's surface to the stratosphere. As a general rule temperature falls as altitude increases. *See* **Atmosphere.**

Troubadours, lyric poets who flourished from the 12th to the end of the 13th cent., chiefly in Provence and the north of Italy. They were often knightly amateurs, and cultivated a lyrical poetry intricate in metre and rhyme and usually of a romantic amatory strain, written in the *langue d'oc. See also* **Jongleurs.**

Trouvère *or* **Trouveur,** mediaeval poet of northern France, whose compositions were of a more elaborate character—epics, romances, fables, and chansons de geste—than those of the troubadour of the south. The poetry was written in the *langue d'oïl.* Flourished *c.* 12th–13th cent.

Truffles are subterranean edible fungi much esteemed for seasoning purposes. There are many species, and they are found in considerable quantities in France and Italy, less commonly in Britain. They are often met with under beech or oak trees, and prefer calcareous soils, but there are no positive indications on the surface to show where they are, and they are not to be cultivated. Hogs, and sometimes dogs, are used to scent them out, the former, by reason of their rooting propensities, being the most successful in the work.

Tsetse, an African dipterous fly belonging to the same family as the house-fly. It is a serious economic pest as it transmits the protozoon causing African sleeping sickness when it pierces human skin in order to suck blood.

Tsunami, a seismic sea wave originating from any one of several submarine geological phenomena such as volcanic explosions, landslides or earth movements. Tsunamis are extremely long waves which travel in the open ocean at speeds up to 640 km/h. In deep water their height is only barely perceptible, but on reaching shallow coastal water they may attain heights of up to 30 m and can cause devastation to low-lying areas (as in 2004 around the Indian Ocean). The Pacific Ocean, whose rim is a seismically active area, is particularly susceptible to tsunamis. Tsunamis are often incorrectly referred to as tidal waves. Scientists are planning to deploy instruments on the ocean floor to predict and track tsunamis.
The devastation and loss of life caused by the 26 December 2004 Indian Ocean tsunami was without equal in modern times (over 225,000 died and thousands are still missing).

Tuatara or **Sphenodon,** a reptile of great antiquity, the sole surviving species of the *Rhynchocephalia,* found in New Zealand. It has a rudimentary third eye on the top of the head; this is called the pineal eye and corresponds to tissue which in mammals forms the pineal gland.

Tube Foot, the characteristic organ of locomotion of starfishes and kindred animals. They are arranged in pairs along the underside of the arms, and their sucker-like ends can grip a surface very tightly. The action of the suckers depends on hydraulic pressure.

Tuesday, the third day of the week, named from the Saxon deity Tuisto, Tiw or Tuesco. To the Romans it was the day of Mars.

Tuileries, a French royal and imperial palace dating from 1564. It was attacked by insurgents in 1792, 1830 and 1848, and was burned down during the Commune of Paris in 1871.

Tumulus, a mound of earth raised over the bodies

of the dead. The mound of Marathon, enclosing the bodies of the Athenians who were killed in the famous battle with the Persians, is a celebrated tumulus. Such mounds were commonly raised over the tombs of the distinguished dead in ancient times, and sometimes enclosed heavy structures of masonry. The Roman "barrows" were tumuli. Evidence of such mounds are frequent in prehistoric remains.

Tuna or **Tunny,** a large marine fish belonging to the mackerel family, frequenting the warm waters of the Atlantic, Pacific and Mediterranean. Tuna fisheries are a major industry. The Japanese appetite for raw tuna (served as *sushi*) is leading to the extinction of the southern bluefin tuna.

Tundra, the vast treeless plains lying in northern N. America and northern Russia where long severe winters and permanently frozen subsoils (permafrost) have resulted in specially adapted plant communities. The summer thaw and impervious permafrost cause waterlogging of lowland areas and marsh plants occur on these sites. In summer the ground cover of lichens and mosses with some flowering plants is distinctive. Stunted willows and birches occur in certain sites.

Tungsten, a hard, brittle metallic element, no. 74, symbol W (it was formerly called wolfram), silver to grey in colour. Its chief ores are wolframite (iron and manganese tungstate) and scheelite (calcium tungstate). Tungsten is alloyed in steel for the manufacture of cutting tools; also in the non-ferrous alloy stellite. Electric lamp filaments are made from tungsten. Tungsten carbide is one of the hardest substances known and is used for tipping tools.

Tunicates. See **Sea Squirts.**

Turbines propelled by steam provide power for the propulsion of many ships, and on land steam turbines are a principal source of power, being used in large central electricity stations, for instance, to convert heat energy into electrical energy. The first gas-turbine ship had its trials in 1947.

Turbot, a large flat fish, highly valued as food. It often attains from 13 to 18 kg in weight. Its flesh is white and firm. It is confined to European waters, and is caught by line or trawl.

Turkey, a fowl of American origin, brought to Europe from America soon after the discovery of that country. It was a domesticated bird in England in the first half of the 16th cent.

Turmeric, spice used to flavour curries which is now believed to have anti-cancer properties.

Turpentine, an oily substance obtained from coniferous trees, mostly pines and firs. It is widely used especially in making paints and varnishes, and also has medicinal properties.

Turquoise, formerly called Turkey-Stone, is a blue or greenish-blue precious stone, the earliest and best specimens of which came from Persia. It is composed of a phosphate of aluminium, with small proportions of copper and iron. India, Tibet, and Silesia yield turquoises, and a variety is found in New Mexico and Nevada. The first specimens were imported through Turkey. Turquoise has been mined since at least 6,000 B.C.

Turtle. See under **Tortoises.**

Turtle Dove, a summer visitor from Africa to southern England. It is a small, slender bird with reddish-brown upper parts, pinkish throat, black tail with white edges, and a repeated purring note.

Tweed. A rough-surfaced fabric of the twilled type, usually all-wool, though cheaper kinds may include cotton. Of a soft, open, flexible texture, it may have a check, twill or herring-bone pattern. Harris, Lewis, Bannockburn and Donegal tweeds are well known.

Twelfth Night is the eve of the feast of the Epiphany. It was once the most popular festival next to Christmas.

Twilight. There are several different classifications of twilight, each of which is based on the angular distance of the Sun below the observer's horizon. Civil twilight begins or ends when the centre of the solar disc is 6° below the horizon, nautical twilight beginning and ending when the centre is 12° below. The brightest stars are visible during nautical twilight. The third is astronomical twilight, at which time stars of 6th magnitude are visible provided the sky is clear. Astronomical twilight starts and finishes when the centre of the

Sun is 18° below the horizon.

Tyburn, a former small tributary of the Thames, which gave its name to the district where now stands the Marble Arch, Hyde Park. Here public executions formerly took place.

Tycoon, the title by which the commander-in-chief of the Japanese army (virtually the ruler of Japan) was formerly described by foreigners. (In Japanese *taikun* means great lord or prince.) The term is now applied, usually in a derogatory sense, to an influential business magnate.

Tynwald, the title given to the Parliament of the Isle of Man, which includes the Governor and Council (the Upper House), and the House of Keys, the representative assembly. This practically constitutes Home Rule, the Acts passed by the Tynwald simply requiring the assent of the Sovereign.

U

Ultramarine, a sky-blue pigment obtained from *Lapis lazuli,* a stone found in Tibet, Iran, Siberia and some other countries. A cheaper ultramarine is now produced by grinding and heating a mixture of clay, sulphur, carbonate of soda and resin.

Ultrasonics, sound waves of frequency so high as to be inaudible to humans, i.e., above 15,000 Hz (Hz is SI unit for cycle per sec.). Ultrasonic waves are commonly produced by causing a solid object to vibrate with a suitable high frequency and to impart its vibrations to the air or other fluid. The object may be a quartz or other crystal in which vibrations are excited electrically, or a nickel component which is magnetically energised. There are numerous technical applications, e.g. submarine echo soundings, flaw detection in castings, drilling glass and ceramics, emulsification. Ultrasonic waves are an important tool of research in physics. Bats produce very loud sounds when they are flying, but at ultrasonic frequencies (20,000 to 150,000 Hz), so that we cannot ourselves hear them.

Ultra-Violet Rays. These are invisible electromagnetic rays whose wavelengths are less than 3900 Å. (Angstrom = one hundred-millionth of a centimetre.) The sun's radiation is rich in ultra-violet light, but much of it never reaches the earth, being absorbed by molecules of atmospheric gases (in particular, ozone) as well as by soot and smoke particles. One beneficial effect of ultra-violet light on human beings is that it brings about synthesis of vitamin D from certain fatty substances (called sterols) in the skin. The wavelengths which effect this vitamin synthesis also cause sun tan and sun burn. Ultra-violet lamps (which are mercury-vapour discharge lamps) are also used for sterilising the air inside buildings, their rays being lethal to bacteria. Many substances fluoresce under ultra-violet light; for instance, zinc silicate glows green, while cadmium borate throws out red light. This phenomenon is applied practically in fluorescent lamps, the light of requisite hue being secured by judicious mixture of the fluorescent materials which coat the lamp.

Umbra, the full shadow of the earth or moon during an eclipse. The term is also used to describe the darker, cooler central region of a sunspot.

Uncia. The Romans took over the Egyptian cubit and divided it into 16 digits as well as into 12 parts called *unciae,* the *uncia* being the origin of the inch.

Unicorn, a fabulous single-horned animal. In heraldry its form is horse-like, with the tail of a lion and pointed single horn growing out of the forehead. In the Middle Ages the unicorn was a symbol of virginity.

Union Jack, the common name for the official 'Union Flag' of the United Kingdom since 1801 (the Union with Ireland). Jack derives from the nautical term for flag.

Union of Great Britain and Ireland was proposed in the Irish Parliament in January 1799 after the 1798 Rebellion and came into force on 1 January 1801. The troubled history of Ireland, associated with the question of self-government, nationalism, land and religion, culminated in the Easter revolution of 1916. A treaty giving the 26 southern counties independence in 1921, as the Irish Free State, was followed by a period of internal dissension. In 1937 a new constitution was enacted in Ireland in which no reference was made to the Crown. This, however, left in force the External Relations Act of 1936 and with its repeal in 1948, Ireland separated itself from the British Crown and thus severed the last constitutional link with the Commonwealth, and became an independent Republic.

Union of Soviet Socialist Republics (USSR). The Union of Soviet Socialist Republics was formally constituted on 6 July 1923, covering most of the old Russian Empire overthrown in the Communist revolution of 1917, minus the territories which formed Finland, Poland, the Baltic Republics and East Prussia. With the fall of communism, it collapsed in 1991.

Union, Treaty of. See **A48**.

Universe, the sum of all potentially observable or knowable things. More and more distant objects are seen to recede at increasing speeds. At certain distances objects are receding at light speed and so they cannot be observed. The study of the universe is called cosmology. See **Section T, Part I.**

Universities are institutions of higher education whose principal objects are the increase of knowledge over a wide field through original thought and research and its extension by the teaching of students. Such societies existed in the ancient world, notably in Greece and India, but the origin of the University as we know it today lies in mediaeval Europe.

The first bodies to become recognised under this description were at Bologna and Paris in the first half of the 12th cent.; Oxford was founded by an early migration of scholars from Paris, and Cambridge began with a further migration from Oxford. Other Universities sprang up all over Europe, including three in Scotland—St. Andrews (1411), Glasgow (1451) and Aberdeen (1494)—which were followed by Edinburgh in 1582. These six bodies remained the only Universities in Great Britain until the foundation in 1826–29 of University and King's Colleges in London (resulting in the establishment of the University of London in 1836) and of the University of Durham in 1832.

The 34 old-established universities in England were: Aston, Bath, Birmingham, Bradford, Bristol, Brunel, Buckingham, Cambridge, The City, Durham, East Anglia, Essex, Exeter, Hull, Keele, Kent, Lancaster, Leeds, Leicester, Liverpool, London, Loughborough, Manchester, Newcastle, Nottingham, Open, Oxford, Reading, Salford, Sheffield, Southampton, Surrey, Sussex, Warwick and York. Other old institutions of university standard were the University of Manchester Institute of Science and Technology; the Manchester Business School; the London Graduate School of Business Studies; Cranfield Institute of Technology; and the Royal College of Art.

Wales used to have one University (The University of Wales with colleges at Aberystwyth, Bangor, Cardiff and Swansea) in addition to the Welsh National School of Medicine, in the Institute of Science and Technology, and St. David's, Lampeter. Scotland had eight: Aberdeen, Dundee (1967), Edinburgh, Glasgow, Heriot-Watt (1966), St. Andrews, Stirling (1967), and Strathclyde (1964), Britain's first technological university. Northern Ireland has two: Queen's University, Belfast and the New University of Ulster at Coleraine. The Open University (OU) received its charter in 1969; it provides degrees and other courses together with radio and television programmes and began its broadcasts in January 1971. More students register with the OU each year than with any other English university.

The Republic of Ireland has the University of Dublin (Trinity College, Dublin), the National University of Ireland, Dublin City University and the University of Limerick among its most famous seats of learning.

In the United States the best known are Harvard (1636), Yale (1701), Princeton (1746), Columbia (1754), Cornell (1865), California (Berkeley), Massachusetts Institute of Technology. In 1972 the European University Institute was established with headquarters in Florence.

In Britain, universities receive aid from the State mainly in the form of grants from the Higher Education Funding Council which over-

sees the distribution of state finance. But they are selfgoverning institutions free from State control. In 1992, the distinction between the former polytechnics and the older universities ended.

The former polytechnics subsequently adopted university names (e.g. Leicester Polytechnic is now the De Montfort University). Financial constraints (as well as other factors) are now producing mergers of universities (e.g. the recent merger of London Guildhall University and the University of North London). Roehampton Institute gained university status in 2001.

The ending of free tuition for students (from September 1998) and the other implications of the 1997 Dearing Report, heralded a revolution in higher education. The debate on "top-up" fees has aroused much passion. In addition, new two-year 'foundation degrees' were planned which began in September 2001. Many smaller colleges and specialist institutions have become universities after changes announced by the Government in July 2004.

In 2005 several former higher education colleges (e.g. Southampton Institute) became universities.

A very different type of organisation is the University of the Third Age (U3A), which is essentially a collective of older people who meet to participate in an exchange of information and ideas. Since its arrival in the UK in 1981, it has grown to 365 groups with 65,000 members. Its national office is at 26 Harrison Street, London WC1H 8JG. See also entries for **Cambridge University, Oxford University** and **London University.**

Unknown Warrior, the tomb of the Unknown Warrior is in Westminster Abbey. In the United States, it is in Arlington National Cemetery. Such tombs serve as a memorial to all the war dead.

Uraninite. See **Pitchblende.**

Uranium, a metallic element, no. 92, symbol U, discovered by Klaproth in 1789 in pitchblende. It is a white metal which tarnishes readily in air. Great developments have followed the discovery that the nucleus of the uranium isotope U^{235} undergoes fission, and uranium minerals have become very important since it was found that atomic energy could be released controllably by taking advantage of fission. Before atomic energy work began to take the major part of the world's output of uranium minerals, the chief users of uranium compounds were the ceramics and textile industries. See also **Nuclear Reactors, Nuclear Fission.**

Uranus. This planet was discovered by Herschel in March 1781. Its diameter is 51,118 km and its mean distance from the Sun is $2,871 \times 10^6$ km. When Voyager 2 visited Uranus in January 1986, it raised the number of known moons orbiting the planet from five to 15 (this total had grown to 21 by 2004). The number of known rings surrounding Uranus was also increased to 11. Uranus has a large axial tilt which means that it rotates on its side. Each pole faces the Sun every half-revolution around the Sun, i.e. every 42 years. See **Section T, Part I and Voyager.**

Urea, the final product in mammals of the breakdown of nitrogenous waste, e.g., excess amino-acids. It is very soluble in water and is excreted in urine. In 1828 Wöhler synthesised urea from inorganic matter. This was the first laboratory synthesis of an organic substance and refuted the idea that living creatures or life force are needed to create such substances.

Ursa Major and **Ursa Minor** ("Greater Bear" and "Lesser Bear"), two celebrated constellations, each of seven stars, in the northern celestial hemisphere, familiar since ancient times. Ursa Major has also been called "the Plough", "Charles's (Charlemagne's) Wain" or "the Wagon". The "Pointers" in this group of bright stars point to the brightest star in Ursa Minor, the Pole Star. Called the Big Dipper and the Little Dipper in the USA.

V

Valency. A term used by chemists to describe the combining ability of an element with respect to hydrogen. Thus oxygen, which forms water, H_2O, with hydrogen is said to have a valency of two, nitrogen (forms ammonia, NH_3) three, and carbon (forms methane, CH_4) four. Chlorine forms hydrogen chloride, HCl, and is said to be monovalent. This empirical approach cannot account for valency in such compounds as carbon monoxide, CO, which appears to require both elements to have the same valency.

With the discovery of the electron it was realised that the concept of valency and chemical bonds is intimately concerned with the electronic structure of atoms, and theories have been advanced to explain why the same element can have different valencies in different compounds. Iron, for example, can have a valency of two (FeCl$_2$, ferrous chloride) or three (FeCl$_3$, ferric chloride). See **Section T, Part II** and **Table of Elements (T56)**.

Valentine's Day (14 February), is a festival in celebration of St. Valentine, one of the Christian martyrs of the 3rd cent. A sweetheart or Valentine is chosen on that day and letters or tokens sent secretly to the object of affection.

Valhalla, in Scandinavian mythology, is the special Paradise to which the souls of warriors slain in battle were transported.

Valkyries, the chosen handmaidens of Odin, appointed to serve at the Valhalla banquets. Their most important office, however, according to the Norse mythology, was to ride through the air at a time of battle and point out the heroes who were to fall. One of these Valkyries is made the heroine of Wagner's opera "*Die Walküre*".

Valve, an electronic device consisting of two or more metal plates (electrodes) usually enclosed in an evacuated glass bulb. One of the electrodes is heated causing electrons to be emitted. If a positive voltage is applied to the other electrode, the electrons will move towards it and the valve must conduct electricity. The current will only flow in one direction as the electrons are emitted only from one direction. A valve with two electrodes is called a diode, but by putting in one or more intermediate electrodes the flow of current can be sensitively controlled and the valves are then called triodes, pentodes, etc., according to the total number of electrodes in them.

Valves originally found extensive applications in amplifiers, rectifiers, oscillators and many electronic devices, but have now been superseded by transistors, which in turn have been replaced by the integrated circuit and the micro-chip.

Vanadium, a scarce metallic element, no. 23, symbol V, whose chief ores are carnotite and patronite. Some iron ores contain it. Most of the vanadium commercially produced finds its way into vanadium steels, which are used for tools and parts of vehicles, being hard, tough and very resistant to shocks. The oxide is used as a catalyst in industry, especially in making sulphuric acid.

Van Allen Belts. One of the most remarkable discoveries made during the IGY, 1957–58, was that the earth is surrounded by a great belt of radiation. Evidence came from *Sputnik II* (which carried the dog Laika) and from the American satellites, *Explorers I* and *III*. The American scientist, J. A. van Allen, was able to explain the puzzling data collected from these satellites. Subsequent observations with deep space-probes showed that there are in fact two zones of high intensity particle radiation surrounding the earth, one concentrated at a distance of about 1,600 km, the other at about 24,000 km. A close relation exists between the shapes of the zones and the earth's magnetic field. Recent evidence suggests that Jupiter also is surrounded by a dense belt of trapped high-energy particles.

Vatican, the Papal residence at Rome, a famous palace on the hill adjacent to St. Peter's. Its museum is a rich treasure-house of literary and artistic objects. Works of Michelangelo glorify the Sistine Chapel.

Vauxhall Gardens, a famous London pleasure resort from the early part of the 18th to the middle of the 19th cent. It was here that many great singers appeared and where the earliest balloon ascents were made.

Venus, the brightest of all the planets, whose orbit lies between the orbits of Mercury and Earth. It is second in order from the sun (*q.v.*). It approaches the earth to within 40 million km. It moves around the sun in the same direction as Earth and the other planets but rotates in the opposite sense. It has been visited by a number of American and Russian probes, some flybys, some

soft-landings, others atmospheric probes. Venus has 90 times the atmospheric pressure of the earth and temperatures of 450°C. It is covered in a very thick cloud mainly of carbon dioxide which some scientists believe acts like a greenhouse trapping the heat from the sun. Complex reactions occur in the atmosphere and the rain consists mainly of sulphuric and hydrochloric acid. The cloud rotates about six times faster than Venus rotates and swirls into the polar regions like giant whirlpools. The *Venus Express*, which went into orbit in April 2006, will collect vital information about the hot, turbulent atmosphere of the planet.

Much information has come from both the Pioneer Venus orbiter and the Magellan probe, which between them have mapped nearly the entire Venusian surface. There are two major continents, Aphrodite Terra, is about the size of Africa, and the smaller Ishtar Terra, about the size of Australia, which consists of a very high plateau (c. 3,300 m) and a mountain range dominated by Maxwell Montes (at 10,600 m higher than Everest). Aphrodite Terra has a deep trench 2,900 m below "sea level". Most of the planet (60 per cent) is relatively flat.

The Magellan probe (1990) revealed a carbon dioxide atmosphere, 100 times thicker than Earth's, with sulphur escaped from volcanoes as well as the longest channel (4,200 miles) in the solar system. It found that there are no asteroid impact craters bigger than 5 miles across.

Venus Fly-trap, a well-known insectivorous plant (*Dionaea muscipula*) occurring in Carolina in damp mossy places. It is related to the Sundew. The leaf is the organ that catches the insects. The leaf blade is in two halves, hinged along the centre line. Each half bears three sensitive hairs called "trigger hairs". When an insect touches a trigger, the two halves of the leaf clap together, trapping the insect between them, when it is digested by a secretion (digestive enzymes) from the leaf, which afterwards absorbs the soluble products.

Vernalization. Seeds which, after being exposed to a low temperature, produce plants that flower earlier than usual are said to have been "vernalized". This technique of seed treatment devised by Lysenko is called vernalization. It is claimed to have been widely used in Russia to obtain cereal crops in places where climatic conditions are favourable for only a short season.

Victoria and Albert Museum, in Kensington, London, was begun in 1852 as the Museum of Ornamental Art at Marlborough House. The present building was completed in 1909. It is one of the great museums of the world for the fine arts. The new British Galleries were opened in 2001.

The V&A also administers Ham House (Richmond) and Osterley Park House. The Museum of Childhood (Bethnal Green) is a branch of the V&A. Apsley House (home of the 1st Duke of Wellington) is also part of the V&A.

Victoria Cross, an order of merit for conspicuous valour, awarded to members of the Army, Navy and Air Force. The first investiture was in June 1857. The VC has been awarded only 1,354 times (the two youngest VCs were aged only 15).

Videotape Recording (VTR), technique for recording television programmes on to magnetic tape. The original means of storing programmes for broadcast or library purposes was by filming productions from high-quality monitors, an expensive and slow process, since the film had to be chemically developed and edited in the conventional way. The difficulty in establishing an instant play-back system along the lines of the sound tape recording system lay in the high speed and large amount of tape needed to accommodate the picture signal. The BBC experimented with a machine called VERA, but it was an American machine, the Ampex VR100, which provided the breakthrough. This recorded the picture across a wider tape rather than along it, and moving at a slower speed. The modern domestic recorder is usually of the VHS standard, while broadcasters use the higher quality systems, such as Betacam. DVDs are now rapidly replacing the older VCRs (whose sales peaked in 1993). The next generation of high-definition DVDs will store up to six times as much data on disc.

Vikings. Scandinavian raiders who from the 8th to the 10th cent. were the terror of northern waters.

Sometimes the Viking raids reached south to the Mediterranean and east to the White Sea. Their leader Rurik founded the first Russian kingdom of Novgorod in A.D. 862. The Icelandic Vikings under Eric the Red discovered Greenland in A.D. 982 and a warm period in world climate allowed many to settle there. Their expeditions took them to Labrador and Newfoundland. In 2000, the 1000th anniversary of Leif Eriksson's voyage to Newfoundland was commemorated. They excelled in shipbuilding, were fine sailors and craftsmen. The name may derive from *vik*, a sheltered deepwater bay now called a *fjord*. The first Viking raid on England was at Lindisfarne monastery in 789 A.D.

Village Green *See* **Commons.**

Vinyl Plastics are polymers made from derivatives of ethylene, examples are polyvinyl chloride (PVC), which is used in making plastic pipes and kitchen utensils, among other things; polyvinyl acetate used in the paint industry and in bonding laminated articles like plywood; and polystyrene (polyvinyl benzene) used in making electrical fittings and for lenses.

Viper, a family of poisonous snakes in which the venom-conducting fangs hinge forward when the snake bites. One species is found in Britain, the common viper or adder.

Visibility is defined by the distance at which the farthest of a series of objects, specially selected to show against the skyline or in good contrast with their background, can be distinguished. Visibility depends chiefly upon the concentration of water or dust particles suspended in the air. Instruments are available to measure the obscurity of the atmosphere more directly, including that at night. A large lapse rate of temperature and a strong wind are favourable to good visibility; a small lapse rate, calm or light wind favourable to bad visibility. Fog is when the visibility is less than 1,000 m; mist or haze when it is between 1,000 and 2,000 m. *See* **Pollution.**

Viscount, a title of rank coming between that of Earl and Baron. The title originally stood for deputy-earl. The first English Viscount was Viscount Beaumont, created in 1440.

Vitamins, name of a group of organic substances found in relatively minute amounts in certain foodstuffs, essential for growth and the maintenance of normal bodily structure and function. The Hungarian biochemist Szent-Györgyi, who first isolated vitamin C or ascorbic acid, defined the vitamin as "a substance that makes you ill if you don't eat it!".

Volcanoes are vents through which magma reaches the surface as lava flows, or as the solid products, *e.g.*, ashes and bombs, of explosive eruption. The vent may be cylindrical or it may be a long fissure. The former type usually builds up cones, *e.g.*, Vesuvius. Notable active volcanoes are Etna, Vesuvius and Stromboli, in Italy; Soufrière on Montserrat; and Mont Pelée on Martinique. The last-named was in violent eruption in 1902, when the chief town of St. Pierre was destroyed.

Volcanic eruptions are sometimes linked with brilliant sunset phenomena, *e.g.*, the Indonesian island of Krakatoa (1883), whose atmospheric and tidal effects were recorded all over the world, and Agung on the island of Bali (1963), which had been dormant for 120 years. In 1991, the eruption of Mt Pinatubo in the Philippines killed 300 people, while in 1997 Montserrat was threatened by the Soufrière eruption.

The huge eruption at Tambora (Indonesia) in 1815 killed an estimated 90,000 people. The eruption of Mt Nyiragongo in 2002 laid waste the Congolese city of Goma. There are towering volcanoes on Mars far higher than any on Earth.

Vole, a small rodent with blunt nose, round face and short tail. Three kinds occur in Britain: the field, the bank and the water vole. The water vole is now Britain's fastest declining mammal.

Volt, the electromotive force unit, named after Alessandro Volta (1745–1827), and defined in terms of the coulomb, the second and the joule.

Voyagers 1 and 2. These spacecraft were launched from Earth on 5 Sept. 1977 and 20 Aug. 1977 respectively as a follow-on mission to the earlier and successful Pioneer 10 and 11 spacecraft.

Both probes were launched towards the planets of the outer solar system. Voyager 1 reached Jupiter in 1979 and flew by the moons Callisto,

Ganymede, Europa and Io. It was then set on a course for Saturn, examining the rings and the satellite Titan, before heading out of the solar system with no further planetary encounters. Voyager 2 also flew to Jupiter and then to Saturn.

The flyby of Saturn by Voyager 2 in Aug. 1981 was carefully planned to obtain the maximum of new information to complement that obtained from Voyager 1 to help understand some of the perplexing new phenomena, and revealed even more new features of this beautiful and still enigmatic planet. Even after its Saturn flyby, the work of Voyager 2 was far from complete: its swing by Saturn redirected it toward Uranus, on which it provided our first close-up data in Jan. 1986, and from there it continued to Neptune in 1989, taking maximum advantage of a unique arrangement of all four of the outer planets, Jupiter, Saturn, Uranus and Neptune, which only occurs once every 200 years. Voyager 1, which would not pass particularly close to any planet after Saturn, carries a multi-lingual goodwill message as well as musical selections to far outside our solar system. It will not reach its nearest star, Sirius, for 360,000 years.

In March 1990, Voyager I beamed back its last colour photographs. By then it was 3,500 million miles from Earth, travelling at 37,000 mph. By 2003, it was 8·4 billion miles from the Sun, reaching the edge of the solar system.

Voyager 2 is now heading out of the solar system and is capable of making and transmitting observations of the solar heliosphere which it is expected to reach before 2005.

Vraic, a name for seaweed in the Channel Islands, where it is extensively used as a manure.

Vulgate, *See* **H3.**

Vulture, a famous bird of prey of two distinctive groups; that of the Old World, whose nostrils are separated by a bony partition, and the New World vulture, which has no such division.

Vultures feed on carrion and are the great scavengers of tropical regions. The European species are the Egyptian vulture, Griffon vulture, Black vulture and Bearded vulture. Vultures have no feathers on the head and neck. Vultures in India are in decline.

W

Wading Birds, *Charadriiformes,* an order of migratory, long-legged, long-billed birds, frequenting marshes and shallow waters. They include the plovers, avocets, stilts, oystercatchers, curlews, godwits, dunlins, sandpipers, redshanks, greenshanks, snipe, woodcocks, the pratincole of the Mediterranean and the sun bittern of tropical America. Many species breed in Britain.

Wagtails, familar long-tailed small birds, the most common British species being the Pied or Water (with sub-species White) Grey and the Yellow (sub-species Blue). Wagtails nest in holes and are active of habit.

Walloons, name given to the French-speaking population of the southern provinces of Belgium, in contrast to the Flemings or Dutch-speaking population of the northern provinces. The Walloon areas contain the mining and heavy industries of the country.

Walpurgis Night, the night before 1 May, when witches were supposed to have liberty to roam. Named after St Walpurgis, an English nun, who went on a mission to Germany in the 8th cent.

Walrus, a very large marine mammal, related to the seals having in the upper jaw two large curved tusks, which average in length from 38 to 60 cm. It lives on bi-valve molluscs, and inhabits the Arctic seas. An adult walrus can exceed 4 m in length and weigh over a tonne.

Wankel Engine *or* **Rotary Engine,** is an internal combustion engine invented by Felix Wankel in the 1930s and greatly developed since by large automobile firms in several countries. The ordinary internal combustion engine has to convert reciprocating motion of the pistons into rotary motion. In the Wankel engine the explosion of the fuel and air mixture drives a moving part (the rotor) directly into rotatory motion, and the rotor itself opens and closes the fuel inlet and exhaust ports. The three spaces between the triangular rotor and its specially shaped housing act successively as intake, compression, explosion and exhaust chambers as the rotor revolves. There are no valves and far fewer moving parts than in an ordinary piston engine. The Wankel engine is claimed to have many advantages in that it is smaller and lighter for a given horse-power, relatively simple, quieter and freer from vibration, and could contribute to pollution control. There are cars now on sale with the Wankel engine and continuous research and development will no doubt test in practice the claim of some protagonists that this engine is the agent of a technological revolution in the automobile.

Warblers, a family of small, lively song-birds closely related to the flycatchers and thrushes. Represented in Britain by about 36 species, including the chiffchaff, one of the earliest spring visitors, willow-wren, wood-warbler, blackcap, garden-warbler, whitethroat, sedge and grasshopper-warbler.

Warsaw Pact. *See* **A48.**

Water is the simplest compound of hydrogen and oxygen. It is formed when an electric spark is passed through a mixture of the gases, and is a product of combustion of all hydrogen-containing compounds, *e.g.*, petrol, coal, coal gas and wood. Water is essential to living matter, and is the medium which carries food to animals and plants. Salts in hard water may be removed by distillation of the water or by a process known as ion-exchange (water softening). Pure water freezes at $0°C$ and boils at $100°C$ and is used as a standard of temperature on this scale. It has a maximum density at $4°C$. Heating water above $100°C$ converts it into steam, which is used under pressure to convert heat energy into useful work, as in electrical power stations and steam engines.

Water gas is a mixture mainly of carbon monoxide and hydrogen formed by blowing steam and oxygen through red-hot coke: it is used as a fuel. Water is one of the very few compounds which freezes from the surface down rather than from the bulk of the liquid up. This property has important consequences on the preservation of life in rivers and lakes when they are frozen. The Drinking Water Inspectorate set up in January 1990 has responsibility for checking that water supplied by the water companies is wholesome and fit to drink when it reaches your home. The privatisation of the water industry, followed by the widespread water shortages during 1995, have caused much debate on the whole question of domestic water supplies. *See also* **Section Y.**

Water Hyacinth (*Eichhornia crassipes*), a beautiful aquatic plant native to Brazil which has spread to other favourable equatorial regions of the world causing havoc on account of its abnormal rate of reproduction away from its natural environment. In recent years it has invaded the Nile and the Congo, forming vast floating carpets which block the channels, clog the paddles of river craft and deoxygenate the water, killing the fish. It is being held in check by spraying with herbicides.

Water Vole. *See* **Vole.**

Waterloo Bridge, crossing the Thames, was built by Rennie, and opened in 1817. It had nine arches, each 120 ft (36 m) span, was built of granite, and had a length (including approaches) of 2,456 ft (749 m). The present bridge, completed in 1942, and formally opened 10 December 1945, is a fine example of reinforced concrete construction. (Architect, Sir Giles Gilbert-Scott.)

Watling Street, the name of the old Roman road which ran from the Channel ports by way of London to Shropshire. *See also* **Roman Roads.**

Watt. A unit of electrical power equivalent to 1 joule of work per second, named after James Watt (1736–1819). *See* **T58–61.**

Waxbill, a small Oriental and African bird of the *Estrildidae* family, with wax-like bill and beautifully variegated plumage. The Java sparrow, and the Blue-breasted waxbill are attractive, but sadly still find their way into cages.

Weasel. A carnivore mammal found in Britain, smallest member of the group including the Stoat, Polecat, and Pine-marten, about 20 cm long. Its fur is reddish on the upper side of the animal, white on the under side; it may all turn white in winter with the exception of the tail.

Weather is generally accepted as being the current state of the atmosphere, particularly as regards its pressure and temperature, wind, cloud and pre-

cipitation. Many other features such as fog, sunshine duration, humidity, pressure tendency, may be added to the list, all items of which are routinely observed by specially instrumented stations usually sponsored by the national meteorological services. Day-to-day changes in the weather as experienced by the individual are due to the passage of circulation systems, many of which bring clearly recognisable areas of "good" (*i.e.*, calm and sunny) weather as frequently occurs in anticyclones and "bad" (*i.e.*, cold, windy, cloudy and rainy) weather. Clearly, the weather in any place at any time is primarily determined by the frequency and intensity of synoptic-scale weather circulation systems (*c.* 3,000 km across). Local weather (over areas of *c.* 100 km) may be heavily influenced by topography, *e.g.*, valley fogs, frost hollows.

Weather Lore. Before instruments were invented to measure atmospheric conditions, man relied on his own observation of wind and sky, behaviour of birds and animals, and came to associate certain phenomena with types of weather. Many popular weather rhymes have survived the centuries, and as long as forecasting is confined to the next few days there is something to be said for them, particularly those dealing with the winds. What is very unlikely is that next year's summer can be predicted from this year's winter, or that one month's weather is related to that of another.

Weaver Bird, the popular name for a large group of finch-like birds belonging to the family *Ploceidae*, found principally in Africa but also in Southern Asia, Australia, and Europe and remarkable for their habit of building nests formed of blades of grass dexterously inter-woven and suspended from the boughs of trees.

Weaving. *See* **Section N.**

Wedding Anniversaries are: first, Paper; second, Cotton; third, Leather; fourth, Fruit and Flowers; fifth, Wooden; sixth, Sugar; seventh, Woollen; eighth, Bronze; ninth, Pottery; tenth, Tin; twelfth, Silk and Fine Linen; fifteenth, Crystal; twentieth, China; twenty-fifth, Silver; thirtieth, Pearl; thirty-fifth, Coral; fortieth, Ruby; forty-fifth, Sapphire; fiftieth, Golden; fifty-fifth, Emerald; sixtieth, Diamond, sixty-fifth, Platinum or Blue Sapphire; seventieth, Platinum; seventy-fifth, Diamond or Gold.

Wednesday, the 4th day of the week, derived its name from Woden or Odin, the Norse god of war.

Weights and Measures. *See* **T58–61.**

Welding is a means of joining together two pieces of material, often metals, by heating the joint until the substances melt locally, run together, and then solidify. The heating can be by burning gas (*e.g.*, oxy-acetylene welding) or electric current (electric arc welding). Techniques exist for welding anything from hair-like wires to massive steel plates. *See* **Soldering.**

Werewolf, a man or woman, who according to mediaeval belief, could be turned by witchcraft or magic into a wolf, eat human flesh or drink human blood and turn into himself again. This belief was widely held in Europe, and similar superstitions prevail among most primitive peoples, *e.g.*, the "leopard man" of certain African tribes. Lycanthropy (from Gr. = wolfman) is a form of madness in which the patient imagines himself a beast.

Westminster Abbey stands on the site of an old church and Benedictine foundation of the 7th cent. It was rebuilt under Edward the Confessor (after 1065), and again under Henry III after 1245, and important additions were made by Edward II, Edward III, Richard II, Richard III and Henry VII, the latter erecting the beautiful eastern chapel in the perpendicular style which bears his name. The west towers and gable were designed by Hawksmoor (1661–1736). The Abbey contains tombs of many sovereigns, of the Unknown Warrior, and many other illustrious persons are commemorated there.

Westminster Cathedral, seat of the Roman Catholic Archbishop of Westminster. It was designed by J. F. Bentley and built betwen 1895 and 1910. It is of red brick, in early Christian Byzantine style with a domed campanile, 283 ft (86 m) high, and a decorative interior.

Westminster Hall, adjoining the House of Parliament, was built as a Banqueting Hall by William Rufus, and many courtly festivals were held there in succeeding centuries. King John established the Law Courts there. It now forms a gigantic hallway, leading to the Houses of Parliament. Charles I, Sir Thomas More, and Warren Hastings were tried there.

Whale, a completely aquatic mammal; the forelimbs are modified to form fin-like paddles and there is virtually no external trace of the hindlimbs.

There are two major groups of whales—the *Toothed Whales,* including the Sperm-whale (Cachalot), Dolphin, Killer-whales and Porpoises; and the *Whalebone Whales.* In the latter a series of whalebone plates grow down from the roof of the mouth, and, being frayed at their edges into a hairy fringe, together constitute a filtering mechanism. The animal takes in sea water containing minute organisms on which it feeds; the mouth is then closed and the tongue raised when the water is forced out through the filter, on which is left the food. As the tongue is lowered, the whalebone plates straighten up, flicking the food on to the tongue, which transfers it to the gut. Most whale oil is obtained from the thick layer of fat under the skin (blubber), but in the Sperm-whale there is a large reserve of oil in the head. One of the major users of sperm oil is the leather industry. Ambergris used in perfumery comes from the intestine of whales. The number of whales that may be killed in a season is limited by International Convention. Today the main whaling nations are Japan, Iceland and Norway.

It is estimated that 2 million whales were killed by humans during the 20th century. In 1994 a whale sanctuary around Antarctica was established by the International Whaling Commission. The sactuary banned commercial whaling in the Southern Ocean for at least 10 years. Sadly, blue whales, the world's largest creatures, have seen their population decimated.

Scientists have found that Beluga whales travel thousands of miles to feast on stocks of cod and halibut after navigating by the stars or Earth's magnetic field. Today the northern right whale is threatened by busy Atlantic shipping lanes.

Whiskers in physics and materials science (*q.v.*) are tiny rods of crystal, thinner than human hair and perhaps 1 cm long. Their importance lies in the fact that such crystals are free from the defects described on **T21**. They are also free from surface cracks and steps. This means they are immensely strong because failures of strength in ordinary solids are due to imperfections and cracks of one kind or another. Large numbers of whiskers of strong solids like graphite or silicon carbide embedded in a matrix of softer matter such as plastic make a very strong new material.

White Ants. *See* **Termites**.

White Elephant, a term in common use to designate a gift that causes the recipient more trouble or cost than it is worth; derived from an old-time custom of the Kings of Thailand who presented a white elephant to a courtier whom it was desired to ruin.

Whitehall Palace, built within sight of Westminster by Hubert de Burgh, Earl of Kent, round about 1240, was the residence of the Archbishops of York until Wolsey presented it to Henry VIII in 1530. From then until 1697, when it was burned down, it continued to be the favourite town residence of royalty, and to the Stuarts especially it was a great centre of court festivities. In those days, with its grounds, it extended from the Strand to the river. The only portion of Whitehall Palace now standing is the Banqueting Hall built by Inigo Jones, on a scaffold projected from the front of which Charles I was beheaded. A block of government buildings has been built on part of the site of the old Palace.

White House, the official residence at Washington of the President of the United States. It was built in 1792, having been designed by an Irishman, James Hoban. In 1814 British troops captured Washington and set fire to the White House.

Whitsuntide, the festival celebrating the descent of the Holy Ghost. It occurs seven weeks after Easter.

Widow Bird, certain species of African weaver birds with predominantly black plumage. In the breeding season the male birds are strikingly beautiful, with scarlet and buff markings and long tail feathers. They are social parasites and trick other birds into rearing their young.

Wig. *See* **Peruke**.

Wigeon, a surface-feeding duck of northern

Europe, known in Britain more as a winter visitor than a nesting bird. It feeds in flocks in the muddy estuaries and has a characteristic "whee-oo" call.

Wildebeest. *See* **Gnu**.

Willow, a water-side-loving tree of the genus *Salix,* to which the osiers belong. The best cricket-bat blades are made from a white willow, *S. alba* var. *caerulea,* a fine tree with bluish-green leaves, mostly found in Essex. Willow is also used for polo balls. Weeping willow, *S. babylonica,* is native to China and is the willow seen on Old China willow-pattern plates.

Wind, air set in motion by special atmospheric conditions, is of various degrees, from a slight rustling breeze to a hurricane. Winds are *constant,* as in trade winds or anti-trade winds; *periodic,* in monsoons and other wind visitations occurring according to influences of season; *cyclonic* and *anticyclonic,* when their motion is spiral: *whirlwinds, hurricanes,* and *tornados,* when high temperature and great density induce extreme agitation.

Ordinarily, a wind is named from the point of the compass from which it blows, or it may be expressed in degrees from true north. The *sirocco,* the *mistral,* and the *simoom* are local forms of winds of great velocity. A *blizzard* is a biting blast of icy temperature.

Britain is the windiest country in Europe. There are currently an ever-growing number of wind-farms in Britain utilising this renewable energy source.

Windmills were in use in the East in ancient times, but were not much seen in Europe before the 13th cent. Wind sawmills were invented by a Dutchman in the 17th cent., and one was erected near the Strand in London in 1633. Great improvements have been made in these mills, especially in the United States, where, by the application of the windshaft principle, much space is saved and the mills can be used for pumping, grinding and other purposes. The Windmill Museum on Wimbledon Common is a popular attraction.

Windows (Old Norse *vindauga* = wind-eye), an opening in a wall of a building to admit light and air, and to afford a view of what is outside. In northern Europe windows, as the derivation of the word implies, were first used for ventilation and glass was not used in private houses before the end of the 12th cent. In early Gothic (12th cent.) windows were still small and narrow, with rounded heads. In Early English (13th cent.) they became longer and the heads pointed. In the Decorated period (14th cent.) windows were mullioned (divided by slender bars into panes) and the pointed heads often traceried.

In Tudor times windows were larger and the bay-window (projecting from the wall) and the oriel window (*q.v.*) were much in vogue; in the late 18th cent. curved bays (called bowwindows) became fashionable. Sash windows (invented by the English) with wooden frames and divided into equal rectangular panes were used in Queen Anne and Georgian houses. Their design was influenced by a passion for symmetry; they were very efficient ventilators. The French window reaches to the floor and has double casements opening as doors. A Dormer window is a vertical window set on the sloping side of a roof. One of the main features of modern architecture is the large area devoted to windows, a development made possible by improved heating systems.

Windsor Castle, the famous British royal residence on the banks of the Thames, as it now stands, was mainly built by Henry III, though a royal residence had existed there from the time of the Conqueror. Additions were made by Henry VIII, Elizabeth and Charles II. Windsor Park and Forest comprise over 5,200 ha. A serious fire in 1992 caused very extensive damage, destroying St. George's Hall and gutting the Queen's Chapel.

Woad, a plant (*Isastis tinctoria*) largely used by ancient Britons for the blue dye obtained from the leaves. It is a biennial plant belonging to the same family (*Cruciferae*) as the wallflower. It is now being considered as a potential source of ink for computer printers.

Wolverine. *See* **Glutton**.

Wolves, well-known carnivorous animals still found in many parts of Europe, but not existing in Britain since the middle of the 17th cent. They usually hunt in packs. In parts of Europe, careful conservation has seen their numbers increase, as in north-west Spain. Grey wolves (Europe's second largest predator after the brown bear) have now returned to Germany.

Women's Institutes (WI) were originally founded in Canada in 1897. The movement spread to Britain, with the first branch opening in Wales in 1915. The organisation is active in rural areas.

Woodcock, a wading bird, valued for its flesh. It is a member of the snipe family, and breeds in Britain. The parent bird is able to carry its young between its thigh and body when flying to and from the feeding spots. It is one of the birds protected by the Game Laws.

Woodhenge, popular name for the traces of an elaborate wooden temple, dating back 5,000 years, located at Stanton Drew in Somerset. Discovered in 1997, archaeologists think nine concentric rings of oak pillars once towered above the site.

Woodpecker, a familiar tree-climbing, insecti-vorous bird of conspicuous plumage, of which four species are found in Britain, the green woodpecker or yaffle (because of its harsh cry), the great spotted, the lesser spotted, and the wryneck. They build in the hollows of trees. Yaffle has a long sticky tongue for licking up ground insects, especially ants. The great and lesser woodpeckers obtain insects by digging into tree trunks with strong, chisel-like bills, spearing the insects with a sharp tongue. The metallic drumming sound made by the birds in spring is thought to be caused by their beaks hammering away at some hard resounding substance.

Wood Pigeon. *See* **Ring Dove.**

Wood's Metal, an alloy with a very low melting point (65°C, which is under 150°F) so that a spoon made of it will melt when used to stir a cup of tea. Contains bismuth 4 parts, lead 2 parts, tin 1 part, cadmium 1 part. Its use as a heat exchanger has now been superseded by silicone oils, which have a wider temperature range.

Woodworm. Four beetles are mainly responsible for woodworm damage: common furniture beetle (*Anobium punctatum*), powder post beetle (*Lyctus brunneus*), death watch beetle (*Xestobium rufovillo-sum*), and house longhorn beetle (*Hylotrupes bajulus*). Particular attention should be paid to wood in damp, dark and out-of-the-way places, and the backs and underneaths of furniture. The most frequent cause of woodworm damage is the common furniture beetle (*q.v.*).

Wool is a fibre, made up of very long protein molecules. It has been largely grown and used in the manufacture of cloth in England since before the Roman invasion. It is grown on the backs of sheep, and is of various kinds, according to the breed of sheep from which it is derived. Wool differs from hair in that it has a wavy, serrated fibre, its curl being a notable characteristic, whereas hair has a smooth surface comparatively free from serratures. Long wools are mostly used for the manufacture of worsted goods, and short wools for woollen cloths, though the improvements in machinery in recent years have enabled manufacturers to utilise short wools to a great extent for dress fabrics as well as for woollens. The finest wools are obtained from the fleece of the Spanish merino sheep. Australia, New Zealand, Argentina and South Africa are among the greatest wool-producing countries. China is the world's largest consumer of wool.

Woolsack, the name given to the seat formerly occupied by the Lord Chancellor in the House of Lords. It is a large square bag of wool, without back or arms, covered with red cloth. At the time when it was first used, in the reign of Edward III, wool was the great staple commodity of the country and, it is said, chosen for the seat of judges as a constant reminder of the main source of the national wealth. The Lord Chancellor was "appointed to the woolsack". Since 2006 the Woolsack has been occupied by the Lord Speaker (a newly-created post filled by election).

World Heritage Sites, established under the World Heritage Convention to secure lasting protection for sites of outstanding universal value. In Britain they include Canterbury Cathedral; Durham Cathedral and Castle; Studley Royal Gardens and Fountains Abbey; Ironbridge Gorge; the prehistoric stone circles of Stonehenge and Avebury; Blenheim Palace; the city of Bath; Hadrian's Wall; the Tower of London; the Palace of Westminster; the islands of St Kilda; Edinburgh Old and New Towns; the North Wales castles and town walls of

Edward I, and the Giants' Causeway, in Northern Ireland. An additional site has been proposed for maritime Greenwich. England's first natural World Heritage Site is the 95-mile 'Jurassic Coast', in Dorset and Devon.

Around the world, UNESCO's sites include the Great Wall of China; the Pyramids and Grand Canyon; the Taj Mahal; Persepolis, the capital of ancient Persia; Australia's Great Barrier Reef and the Inca town on Machu Picchu in Peru. Recently designated sites include Robben Island and the Darjeeling Himalayan railway.

World Population. According to United Nations sources world population has now (2006) reached *c.* 6,450,000,000. More than half the total live in Asia.

Different countries are at different stages in a demographic transition from the stability provided by a combination of high birth rate and high death rate to that provided by a combination of low birth rate and low death rate. Their recent population history and current trend of growth, the age-structure of their population, and consequently their population potential for the near future are all widely different. Most rapid growth is in Africa with rates of over 3 per cent in some countries. In most European countries the rate is less than 1 per cent.

It is estimated that about one in 25 of all human beings who have ever lived are alive today. It took 115 years for the world's population to rise from one to two thousand million; in a further 35 years it rose from two thousand million to three; in only 15 more years from four to five thousand million. It is estimated to reach around 9·3 billion by 2050 and over ten billion by 2080.

Life expectancy in Britain today is 73·8 for men and 79·2 for women (compared to 48 and 51 in 1906). Life expectancy is increasing in Britain. Women are expected to live until the age of 80 and men to 74½ within a few years. Already Britain has the oldest population in the EU. Over 21% of Britons are now over 60 and over 1·1 million are over 85 (compared to 200,000 in 1951). Britain has nearly 9,000 centenarians (2005).

Highest life expectancies in the world for women are currently Japan (82·8), Sweden (81·4) and Hong Kong (81·2). For men, Japan leads with 76·4, Sweden comes second (76·1) and Hong Kong third (75·8). The lowest life expectancies are in such African countries as Sierra Leone (25·9), Niger (29·1) and Malawi (29·4).

The number of centenarians is also rapidly increasing. Japan alone had over 20,500 in 2003 (85 per cent of them women). Living to over 100 will one day be routine (*e.g.* in Japan which will have 1 million centenarians in 2050).

A report published in 1998 by the UN predicts that by 2030 the elderly will make up 40% of the population of Germany and Japan. Projections show the population of Britain will reach 66 million by 2050. *See also* **Section Y**.

Wrasse, a large reef fish. Threatened with extinction because it is a luxury food in Asia.

Wren, a family of small passerine birds possessing upturned tails and most abundant in South America. The British species is an interesting singing bird with a surprising loud note for its size.

X

Xenon a rare gaseous element, no.54, symbol Xe, occurring in minute quantities in the atmosphere, discovered by Sir William Ramsay and M. W. Travers in 1898. *See* **Rare Gases.**

X-Rays were discovered in 1895 by Professor Röntgen, of Wurzburg. X-rays are produced when heavy metal atoms (*e.g.* tungsten) are struck by electrons of sufficient energy. X-rays are now commonly used to examine the internal structure of many opaque objects. In medicine, industry and for security, examination may be conducted without physical invasion. X-rays may also be used to probe the structure of matter, for example the atomic structure of crystals. The discovery in the 1960s that cosmic objects emitted intense X-rays has led to many important discoveries.

Xylem, the woody tissue of higher plants whose function is to conduct water and mineral salts upwards, and to provide mechanical support.

Y

Yacht, a light vessel now much used for pleasure trips and racing. The first yachting club was the Cork Harbour Club, started about 1720; and in 1812 the Royal Yacht Squadron was founded at Cowes. The Royal Thames Yacht Club dates from 1823.

Yak, a curious, long-haired ox, found in Tibet. Used as a beast of burden, and also kept for milk and meat.

Yard, a standard measure of 36 in, the word being derived from the Saxon gyrd, or rod. The yard and pound are now defined by reference to the metre and the kilogram: yard = 0·9144 of a metre; pound = 0·45359237 of a kilogram. By international agreement the metre is defined by reference to the wavelength of krypton-86 light.

Yardies. Jamaican criminal gangs, in some ways similar to the Chinese Triads or Italian mafia.

Yellowhammer, a common British bird of the bunting family, of lemon-yellow and brown plumage. Nests on or near the ground. Recent years have seen its numbers decline. Its nickname is the Scottish canary.

Yeomen of the Guard are a body of Foot Guards established in the reign of Henry VII for the protection of the Royal Person. Yeomen are now about 100 in number, and their duties consist in being present on ceremonial State occasions, the yearly distribution of Maundy Money, and the searching of the vaults of the Houses of Parliament on Guy Fawkes' day.
"Beefeater" is the nickname of both Yeomen of the Guard and Yeomen Warders of the Tower, and they both wear the Tudor style of dress, but with one distinction, the Yeomen of the Guard wear a cross belt, the Warders do not.

Yeti, opinions differ as to whether this is a mythical inhabitant of the Himalayas, a primitive primate or bear. Evidence to date is inconclusive.

Yiddish, language whose basic grammar and vocabulary are Germanic (but it is a complete language in itself). It was the language of most Jews of Eastern Europe before the Second World War.

York Minster, one of the oldest and finest of English cathedrals, is 160 m long, its nave is 73 m broad, and the central tower is 66 m high. The present edifice, in parts, dates back to the 12th cent., but a church stood on the site in the 7th cent. In 1829 it was set on fire by a lunatic named Jonathan Martin.

Young Offenders' Institutions. The Criminal Justice Act 1988 replaced youth custody and detention centre training with the sentence of detention in a young offender institution for all young people aged 15 to 20 whom the courts decided needed custodial treatment. More recently the Crime and Disorder Act 1998 modified this sentence with the creation of the detention and training order, combining custody and community supervision, for young offenders under the age of 18. Detention and training orders came into force in April 2000.

Ytterbium, a chemical, no.70, symbol Yb, element discovered by Urbain in 1907; one of the group of rare earth metals.

Yttrium, a chemical element, no.39, symbol Y, discovered by Mosander in 1842. It is found in a few rare minerals such as gadolinite, xenotine, fergusonite and euxenite. One of the group of rare earth metals.

Z

Zamboni Pile, a dry galvanic battery, which can provide small amounts of high-voltage current over a very long time. At Oxford a couple of Zamboni piles have kept a bell ringing for over a hundred years. These piles in the second world war were perfected and produced in quantity, being the most convenient source of current for infra-red signalling devices.

Zebra, an African quadruped of whitish-grey colour, with regular black stripings, perhaps the most beautiful member of the Equine family. Rather larger than an ass and smaller than the horse, it has a tufted tail, is of light build, wild and fleet of foot. The Zebra may be threatened with extinction—already the fate of the Quagga species—because of its slaughter by man for its beautiful skin. Each year in Africa, zebra undertake a spectacular migration to their breeding grounds.

Zenith, the highest point in the heavens above an observer's head, the opposite pole to the nadir.

Zeppelin, name of the airships developed by Germany, kept aloft by hydrogen. The loss of the *Hindenburg*, which burst into flames in 1937 as it came in to land at Lakehurst, New Jersey, put an end to their popularity.

Zero, the cypher signifying nothing originally came from China. The West is indebted to the Arabs for it, who themselves obtained it from India and passed it to European mathematicians towards the end of the Middle Ages. The zero has also been found in Babylonian cuneiform. The Greeks had no such symbol, which hindered the development of their mathematics. The use of zero led to the invention of decimal fractions and to the later developments in astronomy, physics and chemistry. For absolute zero on the temperature scale *see* **Absolute Temperature.**

Zinc, a familiar metallic element, no.30, symbol Zn, known to the ancients, and used by them in the making of brass. It occurs as the sulphide, carbonate, *etc*. The ores of zinc are crushed, roasted and reduced with coal. In combination with copper it constitutes the familiar alloy called brass, and zinc itself is much used for roofing and other protective purposes.

Zirconium, metallic element, no.40, symbol Zr, was discovered by Klaproth in the sand of the rivers of Sri Lanka in 1789. The crystalline metal is white, soft and ductile; in its amorphous condition it is a blue-black powder. Zirconium is used in atomic reactors as containers for fuel elements, since it does not absorb neutrons.

Zodiac, an imaginary zone or belt of the sky enclosing the circuit over which the principal planets travel. It is divided into 12 equal spaces of 30 degrees each, comprising respectively the 12 signs of the zodiac—Aries, Taurus, Gemini, Cancer, Leo, Virgo, Libra, Scorpio, Sagittarius, Capricornus, Aquarius and Pisces. The idea of the zodiac originated with the Babylonians about 2000 B.C. and passed by way of the Greeks to the Western world. The traditional 12 signs of the zodiac were thrown into turmoil recently when a 13th sign – Ophiucus – was added by astronomers.

Zodiacal Band, a very faint band of light sometimes seen stretching along the ecliptic joining the Zodiacal Light to the Gegenschein and, like them, caused by the reflection of sunlight from interplanetary dust particles.

Zodiacal Light, a faint cone of light occasionally seen stretching along the zodiac from the western horizon after evening twilight or the eastern horizon before morning twilight. It is believed to be due to the scattering of the sun's light by dust particles in orbit round the sun and extending beyond the earth. Recent observations at the high altitudes station at Chacaltaya in the Andes suggest that the dust is travelling round the sun in regular planetary orbits.

Zonda, a warm moist wind in Argentina of great velocity blowing from the north or northwest, and, like the Sirocco in Southern Europe, causing much discomfort. It happens when a depression is moving across the pampas, bringing with it a mass of air from the humid tropics. It is followed by a refreshing wind from the south east.

Zoological Gardens of London were opened in 1828, and belong to the Zoological Society of London. They contain one of the largest collections of living animals in the world (*c*. 5,000 animals and 8,270 invertebrates). The Society maintains an open-air zoo at Whipsnade, on the edge of Dunstable Downs.

Zoology, the branch of science concerned with animal life, embracing many aspects such as anatomy, behaviour, classification, ecology *etc*.

Zulus, one of the peoples of South Africa. Prior to white rule, the Zulus were ruled by a succession of paramount chiefs, reaching the zenith of their powers under King Shaka in the 1820s. Their power was crushed by the British at Ulundi in 1879 (after the Zulus had earlier routed the British at Isandlwana).

SPECIAL TOPIC

SLAVERY AND THE SLAVE TRADE

The Campaign against the Slave Trade and Slavery.

In the course of the 18th century Britain became the world's leading trader in slaves. Between 1770 and 1800 alone, British shipping transported over 900,000 people from Africa to toil in the plantations of the Americas and the Caribbean. But as the century ended there was growing domestic opposition, based on a combination of moral sensibility and changing economic realities. The banning of British participation in the slave trade in 1807 opened the path to a final campaign against the institution of slavery itself.

The Middle Passage.

From the mid-15th to the mid-19th century an estimated 11·7 million slaves underwent the Middle Passage, the journey across the Atlantic. Of these, almost two million were reckoned to have died in the crossing and many in the brutal process of 'seasoning', the initiation into labour and plantation discipline. The captives did not go without a struggle, fighting back on the ships themselves and in the British, Dutch, Spanish, Portuguese and French colonies in the Caribbean and North and South America. In 1804 the Republic of Haiti was established following a successful slave revolution.

The James Somerset Case.

Slavery was often criticised on moral grounds, but it was not until the late 18th century that opposition took an organised form. In 1772 Lord Chief Justice Mansfield ruled that slavery had no basis in English law, ordering the release of James Somerset, a slave who had been brought by his owner to Britain from Jamaica. The radical writer Thomas Paine (1737–1809) wrote in 1775, 'That some wretches should be willing to steal and enslave men by violence and murder for gain, is rather lamentable than strange. But that many civilised, nay, Christianised people should approve, and be concerned in the savage practice, is surprising.'

The Quaker Campaign.

Prominent in the Somerset campaign had been Granville Sharp (1735–1813), who had resigned from the Civil Service because of his support in 1776 for American independence. In 1783 the Society of Friends (the Quakers), of which Sharp was a member, began a systematic campaign against slavery throughout British territories. Quakers were to be among the most active in anti-slavery activity, though members had in the past been slave-owners and slave-traders.

In April 1787 Sharp, with Thomas Clarkson (1760–1846), author of the recently published *An Essay on the Slavery and Commerce of the Human Species, Particularly the African*, and William Wilberforce (1759–1833), a Tory MP, established the Society for Effecting the Abolition of the Slave Trade. Nine of the 12 committee members were Quakers but the bar on their election to Parliament made Wilberforce the campaign's main voice in the House of Commons. Sharp had initially pressed for an all-out fight against slavery but was persuaded by his fellow activists that more could be achieved by concentrating attention on the slave trade.

The Work of Wedgwood and Newton.

Among other leading participants in the Society's work were Josiah Wedgwood (1730–95), a prominent member of the pottery business, and John Newton (1725–1807), a clergyman and former slave trader. Wedgwood produced the Society's seal, a male slave kneeling with his hands raised skywards and the slogan 'Am I not a Man and a Brother?' Newton provided graphic information on the reality of the trade and of conditions on the ships that transported slaves from Africa. Clarkson used his own investigations in Britain's main slaving ports – Liverpool and Bristol – to write *A Summary View of the Slave Trade and of the Probable Consequences of its Abolition* in 1787.

At the centre of the Society's campaign was educating the public, particularly the minority that had the vote, of the barbarity and immorality inherent in trading in human lives. This was to be a preliminary to pressing MPs to support legislation. The Society collected signatures to convince Parliament of the popular support for abolition of the trade.

Olaudah Equiano.

Africans played a vital part in the campaign. Olaudah Equiano (*fl.* 1745–90), a former slave who had become a radical activist in London, published his autobiography, *The Interesting Narrative of the Life of Olaudah Equiano, or Gustavus Vassa, the African: By Himself* in 1790. Though the accuracy of what he wrote is now questioned, Equiano's book was influential for its description of the humiliation and cruelty of kidnap, transportation and slavery. As compelling in gaining sympathy was a work by the freed slave Ottabah Cugoano (dates unknown), *Thoughts and Sentiments on the Evil and Wicked Traffic of the Slavery and Commerce of the Human Species* (1787).

The Wilberforce Bill.

In 1791 Wilberforce presented the first bill to abolish the slave trade. It was defeated in the Commons by 163 votes to 88. Prominent in the opposition were MPs defending the interests of the 'Plantocracy', the largely absentee owners of Caribbean sugar plantations, many of whom were themselves members of the Commons. Arguments concerning the Society's campaign dominated British politics until the declaration of war against France and the egalitarian principles of the French Revolution in 1792 made all reform suspect. In 1788 a society had been established in France to campaign against the slave trade, the *Société des Amis des Noirs*, and slavery was abolished in all French possessions by the National Convention in 1794, to be reinstituted by Napoleon Bonaparte in 1802.

Renewed Agitation.

In 1804 there was a resurgence of anti-slave trade activism in Britain. In 1805 the Commons passed a bill tabled by Wilberforce, only for it to be rejected by the House of Lords. In February 1806 Lord Grenville formed a Whig administration. At the same time, an expansion in British territory in the Caribbean had led to divided opinions among plantation owners about the economic impact of further slave imports. Grenville declared in the Lords that the trade was 'contrary to the principles of justice, humanity and sound policy', while Wilberforce and the Foreign Secretary, the radical Charles James Fox, argued the case in the Commons. The Abolition of the Slave Trade Bill passed through both the Commons and the Lords, receiving the Royal Assent on 25 March 1807.

The 1807 Act.

Under the Act, engagement in the slave trade became illegal throughout the British colonies. Captains of British vessels faced a £100 fine for every captive African found on board. Despite this penalty, and the Royal Navy's attempt to blockade the West African coast, trafficking to the Caribbean continued. In 1811 the government declared participation in the slave trade by British citizens to be piracy and punishable by death.

The African Institution.

Following the ending of the British slave trade campaigners formed the African Institution to persuade other European nations to follow suit. At the Congress of Vienna, which ended the war against Napoleonic France in 1815, slavery was condemned but no effective measures were proposed to end it. However, delegates signed a declaration to cease participation in the trade. The Dutch had already done so in 1814. France followed in 1815 and Portugal gradually over the course of the next 15 years. Spain agreed to withdraw from the trade by treaty with Britain in 1817, but in practice continued involvement until the late 1860s. In 1839 Pope Gregory XVI issued a bull threatening excommunication to any Roman Catholic who trafficked in slaves.

Slavery and the United States.

The United States had ended its own involvement in the trade in 1808 under the Prohibition on Importation of Slaves Act. In the preceding years a number of Northern states, where slavery was of minimal economic importance, had also gone as far as introducing a gradual abolition of slavery. However, over the next half century an estimated 250,000 slaves were illegally imported into the Southern states, where there was a continual demand for their labour on the cotton, tobacco and rice plantations.

The Anti-Slavery Society.

In 1823 campaigners in Britain established the Society for the Mitigation and Gradual Abolition of Slavery Throughout the British Dominions (often known as the Anti-Slavery Society), with Clarkson and Wilberforce once again prominent. They were joined by Thomas Fowell Buxton (1786–1845) and Henry Brougham (1778–1868), both Members of Parliament. In 1825, with Wilberforce's retirement, Buxton became the Anti-Slavery Society's leading parliamentary advocate.

Women Campaigners.

The Anti-Slavery Society's initial aim was to improve slaves' lives by reform of the institution rather than immediate abolition. But increasing pressure from the Society's membership forced the pace. In 1814 a million signature petition had been presented to the Commons calling for slavery to be ended. Now the pressure came from the increasingly influential women activists. Women, denied the vote and any political voice, were at the forefront of organisation in the provinces. Among the most prominent were Elizabeth Heyrick (1769–1831), Mary Honeychurch (1795–1865) and Anne Knight (1781–1862).

In 1824 Heyrick's pamphlet, *Immediate not Gradual Opposition*, criticised the narrow ambitions of the male leadership's stated aims, which then attempted to suppress her views. Nevertheless, in 1830 over 70 women's anti-slavery groups demanded the Anti-Slavery Society adopt a programme of immediate abolition. In 1831 Clarkson broke with the Society to form the Agency Committee to press for an immediate end to slavery, although in practice the two bodies co-operated, for example, in collecting 150,000 signatures for an anti-slavery petition.

The Abolition of Slavery Act, 1833.

In 1832, under the first elections following the expansion of the franchise in the Reform Act, 104 MPs were returned who had pledged themselves to their electors to support the abolition of slavery. The Abolition of Slavery Act received Royal Assent on 24 August 1833, and ended slavery in British possessions from 1 August 1834. Of over 800,000 slaves, mainly in the Caribbean, only those under six years of age were granted their liberty at once. The remainder had to work under 'apprenticeship' for six years. Such was the resistance that this continuing forced labour was abandoned in 1838. The slave owners were further compensated with payments totalling £20 million.

The World Convention on Slavery.

In 1839 Buxton attempted to end what remained of the slave trade at its source. In *The African Slave Trade and Its Remedy* he urged the British government to negotiate treaties with African rulers against the sale of slaves. In the same year Clarkson became founding president of the British and Foreign Anti-Slavery Society, established to campaign for other powers to follow Britain's lead in abolishing slavery. In 1840 the Society organized the first World Convention on Slavery in London.

Two years later Britain and the United States agreed by treaty to mount naval patrols off the West African coast to suppress the slave trade. However, in 1844 a British diplomat in Sierra Leone reported that the trade continued more systematically than ever before.

The Abolition of Slavery in the Americas.

Slavery in the United States, where the numbers of slaves had increased from under half a million on independence in 1783 to almost four million in 1860, remained legal until 1865, the end of the civil war that had been provoked by the election as president of the abolitionist Abraham Lincoln. France had abolished slavery in its colonies in 1848 and the Netherlands in 1863. Slavery was gradually abolished in Central and South America through the 19th century, with Cuba in 1886, and Brazil, 1888, being the last countries to do so, their participation in the slave trade having ended in 1862 and 1851 respectively.

At the Congress of Berlin in 1884, Britain, Germany, France, the United States and other leading European governments agreed to the division of Africa between the European powers, using the campaign against the slave trade and slavery as a moral justification for seizing colonies.

Outposts of Slavery.

Slavery as an institution continued into the 20th century. Korea formally abolished slavery in 1894, but it remained in existence until the 1930s. Portugal retained slavery in her African colonies until 1910, when it was also finally abolished in China. Ethiopia did not abandon slavery until 1942, Saudi Arabia until 1962 and the former French African colony of Mauritania retained it until 1980.

Slavery Today.

According to the campaigning organisation Anti-Slavery International millions of men, women and children continue to lead lives as slaves in the 21st century despite the fact that slavery is prohibited by the 1948 Universal Declaration of Human Rights and the 1956 United Nations Supplementary Convention on the Abolition of Slavery, the Slave Trade and Institutions and Practices Similar to Slavery. Anti-Slavery International gives as examples of the forms that modern slavery takes men forced to work as slaves on Brazilian agricultural estates, women from Eastern Europe tricked into working as prostitutes in the West, and children trafficked between West African countries. In a recent report, *A Global Alliance Against Forced Labour*, the International Labour Organization put the number of enslaved people at over 12 million, the largest proportions in Latin America and poor Asian countries and the majority women and children.

For information on modern slavery, contact Anti-Slavery International, Thomas Clarkson House, The Stableyard, Broomgrove Road, London SW9 9TL. Website: www.antislavery.org.

LITERARY COMPANION

This section provides a concise outline of English Literature from the earliest times to the start of the new millennium. Arranged as a chronological survey, it covers such great poets and writers as Chaucer, Shakespeare, Milton and Dickens as well as the major figures of more recent times. Two Special Topics list winners of selected major literary prizes and some notable prize winning books of the last 25 years.

TABLE OF CONTENTS

LITERARY COMPANION

I. SURVEY OF ENGLISH LITERATURE

OLD ENGLISH LITERATURE

Introduction

The origins of English Literature go back to the period before the Norman Conquest, when a rich literary and cultural tradition, centred in the monasteries that were the repositories of early English Christianity, was developed. While much of the writing that emerged from the monasteries was written in Latin, Old English (or Anglo-Saxon), the language of the Germanic peoples who had first invaded England in the fifth century, emerged as one of the most prestigious early vernacular languages.

Beowulf and Old English Poetry

Old English poetry was mainly written in alliterative verse. It boasts one undisputed masterpiece, Beowulf, a heroic epic probably composed in the eighth century and preserved in a tenth century manuscript. In the first part, the Scandinavian protagonist, Beowulf, successfully defends his uncle's kingdom by killing the monster Grendel and, on the following night, Grendel's mother. In the second part, set fifty years later, Beowulf has himself become king. He once again saves his people, this time by slaying a dragon, but is fatally wounded in the process. Beowulf is considered a great poem, because of its assured epic tone, its moving alliterative verse and its powerful heroic narrative, which involves complex parallels between episodes. It also provides a detailed picture of a pagan Germanic culture, centred on an aristocratic mead hall and kinship loyalties. However, this culture is observed at a time of transition and numerous passages contain a strong vein of Christian morality. Other notable Anglo-Saxon poems also bring Germanic and Christian elements together. They include the elegies, The Wanderer and The Seafarer, The Battle of Maldon, which takes the heroic defeat of an English army by the Danes in 991 as its subject and more generally seems to be a celebration of fighting for a lost cause, poems on Old Testament themes such as Judith and Genesis A and Genesis B and visionary Christian works such as The Dream of the Rood.

Old English Prose

The best-known Old English prose work is the Anglo-Saxon Chronicle, a collection of texts that provides an invaluable historical record of events in the period, narrated in a circumstantial style that lacks the literary merit of the classics of Old English verse. The Chronicle originated in the reign of Alfred the Great, King of Wessex (871–99), a major patron of learning who was responsible for the translation of several important Latin works into English. These include Boethius's Consolation of Philosophy, St. Augustine's Soliloquies and the Ecclesiastical History of the English People by the Venerable Bede, an English monk who lived his life in Northumbria. Bede's History (c. 771) is widely regarded as the most important English work of its kind written before the Renaissance. The prose literature of the Anglo-Saxon period is also notable for homilies and translations of Classical, as well as Christian, texts.

After 1066, as a consequence of Norman rule, Old English lost ground to French and Latin as a literary language, particularly since it existed in numerous regional and local dialects. The records in the Anglo-Saxon Chronicle continue into the twelfth century, but the post-Norman Conquest entries are characterized by linguistic variations, which suggest the increasing fragmentation of the English language in the new political climate.

MIDDLE ENGLISH LITERATURE

The twelfth and thirteenth centuries were a comparatively quiet era in the annals of English literature. In contrast, the fourteenth century saw an efflorescence of writing in the various dialects of English. Foremost among the authors of this period was Geoffrey Chaucer, who wrote in the East Midland dialect of English, which gradually became accepted as the standard form of the language, although orthography and pronunciation continued to be extremely varied. Other major writers of the period included William Langland, the so-called Gawain poet and John Gower, who wrote in English, Latin and French. Towards the end of the medieval period, literature moved into a new phase with the invention of the printing press and one of the books published by the pioneer English printer, William Caxton, was Sir Thomas Malory's masterpiece the Morte D'Arthur, which crystallized many of the concerns of the Age of Chivalry.

Other significant literature of the period includes a broad range of anonymous oral ballads and equally anonymous religious and secular lyrics. The period also saw the beginnings of significant English drama in the shape of morality plays and the cycles of mystery plays, which were popular from the thirteenth to the sixteenth century. Although much of the literature of the medieval era is religious in outlook, reflecting the extent to which social life was shaped by Christian belief, the emergence of a writer such as Chaucer signals a more secular approach that looks forward to the Humanist spirit of the Renaissance. Elsewhere spiritual and secular concerns are not so sharply divided as the modern reader may initially suppose: the mystery plays were performed by trade guilds and included episodes that deviated from their ostensibly devotional purpose. Similarly medieval religious lyrics frequently employ the language of profane love in sacred contexts.

William Langland

Langland's allegorical masterpiece, Piers Plowman exists in three versions, dating from around 1360 to 1387. Little is known about the poet himself, though he wrote in the West Midlands dialect and his work demonstrates a familiarity with parts of modern Worcestershire. The main form of Piers Plowman is a dream vision, but it does not employ this mode consistently. It moves between abstract personification and specific representation of aspects of late fourteenth-century social life. Its dreamer protagonist experiences considerable difficulties as he wrestles with personifications of his moral weaknesses and the poem ends with his realization that his quest for spiritual regeneration must commence all over again. At the same time, through a series of interlocking allegories, it represents the corrupt state of secular society and the Church of the day. The figure of Piers Plowman appears intermittently as an embodiment of the ideal Christian life, as incarnated in a distinctively West Midlands rural form.

The Gawain Poet

Sir Gawain and the Green Knight is the best-known work of a poet who is also believed to have composed three religious allegories, Pearl, Patience and Cleanness, which have survived in the same manuscript. The poems were written in the West Midlands dialect of English in the second half of the fourteenth century. There is no external evidence to corroborate the assumption that all four are the work of a single author, but internal evidence and their common source suggest this. Gawain and the Green Knight is an Arthurian romance written in alliterative verse. Its intricate narrative tells how a mysterious outsider, the green knight, comes to King Arthur's court one New Year's Eve and challenges any of the knights to deal him a single axeblow, to be returned by the green knight a year later. Sir Gawain accepts the challenge and delivers an apparently mortal blow when he decapitates the green knight. However, the knight picks up his head and leaves, reminding Gawain of his promise. The following year Gawain journeys to the knight's home at the Green Chapel and experiences a series of events in which his integrity is tested and finally found partly wanting. He is punished accordingly, when the third of three feints the knight delivers lightly nicks his neck. The main events of the poem have been interpreted as an allegory of seasonal renewal, in which chivalric values are thrown into conflict with an older set of English values associated with pagan traditions of ritual regeneration.

Pearl, *Patience* and *Cleanness* are also moral homilies, but are more obviously Christian. *Pearl* is a dream allegory about death containing a vision of the New Jerusalem from the *Book of Revelation*. *Patience* takes its didactic lesson from the story of Jonah. *Cleanness* (also known as *Purity*) employs a broad range of Old and New Testament references.

GEOFFREY CHAUCER (c. 1343–1400)

Chaucer's Life

In addition to being the foremost English writer of his era, Chaucer held a number of prominent public offices, initially under the patronage of John of Gaunt and his *Book of the Duchess* (c. 1369) is generally considered to be an elegy for Gaunt's wife, Blanche of Lancaster. The son of a London vintner, Chaucer studied at the Inner Temple and saw military service in France during Edward III's campaigns in the Hundred Years War. He held a number of positions at court and travelled abroad on diplomatic missions to France and Italy, which was to be a particularly important influence on his development as a writer and where he may have met Boccaccio and Petrarch. In 1374 he became a customs controller in the port of London. During the last two decades of his life, when he was composing his *magnum opus*, *The Canterbury Tales*, he held appointments as knight of the shire for Kent, Clerk of the King's Works and a deputy forester in Somerset. On his death, he was buried in Westminster Abbey. When Edmund Spenser was laid to rest beside him two centuries later in 1599, their tombs became the basis of Poets' Corner, though Chaucer's burial in the Abbey was not in recognition of his poetic achievement, but because he had been Clerk of Works in the building of Westminster Palace.

Chaucer's Masterpiece

Chaucer's masterpiece, *The Canterbury Tales* (begun c. 1387) comprises the General Prologue, which describes the coming together of a group of travellers about to embark on a pilgrimage to Thomas à Becket's shrine in Canterbury, at the Tabard Inn in Southwark, and twenty-four tales told on the pilgrimage itself: two by the figure of Chaucer himself; the remainder by members of the company. It is often believed to have been inspired by Boccaccio's *Decameron*, in which a hundred tales are told during the course of ten days by ten fugitives from plague-ridden Florence. However, Chaucer does not acknowledge a direct debt to Boccaccio and there are other precedents for linked series of stories in the medieval period. The pilgrims' tavern host, Harry Bailly, proposes that each of them should tell four stories, two on the road to Canterbury and two on the return journey; and he promises the teller of the best tale a free supper. This scheme is never completed and the prize is not awarded, but *The Canterbury Tales* remains the outstanding literary achievement of the fourteenth century, offering a panoramic view of the various orders of society, lay and clerical, with each of the pilgrims being subject to scrutiny by Chaucer's discerning and judicious eye. Incomplete though it is, the series' linking of characters and tales and its exchanges of dialogue between the various pilgrims lend it a degree of dramatic unity rare in such sequences.

The General Prologue provides thumbnail sketches of twenty-one of the pilgrims, each of whom is realized as a rounded figure through a deft and economic choice of characterizing physical and moral qualities. Chaucer's tone varies and while some of the characters are viewed as exemplars of virtue, he characteristically draws attention to their failings through the medium of a laconic irony, which moves between gentle mockery and more savage condemnation and establishes him as the first great English satirist. Similarly, some of the characters, such as "the verray parfit gentil knight", are

rendered as idealized types, but more generally the portraiture of the Prologue is highly individualized and moves away from the allegorical characterization typical of much medieval literature. Its characters provide a vivid cross-section of the society of the period and collectively can be seen as a social microcosm. They include: representatives of chivalric society, such as the knight and his squire; clerical figures, including a monk, a friar and a prioress; and people engaged in a wide variety of secular occupations, among them a lawyer, a miller, a merchant, a cook and a physician. Though the majority of the pilgrims are men and the few female travellers are mainly members of religious orders, Chaucer's ensemble is notable for the presence of one of the most vividly realized female characters in early English writing, the Wife of Bath.

The tales themselves demonstrate a remarkable variety of range, tone and subject-matter. Taken together, they offer an encyclopaedic overview of many of the literary and cultural concerns of the period. They move between tragic romances such as *The Knight's Tale*, narratives that probe complex moral issues, such as *The Franklin's Tale*, parodies such as Chaucer's *Tale of Sir Thopas* and ribald and bawdy comic works, such as *The Miller's Tale*. The predominant metre of the work is rhyming couplets, but again Chaucer's approach is exceptionally diverse: he employs a wide range of verse forms as well as occasionally, as in the *Tale of Melibee*, writing in prose. The tales draw on an extensive range of medieval literary forms, including saints' lives, verse romance, *fabliau* (a tale form, often centred on a battle of wits and containing scatological and other forms of broad comic humour) and homily.

In *The Nun's Priest's Tale*, widely regarded as a work that typifies the ambiguity of Chaucer's tone, an apparently mock-heroic animal fable, which moves between witty playfulness and complex philosophical commentary, ends with a directive to take its pious moral seriously, leaving readers to decide whether to follow this instruction or to view it as an example of Chaucer's sly irony. *The Wife of Bath's Tale* is preceded by a lengthy prologue in which the wife provides an autobiographical account of her life, including details of her five marriages. This draws on anti-feminist literary conventions of the period, but again Chaucer's complexity of tone opens up the possibility of reading the Wife as a prototype feminist. In contrast, her tale, which is taken from the popular medieval story of "the loathly lady", is uncharacteristically serious. It does, however, demonstrate continuity with its prologue, since it is also about women's "maistrie" (or sovereignty) over men, suggesting that Chaucer may be more concerned with thematic links than consistent characterization.

Other Works by Chaucer

After *The Canterbury Tales*, *Troilus and Criseyde* (c. 1385) is generally considered to be Chaucer's finest achievement. Written in rhyme royal, it is a narrative poem of over 8,000 lines, which has been called the first English novel. Set inside Troy during the Trojan War, it describes how the warrior Troilus falls in love with Criseyde, how they are brought together by her uncle and guardian Pandare, how Criseyde subsequently betrays Troilus after they have been separated and how a grief-stricken Troilus is killed in battle. Chaucer appears to have taken the story from Boccaccio's *Il Filostrato*, but he develops his source-material into a highly complex moral fable, notable for the sophisticated rendition of its protagonists' psychologies. Typically Chaucerian in its ambiguity of tone, the poem mainly suggests a lofty, tragic vision of experience, which emphasizes the vanity of human life. However, it also includes comedy, mainly in the characterization of Pandare, and its closing sections contain a series of Christian and other moralizing reflections, which partly negate the tragic view.

Chaucer also wrote numerous other poems, several of which adapted French and Italian models into the English vernacular tradition, which he played a central part in developing. *The Book of the Duchess* and *The Parliament of Fowls* (c. 1380) were inspired by the French tradition of the allegorical dream poem. In the latter, a group of birds engage in a debate about marriage, which contrasts the ideal of courtly love with a more pragmatic approach. In the unfinished *House of Fame* (*c.* 1379), Chaucer parodied aspects of Dante's *Divine Comedy* in a cryptic dream vision, whose purpose remains uncertain. His other works include translations of Boethius's *De Consolatione* (*On the Consolation of Philosophy*) and part of one of the great classics of medieval romance literature, the French *Roman de la Rose*; and the prose work, *Treatise on the Astrolabe*, which is believed to have been written for his son, "little Lewis".

The Ballad

Ballads are short narrative poems of anonymous composition, originally intended to be sung. They customarily express and enforce aspects of the folk imagination and as a consequence of oral transmission, usually exist in several versions. The most popular stanza form employed in ballads involves alternating four-beat and three-beat lines and a similarly alternating rhyme scheme (abab), but ballads also employ numerous other forms. The ballad particularly flourished in Northern England and Scotland from around 1200 to 1700. Popular ballads of the period include "Lord Randal", "Sir Patrick Spens", "Edward", "The Unquiet Grave" and "Thomas Rhymer". Ballads treat a broad range of subjects, but prominent types deal with tragic family themes, romantic love, the supernatural and the exploits of outlaws such as the legendary Robin Hood, whose myth was spread through ballads dating from the fourteenth century.

Morality and Mystery Plays

Often grouped together, morality and mystery plays represent two distinct forms of medieval drama. Morality plays were dramatized allegories of virtues and vices fighting for a human soul. The first morality plays date from the early fifteenth century, but the form continued to be popular in the Elizabethan period at the time of the upheavals brought about by the Reformation. *The Castle of Perseverance* (*c.* 1420), *Mankind* (*c.* 1465) and *Everyman* (*c.* 1510) are the best-known examples of the form. In John Skelton's *Magnyfycence* (*c.* 1515), a late example of the genre, an excessively magnanimous prince is ruined by his generosity, before being educated into more prudent behaviour by qualities such as Good Hope, Circumspection and Perseverance.

In England mystery plays, sometimes also known as "miracle plays", were based on Biblical subjects. (In other parts of Europe the term "miracle plays" was reserved for stories of saints' lives.) Initially mystery plays were staged in churches on religious holidays such as Corpus Christi and Whitsuntide. Later they became more secular and were staged in market places by trade guilds. Hence the use of the name "mystery", which derives from the Middle English word for a skilled trade. Increasingly, the plays were performed as sequences. Cycles of English mystery plays from York, Chester, Coventry and Wakefield have come down to posterity almost intact. They are notable for their blend of simple homiletic instruction and interludes of broad comic portraiture.

Sir Thomas Malory (died *c.* 1471)

One of the earliest books printed in England, Malory's *Morte D'Arthur* (1485; written *c.* 1469) is the greatest English contribution to "the matter of Britain", the widely circulating corpus of stories about the Arthurian legend. Written in prose, the *Morte D'Arthur* is divided into eight tales and twenty-one books. The tales begin with the story of Arthur's birth and early life and the establishment of the Round Table and conclude with a narrative of the collapse of his court, when he discovers his wife Guinevere's adultery with Sir Lancelot, and his subsequent death in battle. The fifth tale, which tells the story of Tristram and Isolde (Tristan and Iseult), occupies almost half the work.

RENAISSANCE LITERATURE

Renaissance Poetry and Prose

During the Renaissance period, writers and thinkers turned to the Greek and Roman classics for cultural inspiration, replacing medieval literature's absorption in Christian and chivalric concerns with a Humanist spirit that encouraged scientific inquiry, a more eclectic approach to learning and an expansionist vigour that was as keen to develop new literary forms as it was to discover new worlds.

Characteristically, Renaissance men, such as Sir Walter Raleigh (*c.* 1554–1618), the famous courtier and adventurer, moved between active involvement in the public life of the day and literary and cultural pursuits, without becoming dilettantes. Raleigh not only wrote accounts of his travels in the *New World*, such as *A Discovery of the Empire of Guiana* (1596), and *The History of the World* (1614), but also a significant body of poetry, notable for its melancholy reflections on the transitory nature of existence. Conversely, John Donne (*see below*), who is best known as a poet, accompanied the Earl of Essex and Raleigh on expeditions against the Spanish. Henry VIII's Lord Chancellor, Sir Thomas More (1478–1535), who was executed for his unbending allegiance to papal authority, produced *Utopia* (1515) which gave a name to the genre of writing about ideal fictional states that had been founded nearly two millennia earlier by Plato's *Republic*.

Sir Thomas Wyatt (*c.* 1503–42) and Henry Howard, Earl of Surrey (*c.* 1517–47) pioneered several of the metres and conventions that became staples of English verse during the next three centuries. They introduced the Petrarchan form of the sonnet and *terza rima*, the three-line stanza used by Dante in the *Divine Comedy*, into English; and Surrey's translation of parts of Virgil's *Aeneid* established blank verse (unrhymed iambic pentameters) as the standard metre of much subsequent English poetry, including Elizabethan dramatic verse and narrative long poems, varying from Milton's *Paradise Lost* to Wordsworth's *Prelude*. Neither Wyatt nor Surrey saw their poems published in their own lifetime. Both were better known for their public activities. So too was another Renaissance man, Sir Philip Sidney (1554–86), whose major works were also published posthumously. His *Astrophel and Stella* (1591) is the most famous of the pre-Shakespearean sonnet sequences. Sidney's *Arcadia* (1590) blends prose romance with verse eclogue to create an idealized, pastoral world, inspired by Virgil and other classical poets.

Edmund Spenser (*c.* 1552–99)

Spenser's masterpiece, *The Faerie Queene* (1590–96) is both a definitive work of the Elizabethan age, drawing on the heroic traditions of classical epic, and the last great English example of a medieval romance. The "queene" of the title is Gloriana, or Elizabeth I, and the poet celebrates her reign and authority in a series of adventures set in the courtly past, in each of which one of her knights exemplifies a particular virtue in action. Spenser invented his own unique nine-line stanza (with the rhyme-scheme ababbcbcc). This became known as the Spenserian stanza and was subsequently used by Romantic poets such as Byron and Keats in an endeavour to recapture the spirit of the medieval world, in a manner not dissimilar from Spenser's attempt to invest his own period with medieval values. Spenser's other works include a pastoral sequence expressing nostalgia for a past golden age, *The Shephearde's Calender* (1579), a collection of love sonnets, *Amoretti* (1595) and the marriage song *Epithalamion* (1595).

Christopher Marlowe (1564–93)

Marlowe preceded Shakespeare as the first great tragic dramatist of the Elizabethan age. He also established the blank verse line as the dominant metre of the drama of the period, refining its use beyond that of its earlier exponents. His plays mostly deal with megalomaniac protagonists, whose obsession with an extreme form of power or knowledge leads to their downfall. *Tamburlaine the Great* (Parts I and II, 1587) narrates the rise and fall of a military overreacher in characteristically hyperbolic language. In *The Jew of Malta* (*c.* 1590) the protagonist, Barabas, is a Machiavellian hero-villain, whose revenge on the Christian society that confiscates his wealth attracts a good deal of sympathy.

More complex in characterization than Marlowe's

earlier tragedies, but less extravagant in its versification, *Edward II* (1592) did much to establish the genre of the Elizabethan historical play. It anticipates Shakespeare's *Richard II* as a tragedy of a weak king betrayed by favourites and a tendency towards histrionic behaviour, though Marlowe places more emphasis on shifting fortune as a cause of tragedy.

Dr Faustus (1594) is a tragedy of damnation, which also anticipates Shakespeare, in this case *Macbeth*, in certain respects. It is, however, more explicitly theological, demonstrating a debt to the medieval morality play (*see above*). It tells the story of the necromancer Faust, who sells his soul to the Devil in return for twenty-four years during which he will enjoy infinite power and knowledge. Though parts of the text are disputed, it contains some of Marlowe's finest verse, including the protagonist's famous response to a vision of Helen of Troy, whom he summons up as an ideal of womanhood: "Was this the face that launched a thousand ships?"; and his poignant monologue as he awaits his tragic fate: "See, see, where Christ's blood streams in the firmament!"

Marlowe's work as a poet includes *Hero and Leander* (1598) and the song "The Passionate Shepherd to His Love" (1599). His outspoken views and notorious private life led to his being accused of atheism, blasphemy and homosexuality. He was allegedly involved in criminal activities on more than one occasion and eventually murdered in a Deptford tavern, possibly as a result of his involvement in espionage, but more probably as a consequence of a dispute over the bill.

The University Wits

"The University Wits" is the name given to the group of writers particularly responsible for the rapid rise of Elizabethan drama as the pre-eminent cultural form of the day during the last two decades of the sixteenth century, but also notable for their achievements in prose. Their plays includes Robert Greene's *Friar Bacon and Friar Bungay* (1589) and George Peele's *The Old Wives' Tale* (1595). Their prose works include John Lyly's romances *Euphues: The Anatomy of Wit* (1578) and *Euphues and His England* (1580) and Thomas Nashe's picaresque *The Unfortunate Traveller* (1594). *The Spanish Tragedy* (1592) by Thomas Kyd, another highly popular play of the late sixteenth century, anticipates Jacobean tragedy in its extensive use of violence and themes of madness and revenge.

Francis Bacon (1551–1626)

One of the leading public figures of the day, Bacon held the offices of Solicitor-General, Attorney-General, Lord Keeper of the Seal and Lord Chancellor of England, before falling from office in disgrace in 1621. He was the central English figure in the movement away from the Scholasticism of the medieval clerics, the dominant intellectual tradition at the beginning of his life, towards the Humanism that came to be seen as the embodiment of the Renaissance spirit. In *The Advancement of Learning* (1605) and *Novum Organum* (1620), he argued for a new spirit of empirical scientific inquiry that would be the scholarly equivalent of the great Elizabethan voyages of discovery.

His other works include the unfinished utopian fiction *The New Atlantis* (1627), in which a group of English sailors discover a Pacific island, where a college of sciences that can be seen as a blueprint for the Royal Society (subsequently founded in England in 1660) flourishes. Some commentators who have cast doubts on Shakespeare's authorship of his plays have asserted the claims of Bacon as a more likely author of "Shakespeare".

WILLIAM SHAKESPEARE (1564–1616)

Shakespeare's Life

Comparatively little is known about the life of England's greatest dramatist. He was born in Stratford-upon-Avon in 1564, probably educated at the local grammar school and in 1582 married Anne Hathaway, who bore him three children: a daughter, Susanna, and the twins Judith and Hamnet, who died at the age of eleven. Some time

between the years 1585 and 1592, Shakespeare left Stratford and pursued a career as an actor and dramatist in London. After initially struggling to establish himself, he became a founder member of one of the leading theatrical companies of the day, the Lord Chamberlain's Men, in 1594 and by the mid-1590s his reputation as the period's leading playwright was assured. His greatest works belong to the latter part of this decade and the first years of the seventeenth century. Many were first performed at the Globe Theatre, built on the south bank of the Thames in 1599, in which Shakespeare was a shareholder. Somewhere around 1613, when the Globe burned down, he appears to have left London and spent the last years of his life in Stratford, where he died and was buried in 1616. The posthumous collection of his plays in the First Folio of 1623 ensured their preservation for posterity, though many also exist in earlier quarto editions. The evidence for precise dating of his plays is often slim. Here they are grouped by period or genre.

Early Plays: 1590–95

Shakespeare's first plays offer glimpses of his later genius, but are frequently indistinguishable from the work of his dramatic contemporaries. The first of the three parts of *Henry VI* is of uncertain authorship, but the plays are among Shakespeare's earliest dramatic work. *Richard III*, a more accomplished history play with a memorable hero-villain, is often grouped with them.

Shakespeare's early comedies frequently take their subjects from classical drama and are heavily reliant on farce and situational humour, often built around disguise, mistakes and trickery. They include *The Comedy of Errors*, *The Taming of the Shrew* and *The Two Gentlemen of Verona*. *Love's Labour's Lost* is a virtuoso satire of inflated language, such as that used in Lyly's *Euphues*, though Shakespeare displays an obvious relish for the wordplay and linguistic excess that are the ostensible objects of his irony.

He also wrote two tragedies during this period. Popular in its own day, *Titus Andronicus*, which has much in common with a play such as Kyd's *Spanish Tragedy* in its use of violence, madness and revenge, is probably Shakespeare's earliest tragedy. *Romeo and Juliet*, the legendary story of the "star-cross'd lovers" who become victims of their feuding Verona families' enmity towards one another, is a more carefully plotted and moving work, which has retained its popularity across the centuries.

History Plays and Roman Plays: 1595–1608

While they ostensibly deal with subject-matter from England's past, Shakespeare's history plays often have an allegorical relevance to Tudor debates about the Constitution and good government. So too do his Roman plays. After the three parts of *Henry VI* and *Richard III*, Shakespeare wrote a second tetralogy of history plays (1595–99). This begins with *Richard II*, a tragic study of a monarch who, like Marlow's *Edward II*, proves unsuited to kingship. The poetic dreamer, Richard, loses his throne to his more pragmatic cousin, Bolingbroke, who becomes Henry IV in the next two plays of the tetralogy. *Henry IV*, Parts I and II are, however, as much concerned with the coming of age of Henry's son, Prince Hal, the future Henry V, as with his own struggles to put down rebellions.

The two plays are also notable for one of Shakespeare's richest comic creations, Falstaff, a larger-than-life character who has affinities with the medieval Lord of Misrule figure, but whose complexity frustrates easy labels. Initially, Prince Hal enjoys Falstaff's convivial company, but when he becomes king at the end of the second part, he disowns him, in a scene which some commentators feel demonstrates his hard-heartedness, in order to assume the duties of his role. In *Henry V*, he takes on the mantle of England's military leader in battles against the French and the play has remained popular as a celebration of nationalism. Falstaff reappears in the comedy *The Merry Wives of Windsor* (c. 1600), allegedly revived at Queen Elizabeth's request.

Shakespeare's histories also include the less highly regarded *King John* (c. 1596) and parts of *Henry VIII* (c. 1612), which was probably a collaboration with John Fletcher.

The Roman plays, *Julius Caesar*, *Antony and Cleopatra* and *Coriolanus*, belong to the years 1599–1608. Like the history plays, *Julius Caesar* has obvious relevance to contemporary debates about government. When Caesar is assassinated, the motivation of his killers is complex. The integrity of their leader Brutus, "the noblest Roman of them all", is never seriously questioned, though the actions taken to avenge Caesar by Mark Anthony, whose oration over his dead body is an outstanding example of persuasive political rhetoric, are also presented sympathetically. In *Antony and Cleopatra*, Antony is torn between the Roman values of reason and political calculation and Cleopatra's Egyptian world of obsessive passion. His love for Cleopatra leads to his neglect of duty, with tragic consequences for both protagonists. *Cymbeline* depicts the tragedy of a Roman hero destroyed by his pride and haughty aloofness from the people.

Comedies: 1595–1600

Shakespeare's most famous comedies, *Much Ado About Nothing*, *As You Like It* and *Twelfth Night*, belong to his middle period (1598–1600). They were preceded by *A Midsummer Night's Dream* (1595–6), a comic fantasy in which a group of rustics stage their version of a tragic love story, with hilarious consequences. The rustics' play is, however, located in a world where serious romantic values have been turned upside down for a single night by fairies. The middle comedies use idealized settings and romantic plots and move between broad humour and a more serious examination of male-female relationships and social attitudes. *Much Ado About Nothing* includes one of Shakespeare's most memorable couples, Beatrice and Benedick, whose verbal sparring makes their relationship much more dramatically animated than that of the play's more conventional romantic lovers, Claudio and Hero. *Twelfth Night* contrasts the values of "cakes and ale" with a more Puritanical approach to social conduct that had come to characterize areas of Elizabethan life. The middle comedies make extensive use of disguise, pretence and mistaken identity. These elements are both a source of humour and a basis for a probing investigation of issues of identity.

The Great Tragedies: 1600–6

Shakespeare's most famous tragedies, *Hamlet*, *Othello*, *King Lear* and *Macbeth*, were written in the early years of the seventeenth century. They are generally regarded as his greatest achievement, containing some of his finest dramatic verse and exploring the ambiguities of human behaviour through a focus on the forces that lead to the downfall of their essentially noble male protagonists.

The plays have generally, though not always, been viewed as tragedies of character rather than fate and each of the heroes has weaknesses that cause his tragedy. Thus the undoing of Othello, a Moorish general in the service of the Venetian Republic, has frequently been attributed to his jealousy and his malleability in the hands of the villain, Iago. However, from another point of view his tragedy can be seen as that of a racial outsider in a European society, which respects his professional abilities but is less generous towards him when he marries a senator's daughter. In a play that can be seen as a companion-piece to this aspect of *Othello*, the tragic-comic *Merchant of Venice* (1596–7), the Jewish moneylender Shylock is also denied the same basic human rights as other Venetians, though he is less sympathetically portrayed than Othello. Hamlet's tragedy has been ascribed to numerous causes, among them his inability to move from introspection to action and his Oedipal love for his mother. Macbeth, a killer-poet who becomes king after murdering those who stand in his way, can be seen as a later version of Richard III. Egged on by his wife, Shakespeare's most compelling female villain, he becomes a personification of the dictum that power corrupts. Shakespeare's most wide-ranging tragedy, *King Lear*, focuses on an ageing protagonist whose lack of self-knowledge prevents him from distinguishing between the hypocrisy of his two elder daughters and the sincerity and love of his youngest. Towards the end

of the play, in a movement which anticipates the mood of Shakespeare's late romances, he learns the truth, but only when he is dying as a "foolish fond old man". *Lear* is, however, more than simply a tragedy of character; it also depicts human beings as the "sport" of the gods, powerless to resist the forces of fate.

Problem Plays: 1601–5

All's Well That Ends Well, *Measure for Measure* and *Troilus and Cressida* have generally been referred to as Shakespeare's "problem plays". They were written around the same time as the great tragedies and have also been called "bitter comedies". The three plays are problematic, not only because of the difficulty of classifying them as any particular form of drama, such as tragedy or comedy, but also because of their complex treatment of moral questions, which are frequently left unresolved. The troubling treatment of sexuality and politics in *Measure for Measure* has increased its popularity in recent decades and it has been seen to have considerable contemporary relevance. *Two Noble Kinsmen* (c. 1613), to which Shakespeare probably contributed, in which case it was his last dramatic work, has also been classified as a problem play.

The Late Romances: 1609–11

In his three late plays, *Cymbeline*, *The Winter's Tale* and *The Tempest*, Shakespeare subsumes tragedy in a larger vision of reconciliation and regeneration, a mood anticipated by a play such as *King Lear*, where the tragic consequences of actions still prove inescapable. Sometimes styled "tragic-comedies", the late romances create a form of drama that is uniquely their own, flouting many of the conventions of both classical and contemporary theatre in the process.

In each of the plays, the protagonist has to come to terms with a sin or omission and manages to do so through the agency of his daughter. *The Tempest*, usually seen as Shakespeare's final dramatic statement, is a particularly enigmatic play, which contains some of his finest poetry. It has been variously interpreted as an allegory of New World colonialism, in which Shakespeare was clearly interested, as a fable about the artistic neglect of worldly responsibilities and as a dramatic treatment of the pastoral contrast between primitive innocence and cultivated experience, which moves beyond a simple opposition between utopian nature and corrupt nurture. The play ends with the magician, Prospero, relinquishing his right to conjure up spirits and declaring "Now my charms are all o'erthrown,/ And what strength I have's mine own", an utterance which has been related to Shakespeare himself, who also appears to be forsaking *his* "art to enchant".

Shakespeare's Poetry

In addition to the plays, Shakespeare also produced a considerable body of non-dramatic verse, including two poems inspired by Ovid: the mythological erotic poem, *Venus and Adonis* (1593), which was his most popular work in his own life-time; and *The Rape of Lucrece* (1594), a narrative poem notable for its portrayal of the protagonist's psychological conflict. Shorter verse ascribed to Shakespeare includes contributions to *The Passionate Pilgrim* (1599), a collection published under his name, the metaphysical poem, "The Phoenix and the Turtle" (1601) and "A Lover's Complaint" (1609).

Shakespeare's *Sonnets* (1609) are his finest achievement in non-dramatic verse. They comprise 154 love poems, probably written between 1592 and 1598, in the fourteen-line verse-form that had been imported into England from Italy. Shakespeare reinvented the form, using the rhyme-scheme ababcdcdefefgg and thus establishing what has become known as the Shakespearean sonnet. The *Sonnets* fall into three main sequences: poems addressed to a young man, a "dark lady" and a rival poet. Sonnets 18 ("Shall I compare thee to a summer's day?") and 130 ("My mistress' eyes are nothing like the sun") are among the most quoted.

SEVENTEENTH-CENTURY LITERATURE

Jacobean Drama

Strictly speaking, "Jacobean drama" refers to plays produced during the reign of James I (1603-25), but the term is used more broadly to describe the theatre of the early seventeenth century, in which the expansionist mood of the Elizabethan age gave way to a more sombre and pessimistic vision, characteristic of the new era.

James came to the throne with the reputation of being a believer in witchcraft, which he had written about in his *Daemonologie* (1597); Robert Burton's *Anatomy of Melancholy* (c. 1621) provided a quasi-scientific classification of various forms of depression; tragedies, full of violence, cynicism and intrigue, captured the mood of Jacobean gloom; and John Marston's tragic-comedy, *The Malcontent* (1604), written in collaboration with John Webster, created the quintessential stage figure of the age, that of the malcontent or cynical outsider. The malcontent also appeared in the character of Bosola in Webster's *Duchess of Malfi* (1623) and even Hamlet can be seen as an early version of the type.

John Webster (c.1580–c.1632) and John Ford (1586–c. 1640)

Despite their reputation for unrelieved cynicism and gloom, vigorous language lends the best Jacobean tragedies as much dramatic energy as their more optimistic Elizabethan forerunners. The most famous tragic playwrights of the period were John Webster and John Ford. Webster's *The White Devil* (1612) and *The Duchess of Malfi* are revenge plays based on historical events with Italian settings. Centred on the political and personal intrigue popularly associated with Renaissance Italy, they achieve their effect through dramatically powerful individual scenes and set-pieces, in which murders, sensational violence, madness and destructive passion loom large.

Ford's best-known plays, *The Broken Heart* (1633) and *'Tis Pity She's a Whore* (1633) place as much emphasis on pathos as tragedy. In *'Tis Pity*, the plot centres on the tragic love of a brother and sister, but the play goes beyond the sensationalism of the incest theme through its use of moving verse and imagery. Other outstanding tragedies of the period include Cyril Tourneur's *Revenger's Tragedy* (1607) and Thomas Middleton and William Rowley's masterpiece *The Changeling* (c. 1622).

Ben Jonson (1572–1637)

Jonson was the leading comic dramatist of the period. His plays *Every Man in his Humour* (1598) and *Every Man out of his Humour* (1599) were first performed in the Elizabethan era, but his best-known work belongs to the Jacobean age, during which he enjoyed royal patronage and wrote a number of court masques with scenery designed by the famous architect Inigo Jones. He is noted for his *Comedy of Humours*, in which particular characters represent an aspect, or Humour, of humanity. Based on early medical beliefs about the forces that determine character (blood, phlegm, melancholy and choler), this approach can be seen as the basis for the type-characters of Restoration Comedy and of later novelists such as Henry Fielding and Charles Dickens.

Jonson's major plays are *Volpone or the Fox* (1605-6), which despite its Venetian setting is generally viewed as a satire on the emergent London merchant classes; and *Epicene, or, The Silent Woman* (1609), *The Alchemist* (1610) and *Bartholomew Fair* (1614), in each of which trickery is an impetus for the action. Jonson also wrote a body of non-dramatic verse, which includes *Epigrams* (1616), *The Forest* (1616) and *The Underwood* (1640), and the tragedy *Sejanus* (1603). The circle of poets who wrote under his influence were known as "the tribe of Ben". They include Robert Herrick, Richard Lovelace and Sir John Suckling.

Francis Beaumont's *The Knight of the Burning Pestle* (1607) is a satire of aspects of contemporary taste, which employs the form of a play-within-a-play. A grocer interrupts the frame-play, "The London Merchant", to insist that his apprentice be given a part. This wish is granted and the apprentice's subsequent appearance as a grocer-errant pokes fun at both middle-class cultural aspirations and chivalric conventions.

The Metaphysical Poets

"Metaphysical" is the term generally used to classify a number of seventeenth-century poets, including John Donne, George Herbert, Andrew Marvell, Thomas Carew, Thomas Traherne, Richard Crashaw, Henry Vaughan and Abraham Cowley. These poets have been called "metaphysical", because of their use of elaborate conceits (metaphors, similes and other forms of imagery) and paradoxes. However, this is only one aspect of their primarily lyric verse technique and there are as many differences between them as there are similarities.

Recent attempts to replace the "metaphysical" label have included calling the poets "the School of Donne" and "the Fantasticks", but these are only marginally more useful terms, particularly since the poets had little sense of themselves as a group. The most famous of all metaphysical conceits is John Donne's comparison, in his poem "A Valediction Forbidding Mourning", of two lovers to the twin points of a compass: the suggestion is that however far they may stray from one another, the lovers remained linked. Other metaphysical images are drawn from cartography, science, Scripture and medicine.

The term "metaphysical" originated in the early seventeenth century with William Drummond, who used it in a censorious way to attack those of his poetic contemporaries who used metaphysical ideas. Towards the end of the century, John Dryden criticized Donne by saying "He affects the metaphysics in his amorous verses . . . where nature only should reign".

In the eighteenth century, writing from a neo classical point of view, founded on a belief in the commonality of human experience, Samuel Johnson attacked the poets' use of extravagant and highly specialized imagery as "a kind of *discordia concors*", in which "the most heterogeneous ideas are yoked by violence together". Johnson's attack contributed to the decline of the poets' reputation. This lasted until an influential 1921 review by T.S. Eliot helped rehabilitate the poets and reclaim "metaphysical" from being a term of abuse. Eliot praised the "metaphysicals" for their "direct sensuous apprehension of thought" and "recreation of thought into feeling", qualities that had been denied them by commentators such as Johnson.

John Donne (1572–1631)

Donne's work can be divided into two main categories: the secular love poetry of his "Songs and Sonnets"; and a body of devotional writing, which includes his "Holy Sonnets" and sermons, that was mainly written in the later part of his life, after he was ordained into the Anglican Church in 1615. He became Dean of St. Paul's in 1621 and was famed as one of the finest preachers of his age. It is, however, mistaken to draw a sharp distinction between the secular and spiritual aspects of Donne's writing.

An attempt to spiritualise the carnal side of his nature characterizes much of his amorous verse and his work is surprisingly modern in the openness and psychological complexity of its treatment of sexual passion. His divine poetry moves in the opposite direction, frequently using physically direct language in spiritual contexts, as when he asks God to ravish his soul. It often expresses doubt, not about Christian doctrine, but about whether the poet himself, as a particular sinner, will be saved from damnation.

Donne's complex metaphysical imagery is tempered by a conversational directness rare among his poetic predecessors and, since the rehabilitation of the metaphysical poets in the early twentieth century, his poetry has been viewed as particularly modern. His most famous love poems include "The Ecstasy", "The Canonization", "The Sun Rising", "The Good Morrow", "The Flea", "A Valediction Forbidding Mourning" and "Go and Catch a Falling Star". His religious writing includes his sonnet to death ("Death be not proud"), his "Hymn to God the Father" and his Meditation 12, from which the phrases "No man is an island" and "Do not ask for whom the bell tolls, it tolls for thee" have passed into the language. Donne also produced numerous epigrams, elegies and some early satirical verse.

George Herbert (1593–1633)

Like Donne's, Herbert's poetry demonstrates metrical variety, conversational directness and a highly imaginative use of conceits. It is, however, more consistently devotional than Donne's. Most of Herbert's work appeared in *The Temple* (1633), a poetic testament in which the various parts are intricately arranged to provide a moving and multi-faceted expression of his Christian faith. It deals with the immature soul's progression towards salvation through immersion in central aspects of Christian belief, including the resurrection, the importance of the sacraments and the need for communal worship.

Herbert is particularly remembered for his two pattern-poems, "The Altar" and "Easter Wings", where the shape of the poem as it appears on the page mirrors its subject, but these are his only poems of this kind. "The Collar" and "Jordan", I and II, are among his other best-known poems. His elder brother, Edward, Lord Herbert of Cherbury, was also a notable metaphysical poet.

Andrew Marvell (1621–78)

Marvell lived through the turbulent years of England's Civil War, occupying a number of political offices, including that of MP for Hull for nearly twenty years. His poetry exhibits a range of styles that both reflect the political vicissitudes of the period and his remarkable personal capacity to capture different moods. Although he excelled as a writer of witty metaphysical verse, his most lasting achievement is his lyric poetry, which includes one of the greatest English love poems, "To His Coy Mistress". His long poem, "Upon Appleton House", which was dedicated to the parliamentarian general, Sir Thomas Fairfax, celebrates the virtues of the rural country house as a retreat from the schisms of seventeenth-century life.

Marvell's capacity to balance opposed perspectives with a judiciousness rare in the period is seen at its best in his "Horatian Ode upon Cromwell's Return from Ireland", which carefully distributes its sympathies between Charles I and the avowed subject of the ode, Cromwell. Marvell was John Milton's assistant during the last years of the Commonwealth period (1657–60) and is credited with having intervened to save Milton from imprisonment and possible execution at the time of the Restoration. In his later years, he deserted the lyric for panegyrics and satires concerned with public issues.

Women Writers of the Seventeenth Century

While seventeenth-century public life was largely the preserve of men and few women writers were published in their own lifetime, recent research has directed attention to the very significant literary achievements of the female authors of the period. Lady Mary Wroth's prose romance *Urania* (1621) achieved a degree of contemporary notoriety through its treatment of court scandals. Today it is more interesting as an early feminist classic. It tells the stories of several women in unhappy marriages or relationships and in search of identities that are independent of men. Margaret Cavendish, Duchess of Newcastle, apologised for her "audacity in writing at all, being a woman", but nevertheless produced twenty-two works in a range of genres, including *Poems and Fancies* (1653) and *The Description of a New World called the Blazing World* (1666), an early science-fiction romance. Dorothy Osborne is noted for a volume of just seventy-seven letters, mainly written to her future husband, Sir William Temple, Jonathan Swift's patron, between 1652 and 1654. Collectively, the letters form a miniature masterpiece that provides a vivid insight into upper-class seventeenth-century domestic life and the writer's own introspective psyche. The prolific Aphra Behn wrote the short novel *Oroonoko, or The Royal Slave* (1688), about an African-born prince, who leads an unsuccessful slave rebellion in Surinam, and numerous dramatic comedies (*see later*).

Restoration Drama

In 1642, when Cromwell and his Puritan supporters, who believed that acting was an immoral pursuit, gained control of Parliament, the London theatres were closed. They did not reopen until the accession of Charles II in 1660. The drama of the next forty years is generally called "Restoration Drama", though there are considerable differences between plays produced in the early part of the period and those staged in the closing decades of the seventeenth century. Comedy was the dominant form of the era, though heroic plays such as Dryden's *Aureng-Zebe* (1676) and his retelling of the Antony and Cleopatra story, *All for Love* (1678), and Thomas Otway's *Venice Preserved* (1682) also made a distinctive contribution to the development of the English theatre of the period.

Restoration Comedy is notable for its use of type-characters, in the tradition of Ben Jonson's *Comedy of Humours* (*see* **M9**). Such types include foppish noblemen, witty young women, rakes, cuckolds, promiscuous wives, country gentlemen and scheming servants. The early comedies of the period reacted against Puritan prudery by depicting cynically amoral upper-class relationships, employing plots centred on sexual and financial intrigues and making extensive use of wit, bawdy and innuendo. Their attitude to gender relations has sometimes been seen as a reflection of the debauchery of the aristocratic society of Charles II's court. William Wycherley's *The Country Wife* (1675), in which a countrywoman newly arrived in London quickly becomes adept in the licentious ways of the capital, is one of the finest examples of this phase of Restoration Comedy. Wycherley's other plays include *The Plain Dealer* (1676).

Wit continues to be a staple of the later plays, but a subtler Comedy of Manners replaces the broad humour of the earlier drama. In William Congreve's *The Way of the World* (1700), the culminating achievement of Restoration comedy, courtship and marriage remain central concerns, but they are explored through a more questioning and sensitive use of witty repartee. Congreve's other comedies include *The Double Dealer* (1693) and *Love for Love* (1695). *The Way of the World* was written in the wake of the Anglican clergyman, Jeremy Collier's *Short View of the Immorality and the Profaneness of the English Stage* (1698), which played a significant part in changing attitudes towards theatrical propriety and decency. Early eighteenth-century comedy was to desert the broad humour of the Restoration play for a more sentimental form of comedy.

Other notable Restoration dramatists include George Etherege, author of *The Man of Mode* (1676), the famous architect Sir John Vanbrugh, who wrote *The Relapse* (1696) and Thomas Southerne, author of *The Wives' Excuse* (1691), which exposes the effects of the sexual hypocrisy of the period on women. In Shakespeare's plays, female roles had been played by boys; in Restoration comedy women's parts were now taken by actresses, one of whom was Charles II's mistress, Nell Gwyn. The period also saw the emergence of a professional woman dramatist, Aphra Behn, whose plays, which include *The Rover* (1677), *The City Heiress* (1682) and *The Lucky Chance* (1686), offer a more serious investigation of gender relations than can be found in most, if not all, of her male contemporaries. Behn's novel *Oroonoko* (*see above*) was dramatized by Southerne in a version first performed in 1695.

John Bunyan (1628–88)

Best-known for *The Pilgrim's Progress*, which remained the most widely read book in the English language, after the Authorized Version of the Bible, until the twentieth century, Bunyan wrote in a plain prose style that anticipates the novel. His first major work, *Grace Abounding to the Chief of Sinners* (1666), describes its author's conversion from a wicked early life and his subsequent call to the ministry. Typical of the Puritan spiritual autobiography of the period, it is a homiletic work, providing an example for others to follow, and has little in common with autobiographies which stress the subject's individuality.

Bunyan spent two periods in Bedford jail (1660–72 and 1675) for unlicensed preaching at a time when divine services could only be conducted according to the forms of the Church of England. He is believed to have written most of the first part of *Pilgrim's Progress* (1678) during his second period of imprisonment. It is a dream allegory which tells the story of an Everyman figure, Christian's journey from the City of Destruction to the Celestial City through such landscapes as the Slough of Despond, the Valley of the Shadow of Death, Doubting Castle and the country of Beulah. This is a "progress" which enacts the individual soul's journey to salvation. Travelling through these varied and difficult surroundings, Christian meets allegorical figures such as Worldly Wiseman, Hopeful and Giant Despair, who represent aspects of both his own character and of contemporary seventeenth-century life. Bunyan's simple, realistic prose has a Biblical quality. Though Christian moves through allegorical terrain, commentators have commented on Bunyan's realism and noted that the contours of his spiritual landscapes resemble those of his native Bedfordshire.

In the second part of *Pilgrim's Progress* (1684), Christian's wife, Christiana, follows in his footsteps, but her journey to heaven is less arduous than his, particularly since she receives more support along the way. This shift in emphasis may reflect Bunyan's desire to focus on the importance of community in the Christian struggle. His other major works, *The Life and Death of Mr Badman* (1680) and *The Holy War* (1682), are also religious allegories.

John Milton (1608–74)

England's greatest epic poet and one of its literature's most extraordinary polymaths, Milton was a Puritan who initially seems to have been drawn to a clerical career, but instead pursued his Christian beliefs and political convictions through the medium of literary works that linked Classical and Christian learning. He suffered from failing eyesight during the 1640s and was completely blind from 1652. The date of his famous "Sonnet on His Blindness" is uncertain, but it probably belongs to the mid-1650s. During the interregnum period he held office as Latin Secretary to the Council of State. In 1660 he published a revised edition of his *Ready and Easy Way to Establish a Free Commonwealth* (1659), a principled if imprudent argument for republicanism at a time when the monarchy was being restored. He was briefly jailed, but escaped a longer period of imprisonment, or possible execution. His masterpiece, the epic *Paradise Lost* (1667), which was probably begun before the Restoration, its sequel, *Paradise Regained* (1671) and his "Greek" tragedy, *Samson Agonistes* (1671), were products of his later years.

Milton's Early Works

Milton's early works include: "Ode upon the Morning of Christ's Nativity" (1629), the masque *Comus* (1637) and "L'Allegro" and "Il Penseroso" (1645; written *c.* 1631), a complementary pair of poems in octosyllabic couplets, which respectively illustrate the qualities of the happy, outgoing man and the melancholy, contemplative man. "Lycidas" (1637), a response to the drowning of Milton's Cambridge contemporary, Edward King, is one of the great English elegies. It expands from being a meditation on a premature individual death into a moving reflection on the transience of human life and the poet's own uncertainties about his personal future, before concluding with an expression of faith in the immortality of the soul. In the 1640s, Milton produced numerous prose pamphlets, including *The Doctrine and Discipline of Divorce* (1643), written shortly after his first wife, Mary, had left him a few weeks after their marriage, and *Areopagitica* (1644), a famous, early defence of freedom of the press.

Milton's Masterpiece

Paradise Lost is written in blank verse and employs many of the conventions of the Greek and Latin epics, including elevated language, a heroic theme, breadth of scope, the Invocation to the Muse (in this case the Greek muse of astronomy, Urania, now transformed into a Christian) and epic similes. The poem's declared purpose is "to justify the ways of God to men", but many critics have seen Milton's Satan as the greatest creation of the poem and taken the view that his use of classical heroic models is at odds with the avowed Christian message of the poem. The most famous expression of this viewpoint is the Romantic poet William Blake's contention that Milton was "a true poet and of the Devil's party without knowing it". If one agrees with such a reading, it lends support to the view that Milton's republican response to the political situation of his day led him, consciously or unconsciously, to adopt a revolutionary attitude towards authority, as represented by God in the poem.

However, although the first two books of *Paradise Lost* depict Satan in heroic terms, its later sections are more centrally concerned with its avowed subject, "man's first disobedience, and the fruit/ of that forbidden tree". They tell the story of Adam and Eve's expulsion from the garden of Eden in a lofty and dignified style which expands outwards from its ostensible subject to provide an encyclopaedic view of human history from a Christian point of view.

Two Diarists: Pepys and Evelyn

The Restoration period is also notable for the work of the two most famous English diarists. The diaries of the naval administrator Samuel Pepys (1633–1703) provide a vivid picture of London life from 1660 to 1669, including accounts of events such as the Coronation of Charles II, the Plague and the Fire of London, as well as demonstrating Pepys's own idiosyncrasies and vanity. His fascination with details and flair for chronicling them makes his writing one of the most illuminating records of the age. The memoirs of his friend, John Evelyn (1620–1706), are less spontaneous, but only slightly less colourful. Beginning rather earlier, they span a longer period, detailing Evelyn's more considered impressions of events from 1657, when Cromwell was offered the Crown, to the Glorious Revolution of 1688.

John Dryden (1631–1700)

Dryden is the quintessential writer of the late seventeenth century, a man who managed to retain royal favour through many of the political changes of the period, as well as producing major work in most of the dominant literary forms of the age. He became Poet Laureate in 1668 and kept this position after converting to Catholicism, when James II succeeded to the throne in 1685. It was only on the accession of William and Mary that he lost the patronage he had enjoyed for more than twenty years. Beginning with *Astraea Redux* (1660), a panegyric celebrating the restoration of the Stuart monarchy, he responded to many of the major public events of the next three decades. *Annus Mirabilis* (1667) demonstrates a similar royalist vision in its treatment of the Dutch War of 1665–6 and the Fire of London. Because of his ability to adapt to different regimes, he has variously been seen as an opportunist and as a man who had the mental flexibility to avoid being compromised by taking up intransigent positions.

The Achievements of Dryden

Dryden was the first great English master of the heroic couplet (rhymed iambic pentameters) and he anticipated Alexander Pope's perfection of this verse form as a vehicle for satire. As a poet, he is best known for his satires. These include *Absalom and Achitophel* (1681; Part II, mainly by Nahum Tate, 1682), an allegory which uses an Old Testament parallel to attack the attempt by the Earl of Shaftesbury and the Duke of Monmouth to replace James, Duke of York as Charles II's heir; and his richest comic work *MacFlecknoe* (1682), a mock heroic poem, lambasting the dramatist Thomas Shadwell and bad art more generally. Dryden also wrote a number of fine Pindaric odes, including "A Song for St Cecilia's Day" (1687) and "Alexander's Feast; or, The Power of Music" (1697), and the didactic religious allegories, *Religio Laici* (1682) and *The Hind and the Panther* (1687). The former defended Anglicanism; the latter Catholicism. His work as a dramatist includes the blank verse heroic plays *All for Love* (*see above*) and *The Conquest of Granada* (1670), which was famously parodied in Buckingham's burlesque play *The Rehearsal* (1671), and a number of tragic-comedies, among them *Marriage à la Mode* (1672).

Dryden is often considered the first major English literary theorist. His *Essay of Dramatick Poesie* (1668) discusses the merits of various forms of drama and justifies his own practice as a dramatist; his *Discourse concerning the Original and Progress of Satire* (1693) examines the appropriateness of the methods of Horace and Juvenal for English satirists and in so doing established the groundwork for one of the key debates of the next century, when Pope produced imitations of Horace and Johnson preferred the model of Juvenal. Dryden was also one of the leading translators of his age, producing an especially fine translation of Virgil's *Aeneid* (1697). His final work, *Fables, Ancient and Modern* (1700), included translations of Homer, Boccaccio and Chaucer.

John Wilmot, Earl of Rochester (1647-80)

Rochester's dissolute aristocratic life-style has led to his being seen as a representative figure of the Restoration period. He was famed as a libertine, drinker and poseur. His verse was noted for its sexual explicitness and poems such as " A Ramble in St. James's Park" enjoyed an underground reputation as pornographic classics. However, Rochester's poetry also has a serious and reflective side and he is one of the first masters of Augustan satirical verse. His most famous poem, "A Satire against Reason and Mankind" (1675), explores tensions between rationalism and sensuality. Rochester also wrote some fine lyric poetry and introduced the form of the classical "imitation" into English verse.

THE EIGHTEENTH-CENTURY NOVEL

Daniel Defoe (1660-1731)

Defoe is generally considered the first great English novelist, since his work is written with a degree of circumstantial realism unprecedented in earlier English prose fiction. He was nearing sixty years of age when his first novel *Robinson Crusoe* (1719) was published. Prior to this he had led an eventful life as a journalist, businessman and political writer, whose publications had included *The True-Born Englishman* (1701), a satirical work praising William III and defending religious minorities, and *The Shortest Way with the Dissenters* (1702), which mocked Anglican intolerance of nonconformists.

The Original Desert Island Novel

The original desert island novel, *Robinson Crusoe* has been interpreted in numerous ways: as a romantic adventure story; as a spiritual autobiography, a secular equivalent of Bunyan's *Grace Abounding*; as an economic success-story that offers a blueprint for capitalism; as one of the modern world's first great do-it-yourself manuals, an account of survival without the usual props of civilization; and, since it is set in the Caribbean, as a narrative of New World utopianism. It was followed by sequels detailing Crusoe's *Farther Adventures* (1719) and *Serious Reflections* (1720) and six other novels, of which *Moll Flanders* (1722) is the best known. Like *Robinson Crusoe*, the novel, which charts Moll's rogue's progress through English society, has also been viewed as both a spiritual autobiography and an economic success-story, though its setting within society makes it superficially very different and finally it is difficult to take the putative religious elements seriously. Nevertheless it offers a striking portrait of the exploits of a woman who has to live by her wits in order to make her way in society and whose situation justifies her resorting to picaroon cunning in the eyes of many readers.

Roxana (1724) tells a similar story of wickedness and repentance, though the penitence is more perfunctory. Defoe's other novels were *Captain Singleton* (1720), *Memoirs of a Cavalier* (1720), *Colonel Jack* (1722) and *A Journal of the Plague*

Year (1722), which made extensive use of documentary records of the 1665 London Plague. In his later years he published the three-volume *A Tour through the Whole Island of Great Britain* (1724-6) and *The Complete English Tradesman* (1725-7).

Samuel Richardson (1689-1761)

Richardson was a middle-aged printer, who became an overnight celebrity when his epistolary novel *Pamela, or Virtue Rewarded* appeared in 1740. Originally conceived as "a series of familiar letters" for "country readers ... unable to indite for themselves", it tells the story of a servant girl who defends her virginity against the advances of her aristocratic master and eventually wins his hand in marriage. The novel established a plot pattern that would become one of the staples of English romantic fiction: the vicissitudes in the relationship between a woman and a man who is her social superior. The first section of *Pamela* is notable for skilful use of the epistolary form for dramatic effect. However, when the letters give way to a journal, much of this immediacy is lost. The second part (1741) depicts Pamela's adaptation to her new social rank and the ways in which she handles her husband's transgressions.

Richardson's Masterpiece

Richardson's masterpiece *Clarissa* (1747-8), originally published in seven volumes and one of the longest novels in the English language, also focuses on the figure of a threatened heroine, this time a woman of higher social rank. Its use of the epistolary form is altogether more complex than that of *Pamela*, with the letters being shared between four main correspondents; and the representation of moral issues and sexual conflict is also more probing and disturbing than in the earlier novel. Clarissa is another personification of virtue, but she is secretly fascinated by the rakish male protagonist, Lovelace, who eventually rapes her. Lovelace, in turn, is one of the most powerfully drawn characters in early English fiction: his struggle to balance his sexual urges with his respect for the virtuous Clarissa demonstrates a psychological complexity that is at variance with the ostensible simplism of Richardson's avowed morality and the tragic outcome can be seen as an indictment of eighteenth-century gender roles.

Richardson also published *Sir Charles Grandison* (1753-4), in which he switched his main focus to the portrayal of male virtue.

Henry Fielding (1707-54)

Fielding was a leading comic dramatist until 1737, when the Licensing Act, generally considered to have been introduced in response to his attacks on the Whig government of the day, imposed censorship on stage performances and put an end to his career as a playwright. He became a reforming magistrate and, along with his brother John, founded Britain's first police force, the Bow Street Runners.

His First Novels

Fielding's career as a novelist began as a response to what he viewed as the hypocrisy and prurience of Richardson's *Pamela*. In his anonymously published parody, *Shamela* (1741), the unprincipled heroine is a whore and trickster, who schemes to entrap her master into marriage. Fielding's first major novel, *Joseph Andrews* (1742), also took its initial inspiration from *Pamela*. In the opening sections, he reversed gender roles to show male virtue, personified by Pamela's brother Joseph, under attack from predatory females. However, parody is discarded in the main part of the novel, where Joseph undertakes a picaresque journey through the countryside with the book's most memorable figure, the Quixotic clergyman Parson Adams. The episodic format of the journey affords Fielding numerous opportunities to engineer comic situations. At the same time, particularly through the character of Adams, he dramatizes a very different kind of morality from Richardson's Puritanism: that of latitudinarian Anglicanism, which placed its emphasis on salvation through good deeds rather than professions of faith.

Fielding's Masterpiece

The same morality informs Fielding's masterpiece *Tom Jones* (1749), which he termed "a comic epic in prose". More generally, the novel is a brilliantly plotted comic picaresque, which provides a panoramic overview of English life in the middle of the eighteenth century. In the central section, a journey through the countryside at the time of the Jacobite rebellion includes a wide-ranging portrait gallery of social types and a series of farcical encounters that shows the influence of Fielding's experience as a comic dramatist. This is framed by sections set in the West Country and London, which suggest that the values of the rural squirearchy are preferable to those of the genteel society of the capital. The novel also propounds a sexual ethic which is in marked contrast to Richardson's conception of "virtue"; the hero Tom is excused for being unfaithful to his beloved Sophie on three occasions on the grounds that he is essentially goodhearted. In the conclusion, the revelation that the "foundling" Tom is really a gentleman secures his promotion in the social hierarchy, just as marriage elevates Pamela, though there is a significant difference in that in Fielding's world nobility remains a matter of birth, not social advancement. *Tom Jones* is also notable for the introductory chapters to its eighteen books, which discourse on a range of subjects, including the novel itself, and in so doing anticipate the self-reflexive style of Sterne's *Tristram Shandy*.

Fielding's other works include: *Jonathan Wild* (1743), an ironic novel which followed Gay's *Beggar's Opera* in attacking prominent public figures, notably the prime minister Robert Walpole, through the guise of a eulogistic account of the "greatness" of a notorious contemporary criminal; *A Journey from this World to the Next* (1743); his last novel, *Amelia* (1751), in which he deserted his customary comic mode of writing for a more Richardsonian consideration of morality in domestic life; and the posthumously published *Journal of a Voyage to Lisbon* (1755).

Tobias Smollett (1721–71)

While Defoe and Fielding had used elements from the Spanish picaresque novel in their fiction, it was the Scottish-born Smollett who became the most significant early English exponent of the genre, which he employed for satirical purposes and social comment. Prior to the publication of his first novel, *Roderick Random* (1748), he had been a surgeon's mate and the novel is particularly notable for its scenes of nautical life. *Peregrine Pickle* (1751), in which the rogue hero moves in a higher social sphere and travels in mainland Europe is often more savage in its satirical attacks and uncompromisingly graphic in its representation of physical characteristics. It was followed by *Ferdinand Count Fathom* (1753), a novel employing mock-heroic and Gothic elements to recount the adventures of its bogus "count", and *Sir Launcelot Greaves* (1760–1), chiefly remembered as an imitation of Cervantes' *Don Quixote*, which Smollett had translated into English, and as the first work by a major novelist to be serialized in a magazine.

His Finest Novel

In his last novel, *Humphry Clinker* (1771), which has generally been viewed as his finest, Smollett uses the epistolary technique to chronicle the picaresque story of a travelling expedition. His characteristically savage representation of the unsavoury and brutal aspects of eighteenth-century life gives way to a more reflective style, though the novel's delineation of a cross-section of British life still includes harsh caricatures. The story is told by a number of letter-writers, with the figure of the elderly squire, Matthew Bramble, who combines misanthropic and sentimental qualities and has sometimes been seen as a mouthpiece for Smollett's own opinions, at the centre. Smollett also published *Complete History of England* (1757–8) and *Travels through France and Italy* (1766).

Laurence Sterne (1713–68)

Like Defoe and Richardson, Sterne came to the novel comparatively late in life. A Yorkshire parson, involved in the ecclesiastical politics of the diocese of York, he, too, achieved overnight fame with the publication of his first major fiction: Volumes One and Two of his novel, *The Life and Opinions of Tristram Shandy* (1760–67), after which he found himself lionized in literary London. *Tristram Shandy* is often regarded as one of the great eccentricities of English literature. Critics such as Dr Johnson, who said, "Nothing odd will do. *Tristram Shandy* did not last long ", have been proved wrong, but Sterne's work does flout most of the conventions that had already come to be associated with the fledgling genre of the novel. An apparently uncompleted nine-volume novel, it is a fictional autobiography in which Tristram sets out to tell the reader everything about his life and opinions, beginning with the night of his botched conception. He does not arrive at the moment of his birth until the third volume and the novel provides a catalogue of false starts, digressions, accidents and comic misfortunes. Despite Tristram's avowed intention to tell his story from beginning to end, it lacks linear progression (it concludes more than four years before it begins), has missing chapters and a blank page and includes very little narrative action.

As such it becomes a kind of parody of the type of fictional autobiography that Defoe writes, in which events, objects and characters are exhaustively described. Yet it succeeds brilliantly as a novel of a completely different kind—a novel about novel-writing—and the Russian formalist critic, Victor Shklovsky, who takes the view that fiction is finally about its own processes, has commented that its self-parody makes it "the most typical novel of world literature".

Sterne is also known for another whimsical, uncompleted novel, *A Sentimental Journey* (1768), which traces the sentimental adventures of its hero, Parson Yorick, in France, poking fun at the accounts of travellers such as Smollett, called Smelfungus here, as it does so. The book owed much of its contemporary appeal to its sentimentality, viewed by Yorick as a form of spontaneous benevolence that spreads outwards from particular individuals to affect all those with whom they come into contact. However, for the modern reader, it is difficult not to view Yorick's sentimental effusions ironically, particularly when they occur in the context of his prurient encounters with women.

Sterne's other writing includes his sermons, published as *The Sermons of Mr Yorick* (1760–69), and the *Journal to Eliza* (written 1767; published 1904).

The Gothic Novel

As a reaction against the neo-classical beliefs that had dominated culture early in the century, the later eighteenth century revived Gothic forms in literature and architecture, preferring to draw its inspiration from a tradition associated with the medieval rather than the classical period. Horace Walpole built his Gothic castle, Strawberry Hill, at Twickenham and wrote a pioneering Gothic novel, *The Castle of Otranto* (1764). William Beckford's *Vathek* (1786) introduced Gothic elements into another fashionable and exotic romantic form, the Oriental tale, and he built a massive Gothic folly, Fonthill Abbey in Wiltshire, which collapsed less than thirty years later. Other prominent Gothic novels of the period include Anne Radcliffe's *The Mysteries of Udolpho* (1794) and Matthew Lewis's *The Monk* (1796).

The staples of the form, on which its individual exponents worked various variations, were quickly established: sensation, mystery, suspense, horror, supernatural happenings, Italian settings, Gothic architecture and persecuted heroines. William Godwin expanded its possibilities by introducing a degree of psychological subtlety that had not hitherto been characteristic of the genre into his more realistic *Caleb Williams* (1794), a novel which is also noteworthy for protesting against the mistreatment of the socially disadvantaged and as an early example of the novel of crime and detection.

The First Gothic Masterpiece

The Gothic novel produced its first undisputed masterpiece in Godwin's daughter, Mary Shelley's *Frankenstein, or the Modern Prometheus* (1818), a novel which dramatizes ethical issues concerning the right to create life with great imaginative power. While there is horror a-plenty in *Frankenstein*, its main appeal lies in the psychology of its protagonists and it is as much concerned with the mental torments of the scientist, Victor Frankenstein, who gives life to the monster for which the numerous popular spin-offs of the book are best known, as with the sufferings of the creature himself.

Other Novelists

Until comparatively recently, the achievements of eighteenth-century women novelists received much less recognition than those of their male contemporaries or their nineteenth-century female successors. Fanny Burney's novels were a notable exception: *Evelina* (1778) followed Richardson in using the epistolary form, taking a young woman's introduction into society as its main theme; *Cecilia* (1782) describes the fortunes of an heiress who is exploited by her guardians. Other important novels by women writers include Fielding's sister Sarah's *David Simple* (1744–53), which challenged the gender norms of the period, Charlotte Lennox's *The Female Quixote* (1752), whose heroine's beliefs about life are modelled on the conventions of French heroic romances, and Elizabeth Inchbald's *A Simple Story* (1791) and *Nature and Art* (1796).

Apart from the fiction of Richardson and Sterne, sentimental novels of the period include Oliver Goldsmith's *The Vicar of Wakefield* (1766), in which the eponymous Dr Primrose has to learn to temper his instinctive magnanimity with worldly wisdom and Robert Mackenzie's *Man of Feeling* (1771), another novel which, while seizing every opportunity to evoke pathos, also cautions against the dangers of ingenuous good-heartedness.

Towards the end of the century, along with Godwin, novelists such as Robert Bage and Thomas Holcroft began to challenge the class assumptions of most earlier fiction. Holcroft's *Anna St. Ives* (1792) offers a variation on the basic plot of *Clarissa* by adding a third main character, a gardener who provides the heroine with an alternative to the aristocratic rake, and in so doing introduced the first proletarian hero into the English novel.

THE ENGLISH AUGUSTANS

Introduction

Writers of the late seventeenth and early eighteenth century who took their inspiration from the classics have frequently been referred to as "The English Augustans". The term derives from an essay by Goldsmith, who used it to suggest a parallel between the Rome of the Emperor Augustus (27 B.C.–14 A.D.) and Queen Anne's England (1702–14). It has been applied more generally to the Restoration era and most of the eighteenth century. Augustan writing is characterized by its emphasis on order, reason and decorum, its admiration for the classics and a belief in the commonality of human experience. In Johnson's words, "Great thoughts are always general and consist in positions not limited by exceptions". The major writers of England's Augustan Age were Dryden, Swift, Pope and Johnson. Gibbon's *Decline and Fall of the Roman Empire* (1776–88), which, in addition to chronicling its historical subject, can be seen as an elegy for the loss of the classical world, is often regarded as the last great Augustan classic.

Jonathan Swift (1667–1745)

Swift was born and brought up in Dublin, but spent his early adulthood moving between England and Ireland, where he served as an Anglican priest from 1694 and was later appointed as Dean of St Patrick's Cathedral in Dublin in 1713. He became increasingly committed to Irish political causes and his pamphlets protesting against English colonial exploitation made him a national hero in Ireland. They include *The Drapier's Letters* (1724), in which he assumed the persona of a Dublin draper to successfully oppose the introduction of a new form of coinage into Ireland, and the savagely ironic "A Modest Proposal" (1729), in which a supposedly moderate speaker exhorts the poor of Ireland to fatten their own children to provide food for the rich, since, after all, they have been metaphorically eaten by their English landlords already. Swift's health failed as he grew older and the ferocity of his satire led to claims that he had gone mad. It seems more likely that the symptoms of his Menière's syndrome, from which he had long suffered, had grown worse with age.

His Two Masterpieces

Perhaps the greatest of all British ironists, Swift's first masterpiece was *The Tale of a Tub* volume (1704), which comprises the title-work, "The Battle of the Books" and "The Mechanical Operation of the Spirit". "The Tale of a Tub" is an elaborate satire on aberrations in modern learning. It includes Swift's famous "Digression on Madness". In which a crazed speaker argues the case for the social and moral usefulness of insanity. While the work's digressions are central, the tale itself is an allegory of three brothers, who represent the Catholic, Anglican and dissenting branches of Christianity, with Swift demonstrating a preference for the Anglican middle way. "The Battle of the Books" stages a mock-heroic battle between ancient and modern volumes in the King's library as a device for debating the relative merits of classical and modern learning. The outcome is left undecided, but at the moment when the work breaks off, the ancients appear to be winning the day.

Swift's second masterpiece, *Gulliver's Travels* (1726), is superficially much more straightforward and its opening part, in which the hero finds himself a giant among the six-inch high people of Lilliput, has had an enduring appeal for children. However, Gulliver's Lilliputian experience also works on a more complex, allegorical level: it offers a satirical critique of contemporary British and European society. This is typical of the work as a whole and, as it continues, the tone of the *Travels* gradually darkens. In Part II, Gulliver visits the land of Brobdingnag, where the formula of Lilliput is reversed, as he finds himself a pigmy among giants. This perspective provides Swift with opportunities to illustrate the grossness of the human body, an aspect of his writing which has led to his being charged with misanthropy. The third part, in which Gulliver visits several places, satirizes what Swift saw as the excesses of modern scientific inquiry, particularly the experiments of the Royal Society. The darkening vision comes to a climax in Part IV, in which Gulliver travels to the land of the Houyhnhmns, a species of super-rational horses, who stand in marked opposition to the other beings that inhabit their country, the bestial and filthy Yahoos. The Yahoos are identified with humankind and by the time Gulliver finally returns home his faith in human nature has collapsed to a point where he prefers the company of his horses to his family.

His Other Works

Swift's other works include the early *Bickerstaff Papers* (1708), in which he parodied the contemporary astrologer, Isaac Partridge by predicting his death and then subsequently, falsely, claiming he was really dead, and *The Journal to Stella* (1710–13), a collection of letters written to Esther Johnson, one of the two women in his life. Swift also produced a considerable body of poetry, mainly written in quatrains, which is generally less assured than his prose. His best known poems include "Baucis and Philemon", "Cadenus and Vanessa" and "Verses on the Death of Dr Swift".

Alexander Pope (1688–1744)

The greatest satirist of his age, Pope is generally regarded as Dryden's heir. Like Dryden he was a neo-classicist who used the heroic couplet to write scathing indictments of what he saw as failings in social and personal morality. In his own day his most popular works were his translations of Homer's *Iliad* (1720) and *Odyssey* (1725–6). Posterity has seen his witty satires as his greatest achievement. As a Catholic in the early eighteenth century, Pope was prevented from attending university and had private tutors. This and his physical make-up—he was approximately four feet six inches high and suffered from poor health throughout his life—led his critics to see Pope's satire as vindictive and personally motivated. In his own view, he was a compulsive moralist, who adhered to Dryden's view that "the true end of satire is the amendment of vices by correction".

Pope's first major poem, *An Essay on Criticism*

(1711), is both his artistic manifesto and an exploration of the state of literature at the time. It outlines his classical humanist creed and his belief that "True wit is Nature to advantage dressed/ What oft was thought but ne'er so well expressed". *Windsor Forest* (1713) is a pastoral celebrating the Peace of Utrecht, which ended the War of the Spanish Succession. In *The Rape of the Lock* (1712; enlarged 1714), Pope used the mock heroic form to poke gentle fun at a prank in Catholic high society and in so doing pointed up the distance between contemporary polite society and the world of classical epic, for example by modelling an account of the heroine's putting on her make-up on Homer's account of the arming of Achilles.

His Debt to Horace

The classical writer to whom Pope was most indebted was Horace and he imitated him in life as well as literature, seeing his own villa on the banks of the Thames at Twickenham as his equivalent of Horace's Sabine farm. His *Essay on Criticism* was modelled on Horace's *Ars Poetica* and he later wrote a series of poems, which imitated Horace's epistles and satires. While each of these poems has a particular addressee and specific satirical targets, collectively they demonstrate a preference for the values of the rural gentry over the newly emergent mercantilist classes. However, their abiding interest owes more to their comic portraiture and mastery of versification than their moral attitudes. *The Essay on Man* (1733–4), a philosophical poem on humanity's place in the universe, which was widely admired in its own day, remains notable for its aphorisms, but its didacticism leads to an unevenness of tone, as conversational passages give way to over-solemn moralizing.

In one sense, Pope's second major mock-epic poem, *The Dunciad* (first version 1728; final enlarged version 1743), is his equivalent of Dryden's *MacFlecknoe*, since, like the earlier poem, it mocks dullness through the use of elevation, and in so doing deflates its subjects, the literary poetasters of the period. However, *The Dunciad* is a work that rises above its mock-heroic origins and ribald comedy to assume the status of serious epic. Its wide-ranging allusions provide a catalogue of contemporary literary and social vices; and its fourth book, added towards the end of Pope's life, is especially notable for references to Milton's *Paradise Lost*, which link the poem's literary dunces to a broader vision of creeping moral chaos and disorder. The poem ends with a lament for the loss of classical humanist values, as the influence of dullness spreads outwards to engulf the whole of society.

Samuel Johnson (1707–84)

Born in Lichfield, Johnson went to London in 1737, along with his pupil David Garrick, who became the leading actor of his age, just as Johnson became its most famous writer. He was far from successful during his first years in the capital and his poem *London* (1738), a Juvenalian satire contrasting the values of the country and the city, expresses his early feelings of disillusionment. He struggled to establish himself as a writer, a predicament which probably led him to identify with his friend Richard Savage, an account of whose life he published in 1744. *The Life of Savage* is both the most immediate and the most polemical of Johnson's biographies: his personal involvement with his subject, whose controversial claim to be the repudiated illegitimate son of the Countess of Macclesfield Johnson fully supported, lend it a vivid first-hand quality lacking in his later *Lives of the English Poets* (1781). Johnson gradually established himself through his work in a range of genres and when George III granted him a royal pension in 1762, his financial position was secure. In later life he became a focal point for London literary life and his influence extended far beyond his own writings. In 1764, along with the artist Sir Joshua Reynolds, he founded the Literary Club, whose members included Garrick, Oliver Goldsmith and Edmund Burke.

His Extraordinary Versatility

Johnson produced significant work in virtually every eighteenth-century literary form. His tragedy *Irene* was staged by Garrick in 1749. As a periodical

essayist, he wrote two essays a week for *The Rambler* from 1750 to 1752 and weekly essays for *The Idler* from 1758 to 1760. As a lexicographer, he compiled his *Dictionary of the English Language* (1755) in eight years, while the French Academy's similar project is said to have taken forty men forty years. It was the first English dictionary to provide etymologies and literary examples of the usage of words as well as definitions, and is particularly remembered for the humour of Johnson's sometimes individualistic definitions. He referred to a lexicographer as "a harmless drudge" and defined oats as "A grain which in England is generally given to horses, but in Scotland supports the people". His alleged prejudice against Scotland lent a particular edge to his relationship with his Scottish biographer, James Boswell, whom he first met in 1763. However, his attitude changed after a journey to Scotland with Boswell, which resulted in Johnson's *Journey to the Western Islands of Scotland* (1775) and Boswell's *Journal of a Tour to the Hebrides* (1785).

Poet, Novelist, Editor and Critic

As a poet, Johnson followed *London* with another Juvenalian satire, *The Vanity of Human Wishes* (1749), his most important poem, in which he takes a lofty, ironic view of human aspirations. His only novel *Rasselas* (1759) is similar in theme. It employs the form of the Eastern Tale to investigate possibilities for human happiness, with the eponymous hero, a prince of Abyssinia, being schooled by the worldly wise philosopher, Imlac, who tells him "Human life is everywhere a state in which much is to be endured, and little to be enjoyed". As an editor, Johnson produced an edition of *Shakespeare's Plays* (1765), more notable for its literary criticism than its elucidation of Shakespeare's texts.

His abilities as a critic also informed his *Lives of the English Poets*, the most comprehensive biographical collection of the century, which combines biography with criticism and a "character" of the poet. The *Lives* vary considerably in direction and quality and while none is as tendentious as the earlier *Life of Savage*, several, such as "The Life of Cowley", in which Johnson attacked the Metaphysical Poets, are openly polemical in their advocacy of a particular attitude or approach. Along with Cowley, the lives of Milton and Pope are among the finest.

Finally, Johnson's reputation owes at least as much to his being the subject of one of the greatest biographies in the English language, Boswell's *Life of Johnson* (1791), which records his witty conversation and personal eccentricities, along with a circumstantial account of his personal and public life that makes him the most fully documented subject in eighteenth-century literature.

Personal Writings

Biography and autobiography came of age in the late eighteenth century. Johnson's *Lives of the English Poets* are often opinionated, but demonstrate an attention to individual detail that had been rare in earlier personal writings. Boswell's *Life of Johnson* is widely regarded as the first modern biography, since it demonstrates an unprecedented attention to researched detail, a commitment to accuracy and an endeavour to treat its subject's life exhaustively. Boswell brings Johnson alive by including details of his mannerisms and records of his *bon mots*, in dramatic scenes, some of which he consciously engineers. He also kept intimate journals of his own life, which remained unpublished until the twentieth century. Best known among these is his *London Journal, 1762–63*, a fascinating companion-piece to the section of the *Life of Johnson* in which he first becomes acquainted with his subject, since it records his private emotions and amorous encounters from the same period.

Gibbon's *Autobiography* (originally entitled *Memoirs of My Life and Writings*, 1796) is an account of the forces that shaped the character of the historian of *The Decline and Fall of the Roman Empire*, written in a detached, ironic style. Other notable personal writings of the age include the diary of Fanny Burney and the letters of Horace Walpole and Lord Chesterfield, whose missives to his natural son collectively come to form a conduct book instructing a young gentleman in matters of breeding, morality and intrigue.

The Periodical Essay

Joseph Addison and Richard Steele's *The Spectator* (1711–14) established the essay as an important genre in its own right. Its essays are notable for their observations on the manners of the period and for their creation of a club, whose members include representatives of various aspects of early eighteenth-century life, with the country gentleman, Sir Roger de Coverley, being the most memorable. The periodical essay flourished throughout the century and important later sequences include Johnson's *Rambler* essays, which range over a broad sweep of subjects, often offering moral instruction, and Oliver Goldsmith's *Citizen of the World* (1760–62), a collection of letters supposedly written by and to a Chinese visitor to London, which provides apparently ingenuous comments on English manners and customs

Poetry of Landscape and Reflection

As the century progressed, classical models for poetry were gradually replaced by approaches that anticipated the Romantic Movement in their concern with Nature, individual emotions, the sublime, rural life and melancholy thoughts. Thomson's *Seasons* (1726–30) looks back to classical pastoral and forwards to the Romantic emphasis on Nature's influence on human sensibilities. Edward Young's *Night Thoughts* (1742–6) is the most famous longer work of the "graveyard poets", whose melancholy meditations on mortality took their inspiration from graveyard settings. The greatest of such poems is Thomas Gray's "Elegy Written in a Country Churchyard" (1751), where the slow, measured verse provides a vehicle for an elegiac meditation on the transience of human life and the particular fate of the humble villagers who are buried in the churchyard.

Village life is also the subject of Goldsmith's *The Deserted Village* (1770), an elegy for rural life which laments the depopulation of the countryside occasioned by the agrarian revolution and the enclosure of common land, and George Crabbe's *The Village* (1783), which took issue with Goldsmith's idealized view of the rural past. William Cowper's finest achievement, *The Task* (1785) is an introspective poem on the pleasures of country life. Other notable eighteenth-century poets whose meditative response to landscape anticipates the Romantics include William Collins, Mark Akenside and Christopher Smart.

Eighteenth-Century Drama

The beginning of the eighteenth century saw a reaction against the licentiousness of Restoration Comedy in favour of a drama that placed its main emphasis on sentimentalism and the cultivation of fine feelings. The cult of sentimentalism continued to exert an important influence on English drama for more than half a century; and representative plays in this genre include Colley Cibber's *The Careless Husband* (1702), Steele's *The Conscious Lovers* (1722) and Richard Cumberland's *The West Indian* (1771).

The early part of the century also saw the growth of a very different kind of drama, the burlesque play. The popularity of the burlesque can be dated back to George Villiers's parody of Restoration heroic drama, *The Rehearsal* (1671), but it assumed new dimensions with the success of John Gay's masterpiece, *The Beggar's Opera* (1728). Ostensibly a satire on the contemporary vogue for Italian opera, Gay's play broadens out into a wide-ranging critique of the social life of the period, in which aristocrats are replaced by highwaymen and merchants by fences. Much of its appeal arose from its lively music, which replaced operatic arias with popular ballads. Other notable burlesques include Gay's *The What d'ye Call It* (1715), Fielding's *Tom Thumb* (1730) and Henry Carey's *Chrononhotonthologos* (1734).

Oliver Goldsmith (1728–74)

Oliver Goldsmith initiated a movement away from sentimental comedy in his essay, "Comparison between Laughing and Sentimental Comedy" (1773), which attacked the vogue for sentimentalism and argued that humour should return to the English stage. His play, *The Good Natur'd Man*

(1768) is a particularly interesting dramatization of the debate about the form that comedy should take, as its hero is both satirized for his foolish magnanimity and genuinely benevolent. Goldsmith's most famous play, *She Stoops to Conquer* (1773), in which a young gentleman mistakes his prospective father-in-law's house for an inn, has had a much more enduring appeal, based as it is on a series of comic misunderstandings that rise above its period and setting.

Richard Brinsley Sheridan (1751–1816)

Goldsmith's contemporary, Richard Brinsley Sheridan, also transcended the conventions of sentimental comedy. His plays employ a broad range of comic effects that derive their humour from situation, character and verbal wit. *The Rivals* (1775), a comedy of manners set in fashionable Bath society, is best remembered for its broad comic characters, particularly Mrs Malaprop, whose habit of confusing similar sounding words (*e.g.* her reference to "an *allegory* on the banks of the Nile") was responsible for the introduction of the term "malapropism" into the language. Sheridan's *The School for Scandal* (1777), a play which redeploys character types from Restoration comedy and makes brilliant use of comic situations, is the finest achievement of late eighteenth-century comedy.

THE ENGLISH ROMANTICS

Introduction

The end of the eighteenth century saw a major shift in literary and cultural taste with the emergence of the Romantic Movement. Its most important characteristics included a belief in the shaping power of the imagination (defined in a range of ways by the various Romantics) rather than reason, a stress on individual experience and a desertion of neo-classical norms in favour of a more emotive and spontaneous approach to life. However, no two major Romantic poets held the same beliefs and Byron's poetic practice was markedly different from those of his contemporaries.

The beginnings of English Romanticism are usually associated with the Lake Poets, Wordsworth, Coleridge and Southey, but it had evolved gradually and Romantic elements can be found in such diverse forms as earlier eighteenth-century poetry of landscape and reflection, the Gothic novel, a growth of interest in the classical notion of the sublime, late eighteenth-century sentimentalism and a fascination with the pictorial, particularly as mediated by Italian landscape painting.

William Blake (1757–1827)

Blake was a writer and artist whose genius developed outside the dominant cultural conventions of his day. Educated at home, he was apprenticed to an engraver at the age of fourteen. He developed a new method of "illuminated printing", in which he blended the text of his poems with colour engravings, and a distinctive symbolism which expressed his highly personal visionary philosophy. His artistic individuality was complemented by his nonconformist views. The son of a dissenter, he was influenced by the beliefs of the Swedish mystic, Emmanuel Swedenborg and the egalitarian political philosophy of his friends and contemporaries, William Godwin and Thomas Paine.

An early volume of *Poetical Sketches* (1783) was followed by his most popular work, the collection of lyrics *Songs of Innocence* (1789), which was expanded to become *Songs of Innocence and Experience* (1795). The latter volume's sub-title indicates its intention to depict "the two contrary states of the human soul" and it includes paired poems, such as "The Lamb" and "The Tyger", which illustrate the dialectical opposition between the Edenic innocence of childhood and the corrupted experience of adulthood. Other poems in the collection include "The Little Black Boy" and "The Chimney Sweeper".

His Mystical Vision

Blake's mystical vision receives extended expression in his numerous prophetic books, where the style is in marked contrast to the apparent simplism of his *Songs*, though profundity and naivety often co-exist. The prophetic books, which he wrote, engraved and published himself, include: *Visions of the Daughters of Albion* (1793), *America: A Prophecy* (1793), *The Book of Urizen* (1794), *The Book of Ahania* (1795), *The Book of Los* and *The Song of Los* (1795), *Jerusalem: The Emanation of the Giant Albion* (1804–20) and *The Ghost of Abel* (1822). Blake was fascinated by *Paradise Lost*, taking the view that "Milton was a true poet and of the devil's party without knowing it". He attacked Milton in his "Los" sequence, which inverts aspects of *Paradise Lost*, and in *Milton: A Poem in Two Books* (1804–8). The latter contains his short poem, "Jerusalem", from which the popular hymn was later taken. Blake's most important prose work, *The Marriage of Heaven and Hell* (1790–93), is a collection of aphorisms, which again demonstrates his belief that "without contraries is no progression".

William Wordsworth (1770–1850)

Wordsworth was university-educated, but the key formative influence on his artistic development, which he describes in his poetic autobiography *The Prelude*, was his early love of Nature, developed during his boyhood in the English Lake District. A walking tour in France, the Alps and Italy and a further visit to France during the first phase of the French Revolution also contributed significantly to the shaping of his poetic sensibility.

His Earliest Verse

The diction of Wordsworth's earliest verse is barely distinguishable from that of most of his contemporaries, but his first major work, *Lyrical Ballads* (1798), to which Coleridge also contributed, signalled one of the most radical changes in English poetry. Unfavourably received on its first appearance, the volume focuses on humble countryfolk, children and dispossessed mothers, describing their lives in a style of cultivated simplicity based on "the language of conversation in the middle and lower classes of society". Among its best-known poems are "We Are Seven", "The Thorn", "Simon Lee" and "The Idiot Boy". It also contains one of Wordsworth's most famous poems, "Lines written a few miles above Tintern Abbey", a meditation on the effect this landscape has had on his "moral being".

In the Preface to the second edition (1800), in which the poem "Michael" was added, Wordsworth provides a manifesto for his kind of Romantic verse, stressing that the principle object of the poems has been "to choose incidents and situations from common life, and to relate or describe them, throughout, in a selection of language really used by men". He explains that "Humble and rustic life was generally chosen, because, in that condition the essential passions of the heart find a better soil in which they can attain their maturity, are less under restraint, and speak a plainer and more emphatic language". He also adumbrates his belief that "all good poetry is the spontaneous overflow of powerful feeling", another facet of his work which represents a marked departure from neo-classical poetic practice.

The Prelude

Wordsworth's finest long poem *The Prelude* exists in two versions (1805 and 1850), neither of which was published in his own life-time. Although it is an autobiography, it places its emphasis on "the growth of a poet's mind" (its sub-title) and Wordsworth dramatizes his own experience as representative of the poetic life. Written in blank verse, it describes his upbringing in the Lake District, his disenchantment with conventional forms of learning, town life and the political philosophy of William Godwin and the French Jacobins, who had been early inspirations to him. Against these, he sets the power of the poetic imagination, acting in communion with a Pantheistic Nature. The poem was intended as an introduction to a long philosophical poem to be called *The Recluse*, but only the second part of this, *The Excursion* (1814), which suffers in comparison with *The Prelude*, was ever completed.

Wordsworth's last major collection of shorter pieces, *Poems in Two Volumes*, was published in 1807. It includes some of his best-loved poems, among them "Daffodils" ("I wandered lonely as a cloud"), his sonnet "Composed Upon Westminster Bridge" ("Earth has not any thing to show more fair") and one of his finest tributes to rural simplicity, "Resolution and Independence", also known as "The Leech-Gatherer". His ode, "Intimations of Immortality from Recollections of Early Childhood", also published in this volume, is both a celebration of childhood innocence and a lament for the loss of the "visionary gleam" that has provided his early poetic inspiration. He published numerous further volumes, including *The White Doe of Rylstone* (1815), *Peter Bell* (1819) and *Sonnets* (1838). He became Poet Laureate in 1843, but virtually all his important poetry had been written in the first half of his life.

Samuel Taylor Coleridge (1772–1834)

Wordsworth's collaborator on the *Lyrical Ballads*, Coleridge had developed a distinctive range of republican and millenarian beliefs, again associated with the optimism of the first phase of the French Revolution, prior to meeting Wordsworth in 1797. Wordsworth's belief in the power of Nature probably influenced his conversation poem "Frost at Midnight" (1798) and during the first year of their friendship he wrote three of his most important poems, "The Rime of the Ancient Mariner", "Christabel" and "Kubla Khan". "The Ancient Mariner" appeared in the *Lyrical Ballads* (1798). Written in ballad metre, it is a tale of crime and absolution, told to a wedding guest, whom the mariner detains to listen to his story. The mariner shoots an albatross, a supposed good omen, during a voyage in the southern seas. When his ship subsequently suffers misfortunes, he is blamed by his crewmates for their sufferings and in the conclusion is absolved by a hermit. The ostensibly simple Christian morality of the ending is undermined by the existential arbitrariness inherent in the poem's depiction of sin and redemption and the mariner's intrusion into the festive occasion of the wedding leaves his auditor "a sadder and a wiser man".

"Kubla Khan" and "Christabel" were published in *Christabel and Other Poems* (1816). The former is a symbolically powerful, but obscure fragment, reputedly produced after a laudanum-induced dream. Its use of luxuriant, oriental imagery creates an evocative Romantic ambience that overshadows any clear meaning, but suggests an allegory about creativity. The equally enigmatic and unfinished "Christabel" is more obviously an allegory, about innocence, which draws on Gothic motifs. "Dejection: An Ode" (1802) begins by expressing sentiments reminiscent of Wordsworth's comments on his waning creative powers in the Immortality Ode and continues by looking for solace in the power of the imagination rather than external Nature. Coleridge's poetic gifts fell away in later life, a decline which has variously been attributed to the ending of his friendship with Wordsworth and his addiction to opium.

His Other Writings

Along with his comparatively small corpus of poems, Coleridge's most important contribution to the development of English Romanticism was his *Biographia Literaria* (1817), an extended prose work which blends autobiography and philosophical deliberations in a haphazard structure that allows him free rein to express his thoughts on life and literature. It is most notable for Coleridge's reflections on the psychology of the creative process, particularly his belief in the imagination's capacity to unify opposing aspects in the human psyche and contemporary society. Its numerous other subjects include a critique of Wordsworth, discussion of the philosophy of Kant and his contemporaries, essays on Shakespeare and advice to aspiring writers. *Table Talk* (1836) is a record of Coleridge's conversations, for which he became famous in later life.

George Gordon Byron, Lord (1786–1824)

From one point of view, Byron was the archetypal English Romantic poet: his public persona perfectly fitted the nineteenth-century's conception of what such a poet should be and his fame throughout Europe was unrivalled. However, his poetry demonstrates little affinity with the more introspective aspects of the Romantic imagination and it is formally the most classical work produced by any of the major English Romantics. An admirer of Pope, Byron wrote much of his early verse in heroic couplets and throughout his work "Romantic" themes are tempered by a witty epigrammatic style that is more characteristic of Augustan verse.

His Early Life

Byron's inheritance of an aristocratic title, a club-foot, sexual abuse by his nurse and an incestuous relationship with his half-sister, Augusta Leigh, all contributed to making his early years markedly different from those of the other English Romantics. After a strict Scottish Calvinist upbringing, he became the sixth Baron Byron and inherited the family estate at Newstead Abbey in Nottingham-shire when he was ten. His reputation as a libertine, atheist and radical idealist began during his time at Cambridge. His first important work was Cantos I and II of Childe Harold's Pilgrimage (1812; Cantos III and IV, 1816 and 1818), a poem in Spenserian stanzas about the European wanderings of a young man disillusioned with his hedonistic life-style. It was followed by a series of hastily written verse tales—The Bride of Abydos (1813), The Giaour (1813), The Corsair (1814) and Lara (1814)—most notable for their development of the figure of "the Byronic hero", a romantic adventurer with a mysterious past. Along with Shelley and Mary Wollstonecraft Godwin, Byron left England in 1816 and after a stay in Switzerland settled in Italy. He died in Greece of fever, having gone there to fight in the Greek struggle for Independence from Turkey.

His Later Period

Most of Byron's best work belongs to his later period. It includes one of his finest shorter poems, The Prisoner of Chillon (1816), the dramatic poem, Manfred (1817), in which the hero is an outcast haunted by past crimes, and the "Venetian tale", Beppo (1818), written in ottava rima, a form which ideally suited his witty imagination. He also employed ottava rima in two of his finest poems, The Vision of Judgement (1822) and Don Juan (1819–24). The Vision is a wickedly funny parody of the Poet Laureate Robert Southey's similarly named poem (1821) about George III's arrival in heaven.

Don Juan, the unfinished thirteen-canto poem for which Byron is best known to posterity, is an epic account of the exploits of the legendary Spanish philanderer. Its use of ottava rima provides Byron with a perfect vehicle for a witty picaresque consid-eration of a range of contemporary philosophical and social issues, as well as ample opportunity to project himself into the complex figure of his pro-tagonist. His play Cain (1821), in which the arche-typal murderer of the Book of Genesis becomes a sympathetic rebel learning about the universe under the instruction of Lucifer, is his most extreme treatment of the figure of the exiled expatriate.

Percy Bysshe Shelley (1792–1822)

Expelled from Oxford, after writing a pamphlet advocating atheism, Shelley was the most reviled of the Romantic poets in his own day. He was also the most intellectually intense of the younger genera-tion of Romantics and his poetry is suffused with a philosophical seriousness not to be found in Byron's work and a seemingly artless spontaneity not to be found in Keats's more direct and controlled imagery. His most famous statement on the imagi-nation comes in his Defence of Poetry (written 1821; published 1840), which sees poets as the "unac-knowledged legislators of the world" and champions the power of inspiration, which he associates with a Platonic view of life. Shelley was an ardent admirer of the Pantheism of "Tintern Abbey", but like Byron he felt that Wordsworth had betrayed his early radicalism. His first important poem, Queen Mab (1813) is a radical attack on a broad range of social targets, including marriage and institutional-ized Christianity, in which the fairy queen of the title looks forward to a future in which society's ills will be cured. Alastor, or the Spirit of Solitude (1816) is a more introspective poem, which depicts an idealist's failure to find an external correlative for his dreams. The Odes, "Hymn to Intellectual Beauty" and "Mont Blanc", also belong to this phase of Shelley's career.

Shelley and Revolutionary Causes

At a time when absolutist governments were being reinstated in several parts of Europe in the wake of the Battle of Waterloo, Shelley wrote various poems and plays supporting revolutionary political causes. The Revolt of Islam (1818), a long poem in Spenserian stanzas, combines a radical political impulse with his idealized belief in human perfectibility. The Cenci (1819) is a verse tragedy based on a Renaissance legend, in which Shelley found a perfect subject for one of his most powerful allegories about resistance to tyranny. His master-piece, Prometheus Unbound (1820), is a passionate lyrical drama, which takes the Greek Titan who rebelled against Jupiter, the king of the gods, as its hero. Rooted in Shelley's Platonic beliefs, the play operates on a number of levels, but is most obviously a socio-political allegory, protesting against all forms of tyranny. Like Byron, Shelley supported the Greek struggle against Turkish rule, and his last completed work, Hellas (1822), was a lyrical drama inspired by this cause.

Epipsychidion (1821) is an autobiographical poem about a Dantean quest for ideal beauty, which also deals with the creative process. Shelley's famous elegy on Keats's death, Adonais (1821), both laments his younger contemporary's passing and pays tribute to his poetic genius, which Shelley believed had not been sufficiently recognized. The poem also reflects Keats's own belief in the immortality conferred by beauty. Shelley's satires include "England in 1819", a vitriolic sonnet on the state of the nation at the end of George III's reign and The Mask of Anarchy (written 1819; published 1832), his most ambitious work of this kind, which responded to the news of the "Peterloo Massacre" of 1819, by equating the government's behaviour in ordering soldiers to shoot peaceful demonstrators for political reform with anarchy.

His shorter poems, which mainly take political freedom and love as their themes, include "Ode to Liberty", "Ode to Naples", "The Cloud", "The Indian Serenade", "Ozymandias", "Ode to the West Wind" and "To a Skylark".

Shelley drowned when his boat capsized in a storm off the coast of Italy, where he had been living since 1818. At the time of his death he was working on another Dantean poem, The Triumph of Life (1824), a dream allegory about the human condition, which breaks off at a point where it appears to be suggesting not the triumph, but the meaninglessness, of life.

John Keats (1795–1821)

The son of a livery-stable manager, Keats became a certificated apothecary in 1816 and subsequently trained as a surgeon, but abandoned this profession to pursue a literary career. His first collection, Poems (1817), which received a hostile critical reception, included "Sleep and Poetry" and the sonnet "On First Looking into Chapman's Homer". It was followed by Endymion (1818), a romance in four books, based on the Greek legend of a shepherd who falls in love with the moon goddess and is spirited away to live with her eternally. Best remembered for its opening line, "A thing of beauty is a joy for ever", Endymion is an uneven allegory about the poet-dreamer's quest for perfection.

His Finest Poetry

Keats's finest poetry appeared a year before his early death in Poems of 1820. This includes three narrative poems dramatizing a conflict between romantic enchantment and a world of colder actual-ity. In "Lamia", a young man's love for a serpent that has taken human shape ends when a philoso-pher calls her by her real name and she reverts to her original identity. In "Isabella or the Pot of Basil", Keats took his story from Boccaccio, using the appropriately Italianate stanza form of ottava rima for his medieval Italian subject. Romantic love is once again destroyed, when the Florentine heroine's beloved is murdered by her proud brothers.

In "The Eve of St Agnes", his most assured longer poem, Keats employed the Spenserian stanza for another medieval subject. Breathing life into the legend that a virgin may see a vision of her lover on St Agnes's Eve, he produced some of his most per-fectly realized physical description to depict a vivid contrast between the wintry cold of external nature and the sensuous warmth of the lovers' interior, in this case allowing the romantic dream world to evade the constraints of everyday reality.

Poems of 1820 also contains Keats's unfinished epic poem, "Hyperion", and the five odes which secured his reputation as one of the greatest of English poets. The richly luxuriant language of the odes embodies Keats's belief in the power of beauty, while also lamenting its transience. "Beauty that must die" is the central theme of "To Autumn" and "To Melancholy". "On a Grecian Urn" suggests the ambiguity of the immortality conferred by art, by reflecting on the paradoxical spring-like situation of two lovers, who transcend death through being depicted on the urn, but whose love remains unconsummated in the frozen stasis of such representation. It culminates with the famous utterance, "Beauty is truth, truth beauty,—that is all/Ye know on earth, and all ye need to know". "To a Nightingale" sees the bird as a symbol of artistic immortality that offers release from "the weariness, the fever, and the fret" of the everyday world. "To Psyche" addresses a neglected pagan goddess who symbolises the human soul made immortal through love.

Seriously ill with tuberculosis, Keats travelled to Italy in late 1820 and died there the following year. He had composed his own epitaph: "Here lies one whose name was writ in water".

Other Romantic Poets

Although he died before the Romantic period, Thomas Chatterton, who committed suicide in 1770 at the age of seventeen, came to be seen as the epitome of Romantic genius, unable to survive in a hostile world. Keats dedicated *Endymion* to him and Wordsworth, referred to him as the "marvellous boy", whose early "gladness" descended into "despondency and madness" ("Resolution and Independence"). Henry Wallis's 1856 Pre-Raphaelite painting further contributed to the growth of the Chatterton myth.

Scotland's most famous poet, Robert Burns, was another important precursor of the Romantic movement, both in his use of ordinary speech in *Poems Chiefly in the Scottish Dialect* (1786), which Wordsworth and Coleridge greatly admired, and for his treatment of rustic and Gothic themes in works such as his finest narrative poem, *Tam o'Shanter* (1791).

Leigh Hunt, who was influential in promoting the reputations of Keats and Shelley, is best remembered for *The Story of Rimini* (1816) and his *Autobiography* (1850). Coleridge's associate, Robert Southey, was held in considerable esteem in his own day and became Poet Laureate in 1813, but his reputation declined after his death. Sir Walter Scott first established his reputation as a writer of historical verse romances and his work in this genre includes *The Lay of the Last Minstrel* (1805) and *Marmion* (1808). John Clare, the "Northamptonshire peasant poet", was acclaimed for his *Poems Descriptive of Rural Life and Scenery* (1820) and subsequently published *The Village Minstrel* (1821) and *The Shepherd's Calendar* (1827), but spent most of his later life in a lunatic asylum, where he continued to write.

Notable Romantic women poets include Hannah More, Charlotte Smith, Ann Yearsley, Mary Robinson, Helen Maria Williams and Felicia Dorothea Hemans, several of whom wrote poems that contributed to the campaign for the abolition of the slave trade. Byron's former lover, Lady Caroline Lamb, wrote *A New Canto* (1819), in which she adopted the persona of Byron and appropriated the style of *Don Juan* in order to mock him, along with a range of targets from contemporary society.

Romantic Prose

In addition to the Preface to the *Lyrical Ballads*, Coleridge's *Biographia Literaria* and Shelley's *Defence of Poetry*, other important non-fictional prose of the Romantic period includes Mary Wollstonecraft's pioneering feminist work, *A Vindication of the Rights of Women* (1792), which makes a powerful case for gender equality and among other things sees "female" characteristics such as submissiveness as the product of nurture rather than nature. William Godwin's *Enquiry Concerning Political Justice* (1793), which set out a philosophy of human perfectibility, was the most influential political treatise of the early Romantic period, but its fame was comparatively short-lived.

Edmund Burke's prose masterpiece, *Reflections on the Revolution in France* (1790), took a conservative stand against the changes effected by the Jacobin revolutionaries and more generally lamented, "The age of chivalry is gone. That of sophisters, economists, and calculators, has succeeded; and the glory of Europe is extinguished forever." Thomas Paine's *The Rights of Man* (1791–2) responded to Burke by justifying the revolutionaries and arguing the case for natural rights shared by all men; and, in its second part, compared the new French and American constitutions with that of Britain, to the detriment of the latter.

Important collections of essays include William Hazlitt's *English Comic Writers* (1819) and *The Spirit of the Age* (1825), a collection of portraits of his contemporaries, and Charles Lamb's *Essays of Elia* (Vol. I, 1823; Vol. II, 1833). Thomas De Quincey's autobiographical *Confessions of an English Opium Eater* (1822; enlarged 1856) describes the effects of his addiction to laudanum and his gradual success in moderating his habit. Keats's letters are notable for his comments on "beauty", "truth" and the Romantic imagination.

EARLY NINETEENTH-CENTURY FICTION

Sir Walter Scott (1771–1832)

The most highly regarded Romantic novelist of the nineteenth century, Scott began his writing career as a poet, achieving critical and popular success with *The Lay of the Last Minstrel* (1805), a six-canto poem in ballad verse based on a traditional story about a sixteenth-century feud in the Scottish Borders. Several further long narrative poems in a similar vein, including *Marmion* (1808) and *The Lady of the Lake* (1810), followed. Scott's first novel *Waverley* (1814) propelled his reputation to new heights and he followed this with several more "Waverley novels", which also offered vivid portraits of various aspects of recent Scottish history: *Guy Mannering* (1815), *The Antiquary* (1816), *The Black Dwarf* (1816), *Old Mortality* (1816), *Rob Roy* (1817), *The Heart of Midlothian* (1818), *The Bride of Lammermoor* (1819) and *A Legend of Montrose* (1819).

Beginning with *Ivanhoe* (1820), a romance set in the England of Richard I's time, Scott extended his prolific talents to fiction that recreated a broader range of historical eras and locations. Novels from this phase of his career include *The Abbot* (1820), *Kenilworth* (1821), *The Fortunes of Nigel* (1822), *Peveril of the Peak* (1822), *Quentin Durward* (1823), *Redgauntlet* (1824) and *The Talisman* (1825). *St Ronan's Well* (1824), a novel of manners set in a Scottish spa, was a rare departure into the nineteenth century. He was knighted in 1820 and continued to be held in high esteem, but suffered financial ruin in 1825 and his novels written after this, which include *Woodstock* (1826) and *The Fair Maid of Perth* (1828), show a falling off in his talent.

The Strength of Scott's Writing

Scott's fiction drew on his reading of ballads and medieval romances and his various other antiquarian interests. Its strengths lie in its atmospheric descriptions of landscape, its vivid depiction of minor characters, its skill in evoking past periods—albeit in a romanticized manner—and its capacity for chronicling historical processes. During his lifetime he was frequently compared with Shakespeare and his reputation remained high throughout the nineteenth century, nowhere more so than in his native Scotland, where he became a cultural icon and a model for Victorian codes of genteel behaviour. Changes in taste, particularly a reaction against the kind of melodramatic romanticism his fiction embodies, subsequently led to a decline in his popularity, though he continues to be respected as a major regional novelist and as the author of memorable shorter poems (originally in his longer works), such as "Lochinvar" and "Breathes There the Man".

Jane Austen (1775–1817)

The daughter of a Hampshire rector, Jane Austen has been described as the first major modern novelist. Her superficially restrained and psychologically subtle fiction is a world away from the expansiveness and magniloquence of Scott, but it has stood the test of time better and today she is the most widely read novelist of her era. Her first piece of extended fiction, *Love and Friendship* (1790), was a burlesque of Richardson and in one sense her work belongs to the counter-tradition of Fielding, since it employs irony to satirize deviations from social norms. However, its range is narrower than Fielding's—it usually deals with "three or four families in a country village", with occasional forays into fashionable town society —and her characterization is more complex.

Her first full-length novel *Northanger Abbey* (posthumously published in 1818) involves a satire on Gothic fiction such as *The Mysteries of Udolpho*, as the heroine Catherine Moreland wrongly imagines that that the house of the title conceals dark secrets. It also engages with the themes that dominate Austen's subsequent fiction: the witty observation of social manners and the moral education of the heroine. The ironic first sentence of *Pride and Prejudice* (1813), "It is a truth universally acknowledged, that a single man in possession of a good fortune, must be in want of a wife", introduces the principal subject of Austen's most famous comedy of manners. The "universally acknowledged" truth in question represents the perspective of Mrs Bennet, the mother of five daughters whom she is anxious to marry off, and courtship and marriage are the pivot on which the plot turns. The central figure is Mrs Bennet's second daughter, Elizabeth, who initially rejects the advances of the seemingly arrogant Fitzwilliam D'Arcy, believing him to be the author of her family's misfortunes, but comes to learn that her prejudice, which has caused her to misinterpret his character, surpasses his pride.

The Success of *Emma*

The heroine of *Emma* (1816) is generally viewed as Austen's most lively creation; she is certainly her most meddlesome. Her efforts to broker a marriage for the illegitimate Harriet Smith, whom she adopts as a protegée, prove disastrous. Her blindness to her own feelings involves a level of self-delusion that outstrips that of either Catherine Moreland or Elizabeth Bennet, but once again the novel charts her moral education and she is finally united with the discerning Mr. Knightley. The heroine of *Mansfield Park* (1814), Fanny Price, is more passive. She is the virtuous poor relative in the house of the well-to-do Bertram family and her integrity offers a sharp contrast to the moral laxity that invades the country house of the title while its patriarch, Sir Thomas Bertram is away in Antigua. The house represents a staple upper middle class English social world, which is contrasted with disorder in the urban worlds of London and Portsmouth. Order is finally restored and Fanny's story has a Cinderella-like happy ending, when her love for Sir Thomas's son, Edmund, results in marriage.

Austen's other major novels, written at the opposite ends of her writing career, *Sense and Sensibility* (1811) and *Persuasion* (1818), both deal with conflicts between love and family obligations and include sections set in fashionable town society.

Thomas Love Peacock (1785–1866)

A close friend of Shelley, whom he often advised on literary and philosophical matters, Peacock is best remembered as a satirical novelist, whose fiction debates and ridicules many of the fashionable social and political attitudes of his day. Several of his novels employ a country house setting, in which a group of guests discuss contemporary intellectual controversies, while the novels themselves incorporate a miscellany of farcical elements, songs and improbable love stories that culminate in incongruously perfunctory happy endings. Novels of this kind include *Headlong Hall* (1816), where the characters represent opposed political and social views and the action ends in four hastily contrived marriages, *Nightmare Abbey* (1818), in which the attitudes of Coleridge, Byron and Shelley are all mocked, *Crotchet Castle* (1831), in which a Coleridge figure is once again included among the satirical portraits, and the later *Gryll Grange* (1860-1), in which a satirical view of mid-Victorian England is juxtaposed with a nostalgic vision of the recent past. His other novels include *Maid Marian* (1822) and *The Misfortunes of Elphin* (1829).

THE VICTORIAN NOVEL

Charles Dickens (1812–70)

Dickens's extraordinary popularity began with the publication of *The Pickwick Papers* (1836-7), which grew from a commission to write a series of sporting sketches and which contains the first of his many memorable characters that have become part of the English popular imagination, Mr Pickwick and his manservant Sam Weller. Prior to this, he had published *Sketches by Boz* (1835-6). *Oliver Twist* (1838) was his first popular masterpiece to combine vivid action and characterization with a critique of the divisions of the class-ridden society of his day, which he felt had been intensified by measures such as the Poor Law of 1834. It was followed by: *Nicholas Nickleby* (1839), which in its scenes set at Dotheboys Hall attacked the harsh regime of contemporary Yorkshire boarding schools; the hugely popular, albeit sentimental *The Old Curiosity Shop* (1841); *Barnaby Rudge* (1841); and *Martin Chuzzlewit* (1843).

The 1840s also saw the publication of the first and best-loved of his Christmas books, *A Christmas Carol* (1843), in which he created the memorable figure of the miser, Ebenezer Scrooge.

His Finest Novels

In the years that followed Dickens produced many of his finest novels: *Dombey and Son* (1848); *David Copperfield* (1850), his most autobiographical work as well as his own favourite novel; *Bleak House* (1853); *Hard Times* (1854), an attack on Utilitarianism set in the fictional northern city of Coketown; *Little Dorrit* (1857); *A Tale of Two Cities* (1859), a novel set during the French Revolution; *Great Expectations* (1861); and *Our Mutual Friend* (1865). All of these novels blend serious social criticism and entertainment, albeit in varying degrees.

Great Expectations, with its rich gallery of characters (the betrayed spinster Miss Havisham, the blacksmith Joe Gargery, the convict Magwitch, the lawyer Jaggers and his clerk Wemmick's Aged Parent among them), keeps these two aspects of his work in perfect balance, as the hero Pip slowly comes to recognize the class snobbery that has made him ashamed of his early origins.

Bleak House, where the interminable case of Jarndyce and Jarndyce serves as a metaphor for the British legal system and *Little Dorrit*, where the bureaucracy of the Circumlocution Office becomes a central symbol of the paralysis at the heart of government, are longer and more complex novels that also show Dickens's talent at its finest.

Dickens and Social Injustice

Dickens's concern with social injustices has often been seen to stem from his early experience of life. His father, on whom he based aspects of Mr Micawber in *David Copperfield*, was jailed for debt in London's Marshalsea prison, which becomes a central setting in *Little Dorrit*. As a consequence of the family's misfortunes, Dickens himself had to work in a blacking factory, where he became aware of the seamier side of London life at an early age.

Dickens has been criticized for his sentimentality, the disorderliness of some of his plots and his tendency to replace character with caricature. He remains one of the greatest storytellers in English literature, a social critic whose reforming fervour played a part in eradicating some of the social ills he dramatized, a writer with a unique flair for bringing the many facets of London life alive in an almost tactile way and the creator of many of the most memorable characters in the English novel.

Arguably the most prodigious genius among Victorian writers, he gave highly popular public readings of his work throughout his career. He collapsed during his final reading tour (1869-70) and died soon afterwards, leaving his last novel, *The Mystery of Edwin Drood* (1870) incomplete.

William Makepeace Thackeray (1811–63)

In the middle of the nineteenth century, when his most successful novel *Vanity Fair* (1847-8) was serialized at the same time as *David Copperfield*, Thackeray's work was frequently compared with that of Dickens, though his popularity with the general public never reached quite the same heights. A satirist of class snobbery, he did not share Dickens's sympathy for the criminalized poor. Thus the picaresque hero of his novel *The Luck of Barry Lyndon* (1844), set in the eighteenth century, is a figure who has more affinities with Fielding's Jonathan Wild than the characters of *Oliver Twist*.

His first major success came with *The Book of Snobs* (1846-7), a collection of portraits originally published in the magazine *Punch*, which casts a critical eye on Victorian class-consciousness.

Vanity Fair and Henry Esmond

Vanity Fair, one of the masterpieces of nineteenth-century "realism", offers a satirical critique of upper middle-class society at the beginning of the nineteenth century. Sub-titled a "novel without a hero", its declared purpose is "to indicate, in cheerful terms, that we are for the most part an abominably foolish and selfish people 'desperately wicked' and all eager after vanities". The machinations of its most memorable character, the scheming Becky Sharp, as she makes her way up the social ladder, attract the sympathy of many readers, in much the same way as Defoe's Moll Flanders' predicament has been seen to vindicate *her* behaviour.

Thackeray admired *The English Humorists of the Eighteenth Century* (the title of a lectures series he published in 1853) and like *Barry Lyndon*, his novel *Henry Esmond* (1852) and its sequel *The Virginians* (1857) were set in this century. *Henry Esmond*, his finest achievement after *Vanity Fair*, deserts the romantic heroism characteristic of much historical fiction in favour of psychological complexity and an ambiguous representation of social forces. At the end of the novel, Henry moves to Virginia and *The Virginians*, which includes scenes set against the backdrop of the American War of Independence, follows the fortunes of later generations of his family.

Other Novels

Thackeray's other novels include *Catherine* (1839-40), the semi-autobiographical *Pendennis* (1850) and *The Newcomes* (1853-5). His fiction frequently employs direct addresses to his readers *e.g.*, "If Miss Rebecca Sharp had determined in her heart upon making the conquest of this big beau, I don't think, ladies, we have any right to blame her". This intrusiveness has seemed dated to some modern readers, but admiration for his comic realism and his satirical exposure of Victorian hypocrisy have helped to re-establish Thackeray's reputation as a major novelist in recent years.

The Brontës

Although *Jane Eyre* (1847) and *Wuthering Heights* (1847) are universally accepted as classics of English fiction, in their own day they were controversial works that challenged the conventions of early Victorian fiction and the social values of the era, particularly with regard to their representation of male-female relationships. Their respective authors, Charlotte (1816-55) and Emily (1818–48) Brontë published their work under names that concealed their gender identity, Currer and Ellis Bell, while their sister Anne (1820–49) wrote under the name of Acton Bell.

Early Life

The sisters grew up in a parsonage in the then-remote village of Haworth on the edge of the Yorkshire moors. As children, they invented their own private fictional worlds, which particularly in the case of Emily seem to prefigure the alternative worlds of their adult writing. They were strongly influenced by the Romantics (particularly Byron)

and their novels introduced a new Romantic dimension into prose fiction, particularly in their emphasis on the interconnectedness of external nature and human character and their use of patterns of unifying organic imagery.

The central situation of Charlotte's masterpiece *Jane Eyre* is a sophisticated version of the plot of Richardson's *Pamela*: Jane is a governess, who finds herself torn between the conflicting claims of passion and restraint, when her employer Rochester, whose "mad" wife, Bertha, is immured in the attic of his house, tries to persuade her into an extramarital liaison. Circumstances finally allow Jane, who takes the view that "Women are supposed to be very calm generally; but women feel just as men feel", to reconcile the forces that threaten to tear her apart and marry Rochester on equal terms, having inherited money of her own. She becomes her "own mistress" and escapes from the position of social inferiority that characterizes the situation of many earlier heroines of English novels.

Wuthering Heights

No such resolution is possible in the story of the love of Cathy and Heathcliff, which dominates Emily Brontë's only published novel, *Wuthering Heights*. Its plot dramatizes a disparity in social background and world-views that drives the lovers apart and the novel reaches a tragic conclusion midway when Cathy dies. Nevertheless the commitment to passion is more total than in *Jane Eyre*: love transcends the grave when, after her death, Cathy's ghost haunts Heathcliff. At the same time, *Wuthering Heights* encompasses several other stories, centred on relationships between the contrasted Linton and Earnshaw families across two generations and reconciliations are achieved at the end. The novel's narrative technique is one of the most complex to be found in English fiction prior to the work of Joseph Conrad and Henry James. Its intricately plotted time-scheme and its two narrators, the outsider Lockwood and the old family servant Nelly Dean, lend credence to what might otherwise seem a far-fetched sequence of events. Charlotte's other novels were *Shirley* (1849), *Villette* (1853) and *The Professor* (1857).

Anne Brontë

Anne Brontë is remembered as the author of *Agnes Grey* (1847), which like *Jane Eyre* deals with the life of a governess, and the darker, more complex *Tenant of Wildfell Hall* (1848). The latter's account of a woman's suffering at the hands of a drunken husband seems remarkably modern, but on its first appearance represented another aspect of the Brontës' fiction that challenged contemporary expectations. Prior to the success of their novels, the three sisters had published *Poems by Currer, Ellis, and Acton Bell* (1846). Emily, who wrote a number of powerful short lyrics on death, is generally considered the finest poet of the three.

Anthony Trollope (1815–82)

Trollope is best remembered for his Barsetshire and Palliser series of novels, but together they constitute less than a quarter of his prolific fictional output. He first became famous with his fourth novel, *The Warden* (1855), which inaugurated the sequence set in the fictional West Country county of Barsetshire. It was followed by *Barchester Towers* (1857), a perceptive study of the impact of social changes on the community, which further augmented Trollope's reputation with the reading public. The other volumes in the series, which benefit from being read as part of the evolving sequence, are *Doctor Thorne* (1858), *Framley Parsonage* (1860-1), *The Small House at Allington* (1862-4) and *The Last Chronicle of Barsetshire* (1866-7). The Barsetshire novels offer a microcosm of English rural society in transition in the mid-Victorian period with a particular insight into ecclesiastical politics. Their particular strength lies in their realistic rendition of "ordinary" events.

Trollope's later fiction, including his Palliser novels, is more concerned with urban society and parliamentary political life. The Palliser novels are *Can You Forgive Her?* (1864-5), *Phineas Finn: The Irish Member* (1867-8), *The Eustace Diamonds* (1871-3), *Phineas Redux* (1873-4), *The Prime Minister* (1875-6) and *The Duke's Children*

(1879–80). Other later novels include *The Claverings* (1866–7), *He Knew He Was Right* (1868–9), *The American Senator* (1876–7) and *Dr Wortle's School* (1880). His longest novel, *The Way We Live Now* (1874–5), a satire on speculative commercialism, is now sometimes regarded as his finest work. Its depiction of stock exchange gambling has given it a particular relevance for contemporary society.

Trollope travelled widely, recording his impressions of other societies in such works as *The West Indies and the Spanish Main* (1859) and *Australia and New Zealand* (1873–4). For most of his life he worked for the post office and, literature apart, has a claim to fame as the man responsible for the installation of the first post box, on Guernsey in 1852.

The Condition of England Novel

Towards the middle of the nineteenth century a sense of the widening gaps between different segments of English society was expressed in a group of novels primarily concerned with what later became known as "the Condition of England". Such novels included Benjamin Disraeli's *Coningsby* (1844) and *Sybil* (1845), Elizabeth Gaskell's *Mary Barton* (1848) and *North and South* (1855), Charles Kingsley's *Alton Locke* (1850) and Dickens's *Hard Times*. Partly inspired by Carlyle's warning that the class divisions created by the Industrial Revolution were a recipe for revolution, Condition of England novels drew attention to disparities between the industrialized north and the more affluent south, the human consequences of mechanization, the need for a more egalitarian educational system and abuses of power occasioned by the new manufacturing industries.

George Eliot (1819–80)

George Eliot (the pen name of Mary Ann Evans) grew up in the English Midlands and her early fiction deals with the lives and loves of ordinary people from the region. It includes the three stories that make up *Scenes of Clerical Life* (1858) and the novels, *Adam Bede* (1859), *The Mill on the Floss* (1860) and *Silas Marner* (1861). *Adam Bede* tells the tragic story of Hetty Sorrel, who murders her illegitimate child. *The Mill on the Floss* is a more autobiographical work, in which the imaginative heroine Maggie Tulliver struggles to find love and self-fulfilment. The shorter *Silas Marner* is a moral fable about a miserly weaver, who is brought back into the human fold by the advent of a small child into his solitary life.

George Eliot's Masterpiece

If Eliot's career had ended here, she would be remembered as a fine regional novelist, with a talent for exploring the intricacies of human motivation, but her subsequent fiction is more ambitious in scope and more penetrating in its analysis of social issues. After broadening her fictional horizons with *Romola* (1862–3), a historical novel set in Renaissance Florence, she subsequently published three novels that were markedly more complex than her early work. *Felix Holt: The Radical* (1866), in which she attempts to emulate the form of a Greek tragic trilogy, is about rural electioneering at the time of the First Reform Bill (1832), a defining moment in British social history. Her masterpiece, *Middlemarch* (1871–2), a novel of epic proportions, is set in the same period. It interweaves four complex stories, to provide an intellectually probing study of "provincial life" during a time of rapid change. Its more memorable characters include Dorothea Brooke, a later more developed version of Maggie Tulliver, her academically sterile husband Casaubon, who is trying to write a "key to all mythologies" and the progressive young doctor, Tertius Lydgate, whose passion for medicine parallels Dorothea's for scholarship. However, its overall effect depends less upon the success of its individual characters than its skill in demonstrating their interaction in the novel's social microcosm.

A similar tone of high seriousness informs *Daniel Deronda* (1874–6), in which two plots gradually converge, with the initially self-centred Gwendolen Harleth finding sustenance in the moral and emotional values of Judaism, a corpus that offers an alternative to her laissez-faire English upbringing.

Robert Louis Stevenson (1850–94)

The Edinburgh-born Stevenson was one of the most prodigious and eclectic talents of nineteenth-century writing, though he is best remembered as the author of classic children's books and one of the great horror stories of English literature, *The Strange Case of Dr Jekyll and Mr Hyde* (1886). *Treasure Island* (1883) with its boy-narrator Jim Hawkins's story of buried treasure and pirates is both a brilliant piece of children's fiction and a novel that suggests the complexities of "evil", one of Stevenson's recurrent themes, in its representation of the figure of Long John Silver. Earlier R.M. Ballantyne's *The Coral Island* (1871) had made a similar use of an island setting for an adventure story that derives much of its appeal from taking a group of boys into unknown territory.

Stevenson's *Kidnapped* (1886) is a darker tale of dispossession, in which the hero David Balfour suffers at the hands of his cruel Uncle Ebenezer. *Dr Jekyll and Mr Hyde* is a study of a split personality, which among other things reflects Victorian unease about the impact of Darwinian theory on beliefs about identity. Other important novels by Stevenson include the sequel to *Kidnapped*, *Catriona* (1893), *The Black Arrow* (1888) and *The Master of Ballantrae* (1889). Suffering from ill health, he left Britain in 1888 and settled in Samoa, enjoying a new lease of literary life. His writing during his Samoan years, which includes the novellas, *The Beach of Falesá* (1893) and *The Ebb-Tide* (1894), protests against the colonial exploitation of the South Seas.

Schoolboy Fiction, Adventure Stories and the Literature of Empire

Unlike Stevenson, the majority of other Victorian writers of adventure stories can be seen as contributing, intentionally or otherwise, to the late Victorian literature of Empire, often developing links between the values instilled in the English public school and subsequent service in the Empire. Classic schoolboy novels that suggest such connections include Thomas Hughes's *Tom Brown's Schooldays* (1857) and Rudyard Kipling's *Stalky & Co* (1899), which closes with its former schoolboys in India. Such writing was also a staple of popular magazines such as the *Boys Own Paper*, where writers like Talbot Baines Reed, later famed for the classic public school novel, *The Fifth Form at St Dominic's* (serialized in the *Boys Own Paper* in 1907), linked team games and a sporting ethic of fair play with Christian morality and charitable work in the Empire.

Haggard and Henty

Rider Haggard's *King Solomon's Mines* (1885), the story of an expedition to find diamonds in southern Africa and its sequels *Allan Quatermain* (1887) and *She* (1887) are notable among the many adventure novels of the period. The heroic thrust of Haggard's work was sometimes seen as a counterforce to naturalism's more pessimistic view of people's capacity to influence their situation. G.A. Henty's numerous tales of heroic virtue, such as *With Clive in India* (1884) and *With Wolfe in Canada* (1887), characteristically link derring-do, Christianity and Empire. Other romances of the period with "exotic" locations include Anthony Hope Hawkins's *The Prisoner of Zenda* (1894), in which Hope created the mythical European country of Ruritania, and W.H. Hudson's *Green Mansions* (1904), a tale set in the South American rain forest.

Earlier Captain Frederick Marryat's stories of sea adventurers had included *Peter Simple* (1834) and *Mr Midshipman Easy* (1836). John Buchan continued the tradition of adventure writing in the early twentieth century with novels such as *Prester John* (1910) and *The Thirty-Nine Steps* (1915).

Novels of Sensation and Mystery

The Victorian vogue for melodrama, sensation and mystery reached its apogee in the novels of Wilkie Collins, whose *The Woman in White* (1860) demonstrates considerable skill in creating suspense. Collins's *The Moonstone* (1868) laid the groundwork for the modern detective novel, though the American Edgar Allan Poe, had pioneered detective fiction in his short stories about August

Dupin, particularly "Murders in the Rue Morgue" and "The Purloined Letter". Dupin was a forerunner of the most famous detective of the nineteenth century, Sir Arthur Conan's Doyle Sherlock Holmes, whose use of deductive reasoning demonstrated a similar fascination with what Poe termed "ratiocination". At the beginning of the twentieth century, the Catholic convert G.K. Chesterton took the figure in a new direction by relating his detective, Father Brown's skill in solving crimes to his capacity to understand evil.

Sir Arthur Conan Doyle (1859–1930)

Holmes and his omnipresent assistant, Dr Watson first appeared in the novels *A Study in Scarlet* (1887) and *The Sign of Four* (1890), but it was the short stories that Conan Doyle wrote for *The Strand Magazine* in the 1890s that secured his popularity. They were collected in *The Adventures of Sherlock Holmes* (1892) and *The Memoirs of Sherlock Holmes* (1894). Doyle killed Holmes off, when he had him plunge to his death at the Reichenbach Falls in Switzerland in a struggle with his arch-enemy Professor Moriarty, but he was forced to resurrect him in response to public demand. The detective reappeared in several subsequent volumes, including Doyle's best-known work, *The Hound of the Baskervilles* (1902) and the short story collections, *The Return of Sherlock Holmes* (1905) and *The Case-Book of Sherlock Holmes* (1927).

The Gothic Novel

At the end of the nineteenth century, the Gothic novel reached new heights in Bram Stoker's classic vampire novel, *Dracula* (1897). Written as a series of first-person narratives that partly help to authenticate its sensational subject-matter, Stoker's novel drew on pre-existing vampire literature to create the figure of the Transylvanian Count who has become the archetypal vampire of the popular imagination. Contemporary reviewers appear to have been blind to the sexual implications of vampirism, which were to become a major part of the *Dracula* myth in the film treatments of the twentieth century.

Thomas Hardy (1840–1928)

Often described as England's one major tragic novelist, Hardy set his work in the fictional West Country region of Wessex, based on his native Dorset. It provided him with an environment that was both very specifically localized and a stage for archetypal human dramas. In all his novels, the human action is played out against a vividly realized rural landscape, which can become a character in its own right. *The Return of the Native* (1878) is set against the landscape of Egdon Heath, described at the outset as having "a lonely face, suggesting tragic possibilities". The setting of *The Woodlanders* (1887), Hintock Woods, is similarly crucial to the action, while the experiences of the heroine of *Tess of the D'Urbervilles* (1891) in a number of different landscapes reflect her situation and state of mind at each particular juncture.

The causes of Hardy's tragic protagonists' downfalls vary. Sometimes, as in *The Mayor of Casterbridge* (1886), where he quotes the dictum, "character is fate", they can be attributed to character flaws: Henchard, the mayor of the novel's title, sells his wife, while drunk. Elsewhere, as in *Tess of the D'Urbervilles*, where Hardy writes in the final paragraph "The President of the Immortals, in Aeschylean phrase, had ended his sport with Tess", fate seems the dominant force. At the same time Tess, like several other Hardy characters, is a victim of the moral conventions of her day and throughout his work, Hardy demonstrates an acute sense of the impact of social forces, particularly moral codes and mechanization, on individuals and agrarian communities. His other major novels include *Under the Greenwood Tree* (1872), *Far from the Madding Crowd* (1874), *The Trumpet-Major* (1880) and *Jude the Obscure* (1896).

Later Novels and Poetry

The later novels, *Tess* and *Jude*, are not without melodrama, but the tragic fates of their protagonists suggest the influence of Naturalism and a belief in social determinism. The sub-title of *Tess*,

"a pure woman", attracted criticism, since in conventional terms its heroine was a "fallen woman"; and the sympathetic representation of extramarital sexual relations in *Jude the Obscure* evoked a similar response. When a copy of *Jude* was burned by a bishop on the grounds of the novel's supposed obscenity, Hardy forsook fiction and turned to poetry, commenting ruefully, "Nobody will be hurt by my poetry, because nobody will read it".

He wrote verse throughout the remainder of his life. His poetry ranges between simple ballads of folk experience that drew on local Dorset traditions, particularly the work of the Dorset poet, William Barnes, and more personal lyrics, notable among which is a series of elegiac poems written after the death of his wife, Emma, in 1912. These were published in *Satires of Circumstance, Lyrics and Poems* (1914). His other poetry includes *Wessex Poems and Other Verses* (1898), *Poems of the Past and Present* (1902) and the epic drama, *The Dynasts* (1903–08).

Naturalism in English Fiction

In the latter part of the nineteenth century, the collapse of traditional belief-systems, the influence of Darwinism and a growing awareness of the effect of environment on character led to the rise of the heightened form of social realism known as "Naturalism". Its major theorist was the French novelist Émile Zola and it was never as important a movement in England as in France and the USA, where its practitioners included Stephen Crane, Frank Norris and Theodore Dreiser. Notable English naturalistic novels of the *fin de siècle* years include George Gissing's *New Grub Street* (1891) and George Moore's *Esther Waters* (1894) and its influence is also apparent in the determinism of Hardy's *Tess* and *Jude*.

The continuing, albeit limited, popularity of Naturalism in the early twentieth century can be seen in Arnold Bennett's novels, such as *The Old Wives' Tale* (1908) and *Riceyman Steps* (1923), which provide meticulously detailed, warts-and-all accounts of the lives of ordinary people. However, for Modernist writers such as Virginia Woolf and D.H. Lawrence, Naturalism was a form of fiction that, despite its care in rendering such details, failed to engage with all that was most vital in human experience. Woolf distanced herself from Bennett in her essay "Mr Bennett and Mrs Brown", in which she argued he completely failed to capture the character of people, such as "Mrs Brown", an ordinary woman in a railway carriage. Lawrence referred to Bennett as "an old imitator", commenting scathingly, "Tell Arnold Bennett that all rules of construction hold good only for novels which are copies of other novels".

VICTORIAN LITERATURE

Elizabeth Barrett Browning (1806–61)

Born in England into a plantation-owning Jamaican Creole family, Elizabeth Barrett became a vehement critic of slavery and other social injustices. Sometimes remembered as the wife of Robert Browning, particularly as represented in the film versions of Rudolf Besier's play *The Barretts of Wimpole Street* (1930), she was a major poet in her own right. She was considered a strong candidate for the post of Poet Laureate when Wordsworth died in 1850 and had a greater reputation as a poet than her husband-to-be when they met in 1845.

Her first volume to attract critical favour was *The Seraphim and Other Poems* (1838). A lung condition she first developed as a child, a spinal injury and grief at her brother's death from drowning in 1838 rendered her an invalid and recluse in the house of her domineering father. *Poems* (1844), which included "The Cry of the Children", secured her reputation and led to the beginnings of her correspondence with Browning. After their elopement and marriage, they moved to Florence, where her health improved and she lived for the remainder of her life.

Her *Sonnets from the Portuguese*, which appeared in *Poems* (1850), is a sequence of forty-four love poems written to Browning, which has no connection with any Portuguese originals. It contains her most famous poem, "How do I love thee,/ Let me count the ways". *Aurora Leigh* (1857) is a verse novel, in which she explores a broad range of social issues, including the "Woman Question", the predicament of the poor, child labour and the role of poetry. Her support for Italian unification informs *Casa Guidi Windows* (1851) and *Poems before Congress* (1860). Her *Last Poems* were published posthumously in 1862. Her popularity declined after her death, but the feminist dimension of her work and its engagement with other social and political issues have occasioned a revival of interest in recent decades.

Alfred, Lord Tennyson (1809–92)

Raised in a Lincolnshire rectory, Tennyson attended Cambridge, where he developed a close friendship with Arthur Hugh Hallam, with whom he subsequently travelled in continental Europe. His *Poems, Chiefly Lyrical* (1830), written under the influence of the Romantics, met with little success, but includes a number of poems for which he is remembered, among them "Mariana", "The Palace of Art" and "The Lady of Shalott", his first important poem on an Arthurian subject. *Poems* (1833) includes "The Two Voices" and "The Lotos-Eaters". Hallam had become engaged to Tennyson's sister, Emily, but died suddenly at the age of twenty-two, and the grief-stricken Tennyson commenced the sequence of 131 elegiac poems that would eventually be published as *In Memoriam: A.H.H.* (1850) in 1833. *English Idyls and Other Poems* (1842) contains some of his finest short poems: "Morte d'Arthur", "Ulysses", "Break, break, break" and "Locksley Hall", a disappointed lover's trochaic monologue, which engages with the state of contemporary society.

His Best-Known Lyrics

The Princess (1847) is a long blank verse poem, containing some of Tennyson's best-known lyrics, including "Tears, Idle Tears". Later satirized by Gilbert and Sullivan in their comic-opera *Princess Ida*, it is an incipiently feminist poem: the eponymous heroine rejects her betrothed and founds a university for women. The lovers *are* eventually united, but the romantic resolution is tempered by a passage which looks forward to their married future in which "man be more of woman, she of man". *In Memoriam* begins as a moving expression of personal loss, but expands outwards to encompass a wide range of philosophical and social issues, progressing from a deep sense of doubt to an affirmation in which new scientific knowledge is reconciled with Biblical teachings. It was published in the year of Wordsworth's death and its immediate popularity was a factor in Tennyson's succeeding him as Poet Laureate.

Tennyson and Queen Victoria

His work was greatly admired by Prince Albert, Queen Victoria's consort, and he became the favourite poet of the Queen herself, who is said to have held his poems second only to the Bible. He eventually accepted a baronetcy from her in 1884. Tennyson's Laureateship led to the writing of poems on such subjects as the death of Wellington (1852), the opening of the International Exhibition of 1862 and, most famously, "The Charge of the Light Brigade" (1854). *Maud* (1855) is a mono-drama about a luckless young man, which inveighs against the materialism of the age and contains a number of popular lyrics.

The *Idylls of the King* (1859–85) is a series of twelve poems on the Arthurian legend, which have the encyclopaedic range of epic poetry and include several self-contained narratives, such as that of Geraint and Enid. They were enormously popular in Tennyson's own day, but have been less well regarded by subsequent critics and the consensus of later opinion has been that his greatest gift was as a lyric poet. However, read as an allegory in which the fortunes of Camelot relate to contemporary society, the *Idylls* offer a fascinating exploration of the changing spirit of the age. *Tiresias and Other Poems* (1885) includes "Locksley Hall Sixty Years After", another expression of personal loss that offers a conservative commentary on the state of the nation, as the speaker attacks the dominance of scientific values and the social consequences of industrialization.

Other work from the period of Tennyson's Laureateship includes the highly popular narrative poem, *Enoch Arden* (1864), *Ballads and Other Poems* (1880) and the plays, *Queen Mary* (1875), *The Cup* (1884) and *Becket* (1884). By the time of his death Tennyson was a public institution, but his reputation had dwindled among his younger contemporaries.

Robert Browning (1812–89)

Browning was born into a nonconformist family in South London and was mainly privately educated. His early work was written under the influence of Shelley, and in poems such as *Paracelsus* (1835), a study of the Swiss alchemist, and *Sordello* (1840), in which he took one of Dante's contemporaries as his subject, he combined metaphysical and poetic inquiry with a talent for dramatizing individual psychologies that was to become one of the main characteristics of his subsequent verse. His greatest achievements were in the form of the dramatic monologue, a genre he made uniquely his own, creating personae with a psychological complexity more normally associated with the novel and rendering them in a range of colloquial and unconventional registers. Most of his finest work in this mode was published in the various parts of *Bells and Pomegranates* (1841–6) and *Men and Women* (1855). It includes "My Last Duchess", "The Bishop Orders His Tomb at St Praxed's Church", "Fra Lippo Lippi", "Bishop Blougram's Apology" and "Andrea del Sarto". His skill as a writer of narrative poems can be seen in "The Pied Piper of Hamelin", "How They Brought the Good News from Ghent to Aix" and "Childe Roland to the Dark Tower Came".

Browning's plays mainly belong to his early period. They include *Pippa Passes* (1841), *A Blot in the 'Scutcheon* (1843) and *Colombe's Birthday* (1844). Some were never intended for performance and generally they show a surer touch in the handling of character than action.

Marriage and Italy

Browning's admiration for Elizabeth Barrett's poetry led him to write to her and they eventually eloped and married in 1846. They settled in Italy, a country which he had first visited in 1838 and which provided the inspiration for many of his most famous works, and lived there until her death in 1861. His "Home Thoughts from Abroad", yearning "Oh, to be in England/ Now that April's there", was written in Tuscany. The serialized publication of *The Ring and the Book* (1868–9), a poem of more than 20,000 lines, in monthly instalments, secured Browning's reputation with a wider reading public. It tells the story of a seventeenth-century Roman murder from several different viewpoints, once again demonstrating his virtuosity in handling dramatized figures, while also covering an encyclopaedic range of subjects.

During his later years Browning's poetic output continued unabated. Notable works from his last two decades include *Red-Cotton Nightcap Country* (1873), *The Inn Album* (1875), *Dramatic Idyls* (1879–80) and *Asolando* (1889). The foundation of the Browning Society in 1881 reflects the adulation in which he was held by a section of the late Victorian reading public. Along with Tennyson, he was regarded as one of the two pre-eminent poets of the period.

Matthew Arnold (1822–88)

The son of Thomas Arnold, the famous headmaster who made Rugby School a model for nineteenth-century middle-class education, Matthew Arnold was a polymath who took a leading role in many of the cultural debates of the Victorian era and became Professor of Poetry at Oxford in 1858. Today he is best known for his literary criticism and writings on the state of English culture. However, his poetry includes some of the finest nineteenth-century lyrics, among them his "Marguerite" poems and his best-known short poem, "Dover Beach" (1867), a powerful expression of the uncertainties of the age, written in melancholy slow-moving verse. Three longer narrative poems, "Tristram and Iseult" (1852), "Sohrab and Rustum" (1853) and "Balder Dead" (1855) respectively turned to medieval, eastern and Norse mythology for heroic subjects, while treating them in an unconventionally sombre vein. Arnold's elegiac poems include "The Scholar-Gipsy" (1853), which laments the impossibility of a simple pastoral response to landscape in the troubled climate of Victorian doubt, and "Thyrsis" (1867), a monody on the death of his friend, Arthur Hugh Clough. *Empedocles on Etna* (1852) is a verse drama.

Arnold's Literary Criticism

Arnold's literary criticism laid the foundations for the development of the subject along detached and "disinterested" lines and was influential in the construction of English literature as an object of academic study in the late nineteenth and early twentieth century. *Culture and Anarchy* (1869) advanced an idealistic view of culture as a kind of secular religion, seeing it as "the best that has been thought and said in the world", a definition that remained popular until the middle of the twentieth century. Written under the influence of Cardinal Newman, his later writings on the religious controversies of the day, which include *Literature and Dogma* (1873), were an attempt to reconcile rationalism and faith. Arnold saw his work as a response to the main movements of Victorian thought that combined the emotion of Tennyson with the intellect of Browning. In his poem "To a Friend", he said of Sophocles that he "saw life steadily, and saw it whole" and his own response to what he viewed as the "sick disease" of contemporary life can be seen as similarly balanced and harmonious.

The Rossettis and the Pre-Raphaelites

Founded in 1848, the Pre-Raphaelite Brotherhood was a movement in art and literature that rejected the prevalent cultural fashions of the day in favour of a return to what it saw as the simplicity of the medieval era. Its members included Holman Hunt, John Everett Millais and Dante Gabriel Rossetti. While its most significant achievements were in painting, its poetry included noteworthy work by Rossetti, who employed archaic language and mystical symbolism and, with the exception of "Jenny" (1870), a ballad about a London prostitute, found its subjects in medieval, particularly Arthurian, legends.

His best-known poem, "The Blessed Damozel" (1850), reflects an idealized Platonic conception of love and was followed by his later painting of the same theme. Rossetti's sister, Christina, is best known for her collection *Goblin Market and Other Poems* (1862). Contemporary critics have found homocrotic tendencies and a tension between sensuality and renunciation in its title-poem, a gnomic allegory about two sisters who exemplify different aspects of nineteenth-century womanhood. Such a tension is typical of much of her poetry, in which a mystical spirituality, born out of her high Anglican faith, co-exists with eroticism. Her verse demonstrates considerable technical virtuosity and she was a particularly accomplished writer of sonnets.

Her later collections include *The Prince's Progress and Other Poems* (1866) and *A Pageant and Other Poems* (1881). Several other poets were associated with the Pre-Raphaelites, though they were not members of the original Brotherhood. These included Algernon Charles Swinburne, George Meredith and William Morris.

Gerard Manley Hopkins (1844–89)

Hopkins was a Catholic convert, who was ordained as a Jesuit priest in 1877. An important poetic innovator, he developed his "sprung rhythm" metre, which attempts to reflect speech rhythms by using a prosody based on the number of stresses (not the feet) in a line, with unaccented syllables being discounted. He combines this distinctive approach to metre with extensive use of alliteration and assonance. His formal innovation was complemented by his ideas on "inscape", the term he coined to describe the distinctive spiritual essence formed by the parts that make up the organic integrity of a thing, and "instress", the energy which secures this coherence and which radiates from the inscape into the mind of its beholder.

"The Wreck of the Deutschland" (written 1876) responds to a shipping disaster, in which five Franciscan nuns were drowned, with a meditation on Christ's passion and an expression of his own faith in God, which links Hopkins's poetic and spiritual beliefs: "His mystery must be instressed, stressed; / For I greet him the days I meet him, and bless when I understand." It was followed by "The Windhover" and "Pied Beauty" (written 1877). His poetry was unknown during his own life-time, but became influential after his friend Robert Bridges's posthumous edition, *Poems* (1918).

Among his other best-known poems are the early "Heaven-Haven" and the late "Carrion Comfort" (one of his "terrible" sonnets) and "That Nature is a Heraclitean Fire", a powerful poetic statement of Christ's immanence in humanity.

Victorian Prose

The rapid social changes caused by the Industrial Revolution and the challenge to traditional beliefs brought about by Darwin's theory of evolution, the Higher Criticism of the Bible and a range of other scientific and intellectual developments led to the emergence of some of English literature's most extraordinary prose writers, whose works combined artistic and cultural concerns with broader social and religious commentary.

Thomas Carlyle (1795–1881)

One of the most influential thinkers of the nineteenth century, Carlyle came from a Scottish Presbyterian background and was strongly influenced by the German philosophical tradition. *Sartor Resartus* (1833–4), an eccentric work, starting from the proposition that clothes represent the provisional nature of the human condition, introduced his mannered prose style, full of neologisms, exclamations and archaisms, which later came to be known as "Carlylese". His fame as a historian was assured with the publication of his *History of the French Revolution* (1837). *On Heroes, Hero Worship and the Heroic in History* (1841) discusses the characteristics of representative heroes, such as Odin, Muhammad, Dante and Rousseau. *Past and Present* (1843), which looks back to medieval times to comment on the situation of the new urban poor, provided an inspiration for certain sections of the working men's movement. However, although his writing is informed by a strong sense of social conscience, Carlyle's anti-democratic identification with heroic leader figures led to a decline in his reputation in the twentieth century.

John Ruskin (1819–1900)

Ruskin's work brings together a broad range of artistic, philosophical and social concerns. He first achieved fame as an art critic with *Modern Painters* (Vol. I, 1843; later volumes, 1846–60). This was followed by *The Seven Lamps of Architecture* (1849) and *The Stones of Venice* (1851–3), the work that best demonstrates his extraordinary capacity for blending specialist art criticism with commentary on the social implications of cultural production. It broadens out from an attack on the romantic sentimentalization of Venetian architecture to contrast the degradation of industrial society's working practices with the labour conditions that existed in feudal times. His work as an art critic championed the Gothic and the paintings of the Pre-Raphaelite Brotherhood.

He became a major campaigner for social reform and was active in a wide range of causes. Like William Morris, he was an advocate of craftsmanship and an opponent of what he saw as the deleterious human consequences of mass production. During his later years he worked on an unfinished autobiography, *Praeterita* (1885–9).

William Morris (1834–96)

The main founder of the Arts and Crafts Movement, Morris pioneered new standards in architecture, interior furnishings, printing, bookbinding, textiles and glasswork. He was associated with the Pre-Raphaelites and like them and like Ruskin, he attempted to counter what he saw as the vulgarity of contemporary taste by returning to medieval practices. Morris's ideas about design were accompanied by strong socialist convictions and he also produced numerous literary works. His poetic sequence, *The Earthly Paradise* (1868–70) is a late Romantic work which draws on Norse and other mythologies. The prose work, *A Dream of John Ball* (1888) looks back to the fourteenth-century Peasants' Revolt to find alternatives to the values of contemporary England; the utopian fantasy, *News from Nowhere* (1890) looks forwards to a socialist future in which craftsmanship has replaced factory production.

The Aesthetic Movement

Another strain in later nineteenth-century thinking came to the fore in the *fin de siècle* aesthetic movement, which rejected the utilitarianism that marked much Victorian intellectual inquiry in favour of a belief in "art for art's sake". This phrase was coined by Walter Pater, in the conclusion to his *Studies in the History of the Renaissance* (1873), but Pater subsequently distanced himself from it.

Pater's best-known work, *Marius the Epicurean* (1885), is a philosophical romance set in ancient Rome, written in his characteristically polished prose. Other prominent figures in the movement included Max Beerbohm, Oscar Wilde and the illustrator Aubrey Beardsley, art editor of the periodical *The Yellow Book* (1894–7), which shocked many of its late Victorian readers with what they saw as its decadence,

Victorian Drama

The nineteenth century was not one of the great ages of the English theatre, but during the Victorian era, plays such as Dion Boucicault's *London Assurance* (1841) and Leopold Lewis's *The Bells* (1871), the story of a man haunted by his death by a murder he has committed, were highly regarded for their melodramatic appeal. Towards the end of the century melodrama became the object of parodies such as Gilbert and Sullivan's *Ruddigore* (1887), while A.W. Pinero's The *Second Mrs Tanqueray* (1893), an attack on the sexual double standards of the day, achieved fame as a more serious treatment of Victorian hypocrisy.

Oscar Wilde (1854–1900)

The hypocrisy of the period is also a prime target of the plays of Oscar Wilde, whose comedy of manners *The Importance of Being Earnest* (1895), in which brilliant epigrams combine with comedy based on mistaken or false identities, is one of the wittiest plays in the English language. Wilde's other comedies, *Lady Windermere's Fan* (1892), *A Woman of No Importance* (1893) and *An Ideal Husband* (1895), are also memorable for their aphorisms and their ingenious manipulation of situation.

Wilde also produced notable work in other genres, including *The Picture of Dorian Gray* (1890), a novel in which the Faustian protagonist sells his soul for eternal youth and which suggests the decadence underlying the genteel facade of polite society, and *Lord Arthur Savile's Crime and Other Stories* (1891). The poem *The Ballad of Reading Gaol* (1898) was a product of his experience serving a two-year sentence in the jail after a conviction for homosexuality.

George Bernard Shaw (1856–1950)

By the end of the nineteenth century, the influence of the Norwegian playwright Henrik Ibsen's naturalistic drama began to be felt in Britain and the early plays of the Irish-born George Bernard Shaw, such as *Arms and the Man* (1894), *The Devil's Disciple* (1897) and *You Never Can Tell* (1899), show the influence of his revolt against the artificiality of nineteenth-century stage conventions.

Shaw was a Fabian socialist, whose dramas of ideas were enlivened by memorable characterization and witty dialogue. His finest plays belong to the first part of the twentieth century. They include *Man and Superman* (1903), *Major Barbara* (1907) and *Pygmalion* (1913), the story of the metamorphosis of a Cockney flower-girl into a lady, from which the musical *My Fair Lady* (1956) was adapted. In *Heartbreak House* (1920), the house of the title suggests the condition of England at the outbreak of World War I and the play's characters are riddled with uncertainties. *Saint Joan* (1923) presents Joan of Arc as a woman born ahead of her time. Shaw's other plays include *Candida* (1897), *Caesar and Cleopatra* (1899), *Captain Brassbound's Conversion* (1900), *The Doctor's Dilemma* (1906),

Back to Methuselah (1922), *The Apple Cart* (1929) and *The Millionairess* (1936). He was awarded the Nobel Prize for Literature in 1925.

W.B. Yeats (1865–1939) and the Irish Literary Renaissance

One of Ireland's greatest poets, Yeats's early work was inspired by traditional Celtic mythology and the beginnings of what was to be a life-long interest in magic and the occult. He was the leading figure in the Irish literary renaissance of the late nineteenth and early twentieth centuries, a movement which endeavoured to counteract the predominantly negative view of the country's culture that was prevalent in his youth and which can be seen as an artistic equivalent of Irish political nationalism. His anthology *The Celtic Twilight* (1893) gave a name to a pre-existing vogue for Gaelic legend and played a significant role in its dissemination.

Yeats's early verse was primarily lyrical. It includes poems such as "The Lake Isle of Innisfree" and "When You Are Old", along with treatments of mythical subjects such as "Fergus and the Druid" and "Cuchulain's Fight with the Sea". In the late 1890s, along with Lady Augusta Gregory and others, he helped found the Irish Literary Theatre, a group dedicated to establishing a national drama, and his play *The Countess Cathleen* (1899) was its first production. The group's efforts resulted in the founding of Ireland's most famous theatrical venue, the Abbey Theatre, which opened in Dublin in 1904. His other plays include his best-known dramatic work, the one-act *Cathleen Ni Houlihan* (1902), which again took its subject from traditional Irish legend, *Deirdre* (1907), *At the Hawk's Well* (1915) and *Purgatory* (1938).

The Later Period

Yeats's later poems blend the lyricism of his early work with a more mature and reflective approach, in which the sometimes gratuitous obscurity of his use of symbols is replaced by a more sustained system of symbolism, based on the Italian philosopher Giambattista Vico's view of history and explained in his prose work, *A Vision* (1937). Many of his major poems appear in the collections, *The Wild Swans at Coole* (1919), *Michael Robartes and the Dancer* (1921) and *The Tower* (1928). Other volumes include *The Wanderings of Oisin* (1889), *The Rose* (1893), *The Wind Among the Reeds* (1899), *The Green Helmet* (1910), *Responsibilities* (1914), *The Winding Stair* (1933) and *Last Poems* (1939). Yeats's finest poems include "Easter 1916", an elegiac response to the political uprising of that year, the powerfully cryptic "Second Coming", in which artistic and political concerns are fused, and two of the greatest poetic meditations on ageing in the English language: "Sailing to Byzantium" and "Among School Children". Yeats became a member of the Irish Senate in the 1920s and was awarded the Nobel Prize for Literature in 1923.

J.M. Synge (1871–1909) and Later Irish Dramatists

Along with Yeats and Lady Gregory, Synge was the other key figure in the movement that led to the opening of the Abbey Theatre. His contribution to the Irish literary renaissance differs from Yeats's in that it lacks obvious political commitment. His plays were inspired by a series of visits to the remote Aran Islands between 1898 and 1902 and are lyrical homages to the individualism and humour of the peasantry of the West of Ireland. They include the one-act *In the Shadow of the Glen* (1903) and *Riders to the Sea* (1904), his masterpiece *The Playboy of the Western World* (1907), in which he achieved his finest representation of the speech of the region, albeit while incurring the wrath of Irish patriots who objected to his debunking of idealized views of the West, and *Deirdre of the Sorrows* (1910), in which he took his subject from Irish mythology.

Subsequent landmarks in Irish theatre include Sean O'Casey's *Juno and the Paycock* (1924), *The Plough and the Stars* (1926) and *The Silver Tassie* (1928), Brendan Behan's *The Quare Fellow* (1954) and *The Hostage* (1958), Brian Friel's *Translations* (1980) and *Dancing at Lughnasa* (1990) and Billy Roche's *Amphibians* (1992).

MODERN FICTION

Henry James (1843–1916)

Along with Joseph Conrad, who was also born in the mid-nineteenth century, James was one of the founding figures of the modern novel in English. The fiction of James and Conrad is modern in its emphasis on the subjectivity of perceptions and the relativism of beliefs and its employment of narrative strategies that reflect this shift in focus. James was also the first great theorist of the modern novel, producing a body of critical work that argued for a movement away from the "loose and baggy monsters" of nineteenth-century fiction towards a more serious "art of fiction" of the kind developed by Flaubert and Turgenev in France. He was a particular pioneer of what he variously called "the point of view", "centres of consciousness" and "scenic reflectors", i.e. the angle of vision from which a narrative is seen and told.

His Early Work

James was born in the United States and his early novels *Roderick Hudson* (1875), *The American* (1877) and *The Europeans* (1878) introduce the subject that dominates much of his fiction, the "international theme": the contrast between English and American manners. *Roderick Hudson* and *The American* both describe the experiences of American innocents abroad in Europe, though ultimately their protagonists suffer very different fates. *The Europeans* reverses the formula by taking "European" American expatriates to Massachusetts and dramatizing the differences between their lifestyles and those of their New England cousins.

In the novella, *Daisy Miller* (1878), James's first notable popular success, another American innocent becomes a victim of European experience, when she flouts social conventions and dies after contracting malaria in the symbolic arena of the Coliseum. The masterpiece of the first phase of James's career, *The Portrait of a Lady* (1881), is the subtlest and most fully developed of his early explorations of the ironies surrounding the encounter between American and European culture and its characters, including the heroine Isabel Archer, and situations are among his most finely drawn.

His Later Work

Innocence and experience also lie at the heart of James novels which desert the international theme, such as *What Maisie Knew* (1897), *The Spoils of Poynton* (1897) and *The Awkward Age* (1899), and his classic "ghost story", *The Turn of the Screw* (1898). *The Turn* uses point of view in a highly complex way, leaving its readers unsure as to whether its narrator-protagonist, a governess figure in the tradition of Jane Eyre, is reliable or unreliable and having to choose between various possible explanations of the apparitions she has "seen", including whether she is really looking at ghosts or hallucinating, possibly because of sexual repression.

In the 1890s James aspired to become a successful dramatist, but after the failure of his play *Guy Domville* (1895) on the London stage, he returned to fiction. In the same decade he wrote most of his best-known short stories, publishing the collections *The Lesson of the Master* (1892), *The Real Thing* (1893), *Terminations* (1895) and *Embarrassments* (1896), which includes "The Figure in the Carpet".

Three Late Masterpieces

In his three late masterpieces, *The Wings of the Dove* (1902), *The Ambassadors* (1903) and *The Golden Bowl* (1904), James returned to variations on the international theme. Written in an often-labyrinthine prose style, they become detective-stories of consciousness, in which the characters struggle to come to terms with hidden forces of betrayal *and* their own capacity for self-deception. His other novels include *Washington Square* (1880), *The Bostonians* (1886) and *The Princess Casamassima* (1886). His volumes of critical prose include *French Poets and Novelists* (1878), *The Art of Fiction* (1885) and *Notes on Novelists* (1914).

H.G. Wells (1866–1946)

Wells's writing blends invention with socialist commentary on the present and future state of society and after World War I he mainly produced novels of ideas that took an increasingly pessimistic view of the direction in which civilization was moving. His beliefs about literature represent an opposite extreme from those of Henry James, with whom he engaged in a debate about the nature and function of fiction. Wells took the view that novels should serve a melioristic function and maintained that their form should reflect the disorderliness of experience; James argued for "selection" rather than "saturation" and for the need for art to shape "reality".

Wells's most significant novels appeared in the early years of his career and fall into two groups: science-fiction romances, mainly written in the 1890s, and social comedies, mainly written in the first years of the twentieth century. His science fiction includes *The Time Machine* (1895), *The Island of Dr Moreau* (1896), *The Invisible Man* (1897) and *The War of the Worlds* (1898). Unlike the slightly earlier science-fiction writing of Jules Verne, where the main interest is in science itself, Wells's work in the genre usually offers allegories of contemporary social situations rather than prophecies of the future or adventure-stories. Thus the story of a Martian invasion of London in *The War of the Worlds* hints at the dangers of imperial complacency.

Wells's social comedies are novels in the tradition of Dickens, which characteristically blend comedy and pathos in their accounts of lower middle-class "little men" struggling to achieve a better life, often through self-education. They include *Love and Mr Lewisham* (1900), *Kipps* (1905), *Tono-Bungay* (1909) and *The History of Mr Polly* (1910).

Joseph Conrad (1857–1924)

Although, like Henry James, Conrad is generally regarded as an English novelist, he was born into a Polish family in a part of the Ukraine that had been annexed by Russia. This and his subsequent twenty-year career as a merchant sailor that travelled to all the world's continents gave him first-hand insight into many forms of imperialism, which would become a central subject in his fiction. His first novel *Almayer's Folly* (1895) did not appear until he was thirty-eight, a year after he had completed his final voyage as a sailor. He was subsequently permanently resident in England, but most of his fiction was set in countries he had visited during his years at sea.

Conrad's Complex Structures

Conrad's fiction creates a relativistic atmosphere by employing complex and unchronological time-structures, multiple points of view and narrators whose reliability is open to question. It reveals an ironic scepticism about human motivation, particularly as manifest in the colonizing enterprises of European nations in the late nineteenth-century phase of imperialist expansion. In his most famous work, the novella *Heart of Darkness* (1902), the narrator Marlow journeys upriver in an unnamed Central African country, clearly based on the Congo, in search of Kurtz, an ivory-trader and supposed emissary of European light, whom it appears has become devilishly corrupt and insane. The story provides an indictment of the economic exploitation involved in colonialism, but has itself been attacked as "racist", particularly by African commentators such as the novelist Chinua Achebe, on the grounds that its Africans are shadowy beings, denied any life of their own. Marlow is also the narrator of another of Conrad's finest works, the novel *Lord Jim* (1900), a tale of lost honour mainly set in the Arabian Sea and Sumatra, and of the short story "Youth" (1902) and the novel *Chance* (1913–14), his first popular success.

Conrad's Masterpiece

Conrad's masterpiece *Nostromo* (1904) is a study of the corrosive power of materialism, set in the fictional South American republic of Costaguana. Again the novel moves between several characters and viewpoints to demonstrate its thesis that "There was something inherent in the necessities of successful action which carried with it the moral degradation of the idea". In *The Secret Agent* (1907), Conrad explores similar issues in a story set in Britain. Its detached, ironic account of an anarchist cell's attempt to blow up the Greenwich Observatory suggests the relationship between corruption in personal and public spheres. Conrad's other novels include *An Outcast of the Islands* (1896), *Under Western Eyes* (1911), *Victory* (1915), *The Rescue* (1920) and *The Rover* (1923).

Much of his best work is in the form of shorter fiction. In addition to "Youth" and *Heart of Darkness*, his novellas and stories include "The *Nigger* of the 'Narcissus'" (1897), "Typhoon" (1902), "Amy Foster" (1903), "The Secret Sharer" (1912) and *The Shadow-Line* (1917), *The Mirror of the Sea* (1906) and *A Personal Record* (1912) are volumes of his reminiscences.

Rudyard Kipling (1865–1936)

Born in Bombay (now Mumbai), Kipling enjoyed an unparalleled reputation as the poet of the British Empire and most of his work expresses supposed virtues of the imperialist ethic, such as self-reliance and courage in adversity. *Plain Tales from the Hills* (1888) and *Soldiers Three* (1888) are collections of his early short stories about Anglo-Indian life; his poems of the same period are collected in *Barrack-Room Ballads* (1892) and other volumes. His masterpiece *Kim* (1901) is a novel of espionage, which transcends the "boy's own" adventure mould in which it is cast to provide an encyclopaedic view of aspects of Indian life, especially during its account of the orphan protagonist's picaresque journey along the Great Trunk Road.

His Children's Books

Kipling was also a highly popular author of children's books and his writing in this genre includes *The Jungle Book* (1894), *The Second Jungle Book* (1895), *Just So Stories* (1902) and *Puck of Pook's Hill* (1906). His other works include the novel, *The Light That Failed* (1890), *Stalky and Co.* (1899) and also a posthumously published volume of autobiography, *Something of Myself* (1937). He became the first English winner of the Nobel Prize for Literature in 1907.

His reputation declined after his death, but with the passage of time it has enjoyed a partial rehabilitation, as more measured assessments have been beyond the stereotyped view of him as a jingoistic imperialist. Although his writing *is* frequently chauvinistic, it demonstrates an insider's sensitivity to aspects of Indian life that was rare among his Anglo-Indian contemporaries. His most famous poems include "Mandalay," "The White Man's Burden", "Gunga Din", "Recessional" and "If" ("If you can meet with Triumph and Disaster/ And treat those two impostors just the same;/ ... you'll be a Man, my son!").

E.M. Forster (1879–1970)

On the surface the five novels E.M. Forster published during his life-time are social comedies in the tradition of Fielding and Jane Austen. Liberal humanist in outlook, they characteristically compare different sets of social mores, both within and outside England. *Where Angels Fear to Tread* (1905) and *A Room with a View* (1908) contrast the intolerance of certain sectors of English middle-class society with the more open-minded attitudes of Italy. In *The Longest Journey* (1907), the Cambridge-educated hero Rickie's experience of marriage and family life ends in tragedy. Forster's most accomplished "English" novel, *Howards End* (1910), is a late Edwardian Condition of England novel, in which ownership of the rural house of the title becomes the central tearing-point of the plot. In a contrast reminiscent of that between city and country values in Jane Austen's *Mansfield Park*, the stability represented by the house is imperilled by a world of "telegrams and anger" that threatens to overtake the more cultured values initially associated with it.

A Passage to India

Howards End's epigraph, "Only connect", typifies Forster's insistence on the need for cultural dialogue and this theme is central to his finest novel, *A Passage to India* (1924), in which symbolic patterns that sometimes suggest mystical connections belie the view that he was simply a writer of social comedies. The novel grew out of his experience in India as secretary and companion to a maharajah, which he wrote about in *The Hill of Devi* (1953). It deals with three aspects of Indian life: the côterie society of an Anglo-Indian Club, whose exclusivity Forster satirizes; the abortive attempt by a liberal Englishman and a Muslim doctor to develop and sustain a friendship; and a more spiritual "Hindu" India, which offers a possibility for "connections" across cultures, where the other areas of contact have failed.

Maurice

After Forster's death, a sixth novel, *Maurice* (1971), written around 1914 but previously suppressed because of its overtly homosexual theme, was published. It partly reshaped views of Forster's earlier fiction, in which marriage and heterosexual love are treated in a manner that is at best conventional and at worst uncomfortable, by suggesting an alternative way of viewing the male friendships in these novels.

Forster also wrote numerous short stories, collected in *The Life to Come* (1972), and an influential study of the novel, *Aspects of the Novel* (1927), notable for its emphasis on "rhythm", the use of recurrent images as a structuring device for fiction and for the distinctions he drew between "flat" and "round" characters and between "story" and "plot". As an example of the latter distinction, he maintained that "The king died and then the queen died" is a story, while "The king died, and then the queen died of grief" is a plot. His numerous essays are collected in *Abinger Harvest* (1936) and *Two Cheers for Democracy* (1951).

James Joyce (1882–1941)

Joyce was born into an Irish Catholic family, but like Stephen Dedalus, the protagonist of his first novel, *A Portrait of the Artist as a Young Man* (1916), he became increasingly disillusioned with the shaping forces of his upbringing, Catholicism, Irish nationalism and family allegiances, and replaced early thoughts of entering the priesthood with a quasi-religious devotion to art. He left Dublin in 1904 and lived in mainland Europe for the remainder of his life. However, all his work is about Dublin and he once said, "if I can get to the heart of Dublin, I can get to the heart of all the cities in the world".

Early Writings

Written in a sparse and unembellished prose style, *Dubliners* (1914) is a collection of short stories about aspects of the city's life. Joyce's declared aim was "to write a chapter of the moral history of my country" and the volume offers an indictment of what he saw as the "paralysis" stifling individual growth in Ireland. The stories generally end with an "epiphany", a sudden moment of revelation, in which characters achieve an awareness hitherto lacking to them.

The main emphasis of *A Portrait of the Artist as a Young Man* is on the growth of the artist, Stephen Dedalus's consciousness. The novel describes his struggle against the forces that threaten to hinder his development and his rejection of the priesthood and is notable for its use of the stream-of-consciousness technique. Beginning with a form of monologue that attempts to convey the thought-processes of a young child, it moves through a range of increasingly complex styles and culminates with Stephen's commitment to an art based on "silence, exile and cunning". By the conclusion, the novel has become an artistic manifesto that prepares the way for the task Joyce was to undertake in his masterpiece, the comic epic *Ulysses* (1922).

His Masterpiece

In the first three sections of *Ulysses*, Stephen Dedalus is once again central and the emphasis is on the problems facing the Joycean artist figure. Subsequently, the main protagonist is the Irish-Jewish advertisement canvasser, Leopold Bloom, an "ordinary man" who is Joyce's modern-day Ulyssses. Bloom provides a focus for representing a broader cross-section of Dublin life and the main part of the novel gives an account of his wanderings through the streets of the city on a single day in 1904, Joyce's equivalent of Homer's narrative of Ulysses' ten-years of travelling in the Eastern Mediterranean.

Ulysses is divided into eighteen sections, each of which is written in a different style, chosen for its relevance to the material it portrays. Joyce also takes the stream-of-consciousness technique further, employing variations suited to the thought-processes of the particular character being portrayed. It concludes with a monologue by its third major character, Bloom's wife, Molly, one of the most fully realized characters in Modernist fiction. Written in an unpunctuated prose that endeavours to mirror the flow of her emotions, Molly's monologue is Joyce's most brilliant *tour de force* in the use of the stream-of-consciousness technique.

Joyce's final novel, *Finnegans Wake* (1939), was his most ambitious. It describes the dreams of H.C. Earwicker, his wife Anna Livia Plurabelle and their children, during the course of a single Dublin night. From this limited vantage point, Joyce expands outwards to encompass an encyclopaedic range of human experience. The novel's dream-like method is indebted to contemporary psychoanalytic theory. It is written in a style full of portmanteau words and neologisms, presenting its readers with a level of difficulty besides which *Ulysses* seems comparatively straightforward.

Virginia Woolf (1882–1941)

Along with Joyce, his exact contemporary, Virginia Woolf pioneered the use of the stream-of-consciousness monologue as a technique for representing the flow of subjective mental processes, which is central to the view of character embodied in her novels. In her essay "Modern Fiction" (1925), she wrote, "Examine for a moment an ordinary mind on an ordinary day. The mind receives a myriad impressions—trivial, fantastic, evanescent, or engraved with the sharpness of steel. From all sides they come, an incessant shower of innumerable atoms, and as they fall ... the accent falls differently from of old."

The technique can be seen at its best in her three finest novels, *Mrs Dalloway* (1925), *To the Lighthouse* (1927) and *The Waves* (1931). As with Joyce's *Ulysses*, the action of *Mrs Dalloway* takes place on a single day, but the focus on the protagonist's consciousness sketches in her previous life through her memories, as well as providing access to her innermost feelings. The intensely subjective action of *To the Lighthouse* takes place on two days ten years apart. These are separated by a short central section, in which catastrophic external events that have taken place in the intervening years are recorded in a shockingly perfunctory way. The novel's characters live in solipsistic mental worlds and loneliness and the difficulty of communication are among its major themes, as is a quest for stability amid the flux of experience. The most experimental of Woolf's novels, *The Waves* follows the lives of six characters from infancy to old age through their own interior monologues, which are punctuated by passages that describe natural phenomena and seasonal changes. Her most extravagant novel, *Orlando* (1928), is a mock-biography of its androgynous protagonist, which ranges across four centuries. Her other novels include *Night and Day* (1919), *Jacob's Room* (1922) and *The Years* (1937).

Woolf and First-Wave Feminism

Woolf's fiction interrogates the gender norms of her day and her non-fiction writing, such as *A Room of One's Own* (1929), in which she specifically discusses the problems facing the female artist, made an important contribution to the first wave of twentieth-century feminism. Its lesser-known sequel, *Three Guineas* (1938), analyses the social and economic exclusion of women, particularly in higher education, and suggests that they could provide a challenge to authoritarianism and the rise of fascism. Her collections of essays include *The Common Reader* (1925), *The Second Common Reader* (1933) and *The Death of the Moth* (1942). Her final novel *Between the Acts* (1941) was published posthumously, after she had committed suicide by drowning herself.

Woolf was a leading figure in the Bloomsbury Group, a circle of writers and artists committed to moving culture beyond what they saw as the narrowness of Victorian artistic and moral standards. Other members included the artist Roger Fry, the economist John Maynard Keynes, the biographer Lytton Strachey and the writers E.M. Forster, Vita Sackville-West and Woolf's husband, Leonard, founder of the innovative Hogarth Press and author of the novel *The Village in the Jungle* (1913).

D.H. Lawrence (1885–1930)

Lawrence shared the Modernist interest in inner mental states, rejecting what he referred to as "the old stable ego of the character" for a view of consciousness founded on the ebb and flow of emotions. Though his fiction is less abstract than that of his Modernist contemporaries, Joyce and Woolf, he also challenged the conventions of earlier fiction. He saw the novel as a genre that "can inform and lead into new places the flow of our sympathetic consciousness" and developed a theory of organic form, in which novels create their own spontaneously developed shape, to embody this.

Sons and Lovers

His semi-autobiographical novel, *Sons and Lovers* (1913), set in the Nottinghamshire mining area where he grew up, is Lawrence's *Portrait of the Artist as a Young Man*, though his artistic technique is very different from Joyce's. It describes the early life and loves of its hero, Paul Morel, particularly his Oedipal feelings for his mother and his relationships with two contrasted women, the puritanical Miriam and the more sensuous Clara. It was followed by two of Lawrence's finest novels, *The Rainbow* (1915) and *Women in Love* (1920). *The Rainbow* deals with the quest of three generations of the Brangwen family to achieve the harmony between flesh and spirit suggested by the image of the rainbow itself. It represents Lawrence's first major development of his ideas on sexual "otherness". *Women in Love* was originally conceived as a sequel to *The Rainbow*, but in its finished form is markedly different in focus and approach, though the two novels share a common character, Ursula Brangwen. In *Women in Love* Lawrence sets the relationships of a central quartet of characters against the backcloth of an England in transition, which he views more pessimistically than in *The Rainbow*.

Lawrence left England in 1919 and subsequently lived in Italy, Ceylon, Australia, Mexico and New Mexico, writing novels set in three of these countries: *Aaron's Rod* (1922) in Italy, *Kangaroo* (1923) in Australia and *The Plumed Serpent* (1926) in Mexico. At their worst, these more hastily composed novels—*Kangaroo* is said to have been written in six weeks—are verbose and art is replaced by overwritten polemic. They share a common concern with "leadership", turning towards "dark gods" and an anti-democratic view of society.

Lady Chatterley's Lover

The sexually explicit accounts of lovemaking and the use of four-letter words in Lawrence's final and most controversial novel, *Lady Chatterley's Lover* (1928), led to its full text being banned in Britain and the United States for thirty years. Then, in 1960, a landmark court case, which had an important effect on English censorship laws, found in favour of an unexpurgated Penguin edition. The novel's graphic account of the titular heroine's turning away from her impotent husband for a passionate relationship with the gamekeeper on his estate marked a return to Lawrence's best work. *The First Lady Chatterley* (1944) and *John Thomas and Lady Jane* (1972) are earlier versions of the novel.

His Shorter Fiction

Lawrence's shorter fiction contains some of his finest writing. His short story collections include *The Prussian Officer* (1914), *England, My England* (1922), *The Woman Who Rode Away* (1928) and *Love among the Haystacks* (1930); his novellas include *The Fox* (1922), *The Ladybird* and *The Captain's Doll* (1923), *St Mawr* and *The Princess* (1925) and *The Virgin and the Gipsy* (1930). His travel-writing includes three books about Italy, *Twilight in Italy* (1916), *Sea and Sardinia* (1921) and *Etruscan Places* (1932), and *Mornings in Mexico* (1927). He also published the novels, *The White Peacock* (1911), *The Trespasser* (1912), *The Lost Girl* (1920) and (with M.L. Skinner) *The Boy in the Bush* (1924).

The Novel in the 1930s and 1940s: Huxley and Orwell

Influenced by the Depression, the rise of Fascism and events such as the Spanish Civil War, novelists of the 1930s turned away from the artistic experimentalism and interest in inner mental status that had characterized the fiction of their Modernist predecessors towards more realistic modes of writing and a more direct engagement with social issues.

Aldous Huxley's novel, *Brave New World* (1932) typifies the period's sense of the threat posed by totalitarianism. George Orwell's *Keep the Aspidistra Flying* (1936) and *Coming Up for Air* (1939) reflect his concern with an England in transition. Huxley's other novels include *Antic Hay* (1923), *Point Counter Point* (1928) and *Eyeless in Gaza* (1936); Orwell also wrote *Burmese Days* (1934) and *A Clergyman's Daughter* (1935).

Subsequently Orwell's critique of society turned to more pessimistic allegorical modes: *Animal Farm* (1945) uses the form of the animal fable for a satirical attack on Stalinist Communism ("All animals are equal, but some animals are more equal than others"), while *Nineteen Eighty-Four* (1949) is a science-fiction novel in the tradition of *Brave New World*, in which a future dystopia offers a thinly-veiled picture of the present.

Christopher Isherwood and Evelyn Waugh

Christopher Isherwood's novels set in the Berlin of the early 1930s, *Mr Norris Changes Trains* (1935) and *Goodbye to Berlin* (1939), a sequence of six diaries and sketches, are witty portraits of "lost" people living in a society moving towards fascism. The opening diary in the latter work contains the famous passage in which Isherwood outlines his quasi-objective narrative method: "I am a camera with its shutter open, quite passive, recording, not thinking". This provided the title for John van Druten's 1951 stage dramatization, which took Isherwood's most memorable character, the cabaret performer Sally Bowles, as its central figure and which provided the basis for the musical *Cabaret* (1966), a work that also drew on Bertolt Brecht and Kurt Weill's *Threepenny Opera* (1928).

Evelyn Waugh's witty portraits of the upper echelons of English society in his novels of the 1930s—*Vile Bodies* (1930), *Black Mischief* (1932), *A Handful of Dust* (1934) and *Scoop* (1938)—established him as the finest satirist of his generation. In his later work, which includes his most popular novel, *Brideshead Revisited* (1945) and his World War II "Sword of Honour" trilogy, *Men at Arms* (1952), *Officers and Gentlemen* (1955) and *Unconditional Surrender* (1961), his characteristic wit is combined with a more elegiac perspective.

Other novelists at the height of their powers during the lean publishing years of the 1940s include Joyce Cary, L.P. Hartley, Elizabeth Bowen, Henry Green and Elizabeth Taylor.

Graham Greene (1904–91)

Beginning with *The Man Within* (1929), Greene's career spanned six decades. In his early "trilogy", *Brighton Rock* (1938), *The Power and the Glory* (1940) and *The Heart of the Matter* (1948), characters wrestle with dilemmas posed by Catholic consciences in varied settings: an English seaside resort, Mexico and West Africa respectively. Many Greene novels achieve their effect through placing their characters in unromantic expatriate situations, including Vietnam in *The Quiet American* (1955), a Congo leper colony in *A Burnt-Out Case* (1961), which takes an Albert Schweitzer-like figure for its protagonist, and Argentina in *The Honorary Consul* (1973). In these novels set in "faraway" places, the plot frequently turns upon an incident in which the central character grapples with a difficult moral choice. *The End of the Affair* (1951) employs a similar pattern for a novel in which the action takes place in London during and just after World War II.

The "Entertainments"

Greene made a distinction between his novels and his "entertainments", several of which were developed as film-scripts. The "entertainments", which draw on the conventions of the thriller, include *Stamboul Train* (1932), *The Confidential Agent* (1939), *The Third Man* (1950), a work set in post-war Vienna and adapted from Greene's screenplay for Carol Reed's highly acclaimed 1949 film, *Loser Takes All* (1955) and *Our Man in Havana* (1958). His numerous other novels include *It's a Battlefield* (1934), *England Made Me* (1935), *The Comedians* (1966), *Travels with My Aunt* (1969), *The Human Factor* (1978) and *Doctor Fischer of Geneva* (1980).

Greene also wrote a number of plays, the travel books *Journey without Maps* (1936) and *The Lawless Roads* (1939) and the autobiographical volumes *A Sort of Life* (1972) and *Ways of Escape* (1980).

Samuel Beckett (1906–89)

Beckett is best known for his absurdist play, *Waiting for Godot* (*En attendant Godot* 1952; English translation 1953), a work devoid of conventional action in which two tramps spend their time in seemingly idle chatter, while they wait for the eponymous Godot, who never arrives. He was also a major novelist in the tradition of his Irish compatriot, James Joyce, whom he followed into exile in Paris. He wrote the majority of his plays and novels in French, subsequently translating them into English.

The protagonists of his finest achievement in fiction, the trilogy of novels, *Molloy* (1951), *Malone Dies* (1951) and *The Unnamable* (1953), probe the limits of language in a struggle to understand their selfhood. The minimalist action of the three novels is pared down to a point where it is virtually nonexistent and fiction's ability to encapsulate external reality is called into question. Beckett also wrote the novels *Murphy* (1938) and *Watt* (1953) and the short story collection *More Pricks than Kicks* (1934). His other plays include *Endgame* (1957), *Krapp's Last Tape* (1958), *Happy Days* (1961) and *Play* (1964). He was awarded the Nobel Prize for Literature in 1969.

Flann O'Brien's whimsical masterpiece *At Swim-Two-Birds* (1939) is a comic novel in the tradition of Joyce and Beckett. It combines realistic scenes from student life with fantasy and folklore in a highly inventive and self-reflexive fictional farrago. O'Brien's other novels were *The Dalkey Archive* (1964) and *The Third Policeman* (1967).

Novelists of the 1950s and 1960s

The changing face of English society in the post-World War II period had a major impact on the novel in the 1950s and early 1960s, when a number of important works dealing with regional, particularly northern, working-class culture appeared. Prior to this, comic novels such as John Wain's *Hurry On Down* (1953) and Sir Kingsley Amis's *Lucky Jim* (1954) had expressed a new generation's cynicism about the pretensions of their elders, albeit from a more privileged social standpoint.

George Orwell's account of his encounter with northern working-class society in *The Road to Wigan Pier* (1937) was a work which, despite its socialist inclinations, had something of the travel-writer's perspective about it, in that it was written from the viewpoint of a visitor to a "depressed" area hitherto unknown to him. In contrast, the post-war generation of working-class novelists wrote from inside the experiences they depicted.

Screen Adaptations

Several of their most important works were adapted for the screen and became major British films in the 1960s. These include John Braine's *Room at the Top* (1957; film 1959), Alan Sillitoe's *Saturday Night and Sunday Morning* (1958; film 1960), Stan Barstow's *A Kind of Loving* (1960; film 1962) and David Storey's *This Sporting Life* (1962; film 1963). The Londoner B.S. Johnson's work, which is currently enjoying a revival, is working-class fiction of a rather different kind. It combines socialist commitment with formal experimentation and metafictive self-consciousness in a manner rare among his contemporaries. In his box-novel *The Unfortunates* (1969), Johnson invites his readers to shuffle the loose-leaf sections before reading. In *Christie Malry's Own Double-Entry* (1973), he playfully parodies classic techniques of English realism.

Other Novelists of the Period

The most ambitious fictional sequence of the period, Lawrence Durrell's *The Alexandria Quartet* (1957–60), a work made up of a triptych of novels that view the same events from different perspectives and a fourth which is a genuine sequel narrating later occurrences, offers a conscious "challenge to the serial form of the conventional novel". Other novelists who produced important work during this period include Muriel Spark, Angus Wilson, Anthony Powell, whose wide-ranging sequence, *A Dance to the Music of Time*, appeared between 1951 and 1975, and Doris Lessing, whose multi-stranded metafictive novel about "free women", *The Golden Notebook* (1962), is an early classic of the second wave of twentieth-century feminism. Margaret Drabble began her career with *A Summer Birdcage* (1963), *The Garrick Year* (1964) and *Jerusalem the Golden* (1967). Anthony Burgess's virtuoso talent ranged over a broad range of subjects, including a trilogy of novels about Malaya (1956–9), futuristic "ultraviolence" in the verbally innovative *A Clockwork Orange* (1962), which achieved cult notoriety after the banning of Stanley Kubrick's 1971 film version, and Shakespeare's life in *Nothing Like the Sun* (1964). Jean Rhys, whose early fiction about the lives of single women in Paris and London appeared in the inter-war years, published her masterpiece *Wide Sargasso Sea*, the story of the "mad" first wife of Mr Rochester in *Jane Eyre* in 1966.

Sir William Golding (1911–93)

Golding's first novel *Lord of the Flies* (1954) is a pessimistic twentieth-century reworking of R.M. Ballantyne's *The Coral Island*, in which a group of boys marooned on a desert island gradually revert to savagery. Like all Golding's novels, it is a moral allegory, which probes below the surface of existence to disclose elemental forces in human nature, which are often evil. *Pincher Martin* (1956) is an even bleaker parable of the predicament of a spiritual castaway, while *The Spire* (1964) is a symbolic fable about the building of Salisbury Cathedral. *Rites of Passage* (1980), which won the Booker Prize, is the first part of a maritime trilogy that concludes with *Close Quarters* (1987) and *Fire Down Below* (1989).

His other novels include *The Inheritors* (1955), *Free Fall* (1959), *The Pyramid* (1967), *The Scorpion God* (1971) and *Darkness Visible* (1979). Golding was awarded the Nobel Prize for Literature in 1983 and knighted in 1988.

Dame Iris Murdoch (1919–99)

Murdoch was a professional philosopher, who produced significant work on existentialism and other philosophical systems concerned with free will and ethics. This is reflected in the central conflicts of her novels, which frequently suggest the limits of human freedom. Set in a remote Celtic landscape, suggestive of the west of Ireland, *The Unicorn* (1963) explores issues of altruism and supposed self-sacrifice, reversing conventional notions of guilt and innocence. *A Severed Head* (1961) is a comedy of sexual manners, in which the multiple and often-unexpected comings together among the limited cast of characters border on farce, but also involve a searching investigation of the ethics of personal relationships.

Other Murdoch novels that have received particular praise include *The Bell* (1958), a novel set in a religious community, and the Booker Prize-winning *The Sea, The Sea* (1978). She was a prolific writer, who had a particular talent for observing both "sacred" and "profane" love with an ironist's eye. Her other novels include *Under the Net* (1954), *An Unofficial Rose* (1962), *The Italian Girl* (1964), *The*

Nice and the Good (1968), *Bruno's Dream* (1969), *An Accidental Man* (1971) and *The Black Prince* (1973).

John Fowles (1926–)

Fowles's reputation mainly rests on *The Magus* (1966; revised version 1977), a powerful and ultimately open-ended *Bildungsroman*, in which reality and illusion are blurred, as the young protagonist is subjected to a seemingly endless series of initiations on a Greek island, and *The French Lieutenant's Woman* (1969), which blends a nineteenth-century story, partly written as a pastiche of a Victorian novel, with self-reflexive commentary on its own processes and the values of the Victorian age. *Daniel Martin* (1977) is a more realistic Condition of England novel, which particularly concerns itself with liberal humanist values. Fowles's other fiction includes the novels *The Collector* (1963), *Mantissa* (1983) and *A Maggot* (1985) and the short-story collection, *The Ebony Tower* (1974). *The Aristos* (1964) is a study in existentialist ethics, which as in Iris Murdoch's novels, are an important area of debate in Fowles's fiction, though he is generally more positive in his assessment of the individual's capacity for choice.

Sir V.S. Naipaul (1932–)

Born in Trinidad, Naipaul came to Britain in 1950 and has lived in the UK ever since, albeit while travelling extensively to research his often acerbic travel-books about "third-world" societies. These include *The Middle Passage* (1962), *An Area of Darkness* (1964) and *Among the Believers* (1981). His best novels include *A House for Mr Biswas* (1961), a tragic-comic novel of epic sweep about its Trinidadian protagonist's attempt to acquire his own house and with it a sense of self-worth, *The Mimic Men* (1967), *A Bend in the River* (1979) and *The Enigma of Arrival* (1987), a novel that blends thinly-veiled autobiography and reflections on the making of the Wiltshire landscape where the protagonist is now living. Beginning with *In a Free State* (1971), which won the Booker Prize, his work has increasingly broken down the distinction between fiction and non-fiction. Naipaul was knighted in 1990, became the first winner of the David Cohen Prize for "lifetime achievement by a living British writer" in 1993 and was awarded the Nobel Prize for Literature in 2001.

Others novelists of the post-World War II generation of Caribbean migrants to Britain included George Lamming, author of *In the Castle of My Skin* (1953), *Water with Berries* (1971) and *Natives of My Person* (1972), and Sam Selvon, whose memorable novels of Caribbean immigrants' lives in London include *The Lonely Londoners* (1956), *The Housing Lark* (1965) and *Moses Ascending* (1975). The British writer, Colin MacInnes chronicles similar experiences in *City of Spades* (1957).

Angela Carter (1940–92)

Carter's fiction, which combines a materialist critique of society with extravagant fantasies, has often been described as magic realist. It draws on a range of non-realist narrative forms, including fairy tale, science fiction allegory, Hollywood wish-fulfilment fantasy, circus performance and the Gothic. Through these forms Carter expresses a feminist desire to elude definition by the norms of patriarchal rationalism, providing a variety of alternative representations of gender and sexuality. Her concern with female desire is to the fore in her early novels, *The Magic Toyshop* (1967), *Heroes and Villains* (1969) and *The Infernal Desire Machines of Dr Hoffman* (1972). The short stories of *The Bloody Chamber* (1979) rework fairy tales by Charles Perrault—such as Bluebeard, Beauty and the Beast and Red Riding Hood—as fables of the unconscious that are frequently concerned with sexuality.

Her other major novels are *The Passion of New Eve* (1977), *Nights at the Circus* (1984) and *Wise Children* (1991). Her most significant non-fiction work is the cultural history *The Sadeian Woman* (1979).

Two Campus Novelists

Sir Malcolm Bradbury and David Lodge both combined successful careers as academics and novelists, developing the genre of the campus novel that had been pioneered in England by Amis's *Lucky Jim*. Bradbury's *The History Man* (1975) satirizes the fashionable, but self-serving side of 1960's culture through the figure of a university lecturer in the newly emergent discipline of sociology. His other academic satires include *Eating People is Wrong* (1959), *Stepping Westward* (1965), *Rates of Exchange* (1982) and *Dr Criminale* (1992).

Lodge's *Changing Places* (1975) and its sequel *Small World* (1984) are more formally innovative satires of academic life. His other novels include *The British Museum is Falling Down* (1965), *Nice Work* (1988), a cleverly plotted latter-day *Condition of England* novel, based around the relationship between the managing director of an engineering firm and a lecturer in English literature, and *Paradise News* (1992).

Two Writers of Fantasy

J.R.R. Tolkien was an academic who made a very different contribution to twentieth-century fiction. His professional expertise in Anglo-Saxon culture informs the mythological landscape of Middle Earth he created for his *Lord of the Rings* trilogy (1954-55). This followed his earlier work *The Hobbit* (1937), in which he introduced the popular characters of the gnome Bilbo Baggins and the wizard Gandalf. Like Mervyn Peake's Gothic *Gormenghast* trilogy—*Titus Groan* (1946), *Gormenghast* (1950) and *Titus Alone* (1959)—*The Lord of the Rings* invents a self-contained fantastic world. Its popularity with readers has increased since Tolkien's death in 1973, making the trilogy a *contemporary* classic.

TWENTIETH-CENTURY POETRY

Poets of World War I

The poetry of the "Great War" gave a new sharpness of perspective to early twentieth-century English verse, which in the preceding years had generally been traditional in both form and theme, as it were celebrating the stability of a seemingly changeless England that was in fact about to disappear forever. Rupert Brooke's question (in his poem "The Old Vicarage, Grantchester"), "And is there honey still for tea?", expresses a mood of Edwardian and Georgian nostalgia that was to be shattered by the advent of the war. Brooke died early in the war, in 1915, and his best-known poem, "The Soldier" ("If I should die think only this of me ..."), conveys an idealistic view of warfare, from which poets who experienced its traumas would soon depart.

Sassoon and Owen

Siegfried Sassoon debunked the romantic attitude to war in poems such as "Counter-Attack", "Does It Matter?" and "Suicide in the Trenches". "Dulce et Decorum Est" by Wilfred Owen, who was killed in November 1918, a week before the Armistice was signed, is only marginally less savage in its ironic indictment of the patriotic ethic that sanctioned the atrocities of the war. Several of Owen's major poems, such as "Anthem for Doomed Youth" and "Strange Meeting", conjure up a nightmarish world, which both reflects the horror of the war and expresses a sense of a more general existential futility. Other important poets of World War I include Isaac Rosenberg and Edward Thomas. World War I poetry by women includes work by Rose Macauley and Edith Sitwell.

T.S. Eliot (1888–1965)

Often regarded as the finest and most influential poet of the early twentieth century, Eliot was also a dramatist and a major critic. He studied philosophy at Harvard, where he first developed his ideas on poetry and the literary tradition. Rejecting the Romantic view of the power of the individual imagination, he favoured a classical model of literary influence and drew on a wide range of sources, including the French symbolist poets, the metaphysicals, Dante and Eastern verse and philosophy. The symbolists were an important influence on *Prufrock and Other Poems* (1917), a volume that takes its title from his *vers libre* study of a little man figure, grappling with the realities of daily routine and ageing.

A Growing Reputation

Eliot settled in England in 1915, where, encouraged by his similarly minded compatriot, Ezra Pound, his poetic talent blossomed. *Poems* (1919), which included "Gerontion", a vivid exploration of the psychology of old age, was followed by his masterpiece, *The Wasteland* (1922), a compressed epic dedicated to Pound, who played a crucial role in editing the poem, cutting it down to half its original length. One of the most influential poems of the twentieth century, it draws on a range of literatures and mythologies, particularly the Grail quest, to suggest the aridity of post-World War I urban life and posits the message of the *Bhagavad Gita* as an alternative to Western materialism. The poem's ellipses, sharp juxtapositions and dense allusiveness were highly innovatory when it appeared.

The Essay Collections

At the same time as Eliot's reputation as a poet was being secured, his essay-collections, *The Sacred Wood* (1920), *Homage to John Dryden* (1924) and *For Lancelot Andrewes: Essays on Style and Order* (1928), established his reputation as a critic. In these he developed his beliefs on the importance of impersonality in art, stressing the need to find an "objective correlative" for the evocation of emotion and, in the highly influential "Tradition and the Individual Talent", arguing that "the most individual parts of [a poet's] work may be those in which the dead poets, his ancestors, assert their immortality most vigorously". In the 1930s Eliot's criticism increasingly turned its attention to broad social issues, deserting the strictly literary for cultural commentary in the tradition of Matthew Arnold.

His later collections include *The Use of Poetry and the Use of Criticism* (1933), *After Strange Gods* (1934), *Notes Towards a Definition of Culture* (1948), *Poetry and Poets* (1957) and *To Criticize the Critic* (1965).

His Religious Ideas

Beginning with *Poems 1909-25* (1925), which includes "The Hollow Men", his poetry became increasingly religious in orientation and in 1927 he became an Anglo-Catholic. His religious ideas were developed in "The Journey of the Magi" (1927) and "Ash Wednesday" (1930) and the major achievement of his later career *Four Quartets* (1943), which brought together "Burnt Norton" (1935), "East Coker" (1940), "The Dry Salvages" (1941) and "Little Gidding" (1942). His children's collection, *Old Possum's Book of Practical Cats* (1939), provided the inspiration for the Andrew Lloyd Webber musical *Cats* (1981).

Verse Drama

In the 1930s, Eliot began to write verse drama in an attempt to revive this neglected genre. His most famous play was *Murder in the Cathedral* (1935), a poetic account of the death of Thomas Beckett.

His other plays include *The Family Reunion* (1939), *The Cocktail Party* (1950) and *The Elder Statesman* (1959). Along with the verse drama of Christopher Fry's *A Phoenix Too Frequent* (1946) and *The Lady's Not for Burning* (1948), his plays made a significant contribution to English theatre during a fairly barren period.

In 1948, Eliot was awarded both the Nobel Prize for Literature and the Order of Merit. His writing apart, he exercised considerable influence on the course of English poetry as a director of the publishers Faber and Faber, though what was perceived as the conservative tendency of his thinking led some of his younger contemporaries to resist the potent influence of poems such as *The Wasteland*.

Ezra Pound (1885–1972)

Like Eliot, Pound was an American expatriate, who settled in Europe, where in the years immediately before World War I he became a leading figure among the Imagists, a movement which advocated experimentation with verse forms, freedom of expression and the use of concise, concrete imagery. He also played an important role in furthering the careers of a number of major Modernist writers, including those of Joyce and Eliot.

Estimates of his own poetry, which can be recondite and obscure, vary, It includes *Personae* (1910), *Homage to Sextus Propertius* (1919) and his most accessible work, *Hugh Selwyn Mauberley* (1920). In 1925, he published the first volume of his *Cantos*, a project on which he would continue to work throughout the remainder of his career. The *Cantos* form a sequence of epic scope, which, like Eliot's work, draws on an eclectic mélange of cultural traditions in an attempt to evolve an aesthetic practice suitable for the modern age. Pound was also a notable translator, producing free, creative translations from the many literatures and cultures that inform the *Cantos*. These include Anglo-Saxon, Chinese, classical Greek, medieval Provençal and Japanese Noh theatre.

He became disillusioned with what he saw as the decadence of post-World War I Europe and, in the 1930s, his artistic elitism drew him towards Italian fascism. During World War II he broadcast propaganda for the Axis. At the end of the war he was indicted for treason and confined to an American hospital after being declared mentally unfit to answer the charges brought against him. On his release in 1958, he returned to Italy, where he lived for the remainder of his life.

Lawrence's Poetry

Though best remembered as a novelist, D.H. Lawrence was a prolific writer who also produced a considerable body of work in other genres: poetry, short stories, novellas, travel books, plays, literary criticism and other non-fictional prose. His poetry employed a theory of expressive form, which again challenged the literary conventions of his day. After some early rhyming verse, written in a rough ballad metre and dealing with his subjects from his Nottinghamshire youth, he mainly wrote imagistic free verse poems, many of which use animal, bird and flower imagery to evoke a sense of communion between humanity and the natural world.

His collections of poetry include *Look! We Have Come Through!* (1917), *New Poems* (1918), *Birds, Beasts and Flowers* (1923), *Pansies* (1929), *Nettles* (1930) and *Last Poems* (1932).

W.H. Auden (1907–73) and the Poets of the 1930s

Auden was the leading figure among a group of writers who attended Oxford in the late 1920s and one of the finest English poets of the twentieth century. His verse is remarkably varied in its subjects, but his early collections, *Poems* (1930), *The Orators* (1932) and *Look Stranger!* (1936), display a recurrent concern with left-wing political causes such as the republican struggle in Spain, which was shared by many of his contemporaries, and post-Freudian psychology. He analyses social issues and sexual repression with a quasi-clinical detachment, using everyday language in an innovative manner, while making encoded references to homosexuality.

The Move to America

Auden moved to the USA in 1939 and deserted the socialist commitment of his 1930's poetry for a more elusive and abstract verse, which partly reflects his return to the Christian beliefs of his early upbringing, but more generally displays a reluctance to being categorized. Subsequent collections include *New Year Letter* (1941; US title *The Double Man*), *For the Time Being: A Christmas Oratorio* (1944), *The Age of Anxiety* (1947), *Nones* (1951), *The Shield of Achilles* (1955), *Homage to Clio* (1960), *About the House* (1965) and *Epistle to a Godson* (1972). With his companion Chester Kallman, he wrote the libretto for Stravinsky's *The Rake's Progress* (1951). Earlier he had collaborated with Christopher Isherwood on the plays, *The Dog beneath the Skin* (1935), *The Ascent of F6* (1936) and *On the Frontier* (1938).

Several of Auden's Oxford contemporaries, including Stephen Spender, C. Day-Lewis, Louis MacNeice, Rex Warner and John Betjeman, went on to become leading poets of their generation. The most important British poet to emerge during the 1940s was the Welsh writer, Dylan Thomas, whose "play for voices" *Under Milk Wood* (1954) was completed shortly before his early death in 1953.

Stevie Smith (1902–71)

Smith's verse is remarkable for its capacity to make poetry out of the everyday, giving voice to the concerns of suburban women and ordinary people more generally with a distinctive and idiosyncratic voice. Her best-known poem, the title-piece of her collection *Not Waving, But Drowning* (1957), in which a dying man says "I was much too far out all my life/ And not waving but drowning", typifies her ability to evoke existential concerns in a casual, seemingly off-hand manner. Smith published her first collection of verse, *A Good Time was Had by All* in 1937 and was also the author of a number of novels, but her reputation grew considerably during her later years, when her public readings of her work, for which she adopted a seemingly naïve girlish persona, attracted a cult following.

Philip Larkin (1922–85) and The Movement

The Movement was the name given to a group of British poets that emerged in the 1950s about the same time as the Angry Young Men of the English stage. They brought a freshness of diction to English poetry, expressing everyday concerns in plain language and traditional verse forms. However, as with the Angry Young Men, their break with earlier literary language was often accompanied by a conservative response to British society. The Movement's poets included Philip Larkin, who was both the finest and the most representative poet of the group, Kingsley Amis, Donald Davie and Thom Gunn. Other notable poets of their generation include R.S. Thomas and D.J. Enright.

Larkin's collections include *The Whitsun Weddings* (1964), and *High Windows* (1974); and the title-poem of the former, "This Be the Verse" and "Church Windows" are among his best-known individual poems. The cool restraint of his verse has been associated with the bleak social climate of post-war England, but it is also expressive of a reticent temperament that was averse to ostentatious displays of emotion.

Ted Hughes (1930–98)

Hughes's work, which introduced a new vitality and urgency into English poetry, has been seen as a reaction against the Movement's devotion to the commonplace. Following in the tradition of D.H. Lawrence's nature poetry, it often uses animals, such as the trickster figure Crow, as anthropomorphic expressions of elemental human instincts operating outside customary social constraints. The poetic intensity of Hughes's verse evokes the raw power of nature and primeval landscapes wounded by the scars of industrialization. His collections include *The Hawk in the Rain* (1957), *Lupercal* (1960), *Wodwo* (1967), *Crow* (1970), *Remains of Elmet* (1979), *Moortown* (1979) and *Wolfwatching* (1989). He became Poet Laureate in 1984. He was preceded in this office by Sir John Betjeman, and succeeded by Andrew Motion.

Marriage to Sylvia Plath

Hughes was married to the American poet Sylvia Plath from 1956 to 1963, when she committed suicide, and his controversial relationship with her has been the subject of several books, including his own poetic sequence, *Birthday Letters* (1998), which has been hailed as one of his finest works. He also produced a number of acclaimed children's books and versions of classical works, including *Tales from Ovid* (1997) and *The Oresteia* (1999).

lished him as one of the most important figures among the new wave of British dramatists. His reputation was further consolidated by his screen-plays for Joseph Losey's films *The Servant* (1963), *Accident* (1967) and *The Go-Between* (1970). Other major Pinter plays include *The Lover* (1963), *The Homecoming* (1965), *Old Times* (1971), *No Man's Land* (1975), *Betrayal* (1978) and *Mountain Language* (1988). His other film scripts include those for notable film versions of *The Caretaker* (1963), *The Birthday Party* (1967) and *The Homecoming* (1973) and the screenplays for several adaptations of novels including *The Quiller Memorandum* (1966), *The French Lieutenant's Woman* (1981) and *The Handmaid's Tale* (1990).

LATER TWENTIETH-CENTURY DRAMA

Angry Young Men and Kitchen Sink Drama

The 1950s saw the emergence of a drama that turned away from the middle-class social worlds that had dominated the English stage in the middle of the twentieth century, in such plays as Sir Terence Rattigan's *The Browning Version* (1948) and *Separate Tables* (1954), towards work that offered a broader range of perspectives. Jimmy Porter, the hero of the first major salvo in this theatrical revolution, John Osborne's *Look Back in Anger* (1956), emerged as an archetypal "angry young man", challenging what he sees as the smug values of an earlier generation. However, Osborne's subsequent plays, which include a nostalgic study of an ageing music hall performer, *The Entertainer* (1957), *Luther* (1961) and *Inadmissible Evidence* (1964), failed to sustain the challenge. Osborne subsequently returned to the character of Jimmy Porter in *Déjà Vu* (1992).

Unlike Osborne, who had received a public school education, Arnold Wesker was born and brought up in a working-class milieu, in London's East End. This provides the subject-matter for his more obviously proletarian trilogy, *Chicken Soup with Barley* (1958), *Roots* (1959) and *I'm Talking about Jerusalem* (1960) and plays such as *The Kitchen* (1959), while *Chips with Everything* (1962) drew on his experience in the RAF.

Set in working-class Salford, Shelagh Delaney's *A Taste of Honey* (1958), a play about a teenage single mother's relationships with her own irresponsible mother, the black sailor who fathers her child, and a gay art student who helps her with her baby, also brought new material onto the English stage. Written while its author was still herself a teenager, the play was first staged by Joan Littlewood's Theatre Workshop, a socialist company committed to broadening the repertory of English theatre and bringing drama to audiences that would not previously have frequented the theatre.

Other notable Theatre Workshop productions included *Oh What a Lovely War* (1963), a musical about World War I devised by Littlewood, which reflected changing attitudes to English society in the post-World War II period and remained popular during the years of protest against the Vietnam War.

Harold Pinter (1930–)

Harold Pinter's technically innovative plays also took British theatre into new territory. They are typically set in claustrophobic environments and, like such plays as Samuel Beckett's *Waiting for Godot* and Jean-Paul Sartre's *In Camera*, deal with bare, existential situations, in which characters appear to be grappling with undefined threats. Their enigmatic, laconic dialogue creates considerable dramatic tension, even as it obscures the possibility of narrative resolution.

His Rise to Prominence

Pinter first came to prominence as the author of *The Room* (1957), *The Birthday Party* (1957), *The Dumb Waiter* (1960) and *The Caretaker* (1960) estab-

Sir Tom Stoppard (1937–)

Stoppard is a Czech-born dramatist, whose highly popular absurdist play *Rosencrantz and Guildenstern are Dead* (1966), in which minor characters from *Hamlet* await their call to action in a manner reminiscent of Beckett's *Waiting for Godot*, immediately established his reputation as one of the cleverest playwrights of his generation. Like his subsequent works, *The Real Inspector Hound* (1968) and *After Magritte* (1970), the play investigates different levels of theatrical reality. *Jumpers* (1972), in which a murder mystery, song and dance and philosophical discussion are brought together, and *Travesties* (1974), in which famous historical figures collaborate on a 1917 production of Oscar Wilde's *The Importance of Being Earnest*, are among his finest work.

Subsequent plays such as *Night and Day* (1978) and the one-act *Dogg's Hamlet* and *Cahoot's Macbeth* (both 1979) move beyond the existential absurdism of his early work to demonstrate a greater concern with social issues. Stoppard's other plays include *Dirty Linen* (1976), *The Real Thing* (1982), *Hapgood* (1988), *Arcadia* (1993), *Indian Ink* (1995), *The Invention of Love* (1997), and *The Coast of Utopia*, (2002), a trilogy about nineteenth-century Russian revolutionaries.

His work for the cinema includes the screenplays for *Brazil* (1985), *Empire of the Sun* (1987), *The Russia House* (1990) and *Shakespeare in Love* (1998), for which he won an Oscar. He was knighted in 1997.

Other Dramatists of the 1960s and 1970s

Joe Orton became something of an icon for the Gay Liberation movement, after his early death in 1967 at the age of thirty-three. His plays, *Entertaining Mr. Sloan* (1964), *Loot* (1966) and *What the Butler Saw* (1969), are black comedies that blend Pinteresque menace with the traditions of more conventional farce to produce a unique postmodern mixture of the bizarre and the outrageous. Orton was murdered by his partner, the playwright Kenneth Halliwell, author of *Little Malcolm and His Struggle against the Eunuchs* (1965), who then took his own life.

Generally considered the most radical dramatist to come to the fore in the 1960s, Edward Bond achieved notoriety when his play *Saved* (1965) was banned, because of a scene in which a baby is stoned. Subsequently, his historical fantasy *Early Morning* (1968) suffered a similar fate. However, the seemingly sensational cruelty of Bond's early work can be seen as a Marxist critique of the deprivation of certain sectors of British society; and it expresses a viewpoint that became more prominent in the ensuing decades. His subsequent plays turn their attention to representing aspects of the literary heritage in equally controversial ways: *Lear* (1971) is a revisionist version of Shakespeare's *King Lear*, which shows the influence of the Theatre of Cruelty that had become popular in the 1960s and Bond returned to Shakespeare for *Bingo* (1973), a play about the Bard's last days. *The Fool* (1975) is a dramatization of the madness of the nineteenth-century poet, John Clare. Bond's other plays include *The Sea* (1973), *The Woman* (1978), *Restoration* (1981), *The Company of Men* (1992) and the television drama *Olly's Prison* (1993).

A Television Dramatist

Dennis Potter established his reputation as one of the leading television dramatists of recent decades with a play about a miner's son who becomes a parliamentary candidate, *Vote, Vote, Vote for Nigel Barton* (1965), and its sequel, *Stand Up, Nigel Barton* (1965). Beginning with *Pennies from Heaven* (1978), which follows the fortunes of a sheet-music salesman in the 1930s, he subsequently became better known for multi-part series that make highly effective use of popular music to express their protagonists' inner feelings, along with the spirit of the decades in which they are set. Like his subsequent series, *The Singing Detective* (1986), which is generally regarded as his most significant achievement, and *Lipstick on Your Collar* (1993), *Pennies from Heaven* uses its musical sequences as surreal counterpoint to the realism of the main action.

Potter's other work includes *Blue Remembered Hills* (1979), a nostalgic play about childhood set in the Forest of Dean where he grew up, and two further series that were screened after his death in 1994: *Karaoke* (1996) and *Cold Lazarus* (1996).

Sir Alan Ayckbourn (1939–)

Ayckbourn's reputation has been two-fold: as a major proponent of English regional theatre, who has been the guiding force behind the success of the Stephen Joseph Theatre in Scarborough; and as a prolific playwright, whose ostensibly light farces have received considerable acclaim through televised productions and on the West End stage. His angst has grown steadily, to a point where it is possible to regard him as a major social commentator, though his theatrical milieu is a world away from that of the more obviously political dramatists of his generation. His plays include *Absurd Person Singular* (1972), the trilogy grouped under the title *The Norman Conquests* (1973), *Bedroom Farce* (1975), *A Chorus of Disapproval* (1984), *A Small Family Business* (1987), *Man of the Moment* (1988) and the two-part *House and Garden* (1999). He was knighted in 1997.

II. SPECIAL TOPICS

LITERARY PRIZES

Introduction

This section provides information on some of the main literary prizes awarded in the UK, along with details of two other important prizes which have numbered British winners among their recipients: the Nobel Prize for Literature and the Commonwealth Writers Prize.

Other important literary prizes around the world include: the Pulitzer Prizes, awarded for Journalism, Letters, Arts and Music in the USA; the Prix Goncourt, France's leading annual award for a work of fiction; the Miles Franklin Award (Australia), given annually 'for the novel or play of the highest literary merit, presenting aspects of Australian life'; the Indian Sahitya Akademi's Awards, which honour work in twenty-two Indian languages; the Governor General's Literary Awards, Canada's pre-eminent literary prizes, awarded annually for work in various categories and administered by the Canada Council; and the Noma Award for Publishing in Africa, a pan-African prize given to an African-published literary, academic or children's book in any of the languages of Africa, 'European or local'.

The Nobel Prize for Literature

The most prestigious literary prize in the world, the Nobel is one of the five annual prizes awarded since 1901 under the terms of the will of the Swedish chemist Alfred Nobel (1833–96). Nobel's will stipulated that one of the prizes should be given to the person who 'in the field of literature shall have produced the most outstanding work in an ideal direction'. British Nobel Literature laureates have included Rudyard Kipling (1907), W.B. Yeats (1923), George Bernard Shaw (1925), John Galsworthy (1932), T.S. Eliot (1948), Winston Churchill (1953), William Golding (1983), V.S. Naipaul (2001) and Harold Pinter (2005).

Winners since 1980 have been:

1980 Czeslaw Milosz
1981 Elias Canetti
1982 Gabriel García Márquez
1983 William Golding
1984 Jaroslav Seifert
1985 Claude Simon
1986 Wole Soyinka
1987 Joseph Brodsky
1988 Naguib Mahfouz
1989 Camilo José Cela
1990 Octavio Paz
1991 Nadine Gordimer
1992 Derek Walcott
1993 Toni Morrison
1994 Kenzaburo Oe
1995 Seamus Heaney
1996 Wislawa Szymborska
1997 Dario Fo
1998 José Saramago
1999 Günter Grass
2000 Gao Xingjian
2001 V.S. Naipaul
2002 Imre Kertész
2003 J.M. Coetzee
2004 Elfriede Jelinek
2005 Harold Pinter

The Man Booker Prize (formerly the Booker Prize)

Established in 1969, the Booker is the UK's leading prize for a work of fiction. It is awarded annually for the best full-length novel written in English by a citizen of the UK or the Commonwealth. It was sponsored for many years by Booker plc. In 2002 the organization and administration of the Prize was transferred to a newly registered charity, the Booker Prize Foundation. The financial services conglomerate, the Man Group, became its new sponsor, renaming it the Man Booker Prize and more than doubling the prize money awarded to the winning book to £50,000, so that at that time the Booker once again became Britain's richest literary prize.

Winners since 1980 have been:

1980 William Golding, *Rites of Passage*
1981 Salman Rushdie, *Midnight's Children*
1982 Thomas Keneally, *Schindler's Ark*
1983 J.M. Coetzee, *Life & Times of Michael K*
1984 Anita Brookner, *Hotel du Lac*
1985 Keri Hulme, *The Bone People*
1986 Kingsley Amis, *The Old Devils*
1987 Penelope Lively, *Moon Tiger*
1988 Peter Carey, *Oscar and Lucinda*
1989 Kazuo Ishiguro, *The Remains of the Day*
1990 Antonia Byatt, *Possession*
1991 Ben Okri, *The Famished Road*
1992 Michael Ondaatje, *The English Patient* and Barry Unsworth, *Sacred Hunger* (joint winners)
1993 Roddy Doyle, *Paddy Clarke Ha Ha Ha*
1994 James Kelman, *How Late It Was, How Late*
1995 Pat Barker, *The Ghost Road*
1996 Graham Swift, *Last Orders*
1997 Arundhati Roy, *The God of Small Things*
1998 Ian McEwan, *Amsterdam*
1999 J.M. Coetzee, *Disgrace*
2000 Margaret Atwood, *The Blind Assassin*
2001 Peter Carey, *True History of the Kelly Gang*
2002 Yann Martel, *Life of Pi*
2003 D.B.C. Pierre, *Vernon God Little*
2004 Alan Hollinghurst, *The Line of Beauty*
2005 John Banville, *The Sea*

Peter Carey and J.M. Coetzee share the distinction of being the only two authors to have won the Prize twice. Prior to winning in 2000, Margaret Atwood had been short-listed on three previous occasions. In 1993, Rushdie's *Midnight's Children* was awarded the Booker of Bookers (the 'Best of Twenty Five Years of the Booker Prize').

The Commonwealth Writers Prize

Established in 1987, the Commonwealth Writers Prize is sponsored by the Commonwealth Foundation and is currently administered by Cumberland Lodge at the invitation of the Book Trust in London. Annual prizes are awarded for the best book and the best first book from each of four Commonwealth regions: Africa; the Caribbean and Canada; 'Eurasia'; and Southeast Asia and the South Pacific (which includes Australasia). Regional winners then go forward to the overall final, which is judged by a pan-Commonwealth jury at a venue that rotates around the Commonwealth.

Winners of the overall prize have been:

1987 Olive Senior, *Summer Lightning* (Jamaica)
1988 Festus Iyayi, *Heroes* (Nigeria)
1989 Janet Frame, *The Carpathians* (New Zealand)
1990 Mordecai Richler, *Solomon Gursky Was Here* (Canada)
1991 David Malouf, *The Great World* (Australia)
1992 Rohinton Mistry, *Such a Long Journey* (Canada)
1993 Alex Miller, *The Ancestor Game* (Australia)
1994 Vikram Seth, *A Suitable Boy* (India)
1995 Louis de Bernières, *Captain Corelli's Mandolin* (UK)
1996 Rohinton Mistry, *A Fine Balance* (Canada)
1997 Earl Lovelace, *Salt* (Trinidad)
1998 Peter Carey, *Jack Maggs* (Australia)
1999 Murray Bail, *Eucalyptus* (Australia)
2000 J. M. Coetzee, *Disgrace* (South Africa)
2001 Peter Carey, *True History of the Kelly Gang* (Australia)
2002 Richard Flanagan, *Gould's Book of Fish* (Australia)
2003 Austin Clarke, *The Polished Hoe* (Canada)

2004 Caryl Phillips, *A Distant Shore* (UK)
2005 Andrea Levy, *Small Island* (UK)

The Orange Prize for Fiction

The Orange Prize was introduced in 1996, to help remedy the perceived neglect of women writers shown by the UK's major literary prizes. It is awarded annually for a novel written by a woman and published in the UK and is open to women of all nationalities.

Winners have been:

1996 Helen Dunmore, *A Spell of Winter*
1997 Anne Michaels, *Fugitive Pieces*
1998 Carol Shields, *Larry's Party*
1999 Suzanne Berne, *A Crime in the Neighbourhood*
2000 Linda Grant, *When I Lived in Modern Times*
2001 Kate Grenville, *The Idea of Perfection*
2002 Anna Patchett, *Bel Canto*
2003 Valerie Martin, *Property*
2004 Andrea Levy, *Small Island*
2005 Lionel Shriver, *We Need to Talk About Kevin*
2006 Zadie Smith, *On Beauty*

The David Cohen Prize

Unlike Britain's other major literary awards, the David Cohen British Literature Prize in the English Language is awarded for lifetime achievement. It has been awarded biennially since 1993 and is funded by the David Cohen Family Trust and the Arts Council, who administer the Prize. Members of the public are invited to nominate winners. A proportion of the prize money (£12,500 in 2005) is allocated to the encouragement of younger writers and readers of the winner's choosing.

Winners so far have been:

1993 V.S. Naipaul
1995 Harold Pinter
1997 Muriel Spark
1999 William Trevor
2001 Doris Lessing
2003 Beryl Bainbridge and Thom Gunn
2005 Michael Holroyd

The Whitbread Book Awards

The Whitbread Book Awards were founded in 1971, with awards being made in five categories: best book, best first book, best biography, best poetry collection and best children's book. Their format changed in 1985, when the Whitbread Book of the Year, widely regarded as Britain's most important literary prize after the Booker, was introduced. Between 1996 and 1998 the Children's Book of the Year was a separate award in its own right. From 1999 to 2001, this separate award continued, but with the Children's Book of the Year subsequently being judged against the other categories for overall Book of the Year. From 2002 it once again became one of five categories, with its winner competing for the overall title of Book of the Year.

The awards are sponsored by Whitbread plc and administered by the Bookseller's Association of Great Britain and Ireland. They are open to authors who have been resident in the UK or Ireland for three years.

Winners of the overall Book of the Year have been:

1985 Douglas Dunn, *Elegies* (Poetry)
1986 Kazuo Ishiguro, *An Artist of the Floating World* (Novel)
1987 Christopher Nolan, *Under the Eye of the Clock* (Biography)
1988 Paul Sayer, *The Comforts of Madness* (First Novel)
1989 Richard Holmes, *Coleridge: Early Visions* (Biography)
1990 Nicholas Mosley, *Hopeful Monsters* (Novel)
1991 John Richardson, *A Life of Picasso* (Biography)
1992 Jeff Torrington, *Swing Hammer Swing!* (First Novel)
1993 Joan Brady, *Theory of War* (Novel)
1994 William Trevor, *Felicia's Journey* (Novel)
1995 Kate Atkinson, *Behind the Scenes at the Museum* (First Novel)

1996 Seamus Heaney, *The Spirit Level* (Poetry)
1997 Ted Hughes, *Tales from Ovid* (Poetry)
1998 Ted Hughes, *Birthday Letters* (Poetry)
1999 Seamus Heaney, *Beowulf* (Poetry)
2000 Matthew Kneale, *English Passengers* (Novel)
2001 Philip Pullman, *The Amber Spyglass* (Children's Book of the Year)
2002 Claire Tomalin, *Samuel Pepys: The Unequalled Self* (Biography)
2003 Mark Haddon, *The Curious Incident of the Dog in the Night-Time* (Novel)
2004 Andrea Levy, *Small Island* (Novel)
2005 Hilary Spurling, *Matisse: The Master* (Biography)

The *Guardian* Fiction Award and The *Guardian* First Book Award

First awarded in 1965, the *Guardian* Fiction Award was one of the UK's most important fiction prizes. It was awarded for both novels and short story collections. In 1999 it was replaced by the Guardian First Book Award, which is not restricted to works of fiction.

Winners of the *Guardian* Fiction Award from 1980 onwards have been:

1980 J.L. Carr, *A Month in the Country*
1981 John Banville, *Kepler*
1982 Glyn Hughes, *Where I Used to Play on the Green*
1983 Graham Swift, *Waterland*
1984 J.G. Ballard, *Empire of the Sun*
1985 Peter Ackroyd, *Hawksmoor*
1986 Jim Crace, *Continent*
1987 Peter Benson, *The Levels*
1988 Lucy Ellmann, *Sweet Desserts*
1989 Carol Lake, *Rose-Hill: Portrait from a Midlands City*
1990 Pauline Melville, *Shape-Shifter*
1991 Alan Judd, *The Devil's Own Work*
1992 Alasdair Gray, *Poor Things*
1993 Pat Barker, *The Eye in The Door*
1994 Candia McWilliams, *Debatable Land*
1995 James Buchan, *Heart's Journey in Winter*
1996 Seamus Deane, *Reading in the Dark*
1997 Anne Michaels, *Fugitive Pieces*
1998 Jackie Kay, *Trumpet*

Winners of the *Guardian* First Book Award have been:

1999 Philip Gourevitch, *We Wish to Inform You that Tomorrow We Will Be Killed with Our Families*
2000 Zadie Smith, *White Teeth*
2001 Chris Ware, *Jimmy Corrigan: The Smartest Kid on Earth*
2002 Jonathan Safran Foer, *Everything Is Illuminated*
2003 Robert Macfarlane, *Mountains of the Mind*
2004 Armand Marie Leroi, *Mutants*
2005 Alexander Masters, *Stuart: A Life Backwards*

The W.H. Smith Award

First conferred in 1959, the W.H. Smith Award is an annual prize whose declared aim is to 'encourage and bring international esteem to authors of the British Commonwealth'. It is awarded to the author whose book, in the opinion of the judges, has made the most significant contribution to the year's literature. Authors from the UK, the Commonwealth, and the Irish Republic are eligible.

Winners since 1980 have been:

1980 Thom Gunn, *Selected Poems, 1959–1975*
1981 Isabel Colegate, *The Shooting Party*
1982 George Clare, *Last Waltz in Vienna*
1983 A.N. Wilson, *Wise Virgin*
1984 Philip Larkin, *Required Writing*
1985 David Hughes, *The Pork Butcher*
1986 Doris Lessing, *The Good Terrorist*
1987 Elizabeth Jennings, *Collected Poems, 1953–1985*
1988 Robert Hughes, *The Fatal Shore*
1989 Christopher Hill, *A Turbulent, Seditious and Factious People: John Bunyan and His Church*
1990 V.S. Pritchett, *A Careless Widow and Other Stories*
1991 Derek Walcott, *Omeros*
1992 Thomas Pakenham, *The Scramble for Africa*

1993 Michèle Roberts, *Daughters of the House*
1994 Vikram Seth, *A Suitable Boy*
1995 Alice Munro, *Open Secrets*
1996 Simon Schama, *Landscape and Memory*
1997 Orlando Figes, *A People's Tragedy: The Russian Revolution*
1998 Ted Hughes, *Tales from Ovid*
1999 Beryl Bainbridge, *Master Georgie*
2000 Melvyn Bragg, *The Soldier's Return*
2001 Philip Roth, *The Human Stain*
2002 Ian McEwan, *Atonement*
2003 Donna Tartt, *The Little Friend*
2004 Richard Powers, *The Time of Our Singing*
2005 Philip Roth, *The Plot Against America*

The T. S. Eliot Prize

The T. S. Eliot Prize is administered by the Poetry Book Society, of which Eliot was a founding member in 1953. It was inaugurated in 1993 to celebrate the Society's fortieth anniversary and is awarded to the best new collection of poetry published in the UK or the Republic of Ireland in the previous calendar year.

Winners have been:

1993 Ciaran Carson, *First Language*
1994 Paul Muldoon, *The Annals of Chile*
1995 Mark Doty, *My Alexandria*
1996 Les Murray, *Subhuman Redneck Poems*
1997 Don Paterson, *God's Gift to Women*
1998 Ted Hughes, *Birthday Letters*
1999 Hugo Williams, *Billy's Rain*
2000 Michael Longley, *The Weather in Japan*
2001 Anne Carson, *The Beauty of the Husband*
2002 Alice Oswald, *Dart*
2003 Don Paterson, *Landing Light*
2004 Michael Sowder, *The Empty Boat*
2005 Mona Lisa Saloy, *Red Beans and Ricely Yours*

NOTABLE LITERARY PRIZE WINNERS

Introductory Note

This special topic deals with twenty of the finest literary prize winners of the last quarter of a century. Its primary emphasis is on books rather than writers. So in the case of Nobel Prize winners, who received this award for their overall output rather than a single work, it focuses on books which received another prize or were specially commended in the Nobel citation.

Salman Rushdie, *Midnight's Children*
Booker Prize, 1981; "Booker of Bookers – for the best novel of the first 25 years of the Prize, 1993

Midnight's Children's narrator Saleem feels that he has been "handcuffed to history", since his personal life has mirrored the first twenty-five years of post-independence Indian history. He has been born at the exact moment of Indian independence in 1947 (Rushdie was born in the same year) and the novel uses this analogy to trace an intricate network of comic parallels between public and private history, with Saleem increasingly viewing himself as a rival to India's Prime Minister, Indira Gandhi.

As the novel moves from the optimism of the Independence era to events connected with the "Emergency" declared by Mrs. Gandhi in the mid-1970s, its mood becomes increasingly sombre and the comedy is supplanted by a more pessimistic political vision.

Midnight's Children stresses the pluralism of contemporary Indian society and brings together a number of non-realist narrative modes, among them traditional Hindu and Islamic storytelling, Latin American magic realism and the hybrid cinematic style of the Bombay Talkie.

Peter Ackroyd, *Hawksmoor*
Guardian Fiction Award, 1985; Whitbread Novel of the Year, 1985

Hawksmoor is an eerie mystery story, which alternates between chapters set in eighteenth- and twentieth-century London. In the eighteenth-century action, Nicholas Dyer, an architect based on the real-life Nicholas Hawksmoor, supervises the rebuilding of seven London churches in the wake of the Fire of London. Opposed to the new spirit of scientific inquiry personified by the work of the Royal Society, Dyer has a belief in older non-rationalist forces. In the twentieth-century action, a detective called Nicholas Hawksmoor attempts to solve seven murders committed on the sites of Dyer's churches. *His* rational inquiries are, however, abortive and as the novel moves towards its chilling climax, the suggestion is that the forces in which Dyer believes have maintained their power across the centuries and are in some way responsible for the murders.

Hawksmoor conflates the genres of crime fiction and ghost story, finally subscribing to a view that suggests the limitations of detection and the abiding nature of incomprehensible evil.

Olive Senior, *Summer Lightning*
Commonwealth Writers Prize 1987: Inaugural Winner

Most of the stories of Senior's first collection, *Summer Lightning*, are set in the late colonial period and focus on child protagonists, several of whom find themselves transplanted into another household, an experience that replicates that of Senior's own Jamaican childhood which involved a similar movement between two social worlds. In the stories, this movement between different worlds enables her to dramatize the competing claims of Jamaica's middle-class and folk cultures and to explore the major forces in her protagonists' socialization, including religion, education, race, colour and class. The title-story, which makes subtle use of a number of controlling images, "Bright Thursdays" and the longer final story, "Ballad", a comic *tour de force*, written in Jamaican Creole, are particularly outstanding.

Toni Morrison, *Beloved*
Pulitzer Prize for Fiction, 1988; Nobel Prize 1993

Set in Kentucky in the middle of the nineteenth century, *Beloved* drew its inspiration from the story of an African American woman who murdered her daughter to save her from becoming a slave. Its time-scheme shifts between past and present, suggesting the extent to which the African American experience is haunted by the trauma of slavery. It is a powerful ghost story, which interweaves a complex account of the psychological effects of guilt with an indictment of the inhumanity of slavery. Sethe's murdered daughter, Beloved, returns from the dead, as a malevolent spirit bent on wreaking revenge on her mother by disrupting her present life and her relationship with her lover Paul D, whom Beloved beguiles with her sexual charms. Eventually the women of the community unite to perform an exorcism which returns Beloved to the spirit-world, a resolution which seems to suggest a partial coming to terms with the nightmare of the slave past.

Like the Holocaust, the horrors of slavery have sometimes seemed to be beyond artistic representation. However, *Beloved*'s use of a non-realistic fictional mode provides a highly effective way of giving voice to the supposedly unspeakable.

Kazuo Ishiguro, *The Remains of the Day*
Booker Prize, 1989

The narrator of Japanese-born Ishiguro's novel, Stevens, is an elderly butler, who has devoted his life to an ideal of service and "dignity". In 1956 he undertakes a journey to the West Country to visit Miss Kenton, the former housekeeper of the stately home in which he works. Along the way he remembers crucial events in his life, most of which are informed by his failure to acknowledge his emotions and the political realities underlying the life-style of his former master, who has had fascist sympathies during the years between the two world wars.

Stevens is a member of a dying breed and *The Remains of the Day* is a quietly ironic Condition of England novel that charts the demise of an aristocratic social order. It is also a powerful study of emotional repression and its understated epiphany comes when Stevens finally meets Miss Kenton and has to acknowledge that his dedication to duty has stifled the feelings they have had for one another.

A.S. Byatt, *Possession*
Booker Prize, 1990

Possession deals with contemporary scholars' attempts to unearth the truth about a relationship between two fictional nineteenth-century poets: Randolph Henry Ash, who is based on Browning and Tennyson, and Christabel LaMotte, an apparent amalgam of Emily Dickinson and Christina Rossetti. Two young academics, Roland Mitchell, an American research assistant working for an Ash expert, and Maud Bailey, a British LaMotte scholar, attempt to piece together the jigsaw of this relationship from various letters and journals. As their quest progresses, their own relationship begins to parallel that of the two poets and when it is revealed that Maud is Christabel LaMotte's great-great-granddaughter, the symmetry is confirmed. *Possession* is part detective novel, part romance quest. It is also a novel about the ethics of literary research, which contrasts the arid, possessive approach of its older authorities on Victorian poetry – both British and American – with the more life-affirming approach to "possession" of the two young researchers, whose relationship becomes a contemporary equivalent of their subjects' passion.

Pauline Melville, *Shape-Shifter*
Guardian Fiction Award, 1990; Commonwealth Writers Prize Best First Book Award, 1991

Melville has been termed a "magic realist" writer, but such a classification obscures the diverse range of fictional modes and voices to be found in her first book, the short-story collection *Shape-Shifter*. Its stories move between coastal Guyana and contemporary London, where Melville mainly deals with the situation of migrants and those living on the fringes of society. The Guyanese stories investigate the efficacy of magic and superstition, while also revealing contemporary political corruption. At first the London stories seem to employ a more realistic method. However, as the volume progresses, they become increasingly surrealistic and in pieces such as "The Truth is in the Clothes" and "You Left the Door Open", the paranormal and the everyday come together in shape-shifting fictional forms that are highly suited to the transformations of identity they depict.

Derek Walcott, *Omeros*
W.H. Smith Award, 1991; Nobel Prize 1992

Omeros is a long narrative poem, which has been seen as a Caribbean version of Homer's epics. However, Walcott has insisted that the poem is not derived from Homer, but rather an autonomous St. Lucian equivalent of *The Odyssey* and *The Iliad*. Its central narrative tells the story of two St. Lucian fishermen, Achille and Hector, who quarrel over a local woman, Helen, a name applied to St. Lucia itself from the era of imperialist expansion onwards. This story is accompanied by an account of the travels of a wandering Odyssean poet, whose journeys provide a means for seeing various aspects of Caribbean history and culture, and the region's relationship with other parts of the world, in a new light.

Other themes include an imaginative return to Africa and a sensitive exploration of the complexities of the white expatriate's role in St. Lucia in the aftermath of Empire. Ultimately the poem's characters seem to merge into a composite persona, a fusion which suggests the extent to which they share a common history. The poem received particular praise in the Nobel citation, when Walcott was awarded the Prize for Literature in 1992.

Michael Ondaatje, *The English Patient*
Booker Prize, Joint Winner, 1992; Canadian Governor General's Award for Fiction, 1992

Set in a semi-ruined Tuscan villa at the end of World War II, *The English Patient* brings together four characters of different nationalities, whose lives, despite their apparent isolation, are indelibly marked by larger public forces, among them the militaristic nationalism of the war and British imperialism in India. At the centre of the narrative lies the dying "English" patient, a mysterious bedridden victim of a plane crash in the North African desert. In memory he revisits the desert where he has been an explorer, engaging in necrophiliac recollections of his lost love. The Tuscan and North African sections of the novel are linked by an emphasis on the ways in which political cartography affects the lives of even those whose desires seem to transcend national categories – the four inhabitants of the villa *seem* to form a supra-national micro-community; the English patient is a Hungarian count – and the closing sections are played out against the background of news of the bombing of Hiroshima.

The popularity of the novel was further enhanced by the success of Anthony Minghella's 1996 film adaptation, which won nine Oscars.

Rohinton Mistry, *Such a Long Journey*
Commonwealth Writers Prize, 1992

Like his earlier short-story collection, *Tales from Firozsha Baag* (1987), Mistry's first novel *Such a Long Journey* is centred on the enclosed world of a Parsi apartment building in Bombay. It combines a despairing humanism with a strong sense of emotional attachment to Bombay. Written in a superficially realistic style, the novel follows the fortunes of Gustad Noble, a bank clerk who becomes embroiled in a tragic-comic web of intrigue and espionage at the time of the 1971 war that led to the creation of Bangladesh. As his surname seems to suggest, Gustad represents the heroism of an ordinary "little man", but *Such a Long Journey* is less sanguine about society at large, offering a scatological vision of Bombay; and, despite hints at the need for pluralism, Gustad's moral struggle revolves around attempts to preserve his insulated community from outside encroachments. The novel is notable for some moving passages on death and traditional Parsi funeral practices.

Graham Swift, *Last Orders*
Booker Prize, 1996

Swift's novel is written as a series of monologues, mainly narrated by four men entrusted with the task of carrying out the "last orders" of the South London butcher, Jack Dobbs, who has asked that his ashes be scattered off the end of Margate Pier. Written in the language of working-class South London, *Last Orders* is an understated study of how people react to mortality and find ways of laying both the dead and their own private fears to rest. Its technique has been compared with *As I Lay Dying* and it shares Faulkner's novel's capacity to blend comedy with pathos. It begins in a South London pub and its characters' journey to the coast takes in a detour about to Canterbury Cathedral. This route is reminiscent of Chaucer's *Canterbury Tales* and while the four travellers initially seem to be unlikely pilgrims, both their journey and the telling of their stories involve rites of passage for them.

Their narratives are complemented by that of Jack's widow, Amy, who declines to accompany them, preferring instead to pay a last visit to her mentally handicapped daughter, whom Jack has never acknowledged. Amy, too, lays ghosts to rest on this day.

Arundhati Roy, *The God of Small Things*
Booker Prize, 1997

The novel's action moves between the early 1990s and 1969. The 1990s action opens with the twins Estha and Rahel being reunited in their home-town in Kerala. In their childhood they have thought of themselves as a "single unity", but they have been separated and have lived elsewhere for over two decades. The 1969 action begins on a day when the seven-year-old twins are being taken to the airport to meet their cousin Sophie Mol, who is arriving from England. Gradually the mysteries surrounding the events that have separated them are explained: their mother has broken caste taboos by having an affair with an "Untouchable", while the twins have been unintentionally involved in the drowning of Sophie Mol. In the later action the twins' intense feelings for one another are consummated in a moment which transgresses "the Love Laws". The novel's intricate time-shifts show how individual lives are affected by "History", but it finally argues for the superior power of "Biology". It is written in an innovative style that makes extensive use of neologisms.

Earl Lovelace, *Salt*
Commonwealth Writers Prize, 1997

Salt deals with various aspects of the social life of multi-ethnic Trinidad, promoting a cross-cultural vision that avoids multicultural platitudes. Most of its characters are Afro-Caribbeans who share a common desire to assert their selfhood in forms that deny the colonial condition of "unfreedom", but Lovelace treats a French Creole and an Indo-Caribbean protagonist with equal empathy. One of the novel's two main figures is a carnivalesque storyteller and much of its success in conveying the individuality of its characters comes from the exuberance of its own story-telling technique.

Salt is set around the time that Trinidad attained Independence in 1962, but its contemporary action is underpinned by a sure sense of Caribbean history and a central chapter delves into the slave past, with Lovelace insisting that this be remembered, since "The tragedy of our time is to have lost the ability to feel loss".

Peter Carey, *Jack Maggs*
Commonwealth Writers Prize, 1998

The novel's eponymous protagonist is loosely based on the character of Magwitch, the convict in *Great Expectations* who, after his transportation to Australia and subsequent emancipation, becomes the mysterious benefactor supporting Pip's lifestyle as a gentleman. However, although this parallel is obvious, *Jack Maggs* has an oblique relationship to Dickens's novel. It places Jack at the centre of its story and renders its equivalent of Pip, Henry Phipps, a shadowy and sinister character, who flees his lodgings when he learns that Jack has returned from Australia. Blending a self-conscious postmodern approach to fiction with Victorian realism, Carey's complex plot also introduces two other main characters who have no equivalents in *Great Expectations*: a Dickensian novelist figure, Tobias Oates, who endeavours to exercise power over Jack, and a maid, Mercy Larkin. Jack finally frees himself from the influence of both Henry and Tobias and returns to Australia, where he and Mercy become the respected founders of a new dynasty, thus reversing the cultural affiliations of *Great Expectations*.

Jackie Kay, *Trumpet*
Guardian Fiction Award, 1998

Trumpet is said to have been inspired by the American jazz musician Billy Tipton, who lived his life as a man, but after his death was revealed to have been a woman. The novel tells the story of fictional black Scottish trumpeter, Joss Moody, who has also been born a woman, but has lived his adult life as a man. It is written in a quietly unsensational style and offers a range of perspectives on Joss's life. Seen, after his death, through the eyes of figures such as a registrar, a doctor and a funeral director, Joss's identity poses problems of classification that raise broader questions about the nature of gender identity. However, *Trumpet* is far more than an investigation of such issues. Its main emphasis is on the grief of Joss's devoted wife Millie and the anger of his foster son Colman, whose initial shock at the discovery that his father was biologically a woman gives way to acceptance. The novel moves towards a poignant climax in which love supplants anger and Colman and his mother are reunited. *Trumpet*'s use of multiple voices to tell its story allows it to offer multiple variations on its theme in a manner which evokes the improvisations of jazz performance.

J.M. Coetzee, *Disgrace*
Booker Prize, 1999; Nobel Prize 2003

Disgrace was Coetzee's second Booker prize-winning novel (he had previously won the Prize in 1983 for *Life & Times of Michael K*) and he was subsequently awarded the Nobel Prize for Literature in 2003. *Disgrace*'s protagonist, David Lurie, is a South African lecturer who loses the respect of his peers and abandons his position, after a brief affair with a student. Like the more humble Michael K, he leaves his urban South African world and journeys into a rural heartland, which provides a more elemental setting for the exploration of moral issues. Gradually, Lurie acquires a degree of

humility, as he comes to terms with the rape of his lesbian daughter by a black South African and learns respect for "the life of animals", another major preoccupation of Coetzee's later fiction. The novel can be read as an allegory of the ethical dilemmas confronting white South Africans in the period after the collapse of apartheid and an investigation of the extent to which free will is compromised by larger historical forces.

V.S. Naipaul, *The Enigma of Arrival*
Nobel Prize, 2001

Prior to receiving the Nobel Prize, Naipaul had won most of Britain's major literary awards including the Booker for *In a Free State* (1971) and the inaugural David Cohen Prize (for lifetime achievement) in 1993. The Nobel Prize citation placed particular emphasis on his novel *The Enigma of Arrival* (1987), a work which on one level is a thinly-veiled autobiography: a personal meditation by a Trinidadian-born writer, whose origins and career correspond closely to Naipaul's own. The novel is, however, much more than this. It is also a book about the changing face of England. The writer is living on Salisbury Plain, an ancient multi-layered landscape, containing numerous "sacred" sites including Stonehenge, Winchester and Victorian churches that are seen as expressive of the Indian Summer of Empire. Initially he views this landscape as immutable, subjectively filtering it through familiar literary and pictorial reference-points, but he gradually comes to realise the extent to which it is a "constructed" location with a transient population, an environment that is a world away from the stereotypically homogeneous England of his imagination.

Yann Martel, *Life of Pi*
Booker Prize, 2002

Brought up in Pondicherry in India, Pi is the son of a zookeeper, who decides to migrate to Canada with his family and his menagerie. When their ship sinks in the Pacific, Pi finds himself the sole human survivor on a lifeboat with a zebra, a hyena, an orang-utan and a 450-pound tiger, named Richard Parker. He witnesses the animals devour one another, before eventually achieving a *modus vivendi* with the surviving animal at the top of this food chain, Richard Parker. After more than 200 days at sea, they reach Mexico, where Richard Parker disappears into the jungle. Pi is questioned by two officials, investigating the sinking of the ship. They refuse to believe his incredible story and so he offers a more plausible alternative, but for most readers his original narrative continues to seem "truer".

Life of Pi blends classic elements from castaway stories of survival with suggestions of religious allegory, deriving from Pi's Hindu-centred belief in three of the world's major religions.

Andrea Levy, *Small Island*
Orange Prize, 2004; Whitbread Book of the Year, 2004; Commonwealth Writers Prize, 2005

Small Island deals with a comparatively neglected period in recent British social history: the 1940s. The novel moves between sections set in "1948" – the date of the arrival of the S.S. *Empire Windrush* at Tilbury, which heralded the beginnings of post-war Caribbean migration to Britain – and "Before". It explores the impact of World War II and the initial difficulties surrounding Caribbean immigration into Britain through the narratives of four characters from the "small islands" of Britain and Jamaica: a Jamaican serviceman in the RAF, who returns to England on the Windrush; his newly married middle-class wife, who joins him in Britain as a comparative stranger; and a complementary white couple, whose lives are also indelibly changed by the war. Levy's compassionate narrative gathers cumulative momentum and emotional force, as the lives of the four protagonists become increasingly intertwined.

Realistic in mode and epic in sweep, *Small Island* also provides a vivid portrait of racism and class discrimination in the RAF in both Britain and India, comparing this with American segregationist attitudes, exemplified by the treatment of American GIs stationed in England during the war.

DICTIONARY
OF
ART

This popular section offers a concise introduction to some of the key terms and movements in the history of art and architecture. A Special Topic looks at Baroque and Rococo art. Readers may also wish to refer to Section B for biographical details of many prominent painters and artists.

DICTIONARY OF ART

References to famous artists (indicated by *q.v.*) are to be found in **Section B, Prominent People**.

A

Abstract art designates paintings, prints or sculptures in which the subject-matter is simplified or schematised to a point that its representational qualities are subordinate to its form and colour. The term is sometimes used loosely to indicate non-objective (*q.v.*) painting.

Abstract Expressionism, a term embracing a diverse group of artists (including Jackson Pollock and Willem de Kooning) working in New York during the 1940s. Their work emphasised the precedence of the creative process over the finished product, giving rise to the name Action Painting (*q.v.*). Although not an organised movement, Abstract Expressionism was influential in Europe and America.

Academy, an official institution concerned with the training of artists and/or the promotion of art. Academies were initially a means of raising the social status of the artist, and they were often under aristocratic or royal patronage. The first art academies in Florence (founded 1563) and Rome (founded 1593) influenced the foundation of other academies throughout Europe in the seventeenth and eighteenth centuries, including France (1648) and England (1768), and in America in the nineteenth century. Academies were increasingly governed by a rigid set of hierarchies and a stultifying training programme, but they nevertheless exerted great influence in Europe and America until the mid-nineteenth century, when excluded artists (such as the Impressionists, *q.v.*) actively rebelled against their authority.

Action Painting is often used synonymously with Abstract Expressionism (*q.v.*), but it refers primarily to a method employed by artists such as Jackson Pollock. It involves applying paint to a canvas in a spontaneous manner, by allowing it to drip or splash. The term suggests that the process of painting itself is the primary concern of the artist.

Aerial perspective, or atmospheric perspective, refers to a sense of depth created by gradations of colour, rather than by the strictly mathematical formulas of perspective (*q.v.*). From the seventeenth century, much landscape painting, including that of Claude (*q.v.*) and Turner (*q.v.*) relies on this method.

Aesthetic Movement does not refer to an organised group of artists. It classifies a general cultural tendency in late nineteenth-century England and, to a lesser extent, America, which encompassed a fascination with morbidity, decadence and sexuality. This cultivation of amorality included the idea of "art for art's sake", which allowed art to exist apart from any moral or didactic purpose. Oscar Wilde (*q.v.*) was the movement's most famous exponent, and the artists James MacNeill Whistler (*q.v.*) and Aubrey Beardsley (*q.v.*) were also considered "Aesthetes".

Aesthetics is a branch of philosophy concerned with concepts of art and beauty. The term was coined in the eighteenth century when the questions of how people perceive art and why they respond to it were considered by theorists such as Johann Joachim Winckelmann, Gotthold Ephraim Lessing (*q.v.*) and Immanuel Kant (*q.v.*).

Alla prima, Italian for "at first", is a method of oil painting which involves applying paint in one session. By avoiding the contrivance of preliminary underdrawing or underpainting, the artist can achieve by this method a sense of spontaneity. This technique was favoured by the Impressionists (*q.v.*).

Altarpiece, an object placed on or behind an altar, usually in a church. Altarpieces generally contain painting or sculpture and devotional or Biblical scenes, which are intended to enhance the spiritual experience of the worshipper. The subject-matter of altarpieces usually consists of images of the Madonna and Child with saints and/ or donors (*q.v.*), or scenes from the life of the Virgin or Christ.

Alto-Relievo, a term applied to sculptured designs which are depicted in prominent relief on a flat surface, technically signifying that the projections exceeds one-half the true proportions of the objects represented. Basso-relievo is carving kept lower than one-half such projection.

Aquatint is a process of engraving which produces tonal effects similar to those of watercolour. It was especially common in England from the late eighteenth century for topographical views, and it has since been used to different effect by such artists as Goya (*q.v.*) and Picasso (*q.v.*).

Architecture, the art and science of building. The provision of shelter for mankind by the orderly arrangement of materials in a manner which expresses man's attitude to living. Until the last hundred years structural methods were limited to timber frames, and columns, lintels, load-bearing walls, arches, vaults, and domes in brick or stone.

From these few basic elements have evolved the great variety of historic styles of building to be found throughout the world. To give but one example, the Greeks created those systems of decorated columns and beams, known as the Orders, which were adapted by the Romans, revived decoratively rather than structurally during the Renaissance and are still used in debased form on the more presumptuous type of modern building. In modern times, however, architecture has taken on a new meaning. Once confined to the rich, in the form of Church, State or Commerce, it is now, with the coming of democracy, recognised as an essential social service for all. This, and the development of new structural techniques and materials (steel, aluminium, sheet glass, reinforced concrete, plastics and plywoods, to name a few), have made the interest in historic styles of less importance.

Modern architecture is the creation of buildings with the highest possible standards of functional performance in terms of efficient planning and structure, good artificial and natural lighting, adequate heating *etc*.

Some recent architectural developments include the Tate Modern, Norman Foster's Jubilee Line station at Canary Wharf and the new National Botanical Gardens in Wales.

Armory Show, an exhibition held in a Regimental Armory in New York in 1913. The presentation of over 1000 works included Impressionism (*q.v.*), Post-Impressionism (*q.v.*) and contemporary European and American painting. It had a radical impact on the development of American modern art.

Art Brut was the name given by Jean Dubuffet to the art of schizophrenics, prisoners and other individuals producing art outside the official and formal institutions and training traditions of the art establishment. Dubuffet believed that such "unsweetened" or untrained art was superior to the contrived and socially controlled productions of "fine artists".

Art Deco, the name given by modern collectors to the decorative style of the 1920s and 1930s; it is derived from the long official name of the Paris Exhibition of 1925, which was almost exclusively devoted to "les Arts Décoratifs". Art Deco runs parallel in time with Functionalism (*q.v.*) but unlike that austere and philosophical style, Art Deco is gay, elegant and even frivolous, being a creation of fashionable Paris. It is related superficially to Cubism, using squares, circles and triangles in interesting combinations for ornament. Another popular motif is the modern girl with her shingled head dancing the tango or drinking cocktails. The style is brash and worldly, but in its best expressions full of charm and vitality. Famous names within the style are the glassmaker Rene Lalique (1860–1945), the fashion designers Gabrielle Chanel and Elsa Schiaparelli, and the decorator and illustrator Erte (Roman de Tirtoff, b. 1829). There has been a revival of Art Deco, in films like "Bonny and Clyde" (1967) or "The Great Gatsby" (1974).

Art Nouveau (German *Jugend Stil*) was prevalent in architecture and decoration in Europe and the USA *c*, 1885–1910. It was rooted in the thoughts of Ruskin and William Morris. In reaction against the impersonal uniformity of industrial products which were flooding the market, artists turned to Nature for their inspiration, choosing organically growing forms, flowers or animals, as motifs for decoration or even for shaping whole objects. Another favourite motif was Romantic Woman with long robes and flowing hair, as interpreted so beautifully by Aubrey Beardsley. The sharply undulating line with a whiplash rhythm is a recurring theme. Famous names are the glassmakers Emile Gallé in France and Louis Comfort Tiffany in New York, the English goldsmith Charles Robert Ashbee (1863–1942), Henry Van de Velde (1867–1942) in Belgium and Charles Rennie Mackintosh (1868–1928) in Scotland, both architects and interior decorators, and in pure architecture Antonio Gaudí of Barcelona (1852–1926) and Victor Horta in Brussels (1861–1946).

Arte Povera literally translates "impoverished art", and it was a term invented by the Italian art critic Germano Celant in the 1960s. It refers to a disposable and Minimal (*q.v.*) art composed of perishable and easily accessible items such as sand and newspaper. Its premise was to detach art from market forces by stripping it of its consumer value, although ironically *Arte Povera* now fetches high prices. Its adherents include Michelangelo Pistoletto and Mario Ceroli.

Arts and Crafts Movement, the English revival of decorative art which began about 1875 as a revolt against the existing vulgarity of internal decoration and furnishings and the pettiness of academic art. Inspired by William Morris and Burne-Jones together with Rossetti, it was strongly influenced by the former's mediaevalism, his hatred of industrialism, and his own version of socialism which included the regeneration of man by handicrafts. His firm of Morris & Co. produced wallpapers, tapestries, furniture, stained-glass windows, carpets and fabrics in a style totally different from that of contemporary Victorian decoration. Morris's Kelmscott Press did much to raise the standards of book design and printing. *See* **Art Nouveau** (above).

Ashcan School, a name given retrospectively to a group of American artists who explored similar themes of city life between *c*, 1908 and the First World War. The original group was dominated by Henri Bellows, but it was later extended to include artists such as Edward Hopper. The name "ashcan" referred to the city dust-bins and thus evocatively defined the group's interest in the ugly side of city life.

Assemblage is a term often used to define a work of art which has been constructed from a variety of found (*q.v.*) materials. It is the three-dimensional equivalent of collage (*q.v.*).

Atelier is the French word for studio, but it refers more specifically to nineteenth-century studios in which a nude model was provided for artists to paint. This type of informal setting was also called an *atelier libre* (free studio), because unlike official art schools, it was open to all. Somewhat confusingly, *ateliers* were also known as academies (*q.v.*), the most notable of which was the Académie Julian, where Matisse (*q.v.*) studied. Although professional artists usually provided tuition, *ateliers* often worked without instructors.

Attribution, a claim that a work is by a specific artist, based on stylistic and documentary evidence.

Automatism is the process of producing a work of art or literature "automatically", or without the intervention of conscious thinking. It was favoured by Surrealist (*q.v.*) artists, who felt that they could use it to tap important subconscious thoughts. Joan Miró and André Masson used this technique most effectively, but only as a starting point for a work of art. The Abstract Expressionists (*q.v.*) embraced automatism more wholeheart-

edly, especially through Action Painting (*q.v.*).

Avant-garde is generally used in reference to art of the late nineteenth and early twentieth centuries, although it is employed loosely for other periods of art history as well. It indicates art which is perceived as "progressive" or which challenges conventions or traditions. The concept helped perpetuate the Romantic notion of the artist as an individual working in opposition to inherited tradition.

B

Baldacchino (baldachin), a canopy placed over an altar or a holy place, such as the location of a saint's relics. Although it could sometimes be a moveable object in holy processions, it was usually a fixed part of a church, as in Bernini's elaborate *baldacchino* in St. Peters, Rome.

Barbizon School, a school of mid-19th-cent. landscape painters whose main tenet was a return to nature with an exact rendering of peasant life and country scenery painted on the spot. It was named after the village of that name in the Forest of Fontainebleau, where its chief members—Millet, Theodore Rousseau, Daubigny and Diaz—made their home. Their practice of painting direct from nature, made them the precursors of Impressionism (*q.v.*).

Baroque, a term used for the art style of the period *c*. 1600–1720 which was the artistic accompaniment of the Jesuit counter-Reformation. Its most obvious characteristics are: (*a*) its emotional appeal and dramatic intensity both related to its deliberate intention as propaganda ("a good picture makes better religious propaganda than a sermon" said one of its exponents); (*b*) in architecture, a style which is heavily and sometimes almost grotesquely ornate, plentifully covered with voluptuous sculpture on which draperies float rather than hang, with twisted and spiral instead of plain or fluted columns, and unnecessary windows or recesses added for ornament rather than use; (*c*) its emphasis on the whole at the expense of the parts such that a building's sculpture merges into its architecture and both into its painting (Baroque paintings are as closely knit as a jig-saw puzzle so that one cannot isolate individual figures as would be possible in a Renaissance one).

Baroque architecture owing to its origin is found mainly in the Catholic countries; Italy, France, Austria, Bavaria, *e.g.*, the Barberini Palace, Rome, designed by its greatest exponent Bernini and others, the Church of the Invalides, Paris. Baroque artists include Caravaggio, Guido Reni, Murillo and Rubens the greatest Northern Baroque painter. The Baroque style merges gradually into Rococo (*q.v.*).

Bas-Relief. ("low relief"), a class of sculptures the figures of which are only slightly raised from the surface of the stone or clay on which the design is wrought.

Bauhaus, a German institution for the training of architects, artists and industrial designers founded in 1919 at Weimar by Walter Gropius, (d. 1969). It was closed by Hitler in 1933 and re-opened at Chicago. The Bauhaus doctrine held that there should be no separation between architecture and the fine and applied arts; that art, science and technology should co-operate to create "the compositely inseparable work of art, the great building". Thus it was an organisation with a social purpose. The original institution, at the instigation of Gropius, included on its teaching staff not only architects and technicians but also such noted artists as Paul Klee and Wassily Kandinsky.

Biedermeier refers to German, Austrian and Scandinavian art produced between the time of Napoleon's defeat (1815) and the period of European revolutions (1848). Its name derives from a conflation of two characters in a satirical Munich magazine, and it is therefore meant to be slightly mocking or pejorative. It signifies a sentimental Realist (*q.v.*) style favoured by the increasingly prosperous middle classes, and practised by such artists as Ferdinand Waldmüller and Carl Spitzweg, especially in landscape and genre (*q.v.*) scenes.

Biomorphic forms are abstract shapes based on organic sources such as plants. In painting and sculpture, biomorphism became popular with Surrealist (*q.v.*) artists such as Yves Tanguy and Jean Arp, who exploited its sexually suggestive nature.

Bitumen is a brown pigment commonly used by English artists in the eighteenth and early nineteenth centuries. It contributes to the richness of a painting's tone, but it darkens over time and causes chemical reactions which ultimately damage the paint surface. *See* Craquelure.

Blaue Reiter, Der (the Blue Rider) was a group of artists based in Munich who banded together in 1912 to challenge the academic conventions of contemporary art. Among their membership were Wassily Kandinsky and Franz Marc, who invented the name to signify their belief in the spiritual significance of horses and the colour blue. An interest in the "Geist", or the inner nature of man, governed their paintings and the themes of their only publications, the *Blaue Reiter Almanac* (1912). They sponsored two travelling exhibitions in 1912 and 1913 which brought together progressive tendencies in European art. Their interest in the spiritual qualities of line and colour made their work an important contribution to Expressionism (*q.v.*).

Bloomsbury Group, a group of British writers and artists most influential between *c.* 1910 and *c.* 1940. One of the members, Roger Fry (*q.v.*), organised the so-called "Post-Impressionist" exhibitions in 1911 and 1912 in which many works by Cézanne (*q.v.*), Van Gogh (*q.v.*) and Gauguin received their first English showing. Fry's insistence on the importance of colour and "significant form" influenced the work of Duncan Grant and Vanessa Bell and fostered an interest in decorative art best seen today in Grant's former Sussex home, Charleston.

Bodegón is Spanish for "tavern". In art, it refers to a type of genre painting (*q.v.*) set in a kitchen and including still-life detail. Velásquez (*q.v.*) produced several *bodegones* early in his career.

Bozzetto, Italian for "sketch", but, more precisely, a model for sculpture made in clay or wax, rather than a sketch for painting.

Brücke, Die (the Bridge), a German Expressionist group formed in Dresden in *c.* 1905. The four original members, Ernst Ludwig Kirchner, Erich Heckel, Karl Schmidt-Rottluff and Fritz Bleyl, were not trained artists, and they cultivated a crude, untutored style as a means of perpetuating their interest in non-European art. They had a strong social consciousness and hoped to foster changes in society through their art, although these ideas were never clearly articulated. Their most notable contribution was a revival of the woodcut (*q.v.*) technique. In *c.* 1911 several members of the group moved to Berlin, and Kirchner began painting scenes of city life which stressed claustrophobia and corruption. Internal dissension led to the dissolution of the group in 1913.

Burin, a tool used in engraving to cut into a metal plate. It is also called a graver. As it must cut directly into the plate, more forceful pressure is applied than is needed with an etching needle, which scratches into a resinous ground.

Burr. In engraving, a metal shaving remaining after a plate has been cut by a burin (*q.v.*). In line engravings (*q.v.*) the burr is scraped away, but in drypoint (*q.v.*) it is often left to create furry tonal effects in the print.

Byzantine Art developed in the eastern part of the Roman empire after Constantine founded the city of Constantinople (A.D. 330). It has many sources—Greek, Syrian, Egyptian and Islamic — and reached its zenith in the reign of Justinian (527–65). The major art form was ecclesiastical architecture, the basic plan of which was Roman—either basilican (symmetrical about an axis) or centralised (symmetrical about a point). Arched construction was developed, and the dome became the most typical feature, although, unlike the Roman dome which was placed on a round apartment, the Byzantine dome was placed on a square one on independent pendentives. Frequently small domes were clustered round a large one as in the case of the great church of Santa Sophia (537), the climax of Byzantine architecture. Usually the churches were small and include those of SS. Sergius and Bacchus, Sta. Irene (in Constantinople),

S. Vitale in Ravenna, and the much later and larger St. Mark's in Venice. Byzantine art also took the form of miniatures, enamels, jewels, and textiles, but mosaics, frescos, and icons (*q.v.*) are its greatest treasures.

C

Cabaret Voltaire was the night club in Zürich in which the European Dadaism (*q.v.*) movement began. During the First World War, artists and intellectuals who were pacifists or dissenters gathered in neutral Switzerland. Among this group Tristan Tzara, Jean Arp and Hugo Ball staged a series of events at the Cabaret Voltaire in 1916 which were intended to express their outrage at the pointlessness of modern life.

Cabinet pictures, small paintings originally intended to be hung in the limited confines of seventeenth-century Dutch bourgeois interiors. These paintings consisted primarily of still-life, landscape or genre (*q.v.*), and their emergence in seventeenth-century northern Europe signalled the new importance of a wealthy art-buying middle-class.

Camden Town Group, an organisation of English artists who broke from the New English Art Club (*q.v.*) in *c.* 1911. Following the example of Sickert's (*q.v.*) works, Harold Gilman, Charles Ginner and Spencer Gore concentrated on painting the ordinary or even ugly aspects of London life. The group was characterised by a common enthusiasm for Post-Impressionism (*q.v.*), which they helped to popularise in England.

Camera obscura, Latin for "dark chamber", is a dark box in which an image is projected through a lens to allow artists to copy it easily. A precursor of photography, the camera obscura was used by such artists as Vermeer (*q.v.*) and Canaletto (*q.v.*) to facilitate a sense of spatial illusion and accuracy in their works.

Caricature, a portrait in which characteristic features are exaggerated or distorted to produce a comic effect. The first true caricatures were made in seventeenth-century Italy by Annibale Carracci. Caricature was popular in eighteenth- and nineteenth-century England, where it became a vehicle for political satire in the hands of James Gillray (*q.v.*) and George Cruikshank (*q.v.*). German artists such as George Grosz and Otto Dix produced a more vicious form of political and social caricature during the 1920s.

Cartoon today signifies a comic strip or children's animation, but in the sixteenth century, it referred to a preparatory drawing which was the same size as the finished work and which was used to plan out the work itself. Raphael's (*q.v.*) cartoons for tapestry (now at the Victoria and Albert Museum, London) are the most famous extant example.

Cassone, Italian for "coffer" or "chest". In fifteenth- and sixteenth-century Italy, cassoni were used for marriage chests, and they were richly, if sometimes crudely, painted, usually with a mythological scene containing a theme of love or marriage.

Chiaroscuro, a term used in painting to denote the disposition of light and shade. Rembrandt is unrivalled as a painter for his contrasts of light and shadows.

Chinoiserie, European decorative designs based on Chinese ornamentation. Chinoiserie was fashionable during the Rococo (*q.v.*) period, especially prevalent in decorative arts, landscape gardening and architecture.

Chromolithography, a type of colour lithography (*q.v.*) in which a separate plate is used to print each colour.

Classicism, like its derivatives "classic" and "classical", is a term often used loosely and inaccurately to refer to the best example of a period or style. In its strictest sense, it signifies an emulation of ancient Greek or Roman art, or the conscious attempt to recall the order and harmony associated with ancient sculpture and architecture. *See* Neo-classical style.

Cloissonism is used to describe the style adopted by Gauguin in the 1880s. It refers to the use of large patches of colour surrounded by outlines, which recall the effects of stained glass windows. The term originally referred to enamel painting.

Collage, objects such as newspaper, string or cloth which are pasted onto paper or canvas. Although it had long been an amateur pastime, this technique was first employed seriously by Picasso (*q.v.*) in *Still Life with Chair Caning* (1912), which signalled a move away from his Analytical Cubist works, towards the creation of Synthetic Cubism.

Collage was also later used satirically or humorously in the works of the German Dada (*q.v.*) artists, such as George Grosz and Kurt Schwitters, and for its startling juxtapositions in the works of Surrealists (*q.v.*) such as Max Ernst.

Colour Field Painting was a style prevalent in America during the 1950s and involving artists such as Barnett Newman, Mark Rothko and Clifford Still. Although included under the umbrella of Abstract Expressionism (*q.v.*), these artists were concerned more with large expanses of pure colour than with the Action Painting (*q.v.*) technique of other Abstract Expressionists such as Jackson Pollock.

Column, in architecture, is an upright solid body serving as a support or decoration to a building. Columns consist of a pedestal, a shaft, and a capital, over which the supported entablature rises. They are named according to the styles of architecture of which they form part, *e.g.* Doric, Tuscan, Ionic, Corinthian or Composite.

Complementary colours are green, orange and violet. They are produced when two primary colours (*q.v.*) are mixed together. Green is the complementary of red as it is produced by mixing blue and yellow; blue is the complementary of orange, and violet is the complementary of yellow.

Conceptual Art is a product of the late 1960s. Artists rejected traditional methods of producing and displaying art, and relied instead on photographs, videos and language to take the place of easel painting. In Conceptual Art, the idea is more important than the finished product.

Constructivism, a Russian art movement initiated by Vladimir Tatlin in *c.* 1913. After visiting Picasso (*q.v.*) in Paris, Tatlin returned to Russia with the idea that a "culture of materials" could result in an art which had social purpose. However, subsequent Constructivists were divided between the concept of art as utilitarian and the idea that art should be pure form. The Russian Revolution in 1917 gave the movement new impetus, but it was condemned by the Soviets in 1922.

Contrapposto is usually used in relation to Italian Renaissance painting and sculpture, although it has been applied more widely. It refers to a twisted torso posture which creates an elegant S-curve. Used most effectively by Michelangelo (*q.v.*) in his *David*, contrapposto became more elaborate and virtuosic in the hands of Mannerist (*q.v.*) artists such as Giambologna.

Conversation piece, an informal group portrait, usually of a family or friends. Its precedents are in Dutch seventeenth-century group portraiture, but it became more popular in eighteenth-century England through the work of such artists as William Hogarth (*q.v.*) and Johan Zoffany. Conversation pieces usually showed a family or friends in a domestic interior or standing before a country seat, and they gave the effect of cultivated informality.

Craquelure, a pattern of cracks which appear on the surface of a canvas when the paint deteriorates.

Cubism, the name of a revolutionary movement in art created in the years 1907–9 by the two painters Picasso and Braque. Rejecting purely visual effects, they approached nature from an intellectual point of view, reducing it to mathematical orderliness. Its respectable grandparent was Cézanne who had once written: "you must see in nature the cylinder, the sphere, and the cone"—a concept which, together with the contemporary interest in Black sculpture, moved the two founders of the movement to experiment with the reduction of natural forms to their basic geometrical shapes. In practice, this meant combining several views of the object all more or less superimposed in order to express the idea of the object rather than any one view of it. The name Cubism was derisive and the movement aroused the same opposition as Impressionism, Fauvism and the later Futurism. Picasso's *Les Demoiselles d'Avignon* (1907; Museum of Modern Art, New York) was his first Cubist painting. Three phases are recognised: (1) Cubism under the influence of Cézanne; (2) high or analytical Cubism (*c.* 1909–12) concentrating on the breaking-down of form to the exclusion of interest in colour; (3) synthetic Cubism (*c.* 1913) making use of *collage* in which pieces of pasted-on paper (illustrations, wallpaper, newspaper) and other materials were used in addition to paint. Amongst other early Cubists were such figures as Metzinger, Gleizes, Gris and Léger.

D

Dadaism (French *Dada* = hobby-horse) was a hysterical and nihilistic precursor of **Surrealism** (*q.v.*), resulting from the shock produced by the first world war. Beginning in Zurich about 1915, it spread to other continental cities, such as Berlin and Paris, dying out in 1922. The movement was deliberately anti-art, destructive, and without meaning; it intended to scandalise by such tricks as "compositions" made out of anything that came to hand—buttons, bus tickets, pieces of wire, bits of tin, *etc.* Other excesses included incoherent poetry, Dada night-clubs, plays, and short-lived newspapers. Many Dadaist painters became Surrealists at a later stage, but where Surrealism is a deliberate attempt to present dreamlike images, Dadaism was sheer anarchism. Leading Dadaists were Hans Arp, Marcel Duchamp, André Breton, Kurt Schwitters and Max Ernst.

Damaskeening, the art of inlaying one metal upon another, largely practised in the East in mediaeval times, in the decoration of sword blades.

Degenerate Art (**Entartete Kunst**), the name given by Adolf Hitler (*q.v.*) to art which he felt was produced by Marxists or Jews and/or which had a negative subject-matter that did not glorify the German people. He contrasted "Degenerate Art" with his favoured brand of Nazi realism, which idealised German Aryan character and culture.

The contrast between these two forms was highlighted in 1937, when a "Degenerate Art" exhibition and a "German Art Exhibition" were held simultaneously in Munich. After these exhibitions, the "degenerate" paintings were either sold to raise money for Germany or destroyed. This label encompassed the art of most modern movements, particularly Expressionism (*q.v.*).

Diorama, a type of large painting invented by Daguerre in 1822. Like the panorama (*q.v.*), the diorama contained effects of atmosphere which were achieved by using translucent canvas, movement and special lighting. Three-dimensional elements, such as real plants or animals were also employed to make the effects of dioramas more convincing. Dioramas were an accessible form of public entertainment in the early nineteenth century.

Diptych can refer to a type of altarpiece created when two panels are hinged together. Unlike triptychs (*q.v.*) and other polyptychs (*q.v.*), diptychs were often small and used for private devotional purposes in the Middle Ages.

Divisionism, the name given to the theory developed by Seurat and others, which suggests that colour placed on a canvas unmixed will give the optical effect of being mixed. The technique of Divisionism has also been called pointillism (*q.v.*) or Neo-Impressionism (*q.v.*). Divisionism also refers to an Italian art movement of the late nineteenth and early twentieth centuries in which such an application of colour is employed.

Donor, a person who has given an altarpiece (*q.v.*) or other devotional image to a church as a means of securing God's grace. The term is most appropriately applied to late Medieval and early Renaissance art in Italy and the North. Artists such as Jan van Eyck (*q.v.*) and Hugo van der Goes included portraits of donors in their altarpieces.

Drip painting, a technique used by Jackson Pollock and other Abstract Expressionists (*q.v.*) which involves applying paint not with a brush but through other methods such as dripping or splashing.

Drypoint, an engraving (*q.v.*) technique used from the late fifteenth century which is similar to etching in its method. To make a drypoint, a copper plate is cut directly, producing a burr (q.v.), which softens the tonal effect. This technique is often used in combination with others, but it has the disadvantage of producing only a limited number of impressions, before the burr is worn away.

E

Earthwork (Land Art), a dispersed tendency in art of the late 1960s, which involved using large expanses of natural spaces. Earth art employs the landscape for artistic purposes and thus opposes the sophisticated industrialisation of city culture. Examples of this genre, such as Robert Smithson's *Spiral Jetty* (1970), need to be seen from aircraft or by means of photography.

Embossing, the art of stamping in relief, letters or designs upon pliant substances.

Empire, the style created in France during the reign of Napoleon in architecture and all the arts. It is austerely classical, making much use of columns, pediments and the like in buildings as well as furniture, with eagles and sphinxes, reminiscent of Napoleon's campaigns, as ornaments. The style is heavy, grandiose and with a strong element of the heroic. A typical monument is the *Arc de Triomphe* in Paris (begun 1806), almost a repetition of a Roman model. In painting Jacques Louis David interpreted the style with heroic subjects taken from mythology or from Napoleon's career. The style was transmitted to the rest of Europe.

Encaustic, an ancient technique of painting in which pigments are submerged in soft hot wax. Examples of the encaustic process can be seen on Egyptian mummy cases. Despite the allure of the technique, there have been very few successful attempts to revive it through the centuries.

Engraving is the art of cutting or otherwise forming designs of pictures on wood, stone, or metal surfaces for reproduction by some method of printing. Wood-engraving was the earliest in the field, dating from the 15th cent. Later, engraving on steel and copper plates was introduced, and mezzotint (q.v.), lithography (q.v.), stipple, aquatint, *etc*. Most modern methods of reproduction are based on photography.

Entablature, that portion of a building which surmounts the columns and extends to the roof of the tympana of the pediments; it comprises the architrave, the frieze and the cornice.

Etching, a print technique in which an acid resistant ground is cut by a thin metal pencil. Parts of the plate are then "stopped out" or covered with a protective material, and the plate is dipped into acid which eats away at the exposed areas. The technique is simpler and more spontaneous than engraving (q.v.) and produces more convincing tonal gradations.

Euston Road School, a group of artists who studied together in the late 1930s at the School of Drawing and Painting on Euston Road in London. The group included William Coldstream, Lawrence Gowing and Victor Pasmore, and they rejected Modernist abstraction and Surrealism (q.v.) in favour of a return to an impressionistic rendering of everyday life.

Expressionism, a modern art movement confined primarily to the non-Latin countries of Europe which sought to give expression to intimate and personal emotions by means of distortions of line and colour and simplified style which carried a greater impact in terms of feeling. Broadly speaking, this has been characteristic of northern art in general. (*See* **Gothic**).

The term is usually used of the modern movement which influenced the Post-impressionists and subsequent movements in France. Tired of the naturalism of the Impressionists, such artists as van Gogh, Gauguin, Matisse and Rouault, together with the Fauvists (q.v.) made use of simple outlines and strong colours.

Apart from Toulouse-Lautrec, the principal Expressionists were Norwegian, like Munch, or German, like the painters of *Die Brücke* and *Der Blaue Reiter* groups. Individual artists were Ensor, Kokoschka, Nolde, Rouault and Soutine. *See also* **Blaue Reiter, Der** and **Brücke, Die.**

F

Fan Tracery, a complicated style of roof-vaulting, elaborately moulded, in which the lines of the curves in the masonry or other material employed diverge equally in every direction. It is characteristic of the late Perpendicular period of Gothic architecture, and may be seen in St. George's Chapel at Windsor and the Chapel of Henry VII at Westminster Abbey.

Fancy picture is a vague term, usually used to define late eighteenth-century English paintings with fanciful subject matter. Gainsborough's (q.v.) idyllic evocations of rural life and portraits of winsome "peasant" children were given this name by his critics. Fancy pictures, unlike genre (q.v.) paintings, are not concerned with the mundane aspects of daily life.

Fauvism (French *Fauve* = wild beast), a term used, at first contemptuously, to describe the work of a group of French painters who first exhibited at the Salon d'Automne in Paris in 1905. The most prominent among them was Henri Matisse. Forms are freely distorted and colours are selected and applied for their emotive power with no necessary reference to the "real" colour of the object in question. Other famous *Fauves* were Derain, Vlaminck and Rouault. By 1908 the group was fading and its members went their separate ways.

Feminist art history, a movement in art-historical scholarship since *c.* 1970 which involves a reassessment of both women artists and of how women were and are perceived in art. Feminist art history challenges the canon of male "genius" artists by questioning the male dominance of art academies and art criticism. Such dominance has caused both the exclusion of women from professional art training and the relegation of women to the subject-matter of painting, or merely the object of male desire. Feminist art history has also been concerned with conflicting problems of gender and class, and with sexual theories, including those of Freud.

Fête galante, or "courtship party", was a name given to the paintings of the French artist Watteau (q.v.) in the early eighteenth century. It refers to a number of courtly paintings by him which show groups of men, women and characters from Italian theatre.

Fontainebleau, School of indicates two "schools" of sixteenth-century European art. The first of these originated in the 1530s, when the French king, Francis I, hired Italian artists to decorate his new palace at Fontainebleau. Artists such as Rosso Fiorentino and Niccolo dell'Abbate produced an elegant, mannered style which was much imitated in painting, sculpture and the decorative arts. The second school of Fontainebleau was a later development of the first.

Foreshortening, a use of perspective related to individual figures or objects, rather than space. Foreshortening was used during the Renaissance (q.v.) by artists such as Mantegna to show their command of illusionism.

Found object (objet trouvé) refers to a natural or man-made object which is displayed as a work of art. Found objects are not made by artists, but artists sometimes use them as a starting point for a creative idea.

Fresco, a painting executed upon plaster walls or ceilings, a technique which has remained unchanged since it was practised by the great Renaissance artists.

Frottage, a technique employed by Surrealist (q.v.) artists such as Max Ernst, which involves placing a piece of paper over an object and rubbing the paper with chalk or charcoal. The impression left on the paper was used as a starting point for a work of art.

Functionalism, in architecture, a movement originated by Le Corbusier, Swiss-born French architect and town-planner, who applied the austere principles of the Purist movement in painting to his own art. From about 1924 he designed in concrete, steel and glass, buildings in which every part had a significance in terms of function on the theory that objects created to carry out their particular function to perfection cannot help being beautiful. "A house is a machine for living in." The style was in vogue between the two wars and it is still the basis of most modern architecture.

Futurism, an Italian school of art and literature initiated by Marinetti, an Italian writer and mountebank friend of Mussolini at a later period. Its origin took the form of a manifesto published in Paris in 1909 in which Marinetti glorified violence, war and the machine age. In its aggression it favoured the growth of fascism. One of the distinctive features of Futurist art was the use of the principle of "simultaneity" in which the same figure (e.g., a woman descending a flight of stairs) is represented in successive positions like film "stills" superimposed on each other. In spite of two further manifestoes it was not until 1911 that the first examples of Futurist painting and sculpture appeared by the artists Severini, Balla and Boccioni. Apart from the principle of simultaneity, Futurism derived from Cubist and Post-impressionist techniques. The movement faded out in the first world war.

G

Genre means literally "type" or "kind", and it signifies the painting of ordinary people or everyday life. Various genre details began appearing regularly in fifteenth and sixteenth-century Netherlandish painting, the most notable examples of which are Pieter Bruegel's peasant subjects. Genre painting became a distinctive class of painting in seventeenth-century Holland, when a prosperous middle-class preferred such accessible images to abstruse historical subjects.

Gesso, an absorbent ground (q.v.) used in Medieval and also Renaissance panel painting. Several layers of gesso were laid onto a surface before the paint was applied. Its brilliant white colour added to the luminosity of these paintings.

Giralda, a beautiful and remarkable surviving example of Arabian art, erected in 1195 at Seville.

Glasgow School refers both to the "Glasgow Boys" and to the followers of Charles Rennie Mackintosh's art nouveau (q.v.) style. The former was a group of Scottish painters influenced by Whistler (q.v.) and the French Impressionists (q.v.) and working in the 1880s and 1890s.

Glaze, a thin transparent layer of paint put over the canvas surface to create a luminous effect. Because the glaze is transparent, it allows layers underneath to shine through.

Gothic, the predominant style of architecture in northern Europe from 12th-15th cent. Its most striking characteristic is the extensive use of the pointed arch, but this is really a mere external reflection of the important structural invention of the 12th cent., that of the rib vault, whereby the whole pressure of the stone vaulting is supported on slim ribs which cross each other at a rising centre. On the outside of the building, the pressure from the vaults is caught up and supported by flying buttresses. A complete Gothic construction gives a marvellous effect of airy lightness also of something striving upwards, towards the heavens, and this is further accentuated when the churches are crowned by lofty towers and spires.

The vital elements of Gothic architecture were first put into use in the abbey church of St. Denis in Paris c. 1140. The style was further developed in a glorious sequence of cathedrals in northern France: Notre Dame in Paris, Rheims, Amiens, Beauvais and others. When, as in Chartres, the windows are filled with stained glass of glowing colours and the doorways flanked with magnificently carved life-size figures of saints and apostles, the whole effect is one of unsurpassed solemnity and grandeur. From France the style spread to other lands in each of which it developed its own characteristics; thus the English churches tended to have massive towers and delicate spires and, as at Salisbury, were often set in open grounds surrounded by lawns; Flemish and Dutch churches were sometimes built of brick as were those in north Germany and Scandinavia; in Spain the Flamboyant style was followed. The main Gothic cathedral in Italy, that of Milan, although begun in 1386 was not completed until the early 19th cent. Late English Gothic is seen, for example, at King's College Chapel, Cambridge, Henry's Chapel at Westminster and St. George's Chapel at Windsor (all c. 1500).

Gothic is also found in secular buildings, e.g., Little Wenham Hall in Suffolk, the castle at Ghent, the town halls of Louvain and Middelburg and the streets of Gothic houses in Bruges still in use today. Virtually Gothic as a style (excluding the "Gothic revival" of 19th cent. England) ended at the close of the 15th cent. Gothic art is best seen in the illuminated manuscripts of the 13th and 14th cent. and in the church sculpture. Its characteristic is a complete departure from the cool, perfectionist realism of classical times with distortion to produce emotional effects. The human figures are not ideal forms but recognisable as people we might meet in the street: yet there was also the element of wild imagination, intricate design and a wealth of feeling which might be grotesque, humorous, macabre, or even obscene. Gothic style also found expression in the decorative arts, retaining its architectural character even in small-scale works like caskets, chalices and the like in metalwork and ivory.

Gouache, a type of watercolour in which the paint is opaque, rather than transparent. It was used commonly in medieval manuscript illumination (q.v.), but was less popular for topographical watercolours produced in the eighteenth and nineteenth centuries. It is also known as body colour.

Grand Manner refers to the elevated style associated with history painting (q.v.). It was discussed by Joshua Reynolds (q.v.) in his Royal Academy discourses of the late eighteenth century. Reynolds described the Grand Manner as an art which stressed general concepts as opposed to particular details.

Greek Art. See **Hellenic Art.**

Grisaille paintings are executed in grey or monochrome. They were often meant to imitate sculpture and were commonly used on the closed panels of altarpieces (q.v.) to create an austere image appropriate for Lent or fast days.

Ground, the substance placed on the surface of a canvas or panel on which the colours are painted. The ground comes between the canvas itself and the paint, and serves both to preserve the painting and create a more satisfactory visual effect.

Group of Seven, a group of Canadian landscape painters who exhibited together in the early 1920s and 1930s. It included Lawren Harris and A. Y. Jackson. Their aim was to create a specifically Canadian brand of modern painting, using familiar Ontario landscapes and an Expressionist (q.v.) colourism.

H

Happening, a seemingly spontaneous event, which takes on qualities of both art and theatre, although it is more ephemeral than art and less coherent than theatre. The term is applied to art of the 1960s which involved performance and required the presence of an audience.

Hatching, the use of parallel lines drawn or painted close together to create tonal effects. Cross-hatching refers to the use of crossed lines for the same purpose.

Hellenic Art. The art of ancient Greece may be roughly divided into three periods: the prehistoric period (c. 1500-1000 B.C.) of the bronze age Mycenaeans; the archaic period (c. 600-500 B.C.); and the classical period (c. 500-300 B.C.). Of the first period centred on Mycenae in Peloponnesus but extending to the coasts of Asia and the city of Troy we can mention only the massive stone gateways and the shaft graves of Mycenae, where the archaeologist Schliemann discovered painted vases, gold cups, bronze swords and ornaments of what had once been a great, if primitive, civilisation. During the archaic period sculpture was the principal form of art expression. The magnificent male and female figures are reminiscent of Egyptian art, but are distinctive in liveliness of facial expression. The vase-paintings of this period became more elaborate, depicting scenes from mythology or ceremonial events. Typical of classical Greek art is the representation of the beautiful and healthy human body deliberately posed and often carrying out heroic or athletic acts. The vast majority of these statues are known to us only through Roman copies. The *Hermes* of Praxiteles (born *c.* 385 B.C.) is possibly the only existing statue which can be assigned with any degree of certainty to an individual artist.

Almost the whole of the Greek genius in architecture was expended on temples which are all basically similar in design—a rectangle with a low-pitched gabled roof resting on side walls. The three orders Doric, Corinthian and Ionic mainly referred to the type of column used, but naturally the whole building was influenced thereby. Some of the main buildings are on the Acropolis, a hill outside Athens, on which stand the Parthenon (from the outer frieze of which the Elgin marbles (*q.v.*), now mostly in the British Museum, were taken), the Erechtheum, famous for its Porch of Maidens, and the gateway known as the Propylaea with its broad flight of marble steps. Apart from that on vases, no Greek painting has come down to us, although Greek painters existed and were noted in their time. All we have are copies in mosaic and fresco made by the Romans, at Naples and Pompeii. Of Greek literature in prose, verse and the drama little can be said here. To the early period (*i.e.*, the archaic age) belong Homer's *Iliad* and *Odyssey*. Hesiod's long poem *Work and Days* and Sappho's love poems, and Pindar's Odes. The period of Pericles in the 5th cent. B.C. produced more great literature than any comparable period in history: the philosophical writings of Plato and Aristotle, the tragedies of Aeschylus, Euripides and Sophocles, the comedies of Aristophanes—all these are still part of the European tradition, and together with Greek architecture played a major part in the Renaissance (*see* **Section J**).

Hellenistic Art, the age of the period of Greek civilisation which began with the conquests of Alexander the Great (356–323 B.C.) and lasted until his former empire (which encompassed most of the Middle East and part of North Africa) was conquered by the Romans in 146 B.C. Culturally it was an important period because it spread Greek culture far beyond its original boundaries—even as far as the north of India, and its centres spread from Athens to the cities of Alexandria in Egypt, Antioch in Syria and Pergamum in Asia Minor. But equally Eastern culture spread to the West: democracy was replaced by absolute monarchy, cosmopolitanism took the place of the Greek tendency to believe that all who were not Greeks were barbarians, and mysticism philosophical took the place of Greek rationalism. This was a sensuous, secular, pleasure-loving, rootless society, and these tendencies were reflected in its art.

Hellenistic sculpture was sensual, effeminate and violently emotional, depicting individuals and not always noble or beautiful ones. (Classical Greek sculpture was idealistic, showed types rather than individuals and appealed to the intellect rather than the emotions.) Some of the best examples came from the school at Pergamum and later from the island of Rhodes, and the titles themselves speak of their nature: *The Dying Gaul, Gaul Slaying his Wife and Himself* and the famous *Laocoön* (representing Laocoön and his two sons being crushed by two enormous serpents). All these date from about 240 to 50 B.C.—for the culture did not immediately end with the Roman conquest.

The great frieze of the altar of the temple in Pergamum depicts a battle between gods and giants with tremendous realism and brutal violence far removed from the serene art of classical times. Portrait sculpture is typical of Hellenistic art, where it may almost be said to have been invented, since such ventures in the past had been idealistic rather than realistic. The great Hellenistic cities were geometrically planned and fine public buildings made their appearance in which the slender and graceful Ionic of the ornate Corinthian columns took the place of the more austere and heavy classical ones. Alexandria was celebrated for its vast libraries and was the centre of a brilliant intellectual life (the Septuagint or Greek translation of the Bible was prepared here). Here too worked the mathematicians Euclid and Archimedes, the physicians Erasistratus and Herophilus, and the geographer Pytheas. But

Hellenistic literature was a pale reflection of the glories of the past and we mention only the comedies of Menander and the pastoral verse of Theocritus of Syracuse.

Hieratic Art, a type of art (typified by the major part of the art of ancient Egypt) which is (*a*) exclusively religious and (*b*) conventionally based on earlier forms and traditions.

History painting represents scenes from the Bible, mythology, ancient history or classical literature which have an elevated or moralising theme. The idea that history painting was the highest form of art was cultivated by the French Academy in the seventeenth century and the Royal Academy of England in the eighteenth

Hudson River School, a loosely linked group of American artists including Thomas Cole and F. E. Church, who practised in the middle of the nineteenth century. They painted mostly landscapes, concentrating on the more remote parts of the north-eastern United States, and they were influenced by the Sublime (*q.v.*) paintings of the English artists Turner (*q.v.*) and John Martin. Their emphasis on a specifically American landscape had a nationalist flavour.

I

Icon, in Byzantine culture, a sacred image of Christ or saints. The reverence for such images often bordered on idolatry and led to the Iconoclastic Controversy of the eighth century. Icons were common in Greek and Russian orthodox churches, and the image itself was interpreted as an intercessor between the worshipper and the holy person depicted.

Iconography, the study of signs and symbols in art, or the interpretation of subject-matter. This practice often involves a reductive unpicking of complex symbolism, and it requires a detailed knowledge of diverse religious, literary and classical sources.

Illuminated MSS. of great value and beauty of decoration exist in most public museums and in many private collections, some of them being of great antiquity, especially those of ancient Egypt executed on papyri. Greek and Latin specimens are also numerous, and the British Museum contains fine examples of all these kinds and also an extensive collection of mediaeval English MSS. Pressure is growing for the 1,300-year-old Lindisfarne Gospels, housed in the British Library, to be returned to Newcastle. They are believed to have been written and painted by just one person, Bishop Eadfrith of Lindisfarne, working around 715–720 in honour of St Cuthbert.

Impasto, paint applied thickly to the surface of the canvas so that the brush strokes themselves are noticeable. This technique was commonly used by artists from the nineteenth century as a means of emphasising the paint surface and thus drawing attention away from the illusionistic qualities of painting.

Impressionism, the most important and influential movement in 19th cent. European painting. It gained its name, at first contemptuously, in 1874 from a picture painted by Claude Monet and named by the artist *Impression: soleil levant*, which showed the play of light on water with the observer looking straight into the rising sun. Although intended to be the ultimate form of naturalism the inspiration of the school had been the scientific study of light with an attempt to render the play of light on the surface of objects.

Feeling that putting a line around a form was bound to cause it to look unnatural, they used bright colours corresponding to the spectrum and unmixed on the palette, and noted that an object of any given colour casts a shadow tinged with the complementary one (*e.g.*, red-green, yellow-blue). Hence bright sunlight was represented in clear yellows and orange with violet shadows. The first Impressionist exhibition held in Paris in 1874 aroused derision with its paintings by Monet, Renoir, Sisley, Pissaro, Cézanne and Degas among others. Impressionism subsequently led to the entirely artistic and anti-naturalist movement of Post-impressionism. Cézanne, who felt that he wanted to produce "something solid and durable, like the art of the museums" was only dubiously impressionist, as were also Degas and Renoir. Of course, in the wider sense of the word (i.e., the recording of an ephemeral impression of a scene), Whistler, Turner and even Rembrandt used the technique.

Intaglio, a term used to describe types of printing such as etching and engraving in which the design on the plate is incised. This is opposed to relief printing, such as woodcuts (q.v.), in which the raised portion creates the design.

International Gothic, a style of art that existed throughout Europe in the late fourteenth and early fifteenth centuries. The style was characterized by an aristocratic elegance and a combination of Gothic (q.v.) mannerism with a new interest in realistic depiction. The style was spread by itinerant artists, and is best typified by Gentile da Fabriano in Italy and the Limbourg brothers in France.

Intimisme refers to the scenes of domestic interiors painted by Edouard Vuillard and Pierre Bonnard (q.v.) in the late nineteenth and early twentieth centuries.

Intonaco, the final layer of plaster onto which frescos are painted. It serves as a protective ground between the other layers of plaster and the paint itself.

J

Junk Art, or Junk Sculpture, was popular in the late 1950s, when artists began using rubbish and other rejected items of consumer culture to create works of art. Generally, Junk Art refers to assemblages (q.v.), such as those produced by Robert Rauschenberg.

K

Kinetic Art denotes works of art which actually move or give the illusion of so doing. An early exponent of kinetic art was the American sculptor Alexander Calder (1898–1976) when he launched his famous "mobiles" in the early 1950s. Since then, constructions which rotate, jump, blink with lights, etc. have been made by many artists and the genre is being further elaborated upon today. Kinetic painters give a visual illusion of movement to their pictures by the use of particular colour contrasts or by a skilful play with spirals, squares, etc. in black and white, sometimes with colours blended in.

Kit-Cat in the early eighteenth century was a name given to a club of Whigs who met in a tavern overseen by Christopher Cat. In artistic terms, the name refers to a series of portraits painted by Godfrey Kneller (q.v.) which represented the Kit-Cat Club members. Kneller's innovatory works were larger than half-length portraits but smaller than whole lengths, and through the inclusion of at least one-hand, they allowed a greater variety of posing than previous small portraits. Kit-Cat later came to refer to a portrait of this size (136" × 28").

Kitchen Sink School was a group of artists, including John Bratby, who produced Social Realist (q.v.) paintings after the Second World War. The name "kitchen sink" referred originally to the concerns of the "Angry Young Man" movement initiated by the playwright John Osborne in 1956. This cultural tendency embraced a strong working-class consciousness as well as post-war disillusionment.

L

Lay figure, a jointed doll or dummy used by portrait painters especially in the eighteenth century. Lay figures could be manipulated to provide a diversity of poses, and they could be dressed to allow a more detailed study of costume. Their use

reflected the general artificiality of portrait painting in eighteenth-century England and the need for short cuts to produce speedy results.

Linocut, a woodcut (q.v.) in which the plate is made from linoleum rather than wood. The soft flexibility of the linoleum allows for an easier process of cutting and larger, bolder effects.

Lithography, the art of drawing on stone and printing therefrom, was discovered by Alois Senefelder about 1796, and was introduced into England a few years later. Many improvements in the art have been made, especially in chrome-lithography and photo-lithography.

Luminism is not a movement as such, but a name given to works produced by American landscape painters in the nineteenth century. Artists such as George Caleb Bingham and the painters of the Hudson River School (q.v.) produced panoramic views dominated by sky. Luminism is also characterised by smooth canvases in which no obvious brush strokes or paint surface could be detected. These qualities distinguished it from the visible brush strokes of the impressionists (q.v.).

M

Macchiaioli, I, a group of Italian artists working mainly in Florence between 1855 and 1865. The name refers to the macchia or patches of colour that they used in their paintings. They were influenced by the Barbizon School (q.v.), and their technique in many ways prefigured that of the Impressionists (q.v.).

Magic Realism refers generally to a type of painting which combines a realistic technique with fanciful or dream-like subject matter, as in the paintings of René Magritte and other Surrealists (q.v.). In its strictest sense, Magic Realism was a type of German realist art produced in the 1920s; it is contrasted with Verism (q.v.), and both are considered aspects of Neue Sachlichkeit (q.v.).

Mannerism, a sixteenth-century art movement, chronologically positioned between the High Renaissance (q.v.) and the later Baroque (q.v.). Unlike these movements, the characteristics of Mannerism are less defined. Generally, Mannerist paintings are distinguished by their sophistication, artificiality and anatomical distortion. They include unusual or brash colours and sometimes their treatment of subject-matter is disturbing. Parmigianino and Giulio Romano (q.v.) produced works considered Mannerist, but the term is also applied to artists such as Tintoretto (q.v.) and El Greco. It has been used equally to refer to sixteenth-century architecture in which playful satires on classical forms are apparent.

Maquette, a clay or wax model for sculpture.

Marxist art history was a development in art-historical scholarship which sought to align art with the economic and political conditions behind its production. Although Marx himself did not tackle the subject of aesthetics, art historians have applied Marx's ideas of class struggle and bourgeois/proletarian conflict to pictures. With the collapse of communism following the fall of the Soviet Union the term is no longer in common usage.

Medium, strictly speaking, is the liquid, whether oil or egg yolk, used with colour pigments to make paint. In a more general sense, it refers to painting, sculpture, charcoal drawing or any other method used by an artist.

Metaphysical Painting (Pittura Metafisica), a name given to the work of Giorgio de Chirico (q.v.) and Carlo Carrà. These two artists met in a military hospital in Ferrara in 1917, where they gave this name to paintings which avoided the mechanical nature of modernist movements such as Cubism (q.v.) in favour of a dream-like evocation of more spiritual concerns. Their works contained unusual combinations of images which were painted in a realistic style, and they employed methods such as perspective (q.v.) drawn from Italian Renaissance painting. The dream imagery of de Chirico was especially influential on the Surrealists (q.v.), particularly those who practised Magic Realism (q.v.).

Mezzotint, a technical method for producing graphic work and works of art. A copper plate is made rough by close cross-hatching, so that a print from it produces an even black. When parts of the cross-hatching are scraped away, these areas will come out white when printed. By skilful use of his tools, the artist or technician can produce pictures finely graded from black to white and with a velvety black as background. The principles of the method were known and practised, for instance, by Rembrandt, but mezzotint became most popular for the reproduction of famous paintings from the end of the 18th cent.

Miniature, a small painting, usually a portrait. The term originally referred to medieval manuscript illumination (*q v*), but by the sixteenth century, it was used to signify small pictures painted on card. Miniatures became especially popular for keepsake portraits in the eighteenth century, and they often parroted the currently fashionable styles of oil painting.

Minimal Art was a movement which began in the United States in the 1960s. As its name implies it involves art, usually sculpture, which is reduced to its most essential form. Examples tend to be assemblages (*q.v.*) composed largely of limited abstract shapes.

Mobile, a type of sculpture popularised by Alexander Calder in the 1930s. Mobiles are composed of flat geometric shapes hung on string and wire and allowed to move, or are moved by mechanical means. If mechanical means are used, mobiles can be considered Kinetic Art (*q.v.*).

Modello, a small preliminary painting used as a "try out" for a larger painting. Unlike sketches, which are often unfinished or merely summary, modelli prefigure the final painting in great detail. In the Renaissance (*see* **Section J**) they were used as a sort of advertisement by artists trying to convince patrons of the worth of their work.

Monotype, as the name suggests, refers to a printing process whereby only one impression can be made from each prepared plate. Monotypes are created by painting in oils directly onto a copper plate and then pressing the plate onto a piece of paper. This process was popular with twentieth-century artists such as Chagall (*q.v.*).

Montage, like collage (*q.v.*) involves the arrangement of diverse images together on a sheet of paper. But montage refers specifically to components which are complete in themselves (*see* **photomontage**), rather than abstract forms.

Mosaic, art of arranging small pieces of coloured glass, marble, or other materials in such a fashion as to produce a decorative pattern. Some of the best examples of Byzantine mosaics are to be seen at Ravenna, Rome, Venice and Sicily.

Mullions, the vertical bars dividing the lights in a window, forming a highly decorative feature in the Tudor period of English Gothic architecture. The cross-beam or horizontal bar of wood or stone in a mullioned window is styled a transom. See **Windows, Section L.**

N

Nabis, the, a group of French painters who followed the Symbolist (*q.v.*) concerns of Gauguin. Between 1889 and 1899, Pierre Bonnard (*q.v.*), Edouard Vuillard and Maurice Denis explored the symbolic possibilities of colour first examined by Gauguin in 1888. They were particularly interested in the use of large patches of colour to convey spiritual intensity. See **Cloissonism.**

Naive Art results from either a real or seeming lack of technical skill. This produces child-like images which offer a very literal form of Realism (*q.v.*). Paradoxically, naive art became popular in the late nineteenth and twentieth centuries, with the work of artists such as Le Douanier Rousseau (*q.v.*). A revival of interest in the simple expression of children's art which characterised modern movements such as German Expressionism (*q.v.*) may be partly responsible for this.

Narrative Art, a type of art popular during the late 19th cent. based on the principle: "every picture tells a story". The term, although often applied derisively, suitably describes many works of considerable artistic merit: *e.g.,* Hogarth's *Marriage à la Mode,* the Bayeux Tapestry, *etc.*

Naturalism in painting has been defined as "a direct and spontaneous approach to nature" —to landscape primarily. Constable, Turner and Boudin were among the great naturalist painters of the 19th cent.

Nazarenes, a group of German artists who worked in Rome in the early nineteenth century. In 1809 Friedrich Overbeck and Franz Pforr formed an artistic organisation called the Brotherhood of St. Luke in Vienna. They carried their interest in the revival of religious art to Rome in 1810, where they moved into an abandoned monastery and were joined by other artists. They hoped to capture the spirit of the Middle Ages through historical and religious subjects, and they were instrumental in the revival of fresco (*q.v.*) technique. Their large scale murals and historical scenes for the German ruling class led them to be associated with the intensification of German nationalism in the nineteenth century.

Neo-Classical Style, term applied to the revival of classical logic and order after the extravagances of Rococo (*q.v.*), beginning in France in the mid-18th cent. and finding expression in architecture and the decorative arts. The style retains some of the daintiness of Rococo, furniture is on a small scale, often gilt, and silks and porcelain favour pastel shades. Straight lines take the place of the wild curvatures of Rococo and classical details like festoons and urn forms are used in many contexts and materials. Its English version is closely associated with the name of the architect Robert Adam whose light and graceful adaptations of Greek and Roman forms were introduced into English country houses. In France the style is sometimes called *Style Louis XVI.* Eventually the Neo-Classical style merges into Empire (*q.v.*).

Neo-Expressionism, or Bad Art, refers to an international art movement of the late 1970s and 1980s involving the revival of Expressionism (*q.v.*) concerns. The prominent artists include George Baselitz and Francesco Clemente.

Neo-Impressionism, a development of Impressionism (*q.v.*) by Seurat and Signac during the 1880s who devised the method of painting known as *pointillism* (the application of pure colours in minute touches to form a composite whole, based on a knowledge of the laws of colour and optics). One of the best-known examples of this technique is Seurat's *Sunday Afternoon on the Grand Jatte.*

Neo-Plasticism was a name used by Mondrian for a type of art which avoids representation in favour of abstraction. Mondrian's principles resulted in canvases which consisted solely of primary colours, black and white, and horizontal and vertical lines. His intention was to create an art which could have meaning for everyone, but paradoxically, his works usually puzzle the uninitiated.

Neo-Romanticism is a British art movement which began before the Second World War. Artists such as John Piper and Graham Sutherland (*q.v.*) initiated a revival of interest in the Romantic landscape painting of William Blake (*q.v.*) and Samuel Palmer (*q.v.*). This concern for evocative native landscapes was a manifestation of pre-war nationalism.

Neue Sachlichkeit, Die (The New Objectivity), a name given by the art dealer G. F. Hartlaub to describe a diverse group of German artists who rejected abstraction during the 1920s. These artists all attempted to represent reality, either through a precise, detailed Magic Realism (*q.v.*) or a satirical and scathing Verism (*q.v.*). The first *Neue Sachlichkeit* exhibition was in 1923.

New Art Club, an organisation formed in 1886 in reaction against the stale practices and politics of the Royal Academy. The members of this group, including Walter Sickert (*q.v.*) and Philip Wilson Steer (*q.v.*) were trained in France, and they preferred the informal *atelier* (*q.v.*) system of education to the rigid strictures of the Royal Academy Schools. Their work was influenced by Whistler (*q.v.*) and Jules Bastien-Lepage.

Newlyn School, the name given to a group of artists who congregated in Cornwall during the 1880s and 1890s. The group included Laura Knight and Stanhope Forbes, and they were particularly concerned with *plein air* (*q.v.*) painting.

Non-Objective Art is the correct name for what is

usually called Abstract Art (*q.v.*). Its name suggests that the representational object has been obliterated, whereas "abstract" implies that the work of art is a simplification or modification of some real object.

Norman Architecture is English Romanesque (*q.v.*), which flourished from the time of the Norman Conquest and was gradually superseded through a transition period (*c.* 1175–1200) by the introduction of the pointed arch characteristic of the Early English (first Gothic style). Typical of Norman churches are the round arches, thick walls, massive cylindrical columns, with throughout the basic pattern of the square and the circle. Some churches (*e.g.*, the Temple church in London or the chapel at Ludlow Castle) are wholly circular. Roofs in the early days were flat and towers, usually placed at the "crossing", were square but occasionally round; the spire of all these towers have perished, but it seems likely that they were squat and pyramidal.

Novecento Italiano, an Italian art movement of the 1920s which encouraged a return to the principles of Italian Renaissance (*see* **Section J**) art. The interest in the Italian past was more than simply a stylistic phenomenon, as it was strongly connected with the nationalist spirit of Fascism. The artists of the group included Mario Sironi and Achille Funi, and they held their first exhibition in the Pesaro Gallery, Milan, in 1922.

Novembergruppe, a group of left-wing Berlin artists formed in 1918. The members, including Max Pechstein, were committed to socialist principles and wanted an art capable of appealing to the masses. The name of the group came from the November Communist uprising in Berlin of that year.

O

Objet trouvé. *See* **Found object.**

Omega Workshops, a cooperative founded by Roger Fry (*q.v.*) in 1913 aimed at producing quality decorative art. The artists of the Bloomsbury Group (*q.v.*), such as Duncan Grant and Vanessa Bell, were involved, and they decorated furniture for a small number of patrons. The impracticalities of their enterprise led to the organisation's demise in 1920.

Op Art, an art based solely on perceptual or optical effects, which was particularly popular in the 1960s. Its practitioners included Bridget Riley.

Oriel Window is a window projected from the front of a building, rectangular, triangular, or pentagonal. The ordinary bay window and bow window are varieties of Oriel. When an Oriel window does not reach to the ground it usually rests upon moulded sills supported by corbels.

Orphism (Orphic Cubism). In response to the monochromatic coldness of Cubism (*q.v.*), the artists Robert and Sonia Delaunay began producing paintings in which colour was fragmented in the same way that the Cubists broke up form. This prismatic treatment of colour was called Orphism by the poet Apollinaire in 1912. Orphism differs further from Cubism in its emphasis on movement and city life, qualities more obviously characteristic of Futurism (*q.v.*). Orphist paintings eventually became totally abstract, but the movement did not last beyond the First World War.

P

Panorama, a circular painting placed inside a large cylinder, in which people can sit or stand. Panoramas could be walked around, or they were moved mechanically to create a sense of total environment. They were invented in Scotland in 1787, and they quickly became a popular form of entertainment. Their subjects included exotic scenes and Picturesque (*q.v.*) landscapes, but they also depicted recent military campaigns during the Napoleonic wars. This latter quality gave panoramas the value of reportage and enhanced their accessibility to a wider public.

Papier collé. French for "pasted paper", a type of collage (*q.v.*) popularised by Braque from 1913. This involved gluing bits of wallpaper or newspaper to a canvas. This process became an important aspect of Synthetic Cubism (*q.v.*), and it was used by Matisse (*q.v.*) for his paper cutouts.

Pastel, a chalk composed of powdered pigments which produces delicate but fragile images. The soft quality of pastel became especially popular in eighteenth-century European portraits.

Pentimento, bits of painting which become visible when the top layer of paint wears away. Often pentimenti signal an artist's earlier rejected experiments, and they are therefore used both as authentication and as a means of studying the processes of work stages of an artist.

Performance Art is a general term referring to a pseudo-theatrical event which is considered art. The agitational demonstrations of the Futurists (*q.v.*), the nonsense recitations of the Dadaists (*q.v.*) and the Happenings (*q.v.*) of the 1960s are all examples of this type of art.

Perspective, a space-creating device used most frequently by Italian Renaissance (*see* **Section J**) artists. Linear or one-point perspective involves mathematically calculating a vanishing point where a series of parallel lines converge. In Renaissance painting, these lines are often created by floor patterns or carefully placed bodies, which lead the eye back into the picture to give a sense of depth. The creation of three-dimensional effects on a two-dimensional surface was particularly important for the Renaissance idea of optical illusionism, although the effect produced by perspective is only approximate to true visual experience. One-point perspective was used less frequently after the fifteenth century, but aerial perspective (*q.v.*) was commonly employed for several centuries afterwards.

Photomontage, a type of montage (*q.v.*) consisting wholly or partly of photographs. This technique was common among the Berlin Dada artists (*q.v.*), who used photographs from fashion magazines and other forms of popular culture to make satirical attacks on the superficiality of Weimar society.

Picturesque, with a capital "p", is an aesthetic term coined in the eighteenth century to describe landscapes which looked "like a picture". Like the Sublime (*q.v.*), the Picturesque was said to instill emotions in the observer, who associated the sight of rough beauty, ruins or irregular landscapes with various sentimental or melancholy moods. In the 1700s the term became the focus of a heated aesthetic debate which included such participants as Richard Payne Knight and Uvedale Price. The growing popularity of Picturesque ideas inspired artists and amateurs to take Picturesque tours, especially in the Lake District and Wales, in order to discover the possibilities in rugged or unusual landscapes.

Pietà (Italian for "pity"), a devotional image of the Virgin Mary with the dead Christ on her lap.

Plein air (French for "open air"), refers to painting out of doors. Before the nineteenth century, landscape painters commonly produced their works in a studio from sketches or studies. The French Barbizon (*q.v.*) painters cultivated the opposing practice of painting outside—a method that was wholeheartedly adopted by the Impressionists (*q.v.*).

Polyptych, an altarpiece (*q.v.*) with more than one panel, such as a diptych (*q.v.*) or triptych (*q.v.*).

Pop Art, a phenomenon of the 1960s and 1970s which involved transforming objects of popular culture into works of art. The movement started in Britain, when a group of artists at the Institute of Contemporary Arts began using images from comic books and advertising in their art. Pop art either attacks modern consumer culture or it glorifies it nostalgically. Its main practitioners were Peter Blake and Richard Hamilton in England and Andy Warhol in America.

Portland Vase, one of the most renowned specimens of ancient art, long in the possession of the Portland family. In 1810 it was loaned to the British Museum. Here it was shattered in 1845 by a stone from a maniac's hand, but has been skilfully restored. It is said to have been found in the 17th cent. in an ancient tomb near Rome. It was purchased from the Barberini family in 1770 by Sir Wm. Hamilton, subsequently sold to the Duchess of Portland. The vase, which is actually a two-handled urn, stands about 25 cm high, is of transparent dark blue glass, ornamented with figures cut in relief in overlaid white opaque glass. It was purchased by the British Museum in 1945. *See* **Glass, Section L.**

Post-Impressionism, a term introduced by Roger Fry to describe the exhibition of paintings sponsored by himself in London (1910–11) officially entitled "Manet and the Post-Impressionists". The exhibition included paintings by Manet, Cézanne, Gauguin, Van Gogh, Seurat, Signac, works by Matisse, Rouault and the *Fauves* (*q.v.*), and sculpture by Maillol. In a second exhibition, held in 1912, Picasso and the Cubists were also represented.

The term therefore refers to the movement in modern art which reacted against the transient naturalism of the Impressionists by concerning itself primarily with colour, form and solidity. Most artists include Cézanne, Van Gogh and Gauguin as the main Post-Impressionists and maintain that it prepared the way for Fauvism, Cubism and Expressionism.

Post-Modernism is a cultural phenomenon. From the end of the Second World War, the failure of Modernism in all of its manifestations was evident, and artists, architects and writers began seeking other solutions to the problems of contemporary life. Post-Modernism is not one style but many styles, and it is often self-referential, playful or parodic. The exact meaning of the term, and those works of art which fall within its parameters, are a subject of continual debate, but a number of post-war developments, such as Happenings (*q.v.*) could be seen to be in its sphere.

Post-Painterly Abstraction was a term invented by the critic Clement Greenberg in 1964 to refer to non-objective (*q.v.*) artists who were not members of the Abstract Expressionist (*q.v.*) movement. The paintings of Kenneth Noland, Frank Stella and others were considered to fall within this definition, as they painted canvases with large patches of colour and which were carefully planned, rather than spontaneous, as in Action Painting (*q.v.*).

Predella, the panel or panels running along the bottom of an Italian Renaissance (*see* **Section J**) painting, and usually containing a series of narrative scenes to complement the main devotional panel of the altarpiece itself.

Pre-Raphaelite Brotherhood was the name given to their school of thought by three British artists, Dante Gabriel Rossetti, J. E. Millais and W. Holman Hunt, who in 1848 revolted against the academic art of their time and advocated a return to the style of the Italian painters prior to Raphael—the simple naturalism of the Primitives, such as Botticelli, Fra Angelico and Filippo Lippi. Thus they avoided the use of heavy shadows and painted on a white ground in bright colours—a technique which aroused the ire of those used to the dark and murky canvases of the contemporary romantic artists. Although they held these principles in common the three members of the "P.R.B.", as it was popularly called, were really quite different in other respects. Thus Rossetti (who for some reason is always thought of as the typical Pre-Raphaelite) produced works of a highly romanticised mediaevalism which, apart from certain aspects of technique, bear not the slightest resemblance to the sentimental naturalism of Millais or the much more dramatic realism of Holman Hunt (*e.g.,* in *The Scapegoat*). The Brotherhood was later joined by a number of lesser artists, but its works are not commonly accepted with enthusiasm today when the general feeling is that they are sentimental and religiose rather than the product of deeply-felt emotions. Ruskin in his writings had defended their work but the movement ended in 1853.

Primitive Art. The word "primitive" has a number of different meanings: (1) the art of prehistoric communities (*e.g.,* the famous animal cave-drawings of the Aurignacians, *c.* 25,000 B.C., at Altamira in Spain); (2) the art of modern primitive communities (*e.g.,* Bushman rock-paintings); (3) child art; (4) peasant art which springs from a spontaneous desire to impart beauty to objects of daily use and shows a tendency towards abstraction. Peasant art has many features in common the world over, the woodcarving of the Norsemen being almost indistinguishable from that of the Maoris; (5) the modern school of primitive painting in which naïveté of presentation is either the aim of a highly sophisticated mind (*e.g.,* the self-taught French painter Le Douanier Rousseau (d. 1910), or arises naturally from a simple one (the American "grandma" Moses (d. 1961) who began to paint in her seventies).

Provenance records the whole history of the ownership of a painting, from its first commission or sale to its present location. A confident provenance is often used to authenticate a work of art, but it can be equally revealing about patterns of taste and art purchase through the centuries.

Purism was a reaction against Cubism (*q.v.*) which drew upon some of Cubism's methods. The term was coined in 1918 when Amédée Ozenfant's book *Après le Cubisme* rejected the "decorative" qualities of Cubist painting, which he felt did not respond properly to the needs of modern industrial society. Purist painters such as Charles-Edouard Jeanneret (Le Corbusier, *q.v.*) and Ferdinand Léger embraced this "machine aesthetic", but it was most influential on architecture.

Putto, a fat naked boy used as a decorative addition to painting and sculpture, especially in the Baroque (*q.v.*) period.

R

Rayonism was a short-lived Russian art movement including the work of Mikhail Larianov and Natalia Goncharova. The ideas behind it were consolidated in the 1913 Moscow Target exhibition. In the exhibition catalogue, Larianov described Rayonism as a combination of Cubism (*q.v.*), Futurism (*q.v.*) and Orphism (*q.v.*). It involved the use of intersecting rays of light, and partial or total abstraction.

Ready-made was a word used by the twentieth-century artist Marcel Duchamp to signify an object selected by an artist to be displayed as a work of art. The artist does not actually produce the work but merely presents it, thus changing the significance of an otherwise ordinary object. A ready-made is less concerned with aesthetic values. The presentation of a ready-made in some ways undermines the whole process of production and display of art and should be considered as a somewhat cynical statement.

Realism is a vague term. As a movement in art it can be said to have started with Gustave Courbet in the mid-19th cent. in his revolt against the classicism of Ingres and the romanticism of Delacroix. He was a man of strong radical views, and like Zola, Balzac and Flaubert in literature, turned to the actuality of everyday life, recording it with frankness and vigour. Some young English painters, notably Bratby, of the "kitchen sink" school, practise what some describe as social realism. In another sense, realism is an attitude concerned with interpreting the essential nature of the subject, revealing truths hidden by the accidentals of ordinary visual appearance. Thus form becomes more significant than content. Beginning with Cézanne and Van Gogh this trend passes on to Cubist and Abstract painting. *See also* **Section J** (philosophy).

Regency Style is the English version of the French Empire (*q.v.*) and approximately covers the period of the regency of Prince George, later George IV, from 1810 to 1820. It is somewhat less austere than the French style, and contains elements of the fantastic and exotic absent from Empire. The most famous monument of Regency style is the Royal Pavilion at Brighton, built for the Prince Regent by John Nash. (Regency style should not be confused with the *Régence* style in France, fashionable during the regency period between the death of Louis XIV in 1715 and the ascent to the throne of Louis XV in 1723. Here the English equivalent is Queen Anne style.)

Relief in sculpture is of three kinds—high relief

(alto-relievo), in which the figures stand out to the extent of one-half of their natural proportions, low-relief *(basso-relievo)* when the figures project but slightly; and middle-relief *(mezzo-relievo)*, when the projection is intermediate.

Renaissance. *See* **Section J.**

Repoussoir is French for "to push back". It signifies an object, usually a tree, which borders the foreground of a picture and draws the eye deeper into the space of a painting. It is especially used in landscape paintings by artists such as Claude *(q.v.)*, where it serves a primarily compositional purpose.

Rococo, an architectural style which was, in effect, the final stage of **Baroque** *(q.v.)*. The name first came into use about 1830 to describe the period 1720–70 and means "shell- shaped" (French *Rocaille)*, since the shell was a favourite motif in Rococo ornamentation. At about the beginning of the 18th cent. the heavy older type of Baroque began to show even less restraint than had characterised it in the past, it became still less utilitarian, and showed a kind of playful light-hearted vitality which manifested itself in a wealth of ornamental invention. Baroque was flamboyant and robust, Rococo dainty, graceful and smiling. Its ornaments are frequently asymmetrical, and in this Rococo is unique among the historical styles of Europe. In architecture Rococo is naturally found in those areas where the Baroque had flourished, *i.e.,* Munich, Prague, Vienna and Dresden. In painting, the best expressions of Rococo are to be seen in the works of the French painters Watteau (d. 1721), Boucher (d. 1770), and Fragonard (d. 1806).

Romanesque Architecture, prevailed throughout Europe from the mid-10th to the 13th cent., and implies an art which developed from that of the Romans. Notable in Romanesque style were the rounded arch and masonry vaulting. Romanesque led to the graceful and more complex Gothic *(q.v.)*. The Italians never regarded Gothic highly and Romanesque churches, generally based on the basilican plan (oblong with double colonnades and a semi-circular apse at the end), continued to be built there until the beginning of the 15th cent. Some of the best examples can be seen at Pisa (11th cent.), Florence (San Miniato, 1013), Lucca (12th cent.) and Milan (the 12th cent. San Ambrogio, most famous of all). In Germany Romanesque architecture flourished longer than in France or England; the most famous churches are in the valley of the Rhine, at Cologne (completely destroyed during the second world war), Mainz and Speyer. In France Romanesque churches are found in Burgundy, Provence and Normandy. *See* **Norman Architecture.**

Romanticism. *See* **Section J.**

S

Sacra conversazione, a type of altarpiece *(q.v.)* which originated in fifteenth-century Italy. It consists of the Madonna and Child with a group of saints standing around her. It departs from the Gothic *(q.v.)* tradition of separating the Madonna from saints in polyptychs *(q.v.)*, and it also allows a greater apparent ease of association among holy figures.

St. Ives painters, a group of artists who congregated in St. Ives, Cornwall, in 1939. The group included Adrian Stokes, Barbara Hepworth and Ben Nicholson *(q.v.)*. Unlike other such artistic colonies, this group was diverse in both style and subject-matter.

Salon, a French organisation that promoted art exhibitions. In 1667 the first salon was the exhibition of works by artists of the Académie Royale, shown in the Salon d'Apollon of the Louvre. There academic artists exhibited occasionally until 1737, when exhibitions became a biennial event. Art exhibitions were consolidated into the academic structure in the eighteenth century through the introduction of juries, which rejected paintings they did not feel appropriate for the Salon. After the French Revolution, the Salon was held every year and became increasingly important in the French art world until the 1860s, when it was challenged by alternative salons *(see* **Salon des Refusés, Salon d'Automne** and **Salon des Indépendants).**

Salon d'Automne, one of the salons formed in competition to the official academy Salon *(q.v.)*. It began holding exhibitions from 1903, the most famous of which was the 1905 exhibition. This included works by Matisse *(q.v.)*, Dérain and Vlaminck which started the "Fauvist" *(q.v.)* movement.

Salon des Indépendants, one of the salons formed in competition to the official academy Salon *(q.v.)*. It began in 1884 on the initiative of the *Société des Artistes Indépendants,* which included among its membership Seurat and Signac. This Salon rejected the jury system of the official Salon and became a major showplace for Post-Impressionist *(q.v.)* painting.

Salon des Refusés, an alternative salon set up in 1863 to house all the paintings rejected by the official Salon *(q.v.)*. It resulted from an intensification of the anger and discouragement of French artists whose works had been consistently rejected by the Salon. To appease them, Napoleon III allowed all rejected works to be exhibited separately. The exhibition induced much derision and distaste in a conservative public, but it became the starting point for a more considered reaction against the French Academy and the hegemony of the official Salon. Manet's *(q.v.) Déjeuner sur l'herbe* was one of the works shown here.

Scumbling, when an opaque colour is applied over an already existing colour but allows the other colour to show through. Scumbling creates a textured or broken effect on the surface of the canvas.

Secession (Sezession), the name given to a series of rebellions against the academic system in Germany and Austria during the 1890s. Throughout Europe at this time, the limitations of academies were becoming apparent to artists who wanted to experiment with new methods, ideas and techniques. The Munich Secession was the first to express this sense of rebellion by turning away from academic classicism towards an art nouveau *(q.v.)* style. Closely following this were the Vienna Secession (beginning 1897), which was also sympathetic to art nouveau, and the Berlin Secession (from 1899) which encouraged an Impressionist *(q.v.)* style.

Secco, Italian for "dry", a term applied to fresco painting. Usually in a fresco, the plaster is painted while wet, but the *secco* method involves waiting for the plaster to dry before painting it. In the Middle Ages and the Renaissance *(see* **Section J),** this technique was usually used for touching up a finished fresco. If it was used exclusively, it caused more rapid deterioration in the painting.

Sfumato, Italian for "smoke", is a term used in the sixteenth century to signify gradations of colour and tone which avoided stark outlines. It was applied especially to the soft tonal effects of Leonardo da Vinci's *(q.v.)* paintings.

Silk screen printing is also called seriography. It is a technique invented in the early twentieth century which involves masking a silk screen with pieces of paper or cardboard and then pressing colour through the screen onto a piece of paper beneath it. Although a skilled designer is necessary for a successful silk screen print, the actual process of making the print can be carried out by anyone.

Sinopia, an earthy red-brown colour used to make a preliminary drawing for a fresco in the Middle Ages and also the Renaissance. The sinopia was applied first, then covered by intonaco *(q.v.)*, which was then painted. It served as a preparatory sketch over which the final painting could be constructed.

Sistine Chapel. *See* **Section L.**

Social Realism, a type of Realism *(q.v.)* concerned not just with style but with subject-matter. The term is applied to paintings of the nineteenth and twentieth centuries which have social or political subtexts, especially of a Leftist variety. Social Realism possibly began with Courbet, whose unapologetic, even heroic, paintings of peasants were especially subversive during a period of political unrest in Europe (*c.* 1848–9). The term has also been used to describe the work of the American Ashcan School *(q.v.)* and the British Kitchen Sink School *(q.v.)*.

Socialist Realism, as opposed to Social Realism *(q.v.)*, had a very specific propagandist purpose. In its strictest sense, it signified the official art of the Communist USSR. It used a Realist (q.v.) style with proletariat subject-matter as a form of instruction to the people. From 1934 until the period of *glasnost*, it was the only official art of the Soviet Union.

Stijl, De, a Dutch art magazine which perpetuated the Neo-Plasticism (q.v.) of Piet Mondrian and Theo van Doesburg. The magazine began in 1917, and its articles stressed pure abstract or non-objective (q.v.) form in painting, sculpture and architecture. Its subsequent influence was primarily in the realm of architecture, and the ideas of *De Stijl* were particularly influential in reforming the Bauhaus (q.v.) when Doesburg visited it in 1923.

Still-life, a type of painting which precludes the depiction of human beings and concentrates on everyday objects such as fruit or flowers. It was popularised in Holland during the seventeenth century, when its immediate appeal was appreciated by the art-buying middle-class, and it continued to be popular throughout the eighteenth and nineteenth centuries, when its most notable practitioners were Chardin (q.v.) and Cézanne (q.v.). Still-lifes (the accepted plural form) often took on emblematic or moralistic meanings, reflecting the vanity or transience of human existence, but despite their potential depth of meaning, they were considered the lowest category of painting by European art academies (q.v.). This relegation of still-lifes also accentuated the repression of women artists, as they were excluded from official training institutions and often painted solely still-lifes.

Sublime, a term which has an ancient origin but was brought into the realm of aesthetics during the eighteenth century. Edmund Burke's (q.v.) *Enquiry Into the Origins of Our Idea of the Sublime and the Beautiful* (1757) postulated an aesthetic category which engaged the emotions. The sublime involved a feeling of awe or terror inspired by overwhelming natural forces. Burke's writings were influential on the growth of Gothic novels, and they were later used to good effect in landscape painting by artists such as Turner (q.v.) and John Martin.

Superrealism (Hyperrealism, Photorealism) describes paintings of the 1970s onwards which attempted to evoke a photographic illusion of reality. In some cases, the artist actually copies a photograph.

Suprematism, a term invented by the Russian artist Kasimir Malevich to describe his non-objective (q.v.) paintings, such as *White on White*. The theory behind Suprematism is complicated and involves an attempt to articulate in visual terms a "fourth dimension". Malevich's first exercises in Suprematism occurred in 1913, and he officially christened the movement in 1915.

Surrealism. The aim of the Surrealist school of painting and sculpture is to overcome the barriers between conscious and unconscious mind, the real and unreal worlds of waking and dreaming. As such it has a long and respectable ancestry, although the term was not in use until 1922 when it was picked by André Breton from Guillaume Apollinaire who had used it in connection with certain works by Chagall. However, Bosch in the 15th cent., Fuseli and Goya in the 18th, and many other purveyors of the weird and fantastic were the forerunners of modern Surrealism. The modern movement has broadly speaking taken two different directions: the first was towards complete fantasy and absurdity which took the form of "found objects"—*e.g.* a bird-cage filled with sugarcubes and a thermometer, a bottle-dryer, a bicycle wheel, or abstract works with strange and apparently irrelevant titles such as Paul Klee's *Twittering Machine*; the second towards highly detailed and realistic paintings of objects placed in strange juxtapositions—*e.g.*, Salvador Dali's trees with limp watches drooping over their branches. On the whole Surrealism has spent its force and become almost respectable.

Symbolism began as a literary term referring to French poetry of the 1850s, but in the 1880s and 1890s it was applied to painting. Symbolist artists rejected the tenets of Impressionism (q.v.), which they saw as too involved with perceptual response. Instead they concentrated on the representation of spiritual and subjective feelings, which often manifested themselves in religious or erotic

subject-matter. Its French exponents included Puvis de Chavannes, Odilon Redon and Gustav Moreau, but the ideas of Symbolism soon spread throughout Europe.

Synthetism refers to the work of Gauguin's followers who, in the 1890s, produced paintings which included large patches of concentrated colour surrounded by black lines, as in Gauguin's *cloisonnism* (q.v.). The root word "synthesis" refers to Gauguin's idea that painting should represent a concentrated synthesis of the artist's emotions. Synthetist artists painted from memory, rather than copied the world before them as the Impressionists (q.v.) had done.

T

Tachisme is sometimes used synonymously with Abstract Expressionism (q.v.), but it strictly refers to a French movement of the 1950s which consisted of paintings composed of large blobs or *taches* of colour.

Tapestry, a fabric largely used in earlier ages for wall decoration and hangings. It was known to the ancient Greeks, but in its modern form came into prominence in the 15th and 16th cent., when it was manufactured in a marked degree of excellence by the weavers of Flanders, especially those of Arras. The manufacture was introduced into England early in the 17th cent., and was attended by considerable success. Nowadays the term is applied to worsted cloths for furniture coverings, and there are also various kinds of tapestry carpets now made. The most famous tapestries of old times were the Aubusson Tapestry and the Savonnerie. The Gobelin Tapestry factory, originated in Paris in the reign of Francis I, is still a national establishment. *See also* Bayeux Tapestry, Section L.

Tempera, a painting technique used commonly by medieval artists before it was superseded by oil painting in the fifteenth century. Tempera is made by mixing powdered colour with egg yolk, egg white or the whole egg to create an opaque paint.

Tondo, Italian for "round", is a circular painting or sculpture. *Tondi* were popular in fifteenth-century Italy.

Triptych, an altarpiece composed of three panels hinged together. This is one of the most common types of altarpieces, as the two outer panels can fold together over the inner panel. The outer panels were thus usually painted on the inside and the outside to allow two different visual effects.

Trompe l'oeil literally means to "fool the eye". It refers to a considered attempt at illusionism that makes it difficult to tell whether or not a painted surface is real. *Trompe l'oeil* devices were commonly used in ceiling painting, and they were employed by the Cubists (q.v.) to create an amusing dissonance between optical space and the perspective distortions of Cubist space.

Tympanum is, in architectural phraseology, the triangular space at the back of a pediment, or, indeed, any space in a similar position, as over window or between the lintel and the arch of a doorway. In ecclesiastical edifices the tympanum is often adorned with sculpture.

V

Varnish is usually painted or sprayed over a finished painting in order to preserve it. Although varnish will help the paint to remain stable, it often darkens over time and paradoxically can cause extreme damage to a painting's surface.

Verism was a name given to the German *Neue Sachlichkeit* (q.v.) artists such as George Grosz and Otto Dix, who produced scathing, and often disturbing, satires on Weimar society during the 1920s.

Vorticism, a British art movement which began in 1913 on the initiative of Wyndham Lewis, Ezra Pound (q.v.) and Edward Wadsworth. The movement brought both Cubism (q.v.) and Futurism (q.v.) into England, as its practitioners were concerned with modern life as well as with the abrogation of the stale stability of established art. From 1914 the artists produced a magazine called *BLAST*, and they held their only exhibition in 1915. The First World War dissipated their momentum.

W

Wanderers, The, a group of nineteenth-century Russian artists who attempted to carry their ideas to the country peasantry. Reacting against the elitism of the Imperial Academy of Arts in St. Petersburg, artists such as Ilya Repin established itinerant exhibitions to show their Social Realist *(q.v.)* paintings of Russian peasant life and Russian history. Founded in 1870, the Wanderers continued to exist until the early twentieth century.

Watercolour, a technique of painting involving water soluble colours. Watercolour creates a transparent effect, as opposed to the opaque effect of gouache, *(q.v.)*, which is particularly useful for landscape painting. It was used by Dürer *(q.v.)* in the early sixteenth century for landscape sketches, but it only became popular at the end of the eighteenth century with the growth of Picturesque *(q.v.)* tourism. The ease of using watercolour made it a particularly appropriate technique for amateurs.

Weaving. The interlacing of two or more threads at right angles to form a fabric is a craft that has been practised since ancient times. The main principle of the weaving loom is the same to-day as it was thousands of years ago; a warp extends lengthwise through the loom, the threads being held in separate regular order by being passed through a reed or "slay", while the weft is crossed through alternating threads of the warp by means of a shuttle which holds the weft. Thus the fabric is built up. Weaving was done by hand up to the early part of the 19th cent., when Cartwright's steam-power loom was introduced. The Jacquard loom for weaving figured designs dates from 1801.

Woodcut, a print technique which involves cutting into a block of wood, inking the block and then pressing it onto a piece of paper. The raised portions of the wood create the design, and the cut portions read as white spaces on the final print. It is one of the oldest printing techniques, and it was used from the fifteenth century. It was superseded by the more efficient method of engraving *(q.v.)*, but it was revived in the early twentieth century by the German Expressionists.

World of Art (Mir Iskusstva), a Russian art magazine and art movement which began in St. Petersburg in 1896. A group of students including Leon Bakst *(q.v.)*, Alexander Benois and Sergei Diaghilev *(q.v.)* intended their magazine to enlighten Russia about progressive European art movements. They reacted strongly against what they perceived as the parochialism of Russian art and attempted to instill the European values of "art for art's sake" in their native country. The movement was most influential in theatre design, particularly the productions in Paris of the *Ballet russe*, which involved innovations of set, costume and movement. The magazine continued to be published until 1905.

SPECIAL TOPIC

ASPECTS OF ART HISTORY
BAROQUE, ROCOCO AND CLASSICISM

The Origins of Baroque

The term "Baroque" has two principal origins. The Italian word *"barocco"* translates "pedantry", and the Portuguese word *"barrocco"* indicates a deformed pearl. The pejorative connotations of each of these words indicates the fact that "Baroque" was originally a derisive classification. Today, it is very difficult to say exactly what Baroque art is, as the word is used as a catch-all for a great variety of European 17th-century art. However, the principal artists of the Baroque period shared the qualities of theatricality, extravagance, dynamism, experimentation and excess.

Caravaggio

The first of these artists, Michelangelo Merisi da Caravaggio (1571–1610) painted religious pictures which were, in some respects, a response to Counter-Reformation complaints about Mannerist painting. Caravaggio's works were accessible, immediate and emotionally appealing, rather than arcane, erudite and fussy. But some of his more daring paintings, such as the *Death of the Virgin* (1605–06) carry this accessibility rather too far. The Virgin in this painting was allegedly modelled on a drowned prostitute, whose distended stomach and dirty feet are all too apparent. The violent aspects of Caravaggio's realism were taken up by his followers, including Artemisia Gentileschi (1593–c. 1652), whose lurid *Judith Slaying Holofernes* (c. 1620) represents blood and violent death.

Bernini

Caravaggio's low-life realism formed a direct contrast to the theatrical exuberance of Gianlorenzo Bernini (1598–1680), who revolutionised the practice of sculpture. For St. Peter's in Rome, Bernini produced the Baldacchino and the Cathedra Petri (begun 1656)—both of which combined elements of sculpture, painting and architecture in a deliberately overwhelmingly display. Bernini's works were intended to glorify the Catholic Church following a period of crisis and reformation.

Rubens

While these developments were occurring in Italy, Peter Paul Rubens (1577–1640) in Antwerp was producing paintings which contained lush colour and dramatic composition. Rubens's position as a respected diplomat gained him access to a number of European courts, and his work was widely respected. The 21 canvases he produced to commemorate the life and marriage of Marie de' Medici (1621–25) include many allegorical figures placed within lavish and crowded compositions. Rubens's interest in loose brushwork became an important consideration for later European art.

17th-Century Painting in Spain and the Low Countries

The uneasy relationship between Spain and the Low Countries underwent a crisis in the late 16th century, when Holland and the other Netherlandish provinces rebelled against their Spanish rulers and formed the Dutch Republic. In reaction against Spain's traditional and rigid Catholicism and aristocracy, the Dutch Republic glorified Protestant virtues and mercantile bourgeois life. These interests stimulated the production of non-religious art forms, such as portraiture, landscape, still-life and genre.

The Genius of Rembrandt

The greatest proponent of portraiture in the 17th century was Rembrandt van Rijn (1606–69). His *Night Watch* (1642) was a group portrait of a militia company, but Rembrandt's imagination transformed it into a lively and active scene. Rembrandt's extravagance and consequent money problems led him to turn to himself as a model in a series of self-portraits which explored gesture, expression and costume. Like Caravaggio before him, Rembrandt created mood in his painting through the use of chiaroscuro, a practice which had a strong impact on later generations of artists. Aside from Rembrandt, Frans Hals (1580–1666) also contributed to the development of portraiture. In single and group portraits, such as the *Laughing Cavalier* (1624), Hals creates an impression of movement and liveliness through loose brushwork.

Genre Painting: Vermeer and Steen

Genre painting in the Dutch Republic was especially popular, as it catered to a desire for compact, familiar scenes of everyday life. The most sophisticated proponent of genre painting was Jan Vermeer (1632–75), but artists such as Jan Steen (1625/6–79) produced equally popular images of low-life characters drinking and cavorting in taverns. Erotic scenes were also popular.

Velázquez

While painting in the Dutch Republic was becoming more and more worldly, the art of the Spanish court continued to cater to the needs of the royal family. Diego Velázquez (1599–1660) was the court painter of Philip IV from 1623, and although many of his works are not flattering, he was popular at the court. His most famous court painting, *Las Meninas* (1656) includes members of the royal family, dwarfs and Velázquez himself, who intrudes through a door at the back of the room. A sense of immediacy and realism pervades the painting, but Velázquez's virtuosity prevented it from becoming mundane or commonplace.

The Rococo in Germany

The extravagance and theatricality of the "High Baroque" period was gradually transformed into the fussy and intricate art of the Rococo. Again, the term "Rococo" has been used loosely to refer to a style of art prevalent in Europe during the first three-quarters of the eighteenth century. In Germany, the Rococo was largely architectural; the predominantly Catholic Bavaria was filled with churches which were more extravagant than those of the Baroque period. For example, Johann Balthasar Neumann's (1687–1753) Vierzehnheiligenkirche (1743–72) dazzles the eyes with a distracting array of architecture, painting, sculpture, illusionism and light.

French Rococo

In France, the Rococo can be seen in both decorative arts and painting. The courtly visions of Jean-Antoine Watteau (1684–1721) consist of both imaginary and real figures cavorting in a fanciful landscape or architectural setting. The *Pilgrimage to the Island of Cythera* (1717) is a typical example of such work: it is set in an artificial world inhabited by beautiful people and theatrical characters. The lush landscapes of Watteau were later exaggerated by Jean-Honoré Fragonard (1732–1806), whose feathery brushwork and fancy themes epitomise the escapism of the Rococo. The sensual lines and brushwork of Rococo were particularly appropriate for erotic subjects, most notably those of François Boucher (1703–70).

The Rococo in England

As in France, the English Rococo was confined primarily to decorative art. However, the painter and engraver William Hogarth (1697–1764)— despite his insistence that he hated anything French—used the curving lines of the Rococo style in his series of engravings *The Marriage à la Mode* (c. 1743). Hogarth also produced the only real art

treatise of the Rococo style: his *Analysis of Beauty* (1753) extolled the serpentine line as the basis of all beauty.

Classicism

From the time of the Renaissance, the revival of the style and subject-matter of ancient sculpture and architecture had been popular among artists. The "rebirth" of the ancient world in the Renaissance was codified in the 17th century by the growth of art academies throughout Europe. The French Academy, founded in 1648 used classical and Renaissance art theory to create a number of rules for painters to follow. This rigid application of formal principles of composition, gesture and expression can be seen in the work of Nicolas Poussin (1593/4–1665). His *Israelites Gathering the Manna* (1639) is an exploration of facial expression and gesture which was later used as a model by artists of the French Academy, such as Charles Lebrun (1619–90). Poussin's intellectual interest in Stoicism and the classical world was shared to a lesser extent by Claude Lorrain (1600–82). Both artists spent time in Italy, and while Poussin studied ancient ruins, Lorrain painted scenes of the Italian countryside. His well-constructed landscapes also followed rules of order and harmony based on classical ideas.

The Neo-classical Movement

The continued admiration for the artefacts of the ancient world came to fruition in the 18th century in architecture, painting, the decorative arts and sculpture. The Neo-classical movement gained impetus when the English architect Robert Adam (1728–92) visited Italy in 1754, and returned with ideas of how to decorate the interiors of country houses. Adam's decorative designs in houses like Kedleston, Derbyshire (c. 1760–70), show his faithful attention to ancient ruins. Also in England, Josiah Wedgwood (1730–95) produced vases which directly imitated Greek black-figure painting, but these well-designed substitutes were mass produced in Wedgwood's factory.

An interest in ancient sculpture was stimulated by the writings of German historian Johann Joachim Winckelmann (1717–68), who admired the spiritual qualities of ancient art. Winckelmann's ideas influenced sculptors such as Antonio Canova (1757–1822), and painters such as Anton Raffael Mengs (1728–79), who attempted to imitate the smooth proportions and balanced grace of ancient art. In England, Sir Joshua Reynolds (1723–92), President of the Royal Academy, tried to encourage artists to elevate their paintings by pursuing classical ideals. His Grand Style portraits, such as *Mrs. Siddons as the Tragic Muse* (1784) show how he could use classical idealism to purify what was otherwise a primarily commercial genre of painting.

The most famous proponent of the Neo-classical style in painting was the French artist Jacques-Louis David (1748–1825). Like Poussin, Lorrain and Winckelmann, David studied in Rome and learned to admire the formal proportions and harmony of classical art. He used these principles in such paintings as the *Oath of the Horatii* (1784), which represents three brothers who are pledging their lives for their country. The moralizing nature of David's paintings was fully in keeping with the idealist principles of Neo-classicism, and David would later contribute to the visual propaganda that emerged during the period of the French Revolution.

THE
WORLD OF
MUSIC

The art of music as it has developed in the Western world, with
an outline historical narrative,
a glossary of musical terms and
an index to composers. The period
covered runs from early secular
music to the vibrant music forms of
the new millennium. A Special Topic
in this edition looks at the life and
music of Dmitri Shostakovich.

TABLE OF CONTENTS

THE WORLD OF MUSIC

In writing this section no special knowledge on the part of the reader is assumed; it is for those who want to know about the history of music, how different styles evolved, and how one composer influenced another. It is a background to music as the science section is a background to science, and just as the latter cannot show the reader the colours of the spectrum but only tell of Newton's experiments and of the relationship between colour and wavelength, so in this section we can only describe human achievements in the world of sound. But knowing something about composers, their work, and when they lived can help to bring fuller understanding and enjoyment when listening to their music.

The section is in four parts:

I. Historical Narrative and Discussion
II. Glossary of Musical Terms
III. Index to Composers
IV. Special Topic

I. HISTORICAL NARRATIVE AND DISCUSSION

The history of music, like that of any people or art, is not one of uninterrupted progress towards some ideal perfection. For five centuries or more music in the West has achieved peaks of accomplishment in one style or another before society has dictated or composers have felt the need for something new and different. Thus Wagner's music-drama *Parsifal*, lasting five hours, is not necessarily a more rewarding work than what Monteverdi achieved in *Orfeo* 250 years earlier. More complex yes, more rewarding—well, that is for the listener to judge.

We must keep this in mind when considering the development of music from a starting point of, say, early plainchant down to the complicated structures of a Schoenberg in our own day. In this development there is no true dividing line between one period and another, nor must simplifying terms such as "classical" or "romantic" be taken too literally.

Introduction.

In the recent past, general histories of music usually started from around 1600 with the implication that earlier music was primitive, and not worth serious consideration. This view has changed, largely as a result of the number of excellent performances and recordings available of medieval music by groups such as Gothic Voices, and the Hilliard Ensemble. These performances show that the music of the 14th and 15th centuries is just as complex and beautiful as anything written afterwards. There are clear parallels between the highly structured works of Machaut and Dufay, and the music of the mid to late 20th century.

Defining Medieval Music.

The term 'medieval' in music usually means the period from approximately AD 900–1500, beginning with the earliest examples of music notation, and ending with the transition to the Renaissance. In the medieval period, most performed music was monophonic (made up from a single line), improvised, and secular, probably with some form of drone. Most church music of the period was also monophonic, in the form of plainchant, with the more elaborate polyphonic settings of the mass reserved for special occasions.

Plainchant.

Plainchant is the fundamental basis of all Western music, and consists of a monodic song setting of the Christian liturgy in free rhythm. In monasteries today it is heard either with equal notes or a long-short rhythmic pattern, as there is no consensus. The pitches used are based on one of the 7 church modes such as the dorian (d, e, f, g, a, b, c, d). All medieval music is modal, the difference with tonal music being that there is much less of a pull to a key centre—it is less 'goal oriented'.

The Evolution of Organum.

In around 900 the first medieval treatise on music was written entitled *Musica Enchiriadis*. This contained some of the first examples of notated polyphonic music (music made up of more than one line), which is called *organum*. This genre evolved as an elaboration of plainchant, increasing the majesty of the liturgy. The first examples of what is termed 'florid organum' occurred in the 12th century in Santiago de Compostela in Spain, and in St. Martial at Limoges in France. Florid organum consists of sustained notes of the plainchant, with florid quicker moving lines over this base. The technique evolved into a highly structured method of composition, which can be seen in the music of the 12th century Notre Dame School in Paris.

Leonin and Perotin.

The two names associated with this school are Leonin (fl. 1175) and Perotin (fl. 1183), although very little is known about their lives. Leonin composed a cycle of two part graduals, alleluias, and responsories for the church year called the *Magnus Liber Organi* (or great book of organi). Perotin expanded this work by composing new substitute sections called *clausulae*, which use the melismatic or florid part of a plainchant as its structural basis or tenor. There are usually 2 or 3 upper voices placed above the tenor, and all the parts move at the same pace. The term 'Tenor' is not the voice type, but the term for the main structural voice, usually the lowest.

The Motet.

The development of the clausula is significant because it creates a greater compositional freedom for the composers of the time, allowing them to display their artistry. The motet evolved from the clausula, and flourished in the 13th and 14th centuries. It consisted of the setting of a new text to an existing clausula, and the name came from the French for word: 'mot'. With the development of the motet, the music became separated from the liturgy, and the words could now be based on love, and politics, as well as spiritual themes.

The Use of Isorhythm.

The main structural feature of the medieval motet is the use of isorhythm. This technique consists of a repeated rhythmic pattern, known as a talea, in the tenor, which is projected onto a repeating pattern of pitches, usually derived from a plainchant known as the color. The other parts created free polyphony around the slower moving tenor, using bare sounding perfect fifths and unisons as the basic harmonic consonance of the music.

The Notation of Rhythm.

The next main musical development in the later 13th century was in the notation of rhythm. Until Franco of Cologne's treatise of 1260 *Ars Cantus Mensurabilis* or 'Art of Measured Song', rhythms had been restricted to a small number of 'modal' patterns. Franco codified a new way of notation which allowed each note to have a number of different durations, creating far more rhythmic flexibility, and establishing the basis of a system that has not fundamentally changed upto the present day.

Ars Nova.

Philippe de Vitry (1291–1361), a French composer and theorist, built upon this in his treatise *Ars Nova* or 'New Technique/Craft' written in 1316, and also in his rhythmically complex motets. Once the term 'Ars Nova' gained currency as a description of the music of the 14th century, the previous period of the Notre Dame School, became described as 'Ars Antique', or 'Old Technique/Craft'. The music of the 14th century became much richer and more varied as a direct result of this innovation of notational practice.

Probably the most significant and versatile composer of this time was the Frenchman Guillaume de Machaut (1300–77). Machaut was a canon, a poet, and secretary to several kings, and his compositional output included secular chansons such as lais, ballades and rondeaux, as well as motets and the seminal *Notre Dame* Mass. The latter, probably a mature work, is very signicant because it was the first time a composer had written a complete mass cycle—a complete setting of the ordinary of the mass. It is an austere but very beautiful work and uses both isorhythmic and discant styles. Discant style is used for the longer texts such as the Gloria, and consists of one note per syllable of text. The isorhythmic movements such as the Kyrie are melismatic, and therefore they have many notes for each syllable.

The Cantus Firmus.

It was not until the following century that the composition of complete mass cycles became the norm. The main innovation in the composition of masses in the 15th century was probably first used in Britain, and is the use of a Cantus Firmus to unify the mass cycle. A Cantus Firmus is a pre-existing melody which is used as the structural basis of the mass, and is usually in the Tenor although it can be found in the other voices. The melody could be plainchant or a well known secular song, such as the French *L'Homme Armé*, which was particularly popular. Another significant shift is the development of more 'tonal' sounding harmonies and cadences.

The Work of Dunstable.

The British composer John Dunstable (1385–1453) was significant in the development of a more consonant and richer harmonic language on the mainland of Europe, particular the use of 3rds and 6ths. The evolution of style can be heard in the music of 15th century composers such as Guillaume Dufay (1400–74), and Josquin des Préz (1440–1521) which paved the way for the rich harmony and polyphony of the Renaissance. The medieval period showed an extraordinary evolution of style and technique, and produced music which is as beautiful and subtle as any work produced in later eras.

The Sixteenth Century.

By the 16th cent. music in England was a steadily expanding art and much encouraged. Music-making in the home was becoming quite the fashion in social circles. The Chapels Royal remained the chief musical centres but the music was changing with the development of new secular forms so that it was not so much religious as a part of life. Composers began their lives as choirboys and received a thoroughgoing education, both theoretical and practical.

Carrying on from where Josquin and his contemporaries left off, Palestrina in Italy, Victoria in Spain, Lassus in the Netherlands, and Byrd in England brought the polyphonic style to its zenith. At the same time, came the rise of the madrigalists, first in Italy, then in the Netherlands; and then the beginnings of instrumental music as it came to be known in the succeeding centuries.

New Methods of Writing.

The vocal composers began to use chordal (homophonic) as well as contrapuntal (polyphonic) methods of writing—examples are Victoria's *Ave Verum Corpus* and Palestrina's *Stabat Mater*—but polyphony was still the fullest most magnificent instrument of composition, as for instance in Byrd's *O Quam Gloriosum* which shows an eager response to the mood and to the inflection of the words in a kind of vocal orchestration. A feature of all these composers' music, but more especially that of Victoria (c. 1548–1611) and Palestrina (1525–94), is its serene simplicity and fervour of utterance. Palestrina was perhaps more spacious in his effects, Victoria the more passionate. How well we can imagine—and sometimes hear—their music resounding down the naves of the great cathedrals of Europe.

The Music of Lassus.

The music of Lassus (c. 1532–94) is distinguished both in sheer amount and in vitality. His mastery in the field of motets was unrivalled, encompassing a wide range of subject and mood. He and his fellow Flemish composers, Willaert, de Monte and Arcadelt, were also expert in the Madrigal, a form popular in Italy and England as well. The Madrigal was a contrapuntal setting of a poem, usually not longer than twelve lines, in five or six parts. The subject (of the poetry) was usually amorous or pastoral. It was a short-lived, but highly prolific vogue. Orlando Gibbons (1583–1625), Thomas Weelkes (c. 1573–1623), and John Wilbye (1574–1638) were the most prominent English exponents.

Instrumental Music.

By the end of the 14th cent. instrumental music began to become something more than mere anonymous dance tunes or primitive organ music. Instruments often accompanied voices, or even replaced them, so that the recorder, lute, viol, and spinet indoors, and sackbuts and shawms outdoors, had already been developed by the time instrumental music came to be written down. Gradually a distinction grew up between what was appropriate to the voice and what was suitable for instruments, Byrd, Gibbons, and Giles Farnaby in England, the great blind keyboard player, Cabezón (1510–66) in Spain, and Frescobaldi (1583–1643) in Italy produced valuable instrumental works. Perhaps the *Parthenia* and the *Fitzwilliam Virginal Book*, collections of Early English Keyboard music, give as fair a representative idea as any of the development of instrumental form at this time.

In chamber music musicians often played collections of dance tunes strung together to make a whole; or they chose fantasies (or "fancies"), where a composer altered a tune as he wished. Then there were sets of variations on a ground, that is a simple tune played over and over again on a bass viol.

As far as brass instruments are concerned, they were often used on festive occasions in spacious halls or in cathedrals. The Venetian composer Andrea Gabrieli (c. 1510-86) was the first to combine voice and instruments and his nephew Giovanni Gabrieli (1557-1612) carried the process further to produce sacred symphonies, often using antiphonal effects.

Drama in Music.

Not until the end of the 16th cent. did anyone begin to think about combining drama and music, and so "invent" the new art we know today as opera. A group of artistic intelligentsia met together in Florence and conceived the idea of reviving the ancient declamation of Greek tragedy. They took Greek mythological subjects, cast them in dramatic form, and set them to music, not in the choral polyphonic style of the Madrigal, but with single voices declaiming dialogue in music. The earliest examples of what was called *Dramma per Musica* were Peri's *Dafne* in 1597 (now lost) and his *Euridice*, in which he co-operated with Caccini. The new style came to its full flowering with the appearance of Monteverdi (1567-1643).

The Music of Monteverdi.

Monteverdi's first opera, *Orfeo*, produced in 1607, is a landmark of dramatic expression, and it is nothing less than a catastrophe that so many of his later operas have been lost. His *Orfeo* provides the basic ground work for the operas of the next two centuries: recitative, accompanied recitative, and aria. His last opera *L'Incoronazione di Poppea*, written when he was at the great age (for those days) of 75, succeeds in its aim of creating a free, fluid form, slipping easily from recitative to arioso and even aria without the strict, closed forms that were to be used in the 17th and 18th cent. He focuses attention to an almost unbelievable extent on character rather than situation. He creates real people with all their faults and foibles—the kittenish, sexually attractive Poppaea, the power-drunk, infatuated Nero, the noble Seneca, and the dignified, rejected empress Octavia. As recent productions have shown these characters leap from the musical page as if they had just been created, each unerringly delineated in musical terms. Only the vocal line, the continuo, and the very incomplete instrumental ritornelli parts have been preserved, but in sensitive, knowledgeable hands tonal variety in the shape of wind and string parts can be added, as we know certain instruments were available to the composer.

Monteverdi's Successors.

Monteverdi's successors were Cavalli (1602-76), Cesti (1623-69) and Stradella (1642-82), who gave the solo voice more and more prominence encouraged by the advent of the castrati's brilliant voices. These artificially created singers had a vogue and popularity similar to "pop" singers of today, fêted wherever they appeared. The aria became more extended and ornate, and dramatic verisimilitude gradually but inexorably took second place to vocal display. An aria was nearly always in *da capo* form, the first section being repeated after a contrasting middle one.

Sixteenth- and Seventeenth-Century Church Music.

Of course, the invention of a new dramatic style affected church music too. The concentration on the vertical aspect of music (homophony) as opposed to the horizontal (polyphony) led to the increasing importance of the voice in religious music. In Italy, it is true, there was the late-flowering, great madrigalist Carlo Gesualdo (1560-1614), whose harmonic daring still astonishes us today, but by 1600 the cantata was coming to replace older forms in church music. In its simplest form this was a story told in accompanied recitative, Giacomo Carissimi (c. 1604-74) was one of the first significant composers of this new form. He too was in on the birth of the oratorio,

whose forerunner was the *sacra rappresentazione* (mystery or miracle play) of early 16th-cent. Florence. Then in the mid-16th cent. St. Philip Neri brought in elements from popular plays on sacred subjects in his services in Rome, designed to hold the attention of youth—rather as certain parsons have tried with "pop" services today. Emilio del Cavalieri (c. 1550-1602) and Carissimi developed the form adding arias and choral movements, omitting actual representation. Alessandro Scarlatti (1660-1725), whose oratorios bear a close resemblance to his operas, brought oratorio to its zenith in Italy.

Heinrich Schütz.

Heinrich Schütz (1585-1672), Bach's great predecessor, was the founder of German church music. His historical place has never been called into question but only in recent times have the intrinsic merits of his own music come to be recognised. He studied with Giovanni Gabrieli in his youth and later came under the influence of Monteverdi, so it was not surprising that he brought Italian ideas across the Alps to Germany and wrote the first German opera *Daphne*, now sadly lost. He also introduced his country to the Italian declamatory style and to the new kind of concertato instrumental writing. But his dramatic religious works were his greatest contribution to musical development. He wrote with a devout intensity, bringing to life the scriptural texts by closely allying his urgent music to the words. His three settings of the Passions—Matthew, Luke, and John—paved the way for Bach's even more remarkable works in this genre.

Two contemporaries of Schütz, Johann Herman Schein (1586-1630) and Samuel Scheidt (1587-1654), were both important figures in German Reformation music.

Seventeenth-Century Music in France and England.

French opera was from the beginning associated with the court ballet. The Italian-born Jean-Baptiste Lully (c. 1632-87) created the characteristic form of the *tragédie lyrique*, which dominated the French musical stage until the mid-18th cent. In Lully's operas the libretto plays a vital role, the text being set in a flexible, naturalistic way, with a less clear distinction between recitative and aria than in Italian opera. The orchestration, chorus and dances assume greater importance than in the contemporary Italian form. In his lifetime, Lully's musical monopoly under Louis XIV limited the outlets for other opera composers. An outstanding opera composed and performed after Lully's death is *Médée* (1693) by Marc-Antoine Charpentier (1643-1704). Charpentier is best known, however, for his church music, of which the *Te Deum* (c. 1691) is a colourful example.

In the instrumental field, the lute music of Denis Gaultier (1603-72) stimulated the development of an idiomatic harpsichord style in the dance suites of J.C. de Chambonnières (1602-72), Louis Couperin (1626-61) and J.-H. d'Anglebert (1635-91).

In England, opera developed from the Masque, an entertainment consisting of dances, songs and poetry, with elaborate stage effects, often incorporated into a drama. Examples are Henry Lawes's (1596-1662) setting of Milton's *Comus* (1634), and *Cupid and Death* (1653) by Matthew Locke (1622-77) and Christopher Gibbons (1615-76). John Blow's (1649-1708) *Venus and Adonis* (c. 1684) is called a masque but is in effect an opera, the whole text being sung.

Henry Purcell.

It was Henry Purcell (1659-95), Blow's pupil, who in *Dido and Aeneas* really exploited the new medium by his power of subtle musical characterisation. Dido's lament "When I am laid in earth" uses typically bold harmonic effects to achieve a remarkable expressive power. These works by Blow and Purcell, however, are exceptions. The favoured form was the semi-opera – essentially a play with a substantial amount of music – to which Purcell contributed some fine examples, such as *The Fairy Queen* (1692).

Purcell's sacred music is also of a high order, representing the culmination of the Restoration style forged from earlier English and newly fashionable Italian and French influences by such composers as Matthew Locke and Pelham Humfrey (1647–74). Purcell's instrumental music includes work in older genres (the Fantasias for viols, which are imaginative, even eccentric, in their approach to harmony and counterpoint); he also adopted the new Italian violinistic style in his Sonatas of Three and Four Parts.

Vivaldi and the Rise of Instrumental Music.

Out of the dance suites popular in the 16th cent. and the beginning of the 17th (known in Italy as the *Sonata da Camera*) developed the concerto. This began as two groups of instrumentalists compared and contrasted with each other as in Giovanni Gabrieli's *Sonata piano e forte*. With Arcangelo Corelli (1653–1713) the concerto grosso took a more definite shape, alternating a solo group of instruments with the main body of strings in three or more contrasting movements. Guiseppe Torelli (1658–1709), Francesco Geminiani (1687–1762) and Tommaso Albinoni (1671–1750) were other notable contributors to the form, but none of the composers so far mentioned has today achieved the popularity of the priest Antonio Vivaldi (c. 1678–1741), himself a violinist, who had at his disposal the orchestra at the Ospedale della Pieta in Venice. The young women at this music school also contributed the vocal side of the concerts there of which there are many descriptions. One says: "They sing like angels, play the violin, flute, organ, oboe, cello, bassoon—in short no instrument is large enough to frighten them . . . I swear nothing is so charming than to see a young and pretty nun, dressed in white, a sprig of pomegranate blossom behind one ear, leading the orchestra, and beating time with all the grace and precision imaginable." For this body, Vivaldi wrote about 500 concertos which maintain a remarkably even quality, but "The Four Seasons" are perhaps the most felicitous.

Organ and Harpsichord.

Meanwhile organ music was advancing rapidly in technique. Girolamo Frescobaldi (1583–1643) and Jan Pieterszoon Sweelinck (1562–1621) wrote works that provided the foundation of the Italian and Northern German schools of organ music. Their ricercares gradually developed into the fugue, a vein so richly mined by Bach. Among their successors the most notable figure before Bach was Johann Pachelbel (1653–1706).

Other keyboard music, especially for the harpsichord, was the particular province of France; and Jean-Philippe Rameau (1683–1764) and François Couperin (1668–1733) were both masters of keyboard style and harmonic invention. They wrote many pieces of subtle charm and exquisite craftsmanship.

Bach (1685–1750).

The two giant figures of Bach and Handel bestride the first half of the 18th cent. Their differences are perhaps greater than their similarities. Bach wrote essentially for himself (although of course, he had to satisfy his employers at Cöthen and Leipzig) while Handel was composing to please his wide public. Bach was a provincial, always remaining in central Germany; Handel was widely travelled. Bach was devoutly religious, almost ascetic; Handel was more a man of the world. They never met.

To summarise Bach's vast output in a short space is virtually impossible. One can only try to distil the flavour of his music. He brought the art of polyphony to the highest pitch of mastery that has ever been achieved or is ever likely to be achieved. In his famous "Forty-Eight" and "the Art of the Fugue" he explored all the fugal permutations of the major and minor keys. At the same time his music rose above technical brilliance to achieve, especially in his organ music, the two Passions, many of the church cantatas,

and the B minor Mass, intense emotional and expressive power. The cantatas, from his Leipzig appointment (1723) onwards, were integrated into the services. They consisted usually of a chorus based on a Lutheran hymn tune, recitatives, several extended arias, and a concluding chorus usually a straightforward version of the hymn tune in which the congregation joined. There are some two hundred of these works and they contain a wealth of comparatively unknown and sometimes even unrecognised beauties. The St. John and the St. Matthew Passion extend these procedures to a grand scale, an Evangelist telling the new Testament story in vivid recitative, the chorus taking the part of the crowd, soloists now dealing in arias on the meaning of the Gospel, and Jesus's words being sung by a bass. Anyone who has heard either of these works well performed cannot help but dismiss from his mind any idea of Bach as a mere dry-as-dust musical mathematician.

In the St. Matthew Passion, every suggestion in the text that can possibly be illustrated by a musical equivalent is so illustrated. The Old Testament Pharasaic law is represented by strict musical forms such as the canon; Christ's sayings are given noble arioso life; and the arias reflect truly the New Testament's compassionate message. Technically the work is a marvel; expressively it is eloquent. The B minor Mass, although it contains borrowings from many of his own works, still stands as a satisfying monumental whole in which Bach's choral writing achieved a new richness, the adaptations being in accord with their new setting.

Bach's Instrumental Music.

Bach's instrumental music, especially the violin concertos and the unaccompanied works for violin and cello, not only show the immense range of his powers but also contain many of his deeper thoughts, whereas the orchestral suites and the Brandenburg concertos are more extrovert, particularly the rhythmically exuberant fast movements.

Bach closes an era—that of the later contrapuntalists—by achieving the *ne plus ultra* in fugal composition; his last, incomplete work, The Art of the Fugue, is evidence of that. In recent years there has been a trend towards playing Bach's music on original instruments of his time (or replicas) and singing it with appropriately sized, sometimes all-male choirs.

Handel (1685–1759).

During his lifetime Handel was far more widely recognised as a great composer than Bach, and his music, unlike Bach's, maintained its place in popular esteem until the re-discovery of Bach and the dominance of the symphony placed Handel somewhat in the background.

During the latter part of the 19th cent. Handel's name was mainly associated with mammoth, anachronistic performances of a small sample of his oratorios at the Crystal Palace and elsewhere in England. In his lifetime these works, and all his other pieces in the genre, were sung by a small choir who were outnumbered by the instrumental players. Over the past few years authentic-sized performances of his oratorios and a revival of interest in his operas have revealed the real Handel, unknown to our grandparents.

The operas were neglected partly because the vocal prowess they required—and which the castrati so brilliantly supplied—was no longer available and because their dramatic life, at least according to 19th- and early 20th-cent. tenets, hardly existed. Now it is realised that this neglect has deprived us of an unending stream of glorious melody and of much daring harmony. But perhaps it is in the hitherto disregarded oratorios, such as *Semele*, that Handel's innate dramatic sense and musical range are to be heard gloriously fulfilled, and the pastoral serenade *Acis and Galatea* is surely one of the most delightful scores ever composed.

Handel was a colourful, imaginative orchestrator, and this can be heard both in his accompaniment to vocal music and in his concerti grossi, op. 3 and 6, the earlier set exploiting a diversity of interesting string and wind combination. In his writing he was at home in a polyphonic or homophonic style as his superb choruses show. His organ concertos, of which he was the "inventor" (to quote a contemporary source), were often played between the acts of his oratorios. They are alternately expressive and exuberant pieces calling for some virtuosity from the player. His occasional works, such as the Water Music and Fireworks Music show his ingenuity in extending the range of the typical 17th cent. suite to serve a particular occasion.

Handel's working life was mostly spent in England where his Italian operas were acclaimed. In the years between his arrival here in 1711 and 1729 he wrote nearly thirty operas. It was only when the public tired of these and his reputation slumped that he turned to oratorio with equal success.

Developing New Styles.

Bach and Handel between them crowned the age of polyphony that had lasted for two hundred years or more. After them, it is hardly surprising that composers began looking for a new style, already anticipated in the music of Rameau and particularly Dominico Scarlatti (1685–1737), whose harpsichord sonatas foreshadowed the classical sonata form that was to dominate music for the next two hundred years. The change in musical style about 1750 was partly the result of a change in musical patronage. Bach was the last great composer to earn his living through being employed by the church. The new patrons were the nobility who liked to have a composer on hand to write for the various evening entertainments of the time. For this purpose the princes and dukes had their own orchestras and their own small opera houses. The music required had to be elegant, formal, *galant*. Haydn was exceptionally fortunate in having an employer, Prince Nicholas of Esterhazy, who allowed him to write more or less as he wished so that he was able to develop symphonic form into something more than a pleasing way of passing an evening.

The early symphonists, culminating in Haydn, broke away from Bach's contrapuntal treatment of the orchestra. Instruments now came to be treated in a more colourful manner according to their particular timbre. The court of Mannheim had an orchestra of a standard unheard hitherto, and Johann Stamitz (1717–57) and his son Karl (1745–1801) influenced the great composers who wore to follow in their footsteps. The composition of their orchestra was flexible, oboes, flutes, and horns often being added to the standard string section. Bach's son Carl Philipp Emanuel (1714–88) added to and developed symphonic and sonata form, especially as regards keys and subjects.

Haydn and Mozart.

These two figures dominate the second half of the 18th cent. as Bach and Handel do the first. In a brief space only a general picture can be presented of their huge output and influence. Of Haydn's 104 symphonies (there may even be others) nearly all are worthy of study and hearing. The craftsmanship is always remarkable, the invention ever new. Indeed without Haydn's harmonic daring or his melodic ingenuity, the even greater symphonic thought of Beethoven would have been impossible: Haydn laid the groundwork on which his successor built towering edifices. A work such as the 93rd symphony in D is typical of his mature style with its searching introduction, powerfully wrought, earnestly argued first movement, beautiful *Largo* and resourceful bustling finale. Haydn did not fight shy of contrapuntal writing: the development section of this symphony's first movement and the finale are evidence of that, but it was only as an integral part of a predominantly homophonic technique.

Mozart's symphonies are not so different in

form from Haydn's but—and this must be a subjective judgment—he put more emotional feeling into his. Nobody could listen to the heart-searching first movement of his 40th symphony without being deeply moved. It was in his final three works in the medium that Mozart brought his symphonic art to perfection, and these obviously had an effect on Haydn's later symphonies written after them. For passion and tenderness contained within a classical form these late symphonies, and many other of Mozart's works, have yet to be surpassed.

Haydn, who has been rightly termed "the Father of the Symphony", was also the founder of the string quartet—perhaps the most perfect, because the most exactly balanced, form of musical expression. The four instruments—two violins, viola, and cello—discuss, argue, commune with each other over the whole gamut of feeling. In his quartets Haydn's mastery of structure is even more amazing than in his symphonies. Mozart's quartets (especially the six devoted to Haydn) and even more his quintets achieve miracles of beauty in sound, nowhere more so than in the first movement of the G minor (his most personal key) quintet. The two late piano quartets show how the piano *can* be ideally combined with strings. His clarinet quintet is also a masterly work.

Haydn did not leave any concertos of consequence. Mozart's, especially those for piano, are among his greatest works. As a brilliant clavier player himself, he showed a consummate skill in writing for the keyboard. Although the instrument he knew was slightly less advanced than the piano today, his concertos call for virtuosity in execution, yet they are as searching in emotional content as the late symphonies and quartets. Indeed the C major concerto (K. 467) and the C minor (K 491) may be said to hold the quintessential Mozart. As well as twenty (mature) piano concertos, Mozart wrote six for the violin, four for the horn, and eighteen others, but none of these, delightful as they are, can be placed in quite the same class.

Of their church music, Haydn's sixteen masses and his oratorios—*The Creation* and *The Seasons* (both late works)—are perhaps more worthy of attention than Mozart's various masses, but we must not forget Mozart's final work—the Requiem or the serene late Motet *Ave Verum Corpus*.

Eighteenth-Century Opera.

Mozart—for many the first great opera composer—did not, of course, create his masterpieces out of nothing. In France, Lully was followed by Rameau (1683–1764), who carried on his tradition of using classical themes but developed a more flexible style of recitative and greatly increased vividness of expression. But it was Gluck (1714–87) who more than anyone broke out of the straitjacket of the now ossified Italian form of opera—dominated by the singer—and showed just what could be achieved in moving human terms. Drama in music really came of age with his *Orfeo e Euridice* (1762), *Alceste* (1767) and *Iphigénie en Tauride* (1779). His simplicity and poignancy of expression were not lost on Mozart.

Meanwhile in Germany a kind of opera called *Singspiel* appeared during the 18th cent. Breaking away from classical themes, mundane stories were told in dialogue and music.

Until quite recently Haydn's operas were dismissed as unworthy representations of his genius but, chiefly through the enlightening efforts of the Haydn scholar, H. C. Robbins Landon, some of his fifteen surviving works in the medium have been successfully revived. They have proved to be perfectly viable for the stage and, especially in the ensembles, full of that delightful invention to be found in the rest of his opus, if on a less fully developed scale. Still as musical drama they inevitably fall far short of Mozart's achievements, for the younger composer seems to have had an instinctive feeling for the stage. Into his operas he poured his most intense, personal music. He vividly portrays the foibles, desires, loves, and aspirations of mankind.

The earlier, immature stage pieces of his youth led to such works as *Lucio Silla* (1772) and *La Finta Giardiniera* (1775) with their first glimpses of the glories to come. His first indubitably great opera is *Idomeneo* (1781). Despite its unpromisingly static plot, *Idomeneo* reveals Mozart's stature through its ability to breathe new life into a conventional *opera seria* form. Though influenced by Gluck it is yet more human and touching in its musical expression. To succeed this Mozart wrote a much more frivolous piece *Die Entführung aus dem Serail*. Stemming from the *Singspiel* tradition, it none the less creates reallife characters who have much charming music to sing.

Mozart's Masterpieces.

After three lesser pieces Mozart embarked on his four masterpieces—*Le Nozze di Figaro* (1786), *Don Giovanni* (1787), *Cosi fan tutte* (1790), and *Die Zauberflöte* (1791).

Figaro, as well as being a delightful comedy, explores more fully than any previous opera situation and character, which find expression in beautiful arias and in two finales of symphonic proportion. In *Don Giovanni*, less satisfactory as a dramatic structure, the range of musical characterisation and insight into human motives is widened still further. *Cosi* lyrically but humorously expresses the follies of love. Mozart could not help but love his characters and his music for them is at one and the same time amusing and heartfelt, *Die Zauberflöte*—The Magic Flute—displays Mozart's deep-felt concern for his fellow men and for truth in an opera of great spiritual strength. Nor has opera any more loveable personality than the birdcatcher Papageno. Mozart's final opera *La Clemenza di Tito*, extolling imperial magnanimity, has never achieved the success or popularity of his other maturer stage works, though it contains much excellent music, and has recently been revived with honour in several opera houses.

Beethoven.

Mozart was the last major composer to depend, to any large extent, on private patronage for his living, and even he left the service of the Archbishop of Salzburg because he could not stand the restrictions imposed on his freedom. Henceforth composers would have to stand on their own two feet with all the advantages (liberty) and disadvantages (lack of security) that implied. Beethoven (1770-1827) was the first such composer of importance.

Although his work is usually divided into three periods, that division is somewhat too arbitrary, for no other composer in history, with the possible exception of Wagner, has shown such a continual development of his genius. Coming at just the right moment in musical history, he crowned the achievements of Haydn and Mozart with music of the utmost profundity of thought and feeling that looks back to its classical heritage and forward to the romantic movement of the 19th cent. His influence on musical thinking and writing is incalculable.

His first period shows his strong melodic gifts and the beginning of his individuality in developing form and structure to suit his own ends and match his particular genius. Unusual keys are explored, unusual harmonic procedures employed. With the "Eroica" (his third symphony) he established his position as a great composer. The unity of purpose he here achieved within a long and diverse structure is truly staggering, even today. In the first movement alone the formal invention and cogency went far beyond what even Mozart had achieved in his "Jupiter" symphony, and the second movement—a vast funeral March—has an overwhelmingly tragic emotional content. But the "Eroica" was followed by six equally great symphonies, each one as varied, as inventive, as unified as the others. The ninth symphony is significant both for its length and its finale. Here Beethoven crowns three superb instrumental movements with a choral movement that, as well as summing up all that has gone

before, expresses in music the joy in existence more ecstatically than any other work.

The burning intensity of Beethoven's genius is just as evident in his chamber music. His quartets are the product of a revolutionary age in which the social graces and formal restraint of the 18th cent. were thrown off in a search for a more personal mode of expression. The early op. 18 set, and the Razoumovsky quartets, op. 59, go even beyond the range of Haydn's and Mozart's works in the medium but it was in his late quartets, his final musical testament, that Beethoven refined and distilled his art for posterity. No words can possibly describe their unique quality, but any and every chance should be taken to make their acquaintance; the effort required will be more than amply rewarded.

The early piano concertos do not reach quite that level of attainment, but the last three, together with the violin concerto, are on a par with the finest of the symphonies and quartets, as well as being considerable tests of the performers' technique. The Triple Concerto for piano, violin, and cello is an unusual and rewarding work.

His Choral Work.

Beethoven's grandest choral work—and one of the most noble in existence—is the Mass in D (*Missa Solemnis*). Its vast scale and sublime utterance often defeat performers, but when it is successfully done there is no more spiritually uplifting experience for the listener, except perhaps Beethoven's only opera, *Fidelio*. This simple escape story was transformed by Beethoven's creative fire into a universal symbol of liberty, the composer identifying himself with the struggle for freedom from tyranny and release from darkness.

Beethoven lived in a period of war and revolution. A passionate believer in the brotherhood of man and in liberty, he was shocked to find his ideals thrown over by revolutionaries-turneddictators. His own tragedy of deafness, which came upon him at the moment of his triumph, nearly submerged him, but in the end he won through and produced the string of masterpieces from the "Eroica" onwards. Hope springing from despair, love from hatred, victory over defeat, these are the unquenchable legacies left by Beethoven.

The Romantic Movement.

Inevitably, the Romantic movement in literature that burst forth about 1800 was bound to have its counterpart in music. And so it was. Breaking the classical bonds, composers such as Schubert, Schumann, Liszt, and Berlioz sought a new freedom in musical expression. Form became of less importance than content; and that content often had literary connections. For their purposes a larger orchestra was needed and supplied, but the miniature, the song especially, because of its very personal connotation, was also a favourite form.

Schubert (1797-1828)—described by Liszt as "the most poetic of musicians"—is perhaps the greatest lyrical genius in musical history. In him the Viennese tradition and influence of Haydn, Mozart, and Beethoven reached its zenith. The song was always Schubert's starting point, so it is hardly surprising that his reputation as a song writer has never been impaired but in his symphonic and instrumental works too it is always his inexhaustible fund of melody that first calls for attention. Nobody could listen to his "Trout" quintet, for piano and strings, his octet, his fifth symphony, or his song cycle *Die Schöne Müllerin* without being enchanted and invigorated by the sheer tunefulness of the music. But there is much more to Schubert than this: his understanding of the possibilities of harmonic change, his grasp of orchestral coloration (in the great C major symphony, for instance), his free use of sonata structure.

Although Mozart, Haydn, and Beethoven had all contributed to the song as an art form, it was with Schubert that it achieved its first full flowering. If he had written nothing but his songs, his place in the musical firmament would be assured. With his *Erlkönig* in 1815 the German *Lied* came of age and from then until the end of his life he wrote more than six hundred songs, hardly a dud among them. Whether it is the charm of *Heiden-röslein*, the drama of *Der Doppelgänger* or the numbed intensity of the *Winterreise* cycle, Schubert unerringly went to the heart of a poet's meaning; indeed he often raised poor verses to an inspired level by his settings.

There is only room to mention one or two other composers, some of them wrongly neglected, who were roughly contemporaries of Beethoven and Schubert: the Czech Dussek (1760–1812), who like Beethoven bridges the classical–romantic gulf, Boccherini (1743–1805), the two Italian opera composers Cimarosa (1749–1801) and Paisiello (1740–1816), the Frenchman Méhul (1763–1817) and the German Hummel (1778–1837).

Weber (1786–1826) lacked Beethoven's energy and constructive powers and Schubert's sheer lyrical profundity, but he is an important figure, especially in the field of opera, where his *Der Freischütz* and *Oberon* led the way to a more flexible, dramatically realistic form of opera. His vivid imagination exactly fitted the new romantic mood abroad. The sheer beauty in the melodic shape of his music is undeniable. His instrumental works are attractive but insubstantial.

Mendelssohn.

Mendelssohn (1809–47) was the civilised craftsman among the Romantic composers. A boy genius—many of his finest works were written before he was twenty—he maintained the importance of classical form while imbuing it with his own affectionate brand of poetic sensibility. His third and fourth symphonies—the "Scottish" and "The Italian"—(and possibly the fifth "The Reformation"), his string quartets (some of which go deeper than the rest of his music), octet, violin concerto, first piano concerto, and of course, the incidental music to "A Midsummer Night's Dream" represent his tidy yet effervescent style at its most winning.

Schumann.

Schumann (1810–56) is less easy to categorise. His early romantic flame was burnt out by some flaw in his intellectual and/or emotional make-up, and his inspiration seems to have declined in later years. No matter, by then he had given us the marvellous song cycles of 1840, an ever fresh piano concerto, many fine piano solos, including the mercurial, popular *Carnaval* and four symphonies, which, if not structurally perfect, contain much lovely music. The joys and sorrows of love and the feeling for natural beauty are all perfectly mirrored in these charming, lyrical works, and in the genial piano quintet.

Romantic Giants: Berlioz and Liszt.

Berlioz (1803–69) and Liszt (1811–86) are the two most typical representative composers of the Romantic era. Both have always been controversial figures, with ardent advocates and opponents either unduly enthusiastic or unfairly derogatory. Berlioz might be termed the perfect painter in music. With an uncanny mastery of orchestral sound he could conjure up the countryside, the supernatural and the historical with the utmost ease. He based his music on the "direct reaction to feeling" and a desire to illustrate literature by musical means. That his technical expertise was not always the equal of his undoubted genius, can be heard in many of his larger works such as the dramatic cantata *The Damnation of Faust* and the dramatic symphony *Romeo and Juliet*, yet most people are willing to overlook the occasional vulgarity for the ineffable beauty of his many fine pages, but brutal cuts in his music, such as are often made in, for instance, his epic opera *The Trojans* only have the effect of reducing the stature of his works. We must accept him, warts and all. Anyone who has seen the two parts of *The Trojans*, presented complete in one evening

at Covent Garden, will realise that Berlioz knew what he was about.

His output is not quantitatively large but includes several monumental works, as well as *The Trojans*, The *Requiem* ("Grand Messe des Morts") requires a tenor solo, huge chorus and orchestra, and brass bands, although Berlioz uses these forces fastidiously. The *Symphonie funèbre et triomphale* calls in its original form, for choir brass, and strings. But Berlioz was just as happy writing on a smaller scale as his exquisite song cycle, to words of Théophile Gautier, *Nuits d'Eté*, shows. Gautier perhaps summed up better than anyone Berlioz's singular talent: "In that renaissance of the 1830s Berlioz represents the romantic musical idea, the breaking up of old moulds, the substitution of new forms for unvaried square rhythms, a complex and competent richness of orchestration, truth of local colour, unexpected effects in sound, tumultuous and Shakespearian depth of passion, amorous or melancholy dreaminess, longings and questionings of the soul, infinite and mysterious sentiments not to be rendered in words, and that something more than all which escapes language but may be divined in music."

During his lifetime Liszt was fêted and honoured not only by his musical colleagues but by the world at large, which idolised him and his piano. Then his reputation took a plunge from which it has only recently recovered. To be sure much of his early music is glitter and gloss, but his symphonies and tone poems—especially the Faust Symphony (both, of course, inspired by literature), and *Orpheus* and *Prometheus*—and his late piano works show that he was an extraordinary harmonic innovator. The piano sonata in B minor brings his romantic, wilful temperament within a reasonably stable, pianistic form, and as such is a landmark in the repertory of the instrument. Liszt's output was prodigious, but the inquiring listener should explore the more original of his compositions already mentioned to appreciate his fertile genius.

Chopin.

Chopin (1810–49) was the master of the keyboard, par excellence. His development of the technical and expressive capabilities of the piano is unique in musical history. His inventive powers were poured out with nervous passionate energy and in a highly individual style through twenty astonishing, possibly agonised years of creative activity before his early death. A Chopin melody, limpid, transparent, singing, can be recognised easily by anyone, but his style gradually developed into something more subtle, more satisfying than pure melody. He took the greatest care of every detail so that any alteration, however small, upsets the perfect balance of his work. His poetic sensibility can be found in any of his works; for his constructive ability we must turn to the Ballades, the B minor Sonata, and the Barcarolle, while the Preludes and Studies blend technical powers and emotional expressiveness in ideal proportions.

Nineteenth-Century Opera.

After Mozart's operas and Beethoven's *Fidelio* the medium might have been expected to decline. Instead it took on a new, if different, lease of life that culminated in Verdi's extraordinary output. Rossini (1792–1868) created a world of exuberant high spirits in his operatic works that are as cheerful and heart-warming today as they were when they were first performed.

He always worked in and around the lyric theatres of Italy and between 1810 and 1830 poured out a stream of works, not all of which can be expected to be masterpieces. However, *Il Barbiere di Siviglia*, *L'Italiana in Algieri*, *La Cenerentola* and *Le Comte Ory* will always delight audiences as long as opera houses exist. Although these works are difficult to sing really well, their vitality and charm can never be submerged even by poor voices or indifferent staging.

His German contemporaries were critical of his confidence and frivolity, but his works show a consistency of invention and an irresistible tunefulness that anyone might envy. In recent years, there has also been a renewed interest in his more serious operas—*Otello* (1816), *La Gazza Ladra* (1817), *Semiramide* (1823), *La Siège de Corinthe* (1820), and *Guillaume Tell* (1829)—which were certainly surpassed in dramatic power by his successors but which nevertheless are not to be despised or neglected.

William Tell, to give it its most popular title, was his last work for the stage although he lived on for nearly forty years in retirement in Paris, scene of many of his greatest successes. There he enjoyed good living, dispensing *bons mots*, and occasionally composing trifles. An exception is the unpretentious *Petite Messe Solennelle*, written originally for soloists, chorus, a harmonium, and two pianos. Rossini later orchestrated it, but he would not allow it to be performed during his lifetime. The first public performance was on 28 February 1869, as near as possible to the 78th anniversary of the composer's birth on Leap Year Day 1792.

Bellini and Donizetti.

In contrast to the mercurial Rossini, Vincenzo Bellini (1801–85) was an exquisite, romantic figure dealing with exquisite, romantic stories, an operatic equivalent to Chopin, who much admired him. His delicate, sinuous vocal line (in the arias) and brilliant acrobatics in the final sections (cabalettas) require singers of the utmost accomplishment to do them justice, although his music is never as florid as Rossini's. His most typical and popular works are probably *La Sonnambula* (1831), *Norma* (1831) and *I Puritani* (1835). The first is a tender, homely country story, the second an almost heroic lyrical drama of sacrifice, and the third a rather unsatisfactory historical story redeemed by its appealing music.

Gaetano Donizetti (1797–1848) was an even more prolific operatic composer than Rossini. He wrote at least 75 works, mostly for the Italian stage, several of which, such as *Alfredo il Grande* or *Emilia di Liverpool*, are never likely to be revived, but during the past few years, with the renewed interest in what are called the *Ottocento operas, many of his more serious work* resuscitated and found as enjoyable in performance as his more frequently heard comedies.

He was a well-grounded musician and although his invention is often criticised for being too tied to the conventions of his day performances often belie this reputation, his dramatic instinct proving sure. *Lucia di Lammermoor*, because of the chances it offers to a coloratura soprano with tragic pretensions, has always held the stage and of late, *Lucrezia Borgia*, *Anna Bolena*, *La Favorita*, and *Poliuto* have all been successfully revived. Of his lighter works, the comedies *L'Elixir d'Amore* and *Don Pasquale* have never declined in popularity. One of his last works was *Linda di Chamounix* (1842) which he wrote for Vienna where it aroused such enthusiasm that the Emperor appointed him Court Composer and Master of the Imperial Chapel.

French Opera.

The taste in Paris was for more and more lavish productions. Following Spontini (1774–1851), whose works were comparatively austere, came Halévy (1799–1862) and Giacomo Meyerbeer (1791–1864) whose operas contain all the ingredients that came to be expected of "Grand Opera"—spectacle, huge ensembles, showpieces for the soloists, and extended, if superfluous ballet. Drawing from Italian, German, and French traditions Meyerbeer's works contained everything the public wanted, yet today they are seldom revived, perhaps because his creative powers were essentially derivative, yet when they are given, operas like *Les Huguenots*, *Le Prophète*, and *L'Africaine* still have the power to fascinate and his influence on his successors, notably Wagner, was considerable.

Verdi.

Italian opera in the 19th cent. culminated in the works of Giuseppe Verdi (1813–1901), who rose from a peasant background to become his country's most noted composer, as well as something of a natural hero during the period of the Risorgimento. His earliest works, indeed, often roused his hearers to patriotic fervour. For instance, *Nabucco* (1841), with its theme of an oppressed people seeking deliverance, was treated as a symbol of the Italians' fight for freedom.

Musically, Verdi developed out of all recognition during the course of his long career. The continuously flowing structure of his last two operas *Otello* and *Falstaff* is very far removed from the start–stop formulas, inherited from his predecessors, of his first works, yet even they are touched, in harmonic subtleties, orchestral felicities, and a sense of drama, by a spark of genius, a burning inspiration that sets him apart from all other operatic composers. *Ernani* (1844), *I due Foscari* (1844), and *Luisa Miller* (1849) all have foretastes of glories to come even if as a whole they are flawed dramas, and these "galley years", as Verdi himself later described them, gave him the essential know-how to produce his later, greater operas, as well as establishing him incontrovertibly as the most popular Italian composer of the time.

Verdi's Masterpieces.

However, it was with *Rigoletto* (1851), *Il Trovatore* (1853), and *La Traviata* (1853) that Verdi first really staked his claim to immortality. In these pieces his increasing dramatic mastery is married to a wonderful flow of lyrical melody, at the same time controlled by a fine musical sensibility. They were followed by four operas—*Simon Boccanegra* (1857), *Un Ballo in Maschera* (1858), *La Forza del Destino* (1862), and *Macbeth* (revised version, 1865)—in which Verdi overcame complexities of story line by his continually developing musical powers. This period is crowned by *Don Carlos* (written for the Paris Opéra, 1867) a masterly exercise in combining private and public situations in a single, grand, and characterful work. In some respects Verdi never surpassed the subtlety of his writing in this opera. *Aida* (1871) carried on the process but the characterisation in this ever-popular piece is less refined than in *Don Carlos*, if the grandeur of the design is more spectacular.

The success of *Otello* (1887) owes nearly as much to the skill of Boito whose literary ability combined with musical knowledge (he was himself a composer) presented Verdi with an ideal libretto for his seamless music in which the drama moves inevitably to its tragic end. Recitative, aria, ensemble are fused in a single, swiftly moving music-drama, which in its very different way equals that of Wagner. *Falstaff* (1893) achieves the same success in the field of comic opera, a brilliant, mercurial ending to a distinguished career. If Verdi had written only these two final masterpieces his place in musical history would have been assured.

Brahms.

Brahms (1833–97) has justly been described as "a romantic spirit controlled by a classical intellect," for while complying with most of the formal regulations of sonata form he imbued them with an emotional content that accorded with his time. Indeed Schumann declared that he was the "one man who would be singled out to make articulate in an ideal way the highest expression of our time."

Perhaps in his chamber music will be found the quintessence of his art. The piano and clarinet quintets, the two string sextets, the horn trio, the violin sonatas all are designed on a large scale yet the expression remains intimate, the design and structure clear.

The symphonies and concertos, though, remain his most popular works; they are part of the solid repertory of every orchestra and most piano and violin players in the world. Their high seriousness, constant lyrical beauty, and control of form are deeply satisfying. They do not provide the extremes of passion and excitement provided by his contemporaries, but their study provides continuous absorption and delight. The double concerto for violin and cello deserves a mention as a unique work in music.

Brahms wrote more than two hundred songs in which the desire for melodic beauty takes precedence over the words and meaning. Many are set to poor poetry, but hidden away are still some unexplored treasures, and the Four Serious Songs, at least, are tragic masterpieces. In a lighter vein the two sets of *Liebeslieder Walzer* for four voices are irresistible. The choral Requiem, too, is a fine work.

Bruckner.

In recent years Bruckner's reputation *vis-à-vis* his great contemporary Brahms has been enhanced in England. The old conception of him as a naïve Austrian unable to grasp the fundamentals of symphonic architecture has died hard, and the prevailing popularity of his grandest works is at last gaining him his rightful place in the 19th-cent. firmament. The nine symphonies and the masses are his chief claim to immortality. They contain melodies of unforgettable beauty, symphonic paragraphs of unparalleled grandeur, and an appreciation of formal development that, though different, is equally as valid as that of Brahms. The movements of his symphonies are long and he often pauses, as if for breath and to admire the scenery, before he reaches the climactic peak of his musical journey. His idiom is best approached by a newcomer to his work through the fourth and seventh symphonies as they are perhaps the easiest to understand, but the fifth, sixth, eighth, and ninth (unfinished) are just as beautiful—and cogently argued—once one has acquired the knack, so to speak, of listening to his music. Most of these works are now to be heard in their original form, stripped of the veneer of "improvements" suggested to the diffident composer by his friends.

The masses, which translate Bruckner's symphonic ideas to the choral plain, and Bruckner's delightful string quintet are worth investigating.

Wagner.

Praised only this side of idolatry by his admirers, unmercifully criticised by his detractors, Richard Wagner (1813–83) is perhaps the most controversial composer in musical history. And so it was bound to be with such a revolutionary figure, whose writings, other than his music, contain, to say the least, dubious theories and whose operas, composed to his own libretti, broke the bonds of the form as known until his time. He regarded music-drama as a fusion of all the arts—music, literature, painting—in one unity. With *The Ring of the Nibelungs* he achieved his purpose; no other work of art has ever tried to encompass the whole of existence. Today, and surely forever, musicians, philosophers, and writers will argue over its meaning, and each age will reinterpret it according to its own lights.

But before he reached this pinnacle of achievement, Wagner gradually transformed opera—through *Rienzi*, *The Flying Dutchman*, *Tannhäuser*, and *Lohengrin*—so that a new mould was fashioned to take what he wanted to pour into it. He introduced the *Leitmotiv*, a musical theme that could be associated with a particular person, situation, or idea, each time it occurred. Slowly he developed the musical form so that the drama could unfold continuously without breaks for arias. By the time he began to write *Tristan and Isolde* and *Die Meistersinger*, he had perfected his methods and had he never undertaken *The Ring* that tragedy and that comedy would have assured him his place in the musical firmament. Indeed, *Die Meistersinger* is considered a masterpiece even by those who are not willing or prepared to accept the rest of the Wagnerian ethos.

The length and complexity of these operas, and of *Parsifal*, a work of unique beauty in spite of certain *longueurs*, means that it is almost essential to prepare oneself by homework, with libretti and records, before attempting to assimilate them in the opera house. The added effort is well worth while for the ultimate musical satisfaction they bring because Wagner was more than an operatic reformer; he opened up a new harmonic language (especially in the use of chromaticism) that was logically to develop into the atonality of the 20th cent.

Wolf.

As Wagner was the culmination of the 19th cent. symphonic and operatic tradition, so Hugo Wolf (1860–1903) summed up, if he did not surpass, the achievements in song-writing of Schubert, Schumann, and Loewe (1796–1869).
Wolf was a lonely, pathetic man. He lived much of his life in poverty, and eventually lost his reason and died of an incurable disease. These circumstances account perhaps for his almost feverish bursts of creative activity, which were also the outward sign of his burning genius. His greatest contributions to the art of *Lieder* were his extraordinary insight into the poet's meaning and the harmonic means by which he heightened the expression of the words. He raised the importance of the piano part even higher than had Schumann, and in some of his songs the vocal part takes the form of a free declamation over a repeated idea in the piano. However, in the main the vocal and piano parts are interweaved with great subtlety, and he unerringly matched the very varied moods of the poems he chose to set.

His greatest creative period was between early 1888 and early 1890 when songs poured from his pen daily—more than 50 settings of the German poet Mörike, 20 of Eichendorff, more than 50 of Goethe, and more than 40 of Heyse and Geibel (the Spanish Song-book). Later he composed songs from Heyse's Italian Song-book and the three Michelangelo sonnets. And the range of his creative understanding was wide, taking in the almost wild passion of the Spanish songs, the humanity and humour of the Italian love songs, the titanic power of *Prometheus* (Goethe), the varying moods of the Mörike book, and the intangible power of the Michelangelo sonnets. There are almost inexhaustible riches here for the inquiring mind to discover. Outside *Lieder*, Wolf's output is small, but it includes a sadly neglected opera, *Der Corregidor*, the Italian Serenade for string quartet (alternatively for small orchestra) and a tone poem *Penthesilea*.

National Movements.

During the course of the 19th cent., alongside the emergence of national political identity, came the rise of nationalism in music, fertilising traditional Western—that is basically German—musical forms with folk material. Of these groups the Russian is certainly the most important, if not the most vital.

Glinka.

Glinka (1804–57) was the first important Russian composer of the national school and, although his two operas *A Life for the Tsar* (sometimes called *Ivan Susanin*) and *Russlan and Ludmilla* are strongly influenced by Italian models, they do introduce Russian song and harmony into the texture. He undoubtedly influenced Borodin (1833–87), Cui (1835–1918), Balakirev (1837–1910), Mussorgsky (1839–81) and Rimsky-Korsakov (1844–1908)—the so-called "Five" of 19th-cent. Russian music. However, each was very much of an individualist too. Borodin was a lecturer in chemistry who wrote in his spare time. His two symphonies, two string quartets led up to his most notable work, the opera *Prince Igor*, left incomplete at his death. Balakirev, a friend and adviser to the rest of the group, wrote little himself, but his orchestral works and the piano fantasia, *Islamey*, are worthy of investigation.

Mussorgsky.

Modest Mussorgsky (1839–81) is today seen as the most important and inspired of "The Five." More than the others he used Russian song and Russian speech as the basis of his operas in which he portrayed the lives and destinies of his own people. Although his capacities were seriously impaired by an uncongenial job, poverty, and drinking, he produced two great operas, *Boris Godunov* and *Khovanshchina*, and another *Sorochintsy Fair* that is immensely enjoyable. *Boris* should be given in its original, with spare orchestration, but more often than not it is heard in Rimsky-Korsakov's more elaborate revision. In any case the opera exists in various versions, none of them necessarily the right one; what is important is to hear it in one or the other because of its great portrayal of Boris's personality set against the background of the Russian people, unforgettably presented in choral outbursts. *Khovanshchina* was completed by Rimsky-Korsakov, *Sorochintsy Fair* by Tcherepnin (although other versions also exist). Mussorgsky's songs explore a new vein of naturalistic vocal declamation. Each of the four *Songs and Dances of Death* is a miniature drama worthy of Wolf, although of course in a quite other idiom. The *Nursery* songs miraculously conjure up a child's world as seen from a child's point of view. Many of the individual songs, the *Sunless* cycle too, should be investigated.

Rimsky-Korsakov.

Rimsky-Korsakov (1844–1908) is perhaps a less attractive figure because so much of his music seems heartless or merely decorative, but this judgment is probably made on the strength of hearing *Shéhérazade* and the *Capriccio Espagnol* a few too many times. Such of his 15 operas as are played evince a (literally) fantastic mind and lyrical vein, and it is a pity that *Sadko*, *The Snow Maiden*, and *The Tsar's Bride*, at least, are not heard more often.

Tchaikovsky.

Peter Ilyich Tchaikovsky (1840–93) is a more universally admired figure than any of "The Five" and his music is indubitably closer to the mainstream than theirs in that it adheres more nearly to Western European forms. His popularity is due to his unhesitating appeal to the emotions and to his tender, often pathetic melodic expression. His lyrical gift is stronger than his sense of architecture, as he himself admitted. Yet his later symphonies—the fourth, fifth, and sixth (the *Pathétique*)—are all cogently enough argued and invigorating, as can be heard in the hands of a conductor willing to emphasise their formal power rather than their tendency towards sentimentality; the orchestral craftsmanship is also superb. The three piano concertos and the violin concerto offer rare opportunities for virtuoso display within a reasonably dramatic structure and his various overtures are always exciting to hear.

The three ballets—*The Sleeping Beauty*, *Swan Lake*, and *Nutcracker* show Tchaikovsky's skill on a smaller and perhaps more congenial scale, but only two of his operas—*Eugene Onegin* and *The Queen of Spades*—survive in regular performance. They demonstrate his ability to delineate character and his always eloquent melodic invention.

Smetana.

The Czech national school is dominated by two composers—Smetana (1824–84) and Dvořák (1841–1904). In his own country Smetana holds a unique position as the father of his country's music—which is remarkable when you consider that he lived in a country that was then under Austrian rule and never spoke the Czech language perfectly. Yet his music is filled with the spirit

of Czech history and national life, and many of his operas, his most important contribution, deal purely with national subjects. The reawakening of interest in things national, after Austria's defeat by Italy in 1859, led to the establishment of a Provisional Theatre in 1862 and Smetana's first opera *The Brandenburgers in Bohemia* was produced there in 1866, but its success was eclipsed by the enormous popularity of *The Bartered Bride*, which appeared the same year. Its melodic charm, lively characterisation and cosy humour have carried it round the world and it is the one Smetana opera to be in the repertory of most opera houses. However, his next opera *Dalibor* (1868) is considered by some authorities as his masterpiece. It is conceived on a heroic scale, and frequently rises to great dramatic heights. His later operas include *Libuše* (1872) a solemn festival tableau, *The Two Widows* (1874), a delightful comedy, *The Kiss* (1876), *The Secret* (1878), and *The Devil's Wall* (1882).

His main orchestral work *Má Vlast* (My Country), written between 1874 and 1879, is a cycle of six symphonic poems nobly depicting the life and legends of his country. He composed only three mature chamber works—an elegiac piano trio, written in 1855 in memory of the death of his eldest daughter, and two string quartets, both autobiographical. The first in E minor (1876)—"From My Life"—tells of his youth and aspirations until a terrible, screeching E in *altissimo* describes the onset of deafness; the second in D minor, sadly neglected, was described by the composer as an attempt to explain the "whirlwind of music in the head of one, who has lost his hearing," and was probably influenced by Beethoven's later music.

Dvořák.

Dvořák combined a fecund melodic gift with an intelligent grasp of structure. His symphonies and chamber music are mostly written in classical form, yet the works are imbued with a spontaneity and freshness that have not lost one whit of their charm over the years.

He wrote nine symphonies and, although only the last three or four are regularly performed, they are mostly mature works, several of which, for instance No. 7 in D minor (formerly known as No. 2) reach a tragic grandeur at times. They are all orchestrated in a masterly way and are full of delightful detail. Dvořák wanted to show that a Brahms could come out of Bohemia—and he succeeded in doing so while maintaining a definitely individual flavour, strongly influenced by natural rhythms.

He wrote three concertos, one each for piano, violin, and cello. The earlier ones are interesting without being quite in the first flight of the composer's output, but the cello concerto of 1895 is perhaps the composer's crowning achievement—warm, mellifluous, romantic.

He wrote chamber music throughout his long creative life. Some of the early works are weak and derivative, but the later string quartets, the "Dumky" trio, and the piano quartet and quintet are expressive and full of unforced invention. Dvořák felt himself somewhat hampered when setting words, nevertheless his *Stabat Mater* and *Te Deum* are both deeply felt choral works and he wrote songs throughout his career, many of them very fine indeed. He wrote ten operas, but only *Rusalka* (1901) is internationally known.

Janáček.

The Moravian composer Leos Janáček (1858–1928) spent most of his life in Brno as a working musician. His music has recently come to be recognised as some of the most original written in the past hundred years. His operas, in which he closely followed the inflection of the speech of his native land, are his finest works. Over the score of his last opera, *From the House of the Dead*, he wrote the words "In every human being there is a divine spark", and it is this deep love of humanity that permeates all his works. Of his operas *Kátya Kabanová* (1921) and *The Cunning Little Vixen* (1924), the *Makropoulos Affair* (1926), and *From the House of the Dead* (adapted from a Dostoyevsky novel, 1928) are the most important and they have all been produced in Britain in recent years. His original genius is self-evident in all of them.

Among his orchestral works *Taras Bulba* and *Sinfonietta* should be noted, and his two string quartets, very difficult to play, should be better known. The song cycle, *Diary of one who has disappeared*, for tenor, contralto, and three female voices with piano, and the Glagolithic Mass contain music of much expressive beauty.

Hungary: Bartók and Kodály.

The Hungarian musical outburst came somewhat later than that of other countries. Its great figure is Bela Bartók (1881–1945) who, as well as being a national figure, has proved an influential composer in the whole of 20th-cent. music. His mind was full of folk music, but it was transmuted by his strongly personal style and powerful intellect into something highly original. His music is tense and volatile but this restlessness is sometimes relieved by a kind of other-wordly, ethereal lyricism, as in the lovely slow movements of his quartets.

Bartók was affected as much by the musical innovations of Debussy and Stravinsky (*see below*) as by East European, notably Magyar, folk music. Many of his works are an attempt to meld the two.

The most important part of his output is undoubtedly his string quartets which cover most of his creative life. To this intimate form he confided his personal innermost thoughts and in it conducted his most far-reaching musical experiments, thereby extending its boundaries beyond anything previously known. As with Beethoven's late quartets many of Bartók's rely on organic or cyclic development while remaining just within the laws of classical form. As Mosco Carner puts it, "For profundity of thought, imaginative power, logic of structure, diversity of formal details, and enlargement of the technical scope, they stand unrivalled in the field of modern chamber music."

The most important of his orchestral works are the three piano concertos, of which the first two are harsh and uncompromising, and fiendishly difficult to play, while the third, written in 1945, is mellower and more diatonic. The second violin concerto (1937–8) shows the various elements of Bartók's style in full flower, by turns exuberant, passionate, and brilliant. The *Music for Strings, Percussion and Celesta* (1937) is remarkable for its strange sonorities and its fascinating texture. The *Concerto for Orchestra* (1944) is more immediately appealing and again shows the composer in complete command of a large canvas. Of the piano works *Mikrokosmos* (1935) and the sonata for two pianos and percussion (1937) are worth investigating.

His chief stage pieces are *The Miraculous Mandarin* (1919), a harsh, cruel ballet which drew appropriately dramatic music from the composer, and the opera *Duke Bluebeard's Castle* (1911), a luscious, original score that makes one regret that he wrote no more operas later in his career.

Kodály (1882–1967) was from early years closely associated with Bartók and with him collected Hungarian folk melodies using many of them in his music. He worked in many forms and the more important of his works are the *Peacock Variations* for orchestra, the choral *Psalmus Hungaricus* and *Te Deum*, The *Dances of Galánta*, and the opera *Háry János*, and the sonatas for cello and for unaccompanied cello.

Sibelius, Nielsen and Grieg.

Among Scandinavian composers the Finn Jean Sibelius (1865–1957) and the Dane Carl Nielsen

(1865–1931) are outstanding. Sibelius is a lone northern figure ploughing his own furrow oblivious or, at any rate, ignoring the unusual developments that were taking place in Central Europe, yet his seven symphonies are strong as granite, honest, rugged works that will undoubtedly stand the test of time. They are not by any means all similar in mood, or even form. The first is very much influenced by Tchaikovsky and Borodin, the second and third show a more personal style developing, the fourth is terse and tragic, the fifth lyrical, bright, and lucid; the sixth is perhaps most typically Sibelian in its evocation of primeval nature, and the seventh—in one continuous movement—is a more purely abstract piece, notable for its structural logic and the grandness of its themes. The violin concerto is the most easily understood of the composer's main works and has a grateful part for the soloist.

The tone poems *The Swan of Tuonela*, *Pohjola's Daughter*, *En Saga*, *Night Ride and Sunrise*, *The Bard*, and *Tapiola* uncannily evoke the icy words of the legends of the far north, and the primeval forces of nature. Sibelius's one string quartet *Voces Intimae* and many of his songs are worth hearing too. His music, reviled in some quarters during the 1950s, has since been restored to favour, and seems to be enjoyed again by critics and the general public alike.

Carl Nielsen (1865–1931) is another individualist. His six symphonies, like Sibelius's seven, are the most important part of his output, but whereas Sibelius was dealing with a huge, uninhabited northern landscape, Nielsen is more friendly and serene in his music, which is seldom forbidding, always inventive, throwing a new light, through unusual ideas about harmony, structure and tonality, on traditional forms. He also wrote highly individual concertos for the flute and clarinet, four string quartets and two operas—the dramatic, rather Brahmsian *Saul and David* (1902) and a delightful comedy, *Maskarade* (1906), full of lyrical music.

Edward Grieg (1843–1907), the Norwegian composer, was essentially a miniaturist whose range of feeling was not wide but whose music is always gentle and appealing. His most notable works are the romantic piano concerto, the atmospheric incidental music to Ibsen's play *Peer Gynt*, the charming Lyric Suite, and the small piano pieces

Elgar and the English Revival.

After the death of Purcell there is hardly a name in English music worth speaking of until the 19th cent. when Hubert Parry (1848–1918) and Charles Villiers Stanford (1852–1924), actually an Irish man, led a revival. Their music is seldom heard today, but their pioneer work paved the way for Edward Elgar (1857–1934). Although all were influenced by Brahms they nevertheless managed to establish a new English tradition that has been carried on in our own day. Elgar's symphonies are both laid out on a grand, leisurely scale and they are both eloquent and exhilarating. His violin concerto has an elegiac slow movement as has the glorious cello concerto and both contain many fine opportunities for the soloist. The cello concerto is as appealing a work as any by Elgar expressing his innermost thoughts. His *Enigma Variations* are a series of portraits in sound of his friends, but there is another overall theme to go with them that has never been identified. This has not prevented the work from becoming Elgar's most popular, not surprisingly when one considers its charm and melodiousness.

Three other orchestral pieces that should not be neglected are his symphonic study *Falstaff*, a many-sided musical picture of the Fat Knight, and the overtures *Cockaigne*, a happy evocation of London, and *In the South*, inspired by a visit to Italy. His three late chamber works, written when he was 61, are reticent, economic pieces that remove any misconception of Elgar as a bombastic composer. His songs are mostly feeble, but the oratorios, notably *The Dream of Gerontius*, show the composer's ability to control a large canvas.

French Music.

The Belgian César Franck (1822–90) was the main figure in mid-19th-cent. France. His influence spread even wider than his music of which only the D minor Symphony, the Symphonic Variations for piano and orchestra, the piano quintet, and the violin sonata are likely to be encountered today. The leading French opera composers of that time were Gounod (1818–93), Bizet (1838–75) and Massenet (1842–1912). Gounod's *Faust*, Bizet's *Carmen* (composed just before his untimely death when he caught cold after a swim) and Massenet's *Manon* all retain a deserved place in the repertory; each is a well-judged mini-drama unafraid of romantic ardour and forceful, histrionic strokes. Some of Massenet's other numerous operas, such as *Werther* and *Don Quichotte*, have enjoyed a revival in recent years.

Debussy.

Concurrently with similar movements in French painting and poetry came the French Impressionist composers at the end of the 19th cent. Their leader—and one of the great seminal forces of modern music—was Claude Debussy (1862–1918). His aim was to capture a mood or sensation, and he did that by more or less inventing a fresh system of harmony using a whole-tone scale, unusual chords, and by creating in the orchestra new, highly personal textures—there is no mistaking the Debussy idiom once you have heard at least one piece by him. His impressionistic style did not lead him, however, to abandon form as some have suggested, and his main works are just as closely organised as those by classical German composers. His music is sensuous and poetic yet nearly always structurally satisfying as well.

His reputation, at least with the general musical public, rests largely on his orchestral music, a few piano pieces and his only opera *Pelléas et Mélisande*. *La Mer* is a scintillating evocation of the sea in all its moods; *Nocturnes*, *Images*, and *Prélude à l'Après-midi d'un Faune* exactly suggest different places, times, moods—the "Iberia" and "Gigues" sections of *Images*, calling to mind respectively the spirit of Spain and the flickering light of a rainy English night. *Pelléas*, based on a Symbolist drama by Maeterlinck, tells a story of love, jealousy, and murder in predominantly restrained yet emotionally loaded terms. It is an elusive original work that has no predecessor or successor. Intensely atmospheric, rivetingly beautiful, it weaves an irresistible spell over the listener.

Debussy's chamber music is unjustly neglected. His string quartet (1893) was one of the first works in which he displayed his new and strange world of sound, and the three late sonatas, one for violin, one for cello, and the third for flute, viola, and harp are elliptical, compressed pieces which seem to be questing disjointedly into new regions of sound. His songs too, are worthy of investigation, and his piano music, especially the twenty-four Preludes and some of the shorter pieces, contain some of his most imaginative and original ideas and thoughts.

Gabriel Fauré (1845–1924) is a difficult figure to place. He lived through all kinds of musical revolutions yet they seemed to affect the character of his work very little. He has never been, and is never likely to be, a widely known or popular composer, yet his music has a reticence and delicacy that is very appealing. Despite his dreamy, retiring art he was not a recluse, but a very sociable man.

He was content with forms as he found them, but he imbued them with a very personal, human style. Perhaps his art is best heard in his songs. They are not overtly passionate or dramatic but the long, sinuous melodies and subtle harmonies are exquisitely wrought. Of the song-cycles, *La Bonne Chanson*, *Cinq Mélodies*, *Le Chanson d'Eve*, and *L'Horizon Chimérique* are best known. The last written in 1922, when the composer was seventy-seven, is a beautiful setting of words by a soldier killed in the first World War. There are also many remarkable single songs, many of them settings of poems by Verlaine. His opera *Pénélope*, based on the classical heroine, is unjustly neglected.

He wrote few orchestral pieces, but the *Ballade* for piano and orchestra and the *Pavane* are among his most typical, and delicate compositions, and his outstanding piano music, modelled on Chopin's, includes Nocturnes, Impromptus, and Barcarolles. His chamber music covers more than half a century from the violin sonata of 1876 to the string quartet written the year he died. In that period he composed two piano quartets, two piano quintets, another violin sonata and two cello sonatas, the later works failing to show quite the unforced lyrical grace of the earlier ones. Perhaps Fauré is best approached with the first piano quartet, a charming, easily assimilated work, and the beautiful choral *Requiem*.

Saint-Saëns (1835–1921), an accomplished, cultivated musician, has had a "bad press" but his craftsmanship, as displayed in his symphonies, concertos, and *Samson et Dalila* (one among his 12 operas) is not to be despised.

Henri Duparc (1844–1933), despite a very long life, is known today only for a group of songs he wrote before he was forty. They are among the most emotionally direct yet tasteful melodies ever written. Paul Dukas (1865–1935) is another figure off the beaten track, as it were. He, too, is known only for a handful of compositions. He was strongly influenced by Vincent d'Indy (1851–1931) and the school who strongly opposed Debussy's new ideas, yet he could not help but come under Debussy's spell. Dukas's one great work is his opera *Ariane et Barbe-Bleue*, the text adapted from a Maeterlinck play written with the composer in mind.

Maurice Ravel (1875–1937), a pupil of Fauré, followed in Debussy's footsteps, although his later pieces were more ascetic. Indeed, he was one of the most fastidious of composers, always seeking, and often finding, artistic perfection. The works he wrote before 1918 are definitely of the Impressionist School and it would be difficult to imagine more beautiful sounds than are to be found in the ballet *Daphnis et Chloé*, in the song-cycle *Shéhérazade*, and the piano fantasy *Gaspard de la Nuit*. His first style was summed up in the A minor piano trio (1915). In his later music Ravel was struggling, not always successfully, to keep up with new developments such as jazz and atonality. The piano concerto, for instance, shows very strongly the influence of jazz.

Outstanding orchestral works of his, other than *Daphnis* are *Rapsodie espagnole* (1907), *La Valse* (1920), a sumptuous evocation of the Vienna waltz, and the ever-popular *Boléro*. Two chamber works, besides the trio, are masterpieces—the string quartet (1902–3) and the Introduction and Allegro for Harp, String Quartet, Flute, and Clarinet. This Septet composed in 1906, ravishes the senses with magical sound.

Ravel's piano pieces are perhaps his most notable contribution to music, combining an extraordinary feeling for the instrument's technical possibilities with the sensibility of a Chopin, and in this field *Jeux d'eau*, *Miroirs*, and *Ma Mère l'Oye*, all written just after the turn of the century, come very close to the perfection of *Gaspard de la Nuit*. His songs show his unusual appreciation of the need to fuse poetic and musical values, and he set exotic poems for preference. His output in this field includes the cycle *Histoires naturelles* (1906), acutely observed settings of five poems about birds and animals; *Cinq Mélodies populaires grecques* (1907), charming settings of Greek folk songs; *Trois Poèmes de Mallarmé* (1913); and *Chansons madécasses* (1926), suitably exotic settings of three poems by an 18th-cent. Creole poet called Parny. Finally in 1932 came *Don Quichotte à Dulcinée*, three poems by Paul Morand, Ravel's last composition.

Ravel wrote two operas—the slight but moderately amusing *L'Heure espagnole* (1907), nicely orchestrated in a faintly and appropriately Spanish style and *L'Enfant et les Sortilèges* (1925) to a story by Colette, a delicious fantasy about a naughty child who gets his due punishment for tormenting animals and destroying furniture.

French music after Debussy and Ravel was dominated by the slighter composers known as *Les Six*, the most important of whom were Arthur Honegger (1892–1955, Swiss born), Darius Milhaud (1892–1974) and Francis Poulenc (1890–1963). Each has contributed music of some wit and charm to the repertory. They were influenced by Erik Satie (1866–1925), an eccentric but interesting figure who wrote works with odd titles such as *Three Pear Shaped Pieces*. His music is entirely unsentimental, often ironic.

Spain.

Felipe Pedrell (1841–1922) has been aptly described as the midwife of Spanish nationalist music. As a musicologist and teacher he strongly influenced the two main composers of the school, Manuel de Falla (1876–1946) and Enrique Granados (1867–1916). Falla's output was not large and most of it was written around the years of the first world war. The pre-war years were spent in Paris where Falla came under the influence of Debussy. However his style is individual and evokes all the passion and gaiety of his native land. Perhaps his most typical works are in two ballets *Love the Magician* (1915) and *The Three-Cornered Hat* (1919). The opera *La Vida Breve* (1905) despite its weak libretto also has much appeal. The vivacity and smouldering passion at the heart of the country's character is conjured up by the *Seven Popular Songs* (1914) and the *Nights in the Gardens of Spain* (1916) for piano and orchestra. His later works, especially the harpsichord concerto of 1926, show Falla tending towards a less ebullient, more restrained style. The second opera, *Master Peter's Puppet Show* (1923) is a miniaturist work, refined and intense. His third opera *Atlantida*, left unfinished at his death, was completed by his pupil Ernesto Halffter and first staged in 1962.

Granados was perhaps a more restrictedly Spanish composer than Falla, but his music is unfailingly attractive and deserves to be better known. The opera *Goyescas* (1916) is most famous for the second interlude and opening of Act III—*La Maja y el Ruiseñor* (The Lover and the Nightingale), a haunting, sinuous melody for soprano, generally heard in its original form as a piano solo.

The chief claim to fame of Albéniz (1860–1909) is *Iberia*, masterly descriptive pieces for piano. Many of his other piano works are now more well known in the form of very effective guitar arrangements.

Turina (1882–1949), attempted a more cosmopolitan style, but his most often heard music is typically Spanish.

The Late German Romantics.

While composers such as Debussy, Sibelius, Stravinsky and Schoenberg (see below for the latter pair) were striking out along new paths, Richard Strauss (1864–1949) continued in the trend of 19th-cent. German composers; he was the tradition's last great figure. At least two of his operas—*Salome* and *Elektra*—were considered shocking at the time, but today we can hear that they are essentially big-scale, romantic works—natural successors to Wagner's—however startling the harmonies may once have seemed.

If Strauss did not achieve the granite intellectual greatness of Beethoven or Wagner, there is no denying his melodic genius and powers of fertile invention which overlaid the streak of vulgarity and inflation in his musical make-up. His first outstanding achievement was in the field of the symphonic poem, where he carried the work of composers such as Liszt and Berlioz to its logical conclusion. Starting with *Don Juan* in 1888 and ending with *Sinfonia Domestica* in 1903 he wrote a series of kaleidoscopic works, full of enormous vitality, endless melody, and fascinating orchestration. The most easily assimilated—and the most popular—are *Don Juan* and *Till Eulenspiegel* but some of the longer works, notably *Also Sprach Zarathustra* (based on Nietzsche's

prose poem) and *Don Quixote* (based, of course, on Cervantes's great work) will reward the persistent, inquiring mind with long hours of enthralled listening. Other works sound somewhat dated in their bombastic over-confidence, though Strauss's skill in composition seldom flagged at this stage of his long creative career. The symphonic poems all tell something of a story usually based on a literary source, but it is not essential to the enjoyment of the music to know what this is, although it may be helpful.

The Reputation of Strauss.

Strauss's reputation is even more solidly based on his fifteen operas, the earliest of which *Guntram* was first performed in 1894, the last, *Capriccio*, in 1942. During these years the essentials of Strauss's style changed little, though it became very much more refined as the years passed. His first operatic period ended with the violent, sensual tragedies *Salome* (1905) and *Elektra* (1909), the latter being his first collaboration with his chief librettist, Hugo von Hofmannsthal. Then came their unique *Der Rosenkavalier* (1911), which filters the charm and the decadence of 18th-cent. Vienna through early 20th-cent. eyes. This was followed by *Ariadne auf Naxos* (1912). Originally intended to be given after Molière's *Le Bourgeois Gentilhomme*, it was later presented (1916) without the play but with an amusing Prologue, written by von Hofmannsthal. *Die Frau ohne Schatten* is the most grandiose result of the Strauss-Hofmannsthal partnership. It is a complex psychological allegory, but Strauss's contribution is not on as consistently lofty a level as is his librettist's. *Intermezzo* (1924), which has a libretto by Strauss himself, is a largely autobiographical domestic comedy, which has lately gained in reputation as a compact, charming piece. With *Die Aegyptische Helena* (1928), an opera on a mythical theme, and *Arabella* (1933), another sensuous Viennese comedy, the Strauss-Hofmannsthal collaboration ended on account of the librettist's death. Strauss then wrote *Die Schweigsame Frau* (1935) to a libretto by Stefan Zweig, based on a play by Ben Jonson, and *Friedenstag* (1938), *Daphne* (1938)—a beautiful opera—and *Die Liebe der Danae* (written 1938–40) with Josef Gregor as librettist. His swan-song was *Capriccio*, a dramatisation of the old argument about the relative importance of words and music in opera. The libretto is by the conductor Clemens Krauss and the opera, a serene, melodious work, was a fit end to a great operatic career.

However, Strauss went on composing till nearly the end of his life, adding a group of late orchestral pieces to his already large catalogue of works. The *Metamorphosen* for 23 solo string instruments, is probably the best of these. During his long creative career he wrote numerous songs, many of them, such as *Morgen, Wiegenlied* and *Ruhe, meine Seele* of surpassing beauty.

Other notable figures in German music at this time were Max Reger (1873–1916), a somewhat ponderous but highly accomplished composer who, in a quarter of a century of creative life, wrote more than 150 works, of which his sets of variations, his piano concerto, and chamber music are probably the most impressive. Hans Pfitzner (1869–1949), another German traditionalist, is chiefly remembered today for his opera *Palestrina*, about events, now known to be spurious, in the life of the 16th-cent. Italian composer.

Gustav Mahler.

Gustav Mahler (1860–1911), the Austrian Jewish composer, is one of the most important figures in 20th-cent. music. In a sense he bridges the gulf between the late Romantics, who were tending more and more towards chromaticism and away from established key relationships, and the atonalists, who abandoned the key system entirely. His detractors maintain that his inflation of allegedly banal Viennese beer-house music to unheard-of lengths rules him out of court as a serious writer. His admirers would claim that his music encompasses the whole of life in enormous, valid structures. The truth, if truth there be, perhaps lies somewhere in between: if his material does not always justify the length of his symphonies, and if there are occasional imperfections and *longueurs*, these shortcomings are worth enduring for the sake of the depth of utterance, the humanity and the poetry of the great pages.

His music is undoubtedly best approached through his songs, where the words force him to discipline his wide-ranging vision. *Lieder eines fahrenden Gesellen* (1884), to his own words, *Kindertotenlieder* (1901 4), to poems by Rückert, and some individual songs perfectly relate words to music, and are all of a poignant loveliness. Similarly *Das Lied von der Erde* (1908), especially the last of the six songs, is a touching farewell to the world, nobly expressed.

Mahler's Symphonies.

The ten symphonies, however, are Mahler's most impressive legacy to posterity. They are almost impossible to characterise briefly so vast are they in terms of both length and variety. The first, fourth and ninth are probably the easiest to grasp but the fifth, sixth and seventh, despite flaws, contain some of his most awe-inspiring conceptions. The second and third, both of which use soloists and chorus, are revolutionary in orchestration and structure; they both try, inevitably without complete success, to carry out the composer's dictum, "a symphony should be like the world—it must contain everything." The eighth is even more gargantuan, but as in all Mahler's work size does not mean loss of clarity or an overloading of the structure. Part one—a mighty choral invocation—is a visionary setting of the mediaeval hymn *Veni Creator Spiritus*. Part two, which incorporates adagio, scherzo, and finale in one, is a setting of the final scene of Goethe's *Faust*. Until recently all of Mahler's unfinished tenth symphony that was ever performed was the Adagio, but the musicologist and Mahler scholar, the late Deryck Cooke, provided a performing version of the symphony to critical and popular acclaim during the 1960s and thus added a noble, and also optimistic epilogue to the Mahler opus. The debate over the quality of Mahler's music is likely to continue; one fact, however, that cannot be gain-said is his popularity with an ever-increasing audience, largely made up of young people. There must be something in his uncertainty and intense self-inquiry that appeals.

Schoenberg and the Second Viennese School.

Arnold Schoenberg (1874–1951) revolutionised Western music by his twelve-note method—a system which uses all the notes of the chromatic scale "and denies the supremacy of a tonal centre," as Schoenberg himself puts it. This serial technique of composition, as it is commonly called, naturally sounds strange to an ear acclimatised to music written, as it were, with a home base, but Schoenberg and his disciples Berg and Webern showed that the system could produce works that were something more than mere intellectual exercises. None of the recent advances in music would have been possible without Schoenberg.

Schoenberg always considered himself as much as a composer as a theorist or teacher, and his works are supposed to appeal as much to the emotions as to the intellect, although to be understood they do, of course, require the listener's concentrated attention. To appreciate how his ideas developed it is necessary to hear first his pre-atonal music, such as the *Gurrelieder* (1900–1) and *Verklärte Nacht* (1899), in which he carried Wagnerian chromaticism to extreme lengths. The *Gurrelieder*, in particular, is a luxuriant, overblown work that shows the Wagnerian idiom in an advanced stage of decay, in spite of many beautiful pages of music. In his succeeding works the feeling of tonality began to disappear until in the Three Piano Pieces (opus 11), of 1909, he finally rejected tonality, although the new 12-note scheme is not yet evident; traces of the old order can still be heard. The succeeding works were mostly short, highly compressed, and very expressive. Schoenberg was reaching out for a new system, which would "justify the dissonant character of

these harmonies and determine their successions." By 1923 he had formulated his 12-note system and the Five Piano Pieces (opus 23), and the Serenade (opus 24) of that year, can thus be considered the first works that used a note-row as the fundamental basis of their composition. Between 1910 and 1915, however, the Russian composer Alexander Skryabin (1872–1915) had attempted to define a new method of composition of his own employing the "mystic chord" of ascending fourths, but his scheme proved comparatively abortive when compared with Schoenberg's. Josef Hauer (1883–1959) also developed a 12-note system which he propounded in 1919 and he always considered himself, rather than Schoenberg, as the true founder of the system. He later worked out a system of tropes (*i.e.*, half-series of six notes).

Schoenberg's Later Work.

To return to Schoenberg, in later works he shows much more freedom and assurance in the use of his system. The wind quintet (1924), the Variations for Orchestra, opus 31 (1927–8), the third (1926), and fourth (1936) string quartets, and the string trio (1946) are modern classics of their kind; they require concentrated listening and a degree of understanding of the unfamiliar style of composition. The set of songs with piano *Das Buch der hängenden Gärten* (opus 15), written in 1908, *Pierrot Lunaire*, opus 21 (1912) and the Four Songs, opus 22 (1913–14) provide a kind of bridge between tonality and atonality that the adventurous mind should cross. The monodrama *Erwartung* (1909) is another fascinating work, but perhaps the unfinished *Moses and Aaron* (1932) is Schoenberg's masterpiece as its production at Covent Garden in 1965 showed. Here, for certain, the composer matched his obvious intellectual capacities with an evident emotional content and managed to combine *Sprechgesang* (speech-song) and singing with a real degree of success.

It is only in recent years that Schoenberg's music has had a real chance to make its mark through the essential prerequisite of frequent performance. If his idiom now seems approachable, and a reasonably natural outcome of late 19th-cent. developments, it is perhaps because other, more recent composers have extended the boundaries of sound much further.

Disciples of Schoenberg.

Schoenberg's two most respected disciples were Anton Webern (1883–1945) and Alban Berg (1885–1935). Webern's output is small, reaching only to opus 31, and many of his works are very brief. They are exquisitely precise, and delicate almost to a fault. He was trying to distil the essence of each note and in so doing carried the 12-note system to its most extreme and cerebral limit. His music has often been described as pointillist in the sense that one note is entirely separated from the next, there being little discernible melody. Beyond Webern's music, there is indeed the sound of nothingness, and he was rightly described during his lifetime as the "composer of the *pianissimo espressivo*". In his later works, Webern tended towards a strict, and often ingenious use of form and the Variations for Orchestra of 1940 are a good example of this and of his delicacy of orchestration. Webern's influence has perhaps been greater than the impact of his own music, even though he has had no direct successor.

Berg's music is much more accessible. Like Webern his total output was not large, but nearly all his works are substantial additions to the repertory. He is also the directest link between Mahler and the second Viennese School, as Mahler's music influenced him strongly. He studied with Schoenberg from 1904 to 1910. His music is more intense, more lyrical, and less attenuated in sound than Schoenberg's or Webern's. His humanity and abiding compassion can be heard most strongly in his finest opera *Wozzeck* (1925) and his violin concerto (1935), written as an elegy on the death of Manon Gropius, a beautiful 18-year-old girl. Both works are very carefully designed yet formal considerations are never allowed to submerge feeling, and the note-row is fully integrated into the structure.

Both *Wozzeck* and the unfinished but rewarding *Lulu* are concerned with society's outcasts who are treated with great tenderness in both operas. The later work is entirely dodecaphonic, all the opera's episodes being based on a theme associated with Lulu. Between these operas Berg wrote the highly complex Chamber Concerto for piano, violin, and thirteen wind instruments (1925) and the expressive Lyric Suite (1926). Among his other works the Seven Early Songs (1908–9) and the concert aria *Der Wein* (1929) are notable.

Stravinsky.

Igor Stravinsky (1882–1971) was another vital figure in 20th-cent. music. If his influence has been in quite another and perhaps less drastic direction than Schoenberg's it is hardly less important. Indeed, future musical historians may consider his achievement the more significant. He has been compared with the painter Picasso in his almost hectic desire to keep up with the times, yet, although he wrote in a number of very different styles over a period of fifty years, every work of his is stamped with his own definitive musical personality. His most revolutionary and seminal work is undoubtedly *The Rite of Spring* (written for the ballet impresario Diaghilev), which caused a furore when it first appeared in 1913, and although it no longer shocks, the rhythmical energy, the fierce angular thematic material, and the sheer virtuosity of the orchestration will always have the power to excite new audiences. Before *The Rite* Stravinsky had written two ballets for Diaghilev—*The Firebird* and *Petrushka*—that are no less filled with vitality and new, albeit not so violent, sounds. During the next thirty years Stravinsky wrote a series of ballet works, gradually becoming more austere and refined in composition. *Apollo* (1928) and *Orpheus* (1947) belong among his best scores.

The Versatility of Stravinsky.

Stravinsky did not confine himself in stage works to the ballet. *The Nightingale* (1914) is a charming, early opera; *The Soldiers Tale* (1918) is a witty combination of narration, mime, and dance; *Les Noces* (1923) is a concise, original choreographic cantata for soloists and chorus; *Oedipus Rex* (1927) is a dignified version of the Sophocles play, which can be staged or given on the concert-platform; either way it is a moving experience. *Perséphone* (1934), a melodrama for reciter, tenor, chorus, and orchestra is an appealling, lucid score. After the war his most important stage work by far was *The Rake's Progress* (1951), with a libretto by W. H. Auden and Chester Kallman. This fascinating opera is deliberately based on 18th-cent. forms and the music itself is neo-classical, always attractive, often haunting.

Stravinsky was no laggard in writing for the concert-platform either. The finest of his orchestral pieces are probably the fervent choral *Symphony of Psalms* (1930), the violin concerto (1931) and the aggressive compact Symphony in Three Movements (1945). Of his chamber music the octet (1923), a duo concertant (1932), and septet (1952) are probably the most important, but no piece, even the dryest and most pedantic, is without redeeming features.

Stravinsky is often thought of as an aloof, detached figure. He has been castigated for his lack of lyrical warmth. But in spite of his own professed desire to drain his music of specific emotion, craftsmanship and originality, often with a strange other-worldly beauty added, are unmistakably there throughout his many scores.

Busoni.

Italian music in the early part of the century was dominated by two very different composers—Ferruccio Busoni (1866–1924) and Giacomo Puccini (1858–1924). Busoni is a difficult figure to place. His austere, intellectual power is never called in question, but he seldom, if ever, succeeded in translating his technical prowess into altogether successful compositions. We can admire the strength, honesty, and often beauty of such works as his huge piano concerto (1903–4), *Fantasia Contrappuntistica* (1912)—for piano solo—and his unfinished opera *Doktor Faust* without ever capitulating to them entirely. None the less, it has to be admitted that those who have studied his music closely have always fallen completely under his spell. In style his music is anti-Romantic and often neo-Classical yet he was an ardent admirer of Liszt and more especially of Liszt's realisation of the possibilities of the pianoforte. Busoni, himself a great pianist, carried on where Liszt had left off in his own piano music, in which form and expression often find their perfect balance. *Doktor Faust* is undoubtedly his most important opera but *Die Brautwahl* (1908–10) and *Turandot* (1917) have many points of interest too.

Puccini.

Puccini's *Turandot*—his last opera—is a much grander version of the same Gozzi fable and the culmination of this great opera composer's work. His achievement is at an almost directly opposite pole to Busoni's. Not for him the severity or intellectuality of his contemporary. He sought and found an almost ideal fusion of straight-forward lyricism and dramatic truth. His music unerringly follows the pathos and passion of the stories he sets and all his characters "live" as human beings. That, and his abundant flow of easy, soaring melody, are the reasons for his immense popular success, unequalled by any other 20th-cent. composer. Whether it is the pathetic Mimi (*La Bohème*—1896) and Cio-Cio-San, (*Madam Butterfly*—1904), the evil Scarpia (*Tosca* —1900), the cunning Schicchi (*Gianni Schicchi*— 1918), the ardent Rodolfo (*La Bohème*) and Cavaradossi (*Tosca*), or the ice-cold Turandot (*Turandot*—1926). Puccini's musical characterisation is unfailing. And he backs his *verismo* vocal writing with an orchestral tissue that faithfully reflects the milieu of each opera, for instance, Japanese for *Butterfly*, Chinese for *Turandot*, while never losing his particular brand of Italian warmth. His orchestration is always subtle and luminous.

Other Italian composers who wrote operas in the *versimo* style of Puccini were Leoncavallo (1858–1919), Mascagni (1865–1945), and Giordano (1867–1948). Mascagni's *Cavalleria Rusticana* and Leoncavallo's *Pagliacci* are both widely performed.

Prokofiev, Shostakovich, and Rachmaninov.

Sergey Prokofiev (1891–1953) spent part of his creative life in his native Russia, part of it (1918–34) abroad, mostly in Paris. His early music, apart from the popular Classical Symphony (1916–17) tended to be acid and harsh, but on his return to Russia his style, though still frequently satirical, became warmer, more Romantic. The third piano concerto (1917) and the second symphony (1924) are good examples of the former period, the ballets *Romeo and Juliet* (1935) and *Cinderella* (1941–4) and the fifth (1944) and sixth (1946) symphonies of the latter. His music gives the impression of immense rhythmical energy, as in the outer movements of several of his nine piano sonatas, but this fierce drive is often leavened by the soft, wistful lights of his slow movements. His second string quartet (1941), perhaps, presents all the elements of his music in the kindest light.

His strong leaning towards fantasy and mordant parody is felt in his earlier operas *The Love of the Three Oranges* (1921) and *The Fiery Angel* (1922–5). Towards the end of his life much of Prokofiev's music fell into official disfavour.

Dmitri Shostakovich (1906–75) also suffered from attacks on his style. He had to conform to Stalin's requirements for writing music, but he survived and continued to produce music of universal significance, for example, his later string quartets. Like Prokofiev, his music falls into two very distinct styles: one humorous and spiky, the other intense, very personal and often large-scale in its implications. Not all his symphonies reach the expressive depths of numbers one, five, six, eight, ten and fourteen, but they all have rewarding passages, and his violin and cello concertos are of high quality. He also wrote fifteen string quartets, a piano quintet (an attractive piece) and two operas: the satirical *The Nose* (1930) and *Katrina Ismailova* (1934, revised 1959), originally known as "Lady Macbeth of Mtsensk."

Although Sergey Rachmaninov (1873–1943) was born in Russia, he left his home country in 1918, disliking the Soviet régime, and lived mostly in Switzerland and the United States. His music is chiefly notable for its Romanticism, nostalgic melody, nervous energy and, in the piano works, its opportunities for displays of virtuosity. The first three piano concertos, the third symphony, the piano preludes, and the Rhapsody on a theme of Paganini, are his most typical and attractive works, and many of his songs are touching and beautiful. He wrote three operas.

Weill and Hindemith.

Kurt Weill (1900–50) is chiefly known for his sociopolitically pointed operas, such as *Die Dreigroschenoper* (1929), *Mahagonny* (1929), *Der Jasager* (1930) and *Happy End* (1929), all effective works on the stage, and for his particular brand of brittle, yet fundamentally romantic music. His influence on later composers has been considerable.

Paul Hindemith (1895–1963) in his later years wrote in a strictly tonal, often neo-classical idiom, after being one of the most advanced intellectuals of his time. As well as many chamber and orchestral works, he wrote three formidable operas: *Die Harmonie der Welt*, *Cardillac* and *Mathis der Maler*.

Ives and Copland.

Charles Ives (1874–1954) is generally recognised as the first American composer of major stature. Most of his works were composed before about 1920, while he was pursuing a successful career in insurance. Ives' music is noted for its thorough-going electicism and his refusal to be bound by rules and conventions. His work anticipates many 20th century techniques, such as polytonality and polyrhythm, which he seems to have arrived at independently of others. Folk song, hymn tunes, dance music and the sound of the brass band all appear in his compositions, many of which are evocative of his New England background (*e.g. Three Places in New England*, the *Holidays Symphony*, the *Concord* Sonata). It was not until the 1930s that Ives began to achieve recognition, but his influence on later American composers can hardly be exaggerated.

Aaron Copland (1900–90) was a composer who had absorbed a variety of influences—from his Jewish background, contemporary Europe, American folk music and jazz, Latin American music— while writing music which is instantly recognisable as his own in its clean textures and taut rhythms. Early works such as the Piano Concerto (1927) show the use of jazz styles, while the Piano Variations (1930) combine inventiveness and technical discipline in a tough, concentrated and highly dissonant piece. A move towards a simpler, more immediately appealing idiom is evident in pieces like *El Salón México* (1936), and the ballets *Billy the Kid* (1938), *Rodeo* (1938) and *Appalachian Spring* (1944) and the Third Symphony (1946). These works remain Copland's most popular and frequently performed pieces. A number of works from the 1950s and 1960s experiment with serial techniques, while retaining his individual voice.

Vaughan Williams, Holst and Delius.

The twentieth century revival of music in England owes much to Ralph Vaughan Williams (1872–1958) and Gustav Holst (1874–1934). The English folk song revival, associated with Cecil Sharp, was in full swing during their formative years, and both composers produced arrangements of folk songs as well as assimilating the folk idiom into their own styles. The influence of 16th century polyphony is also strong in Vaughan Williams' music, the most obvious example being the *Fantasia on a Theme by Thomas Tallis* (1909). Vaughan Williams' strongest works (*e.g.* the first, fourth, fifth and sixth symphonies, the ballet *Job*, the choral *Dona Nobis*

Pacem) show his characteristic alternation of the forceful and the contemplative.

Holst was a more enigmatic figure. Only his suite *The Planets* and the choral work *The Hymn of Jesus* have established themselves in the regular repertory, but his bold harmonic experiments and the austerity, even mysticism, of his style as heard in the opera *Savitri* and the orchestral piece *Egdon Heath* are perhaps more typical of this composer.

Frederick Delius (1862–1934) was the major English composer to fall under the sway of French impressionism, though his English (north country) background, his friendship with Grieg, and the time he spent in America all contributed to the formation of his musical style. He lived in France from 1888 onwards. His most important works are the atmospheric tone-poems for orchestra, such as *Brigg Fair*, the vocal and orchestral *A Mass of Life*, *Sea Drift* and *Appalachia*, and the opera *A Village Romeo and Juliet*.

Sir William Walton.

Sir William Walton (1902–83) became known as an *enfant terrible* with the witty and irreverent *Facade* (1923) for speaker and chamber orchestra (with words by Edith Sitwell). The poetic Viola Concerto (1929) shows another side of his musical character. His First Symphony (1934–5) is an arresting, dramatic score and the colourful oratorio *Belshazzar's Feast* (1931) is a landmark in choral music. Walton's rhythms show the influence of jazz and of Stravinsky but he is generally felt to be a quintessentially English composer. An Elgarian element is clear in such occasional pieces as the coronation marches *Crown Imperial* (1937) and *Orb and Sceptre* (1953).

Benjamin Britten.

Benjamin Britten (1913–76) did as much as anyone to establish English music on the forefront of the international stage. Much of his music seems to have an immediate appeal to large audiences and certainly his many stage works earned him quite exceptional prestige both at home and abroad. *Peter Grimes* (1945), *Billy Budd* (1951), *Gloriana* (1953), *A Midsummer Night's Dream* (1960) all show his mastery of stage technique and the first two are also moving human documents. On a smaller scale he has achieved as much with his chamber operas—*The Rape of Lucretia* (1946), *Albert Herring* (1947), *The Turn of the Screw* (1954)—and the three Parables for Church Performance—*Curlew River* (1964), *The Burning Fiery Furnace* (1966) and *The Prodigal Son* (1968). His operatic output was crowned by *Death in Venice* (1973). If he had written nothing else, these dramatic works would have marked him out as a composer of outstanding imaginative gifts. In addition to these, however, the choral works culminating in the *War Requiem* (1962), the various song cycles written, like so much else, for his friend Peter Pears, the *Serenade* for tenor, horn and strings, *Nocturne* for tenor and orchestra, the three *Canticles*, and the *Spring Symphony* are further evidence of both his intense emotional commitment and his technical skill. Despite the strong influence of such composers as Purcell, Schubert, Verdi, Mahler and Berg, his style is entirely his own; his musical personality combines, it has been said, "a deep nostalgia for the innocence of childhood, a mercurial sense of humour and a passionate sympathy with the victims of prejudice and misunderstanding."

Sir Michael Tippett.

This last quality was also evident in the emotional make up of Sir Michael Tippett (1905–98), as expressed in such works as the oratorio *A Child of our Time* (1941) one of his earliest successes, which shows both his compassion and his ability to write on a large scale. This and the Concerto for Double String Orchestra (1939) remain his most popular works. Tippett was open to a wide range of influences, both musical (from English Madrigals, Monteverdi and Beethoven to Negro spirituals and jazz) and non-musical (*e.g.* the ideas of Jung). His early style—often richly lyrical and affirmative of the continued power of tonality—reached its culmination in his allegorical opera *The Midsummer Marriage* (1952), the Piano Concerto (1955) and the Second Symphony (1957). A new style, spare and incisive, with structure arising from the juxtaposition of contrasting ideas rather than from a process of development, was evident in his second opera, *King Priam* (1961) and its offshoots, the Second Piano Sonata (1962) and the Concerto for Orchestra (1963). The mystical, ecstatic *The Vision of St. Augustine* (1965), a complex, difficult but rewarding work, is one of his finest from this period. The opera *The Knot Garden* (1970) exemplifies again Tippett's concern with human relationships and the need for self-knowledge. Tippett never ceased to explore and experiment; his inspiration still seems as fresh as ever. His most recent works, *The Mask of Time*— a huge choral piece—and the Fourth Piano Sonata (1984) have something of the quality of summarising statements about the musical and non-musical concerns of a lifetime.

Olivier Messiaen.

Amongst the many schools and groups of composers in the twentieth century, two major figures stand apart, Olivier Messiaen (1908–92) and Elliott Carter. Both born in 1908, each is an individualist of great influence and stature who has pursued his own path to a personal style of composition.

A devout Catholic, Messiaen viewed himself as a theological composer and music as a medium for a profound communication, celebration and contemplation of the love and mystery of God. Few of his works are liturgical but most have religious and doctrinal themes, for example *La Nativité du Seigneur* (1935) for organ and *Vingt Regards sur l'Enfant-Jésus* (1944) for piano. Messiaen was inspired to compose by hearing the music of Debussy. This influence can be particularly seen in Messiaen's flexible rhythms, sensitive scoring and use of timbre. Indeed, he identifies sounds with colours and views composition as painting. The other major early influence was that of the East, particularly Indian music.

Messiaen often uses Hindu rhythmic patterns alongside Greek poetic metres, plainsong and other medieval techniques and Stravinskian devices. The sum of these can be seen in *Quatuor pour le fin du temps* for violin, clarinet, cello and piano which he composed in a prisoner of war camp in 1940. A very complex work, it reflects the primacy Messiaen gives to rhythmic control. Its overwhelming impression however is of lush and exotic sounds and textures. Similarly, the vibrant colours and rhythms of the massive *Turangalila-symphonie* (1946–8) for orchestra effectively realise the ideas of life and vitality embodied in the Sanskrit title.

Elements of Messiaen's Music.

After *Turangalila*, Messiaen adopted a less luxurious style. It was works such as the *Livre d'orgue* (1951) which profoundly influenced many young composers of post-war years in the use of systematic transformations of rhythm and dynamics using a system of modes in a quasi-serial fashion. For Messiaen it is the seven harmonic modes, inspired by Debussy, Liszt and the Russian "Five", which are perhaps more important because they give his music its unique sound quality.

The 1950s saw the integration of the final element crucial to Messiaen's music; birdsong. A keen ornithologist, he collected and accurately notated the songs of many birds for incorporation into compositions. *Catalogue d'oiseaux* (1951–8) is a collection of thirteen piano pieces featuring French bird songs.

Since 1960, his style has become less complex to the ear. To encounter the many elements of his music one can do little better than to listen to *La Transfiguration de Notre Seigneur Jésus-Christ* (1963–9) for one hundred voices, seven instrumental soloists and a large orchestra. Its subject is the mystery of God, his relationship with man and nature as a revelation of God. Messiaen draws upon all his compositional techniques in a spellbinding and overwhelming work that is a profound affirmation of faith. It is fitting that his most recent work is a vast opera (1973–83), *St François d'Assise* about the saint who is best known for his great spirituality and for gaining inspiration and insight from nature.

Elliott Carter.

Carter's reputation is based on a small number of works. He has concentrated on problems of language and structure in a dramatic context unlike Messiaen's preoccupations with colour and the communication of religious truths. Carter's early works reflect a variety of influences: Stravinsky, Hindemith and the English Virginalists. He consciously aimed at a simple, lyrical, accessible style, for example, in the ballet, *Pocahontas* (1938–9) and *Holiday Overture* (1944). During those war years however there occurred a change of direction. The Piano Sonata (1945–6) saw the start of a compositional style where instruments were endowed with personalities who act as protagonists in a drama. His ideas crystallised in the *String Quartet No. 1* (1950–1) after an absorbing study of the music of Ives, Cowell and African and Oriental music. It led to the use of very complex rhythmic relationships and a very tightly-knit pitch structure that could be traced back to a simple and small source, in this case a four-note chord. After this Carter refined his portrayal of his dramatis personae such that in *String Quartet No. 2* (1959) his players each have a separate personality defined by melodic material, gestures and rhythms. They converse, argue and enact that work's dramatic programme. *String Quartet No. 3* (1971) marked a shift in approach. Although the players were still "personalities", the work relied heavily on the use of contrast between strict and flexible writing between members of two duos. The *Symphony of Three Orchestras* (1975–7) and *Triple Duo* (1983) continue to explore the possibilities of simultaneous presentation of independent and sometimes unrelated processes

THE AVANT GARDE SINCE 1945

The early post-war years saw a renewed interest in "twelve-note techniques" otherwise known as "serialism". Composers like Stravinsky and Dallapiccola (1904–75), who had shunned serialism in earlier years, began to experiment and absorb serial techniques into their musical style. Stravinsky, for example, in works such as *Threni* (1957–8) explored ideas of varied repetition both of small ideas and large sections, in a serial context. A clear example to listen to is the fifteen-minute *Requiem Canticles* (1964–6). During the progression from its Prelude to Postlude, one can hear the piece subtly develop. The succeeding movements, and phrases within movements, slightly alter that which has gone before, evolving into something fresh.

Serialism.

This period also saw the emergence of a new generation of composers, keen to jettison the past and begin anew. Serialism was a favoured tool, its revival stemming from Paris, where Webern's pupil René Leibowitz was teaching, and the USA where Schoenberg had fled from Nazi Germany. The American Milton Babbitt (b. 1916) was much concerned with codifying serial techniques. His younger European contemporaries Pierre Boulez (b. 1925) and Karlheinz Stockhausen (b. 1928) sought to increase the number of musical elements that could be controlled by a predetermined method. They sought to emulate the rigorous methods of Webern, hoping to control not only pitch, but also rhythm, timbre *etc*. In doing so they hoped to create an impersonal, emotionally restrained music.

Attention went first to controlling rhythm. Forerunners of this control can be seen in movement three of Berg's *Lyric Suite* and in Webern's Op.30 Variations. However, the catalyst came from Messiaen. He inspired his pupil Boulez to explore the possibilities of rhythmic and dynamic serialism in his Second Piano Sonata (1948). The performance of Messiaen's *Modes de valeurs et d'intensités* (1949) at the Darmstadt Summer School proved decisive for Stockhausen. Although not serial, the piece established scales of pitch, length of note (duration), loudness and attack. The 1950s were to see this potential for serialism taken to extremes. Boulez reached "total serialism" in *Structures 1a* for piano. However, having attained it he soon became frustrated with its restrictions. Some of the more fantastic and exotic elements were allowed to reappear. *Le Marteau sans Maître* (1952–4) for mezzo-soprano and six instruments is a masterly setting of three surreal poems by René Char, with instrumental interludes. It is the contrasts of timbres, of flexible and regular pulsing rhythms, of sound and silence that are spellbinding. The virtuosic serial workings are hidden.

The Achievement of Total Serialism.

Stockhausen reached total serialism in *Kreuzspiel* (1951) for oboe, bass clarinet, piano and percussion. Each note's pitch, length, dynamic and timbre are part of a predetermined plan. All are concerned with "Kreuzspiel" or "crossplay". Its various processes reverse or change over throughout so that at the end we have returned full circle. The effect is of clearcut lines where each note is weighted. However, despite the intention of the composer, the effect is not unemotional, especially with the insistent throbbing of the percussion, and the piece builds to a series of climaxes before dying away. *Punkte* (points) (1952) for orchestra finds each note being treated as an isolated point of sound. It illustrates some of the problems of total serialism; often very difficult to play, it can be monotonous or lack focal points, appearing to be random rather than rigorously controlled. Stockhausen therefore transferred his attention to using not points but bursts of sound and moved towards possibly his most significant contribution to music, "moment form". There, different aspects of a note, chord or sound are suspended in eternity for contemplation and re-examination. Works became longer, slower and had a greater emphasis on colour and the effects of spatial separation, both between sounds and between their sources. *Carré* (1959–60) uses four orchestras between which chords move and evolve. Although unifying principles in pitch content *etc.* might be present, "strict" serialism had been gently left behind, until *Mantra* (1970). This work for two pianos, percussion and two electronic ring modulators is totally based on a thirteen-note row, the mantra, with a different duration, mode of attack and dynamic for each note. These permeate the whole piece. For example, each of the thirteen portions is allotted to one of the thirteen types of attack. The work's climax is the coda where the 156 versions of the mantra used are rushed through in a few minutes. The work is important, not only as marking a return to serialism and notated music, but also in its rediscovery of melody.

Later Serialism.

Since the 1960s serialism and integral serialism have had less of an influence in Europe, although they have continued to hold a fascination for American composers such as Milton Babbit (b. 1916). Composers have used the underlying concept of serialism (*i.e.* using a systematic approach to detailed structuring) without using the technique in any strict sense. Examples of this include Maxwell Davies's use of magic number squares (*see below*), and Harrison Birtwistle's use of random numbers to generate rhythmic and melodic elements. The Hungarian composer György Ligeti (1923–2006) used very tightly controlled canonic music which he described as 'micropolyphony' which, though not serial, has a similarly organised and systematic approach. One of the reasons for the use of systems is to take some of the decision-making out of the compositional process. Birtwistle has said that he would seize up if he had to make all the decisions in his music.

Mathematics and Music.

The younger generation of composers have often used mathematical systems for composing which are not necessarily serial. A good example is Sir Peter Maxwell Davies (b. 1934). The use of durational ratios, ciphers and magic squares features prominently in his work, partly reflecting his interest in medieval music. A magic square is a number square

where the sum of any line is the same. This becomes the basis for a composition by assigning notes to the numbers—a technique that Davies has often used since the mid-1970s. For example, in *Ave Maris Stella* (1975), each of the nine movements uses a different transformation of the square and follows a characteristic route through the square. The work is governed by the square at all levels: it even determines the precise length of each movement. Far from being a mathematical exercise however the piece shows masterly control which is particularly revealed in its drama and the beauty of its colours.

Mathematical processes of a different type have been taken up by the Greek, Xenakis (b. 1922), possibly because of his original training as an engineer and architect in France. His rejection of serialism led to the use of "stochastic" principles, derived from the mathematical laws governing probability. He also applied mathematical set theory to composition. The use of these ideas however is not audible. In *Nomos Alpha* (1965) for solo cello, for example, it is the use of contrasts, texture *etc.*, which give shape and form for the listener.

Eastern Influences.

Although for many serialism represented the way of reviving music after the excesses of romanticism, some looked beyond Europe to the East. John Cage (1912–92) found inspiration there, studying Zen Buddhism in the early 1950s. By using the "chance operations" of the Chinese *I Ching* (Book of Changes) Cage brought a new radical approach to Western music. *Music of Changes* (1951) for piano is fully notated but its content is the result of operations where chance has a role. The use of "indeterminacy" or "chance" gave the performer an active role in determining the course of a piece. This might come about by providing "graphic notation"—an artist's impression of what the piece might sound like. Thus Earle Brown's *December 1952* is a visual design to be realised on any instrument as the performer sees fit. Alternatively the composer could give the performer control over the order of sections or their content. *Twenty-five pages* (1953) by Brown is for one to twenty-five pianos. Each person has twenty-five pages and may arrange them in any order before commencing. Thus music was no longer to be necessarily a progression of fixed and immutable steps to an endpoint. This and other traditional concepts about music were challenged in Cage's most well-known outrage, *4' 33"*. The performer does not play any notes at all. The music consists of the sounds in the environment that occur during a period of four minutes and thirty-three seconds.

Chance and Indeterminacy.

In 1957, both Stockhausen and Boulez took to chance having realised that total control was an impossibility. The more rigorous the control of musical elements, the more impossible it became to realise it accurately. Stockhausen's first experiment with chance techniques was Piano Piece XI which is a single page with nineteen fragments of music. They may be played in any order but the tempo, dynamic and attack must be that shown at the end of the previous fragment. After one fragment has been played three times the work ends. Boulez's Third Piano Sonata was less free. There the choices are in the nature of varying routes through the piece. Boulez saw his music as using a form of control that is not random but akin to throwing a dice. Limited choices in the combination of instruments and their choice of lines form the basis of *Pli selon pli* (1957–65) for soprano and orchestra, offering Boulez a way "to fix the infinite".

For Stockhausen, chance has been a way to encourage performer participation and the development of "intuitive music-making". In *Prozession* (1967) for example, performers react to what is going on guided by plus or minus signs in the score which denote whether the response should be positive or negative. It has worked well in combination with the ideas behind moment form. *Stimmung* (1968) is a 45 minute meditation on one chord whose parts and overtones emerge and merge into the whole, punctuated by erotic poems, magic numbers and words which are delivered in response to chance operations. The culmination of these ideas may be seen in *Aus den Sieben Tagen* (1968) where the score for each of the seven movements is a short poem.

Witold Lutoslawski.

Use of indeterminacy does not necessarily have to be so extreme. For Witold Lutoslawski (1913–93) use of controlled chance techniques has provided a way for composing without embracing serialism. During 1955–60 Lutoslawski evolved a harmonic language which used twelve-note chords for expression and colour. In 1960 he heard a performance of Cage's Piano Concerto and realised that he could use chance techniques to add a rhythmic freedom and new types of texture to his music. The exact combination of sounds at any given moment is often a matter of chance but the overall effect is planned. Textures are created by the constant repetition of small melodic ideas and simple rhythms in different parts, creating a kaleidoscope of sound, and by lines of counterpoint set off against each other, often sliding from one note to another blurring the transition between chords. The music of Lutoslawski is a fine example of the use of chance as a tool in compositions which still have strong links to tradition. The direction and drama of works such as *Mi-Parti* (1976) and his Third Symphony (1983) are firmly in the composer's hands, relying heavily on his skilful sense of harmonic movement, use of colour and proportion. Only small rhythmic details are left to chance.

The Music of Ligeti.

Ligeti's music often sounds as if it were chance-like but in fact his massive textural structures of the 1960s are controlled by highly organised arhythmic canons. Each instrument or voice follows the same line of notes but with different rhythmic values. The listener hears a kaleidoscopic and ever-changing background cluster. Works from this period include: *Atmosphères* for orchestra (1961), *Requiem* (1963–5) and *Lux Aeterna* for voices (1966). Ligeti's music was made famous when the above works were used (without the composer's permission) by Stanley Kubrick in his film *2001: a Space Odyssey*. Ligeti's music since the 1970s shows a rediscovery of elements that he had previously shunned such as melody, harmony and even tonality/modality. Typical examples include Horn Trio (1982), Piano Concerto (1988) and Violin Concerto (1992) which show influences from African music, fractal geometry and the piano music of the American Conlon Nancarrow (1912–97). The rediscovery of previously rejected elements can also be seen in the music of the Polish composer Krzysztof Penderecki (b. 1933) and Luciano Berio (1025–2003) and can be seen as a symptom of the existence of Post-Modernism in music.

Electronic Music.

An important part of the post-war struggle with musical language has been the development of electronic means to generate, manipulate and record sounds. Its pioneer was the Frenchman Edgard Varèse (1883–1965). Before the war he had been an independent and radical composer much concerned with the exploration of new sounds. This had led to an emphasis on the exploitation of percussion effects in works such as *Intégrales* (1924–5) and *Ionisation* (1933). The following work *Ecuatorial* (1934) explored further, using primitive electrically generated sounds produced by two Ondes Martenot. However the catalyst for further development was the invention of the tape recorder which provided an easy means to store sounds that could then be rearranged by cutting and rejoining the tape in different ways. Varèse explored these possibilities in *Déserts* (1949–54) which alternated recorded and instrumental sounds in an atmospheric work which really seems to conjure up the aridity and emptiness of the desert. Recorded sound offered the possibility of creating illusions of aural space by technical manipulation and by judicious positioning and control of loudspeakers. This is a fundamental part of Varèse's great masterpiece, *Poème Electronique* (1958) which used soprano, chorus, bells, organs and artificial sounds. Its spatial effects were achieved by

using many loudspeakers positioned around a specially designed pavilion at the 1958 Brussels Exhibition.

Generally, electronic music-making required a studio and the 1950s saw the setting up of important studios in Paris and Cologne. In Paris Pierre Schaeffer (1910–95) pioneered "musique concrète" which used altered and rearranged natural sounds, for example, the sound of a steam train, to create a musical piece. At Cologne where Stockhausen worked, the emphasis was on new synthetic sounds.

The Potential of Electronic Music.

Electronic music had the potential to generate complex, accurate serial structures through precise electronic operations. Boulez's studies in this however did not satisfy him and he neglected the medium until 1970 when he became Director of IRCAM (*Institut de Recherche et de Coordination Acoustique/Musique*). Stockhausen however found electronic music an ideal medium to create a musical unity far beyond that of serialism; pitch, timbre, rhythm and form could be seen as different aspects of the same thing—vibration. He did not restrict himself to pure synthetic sounds and in 1955–6 created perhaps his most well-known electronic work, *Gesang der Jünglinge*.

With *Kontakte* (1958–60) for piano, percussion and tape, Stockhausen began an exploration of the interplay between live performers and electronic sound which still preoccupies him today. The work explores "contact" between real and artificial sounds and between the elements of music. Compared to pure electronic music, the presence of the live performers made it easier to listen to, providing a visual focus and making each performance unique. The next step was to create "live" electronic music where performers created their electronic sounds on stage. Cage had already begun this in 1960 with *Cartridge Music*. Unlike Stockhausen's first attempt, *Mikrophonie I* (1964–5), *Cartridge Music* gives much freedom to the performer in creating the electronic effects. A desire to create a world music led to one of the most vast electronic works to date, *Hymnen* (1966–7), a two-hour work for quadraphonic tape or tapes, soloists and optional symphony orchestra. Stockhausen constructed it out of national anthems from all over the world. Inspired by the occult *Urantian Book*, he became more ambitious still, seeking a galactic music. *Sirius* (1977) for four soloists and electronic music deals with the arrival on earth of four visitors from the star Sirius.

In America, developments have followed a different course. There, the use of computer synthesised sounds has been the main interest because of the computer's superior control and accuracy. It has allowed the continuation of abstract composition where complicated operations are achieved simply and effectively.

Minimalism.

The transformation of existing material on tape has been a crucial part of an American movement dating from the 1960s known as "Minimalism". Its chief exponents are Steve Reich (b. 1936), Philip Glass (b. 1937), Terry Riley (b. 1935) and La Monte Young (b. 1935). Minimal music uses material which is limited in pitch, rhythm and timbres; the elements are subjected to simple transformations relying heavily on repetition. Of great importance are the subtle evolution from one idea to another as repetitions are modified, and the use of "phasing" techniques. Phasing is the effect of altering the rate of repetition between parts repeating the same material so that it is no longer synchronised. The effect of works such as *Drumming* (1971) by Reich may appear long and non-dramatic. However, the listener is not expected to concentrate all the time but to become aware of a piece's various elements and processes. The music's patterns will change as the listener's attention shifts from one aspect to another. As in moment form, minimalist works owe much to Indian concepts of time as a circular rather than linear phenomenon. In recent years, the minimalists have developed their style and there are greater differences between the four. Philip Glass has written several operas, *Einstein on the Beach* (1975), *Satyagraha* (1980), *Akhnaten* (1983), *The Making of the Representative for Planet 8* (1986), *The*

Fall of the House of Usher (1988), *1000 Airplanes on the Roof* (1988) and *The Voyage* (1992). Other works by Reich include *Different Trains* (1988) for String Quartet and tape, *The Cave* (1993) a multimedia extravaganza and *The Four Sections* (1987) for full orchestra.

Music Theatre.

During the early post-war years many composers were grappling with the tools of composition. Only more "traditional" writers such as Britten, Tippett and Hans Werner Henze (b. 1926) were engaged in writing opera. By 1970 however, most composers were including elements of theatre in their work even if they were not necessarily engaged in writing full-scale operas.

One of the major composers of "traditional" opera has been Henze. His first three operas draw heavily on the past. For example, *Boulevard Solitude* (1952) updates the story of Manon, a nineteenth-century favourite. After moving to Italy in 1953, Henze's stance appeared more traditional still as lyrical elements became more dominant in contrast to the abstract athematic style of contemporaries such as Stockhausen. Increasingly Henze's operas began to reflect his preoccupation with socialism. The *Bassarids* (1966), for example, examines through a mythological guise the precipitation of social upheaval and disruption. The oratorio *Das Floss der "Medusa"* (1968) is dedicated to Che Guevara and provoked such struggles between police and left-wing students at its premiere that Henze went to Cuba for a year. There he was inspired to write *El Cimarrón* (1969–70), a vocal monologue portraying a Cuban runaway slave accompanied by flute, guitar and percussion. For a while, Henze continued to reject the traditional opera format because of its bourgeois overtones, preferring a more intimate, chamber style. But in 1976 Henze returned to opera with *We come to the River*. It reflected a renewal of Italianate lyricism, the exploitation of opera's full potential and a less overt political message.

Exponents of Music Theatre.

Luigi Nono (1924–90) also exploited theatre for political ends, beginning with *Intolleranza* (1960). However he found greater resource than Henze in contemporary developments, taking full advantage of the opportunities offered by electronics. *Contrappunto dialettico della mente* (1967–8) includes the sounds of political demonstrations. Like Henze, Nono also returned to the opera house after a long break from large-scale opera with *Al gran sole carico d'amore* (1972–4), which consolidated the techniques he had developed in the previous decade.

"Theatre" was a dominant characteristic in the works of Luciano Berio (1925–2003). One of his most famous works is *Circles* (1960) for female voice, harp and percussion. The virtuosic technique used there and in other works was inspired by the phenomenal vocal elasticity of his then wife, Cathy Berberian. "Circles' are depicted at many different levels in the work's structure and content. More importantly, these are underlined by the singer moving about the stage during the performance. Berio's next few works became overtly political, culminating in *Laborintus II* (1965) which was intended as an attack on capitalism via a musical collage and extracts from Dante's *Inferno*. Many of Berio's larger scale works since *Laborintus II* have been theatrical in their virtuosity and instrumental technique. For example, *Sequenza IV* (1965) demands a pianist with very agile feet. This type of dramatic gesture is much seen in Stockhausen's work, particularly those written for his own music ensemble, for example, *Solo* (1966). Since *Alphabet für Liege* (1972) his work has become increasingly theatrical and from 1978, Stockhausen has been working on an opera project *Licht*. Twenty years earlier, such a project would have been unthinkable.

Sir Peter Maxwell Davies.

The small-scale synthesis of text, music and gesture characteristic of Berio has greatly influenced British work in music theatre, notably the work of Sir Peter Maxwell Davies and Sir Harrison Birtwistle. Davies' work is very powerful particularly through its use of parody and wild use of outrageous gesture. *Vesalii Icones* (1969) uses a naked male dancer portraying parts of the Stations of the Cross and scenes from the anatomy text by Vesalius. It is a good example of parody, particularly of what Davies views as nineteenth-century grossness—it includes a vile distortion of a Victorian hymn tune which turns into a foxtrot, both played on a honky-tonk piano. Many of his works feature a single vocal soloist, with instrumental back up, who plays the part of a crazed, obsessive individual. For example, *Eight Songs for a Mad King* (1969) features the instrumentalists in giant bird cages who must suffer the mad ravings of George III played by the singer.

Davies has written three full-scale operas to date, *Taverner* (1962–8) and *The Martyrdom of St. Magnus* (1976) and *Resurrection* (1987). *Taverner* deals with two fundamental preoccupations of Davies—the nature of faith and betrayal—and uses both musical and dramatic parody to convey its message. *St. Magnus* was written after Davies moved to Orkney. It reflects a change in style, uses only a small orchestra and is for production "in the round". Recently Maxwell Davies has explored the traditional orchestral sound world. In 2004 he was appointed Master of the Queen's Musick.

Sir Harrison Birtwistle.

Birtwistle's first major dramatic work was a chamber opera, *Punch and Judy* (1966) which uses grotesque and violent gestures. However, while Davies' roots may lie with early Schoenberg, Birtwistle has found inspiration in the clear-cut lines and ritualism of Stravinsky. Possibly his most significant work to date is *The Mask of Orpheus* (1973–5 and 1981–3). He has written a further three operas: *Gawain* (1981–91); *The Second Mrs. Kong* (1994) and *The Last Supper* (2000). Birtwistle was made a Companion of Honour in 2001.

MUSIC OF THE 1990s

Brian Ferneyhough (b. 1943) is continuing to expand the chamber music repertoire using traditional structures as a framework for music in which micro-tones play an increasingly important part. A significant part of his output before 1990 is the group of seven compositions, *Carceri d'invenzione* (1981–6), 'dungeons of invention' referring to the etchings of Piranesi. He has become the focus of a style of composition named 'the New Complexity' which pushes the techniques of players to their limits and creates extremely complex textures.

Robin Holloway (b. 1943) has also been active in composing smaller scale works, often lyrical, of which recent examples are his *Viola Concerto* (1985) and the bleak *Ballad* for harp and chamber orchestra (1985). Nigel Osborne (b. 1948) has used electronic and non-Western music in his work, gravitating recently towards vocal works. 1986 saw the premiere of his theatre piece, *Hells Angels*. Other recent operas are *Where the Wild Things Are* (1984) and *Higglety, Pigglety Pop!* (1985) by Oliver Knussen (b. 1952) which attracted acclaim for a young composer already noted for his symphonies, vocal and chamber work. Tim Souster (1943–94) has been active in composing and promoting electronic music of all types, some influenced by rock music. A recent example is his *Quartet with Tape* (1985).

Choral Music. Meanwhile choral music is flourishing with new works by Paul Patterson (b. 1947) which often involve new types of notation and vocal technique, and several ritualistic works by Sir John Tavener (b. 1944), inspired by his Eastern Orthodox faith. For example *Doxa* (1982) sets a single word from the Eastern liturgy. A meteoric rise to fame has been achieved by George Benjamin (b. 1960) starting with *Ringed by the Flat Horizon* (1980) written while still at Cambridge.

Diversity of Approach.

The emerging British composers of the 1980s and 1990s are diverse in their compositional approaches and interests. One feature they do have in common is an eclecticism drawing from a wide range of sources such as football chants (Turnage), jazz (Butler) and Celtic culture (MacMillan and Weir). There is also a trend towards greater approachability in the style and language of their music. There has been a realisation that audiences have been alienated in the past, and composers have attempted to make their music more communicative. One manifestation of this is the apparent 'rediscovery' of tonality or modality.

Some Contemporary Composers.

Mark-Anthony Turnage (b. 1960) is one of the most characteristic and popular composers of his generation. He uses material from popular culture in his music (like Martland and MacMillan) including rhythmic and melodic elements, which can be most clearly seen in his controversial opera *Greek* (1990), a setting of Steven Berkoff's play. His rich and colourful orchestration can be heard in his orchestral works such as *Three Screaming Popes* (1989), *Momentum* (1990–1), *Drowned Out* (1993) and his highly successful latest opera *The Silver Tassie* (1997–9).

James MacMillan (b. 1959) is a part of the general rebirth of the arts in Scotland and shows something of his Celtic heritage in such works as *The Confessions of Isobel Gowrie* (1990) which explores a wide range of Scottish traditional music. His music since *Litanies of Iron and Stone* (1987) shows an increase in rhythmic drive, perhaps influenced by his interest in rock music, and also an increasing approachability. His major compositions since *Litanies* have mostly used external political or religious subjects as inspiration, for example *The Exorcism of Rio Sumpul* (1989) which is based on a helicopter raid on a village in El Salvador. His musical language is characterised by colourful instrumentation, a powerful rhythmic drive and an eloquent lyricism, which can be seen clearly in his popular *Veni Veni Emmanuel* (1993) written for the percussionist Evelyn Glennie. His first full-scale opera was *Ines de Castro* (1995) which was first performed by Scottish Opera at the 1996 Edinburgh Festival. His most recent large scale work is his Second Symphony (1999) written for the Scottish Chamber Orchestra.

Judith Weir (b. 1954) also makes reference to her Celtic heritage in her music. Her main compositional output is in the area of opera and music drama. *A Night at the Chinese Opera* (1987) is perhaps her best known work to date and is evidence of her interest in Chinese Yuan dramas. Her two later operas use magical stories: *The Vanishing Bridegroom* (1990) is based on 3 linked Scottish folktales, and *Blond Eckbert* (1994, for the English National Opera) on a fairytale by the German Romantic writer Ludwig Tieck. Her musical language shows influences from folk music, tonality and composers such as Stravinsky, Janacek and Peter Maxwell Davies.

Martin Butler (b. 1960) like MacMillan has shown a shift in his musical language from a Modernist approach to one which is more eclectic and expressive. As he states: "Recent examples of mine have drawn, more or less directly, on Irish and bluegrass fiddle music, Latin salsa and dance music, and various types of jazz." Examples showing these influences include *Jazz Machines* (1990) for chamber ensemble, *Bluegrass Variations* (1988) for violin, and *Tin Pan Ballet* (1986) for ensemble and DX7 synthesiser. His most substantial work to date is his opera *Craig's Progress* (1994) which uses the "twin inheritances of opera and comic books".

Steve Martland (b. 1959) is a key figure of radical minimalism in Britain and owes much of his musical development to his studies with Louis Andriessen at the Royal Conservatory in The Hague. His music, like that of MacMillan, is strongly shaped by his socialist politics and is characterised by uncompromising aggression and bold sonorities. Like Andriessen he explores hocketing techniques in works like *Drill* (1987) and *Birthday Hocket* (1989), both for 2 pianos. His larger scale works include *Babi Yar* (1983) for large orchestra in 3 groups and *Crossing the Border* (1990–91) for String Orchestra.

The New Millennium.

With the advent of the new millennium it is tempting to identify the direction that contemporary music is taking, and who might be the composers to

watch. The major shift in contemporary music over the last 20 years is towards a more tonal/modal music with a parallel shift towards greater comprehensibility. It is likely that successful composers in the future will be those who communicate directly with their audience. Some of the British composers discussed earlier, such as Weir and Turnage, show this characteristic, although this is not to suggest that their music is without depth or artistic richness.

There will also be a continued interest of composers into popular idioms and an exploration of the grey areas in between. Minimalism and Post-Minimalism, which explore the interesting area of contemporary music, popular music and world music, will continue to thrive and evolve into more sophisticated and varied forms. It would be wrong to suggest that the tougher, more modernist style of music will disappear in the next millenium; diversity of style and pluralism will continue to be a defining characteristic of New Music. Some of the most innovative current composers and stylistic groupings will be outlined below.

Popular Minimalism: Michael Nyman.

The British composer Michael Nyman (b. 1944) is an example of a composer who writes music which cannot be easily categorised, as it consists of an amalgam of Minimalism, Baroque Ground Bass and Popular rhythms. Nyman's most characteristic works have been those written for Peter Greenaway's films such as *The Draughtsman's Contract* (1982), *A Zed and Two Noughts* (1985) and *The Cook, The Thief, His Wife, and Her Lover* (1989) which show a powerful and distinctive style. Nyman's music for *The Piano* (1992), directed by Jane Campion, is less hard-edged and original than his earlier works, but it does suit the film and has brought him much popularity. His non-film music includes: the chamber opera *The Man Who Mistook His Wife for a Hat* (1987) based on the case study by the psychiatrist Oliver Sacks and the music of Schumann; The Piano Concerto (1993) based on the music from *The Piano*; and three string quartets (1985, 1988 & 1990). His latest major work is the Double Concerto (1997) for saxophone, cello and orchestra; quite an unusual and innovative combination.

Post-Minimalism: John Adams.

The American composer John Adams is considered to be a significant innovator in the Minimalist genre. His recent style could be better classified as Post-Modernist or perhaps Post-Minimalist as he avoids the austere Minimalism of Steve Rich or Philip Glass, in favour of a richer and more backward looking style. *Grand Pianola Music* (1981) for chamber orchestra, 3 sopranos and 2 solo pianos is an example of this more eclectic approach using jazz-like harmony and a banal tune at the end which is alarmingly reminiscent of Beethoven's *Ode to Joy*.

Adams, like Glass, has latterly explored the larger canvas of opera using relatively recent historical events for the plots. Examples include: *Nixon in China* (1987) which outlines the historic meeting between President Nixon and Chairman Mao; and *The Death of Klinghoffer* (1991) which highlights the eternal clash of the Arabs and the Jews. What Adams's music shows above all is the increasing pluralism in the styles of contemporary music which include popular idioms and also the raiding of past musical genres to create a fascinating blend of disparate materials.

The Modernists: Birtwistle, Stockhausen, Boulez.

Modernist composers, who reject the notion that there are 'easy answers' in art, will continue to have a significant role in contemporary music. The leading 'Modernists' include Stockhausen, Boulez, Birtwistle, Xenakis, Ligeti, and Ferneyhough. Their music is very diverse in style but they have a common commitment to atonal music, the use of systems in their music and an avoidance of the approachability of the Post-Modernists like Holloway or the American David Del Tredici (b. 1937), or the Mystics such as Pärt, Tavener or Górecki.

Harrison Birtwistle is a British composer who has continued to use an uncompromising, non-tonal and often very aggressive musical language. He is also a figure who is seen as the most original and distinctive voice of his generation. His musical development can be seen as the gradual evolution of one basic approach which shows increasing refinement of technique, but without changing his main focus on the issue of the structuring time. His most recent works include: *Earth Dances* for large orchestra (1985–6) which shows a complex layering of strata, like the earth's crust; *Gawain* (1991), an opera based on a Middle English Romance about courtly chivalry among knights; and *The Second Mrs Kong* (1994) which explores a confusing plethora of film and mythic characters.

In the 1995 last night of the Proms, John Drummond, the controller of Radio 3, had the audacity to commission Birtwistle to write *Panic* for John Harle, the saxophonist. The result was a wild and virtuoso work which sounds almost like free jazz. It caused uproar in the press as it brought an example of modernist violence into what is usually a cosy, musically mediocre and blatantly jingoistic event.

Other Modernists have perhaps fared less well in the 1980s and 1990s. Boulez, the archetypal Modernist, seems to be rewriting old works such as the orchestral *Notations* (1977–) or continuations of existing works such as the recent reworking of *explosante-fix* (1993).

Stockhausen has continued with his seven opera project *Licht* which he began in 1977 and has become increasingly isolated, working with a very close-knit group of players, including several of his family members. All his compositional work is focused on *Licht* which has much in common with Wagner's *The Ring* – however *Licht* seems to lack the unity and perhaps the consistency of *The Ring*. It would appear that Stockhausen is no longer the innovator of the 1960s and 1970s, and has perhaps lost his direction.

Mystics and the New Simplicity: Arvo Pärt.

As part of the shift towards a greater comprehensibility in music, a number of composers have written music imbued with mysticism, usually allied to an increased religious devotion. Arvo Pärt (b. 1935), the Estonian, is an example of a composer whose earlier works are in the Modernist serial tradition but who had a change of heart in the late 1960s. At this time he made an intensive study of Gregorian Chant, 13th Century Notre Dame Organum, and Renaissance Polyphony. "Gregorian Chant has taught me what a cosmic secret is hidden in the art of combining two or three notes." he said in 1988.

He managed to incur the wrath of the old communist authorities throughout his career, firstly as a serial composer, then as a composer using religious texts, and finally, when Western Serialism was becoming accepted in the 1970s, he shifted to a new simplicity in his music. His most significant works in the later style include: *Tabula Rasa*, a double concerto for two violins (1977); *Passio* for voices and instruments (1982); *Stabat Mater* for Soprano, Alto and strings (1985); and *Litany* for soloist, choir and orchestra (1994).

Other composers who have embraced a mystical and simple approach in their music include: Sir John Tavener (b. 1944) the British composer who rediscovered his Greek Orthodox roots; Henryk Górecki (b. 1933), the Polish composer whose Symphony No. 3 (1976) was a chart hit; and the Georgian symphonic composer Giya Kancheli (b. 1935).

POPULAR MUSIC AND JAZZ

The evolution of popular music and jazz is arguably the most far-reaching musical development of recent times. Many of the world's population have heard of Michael Jackson, or The Beatles, but few will have heard of such significant musical figures as Arnold Schönberg or Pierre Boulez. The audience for contemporary classical or 'art' music is an ever-shrinking one, and only styles which have links with popular music, such as minimalism, or look to the past, such as post-Modernist/ neo-Romantic music, have any significant audience. Therefore popular music could be considered by future musicologists as the most significant musical genre of the twentieth century.

The term 'popular music' is problematic as not all popular music is actually that popular or commercial, but it has come to mean music which has its roots in the blues. Popular music is aimed at the whole spectrum of the population, whereas classical or 'art' music has always had a following among the educated middle classes, and therefore could be considered elitist. The roots of present day popular music include folk song, African music, ballads blues, jazz, and ragtime as well as elements of Western classical music. The development of blues, jazz and popular music will be outlined below.

The Blues: Origins.

The origins of the blues are a mixture of African influences brought by the slaves to North America, work songs used on the plantations, and Western musical elements. The work songs were sung by the slaves as they worked and had a call and response pattern. One man would sing the verse and the rest of the workers would reply with a chorus. The style of singing was different from the Western approach as it included growls, cries, and falsetto avoiding a pure tone. Rhythm is also a more developed feature in African music and the blues and jazz show traces of this.

The field holler was a variety of work song which was sung by a lone worker and consisted of a long, tremulous one or two line call, often in falsetto, and comparatively free in form. This type of call has been recorded in the savannah parts of West Africa. Other elements contributing to the origins of the blues include reels, dances, and jigs of Anglo-Scottish-Irish origin with African rhythmic elements and tuning, played on banjos (a descendant of the African *bania*) and fiddles. European-influenced song forms were also adopted by the Black Americans in the nineteenth century.

The Structure of the Blues.

The structure of the blues may have been heavily influenced by ballads such as *Railroad Bill* which was popular among black vocalists of the nineteenth century. This had the form of a couplet with a rhyming third line as a chorus. In blues the couplet was replaced with a repeated line:

See, see rider, see what you have done,
See, see rider, see what you have done,
You've made me love you, now my man done come.

The basic blues structure consisted of three lines within a 12 bar stanza and the rhyme schemes included aaa, abb, abc but aab predominated. The chord sequence, which was usually played by the guitar, can be described as follows (one chord per bar in the key of C major):

I (CEG), I, I, I, IV (FAC), IV, I, I, V⁷ (GBDF),
IV, I, V⁷ (last line I).

This is the most simple form and there are many variants.

The scale used by blues vocalists and instrumentalists is called the blues scale, because of the flattened or 'blue' notes. In the key of C major, the simplest scale consists of C E♭ F G B♭ which is also a pentatonic scale found in much folk music. The 'blue' notes are the E♭ and B♭ although a vocalist may not bend the notes exactly to these pitches.

The rhythmic language of the blues is also significant and includes syncopation, a displacement of the beat, and 'swung' quavers, consisting of the first quaver of a pair being longer and heavier than the second, rather than being equal as in classical music. Many of the above technical features, such as the 12 bar blues sequence, the blues scale, and the rhythmic style, can be observed in jazz and popular music.

Early Blues Singers.

The term 'blues' relating to song probably did not emerge until after 1900, but the original sixteenth century meaning was 'a condition of melancholy or depression' which describes the nature of many blues lyrics. The early blues singers, based in the South of the United States, worked in 'medicine shows' to attract buyers for dubious patent medicines. Wandering blues singers, rather like the French medieval troubadours, sang and played for their living, and helped to disseminate the blues in the early years of the present century. By 1910 white folk song collectors had noted the existence of the blues and in 1912 *Dallas Blues* by Hart Wand and Lloyd Garret was published the first published example.

It is unlikely that the large number of published blues songs had a major effect on blues singers as few could read music. Probably the blues were passed on orally, and later, through recordings. The blues originated in the South, known as the Delta Blues, but in the 1920s blues singers moved North to record, along with the jazz musicians.

Classic Blues.

Mamie Smith (1883–1946) was the first black singer whose records were sold to the black public. *Crazy Blues*, which was recorded in 1920 and sold 75,000 copies in one month, made her a fortune and encouraged other black singers to follow her example, recording specifically for black listeners on what were dubbed 'race records'.

The term 'Classic Blues' refers to the songs of women singers based in New York and Chicago, particularly the larger-voiced contraltos who focused on blues and were backed by jazz musicians. Gertrude 'Ma' Rainey (1886–1939) was a significant example who was closest to the folk tradition. She was known as the 'Mother of the Blues', worked with Louis Armstrong on *Jelly Bean Blues* (1924), and made over 100 records in five years.

Bessie Smith (1894–1937) is probably the best known blues singer and her recording of *Down Hearted Blues* (1923) established her as the most successful black artist of the time. Her singing showed a powerful, emotional involvement, particularly noticeable in her slow blues songs.

The Blues since the 1930s.

The poor conditions of the Depression may have partly triggered a more aggressive and powerful blues sound in the 1930s, with larger bands and the introduction of drummers and electrical amplification. This style of blues has been described as 'Urban Blues' and the guitarist Big Bill Broonzy (1893–1958) was an important exponent. In the early 1930s he added a trumpet, clarinet, a second guitar and a bass to make his Memphis Five Band, later adding a drummer. This created a music which had the drive needed for dancing. Other pioneers of Urban Blues include Tampa Red with his Chicago Five.

The evolution of blues into an ensemble-based genre continued after the war with singers like Muddy Waters (1915–83) and B.B. King (b. 1925). King, while remaining true to the blues form, explored aspects of jazz, gospel, and soul, with an innovative and expressive guitar technique. The blues have continued to have a significant role in music, but the genre has been largely absorbed into popular music.

The Origins of Jazz.

It is difficult to give a comprehensive definition of jazz because of the variety of different styles within the genre. Generally, jazz shows a heightened preoccupation with rhythm, an emphasis on free improvisation, and usually a tonal/modal basis. Jazz emerged around the same time as the blues, and shares some of the latter's origins. Jazz has also had a significant influence on 'classical' composers, examples including Milhaud's *Le Creation du Monde* and Stravinsky's *Ragtime*.

Jazz originated in New Orleans around 1900, although the precise nature of the music played at that time is unclear because the earliest recording was made in 1917 by the white Original Dixieland Jazz Band. New Orleans jazz consisted of dense counterpoint from the front line wind instruments: saxophone, cornet, clarinet, and trombone, using material from the blues, marches or ragtime. The melody was usually embellished on the cornet with a higher counter-melody on the clarinet or saxophone. The rhythm section consisted of a piano, guitar or banjo playing the harmony, the drummer

playing syncopated march rhythms, and a tuba or bass saxophone playing the bass line. There were short breaks for improvised solos from the wind players.

In the 1920s and 1930s the most innovative jazz musicians worked in Chicago and New York, and there was a musical shift towards more complex harmony, with a more subtle approach to improvisation. This can be seen in Bix Beiderbecke's (1903–31) cornet playing, for example *Davenport Blues* (1925) which shows a more expanded and imaginative approach to the improvised solo. Louis Armstrong (1901–71) with his Hot Five and Hot Seven had a more aggressive and rhythmically adventurous approach, which had a greater impact on the style. Other significant bands that moved to Chicago in the 1920s include King Oliver's Creole Jazz Band and Jelly Roll Morton's band.

The 1920s.

In the 1920s another strand emerged known as orchestral jazz which can be seen in Fletcher Henderson's (1897–1952) band, partly due to the work of his arranger Don Redman. His approach to arranging was to use the sections: saxophones, brass (trumpets and trombones), and a rhythm section of banjo, tuba, piano and drums. Henderson created a combination of arranged big band sound with swinging jazz solos by such players as Louis Armstrong. The term 'swing' describes the bands of the 1930s onwards, and also refers to the rhythmic approach where all quavers are 'swung' in a triplet rhythm. The difference between the 'swing' bands and their precursors is that the former had a greater control of the arrangement, and a tighter and more unified rhythm.

Duke Ellington.

Duke Ellington (1899–1974) and his Orchestra had a major impact on the development of big band composition, exploring a new range of expression. His compositions include miniature tone-poems such as *Daybreak Express* (1933), recompositions such as *Ebony Rhapsody* (1934) based on Liszt's *Hungarian Rhapsody No. 2* and solo concertos like *Clarinet Lament* (1936).

Benny Goodman (1909–86) was the significant white band leader of the period and succeeded in transforming Fletcher Henderson's approach with a more classically-based accuracy. He kept the swing element but removed the more adventurous approach to expression and note bending of the black bands.

Bebop.

In the 1940s a new style appeared called 'Bebop' or 'Bop' which consisted of complex, jagged, and stabbing harmonies, combined with free flowing scalic improvisation. The finest exponent of bebop was the alto saxophonist Charlie Parker (1920–55). He generally worked in small ensembles and played breathtaking improvisations of chromatic and irregular melodies, using rhythms which contradicted the underlaying pulse. Other important bebop players include the trumpeters Dizzy Gillespie and Miles Davis, and the pianist Thelonious Monk, all of whom played with Parker. Bebop marked a radical shift in the development of jazz as it allowed a much freer mode of expression, comparable with contemporary 'art' music.

Cool, Free Jazz and Fusion.

Miles Davis (1926–91) is unusual among jazz musicians as he successfully transformed his style several times, including swing, bebop, cool, modal jazz, fusion and funk. *The Birth of the Cool* (1949–50) with his own 9-piece band created a new sound which eschewed the frenetic activity of bebop for a drier, mellower, and 'cooler' sound. Other musicians working in this almost classical chamber of music style included Lennie Tristano and Gill Evans. In *A Kind of Blue* (1959) Davis continued his development into modal jazz where long stretches of music are based on one chord, with the improvised solos on a compatible mode.

The next step entailed removing the chord progressions completely, which Ornette Coleman (b. 1930) did in his 'free jazz' by removing harmony instruments from his groups. In addition, tempo and the time signature are variable in his work, giving his music a very fluid rhythmic flow. *Free Jazz* (1960) is Coleman's seminal recording, and his work was continued by the pianist Cecil Taylor and the trumpeter Don Cherry.

In the 1960s 'pop music' dominated the musical scene and in this period the use of electronics and musical elements from rock 'n' roll can be observed. Miles Davis' *Bitches Brew* (1960) is a good example of the fusion of jazz and rock. From 1970 to the present day the jazz scene has similar characteristics to that of contemporary 'art' music in the multiplicity of coexisting styles. This makes it difficult to identify a clear direction of development. The most innovative current jazz performers include the pianist Keith Jarrett, George Russell, Anthony Braxton and Evan Parker.

Popular Music: Origins.

Popular Music can be defined as music which is aimed at the populace rather than an elite. Its abbreviated form 'pop', has been used since the 1950s, although one early use of this word was for a popular concert – first recorded in 1862. Popular music of the eighteenth and nineteenth centuries was briefer, simpler, and lighter than contemporaneous classical music.

In the early twentieth century, song writers such as Jerome Kern, Irving Berlin, George Gershwin, and Cole Porter, continued to develop the popular song often using 32 bar ballad form. This consisted of an introductory verse of 16 or 32 bars followed by a more memorable and lyrical chorus of 32 bars constructed of 4×8 bar sections: AABA. The songs were more imaginative than the above formula suggests and used sophisticated harmony influenced by both jazz and classical music. Tin Pan Alley was the area in New York City where many popular songs from the 1920s to 1950s were composed and published. 'Popular music' is now generally used for music since the 1950s with roots in rock 'n' roll, covering music as diverse as 'The Sex Pistols' and Cliff Richard.

Rock 'n' Roll and Rock.

Rock 'n' roll is a form of rhythmicised blues, evolving from rhythm and blues, and was meant for dancing. Its tempo was fast and furious, the words were largely sexually based, the dynamic was loud, and the vocal style aggressive and semi-shouted. The instrumentation was dominated by electric guitars, saxophones, and a powerful rhythm section of drums, piano and bass, with a strong emphasis on the first beat of each bar. Successful American performers include Bill Haley and his Comets, Jerry Lee Lewis, Elvis Presley, Chuck Berry and Little Richard.

The 1960s: The Beatles.

In the early 1960s rock 'n' roll was revitalised by the emergence of new bands including the Beach Boys in the US and British groups such as the Beatles, the Rolling Stones, and the Who. These groups helped to transform the genre into a more varied and sophisticated form which became 'rock'.

The main features of 'rock' were developed in California by the Byrds and other bands in San Francisco. Rock had the flexibility and potential to create more varied and complex structures. The Beatles illustrated this greater sophistication in albums such as *Revolver* (1966) and *Sgt. Pepper's Lonely Hearts Club Band* (1967). Their contribution to the development of popular music was immense through the unfolding of a varied and distinctive musical language, and also their evolution of studio techniques, including multi-tracking and sound processing. They disengaged their music from the 'live performance' which would have been impossible for many of their best recorded songs. The basic characteristics of rock are an instrumentation of electric guitars, bass guitar, keyboard and drums; a fast, pounding rhythm from the bass and drums; and rather egocentric performances.

Heavy Metal, Punk and Reggae.

Heavy metal was developed from the blues progressions of the late 1960s by 'power trios' like Cream and the Jimi Hendrix Experience. It consisted of guitar-based rock with highly amplified and virtuosic guitar and bass, creating a 'wall of sound'. In the 1970s heavy metal bands included Deep Purple, Steppenwolf and Black Sabbath who were followed by the new wave of British bands such as Def Leppard and Iron Maiden. Live performance is very important for heavy metal, as fans enjoy interacting with the performers.

Punk was a term originally given to garage-based US rock of the 1960s, but was more famously used for music in 1976 played by the British bands, Sex Pistols, Clash, and Buzzcocks, who had been influenced by Richard Hell, and Patti Smith playing in New York City. Punk attempted to make rock 'dangerous' again, consisting of aggressive, anti-establishment lyrics, very basic guitar-based rock played at great speed. Punk evolved into New Wave which has similar energy but with more finesse and musical technique. Examples include Blondie and Talking Heads.

Reggae also emerged in the 1970s consisting of a Jamaican pop style developed from Ska (a shuffling hybrid of rhythm and blues) and Mento. The music is much slower and more sensuous than other popular genres and has a hypnotic, bass-dominated sound, a 'chopped off' beat, and often a lyrical and expressive vocal line. Bob Marley was the most impressive performer, along with Desmond Dekker and Jimmy Cliff.

Disco, House and Techno.

In the last 20 years music for dancing has become prevalent through the Discotheque and latterly the 'Rave'. Disco consists of a thumping bass drum on each beat of the music and is considered a debased form of pop music. It was promoted by the film *Saturday Night Fever* (1977) and is a relatively simple style, making use of drum machines and a relatively simple rhythm give it an anonymous quality.

House is based on Disco and consists of the warm, feel-good music of the late 1980s. The term comes from the use of warehouses for performance, and it originated in Chicago with Frankie Knuckles.

Techno, originating in Detroit, was also a development of the 1980s. It is a percussion-based electronic dance music, with stripped-down drum beats and bass lines. UK labels include Rising High and Warp and successful groups are Prodigy, Orbital, and L.F.O.. Most techno uses a 'groove' or movement by repetition, which builds up an evolving musical texture in a similar way to minimalist music.

Grunge.

Originating in Seattle during the mid-1980s, the grunge movement has largely usurped traditional heavy metal to become one of the most influential rock sounds of the 1990s. Essentially a mixture of blues-based chord progressions, punk-like energy levels and nihilistic lyrical content, the typical grunge song contrasts quieter, contemplative verses against raging, aggressive choruses. To achieve the deep and sinister sound at the heart of the music, grunge performers often de-tune their guitars and basses from standard concert pitch by up to two whole tones.

Since the movement came to world-wide prominence in 1992, grunge's most commercially successful acts have included Pearl Jam, Soundgarden and Alice In Chains. But by far the most important band to emerge from the genre was Seattle-based group Nirvana, whose second album, *Nevermind*, encapsulated much of grunge's intrinsic appeal. Unfortunately, Nirvana's singer/songwriter Kurt Cobain reacted badly to the demands of fame and subsequently took his own life in 1994. He has since become a cultural icon to disaffected teenagers everywhere. Though its forward momentum was temporarily checked by Cobain's death, grunge continues to grow with newer groups such as Live, Bush, Ash and Korn all expanding on the form's more dominant musical themes.

Brit-Pop.

After a particularly uneventful period in the history of British pop, a slew of similarily themed bands emerged in 1993 and commercially re-invigorated the domestic music scene. Taking their blueprint from the sounds and styles of the 1960s—with the music of The Beatles and The Kinks a clear reference point—groups such as Manchester's Oasis, London's Blur and Sheffield's Pulp all but dominated the UK charts in the 1990s. In direct opposition to America's grunge movement, the lyrical content of much of Brit-Pop is optimistic in nature, with images of casual hedonism and wry social commentary well to the fore.

Conversely, as the genre continues to evolve, emergent acts such as Radiohead and The Verve are directly challenging the more formulaic aspects of the Brit-Pop sound. More 'rock' than 'pop', these groups employ odd time signatures, thicker orchestral textures and lyrical themes of paranoia and rigorous self-examination to inform their music. The result of such experimentation has meant that original Brit-Pop acts have been forced to re-evaluate their position and explore wider musical themes in an effort to compete.

Boy Bands.

One of the more interesting developments to come out of the popular music scene in recent years has been the increasing proliferation of boy/girl bands. Unlike most pop acts that hone their musical craft in rehearsal rooms and concert halls over a period of years, the majority of boy/girl bands are 'manufactured', with group members brought together by prospective managers through the process of audition.

As record producers and professional song-writers often provide these acts with their material, the skills required of the average boy/girl band member differ greatly from more traditional groups. In place of instrumental prowess, they must be youthful in appearance, able dancers and reasonably proficient singers. When marketed properly, these acts have achieved huge chart success, finding a dedicated fanbase consisting not only of teenagers, but also children as young as five or six.

A sterling example of a successful boy band was Take That, who enjoyed an almost Beatles-like public profile until their break-up at the start of 1996. (After his departure from Take That, Robbie Williams went on to achieve great acclaim as a soloist, reaching new pinnacles in his career). Interestingly, a 'Samaritans Hotline' was established to help fans deal with their dissolution. Nonetheless, within months, Take That had been replaced in the public's affections by two more boy bands, Boyzone and the Backstreet Boys.

Girl Bands: The Spice Girls.

By far the most commercially profitable of the all girl groups has been the Spice Girls, who dominated both the UK and US charts with their blend of soulful melodies and appealing dance routines. Their simple mantra of 'Girl Power' has also become a catchphrase for many teenagers.

Though boy and girl bands offer little in developmental terms to the course of popular music, their success indicated a trend towards a more generalised form of entertainment within the pop scene, where the ability to dance well was as highly prized as a fine singing voice.

Jungle.

Jungle is a loose term used to describe a frenetically paced form of dance music that originated in the UK 'rave/club' scene in the early 1990s. Like Techno music, jungle is percussion based and reliant on the use of drum machines and synthesisers to provide its centralised core. Yet, where it differs from techno and house music is in the profound absence of mid-range frequencies, with virtually no vocals or guitar used to enhance melody. Instead, both bass and treble frequencies are heavily compressed, creating a thunderous, filtered sound. To add to the sense of musical drama, jungle moves at a pace of approximately 156–180 BPM (beats per minute), almost double the speed of the average pop song. Some of jungle music's more notable performers include Tricky and Goldie.

Drum and Bass.

Drum and bass is similar to jungle music in that it relies heavily on rhythm to enforce its point. However, in stark contrast to jungle's more repetitive approach, drum and bass often manipulates time signatures, speeding the beat up and down at irregular intervals to create a jarring musical effect. Because it compresses and stretches four bar progressions, drum and bass is often compared to jazz/bebop in terms of musical sensibility and performance. Roni Size is considered to be Great Britain's leading exponent of the drum and bass style.

Ambient.

Ambient is one of the most recent musical genres to emerge from the UK club scene. Effectively, it is a music of texture, where minimalist drum machine patterns and pulsating synthesisers are employed to invoke a sense of atmosphere and general relaxation. Less frenetic than either jungle or drum and bass, ambient is often played in smaller rooms within clubs, enabling the 'raver' a much needed opportunity to relax after an energetic night's dancing. Leading ambient acts include Black Dog, Plaid and Future Sound of London.

II. GLOSSARY OF MUSICAL TERMS

A. Note of scale, commonly used for tuning instruments.

Absolute Music. Music without any literary descriptive or other kind of reference.

A Capella. Literally "in the church style." Unaccompanied.

Accelerando. Quickening of the pace.

Accidental. The sign which alters the pitch of a note; ♯ (sharp) raises and a ♭ (flat) lowers note by one semitone, ✗ (double sharp) and ♭♭ (double flat) alter by two semitones.

Accompaniment. Instrumental or piano part forming background to a solo voice or instrument that has the melody.

Ad lib. (L. *ad libitum*). Direction on music that strict time need not be observed.

Adagio. A slow movement or piece.

Aeolian mode. One of the scales in mediaeval music, represented by the white keys of the piano from A to A.

Air. A simple tune for voice or instrument.

Alberti Bass. Characteristic 18th century keyboard figuration derived by splitting chord(s) of an accompanying part. Tradition credits Alberti as its inventor.

Allegretto. Not quite so fast as *Allegro*.

Allegro. Fast, but not too fast.

Alto. An unusually high type of male voice; also the vocal part sung by women and boys with a low range.

Ambrosian Chant. Plainsong introduced into church music by St. Ambrose, bishop of Milan (d. 397), and differing from Gregorian chant.

Andante. At a walking pace, not so slow as *Adagio* nor as fast as *Allegretto*.

Animato. Lively.

Answer. Entry in a fugue or invention which imitates or "answers" the theme at a different pitch.

Anthem. Composition for use in church during a service by a choir with or without soloists.

Antiphonal. Using groups of instruments or singers placed apart.

Appoggiatura. An ornament consisting of a short note just above or below a note forming part of a chord.

Arabesque. Usually a short piece, highly decorated.

Arco. Direction for string instruments to play with bow.

Aria. Vocal solo, usually in opera or oratorio, often in three sections with the third part being a repeat of the first. An *Arietta* is a shorter, lighter kind of aria.

Arioso. In the style of an aria; halfway between aria and recitative.

Arpeggio. Notes of a chord played in a broken, spread-out manner, as on a harp.

Ars antiqua. The old mediaeval music, based on organum and plainsong, before the introduction of *Ars nova* in 14th cent.

Ars Nova. New style of composition in 14th century France and Italy. It has greater variety in rhythm and independence in part-writing.

Atonal. Not in any key; hence *Atonality*.

Aubade. Morning song.

Augmentation. The enlargement of a melody by lengthening the musical value of its notes.

Ayre. Old spelling of *air*.

B. Note of scale, represented in Germany by *H*.

Bagatelle. A short, generally light piece of music. Beethoven wrote 26 Bagatelles.

Ballad. Either a narrative song or an 18th-cent. drawing-room song.

Ballade. A substantial and dramatic work, often for piano. Notable examples are by Chopin and Brahms.

Ballet. Stage entertainment requiring intrumental accompaniment; originated at French court in 16th and 17th cent.

Bar. A metrical division of music; the perpendicular line in musical notation to indicate this.

Barcarolle. A boating-song, in particular one associated with Venetian gondoliers.

Baritone. A male voice, between tenor and bass.

Baroque. A term applied, loosely, to music written in the 17th and 18th cent., roughly corresponding to baroque in architecture.

Bass. The lowest male voice; lowest part of a composition.

Bass Drum. Largest of the drum family, placed upright and struck on the side.

Bassoon. The lowest of the woodwind instruments, uses double reed.

Beat. Music's rhythmic pulse.

Bel canto. Literally "beautiful singing"—in the old Italian style with pure tone and exact phrasing.

Berceuse. Cradle song.

Binary. A piece in two sections is said to be binary in form. The balance is obtained by a second phrase (or section) answering the first.

Bitonality. Use of two keys at once.

Bow. Stick with horsehair stretched across it for playing string instruments.

Brass. Used as a collective noun for all brass or metal instruments.

Breve. Note, rarely used nowadays, with time value of two semibreves.

Bridge. Wood support over which strings are stretched on a violin, cello, guitar, *etc*.

Buffo(a). Comic, as in *buffo bass* or *opera buffa*.

C. Note of scale.

Cabaletta. Final, quick section of an aria or duet.

Cadence. A closing phrase of a composition or a passage, coming to rest on tonic (key note).

Cadenza. Solo vocal or instrumental passage, either written or improvised, giving soloist chance to display technical skill to audience.

Calando. Becoming quieter and slower.

Canon. A piece or section of music resulting from one line of music being repeated imitatively in the other parts which enter in succession.

Cantabile. Song-like, therefore flowing and expressive.

Cantata. Vocal work for chorus and/or choir.

Cantilena. Sustained, smooth melodic line.

Cantus firmus. Literally "fixed song." Basic melody from 14th to 17th cent., around which other voices wove contrapuntal parts.

Canzonet. Light songs written in England *c.* 1600.

Carillon. A set of bells in tower of church, played from a keyboard below.

Carol. Christmas song.

Castrato. Artificially-created male soprano and alto, fashionable in 17th and 18th cent. (The castration of vocally gifted boys prevailed in Italy until the 19th cent.)

Catch. A part-song like a round, in vogue in England from 16th to 19th cent.

Cavatina. An operatic song in one section, or a slow song-like instrumental movement.

Celesta. Keyboard instrument with metal bars struck by hammers.

Cello. Four-stringed instrument, played with bow, with a bass range. Comes between viola and double bass in string family.

Cembalo. Originally the Italian name for the dulcimer, but sometimes applied to the harpsichord.

Chaconne. Vocal or instrumental piece with unvaried bass.

Chamber Music. Music originally intended to be played in a room for three or more players.

Chanson. Type of part-song current in France from 14th to 16th cent.

Chant. Singing of psalms, masses, *etc.*, in plainsong to Latin words in church.

Choir. Body of singers, used either in church or at concerts.

Chorales. German hymn tunes, often made use of by Bach.

Chord. Any combination of notes heard together. *See also* Triad.

Chording. Spacing of intervals in a chord.

Chorus. Substantial body of singers, usually singing in four parts.

Chromatic. Using a scale of nothing but semitones.

Clarinet. Woodwind instrument with single reed in use since mid-18th cent.

Clavichord. Keyboard instrument having strings struck by metal tangents, much in use during 17th and 18th cent. as solo instrument.

Clavier. Used in German (*Klavier*) for piano, in England for any stringed keyboard instrument.

Clef. Sign in stave that fixes place of each note.

Coda. Closing section of movement in Sonata form.

Coloratura. Term to denote florid singing.

Common chord. *See* Triad.

Common Time. Four crotchets to the bar, 4/4 time.

Compass. Range of notes covered by voice or instruments.

Composition. Piece of music, originated by a composer's own imagination; act of writing such a piece.

Compound Time. Metre where beats are subdivided into threes rather than twos.

Con Brio. With dash.

Concert. Public performance of any music.

Concertato. Writing for several solo instruments to be played together.

Concerto. Work for one or more solo instruments and orchestra.

Concerto grosso. Orchestral work common in 17th and 18th cent. with prominent parts for small groups of instruments.

Concord. Opposite of discord, *i.e.*, notes that when sounded together satisfy the ear. (Conventional term in that its application varies according to the age in which one lives.)

Conduct. To direct a concert with a baton.

Consecutive. Progression of harmonic intervals of like kind.

Consonance. Like Concord.

Continuo. Bass line in 17th and 18th century music. Played by a bass instrument and keyboard, the latter improvising on the indicated harmonies.

Contralto. A woman's voice with a low range.

Counterpoint. Simultaneous combination of two or more melodies to create a satisfying musical texture. Where one melody is added to another, one is called the other's counterpoint. The adjective of counterpoint is contrapuntal.

Counter-tenor. Another name for male alto.

Courante. A dance in triple time.

Crescendo. Getting louder.

Crook. Detachable section of tubing on brass instruments that change the tuning.

Crotchet. Note that equals two quavers in time value.

Cycle. Set of works, especially songs, intended to be sung as group.

Cyclic form. Form of work in two or more movements in which the same musical themes recur.

Cymbal. Percussion instrument; two plates struck against each other.

D. Note of scale.

Da Capo (abbr. D.C.). A *Da Capo* aria is one in which the whole first section is repeated after a contrasting middle section.

Descant. Additional part (sometimes improvised) sung against a melody.

Development. Working-out section of movement in sonata form. *See* Sonata.

Diatonic. Opposite of chromatic; using proper notes of a major or minor scale.

Diminished. Lessened version of perfect interval, *e.g.*, semitone less than a perfect fifth is a diminished fifth.

Diminuendo. Lessening.

Diminution. Reducing a phrase of melody by shortening time value of notes.

Discord. Opposite of concord, *i.e.*, notes that sounded together produce a clash of harmonies.

Dissonance. Like discord.

Divertimento. A piece, usually orchestral, in several movements; like a suite.

Dodecaphonic. Pertaining to 12-note method of composition.

Dominant. Fifth note of major or minor scale above tonic (key) note.

Dorian Mode. One of the scales in mediaeval music, represented by the white keys on the piano from D to D.

Dot. Placed over note indicates staccato; placed after note indicates time value to be increased by half.

Double bar. Two upright lines marking the end of a composition or a section of it.

Double bass. Largest and lowest instrument of violin family; played with bow.

Drone bass. Unvarying sustained bass, similar to the permanent bass note of a bagpipe.

Drum. Variety of percussion instruments on which sound is produced by hitting a skin stretched tightly over a hollow cylinder or hemisphere.

Duet. Combination of two performers; composition for such a combination.

Duple Time. Metre in which there are two beats to a bar.

Dynamics. Gradations of loudness or softness in music.

E. Note of scale.

Electronic. Term used to describe use of electronic sounds in music.

Encore. Request from audience for repeat of work, or extra item in a programme.

English horn (*Cor anglais*). Woodwind instrument with double reed of oboe family.

Enharmonic. Refers to use of different letter names for the same note, *e.g.* F and E♯. Often exploited to achieve modulation between distantly related keys.

Ensemble. Teamwork in performance; item in opera for several singers with or without chorus; a group of performers of no fixed number.

Episode. Section in composition usually divorced from main argument.

Exposition. Setting out of thematic material in a sonata-form composition.

Expression marks. Indication by composer of how he wants his music performed.

F. Note of scale.

False relation. A clash of harmony produced when two notes, such as A natural and A flat, are played simultaneously or immediately following one another.

Falsetto. The kind of singing by male voices above normal register and sounding like an unbroken voice.

Fanfare. Flourish of trumpets.

Fantasy. A piece suggesting free play of composer's imagination, or a piece based on known tunes (folk, operatic, *etc.*).

Fermata. Pause indicated by sign ⌒ prolonging note beyond its normal length.

Fifth. Interval taking five steps in the scale. A perfect fifth (say, C to G) includes three whole tones and a semitone; a diminished fifth is a semitone less, an augmented fifth a semitone more.

Figure. A short phrase, especially one that is repeated.

Fingering. Use of fingers to play instrument, or the indication above notes to show what fingers should be used.

Flat. Term indicating a lowering of pitch by a semitone, or to describe a performer playing under the note.

Florid. Term used to describe decorative passages.

Flute. Woodwind instrument, blown sideways. It is played through a hole, not a reed. Nowadays, sometimes made of metal.

Folksong. Traditional tune, often in different versions, handed down aurally from generation to generation.

Form. Course or layout of a composition, especially when in various sections.

Fortissimo. Very loud.

Fourth. Interval taking four steps in scale. A perfect fourth (say, C to F) includes two whole tones and a semitone. If either note is sharpened or flattened the result is an augmented or a diminished fourth.

Fugato. In the manner of a fugue.

Fugue. Contrapuntal composition for various parts based on one or more subjects treated imitatively but not strictly.

G. Note of scale.

Galant. Used to designate elegant style of 18th cent. music.

Galliard. Lively dance dating back to 15th cent. or before.

Gavotte. Dance in 4/4 time, beginning on third beat in bar.

Giusto. Strict, proper.

Glee. Short part-song. See **L46**.

Glissando. Rapid sliding scales up and down piano or other instruments.

Glockenspiel. Percussion instrument consisting of tuned steel bars and played with two hammers or keyboard.

Grace note. See Ornament.

Grave. In slow tempo.

Grazioso. Gracefully.

Gregorian Chant. Plainsong collected and supervised mainly by Pope Gregory (d. 604).

Ground Bass. A bass part that is repeated throughout a piece with varying material on top.

Guitar. Plucked string instrument of Spanish origin, having six strings of three-octave compass.

H. German note-symbol for B.

Harmony. Simultaneous sounding of notes so as to make musical sense.

Harp. Plucked string instrument of ancient origin, the strings stretched parallel across its frame. The basic scale of C flat major is altered by a set of pedals.

Harpsichord. Keyboard stringed instrument played by means of keyboard similar to a piano but producing its notes by a plucking, rather than a striking action.

Homophonic. Opposite of polyphonic, *i.e.*, indicated parts move together in a composition, a single melody being accompanied by block chords, as distinct from the contrapuntal movement of different melodies.

Horn. Brass instrument with coiled tubes. Valves introduced in 19th cent. made full chromatic use of instrument possible.

Imitation. Repetition, exactly, or at least recognisably, of a previously heard figure.

Impromptu. A short, seemingly improvised piece of music, especially by Schubert or Chopin.

Improvise. To perform according to fancy or imagination, sometimes on a given theme.

In alt. The octave above the treble clef; *in altissimo*, octave above that.

Instrumentation. Writing music for particular instruments, using the composer's knowledge of what sounds well on different instruments.

Interlude. Piece played between two sections of a composition.

Intermezzo. Formerly meant interlude, now often used for pieces played between acts of operas.

Interval. Distance in pitch between notes.

Ionian mode. One of the scales in mediaeval music, represented on piano by white keys between C and C, identical therefore to modern C major scale.

Isorhythmic. Medieval technique using repetitions of a rhythm but with different notes. Much used in 15th century motets. See **P4**.

Jig. Old dance usually in 6/8 or 12/8 time.

Kettledrum (It. pl. *Timpani*). Drum with skin drawn over a cauldron-shaped receptacle, can be tuned to definite pitch by turning handles on rim, thus tightening or relaxing skin.

Key. Lever by means of which piano, organ, *etc.*, produces note; classification, in relatively modern times, of notes of a scale. Any piece of music in major or minor is in the *key* of its tonic or keynote.

Keyboard. Term used to describe instruments with a continuous row of keys.

Key-signature. Indication on written music, usually at the beginning of each line, of the number of flats or sharps in the key of a composition.

Kitchen Department. Humorous term for percussion section of an orchestra.

Lament. Musical piece of sad or deathly significance.

Largamente. Spaciously.

Largo. Slow.

Leading-motive (Ger. *Leitmotiv*). Short theme, suggesting person, idea, or image, quoted throughout composition to indicate that person, *etc.*

Legato. In a smooth style (of performance, *etc.*).

Lento. Slow.

Libretto. Text of an opera. See **L66**.

Lied (pl. *Lieder*). Song, with special reference to songs by Schubert, Schumann, Brahms, and Wolf.

Lute. String instrument plucked with fingers, used in 15th- and 16th-cent. music especially.

Lydian mode. One of the scales in mediaeval music, represented by white keys of piano between F and F.

Lyre. Ancient Greek plucked string instrument.

Madrigal. Contrapuntal composition for several voices, especially prominent from 15th to 17th cent.

Maestoso. Stately.

Major. One of the two main scales of the tonal system with semitones between the third and fourth, and the seventh and eighth notes. Identical with 16th-cent. Ionian mode.

Mandolin(e). Plucked string instrument of Italian origin.

Manual. A keyboard for the hands, used mostly in connection with the organ.

Master of the King's (or Queen's) Musick. Title of British court appointment, with no precise duties.

Melisma. Group of notes sung to a single syllable.

Mélodie. Literally a melody or tune; has come to mean a French song (cf. German Lied).

Metronome. Small machine in use since the beginning of the 18th cent., to determine the pace of any composition by the beats of the music, e.g., =60 at the head of the music indicates sixty crotchets to the minute.

Mezzo, Mezza. (It. = "half ") Mezza voce means using the half voice (a tone between normal singing and whispering). Mezzo-soprano, voice between soprano and contralto.

Minim. Note that equals two crotchets in time value.

Minor. One of the two main scales of the tonal system (cf. major), identical with 16th-cent. Aeolian mode. It has two forms—the harmonic and melodic, the former having a sharpened seventh note, the latter having the sixth and seventh note sharpened.

Minuet. Originally French 18th-cent. dance in triple time, then the usual third movement in symphonic form (with a contrasting trio section) until succeeded by scherzo.

Mixolydian mode. One of the mediaeval scales represented by the white keys on the piano from G to G.

Modes. Scales prevalent in the Middle Ages. See Aeolian, Dorian, Ionian, Lydian, Mixolydian, Phrygian.

Modulate. Changing from key to key in a composition, not directly but according to musical "grammar".

Molto. Much, very; thus allegro molto.

Motet. Sacred, polyphonic vocal composition. More loosely, any choral composition for use in church but not set to words of the liturgy. See P3.

Motive, motif. Short, easily recognised melodic figure.

Motto. Short, well-defined theme recurring throughout a composition, cf. Idée fixe in Berlioz's Symphonie Fantastique.

Movement. Separate sections of a large-scale composition, each in its own form.

Music drama. Term used to describe Wagner's, and sometimes other large-scale operas.

Mutes. Devices used to damp the sound of various instruments.

Natural (of a note or key). Not sharp or flat.

Neoclassical. Clear-cut style, originating during 1920s, that uses 17th and 18th century forms and styles. It constituted a reaction to the excesses of romanticism.

Ninth. Interval taking nine steps, e.g., from C upwards an octave and a whole tone to D.

Nocturne. Literally a "night-piece" hence usually of lyrical character.

Nonet. Composition for nine instruments.

Notation. Act of writing down music.

Note. Single sound of specified pitch and duration; symbol to represent this.

Obbligato. Instrumental part having a special or essential rôle in a piece.

Oboe. Woodwind instrument with double reed, descended from hautboy; as such, in use since 16th cent., in modern form since 18th cent.

Octave. Interval taking eight steps of scale, with top and bottom notes having same "name"; C to C is an octave.

Octet. Composition for eight instruments or voices.

Ondes Martenol. Belongs to a class of melodic instruments in which the tone is produced by electrical vibrations controlled by the movement of the hands not touching the instrument.

Opera. Musical work for the stage with singing characters, originated c. 1600 in Italy.

Opera buffa (It.), **Opéra bouffe** (Fr.). Comic opera (in the English sense), not to be confused with Opéra comique (Fr.) which is opera with spoken dialogue and need not be humorous.

Opera seria. Chief operatic form of 17th and 18th cent., usually set to very formal librettos, concerning gods or heroes of ancient history.

Operetta. Lighter type of opera.

Opus (abbr. Op.). With number following opus indicates order of a composer's composition.

Oratorio. Vocal work, usually for soloists and choir with instrumental accompaniment, generally with setting of a religious text.

Orchestra. Term to designate large, or largish, body of instrumentalists originated in 17th cent.

Orchestration. Art of setting out work for instruments of an orchestra. To be distinguished from Instrumentation (q.v.).

Organ. Elaborate keyboard instrument in which air is blown through pipes by bellows to sound notes. Tone is altered by selection of various stops and, since the 16th cent., a pedal keyboard has also been incorporated.

Organum. In mediaeval music a part sung as an accompaniment below or above the melody of plainsong, usually at the interval of a fourth or fifth; also, loosely, this method of singing in parts.

Ornament. Notes that are added to a given melody by composer or performer as an embellishment.

Overture. Instrumental introduction or prelude to larger work, usually opera. Concert overtures are simply that: i.e., work to be played at start of a concert.

Part. Music of one performer in an ensemble; single strand in a composition.

Part-song. Vocal composition in several parts.

Passacaglia. Composition in which a tune is constantly repeated, usually in the bass.

Passage. Section of a composition.

Passion. Musical setting of the New Testament story of Christ's trial and crucifixion.

Pastiche. Piece deliberately written in another composer's style.

Pavan(e). Moderately paced dance dating from 16th cent. or earlier.

Pedal. Held note in bass of composition.

Pentatonic. Scale of five consecutive notes, e.g., the black keys of the piano.

Percussion. Collective title for instruments of the orchestra that are sounded by being struck by hand or stick.

Phrygian Mode. One of the scales of mediaeval music, represented by the white keys on piano from E to E.

Piano. Soft, abbr. p; pp=pianissimo, very soft; instrument, invented in 18th cent., having strings struck by hammer, as opposed to the earlier harpsichord where they are plucked. The modern piano has 88 keys and can be either "upright" (vertical) or "grand" (horizontal).

Pianoforte. Almost obsolete full Italian name for the piano.

Pitch. Exact height or depth of a particular musical sound or note.

Pizzicato. Direction for stringed instruments, that the strings should be plucked instead of bowed.

Plainchant, Plainsong. Mediaeval church music consisting of single line of melody without harmony or definite rhythm. *See* **P3**.

Polka. Dance in 2/4 time originating in 19th cent. Bohemia.

Polonaise. Polish dance generally in 3/4 time.

Polyphony. Combination of two or more musical lines as in *counterpoint*.

Polytonality. Simultaneous use of several keys.

Postlude. Closing piece, opposite of Prelude.

Prelude. Introductory piece.

Presto. Very fast. *Prestissimo.* Still faster.

Progression. Movement from one chord to next to make musical sense.

Quartet. Work written for four instruments or voices; group to play or sing such a work.

Quaver. Note that equals two semiquavers or half a crotchet.

Quintet. Work written for five instruments or voices; group to play or sing such a work.

Rallentando. Slowing down.

Recapitulation. Section of composition that repeats original material in something like its original form.

Recitative. Term used for declamation in singing written in ordinary notation but allowing rhythmical licence.

Recorder. Woodwind instrument, forerunner of flute.

Reed. Vibrating tongue of woodwind instruments.

Register. Set of organ pipes controlled by a particular stop; used in reference to different ranges of instrument or voice (*e.g.*, chest register).

Relative. Term used to indicate common key signature of a major and minor key.

Répétiteur. Member of opera house's musical staff who coaches singers in their parts.

Rest. Notation of pauses for instrument in composition, having a definite length like a note.

Retrograde. Term used to describe a melody played backwards.

Rhapsody. Work of no definite kind with a degree of romantic content.

Rhythm. Everything concerned with the time of music (*i.e.*, beats, accent, metre, *etc.*) as opposed to the pitch side.

Ritornello. Passage, usually instrumental, that recurs in a piece.

Romance, Romanza. Title for piece of vague song-like character.

Romantic. Term used vaguely to describe music of 19th cent. that has other than purely musical source of inspiration.

Rondo. Form in which one section keeps on recurring.

Rubato. Manner of performing a piece without keeping strictly to time.

Sackbut. Early English name for trombone.

Saxophone. Classified as wind instrument, although made of brass, because it uses a reed.

Scale. Progression of adjoining notes upwards or downwards.

Scherzo. Literally "a joke". Often used as a light movement in the middle of a sonata type work.

Score. Copy of any music written in several parts.

Second. Interval taking two steps in scale, *e.g.*, C to D flat, or to D.

Semibreve. Note that equals two minims or half a breve.

Semiquaver. Note that equals half a quaver.

Semitone. Smallest interval commonly used in Western music.

Septet. Composition for seven instruments or voices.

Sequence. Repetition of phrase at a higher or lower pitch.

Serenade. Usually an evening song or instrumental work.

Seventh. Interval taking seven steps in the scale.

Sextet. Composition for six instruments or voices.

Sharp. Term indicating a raising of pitch by a semitone.

Shawm. Primitive woodwind instrument, forerunner of oboe.

Simple time. Division of music into two or four beats.

Sinfonietta. Small symphony.

Sixth. Interval taking six steps in the scale.

Solo. Piece or part of a piece for one performer playing or singing alone.

Sonata. Term to denote a musical form and a type of composition. In *sonata form* a composition is divided into exposition, development and recapitulation. A *sonata* is a piece, usually for one or more players following that form.

Song. Any short vocal composition.

Soprano. Highest female voice.

Sostenuto. Sustained, broadly.

Sotto voce. Whispered, scarcely audible, applied to vocal as well as instrumental music.

Spinet. A small keyboard instrument belonging to the harpsichord (*q.v.*) family.

Sprechgesang. (Ger. Speech-song.) Vocal utterance somewhere between speech and song.

Staccato. Perform music in short, detached manner.

Staff. Horizontal lines on which music is usually written.

Stop. Lever by which organ registration can be altered.

String(s). Strands of gut or metal set in vibration to produce musical sounds on string or keyboard instruments. Plural refers to violins, violas, cellos, and basses of orchestra.

Study. Instrumental piece, usually one used for technical exercise or to display technical skills, but often having artistic merits as well (*e.g.*, Chopin's).

Subject(s). Theme or group of notes that forms principal idea or ideas in composition.

Suite. Common name for piece in several movements.

Symphony. Orchestral work of serious purpose usually in four movements, occasionally given name (*e.g.*, Beethoven's "Choral" symphony).

Syncopation. Displacement of musical accent.

Tempo. Pace, speed of music.

Tenor. Highest normal male voice.

Ternary. A piece in three sections is said to be in ternary form. The balance is obtained by repeating the first phrase or section (though it need not be exact or complete) after a second of equal importance.

Tessitura. Compass into which voice or instrument comfortably falls.

Theme. Same as *subject* but can also be used for a whole musical statement as in "theme and variations."

Third. Interval taking three steps in scale.

Time. Rhythmical division of music.

Timpani. *See* Kettledrum.

Toccata. Instrumental piece usually needing rapid, brilliant execution.

Tonality. Key, or feeling for a definite key.

Tone. Quality of musical sound; interval of two semitones.

Tonic Sol-fa. System of musical notation to simplify sight-reading.

Transcribe. Arrange piece for different medium, instrument, or voice than that originally intended.

Transition. Passage that joins two themes of sections of a composition.

Transpose. To move a musical idea, theme or piece to a different key from its original.

Treble. Highest part in vocal composition; high boy's voice.

Triad. Three note chord. Usually consists of a note and those a third and fifth above.

Trio. Work written for three instruments or voices; group to play or sing such a work.

Trombone. Brass instrument with slide adjusting length of tube.

Trumpet. Metal instrument of considerable antiquity; modern version has three valves to make it into a chromatic instrument.

Tuba. Deepest-toned brass instrument with three or four valves.

Twelve-note. Technique of composition using full chromatic scale with each note having equal importance. Notes are placed in particular order as the thematic basis of works.

Unison. Two notes sung or played together at same pitch.

Valve. Mechanism, invented in early 19th cent. to add to brass instruments allowing them to play full chromatic scale.

Variation. Varied passage of original theme. Such variations may be closely allied to or depart widely from the theme.

Verismo. Term to describe Italian operas written in "realist" style at the turn of this century.

Vibrato. Rapid fluctuation in pitch of voice or instrument. Exaggerated it is referred to as a "wobble" (of singers) or tremolo.

Viol. String instrument of various sizes in vogue until end of 17th cent.

Viola. Tenor instrument of violin family.

Violin. Musical four-string instrument, played with bow, of violin family, which superseded viol at beginning of 18th cent.

Virginals. English keyboard instrument, similar to harpsichord of 17th and 18th cent.

Vivace. Lively.

Voluntary. Organ piece for church use, but not during service.

Waltz. Dance in triple time, fashionable in 19th cent.

Whole-tone scale. Scale progressing by whole tones. Only two are possible, one beginning on C, the other on C sharp.

Xylophone. Percussion instrument with series of wood bars tuned in a chromatic scale and played with sticks.

Zither. String instrument laid on knees and plucked. Common in Central-European folk music.

III. INDEX TO COMPOSERS

IV. SPECIAL TOPIC

DMITRI SHOSTAKOVICH
THE COMPOSER, HIS MUSIC AND HIS TIMES

Introduction.

This article deals with one of the foremost Russian composers of the 20th century, a musician whose whole career has been bound up with his nation's history and its cultural politics. His formative years were overshadowed by war and revolution. A relatively free and experimental period in musical life was followed in the late 1920s by the dominance of a "proletarian" movement demanding simplicity from composers; this in turn gave way in 1932 to the establishment of Communist Party control over music through the Union of Composers and the doctrine of "socialist realism". Stalin's terror, World War II, renewed repression and the post-Stalin "thaw" all left their mark. Shostakovich was at various times both the victim of official censure and the recipient of official honours and privileges. He produced pieces to order which satisfied the authorities; he also wrote music which spoke eloquently to his fellow-citizens and in which he expressed himself honestly.

The Early Years: 1906–26.

Dmitri Dmitrievich Shostakovich was born in St. Petersburg on 25 September 1906, the second of three children of a middle-class family. Music played an important part at home, but it was not until the age of nine that Dmitri was persuaded by his mother to take piano lessons. His precocious talent soon became apparent. He possessed absolute pitch and a prodigious musical memory. Progress as a pianist was rapid: at the age of 11 he had mastered all of Bach's 48 Preludes and Fugues. He also began composing. In autumn 1919 he enrolled as a student at the Petrograd Conservatoire. Here he received a thorough traditional musical training and joined with like-minded students in exploring new music.

His father's death in February 1922 left his family in straitened circumstances. Employment from October 1924 as a pianist for silent films provided some income; although Shostakovich considered it drudgery, it helped to develop his skill in musical characterisation and satire. Performances of his compositions in Moscow widened his circle of musical supporters, and he came to the attention of Marshal Tukhachevsky, a music-lover as well as a leading figure in the Red Army. Tukhachevsky gave financial support to the young composer and his family. In July 1925 Shostakovich completed his graduation piece for the Conservatoire, his 1st Symphony. Premièred on 12 May 1926, it was an instant success; Shostakovich referred to that date as his "second birth".

First Successes: 1926–36.

The 1st Symphony brought recognition not only in Russia but also in the West. Within a year Bruno Walter conducted it in Berlin, and conductors like Toscanini and Klemperer soon programmed it. Shostakovich now turned in a distinctly experimental direction in piano works like the First Sonata (1926) and *Aphorisms* (1927). The 2nd Symphony (originally entitled "To October: a Symphonic Dedication") was an official commission (1927) to celebrate the tenth anniversary of the Bolshevik revolution. A single-movement work, its first part shows Shostakovich's modernist style, with some dense, complex writing; in the second part this gives way to a setting for chorus (heralded by a factory siren) of a propagandist text, ending with the shouted words: "October, the Commune, Lenin!". The 3rd Symphony of 1929 ("The First of May") is constructed along similar lines.

Shostakovich's friendship with the musicologist Ivan Sollertinsky began in 1927 and lasted until Sollertinsky's death in 1944. In particular, Sollertinsky directed Shostakovich to the music of Mahler, with whom he found an immediate affinity. Mahler's irony, his use of popular idioms and his overt emotionalism all find their parallels in Shosta-

kovich. It was also in 1927 that Shostakovich met Nina Varzar, a Physics student whom he married in 1932; they were to have two children.

During the late 1920s and early 1930s Shostakovich was occupied with composing music for stage and film. His first opera, *The Nose*, based upon a short story by Gogol, gave full scope for his satirical sense and musical inventiveness (for example, it contains an entr'acte for unpitched percussion alone); the approach to vocal writing and text-setting is highly individual, although rooted in the practice of 19th-century Russian composers like Mussorgsky: "the vocal parts", Shostakovich wrote, "are built upon speech inflections." Produced in 1930, the opera met with considerable critical hostility, and for the first time Shostakovich was accused of "formalism".

In 1929 he collaborated with the experimental theatre director Vsevolod Meyerhold, providing incidental music for his production of Mayakovsky's play *The Bedbug*. Many of his scores around this time, however, were for propagandistic works. The culmination of these years of writing music for dramatic purposes was the opera *Lady Macbeth of the Mtsensk District*, completed in 1932, based on a story of adultery and murder in provincial Russia by the 19th-century writer Nikolai Leskov. Productions in both Leningrad and Moscow opened in January 1934; the opera was immensely successful with audiences and critics, and received numerous performances over the next two years. It was also given in venues abroad. Shostakovich was established as the Soviet Union's leading opera composer.

The Mature Composer: 1936–48.

A new production of *Lady Macbeth* opened at Moscow's Bolshoi Theatre in December 1935. On 26 January 1936 Stalin and a group of colleagues attended a performance; they left before the final Act. Two days later an unsigned article, "Muddle Instead Of Music", appeared in *Pravda*, condemning the opera for its musical style and its treatment of the subject-matter. The author (possibly Stalin himself) wrote: "From the very first moment, listeners are stunned by the deliberately dissonant and confused stream of sounds . . . Singing is replaced by screaming . . . The music quacks, hoots, pants and gasps in order to express the love scenes as naturally as possible." The composer was warned that the matter "could end badly." Another article on 6 February attacked Shostakovich's ballet *The Limpid Stream*.

Shostakovich completed his 4th Symphony later that year and it went into rehearsal, but he withdrew it in November before the scheduled first performance. (The symphony was eventually performed in 1961; a revised version of *Lady Macbeth*, entitled *Katerina Izmailova*, was staged in 1963.) A change of style was a political necessity, but Shostakovich had already been moving in that direction in the 1st Piano Concerto (1933) and the Cello Sonata (1934). The 5th Symphony – "a Soviet artist's creative response to just criticism" – met official requirements in terms of an accessible style and an apparently "positive" conclusion; its première (21 November 1937) was a triumph.

In 1938 Shostakovich composed the first of his fifteen string quartets, and his developing interest in chamber music is also shown in the Piano Quintet (1940) and the 2nd Piano Trio (1944, dedicated to the memory of Sollertinsky).

The USSR joined World War II following the Nazi attack of June 1941; the siege of Leningrad began on 30 August. Shostakovich worked on his 7th Symphony in Leningrad through the first month of the siege. In October he was evacuated to Kuibyshev in the Urals, where he completed the symphony; it was first performed there on 5 March 1942. Performances followed in Moscow and in Leningrad itself. A microfilm of the score was flown to the West where conductors in the UK and USA were eager to programme it. Sir Henry Wood conducted it in London in June, followed by Toscanini in a nationwide broadcast in the USA in July. Another "war" symphony, the tragic, pessimistic

8th, appeared in 1943. The 9th Symphony of 1945 – a "merry, light-hearted scherzo-symphony" as Shostakovich called it – was the very opposite of the kind of monumental work which the authorities might have expected for the celebration of victory. Nevertheless, Shostakovich's 40th birthday year in 1946 was marked by the award of the Order of Lenin and his third Stalin Prize for the 2nd Piano Trio (he had previously won prizes for the Piano Quintet and the 7th Symphony).

The relatively relaxed artistic atmosphere of the war years was changing, however. Andrei Zhdanov, Stalin's right-hand man in cultural matters, had already promulgated party decrees on literature in 1946, attacking leading writers like Pasternak and Akhmatova. He now turned his attention to music.

The Mature Composer: 1948–62.

On 10 February 1948 a resolution of the Central Committee of the Communist Party condemned Shostakovich, Prokofiev, Khachaturian and other leading composers for "formalistic distortions and anti-democratic tendencies alien to the Soviet people." At a subsequent conference of the Composers' Union, the 8th Symphony was one of the works picked on for criticism: Shostakovich was accused of having "fallen victim to his ultra-individualistic conception of life" and dwelling "too much on the dark and fearful aspects of reality." He lost his teaching posts at the Leningrad and Moscow Conservatoires; much of his music was blacklisted.

He had no alternative but to accept, outwardly, the Party's judgement. New works which could not be performed in the current climate – the 1st Violin Concerto and the song-cycle *From Jewish Folk Poetry* of 1948, the 4th String Quartet of 1949 – were kept "in the desk drawer" to await better times. "Safe" compositions in the required style and on approved subject-matter helped his rehabilitation: *The Song of the Forests* (1949), *Ten Poems and Texts by Revolutionary Poets* (1951), *The Sun Shines over Our Motherland* (1952). In March 1949, at Stalin's personal insistence, Shostakovich attended, unwillingly, a "Peace Congress" in New York. More happily, the Bach bicentenary celebrations in Leipzig in 1950 provided the impetus for the composition of the 24 Preludes and Fugues, completed in February 1951.

Stalin's death in 1953 and the subsequent De-Stalinisation campaign resulted, albeit intermittently, in an easing of the pressures upon artists. Shostakovich's 10th Symphony, a highly personal work, was written in that year and marks his return to symphonic composition. Professionally the following decade was very successful. He received the Lenin Prize on his 50th birthday. Major works include the 11th Symphony ("The Year 1905") and the 2nd Piano Concerto of 1957, the 1st Cello Concerto (1959), the 8th String Quartet (1960) and in 1961 the 12th Symphony ("The Year 1917 – to the memory of Vladimir Ilyich Lenin"). In 1960, in response to pressure from above, Shostakovich joined the Communist Party.

His wife Nina died in 1954, and in 1956 he remarried; the marriage was unhappy, ending in divorce in 1958. In 1962 he remarried again; his third wife, Irina, provided support and domestic tranquillity for the increasingly frail composer.

The Late Period, 1962–75.

As the leading Soviet composer, Shostakovich continued to receive awards and honours in the USSR and abroad; yet during this late period his music became more uncompromising and personal. Vocal writing was a preoccupation, not only in a number of song-cycles but also in two symphonies; his choice of subject-matter and texts was sometimes controversial. The 13th Symphony (1962) contains settings of poems by Yevgeni Yevtushenko, including *Babi Yar*, the famous indictment of anti-Semitism. The 14th Symphony (1969), dedicated to Benjamin Britten (with whom Shostakovich had formed a mutually admiring friendship) sets texts by various poets on the subject of death; mortality increasingly obsessed Shostakovich during these years. From the mid-1960s he experimented with the inclusion of twelve-note rows in his music, to provide a contrast with tonal themes (as in the 12th String Quartet, 1968) or to undermine radically the sense of tonal security (as in the extra-

ordinary 13th String Quartet, 1970).

The cycle of symphonies ends with the enigmatic 15th (1971) and the string quartets with the 15th (1974), a series of slow movements. Shostakovich's last work is the Viola Sonata (whose lengthy final slow movement pays homage to Beethoven), completed shortly before his death. He died in hospital on 9 August 1975 of lung cancer.

Shostakovich and the Soviet Régime.

The official obituary of Shostakovich referred to him as "a faithful son of the Communist Party" who "devoted his entire life to the development of Soviet music, reaffirming the ideals of socialist humanism and internationalism." This view of Shostakovich, as a fundamentally loyal Soviet citizen, was broadly accepted in the West during his lifetime. In 1979 a book was published giving a quite different picture of the composer – *Testimony: the memoirs of Dmitri Shostakovich as related to and edited by Solomon Volkov*. Volkov, a young Soviet musicologist, claimed to have had conversations with Shostakovich between 1971 and 1974 in which the composer reminisced frankly about his life and times; Volkov wrote these up and Shostakovich put his signature to each of the eight chapters. Shostakovich insisted that the "memoirs" should only be published after his death. Volkov emigrated to the USA in 1976. The published book is a translation of his typescript. It shows Shostakovich as a bitter, often cynical man, unremittingly hostile to the régime under which he lived and worked. "Looking back I see nothing but ruins, only mountains of corpses . . . the horrible disillusionment that I had to face . . . the bitterness that has coloured my life grey."

Controversy has surrounded *Testimony* since its publication. There are two issues: authenticity – are these "memoirs" actually what Volkov claimed them to be? And truth – do they in any case represent Shostakovich's views? As to the first, there is evidence that the situation is more complex than claimed; in particular, it has been shown that the pages which Shostakovich actually signed consist of word-for-word transcriptions of rather innocuous material which had already been published in his lifetime. However, the reader of *Testimony* certainly does not get the impression that it is a fabrication.

Dissident or Conformist?

Was Shostakovich a "closet dissident" or a conformist? The likely answer is that he was something of both. Certainly from personal experience he could have had no illusions about the nature of the régime: relatives were arrested in the 1930s; a student friend, Mikhail Kvadrin, the original dedicatee of the 1st Symphony, was shot in 1929 as a "counter-revolutionary"; Marshal Tukhachevsky was executed in 1937 in Stalin's purge of the Red Army; the director Meyerhold was arrested in 1939 and killed in 1940. During these years Shostakovich cannot ever have felt safe, but he survived. The régime recognised the usefulness of having a composer of Shostakovich's stature playing a rôle in cultural life, and he was willing to accommodate himself to the régime's demands, both in Stalin's time and afterwards.

This accommodation was not only musical: it also involved a willingness to read speeches prepared for him and to sign letters which, by his own admission, he had often not read. His contempt for officialdom, however, found musical expression in the *Antiformalist Rayok* (the untranslatable "rayok" means something like "peepshow"), a kind of satirical vaudeville begun in 1948 and added to intermittently over many years. It was eventually performed in September 1989.

Political and Personal Meaning in Shostakovich's Music.

The question of "meaning" in Shostakovich's music is not an easy one. To take the 7th Symphony as an example: Shostakovich provided descriptions of this work in the approved "socialist realist" style – "a symphony about our epoch, about our people, about our sacred war, about our victory." Even there is calculated ambiguity: "our epoch, our people" could refer to the Soviet people under Stalin as well as to the Leningraders threatened by Hitler. If *Testimony* is to be believed, the symphony was "planned before the war, and, consequently, it simply cannot be seen as a reaction to Hitler's attack . . . It's not about Leningrad under siege, it's about the Leningrad that Stalin destroyed and that Hitler merely finished off."

Shostakovich expressed himself against simplistic programmatic interpretations of music: "When a critic . . . writes that in such-and-such a symphony Soviet civil servants are represented by the oboe and clarinet, and Red Army men by the brass section, you want to scream!" This comment from 1933 should also act as a warning against post-*Testimony* attempts to read straightforward anti-Soviet stories into Shostakovich's music.

The Use of Codes.

However, he certainly believed that music carried meaning, and his use of quotations and musical "codes" encourages a search for "messages", often of a personal nature. For example, his initials D.Sch. (from the German transliteration D. Schostakowitsch) generated a musical motto, D-Es-C-H (the German version of the notes D-E flat-C-B). He used this extensively in the 10th Symphony; in the 3rd movement he also introduced a repeated motif on the horn consisting of the notes E-A-E-D-A; this is derived from the first name of Elmira Nazirova, a former student with whom he had maintained an emotionally intense correspondence. Evidently there is an autobiographical "subtext" here.

Another case is the 8th String Quartet. This has the dedication "In memory of the victims of fascism and war", and was apparently inspired by a visit to Dresden; but Shostakovich admitted its personal significance in a letter to his close friend Isaak Glikman: "When I die it's hardly likely that someone will write a quartet dedicated to my memory. So I decided to write it myself. One could write on the frontispiece, 'Dedicated to the author of this quartet'." There is evidence that his unhappiness at having to join the Communist Party lies behind the composition of this work; it has been described as "an apologia . . . to his own conscience." The D-S-C-H figure is omnipresent in the quartet, but there are also quotations from the 1st, 5th and 10th Symphonies, the 1st Cello Concerto, the 2nd Piano Trio (a "Jewish" theme), *Lady Macbeth*, and a revolutionary song "Tormented by the Weight of Bondage". What matters for the listener about this music, however, is less its precise autobiographical significance than its emotional intensity and its structural power.

Conclusion.

Shostakovich's best-known works have never lacked popularity in the West. However, in the mid-20th century academic musicologists and "modernist" composers tended to disregard his work, which was perceived as too bound by traditional musical forms and tonal language. A change in the musical climate from the 1970s has led to a revaluation. In his centenary year it is safe to say that the range and complexity of Shostakovich's music is receiving due recognition, and that his standing as a great, and central, figure in 20th-century music is now fully established.

THE CINEMA

This section provides a brief but wide-ranging introduction to the world of the cinema. It includes sections on how the cinema has evolved, notes on many famous directors, actors and actresses as well as a wide-ranging glossary of film terms and lists of the Oscar Winners.

TABLE OF CONTENTS

THE CINEMA

1. THE EVOLUTION OF THE CINEMA

HISTORICAL BACKGROUND

The Lumière Brothers

It was in December 1895 that the Lumière brothers, Louis and Auguste, organised what is generally regarded as the first exhibition of "moving pictures" for admission money. The event was really the culmination of numerous photographic developments that had taken place over the preceeding decades. These included Eadweard Muybridge's famous photographs of horses in motion in 1871; Etienne Julius Marey's development of a so-called "photographic rifle" with which he could take ten pictures a second (the term "shooting" for a film is commonly thought to derive from this); George Eastman's launch in 1888 of the Kodak camera and his development of the celluloid roll film; and Thomas Edison's production in 1891 of the 35mm film and, with his brilliant assistant W.K.L. Dickson, the development of the Kinetoscope which showed photographic moving pictures in a peepshow.

Georges Méliès

The Lumière brothers owned a factory that manufactured cameras and photographic equipment and envisaged the motion picture primarily as an extension and promotion of this. Their work, mostly documentary with a number of comic or light dramatic set-pieces, is seen as a major precursor of realism in the cinema. Roughly contemporary with them was the stage magician, Georges Méliès who made the first trick films, using a variety of artificial devices and special effects to tell entertaining science and pseudo-historic tales. In some ways, the Lumières and Méliès exemplify the two major tendencies to which the cinema has been drawn throughout its history: film as magic carpet (the Méliès tradition) or film as window on the world (the Lumière tradition), film as dream or film as document.

The Coming of Sound

Despite many short-lived innovations (such as three-dimensional cinema, which necessitated the wearing of a special pair of spectacles), the technical battery of cinema has remained in many respects remarkably moderate. Special effects, the development of sophisticated animation techniques, quadrophonic sound in certain large city-centre cinemas, and an increasingly sophisticated range of colour techniques are all quantitative rather than qualitative modifications, and plans to enlarge the sensory battery of cinema through pumping appropriate scents in the cinema (and even providing spectators with suitable tactile stimuli) have never developed in any sustained way. The major date in the history of the medium remains 1927, the year of the first sound film (*The Jazz Singer*, with Al Jolson).

Sound was fiercely resisted (by Charlie Chaplin among others), but its possibilities were so rapidly recognised, not least by Rene Clair and Alfred Hitchcock who both made early innovatory use of it, that its survival was never long in jeopardy.

Introduction of Colour

As well as sound, another major technical development was in colour photography. Film prints had been tinted from the earliest days (a fact worth bearing in mind when it is sometimes assumed that all silent films were monochrome) but colour of a high technical standard did not become widely used until after the Second World War. Colour first tended to be used for fantasy or adventure genres or spectaculars such as *Gone With the Wind* (1939), and it was not until the mid 1960s that sales of film to television more or less demanded that every film be made in colour. Nevertheless, there are a number of films that continue to be filmed in black and white, not out of a hostility to colour, but for purposes of, for example, nostalgia (as in Woody Allen's *Manhattan*, 1979 or *Purple Rose of Cairo*, 1985), brutal realism (Scorsese's *Raging Bull*, 1980), pastiche and homage (Tim Burton's *Ed Wood*, 1994) and of dramatic newsreel evocation (as in Spielberg's *Schindler's List* of 1993, with its momentary bursts of colour). Colour has also often been used expressively: for example, to evoke a mood (as in Antonioni's *Red Desert* of 1964) or as dramatic motif (the menacing use of red in Nicolas Roeg's *Don't Look Now* of 1973) or to suggest a process of ironic distancing from a set of stylistic conventions (as with the deliberately lurid colours in Douglas Sirk's melodramas). Although its use has sometimes been unimaginative and blandly naturalistic, colour has become a rich and important part of cinematic language and it has been shown that it can co-exist with black and white, sometimes even in the same film.

Other Technical Developments

Another technical development was that of the big screen—in processes such as Cinerama, Cinemascope, Todd-AO—particularly associated with the fifties and sixties, when Hollywood's response to the threat of television was not necessarily to make movies better but at least to make them wider. Many directors hated this development, feeling that the new screen shape was only suitable for filming duck-shoots or dachshunds and not permitting the kind of concentrated detail a director had formerly required. "You can't get a close-up of a finger nail," commented Alfred Hitchcock disdainfully. Nevertheless, a director like Nicholas Ray (who had noted that every technical advance of the cinema had generally been greeted with dismay) demonstrated in a film like *Rebel Without a Cause* (1955) that it was possible to use colour and widescreen for eloquently expressive purposes. A film like Kenneth Branagh's *Hamlet* (1997) was made in 70mm in an attempt to emulate the visual splendour of epics of three decades earlier, such as *Lawrence of Arabia* (1962).

Recent Technology

In recent years, video technology had made it more possible for new film-makers to engage in comparatively inexpensive, independent and experimental work: experienced directors such as Antonioni, Godard and Chris Marker have also made use of this. But the major advances in the last decade have been in the area of special effects as generated by new technologies of computer animation. These have brought new virtuosity into the realm of the Disney cartoon; new visual wonders into spectaculars such as *Jurassic Park* (1993), *Men in Black* (1997) and *Gladiator* (2000); and fresh tricks of illusion in their capacity seamlessly to blend live-action and animation or computer re-touching, as seen in the films of Robert Zemeckis such as *Who Framed Roger Rabbit* (1988) and *Forrest Gump* (1994). The downside of this is the danger that technology for its own sake might come to overwhelm narrative, characterisation, artistic creativity: precisely those qualities which made cinema not simply one of the technological wonders of the twentieth century but its major new art form.

MAJOR DATES AND THEIR SIGNIFICANCE

1895

On 28 December, the Lumière brothers gave the first paying show of films, at the Grand Café in Paris—a programme of documentary and comedy shorts.

1896

2 February—the Lumière programme screened at the Regent Street Polytechnic in London, the first film-show in Britain. Later that year, the British film pioneer, R. W. Paul made a celebrated film of the Derby.

1903

Edwin S. Porter made the most famous of all early silent films, *The Great Train Robbery*, credited as being the first Western and the first film to tell a story. Porter was later to direct a film called *Rescued From an Eagle's Nest* (1907), the leading role being taken by a young actor called Lawrence Griffith who was later to change his initials to DW and his profession to director.

1909

The theatrical producers Klaw and Erlanger forbade their contracted actors to appear in films—a sign both of the way theatre looked down on the movies but also feared their competition.

1910

D. W. Griffith made a film in California, partly to avoid the prohibitive actions against independents by the New York based Motion Pictures Patent Company and partly because of the more favourable climate for filming. It marked the beginning of what was to become Hollywood.

1911

The first fan magazines, *Motion Picture Story Magazine* and *Photoplay* began publication in the USA. The era of the star was about to emerge, particularly when, in an elaborate publicity stunt, the independent producer Carl Laemmle named the Biograph girl as Florence Lawrence.

1912

Adolph Zukor established the Famous Plays Film Company and had a big success with the distribution of *Queen Elizabeth* starring the legendary Sarah Bernhardt. "Mister Zukor," she told him, "you have put the best of me in pickle for all time."

1913

Mack Sennett made his first films from Keystone studios.

1914

The release of the first Chaplin film, *Making a Living*. His first appearance as the Tramp occurred shortly after in *Kid Auto Races at Venice*.

1916

The release of D. W. Griffith's *Intolerance*, whose narrative and technique baffled early audiences but which was to prove an enormous influence on future film makers, such as Eisenstein and Pudovkin.

1917

Chaplin signed a million dollar contract making him the highest paid screen star up to this point.

1919

United Artists formed, with Chaplin, Mary Pickford, Douglas Fairbanks and D. W. Griffiths as partners.

1921

Roscoe "Fatty" Arbuckle was charged with the rape and murder of Virginia Rappe. Although later acquitted on all charges, his career never recovered and it was one of several scandals to rock Hollywood in the early 1920s—*e.g.* the unsolved murder of the director William Desmond Taylor in 1922, the death through morphine addiction of the actor Wallace Reid in 1923. The Arbuckle scandal "drew the lightning on us all " said Gloria Swanson. It reflected the sometimes morbid fascination of the public and the press with film stars that was later to become recognised as part of the price of fame and to have an impact on the development of some film careers (*e.g.* Chaplin, Ingrid Bergman, Marilyn Monroe).

1922

Lenin told the People's Commissar for Education: "Of all the arts, for us cinema is the most important." Robert Flaherty makes *Nanook of the North*, often seen as the first great documentary film.

1925

Director Mauritz Stiller and actress Greta Garbo left Sweden for Hollywood. The year of Eisenstein's film, *The Battleship Potemkin*, revolutionary in both theme and technique.

1927

The dawn of sound. Al Jolson's "You ain't heard nothing yet" in *The Jazz Singer*, were the first words spoken on a film soundtrack.

1928

Mickey Mouse made his first appearance in *Plane Crazy*.

1929

The Great Depression hit the American stock market, but cinema proved resilient

1933

Following Adolf Hitler's rise to power, Joseph Goebbels became Minister for Information in Germany and assumed total control over the national cinema. Acclaimed director of *Metropolis* (1926) and *M* (1931), Fritz Lang was invited to become head of the national film industry: instead he emigrated to America.

1936

Hollywood's Anti-Nazi League was founded, foremost amongst its members being Dorothy Parker, Fritz Lang and Fredric March. (A decade later the League will be denounced by the newly constituted House UnAmerican Activities Committee as a Communist front.)

1938

Former child star Jackie Coogan (immortalised in Chaplin's *The Kid* of 1921) sued his mother and stepfather for the recovery of earnings in his period of popularity. He won the case but the money was swallowed up in legal costs. (Fifty years on, star of *Home Alone* Macaulay Culkin would experience not dissimilar problems).

1939

The outbreak of the Second World War was marked by the banning of Renoir's *La Règle du Jeu* in France and the departure of many European directors for Hollywood. Fritz Lang had already left; Renoir left France in 1940. A golden year for Hollywood cinema, culminating in the huge success of *Gone with the Wind*.

1940

Tom and Jerry appeared in their first movie, *Puss gets the Boot* and Bugs Bunny asked "What's up, Doc?" in *A Wild Hare*. Meanwhile the British Ministry of Information took over the GPO Film Unit and proceeded to sponsor a major series of wartime documentaries.

1941

Germany invaded Russia, and the entire Soviet industry turned itself over to the war effort. In Hollywood there were two remarkable directing debuts: Orson Welles's *Citizen Kane* and John Huston's *The Maltese Falcon*.

1942

First use of the term "neo-realism" by the Italian critic Umberto Barbaro. Marcel Carné began work on *Les Enfants du Paradis* which took three years to make. One of the reasons for this was that it kept cast and production-team away from the fighting.

1946

The opening of the first Cannes Film Festival—originally planned for 1939 but postponed on account of the war. The peak year for box-office attendance in America (4,500 million entries)..

1947

The US House UnAmerican Activities Committee (HUAC) began hearings in Los Angeles to root out "Communists" (*i.e.* liberals) in the industry. The investigation, begun on 18 October, wreaked enormous personal, financial, and artistic havoc. Cheryl Crawford, Elia Kazan and Lee Strasberg opened the Actors' Studio (home of 'The Method') in New York.

1948

French critic Alexandre Astruc predicted that the cinema would become "a means of writing just as flexible and subtle as written language", in an article that would have a tremendous impact on the French *Nouvelle Vague* directors.

1949

The release of Henry Cornelius's *Passport to Pimlico*, Alexander Mackendrick's *Whisky Galore* and Robert Hamer's *Kind Hearts and Coronets* highlighted a series of distinctive films emanating from Michael Balcon's Ealing Studios, whose humour and superb cast of character-actors ensured their success until the last of the great comedies (*The Ladykillers*) six years later.

1951

Akira Kurosawa's *Rashomon* won the Golden Lion at the Venice Film Festival, introducing the West to Japanese cinema.

1952

Charlie Chaplin, in England for his film *Limelight*, learned his re-entry permit to America had been rescinded, beginning a twenty year period of exile from that country. Twentieth Century Fox announced the imminent launching of their new wide screen system, Cinemascope. 3-D was invented, one of its few successes being *House of Wax*, directed by the one-eyed Andre De Toth.

1956

Satyajit Ray's *Pather Panchali* won a major award at the Cannes Festival, although a young French critic walked out of the screening declaring he was not interested in a film about Indian peasants: his name was Francois Truffaut.

1959

Francois Truffaut's *Les Quatre Cents Coups* and Godard's *Breathless* inaugurated what came to be known as the French *Nouvelle Vague*.

1960

Kirk Douglas (with *Spartacus*) and Otto Preminger (with *Exodus*) effectively ended the "anti-communist" blacklist when they employed as screenwriter the formerly blacklisted Dalton Trumbo. Antonioni's *L'Avventura* was noisily barracked at the Cannes Film Festival: within eighteen months, he was to be the most fashionable and esteemed director in Europe.

1961

Luis Buñuel was invited to return to Spain; he did so with *Viridiana*, infuriating the Franco régime.

1962

In a poll of a hundred critics circulated by *Sight and Sound* magazine, *Citizen Kane* was voted the best film ever made, a position it has retained in each succeeding decade in which the poll was conducted.

1968

The year of the Russian invasion of Czechoslovakia, the intensification of protest against the American war in Vietnam, the "May events" in Paris had important repercussions for the cinema. The Cannes Film Festival ended abruptly when there were demonstrations in support of student protests. In America, the youth rebellion movie of the fifties took on a new lease of life, culminating in the success of Dennis Hopper's *Easy Rider* (1969).

1975

Steven Spielberg had a huge box-office success with *Jaws*, to be topped two years later by his friend and fellow "movie brat" George Lucas, with *Star Wars*. (Both films were to be immensely influential in future Hollywood thinking, particularly about the revenue to be made from merchandising spin-offs and the concept of the summer 'blockbuster'.) Nagisa Oshima's *Empire of the Senses* surpassed even Bernardo Bertolucci's 1973 *Last Tango in Paris* for sexual frankness.

1980

A new version of Abel Gance's *Napoleon*, reconstructed by the film-maker and historian Kevin Brownlow, was shown to great acclaim in England.

1987

Bernardo Bertolucci's *The Last Emperor* became the first Western film to be shot in Beijing. It coincided with a new Western interest in Chinese film.

1988

Krzysztof Kieslowski's *A Short Film About Killing* (U.S. title: *Thou Shalt Not Kill*) was voted best film at the first European Film Awards.

1995

Cinema celebrated its centenary.

1996

Mike Leigh's *Secrets and Lies* won the Golden Palm at the Cannes Film Festival and the director celebrated his victory as a comeback for the modestly priced film that deals with human values. By way of contrast, a Hollywood epic about alien invasion, *Independence Day*—a B-picture in all but inflated cost and special effects grandeur—became the box-office blockbuster of the summer. The death was announced of Krzysztof Kieslowski, arguably the greatest director of the last decade.

1997

The music magazine *Gramophone* gave an award to a recording by Joel McNeely and the Royal Scottish National Orchestra of Bernard Herrmann's complete score for Hitchcock's *Vertigo*—a sign of the new respect being accorded by musicologists and critics to film music.

1998

The death of director Akira Kurosawa, one of the giants of post-war cinema. The success of Spielberg's *Saving Private Ryan* sparks a new interest in films about World War Two.

1999

Box office success of *Shakespeare in Love* which goes on to win 7 Oscars. Death of Japanese filmmaker Keisuke Kinoshita, a prolific contemporary of Akira Kurosawa, and also Stanley Kubrick, a reclusive master director whose last film, *Eyes Wide Shut* (1999) divided critics. The centenary of Alfred Hitchcock's birth is widely commemorated; Carol Reed's *The Third Man* (1949), scripted by Graham Greene, is voted the best British film of the century in a poll conducted by the British Film Institute.

2000

British theatre director Sam Mendes wins an Oscar for his first film, *American Beauty*. Meanwhile two of the major European talents of the 1990s, Spain's Pedro Almodovar and Denmark's Lars von Trier are also rewarded. Almodovar's *All About My Mother* wins the best foreign film Oscar; Von Trier's

Dancer in the Dark controversially wins the Golden Palm at Cannes.

2001

Death of American film producer/director Stanley Kramer whose films included *The Wild One* and *High Noon*. US-based director, Ang Lee makes a huge crossover success, an arthouse martial arts movie, *Crouching Tiger, Hidden Dragon*, that wins four Oscars. Steven Spielberg completes *A.I.*, the film on which Kubrick was working when he died.

2004

Lord of the Rings: Return of the King triumphs at Oscars. Mel Gibson's *The Passion of the Christ* arouses much controversy for its violence and alleged anti-Semitism, but is a huge commercial success. Michael Moore's *Fahrenheit 9/11* becomes the first documentary to take $100 million at the box-office.

2006

Despite widespread acclaim for *Brokeback Mountain*, the gay cowboy film, the award for Best Film goes to *Crash*. Ang Lee (who directed *Brokeback Mountain*) gets Best Director.

2. THE LEADING CINEMA DIRECTORS

Allen, Woody (b. 1935)

Woody Allen first achieved star status as an actor in movies he himself directed, playing a walking worry-bead who wore his urban anxiety like a red badge of courage. Films like *Take the Money and Run* (1969), *Bananas* (1971) and *Love and Death* (1975) seemed to align him with prior film farceurs like his favourite, Bob Hope. He became more ambitious and intellectual, with films such as *Annie Hall* (1977) and *Stardust Memories* (1980) being anguished as well as amusing self-portraits, and *Interiors* (1978) being a study of family breakdown closer to Chekhov than Chaplin. Films such as *Zelig* (1983) and *The Purple Rose of Cairo* (1985) have shown him to be the technical equal of any contemporary American director, whilst *Hannah and her Sisters* (1986) and *Crimes and Misdemeanours* (1989) have the philosophical density of a Russian novel.

However, after *Husbands and Wives* (1992) and a bitter and much publicised split with his partner Mia Farrow, he has returned to comedy, spicing the humour with considerable formal adventurousness for a dwindling but loyal following.

Almodovar, Pedro (b. 1951)

The most acclaimed Spanish director since Luis Buñuel, Almodovar came to international attention with *Women on the Verge of a Nervous Breakdown* (1988), which won numerous awards and was a typical example of what has since been called "Almodrama"—emotionally extravagant and sexually outrageous stories that revel in passionate extremes and narrative quirkiness. A film-maker of the post-Franco era whose work has tended to ignore or reject his country's political past, Almodovar's recent films have shown a new depth and compassion in their exploration of the hidden by-ways of love. *Talk to Her* (2002) won him a best screenwriting Oscar. Other key films: *Matador* (1986), *Tie Me Up! Tie Me Down!* (1990), *High Heels* (1991), *Live Flesh* (1998), *All About My Mother* (1999), *Bad Education* (2004).

Altman, Robert (b. 1925)

Innovative, iconoclastic director who shot to prominence with the military comedy *M:A:S:H* (1970), and then proceeded to subvert some of America's major film genres, notably in his western *McCabe and Mrs. Miller* (1971), which was more

about the rise of capitalism than the growth of civilisation, and in his private-eye movie, *The Long Goodbye* (1973), where he debunked Raymond Chandler's knight-errant hero, Philip Marlowe. His epic and ironic fresco on the American Dream, *Nashville* (1975) was a highpoint of his career. Since then he has become ever more esoteric and experimental. Nevertheless, in films like his imaginative realisation of the play, *Come Back to the Five and Dime, Jimmy Dean, Jimmy Dean* (1982), and the made-for-TV biopic of Van Gogh, *Vincent and Theo* (1990), he has shown he can still spring some surprises. His Hollywood satire, *The Player* (1992) was his most acclaimed film for a decade; his ambitious adaptation of Raymond Carver short stories, *Short Cuts* (1994) was no less impressive; and his country house satire *Gosford Park* (2001) was both a critical and commercial success.

Antonioni, Michelangelo (b. 1912)

Antonioni was the director who made alienation fashionable in the early 1960s with his trilogy *L'Avventura* (1960), *La Notte* (1961) and *The Eclipse* (1962), which explored the gap between his characters' material affluence and their spiritual impoverishment. He also gave alienation a palpable visual form, each shot an eloquent comment on the tension between protagonist and environment. These films remain his greatest achievement, and in Monica Vitti he found a leading lady whose haunted performances greatly enhanced the emotional impact of his work. His other major films include *Le Amiche—The Girl Friends* (1955), *The Red Desert* (1964), *Blow-Up* (1966) and *The Passenger* (1975). Although disabled by a stroke he made a remarkable comeback with *Beyond the Clouds* (1996), a prize-winner at the Venice Festival.

Bergman, Ingmar (b. 1918)

The definitive example of the film artist, by virtue of the maturity and complexity of his themes and of the control he has had over all aspects of his films—writing, casting *etc*. Since he established his international reputation with a trio of masterly works in the 1950s—*Smiles of a Summer Night* (1955), *The Seventh Seal* (1956) and *Wild Strawberries* (1957)—he enjoyed almost complete creative freedom. Films like *The Seventh Seal*, *Through a Glass Darkly* (1960) and *Winter Light* (1962) test the validity of an individual's religious faith in a world of fearful cruelty, whilst a masterpiece like *Persona* (1966) is a revelatory study of character and creativity, superbly acted by Bibi Andersson and Liv Ullmann. There are those who criticise Bergman for the narrowness of his social range, his limited political vision, his spiritual masochism. But to Bergman the camera eye is the window of the soul and few have probed more deeply to the roots of human personality. And it is not all Scandinavian gloom. In *Fanny and Alexander* (1983), he created a wonderful reminder of his story-telling gifts, his rich visual sense, and his capacity to embrace life with all its pain, perils, and pleasures.

Bergman's autobiography, *The Magic Lantern* was published in 1988; and his screenplay about the early life of his parents, *Best Intentions* (1992) was memorably filmed by Bille August. Another screenplay, *Faithless* (2000) has been recently directed by Liv Ullmann.

Bertolucci, Bernardo (b. 1940)

The Italian Communist Party evolved in the seventies the conception of the "historic compromise"—a tactical alliance on the part of a self-styled revolutionary party with progressive reformist forces. Bertolucci's aesthetic strategy can be seen as an (unconscious?) embodiment of this—a "message" of revolution often clothed in the glossy, star studded forms of bourgeois Hollywood cinema, as in the two-part *1900* of 1976. Likewise, in *Last Tango in Paris* (1972), the brutal sexual frankness for which the film rapidly became notorious is cushioned by the reassuring Hollywood deep-orange glow in which the scenes are shot and the presence of attested Hollywood rebel Marlon Brando. He won an Oscar for the opulent epic, *The Last Emperor* (1987), and *The Dreamers* (2003) was a return to form, but his best films to date are his early works—*Before the Revolution* (1964), *The Spider's Stratagem* (1970), *The Conformist* (1970)— which combine an incisive political and psychological analysis with a poetic and lyrical style.

Bresson, Robert (1907-99)

The most reclusive and rigorous of French directors, Bresson expressed his religious themes through a style of pared-down purity. He rejected plot and for the most part used non-professional actors, because acting is for the theatre, he believed, and what he was after was inner truth. His most famous film is *Diary of a Country Priest* (1950), but other works such as *A Man Escaped* (1956), *Pickpocket* (1959), *Balthazar* (1966) and *L'Argent* (1982) expressed his individuality equally strongly.

Brooks, Richard (1912-92)

Leading writer-director of the postwar American cinema. Author of the novel on which the film *Crossfire* (1947) was based and co-writer on Huston's powerful allegory *Key Largo* (1948), Brooks made his directing debut in 1950 and became a specialist in accessible, highly charged adaptations of literary classics. His best film is *Elmer Gantry* (1960), an incisive dissection of American evangelism that won Oscars for Brooks (as screenwriter) and its star, Burt Lancaster and features the characteristic Brooks protagonist: a dynamic, divided individualist treading a tightrope between redemption and damnation. Key films: *Blackboard Jungle* (1955), *Cat on a Hot Tin Roof* (1958), *Sweet Bird of Youth* (1962), *Lord Jim* (1965), *The Professionals* (1966), *In Cold Blood* (1967).

Buñuel, Luis (1900-83)

Buñuel began his career by collaborating with Salvador Dali on a surrealist short, *Un Chien Andalou* (1928) and then scandalised audiences with *L'Age d'Or* (1930), which attacked the Church ("Thank God I'm an atheist," Buñuel declared) and bourgeois morality (which Buñuel always found deeply immoral). A powerful, hallucinatory film about violence and poverty in the slums, *Los Olvidados* (1950) launched a second phase of his career, and his religious assaults were continued in *El* (1953), which equated religious orthodoxy with emotional repression, and *Nazarin* (1958) and *Viridiana* (1961), which showed the impossibility of

a modern Christ surviving in today's society. In his final years, he took pleasure not so much in savaging the bourgeoisie as in, metaphorically speaking, poisoning their food, serving them a dainty cultural dish with a sinister undertaste. *Belle de Jour* (1967), *Tristana* (1970) and *The Discreet Charm of the Bourgeoisie* (1972) are all slyly subversive, surreal works, dealing with the split between appearance and reality, decorum and desire. He believed man was unconsciously a slave to custom and to social orthodoxy and, with his enthusiasm for symbols and the world of dreams, which reveal the hidden fears and desires of modern man, Buñuel did everything in his power to shock man out of his complacency. His impish spirit was also revealed in his appropriately liberating autobiography, *My Last Breath*, published in 1983.

Campion, Jane (b. 1955)

A graduate of the Australian Film, TV and Radio School who made a stir with her short film *Peel* (1982). Her first features, *Sweetie* (1989) and *An Angel at my Table* (1990), an imaginative bio-pic of writer Janet Frame, were highly acclaimed, and she became the first ever woman director to win the Golden Palm at Cannes for her film *The Piano* (1993).

Capra, Frank (1897-1991)

The films of Sicilian-born Frank Capra embodied the American Dream. His major works were comedies with a strong moral lesson, and their message of optimism over adversity cheered up audiences during the Depression. His films were essentially variations on David and Goliath, with the common man victorious over seemingly insurmountable odds. His main characters, such as Cary Cooper's Mr. Deeds in *Mr. Deeds Goes To Town* (1936) or James Stewart's Mr. Smith in *Mr Smith Goes to Washington* (1939) were innocent idealists who vanquished the cynical, the crooked and the corrupt. After winning three directing Oscars in the 1930s, Capra never recovered his popularity after World War Two and retired after *A Pocketful of Miracles* in 1961. His testament is the aptly entitled *It's A Wonderful Life* (1946), a beautiful fantasy, with dark undertones, on the typical Capra theme that no man is born a failure.

Carné, Marcel (1909-96)

Carné occupied a role in the immediately pre-war cinema in many ways similar to that of Antonioni in the early sixties—the poet of an age's style of despair, whose fatalism receives tangible support and embodiment from the skilful use of decor and architecture. In Carné's case these were entirely studio-bound (his mature masterpieces eschewed location filming entirely), which may be one reason why his output has dated compared with, say, Renoir's. But *Quai des Brumes* (1938) and *Le Jour Se Leve* (1939) provide atmospheric frameworks for the acting of Jean Gabin, and *Les Enfants du Paradis* (1945), the three-and-a-half-hour tale of lost love and cynicism in the theatrical world of nineteenth-century Paris, remains exciting through its amalgam of "period" style and a tortured consciousness evocative of the time at which it was made. With Rene Clement (director of *Jeux Interdits*, 1952) and Henri-Georges Clouzot (maker of *Wages of Fear*, 1952 and *Les Diaboliques*, 1955) Carné fell out of fashion at the time of the less studio-and-script-bound films of the *Nouvelle Vague*, but in 1979, French critics voted *Les Enfants du Paradis* as the best French film ever made.

Cassavettes, John (1929-89)

Actor-director who, with associates such as his actress-wife Gena Rowlands and actor-friends such as Peter Falk and Ben Gazzara, made offbeat films that focused more on intimate relationships than exciting narrative. Improvisational and unashamedly indulgent, the films have been an inspiration to independent film-makers wishing to eschew the mainstream. Films include: *Shadows* (1960), *Faces* (1968), *Husbands* (1970), *A Woman Under the Influence* (1974), *Killing of a Chinese Bookie* (1976), *Love Streams* (1982).

Chabrol, Claude (b. 1930)

Like Godard and Truffaut, Chabrol first distinguished himself as an abrasive and articulate critic on the magazine *Cahiers du Cinema* before branching into direction. With Eric Rohmer (later also to become a director), he also wrote an influential book at this time on the films of Alfred Hitchcock. Hitchcock has been a strong influence on Chabrol's films, which are often cynical detective stories or psychological suspense thrillers set against carefully observed French provincial settings. He is a cool anatomist of the darkest charms and deadly passions of the bourgeoisie. His key films include *Les Cousins* (1958), *Les Bonnes Femmes* (1960), *Leo Riohos* (1968), *La Femme Infidele* (1969), *Killer!— Que la Bete meure* (1969), *Les Noces Rouges* (1973) and his best film, *Le Boucher* (1970). Recent work, such as *Judgment in Stone* (1994), adapted from a novel by Ruth Rendell, and *Merci Pour Le Chocolat* (2000) shows he has lost none of his animosity towards the bourgeois nor his capacity to disturb.

Chen, Kaige (b. 1952)

With Zhang Yimou, the leading director of the so-called 'fifth generation' of film makers who graduated from the Beijing Film Academy in 1982, following its re-opening after Mao Tse-Tung's Cultural Revolution. His first film, *Yellow Earth* (1984) made an impact in the West comparable to that of *Rashomon* and *Pather Panchali* in its revelation of a new national cinema, and his reputation was consolidated by *Farewell My Concubine* (1993), which shared the top prize at Cannes with *The Piano* and was nominated for an Oscar. However, his first Hollywood film, *Killing Me Softly* (2002) has been widely deemed a soft-porn disaster. Other films: *The Big Parade* (1985), *King of the Children* (1987), *Life on a string* (1991), *Temptress Moon* (1997), *The Emperor and the Assassin* (2000).

Clair, Rene (1898–1981)

The first and still the greatest European musical director. His early interest in asynchronous sound (*i.e.* that which does not always correspond to what we see going on on the screen) led him to attach equal importance to natural noise and music and to dialogue in his early sound films (such as *Sous les Toits de Paris* of 1930). A delight in dance—the choreographed quality of fights, chases and crowd scenes—permeates his two most successful works, *Le Million* and the simplistic but vivacious satire on industrialisation, *A Nous la Liberté* (both 1931) which greatly influenced Chaplin's *Modern Times*.

Cocteau, Jean (1889–1963)

Cocteau was a poet who expressed himself variously in fiction, drama, painting and drawing as well as through the cinema. *Beauty and the Beast* (1946) was an imaginative telling of the familiar tale, with Jean Marais both frightening and poignant as the Beast. In *Orphée* of 1950 he produced one of the cinema's unquestioned fantastic masterpieces, using mirrors as links between the world of the living and that of the dead to great effect, and playing upon the connection between love and death in a way that must have influenced the makers of *Last Year in Marienbad* (Resnais and Robbe-Grillet) eleven years later.

Coen, Joel (b. 1958)

With his brother Ethan (who co-writes and produces), Joel Coen has fashioned some of the most original modern American films, darkly comic, densely plotted dramas that blend passion with pastiche. Key films: *Blood Simple* (1983), *Raising Arizona* (1987), *Miller's Crossing* (1990), *Barton Fink* (1991), *Fargo* (1996), *O Brother, Where Art Thou* (2000), *The Man Who Wasn't There* (2001).

Coppola, Francis Ford (b. 1939)

The Godfather of modern American cinema, confidante and father-figure to the new generation of directors (such as George Lucas and Steven Spielberg) who emerged from film school to storm Hollywood in the early 1970s. Coppola's *The Godfather* (1972) and *The Godfather, Part II* (1974) combined the sweep of a dynastic family melodrama with a mature political analysis of corporate America. The former restored Marlon Brando to superstardom; the latter made stars of Al Pacino and Robert De Niro. Two other major films of the decade were *The Conversation* (1974), a tale of treacherous tapes and an atmosphere of paranoia that evoked Watergate; and *Apocalypse Now* (1979), in which America's incursion into Vietnam was interpreted as a mad, metaphysical journey into the heart of darkness. Since then Coppola has seemed something of a lost soul, marking time for hisple ration, marking time and, with *Godfather III* (1990) and a revised, extended version of *Apocalypse Now* (premiered at Cannes in 2001) revisiting old haunts.

Costa Gavras, Constantin (b. 1933)

The cinema's specialist director of the political thriller, throwing up large social issues of corruption and responsibility under the guise of suspense melodrama. He achieved international prominence with *Z* (1969), an indictment of the repressive regime in Greece, and he has had equal success in the mainstream commercial cinema, particularly with *Missing* (1982) and *Music Box* (1989). His most recent film is *Amen* (2002), a typically controversial critique of the Catholic church's failure to attack the Holocaust.

Cronenberg, David (b. 1943)

Canada's most controversial film export, whose early reputation was made with stomach-churning, mind-exploding horror films. Critical respectability came with *The Fly* (1986) and *Dead Ringers* (1988), which married the gore with intellect and compassion, but controversy flared again over his adaptation of J. G. Ballard's notorious novel about eroticism and the automobile, *Crash* (1996). *Spider* (2002) was shown to great acclaim at the Cannes Film Festival.

Cukor, George (1899–1983)

Cukor came to Hollywood from directing on the New York stage, and this theatrical background was an important clue to his work. His films were often adaptations of plays, like *Gaslight* (1944); he was always intrigued by theatrical people indulging a flair for the dramatic, either on stage, like Ronald Colman in *A Double Life* (1947), or in a courtroom, like Spencer Tracy and Katherine Hepburn in *Adam's Rib* (1949); and his films are particularly remembered for their performances, *e.g.* Greta Garbo's in *Camille* (1937) or Judy Garland's in *A Star is Born* (1954). Cukor was one of the most civilised of Hollywood directors, versatile and visually stylish, but particularly revelling in the sex-war comedies of Tracy and Hepburn, such as *Adam's Rib* and *Pat and Mike* (1952).

Curtiz, Michael (1888–1962)

Hungarian-born super-professional of Hollywood's heyday. He began his association with Warner Brothers in 1926, making over a hundred films there of every conceivable genre and with stars such as Errol Flynn, James Cagney and Humphrey Bogart. His famous films include *Angels With Dirty Faces* (1938), *Yankee Doodle Dandy* (1942), *Mildred Pierce* (1945) and the immortal *Casablanca* (1943).

De Mille, Cecil B. (1881–1959)

An innovative director in the silent era, Cecil B. De Mille became indelibly associated in his later career with bigness in the movies. His gigantic epics include *The Sign of the Cross* with Charles Laughton in 1932, and two spectacularly tasteless versions of *The Ten Commandments* (1923 and 1956). The films themselves matter less nowadays than the reputation for scale and the consistently successful box-office returns. Joseph L. Mankiewicz's observation on de Mille is worth quoting: "He had his finger up the pulse of America."

De Sica, Vittorio (1902–74)

Although he began his screen career as an actor, Vittorio De Sica is remembered principally for a remarkable group of films he made immediately after World War II, collaborating with writer Cesare Zavattini on works which are regarded as key examples of Italian neo-realism; *Shoeshine* (1946), *Bicycle Thieves* (1948) and *Umberto D* (1952). These sympathetic studies of the poor were heavily criticised in their own country (for political simplemindedness by the Left and for unflattering and unpatriotic portraiture of Italy by the Right) but were widely acclaimed abroad. With the decline of neo-realism in the early 1950s, De Sica was never to scale the same heights, though he did direct Sophia Loren to an Oscar winning performance in *Two Women* (1961), and experienced critical acclaim for two of his final films, *The Garden of the Finzi Continis* (1971) and *A Brief Vacation* (1973).

Dreyer, Carl Theodor (1889–1968)

Dreyer is still regarded as the greatest artist in the history of Danish cinema, though it was in France that he directed his first masterpiece, *The Passion of Joan of Arc* (1928), with its remarkable leading performance by Renee Falconetti in her only screen role. The austerity and apparent Protestant guilt that pervade his work compare interestingly with Robert Bresson's Catholic severity. Dreyer's last film, *Gertrud* (1964) was disgracefully derided at its premiere, but it is now regarded as one of his finest works, both for its steady satire of the bourgeoisie and its sympathy with women and hatred of their oppression. The slowness of his work still causes difficulty, but the fantastical quality of *Vampyr* (1932), and the undercutting of fanaticism in *Days of Wrath* (1943) and *Ordet/The Word* (1955) are nowadays widely appreciated.

Eisenstein, Sergei (1898–1948)

A prominent theorist as well as practitioner, Eisenstein's Marxist awareness of society as founded upon conflict rather than harmony led him to develop a theory of montage, or meaning built up by collision and clash of images. This theory found illustration in what are at the same time highly effective Socialist propaganda films: *The Battleship Potemkin* of 1925, whose massacre-sequence on the steps of the port of Odessa is among the most famous in cinematic history; *October* of 1927 (in which the Menshevik or moderate leader Kerensky is denigrated when his image is followed by that of a peacock—an example of the montage technique); and the more contorted and baroque *Ivan the Terrible* (Part one, 1942; Part two, 1945). This last caused Eisenstein to fall into disfavour with Stalin (who may have taken the portrait of the tyrant Ivan to be a reflection upon himself), and the financial difficulties and persecution because of his homosexuality led to his premature death of a heart attack. "Of all the arts", said Lenin, "for us the cinema is the most important". In Soviet Russia its most important voice was Eisenstein who, in finding filmic forms to express collectivism and brotherhood, gave substance to a national ideology.

Fassbinder, Rainer Werner (1946–82)

Phenomenally prolific director of the German cinema of the 1970s, Fassbinder's films at their best combined the political commitment of a Godard with the heady melodrama of a Hollywood director he much admired, Douglas Sirk. His best film is probably *The Marriage of Maria Braun* (1979), an extraordinary allegory of the history of post-war Germany with a magnetic leading performance from Hanna Schygulla. The best films in his melodramatic style are *The Merchant of Four Seasons* (1972), *The Bitter Tears of Petra von Kant* (1972), *Fear Eats the Soul* (1974) and *Veronika Voss* (1981).

Fellini, Federico (1920–93)

Fellini was an example of the director as star, delighting in treading a thin line between self-expression and self-indulgence. The films recall his early experience in the circus and as a cartoonist, being populated by grotesques and having a unique mixture of risk and spectacle, fantasy and fact. *I Vitelloni* (1953), a semi-autobiographical account of his wastrel adolescent days, established Fellini's reputation; it was enhanced by the international success of his next film, *La Strada* (1954), a parable of body and spirit, love and salvation. With *La Dolce Vita* (1960), a sensational view of contemporary Roman society, Fellini entered his decadent

phase, which was to be continued in such films as *Fellini Satyricon* (1969) and *Fellini's Casanova* (1976). His most highly regarded films are his most autobiographical, *8½* (1963), in which a film director encounters a creative crisis and ransacks his past for inspiration, and *Amarcord* (1973) which is a remembrance of his childhood.

Flaherty, Robert (1884–1951)

Often referred to as the "father of film documentary", Flaherty was actually as much a Romantic as a realist. He has been criticised for the political absences in his movies but he was not a polemicist but a poet, making films that were either hymns to a vanishing way of life or recorded elemental struggles between Man and Nature. His best films were his first, and last: respectively, *Nanook of the North* (1922) and *Louisiana Story* (1948).

Ford, John (1895–1973)

"My name's John Ford," he said. "I make Westerns." He not only made them: he transformed them into poetic statements of the American spirit. Particularly celebrated are those he made starring John Wayne: *Stagecoach* (1939), an odyssey of Western outcasts across hostile Indian territory; *The Searchers* (1956), in which Wayne's bitter racialism is eventually tamed; and *The Man Who Shot Liberty Valance* (1962) which pits Wayne against James Stewart. But he also excelled with Henry Fonda (*Drums Along the Mohawk* of 1939), and in non-Western films (*The Grapes of Wrath*, 1940). His greatest limitation is that he is pre-eminently a man's director, whose bourbon-soaked camaraderie and stress on tough, determined action in some of his less successful films palls rapidly. His greatest strengths are as the unsurpassed chronicler of pioneering America and as the sympathetic observer of the endurance of the common people; and his insights into prejudice, injustice and the tragedy of destroyed families. "This is the West, sir", says the newspaper editor of *Liberty Valance*. "When the legend becomes fact, print the legend". Ford printed the legend better than anyone. Other key films: *The Informer* (1935), *My Darling Clementine* (1946), *Fort Apache* (1948), *The Quiet Man* (1952).

Forman, Milos (b. 1932)

Forman was one of a group of directors of the so-called Czech New Wave of the 1960s, whose comedies such as *A Blonde in Love* (1965) and *The Fireman's Ball* (1967) audaciously satirised authority, both parental and political. In Paris in 1968 when the Soviet tanks rolled into Prague and there was a clampdown on artistic expression, Forman eventually emigrated to America, where he has continued to score notable successes with offbeat films, most famously with *One Flew Over the Cuckoo's Nest* (1975) and *Amadeus* (1984).

Fuller, Samuel (1912–97)

A ferocious action director, castigated as neo-Fascist by his adversaries and lauded by his advocates for the tough, unsparing economy and desperate honesty of his work. Fuller worked across different genres, including the spy-thriller (*Pickup on South Street*, 1953) and the Western (*Run of the Arrow*, 1957). In *Shock Corridor* of 1963, his finest and most revelatory work, he combined the investigative-journalist picture with the drama of psychological horror to create an unnerving dissection of American prejudices and fears. His later films were few and far between, though *White Dog* (1983) showed that, given the opportunity, Fuller had lost none of his bite. His was tabloid cinema, done with tremendous verve, and admired by modern directors such as Scorsese and Tim Robbins.

Gance, Abel (1889–1981)

"The day of the Image has arrived", proclaimed Abel Gance at the triumphant premiere of his five-and-a-half-hour epic, *Napoleon* (1927), which deployed superimposition, slow-motion, split-screen, colour, and a triple-screen process, Polyvision, that anticipated Cinerama by nearly thirty years. Alas, Gance was mistaken: sound was round the corner and the visual innovations of *Napoleon* were rendered virtually obsolete before they had begun. Not until the film's restoration in 1980 was Gance's achievement appreciated and his own reputation restored as one of the great innovators of the silent screen.

Godard, Jean-Luc (b. 1930)

"We are the children of Marx and Coca-Cola", claimed Godard in the 1960s, when he seemed the most radical, innovative and controversial director in world cinema. Nowadays we are probably the children of McDonald's and market forces and his ideas and formal experiments seem correspondingly less urgent, more marginal. The turning-point was *Weekend* (1967), an apocalyptic black-comedy of chaos and cannibalism, of social and cultural breakdown. From his early films, which were often love letters to the Hollywood cinema, he had moved to an alternative political cinema that seemed to demand not audiences but disciples. His influence on all spheres of alternative, independent, avant-garde film theory and practice continues to be immense. Other key films: *Breathless* (1959), *Vivre sa Vie* (1962), *Le Mepris-Contempt* (1963), *Une Femme Mariee* (1964), *Pierrot le Fou* (1965), *Tout Va Bien* (1972).

Griffith, D. W. (1875–1948)

Griffith more than any other individual was responsible for the cinema moving from short one and two-reelers to the grand epic scale. *The Birth of a Nation* (1915), despite overt racism, was the most exciting attempt the cinema had hitherto made to capture and reconstruct the course of historical events, and broke all box-office records as well as profoundly influencing Eisenstein. Its successor, *Intolerance* (1916), was even more grandiose and cost unimaginable sums by the standards of those days. Apart from *Broken Blossoms* (1919) and *Way Down East* (1920), Griffith's later films were undistinguished and his career ended in a prolonged, drink-sodden decline. Although sometimes criticised for his Victorian melodrama, Griffith is more properly remembered for his popularisation of feature-length narrative; his revelation of the creative possibilities of montage; and his encouragement of a new subtlety and realism in screen performance. He was the first figure to give this new mass medium intellectual respectability.

Hamer, Robert (1911–63)

The problem child of Ealing studios, whose career was to decline due to alcoholism and what producer Michael Balcon was to call Hamer's "self-destructive streak", but who was responsible for at least three classics of British film: "The Haunted Mirror" episode from *Dead of Night* (1945); the neo-realist melodrama about the London underworld, *It Always Rains on Sunday* (1947); and, above all, the black comedy, *Kind Hearts and Coronets* (1949) in which Dennis Price purrs through some of the most suavely literate dialogue in British cinema as he attempts to kill off eight Alec Guinnesses on his way to a dukedom.

Hawks, Howard (1896–1977)

One of the most versatile and consistent operators within the Hollywood studio system. Whatever genre he worked in, it was transmuted and made more ambiguous. Thus the Western *Rio Bravo* (1959) contains a minimum of big-scale outdoor action and a maximum of charged conversation; private-eye classic *The Big Sleep* (1946) is concerned with Bogart's process of ironic self-discovery rather than with who-dunnit (a question to which Hawks himself never worked out the answer); and the action in the civil-aviation drama *Only Angels Have Wings* (1939) takes place predominantly on the ground. His comedies, notably those with Cary Grant, hilariously subvert sex stereotypes, as in *Bringing Up Baby* (1938), *His Girl Friday* (1940) and *I Was a Male War Bride* (1949).

Herzog, Werner (b. 1942)

One of the most exciting of the new German directors in the 1970s, his treatment of madness is particularly penetrating. This is normally undertaken within the context of a part-historical, part-

fictional society, as with the paranoia of the sixteenth-century Amazon conquistador in *Aguirre, Wrath of God* (1972), the scandalous insights of the supposed "savage" in *The Enigma of Kaspar Hauser* (1974), and the odd symbiosis between predator and victim in his Murnau remake *Nosferatu the Vampyre* (1978). "Dreams move mountains", says Herzog: it is his philosophy of film-making.

Hitchcock, Sir Alfred (1899–1980)

For half a century Hitchcock was the acknowledged master of mystery and suspense, whose godly planned delight in playing on his audience's nerves has occasioned violent disagreement between those who see him as the medium's leading exponent of predestination and those for whom he is but a limited practical joker in bad taste. *Psycho* (1960) remains the most notorious film, less now perhaps for the murder of Janet Leigh in her shower than for the *coup de grace* when the murderer's "real identity" is revealed near the end. *North by North-West* of the previous year is among his most accomplished works, a comic spy-thriller based (like so much that is funniest in Hollywood cinema) on a mistake involving the identity of Cary Grant.

Sexually perverse or tabooed areas which the conventional narrative cinema perforce ignored or treated as marginal assume central (though often implicit) places in his work, *cf.* the latent homosexuality in *Strangers on a Train* (1951), the Grand Guignol parody of an Oedipus complex in *Psycho* and the treatment of repression and the traumatic return of what has been "forgotten" (*i.e.* repressed) in *Marnie* (1964). In recent years his early English films have been revalued and upgraded, and the sexual politics of his films have been earnestly analysed.

He continues to fascinate because of the multi-sided personality of his work, which reveals at once the mask of a joker of genius, a nihilist, a Catholic moralist, a Freudian sexual psychologist and, in his greatest work, *Vertigo* (1958) an anguished romantic. He was more than the "master of suspense": he made murder into an art form. Other key films include: *Blackmail* (1929), *The Thirty-Nine Steps* (1935), *Sabotage* (1937), *The Lady Vanishes* (1938), *Rebecca* (1940), *Shadow of a Doubt* (1943), *Notorious* (1946), *Rope* (1948), *Rear Window* (1954) and *The Birds* (1963).

Huston, John (1906–87)

1941 marked two of the most sensationally successful debuts in directorial history—Orson Welles with *Citizen Kane* and Huston's *The Maltese Falcon*, an elegantly perverse private-eye tale in which double-crosses occur at a bewildering rate, thereby setting the mould for the *film noir* that was so prominent later in the decade. Huston's career intermittently maintained this initial impetus, though public and critical reception of his works was not always judicious: *Freud: The Secret Passion* (1962), a remarkable drama ahead of its time, was ill received, whereas *The African Queen*, for which Bogart won an Oscar in 1952, is an overrated, though entertaining, film. Huston was intrigued by over-reachers, people who pursue their dreams to the point of obsession. Even when their obsessions blow up in their faces, as they do in two of his best films, *The Treasure of the Sierra Madre* (1948) and *The Man who would be King* (1975), Huston is still impressed by the grandeur of human aspiration, by the ironies of courage and cowardice, by the stirring way humanity challenges its fate.

His work was uneven but his career ended on a high note: a typically literate adaptation of a literary classic, *Under the Volcano* (1984); an impish Mafia black comedy, *Prizzi's Honor* (1985); and a serene rendering of James Joyce's elegiac short story, *The Dead* (1987).

His direction also helped win Oscars for his family: for father Walter in *Sierra Madre*, and for daughter Anjelica in *Prizzi's Honor*. Other key films: *Key Largo* (1948), *Moby Dick* (1956), *The Misfits* (1961), *Reflections in a Golden Eye* (1967), *Fat City* (1972), *Wise Blood* (1979).

Kazan, Elia (1909–2003)

Dynamic director who founded the Actor's Studio with Lee Strasberg and is responsible for bringing the Method style of acting into the American cinema. His association on three films with Marlon Brando—*A Streetcar named Desire* (1951), *Viva Zapata* (1952) and *On the Waterfront* (1954)—was significant for its establishment of the prototype Kazan hero: a rebel, anguished and ambivalent about his personal situation and social responsibilities but with a tremendous drive to solve his problems. *On the Waterfront* was particularly controversial for its so-called "glorification of the informer" (an ex-Communist, Kazan had named names to the House UnAmerican Activities Committee in 1952). He also directed James Dean in *East of Eden* (1955), Montgomery Clift in *Wild River* (1960) and Robert De Niro in *The Last Tycoon* (1976), though in his later years he occupied himself mainly in writing novels and a revelatory autobiography, *A Life*. Amid much controversy, he was awarded an honorary Oscar in 1999.

Kiarostami, Abbas (b.1940)

A leading figure of the new Iranian cinema. *Close-Up* (1989), an ironic and technically adroit story (based on fact) of a movie fanatic who impersonates a film director, first brought him to the attention of critics in the West. Since then, his films have been widely praised for their humanistic observation (often compared with that of directors such as Renoir, De Sica and Satyajit Ray) and their sympathetic insights into modern Iranian society. Key films include: *The Traveller* (1974), *Where is My Friend's House?* (1987), *Homework* (1989), *And Life Goes On* (1992), *A Taste of Cherry* (1997), *The Wind Will Carry Us* (1999), *Ten* (2002).

Kieslowski, Krzysztof (1941–96)

The greatest Polish directors, like Andrzej Wajda and Krzysztof Zanussi, see cinema as the nation's social conscience, the art-form that most courageously interrogates the country's moral and political values. Kieslowski was in that tradition and is best known abroad for his contemporary TV films on the theme of the Ten Commandments, two of which were expanded to feature-film length: *A Short Film About Killing* (1988) and *A Short Film About Love* (1989); and for his *Three Colours* trilogy, *Blue* (1993), *White* (1993) and *Red* (1994), which for some critics represents the finest achievement of European cinema in the 1990s. Other key films include: *Camera Buff* (1979), *No End* (1984), *The Double Life of Véronique* (1991).

Kubrick, Stanley (1928–99)

For Kubrick, the cinema was a laboratory for observation and experiment and his findings provoked more critical debate than any American director since Orson Welles. Two films in the 1960s particularly confirmed his extraordinary gifts: the nuclear comedy, *Dr. Strangelove* (1964), which showed the tension between man and the machine; and his sci-fi epic, *2001: A Space Odyssey* (1968), a vast enigmatic meditation on evolution and the degree to which man has been mastered by the technology he has created. His following two films, *A Clockwork Orange* (1971) and *Barry Lyndon* (1975) were amongst the most controversial of the next decade, the former for its violence in depicting the issue of free-will, the latter for its sumptuousness in anatomising high society at the end of the eighteenth-century. Many were disappointed with his labyrinthine horror film, *The Shining* (1980) and his Vietnam movie *Full Metal Jacket* (1987), but until his death he remained a key figure in modern film, analysing the tensions between the individual and history, man and science, language and social conditioning with a disturbingly clinical detachment. Other key films: *Paths of Glory* (1957), *Lolita* (1962) and *Eyes Wide Shut* (1999).

Kurosawa, Akira (1910–98)

Kurosawa was the first Japanese director to make a major impact on Western audiences with *Rashomon*, the recounting of a rape and murder from four separate perspectives, which was the great success of the Venice Film Festival in 1951. Compared to such as Mizoguchi and Ozu his work looks Westernised, but this can be of positive benefit, as in the Samurai "Westerns" he made with the actor Toshiro Mifune, where classic Western plot-

schemes are translated into stylised Japanese settings (*The Seven Samurai*, 1954; *Sanjuro*, 1962). He has made highly praised adaptations of Shakespeare, *Throne of Blood* (1957), a version of *Macbeth*, and *Ran* (1985), an interpretation of *King Lear*. Psychological extremes always excited Kurosawa, and his pulsating visual style can be understood in terms of finding a powerful visual pattern to reflect the feverish inner intensity of his characters. But one should not overlook the strong humanist vein in Kurosawa, expressed most movingly in *Living* (1952). Other key films: *Drunken Angel* (1948), *The Idiot* (1951), *I Live in Fear* (1955), *The Lower Depths* (1957) and *Kagemusha* (1980).

Lang, Fritz (1890–1976)

Lang began as a leading exponent of German Expressionism, with the psychodrama *M* (1931), starring Peter Lorre as the self-hating child murderer, and *Metropolis* (1926), a science-fiction evocation of a nightmarish industrial city of the future. Goebbels was very taken with the latter film, and offered Lang the job of film-propaganda director to the Third Reich. Instead, he fled to America, and proceeded to provide auteurist critics with one of their juiciest test-cases by adapting his preoccupations with fate, revenge, and the social outcast to the turbulent American society of the pre-war and wartime years (*Fury*, 1936; and *Ministry of Fear*, 1944), and to genres such as the Western (*Rancho Notorious* in 1952) and the gangster film (*The Big Heat* in 1953). Two Edward G. Robinson performances—as a Professor implicated in murder in *The Woman in the Window* (1944) and as an artist infatuated with a prostitute in *Scarlet Street* (1945)—embody to perfection the typical Lang hero, trapped by personality, circumstance and environment. He is still arguably the most formidable pessimist in film history, and his presentation of fear and alienation in the modern metropolis was profoundly influential on, among others, Godard, Hitchcock and Kubrick.

Lean, Sir David (1908–91)

The popular cinema's master story-teller. In *Brief Encounter* (1945), he made the British cinema's greatest love story; his Dickens' adaptations, *Great Expectations* (1946) and *Oliver Twist* (1948) have never been surpassed; and with *The Bridge on the River Kwai* (1957), *Lawrence of Arabia* (1962) and *Doctor Zhivago* (1965), he managed to align epic perspectives with intimate and intense characterisation. After the failure of *Ryan's Daughter* in 1970, his reputation slumped: "bourgeois impersonality" was the label given to his films. But the success of *A Passage to India* (1984) helped to force a re-evaluation of his work and recognise its individual qualities: the emotional repression of his heroines; the visionary madness of his heroes; the spirit of place that pulses in his films; and his sensitivity to the erratic, exotic emotions that lurk beneath the surface of English propriety. Other key films include: *The Sound Barrier* (1952), *Hobson's Choice* (1954) and *Summer Madness* (1955).

Lee, Ang (b.1954)

Emigrating from his native Taiwan to America in 1978 and learning his film craft at New York's University Film School, Ang Lee has amassed the most varied and accomplished body of work of any director of the last decade. It ranges from domestic drama to a western; from martial arts to Jane Austen; from low-key comedy of observation, like the delightful *Pushing Hands* (1992), to high-tech comic-strip fantasy such as *Hulk* (2003) ; and from the visual splendour of *Crouching Tiger, Hidden Dragon* (2000) to the psychological depth of *The Ice Storm* (1997). Other key films: *The Wedding Banquet* (1993), *Eat Drink Man Woman* (1994), *Sense and Sensibility* (1995), *Ride with the Devil* (1999).

Leigh, Mike (b. 1943)

English director of growing international reputation after his success with *Secrets and Lies* (1996), a tragi-comic study of family relationships that is Leigh's forte. He had made his first film as far back as 1971, but only in the last decade has he been able to develop some cinematic continuity. Cineastes cherish his quirky insight into character and his sharp, sometimes astringent, satire of middle-class mores. Key films: *Bleak Moments* (1971), *High Hopes* (1988), *Life is Sweet* (1990), *Naked* (1993), *Career Girls* (1997), *Topsy Turvy* (1999), *All or Nothing* (2002) and *Vera Drake* (2004).

Leone, Sergio (1921–89)

Leone will always be remembered as the director who re-invigorated the western genre in the 1960s and made a star of Clint Eastwood. His spaghetti westerns—*A Fistful of Dollars* (1964), *For a Few Dollars More* (1965), *The Good, the Bad and the Ugly* (1966)—were an iconoclastic blend of parody and anti-heroism that appealed to a distrustful, anarchic age. His later films, *Once Upon a Time in the West* (1968) and *Once Upon a Time in America* (1984) were operatic meditations on the western and the gangster film respectively, both majestic and self-reflexive.

Loach, Ken (b. 1936)

Untamed radical film-maker who cut his teeth on social realist TV dramas, notably the massively influential *Cathy Come Home*, and then brought the same intensity to his feature films, most memorably in *Kes* (1969), a work much admired for its social critique and documentary-style technique by directors such as Kieslowski. Like Mike Leigh, Loach experienced a new lease of life in the 1990s, twice winning the European Film of the Year Award—for *Riff-Raff* (1990) and *Land and Freedom* (1995)—without compromising his vision, integrity or socialism.

Losey, Joseph (1909–84)

There were several Joseph Loseys: the American Losey renowned for cogent moral fables such as *The Prowler* (1951) before the McCarthyist blacklist forced him out of America; the British Losey in which, with collaborators like actors Stanley Baker and Dirk Bogarde and writer Harold Pinter, he analysed the sexual mores and class corruption of English society, as in *The Servant* (1963), *Accident* (1967) and *The Go-Between* (1971); and the European Losey of the final phase of his career, when he adapted classics such as *A Doll's House* (1973) or Mozart's *Don Giovanni* (1980) or offered trenchant insights into recent political history, as in *The Assassination of Trotsky* (1972) and *Mr. Klein* (1976). With a style often verging on the baroque, Losey tackled a variety of subject matter, but the themes were consistent: the hypocrisy and deceit of dominant social and sexual attitudes. He was the most Brechtian of directors and had one of the most lucid intellects in movies. Other key films include: *The Boy with Green Hair* (1948), *Blind Date* (1959), *The Criminal* (1960), *King and Country* (1964) and *Secret Ceremony* (1968).

Lubitsch, Ernst (1892–1947)

The master of sophisticated sex comedy who, in Billy Wilder's phrase, "could do more with a closed door than most modern directors can do with an entire bedroom". Born in Berlin, Lubitsch brought a European flavour to Hollywood farce, satirising the pretension and insensitivity that sometimes go with wealth and position. His best remembered films are *Ninotchka* (1939), in which Garbo laughs, and *To Be or Not to Be* (1942), in which Jack Benny plays Hamlet. They are not only comedies: they are fervent anti-Nazi satires made at a time when Lubitsch must have known that the Europe of his youth, so lovingly evoked on screen, was being destroyed forever. Other key films: *Trouble in Paradise* (1932) and *The Shop Around the Corner* (1940).

Lumet, Sidney (b. 1924)

The most enduring of the generation of directors (including John Frankenheimer, Martin Ritt and Franklin Schaffner) who graduated to the cinema in the 1950s after learning their craft on television. Lumet's first film, the jury-room drama, *12 Angry Men* (1957) was an instant classic, and his best films have often returned to the themes of justice, law and order, civic corruption and abuse of police power. A child actor on stage, he has developed a powerful rapport with actors and some of his films rival Kazan's in the skill and intensity of the perfor-

mances. Arguably over-prolific, undeniably humourless, Lumet has nevertheless amassed a powerful body of work that testifies to his talent, professionalism and liberal values. Key films include: *Long Day's Journey into Night* (1962), *Fail Safe* (1964), *The Hill* (1965), *Dog Day Afternoon* (1975), *Prince of the City* (1981), *The Verdict* (1982), *Running on Empty* (1987).

Lynch, David (b. 1946)

One of the modern cinema's most unnerving directors. He achieved instant notoriety with the gruesome *Eraserhead* (1976); had a deserved success with the compassionate *The Elephant Man* (1980); but has since polarised critical opinion with such films as *Wild at Heart* (1990) and *Lost Highway* (1997), psychologically challenging or pretentiously incoherent, according to taste. His most fully achieved works to date are *Blue Velvet* (1987), a nightmarish investigation of the dark sexual secrets of 'typical' small-town America; and *Mulholland Drive* (2001), a mysterious mesmerising look at the American Dream.

Mackendrick, Alexander (1912–93)

The most consistently brilliant of the Ealing directors, making four of its most successful and enduring comedies: *Whisky Galore* (1949), *The Man in the White Suit* (1951), *The Maggie* (1954) and *The Lady-Killers* (1955). His American debut—an exposé of yellow journalism—*Sweet Smell of Success* (1957) was also remarkable, but after a series of abortive projects in the 1960s, Mackendrick retired from directing to become Dean of the film department of the California Institute of the Arts. He left behind a fine body of work, notable for its extraordinary insights into the world of children, its fascination with the dangers of innocence, and its mordant observation of the intricate yet inevitable ways in which humans fail to communicate. Other key films: *Mandy* (1952), *Sammy Going South* (1963) and *A High Wind in Jamaica* (1965).

Malle, Louis (1932–95)

Formerly an assistant to Robert Bresson and Jacques Cousteau, Louis Malle developed into one of the most esteemed of international directors. He made films as dashing as *Zazie dans le Metro* (1960), as disturbing as *Lacombe Lucien* (1973), as atmospheric as *Atlantic City* (1980), and as moving as *Au Revoir les Enfants* (1987). Malle often challenged the norms of society and the boundaries of cinema, exploring such risky subjects as eroticism (in *Les Amants* in 1958), incest (in *Murmur of the Heart* in 1971) and child prostitution (in *Pretty Baby* in 1979) and yet still achieving popular success and critical acclaim. Isolation and social alienation were recurrent themes, fittingly so perhaps for one of the least predictable and most individualistic film-makers of modern times. Other key films include: *Lift to the Scaffold* (1957), *Le Feu Follet* (1963), *My Dinner With Andre* (1982) and *Damage* (1992).

Mankiewicz, Joseph L. (1909–93)

To those who find Mankiewicz's films too wordy, he replied: "There can never be an excess of *good* talk". Mankiewicz was one of the most eloquent of Hollywood's writer directors, who began by writing dialogue for W. C. Fields and, he claims, Rin-Tin-Tin (an unused screen-play about a dog that hates its master, a familiar Mankiewicz theme). His greatest period was during the ten years after the War, in which he won the writing and directing Oscars for two consecutive years (for *A Letter to Three Wives* in 1949 and *All About Eve* in 1950) and also made Hollywood's best Shakespearian film (*Julius Caesar* in 1952). His career never really picked up momentum after his labours on the mammothly expensive *Cleopatra* (1963), though he was proud to claim that his last film *Sleuth* (1972) is the only film ever to have its entire cast—*i.e.* Laurence Olivier and Michael Caine—nominated for Oscars. There are a lot of interesting recurrent motifs in Mankiewicz—generation conflict, ghosts from the past that will not stay dead—and nobody has made more haunting use of the flashback. Other key films: *The Ghost and Mrs. Muir* (1947), *Five Fingers* (1952), *The Barefoot Contessa* (1954) and *Suddenly Last Summer* (1959).

Mann, Anthony (1909–67)

Anthony Mann is best remembered for a series of Westerns he made with actor James Stewart, which were striking for their dramatic use of landscape and the psychological instability of their heroes. In *Winchester 73* (1950), *Bend of the River* (1952), *The Naked Spur* (1953), and *The Far Country* (1955), Stewart plays an ostensibly noble but actually neurotic hero who, whilst undertaking a perilous journey across a treacherous landscape, must also root out the evil in himself. Mann also made fine thrillers, a classic epic (*El Cid* in 1961) and even a stylish musical (*The Glenn Miller Story* in 1954) but it was the Mann of the Western that really showed his quality as a director. Other key films: *The Man from Laramie* (1955), *Man of the West* (1958) and *The Fall of the Roman Empire* (1964).

Melville, Jean-Pierre (1917–73)

Melville was something of a father figure of the *Nouvelle Vague* because of his economical and independent production methods. He made an exemplary adaptation of Jean Cocteau's novel *Les Enfants Terribles* (1950). However, he is most celebrated for a series of poetic, stylised existential gangster films, among them *Second Breath* (1966), *The Samurai* (1967), and *The Red Circle* (1970), which particularly took their inspiration from Melville's favourite director, John Huston. (Melville had chosen his pseudonym after his favourite author, Herman Melville: his actual surname was Grumbach). Perhaps his masterpiece, though, and certainly his most personal film, is *Army of the Shadows* (1969), a film about the French Resistance that drew on his own personal experience in the war.

Minnelli, Vincente (1910–86)

The name Vincente Minnelli is synonymous with the MGM musical—*Meet Me in St. Louis* (1944), *An American in Paris* (1951), *The Band Wagon* (1953), *Gigi* (1958) and others. Yet he was also adept at comedy, and did some remarkably intense melodramas, of which *Lust for Life* (1955), his bio-pic of Van Gogh, and *The Bad and the Beautiful* (1952), his glittering dissection of Hollywood ruthlessness, are particularly notable. He was interested in the plight of the artist in society, and the superiority of the world of imagination to that of reality. Hollywood's Dream Factory proved a most congenial environment for this most elegant of stylists. Other key films: *The Pirate* (1948), *Madame Bovary* (1949), *Father of the Bride* (1950). *Brigadoon* (1953), *The Cobweb* (1955) and *Some Came Running* (1958).

Mizoguchi, Kenji (1898–1956)

For many, Mizoguchi is the greatest of all Japanese directors, but his films are still not that well known in the West. The most famous is *Ugetsu Monogatari* (1953), a ravishingly beautiful tale of ghosts and greed. Its articulation of history and fantasy, its lyrical style and its commitment to the treatment of women as equals are characteristic of the director. Other films include: *The Story of the Last Chrysanthemums* (1939), *The Life of Oharu* (1952), *Sansho the Bailiff* (1954).

Murnau, F. W. (1889–1931)

Murnau is renowned for three classics of silent film: *Nosferatu* (1922), the cinema's first version of the *Dracula* story and still the most frightening; *The Last Laugh* (1924), credited as being one of the few silent films to dispense with titles and remarkable for its fluid camera movement; and *Sunrise* (1927), his first American film. Tragically he was killed in a car crash in 1931.

Olmi, Ermanno (b. 1931)

An Italian director whose work is characterised by a sympathy for the working man and by a concern for human dignity. In films such as *Il Posto* (1961) and *The Tree of Wooden Clogs* (1979), he has kept the spirit of neo-realism alive.

Ophuls, Max (1902–57)

For a long time regarded as a talented minor director of exquisite trifles, Ophuls has been reinstated by modern—notably feminist—criticism to his rightful place as one of the greatest of forties and fifties directors. *Lola Montès* (1955) was his last film, about the beautiful "adventuress" who allows herself to be put on display in a circus ring at the end of her career. The swooping camera-movements and awareness of how feminine sexuality necessarily connotes being an object to be looked at are in evidence too in *Madame de . . .* (1953), as well as in the films he made in Austria, Germany and France before setting out to pursue his career in Hollywood. His best American film was the beautiful tragic romance, *Letter from an Unknown Woman* (1948); whilst both *Caught* (1949) and *The Reckless Moment* (1949) took conventional women's magazine material and, through intense visual style, transformed them into tense and subversive comments on romantic obsession and domestic imprisonment.

Oshima, Nagisa (b. 1932)

His name became familiar to most filmgoers only with *Ai No Corrida* (otherwise *Empire of the Senses*) in 1975. An innkeeper and his ex-servant make untiring love until she, at his behest, strangles him in the moment of orgasm. The much-touted erotic frankness—certainly far less surrogate than that in *Last Tango in Paris*—assumes its importance only when seen in conjunction with the film's critique of the situation of women in Japanese society. In his first international film, *Merry Christmas, Mr. Lawrence* (1983), he explored the strange bond which grows between a Japanese captain and a British prisoner of war: a variation of his typical themes of forbidden passion, and his preoccupation with society's "enemies" whose psychology he seeks to understand. More recently he completed a documentary for the BBC, *My Mother's Place* (1991), which gives a fascinating account of his background. Other key films: *Diary of A Shinjuku Thief* (1968), *Boy* (1969), *The Ceremony* (1971) and *Empire of Passion* (1978).

Ozu, Yasujiro (1903–63)

Like Mizoguchi, Ozu is a director long known to the Western public through one work—*Tokyo Story* of 1953, about a visit paid by an elderly couple to their children in the capital. Ozu's style is slow, his narrative-lines not exactly eventful, his photography from a low level (the seated position traditional for social intercourse in Japan) perhaps difficult for Westerners to adjust to. But now he is accepted as one of the most important innovators in film language, for the way in which his small-scale stories distil much that is important in Japanese life and history, and for the separating out of individual actions and gestures so that spectators have time fully to appreciate their implications. Key films include: *I Was Born But . . .* (1932), *There was a Father* (1942), *Late Spring* (1949), *Early Summer* (1951), *Good Morning* (1959) and *An Autumn Afternoon* (1962).

Pasolini, Pier Paolo (1922–76)

Pasolini's notorious death—murdered by a homosexual pick-up—could almost have been engineered as a publicity stunt to launch his final film, *Salo or the 120 Days of Sodom* (1976), in which the combination of intense and complex visual lucidity with a recoiling from the tyrannies of the twentieth century already evident in *Pigsty* (1969) reaches its zenith. Ideological revulsion from the present and an interest in the possibilities of film language motivate Pasolini's curious "Marxist-Freudian-Catholic" rewritings of classics for the screen—*Medea* (1969) and *The Decameron* (1971). His complex artistry is seen at its best in his first film, *Accatone!* (1961) and *The Gospel According to St. Matthew* (1964), an austere rendering of the Biblical story far removed from the Hollywood epic, and movingly attempting to reconcile Pasolini's Marxist political outlook with his religious mysticism.

Peckinpah, Sam (1925–84)

Peckinpah was a Hollywood maverick, associated with scenes of graphic violence photographed in loving slow motion. In fact, he had something of the visual lyricism and raucous male humour of John Ford, though whereas Ford disclosed the poetry behind America's pioneering past, Peckinpah explored its passions and perversions as well. He will always be remembered for *The Wild Bunch* (1969), his radical, revisionist Western that majestically dragged the genre, kicking and screaming, into the 20th century. Other key films: *Guns in the Afternoon* (1962), *Major Dundee* (1965), *Straw Dogs* (1971), *Pat Garrett and Billy the Kid* (1973) and *Cross of Iron* (1977).

Penn, Arthur (b. 1922)

An abrasive stylist, notable for his subversive way with popular film genres, his investigation of the reality behind legendary figures, and his insertion of counter-culture attitudes into mainstream movie-making. Key films: *The Left-Handed Gun* (1958), *The Miracle Worker* (1962), *Bonnie and Clyde* (1967), *Alice's Restaurant* (1969) and *Night Moves* (1975).

Polanski, Roman (b. 1933)

From early Surrealist shorts, Polanski moved into feature-length dramas of sexual tension with *Knife in the Water* (1962) and *Repulsion* (shot in England in 1965). The reputation for kinkiness he thereby gained was tragically highlighted when his wife, the actress Sharon Tate, was butchered by crazed followers of Charles Manson in 1969. His major box-office success has been the private-eye drama *Chinatown* (1974), in which Polanski himself slits open the nose of the character played by Jack Nicholson. He also breathed flesh and blood into the horror film with *Rosemary's Baby* (1968) and fresh life into the filmed literary classic with *Tess* (1979). His traumatic life has been recounted in his autobiography, *Roman*. His recent film, *The Pianist* (2002) was a remarkable return to form and won him an unexpected Oscar as best director. Other key films: *Cul-de-Sac* (1966), *Macbeth* (1971), *The Tenant* (1976) and *Oliver Twist* (2005).

Powell, Michael (1905–90) and Pressburger, Emeric (1902–88)

British cinema's most full-blooded fantasists, who peaked in the 1940s with such passionate and visually imaginative films as *The Life and Death of Colonel Blimp* (1943), *I Know Where I'm Going* (1945), *A Matter of Life and Death* (1946), *Black Narcissus* (1947) and their greatest success, *The Red Shoes* (1948). From the late 1950s, Powell went solo and created an enormous furore with *Peeping Tom* (1960), which was critically reviled at the time but has since attained classic status and is deeply admired by cineastes and fellow directors such as Martin Scorsese.

Preminger, Otto (1906–86)

Talented tyrant who thrived on controversy, whether it involved the use of "naughty" words in *The Moon is Blue* (1953) or the depiction of the world of the drug addict in *The Man with the Golden Arm* (1955). His best films are the detective thriller, *Laura* (1945), one of a number of Preminger's features about mysterious, irresistible women who lure men to their doom; and the courtroom drama *Anatomy of a Murder* (1959), a masterpiece of objectivity and ambiguity. Other films: *Angel Face* (1953), *Carmen Jones* (1954), *Bonjour Tristesse* (1957), *Advise and Consent* (1962), *The Cardinal* (1963).

Ray, Nicholas (1911–78)

Ray was one of the most inventive and consistent of Hollywood action directors, whose rhetorical question summed up his philosophy of cinema: "If it were all in the script, why make the film?" *Rebel Without A Cause* (1955) blazed the trail for a host of movies about rebellious youth, but the dignity of James Dean's performance and the symbolic richness of Ray's *mise-en-scene* have caused it to survive longer than most of its imitators. He enjoyed success also with Bogart, *In a Lonely Place* (1950) and Robert Mitchum, *The Lusty Men* (1952). The critics of *Cahiers du Cinema* particularly championed Ray's more extreme stylistic exercises, such as the feminist Western, *Johnny Guitar* (1954) and the baroque gangster film, *Party Girl* (1958). Alienated youth, the rebel, the outsider: these were the figures with whom Ray identified, sometimes

melodramatically, often poetically. Other key films: *They Live By Night* (1948), *Knock on Any Door* (1949), *On Dangerous Ground* (1952), *Bigger Than Life* (1956) and *Bitter Victory* (1957).

Ray, Satyajit (1921–92)

Pather Panchali of 1955 introduced Indian cinema to a wider audience, and launched a highly successful trilogy, completed by *Aparajito* of 1957 and *The World of Apu* of 1959. The withdrawn, analytical style of Ray's output expanded with some of his work in the seventies (see *Company Limited*, 1972) to a greater awareness of the problems of Westernised India. His films were rooted in the tradition of the humanist documentary, influenced by the social concern of Italian neo-realists, and inspired by the natural lyricism of a director like Jean Renoir. Other key films: *The Music Room* (1958), *Charulata* (1964), *Days and Nights in the Forest* (1970), *The Middle Man* (1976), *The Chess Players* (1977) and *The Home and the World* (1984).

Reed, Sir Carol (1906–76)

Reed's reputation as one of the key directors of post-war cinema rests on a small number of films: the Expressionist, *Odd Man Out* (1947), the last day-in-the-life of an IRA man on the run, and two adaptations of Graham Greene stories, *The Fallen Idol* (1948) and *The Third Man* (1949). Overall his films are notable for a self-effacing craftsmanship, a sympathy with the world of children, and a fascination with confrontations between innocence and experience. He won an Oscar for *Oliver!* (1968). Other key films include *Outcast of the Islands* (1951), one of the cinema's best adaptations of Conrad; and *The Man Between* (1953), using its post-war Berlin setting less evocatively than post-war Vienna in *The Third Man* but a gripping human drama nonetheless.

Renoir, Jean (1899–1979)

A career spanning nearly fifty years included one of the first great dramas to be shot entirely on location, *Toni*, made with a largely non-professional cast in the South of France in 1935; two magnificent performances from Michel Simon, in *La Chienne* (1931) and *Boudu Sauve Des Eaux* (1932); a period funded by the Left-wing Popular Front that produced the film about a workers' cooperative, *Le Crime de Monsieur Lange* (1935); and a forties and fifties output as an exile in Hollywood of considerable merit, including *The Southerner* of 1945. These would be enough to mark Renoir out as an all-time cinema great even were it not for his two pre-Second-World-War masterpieces, *La Grande Illusion* (1937), a drama set in a POW camp, and the matchless *La Regle du Jeu* of 1939. This savage and frequently hilarious drama of love, class-antagonism, and the ambiguous corruption of aristocratic style so quickly achieved recognition as a masterpiece that it requires an effort now to remind ourselves that it was banned on first release, so clear was its scathing criticism of French society.

Resnais, Alain (b. 1922)

Resnais began as a documentarist, and made his first feature film in 1959—*Hiroshima Mon Amour*, from a screenplay by the novelist Marguerite Duras. *Hiroshima*'s concern with the interaction of time, place and memory was taken up and amplified in *Last Year in Marienbad* (1961), where there is no reassuring continuity of character or coherence of time or space other than that imposed ambiguously, from moment to moment by the "eternal present" of the screen. Speculation about *Marienbad* reached quasi-metaphysical heights that have frequently tended to obscure the dazzling frozen eroticism of its *mise-en-scene*, its masterful exploitation of the dreamlike aspect of film-watching, and the performances of Georgio Albertazzi and Delphine Seyrig. Memory and imagination have continued to be important preoccupations in his work, and he remains one of the great "modernist" innovators of contemporary cinema, continually exploring new areas of expression. Key films: *Night and Fog* (1956), *Muriel* (1963), *Providence* (1977) and *L'Amour a Mort* (1984).

Rosi, Francesco (b. 1922)

Rosi began as an assistant to Luchino Visconti and is perhaps best known as the maker of the Placido Domingo film of *Carmen* (1984). But his natural home is the world of political corruption and paranoia, and no modern film-maker can match him for his trenchant critique of the institutions of power. His most important films in this vein are *Salvatore Giuliano* (1961), *Hands Over the City* (1963), *The Mattei Affair* (1972). *Illustrious Corpses* (1976), *Christ Stopped at Eboli* (1979) and *Three Brothers* (1981).

Rosselini, Roberto (1906–77)

A key figure in the Italian neo-realist movement, whose early films were made on shoestring budgets and in often difficult conditions (*e.g. Rome, Open City*, 1945, about the anti-Fascist Resistance, shot when Mussolini's troops were still occupying Rome). *Voyage in Italy* (1953), in its open-endedness and preoccupation with George Sanders' and Ingrid Bergman's fluctuating senses of cultural alienation, foreshadowed the hesitant psychological explorations of Antonioni. Other key films: *Germany Year Zero* (1948), *Stromboli* (1949) and *The Rise of Louis XIV* (1966).

Rossen, Robert (1908–66)

One of the most socially aware of Hollywood directors who made his mark in the late 1940s with a hard-hitting boxing saga *Body and Soul* (1947), which was actually an allegory of capitalist corruption, and the Oscar-winning *All the King's Men* (1949), an indictment of creeping political Fascism. But then, hounded by the House UnAmerican Activities Committee for his Communist affiliations, he finally recanted and named names. He was able to work again but became, according to friends, a haunted, withdrawn individual. But his last two films were remarkable returns to form: a study of character and courage around the pool table, *The Hustler* (1961), and a study of madness, *Lilith* (1964), which was condemned on its first release but has gained an underground reputation as one of the most lyrical films of the American cinema.

Sautet, Claude (1924–2000)

Highly regarded French director who began as a screenwriter and who belatedly secured recognition as a subtle anatomist of human behaviour through the international success of *Un Coeur en Hiver—A Heart in Winter* (1993) and *Nelly and M. Arnaud* (1995). Other key films: *Les Choses de la Vie—The Things of Life* (1970), *Cesar et Rosalie* (1972), *Une Histoire Simple—A Simple Story* (1978).

Scorsese, Martin (b. 1942)

Arguably the most exciting of modern American film-makers. His movies are notable for their restless camera movement which reflects the inner tension of the characters. He has collaborated particularly closely with actor Robert De Niro, forging the most important actor-director partnership in American film since Brando and Kazan in the 1950s. Together they have made emotionally lacerating films about troubled masculinity and with a religious sense of redemption. Sometimes criticised for misogyny, his films are among the most disturbing and challenging of mainstream cinema. Key films: *Mean Streets* (1973), *Taxi Driver* (1976), *Raging Bull* (1980), *The King of Comedy* (1983), *After Hours* (1985), *Goodfellas* (1990) *Cape Fear* (1991), *The Age of Innocence* (1993), *Casino* (1995), *Kundun* (1997), *Bringing Out the Dead* (1999), *The Gangs of New York* (2002) and *The Aviator* (2004).

Siegel, Don (1912–91)

Siegel learnt his craft as head of montage at Warners before gaining a reputation on low budget thrillers such as *Riot in Cell Block 11* (1954), *Baby Face Nelson* (1957) and *The Line Up* (1958), that combined sharp observation of the social outsider with a real flair for staging violent action. The sci-fi classic *Invasion of the Body Snatchers* (1956) and a brilliant re-make of *The Killers* (1964) cemented his cult status, and his career achieved a decisive upturn through his association on five films with Clint

Eastwood, notably on *Dirty Harry* (1971), where they created arguably the most controversial anti-hero of postwar cinema. Other key films: *Hell is for Heroes* (1962), *Madigan* (1968), *The Beguiled* (1971), *The Shootist* (1976) and *Escape from Alcatraz* (1979).

Siodmak, Robert (1900–73)

Siodmak made his directing debut on the low budget German film, *Menschen am Sontag-People on Sunday* (1929), a work that has become famous for also launching the careers of directors Billy Wilder and Fred Zinnemann and cameraman Eugene Schufftan. Like them, Siodmak moved to Hollywood, and he did his best work during the 1940s, making a number of fatalistic, visually gloomy dramas that are acknowledged as classics of film noir or Grand Guignol suspense: *Phantom Lady* (1944), *The Spiral Staircase* (1945), *The Killers* (1946), *Cry of the City* (1948), *Criss Cross* (1949).

Sirk, Douglas (1900–87)

Long regarded as a curiosity, Sirk was a Danish expatriate whose melodramas, richly shot and distinguished by narrative flamboyance, were at first treated with mild condescension. *Written on the Wind* (1956) was among the first to gain serious acceptance, with its dramatisation of the conflicts within a wealthy oil family whose problems (alcoholism, instability, sexual promiscuity) were sympathetically presented in a highly-coloured style that still managed to eschew portentousness.

His other works, notably *All That Heaven Allows* (1955) and *Imitation of Life* (1959), also began to receive more serious and sympathetic treatment as ironic and subversive critiques of middle-class America: they had a profound influence on the work of Fassbinder and inspired the recent film, *Far from Heaven* (2002). Other key films: *There's Always Tomorrow* (1956), *Tarnished Angels* (1957) and *A Time to Love and A Time to Die* (1958).

Spielberg, Steven (b. 1947)

The most successful director in the history of cinema, notably for four films: *Jaws* (1975), *Close Encounters of the Third Kind* (1977), *E.T.—the Extra-Terrestrial* (1982) and *Jurassic Park* (1993). His films are basically about ordinary people in extraordinary situations, and he directs these with a witty eye for the mores of American suburbia, a tremendous flair for suspense, and an unusually sympathetic presentation of the relationships between mothers and children. Recently a new maturity has come into his work with *The Color Purple* (1985), *Empire of the Sun* (1987) and *Schindler's List* (1993), his unexpected powerful film of the holocaust. Often attacked for sentimentality, his work has been defended by the novelist J.G. Ballard, who has described Spielberg as the "Puccini of cinema – too sweet for some tastes, but what melodies, what orchestrations, what cathedrals of emotion ..." Other key films: *Duel* (1971), *The Sugarland Express* (1974), *Raiders of the Lost Ark* (1981), *Amistad* (1997), *Saving Private Ryan* (1998), *Minority Report* (2002) and *The War of the Worlds* (2005). Awarded Honorary Knighthood, 2001.

Stevens, George (1904–75)

Beginning his career as a cameraman on Laurel and Hardy shorts, Stevens' early reputation as a director was in comedy: *Woman of the Year* (1942) and *The More the Merrier* (1943). But his war experience, which included being part of the American force that liberated Dachau, changed his sensibility: comedy receded and his films became full of a feeling of tragic sacrifice. *The Diary of Anne Frank* (1959) is his memorial to the war dead. His own movie monument is probably a trio of films that encapsulates his sympathy for the outsider and constitutes his epic reassessment of the American Dream: *A Place in the Sun* (1951), *Shane* (1953), and *Giant* (1956). Other key films: *Alice Adams* (1935), *Gunga Din* (1939), *Talk of the Town* (1942), *I Remember Mama* (1948) and *The Greatest Story Ever Told* (1965).

Stone, Oliver (b. 1946)

Vietnam vet turned polemicist director. He turned his Army experience into compelling cinema in *Platoon* (1986) and *Born on the Fourth of July* (1989), for which he won directing Oscars, and his bio-pics of *JFK* (1991) and *Nixon* (1995) were powerfully paranoid assaults on the American political system. Often derided for the extreme views and excessive violence of his films, Stone has been nonetheless a provocative presence in modern cinema. Other key films: *Salvador* (1985), *Wall Street* (1987), *Natural Born Killers* (1995).

Sturges, John (1911–92)

One of the finest directors of westerns during one of the genre's golden eras, the 1950s. His masterpiece is *Bad Day at Black Rock* (1955), which is both modern western and suspense thriller, and his other fine contributions to the genre include: *Escape from Fort Bravo* (1954), *Gunfight at the O.K. Corral* (1957), *The Law and Jake Wade* (1958), *Last Train from Gun Hill* (1959), and *The Magnificent Seven* (1960).

Sturges, Preston (1898–1959)

One of the first great writer-directors of the sound era in Hollywood, Sturges sold his screenplay *The Great McGinty* (1940) to Paramount for ten dollars on the condition he was allowed to direct. It was the first of eight comedies he wrote and directed within four years, each of which was interesting, some of which—*The Lady Eve* (1941), *Sullivan's Travels* (1942), *Palm Beach Story* (1942)—are classics. His comedies are distinguished by a frantic pace, tremendous ingenuity of dialogue and situation, and an air of shrill desperation. His characters comprise hapless millionaires, seductive gold-diggers and frustrated inventors, all whipped together in a sustained assault on what Sturges saw as all-American sacred cows.

Tarantino, Quentin (b.1963)

Former video store clerk and movie fanatic who became the most copied and discussed cult director of the 1990s. His first film, *Reservoir Dogs* (1991), about a heist that goes wrong, showed his gift for sharp dialogue and ingenious story-telling, but it was his second, *Pulp Fiction* (1994) that really caught the popular, post-modernist imagination. This underworld tale, with its outrageous violence, narrative surprises and subversively playful tone amidst the pervasive amorality, has since been much imitated but never equalled—not even, to date, by Tarantino himself, though his two-part *Kill Bill* (2002) attracted much attention.

Tarkovsky, Andrey (1932–86)

The greatest Soviet film-maker since Eisenstein—and the resemblance ends there. Tarkovsky found his inspiration not in the spirit of the Russian Revolution but in the spirituality of the classic Russian novel, and the questions his films posed were not about the nature of political power but about the possibilities of personal salvation. This inevitably brought him into conflict with the Soviet authorities, who disliked the unsocialist, surreal, avant-garde qualities in films such as *Andrei Rublev* (1966) and *Mirror* (1974). They also took exception to Tarkovsky's thinly concealed allegory of the struggles of the artist in a repressive society. His last films were made in exile, and his final film, *The Sacrifice* (1985), a typically hallucinatory drama about a dream of nuclear holocaust averted, was one of his most movingly accessible and affirmative. A dreamer, a poet, a prophet, Tarkovsky's provocative and challenging thoughts on cinema were published in his book, *Sculpting in Time* (1987). Other key films: *Ivan's Childhood* (1962), *Solaris* (1971), *Stalker* (1979) and *Nostalgia* (1982).

Trier, Lars von (b.1956)

A signatory to the Dogme 95 manifesto (*see* **Q28**) which rejected cinema artifice and extravagance, von Trier has nevertheless made films of prodigious imagination and experimentation that have provoked extreme critical reaction, both for and against. Few would deny his claim to be the most important Danish film-maker since Carl Dreyer. Key films: *The Element of Crime* (1984), *Europa* (1991), *The Kingdom* (1994), *Breaking the Waves* (1996), *The Idiots* (1998), *Dancer in the Dark* (2000), *Dogville* (2003).

Truffaut, Francois (1932–84)

With Godard, one of the outstanding early names of the so-called French "New Wave". Truffaut's early work reveals a delight in the possibilities of the cinematic medium (notably in evoking situations of emotional fluidity and ambiguity) that is often exhilarating, as in *Shoot the Pianist* (with Charles Aznavour, 1960) and his masterpiece, *Jules et Jim* (1961). This deals with a menage a trois in the France of the beginning of the century, portrayed with tragic irony and a light yet serious treatment of historical and cultural influences on the relationship between Catherine (Jeanne Moreau) and her two lovers, the German Jules and the Frenchman Jim. His first feature film, *The 400 Blows* (1959) drew on his own difficult childhood and delinquent adolescence, and later films like *L'Enfant Sauvage* (1970) also deal sensitively with the world of childhood. He also made films like *Fahrenheit 451* (1965) and *The Bride Wore Black* (1968) in homage to Hitchcock. In the 1970s he made two of his most haunting films on his favourite theme of romantic obsession, *The Story of Adele H* (1975), and *The Green Room* (1978), but he also made one of the most affectionate of all films about film-making, *Day for Night* (1973). Truffaut loved movies and his death left cineastes feeling that they had lost a member of the family.

Vertov, Dziga (1896–1934)

Often seen as the great documentary director, as Eisenstein was the great feature director, of the early Bolshevik Russian days. His principal work is *The Man with a Movie Camera* (1929), an exhilarating exploration of the relationship between the camera, the person holding it, and the subject-matter being filmed.

Vidor, King (1894–1982)

A pioneer of the cinema, responsible for two of the masterpieces of American silent film, the World War One drama, *The Big Parade* (1925), and the urban realist classic, *The Crowd* (1928). His films of the sound era were less distinguished, curiously at their most impressive when he foresook realism in favour of melodrama. Key films include: *Hallelujah* (1929), *Our Daily Bread* (1934), *Stella Dallas* (1937), *The Citadel* (1938), *Duel in the Sun* (1947), *Ruby Gentry* (1952), *War and Peace* (1956).

Vigo, Jean (1905–34)

A great Surrealist director, whose early death from tuberculosis meant that he produced only two feature films, both masterpieces: *Zero de Conduite* (1933), an account of a rebellion in a repressive boys' school whose fragmentary, night-marish quality (partly a result of the tight conditions under which it was shot) is exceptional, and *L'Atalante* (1934), about a honeymoon on a barge, a haunting blend of lyricism and realism.

Visconti, Luchino (1906–77)

The most emotive and extravagant of the Italian neo-realists. Visconti came to attention with *La Terra Trema* (1948), about Sicilian fishermen; a mixture of tragic fatalism and concern for social change characteristic of Visconti pervades this, as it does the operatic *Rocco and his Brothers* of 1960 and his adaptation of the novel by Lampedusa, *The Leopard* (1963). Aristocrat yet communist, arthouse director who loved working with stars (like Dirk Bogarde and Burt Lancaster), Visconti was a strange mixture of extremes. His films dealt with forbidden passions; tormented heroes imprisoned by the standards of a society they despise; and superficially cultured ways of life in their death- throes. Nobody recreated the past more sumptuously on the screen than Visconti nor photographed doom more voluptuously. Other key films: *Ossessione* (1942), *Senso* (1954), *The Damned* (1969), *Death in Venice* (1971), *Ludwig* (1972) and *Conversation Piece* (1974).

Von Sternberg, Josef (1894–1969)

The supreme exponent of cinema as icon, of the image whose lavish and elaborate composition is its most immediately apparent justification. Yet his films are astounding essays on the infinite varieties of love, in which the love object (invariably Marlene Dietrich) is alternately the exploited victim or the tyrannical temptress. He never created real worlds: his films are stylised sound stages of dream and desire. Key films: *The Blue Angel* (1930), *Morocco* (1930), *Shanghai Express* (1932), *The Scarlet Empress* (1934) and *The Devil is a Woman* (1938).

Von Stroheim, Erich (1885–1957)

"By God I told them the truth" said Stroheim of his classic film *Greed* (1923). Unfortunately for MGM, he told it at excessive length, and the film was cut from 42 to 10 reels in length. Stroheim's career as director never recovered from this. But John Grierson was to call him "the director of directors", for his unflinching realism and fanatical attention to detail. Billy Wilder thought he was ten years ahead of his time, though Stroheim contradicted him: "No—twenty". Key films: *Foolish Wives* (1922), *Merry-Go-Round* (1923) and *Queen Kelly* (1928).

Wajda, Andrzej (b. 1926)

Perhaps the most important film-maker Poland has ever produced. Wajda grew up in Poland during the Nazi occupation and his famous trilogy—*A Generation* (1955), *Kanal* (1956) and *Ashes and Diamonds* (1958)—records the wartime suffering and courage and the scramble for political power that followed the liberation. *Ashes and Diamonds*, in particular, with its charismatic performance by Zbigniew Cybulski, exemplifies Wajda's fascination with heroes who refuse to follow the tide of history and attempt to shape their own destinies through extreme action. For a time, history took second place to psychology and symbolism in his work. But in the mid 1970s, he returned head-on to contemporary issues, tackling the theme of censorship, political blackmail and the film-maker's responsibilities in *Man of Marble* (1976), and celebrating the rise of Solidarity in *Man of Iron* (1980) in a tone of prophetically precarious optimism. Wajda's films have often been set in transitional periods where one era has died and another is struggling to be born. His own career has also been subject to the turbulent tides of history, facing censorship, exile and rejection, but his achievements stand as an inspiring example of artistic talent surviving against difficult odds. Other key films: *Innocent Sorcerers* (1961), *Everything for Sale* (1968), *The Wedding* (1973), *The Conductor* (1980) and *Korczak* (1088).

Welles, Orson (1915–85)

Welles made his debut with *Citizen Kane* in 1941; over sixty years later, it is still a popular choice as the best film ever. Innovatory in film language (in its bold and extensive use of "deep-focus"—the camera plunging into the imaginary "depth" of the screen), suggestive in its plot (about a tycoon, modelled on William Randolph Hearst, whose public success is seen as a remedy for private unhappiness), electric in the quality of its camerawork and ensemble acting, and with its finale (the "secret" of Kane's life—the name of his confiscated childhood sledge, Rosebud) the most ironically well-kept secret in cinema history, the film succeeded on so many levels that hindsight almost suggests that Welles's subsequent career had to be an anticlimax. He filmed Shakespeare (*Macbeth*, 1948, *Othello*, 1952, *Chimes at Midnight*, 1966), Kafka (*The Trial*, 1963) and a "documentary" about forgeries (*F. for Fake*, 1975), none to the effect of *Kane*. Nevertheless the qualities of his other films should not be overlooked: the tenderness of *The Magnificent Ambersons* (1942), the *film noir* virtuosity of *Lady from Shanghai* (1948), the magisterial study of police corruption in *Touch of Evil* (1958). It is tempting to see *Kane* as a prophetic study of promise unfulfilled, and Welles's career certainly had more than its share of disappointments and frustrations. But he still remains a giant of the cinema, probing themes of power and corruption with that virtuoso camera style that he said "describes that sense of vertigo, uncertainty, lack of stability, that melange of movement and tension that is our universe".

Wenders, Wim (b. 1945)

One of the major figures of the "New German Cinema" of the 1970s, cooler and less didactic than Fassbinder, more streetwise and less anti-American than Herzog. His ambivalent response to America's "Coca-colonisation" of Europe was explored in *The American Friend* (1977), which had guest roles for Nicholas Ray and Samuel Fuller; and films such as *The Goalkeeper's Fear of the Penalty* (1972) and *Kings of the Road* (1976) elaborated his interest in the alienation of the modern environment and the rootlessness of modern man. Wenders' films commonly start from place rather than plot and it is no surprise that his biggest international success to date is *Paris Texas* (1984), a film as remarkable for its disorienting landscape as its characters or story.

Wilder, Billy (1906–2002)

"It's not important that a director knows how to write," said Billy Wilder, "but it is important that he knows how to read." Fleeing from Nazi Europe and becoming a Hollywood screenwriter for, among others, Ernst Lubitsch, Wilder became a director in order to protect his own scripts. *Double Indemnity* (1944), *The Lost Weekend* (1945) and *Sunset Boulevard* (1950) were wonderfully macabre demonstrations of his talents, and films like *Some Like it Hot* (1959) and *The Apartment* (1960) consolidated his reputation as the sharpest satirist in Hollywood, with an unusually mordant view of human nature that did not, however, preclude the possibility of redemption. *Sabrina* (1954) and *Avanti!* (1972) showed the melting of American materialism by European romanticism. His care for structure, his unceasing verbal wit and the intelligence of his character development made Wilder's overall achievement the equal of any Hollywood director's of the sound era. Other key films: *Ace in the Hole* (1951), *Stalag 17* (1953), *Witness for the Prosecution* (1957), *One, Two, Three* (1961), *The Fortune Cookie* (1966), *The Private Life of Sherlock Holmes* (1970) and *Fedora* (1978).

Wong, Kar-Wei (b.1958)

Major figure of Hong Kong cinema, a director who specialises in visually exquisite, emotionally delicate stories of unrequited, unconsummated or understated love. This is seen to particularly exhilarating effect in *Chungking Express* (1994), his most famous film to date and one of the best films of the 1990s. Other key films: *As Tears Go By* (1988), *Fallen Angels* (1995), *Happy Together* (1997), *In the Mood for Love* (2000) and *2046* (2004).

Wyler, William (1902–81)

One of the master craftsmen of Hollywood film. As well as winning three Oscars for himself (for *Mrs. Miniver*, 1942; *The Best Years of Our Lives*, 1946; and *Ben-Hur*, 1959), Wyler elicited more than a dozen Oscar-winning performances from his casts. Although he could handle the epic canvas as well as anyone, his forte was for drama in a confined setting and struggles for territorial advantage in a marriage or family. *The Little Foxes* (1941), *The Heiress* (1949) and *Carrie* (1952) are all masterpieces of domestic claustrophobia. Whilst his heroes tended to be withdrawn figures, needing to be convinced of the necessity for action (like the pacifist hero of *The Big Country*, (1958)), his heroines are more often dynamic creatures, kicking against the constraints of a masculine world. No wonder he was Bette Davis's favourite director and directed her in some of her best films: *Jezebel* (1938), *The Letter* (1940) and *The Little Foxes*. Although recurrent patterns and themes are discernible in his films (unrequited love, class confrontations between the complacent and the envious), he tended, like Huston, to subordinate his personality to the requirements of the story. For this reason, he is often been underestimated by *auteurist* critics. But if a great director is simply someone who has made a number of great films, Wyler was a great director. Other key films: *Dodsworth* (1936), *Wuthering Heights* (1939), *Roman Holiday* (1952) and *The Children's Hour* (1961).

Yimou, Zhang (b. 1950)

One of the key figures of modern Chinese cinema,

an actor and cameraman (on Chen Kaige's *Yellow Earth* and *The Big Parade*) before turning to direction. Behind the sumptuous visual surfaces of his films lurk some telling observations on politics and patriarchy that have sometimes antagonised the Chinese authorities. His films also made a major star of his then leading actress Gong Li, whose characterisation often and excitingly subvert the stereotype of female submissiveness. The epic adventures *Hero* (2003) and *House of Flying Daggers* (2004) have both proved an unexpected cross over success. Key films: *Red Sorghum* (1988), *Ju Dou* (1990), *Raise the Red Lantern* (1991), *The Story of Qui Ju* (1992), *Shanghai Triad* (1995), *Not One Less* (2000).

Zinnemann, Fred (1907–97)

Born in Vienna, Zinnemann came to America in 1929, but his career did not really take off until *The Search* in 1948, a story of European children orphaned by the war and which presaged a number of his films about the impact and aftermath of war. But it was the western *High Noon* (1952) that established both Zinnemann's reputation and his fundamental theme: that of individual conscience. At considerable personal risk but on a point of principle, a character takes a stand against a community or institution that wishes him to compromise and conform: it is the theme also of *From Here to Eternity* (1953), *The Nun's Story* (1959) and *A Man for All Seasons* (1966). Unusually for Hollywood, these were dramas of reaction, not action, and with melancholy rather than happy endings. Their critical and commercial success testified to Zinnemann's skill at popularising complex themes without compromising his vision. Other key films: *The Seventh Cross* (1944), *Act of Violence* (1949), *Member of the Wedding* (1952), *Day of the Jackal* (1973) and *Julia* (1977).

3. FAMOUS SCREEN ACTORS AND ACTRESSES

Andrews, Dame Julie (b. 1935)

The archetype of screen virtue who reached her peak of popularity in the mid-1960s with *Mary Poppins* (1964) and *The Sound of Music* (1965), in both of which her "English rose" image and pure singing voice enchanted audiences. She later made a number of films for her second husband, director Blake Edwards, but without the same success.

Arbuckle, "Fatty" (1887–1933)

Superb silent comedian whose career was ruined when accused of the rape and murder of a starlet Virginia Rappe at a wild Hollywood party in 1921. Although completely cleared of all charges, Arbuckle was never allowed to appear on the screen again (the whole story is told in David Yallop's book, *The Day the Laughter Stopped*). Buster Keaton, who owed his start in movies to Arbuckle, said he learnt everything about film from him.

Astaire, Fred (1899–1987)

"Can't act, slightly bald, can dance a little", was the verdict of the screen test of Astaire, who, in partnership with Ginger Rogers, was to become the most stylish screen dancer in Hollywood history. He starred in such classic musicals as *Top Hat* (1935), *Swing Time* (1936), *Easter Parade* (1948) and *Funny Face* (1956). Turned to straight acting in his later career with such effect that Spencer Tracy felt threatened and sent the following wire to his friend: "You stop acting or I'll start dancing!"

Bacall, Lauren (b. 1924)

Bacall was one of the first examples of Hollywood's skill at playing on-and-off screen personas off against each other. Opposite Humphrey Bogart in *To Have and Have Not* (1944), she enchanted him on the screen as she did in real life while the film was being shot. (They were later to be married.) Her performance there is a remarkably knowing and ironic one (particularly in the famous scene where she tells Bogart how to whistle for her if he wants anything), and she was to play similar roles opposite him in *The Big Sleep* (1946), *Dark Passage* (Delmer Daves, 1947) and *Key Largo* (John Huston, 1948). Although she was never really able to repeat her success with Bogart, her persona in these films is interesting as a contrast to the submissive view of women often purveyed by Hollywood. She has been a great survivor and was nominated for an Oscar for her performance in Barbra Streisand's *A Mirror has Two Faces* (1996).

Bardot, Brigitte (b. 1934)

"Created" by her then-husband Roger Vadim in *And God Created Woman* (1956), Bardot epitomised a certain popular view of French female sexuality—poutingly sensual, sporting a St. Tropez suntan and little else besides, as ardent and capricious in her off-screen romances as in those for the cameras. In Julien Duvivier's *La Femme et le Pantin* (1958) and Vadim's *Warrior's Rest* (1962) she exploited this role to perfection; but she did show that she had some acting ability in *Le Mepris*, made for Jean-Luc Godard in 1963, in *Viva Maria* (1965) for Louis Malle, and in *La Verité* (1960) for Henri-Georges Clouzot. Retired from the screen to devote herself to ecological issues.

Beatty, Warren (b. 1937)

Many people think of Beatty's career as beginning with *Bonnie and Clyde* (Arthur Penn, 1967), in which his performance as the debonair yet sexually insecure bandit Clyde steals the show. But he sprang to prominence as early as 1961 (Elia Kazan's *Splendour in the Grass*), and has appeared infrequently, but always to great effect, ever since, his best post-Bonnie performance perhaps being the gambler McCabe in Altman's *McCabe and Mrs. Miller* (1971). Directorial ambitions then preoccupied him more than acting, and he won an Oscar for the direction of *Reds* (1981). Recently appeared as a controversially honest politician in *Bulworth* (1998)—a role he has sometimes threatened to play in real life.

Belmondo, Jean-Paul (b. 1933)

Belmondo sprang to fame with his performance as the confusedly amoral Michel Poiccard in Godard's *Breathless* (1959). This earned him recognition as one of the first "anti-heroes" of the European cinema, concerned with discovering himself through action and, in his second masterpiece for Godard, *Pierrot le Fou* (1965), contemplation as well. Both films featured Belmondo "betrayed", ostensibly by the women he chose (Jean Seberg and Anna Karina respectively), but as much by his own insecure openness. His later work (including *Borsalino* for Deray in 1970, and *Stavisky* for Resnais in 1974) tended to be glossier and more spectacular, to the detriment of the "anti-hero" persona, though he scored a big personal success in Claude Lelouch's updating of *Les Miserables* (1994).

Bergman, Ingrid (1915–82)

Enticed, like Greta Garbo, from Sweden to Hollywood at the end of the thirties, Bergman became one of Hollywood's star actresses, particularly in exotic "European" roles like that of Humphrey Bogart's lost *grand amour* in Michael Curtiz's *Casablanca* (1943) and in three films for Hitchcock, *Spellbound* (1945), *Notorious* (1946) and *Under Capricorn* (1949). She went on to freelance in Europe in the fifties, notably for Roberto Rosselini (whom she married), in neo-realist classics such as *Stromboli* (1950) and *Voyage in Italy* (1953). Made a triumphant comeback to Hollywood in *Anastasia* (1956), and in her later years had great success in *The Murder on the Orient Express* (1974), for which she won her third Oscar, and in Ingmar Bergman's *Autumn Sonata* (1978).

Binoche, Juliette (b. 1964)

Born in Paris, Juliette Binoche has become one of the star actresses of modern European cinema, whose screen aura of wounded sensuality has been deployed to powerful effect by major directors such as Louis Malle in *Damage* (1992), Krzysztof Kieslowski in *Three Colours:Blue* (1993) and Michael Haneke in *Code Unknown* (1999). She enhanced her international profile with an Oscar-winning performance as the nurse in *The English Patient* (1996) and also scored a personal success in the popular romance, *Chocolat* (2000).

Bogarde, Sir Dirk (1921–99)

It takes an effort to remind ourselves that the Bogarde who destroyed by his death-wish passion for a young boy in Visconti's *Death in Venice* (1971) began his acting career in British comedy and melodrama and acquired real prominence as the accident-prone medical student in the "Doctor" films of the late fifties. His fine performance as a homosexual barrister in *Victim* (1960) marked a turning point and Joseph Losey exploited his dramatic acting talent in *The Servant* (1963), which played off his British reserve against a highly-charged situation as Losey was also to do in *Accident* (1967). The association with Visconti confirmed him as one of the screen's subtlest and most accomplished actors.

Bogart, Humphrey (1899–1957)

One of the all-time superstars. Bogart began as a stage actor and graduated to screen stardom with one of his theatre roles, the psychopathic gangster in Mayo's *The Petrified Forest* (1936). He became famous in the forties as an "outsider" figure, caught up in corrupt or devious situations from which he tried to stay aloof through a basic decency masquerading as hard-bitten cynicism. *Casablanca* (Michael Curtiz, 1943) revealed the persona to have a soft heart, in the scenes where he drinks to forget his love for Ingrid Bergman—or rather to remember it—and where he sacrifices it in the airport scene at the end with the immortal: "Here's looking at you, kid". For Howard Hawks he made *To Have and Have Not* in 1944 and *The Big Sleep* in 1946, both with Lauren Bacall and both exploiting the same persona. Small wonder that fifties anti-hero Belmondo elevated him to a god in *Breathless* (Godard, 1959), as did Woody Allen in a different way in *Play it Again, Sam* (1972). Closely associated with director John Huston, for whom he made six films, including *The Maltese Falcon* (1941), *The Treasure of the Sierra Madre* (1948) and the film for which he won his Oscar, *The African Queen* (1951).

Bow, Clara (1905–65)

Known as the "It" girl because of her enormously popular personal success in the film *It* (1927). Epitomised the "Roaring 20s" during the silent era but her career then foundered because of sound, scandals and mental illness. She was the Monroe of her time: a sad fate.

Brando, Marlon (1924–2004)

Brando came to the cinema from the stage, a leading proponent of the "Method" school of acting which relied upon naturalistic empathy with the part rather than careful professional stylisation. Laconic violence, often tending to the inarticulate, was his early stock-in-trade, exemplified in *A Streetcar Named Desire* (1951) and *On The Waterfront* (1954), both directed by Elia Kazan. Other rebels vied with Brando in the late fifties and sixties, and his career went into an eclipse from which it was rescued by two very different, but remarkable, performances as men aware that they have passed their personal peak—the Mafioso Don Corleone in Coppola's *The Godfather* (1972), and the self-loathing American in Bertolucci's *Last Tango in Paris* (1973). He later tended to confine himself to expensive guest performances in movies like *Superman* (1980), though he gave a superb character performance as a Scottish liberal lawyer in the anti-apartheid drama, *A Dry White Season* (1989). Published a much publicised autobiography in 1994.

Brooks, Louise (1906–85)

Magnetic star whose film fame rests mainly on one charismatic performance: as Lulu in G. W. Pabst's *Pandora's Box* (1929). She retired from the screen in the early 1930s and led a reclusive life, though briefly surfaced to write a marvellous book of memoirs, *Lulu in Hollywood*.

Burton, Richard (1925–84)

Burton was initially a leading stage Shakespearian, but better-known to the film-going public for his flamboyant romance with Elizabeth Taylor. His performance as the verbally aggressive college professor in Mike Nichols's *Who's Afraid of Virginia Woolf ?* (1966) marked him out as a great screen actor, as did his performance in *The Spy who came in from the Cold* (1965). He was nominated seven times for the coveted Oscar without winning: his last performance was as the sinister interrogator O'Brien in the 1984 screen adaptation of George Orwell's *1984*.

Cagney, James (1899–1986)

Pugnacious leading man who started out as a dancer but whose energy and vitality made him ideal for the dynamic gangster movies of the 1930s, such as *Public Enemy* (1931), *Angels with Dirty Faces* (1938) and *The Roaring Twenties* (1939). Won an Oscar for *Yankee Doodle Dandy* (1942) but his most memorable characterisation was probably as the psychopathic, mother-fixated Cody Jarrett in Raoul Walsh's *White Heat* (1949).

Caine, Sir Michael (b. 1933)

Durable, dependable British star who, rather like Robert Mitchum, conceals his range and professionalism beneath a deceptively languid style. Came to the fore in the 1960s, particularly for his performance in the title role of *Alfie* (1966): thereafter he has remained in demand through a skilful balance of the commercial with the more challenging. Won supporting actor Oscars for *Hannah and Her Sisters* (1986) and *The Cider House Rules* (1999). Other important films include *Zulu* (1964), *Get Carter* (1971), *The Man Who Would be King* (1975), *Educating Rita* (1983), *Little Voice* (1998), *The Quiet American* (2002).

Chaplin, Sir Charles (1889–1977)

Still the most famous film star and director in the history of movies. His creation of the "little man"— the wistful tramp figure who fantasises his way out of the hardships of life—achieved success on an unprecedented scale and effectively made the transition from silent shorts to feature-length films, the most famous being *The Gold Rush* (1925). He fought hard against the coming of sound, refusing to use any apart from music and sound effects in *City Lights* (1931), where the blend of slapstick and suspense was particularly well achieved. His later films, like *Modern Times* (1936), *The Great Dictator* (1940) and *Monsieur Verdoux* (1947) were infused with his socialist political sympathies which set him at odds with the American authorities and led to his exile in 1952. His reputation plummeted after his death, but he remains the most significant and creative film comic of the twentieth century.

Christie, Julie (b. 1941)

Beautiful British actress who shot to international stardom with her performance in *Darling* (1965) and *Doctor Zhivago* (1965). Her best films include *Petulia* (1968), *The Go-Between* (1971), *McCabe and Mrs. Miller* (1971) and *Don't Look Now* (1973). In recent years, she has developed into a character actress of stature, particularly with her performances in *Hamlet* (1997) and *Afterglow* (1997).

Clift, Montgomery (1920–66)

Clift now enjoys a vogue as one of the great Hollywood victims, destroyed by drink, pills and inability to come to terms with his homosexuality. This litany should not obscure the fact that he was a tremendously gifted screen actor, as a tormented priest in *I Confess* (Hitchcock, 1952), as a cowboy opposite John Wayne in Hawk's *Red River* (1948), or with Clark Gable and Marilyn Monroe in that most macabre of pictures (it marked the end of virtually all its stars' careers), John Huston's *The Misfits* of 1961. Other key performances include *A Place in the Sun* (Stevens, 1951), *From Here to Eternity* (Zinnemann, 1953) and *Freud* (Huston, 1962). Speaking of his tormented personality, Marilyn Monroe once commented: "He's the only person I know who's in worse shape than I am."

Connery, Sir Sean (b. 1930)

Connery achieved early fame as the first of the screen James Bonds, but has been recognised as one of the best character-actor stars of modern cinema. Won an overdue Oscar for *The Untouchables* (1987) and has also given fine performances in such films as Hitchcock's *Marnie* (1964), *The Hill* (1965), *The Man Who Would be King* (1975), *Robin and Marian* (1976), *Cuba* (1979) and *The Name of the Rose* (1987). Knighted in New Year Honours, 2000.

Cooper, Gary (1901–61)

Cooper embodied quintessential American decency—not blustering like Wayne nor cynical like Bogart. His most famous roles are as the decent lad up from the country putting sophisticates to shame in *Mr. Deeds Goes to Town* (Frank Capra, 1936), the pacifist soldier in Hawks's *Sergeant York* (1941), and the lone sheriff in Zinnemann's *High Noon* (1952) confronting four gunmen out for revenge.

Crawford, Joan (1906–77)

The leading unhappy-in-love female star of the thirties and early forties (as in Cukor's *The Women* of 1939), Crawford won an Oscar for *Mildred Pierce* (Michael Curtiz, 1945). In later life a successful and immensely wealthy businesswoman, she was better known perhaps as a star than for any individual performances, and as the subject of her daughter's sensational memoir, *Mommie Dearest*, filmed in 1981 with Faye Dunaway as Crawford. Played masochist to Bette Davis's sadist in *Whatever Happened to Baby Jane?* (1962).

Crowe, Russell (b. 1964)

Like Mel Gibson before him, Crowe established a successful film career in Australia before moving to Hollywood. Such roles as the policeman in *L.A. Confidential* (1997) and the Roman hero of *Gladiator* (2000) seemed to type him as a virile leading man of the old school, but he has also shown himself adept at character roles, such as the mentally unstable mathematician in *A Beautiful Mind* (2001) and, particularly, as the whistle-blower in Michael Mann's critique of the tobacco industry, *The Insider* (1999).

Cruise, Tom (b. 1962)

Of the group of young American actors who shot to fame in the 1980s and were known collectively as the "brat pack", Cruise has proved to be the most durable, combining good looks with career shrewdness. He has had his glossy hits like *Top Gun* (1986) and *Mission Impossible* (1995) but he has also, as learning experience, played unselfish supporting roles to two Oscar-winning performances—Paul Newman's in *The Color of Money* (1986) and Dustin Hoffman's in *Rain Man* (1988). The benefit of such experience can be seen in his own Oscar-nominated performances in *Born on the Fourth of July* (1989), *Jerry Maguire* (1996), *Magnolia* (1999) and his work with Stanley Kubrick on that director's final film, *Eyes Wide Shut* (1999).

Davis, Bette (1908–89)

"Nobody's as good as Bette when she's bad" was the slogan coined for Bette Davis, who excelled at playing dynamic or queen-bitch heroines. Among her major screen performances were three for William Wyler, *Jezebel* (1938), *The Letter* (1940) and *The Little Foxes* (1941), and when her career seemed destined for oblivion in the late 1940s, she returned with one of the classic characterisations of the screen, as the dominating actress Margot Channing in *All About Eve* (1950). Her autobiography *The Lonely Life* (1962) is one of the frankest and most intelligent of any screen star.

Day, Doris (b. 1924)

Pure, wholesome singing star who achieved her peak of popularity in the 1950s and early 1960s, particularly in a series of romantic comedies she made with Rock Hudson, including *Pillow Talk* (1959), *Lover Come Back* (1962) and *Send Me No Flowers* (1964). Appropriated by the feminists, who admire her screen persona for its career-woman independence and its healthy suspicion of male seductive stratagems. Certainly someone who can upstage performers such as James Cagney (in *Love Me or Leave Me*, 1954), James Stewart (in *The Man Who Knew Too Much*, 1956) and Clark Gable (in *Teacher's Pet*, 1958) was no mean actress.

Dean, James (1931–55)

Dean made three starring feature roles before his death in a car crash in 1955. But those three, and particularly *Rebel Without a Cause* for Nicholas Ray in 1955, were enough to establish him as Hollywood's leading rebel (along with Brando—and how fascinating subsequent rivalry between their careers would have been). In *Rebel* Dean showed himself as a gentler, more idealistic figure than Brando, particularly in his "adoption" of the young runaway Sal Mineo. In *East of Eden* (Kazan, 1955), it is again his idealism that leads him to look out his mother, now running a whore-house, with disastrous results. In *Giant* (Stevens, 1956) he is an independent cowboy whose discovery of oil on his land will transform him into an isolated tycoon.

De Niro, Robert (b. 1943)

Arguably the finest American screen actor since Brando, noted for the dedication with which he immerses himself in his roles (*e.g.*, his gaining sixty pounds in weight to play the role of Jake LaMotta in decline in *Raging Bull*). He has had a particularly important collaboration with director Martin Scorsese, for whom he has turned in some of his finest studies of violent yet tortured masculinity: *Mean Streets* (1973), *Taxi Driver* (1976), *Raging Bull* (1980), *Cape Fear* (1991), *Casino* (1995). Other important films include: *The Godfather Part II* (1974), *The Deer Hunter* (1978).

Dietrich, Marlene (1902–92)

Overnight fame came Dietrich's way when Joseph von Sternberg cast her as the sensuous and manipulative night-club singer Lola in *The Blue Angel* (1930). She manipulates Emil Jannings's school teacher there as Sternberg's camera manipulates her (and us, the spectators), through a sequence of lushly masochistic masterpieces including *The Scarlet Empress* (1934). Her post-Sternberg career diversified into cabaret performance, and her subsequent movies, including *The Flame of New Orleans* for Rene Clair in 1941 and *Rancho Notorious* for Fritz Lang in 1952, did not attain the same heights as her work for Sternberg, though she gave striking performances in two Billy Wilder films, *A Foreign Affair* (1948) and *Witness for the Prosecution* (1957), and a memorable cameo in Welles's *Touch of Evil* (1958).

Douglas, Kirk (b. 1916)

Dimpled-chin he-man of the American screen, who excelled in roles of unscrupulous, ambitious anti-heroes, such as those in *Champion* (1949), *Ace in the Hole* (1951) and *The Bad and the Beautiful* (1952), though a more sensitive and tormented side to his persona is also seen in such films as *Lust for Life* (1955), in which he plays Van Gogh, and *Paths of Glory* (1957). The father of successful screen actor and producer, Michael Douglas.

Eastwood, Clint (b. 1930)

Eastwood is in the great tradition of stars like John Wayne and Gary Cooper who projects pure Americanism and rectifies wrongs, though in a more ferocious manner than his predecessors. Became a star for his "Man With No Name" characterisation in Sergio Leone's violent, stylised "Dollars" westerns; and became a superstar after playing the tough cop in *Dirty Harry* (1971). Sometimes attacked for their Fascist overtones, Eastwood's films have also been praised for their strong female roles, Eastwood's willingness to examine his own screen persona, and their engagement with contemporary issues. Eastwood is also a talented director, sometimes starring in his own films (*e.g. The Outlaw Josey Wales*, 1976) and sometimes not (*Bird*, 1988), *Mystic River*, (2003). His revisionist Western *Unforgiven* (1992) was widely acclaimed as a classic and won him a directing "Oscar", as did the sensitive drama, *Million Dollar Baby* (2004).

Fairbanks, Douglas (1883–1939)

The supreme action hero of silent cinema, excelling in such features as *The Three Musketeers* (1921), *Robin Hood* (1922) and *The Thief of Bagdad* (1924). Age and sound took their toll of his popularity as did his divorce from Mary Pickford in 1936, after a marriage of sixteen years. But during the silent era, nobody epitomised screen heroism more exuberantly.

Fields, W. C. (1879–1946)

Fields is the polar opposite of Chaplin as a screen comedian, in that, while the "little fellow" courts audience affection, Fields does everything in his drunken, misogynistic, mean, cynical, ill-tempered power to repel it. Through such titles as *Mrs. Wiggs of the Cabbage Patch* (Norman Taurog, 1934) and *Never Give a Sucker an Even Break* (Edward Cline, 1941), he paraded preposterous situations (usually of his own invention), and a battery of dislikes that included wives, children, domestic animals and authority figures. His best films were *It's A Gift* (1935) and *The Bank Dick* (1940). When discovered on his death-bed reading the Bible, he explained that he was "looking for loopholes".

Finch, Peter (1916–77)

Rugged yet subtle screen performer, who won the British Academy Award four times for his performances in *A Town Like Alice* (1956), *The Trials of Oscar Wilde* (1960), *No Love for Johnnie* (1961) and *Sunday, Bloody Sunday* (1971). He won a posthumous Oscar for his performance in *Network* (1976).

Finney, Albert (b. 1936)

Finney made a big impression with his first screen performances in such films as *Saturday Night and Sunday Morning* (1961) and *Tom Jones* (1963), and was hailed as "a second Olivier". But, unlike Richard Burton, he preferred to eschew screen stardom in favour of theatrical work. The most powerful of his later film performances has been as the drunken Consul in Huston's adaptation of Malcolm Lowry's novel, *Under the Volcano* (1984). Co-starred with Julia Roberts to fine effect in *Erin Brockovich* (2000).

Fonda, Henry (1905–82)

One of the major Hollywood leading men of the late thirties and forties, with distinguished starring roles for Fritz Lang (as the runaway in *You Only Live Once*, 1937) and John Ford (in *Young Mr. Lincoln* and *Drums Along the Mohawk*, both 1939, and *The Grapes of Wrath* (1940). His honest and conscientious stance was just right for the immediate pre- and post-war years. After a lull in his screen career, he made a successful comeback in such films as *Mister Roberts* (1955), *Twelve Angry Men* (1957) and *The Best Man* (1964), and won a long-awaited Oscar for his last film, *On Golden Pond* (1981), co-starring with his daughter Jane.

Fonda, Jane (b. 1937)

Began her career in "sex-symbol" roles—in Hollywood and for her then husband Roger Vadim—that now appear incongruous in the light of her progressive political position (Edward Dmytryk's *Walk on the Wild Side*, 1962; Vadim's *Barbarella*, 1968). Her involvement with the women's movement and anti-Vietnam campaigns took her into such films as *Klute* (Pakula, 1971), where she plays a prostitute who regards herself as "the only truly liberated woman". She won an Oscar for *Klute* and won again later in the decade for *Coming Home* (1978), confirming herself as one of the most accomplished of screen actresses.

Ford, Harrison (b. 1942)

Recently voted the world's most popular film star, a well-earned reward for an actor whose career had begun with discouraging slowness. The turning point came with his role as Han Solo in *Star Wars* (1977) and his stardom was augmented when he became Steven Spielberg's Indiana Jones, a characterisation said to be much admired by Burt Lancaster for its difficult combination of athleticism and wit. An accomplished actor in both romantic comedy and complex character roles (*e.g.* in *Witness* and *The Mosquito Coast*), he is liked best by the public as a taciturn action man of the old school, even when, as in the film *Air Force One* (1997), he also happens to be President of the United States of America.

Foster, Jodie (b. 1962)

Child star who has developed into one of the foremost feminist talents of the cinema. Played a precocious moll in the child gangster spoof, *Bugsy Malone* (1976) and then created a furore with her role as an under-age prostitute in *Taxi Driver* (1976), fanned even further when an attempted assassination of President Reagan was said to have been inspired by the gunman's infatuation with Foster's role in that movie. She survived the attendant notoriety to develop into one of the modern screen's most adventurous actresses, winning Oscars for her performances as a rape victim in *The Accused* (1988) and a feisty female investigator in *Silence of the Lambs* (1991). She can direct too.

Gabin, Jean (1904–76)

In many ways Gabin was for the French cinema of the thirties and forties what Gary Cooper or Henry Fonda were for Hollywood—the stoically decent man of the people whose malediction sprang from his very ordinariness. He excelled for two directors in particular: Marcel Carné for whom he played a deserter in *Quai des Brumes* and a workman in *Le Jour se Leve* (1938 and 1939 respectively), both of whom meet violent deaths as a result of falling in love, and Jean Renoir, in whose *La Bete Humaine* (1938) he was an engine-driver vainly struggling against homicidal urges. A less doom-laden performance, but one that revealed his particular strength as an ensemble player as well as a "star", was also for Renoir, as one of the soldiers who escape from a POW camp in *La Grande Illusion* (1937).

Gable, Clark (1901–60)

Gable was Hollywood's number one heartthrob in the years immediately preceding the war. His open-handed cheerfulness and easy-going Americanism now might appear dated, but they bowled over a long list of leading ladies, including Claudette Colbert (in Frank Capra's *It Happened One Night*, 1934) and Vivien Leigh (in the Fleming/Cukor/Wood success *Gone with the Wind*, 1939). He is proof that Hollywood male chauvinism did not need the bullying qualities of a John Wayne to make its mark. He gave perhaps his greatest performance in his last film, *The Misfits* (1961).

Garbo, Greta (1905–90)

A career that lasted only seventeen years and a reclusive retirement combined to create the "Garbo myth" of world-weary, capricious and lonesome sensuality, which must be one of the most potent in cinema history. She moved from Sweden to Hollywood under the aegis of the director Mauritz Stiller in 1926, to become MGM's major star, whose every move was heralded by a barrage of studio publicity (thus, "Garbo talks!" before Clarence Brown's *Anna Christie* in 1930, and "Garbo laughs!" before *Ninotchka*, made for Ernst Lubitsch in 1939). Unlike her romantic co-star in the silent period, John Gilbert, Garbo triumphantly made the transition to talkies, her greatest successes being in *Queen Christina* (1934) and *Camille* (1937). But after the disaster of *Two-Faced Woman* (1941) she retired from the screen.

Garland, Judy (1922–69)

A prominent teenage star who became famous through her performance in *The Wizard of Oz*

(Victor Fleming, 1939), where she first performed the song whose soaring yearning was to become her hallmark—"Over the Rainbow". She starred in musicals for her then-husband, Vincente Minnelli (including *Meet Me in St. Louis*, 1944), but the pattern of breakdown, emotional turmoil, and abuse of barbiturates had set in by the beginning of the fifties. Stage appearances and nervous breakdowns between them crowded out her mature film career, though her performance in *A Star is Born* (1954) was a tour-de-force.

Gibson, Mel (b. 1956)

The most interesting young actor of his period,' said Franco Zeffirelli when casting Mel Gibson as Hamlet. An odd role ostensibly for the star of action extravaganzas like *Mad Max* (1979) and *Lethal Weapon* (1987) but then again, perhaps not: all are heroes unhinged by violent destruction of their family lives and who affect an antic disposition to cope with their torment. Gibson is good at character extremes, as well as being a competent director and a glamour film star of a kind rarely seen since the 1930s. Though actually born in New York, his first film successes were in Australia, but like director Peter Weir, for whom he starred in *Gallipoli* (1981) and *The Year of Living Dangerously* (1983), he moved to Hollywood in the early 1980s and has not looked back. Won a directing Oscar for *Braveheart* (1995) and created enormous controversy with a personal project inspired by his religious beliefs, *The Passion of the Christ* (2004).

Gish, Lillian (1896–1993)

The longest career of movie actors—from D. W. Griffith's *An Unseen Enemy* (1912) through to Lindsay Anderson's *The Whales of August* (1987). She radiated innocence for Griffith in *The Birth of a Nation* (1915) and *Intolerance* (1916), before leaving his Biograph company to make more money, first for Inspiration and then for MGM. During the sound era, her screen appearances were intermittent, though she was particularly effective as the brave schoolma'am facing up to Robert Mitchum's demonic preacher in *The Night of the Hunter* (1955). Her performances in Griffith's *Broken Blossoms* (1919) and Victor Seastrom's *The Wind* (1928) are among the greatest of the silent film era.

Grant, Cary (1904–86)

His British origin shows in his debonair style and curious "mid-Atlantic" accent (imitated by Tony Curtis in Billy Wilder's *Some Like it Hot*, 1959). Beneath his gentlemanly urbanity, frenzy, even insanity, never seem far away, which accounts for the matchless ambiguity of his greatest performances—as the suspected wife-murderer in Hitchcock's *Suspicion* (1941), as baiting foil to Mae West in Wesley Ruggles's *I'm No Angel* (1933), as advertising man pursued across America by spies in *North by North-West* (Hitchcock, 1959), and above all the victim of the insecurity that stems from sex-stereotyping in the magnificent comedies he made opposite various leading ladies for Howard Hawks—*Bringing Up Baby* (with Katharine Hepburn, 1938), *His Girl Friday* (with Rosalind Russell, 1940), and *I Was a Male War Bride* (with Ann Sheridan, 1949). Small wonder that he won an Oscar in 1970 for "sheer brilliance".

Guinness, Sir Alec (1914–2000)

Guinness came to prominence as a screen actor in the great Ealing comedies, notably *Kind Hearts and Coronets* (1949), *The Man in the White Suit* (1951), *The Lavender Hill Mob* (1952), and *The Ladykillers* (1955). He also developed a close working relationship with David Lean, and won an Oscar for his superb performance in Lean's *The Bridge on the River Kwai* (1957). An actor of unobtrusive subtlety and infinite resource, he achieved his biggest popular success in *Star Wars* (1977) but more representative of his skills were his masterly characterisations in such films as *Tunes of Glory* (1960) and *Little Dorritt* (1987).

Hackman, Gene (b. 1931)

One of the most durable and dependable character stars of modern American cinema., at home in comedy but at his best when giving subtle emotional colouring to 'average' men with a darker side to their natures. His most famous role is still probably that of the rebellious rule-breaking cop, 'Popeye' Doyle in *The French Connection* (1971), for which he won an Oscar, as he did also for his performance as the sadistic sheriff in Clint Eastwood's *Unforgiven* (1992). But his exceptional performances are legion: *The Conversation* (1974), *Night Moves* (1975), *Eureka* (1982), *Under Fire* (1983), *Target* (1985), *Mississippi Burning* (1988), *Class Action* (1991).

Hanks, Tom (b. 1956)

Popular leading man of the last decade in both comedy and dramatic roles, who became the first actor since Spencer Tracy to win the Best Actor Oscar in consecutive years: for *Philadelphia* (1993) and *Forrest Gump* (1994). His acceptance speeches have become something to be feared, however: in one, he inadvertently 'outed' a former drama teacher. Other key films: *Big* (1988), *Sleepless in Seattle* (1993), *Apollo 13* (1995), *Saving Private Ryan* (1998) and *Road to Perdition* (2002).

Hepburn, Audrey (1929–93)

Enchanting elfin actress who won an Oscar in her first starring role, *Roman Holiday* (Wyler, 1953). She then proceeded to bewitch some of Hollywood's most eminent senior citizens—Humphrey Bogart in *Sabrina* (1954), Gary Cooper in *Love in the Afternoon* (1957), Cary Grant in *Charade* (1963), Rex Harrison in *My Fair Lady* (1964). An adept comedienne, she also proved herself a formidable dramatic actress in *The Nun's Story* (1959), *The Children's Hour* (1961) and *Robin and Marian* (1976). She then virtually retired though Spielberg cast her appropriately as an angel in *Always* (1989).

Hepburn, Katharine (1909–2003)

The most intelligent and astringent of all screen comediennes—if not all screen actresses. She remained resolutely outside the mould of female stardom, regarded for years as box-office poison and relying on her mind rather than her body for impact. Her most celebrated films are those made with her long-time off-screen lover, Spencer Tracy—notably *Adam's Rib* and *Pat and Mike* for George Cukor (1949 and 1952 respectively), and *State of the Union* for Frank Capra in 1948. But her warm sharpness was equally in evidence with Cary Grant (*Bringing Up Baby* for Hawks in 1938) and Humphrey Bogart (*The African Queen* for John Huston in 1951). Winner of four best actress Oscars (more than any other recipient), she published a set of autobiographical memoirs, *Me* (1991). Her greatest screen performances include *Alice Adams* (1935), *Summer Madness* (1955), *Suddenly Last Summer* (1959) and *Long Day's Journey into Night* (1962).

Heston, Charlton (b. 1923)

Heston's first starring role was in C. B. DeMille's circus epic, *The Greatest Show on Earth* (1952). He has since specialised in epic roles, bringing dignity and integrity to the genre, particularly in his title performances in *Ben Hur* (1959) and *El Cid* (1961). His historical roles range from Cardinal Richelieu to General Gordon, from Moses to Michelangelo: his best modern film role was probably been in Welles's *Touch of Evil* (1958). He has also excelled in westerns, notably in *The Big Country* (1958) and *Will Penny* (1968).

Hoffman, Dustin (b. 1937)

Earnest, intense method actor whose perfectionism has sometimes driven co-stars to distraction (Olivier: "Dustin is very talented—but why doesn't he just act?") but has certainly produced the goods—Oscars for his performances in *Kramer vs. Kramer* (1979) and *The Rain Man* (1988). Other important roles: *The Graduate* (1967), *Lenny* (1974), *All the President's Men* (1976), and *Tootsie* (1982).

Holden, William (1918–81)

Handsome leading man of the 1940s who was rescued from bland B-picture roles by Billy Wilder, who cast him as a screen writing gigolo in *Sunset*

Boulevard (1950) and as a captive capitalist in *Stalag 17* (1953), for which Holden won an Oscar. After a lean spell in the 1960s, his career revived with his splendid leading performance in *The Wild Bunch* (1969), and before his death, he gave further thoughtful characterisations in *Network* (1976) and *Fedora* (1978). Other key roles: *Golden Boy* (1939), *Sabrina* (1954), *Picnic* (1955) and *The Bridge on the River Kwai* (1957).

Hopkins, Sir Anthony (b. 1937)

Theatrically trained, Hopkins is sometimes seen as the natural successor to Richard Burton and Sir Laurence Olivier: indeed, he dubbed Olivier's voice when *Spartacus* was re-released in an extended version. For all his versatility and skill, however, he seems likely to be remembered most for his performance as a monster, the cannibalistic Hannibal Lecter in *The Silence of the Lambs* (1991). Other key performances: *The Lion in Winter* (1968), *Juggernaut* (1974), *The Elephant Man* (1980), *The Bounty* (1984), *Howards End* (1992), *The Remains of the Day* (1993), *Nixon* (1995), *Amistad* (1997).

Howard, Trevor (1916–87)

Leathery character actor of the British film, reputedly Graham Greene's favourite. Capable of acting just about anyone off the screen, which might be the reason that he only rarely got the parts (and therefore the recognition) that he deserved. Important films include: *Brief Encounter* (1945), *The Third Man* (1949), *Outcast of The Islands* (1951), *The Key* (1958), *Sons and Lovers* (1960), *Mutiny on the Bounty* (1962) and *Ludwig* (1972).

Hudson, Rock (1925–85)

Solid Hollywood leading man who sprang back into the public eye in the 1980s because of his death from AIDS. This rather contradicted his screen image as the all-American romantic hero. An effective screen actor in dramas such as *Giant* (1956) or comedies such as *Send Me No Flowers* (1964), he had, in retrospect, his most resonant role in John Frankenheimer's sci-fi horror film, *Seconds* (1966), where a dissatisfied middle-aged man fakes his own death and, through plastic surgery, starts a new life looking like Rock Hudson—and finds that soul-destroying also.

Huppert, Isabelle (b. 1955)

She came to prominence with a beautiful performance in *The Lacemaker* (1977), playing an unaffected girl whose emotional vulnerability leads to a complete mental breakdown after an unhappy love affair. The fragility seemed so natural and believable that one has since been often taken aback by her range and resource, particularly in some of her films for Claude Chabrol, where she has revealed surprising ferocity behind the freckle-faced exterior. A recent performance in Michael Haneke's *The Piano Teacher* (2001), where she plays a music teacher with secret sado-masochistic tendencies, is a *tour-de-force*.

Jannings, Emil (1884–1950)

A king of the German silent cinema, but ruined by the coming of sound (which showed up his thick accent) and also his collaboration with the Nazis. His massive self-sentimentalisation and Prussian obsession with lost status were triumphant in Murnau's *The Last Laugh* (1924), and even more so in his role as the puritanical schoolteacher Professor Rath, destroyed by his passion for Marlene Dietrich's Lola in Sternberg's *The Blue Angel* (1930). This performance remains the greatest monument of male sexual humiliation in cinema history. He epitomised silent film acting at its most Expressionist and expressive, though Luis Buñuel said he preferred Buster Keaton.

Karloff, Boris (1887–1969)

Here again on- and off-screen personas interacted intriguingly. Mild mannered English cricket-loving gentleman William Henry Pratt became the best-known horror star in Hollywood history with his performance as the blundering yet tender-hearted monster in James Whale's *Frankenstein* in 1931.

Thenceforth his legendary status was secure, and augmented by his work for Karl Freund (*The Mummy* of 1932) and Charles Vidor (*The Mask of Fu Manchu*, 1932). As moving as his performance in *Frankenstein* in many ways is his valedictory appearance in Peter Bogdanovich's *Targets* (shot in the year of his death) where he plays a retired Hollywood horror star whose essential kindness is appalled by the horror of American society.

Keaton, Buster (1895–1966)

Arguably the greatest director and the greatest actor of the American silent era. As an actor, Keaton's deadpan appearance, often almost suicidal insistence on choreographing and carrying out all his own stunts, and awareness of the element of fantasy identification in cinema have ensured that his performances remain consistently exciting and do not date. As a director, he masterfully exploited the relationship between man and machine—driver/train and actor/camera—in *The General* of 1926, and that between cinema and dream in *Sherlock Junior* of 1924. His career was undermined as much by the classic Hollywood afflictions—marital problems and heavy drinking—as by the coming of sound. But his reputation has soared since his death, and works such as *Our Hospitality* (1923), *Seven Chances* (1925), *The Navigator* (1927) and *Steamboat Bill Jr.* (1928), along with his aforementioned films, are now regarded as comedy classics. Appeared alongside Chaplin in an unforgettable routine in the latter's *Limelight* (1952).

Kelly, Gene (1912–96)

The most inventive and adventurous actor-choreographer of the American screen. Rival to Fred Astaire as Hollywood's dancing master, Kelly was even more creative in furthering the boundaries of the film musical, particularly in a trio of magnificent musicals he co-directed with Stanley Donen: *On the Town* (1949), *Singin' in the Rain* (1952) and *It's Always Fair Weather* (1955).

Kelly, Grace (1928–82)

Aloof but elegant leading lady who made her first major impression as Gary Cooper's Quaker wife in *High Noon* (1952) and then as the archetypal Hitchcockian ice-cool blonde in *Dial M for Murder* (1954), *Rear Window* (1954) and *To Catch a Thief* (1955). Her dramatic prowess was revealed in her Oscar-winning role in *The Country Girl* (1954) but she gave up stardom for royalty when she married Prince Rainier of Monaco in 1956.

Kerr, Deborah (b. 1921)

One of the most versatile and sensitive of British screen actresses, whose persona of "English rose" was changed when she played the nymphomaniac wife of an Army Captain in *From Here to Eternity* (1953). She has seemed at her best either when playing nuns with a hint of neurosis—*Black Narcissus* (1947), *Heaven Knows, Mr. Allison* (1957)—or prim teachers or governesses wrestling privately with emotional repression—*The King and I* (1955), *Tea and Sympathy* (1956), *The Innocents* (1961).

Kidman, Nicole (b. 1968)

Formerly married to Tom Cruise, she seems to share Cruise's ability to choose her roles with some shrewdness. As a consequence, she has matured into a screen actress of considerable subtlety and force. She won an Oscar for her portrayal of Virginia Woolf in *The Hours* (2002). Other important films: *Dead Calm* (1989), *Malice* (1993), *To Die For* (1995), *Portrait of a Lady* (1996), *Eyes Wide Shut* (1999), *Moulin Rouge* (2001), *The Others* (2001), *Dogville* (2003).

Lancaster, Burt (1913–94)

Acrobat turned actor, who revealed a sensitive interior behind his action-man mask. He won an Oscar for his role as a religious charlatan in *Elmer Gantry* (1960), and a Venice Festival award for a more introvert performance in *Bird Man of Alcatraz* (1962). "A deeply mysterious man" was the verdict on him of Luchino Visconti, who directed him to great effect in *The Leopard* (1963) and *Conversation*

Piece (1974), and he triumphed also under Louis Malle in *Atlantic City* (1980). He had a career of fascinating contrasts, between swashbuckling and sensitive roles. Other key films include: *The Killers* (1946), *The Crimson Pirate* (1952), *From Here to Eternity* (1953), *Sweet Smell of Success* (1957), *1900* (1976) and *Twilight's Last Gleaming* (1977).

Laughton, Charles (1899–1962)

Bulky actor of phenomenal power and range, with the occasional tendency to ham but also capable of producing magical effects with a sympathetic director It is sometimes thought that his heyday was in the thirties, when he excelled in *The Private Life of Henry VIII* (1933), *Ruggles of Red Gap* (1935), *Mutiny on the Bounty* (1935) and *The Hunchback of Notre Dame* (1939). But he was no less remarkable in later films such as *Hobson's Choice* (1953), *Witness for the Prosecution* (1957), *Spartacus* (1960) and *Advise and Consent* (1962). There is a sense of relish about his greatest acting, whether playing saint or sadist. One should not forget also his one and only film as director, an altogether remarkable, poetic thriller *The Night of the Hunter* (1955) that constitutes one of the most extraordinary directing debuts in cinema history.

Laurel (1890–1965) and Hardy (1892–1957)

The first great comedy partnership in films, and never surpassed. Their films usually involve frantic attempts to gain social acceptance (*e.g.* as pianomovers or salesmen), that lead to the disasters ruefully described by Hardy as "another nice mess". Their features, including *Pack Up Your Troubles* (Marshall and Raymond McCarey, 1932) and *A Chump at Oxford* (Alfred Goulding, 1940), retain the personas—sly and skinny Stan and overweight Ollie trying to cling on to his dignity—almost intact. The comedy of failure in its purest, most unpretentious form. Key films include: *Big Business* (1929), *The Music Box* (1932), *Sons of the Desert* (1934), *Way Out West* (1937).

Leigh, Vivien (1913–67)

Fragile and exquisite English actress who remarkably scored her greatest film triumphs in two quintessentially American roles: as Scarlett O'Hara in *Gone With the Wind* (1939) and as Blanche DuBois in *A Streetcar Named Desire* (1951). Married to Laurence Olivier in 1940, her later career was blighted by physical and mental illness. She was divorced from Olivier in 1960, and her last major film roles were in *The Roman Spring of Mrs. Stone* (1961) and *Ship of Fools* (1965).

Lemmon, Jack (1925–2001)

Consummate film actor who is probably most associated in the public mind with a series of sublime comedy characterisations in films of Billy Wilder, such as *Some Like it Hot* (1959), *The Apartment* (1960), *The Fortune Cookie* (1966), and *Avanti!* (1972). But he was an equally forceful straight actor, as films such as *Days of Wine and Roses* (1962), *The China Syndrome* (1979), *Missing* (1982) and *Glengarry Glen Ross* (1992) demonstrate. The screen's best tragi-comedian since Chaplin.

Loren, Sophia (b. 1934)

Epitomises the stereotype of Latin female sexuality for the moviegoer, much as Marcello Mastroianni did for the male. She began for Hollywood in ripely sensual roles (*e.g. Desire under the Elms* for Delbert Mann in 1958), before moving on to more demanding dramatic parts, such as Vittorio de Sica's *Two Women* for which she won an Oscar in 1961.

Lorre, Peter (1904–64)

Among his best-known films there is only one in which he actually starred: *M* for Fritz Lang in 1931, where he portrayed a demented child-murderer, contorting his features as much as Lang's direction contorted the screen images. But he became one of Hollywood's most memorable supporting actors, as the crazed hitman in Huston's *The Maltese Falcon* (1941), and for Michael Curtiz (in *Casablanca* of 1943 and *Passage to Marseilles* of 1944) and Frank Capra (*Arsenic and Old Lace*, 1944). Like Karloff

but in a very different way, he excelled at suggesting sensitivity beneath the contortions of horror and malice.

Maclaine, Shirley (b. 1934)

Prodigiously talented dancer-cum-comedienne-cum dramatic actress. Won an Oscar for *Terms of Endearment* (1983), but her best films are the early ones: *The Trouble With Harry* (1955), *Some Came Running* (1958), *The Apartment* (1960), *The Children's Hour* (1961) and *Sweet Charity* (1969).

March, Fredric (1897–1975)

One of Hollywood's finest character actors, particularly when portraying ostensibly decent men with darker sides to their personalities. This was shown to particular effect in *Dr. Jekyll and Mr. Hyde* (1932) but was also a feature of some other of his major roles: *Les Miserables* (1935), *The Best Years of our Lives* (1946), *Death of a Salesman* (1952), *Executive Suite* (1954) and *The Desperate Hours* (1955).

Marx Brothers: Chico (1887–1961), Harpo (1888–1964), Groucho (1890–1978)

Hollywood's undammable great comic family. Groucho's undammable flow of insult and wisecrack, Chico's illogicalities and prevarications (delivered in a heavy mock-Italian accent), and Harpo's mute mime form an unbeatable trio, whether in the early Paramount features (such as *Duck Soup* for Leo McCarey in 1933) or in their later work for MGM, where musical and romantic interludes irksomely break up the stream of comedy (as in *A Day at the Races*—Sam Wood, 1937). Their most popular film, and Groucho's favourite, was *A Night at the Opera* (1935). (Another brother Zeppo appeared in some of their earlier films, either as an improbable romantic lead or even, in *Horse Feathers* of 1932, as Groucho's son.)

Mason, James (1909–84)

Mason's style migrated successfully from the British industry (as in *Odd Man Out*—Carol Reed, 1947) to Hollywood and the international circuit. He was an urbane villain for Hitchcock in *North by North-West* (1959), and a suitable articulate and obsessed lover for *Lolita* (Stanley Kubrick, 1962), somewhat removed from the persona of the romantic sadist with which he had first shot to fame (in *The Man in Grey*, 1943 and *The Wicked Lady*, 1945). One of those screen actors like Trevor Howard or David Niven who seemed incapable of giving a bad performance, however bad the film was around him. When the film was good—like, say, *Five Fingers* (1952), *A Star is Born* (1954), *The Pumpkin Eater* (1964), *The Verdict* (1982)—he could be quite exceptional.

Mastroianni, Marcello (1924–96)

The ultimate listless Latin lover, who seems wearied by the very thought of all the women to whom he is supposed to appeal. This quality in fact enables his screen persona to work quite subversively against the macho ideal of Hollywood, as in Fellini's *La Dolce Vita* (1960), where he plays a disillusioned journalist, or Antonioni's *La Notte* (1961), as the exhausted husband of Jeanne Moreau. His finest performance remains that in Fellini's *8½* (1963), as the film director (an obvious alter ego to Fellini), whose very prostration and inability to organise his neuroses into cinematic form at the end provide the mainspring that enables him to do so. The films with Fellini and Antonioni remain his best-known work. His later successes included *Macaroni* (1985), opposite Jack Lemmon; *Ginger and Fred* (1986), for Fellini; and a particularly intense performance in *The Beekeeper* (1986) for Greece's major contemporary director, Theo Angelopoulous.

McQueen, Steve (1930–80)

Supercool but smouldering anti-hero and loner, McQueen became a star after his POW antics on a motorbike in John Sturges' *The Great Escape* (1963). Best remembered for action roles like *The Magnificent Seven* (1960) or *Bullitt* (1968), McQueen was showing signs of greater artistic ambition towards the end of his life, producing as well as starring in an adaptation of Ibsen's *An Enemy of the People* (1979) and contributing a finely shaded, poignant performance in the elegiac Western, *Tom Horn* (1980).

Mifune, Toshiro (1920–97)

Japanese actor whose robust style, ironic as well as dramatic, was indelibly associated with the films he made for Kurosawa, including *Seven Samurai* (1954), *Throne of Blood* (1957) and *Yojimbo* (1961). He also appeared in the occasional Hollywood film, most notably opposite Lee Marvin in *Hell in the Pacific* (1969).

Mitchum, Robert (1917–97)

A deceptively outstanding film actor whose lazy style concealed enormous range and prodigious depth. Directors as exacting as John Huston (*Heaven Knows Mr. Allison*, 1957) and Fred Zinnemann (*The Sundowners*, 1960) testified to Mitchum's exceptional abilities. Only once nominated for an Oscar (for *The Story of G.I. Joe*, 1945), his memorable performances include *Pursued* (1947), *Build My Gallows High* (1947), *The Lusty Men* (1952), *The Night of the Hunter* (1955), *Cape Fear* (1962), *Ryan's Daughter* (1970), *The Friends of Eddie Coyle* (1973), *The Last Tycoon* (1976).

Monroe, Marilyn (1926–62)

Not the original cinematic sex symbol—that distinction belongs to Mary Pickford or Rudolph Valentino—but Monroe is certainly the best-known. Nowhere else have the on-and-off screen persona interacted to such devastating, and finally destructive, effect. She began as a "dumb blonde" in the early fifties before producers and directors recognised in her vulnerability and ambivalent attitude towards her own sexuality—pride tempered by the desire to be appreciated for something more—outstanding qualities. Her best films remain comedies in which her ambivalence was played upon to enrich the texture of the movies: *Bus Stop* for Joshua Logan in 1956, and for Billy Wilder, *The Seven-Year Itch* of 1955, and *Some Like It Hot* in 1959. She gave an extraordinary dramatic performance in Huston's *The Misfits* (1961), but was dismissed from her final project (Cukor's *Something's Got to Give*) for unreliability in 1962, and not long afterwards committed suicide. Revelations of her off-screen loneliness and the mysterious circumstances of her death went to fuel what is still Hollywood's most potent and macabre legend.

Moreau, Jeanne (b. 1928)

Described as the "thinking man's actress", and whose name was synonymous with some of the greatest and most controversial European art movies of the late fifties and early sixties: Malle's *The Lovers* (1958), Truffaut's *Jules et Jim* (1961), Antonioni's *La Notte* (1962) and Buñuel's *Diary of a Chambermaid* (1964).

Newman, Paul (b. 1925)

Blue-eyed boy of modern American film, exceptionally good looking and a considerable actor to boot. Early Oscar-nominated performances in *Cat on a Hot Tin Roof* (1958), *The Hustler* (1961), *Hud* (1963) and *Cool Hand Luke* (1967) testified to Newman's great skill in revealing an attractive, adventurous side to roles which, in other hands, could have seemed unsympathetic and morbid. He finally won his Oscar for *The Color of Money* (1986), Scorsese's sequel to *The Hustler*. He has also proved himself a sympathetic director, particularly of his actress-wife Joanne Woodward, in films such as *Rachel, Rachel* (1968) and *The Glass Menagerie* (1987).

Nicholson, Jack (b. 1937)

Nicholson broke into public prominence with his performance as the alcoholic ne'er-do-well in Hopper's *Easy Rider* (1969), and has remained at the top ever since with sardonic yet often tender performances. The versatility that often goes with understatement has enabled him to give outstanding performances as a drop-out classical musician (Bob Rafelson's *Five Easy Pieces* in 1970), a private eye (Polanski's *Chinatown* in 1974), a rebel in a mental hospital (Milos Forman's *One Flew Over The Cuckoo's Nest*, 1975), a cynical writer (James L. Brooks' *As Good as it Gets*, 1997) a retired cop (*The Pledge*, 2001), and a widower reappraising his life (*About Schmidt*, 2002).

Olivier, Sir Laurence (1907–89)

Perhaps the most exciting and respected actor of his generation, Olivier will first be remembered and revered for his achievement as actor and director in bringing Shakespeare to vivid life on screen with *Henry V* (1944), *Hamlet* (1948) and *Richard III* (1955). But his most subtle screen acting was to be found in two films he made for Wyler, *Wuthering Heights* (1939) and *Carrie* (1952), and one for Hitchcock, *Rebecca* (1940). His last major film role was in Mankiewicz's *Sleuth* (1972).

Pacino, Al (b. 1940)

Born in New York of Sicilian descent and an apostle of the great acting teacher Lee Strasberg, Pacino shot to prominence with his performance as Michael Corleone in *The Godfather* (1972), a role he was to repeat and refine in two sequels. An actor of great resource and range, he now rivals DeNiro as the most admired American screen actor since Marlon Brando. Key films include: *Godfather II* (1974), *Dog Day Afternoon* (1975), *Scarface* (1983), *Glengarry Glen Ross* (1992), *Heat* (1996), *Looking for Richard* (1996), *The Insider* (1999) and *Insomnia* (2002).

Peck, Gregory (1916–2003)

Archetypal screen symbol of liberal integrity, particularly embodied in his performance as the lawyer defending an unjustly accused Negro in *To Kill a Mockingbird* (1962), for which he justly won an Oscar. Other important films: *Gentleman's Agreement* (1947), *The Gunfighter* (1950), *Roman Holiday* (1953), *Moby Dick* (1956), *The Big Country* (1958), *The Stalking Moon* (1968) and *I Walk the Line* (1970).

Pickford, Mary (1893–1979)

The sentimentality of Pickford's early performances for D. W. Griffith between 1909 and 1912, and her peak period as "America's Sweetheart" when married to Douglas Fairbanks (*Daddy Long Legs* for Marshall Neilan in 1919, *Pollyanna* for Paul Powell in 1920) are considerably less interesting today than her ideological role as what Basil Wright has dubbed the "hearth goddess" of domesticity and her early status as one of the first multi-millionaire film stars.

Poitier, Sidney (b. 1924)

Ground-breaking black actor, one of the first to attain Hollywood star status. Poitier won an Oscar for a now virtually forgotten movie, *Lilies of the Field* (1963), and is better remembered for such films as *The Defiant Ones* (1958), *In The Heat of the Night* (1967) and *Guess Who's Coming to Dinner* (1967). Also an accomplished director, though definitely in the commercial mainstream rather than in the radical alternative lane chosen by the new generation of black American directors such as Spike Lee and John Singleton.

Rains, Claude (1889–1967)

Soft-spoken, diminutive actor whose first screen triumph was in a part in which his face was only shown in the very last shot: namely, the eponymous hero of *The Invisible Man* (1932). A favourite co-star of Bette Davis, he was incomparable at portraying suave villainy, notably in *The Adventures of Robin Hood* (1938) and, of course, *Casablanca* (1943), but, for all his seeming dryness, he could also give uncommon intensity to the feelings of scorned love: his performances as the humiliated husbands in Hitchcock's *Notorious* (1946) and Lean's *The Passionate Friends* (1949) throb with a poignant romantic anguish.

Redford, Robert (b. 1937)

Redford is distinguished from his "peer-group" stars such as Beatty and Nicholson by a resolute rejection of the trappings of stardom. Athletically handsome (like John Wayne he went to university on a sports scholarship), he struck gold with *Butch Cassidy and the Sundance Kid* (George Roy Hill, 1969), and created perhaps his most successful dramatic role in the Scott Fitzgerald adaptation, *The Great Gatsby* for Jack Clayton in 1974. His directing debut, *Ordinary People* (1980) won him an Oscar but his most lasting monument might well be the Sundance Institute, which he founded in 1980 and which has since become a training ground and launching pad for some of America's finest young independent film makers.

Roberts, Julia (b. 1967)

Former model who has developed into one of the star actresses of the last decade, culminating in her critically acclaimed, Oscar winning performance in *Erin Brockovich* (2000). Other key films: *Pretty Woman* (1990), *Sleeping with the Enemy* (1990) and *Everyone Says I Love You* (1996).

Robinson, Edward G. (1893–1973)

Robinson made his name in gangster film roles such as *Little Ceasar* (1931) and as Johnny Rocco in Huston's *Key Largo* (1948). But he was actually a highly skilled actor in a variety of parts, at his best perhaps in two psychological dramas for Fritz Lang, *Woman in the Window* (1944) and *Scarlet Street* (1945); as the insurance investigator in Wilder's *Double Indemnity* (1944); and as a roguish diamond smuggler in Mackendrick's *Sammy Going South* (1963).

Schwarzenegger, Arnold (b. 1947)

Born in Graz, Austria, Schwarzenegger was a champion body-builder before he turned to acting in roles that exploited both his physique and his robotic histrionics. His persona has essentially been that of a slow-witted, thickly accented superhero whose muscle power far exceeds his intellect, and he has maintained a mass following not only through his screen heroics but also a genial willingness to poke fun at his own image. Married to the niece of President of John F. Kennedy, he has recently been elected Republican Governor of California. Main films: *Stay Hungry* (1976), *Conan the Barbarian* (1982), *The Terminator* (1984), *Total Recall* (1990).

Scott, George C. (1926–99)

On his day, one of the screen's most powerful and exciting actors. His first important role was as a razor-sharp prosecutor in Preminger's *Anatomy of a Murder* (1959), putting James Stewart on his mettle, and he followed it with an equally incisive characterisation as the sinister, Mephistophelian gambler in *The Hustler* (1961) who covets Paul Newman's soul. A dazzling comic turn as a war-mongering General in Kubrick's *Dr Strangelove* (1964), contemplating global annihilation with a sort of maniacal glee, revealed his acting range, as did his subtle, moving performance in Richard Lester's *Petulia* (1968) as a doctor experiencing a mid-life crisis in a late 1960s America that is itself about to implode. As forthright off the screen as on, he turned down his Oscar for *Patton* (1970) out of distaste for what he called the demeaning "meat parade" of the Awards ceremony.

Signoret, Simone (1921–85)

Classy French actress who excelled at playing lovelorn women, most memorably in Jacques Becker's *Casque d'Or* (1952) and Jack Clayton's *Room at the Top* (1959). Among her other important films are *La Ronde* (1950), *Les Diaboliques* (1955), *The Army of the Shadows* (1969) and *Madame Rosa* (1977).

Stanwyck, Barbara (1907–90)

Vibrant, strong actress, much appreciated by directors such as Capra, DeMille, Lang, Sirk for her utter professionalism. Her stock-in-trade was as a hard-as-nails heroine who knew her own mind and was sometimes not to be trusted. Nominated for an Oscar four times without winning (for *Stella Dallas*, 1937; *Ball of Fire*, 1942; *Double Indemnity*, 1944; and *Sorry, Wrong Number*, 1948), she was finally given an honorary Oscar in 1982. Other key films: *The Bitter Tea of General Yen* (1933), *Annie Oakley* (1935), *The Lady Eve* (1941), *The Furies* (1950), *There's Always Tomorrow* (1956).

Stewart, James (1908–97)

Directors found complex uses for the slow drawl and shy demeanour of this adroit screen actor: all-American integrity, in his films for Capra (*Mr. Smith goes to Washington*, 1939; *It's A Wonderful Life*, 1946); seething inner intensity in his Anthony Mann westerns; and romantic vulnerability in his Alfred Hitchcock movies, most disturbingly and tragically so in *Vertigo* (1958). A versatile performer, who combined exceptional dramatic power, seen at its best in Preminger's *Anatomy of a Murder* (1959), with a flair for comedy: his performance in the latter vein in Cukor's *Philadelphia Story* (1940) won him an Oscar.

Streep, Meryl (b. 1951)

One of the leading ladies of the modern screen, who at one stage seemed to snatch all the big parts, whether they be English, Danish, Polish, or Australian, let alone American. She might not always move the heart, but the acting intelligence and technique are formidable. Her key films include: *The Deer Hunter* (1978), *Kramer Vs. Kramer* (1979), *The French Lieutenant's Woman* (1981), *Sophie's Choice* (1982), *Out of Africa* (1985), *The Bridges of Madison County* (1995), *The Hours* (2002).

Swanson, Gloria (1897–1983)

Perhaps the most glamorous of silent screen stars, particularly in her films for Cecil B. DeMille, like *Male and Female* (1919). She lost much of her wealth when producing *Queen Kelly* (1928), a film she stopped in mid-production owing to director Erich von Stroheim's extravagance: and talkies proved a problem. However, she made a triumphant return to the screen as Norma Desmond in Billy Wilder's *Sunset Boulevard* (1950), as the former silent star dreaming of a comeback. When the brash screenwriter says she used to be big, she snaps back imperiously: "I *am* big. It's the pictures that got small."

Tati, Jacques (1908–82)

Like Keaton, Tati's claim to fame is based on his direction as much as on his acting. Indeed it could be said that the two in a sense came into conflict in his later career, his directorial skill and concern with elaborate mechanised set-pieces causing his output to be irregular and often working against his lanky, absent-minded quality as a clown. *Mr. Hulot's Holiday* (1953) remains one of the greatest silent comedies in cinema history (sound was actually added after shooting, but its contribution to the comic impact is minimal), and Tati's greatest achievement in that film is perhaps the way in which he manages to render a specifically French social stereotype—the would-be sporting bourgeois on a seaside holiday—appealing to a much wider audience. Later films like *Mon Oncle* (1958), *Playtime* (1968) and *Traffic* (1971) have an almost mathematical precision in their comedy lay-out and a serious underlying theme: the decline of individuality in an age of mechanisation.

Taylor, Dame Elizabeth (b. 1932)

Taylor started out as a child-star in Clarence Brown's *National Velvet* (1944) before becoming one of the major Hollywood sex symbols of the fifties, dark and sultry in Richard Brooks's *Cat on a Hot Tin Roof* (1958) and Mankiewicz's *Suddenly Last*

Summer (1959). After her marriage to Richard Burton off-and-on screen persona were profitably played off against each other, this culminating in her Oscar-winning performance in Mike Nichols's *Who's Afraid of Virginia Woolf!* (1966). Directors like George Stevens and Joseph Losey spoke glowingly of her skill as a screen actress, but it is as a star that she has excelled, and nobody has symbolised celluloid glamour more seductively. From being its loveliest child star, Elizabeth Taylor can now be fairly regarded as Hollywood's Queen Mother. Other important films: *Father of the Bride* (1950), *A Place in the Sun* (1951), *Butterfield 8* (1960), *Cleopatra* (1963), *Reflections in a Golden Eye* (1967) and *Secret Ceremony* (1968).

Temple, Shirley (b. 1928)

The most famous of all child stars, precociously talented at singing, dancing and emoting. The top box-office attraction of 1938, she was a has-been by 1940, and has spent her adult life engaged not in movies but in Republican politics. Main films include: *Little Miss Marker* (1934), *Wee Willie Winkie* (1937) and *Rebecca of Sunnybrook Farm* (1938).

Tracy, Spencer (1900–67)

Tracy successfully embodied in the thirties and forties certain "all-American" qualities—bluff decency, perceptive kind-heartedness, the "Honest Joe" syndrome—marked in such movies as Fritz Lang's *Fury* (1936) and Frank Borzage's *Big City* (1937). With Katharine Hepburn, he formed one of the archetypal American-movie couples. They strike sparks off each other in *Adam's Rib* and *Pat and Mike* for George Cukor (1949 and 1952 respectively), and in work for such directors as George Stevens and Frank Capra. An actor's actor, so natural that he seemed not to be acting at all, he was greatly admired by his peers, not least by Laurence Olivier, who commented: "I've learned more about acting from watching Tracy than in any other way. He has great truth in everything he does." His films included: *San Francisco* (1936), *Captains Courageous* (1937), *Boys' Town* (1938), *Woman of the Year* (1942), *Father of the Bride* (1950), *The Actress* (1953), *Bad Day at Black Rock* (1955), *Inherit the Wind* (1960) and *Judgment at Nuremberg* (1961).

Valentino, Rudolph (1895–1926)

Valentino was one of the first major Hollywood sex symbols whose funeral after a premature death from peritonitis was followed by thousands of sobbing fans. This now seems ironic due not only to changes in film fashions and sexual coding that make his savagely passionate oriental in *The Sheik* (George Melford, 1921) appear passé, but also to subsequent revelations about his unconsummated first marriage, homosexual tendencies and domination by his second wife, who took charge of his career and mismanaged it abominably. To women he symbolised exotic eroticism; to men, to quote an infamous *Chicago Tribune* editorial, a "painted pansy". His premature death (which is often a smart career move, as one cynical journalist remarked) only fanned the legend and the controversy. Other important films: *The Four Horsemen of the Apocalypse* (1921), *Blood and Sand* (1922) and *Son of the Sheik* (1926).

Wayne, John (1907–79)

Wayne remains perhaps Hollywood's greatest, most loved and most hated star. Loved, by Western fans the world over for performances that set the mould for the horseback hero—big physically and spiritually, charismatically dominating with men, awkward and latently sentimental with women, always coming out on top in a crisis. Hated, for his uncompromising right-wing political stance which led him to endorse the McCarthyite persecutions of the fifties and to give active support to the American invasion of Vietnam, even making a film—*The Green Berets* (1968)— in support of it. As an actor, Wayne revealed in his best parts more sensitivity than he often cared to off-screen—as the outlaw Ringo in Ford's *Stagecoach* (1939) who ends up with the prostitute Dallas, as the tamed Comanche-hater Ethan Edwards in Ford's *The Searchers* (1956), who walks off into the barren landscape at the end, and as the sheriff in Hawks's *Rio Bravo* (1959), holding a motley posse together by force of personality. He won an Oscar for *True Grit* (1969). Other important films: *Fort Apache* (1948), *Red River* (1949), *She Wore a Yellow Ribbon* (1949), *Sands of Iwo Jima* (1950), *The Quiet Man* (1952), *The Man Who Shot Liberty Valance* (1962) and *The Shootist* (1976).

West, Mae (1892–1980)

"I was Snow White—but I drifted." So said Mae West, whose raunchy style was seen at its best on film in *She Done Him Wrong* (1933) and *I'm No Angel* (1933). This blousy buxom blonde appealed to men because of her sex-appeal, and to women because of the way she seized the sexual initiative from the male and sent up his desires. Unfortunately the production code of 1934, which laid down strict guidelines on the treatment of sex on film, inhibited Miss West's screen career. Other key films include: *Belle of the Nineties* (1934), *My Little Chickadee* (1940).

4. GLOSSARY OF FILM TERMS

Art director, technician responsible for the designing of the sets

Art-house film, a film commonly thought by critics to have artistic merit and often shown at specialist rather than mainstream cinemas.

Auteur, literally French for 'author', but generally a complimentary term bestowed by critics on a director whose films are deemed to exhibit stylistic and thematic distinctiveness and distinction. The so-called 'auteur theory', popularised in France in the 1950s, ascribed overall responsibility for the creation and quality of a film to its director, thereby renewing critical analysis of much previously neglected Hollywood work. The *'politique des auteurs'* (policy of authors) was first stated by François Truffaut in the January 1954 issue of *Cahiers du Cinema*; the main exponent of the auteur theory in America was the critic Andrew Sarris.

Back lighting, lighting directed at the camera from behind the subject, which is therefore silhouetted.

Back projection, background scene projected onto a screen behind the action to give the impression the actors are on a real location. A convention of classic Hollywood cinema that can now look dated, it became a source of keen critical debate in Hitchcock's *Marnie* (1964), where its perceptible use was both attacked for technical sloppiness and defended as expressively appropriate and meaningful.

Best boy, the main assistant to a film's chief electrician.

Bio-pic, a film about the life of a real person. It was a kind of film particularly popularised by Warner Brothers in the 1930s *e.g. The Story of Louis Pasteur* (1936) and *The Life of Emile Zola* (1937). Writers, sportsmen, composers, scientists, painters have all come under the spotlight: recent real-life subjects whose life and work have inspired successful films range from Virginia Woolf to

Mohammed Ali.

B-picture, generally a modest, low-budget production that, during the cinema's peak of popularity between 1930 and 1960, preceded the main feature. Often of low quality (one remembers the mortifying comment in the 1957 British comedy, *The Smallest Show on Earth*: 'She was as pretty as a picture- a B-picture, mind you'), B-pictures could sometimes prove to be useful training grounds for directors (*e.g.* Fred Zinnemann) who were to move on to bigger things, and some of the films were to become cult classics.

Camera angle, looking up, looking down, tilted (the latter used particularly strikingly in Carol Reed's 1949 classic, *The Third Man* to suggest a world out of joint).

Cannes Film Festival, the most glamorous of the annual international film festivals, generally taking place in May and whose top prize, the 'Golden Palm' gives its recipient valuable prestige and publicity.

CGI, or computer generated images, as seen to spectacular effect in such films as *Jurassic Park* (1993), *Toy Story* (1995), and *Gladiator* (2000). As George Lucas told Martin Scorsese during the shooting of his lavishly expensive *Gangs of New York* (2002): 'Sets like that can be done with computers now.'

Chiaroscuro, a striking or stylised use of light and shadow.

Cinemascope, a wide-screen process developed by Twentieth Century Fox and first used for their religious epic, *The Robe* (1953).

Cinema verité, literally 'cinema truth': it signified a kind of documentary cinema that used lightweight, hand-held equipment, minimal crews and interview techniques on real locations.

Crane shot, a shot where the camera is mounted on a crane and rises above the ground to offer an aerial perspective on the action. A famous example is the shot in Fred Zinnemann's *High Noon* (1952), where the crane shot of the Marshal in the empty street prior to his confrontation with the four outlaws emphasises his isolation, rejection and vulnerability.

Crosscutting, cutting back and forth from one action to another, giving the impression of parallel action and the events happening simultaneously or one event commenting on the other. Famous examples include the finale of D W Griffith's *Intolerance* (1916), where the chase to save the pardoned hero from execution in the modern story is crosscut with Christ's procession to Calvary; and the scene in Francis Ford Coppola's *The Godfather* (1972), where the baptism of Michael Corleone's godson is crosscut with the violent elimination of Corleone's Mafia rivals.

Cult movie, a film which gathers an underground reputation as a classic because of its appreciation by a specialist audience of followers, often in defiance of mainstream taste.

Cut, change from one shot to another. *See also* **Crosscutting** and **Match cut**.

Day for night, a technique used for shooting night sequences during daytime with the use of special lens filters. Alluded to in François Truffaut's film about film-making, *La Nuit Americaine—Day for Night* (1973)

Deep focus, a photographic technique in which objects far away from the camera as well as those in the foreground of the frame are in focus at the same time. It was particularly associated with the cameraman Gregg Toland and his work on the 1940s films of Orson Welles (*Citizen Kane*) and William Wyler (*The Little Foxes, The Best Years of our Lives*). It was considered to be an enhancement of film realism by the influential French film theorist, André Bazin.

Director's cut, a re-edited version of a classic film that supposedly restores, or more closely represents, the director's original intentions. Examples include David Lean's *Lawrence of Arabia*, Sam Peckinpah's *Pat Garrett and Billy the Kid* and Ridley Scott's *Blade Runner*.

Dissolve, a visible transition where one shot fades out as another fades in. A powerful example occurs in Hitchcock's *The Wrong Man* (1957), where Hitchcock slowly dissolves from a shot of unjustly accused Henry Fonda as he prays for help to that of the actual criminal about to attempt a robbery that will clear Fonda's name.

Documentary, a term first coined by John Grierson when describing Robert Flaherty's film about the daily life of a Polynesian youth, *Moana* (1926). It

derived from the French word *documentaire*, which the French used to describe travelogues, but it has come to be applied to all non-fiction films that show real events and people, albeit covering a wide variety of styles.

Dogme 95, a manifesto by key Danish film-makers such as Lars von Trier and Thomas Vinterberg, which eschewed the cinema of spectacle and special effects and lauded the 'inspiration of limitation' (natural sound, location shooting, hand-held camerawork *etc.*) An antithesis to the *Titanic* kind of cinema, its practice was short-lived—seen at its best in Vinterberg's *Festen* (1995) and its most controversial in von Trier's *The Idiots* (1998)—but, as the British director Michael Winterbottom commented, 'it was attractive as a polemic or provocation.'

Ealing comedy, a series of British comedies made at Ealing studios in West London that poked fun at bureaucracy, officialdom and the quaintness of British character. Its heyday was between 1949 and 1955, framed by the two darkest and most subversive achievements of the genre, Robert Hamer's *Kind Hearts and Coronets* and Alexander Mackendrick's *The Ladykillers*.

Establishing shot, opening shot of a scene that establishes the location or setting.

Fade in/Fade out, an optical device whereby the image appears/disappears gradually.

Film noir, films with a grim urban setting that deal mainly with dark and violent passions (often triggered by a seductive *femme fatale*) in a downbeat way. The term was applied by French critics to American thrillers of the 1940s, particularly those directed by European émigrés like Billy Wilder (*Double Indemnity*), Robert Siodmak (*The Killers*) and Fritz Lang (*Woman in the Window, Scarlet Street*), who intensified their themes with distorted imagery and stylised use of lighting and shadow that also owed something to German Expressionism (*see below*).

Fish-eye lens, a lens with such a wide angle that it distorts the image: used particularly effectively by cameraman James Wong Howe in John Frankenheimer's *Seconds* (1966) to enhance the horror of Rock Hudson's final journey to the operating table.

Flashback, scene or shot that disrupts the chronological narrative of a film to show events that happened in the past or before the main story began.

Flashforward, scene or shot that interrupts the chronological flow of a narrative to show future events.

Free cinema, a documentary movement in England in the 1950s that was a precursor of the British New Wave films of the early 1960s and was a springboard for the careers in film of directors such as Lindsay Anderson, Karel Reisz and Tony Richardson, who wished to bring a grittier honesty and realism to their portrait of English society.

Freeze frame, a shot where the action is 'frozen' into stillness, as in the famous endings of François Truffaut's *Les Quatre Cents Coups* (1959), George Roy Hill's *Butch Cassidy and the Sundance Kid* (1969), and Ridley Scott's *Thelma and Louise* (1992).

Gaffer, the chief electrician on a production.

Genre, a type or class of film (*e.g.* the musical, the western).

German expressionism, a style of film common in Germany in the twenties, typified by dramatic lighting, distorted sets, symbolic action and characterisation, as in, for example, Robert Wiene's *The Cabinet of Dr Caligari* (1919).

Hammer horror, English horror films from Hammer studios which made stars of regulars such as Peter Cushing and Christopher Lee and cult figures of directors such as Terence Fisher.

Hays Office, essentially the body that regulated what constituted good taste and acceptable behaviour on screen during the heyday of Hollywood. It was run by a former lawyer and conservative politician, Will Hays, and was the creation of the studio moguls in 1930, designed to improve the image of Hollywood after a series of highly publicised scandals about 'immoral' behaviour. The so-called Hays Code had an enormous influence on the content of Hollywood films until its termination in 1966.

Hollywood Ten, the ten artists who were imprisoned for contempt of Congress in 1948 when they refused to disclose their political affiliations to the

House UnAmerican Activities Committee (HUAC) during its infamous investigation into so-called 'Communist infiltration into the Hollywood motion picture industry'. The investigation provoked a climate of fear and period of blacklisting that permanently scarred the film community.

The ten individuals were producer-director Herbert Biberman, director Edward Dmytryk, producer-writer Adrian Scott, and writers Alvah Bessie, Lester Cole, Ring Lardner Jr., John Howard Lawson, Albert Maltz, Samuel Ornitz and Dalton Trumbo.

Kuleshov experiment, a montage experiment by the early Soviet director, Lev Kuleshov, which juxtaposed shots of the actor, Ivan Mozhukin with different objects to generate different meanings—*i.e.* the same expression of the actor juxtaposed with a shot of a child, a plate of soup, a coffin, was read by audiences to express tenderness, hunger and grief, respectively. In other words, the meaning was not in the shot itself but in the combination of images, showing the power of editing to alter perception. Subsequent film theorists have cast doubt on the claims and even existence of this experiment, but it did influence attitudes to the cinema and montage and a film such as Hitchcock's *Rear Window* (1954) could be said to derive its whole editing style from this 'experiment'.

MacGuffin, a term associated with Alfred Hitchcock and applied to a plot device that is of little interest in itself but is there simply to generate the action (like the microfilm that James Mason is trying to smuggle out of the country in *North by Northwest*).

Match cut, two shots linked by some aural or visual connection, like the moment in Stanley Kubrick's *2001:A Space Odyssey* (1968), where a bone tossed in the air by a primordial ape is visually displaced by the shot of a spinning spacecraft, or the moment in Nicolas Roeg's *Don't Look Now* (1973), where the director cuts from the wife's scream on seeing her dead daughter to the drill her husband is using in his reconstruction work on the church in Venice, a sound match and cut that, as Roeg said, fires the viewer like a bullet into the future.

Method acting, a style of acting influenced by the teachings of Konstantine Stanislavsky (1863-1938), which aimed to increase the realism of a performance by encouraging the actor to draw on his or her personal experiences to 'become' the character. Closely associated with the Actors' Studio in New York, it came to public attention in the 1950s through the striking and influential performances of actors such as Marlon Brando, James Dean and Paul Newman.

Mise-en-scene, literally, 'staging'—the way in which the elements and components in a film are arranged and encompassed by the camera, or the term normally used to denote that part of the cinematic process that takes place on the set, as opposed to montage, which takes place afterwards.

Montage, the juxtaposition of material (successive shots, or items within a shot) to suggest meaning—as when Eisenstein in *Battleship Potemkin* (1925) evokes anger at the massacre on the Odessa Steps by showing three successive shots of stone lions in various positions, shot to look as though they are one lion rising to its feet and roaring its fury. Or simply another word for a film's editing.

Movie brats, a new generation of Hollywood directors, many of them from film school, who exploded onto the scene in the early 1970s—(*e.g.* George Lucas, Brian DePalma, Martin Scorsese, Steven Spielberg).

Narration, the various means by which the events of the plot can be placed before the viewer. Also used of voice-over narration, a technique particularly associated with the fatalism of film noir, like that of the mortally wounded hero in *Double Indemnity* (1944) as he confesses his crime into a dictaphone, or that of the writer in *Sunset Boulevard* (1950), who, lying dead at the bottom of a movie star's swimming pool, reflects on how he got there.

Narrative, structured series of events, linked by cause and effect, that provides the film's plots.

Nickelodeon, a makeshift movie theatre in the early

days of cinema, so called because the admission price was only a nickel.

Neo-realism, connected with movement out of the studio, shooting on real locations, absence of a script and/or non-professional casts, all designed simultaneously to cut costs and increase the impression of spontaneity and real life. Inaugurated by Renoir but particularly associated with Italian directors of the immediate post-war period (Rossellini, Visconti, DeSica), who rejected the escapism of the national cinema to make films that reflected contemporary social conditions.

Nouvelle Vague, a term for a loose heterogeneous group of young French film critics (including Chabrol, Godard and Truffaut), who went into direction in the late 1950s and early 1960s and created an enormous impact with their experimental style and their laconic sense of existential amorality.

Pan, a shot where the camera looks around from a stationary position. It can be used for dramatic effect, as in John Ford's *Stagecoach* (1939), when a brief panning shot reveals the presence of an Indian war party just when the stagecoach seems to be heading for safety; or, more elaborately, in John Frankenheimer's *The Manchurian Candidate* (1962), where a 360-degree panning shot introduces the film's famous brainwashing sequence.

Point of view shot, a shot where the action is seen through the eyes of a particular character, the shot generally preceded or followed by the shot of the character looking. Used with particular effectiveness by Hitchcock in films such as *Rear Window* and *Vertigo* (1958). Robert Montgomery's *Lady in the Lake* (1948) also experimented with a subjective camera by showing us only what the leading character saw and only showing the character himself in mirror shots.

Screwball comedy, a type of comedy particularly popularised by directors like Howard Hawks and Preston Sturges in the 1930s and early 1940s and characterised by frantic action, rapier wit, and a couple in a bizarre situation. Fine examples would include: Capra's *It Happened One Night* (1934), Hawks's *Bringing Up Baby* (1938) and Sturges' *Palm Beach Story* (1942).

Silent period, roughly that period of film history between the Lumières in 1895 and *The Jazz Singer* in 1927, when most films were shot without sound, although, when exhibited, were often supported by sound effects and live piano accompaniment.

Sleeper, a term used of a film which initially escapes attention but gradually acquires a following, either cult or commercial.

Sneak preview, a tryout of a film to gauge audience reaction. In some notorious cases, such as Orson Welles's *The Magnificent Ambersons* (1942) and John Huston's *The Red Badge of Courage* (1951), the disastrous preview response caused the studios to panic and butcher the films through desperate re-editing.

Spaghetti western, a western made in Italy by Italian film-makers, which commonly stylises the action and often parodies genre conventions. They became particularly popular in the 1960s because of the successful association on the 'Dollars' films of actor Clint Eastwood and director Sergio Leone.

Storyboard, series of sketches of the shots that comprise a scene and a useful reference for a director when shooting particularly complicated pieces of action.

Ten-minute take, a ten-minute sequence filmed in a single take without cuts. Particularly associated with Alfred Hitchcock and his deployment of the technique in *Rope* (1948) and *Under Capricorn* (1949).

Tracking shot, camera moves forward or backwards in order to follow subject, a technique taken to an extreme in the elaborate three-minute continuous shot that opens Orson Welles's *Touch of Evil* (1958) and to which Robert Altman pays homage in *The Player* (1992).

Zoom shot, a shot during which the focal length of the lens is adjusted and gives the impression of optical motion without moving the camera backwards or forwards. The zoom lens has been used to particularly expressive effect by directors such as Robert Altman and Stanley Kubrick.

5. THE OSCAR WINNERS

Introduction

The film industry's most glittering prize remains the Hollywood Academy Award, or "Oscar'. The "Oscar' came about as a result of the formation of the Academy of Motion Picture Arts and Sciences in 1927. The Academy thought it would gain additional prestige and publicity if it gave out annual awards for artistic and technical merit. The first awards ceremony was in May 1929 and was a modest affair. Nowadays the ceremony is a lavish spectacle watched by countless millions on TV.

The Oscar itself is a gold-plated statuette of a knight holding a crusader's sword and standing on a reel of film whose five spokes symbolise the original branches of the Academy (actors, directors, producers, technicians and writers). Legend has it that the name comes from a secretary Margaret Herrick, later an executive director of the Academy, who commented one day that the statuette "reminds me of my uncle Oscar".

Oscar Records

Ben-Hur (1959), *Titanic* (1997) and *Lord of the Rings* (2003) hold the record number of Oscars—11. *West Side Story* (1961) won 10; *Gone With the Wind* (1939), *Gigi* (1958), *The Last Emperor* (1987) and *The English Patient* (1996) each won nine. Katharine Hepburn has won more major acting Oscars than any other star (4). Bette Davis, Luise Rainer, Olivia de Havilland, Ingrid Bergman, Glenda Jackson, Jane Fonda, Sally Field, Elizabeth Taylor, Jodie Foster and Hilary Swank have won Best Actress twice; Spencer Tracy, Fredric March, Gary Cooper, Marlon Brando, Dustin Hoffman, Jack Nicholson and Tom Hanks have done the same as Best Actor.

Best Actor

1927–28	Emil Jannings, *The Way of All Flesh*
1928–29	Warner Baxter, *In Old Arizona*
1929–30	George Arliss, *Disraeli*
1930–31	Lionel Barrymore, *A Free Soul*
1931–32	Fredric March, *Dr Jekyll and Mr Hyde*; Wallace Beery, *The Champ* (tie)
1932–33	Charles Laughton, *Private Life of Henry VIII*
1934	Clark Gable, *It Happened One Night*
1935	Victor McLaglen, *The Informer*
1936	Paul Muni, *Story of Louis Pasteur*
1937	Spencer Tracy, *Captains Courageous*
1938	Spencer Tracy, *Boys Town*
1939	Robert Donat, *Goodbye Mr Chips*
1940	James Stewart, *The Philadelphia Story*
1941	Gary Cooper, *Sergeant York*
1942	James Cagney, *Yankee Doodle Dandy*
1943	Paul Lukas, *Watch on the Rhine*
1944	Bing Crosby, *Going My Way*
1945	Ray Milland, *The Lost Weekend*
1946	Fredric March, *The Best Years of Our Lives*
1947	Ronald Colman, *A Double Life*
1948	Laurence Olivier, *Hamlet*
1949	Broderick Crawford, *All the King's Men*
1950	José Ferrer, *Cyrano de Bergerac*
1951	Humphrey Bogart, *The African Queen*
1952	Gary Cooper, *High Noon*
1953	William Holden, *Stalag 17*
1954	Marlon Brando, *On the Waterfront*
1955	Ernest Borgnine, *Marty*
1956	Yul Brynner, *The King and I*
1957	Alec Guinness, *The Bridge on the River Kwai*
1958	David Niven, *Separate Tables*
1959	Charlton Heston, *Ben-Hur*
1960	Burt Lancaster, *Elmer Gantry*
1961	Maximilian Schell, *Judgment at Nuremberg*
1962	Gregory Peck, *To Kill a Mockingbird*
1963	Sidney Poitier, *Lilies of the Field*
1964	Rex Harrison, *My Fair Lady*
1965	Lee Marvin, *Cat Ballou*
1966	Paul Scofield, *A Man for All Seasons*
1967	Rod Steiger, *In the Heat of the Night*
1968	Cliff Robertson, *Charly*
1969	John Wayne, *True Grit*
1970	George C. Scott, *Patton* (refused)
1971	Gene Hackman, *The French Connection*
1972	Marlon Brando, *The Godfather* (refused)
1973	Jack Lemmon, *Save the Tiger*
1974	Art Carney, *Harry and Tonto*
1975	Jack Nicholson, *One Flew Over the Cuckoo's Nest*
1976	Peter Finch, *Network*
1977	Richard Dreyfuss, *The Goodbye Girl*
1978	Jon Voight, *Coming Home*
1979	Dustin Hoffman, *Kramer vs. Kramer*
1980	Robert DeNiro, *Raging Bull*
1981	Henry Fonda, *On Golden Pond*
1982	Ben Kingsley, *Gandhi*
1983	Robert Duvall, *Tender Mercies*
1984	F. Murray Abraham, *Amadeus*
1985	William Hurt, *Kiss of the Spider Woman*
1986	Paul Newman, *The Color of Money*
1987	Michael Douglas, *Wall Street*
1988	Dustin Hoffman, *Rain Man*
1989	Daniel Day-Lewis, *My Left Foot*
1990	Jeremy Irons, *Reversal of Fortune*
1991	Anthony Hopkins, *The Silence of the Lambs*
1992	Al Pacino, *Scent of a Woman*
1993	Tom Hanks, *Philadelphia*
1994	Tom Hanks, *Forrest Gump*
1995	Nicolas Cage, *Leaving Las Vegas*
1996	Geoffrey Rush, *Shine*
1997	Jack Nicholson, *As Good As It Gets*
1998	Roberto Benigni, *Life is Beautiful*
1999	Kevin Spacey, *American Beauty*
2000	Russell Crowe, *Gladiator*
2001	Denzel Washington, *Training Day*
2002	Adrien Brody, *The Pianist*
2003	Sean Penn, *Mystic River*
2004	Jamie Foxx, *Ray*
2005	Philip Seymour Hoffman, *Capote*

Best Actress

1927–28	Janet Gaynor, *Seventh Heaven*
1928–29	Mary Pickford, *Coquette*
1929–30	Norma Shearer, *The Divorcee*
1930–31	Marie Dressler, *Min and Bill*
1931–32	Helen Hayes, *Sin of Madelon Claudet*
1932–33	Katharine Hepburn, *Morning Glory*
1934	Claudette Colbert, *It Happened One Night*
1935	Bette Davis, *Dangerous*
1936	Luise Rainer, *The Great Ziegfeld*
1937	Luise Rainer, *The Good Earth*
1938	Bette Davis, *Jezebel*
1939	Vivien Leigh, *Gone With the Wind*
1940	Ginger Rogers, *Kitty Foyle*
1941	Joan Fontaine, *Suspicion*
1942	Greer Garson, *Mrs Miniver*
1943	Jennifer Jones, *The Song of Bernadette*
1944	Ingrid Bergman, *Gaslight*
1945	Joan Crawford, *Mildred Pierce*
1946	Olivia de Havilland, *To Each His Own*
1947	Loretta Young, *The Farmer's Daughter*
1948	Jane Wyman, *Johnny Belinda*
1949	Olivia de Havilland, *The Heiress*
1950	Judy Holliday, *Born Yesterday*
1951	Vivien Leigh, *A Streetcar Named Desire*
1952	Shirley Booth, *Come Back, Little Sheba*
1953	Audrey Hepburn, *Roman Holiday*
1954	Grace Kelly, *Country Girl*
1955	Anna Magnani, *The Rose Tattoo*
1956	Ingrid Bergman, *Anastasia*
1957	Joanne Woodward, *The Three Faces of Eve*
1958	Susan Hayward, *I Want to Live*
1959	Simone Signoret, *Room at the Top*
1960	Elizabeth Taylor, *Butterfield 8*
1961	Sophia Loren, *Two Women*
1962	Anne Bancroft, *The Miracle Worker*
1963	Patricia Neal, *Hud*
1964	Julie Andrews, *Mary Poppins*
1965	Julie Christie, *Darling*
1966	Elizabeth Taylor, *Who's Afraid of Virginia Woolf?*
1967	Katharine Hepburn, *Guess Who's Coming to Dinner*
1968	Katharine Hepburn, *The Lion in Winter*; Barbra Streisand, *Funny Girl* (tie)
1969	Maggie Smith, *The Prime of Miss Jean Brodie*

1970	Glenda Jackson, *Women in Love*		1970	*Patton*, 20th Century-Fox
1971	Jane Fonda, *Klute*		1971	*The French Connection*, 20th Century-Fox
1972	Liza Minnelli, *Cabaret*			
1973	Glenda Jackson, *A Touch of Class*		1972	*The Godfather*, Paramount
1974	Ellen Burstyn, *Alice Doesn't Live Here Anymore*		1973	*The Sting*, Universal
			1974	*The Godfather, Part II*, Paramount
1975	Louise Fletcher, *One Flew Over the Cuckoo's Nest*		1975	*One Flew Over the Cuckoo's Nest*, United Artists
1976	Faye Dunaway, *Network*		1976	*Rocky*, United Artists
1977	Diane Keaton, *Annie Hall*		1977	*Annie Hall*, United Artists
1978	Jane Fonda, *Coming Home*		1978	*The Deer Hunter*, EMI
1979	Sally Field, *Norma Rae*		1979	*Kramer vs. Kramer*, Columbia
1980	Sissy Spacek, *Coal Miner's Daughter*		1980	*Ordinary People*, Paramount
1981	Katharine Hepburn, *On Golden Pond*		1981	*Chariots of Fire*, Fox
1982	Meryl Streep, *Sophie's Choice*		1982	*Gandhi*, Columbia-Warner
1983	Shirley MacLaine, *Terms of Endearment*		1983	*Terms of Endearment*, Paramount
1984	Sally Field, *Places in the Heart*		1984	*Amadeus*, Columbia-Warner
1985	Geraldine Page, *The Trip to Bountiful*		1985	*Out of Africa*, Universal
1986	Marlee Matlin, *Children of a Lesser God*		1986	*Platoon*, Orion Pictures
1987	Cher, *Moonstruck*		1987	*The Last Emperor*, Columbia
1988	Jodie Foster, *The Accused*		1988	*Rain Man*, United Artists
1989	Jessica Tandy, *Driving Miss Daisy*		1989	*Driving Miss Daisy*, Warner Bros.
1990	Kathy Bates, *Misery*		1990	*Dances with Wolves*, Guild
1991	Jodie Foster, *The Silence of the Lambs*		1991	*The Silence of the Lambs*, Orion Pictures
1992	Emma Thompson, *Howards End*		1992	*Unforgiven*, Warner Bros.
1993	Holly Hunter, *The Piano*		1993	*Schindler's List*, Universal
1994	Jessica Lange, *Blue Sky*		1994	*Forrest Gump*, Paramount
1995	Susan Sarandon, *Dead Man Walking*		1995	*Braveheart*, Paramount/20th Century-Fox
1996	Frances McDormand, *Fargo*		1996	*The English Patient*, Miramax
1997	Helen Hunt, *As Good As It Gets*		1997	*Titanic*, 20th Century-Fox/Paramount
1998	Gwyneth Paltrow, *Shakespeare in Love*		1998	*Shakespeare in Love*, Miramax Films/Universal
1999	Hilary Swank, *Boys Don't Cry*			
2000	Julia Roberts, *Erin Brockovich*		1999	*American Beauty*, DreamWorks
2001	Halle Berry, *Monster's Ball*		2000	*Gladiator*, DreamWorks/Universal Studios
2002	Nicole Kidman, *The Hours*		2001	*A Beautiful Mind*, DreamWorks/Universal Studios
2003	Charlize Theron, *Monster*			
2004	Hilary Swank, *Million Dollar Baby*		2002	*Chicago*, Miramax/Buena Vista International
2005	Reese Witherspoon, *Walk the Line*		2003	*Lord of the Rings: Return of the King*, New Line Cinema
			2004	*Million Dollar Baby*, Warner Bros.
			2005	*Crash*, Lions Gate

Best Film

1927–28 *Wings*, Paramount
1928–29 *Broadway Melody*, MGM
1929–30 *All Quiet on the Western Front*, Universal
1930–31 *Cimarron*, RKO
1931–32 *Grand Hotel*, MGM
Special: *Mickey Mouse*, Walt Disney
1932–33 *Cavalcade*, 20th Century-Fox
1934 *It Happened One Night*, Columbia
1935 *Mutiny on the Bounty*, MGM
1936 *The Great Ziegfeld*, MGM
1937 *Life of Emile Zola*, Warner
1938 *You Can't Take It With You*, Columbia
1939 *Gone With the Wind*, Selznick International
1940 *Rebecca*, Selznick International
1941 *How Green Was My Valley*, 20th Century-Fox
1942 *Mrs Miniver*, MGM
1943 *Casablanca*, Warner
1944 *Going My Way*, Paramount
1945 *The Lost Weekend*, Paramount
1946 *The Best Years of Our Lives*, Goldwyn, RKO
1947 *Gentleman's Agreement*, 20th Century-Fox
1948 *Hamlet*, Two Cities Film. Universal International
1949 *All the King's Men*, Columbia
1950 *All About Eve*, 20th Century-Fox
1951 *An American in Paris*, MGM
1952 *Greatest Show on Earth*, Cecil B. De Mille, Paramount
1953 *From Here to Eternity*, Columbia
1954 *On the Waterfront*, Horizon-American Corp. Columbia
1955 *Marty*, Hecht and Lancaster's Steven Productions UA
1956 *Around the World in 80 Days*, Michael Todd Co. UA
1957 *The Bridge on the River Kwai*, Columbia
1958 *Gigi*, Arthur Freed Production, MGM
1959 *Ben-Hur*, MGM
1960 *The Apartment*, Mirisch Co. UA
1961 *West Side Story*, United Artists
1962 *Lawrence of Arabia*, Columbia
1963 *Tom Jones*, Woodfall Prod. UA-Lopert Pictures
1964 *My Fair Lady*, Warner Bros.
1965 *The Sound of Music*, 20th Century-Fox
1966 *A Man for All Seasons*, Columbia
1967 *In the Heat of the Night*, United Artists
1968 *Oliver*, Columbia
1969 *Midnight Cowboy*, United Artists

Best Director

1927–28 Frank Borzage, *Seventh Heaven*
Lewis Milestone, *Two Arabian Knights*
1928–29 Frank Lloyd, *The Divine Lady*
1929–30 Lewis Milestone, *All Quiet on the Western Front*
1930–31 Norman Taurog, *Skippy*
1931–32 Frank Borzage, *Bad Girl*
1932–33 Frank Lloyd, *Cavalcade*
1934 Frank Capra, *It Happened One Night*
1935 John Ford, *The Informer*
1936 Frank Capra, *Mr Deeds Goes to Town*
1937 Leo McCarey, *The Awful Truth*
1938 Frank Capra, *You Can't Take It With You*
1939 Victor Fleming, *Gone with the Wind*
1940 John Ford, *The Grapes of Wrath*
1941 John Ford, *How Green Was My Valley*
1942 William Wyler, *Mrs Miniver*
1943 Michael Curtiz, *Casablanca*
1944 Leo McCarey, *Going My Way*
1945 Billy Wilder, *The Lost Weekend*
1946 William Wyler, *The Best Years of Our Lives*
1947 Elia Kazan, *Gentleman's Agreement*
1948 John Huston, *Treasure of the Sierra Madre*
1949 Joseph L. Mankiewicz, *A Letter to Three Wives*
1950 Joseph L. Mankiewicz, *All About Eve*
1951 George Stevens, *A Place in the Sun*
1952 John Ford, *The Quiet Man*
1953 Fred Zinnemann, *From Here to Eternity*
1954 Elia Kazan, *On the Waterfront*
1955 Delbert Mann, *Marty*
1956 George Stevens, *Giant*
1957 David Lean, *The Bridge on the River Kwai*
1958 Vincente Minnelli, *Gigi*
1959 William Wyler, *Ben-Hur*
1960 Billy Wilder, *The Apartment*
1961 Jerome Robbins, Robert Wise, *West Side Story*
1962 David Lean, *Lawrence of Arabia*
1963 Tony Richardson, *Tom Jones*
1964 George Cukor, *My Fair Lady*
1965 Robert Wise, *The Sound of Music*
1966 Fred Zinnemann, *A Man for All Seasons*
1967 Mike Nichols, *The Graduate*
1968 Sir Carol Reed, *Oliver*
1969 John Schlesinger, *Midnight Cowboy*
1970 Franklin J. Schaffner, *Patton*

1971	William Friedkin, *The French Connection*	1988	Barry Levinson, *Rain Man*
1972	Bob Fosse, *Cabaret*	1989	Oliver Stone, *Born on the Fourth of July*
1973	George Roy Hill, *The Sting*	1990	Kevin Costner, *Dances with Wolves*
1974	Francis Ford Coppola, *The Godfather, Part*	1991	Jonathan Demme, *The Silence of the Lambs*
	II	1992	Clint Eastwood, *Unforgiven*
1975	Milos Forman, *One Flew Over the Cuckoo's*	1993	Steven Spielberg, *Schindler's List*
	Nest	1994	Robert Zemeckis, *Forrest Gump*
1976	John Avildsen, *Rocky*	1995	Mel Gibson, *Braveheart*
1977	Woody Allen, *Annie Hall*	1996	Anthony Minghella, *The English Patient*
1978	Michael Cimino, *The Deer Hunter*	1997	James Cameron, *Titanic*
1979	Robert Benton, *Kramer vs. Kramer*	1998	Steven Spielberg, *Saving Private Ryan*
1980	Robert Redford, *Ordinary People*	1999	Sam Mendes, *American Beauty*
1981	Warren Beatty, *Reds*	2000	Steven Soderbergh, *Traffic*
1982	Richard Attenborough, *Gandhi*	2001	Ron Howard, *A Beautiful Mind*
1983	James L. Brooks, *Terms of Endearment*	2002	Roman Polanski, *The Pianist*
1984	Milos Forman, *Amadeus*	2003	Peter Jackson, *Lord of the Rings: Return of*
1985	Sydney Pollack, *Out of Africa*		*the King*
1986	Oliver Stone, *Platoon*	2004	Clint Eastwood, *Million Dollar Baby*
1987	Bernardo Bertolucci, *The Last Emperor*	2005	Ang Lee, *Brokeback Mountain*

SPECIAL TOPIC

RADICAL CINEMA

Introduction

Graham Greene, sometime satirist of the Secret Service and scourge of political dictatorships, saw his task as a novelist to be, as he put it, "a piece of grit in the State machinery." Radical cinema might be said to aspire to a similar function. It attempts to be non-conformist in an industry given over to conformity. It is designed to provoke more than placate. Stylistically it can subvert the usual way of showing things or telling stories; thematically it can challenge traditional views or institutions. In short, it can be a vehicle that reflects the need for social and cinematic change. Unconventional almost by definition, it need not necessarily be unpopular or marginal, since it might be a refreshing antidote to the mainstream or fortuitously catch a shifting mood.

Precursors of Modern Radicalism

One way of thinking about radicalism in the cinema could involve looking at those film movements which emerged at a particular time to shake up the cinema conventions of the time. A starting-point would be the Soviet cinema of the 1920s. When Lenin declared that "for us, of all the arts, cinema is the most important", he was not thinking of its aesthetic properties so much as its potential for propaganda, a new medium that could express the ideology of a post-revolutionary society. Directors such as Lev Kuleshov and Vsevolod Pudovkin experimented with montage to increase the expressiveness of film and explore how it might be used to manipulate audiences, whilst the documentary film-maker Dziga Vertov sought to demonstrate how cinema could do more than simply tell stories but also capture truth and reflect on its own methods.

Sergei Eisenstein

However, it was Sergei Eisenstein who made the biggest impact. In the legendary Odessa Steppes sequence of *Battleship Potemkin* (1925), where Cossack soldiers attack innocent civilians, Eisenstein dynamically and dialectically deployed his montage to mount a devastating protest on behalf of the people against the tyranny of their oppressors. The power of the sequence was such that, momentarily, it made revolutionaries of us all—enough indeed to lead to the banning of the film in many parts of Europe lest it stirred revolt.

Italian Neo-realism

Although lacking Eisenstein's stylistic adventurousness and polemical passion, the Italian neo-realist movement that flourished for a decade or so after World War Two had certain features in common with the Soviet example: the preference for shooting on location (necessitated anyway by the destruction of the studios during the war), the use of non-actors as a strategy to make the common people its heroes. Roberto Rossellini, whose film *Rome – Open City* (1945) had the immediacy of documentary in its depiction of the struggle of the Resistance against Nazi occupation, described neo-realism as not so much a style as a moral standpoint: it brought recent reality vividly to the screen in order to expose evils and injustice and to urge for change. "Each of us felt the wild urge to sweep away all the worn-out plots of the Italian cinema," said Vittorio de Sica, "and to set up our cameras in the midst of real life, in the midst of all that struck us with dismay."

De Sica's most famous film, *Bicycle Thieves* (1948) took a simple theme—a man's livelihood for his work is threatened when the bicycle he needs for his work is stolen—but turned it not only into a poignant study of the loss of human dignity but into an unflinching portrayal of poverty and suffering. The film was informed by a passionate anger against social conditions that reduce decent people to desperate measures.

The British New Wave

As a movement, neo-realism managed to antagonise factions on both sides of the political divide. The Right disliked its unflattering portrayal of the country; the Left thought it lacked political analysis. However, de Sica claimed he was never aiming to propose political solutions but to make people feel for poverty's victims. The movement declined in the 1950s but something of its spirit lived on in the British Free Cinema documentary movement of the mid-1950s that took its camera out into the streets and looked honestly at working-class life, in contrast to a national cinema that it saw as moribund, conservative and class-bound.

One of the Free Cinema directors, Karel Reisz, was to make one of the earliest and greatest films of the so-called British New Wave, *Saturday Night and Sunday Morning* (1960), a work which brought a fresh realism and regionalism into British film; another, Lindsay Anderson, was also to make a striking debut with a film in the same vein, *This Sporting Life* (1963).

Always an astringent and iconoclastic voice in his attacks on what he saw as the emotional and political conservatism and timidity of most British cinema, Anderson was to have his biggest success at the end of the decade with a denunciation of the British public school system, *If . . .* (1968), whose exhilarating anti-authoritarianism seemed in tune with the mood of protest and anarchy that rocked society in 1968.

Nouvelle Vague

If the British New Wave struck a chord with its portrayal of angry young men in Northern surroundings rejecting the values of an earlier generation, the French Nouvelle Vague was even more influential. Many of the young directors here, including François Truffaut, Jean-Luc Godard and Claude Chabrol, had begun as fiercely committed film critics for the magazine *Cahiers du Cinema* who had dismissed the cinema of their elders as outmoded, overly literary and old-fashioned (with a few honourable exceptions such as Renoir). They carried that fervour into their early films, which were liberating both in subject matter (as in Truffaut's daring depiction of a ménage-a-trois in his 1961 film, *Jules et Jim*) and in method (as in Godard's *Breathless* of 1960 whose jumpy, insolent style seemed, in one critic's words, "like a hand-grenade tossed into the audience").

As the decade developed, Truffaut's films became more conventional, whilst Godard's became more overtly political, culminating in his apocalyptic vision of social and cultural breakdown, *Weekend* (1967). The political convulsions of 1968 radicalised him still further and indeed had their impact also on critical practice, *Cahiers du Cinema* completely redefining its approach to film in ideological terms and finding new resonance and relevance in earlier theorists and practitioners such as Eisenstein and Vertov.

New German Cinema

During the 1970s a film movement that attracted particular attention was the new German cinema. One of its characteristics was a critical reassessment of the country's recent past and of the kind of society created by the post-war economic miracle. Three key, contrasting figures were Rainer Werner Fassbinder, Werner Herzog and Wim Wenders.

From his perspective as a gay film-maker, Fassbinder made anguished melodramas about social and sexual prejudice and oppression, such as *Fear Eats the Soul* (1973), which was much influenced by a Hollywood director he greatly admired, Douglas Sirk. Herzog's sympathies were with the visionaries, eccentrics and outsiders whom so-called "normal" society rejects: *The Enigma of Kaspar Hauser* (1975) is his most poignant elaboration of that theme. Wenders' best films, such as *Kings of the Road* (1976) and *The American Friend* (1977), investigated the impact of American culture on post-war Germany and how America had, in his phrase, "colonised our subconscious".

The Reaction Against Hollywood

Wenders' films were a reminder that much of the cinema talked about here defined its radicalism, whether it be stylistic, ideological or political, as a reaction against Hollywood values and practice. It is worth noting, however, that there existed within the Hollywood system a tradition of radicalism of its own that was struggling to find a voice. Young men, whose political sensibilities had been forged by the Depression, Roosevelt's New Deal politics and opposition to European Fascism, began their directing careers in the mid-1940s with a real social zeal and were not afraid to launch trenchant critiques of some unsavoury aspects of American society, for example, prejudice in Joseph Losey's *The Boy with Green Hair* (1947); anti-Semitism in Edward Dmytryk's *Crossfire* and Elia Kazan's *Boomerang* (both 1947); or capitalistic greed in Robert Rossen's *Body and Soul* (1947) and Abraham Polonsky's *Force of Evil* (1948).

The McCarthyist Repression

However, in the McCarthyist era, such expressions of dissent were seen as un-American, and all of these directors were either to be blacklisted and forced into exile or compelled to recant their previous political convictions and turn informer to the HUAC (the House of UnAmerican Activities Committee). The most overtly left-wing American film of this period, *Salt of The Earth* (1954), made by one of the Hollywood Ten, Herbert Biberman after his release from prison, had to be filmed in Mexico and was denied an American screening for years. In the 1950s, it was left to non-conformist auteurs such as Nicholas Ray and Douglas Sirk, and even Howard Hawks and Alfred Hitchcock, to express an ambiguous or hostile relationship to the dominant ideology but in a subtly oblique and cleverly entertaining way.

Other Radical Champions

In a brief survey of this kind, it would be impossible to name all the film-makers who would warrant a mention under this heading. In the 1960s, Nagisa Oshima in Japan, Glauber Rocha in Brazil, and Bernardo Bertolucci in Italy made films that incisively interrogated the values of their society. So did the German director Margaretha von Trotta in the 1970s and the Dutch film-maker Marleen Gorris in the 1980s from their particular feminist positions. The films of Spike Lee offered an alternative, authentic and penetrating insight into the experience of black Americans, particularly the magnificent *Do the Right Thing* (1989).

Nowadays, directors such as Lars von Trier (Denmark), Abbas Kiarostami (Iran) and Ken Loach and Mike Leigh (England) can be relied on for a different perspective on perceived norms, making films that enlarge human sympathies and make us think afresh about the cinema's social and political responsibilities.

Because film is an industry dominated by America and designed to maximise its profits, it follows that most of the product will be safe rather than risky; geared towards escapism more than enquiry; and dedicated more towards making money than questioning values. On the other hand, who would have thought that an American documentary, disloyally attacking its President's foreign policy in an election year, would make over $100 million on release? Michael Moore's *Fahrenheit 9/11* (2004) did not affect the Presidential outcome, but it was at least a heartening sign that, in a conservative industry, an eloquent and enquiring radical voice can still make itself heard even if not necessarily heeded.

SPORTING COMPANION

This section provides a wide-ranging variety of tables giving numerous recent winners of major popular sporting competitions, both domestic and international. The results included here range from Association Football to the Grand National.

SPORTING COMPANION

AMERICAN FOOTBALL

WORLD CHAMPIONSHIP SUPERBOWL WINNERS

I (1967)	Green Bay Packers	XXI (1987)	New York Giants
II (1968)	Green Bay Packers	XXII (1988)	Washington Redskins
III (1969)	New York Jets	XXIII (1989)	San Francisco 49ers
IV (1970)	Kansas City Chiefs	XXIV (1990)	San Francisco 49ers
V (1971)	Baltimore Colts	XXV (1991)	New York Giants
VI (1972)	Dallas Cowboys	XXVI (1992)	Washington Redskins
VII (1973)	Miami Dolphins	XXVII (1993)	Dallas Cowboys
VIII (1974)	Miami Dolphins	XXVIII (1994)	Dallas Cowboys
IX (1975)	Pittsburgh Steelers	XXIX (1995)	San Francisco 49ers
X (1976)	Pittsburgh Steelers	XXX (1996)	Dallas Cowboys
XI (1977)	Oakland Raiders	XXXI (1997)	Green Bay Packers
XII (1978)	Dallas Cowboys	XXXII (1998)	Denver Broncos
XIII (1979)	Pittsburgh Steelers	XXXIII (1999)	Denver Broncos
XIV (1980)	Pittsburgh Steelers	XXXIV (2000)	St Louis Rams
XV (1981)	Oakland Raiders	XXXV (2001)	Baltimore Ravens
XVI (1982)	San Francisco 49ers	XXXVI (2002)	New England Patriots
XVII (1983)	Washington Redskins	XXXVII (2003)	Tampa Bay Buccaneers
XVIII ((1984)	Los Angeles Raiders	XXXVIII (2004)	New England Patriots
XIX (1985)	San Francisco 49ers	XXXIX (2005)	New England Patriots
XX (1986)	Chicago Bears	XL (2006)	Pittsburgh Steelers

ASSOCIATION FOOTBALL

WORLD CUP WINNERS

1930	Uruguay	1962	Brazil	1986	Argentina
1934	Italy	1966	England	1990	West Germany
1938	Italy	1970	Brazil	1994	Brazil
1950	Uruguay	1974	West Germany	1998	France
1954	West Germany	1978	Argentina	2002	Brazil
1958	Brazil	1982	Italy	2006	Italy

South Africa hosts the 2010 World Cup.

EUROPEAN CHAMPIONS

1960	USSR	1976	Czechoslovakia	1992	Denmark
1964	Spain	1980	West Germany	1996	Germany
1968	Italy	1984	France	2000	France
1972	West Germany	1988	Holland	2004	Greece

EUROPEAN CHAMPIONS CUP WINNERS

1955–6	Real Madrid	1972–3	Ajax Amsterdam	1989–90	AC Milan
1956–7	Real Madrid	1973–4	Bayern Munich	1990–1	Red Star Belgrade
1957–8	Real Madrid	1974–5	Bayern Munich	1991–2	Barcelona
1958–9	Real Madrid	1975–6	Bayern Munich	1992–3	Marseille
1959–60	Real Madrid	1976–7	Liverpool	1993–4	AC Milan
1960–1	Benfica	1977–8	Liverpool	1994–5	Ajax Amsterdam
1961–2	Benfica	1978–9	Nottingham Forest	1995–6	Juventus
1962–3	AC Milan	1979–80	Nottingham Forest	1996–7	Borussia Dortmund
1963–4	Inter Milan	1980–1	Liverpool	1997–8	Real Madrid
1964–5	Inter Milan	1981–2	Aston Villa	1998–9	Manchester United
1965–6	Real Madrid	1982–3	SV Hamburg	1999–00	Real Madrid
1966–7	Glasgow Celtic	1983–4	Liverpool	2000–01	Bayern Munich
1967–8	Manchester United	1984–5	Juventus	2001–02	Real Madrid
1968–9	AC Milan	1985–6	Steaua Bucharest	2002–03	AC Milan
1969–70	Feyenoord	1986–7	FC Porto	2003–04	FC Porto
1970–1	Ajax Amsterdam	1987–8	PSV Eindhoven	2004–05	Liverpool
1971–2	Ajax Amsterdam	1988–9	AC Milan	2005–06	Barcelona

EUROPEAN CUP–WINNERS' CUP WINNERS (until 1999)

1960–1	Fiorentina	1973–4	FC Magdeburg	1986–7	Ajax Amsterdam
1961–2	Atletico Madrid	1974–5	Dynamo Kiev	1987–8	Mechelen
1962–3	Tottenham Hotspur	1975–6	Anderlecht	1988–9	Barcelona
1963–4	Sporting Lisbon	1976–7	Hamburg SV	1989–90	Sampdoria
1964–5	West Ham United	1977–8	Anderlecht	1990–1	Manchester United
1965–6	Borussia Dortmund	1978–9	Barcelona	1991–2	Werder Bremen
1966–7	Bayern Munich	1979–80	Valencia	1992–3	Parma
1967–8	AC Milan	1980–1	Dynamo Tbilisi	1993–4	Arsenal
1968–9	Slovan Bratislava	1981–2	Barcelona	1994–5	Real Zaragoza
1969–70	Manchester City	1982–3	Aberdeen	1995–6	Paris St Germain
1970–1	Chelsea	1983–4	Juventus	1996–7	Barcelona
1971–2	Glasgow Rangers	1984–5	Everton	1997–8	Chelsea
1972–3	AC Milan	1985–6	Dynamo Kiev	1998–9	Lazio

UEFA CUP WINNERS

1957–8	Barcelona	1975–6	Liverpool	1992–3	Juventus
1959–60	Barcelona	1976–7	Juventus	1993–4	Inter Milan
1960–1	AS Roma	1977–8	PSV Eindhoven	1994–5	Parma
1961–2	Valencia	1978–9	Borussia	1995–6	Bayern Munich
1962–3	Valencia		Moenchengladbach	1996–7	Schalke
1963–4	Real Zaragoza	1979–80	Eintracht Frankfurt	1997–8	Inter Milan
1964–5	Ferencvaros	1980–1	Ipswich Town	1998–9	Parma
1965–6	Barcelona	1981–2	IFK Gothenburg	1999–00	Galatasaray
1966–7	Dynamo Zagreb	1982–3	Anderlecht	2000–01	Liverpool
1967–8	Leeds United	1983–4	Tottenham Hotspur	2001–02	Feyenoord
1968–9	Newcastle United	1984–5	Real Madrid	2002–03	FC Porto
1969–70	Arsenal	1985–6	Real Madrid	2003–04	Valencia
1970–1	Leeds United	1986–7	IFK Gothenbug	2004–05	CSKA Moscow
1971–2	Tottenham Hotspur	1987–8	Bayer Leverkusen	2005–06	Seville
1972–3	Liverpool	1988–9	Napoli		
1973–4	Feyenoord	1989–90	Juventus		
1974–5	Borussia	1990–1	Inter Milan		
	Moenchengladbach	1991–2	Ajax Amsterdam		

ENGLISH FOOTBALL LEAGUE CHAMPIONS (since 1953)

1953–4	Wolverhampton Wanderers	1980–1	Aston Villa
1954–5	Chelsea	1981–2	Liverpool
1955–6	Manchester United	1982–3	Liverpool
1956–7	Manchester United	1983–4	Liverpool
1957–8	Wolverhampton Wanderers	1984–5	Everton
1958–9	Wolverhampton Wanderers	1985–6	Liverpool
1959–60	Burnley	1986–7	Everton
1960–1	Tottenham Hotspur	1987–8	Liverpool
1961–2	Ipswich Town	1988–9	Arsenal
1962–3	Everton	1989–90	Liverpool
1963–4	Liverpool	1990–1	Arsenal
1964–5	Manchester United	1991–2	Leeds United
1965–6	Liverpool	1992–3	Manchester United
1966–7	Manchester United	1993–4	Manchester United
1967–8	Manchester City	1994–5	Blackburn Rovers
1968–9	Leeds United	1995–6	Manchester United
1969–70	Everton	1996–7	Manchester United
1970–1	Arsenal	1997–8	Arsenal
1971–2	Derby County	1998–9	Manchester United
1972–3	Liverpool	1999–00	Manchester United
1973–4	Leeds United	2000–01	Manchester United
1974–5	Derby County	2001–02	Arsenal
1975–6	Liverpool	2002–03	Manchester United
1976–7	Liverpool	2003–04	Arsenal
1977–8	Nottingham Forest	2004–05	Chelsea
1978–9	Liverpool	2005–06	Chelsea
1979–80	Liverpool		

Titles won since Football League began in 1888

18	Liverpool	3	Blackburn Rovers, Chelsea, Huddersfield Town,
15	Manchester United		Leeds United, Wolverhampton Wanderers
13	Arsenal	2	Burnley, Derby County, Manchester City,
9	Everton		Tottenham Hotspur, Portsmouth,
7	Aston Villa		Preston North End
6	Sunderland	1	Ipswich Town, Nottingham Forest,
4	Newcastle United, Sheffield Wednesday		Sheffield United, West Bromwich Albion

ENGLISH FOOTBALL ASSOCIATION CUP WINNERS (since 1953)

1953–4	West Bromwich Albion	1980–1	Tottenham Hotspur
1954–5	Newcastle United	1981–2	Tottenham Hotspur
1955–6	Manchester City	1982–3	Manchester United
1956–7	Aston Villa	1983–4	Everton
1957–8	Bolton Wanderers	1984–5	Manchester United
1958–9	Nottingham Forest	1985–6	Liverpool
1959–60	Wolverhampton Wanderers	1986–7	Coventry City
1960–1	Tottenham Hotspur	1987–8	Wimbledon
1961–2	Tottenham Hotspur	1988–9	Liverpool
1962–3	Manchester United	1989–90	Manchester United
1963–4	West Ham United	1990–1	Tottenham Hotspur
1964–5	Liverpool	1991–2	Liverpool
1965–6	Everton	1992–3	Arsenal
1966–7	Tottenham Hotspur	1993–4	Manchester United
1967–8	West Bromwich Albion	1994–5	Everton
1968–9	Manchester City	1995–6	Manchester United
1969–70	Chelsea	1996–7	Chelsea
1970–1	Arsenal	1997–8	Arsenal
1971–2	Leeds United	1998–9	Manchester United
1972–3	Sunderland	1999–00	Chelsea
1973–4	Liverpool	2000–01	Liverpool
1974–5	West Ham United	2001–02	Arsenal
1975–6	Southampton	2002–03	Arsenal
1976–7	Manchester United	2003–04	Manchester United
1977–8	Ipswich Town	2004–05	Arsenal
1978–9	Arsenal	2005–06	Liverpool
1979–80	West Ham United		

Wins since FA Cup began in 1872

11 Manchester United
10 Arsenal
8 Tottenham Hotspur
7 Aston Villa, Liverpool
6 Blackburn Rovers, Newcastle United
5 Everton, The Wanderers, West Bromwich
　Albion
4 Bolton Wanderers, Manchester City,
　Sheffield United, Wolverhampton
　Wanderers

3 Chelsea, Sheffield Wednesday, West Ham
　United
2 Bury, Nottingham Forest, Old Etonians,
　Preston North End, Sunderland
1 Barnsley, Blackburn Olympic, Blackpool,
　Bradford City, Burnley, Cardiff City, Charlton
　Athletic, Clapham Rovers, Coventry City,
　Derby County, Huddersfield Town, Ipswich
　Town, Leeds United, Notts County, Old
　Carthusians, Oxford University, Portsmouth,
　Royal Engineers, Southampton, Wimbledon

FOOTBALL LEAGUE & FA CUP 'DOUBLE' WINNERS

1888–9	Preston North End	1985–6	Liverpool	1998–9	Manchester United
1896–7	Aston Villa	1993–4	Manchester United		(and also European Champions
1960–1	Tottenham Hotspur	1995–6	Manchester United		Cup)
1970–1	Arsenal	1997–8	Arsenal	2001–02	Arsenal

ENGLISH FOOTBALL LEAGUE CUP (WORTHINGTON, now CARLING, CUP) WINNERS

1960–1	Aston Villa	1983–4	Liverpool
1961–2	Norwich City	1984–5	Norwich City
1962–3	Birmingham City	1985–6	Oxford United
1963–4	Leicester City	1986–7	Arsenal
1964–5	Chelsea	1987–8	Luton Town
1965–6	West Bromwich Albion	1988–9	Nottingham Forest
1966–7	Queen's Park Rangers	1989–90	Nottingham Forest
1967–8	Leeds United	1990–1	Sheffield Wednesday
1968–9	Swindon Town	1991–2	Manchester United
1969–70	Manchester City	1992–3	Arsenal
1970–1	Tottenham Hotspur	1993–4	Aston Villa
1971–2	Stoke City	1994–5	Liverpool
1972–3	Tottenham Hotspur	1995–6	Aston Villa
1973–4	Wolverhampton Wanderers	1996–7	Leicester City
1974–5	Aston Villa	1997–8	Chelsea
1975–6	Manchester City	1998–9	Tottenham Hotspur
1976–7	Aston Villa	1999–00	Leicester City
1977–8	Nottingham Forest	2000–01	Liverpool
1978–9	Nottingham Forest	2001–02	Blackburn Rovers
1979–80	Wolverhampton Wanderers	2002–03	Liverpool
1980–1	Liverpool	2003–04	Middlesbrough
1981–2	Liverpool	2004–05	Chelsea
1982–3	Liverpool	2005–06	Manchester United

SCOTTISH FOOTBALL LEAGUE CHAMPIONS (since 1953)

1953–4	Celtic	1971–2	Celtic	1989–90	Rangers
1954–5	Aberdeen	1972–3	Celtic	1990–1	Rangers
1955–6	Rangers	1973–4	Celtic	1991–2	Rangers
1956–7	Rangers	1974–5	Rangers	1992–3	Rangers
1957–8	Hearts	1975–6	Rangers	1993–4	Rangers
1958–9	Rangers	1976–7	Celtic	1994–5	Rangers
1959–60	Hearts	1977–8	Rangers	1995–6	Rangers
1960–1	Rangers	1978–9	Celtic	1996–7	Rangers
1961–2	Dundee	1979–80	Aberdeen	1997–8	Celtic
1962–3	Rangers	1980–1	Celtic	1998–9	Rangers
1963–4	Rangers	1981–2	Celtic	1999–00	Rangers
1964–5	Kilmarnock	1982–3	Dundee United	2000–01	Celtic
1965–6	Celtic	1983–4	Aberdeen	2001–02	Celtic
1966–7	Celtic	1984–5	Aberdeen	2002–03	Rangers
1967–8	Celtic	1985–6	Celtic	2003–04	Celtic
1968–9	Celtic	1986–7	Rangers	2004–05	Rangers
1969–70	Celtic	1987–8	Celtic	2005–06	Celtic
1970–1	Celtic	1988–9	Rangers		

Titles won since League began in 1890

51	Rangers	4	Aberdeen, Hearts, Hibernian	1	Dundee, Dundee United, Kilmarnock,
40	Celtic	2	Dumbarton		Motherwell, Third Lanark

SCOTTISH CUP WINNERS (since 1959)

1959–60	Rangers	1975–6	Rangers	1991–2	Rangers
1960–1	Dunfermline Athletic	1976–7	Celtic	1992–3	Rangers
1961–2	Rangers	1977–8	Rangers	1993–4	Dundee United
1962–3	Rangers	1978–9	Rangers	1994–5	Celtic
1963–4	Rangers	1979–80	Celtic	1995–6	Rangers
1964–5	Celtic	1980–1	Rangers	1996–7	Kilmarnock
1965–6	Rangers	1981–2	Aberdeen	1997–8	Hearts
1966–7	Celtic	1982–3	Aberdeen	1998–9	Rangers
1967–8	Dunfermline Athletic	1983–4	Aberdeen	1999–00	Rangers
1968–9	Celtic	1984–5	Celtic	2000–01	Celtic
1969–70	Aberdeen	1985–6	Aberdeen	2001–02	Rangers
1970–1	Celtic	1986–7	St Mirren	2002–03	Rangers
1971–2	Celtic	1987–8	Celtic	2003–04	Celtic
1972–3	Rangers	1988–9	Celtic	2004–05	Celtic
1973–4	Celtic	1989–90	Aberdeen	2005–06	Hearts
1974–5	Celtic	1990–1	Motherwell		

Wins since Scottish Cup began in 1873

33	Celtic	2	Dunfermline Athletic, Falkirk, Hibernian,
31	Rangers		Motherwell, Renton, Third Lanark
10	Queen's Park	1	Airdrieonians, Dumbarton, Dundee, Dundee
7	Aberdeen, Hearts		United, East Fife, Morton, Partick Thistle, St
3	Clyde, Kilmarnock, St Mirren, Vale of Leven		Bernard's

SCOTTISH LEAGUE CUP WINNERS (CIS INSURANCE CUP)

1946–7	Rangers	1966–7	Celtic	1986–7	Rangers
1947–8	East Fife	1967–8	Celtic	1987–8	Rangers
1948–9	Rangers	1968–9	Celtic	1988–9	Rangers
1949–50	East Fife	1969–70	Celtic	1989–90	Aberdeen
1950–1	Motherwell	1970–1	Rangers	1990–1	Rangers
1951–2	Dundee	1971–2	Partick Thistle	1991–2	Hibernian
1952–3	Dundee	1972–3	Hibernian	1992–3	Rangers
1953–4	East Fife	1973–4	Dundee	1993–4	Rangers
1954–5	Hearts	1974–5	Celtic	1994–5	Raith Rovers
1955–6	Aberdeen	1975–6	Rangers	1995–6	Aberdeen
1956–7	Celtic	1976–7	Aberdeen	1996–7	Rangers
1957–8	Celtic	1977–8	Rangers	1997–8	Rangers
1958–9	Hearts	1978–9	Rangers	1998–9	Rangers
1959–60	Hearts	1979–80	Dundee United	1999–00	Celtic
1960–1	Rangers	1980–1	Dundee United	2000–01	Celtic
1961–2	Rangers	1981–2	Rangers	2001–02	Rangers
1962–3	Hearts	1982–3	Celtic	2002–03	Rangers
1963–4	Rangers	1983–4	Rangers	2003–04	Livingston
1964–5	Rangers	1984–5	Rangers	2004–05	Rangers
1965–6	Celtic	1985–6	Aberdeen	2005–06	Celtic

SCOTTISH LEAGUE, SCOTTISH CUP AND LEAGUE CUP "TREBLE" WINNERS

1948–9	Rangers	1975–6	Rangers	2000–01	Celtic
1963–4	Rangers	1977–8	Rangers	2002–03	Rangers
1966–7	Celtic	1992–3	Rangers		
1968–9	Celtic	1998–9	Rangers		

ATHLETICS

OLYMPIC CHAMPIONS (SINCE 1952)

Men's 100m
1952	Lindy Remigino (USA)
1956	Bobby Morrow (USA)
1960	Armin Hary (FRG)
1964	Robert Hayes (USA)
1968	James Hines (USA)
1972	Valeriy Borzov (USSR)
1976	Hasely Crawford (Tri)
1980	Allan Wells (UK)
1984	Carl Lewis (USA)
1988	Carl Lewis (USA)
1992	Linford Christie (UK)
1996	Donovan Bailey (Can)
2000	Maurice Green (USA)
2004	Justin Gatlin (USA)

Men's 200m
1952	Andrew Stanfield (USA)
1956	Bobby Morrow (USA)
1960	Livio Berruti (Ita)
1964	Henry Carr (USA)
1968	Tommie Smith (USA)
1972	Valeriy Borzov (USSR)
1976	Donald Quarrie (Jam)
1980	Pietro Mennea (Ita)
1984	Carl Lewis (USA)
1988	Joe DeLoach (USA)
1992	Michael Marsh (USA)
1996	Michael Johnson (USA)
2000	Konstantinos Kenteris (Gre)
2004	Shawn Crawford (USA)

Men's 400m
1952	George Rhoden (Jam)
1956	Charles Jenkins (USA)
1960	Otis Davis (USA)
1964	Michael Larrabee (USA)
1968	Lee Evans (USA
1972	Vincent Matthews (USA)
1976	Alberto Juantorena (Cub)
1980	Viktor Markin (USSR)
1984	Alonzo Babers (USA)

1988	Steve Lewis (USA)
1992	Quincy Watts (USA)
1996	Michael Johnson (USA)
2000	Michael Johnson (USA)
2004	Jeremy Wariner (USA)

Men's 800m
1952	Malvin Whitfield (USA)
1956	Thomas Courtney (USA)
1960	Peter Snell (NZ)
1964	Peter Snell (NZ)
1968	Ralph Doubell (Aus)
1972	David Wottle (USA)
1976	Alberto Juantorena (Cub)
1980	Steve Ovett (UK)
1984	Joaquim Cruz (Bra)
1988	Paul Ereng (Ken)
1992	William Tanui (Ken)
1996	Vebjorn Rodal (Nor)
2000	Nils Schumann (Ger)
2004	Yuri Borzakovski (Rus)

Men's 1500m
1952	Josef Barthel (Lux)
1956	Ron Delany (Ire)
1960	Herbert Elliott (Aus)
1964	Peter Snell (NZ)
1968	Kipchoge Keino (Ken)
1972	Pekka Vasala (Fin)
1976	John Walker (NZ)
1980	Sebastian Coe (UK)
1984	Sebastian Coe (UK)
1988	Peter Rono (Ken)
1992	Fermin Cacho (Spa)
1996	Noureddine Morceli (Alg)
2000	Noah Ngeny (Ken)
2004	Hicham El Guerrouj (Mor)

Men's 5000m
1952	Emil Zatopek (Cze)
1956	Vladimir Kuts (USSR)
1960	Murray Halberg (NZ)
1964	Robert Schul (USA)

1968 Mohamed Gammoudi (Tun)	
1972 Lasse Viren (Fin)	
1976 Lasse Viren (Fin)	
1980 Miruts Yifter (Eth)	
1984 Saïd Aouita (Mor)	
1988 John Ngugi (Ken)	
1992 Dieter Baumann (Ger)	
1996 Venuste Nyongabo (Bur)	
2000 Millon Wolde (Eth)	
2004 Hicham El Guerrouj (Mor)	

Men's 10,000m
1952 Emil Zátopek (Cze)
1956 Vladimir Kuts (USSR)
1960 Pyotr Bolotnikov (USSR)
1964 William Mills (USA)
1968 Naftali Temu (Ken)
1972 Lasse Viren (Fin)
1976 Lasse Viren (Fin)
1980 Miruts Yifter (Eth)
1984 Alberto Cova (Ita)
1988 Brahim Boutayeb (Mor)
1992 Khalid Skah (Mor)
1996 Haile Gebrselassie (Eth)
2000 Haile Gebrselassie (Eth)
2004 Kenenisa Bekele (Eth)

Men's Marathon
1952 Emil Zátopek (Cze)
1956 Alain Mimoun (Fra)
1960 Abebe Bikila (Eth)
1964 Abebe Bikila (Eth)
1968 Mamo Wolde (Eth)
1972 Frank Shorter (USA)
1976 Waldemar Cierpinski (GDR)
1980 Waldemar Cierpinski (GDR)
1984 Carlos Lopes (Por)
1988 Gelindo Bordin (Ita)
1992 Hwang Young-jo (SKo)
1996 Josiah Thugwane (SA)
2000 Gezaghne Abera (Eth)
2004 Stefano Baldini (Ita)

Men's 3000m Steeplechase
1952 Horace Ashenfelter (USA)
1956 Christopher Brasher (UK)
1960 Zdzislaw Kryszkowiak (Pol)
1964 Gaston Roelants (Bel)
1968 Amos Biwott (Ken)
1972 Kipchoge Keino (Ken)
1976 Anders Gärderud (Swe)
1980 Bronislaw Malinowski (Pol)
1984 Julius Korir (Ken)
1988 Julius Kariuki (Ken)
1992 Matthew Birir (Ken)
1996 Joseph Keter (Ken)
2000 Reuben Kosgei (Ken)
2004 Ezekiel Kemboi (Ken)

Men's 110m Hurdles
1952 Harrison Dillard (USA)
1956 Lee Calhoun (USA)
1960 Lee Calhoun (USA)
1964 Hayes Jones (USA)
1968 Willie Davenport (USA)
1972 Rodney Milburn (USA)
1976 Guy Drut (Fra)
1980 Thomas Munkelt (GDR)
1984 Roger Kingdom (USA)
1988 Roger Kingdom (USA)
1992 Mark McKoy (Can)
1996 Allen Johnson (USA)
2000 Anier Garcia (Cub)
2004 Liu Xiang (Chi)

Men's 400m Hurdles
1952 Charles Moore (USA)
1956 Glenn Davis (USA)
1960 Glenn Davis (USA)
1964 Rex Cawley (USA)
1968 David Hemery (UK)
1972 John Akii-Bua (Uga)
1976 Edwin Moses (USA)
1980 Volker Beck (GDR)
1984 Edwin Moses (USA)
1988 Andre Phillips (USA)
1992 Kevin Young (USA)
1996 Derrick Adkins (USA)
2000 Angelo Taylor (USA)
2004 Felix Sanchez (Dom)

Men's High Jump
1952 Walter Davis (USA)
1956 Charles Dumas (USA)
1960 Robert Shavlakadze (USSR)
1964 Valeriy Brumel (USSR)
1968 Dick Fosbury (USA)
1972 Jüri Tarmak (USSR)
1976 Jacek Wszola (Pol)
1980 Gerd Wessig (GDR)
1984 Dietmar Mögenburg (FRG)
1988 Gennadiy Avdeyenko (USSR)
1992 Javier Sotomayor (Cub)
1996 Charles Austin (USA)
2000 Sergey Kliugin (Rus)
2004 Stefan Holm (Swe)

Men's Pole Vault
1952 Robert Richards (USA)
1956 Robert Richards (USA)
1960 Donald Bragg (USA)
1964 Frederick Hansen (USA)
1968 Bob Seagren (USA)
1972 Wolfgang Nordwig (GDR)
1976 Tadeusz Slusarski (Pol)
1980 Wladyslaw Kozakiewicz (Pol)
1984 Pierre Quinon (Fra)
1988 Sergey Bubka (USSR)
1992 Maksim Tarasov (CIS/Rus)
1996 Jean Galfione (Fra)
2000 Nick Hysong (USA)
2004 Tim Mack (USA)

Men's Triple Jump
1952 Adhemar Ferreira da Silva (Bra)
1956 Adhemar Ferreira da Silva (Bra)
1960 Jozef Schmidt (Pol)
1964 Jozef Schmidt (Pol)
1968 Viktor Saneyev (USSR)
1972 Viktor Saneyev (USSR)
1976 Viktor Saneyev (USSR)
1980 Jaak Uudmäe (USSR)
1984 Al Joyner (USA)
1988 Khristo Markov (Bul)
1992 Mike Conley (USA)
1996 Kenny Harrison (USA)
2000 Jonathan Edwards (UK)
2004 Christian Olsson (Swe)

Men's Long Jump
1952 Jerome Biffle (USA)
1956 Gregory Bell (USA)
1960 Ralph Boston (USA)
1964 Lynn Davies (UK)
1968 Bob Beamon (USA)
1972 Randy Williams (USA)
1976 Arnie Robinson (USA)
1980 Lutz Dombrowski (GDR)
1984 Carl Lewis (USA)
1988 Carl Lewis (USA)
1992 Carl Lewis (USA)
1996 Carl Lewis (USA)
2000 Ivan Pedroso (Cub)
2004 Dwight Phillips (USA)

Men's Shot
1952 Parry O'Brien (USA)
1956 Parry O'Brien (USA)
1960 William Nieder (USA)
1964 Dallas Long (USA)
1968 Randy Matson (USA)
1972 Wladyslaw Komar (Pol)
1976 Udo Beyer (GDR)
1980 Vladimir Kiselyov (USSR)
1984 Alessandro Andrei (Ita)
1988 Ulf Timmermann (GDR)
1992 Mike Stulce (USA)
1996 Randy Barnes (USA)
2000 Arsi Harju (Fin)
2004 Yuri Belonog (Ukr)

Men's Discus
1952 Sim Iness (USA)
1956 Al Oerter (USA)
1960 Al Oerter (USA)
1964 Al Oerter (USA)
1968 Al Oerter (USA)
1972 Ludvik Danek (Cze)
1976 Mac Wilkins (USA)
1980 Viktor Rashchupkin (USSR)
1984 Rolf Danneberg (FRG)
1988 Jürgen Schult (GDR)
1992 Romas Ubartas (Lit)
1996 Lars Riedel (Ger)
2000 Virgilijus Alekna (Lit)
2004 Virgilijus Alekna (Lit)

Men's Javelin
1952   Cyrus Young (USA)
1956   Egil Danielsen (Nor)
1960   Viktor Tsibulenko (USSR)
1964   Pauli Nevala (Fin)
1968   Janis Lusis (USSR)
1972   Klaus Wolfermann (FRG)
1976   Miklós Németh (Hun)
1980   Dainis Kula (USSR)
1984   Arto Harkönen (Fin)
1988   Tapio Korjus (Fin)
1992   Jan Zelezny (Cze)
1996   Jan Zelezny (Cze. Rep)
2000   Jan Zelezny (Cze. Rep)
2004   Andreas Thorkildsen (Nor)

Men's Hammer
1952   József Csermak (Hun)
1956   Harold Connolly (USA)
1960   Vasiliy Rudenkov (USSR)
1964   Romuald Klim (USSR)
1968   Gyula Zsivótzky (Hun)
1972   Anatoliy Bondarchuk (USSR)
1976   Yuriy Sedykh (USSR)
1980   Yuriy Sedykh (USSR)
1984   Juha Tiainen (Fin)
1988   Sergey Litvinov (USSR)
1992   Andrey Abduvaliyev (CIS/Tjk)
1996   Balazs Kiss (Hun)
2000   Szymon Ziolkowski (Pol)
2004   Koji Murofushi (Jap)

Men's Decathlon
1952   Robert Mathias (USA)
1956   Milton Campbell (USA)
1960   Rafer Johnson (USA)
1964   Willi Holdorf (FRG)
1968   Bill Toomey (USA)
1972   Nikolay Avilov (USSR)
1976   Bruce Jenner (USA)
1980   Daley Thompson (UK)
1984   Daley Thompson (UK)
1988   Christian Schenk (GDR)
1992   Robert Zmelik (Cze)
1996   Dan O'Brien (USA)
2000   Erki Nool (Est)
2004   Roman Sebrle (Cze)

Men's 20km Walk
1960   Vladimir Golubnichiy (USSR)
1964   Kenneth Matthews (UK)
1968   Vladimir Golubnichiy (USSR)
1972   Peter Frenkel (GDR)
1976   Daniel Bautista (Mex)
1980   Maurizio Damilano (Ita)
1984   Ernesto Canto (Mex)
1988   Jozef Pribilinec (Cze)
1992   Daniel Plaza (Spa)
1996   Jefferson Perez (Ecu)
2000   Robert Korzeniowski (Pol)
2004   Ivano Brugnetti (Ita)

Men's 50km Walk
1952   Giuseppe Dordoni (Ita)
1956   Norman Read (NZ)
1960   Don Thompson (UK)
1964   Abdon Pamich (Ita)
1968   Christophe Höhne (GDR)
1972   Bernd Kannenberg (GDR)
1980   Hartwig Gauder (GDR)
1984   Raúl Gonzales (Mex)
1988   Vyacheslav Ivanenko (USSR)
1992   Andrey Perlov (CIS/Rus)
1996   Robert Korzeniowski (Pol)
2000   Robert Korzeniowski (Pol)
2004   Robert Korzeniowski (Pol)

Men's 4 × 100m Relay
1952	USA	1980	USSR
1956	USA	1984	USA
1960	West Germany	1988	USSR
1964	USA	1992	USA
1968	USA	1996	Canada
1972	USA	2000	USA
1976	USA	2004	UK

Men's 4 × 400m Relay
1952	Jamaica	1980	USSR
1956	USA	1984	USA
1960	USA	1988	USA
1964	USA	1992	USA
1968	USA	1996	USA
1972	Kenya	2000	USA
1976	USA	2004	USA

Women's 100m
1952   Marjorie Jackson (Aus)
1956   Betty Cuthbert (Aus)
1960   Wilma Rudolph (USA)
1964   Wyomia Tyus (USA)
1968   Wyomia Tyus (USA)
1972   Renate Stecher (GDR)
1976   Annegret Richter (FRG)
1980   Lyudmila Kondratyeva (USSR)
1984   Evelyn Ashford (USA)
1988   Florence Griffith-Joyner (USA)
1992   Gail Devers (USA)
1996   Gail Devers (USA)
2000   Marion Jones (USA)
2004   Yuliya Nesterenko (Bel)

Women's 200m
1952   Marjorie Jackson (Aus)
1956   Betty Cuthbert (Aus)
1960   Wilma Rudolph (USA)
1964   Edith Maguire (USA)
1968   Irena Szewinska (Pol)
1972   Renate Stecher (GDR)
1976   Bärbel Eckert (GDR)
1980   Bärbel Wöckel (née Eckert) (GDR)
1984   Valerie Brisco-Hooks (USA)
1988   Florence Griffith-Joyner (USA)
1992   Gwen Torrance (USA)
1996   Marie-Jose Perec (Fra)
2000   Marion Jones (USA)
2004   Veronica Campbell (Jam)

Women's 400m
1964   Betty Cuthbert (Aus)
1968   Colette Besson (Fra)
1972   Monika Zehrt (GDR)
1976   Irena Szewinska (Pol)
1980   Marita Koch (GDR)
1984   Valerie Brisco-Hooks (USA)
1988   Olga Bryzgina (USSR)
1992   Marie-José Pérec (Fra)
1996   Marie-Jose Pérec (Fra)
2000   Cathy Freeman (Aus)
2004   Tonique Williams (Bah)

Women's 800m
1960   Lyudmila Shevtsova (USSR)
1964   Ann Packer (UK)
1968   Madeline Manning (USA)
1972   Hildegard Falck (FRG)
1976   Tatyana Kazankina (USSR)
1980   Nadezhda Olizarenko (USSR)
1984   Doina Melinte (Rom)
1988   Sigrun Wodars (GDR)
1992   Ellen van Langren (Hol)
1996   Svetlana Masterkova (Rus)
2000   Maria Mutola (Moz)
2004   Kelly Holmes (UK)

Women's 1500m
1972   Lyudmila Bragina (USSR)
1976   Tatyana Kazankina (USSR)
1980   Tatyana Kazankina (USSR)
1984   Gabriella Doria (Ita)
1988   Paula Ivan (Rom)
1992   Hassiba Boulmerka (Alg)
1996   Svetlana Masterkova (Rus)
2000   Nouria Merah-Benida (Alg)
2004   Kelly Holmes (UK)

Women's 5000m*
1984   Maricica Puica (Rom)
1988   Tatyana Samolenko (USSR)
1992   Yelena Romanova (CIS/Rus)
1996   Wang Junxia (Chn)
2000   Gabriela Szabo (Rom)
2004   Meseret Defar (Eth)

*This event was 3000m before 1996.

Women's 10,000m
1988   Olga Bondarenko (USSR)
1992   Derartu Tulu (Eth)
1996   Fernanda Ribeiro (Por)
2000   Derartu Tulu (Eth)
2004   Xing Huina (Chi)

Women's Marathon
1984   Joan Benoit (USA)
1988   Rosa Mota (Por)

1992 Valentina Yegorova (CIS/Rus)
1996 Fatuma Roba (Eth)
2000 Naoko Takahashi (Jpn)
2004 Mizuki Noguchi (Jap)

Women's 80m Hurdles*
1952 Shirley Strickland (Aus)
1956 Shirley Strickland (Aus)
1960 Irina Press (USSR)
1964 Karin Balzer (GDR)
1968 Maureen Caird (Aus)
*Event defunct since 1968. Now 100m

Women's 100m Hurdles
1972 Annelie Ehrhardt (GDR)
1976 Johanna Schaller (GDR)
1980 Vera Komisova (USSR)
1984 Benita Fitzgerald-Brown (USA)
1988 Yordanka Donkova (Bul)
1992 Paraskevi Patoulidou (Gre)
1996 Lyudmila Engquist (Swe)
2000 Olga Shishigina (Kaz)
2004 Joanna Hayes (USA)

Women's 400m Hurdles
1984 Newal El Moutawakil (Mor)
1988 Debbie Flintoff-King (Aus)
1992 Sally Gunnell (UK)
1996 Deon Hemmings (Jam)
2000 Irina Privalova (Rus)
2004 Fani Halkia (Gre)

Women's High Jump
1952 Esther Brand (SAf)
1956 Mildred McDaniel (USA)
1960 Iolanda Balas (Rom)
1964 Iolanda Balas (Rom)
1968 Miloslava Rezková (Cze)
1972 Ulrike Meyfarth (FRG)
1976 Rosemarie Ackermann (GDR)
1980 Sara Simeoni (Ita)
1984 Ulrike Meyfarth (FRG)
1988 Louise Ritter (USA)
1992 Heike Henkel (Ger)
1996 Stefka Kostadinova (Bul)
2000 Yelena Yelesina (Rus)
2004 Yelena Slesarenko (Ukr)

Women's Long Jump
1952 Yvette Williams (NZ)
1956 Elzbieta Krzesinska (Pol)
1960 Vyera Krepkina (USSR)
1964 Mary Rand (UK)
1968 Viorica Viscopoleanu (Rom)
1972 Heide Rosendahl (FRG)
1976 Angela Voigt (GDR)
1980 Tatyana Kolpakova (USSR)
1984 Anisoara Stanciu (Rom)
1988 Jackie Joyner-Kersee (USA)
1992 Heike Drechsler (Ger)
1996 Chioma Ajunwa (Nig)
2000 Heike Drechsler (Ger)
2004 Tatyana Lebedeva (Rus)

Women's Discus
1952 Nina Ponomaryeva (USSR)
1956 Olga Fikotová (Cze)
1960 Nina Ponomaryeva (USSR)
1964 Tamara Press (USSR)
1968 Lia Manoliu (Rom)
1972 Faina Melnik (USSR)
1976 Evelin Schlaak (GDR)
1980 Evelin Jahl (née Schlaak) (GDR)
1984 Ria Stalmach (Hol)
1988 Martina Hellmann (GDR)
1992 Maritza Marten (Cub)
1996 Ilke Wyludda (Ger)

2000 Ellina Zvereva (Blr)
2004 Natalya Sadova (Rus)

Women's Javelin
1952 Dana Zátopková (Cze)
1956 Inese Jaunzeme (USSR)
1960 Elvira Ozolina (USSR)
1964 Mihaela Penes (Rom)
1968 Angéla Németh (Hun)
1972 Ruth Fuchs (GDR)
1976 Ruth Fuchs (GDR)
1980 Maria C. Colon (Cub)
1984 Tessa Sanderson (UK)
1988 Petra Felke (GDR)
1992 Silke Renk (Ger)
1996 Heli Rantanen (Nor)
2000 Trine Hattestad (Nor)
2004 Osleidys Menendez (Cub)

Women's Heptathlon
1984 Glynis Nunn (Aus)
1988 Jackie Joyner-Kersee (USA)
1992 Jackie Joyner-Kersee (USA)
1996 Ghada Shouaa (Syr)
2000 Denise Lewis (UK)
2004 Carolina Kluft (Swe)

Women's 20km Walk
1992 Chen Yueling (Chn)
1996 Yelena Nikolayeva (Rus)
2000 Liping Wang (Chn)
2004 Athanasia Tsoumeleka (Gre)

Women's 4 × 100m Relay
1952 USA
1956 Australia
1960 USA
1964 Poland
1968 USA
1972 West Germany
1976 East Germany
1980 East Germany
1984 USA
1988 USA
1992 USA
1996 USA
2000 Bahamas
2004 Jamaica

Women's 4 × 400m Relay
1972 East Germany
1976 East Germany
1980 USSR
1984 USA
1988 USSR
1992 CIS (united team)
1996 USA
2000 USA
2004 USA

Women's Triple Jump
1996 Inessa Kravets (Ukr)
2000 Tereza Marinova (Bul)
2004 Françoise Mbango (Cam)

Women's Pole Vault**
2000 Stacy Dragila (USA)
2004 Yelena Isinbayeva (Rus)

Women's Hammer**
2000 Kamila Skolimowska (Pol)
2004 Olga Kuzenkova (Rus)
**Completely new events in 2000

BADMINTON

WORLD CHAMPIONS

	MEN	WOMEN
1977	Flemming Delfs (Denmark)	Lene Koppen (Denmark)
1980	Rudy Hartono (Indonesia)	Wiharjo Verawaty (Indonesia)
1983	Icuk Sugiarto (Indonesia)	Li Lingwei (China)
1985	Han Jian (China)	Han Aiping (China)
1987	Yang Yang (China)	Han Aiping (China)
1989	Yang Yang (China)	Li Lingwei (China)
1991	Zhao Jianhua (China)	Tang Jiuhong (China)
1993	Joko Suprianto (Indonesia)	Susi Susanti (Indonesia)
1995	Heryanto Arbi (Indonesia)	Ye Zhaoying (China)
1997	Peter Rasmussen (Denmark)	Ye Zhaoying (China)
1999	Sun Jun (China)	Camilla Martin (Denmark)
2001	Hendrawan (Indonesia)	Gong Ruina (China)
2003	Xia Xuanze (China)	Zhang Ning (China)
2005	Taufik Hidayat (Indonesia)	Xingfang Xie (China)

ALL-ENGLAND CHAMPIONS (since 1953)

	MEN	WOMEN
1953	Eddie Choong (Malaya)	Marie Ussing (Denmark)
1954	Eddie Choong (Malaya)	Judy Devlin (USA)
1955	Wong Peng Soon (Malaya)	Margaret Varner (USA)
1956	Eddie Choong (Malaya)	Margaret Varner (USA)
1957	Eddie Choong (Malaya)	Judy Devlin (USA)
1958	Erland Kops (Denmark)	Judy Devlin (USA)
1959	Tan Joe Hok (Indonesia)	Heather Ward (England)
1960	Erland Kops (Denmark)	Judy Devlin (USA)
1961	Erland Kops (Denmark)	Judy Hashman (née Devlin) (USA)
1962	Erland Kops (Denmark)	Judy Hashman (USA)
1963	Erland Kops (Denmark)	Judy Hashman (USA)
1964	Knud Nielsen (Denmark)	Judy Hashman (USA)
1965	Erland Kops (Denmark)	Ursula Smith (England)
1966	Tan Aik Huang (Malaya)	Judy Hashman (USA)
1967	Erland Kops (Denmark)	Judy Hashman (USA)
1968	Rudy Hartono (Indonesia)	Eva Twedberg (Sweden)
1969	Rudy Hartono (Indonesia)	Hiroe Yuki (Japan)
1970	Rudy Hartono (Indonesia)	Etsuko Takenaka (Japan)
1971	Rudy Hartono (Indonesia)	Eva Twedberg (Sweden)
1972	Rudy Hartono (Indonesia)	Noriko Nakayama (Japan)
1973	Rudy Hartono (Indonesia)	Margaret Beck (England)
1974	Rudy Hartono (Indonesia)	Hiroe Yuki (Japan)
1975	Sven Pri (Denmark)	Hiroe Yuki (Japan)
1976	Rudy Hartono (Indonesia)	Gillian Gilks (England)
1977	Flemming Delfs (Denmark)	Hiroe Yuki (Japan)
1978	Liem Swie King (Indonesia)	Gillian Gilks (England)
1979	Liem Swie King (Indonesia)	Lene Koppen (Denmark)
1980	Prakash Padukone (India)	Lene Koppen (Denmark)
1981	Liem Swie King (Indonesia)	Sun Ai Hwang (South Korea)
1982	Morten Frost (Denmark)	Zang Ailing (China)
1983	Luan Jin (China)	Zang Ailing (China)
1984	Morten Frost (Denmark)	Li Lingwei (China)
1985	Zhao Jianhua (China)	Han Aiping (China)
1986	Morten Frost (Denmark)	Kim Yun-Ja (South Korea)
1987	Morten Frost (Denmark)	Kirsten Larsen (Denmark)
1988	Ib Frederiksen (Denmark)	Gu Jiaming (China)
1989	Yang Yang (China)	Li Lingwei (China)
1990	Zhao Jianhua (China)	Susi Susanti (Indonesia)
1991	Ardy Wiranta (Indonesia)	Susi Susanti (Indonesia)
1992	Liu Jun (China)	Tang Jiuhong (China)
1993	Heryanto Arbi (Indonesia)	Susi Susanti (Indonesia)
1994	Heryanto Arbi (Indonesia)	Susi Susanti (Indonesia)
1995	Poul-Erik Hoyer Larsen (Denmark)	Lim Xiaoqing (Sweden)
1996	Poul-Erik Hoyer Larsen (Denmark)	Bang Soo-Hyun (South Korea)
1997	Dong Jiong (China)	Ye Zhaoying (China)
1998	Sun Jun (China)	Ye Zhaoying (China)
1999	Peter Gade Christensen (Denmark)	Ye Zhaoying (China)
2000	Xia Xuanze (China)	Gong Zhichao (China)
2001	Pulella Gopichand (India)	Gong Zhichao (China)
2002	Hong Chen (China)	Camilla Martin (Denmark)
2003	Muhammad Hafiz Hashim (Malaysia)	Mi Zhou (China)
2004	Dan Lin (China)	Ruina Gong (China)
2005	Hong Chen (China)	Xingfang Xie (China)

BASEBALL

WORLD SERIES WINNERS (POST WAR)

1946	St Louis Cardinals	1954	New York Yankees	1962	New York Yankees
1947	New York Yankees	1955	Brooklyn Dodgers	1963	Los Angeles Dodgers
1948	Cleveland Indians	1956	New York Yankees	1964	St Louis Cardinals
1949	New York Yankees	1957	Milwaukee Braves	1965	Los Angeles Dodgers
1950	New York Yankees	1958	New York Yankees	1966	Baltimore Orioles
1951	New York Yankees	1959	Los Angeles Dodgers	1967	St Louis Cardinals
1952	New York Yankees	1960	Pittsburgh Pirates	1968	Detroit Tigers
1953	New York Yankees	1961	New York Yankees	1969	New York Mets

BASEBALL

1970	Baltimore Orioles	1982	St Louis Cardinals	1994	No Competition
1971	Pittsburgh Pirates	1983	Baltimore Orioles	1995	Atlanta Braves
1972	Oakland Athletics	1984	Detroit Tigers	1996	New York Yankees
1973	Oakland Athletics	1985	Kansas City Royals	1997	Florida Marlins
1974	Oakland Athletics	1986	New York Mets	1998	New York Yankees
1975	Cincinnati Reds	1987	Minnesota Twins	1999	New York Yankees
1976	Cincinnati Reds	1988	Los Angeles Dodgers	2000	New York Yankees
1977	New York Yankees	1989	Oakland Athletics	2001	Arizona Diamondbacks
1978	New York Yankees	1990	Cincinnati Reds	2002	Anaheim Angels
1979	Pittsburgh Pirates	1991	Minnesota Twins	2003	Florida Marlins
1980	Philadelphia Phillies	1992	Toronto Blue Jays	2004	Boston Red Sox
1981	Los Angeles Dodgers	1993	Toronto Blue Jays	2005	Chicago White Sox

Wins since World Series began in 1903

26	New York Yankees	
9	St Louis Cardinals	
6	Boston Red Sox	
5	Cincinnati Reds, Los Angeles Dodgers, New York Giants, Philadelphia Athletics, Pittsburgh Pirates	
4	Detroit Tigers, Oakland Athletics	
3	Baltimore Orioles, Chicago White Sox	
2	Atlanta Braves, Chicago Cubs, Cleveland Indians, Florida Marlins, Minnesota Twins, New York Mets, Toronto Blue Jays	
1	Anaheim Angels, Arizona Diamondbacks, Brooklyn Dodgers, Kansas City Royals, Milwaukee Braves, Philadelphia Phillies, Washington Senators	

BASKETBALL

WORLD CHAMPIONS

MEN

				WOMEN				
1950	Argentina	1978	Yugoslavia	1953	USA	1979	USA
1954	USA	1982	USSR	1957	USA	1983	USSR
1959	Brazil	1986	USA	1959	USSR	1987	USA
1963	Brazil	1990	Yugoslavia	1964	USSR	1990	USA
1967	USSR	1994	USA	1967	USSR	1994	Brazil
1970	Yugoslavia	1998	Yugoslavia	1971	USSR	1998	USA
1974	USSR	2002	Yugoslavia	1975	USSR	2002	USA

NBA CHAMPIONS (since 1980)

1980	Los Angeles Lakers	1989	Detroit Pistons	1998	Chicago Bulls
1981	Boston Celtics	1990	Detroit Pistons	1999	San Antonio Spurs
1982	Los Angeles Lakers	1991	Chicago Bulls	2000	Los Angeles Lakers
1983	Philadelphia 76ers	1992	Chicago Bulls	2001	Los Angeles Lakers
1984	Boston Celtics	1993	Chicago Bulls	2002	Los Angeles Lakers
1985	Los Angeles Lakers	1994	Houston Rockets	2003	San Antonio Spurs
1986	Boston Celtics	1995	Houston Rockets	2004	Detroit Pistons
1987	Los Angeles Lakers	1996	Chicago Bulls	2005	San Antonio Spurs
1988	Los Angeles Lakers	1997	Chicago Bulls		

BOWLS

WORLD OUTDOOR CHAMPIONS

Men's Singles

1966	David Bryant (Eng)	1988	David Bryant (Eng)
1972	Maldwyn Evans (Wal)	1992	Tony Allcock (Eng)
1976	Doug Watson (SAf)	1996	Tony Allcock (Eng)
1980	David Bryant (Eng)	2000	Jeremy Henry (Ire)
1984	Peter Belliss (NZ)	2004	Steve Glasson (Aus)

Women's Singles

1969	Gladys Doyle (PNG)	1988	Janet Ackland (Wal)
1973	Elsie Wilkie (NZ)	1992	Margaret Johnston (Ire)
1977	Elsie Wilkie (NZ)	1996	Carmelita Anderson (NZ)
1981	Norma Shaw (Eng)	2000	Margaret Johnston (Ire)
1985	Merle Richardson (Aus)	2004	Margaret Johnston (Ire)*

*The first woman to win the title three times.

CRICKET

For a note on the history of **The Ashes**, *see* **L10**.

WORLD CUP*

1975	West Indies	1992	Pakistan
1979	West Indies	1996	Sri Lanka
1983	India	1999	Australia
1987	Australia	2003	Australia

*The 2007 World Cup takes place in the West Indies.

COUNTY CHAMPIONSHIP (POST WAR)

1946	Yorkshire	1965	Worcestershire	1985	Middlesex
1947	Middlesex	1966	Yorkshire	1986	Essex
1948	Glamorgan	1967	Yorkshire	1987	Nottinghamshire
1949	Middlesex	1968	Yorkshire	1988	Worcestershire
	Yorkshire	1969	Glamorgan	1989	Worcestershire
1950	Lancashire	1970	Kent	1990	Middlesex
	Surrey	1971	Surrey	1991	Essex
1951	Warwickshire	1972	Warwickshire	1992	Essex
1952	Surrey	1973	Hampshire	1993	Middlesex
1953	Surrey	1974	Worcestershire	1994	Warwickshire
1954	Surrey	1975	Leicestershire	1995	Warwickshire
1955	Surrey	1976	Middlesex	1996	Leicestershire
1956	Surrey	1977	Kent	1997	Glamorgan
1957	Surrey		Middlesex	1998	Leicestershire
1958	Surrey	1978	Kent	1999	Surrey
1959	Yorkshire	1979	Essex	2000	Surrey
1960	Yorkshire	1980	Middlesex	2001	Yorkshire
1961	Hampshire	1981	Nottinghamshire	2002	Surrey
1962	Yorkshire	1982	Middlesex	2003	Sussex
1963	Yorkshire	1983	Essex	2004	Warwickshire
1964	Worcestershire	1984	Essex	2005	Nottinghamshire

Wins and shared wins since Championship began in 1864

34	Yorkshire	6	Essex, Warwickshire
22	Surrey	5	Worcestershire
20	Nottinghamshire	4	Gloucestershire
13	Middlesex	3	Glamorgan, Leicestershire
12	Lancashire	2	Hampshire
7	Kent	1	Derbyshire, Sussex

C & G CUP (formerly NATWEST BANK TROPHY)

1963	Sussex	1978	Sussex	1993	Warwickshire
1964	Sussex	1979	Somerset	1994	Worcestershire
1965	Yorkshire	1980	Middlesex	1995	Warwickshire
1966	Warwickshire	1981	Derbyshire	1996	Lancashire
1967	Kent	1982	Surrey	1997	Essex
1968	Warwickshire	1983	Somerset	1998	Lancashire
1969	Yorkshire	1984	Middlesex	1999	Gloucestershire
1970	Lancashire	1985	Essex	2000	Gloucestershire
1971	Lancashire	1986	Sussex	2001	Somerset
1972	Lancashire	1987	Nottinghamshire	2002	Yorkshire
1973	Gloucestershire	1988	Middlesex	2003	Gloucestershire
1974	Kent	1989	Warwickshire	2004	Gloucestershire
1975	Lancashire	1990	Lancashire	2005	Hampshire
1976	Northamptonshire	1991	Hampshire		
1977	Middlesex	1992	Northamptonshire		

SUNDAY LEAGUE WINNERS (currently the TOTESPORT NATIONAL LEAGUE)

1969	Lancashire	1982	Sussex	1995	Kent
1970	Lancashire	1983	Yorkshire	1996	Surrey
1971	Worcestershire	1984	Essex	1997	Warwickshire
1972	Kent	1985	Essex	1998	Lancashire
1973	Kent	1986	Hampshire	1999	Lancashire
1974	Leicestershire	1987	Worcestershire	2000	Gloucestershire
1975	Hampshire	1988	Worcestershire	2001	Kent
1976	Kent	1989	Lancashire	2002	Glamorgan
1977	Leicestershire	1990	Lancashire	2003	Surrey
1978	Hampshire	1991	Nottinghamshire	2004	Glamorgan
1979	Somerset	1992	Middlesex	2005	Essex
1980	Warwickshire	1993	Glamorgan		
1981	Essex	1994	Warwickshire		

BENSON & HEDGES CUP WINNERS

1972	Leicestershire	1983	Middlesex	1993	Derbyshire
1973	Kent	1984	Lancashire	1994	Warwickshire
1974	Surrey	1985	Leicestershire	1995	Lancashire
1975	Leicestershire	1986	Middlesex	1996	Lancashire
1976	Kent	1987	Yorkshire	1997	Surrey
1977	Gloucestershire	1988	Hampshire	1998	Essex
1978	Kent	1989	Nottinghamshire	1999	Gloucestershire
1979	Essex	1990	Lancashire	2000	Gloucestershire
1980	Northamptonshire	1991	Worcestershire	2001	Surrey
1981	Somerset	1992	Hampshire	2002	Warwickshire*
1982	Somerset				

*This was the last Benson & Hedges final after 31 years.

This newest ECB domestic cricket competition was first won in 2003 by Surrey Lions who convincingly beat Warwickshire Bears by 9 wickets. In the semi-finals, Warwickshire Bears beat Leicestershire Foxes and Surrey Lions beat Gloucestershire Gladiators by just 5 runs.

Winners

2003 Surrey Lions
2004 Leicestershire Foxes

2005 Somerset

CYCLING

TOUR DE FRANCE

1982	Bernard Hinault (Fra)	1994	Miguel Indurain (Spa)
1983	Laurent Fignon (Fra)	1995	Miguel Indurain (Spa)
1984	Laurent Fignon (Fra)	1996	Bjarne Riis (Den)
1985	Bernard Hinault (Fra)	1997	Jan Ullrich (Ger)
1986	Greg Lemond (USA)	1998	Marco Pantani (Ita)
1987	Stephen Roche (Ire)	1999	Lance Armstrong (USA)
1988	Pedro Delgado (Spa)	2000	Lance Armstrong (USA)
1989	Greg Lemond (USA)	2001	Lance Armstrong (USA)
1990	Greg Lemond (USA)	2002	Lance Armstrong (USA)
1991	Miguel Indurain (Spa)	2003	Lance Armstrong (USA)
1992	Miguel Indurain (Spa)	2004	Lance Armstrong (USA)
1993	Miguel Indurain (Spa)	2005	Lance Armstrong (USA)*

*In 2005 Lance Armstrong announced his retirement, following a record seven successive victories.

GOLF

MAJOR TOURNAMENT WINNERS (POST WAR)

	The Open	US Open	US Masters	PGA
1946	S Snead (USA)	L Mangrum (USA)	H Keiser (USA)	B Hogan (USA)
1947	F Daly (GBR)	L Worsham (USA)	J Demaret (USA)	J Ferrier (USA)
1948	H Cotton (GBR)	B Hogan (USA)	C Harmon (USA)	B Hogan (USA)
1949	B Locke (SAf)	C Middlecoff (USA)	S Snead (USA)	S Snead (USA)
1950	B Locke (SAf)	B Hogan (USA)	J Demaret (USA)	C Harper (USA)
1951	M Faulkner (GBR)	B Hogan (USA)	B Hogan (USA)	S Snead (USA)
1952	B Locke (SAf)	J Boros (USA)	S Snead (USA)	J Turnesa (USA)
1953	B Hogan (USA)	B Hogan (USA)	B Hogan (USA)	W Burkemo (USA)
1954	P Thomson (Aus)	E Furgol (USA)	S Snead (USA)	C Harbert (USA)
1955	P Thomson (Aus)	J Fleck (USA)	C Middlecoff (USA)	D Ford (USA)
1956	P Thomson (Aus)	C Middlecoff (USA)	J Burke (USA)	J Burke (USA)
1957	B Locke (SAf)	D Mayer (USA)	D Ford (USA)	L Herbert (USA)
1958	P Thomson (Aus)	T Bolt (USA)	A Palmer (USA)	D Finsterwald (USA)
1959	G Player (SAf)	B Caspar (USA)	A Wall (USA)	B Roseburg (USA)
1960	K Nagle (Aus)	A Palmer (USA)	A Palmer (USA)	J Hebert (USA)
1961	A Palmer (USA)	G Littler (USA)	G Player (SAf)	J Barber (USA)
1962	A Palmer (USA)	J Nicklaus (USA)	A Palmer (USA)	G Player (SAf)
1963	B Charles (NZL)	J Boros (USA)	J Nicklaus (USA)	J Nicklaus (USA)
1964	T Lema (USA)	K Venturi (USA)	A Palmer (USA)	B Nichols (USA)
1965	P Thomson (Aus)	G Player (SAf)	J Nicklaus (USA)	D Marr (USA)
1966	J Nicklaus (USA)	B Casper (USA)	J Nicklaus (USA)	A Geiberger (USA)
1967	R De Vicenzo (Arg)	J Nicklaus (USA)	G Brewer (USA)	D January (USA)
1968	G Player (SAf)	L Trevino (USA)	B Goalby (USA)	J Boros (USA)
1969	T Jacklin (GBR)	O Moody (USA)	G Archer (USA)	R Floyd (USA)
1970	J Nicklaus (USA)	T Jacklin (GBR)	B Casper (USA)	D Stockton (USA)
1971	L Trevino (USA)	L Trevino (USA)	C Coody (USA)	J Nicklaus (USA)
1972	L Trevino (USA)	J Nicklaus (USA)	J Nicklaus (USA)	G Player (SAf)
1973	T Weiskopf (USA)	J Miller (USA)	T Aaron (USA)	J Nicklaus (USA)
1974	G Player (SAf)	H Irwin (USA)	G Player (SAf)	L Trevino (USA)
1975	T Watson (USA)	L Graham (USA)	J Nicklaus (USA)	J Nicklaus (USA)
1976	J Miller (USA)	J Pate (USA)	R Floyd (USA)	D Stockton (USA)
1977	T Watson (USA)	H Green (USA)	T Watson (USA)	L Wadkins (USA)
1978	J Nicklaus (USA)	A North (USA)	G Player (SAf)	J Mahaffey (USA)
1979	S Ballesteros (Spa)	H Irwin (USA)	F Zoeller (USA)	D Graham (Aus)
1980	T Watson (USA)	J Nicklaus (USA)	S Ballesteros (Spa)	J Nicklaus (USA)
1981	B Rogers (USA)	D Graham (Aus)	T Watson (USA)	L Nelson (USA)
1982	T Watson (USA)	T Watson (USA)	C Stadler (USA)	R Floyd (USA)
1983	T Watson (USA)	L Nelson (USA)	S Ballesteros (Spa)	H Sutton (USA)
1984	S Ballesteros (Spa)	F Zoeller (USA)	B Crenshaw (USA)	L Trevino (USA)
1985	S Lyle (GBR)	A North (USA)	B Langer (WGR)	H Green (USA)
1986	G Norman (Aus)	R Floyd (USA)	J Nicklaus (USA)	B Tway (USA)
1987	N Faldo (GBR)	S Simpson (USA)	L Mize (USA)	L Nelson (USA)
1988	S Ballesteros (Spa)	C Strange (USA)	S Lyle (GBR)	J Sluman (USA)
1989	M Calcavecchia (USA)	C Strange (USA)	N Faldo (GBR)	P Stewart (USA)
1990	N Faldo (GBR)	H Irwin (USA)	N Faldo (GBR)	W Grady (Aus)
1991	I Baker-Finch (Aus)	P Stewart (USA)	I Woosnam (GBR)	J Daly (USA)

1992	N Faldo (GBR)	T Kite (USA)	F Couples (USA)	N Price (Zim)
1993	G Norman (Aus)	L Janzen (USA)	B Langer (GER)	P Azinger (USA)
1994	N Price (Zim)	E Els (SAf)	J M Olazabal (Spa)	N Price (Zim)
1995	J Daly (USA)	C Pavin (USA)	B Crenshaw (USA)	S Elkington (Aus)
1996	T Lehman (USA)	S Jones (USA)	N Faldo (GBR)	M Brooks (USA)
1997	J Leonard (USA)	E Els (SAf)	T Woods (USA)	D Love (USA)
1998	M O'Meara (USA)	L Janzen (USA)	M O'Meara (USA)	V Singh (Fij)
1999	P Lawrie (GBR)	P Stewart (USA)	J M Olazabal (Spa)	T Woods (USA)
2000	T Woods (USA)	T Woods (USA)	V Singh (Fij)	T Woods (USA)
2001	D Duval (USA)	R Goosen (SAf)	T Woods (USA)	D Toms (USA)
2002	E Els (SAf)	T Woods (USA)	T Woods (USA)	R Beem (USA)
2003	B Curtis (USA)	J Furyk (USA)	M Weir (Can)	S Micheel (USA)
2004	T Hamilton (USA)	R Goosen (SAf)	P Mickelson (USA)	V Singh (Fij)
2005	T Woods (USA)	M Campbell (NZ)	T Woods (USA)	A Cabrera (Arg)

The 2006 season opened with Phil Mickelson taking the US Masters and the Australian Geoff Ogilvy taking the US Open.

RYDER CUP WINNERS (POST WAR)

USA v Great Britain

1947	Portland, Oregon	USA	1963	Atlanta, Georgia	USA
1949	Ganton, England	USA	1965	Southport, England	USA
1951	Pinehurst, North Carolina	USA	1967	Houston, Texas	USA
1953	Wentworth, England	USA	1969	Southport, England	Tied
1955	Thunderbird, California	USA	1971	St Louis, Missouri	USA
1957	Lindrick, England	Great Britain	1973	Muirfield, Scotland	USA
1959	Elorado, California	USA	1975	Laurel Valley, Pennsylvania	USA
1961	Royal Lytham, England	USA	1977	Royal Lytham, England	USA

USA v Europe

1979	Greenbrier, West Virginia	USA	1993	The Belfry, England	USA
1981	Walton Heath, England	USA	1995	Oak Hill, New York	Europe
1983	PGA Course, Florida	USA	1997	Valderrama, Spain	Europe
1985	The Belfry, England	Europe	1999	Brookline Country Club, Boston	USA
1987	Columbus, Ohio	Europe	2002	The Belfry, England	Europe
1989	The Belfry, England	Tied	2004	Detroit, USA	Europe
1991	Kiawah Island, South Carolina	USA			

Wins since competition began in 1927: USA 24; GB/Europe 9; Tied 2.

GREYHOUND RACING

THE DERBY WINNERS (POST WAR)

Year	Greyhound	Year	Greyhound
1945	Ballyhennessy Seal	1976	Mutts Silver
1946	Monday's News	1977	Balliniska Band
1947	Trev's Perfection	1978	Lacca Champion
1948	Priceless Border	1979	Sarah's Bunny
1949	Narrogar Ann	1980	Indian Joe
1950	Ballymac Ball	1981	Parkdown Jet
1951	Ballylanigan Tanist	1982	Laurie's Panther
1952	Endless Gossip	1983	I'm Slippy
1953	Daws Dancer	1984	Whisper Wishes
1954	Paul's Fun	1985	Pagan Swallow
1955	Rushton Mack	1986	Tico
1956	Dunmore King	1987	Signal Spark
1957	Ford Spartan	1988	Hit-the-Lid
1958	Pigalle Wonder	1989	Lartigue Note
1959	Mile Bush Pride	1990	Slippy Blue
1960	Duleek Dandy	1991	Ballinderry Ash
1961	Palm's Printer	1992	Farloe Melody
1962	The Grand Canal	1993	Ringa Hustle
1963	Lucky Boy Boy	1994	Moral Standards
1964	Hack Up Chieftain	1995	Moaning Lad
1965	Chittering Clapton	1996	Shanless Slippy
1966	Faithful Hope	1997	Some Picture
1967	Tric-Trac	1998	Tom's the Bes
1968	Camira Flash	1999	Chart Kin
1969	Sand Star	2000	Rapid Ranger
1970	John Silver	2001	Rapid Ranger
1971	Dolores Rocket	2002	Allen Gif
1972	Patricia's Hope	2003	Droopys Hewitt
1973	Patricia's Hope	2004	Droopys Scholes
1974	Jimsun	2005	Westmead Hawk
1975	Tartan Khan	2006	Westmead Hawk

HOCKEY

MEN'S WORLD CUP CHAMPIONS	
1971	Pakistan
1973	Holland
1975	India
1978	Pakistan
1982	Pakistan
1986	Australia
1990	Holland
1994	Pakistan
1998	Holland
2002	Germany

WOMEN'S WORLD CUP CHAMPIONS	
1974	Holland
1976	West Germany
1978	Holland
1981	West Germany
1983	Holland
1986	Holland
1990	Holland
1994	Australia
1998	Australia
2002	Argentina

HORSE RACING

MAJOR RACE WINNERS (since 1950)

GRAND NATIONAL WINNERS		DERBY WINNERS
1950	Freebooter	Galcador
1951	Nickel Coin	Arctic Prince
1952	Teal	Tulyar
1953	Early Mist	Pinza
1954	Royal Tan	Never Say Die
1955	Quare Times	Phil Drake
1956	ESB	Lavandin
1957	Sundew	Crepello
1958	Mr What	Hard Ridden
1959	Oxo	Parthia
1960	Merryman II	St Paddy
1961	Nicolaus Silver	Psidium
1962	Kilmore	Larkspur
1963	Ayala	Relko
1964	Team Spirit	Santa Claus
1965	Jay Trump	Sea Bird II
1966	Anglo	Charlottown
1967	Foinavon	Royal Palace
1968	Red Alligator	Sir Ivor
1969	Highland Wedding	Blakeney
1970	Gay Trip	Nijinsky
1971	Specify	Mill Reef
1972	Well to Do	Roberto
1973	Red Rum	Morston
1974	Red Rum	Snow Knight
1975	L'Escargot	Grundy
1976	Rag Trade	Empery
1977	Red Rum	The Minstrel
1978	Lucius	Shirley Heights
1979	Rubstic	Troy
1980	Ben Nevis	Henbit
1981	Aldaniti	Shergar
1982	Grittar	Golden Fleece
1983	Corbiere	Teenoso
1984	Hallo Dandy	Secreto
1985	Last Suspect	Slip Anchor
1986	West Tip	Shahrastani
1987	Maori Venture	Reference Point
1988	Rhyme'n'Reason	Kahyasi
1989	Little Polveir	Nashwan
1990	Mr Frisk	Quest for Fame
1991	Seagram	Generous
1992	Party Politics	Dr Devious
1993	–	Commander in Chief
1994	Miinnehoma	Ehrhaab
1995	Royal Athlete	Lammtarra
1996	Rough Quest	Shaamit
1997	Lord Gyllene	Benny The Dip
1998	Earth Summit	High-Rise
1999	Bobbyjo	Oath
2000	Papillon	Sinndar
2001	Red Marauder	Galileo
2002	Bindaree	High Chaparral
2003	Monty's Pass	Kris Kin
2004	Amberleigh House	North Light
2005	Hedgehunter	Motivator
2006	Numbersixvalverde	Sir Percy

ICE HOCKEY

WORLD CHAMPIONS (POST WAR)

1947	Czechoslovakia	1967	USSR	1987	Sweden
1948	Canada	1968	USSR	1988	USSR
1949	Czechoslovakia	1969	USSR	1989	USSR
1950	Canada	1970	USSR	1990	USSR
1951	Canada	1971	USSR	1991	Sweden
1952	Canada	1972	Czechoslovakia	1992	Sweden
1953	Sweden	1973	USSR	1993	Russia
1954	USSR	1974	USSR	1994	Canada
1955	Canada	1975	USSR	1995	Finland
1956	USSR	1976	Czechoslovakia	1996	Czech Republic
1957	Sweden	1977	Czechoslovakia	1997	Canada
1958	Canada	1978	USSR	1998	Sweden
1959	Canada	1979	USSR	1999	Czech Republic
1960	USA	1980	USA	2000	Czech Republic
1961	Canada	1981	USSR	2001	Czech Republic
1962	Sweden	1982	USSR	2002	Slovakia
1963	USSR	1983	USSR	2003	Canada
1964	USSR	1984	USSR	2004	Czech Republic
1965	USSR	1985	Czechoslovakia	2005	Czech Republic
1966	USSR	1986	USSR	2006	Sweden

Wins since competition began in 1920

24	USSR	6	Czechoslovakia and Czech Rep.	1	Finland, Britain, Russia,
13	Canada	3	USA		Slovakia
8	Sweden				

NHL STANLEY CUP WINNERS

1982	New York Islanders	1995	New Jersey Devils
1983	New York Islanders	1996	Colorado Avalanche
1984	Edmonton Oilers	1997	Detroit
1985	Edmonton Oilers	1998	Detroit
1986	Montreal Canadiens	1999	Dallas
1987	Edmonton Oilers	2000	New Jersey Devils
1988	Edmonton Oilers	2001	Colorado Avalanche
1989	Calgary Flames	2002	Detroit Red Wings
1990	Edmonton Oilers	2003	New Jersey Devils
1991	Pittsburgh Penguins	2004	Tampa Bay Lightning
1992	Pittsburgh Penguins	2005	Not held
1993	Montreal Canadiens	2006	Carolina Hurricanes
1994	New York Rangers		

ICE SKATING

WORLD CHAMPIONS (since 1967)

	Men		Women
1967	E Danzer (Aut)		P Fleming (USA)
1968	E Danzer (Aut)		P Fleming (USA)
1969	T Wood (USA)		G Seyfert (GDR)
1970	T Wood (USA)		G Seyfert (GDR)
1971	O Nepela (Cze)		B Schuba (Aut)
1972	O Nepela (Cze)		B Schuba (Aut)
1973	O Nepela (Cze)		K Magnussen (Can)
1974	J Hoffmann (GDR)		C Errath (GDR)
1975	S Volkov (USSR)		D De Leeuw (Neth)
1976	J Curry (GBR)		D Hamill (USA)
1977	V Kovalyev (USSR)		L Fratianne (USA)
1978	C Tickner (USA)		A Potzsch (GDR)
1979	V Kovalyev (USSR)		L Fratianne (USA)
1980	J Hoffmann (GDR)		A Potzsch (GDR)
1981	S Hamilton (USA)		D Biellmann (Swi)
1982	S Hamilton (USA)		E Zayak (USA)
1983	S Hamilton (USA)		R Sumners (USA)
1984	S Hamilton (USA)		K Witt (GDR)
1985	A Fadeyev (USSR)		K Witt (GDR)
1986	B Boitano (USA)		D Thomas (USA)
1987	B Orser (Can)		K Witt (GDR)
1988	B Boitano (USA)		K Witt (GDR)
1989	K Browning (Can)		M Ito (Jap)
1990	K Browning (Can)		J Trenary (USA)
1991	K Browning (Can)		K Yamaguchi (Jap)
1992	V Petrenko (Ukr)		K Yamaguchi (Jap)
1993	K Browning (Can)		O Baiul (Ukr)
1994	E Stojko (Can)		Y Sato (Jap)
1995	E Stojko (Can)		L Chen (Chi)
1996	T Eldredge (USA)		M Kwan (USA)
1997	E Stojko (Can)		T Lipinski (USA)
1998	A Yagudin (Rus)		M Kwan (USA)
1999	A Yagudin (Rus)		M Butyrskaya (Rus)
2000	A Yagudin (Rus)		M Kwan (USA)
2001	E Plushenko (Rus)		M Kwan (USA)
2002	A Yagudin (Rus)		I Slutskaya (Rus)
2003	E Plushenko (Rus)		M Kwan (USA)
2004	E Plushenko (Rus)		S Arakawa (Jap)
2005	S Lambiel (Swi)		I Slutskaya (Rus)

LAWN TENNIS

GRAND SLAM CHAMPIONSHIP WINNERS – MEN (since 1948)

	Wimbledon	US Open	French Open	Australian Open
1948	B Falkenberg (USA)	R Gonzales (USA)	F Parker (USA)	A Quist (Aus)
1949	T Schroeder (USA)	R Gonzales (USA)	F Parker (USA)	F Sedgman (Aus)
1950	B Patty (USA)	A Larsen (USA)	B Patty (USA)	F Sedgman (Aus)
1951	D Savitt (USA)	F Sedgman (USA)	J Drobny (Egy)	D Savitt (USA)
1952	F Sedgman (Ans)	F Sedgman (Aus)	J Drobny (Egy)	K McGregor (Aus)
1953	V Seixas (USA)	T Trabert (USA)	K Rosewall (Aus)	K Rosewall (Aus)
1954	J Drobny (Egy)	V Seixas (USA)	T Trabert (USA)	M Rose (Aus)
1955	T Trabert (USA)	T Trabert (USA)	T Trabert (USA)	K Rosewall (Aus)
1956	L Hoad (Aus)	K Rosewall (Aus)	L Hoad (Aus)	L Hoad (Aus)
1957	L Hoad (Aus)	M Anderson (Aus)	S Davidson (Swe)	A Cooper (Aus)
1958	A Cooper (Aus)	A Cooper (Aus)	M Rose (Aus)	A Cooper (Aus)
1959	A Olmedo (USA)	N Fraser (Aus)	N Pietrangeli (Ita)	A Olmedo (USA)
1960	N Fraser (Aus)	N Fraser (Aus)	N Pietrangeli (Ita)	R Laver (Aus)
1961	R Laver (Aus)	R Emerson (Aus)	M Santana (Spa)	R Emerson (Aus)
1962	R Laver (Aus)	R Laver (Aus)	R Laver (Aus)	R Laver (Aus)
1963	C McKinley (USA)	R Osuna (Mex)	R Emerson (Aus)	R Emerson (Aus)
1964	R Emerson (Aus)	R Emerson (Aus)	M Santana (Spa)	R Emerson (Aus)
1965	R Emerson (Aus)	M Santana (Spa)	F Stolle (Aus)	R Emerson (Aus)
1966	M Santana (Spa)	F Stolle (Aus)	T Roche (Aus)	R Emerson (Aus)
1967	J Newcombe (Aus)	J Newcombe (Aus)	R Emerson (Aus)	R Emerson (Aus)
1968	R Laver (Aus)	A Ashe (USA)	K Rosewall (Aus)	B Bowrey (Aus)
1969	R Laver (Aus)	R Laver (Aus)	R Laver (Aus)	R Laver (Aus)
1970	J Newcombe (Aus)	K Rosewall (Aus)	J Kodes (Cze)	A Ashe (USA)
1971	J Newcombe (Aus)	S Smith (USA)	J Kodes (Cze)	K Rosewall (Aus)
1972	S Smith (USA)	I Nastase (Rom)	A Gimeno (Spa)	K Rosewall (Aus)
1973	J Kodes (Cze)	J Newcombe (Aus)	I Nastase (Rom)	J Newcombe (Aus)
1974	J Connors (USA)	J Connors (USA)	B Borg (Swe)	J Connors (USA)
1975	A Ashe (USA)	M Orantes (Spa)	B Borg (Swe)	J Newcombe (USA)
1976	B Borg (Swe)	J Connors (USA)	A Panatta (Ita)	M Edmondson (Aus)
1977	B Borg (Swe)	G Vilas (Arg)	G Vilas (Arg)	R Tanner (USA)
1978	B Borg (Swe)	J Connors (USA)	B Borg (Swe)	G Vilas (Arg)
1979	B Borg (Swe)	J McEnroe (USA)	B Borg (Swe)	G Vilas (Arg)
1980	B Borg (Swe)	J McEnroe (USA)	B Borg (Swe)	B Teacher (USA)
1981	J McEnroe (USA)	J McEnroe (USA)	B Borg (Swe)	J Kriek (SAf)
1982	J Connors (USA)	J Connors (USA)	M Wilander (Swe)	J Kriek (SAf)
1983	J McEnroe (USA)	J Connors (USA)	Y Noah (Fra)	M Wilander (Swe)
1984	J McEnroe (USA)	J McEnroe (USA)	I Lendl (Cze)	M Wilander (Swe)
1985	B Becker (WGR)	I Lendl (Cze)	M Wilander (Swe)	S Edberg (Swe)
1986	B Becker (WGR)	I Lendl (Cze)	I Lendl (Cze)	—
1987	P Cash (Aus)	I Lendl (Cze)	I Lendl (Cze)	S Edberg (Swe)
1988	S Edberg (Swe)	M Wilander (Swe)	M Wilander (Swe)	M Wilander (Swe)
1989	B Becker (WGR)	B Becker (WGR)	M Chang (USA)	I Lendl (Cze)
1990	S Edberg (Swe)	P Sampras (USA)	A Gomez (Ecu)	I Lendl (Cze)
1991	M Stich (Ger)	S Edberg (Swe)	J Courier (USA)	B Becker (Ger)
1992	A Agassi (USA)	S Edberg (Swe)	J Courier (USA)	J Courier (USA)
1993	P Sampras (USA)	P Sampras (USA)	S Brugera (Spa)	J Courier (USA)
1994	P Sampras (USA)	A Agassi (USA)	S Brugera (Spa)	P Sampras (USA)
1995	P Sampras (USA)	P Sampras (USA)	T Muster (Aut)	A Agassi (USA)
1996	R Krajicek (Hol)	P Sampras (USA)	Y Kafelnikov (Rus)	B Becker (Ger)
1997	P Sampras (USA)	P Rafter (Aus)	G Kuerten (Bra)	P Sampras (USA)
1998	P Sampras (USA)	P Rafter (Aus)	C Moya (Spa)	P Korda (Cze)
1999	P Sampras (USA)	A Agassi (USA)	A Agassi (USA)	Y Kafelnikov (Rus)
2000	P Sampras (USA)	M Safin (Rus)	G Kuerten (Bra)	A Agassi (USA)
2001	G Ivanisevic (Cro)	L Hewitt (Aus)	G Kuerten (Bra)	A Agassi (USA)
2002	L Hewitt (Aus)	P Sampras (USA)	A Costa (Spa)	T Johansson (Swe)
2003	R Federer (Swi)	A Roddick (USA)	JC Ferrero (Sp)	A Agassi (USA)
2004	R Federer (Swi)	R Federer (Swi)	G Gaudio (Arg)	R Federer (Swi)
2005	R Federer (Swi)	R Federer (Swi)	R Nadal (Sp)	M Safin (Rus)
2006	R Federer (Swi)	—	R Nadal (Sp)	R Federer (Swi)

GRAND SLAM CHAMPIONSHIP WINNERS – WOMEN (POST WAR)

	Wimbledon	US Open	French Open	Australian Open
1946	P Betz (USA)	P Betz (USA)	M Osborne (USA)	N Bolton (Aus)
1947	M Osborne (USA)	L Brough (USA)	P Todd (USA)	N Bolton (Aus)
1948	L Brough (USA)	M Du Pont (USA)	N Landry (Fra)	N Bolton (Aus)
1949	L Brough (USA)	M Du Pont (USA)	M Du Pont (USA)	D Hart (USA)
1950	L Brough (USA)	M Du Pont (USA)	D Hart (USA)	L Brough (USA)
1951	D Hart (USA)	M Connolly (USA)	S Fry (USA)	N Bolton (Aus)
1952	M Connolly (USA)	M Connolly (USA)	D Hart (USA)	T Long (USA)
1953	M Connolly (USA)	M Connolly (USA)	M Connolly (USA)	M Connolly (USA)
1954	M Connolly (USA)	D Hart (USA)	M Connolly (USA)	T Long (USA)
1955	L Brough (USA)	D Hart (USA)	A Mortimer (GBR)	B Penrose (Aus)
1956	S Fry (USA)	S Fry (USA)	A Gibson (USA)	M Carter (Aus)
1957	A Gibson (USA)	A Gibson (USA)	S Bloomer (GBR)	S Fry (USA)
1958	A Gibson (USA)	A Gibson (USA)	Z Kormoczy (Hun)	A Mortimer (GBR)
1959	M Bueno (Bra)	M Bueno (Bra)	C Truman (GBR)	M Reitano (Aus)
1960	M Bueno (Bra)	D Hard (USA)	D Hard (USA)	M Smith (Aus)
1961	A Mortimer (GBR)	D Hard (USA)	A Haydon (GBR)	M Smith (Aus)
1962	K Susman (USA)	M Smith (Aus)	M Smith (Aus)	M Smith (Aus)
1963	M Smith (Aus)	M Bueno (Bra)	L Turner (Aus)	M Smith (Aus)
1964	M Bueno (Bra)	M Bueno (Bra)	M Smith (Aus)	M Smith (Aus)
1965	M Smith (Aus)	M Smith (Aus)	L Turner (Aus)	M Smith (Aus)

1966	B-J King (USA)	M Bueno (Bra)	A Jones (GBR)*	M Smith (Aus)
1967	B-J King (USA)	B-J King (USA)	F Durr (Fra)	N Richey (USA)
1968	B-J King (USA)	M Court (Aus)*	N Richey (USA)	B-J King (USA)
1969	A Jones (GBR)*	M Court (Aus)*	M Court (Aus)*	M Court (Aus)*
1970	M Court (Aus)*	M Court (Aus)*	M Court (Aus)*	M Court (Aus)*
1971	E Goolagong (Aus)	B-J King (USA)	E Goolagong (Aus)	E Goolagong (Aus)
1972	B-J King (USA)	B-J King (USA)	M Court (Aus)*	V Wade (GBR)
1973	B-J King (USA)	M Court (Aus)*	B-J King (USA)	M Court (Aus)*
1974	C Evert (USA)	B-J King (USA)	M Court (Aus)*	E Goolagong (Aus)
1975	B J King (USA)	C Evert (USA)	C Evert (USA)	E Goolagong (Aus)
1976	C Evert (USA)	C Evert (USA)	S Barker (GBR)	E Cawley (Aus)*
1977	V Wade (GBR)	C Evert (USA)	M Jauseovec (Yug)	K Reid (Aus)
1978	M Navratilova (Cze)	C Evert (USA)	V Ruzici (Rom)	C O'Neill (Aus)
1979	M Navratilova (Cze)	T Austin (USA)	C Evert (USA)	B Jordan (USA)
1980	E Cawley (Aus)*	C Evert (USA)	C Evert (USA)	H Mandlikova (Cze)
1981	C Evert (USA)	T Austin (USA)	H Mandlikova (Cze)	M Navratilova (USA)
1982	M Navratilova (USA)	C Evert (USA)	M Navratilova (USA)	C Evert (USA)
1983	M Navratilova (USA)	M Navratilova (USA)	C Evert (USA)	M Navratilova (USA)
1984	M Navratilova (USA)	M Navratilova (USA)	M Navratilova (USA)	C Evert (USA)
1985	M Navratilova (USA)	H Mandlikova (Cze)	C Evert (USA)	M Navratilova (USA)
1986	M Navratilova (USA)	M Navratilova (USA)	C Evert (USA)	—
1987	M Navratilova (USA)	M Navratilova (USA)	S Graf (WGR)	H Mandlikova (Cze)
1988	S Graf (WGR)	S Graf (WGR)	S Graf (WGR)	S Graf (WGR)
1989	S Graf (WGR)	S Graf (WGR)	A Sanchez (Spa)	S Graf (WGR)
1990	M Navratilova (USA)	G Sabatini (Arg)	M Seles (Yug)	S Graf (WGR)
1991	S Graf (Ger)	M Seles (Yug)	M Seles (Yug)	M Seles (Yug)
1992	S Graf (Ger)	M Seles (Yug)	M Seles (Yug)	M Seles (Yug)
1993	S Graf (Ger)	S Graf (Ger)	S Graf (Ger)	M Seles (Yug)
1994	C Martinez (Spa)	A Sanchez (Spa)	A Sanchez (Spa)	S Graf (Ger)
1995	S Graf (Ger)	S Graf (Ger)	S Graf (Ger)	M Pierce (Fra)
1996	S Graf (Ger)	S Graf (Ger)	S Graf (Ger)	M Seles (USA)
1997	M Hingis (Swi)	M Hingis (Swi)	I Majoli (Cro)	M Hingis (Swi)
1998	J Novotna (Cze)	L Davenport (USA)	A Sanchez (Spa)	M Hingis (Swi)
1999	L Davenport (USA)	S Williams (USA)	S Graf (Ger)	M Hingis (Swi)
2000	V Williams (USA)	V Williams (USA)	M Pierce (Fra)	L Davenport (USA)
2001	V Williams (USA)	V Williams (USA)	J Capriati (USA)	J Capriati (USA)
2002	S Williams (USA)	S Williams (USA)	S Williams (USA)	J Capriati (USA)
2003	S Williams (USA)	J Henin-Hardenne (Bel)	J Henin-Hardenne (Bel)	S Williams (USA)
2004	M Sharapova (Rus)	S Kuznetsova (Rus)	A Myskina (Rus)	J Henin-Hardenne (Bel)
2005	V Williams (USA)	K Clijsters (Bel)	J Henin-Hardenne (Bel)	B Williams (USA)
2006	A Mauresmo (Fra)	—	J Henin-Hardenne (Bel)	A Mauresmo (Fra)

* Players who have won before under maiden names:
A Jones as A Haydon, M Court as M Smith, E Cawley as E Goolagong

DAVIS CUP WINNERS (POST WAR)

1946	USA	1966	Australia	1986	Australia
1947	USA	1967	Australia	1987	Sweden
1948	USA	1968	USA	1988	West Germany
1949	USA	1969	USA	1989	West Germany
1950	Australia	1970	USA	1990	USA
1951	Australia	1971	USA	1991	France
1952	Australia	1972	USA	1992	USA
1953	Australia	1973	Australia	1993	Germany
1954	USA	1974	South Africa	1994	Sweden
1955	Australia	1975	Sweden	1995	USA
1956	Australia	1976	Italy	1996	France
1957	Australia	1977	Australia	1997	Sweden
1958	USA	1978	USA	1998	Sweden
1959	Australia	1979	USA	1999	Australia
1960	Australia	1980	Czechoslovakia	2000	Spain
1961	Australia	1981	USA	2001	France
1962	Australia	1982	USA	2002	Russia
1963	USA	1983	Australia	2003	Australia
1964	Australia	1984	Sweden	2004	Spain
1965	Australia	1985	Sweden	2005	Croatia

Wins since competition began in 1900

31	USA	2	Spain
28	Australia or Australasia	1	Croatia, Czechoslovakia, Italy,
9	Great Britain or British Isles, France		Russia, South Africa
7	Sweden		
3	Germany or West Germany		

MOTOR CYCLING

WORLD SUPERBIKE CHAMPIONSHIP (since 1990)

1990	Raymond Roche (Fra)	Honda	1998	Carl Fogarty (Eng)	Ducati
1991	Doug Polen (USA)	Ducati	1999	Carl Fogarty (Eng)	Ducati
1992	Doug Polen (USA)	Ducati	2000	Colin Edwards (USA)	Ducati
1993	Scott Russell (USA)	Ducati	2001	Troy Bayliss (Aus)	Ducati
1994	Carl Fogarty (Eng)	Ducati	2002	Colin Edwards (USA)	Ducati
1995	Carl Fogarty (Eng)	Ducati	2003	Neil Hodgson (Eng)	Ducati
1996	Troy Corser (Aus)	Ducati	2004	James Toseland (Eng)	Ducati
1997	John Kocinski (USA)	Honda	2005	Troy Corser (Aus)	Suzuki

MOTOR RACING

FORMULA ONE WORLD CAR CHAMPIONSHIP

	Driver		Car	Constructors Cup
1950	Giuseppe Farina	Italy	Alfa Romeo	
1951	Juan Manuel Fangio	Argentina	Alfa Romeo	
1952	Alberto Ascari	Italy	Ferrari	
1953	Alberto Ascari	Italy	Ferrari	
1954	Juan Manuel Fangio	Argentina	Maserati/Mercedes	
1955	Juan Manuel Fangio	Argentina	Mercedes-Benz	
1956	Juan Manuel Fangio	Argentina	Lancia-Ferrari	
1957	Juan Manuel Fangio	Argentina	Maserati	
1958	Mike Hawthorn	Great Britain	Ferrari	Vanwall
1959	Jack Brabham	Australia	Cooper-Climax	Cooper-Climax
1960	Jack Brabham	Australia	Cooper-Climax	Cooper-Climax
1961	Phil Hill	USA	Ferrari	Ferrari
1962	Graham Hill	Great Britain	BRM	BRM
1963	Jim Clark	Great Britain	Lotus-Climax	Lotus-Climax
1964	John Surtees	Great Britain	Ferrari	Ferrari
1965	Jim Clark	Great Britain	Lotus-Climax	Lotus-Climax
1966	Jack Brabham	Australia	Brabham-Repco	Brabham-Repco
1967	Denny Hulme	New Zealand	Brabham-Repco	Brabham-Repco
1968	Graham Hill	Great Britain	Lotus-Ford	Lotus-Ford
1969	Jackie Stewart	Great Britain	Matra-Ford	Matra-Ford
1970	Jochen Rindt	Austria	Lotus-Ford	Lotus-Ford
1971	Jackie Stewart	Great Britain	Tyrell-Ford	Tyrell-Ford
1972	Emerson Fittipaldi	Brazil	Lotus-Ford	Lotus-Ford
1973	Jackie Stewart	Great Britain	Tyrell-Ford	Lotus-Ford
1974	Emerson Fittipaldi	Brazil	McLaren-Ford	McLaren-Ford
1975	Niki Lauda	Austria	Ferrari	Ferrari
1976	James Hunt	Great Britain	McLaren-Ford	Ferrari
1977	Niki Lauda	Austria	Ferrari	Ferrari
1978	Mario Andretti	USA	Lotus-Ford	Lotus-Ford
1979	Jody Scheckter	South Africa	Ferrari	Ferrari
1980	Alan Jones	Australia	Williams-Ford	Williams-Ford
1981	Nelson Piquet	Brazil	Brabham-Ford	Williams-Ford
1982	Keke Rosberg	Finland	Williams-Ford	Ferrari
1983	Nelson Piquet	Brazil	Brabham-BMW	Ferrari
1984	Niki Lauda	Austria	McLaren-TAG	McLaren-Porsche
1985	Alain Prost	France	McLaren-TAG	McLaren-TAG
1986	Alain Prost	France	McLaren-TAG	Williams-Honda
1987	Nelson Piquet	Brazil	Williams-Honda	Williams-Honda
1988	Ayrton Senna	Brazil	McLaren-Honda	McLaren-Honda
1989	Alain Prost	France	McLaren-Honda	McLaren-Honda
1990	Ayrton Senna	Brazil	McLaren-Honda	McLaren-Honda
1991	Ayrton Senna	Brazil	McLaren-Honda	McLaren-Honda
1992	Nigel Mansell	Great Britain	Williams-Renault	Williams-Renault
1993	Alain Prost	France	Williams-Renault	Williams-Renault
1994	Michael Schumacher	Germany	Benneton-Ford	Williams-Renault
1995	Michael Schumacher	Germany	Benneton-Renault	Benneton-Renault
1996	Damon Hill	Great Britain	Williams-Renault	Williams-Renault
1997	Jacques Villeneuve	Canada	Williams-Renault	Williams-Renault
1998	Mika Hakkinen	Finland	McLaren-Mercedes	McLaren-Mercedes
1999	Mika Hakkinen	Finland	McLaren-Mercedes	Ferrari
2000	Michael Schumacher	Germany	Ferrari	Ferrari
2001	Michael Schumacher	Germany	Ferrari	Ferrari
2002	Michael Schumacher	Germany	Ferrari	Ferrari
2003	Michael Schumacher	Germany	Ferrari	Ferrari
2004	Michael Schumacher	Germany	Ferrari	Ferrari
2005	Fernando Alonso*	Spain	Renault	Renault

*Fernando Alonso became the youngest-ever winner.

ROWING

THE UNIVERSITY BOAT RACE

The Boat Race is run over 4 miles 374 yards. The record time is held by Cambridge (16 min., 19 secs in 1998).

1946	Oxford	1975	Cambridge
1947–51	Cambridge	1976–85	Oxford
1952	Oxford	1986	Cambridge
1953	Cambridge	1987–92	Oxford
1954	Oxford	1993–9	Cambridge
1955–8	Cambridge	2000	Oxford
1959–60	Oxford	2001	Cambridge
1961–2	Cambridge	2002	Oxford
1963	Oxford	2003	Oxford
1964	Cambridge	2004	Cambridge
1965–7	Oxford	2005	Oxford
1968–73	Cambridge	2006	Oxford
1974	Oxford		

Overall results since race began in 1829

Cambridge   78   Oxford 73   Dead Heat 1

RUGBY LEAGUE

LEAGUE CHAMPIONS (since 1954)

1953–4	Warrington	1975–6	Salford
1954–5	Warrington	1976–7	Featherstone Rovers
1955–6	Hull	1977–8	Widnes
1956–7	Oldham	1978–9	Hull Kingston Rovers
1957–8	Hull	1979–80	Bradford Northern
1958–9	St Helens	1980–1	Bradford Northern
1959–60	Wigan	1981–2	Leigh
1960–1	Leeds	1982–3	Hull
1961–2	Huddersfield	1983–4	Hull Kingston Rovers
1962–3	Swinton/Hunslet	1984–5	Hull Kingston Rovers
1963–4	Swinton/Oldham	1985–6	Halifax
1964–5	Halifax	1986–7	Wigan
1965–6	St Helens	1987–8	Widnes
1966–7	Wakefield Trinity	1988–9	Widnes
1967–8	Wakefield Trinity	1989–90	Wigan
1968–9	Leeds	1990–1	Wigan
1969–70	St Helens	1991–2	Wigan
1970–1	St Helens	1992–3	Wigan
1971–2	Leeds	1993–4	Wigan
1972–3	Dewsbury	1994–5	Wigan
1973–4	Salford	1995–6	Wigan
1974–5	St Helens		

Wins since competition began in 1906
17 Wigan
7 Huddersfield, St Helens
6 Hull, Salford
5 Hull Kingston Rovers

4 Swinton
3 Halifax, Leeds, Oldham, Warrington, Widnes
2 Bradford Northern, Hunslet, Leigh, Wakefield Trinity
1 Batley, Dewsbury, Featherstone Rovers, Workington Town

SUPER LEAGUE

1996	St Helens Saints	2001	Bradford Bulls
1997	Bradford Bulls	2002	St Helens Saints
1998	Wigan Warriors	2003	Bradford Bulls
1999	St Helens Saints	2004	Leeds Rhinos
2000	St Helens Saints	2005	Bradford Bulls

CHALLENGE CUP WINNERS (POST WAR)

1946	Wakefield Trinity	1976	St Helens
1947	Bradford Northern	1977	Leeds
1948	Wigan	1978	Leeds
1949	Bradford Northern	1979	Widnes
1950	Warrington	1980	Hull Kingston Rovers
1951	Wigan	1981	Widnes
1952	Workington Town	1982	Hull
1953	Huddersfield	1983	Featherstone Rovers
1954	Warrington	1984	Widnes
1955	Barrow	1985	Wigan
1956	St Helens	1986	Castleford
1957	Leeds	1987	Halifax
1958	Wigan	1988	Wigan
1959	Wigan	1989	Wigan
1960	Wakefield Trinity	1990	Wigan
1961	St Helens	1991	Wigan
1962	Wakefield Trinity	1992	Wigan
1963	Wakefield Trinity	1993	Wigan
1964	Widnes	1994	Wigan
1965	Wigan	1995	Wigan
1966	St Helens	1996	St Helens
1967	Featherstone Rovers	1997	St Helens
1968	Leeds	1998	Sheffield Eagles
1969	Castleford	1999	Leeds Rhinos
1970	Castleford	2000	Bradford Bulls
1971	Leigh	2001	St Helens
1972	St Helens	2002	Wigan
1973	Featherstone Rovers	2003	Bradford Bulls
1974	Warrington	2004	St Helens
1975	Widnes	2005	Hull

Wins since competition began in 1897
17 Wigan
11 Leeds
9 St Helens
7 Widnes
6 Huddersfield
5 Halifax, Wakefield Trinity, Warrington
4 Bradford Northern, Castleford

3 Batley, Featherstone Rovers, Hull, Oldham, Swinton
2 Bradford Bulls, Broughton Rangers, Dewsbury, Hunslet,Leigh
1 Barrow, Hull Kingston Rovers, Rochdale Hornets, Salford, Sheffield Eagles, Workington Town

WORLD CUP WINNERS

1987	New Zealand	1999	Australia
1991	Australia	2003	England
1995	South Africa		

In 2007 the World Cup will be hosted by France. The hosts in 2011 are New Zealand (who hosted the first World Cup in 1987).

SIX NATIONS CHAMPIONSHIP WINNERS (POST WAR)*

1947	England	1967	France	1986	France
1948	Ireland	1968	France		Scotland
1949	Ireland	1969	Wales	1987	France
1950	Wales	1970	France	1988	France
1951	Ireland		Wales		Wales
1952	Wales	1971	Wales	1989	France
1953	England	1972	No competition	1990	Scotland
1954	England	1973	England	1991	England
	France		France	1992	England
	Wales		Ireland	1993	France
1955	France		Scotland	1994	Wales
	Wales		Wales	1995	England
1956	Wales	1974	Ireland	1996	England
1957	England	1975	Wales	1997	France
1958	England	1976	Wales	1998	France
1959	France	1977	France	1999	Scotland
1960	England	1978	Wales	2000	England
	France	1979	Wales	2001	England
1961	France	1980	England	2002	France
1962	France	1981	France	2003	England
1963	England	1982	Ireland	2004	France
1964	Scotland	1983	France	2005	Wales
	Wales		Ireland	2006	France
1965	Wales	1984	Scotland		
1966	Wales	1985	Ireland		

*The competition was the Five Nations Championship prior to 2000.

Wins and shared wins since Championship began in 1883:
England 35   Wales 34   Scotland 22   France 23   Ireland 18

Grand Slam Winners:		Triple Crown Winners:	
England	12	England	23
Wales	6	Ireland	1
France	8	Scotland	10
		Wales	18

HEINEKEN CUP

1996	Toulouse	2000	Northampton	2004	Wasps
1997	Brive	2001	Leicester	2005	Toulouse
1998	Bath	2002	Leicester	2006	Munster
1999	Ulster	2003	Toulouse		

POWERGEN CUP WINNERS (formerly TETLEY BITTER CUP)

1972	Gloucester	1984	Bath	1996	Bath
1973	Coventry	1985	Bath	1997	Leicester
1974	Coventry	1986	Bath	1998	Saracens
1975	Bedford	1987	Bath	1999	Wasps
1976	Gosforth	1988	Harlequins	2000	Wasps
1977	Gosforth	1989	Bath	2001	Newcastle
1978	Gloucester	1990	Bath	2002	London Irish
1979	Leicester	1991	Harlequins	2003	Gloucester
1980	Leicester	1992	Bath	2004	Newcastle
1981	Leicester	1993	Leicester	2005	Leeds
1982	Gloucester & Moseley	1994	Bath	2006	Wasps
1983	Bristol	1995	Bath		

GUINNESS (formerly ZURICH) ENGLISH LEAGUE CHAMPIONS

1987–8	Leicester	1994–5	Leicester	2001–02	Leicester
1988–9	Bath	1995–6	Bath	2002–03	Wasps
1989–90	Wasps	1996–7	Wasps	2003–04	Wasps
1990–1	Bath	1997–8	Newcastle	2004–05	Wasps
1991–2	Bath	1998–9	Leicester	2005–06	Sale Sharks
1992–3	Bath	1999–00	Leicester		
1993–4	Bath	2000–01	Leicester		

SNOOKER

WORLD PROFESSIONAL CHAMPIONS*

1976	Ray Reardon (Wales)	1992	Stephen Hendry (Scotland)
1977	John Spencer (England)	1993	Stephen Hendry (Scotland)
1978	Ray Reardon (Wales)	1994	Stephen Hendry (Scotland)
1979	Terry Griffiths (Wales)	1995	Stephen Hendry (Scotland)
1980	Cliff Thorburn (Canada)	1996	Stephen Hendry (Scotland)
1981	Steve Davis (England)	1997	Ken Doherty (Ireland)
1982	Alex Higgins (Northern Ireland)	1998	John Higgins (Scotland)
1983	Steve Davis (England)	1999	Stephen Hendry (Scotland)
1984	Steve Davis (England)	2000	Mark Williams (Wales)
1985	Dennis Taylor (Northern Ireland)	2001	Ronnie O'Sullivan (England)
1986	Joe Johnson (England)	2002	Peter Ebdon (England)
1987	Steve Davis (England)	2003	Mark Williams (Wales)
1988	Steve Davis (England)	2004	Ronnie O'Sullivan (England)
1989	Steve Davis (England)	2005	Shaun Murphy (England)
1990	Stephen Hendry (Scotland)	2006	Graeme Dott (Scotland)**
1991	John Parrott (England)		

*Currently (2006) sponsored by 888.com.
**After the longest Final in Crucible history.

SWIMMING

OLYMPIC CHAMPIONS (since 1952)

Men's 50m Freestyle

1988	Matt Biondi (USA)
1992	Aleksandr Popov (CIS)
1996	Aleksandr Popov (Rus)
2000	Anthony Ervin (USA)
2004	Gary Hall (USA)

Men's 100m Freestyle

1952	Clarke Scholes (USA)
1956	Jon Henricks (Aus)
1960	John Devitt (Aus)
1964	Don Schollander (USA)
1968	Mike Wenden (Aus)
1972	Mark Spitz (USA)
1976	Jim Montgomery (USA)
1980	Jorg Woithe (GDR)
1984	Howdy Gaines (USA)
1988	Matt Biondi (USA)
1992	Aleksandr Popov (CIS)
1996	Aleksandr Popov (Rus)
2000	Pieter van den Hoogenband (Neth)
2004	Pieter van den Hoogenband (Neth)

Men's 200m Freestyle

1968	Mike Wenden
1972	Mark Spitz (USA)
1976	Bruce Furniss (USA)
1980	Sergey Koplyakov (USSR)
1984	Michael Gross (FRG)
1988	Duncan Armstrong (Aus)
1996	Danyon Loader (NZ)
2000	Peter van den Hoogenband (Neth)
2004	Ian Thorpe (Aus)

Men's 400m Freestyle

1952	Jean Boiteux (Fra)
1956	Murray Rose (Aus)
1960	Murray Rose (Aus)
1964	Don Schollander (USA)
1968	Mike Burton (USA)
1972	Brad Cooper (Aus)
1976	Brian Goodell (USA)
1980	Vladimir Salnikov (USSR)
1984	George DiCarlo (USA)
1988	Uwe Dassler (GDR)
1992	Yevgeniy Sadoviy (CIS)
1996	Danyon Loader (NZ)
2000	Ian Thorpe (Aus)
2004	Ian Thorpe (Aus)

Men's 1500m Freestyle

1952	Ford Konno (USA)
1956	Murray Rose (Aus)
1960	John Konrads (Aus)
1964	Bob Windle (Aus)
1968	Mike Burton (USA)
1972	Mike Burton (USA)
1976	Brian Goodell (USA)
1980	Vladimir Salnikov (USSR)
1984	Michael O'Brien (USA)
1988	Vladimir Salnikov (USSR)
1992	Kieren Perkins (Aus)
1996	Kieren Perkins (Aus)
2000	Grant Hackett (Aus)
2004	Grant Hackett (Aus)

Men's 100m Backstroke

1952	Yoshinobu Oyakawa (USA)
1956	David Theile (Aus)
1960	David Theile (Aus)
1968	Roland Matthes (GDR)
1972	Roland Matthes (GDR)
1976	John Naber (USA)
1980	Bengt Baron (Swe)
1984	Rick Carey (USA)
1988	Daichi Suzuki (Jap)
1992	Mark Tewksbury (Can)
1996	Jeff Rouse (USA)
2000	Lenny Krayzelburg (USA)
2004	Aaron Peirsol (USA)

Men's 200m Backstroke

1964	Jed Graef (USA)
1968	Roland Matthes (GDR)
1972	Roland Matthes (GDR)
1976	John Naber (USA)
1980	Sándor Wladár (Hun)
1984	Rick Carey (USA)
1988	Igor Polyanskiy (USSR)
1992	Martin López-Zubero (Spa)
1996	Brad Bridgewater (USA)
2000	Lenny Krayzelburg (USA)
2004	Aaron Peirsol (USA)

Men's 100m Breaststroke

1968	Don McKenzie (USA)
1972	Nobutaka Taguchi (Jap)
1976	John Hencken (USA)
1980	Duncan Goodhew (UK)
1984	Steve Lundquist (USA)
1988	Adrian Moorhouse (UK)
1992	Nelson Diebel (USA)
1996	Frederik Deburghgraeve (Bel)
2000	Domenico Fioravanti (Ita)
2004	Kosuke Kitajima (Jap)

Men's 200m Breaststroke

1952	John Davies (Aus)
1956	Masaru Furukawa (Jap)
1960	William Mulliken (USA)
1964	Ian O'Brien (Aus)
1968	Felipe Munoz (Mex)
1972	John Hencken (USA)
1976	David Wilkie (UK)
1980	Robertas Zhulpa (USSR)
1984	Victor Davis (Can)
1988	József Szabó (Hun)
1992	Mike Barrowman (USA)
1996	Norbert Rozsa (Hun)
2000	Domenico Fioravanti (Ita)
2004	Kosuke Kitajima (Jap)

Men's 100m Butterfly

1968	Doug Russell (USA)
1972	Mark Spitz (USA)
1976	Matt Vogel (USA)
1984	Michael Gross (FRG)
1988	Anthony Nesty (Sur)
1992	Pablo Morales (USA)
1996	Denis Pankratov (Rus)
2000	Lars Froedlander (Swe)
2004	Michael Phelps (USA)

Men's 200m Butterfly

1956	William Yorzyk (USA)
1960	Mike Troy (USA)
1964	Kevin Berry (Aus)
1968	Carl Robie (USA)
1972	Mark Spitz (USA)
1976	Mike Bruner (USA)
1980	Sergey Fesenko (USSR)
1984	Jon Sieben (Aus)
1988	Michael Gross (FRG)
1992	Melvin Stewart (USA)
1996	Denis Pankratov (Rus)
2000	Tom Malchow (USA)
2004	Michael Phelps (USA)

Men's 200m Individual Medley

1968	Charles Hickcox (USA)
1972	Gunnar Larsson (Swe)
1984	Alex Baumann (Can)
1988	Tamás Darnyi (Hun)
1992	Tamás Darnyi (Hun)
1996	Attila Czene (Hun)
2000	Massimiliano Rosolino (Ita)
2004	Michael Phelps (USA)

Men's 400m Individual Medley

1964	Richard Roth (USA)
1968	Charles Hickcox (USA)
1972	Gunnar Larsson (Swe)
1976	Rod Strachan (USA)
1980	Aleksandr Sidorenko (USSR)
1984	Alex Baumann (Can)
1988	Tamás Darnyi (Hun)
1992	Tamás Darnyi (Hun)
1996	Tom Dolan (USA)
2000	Tom Dolan (USA)
2004	Michael Phelps (USA)

Men's 4 × 100m Freestyle Relay

1964	USA	1992	USA
1968	USA	1996	USA
1972	USA	2000	Australia
1984	USA	2004	South Africa
1988	USA		

Men's 4 × 200m Freestyle Relay

1952	USA	1980	USSR
1956	Australia	1984	USA
1960	USA	1988	USA
1964	USA	1992	CIS
1968	USA	1996	USA
1972	USA	2000	Australia
1976	USA	2004	USA

Men's 4 × 100m Medley Relay

1960	USA	1984	USA
1964	USA	1988	USA
1968	USA	1992	USA
1972	USA	1996	USA
1976	USA	2000	USA
1980	Australia	2004	USA

Men's 3m Springboard Diving

1952	David Browning (USA)
1956	Robert Clotworthy (USA)
1960	Gary Tobian (USA)
1964	Kenneth Sitzberger (USA)
1968	Bernard Wrightson (USA)
1972	Vladimir Vasin (USSR)
1976	Phil Boggs (USA)
1984	Greg Louganis (USA)
1988	Greg Louganis (USA)
1992	Mark Lenzi (USA)
1996	Ni Xiong (Chn)
2000	Ni Xiong (Chn)
2004	Bo Peng (Chn)

Men's 10m Platform Diving

1952	Samuel Lee (USA)
1956	Joaquin Capilla (Mex)
1960	Robert Webster (USA)
1964	Robert Webster (USA)
1968	Klaus Dibiasi (Ita)
1972	Klaus Dibiasi (Ita)
1976	Klaus Dibiasi (Ita)
1980	Falk Hoffmann (GDR)
1984	Greg Louganis (USA)
1988	Greg Louganis (USA)
1992	Sun Shuwei (Chn)
1996	Dimitri Sautin (Rus)
2000	Liang Tian (Chn)
2004	Hu Jia (Chn)

Men's Synchronised 3m Springboard Diving***

2000	China
2004	Greece

Men's Synchronised 10m Platform Diving***

2000	Russian Federation
2004	China

***New events in 2000

Women's 50m Freestyle

1988	Kristin Otto (GDR)
1992	Yang Wenyi (Chn)
1996	Amy van Dyken (USA)
2000	Inge de Bruijn (Neth)
2004	Inge de Bruijn (Neth)

Women's 100m Freestyle

1952	Katalin Szöke (Hun)
1956	Dawn Fraser (Aus)
1960	Dawn Fraser (Aus)
1964	Dawn Fraser (Aus)
1968	Jan Henne (USA)
1972	Sandra Neilson (USA)
1976	Kornelia Ender (GDR)
1980	Barbara Krause (GDR)
1984	Nancy Hogshead (USA) / Carrie Steinseifer (USA)
1988	Kristin Otto (GDR)
1992	Zhuang Yong (Chn)
1996	Le Jingyi (Chn)
2000	Inge de Bruijn (Neth)
2004	Jodie Henry (Aus)

Women's 200m Freestyle

1968	Debbie Meyer (USA)
1972	Shane Gould (Aus)
1976	Kornelia Ender (GDR)
1980	Barbara Krause (GDR)
1984	Mary Wayte (USA)
1988	Heike Friedrich (GDR)
1992	Nicole Haislett (USA)
1996	Claudia Poll (Costa Rica)
2000	Susie O'Neill (Aus)
2004	Camelia Potec (Rom)

Women's 400m Freestyle

1952	Valéria Gyenge (Hun)
1956	Lorraine Crapp (Aus)
1960	Chris Von Saltza (USA)
1964	Virginia Duenkel (USA)
1968	Debbie Meyer (USA)
1972	Shane Gould (Aus)
1976	Petra Thümer (GDR)
1980	Ines Diers (GDR)
1984	Tiffany Cohen (USA)
1988	Janet Evans (USA)
1992	Dagmar Hase (Ger)
1996	Michelle Smith (Ire)
2000	Brooke Bennett (USA)
2004	Laure Manaudou (Fra)

Women's 800m Freestyle

1968	Debbie Meyer (USA)
1972	Keena Rothhammer (USA)
1976	Petra Thümer (GDR)
1980	Michelle Ford (Aus)
1984	Tiffany Cohen (USA)
1988	Janet Evans (USA)
1992	Janet Evans (USA)
1996	Brooke Bennett (USA)
2000	Brooke Bennett (USA)
2004	Ai Shibata (Jap)

Women's 100m Backstroke

1952	Joan Harrison (SAf)
1956	Judy Grinham (UK)
1960	Lynn Burke (USA)
1964	Cathy Ferguson (USA)
1968	Kaye Hall (USA)
1972	Melissa Belote (USA)
1976	Ulrike Richter (GDR)
1980	Rica Reinisch (GDR)
1984	Theresa Andrews (USA)
1988	Kristin Otto (GDR)
1992	Krisztina Egerszegi (Hun)
1996	Beth Botsford (USA)
2000	Diana Mocanu (Rom)
2004	Natalie Coughlin (USA)

Women's 200m Backstroke

1968	Pokey Watson (USA)
1972	Melissa Belote (USA)
1976	Ulrike Richter (GDR)

1980	Rica Reinisch (GDR)
1984	Jolanda de Rover (Neth)
1988	Krisztina Egerszegi (Hun)
1992	Krisztina Egerszegi (Hun)
1996	Krisztina Egerszegi (Hun)
2000	Diana Mocanu (Rom)
2004	Kirsty Coventry (USA)

Women's 100m Breaststroke

1968	Djurdjica Bjedov (Yug)
1972	Catherine Carr (USA)
1976	Hannelore Anke (GDR)
1980	Ute Geweniger (GDR)
1984	Petra Van Staveren (Neth)
1988	Tania Dangalakova (Bul)
1992	Yelena Rudkovskaya (CIS/Bls)
1996	Penelope Heyns (SA)
2000	Megan Quann (USA)
2004	Xuejuan Luo (Chi)

Women's 200m Breaststroke

1952	Eva Székely (Hun)
1956	Ursula Happe (FRG)
1960	Anita Lonsbrough (UK)
1964	Galina Prozumenshchikova (USSR)
1968	Sharon Wichman (USA)
1972	Beverley Whitfield (Aus)
1976	Marina Koshevaya (USSR)
1980	Lina Kachushite (USSR)
1984	Anne Ottenbrite (Can)
1988	Silke Hörner (GDR)
1992	Kyoko Iwasaki (Jap)
1996	Penelope Heyns (SA)
2000	Agnes Kovacs (Hun)
2004	Amanda Beard (USA)

Women's 100m Butterfly

1956	Shelley Mann (USA)
1960	Carolyn Schuler (USA)
1964	Sharon Stouder (USA)
1968	Lynette McClements (Aus)
1972	Mayumi Aoki (Jap)
1976	Kornelia Ender (GDR)
1980	Caren Metschuck (GDR)
1984	Mary T. Meagher (USA)
1988	Kristin Otto (GDR)
1992	Qian Hong (Chn)
1996	Amy van Dyken (USA)
2000	Inge de Bruijn (Neth)
2004	Petria Thomas (Aus)

Women's 200m Butterfly

1968	Ada Kok (Neth)
1972	Karen Moe (USA)
1976	Andrea Pollack (GDR)
1980	Ines Geissler (GDR)
1984	Mary T. Meagher (USA)
1988	Kathleen Nord (GDR)
1992	Summer Sanders (USA)
1996	Susan O'Neil (Aus)
2000	Misty Hyman (USA)
2004	Orylia Jedrzejczak (Pol)

Women's 200m Individual Medley

1968	Claudia Kolb (USA)
1972	Sharon Gould (Aus)
1984	Tracy Caulkins (USA)
1988	Daniela Hunger (GDR)
1992	Lin Li (Chn)
1996	Michelle Smith (Ire)
2000	Yana Klochkova (Ukr)
2004	Yana Klochkova (Ukr)

Women's 400m Individual Medley

1964	Donna De Varona (USA)
1968	Claudia Kolb (USA)
1972	Gail Neall (Aus)
1976	Ulrike Tauber (GDR)
1980	Petra Schneider (GDR)
1984	Tracy Caulkins (USA)
1988	Janet Evans (USA)
1992	Krisztina Egerszegi (Hun)
1996	Michelle Smith (Ire)
2000	Yana Klochkova (Ukr)
2004	Yana Klochkova (Ukr)

Women's 4 × 100m Freestyle Medley

1952	Hungary
1956	Australia
1960	USA
1964	USA
1968	USA
1972	USA
1976	USA
1980	East Germany
1984	USA
1988	East Germany
1992	USA
1996	USA
2000	USA
2004	Australia

Women's 4 × 100m Medley Relay

1960	USA
1964	USA
1968	USA
1972	USA
1976	East Germany
1980	East Germany
1984	USA
1988	East Germany
1992	USA
1996	USA
2000	USA
2004	USA

Women's 3m Springboard Diving

1952	Pat McCormick (USA)
1956	Pat McCormick (USA)
1960	Ingrid Krämer (GDR)
1964	Ingrid Engel (née Krämer) (GDR)
1968	Sue Gossick (USA)

1972	Micki King (USA)
1976	Jennifer Chandler (USA)
1980	Irina Kalinina (USSR)
1984	Sylvie Bernier (Can)
1988	Gao Min (Chn)
1992	Gao Min (Chn)
1996	Mingxia Fu (Chn)
2000	Mingxia Fu (Chn)
2004	Jingjing Guo (Chn)

Women's 10m Platform Diving

1952	Pat McCormick (USA)
1956	Pat McCormick (USA)
1960	Ingrid Krämer (GDR)
1964	Lesley Bush (USA)
1968	Milena Duchkova (Cze)
1972	Ulrika Knape (Swe)
1976	Elena Vaytsekhovskaya (USSR)
1980	Martina Jäschke (GDR)
1984	Zhou Jihong (Chn)
1988	Xu Yanmei (Chn)
1992	Fu Mingxia (Chn)
1996	Fu Mingxia (Chn)
2000	Laura Wilkinson (USA)
2004	Chantelle Newbery (Aus)

Women's Synchronised 3m Springboard Diving*

2000	Russian Federation
2004	China

Women's Synchronised 10m Platform Diving*

2000	China
2000	China

***New events in 2000

YACHTING

AMERICA'S CUP

Background Note: In 1851 the Royal Yacht Squadron put up for competition a silver cup that has become the most famous trophy in yachting. In that year the New York Y.C. sent the schooner *America* across the Atlantic to compete in a 53-mile (85 km) race round the Isle of Wight; it captured the trophy which now bears its name. Until 1983 none of the many challenges by yachtsmen from Great Britain, Canada, and latterly, Australia, had been successful. In that year, however, in Rhode Island Sound *Australia II*, skippered by John Bertrand, won on the 25th challenge. The triumph was short-lived. The 1992 winner was Bill Koch's *America³* which claimed the prestigious trophy 4–1. In 1995 the New Zealand yacht *Black Magic* achieved a sensational 5–0 victory over the Americans.

In 2000 the holders, New Zealand, successfully defended their title. In 2003 the Cup was won by the Swiss yacht *Alinghi* (the first-ever European victory in the history of the competition).

Winners (since 1960)

Year	Yacht	Skipper
1962	*Weatherly* (USA)	Emil Mosbacher Jr
1964	*Constellation* (USA)	Bob Bavier Jr
1967	*Intrepid* (USA)	Emil Mosbacher Jr
1970	*Intrepid* (USA)	Bill Ficker
1974	*Courageous* (USA)	Ted Hood
1977	*Courageous* (USA)	Ted Turner
1980	*Freedom* (USA)	Dennis Conner
1983	*Australia II* (Aus)	John Bertrand
1987	*Stars & Stripes* (USA)	Dennis Conner
1988	*Stars & Stripes* (USA)	Dennis Conner
1992	*America* (USA)	Bill Koch
1995	*Black Magic* (NZ)	Russell Coutts
2000	*NZL 60* (NZ)	Russell Coutts
2003	*Alinghi* (Swi)	Russell Coutts

ADMIRAL'S CUP (since 1975)

Year	Country	Year	Country
1975	UK	1991	France
1977	UK	1993	Germany
1979	Australia	1995	Italy
1981	UK	1997	USA
1983	West Germany	1999	Netherlands
1985	West Germany	2001	Cancelled
1987	New Zealand	2003	Australia
1989	UK	2005	Cancelled

THE WORLD
OF SCIENCE

A wide-ranging picture of scientific
discovery, designed to explain some
of the most important ideas in
astronomy, physics, chemistry, biology, genetics and human evolution.
It also aims to give some account of
current research in various fields.
This edition includes Special Topics
ranging from the minerals of the
world to mobile phones and from
fossil evidence of evolution to optical storage. Also included is a variety
of useful scientific tables. Readers
will also find many definitions of
scientific terms in the General
Information section.

TABLE OF CONTENTS

THE WORLD OF SCIENCE

In Parts I, II, and III the inanimate universe is described. This is the domain of cosmology, astronomy, geology, physics, and chemistry. There are already many interesting links which join this realm to that of the living and make it difficult to say where the boundary lies. Nevertheless it is still convenient to accord biological science and human evolution two separate chapters, IV and V. Part VI provides some useful scientific tables. Part VII consists of articles on topics of current interest.

I. THE UNIVERSE—ASTRONOMY AND COSMOLOGY

LOOKING AT THE UNIVERSE

We can observe the universe in many different ways. First, there are waves of visible light together with invisible rays of somewhat longer (infra-red) and somewhat shorter (ultra-violet) wavelengths. These waves show us the bright astronomical objects and, to make use of them, astronomers have constructed telescopes of great power and precision backed up with cameras, spectroscopes, and numerous auxiliaries. The biggest telescope in the world is the 10 m reflector based at Mauna Kea in the United States. The earth's atmosphere acts as a distorting and only partially transparent curtain and the erection of telescopes on satellites is beginning to extend optical telescope performance significantly. Indeed, the Hubble Space Telescope, launched in 1990, has already dramatically expanded our knowledge of the universe.

Secondly, there are radio waves of much longer wavelength than light. Radio telescopes are sensitive radio receivers with specialised aerial systems. The scientific stature of modern radio astronomy was emphasised by the award in 1974 of the Nobel Physics Prize to two Cambridge radio astronomers, Ryle and Hewish.

Other types of radiation reach the earth from outer space but do not necessarily penetrate the atmosphere. With the advent of satellite-borne detectors, mountain-top telescopes of increasing sophistication and apparatus buried in deep mines, new facets of X-ray, gamma-ray, optical UV and infrared astronomy are now rapidly deepening our knowledge of the nature of the universe and of the violent processes by which galaxies as well as individual stars and planetary systems evolve.

Gravitational Wave Astronomy

Currently, a new area of astronomy called gravitational wave astronomy is being researched. It is predicted by Einstein's general theory of relativity and measures the wobble in space-time caused as massive bodies are accelerated or disturbed.

Great Distances and Large Numbers

To visualise the immense scale of the universe is almost as much a problem for the scientist as for the layman. The conventional shorthand is to express 1,000 as 10^3; 1,000,000 as 10^6. On this scale the earth is 1.496×10^8 km away from the sun. Concorde, for example, the world's fastest airliner, took about $3\frac{1}{2}$ hours to travel 5,000 km from London to New York. The "Viking" spacecraft in 1976 took just over a year to travel the 200 million km to Mars.

These distances are minute by comparison with the distance even to the nearest star, Proxima Centauri, some 4×10^{13} km away. This distance is more conveniently expressed in terms of the travel time of light itself. With a velocity of nearly 300,000 km per second, in a year light travels about 9.46×10^{12} km. The distance to Proxima Centauri is therefore 4·2 light years. Even this distance, enormous on our terrestrial scale, is a small cosmic distance. The diameter of our Galaxy is about 10^5 light years, while the most distant objects yet observed lie over 1.3×10^{10} light years away. Some astronomical distances are shown on T8.

PLANETS, STARS AND GALAXIES

The Solar System

The earth is the third, counting outward, of nine planets revolving in nearly circular orbits round the sun. Some of their particulars are given in the Table (T8). The sun and its planets are the main bodies of the solar system. Mainly between the orbits of Mars and Jupiter revolve numerous small bodies—the minor planets or asteroids, the largest of which, Ceres, is only 947 km in diameter. Apart from these, the solar system is tenuously populated with particles varying in size from about a micron (10^{-6} m) to hundreds of metres in diameter. Some of these objects collide with the earth's atmosphere. The smaller particles (micrometeoroids) are too small to be visible. Larger particles (meteoroids) cause the phenomenon known as meteors (commonly referred to as 'shooting stars') when they burn up at around 100 km altitude. The particle collides with air molecules. This causes frictional heating which usually results in complete vapourization of the particle. Even larger chunks, of rocky or iron composition, cause the rare and brilliant fireballs, some of which survive their high-speed flight through the earth's atmosphere and may later be recovered. Such objects (meteorites) are very important, providing examples of extraterrestrial rocks, and thus giving the composition of some of the most primitive material left in the solar system. Collisions with very large meteorites (or small asteroids) are now, fortunately, very rare. However, the large meteorite crater in Arizona is one recent reminder that such collisions still occur, although much less frequently now than earlier in the history of the planetary system. The surfaces of Mercury, the Moon, Mars, and Venus together with those of many other planetary satellites still show the scars from collisions with a multitude of objects of up to tens of km in diameter.

Comets

Comets are fascinating objects which, from time to time, provide a spectacular sight. More than 700 comets have been observed so far, and about six new ones are discovered each year. At the heart of every comet is a small nucleus. In 1986 the Giotto space probe revealed that Halley's comet has a potato-shaped nucleus measuring 15 km by 10 km. This nucleus consists of ices of various gases, chiefly water, interspersed with dust particles. In their highly elliptical orbits comets spend most of their life at great distances from the sun, where the temperature is very low because of the feeble solar radiation, so that all the "icy" materials are solid. Periodically, when each comet returns to the inner parts of the solar system, the increasing solar radiation heats the surface layers, evaporating the volatile ices, which carry the surface dust away from the comet nucleus. Solar-radiation pressure, acting on the dust constituents, and the solar wind acting on the ionised constituents, form the gigantic cometary tails which may reach 2×10^8 km in length—larger than the radius of the earth's orbit. The dramatic impact of the fragments of Comet Shoemaker-Levy 9 on the dark side of Jupiter in 1994 created spots on the planet's surface that were as big as the earth's diameter and that lasted for seven weeks.

The Sun

The sun itself is a dense, roughly spherical mass of glowing matter, 1,392,000 km across. Its heat is so intense that the atoms are split into separated electrons and nuclei and matter in such a state is called plasma. At the sun's centre the temperature has the unimaginable value of about 15 million degrees Centigrade (a coal fire is about 800°C). Under such conditions the atomic nuclei frequently collide with one another at great speeds and reactions occur between them. The sun consists largely of hydrogen and, in the very hot plasma, the nuclei of hydrogen atoms interact by a series of reactions whose net result is to turn hydrogen into helium. This is a process which releases energy just as burning does, only these nuclear processes are incomparably more energetic than ordinary burning. In fact, the energy released is great enough to be the source of all the light and heat which the sun has been pouring into space for thousands of millions of years.

The Solar Wind

Emerging from the sun and streaming past the earth is a "solar wind" of fast-moving electrons and protons (T11) whose motion is closely linked with the behaviour of an extensive magnetic field based on the sun. In fact, the region round the sun and extending far into space past the earth is full of complex, fluctuating particle streams and magnetic fields which interact with planetary atmospheres causing, among other things, auroras and magnetic storms.

Stars

In colour, brightness, age, and size the sun is typical of vast numbers of other stars. Only from the human point of view is there anything special about the sun—it is near enough to give us life. Even the possession of a system of revolving planets is routinely observed in other stars.

No star can radiate energy at the rate the sun does without undergoing internal changes in the course of time. Consequently stars evolve and old processes in them give rise to new. The exact nature of stellar evolution—so far as it is at present understood—would be too complex to describe here in any detail. It involves expansion and contraction, changes of temperature, change of colour, and change in chemical composition as the nuclear processes gradually generate new chemical elements by reactions such as the conversion of hydrogen to helium, helium to neon, neon to magnesium, and so on. The speed of evolution changes from time to time, but is in any case very slow compared with the pace of terrestrial life; nothing very dramatic may occur for hundreds of millions of years. Evidence for the various phases of evolution is therefore obtained by studying many stars, each at a different stage of its life. Thus astronomers recognise many types with charmingly descriptive names, such as supergiants, blue giants, sub-giants, red, white and brown dwarfs.

The path of stellar evolution may be marked by various explosive events. One of these, which occurs in sufficiently large stars, is an enormous explosion in which a substantial amount of the star is blown away into space in the form of high-speed streams of gas. For about a fortnight, such an exploding star will radiate energy 200 million times as fast as the sun. Japanese and Chinese (but not Western) astronomers recorded such an occurrence in A.D. 1054, and the exploding gases, now called the Crab nebula, can still be seen in powerful telescopes and form a cloud six or seven light-years across. While it lasts, the explosion shows up as an abnormally bright star and is called a supernova. In late February 1987 a spectacular supernova was observed in our nearby galaxy the Large Magellanic Cloud. At a distance of only 1.7×10^5 light years this supernova was the closest to the Earth for over 400 years. Many theories have been confirmed by the findings.

Groups of Stars

It is not surprising that ancient peoples saw pictures in the sky. The constellations, however, are not physically connected groups of stars but just happen to be patterns visible from earth. A conspicuous exception to this is the Milky Way, which a telescope resolves into many millions of separate stars. If we could view the Milky Way from a vast distance and see it as a whole we should observe a rather flat wheel of stars with spiral arms something like the sparks of a rotating Catherine wheel. This system of stars is physically connected by gravitational forces and moves through space as a whole; it is called a galaxy.

The Galaxy is about 10^5 light-years across and contains roughly 10^{11} stars. An inconspicuous one of these stars near the edge of the wheel is our sun; the prominent stars in our night sky are members of the galaxy that happen to be rather near us. Sirius, the brightest, is only 8·6 light-years away, a trivial distance, astronomically speaking.

The galaxy does not contain stars only, there are also clouds of gas and dust, particularly in the plane of the galaxy. Much of the gas is hydrogen, and its detection is difficult. However, gaseous hydrogen gives out radio waves with a wavelength of 21 cm. Radio telescopes are just the instruments to receive these, and workers in Holland, America, and Australia detected the gas clouds by this means. In 1952 they found that the hydrogen clouds lie in the spiral arms of the galaxy, and this is some of the strongest evidence for the spiral form.

Another important feature of the galactic scene is the weak but enormously extensive magnetic field. This is believed to have an intimate connection with the spiral structure.

Globular Clusters

Around the spiral arms, and forming part of the galaxy, are numerous globular clusters of stars. These are roughly spherical, abnormally densely packed, collections of stars with many thousands of members. Because of its form and density, a globular cluster may be assumed to have been formed in one process, not star by star. Thus all its stars are the same age. This is of great interest to astronomers, because they can study differences between stars of similar age but different sizes.

The 21cm radio waves that are given out by hydrogen also gave a startling and wholly unexpected finding. The outer reaches of our galaxy (and others) were seen to be rotating at a constant velocity. This implies that the mass is not concentrated in the centre, as might be expected, but is distributed in a large dark halo extending up to five times the radius of the visible part of the galaxy. The total mass of the Galactic halo is unknown but it is thought to contain at least ten times as much matter than the visible material in the galaxy.

Currently, astronomers are left with the rather fundamental question: what is the majority of the galaxy made of? There are presently a number of competing theories. It may be composed of compact sub-stellar material (such as brown dwarfs or neutron stars) known collectively as MACHOs or some kind of weakly interactive massive particle.

Galaxies

One might be forgiven for assuming that such a vast system as the galaxy is in fact the universe; but this is not so. In the constellation of Andromeda is a famous object which, on close examination, turns out to be another galaxy of size and structure similar to our own. Its distance is given in the table (T8). The Andromeda galaxy is the same basic structure as our own, but roughly half as big again. The Milky Way, the Andromeda nebula, and about two dozen other galaxies form a cluster of galaxies called the Local Group. It is indeed a fact that the universe is populated with groups, clusters and superclusters, of galaxies. A cluster may contain two or three galaxies, but some contain thousands.

By about 1920 it was known that there were at least half a million galaxies, and with the advent of the 2·54 m. Mt. Wilson telescope this number rose to 10^8 and has now been increased further by larger telescopes which can see out to distances greater than 10^{10} light years. Through the powerful telescopes the nearer galaxies reveal their inner structures. Photographs of galaxies are among the most beautiful and fascinating photographs ever taken, and readers who have never seen one should hasten to the nearest illustrated astronomy book. Most galaxies have a spiral or elliptical structure but about 2 per cent have peculiar wisps and appendages. Some galaxies are strong emitters of radio waves. A recently discovered type of galaxy is the starburst galaxy. This is an otherwise normal galaxy in which huge numbers of stars are forming in a small volume at its centre.

Rather alarmingly there is an increasingly large amount of information from observations of groups and superclusters of galaxies that they contain significant amounts of dark matter. In a similar way that the mass of the Sun can be calculated by the orbits of the planets, the mass of a galactic group can be found by observing the orbits of galactic members. By observing the galaxies and applying well understood Newtonian mechanics the mass of many clusters has been found.

There seems to be an even larger proportion of dark matter than that found in lone galaxies. This implies that the entire universe is mostly composed of dark matter interacting with ordinary matter only though the force of gravity. Currently there are about 30 major international dark matter experiments trying, quite simply, to discover what the universe is made of.

The Expanding Universe

Two discoveries about galaxies are of the utmost importance. One is that, by and large, clusters of galaxies are uniformly distributed through the universe. The other is that the distant galaxies are receding from us.

How is this known? Many readers may be familiar with the Doppler effect first discovered in 1842. Suppose a stationary body emits waves of any kind and we measure their wavelength, finding it to be L cm. Now suppose the body approaches us; the waves are thereby crowded together in the intervening space and the wavelength appears less than L; if the body recedes the wavelength appears greater than L. The Austrian physicist, J. Doppler (1803–53), discovered the well-known change of pitch of a train whistle as it approaches and passes us. The same principle applies to the light. Every atom emits light of definite wavelengths which appear in a spectroscope as a series of coloured lines—a different series for each atom. If the atom is in a receding body all the lines have slightly longer wavelengths than usual, and the amount of the change depends uniquely on the speed. Longer wavelengths mean that the light is redder than usual, so that a light from a receding body shows what is called a "red shift." The speed of recession can be calculated from the amount of red shift.

Hubble's Law

It was the American astronomer, V. M. Slipher, who first showed (in 1914) that some galaxies emitted light with a red shift. In the 1920s and 1930s the famous astronomer E. Hubble (1889–1953) measured both the distances and red shift of many galaxies and proved what is now known as Hubble's Law about which there is now some controversy. This states that the speed of recession of galaxies is proportional to their distance from us. This does not apply to our neighbours in the Local Group, we and they are keeping together. Hubble's Law has been tested and found to hold for the farthest detectable galaxies; they are about 7×10^9 light-years away and are receding with a speed approaching that of light.

The expansion of the universe does not imply that the Local Group is the centre of the universe —from any other viewpoint in the universe Hubble's Law would also be valid, and the distant galaxies would, similarly, all appear to be rapidly receding.

The Big Bang Theory

One possible implication of this most exciting scientific discovery is that, if the galaxies have always been receding, at an early time they must have been closer together. We can calculate that about 10^{10} years ago all the matter of the universe could have been densely packed.

This is called the big bang theory. The central questions of cosmology now concern the ultimate fate of the universe, its size, age and composition. Telescopes of ever increasing sophistication on the Earth and in space are beginning to address these fundamental questions.

Quasars, Pulsars and Black Holes

In November 1962 Australian radio astronomers located a strong radio emitter with sufficient precision for the Mt. Palomar optical astronomers to identify it on photographs and examine the nature of its light. The red shift was so great that the object must be exceedingly distant; on the other hand it looked star-like, much smaller than a galaxy. By the beginning of 1967 over a hundred of these objects had been discovered and other characteristics established, such as strong ultraviolet radiation and inconstancy, in some cases, of the rate at which radiation is emitted. Not all of these so-called quasars are strong radio emitters; some show all the other characteristics except radio emission. It has been estimated that the "quiet" kind are about a hundred times more numerous than the radio kind. One great problem here is: how can such relatively small objects generate such inconceivably great amounts of energy that they appear bright at such huge distances? Recent observations suggest that quasars are only the central visible part of an otherwise undetected galaxy. There may also be a massive black hole near the quasar centre.

Late in 1967, while investigating quasars, Cambridge radio astronomers discovered pulsars, a new type of heavenly body. Their characteristic is the emission of regular pulses of radio waves every second or so. A pulsar in the Crab nebula has a repetition rate even faster—about 1/30 sec—and it follows that pulsars must be very small bodies little if at all bigger than the Earth.

The Fate of Evolving Stars

The existence of such small bodies raises again the problem of the ultimate fate of evolving stars. Much depends on their mass because this determines how strong the inward pull of gravity is. For a star to be at least temporarily stable the inward pull must be balanced by an outward pressure. In the sun this is the pressure of the burning hydrogen and the resulting average density is about 1·4 times that of water (**Table, T8**). In some stars the inward pressure is so great that collapse proceeds until it is balanced by a different type of outward pressure that sets in when electrons and atomic nuclei are forced into proximity. Stars so formed are the "white dwarfs". They are millions of times denser than the sun—"a matchbox of their matter would weigh a ton"— and they are very small though not small enough to be pulsars. The latter are now generally thought to be a million times denser even than white dwarfs and to consist largely of tightly packed neutrons. Such bodies are called neutron stars.

Other Debates

Could the tendency of a massive star to fall inwards ever be so great that no outward pressure known to physics would suffice to balance it? Apparently it could! Many astrophysicists now hold on theoretical grounds that such a gravitational collapse could create a high density object whose gravitational field would be too strong to allow anything—including light waves—ever to leave the body. Such hypothetical objects are called "black holes" because, light and other signals being unable to emerge from them, their matter has literally disappeared from view. Black holes could be detected by the disturbance their gravitational attraction causes to neighbouring visible stars and also because atoms attracted by the black hole should emit intense X-rays before falling so far in that they too disappear into the black hole. Both of these detection methods led some astronomers to conjecture that there is a black hole in the constellation Cygnus. There is another promising candidate for a black hole in the Large Magellanic Cloud. The theory of gravitational collapse raises profound and unsolved problems about our physical concepts.

In 1995 scientists discovered compelling evidence of the existence of the biggest black hole ever found, with a mass equivalent to 40 million of our suns. Even larger black holes of up to 1000 million solar masses may reside in the centres of some galaxies.

THE ORIGIN, DEVELOPMENT AND ULTIMATE FATE OF THE UNIVERSE

Scientists can only attempt to explain the universe by relating its observable structure to the features predicted by alternative theories of its origin and development. The time span of all our observations of the Cosmos is very small by comparison with the lifetime of the universe (more than 10^{10} years). Also, contrary to many other scientific disciplines, it is impossible to repeat the "experiment", under controlled conditions. We must, therefore, explore the evolution of the universe by using the fact that light from the most distant galaxies has taken about 10^{10} years to reach us, thus providing us with a crucial, if tantalisingly remote and thus indistinct, view of the universe at a much earlier epoch.

Models of the Universe

Several models of the universe have been based on Einstein's theory of General Relativity (**T17**). Einstein's equations may be solved to predict the evolution of the universe. However, there is a spectrum of solutions which vary from a continuous and indefinite expansion at the present rate to an eventual slowing and subsequent contraction to a dense state, again in the distant future, which hints at a "pulsating" universe.

The Formation of Galaxies and Stars

On any theory of the universe, some explanation has to be found for the existence of clusters of galaxies. In all theories galaxies condense out from dispersed masses of gas, principally hydrogen. It is believed on theoretical grounds each galaxy could not condense into one enormous star but must form many fragments which shrink separately into clusters of stars. In these clusters many stars, perhaps hundreds or thousands or even millions, are born. A small cluster, visible to the naked eye, is the Pleiades. The Orion nebula, visible as a hazy blob of glowing gas in the sword of Orion, is the scene of much star-forming activity at present. However, the best evidence yet for witnessing the birth of a star comes from observations by the Infrared Astronomical Satellite (IRAS). Deep within a gas and dust cloud called the Ophiuchus dark nebula, matter is falling inward in a manner predicted by contemporary theories of star formation. At the centre of this collapsing cloud there seems to be an embryonic star perhaps only 30,000 years old.

The Evolutionary Theory

According to the Evolutionary theory the "initial dense state" consisted of very hot plasma in a state of overall expansion. The expanding plasma was both cooling and swirling about. The random swirling produces irregularities in the distribution of the hot gas—here it would be rather denser, there rather less dense. If a sufficiently large mass of denser gas happened to occur, then the gravitational attraction between its own particles would hold it together and maintain its permanent identity, even though the rest of the gas continued to swirl and expand. Such a large mass would gradually condense into fragments to become a cluster of galaxies.

Revolutionary Discoveries

The 1960s witnessed revolutionary developments in both observational and theoretical astronomy. For example, it now seems agreed that remote sources of radio waves are more abundant the weaker their intensity. This strongly suggests that they are more abundant at greater distances. Thus the universe is not *uniform* as the original steady-state theory prescribed. Since greater distances correspond to earlier times, any extra abundance of objects observed at the greater distance means that the universe was denser in its younger days than now. This favours an evolutionary theory of the universe.

The same theory requires that the initial dense state of the universe—aptly christened "the primaeval fireball"—should contain intense electromagnetic radiation with a distribution of wavelengths characteristic of the high temperature. As the fireball, *i.e.* the universe, expanded over a period of about 10^{10} years it cooled, and one feature of this process is that the wavelengths of the radiation increase and their distribution becomes characteristic of a much lower temperature. In fact, the wavelengths should now be concentrated round about 1 mm to 1 cm (corresponding to about $-270°C$) and the radiation should approach the earth uniformly from all directions. Radiation just like this was detected in the 1960s by extremely sensitive instruments both at ground-based observatories and flown from balloon payloads high in the earth's atmosphere— above most of the water vapour and other constituents which interfere with such delicate observations. This "microwave background" radiation appears to be "cosmological", and thus supports strongly the evolutionary or "Big Bang" theory as opposed to the "Steady-State" theory, which cannot rationally explain the radiation.

In 1992 data from the Cosmic Background Explorer (COBE) satellite strengthened the Big Bang theory still further. Minute variations in the temperature of the background radiation across the sky help to show that the distribution of matter in the early universe could act as a blueprint for the future large-scale structures we can observe today. In 2003 a satellite called MAP was due to re-measure the cosmic background radiation in exquisite detail. This satellite will bring exciting new discoveries.

The Formation of the Chemical Elements

A stable nucleus is one that lasts indefinitely because it is not radioactive. There are 274 known kinds of stable atomic nuclei. These nuclei are the isotopes (*q.v.*) of 81 different chemical elements; the other elements, including, for example, uranium and radium, are always radioactive. Some elements are rare, others abundant. The most common ones on earth are oxygen, silicon, aluminium, and iron. However, the earth is rather atypical. It is especially deficient in hydrogen, because the gravitational attraction of our small planet was not strong enough to prevent this very light gas from escaping into space.

It is possible to examine the chemical constituents of meteorites and to infer the composition of the sun and other stars from the spectrum of the light they emit. By such means, the conclusion has been reached that 93% of the atoms in our galaxy are hydrogen, 7% are helium; all the other elements together account for about one in a thousand atoms. A glance at the Table of Elements (*see* **T56**) will show that hydrogen and helium are two of the lightest elements: they are in fact the two simplest. The problem is to explain how the heavier chemical elements appear in the universe at all. It is here that a fascinating combination of astronomy and nuclear physics is required.

Energy

We have already referred to the fact that the energy radiated from the sun originates in nuclear reactions which turn hydrogen into helium. Why is energy given out? To answer this question we note that nuclei are made up of *protons* and *neutrons* (*q.v.*). These particles attract one another strongly—that is why a nucleus holds together. To separate the particles, energy would have to be supplied to overcome the attractive forces. This amount of energy is called *binding energy* and is a definite quantity for every

T7

kind of nucleus. Conversely, when the particles are brought together to form a nucleus the binding energy is *released* in the form of radiations and heat. Different nuclei consist of different numbers of particles, therefore the relevant quantity to consider is the *binding energy per particle*. Let us call this B. Then if elements of *high* B are formed out of those of *low* B there is a *release* of energy.

Now B is small (relatively) for light elements like lithium, helium, and carbon; it rises to a maximum for elements of middling atomic weight like iron; it falls again for really heavy elements like lead, bismuth, and uranium. Consequently, energy is released by forming middleweight elements either by splitting up heavy nuclei ("nuclear fission") or by joining up light ones ("nuclear fusion").

The Study of Fusion Processes

It is the latter process, fusion, that is going on in stars. The fusion processes can be studied in physics laboratories by using large accelerating machines to hurl nuclei at one another to make them coalesce. In stars the necessary high velocity of impact occurs because the plasma is so hot. Gradually the hydrogen is turned into helium, and helium into heavier and heavier elements. This supplies the energy that the stars radiate and simultaneously generates the chemical elements.

The Heaviest Elements

The very heavy elements present a problem. To form them from middleweight elements, energy has to be *supplied*. Since there is plenty of energy inside a star, a certain small number of heavy nuclei will indeed form, but they will continually undergo fission again under the prevailing intense conditions. How do they ever get away to form cool ordinary elements, like lead and bismuth, in the earth? One view links them with the highly explosive supernovæ, to which we have already referred earlier. If the heavy elements occur in these stars the force of the explosion disperses them into cool outer space before they have time to undergo the fission that would otherwise have been their fate. The heavy elements are thus seen as the dust and debris of stellar catastrophes. The view is in line with the steady-state theory, because supernovæ are always occurring and keeping up the supply of heavy elements. In the evolutionary theory some of the generation of elements is supposed to go on in the very early stages of the initial dense state and to continue in the stars that evolve in the fullness of time. It cannot be claimed that the origin of the chemical elements is completely known, but we have said enough to show that there are plausible theories. Time and more facts will choose between them.

The Formation of the Planets

Precisely how the planetary system was formed is still not understood in detail. From extremely precise observations of the movements of some nearby stars, it seems certain that other planetary systems occur among our stellar neighbours. By inference, it is thus probable that among certain classes of stars, planetary systems are very common throughout the universe.

Two other facts are crucial for any theory of planetary system formation. First, all the planetary orbits lie nearly in the plane perpendicular to the axis of rotation of the sun. The planets' rotations about the sun are all in the same direction and their axes of rotation, with two exceptions (Venus and Uranus), are close to the polar axis of their orbit planes, and in the same sense as their orbital rotation about the sun. Secondly, there is a very strong inverse correlation between planetary distance from the sun and the planet's mean density, particularly if the correct allowance is made for the effects of gravitational compression in the deep interiors of planets (greater in large than in small planets).

Rather than theories which would place plan-

etary formation as either the random collection of pre-formed planets by the sun in its path through the galaxy or as the consequence of a very near encounter between our sun and another star, it is now generally believed that the origin of the planetary system (and most of the satellites, etc.) was a direct consequence of the process which originally formed the sun.

As the primæval solar nebula contracted, to conserve angular momentum, its rotation rate increased, and a diffuse equatorial disk of dust and gas formed. In the cold outer region (10–20° K) of this disk, all materials except helium and possibly hydrogen could readily condense on dust particles. Near the centre the temperature was higher, increasingly so as the proto-sun heated up, initially by the energy released by its gravitational contraction and, later, by the thermonuclear processes.

The Process of Accretion

Within this rotating and swirling disk of gas and dust, the process of accretion proceeded. Low-velocity collision between dust particles from time to time allowed larger particles to be created, composed of a mixture of the heavier elements and also the "icy" materials, particularly so in the colder outer regions where more of the "ices" were in a frozen state. Virtually our only information comes from detailed study of meteorites and from spectroscopic observation of comets. Eventually rocks of the size of centimetres, metres, and even kilometres were built up in this way. The build-up, controlled by low-velocity collisions, particularly of "sticky" materials, and also by electrostatic charges, was, at all times, however, moderated by occasional destructive high-velocity collisions. The relatively high viscosity of the dust and gas mixture throughout the disk must have been very important in producing a relatively uniform, rotational motion throughout the disk. When "rocks" a few kilometres in size had been created new factors became important. Gravitational forces firstly increased the capacity of the larger "rocks" to accrete additional dust and smaller particles and, secondly, allowed some retention of material after even high-velocity collisions which would have destroyed smaller pieces.

The Giant Planets

The next stage is possibly the most difficult to model. Within a relatively uniform disk containing large numbers of rocks up to a few kilometres in diameter mixed within the residual dust and a large amount of gas, and extending to well outside Pluto's orbit, a small number of massive planets were formed. Some debris now remains as the comets and asteroids; however this debris and all the major planets, including the massive Jupiter, represent in total only a very small percentage of the original material of the solar nebula which was not condensed to form the sun.

It would appear that relatively quickly, during a period of 10^7 or 10^8 years, the large numbers of kilometre-sized objects, by collision and mutual gravitational attraction, formed the nuclei of the present planets and probably, in most cases, their major satellites also, in orbits relatively similar to their present ones. The planet-building process was most efficient at distances from the sun corresponding to the present orbits of Jupiter or Saturn, a compromise between temperature decreasing with distance from the sun, allowing a greater percentage of the total material to be solid and thus available for accretion, and density of material being greater closer to the sun.

The Jovian Planets

The outer or "Jovian" planets must have grown quickly, sweeping up hydrogen and helium gas as well as solid particles. Closer to the sun, the "icy" materials, still mainly in gaseous form, could not contribute very significantly to the

THE SOLAR SYSTEM

	Mean distance from Sun (millions of km)	Diameter km	Period of Revolution**	Average density (water = 1)	Number of Satellites
Sun	—	1,392,000	27·30 d	—	—
Mercury	57·9	4,878	87·97 d	5·4	0
Venus	108·2	12,104	224·70 d	5·2	0
Earth	149·6	12,756	365·26 d	5·5	1
Mars	227·0	6,705	686·98 d	?·0	2
Jupiter	778·3	142,985	11·86 y	1·3	61*
Saturn	1,427	120,537	29·46 y	0·7	31*
Uranus	2,869·6	51,119	84·01 y	1·3	21*
Neptune	4,496·6	50,538	164·79 y	1·8	11*
Pluto***	5,900	2,320	248·59 y	1·1	1

*These planets also have planetary rings. **d = days   y = years. ***Scientists are now calling Pluto (and the other bodies at the edge of the solar system such as Sedna and Quaoar) trans-Neptunian planets.

initial accretion process, so that only smaller planets could form. Owing to their smaller mass, gravitational field and thus lower "escape velocity," they were only able to accrete a small proportion of the heavier gas present within the inner part of the solar system. Thus, at present, these "terrestrial" planets are much denser than the outer "Jovian" planets, much smaller in size, and contain very little hydrogen or helium. The planet-building process was probably ended by two factors: the gravitational disruptive effect of the planets already formed and the enhanced "solar wind" of the young sun, which swept much of the residual dust and gas out of the solar system.

Before the process was complete, however, the gravitational energy released by the material falling onto the proto-planets plus the radioactive heating of short-lived isotopes present at the time of planetary formation were responsible for melting most of the bodies of the planets and probably all the larger satellites and asteroids. This process allowed gravitational segregation of denser and lighter materials within the planets, and the production of the core, mantle and crustal regions of each of the terrestrial planets. Long after the dust and gas were driven from the solar system and the planet surfaces cooled and solidified, the residual larger rocks and asteroids, of which enormous numbers were originally still present, continued to be swept up by each of the planets. The record of this violent stage of the solar system's development can still be seen in the saturation cratering observed on the Moon, Mercury, and Mars.

Recent Discoveries

In the past four decades, direct space exploration, using automated space probes (and manned spacecraft in the case of the Moon) has enormously increased our knowledge of the solar system. Notable have been the Viking, Pioneer and Voyager projects. The five space probes to Halley's comet in 1986 were also a huge success. Important discoveries have continued to be made by ground-based telescopes that are now comparable in some wavebands to the Hubble Space Telescope thanks

to increasing sophisticated techniques such as the adaptive optics system that accounts for atmospheric ripples. More recently a large number of scientific missions have been launched including the X-ray multimirror telescope (XMM) to observe the universe, the Cluster II satellites observing the Earth's plasma environment, the Cassini mission to Saturn which is also carrying the Huygens probe to be dropped into Titan's atmosphere, the Mars Pathfinder mission, the Galileo trip to Jupiter, the Ulysses probe investigation of the Sun and the repaired Hubble Space Telescope. All have generated great quantities of exciting new scientific data.

THE EARTH

The Earth is the third of nine planets in the Solar System, orbiting the Sun at a distance of approximately 150 million kilometers. The Earth has the shape of a slightly flattened sphere, with an equatorial radius of 6378 km and a polar radius of 6357. It has a mass of $5·97 \times 10^{24}$ kilograms, a density of about 5·5 grams per cubic centimeter, and an average surface gravitational acceleration of 9·8 meters per second per second.

Internal Structure of the Earth

Although the Earth has an average density of 5·5 g/cc, most rocks on the surface range in density from about 2·5 to 3·3 g/cc. This indicates that the Earth is not a homogeneous body and must contain denser material within. In fact, the solid Earth (that is, the Earth excluding the hydrosphere, biosphere, and atmosphere) is divided into three layers that are distinct in composition and physical properties: crust, mantle, and core.

Core, Mantle and Crust

By these findings, and by many others, a picture can be built up of the internal structure of the earth. The core is composed of iron–nickel alloy. It is liquid at the outside, but contains a solid inner core of radius about one-fifth of that of the earth. For a further discussion, see Geology, T47–8.

SOME ASTRONOMICAL DISTANCES

(1 light-year = $9·46 \times 10^{12}$ km).

Object	Distance from Earth (light-years)	Velocity of recession (km per second)	Object	Distance from Earth (light-years)	Velocity of recession (km per second)
Sun	$1·6 \times 10^{-5}$	—	Andromeda Galaxy	$2·2 \times 10^6$	−299
Nearest star (Proxima Centauri)	4·2	—	Galaxy in Virgo	$7·5 \times 10^7$	1,200
Brightest star (Sirius) .	8·6	—	Galaxy in Gt. Bear	10^9	14,900
Pleiades . . .	410	—	Galaxy in Corona Borealis	$1·3 \times 10^9$	21,600
Centre of Milky Way .	$3·0 \times 10^4$	—	Galaxy in Bootes	$4·5 \times 10^9$	39,300
Magellanic clouds (the nearest galaxies) .	$1·6 \times 10^5$	—	Very remote quasi stellar object	$\sim 1·2 \times 10^{10}$	~280,000

Continents and Oceans

If the surface of the Earth were level, the sea would cover the entire planet. So why are there continents and oceans? One reason is buoyancy. The continental crust and oceanic crust are fundamentally different. The continental crust is thick and relatively light, while the oceanic crust is thin and dense. As a result, the continental crust floats high on the mantle in the same way that a huge, empty ocean liner floats high in the water, whereas the oceanic crust acts more like an overloaded barge.

The state of gravitational equilibrium of the crust is known as *isostasy*, and the flexing of the crust in response to loads imposed or removed from it is known as *isostatic adjustment*. Just as ships and icebergs have a submarine keel that keeps them in balance, so does thick continental crust. The Himalayas, for example, rise almost 9 km above sea level, but *descend* more than 60 km below sea level. It is also this isostatic adjustment that allows rocks that form at depths of many kilometres to buoy up as the rocks above them erode away.

Materials of the Earth: Minerals and Rocks

Rocks are solid, naturally-occurring pieces of a planet. Most rocks are composed of one or more minerals (coal is composed of organic material, but it is still considered to be a rock). A mineral is a naturally-occurring, generally inorganic material with a specific chemical composition and a definite crystalline structure (its molecules are arranged in an orderly, repeating pattern). Although water is natural and has a specific composition, it is not a mineral because it is liquid and therefore not crystalline; water ice, however, is a mineral because it has a crystalline structure.

Minerals

More than 3500 minerals have been discovered so far, but only about 100 are common in the crust. There are a number of groups of minerals, including carbonates, sulfides, phosphates, and native elements, but the largest group by far is the silicates. Silicates are all composed of silicon-oxygen molecules combined with other elements. In fact, there is much more oxygen in the Earth's crust than there is in the atmosphere. See T70 for a further discussion.

Groups of Rocks

There are three groups of rocks on Earth: igneous, sedimentary, and metamorphic. Igneous rocks form from the solidification of molten rock, either on the surface (volcanic, or extrusive, rocks) or underground (plutonic, or intrusive, rocks). Sedimentary rocks form when sediments (e.g., sand and mud) lithify, or turn to stone. Sediments may be a) mechanical: derived from the physical breakdown of other rocks (e.g., sand); b) chemical: precipitated from solution (e.g., salt); or c) organic: derived from living things (e.g., chalk, peat). Metamorphic rocks form when other rocks are subject to heat or pressure that alters the mineralogical composition or the texture of the rock.

The Rock Cycle

Geologists often refer to the *rock cycle*, the continuous alterations of rocks from one type to another. An igneous rock is broken down by weather and gravity; its pieces accumulate elsewhere as a sediment, the sediment is buried and lithified to form a sedimentary rock; the sedimentary rock is buried further and subject to tremendous heat and pressure; new minerals grow and a metamorphic rock forms; part of the metamorphic rock melts; the molten rock solidifies to form a new igneous rock.

The importance of rocks to earth science is not simply that they give us an indication of the composition of the Earth, but that they are windows into the past. Each type of rock forms in a particular environment. For instance, limestone forms in warm shallow seas, salt in hot deserts, and granite deep underground. Thus the presence of limestone indicates that the area was once a shallow sea, salt that it was once a desert, and granite that thousands of meters of rocks have eroded away to expose the rock below. James Hutton, the founder of modern geology, refered to rocks as "God's books," which tell the story of the Earth.

Age and Origin of the Earth

The current theory of planet formation states that the Sun and planets accreted from a rotating cloud of dust and gas that contracted under the force of gravity about 4·56 billion years ago. Most of the material went in to making the Sun, while the remaining dust and gas accumulated to form rocks, then small bodies known as *planetesimals*, and finally planets. Because of the reworking of rocks on Earth, there are most likely no pieces left of the primitive Earth. The oldest rock dated so far is a 3·96 billion-year-old gneiss from Canada, while the oldest mineral grain is a 4·2 billion-year-old zircon grain from Australia. The 4·56 billion-year-old age of the earth is inferred from the ages of primitive meteorites, which are thought to be relics of the early solar system.

The Rest

There is a lot more to the study of the Earth than has been possible to set down here. The oceans, the atmosphere, and the rocks of the crust all interact with one another in their development in a complex way. The surface of the earth has gradually changed as life has evolved over thousands of millions of years and ice ages have come and gone, changing the surface again and again. Just as important is the economic potential of the earth, on which we depend for all of our energy and all raw materials. This section has given the basic framework within which such further investigations are carried out, to help the reader understand as he reads more widely.

II.   PHYSICS—THE FUNDAMENTAL SCIENCE
OF MATTER

WHAT PHYSICS IS ABOUT

Introduction

Anyone compelled by curiosity or professional interest to look into contemporary journals of pure physics research is soon struck by the fact that the traditional division of physics into "heat, light, sound, electricity, and magnetism" has become very blurred.

Current Divisions of Physics

Two different, though complementary, sections can be distinguished. First, there is the physics concerned with the properties of matter in bulk, with solids, liquids, and gases, and with those odd but very important substances, such as paints, plastic solutions, and jelly-like material, which are neither properly solid nor liquid. In this vast domain of physics questions like this are asked: Why is iron magnetic, copper not? What happens when solids melt? Why do some liquids flow more easily than others? Why do some things conduct electricity well, others badly, some not at all? During the last century, particularly the last few decades, it has become clear that such questions can be answered only by raising and solving others first. In particular, we must ask: (i) Of what nature are the invisible particles of which matter is composed? and (ii) How are those particles arranged in bulk matter?

The first of these two questions has generated the second major category of modern physics: this is the physics of particles and of the forces that particles exert on each other. In this field which represents science at its most fundamental questions like this are asked: If matter is composed of small units or particles, what are they like? How many kinds of particle are there? Do the particles possess mass? electric charge? magnetism? How do the particles influence each other? How can their motion be described and predicted?

The discussion which follows has been divided into two main parts (1) **Particles and Forces**, and (2) **The Properties of Matter in Bulk**, with part (1) describing the microscopic structure of matter and part (2) its macroscopic properties.

PARTICLES AND FORCES

Aristotle to Newton

The inference that matter should be composed of small particles or atoms originated, it is true, in classical times. The atomic idea was an attempt to solve the age-old problem of matter and its peculiar properties. The ancients had provided themselves with two solutions to the problem of matter:

(i) The theory of the four elements (earth, water, fire, air), from which all different forms of matter were composed by selecting different ratios of the four ingredients. This approach had been used by traditional philosophy and was adopted by Aristotle.
(ii) The theory of atomism which postulated the existence of atoms and empty space.

Atomism remained very much in the background in the development of Western Science and persisted even longer in the Arab world. The idea that matter is composed of "small units" was in reality forced into the mental development of mankind by the repeated application of the process of dimension halving. By the time of Newton atomism had come to the fore and Newton con-

sidered that God had made the Universe from "small indivisible grains" of matter. Nevertheless, the search for the "philosopher's stone" was still, in the seventeenth century, the main pursuit of many scientists, but the new chemistry of the seventeenth century made use of atomistic concepts. Newton's physics was a mechanics concerning particles in a vacuum and when Boyle described his gas law (i.e., Pressure × Volume is constant at a fixed temperature) he visualised matter as composed of particles with specific qualitative properties. It was, of course, the advance of experimental techniques which enabled scientists to test ideas and theories on the nature of matter.

Dalton and Atomic Theory

The modern view of atomism need be traced no farther than the beginning of the nineteenth century when Dalton and his contemporaries were studying the laws of chemical combination using precise weighing techniques. By that time the distinctions between elements, compounds, and mixtures are already made. Compounds and mixtures are substances which can be separated into smaller amounts of chemically distinguishable constituents. Elements (see end of Sec.) cannot be so divided. In a mixture the components may be mixed in any proportion and sorted out again by non-chemical means. In a compound the elements are combined in fixed proportions by weight. This last fact gives the clue to atomic theory.

Dalton pointed out that the fixed combining weights of elements could easily be explained if the elements consisted of atoms which joined in simple numerical ratios, e.g., 1 atom of element A with one of B, or one of B with two of C, and so on. For instance, 35·5 g of chlorine combine with 23·0 g of sodium to make 58·5 g of ordinary salt. If we assume one atom of chlorine links with one of sodium, then the atoms themselves must have weights in the ratio 35·5 to 23·0. This turns out to be consistent with the combining weights of chlorine and sodium in all other compounds in which they both take part. Sometimes two elements combine in several different proportions by weight. But this is easily explained by assuming that the atoms link up in a variety of ways e.g., one iron atom with one oxygen, or two irons with three oxygens, or three irons with four oxygens. Then the three different combining proportions arise from the three different numbers of atoms, using in each case the same ratio of oxygen atom weight to iron atom weight.

Atomic Weight

Over the century and a half since Dalton, these ideas have been repeatedly tested by chemical experiments. Nobody now doubts that every chemical element has atoms of characteristic weight. The atomic weight or more properly the relative atomic mass, of an element is by international agreement expressed relative to one isotope (see below) of carbon, namely carbon-12 which is given the relative mass of twelve. These numbers are only ratios; the real weight of one single oxygen atom is $2·7 \times 10^{-23}$ g.

Valency

That the combinations of atoms in definite proportions was necessary to produce compounds, or more correctly molecules, was known from 1808. The reason why only one atom of sodium and one of chlorine was required to produce one molecule of salt was unknown. Further the seemingly odd combinations of two atoms of hydrogen (H) with one of oxygen (O) to give water (H_2O), while only one atom of hydrogen could combine with chlorine to give hydrogen chloride (HCl) could not be explained. This situation was not resolved until around 1860, when the chemical formulae of many molecules were known. It was then discovered that homologies existed in the elements, for example the series Na, K, Rb, Cs, or Fl, Cl, Br, I, and this culminated in the Periodic Table of the elements (see end Sec.). The valency of an atom was determined by its position in the periodic table and determined by the number of electrons (*see below*) which the atom has orbiting its nucleus. Atoms combined to form molecules in a manner which maintained the number of "valence" electrons in a stable grouping of 2, 8, or 18 (*see later*). For example, sodium has one valence electron and chlorine seven, therefore the combination NaCl gives the stable grouping of eight; hydrogen has one and oxygen six, hence it requires two atoms of hydrogen and one of oxygen to give one stable molecule, H_2O. Other more complicated molecular structures and types of bonding between atoms are dealt with in the chemistry section. This discovery of particles smaller than the atom itself was necessary to fully comprehend the nature of valency in atomic combinations.

J. J. Thomson and the Electron

Matter is electrically uncharged in its normal state, but there exist many well-known ways of producing electric charges and currents—rubbing amber, or rotating dynamos, for example. It is therefore necessary to have some theory of electricity linked to the theory of matter. The fundamental experiment in this field was made by J. J. Thomson when, in 1897, he discovered the electron. If you take two metal electrodes sealed inside a glass vessel and if the pressure of the air is reduced from atmospheric pressure, 76 cm of mercury, to 1 mm of mercury by mechanical pumping and then a high voltage, several kilo-volts, is applied to the electrodes, the negative electrode emits a "radiation" which causes the walls of the tube to glow. The rays are called cathode rays. The discovery of the electron was essentially a clarification of the nature of cathode rays. Thomson showed that they were streams of particles with mass and negative electric charge and a general behaviour unlike any other atomic particle known at that time. The importance of this discovery for the world of science cannot be overestimated, and its technical progeny are in every home and factory in X-ray machines, television tubes, and all electronic devices.

Rutherford–Bohr Atom

Since the electrons emerge from matter, they are presumably parts of atoms. The relation between the negative electrons and the positively charged constituents of matter was elucidated by the great experimenter Rutherford and the great theoretician Bohr. Their work, just before the First World War, showed that the positive charge, together with almost all the mass, is concentrated in the central core or nucleus of the atom about which the very light-weight electrons revolve. The diameter of an atom is about 10^{-8} cm, roughly one three-hundred-millionth part of an inch. The central nucleus has a diameter about 10,000 times smaller still. The nucleus and the electrons hold together because of the electric attraction between them. The positive charge of the nucleus is responsible for holding the electron in the region of space around the nucleus. The electrostatic Coulomb force, if left on its own would quickly attract the electrons into the nucleus but since the electrons move in orbits, circular and elliptical, they experience an outward centrifugal force which balances the inward electrostatic force. The mechanism is similar to that which holds the earth in orbit around the sun, only here a gravitational force replaces the effect of the Coulomb force. Modern theories of the electronic structure of atoms are quantum mechanical (*see below*).

At this stage work could, and did, go on separately along several different lines:

(i) Electrons could be studied on their own. Nowadays the handling of beams of electrons

of all sizes and intensities has become a major branch of technology.

(ii) The nucleus could be treated as a special problem, and this led to the mid century flowering of nuclear physics, to the atomic bomb, and to nuclear power.

(iii) The behaviour of electrons in the atom could be analysed; this is the great domain of atomic physics which spreads into many other sciences as well.

Volumes have been written about these three fields, but we can spare only a few lines for each.

The Electron

Electrons are expelled from solids by light, heat, electric fields, and other influences. It has therefore been possible to study beams of electrons on their own *in vacuo*. Electrons inside matter, either as constituents, or temporarily in transit, can also be observed by their innumerable effects. These observations all show the particles to be indistinguishable one from another; all electrons are the same wherever they come from. They have a definite mass (9.11×10^{-28} g), a negative electric charge, a magnetic moment, and a "spin" (intrinsic rotatory motion). No one has ever subdivided an electron or obtained an electric charge smaller than that on one electron. The electronic charge is therefore used as a basic unit of charge in atomic physics. The electron has come to be the best known of all the "fundamental particles." It is now used in research as a probe for studying the structure of matter, for which it is ideally suited, since it is very much smaller than an atom. A whole field of electron-scattering research which studies the nature and structure of solids, liquids, and gases is being actively conducted in many laboratories.

The Nucleus

The early research programmes in nuclear physics were greatly facilitated by the occurrence in nature of certain unstable (radioactive) nuclei which emit fast-moving fragments. The latter can be used as projectiles to aim at other nuclei as targets; the resulting impacts yield much valuable information. This technique still dominates nuclear physics, though nowadays the projectiles are artificially accelerated by one or other of the large costly machines designed for the purpose.

Protons and Neutrons

The most important early discovery was that the nucleus consists of two types of fundamental particle—the positively charged *proton* and the electrically neutral *neutron*. These two are of nearly equal mass (about 1,800 times that of the electron), and like electrons, have a magnetic moment and spin. The proton charge is equal to the electron charge, though opposite in sign. Consider a moderately complex nucleus like that of iron. This usually has 30 neutrons and 26 protons. Its atomic weight therefore depends on the total number of neutrons plus protons, but the total charge depends only on the number of protons—called the *atomic number*. The latter is denoted by Z while the total number of neutrons plus protons is called the *mass number* and denoted by M. A species of nucleus with given values of Z and M is called a *nuclide*. Z is also the number of electrons in the atom, since the atom as a whole is electrically neutral. The atomic number determines the chemical nature of the atom (*see below*), so that by altering the number of *neutrons* in a nucleus we do not change the chemical species. It is therefore possible to find—and nowadays to make—nuclei of the same element which nevertheless differ slightly in weight because they have different numbers of neutrons. These are called *isotopes*. Iron isotopes are known with anything from 25 to 36 neutrons, but all have 26 protons. Thus a set of isotopes consists of the various nuclides that have the same Z but different M's.

When the atomic properties of isotopes are measured it is found that small, hyperfine differences in the motions of the electrons around the respective nuclei exist. These result from the different total spin of the isotopes and its effect on the orbiting electrons. This influence of atomic properties by nuclear effects is important in that it provides a link between different fields of research.

Stable Nuclides

The protons and neutrons in a nucleus are bound together by strong forces called *nuclear forces*. In many cases, the forces are so strong that no particles ever escape and the nucleus preserves its identity. There are two hundred and seventy-four different combinations of neutrons and protons of this kind, and they are called the *stable nuclides*. The earth is largely composed of such stable nuclides, because any unstable ones have, in the course of time, spontaneously broken up into stable residues. Nevertheless, there are some unstable nuclei left on earth. They give rise to the phenomenon of radioactivity which was discovered by Becquerel in 1893.

Unstable Nuclides: Radioactivity

Becquerel found that certain chemicals containing uranium gave off rays capable of blackening a photographic plate, and shortly afterwards Marie and Pierre Curie discovered other substances, including radium, which produce similar but stronger effects. By now, about fifty chemical elements having radioactive properties are known to exist on earth, some, like radium, being strongly radioactive, others, like potassium, being so weak that the radiations are difficult to detect. These are called the *natural radioactive nuclides*.

The main facts about radioactivity are as follows: it is a *nuclear* phenomenon and (with minor exceptions) proceeds quite independently of whatever the electrons in the atom may be doing. Thus, the radioactivity of an atom is not affected by the chemical combination of the atom with other atoms, nor by usual physical influences like temperature and pressure. The radioactivity consists of the emission by the substance of certain kinds of rays. The early workers, Rutherford being the giant among them, distinguished three kinds of rays labelled α, β, and γ. These are described below. Whatever kind of ray is examined, it is found that the radiation from a given sample decreases gradually with time according to a definite law which states that the intensity of radiation decreases by half every T seconds. The number T, called the half-life, is constant for each radioactive material, but varies enormously from substance to substance. For instance, radium decreases its activity by a half every 1,602 years, whereas the half-life of one of the astatine isotopes is about 0.1×10^{-6} sec.

Radioactive Emissions

The three most well-known types of radioactive emission are quite distinct from one another.

(i) **α-rays** or α-particles consist of two protons and two neutrons bound together. They are ejected from the radioactive nucleus with one of several well-defined speeds. These speeds are high, often of the order 10^9 cm per sec. Two protons and two neutrons are the constituents of the nucleus of helium, and α-particles are thus fast-moving helium nuclei.

(ii) **β-rays** are moving electrons. They may emerge from their parent nucleus with any speed from zero to a definite maximum. The maximum speed often approaches that of light, and is different for each isotope. The electron has a positively charged counterpart, the positron (see below), and β-rays are sometimes positrons. To distinguish the two cases, the symbols β^- and β^+ are used. The naturally occurring β-radiations are almost all β^-.

(iii) **γ-rays** travel with the speed of light because they are in fact electromagnetic waves differing from light only in the extreme shortness of their wavelength. They have no electric charge.

It is unusual, though not unheard of, for the same radioactive substance to emit both α- and β-rays. On the other hand, γ-rays frequently accompany either α or β-rays.

γ-rays pass through matter easily; in fact, they are extra penetrating X-rays. α-rays can be stopped by thin sheets of tissue paper. α-rays brought to rest pick up a pair of electrons from the surrounding matter and become neutral helium atoms, and helium gas from this source is consequently found imprisoned in certain radioactive rocks. β-rays are intermediate in penetrating power between α- and γ-rays.

We must now try to interpret these observations.

Radioactive Disintegration

A nucleus is a collection of neutrons and protons interacting with each other and possessing collectively a certain amount of energy. Just as some human organisations lose their coherence if they accept too many members, so nuclei can remain stable only if (i) the total number of particles is not too great, and (ii) neutrons and protons are there in suitable proportions. Radioactive nuclei are the ones for which either or both these conditions do not hold. Sooner or later such nuclei eject a fragment, thus getting rid of some energy they cannot contain. This is called a *radioactive disintegration*, and the fragments are the α-, β-, and γ-rays. α-emission relieves a nucleus of two neutrons and two protons and some energy; γ-emission simply carries off excess energy without altering the number or kind of particles left behind. β-emission is more complicated. There are no electrons normally present in a nucleus, but they are suddenly created and explosively emitted if a neutron changes into a proton; positive electrons are similarly generated if a proton changes into a neutron. β-emission is therefore a mechanism for changing the ratio of protons to neutrons without altering the total number of particles.

Both α- and β-emission change the Z of a nucleus, and the product, or daughter nucleus, is a different chemical element. α-emission also changes the M. It might happen that the daughter nucleus is unstable, in which case it too will disintegrate. Successive generations are produced until a stable one is reached. Part of such a family tree is shown below. The symbols above the arrows show the kind of rays emitted at each stage, the figures are the mass numbers, M, and the names and symbols of chemical elements can be found on T56-7.

$$U^{238} \xrightarrow{\alpha} Th^{234} \xrightarrow{\beta} Pa^{234} \xrightarrow{\beta} U^{234} \xrightarrow{\alpha} Th^{230} \xrightarrow{\alpha}$$

$$Ra^{226} \xrightarrow{\alpha} Rn^{222} \xrightarrow{\alpha} Po^{218} \xrightarrow{\alpha} Pb^{214} \xrightarrow{\beta} Bi^{214} \xrightarrow{\beta}$$

$$Po^{214} \xrightarrow{\alpha} Pb^{210} \xrightarrow{\beta} Bi^{210} \xrightarrow{\beta} Po^{210} \xrightarrow{\alpha} Pb^{206}$$
(Pb^{206} is stable lead).

This family exists naturally on earth, because the head of the family, U^{238}, has so long a half-life (4.5×10^9 years) that there has not yet been time enough since its formation for it to have disappeared.

Artificial Radioactivity

Nowadays many new radioactive isotopes can be man-made. All that is required is to alter the M or Z (or both) of a stable isotope to a value which is incompatible with stability. The means for doing this is *bombardment*, i.e., stable nuclei are exposed to the impacts of atomic particles such as streams of protons from an accelerator, or neutrons in an atomic reactor, or simply the α-particles from another radioactive substance.

The new material is called an *artificially radio-active isotope*. Artificial radioactivity is not different in kind from that of the naturally radio-active substances, but the half-lives are usually on the short side. Indeed, the isotopes in question would exist in nature but for the fact that their short half-lives ensured their disappearance from the earth long ago.

Suppose a piece of copper is exposed to the intense neutron radiation in an atomic reactor. The more abundant of the two stable isotopes of ordinary copper has thirty-four neutrons and twenty-nine protons (*i.e.*, $Z = 29$, $M = 63$). In the reactor many (not all) of these nuclei absorb a neutron, giving an unstable copper nucleus with $Z = 29$, $M = 64$. When removed from the reactor the specimen is observed to be radioactive with a half-life of 12·8 hours. It is somewhat unusual in that it gives out both β^- and β^+ rays. Some nuclei emit electrons, leaving a daughter nucleus with one more positive charge than copper, *i.e.*, a zinc nucleus ($Z = 30$, $M = 64$). One neutron has become a proton, and the re-sulting zinc nucleus is stable. The others emit positrons, leaving behind a nucleus in which a proton has been turned into a neutron ($Z = 28$, $M = 64$); this is a stable nickel nucleus. The overall process is one example of the artificial transmutation of the chemical elements which is now a commonplace of nuclear physics. It was first discovered by Irene and Frederick Joliot-Curie in 1934.

Lack of a Complete Theory

Consider now a collection of, say, one million radioactive nuclei of the same kind. It is im-possible to tell exactly when any one of them will disintegrate; it is a matter of chance which ones break up first. All we know is that, after a time equal to the half-life, only a half a million will survive unchanged. In general, the more excess energy a nucleus has, the more likely it is to break up, and therefore the shorter the half-life of that particular nuclear species. In principle, to cal-culate the half-life theoretically, one would have to have a reliable theory of nuclear forces and energies. This is still being sought after, so it is probably fair to say that while the laws of behaviour of radioactive isotopes are well and accurately known, the *explanation* of this behaviour in terms of the properties of protons and neutrons is by no means complete.

Nuclear Fission—Chain Reaction

A discovery important not just for nuclear physics but for the whole of mankind was made by Hahn and Strassman in 1939. This was the dis-covery of nuclear fission in uranium. One of the natural isotopes of uranium is an unstable one, U^{235}, with 143 neutrons and 92 protons. It norm-ally shows its instability by emitting α- and γ rays. If uranium is bombarded with neutrons, some U^{235} nuclei temporarily gain an extra neutron, which makes them even less stable. This they show by splitting into two roughly equal parts, called fission fragments, together with two or three neutrons. There are two highly important things about this disintegration. One is that the two or three neutrons can promote further disintegrations in other uranium nuclei, and the process can therefore be self-propagating: it is then called a *chain re-action*. The other is that the total mass of the fission products is less than that of the original nucleus. This mass difference does not disappear without trace; it turns into energy according to a formula discussed later.

Nuclear Fusion

The ability of two light nuclei to combine and form a heavier nucleus is called fusion. A reac-tion of this nature does not form a chain process but proceeds in singly induced reactions. A typical fusion reaction is the formation of a helium nucleus (mass 3) from two deuterium nuclei which are made to collide at an energy of 60 keV (speed of $2·4 \times 10^6$ m/s)

i.e., $^2D_1 + {}^2D_1 \rightarrow {}^3He_2$ (0·82 meV) + n(2·45 meV)

where the $^3He_2$ particle has kinetic energy of 0·82 meV and the free neutron has free kinetic energy of 2·45 meV. This type of reaction is exo-energetic, the additional kinetic energy coming from the tighter binding of the nucleus in ^3He than in the two separate deuterium nuclei. The energy released in this form of nuclear reaction is much more than that in a fission process and is respon-sible for the emitted energy of the sun which burns hydrogen to form helium.

Applications of Nuclear Reactions

The world has two uses for the energy released in nuclear reactions:

(1) nuclear weapons;
(2) nuclear power plants.

The only nuclear bombs to be used in anger employed the fission chain reaction proceeding at a rapid rate which quickly becomes uncontrollable and produces a tremendous explosion. The second generation of nuclear warhead uses the fusion reaction, which is initiated by a fission-reacting detonator to produce an even more des-tructive blast. The third generation of nuclear warhead uses the large flux of very energetic neutrons to kill biological material, but the blast effect is essentially zero, hence attacks with neutron bombs leave most non-biological material and structures intact.

In the second application the nuclear fission process is controlled to provide a constant source of energy to drive turbines which produce elec-tricity.

Both uses represent epoch-making technical achievements, but mankind has yet to show itself capable of bearing sanely the burden of respon-sibility which nuclear physicists have laid upon it. One thing is certain: the discoveries will not cease. Already, other fissionable elements have been made and used; new chemical elements have been created; nuclear plants ("atomic piles") have stimulated great demands for new materials that will stand the heat and radiation inside the reactor, and this promotes research in other fields of science; irradiation inside an atomic pile gives new, and potentially useful properties to old materials; nuclear power drives ships and submarines. It is difficult to write even briefly about contemporary nuclear physics without feel-ing keenly the ambiguity of its powerful promises.

Atoms

A nucleus surrounded by its full complement of electrons is an electrically neutral system called an atom. Neither the atom as a whole, nor its nucleus, counts as a "fundamental particle" because either can be subdivided into more elementary parts, thus:

atom → electrons + nucleus → electrons + neutrons + protons

The chemical identity of the atoms of a given element, which was Dalton's key idea, depends entirely on the number and motion of the elec-trons. For example, the simplest element, hydrogen, has one proton for a nucleus, and one electron. The latter is comparatively easily detached or disturbed by the electric forces exerted by neighbouring atoms, consequently hydrogen is reactive chemically, *i.e.*, it readily lends its electron to build chemical structures with other equally co-operative elements. The second element, helium, has a nucleus of two protons and two neutrons; outside are two electrons in a particularly stable arrangement. Both electrons orbit the nucleus in the same spacial orbit, but with their spin directions oppo-site and at 90° to the plane through the nucleus and the electrons. This pair of electrons is so difficult to disarrange that the special name of closed shells has been coined to cover such cases.

The fact that two electrons can be present in the same orbit is only possible if their spins are anti-parallel (Pauli Exclusion Principle). In the case of a stable group of eight electrons they arrange themselves in groups of two and their spins antiparallel. Helium with its closed shell will not react chemically, whereas hydrogen, which has an open shell of only one electron, will react very quickly with other atoms.

As the nuclear charge increases, different electron arrangements of greater or lesser stability succeed one another, with every so often a closed shell corresponding to one of the chemically inert gases neon, argon, xenon, krypton.

Such considerations, pursued in sufficient detail, enable atomic physics to account for all the differences and similarities among the chemical elements and, in principle at least, for all other facts of chemistry as well.

Ions

Changes in the atomic properties of an atom are accomplished by altering the position of any electron from one orbit to another. In the limit when an electron is completely removed from the atom, leaving it positively charged, the atom is said to be ionised and is called a positive ion. An atom can be singly or multiply ionised up to a level equal to the number of electrons existing in the neutral atom. In addition, atoms can, through distortion of the existing electrons, accept an additional electron and become negative ions. These can be formed in a resonance scattering process and exist only for life-times of only 10^{-14}s or be formed by chemical reactions. The roles played by negative and positive ions in the upper atmosphere of the earth and stellar atmospheres have been of special interest to atomic physicists since the 1930s.

Maxwell and Electromagnetic Waves

Atoms are held together by the electric attraction of the nucleus for the electrons. Finer details of atomic behaviour depend on the magnetic moments of the particles. Any moving charged particle gives rise to magnetic effects, and in the dynamo a coil moving in a magnet produces an electric current. It can be seen therefore that electric and magnetic phenomena are intimately linked. Any region of space subject to electric and magnetic influences is called an *electromagnetic field*.

In 1862, before the discovery of the electron, Maxwell, while still in his twenties, had perfected a general theory of the electro-magnetic field. This theory today still describes correctly almost all electro-magnetic phenomena. The elegance of this theory is difficult to appreciate, but it alone was the only theory of pre-twentieth century physics which satisfied the prerequisites of Einstein's relativity theory (1905), *i.e.*, inherent in its structure was the concept of relativistic invariance. *Inter alia*, he proved that disturbances in the electric and magnetic conditions at one place could be propagated to another place through empty space, with a definite velocity, just as sound waves are propagated through air. Such electromagnetic disturbances in transit are called *electromagnetic waves*, and their velocity turned out experimentally to be the same as that of light and radio waves—which was a decisive argument to show that both of these phenomena are themselves electro-magnetic waves.

Einstein and Photons

In the years between about 1900 and 1920 this view was upset by Planck, Einstein, Millikan, and others, who focused attention on phenomena (radiant heat, photoelectricity) in which light behaves like a stream of particles and not at all like waves. A wave and a particle are two quite different things, as anyone will admit after a moment's contemplation of, say, the ripples on a pond and a floating tennis ball. The acute question was: is light like waves or particles?

Theoretical physicists have devised means of having it both ways. To say that light behaves as particles means that the waves of the electro-magnetic field cannot have their energy subdivided indefinitely. For waves of a given frequency, there is a certain irreducible quantity of energy that must be involved whenever light interacts with anything. This quantity is the product $h\nu$ where ν is the frequency and h is a constant named after Planck. Each such unit

is called a *quantum of the electromagnetic field* or a *photon* and is counted as one of the fundamental particles. Frequencies and wavelengths vary widely. Typical wavelengths are: radio—hundreds or thousands of metres; radar—a few centimetres; visible light—5 × 10^{-5} cm; X-rays—10^{-8} cm.

De Broglie and Particles

Since it seemed possible to attribute particle properties to electro-magnetic waves, then why not associate wave properties with particles. If an electron (mass m) is travelling with a velocity of v cm/s, then De Broglie (1923) suggested that its characteristic wavelength would be given by the relation mv $\lambda = h$; for example if $v = 10^8$ m/s, $m = 9 \times 10^{-31}$ kg, $h = 6\cdot626^{-34}$ joules-seconds, then $\lambda = 7\cdot36 \times 10^{-7}$ m, which is the same wavelength as red light. This proposal was confirmed in 1927 by Davisson and Germer when they showed that electrons could produce diffraction, a property until then only associated with light. These wave-like properties are now known to exist for all particles, and we now consider a particle with momentum mv to behave like a wave of wavelength $\lambda = h/mv$.

De Broglie made his revolutionary assertion in his doctoral thesis, and his examiners were so uneasy about the validity of the hypothesis that they were prepared to fail the young man in his examination. Happily for De Broglie, Einstein was visiting that particular university and he was asked his opinion of the idea; his reply ensured success for De Broglie and saved the examiners from future embarrassment.

Molecules

Electrical attractions and interactions of various kinds can cause atoms to combine with each other or themselves to form molecules. Two similar atoms, say hydrogen, combining to form the homonuclear diatomic molecule H_2, while two different atoms, hydrogen and chlorine, will form a heteronuclear diatomic molecule HCl. Molecules have a wide range of complexity, from simple pairs of atoms to highly intricate spirals and chains composed of thousands of atoms. The biological basis of all life is, of course, molecular in both origin and function.

Excited Atoms

Like nuclei, atoms, when given excess energy (insufficient to ionise them), will absorb the energy in one of the electrons, which is then displaced from its equilibrium state to a state (or orbit) of higher energy. It will remain there for typically 10^{-8} seconds before returning to its equilibrium position with the excess energy being emitted as light. The time an atom remains in its excited state can exceed 10^{-8} seconds; lifetimes of 0·1 second are known, and these metastable states are prevented by the atomic properties of the atom from decaying quickly to their equilibrium states. The colour of the light emitted is characteristic of the atom involved, with the more energetic transitions giving blue light while the less energetic transitions give red light. Hence the emitted colour (or wavelength) of the light can be used for chemical identification and study of the various transition probabilities in atoms.

Herein lies the explanation of innumerable natural and technical phenomena, such as the colours of glowing gases whether they exist in the sun and stars, in aurora, or in street-lamps and neon signs. Herein also lies the reason for the importance of spectroscopy, which is the study of the characteristic radiation from excited states for spectroscopy is not only a useful tool for the chemical identification of substances ("spectroscopic analysis") but was one of the main routes along which twentieth-century physicists broke through to a knowledge of the inner nature of the atom.

Forces in Nature

Nature uses four, at high energies three, different forces to make one particle interact with another. The weakest force is **gravity** which although present at all particle interactions, is insignificant in atomic and nuclear interactions. Gravity controls the mass distribution in the universe and the force has an infinite range of interaction.

The **electric force** which also has an infinite range of interaction is much stronger than the gravitational force and is responsible for the binding forces inside atoms by the attraction of nuclei for electrons.

Inside the nucleus two types of interaction take place which require different forces for their existence:

(1) the forces which hold neutrons and protons together in the nucleus and this is the **strong force**, and
(2) the **weak force** which controls the changes in charge state of nucleons, e.g., the β-decay process when a neutron in a nucleus changes into a proton with the ejection of an electron is controlled by the weak force.

Both these nuclear forces are short-range with their radius of influence approximately 10^{-13} cm, with the weak force acting on all matter and the strong force acting on quarks only. In today's parlance, gravity will act on any particle with mass, the electric force on any particle with charge, the strong nuclear on quarks and the weak nuclear on quarks and leptons (see below).

Quarks appear to experience short-range freedom of movement combined with a long-range binding. The proton, i.e., the nucleus of atomic hydrogen, is composed of three quarks which move about freely within the shell of the proton; only when one quark tries to escape across the boundary of the proton does it experience a force which rebinds into the proton. Before we discuss further the interactions of these forces we must describe the range of particles which exist in physics.

Elementary Particles

When considering the word elementary in this context the reader should be wary of thinking that it implies some degree of absoluteness. The elementary mass of any particular particle is always highly qualified and subject to change. When a particle is discovered physicists measure its properties, i.e., mass, electric charge, and spin, and determine which of the four forces to which it is subject. In addition, its life time must be determined to see if the particle is stable or only a transient particle which will break up into other particles. The life-times of unstable particles are extremely short, ranging from 10^{-17}s to 10^{-21}s, and it is debatable if a particle which lasts only for 10^{-21}s should be called a particle. Generally now such short-lived particles are called resonances which are produced in an interaction which is only a step to the final product.

Classification of Particles

The rudimentary classification of particles is into four groups:

(1) **Gauge bosons**
(2) **Leptons**
(3) **Mesons**
(4) **Baryons**

All particles have an anti-particle which has the same mass but opposite charge as the real particle, the only exception being the photon, which is its own anti-particle and forms a group on its own. The leptons (electron, muon, and neutrino) form a stable group of particles and do not react to the strong nuclear force. This group of particles, and the photon, are perhaps the most fundamental of all particles. The mesons are unstable particles and (as will be seen later) exist only to act as a means which enables nucleons to interact with each other. They are subjected to the strong nuclear force. All particles heavier than the proton are called baryons, every one of them, except the proton, is unstable in some degree, and a vast

number of them are known. Only a few are listed in the Table on the next page.

Mesons and baryons are collectively called hadrons. All of these unstable particles have been detected either in the cosmic flux falling on the earth or produced in the very high energy accelerating machines in Europe, the USA etc.

Strangeness

Some particles have long life-times $\sim 10^{-9}$ s, which is much larger than that encountered normally. Particles which possessed these long life-times were called "strange". Strangeness describes not a new property of matter but a different quality of matter which persists long enough to enable that particle to engage in strong nuclear-force interactions. Hence strangeness does not persist indefinitely. The decay of a strange particle into other particles with the abolition of strangeness proceeds via the weak nuclear force. The strange (and doubly strange) particles form highly symmetrised shapes when combined with non-strange particles. The pattern itself does not explain anything, but the underlying theory, known as Group Theory, does indicate by symmetry arguments which particle should be necessary to form a complete group. This mathematical procedure had a resounding success when it predicted the existence of a triply strange particle known as "omega minus". The organisation of particles according to properties of mass, spin, and strangeness in groups is now only an organisation exercise, and it will not tell us anything about the composition of nucleons.

Interactions of Particles

The method by which atomic, nuclear, and sub-nuclear particles interact is via the exchange of energy which can be considered as a particle exchange. The interaction between electric charges proceeds by the exchange of photons. For example, two charges feel each other by one charge emitting a photon which interacts with the second charge. Since the electric force has infinite range, its force-carrying particle has zero mass. The same criteria apply in the gravitational force, where the graviton is the particle which carries the force effect between particles of matter. Since the weak and strong forces are short-range, then their force-carrying particles have finite masses. The weak force is transmitted by W and Z particles and the strong force can be considered as transmitted by mesons. The quarks also interact via the strong force, here carried by gluons (mass at present unknown), which also feel the force themselves. Strangeness is conserved in strong nuclear reactions but not in weak ones.

A theory which combines the electric and weak forces into a single interaction has predicted the masses of the W and Z particles to be around 82 and 93 GeV respectively. Back in 1983 experimental evidence was found by international groups at CERN for the existence of the W particle with the predicted mass thereby giving considerable support to this theory. A long term aim is to unify all the known forces of nature into a single interaction.

Quarks

The stability of the leptons contrasts sharply with the instability of the hadrons (excepting the proton), and this as well as other things had led physicists to consider that all hadrons were composed from different combinations of yet undiscovered particles. Gell-Mann first postulated the existence of three particles from which the nucleons, mesons, and hence all hadrons are composed. These "new" particles are attributed with fractional electric charges of $+\frac{2}{3}$, $-\frac{1}{3}$, and $-\frac{1}{3}$ of the electron charge. The particles were called quarks. The name quark was taken from the novel Finnegans Wake by James Joyce, the meaning of which is obscure, but is perhaps appropriate, but as students of Joyce will know, quark means "non sense", and other interpretations as to its meaning, such as the "sound of seagulls" or "quarts" are wrong. The three

SOME MEMBERS OF THE ATOMIC FAMILY

The numbers in brackets after the name denote first the electric charge and second, the mass. The charge on an electron is counted as −1 unit and the electron mass as +1 unit. Thus (+1,207) means the particle has a positive charge of 1 unit and a mass 207 times that of the electron.
The mass energy of an electron is 0·51 MeV, hence conversion to mass energies can be made by multiplying the given mass by 0·51. Thus the muon has a mass energy of 106 MeV. Note: the letter M is used to denote quantities of millions and the letter G to denote quantities of thousand of millions.

Photon (0, 0)	A quantum of electromagnetic radiation, *e.g.*, light, X-rays, γ-rays. The concept was introduced by M. Planck in 1900 when he described the emission of light as taking place in "packets" rather than in a steady stream. The energy of a photon is proportional to the frequency of the radiation and inversely proportional to the wavelength.

Leptons

Electron (−1, 1)	Discovered by J. J. Thomson in 1897. The number of orbital electrons in an atom determines its chemical properties. Actual rest mass = 9·1 × 10^{-28} g. Emitted as β-rays by some radioactive nuclei. A stable particle.
Positron (+1, 1)	Positive counterpart or, "anti-particle", to the electron. Predicted theoretically by P. A. M. Dirac in 1928 and first discovered in cosmic rays by C. D. Anderson in 1932. Emitted as β-rays by some radioactive nuclei. When positrons and electrons collide they usually annihilate each other and turn into γ-rays; consequently, positrons only last about 10^{-10} sec. within ordinary matter, but are stable in isolation.
Neutrino (0, 0) and **Anti-neutrino** (0, 0)	These particles travel with the speed of light and are distinguished from one another by the relation of their spin to their direction of motion. A neutrino is emitted with the positron during positive β-decay; and an anti-neutrino with the electron during negative β-decay. Their interaction with matter is extremely slight. First postulated by Pauli in 1933 and detected in 1956. π-meson decay also produces neutrinos and anti-neutrinos but in 1962 it was proved experimentally that these are a different species. Thus there are two kinds of neutrino each with an anti-neutrino. All these particles are distinguished from photons by having different spin.
Muon (±1, 207)	Similar to, but heavier than, the electron and positron; disintegrates into electron (or positron if positive) + neutrino + anti-neutrino.

Mesons

Pion (±1, 273) or (0, 264)	The π-meson. Charged pions decay either into muons and neutrinos or into electrons and neutrinos. Neutral pions decay into γ-rays, into "positron-electron pairs", or both. Pions are intimately connected with nuclear forces, *i.e.*, with the "strong" interaction.
Kaon (±1, 966) or (0, 974)	The K-mesons. These decay in many different ways producing other mesons, electrons, and neutrinos.

Baryons

Proton (+1, 1836·1)	The positively-charged constituent of nuclei; the hydrogen nucleus is one proton. Fast-moving protons occur in cosmic rays. Does not spontaneously disintegrate.
Anti-proton (−1, 1836·1)	Negative anti-particle of the proton. Its existence was long suspected. Artificially produced and detected for the first time in 1955. Will react with the proton to produce pions or kaons.
Neutron (0, 1838·6)	Discovered by J. Chadwick in 1932. The neutral constituent of nuclei. When free it spontaneously disintegrates into a proton, an electron, and an anti-neutrino, after an average lifetime of about 18 minutes. Passes through matter much more easily than charged particles.
Anti-neutron (0, 1838·6)	The anti-particle of the neutron from which it is distinguished by properties connected with its magnetic moment and spin. Will react with neutron to produce pions or kaons.
Lambda Particle (0, 2183)	Discovered in 1947. Decays into proton plus pion.
Sigma Particle (0 or ±1; about 2330)	Various modes of disintegration, producing neutrons, protons, mesons and lambda particles.
Omega Particle (±1, 3272)	Predicted by scientists and duly discovered at Brookhaven, New York, in 1964.
Psi Particle (0, about 6100)	Discovered independently by two laboratories in the USA 1974. Still under intensive study.

quarks were called up, down, and strange and have the properties given in the Table below:

Name	charge	spin	mass-energy (MeV)
up	$+\frac{2}{3}$	$\frac{1}{2}$	336
down	$-\frac{1}{3}$	$\frac{1}{2}$	338
strange	$-\frac{1}{3}$	$\frac{1}{2}$	540

These particles interact with each other via the strong force. Hence it can be seen that by taking different combinations of quarks, different hadrons can be built up. For example, the proton is two up quarks and one down, the neutron is two down and one up. The simplicity of this system can be appreciated, but the only experimental evidence to support the existence of quarks is indirect.

No one has yet isolated a single quark! Many scientists are seeking ways to produce and detect them, but as yet (2002) no claims have stood the test of scrutiny. Further theoretical and experimental evidence has proved the existence of three more quarks, known as top, bottom and charmed (see below). These six elementary particles are complimented by six equivalent anti-matter particles, each with the opposite charge of its mate.

The K-mesons, for example, are composed of a quark and an anti-quark either with the spins of the two quarks aligned parallel to give a net spin of one, or aligned antiparallel to give a net spin of zero. The charges +1, −1, and 0 are simply determined by selecting the correct combination of up and down quarks.

Charm

In the quest to unite the weak and electric forces, theoreticians were forced to introduce yet another new particle into the quark family. This was a charmed quark with charge +⅔. The four members of the quark family had seemed then to be symmetrical with the four members of the lepton group (electron, muon, and two neutrinos). Since the charmed quark had charge +⅔ and mass of 1,500 MeV, it could simply replace the up quark as a building brick in nucleons to produce charmed matter. For example, by replacing the up quark in a proton and a meson by a charmed quark we get a charmed proton and a charmed meson. The first experimental evidence of the existence of charm was obtained by the high-energy physics group at University College, London, working at CERN laboratory, when they established the existence of "a neutral current interaction" in neutrino scattering experiments. Although "naked" charm has never been detected, charmed mesons (masses of 1,865 and 2,020) have been detected by the SPEAR laboratory in USA and charmed anti-protons have also been detected with masses of 2,260 MeV. The experimentally determined masses are in sufficient agreement with theory to confirm the existence of the charmed quark. Theoretical proof for the existence of two more quarks, top and bottom, soon followed and by 1995 both had been discovered by experimentalists.

As a whole, this theory of elementary particles is called the standard model and has become generally accepted. Scientists are not happy to rest with this, however, because the number of unspecified parameters involved (the standard model has about 20 of these) seems too many for a fundamental theory. The search is on for deeper patterns and symmetries to explain matter.

The Higgs Particle

Since the discovery of the top quark, physicists have concentrated their efforts on tracking down an even rarer particle called the Higgs. Finding it would not only continue to validate the standard model, but would also help theorists explain the existence of mass. Since the US government decided to stop funding its expensive Superconducting Supercollider project, the search is wholly in the hands of the Europeans at CERN.

QUANTUM THEORY AND RELATIVITY

In our discussion of the nature of the various particles in physics we have alluded to them as being classified with well-defined sizes and weights. Of course, once we consider the physics of matter on a scale which is smaller than that of our everyday comprehension, then the classical physics of Newton is insufficient and we must use quantum physics. In the atomic region of reality we are again faced with the problem of indivisibility where the Greeks stopped their thinking and called the smallest particles of the universe atoms.

Today we know that each separate particle is composed of a definite amount of energy, and the larger the particle, i.e., the more energy it is composed of, the easier it is to detect. We also know that the exchange of force between nucleons is carried by particles and that this inchangeability between mass and energy is a reality of quantum theory. To see this more fully we must realise that quantum theory rests on the theory of measurement! If a particle, of any type or structure, is composed of an amount of energy ΔE, then it is necessary to make measurements on it for a certain minimum time before it is detected. This minimum time Δt is given by the equation $\Delta E \times \Delta t \geq h$, where h is Planck's constant divided by 2π; hence it can be seen that the smaller ΔE, then the longer a measurement must be made to detect the particle. Correspondingly, the time of measurement itself introduces an uncertainty, ΔE, in the energy of the particle. As well as the parameters ΔE and Δt, a particular physical event can be expressed in terms of its momentum p and position q, and these can also be expressed in a relationship as $\Delta p \times \Delta q \geq h$. Hence one can ask at what position in space, q, is a particular particle with momentum p? Or what exactly is the wavelength of a wave? It may be thought that the first question cannot reasonably be asked of a wave nor the second of a particle, but bearing in mind the dual roles of particles and waves discussed earlier, then those questions can be interchanged.

The Heisenberg Uncertainty Principle

We know that electrons behave both as particles and waves. Since electrons have something in common with both, one question cannot be answered precisely for electrons without ignoring the other; alternatively, both questions can be given an imprecise answer. As the wavelength of electrons is intimately connected with their speed, one has to accept an accurate knowledge of the speed (wavelength) and ignorance of position, or the converse, or inaccurate knowledge of both. This is the famous Heisenberg Uncertainty Principle.

Quantum theory is a set of mathematical rules for calculating the behaviour of fundamental particles in accordance with the Uncertainty Principle. In spite of its equivocal-sounding name, the principle has led to an enormous increase in the accuracy with which physical phenomena can be described and predicted. Quantum theory includes all that previous theories did and more.

Quantum theory grew up in the same epoch as the Theory of Relativity. Heroic attempts have been made to combine the two, but with only partial success so far. Relativity is concerned with all motion and all physical laws, but its characteristic manifestations occur only when something is moving with nearly the velocity of light. Quantum theory is likewise all-embracing, but its typical phenomena almost always occur when something on the minute atomic scale is in question. Consequently, the vast majority of everyday mechanics needs no more than the classical theory laid down by Newton, which is neither relativistic nor quantum.

Relativity

Historically, relativity grew out of attempts to measure the speed with which the earth moved through that hypothetical medium called the ether, which was supposed at that time to be the bearer of light waves. To take a simple analogy: sound waves travel through still air with a certain definite speed, v. If you move through the air with speed v' towards oncoming sound waves, they will pass you at the speed $v + v'$. Michelson and

Morley, in their celebrated experiment of 1887, failed to find the corresponding behaviour on the part of light. This is so important an experiment that it has been repeated, and repeatedly discussed ever since. In October 1958 the latest and most accurate confirmation of the Michelson-Morley result was announced. It seems as if light always travels with the same speed relative to an observer, however fast he moves relative to anything else. Einstein put it this way: two observers moving with any constant velocity relative to each other will always agree that light travels past them at the same speed, this speed is denoted by c, and is approximately 186,000 miles per second.

It should be remembered that the limiting value of the velocity of light in relativity is a postulate introduced by Einstein not a conclusion which the theory provides. There may exist forms of matter which can travel faster than light!

Nevertheless, the postulate that the maximum velocity encountered in the universe is c, logically developed, leads to remarkable conclusions. For instance: if you walk from tail to nose of an aircraft at 4 mph and the plane is receding from me at 300 mph, then you recede from me at 304 mph "Common sense", Newton, and Einstein would all agree on this. But if you could walk at $0.25c$ and the plane moved at $0.5c$, the Newtonian mechanics would give your recession speed as $0.75c$, whereas Einsteinian relativity would give about $0.67c$. Although at the everyday speed of 300 mph, the disagreement, though present in principle, is absolutely negligible, at speeds near that of light it is very pronounced. Many experiments show that the relativity answer is right.

Equivalence of Mass and Energy

The most famous consequence of relativity theory from which we derive benefit is the knowledge that mass can be converted into energy. The amount of energy, E, which can be derived from a given mass, m, of any type of material is given by the celebrated equation $E = mc^2$. If we take one gram of ash and convert it into the free energy of which it is composed we would get 10^8 kilowatts of power, sufficient to heat 15 houses for a year. The heat provided by the material which produced the ash is equivalent to that obtained from burning a single furnace. The massive energy released by $E = mc^2$ has been demonstrated in the power of nuclear weapons, but this energy has also been put to peaceful uses in nuclear-powered electricity generating stations.

In fundamental particle physics the masses of particles were always expressed in units of mass energy using $E = mc^2$ as the conversion equation. This is a matter of convenience from the realisation that mass is simply a condensed form of energy. The mesons which are the force-exchanging particles in the strong interaction have a mass energy of approximately 130 MeV, which is equivalent to a real mass of only 210^{-26} grams. The energy of the sun is provided by the conversion of real mass into light energy through thermonuclear fusion processes.

Mass and Rest Mass

The concept of mass is not a simple idea to grasp, for as we have seen, the mass of a body which is at rest is equivalent to its inherent latent energy. Further complications and interpretations arise when the body starts moving and its mass is no longer necessarily a constant quantity.

A stationary body can be observed to have a mass called its *rest mass*. If the body moves, it has energy of motion and therefore, according to Einstein's mass-energy equation, it increases its mass. Mass thus depends on speed, but in such a way that there is very little change unless the speed approaches that of light. Many experiments on atomic particles demonstrate this. The interesting question now arises: do all fundamental particles have rest mass? or do some have mass derived solely from their energy? The answer appears to be that photons and neutrinos have no rest mass; all other particles have. The Table on **T16** gives their rest masses.

Special Theory of Relativity

The mathematical development of Einstein's ideas, leading to the conclusions just referred to, constitutes the Special Theory of Relativity. Stated more generally, the theory raises the question whether two observers in uniform relative motion could ever detect, as a result of their relative speed, any difference in the physical laws governing matter, motion, and light. To this, Special Relativity answers No. The detailed theory involves special consideration of the results the two observers would obtain when measuring (i) the spatial distance, and (ii) the time interval, between the same two events. It turns out that they would not agree on these two points. They would agree, however, on the value of a certain quantity made up jointly of the spatial distance and the time interval in a somewhat complex combination. The intimate mixture of space and time in this quantity has led to the treatment of the three space dimensions and time on an equivalent footing. Hence the frequent references to time as the "fourth dimension". Minkowski devised an extremely elegant presentation of relativity theory by using an extension of ordinary geometry to four dimensions. A line drawn in his four-dimensional space represents the path of a particle in space and time, i.e., the whole history of the particle. Thus the movement of particles in the ordinary world is turned into the geometry of lines in Minkowski's four-dimensional world of "space–time".

General Relativity and Gravitation

In 1915, 10 years after the publication of the Special Theory of Relativity, Einstein published his theory of General Relativity. This apparently innocuous extension of the ideas of special relativity to include accelerated relative motion opened up new and difficult fields of mathematical complexity which, when solved, enabled Einstein to include gravitation in the theory. In discussing the physics of atomic, nuclear, and subnuclear particles, we did not include the effect of the gravitational force, since in relation to the Electric, Weak and Strong forces it is extremely small and can be neglected in the discussion of the structure of matter but not in the discussion of astronomical problems and the movements of large-scale electrically uncharged bodies.

It has been usual, ever since Newton, to say that two bodies of mass m_1 and m_2, separated by a distance r attract one another with a force proportional to $m_1 m_2/r^2$. This is Newton's inverse square law of gravitation which explains the movements of planets and comets and the falling to earth of an apple from a tree.

The apple's fall is accelerated, and we observe this by noting its position relative to us, and by timing it with some sort of clock. This system of location in space and time may be called our "frame of reference". We therefore assert that, in our frame of reference, the apple falls down with an acceleration which Newton saw no alternative but to attribute to a thing called gravitational attraction. Galileo had shown that *all* bodies fall with the same acceleration at all points, and we we can now rephrase this by saying that in our frame of reference there is a constant gravitational attraction or *uniform gravitational field*. (This last statement and Galileo's demonstration only refer strictly to points fairly near the earth's surface; at greater distances the gravitational field decreases and is therefore not uniform.)

Now suppose a collection of falling bodies is observed by us and an intelligent creature, designated C, inhabits one of them. C has his own frame of reference fixed relative to him and we have ours fixed relative to us. In *C*'s frame neither his own body, nor any of the others, is accelerated, and therefore he has no reason to suppose a gravitational force is acting on them. We have, therefore, the following situation:

(i) in our frame, fixed relative to us, we find all the bodies falling subject to a gravitational pull;

(ii) in C's frame, undergoing accelerated fall relative to us, no gravitational field is apparent to C.

It looks, therefore, as if one has only to choose the correct frame of reference for the measurements in order to remove the need for any assumptions about the existence of gravitational fields. This is a simple illustration of the connection between gravitation and frames of reference for the measurement of space and time. Einstein's General Theory of Relativity extends this to cover non-uniform gravitational fields and shows that what Newton taught us to call the gravitational field of material bodies is better thought of as a peculiarity of the space and time in the neighbourhood of such bodies. Since space-time, as we mentioned above, can be expressed in geometrical terms, Einstein has transformed the theory of gravitation into an exercise (a difficult one) in the geometry of space-time. Other physicists, in Einstein's tradition, are trying to turn *all* physics into geometry, but no one knows whether this is really feasible.

All this abstruse work is much more than a demonstration of mathematical power and elegance. Observable phenomena which fall outside the scope of Newton's theory of gravitation are accounted for by relativity. One is the small but definite discrepancy between the actual orbit of the planet Mercury and the predictions of Newton's theory. Another is the effect of a gravitational field on the wavelength of light emitted by atoms. Similar atoms in different places in a gravitational field emit radiations with slightly different wavelengths. For example, the light from an atom in the intense field of a star should have slightly longer wavelength than the corresponding light from an atom on earth. This effect has always proved very difficult to detect with certainty. However, Einstein's prediction was verified with moderate accuracy in 1960.

Quantum Theory and Relativity Combined

The atomic family table refers to "antiparticles". The theory which first introduced such things in 1934 is due to the Cambridge physicist Dirac and was epoch-making. Dirac conceived an equation to describe the motion of electrons subject to the laws of both quantum theory and relativity. His achievement was thus to synthesise these two great ideas. The spin of the electron was originally a supposition that helped to make sense of spectroscopic observations of light emitted from atoms. Dirac's equation made spin a logical consequence of the union of relativity and quantum theory. Perhaps even more important was the brilliant inference that the equation for the electron implied the existence of another particle having the same mass and spin but with a positive instead of a negative electric charge. This object is called the electron's antiparticle and is now well known as a positron. Every particle is now believed to imply an antiparticle, so it is conceivable that the universe could have been (but isn't) an anti-universe, *i.e.*, all the electrons and protons might have been positrons and antiprotons and so on. The laws of physics would still have been applicable, however. The gravitational force has an infinite range and therefore its force-carrying particles must travel at the speed of light. The graviton is the name of the particle which transmits the gravitational force between bodies with mass. To date (2000) no experiment has detected the existence of gravitons which are the postulated quanta of gravitational waves. There is an exact analogy between photons, the quanta of electro-magnetic radiation, and gravitons.

Conservation Laws

If charged particles interact, then it is found that the amount of electric charge existing after the reaction is the same as that which existed before the event. This is called the law of the conservation of charge. Many other conservation laws exist in physics, *e.g.*, conservation of mass energy, angular momentum, linear momentum, and other more abstruse conservation laws exist in particle physics, *e.g.*, conservation of baryons, leptons, strangeness, isotopic spin, and parity. The last three conservation laws listed have been found to have a limited jurisdiction, and the violation of parity in the weak interaction was a great surprise to physicists.

Any reader who looks in a mirror knows that the left- and right-hand sides of his face are interchanged in the image. Fortunately mirrors do not also turn the image upside down, but, if they did, the face would then have undergone what is called "a parity transformation". A screwdriver driving a right-handed screw downwards becomes, on parity transformation, a screwdriver driving a left-handed screw upwards. The law of conservation of parity is a way of asserting that any physical process that goes on in the world could equally well go on—obeying the same laws—in a parity transformed world. There is nothing left-handed that does not in principle have a right-handed counterpart.

For many years this belief was strongly held. It came as something of a shock when, in 1957, after theoretical proposals by Lee and Yang in America, Wu and co-workers proved that parity was not always conserved. To understand Wu's experiment, we must recall that nuclei can have intrinsic spin. Suppose the axis of spin were downwards into the page and the rotation were suitable for driving an ordinary screw into the page. Then Wu showed that beta-rays from such a nucleus are emitted *preferentially upwards*, *i.e.*, against the direction of travel of the screw. The parity transformed version of this would have the beta-rays preferentially emitted in the same direction as the travel of the screw and, if parity is conserved, this process would happen too. But it does not. If the beta rays in the experiment had been emitted in equal numbers up and down, then the parity transformed version would have had this feature too, and thus parity would have been conserved.

A reprieve for the standard model came when P symmetry was combined with a transformation of charge. But when this new CP symmetry was also found to break down, scientists were forced back to their accelerators to search for either another patch to, or an alternative for, the standard model.

Conclusion

Over a century's development of the atomic ideas has brought a progressive, if jerky, increase in the mathematical precision of the theories. In some fields of particle physics, observations to one part in a million, or even better, can be explained, to that level of accuracy, by the existing theories. At the same time, however, the theories have lost visual definition. An atom as an invisible but none the less solid billiard ball was easy enough; so was a light wave conceived like a sound wave in air. Even after Rutherford, an atom consisting of a miniature solar system merely exchanged the solid billiard ball for a system of revolving billiard balls and was no great obstacle to visualisation. But since quantum theory and the Uncertainty Principle, every unambiguous visualisation of fundamental wave-particles leaves out half the picture, and although the electrons are in the atom, we can no longer represent them in definite orbits. The moral seems to be that visualisation is unnecessary, or at best a partial aid to thought.

THE PROPERTIES OF MATTER IN BULK

One of the most obvious and at the same time most wonderful things about the properties of matter is their great variety. Think of air, diamond, mercury, rubber, gold, pitch, asbestos *etc*. Even the differences of state of the same chemical substance are remarkable enough, ice, water, and steam, for example. One of the aims of physics is to reach an understanding of all these different properties by explaining them in terms of the behaviour of the particles discussed in the previous section.

The great success with which this imposing

programme has been carried out indicates the maturity of physics. It is difficult to think of any major property of matter in bulk for which there is not some attempted theoretical explanation, though future physicists will no doubt regard some present-day theories as rudimentary or incorrect.

Physics, Statistics, and Thermodynamics

Take a number equal to the population of London, multiply it by itself, and multiply the product by another million. The answer is about the number of molecules in 1 cubic centimetre of ordinary air. They are constantly moving about and colliding with one another. Even if the nature of the molecules and their laws of motion were perfectly understood, it would clearly be impracticable to calculate the exact paths described by each particle of so vast an assembly. This difficulty brought into being a whole branch of physics concerned with calculating the overall or average properties of large numbers of particles. Just as statisticians will provide the average height, income, expectation of life, and so on, of the population of London, without knowing everything about every individual, so statistical physicists can work out average properties of molecules or atoms in large groups. This important branch of physics is called *Statistical Mechanics*. It was founded in the nineteenth century by Maxwell, Boltzmann, and Gibbs and is still being actively developed.

Consider now all the molecules in 1 cubic centimetre of air contained in a small box. They are continually bombarding the walls of the box and bouncing off. This hail of impacts (it is actually about 10^{23} impacts per square centimetre per second) is the cause of the pressure which the gas exerts against the walls of the box. Now suppose we pump air in until there is twice as much as before, though the box is still the same size and at the same temperature. This means that the density of the gas (*i.e.*, the mass of 1 unit of volume) has doubled. We should now expect twice as many impacts per second on the walls as before, and consequently twice the pressure. We therefore arrive at a conclusion that, if the volume and temperature are constant, the pressure of a gas is proportional to its density. This is one of the simplest statistical arguments that can be checked against observation; in fact, it stands the test very well.

Heat, Temperature, and Energy

The proviso about the temperature remaining the same is an important one for the following reason. In the nineteenth century there was much discussion about the nature of heat. To Joule we owe the now well-established view that heat is equivalent to mechanical work. In one of his experiments, in the 1840s, the work necessary to rotate paddle wheels against the resistance of water in a tank generated heat that caused a slight rise in the temperature of the water. Joule found out exactly how much work was equivalent to a given quantity of heat. However, one can do other things with work besides generate heat; in particular, work creates motion, as when one pushes a car. Bodies in motion possess a special form of energy, called kinetic energy, which is equal to the work done in accelerating them from a state of rest. We have, then, three closely connected ideas: work, heat, and kinetic energy. Now according to the views of the nineteenth century, which are still accepted, any heat given to a gas simply increases the kinetic energy of its molecules; the hotter the gas, the faster its molecules are moving. If, therefore, the gas in our box is allowed to get hotter, there is an increase in molecular speed, and the impacts on the walls become correspondingly more violent. But this means the pressure increases, so we have another law: if the density remains the same, the pressure increases if the temperature does.

Laws of Thermodynamics

Such considerations as these have been pursued with great elaboration and subtlety. The notions of heat, temperature, energy, and work—familiar but vague in everyday life—have been given precise definitions, and the relations between them have been enshrined in the Laws of Thermodynamics. Enshrined is perhaps a suitable word, because these laws are so soundly and widely based on experimental results that they have greater prestige than any others in physics. If any proposed physical law comes in conflict with thermodynamics then so much the worse for that law—it has to be revised. It is sometimes asserted that no one is properly educated who does not understand the Second Law of thermodynamics. We cannot, therefore, leave this section without at least stating the two best known thermodynamic laws:

First Law: *If any physical system is given a quantity of heat, and if the system performs some work, then the energy of the system increases by an amount equal to the excess of heat given over work done.* This law asserts that heat, energy, and work are convertible one into the other, and that all such transactions balance exactly. This is one form of a principle accepted as fundamental in all science, *viz.*, the Principle of the Conservation of Energy, according to which energy can never be created or destroyed, but only changed from one form to another.

Second Law: *It is impossible to make an engine which will continuously take heat from a heat source and, by itself, turn it all into an equivalent amount of mechanical work.* In fact, all engines which produce work from heat—steam engines for example—always use only a fraction of the heat they take in and give up the rest to some relatively cool part of the machine. The Second Law makes this obligatory on all work-from-heat devices. This statement of the Second Law has an engineering ring about and, indeed, it arose from the work of the nineteenth-century French engineer Carnot. Nevertheless, it can be rephrased in terms of the concept of entropy, and has been applied with unbroken success to all fields of science involving the transfer of heat and allied matters. It sets a definite limit to the kinds of physical and chemical process that can be conceived to take place. Nothing has been known to contravene it.

The States of Matter

The molecular motion in gases has been referred to in the previous section. Tacitly it was assumed that each molecule acted independently of all others, except that collisions occurred between them. In reality, molecules exert attractive forces on one another and, if a gas is cooled so that molecular movements become relatively sluggish, a time comes when the attractive forces succeed in drawing the molecules close together to form a liquid. This process is called condensation.

The molecules in a liquid are packed tightly together and they impede each other's movements. On the other hand, movement still persists, and the molecules struggle about like people in a milling crowd. Besides wandering about, the molecules vibrate. These motions represent the energy contained in the liquid.

The fact that the molecules, though irregularly packed, can still slip past one another and move from place to place, explains the essential property of liquids that distinguishes them from solids—ability to flow. As a matter of fact, although the rather vague assertion that in a liquid molecules are irregularly packed would be generally accepted, there is no agreed opinion on what the irregularity is actually like. Indeed, not only the precise structure of liquids, but the theory of liquids in general, is fraught with such considerable mathematical difficulties that the liquid state is much less well understood than the solid or gaseous.

Most solids are crystals. The popular idea of a crystal is of something which has a more or less regular geometrical form with faces that shut in the light—like snowflakes or gems. However, crystallinity really depends on a regular inner pattern of the atoms, and may or may not show itself on the visible surface. A lump of lead, for example, is crystalline, despite its appearance.

The actual arrangement of the atoms in a crystal can be extremely complex. Some are quite simple, however. The largest model of a crystal structure must surely be the 400-ft. "Atomium" building in the 1958 Brussels Exhibition. This consisted of eight balls, representing atoms, situated at the corners of a cube, and one more ball exactly in the middle. Imagine this repeated in all directions so that every ball is the centre of a cube whose corners are the eight neighbouring balls. This is known to crystallographers and physicists as the "body-centred cubic structure"; it is the actual arrangement of atoms in iron, sodium, chromium, and some other metals. If every ball, instead of being the centre of a cube, were the centre of a regular tetrahedron (a solid figure with four equal triangular faces), and had its four neighbours at the corners of the tetrahedron, then we should have the "diamond structure". This is how the carbon atoms are arranged in diamonds.

In crystals the atoms are locked into a regular ordered structure by attractive forces which give the solid its rigidity and prevent it from flowing. The atoms are so close together that any attempt to press them closer involves crushing or distorting the atoms—a process they resist strongly. This explains why solids (and liquids too) are so difficult to compress. Gases can easily be compressed because there is so much space between the molecules.

Distinction of Solid and Liquid

The distinction between solid and liquid is not so sharp as is commonly supposed. A lump of dough will not bounce, but is plastic; a steel ball-bearing is very elastic and bounces excellently, but one cannot mould it in the fingers. Neither dough nor steel qualifies for description as a liquid. There are, however, substances which can be moulded like plasticine into a ball that will then bounce very well on the floor like an elastic solid, and finally, if left on a flat table, will spread into a pool and drip off the edge like a liquid. There is no point in trying to force such things into rigid categories. One may say instead that for short, sharp impacts the material behaves like an elastic solid, but under long-sustained forces it flows like a liquid. The properties of these, and many other anomalous materials, are increasingly engaging the attention of those who study the science of flow—rheology. It is interesting to see how many familiar and important materials exhibit peculiar rheological behaviour—paint, dough, ball-pen ink, cheese etc.

Inside a Crystalline Solid

We now return to our wallpaper analogy. Suppose we have walls papered with a regular pattern of, say, roses, fuchsias, and green leaves. These represent the different kinds of atoms in the solid. Careful observation shows that the whole pattern is shimmering. The flowers and leaves are not stationary, but are undergoing slight random oscillations about their proper positions. In a crystal these movements are called thermal vibrations, and are never absent. The hotter the crystal, the more the vibration, and at a high enough temperature the vibrations become so great that the atoms get right out of position and the pattern disappears altogether, i.e., the crystal melts. Thermal vibrations are essential to the theory of solids, and are responsible for numerous physical properties.

Next we note something extraordinary about some of the papered walls. On these the paper has been hung in irregular patches fitted together like a not very well-made jig-saw puzzle. Lines of roses which should be vertical are horizontal in some patches, oblique in others. This represents the situation in most ordinary solids, for they consist of many small pieces of crystal irregularly packed together. Such material is called poly-crystalline, and the small pieces are crystal grains. Crystal grains may be almost any size, sometimes visible to the naked eye, as often on galvanised iron.

However, on one wall, we see excellent regularity and no obvious patches at all. The physicist would call this a single crystal, and several techniques exist for preparing them. Natural single crystals can be found, and there are some

beautiful large single crystals of rock salt. But on examining the single crystal wall closely, we find a number of places where the paperhanger has failed to make adjacent pieces register perfectly—there is a slight disjointedness. This occurs in real single crystals, and the line along which the structure fails to register is called a dislocation. These are much studied by physicists because of their bearing on the mechanical properties of solids, on the yielding of metals under strong stress, for instance.

Types of Impurity

This by no means exhausts the possibilities of the wallpaper analogy; several other phenomena can be found. For example, in a place where there should be a fuchsia there is actually a daffodil—something completely foreign to the pattern. Or perhaps a small wrongly shaped leaf is jammed between the proper leaves in a place that should really be blank. These represent chemical impurity atoms. The first is called substitutional, because it occupies the position of an atom that should be there, the second is called interstitial, because it does not. Substitutional impurities of indium metal, deliberately added to the semi-conductor silicon, make possible the manufacture of transistors (see Section L). Some steels derive their valuable properties from interstitial carbon atoms within the iron pattern.

What physicists call a vacancy would occur if a flower or leaf were simply missing. Remembering that all the atoms are vibrating, we should not be surprised if occasionally an atom jumps into a neighbouring vacancy if there happens to be one, i.e., the atom and the vacancy change places. Later this may occur again. In the course of time, a rose which was near the ceiling may make its way to the floor by jumping into vacant rose positions when they occur near enough. This process, which the physicist calls diffusion, is also analogous to the game in which numbers or letters can be moved about in a flat box because there is one vacant space to permit adjustment. The more vacancies there are in a crystal, the faster diffusion occurs. It is very slow in solids, but is nevertheless evidence that apparently quiescent materials are really internally active.

Metals, Electricity, and Heat

There is ample evidence that inside metals there are large numbers of free electrons. To illuminate this statement let us take sodium metal as an example. One single sodium atom has a nucleus with eleven protons; there are therefore eleven electrons in the atom. The outermost one is easily detached, leaving a positively charged sodium ion behind. We may think of these ions arranged in the three-dimensional pattern characteristic of sodium crystals. It is the same as the iron structure previously described. The detached electrons, one per atom, occupy the spaces in between. The usual metaphor is that the structure of ions is permeated by a "gas" of electrons. Like all visualisations of fundamental particles, this must be taken as a rough approximation. The important point is that the electrons in the gas are not bound to individual atoms but may wander freely about the crystal, hindered only by the collisions they make with the vibrating ions.

This is the picture as it appeared to physicists of the first decade of this century, and we can explain many properties of metals with it. Naturally the theory has developed greatly since then, thanks to the great work of Lorentz, Sommerfeld, and Bloch; it now relies heavily on quantum theory, but it is surprising how little violence is done to modern ideas by the simple picture we are using.

The free electrons move randomly in all directions at thousands of miles per hour. If the metal is connected across a battery it experiences an electric field. Electrons are negatively charged particles, and are therefore attracted to the electrically positive end of the metal. They can move through the metal because they are free; this flow is not possible to those electrons which remain bound to the ions. The function of the battery is to keep the flow going and, for as long

as it is going, it is the electric current.
The flow of electrons is not unimpeded. They
constantly collide with the ions and are deflected
from the path of flow. This hindrance is what
the electrician calls *electrical resistance*. The
electric force, due to the battery or a dynamo,
accelerates the electrons, thus giving them extra
energy; but they lose this to the ions at collisions
because the ions recoil and vibrate more than
before. The net effect of innumerable collisions
is to increase the thermal vibrations of the ions,
i.e., to make the metal hotter. This is the
explanation of the fact well known to every user of
electric irons; that electric current heats the
conductor. If a strong current is passed through
a wire, the heating is so great the wire glows, as in
light bulbs, or melts and breaks, as in blown fuses.
If one end of a metal rod is heated we soon feel
the heat at the other end; metals are excellent
thermal conductors. This is because the mobile
free electrons carry the heat energy down the rod,
passing it on to the ions by colliding with them.
Substances without free electrons cannot do this,
nor can they conduct electricity well; we have, in
the free electrons, an explanation of the fact that
the good electrical conductors are the good heat
conductors. For technical purposes, it would be
useful to have electrical insulators that would
conduct heat well, and *vice versa*; but this is almost
a contradiction in terms, and one can only compromise.

Non-conductors and Semi-conductors

There are some elements, and numerous compounds in which all the electrons are so tightly
bound to their parent atoms that free electron
flow is impossible. These materials are electrical
and thermal insulators.
Let us return to our sodium atom. It readily
loses its outer electron, forming a positive ion.
The ion is very stable; indeed, its electron
arrangement resembles the "closed shell" belonging to the inert gas neon. The chlorine atom, on
the other hand, would have a very stable structure,
resembling the inert gas argon, if only it could be
given one extra electron to complete the closed
shell. If the outer sodium electron were given to
a chlorine atom we should have two stable ions,
one positive and one negative. These would then
attract and form a compound. This is
just how common salt, sodium chloride, is formed,
and its crystals consist of a regular network of
alternate sodium and chlorine ions. As all the
electrons are bound to ions, it is not surprising
that salt will not conduct electricity or heat to any
appreciable extent. Not all insulating compounds are built on this pattern, but all have
structures which bind the electrons tightly.

We saw earlier that Nature does not permit
a hard-and-fast distinction between solids and
liquids; nor does she between conductors and
insulators. Back in the 19th century, Faraday knew
of substances which would conduct electricity, but
rather badly. A common one is the graphite
in pencils. Others are the elements selenium,
germanium, and silicon, and a considerable number
of compounds. Such substances are called semiconductors.

Semi-conductors conduct badly because they
have so few free electrons, many thousands of
times fewer than metals. In very cold germanium—say, 200 degrees below freezing—all the
electrons are tightly bound to atoms and the
substance is an insulator. It differs from normal
insulators in that, on warming it, the gradually
increasing thermal vibration of the crystal
detaches some of the electrons, for they are only
moderately tightly bound. The warmer the
crystal becomes, the more of its electrons become
detached and the better it conducts electricity.
By about the temperature of boiling water,
there are so many freed electrons that conduction
is moderately good, though less good than in
metals. This is basic semi-conductor behaviour.
Because transistors were made of germanium,
and because they were of such great technical
importance, more knowledge has accumulated
about germanium than about any other material.
See also **Transistor, Section L.**

Magnetism

The most important thing about magnetism is
that it is inseparably connected with electricity.
Oersted showed this in July 1820, when he
deflected a magnetic compass needle by passing an electric current through a wire near it.
Since then, many experiments have shown that
wherever a current flows there will certainly be a
magnetic field in the surrounding space. The
laws of this are very well known now—they are
the Maxwell equations previously referred to.
Most people first meet magnetism when they pick
up pins with a magnet. Where is the electricity
here? What is a magnet?
The explanation of magnetism exemplifies
beautifully the technique of explaining the bulk
properties of matter in terms of fundamental
particles. In the atoms the electrons are moving,
and a moving electric charge constitutes an
electric current. Therefore each moving electron
is a tiny source of magnetism. It does not immediately follow that every atom is a source of
magnetism because it might—and often does—
happen that the magnetic effect of different
electrons in the atom cancel out. In helium
atoms, for example, the two electrons have equal
but opposed magnetic effects. Nevertheless,
some atoms and ions have a net effect called
their *magnetic moment*. This simply means they
behave like tiny magnets. Crystals containing
such atoms will be magnetic, though the magnetism is much weaker than in ordinary magnets
because the different atoms largely annul one
another's effects. In a very limited number of
crystals, however, the magnetic ions act on one
another in a special way which forces all the
atomic magnets to point in the same direction.

Ferromagnetism

The total effect of many co-operating atoms is
very strong and the crystal becomes what we
normally call a magnet. Iron acts like this, so
do cobalt and nickel, the rarer elements gadolinium and dysprosium, and a fair number of alloys.
On the whole, this behaviour, which is called
ferromagnetism, is very rare. The reason for the
co-operation of all the atoms is not to the
explanation of everyone's satisfaction yet, though
the key idea was given by Heisenberg in 1928.
In the section dealing with the electron it was
pointed out that every electron has an *intrinsic*
magnetic moment. This is in addition to any
effect simply due to the electron's motion round
a nucleus. The net effects of ions are therefore
partly due to the intrinsic magnetism of
electrons. In the ferromagnetic metals the latter
is by far the most important contribution. Thus
we pick up pins, and benefit from magnets in
other ways, because innumerable fundamental
particles act in co-operation for reasons that are
still somewhat obscure. It is interesting to ask
whether the electrons responsible for magnetism
are the same free electrons that allow the metals
to conduct electricity. It is thought not.
We are accustomed to think of magnets as
metallic. Nowadays a number of non-metallic magnets are made. They are called *ferrites*, and some are
insulators and some are semi-conductors. The combination of magnetism and insulation is technically
very valuable in radio, radar, and other applications. The explanation of ferrite behaviour is
related to that of metallic ferromagnetism, but is
not the same.

Conclusion

The aim of the second part of this account of
physics is to show how our conception of fundamental particles allows us to build theories of the
properties of matter. This very aim shows that
the two "major divisions" of physics referred to
at the beginning are divided only in the way that
labour is divided by co-operating workers to lighten
the task. For the task of physics is a very great
one—no less than to explain the behaviour
of matter; and since the universe, living and
inanimate, is made of matter, physics must
necessarily underlie all the other sciences.

III. THE WORLD OF THE CHEMISTS

WHAT CHEMISTRY IS ABOUT

Chemistry is the scientific study of the preparation, composition and architecture of chemical compounds, and of the modes and mechanisms of their transformations or reactions. Natural (and other) processes can be classified as *physical*, in which no chemical reactions occur, for example water running down a hill, and *chemical* if changes occur in the chemical compounds involved. Common examples are the burning of fuel, whether in a biological cell, an internal combustion engine, or a lowly domestic grate. Biological changes at the molecular level in plants and animals generally consist of many chemical reactions, as do some geological changes in rocks and deposits. Chemistry therefore is rooted in physics and interpenetrates biology (biochemistry) and geology (geochemistry). Some of the main sub-divisions of chemistry are delineated in the Table. Chemists not only aim to discover new reactions by trial and error, but by seeking to understand chemical change aspire to design new compounds and reactions. New reactions can be used to produce useful physical *effects* in new ways—like light from the cold chemical candle (chemiluminescence) as the firefly does, and electricity from more efficient batteries and from fuel cells—or to produce new *synthetic products*. These can be faithful copies of compounds like penicillin which have been discovered first in nature, or completely new, invented, compounds like sulphonamide drugs. This research activity, which is mainly centred in the Universities, is the basis of a large chemical industry, one of the major manufacturing industries. Other branches which deal with more restrictive topics or use combinations of the above for specific goals have names which are self-explanatory, for example:—analytical chemistry, colloid chemistry, pharmaceutical chemistry, chemistry of dyes, petroleum chemistry, polymer chemistry, environmental and medicinal chemistry.

ELEMENTS AND COMPOUNDS

Elements

The reader will find a description of the formation of chemical elements in Part I. They are listed alphabetically in the Table of Elements (with their chemical symbols) and in order of atomic number in the Periodic Table. Other details may be found in Section L. They vary widely in natural abundance terrestrially.

In the earth's crust the most abundant elements are oxygen (O), silicon (Si), aluminium (Al), and iron (Fe). Our familiarity with them varies too, not only because of the rarity of some (thulium, Tm, and radium, Ra) and the artificiality of a few (plutonium, Pu) but because we meet some only in combination with other elements and not in their elemental state, for example, fluorine (F) in fluorides. The most familiar non-metallic elements besides oxygen and nitrogen in their gaseous molecular states (O_2 and N_2) are probably carbon (C), as graphite (or diamond!) and sulphur (S). Among the metallic elements most people know aluminium (Al), tin (Sn) and lead (Pb) from the main groups of the Periodic Table, and the transition metals: iron (Fe), chromium (Cr), nickel (Ni) as well as copper (Cu) and the precious metals silver (Ag), gold (Au) and platinum (Pt). Increasingly familiar because of their use in semi-conductors are the metalloids silicon (Si) and germanium (Ge).

Compounds

Most terrestrial matter as we know it can be classified in terms of the chemical compounds it contains, *i.e.*, is a mixture of compounds. Each compound consists of chemical elements in combination, the relative amount of each being characteristic and definite (Law of Constant Composition). Compounds vary not only in the number of elements combined but also in their proportions: carbon dioxide has twice as much oxygen per carbon as carbon monoxide (*see* atoms and molecules).

The properties of a compound can be, and normally are, very different from the properties of the elements it contains, a fact not commonly recognised in the popular imagination, witness phrases like—"it's good for you, it's got iron in it". This does not mean that elemental metallic iron is present but rather that some seemingly beneficial compound of iron is present. The ambiguity is that although iron is essential to human life in the form of haemoglobin in the blood, it also can form highly poisonous compounds. Similarly arsenic (As), although notoriously poisonous as the element and in some of its compounds, was nevertheless contained in one of the first chemotherapeutic drugs ever produced, salvarsan. The point can be further illustrated with sodium chloride, a water-soluble white crystalline solid, which is a compound of the very reactive metal sodium, and of chlorine (known as a poisonous green gas). Similarly diamond (a particular elemental form, or allotrope, of carbon) is one of the hardest known substances but may be combined with hydrogen (the highly inflammable gas which can combine with oxygen gas to give water), to give thousands of different derivatives which include benzene (a liquid), methane (a gas) and various hydrocarbon waxes and polishes.

ATOMS AND MOLECULES

Atoms vary in weight, structure and size from one element to the next, as discussed earlier. Molecules are made from whole numbers of atoms in combination. A particular molecule is characterised by the number of atoms of each of its constituent elements. It has a characteristic weight

MAIN DIVISIONS OF CHEMISTRY

	Elements, Compounds and reactions involved	Examples
Organic Chemistry	Carbon in combination mainly with H, O, N.	Natural products Carbohydrates Steroids Proteins
Inorganic Chemistry	All elements and compounds not covered in organic chemistry. Minerals and salts.	Inorganic polymers (*e.g.*, silicones) Transition metal complexes Organometallic compounds
Physical Chemistry	Mathematical and physical descriptions of organic and inorganic compounds and reactions.	Electrochemistry Chemical thermodynamics Molecular spectroscopy Photochemistry
Biochemistry	The chemistry of biological systems	Enzymes Biosynthesis.

called its *molecular weight* (the sum of the weights of the atoms in it), and a characteristic three dimensional structure (*see below*).

An aggregate of molecules of the same type is a chemical compound, so that the molecule is to a compound as the atom is to an element.

The Mole

It is frequently very useful to know when the amounts of two compounds are the same, not in terms of their masses but in terms of the number of molecules each contains, since chemical reactions occur at the molecular level and involve small relative numbers of molecules of the reacting species at each step. Avogadro first suggested that equal volumes of gases under identical conditions contained equal molecular numbers and it followed that if the weights of two substances were in the ratio of their relative molecular masses (molecular weights) then they too contained equal numbers of molecules. The approximate molecular weights of water (H_2O) and ethanol or ethylalcohol (C_2H_5OH) are 18 and 46 respectively and so 18 g of water for example contain the same number of molecules as 46 g of ethanol.

The amount of substance referred to in each case is called 1 mole. For any compound the weight of 1 mole is equal to the gramme molecular weight. Molecular weights (or relative molecular masses) are now referred to the carbon-12 atomic scale. The modern definition of the mole therefore is that it is the amount of substance which contains the same number of elementary particles as there are atoms in twelve grammes of carbon-12. This number, called Avogadro's number, is $6·022\,169 \times 10^{23}$.

Molecular Structure and Isomers

Modern spectroscopic and diffraction methods have enabled the details of molecular structures to be accurately determined not only with respect to the distances between atoms (normally in the range 1–5 Å ", *i.e.*, 100–150 pm for adjacent atoms) and the angles which define the structure, but also with respect to the various internal motions (vibrations and rotations).

Sometimes two (or more) different compounds have the same molecular weight (and are called, therefore, *isomers*) but have different molecular structures in which the same atoms are arranged in different relative positions, and hence have different properties. If two isomeric structures are related as left and right hands are related, the isomers are stereoisomers of a particular class called enantiomers. An example is glucose. Even such subtle variation as this produces differences in properties which can be crucial in biological function or drug metabolism.

A familiar simple example of *structural* isomers are ethylalcohol (or ethanol) and dimethyl ether of formula C_2H_6O. They each can be represented by the structural formulae

$$CH_3-CH_2-OH \text{ and } \begin{matrix} CH_3 \\ \diagdown \\ O \\ \diagup \\ CH_3 \end{matrix}$$

in which the lines represent some of the *covalent chemical bonds* (*see below*). It is these interatomic forces which hold the atoms in specific spatial arrangements. Some examples are shown on **T25**.

CHEMICAL BONDING

The number of possible arrangements of a given set of atoms is limited since each type of atom (each element) is capable of forming only a limited number of bonds, equal to its *valency*. The valency varies from element to element; hydrogen has a valency of one (exceptionally two); oxygen, two; nitrogen, three; and carbon four (hence the molecular formulae H_2, H_2O, NH_3 and CH_4 for hydrogen, water, ammonia and methane respectively).

In some compounds two atoms may be joined by a *multiple bond* so that the valency number may be reached. Examples are the double and triple bonds in ethylene (ethene) and acetylene (ethyne respectively):

$$CH_2 = CH_2 \text{ and } CH \equiv CH$$

The modern theory of chemical bonding is electronic. Bonds are formed:

(i) by the sharing of electrons in pairs between two bonded atoms (*covalent* bonding); or

(ii) by the transfer of an electron from one atom to another to form oppositely charged ions (*ionic* bonding).

The ionic situation is electrically *polar* whereas pure covalent bonds have no polarity. If, however, the shared electrons are not shared equally between the bound atoms some effective electron transfer occurs and the bond has some polar character. Covalent bonds between *dissimilar* atoms are generally polar. If one of the two atoms provides *both* the shared electrons, the polarity is particularly high and the bond is called *dative covalent*.

VALENCIES OF THE ELEMENTS

Electronic Theory of Valency

These ideas of the chemical bond lead to a ready explanation of the valencies of the elements (which are periodic if the elements are arranged in order of atomic number) when combined with knowledge of the electronic structure of atoms.

In the original Bohr theory the electrons of atoms move in well defined orbits arranged in shells. The known elements use seven shells, and each element has its unique number of electrons equal to the atomic number, Z ranging from 1 in hydrogen to 103 in lawrencium. Each element also has its unique arrangement of its electrons in these shells. The build-up of electrons in the above sequence follows well-defined rules. The resulting electron configuration of the elements is an important starting point for a discussion of valency. The shells each have a limited capacity and the numbers of electrons that can be accommodated in the first four labelled 1, 2, 3, 4 (or sometimes K, L, M, N) are 2, 8, 18, 32 respectively. Each of these shells has sub-shells of which there are four main types designated s, p, d and f which can contain 2, 6, 10 and 14 electrons respectively. If all the orbits in a shell have electrons actually present in them the shell is filled or closed and this confers on the shell an unusual stability or inertness. Conversely, unfilled shells lead to activity and the electrons in the incompletely filled shells largely determine the chemical and physical properties of the element and are responsible for the combination of atoms to form molecules. These electrons are referred to as *valence electrons*. The inner shell, *i.e.*, the one nearest the nucleus, can accommodate only two electrons (the element helium has just that number) and the next two shells can hold eight each.

Electropositive Elements

Large atoms, *e.g.*, lead, radium, have many filled shells and, subject to special exceptions, the general rule is that the inner shells are the filled ones and the outer shell may be incomplete. Elements which have equal numbers of electrons in their outer shell resemble each other and come in the same Group of the Periodic Table. Thus the elements with complete electronic shells are chemically unreactive gases, *e.g.*, argon and neon (minor constituents of the atmosphere). Elements with just one electron in the outer shell are highly reactive metals, *e.g.*, sodium and potassium which lose this electron readily to give monopositive ions, *e.g.*, Na^-. These elements are called electropositive. Contrariwise elements with just one electron too few are electronegative and readily gain one electron either by sharing, or by capture (to form anions, *e.g.*, Cl^-).

More generally, at least for the light elements of Periods 2 and 3 of the Periodic Table, the valence of an element is given by the Group Number, N, *i.e.*, the number of valence electrons which must be lost by the electropositive metals, or by $8-N$, the number of electrons which electronegative elements need to gain.

VALENCE ELECTRONS (N) AND VALENCY (V)

N = 1	2	3	4	5	6	7	8
V = 1	2	3	4	3	2	1	0
Hydrogen							Helium
Sodium	Magnesium	Aluminium	Carbon	Nitrogen	Oxygen	Fluorine	Neon
Potassium	Calcium	Gallium	Silicon	Phosphorus	Sulphur	Chlorine	Argon
			Germanium	Arsenic		Bromine	
			Tin			Iodine	
Barium			Lead				

←————————Metals————————→ ←————————————————→ Non-metals:
Positive ions   Covalent   Negative ions
                                 compounds   or covalent compounds

The covalence of an electronegative element is increased by one if it loses one electron to form a positive ion, and decreased by one if it gains an electron. Thus nitrogen with a covalence 3 can give either N^- which can form 4 covalent bonds (in the ammonium ion, NH_4^-) or the N^- ion with a covalency of 2 (e.g., NH_2^-). Similarly oxygen can give H_3O^-, the hydroxonium ion (the acid principle in water), H_2O (water itself), and OH^- (the hydroxyl ion).

IONIC BONDS, SALTS AND ACIDS

These bonds are normally formed between electropositive elements (at the left of the Periodic Table, e.g., sodium and potassium) and electronegative elements (at the right of the Periodic Table, e.g., oxygen, fluorine, chlorine). The ionic charge may be determined from the valency: Na^+, Mg^{++}, Al^{+++}; O^-, Cl^-.

Ions may contain a number of atoms, as shown by many of the common anions: hydroxyl, OH^-; nitrate, NO_3^-; sulphate, SO_4^-; carbonate CO_3^-. Ionic solids formed from a metal ion and one of these anions are called salts and are derived from the parent acid in which the anion is bound to a hydrogen ion (or ions): HNO_3, nitric acid; H_2SO_4, sulphuric acid. Sulphuric acid can form two series of salts, one called normal based upon the SO_4^{--} ion and a second (called acid salts since they contain a hydrogen) based upon the HSO_4^- ion. Phosphoric acid, H_3PO_4, has three series of salts. A substance which reacts with an acid to form a salt and water as the only products is called a base. An example is sodium hydroxide, NaOH (caustic soda). The Lewis definitions of acid and base are given below.

The ionic forces are less directional in character than covalent bonds are, but in solids the ions are in regular fixed arrangements (see Part II). Each anion is surrounded by cations and is attracted to them by electrostatic Coulomb forces. These are of long range and so the anion is attracted not only to the closest cations. Additionally each cation is surrounded by anions so that the bonding is not localised. The whole solid therefore is like a giant molecule and is not easily broken down by melting. This contrasts with covalent compounds in which the forces between molecules are small, the main attractions being within the molecule.

The structures adopted depend upon the relative numbers of the anions and cations (which are determined by ionic charges) and by the relative ionic sizes, which have been deduced from X-ray diffraction measurements.

COVALENT BONDS

In the simple theory the shared electron pairs are localised between two atoms. Multiple bonds result when there are more pairs shared. The multiplicity (or bond order) is then integral. The theory may be extended by admitting that an electron pair may be shared between more than two atoms in delocalised bonding which can then give rise to fractional bond orders. The best example is benzene (and graphite) where nine pairs

of electrons are shared between six carbon-carbon bonds giving a bond order of 1·5.

Modern Theories

Modern theories of valency make use of the concepts of quantum mechanics (see T17) in which each of the well-defined electron orbits of the s, p, d and f electrons in the Bohr theory is replaced by the idea of the electron cloud with a spatial electron density and distribution. Each of these electron clouds (now called an orbital) has a definite shape depending upon the type of electrons. The orbitals of s electrons are of spherical shape with a density that falls off with the distance from the nucleus. The peak density occurs at the old Bohr radius. Electrons of the p type have orbitals with double lobes giving the figure of eight or dumbell shape. There are three such orbitals in every shell except the first and they are arranged mutually at right angles. Each one can contain two electrons giving a total of six. The d orbitals are five in number. Each again can contain two electrons giving a total of ten. Four of these d orbitals have shapes like four-leaf clovers, whereas the fifth has two lobes, rather like the p orbitals but with the addition of a torus or doughnut. The shapes of the f orbitals are even more complicated. It is the shape of these orbitals and their relative spatial arrangement which gives the covalent bond its directional character.

Molecular Orbital

The idea of electron sharing between two atoms becomes the notion of overlap of an orbital on one atom with an orbital on another to give a bonding molecular orbital which can contain the pair of shared electrons. The bond energy is a maximum when this overlap is optimum and this occurs when the atoms are in certain definite positions thus giving the molecule its own characteristic shape.

Molecular Shape

For elements from the second row of the Periodic Table the number of electrons in the valence shell can be eight arranged in four pairs of orbitals (one 2s and three 2p orbitals). These orbitals can be combined or hybridised to give the basic tetrahedral shape (see Fig. 1). Each of these can overlap with say an orbital of a hydrogen atom (the 1s) to give a bonding orbital which can accommodate two electrons. Alternatively each orbital can, if the atom has enough electrons, contain two non-bonding electrons called a lone pair. The basic molecular shapes of methane (CH_4), ammonia (NH_3), and water (H_2O) may then be rationalised as in Fig. 1.

The bond angle in methane is the tetrahedral angle (109° 28'). The angles in ammonia (107° 18') and water (104° 30') are smaller probably because the lone pair orbital is slightly more repulsive than the bonding orbital is. This closes down the angles between the bonds.

The lone pairs may be used to bind the hydrogen ions from acids to give tetrahedral NH_4^- and pyramidal H_3O^-. It is the lone pairs therefore which give ammonia and water their basicity. In the modern concept of acids and bases due to Lewis, a base is an electron donor and an acid becomes an electron acceptor. This definition of an acid includes the older idea of it as a hydrogen ion

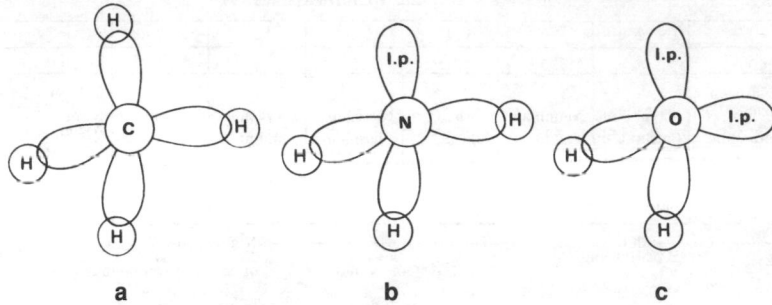

a   b   c

Fig. 1. The spatial arrangements of the atoms and orbitals in (a) methane (CH_4), (b) ammonia (NH_3) and (c) water (H_2O). The basic shape is tetrahedral and the hybridised orbitals are lone pair orbitals (l.p.) and bonding orbitals.

producer in that the hydrogen ion is an electron acceptor but it is more general—a Lewis acid need not be a protic acid.

Bond Lengths

Many covalent bond distances have been measured and each may be apportioned between the bound atoms to give a self-consistent set of covalent bond-radii for each element which can be used in predictions of molecular structures. These radii vary inversely with the bond order involved. Thus the carbon-carbon bond length varies from 154 pm (*i.e.*, 10^{12}m) for C−C to 135 pm for C=C.

Bond Energies

Bonds differ in their strength depending upon the atoms and the bond order. A double bond between two given atoms is stronger than a single bond but generally not as strong as two single bonds. Thus "unsaturated" compounds, which contain multiple bonds, will tend to form "saturated" compounds containing only single bonds since the energetics are favourable.

Functional Groups

Compounds may be further classified according to certain persistent groups of atoms which have a residual valency and can combine with other groups. Thus the methyl group (CH_3) related to

methane (CH_4) by the removal of a hydrogen atom can combine with other atoms or groups of valency one: methyl chloride (chloromathane), CH_3Cl; methyl alcohol (methanol), CH_3OH; dimethyl ether, CH_3OCH_3. Common functional groups are shown in the table.

CHEMICAL ENERGETICS

Chemical reactions are accompanied by energy changes which can be utilised as heat (in fires) or mechanical work (in explosions or rockets), or to produce electric current in batteries. Chemical compounds can therefore be said to store energy and to possess "internal energy". The energy can be thought of as being stored in the chemical bonds. The energy change (at constant volume) in a reaction is then a result of changes (denoted ΔU) in the nett internal energy of the reactants and products by the law of the conservation of energy. If the conditions are those of constant pressure, the energy change is due to overall changes in a closely related properly called enthalpy (ΔH).

It was at one time thought that reactions would proceed only if energy was given out (*exothermic* processes). Although this is now known to be true at the lowest temperature, in other cases a second consideration, the entropy term, needs to be considered, as the existence of *endothermic* changes confirms. A new "energy" term defined

SOME CLASSES OF SIMPLE ORGANIC COMPOUNDS		
Name	**General Description and Formula**	**Examples**
Alkanes (or paraffins)	"Saturated" hydrocarbons of the general formula C_nH_{2n+2} Contain single bonds only	methane (CH_4) butane (C_4H_{10})
Alkenes (olefins)	"Unsaturated" hydrocarbons of general formula C_nH_{2n} Contain double bonds	ethylene (C_2H_4) styrene ($C_6H_5.C_2H_3$)
Alkynes (acetylenes)	"Unsaturated" hydrocarbon of general formula C_nH_{2n-2} Contain triple bonds	acetylene (C_2H_2)
Alcohols	Contain the OH group, bound for example to an alkyl group $C_nH_{2n+1}OH$	methylalcohol (CH_3OH) ethylalcohol (C_2H_5OH)
Ketones	Contain the C=O group $C_nH_{2n+1}C=O$	acetone ($(CH_3)_2CO$)
Aldehydes	Contain the CHO group	formaldehyde (HCHO) acetaldehyde (CH_3CHO)
Aromatic hydrocarbons	Ring compounds with reactions similiar to the proto type, benzene (C_6H_6)	napthalene ($C_{10}H_8$) anthracene ($C_{14}H_{10}$)
Phenyl compounds	Derivatives of the phenyl group, C_6H_5	phenol (C_6H_5OH) aniline ($C_6H_5NH_2$)
Heterocyclic compounds	Ring compounds containing mainly carbon atoms and one or more other atoms, *e.g.*, nitrogen	pyridine (C_5H_5N) thiophene (C_4H_4S)

to contain the entropy consideration and called the Gibbs Free Energy, G, may then be used. Natural or "spontaneous" processes are accompanied by a decrease in the nett value of G, and systems tend to assume whichever state has the lowest value of G.

Chemical Equilibrium

Certain chemical changes, like physical changes such as raising and lowering weights, or freezing and melting water, may be easily reversed. The forward and backward reactions which are proceeding continuously can then be made to balance out, given enough time, and the system is said to be in equilibrium.

Suppose that X and Y when mixed are partially converted to Z and an equilibrium mixture is obtained under certain defined conditions. The relative amounts $[X]$, $[Y]$, etc., are then definite and governed by the equilibrium constant defined as

$$K = \frac{[Z]}{[X][Y]}$$

Putting it in another way, if we know K we can predict the relative amounts of products and reactants, i.e., the extent to which the reaction proceeds. K in turn depends upon the change in Gibbs Free Energy for the reaction:

$$\Delta G = -RT \ln K$$

where R is the gas constant, and T the absolute temperature, and $\ln$ denotes the natural logarithm.

Chemical Thermodynamics

The efficiency of a reaction therefore can be predicted theoretically since values for ΔG can frequently be calculated from tabulated values of ΔH and ΔS. Such studies constitute *chemical thermodynamics*, the branch of thermodynamics applied to chemical reactions. It is an essential consideration in industrial processes.

Bond Enthalpies

The enthalpy (q.v.) of a molecule can be thought of as the sum of the enthalpies associated with each covalent bond, for each of which there is a characteristic value. Determination and tabulation of these bond energies helps in the prediction of enthalpy changes in new reactions involving covalent molecules. Similarly for ionic solids.

THE SPEED OF REACTIONS—CATALYSIS

A good analogy to illustrate the difference between chemical thermodynamics and kinetics is the downhill flow of water. The water will seek the lowest point where it has the lowest potential energy, and in an analogous way a reaction will try to proceed to the state with the lowest Gibbs Free Energy. However, the speed of both water flow and reaction will depend upon a large number of factors, particularly the available *pathway* (or reaction mechanism). Indeed water at the top of a mountain or in a domestic bath may not flow down at all if a suitable path is blocked say by a hillock (or bath plug). The unblocking may involve the expenditure of energy, for example to lift the water over the dam (or pull out the plug).

Activation Energy

In reactions this type of energy is called the *activation energy*. It can be supplied in a number of ways (see below) such as heating. Sometimes it is small and (thankfully) at other times it is large enough that thermodynamically feasible reactions do not occur at all quickly. Each of us is, in fact, *thermodynamically* unstable with respect to our combustion products, mainly CO_2 and H_2O, i.e., we should burn (!), but fortunately we are *kinetically* stable.

Catalysts

A *catalyst* is a substance which will provide an alternative reaction pathway of low activation energy, i.e., it can speed up a reaction, without itself being consumed in the process. The analogy for the water flow would be a tunnel through the hillock. Catalysts are very important industrially, for example, in the manufacture of sulphuric acid (using platinised asbestos or vanadium pentoxide), in the Haber process for ammonia used for fertilisers (iron derivatives), and in the "cracking" of crude oil to give lighter oils (aluminium oxide). Natural catalysts are called *enzymes* (q.v.).

CLASSIFICATION OF REACTIONS

Chemical change can be brought about by a variety of techniques used separately or together:
mixing of single substances
heating single substances or mixtures
electrolysing solutions
exposure to light or radiation
addition of catalysts.

The changes can be classified according to the results produced:

Dissociation—breakdown into simpler substances or ions

Addition—in which one type of molecule or ion is added to another

Polymerisation—reaction of a substance (monomer) with itself to produce larger molecules of the same composition (polymer)

Substitution—in which one particular group in a molecule is replaced by another

Elimination—in which one particular group in a molecule is lost

Exchange—in which two groups are mutually substituted one by the other

Oxidation—removal of electrons (increase of oxidation number), e.g., Fe^{++} ferrous ion is oxidised to ferric, Fe^{+++}

Reduction—the converse of oxidation

Classification by Molecular Mechanism

More significantly modern classifications are based upon the precise *molecular mechanism* employed. Examples are

Nucleophilic attack—where an electron-rich reagent attacks a position of low electron density in a molecule

Electrophilic attack—where an electron-depleted reagent—an electrophile (for example, a positive ion)—attacks a position of high electron density

Bimolecular reaction—one which involves two molecules unlike a monomolecular reaction which involves only one in each step

Precise descriptions can be built up: substitution, nucleophilic, bimolecular.

ELECTROLYTES, ELECTROLYSIS AND ELECTROCHEMICAL CELLS

Electrolytic Solutions

Ionic solids can dissolve in some solvents especially if each has a high dielectric constant to cut down the force of attraction between oppositely charged ions. The process can be assisted by solvation of the ions and also by the entropy changes which favour the less ordered state of affairs—the liquid rather than the ordered solid.

Electrolysis

The oppositely charged ions are capable of independent movement and the application of an electric potential from an external battery or source of direct current to electrodes in the solution will cause the ions to move. The positive ions (cations) will move to the negatively charged electrode (the cathode) and the negatively charged ions (anions) to the positively charged anode. At the electrodes chemical changes occur and ions may be converted to uncharged species and deposited: for example, sodium ions (Na^+) to sodium metal, Na. This process is referred to as electrolysis. Faraday discovered two laws of electrolysis: (i) the amount of any substance deposited (or dissolved) is proportional to the amount of electricity used; (ii) the relative amounts of substances deposited by the same quantity of electricity are in the ratio of their *equivalent weights*.

For any ion discharged below a certain value of the applied voltage the *discharge voltage* is small. In an electrolyte containing many different ionic species therefore, each ionic discharge will occur only as the appropriate potential is reached. For solutions of acids, hydrogen (formed from H^+ ions) is discharged at the cathode, and oxygen (formed from OH^- ions) at the anode. Electrolysis is important commercially for the refining of metals, electroplating, and in the production of many basic chemicals.

Electrochemical Cells

Ever since 1800 when Volta produced an electric battery consisting of alternate plates of silver and zinc separated by cloth impregnated with salt, the search for new batteries has been continuous. In each new battery a different chemical process is harnessed to produce electrical energy. The battery must not only be feasible according to the laws of thermodynamics, but must be practicable and cheap for widespread consumer use.

The voltages developed in any battery can be predicted from a knowledge of the two processes occurring: one at the cathode and the other at the anode. Voltages can be ascribed to each of these "half cells" according to the chemical reaction which occurs and the condition used, for example concentrations of the reactants (the so-called "standard electrode potentials"). The voltage of any combination of two half cells is the sum of the half-cell voltages. Furthermore each of these voltages is related to the change in the Gibbs Free Energy for its reaction and can, in theory, therefore be predicted thermodynamically.

CHEMISTRY IN MODERN LIFE

Chemistry plays a crucial role in modern life, not least in the third world, as well as in the more developed nations. In the UK chemistry has been studied, developed and put to practical use as well as anywhere in the world in modern times. It is no accident that the largest specialised scientific society in the UK is the Royal Society of Chemistry (RSC) and that its forerunner, The Chemical Society, lays claim to being the oldest in the world.

The high quality of chemical science at the crucial level of basic research is indicated by the remarkable frequency with which the Nobel Prize in Chemistry has come to the UK The success is not confined to academic activity but, surely as a consequence, it extends to the economic life of the nation.

The UK Chemical Industry

The UK chemical industry is among the largest in the world and one of the most successful. In December 2000 it employed 238,000 people in over 3,400 companies with product sales of £32 billion. In national statistics it is included in the manufacturing sector alongside other sectors which have a high chemical component such as petroleum and petroleum products. Its output covers a very wide range. The so called "basic chemicals", such as sulphuric acid, which are utilised in the manufacturing processes of other sectors.

In agriculture chemicals are not only important in the form of bulk products such as fertilizer, without which modern agriculture could not operate efficiently, but also for the 'finer' chemicals such as herbicides and insecticides. Manufactured synthetic polymers and plastics are omnipresent in modern life, for example in architecture and building as well as in many familiar household products and uses. The list here is long and includes moulded casings for televisions and other electronic and electrical products, kitchen utensils, all forms of coverings from paints and varnishes to fabrics. Then there are the "finer" chemicals: cosmetics and pharmaceuticals, ranging from vanity products to the birth control pill and life-saving synthetic drugs. Petroleum products from oil cover an extremely wide range. Petroleum is a most valuable "feed stock" for other products and in this use it is arguably more unique and precious than as a fuel or energy source.

Chemistry Today

Nevertheless, chemistry has had as bad a press recently as other basic physical sciences have had, with the consequence that universities are lining up to close their chemistry departments. The Royal Society of Chemistry has found that the percentage of 18-year-olds studying A-level chemistry has fallen from just over 7 per cent in 1995 to less than 5 per cent in 2003. In the popular mind, chemistry has become associated with pollution resulting from the manufacturing, use and misuse of synthetic chemicals, as well as industrial accidents. Indeed, the word "chemical" has been used increasingly in a pejorative way, even in informed broadcasting and reportage.

Thus chemical fertilizers (meaning synthetic fertilizers) are distinguished falsely from organic fertilizers. This sort of practice ignores the fact that we ourselves consist of, use, rely on, are surrounded by naturally occurring chemicals, organic and inorganic, as well as the useful man-made synthetics.

IV. BIOLOGY—THE SCIENCE OF LIFE

WHAT BIOLOGY IS ABOUT

Biology embraces the study of all living things which exist on earth at the present time and also the recognisable remains of those that are extinct. Living things or organisms range from the apparently simple micro-organisms such as viruses and bacteria to the largest animals and plants.

Living Processes

The enormous variation and complexity of living processes make the task of understanding and defining life a very difficult one. Every living organism undergoes continual physical and chemical changes which, in spite of their diversity, are referred to as the metabolism of the organism. Metabolism involves the processing of food materials, the production of waste products, and all the intermediate stages between these whereby energy and matter are provided for the operation, maintenance, and growth of the organism. These reactions are under very exact chemical or nervous control at every stage and can be slowed down or speeded up as the need arises. Thus the organism can react to changes in the environment in which it lives, adjusting its activities in relation to the external changes. Finally, organisms can reproduce either in an identical or very slightly modified form. In this process new individuals are produced and the species continues to survive. Differences between offspring and parents can, under certain circumstances, act cumulatively over many generations and so form the basis of evolutionary change in which new species of organism are ultimately formed. Viruses occupy a middle ground between biology and chemistry, as do the more recently discovered transposons, which are organisms in the genetic sense of undergoing replication but are so simple that they are amenable to chemical analysis. However, since these are intimately dependent on cellular organisms, they are included in the study of biology rather than chemistry.

Molecular Biology

It has been evident for many years that the most fundamental aspects of these living processes occur in basic structural units known as cells. The study of living processes at the molecular and cell level has been given a tremendous impetus in recent years by the advent of new techniques which enable microscopic and submicroscopic parts of cells to be examined. Physicists, chemists, and mathematicians have found themselves working alongside biologists in this field and several of the very notable advances have been made by physical scientists. Molecular biology is a term frequently used in describing this rapidly expanding and fascinating field of research. A lengthy discussion of this topic can be found on **T62–68.**

EVOLUTION

Introduction.—The idea that species of living organisms could change over long periods of time was considered by some Greek writers and, much later, by the Frenchmen Buffon and Lamarck at the end of the 18th cent. Further, the work of the 18th cent. geologists such as James Hutton and William Smith provided a basis without which the major contribution of Darwin, the great 19th cent. naturalist, would have been impossible. Hutton showed that the earth's surface had undergone prolonged upheavals and volcanic eruptions with consequent changes in sea level. This implied that the earth was much older than had previously been supposed. Smith developed a method of dating the geological strata by means of the fossils found in them and demonstrated that widely different types of animals

and plants existed at different periods of the earth's history. Later in this section (**T68–70**) a more detailed picture is presented of the geological record of evolution.

These discoveries conflicted with the Biblical account in the book of Genesis and, although various attempts were made to explain them away or discredit them, it became abundantly clear that through millions of years life has been continually changing, with new species constantly arising and many dying out.

The Evidence for Evolution

1. The Geological Record.—It has already been pointed out that successively younger rocks contain fossil remains of different and relatively more complex organisms. The spore-bearing plants preceded the gymnosperms and the angiosperms arose much later. Similarly in the vertebrate series the fish appeared before the amphibia which were followed by the reptiles and later by the air breathing, warm-blooded birds and mammals.

On a more restricted level the evolution of the horse has been worked out in great detail from the small *Eohippus* which was about a foot high and had four digits on the forefeet and three on the hind-feet to the large one-toed animal living today. However, such complete series are rare and the geological record is very incomplete. There are a number of gaps, particularly between the major groups of organisms. No satisfactory fossil evidence is known of the ancestors of the angiosperms so perhaps they did not grow in conditions which favoured their preservation as fossils.

On the other hand, *Archæopteryx* provides an indisputable link between the reptiles and the birds. For a fuller discussion of these topics, *see* **Special Topic, The Geological Record (T68).**

Although we talk about the age of fishes, the age of reptiles and so on it must be emphasised that these are the periods during which particular groups were abundant or even dominant. Each group probably originated many millions of years before it became widespread. Further, some groups, such as the giant reptiles and the seed-ferns, died out completely whereas others, the fishes and true ferns for example, are still common today although many fishes and ferns that exist today are very different from those of the Devonian and Carboniferous periods. On the other hand some species, *e.g.* the maidenhair tree, have remained unaltered for many millions of years.

2. Geographical Distribution.—Nearly all the marsupials or pouched mammals are found in the Australian continent which was cut off from the mainland about 60 million years ago. All the fossil evidence indicates that at that time the eutherian or placental mammals did not yet exist. The marsupials are the only naturally occurring mammals in Australia but since the isolation of the continent the group has given rise to a large number of species very similar in appearance to those which evolved elsewhere in the world among the eutherian mammals. There are marsupials which look like wolves, dogs, cats and squirrels; yet they have no close biological relationships to these animals. Further, some marsupials such as the kangaroos have evolved which are unlike any other creatures in the rest of the world. Quite clearly the isolation of Australia so long ago has resulted in the evolution of these distinct types, just as Darwin found in the Galapagos islands where each has its own distinct flora and fauna which differ also from those of the S. American mainland.

3. Anatomy.—The comparative study of the development and mature structure of the mammalian body provides much evidence that all the species have evolved from a single ancestral stock.

Although the arm of an ape, the leg of a dog, the flipper of a whale and the wing of a a bat appear very different externally they are all built on the same skeletal plan. It would be difficult to explain such similarities unless they had all evolved from a common type. There is also evidence that the early development of an animal recapitulates its biological history to a certain extent. For example, the gill slits found in fish are formed during the early stages in the development of a mammal although later they disappear. Finally, apparently useless vestigial structures sometimes occur which would be inexplicable unless regarded in the light of an evolutionary history. In man a small appendix and vestiges of a third eyelid occur but these are functionless although in other animals such structures are well developed and functional, e.g., the appendix in the rabbit.

4. Human Selection.

During his brief history on earth modern man has continually selected and bred animals and plants for his own use. We have only to look at the various breeds of dogs which have been developed from a single wild type to see that under certain circumstances great structural divergence can occur in a species even in a relatively short time. The advent of genetic engineering may represent a qualitatively new form of evolution: many can now bypass the slow process of natural selection for small beneficial alterations in a species by rapid laboratory screening for dramatic changes selected to his advantage.

The Darwinian Theory of Evolution.

Darwin amassed a great deal of information such as that outlined above which convinced him that evolution of life had taken place over millions of years. His was the first real attempt to collect all the evidence scientifically and no other satisfactory alternative explanation of all the facts he presented has been proposed. Perhaps even more important was his attempt to explain how evolution had actually occurred. He published his theory after many years of work in his book The Origin of Species by Means of Natural Selection in 1859. Some of his ideas have since been modified owing to our increased knowledge of genetics but they are so important that it is worth-while recounting his theory.

1. The Struggle for Existence.—It is clear that in nature there is a severe struggle for existence in all animals and plants. Over a period of time the number of individuals of a species in a given community does not vary greatly. This implies that the number of progeny which survive to become mature breeding individuals more or less replaces the number of mature ones that die. Generally speaking the reproductive output of a species is much greater than this. For example, a single large foxglove plant may produce half a million seeds each one of which is potentially capable of giving rise to a new individual. Obviously nearly all the progeny die before reaching maturity and the chance of any single one surviving is very remote.

2. Variation.—The individuals of any generation of human beings obviously differ from one another and such differences are found in other organisms. It is clear that they vary considerably in structure, colour, activity and so on. Darwin also pointed out that generally these variations were passed on from one generation to the next, for example, the children of tall parents tend to grow tall.

3. Survival of the Fittest.—If there is an intense struggle for existence in their natural environment among individuals of a species having different characteristics, those which are best "fitted" to a given set of conditions are most likely to survive to maturity. These will reproduce and the features which enabled them to survive will be passed on to their offspring. This process is liable to continue and a species will become better adapted to its environment.

4. Natural Selection.—Over a long period of time the environment of a given species is never stable but will change in various ways. As it does so

the characters which best fit the individuals to the changed environment will be selected. If an environmental change affects only part of the range occupied by a species, the populations living in different parts may adapt and come to differ so much that they are no longer able to interbreed, with the result that the original species has now become two distinct species.

Darwin and Lamarck.

Darwin pictured evolution as a slow continuous process with natural selection operating on the small inheritable variations found between the individuals of a species which were undergoing intense competition. This neglects the important effect of the environment on the growth and structure of the individual. It is obvious that external conditions will affect the development of an organism, for example the effect of various soil conditions on the growth of a plant or the amount of food material available to an animal. Lamarck maintained that the characters acquired by an individual owing to the effect of its environment could be passed on to its offspring. Undoubtedly characters are acquired by the individual during its growth but in spite of many attempts to prove otherwise no experiments have been done which prove conclusively that these are inherited by the offspring. Thus Lamarck's theory that evolution has occurred by the inheritance of acquired characters is not widely acceptable today.

Neodarwinism

Darwinism received something of a setback during the early years of modern genetics. There did not seem to be much in common between the large mutations studied by geneticists and the small continuous variations which Darwin thought were the basic material upon which selection acted. With time, it became evident that not all mutations are large in their effects and that much of the continuous variation which occurs does indeed have a genetic basis. Mathematicians such as J. B. S. Haldane and Sewall Wright showed that even very small selective advantages would cause genes to spread throughout populations as the generations passed by. Further development of this idea has led to the 'selfish gene' model, in which the struggle for existence, variation and survival of the fittest operate at the level of genes rather than whole animals, which are relegated to the role of mere vehicles allowing the expression of genes and, thus, the struggle between them. Experiments and observations on natural populations showed that evolution—seen as progressive, adaptive genetic change—does indeed occur today. For example, the proportion of dark-coloured moths has greatly increased in many areas where smoke pollution occurs, as a result of predation by birds on the now more obvious light forms. Again, many pest insects have evolved genetic resistance to the insecticides used to attack them. Increases in the available fossil information suggest that evolution occurs in fits and starts, with long periods of stability alternating with short periods of rapid change. This is called the punctuated equilibrium model, and the 'punctuations' may be associated with sudden changes in climatic conditions.

GENETICS

Mendelism

Genetics is the study of the mechanisms of the hereditary process. Modern genetics began with the experiments of Gregor Mendel, an Austrian monk in 1865. He studied the inheritance of different factors in peas by crossing different strains and counting the numbers of plants with different characters in the succeeding generations.

In one experiment Mendel crossed peas with round seeds with peas having wrinkled seeds. All of the offspring (known as the "first filial" or F1 generation) had round seeds. Mendel allowed these plants to pollinate themselves, and then measured the characteristics of their offspring (the F2 generation). There were 5,474 round-seeded plants and 1,850 wrinkled-seeded plants in the F2 generation, a ratio of very nearly three to one. The character of roundness can be described as being "dominant" over the "recessive" character of wrinkledness.

In order to explain his results Mendel suggested
that the characters of roundness and wrinkledness
were determined by particulate factors (now called
genes), and that each plant possessed two genes
for each feature. Suppose the gene for roundness
is *A* and that for wrinkledness is *a*. Then the
parental plants in Mendel's experiment will be
represented by *AA* (round seeds) and *aa* (wrinkled
seeds). The gametes (the ovules and the sperm
nuclei of the pollen grains) will be *A* and *a* respectively. When these combine to form the F1
generation they will produce plants with the
genetic constitution *Aa*. Both male and female
gametes of the F1 generation are then of the two
types *A* and *a*, and these can combine, on self-
pollination, in four different ways:

F1	male gamete	female gamete	F2
	A	*A*	*AA*
Aa	*A*	*a*	*Aa*
	a	*A*	*aa*
	a	*a*	

The individuals of the F2 generation will thus have
genetic constitutions of *AA*, *Aa* and *aa* in the
approximate proportions 1 : 2 : 1. Since both *AA*
and *Aa* individuals have round seeds, the ratio of
round-seeded plants to wrinkled-seeded plants
will be about three to one, which indeed it is.

Mendel's results were ignored for many years
until their rediscovery at the start of the 20th
century. Mendelian ratios were then found to
govern inheritance in a large number of other
cases, such as coat colour in rabbits and cattle,
and white eyes and other characteristics in the
fruit fly *Drosophila*. In other cases characteristics
are governed by more than one set of genes so
the simple mathematical relationships are obscured. This occurs in quantitative features,
such as yield in crop plants and weight in animals.

Application of modern statistical methods to
Mendel's results suggest that they were subjected to
certain 'massaging'—they are in fact simply too
good to be true. However, many repeats of his
experiments have shown that his conclusions are
indeed statistically valid.

Chromosome Theory

The chromosomes are dark-staining filaments
which, as we shall see later, can be observed in the
nucleus at cell division. Their behaviour was
described in the nineteenth century, but it was not
clear what their function was. After the rediscovery of Mendel's work, Sutton suggested that
the genes are carried on chromosomes, since the
observed behaviour of the chromosomes corresponded very well with the theoretical behaviour
of Mendel's factors.

Further evidence for the chromosome theory of
inheritance came from study of the phenomenon
known as sex-linkage, in which the expression of
a gene depends upon the sex of the individual
in which it is found. Haemophilia in man, for
example, is a hereditary disease which is normally
found only in males, although it is clear that females can act as carriers (Queen Victoria was one,
since one of her sons, three of her grandsons and
seven of her greatgrandsons were haemophiliacs).
Cytological study shows that there is one pair of
chromosomes which differ in the two sexes. In
the female (in man and most animals) the two
chromosomes of this pair are similar and are known
as the X chromosomes. In the male one of these
is replaced by a much smaller Y chromosome.
Hence recessive genes which are found on only
one X chromosome are expressed in the male,
since there is no other dominant gene present. A
female haemophiliac would have haemophilia
genes on both X chromosomes; this could only
arise from a carrier mother and a haemophiliac
father, a very rare occurrence.

Modern Research

In recent years it has become clear that chromosomes are composed largely of the DNA molecules
of the cell nucleus (*q.v.*), to be discussed later. And

since it has become evident that genes are DNA
molecules, we now have a firm chemical basis for
the assumption that genes are carried on chromosomes. Genetics has thus to some extent become a
branch of molecular biology. (*see* T62–8).

Mutations

Sometimes a DNA molecule may not replicate
itself exactly during the process of cell division.
When this happens the gene which it constitutes
has changed its character so as to produce a difference effect when expressed in the individual
organism. Such a change is known as a gene
mutation. It seems likely, for example, that
Queen Victoria's haemophilia gene arose as a
mutation in herself or in her mother. Mutations,
as we shall see, are of vital importance in providing
the genetic variation upon which evolutionary
selection can act.

The frequency with which mutations occur is
increased by certain chemicals and by ionising
radiation. Hence the need for caution in exposing the body to X-rays and to radioactive materials, and the concern over the possible genetic
effects of radioactive waste from power stations
and from military testing programmes.

THE CELL

Cells were first seen in 1665 by Robert Hooke
when he looked at a piece of cork under his
primitive microscope. It was not until 1839,
however, that Schlieden and Schwann produced
the cell doctrine which visualised the cell as both
the structural and functional unit of living organisation. Viruses constitute a difficulty since in many
ways they are intermediate between living and dead
matter. They are absolutely dependent on cells of
other organisms for their continued existence.
Outside living cells they are inert molecules which
may take a crystalline form. Inside a host cell, however, they become disease-producing parasites
which multiply and show many of the other properties of living organisms. They are minute and
lack the complex organisation usually associated
with cells. Notwithstanding their somewhat
ambiguous position, the viruses are often treated
as though they were single cells or parts of cells
and their extreme simplicity has made them ideal
material for many types of research at this level.

Structure and Function of Cells

Though the constituent cells of a multicellular
organism are usually specialised to perform particular functions, they have a great many features in
common. The cell is often said to be made up of a
substance called protoplasm, a term for the fundamental material of life which dates from the 19th
cent. Protoplasm has two main constituents, the
cytoplasm and the nucleus, and is bounded on the
outside by a cell or plasma membrane. Plant
cells generally have an additional wall composed
primarily of cellulose and used for support. The
nucleus is the controlling centre of the cell and has
rather limited metabolic capabilities. The cytoplasm contains various organelles which operate to
produce energy and new cell structure during the
normal metabolism of the cell.

Cells take up the raw materials for metabolism
through the cell membrane from extracellular
fluid which surrounds them. The nutrients include carbohydrates, fats, proteins, minerals,
vitamins, and water. Fats and carbohydrates are
important principally as sources of energy, though
both types of compound are found in permanent
cell structure. Proteins are complex substances of
high molecular weight which contain nitrogen in
addition to the carbon, hydrogen, and oxygen
found in the other compounds. They are of
fundamental importance in the structure and
function of the cell and are built up of a number
of simple nitrogen-containing organic molecules
called amino acids. There are twenty amino
acids occurring commonly in nature so that the
number of possible combinations in large protein
molecules is quite clearly enormous. A group of

proteins whose significance is well established are the enzymes which are the catalysts of chemical reactions in living cells. Each enzyme will control and speed up a specific reaction even though it is present in very small amounts and is usually unchanged at the end of the process. A large number of inorganic mineral salts are essential for cells to function normally. Some, such as sodium, potassium, and calcium salts, are needed in considerable quantity; others are required only in trace amounts and these include iron, copper, and manganese. The trace elements are usually important constituents of enzyme systems. Vitamins are also necessary in very small amounts and many act as 'co-enzymes', i.e. molecules which must bind to an enzyme before the enzyme is able to catalyse its specific reaction.

I. CYTOPLASM

For a long time cytoplasm was thought to be a homogeneous and structureless substrate in which enzymes occurred as part of a general colloidal system. With the refinement of techniques such as electron microscopy and ultracentrifugation, more and more identifiable components have been found within the cytoplasm. It now seems certain that the material other than these recognisable particles is not a structureless matrix but a highly organised and variable complex, organised around a network of protein filaments called the cytoskeleton, which is responsible for maintaining the internal distribution of organelles and also for cell movements, as in amoebae.

Mitochondria and Oxidation

Mitochondria vary in shape from cylindrical rods to spheres and in size from 0.2 to 3.0 μm. When seen in the living cell they are in constant motion. The whole structure is enclosed within a thin double membrane, the inner layer of which is thrown into folds extending across the central cavity of the mitochondrion and dividing it into small chambers. The function of mitochondria is to provide energy for the reactions of the rest of the cell. Almost the whole machinery for the oxidation of foodstuffs is to be found in the mitochondria. Slight damage to the mitochondrion will render it unable to carry out a complete cycle of oxidative processes. Destruction of parts of the double membrane system prevents the production of energy-rich phosphate bonds in adenosine triphosphate (ATP) in which energy is stored and transported about the cell.

Chloroplasts

Chloroplasts are particles found in cells in the green parts of plants, in fact they contain the green pigment called chlorophyll. They are involved in the process known as photosynthesis in which energy absorbed from light is used to synthesise carbohydrates from carbon dioxide and water, oxygen being formed as a byproduct.
Chloroplasts are disc-shaped or flat ellipsoids from 2 to 20 μm across, possessing a complex structure which in many ways is reminiscent of that found in mitochondria. A typical double membrane surrounds the structure and the inside is made up very largely of a stack of discs consisting of paired membranes connected at their ends to form closed systems. This seems to be a further development of the type of lamellated structure seen dividing the central cavity of a mitochondrion. The chlorophylls and other pigments, such as the orange yellow carotenoids, seem to be arranged in layers a single molecule thick in the chloroplast discs so that they are maximally exposed to light.

Photosynthesis

Photosynthesis is probably the most important of all biological reactions, and can be regarded as the basis of all higher life, and is responsible for producing the oxygen required for efficient metabolism. The whole animal population of the world, including man, is dependent on plants for food since even the meat-eating carnivores prey upon herbivores.
Although scientists continue to make efforts to produce adequate food materials from simple compounds, there is still no better machinery known for doing this than the plant cell. Man is dependent on photosynthesis for his supplies of food and also for much of his fuel, since much of the combustible material removed from the earth is of plant origin.

Ribosomes

Ribosomes, which are tiny granules composed of protein and RNA, are found in the cytoplasm, both free and attached to the surface of a system of membrane tubules called the endoplasmic reticulum, which permeates most of the cell. Ribosomes are responsible for the synthesis of proteins, which are bound to the endoplasmic reticulum and inject their proteins into the system of tubules as they are synthesised. The proteins can then be folded into the correct three-dimensional structure, modified by addition of sugar units, and transported to other parts of the cell. Some proteins accumulate in a special part of the endoplasmic reticulum, the Golgi apparatus, which lacks attached ribosomes and from which small vesicles bud off and later fuse with the plasma membrane to release their contents to the outside of the cell.

Nucleic Acids

The term nucleic acid covers a class of substances, usually of great complexity, built up from smaller units called nucleotides. Each nucleotide consists of a base, united to a sugar, in turn united to phosphoric acid. Nucleotides are joined together in a linear fashion by means of the phosphoric acid residues to form a chain from which the bases project at right angles into the centre of the double helix formed by two DNA molecules. Two types of sugar are found in naturally occurring nucleic acids and these are the ribose of RNA and the deoxyribose of deoxyribonucleic acids (DNA). We shall return to the latter when the nucleus is considered. Four nitrogen-containing bases occur in nucleic acids and in RNA—adenine, cytosine, guanine, and uracil. In DNA the uracil is replaced by thymine.

Protein Synthesis

RNA is predominantly manufactured in the nucleus and subsequently moves out into the cytoplasm. There are three major types of RNA, and all are involved in synthesising proteins. Ribosomal RNA, or rRNA, combines with a number of proteins to form the ribosomes, which act as the assembly line for proteins. Messenger RNA, or mRNA, carries a copy of the structural information encoded by a particular gene and, once in the cytoplasm, associates temporarily with ribosomes to have this information 'translated' into the structure of the protein. Transfer RNA, or tRNA, has a characteristic 'clover-leaf' structure, and picks up amino acids from the cytoplasm and carries them to the ribosome for addition to a growing protein chain. The information in genes and hence in the mRNA molecule is encoded as sequences of three of the nucleotide bases; each such codon tells the ribosome to add a particular amino acid to the protein it is making. Thus, as the ribosomes slide along the mRNA molecule, it stops at each codon, waits for the correct tRNA to arrive with the required amino acid, transfers the amino acid from the tRNA molecule to the growing protein, releases the used tRNA, and moves along to the next codon. mRNA molecules contain a number of special 'signal sequences' to tell the ribosome where to start and stop reading its instructions.
Nucleic acids are composed of four different nucleotide bases, while proteins are made using 20 different amino acids; mRNA molecules also need at least one codon as a 'start here' sign and another as a 'stop' sign. Clearly, a code of one base per amino acid would only be able to make proteins with four amino acids; a code of two bases per amino acid would be able to encode 16 amino acids, which is still insufficient. A code using three bases per amino acid can encode 64 amino acids, which is far more than enough, but is nonetheless the mini-

mum that can be used. The genetic code is thus 'redundant', and most amino acids can be specified by more than one codon. Examination of the genetic code showed that redundancy is organised in such a way as to minimise the effects of changes in DNA nucleotides (mutation): thus, the amino acid valine has four codons, GUA, GUU, GUC and GUG, and changes in the last base will have no effect on the protein synthesised. Changes in the first position also have relatively minor effects, because all codons with U in the second position code for amino acids with only slightly different physical and chemical properties. Thus, evolution has taken great care to develop and maintain an optimal system for its own operating.

Cell Membrane

Though the cell membrane plays a most vital part in regulating what can enter and leave the cell, it remains rather poorly understood. It consists of two layers of lipid molecules with protein and other large molecules embedded within it. These protein molecules have many functions, including attachment of cells to each other, signalling the occurrence of extracellular events to the inside of the cell, and transport of water and other molecules into and out of cells. The first of these depends on the proteins and other molecules of different cells recognising each other and having the ability to join together; other adhesion molecules fix cells to various surfaces. Changes in cell recognition proteins are thought to be important in the spread of cancer cells through the body. Signalling functions involve proteins that pass right through the cell membrane and have, on the part exposed outside the cell, the ability to bind specific chemical compounds, such as hormones and neurotransmitters. When this occurs, the physical structure of the transmembrane protein changes, and this change is recognised by other proteins attached to the inner surface of the membrane.

This then induces an alteration in catalytic activity, for example increasing the production of cyclic adenosine mononucleotide (cAMP), which then diffuses to other parts of the cell to initiate changes in the activity of the cell. Such changes include increases in membrane permeability for sodium or potassium (as in nerve cells), increases in corticosteroid synthesis (as in adrenal cells), and many others.

Second Messengers

The intermediate molecules such as cAMP in the example above are termed 'second messengers'. Transport of many substances, particularly metal ions (sodium, potassium, calcium) and sugars is mediated by membrane proteins which form pores through the membrane. These pores are of different sizes and chemical properties, which allows each pore type to be specific for a given chemical compound; this allows cells to regulate the composition of their contents very precisely. In many cases, regulation is by processes more complex than simple diffusion through a pore that can open and close; some pore proteins can actively pump ions across membranes, to give higher or lower concentrations inside the cell than outside. Such processes can be monitored by impaling cells with microscopic glass electrodes and measuring the voltages across their membranes; manipulation of the external conditions (*e.g.* removing calcium ions and adding substances known to open or close particular types of pore) can be used to determine which pores are active in a given type of cell and see how pore activity changes during biochemical and physiological processes such as conduction of nerve impulses.

II. NUCLEUS

The main regions of the nucleus are the surrounding nuclear membrane, a mass of material known as chromatin, and a small sphere called the nucleolus. The nuclear membrane is a double structure very much like the membranes of the cell surface and endoplasmic reticulum. Suggestions have been made that these membranes are continuous at some regions within the cell. The status of chromatin was in doubt for many years. Light microscope studies reveal very little structure in the nucleus until the time when the cell is preparing for, and undergoing, division or mitosis. At this time a number of discrete double strands, the chromosomes, are revealed by virtue of their chromatin content—the material stains heavily with basic dyes.

The nucleolus is a specialised region containing copies of the genes encoding ribosomal RNA, and are sites of intensive production of the latter. Thus, cells engaged in high levels of protein synthesis have a more developed nucleolar apparatus.

Cell Division

During division of body cells (mitosis) the chromosomes behave in regular and recognisable sequence. In the first stage called prophase they appear and at the same time the nuclear membrane breaks down. Next, in metaphase, the chromosomes become arranged across the equator of a spindle-shaped collection of fibrils which appears in the area formerly outlined by the nucleus. Then follows anaphase in which the two threads of each chromosome, the chromatids, move to opposite poles of the spindle. Finally in the last stage, telophase, nuclear membranes are formed round the two separate collections of chromosome material and the cytoplasm itself divides into two. Thus two cells are formed each containing the same number of chromosomes as the parent and the cells enter a period of rest, or interphase, between divisions. During interphase the chromatin material disappears as the DNA spreads through the nucleus, the high level of organisation observed during cell division no longer being needed.

Division of germ cells (oocytes, sperm cells) is more complex, and occurs by the process of meiosis. This will not be described in detail here, but the essential point is that the parent cell has two sets of chromosomes, one inherited from the mother and one from the father. During meiosis, these are cut and rejoined to each other to produce 'mosaic' chromosomes, and one set is distributed to each of the two daughter cells. A new organism is formed when a sperm cell delivers its one set of chromosomes to complement the one set present in an egg cell to produce a new cell with two sets, from which the new organism develops.

Genes

These are the elements which contain all hereditary information and the medium whereby hereditary features are transmitted from one cell to the next, either in the same organism or from parents to offspring via the fertilised egg. Experiments indicated that the same genes always occupy the same position on chromosomes and this really demands a structural continuity through the life of the cell. Thus, the DNA which is loosely packed during interphase is 'condensed' into chromosomes for cell division by attachment of the necessary proteins; after division, the chromosomes are decondensed to allow the DNA to return to its normal function of specifying the metabolic activity of the cell.

One of the most fundamental problems in biology since the discovery of inheritance by means of genes has been the chemical nature of the genes and how genes are passed from generation to generation in such a way as to explain Mendelian inheritance. Genes have been shown to consist, at the chemical level, of DNA, and the structure of the DNA molecule was established by Watson and Crick. For an introduction to the structure of this molecule, *see* **T62**. This will inform the reader that DNA molecules are usually double-stranded, *i.e.* composed of two linear molecules arranged side by side. This is the explanation for a number of studies which showed that the proportions of the four nucleotide bases in DNA molecules from most sources follow a certain ratio, which results from pairing of A bases in one strand with T bases in the other and vice versa, and C bases in one strand pairing with G bases in the other and, again, vice versa.

The contribution of Watson and Crick, along with their under-known colleague Rosalind Franklin, was to show that two linear DNA molecules joined together to form a double helix. (*see* FIG 1) illustrates the complementary nature of the DNA molecule; the A-T and G-C pairs have different 'lock-and-key' structures which are responsible for the specificity of base pairing.

Importance of Recent Discoveries

The importance of these discoveries is that they provided the structural basis for our understanding of the mechanisms by which a long molecule, about 1 m of DNA in every human cell, can carry out its functions of transcription, replication and repair. These are all copying operations, involving the

transmission of genetic information: organisms are the expression of information and DNA is the store of that information. The information is copied to make RNA (transcription, for making proteins and thus bodies), to make DNA (replication, to make offspring), and to correct errors in one of the two strands (repair, to protect against mutation).

This molecular theory of genetics has received extensive support, much of it in the form of complex and often subtle laboratory investigations. More dramatic support was provided by Khorana and his group when they started from simple chemicals bought in bottles and used a limited number of enzymes to assemble a bacterial tRNA gene. The artificial gene was found able to carry out many of the functions of the natural gene. Similar studies have resulted in the construction and manipulation of synthetic genes encoding a number of other molecules, particularly hormones. However, these are not generally used methods, because it is usually easier to take a ready-assembled gene from an organism which has built it for us.

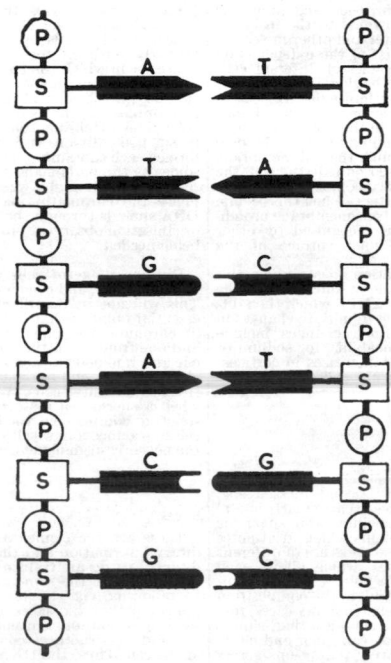

Fig. 1. A portion of a DNA molecule showing how it is made up of two strands of nucleotides. Each nucleotide consists of a base, which may be Adenine (A), Thymine (T), Guanine (G), or Cytosine (C), united to the Pentose Sugar, Deoxyribose (S), in turn joined to Phosphoric Acid (P). The nucleotides are linked through the phosphoric acid groups. The two strands are held together by hydrogen bonds between bases, adenine linking only with thymine, and guanine only with cytosine. They are twisted round each other so that the molecule is in the form of a double helix.

Note: Readers may wish to refer to **T62–8** for a Special Topic devoted to recent developments in the field of modern molecular biology. There is also a glossary of terms on **T66** which may provide help for readers new to this important area of modern biology.

MULTICELLULAR ORGANISATION

It is axiomatic, if evolutionary theory is accepted, that in the course of very long periods of time there has been a general change in multicellular organisation from the simple aggregation of cells with little individual differentiation, to the highly specialised and differentiated cells and tissues seen in complex animals and plants.

Furthermore the complex organisation must be built up in the lifetime of each animal or plant from the single-celled stage of the fertilised egg. The essential problems in development are: (1) how is the smooth succession of shape changes produced during cell division so that an appropriate and recognisable end product is reached?; (2) how do the cells *differentiate* during this temporal sequence so that those which form part of the eye, say, are different from those of liver?

Differences in Development

There are some important differences in the method of development in animals and plants. In animals there tends to be a relatively short period during which the basic structure is produced and after which growth, repair, and replacement may cause adjustment rather than major change. In higher plants, on the other hand, the apical regions of both roots and shoots remain in a permanently embryonic state and add material, which then differentiates, in a continuous process throughout the life of the plant. In spite of these differences—and in any case there are many exceptions—the two main problems in development are similar in both animals and plants.

Work on Animal Development

A great deal of work has been done on animal development since this takes place in a fairly stereotyped way during a short period of time. The fertilised egg of an animal divides in such a way as to form a hollow ball of cells, the blastula, which folds in on itself to produce a two-layered sac, the gastrula. A third layer, the mesoderm, is now added between the two layers, known as ectoderm on the outside, and endoderm on the inside. At this stage much of the animal's basic structure is established. Many aspects of this orderly sequence can be explained in terms of specific adhesive properties of cells, so that a cell will stick to others of the same type but not to unrelated types. Other mechanical properties such as elasticity, particularly in surface layers, are important in maintaining shape and producing appropriate changes during processes when one layer is folded in on another. Why cells should have the different physical properties necessary to produce an integrated whole embryo is not known, but certainly it cannot be thought that every cell has an absolutely fixed constitution and therefore a predetermined role in development. Large parts of developing embryos can be removed in early stages and their places taken by remaining cells so that intact organisms are still produced.

Formation of Specialised Tissues

This is essentially a problem in the regulation of gene activity since each cell division generally produces daughter cells which are genetically identical. It seems likely therefore that instructions are carried on the chromosomes to cope with all requirements of the organism, but that in specialised cells only a small fraction of this full potential is realised. For a long time embryologists have known that egg cytoplasm shows regional differences which make identical nuclei behave differently, and it is thought that regional cytoplasm can in some way control gene activity. Techniques for the transplantation of nuclei in developing frog embryos have been perfected and it has been possible to put a nucleus from an intestinal cell of a tadpole into an enucleate egg. The egg will go on to develop normally even though its nucleus came from a fully specialised cell derived from endoderm. The embryo will form blood and muscle from the mesodermal layer and all the other components of an organism,

under the influence of a nucleus which normally would have produced none of these things. One can conclude that all the genes are present, even in the nuclei of specialised cells, but that they have to be placed in a suitable cytoplasmic environment in order to be activated. Similar nuclear transplantation experiments indicate that genes can be "turned off" as well as "turned on" by an appropriate cytoplasmic environment, even though the nuclei come from cells which are so specialised as to stop dividing. Chemical signals secreted by cells in particular parts of the embryo are known to play a major role in directing the differentiation of nearby cells to form a variety of body structures. The cells receiving these signals respond differently to the local concentrations of these chemicals.

A study of cell differentiation and the development of multicellular organisation leads us to the view that, important though the nucleus and its genes are in controlling cell activity, an integrated organism is the result of complex interactions between its constituent cells and between the cytoplasm of those cells and their nuclei.

THE CLASSIFICATION OF ORGANISMS

It was clear to the biologists of the 17th cent. that animals and plants could be fitted into different groups or species. John Ray, a leading biologist of the day, defined a species as a group of individuals capable of interbreeding within the group. This criterion, with its corollary that a species is reproductively isolated from organisms outside the group, has survived more or less unchanged to the present day. The early workers also saw that some species were very similar to one another while others were obviously dissimilar. Systems of classification based on the similarities and differences were drawn up so that all organisms could be fitted into an orderly scheme and species could be given names in accordance with the scheme. The most famous collector and classifier was the Swede, Linnaeus. A very large number of animals and plants are known by the names given to them by Linnaeus.

Systematics, as this type of study is called, acquired a new significance after Darwin and the theory of evolution. The most satisfactory classification became one which reflected the evolution of the organisms classified, a so-called natural classification. It is not always easy to produce because ancestral types tend to become extinct and the problem then becomes one of reconstructing a whole branching system when only the ends of the branches are known. A great deal of the work on systematics has, of necessity, to be done on museum specimens which may be fossils or material preserved in some way by the collectors. The biological criterion of reproductive isolation cannot be used to define a species when the only available representatives are in a preserved state. In this case the scientist must resort to an assessment of structural differences in an attempt to decide whether two organisms are of different species. Other fossil evidence found at the same site as the fossil being classified is often important, in that it can provide evidence of biological and behavioural characteristics such as the type of food consumed and nest-building activity. In recent years computer techniques have been used to compare large numbers of structural differences between groups of animals or plants, as well as physiological and biochemical characteristics. All these techniques have led to the realisation that even the species cannot be regarded as a static point in an evolutionary pattern. Some species die out and others arise as the environment changes.

When the systematist shifts his attention to the higher levels of classification the problems are just as great as at the species level. Different species having features in common can be grouped together into genera, genera into families, families into orders, orders into classes, and classes into phyla. The dividing lines between different groups at all levels is always difficult and in the final analysis somewhat arbitrary since at these levels we do not have any biological criterion such as exists for the species. The evolutionary status of the larger groups is also poorly defined. Many are now recognised to be polyphyletic, which is to say that there are several main evolutionary lines running right through the group.

THE ANIMAL KINGDOM

The animal kingdom is divided into about 24 large groups or *phyla* though the number varies between different classifications. Ten of the more important *phyla* are listed below.

1. Protozoa.—Microscopic, unicellular forms of great variety. Some may have more than one nucleus and others form colonies. Many are able to swim by waving hair-like flagella or cilia. Others move by putting out extensions of the body or pseudopodia into which the rest of the body then flows. Protozoa are found in the sea, in fresh water and in the soil. Some are parasitic and cause important diseases in animals and man such as sleeping sickness and malaria.

2. Porifera.—Sponges. Very primitive, multicellular animals whose cells display considerable independence of one another. Largely marine. The body which may become branched and plant-like is supported by a framework of spicules and fibres. The bath sponge is the fibrous skeleton of certain species.

3. Coelenterates.—Hydra, jellyfish, sea anemones, corals. Simple animals which have a body only two cells thick surrounding a gut cavity with a single opening to the outside. Largely marine. Many are colonial. Coral reefs are formed from the calcareous skeletons of these animals.

4. Platyhelminths.—Flatworms, which are free living in water, and liver flukes and tapeworms, which are parasitic. A third, solid block of cells, the mesoderm, has been developed between the two layers of cells seen in the coelenterates. A simple gut may be developed and the reproductive system is complex especially in the parasitic forms.

5. Nematodes.—Roundworms. The body is smooth and pointed at each end. Some of the most numerous and widespread of all animals. Free living in all environments and parasitic in practically all groups of plants and animals. The same level of complexity as the Platyhelminths.

6. Annelids.—Segmented worms such as earthworms, marine worms and leeches. A system of spaces, the body cavity, is developed in the mesoderm so that movements of the main body of the animal and movements of the gut become more or less independent. Digestive, excretory, circulatory, nervous and reproductive systems are all well developed.

7. Arthropods.—A very large, diverse and important group of animals which includes crustaceans such as crabs, shrimps and water fleas; myriapods, such as centipedes and millepedes; insects; and arachnids, such as spiders and scorpions. The arthropods show many of the developments seen in annelids and in addition they possess a jointed, hard *exoskeleton*. Paired appendages grow out from the segments of the body and form antennae, mouth parts, walking legs, etc. The muscles within the skeleton are able to exert a fine control over the movement of the appendage. In order to grow these animals have to shed the exoskeleton periodically. Around 80 per cent of all animal species alive today are arthropods.

8. Molluscs.—Mussels, clams, oysters, squids, octopods and snails. Complex body form but somewhat different from annelid-arthropod type.

Unsegmented body protected by shell which is variously developed in different types. It forms two valves in mussels and oysters, a spiral structure in snails, is reduced and internal in squids and completely lost in octopods.

9. Echinoderms.—Starfish, brittle stars, sea cucumbers, sea urchins, and sea lilies. All marine and all radially symmetrical, usually with five radii. Completely unlike the other advanced, major groups. Circulatory, excretory and nervous systems differently developed. Locomotion and feeding by means of hundreds of tube feet projecting from under surface.

10. Chordates.—Sea squirts, Amphioxus, fish, amphibia, reptiles, birds and mammals. Segmented animals which at some stage in their life have gill slits leading from pharynx to the outside and a supporting notochord from which, in all chordates except sea squirts and Amphioxus, is developed a vertebral column or backbone.

Those animals with a backbone are commonly referred to as vertebrates, *all* those without as invertebrates. These are obviously names of convenience having no phylogenetic significance since they lump together totally unrelated phyla in one case and align these with a part of a single phylum in the other. The vertebrates have been investigated more completely than any other animals because of their direct structural and functional relationship with man himself. There are five well defined classes which are listed below.

The first vertebrates were the fish and from them came the amphibia. The amphibia gave rise to the reptiles and both birds and mammals evolved from different reptilian stock.

(a) Fish

Cold blooded, aquatic animals breathing by means of gills. Sharks, rays and dogfish belong to a group known as the elasmobranchs characterised by a skeleton made of cartilage. Bony fish, most of them in a group called the teleosts, include almost all the fresh water fish and the common marine fish such as cod, mackerel, plaice, herring, *etc.*

(b) Amphibia

Cold blooded, more or less terrestrial animals which have to return to water to breed. Five-fingered limbs are developed in place of the fins of fish. The egg hatches into a tadpole larva which is aquatic and breathes by gills. At metamorphosis the larva changes into the terrestrial adult which possesses lungs. Some amphibia such as the axolotl may become sexually mature as a larva and so never metamorphose into the adult. The class includes newts, salamanders, frogs and toads.

(c) Reptiles

Cold blooded and terrestrial. These animals do not return to water to breed because they have an egg with a relatively impermeable shell containing the food and water requirements of the developing embryo. There is no larval stage. Present day reptiles such as lizards, snakes and crocodiles are all that remains of a tremendous radiation of dinosaur-like creatures which occurred in the Mesozoic period.

(d) Birds

Warm blooded and adapted for aerial life. The characteristic feathers are both to insulate the body against heat loss and to provide the airfoil surfaces necessary for flight. The birds are an astonishingly uniform group and show less diversity of structure than much lower classification categories (*e.g.*, the teleosts) in other classes. The relationships of the 8,000 or more species of bird are difficult to establish because of this uniformity. It is clear that the flightless forms such as the ostrich are primitive and that the penguins are also in a separate category but the typical modern birds are classified in a large number of rather arbitrary orders. About half of all the known species are placed in one enormous order called the Passeriformes or perching birds.

(e) Mammals

Warm blooded animals which have been successful in a tremendous variety of habitats. Mammals are insulated from the environment by the characteristically hairy and waterproofed skin. They are, with two exceptions, viviparous which means that their young are born alive and in typical mammals at an advanced stage of development. In the marsupials of Australia the young are born at an early stage and transferred to a pouch where they develop further. The two exceptions referred to are primitive monotreme mammals known as the duck-billed platypus and spiny ant-eater and these animals lay eggs. The young of mammals are suckled by means of the milk-producing mammary glands. The mammals include aquatic whales and dolphins, hoofed ungulates, flesh eating carnivores, rodents and insectivores, the aerial bats, and the tree-climbing primates to which man himself belongs.

There are around 5,000 species of mammals on the planet today (and around 2,000 of them are rodents).

Modern geneticists now put all placental mammals into four great groups—Afrotheria, Laurasiatheria, Xenarthra and Glires-Euarchonta. The surprising bedfellows brought about by this new grouping may cause biologists to redraw traditoonal classifications.

THE PHYSIOLOGY OF ANIMALS

In multicellular animals cells are of various types, constituting distinct tissues and organs which perform special functions in the body. Although each cell has its own complex metabolism there must be coordination between cells forming special tissues and between the tissues which form the whole organism in order for the body to function efficiently. The study of these functional interrelationships at the tissue and organism level of organisation is the province of the physiologist.

1. Movement, Fibrils and Skeletons

(a) Muscles.—The prime movers in almost all animal movement are large protein molecules in the form of microscopic fibrillar threads. These fibrils convert the chemical energy stored in the high energy phosphate bonds of ATP into mechanical energy. In the long, thin cells forming the muscles of animals, it has been discovered that there are two sets of fibrils, one formed of a protein called myosin, the other of actin, arranged in a regular, interdigitating fashion. When the muscle contracts the fibrils slide past one another so that, although the fibrils themselves do not change in length, the muscle as a whole develops tension and shortens. Fine bridges extend from the myosin fibrils to attach on to the actin and it is here that the conversion of chemical to mechanical energy goes on.

(b) Skeletons.—In order for muscles to work effectively it is necessary for them to operate in some sort of skeletal system. Contraction but not relaxation is an active process; muscles are usually arranged in antagonistic pairs so that one muscle can extend the other. A skeleton also provides a system of levers so that the muscles can do work against the environment in an efficient manner. A simple type of skeleton found in fairly primitive animals is the hydrostatic system of coelenterates and worms. Here the animal can be thought of as a fluid-filled bag or tube which can change shape but whose volume remains constant. By contraction of circular

muscles the tube will become long and thin and conversely contraction of longitudinal muscles makes the tube short and fatty. Examination of an earthworm will demonstrate how alternating waves of activity of this type passing from head to tail can move the animal over the ground. The earthworm shows an advance over the simplest systems because the hydrostatic tube is broken up into small units by the segmentation of the body. This makes local responses possible. The next advance to be seen is the development in animals such as arthropods and vertebrates of a firm skeleton to which muscles are directly attached. The skeleton can then be used to support the body and to engage the environment. It seems to matter little whether an endoskeleton (vertebrates) or exoskeleton (arthropods) is developed since in both cases a tremendous radiation of fins for swimming, legs for walking and wings for flying can be seen. However in other respects these two types of skeleton show significant differences. The exoskeleton for example offers more protection than the endoskeleton while apparently setting an upper size limit. All the really big animals have endoskeletons.

(c) Cilia.—Fibrillar systems are also seen in the hair-like cilia which project from the surface of some cells. Cilia are important in a number of ways. They are the organelles of movement in many protozoa, they are used to produce water currents past the bodies of some aquatic animals, and they are of great importance in moving fluid within the body of almost all animals. They beat in a regular fashion, the effective stroke being accomplished with the cilium held straight out from the surface and the recovery stroke with the cilium flexed at the base.

2. Feeding

All animals require complex organic substances, proteins, fats and carbohydrates, together with small amounts of salts and vitamins. These materials are obtained by eating the dead bodies of plants and other animals. They are taken into the alimentary canal and there broken down or digested by enzymes into simpler, soluble amino acids, sugars and fatty acids. These substances are absorbed and distributed to various parts of the body where they are used in cell metabolism (q.v.) or stored for future use. Many animals, called macrophagous feeders, take in relatively large masses of food. Some such as frogs and snakes swallow their food whole, but many break it up first. Arthropods have modified appendages arranged round the mouth for cutting, some molluscs have a rasp-like radula with which to scrape off particles, and many mammals break up their food with jaws and teeth. The teeth are usually well adapted to the type of food. Carnivores have large, sharp canines, premolars and molars with which to tear the flesh of the prey, fish-eating seals have small peg like teeth to grip the fish and herbivorous ungulates have flat grinding teeth with which they break up hard plant material.

In contrast, microphagous feeders collect small particles of food material from the environment by continuous filtration. In bivalve molluscs and many marine worms water currents are produced by beating cilia. Food is trapped within the confined space through which the water flows by means of a plentiful supply of sticky mucus in the filtering region. Some crustacea use fine hairs to sieve off food material, often from water currents created by the swimming movements. The most startling of filter feeders is the whalebone whale. As the whale swims forward a stream of water flows in at the front of the mouth and out at the sides via sheets of whalebone which filter off the organisms on which the animal feeds. Though macrophagy seems to favour the attainment of larger size there are exceptions! Another type of particulate feeding is those animals which eat deposits of detritus as do many worms. Finally some animals take in only soluble food materials. These include fluid feeders like the tapeworm which absorb substances over the surface of the body, and insects such as the aphid with sucking mouth parts.

3. Respiration. Gills, Lungs and Tracheae

All living cells respire and remain alive only if supplied with oxygen. In a multicellular body, however, many cells are remote from the oxygen of the environment and the need arises for an efficient respiratory system by which oxygen can be taken up and carbon dioxide released. In addition a circulatory system is necessary to transport the oxygen to and from the respiring cells.

(a) Simple Gas Exchange Systems

Animals such as protozoa do not need special structure for gas exchange. Diffusion over the whole body surface ensures an adequate supply of oxygen. Much larger animals such as earthworms also find it possible to rely on diffusion alone, partly because their consumption of oxygen is fairly low, and partly because their bodies are permeable all over. For various reasons most animals restrict the permeability of the outer layers of the body and under these conditions special respiratory areas have to be developed.

(b) Gas Exchange in Water

Aquatic animals, except those such as whales breathing at the surface, have to obtain their oxygen from the supplies which are dissolved in the water. This presents several problems because water is a dense medium, there is not a lot of oxygen in solution, and its diffusion rate is low. For these reasons there is a surprising functional uniformity in gill systems and they are very different from lungs. Gills are fine, finger-like processes with a good blood supply which are held out in a water stream. The water current is brought very close to the gill filaments so that the length of diffusion pathway for oxygen is minimal. There is a "counter current" flow of water and blood so that the water containing most oxygen comes into contact with the blood just leaving the gill. This ensures that most of the oxygen can be transferred from water to blood through the thin gill cells. The efficiency of "counter current" systems is well known to the engineer but they were invented by aquatic animals long before they were by man. These features can be seen in the gills of molluscs, crustacea and fish. The pumping devices which maintain the water currents also operate economically. Flow is maintained in crustacea by appendages modified to form beating paddles, in many molluscs by ciliary movement, and in fish by the operation of a double pump in mouth and opercular cavities. In almost all cases there is a continuous current over the gills, the water coming in one way and going out another. Thus the animal avoids reversing the flow with the consequent waste of energy in accelerating and decelerating a large mass of water. Fish, for example, take water in at the mouth and force it out through the gill slits (sharks) or operculum (teleosts).

(c) Gas Exchange in Air

Air breathing animals do not encounter these problems since the medium is less dense, contains a great deal (21%) of oxygen and diffusion rates are high. Lungs are therefore in the form of sacs whose walls are well supplied with blood. The area of the walls may be increased by folding so that the lung becomes spongy and full of minute air spaces called alveoli where the gas exchange goes on. Only the main airways receive fresh air as the lung expands; oxygen is renewed in the alveoli by diffusion. Ventilation of the lung is accomplished by a tidal flow of air in and out of the same tubular opening known as the trachea. The actual ventilating mechanism varies in different animals. In the amphibia for example air is forced into the lungs when the floor of the mouth is raised with the mouth and nostrils shut. The lungs are emptied by elastic recoil and by lowering the floor of the mouth. Higher vertebrates use a costal pump which changes the volume of chest and lungs by movements of the ribs. This change in volume is further assisted in mammals by the diaphragm, a sheet of muscle which lies beneath the lungs and separates thorax and abdomen. In many animals sound producing organs are associated with the lungs and trachea. The larynx is a vocal organ in frogs, some lizards, and most notably mammals. In birds voice production takes place in the syrinx situated further down at the base of the trachea.

A completely different gas exchanging system is seen in insects. Branching tubes, known as tracheae, run throughout the body and carry oxygen directly to the cells without the intervention of a blood system. The tracheae communicate with the outside world via a series of holes called spiracles. Although the main tubes may be actively ventilated, diffusion in the system accounts for a large part of the movement of oxygen between the outside world and cells.

4. Circulation

In the larger animals a transport system is necessary to convey materials about the body and in many it is in the form of a blood system. Blood systems are of two types, closed and open.

(a) Open Systems

In an open circulatory system blood is pumped from the heart into a few major arteries but these very quickly give way to large tissue spaces or sinuses so that the tissues and organs of the body are directly bathed in blood. Blood flows slowly from the sinuses back to the heart. Both mollusc and arthropods possess an open system.

(b) Closed Systems

In a closed system blood is pumped round the body in a branching network of arteries and comes into contact with tissues and cells via very thin walled vessels called capillaries. Substances diffuse into and out of the blood through capillary walls. From capillaries, blood enters the veins and so returns to the heart. Blood flow in the tubes of a closed system is much more brisk and blood pressures tend to be higher than in an open system. In annelids the closed system is fairly simple with a vessel above the gut in which blood moves forward connecting to one below in which blood moves backwards. The blood is pumped by peristaltic contraction of the vessels and this system is the precursor of a localised pump. Simple hearts are in fact seen in some annelids.

In vertebrates a well defined heart is always present, situated ventrally at the level of the forelimbs. In fish there is a single auricle and ventricle and the latter pumps blood directly to the gills. From the gills the blood is collected into a dorsal aorta which then branches to serve the rest of the body. Associated with the development of lungs and loss of gills in the tetrapods, we see a progressive modification of this simple pattern. The most posterior gill vessel is taken over as the lung or pulmonary artery and slowly a completely separate circuit evolves. This involves the division of the single heart into right and left sides, the former pumping blood to the lungs and the latter to the body. In the birds and mammals where the division is complete the system can be seen to be functionally satisfactory. Blood flows along the following route: left auricle to left ventricle, to body, to right auricle, to right ventricle, to lungs, to left auricle, and so on. Thus blood charged with oxygen in the lungs returns to the heart before being pumped to the body.

(c) Function of the Blood

Most of the materials transported by the blood such as nutrients, waste materials and hormones are carried in solution in the plasma. The respiratory gases, oxygen and carbon dioxide, are present in greater quantity than would be possible if they were in simple solution. Carbon dioxide is carried in the form of bicarbonate and oxygen combines with blood pigment. The best known blood pigment is haemoglobin which is found in a variety of animals and gives the red colour to blood. When oxygen is present in high concentration, as it is in the lungs, combination occurs to give oxyhaemoglobin. If the concentration of oxygen is low, as it is in the tissues, dissociation occurs and oxygen is given off leaving reduced haemoglobin. Carbon monoxide will combine more readily than oxygen with haemoglobin so that in carbon monoxide poisoning the blood cannot transport oxygen. The haemoglobin of vertebrates is contained in high concentration in red blood corpuscles. The amount of haemoglobin and, hence, oxygen carried is greater than if the pigment is not in corpuscles. In mammals the oxygen carrying capacity of blood is thirty times that of a similar quantity of water. Other blood pigments are the blue haemocyanin found in crustacea and molluscs, and the violet haemerythrin found in some worms. Also present in the blood are various types of white corpuscle which are part of the defence mechanism of the body and ingest invading bacteria. Special blood proteins such as fibrinogen, causing clot formation, and antibodies effective against foreign substances occur in the plasma.

5. Excretion, Ionic Regulation and Kidney Tubules

As the chemical reactions included under the term metabolism proceed, so numerous waste products accumulate. The most important of these are compounds containing nitrogen, such as ammonia, urea and uric acid, arising from the use of protein as an energy source. In terrestrial animals they are removed from the blood by the kidney. The basic unit of a kidney is the tubule; in worms these tubules are not concentrated into a solid kidney but occur, a pair in every segment, right down the body. The kidney tubule begins with an end sac, corpuscle or funnel which is closely associated with the body cavity or the blood system. Fluid is filtered from the body cavity or blood into the corpuscle whence it passes to the tubule proper. During passage down the tubule, useful materials are reabsorbed through the tubule cells into the blood. Unwanted materials remain and pass to the outside world.

Although it is usual to think of kidney function being primarily one of nitrogenous excretion, it is quite common to find that in aquatic animals the kidneys are hardly used for this purpose. In these animals the tubules are primarily concerned in regulating the salt and water levels in the body, nitrogenous wastes being eliminated by diffusion through any permeable surface. In fresh water for example all animals have osmotic problems since the body fluids have a much greater osmotic pressure than the environment. Water tends to enter the body and salts tend to leave. Fresh water animals produce large quantities of very dilute urine, filtering off a lot of blood plasma into the tubules but reabsorbing all wanted materials including the invaluable salts. Fresh water crustacea, molluscs and fish all possess tubules of different morphology which show very similar functional properties.

Different environmental conditions impose different demands on the osmotic and ionic regulating machinery. In very dry conditions, such as in deserts, it is obviously of advantage to reabsorb as much water from the tubule as possible. All animals do this but it is interesting that only birds and mammals have discovered the secret of so concentrating the urine that its salt concentration is higher than that in the blood. This is done by means of a hairpin-like loop in the tubule called the Loop of Henle, another counter current device.

6. Co-ordinating Systems

Overall co-ordination of the animal's body, so that it functions as a whole and reacts appropriately to environmental changes, is largely the province of two systems, one chemical or hormonal, the other nervous. In one respect these are systems for homeostasis, that is for preserving the *status quo*, in spite of considerable environmental fluctuation. Paradoxically they can also initiate change as, for example, one can see in the daily repertoire of complicated behaviour patterns produced by almost any animal.

(a) Nervous Systems

(i) Sensory Information

Before appropriate reactions can be produced to any stimulus it is necessary to measure its intensity, position, duration and, most important, character. This is done by sense organs which are usually specialised to receive stimuli of a single modality or character. Thus photoreceptors detect light, mechanoreceptors detect mechanical disturbance and chemoreceptors detect specific chemicals. In all cases the sense organs produce a message about the stimulus in the form of nerve impulses which travel up the nerve from the sense organ to the rest of the nervous system. Change of stimulus intensity is usually signalled as a change in frequency of nerve impulses. The position of the sense organ which is active indicates the position of the stimulus within or without the body. The duration of the repeated discharge of nerve impulses indicates the duration of the stimulus.

(ii) Simple Networks

The simplest type of nervous system is the network of interconnected nerve cells (neurones) found in the coelenterates. Branching processes of the nerve cells communicate with neighbouring processes at special regions called synapses. Quite complicated behaviour is possible even with this relatively simple system. If a sea anemone is prodded violently it will close up equally violently, showing that activity has spread throughout the network. If it is tickled gently it will respond with local contractions around the site of stimulation. The movements of feeding and locomotion are very delicately performed at appropriate times.

(iii) Central Nervous Systems

In the majority of animals all the nerve cells tend to become collected into a solid mass of tissue referred to as a central nervous system (CNS). Within the mass the nerve cells are interconnected via synapses in the same way as in a nerve net. The connexions with sense organs and muscles are made via long processes called axons. Numbers of axons are usually bound together with connective tissue to form a nerve trunk. In annelids and arthropods the CNS is seen as a ventral cord lying beneath the gut with a swelling or ganglion in each segment of the body. In molluscs, the ganglia are usually more closely grouped around the oesophagus, with the possible provision of a pair of ganglia further back in the viscera. Vertebrates possess a dorsal nerve cord which is uniform in diameter and not ganglionated, though nerves emerge from it in a segmental fashion. The segmental nerves arise in two separate bundles or roots. The dorsal root is made up entirely of sensory nerves conveying information to the CNS. The ventral root consists of motor nerves which convey nerve impulses to the muscles of limbs and alimentary canal together with other effector organs such as glands.

(iv) Reflexes

A reflex, in which stimulation of a sense organ or sensory nerve results in the almost immediate contraction of a muscle, is the simplest type of CNS activity. Reflexes have been studied in all animals but the best known ones can be seen in frogs, cats, dogs, and sometimes humans. The very simplest is the stretch reflex, in which a stretched muscle is made to contract by activity coming into the CNS from stretch receptors in the muscle. The activity is relayed directly to the motor neurones of the muscle concerned, making them active and thus causing the muscle to contract. This reflex is monosynaptic, i.e. there is only the single synaptic connexion between sensory nerve and motor neurone. The knee jerk in humans is a stretch reflex, the stretch being caused by hitting the muscle tendon as it passes over the knee. Much of the recent work on reflexes has been done on this simple system, notably by Eccles. The flexor reflex, which is seen as the sudden withdrawal of a limb from any painful stimulus, is more complicated. Although the stimuli may vary, the withdrawal response is always accomplished by contraction of flexor muscles which bring the limb in towards the body. The reflex is polysynaptic, *i.e.* several intermediate neurones connect the sensory nerves through to the motor neurones. More complicated still is the scratch reflex in which an animal is made to scratch its flank in response to an irritation or tickling in that region. This reflex demonstrates some of the more involved properties of the CNS For example a dog will continue to scratch for a time after the tickling has stopped, so that the CNS must continue to be active in the absence of sensory stimulation. This has been called after-discharge.

(v) The Brain

The CNS functions in a more complicated way than is suggested by study of the reflexes and most of these higher activities are co-ordinated by the brain. A greater condensation of neurones is seen at the front end of the CNS of all animals because of the larger numbers of sense organs in that region. Brains, which become the dominant part of the CNS, can be seen in arthropods, molluscs and vertebrates. The close association with sense organs is illustrated by the vertebrate brain which is divided into three regions: (a) forebrain (nose), (b) midbrain (eye) and (c) hindbrain (ear and taste). However, the brain is much more than a relay station for these stimulus modalities and it receives information from other parts of the body via the spinal cord. All this information is correlated and activity patterns initiated and transmitted to appropriate regions. In lower vertebrates, the roof of the midbrain (the optic tectum) is the important correlation centre and its effectiveness has been well established in studies on instinct and learning in fish. Another region of the brain of importance in all vertebrates is a dorsal upgrowth of the hindbrain called the cerebellum. This is a motor co-ordinating centre which ensures that all activities are performed in a smooth and well balanced way by the muscles and limbs of the body. In reptiles, the forebrain begins to take over the correlation role and in mammals this development reaches its peak in the cerebral cortex. In man the cortex overshadows the rest of the brain and contains some 1,000,000,000 neurones. It is easy to see the magnitude of the problem of understanding a system of this complexity. The bee's brain with far, far fewer cells can initiate complicated behaviour such as the hive dances. The possibilities offered by the human cortex seem vastly greater, though they are often realised in ways which give cause for concern. At the moment it would be quite impossible to build a computer with the properties of the human brain, though the first steps have been taken with the development of 'neural networks' of computers, which display a limited amount of learning and integration skills.

(b) Hormonal Regulation

Many aspects of an animal's metabolism are regulated, not by the nervous system, but by specific chemical signals known as hormones which are circulated in the blood stream. Growth, carbohydrate metabolism, salt balance, activity of ovaries and testes and their associated structures, and colour change are all regulated in some way by hormones. The substances are secreted by endocrine glands or ductless glands as they are often called. The important endocrine glands in vertebrates are the thyroid, parathyroid, adrenal, pancreas, the sex glands, and the pituitary.

In the past the endocrine and nervous systems were regarded as exerting an independent control in slightly different functional areas of the body. It is clear now that the integration of the two systems is much greater than was formerly envisaged and in vertebrates is accomplished through the pituitary gland. Secretions of this gland regulate almost all other endocrine glands and the secretions of the pituitary are either produced in the CNS with which it is directly connected or are controlled by CNS secretions. An astonishing, parallel development of other neurosecretory systems, such as those of the pituitary, has been found in a variety of animals and in all types the neurosecretory organ complex is the dominant endocrine gland of the body. In crustacea the so-

called X organ complex found within the eyestalk, and in insects neurosecretory cells connecting to the corpora cardiaca glands, occupy the functional position of the vertebrate pituitary. They all regulate growth, metabolism and reproductive physiology, either directly or through the medication of other endocrine glands.

7. Animal Behaviour

In discussing the nervous system we have already dealt with simple mechanisms such as the reflex. Very much more complicated are the instinctive and learned patterns of behaviour which are studied by animal psychologists and ethologists.

(a) Instinct

Instinct is inborn behaviour which does not have to be learnt and is usually performed in a stereotyped way. For example a gull will retrieve an egg taken out of its nest by shovelling it back with the underside of its beak. The gull will never replace an egg in its nest in any other way, for example by using a wing or leg, and once it has begun a retrieval it will usually continue the movements back to the nest even though the egg is taken away. An instinctive behaviour pattern is triggered off by a particular stimulus or "releaser" which may be a very small part of the total environment. A male stickleback will attack a very crude model with a red belly but will not attack an exact model without it. The red underside appears to be a much more important stimulus than general shape. A particular instinctive pattern cannot always be elicited and the reaction of an animal very largely depends on when the behaviour was last produced. The longer the time that elapses, the easier it is to trigger off the instinctive pattern until eventually it may appear in the absence of an appropriate set of environmental circumstances.

(b) Learning

Learning is that behaviour acquired during the organism's lifetime as a result of experience. Evidence of learning has been seen in many animals from worms upwards though, as might be expected, the more complicated types of learning are found only in those animals with elaborate nervous systems. A simple type of learning is seen when an animal, upon repeated exposure to a stimulus, gradually decreases the normal response which is usually one of flight, until eventually the response may disappear completely. This process is called habituation. More complex are the *conditioned reflexes*, which were first discovered by Pavlov.

In these an animal can in some way connect a conditioned stimulus such as a bell, with an unconditioned stimulus such as meat, so that eventually it salivates when the bell is rung. Trial and error learning of the type needed to be successful in running a maze is more complicated still. In this there is a retrospective element because the reward at the end of the maze comes after all the responses. Many animals can run mazes but the white rat has been extensively used in experiments of this nature and there is a huge literature on this one animal. A final category of learning can be called insight learning; in this an animal shows evidence of resolving a new problem without trial and error. This type of learning involves the perception of relations between different parts of the environment and though there may be examples in arthropods and molluscs the clearest evidence of it is seen in the behaviour of birds and mammals.

8. Reproduction

A single animal may live for a short or long time, but eventually it dies, and the continuance of the species is dependent upon reproduction. Some protozoa, such as *Amoeba*, reproduce asexually by the simple division of the cell to produce two new individuals. Asexual reproduction also occurs in some coelenterates, such as jelly-fish, in which there is an alternation of sexual and asexual generations. However, the vast majority of animals only reproduce sexually.

This involves the fusion of two cells, the gametes, produced by adult individuals, and each zygote thus formed develops into an individual of the next generation. The gametes are of two kinds, the large, spherical, immobile ova produced by the female gonad or ovary and the much smaller motile sperms produced by the male gonad or testis. The motility of the sperms helps them to reach the passive ovum, which contains food reserves to support the early development of the embryo.

Worms.—The flat worms, particularly parasitic forms, have complicated life cycles, and many are hermaphrodite, *i.e.*, each individual has both male and female organs. Cross-fertilisation usually occurs, the sperms from one worm being introduced into the female duct of another. The round worms are unisexual, and internal fertilisation also occurs. Of the annelids the polychaete worms are unisexual, but the ova and sperms are shed into the sea, where fertilisation takes place. However, *Lumbricus* and the leeches are hermaphrodite, cross-fertilisation takes place and the eggs are laid in cocoons.

Arthropods.—Many crustacea are unisexual, though the sedentary barnacles are hermaphrodite. Internal fertilisation may occur, but in the crabs and crayfish pairing takes place and the sperms are deposited on the tail of the female. When the eggs are shed they become fertilised and remain attached to the abdominal appendages. Most crustacea have motile larval stages into which the eggs first develop. In *Daphnia*, the water-flea, parthenogenesis sometimes occurs, *i.e.*, the eggs develop without being fertilised. The sexes are separate in the arachnida and there are usually no larval stages except in the primitive king-crabs. The insects are also unisexual, and the fertilised eggs are laid after copulation. In some, *e.g.*, dragon-flies, an immature nymph similar to the adult is formed, but in flies, beetles, moths, and many others the egg hatches into a larval form. This then develops into a pupa, from which the final adult or imago is produced. In the social ant's nest the workers are sterile females with large heads, reduced eyes, and no wings. The males and queens are winged, and insemination of the latter occurs during the "nuptial" flight.

Molluscs and Echinoderms.—Most lamellibranchs are unisexual, although some species of scallops and oysters are hermaphrodite. There are motile larval forms, and in the swan mussel, *Anodonta*, the larvae develop in the mantle cavity of the parent and when liberated become attached to the gills or fins of fish, where they remain parasitic for some time. Some gastropods are unisexual, but the slugs and snails are hermaphrodite. In the latter cross-fertilisation occurs, the two approaching snails being stimulated to copulate by firing small sharp darts of calcium carbonate into each other. The echinoderms are unisexual, and fertilisation takes place in the sea. The egg first develops into a ciliated larval form.

Vertebrates.—The sexes are always separate in the vertebrates. In some cartilaginous fish, *e.g.*, dogfish, internal fertilisation occurs and the eggs are laid in protective sacs. In contrast, the bony fish shed ova and sperms into the water, where fertilisation takes place. Although pairing may take place in amphibia, fertilisation occurs in water, and there is usually an aquatic larval stage. The reptiles, birds, and mammals are independent of water for fertilisation, as copulation takes place and the sperms from the male are introduced directly into the female. Most reptiles and all birds lay eggs with hard shells. Development of the embryo in marsupial mammals begins in the female uterus, but is continued in a ventral pouch which surrounds the teat of the mammary gland. In the two living species of monotreme mammals the eggs are incubated in a similar pouch. Finally, in the eutherian mammals the embryo develops in the female uterus and is born at an advanced stage.

Diversity of Sexual Reproduction.—This brief survey will give some idea of the diversity of sexual reproduction in animals. External fertilisation is very much a matter of chance, and large numbers of gametes are produced which offset the great losses of gametes and embryos that this method involves. Internal fertilisation is more certain, and is also independent of external water—an important factor in land animals. In vertebrates particularly there is increase in the care of the young by the parents, involving the development of characters of behaviour as well as those of structure. Some fish lay their eggs in holes or nests which are protected by the male. Similarly, a few frogs build nests, while others carry the eggs about. The eggs of birds require a constant high temperature for their development, and they are usually incubated by the parents. After hatching the young are fed and guarded by the parents until they can leave the nest and fend for themselves. In the eutherian mammals the embryos are attached to the uterus wall by the placenta, *via* which food materials pass from the mother. The period of gestation is long, and after birth the young are supplied with milk from the mother until they are weaned and can feed themselves. Another feature in mammals is the period of "childhood" during which they play and learn and are protected and fed by their parents. The internal fertilisation, internal development, and care and protection of the young after birth which is so conspicuous in the higher vertebrates results in the reduction of losses during the vulnerable embryonic and young stages, and in consequence relatively few progeny are produced by a pair of individuals.

THE PLANT KINGDOM

There are various ways in which the main classes of the plant kingdom can be grouped, but a simple, up-to-date arrangement is given in the chart. Vascular plants are often known as the *Tracheophyta* because they all possess woody conducting elements. These are absent in non-vascular plants, and the fungi and algæ are often called *Thallophyta*, *i.e.*, they have a relatively simple plant body or thallus. Many of the bryophytes also possess a thallus, but in some there is a stem bearing leaves, although a true vascular system is absent. Many thallophytes are aquatic, whereas the tracheophytes are mostly land plants in which the development of woody tissues can be related to the attainment of the land habit as the plant kingdom evolved. However, the chart should not be taken as indicating the evolutionary relationships of the various groups. It is more a convenient arrangement which reflects the relative complexity of the plant body.

1. Bryophyta.—These are the liverworts (Hepaticæ) and the mosses (Muscineæ). They are all small plants characterised by a sharply defined life-cycle. This consists of an alternation of generations, the "plant" being a gametophyte bearing sex organs. The latter are multicellular, the female archegonium containing a single stationary ovum and the male antheridium producing many motile sperms. The latter are released and swim in water to the archegonium, where fertilisation takes place. After this a sporophyte is formed which is always dependent on the gametophyte and never becomes free living. The sporophyte usually consists of an absorbing foot buried in the tissue of the gametophyte and a stalk or seta bearing at the top a single sporangium. In many mosses this is a complex structure with hygroscopic teeth which move apart only when dry, thus releasing the minute spores only when conditions are suitable for their dissemination in the air. The bryophytes are of little economic importance, and may be looked upon as an evolutionary side-line. However, they occupy suitable "niches" in many plant communities, and species of the bog-moss *Sphagnum* cover large areas where rainfall is high.

2. Psilopsida.—This is a small group of primitive, vascular, spore-bearing plants. Its only living representatives are two rare genera of the southern hemisphere. However, a number of fossil forms are known from the Devonian period. The best known are those found in the chert at Rhynie in Scotland. The plants are excellently preserved, and their internal structure can be easily seen.

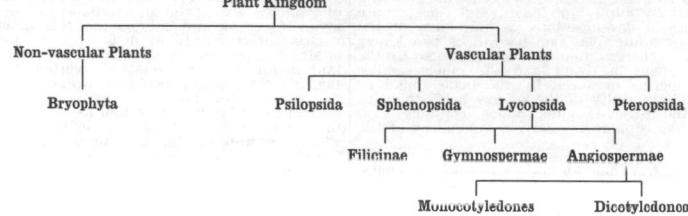

They were probably marsh plants with prostrate and erect leafless stems, although *Asteroxylon* had simple leaves.

3. Sphenopsida.—The only living members of this group are about twenty-five species of horsetails (*Equisetum*). In the Carboniferous period many tree forms existed (*e.g.*, *Calamites*), the remains of which are very common in coal deposits.

4. Lycopsida.—In the Carboniferous period the tree clubmosses were also prominent members of the forests (*e.g.*, *Lepidodendron*). They often reached 30m in height, were branched or unbranched, and had large simple leaves. They also had extensive root systems. The only living members belong to a few genera of small herbaceous clubmosses, such as *Lycopodium* and *Selaginella*. Like the true mosses, they have an alternation of generations, but the elaborate plant with stem, leaves, and roots is the sporophyte, and the gametophyte is very small. In *Lycopodium* only one kind of spore is produced, and the resultant gametophyte is bisexual. *Selaginella* produces numerous small microspores which give rise to the very reduced male gametophytes and motile sperms and the few large megaspores which produce the female gametophytes. The latter are formed within the megaspore wall, which splits to allow the sperms to reach the small archegonia.

5. Filicinae.—These are the true ferns, which in some classifications are put with the horsetails and clubmosses in the Pteridophyta or vascular cryptogams (*i.e.*, vascular plants without seeds). The ferns have a long fossil history, and remains very similar to the living Royal ferns (*Osmunda*) are known from the Carboniferous. The ferns are widespread and particularly abundant in tropical forests. The majority are herbaceous perennial plants, but a few are aquatic, and there are some tree ferns, which may reach 6 m in height. Most ferns possess a stem bearing roots and large leaves or fronds. The plant is the sporophyte and produces numerous spores in sporangia borne on the fronds. Each spore gives rise to a minute green free-living gametophyte known as the prothallus, which bears the archegonia and antheridia. After fertilisation a young sporophyte develops, which at first draws nourishment from the prothallus. Thus, as in the Bryophyta, external water is essential for the motile sperms to swim in, and there is a clearly defined alternation of generations, but the sporophyte is a complex independent plant, and the gametophyte is reduced though free-living.

6. Gymnospermae.—These were the dominant land plants in the Mesozoic era, although fossil remains are found as far back as the Devonian. The living members still form large forests in the north temperate regions. They are mostly tall evergreen trees with roots, stems, and small leaves. The conifers include the pines (*Pinus*), larches (*Larix*), and yews (*Taxus*). The cycads are a relic group of tropical plants with thick, unbranched trunks and large fern-like leaves. The maiden-hair tree of Japan (*Ginkgo biloba*) has also had a long geological history. Another interesting gymnosperm is *Metasequoia*, a genus well known to palaeobotanists. In 1948 a few living specimens were found in a remote area of China. Seeds were collected and plants are now being grown in botanical gardens all over the world. The gymnosperms are characterised by the production of "naked" seeds, which are usually born on cones. The male pollen grains, which are equivalent to the microspores of *Selaginella*, are carried by wind to the ovule of the female cone. The pollen germinates and the pollen tube carries the male gametes to the reduced archegonia borne on the female prothallus, which, unlike those of the ferns, is retained within the ovule on the parent plant. After fertilisation an embryo is formed, the prothallus becomes the food store or endosperm, and the outer part of the ovule becomes the seed coat. The cycads and *Ginkgo* retain a primitive feature in that the male gametes are motile and they swim to the archegonia from the pollen tube.

7. Angiospermae.—The apparent sudden rise of the angiosperms in the Cretaceous period is still the "abominable mystery" it was to Darwin. Various suggestions have been put forward, but nothing definite is known about the origin of the group. The angiosperms or flowering plants are now the dominant group over most of the land surface of the earth, and at least 250,000 species are known. Apart from the natural vegetation, the majority of our crop and garden plants are angiosperms. They occur in every type of habitat and range in form from gigantic trees to minute plants, such as the duck-weeds. Some are climbers, others succulents, and a number have reverted to the aquatic habit. Although most possess chlorophyll, a few are partial (*e.g.*, mistletoe) or complete parasites (*e.g.*, dodder).

Flower, Fruit and Seeds.—The diagnostic feature of the group is the production of seeds, which are completely enclosed within the female part of the flower, the ovary. Basically a flower is a short reproductive shoot which bears several whorls of lateral organs. At the base are several, often green, protective sepals forming the calyx, and above this are the often brightly coloured petals of the corolla. Within this are the stamens of the androecium or male part of the flower. Centrally is the female gynoecium of one or more carpels containing the ovules. The parts of the flower may be free, as in the buttercup, or fused together. In many species the petals are fused (sympetalous), the stamens are borne on the corolla (epipetalous), and the carpels are fused to form a compound gynoecium (syncarpous). The stamens possess anthers, which produce pollen grains. These are shed and carried by insects or wind to the receptive stigmas of the carpels. Each produces a tube which grows down the style to the ovary and enters an ovule. The ovule is a complex structure containing an ovum and a primary endosperm nucleus. Two male nuclei are discharged from the pollen tube, one fuses with the ovum and the other fuses with the primary endosperm nucleus. After this "double fertilisation" an embryo is formed which is embedded in the nutritive endosperm and the outer tissues of the ovule form the seed coat or testa. The ovary of the carpel develops into the fruit containing the seeds.

Fruits are of various kinds, being either *dehiscent* and opening when mature to release the seeds or *indehiscent*, with a succulent or dry wall. The indehiscent fruits are shed as a whole, and often contain only a single seed. Seeds and fruits show great variation in structure, and often have adaptations assisting dispersal. Some have hairs or wings which aid wind dispersal, whereas others have hooks or are sticky and are transported by animals. Some have flotation devices and may be carried a great distance from the parent plant by water. Seeds vary in size from the microscopic seeds of orchids to those of the double coconut, which may weigh 18 kg. Only about 10% of the weight of a seed is water, and the embryo, although alive, is dormant. The bulk of a seed consists of stored food material, commonly fats or starch and proteins, which may be contained in the endosperm surrounding the embryo, although in some species the endosperm is absorbed during seed development and the food is stored in the one or two swollen seed leaves or cotyledons of the embryo.

Classification of Flowering Plants.—John Ray (1627–1705) was the first botanist to recognise the two great divisions of the angiosperms—the dicotyledons with two seed leaves and the monocotyledons with only one. This primary division of the flowering plants is still recognised. Other differences are also found between the two groups. The dicotyledons usually have net-veined leaves and the floral parts are in fours or fives, whereas the monocotyledons usually have leaves with parallel veins and the floral parts are in threes.

Reclassification of Plants

The world's flowering plants were reclassified in 1998 on the basis of their genetic similarity. Previously, the classification of plants had been largely based on their morphology (physical characteristics). New DNA techniques enabled the study of genetic similarity to be incorporated into plant classification. The more similar the patterns within genes, the more recently two species have diverged.

The New System

The addition of sophisticated genetic analysis has allowed relationships to be clarified and evolutionary patterns to be more clearly understood. The new classification, which draws together several lines of evidence, arranges plants that have evolved from the same ancestor in supra-familial groups, or *clades*. A total of 462 Families and 40 Orders of flowering plants are now recognised.

As a result, it is known, for example, that the lotus flower is more closely related to the plane tree than the water-lily, to which it bears a striking resemblance. Orchids are not related to lilies but to the Hypoxidaceae, or yellow stargrasses. The papaya is related to the cabbage. Roses are related to nettles, blackthorns and figs.

For the first time, there is a true scientific basis for classification; a dataset visible to all researchers

THE PHYSIOLOGY OF PLANTS

Some of the fundamental differences between animals and plants can be ascribed to the ways in which the two groups of living organisms satisfy their requirements for food material. In a simple way at least, an animal can be thought of as a mobile gastro-intestinal tract which is highly specialised to search out and receive food in convenient, concentrated packets. In typical land plants, however, a quite different organisation exists because the organic nutrition is based on the process of photosynthesis in which carbon dioxide from the air is combined with water from the soil to form simple carbohydrates. An expanded foliage system is necessary to absorb carbon dioxide and to expose the photosynthetic pigment, chlorophyll, to sunlight. Similarly, an expanded root system is needed to absorb the other ingredients of nutrition, water and mineral salts, from the soil. The work of the plant physiologist is devoted to understanding the functional relationships between these two expanded systems of root and shoot.

The Spread of Roots

In addition, the physiologist is concerned with the progressive elaboration of root and shoot as the plant grows. Plants show much less specialisation of their cells into discrete tissues and organs than do animals and they also retain special areas,

at root and shoot tips for example, where new cells are added to the structure throughout the life of the plant. In some cases whole plants can be regenerated from very few cells taken almost anywhere from a growing plant body. The orderly regulation of growth and differentiation is thus a basic property of much plant tissue.

1. Movement of Solutes and Water

The movement of water and inorganic solutes in a plant is primarily upwards from the roots where they are absorbed, to the leaves or growing regions where evaporation of water or the use of both water and salts occurs. Water and inorganic ions permeate freely through the cell walls and air spaces of the more peripheral cells of the roots. Equilibrium is established between the insides of cells in this region and the water and salts outside, water tending to enter by osmosis and the salts by diffusion or active transport. Increase in cell volume which would be caused by continual influx of materials is, of course, restricted by the inextensible cell wall. In the centre of the root is a region packed with the specialised conducting tissues called xylem and phloem. These form continuous channels through the root and into the shoot and clearly serve for the conduction of water and substances in solution. In the root this central region is separated from the more peripheral tissue by a single layer of cells, the endodermis. The endodermal layer can actively pump water and salts from the outer regions through into the longitudinal conducting strands of, in this case, the xylem. Evidence for this pumping activity can be seen in the exudation of liquid from the base of a plant stem cut close to ground level. In some cases pressures of 8 to 10 atmospheres have been generated in roots as a result of the pumping action of the endodermal cells.

Transpiration

Water is also moved up a plant by forces generated in the leaves. Constant evaporation from the walls of leaf cells, both on the surface and within the substance of the leaf, causes loss of water from the plant. The process is called transpiration and, within limits, the plant can control transpiration rate by regulating the ease with which water-saturated air passes to the exterior through perforations in the leaf surface called stomata. The diameter of these apertures can be regulated by movements of guard cells surrounding the stomatal openings. Loss of water from the leaf cells is made good by withdrawing more water from the xylem elements within the leaves and stem of the plant. Cohesive forces between water molecules prevent the continuous water columns within the xylem from breaking. The net result is that water is drawn up the stem as transpiration occurs in the leaves. Considerable suction pressures have been measured by suitable manometer systems attached to the cut stems of actively transpiring plants. In addition materials such as dyes or radioactive isotopes have been followed as they move up the conducting xylem vessels at rates which can usually be related to the rate of transpiration.

2. Movement of Organic Substances

The organic substances, whose site of manufacture is primarily in the leaves, have to be distributed to the rest of the plant body. It is thought that a second conducting system, the phloem, is mainly responsible for the distribution of these materials in solution. Ploem is found as a layer of tissue to the outside of the xylem vessels in a plant stem. It consists of conducting cells which are rather different from those of the xylem, which serve, as we have seen, mainly in the transport of water and salts. Whereas xylem tissues are composed of dead cells whose cell walls form effective longitudinal conducting channels, phloem is made up mainly of living cells. Elements called sieve tubes are the most important conducting cells in phloem and, during the initial stages of differentiation, a sieve tube has a full complement of cytoplasm and cell organelles. Later differentiation sees the protoplasmic structures break down, but even in mature sieve tubes protoplasmic strands join through the perforated ends of adjacent cells and may extend longitudinally through the conducting elements.

Ringing experiments in which a complete ring of phloem is cut from the outside of a plant, provide evidence of the tissue's function in longitudinal conduction of carbohydrates. Sugars accumulate above such a ring but not below it. Samples of fluid taken from sieve tubes have also revealed high concentrations of carbohydrates in the sap. The method used to obtain such samples is very ingenious. Several aphids (insects such as green fly) are known which parasitise the phloem translocation channels of plants. The aphid is allowed to insert its stylet tip into the phloem vessels and is then anaesthetised and cut off the inserted stylet. Sap exudes from the stylet stump and can be collected and analysed.

3. Growth

Growth is usually, but not always, thought of as involving increase of size as measured by length, volume, or weight. In these terms any unit in a plant, whether root, shoot or fruit would follow a sigmoid growth curve with growth starting slowly, then speeding up, before finally slowing down at maturity leading on to death. Growth may also be considered as an increase in the number of cells, an increase in substances such as water, protein or DNA in the growing system, or an increase in complexity of organisation.

(a) The **organisation of growth**, no matter how it is measured, presents a number of interesting problems. In the first divisions of a fertilised egg, all cells divide. Very soon this property becomes localised, polarity is established, and the young embryo develops a shoot tip and a root tip. These have then become discrete regions of cell division. The cells behind them cease active division, enlarge by developing large vacuoles and form mature plant tissue. A circular strand of dividing tissue, called the cambium, is left in the stem between differentiated xylem and phloem. The cambium is responsible for growth in girth. The acquisition of polarity has far-reaching consequences, for the behaviour of a shoot tip is very different from that of a root. The shoot tip, for example, gives rise to leaf cells with photosynthesising chloroplasts and it grows upwards away from gravity and towards light. The root tip gives rise to cells which absorb salt and water, and it grows towards gravity and away from light.

(b) Quite a lot is known about the **mechanisms which regulate growth** by cell enlargement in the regions behind the actively dividing tips. Cell enlargement is achieved by the secretion of water and solutes to form a substantial vacuole within the cell, thus causing an overall increase of volume and expansion of the cell wall. The degree of enlargement is affected by external stimuli such as light and gravity, producing the differential growth patterns seen when plants orientate to these stimuli. Substances, called plant hormones or auxins, are now known to be produced at the growing apex and to move back causing vacuole formation in the actively elongating region. The distribution of auxin is affected by light or gravity so that the plant will turn towards or away from the stimulus. Indoleacetic acid is the active growth substance occurring naturally in many plants. Several man-made substances are also effective and are widely used as weedkillers. Evidence is also accumulating to show that a group of substances exists in plants to control cell division, just as auxins regulate cell enlargement.

Monera, Protista and Fungi

Monera

Monera are simple single-celled organisms lacking a clearly defined nucleus and membrane-bound sub-cellular organelles such as mitochondria and chloroplasts; they constitute the prokaryotes, or bacteria, archebacteria and blue-green algae. Many authors believe that the archebacteria should be placed in a kingdom of their own. This is a vast group of minute organisms of very simple structure. They are spherical or rod shaped and may exist as separate cells, some species being motile, or as long chains or irregular masses. There is a wall of complex composition, and cytoplasm which contains glycogen and fat. Electron-microscope studies have revealed the presence of structures which appear to consist of nuclear material. Multiplication is by simple division, which may take place very rapidly. For example, Bacillus subtilis can divide every 20 minutes, so that in 8 hours a single cell may give rise to 16 millions. Limited sexual processes also occur. Bacteria can survive unfavourable conditions by producing a resistant spore within the cell. They do not possess chlorophyll, though a few are pigmented. Most obtain their food already formed, and are thus either saprophytes or parasites. The saprophytic bacteria occupy a vital position in the living world. They are responsible for most of the decay of dead organic matter, and it has been truly said that without them the surface of the earth would soon become completely covered with the dead bodies of animals and plants.

Bacteria also play a vital part in the circulation of nitrogen in nature. By breaking down organic material, ammonia is released and ammonium carbonate is formed in the soil. This is oxidised by other bacteria to form nitrates, which can be absorbed by plants again. Yet other bacteria can "fix" atmospheric nitrogen, and one species, Rhizobium leguminosum, occurs in the root nodules of the pea plant. Such plants are often grown on poor soils and ploughed in, thus improving the fertility of the soil. The parasitic bacteria are also of great importance, as they are responsible for many diseases of plants, animals, and man.

Protista

This kingdom consists of algae other than the blue-gree algae, along with protozoa and slime moulds. They are mostly unicellular, microscopic, non-vascular organisms; many are motile by virtue of flagella, cilia and pseudopodia.

These are essentially aquatic organisms which contain chlorophyll. They range from microscopic forms to the large seaweeds. The green algae (Chlorophyceae) live mostly in fresh water and may be unicellular, motile or non-motile, or filamentous, though a few found in tropical seas are more complex. The brown algae (Phaeophyceae) are mostly seaweeds which possess a brown pigment, fucoxanthin, which masks the green chlorophyll. They include the bladder-wracks (Fucus) and kelps (Laminaria) of our coasts and the seaweeds which form dense floating masses over hundreds of square miles of the Sargasso Sea. Another group is the red algae (Rhodophyceae), mostly seaweeds of delicate form, the unicellular motile diatoms (Bacillariophyceae). All algae possess unicellular reproductive organs. Various types of life cycle occur, the most complex is found in the red algae.

Fungi

These are multicellular non-vascular organisms, (forming mycelia with low levels of differentiation into tissues, and more highly differentiated replicative bodies (e.g. mushrooms). None contains chlorophyll. Hence, like the bacteria, they are either parasites on other living plants and animals or saprophytes which live on dead organic matter. Some are unicellular aquatic plants, but many have a body called a mycelium composed of many branched threads or hyphæ. In the higher fungi (e.g., toadstools, bracket fungi, and puff-balls) complex reproductive structures are formed which produce spores. In the aquatic species these may be motile, but the majority form minute, airborne spores. The spore output is often very great, and a single mushroom may produce 1,800 million spores. Some fungi are serious diseases of crop plants, such as potato blight and wheat rust.

ECOLOGY

Ecosystems

The important branch of biology which deals with the relationship between living organisms and their environment must now be considered. Living organisms and the physical environment in which they exist form what is termed an ecosystem. Obviously it would be possible to regard the whole world as a giant ecosystem, though for purposes of study it would be extremely unrewarding and impractical. A pond, a rocky or sandy shore, a forest, and a peat bog are examples of ecosystems on a somewhat smaller scale, possessing different properties and containing populations of animals and plants that are different both in number of individuals and in species represented. The ecologist seeks to understand why a particular species is present in certain numbers in an ecosystem in terms of that species' interaction with all other living organisms (*biotic*) and with the physical (*abiotic*) factors of the ecosystem.

1. Abiotic Factors

All living organisms will show ranges of tolerance for abiotic factors such as temperature, humidity, salinity, oxygen levels, amount of light, etc. Clearly, if any factor in the environment moves outside the range of tolerance of a species, it becomes limiting for that particular species which is then excluded from the environment. Within the range of tolerance there will be an optimum value for each abiotic factor at which a species will survive best.

There is not a firm line separating suitable and unsuitable environments, but rather a steady shift from optimum values into conditions in which an organism finds it more and more difficult to survive.

One of the most important abiotic factors in an environment is the nature of the substrate upon or within which an organism moves and settles.

(*a*) **The Terrestrial Environment.**—Soil is the commonest substrate for terrestrial organisms. Particle sizes, ranging from the coarsest gravel soils, through sands and silts to the finely textured clays, have extensive effects on the flora and fauna of any area. Coarsely textured soils are obviously penetrated most easily by roots and by soil animals. Soils of this type also allow the rapid movement of water and soil gases, but they have the serious disadvantage of poor water retention. The level at which water saturation occurs is known as the water table and is an important abiotic factor. The terrestrial environment tends on the whole to dehydrate organisms and there is always a marked dependence on water supplies.

Soil characteristics also vary with depth. A vertical section through any soil is referred to as its profile and has considerable bearing on the ecosystems in which the soil is involved. The layers, or horizons, of a soil profile vary enormously from one soil to another. Below a surface layer of organic debris one can, in general terms, distinguish a layer of soil from which substances have been leached (A horizon), soil containing the leached-out substances from the layer above (B horizon), the weathered parent material (C horizon), and finally the parent rock or some other stratum beneath the soil (D horizon).

Humus, which is formed from animal and plant remains is of great importance in providing food for soil organisms and chemical elements such as nitrogen, phosphorus, and calcium for plant growth. It is also important in maintaining good soil structure and, though inorganic fertilisers can supply chemical elements, they have little or no effect on structure. Soil requires careful cultivation, and structure is easily disturbed by such things as heavy farm machinery, which can lead to the creation of impermeable layers with the disastrous exclusion of oxygen and oxygen-consuming organisms.

(*b*) **The Aquatic Environments.**—Marine and freshwater environments together cover more than 75 per cent of the earth's surface and, since they can be occupied throughout their entire depth, offer a much greater volume of living space than does the land. There is only a slight difference between the density of water and of living tissues, so that the bodies of aquatic organisms are very largely supported by the environment and do not need strong woody stems or powerfully muscled limbs to hold them up. Water has a high specific heat, which means that large amounts of heat are needed to raise its temperature. The result is that aquatic environments tend to show much smaller fluctuations in temperature than the terrestrial ones. In general, the larger the volume of water the smaller are the fluctuations in temperature, and so the fauna and flora of the oceans will not show wide temperature tolerance, whereas that of small pools will, but in neither case will the tolerance be so great as that shown by many terrestrial forms. Oxygen and carbon dioxide concentrations are very different in water and in air and are also variable from one aquatic environment to another, making them suitable for the support of different fauna and flora.

Salt Concentration

An important difference between the sea and freshwater is seen when their salt concentrations are determined. Organisms in fresh or in sea water face quite dissimilar problems in osmotic and ionic regulation. Life evolved originally in the sea and the salt concentration in the blood of marine molluscs, crustaceans, and echinoderms, for example, is about the same as in sea water itself. Marine organisms have, on several occasions in the course of their evolution, moved into freshwater. Representatives of the worms, crustaceans, molluscs, and vertebrates have all independently invaded this very dilute habitat. What is more, all these animals show approximately the same types of modification to cope with the change. Their outer layers, in the main, become impermeable and the salt concentration of their blood is reduced considerably and to a spectacularly low level in the freshwater mussel. The kidneys become enlarged and produce a large volume of dilute urine. By these means freshwater animals can cut down loss of their salts. It is interesting that all terrestrial vertebrates, including the mammals have retained a salt concentration in their blood of about half the seawater level and this is partly attributable to their freshwater ancestry. The ultimate development of salinity tolerance is seen in such animals as the salmon and eel which move from fresh to salt water and back again during their life cycle.

2. Biotic Factors

(*a*) **Associations between Organisms.**—No organism can be considered to be independent of any other organism in an ecosystem but in some cases close associations of various types can be developed between different species or different members of the same species.

Commensalism is an association which benefits one member but has little effect on the other. Small organisms can live within the protective covering offered by a larger individual, as, for example, commensal crabs living within the shell of some species of oyster.

Symbiosis is a somewhat closer association in which both members benefit, as do certain species of green algae and the coelenterates in whose body tissues they live. The algae are protected and the coelenterates benefit from the food produced by the photosynthetic plant. Some symbiotic organisms are unable to survive outside the association. The lichens which are associations of algae and fungi, are examples of this type of symbiosis, as are some of the food-processing micro-organisms together with the animals in whose intestinal tracts they live.

Social animals. In some cases animals of the same species form social groups in which co-operative effort and division of labour makes them more successful in exploiting a particular environment. Social development is most obvious among certain insects such as termites, ants, wasps, and bees, and among the vertebrates. Social organisation in these groups may lead to the development of different behaviour patterns and ultimately, as in ants and bees, for example, to the evolution of a variety of structural modifications so that different castes are recognisable.

Parasitism. Not all associations are of mutual benefit and when one organism becomes sufficiently specialised so that it can live successfully on materials extracted from another, the latter is always adversely affected. Parasites, by causing disease in, and sometimes the death of, the host, can influence population growth and size. Important groups are bacteria, protozoa, fungi, nematodes (roundworms), and platyhelminths (tapeworms and liver flukes). Viruses are also important disease-producing agents which are incapable of an independent existence outside the cells of the host and utilise the host cell's metabolic pathways directly to synthesise new virus material.

Control of Parasites. Many parasites (and other pests which may disturb the comfort and health of man) can now be controlled to some extent, and, for a variety of reasons, such control procedures have extensive effects on the ecosystems involved. The regulation of some bacterial parasites by means of antibiotics, and control of the insect vectors of organisms such as the malaria parasite by means of insecticides, have both been important factors in the increase in human population. Though the beneficial effects of pest control of all types are clear, the process is not without its difficulties and dangers. Indiscriminate use of many chemical agents has led to the development of resistant strains. In any group of organisms, some will naturally be more resistant to a pesticide or antibiotic than others and these will be the survivors of any treatment that is less than totally effective. They will form the breeding stock for subsequent generations and so progressively more and more resistant types will evolve. Thus, there are now many strains of bacteria resistant to penicillin and other antibiotics.

Parasite Resistance. Even more alarming is the recent discovery that this resistance can be transferred in an infective way between bacteria of different species. Another complication associated with chemical control is that the agent concerned frequently affects a wide spectrum of organisms, including those that are in no sense injurious to man or his crops. Thus DDT kills bees and other pollinating insects unless its application to a crop is very precisely timed. In addition, the accumulation of quantities of chlorinated hydrocarbons such as DDT in the environment is known to have an injurious effect on organisms other than insects. Because these chemicals are broken down very slowly they now form a serious problem in environmental pollution.

Specific Pesticides. Agents such as DDT are now being replaced with much more specific pesticides which inhibit particular stages of development of particular species of pests, *i.e.* growth regulators. Biological control is also becoming much more widely used, and is based on introduction of species which are specific predators of local pest populations.

(b) **The Food Factor.**—Plants are the ultimate source of organic food for all animals. The most important food plants are those capable of photosynthesis in which organic material is synthesised from carbon dioxide and water, using radiant energy from the sun to drive the reaction.

Food Chains. Plants are eaten by herbivores which in turn are eaten by carnivores. It is possible to see many such sequences, called food chains, in all ecosystems. For example, in the open sea, green algae are the important photosynthetic organisms; these are eaten by a small crustacean, *Calanus*, which in turn forms a large part of the diet of the herring. Feeding relationships are usually of much greater complexity than is suggested by a simple food chain. Thus, *Calanus* represents about 20 per cent of the herring's diet but it is also eaten by many other marine animals as well. For example, it forms about 70 per cent of the total diet of larval sand eels. The larval eels are eaten in turn by the herring and may form 40 per cent of its diet. Because an animal's diet is usually quite varied and one species of animal or plant may be part of the food of a wide range of different animals, interactions are set up which are referred to as food webs.

However, for general comparative purposes it is possible to disregard the detail of species and to group together all organisms with similar food habits. When this is done a relationship known as pyramid of numbers often appears in which organisms at the base of a food chain (the primary producers) are extremely abundant, while those at the apex (the final consumers) are relatively few in number.

Productivity. The validity of using numbers of individuals in such an analysis is often open to question, especially when ecosystems are to be compared. For example, a comparison between numbers of herring and numbers of whales as final consumers in two pyramidal systems is not very informative. This difficulty is partially overcome by using estimates of the total weight (biomass) of organisms at each level rather than their number. Even this has disadvantages because determinations of biomass give a measure of the amount of material present at any one time (the standing crop) but give no indication of the amount of material being produced or the rate of its production (the productivity). In some parts of the sea, for example, the biomass of small animals forming the zooplankton is greater than that of the plant life or phytoplankton on which it depends for food.

This seems to contravene the pyramid concept. However, the rate of production of new material by the phytoplankton is very much greater than by the zooplankton so that, if taken over a year, the total amount of plant material produced would far exceed the total production of animal material. Productivity is a concept of great practical and theoretical importance. It may be determined in terms of the actual organic material produced in an area over a set period of time or, more usefully, in terms of the amounts of energy transferred and stored at each food level, again over a set period of time.

Photosynthetic Efficiency Under natural conditions only 1 to 5 per cent of the light falling on a plant is converted by its photosynthetic system into chemical energy contained in the material of its tissues. Similarly herbivores which consume plants will pass on to their predators only some 10 per cent of the energy contained in the plant material they eat.

These low values for photosynthetic efficiency and ecological efficiency respectively are due to the fact that most of the energy appears as heat during the metabolic reactions needed to sustain life and only a small amount is incorporated into new tissue.

It is easy to see that the form of a pyramid of numbers can be explained in terms of low ecological efficiency, as can the observation that a food chain rarely has more than five links. The loss of energy at each stage must mean that each succeeding stage becomes smaller and smaller in number and that the number of stages is severely limited.

Human Population Growth. The explosion of the population of the world, together with recent trends, and its impact on natural habitats, is discussed in **Section Y, The Environment.**

GEOLOGICAL SCIENCE

The Science of Geology

Geology deals with the composition and structure of the Earth, the physical processes which act upon that composition and structure, and the history of change and development the planet has undergone since its formation, 4·6 billion years ago.

Early Geological Explanations

Attempts to explain the puzzles of the Earth's structure and dynamic processes go back to the very beginnings of scientific endeavour. Long before the marine origin of the Himalayas came to the attention of science, for example, classical scholars were attempting to explain similar evidence of marine origin in European mountains. In the 6th century B.C. Xenophanes of Colophon concluded that since seashells (fossil seashells, that is, though not then known as such) were embedded in the rocks of mountain ranges far from the coast, the Earth and the sea must once have been mixed up together. With regard to earthquakes and volcanoes, Aristotle (384–322 B.C.) concluded that they were caused by hot winds that forced their way through fractured rocks deep underground and occasionally burst through weak spots in the Earth's surface.

For many centuries, the true explanations of geological phenomena were simply beyond the reach of human enquiry. Direct knowledge of the Earth's geology remained meagre until research in the 20th century.

Modern Geological Knowledge

The fundamental aspects of the dynamic processes that raise mountains from the sea, cause volcanoes to erupt and earthquakes to fracture the landscape have only become known since the 1960s.

The problem has always been access. The Earth's terrestrial surface is a tiny fraction of its total mass (if the Earth was reduced to the size of a globe 50 cm in diameter, the portion accessible to direct observation through even the deepest mines and boreholes would be less than 1 millimetre thick). But, although scientists cannot examine the interior of the Earth directly, the seismograph (much developed from its Chinese progenitor) and associated instrumentation ultimately has enabled them to describe its internal structure with some certainty: seismic waves are bent to varying degrees by the varying density of material as they pass through the Earth, and analysis of these variations defines the type of materials present and the depths at which they occur.

The Earth's Structure. The Earth is an almost spherical body with an equatorial radius of 6378km, and slightly less along its polar axis (due to the flattening of the poles). Seismic investigations have shown that the Earth is made up of three layers which are distinguished one from another by their composition and density. The central *core* of the Earth is the densest of the three; the surrounding *mantle* is a thick shell of less dense rocky material, and above the mantle lies the thinnest, least dense and outermost layer, the *crust*.

The Core. At the centre of the Earth lies the core, a dense mass of iron and nickel with a radius of 3486 km. As there is no way to sample the core, its composition and properties are inferred from seismic studies, astronomical data (the way the Earth interacts with other bodies is affected by the density structure of the planet), and meteorites. (Iron meteorites, which are composed of a mixture of iron and nickel, were thought to come from the cores of asteroids that were smashed apart in collisions with other asteroids.)

The core is divided into two layers. The outer core, which extends to a depth of 5144 km, is liquid. It is thought that the convection of this metallic liquid creates the Earth's magnetic field. Although the inner core is hotter than the outer core, it is under more pressure and is therefore solid. Scientists have now discovered that the Earth's inner core is rotating faster than the rest of the planet. No one is certain of the temperature at the centre of the Earth. It may be 4000°C–5000°C, or could be as high as 8000°C.

The Mantle. The thick shell of rocky material which surrounds the core. No one has sampled the mantle directly. Knowledge of its composition and structure comes from a number of sources. Volcanoes occasionally erupt pieces of mantle known as mantle xenoliths, which are primarily composed of dense iron and magnesium-rich (*mafic*) minerals such as olivine and pyroxene. Experiments that simulate the high pressures and temperatures in the mantle have given us a better idea of what minerals can exist there. Geochemical studies of igneous rocks such as basalt, which are thought to be derived directly from the mantle, are also of use in calculating its composition. Seismic studies have given us a view into the physical properties. The velocity of energy waves (seismic waves) traveling through the Earth after an earthquake or explosion depends on the properties of the rock (*e.g.*, density) they are traveling through. Using an array of seismometers recording seismic waves arriving at many different points on the surface, geophysicists can "image" the structure of the crust, mantle, and core.

The mantle is believed to be ultramafic in composition throughout, although the exact mineral assemblage changes with depth as pressure and temperature increase. In addition, there are probably slight differences in composition between the upper and lower sections of the mantle. In places (*e.g.*, below some volcanoes), the mantle is partially molten, but in general, although it is extremely hot, it is solid.

The Crust. The rocky outer shell of the Earth on which all known organisms live and the oceans lie is known as the crust. There are two fundamentally different types of crust: *continental crust*, which makes up the continents; and *oceanic crust*, which underlies the oceans. Continental crust is composed of a wide array of rock types, and has an average composition of that of a granitic rock, with an overall density of about 2·5 g/cc. Continental crust is on average 35 km thick, but is quite thin under some low plains and valleys, and as thick as 70 km under high mountain ranges. Oceanic crust, on the other hand, is composed primarily of the volcanic rock basalt overlain by sediments, and has an average density of about 3 g/cc. It covers 60% of the Earth's surface, but is much thinner than continental crust, on average 7 km. Overall, the crust is relatively cool and brittle, but its properties change with depth. Pressure increases by 300 atmospheres per km, and temperature increases by 25°C/km near the surface.

Plate Tectonics. Perhaps the most fascinating long-term change the surface of the Earth undergoes is that of *plate tectonics*. Plate tectonics is the theory that ascribes the large-scale structures of the Earth's crust (*e.g.*, mountain ranges, rift valleys, continents, and ocean basins) to the interaction of brittle pieces, or *plates*, of crust and upper mantle as they move about on ductile mantle below.

Most evidence of plate tectonics can be found at plate boundaries (or former plate boundaries), where plates are moving against one another. There are three kinds of active plate boundaries: *divergent margins*, where plates are moving apart; *convergent margins*, where plates are moving towards one another; and *transform margins*, where plates are sliding past each other. Each kind of margin is characterized by distinct topography and a particular type of seismic and volcanic activity.

Mechanism of Plate Tectonics.

The mechanism that drives plate tectonics has been a problem since continental drift was first expounded by Alfred Wegener in 1912. The prevailing theory is that the plates are riding around on convection currents in the mantle. Although the mantle is solid, it is extremely hot and under enormous pressures. Over long periods of time, it acts as a fluid. Its behaviour is somewhat analogous to pitch, which shatters when hit quickly with a hammer, but will flow under the force of gravity if left to sit for a while. The convection of the mantle is driven by temperature differences. Hot, buoyant material near the core rises, while cooler, denser material near the surface descends. It is thought that there are a number of large-scale convection cells in the mantle, which drive the plates in different directions above. The heat that drives convection comes from the decay of radioactive elements, and from the heat left over from the Earth's accretion 4.56 billion years ago. There are still many unanswered questions as to the precise nature of mantle convection and exactly how it translates into plate movement.

The Composition of the Earth's Crust. The many different kinds of *rock* found in the Earth's crust are each an assemblage of one or more minerals. A mineral, in its turn, is a discrete solid substance consisting of chemical elements, with a specific chemical composition and a characteristic crystal structure. Iron, for instance, is an element (Fe); iron oxide is a mineral (Fe_3O_4); iron ore is a rock composed of iron and other minerals. More than 3700 minerals have been identified, but of these about 20 make up more than 95 per cent of the Earth's crust. And of the elements, 12 comprise 99·23 per cent of the total crust mass. Thus the crust consists of a limited number of minerals in which one or more of the 12 abundant elements is an ingredient. Oxygen is the most abundant element, comprising 45·20 per cent by weight of the crust, followed by silicon (27·20 per cent), aluminium (8·00 per cent) and iron (5·80 per cent).

The Rocks. The rocks of which the Earth's crust is composed, though numerous in their different mineral composition, can be grouped in just three families, distinguished one from the other by the manner in which they were formed.

(i) **Igneous rocks** (from the Latin *ignis*, fire). Igneous rocks are those which were formed from the cooling and solidification of *lava*, the molten rock which erupts from volcanoes. Basalt is the most common igneous rock, comprising about 80 per cent of all lava erupted by volcanoes.

(ii) **Sedimentary rocks.** Those rocks which are formed by the settling and consolidation of materials that had previously existed in some other form. Most originated as loose particles that were eroded from their parent material and transported in suspension by wind, water or ice to some other location, where they were deposited and subsequently consolidated into sedimentary rock – sandstone is a typical example, shale is another. Others were originally organic material, which as it died and decomposed formed beds of sedimentary rock. Limestone, for example, was originally the shells and remains of marine animals; coal is a combustible sedimentary rock, more than 50 per cent of which is decomposed plant matter.

(iii) **Metamorphic rocks.** From the Greek *meta* (meaning change, and *morphe*, meaning form: thus, change of form) are those rocks which have been changed from their original form (either igneous or sedimentary) into something else by the effects of temperature, pressure, or both. The process is analogous to that which occurs when a clay pot is fired in the kiln. The high temperatures trigger a series of chemical reactions in the tiny mineral grains that make up the clay. New compounds form, and the soft malleable clay becomes hard and rigid. Marble is a metamorphic rock, transformed by heat and pressure from the irregularities of sedimentary limestone into a glistening mass of uniformly sized, interlocking grains of soft calcite.

Earth History. See **T68.**

V.   HUMAN EVOLUTION

THE STORY OF HUMAN EVOLUTION

Introduction

New discoveries are constantly causing our views on the fascinating story of human evolution to be revised. The recent find of Sahel Man in Chad, a 'missing link' provisionally dated to *c.* 7,000,000 B.C. could suggest that the very first hominids did not develop in the Rift Valley of Kenya and Ethiopia (often called the Cradle of Civilisation) but in fact 1,500 miles west.

The 'Hobbit' Discovery

Similarly, the widely-reported discovery of the 'Hobbit', the skeleton of a new and completely unexpected species of tiny humans from the remote Indonesian island of Flores, suggests that this very small metre-tall human shared the planet with other humans around 18,000 years ago – not long before the dawn of recorded history.

Yet other discoveries have found the oldest fossil remains of humans so far unearthed in Europe (dated to *c.* 33,000 B.C.) in a cave in the Carpathian mountains of Romania. It is all a constantly changing scene.

Systematics

The study of systematics (*q.v.*) shows us that the relationships which form the basic structure of zoological classification set every species in the context of a greater whole—genus, family, order, and so on. *Homo sapiens* is no exception. Man is not the end-product of the entire evolutionary process, as is commonly supposed. On the contrary, man's place in nature is at the end of a relatively short line radiating from among the millions which have evolved since life on Earth began.

The Origin of the Primates

The primates are essentially tropical animals. With the exception of humans, virtually all living species are arboreal, and 80 per cent of them are found in the tropical rain forests. Their most distinctive characteristic is the very general and unspecialised nature of their anatomical structure, and the highly specialised and adaptable nature of their behaviour. While other mammals evolved specialised physical characteristics (the giraffe's long neck, for example), the primates have retained the basic structure of the ancestral mammalian form and have instead adapted their behaviour to suit prevailing circumstances. The human hand is a case in point—it has the same number of bones operated by the same arrangement of muscles as the arboreal primates possessed 45 million years ago, yet the human hand serves a much greater variety of uses.

Early Fossil Evidence

The fossil evidence indicates that primates have existed for at least 70 million years. They were one of the groups of placental mammals which survived the mass-extinction event which closed the Cretaceous period of geological time, about 65 million years ago. The dinosaurs were among those which disappeared with that event, and their passing marks the end of the epoch known as the age of the reptiles. Some reptiles survived, of course, but with the declining prominence of the dinosaurs the mammals flourished, heralding the age of the mammals with a burst of adaptive radiation which eventually took them into every ecological niche which the dinosaurs had previously occupied.

The Early Mammals

The early mammals had lived in the shadow of the dinosaurs for more than 100 million years before the Age of the Reptiles came to a close. They were small (typically about 10 cm long), and occupied parts of the environment that the large reptiles could not reach—the nocturnal world, for instance, (a temporal dimension in which the cold-blooded reptiles could not function), and rocky crags, holes and forest undergrowth. Here they evolved a high degree of sensory perception. Sight, sound, touch and smell assisted their capture of the invertebrate prey upon which they largely subsisted; integration of cerebral and physical equipment was crucial, and while the later evolution of the dinosaurs was concerned primarily with physical structure, that of the early mammals was concerned with the development of brain and behaviour. This equipped them well for the radiation which followed.

Of the various habitats available to the mammals as the age of the reptiles drew to a close, the ancestors of the primates took to the trees. Here they found a rich and varied diet—leaves, buds, fruit, insects, birds' eggs and nestlings—but also a suite of new demands. Life in the trees called for a shift in the emphasis of the mammals' environmental awareness. While the nose had probably been the most important organ of ground-dwelling mammals, the eyes were more crucial in the trees.

The Development of Arboreal Mammals

Because a tree is a spatially restricted environment, an arboreal animal needs to be particularly aware of its whereabouts. It must know if a potential predator is in the same tree, and if a fruit is at the end of a safe branch. It must be able to see clearly and judge distances accurately as it moves through the branches. These requirements favoured the evolution of stereoscopic vision, which was further enhanced by the advent of colour vision.

Life in the branches also called for greater agility. An ability to flex the paws and grasp things was advantageous; digits evolved into fingers, claws into fingernails. Front limbs became principally a means of holding on, while the rear limbs served as a means of propulsion and also of static support. Thus the animals could leap safely about the trees, and also could sit with the spine erect, the head turning with a perceptive eye, the ears twitching.

It can be supposed that the attributes favouring an arboreal existence also promoted yet more cerebral development. A large brain relative to body size evolved; accommodating a larger brain required some restructuring of the skull, which in turn was affected by the masticatory demands of the foods which the animals ate—fruit, leaves, insects, meat. Such an omnivorous diet calls for neither the specialised canines and slicing teeth of the carnivores, nor the grinding molars of the herbivores. The ancestral set of general all-purpose teeth was retained. The jaws broadened and shortened, the face flattened, the eyes looked forward and the expanding brain took up more and more room at the back of the skull. These interactive and interdependent features evolved over millions of years, a mosaic of cause and effect from which evolved the order of mammals known as the primates.

In basic zoological terms, the primates which evolved from the early arboreal mammals are distinguished from all other placental mammals by the fact that they have retained the four kinds of teeth found in ancestral mammals (incisors, canines, premolars and molars); they can hold things between finger and thumb, they have frontally directed eyes and have a large brain, relative to body size. They are represented today by 193 living species, all but one of which are covered with hair.

Hominid Ancestry

The broadest categories of the primate order were also the earliest to have existed in evolutionary time, and the divisions were created principally by the geographic isolation resulting from the breakup of Gondwanaland, the supercontinent on which the primates had originated. Thus, the tarsier suborder became confined to the islands of Indonesia and the Philippines, and the prosimian suborder is best represented today by the lemurs of Madagascar, where the infraorder has been isolated for close on 60 million years. Another infraorder of prosimian, represented by the pottos, lorises and bushbabies, remained on continental Africa and Asia, and has found isolation in a nocturnal way of life as other primates adopted a diurnal lifestyle.

Isolation similarly split the anthropoid suborder when the landmass of South America broke away from Gondwanaland about 40 million years ago, carrying with it the primate stock which evolved into the platyrrhines—the New World monkeys. Subsequently, the catarrhine stock left on Gondwanaland split into its two main groups, probably along the lines of diverging dietary preferences. One group adopted a mainly herbivorous diet and gave rise to the Old World monkeys or cercopithecoids (represented today by the baboons and the colobines), while the other retained a more omnivorous diet and produced the hominoids (gibbons, apes and humans).

Dating the Hominid Line

The precise dates at which these splits occurred are uncertain, but the fossil evidence suggests that the hominoid line is at least 25 million years old. A putative ancestor from that time has been found in the Fayum, south west of Cairo. The land is arid desert now, but 25 million years ago it was tropical rain forest and swampland, laced with broad meandering rivers. Scientists excavating fossil beds in the region have recovered the remains of a creature which is described formally as *Aegyptopithecus zeuxis*, though it is more colloquially known as the "dawn ape". Jaws and teeth, a skull and the skeletal parts of several individuals suggest that *Aegyptopithecus* was diverse and very generalised in its physical form. Experts have reconstructed from the fossil evidence a picture of a small arboreal primate, about the size of a domestic cat, with a sinuous back, long limbs, and all four feet capable of both grasping branches and conveying food to the mouth. The eyes looked forward, indicating stereoscopic vision, and the brain was larger in proportion to bodyweight than that of any other mammal then alive.

Early Species

The descendants of *Aegyptopithecus* and its kind appear to have been very successful in evolutionary terms. More than 50 species are known from the fossil record, and hence palaeoanthropologists are inclined to refer to the Miocene (the geological period extending from 26 million to 8 million years ago) as the age of the ape. One of these species, *Proconsul africanus*, is believed to represent the line which led to the modern apes and humans.

First described from a nearly complete face and partial skull discovered by Mary Leakey on Kenya's Rusinga Island, Lake Victoria, in 1948, *Proconsul* was a tree-dwelling animal about the size of a baboon which roamed East Africa about 18 million years ago, sometime after the monkey and ape lines had diverged. More remains were recovered during the 1970s, enabling scientists to reconstruct a skeleton that was essentially 75 percent complete. The result showed an unexpected mixture of characteristics. *Proconsul* had a backbone resembling that of the gibbon, shoulder and elbow joints like those of the chimpanzee, and the wrists of a monkey. Overall, *Proconsul* is quite unlike any living ape, but could be ancestral.

Migration from Africa

Around 17 million years ago, the African continental plate butted up against Europe, raising high mountains and creating a landbridge across which many African animals migrated into Eurasia for the first time. Among them were apes whose fossil remains have also been proposed as candidates for the ancestry of the ape and human lines. *Dryopithecus* was found in Greece, *Ramapithecus* and *Sivapithecus* in the Siwalik Hills of northern Pakistan. The fossil evidence was fragmentary, but for many years *Ramapithecus*, dating from 14 million to 7 million years ago, was almost universally accepted as the earliest known ancestor of the human line. During the early 1980s, however, the discovery of more complete ramapithecine remains showed that it and the sivapithecines are more likely to represent ancestors of the orang-utan on their evolutionary and migratory journey to the south-east Asian islands where they are found today. Consensus opinion now rates the dryopithecines as close cousins headed for extinction, and regards Africa as the cradle of mankind.

The Emergence of Mankind

The question of human origins has intrigued every generation. Charles Darwin himself added a biological dimension with the publication of *The origin of species* in 1859. The controversy aroused by Darwin centred very largely around the mistaken idea that the theory of evolution implied that humans were descendants of the apes. This mistake is still encountered with surprising frequency, even though Darwin's original work and the many studies conducted since then all make the evolutionary proposition quite clear: humans are not descended from the apes, the two branches evolved simultaneously from a common ancestor which existed sometime in the past.

Among evolutionists, the question of human origins is basically a question of when the divergence of the ape and human lines occurred, and what the common ancestor looked like. For the greater part of the time since Darwin's day it has been assumed that the answers to these questions would be supplied by the fossil remains of the ancestral forms which might be recovered from geological deposits of ever-greater antiquity—if only those fossils could be found. Thus began the search for the missing link, as it became popularly known. By the 1960s the results of these fossil hunts had provided the basis for a widely-accepted scenario in which humans had evolved from *Ramapithecus* on a line which had split from the apes some 30 million years ago. Since the 1960s, however, this fossil-based scenario has been displaced by one based on biochemistry which puts the human/ape split at just 5 million years ago.

Modern DNA Evidence

Instead of studying fossil bones, biochemists have used the genetic material (DNA—deoxyribonucleic acid) of related living species to measure the amount of time which has passed since they diverged from a common ancestor. This work is based on three findings: first, DNA accumulates random mutations and changes over time which are evident in the protein structure of all individuals of a species. Second, as two lineages diverge from a common ancestor, each lineage accumulates changes in its DNA which are different from those of the other. Third, the accumulation of changes tends to occur at a regular, almost clocklike rate through time. Clearly, the greater the differences, the longer the divergence, and biochemists have thus been able to put a timescale on the divergence of the apes and humans. The orang-utan split away from the African hominoid stock about 12 million years ago, and the gorilla lineage diverged from the common ancestor of apes and humans about 8 million years ago. The chimpanzee and human lineages were the most recent to diverge from the common ancestor, their split having occurred about 5 million years ago.

Origin of the Hominid Lineage

In one sense the facts of human origins can be reduced to a series of dates at which humans and related species diverged from their common ancestors. But an intriguing question remains even then: what caused the splits; why did the species diverge from their common ancestor?

A species is the result of reproductive isolation. If the individual members of a viable breeding population reproduce only among themselves for any length of time, the genetic changes which accumulate with each generation will eventually produce a closely-related population which is significantly different from both its ancestral stock and the other descendants of that stock. If the process continues long enough a discrete species will have evolved, one which can only produce fertile

offspring among its own kind. It can be supposed with some certainty that the reasons for the isolation which provoked speciation lay in the prevailing ecological circumstances of the time. Food supply would have been a primary factor, and this would have been susceptible to other factors such as climatic variation, the incursion of competing animals, climatic changes, or simply the pressures of a growing population.

Divergence of Gorillas and Chimpanzees

Any one or a combination of these ecological factors could have moved a viable breeding population into reproduction isolation where they might evolve into a discrete species. Migration is the most obvious course by which such isolation could have been achieved—but not the only one. Exploiting an alternative food resource, or adopting different social strategies could have achieved a similar degree of isolation even in close proximity with the ancestral population.

Precisely why the gorilla, chimpanzee and human lineages diverged between 8 million and 5 million years ago is not known. It may have been a consequence of the major climatic fluctuations which occurred during that time, when the overall pattern ranged from hot and dry to wet and very cold. The tropical forests retreated to the equatorial region, woodlands became dominant and grasslands proliferated. And with the changes in vegetation the composition of resident animal populations changed too. Many species became extinct, particularly among the browsers, while the grazers became more numerous. Doubtless the common ancestor of apes and humans was also affected by these developments, but the only certainties are that divergence and speciation occurred during that time, and that the distinctive characteristics of the living species can be considered as adaptations which proved advantageous to a reproductively isolated population.

Distinctive Human Characteristics

The distinctive characteristics of humans are the adaptation to a terrestrial way of life and bipedal locomotion; the much reduced face and jaws, and the greatly enlarged brain. In evolutionary terms, bipedalism was the crucial development, and it has been suggested that this was a consequence of the climatic changes which reduced the forest area and thereby increased competition for its resources. Under pressure from other arboreal primates, the human ancestor found a niche on the savannah. Whatever the case, bipedalism offered extensive evolutionary advantages. This was not because bipedalism itself is a particularly effective means of locomotion but rather because it freed forelimbs from locomotor functions and made them available for other purposes. One of the most important of these was the use of tools, and subsequently toolmaking. When the ancestral hominids first colonised the terrestrial habitat they had few inbuilt defence mechanisms and the ability to use stones, sticks and bones to ward off predators must have been of considerable survival value (as has been observed among present-day chimpanzees when they take to the ground). Initially used for defence, tools eventually were used in attack, heralding the adoption of a hunting mode of life. Toolmaking is also thought to have been one of the practices which favoured the development of language, and, since toolmaking called for fine manipulative skills, hand and brain evolved together; particularly those parts of the brain concerned with precise motor control and tactile sensation.

Advantages of Bipedalism

Another consequence of freeing the forelimbs through bipedalism was that carrying became so much easier. Thus food and other items could be carried over considerable distances and this facilitated the establishment of a home base. Perhaps even more important, the human infant could be carried in its mother's arms and held close to her body, allowing a much closer and more intimate relationship between mother and child than is possible in other animals. In terms of its physical development, the human infant is born in a very immature state; in part because of the limitations to the size of the birth canal imposed by the demands of bipedalism, but especially because of the large brain size of adult humans. It is therefore long dependent upon parental care. This raises problems in a society where pregnant women and nursing mothers become dependent upon the group for food. Social bonds were forged in response, and it has been argued that the evolution of the particular form of reproductive cycle found in humans, in which the female is receptive to the male throughout most of her menstrual cycle should be seen as a means of ensuring that a male will be willing to assume responsibility for females and offspring.

FOSSIL EVIDENCE OF HUMAN EVOLUTION

A fundamental premise of palaeoanthropology (the study of man in times past) rests on the contention that unequivocal evidence of human evolution would be found in fossils of known antiquity linking modern man to extinct ancestor. Ideally, the fossils should comprise a series of complete skeletons from a precisely dated sequence of time: this would enable scientists to trace the evolutionary development of humans with complete certainty. But the arbitrary nature of the fossilization process virtually eliminates all chance that such an ideal could ever be achieved or even approached. Far from ideal, palaeoanthropology has had to work with a slowly accumulating collection of diverse and often very fragmentary specimens ever since it became an established discipline in the mid-19th century. In the first fifty years only five specimens were discovered; another twenty-five years passed before a dozen were known, and even today the significant specimens could all be accommodated on a billiard table. The fossils have come from Europe, the Far East and Africa; they span over 3 million years, but as clues to the process of human evolution during that time they represent a minute fraction of mankind's potential ancestry. It has been calculated that ten skulls from East Turkana in Kenya (an exceptional collection covering 1 million years), for example, represent only one individual in every 100 million.

Problems of Evidence

The shortage of evidence is compounded by other problems. Uncertainties concerning age, for instance, mean that differing features which may represent evolutionary change over time cannot be placed in chronological order. And many fossils are so broken, distorted or incomplete that unequivocal interpretation of their significance is rarely possible. In such cases, different authorities may emphasize the importance of different features with equal validity, and the points distinguishing their interpretations may be so slight that each depends as much upon the proponent's beliefs about the course of human evolution as upon the evidence presented.

Beliefs have always been an important component of palaeoanthropological debate, and for many years they centred around the question of the order in which humans had acquired the characteristics which distinguish them from other primates. Which came first—the restructuring of the jaw and speech? The erect posture and bipedal gait? The enlargement of the brain? Two broad groupings developed in the science—one believing that enlargement of the brain had been the prime mover; the other contending that bipedalism had led the way—and as each new fossil was discovered it was immediately assessed according to those propositions. Neanderthal Man (1857) was initially dismissed as non-human on the basis of the shape and proportions of its brain; Java Man (1891) was promoted as small-brained but bipedal and dubbed *Homo erectus* because a thighbone was found in the same deposit as the skull; Piltdown Man (1912) was a forgery which found widespread acceptance because its large brain and apelike jaw confirmed the beliefs of

prominent authorities; *Australopithecus* (1925) was rejected as a candidate for human ancestry because its small brain did not match the expectations of the day.

Subsequent discoveries, including fossils and a trail of fossilized footprints, have shown that hominids were fully bipedal more than 3.6 million years ago, though the configuration of skull and jaw remained distinctly apelike for some time thereafter, while brainsize did not begin to approach modern proportions until 1.5 million years ago.

Finding the Fossils

Fossils (from the latin *fossilis*, meaning dug up) are the end products of a process in which organisms are buried and infiltrated by minerals which replace them, molecule by molecule, until, where organic material existed before, stone remains, exactly preserving the form of the original. Fossils have been the source of virtually all that is known about the evolution of life—from the oldest known forms (microscopic fossil algae dating back to 3.5 billion years) to modern times.

For an organism to become fossilized it must first of all be entrapped in a suitable material, away from the attention of scavengers and decomposers. Aquatic organisms comprise by far the greatest number of fossils, not only because they have been more numerous throughout the history of life, but also because the seabed or lake bottom favours fossilization. Terrestrial organisms are less commonly found as fossils (most are consumed or decomposed by other creatures soon after death), and hominid fossils are among the rarest of all. Palaeoanthropologists wishing to find the fossil remains of early humans are limited by two major factors. First, humans evolved in the comparatively recent past and were not numerous until recent times—which means that the total number available for fossilization must always have been relatively small. Second, their way of life and the terrain they occupied were unlikely to favour the fossilization of their remains, and there are few places in the world where fossil beds of a suitable age and composition are exposed.

Early European Sites

In scouring the world for potential fossil deposits, palaeoanthropologists have found ancient caves to be a most productive source of fossils (and not only of hominids). Whether originally used as shelters, or as dens to which predators such as leopards or hyenas may have retreated with their victims, bones left in the cave did not decay, but were fossilized as debris and rockfalls filled the caves. The first hominid fossils ever known to science were discovered at cave sites in Europe—Cannstadt in Germany (c.1700); Koestritz, Upper Saxony (1820); Kent's Cavern, Devon (1829); Engis in Belgium (1833), Gibraltar (before 1848), Neanderthal in Germany (1857). Several of the discoveries made before Darwin published his theory of evolution in 1859 received little notice at the time of discovery; some were lost. Investigations moved to the Far East at the end of the 19th century, where *Homo erectus* was recovered from riverbed deposits in Java (1891), and again in cave deposits near Peking (Beijing) during the 1920s.

Fossil Discoveries in Africa

Cave sites in South Africa have also proved to be a good source of hominid fossils. Alerted in the 1920s by quarrymen exploiting the lime-rich infills of ancient cave systems in the dolomitic hills, palaeoanthropologists have since recovered a number of important fossils from these sites.

The famed fossil sites of East Africa are predominantly volcanic in origin; the ash settling from eruptions associated with the formation of the Rift Valley having created conditions that were particularly suitable for the fossilization of bone. At Olduvai Gorge in Tanzania, where an ancient lake basin was inundated by successive eruptions of ash and subsequently drained by geological faulting, a river has sliced through the deposits to reveal much evidence of the hominids who frequented the area from at least 2 million years ago. Volcanic eruptions similarly preserved the 3.6 million year old footprint trail at Laetoli, near Olduvai.

As at Olduvai, volcanic activity and a lakeside environment were also responsible for the preservation of hominid fossils dating from 3.1 million years ago which have been found in the Afar depression of Ethiopia, and those dating from 1.8 million years ago found in the Koobi Fora region of the Lake Turkana basin, northern Kenya.

Hominid fossil sites may be discovered by chance or by a geological survey which deliberately acts out to locate cave sites or sedimentary beds of an age and situation which renders them likely to contain hominid remains. In cave sites the fossils are nearly always embedded in a hard calcrete matrix from which they are removed by careful preparation after the rock has been removed from the cave. Open sedimentary beds often extend over many hundreds of square kilometres and specific sites worthy of excavation are usually identified by foot surveys leading to the discovery of fossil bone eroding from the side of a watercourse, or a steep slope cutting into the fossil deposits.

Assessing the Age of Hominid Fossils

The age of a fossil is of paramount importance to the palaeoanthropologist in the assessment of its evolutionary significance. Until the late 1950s scientists could do no more than assess the age of their finds in *relative* terms, that is according to the kinds of other fossil animals found in the same deposit or sequence of deposits. The fossil record as a whole gives a broad picture of the order in which various animal forms have evolved and become extinct through the course of geological time. Hominid fossils are not found among the remains of dinosaurs, for instance, so must be younger; on the other hand, they must be older than any extinct animals (such as hyenas and pigs) which may be found in deposits overlaying the hominid beds.

Relative dating was always of limited use to palaeoanthropologists since human evolution occurred in a recent and extremely brief period of geological time (if the whole of Earth history was condensed into 24 hours, man would have existed for little more than one minute). Estimates of the fossils' age in years were made from time to time, but they were rough estimates based on guesses of how fast evolution proceeds, and of the rate at which sedimentary deposits accumulate. Most underestimated the actual ages which were given when developments during the 1950s, enabled geochronologists to give an *absolute* date for hominid fossil deposits.

Methods of Dating

Several methods of absolute dating have been applied to the study of fossil man:

Radiometric Dating is based on the principle that a radioactive "parent" element decays into a stable "daughter" element at a constant rate. Once the rate of decay is known, the age of a sample can be calculated from the ratio of parent to daughter elements which it contains. It should be noted that it is not the fossils themselves that are dated, but the deposits in which they are found. The cave sites of South Africa and elsewhere are devoid of materials suitable for radiometric dating, but the volcanic beds of East Africa have proved especially informative in this respect because they contain the minerals necessary for the *potassium-argon* dating method, which measures the ratio of the radioactive isotope of potassium, K-40, to its decay product, the gas argon 40. Potassium-argon is used for the absolute dating of deposits between 230,000 and 26 million years old, which makes it particularly suited to the needs of palaeoanthropologists.

Fission-Track Dating: a method in which the age of a specimen is assessed from the tracks made by the fission of uranium atoms within them. The density and number of tracks already present in the specimen are compared with those produced when the specimen is exposed to neutron radiation in the laboratory. This comparison provides the basis for an estimate of age.

Radiocarbon Dating: the radioisotope carbon-14 accumulates in living tissue, but begins to decay after death. The rate of decay is known, and so the proportion of carbon-14 remaining in a specimen is a measure of the time which has passed since the organism ceased to live. After about 50,000 years, however, so little carbon-14 remains that dating becomes impossible. This limited timespan makes the methods of little use to palaeoanthropologists, but it has proved immensely useful to archaeologists in the dating of wood and other organic materials.

Thermoluminescence: with the passage of time, certain substances accumulate energy in the form of electrons trapped at defects in the crystal lattice of their constituent minerals. When the materials are heated this energy is given off as a "puff " of light (thermoluminescence, or TL); the intensity of that light is a measure of how long the energy had been accumulating in the material, and this can be set against a known timescale to give an estimate of the material's age. The method has been particularly useful in dating archaeological finds such as pottery, where it is certain that the firing process reset the material's TL clock to zero when the pot was made, but it has also been used to date flints that were dropped in early man's campfires. These go back to 100,000 years ago.

Geomagnetic Dating (also known as **palaeomagnetic dating**): makes use of the fact that the Earth's magnetic field has changed direction many times in its history. When metals are deposited in sediments they align with the prevailing magnetic field, which is then effectively "fossilized" as the sediments harden. The record of these directional changes through geological time establishes a sequence of broad time-segments which can be used for dating deposits directly, or as a check of other methods.

THE FOSSIL LINEAGE

From the earliest days of palaeoanthropological research, investigators have tended to consider the fossils in chronological order (on either the relative or the absolute timescale), from oldest to youngest, and to describe the differences between them as progressive evolutionary changes which have led, ultimately, to modern man. So long as the number of hominid fossils remained small, and the temporal distance between them large, this attractively simple scheme remained valid, inculcating a general readiness to believe that human evolution had been a straightforward single-line affair, unwaveringly directed towards its ultimate expression: *Homo sapiens sapiens* and contentious only in the matter of which human attributes were acquired first— restructuring of the jaw, the bipedal gait, or the large brain?

A Single-Line Sequence?

Straightforward and attractive, yes, but contradicting the evidence of evolution in many other mammalian lineages. The fossil remains of pigs, horses, and antelopes, for example, display a tremendous amount of variation, not only through the geological sequence, but also at any given point on it, indicating that their evolution had been more of a radiation than a single line, with extinctions and proliferations of species occurring at many points in their evolutionary histories. Indeed, the frequency of extinction and speciation found in the fossil record of most organisms whose remains have been found suggests that such patterns are the rule. Why should humans be the exception?

The answer emerging from the tremendous advances made in palaeoanthropological research over the past thirty years is that they are not. Though the total number of fossil hominids is small (as was the total number of hominids available to be fossilized, especially when compared with the size of living pig, antelope and horse populations), it shows that there have been extinctions and speciations during the course of human evolution too.

The fossil hominids discovered so far date from over 5.5 million years ago to less than 30,000. This survey presents them in a series of broad groupings which represents both a chronological sequence and a presumed evolutionary progression, but it should be noted that the relationship of one fossil to another is not always a matter of universal agreement. A brief account of the discovery and initial description of each is given below.

The Australopithecines: The Oldest Hominids

Recent discoveries in Ethiopia and Kenya have suggested that established theories may underestimate the age of our earliest ancestors by as much as two million years. The lineages of these new specimens are, however, not universally accepted. Notwithstanding this, the group called the *Australopithecines* represent the oldest group of hominids, dating from 3.7 to 1.6 million years ago. Most authorities now accept four species—*Australopithecus afarensis*, *A. africanus*, *A. boisei* and *A. robustus*. The taxon was created in 1925 by Raymond Dart (1893–1988), professor of anatomy at the Witwatersrand University in South Africa, to accommodate a fossil skull which had been sent to him following its discovery during blasting activities at a lime quarry near Taung, in the northern Cape Province. The specimen comprised the greater part of a juvenile skull, together with a endocast of the right half of the brain (formed by the petrification of sediments which had filled the cranium after death). The face was complete and undistorted, with large rounded orbits, flattened nasal bones and a forward jutting jaw. Though the overall configuration of the specimen was essentially apelike, Dart noted several features which in his view made it more likely to represent the hominid lineage. The dental arcade was parabolic (it is more U-shaped in the apes); the erupting permanent teeth had a hominid cusp pattern; the braincast displayed certain hominid characteristics, and the foramen magnum (the hole in the base of the skull through which the spinal cord joins the brain) was set well forward beneath the skull, indicating that the head had been held erect at the top of the spine as in humans, and implying that the creature had been bipedal. In apes the foramen magnum is more to the rear of the skull and the head is slung forward, as befits their quadrupedal gait.

The Dart Controversy

When Dart published his conclusions he claimed that his *Australopithecus africanus* (the southern ape of Africa) represented an early stage of human evolution. The claim was rejected, principally because it contradicted prevailing views. No evidence of early man had been found in Africa until then, and consensus opinion held that man had evolved in Asia or Europe, where the known fossils had been found. Furthermore, *A. africanus* had a small brain and a jaw of hominid configuration, which directly contradicted the faked Piltdown skull then still reinforcing the contention that a large brain and ape-like jaw would have characterised the earliest human ancestors. The leading authorities of the day dismissed *Australopithecus* as an ape, and nothing to do with human evolution.

The Work of Robert Broom

More than a decade later, in 1936, a retired Scots medical doctor and palaeontologist, Robert Broom (1866–1951), decided to look for more specimens of *Australopithecus* and re-investigate the matter of its relationship to human evolution. Broom was then 69. By the time he died in 1951 at the age of 84, he and his associates had recovered numerous australopithecine fossils from cave sites at Sterkfontein, Swartkrans and Kromdraai near Pretoria, in the Transvaal. Broom's findings confirmed Dart's assertion that the australopithecines were good candidates for the ancestry of man. Though Broom tended to create a new taxon for each of his finds, it soon emerged that two species were represented: the lightly-built *A. africanus*, which includes the Taung specimen and is often referred to as the *gracile* australopithecine; and the heavily-

built *A. robustus*, the robust australopithecines. Mean brain size is estimated to have been 450 cc for *A. africanus*; 500 cc for *A. robustus*.

Dating the South African fossils has always been a problem, due to the confused geology of the infills and a lack of materials suitable for dating. The current consensus view suggests a date of about one million years ago, though some authorities claim that two million could be nearer the mark.

The Work of the Leakey Family

In 1959 Louis Leakey (1903–72) and his wife, Mary (1913–96), recovered an almost complete skull, lacking the mandible, from deposits at Olduvai Gorge in Tanzania subsequently dated at 1.7 million years by the potassium-argon method. Though the skull showed definite affinities with the robust australopithecines from South Africa, it was thought to differ sufficiently to merit the creation of a new genus: *Zinjanthropus* (East African man), with the species name *boisei* honouring a benefactor. Subsequently the generic distinction has been dismissed and the specimen is now known as *Australopitheus boisei*.

Since 1969 teams under the direction of National Museums of Kenya Director, Richard Leakey (1944–), have recovered numerous australopithecine fossils with both gracile and robust affinities from 1.4 to 1.8 million year old deposits at East Turkana, northern Kenya. In 1985, the same team recovered a robust australopithecine skull from 2.5 million year old deposits on the west shore of Lake Turkana.

Between 1973 and 1977 joint French and American expeditions recovered large numbers of gracile australopithecine fossils from deposits dated at 2.6 to 3.3 million years ago in the Afar depression region of north-eastern Ethiopia. The fossils proved to be remarkably similar to others found at Laetoli, near Olduvai Gorge, by Mary Leakey in 1974–5 which were dated at 3.6 million years. In publishing the Afar findings, Donald Johanson, (1943–) and his co-authors concluded that the Afar and Laetoli material represented a single species which was sufficiently distinct from existing species to merit the creation of a new taxon: *Australopithecus afarensis*. Mary Leakey objected to this conclusion.

The fossil hominids discovered at Laetoli came from the same age deposit as a trail of fossilised footprints, and this circumstantial evidence invites the inference that the trail was made by those same hominids –*A. afarensis*. Evidence has been adduced for and against, but the issue remains contentious.

The Affinities of the Australopithecines

The South African discoveries established the australopithecines as viable candidates for the early ancestry of man, while fossils from East Africa and Ethiopia have shown that the species were widely dispersed through Africa between 3.7 and 1.6 million years ago. The distinction between the robust and gracile species is considered to represent differences in diet, the heavier teeth and facial build of the robust australopithecines reflecting the masticatory demands of an herbivorous diet while the lightly-built gracile australopithecines were adapted to a less demanding omnivorous diet. This distinction is presumed to represent a dietary specialization which led the robust australopithecines away from the ancestral australopithecine stock and ultimately to extinction, while the gracile line continued and thus represents the earliest known stage of hominid evolution.

Several schemes of australopithecine phylogeny (the evolutionary history of the group) have been proposed, their suggestions as to the manner by which the australopithecines evolved among themselves and ultimately into *Homo* differing principally on the questions of whether or not *A. afarensis* is accepted as a valid species, and whether the Afar and Laetoli fossils represent a single species or two distinct species. But despite their differences, no scheme denies that the australopithecines represent a pre-human phase of hominid evolution during which considerable advances were made in the development of the upright stance and bipedalism, and in the modification of the dentition, while expansion of the brain proceeded slowly; and many agree that the next stage of human evolution is represented by *Homo habilis*.

HOMO HABILIS

The taxon was created by Louis Leakey and his co-authors in a 1964 *Nature* paper describing hominid remains excavated at Olduvai Gorge in 1961 from deposits dated at 1.7 million years by the potassium-argon method. The fossils comprised a lower mandible, skull fragments, and a group of handbones. They were found in association with stone tools, and this was a persuasive factor in the authors' decision to assign the fossils to the genus *Homo*, since no tools had ever been found in-controvertibly associated with the australopithecines and it was generally considered that man by definition was a toolmaker. Hence the name, *Homo habilis*, colloquially translated as "handy man".

Further remains of *Homo habilis* were found at Olduvai in succeeding years, including teeth, limb bones and a badly crushed and distorted skull. Richard Leakey's team at East Turkana discovered the skull known as 1470 (from its museum accession number KNM-ER 1470), which is informally described as *Homo habilis*, as are sundry other finds from East Turkana. Remains assigned to *Homo habilis* have also been recovered from excavations at the Swartkrans and Sterkfontein cave sites in South Africa, and at deposits in the Omo river basin in southern Ethiopia. In 1986, a new survey of the Olduvai Gorge deposits (led by Donald Johanson), recovered numerous fragments of skull, jaw and limb representing a single individual, which was subsequently assigned to *Homo habilis*.

The fossil evidence of *Homo habilis* recovered to date gives the species wide distribution through Africa, and a timespan dating from 2.1 to 1.8 million years ago. The species' mean brainsize is estimated to have been 750 cc.

The Affinities of Homo Habilis

Though the significance of the fossils was widely acknowledged, and the association of stone tools as a definition of man not questioned, *Homo habilis* did not find universal acceptance when the species was first proposed in 1964. All agreed that stone tools and an enlarged brain represented a significant step in the human direction, but some critics felt that the Olduvai material was insufficient evidence upon which to found a new species; others felt that if the material were to be assigned to a new species it should be within the genus *Australopithecus*, not *Homo*. The specimen certainly possessed a blend of gracile australopithecine and *Homo* characteristics which might be supposed to present an intermediary stage between the two, but critics observed that in the then prevailing state of knowledge there was insufficient temporal and morphological space for a new species between *Australopithecus* and *Homo erectus* (the latter is generally accepted as the immediate antecedent of modern humans, *see below*). Louis Leakey, however, firmly believed that both *Australopithecus* and *Homo erectus* were aberrant offshoots from the hominid line which became extinct, and his promotion of *Homo habilis* as the oldest representative of the human line must be seen in the light of this belief.

The Status of Homo Habilis

The status of *Homo habilis* itself has not been much clarified in the four decades since it was first described. Two main issues have arisen: First, the discovery of *Homo erectus* fossils from 1.6 million year deposits at East Turkana indicates that *Homo habilis* was one of at least three hominid species alive at that time (the other was *A. robustus*), which questions its status as an ancestor of *H. erectus*. Second, the *Homo habilis* fossils discovered at Olduvai in 1986 by Johanson and his team show a considerable degree of affinity with the *Australopithecus afarensis* material dating from more than 3.5 million years ago, which suggests that the ancestral form remained unchanged for a very long time, and that the *Homo* characteristics evident in later specimens of *H. habilis* must have evolved very quickly.

At the heart of these difficulties lie a number of different definitions of what it means to be human. Recent research hopes to move the debate forward by restricting the definition to criteria which can be measured or reliably inferred from fossil remains. The evidence suggests that *Homo habilis* is still more of an idea in an evolutionary scheme than a well-defined example of anatomical fact linking one species to another. Only more evidence and rigorous analysis of early hominid variation will resolve the question of its status.

HOMO ERECTUS

The most widespread and longest-surviving of the fossil hominids. Remains have been found in north and east Africa, Europe, Indonesia and China. The fossils date from 1.6 million years ago (West Turkana) to less than 300,000 years (China). Mean brain size ranges from 900 cc in early specimens to 1100 cc in late specimens.

The first known specimens were described by Eugene Dubois (1858–1940) in 1894 and included a calotte (the cranial vault) and a complete femur (thighbone) excavated from sedimentary deposits comprising freshwater sandstones, conglomerates and volcanic material at a bend of the Solo river in Central Java, Indonesia. The cranial capacity was relatively small (900 cc) while the femur was entirely human, and this combination led Dubois to assign the fossils to a new species: *Pithecanthropus erectus*, meaning erect ape-man, while the specimen became popularly known as Java Man. When fossils of similar configuration were found in China (Peking Man) both the Java and Peking material was assigned to the taxon *Homo* with sub-specific distinctions made for the Java (*Homo erectus javensis*) and Peking material (*Homo erectus pekinensis*). Subsequently, sub-specific distinctions were dropped and the taxon became known as *Homo erectus*.

Remains displaying *Homo erectus* characteristics have been recovered in Europe from sites in Germany (both East and West), Hungary, Greece, and France, and in 1960 a skull found at Olduvai Gorge extended the range of the species to Africa. Subsequently, further remains were found in Morocco and Algeria, in the Omo river basin of Ethiopia, and the Lake Turkana basin, northern Kenya.

The Turkana Boy

In 1985 a virtually complete *Homo erectus* skeleton was found in deposits on the western side of Lake Turkana dated at 1.6 million years old. The remarkable preservation of the specimen is thought to be the result of the body having sunk quickly into lake silts after death. The skeleton is immature, its development matching that of a modern 12 year old. Estimates based on its limb size and modern growth rates suggest that the individual would have stood 1.68 m tall as an adult. Cranial capacity is as yet undetermined, but clearly relatively low. The forehead is low and recedes, as does the chin.

The Affinities of Homo Erectus

Though *Homo erectus* is well positioned in time to be both a descendent of earlier hominid forms and an ancestor of modern humans, several questions arise from its distribution and physical characteristics. Some authorities argue that the Asian and African forms are so distinct that the latter should not be assigned to *Homo erectus*. Others have suggested that the species represents a side branch of human evolution which became extinct, and its co-existence with *Homo habilis* at East Turkana indeed could be seen as reason for dismissing it from the human line.

There is also continuing debate on whether the relatively incomplete material from Europe represents the "true" *Homo erectus* or a group that should be more closely aligned to modern humans. This in turn raises the question of the *Homo erectus/Homo sapiens* transition: was this a gradual change, as some authorities see demonstrated in the Omo material? Or was there a long period of stasis followed by abrupt change?

ARCHAIC HOMO SAPIENS

A term applied to specimens which might be said to exemplify the *Homo erectus/Homo sapiens* transition mentioned above, and also integral to the proposition that modern man evolved in Africa in the relatively recent past. The definitive specimen (Rhodesia Man) was discovered in the course of mining operations at Kabwe, Zambia in 1921, and comprises a complete cranium, teeth and skeletal fragments. Recent appraisal of the site and associated finds has suggested that the remains date from at least 125,000 years ago. Cranial capacity is 1280 cc, indicating an enlarged brain. Numerous other specimens assigned to the group have come from more than 30 sites spanning Africa from north to south and covering a timespan ranging from 500,000 to 30,000 years ago. Some display features characteristic of the ancestral hominids, others are entirely modern. An age of about 100,000 years has been given to comparable forms known from Qafzeh in Israel, but all other evidence of anatomically modern man known from outside Africa is significantly younger. This is seen as indicating that modern man originated in Africa and migrated from the continent to populate the rest of the world not more than 200,000 years ago.

NEANDERTHAL MAN

The first specimen was discovered by quarrymen clearing a cave in the Neander valley, near Dusseldorf in 1857. Following its classification as a distinct species in 1864, *Homo neanderthalensis* soon became symbolic of the popular view of early man as an inferior and degenerate version of modern man. Based at first on a shortage of evidence and a determination to believe in the purity of the human line, this misconception was later reinforced by the distinguished palaeontologist Marcellin Boule (1861–1942) in a series of reports on Neandertal remains found in cave sites at La Chapelle-aux-Saints and La Ferrassie between 1908–1912. Boule interpreted skeletal deformities as indicative of an habitual slouching gait and concluded that Neanderthal Man was every bit as degenerate as had been popularly supposed. Subsequent studies have shown that the deformities were the result of arthritis and that the Neanderthals were a sturdy and successful race, well-adapted to the environmental conditions of their time.

Features of Neanderthal Man

Discoveries of Neanderthal fossils at Engis in Belgium (1832), and Gibraltar (before 1848) predated the original find, and further remains have been found in Europe, Iraq and Israel. Bone structure and stout muscular attachments indicate that the Neanderthals were generally short and thick-set, with large feet and hands and a body form similar to that of modern cold-adapted people. Average brain size was over 1400 cc (some 10 percent larger than modern human, relative to body size) and exceeded 1700 cc in some large males. Dating of the fossil sites indicates that the Neanderthals lived from about 130,000 to 35,000 years ago. Thus they appear to have been a well-adapted and successful group of hunters and gatherers who ranged across Europe with the advance and retreat of the Ice Age.

The Affinities of Homo Neanderthalensis

Anatomical characteristics evident in both the Neanderthals and *Homo erectus* indicate that the two shared a common ancestry and possibly even a direct line of descent, but their relationship to modern man is far less clear. There are common characteristics, but much more that is different between the two forms. Moreover, it is generally felt that the proximity of the dates at which the Neanderthals disappeared and the modern humans became prevalent leave too little time for evolution to have effected the change from one to the other. After 100,000 years of unchallenged existence, the Neanderthals disappeared between 35,000 and 30,000

years ago. Only the remains of people anatomically indistinguishable from modern humans have been recovered from more recent sites.

The Neanderthal Problem

This transition from Neanderthal to anatomically modern man poses what has become known as the "Neanderthal Problem": what happened to the Neanderthals in Europe? Only one of three explanations could apply: either the Neanderthals themselves were transformed into modern humans by a very rapid process of evolution, or they were overrun and replaced by modern humans who moved into Europe from some other point of origination, or they interbred with modern human immigrants and their distinctive characteristics were lost in the process. All three explanations have had their advocates. Argument and counter-argument have been pursued at length over the last century, but genetic research (*see below*) indicating that modern humans originated in Africa and left the continent relatively recently strongly suggests that replacement was probably responsible for the disappearance of the Neanderthals. This need not have been a violent process. Some interbreeding also could have been involved, and the principal factor could have been better adaptation, perhaps of a behavioural or social nature. It has been suggested, for instance, that speech and enhanced social communication could have given the modern humans adaptive advantages in the changing, post-Ice Age climate of Europe which increased their reproductive rate and population growth while Neanderthal numbers declined to the point of extinction.

HOMO SAPIENS SAPIENS

Fossil remains of anatomically modern humans are known from sites in Europe, Africa, the Near East, Asia and Australia. The first and most famous to be found was Cro-Magnon Man, unearthed in the Dordogne region of France in 1868 and dating from about 40,000 years ago. Fragmentary fossils of a wholly modern form recovered from a cave at the Klasie's river mouth in South Africa date back to more than 100,000 years ago, while those from the Mungo site in Australia are from 32,000 years ago. On present knowledge, these two finds represent the greatest time-depth and geographic dispersal of early modern humans.

The dispersal of modern humans appears to have been rapid between 30,000 and 20,000 and became especially so with the domestication of animals and crop plants from about 10,000 years ago. Migration into the Americas was delayed until a landbridge across the Bering Straits opened through glacial ice about 18,000 years ago, but excavations have shown that modern humans were well-established in north America soon thereafter and had spread as far south as the Chilean Andes by 12,000 years ago.

The spread and proliferation of anatomically modern humans is inextricably linked with the development of technological skills, art, and circumstantial evidence of social interaction. While the Neanderthals employed a stone tool technology little improved from earlier forms, the anatomically modern humans introduced the flint-flaking techniques by which a greater variety of tools were made. Personal adornment and careful burial of the dead were features of their lifestyle not evident among the Neanderthals, and cave paintings speak eloquently of their perceptive talents.

More recent studies of mitochondrial DNA, which is inherited strictly through the maternal line because the sperm does not contribute mitochondria to the fertilised egg cell, show that modern humans can trace their ancestry to a single female, commonly referred to as Eve, a member of a population living in Africa some 150,000 years ago.

VI. SCIENTIFIC TABLES
TABLE OF ELEMENTS

Element (Symbol)	Atomic Number	Atomic Weight	Valency	Element (Symbol)	Atomic Number	Atomic Weight	Valency
actinium (Ac)* ...	89	227		molybdenum (Mo).......		42	95·94
aluminium (Al) ..	13	26·9815	3				
americium (Am)* .	95	243	3, 4, 5, 6	neodymium (Nd)	60	144·24	3
antimony (Sb) ...	51	121·75	3, 5	neon (Ne).....	10	20·17	0
argon (Ar).....	18	39·944	0	neptunium (Np)*	93	237	4, 5, 6
arsenic (As).....	33	74·9216	3, 5	nickel (Ni).....	28	58·71	2, 3
astatine (At)* ...	85	210	1, 3, 5, 7	niobium (Nb)....	41	92·906	3, 5
				nitrogen (N)	7	14·0067	3, 5
barium (Ba)	56	137·34	2	nobelium (No)* ..	102	254	
berkelium (Bk)* ..	97	247	3, 4				
beryllium (Be) ...	4	9·0122	2	osmium (Os)	76	190·2	2, 3, 4, 8
bismuth (Bi)	83	208·980	3, 5	oxygen (O)	8	15·9994	2
boron (B)	5	10·811	3				
bromine (Br)	35	79·904		palladium (Pd)...	46	106·4	2, 4, 6
				phosphorus (P)...	15	30·9378	3,5
cadmium (Cd) ...	48	112·40		platinum (Pt) ...	78	195·09	2, 4
				plutonium (Pu)*..	94	244	3, 4, 5, 6
calcium (Ca)	20	40·08	2	polonium (Po)* ..	84	210	
californium (Cf)* .	98	251		potassium (K) ...	19	39·102	1
carbon (C)......	6	12·0111	2, 4	praseodymium			
cerium (Ce).....	58	140·12	3, 4	(Pr)	59	140·907	3
caesium (Cs)	55	132·905	1	promethium			
chlorine (Cl).....	17	35·453	1, 3, 5, 7	(Pm)*	61	145	3
chromium (Cr) ...	24	51·996	2, 3, 6	protactinium			
cobalt (Co)	27	58·9332	2, 3	(Pa)*	91	231	
copper (Cu)	29	63·546	1, 2				
curium (Cm)*....	96	247	3	radium (Ra)*....	88	226	2
				radon (Rn)*.....	86	222	0
dysprosium (Dy) .	66	162·50	3	rhenium (Re)....	75	186·2	
				rhodium (Rh) ...	45	102·905	3
einsteinium (Es)* .	99	254		rubidium (Rb)...	37	85·47	1
erbium (Er).....	68	167·26	3	ruthenium (Ru)..	44	101·07	3, 4, 6, 8
europium (Eu) ...	63	151·96	2, 3				
				samarium (Sm) ..	62	150·35	2, 3
fermium (Fm)*...	100	253		scandium (Sc) ...	21	44·956	3
fluorine (F)	9	18·9984	1	selenium (Se)....	34	78·96	2, 4, 6
francium (Fr)*....	87	223	1	silicon (Si)......	14	28·086	4
				silver (Ag)......	47	107·870	1
gadolinium (Gd)..	64	157·25	3	sodium (Na)	11	22·9898	1
gallium (Ga)	31	69·72	2, 3	strontium (Sr) ...	38	87·62	2
germanium (Ge)..	32	72·59	4	sulphur (S)	16	32·064	2, 4, 6
gold (Au)	79	196·967	1, 3				
				tantalum (Ta) ...	73	180·947	5
hafnium (Hf)....	72	178·49	4	technetium (Tc)* .	43	99	6, 7
helium (He).....	2	4·0026	0	tellurium (Te) ...	52	127·60	2, 4, 6
holmium (Ho)....	67	164·930	3	terbium (Tb)	65	158·925	3
hydrogen (H)....	1	1·00797	1	thallium (Tl)	81	204·37	1, 3
				thorium (Th)....	90	232·038	4
indium (In)	49	114·82	3	thulium (Tm)....	69	168·934	3
iodine (I)	53	126·904	1, 3, 5, 7	tin (Sn).......	50	118·69	2, 4
iridium (Ir)	77	192·2	3, 4	titanium (Ti)	22	47·90	3, 4
iron (Fe).......	26	55·847	2, 3	tungsten (see wolfram)			
krypton (Kr)	36	83·8	0	uranium (U)	92	238·03	4, 6
lanthanum (La) ..	57	138·01	3	vanadium (V) ...	23	50·942	3, 5
lawrencium (Lr)* .	103	257					
lead (Pb).......	82	207·19	2, 4	wolfram (W)	74	183·85	6
lithium (Li).....	3	6·941	1				
lutetium (Lu)....	71	174·97	3	xenon (Xe)	54	131·30	0
magnesium (Mg)..	12	24·305	2	ytterbium (Yb) ..	70	173·04	2, 3
manganese (Mn)..	25	54·9380	2,3,4,6,7	yttrium (Y).....	39	88·905	3
mendeleevium							
(Md)*	101	256		zinc (Zn).......	30	65·37	2
mercury (Hg)....	80	200·59	1, 2	zirconium (Zr) ...	40	91·22	4

* In the cases of these elements, which are very rare or not found in nature, but have been artificially prepared, atomic weight in the chemical sense is meaningless; the integral mass of the most stable isotope known is given

Note: In 1961 the isotope of carbon-12 replaced oxygen as a standard, the weight of its atom being taken as 12. This change has meant a slight adjustment in atomic weights from the old chemical scale

The new elements with an atomic number higher than that of uranium 238 (element 92) are termed Transuranics

GAS LAWS

The Perfect or Ideal Gas Law: $pV = nRT$
where n is the number of moles in volume V at pressure p and absolute temperature T, and R is a universal constant

Van der Waals' equation: $\left(p + \dfrac{a}{V^2} \right)(V - b) = nRT$

where a and b are constants, different for each gas.

PERIODIC TABLE

GROUP	1A	2A	3B	4B	5B	6B	7B	8			1B	2B	3A	4A	5A	6A	7A	0
Period	Alkali metals	Alkaline earth metals		← Transition metals →							Noble metals							Inert gases
1	1 **H** 1·00797																	2 **He** 4·0026
2	3 Li 6·941	4 Be 9·0122											5 **B** 10·811	6 **C** 12·0111	7 **N** 14·0067	8 **O** 15·9994	9 **F** 18·9984	10 **Ne** 20·179
3	11 Na 22·9898	12 Mg 24·305											13 Al 26·9815	14 *Si* 28·086	15 **P** 30·9738	16 **S** 32·064	17 **Cl** 35·453	18 **Ar** 39·948
4	19 K 39·103	20 Ca 40·08	21 Sc 44·9559	22 Ti 47·90	23 V 50·942	24 Cr 51·996	25 Mn 54·938	26 Fe 55·847	27 Co 58·933	28 Ni 58·71	29 Cu 63·546	30 Zn 65·37	31 Ga 69·72	32 *Ge* 72·59	33 *As* 74·9216	34 *Se* 78·96	35 **Br** 79·904	36 **Kr** 83·80
5	37 Rb 85·4678	38 Sr 87·62	39 Y 88·9059	40 Zr 91·22	41 Nb 92·9064	42 Mo 95·94	43 Tc 99	44 Ru 101·07	45 Rh 102·905	46 Pd 106·4	47 Ag 107·870	48 Cd 112·40	49 In 114·82	50 Sn 118·69	51 *Sb* 121·75	52 *Te* 127·60	53 **I** 126·904	54 **Xe** 131·30
6	55 Cs 132·905	56 Ba 137·34	57 La* 138·91	72 Hf 178·49	73 Ta 180·947	74 W 183·85	75 Re 186·2	76 Os 190·09	77 Ir 192·2	78 Pt 195·09	79 Au 196·967	80 Hg 200·59	81 Tl 204·37	82 Pb 207·19	83 Bi 208·980	84 *Po* 210	85 **At** 210	86 **Rn** 222
7	87 Fr 223	88 Ra 226	89 Ac† 227															

PERIODIC TABLE OF THE ELEMENTS

Key to Chart

Atomic Number →   1
Symbol →   B
Atomic Weight →   10.811

* Lanthanides (*see* L72)

58 Ce 140·12	59 *Pr* 140·907	60 *Nd* 144·24	61 Pm 145	62 Sm 150·96	63 Eu 151·96	64 Gd 157·25	65 Tb 158·925	66 Dy 162·50	67 Ho 164·930	68 Er 167·26	69 Tm 168·934	70 Yb 173·04	71 Lu 174·97

† Actinides (*see* L8)

90 Th 232·038	*91 Pa 231*	92 U 238·03	93 Np 237	94 Pu 244	95 Am 243	96 Cm 247	97 Bk 247	98 Cf 251	99 Es 254	100 Fm 253	101 Md 256	102 No 254	103 Lr 257

Roman type—metals
Italic type—semiconductors }
Bold type—non-metals

These designations refer to the normal materials usually at room temperature. Processes like heating or compressing can turn metals into insulators and vice versa.

Note: It is possible by artificial methods such as bombardment by other nuclei to produce elements with atomic numbers greater than 103. However the very heavy elements tend to be unstable and decay spontaneously into lighter elements. Because the lifetime of such elements is short no element with an atomic number greater than Uranium (92) occurs naturally on earth.

MEASURES, UNITS AND METROLOGY

Introduction

Before any quantity can be measured one must decide on the *units* used for measurement. For example, a 2 lb loaf of bread when weighed in ounces will give 32, *i.e.* 2 × 16. This is because there are 16 oz in a pound. It would be incorrect to say the weight of the loaf is 2 or 32. We say it is 2 lb or 32 oz and we can convert from one unit to another by knowing the ratio of their sizes.

If a standard pound is kept somewhere this can be used to calibrate other standard weights using accurate scales. These in turn can be used to calibrate other weights which in turn can be compared with the loaf with scales in order to weigh the bread.

The International Prototype Kilogram

Nowadays, for scientific purposes, weights are compared with that of the *international prototype kilogram*, kept at Sèvres in France. For a long time the length of an object was obtained by making a comparison, direct or indirect, with the standard metre if using the metric system or the standard yard if using the Imperial system. The standard metre was the length between two notches on a metal rod, kept at a controlled temperature, at Sèvres. Time is measured in seconds, which at one time was defined as a certain fraction of the tropical year.

Definitions of this kind are unsatisfactory for two reasons. First, the tropical year is not constant and even the most carefully kept metal rods are liable to change their dimensions over a long period of time. Secondly, it is not always convenient to do a comparison with an object kept in France. Nowadays every effort is made to define units in terms of some fundamental property of matter which is reproducible everywhere and does not require comparison with one particular object. The second is now defined using an atomic clock and can be measured to an accuracy of 1 part in 10^{12}. Variations in the rotation of the earth are far greater than this. The metre is nowadays defined in terms of the distance light travels in one second. Although the kilogram could likewise be defined in terms of some fundamental quantity of matter, such as insisting the mass of an electron is $9.1083 × 10^{-31}$ kilogram, this quantity is only known to about 2 parts in 10^5. Comparisons with the standard kilogram can lead to an accuracy of the order 10^{-9}, so at present this definition of the kilogram stands.

The scientist nowadays mainly uses the SI system of units. SI is short for "Système International d'Unités" and it is a system of metric units which has come into international use through the agency of such bodies as the General Conference of the International Bureau of Weights and Measures and the International Organisation for Standardisation (ISO) in whose work Britain participates.

Definitions of the Base Units

The system uses the *base quantities* listed below:

Quantity	Name of unit	Symbol of unit
Length	metre	m
Mass	kilogram	kg
Time	second	s
Electric current	ampere	A
Thermodynamic temperature	kelvin	K
Luminous intensity	candela	cd
Amount of substance	mole	mol

The seven SI base units are defined as follows:

The **metre** is the length travelled by light in a vacuum in 1/299 792 458 sec. (*See* **Metre, Section L**).

The **kilogram** is the mass of the international prototype of the kilogram (*q.v.*). Scientists use the word 'mass' where the layman would say "weight". Strictly speaking, weight is not a base quantity and is a measure of *force*.

The **second** is the duration of 9 192 631 770 periods of the radiation corresponding to the transition between the two hyperfine levels of the ground state of the caesium-133 atom (*See* **Clock, Section L**).

The **ampère** is that constant current which, if maintained in two straight parallel conductors of infinite length, of negligible circular cross-section, and placed 1 metre apart in vacuum, would produce between these conductors a force equal to $2 × 10^{-7}$ newton per metre of length.

The **kelvin**, unit of thermodynamic temperature, is 1/273.16 of the thermodynamic temperature of the triple point of water (*See* **Absolute Temperature, Section L**).

TABLE I

Quantity	Name of SI unit	Symbol	SI unit in terms of base units or derived units
frequency	hertz	Hz	$1\ Hz = 1\ s^{-1}$
volume	stere	st	$1\ st = 1\ m^3$
density	kilogram per cubic metre		$kg\ m^{-3}$
velocity	metre per second		$m\ s^{-1}$
force	newton	N	$1\ N = 1\ kg\ m\ s^{-2}$
pressure, stress	pascal	Pa	$1\ Pa = 1\ N\ m^{-2}$
viscosity (dynamic)	pascal second		$Pa\ s$
work, energy, quantity of heat	joule	J	$1\ J = 1\ N\ m$
power	watt	W	$1\ W = 1\ J\ s^{-1}$
quantity of electricity	coulomb	C	$1\ C = 1\ A\ s$
electric potential, EMF	volt	V	$1\ V = 1\ W\ A^{-1}$
electric field	volt per metre		$V\ m^{-1}$
electric capacitance	farad	F	$1\ F = 1\ C\ V^{-1}$
electric resistance	ohm	Ω	$1\ \Omega = 1\ V\ A^{-1}$
electric conductance	siemens	S	$1\ S = 1\ \Omega^{-1}$
magnetic flux	weber	Wb	$1\ Wb = 1\ V\ s$
magnetic flux density	tesla	T	$1\ T = 1\ Wb\ m^{-2}$
inductance	henry	H	$1\ H = 1\ V\ s\ A^{-1}$
magnetic field	ampère per metre		$A\ m^{-1}$
luminous flux	lumen	lm	$1\ lm = 1\ cd\ sr$
luminance	candela per square metre		$cd\ m^{-2}$
illuminance	lux	lx	$1\ lx = 1\ lm\ m^{-2}$
heat flux density, irradiance	watt per square metre		$W\ m^{-2}$
heat capacity	joule per kelvin		$J\ K^{-1}$
specific heat capacity	joule per kelvin per kilogram		$J\ kg^{-1}\ K^{-1}$
thermal conductivity	watt per metre per kelvin		$W\ m^{-1}\ K^{-1}$

The **candela** is the luminous intensity, in the perpendicular direction, of a surface of 1/600 000 square metre of a black body at the temperature of freezing plantinum under a pressure of 101 325 newtons per square metre. Luminous intensity is a property of a *source* and is the amount of luminous flux (light) it throws out per steradian.

The **mole** is the amount of substance of a system which contains as many elementary entities as there are atoms in 0·012 kilogram of carbon 12. Since this number is approximately 6·022 17 × 10²³ a mole of hydrogen molecules, for example, is approximately this number of hydrogen molecules.

In addition to the base units, two SI *supplementary* units are listed below:

Quantity	Name of unit	Symbol of unit
Plane angle	radian	rad
Solid angle	steradian	sr

They are defined as follows:

The **radian** is the plane angle between two radii of a circle which cut off on the circumference an arc equal in length to the radius.

The **steradian** is the solid angle which, having its vertex in the centre of a sphere, cuts off an area of the surface of the sphere equal to that of a square with sides of length equal to the radius of the sphere.

Derived Units

Most quantities that occur in nature are *derived quantities* and are measured in *derived units*. Speed is a derived quantity which can be measured in metres/sec, so that the units of speed involve the definition of two base units, *i.e.* metres and seconds. It is said that speed has the dimensions of [length]/[time], also written $[L][T]^{-1}$, since the metre is a measure of length and the second is a measure of time. In any equation in science the dimensions of both sides must always be the same and this is often a useful check of whether the equation is correct. If a mile = 1609·3 metre and an hour = 3600 sec, one mile/hr = 1609·3/3600 m s⁻¹. Conversions between any unit and any other unit which measures the same quantity can be similarly obtained.

Table I gives a list of some important derived quantities that occur in nature and in the fourth column the SI unit that is used to measure it. Some of these derived units have a name (usually that of a famous scientist) and a symbol which are given in the second and third columns. Thus for example, the SI unit of force is a kilogram metre sec⁻², but this unit is also given the name of a newton. A force of 5 kg m s⁻² is 5 newton, which can be written "5N".

Multiples and Fractions of Units

Within the SI system there are special prefixes for forming multiples and sub-multiples of its units.

Factor by which the unit is multiplied	*Prefix*	*Symbol*
10¹²	tera	T
10⁹	giga	G
10⁶	mega	M
10³	kilo	k
10²	hecto	h
10	deca	da
10⁻¹	deci	d
10⁻²	centi	c
10⁻³	milli	m
10⁻⁶	micro	m
10⁻⁹	nano	n
10⁻¹²	pico	p
10⁻¹⁵	femto	f
10⁻¹⁸	atto	a

Examples: one thousandth of a metre is one millimetre (1 mm); one million volts is one megavolt (1 MV). These prefixes are *recommended* but other multiples and sub-multiples will be used when convenient, *e.g.*, the centimetre (cm), the cubic decimetre (dm³).

The following is a selection of points to note:
(i) The name litre now means 1 cubic decimetre or 10⁻³m³ and is a measure of volume.

(ii) Days, hours, and minutes are still used to measure time, though some scientists may prefer to use kiloseconds, etc.
(iii) The SI unit of plane angle is the radian (rad), but degrees, minutes and seconds are still used as well. $1° = \dfrac{\pi}{180}$ rad.; 1 rad
= 57·295 78° = 57° 7′ 44·81″
(iv) A Celsius temperature, say 15 degrees, is written 15°C; note that 15C would mean 15 coulombs.

The Imperial System of Units

The SI system is not the only system of units in use today, although it is the one most favoured by scientists. The Imperial system is widely used in the UK and other English speaking countries and some Imperial weights and measures are given below:

Length

1 nail	= 2¼ in
1 link	= 7·92 in
12 in	= 1 ft
3 ft	= 1 yd
22 yd	= 1 chain
10 chains	= 1 furlong
8 furlongs	= 1 mile = 1760 yd = 5280 ft

Area

1210 yd²	= 1 rood
4 roods	= 1 acre = 4840 yd²
640 acres	= 1 mile²

Volume

1728 in³	= 1 ft³
27 ft³	= 1 yd³

Capacity

4 gills	= 1 pint
2 pints	= 1 quart
4 quarts	= 1 gallon
2 gallons	= 1 peck
4 pecks	= 1 bushel
8 bushels	= 1 quarter
36 bushels	= 1 chaldron
1 gal	= 277·274 in³

Weight (Avoirdupois)
(System used in commerce)

1 dram	= 27 343 75 grains
16 drams	= 1 oz = 437·5 grains
16 oz	= 1 lb = 7000 grains
14 lb	= 1 stone
28 lb	= 1 quarter
4 quarters	= 1 cwt = 112 lb
20 cwt	= ton = 2240 lb

Troy Weight

1 pennyweight	= 24 grains
480 grains	= 1 ounce

The only unit of troy weight which is legal for use in trade in Britain is the ounce Troy, and weighings of precious metal are made in multiples and decimals of this unit.

The term *carat* is not a unit of weight for precious metals, but is used to denote the quality of gold plate, etc., and is a figure indicating the number of 24ths of pure gold in the alloy, *e.g.*, a 9 carat gold ring consists of nine parts of pure gold and fifteen parts of base metals.

Nautical Measures

1 nautical mile = 6080 ft = 1853·18 m
1 knot = 1 nautical mile per hour = 1·151 mile/h

Note.—In future the international nautical mile of 1852 m will be used.

Note.—The British Pharmaceutical Code and the

British National Formulary—the official works of medicinal reference—no longer contain the apothecaries' units of measurement since medicine is now measured in metric units. Prescriptions are in 5 millilitre (*ml*) units; medicine bottles are in six sizes from 50 to 500 m*l*.

Selected Conversions between Units

Length

1 inch	= 2·54 cm
1 foot	= 30·48 cm
1 yard	= 0·9144 m
1 mile	= 1609·344 m
1 fathom	= 6 feet
1 nautical mile	= 1852 m
1 fermi	= 1 fm (femtometre)
1 X unit	= 0·1002 pm (pico-metre)
1 angstrom	= 100 pm
1 micron	= 1 μ m
1 astronomical unit	= 149·6 Gm
1 light year	= 9460·70 Tm
1 parsec	= 30,857 Tm
	= 3·26 light years

For Angstrom, Light year, Parsec, Astronomical Unit *see* **Section L.**

Area

1 hectare (ha)	= 10^4 m2 = 2·471 acre
1 acre	= 0·404686 ha
1 acre	= 4840 yd^2 which is approximately 70 yards square
1 mile^2	= 258·999 ha = 2·58999 km^2
1 barn	= $10\Omega^{28}$ m^2 (measure of nuclear cross-section)

Volume

1 litre (l)	= 0·001 m^3
1 gallon UK	= 4.546 092 1
1 gallon UK	is the volume of 10 lb water at 62° F
1 pint	= 0.568 l which is approximately 4/7 l
1 gallon US	= 0·8327 gallon UK

Mass and Weight

1 oz	= 0·02835 kg
1 lb	= 0·453 592 37 kg
1 cwt	= 50·80 kg
1 ton	= 2240 lb = 1016 kg = 1·016 tonne
1 tonne	= 1000 kg

Angle

		degree	minute	second	radian	revolution
1 degree	= 1		60	3600	$1·745 \times 10^{-2}$	$2·778 \times 10^{-3}$
1 minute	= $1·667 \times 10^{-2}$		1	60	$2·909 \times 10^{-4}$	$4·630 \times 10^{-5}$
1 second	= $2·778 \times 10^{-4}$		$1·667 \times 10^{-2}$	1	$4·848 \times 10^{-6}$	$7·716 \times 10^{-7}$
1 radian	= 57·30		3438	$2·063 \times 10^5$	1	0·1592
1 revolution	= 360		$2·16 \times 10^4$	$1·296 \times 10^6$	6·283	1

1 rt angle = 90° 1 grade = 0·01 rt angle

Time

		second	minute	hour	solar day	year
1 second	= 1		$1·667 \times 10^{-2}$	$2·778 \times 10^{-4}$	$1·157 \times 10^{-5}$	$3·169 \times 10^{-8}$
1 minute	= 60		1	$1·667 \times 10^{-2}$	$6·944 \times 10^{-4}$	$1·901 \times 10^{-6}$
1 hour	= 3600		60	1	$4·167 \times 10^{-2}$	$1·141 \times 10^{-4}$
1 solar day	= 86400		1440	24	1	$2·738 \times 10^{-3}$
1 year	= $3·156 \times 10^7$		525,900	8766	365·24	1

Force

		newton	dyne	poundal	kg force	pound force
1 newton	= 1		10^5	7·233	0·1020	0·2248
1 dyne	= 10^{-5}		1	$7·233 \times 10^{-5}$	$1·020 \times 10^{-6}$	$2·248 \times 10^{-6}$
1 poundal	= 0·1383		13830	1	0·01410	0·03108
1 kg force	= 9·807		980700	70·93	1	2·205
1lb force	= 4·448		$4·448 \times 10^5$	32·17	0·4536	1

Energy, Work, Heat

		joule	kW. hr	ft lb	calory	B.t.u
1 joule	= 1		$2·778 \times 10^{-7}$	0·7376	0·2389	$9·478 \times 10^{-4}$
1 kW. hr	= $3·600 \times 10^6$		1	$2·655 \times 10^6$	$8·598 \times 10^5$	3412
1ft lb	= 1·356		$3·766 \times 10^{-7}$	1	0·3238	$1·285 \times 10^{-3}$
1 calory	= 4·187		$1·163 \times 10^{-6}$	3·088	1	$3·968 \times 10^{-3}$
1 B.t.u.	= 1055		$2·931 \times 10^{-4}$	778·2	252	1

1 kW. hr (kilowatt hour) is 1 unit (Board of Trade unit) as measured by the electricity meter.
1 B.t.u. is a British thermal unit and is the amount of heat required to raise the temperature of 1 lb of water by 1° Fahrenheit.
1 Therm is 100 000 B.t.u. and is equivalent to the heat generated by 29·3 units of electricity.
1 calorie is the heat required to raise the temperature of 1 gm of water by 1° C. The calorie as used by weightwatchers is actually 1000 calories as defined above.
1 erg is 10^{-7} joule.
1 electron volt (eV) is $1·6 \times 10^{-19}$ joule.

Pressure

	pascal	millibar	atmosphere	torr	lb/sq in
1 pascal	= 1	0·01	$9·869 \times 10^{-6}$	$7·501 \times 10^{-3}$	$1·450 \times 10^{-4}$
1 millibar	= 100	1	$9·869 \times 10^{-4}$	0·7501	0·01450
1 atmosphere	= 101 300	1013	1	760	14·7
1 torr	= 133·3	1·333	$1·316 \times 10^{-3}$	1	0·01934
1 lb/sq in	= 6895	68·95	0·06805	51·72	1

1 pascal = 1 newton/sq metre = 10 dyne/sq cm
1 torr is the pressure due to 1 mm of mercury.
By atmosphere is meant "standard atmosphere" which is 760 mm or 29·92 inches of mercury.

Temperature

The Celsius scale is the same as the Centigrade scale. To convert from degrees Fahrenheit (°F) to degrees Celsius (°C), subtract 32 from the temperature in Fahrenheit and multiply by 5/9. To convert from Celsius to Fahrenheit multiply the temperature in Celsius by 9/5 and add 32. Applying this rule we obtain:

0° C = 32° F	20° C = 68° F
5° C = 41° F	25° C = 77° F
10° C = 50° F	30° C = 86° F
15° C = 59° F	35° C = 95° F

37° C (normal body temperature) is 98·6 ° F.

The absolute zero temperature (lowest possible temperature) is −273·15° C.

To convert from ° C to degrees Kelvin (° K) add 273·15 to the temperature in Celsius so that the absolute zero is 0° K.

To obtain the temperature according to the Rankine scale add 459·69 to the temperature in Fahrenheit. 0° Rankine is the absolute zero.

The cgs System in Electromagnetism

The centimetre gram second (cgs) system of units is favoured by some scientists (notably theoretical physicists). There are in fact two sets of cgs units: electrostatic units (esu) and electromagnetic units (emu). Electrostatic units are sometimes given the prefix *stat* and electromagnetic units sometimes given the prefix *ab*. Thus voltage can be measured in statvolts (esu) or abvolts (emu) as well as in volts (SI).

These two systems do not normally treat charge or current as base quantities as the SI system does but as derived quantities. In the electrostatic system the unit of electric charge, the statcoulomb is defined so that one statcoulomb of charge placed at a distance of 1 cm from another statcoulomb of electric charge in a vacuum repels it with a force of 1 dyne. In the electromagnetic system the abampere is such that if two parallel wires in a vacuum 1 cm apart both carry a current of 1 abampere the force between them is 2 dynes per cm length of wire. Also the force between two magnetic poles of unit strength one centimetre apart in a vacuum is one dyne.

These two systems usually treat permittivity and permeability as dimensionless quantities, unlike the SI system.

In the table below c = $2·997\ 925 \times 10^{10}$ and is the speed of light in cm s⁻¹.
The symbol "≏" means "is approximately equal to".
Thus c ≏ 3×10^{10} cm s⁻¹.

Quantity	SI Unit			emu	esu
Current	ampere	A	1 abampere = 10A	1 statampere = 1 abamp/c	
				1 amp ≏ 3×10^9 statamp	
Charge	coulomb	C	1 abcoulomb = 10 C	1 statcoulomb = 1 abcoulomb/c	
EMF	volt	V	1 abvolt = 10^{-8} V	1 statvolt = c abvolt ≏ 300 V	
Capacitance	farad	F	1 abfarad = 10^9 F	1 statfarad = 1 abfarad ×c⁻²	
				1 F ≏ 9×10^{11} statfarad	
Permittivity	F m⁻¹			1 ccu/1 SIU = $10^{11}/(4\pi\ c^2)$.	
				Since the permittivity of a vacuum in esu is 1 this is equivalent to saying the permittivity of a vacuum in SI units = $10^{11}/(4\pi c^2)$ ≏ $1/(36\pi \times 10^9$.	
Magnetic field	A m⁻¹		1 oersted (emu) = $10^3/(4\pi)$ Am⁻¹		
Magnetic flux density	tesla	T	1 gauss (emu) = 10^{-4} tesla. 1 gauss is equivalent to a magnetic field of 1 oersted in a vacuum		
Magnetic flux	weber	Wb	1 maxwell (emu) = 10^{-8} Wb		
Inductance (self or mutual)	henry	H	1 abhenry = 10^{-9}H		
Permeability	H m⁻¹		1 emu/1 SIU = $4\pi \times 10^{-7}$. Since the permeability of a vacuum in e.m.u. is 1, this equivalent to saying the permeability of a vacuum in SI units = $4\pi \times 10^{-7}$.		

Units Related To Radioactivity

Radioactivity is the spontaneous disintegration of atomic nuclei to form lighter nuclei and to simultaneously emit fast moving particles. These particles are usually either α particles, electrons, neutrons, X rays or γ rays, the latter two being photons. These particles constitute radiation and can have a profound effect on the materials through which they pass, e.g. causing cancer in humans. Units are required to define the amount of radioactivity, exposure to radiation, absorbed dose of radiation and effective absorbed dose of radiation by human tissue.

The Becquerel

The SI unit of radioactivity is the *becquerel* (Bq), which is the number of disintegrations per second. It is a measure of the amount of radioactive material present.

The emitted particles cause ionisation in a substance through which they pass. If this substance is a gas an electric field can be used to collect the ionised particles at electrodes before they recombine and enable the amount of ionisation produced to be measured. The number of SI units of exposure to radiation is the number of coulombs of electricity that would be produced in a kilogram of dry air by the radiation. The SI unit of exposure to radiation is the *coulomb* per kilogram.

Since the particles are fast moving they have energy. If they are absorbed by the medium through which they pass this energy is transmitted to the medium. The number of SI units of absorbed dose of radiation is the number of joules produced in a kilogram of this medium. The SI unit of absorbed dose of radiation is called the *gray* (Gy).

Some of the absorbed particles have more effect on human tissue than others. Each type of particle has a factor and the effective absorbed dose of radiation is the absorbed dose times the quality factor (q.v.) which is a weighted sum of the quality factors for each of the component particles.

For α particles q.v. = 20, for neutrons q.v. = 10, for electrons, X rays and γ rays q.v. = 1. The SI unit of effective absorbed radiation dose is the Sievert (Sv).

Number of Sv = Number of Gy $\times$ q.v.

Non SI units are also used to measure these quantities. The conversions are as follows:

     1 Curie (Ci) = 3.7×10^{10} Bq
     1 Roentgen (R) = 2.58×10^{-4} C kg^{-1}
     1 rad = 10^{-2} Gy
     1 Roentgen Equivalent Man (REM) = 10^{-2} Sv

Quantity units	Name of SI unit	Symbol	SI unit in terms of base or derived
Radioactivity, disintegrations per second	becquerel	Bq	s^{-1}
Exposure to radiation	coulomb/kilogram		C kg^{-1}
Absorbed dose of radiation, joule/kilogram	gray	Gy	J kg^{-1}
Effective radiation dose absorbed by tissue	sievert	Sv	J kg^{-1}

VII. SPECIAL TOPICS

MODERN MOLECULAR BIOLOGY

All the structures and functions of living organisms are determined by their genes. Changes in genes lead to changes in structure and/or function, which can result directly in a variety of diseases, including inherited diseases and cancer. Genes are also important in infectious disease, because the properties of the bacteria and viruses that cause disease are determined by their genes. The science of molecular biology allows us to study individual genes and the effects of changes within them. Studies of genes have given us a greater understanding of many diseases, as well as new methods for their diagnosis and treatment, and have also allowed us to start manipulating organisms ranging from viruses to animals to improve our ability to exploit them in biotechnology. Other areas in which molecular biology is important include the understanding of body development and of the evolutionary relationships between different organisms.

The Historical Background

The technology to investigate our genes has been developed over the last 60 years to the extent that we can now manipulate human genes in vitro and use them to treat genetic disease. This achievement is a result of advances in molecular biology which allows complicated biological systems to be investigated by studying their genes. The spin off will enable mankind to understand the genetic basis of disease, to synthesise gene products commercially using biotechnology, to investigate the genetic diversity of living systems and to determine the evolutionary links between organisms. What follows is a historic account of the events leading to the establishment of modern molecular biology and the subsequent use of this technology to diagnose and eventually treat human genetic disease. The table (**T63**) highlights the development of recombinant DNA technology, the "tools of the trade".

Although nucleic acids were discovered in the 19th century by Miescher, the development of modern molecular biology starts in 1944 when Avery and co-workers at the Rockefeller Institute in New York demonstrated for the first time that genetic information is held in nucleic acid not protein as previously believed. Nucleic acids, deoxyribonucleic acid (DNA) and ribonucleic acid (RNA) are information molecules allowing the genetic identity of an organism to be stored, retrieved and copied. DNA is the gene store found mainly in the chromosomes within the nucleus and is duplicated during cell division. RNA occurs mainly in the nucleolus, a structure within the cell to aid the transfer of genetic information from genomic DNA to the synthesis of functional proteins, a process called gene expression.

The Work of Watson and Crick

In 1953 Watson and Crick, working in Cambridge, proposed the double helical structure of DNA based on their interpretation of X-ray diffraction studies of Wilkins and Rosalind Franklin. The attraction of the proposed structure was that it accounted for the ability of the molecule to reproduce itself in such a manner that an identical replica of itself would be formed at each cell division.

DNA is composed of long chains of molecules called nucleotides which form each strand. The nucleotides are composed of a base (adenine, thymine, guanine and cytosine), a sugar (deoxyribose) and a phosphate molecule. The arrangement of bases in the DNA is not random: guanine in one strand pairs with the cytosine in the other strand and adenine always pairs with thymine. At nuclear division the two strands of DNA molecules separate and each chain is then copied using specific base pairing to generate a complementary strand. In 1957 Kornberg discovered DNA polymerase, the enzyme that copies strands of DNA during DNA replication.

The Composition of the Human Genome

The human genome is made up of 23 pairs of chromosomes. Each chromosome contains a single molecule of DNA between 50–250 million nucleotide base pairs long. Therefore the human haploid genome is 3 thousand million base pairs long. What is the link between nucleotide and amino acid

MILESTONES IN RECOMBINANT TECHNOLOGY, 1869–2005	
1869	Miescher isolated DNA for the first time.
1944	Avery proved that genetic information is carried by DNA rather than protein.
1953	Watson and Crick demonstrated the double-helical structure of DNA based on X-ray results of Franklin and Wilkins.
1957	Kornberg discovered DNA polymerase, the enzyme that copies strands of DNA (DNA replication).
1961	Marmur and Doty discovered that DNA single strands can reform the double-helical structure, establishing that nucleic acids can be specifically identified by renaturation reactions.
1966	Nirenberg, Ochoa, and Khorana elucidated the genetic code.
1967	Gellert discovered DNA ligase, the enzyme used to join DNA fragments together.
1970	Khorana synthesis of the first gene.
1970	Temin and Baltimore reverse transcriptase discovered RNA to DNA.
1970	Nathans and Hamilton Smith characterisation of DNA restriction nucleases, leading to their later purification and use of DNA sequence.
1972	Jackson first recombinant DNA molecules generated.
1972–73	DNA cloning techniques were developed by the laboratories of Boyer, Cohen, Berg and their colleagues at Stanford University and the University of California at San Francisco.
1975	Southern developed gel-transfer hybridisation for the detection of specific DNA sequences.
1976	Kan, Golbus and Dozy first prenatal diagnosis using a gene specific probe.
1975–77	Sanger and Barrell and Maxam and Gilbert developed rapid DNA-sequencing methods.
1977	Jeffries and Flavell discovery of gene splicing.
1977	Itakura somatostatin synthesised using recombinant DNA.
1979	Burrell first recombinant vaccines.
1981–82	Palmiter and Brinster produced transgenic mice.
1985	Mullis and co-workers invented the polymerase chain reaction (PCR).
1985	Development of DNA fingerprinting.
1986	Start of the genome project.
1989	Cystic fibrosis gene identified.
1990	Gene therapy for the adenine deaminase gene.
1990–99	Intense development of modified organisms including plants with resistance to viruses, insects, and herbicides, with modified storage properties, modified protein and oil contents, and expressing animal proteins. Development of transgenic animals secreting therapeutic proteins in milk. Development of recombinant vaccines using different host bacteria and viruses, some for multiple immunising properties. Cloning of a sheep from a somatic cell and development to adulthood (cloning performed in 1990). First reproducible cloning of a mammal from adult cells (of mice) by scientists at University of Hawaii (1998). Entire genetic blueprint of the nematode worm decoded (1998).
2000	First human genome draft announced. Leprosy, meningitis and fruit fly genomes completed.
2003	Entire human genome sequenced. Birth of Idaho Gem, the world's first cloned mule and Prometea, first cloned horse.
2005	World's first nerve stem cells made from human stem cells. Scientists hail successful transplantation of human chromosome 21 into mice.

sequence and how many genes can such a large genome code for? The first successful attempt to break the genetic code was made by Nirenberg and Matthaei in 1961 while working in the National Institute of Health in the United States. Later it was shown that the genetic information in DNA molecules was stored in the form of triplet codes, a sequence of three nucleotide bases determines the identity of one amino acid; by 1966 a complete genetic code for all twenty amino acids had been established. In 1970 Khorana and his colleagues succeeded in synthesising a gene in vitro for the first time by assembling its constituent base pairs or sequence using DNA polymerase. Another important discovery by Marmur and Doty (1961) was the denaturation and renaturation properties of nucleic acids. High temperature can be used to separate DNA strands and when allowed to cool the DNA helix reforms by complementary base pair alignment. Therefore the information retained in the order of the nucleotide bases controls the specific identity of genes. Analysis of human DNA using renaturation experiments showed that a large proportion of the DNA is made up of repetitive sequences that do not code for genes. Thus although the genome is very large and could code for millions of genes the actual number is nearer thousands.

Recombinant DNA Techniques

During the 1970s recombinant DNA techniques emerged as further analysis of nucleic acids and associated enzymes expanded. In 1970 Nathans and Hamilton Smith discovered a group of enzymes which occur in micro-organisms and they are now referred to as Class II restriction endonucleases. These enzymes were found to cleave the DNA molecule at sequence specific sites. It meant that DNA fragments of reproducible size could be produced and that DNA fragments containing a particular gene, for example, could be cut out from the rest of the DNA molecule.

The discovery of another enzyme which was subsequently proved to be of immense value in cloning genes was made by Temin and independently by Baltimore (1970). Genetic information is usually transferred from DNA to RNA by a process referred to as transcription and then the messenger RNA(mRNA) migrates into the cytoplasm where this genetic information is translated into protein. However, Temin and Baltimore and their colleagues showed that in retroviruses genetic information could flow in the reverse direction from RNA to DNA. This is referred to as RNA-directed DNA synthesis and the enzyme responsible is called reverse transcriptase. This enzyme provides a method of making a complementary copy of a gene referred to as complementary DNA(cDNA) and mRNA is converted to cDNA by the enzyme. For example, red blood cells contain only globin mRNA and therefore if this mRNA is reverse transcribed it is possible to make a globin cDNA copy. Other examples include using mRNA from the pancreas to clone the insulin gene. Globin cDNA is now used extensively to diagnose various haemoglobin abnormalities in the foetus and recombinant insulin is now used to treat insulin-dependent diabetes. Many other cDNAs have since been synthesised and sequenced and these find wide applications in the biotechnology industry.

Cloning Human Genes

Cloning of the cDNA for genes was developed from the experiments joining recombinant DNA fragments using the "sticky" or cohesive ends produced by some of the restriction enzymes to produce biologically functional hybrid DNA molecules.

The two molecules are joined together by DNA ligase, an enzyme discovered by Gellert in 1967 which bonds the sugar phosphate molecules together.

The First Experiments

The first successful recombinant experiments were achieved in Edinburgh by Jackson in 1972. They were followed by the introduction of plasmid vectors to carry fragments of foreign DNA. Plasmids are naturally occurring small circular pieces of DNA found in the cytoplasm of bacteria. They are extrachromosomal and replicate independently of the host bacterial genomic DNA. By using a restriction endonuclease that cuts the plasmid DNA at a single site, the plasmid can be opened up and a foreign piece of DNA with the same restriction endonuclease sites inserted. Once ligated together the new recombinant plasmid can be introduced into a bacterial host and cloned. This is in fact the actual recombinant part of the process. In 1973 Boyer, Cohen and Berg constructed the first plasmid using a recombinant DNA technique, this plasmid is referred to as pSC101; p for plasmid, SC after its originator Stanley Cohen. Later, other plasmids were developed, perhaps the most important being pBR322, BR after the originators Bolivar and Rodriguez. If cDNA sequences are inserted into a plasmid designed or engineered to express the cDNA then recombinant protein can be produced and purified. To date a large variety of vectors have been constructed to clone and express genes in different organisms including bacteria, yeast, mammalian cells and plant cells. In order to clone large fragments of DNA, vectors have been designed from viruses and chromosomes. For example, yeast artificial chromosomes (YACs) have been used to clone large pieces of human DNA millions of nucleotides long.

The Work of Southern

In 1975 Southern in Edinburgh pioneered a technique which proved essential for the subsequent developments in this field. If DNA is extracted from human tissues or cells, this DNA contains thousands of genes of the host organism. These genes must be selected or identified from the millions of fragments of DNA digested by restriction enzymes. How can a particular gene or nucleic acid sequence be identified among all this DNA? The first step is to separate the restricted fragments of DNA on an agarose gel, which results in the fragments separating under an electric current according to their size, smaller fragments migrating further than larger fragments. Among these fragments will be the ones containing the genes of interest. Southern's technique was to transfer the DNA fragments from the gel with an alkali buffer onto a nitrocellulose filter. This allows the fragments to be permanently fixed to the filter. The specific fragments can then be identified by hybridising a radiolabelled probe of nucleic acid fragments to the filter, where they will form double stranded molecules with their complementary strands. These hybrids are then displayed by autoradiography by exposing the filter to an X-ray film in the dark, radiolabelled bands on the X-ray film demonstrate the presence of DNA homologous to the probe. Modifications of this method can be used to identify mRNAs from total RNA extracted from cells or tissues using solvents. Hybridisation of probes to RNA filters is called Northern blotting and is used to assess which genes are expressed in different cells or tissues.

Diagnosis of Genetic Disease

The methods developed for identifying genetic change using Southern blotting were the forerunner for prenatal diagnosis of genetic disease whereby certain genetic disorders in the foetus can be detected early in pregnancy. If the foetus proves to be affected with the genetic defect the parents may opt to have the pregnancy terminated. On the other hand, if the foetus proves to be unaffected the pregnancy is allowed to continue. In this way the parents can be sure that the child they will have will not be affected with an inherited genetic disorder. The usual procedure is to remove a small amount of amniotic fluid which surrounds the foetus by transabdominal amniocentesis or alternatively a small sample of the placenta called chorionic villi. Both procedures are safe in competent hands and carry very little risk to the foetus. By looking for chromosomal changes in the foetal DNA it is possible to diagnose a variety of genetic diseases. Also, by making DNA from the foetal or placental sample it is possible to detect genetic change. This was first described in 1976 by Kan, Golbus and Dozy. They were able to show if the foetus was affected by α thalassaemia, a disorder in which the α-globin genes are deleted. This was observed by reduced hybridisation with the appropriate α-globin cDNA probe prepared from reticulocyte mRNA using reverse transcriptase.

This represented a major step forward in the field of prenatal diagnosis. It is now possible not only to identify a variety of genetic defects but also to give prenatal counselling giving parents the risk of having a genetically abnormal child and with the choices that incurs. In 1977, a year after Kan's report, there appeared two new and relatively simple methods for rapidly sequencing the bases in a DNA molecule. One of the methods was developed in the MRC Laboratory of Molecular Biology at Cambridge by Sanger and Barrell and the other at Harvard University by Maxam and Gilbert. The DNA sequencing methods evolved by these workers meant that given a piece of DNA it was now possible to analyse its nucleotide base sequence. This was to have far-reaching consequences.

Gene Structure Discoveries

It was also at this time that recombinant DNA technology led to major discoveries concerning gene structure. It had always been assumed that genes were discrete and contiguous structures of DNA which coded for particular enzymes or peptides. However, in 1977 Jeffries and Flavell published the first report on the structure of a gene from a higher organism, i.e. the rabbit globin gene. It was found that the genes were in fact rarely contiguous stretches of DNA. It turned out that at least in higher organisms, almost all the genes are interrupted by so-called intervening sequences or introns, the remaining parts of the genes separated by introns being called exons. This led to the concept of gene splicing, subsequently it has been shown that during transcription the precursor RNA derived from introns is excised and the precursor RNA from non contiguous exons are spliced together to form functional mRNA. Thus exons and not introns specify the primary structure of the gene product. This finding was to have far reaching consequences particularly with regard to the use of DNA technology in biosynthesis.

Biosynthesis of Human Protein

At the same time as the fine details of gene structure were beginning to be revealed the first biosynthesis of a human protein using DNA technology was reported by Itakura in 1977 and the first genetic engineering firm Genentech Incorporated in the United States was founded specifically to develop recombinant DNA methods for making medically important drugs. Itakura and his colleagues successfully obtained the bacterial expression of a cloned gene for somatostatin, a peptide hormone which among other things inhibits growth hormone and is used for the treatment of children with excessive growth. From knowing the amino acid structure of somatostatin they were able to infer the nucleotide base composition of its gene. This was relatively easy because somatostatin contains only 14 amino acids. The assembled synthetic gene, along with various regulators, was then inserted into the plasmid pBR322 and cloned in bacterium Escherichia coli. Since the first step many other valuable hormones and proteins have been synthesised using DNA technology. For example, Goeddel and his colleagues at Genentech published details of their successful synthesis of human insulin in 1979. Subsequently marketing approval for the genetically engineered insulin was obtained by the Eli Lilly Corporation in 1982 and is now available for the treatment of diabetes.

Factor VIII is another medically important gene essential for the treatment of haemophilia. This gene has also been cloned and expressed as a recombinant protein. The gene presented major cloning difficulties because the full length cDNA could not be synthesised so the gene had to be assembled from genomic DNA by cloning the many exon fragments into the vector in the correct order, a feat which took 8 man years.

The Human Genome Project

As more experience was gained in cloning DNA sequences and confidence in the techniques grew the feasibility of possibly cloning DNA sequences from the entire human genome began to be entertained. The fragments produced by restriction enzymes and cloned into appropriate vectors could be stored and in this way a so-called library of individual genome could be produced. The pioneers in this regard were Maniatis and his colleagues in California, who reported the first successful construction of a gene library in 1978 and this was to prove extremely valuable for subsequent research. Currently DNA libraries are available for many organisms.

The human genome project had the aim of identifying and sequencing all DNA libraries. This project became feasible with the development of automated DNA sequencing and computer analysis of the very large sequence database. The entire human genome was sequenced by April 2003.

The HapMap Project

The successor to the Human Genome Project is the International HapMap Project. This international venture has begun to chart the genetic variation in populations in Asia, Africa, Europe and North America. The first full draft was published in October 2005.

The Identification of Genetic Disorders

Recombinant DNA technology had been so far used to detect defined genetic disorders in the foetus by demonstrating an abnormality in amniotic fluid cell DNA using gene specific probes. However, in many genetic disorders the identity of the basic biochemical defect is unknown and therefore a specific gene probe cannot be produced. Kan and Dozy in 1978 showed that an entirely different approach was feasible. The new approach depended on demonstrating that the disease producing gene is very closely linked to a particular restriction enzyme recognition site. It is known that variations in DNA sequence occur randomly throughout the entire genome and are apparently without any ill effects. These variations result in a loss of existing restriction sites or acquisition of new restriction sites. Such changes in DNA sequence mean that fragments produced by a particular restriction enzyme will be of different lengths in different people and they can be recognised by different mobilities on electrophoresis. They are referred to as restriction fragment length polymorphisms and are inherited as simple genetic traits obeying Mendelian laws of inheritance. If a disease producing gene could be shown from family studies to be closely linked to a restriction fragment length polymorphism then it would provide a method of detecting the disease without actually knowing anything about the gene itself. Kan and Dozy found that restriction enzyme DNA fragments incorporating the β globin gene were of different sizes depending on whether the chromosome carried the normal gene or the gene for sickle cell anaemia. Much work is currently directed towards finding such linkages using a variety of genetic markers. The repetitive DNA found throughout the genome has proven useful in this respect as micro-satellite DNA repeats show extensive variation and can be used to map most genetic traits.

Successful Gene Cloning

By the late 1970s reports of successful gene cloning were becoming almost an everyday occurrence. One of particular importance was a report in early spring of 1979 by Burrell and his colleagues, then working in Edinburgh, of a successful cloning of the hepatitis B viral antigen. This was followed shortly afterwards by similar reports in the Pasteur Institute in Paris and Stanford Medical School in California. The importance of this work was that it opened up the possibility of producing an effective and safe vaccine against a relatively common disease which on occasions can lead to chronic ill health and even death. Following these reports DNA technology also began to be used to produce other viral antigens for use in developing vaccines as well as important biologically active proteins such as interferon. The production of vaccines and cellular proteins is a major commercial use for recombinant DNA technology. Though the emphasis has been so far largely on DNA in relation to medicine, at the same time significant developments were also taking place in relation to agriculture and animal husbandry, for example the successful cloning of viral antigens of the foot and mouth disease by Clyde and his colleagues.

Advances with Cancer Genes

The year 1982 saw the publication of the first attempts to isolate, clone and characterise human cancer genes, in this case a gene associated with bladder cancer. DNA was extracted from cancer cells, fragmented with restriction enzymes and then applied to a special line of cultured mouse fibroblasts referred to as NIH3T3. In tissue culture these cells became transformed and formed clumps rather than a flat single layer of cells when exposed to the whole tumour cell DNA from the cancer tissues. When the specific fragments of DNA capable of transforming NIH3T3 cells were identified the genes they contained were termed cancer genes or oncogenes. We all carry such genes and there is much speculation and interest at present in trying to find out how they may become activated. Another type of gene associated with cancer has been identified recently from cancers which show a hereditary form. These genes are called tumour suppressor genes as they normally prevent the development of cancer. Studies of hereditary cancers (such as retinoblastoma, Wilm's tumour and familial adenomatous polyposis) have identified the genes by linkage analysis providing a screening method to detect individuals at risk of developing these forms of cancer. Many problems still remain to be answered, in particular how oncogenes and tumour suppressor genes can lead on to cancer.

Transgenes

One way of investigating an abnormal gene or cancer associated gene is to test its function by reinserting it into an organism and see what effect it has. By replacing the normal gene with the altered gene the function of the mutant protein can be tested. Palmiter and Brinator in 1982 injected linear DNA containing the gene of interest into fertilised mouse eggs which developed into mice with the foreign gene in many of their cells. Animals with the foreign gene in the germ line cells were then used to pass the foreign gene on to their progeny, creating permanently altered animals called transgenic organisms. The foreign genes are called transgenes. This approach can also be used to target and inactivate genes of interest producing "knockout" experiments which answer questions about the importance of a specific gene to normal growth.

Advances in DNA Technology

By 1985 the availability of purified DNA polymerases and chemically synthesised DNA oligonucleotides has made it possible to amplify and clone specific DNA sequences rapidly without the need for living cells. The technique, called polymerase chain reaction (PCR) was invented by Mullis and co-workers in 1985 and allows the DNA from a selected gene or region of the genome to be amplified a thousand million fold provided that part of the nucleotide sequence is known. The principle of the technique is to double the amount of DNA in reaction cycles. Each cycle heat denatures the DNA producing single strands, followed by the oligonucleotide primers hybridising with the target complementary sequences as the DNA solution cools, followed by the synthesis of complementary DNA from the primer using the single strand as a template. By repeating the cycle 20–30 times and by using an enzyme which is able to withstand the high denaturation temperatures the DNA is amplified exponentially. Therefore the PCR is very sensitive so even DNA from single cells can be amplified and visualised using this method.

The method has replaced many of the original DNA techniques for cloning specific genes and detecting genetic mutations, and it can be used to amplify RNA by first transcribing them into DNA with reverse transcriptase. It can be applied to the diagnosis of genetic diseases and to the detection of low levels of microbial infection. It can also be used to amplify genes from single cells taken at the first stages in the development of the embryo, improving early detection of genetic abnormalities. It has great promise in forensic medicine as a means of analysing minute traces of blood or other tissues and identifying the person from whom they came by their genetic "DNA fingerprint" using mini and micro satellite sequences.

The Future

The most important medical application for this technology is its eventual use to treat genetic and other disease directly by gene therapy. Human genetic engineering raises unique safety, social, and ethical concerns. The first successful therapy was carried out in the National Institute of Health in the United States in 1990 on a 4-year-old girl suffering from adenosine deaminase (ADA) deficiency. Patients with ADA deficiency have a defect in DNA metabolism which affects growth of their immune system. By infecting the patient's cultured lymphocytes with a retrovirus containing the normal recombinant ADA gene the defect was treated and the healthy cells were returned to the patient's blood. In future gene therapy will be used to treat cancer and acquired immune deficiency syndrome as well as a variety of genetically inherited diseases.

This brief history of the developments which have led to the establishment of modern molecular biology has only outlined some of the principal techniques and applications. The ability to manipulate our own genes will have far reaching consequences which we are only just realising.

GLOSSARY OF GENETIC TERMS

Biotechnology A set of methods for using living organisms to make a variety of products, including alcoholic drinks, bread and medical drugs.

Blotting A method of detecting specific nucleic acid sequences. A mixture of molecules is separated by size on a gel made of agarose, and a filter made of nylon or nitrocellulose is then placed on the gel, so that the nucleic acid molecules bind irreversibly to the filter. A nucleic acid of known sequence, which has been radioactively labelled, is then incubated with the filter so that the labelled nucleic acid sticks ("hybridises") with molecules of complementary sequence attached to the filter, so that the latter can be detected and the size can be measured. When DNA is attached to the filter, the procedure is called Southern blotting after its inventor; when RNA is attached to the filter, it is called Northern blotting. A similar method exists for proteins, using antibodies to detect specific proteins, which is called Western blotting.

cDNA An abbreviation for complementary DNA, which is a DNA "copy" of an mRNA molecule extracted from a cell; this is often the first step in cloning a gene, and is carried out using reverse transcriptase.

Chromosomes Chromosomes are structures found in the nuclei of plant and animal cells and consist of the cell's DNA, along with a number of specialised proteins. The functions of the chromosome are to minimise the space occupied by the DNA—in mammalian cells, up to 2 m of DNA has to be packed into a nucleus only 4–10 μm in diameter—and to distribute newly synthesised DNA to the daughter cells after cell division. Somatic cells (i.e. cells not specialising in reproduction) of different species contain different numbers of chromosomes, e.g. man (46), cat (38), mouse (40), honey bee (16), Drosophila fruit fly (8), and potato (8). The chromosomes in each case consist of 2 sets of paired chromosomes; reproductive cells contain only 1 set of chromosomes, and are thus described as haploid. Bacteria contain a single chromosome, which is much simpler than the chromosomes of higher organisms, and is circular.

Cloning The production of genetically identical copies of a biological material, for example starting from a single cell. In recombinant DNA technology, cloning consists of joining a DNA molecule to a vector (q.v.) and putting the resulting recombinant molecule into a bacterium, where the vector then allows large quantities of the DNA molecule of interest to be made.

Cytoplasm See **T32**.

Denaturation In general, the breakup of the higher structure of a biological polymer. For example, egg white becomes opaque on cooking because of denaturation of the protein albumin, caused by heat. In nucleic acids, denaturation refers to the breakage of the hydrogen bonds between the nucleotide bases that hold the two strands of a double-stranded DNA molecule together; heating a double-stranded molecule causes the two strands to separate (this is also called "melting"). If a solution of denatured DNA molecules is allowed to cool slowly enough for the separated strands to bump into each other, the double helix re-forms; this is called renaturation, and only occurs when the base sequences of two DNA molecules are complementary to each other (see **Nucleic Acids**). Double-stranded molecules consisting of one DNA strand and one RNA strand ("heteroduplexes") can also be formed by this method.

Deoxyribonucleic Acid (DNA) See **Nucleic Acid, T67**.

DNA Fingerprinting DNA fingerprinting consists of examining repetitive DNA in the genome for variations in the lengths of restriction fragments. The DNA from the genome is cut with a restriction enzyme known to cut repetitive sequences into short pieces and is then used in blotting experiments using probes that hybridise to the repetitive sequences. Every individual has his own pattern, so that fingerprinting can match blood to a particular person, and patterns are inherited from parent to child, allowing the method to identify relationships between individuals.

Exon See **Intron, T67**.

Gene A unit of genetic information, i.e. the DNA sequence encoding one protein or RNA gene product.

Gene Expression The process of making a product (protein or RNA) from a gene. Regardless of the gene product, the first step consists of transcribing the DNA to make an RNA copy; this can be the final product, or it can be translated to make a protein molecule.

Gene Product When the information in a gene is copied, the final product is either a protein or an RNA molecule. The term gene product includes both of these. It does not usually include messenger RNA (mRNA), which is an intermediate between the DNA of the gene and the final protein.

Genetic Code Sequence information in genes is used to specify amino acid sequences in proteins. There are four bases in nucleic acids and 20 amino acids in proteins, so a direct one-to-one correspondence is not possible. Groups of two bases could only store information about eight amino acids. Three bases (a "codon") can store information about 64 amino acids; this is the code that is used. Since there are only 20 amino acids in proteins, the code is quite redundant, most amino acids being represented by 2, 3 or 4 different codons, though these codons are generally related, e.g. GGA, GGT, GGC, and GGG all encode the amino acid glycine. Three of the 64 codons have the special function of telling ribosomes that the protein it is making has come to an end; these are called "stop codons".

Genetic Disease A disease caused by a defect in a gene (i.e. a mutation) or in a chromosome. A well known example of a genetic disease caused by a point mutation is cystic fibrosis. Some types of leukaemia are associated with a chromosomal defect, where the long arms of chromosome 21 are shorter than normal (this is called the Philadelphia chromosome).

Genetic Diversity The number of different alleles in a population. An allele is an individual's version of a particular gene, so the larger and more varied a population, the more different versions of a given gene it will contain, and the greater will be its genetic diversity. The importance of genetic diversity is that a larger allele pool makes a species better able to adapt to changing conditions.

Genome The total set of genetic information in an organism. Physically, the genome corresponds to the sum of all the chromosomes in a cell, i.e. all the DNA that the cell contains. The genome thus consists of all the genes encoding proteins and RNA molecules, as well as large amounts of non-coding or silent DNA. Much of this is made of repeated DNA sequences, which can be classified into a number of families.

Haploid Most animal cells contain two pairs of chromosomes—one from the father and one from the mother, and are called diploid. Reproductive cells (spermatozoa and oocytes) contain only one set of chromosomes and are called haploid. When a spermatozoon and an oocyte fuse, the resulting cell becomes diploid and develops into a new animal. A similar process occurs in plants.

Human Genome Project See L54 and T65.

In vitro Used of an experiment that is not carried out in a living body.

In vivo Used of an experiment carried out in a living body.

Intron The nucleic acid sequence of a gene is often much longer than needed to encode the protein or RNA product of that gene. The part of the gene containing protein-encoding information is found to be split up into sometimes numerous small pieces called exons, which are separated by non-coding pieces called introns. Transcription produces an RNA copy (a pre-mRNA) containing both exon and intron sequences. Before the mRNA migrates out of the nucleus, the parts of the pre-mRNA corresponding to the introns are removed, a process called splicing.

Ligase An enzyme that is used in recombinant DNA technology for joining the ends of two DNA molecules together, usually after renaturation of sticky ends. Ligase is involved in the replication and repair of DNA.

mRNA An RNA molecule that is a copy of the base sequence of a gene, and carries that sequence from the nucleus to the cytoplasm to instruct the ribosomes to make a protein of the correct amino acid sequence.

Mutation A change in the sequence of bases in a gene. This can be a change from one base to another (point mutation), or loss or addition of one or more bases from or to a gene sequence (deletions and insertions respectively). Changes which do not alter the structure of the gene product, e.g. mutations in exons and mutations in codons that do not alter the amino acid encoded by those codons, are called silent mutations.

Nucleic Acids Biological polymers consisting of a chain of sugars joined by phosphate groups, where each sugar carries a nucleotide base. There are two important nucleic acids, deoxyribonucleic acid (DNA), which is the chemical of which genes are made in most organisms, and ribonucleic acid (RNA), of which three types (mRNA, rRNA and tRNA) are involved in protein synthesis; some viruses carry their genes in the form of RNA. Nucleic acids store information in the sequence of chemical bases attached to the sugars; the bases in DNA are adenine (A), thymine (T), cytosine (C) and guanine (G), while those in RNA are the same except that uracil (U) replaces thymine. The two ends of a nucleic acid molecule are different; one is called the 5'-end and the other is called the 3'-end.

DNA is usually double-stranded; that is, two DNA molecules are linked together side by side and pointing in opposite directions as a double helix, joined by hydrogen bonds between the bases, which point towards the centre of the helix. Because of the chemical structures of the bases, C can only form hydrogen bonds with G and vice versa, T and G can only form bonds with A, while A forms hydrogen bonds with T in DNA and with U in RNA. Thus, if the sequence of bases in one of the two strands in a double-stranded DNA molecule is 5'-CATTG-3', the "complementary" sequence in the other strand will be 3'-GTAAC-5'. The RNA sequence complementary to this DNA sequence will be 3'-GUAAC-5'. Two molecules that have similar sequences are said to be homologous.

Nucleolus A structure within the nucleus, consisting of copies of the cell's ribosomal RNA genes, which are sometimes needed in larger numbers than can be provided within the chromosomes, i.e. when cells have to synthesise large quantities of protein and thus need large numbers of ribosomes.

Nucleotides Nitrogen-containing bases attached to a sugar phosphate. See **Nucleic Acids**.

Oligonucleotides Very short nucleic acid molecules. Oligonucleotides are often used as the probes in blotting studies and other recombinant DNA techniques, because oligonucleotides of known sequences can easily be made in the laboratory.

Oncogenes A number of cancers have been found to be caused by viruses. The ability of a virus to cause cancer is conferred upon it by special genes, which are called oncogenes. Oncogenes are usually related to normal cellular genes involved in regulation of cell growth, and cancer due to oncogenes can be thought of as resulting from the abnormal expression of a normal gene.

Peptides Very short proteins.

Plasmid A small circular DNA molecule containing a replication origin (it is thus a replicon) commonly found in bacteria. Plasmids are widely used in recombinant DNA technology as vectors for cloning DNA fragments because of their small size. In nature, plasmids are responsible for a considerable proportion of bacterial antibiotic resistance—moving from cell to cell, they carry antibiotic resistance genes with them.

Polymerase Chain Reaction (PCR) A method for synthesizing relatively large amounts of a nucleic acid of known sequence, using polymerase enzymes and oligonucleotides.

Proteins Biological polymers made of amino acids, of which 20 are used in living organisms. The properties of a particular protein depend on the sequence of amino acids of which it is made, and this sequence is determined by the sequence of nucleotide bases in the gene corresponding to the protein. Proteins can be structural (e.g. collagen) or they can be enzymes, which catalyse chemical reactions. Some proteins, such as haemoglobin, have the special function of transporting other chemicals around the body.

Recombinant DNA Technology A more precise term for genetic engineering.

Repetitive Sequences Much of the DNA in the genome of a higher organism does not contain genes, but consists of apparently functionless sequences, some of which are repeated head-to-tail. Genomes contain a number of families of related repeats, and up to 20% of the genome can consist of sequences present at up to 1,000,000 repeated copies.

Replicon A DNA molecule that is able to replicate in a cell. In order to do this, the molecule needs to carry a special sequence called a replication origin, which is the point at which synthesis of new copies of the DNA begins.

Restriction Endonucleases Enzymes found in bacteria that cut DNA molecules; their function is to protect bacteria against infection from viruses. Class II restriction enzymes, the group which is important in recombinant DNA techniques, bind to a short (usually 4 or 6 bases) sequence and cut the DNA in or close to the recognition sequence.

Bacteria protect themselves against their own restriction enzymes by chemically modifying their DNA. Restriction enzymes allow DNA molecules whose sequences are known to be cut at predetermined positions. Many enzymes cut the two strands of a DNA molecule in slightly different places, to leave single-stranded overhangs ("sticky ends"); these can be renatured to join pieces of DNA together in a specific way.

Retrovirus A virus which stores its genetic information in the form of RNA instead of DNA; several are tumour-inducing viruses, and the viruses associated with AIDS are retroviruses. Replication of these viruses starts with making a DNA copy of the RNA genome, using the enzyme reverse transcriptase.

Reverse transcriptase A viral enzyme found in some viruses that use RNA instead of DNA for their genomes. This enzyme is an RNA-dependent DNA polymerase, and makes a DNA copy of the viral RNA, which is the first step in the replication of such viruses.

Ribonucleic acid (RNA) *See* **Nucleic Acids.**

Splicing *See* **Intron.**

Transcription The process of copying a DNA molecule to make a complementary RNA copy of a gene. Transcription occurs in the nucleus of higher organism cells, and is carried out by enzymes called DNA-dependent RNA polymerases.

Transgene A foreign gene inserted into a higher organism (animal or plant). This is done by inserting the gene into the organism at an early stage of embryonic development; since all the cells of the adult come from these early embryo cells, all adult cells will contain the inserted gene. Such organisms are called transgenic animals or plants.

Translation The process of converting a gene sequence in the form of mRNA into a protein sequence. Translation is carried out by ribosomes.

Vector In recombinant DNA technology, a replicon that is used for cloning DNA sequences. Vectors are usually small and simple replicons, *i.e.* plasmids and bacteriophages.

THE GEOLOGICAL RECORD

Earth History

Earth's history is long, at least 4,600 million years. This stretch of time is virtually impossible to visualise but an analogy may make it more comprehensible. Imagine that Earth time has been but a single 24 hour day. If the Earth came into being at time zero, 0:00:00, then bombardment by meteorites would have lasted until 3am; there would not have been enough stability for the origin of life until 4am: 5:36am would see the first fossils and traces of bacteria. It would be well past noon before single celled algae appeared and seaweeds not until 20:28pm: 20 minutes later there were jelly fish; trilobites dominated the sea floor by 21:04pm. Plants reached the land by 21:52pm and coal swamps flourished by 22:24pm. Then, 32 minutes later the dinosaurs dominated, to be replaced by mammals at 23:39pm. Not until a minute to midnight did Humans come on the scene.

How Palaeontologists Date Fossils

How can Palaeontologists (geologists that study past life) have any idea about relative dates? Each layer of sedimentary rock (*see* **T48**) contains clues to the environment in which that sediment was laid down. This is based on one of the fundamental principles of Geology, that the present is the key to the past, that by studying the sediments in today's environment, one can conclude that the same sediments lithified (cemented into rock) and would have been deposited under similar conditions in the past.

Sedimentary rocks also hold clues to the life forms of the time through the fossils that they contain; some rocks such as a coral limestone will be rich in fossils since coral reefs support a wide variety of creatures; the harsh conditions of a hot desert are not conducive to life. Rocks can be dated by radioactive isotopes so, putting all this evidence together, it is possible to reconstruct the *palaeoenvironment* (past environment) and the community (assemblage) of species that was living in it. Molecular biology has made dating proteins another possibility.

However, the fossil record does not contain all creatures that have ever lived for, to be preserved as a fossil, an organism must have hard parts such as bone or shell. Only in rare circumstances can jellyfish or bacteria be preserved if the sediments were fine and burial very quick, perhaps by a submarine mudslide, so that currents or waves had no chance to stir up the delicate remains.

Main Geological Eras

The table set out later (**T69**) is a history of life on Earth, a time chart summarising the main stages in Earth's history. There are four major chunks of time called Eras, based on the differences in animal groups present in each one: Azoic (no life), Palaeozoic (ancient animals), Mesozoic (middle animals) and Caenozoic (recent animals). The earliest times are conventionally shown at the bottom, in line with another fundamental principle, the Law of Superposition which states that in an undisturbed sequence, a layer of rock will be younger than the ones below it and older than those above it.

Hand in hand with this law is the Law of Fossil Succession, that plants and animals that have parts hard enough to survive burial and compaction change through time and that where there are the same kinds of fossils and assemblages (groups of species together) in rocks of different locations, then they are of the same age. As exploration and technology, such as the scanning electron microscope, advance so the scope for reading the rocks increases, interpretations change and what is written here becomes out of date.

The Development of Life

The development of life on Earth has been neither smooth nor gradual. There have been times of abundance balanced by times of major extinctions, of which there have been at least five. Long periods of gradual evolution are punctuated by brief periods of rapid change, either in proliferation, as the explosion of life forms in the Cambrian seas, or in extinction, as the virtual disappearance of the dinosaurs some 70 million years ago which has so captured the popular imagination and occupied many palaeontologists in debate as to its cause. Changes in palaeogeography, as the continents have shifted positions relative to each other, have prompted radiation or extinction, migration and mixing.

The Origin of Life

How did life originate? The answer can probably only ever be conjectural. It is commonly thought that complex organic molecules, amino acids, synthesized naturally in Precambrian oceans. These basic ingredients of proteins would have had favourable environments of high energy from both the sun (no ozone layer to screen out UV rays) and warm water from volcanic hydrothermal vents. The earliest known fossils are those of prokaryotic cells (small with no nuclei) in the anaerobic (without oxygen) oceans. By 1000 million years ago (mya) eukaryote cells (large, membrane bounded nuclei containing chromosomes) were well established. Here was an opportunity for evolution, since these cells reproduced sexually allowing genetic material to mix and mutate.

To have life means having the ability to reproduce; reproduction requires the passing on of genetic information. This is done on Earth today by the very complex protein substance, DNA (deoxyribonucleic acid). (*see* **Nucleic acid, T67**) Gradually microbes became more complex and

TABLE: GEOLOGICAL TIME SCALE

ERA		AGE (MYA, million years ago)	CHARACTERISTICS
CAINOZOIC	QUATERNARY		Modern humans
		2	
	TERTIARY		Mammals & flowering plants diversify. Earliest hominids.
		65	
MESOZOIC	CRETACEOUS		Dinosaurs included in major extinction. Flowering plants common.
		145	
	JURASSIC		Early birds & mammals. Dinosaurs abundant.
		205	
	TRIASSIC		First dinosaurs & mammals. Coniferous trees common.
		250	
PALAEOZOIC	PERMIAN		Mass extinction of many marine species, including trilobites.
		290	
	CARBONIFEROUS		First winged insects. Large primitive trees. First reptiles.
		360	
	DEVONIAN		First seed-bearing plants (ammonoids). Early tetrapods. First amphibians and insects.
		410	
	SILURIAN		First jawed fish, first upright plant.
		440	
	ORDOVICIAN		First land plants and early fish. First jawless vertebrates.
		500	
	CAMBRIAN		Trilobites dominant. First molluscs.
		570	
PRECAMBRIAN	PROTEROZOIC		First invertebrates & multi-celled/ soft-bodied organisms.
		2,500	
	ARCHÆAN		Bacteria/single celled organisms.
		3,800	Oldest known fossils.
	ORIGIN OF EARTH	4,550?	

colonial, by 3000 mya creating layered structures called *stromatolites*; these still form today at places such as Hamlyn Pool in Western Australia.

Proterozoic Era Discoveries

The late Proterozoic has been an empty mystery but modern finds are constantly filling in this gap. For example, Ediacara chert from Australia has revealed flat bodied creatures only 0.1mm in size, 610 to 510 million years old. Alongside these are fossils that look like feathery fronds up to a metre long. Others are pouchlike with no recognisable circulatory or nervous system; it is thought that their air-mattress appearance was due to fluid-filled hydraulic support. These have now been discovered in rocks world wide, but were they a life form that failed or the ancestors of modern species? Amongst these fossils have been found trails and holes left by metazoans; it seems that these had been burrowing in sediments since 1000 mya. What seems certain is that early bacteria developed in the absence of oxygen; the blue-green algae (cyanobacteria) released this vital gas into the oceans and atmosphere, setting the stage for Biology's Big Bang.

The Early Cambrian Period

In the early Cambrian period the world recovered from a severe glaciation (nicknamed Snowball Earth) and shallow seas flooded the continents. (There was an extraordinary radiation of life forms; almost every major group of animals appeared then, 540–500 mya. Indeed, so rapid was this radiation, current research puts it at only 10–20 million years, that it suggests another kind of evolution in very short time periods in addition to the more steady Darwinian one.

The cause of this dramatic explosion is a matter of Geological conjecture. Had the cyanobacteria established so much oxygen that more complex life was possible? Was it that so many new species created more diverse food chains (*see* **Ecosystems, T45**) such that there was increasing competition in the predator and prey relationship so adaptation was necessary for survival?

The Cambrian Explosion

The Cambrian explosion of life produced important marine creatures such as brachiopods (bivalved marine animals whose valves are not identical) and trilobites (rather like woodlice in appearance, bodies in three sections), with eyes as well developed as any modern insect, in abundance.

Significantly, these creatures had made an advance by developing shells. These gave support for muscles and protection against new predators, something that pre-Cambrian Ediacara species would not have needed.

Astonishingly, every design for a body plan that has ever existed (there are eight main ones) came into being then, and no new ones have appeared since though many minor ones became extinct in the first major extinction recorded in the rocks at the end of the Cambrian Period. This extinction after such diversity indicates that maybe extinctions do not need a major external cause such as Ice Ages or asteroids after all; perhaps a small evolutionary step creates an advantage to one species that upsets the balance of a whole ecosystem.

The Appearance of Fish

Fish first appear in the fossil record in the Ordovician. Their soft bodies were armoured by external skeletons. By Silurian times, a group of fish emerged with internal skeletons and body armour reduced to scales. By late Devonian times, 370 mya, there were lobe finned fishes that had stout bony supporting appendages, unlike the ray finned fishes (such as trout or salmon of today) that have much thinner bone structures arranged as a fan in their fins. Some of these lobe fins had one upper and two lower bones similar to those of tetrapods (four jointed legged, land living vertebrates); indeed, the first tetrapods evolved in the Devonian, about 360 mya and were the forerunners of amphibians.

The Evolution of Plants

If animals were to occupy the land surface, then plants must have got there first or else there would have been no food source to sustain them. Early plants evolved in water, using currents for reproduction, but in the Silurian, or even earlier than that, there was greening of the land with a skin of cyanobacteria. Once plants developed the capacity to live on land, with spores with walls and stems and leaves with cuticles that would prevent drying out, stomata to control gas exchange, vascular system to circulate water and tough polymers such as lignin to prevent collapse, then invasion was possible. Mosses and liverworts were probably the first: these have different combinations of land requirements, but not all of them.

Developments in the Devonian Era

The oldest known vascular land plant is Cooksonia found in Silurian rocks in Wales and Ireland, only a few millimetres long; by the Devonian they were several centimetres. Other Devonian plants reached 8 metres in height; Carboniferous ones were even taller, the clubmoss Lepidodendron was 50 metres or more and the horsetail, Calamites, was 20 metres. These forests decayed into the coal deposits found today from Pennsylvania to Poland. They contain fossils of insects with 50cm wing spans rather like giant dragonflies. Gymnosperms, seed bearing plants, first arose in the Devonian; they include seed ferns and the most successful conifers that first carried their cones in the Carboniferous forests.

Early Cretaceous was brightened by the first Angiosperms, flowering plants where the ovule is protected, not naked as in the gymnosperms. They have been successful; their almost identical descendants dominate today's plant life.

The Development of Amphibians

The development of amphibians had marked a significant step towards animal life colonising land. They appeared in two major groups, frogs and toads in the Triassic and newts and salamanders in the Jurassic. To move out from water, amphibians had to solve several problems, impermeable skin, air breathing lungs instead of gills, and skeletal support, especially a rib cage to hold up the internal organs—bodies are not weightless on land as they are in water. However, they could not spread far onto land, needing swampy conditions for their eggs. The first recorded reptile was found in Carboniferous tree trunks where it had gone in quest of insects. Reptilian success stems from laying eggs that could keep themselves wet, with amniotic fluid enclosed in a shell. By the Permian, when hot, dry conditions did not favour amphibians, reptiles on land spread wide and grew ever larger.

The Mesozoic Era: Age of the Dinosaur

The next era, the Mesozoic, is most distinguished in the popular imagination by the dinosaurs. There are two important branches in the structure of these reptiles, the Saurischians (lizard-hipped) and the Ornischians (bird-hipped). The saurischians had a pelvis with a pubic bone pointing forward and downwards; the group included the giant vegetarians such as Diplodocus and Brachiosaurus and the carnivorous (meat eating) hunters like Tyrannosaurus Rex and Allosaurus.

It has been accepted for more than a century now that birds are descendants of dinosaurs. The first specimen of the link between them, the famous Archaeopteryx, was discovered in Germany in 1861. The creature had a mouthful of teeth, claws on its wings, long bony tail but also something new in the fossil record, feathers. Archaeopteryx is very similar to dinosaurs of the bird-hipped group that includes the equally famous Velociraptors. There are constantly new fossil finds that help to "flesh out" the evolution of the birds. As tall plants produced layers of vegetation, gliding and then fflight became a major way of life (a successful one; 70% of all animal species alive today are insects).

The First Reptiles

Contemporary with the dinosaurs, and poised to assume their dominant role, were warm blooded mammals. The first reptiles with mammal-like features appeared in the Upper Carboniferous, but by Late Triassic, 210 mya, the first true mammals are found. Mammals have dispensed with the need to lay eggs outside of their bodies. There are two ways of doing this; the marsupials give birth to tiny, helpless young that must spend months in a pouch suckling milk. Today the marsupials have reached their greatest variety in Australia, isolated by the separation of continents and free from disturbance by placentals, until invasion by humans.

Placental mammals retain young in the womb for longer, nourished by blood through the placenta. The earliest placentals are Cretaceous but they could not diversify until dinosaurs were no longer competition. Then they rapidly radiated to reach twenty orders in the Palaeocene, the ancestors of all modern groups and others now extinct. These include carnivores, insectivores, rodents, ungulates (like pigs, camels, hippo and cattle) and primates. From these primates, first seen in the Cretaceous, emerged hominids. (see **Human Evolution T48–55**).

Summary and Conclusions

This outline of the History of Life on Earth is by no means the definitive story. With each new discovery, of new specimens or from closer examination of existing ones, some chapters will be rewritten. More evidence will be amassed for the causes of major extinctions. There is already substantial support for the impact of an asteroid near the Yucatan Peninsula, to have done for the dinosaurs, with layers of ash corresponding to vast areas of forest fires that would have been the direct result of a hit, abnormally high levels of iridium, a usually rare mineral that is carried by asteroids, and shocked quartz, crystals that are fractured by the shock waves of a massive impact. But so also is there evidence for vast outpourings of lava, the sulphurous and chlorine gasses accompanying which would have poisoned the atmosphere.

Whatever the cause, the elimination of the giant reptiles cleared the stage for the dominance of mammals culminating in the hominids that finally gave rise to Homo Sapiens, the only known species with the consciousness to ask questions about his own origins.

THE MINERAL WORLD

Note

Readers may wish to consult **T47–8** for an outline article on geology, including a description of the main types of rocks and their evolution.

Introduction

Minerals are the constituents of rocks. Every rock has minerals as its building blocks and the nature of these minerals determines the character of the final rock. There are over 3,600 different minerals known to geologists but only six of these are common in rocks – olivine, quartz, feldspar, mica, pyroxene and amphibole. Some specimens are spectacular; varieties of quartz can be over a metre in size. Some minerals are so beautiful that they are valued as gemstones, such as ruby and emerald, varieties of corundum and beryl respectively; others are earthy and rather dull looking yet have huge economic importance, such as hematite and limonite (two types of iron ore).

Types of Minerals

Minerals are naturally occurring solid elements or combination of elements; very few elements occur simply on their own (copper, silver and gold are good examples of ones that do) so most minerals are compounds of ions bonded together with an atomic structure. For example, copper is frequently found bonded together with carbonate, $CuCO_3$, as the pretty green mineral malachite or in a brassy one called chalcopyrite where iron is included in the copper carbonate. The presence of some hydroxide in the chemical bonding will result in the glorious blues of azurite.

Chemical Composition of Common Minerals

Each specific chemical composition does not vary, no matter how small the fragments into which a piece may be broken, because that composition is a fixed ratio. Take quartz, one of the most common of all minerals; its chemical formula is SiO_2, which means that for every one silica atom there are two of oxygen. This one:two ratio is constant for all quartz. Each mineral, to a greater or lesser degree, forms crystals that have a distinctive geometry, such as cubes or prisms, whose faces follow the atomic structure of the molecules making up that mineral. A surprising example of how atomic structure affects a mineral's characteristics comes by comparison of graphite with diamond. Both are composed of carbon but in diamond, the carbon atoms are arranged in a cubic lattice, internally so strong that diamond is the hardest known mineral. In graphite, on the other hand, the carbon atoms are weakly bonded together in flat sheets so that it is soft with a greasy feel. The difference is a result of the position in which the carbon grew. Diamond's strength is a result of greater depth; it forms at the equivalent of 150 km or more deep in the Crust.

Constant Characteristics

Since the chemistry of each mineral does not vary, there is a distinctive set of constant characteristics by which each can be identified, such as colour, hardness, lustre, streak on an unglazed tile, form, cleavage (the preferred direction in which a mineral breaks) and density. A good textbook on minerals will describe fully these features but three common examples will illustrate the point. Calcite, quartz and halite are three common, normally colourless minerals which have a non-metallic lustre. Lustre is the way in which a mineral reflects light; it might be metallic, vitreous like glass, pearly, resinous or greasy, looking as if it were coated with oil. One of the first tests to do to tell them apart is hardness, the ability to withstand scratching, which is assessed using Moh's Scale of Hardness.

Hardness: The Moh Scale

Moh was an Austrian geologist who listed ten minerals from the softest, Talc, to the hardest known, Diamond, and assigned them values of 1 to 10 (1 is Talc, 2 Gypsum, 3 Calcite, 4 Fluorite, 5 Apatite, 6 Orthoclase, 7 Quartz, 8 Topaz, 9 Corundum, 10 Diamond). A finger nail is hardness 2·5 so anything that it can scratch will be softer than that; likewise, a steel blade is hardness 6·5 so anything that it will scratch is softer than it and anything that will scratch it is harder than steel. Calcite will scratch halite which has a hardness of 2. In terms of crystal form all three are different, quartz having well formed six-sided prism shaped ones, calcite has rhombohedral and halite has perfect cubic ones. If the crystals are broken, then both halite and calcite will have perfect cleavage, meaning that they split in planes parallel to the crystal faces; quartz does not have any cleavage and broken faces will be rough or look like the curves of a shell.
Streak is not a significant test for these three, unlike haematite which, though it may look grey or brown, leaves a red streak on a tile. However, there are individual clues which readily distinguish the halite from the calcite (the crystal form and hardness leaves us in no doubt about quartz). In a clear and well formed piece of rhomboidal calcite, any image put under it will be double refracted (two images will be seen slightly overlapping). Also, all forms of calcite will fizz with dilute hydrochloric acid. Halite has one unique characteristic, its taste of salt.

Colours

Quartz has been described above and is the only one of the six that is not a whole family of minerals

although it has several varieties, distinguished by colour, such as rose quartz which is pink and amethyst, purple. These beautiful colours are the result of trace impurities of atoms such as iron or titanium. In large masses, it can be milk white. Where quartz has precipitated from water, it is fine grained with chalcedony an important variety, called agate when it is decoratively colour banded and flint when it is grey and breaks with a conchoidal fracture resembling the growth rings of a shell.
Olivines are pale yellow-green magnesium iron silicates, with vitreous lustre and hardness of 6·5 to 7. The *Pyroxenes* are a diverse family ranging from dark green to black. *Amphiboles* are ferromagnesian silicates of which hornblende is the most common.

Feldspar, Mica and Calcite

Feldspars are a group of aluminium silicate minerals that account for 60 % of all minerals in the Earth's crust, common in oceanic crust and, with quartz, comprising 75 % by volume of the continents. The strange name is Swedish and means "field mineral", a reference to the frequency with which it needed clearing from farmland. Feldspar family minerals are not glassy like quartz but appear porcelainic and dull. There are two common types, either orthoclase which is red, pink or whitish, or plagioclase, green, dark grey or white in colour but *striated* (scratched in parallel grooves). When feldspars break, they do so along flat, rectangular faces.

Mica has black/shiny (biotite) and white/pearly (muscovite) forms but both are distinctive because they can be peeled into thin, flat, transparent sheets.

Calcite is a carbonate, not a silicate, but, though of little significance in terms of the whole crust, it is common in sedimentary rocks at the surface.

Igneous Rock Granite

Igneous rock granite (*see* **T**48) is a good example to show how minerals form the building blocks of rocks since all the crystals, whether well- or partly-formed, are clearly visible to the naked eye. There are interlocking crystals of feldspar, mica and quartz; usually the feldspar has the best developed crystals because it was the first mineral to begin to crystallise out from the molten magma. Quartz forms at the lowest temperature and so it "fills in" between the pre-existing solids. Often minerals grow in restricted spaces and so perfect faces cannot form. Much more important to a geologist is the angle between the faces which will be constant, in the case of quartz, 60 degrees, no matter what the size of those faces.
Ore minerals have economic importance. Iron as an oxide, either Fe2O3 Haematite or Fe2O4 Magnetite, the only mineral that will swing a compass needle, and with sulphur as pyrite. Others include Bauxite (aluminium) *etc.*

MOBILE PHONE CONCERNS

The Background

The number of mobile phones in use in the UK has now passed 50 million. Increasingly, the new handsets are being used not just for voice communication, but also to download data from the internet, images and – with the advent of the "third generation" (3G) phones – full video communication. To support this growing demand, an expanding network of over 35,000 base stations has been built across the country. At the same time, there has been a growth in concern and suspicion over the possible negative health effects of these new technologies.
In essence, mobile phones – and the base stations they communicate with – work as simple radio transmitters and receivers. They produce the same electromagnetic waves which we use – at differing

frequencies – to broadcast radio and television, or to heat food in a microwave oven. The question is one of degrees. Are the exposure levels used in mobile phone communications safe? The consensus of scientific opinion is that they are, but scepticism in the public remains.

Monitoring the Risks

A number of national and international bodies monitor the scientific research into the potential risks in order to fix maximum exposure levels. In the UK, the National Radiological Protection Board (NRPB) has adopted safety limits set out by the International Commission on Non-Ionizing Radiation Protection (ICNIRP). The quantity that is being measured is the Specific Absorption Rate (SAR) that shows how much energy is absorbed by the body over a specified time. The current ICNIRP guidelines are for a SAR of no more than 2 watts per kilogram.

Handsets

The power of radio transmission falls away rapidly at a distance. This means that even in a room full of phones, exposure levels could still be very low (a SAR of just fractions of a watt per kilogram). However, when placed at the ear to make a call, obviously a handset will have a much greater effect on the head. Methods of measuring this effect have differed, but a newly accepted standard shows that no phone currently on sale in the UK generates a SAR greater than 1·5 watts per kilogram. To some, this seems dangerously close to the guideline limit of 2. Remember though that the limit already has a conservative safety factor built in (the ICNIRP applies a safety factor of 50 for exposure levels on the general public. *i.e.* the real limit – where effects of the exposure would be expected to start – is more like 100 watts per kilogram). Also, the SAR values quoted are for peak outputs. In many situations the handset will operate at a much lower level. For example, when signal strength is good, power is saved by broadcasting at a weaker signal.

SAR values for the different handsets are available for comparison. An industry body called the Mobile Manufacturers Forum lists the SAR values on their website at http://www.mmfai.org.

Base Stations

The location of mobile phone base stations in the UK is often the source of controversy. Local residents often worry about exposure levels, health and the effect on property prices. Because of the difficulty in measuring absorption by the whole body, the guideline limits set out are not in terms of the SAR, rather a more complex power density score. This is further complicated by the fact that different power densities are set for different frequencies of broadcast (to reflect, for example, the fact that our bodies will interact less with certain signals, such as the new 3G range). To make the measurements simpler, levels are quoted in terms of the fraction of the guideline limit. The encouraging news is that nearly all surveys of exposure in public areas have found levels to be only fractions of a per cent of the guideline limit.

One interesting consequence of the research even suggests a possible benefit of living close to a base station, for anyone who is themselves a user of a mobile phone. Close proximity means a better signal, which means your handset will step down the power of its own transmission, reducing the amount of energy it radiates to the body.

Precautionary Approach

Despite the upbeat analysis from the industry and its advisory bodies, it remains true that – as with any new technology – it is impossible to say for sure that there are no long-term problems. For example, most of the emphasis has been on the thermal effects of the fields; what if other subtle interactions are going on inside cells? Also, many people think it is too simplistic to set a single safety level; what if some members of the population are particularly susceptible? In recognition of these additional concerns, bodies such as the NRPB recommend a precautionary approach to mobile phone usage. Adults are encouraged to use their phones less and to favour a hands free kit. The recommendation for children under the age of eight, who may be most affected by any yet to be determined factors, is not to use a mobile phone at all.

Like many other international bodies, however, the thing that the Board would most like to see is much more research in the area so we can understand more precisely what the issues are.

SCIENCE NEWS AND NOTES

Optical Storage

Over the past two decades, we have become familiar with the *compact disc* (CD) and, more recently, the *digital versatile disc* (DVD). These are examples of optical storage. Their popularity is due to a combination of structural stability and high storage capacity, whilst also able to be rewritten.

A CD consists of a series of pits which encode the digital information stored on it. These pits are produced by injection moulding in a mass-produced read-only disc, or by laser ablation in a disc produced as a one-off, for example in a home computer. The pits in a rewritable disc are created by modifying a special polymer from its crystalline state to its amorphous state. In each case, however, the method of reading the data is the same. Light from a laser is focused by a small lens to a tiny spot which is the same size as the pit. The light reflects back through the lens and is detected. The pits reflect light less well than the areas around them, allowing them to be distinguished.

Increasing Storage Capacity

A CD can hold 650 Megabytes of information per layer. One way of increasing the storage capacity would be to reduce the size of the pits. This demands that the laser beam be focused to a smaller spot, which can be achieved by changing the colour of the laser light or by improvements to the lens. CDs are designed for lasers with a wavelength of 780 nanometres (infra-red). DVDs work with a laser at a wavelength of 650 nanometres (red), allowing an eight-fold increase in storage to 4·7 Gigabytes (GB). This improvement followed the development of cheap and compact lasers at shorter wavelengths.

Compact blue lasers with a wavelength of 405 nanometres have now been developed and will be used by the next generation of optical discs, called *Blu-ray discs*, giving a further increase in storage capacity to 50 GB for a double-layer disc. A further enhancement to 250 GB per layer is anticipated by giving the pits an angular substructure. Importantly, equipment for reading each of these discs is compatible with older types.

The idea of holographic storage is discussed below.

Holography

Two properties of a wave are its *intensity* and its *phase*. Considering a wave on the sea, the intensity of the wave is related to its height at a specific point, while the phase indicates the relative position of that point to the wave crests. A camera measures the intensity of light waves from a scene. The resultant photograph is a two-dimensional representation of that three-dimensional scene. The third dimension is lost because phase information is not recorded.

In holography, coherent light waves from a scene and from a light source (the *reference wave*) cross each other and interfere. (Light is said to be coherent if the waves within it have the same phase.) This means that the two waves add or subtract, depending on their phases, giving a pattern of speckles. Imaging this pattern – the *hologram* – allows us to record both intensity and phase information. To reconstruct an image of the scene subsequently, it is only necessary to shine a reference wave on the hologram.

We are familiar with holograms as security

devices on credit cards. An interesting application under development is optical storage. CDs and DVDs are limited in the amount of information that they can store by their surface area, while the rate at which they can be read is low because each pit is read separately. In contrast, many superimposed holograms could be recorded throughout the thickness of the disc and each hologram, equivalent to perhaps a million pits, could be read in one go. Materials exist which would make both write-once and rewritable storage.

If a hologram is illuminated by light equal to the scene originally imaged, then it is the reference wave that is reconstructed instead. When multiple holograms are illuminated by information-rich light, the holograms which correspond most closely to that information will reconstruct the brightest reference waves. This gives holographic storage the particular advantage that it may be searched by content.

Depth-Resolved Imaging

A second promising application is depth-resolved imaging. Light is scattered by, for example, body tissue, making it difficult to see objects under our skin. A small proportion of the light is not scattered, however, and could be used to produce an image if it could be separated. Holography provides a solution because only the non-scattered light reaches the detector within the coherent time of the laser illumination and contributes to the hologram. The depth imaged can be adjusted by changing the path length of the reference beam. Devices exist that can be used to write and read the holograms in real time.

Quantum Computing

Information in computers is in the form of *bits*, which can have one of two values: "0" or "1". (In practise, these values correspond, say, to preset levels of electrical voltage.) During the past few decades, computers have become part of everyday life. Their increasing pervasiveness is due in large part to their speed of operation, which is however, fundamentally limited by the serial processing of individual bits. Parallel processing of the bits would give computers new capabilities and allow them to operate even faster.

Qubits

In quantum mechanics, the strange paradox of Schrödinger's Cat is that a particle (or cat) in a sealed box can be simultaneously in two states (dead and alive) until we look inside it. Quantum bits, known as *qubits*, are just the same – their value can be 0, 1 or both at the same time: the *superposition* state. Qubits can be, for example, photons or atoms. Similarly, when we come to measure a qubit in the superposition state, it will have a value of 0 or 1. A system will retain its ability to have such states as long as no measurement takes place; this characteristic is called *quantum coherence*. In addition, systems can be *entangled*, that is to say they hold properties not present in the individual constituent parts. When entangled superpositions of qubits form the input to a quantum computer, the output is a superposition of the results for each input qubit. This parallel processing is the driving force behind research in quantum computing, one of the most active areas in contemporary physics.

At present, there is no physical quantum computer, in part because it is difficult to manufacture large numbers of satisfactory qubits. However, the key concepts have been demonstrated experimentally and a real quantum computer is the goal.

Bioglass

When a foreign object is introduced into the body, whether as small as a virus or as large as a hip prosthetic implant, the body makes a response (inflammation) and tries to reject it. In the latter case, a hard fibrous capsule envelops the hip prosthesis where it is in contact with the bone and soft tissues. Because the two are therefore poorly integrated, they move against each other and further damage to the surrounding tissue occurs. As a result, the prosthesis must be replaced after

around ten years. An ideal prosthesis would be chemically bonded to the tissue, such that the bond is at least as strong as the tissue and prostheses themselves.

Indeed, some glass and glass-ceramic materials have been discovered that are not rejected by the body, but which are actively incorporated. Glass consists of a mixture of mineral oxides, the proportions of which are varied for different tasks. A simple glass, used for windows and bottles, consists of oxides of silicon, calcium, sodium and phosphorous. Depending on their proportions, such a glass will elicit the same fibrous response as a standard bone prosthesis, be resorbed or bonded to bone – when it is termed *bioglass*.

Bone consists of a dense fibre network of the protein collagen onto which is bound crystals of hydroxyapatite. This is a mineral largely consisting of calcium phosphate, whose elements are also found in glass. Indeed, when pieces of bone and bioglass are brought into contact in a physiological environment, a series of chemical reactions takes place producing a transition layer between the two which contains hydroxycarbonyl apatite derived from the glass. The collagen fibres from the bone bind strongly to bioglass and are locked into the bond as the apatite grows around them. This is similar to the processes which occur in order for collagen fibres in ligaments and tendons to bind to bone.

For a very restricted range of glass compositions, bioactive glasses will bond not only to bone, but also the soft tissues which surround them. Such a bioglass is then suitable for use as a prosthesis and is currently used in a number of non-load bearing applications including eye socket reconstruction, periodontal repair and ossicle (the bones in the middle ear) prostheses.

Advances in Robotics

The recent successes of Nasa's Rover Mission to Mars have amply demonstrated many of the latest advances in the field of robotics. None of the predecessors of the *Spirit* and *Opportunity* robots – dating right back to the early Russian moon rover *Lunokhod* – had anything like their degree of sophistication or autonomy. With stereoscopic cameras and a range of other detectors harvesting a vast quantity of data for the scientists back on earth, these 'Robot Geologists' travel on six independently steered wheels and can examine rock samples using drill bits and microscopes at the end of a titanium arm.

Technologies from a robotic arm developed on another space mission, the International Space Station, have been tested in a very different field. Testing has now begun on a Canadian robot designed to help conduct brain surgery. Always operating under the control of an experienced surgeon, the two arms of the robot have the ability to make extremely precise movements and also provide high levels of monitoring and observation, thanks to integrated 3D video cameras and Magnetic Resonance (MR) scanning equipment. It is hoped that these tools will allow the surgeon to navigate with far more precision inside the brain.

New Map of the Universe

Despite Nasa's cancellation of its essential servicing mission and the likely slow demise of the instrument that will follow, the Hubble space telescope continues to be our foremost tool in examining the very oldest and furthest objects so far discovered. Through this telescope, and other radio and optical telescopes on the ground, we have amassed huge amounts of information about the structures that we share the universe with. Mapping this information presents a great challenge, but a recent attempt by astronomers in the United States has managed to put the entire thing down on a single piece of paper. Just as the first cartographers found ways to draw the curved surface of the globe on a flat page, the creators of the new map use a simplification – or projection – that, while obviously loosing some information about three-dimensional positions, still preserves many characteristics of the layout of the universe, including local shapes. One of the features that can clearly be seen on the map is the Sloan Great Wall, a 1·37 billion light years long collection of galaxies – the largest observed structure in the universe.

Superfluids and Superconductors

The importance of the strange behaviour of superfluids and superconductors has been recognised by many in the scientific community, including those that are responsible for awarding the Nobel prize (from the prize given to Heike Kamerlingh Onnes for his discovery of superconductors in 1910, through to the prize for physics that went to research in this area in 2003). To produce these effects, materials often need to be cooled very close to absolute zero, so that their atoms derive almost no motion at all from their heat. In these situations quantum physical effects take over. Fluids, which usually have at least some measure of viscosity or stickiness, suddenly loose all their resistance to internal movement. Once stirred, a superfluid will experience no drag and so will continue to circulate forever. Similarly, a material which can carry a current, should it enter a superconducting state, will suddenly loose all electrical resistance.

Supersolids?

It is possible that yet another new type of matter has been observed recently too, that of the 'supersolid'. Researchers working with a porous form of glass (filled with highly cooled and pressurised helium) found that a spinning disc of their new material would begin to move much more easily at a particular temperature. It is thought that strong coherence between adjacent atoms in the lattice of such a solid could permit such frictionless behaviour.

DICTIONARY
OF
COMPUTING

This brief section in *Pears* provides a concise glossary of many of the key terms currently in use in the fast-changing world of computers, information technology and the communication revolution in the new century.

DICTIONARY OF COMPUTING

A

Access Time. In a disc drive or other mass storage device, this is the time taken to find and retrieve a particular piece of information, or block of data. For a disc drive it is the time taken up by the lateral motion of the head assembly (seek time) and waiting for the disc to rotate sufficiently for the area of interest to be under the head (rotational latency).

Ack. Abbreviation of Acknowledge. One of the characters transmitted for the purposes of handshaking in a data transfer. The character is sent back to the transmitting device by the receiving device to confirm that the last block of data has been received.

ActiveX. An adaptation of Microsoft's "Object Linking and Embedding" (OLE) technology which allows small programs, called "Controls" to be run from within HTML pages on the World Wide Web. The programs provide additional functionality beyond that contained within the HTML standard. Ideally the running of the Control is handled by the browser, requiring no additional action on the part of the user. It can provide similar functionality to Java.

ADC. *See* **Analogue to Digital Converter.**

ADSL. An abbreviation of Asymmetric Digital Subscriber Line (or Loop). A method of transmitting both digital and voice signals over an analogue telephone line. The digital transfer is optimised such that the bandwidth for receiving data is considerably greater than that available for transmitting data. The absolute bandwidth is limited by the quality of the subscriber's line, and is variable. Typically the data rate from the subscriber will be up to 640 kilobits per second, while data incoming to the subscriber will be up to 9 megabits per second. It is ideally suited for provision of Internet access through a telephone line, being much faster than a standard modem connection. *See also* **Data Rate, Modem.**

AI. *See* **Artificial Intelligence.**

AIFF. Abbreviation of Audio Interchange File Format. A method for storing and distributing audio as computer data, developed by Apple Computers for their Macintosh range and adopted by other companies. Unlike the AU standard the Apple system uses linear encoding. It is also used for exchanging soundfiles over the Internet. *See also* **AU, WAV.**

Algorithm. In a computer, a sequential group of rules which, taken as a whole, will solve a specific problem. Each rule is sufficiently unambiguous that it can be executed by a machine. The algorithm can be considered as a symbolic representation of the problem. Generation of the algorithm is one of the stages of writing a computer program. The more accurately the algorithm models the problem, the more effective will be the program which results from it.

Algorithmic Composition. The use of, or a facility within, software to help music composition. Essentially computer generated music. Sometimes called Computer Aided Composition.

Aliasing. In digital video systems (especially computer screens) an effect that occurs to a greater or lesser extent when a curve is displayed on a video screen. On close inspection it is possible to see that the curve is approximated by jagged steps or "jaggies". The term is also used to describe a type of unwanted noise generated in digital audio systems if the sampling rate is less than twice the highest frequency found in the wanted signal.

Alpha Test. *See* **Bug.**

Analogue to Digital Converter. The encoding part of a digital device whose function is to sample an analogue signal such as sound or video and derive a numeric (binary) value from it at regular intervals.

Anti Virus. Software to provide a solution to virus programs. Often, such programs work in an organic manner, inhibiting reproduction prior to elimination. The anti virus software may either be used as a response to a specific infection and employed thereafter, or may be working constantly in the background. This background scanning of the computer's facilities will only interrupt the user upon finding something that is undesirable and that requires the software to resolve.

Apple. A brand of personal computer. Apple is the main competitor on hardware and operating system to the IBM PC clones and Windows, respectively. Apple is known for its trend setting and stylish design.

Applets. *See* **Java.**

Artificial Intelligence. The concept (almost an article of faith for some) that computers will be able to, or can now, behave in a manner that resembles human intelligence, in that they will be able to learn to perform a task rather than require programming, be able to adapt to changing levels or types of input, perform deductively or reason and possibly even imagine. More strictly the branch of computer science which deals with such problems as pattern recognition and knowledge based or expert systems. Many new technologies are contributing to developments in this area including neural networks (one neural network now exists with 40 million artificial nerve cells) and bioelectronics.

ASCII. Acronym from American Standard Code for Information Interchange. One of a number of standard systems which determine how a specific character is represented by a specific binary numeric value in a computer. Thus the character "A" is represented by the number 65. ASCII is a seven bit code and thus allows 128 characters to be uniquely defined. The intention was to ensure that text data could be transmitted from one machine to another. There is a so called extended ASCII which is an eight bit version of ASCII used by IBM for its PCs. *See also* **UKASCII, EBCDIC.**

ASIC. Acronym from Application Specific Integrated Circuit. Essentially an integrated circuit (usually LSI) which has been manufactured to have a particular function, and which might replace an assembly of general purpose ICs which did the same job *e.g.* the image processing circuitry in a printer.

Asynchronous. A form of data transfer between two devices which have separate, free running clocks. In order to ensure that data are not missed, each byte is preceded by a start bit and succeeded by a stop bit. RS232C is asynchronous.

Attachment. An additional enclosure to an email, that does not form part of the message. An attached file is often signified by a paper clip sign.

AU. Abbreviation of AUdio. A method for storing and distributing audio as computer data, developed by Sun Computers and adopted by other companies. It is also used for exchanging soundfiles over the Internet. Unlike the AIFF standard, the Sun AU system uses a logarithmic encoding scheme for its 8-bit formats; this is akin to audio compression and results in an apparently increased dynamic range equivalent to about 12-bit linear encoding at the expense of added noise. *See also* **AIFF, WAV.**

AV. Abbreviation of Audio Visual. Sometimes applied to computer systems which are optimised for processing sounds and images, for Multimedia work *etc.*

B

Back Up. (1) A copy of data which has been taken from a computer system and is stored separately from it. The intention is that the data can be restored to the computer in case of any accidental loss of the original. The back up can take the form of any type of memory such as floppy disc, RDAT *etc.* (2) A source of power such as a battery used when the main source of power has been removed. Normally encountered in devices such as synthesisers *etc.* whose memory contents are preserved by an internal battery when the device is switched off.

BASIC. Acronym from Beginner's All-purpose Symbolic Instruction Code. *See* **High Level Language.**

Baud Rate. The rate at which data are transmitted, and encountered with reference to MODEMs, Fax *etc.* If methods such as data compression and error correction are not being used then Baud Rate can be synonymous with bits per second (BPS), and related to the number of characters per second. In general it requires 10 bits to transmit a character such as a letter "A" (8 bits plus 1 start and 1 stop bits). So in these circumstances the character rate is one tenth the Baud Rate or BPS. However data compression can have the effect of representing more characters with the same or fewer bits, so the relationship between Baud Rate and character rate becomes less simple particularly at higher data rates.

Beta Test. See **Bug.**

Bidirectional. A form of data transfer which allows a device to receive and transmit data simultaneously. Also called Full-Duplex. The ability to receive only or transmit only at any given time is called Half Duplex.

Binary. A way of representing numbers using only two symbols "0" & "1". The system is described as a base 2 numbering system and follows the same rules as the more familiar base 10 or decimal system. In decimal each column is 10 times bigger than the one to its right (1000, 100, 10, 1). In Binary each column is 2 times bigger (8, 4, 2, 1). Any decimal number can be represented in binary although it may require more columns. In binary the columns are called Binary digITs or BITS for short. It is used by computers as it is easy to tell whether a voltage is present ("on" or "1") or not ("off" or "0"). Because of the relatively large number of columns or bits used to represent numbers, binary numbers are sometimes compressed by presenting them in hexadecimal (base 16) form, whereby one hexadecimal digit represents four binary digits.

bis. French for "again", a suffix added to some CCITT V-series standards to indicate derivation. For example V.32bis is a fast (14,400 BPS) derivative of the V.32 standard (9,600 BPS).

Block. In a mass storage device such as a disc drive, the smallest amount of data that can be accessed is called a block, it being more efficient to store a fixed minimum amount. A block is typically 512 or 1024 bytes. Also used in a general way to describe an amount of data being transmitted or processed.

Bluescreen. A text only screen with white characters against a blue background. Indicative of a Fatal Error from which the computer cannot recover without restarting, and sometimes indicative of a more serious error requiring hardware replacement.

Bluetooth. A method of wireless transmission of communications between devices such as a mobile telephone and a hands-free earpiece. It is based around radio transmissions, which have a strictly limited range.

BPS. Abbreviation of Bits Per Second. See **Data Rate.**

Broadband. The next step in the communications revolution. A high-capacity technology becoming available over adapted telephone lines, via fibre-optic cable and by wireless systems. It can carry greater volumes of data at speeds up to 40 times faster than current systems.

Browser (also Web Browser). A software interface between user and an object, usually Internet downloads. A Web Browser consists of, among other things, a viewing area, navigation buttons, drop down menus and a URL bar. See also **URL.**

Bubble Printer. See **Printer.**

Buffer. An area of memory used for temporary storage of data, particularly as an intermediate stage between two devices which operate at different speeds. The presence of the buffer allows the data to be held until the slower device is ready to accept it.

Bug. A fault, defect or error in computer hardware or, more usually, software, which results in incorrect operation. To some extent bugs are inevitable. Indeed there is a body of mathematical thought which suggests that it is not possible to prove that a program is without error (this is an important issue for software controlled systems which are required to be 'intrinsically safe' such as flight automation and nuclear or chemical process control). For this reason most software houses can only rely on a two tier testing of their products. In-house or Alpha tests are designed to check that the program functions according to the design specification, and external Beta tests are intended to check that the program doesn't do anything which was not part of the design specification, like format the user's hard disk. Beta testers are usually trusted 'power users' who will put the program through its paces and report faults only to the authors of the software. A computer system which exhibits bugs is sometimes described as 'flaky'.

Bulletin Board. A computer fitted with a MODEM which allows similarly equipped people to make contact and to download information, software etc. from that computer to their own. The process of making the initial contact is usually called "Logging On". These often have a sort of club atmosphere as they tend to be aimed at people with a particular interest. Many universities etc. have them and they are a good source of the cheap software sometimes called shareware.

Burn. The process of transferring data to CD-R. The name derives from the use of a laser beam within the CD re-writer to "burn" pits onto the metallic surface of the CD to represent binary codes.

C

CAD. Acronym from Computer Aided Design. The D is also variously taken to stand for Drawing, Draughting and Dealing (stock markets). Other Computer Aided areas include CAEngineering, CAManufacture or Music and CAComposition.

Cancel. One of the characters transmitted for the purposes of handshaking in a data transfer. The character is sent back to the transmitting device by the receiving device to indicate that the receiver wants the transmission to cease.

Card. An alternative description for a printed circuit board.

Carrier. A signal which can be changed (modulated) in such a way that the changes in the signal can represent information. For example a continuous tone can be changed in pitch between a high and low pitch. These changes in pitch then effectively become binary data which can be used to represent text or images etc. Such a system could be described technically as a "frequency modulated carrier", and is the basic method whereby Modems and fax machines work.

CAV. Abbreviation of Constant Angular Velocity. In a mass storage device such as a disc drive, it refers to the fact that the disc rotates at a constant speed. This means that the data rate will increase for a track at the edge of a disc and decrease for a track in the centre of the disc, in much the same way as the outside pair of skaters in a line spinning around a central skater will be going much faster than the pair on either side of the central skater, although the speed of rotation of the line of skaters is constant. See also **CLV.**

CCITT. Abbreviation of Consultative Committee for International Telephone and Telegraph. A body which defines international standards for communication systems, such as fax machines, modems etc. Individual standards are often identified by V number prefix e.g. V.22, V.34bis, V.42 etc.

CD. Abbreviation of Compact Disc. A digital audio storage medium consisting of a 5 inch disc upon which digital audio data are recorded in a manner which allows them to be read by an optical laser for replay.

CD+MIDI. A type of CD ROM which includes both digital audio data and MIDI data. This means that a recording of the sound of a musical performance and the MIDI data which were used to generate the performance, are simultaneously available to the user, although in some cases the MIDI data might be for additional musical parts which do not appear in the sound recording. In any case this allows the user to "play with" the performance by choosing different sounds etc. on their MIDI network.

CD-I. Abbreviation of Compact Disc-Interactive. A system whereby images (maps, pictures etc.), text and sound are placed on a CD, along with a program which enables a computer to present all this information to a user in an interactive manner. A typical example might be an map disc, combining maps with pictures of locations on the map, text which describes the locations and the sounds which are heard at those locations etc. In principle anybody can access the information at will. In practise, there are often limitations on what is possible. See also **Interactive.**

Checksum. A simple means of error detection employed in data transfer between devices in a network. The checksum is a numeric value which is the result of some calculation performed on the data which are being transmitted. It might simply be the sum total of all the data, but other, more elegant methods tend to be used. The resulting value is then transmitted along with the block of data. The receiving device will then perform the same calculation on the data and compare its result with the checksum it has received. If there has been no error in the transmission (*i.e.* no data have been lost or changed) the checksum values will be identical. If the receiving device produces a different result, it will normally request that the data be sent again. In general the checksum can only tell a receiving device that a transmission error has occurred, it does not carry sufficient information to allow the error to be corrected. This limits the usefulness of checksums to data transfers which are non-real time *i.e.* it doesn't matter how long it takes the data to be transmitted. In situations where the data have to meet a deadline *e.g.* the digital to analogue converter in a CD player it is desirable to be able to detect and correct the error. *See also* **Error Correction**.

Chip. *See* **Integrated Circuit**.

CIRC. Acronym from Cross Interleaved Reed-Solomon Code. *See* **Error Correction**.

CISC. Acronym from Complex Instruction Set Computer (pronounced "sisk"). Essentially a microprocessor which has an elaborate and powerful instruction set which is ideal for implementing a general purpose microcomputer such as a PC. *See also* **RISC**.

Clipboard. In a computer, a temporary memory area which can be used to store sections of text or pictures, so that they can be moved within the current program, or transferred from one program to another. The clipboard generally holds only one thing at a time and this will usually not be preserved if the computer is switched off. *See also* **Copy**, **Cut** and **Paste**.

Clock. In a computer, a high frequency (typically 5 Mhz or more) oscillator which generates a pulse wave. This is used as a timing reference to ensure that each of the separate sections of the computer (memory, CPU *etc.*) operate in a synchronised manner. The clock rate can be a very crude indicator of the performance of the computer.

Clone. A term used to describe a device which offers the same facilities and compatibility as an established product made by a different manufacturer. Most commonly encountered to describe IBM-PC type computers made by companies other than IBM *etc.*

CLV. Abbreviation of Constant Linear Velocity. In contrast to CAV a mass storage system that has a disc whose speed varies, thus keeping the data rate at the head constant irrespective of the head's position on the disc. CD is an example of this method.

Coding. The process of altering the form of a signal or data. There are normally two complementary stages: encoding is the process which converts from the original to the new form, decoding is the process which converts back from the new to the original form. Coding methods are adopted for a number of reasons: to standardise data to make it easy to transfer between otherwise incompatible machines; to protect the data from errors which might occur during transfer (Error Correction); to reduce the size of the data file (Data Compression); or to make the data unreadable by the unauthorized (Encryption).

.com (pronounced **dot com**). A generic term for any business either based on the Internet or with a Web presence. It has increasingly been associated with the negative aspects of the .com bubble.

Compact Disc. *See* **CD**.

Compiler. A program that takes the "raw" code of a programming language and converts it into a executable program. *See also* **.exe**.

Compression Ratio. In data compression the ratio of uncompressed to compressed data. An indication of the saving in storage or increase in transmission speed which the data would otherwise require.

Computer. A device, usually electronic (the hardware), which processes data which are input, according to a set of instructions (the program or software) to produce data which are output. Almost all available computers conform to "von Neumann" architecture, which means, in essence, that they perform instructions one after the other and cannot do more than one thing at a time, although they may do serial operation so quickly that it appears parallel to our sluggish minds. Computers can be broadly classed according to speed or power in decreasing order: supercomputers, mainframes, minicomputers and microcomputers or personal computers (PCs). However the distinctions are not always clear cut; many personal computers are classed as micros, but are as powerful or fast as mainframes of a few years ago. For example the engine management systems of some cars have greater computing power and memory than the mainframes which ran the early Apollo space shots. The main computers found in UK homes, schools and businesses are the IBM PC and its "clones", and the Apple Macintosh. Acorn (especially in schools), Atari and Amiga also have some share of the computer market. Many pieces of technology available today, from cars to microwave ovens, also have considerable computer capability.

Computer Generations. Computers can be categorised according to power and type of technology into "generations" in the sense that each new generation is different from the last by virtue of some improvement in technology or design. Thus: first, *c.* 1951 using valve technology & magnetic or paper tape storage; second, *c.* 1961 using transistor technology and having separate systems to handle input & output thus freeing the CPU and programmable via a high level language; third, *c.* 1965 using SSI & MSI ICs and using hard disc storage, thus reducing physical size and improving reliability; fourth *c.* 1984, using LSI & VLSI technology and allowing networking and multitasking; fifth, 1990s, using VLSI technology, parallel processing using RISCs or Transputers, for artificial intelligence (AI) and expert systems applications.

Contiguous. Literally meaning "alongside" from Latin *contigere*, to touch. In a mass storage device such as a hard disc, it refers to the practice of allocating blocks of data that are physically next to one another on the disc. This is advantageous as it means that once a track on the hard disc has been accessed, the head need not be stopped again until that track has been completely read.

Controls. *See* **ActiveX**.

Copy. In a computer, a command which places a previously selected section of text or picture in the clipboard so that it may be repeated elsewhere, either within the current program or another. *See also* **Cut**, **Paste**.

Copy Protection. A term most commonly used to describe any of various systems designed to prevent multiple copies being made of an original, or less commonly, a system such as the knock-out tabs on audio and video cassettes or the write-protect shutters on floppy disks and RDAT cassettes, which prevents inadvertent overwriting of an original. In the former sense with application to proprietary software it includes the use of hardware dongles, keys or registered user-passwords. *See also* **Encryption**, **Hacking**.

CPU. Abbreviation of Central Processor Unit. In a computer, the device or integrated circuit that actually carries out the computing processes.

CRC. Abbreviation of Cyclic Redundancy Checking. A method of error detection employed in data transfers such as FTP. The greater the number of bits used to define the CRC, the more reliable it is. ZMODEM uses a 32 bit CRC which is more reliable than the 16 bit CRC of XMODEM.

Cripple Ware. An ironic term which describes versions of computer software with some crucial features disabled (they might not load or save data, or they might quit after a short period of running). Often issued free to demonstrate the software to potential users.

CRT. Abbreviation of Cathode Ray Tube. A large valve used to display TV pictures or computer data.

Ctrl Alt Delete. A method of getting to the Task Manager menu in Windows. Commonly used to get around stalled or malfunctioning programs. Also common for accessing log-on menus in network based PCs.

CTS. *See* **RS232C**.

Cursor. The position on a computer monitor, usually indicated by a solid or flashing mark, where text *etc.* will appear or can be changed. On some systems the cursor can be moved with a mouse or trackerball *etc.*

Cut. In a computer, a command which places a previously selected section of text or picture in the clipboard and simultaneously removes it from its current position, so that it may be moved elsewhere, either within the current program or another. *See also* **Copy**, **Paste**.

Cylinder. A term used by some manufacturers to refer to the entire surface of a data disk. The two sides of a floppy disk are considered by them to be like the surfaces of two separate cylinders. In a hard disk with several platters the cylinder is a set of tracks which coincide vertically on the platters.

D

DAC. *See* **Digital to Analogue Converter.**
Daisy Chain. A type of network whereby devices are connected one behind the other. In a network of seven devices a message generated by device 1 for device 7 is passed through (and ignored by) devices 2 to 6. SCSI is an example of this.
DAT. *See* **RDAT.**
Data. The information operated on by a computer as it executes a program. In general the data inside a computer are intended to be a representation of some aspect of the "real" world, that is, the data are symbolic. In digital audio the data represent sound. In digital video the data represent an image. Data is strictly a plural noun, the singular being datum.
Data Cartridge. Essentially a RAM or ROM integrated circuit packaged in a plastic box or thin card, which plugs into a computer or other device. This allows alternative versions of the device's internal memory to be stored, or new software *etc.* to be added to the device. PCMCIA is an example of this.
Data Compression. A process whereby the quantity of data required to represent some real world thing such as a sound or picture, is reduced by a variety of more or less successful means, so that the data occupy less space in a mass storage device, or can be transmitted in a shorter time. Most systems which do this operate with a compression ratio of between 2:1 and about 4:1. For data which represent text the process has little deleterious effect, but as you don't generally get something for nothing, you would be wise to expect some reduction in the quality of the sound or picture upon conversion from the data compressed form. Luckily humans are remarkably tolerant of "lossy" data compression.
Data Protection Act. UK legislation governing the storage and use of data about consumers or individuals. Based around five founding tenets and passed in 1998 as a response to EU legislation.
Data Rate. The rate at which data are transferred from one place (*e.g.* a hard disc) to another (*e.g.* a computer). It is usually measured in Bits Per Second or kilobits per second (kb/S), but occasionally (and less meaningfully) in bytes per second. Sometimes called transfer rate.
Database. A category of computer software which allows a user to collect information or data about a number of different types of things, and keep it in a standard format. The user can then search through the information to find specific items of interest. The term is also used to refer to the collection of data itself. Properly speaking the total collection of information is called a datafile, the datafile is divided into records, where each record is a unique set of information *e.g.* an entry in the address book for s specific person. Each record is divided into fields, where each field is a particular unit of information *e.g.* a telephone number, a county, or a post code. Databases are useful for purposes other than address lists: stock control and statistical research are common uses.
DCD. *See* **RS232C.**
DCE. *See* **DTE.**
Decoding. *See* **Coding.**
Default. The condition adopted by a device when it is first powered up and has not yet received instructions which would cause any change to the condition. Most machines will simply be in whatever condition they were in prior to being powered down. Others will be completely blank, or in some more or less useful predetermined condition set by the manufacturers.
Desktop. A generic name for a type of personal computer system with separate components joined by cables, that is large enough to occupy part of your desk. Originally coined to distinguish between such devices and larger stand alone mainframes and minicomputers *etc.* The term is also used to refer to an abstract "desktop" environment represented on a computer screen by some user interfaces such as Windows or the Apple Desktop.
Desktop Publishing. Also called DTP. A category of computer software which allows a user to generate complex and finished documents such as magazines, books, display adverts, brochures *etc.* The user will be able to do such fancy things as "flow" the text

around a picture so that it follows the boundary of the image, as well as the more mundane aspects of layout and style. Although superficially similar to a word processor, it is optimised to the creation and altering of layouts *i.e.* where text goes, rather than the initial keying of the text. It is not common to find a DTP software with a spelling checker, although this feature is common on word processors. Therefore the DTP software will normally be used to produce a layout or template into which the text, previously generated by a word processor, will be imported.
Digital Domain. An imaginary land where everything is described in terms of numbers. Thus when a signal is converted into digital form and then modified by the application of arithmetic so that the signal is altered in some way, for example, to reduce the amount of red in a colour picture, this is said to take place in the digital domain. If the digital data which represent a picture are transferred from one piece of equipment to another without conversion, the transfer is said to take place in the digital domain.
Digital Signal Processing. The modification of a signal which has first been converted into digital data, involving the application of arithmetic to the numbers which represent the signal. For example if a sound has been converted into digital form, making all the numbers 45% bigger will increase the amplitude of the sound, thus implementing a digital amplifier. In principle any process (tone control, *etc.*) can be applied to a sound in this way. The process can be also used to generate sounds from scratch, instead of relying on an existing set of data. This is the principle of most digital synthesisers. Similar processing can be applied to digital images, for example to reduce the amount of blue in a picture, or to increase contrast. Often shortened to DSP.
Digital to Analogue Converter. The decoding part of a digital device whose function is to sample binary values, at regular intervals and derive an analogue signal from them.
DIMM. Acronym for Dual In-line Memory Module. A collection of RAM chips mounted in two in-line blocks on a printed circuit board with a row of metal contacts along one edge. The modules have a different wiring arrangement in comparison to SIMM which allows a 128 bit data path. *See also* **RAM, SIMM.**
DIP Switch. An array of miniature (and fiddly to operate) switches, usually in groups of eight, which are sometimes fitted to devices to allow the user to preset certain functions for that device. DIP is an acronym from Dual In-line Package, a standard method of packaging components or circuits inside an oblong plastic or ceramic case with two rows of metal legs or pins, one on each of the long sides of the rectangle.
Direct to Disc Recording. The practice of recording digital audio data (or more recently video data) to a hard disc for later replay or editing.
Directory. In computer systems a term used to describe a collection of files in a mass storage device such as a hard disc. In its simplest form it may consist of a list of files. In more elaborate forms it may adopt a hierarchical structure with multiple directories being connected together like the branches of a tree. A directory may then have sub-directories in the same way as a branch has sub branches or twigs. From this metaphor the lowest level of a branched directory system is called the root or root directory.
Dither. (1) Dithered, Dithering *etc.* In digital video, a method of interpolating colour information between adjacent pixels, so that for example, an 8-bit imaging system with only 256 discrete colours can apparently represent the greater colour range of an image stored with more bits per pixel. (2) In digital audio, the principle of adding a small amount of random white noise to the signal with the intention of reducing the distortion which occurs when the signal level falls between resolution steps close to zero, *i.e.* those encoded by the LSB. *See also* **Quantisation Error.**
DMA. Abbreviation of Direct Memory Access. Many computers require that the CPU spend some of its precious time looking after the movement of data in and out of the memory. If a computer uses DMA the memory is controlled by a dedicated processor (MMU) which frees the processor from this tedious task. This has the effect of speeding up the task that the CPU is trying to carry out.

Dongle. A piece of hardware whose presence is required and verified by a piece of software before that software will run at all or, in some cases, become fully functional. It is one of a number of systems of copy protection. Usually it takes the form of a cartridge containing a ROM of some sort or a custom IC, which plugs into a socket on the computer. If the dongle is a ROM, it will probably contain a serial number which matches that of the software. If it contains a custom IC this will usually perform a mathematical function on a value generated by the software, the result of which is already known to the software. If the software gets the wrong answer (which includes no response) it may not load or it may start up in a 'demo mode' where it runs but with key features, such as the ability to load or save files, inhibited. *See also* **Hacking.**

DOS. Acronym from Disc Operating System. Often used as a short form of various operating systems for IBM PCs. *See also* **Operating System.**

Dot Matrix. *See* **Printer.**

Dot Pitch. *See* **DPI.**

Download. The transfer of a file, most commonly a web page, from host computer (the server) to the client computer for viewing or use upon the client computer.

DPI. Abbreviation of Dots Per Inch. An indication of the resolution of graphic imagers, such as computer monitors and printing systems. The higher the number, the greater the ability to show fine detail. Most laser printers operate at 300 DPI and this is quite adequate for most purposes, typesetting quality printers operate at 1200 or more DPI.

DSL. Digital Subscriber Line.

DSP. *See* **Digital Signal Processing.**

DSR. *See* **RS232C.**

DTE. Abbreviation of Data Terminal Equipment. A class of equipment, most commonly computers or printers, which can be directly connected via the RS232C interface to DCE (Data Communication Equipment) such as MODEMs.

DTP. *See* **Desktop Publishing.**

DTR. *See* **RS232C.**

DVD. An optical storage medium akin to the CD but with much greater storage capacity. The greater storage capacity, 4.7 Gigabytes as opposed to 700 Megabytes, is due to greater accuracy in the laser that reads the disc allowing much higher density of the pits upon the surface of the DVD that signify binary digits of data.

Dynamic HTML. A rather nebulous term for technologies which add functionality to standard HTML such as JavaScript, Java, ActiveX *etc.*, as well as for features of the "official" HTML fourth generation. Such functionality can include altering a previously displayed image or playing a sound when the mouse pointer is passed over the image *etc.* The effect is to make the page more "interactive" with the user. *See also* **HTML.**

E

EBCDIC. Acronym from Extended Binary Coded Decimal Interchange Code (pronounced "ebsdick").

e-commerce. the practice of conducting business via the Internet, particularly applied when the business has no conventional outlets. Prime examples are businesses such as "amazon.co.uk".

EIDE. *See* **IDE.**

Email. Abbreviation of Electronic-MAIL. The use of computers, as communication devices for sending text, graphics, or other data such as MIDI files or software *etc.* Particularly used with reference to computer communication over telephone lines using MODEMs. First created in a US computer lab in 1971. *See also* **Bulletin Boards.**

Emulator. A system of software and/or hardware which allows a computer to run applications written for a different type of computer. In general, but not always, the application will run at a slower speed on the emulating computer than it would on its intended platform.

Encoding. *See* **Coding.**

Encryption. The alteration of a piece of information by some coding process so as to make it secure from unauthorised users, or to allow recovery from errors which might otherwise occur, when the information is transmitted from one place to another. *See also* **Error Correction, Hacking, Password Protection.**

EPROM. Acronym from Erasable Programmable Read Only Memory. A type of memory which can be written to once, read many times and subsequently erased, which distinguishes it from ROM and other types of WORM, (although erasure generally involves removing the EPROM from its circuit). The most common erasure method is exposure to strong ultra violet light for an hour or more. There is also EEPROM where the first E stands for electronic and specifies an electronic method of erasure.

Erase. The removal of the recorded data from a data storage device, such as a floppy disc or hard disc. In practice the actual data are not erased, but the directory area of the storage device, which keeps a record of where data are, is erased. As it is no longer possible to find the data, they might just as well not be there. Systems that allow an unerase, are able to reconstruct the directory, and therefore find the data, as long as no new data have been recorded since the erasure was carried out. Also the removal of data from a memory device such as EPROM, although generally this cannot be undone.

Error Correction. A process whereby data which are being transferred from one computer to another, particularly via MODEM, can be protected against minor errors. The system is also used internally on some pieces of equipment such as CD and CD-ROM players. The data have extra pieces of information in the form of known "keywords" added to them. These extra pieces of data are interleaved or combined with the original data in such a way that if there is a problem in the data path (*e.g.* noise on the 'phone line or a scratch on the CD surface) which leads to the keyword becoming corrupted, the error can in most cases (but not always) be corrected. This is possible because of the interleaving method, the fact that the keyword is known, and therefore the precise way in which the data have been altered can be worked out and reversed. Methods include Microcom Network Protocol (MNP) and Cross Interleaved Reed-Solomon Code (CIRC).

.exe. A file extension that denotes that the file is executable, a program in its own right. Often an indication of a suspicious program being present where an attachment should only be usable in conjunction with another program.

Executable. Said of any file which contains instructions or commands that can be carried out by a computer, *i.e.* the file contains some sort of computer program.

Expansion Slot. A socket provided on a piece of equipment, usually a computer, which allows additional hardware components to be added.

Export. In a computer, the act of placing data generated by the current program into a file which can be accessed by another program. This will be possible only if the data are formatted in a way the other program understands. This leads to a number of standardised file formats, such as TIFF and PICT for graphic images, AIFF and WAV for audio files and SYLK for database/spreadsheet files.

F

Fibre Optic. A method of data transmission in which a light beam (usually generated by a laser) is shone along a thin glass or plastic "cable". The light beam is turned on and off very rapidly in order to represent the bits of the digital word. The system can carry a much greater rate, and therefore amount of data, than most conventional electronic means, and is virtually immune to electromagnetic interference (EMI).

File. In a computer, a quantity of data which have been previously stored in such a way that they can be retrieved in the future. The storage will probably be a floppy disc or hard disc. In general the file is identified by a name which must be unique, unless it is the intention of the user to overwrite (and therefore destroy) the existing data with a new set. The act of creating such a file is called "saving" or "closing", while the act of retrieving the data in the file is called "opening".

File Extension. The combination of a dot followed by three letters to denote what type of file is present, or what package it was made in. Not to be confused with the Internet addresses of the type ".com".

File Sharing. The practice of creating a temporary peer-to-peer network between two (usually) private

PCs over the Internet. This is commonly for the exchange, without charge, of music, film or software stored on one of the PCs. It is almost always in contravention of copyright and piracy laws.

Firewall. A software application, or a hardware device, to try to prevent unwanted material accessing a computer. Most firewalls work by examining what may be concealed within seemingly innocuous codes or files. If anything suspicious is found, the files are quarantined and the user notified.

Firmware. In a computer system the physical medium in which the software is contained e.g. a floppy disc, ROM or magnetic tape, as distinct from either the abstract form of the software itself, or the hardware which is controlled by it.

Flaky. See **Bug.**

Floppy Disc. A device for long term storage of computer data. The device is so called because of the floppy plastic disc surfaces which it uses rather than the hard metal surfaces used in hard discs. These plastic surfaces have a lower density of storage and slower speed of operation than hard discs. Floppy discs start at about 300 Kilobytes and currently go up to about 1.4 Megabytes.

FLOPS. Acronym from FLoating-point OPerations per Second. An indication of the numeric processing or "number crunching" speed of a computer. See also **MIPS.**

Flow Control. See **Handshaking.**

Font. A collection of symbols (usually letters, numbers etc.) of a given design, in a particular style and point size. Part of a typeface. e.g. "Times" is a typeface, whereas "12pt. Times Bold" is a font of the Times typeface.

Fragmentation. A condition of random access disc drives, particularly hard discs etc., whereby long use and the pattern of erasure and writing will result in a file being discontiguous or fragmented, i.e. distributed over several areas of the disc instead of one contiguous file. The overhead of hunting around the disc and gathering up the various separate sections of the file will slow down its retrieval. Disc optimising software is available which can defragment a hard disc by shuttling the various file sections around into complete, contiguous files all at one "end" of the disc, with all the empty sections joined together at the other end.

FSK. Abbreviation of Frequency Shift Keying. A method of transmitting computer data via media which normally accommodate audio signals (e.g. telephone lines or audio tape), using two distinct frequencies to represent the binary states "on" & "off" of digital signals. It was quite commonly used in the early 1980s as the primary means of storing computer data, before disc drives became popular and is occasionally encountered as a system for "backing-up" disc drives.

FTP. Abbreviation of File Transfer Protocol. A system of data transfer which checks for errors in the data. If any are detected the receiver requests the data be present in the hope that the error will not occur again. The error checking method is Cyclic Redundancy Checking (CRC). Varieties of FTP include ZMODEM which uses a 32 bit CRC and flow control, and XMODEM, which uses a 16 bit CRC and does not require flow control. FTP is most commonly encountered on the Internet.

Full Duplex. See **Bidirectional.**

G

GEM. See **Operating System.**

GIF. Abbreviation of Graphic Image Format. A file format for transferring images as computer data. It indexes the colour information of the image according to a colour table with a range of 256 or fewer colours. It is perhaps less suitable for photographic type images which typically have many millions of colours but is perfectly suitable for artwork. It is one of a number of graphic formats used on the Internet. See also **JPEG.**

Gigabyte. 1,073,741,824 bytes. Not 1,000,000,000 as you might expect, but the nearest power of 2 which is close to a billion. This is a result of the influence of binary numbers on computer engineers.

GIGO. An abbreviation of Garbage In, Garbage Out. A comment upon the limitations of computers and their lack of human traits such as interpretive skill.

GIPS. Acronym from Giga Instructions Per Second.

See also **MIPS.**

GPS. Abbreviation of Global Positioning System. A network of 24 satellites used to provide information about the location of a person or object on the earth's surface. The satellites each contain atomic clocks and transmit synchronised radio signals. A GPS receiver will compare the signals from as many as six of the 24 satellites and by calculating the relative delay between these signals (arising because of their varying distances from the object or person), will arrive at a grid reference for the location. For commercial GPS this is accurate to about 30 metres. Military versions are said to be accurate to about a metre.

Graphic User Interface. The ability of a device such as a computer (usually a function of the operating system) to symbolise and represent objects or concepts as pictures on a monitor which can be manipulated using a mouse or keyboard etc., as opposed to the text based interfaces of older technologies such as UNIX, or PC-DOS used on IBM PCs. It is considered more intuitive and easier to use, especially by computer novices.

Graphics. The use of pictures (as opposed to text) on a monitor by a computer. This very often has the advantage of making the computer more understandable or intuitive to use. Also the manipulation of pictures or video images by a computer.

GSM. Abbreviation of Global System for Mobile Communications. This is an international standard for transmission of digital signals to mobile phones. GSM makes possible enhanced services such as SMS and WAP. See also **SMS, WAP.**

GUI. See **Graphic User Interface.**

H

Hacking. Originally a term derived from 'hack', to describe an emergency or temporary modification of a computer system to fix a bug, but more recently used in the specific context of unauthorised modification of a computer system, and by extension any unauthorised access of such a system. Hacking became a cult underground activity in the late 1970s and early 1980s as many amateur (and professional) computer users found that they could access or 'hack into' systems which controlled billing of telephone and other utility services for their financial benefit, as well as cause general mayhem irrespective of benefit to themselves. A war of attrition has developed between hackers and their opponents who seek to ensure that distributed information systems (national and international telephone and data networks) remain secure, with each in turn leapfrogging the other. Hacking is also used to describe the practise of removing or bypassing copy-protection systems such as dongles from computer software to facilitate piracy. See also **Virus.**

Half Duplex. See **Bidirectional.**

Handshaking. In data transmission, the process of checking that a receiving device is ready to receive or that a transmitting device is ready to transmit. Or the method whereby such checking takes place. It is the principal means of stopping and starting the data transmission, a process otherwise known as "flow control". Two types are commonly described: Hardware handshaking where the data cable has conductors in addition to the normal receive and transmit wires, and which carry flow control signals in the form of changing voltage levels; and Software handshaking where particular codes called "X On" and "X Off" are sent in amongst the normal data stream. From this explanation it should be apparent that hardware handshaking is more expensive to implement as the data cable requires more connections. However it is essential for high speed data transfers or those which use error correction or data compression.

Hard Copy. Words or images printed on paper as opposed to soft-copy which has the same data but printed on a computer screen.

Hard Disc. A device for long term storage of computer data. The device is so called because of the hard metal disc surfaces which it uses rather than the floppy plastic surfaces used in floppy discs. These metal surfaces allow much greater density of storage and much higher speed of operation than floppy discs. Hard discs start at about 80 Megabytes and currently go up to about 9 Gigabytes (equivalent to about 10,000 floppies). Very large hard discs (above say 1 Gigabyte) are only usually encountered where large amounts of digital audio or video are being stored in "direct-to-disc recording".

Hardware. The electromechanical parts of a system, especially a computer system where the term is used to draw a distinction between the physical machine, the firmware and the abstract software that instructs it.

Header. Additional data which prefix a block of data either in a stored file or for the movement of data between devices. These data usually represent a description of the block of data which then follows. Postscript files which define the appearance of text and images for printers *etc.* use headers.

Hexadecimal. A numbering system using base 16. It is often used to represent equivalent binary values as the hexadecimal form is more convenient since one hexadecimal digit is equivalent to four binary digits. The system requires 16 different symbols and these are derived using the normal 0–9 supplemented by the letters A–F. *e.g.* the decimal number 1310 is represented by D16 in hexadecimal.

High Level Language. A computer programming language that is reasonably close to ordinary human language. Its significance is best understood by comparing it to low level language. This is the language the CPU understands, more specifically each program instruction corresponds to a machine code instruction executed in a single machine cycle. In a high level language, a single instruction that might read PRINT "so and so" would have to be compiled or interpreted by an interim process into a number (possibly hundreds) of machine code instructions, which are then executed. While it is possible, if laborious, to program in a low level language, a programmer will prefer to work with a high level language as it more closely resembles the language used in everyday thinking. Basic, Forth, Lisp and Pascal are high level languages.

Hotmail. The Microsoft Corporation's own web-based email service. It is often seen as the market leader and instigator of market trends, such as commercialisation, charges for storage capacity and mass spamming.

HTML. Abbreviation of HyperText Mark-up Language. A system of "tags" which are embedded into the text of a document intended for the World Wide Web. The tags control the way the document is laid out and displayed, as well as allowing graphics and even sounds to be included in the pages. The most powerful feature of HTML as originally developed by Dr. Tim Berners-Lee at CERN, was the inclusion of tags which allow linking between HTML documents. The simplest of such links is the highlighting (perhaps by a different colour, or underlining) of a word or phrase. This marks the text as a referential "Link" to another document which can be activated by a mouse click. When activated the text of the linked document is called replacing the current document. Since its inception in 1990 HTML has evolved through a number of generations, each one providing new functionality to Web pages. Unfortunately these changes have occasionally been browser-led with the leading browser suppliers adding unofficial, idiosyncratic and competing features to HTML as implemented by their browser. In some cases these are adopted into the official HTML standard. Such leapfrogging can be confusing for HTML authors. The current fourth generation caters for so called Dynamic HTML with such features as cascading style sheets and support for objects implementing JavaScript, Java Applets or ActiveX Controls.

HTTP. Abbreviation of HyperText Transfer Protocol. An Internet protocol for specifying World Wide Web documents. It typically appears at the beginning of a web page URL.

Hyperlink. A method of direct referral from one web page to another. Hyperlinks can be text or graphical, within a web site or referring to another separate web site.

Hypertext. A system available to a computer user which can store a large amount of data as a database and which has a user interface that allows so called "interactive" access to the data. In practise this might mean that the user does not have to approach the stored data in any sequential way, but can hop intuitively from one area to another. It might also mean that data is presented in a hierarchical manner, such that the most obvious bits are presented first and the user can then request that a particular section be expanded to provide more information about that specific area. The interface may present pictures as well as text. The WWW is a hypertext system.

I

Icon. A form of graphics where a picture is used by a computer to symbolise some sort of job carried out by the program. For example a picture of a wastebasket may be present on the monitor, any object placed in the wastebasket will be deleted. In general any picture which can be manipulated as a unit is an icon.

IDE. Abbreviation of Integrated Drive Electronics. A system for interfacing hard disc drives *etc.* which is used by IBM PCs and clones. The essential feature of IDE is the fact that the intelligent electronics are integrated on the disc drive as opposed to being carried on a separate card plugged into the PC's expansion slots. EIDE (Enhanced IDE) overcomes some limitations of speed and storage capacity of the earlier standard. It is effectively an alternative to SCSI.

Imagesetter. *See* Printer.

Import. In a computer, the act of placing data generated by another program into the current program. This will be possible only if the alien data are formatted in a way the current program understands.

Information Technology. *See* IT.

Inkjet. *See* Printer.

Instruction Set. A complete set of all possible instructions that a microprocessor can carry out. In the early years of microprocessor design the emphasis was on producing a wide variety of powerful and extended instructions, but it was found that programmers tended to use a small number of basic (forgive the pun) instructions to do almost every job. The recent fashion in certain applications has been to restrict the number of instructions to these basic functions, as the fewer instructions a microprocessor has, the faster it can execute any given instruction. This approach is particularly suited to microprocessors built into a product that has a specific purpose such as a printer and microprocessors using this approach are described as RISC. However if the microprocessor is going to live in a general purpose machine like a personal computer, where versatility takes precedence over speed of execution, it is convenient to have as elaborate an instruction set as possible and microprocessors using this approach are described as CISC.

Integrated Circuit. A method of compacting electronic circuits into a small space. This is achieved by manufacturing several tens, hundreds, thousands or even hundreds of thousands of diodes, transistors, *etc.*, more or less simultaneously onto one common semiconductor base called a substrate. There exist rough divisions of scale *i.e.* how many devices are present of SSI, MSI, LSI, VLSI. The components are joined by tiny tracks which are separated by distances comparable to wavelengths of light. This is the reason it is possible to see rainbow-like reflections off the surface of an IC. Connections to the outside world are made through tiny single strand wires much thinner than human hair. The complete assembly is typically only a millimetre or two square and is extremely fragile. In order to make the IC easy to handle and more robust it is generally packaged in some plastic material with the tiny wires welded to flat pins, which are then arranged in rows on the sides of the package. All manner of useful circuits from amplifiers to computers are available in this form.

Integrated Package. In a computer, a collection or suite of software, which combines the most common types of business software (usually database, word processor and spreadsheet). The package should be designed so that data from one program can be easily transferred to another within the package. This would allow a standard or form letter to be keyed in the word processor, but with blanks for personal names *etc.* The personal names would be held in the database database and would be added to the form letter during printing. This allows the user to send essentially the same letter, but personalised, to each customer, without the otherwise tedious task of manually filling in the name.

Intel. The best known and largest of the companies making IBM compatible PC microprocessors. Founded by Gordon Moore. It is of such importance in the market that television and other adverts routinely make space to advertise that the Intel brand is incorporated into the advertised product.

Interactive. In computing and media-speak, a two way communication process, with "mutual and simultaneous activity on the part of both participants" (Andrew B. Lippman) which has the following features: Interruptibility, one participant can interrupt the other without having to wait until the end of the current topic; infinite destination, the direction of the interaction can lead anywhere, not just to specific preprogrammed destinations. A lecture is not usually interactive, a conversation with a friend often is. Humans are very good at interaction, computers currently are not very good. Interactive is a vogue or hype word at the moment, however, few of the systems are properly interactive in the above sense. Some CD-I systems feature city maps which at first glance are very impressive. The user can "navigate" up a street and turn left (or right) into another street at will and see the correct buildings going past. Entering buildings is not however possible as the CD does not contain information about them. Such a system is interruptible, but has finite destinations, so it is not truly interactive. But it is a start. The projected major area for interactivity is computer aided learning. *See also* **Virtual.**

Interface. That which joins, or the point of connection of two joined things. Usually used to refer to electrical connections and their associated data structure such as MIDI, or more abstractly, in the sense of user interface the environment (graphic images on a monitor, front panel switches, keyboard *etc.*) in which a human communicates with a machine.

Interlaced Scan. A method of displaying an image on a video screen or monitor using two or more complete scans of alternate lines of the image area. For example the system might scan (display) the even numbered lines and then return to the top of the image and scan the odd numbered lines. As there is a persistence effect both in the imaging system and the human eye then given a suitably fast refresh rate the image appears complete. Interlace is sometimes used as a synonym for "interleave" with reference to data systems.

Interleaving. A method of arranging, or rearranging, data according to some systematic rule, to increase the efficiency of a data storage device, or so that the data may be protected during transmission. *See also* **Error Correction.**

Internet. A global network of interconnected computers. Originally conceived as a "fault tolerant" method of connecting America's military computers, the system is now widely used and serviced by academic institutions, businesses and individuals. The system is a collection of computers connected by local national networks (including the telephone system) to Network Servers which are in turn connected internationally. It is hard to estimate the numbers of computers involved but currently it is probably at least 20 million and could be as many as 100 million. In any case it is set to increase in size. It is used for electronic mail (E-Mail); forums or newsgroups where particular interests or hobbies can be discussed; as well as publishing and broadcasting of information, software, audio and video. The World-Wide Web (WWW or W³) is a system for displaying information on the Internet in a graphic (as opposed to purely textual) manner, with intelligent or "hypertext" links between different areas of the Internet.

IO Device. *See* **Peripheral.**

ISDN. Abbreviation of Integrated Services Digital Network. A standard which allows high capacity direct data transfers through the telephone and other telecommunications networks obviating the need for MODEMs *etc.*

ISP. Abbreviation of Internet Service Provider, companies providing us with access to the Internet. Such companies may offer services such as website design, web hosting and telephone support on technical matters.

IT. Abbreviation of Information Technology. A generic term for all types of devices involved with information processing, storage, recovery *etc.* In general (especially educational) usage it simply means "computer-stuff".

J

Java. A programming language developed by Sun Microsystems which produces platform independent programs (in principle they can be made to run on any computer), called "Applets" which can be run from within HTML pages on the World Wide Web. Applets provide additional functionality beyond that contained within the HTML standard. Ideally the running of the Applet is handled by the browser, requiring no additional action on the part of the user. It can provide similar functionality to ActiveX.

JavaScript. In essence it can be considered a subset of Sun Microsystems Java programming language. It was developed by Netscape Communications Corp., to provide additional functionality to HTML pages on the World Wide Web beyond that contained within the HTML standard (so called "Dynamic HTML"). Unlike Java, a fully fledged programming language which produces stand alone applications (Applets) which are called and run by an HTML tag, JavaScript is a scripting language which is understood and implemented directly by the browser which is displaying the HTML page containing the script. In this way it can be seen as an extension of the HTML standard as it allows HTML authors to control how the browser responds to the user's interaction with the page, even, for example, generating web pages on the fly according to the user's requirements. It was standardised by the European Computer Manufacturers Association (ECMA) in June 1997.

JPEG. Abbreviation of Joint Photographic Expert Group. A committee of scientists, programmers, mathematicians *etc.*, which formed to specify the standard also known as JPEG, for a data-compression based graphic image file format, which would make it possible to transfer near photographic quality images as computer data. The system works by removing as much redundant information (large areas of the same shade on a balloon, for example) from the image as possible, thereby reducing the file size required to store the image and the bandwidth required to transmit it. It is "lossy" compression method in that some information about the image is thrown away. Usually when creating JPEG files the user has control over the compression ratio. Increasing the compression reduces the file size, and reduces the quality of the image. Some images will compress considerably with barely imperceptible loss of quality while other more complex images will not compress well at all. It is one of a number of graphic formats used on the Internet. *See also* **GIF, MPEG.**

K

kb/S. Abbreviation of Kilobits Per Second. *See* **Data Rate.**

Keyboard. A collection of keys in a staggered but broadly rectangular pattern, which are differentiated by symbols, and which forms a means of input of data into a computer. There are a number of stories which purport to explain the apparently irrational order of symbols in the keyboard layout (in America, Britain and much of Europe this layout is called QWERTY—from the top left row of keys). The most common of which suggests that they were laid out in this manner to slow enthusiastic operators so as to prevent jamming of the mechanism. This is fairly unlikely as even a slow typist can jam a manual machine. More likely is the explanation that one of the original manufacturers operated schools to train typists on their layout. As their layout was different from that of their rivals they increased sales by creating a work force of trained typists who would only work on one layout, forcing prospective employers to purchase machines of that type. Various attempts have been made to improve the efficiency and ergonomics (*see* **RSI**) of keyboards and these have produced quite suitable devices such as the almost eponymous MOLD keyboard that looks just like a jelly mould. In general these have not been very successful due to the historic and universal establishment of the existing layout.

Keyboard Shortcuts. Combinations of particular keys on a computer keyboard which have the same effect as using a mouse to select a function or facility from a menu in a WIMP environment. Usually they will be mnemonic. For example, pressing the 'Control' key and the 'S' key simultaneously will have the same effect as selecting 'Save' from the 'File' menu. Likewise 'Command C' might be the same as selecting 'Cut' or 'Command P' might be the same as 'Print'.

Kilobyte. 1,024 bytes. Not 1,000 as you might expect, but the nearest power of 2 which is close to a thousand. This is a result of the influence of binary numbers on computer engineers.

L

LAN. Stands for Local Area Network. Indicates a network within a specific geographical proximity and usually under the control of one organisation. *See also* **WAN**.

Laser Printer. *See* Printer.

LCD. Abbreviation of Liquid Crystal Display. A type of flat monitor, which is used on some computers (particularly those designed to be portable). Often monochrome, but more recently allowing colour display.

Least Significant. The rightmost value in any number system. In the decimal number 5,463, three is the least significant number as subtracting it would not make much difference to the value. *See also* **LSB**.

Line Printer. *See* Printer.

LINUX. An alternative operating system to Microsoft Windows. It is notable for a number of reasons. As a product of the Open Source movement, it is essentially free (other than production and distribution costs). It was also programmed by individuals using the Internet for communication. It is named after the instigator of the project, Linus Torvalds, who originally sought to write his own version of the UNIX operating system, hence Linus's Unix. Other notable points include its arguable superiority and stability over the version of Windows against which it was released.

Long Word. *See* **Word**.

LSB. Abbreviation of Least Significant Bit. The rightmost bit or column of a binary number. So called because it has the least effect on the result of any sum involving the number. Occasionally in 16 bit or more (*i.e.* multi byte) systems it may be taken to stand for Least Significant Byte when referring to the rightmost byte for similar reasons. LSN is Least Significant Nibble.

LSI. Abbreviation of Large Scale Integration. An integrated circuit which contains about 1,000–90,000 active elements. *See also* **MSI, SSI, VLSI**.

M

Machine Code. In a computer, the numbers which represent individual instructions which can be executed by the CPU in a small number (1–4) of clock cycles. It is the lowest level at which a human programmer can work (inside a microprocessor there is a lower level called microcode, which the chip uses to perform the specific function, but this is built into the chip at the time of manufacture and is transparent to the programmer).

Magneto Optical. A method of mass storage in the form of a disc drive with removable discs held in cartridges. When writing information the system utilises a laser to heat the disc's surface thus altering its magnetic properties. The same laser or another can then scan the disc whose reflectivity is changed according to the pattern of magnetism laid down by the writing process. Once written the cartridges can be removed from the drive, which is advantageous in applications where data-portability is required.

Mainframe. A type of computer (strictly speaking of the third generation) which was first introduced in the mid-1960s and which took advantage of the (then) new SSI & MSI technologies. Machines of this type include the ICL 1900 series and IBM 300 series. More generally the term is used for a physically large computer which is located centrally to a network of users, each with their own terminal.

Mass Storage. A device or system for storing large amounts of data. There is a historical progression

in the meaning of Mass in this context. Ten years ago a computer might have had "mass storage" of only 100 Kilobytes. "Mass" at the moment probably means more than 80 Megabytes, as the smallest hard disc that is worth making is about this size.

Master. In a system of devices, it is sometimes useful to have one device which governs the operation of the others (particularly as regards a timing reference, for example). This device is nominated the Master, the other devices become "slaves".

Megabyte. 1,024 Kbytes or 1,048,576 bytes. Not 1,000,000 as you might expect, but the nearest power of 2 which is close to a million. This is a result of the influence of binary numbers on computer engineers.

Memory. An area in a device such as a computer, where data are stored prior and subsequent to some manipulation determined by the program which the device executes. The memory can be in a variety of forms, such as semiconductor, magnetic tape, CD, floppy or hard disc. Memory is functionally classified according to whether data can only be read from memory (ROM) or can be both read and written (WORM, RAM), irrespective of the material form the memory takes.

Menu. In a computer system, the presentation to the user of a list of options, from which a choice may be made.

Microcomputer. A type of computer which is based on a microprocessor and which will probably include the keyboard and monitor in the same (or closely linked) package. The term is more or less synonymous with personal computer, or rather, a PC is a type of microcomputer.

Microprocessor. An integrated circuit (usually LSI) which has the function of the central processing unit (CPU) of a computer. It is the mass produced nature and comparative cheapness of these ICs which have contributed to the stupendous growth of information technology since the mid 1970s.

MIDI. Acronym from Musical Instrument Digital Interface. An internationally agreed standard of electronic hardware and language of commands, which allows musical (and increasingly non-musical such as lighting) equipment to be controlled and manipulated in a useful manner. It can also be defined as a system for encoding a musical performance digitally in such a way as it can be stored, manipulated and replayed on a computer. But it should be understood that it is only the instructions necessary to carry out the performance and related aspects which are encoded digitally and not the sound of the performance itself. Multimedia or "AV" (audio-visual) computers often implement MIDI.

Minicomputer. *See* **Computer**.

MIPS. Acronym from Million Instructions Per Second. Invariably prefixed by a number *e.g.* 400 mips, and intended to give some indication of the performance of a computer (usually one in the supercomputer class). However the indication can be misleading, as it does not take account of factors such as access time to memory or storage devices. As a result some computer engineers wryly explain it as "Meaningless Indicator of Performance Speed". As technology improves GIPS is becoming more common (Giga is 1,000,000,000 or a billion).

MMU. Abbreviation of Memory Management Unit. *See* DMA.

MNP. Abbreviation of Microcom Network Protocol. Proprietary standards for Error Correction (MNP2-4), or Data Compression (MNP5) for use with communication devices such as modems and adopted into CCITT V.42 and V.42bis.

MODEM. Acronym from MOdulator/DEModulator. A device which allows digital data to be transmitted and received via a standard voice or telephone line. It essentially uses FSK (*q.v.*) as a means of converting the digital data into an audio signal suitable for a voice line. Data rates for MODEMs vary from between 300 to 28,800 BPS, although by employing data compression equivalent transfer rates as high as 115,200 BPS can be achieved.

Most Significant. The leftmost value in any numbering system. In the decimal number 5,463, five is the most significant number as subtracting it would make a great difference to the value. *See also* **MSB**.

Motherboard. A printed circuit board that forms the main component onto which all other components in a PC, for example the hard drive, processor and power supply unit, are connected. The motherboard facilitates the smooth operation of all components and peripherals.

Mouse. A hand operated control which is free to travel across a horizontal surface. In its most common form, it consists of a ball in a frame which rolls over the surface when the mouse is moved. Movement of the ball in two dimensions is transmitted to sensors inside the mouse. The movement is interpreted and used to position a cursor on a computer monitor. It is usually fitted with one or more switches, the pressing of which will select or activate an area of the computer monitor currently under the cursor. Essentially it is an upside down tracker ball and is used instead of a tracker ball or joystick. Other forms have no ball but work optically by shining a pulsed LED at a semi-reflective surface. Lines printed on the surface decrease the intensity of the reflected light and this interference in the pulse rate is interpreted as movement.

MP3. MP3 is a subset of the MPEG-1 standard (its full title is MPEG-1 audio layer 3) and is used to transfer audio files between computers, most typically via the Internet. The maximum compression ratio can be about 12:1. This is considered to have very little noticeable effect on the content of the file which is usually music. There is some controversy surrounding MP3 as it is known that it is used to distribute pirated copies of music CDs. A program called a ripper is used to copy the music data on a CD onto a computer's hard disc where an encoder program achieves the data compression and formatting of the MP3 file. As indicated above the MP3 file might be as little as 8% of the size of the unencoded audio file. A number of manufacturers produce portable MP3 players which can be used to replay MP3 files downloaded from a computer. *See also* **MPEG.**

MPEG. Abbreviation of Motion Picture Expert Group. A committee of scientists, programmers, mathematicians *etc.*, formed to specify the various standards for data-compression based graphic image and audio file formats. The MPEG-1, MPEG-2, MPEG-3 and MPEG-4 standards make it possible to transfer moving images such as film, or video, as well as audio, as computer data. In some ways it is an extension of the still image JPEG standard. It is one of a number of moving-image formats used on the Internet. *See also* **JPEG, MP3, QuickTime.**

MSB. Abbreviation of Most Significant Bit. The leftmost bit or column of a binary number. So called because it has the most effect on the result of any sum involving the number. Occasionally in 16 bit or more (*i.e.* multi byte) systems it may be taken to stand for Most Significant Byte when referring to the left-most byte for similar reasons. MSN is Most Significant Nibble.

MSDOS. *See* **Operating System.**

MSI. Abbreviation of Medium Scale Integration. An integrated circuit which contains about 100–900 active elements. *See also* **LSI, SSI, VLSI.**

Multimedia. The mixed use of text, visual images and sound by a computer or other system, or the integration of music, picture and other effects during a presentation.

Multiplexer. A device which switches an input sequentially or in some other ordered fashion between a number of outputs or vice versa. This occurs in some computer communication systems as well as between components inside a computer.

Multisync. A term used to describe the facility of some computer monitors to display output from several different computer platforms without hardware modification.

Multitasking. A much abused phrase intended to suggest the ability of a computer to carry out more than one job simultaneously. In fact von Neumann architecture computers (which includes almost all currently in use) are serial operators and can only execute one instruction at a time. At best, all you can say is that the separate jobs are done sufficiently quickly that a human considers them to be almost simultaneous. In practice multi-tasking requires more memory and processor speed than is commonly found in domestic and even full scale business computers. Although these technologies are improving all the time, even research level computer workstations slow down noticeably when given more than one task to perform. The term is frequently used to describe a process whereby, once loaded, different software packages can coexist in a computer allowing the user to switch from one task to another. However in this case the previous task is generally suspended or at least given very low priority.

N

Nak. Abbreviation of Not Acknowledged. One of the characters transmitted for the purposes of handshaking in a data transfer. The character is sent back to the transmitting device by the receiving device to inform it that the last block of data has not been received without error and that it should be retransmitted. *See also* **Ack.**

Nibble. In computers and digital systems a group of four bits, *i.e.* half a byte (evidence that computer engineers do possess a rudimentary sense of humour!).

Non Volatile Memory. In a computer system, a type of memory whose contents will be retained during the time that the system is unpowered. This is either due to the presence of an alternative or back up source of power such as a battery (especially in the case of semiconductor memory), or because the memory is magnetic and does not require power to maintain the contents.

Non-executable. Said of any file which contains no instructions or commands that can be carried by a computer, *i.e.* the file contains data only.

Null Modem. A type of cable which can be used to connect equipment of the same type (such as two computers) together for data transfer. The cable is wired with "crossover" connections *i.e.* the transmit pins at each end are not connected together as is usual but instead are connected such that the transmit pin at one end is connected to the receive pin at the opposite end *etc.* The effect is to persuade each computer that it is connected to a MODEM.

O

Off Line. In a network of devices, the condition of any device which is unable to receive or transmit a signal.

On Line. In a network of devices, the condition of any device which is able to receive or transmit a signal.

Open Source. A movement within software and involving software programmers that believes that the end user of the product has the right to see the constituent parts of the product that they use. This generally means the source code, or written program instructions that, when compiled, creates software. Most famous of the Open Source products is LINUX. LINUX versions are delivered with the original source code available to read on a CD. One of the virtues of this approach is the ability to customise, or to make more responsive, the program according to the user's individual needs.

Operating System. The part of a computer's software which looks after housekeeping tasks such as updating the monitor 75 times a second, opening and closing disc files, checking the keyboard for key presses *etc.*—the really mundane stuff. The OS is usually stored in a chip in the computer or has to be loaded from disc or some combination of these. Without an operating system the computer will not run any other software unless the author undertakes these chores as well as the main function of his software. Sometimes authors feel that they can speed up the operation of their software if they hijack these routine tasks and do them in a different way. This leads to incompatibility problems if the computer manufacturer improves their OS. This was the problem with some software when Microsoft recently introduced Windows '95 which had such improvements. GEM (Graphic Environment Manager), MS-DOS (Micro Soft Disc Operating System), TOS (Tramiel Operating System), PC-DOS, C/PM and the Apple Desktop are all operating systems of various levels of complexity.

Opto Isolator. A method of passing a signal via a light path thus avoiding a direct electrical connection between a transmitting device and a receiving device. This presents voltage spikes generated in one device finding their way into another, and stops earth loops forming. The unit consists of a light source (a LED) and a light detector (a phototransistor) enclosed in a sealed box (the whole package looks just like a normal IC). The incoming signal is used to turn the light source on and off. The light shines on the detector which has an output signal when it sees the light and changes the output when it doesn't. It is specified for use in MIDI connections and other types of "current loop" data connections between computers.

OS. *See* **Operating System.**

P

Parallel Data. A method of sending computer data whereby all bits of the digital word are sent simultaneously. This is generally more expensive as the connectors involved have to have a pin for each bit plus a few pins for ground, handshaking *etc.* However parallel data transfers are typically ten or more times faster than electrical serial methods. SCSI and Centronics are examples of parallel data standards.

Parity Bit. A bit added to a data word to provide a simple form of error checking. The bits of individual data words, when summed, will give either an odd or even value. The parity bit can be set to an odd or even value and added to the data word so that all words become, say, odd (or even). If the parity is even and the receiving device sees a data word which sums to an odd value, this must be because the data have become corrupted. In practice this may be merely ignored or a request may be made by the receiving device to instruct the transmitting device to resend the defective word.

Password Protection. A method of obtaining access to a computer system or file on a system, which requires the user to provide an input when requested in the form of a word which (in theory at least) is known only to authorised users. Often these are ludicrously easy to bypass. A major accounting software is shipped with the password "LETMEIN". This is rarely altered by users, with the result that many using this software have the same password. Most common passwords chosen by people are: dog, cat or goldfish's name, mother's maiden name, wife's maiden name, date of birth, social security number, user's first name and "Open Sesame". Needless to say this all makes the hacker's job rather trivial. *See* **Hacking.**

Paste. In a computer, a command which places a section of text or picture, previously placed in the clipboard, at the current cursor position. *See also* **Copy, Cut.**

PC. *See* **Microcomputer.**

PCMCIA. Abbreviation of Personal Computer Memory Card International Association. A formalised interface initially intended to provide a means of expanding the memory of computerised equipment with plug-in cards of RAM or ROM, now also used to provide additional facilities such as a MODEM *etc.*

PDA. Abbreviation for Personal Digital Assistant, a small handheld electronic organiser device. Many now connect to the mobile Internet.

Pentium. A trademark of the Intel Corporation's generations of processors.

Peripheral. In a computer system a device which either allows input to or output from the system or both apparently simultaneously. A printer or a monitor are output devices, a mouse or keyboard are input devices, while a disc drive is an input/output or IO device. Other peripherals include scanners, tape data storage devices, liquid crystal displays (LCD) *etc.*

Pixels. Derived from Picture Cells, the individual dots from which an image is produced on a computer monitor. Pixels can be categorised by bit depth which is another way of describing the number of light levels or colours the pixel can emit. 1-bit pixels are monochrome as they are either on or off. 4-bit pixels can display 16 shades of grey or colour. A 24-bit pixel can display in excess of 16.7 million shades of grey or more usually colour. This is arguably very many more than the average human can actually discriminate.

Platform. A term used instead of computer, when it is desirable to include all computers of a general type and their clones rather than specific models. For example an application will be described as running on the "Mac Platform", while an operating system like UNIX which can run on many different types of computer may be described as "Multi-Platform".

Pop-up. A self-contained Internet page, somewhat smaller than the browser screen, triggered by an event, usually the accessing of a host page. These pop-ups are usually advertising adult orientated products. They are seen as so irritating that many Internet browsers have blocking devices incorporated into them.

Port. An input or output socket on a device such as a computer.

Printer. An output device used by a computer to render text and graphics onto paper or acetate *etc.* A number of technologies are available. Impact printers such as Dot Matrix form images using metal components which press an ink ribbon onto the page. These are generally low resolution <100 DPI. Other technologies which spray ink (inkjet) or explode ink bubbles (bubblejet) onto the paper can achieve higher resolutions, ≥300 DPI, and colour operation. Laser printers generate a negative image on a cylinder or drum using a variable electrostatic charge. This rotates past a dry powder ink or toner cartridge attracting the ink particles to the charged areas of the surface. The paper is passed over this drum where it picks up the particles. It is then heated causing the particles to fuse and coalesce into a permanent image. Laser printers range between 300 and 2400 DPI and can produce colour images. The highest resolution laser printers are sometimes called imagesetters.

Programmer. A person who writes software for computers.

PROM. A form of memory which can be programmed once only and not erased. *See also* **EPROM, ROM, WORM.**

Q

Quantisation Error. In computer systems and often with particular reference to digital audio, the number of bits a system uses to describe numbers (the word size) sets the limit to the maximum count or resolution of the system, and this consequently determines the maximum accuracy with which, for example, audio signals can be described digitally. With 4 bits it is possible to divide the amplitude of a signal into 16 quantisation steps. Thus a signal whose peak amplitude was 2 volts would be described in steps 125 mV apart. Signal levels which fall between these steps are not recorded (the quantisation error), and the signal is therefore distorted by the quantisation process. This distortion manifests itself as noise for large signals and as harmonic distortion at signal levels close to zero. In practice the resolution determines the signal to noise ratio and by extension the dynamic range of the encoded signal. In general the greater the number of bits the digital audio system uses to encode the signal, the greater the dynamic range.

QuickTime. A proprietary system of storing and distributing "moving-image with sound" or "Multimedia" files. It was developed by Apple Computers and is used on the Internet and CD-ROMs. The system supports replay of Standard MIDI Files conforming to the general MIDI (GM) format. Extensions to the system allow interactive "browsing" of 3D graphic environments. *See also* **MPEG.**

QWERTY. Acronym formed from the first six letters of the top letter row in a standard keyboard layout, used to describe a keyboard having that standard layout, as opposed to say the AZERTY layout used in some European countries.

R

RAM. Acronym from Random Access Memory. Essentially any form of memory which allows you to write new data into it at random, unrelated locations. Unlike say a tape recorder where things are stored sequentially. Generally used specifically to refer to semiconductor memory (chips), although strictly speaking disc drives are also RAM. *See also* **Virtual.**

RDAT. Acronym from Rotary head Digital Audio Tape. A standard for digital audio recording as well as a mass storage medium for backing up hard discs *etc.* The system employs a rotating head mechanism similar to that of video recorders, to record two channels of 16 bit digital audio information plus subcode and track information. The tape is housed in a case similar to a video cassette though much smaller. Maximum continuous record time for a cassette is 2 hours at standard play and four hours at long play with reduced quality. In data storage applications densities in excess of 4 Gigabytes can be achieved per tape.

Refresh Rate. The number of times per second that a complete screen image displayed on a monitor is "rewritten". It is expressed in Hz. Refresh rates of less than about 60 Hz are likely to "beat" with the mains line frequency and cause a low frequency flicker, which can be uncomfortable to look at for any length of time and may even precipitate epileptic fits in those prone to them.

Removable Storage. A method of data transfer using devices of higher capacity and greater robustness than media such as the floppy disc. Usually refers to the transfer of data via USB ports with resulting benefits of speed of data transfer.

Retrofit. The process of adding facilities to a device after it has been manufactured or even sold. The retrofit may be a software update in the form of an EPROM or ROM, but is more usually a complete circuit board. For example the fitting of memory or sound expansion boards etc.

RISC. Acronym from Reduced Instruction Set Computer. Essentially a microprocessor which only implements a few instruction types. It is then able to execute these instructions much more quickly than a more general microprocessor, as there are fewer possibilities for it to look up each time an instruction is to be executed. The increased speed of operation is very desirable for processing digital audio and video data, and these ICs are often used in devices which are designed to perform a specific function. See also **Instruction Set, CISC**.

ROM. Acronym from Read Only Memory. Essentially any form of memory which allows you to read information or data from it, but not to write or add new memory information or data to it. Thus a prerecorded audio cassette (with its record tabs broken out) is a ROM. Generally used specifically to refer to semiconductor memory (chips). See also **EPROM, PROM**.

Root Directory. See Directory.

Rotational Latency. See Access Time.

RS232C. A serial data transfer or communications standard commonly adopted on personal computers. The standard defines cable connections for Transmit, Receive data lines and Signal ground. In addition, Request to Send (RTS) and Clear To Send (CTS) signals are used for "Handshaking", and Data Carrier Detect (DCD), Data Set Ready (DSR), Data Terminal Ready (DTR) for MODEM control. It has to be said that the standard is not straightforward or uniformly implemented with the result that DCD, DSR, and DTR are sometimes used by some manufacturers for Handshaking.

RSI. Abbreviation of Repetitive Strain Injury. A medical term used to describe the process of accumulating "insults" to an area of tissue, usually tendon, ligament or muscle, by overuse or awkward use to the extent that the tissue becomes injured through inflammation or rupture. It has previously been most commonly found in athletes etc. but most recently associated with computer keyboard operators, especially those who make constant use of keyboard short cuts that require several keys to be depressed simultaneously. The achievement of this often requires operators to overflex tendons and other tissues in the hand and wrist. As the resulting injury can lead to loss of livelihood, RSI is increasingly cited in industrial injury compensation cases.

RTS. See RS232C.

S

Sample. In analogue to digital conversion, one instantaneous digital measurement of the analogue signal. As the sample value is expressed in binary there is a correlation between samples and bytes. However the precise relationship depends on a number of factors (the resolution of the converter and the number of simultaneously converted signal channels). For a 16 bit converter a sample is two bytes, for a 12 bit converter a sample is 1.5 bytes, for a 16 bit two channel converter a sample is 4 bytes etc.

Sampling Rate. The rate at which samples of an analogue signal are encoded or decoded by a digital device. The higher the sampling rate is set during the encoding process the greater the bandwidth of signal it is possible to record without error.

Scanner. A computer input device which is the functional opposite of a printer. It "looks at" or scans an existing image and inputs the information in the image into a computer.

Scroll. Originally a facility on a computer monitor that allowed the user to move a large text or image up or down to bring the previous or next section of it into view, rather like rolling the top part of a paper scroll while simultaneously unrolling the bottom part. Now extended to describe such movements in both dimensions (up/down, left/right). It is a common feature of graphic user interfaces such as Apple's Desktop or Microsoft's Windows.

SCSI. Acronym from Small Computer Systems Interface (pronounced "scuzzy" to rhyme with fuzzy). An agreed standard of hardware and command language, which allows data communication between components in a computer system. Primarily used for hard disc drives and other volume data storage devices, but also used for scanners and other types of devices. As the interface is a parallel type it is capable of high speed operation.

Search Engine. A web based utility that is able to locate instances of a word or phrase submitted via a data entry box. The utility program is hosted on powerful servers that search indexes in a database for "hits". The accuracy of searches can be increased using inverted commas, &, NOT and other logical operators.

Sector. A subdivision of the surface of a data disc consisting of a number of blocks. In a hard disc with several platters the sector is a number of blocks in a vertical "slice" through the platters.

Seek Time. See Access Time.

Sequencer. A stand alone device, or a category of computer software, which allows a user to create, edit and (sometimes) print music by recording and playing back MIDI messages. While these are most commonly musical performance messages in theory any MIDI messages may be recorded. In practice they generally behave like tape recorders, in that they have a number of "tracks" and "transport controls" etc. Drum machines generally contain some sequencer capability. As regards printing of music or scorewriting, sequencers sometimes include this ability (in a rudimentary form), while scorewriters can often "play" (in a rudimentary manner) the score like a sequencer, but each is usually optimised to its own task. So it is sensible to record and edit a piece of music on a sequencer and then export the data to a scorewriter so that its appearance in notation can be edited separately.

Serial Data. This is a format for sending computer data whereby all bits of the digital word are sent one after the other. This is generally cheaper as the connectors involved only need one transmit pin and one receive pin plus ground. However serial data transfers are typically ten times slower than parallel methods. RS232C uses a serial data format. Fibre optic data transfers are also serial but can run at very much higher speeds than electrical serial methods and can surpass even parallel interfaces.

Server. A piece of hardware similar to a desktop PC, but with much greater memory capacity. The purpose of the server is the storage of information for the use of the server's clients. Clients are almost always normal PCs. The server is the fundamental component of the Client-Server network, where the server coordinates and services requests from PCs. Servers may be allocated specific single tasks, for example a print server or a web server.

Shareware. Term used to describe software which is available in such a way that it can be tried without purchase, and only paid for if found to be useful. The cost of such software is often nominal, amounting to little more than a few pounds or dollars. Usually the application when run displays a page giving the address of the author and the nominal figure for payment. It is essentially an "honesty system" which relies on the good will of the author and potential users. Many people unfortunately abuse the system and use the software without payment. This is obviously a shame, and in fact counter productive as the author when contacted and paid will often forward an improved version of the software and register the user for similar upgrades at nominal cost. Shareware is not in the public domain.

SIMM. Acronym for Single In-line Memory Module. A collection of RAM chips mounted on a printed circuit board with a row of metal contacts along one edge. About 100 mm by 20 mm in size the modules carry up to 32 MB. *See also* **DIMM, RAM**.

Slave. In a system of devices, it is sometimes useful to have a number of devices which are subordinate in operation to one other device (particularly as regards a timing reference, for example). These devices are nominated slaves, the other device becomes the "master".

Smart Card. A thin plastic card which encapsulates a memory chip, used for storing data. Smart cards are used in mobile phones, to store telephone numbers and PINs. They can be used in other ways, for example to carry an individual's medical records. In this application a person always has their medical record with them (probably in their wallets as smart cards can resemble credit cards), so that, in emergency, their record can be accessed by a doctor equipped with a suitable reader. They could also be used as a form of electronic cash, with the card being used to store a balance of credits which reduces when something is purchased. However complex security issues are delaying wide acceptance of this application.

SMS. Abbreviation for Short Message Service. This allows a text message to be received and displayed on a GSM mobile phone in the manner of a pager. If the phone is switched off the message is held in the GSM system until the phone becomes available again. *See also* **GSM**.

Software. The abstract form of the instructions which determine how the hardware of a computer system functions, *i.e.* a list of instructions that the computer will perform in sequence, so as to perform some useful task. The program is written by a programmer after analysing the problem to be solved, then identifying those instructions from the instruction set which will help solve the problem and assembling them into the right order. For any given task which it is desirable for a computer to carry out, there is probably an infinite number of methods resulting in a "correct" solution. Programming is something of an art. While apparently a scientific and logical process, the best and most elegant programs are often written by people with a good intuitive "feel" for the way problems work. Programs which do not work well probably result from a poor definition of the problem. There is some mathematical evidence to suggest that it is not possible to write a piece of software which contains no errors.

Soundcard. A printed circuit board which can be plugged into the expansion sockets of a personal computer and which considerably improves the ability of the computer to produce sound effects or music. These are often described by the prefix 8-bit, 16-bit *etc.* In general the higher the number the better the quality of sound. In a well designed 16-bit soundcard the quality should compare favourably with CD standard recordings. Soundcards occasionally add MIDI compatibility to the computer and many can act as samplers by making short term digital recordings of sounds for replay by the computer or from an external MIDI controller such as a master keyboard.

Spam. The unwanted email automatically generated and sent over the email system. Spam depends upon automation in email address selection via custom-made address writing programs *e.g.* johnsmith@amadeup.com being an easy to guess and generate name. Spammers are almost always commercial and work upon very small margins of profit, one reply out of one thousand messages sent making the practice profitable. Spam can often be partially defeated by inserting characters into an address that would not be found in a conventional name.

Spreadsheet. A category of computer software which allows a user to generate tables of arithmetic calculations. It will normally be used for such things as keeping track of income and expenditure. It consists of a grid of cells, in rows and columns, which may be independent or which may be related to one another by a mathematical formula or calculation. Cells may also be labelled. Thus the cell at the bottom of a column might be called "Total" and represent the sum of all cells above it, so that any numbers placed in a cell higher than Total will be added together automatically, the result appearing in the Total cell. Its usefulness lies in the fact that having established a set of mathematical relationships (which might represent the cash flow for a company) it is possible to alter specific values

temporarily to see what the overall effect of that change is. Essentially a database optimised for number handling.

SSI. Abbreviation of Small Scale Integration. An integrated circuit which contains about 10–90 active elements. *See also* **LSI, MSI, VLSI**.

Start Bit. In serial data transmission (particularly asynchronous) the use of an extra bit which precedes the data bits and which serves to "wake up" the receiving device in readiness for the data which follow.

Stop Bit. In serial data transmission (particularly asynchronous) the use of an extra bit which succeeds the data bits and which serves to indicate to the receiving device that the data have stopped and that it may now rest.

Supercomputer. A computer whose speed of operation is close to the current maximum possible. Typically in 400–800 MIPS range. Some available technologies and the use of parallel processing will extend this above 1 GIPS in the immediate future. *See also* **Computer**.

SVGA. Abbreviation of Super Video Graphics Adaptor. An enhanced standard system for displaying text and images with higher quality (than VGA) on a computer monitor, widely used by IBM PCs *etc.*

T

Tail. Additional data which suffix a block of data either in a stored file or for the purposes of data transfer between devices. These data usually serve the function of a "full stop" to the block of data which precedes them.

Terminal. In a computer system, particularly a mainframe type, a remote keyboard and monitor and sometimes printer, which allows a user of the system to communicate with the computer. It is an input/output or IO device.

TOS. *See* **Operating System**.

Tracker Ball. A hand operated control in the form of a captive but free rolling ball which allows simultaneous movement in two axes (X and Y) and which allows the user (who rolls the ball around in its frame) to define a unique position within the limits of movement of the control. Essentially it is a mouse mounted upside down. Sometimes used on computers instead of a mouse or joystick, to define the position of a cursor on the monitor. It is sometimes fitted with one or more switches, the pressing of which will select or activate an area of the computer monitor currently under the cursor.

Transfer Rate. *See* **Data Rate**.

Trojan Horse. A term used to describe a computer program which is concealed in some way and is unknowingly executed, sometimes with unpleasant results. It might take the form of a functionally useful and desirable application which contains a second program which operates as an unseen background activity of the first, or it may be a text file *etc.* which includes executable code. The latter situation is sometimes a problem on the Internet, where hackers might place a desirable file *e.g.* a picture, on the Internet, which when accessed by the unwary promptly returns the user's passwords, account details *etc.* to an address elsewhere on the Internet for the benefit of the hackers. They are not generally viruses. *See also* **Virus**.

U

UART. Acronym from Universal Asynchronous Receiver Transmitter. An integrated circuit that carries out the function of asynchronous, bidirectional communication between a microprocessor and a serial interface. It allows data to be transferred into or out of a microprocessor based equipment. It is commonly used on equipment which implements the RS232C and MIDI standards.

UKASCII. A variant of ASCII which takes account of (among other things) the fact that British people do not use the character "#" but do require the character "£" which is not normally part of ASCII. Thus the character represented by the decimal value 35 in an American computer is #, while the same value in a British computer produces £.

Undo. An interface button often viewed as the most important since it allows the user to rescind the previous action.

UPS. Abbreviation of Uninterruptible Power Supply. A type of power supply which can continue to provide power despite a momentary interruption or even complete failure of the mains supply to it. This is achieved by trickle charging batteries in the power supply while monitoring the mains supply for failures. If a failure is detected the batteries can be instantaneously connected to the load, through an "inverter" circuit that converts the DC of the batteries to the AC typical of mains supplies. The intention is not to replace a failed mains supply indefinitely, but simply for long enough that the connected equipment such as a computer can be "shut down" in a methodical and safe manner without loss of data *etc.*

URI. Abbreviation of Universal Resource Identifier. A generic way of referring to any address or name used to identify an object on the Internet. A URL is an example of a URI. But it is commonplace for these abbreviations to be used interchangeably. *See also* **URL.**

URL. Abbreviation of Uniform Resource Locator. The URL of a web page is the unique addressing of the page, for example "amadeup.com". The URL is a synonym for the DNS entry to identify the site, thus www.amadeup.com will have an Internet Protocol address easier to use for computers but less easy to recollect for the user.

USB. Stands for Universal Serial Bus. A port for devices that are external to the PC, to communicate with the PC. Renowned for the speed of data transfer between device and the PC.

V

V.17, V.21, V.22, V.29, V.32bis, V.42 *etc.* Various communication standards recommended by the Consultative Committee for International Telephone and Telegraph (CCITT), V.17, V.21, V.29 are Facsimile standards, while V.22, V.32, V.32bis and V.34 are MODEM standards. V.42 and V.42bis are respectively Error Correction and Data Compression standards.

V.Fast Class. A proprietary standard for high speed (28,800 BPS) data transfer, mutually agreed by a number of MODEM manufacturers, who couldn't wait for the CCITT to finish their lunch break. It was subsequently adopted by CCITT as V.34.

V.FC. *See* **V. Fast Class.**

Vapourware. An ironic term to describe promised features in software or hardware which never actually get implemented.

VGA. Abbreviation of Video Graphics Adaptor. A standard system for displaying text and images on a computer monitor, widely used by IBM PCs *etc.*

Virtual. In computing, said of a facility or quality that appears to a user to exist and functions as if it did, but in fact does not. For example in Virtual Memory, a section of a mass storage device, such as a hard disc, is set aside and used by the computer's operating system as if it were the computer's main work memory or RAM. "Virtual Reality" is used to describe a system that simulates, and allows interaction with, an environment that is different to the one the user is in. This has obvious potential in the entertainments industry but has other applications. For example, in hazardous environments in the nuclear and chemical industries a real technician in a safe place with a VR system could control a robot remotely in a dangerous place.

Virus. A form of computer software which in operation has the ability to make copies of itself in new locations within a computer (in RAM, hard disc, or floppy discs inserted subsequently). This is occasionally harmless, but some viruses have pernicious effects which range from mere blanking of the computer screen to wholesale erasure of data. The problem can be acute if a virus is introduced to a computer which is part of a large network, as it can quickly spread throughout the network. It has to be said that there is considerable media hyperbole about viruses and some of the horror stories of viral incidents have

not stood the test of a few minutes investigation. The origin of the first computer virus has likewise entered the realm of modern myths, but is generally attributed to a pair of brothers in Pakistan, involved in computer piracy of commercial software, who developed a virus to ensure that their illegal copies would not in turn be recopied. *See also* **Trojan Horse.**

VLSI. Abbreviation of Very Large Scale Integration. An integrated circuit which contains about 100,000 active elements. *See also* **LSI, MSI, SSI.**

W

W³. *See* **Internet.**

WAIS. Abbreviation of Wide Area Information Search. An Internet protocol for specifying remote database search criteria. This allows Internet users to search for keywords in one or more of the many useful databases available over the Internet.

Wait. One of the characters transmitted for the purposes of handshaking in a data transfer. The character is sent back to the transmitting device by the receiving device to indicate that the receiver wants the transmitter to pause. The transmission will then continue when the receiver sends an ack, or it will be stopped altogether if the receiver sends a cancel.

WAN. Stands for Wide Area Network. Indicates a network that can potentially span continents and can be flexible over the number and location of PCs that are on it. An example of a WAN is the Internet. *See also* **LAN.**

WAP. An acronym of Wireless Application Protocol, an international standard for wireless communication of data. Most certainly used to provide internet access for mobile phones.

WAV. Derived from "Windows Wave". A standard (almost) with many variants for storing and distributing audio as computer data. It was developed by Microsoft and IBM. It is also used for exchanging soundfiles over the Internet. It allows data compression of the audio data resulting in smaller file sizes and reduced bandwidth requirement, albeit with arguably reduced sonic quality. Various data compression methods are used causing occasional problems in recognition of the files between different computers. *See also* **AIFF, AU.**

Web Mail. Any mail service provided for users of a particular web site, for example yahoo.co.uk. It is distinct from other email provision in that users are not dependant upon being located at a specific PC. Web Mail is particularly popular with those travelling and therefore unable to guarantee conditions suitable for a laptop computer.

WIMP. Acronym from Windows, Icons, Mouse Pointer. A generic term used to describe any graphic user interface which employs these features in its operating system.

Window. In a computer, one of a number of areas of the monitor which can present information that is independent of and separate from another window or area on the same monitor. The dimensions of the window can generally be adjusted or "sized". This will result in more or less information being visible, or the information may be scaled to match the size of the window. A window may also be "opened" or "closed". Windows may present information about different parts of a single program, thus allowing the user to select the displays which are most relevant to their use of the program, or the windows may contain information from different programs, allowing information to be "copied" from one window and "pasted" into another.

Windows. The proprietary name used by Microsoft for their WIMP operating system for IBM-PC and compatible computers.

Word. In computers and digital systems the number of bits used by the system to define a single numerical value or sample. This indicates the resolution of number representations in the computer. An 8 bit word is 1 byte, a 12 bit word is 1.5 bytes, a 16 bit word is 2 bytes. However in general usage a word is considered to be 2 bytes unless otherwise qualified. 32 bits is often called a "long word".

Word Processor. Also called WP. A category of computer software which allows a user to generate and edit text documents, essentially a computerised pencil, paper and rubber. Initially used to create simple documents such as letters, but not complex documents such as newspapers or magazines, these programs are increasingly becoming more sophisticated and are now more likely to allow a user to place pictures within the text and format the text into a complex layout typical of a published magazine or book. To this extent there is no longer a clear cut line between WP software and desktop publishing software. However WP is normally optimised to the keying and altering of text, rather than to questions of layout (most WPs have spelling checkers, a feature which tends to be absent on desktop publishing software), so it is still common (and more sensible) to generate the text in the word processor and export it to the desktop publishing software.

Workstation. Describes a single device which contains a number of functions normally executed by a number of different devices, for example a powerful, self-contained system with adequate mass storage and graphics capability (as opposed to a terminal linked to a mainframe or file server).

World Wide Web. *See* **Internet**.

WORM. Write Once Read Many. Essentially any form of memory which allows information or data to be stored or saved once only, but the information can be read as many times as you like (until it wears out). Recordable CDs are an example of this. ROM also comes under this heading.

WP. *See* **Word Processor**.

WWW. *See* **Internet**.

X

X On/X Off. Abbreviation of transmitter on/transmitter off. The two codes used for software handshaking or flow control in computer communications or data transfers. It is used as an alternative to hardware handshaking, sometimes to reduce the cost of implementation as these cables can then be omitted. It is wise not to use X on/X off for high speed data transfers or those which use error correction or data compression.

XMODEM. *See* **FTP**.

Z

Zip Drive. Proprietary system of mass storage which utilises 100MB removable magneto-optical (MO) storage on 3·5″ cartridges.

ZMODEM. *See* **FTP**.

THE ENVIRONMENT

This popular section provides a concise introduction to some of the key environmental issues facing the world in which we live. Subjects covered range from air pollution and endangered wildlife habitats to world ocean resources and from global hunger to the history of deadly pandemics. Also included are a glossary of key terms, a wide-ranging chronology of recent events and a concise history of the green movement.

TABLE OF CONTENTS

1. GLOSSARY OF ENVIRONMENTAL TERMS

Acid Rain. *See* Section L.

Agenda 21. A 'blueprint' for sustainable development, agreed at the 1992 Earth Summit. Its aims are to integrate conservation and development in order to improve the quality of human life, whilst minimising the depletion of natural resources.

Atmosphere. *See* Section L.

Bioaccumulation. The build up of pollutants within the tissue of an organism.

Biodiversity. From biological diversity. The variety, distribution and abundance of plants, animals and micro-organisms. Includes genetic, taxonomic, and ecosystem components.

Biodiversity Convention. Document agreed at the 1992 Earth Summit, obliging signatories to prevent the depletion of biological resources. The USA was the only government not to sign.

Biosphere. *See* Section L.

Blue-green algae. *See* Cyanobacteria.

Carcinogen. An agent that is capable of causing cancer in animals.

Chlorofluorocarbons (CFCs). Compounds composed of carbon, fluorine, and chlorine. Used in aerosol propellants, refrigerants, and packaging. Unstable in upper atmosphere and considered to be responsible for the destruction of ozone. Chlorofluorocarbons are also powerful greenhouse gases.

CITES (Convention on International Trade in Endangered Species). 1973 agreement prohibiting or restricting the international trade in species threatened with extinction.

Clone. Cells or organisms which are genetically identical to each other.

Conservation. 1. The control of human activities in order to maintain biodiversity and sustain ecological processes. 2. The management of natural resources in order to prevent their depletion.

Coral. *See* Section L.

Coral Reef. A ridge on the sea bed created by the gradual build up of the calciferous skeletons of colonial coral. One of the most fertile ecosystems, rich in biodiversity, coral reefs are under threat from pollution and rising sea temperatures.

Cyanobacteria (blue-green algae). Single celled organisms capable of photosynthesis. Widely distributed in both salt and fresh water. Can reproduce at high rates forming huge blooms which may consume so much oxygen that other aquatic organisms die.

Deforestation. The clearing of all trees and undergrowth from an area, in order to harvest timber or develop land for other purposes. Deforestation can lead to soil erosion and may contribute to increasing levels of carbon dioxide in the atmosphere.

Desertification. The conversion of arid or semi-arid land into desert, caused by factors such as drought, over-grazing and over-cultivation.

Drought. Period of abnormally low rainfall which leads to water shortages and damage to vegetation. *See also* L32–3.

Earth Summit. Also known as the United Nations Conference on Environment and Development (UNCED). 178 Heads of Government met in Rio de Janeiro, Brazil, in June 1992 to discuss the environmental consequences of development. Key agreements include the Rio Declaration, conventions in Biodiversity and Climate Change, a declaration on Sustainable Development and Agenda 21.

Ecology. The relationships between organisms, their interactions with the environment, and the scientific study thereof. *See also* T45.

Ecosystem. A community of living organisms, their non-living environment, and the processes by which they interact.

Ecotourism. Tourism with the particular purpose of visiting areas of unspoilt natural beauty, which are rich in wildlife.

Eco-warrior. A person prepared to take direct action to prevent environmentally damaging activities.

El Niño. A movement of warm water across the Pacific Ocean from east to west, caused by a change in wind direction above the equator (Southern Oscillation). The two events are collectively referred to as ENSO (El Niño Southern Oscillation).ENSO results in unusually high temperatures along the east coast of South America for up to a year. It is thought to have important effects on global weather patterns. *See also* Y7.

Endangered Species. A species that is likely to become extinct if the factors causing its decline are not addressed. *See* Y10–12.

Environment Agency. *See* Section L.

Environmental Impact Assessment. A prior evaluation of the environmental consequences of a human activity.

Eutrophication. The enrichment of a water body with nutrients, especially nitrogen and phosphorus. It can promote the growth of algae, subsequently leading to deoxygenation of water and the death of aquatic organisms. Can occur naturally, but is commonly caused by slurry, sewage and fertilisers from agricultural land.

Extinction. The destruction of all the members of a particular species. Over-harvesting and habitat loss are now the main causes of extinction.

Fertilizer. Any substance that contains chemical elements essential for plant growth. Added to soil to increase fertility.

Food Chain. A series of organisms linked to each other by their food requirements. A typical food chain would be: green plant → herbivore → carnivore.

Fossil Fuels. Fuels extracted from the earth and derived from the remains of ancient organic material. Include coal, crude oil and natural gas.

Gaia Hypothesis. The theory proposed by James T. Lovelock which considers the earth to be one organism that controls its own regulatory systems.

Genetic Engineering. Altering the DNA (genetic material) of an organism to confer a specific characteristic upon it. Applications include the production of antibiotics and hormones, and improving the yield of crops. There is concern over the environmental, ethical and safety implications of genetic engineering.

Global Warming. Human induced warming of the atmosphere, caused by increased absorption of radiation by "greenhouse gases". Global temperature has risen by 0·5°C since the start of the twentieth century. If this trend continues, it could cause droughts, flooding, etc. *See* Y6.

Green Revolution. A system of agricultural development, instigated by the United Nations Food and Agriculture Organisation (FAO). Its key component is the use of new crop varieties with improved yields, requiring high external inputs of water, pesticides and fertilisers. The use of these varieties increased food production by 2% per year between 1961 and 1980.

Greenhouse Effect. The ability of the atmosphere to prevent the escape of the earth's long wave radiation. Without the greenhouse effect, the temperature of the earth's surface would be -23°C. Over the past century, human emission of greenhouse gases has caused the phenomenon of increased global warming. *See* Y6.

Greenhouse Gases. Constituents of the earth's atmosphere that absorb long-wave radiation, thereby causing its temperature to increase. Chlorofluorocarbons (CFCs), carbon dioxide (CO_2), water vapour, methane (CH_4) and nitrous oxide (N_2O) are all greenhouse gases. The combustion of fossil fuels and deforestation are thought to be causes of currently increasing CO_2 levels.

Heavy Metals. Metals with a high relative atomic weight, such as lead, mercury and cadmium. They are often toxic and can accumulate in plant and animal tissues.

Keystone Species. An organism, usually a large mammal, which plays an important role in ecological processes. The loss of a keystone species can threaten ecosystem integrity and cause the extinction of other species.

Kyoto Conference. *See* **Y6–7.**

Marine Nature Reserve (MNR), sea areas within territorial waters, to conserve marine fauna, flora *etc.* Lundy Island (England) and Skomer Island (Wales) are examples.

Nuclear Power. *See* **L79.**

Organic Farming. A form of farming that does not use industrially produced, synthetic chemicals, such as pesticides, fertilisers, growth regulators or livestock feed additives.

PCBs. *See* **Polychlorinated Biphenyls.**

Pesticides. A generic term for any substance used to reduce or eliminate pests—organisms that compete with humans for resources. The most common pesticides are: insecticides, herbicides, nematicides, rodenticides and fungicides. They can be very simple elements such as copper or highly complex chemical compounds like DDT. Currently about 1000 pesticides are used globally. They have contributed to the increase in world food production and the reduction of some insect born diseases but have also been responsible for the poisoning of humans and animals.

Pollution. The contamination of the environment with hazardous or undesirable substances, radioactivity or noise. Generally refers to human activities although natural pollution can occur. *e.g.* volcanic ash.

Polychlorinated Biphenyls (PCBs). Very stable synthetic chemicals manufactured for insulation and lubrication purposes. Are toxic and persist in food chains. Their manufacture has been banned in many countries since the late 1970s.

Precautionary Principle. A guide to policy making aiming for the prevention, rather than cure, of environmental damage. It recognises that there is a degree of uncertainty in human interventions in ecological processes. To prevent environmental crises, the worst possible effect of an action should be anticipated. Lack of scientific certainty should not delay measures to protect the environment.

Rainforest. Dense, mainly evergreen forest which is found in areas of high rainfall within the tropics. Rainforests are highly complex ecosystems and contain as many as 30 million species of plants and animals. *See also* **Y12.**

Renewable Energy. Energy generated from natural resources that are not depleted as a result. Energy sources include water, wind and the sun.

Rio Declaration. 27 principles for sustainable development, agreed at the 1992 Earth Summit. They include references to the eradication of poverty, the strengthening of environmental legislation and the development of environmental impact assessment.

Soil Erosion. The removal of topsoil by wind or water that exceeds the rate at which soil is being produced by weathering. The effect can be accelerated by human activities such as deforestation, poor land management, and overgrazing.

Special Areas of Conservation (SAC). These areas of environmental sites of importance have now replaced Sites of Special Scientific Interest. In Britain they include woods (such as Windsor Forest and Great Park), mountains and moorlands (Ben Nevis, the Cairngorm plateau, Rannoch Moor *etc.*) and whole river systems.

Sustainable Development. A theoretical process of social and economic change, which meets the need of the present generation without compromising the ability of future generations to meet their own needs. It is based on the exploitation of renewable resources at levels that do not cause depletion.

World Population. *See* **L117 and Y14.**

2. CHRONOLOGY OF ENVIRONMENTAL MOVEMENT

Introduction.

The roots of the environmental movement can be found in the nineteenth century. Industrialisation and its associated pollution were taking their toll on human health, leading for calls to protect air and water quality.

However, it was not until the 1960s that the environmental movement gained mass popularity and a strong political voice. There were protests against nuclear weapons and demands for protection of the natural world. Many environmental groups were founded during this era, and advances were made in the development of legislation protecting the environment.

During the 1980s and 1990s, attention focussed on the global nature of environmental problems such as global warming, acid rain and the extinction of species. Now, in a new century, this is leading to an increased awareness of the need for international co-operation and the first attempts to protect the environment on a global scale.

1946 International Convention on the Regulation of Whaling. Established the International Whaling Commission

1948 Foundation of the World Conservation Union (IUCN), a body which acts as a link between 55 states, 100 government agencies and non-governmental organisation

1949 Foundation of the Nature Conservancy, in the USA, to conserve and restore natural areas including Tall Grass Prairies and the Florida Everglades

1952/53 Perhaps 12,000 people die as a direct result of smog in London

1956 Clean Air Act; established measures to control smoke emissions in cities

1957 Core of a nuclear reactor at Windscale caught fire, leading to a major release of radioactivity

1959 Antarctic Treaty. Provided protection for the flora and fauna of the Antarctic

1961 Establishment of the World Wildlife Fund (WWF), with the aim of protecting endangered species. It later changed its name to the World Wide Fund for Nature, and broadened its objectives to include habitat conservation and sustainable development

1962 Publication of *Silent Spring*, by Rachel Carson, highlighting the dangers of pesticide use to wildlife

1963 Treaty Banning Nuclear Weapon Tests in the Atmosphere, in Outer Space, and Under Water

1964 Agreed Measures on the Conservation of Antarctic Fauna and Flora

1967 *Torrey Canyon* spilt 100,000 tonnes of crude oil off Cornwall

1968 Further Clean Air Act extended and improved the 1956 Act. Introduced the Tall Stacks Policy, which increased the dispersal of pollutants, improving air quality locally, but creating problems such as acid rain further afield
180 kg of plutonium discharged into the Irish Sea from the Sellafield nuclear reprocessing plant
"The Tragedy of the Commons" by Garrett Hardin published in *Science*, stimulating debate over the sustainability of the continued use of common property resources

1969 Foundation of Friends of the Earth, an environmental pressure group renowned for the quality of its research into green problems
Publication of the first British green consumer guide

1970 Department of the Environment established

The Environmental Protection Agency was established in the USA
Clean Air Act, USA
Launch of *The Ecologist*

1971 Royal Commission on Environmental Pollution in the United Kingdom established in order to monitor pollution independently
Foundation of *Greenpeace*, in north America, an organisation committed to non-violent but confrontational defence of the environment. Their first campaign was a protest against a nuclear test on Amchitka island in the Pacific Ocean
Convention on Wetlands of International Importance especially as Waterfowl Habitat (Ramsar Convention) IUCN/IWRB. Almost 200 million hectares are now protected under this convention

1972 United Nations Conference on the Human Environment (Stockholm). The first global conference focussing on environmental concerns. It accepted the principle of stopping transnational pollution and led to the formation of the United Nations Environmental Program (UNEP)
Convention on the Prevention of Marine Pollution by Dumping of Wastes and Other Matter (London Dumping Convention); prohibits or restricts dumping of listed substances at sea
Foundation of the British branch of Greenpeace
Convention concerning the Protection of the World Cultural and Natural Heritage (World Heritage Convention). Parties endeavour to protect and study their natural and cultural heritage by the establishment of World Heritage Sites

1973 Foundation of the Green Party (initially called the People Party, then the Ecology Party)
UNEP Convention on International Trade in Endangered Species (CITES). Convention restricting or prohibiting international trade in almost 500 species, which are at risk of extinction because of over-exploitation. It has been signed by 125 nations
Establishment of the Nature Conservancy Council in Britain, to conserve flora, fauna and geological features, through the designation of Sites of Special Scientific Interest (SSSIs).

1976 Dioxin released after an explosion at Seveso, northern Italy

1978 *Amoco Cadiz* spill 200 million litres of crude oil, contaminating 180 miles of the coast of Brittany

1979 Partial core meltdown in a nuclear reactor at Three Mile Island, Pennsylvania
Convention on Long Range Transboundary Air Pollution
Convention on the Conservation of Migratory Species of Wild Animals (Bonn Convention)

1980 IUCN/UNEP World Conservation Strategy highlighted the loss of species and the need for habitat preservation. However, it did not challenge existing economic exploitation and failed to address issues of sustainability
Convention on the Conservation of Antarctic Marine Living Resources (CCAMLR). Drafted in response to over-fishing in Antarctic waters, this convention entered into force in 1982. It encourages the conservation of the marine ecosystem of the Antarctic

1982 First reports of a hole in the ozone layer over Antarctica
UN Convention on the Law of the Sea (LOS Convention): obligates parties to protect the marine environment

1983 International Tropical Timber Agreement: establishes the International Tropical Timber Organisation and provides a framework for co-operation between tropical timber producing and consuming nations, with the aim of ensuring that tropical timber is harvested sustainably

1984 In Bhopal, India, 40 tonnes of methyl isocyanate leaked from a Union Carbide chemical plant, leading to the formation of a toxic gas cloud which drifted into a residential area. At least 2,500 people died as a result and a further 200,000 suffered major health problems
Formation of the '30% Club'. Some of the industrialised nations agreed to cut sulphur dioxide emissions by 30% of 1980 level by 1993

1985 Helsinki Protocol on the Reduction of Sulphur Emissions of their Transboundary Fluxes by at least 30%
Vienna Convention for the Protection of the Ozone Layer (Vienna Convention)—UNEP.
Action Plan for Biosphere Reserves
Wildlife and Countryside Act passed

1986 International moratorium on commercial whaling
30 tons of pesticides and dyes were released into the River Rhine after a fire at the Sandoz chemical plant, Basel
Launch of the Rainforest Action Network
Explosion in a nuclear reactor at Chernobyl

1987 Brundtland Report. First introduced the concept of sustainable development
Montreal Protocol on Substances that Deplete the Ozone Layer (Montreal Protocol): entered into force in 1989

1988 Establishment of UN Intergovernmental Panel on Climate Change (IPCC)
European Community agrees to cut emissions from large power stations by 2003
Sofia Protocol concerning the Control of Emissions of Nitrogen Oxides or their Transboundary Fluxes

1989 *Exxon Valdez* ran aground and released 11 million gallons of crude oil into Prince William Sound, Alaska: 250,000 sea-birds, as well as sea otters and other animals were killed
Convention on the Control of Transboundary Movements of Hazardous Wastes (Basel Convention)

1990 Ban on the international trade in ivory came into effect

1991 World Conservation Strategy for the 1990s (IUCN, UNEP, WWF)
Protocol to the Antarctic Treaty was concluded, designating Antarctica as a natural reserve, and prohibiting all mineral extraction

1992 United Nations Conference on Environment and Development (UNCED). Also known as the Rio Earth Summit. It established a Sustainable Development Commission, and produced the Rio Declaration, Agenda 21, and Conventions on climate change and biodiversity

1996 Comprehensive Nuclear Test Ban Treaty
French test nuclear weapons in Pacific

1997 Kyoto Conference on Climate Change: formulated the Kyoto Protocol, committing industrial nations to reduce greenhouse emissions by at least 5% below 1990 levels by 2008–2012

1998 Convention on Access to Information, Public Participation in Decision-making, and Access in Justice in Environmental Matters

2000 Increased evidence of global warming in the Arctic. Failure of UN Climate Convention at The Hague (*see* **Y7**). UK Government published Rural White Paper.

2001 Meteorological Office confirms 2001 to be the second warmest year on record in the UK, but 2002 soon takes over this accolade

2002 Johannesburg Earth Summit (Sept.) (*see* **Y8**). Oil spillage from *Prestige* threatens coasts of Spain and Portugal

2003 World Water Forum meets in Japan. Russia fails to ratify Kyoto Treaty

2004 Russia at last ratifies Kyoto Treaty. Devastation of Indian Ocean coastline by tsunami which leaves 225,000 dead.

2005 Massive destruction from Hurricane Katrina in New Orleans and Mississippi delta. Montreal Conference on environment (Dec.) (*see* **Y7**).

3. CURRENT ENVIRONMENTAL ISSUES

GLOBAL WARMING AND SUSTAINABILITY.

It may be thought incongruous to describe climate change as a current environmental controversy. It is after all nothing new. The last Ice Age finally retreated from Britain perhaps only some 12,000 years ago, and the North African coastal plains, much of which are now desert, were the granary of the Roman Empire. What, though, is new is the speed of change and the risk it poses that eco-systems will be unable to adapt at the same rate. The fears of some members of the UN Intergovernmental Panel on Climate Change that southern Africa could face a 100-year drought, and that it is the climate refugee rather than the political refugee who will characterise the 21st century, convey the scale of that risk. Even if there is overall adaptation, localised impacts could still be severe. For example, any diversion of the Gulf Stream could give the United Kingdom a climate akin to that of Labrador.

The Impact of Climate Change.

The impact of climate change to date is, however, anything but speculative. Figures released by Munich Re, one of the world's largest reinsurance companies, at the end of December 1998, indicated that natural disasters across the globe were now three times as frequent as when the company started to monitor them 25 years ago. The human cost of some 50,000 deaths in 1998 alone is high, but the economic cost is even higher. Floods during the year were responsible for 85% of economic losses of some £60 billion, nine times more in real terms than 25 years earlier. As one direct consequence, large tracts of low-lying land across the globe are rapidly becoming uninsurable with highly adverse consequences for countries, notably those in the Caribbean, parts of Asia and the Pacific, dependent on inward investment for tourism and other forms of economic development.

Recent High Temperatures.

The nine hottest years globally since records began in the 1860s have now occurred since 1990. In descending order, they are 1998, 2002, 2001, 1997, 1995, 1990 and 1999 (joint), and 1991 and 2000 (joint). It is thought that 2005 will prove to have been the hottest globally on record. The ten summers 1994–2003 are believed to have been Europe's hottest decade in more than 500 years. Europe and Asia both suffered from extreme temperatures, with southern France recording temperatures of over 40°C (104°F), some 5–7°C above average. Switzerland had its hottest June for 250 years. Ironically, the River Elbe, the scene of catastrophic flooding in 2002, experienced such low water levels that navigation had to be suspended. In Britain in August, the London area broke the 100°F (37.9°C) barrier for the very first time. In India, the pre-monsoon heatwave produced peak temperatures of 45°C, some 2–5°C above average. On the other hand, the USA suffered from 562 tornadoes in May, beating the previous monthly record of 392 in June 1992.

Although the temperature variations involved may appear modest in themselves, they need to be set against the estimate that the last Ice Age was provoked by average temperatures only 4–5°C lower than those with which we are familiar. The sensitivity of the human body to very small fluctuations in blood temperature may be a useful parallel.

The Phenomenon of Global Warming.

Climate change is a comprehensive term for the changes arising from the phenomenon of global warming generated by the build up of what are known as "greenhouse gases" in the atmosphere. The best known of those "greenhouse gases" is carbon dioxide (CO_2), and the first area of controversy, which is essentially scientific, is the actual rate of change and the extent to which it is man-made. The Intergovernmental Panel on Climate Change currently estimates that warming is occurring at a speed of between 1.4°C and 5.8°C every century, rates which may sound modest but which at the higher end of the scale could raise sea levels by up to one metre in the same period. Scientific opinion increasingly supports estimates at the higher end of the range, but the argument is far from closed. Similarly, there is growing but not unanimous acceptance that global warming is being accelerated by greenhouse gas emissions from the burning of fossil fuels, particularly coal and oil, with natural gas as a lesser but still major contributor.

Although most greenhouse gas emissions are produced by domestic households, industry, commerce and agriculture, road transport is responsible for 21% and that proportion is increasing. Improvements in the domestic and industrial sectors are steadily being outweighed by the increasing levels of use of cars and lorries. Even the substantial gains of 50% or more in fuel efficiency over the last 20 years have been outweighed by longer journeys and the preference for more powerful models. The net result has been that CO_2 emissions from road vehicles have increased by 70%–80% throughout the European Union alone in the last 20 years.

Rising Sea Levels.

Rising sea levels are a daunting threat not only to countries like Bangladesh, where more than 100 million people live on land barely above sea level, but also to those extensive areas of north western Europe like East Anglia, the Netherlands and the German coastal plain where the land drainage of centuries past has caused the soil to dry out and shrink, putting much land significantly below the present sea level. A study published in November 2005 showed that global sea levels were rising twice as fast as they had been 150 years previously.

Recent years have been the warmest for over a century, and both droughts and flooding have grown in frequency. February 1995 saw the breaking away of an Antarctic iceberg the size of Oxfordshire.

Although the flooding experienced across much of England in the Autumn of 2000 narrowly spared the historic centre of York, it devastated many smaller towns, including Lewes, the county town of East Sussex, and a large number of villages. Infinitely more severe, however, was the flooding of the catchment areas of the Danube and the Elbe in August 2002, which caused incalculable damage in Austria, the Czech Republic and eastern Germany. The historic cultural cities of Salzburg, Prague and Dresden were amongst the areas hardest hit. Germany's Green foreign minister considered that 10 years of reconstruction in Saxony had been undone by rainfall of perhaps once in a thousand years severity.

The 1992 Rio Conference.

Such anxieties had been aired at the United Nations Conference on Environment and Development held in Rio in 1992, and led to the drafting of the Convention on Climate Change. The European Union for its part had earlier agreed after much argument to stabilise CO_2 emissions at 1990 levels by the year 2000. The results of these initiatives, in themselves fairly undemanding, remain modest. The EU target was only narrowly met despite the substantial contribution made in some countries, notably the UK, by the substitution of natural gas for coal to generate electricity, although that change is controversial for other reasons. Some observers also fear that emissions will rise steeply in the coming years as public opinion, notably in Germany, refuses to countenance the building of another generation of nuclear power stations and much reliance again has to be placed on coal.

Carbon Taxation.

Greenhouse gas emissions are unlikely to be stabilised let alone reduced unless fuel use becomes more expensive, which in practice means taxation of energy generated from fossil fuel sources. Although such taxation has the potential to be popular as one facet of a movement away from taxing incomes and employment towards taxing resource consumption, which would help to reduce unemployment, it will be seen as a regressive additional burden unless it forms part of a comprehensive redistributive package. Moreover, it is feared by many in industry, particularly in fields such as chemicals where energy use is high, by governments such as those of Japan and the US which are apprehensive of the impact on their competitiveness, by developing countries who fear their development might be stifled, and by the oil producing countries who do not wish to see a reduction in the sales of what may be their sole significant export.

Taxation in some form is, however, almost certain to come because the challenge of climate change will not go away. Indeed, modest initiatives have been taken in the United Kingdom with the introduction of the Climate Change Levy (CCL), and in Germany.

The Kyoto Conference.

It is not surprising against this overall background that the third conference of the 150 parties to the Convention on Climate Change, held in Kyoto, Japan, in December 1997, was politically charged. The European Union, strongly supported by the Association of Small Island States, urged a target of a 15 per cent reduction in emissions of three key greenhouse gases by the year 2010 with Britain being ready to reduce its emissions by 20 per cent in any event. America and Canada were initially unwilling to envisage any reduction at all, although America expected China and India to commit themselves to future reductions. China and the G7 group of developing nations, on the other hand, called for reductions of 35 per cent by the wealthier countries by the year 2020.

It is perhaps remarkable in these circumstances that any agreement was reached at all, even if it was dubbed second-rate. A Protocol was nevertheless adopted stipulating a binding target of a 5·2 per cent average reduction by the major industrialised countries on 1990 levels of emissions of a "basket" of six greenhouse gases by the years 2008–12. The different regions will, however, receive differential treatment. The EU will make a reduction of 8 per cent as will most of the countries of central and eastern Europe, countries one of 7 per cent, and Japan and Canada 6 per cent. New Zealand, Russia and the Ukraine will stabilise emissions at 1990 levels but Australia will be allowed an increase of 8 per cent. No emission reductions are required of the developing countries, but America did, however, gain acceptance of the controversial concept of "carbon trading" between developed and developing countries, which is on the one hand a politically realistic approach but on the other a disincentive to real domestic change—a case of do as I say, rather than do as I do.

The Hague and Marrakesh Conferences.

The future of the Protocol was, however, put in doubt by the sixth conference of the parties in The Hague in November 2000 which collapsed in chaos. The key point at issue was the extent to which carbon trading, and other flexible mechanisms such as "carbon sinks", could be used to offset national emission targets. One group of countries, led by the EU, maintained that recourse to such mechanisms should be restricted to a maximum of 50 % of the national targets, while others, led by the US, argued that any such limitation was unreasonable and wanted even the greenhouse gas absorption capacity of their existing agriculture to be taken into account.

This gap in outlook proved unbridgeable, and in spring 2001 President Bush took the American position to its logical conclusion by withdrawing from the whole Kyoto agreement. Although many feared that that would spell the end of the Protocol, the seventh conference of the parties to the Convention in Marrakesh, Morocco, in November 2001, finally succeeded in reaching a compromise on implementation.

The future of the Protocol long remained in doubt. To enter into force, it had to be ratified by 55 % of its signatory nations, representing 55 % of global emissions at 1990 levels. In practice that made Russian ratification essential, but it was not until November 2004 that Russian ratification was actually achieved. The Protocol duly came into force as a binding treaty on 16 February 2005.

Outlook.

The Kyoto Conference decisions represent a considerable advance on the non-binding undertakings entered into at Rio in 1992, but their adequacy is controversial. For those who still doubt the extent to which man is responsible for global warming, they are a gratuitous economic hurdle. For the much larger number who accept that humanity is accelerating a natural phenomenon, they are a very weak response. A reduction in emissions of greenhouse gases of 5·2 per cent on 1990 levels by the developed countries by 2008–12 has to be set against the estimate of the Intergovernmental Panel on Climate Change in 1990 that a global reduction of 60 per cent in carbon dioxide emissions was required then, if the atmosphere was to enjoy a stable equilibrium. Moreover, that estimate had risen by 1999 to 70 per cent.

The Montreal Conference.

The eleventh conference of the parties held in Montreal in December 2005 threatened to be the most rancorous yet, but finally came to an agreement which was praised by delegates and environmentalists alike. The initially highly obstructive Americans appeared to realise the risks of their isolation, not least after a surprise visit from former President Clinton, and the parties could finally agree to launch negotiations on the future strengthening of international co-operation in the fight against climate change, and to make the Kyoto Protocol itself legally binding. The opening of the door to a post-Kyoto agreement was indeed to be welcomed, but the cynical observation of *The Independent* newspaper should not be overlooked: "Since the summit began (11 days previously), the seas have risen by 0·077mm, 1,176 million barrels of oil have been pumped, 80,000 hectares of forest have been destroyed, and 907 million tons of greenhouse gases have been discharged."

The Global Perspective.

Although the average Briton might still instinctively react that such an increase for the traditional holiday month was a positive asset, the global reality is very different from the perspective of the Pacific and the Caribbean. Some twenty states including the Maldives, the Cook Islands, Nauru, Kiribati, the Seychelles, Antigua, Barbuda and the Federated States of Micronesia are at risk of becoming uninhabitable through the saline pollution of all water supplies or through simply being submerged. One of the leading members of the islands' lobbying body, the Association of Small Island States (Aosis), is the Marshall Islands with an average height above sea level of 6-feet and a maximum height of 20-feet but with a population of 56,000. It is projected that 80 per cent of the main island and its capital will be under water within a century, which has led to the preparation of a strategy of total evacuation and abandonment.

Precedent is not encouraging for the ready welcome of such refugees, and even if they do receive a welcome their national culture will almost certainly be lost. The possible host nations may also have problems of their own. Vulnerable coastal cities range from New Orleans in the USA to Bangkok, Hong Kong, Shanghai and Tokyo in Asia.

El Niño.

The most dramatic recent expression of the destructive potential of global warming, however, has been provided by El Niño, although its precise relationship with the wider global phenomenon is the subject of scientific argument. El Niño is a complex of storms and hurricanes routinely generated at five to six year intervals by the warming of the Pacific. An area of warm water comparable in size to the continent of Europe is displaced from off Indonesia towards the South American coast 3,000 miles away, and instead of provoking the familiar south-east Asian monsoon it brings torrential rain and floods the length of the western littoral of the Americas. Moreover its scale is such that it disrupts weather patterns as far away as Africa.

Although the phenomenon is ancient, it appears

to be growing in frequency and intensity, fuelling speculation that it is being aggravated by global warming. Research published in 2001 shows that it is now stronger than at any other time in the last 130,000 years. The rise of 5°C in the surface water temperature of the Pacific in 1997 was expected to provoke rainfall 200 per cent of normal before Christmas and 300 per cent afterwards along the Pacific seaboard of the United States. In an apparently perverse contradiction, it can provoke compensating snowstorms and blizzards further inland.

El Niño returned to haunt Australia in 2002, provoking the worst drought for a century. The production of both wheat and barley was predicted to fall by more than 50%, and the overall cost to the economy was likely to be some £2 billion.

Devastation in America.

Despite earlier predictions by meteorologists that El Niño would continue to disrupt global weather conditions until May 1998, there is good reason to believe that it contributed to two later phenomena. In accordance with the expectation that the eastern seaboard of the United States would experience the reverse of the western, July 1998 saw one of the worst droughts in Texan history, with temperatures in Dallas remaining at 37°C (100°F) for the whole month. The drought was then followed by torrential rains resulting in floods which affected a quarter of the state's territory. This faded into insignificance, however, against the impact of Hurricane Mitch on Honduras and neighbouring Nicaragua at the beginning of November 1998. Central America's worst storm on record, during which the equivalent of perhaps three years' rainfall fell in just four days, killed up to 10,000 people in Honduras, central America's poorest state, and rendered some 800,000 people, more than 10 per cent of the population, homeless. It also destroyed some 70 per cent of agricultural output, with preliminary estimates suggesting that loss alone would amount to some £1·2 billion, equivalent to more than 60 per cent of annual national income.

The World Summit in Johannesburg.

The issues of crippling indebtedness in the developing world highlighted by such disasters, and of the appropriate response stimulated a series of international gatherings in 2002 of which the World Summit in Johannesburg in August–September attracted by far the most attention.

The reality proved to be better than feared but was still widely criticised by environmentalists for the weakness of its undertakings. The most important commitment by the nations of the world was to halve the number of people without access to drinking water and sanitation by 2015, but the right to drinking water was a repetition of the UN Millennium Declaration, and the political will to achieve either was unconvincing. More impressive in some respects was the new agreement to phase out the use of toxic chemicals by 2020, but it remained a non-binding commitment for individual countries. Most of the other goals, like reducing deaths of under-fives by two-thirds by 2015, slowing or stopping biodiversity loss by 2010, and reducing the prevalence of HIV/AIDS among 15 to 24-year-olds by 2005, were reiterations of previous goals, or, like stopping overfishing by 2015 and substantially increasing the use of renewable energy sources, were new goals but without either timetables or targets. The one exception was the agreement to establish a network of international marine reserves by 2012.

The position was no better with regard to debt, aid and poverty, which many saw as being the key challenges of the Summit. The agreement to reduce the unsustainable burden of debt was a reiteration of the Monterrey Consensus in March and the agreement to increase development aid to 0·7% of GDP in developed countries was a reiteration of the agreement at the International Conference on Financing and Development, and the resolution to halve by 2015 the number of people living on under $1 a day a restatement of the UN Millennium Declaration. None of these committed anybody to actually doing anything. For further discussion, see **The Hungry Planet, Y22.**

The Crucial Failure.

The key failure of the Summit, though, was its failure to pursue its ostensible aim of building on the foundations for a more sustainable future laid at Rio ten years previously. It was "Rio +10" in name only. The sense shown of mutual self-interest in the welfare of the planet was minimal. The important question is whether this failure represents a short-term or a long-term reversal. The approach of the US was extraordinarily negative with President Bush being praised by oil industry interests for not attending the Summit, as it "will provide a global media stage for many of the most irresponsible and destructive elements in critical economic and environmental issues. Your presence would help publicise various anti-freedom, anti-people, anti-globalisation and anti-western agendas."

Anger at US Obstruction.

US delegates also opposed certain human rights clauses because the US religious right feared that they could be used to justify abortion and birth control. The reward was the repeated jeering, slow hand-clapping and walk-outs which accompanied the US Secretary of State's address during the closing session. The world's delegates simply could not believe Colin Powell's assertion that "President Bush and the American people have an enduring commitment to sustainable development".

The growth in US military hegemony could come to be seen in retrospect as less important than this loss of leadership, not just on the environmental issues of the World Summit but on a host of other political and social issues ranging from birth control and capital punishment to liability for war crimes. Not least, the US economy is to be denied the environment-related stimulus to technological advance on which its future competitiveness depends.

WORLD WATER RESOURCES.

The Background.

"Water, water, everywhere nor any drop to drink." The lament of Coleridge's Ancient Mariner memorably summarises the essential dilemma of water. In global terms there is an abundance, but in national and regional terms there can be dramatic deficiencies in availability, distribution, predictability and quality. A fifth of all the world's population, for example, lacks access to safe drinking water, a proportion which is set to increase. By 2025, an estimated 2·7 billion people (a third of the global population) will live in regions which face severe water shortages. Those opposing propositions can be reconciled in part by technology but only at a price. It is the interplay of these considerations, and in particular of distribution, quality and cost, which makes water such a political topic at every level.

The Paradox.

The literal abundance of water is not always appreciated, but it has been calculated that the earth contains some 1·4 billion cubic kilometres of it. The difficulty is that most of it is either saline in the seas and oceans, buried deep underground or frozen in the polar ice caps. We all know, perhaps from experiments as children, that we cannot drink salt water. Neither can the other mammals. Salt is also poisonous to the crops on which we depend, and land recently flooded by, or reclaimed from, the sea is infertile. Moreover, man needs clean water. The general absence of bacteria in drinking water supplies, and the consequent decline in such water-borne diseases as cholera and typhus, is one of the more important reasons behind our life expectancy being perhaps treble that of our earlier ancestors.

Access to Water.

In current day-to-day living, therefore, we are concerned with access to water fresh enough for agricultural use and for use as drinking water after treatment. The prime source of such fresh water is rain, either collected direct in storage tanks ranging from the water butt to the reservoir or, more normally, from rivers or subsurface water-retaining rock strata (aquifers) such as chalk. The use of aquifers, which are often vast in capacity and do not suffer losses from evaporation, makes a large contribution to ensuring the predictability of supplies in areas of moderate, but sometimes erratic, rainfall like much of north-western Europe. They also underlie the desert oases, some of which like Tashkent in central Asia support very large cities.

The use of aquifers, however, does not obviate the initial need for rain, and we all know of the contrast between the heavy falls of the tropics and the aridity of the Sahara or the Gobi, and of the disaster in the years when the monsoon fails. What we usually appreciate less is that the *distribution* of rainfall across even England and Wales is sufficient to have a considerable impact on the availability of drinking water supplies. This is not just because precipitation ranges from the more than 40 inches of the west coast to the less than 20 inches of parts of the east coast, but because growing plants absorb up to 18 inches of the rain that falls. In practice, therefore, a notoriously rainy city such as Manchester has an area water supply potential perhaps ten times greater than that of, say, Southend at the mouth of the Thames estuary. Such unpopular measures as hosepipe bans will inevitably be more likely in those areas where the margin of available water is particularly low or where the capacity of the underlying aquifers is limited.

Man's Need for Water.

Man has traditionally responded to these realities by settling where fresh water was plentiful—in the river valleys, near natural springs and adjacent to lakes. Indeed the growth of advanced civilisation is synonymous with the Nile, the Tigris and the Euphrates, the Indus, and other great rivers. Such civilisations, however, were based on comparatively small populations, modest living standards for the great majority and the limitation of water-consuming technology to the irrigation ditch and bucket. The Egyptian bucket or 'shadouf' remains, but otherwise all has changed in developing and developed world alike. The world's population passed 6 billion in 1999, and the rate of growth is easy to appreciate from national statistics. Egypt's estimated population of 44 million in 1981 is now (2003) more than 69 million. China has probably added a quarter of a billion people to its population over the same period. Such growth is paralleled in developing countries world-wide. No less significant, though, is the increase in living standards and the associated increase in water consumption. The bath, the shower, the washing machine and the flush toilet are the norm in the developed world, and increasingly so in the developing one. The dishwasher and the garden sprinkler are not far behind. In their traditional form, at least, all consume much more water than is commonly appreciated. The consequence is that the global demand for water has trebled since 1950.

The Exhaustion of Current Supplies.

Against this background it is easy to appreciate that the traditional sources of fresh water are fast approaching exhaustion. In some places the critical point has already been reached. The Aral Sea, now the earth's fourth largest lake, is now half the size it was only thirty years ago because of excessive abstraction from the rivers Amu Darya and Syr Darya (Oxus and Jaxartes). The Colorado River in the USA usually runs dry before it reaches the sea. Many other famous rivers are running at critically low levels. Of equal importance is the wide-spread fall in water table levels, with the level under Beijing, as just one example, having fallen by 37 metres in as many years. Groundwater in the Arabian peninsula could be exhausted within another 50 years. The long-term implications are obvious, but major problems in the shorter term include land subsidence and the pollution of the remaining fresh water deposits by salt water drawn in from the sea by subterranean vacuum pressure.

Consequences of Water Shortages.

The economic and political consequences of these developments are considerable and could easily prove catastrophic. Less accessible water is usually more expensive water, as ever deeper aquifers have to be tapped, larger and more numerous river regulation dams have to be built, and more dependence is placed on marginal supplies needing blending and more extensive prior treatment. It is the political consequences, however, which are the most sobering. Many of the world's famous rivers are shared between mutually suspicious neighbours, with control of the all-important headwaters sometimes lying with unstable or traditionally hostile states.

Ethiopia and the Sudan hold the key to the Nile, Turkey to the Euphrates, and Israel to the Jordan, to the potential detriment of Egypt, Syria and Iraq, and the state of Jordan respectively. Egypt has already threatened to bomb Ethiopia if it proceeds with plans to use the waters of the Blue Nile for irrigation projects. Israel has already broken commitments to Jordan, and Turkey has plans for a hydro-electric scheme which could reduce the flow of the Euphrates into Syria by 35%.

International Water Disputes.

Moreover, bitter disputes have also arisen away from the more obvious centres of tension. Mexico has been refused more water from the Rio Grande by the United States and the extremely contentious Gabcikovo-Nagymaros hydroelectric dam project on the Danube, inherited from the Communist era, was finally referred by Hungary and Slovakia to the International Court of Justice. It is not difficult to appreciate the concern of many observers that such disputes in areas already tense, like the Middle East, could easily lead to war.

Those fears may well turn out to have been justified, but the reality of water is complicated by the impact of human activity in other spheres and by the availability of practicable, albeit sometimes expensive, technological solutions. Human activity uses water and the more sophisticated it becomes the more it tends to use. At the same time, whilst it cannot literally create water, it can certainly concentrate and redirect its flows. The positive face is irrigation, the negative face is ill-considered drainage, often associated with agricultural or residential development, causing flooding downstream.

The chain of cause and effect can be a long one. Low-lying Bangladesh at the mouth of the Ganges is increasingly exposed to ever more flooding as a result of increased run-off into the river following deforestation a thousand miles away in Nepal and northern India. Flood prevention schemes for the Rhine in Germany have led to flooding downstream in the Netherlands, and in Britain too much housing has been built on natural flood plains which contain rather than discharge water. Many parts of the world are increasingly exposed to the risk of too much and too little water at one and the same time.

The Impact of Global Warming.

All these considerations, however, are likely to be marginalised by the impact of global warming (*see* **Y6**). Scientific opinion on the rate of warming increasingly favours estimates at the upper end of the scale, and researchers at the UK Meteorological Office now suspect that warming will accelerate significantly from 2050 as natural carbon absorption systems begin to fail. It is clear that warming will raise sea levels and that the polar ice cap melts and that traditional weather patterns will change significantly. It is, though, almost impossible to predict what the more localised impact will be. It is nevertheless likely to be drastic. Heavy rain could become characteristic of the Sahara and the Gobi. The temperate lands of northwestern Europe could become a dustbowl. Nobody knows, but it seems likely that nature will give relief to some present areas of acute water shortage while seriously worsening others.

The Management of Demand.

The level of adaptation required will strain economic and political systems to their limits, but the likely response of the developed world can already be discerned. Whereas a growing demand for water was once welcomed as evidence of growing public health—it is not so many decades since those rehoused from slum dwellings were wont to keep the coal in the bath—it is now to be discouraged. The UK government, for one, effectively decided nearly 20 years ago now that the era of major water engineering projects, culminating in Northumberland's Kielder Water, was over. The management of demand can in practice be achieved either through the price mechanism or through technical solutions or a combination of both. Reliance on the price mechanism does, however, have its difficulties. Specific charges can be levied for connections to hosepipes or garden swimming pools, but higher prices in general will not have an impact in the absence of metering. Metering accords with the strand in governmental thinking which now sees water as a product rather than a service, but both the practical reality and the philosophy have their critics. Although metering is widespread in Europe it has always been comparatively rare in Britain. It is expensive to install and the meters, compared with those for gas and electricity, are less reliable and need more maintenance. Critics of the philosophy argue that water is a basic human need and that the application of market principles is simply inappropriate. Not dissimilar arguments are familiar from the debates over the funding of health, education and transport.

Higher Quality Standard.

Both sides, however, have to recognise the reality that the higher quality standards demanded by the public and enforced by EU directives have made water more costly. Rain may be free, but collecting it when it falls, treating it and distributing it to homes and businesses, and taking it back as sewage and again treating it to make it fit for re-use, is very expensive. More attention could, therefore, be paid to some technical solutions. Although domestic appliances are much more water efficient than they once were, yet more could be done. It is little appreciated that the traditional flush toilet consumes 9 litres with each flush while a water saving equivalent consumes only 3·75 litres, equivalent to an estimated saving of 40 tonnes of water for an average household annually. Moreover, the toilet is responsible for 35% of all domestic water use. It also has to be remembered that all the water coming into a UK household has been expensively treated to drinking water standard. One body of opinion argues that it is a waste of both money and natural resources to treat all water in this way, and that houses should be equipped with two water supply systems—one of drinking water and one of much lower quality "grey" water suitable for washing the car and the floor and for flushing the toilet.

Such an innovation would have a high initial capital cost but would save money in the longer term, and ideas of cost, value and ownership may have to be modified if the global problem of water is to be resolved in the longer term. Water tends to be seen as national property. Within the UK, Welsh nationalist opinion has long resented the abstraction of Welsh water to supply English Liverpool without compensating payment. When the Syrians requested more water from the Euphrates, the Turks responded: "We do not say they should share their oil resources. They cannot say they should share our water resources." Water, however, is a human necessity in a way that oil is not, and although it may be feasible to imagine oil-rich countries purchasing water, their oil is finite and many of the world's poorest countries are equally poor in water resources. Moreover, the potential cost of fighting over water and of coping with the very many refugees is so high that a measure of sharing may come to be seen as self-interested. One fighter plane can cost as much as supplying 100,000 people with fresh water.

Conclusions.

Such considerations must not, however, totally distract us from our initial reality: the globe has an abundance of water. Some of the technology needed to secure it is expensive. The most obvious is the desalination of sea water, but the cost is falling and the application of solar power or even of nuclear fusion, as distinct from fission, could make it routine in the longer term. Supplies can be pumped up from deeper levels, and may even have to be for other reasons. London, for example, is threatened by a water table rising at the rate of two metres a year consequent upon the cessation of pumping for industrial purposes. Thames Water argues that the use of such contaminated water would not be cost-effective, but that depends on who pays for the likely damage to basements and the London Underground if it is not used. Global warming is melting the polar ice caps, and engineers have toyed with the possibility of towing icebergs to water-deficient regions.

Other possibilities, however, are remote from science fiction, notably the reduction of waste. In the UK, for example, leakage from distribution mains has traditionally represented more than a quarter of all treated water. A world critically short of water may have to regard garden swimming pools and ornamental ponds as unacceptable luxuries. Less controversially, there seems a real prospect of developing seeds and plants which can grow in saline soils.

The key questions are whether both the liberal democratic political system and the market economic system will be able to rise to challenges of this magnitude. The evidence is not always encouraging, but the verdict must remain open.

ENDANGERED SPECIES.

The first decade of the new century is witnessing an alarming increase in the number of species threatened with likely extinction. The World Conservation Union's Red List of Threatened Species (published in November 2003) reported that the nomadic Saiga antelope, the wild Bactrian camel and the Ethiopian water mouse are among 121 species to join the endangered list.

Others have fared even worse. Since the start of the new century, five creatures have been officially declared extinct—from the Reunion Island sheldgoose to the sea mink and two types of hippo. No less than 11,167 assorted plants and animals are at risk of joining the list of long-vanished species.

Vulnerable Species.

The rarity of a species can be evaluated in terms of its geographical range, its habitat specificity, and the size of its local and total population. Some species are especially vulnerable to extinction:

1) **Geographically restricted species.** Some species occur over a very limited range. Physical, biological or climatic factors can all restrict the distribution of a species.

2) **Highly specialised species.** Species that are highly adapted to specific habitats are less resilient to environmental change than are habitat generalists. Examples are hardwood trees and many large mammals, such as rhino, elephant, tigers and whales. Once depleted, their populations are slow to recover.

3) **Intrinsically rare species.** Some species do not occur at high abundance, even when environmental conditions appear favourable. Most rainforest species are intrinsically rare, in that each species constitutes a low percentage of the community as a whole. There is therefore a high risk of local extinction if habitat is lost.

Causes of Extinction.

Climatic change has been a major factor in driving speciation and extinction throughout the history of the earth. Today, however, the causes of extinction stem from the growing human population and the increasing scale of human influence on the environment. The main causes of extinction are over-exploitation and the loss or alteration of habitats.

Population depletion may cause a reduction in

genetic variation, reducing the species' ability to adapt to changing conditions. Depleted populations may enter the extinction vortex, which means that they decline more rapidly as their diminishing population becomes less fit for survival and reproduction. Small populations are vulnerable to extinction because of random events, such as outbreaks of disease or extreme weather conditions. It is thought that each species has a minimum viable population size, below which it cannot recover (the "Allee effect").

Habitat Loss, Degradation or Alteration.

Loss of habitat is the main threat to species today. Tropical rainforests contain over half of the world's species. Over 50 million acres of tropical rainforests are lost every year. 60–85% of forest in Madagascar has been destroyed, with the loss of untold numbers of endemic plants and animals. Other species-rich habitats, such as coral reefs and coastal wetlands are also being rapidly destroyed.

Industrialisation, urbanisation and large-scale development have caused habitat destruction on a massive scale. Mankind can now drastically alter habitats through large-scale technology, such as the drainage of wetlands and the development of hydroelectric power-schemes. Clear-felling of forests has resulted in erosion and has caused siltation of river systems. Intensive agriculture involves the establishment of monocultures, which almost entirely exclude wildlife habitat.

Industry, agriculture, transport and human settlements are all sources of pollution. Pollution of the environment can occur on a local or an international scale. The discharge of pesticides, fertilisers, sewage, and chemical waste into the environment can cause serious degradation of habitats. The effects of particular toxins may become intensified throughout the food chain because of bio-accumulation. In the Amazon basin, mercury from gold-mining processes is polluting river systems and endangering the health of plants, animals and humans.

The introduction of exotic species can have serious consequences for the native flora and fauna. The introduction of the Nile Perch to Lake Victoria drove half of the indigenous fish species to or near to extinction. Some species are introduced as biological control agents, but have deleterious effects on non-target species. In the future, global warming and the associated changes in habitat will influence the distribution and abundance of species.

Over-Exploitation.

Animal and plant populations are over-exploited if they are harvested at a faster rate than they can replenish themselves. Some examples are given below.

Open access resources, such as some fisheries, are especially vulnerable to over-exploitation. Individual users do not benefit from restricting their level of harvesting; someone else will simply take what is left behind. It is this phenomenon, known as the fisherman's dilemma, which led to the devastation of whale populations and some fish stocks. The population of blue whales was once 228,000. There are now less than 12,000 and it is not known whether their population can ever recover.

Local over-exploitation can occur where communities that depend on subsistence harvesting outstrip the resources available to them. For example, in parts of India, gathering of fuel wood is degrading forests and having detrimental effects on wildlife. Human populations in some areas are growing more quickly than the resources on which they depend. This is a problem of equity and distribution, rather than a lack of resources *per se*. 80% of the world's resources are consumed by 20% of its population.

The Endangered Species Convention (CITES).

The Convention on International Trade in Endangered Species (CITES) is an attempt to protect endangered species from over-harvesting. Species are afforded different levels of protection according to how at risk they are from international trade. CITES prohibits international trade in species which are in danger of extinction. It also restricts trade in those species that could become threatened with extinction if trade continues. However, enforcement remains a problem and many signatories lack the will or resources to prevent illegal trade. Unfortunately, as species become rare, their market value increases, creating an incentive to poach. Three sub-species of tiger are already extinct because of the high value of their bones which are used in traditional Chinese medicines. Black rhinos have been hunted to the brink of extinction because of the value of their horns. There are now less than 2,500 in the wild.

In a free market, demand for a product is mainly determined by its price. Trade restrictions, such as those recommended by CITES are essential in preventing the over-exploitation of species because market forces are not linked to the regeneration rate of populations. The aggressive defence of free trade is seriously hampering efforts to prevent the over-exploitation of natural resources. For example, the United States banned the import of Mexican tuna, on the grounds that Mexico had not taken steps to reduce the number of dolphins killed during tuna harvesting. The ban was deemed illegal under the General Agreement on Tariffs and Trade (GATT).

Why Conserve Species?

Humans utilise less than 1% of living species. Medicine, agriculture and industry could all potentially benefit from these unexplored resources. There are between ten million and thirty million species on earth, the vast majority of which are insects.

Species and their ecosystems maintain the earth's essential life-support systems, such as the atmosphere, water resources and soil structure. The loss of a "keystone" species may have unforeseen consequences for other species and the ecosystem as a whole. In addition, species loss restricts our ability to deal with problems and adapt to change. It also represents the loss of a key to understanding and maintaining the environment on which we depend.

Aside from utilitarian arguments, humans gain aesthetic, educational, recreational and psychological benefits from wildlife. Many people believe that we have a moral duty to safeguard the environment.

The Options for Rare Species Conservation.

The long-term survival of species depends on the maintenance of a suitable habitat. Many human activities are incompatible with habitat conservation and it is therefore essential to control development in some regions if viable populations of wildlife are to survive. A comprehensive system of protected areas is required to ensure that representative habitat types and fragile ecosystems are not destroyed. Protected areas can reduce the threats to rare species, contribute to conserving the diversity of a region and provide a supply of natural resources and additional income from tourism.

Ideally, protected areas encompass entire ecosystems, ensuring that essential ecological processes, such as water and nutrient cycling, are protected. However, this is not always possible in practice. A general rule is that reserves must be able to accommodate a viable population of those species at the top of the food chain. These species, which include top carnivores, birds of prey, and other megafauna, require the largest area. Providing space for them also protects many other species lower down the food chain.

Only 10% of land is currently protected. An isolated reserve, surrounded by land hostile to wildlife, is effectively an island. The populations within it are vulnerable to extinction in the same way as true island species. In some cases, the problem can be solved by protecting corridors of habitat, which link reserves together and allow the migration of species.

A more integrated approach to development, encompassing environmental impact assessment, may improve the prospects for the survival of wildlife outside of protected areas. Land-use planning, agricultural and forestry practice and pollution control are all crucial issues in habitat conservation. In some cases, it may be possible to integrate conservation and human activities. For example, in the

Sierra de Manantlan Biosphere Reserve, Mexico, traditional agricultural systems help to maintain habitat heterogeneity.

Ex-situ Conservation.

Ex-situ conservation is the preservation of species outside of their natural habitat, in botanic gardens, arboreta, aquaria and zoos. It is generally accepted that the long-term survival of a species cannot be ensured by *ex-situ* conservation. *Ex-situ* methods can, at best, provide a safety net in case *in-situ* conservation fails.

Botanic gardens, arboreta and seed banks can provide research, education and amenity value. Difficulties include ensuring the survival of species in an alien climate, and the long-term viability of stored seeds. *Ex-situ* populations of plants could provide the basis for the restoration of degraded habitat and the establishment of wildlife corridors. In the USA, an area of tallgrass prairie has been restored, following research into habitat restoration at the Madison Arboretum, University of Wisconsin.

Aquaria and zoos can provide amenity and research possibilities. They may also help to raise public awareness about conservation. However, the practical conservation value of zoos is constrained by physical and biological factors. Most zoos do not have space for viable populations of large animals. It is therefore necessary for zoos to exchange animals or their genetic material in order to avoid inbreeding depression. There are 500 zoos which contribute to the International Species Inventory System (ISIS) which maintains a database for zoos who wish to swap bloodlines.

Welfare Problems in Captivity.

There are welfare problems in keeping some animals in captivity. For example, many zoos do not keep elephants, because it is impossible in captivity to provide them with the space and social structure essential to their well-being. Some animals do not successfully breed or rear their young in captivity. Many captive-bred animals lack the skills and behaviour necessary for survival in the wild. There have been just 16 successful reintroductions of captive bred mammals, birds and reptiles to the wild. Most animals kept in zoos have healthy wild populations and no conservation benefit is derived from breeding them in captivity. Capture of wild individuals for use in breeding programmes can disrupt and deplete natural populations. Over-all, the funds and energy devoted to captive breeding may be more effectively spent on *in-situ* conservation.

The Future.

Our ability and willingness to conserve rare species are influenced by technical, economic and ethical considerations. In the past, legislation protecting wildlife and the environment has developed in response to crises. However, as our understanding of ecosystems improves, it may become possible to predict the environmental consequences of human activities more reliably. A precautionary approach to development could help to prevent the environmental disasters we have witnessed in recent decades.

The integration of ecological knowledge and the potential benefits of conservation into land-use planning and economic analysis would reduce the threats to species. Better understanding of the environmental consequences of consumption may encourage a more responsible attitude to natural resource use.

International co-operation is essential in preventing over-exploitation and protecting habitats across international boundaries. Over 150 nations have signed the Biodiversity Convention, thus making a commitment to conserving biological diversity.

HABITATS IN DANGER.

A habitat is the environment in which an organism lives. Though people often speak of the habitat of a particular species, habitats can be more realistically considered as functional units, consisting of a community of living organisms, and their non-living environment. Living (*biotic*) factors include the structure provided by plants and animals, and the interactions between them, such as herbivory, predation and competition. The climate, geology, and topography of an area are important non-living elements of a habitat.

Why are Habitats different?

The characteristics that distinguish different habitats result from a combination of factors, which operate at different scales. On a global scale, climate is the main determinant of habitat type, the two most important factors being temperature and rainfall. Factors such as soil type and topography operate over smaller scales, influencing the availability of water and nutrients, amongst other factors. On an even smaller scale, the distribution of organisms within the habitat creates a mosaic of micro-habitats.

There are various ways of differentiating between habitats, but perhaps the most useful one is based on climatic as well as biological factors. In general, more species can survive at the equator than at the poles. Only species adapted to severe cold can survive in the polar regions, whereas many species can thrive in the warm, moist atmosphere of the tropics. There is therefore a general, latitudinal gradient in species diversity. More complex patterns of habitat diversity are superimposed on this, due to variations in rainfall, topography and the interactions between species. The result is that species and habitats are not distributed uniformly throughout the globe.

Bioclimatic zones (or *biomes*) contain a characteristic assemblage of plants and animals. Since it is the plants that provide the physical structure, biomes are generally described in terms of their plant communities. It is convenient to give these plant communities different names and to treat them as distinct entities. In reality, the boundary between biomes may not be sharply defined. On moving from one biome to another, some species will be lost and others gained, until the habitat has completely changed in character.

Threats to Habitats.

The threats to habitats are as varied as the habitats themselves; different plant and animal communities vary in the vulnerability to disturbance and their ability to recover from it. In general, however, the increasing human population and its spread into marginal areas is placing increasing strain on soil and water resources, and is creating serious pollution problems.

Agriculture, industry and forestry operations are causing damage to habitats throughout the world. Over-harvesting of some species and introduction of others can have unforeseen consequences for the stability of ecosystems. Global climate change is a major threat to the long-term future of many habitats. A change in temperature or rainfall pattern will alter not only the physical environment, but also the distribution of species.

Some major habitats, and the threats to them, are described below.

Tropical Rainforests.

Tropical rainforests are located in South America, West and Central Africa and South-East Asia, some 10° north and south of the equator, where rainfall is distributed evenly throughout the year. They are characterised by their extremely high species diversity, and the complex structure of their plant communities. Their tallest trees often exceed 30m in height, and as many as five other layers of trees may grow beneath them, so that very little light reaches the forest floor. Smaller plants therefore tend to be climbers or epiphytes, which grow on other plants. They grow in regions of high rainfall (1750–2500mm per year). The warm, moist conditions facilitate the decomposition of plant and animal remains. The soil layer therefore tends to be thin and is easily lost to erosion if tropical forests are clear-felled.

Tropical rainforests are home to a profusion of plant and animal life. It is thought that they contain between 2·5 million and 30 million species, only a small proportion of which have been described by science. Tropical rainforest species represent a vast, largely untapped potential for medicinal products. They are essential in maintaining climatic stability, by generating oxygen and storing carbon. They also maintain rainfall patterns by encouraging cloud formation.

Many valuable timber species such as mahogany, teak and ebony grow in rainforests. Rainforests grow in some of the poorest countries in the world. The need to earn foreign currency drives the harvesting and sale of rainforest trees. Potentially valuable timber often ends up as matchsticks, charcoal, or toilet-roll. Some countries are forced by debt to hand over logging rights to their creditors.

Around 75 million hectares of tropical rainforest are felled every year, and the subsequent loss of soil cover may prevent them from ever recovering. As well as timber harvesting, tropical forests are cleared for cattle ranching, cultivation of cash crops and for shifting agriculture. Global warming also threatens the integrity of rainforests, potentially disrupting the rainfall regimes on which they depend.

Savannas.

Savannas are those habitats characterised by grassland with scattered trees and shrubs. They cover about 15% of the earth's land surface. They occur in areas with seasonal rainfall, and are strongly influenced by the occurrence of fire and grazing. Their structure can be very dynamic; the proportion of tree cover varies dramatically in response to variation in fire and grazing pressure. They tend to occur in the semi-arid tropics, for example at the borders between tropical deciduous forests and deserts. The most familiar are found in Africa, where they are home to some of the world's most spectacular wildlife, such as elephant, rhino, giraffe, zebra, lion and buffalo.

They also occur to the north and south of the Amazon Basin rainforest, and in some temperate areas.

Threats to savannas include over-grazing by domestic livestock, and conversion to farmland for the cultivation of crops. Over-harvesting of herbivores for subsistence purposes has greatly reduced their density outside of protected areas. In some regions, loss of habitat, hunting pressure and the disruption of migratory routes has concentrated the remaining animals at high densities into protected areas. Some argue that these areas do not contain sufficient food and water resources to sustain the current population densities.

Deserts.

Deserts are characterised by their low rainfall and high daily temperatures. They occur mainly in the horse latitudes, which is the region between 30° and 40° north and south of the equator. Some desert regions receive no rainfall for years at a time.

Others do receive rainfall, but the high temperatures cause immediate evaporation of the water, so it is not available for plant growth. Few plants can grow in these conditions, and those that do possess special adaptations for resisting drought. Desert animals, too, possess an array of behavioural and physical adaptations to their environment. These unique ecosystems are extremely fragile and may take centuries to recover from a period of disturbance. On the other hand, desert-like conditions are being created in areas where overgrazing and diversion of water for agriculture are degrading more productive habitats.

Temperate Grasslands.

Temperate grasslands occur between 30° and 60° in areas where rainfall is too low to support trees. They once covered 40% of the earth's surface. Grasses and sedges dominate their vegetation, making them an important habitat for grazing animals, as well as birds. In the more arid regions of this biome are the desert grasslands in warm areas, and the shortgrass plains, or steppe, in colder latitudes.

Wetter areas can sustain a larger, above-ground biomass, for example the tallgrass prairies of North America, the pampas of South America, the veldt of South Africa and the puszta of eastern Europe. The dominant grasses in these habitats are peren-

nials, which are adapted to withstand grazing by herbivores. Their growing tissue is located below ground, a feature known as a basal meristem. They can therefore withstand repeated loss of their foliage by grazers. Woody plants, on the other hand, cannot recover so easily from such damage, since the growing part of the plant is located at the tips of the stems, and is therefore lost by grazing. Grazing by wild herbivores therefore tends to prevent the encroachment of scrub.

Over-grazing by domestic animals, however, can lead to the degradation and loss of grassland habitats. Over-grazing can completely destroy the grass and herb layer, exposing bare soil and leading to erosion and scrub encroachment.

Most of the biomass in a grassland lies below ground. As a result, they tend to have deep fertile soils, and have been targeted for agricultural development. Over half of the world's naturally occurring grassland has been ploughed up for arable crops, or has been "improved" by the introduction of species and the addition of fertilisers, leading to a loss of diversity. Afforestation also threatens some grasslands, notably the Spanish steppes.

Temperate Deciduous Forests.

This biome occurs throughout the temperate latitudes, in areas with sufficient rainfall to support large trees. They occur in North America, western Europe and parts of eastern Asia. Though they are variable in structure and species composition, all of their main tree species are dormant and leafless during winter. This can allow a highly diverse understory to develop during the spring, before the leaf canopy causes shade. Deciduous trees are important habitats for insects and bird life.

Many of the species typical of temperate deciduous forests, such as oak and beech, are slow-growing. Over-harvesting of commercially important species and the accompanying destruction of associated vegetation has degraded or destroyed much of this habitat. Over half of Britain's ancient woodlands were destroyed between 1930 and 1990, to make way for plantations of faster growing species, such as sitka spruce.

Effects of Acid Rain.

During the 1980s, concern grew over the effects of "acid rain" on forests, particularly those of Scandinavia, Germany and parts of North America. The burning of fossil fuels in the industrial areas generated sulphur dioxide (SO_2) and oxides of nitrogen (NO_x), causing the formation of sulphuric and nitric acids in rainwater. The Convention on Long Range Transboundary Air Pollution is an international agreement aiming to limit emissions of airborne pollutants such as SO_2 and NO_x. Measures to control sulphur emissions have met with some success, and the problem of acid rain seems to be abating in some regions. However, it is still a problem in eastern Europe and may become worse again as more countries become industrialised.

Coral Reefs.

Coral reefs occur in the warm, shallow waters of the tropics, covering approximately 60,000 square kilometres. They are found in shallow waters, up to 30m in depth. They are the most diverse marine habitat. Their structure is provided by the calcareous skeleton of tiny animals. These animals live in colonies. Each coral polyp contains symbiotic algae, which use the energy of sunlight to make sugars, thus providing energy for the coral organism. As the polyps die, their skeletons build up and form a reef. The complex structure of the reefs provides a home for a vast array of marine organisms, making the coral reef one of the most spectacular and beautiful environments on earth. An estimated 60% of coral reefs are now under threat.

In recent years there have been massive die-offs of coral reef communities, accompanied by "bleaching" or loss of colour in coral organisms. This effect is caused by the death of the algae which live within the coral cells. It is thought that the causes of bleaching are slight increases in temperature, which disrupt the fragile balance between the algae and their hosts. Global warming is therefore a major threat to the future of coral reefs.

Reefs are also damaged by the tourist industry, which causes direct physical disturbance, and generates indirect threats by the collection and sale of coral as souvenirs. Destructive fishing methods, including the use of dynamite, have also destroyed large areas of coral. The trade in tropical fish is also responsible for further disruption of coral reef ecosystems.

Coral reefs can also suffer because of environmental degradation in terrestrial biomes. Deforestation and erosion can massively increase the amount of particles in river systems. If these particles reach the sea and are deposited on reefs, they can smother the reef system, preventing light from reaching the reef and thus starving it of essential nutrients.

Wetlands.

The term "wetlands" encompasses a variety of habitats including swamps, marshes, fens and estuaries. They are all dominated by the presence of water, which may be temporary or permanent. They are an important habitat for fish and other wildlife, and are essential resting points for migratory birds. They also fulfil important ecological functions, such as trapping sediments and reducing erosion and flooding.

Wetlands were once considered practically worthless in human terms and many were drained to make way for agriculture and other developments. However, by the late 1960s, their ecological importance was recognised, and in 1971, the Convention on Wetlands of International Importance (the Ramsar Convention) was drawn up in order to protect wetlands of international importance. The Ramsar Convention lists 400 sites of conservation, covering an area of 193 million hectares.

Habitat Conservation.

Habitats and the threats to them are international concerns. International legislation and co-operation therefore provide the key to safeguarding their future. Examples of agreements protecting specific habitats can be found in the section above. In addition, the following can be mentioned.

* The *Convention concerning the Protection of the World Cultural and Natural Heritage* was agreed in 1972, and has now been signed by over 140 nations. It identified world heritage sites and established a fund for protecting them.

* The *Biodiversity Convention* is a product of the 1992 Earth Summit (United Nations Conference on Environment and Development). It obliges signatories to prevent the depletion of biological resources and provides guidelines for doing so. Although its language could be stronger, it provides a first step for a co-ordinated, global attempt at preventing the destruction of habitats and species. It was signed by all 150 participating nations, apart from the United States of America.

TRENDS IN WORLD POPULATION.

Introduction.

The Universal Declaration of Human Rights adopted by the United Nations in 1948, and similar declarations before and since, assert that man has the right to life, liberty and security of the person. Few would argue, at least in principle, but in practice any such right is threatened on all sides. Those threats fall into distinct, if overlapping, categories.

The first threat is posed by the sheer size and rate of growth of population, which raises the issue of whether the globe has the resources to support them. The second is posed by the danger of disease, notably AIDS. The third threat is posed by the uncertainty as to whether established interests will have sufficient sense of the common human interest to allow enough redistribution of advantage to avoid ongoing warfare over land and resources.

Concerns over Population Growth.

Concern at population growth is not new. Malthus first responded to it in the eighteenth century by predicting that, as soon as the demands of a growing population approached the limits of the economy to supply them, warfare would break out and last until the population had been reduced to a sustainable level.

The concern proved needless at the time, because Malthus did not appreciate the extent to which economic limits were extendable and how applied science could increase agricultural productivity, but fears continue to be expressed that the world of our own time is growing and consuming at a rate which is literally unsustainable. The raw facts are daunting. When Malthus was writing his famous essay in 1798, the earth's population numbered probably less than 1 billion. By the 1960s it had reached 3.6 billion and it now stands at 6 billion. It is clearly true that this has not yet caused global famine: the very real famines with which we are familiar are comparatively localised and often associated with protracted warfare. The traditional great famines of China and India appear to have receded into history.

Nevertheless two very real fears remain. The first is that many of the agricultural practices employed to feed 6 billion people today, and who knows how many tomorrow, are unsustainable in the longer term because they are using up natural resources at a rate faster than they can be replenished. Such critics will point to the pollution of watercourses, the contamination of land, and diseases such as BSE in cattle, which are alleged by many to be the consequence of industrialised farming methods.

They can also point to the seriously depleted stocks of such a staple as cod, resulting from decades of over-fishing. The second is that not only has the world's population doubled in perhaps half a century, but its consumption patterns also have dramatically altered. The developed world takes ever more sophisticated consumer goods for granted, and the developing world is determined to catch up. The "Living Planet Report 2000", published by the World Wide Fund for Nature and the United Nations Environment Programme, argues that the demands being placed in many parts of the West and in the Middle East on the resources of the sea and the land are such that they may have run out by 2075.

Disease and Poor Health.

The threat posed by disease is readily overlooked. The traditional mass killers such as cholera and typhoid have indeed been brought under control, although others like tuberculosis remain challenging, but AIDS is expanding to fill the gap. The disease is not advancing in Europe and North America in the way that was first feared, although it has claimed some distinguished victims, but it is advancing in sub-Saharan Africa at an alarming rate and is already the largest cause of death. Many observers fear that it could prove as disastrous there as the Black Death was in fourteenth-century Europe.

Less dramatic, but in some ways as significant, is premature death from poor health and deteriorating conditions. Life expectancy in the developed world with its better health care has long been well ahead of that in the developing world, but what is new is the plummeting life expectancy in parts of the former Soviet bloc consequent upon the fall of Communism in 1990. The great decline in health care standards, coupled with the recourse to alcohol and cigarettes of those unemployed or otherwise suffering from the devastated economy, means that the life expectancy of the average Russian male is now only 59 compared with the 72·1 years of the average British male or the 76·2 years of the average Japanese male. Fewer than half of the Russian boys now aged sixteen can expect to see the age of sixty: a proportion lower than 100 years ago. On the basis of present trends the Russian population will have fallen by 39 million by the year 2025, in addition to the fall of 6 million already experienced since 1990.

Some experts believe that, for similar reasons, the population of the rest of eastern Europe could fall by as much as half within the next 50 years.

Distribution of World Population.

The third threat is much more difficult to assess, but may well prove to be the most significant. It is not just a question of how much the world's population is growing but of where it is growing and why, and whether the rate of growth will continue. Why is it stagnant or even falling in some regions? What relationship does the birth rate have with changing family patterns in much of the developed world and what is the real significance of those changes in the longer term?

Changing World Distribution.

The great change in the distribution of the world's population is easy to illustrate. In 1950, the population of Europe was two and a half times that of Africa, now at 729 million it is lower than Africa's 749 million. In 1950, Europe and North America contained 28·5 % of the world's population; it is estimated that by 2050 that proportion will have fallen to 11·5 %. In 1950, Britain was the ninth largest country in the world in population, but by 2050 it is likely to be thirtieth.

EU Population Projections.

The United Nations predicted in 2003 that the population of the EU could fall by as much as 88 million, if current replacement trends continue for a further 15 years. Only the United Kingdom and France are projected to grow, with the British population rising by 7·5 million people to 66·2 million by 2050, and the French population rising by 5 million over the same period, as a result of both immigration and high birth rates.

Around 40 % of the world's population is now either Chinese or Indian. Whether those trends will continue is a much more difficult question. It is true that the world's population has grown by an awesome 62 % in the last 30 years, but that overall statistic hides the fact that the rate of increase appears to have peaked in about 1970. Even if the rate of growth does decelerate, however, and some sort of stability is achieved, the world's population could still reach 8.9 billion by 2055 compared with some 6 billion today. Scientists are currently (2004) predicting that the growth in world population may peak at 9 billion around 2070. It will then decrease, but simultaneously grow older. One prediction is that by 2100 45 per cent of the population of Western Europe will be aged over 60.

Agents of Population Growth.

Population growth is driven by two distinct components which may overlap but are still essentially separate. The first is the age at which people die and the second is the rate at which they are born. The age at which people die is by far the more predictable, because the rate at which health care can be improved is, within limits, controllable. It is not normal for the trend to go into abrupt reverse in the way it has in Russia, and it is unlikely that the increase in life expectancy worldwide over the last 50 years, of from 46 to 66 years, will be reversed unless disaster strikes.

The birth rate, however, is only very imperfectly understood. It is broadly true that it is traditionally high when there is an expectation that many children will not survive infancy or when children are likely to be one's sole source of support in old age. Religious traditions may encourage procreation and discourage birth control. The rate normally falls as the poorer social groups become wealthier and seek to give their children opportunities which their own parents had not been able to afford for them. It sometimes seems that the rate falls when a country lacks confidence in the future, with Britain in the 1930s a possible case in point. All of these possibilities, however, match the reality imperfectly at best. There is no obvious reason, for example, why France's population remained relatively stagnant throughout the nineteenth century whereas Britain's grew by leaps and bounds. Likewise, there is no obvious reason now why the birth rates in both modern Germany and modern Italy are insufficient to maintain population in the longer term, whereas the rate in India is so high that India is likely to have more people than China within 40 years. When the rate is the equivalent of a baby born every two seconds, it may be dangerous to presume that the rate of increase worldwide has indeed peaked. What is the real significance of the statistic that children in the West are increasingly likely to be born out of wedlock, with the proportion in Europe ranging from 55 % in Sweden to 8 % in Italy?

The Trend to Urbanisation.

What is clear is that these different rates are sustaining or increasing existing patterns of disadvantage. Half of India's adults are already illiterate, more than half its children undernourished, and a third of its population living below the poverty line. They are also promoting an ever more urban world. Whereas the average contribution of the world's more developed regions to global urban population growth was only some 15 % over the last thirty years, Africa is expected to contribute 25 % and Asia 60 % of the global increase in the period 2000–2030. It is expected that 2006 will be the first year in which the number of urban dwellers worldwide exceeds that of rural dwellers.

Such changes will push human resilience and adaptability to the limit. It seems inevitable that countries like Bangladesh, with 2,244 people to the square mile already, compared with Europe's highest figure of 978 to the square mile in the Netherlands, will see growing emigration.

The phenomenon of climate change will be a further complicating factor. Both Bangladesh and the Netherlands could succumb to rising sea levels quite rapidly, whereas some less promising areas like Central Asia could become more inviting. Sub-Saharan Africa, where so much population growth is predicted, could succumb to desertification. We do not know, but a renewed period of mass human migration seems a very real possibility.

THE GREEN MOVEMENT: A HISTORY

Introduction.

Any history of the Green Movement should perhaps really be entitled a history of green movements, because the modern umbrella term covers a range of concerns of very different origins and of groups with very different, and sometimes contradictory, priorities.

The oldest strand of concern is probably religious. It is rooted in the awareness of man at a very early stage in his development that he is dependent on the forces of nature, and on his attempts to placate those forces by religious ceremonial and worship. The sun, the moon, the stars, the weather, mountains, rivers and much more modest features such as trees were all seen as gods, goddesses and spirits with distinct powers of their own. Such qualities are immediately recognisable in the divinities of Classical and Nordic mythology: Jupiter with his thunderbolt, Thor (whom we remember every week in Thursday and the Germans even more vividly in *Donnerstag*, literally thunder day) with his hammer which made thunder, and the nereids and dryads which dwelt in the waters and woods of Classical Greece.

In Europe, such perceptions were overshadowed by the arrival of Christianity, but they did not disappear. They are reflected in the familiar Harvest Festival, in the decoration of Christmas trees, and in legend and fairy tale in the elves and pixies and the ubiquitous Green Man whose memory is recorded in the name of countless pubs across the country. More significantly perhaps is the rich vein of European, and particularly English, poetry which has seen nature as having a spiritual dimension. For poets such as Shelley, God lived in nature, not at some heavenly remove, and certainly not in the city. In India, where Hinduism remained dominant, its gods, who were ultimately those of Classical Europe, were never displaced in the public mind from natural objects of which the cow and the River Ganges are the most familiar.

The Spiritual in Nature.

This sense of the spiritual in nature seems to be a growing rather than a diminishing force, and may be associated with the general decline in the appeal of organised religion which is characteristic of most of modern Europe and certainly of Britain. It is associated most obviously with remote and untouched areas, such as Dartmoor, the Pennines and the Scottish Highlands, but it is reflected in any common or wood where people go "to seek refreshment" or "to get away from it all". In Sweden it is reflected in a public opinion which rejects further exploitation of the wilderness which comprises the north of the country in the form of, say, hydro-electric schemes.

In Britain and Europe as a whole it is reflected in that vein of environmental thinking which argues that man has no more right to exploit the planet than has any other species. At a less sober level, it was reflected in the celebrated response of Percy Thrower, the one-time BBC gardening expert, to the question of how he managed to grow such wonderful blooms "I just talks to 'em"!

Christian Attitudes.

It would be wrong though to discuss the nebulous but important subject of the wider religious impulse to environmentalism in purely animist or, arguably, pagan terms. The specifically Roman Catholic contribution to the European debate since the 1970s has exercised major influence on the policies of the Christian Democrats, the mainstream right-wing party in Germany, in particular. It is not coincidental that Dr Klaus Töpfer, the present head of the United Nations Commission for Sustainable Development, was formerly Germany's Christian Democrat environment minister. For these Roman Catholic thinkers, conserving and protecting the natural environment is literally conserving and protecting God's creation and hence a religious duty. It is in marked contrast to the older Christian tradition which looked back to the divine declaration in the Book of Genesis that man should have dominion over the earth. It is that interpretation of the divine purpose which has led the Vatican to look favourably, for example, on the controversial development of genetically modified foods.

The Political Dimension.

If the oldest strand of green concern is religious, the newest is political, and although Green Party political thinking is significant for Britain, its roots lie in continental Europe and in Germany in particular for two distinct reasons. The first is that postwar Germans saw their country as the almost certain theatre of conflict in any nuclear war between the Soviet Union and the United States and many of them reacted by opposing not only nuclear armaments, as did CND in Britain, but also the whole nuclear concept, including power generation.

Chernobyl and Nuclear Power.

Such fears were, of course, reinforced by the disaster at the Chernobyl nuclear power station in the Ukraine. Members of Green parties everywhere are almost viscerally opposed to nuclear power and perhaps underestimate the dangers of global warming in consequence. In Germany, the phasing-out of nuclear power was a non-negotiable precondition for the Green Party to enter into coalition with Chancellor Schröder's Social Democrats in 1998.

Acid Rain.

The second reason for the emergence of European Green parties was the realisation, in Germany in particular, that acid rain, the dilute sulphuric acid which falls when sulphur dioxide combines with cloud-borne water vapour, was killing large swathes of the forests, which the Germans see almost as a symbol of national identity. It was a problem which affected Europe as a whole and still does, but was concentrated in Germany because it was ringed by the heavily polluting industries of the then Soviet bloc, which were highly dependent on sulphurous brown coal. Environmental degradation and its relationship with industrial power rapidly became a party political issue.

Green Political Parties.

Such environmental concerns readily combined with the spirit of rejection by educated youth of the perceived compromises and insincerities of the older generation in its approach to fascism, associated with the student rebellions of 1968, to create a dynamic political movement which has readily absorbed other movements, such as those for female emancipation and against discrimination generally, to create a party with no real British parallel. Although the Green Party in Britain has registered some significant successes, particularly at the local

level, and is represented, as a result of proportional representation, in the European Parliament, it remains a comparatively marginal force. Its focus has been essentially on such community concerns as health, on conservation and environmental protection and on the more localised satisfaction of needs. When the Prince of Wales declared in his 2000 Reith Lecture that "we should seek to work with the grain of Nature in everything we do, for the natural world is the envelope that contains, sustains and provisions the economy not the other way round", he was promoting, designedly or otherwise, a vision very close to that of the Green Party

The Greens and the EU.

The direct impact of the Greens in the party political sense on Britain has been exercised in practice through the influence of the European Green parties in the European institutions, including the European Parliament and particularly the council of ministers, which lay down the EU-wide environmental policy by which Britain is bound. Existing and future legislation on everything from emission standards to water quality and from recycling to environmental impact assessment is made in gatherings in which Greens have a powerful, and in the past sometimes a dominant, influence. The German environment minister, 1998–2005, Jürgen Trittin, was one such Green.

The Green Movement in Britain.

The organised green movement in Britain, in contrast, has traditionally been non-political, and has indeed prided itself on being so. It has taken the form of pressure groups established to counter a wide range of perceived threats, of which the Council for the Protection of Rural England (CPRE) is one of the oldest and best-known, or to promote a particular environmental philosophy, with Greenpeace being perhaps the most radical. Although many such groups, including Greenpeace and the World Wide Fund for Nature (WWF), are part of wider European and sometimes global groupings, and are members of the European Environmental Bureau (EEB) which is officially recognised as a partner by the European Commission, they represent a distinctively English approach. Many, like the Royal Society for the Protection of Birds (RSPB), are mass organisations, far larger in numbers than political parties or trade unions, and exercise informally much greater influence on government than is often recognised. The concept of the New Town, for example, which saw the large-scale creation of new communities on the basis of small existing towns like Crawley and Harlow in the post-war era and reached its logical conclusion in the foundation of the completely new city of Milton Keynes, can be traced back to the influence of the Town and Country Planning Association. This popularised the ideas of Ebenezer Howard, the inspiration behind Letchworth and Welwyn Garden Cities in Hertfordshire a century ago.

Conservation of the Environment.

These pressure groups are partnered, again in a particularly English way, by a range of non-governmental organisations responsible for conserving and preserving the nation's environmental assets, of which the National Trust is by far the best known. Its holdings range from wild natural assets, like the Giant's Causeway in Northern Ireland, the long stretches of British coastline acquired under Enterprise Neptune and vast tracts of moorland, to stately homes and more modest domestic buildings of historic interest. Some of its latest and more controversial acquisitions, like the two Beatles' homes in Liverpool, have widened its remit beyond any normal definition of environmental conservation although its even more recent preservation of some of the last back-to-back dwellings in Birmingham is perhaps a salutary reminder of the meaning of a black environment. It is also a reminder of the extent to which the foundation of so many of both the voluntary and the more official environmental organisations was rooted in concern at the consequences of both the agricultural and industrial revolutions.

Epping Forest.

One of the earliest initiatives was the vesting of Epping Forest, Essex, on the edge of what is now Greater London, in the Corporation of London, in 1878, for the benefit of the public. It had been stimulated by the enclosure of half the previous Forest between 1851 and 1871 alone. The years before the Second World War saw similar urgent action by the National Trust to purchase extensive areas of the Surrey Hills to protect them from residential development.

Current Developments and Concerns.

It was suggested in the beginning that any history of the Green Movement was really a history of very different green movements, and that is indeed so but it also has to be recognised that the Green Movement has a salience today that it did not have fifty, or even forty, years ago. In part, as with Green political parties, this is the result of the specific historical developments discussed, but three wider forces have been at work which have reinforced and served to interconnect these movements. The whole has become far more than the sum of the parts.

One such force has been the growing realisation that the earth's physical resources are finite. This realisation was first popularised by D. H. and D. L. Meadows in their best-seller, *The Limits to Growth*. Their methodology has been found faulty, as the authors have recognised in their later publications, and many critics have argued that an almost infinite range of substitutes for scarce resources can always be developed in the case of need. Nevertheless, political and public opinion has moved decisively against the environmentally destructive "throw-away society" of the 1960s.

The second such force is the parallel realisation that the globe is a single eco-system, and that pollution is not the localised phenomenon it was once thought to be. Another best-seller, Rachel Carson's *Silent Spring*, combined with advancing scientific knowledge to spread the realisation that neither high chimneys nor long sea outfalls reduced pollution to innocuous levels. The acid rain falling across Europe was imposing enormous costs.

The last and third of the forces returns us to the beginning: the semi-religious sense of man as part of, rather than apart from, nature. It gained new life from an appreciation that the high living standards which were increasingly becoming the norm in the developed world presumed high environmental standards as much as they did high medical standards. It regenerates the sense of a duty of care which is ultimately the most pervasive of motivations.

THE ENERGY DEBATE.

A Turbulent Background.

The year 2006 began as a turbulent one in the UK energy sector, with continuing major uncertainties in the Middle East and longer-term fears as to security of supply and the impact of the dramatic rate of growth of the Chinese economy. This turbulence is attributable to both domestic and international, mainly European, factors, but it has been reflected for some parallel reasons in the US, where Enron, the utilities conglomerate, crashed spectacularly in 2001.

This turbulence can be attributed ultimately to the interaction of two very broad forces, which are ultimately perhaps irreconcilable. The first is the pressure from consumers for ever lower unit prices, which was given enormous impetus by the introduction of competition on the privatisation of coal, electricity and gas, and which was indeed one of the motives of privatisation. It is a pressure being intensified by the current drive across the European Union single market to liberalise energy markets, which again intensifies that wider response of diversification of interests on the one hand and incorporation within ever larger holding companies on the other, which we define as globalisation. The second broad force is the growth in concern about the long-term impact of these trends and their implications for the global and national resource base, for international commitments, and for national security.

Privatisation and Liberalisation.

When the UK's nationalised and unified electricity and gas undertakings were privatised and broken up in the 1980s, it was on the basis of certain, necessarily untested, assumptions. It was argued that competition would stimulate greater efficiency and reduce costs, and that it should be promoted at the expense of co-ordination and integration, even when the existing structure was recognised as highly efficient, as was the case with British Gas. It was also argued that market forces would allocate resources more efficiently than any government could do, and that ministers should gladly abdicate responsibility for deciding on the relative contribution to UK electricity generation of coal, natural gas, nuclear and renewable resources. Not least, it was argued that the energy sector would benefit from the injection of the private capital which it was denied under state ownership. The public interest could be protected against what would remain unusually dominant companies by an independent regulator with the power to intervene in investment and charging decisions.

At one level these expectations were met. Prices did fall, the Department of Energy was wound up without incident, and private capital flowed in. Privatisation was held to be a great success.

Similar, though not identical, considerations are powering the current drive to liberalise energy markets within the EU. Although power generators may remain in public ownership, they, like those in private ownership, must increasingly compete for business on a level playing field with no regard to national borders. Traditional powerful national monopolies, like Electricité de France, are under attack and may be privatised in due course.

The Costs of Privatisation.

Privatisation and liberalisation, however, have brought their own costs, some of which are only becoming apparent with time. Competition on the basis of unit prices has directed attention away from energy conservation and efficiency, which often have the potential to reduce overall expenditure on energy to a much greater degree. It is perfectly possible, for example, to design a normal house with sufficient insulation to ensure that it needs energy for heating on only a few days a year. In practice, however, many major UK housebuilders are currently erecting homes whose energy efficiency is no greater than that of the Swedish homes of 60 years ago. Similarly, great energy savings can be achieved by orienting properties for maximum solar gain.

Unpredictable energy prices have also undermined attempts to popularise combined heat and power (CHP) or cogeneration, which is normally accepted as the most effective approach to energy use. It is common in north-western Europe and Scandinavia, where homes are normally connected to an adjacent heating plant and often benefit from the waste heat of local industry. Competition on the basis of unit prices inevitably encourages usage and wastage of what is, in fact, a very valuable resource.

The "Dash for Gas".

More dramatic, however, has been the impact of the drive for ever-lower prices on the structure of energy generation itself. The comparatively high price of coal, particularly home-produced coal, prompted the newly privatised electricity generation companies to switch to natural gas, which was both cheaper and abundant under the coastal shelf around the UK. The so-called "dash for gas" ended the long rule of "King Coal" as the UK's dominant source of primary energy, a development which was welcome to the Conservative government of the time, which remembered all too clearly the bitter struggles with the miners of the 1970s and 1980s and was now being given also a painless means of complying with the growing international pressures to reduce greenhouse gas emissions. (*See* Climate Change, Y6.)

Nuclear Power Generation.

The UK's nuclear power generation industry, similarly privatised, enjoyed an even greater advantage in this respect because it emits no greenhouse gases at all, whereas natural gas certainly does though to a lesser degree than coal. Privatisation, however, revealed what many opponents of nuclear power had long suspected, namely, that it was a comparatively expensive way of generating electricity and of questionable commercial viability. It had also been the beneficiary of some £10 billion at current prices in research funding since the 1950s. This problem has become ever more acute as electricity prices have been driven ever lower by the forces of competition and technology and, increasingly, of liberalisation of EU energy markets. British Energy accordingly teetered on the edge of bankruptcy throughout 2002 and was only saved by a controversial emergency loan of £650 million from the UK government. It was claimed in justification of the loan that it was a bridging measure pending restructuring, and it was backed up by legislation permitting the government to renationalise British Energy or indeed any other privatised electricity company.

The final restructuring plan approved in September 2004 involved total aid from the British government of £3·4 billion.

Restructuring and Consolidation.

The reaction of the market to all these challenges has been the continued restructuring of the energy generation industry. Companies have been bought and sold, broken up and consolidated, in the interests of profitability and shareholder value. Essentially regional companies have become part of multinational corporations or allied with companies with interests remote from their own. Investment has been determined by potential profitability rather than by any concept of social value. It is a strange consequence of the policies of a Conservative government determined to defend national sovereignty, that so much of the UK energy sector is now in foreign, and indeed German, hands. Powergen, the UK's largest electricity supplier, and N Power, its rival, for example, are both German-owned, while London Electricity is in French ownership. Company manoeuvring can seem reminiscent of the power play of medieval monarchs arbitrarily exchanging their territories.

Growing Criticisms of Privatisation.

These developments have highlighted the weaknesses in some of the arguments made for privatisation. On the one hand, a government simply cannot in practice abdicate responsibility for decisions in the energy sector which are critical to the whole economy. British Energy's nuclear power stations generated some 21 % of all the UK's electricity needs and could not be allowed to stop trading in the manner of an indebted high street retailer. On the other, the internal affairs of international corporations may well be beyond the scope of public inquiry. The chief executive of *The New York Times* has written, with reference to the collapse of Enron, that it is far easier to investigate governments than businesses: "The press is aided by laws that provide reporters with access to government meetings and documents. But much of what happens in corporations goes on behind closed doors".

More fundamentally still in some respects, experience has shown the limitations of creating artificial markets where real markets do not exist. In the energy sector, as on the railways and in the National Health Service, integrated systems were broken up in the belief that bargaining between the providers and consumers of services would drive up standards by harnessing the acknowledged capacity of the market to allocate resources efficiently. This belief, which was ultimately attributable to Treasury thinking, has, however, proved wanting in practice. In the railways it has led to the abnegation of direct responsibility for such crucial matters as safety; in the National Health Service it led to distortions in care which were found unacceptable.

In the energy sector it led first to such contentious decisions as the separation of gas extraction and gas distribution, which many considered damaged the industry's effectiveness and which certainly reduced the value of the investments of the early shareholders and subsequently led to a wholesale market in electricity in which competition has on occasion driven prices down to unsustainably low levels. By October 2002 electricity prices had fallen by almost 40 % from their 1998 level, prompting Powergen to describe the market as "bust".

Shortage of Generating Capacity.

Ironically, the market forces which have hitherto forced prices down may be coming to work in reverse. Many in the industry are concerned at the growing shortage across Europe of modern generating capacity and the lack of investment in the associated infrastructure, which is inherently unprofitable. They fear widespread blackouts unless government intervenes to encourage the construction of new power stations.

Pressing Current Problems.

The overall situation did, however, change quite radically during 2004. The war in Iraq, the escalation in the demand for oil by China, its headlong economic growth, and diminishing national reserves combined with a number of other factors to point towards an end to the era of cheap energy. Domestic gas prices rose by some 10 % and many sectors of British industry had to cope with increases of up to 30 % in electricity and gas prices in the early months of the year. It was being predicted that the introduction of a European-wide emissions trading scheme in January 2005 to meet Britain's commitments under the Kyoto Protocol could push electricity prices up by a further 40 % by 2010.

Neither the UK nor any other EU government can leave the market to recover equilibrium at some indefinite time in the future of its own choosing. Once lost, industries like coal mining and nuclear power generation are gone, probably for good. Large scale financial crashes like that of Enron also pose a threat to the stability of the banking system. The risks of war in the Middle East and of terrorist attacks have served to strengthen fears of either greatly increased oil prices or of interruptions to supply, or indeed both, which underline the importance of reliable supplies of electricity. Nuclear generation, though, is the subject of wide suspicion across the EU, except in France and Finland, and most countries, notably Germany, are phasing it out.

All EU countries, however, are committed under the Kyoto Protocol to reducing their greenhouse gas emissions (*see* **Climate Change, Y6**), which precludes a switch back to coal unless emissions are reduced disproportionately in some other sector, most obviously transport. The UK and Germany are in any event the only EU member states which still generate a significant proportion of their electricity from coal. Natural gas has been consumed at a rate which can only be described as imprudent, and the EU now envisages that it will have to import 70 % of its needs by 2020.

Renewable Energy Sources: Wind and Tides.

If national or EU security of supply is to be guaranteed that leaves only renewables to fuel electricity generation, and it is the EU target to generate 12 % of its electricity needs from renewable sources by 2010. The UK has gone further with a target of 20 % by 2020. In British conditions that means primarily wind energy, and the number of wind farms is expanding rapidly. Plans are well advanced for the world's biggest onshore wind farm on the Hebridean island of Lewis, with an ultimate capacity of 2000 megawatts, the equivalent of two nuclear power stations. Their impact on the landscape, however, can be unwelcome and they are increasingly being constructed out to sea. Their true potential is contested.

A recent report from the Royal Academy of Engineers argues that the government's plans vastly overestimate the capacity of the UK's engineering base to construct and connect the tens of thousands of turbines required. One of the report's authors has suggested that 10 % would be a more realistic renewables target. Harnessing tidal energy is highly attractive in principle and has been undertaken successfully in some locations but is generally regarded as presenting insuperable problems. Energy crops to produce bioethanol, which can be used mixed with or as an alternative to petrol, avoid such technical problems and are favoured in France, where they are seen as an answer to the abandonment of the land by farmers whose traditional produce is no longer required. Nevertheless, environmentalists have often been unsympathetic, expressing what can seem excessively negative concerns about the effect on the soil.

A Continuing Debate.

It is not surprising against this background that the arguments over the future for energy policy are so intense. The UK government is being lobbied by the industry to authorise the construction of three new nuclear stations, most plausibly on the existing sites at Hinckley, Somerset, Hunterston, Ayrshire, and Sizewell, Suffolk. Environmentalists are lobbying equally vigorously for the UK to follow the German example and phase out nuclear power altogether. The same arguments are dividing the EU institutions, not least the European Commission.

Arguably the most important question, though, is not being posed. Quite simply: can Europe, including Britain, demand the lowest possible prices and security of supply at one and the same time? The evidence suggests not, or at least not on any sustainable basis.

Current Developments.

The arguments intensified during 2005 and early 2006, but agreed solutions receded rather than progressed. Fears grew that gas supplies would be inadequate if the winter of 2005–6 proved to be as severe as some predicted, and tensions between Russia and Ukraine over gas prices were a reminder of Europe's vulnerability. Some in energy-intensive industries such as chemicals called on government once more to be involved in the energy market to protect national competitiveness.

The demand for gas and oil by China continued to grow at an extraordinary rate, confirming forecasts by the International Energy Agency that the global demand for oil would increase by almost half over the next 25 years. China's own demand has doubled over the last 10 years, and it is now the world's second largest importer.

The biggest surprise was the apparently sudden conversion of the UK prime minister, Tony Blair, to the cause of nuclear power in November 2005. It prompted support and dissent in equal measure, although it also helped to draw attention to technologies such as clean coal burning and carbon sequestration which have hitherto been comparatively neglected.

The future remains uncertain.

4. SPECIAL TOPICS

THE TRANSPORT CHALLENGE

The Background: Road and Rail Imbalance.

One of the more striking features of the transport debate as the year 2006 opened was the persistence of problems to which Britain had been unable, or unwilling , to find answers for more than fifty years. In particular, there had been a continuing failure to address the consequences of the imbalance in financing whereby road infrastructure was provided free to the user but rail infrastructure was partly paid for by the rail passenger. This fundamental imbalance had predictably stimulated the use of cars and lorries and the demand for more road space, and discouraged the use of the railways. The closure of rural branch lines had started as early as the 1920s.

Attempts to modify this imbalance had been limited in scope and sporadic in application. The road tax which had been designed initially to raise funds for road construction had become divorced from that purpose, and was in any event too low to meet more than a fraction of the actual cost and bore no relationship to miles travelled. The railways had last been able to recover their costs in 1947 and needed blanket revenue support, but there was little attempt to justify support for specific routes as keys to, say, industrial, regional or tourist development. Support was popularly denigrated as subsidy and, as such, something to be phased out wherever possible. The same problem was to face the bus industry as the growth in private motoring progressively undercut its high early profitability.

Lack of Rail Investment.

Investment in the railways, though not in the roads, was sporadic and not always coherent. New diesel trains dramatically improved branch line services following the Modernisation Plan of the 1950s, only to become redundant with the large-scale route closures of the Beeching Plan just a few years later. Investment was also generally inadequate. The rate of mainline electrification lagged some twenty years behind that in most of Britain's European neighbours.

The Environmental Consequences.

The consequences of this imbalance were both clear to see and unpopular. Town centres across the country were damaged, sometimes irreparably, by road widening schemes and the insertion of new inner relief roads. The Buchanan Report, which had preached the separation of car and pedestrian as the key to the town of the future, was all too often misinterpreted to put the interests of the car before the interests of the pedestrian. Cities like Birmingham discovered that they had rendered their centres inaccessible except through uninviting and potentially dangerous subways. Most continental European cities were wiser and buried their cars rather than their citizens.

The problem of imbalance also had a substantial social dimension because a large proportion of the population did not have access to a car, and public transport was vital to its participation in society. It is a problem which has intensified in many parts of the country as public transport has diminished and families have needed two or even three cars for basic daily living.

New Environmental Concerns.

These familiar unresolved problems have been joined over the last twenty years by newer ones. The growing awareness of the rate at which the developed world is consuming the earth's stock of non-renewable natural resources, and concern, even alarm, at the rate of global warming (see **Y6**), have combined to increase the pressures in favour of more sustainable forms of transport; forms of transport which carry the most people for the least energy per person per mile. In practice, and in British conditions, this normally means public transport and preference for rail over road in view of its superior environmental performance, provided reasonable loadings can be achieved. Those pressures have been reinforced by growing concerns at the effect of vehicular emissions on human health in congested urban situations. One positive response has been the rebirth of the once despised tram as light rail transit, incorporating new tracks in city centres, the conversion of less used suburban railways, and usually extensions out to new developments or even further afield. The pioneering Tyne and Wear Metro had reached as far as Sunderland by 2002.

Further development has, however, been put in serious question by the government's refusal in 2005 to authorise the proposed scheme linking Portsmouth and Gosport, and its scepticism about the merits of a number of other schemes.

Despite the popularity of such encouraging developments, the overall pattern has been adverse. Growing prosperity and the failure to reflect the cost of road provision and environmental impact in fuel prices has continued to stimulate unsustainable demands for mobility. Whereas the average Briton travelled five miles a day in 1950, he or she now travels 30 miles a day and by 2025 is likely to travel 60 miles a day. The distance travelled specifically by car is likely to increase by 17% by as soon as 2010. Comparable approaches to charging, which mean that under the provisions of the 1944 Chicago Convention aircraft kerosene is subject to no fuel tax at all, combined again with prosperity, have led to a parallel explosion in the demand for air travel.

The Relocation of Business.

Equally significant has been the stimulus given to business distribution over ever larger distances to exploit economies of scale. These trends are self-reinforcing. Low fuel prices underpin dispersed patterns of settlement dependent on out-of-town supermarkets for their every need. The failure to include the full range of costs in prices, or to "internalise the externalities" as it is technically known, means that the market is giving perverse price signals. For many, the motor car has moved from being a luxury to being a necessity. These perverse signals have counted for far more in practice than any specific transport initiative.

The Decline of Public Transport.

The losers have been public passenger transport and rail-borne freight. To be effective, not to mention economical, public provision needs concentration not dispersal. The new city of Milton Keynes, conceived in the 1960s and 1970s when acceptance of the car as the transport of the future was at its most unqualified, is built like Los Angeles on a grid pattern without the concentrated focal points of traditional urban centres. It remains singularly difficult to serve by public transport.

Public transport has also suffered in practice from the application of arguable political dogma. Faith in the efficacy of market forces led to the mass privatisation and deregulation (outside London) of bus companies and, contrary to European practice and the advice of most transport experts, to the deliberate breaking up of integrated transport networks. This dismantling of long efforts at integrated provision distressed the conurbations and particularly alarmed Newcastle which had invested heavily not just in the Tyne and Wear light rail network but in the associated road/rail interchanges. The results were mixed. Levels of public subsidy were reduced overall, but bus patronage outside London continues to fall and only skeleton services serve large areas of rural Britain.

Deregulation of Bus Services.

Competition from deregulated bus services is one of the reasons why Britain's light-rail networks have been less viable commercially than had been hoped.

Bus stations and the associated facilities were widely sold off as valuable real estate. On the other hand, the more effective bus operators absorbed their rivals with unexpected speed and established new co-ordinated networks of their own, sometimes assisted by the county councils who enjoyed extensive permissive powers.

Labour Government Policy since 1997.

When the new Labour government came to power in 1997, therefore, it was faced with a considerable challenge. An ever more dispersed and mobile population was wedded to the use of the private car but recognised, albeit reluctantly in many cases, that the car was causing serious damage to urban quality of life, that attempting to conquer congestion by yet more road building was both self-defeating and unpopular, and that public transport was a necessity. The government also had to recall that a substantial proportion of the population did not have access to a car.

It was also faced with a railway system which had not only been privatised but restructured in accordance with the same political and Treasury thinking as had broken up the previous nationalised monopolies in the energy sector. The logic, however, had been pressed much further. Track, signalling and major stations had been passed to a new company, Railtrack, and train operation franchised to twenty-five nominally competing train operating companies, many of which were reminiscent in area of the companies prior to grouping in 1923. The trains themselves had been transferred to new leasing companies and maintenance of both trains and track to established civil and mechanical engineering companies, which were anxious to diversify into rail.

In practice, a number of these functions including customer relations, station security and track maintenance had been widely subcontracted. This splintered structure was held together in theory by a raft of contractual obligations under the scrutiny of a director of franchising and a rail regulator. As with the energy sector, it was argued that private sector finance and initiative would improve the level of service to the passenger and progressively reduce, and ultimately obviate, the need for government subsidy. The Labour Party in opposition had voted against privatisation and originally proposed to renationalise at least in part by the simple expedient of not re-letting franchises, but had fallen silent in the face of the very heavy costs involved.

The 1998 White Paper.

The new government's initial response to these very different challenges was bold, at least in theory. A White Paper published in July 1998 proposed ambitious targets for reducing dependence on the car and for promoting public transport. One in ten motorists were to be persuaded to give up their cars and the rest to use public transport more often. Motorists would be charged for workplace parking and for driving into city centres, and the money so raised, estimated at £1 billion annually by 2006, would be ploughed back into local public transport. Partnerships would be encouraged between local authorities and bus companies. A new Strategic Rail Authority would absorb the functions of the franchising director and work towards greater coherence across the rail industry. John Prescott, as secretary of state for the environment, transport and the regions, maintained: "After 20 years in the wilderness, this is the day transport policy bursts into the light of a new dawn. There is a clear mood for change and I am in a mood to deliver it."

Shortcomings of the White Paper.

Although such an approach had the potential to be genuinely popular, it ran counter to many powerful and vocal interests, and had no chance of success without real political commitment. It was doubtful whether that existed except in the person of Mr Prescott, even in the beginning. Some of the most valuable draft proposals, like taxes on parking spaces at out-of-town supermarkets, had already been omitted from the final White Paper under the influence, it was believed, of the prime minister himself.

In fact, most of these changes needed legislation which did not feature prominently in the government's legislative timetable. The Strategic Rail Authority was established in due course and permissive powers granted to local authorities to introduce congestion charges, but little else. As one newspaper had perceptively commented: "The most likely outcome is that nothing much will change before Mr. Prescott qualifies for his bus pass."

The Impact of External Events.

Events proved more significant. A rise in global oil prices stimulated protests in France, Germany and then Britain in August-September 2000, orchestrated by the road haulage industry demanding relief from fuel taxes. Hauliers threatened to blockade oil depots, and could count on wide tacit support from a public for whom cheap motoring had come to be seen almost as a right. Attempts to reflect the true environmental cost of motoring in fuel prices were abandoned with the British government's abolition of the fuel price escalator, which had increased the price of fuel at a rate greater than the rate of inflation and had been an environmentally friendly initiative of the previous Conservative government. The priority, widely attributed to the prime minister himself, was to conciliate "middle England".

The limitations of this somewhat supine approach to policy were, however, rapidly underlined by the torrential rains and heavy flooding of October 2000. If they could not be proved to be the consequence of global warming, they were at the very least in accord with its predicted consequences. The severe weather also exposed the grave weaknesses in the chosen style of rail privatisation, which were further cruelly emphasised by the accident at Hatfield the same month. The diffusion of responsibility and the reliance on legal rather than administrative relationships meant in practice that the lines of authority were confused and nobody dared to take responsibility for fear of incurring legal liability. Railtrack literally lost its nerve and abruptly closed the whole network one morning, leaving countless numbers of passengers stranded until it rescinded its decision equally abruptly an hour or two later.

The Hatfield Crash.

It was the core subject of safety, however, which was to seal Railtrack's fate as a commercial company. The damaging admission after the Hatfield crash that the company had known about the unsatisfactory condition of the track for months, and the evidence after the Ladbroke Grove crash of October 1999 in which 31 people died that it had ignored repeated warnings as to the visibility of the crucial signal, persuaded public opinion that the company was putting profit before safety. Its supervision of its maintenance contractors and their supervision of their sub-contractors were found wanting, and timetables were disrupted for months after Hatfield as stringent speed limits were placed on many miles of track right across the network.

The resulting claims for compensation from the train operating companies turned what had been regarded as the most copper-bottomed of concerns, with an unlimited capacity to generate profit from track access charges and its vast property portfolio, into a highly vulnerable company dependent for its survival on government support.

The Collapse of Railtrack.

That support, though, was further eroded by the emerging evidence that the new market relationships and the compensation culture were pushing prices up not down. It was authoritatively estimated that it was costing Railtrack three times as much in real terms to upgrade a mile of track as it had cost British Rail. The estimated cost of upgrading the West Coast mainline escalated from £2 billion to £13 billion in three years. It was no surprise when support was abruptly withdrawn by Stephen Byers, the then secretary of state for transport, in circumstances which remain controversial, and the company passed into receivership. A restructuring of the rail industry had been rendered virtually inevitable not only to preserve Railtrack's infrastructure assets but also to restore public confidence in rail transport generally. Some on the left called for total renationalisation but government remained preoccupied by the question of cost.

The structure which was emerging, however, was probably closer to shadow renationalisation than to the direction by market forces originally envisaged on privatisation. Overall direction was being exercised by a much enhanced Strategic Rail Authority, which had taken over responsibility for infrastructure investment. Railtrack had come out of receivership as a "not for profit" company, Network Rail, poised between the public and private sectors.

The train operating companies remain, but are to be reduced in number with shorter franchises of five-eight years rather than twenty. "Excessive" profits will be clawed back for investment in the network. The franchise reorganisation marks the end of their potential involvement in infrastructure investment, and also seeks to rationalise their areas so that most of the London terminals will be served by just one franchise. Freight traffic is not affected.

Developments in 2003.

A precedent was set in 2003 when the franchise of Connex South-Eastern, serving south-east London and Kent, was terminated prematurely on the grounds of poor financial management.

It was also decided by Network Rail during the year that rail maintenance should be taken back in house.

Prospects and Retrospect.

In 2004, however, the government changed its position. A White Paper published in July proposed the abolition of the Strategic Rail Authority, after just four years, and the transfer of its powers to Network Rail on the one hand and the Department for Transport on the other. Moreover, the role of the regulator in determining the level of subsidy to the railways would be reduced.

Although some of these moves may be seen as being in the right direction, there is also a sense in which we have turned full circle only to return to an worse starting point. Overall passenger numbers have increased by a third since privatisation as a consequence of economic prosperity, some excellent trains have been introduced and some real advances in timetabling achieved, particularly perhaps on cross-country routes, but change and uncertainty from the run-up to privatisation to the present day have delayed stock replacement and confused project planning. Much skilled labour has either gone abroad or left the industry. There are many proposals in the pipeline, some of which would bring revolutionary benefits, notably a new high-speed rail line from London to the north which could reduce the journey time from London to Manchester or Leeds to less than 90 minutes. The closed links between Oxford and Cambridge, and Matlock and Buxton, could be advantageously reopened. Many of these proposals, however, like London's Thameslink 2000 and Cross-Rail, now the east-west route, and the private proposal for a dedicated freight route down the spine of England to the Channel Tunnel, have made little progress for years. Nearly all the £34 billion of public money promised up to 2010 has already been allocated. Only the separately financed Channel Tunnel high-speed rail link is advancing. The comparison with France in particular is cruel.

The day to day reality is often discouraging. Up to ten train operating franchises including ScotRail and Central Trains were in financial difficulties in 2002. The promise of 140mph trains running on the West Coast main line, Britain's busiest railway, by 2005 has been abandoned. The rail freight companies are having little success in attracting goods which currently travel by road. The Potters Bar derailment of 2002, which renewed fears as to the quality of rail maintenance work, combined with collapsing global share prices, has put serious question marks over the ability of the private sector to raise capital for investment. Its failure, or un-willingness, to raise the 50% of the £60 billion to be pumped into rail improvements under the 10-year strategy of 2001 could put the whole plan at risk.

A Gridlocked Debate?

The conduct of the transport debate has proved circular. Despite John Prescott's White Paper, any serious attempt to move traffic from road to rail or to integrate environmental considerations into transport planning has been stillborn. The first annual audit of the government's 2010 Transport Plan published in May 2002 showed that progress in meeting the Plan's targets bore little relationship to reality and was in many sectors negative. The Plan's targets for increased rail travel were simply withdrawn in July 2004. The Plan was in any event vastly less radical than the 1998 White Paper. The number of cars on the roads has risen by three million since 1997, enough to stretch from London to Sydney. The government's target has moved from reducing dependence on the car to reducing the rate of growth of car travel and reducing traffic congestion by 6% by 2010 to accepting that congestion will increase by up to 20% by the same date.

Any action to reduce congestion, moreover, will be undertaken by local authorities without the support of central government, and it is Ken Livingstone as Mayor of London who has risen to that pioneering challenge. A £5 congestion charge per day became payable to drive into central London with effect from 17 February 2003. Gridlock seems to be anticipated elsewhere. Other responses are all too familiar. £100 million is to be spent on widening parts of London's orbital motorway, the M25, to up to 12 lanes. Government studies recommend major road widening programmes. Ominously, even the 2004 White Paper is echoing the surely discredited Beeching approach of substituting buses for "uneconomic" railway lines.

Moreover, in January 2003, the Strategic Rail Authority announced that more than £10 billion of rail projects would be cancelled or postponed, and, in February, that service cuts would be introduced in May, admitting that they would encourage passengers to switch to their cars.

As Roger Ford, the technical editor of *Modern Railways* said in October 2003: "The railway now needs three times the subsidy received by British Rail and yet performance is significantly worse." Figures released by the Strategic Rail Authority in July 2004 showed that "three times" had increased to "five times". It is all a sorry saga.

THE HUNGRY PLANET

The Background.

One of the less happy side-effects of the tide of events unleashed by the 11 September attack on the World Trade Centre in New York and the Anglo-American invasion of Iraq in 2003 has been the distraction of the world's attention from underlying global challenges which affect far more people than terrorism ever has in the past or is likely to do in the future. Amongst those challenges are world water resources, world population trends and climate change, as discussed elsewhere in this section. But closely related to all three, and in some ways even more fundamental, is the problem of hunger.

The Paradox.

It is a challenge which the world as a whole is minded to overlook for a wide range of very different reasons. On the one hand it is a problem of which the developed world has had no direct experience since at least the immediate aftermath of the Second World War. Indeed the developed world's problems have tended to be the reverse: the obesity caused by over-, or imprudent, eating, which is most prevalent in the US but widespread in Britain also, and the overproduction associated with the EU's Common Agricultural Policy. Even conditions like the anorexia from which some young women suffer arise in a world of plenty. Parts of the West may be familiar with water shortages, usually in the form of hosepipe bans, but they are not familiar with food shortages.

The Distribution of Hunger.

On the other hand, although the UN Food and Agriculture Organisation (FAO) estimates that *c.* 815 million people worldwide suffer from hunger, their distribution is very uneven, as is the percentage of the population affected in the countries concerned. Although many millions of people still eat inadequately in India and much of Latin America and, with the demise of communism, have come to do so across what was the Soviet Union, the focal points of widespread malnutrition in Asia are the generally inaccessible states of Afghanistan, Cambodia, North Korea, and Tadjikistan, which share a history of civil conflict. Statistics are for obvious reasons somewhat conjectural, but are normally in the range of 40–60% of the population affected.

The Political Aspect: The Example of Africa.

What those statistics do underline is that to a much greater degree than population trends or water resources, or even perhaps global warming, hunger is a political rather than an environmental problem. Of no part of the world is this as true as of Africa, where global rates of malnutrition are overwhelmingly concentrated. All too often those rates are related to the wars which have bedevilled the continent since the general triumph of the independence movements of the 1960s. On some estimates, Somalia, which has almost ceased to exist as a state, is the hungriest country on earth, with three-quarters of its population suffering from malnutrition. It is easy to blame the Africans for creating their own problems through ambition, corruption and greed, and such interpretations have led many developed countries to make "good governance" a pre-condition of any further aid.

When the late President Bokassa of the Central African Republic is believed to have been a cannibal and when Nigeria is often categorised as the most corrupt nation in the world in which to do business, such criticisms must carry great weight, but at best they are only part of the story. Many of the wars have been prolonged, provoked even, by western and, in their time, Soviet and South African interests, and the most unprepossessing of African leaders, including Bokassa, have not found it difficult to cultivate western patrons, in either business or government circles. Some dictators simply copied the example set by their previous colonial masters. The Belgian Congo was for decades the private property of the king of the Belgians and President Mobutu similarly turned what had become Zaïre into his own personal estate.

The Colonial Inheritance.

Furthermore many, if not most, of the African states to be found on a modern map are artificial creations of the former colonial empires, who, as in the Middle East, were concerned with their imperial strategies rather than with cultural, ethnic, tribal or religious loyalties. If the former colonial powers cannot be held directly responsible for the religious wars of the Sudan or the tribal wars of Rwanda and Uganda, they cannot claim total innocence either.

Not least, the droughts and other extreme conditions, which have repeatedly caused crisis in much of eastern Africa and elsewhere, have almost certainly been worsened by the global warming which has been provoked by the actions of the developed world, not by those of Africans.

A not dissimilar rather judgemental approach is also often heard with respect to the incidence of AIDS, the continent's greatest killer, which often contributes to hunger indirectly by striking down the economically active members of a family. It is a moralism which can be placed on its head when Africans accuse western pharmaceutical firms of profiteering over the sale of the remedial drugs.

Charges and Counter-Charges.

All such charges and counter-charges, however, tend to detract attention from deeper African realities. For all the imaginings of nineteenth-century explorers, and writers like Rider Haggard, Africa is not naturally an exceptionally wealthy continent.

Moreover, the consequences of exploiting some of its most valued resources, like diamonds, have actually sometimes proved negative. The personal greed provoked in Sierra Leone was such that the nation was destabilised to the point of collapse, and it now has the unenviable distinction of being the world's poorest country, with GDP per capita of US$448 (2002). A number of other countries, including some which have been competently run, have been highly dependent on exports of particular crops or minerals, and have found themselves to be highly vulnerable to fluctuations in world markets.

Africa's Poorest Nations.

The consequences of this malign combination of western cynicism, widespread African corruption and mismanagement and, some would add, ill-conceived policies from the World Bank and the International Monetary Fund (IMF) are sobering. Of the world's 50 poorest countries 34 are in Africa, and the ten poorest are all in Africa: Sierra Leone, Tanzania, Burundi, Malawi, Ethiopia, Sudan, Guinea-Bissau, Congo, Niger and Mali in ascending order, with the latter enjoying a GDP of US$753 per capita, $53 less than the Yemen which is the world's poorest country outside Africa. Most of Africa's 800 million people live in poverty and the gap between them and the rest of the world is widening. Whereas Asia some 40 years ago looked like the world's most vulnerable continent, the reverse has proved to be the case.

Statistics on Hunger.

Figures for hunger are little more encouraging. Calculated as the percentage of the population defined as undernourished under UN criteria, in the period 1996–98 ten of the world's twelve hungriest countries are in Africa, headed by Burundi with 68 %. Eritrea with 65 %, the Democratic Republic of Congo (formerly Zaire/Belgian Congo) with 61 %, and Mozambique with 58 % are all characterised, as is Haiti in the Caribbean, by having more than half their population undernourished. Ethiopia with 49 %, Niger with 46 %, Zambia with 45 %, Angola with 43 %, and Kenya and Sierra Leone, both with 43 %, are, as is Mongolia with 45 %, only better on strictly comparative terms. The precise ordering of nations can vary with the definition adopted but the overall picture does not change.

A quarter of Africa's whole population is defined under UN criteria as undernourished. Such proportions are actually worse than they appear, because Arab North Africa is in a very much more favourable position than elsewhere. Malnutrition in Algeria and Egypt, for example, with some 95 million people between them, is only 4–5 %.

The Prevalence of AIDS.

The problems of hunger and poverty are worsened by the prevalence of AIDS, which contributes to low African life-expectancy and is prevalent in some of the poorest countries although it is not confined to them. The world's highest HIV rate of 35·8 %, for example, is in Botswana, which is usually considered well governed and where malnutrition is at the comparatively low level for sub-Saharan Africa of 27 %. HIV is indeed concentrated in southern Africa with the next most affected countries being Swaziland with 25·3 %, Zimbabwe with 25·1 %, Lesotho with 23·6 %, Zambia with 20 %, South Africa with 19·9 %, Namibia with 19·5 % and Malawi with 16 %. Kenya and the Central African Republic (somewhat further north) follow with figures of 14 % and 13·8 % respectively. Overall, some 28 million Africans are suffering from AIDS, nearly three-quarters of the world total of 40 million.

Life-Expectancy Rates.

These alarming figures are reflected in the very low life-expectancy of most Africans. Whereas Algerians have an HIV incidence of just 0·1 % and a life-expectancy of 71 years, and Egyptians one of 0·02 % and an expectancy of 67·5 years, few black African countries have an average life-expectancy of more than 50 years, Ghana being in the lead with an average of 56·9 years. At the bottom, Zimbabwe can offer only 39·9 years, Sierra Leone 39·2 years, Botswana 39, Malawi 38·8, and Zambia just 38 years.

Problems in Zimbabwe and South Africa.

Some of the causes and the consequences are actually worsening. The reaction against colonialism has, after initial decades of comparative calm, totally destabilised Zimbabwe, formerly Southern Rhodesia, and provoked the seizure of land without compensation, the suppression of civil rights, and economic and social disorder. Despite its brave start as a multi-cultural, multi-ethnic republic, South Africa will face daunting threats for years to come. Black-white divisions surface all too readily, as was seen in the divide within the Commonwealth over the future status of Zimbabwe.

More generally, Africa is suffering from a brain drain as so many of its limited pool of educated and professional people see their future in America or Europe. Probably nothing would help African stability more than the consolidation of its frequently embryonic middle class.

Searching for Solutions.

If describing the problems of hunger and disease is straightforward, and there is a broad consensus on the underlying causes, solutions are both very much harder and very much more contentious. Greater democracy would probably reduce corruption and malpractice but might actually aggravate the religious and tribal tensions which lie just below the surface in so many countries. An extensive redrawing of national boundaries might produce more homogeneous states, but at the expense of long drawn-out uncertainty at best and chaos at worst.

Alternatively, one of the larger countries, most obviously South Africa or Nigeria, might succeed in overcoming its daunting problems and act as a beacon for its weaker neighbours. The whole population of Africa is after all appreciably less than that of either India or China.

Some argue that the greatest need is for a new culture of risk to overcome the conservatism engendered by traditional responses to Africa's frequently difficult environment and entrenched in tribal traditions.

Africa and the Developed World.

Perhaps the biggest question mark hangs over Africa's future relations with the developed world. Many argue that Africa is actually being held back by western policies, not least the European Union's Common Agricultural Policy, which makes it harder for African agricultural exports to penetrate EU markets. However strong the arguments may be against dumping, there does, though, seem to be a certain illogicality in arguing that Africa should export foodstuffs to the West when it cannot feed itself. It is also highly questionable from an environmental perspective whether Europe should import vegetables which it can often grow on its own doorstep from thousands of miles away.

Differing interpretations are also possible of the impact of economic globalisation. For some observers Africa is a victim because globalisation is a process which inevitably punishes the weak. For others, the problem is that globalisation has bypassed Africa and the answer is to embrace it.

Current Developments.

The countries of the developed world remain ambivalent in their policies. Some, joined more recently by Libya, continue to exploit patron and client relationships which retain a neo-colonial flavour, and in which business can be as active as government. The same countries, however, can form part of a wider consensus that Africa needs aid of many kinds, and not just financial, if it is to participate fully in the wider world of the twenty-first century. It is a daunting thought that the GDP of the whole of Africa at $420 billion is just 1·3 % of the world total, and significantly less than that of Mexico.

Future Aid Requirements.

The consensus, however, starts to fray over questions of implementation. Official development aid to the countries of sub-Saharan Africa actually fell from $16·1 billion in 1996 to $12·7 billion in 1999 and 2000. In contrast, the African leaders themselves called under the New Partnership for Africa's Development (Napad) proposals of 2002 for $64 billion (£45 billion) a year for the next 15 years in a package of aid, accelerated debt relief, and investment, to generate the annual economic growth of 7 % which they considered necessary to reverse the continent's fortunes. In return, they promised to weed out economic mis-management, corruption and dictatorship with a commitment to multiparty democracy, good government, the rule of law, and policies conducive to economic growth.

The likelihood of either the funds requested or the good governance promised materialising are slender. In practice it might be better to concentrate on more modest but more readily achievable goals such as improvements in education, health, institutional capacity and wealth distribution on the one hand and basically honest and representative government on the other. The elimination of hunger and malnutrition has more to do with ending bad practice than with ambitions for economic growth, whatever other benefits that might bring.

New Hopes in 2005.

In comparison, at least with earlier years, 2005 did bring a measure of new hope for relations between Africa and the developed world. Spurred on to no small degree by Bob Geldof's "Make Poverty History" campaign, the G7 meeting of finance ministers in June and the G8 summit in Gleneagles, Scotland, in July under Tony Blair's chairmanship agreed to cancel £22 billion in debt owed by the world's 18 poorest countries, 14 of them in Africa. It also agreed to increase the level of aid, although not to the degree sought by campaigners. The US in particular stressed that increases in official aid were dependent on their being spent on health and education, and on a reduction in corruption.

Less progress, however, was made on agreeing to reduce the subsidies paid to farmers in the developed world, and on opening markets. These were the subject of further negotiation under WTO auspices in Hong Kong in December, when a very modest compromise was only achieved with the greatest difficulty.

GLOBAL OCEAN RESOURCES

Introduction.

Oceans are characteristic of the planet Earth. Roughly 72% of the Earth's surface is covered by seawater, at depths from a few inches to over 35,000 feet. The seas are critical to atmospheric, chemical and geological processes, and it is impossible to imagine any part of the Earth functioning without them, including life as we know it. Most of the world's 6·4 billion people live within 200 miles of the sea, with two-thirds of the world's countries laying claim to parts of its coastline.

Essential functions aside, the oceans can be envisaged as the greatest resource available to humankind, providing food, products, power and services like waste disposal on a scale that was long assumed to be limitless. However, the growth of world population and consumption in recent centuries, fuelled by technology, now challenges this assumption. Many fisheries, industries and ecosystems are at or near collapse with little hope for recovery. As its resources dwindle humanity needs to manage them with great care to meet first immediate, and then future, needs. If this can be done, 'the seas' wealth may prove to be sustainable after all.

Marine Fisheries and Aquaculture.

The world's annual marine fish and shellfish catch is around 90 million tons, with a first sale value of about $US 50 billion. Over 70% is used in human consumption, accounting for a third of the animal protein consumed in the developing world (somewhat less in the remaining countries). There are now thought to be around a million fishing vessels worldwide, from tiny canoes to huge factory/freezer ships. Shellfish and other invertebrates are also harvested and can fetch higher prices than fish by weight as delicacies for particular markets. Algae are also used as food or as emulsifiers or abrasives in products from ice cream to toothpaste and cosmetics.

Much of this exploitation has been made possible by stronger vessels, diesel engines, improved fishing gear, sonar, aerial and satellite fish-finding techniques and better preservation techniques. Fishing fleets were formerly free to roam the high seas, but in the 1970s disputes helped lead to the division of the oceans into exclusive economic zones under the control of seaboard states.

Maximum Sustainable Yield.

The world annual catch is thought to be more than 80 percent of the fish the oceans actually produce in an average year. Immediately it is clear that we must be taking somewhere near the maximum that will allow the process to be sustainable at current levels. This maximum sustainable yield (MSY) is a preoccupation of all who manage and work in fisheries of whatever size. In major fisheries, scientists assess stocks and advise policy-makers on how to limit and protect the fishery. However, fish stocks can only be assessed indirectly, by surveys

and catch reports, so there is always uncertainty, and natural fluctuation in populations means catch limits (quotas) must be strictly adhered to and always reassessed. Lobbying from struggling fishermen unhappy with the limits means that conflict between scientists and managers is common.

Exploitation and Over-Exploitation.

The sequential stages of development, full exploitation, over exploitation and collapse (when it becomes unprofitable or impossible to find the target species) have been seen in one fishery after another in recent decades. After collapse, recovery is possible but over-exploitation is likely to cause a second collapse. The North Sea cod fishery is a example of one that may be entering the collapse phase. In 2003, North Sea cod were less numerous than at any time in the last 20 years, with scientists predicting a fisheries collapse similar to that experienced off Newfoundland in the early 1990s. The number of young cod (that replenish the population) found by surveys has been at or below the long-term average since the mid-1980s.

The advisory International Council for the Exploration of the Sea (ICES) has recommended that exploitation rates be curtailed considerably and at once, in order to reduce the risk of collapse. Fisheries that have collapsed include Canadian cod stocks (1992) Chilean loco (1989) and the Galapagos sea cucumber (1997, only 5 years after fishing began). According to the United Nations' Food and Agriculture Organisation, even now 69% of the world's commercial marine fish stocks are "fully exploited, over-fished, depleted, or slowly recovering."

Aquaculture.

The ancient Greeks maintained fish farms, but until recently, almost all marine fish and seafood were wild-caught animals. Much still is, making fish the only non-agricultural product in the diet of most Westerners, but fish and invertebrate farming (aquaculture) is expanding greatly to meet current economic demands. Many marine species are hard to corral and keep, and problems of diet and disease control must be overcome. Appropriate sites like sheltered lochs or mangroves must also be found, but from then on the economic rewards can be great. Recent developments include breeding successfully and genetically to speed growth or improve flavour. Many of the issues surrounding marine livestock are similar to those in the debates over conventional agriculture.

Marine Biodiversity.

Biological diversity (biodiversity) is the source of sustenance for all people and of fascination for many. Scientists are still struggling to understand just how essential a part diversity plays in the functioning of ecosystems and global cycles. Nowhere is this interconnection more prevalent than in the oceans. Every marine organism shares a single body of water with every other. The viscous nature of water allows nutrients and organisms to travel through it in three dimensions, and the vast range of different seabed types mean that all manner of animals and plants can make a living under the sea. All 35 major groups of animals (phyla) are represented in the sea compared to the 11 found on land. Current estimates put the number of known marine species at 300,000, with at least 500,000 remaining to be found and described if discoveries continue to be made at current rates. In 2004, for example, new marine life was discovered by the Norwegian-led Mid-Atlantic Ridge survey. Many marine forms never move at all once they have found a resting place; whereas some oceanic fish or larger whales appear to roam endlessly, often to places too remote to track them. But like all life, all are dependent on certain habitats.

Marine Habitats.

Habitats themselves are diverse in the seas, ranging from the "water deserts" of the open ocean, the sediments of continental shelves by the lightless abyssal plains and trenches. Nearer coasts, coral reefs, rocky and sandy shores, mudflats and mangroves occur, each with their own characteristic species. In 1977, new ecosystems were discovered around hydrothermal vents (underwater hot springs) that supported unique communities of life independent of the sun's energy, and these are thought by some scientists to be similar to the places life first evolved.

Marine biodiversity is highest around the Indonesian archipelago, thought to be the point of origin of many modern coastal species, and decreases away from there. Unlike on land, temperate areas are not necessarily less diverse than the tropics, particularly in the south. The seas under the Antarctic ice have a rich complement of species, many found nowhere else. Diversity is generally higher in coastal areas (with their broader range of habitats) and on the seafloor than in open water.

Within each habitat, diversity can vary across zones dictated by waves, sunlight and competition for space. Nevertheless there is no part of the sea that does not support organisms that are remarkable for their productivity, specialisation, or beauty. Much of this life is under threat of local or total extinction from overfishing, habitat destruction, pollution and climate change, and great efforts will have to be made to prevent the most vulnerable species from becoming totally lost to future generations.

Marine Mineral Wealth.

Most of the 92 naturally occurring elements are found in seawater, but at very low concentrations. The seafloor is much more attractive as a mineralogical resource. Raw materials such as sand, gravel, phosphorite (for fertiliser and industry) and coral abound, and where accessible can be exploited. Also present are rare heavy minerals and ores like gold, magnetite, diamond, and tin. Particles of these may accumulate as water movement separates them from other sediments. Manganese nodules are widely distributed over the Pacific seabed and contain cobalt, copper or nickel that could be valuable enough to pay for their extraction and processing as land-based supplies run out.

Power from the Oceans.

The oceans are also a source of energy wealth. Fossil fuels (coal, oil, and natural gas) are products of past biological growth. Oil and gas are abundant at the bottom of the seas where they formed from the remains of marine life at immense geological pressures. But the processes that generate fossil fuels are too slow to rely on as an energy source forever (some estimate that we have only a few decades' worth of fossil fuel left at current consumption rates, others that the shortage has already begun to be felt). Fossil fuels also produce atmospheric and other pollutants that are potentially contributing to the recent and projected rise in global average temperatures (the "greenhouse effect") the consequences of which are likely to be dire. The search for renewable, clean and efficient energy sources frequently turns its attention to the oceans.

Because the oceans cover more of the Earth's surface than the land, they have even greater potential as a site and source for renewable energy. This can be derived from the sun, either directly, as solar power, or indirectly. Indirect sources of solar energy include the heat stored in warm surface waters, the winds (which are driven by the sun's warming of the atmosphere), and waves and ocean currents (in turn driven by the winds). Uniquely in the seas, the moon can also be tapped to provide energy, as the vast volumes of water moved by the tides are created by the gravitational pull of the moon, sun and Earth in the solar system.

Thermal Power.

Some 90% of the area of the tropics is covered by sea, most of it open ocean. Solar energy throughout the year heats the surface waters to a temperature several degrees above the colder water below. Ocean Thermal Energy Conversion (OTEC) is a little exploited means of evaporating fluids like liquid propane or ammonia using warm surface water and allowing the resulting gas to drive turbines. The liquids are condensed and recycled using cooler water

pumped up from below. An advantage of this process is that ammonia itself could be produced using the energy for use in agriculture and industry. A disadvantage is the high capital cost of developing suitable plants in the form of huge ocean-going vessels.

Wind Power.

Wind energy is reasonably reliable and renewable, and works simply by allowing the turning of a "windmill" or turbine to generate electricity. In the sea there is also the option of putting the turbines underwater to obtain hydroelectric power from wind-driven currents. In the short-term, wind turbines in the remote ocean may at least prove to be free of the "eyesore" and noise controversies that have made the technology divisive (as currently seen in rural parts of Britain). One disadvantage is that some parts of the seas are extraordinarily windy – perhaps to a point that makes the building and maintenance of these systems commercially unviable.

Wind also makes waves in the sea, triggering circular movements of water that can grow tremendously as they travel and dissipate only when they reach suitable obstacles like coastlines. The complex motion of waves (which look deceptively like simple undulations from land) contains great energy but is difficult to harness efficiently. Turbine-based generators can be shown to be reliable but great care must be taken to site them so as not to interfere with the natural coastal processes of erosion and deposition.

Tidal Power.

Tides are essentially waves thousands of kilometres long and up to 15 metres high, but they appear to us only as a rise, fall or rushing of water. Harnessing this movement of water to provide power is theoretically possible, but, like most potential renewable sources, the technology is somewhat speculative and subject to its own particular problems. Tidal turbines would generate power only at certain times in a 24-hour period, with some needing to be stored, and ideally also be able to turn in either direction (for a rising and falling tide). The best sites are in strongly tidal inlets or estuaries, such as the Severn Estuary (UK) or Bay of Fundy (USA). Such plants would need a big engineering commitment, whether they take the form of massive barrages (as on the Rance River in France) or other structures. But the potential is there for us to use.

AIR POLLUTION

Introduction.

From certain points of view, the most interesting quality of air pollution is that it is a matter of public concern in Britain at all. A cynic who remembered the London smog of 1952 or the industrial grime of earlier decades, or who was familiar with the toxic atmospheres of industrialising Asia in the present day, might feel it was much ado about nothing. In one sense this is true. Present levels of concern reflect the escalation in the public demand for a healthy environment rather than any consciousness of a decline in air quality.

There is the further problem that certain environmentally significant emissions are not, strictly speaking, emissions of pollutants at all. The greenhouse gases, carbon dioxide and methane, whose importance is described in the earlier section on climate change (**Y6**), are neither "dirty" nor directly injurious to health. Nor were the chlorofluorocarbons (CFCs) which were used in aerosols and refrigerators before they were phased out under the Montreal Protocol of 1987: their significance lay in their thinning of the ozone layer which blocks some of the sun's ultra-violet rays, which cause skin cancers.

Smoking.

Pollutants proper (derived from the Latin *polluere*

meaning "to soil") nevertheless represent an important challenge, partly because the linkage with health is now very much better understood. Of no form of air pollution is this truer than of smoking. It is becoming increasingly hard to remember that only forty years ago smoking was as natural to the great majority of people as eating and drinking. Moreover it was a source of sexual allure for men and women alike: the rugged male was as incomplete without his cigarette as was the vamp without her cigarette holder. The pipe was associated with reliability and trustworthiness — a connection which British prime ministers as different as Baldwin, Attlee and Wilson exploited to the full.

The reality was rather different. The nicotine in cigarettes is an addictive drug and it was not difficult to find smokers of 40 cigarettes a day and more. The cartoon character, Andy Capp, mirrors the habit to perfection. It was not widely appreciated that even people's external appearance would be seriously affected for the worse. The face could suffer extreme wrinkling and the formation of disfiguring craters and ridges. The famous poet, W. H. Auden, was one very prominent example in his later years. The internal effects were more dramatic and more serious. To a degree then little appreciated, smoking was causing a wide range of respiratory diseases including emphysema, which makes it difficult for the victim to breathe, and, most serious of all, lung cancer.

The Hazards of Passive Smoking.

What was not appreciated at all was that not just active smoking but also passive smoking – inhaling the cigarette fumes of others – could be hazardous. When one recalls such phrases as "smoke-filled rooms", a very literal description of the working environment of groups such as journalists and trade union negotiators, this may seem less surprising, but it was much harder to associate hazard with the more subdued smoking associated with public transport and restaurants. Nevertheless, medical and scientific research established that what had been seen as at most a low-level social nuisance was in reality a significant form of air pollution bringing in its train all the ailments associated with active smoking. In consequence, ever tighter constraints have been placed on smoking in public places with the added motivation, following the escalator fire at Kings Cross Underground station, of protecting public safety. The Republic of Ireland has gone as far as imposing a blanket ban on smoking in all public places including its famous pubs, and Britain has banned it on the great majority of its trains, in enclosed stations, extending to the whole of the London Underground, and is now to follow the Irish example and ban it in all public places. Increasing constraints have been placed on all forms of tobacco advertising, producing an indirect, and to the un-initiated incomprehensible, style of advertising, which is almost an art form in its own right. The European Union has given serious consideration to a total ban on all forms of tobacco advertising, but perversely continues to subsidise the crops of Greek tobacco farmers under the Common Agricultural Policy.

The Problem of Household Chemicals.

Another form of "domestic" air pollution which is increasingly suspect is that generated by household chemicals. Although it has been known for many years that the burning-off or rubbing-down of old paint surfaces with a high lead content can generate noxious fumes, it is now feared that such familiar products as the disinfectant used by 87·5% of households, bleach, air freshener and window cleaner can cause children to wheeze persistently which renders them more likely to become asthmatic. The incidence of asthma has tripled since the 1970s and the total number of regular sufferers in Britain is now put at some 1·4 million people. The precise linkage is uncertain, but the volatile chemical compounds and the formaldehyde in the household products may play a role in causing the relevant allergies. A further difficulty lies in our incomplete understanding of the relationship between asthma and air pollution more generally but, as will be discussed below, vehicular pollution appears to be a significant factor.

The Role of Asbestos.

This review of "domestic" or localised sources of air pollution should, however, finish by noting the dangers of asbestos, which was widely used in buildings, primarily as a fire inhibitor, until the 1960s and 1970s. It is now known, however, that the minute fibres spread wherever it is used are highly carcinogenic, or cancer causing, and it is now removed whenever possible, under the strictest safety obligations. The EU Commission's Berlaymont headquarters in Brussels is just one well-known building which had to be closed for some years while its asbestos was being stripped out.

Smog Pollution.

At the opposite extreme from these personally or "domestically" generated forms of air pollution are those from industrial and transportation sources, which are again associated with lung cancer and such respiratory complaints as asthma, bronchitis and emphysema. The comparative significance of these different sources of air pollution has changed significantly over the years. The type of pollution associated with the London smog of 1952 to which reference was made at the beginning, and which killed an estimated 12,000 people, was directly related to the emission of soot from the burning of coal. It was largely ended by the passing of the Clean Air Acts, which required the substitution in urban areas of such smokeless fuels as coke and coalite. From 1955 onwards, the railways progressively phased out the steam locomotive which had similarly deposited large quantities of soot in the areas through which it passed.

Attacking Industrial Pollutants.

The emission of pollutants from other industrial sources has also been progressively tightened up over the last 50 years, not least because of the influence of EU environment policy. The Large Combustion Plant directive set much more stringent standards for the emission of pollutants like nitrogen and sulphur compunds from installations such as power stations, and greatly encouraged the fitting of flue gas desulphurisation systems (FGD) – an expensive but effective means of reducing the sulphur released as sulphur dioxide from the burning of coal. Some coal industry sources argue in addition that if Britain were to invest in clean coal technology rather than wind farms it could meet its commitment under the Kyoto Protocol to reduce greenhouse gas emissions for £6 billion rather than £9 billion.

Acid Rain.

Be that as it may, sulphur dioxide (SO_2) in the atmosphere combines with the water vapour in the clouds to fall as dilute sulphuric acid (H_2SO_4), popularly known as acid rain. As noted in the accompanying piece on the History of the Green Movement, the consequences of acid rain were most dramatically perceived in West Germany where the phenomenon of forest death quickly mobilised public opinion. West Germany was particularly vulnerable because the coals of its neighbours, Czechoslovakia and Poland, were high in sulphur, as was, only even more so, the sub-surface brown coal or lignite on which East Germany was almost totally dependent. The damage was confined neither to West Germany nor to trees. Acid rain was estimated to cause US$9·5 billion damage to metals and building stones across Europe every year. Very substantial reductions in sulphur emissions followed the fall of communism in central and eastern Europe and the large-scale closing down of former East German industry, but forest death remains a serious problem. It is concentrated in central and eastern Europe but Britain is far from exempt. Figures published jointly by the UN Economic Commission for Europe and the European Commission in the summer of 2001 showed that one quarter of all Europe's forest trees were suffering severely.

The "Dirty Man of Europe"?

Moreover, British industry has its own history of pollution. Emissions from north-eastern England were soon blamed by Scandinavian scientists for the acidification of the Swedish lakes from the 1970s onwards – a charge which the British long indignantly rejected but were eventually obliged to concede. As recently as 1990, a polemical report by Greenpeace described Britain as the "dirty man of Europe", noting in particular that it was the largest sulphur dioxide polluter in western Europe. Public pressure arising from such bad publicity and, not least, the increasingly strict requirements of EU directives has since led to substantial improvements.

Transport and Pollution.

Pollution does, however, remain a problem, albeit not a dramatic one, primarily because of developments in the transport sector, in Britain, in Europe and world-wide. Put at its simplest, ever stricter standards are being outweighed by ever greater levels of usage. Emissions per mile of nitrous oxides (NO_x), carbon monoxide (CO) and sulphur dioxide (SO_2) by lorries and cars of specific engine capacity have steadily fallen across the EU to comply with the ever stricter EU directives.

Those on the maximum sulphur content of fuel oils and on maximum auto emissions are the most recent. Catalytic converters for the reduction of SO_2 emissions are now mandatory for new vehicles. Similarly, leaded petrol has been largely phased out. Auto engines, however, have grown larger, cars and lorries have become more numerous and they are being driven much further. The fall of the Iron Curtain has given a great boost to trans-European road traffic and the European Commission estimates that EU road freight will increase by 38 % in the first twelve years of the present century. The European pattern is being replicated explosively in China and elsewhere in the developing world.

The Emission of Particulates.

The root of the impact on health of air pollution, whether from industrial or transportation sources, appears to lie in the emission of very fine particles less than 2·5 microns thick, known as particulates. Studies have shown that mortality rates can increase by 6 % for every additional ten microgrammes of such particulates in a cubic metre of air and that they could be responsible for nearly 4,000 of the deaths from lung cancer in Britain every year.

The prime source of such particulates is diesel fuel used in lorries and many cars, and ever stricter maximum emission levels are being enforced under EU environmental legislation, with particle traps being obligatory on new buses and lorries from 2006. Tracking the direct route of the health impact, however, is not straightforward. One set of studies on London cyclists, for example, found that their exposure to particulates appeared to be much lower than that of passengers on the Underground. The incidence of asthma can be similarly perverse, with comparatively high levels normally being associated with areas of high traffic flow but sometimes also with quite remote rural areas.

The Air Pollution Information Service.

In response to public concern over air pollution, the British government, like those of most of our neighbours, has introduced an air pollution information service available through TV teletext pages, freephone and the Internet, which reports levels of the five main air pollutants that can cause immediate health effects. Those five are, as already discussed, sulphur dioxide, nitrogen dioxide, ground level ozone (a pollutant created by the interaction of nitrogen dioxide, sunlight, and petrol fumes), carbon monoxide and particles. Levels of these pollutants are normally unlikely to be high in modern Britain, but the combination of high summer temperatures and very heavy traffic in some cities of southern Europe and the United States has sometimes produced such concentrations of them, particularly ozone, that drastic traffic limitation measures have had to be temporarily introduced. The simplest and best-known is probably the banning on alternate days of vehicles with odd and even registration numbers.

The Warning from Chernobyl.

Reference should perhaps be made finally to a very different form of air pollution which is not within normal experience, and which is not strictly air pollution at all, namely nuclear radiation. Although Chernobyl mercifully remains the world's only really serious nuclear accident, its fall-out was carried across the whole of Europe and beyond, and helps to place other air pollution concerns in a wider perspective.

THE GLOBALISATION OF FOOD

A Climate of Concern.

The expression of concern at the quality and safety of food has been a feature of recent years. The controversies over foot and mouth, BSE, and GM foods, and, to a lesser degree, over animal welfare and even hunting, have generated a pervasive sense of uncertainty, and sometimes anxiety, over whether what we eat is good for us. Public faith in the protection offered by the Food Standards Agency is limited, possibly because its relations with environmental groups have been poor. Our anxiety can come to a head when disease breaks out or when a dangerous additive finds its way inadvertently into the food chain, but for most of the time it is actually very unfocused.

The reasons for that lack of focus are not difficult to understand. Our food is probably more attractively packaged and presented, and more varied, than it has ever been. Much of it is very competitively priced. Concern over food content can easily be seen as a southern, middle-class obsession of little relevance to the majority of families, for whom convenience and economy are all-important.

The Industrialisation and Globalisation of Food Production.

Those reactions may be valid in themselves, but they do tend to deflect attention from the highly industrial nature of modern food production, processing, distribution and sale. Moreover, food, in common with all other industries, is being exposed to a globalisation process which sources supplies from ever further afield in its drive to satisfy consumer demand at the lowest possible cost.

The environmental and social implications of this increasing globalisation of food production are likely to be even more radical than those of the globalisation of industrial production, however, because the production of food affects so much more directly the land we live on and ultimately depend on. Few people would probably accept the logic of those who would close down the whole of British farming, rather as cotton weaving and to a large extent coal mining were closed down in earlier years, rely totally on allegedly cheaper food imports, and convert the British landscape to forest.

Implications for Health.

No effect, however, is as direct as that on human health. Bad food, which encompasses bad eating habits as much as questions of product quality, is a national problem which is only slowly receiving the attention it deserves. A high proportion of children are now clinically obese and, more worryingly still, experts predict that they will remain so for the rest of their lives. Although such extremes as the deep-fried Mars bar may remain restricted to parts of Scotland, high-fat and high-salt crisps feature prominently in the diets of the majority. The television has replaced the dining table for many families, encouraging the use of fast food snacks of low nutritional value.

These trends are, of course, shaped to no small degree by cultural and social factors remote from globalisation. It is also important not to become overly romantic about the diets and eating habits of the past, which in Britain at least could be limited indeed for the great majority. Fish, meat and vegetables are still good for you even if they come from the other side of the globe. In times of economic hardship, like those experienced during the great slump of the 1920s and 1930s, malnutrition was so serious a problem in parts of industrial Britain that the government feared for the country's ability to raise an army fit enough to defend the country and introduced free milk for all schoolchildren as a palliative.

Merits of Locally-sourced Food.

Nevertheless, the linkages between the increasingly industrial style of food production, processing and distribution, the globalisation of sourcing, and concerns over food quality and safety are real. No less real are their linkages with questions of global development on the one hand and with the future of the countryside in Britain and other developed countries on the other. That linkage can be expressed most clearly in the form of a simple proposition: all other things being equal, the fresher the food the better it is for you and the better it tastes. And freshness is not just a question of appearance at point of sale. It involves the chilling or freezing or treating which may have been necessary to secure that freshness between farm and shop. The pumping of water into bacon and poultry to make them look plumper is so commonplace that it does not attract notice. Some processed meat can contain as little as 37% meat. There can be little doubt that the best produce will come from known local sources, with as localised a system of distribution as possible and with the minimum of preservatives. It is a pattern which is still clearly discernible across much of France and which the French seek tenaciously to defend.

The Distribution Network.

It is often not appreciated just how different British practice often is. Milk is regularly distributed having travelled some hundreds of miles between the cow, the treatment plant, a hierarchy of supply centres, and the shop or doorstep. Every ton of food travels an average of 59 miles by road. Needless to say, the wider environmental cost of such industrial-style distribution systems is high. The total bill for food miles in Britain is £3·7 billion, including £1·3 billion on associated shopping by car. Other consequences verge on the bizarre: every year, Britain imports 0·41 million tons of milk only to export 0·43 million tons and imports 120,000 sheep only to export 130,000.

Patterns in Europe.

French agriculture, as much as British, has obviously had to adjust to what can only be described as a second agricultural revolution, which means that far more food can be produced from far less land and with far less labour than ever before. Mirroring what had happened in Britain in the nineteenth century, the French agricultural labour force dropped from 4·1 million in 1960 to 1·1 million by 1992. The countries of southern and eastern Europe are seeing the same pattern of development. Nevertheless, nineteenth-century Britain diverged from continental Europe in some significant respects. Confident in its industrial productivity and in the protection of its trade routes by the Royal Navy, and not least in such new technologies as refrigeration and food tinning, it imported cheap food in bulk from the Americas and the then Empire to satisfy the demand from its manufacturing cities, and allowed British agriculture to decline. The corollary of cheap food was the depopulation of the countryside and a rural decline which lasted until the Second World War. Whereas nineteenth-century Denmark, for example, invested in agricultural training institutes to develop quality and yields, with the result that Danish bacon is a feature of any British supermarket today, Britain preferred to pay for food imports with industrial exports. The lasting result is that the British consumer has arguably unrealistic expectations of the proper price of quality food.

The Power of the Supermarket.

The beneficiary has been the supermarket as the form of retailing most suited to the mass distribution of food at the lowest possible prices. The phenomenal rise and rise of a chain such as Tesco can only elicit admiration as an expression of business acumen and drive. The downsides of the supermarket phenomenon, however, are many. One is the weak bargaining position of the individual British farmer as supplier. The supermarket chains have so cut their margins in ever more ruthless competition with each other that there may be little left for the producer, who can often only respond by adopting an equally industrial approach. In practice many farmers simply give up. Not dissimilarly, local food shops even in towns of some size are disappearing rapidly. A city like Chichester, for example, the county town of West Sussex and with a population of some 25,000, long had no independent greengrocer and just one independent butcher. The baleful effects of the decision of Nicholas Ridley, then Secretary of State for the Environment, to override warnings that large out-of-town hypermarkets would drain the life out of town centres, are growing rather than shrinking.

The Growth in Imports.

A further consequence of mass production retailing, as of mass production business in other spheres, has been the growth in the import of supplies. Supermarket shelves groan under vegetables from Africa, fruit from Africa, Asia and the Americas, fish from Oceania and meat from Latin America. Brazil is rapidly emerging as a major world meat supplier. In part this is to be welcomed. Oranges and lemons, coffee and tea, have been valued imports for centuries to the benefit of all concerned. One may, however, be less relaxed about imports which are driving out home produce only because of the logic of mass production. The general disappearance of the once ubiquitous Kentish cherry in favour of American and Turkish substitutes, and the fading of the "Garden of England" with it, is surely no small matter?

A World Gone Mad?

Some substitutes seem simply unnecessary, like Hungarian gooseberries, or ultimately comic, like the expensive import by air of blackberries from Mexico when they can be gathered in profusion for nothing from the domestic or rural bramble. Less comic may be the impact on the country concerned of mass food exports. It is difficult to see wisdom in, for example, an arid country like Jordan exporting runner beans to Britain, and the growth in stock breeding in Brazil, to which reference has already been made, which is leading to the widespread destruction of rainforest with serious implications for global climate change. The recourse to fish from New Zealand waters to compensate for diminishing fish stocks in Northern European waters has simply widened the problem by putting New Zealand species, such as the orange roughy, at risk. The expansion of horticultural production on the dry Mediterranean coast of Spain stimulated plans, now shelved, for the mass transfer of water from the wet Atlantic coast, which many regarded as environmentally catastrophic.

Concern Over Standards.

Not least, and of direct relevance to the initial remarks on concern over the safety of food, such globalised sourcing can give rise to doubts over the standards under which produce has been grown or reared. The globalisation and industrialisation of food production is also uncannily similar to the manufacture of, say, a car in that the end product has a wide range of components from quite unrelated sources. Parma ham is defined as such by the final treatment of the meat, but the pig may have been reared far from Italy and its feed produced in yet another country again. The problem of quality control is obvious, with polluted feed having been suspected as the cause of Britain's last epidemic of foot and mouth disease.

The Globalisation Argument.

The proper response to these challenges is highly contentious. For most orthodox economists, global markets and product specialisation spell greater prosperity for all and the challenge is to integrate the undeveloped countries in the global trading system. The British prime minister, Tony Blair, strongly agrees. Critics, however, including charities like Christian Aid, argue equally strongly that globalisation causes disproportionate suffering to the most vulnerable. Perhaps it is appropriate to repeat an earlier point. Trade in food is not perhaps quite the same as trade in manufactures.

Other Possibilities.

Such considerations underlie the growing popularity of farmers' markets, which benefit the producer by excluding the middle-man (or more accurately middle-men), and benefit the consumer by offering food with all the health and taste advantages of locally sourced produce, albeit not at rock-bottom prices. By their nature, however, such outlets are only open occasionally, usually on alternate Saturday mornings. This seems likely to continue to restrict their impact, unless farmers work on the more co-operative basis familiar from Switzerland but hitherto undeveloped in Britain.

Another recognisable development is the direct sale of local produce to local shops and supermarkets, although it is a development generally restricted to the more expensive outlets. It is a development which is hindered in Britain compared with France, Germany or Italy by the historically low level of regional consciousness, but it is being promoted by a range of tourism-oriented bodies like the National Trust.

It would be nice to add that the most promising development in the provision of healthy food is the comparative popularity of organic produce, but unfortunately this is not the case. Quite apart from the arguments of those critics who allege that some officially sanctioned organic methods are negative rather than positive in their impact, the current weakness of organic food in Britain is that it is 70-80% imported — by definition the reverse of local.

Other possible solutions to the problem of farm viability, like the traditional German family farm run by family members who share in agricultural labour while having other urban employment, have never been common in Britain.

The Common Agricultural Policy.

These arguments are at their most familiar to the British citizen and consumer in the arguments over the European Union's Common Agricultural Policy, which guarantees Europe's farmers minimum prices for their produce which are higher than world prices. It is a very blunt instrument which rewards high-volume producers who may well be wealthy, like the Prince of Wales, but also offers a lifeline to a host of small farmers Europe-wide. The Policy's abolition would mark the end of the substantial subsidy being paid by Britain's consumers to Europe's farmers and also the end of many of the barriers to entry faced by poor farmers in the developing world. It could also, though, mark the end of much European agriculture, the abandonment of the land to development or scrub, and the sourcing of food from ever further afield. The possible consequences could be presaged by the recent agreement over sugar where the abandonment of control will mean a reduction in prices of one-third, the reduction of European beet production by a quarter and its termination in Greece and Ireland, the loss of 100,000 jobs, the exchange by the EU of the status of exporter for that of importer, and the probable abandonment of production in the former British and French African and Caribbean colonies. The beneficiaries will be Australia, Thailand, Brazil and some of the poorest African countries.

PANDEMICS

Introduction.

It was unclear as 2006 dawned whether Avian Flu would become the pandemic (mass epidemic) feared by some experts, with a death toll under the worst scenario of up to perhaps 150 million worldwide,

600,000 in Britain and 1·9 million in the US, or whether it would be a false alarm. As of end-March, 100 people had died across the world from the disease, and it had reached France in its westward march. In April 2006 the first confirmed case was reported in Scotland.

Its further spread would depend on the skill, and luck, of the World Health Organisation, the European Commission and national medical authorities in devising and implementing counter-measures. If they were successful, it could be of little more significance, except to an unfortunate few, than the dreaded millennium computer bug whch singularly failed to bring business to the predicted standstill.

Avian Flu is, however, a reminder that the world remains vulnerable to the pandemics which have afflicted it in the past, of which the Black Death of the fourteenth century is probably the most familiar. Comparison with Avian Flu does, however, reveal equally remarkable differences and similarities. The great similarity is that both originated in China. The differences relate to scale. By Spring 2006 there appeared to be some grounds for cautious optimism.

The Black Death.

The impact of the Black Death was quite staggering. Some 25 million people, equivalent to roughly a third of the total population, may have died across Europe as a whole and the population size of western Europe did not recover for more than 150 years. England's population dropped by perhaps half. The economic consequences were profound. About 1,000 English villages effectively disappeared, and the whole feudal system was shaken, and ultimately undermined, by the new shortage of labour which stimulated the substitution of wages for the traditional obligatory labour services. Even the position of the church was shaken by the new personal obsession with death. These economic and social consequences could take on a specifically revolutionary aspect. It is surely not coincidental that the later fourteenth century in England also saw John Ball's radical question: "When Adam delved [dug] and Eve span, who was then the gentleman?", the subsequent rebellion led by Wat Tyler, and Wycliffe's pioneering translation of the Bible into English.

The Great Plague of 1665.

Yet a further difference, one must hope, from even a severe epidemic of Avian Flu is that the Black Death readily recurred for more than 50 years. In this, it was highly similar to the more familiar bubonic plague with which it was probably clinically identical. The Great Plague of London of 1665 was a particularly severe outbreak of an underlying disease and would probably have recurred if it had not been for the chance of the Great Fire the following year. Even if it was very localised in comparison with the Black Death, the consequences for Londoners were severe. Perhaps 70,000 out of an estimated population of 460,000 died. Such modern London districts as Finsbury contain the sites of the plague pits into which the bodies of victims were thrown in unceremonious haste.

The Example of Eyam.

In their desperate attempt to escape the disease many who were already unknowingly infected fled to the countryside only to take the disease there with them. Perhaps as a result, remote Eyam in Derbyshire was to suffer more than London, with 260 deaths out of a population of 350. Nevertheless, the Great Plague, unlike the Black Death, was essentially a localised rather than a national, let alone international, phenomenon. The two did, however, share a social effect which would, no doubt, be shared by Avian Flu, if it did indeed spread. They attacked all classes equally. Popes and royalty were as vulnerable as craftsmen and serfs. The differing extent to which vaccines have been developed and ordered could, however, lead this time to substantial variations between nations.

Advances in hygiene and medicine as well as in building techniques have kept plague-related pandemics at bay across Europe in subsequent centuries. Other pandemics have, nevertheless, broken out in particular circumstances. The influenza which swept the weakened globe after the First World War killed up to 50 million people, many more than had the military hostilities themselves. Virologists consider the strain, which was of avian origin, to have been a faster, more powerful and more efficient killer than even bubonic plague.

The AIDS Pandemic.

A question mark must hang over the future impact in Europe of AIDS, as much as over that of Avian Flu. Despite earlier fears, it has remained, at least in North America as well as in Europe, so far largely confined as a killer to the homosexual community. AIDS is, however, a timely reminder that in sub-Saharan Africa, a pandemic is currently raging which is killing populations in Black Death proportions (and it is not confined to the homosexual community). Life expectancy has dropped to below 40 years in countries such as Zambia and Zimbabwe respectively. Medical resources are likely to remain far too thinly spread to meet the challenge. Africa is, however, also a reminder that pandemics are only part of the drama. Endemic diseases such as malaria still kill millions in tropical regions. Some 6 million children alone have died from it since 1997. In such a context, Avian Flu may or may not turn out to have been a relatively minor medical footnote.

MEDICAL
MATTERS

Here we give a brief summary of modern medical knowledge for a wide variety of the most common illnesses. The section also looks at some medical problems of our contemporary society, from diabetes to drug abuse. It must not be allowed to replace your doctor, who should be consulted immediately if you are worried. The main index at the end of *Pears* provides an easy reference guide.

TABLE OF CONTENTS

MEDICAL MATTERS

PART I. INTRODUCTION.

MEDICINE AT THE MILLENNIUM.

An Age of Progress.

Much in medicine which is now taken for granted (that for the majority of diseases caused by identifiable organisms there is a specific drug treatment, for example) was undreamed of even as recently as 60 years ago. Progress in diagnosis, in preventive medicine and in treatment, both medical and surgical, has been so rapid as to be almost breathtaking. A doctor retiring from active practice this year has seen smallpox completely eradicated, poliomyelitis practically banished (at least from the UK), tuberculosis become curable, coronary artery disease relievable surgically and he will have witnessed the dramatic progress in the field of molecular biology and in the research by immunologists and geneticists into their efforts to control parasitic diseases like bilharzia, malaria and river blindness that affect millions of people in the Third World. One aspect of medicine and medical thinking still resistant to progress in understanding in spite of continued research is the effect of mind on body.

The Effect of Mind on Body.

Many of us still like to think that our bodies are just something we have got into, like cars, that ill-health is simply something that has "gone wrong" in one system or another and that therefore provided we find the appropriate expert (a chest physician, a gastro-enterologist or an ophthalmic surgeon, for example) to correct the fault, we will recover. Whereas that idea holds good for a broken leg, for instance, with many diseases the idea that mind can be totally separated from the "defective" part just isn't good enough. You cannot simply divorce your stomach, your bowels, your liver or your heart from your "self". They are all part of you and react, as you yourself react, to all the stresses and anxieties, fears and worries and the hundred and one other factors that are part and parcel of modern living. It is true that most of your stomach can be removed, your gall-bladder entirely so and with the aid of a dialysing machine or a transplant you can get by without your kidneys. As with your car, old or diseased parts can be repaired or totally replaced; even your heart, conventionally the very "seat" of the emotions. *Mens sana in corpore sano* a sound mind in a sound body. Your body and its many parts may be helped to normal function by modern medicines and surgery but, in general, it will only stay that way if you can rid yourself of all those emotional blemishes—anger, frustration, fear, worry and anxiety—which trouble you. Easier said than done, of course, but a good physician can help with good advice, with medicines if necessary—or simply with his ear. Emotional stress can not only inhibit healing of such things as duodenal or gastric ulcers but may even *cause* them. There are many diseases now recognised which are known to be associated with stress factors if not actually caused by them. Mainly these are diseases of the digestive tract or of the heart and blood vessels and you will find some of them discussed in the appropriate sections.

The state of the mind has more influence on bodily functions than you might think and recovery from many serious conditions can be slowed or hastened, depending on your state of mind. Every doctor has had experience of the patient who "loses the will to live", a situation which is unfortunately commoner than the reverse.

Preventive Medicine.

A word about preventive medicine—or helping yourself to health. A great deal of nonsense has been talked about the healthy life; at one time we were told to take eighteen chews to each bite, to do deep breathing, to take plenty of exercise, to get lots of fresh air, to eat regularly (or to indulge in peculiar diets). But more recently eminent doctors have cast doubt on most of these fancies. Moderate exercise is necessary to health, but athletes who indulge in violent exercise have not always been noted for longevity. Fresh air is pleasant and stimulating, but, where actual breathing is concerned, it is no better than the air in most rooms, though secondary smoking is now considered to be harmful. Certainly, one of the problems of our time is air pollution, but at present we are considering ordinary fresh air in comparison with the air indoors, and, in this case, the experts say there is little difference so far as health is concerned.

Diet and Sleep.

A balanced diet containing correct amounts of the basic food substances is essential, but there is no evidence that when, or at what intervals, you eat makes the slightest difference—unless you are a sufferer from stomach ulcer, in which case it is necessary that the intervals between meals should not be too long. The whole business of having meals at fixed intervals is nothing but a social convention, and in modern life obviously a matter of convenience.

Sleep, too, is a necessity. But different people require different amounts of sleep. Some manage on as little as three hours, others need ten or more.

In a number of studies of men and women who lived to a ripe old age it was found that the only factors in common between them were that they had a good balanced diet of healthy food, that they had contented minds, and that they were interested in something which gave them an aim in life. They also came of long-lived families—for living a long and healthy life depends partly upon heredity.

So the main rules of health are:

(1) Don't abuse your body—*i.e.*, exercise it, feed it sensibly and in moderation and don't poison it with cigarette smoke (yours or anyone else's), with alcohol or with other drugs

(2) Think positively about health—make it a purpose for living

(3) Turn your thoughts away from those bodily functions (digestion, circulation, breathing and so on) which can look after themselves. Introspection leads to hypochondriasis, and

(4) Choose your parents for *their* longevity!

THE DEVELOPMENT OF MEDICINES.

A great surgeon, the first of the moderns, was Ambrose Paré, who died in 1590, and one of his best known sayings was: "I apply the dressing, but God heals the wound." He was quite right; for until about sixty years ago, or even less, all the physician could do was to put the patient in as favourable a state as possible to enable his body to cure itself. That is to say, there were hardly any specific drugs—drugs that had a direct effect on the disease. There were quinine, discovered by the Spaniards in America, which was specific for malaria, and there were iron (specific for anaemia) and digitalis (specific for certain types of heart disease), but otherwise nothing until the nineteenth century, when Paul Ehrlich discovered salvarsan, which is specific for syphilis. Ehrlich died in 1914, having conceived the brilliant idea of drugs, which he described as "magic bullets"—*i.e.*, drugs which, like bullets, would be aimed at the real cause of the disease. They would, that is to say, be specific.

The Advent of Penicillin.

Since then a large number of such drugs have been discovered. For example, the antibiotics, such as penicillin, discovered in 1928 by Fleming at St. Mary's Hospital, Paddington. Later, Florey and Chain in Oxford, helped in the war years by the vast resources of the American pharmaceutical industry, were able to make penicillin available to the public in sufficient quantities by new techniques of production. Penicillin is practically non-poisonous (although it is possible to become allergic to it, sometimes with serious results). It can kill some germs in a dilution of one part of penicillin to one million parts of water; it is effective against streptococci, the cause of blood-poisoning, sepsis in wounds, and many other diseases; and also against the germs of gonorrhoea, meningitis of certain types, and syphilis—penicillin is typically active at 1–10 ug/ml *i.e.* 1–10 parts per million. Blood-poisoning, whether from wounds or childbirth, used to be almost incurable—now the rate of cure is 80–90 per cent.; gonorrhoea has an almost 100 per cent. rate of cure. In pneumonia the rate is 90 per cent., and early syphilis can be cured in a week, instead of the previous two to three years.

New Types of Drugs.

But that was only the beginning. Other antibiotics—streptomycin, tetracycline, erythromycin, and many others—have greatly reduced the terrible scourges of the human race, in particular, in the case of streptomycin, tuberculosis. The sulpha group of drugs—sulphadiazine, sulphadimidine, *etc.*—have also proved a great boon. Then there are the new drugs which have created a revolution in psychiatry—the tranquillisers which relieve anxiety, the drugs which clear up certain types of depression, and substances such as chlorpromazine which make it possible to nurse formerly violent patients in the wards of a general hospital. The antihistamine drugs help in allergies, anticoagulants are of value after heart attacks and levodopa mitigates some of the distressing features of Parkinson's Disease.

The Safety of Drugs.

No drug, old or new, is completely safe—if we define "safe" as meaning having absolutely no potential for harm. The household aspirin, widely used in a variety of conditions for its analgesic (pain-relieving) and antipyretic (fever-reducing) qualities, can cause bleeding from the stomach and small intestine. Phenacetin, at one time a component of compound codeine tablets but now withdrawn, can—with prolonged use—damage the kidney. Chloramphenicol, a powerful antibiotic effective in typhoid fever, typhus and whooping cough, can damage the blood-forming cells of the bone marrow producing an agranulocytosis which can be fatal.

Clearly, in any one case, the doctor must weigh up the advantages and disadvantages of this or that drug before prescribing. Minor, self-limiting illnesses do not require potent, potentially toxic remedies. Chloramphenicol is rarely justified in whooping cough, but would never be withheld from a patient with typhoid fever.

Humans make up a unique species. A new chemical compound promising in animal experiments, for example, as an anti-inflammatory agent, apparently safe when given, say, to mice in a dose 100 times that required to produce that anti-inflammatory effect may, over a long period of time in us, not only have no effect but make his hair fall out or perhaps cause retention of urine. Nevertheless, some animal species do react like man, or vice versa, and it is possible to make reasonably accurate extrapolations from animals to man in terms of drug effect. It is also possible to estimate the toxicity of a drug on humans from its toxicity in certain animal species, but the ultimate test comes only when it is given to us.

The Thalidomide Tragedy.

Thalidomide was unique. In every animal test used throughout the drug industry at that time—it was introduced in the late 1950s—it had a clean bill of health. It was chemically related to other drugs which had been in use for a long time. Overdosage with other sedatives such as the barbiturates was common at that time, although less so now. Overdosage with thalidomide was unlikely to prove fatal. It was marketed in Europe and in Britain as a "safe sedative". The tragic results that followed its ingestion by women in the early weeks of pregnancy are now well known. Babies were born with severe deformities of limbs, internal organs or both. That effect could not have been foretold from any animal tests then in use. Since that date new drugs have been subjected to rigorous testing in various animal species to check the effect on foetal development as a statutory requirement, along with the older tests for toxicity which had always been undertaken by reputable drug companies.

Marketing of New Drugs.

The thalidomide disaster of the early 1960s led directly to the setting up of regulatory drug agencies in most countries of the world. In Britain the introduction and clinical testing of new compounds is controlled by the Medicines and Environmental Health Division of the Department of Health and Social Security, statutory machinery set up by the Medicines Act 1968, which followed the purely voluntary scheme of control under what was known as the Dunlop Committee after Sir Derrick Dunlop, its first chairman.

The development and introduction of new drugs is now very strictly controlled. No new drug can be marketed in Britain without the Medicines Commission being satisfied about its efficacy and its safety. We would need space in this edition almost the size of the complete Medical Section to describe fully the workings of the Commission and the limitations that the requirements of the Medicines Act inevitably place on the development and introduction of new remedies. The time from the initial synthesis of a novel compound likely to be of value to its eventual appearance in the pharmacy on prescription is now eight to 10 years. The cost is measured in millions of pounds because, for each successful drug, there will have been many thousands of unsuccessful ones.

The Control of New Drugs.

Briefly, no new drug or modification of an old one can be sold, whether or not on prescription, unless it has been granted a product licence by the Department of Health and Social Security through its Medicines and Environmental Health Division. Many stages have to be passed to acquire that licence, from the granting of certificates to allow the drug to be tested initially in a limited way in patients in a strictly controlled manner by investigators approved by the Commission, to permission for extension of those trials at a later date to include larger numbers of patients or more investigators, to perhaps a "monitored release"—that is, to enable its use in, say, hospitals only—to the final release on the granting of a full product licence. Thus, the Medicines Commission has control at all stages.

Furthermore, all the stages are dependent on production of evidence relating to the safety and efficacy of the drug, evidence which may take the drug company months, sometimes years, to produce and which, of course, must be acceptable to the Commission. Trials may be stopped at any time, for example, if evidence of side effects of an undesirable nature come to light during clinical testing, or when evidence from some other similar compound indicates a likely risk in the use of the drug in question. Of course, "acceptable" means that the strict criteria which have been laid down by the specialist committees appointed to deal with all the various aspects of drug development, such as toxicology, adverse reactions and so forth, have been met. Experts serve on these committees which meet regularly, but the day-to-day running of the Medicines Commission is in the hands of full-time medically qualified personnel as well as pharmacists, pharmacologists and toxicologists. In addition, outside consultant opinion can be sought.

Surveillance of Side Effects.

As well as all these rigid controls on development and testing in the early stages, there is also a scheme of surveillance for untoward side effects. These are the action, or actions, of a drug apart from its main one. Take the well-known side effect of drowsiness which occurs with certain antihistamine drugs: the main action, the one for which the drug is prescribed, is the mitigation of the effects of allergy, such as urticaria. Drowsiness would be an unwanted effect if the patient is not incapacitated and is able to do his usual job. On the other hand, some antihistamines have an appetite-stimulating effect which could, of course, be a useful attribute in certain situations or even allow the drug to be used solely for that purpose, the anti-allergic effect then being incidental.

New Surgical Advances.

Mention must of course be made of the surgical advances and progress in anaesthesia. Hardly a week goes by without operations being undertaken which seemed inconceivable even as short a time as 40 years ago. Transplantation and re-plantation (the re-attachment of severed limbs) are regularly reported; haemodialysis (the 'cleansing' of blood in patients with irreversible kidney disease) is now often undertaken in the patient's own home where, with appropriate adaptation and the modern kidney machine, he or she can run the procedure—single-handed in many instances—and still keep his or her job; and the laser beam is used to deal with detached retinas or to obliterate tiny, microscopic blood vessel 'bubbles' (aneurysms) in the back of the eye while the patient is conscious and cooperative. The list grows daily.

Social Medicine and Social Health.

What did the twentieth century contribute to the concept of social health? Well, of course, there was a very great deal of legislation along the lines initiated by 19th century pioneers such as Edwin Chadwick to control disease, and a great many other measures have been introduced concerned with the idea of positive health—not merely preventing bad health, but trying to bring about the highest possible state of good health. Orange juice, milk, and good meals for school-children brought about a transformation in child health which became apparent to the least observant. And the National Health service of today is in the direct line of descent from early nineteenth-century legislation.

But in future years it is probable that the main achievement of the twentieth century will prove to have been its extension of the term "social health" to cover every aspect of community life, not only in such subjects as bodily health and its control of social means, but also such problems as mental illness, crime, delinquency, drug addiction, and so on. What we are now asking ourselves is:

how far are these problems produced by society itself, and if this is the case, how far can we go in preventing them by social means?

Community medicine takes the view that these problems can never be dealt with solely by moralising and retribution, but only by dispassionately analysing causes and dealing with them. In today's world we have developed a social conscience. Not always, it is true, a very well-informed social conscience, but at least this is a good beginning. There are organisations for dealing scientifically with delinquency, for dealing with problem children, for spreading knowledge about cancer in order to show people that it can be successfully treated if taken in time.

NATIONAL HEALTH SERVICE (NHS).

Among developments in the National Health Service during the 1990s was the introduction of *The Patient's Charter* from 1 April 1992. As from this date patients were given three important new rights:

* to be given detailed information on local health services, including quality standards and maximum waiting times. Patients can get this information from their health authority, GP or Community Health Council;

* to be guaranteed admission for virtually all treatments by a specific date no later than two years from the day when a consultant places you on a waiting list. Most patients will be admitted before this date.

* to have any complaint about NHS services—whoever provides them—investigated, and to receive a full and prompt written reply from the chief executive of your health authority or general manager of your hospital. If you are still unhappy, a patient may take the case up with the Health Service Commissioner.

Standards of Service.

In addition to a patient's rights, the NHS is committed to a number of *standards of service*. These currently include:

* respect for privacy, dignity and religious and cultural beliefs;

* arrangements to ensure everyone, including people with special needs, can use the services;

* information to relatives and friends about the progress of your treatment, subject, of course, to your wishes;

* an emergency ambulance should arrive within 14 minutes in an urban area, or 19 minutes in a rural area;

* when attending an accident and emergency department, you will be seen immediately and your need for treatment assessed;

* when you go to an outpatient clinic, you will be given a specific appointment time and will be seen within 30 minutes of it;

* your operation should not be cancelled on the day you are due to arrive in hospital. If, exceptionally, your operation has to be postponed twice you will be admitted to hospital within one month of the second cancelled operation;

* a named qualified nurse, midwife or health visitor responsible for your nursing or midwifery care;

* a decision should be made about any continuing

health or social care needs you may have, before you are discharged from hospital.

The NHS Website.

If you need to find out more about NHS services, www.nhs.uk is the official NHS website that can help you. It provides free, basic information such as addresses, maps and contacts for NHS organisations. In addition, www.nhs.uk holds information about what the NHS has to offer and how you can get access to these services.

Through this simple, easy-to-remember website you can:

* access NHS Direct Online for health advice;

* get the latest news about the NHS and current health campaigns;

* find out how to have your say about NHS services;

* learn about the history and structure of the NHS; and;

* look up performance facts and figures.

Prescription Charges.

Currently (June 2006) a charge of £6·65 is payable in England for prescriptions (except for contraceptives which are not charged). Prescription charges are lower in Wales. There are, however, important categories of people exempt from charges. These include children under 16, full-time students under 19 as well as men and women aged 60 or over. Pregnant women who hold an exemption certificate are also included. Diabetics are exempt. Certain people on income support and other benefits are also exempt. Check booklet HC11 available from Post Offices.

The General Medical Council (GMC).

The General Medical Council regulates the medical profession in the United Kingdom. It sets the qualifications and standards required to be registered as a doctor. If found unsafe or unfit it can restrict a doctor's medical practice. Patients may complain directly to the General Medical Council.

British Medical Association.

The British Medical Association has over 126,000 members including about 80% of the UK's practising doctors. It represents their interests, and its roles include publishing the *British Medical Journal*. This respected medical journal is available free on the Internet (*www.bmj.com*) together with an accompanying electronic discussion forum.

Primary Care.

Primary care describes the service you receive from the NHS staff who look after your health needs in the community. This includes your family doctor, health visitor, community nurse, community pharmacist, optician, dentist, physiotherapist *etc.*

A Primary Care Trust (or PCT for short) is a local NHS organisation, which receives money from the Government to plan and provide health services for local people. The PCT's main aim is to improve the health of local people and deliver the best quality healthcare for the population.

The Local GP.

There are currently (2006) around 32,000 NHS GPs in the UK and around 10,500 surgeries. The average size of a GP's list is c.1,850. On average, each practice in Britain has 3·75 GPs. It is estimated that about 80 per cent of the population see their GP at least once a year.

The Health Service Ombudsman.

The Health Service Ombudsman looks into complaints made by or on behalf of people who have suffered because of unsatisfactory treatment or service by the NHS. He is completely independent of the NHS and the government. His services are free.

The Ombudsman also looks into complaints against private health providers, but only if the treatment was funded by the NHS. He can also investigate complaints about other services provided on behalf of the NHS.

Anybody wishing to complain to the Ombudsman must first have put their complaint to the NHS organisation or practitioner concerned, such as the hospital trust, Health Authority, the GP or the dentist. They will give you full details of the NHS complaints procedure and will try to resolve your complaint. If you are still dissatisfied once you have exhausted the NHS complaints procedure you can complain to the Ombudsman.

To find out more about the NHS complaints procedure, pick up a leaflet from any NHS organisation, the NHS website or your GP or dentist's surgery.

The European Health Insurance Card.

The free E111 form which entitled you to free or reduced-cost state healthcare if you fell ill or had an accident while travelling in a European Union (EU) country has now been replaced with the European Health Insurance Card from 1 January 2006. The card is free and can be applied for on 0845-606 2030 or online at www.dh.gov.uk/travellers.

PART II. DISEASES ARRANGED BY CAUSE OR BODY SYSTEM AFFECTED

THE INFECTIOUS DISEASES.

Introduction.

Infectious diseases are those which are caused by an invasion of the human body by organisms from outside (the word "organism" simply means living things, and we are using this word because, as will be seen later, it is not only what are known as "germs" which can cause infection). We know, too, that what is generally typical about this group is: (*a*) that the disease can be passed on from one person to another, and (*b*) that it is usually accompanied by a raised temperature or fever. Now (*a*), of course, is always true, because the definition of an infectious disease is one that can be passed on to others, but (*b*) is not always true, because a few infections produce little or no temperature, and also because it is possible to have a raised temperature (again in only a few cases) without any infection. For example, certain types of brain injury, tumour, or haemorrhage can produce a raised—or lowered—temperature, and so can the injection of some foreign substance such as milk into the muscles. This is known as "protein shock," and was at one time used in the treatment of certain illnesses.

Finally, solutions of dead germs, such as the antityphoid vaccine given to protect troops in wartime, may lead when injected to very high temperatures. But, by and large, we are entitled to suppose that the patient with a raised temperature is probably suffering from an infection.

Types of Infection.

As we have seen, it is not only germs which cause infections—so from now on we shall give germs their proper name of "bacteria." Here is a list of the chief offenders which are liable to attack our bodies: bacteria, viruses, fungi, amoebae, worms and other parasites.

Bacteria are tiny living things which can be seen only under a fairly powerful microscope. Some are grouped like bunches of grapes (*staphylococci*) or in strings or chains (*streptococci*). They are given these names because "staphylos" is the Greek word for a bunch of grapes, and "streptos" means a chain. Yet others are comma-shaped (such as the cholera vibrio), or shaped like a drumstick—a rod with a small knob at the end (the tetanus bacillus, which causes lockjaw).

Types of Bacteria.

It would be a mistake to think that all bacteria are harmful; for without some species we could not survive for long. Indeed, a human being carries around ten times as many bacterial cells as human cells. Our guts team with them. Bacteriologists divide them according to their behaviour in the human body into three groups: saprophytic, parasitic or pathogenic, and symbiotic. The *saprophytic* organisms are the bacteria normally found in the skin, mouth, and intestines; they do us neither harm nor good. The *parasitic*, or as they are more usually called, pathogenic (*i.e.*, disease-producing) organisms, are the harmful ones with which we are naturally more concerned. Lastly, there are the *symbiotic* organisms, which, whilst taking something from the body, give something in return. For example, cattle would not be able to digest the cellulose of the grass they eat were it not for helpful bacteria in the lower parts of the intestines, and there are certain bacteria in the large intestine of man which produce vitamins.

Characteristics of Bacteria.

Bacteria have two peculiar characteristics: each reproduces by splitting into two separate individuals as often as every twenty minutes in favourable circumstances like an open wound. If no bacterium were destroyed, one individual could produce a mass of bacteria larger than the whole world in a matter of a few weeks (since each of the offspring also divides into two, which in turn divide again— the progression goes: one gives birth to two, these two to four, the four to eight, eight to sixteen, sixteen to thirty-two, and so on—you will see, if you work it out, that in a short period the figure becomes astronomical). Fortunately, most bacteria do not find themselves in ideal conditions, so for the present the world is safe! The other curious thing about bacteria is that, barring accidents, they are potentially immortal. Under ideal conditions in which no bacteria were killed, none would die; for a bacterium there is no death from old age, no corpse except when it is actively destroyed. It simply goes on dividing, dividing, and subdividing for ever.

How, then, are bacteria destroyed? Briefly, the answer is that most are destroyed by the natural defences of the body of whatever host they are preying on; others are destroyed by antiseptics and the new drugs; and many are destroyed when they are excreted from the body in the sputum or through the bowels and land in places where they are dried up and cannot survive —although some bacteria in such circumstances can form what are called "spores," rather like the seeds of plants, so making it possible for them to survive in a state of suspended animation for months on end until picked up accidentally by another unfortunate host. Finally, bacteria, in addition to all these possibilities, face another danger: they may themselves develop disease.

Bacteriophages.

This disease is caused by even more minute organisms known as bacteriophages (viruses which affect bacteria), discovered by F. W. Twort in 1915. Attack by bacteriophage causes whole groups of bacteria (known as "colonies") to disintegrate and become harmless.

Although bacteriophage have been used in the treatment of some diseases in human beings, this method has now been largely given up, since the new drugs are infinitely more effective.

Other Spirochaetes, like bacteria, are minute organisms, but differ in being shaped somewhat like a corkscrew and in being able to move. Their progress is produced by a sideways wriggling motion. The two main diseases caused by spirochaetes are syphilis and leptospirosis.

Leptospirosis is carried by rats, and is common in those who work in mines. It is now rare in Britain, but still occurs in Egypt, and Malaysia; the infection is passed through the skin where the excreta of infected rats mingles with water on damp ground in the mine where miners kneel. Infection may also occur through eating infected food.

Viruses.

Unlike bacteria, viruses are too small to be seen under an ordinary microscope. They can, however, be photographed in some cases under an electron microscope, which uses a magnetic field instead of a glass lens and a stream of electrons in place of a beam of light. Viruses cause such diseases as measles, mumps, poliomyelitis, smallpox, and chickenpox—not to mention such plant and animal diseases as tobacco mosaic disease and foot-and-mouth disease, which often have serious economic consequences. Other virus diseases are swine fever in pigs, influenza in Man, and myxomatosis in rabbits. They also cause the common cold.

Characteristics of Viruses.

The main characteristics of viruses are, first, that they can only grow in living cells—unlike bacteria, which readily grow in the laboratory on plates containing a jelly made from meat, broth, gelatin, milk, and other delicacies. The scientist, therefore, must keep them in portions of living tissue kept alive outside the body. Secondly, many are so small that they pass through the pores of the finest filter. Thirdly, a first attack usually produces immunity for life. Second attacks of the common virus diseases mentioned above are very rare; but unfortunately, this rule does not apply to influenza or the common cold. Fourthly, there is reason to believe that viruses represent an extraordinary intermediate stage between the living and non-living; they can, for instance, be produced in crystalline form and yet are just as dangerous when "thawed out." Lastly, the virus diseases have proved for the most part to be little affected by the new antibiotics and other drugs, although vaccination in smallpox and the injection of sera from infected patients in other infections may give immunity for longer or shorter periods, and progress has been made in developing drugs to combat some viruses, such as herpes viruses and the AIDS virus.

The two great practical problems that doctors face with viruses are: (i) many viruses are unknown because of the difficulty of growing them outside the body in suitable tissue culture. They cannot therefore be conveniently identified in specimens from the patient, as bacteria can; and (ii) most are unaffected by antibiotics like penicillin. It has been a great step forward to grow viruses artificially in tissue culture, in which they are identified indirectly by the effects they have on the cultured *cells*. But since we do not know exactly how to grow some viruses (like those of infective hepatitis) many have still not been seen.

When we recover from a viral illness like chickenpox, we probably do so by producing virus-killing substances such as interferon inside our own cells. Scientists are currently searching for these substances in case they can be used, like penicillin, to cure viral disease.

Fungi.

Some infections are caused by fungi— that is to say organisms belonging to the same group as moulds, mushrooms, and toadstools. Penicillin and some other antibiotics are produced from moulds, so, as in the case of bacteria, some fungi are helpful; they even help to destroy each other, as bacteria do. For example actinomyces, which can cause infection of the jaw and other tissues, is destroyed by penicillin.

Most fungal infections are trivial and limited to the skin. But, although trivial, they can be unsightly and uncomfortable. Ringworm of the scalp, dhobie itch—an infection of the groin spread by infected underclothing—and so-called "athlete's foot" are caused by a fungus.

Amoebae. Amoebae are small, single-cell organisms, the largest of which (a harmless type found in stagnant ponds in Britain and elsewhere) is just visible to the naked eye. It is about the size of the head of a pin. Amoebae move, in the species which are capable of moving, by pushing forward a part of the cell in the appropriate direction and causing the rest to flow into the advancing portion. Like bacteria, they reproduce by dividing into halves, each of which becomes a new amoeba.

The main human disease caused by amoebae is amoebic dysentery (not to be confused with bacillary dysentery).

Parasites. These may live on the skin like lice (which can carry typhus) or fleas (carriers of plague) or the parasites of scabies which burrow into the skin, or they may live part of their time in the blood or other tissues, like malaria. They often have complicated life-cycles involving other hosts (like mosquitoes) at certain stages of development.

Worms. Worms are intestinal parasites, but the only common types found in Britain are threadworms, the tiny thread-like worms which cause irritability and itching in the skin of children, less often in adults; round-worms, somewhat resembling the ordinary garden earthworm, which seldom lead to symptoms; and tapeworms, which may reach a length of 3 or even 6 m. Many parasitic worms (like parasites elsewhere) lead a double life—they spend part of their life in the human intestine and the other part in the muscles of another animal. The tapeworm, for example, whilst in the human intestine, lays eggs which pass out of the body in the excreta, and are then swallowed by pigs, especially in those parts of the world where human excreta are used as manure in the fields. In the pig, the eggs form cysts in the muscles—meat infected in this way is known as "measly pork"—and when, in turn, the meat is eaten by man, the process in the intestine begins all over again.

Russian Tape-worm. Less common types include the Russian tape-worm; this type is spread by caviare or undercooked infected fish. The small, leaf-shaped liver fluke lays eggs which are passed into canals or pools in tropical countries in the urine of infected people, hatch out and enter a water snail, and finally leave the snail in the form of small parasites which pierce the skin of bathers, whence they pass to the liver and subsequently the bladder and rectum. This is a serious condition, as is also *filariasis* (another tropical disease), for which, unlike bilharzia—caused by the liver fluke—no cure is known. The tropical disease known as *loa-loa* is caused by a variety of filaria.

How the Infection is Spread.

Infection is spread in many ways, some of which have already been mentioned. In the common fevers found in Europe and elsewhere one of the most frequent ways is by *droplet infection*—that is to say, by minute drops carrying the germs which are coughed or sneezed into the air by someone already suffering from the disease. Such droplets can be projected into the air for 3m or more, and when breathed in by someone within range infection may result. Next commonest mode of spread is perhaps by *infected food, water*, and the dirty hands of those who prepare food: cholera, dysentery, food-poisoning, and typhoid are spread in this way. Spread by *direct contact* is found in the venereal diseases (usually, but not always, spread by sexual intercourse with someone who already has the disease), and, of course, lice,

fleas, and other parasites, including the scabies mite, are spread by contact with the infested individual—or sometimes with his clothes or bed linen. Spread through an *intermediary host*, whether it be lice, fleas, or mosquitoes carrying infection, or the various means adopted by worms, has already been described above, so no more need be said. Lastly, the infection may result from *bacteria already within the body*; for example, Escherichia coli, which lives in the large intestine is harmless there, but if it gets into the bladder or the ureters (the tubes leading from kidney to bladder) a quite unpleasant result may follow in the form of cystitis or pyelonephritis.

How the Body Deals with Infection.

The body has many mechanisms of defence against intruders; these can generally be divided into two types. First, non-specific defence substances such as lysozyme, an enzyme that digests bacterial cell walls, are present in many body fluids, and a system of blood proteins known as the complement cascade punches holes in bacteria to kill them. Interferons and other so-called cytokines are produced when the body's cells are damaged by infection and help other cells to resist infection. A class of blood cell, known as macrophages, responds to infection and other damage by migrating to the affected part of the body and swallows bacteria and cell debris for destruction by the powerful enzymes that they contain. Secondly, specific defences are stimulated by infection: one class of lymphocytes produces antibodies, which recognise particular parts of bacteria and viruses, neutralising them and marking them out for destruction. Another class of lymphocytes hunts for foreign cells and kills them by a variety of methods, bursting them open and leaving debris for the macrophages to clear away.

Immunity can be induced by immunisation, which can be active or passive. In active immunisation, a vaccine is injected into the body to simulate the first time the body is infected with a disease-causing agent. Vaccines are made either from dead bacteria or viruses or from specially adapted strains which have lost their ability to cause disease. Passive immunisation is used when a person has already been exposed to a disease or when an effective vaccine is not available, and consists of injections of specific gamma-globulin obtained from the blood of a patient who has recently recovered from the disease concerned.

Immunology is one of the fastest-growing areas of medical research, as there are still many infectious diseases which are difficult to treat with antibiotics, and manipulation of the immune system has great potential in the fight against cancer.

Antiseptics.

The earliest antiseptic was carbolic acid, used by Lister in his operating-theatre in the form of a fine spray directed throughout the operation on the wound, or sometimes in the form of steam from a kettle containing a solution of carbolic. But carbolic is dangerous, and since Lister's time many more useful antiseptics have been discovered. Acriflavine, thymol, and other old favourites have been discarded too. The various forms of carbolic are still used to disinfect drains, but, to tell the truth, the use of antiseptics nowadays is very limited. In surgery the *antiseptic* method has given way to the *aseptic* method—instead of fighting sepsis we see to it that no possibility of sepsis is present before operating; all instruments, the surgeons' and nurses' hands, the skin, are sterilised—the instruments by boiling, the dressings by dry heat, the hands by soap and water, and almost the only antiseptic used is to clean the patient's skin in the area to be operated on.

Antiseptics are used as first-aid treatment for cuts and wounds, but should be applied only once as a general rule—that is, when the wound is first received. The trouble with antiseptics is that as well as killing germs they also kill the surrounding tissues, which antibiotics never do.

Antibiotics.

Some antibiotics—penicillin, streptomycin, erythromycin and so on—have already long been used by doctors. In recent years many others have been introduced—ampicillin, gentamicin, cephalexin. Indiscriminate use of these drugs (e.g. for trivial complaints) has led to problems, the most important being the development of resistance by previously sensitive organisms. It is not always convenient or possible to be able to identify the particular germ responsible for an infection and determine to which drug it is sensitive, but if there is an initial clinical response, it can be assumed that the "right" drug has been used. It is important to have a full course of treatment—which usually means ten days minimum.

Other problems are hypersensitivity (allergic) reactions which can take many forms. Once hypersensitivity to one of the antibiotics has been identified (penicillin hypersensitivity is not rare) the patient must be made aware of this, and so protect himself from unwitting prescribing by another doctor. Hospital and GP records are clearly marked in such instances but it is very important that the patient himself knows.

Antibiotics are only available on prescription, at least in the UK, but medicine cupboards are full of them, accumulated from unfinished courses. Self-prescribing is tempting but ill-advised; antibiotics must always be given under medical supervision. Side effects are common and some are dangerous. Repeated use may lead to rapid overgrowth of fungi e.g. thrush (Candida albicans) normally present in harmless numbers in the alimentary tract with serious, sometimes fatal results.

General Treatment of Fevers.

Fevers, a rise in body temperature above normal, may be noticeable either by a flushed face or by alternate sensations of heat and cold. A patient with a high temperature may have shivering attacks known as "rigors." Tell the doctor.

A high temperature does not necessarily (especially in a child) mean that the trouble is serious but the lay person should always treat it as such and certainly call a doctor if the patient is a child or an elderly person. The majority of fevers are of a viral origin and usually self limiting. The patient tends to improve rapidly once the temperature is controlled.

Even the trained physician finds it difficult to tell one fever from another in the early days; for most of the common fevers begin in more or less the same way. It is only when a rash or some other more definite sign becomes evident that a certain diagnosis can be made, and these may not show themselves until the patient has been feeling "run-down" and fevered for some days. A clinical thermometer is a useful tool and inexpensive to buy. Control of temperature is important, especially in young children, where a high fever may produce a convulsion. A febrile convulsion is a frightening experience for any parent, particularly as their child may have seemed quite well a few minutes previously. High temperature, twitching, and increased irritation may herald the onset.

Emergency management involves keeping the child on its side to avoid inhalation of vomit, clearing debris around his mouth, removing his clothes and sponging him with lukewarm water. Get someone to summon medical help, but never leave an unconscious child alone. Above all, do not panic as the initial episode will usually soon pass.

Briefly, then, the way to treat a fever in the early stages before the doctor comes, and before one knows exactly what is wrong, is as follows:

(1) Put the patient to bed. The child is probably better on the living room sofa where he will feel less isolated and is more easily observed.

(2) Give plenty of clear fluids; water, water and fruit juice, weak tea or lemonade.

(3) Give small amounts of easily digested food but only if the patient requires it.

Aspirin is no longer recommended for the treatment of feverish children, and should not be given to children under 12 years of age. This is because it has been linked to the development of "Reye's Syndrome", an acute encephalopathy or inflammation of the brain with delirium, convulsions and coma. Although very rare, "Reye's Syndrome" carries a high mortality.

Adults with a history of peptic ulcer or chronic indigestion should also avoid aspirin because of the possible risk of a gastro-intestinal bleed.

Paracetamol is now the treatment of choice to reduce temperature and relieve headache and elixir preparations are available for children. The dose may be repeated 4/6 hourly and there are no gastro-intestinal side effects.

Medicines containing Paracetamol should be stored in a safe place as overdosage, accidental or otherwise, may cause liver damage without initial drowsiness or loss of consciousness. Symptoms may not be apparent for a number of days.

Other methods of cooling a feverish patient involve removing excess clothing, administering tepid baths or sponging with lukewarm water. Simply standing at an open door and allowing the cool outside air to waft around the feverish child, or the use of fans, can have an immediate effect.

THE INFECTIOUS FEVERS.

The remarks made above apply to the management of any fever, and we are now going to discuss particular infectious diseases, beginning with the common childhood fevers, then passing on to less common ones, tropical diseases, and worm and parasitic infestations.

The common infectious fevers are caused by bacteria or viruses, and it is useful to know the meaning of the following terms: incubation period is the time which elapses between being infected and developing symptoms; prodromal period is the time which elapses between the end of the incubation period and the appearance of a rash; quarantine period, the maximum time during which a person who has been in contact with the infection may develop the disease—it is usually two days more than the incubation period; isolation period the time a patient is supposed to be isolated.

Virus Diseases.

First, we shall take the common virus diseases, measles, chickenpox, and rubella or German measles, then the other virus diseases, mumps, infective hepatitis, viral pneumonia, and some less common conditions which do not always produce a typical rash as in the case of the first three.

In nearly all of these fevers there is a long incubation period, and one infection gives immunity for life.

Measles. The incubation period is 10–11 days. The first sign is the appearance of symptoms rather like a severe cold. The eyes become red, and exposure to light is unpleasant, the nose runs, the throat becomes inflamed, and a dry, harsh cough develops. There may be headache and the temperature rises to 39°C or more. Usually the patient is a child, and especially typical is the development of so-called Koplik's spots, which are small, bluish-white, raised spots seen on the inside of the cheek at the back of the mouth. The rash begins on the fourth day of the prodromal period, i.e., 14 days after the initial infection. It shows on the forehead and behind the ears, spreading within a day downwards over the whole body; in another two days it starts to disappear, but often leaves behind a sort of brownish staining which may last for one to two weeks.

Measles can be serious, especially in very young children because of its complications, such as bronchopneumonia and infection of the ear, which can now be treated with antibiotics. These drugs have no effect on the measles virus, but only on the secondarily invading bacteria which have invaded the lungs and ear during the illness. The illness can be attenuated or lessened by injection of antibodies (gamma globulin) from an immune adult, and this is often worth while in the very young. Since the MMR vaccine was introduced in 1988, measles has almost disappeared in Britain but the number of cases is now rising.

Rubella or German Measles. Incubation period 14 19 days. A mild fever, similar to measles except that the rash is usually the first sign that anything is wrong, and the temperature is rarely above 38°C. The eyes may be pink, and there are enlarged glands at the back of the neck. The rash disappears completely in thirty-six hours. There are no complications.

German measles, in itself, is harmless, but if a woman gets the disease in the early months of pregnancy malformations in the child may appear at birth. Vaccination is advised if a girl has not contracted the disease by the time she reaches puberty. There is no special treatment except the general rules for fevers given above.

Chickenpox. Incubation period 14–15 days, but may be more variable. In children chickenpox is a mild fever which begins with the appearance of tiny blisters on the chest and back. These later spread outwards to the legs, arms and face, and cause itching. Treatment is the general one for fevers already described. Calamine lotion or dusting powder will be helpful for the irritation, and the child's nails should be cut short to prevent scratching and infection of the spots. Whereas children are usually little bothered by chickenpox, young adults may be much more drastically affected—a temperature of 40°C is not uncommon, and then there may be severe headache.

Shingles is a disease that sometimes follows chickenpox – usually by many years, and results from reactivation of the chicken pox virus, which 'hides' in the spinal cord after a childhood infection.

Mumps. Incubation period 17–18 days. The typical appearance of mumps is a swelling in the salivary glands in front of the ears which makes the face look full. This causes pain later on, and it may be difficult to open the mouth. Temperature is not usually high (about 38°C). Although uncomfortable, mumps is rarely dangerous, but orchitis—swelling of the testicles—is sometimes a complication, especially if the infection occurs beyond childhood. Fluid diet should be given if eating is painful, with mouth-washes, and rest in bed. The number of mumps cases is rising rapidly.

Infective Hepatitis. "Hepatitis" means inflammation of the liver, and infective hepatitis, which is much the commonest cause of jaundice in young adults, is a viral infection of the liver. The main symptoms are fever, followed by jaundice, which is first noticed in the whites of the eyes as yellow staining, then in the skin. The urine becomes coloured also, and this is most easily noticed if, on shaking in a bottle, the froth shows coloration. If the froth remains white, no jaundice is present. Treatment is a matter for the doctor, but great care should be taken, both by the patient and those in contact with him, to wash the hands thoroughly after urinating or defaecating, after handling utensils from the sickroom, and both before and after eating; for the disease is very infectious.

Hepatitis A is spread in faeces (i.e. by poor hygiene), while Hepatitis B and C are spread in blood or saliva (e.g. needle sharing). There is a vaccine available for Hepatitis A and B, and people at risk of exposure to infected people should consider it. Almost 500,000 people in Britain have Hepatitis C, but only one in ten know they are infected. There is no vaccine for Hepatitis C as yet. Hepatitis C was identified in 1988.

Hepatitis A is one of a set of viral diseases of the liver, of which seven – Hepatitis A to G – have now (2006) been identified. It is likely more viruses will be identified.

Viral Pneumonia. Pneumonia is usually caused by bacteria, and when we speak of pneumonia, that is the type we ordinarily refer to. Viral pneumonia can be caused by a variety of viruses. There is no specific treatment so far, and since diagnosis is a specialist matter little more need be said except that the symptoms in general resemble those of ordinary pneumonia. Although there is no specific treatment for virus infections of the lungs, it is always worth while trying antibiotics in view of the possibility that the lung condition may be caused by a secondary invasion of bacteria.

Influenza. While serious epidemics of influenza take the form of a very dramatic and often fatal disease—for example, the epidemic of "Spanish 'flu" which followed the First World War killed more people than the actual fighting— the milder type more usually seen is difficult to distinguish from the common cold. In fact, many people who complain of "a dose of the 'flu" are suffering from simple colds.

However, a sudden onset, aching in the muscles of the back and legs, and redness of the eyes, would suggest influenza, and especially typical is the depression and weakness which follow influenza but not a cold. The measures suggested above for the general treatment of fever should be applied; but the depression and weakness which follow influenza may need special treatment by the doctor. Effective vaccines are now available, and are particularly recommended for the elderly, though immunisation must be carried out each year to overcome the propensity of influenza viruses to change the proteins in their "coats."

Colds and Sinusitis. Although we all think we know what a "cold" is, the issue is not so simple; for the symptoms of fever, running nose, and a run- down, "headachy" feeling are found in many illnesses. They may be observed, as we have seen, in the early stages of measles before the arrival of the rash, or in a number of other fevers, such as whooping cough. Mild attacks of influenza (see above) may resemble the common cold, and blocking of the nose with discharge and fever may be due to sinusitis—although here there is usually pain above, between, or below the eyes.

Colds can be caused by any one of more than 100 different viruses known as "rhinoviruses" This is why a single cold does not confer immunity on the sufferer. It is probable that you will not catch a cold from the same virus, at least for the rest of the year, but there are all those others waiting to infect you with other colds in buses, tubes, and other crowded places.

Like all infections, do not forget that the best way to avoid them is to keep generally well, and in a good nutritional state. It is unlikely that adding vitamins or mineral supplements to normal diet will do any good at all provided you are eating sensibly.

Polio, or Infantile Paralysis as it used to be known, is caused by a virus which has a particular affinity for the nerve cells of the spinal cord and which results in paralysis of those muscles under the control of the particular group of cells infected. Rarely, the infection is widespread in the nerve tissue causing paralysis of muscles of swallowing and respiration as well as those of the trunk and limbs. The usual pattern is for a single muscle group to be affected, for example, the muscles controlling the movements of the arm at the shoulder. Such paralysis may be transient with complete recovery, partial with some residual weakness, or total, leaving a "flail limb" which is wasted and powerless.

At one time in this country epidemics of poliomyelitis were common, mainly affecting children and young adults. There is no doubt that mild forms of the disease were always occurring in very young children, forms never diagnosed as such but conferring a natural immunity in later life.

In common with other infections, poliomyelitis

begins with a mild or moderate fever, with a sore throat, headache, nausea and perhaps actual vomiting, some five to 10 days after contact with the virus. There may be rigidity of the neck muscles. Paralysis, if it occurs, will become apparent about the second or third day of illness. This stage may last two or three weeks, by which time the temperature will have subsided and the paralysis started to improve. There is no specific treatment and medical care is confined to symptomatic relief. Difficulty with swallowing and breathing calls for special nursing measures. In severe cases, artificial means of maintaining respiration may have to be continued for months, or for the rest of the patient's life. Many severely paralysed polio victims of the post-war epidemics —the self-styled "responauts"—depend for their lives on artificial respirators ("iron lungs").

With the development of the oral vaccine early in the 1960s, and its introduction into the immunisation schedule in this country, the disease has now virtually disappeared from Great Britain.

Smallpox. In previous editions we stated that "since the introduction of vaccination it (smallpox) is comparatively rare in industrialised countries." In the 88th edition we reported that smallpox (*variola major*) had now been eradicated throughout the world. The less serious form of the disease, *variola minor*, is still found in some parts of Africa, but all the signs are that it, too, will soon be eradicated. The last case of *variola major* occurred in Bangladesh in 1975, except for at least one accidental infection in England in the 1980s. With the disappearance of the disease vaccination will become unnecessary; however, the World Health Organisation is planning to store vaccine (which can be done almost indefinitely at a temperature of $-20°C$) in sufficient quantities to vaccinate many millions of people should the need ever arise again.

Glandular Fever. Sometimes called infectious mononucleosis, since one of its features is an increase in a certain type of white cell—the monocyte—and a change in its microscopic characteristics. It is caused by a virus (the Epstein-Barr), predominantly affects young children and adults and although often taking a protracted course, it is not in itself a serious infection. The main symptoms are fever, enlargement of lymph glands in the neck and a sore throat. A transient body rash may be seen occasionally, particularly during or after the treatment of the sore throat with penicillin or one of its synthetic cousins such as ampicillin. Diagnosis without laboratory tests on the blood (the Paul-Bunnel test) may not be easy although the combination of sore throat, swollen neck glands and a rash is highly suspicious. The disease is self-limiting and there is no treatment.

Rabies. Finally, we shall deal very briefly with a number of less common virus diseases, beginning, as is appropriate, with *hydrophobia* or *rabies*, since it was in this infection that the great French scientist Louis Pasteur (1822–95) showed the possibility of prevention by vaccination.

Rabies is spread by the bite of infected animals, usually dogs, cats, or wolves, who are driven mad by the disease; in Trinidad, however, it has been spread by vampire bats. It is thus a classic *zoonosis*, an illness transmitted from animals to people. Those who are bitten usually show no symptoms for six weeks or more, but sooner or later convulsions and delirium arise, which within four to five days are fatal. In essence, rabies is a form of brain inflammation. Around 70,000 people a year die of the disease, 40,000 in India.

There is no cure once the symptoms have developed, but antirabies serum, followed by antirabies inoculation as soon as possible, prevents illness in the majority of cases. Dogs should be muzzled in areas where the disease is common, but quarantining imported dogs has made the infection almost unknown here. Effective immunisation is now available.

Leishmaniasis, or Sandfly Fever, **Dengue,** or break-bone fever, and **Trench Fever** are all somewhat similar conditions in that they resemble influenza and are rarely fatal. They are all due to viruses, spread in the first case by sandflies in tropical climates; in the second by mosquitoes in tropical climates; and in the third by lice in temperate climates. They are all typical "soldiers' diseases"; the first two were common in the Middle East and Far East during the last War, the third during the First World War in France.

Yellow Fever. Yellow fever is carried by a mosquito known as Aedes, common in South and Central America and in African ports. For its spread, it therefore needs: a hot climate, the Aedes mosquito, and an infected person.

In yellow fever there is a sudden high temperature, aching of limbs and head, jaundice, and black vomit; the pulse-rate falls as the fever rises. Previous vaccination seems to be preventive if undertaken in time.

Ebola haemorrhagic fever is an illness with a high mortality and no specific treatment. Only a few outbreaks have been reported, but as it is spread person to person strict quarantine is required.

AIDS. AIDS stands for acquired immunodeficiency syndrome, and is caused by the human immunodeficiency virus (HIV). AIDS has become a terrible affliction for the human race, and was first described in 1981. In some areas of the world, such as southern Africa, AIDS is becoming the scourge of the 21st century.

The statistics are frightening. Since 1981, over 20 million people have died from AIDS. Over 40 million have now (2006) become infected. There are 15 million children worldwide who have lost one or both parents to AIDS. Over 5 million people have AIDS in South Africa and also India, while Nigeria has 3,600,000.

Infection occurs by intercourse, the anal variety apparently being the more dangerous, by direct transmission through infected blood, and congenital transmission from mother to baby.

Thus, the major risk factors for AIDS are male homosexuality, needle sharing by intravenous drug abusers, haemophilia, and having an infected mother. Heterosexual intercourse is also an important mode of spread, especially among prostitutes, who are the most promiscuous members of communities. AIDS can be avoided by restricting sexual relations to the one you trust, and by avoiding *any* contact with other people's blood.

HIV damages the T-lymphocytes that are responsible for protecting the body against infection, with the result that the sufferer becomes prey to a variety of otherwise rare infections such as *Pneumocystis carinii* pneumonia, as well as some rare tumours, particularly Kaposi's sarcoma and lymphomas. The incubation period can be very long, and the first signs are often lethargy, weight loss and swelling of the lymph glands.

There is as yet no effective vaccine; treatment consists of taking a number of different anti-viral and enzyme inhibiting drugs. These have numerous side-effects and the treatment remains to be optimised. Long term success rates are unclear.

Conclusion.

There is no specific cure for most viral diseases, though several can be prevented by immunisation or by social control of the creatures carrying the virus and by the use of common day-to-day hygiene, and drugs are beginning to be introduced against a few viruses. Incubation periods are generally of the order of days, though in the case of the AIDS virus can be measured in years. Where active immunisation is not available, passive protection with gamma globulin is often an effective alternative.

Bacterial Diseases.

Bacterial diseases differ from virus infections in a number of respects; their incubation period tends to be shorter: having the disease once does not often confer lifelong protection; and unlike virus diseases, most bacterial diseases respond to one of the antibiotics or sulphonamides. In some cases it is possible to inoculate against the disease to prevent it occurring, as is possible with some of the virus diseases.

Scarlet Fever and Other Streptococcal Infections.

In the days, not so long ago, before the arrival of chemotherapy (sulphonamides and antibiotics), streptococci were very much feared and even caused a high mortality, particularly in such susceptible groups as children, and mothers and babies in maternity hospitals. They are still taken very seriously in the latter and rightly so, although one wonders how much of the mystique is simply a hangover from the days when many mothers died from "childbed fever." All signs of infection, such as fever, during the puerperium (the period following childbirth) must be promptly dealt with by a doctor, and only occasionally now is there real cause for anxiety provided treatment is prompt.

Scarlet fever is much less common and very much less serious an illness than it used to be, partly because of the effective treatments available today, but also because of a definite but unexplained reduction in its severity. Perhaps the streptococcus has changed, and certainly the improved physical condition of people who are now much better fed and housed than they were, has helped to ward off the terrors of this disease as of so many other infections.

The disease, which is more common in children, begins with a sore throat and rash. Nowadays treatment with antibiotic drugs usually produces fast recovery in the patient.

The importance of streptococcal infections has shifted from the initial infection, such as a sore throat, to some serious conditions which occasionally arise as a result of some form of delayed sensitivity to the bacteria. Acute rheumatism or rheumatic fever (not to be confused with ordinary aches and pains nor with rheumatoid arthritis) occasionally arise in people who have had a sore throat a few weeks before. Since the streptococcus is not the direct cause of the damage which may consequently occur in the heart or kidney, the antibiotics are no answer except sometimes to keep off further streptococcal invasions.

Diphtheria.

This used to be an extremely serious disease, but immunisation has made it almost unknown; it is important, therefore, that all children should be immunised. Many modern doctors have never seen a case because it has become so rare, and in spite of the propaganda of certain ill-informed people, this saving of children's lives is entirely the result of nationwide inoculation.

The following description is of historic interest only, and will remain so if a high level of inoculation is kept up by parents.

In a typical case of diphtheria the incubation period is about three days; the patient is a child who becomes ill and pale-looking (i.e., the onset is not sudden, as in many fevers, but insidious); the temperature is only slightly raised to, perhaps, 37° or 38°C, and although there may be no complaint of sore throat, examination will reveal inflammation with—and this is typical of diphtheria —a grey membrane spread over the tonsils, the palate, and the back of the mouth generally. The diphtheria germ does not spread within the body. It stays at the place where it entered (in this case the throat) and sends its toxins throughout the body.

Even after the acute phase is over the patient must not be allowed to walk, because the diphtheria toxin is particularly poisonous to the heart. The ordinary rule is at least one or two months in bed.

Diphtheria also occurs in the larynx—in preinoculation days many children choked to death with this form of the infection; in the nose; and, although this is not generally known, wounds can be infected.

Diphtheria may lead to paralysis of the throat, with difficulty in speaking or swallowing, and paralysis of the eyes or limbs; these are due to neuritis caused by the influence of the toxin on the nerves.

Whooping Cough.

For many years whooping cough has been regarded merely as a bother to the patient and a nuisance to others, as, in fact, a trivial disease. Unfortunately, this is not so; because statistics show that it caused more deaths than polio, diphtheria, scarlet fever, and measles put together.

Whooping cough begins in a child as an ordinary cold with cough and slight fever, and this stage lasts for a week or ten days. Then the "paroxysmal stage" begins as a series of coughs following in rapid succession, during which time the patient is unable to breathe. The "whoop" is caused by the noisy indrawing of breath when the fit stops. The face may become blue and congested. Bronchitis is usually present, and bronchopneumonia may result as a complication, so inoculation of all children before the disease has a chance to strike them is most important.

Once whooping cough has begun, there is no specific treatment, although modern drugs can reduce the frequency of the fits of coughing. The antibiotic chloramphenicol has been used for this disease, but the general opinion is that it is ordinarily of little benefit. Chinese physicians once described whooping cough as the "hundreddays cough," and the cough may, indeed, continue for at least a hundred days. There is an effective vaccine.

Typhus.

This disease used to be known as "jail fever," because it was frequent in prisons; but overcrowding, poverty, and bad hygienic surroundings anywhere are suitable conditions for epidemics of typhus. Improved conditions in industrialised countries have made it unusual, since typhus is carried from one person to another by infected body lice. It is due to the organism *Rickettsia prowazekii*, a very small type of bacterium.

Typhus comes on suddenly with a rise in temperature to about 39°C, but within four days it may be as high as 42°C. There may, or may not, be a rash at this time, and in the second week, when the temperature is at its highest, there is delirium, weakness, and a feeble pulse. The typical typhus rash appears about the fifth day as reddish blotches on the chest, abdomen, and wrists.

Typhus is, needless to say, very serious but responds to modern antibiotics. Preventive measures are directed towards eradicating lice.

Psittacosis.

This disease which is of interest mainly in that it is spread by birds of the parrot group, such as parrots, lovebirds, macaws, and the rest is caused by chlamydia, which are similar to bacteria. It occasionally occurs here in people who have been in contact with birds of this type, and is serious both to the bird and to its owner. Quarantine regulations greatly reduced the risk of infection in Britain. Concern over renewed outbreaks, not only of psittacosis but a number of economically important diseases such as fowl pest, led to their reintroduction in 1976.

The symptoms of psittacosis are fever, cough, and bronchitis. The disease is especially dangerous to old people, but it responds to the same antibiotics as typhus.

Tuberculosis.

No disease is more difficult to describe than tuberculosis; for, like the Streptococcus or the Staphylococcus, the tubercle germ can attack many different parts of the body and manifest itself in many ways. Furthermore, it is a widely spread disease, infecting not only humans but also cattle, birds and reptiles. In Britain, even now, around 6,000 people are still diagnosed with TB each year. Worldwide, TB affected 8·7 million people in 2004. But here we shall be concerned with those types common to man—the human and bovine (*i.e.*, the type found in cattle which can be spread to man by infected milk).

The tubercle bacillus is particularly hardy, so that when coughed or spat out on the ground it continues to be infectious for a long time. Infection is therefore caused by: (*a*) drinking infected milk; (*b*) droplet infection from aerosols produced by coughing; (*c*) breathing in infected dust. In other words, tuberculosis is caused by absorption through either the lungs or the intestines; the former is common in adults, the latter in children.

The question arises: what conditions predispose to TB—why do some people get over the early infection and others not? There are two answers to this question: one is certain—that those who are impoverished and do not get enough food are liable to TB; the second is not so certain—that mental stress plays some part. Stress causes a general reduction in immunity, predisposing the body to several infections including TB.

In children, lung tuberculosis is not common, but tuberculosis of the bones and glands is, as is also infection in the abdomen, the kidney or spine, and, worst of all, tuberculous meningitis. These are often of the bovine type from infected milk. Ordinarily, TB in children is less serious than adult infections; but tuberculous meningitis used to be almost invariably fatal until streptomycin was discovered.

Adult Tuberculosis usually occurs in the lungs or the pleura—the thin membrane surrounding the lungs. In younger people miliary tuberculosis, which is a form of TB blood-poisoning or septicaemia, is a very serious condition, and the infection spreads throughout the whole body in a few weeks.

Lung infection begins gradually in someone who has previously felt unwell. There may be cough, and later blood-stained sputum (although blood which is coughed up does not necessarily prove that TB is present). Whatever means of treatment is used, the struggle between disease and patient is likely to be fairly long, but the outlook is now good. The closure of the Swiss sanatoria is due partly to modern disbelief that air in one place is better than that in another, but mainly to improved treatment.

Prevention depends on legal action ensuring tuberculosis-free herds of cattle; on control of spread of the disease by those "open" cases who carry germs in their sputum; on the use of vaccination in childhood with BCG vaccine (which you can ask your doctor about).

Many methods are used in treatment. TB is now a fairly rare disease in developed countries, but there are worries that the emergence of antibiotic resistant strains will lead to an upsurge in its frequency. This happened in New York in 1989 and doctors fear it could happen in such cities as London. There are skin tests to show any susceptibility to TB. In 2004 the first new TB vaccine for 80 years completed safety trials.

Septicaemia. Commonly known as "blood-poisoning." This occurs generally by spread from some septic area such as a wound (or even a small prick), after childbirth, or any place where certain germs have got admission to the body. The most usual germ is the Streptococcus, although the pneumococcus—which ordinarily causes pneumonia—and the Staphylococcus may also cause septicaemia.

In septicaemia, the bacteria damage the blood vessels, allowing blood to leak out under the skin. This leaking causes marks on the skin – a rash of red or brown pin prick spots, purple bruises or blood blisters – and reduces the amount of blood reaching vital organs such as the heart and brain.

Fever comes on suddenly and rises rapidly with headaches, sweating, and shivering. The patient is obviously very ill, and later there is wasting and delirium. The white blood cells increase in number. Septicaemia sometimes occurs without any apparent local infection in those who are weak and debilitated.

Pyaemia is a type of septicaemia which leads to the formation of numerous abscesses throughout the body. Its symptoms are the same as described

above, except that the causative germ is usually the Staphylococcus, and abscesses are found which may need surgical treatment.

However, in both conditions the state of affairs has been revolutionised by the use of antibiotics; cure is now the rule rather than the exception.

Septicaemia should be suspected when any small wound or cut is followed by high temperature and the symptoms described above.

"Toxaemia" is the word used when the germs stay in their original position and go on to produce symptoms by spreading their toxins throughout the body. Tetanus, diphtheria, and some kinds of childbirth infection come into this category; the symptoms may vary from mild disturbance to severe illness.

Meningitis means inflammation of the meninges, the covering which, like a layer of plastic, lies over the brain and spinal cord, just as the pleura covers the lungs and the peritoneum covers internal organs in the abdomen. (Hence inflammation of the pleura is known as pleurisy, and inflammation of the peritoneum as peritonitis.)

Various germs may cause meningitis, for example, some viruses, the bacillus of tuberculosis, the pneumococcus, which ordinarily causes pneumonia, and the Streptococcus or Staphylococcus, but often the word refers to *meningococcal meningitis* (caused by the Meningococcus bacteria) occurring at times as an epidemic.

It is commonest in the years from infancy to the early twenties, and begins suddenly with headache, vomiting, and fever. The temperature rises quickly, and pain develops in the back and legs; on the second or third day a rash appears on the body, and particularly on the inside of the thighs. Later there is stiffness of the neck, the head may be drawn back, vomiting persists, and the headache can be so severe as to cause the patient to scream with pain.

Fortunately, this type of meningitis (and most of the others) respond to treatment with antibiotics, so the risks are now very much less.

New vaccines are being introduced, but these do not protect against all types of meningococcal meningitis. One new vaccine now available protects against group C meningitis and septicaemia.

Pneumococcal Meningitis is an unusual complication of pneumonia, and the septic types (*streptococcal* or *staphylococcal*) arise either following an infected fracture of the skull or from infection of the ear or mastoid.

Tuberculous Meningitis has already been mentioned; originally always fatal, it is now treatable with streptomycin.

All these diseases are very much a matter for specialist and hospital treatment, but it is worth while mentioning viral meningitis, in which, although all the symptoms of meningitis are present, recovery without specific treatment is invariable.

Tetanus is usually known as "lockjaw" because there may be difficulty in opening the mouth, although this is simply part of a spasm of all the muscles of the body. The tetanus bacillus is found in rich soil—hence the disease is less common in desert areas—and tetanus resembles rabies in that: (*a*) it enters at a wound; (*b*) it affects the nervous system; (*c*) it results in fits and ultimately death.

However, active immunisation with TT (tetanus toxoid) has resulted in the disease becoming uncommon, and even when developed, treatment with antitoxin, sedatives, muscle relaxants, and antibiotics may lead to cure.

The bacillus is anaerobic (*i.e.*, does not use oxygen) and is most likely to occur in such situations as when a man digging manure or working in his garden sticks a fork through his foot.

Brucellosis falls into two types: melitensis, which infects goats, and abortus, cattle and pigs. Man gets the disease by reason of close contact with or drinking the milk of infected animals. (The name abortus is given because abortion is produced in cattle and sows.)

In the past, brucellosis was sometimes known as undulant fever, as the fever goes up and down for two to three weeks; it may then go down and rise again, persisting for many months. The disease may occur in Britain, but modern drugs are on the whole successful in dealing with it. A striking feature of the disease is the combination of a high temperature with an appearance of relative well-being.

Another disease carried by mammals is **Glanders** or **Farcy**, spread by horses. In glanders there is discharge from the nose and sometimes pneumonia. Occasionally the disease is fatal. In farcy abscesses form, usually along the lymph vessels. Both conditions are very contagious, and treatment is a matter for a specialist; infected horses should be destroyed.

Cholera. Cholera could be classified under the head of food-poisoning, because it is mainly spread by infected water (however, like typhoid, it can also be spread by flies, infected food, and carriers); it could also be classified as a tropical disease, since, although it used to be found in Europe, it is now mainly rife in India.

Cholera is caused by a vibrio, which is a spiral bacterium, and can be prevented by early inoculation and care over food supplies—boiling water and milk, washing uncooked foods in chlorinated water, and keeping flies away.

The fever begins in the usual way with a short incubation period, followed by abdominal pain, severe vomiting, and diarrhoea. Later with the loss of fluid from the body there may be cramps in the muscles, diarrhoea increases, and the motions become of the typical "rice-water" type —*i.e.*, there is no solid matter, and the appearance is that of water to which a little milk has been added. This stage is followed by collapse, with low pulse and cold hands and feet. Death, if adequate treatment is not available, results in about 70 per cent. of cases. Cholera can generally be survived simply by replacing the water and salts lost in the diarrhoea, along with antibiotic therapy.

Anthrax. The bacillus of anthrax, like that of tuberculosis, can exist outside the body for long periods, and, like that of tetanus, then takes the form of spores or seed-like bodies. It is spread by infected cattle and horses, which get the disease from eating grass containing spores.

In human beings the form the disease takes depends on where the germ alights. Cutaneous (or skin) anthrax arises from cuts or fly bites, which may cause a large sore like a boil. It is usually curable with antibiotics. Inhalation anthrax sometimes develops in those who inhale the dust from infected hides or wool (hence the name 'wool-sorters' disease," which is a form of bronchitis with blood-stained sputum); it may arise through eating infected meat, causing intestinal anthrax.

Both intestinal and inhalation anthrax are often fatal, but now the genetic code of anthrax has been cracked there is new hope for a cure.

Food Poisoning Diseases.

Strictly speaking there is no such thing as "food poisoning" if one is thinking of "poisoning" in terms of anything apart from germs. But not so long ago it used to be thought that decomposition of food in itself produced poisons known as "ptomaines" which were deadly to those who swallowed them. All food poisoning is caused by infection of food with bacteria and by no other cause—unless of course, we are thinking of the kind of poisoning which is the concern of the lawyer rather than the doctor!

Here we are considering those diseases which are commonly spread by contaminated food or drink. The classification is not scientific, but then no scientific classification has as yet been devised. First, we shall deal with typhoid, paratyphoid, and dysentery—uncommon here in Britain, although Sonné dysentery is fairly frequent. Then there is gastro-enteritis (which means irritation of

the stomach and intestines), which is caused by staphylococci and the germs of the salmonella group, and lastly botulism, which is rare.

Typhoid and Paratyphoid. These diseases are spread by infected water, food, or hands—especially uncooked food, such as milk, salads, oysters, and shellfish. Flies, too, play some part in spreading the disease. Some people are "carriers" and carry and excrete the germs without being themselves affected; for example, "Typhoid Mary," a carrier in the USA in the early years of the 20th century.

The influence of Chadwick's propaganda for pure water supplies is shown by the fact that deaths from typhoid, still 332 per 1,000,000 in 1870, fell to 198 per 1,000,000 by 1900. In the 1920s the death-rate was only 25 per 1,000,000, and now it is even less.

Typhoid fever begins like most fevers with headache, raised temperature, and general feeling of unwellness. This stage lasts about a week, and then the rash appears in the form of rose-red spots on the front of the chest and abdomen and on the back. In the second week there is great weakness, sometimes diarrhoea, flatulence, and mental dullness, together with dry and cracked lips and tongue. The third week is the week, in hopeful cases, of gradual decrease in temperature and other symptoms, and the fourth week is the week of convalescence. Complications are perforation of the intestine (which needs surgical treatment), delirium, and bronchitis. Treatment is with chloramphenicol.

Dysentery. Dysentery may be caused either by a bacterium or an amoeba; the first type is known as bacillary dysentery, the latter as amoebic dysentery (which is dealt with under tropical diseases). Infection is spread in much the same way as in typhoid. There is high fever, abdominal pain, and diarrhoea, at first consisting of faecal matter, then blood and mucus. In severe cases the death-rate used to be over 20 per cent. Dysentery is caused by several species of bacteria of the genus *Shigella*.

However, in all these infections sulphaguanidine, ampicillin or tetracycline bring rapid relief, but care must be taken to avoid infection of other people.

Diarrhoea and Vomiting. Leaving out typhoid and paratyphoid fevers and dysentery, there is a common group of infections known as "D&V"—diarrhoea and vomiting. In Britain D&V is now mostly due to:

    (1) Salmonella infection.
    (2) Staphylococcal infections.
    (3) Other bacteria, ordinarily harmless, such as Escherichia coli, when present in sufficient numbers.
    (4) Various viral infections, *e.g.* rotavirus.

Salmonella Infections are the most serious of this group; they affect the small intestine and produce vomiting, severe abdominal pain, and diarrhoea. These symptoms occur about one day after eating infected food and usually clear up within about two weeks, but occasionally death results. Salmonella bacteria are most likely to be found in meat, egg powder, vegetables, and ducks' eggs. The number of cases rose greatly in the 1980s and 1990s and about 100,000 cases are now reported annually.

Staphylococcal Food Poisoning has greatly increased in recent years, so it is important to know what circumstances are likely to cause it. Staphylococci are liable to grow in milk products, such as ice-cream and cream buns. Food poisoning from staphylococci is seldom severe, and recovery takes place in about a week. Nevertheless, it is extremely infectious, and causes a great deal of lost time in industry and temporary illness in institutions; for it is in such situations that it is most likely to occur. The reason for the increase in staphylococcal food poisoning has nothing to do, as many people suppose, with greater use of canned foods, but it has much to do with the greater use of communal feeding and canteen meals. It is *possible* for bacterial toxins in infected food to bring about illness even when the canning process has killed the bacteria, but it is certainly extremely rare. Canned foods, in fact, are much safer than so-called "fresh" foods in this respect—except when they have been opened, left about, and then re-heated. The same applies to the re-heating of any kind of food.

The real enemy is the canteen worker with a boil, a discharging nose, dirty hands, or a septic finger. Occasionally food may be infected in the larder by rats or mice, but the sort of canteen or restaurant where this can happen has little to commend it. Frankly, these infections are caused by dirty or stupid people who do not realise that their sore finger or boil can become someone else's diarrhoea and vomiting. Where children are concerned, the outlook is potentially more serious. Infection is much more common in artificially fed babies or in older children who eat infected ice-cream. However trivial the condition may seem, diarrhoea and vomiting with fever in a child should never be ignored. Those in charge of canteens or restaurants must ensure that staff is supervised, that anyone with a septic infection is put off duty, and that all know about washing after visiting the lavatory and absolute cleanliness.

Bacilli normally present in the intestine, such as Escherichia coli, can cause infections if absorbed in large amounts, or if of a different strain from those in the patient's intestine. They are not usually serious.

Botulism. Now uncommon, botulism is caused by a germ, clostridium botulinum, which is peculiar in that, like tetanus, its poison attacks the nervous system rather than the intestines, resulting in fits, double vision, paralysis beginning in the face and spreading downwards, and difficulty in swallowing. It is found in tinned fruits or vegetables containing the toxin even when the germ has been killed, but, as we have already seen, the toxin comes from the bacilli, not from decomposition of food as such (in fact, food does not decompose in the absence of germs). Death is common in botulism, but an antitoxin is now available which, if used in time, can cure the disease.

The botulinum toxin, which paralyses muscles, has found some medical uses. "Botox" is being used as a cosmetic treatment injected into the forehead to reduce obvious wrinkles. It may have a more valuable medical role in overcoming muscle rigidity accompanying a number of medical conditions.

Diseases Caused by Fungi.

Numerous fungi are pathogenic (*i.e.* cause disease), and fungal diseases may be primary or secondary to other diseases; allergies to fungi are also important. The most common fungal disease is candidiasis, which is infection with the imperfect yeast-like fungus *Candida albicans*, this frequently infects the feet (athlete's foot), the mouth and the vagina, producing local itching as the main symptom.

Ringworm or **tinea**, despite its name, is not caused by worms but fungi which cause ring-shaped pigmented patches on the skin, sometimes covered with vesicles or scales.

Actinomycosis, a disease caused by bacteria which superficially resemble fungi, is a serious but treatable condition with inflamed lymph glands around the jaw or ulcerating sores on the skin; it can also affect the lungs, intestines and brain.

The Venereal Diseases.

The venereal diseases are those caused—or at least that is what the name means—by the goddess of love, Venus. Venus, of course, causes a great deal of trouble, but venereal disease is not necessarily the worst she can do. Sexually transmitted disease (Venereal Disease) is spread by sexual intercourse with an infected person (or with intimate acts associated with it—*e.g.*, "oral sex"). Promiscuity therefore increases the risk. Not all lesions in, on or around the genitals are necessarily venereal disease. If in doubt consult your own doctor or attend one of the many special clinics which can be found in most cities. Their location is usually advertised in conveniences and other public places. Always act promptly.

Gonorrhoea is the result of an infection by the gonococcus (*Neisseria gonorrhoeae*) and ordinarily comes on after an incubation period of three to seven days. However, babies can get an infection of the eyes, known as ophthalmia neonatorum, from their mother if she is infected, and gonorrhoea in young children is often the result of being in contact with infected towels or clothes. The disease in adults is evident when there is a thick, creamy discharge from the sexual organs and sometimes pain on passing water; in infants ophthalmia is prevented by the use of silver nitrate eye-drops at birth. Gonorrhoea is fairly easily cured by the use of sulpha drugs or penicillin; but unfortunately venereal disease is increasing in recent years and drug-resistant forms are becoming more common.

Syphilis is a serious venereal disease caused by a spirochaete (*Treponema pallidum*). Stories about lavatory seats are simply stories, although it is occasionally possible to get syphilis by other than sexual means. But this is very unusual, although kissing can spread the disease. Children, too, can be born with syphilis (the so-called *congenital syphilis*).

Adult syphilis begins with a sore, known as a hard chancre, at the point where the spirochete of syphilis has entered; this may be on the lips, through kissing; on the sexual organs, through intercourse; and very rarely, as explained above, elsewhere. In a short time the chancre disappears and all may seem to be well, but this primary stage is followed by a secondary stage with sore throat, a rash, headache, and enlargement of glands. This, if left alone, also clears up, but is followed by the tertiary stage, in which a chronic infection develops in some part of the body which, presumably, is most susceptible in the particular individual. Thus there may be chronic syphilis of the skin, the bones, the heart, liver, or nervous system.

Syphilis, in common with other sexually-transmitted diseases, is growing fast in Britain.

Tabes Dorsalis. In the nervous system, the commonest forms are the two diseases of *tabes dorsalis*, in which the spinal cord is infected, and GPI (general paralysis of the insane), in which the brain and mind are affected.

In congenital syphilis the pregnant mother gives her child syphilis. Such infants are often stillborn or premature, they look wizened, like little old men, and amongst other symptoms are eye disease, "snuffles," a flattened nose, and when the adult teeth appear the front ones may be notched at the biting surface.

It was for syphilis that Ehrlich produced his "magic bullet"—an arsenical drug, known as salvarsan, which could attack the organism selectively without harming the body and was the first of the modern specific drugs. Present-day treatment is with penicillin. GPI was once treated with malarial therapy with some success. Penicillin alone is often adequate.

Chancroid produces small septic ulcers around the sex organs, with swelling of the local glands in the groin, which may suppurate. It is caused by a bacillus, and can usually be cleared up by antibiotics within a week. Scabies and lice often pass from one body to another during sexual intercourse, but are not usually thought of as venereal in origin, although in many cases they are.

Herpes virus infections may be oral ("Cold sores") or genital. These recurrent sores appear particularly at times of physical or emotional stress. They are not curable, but medicines may shorten episodes.

HIV/AIDS (see **Z11**) may be spread by sexual intercourse, or by blood. The use of condoms reduces the risk of sexual transmission.

Tropical Diseases.

Nothing is more difficult than to define the term "tropical diseases." One might define them as the diseases which occur in tropical climates—but then measles occurs there too; and if they are defined as those diseases which are found *only* in the tropics, the solution is no easier, since leprosy, cholera, smallpox, and typhus are usually listed as tropical diseases, yet were found in this country until fairly recently—and the odd case still is.

But what a story could be told about the conquest of those infections which were—and many still are—the scourge of humanity! One day when generals and dictators are forgotten we shall remember that great international army of physicians and bacteriologists who have saved millions of lives and infinitely reduced human suffering: Koch and Ehrlich of Germany, Pasteur and Roux of France, Ross and Jenner of Britain, Reed of America, Noguchi of Japan, and many others.

Relapsing Fever, common in India and Africa, may be louse- or tick-borne; the germ is a spirochaete, similar to that of syphilis, but the disease is non-venereal. Relapsing fever gets its name from the fact that the temperature remains high (39°–41°C) for about a week, returns to normal for a week, and rises again. There may be three to five relapses of this sort. Penicillin is effective; lice or ticks must be eradicated.

Leptospirosis (also known as Weil's disease), is also caused by a spirochaete, and spread by rats. Now it is rarely found in Europe, although it occurred in the trenches during the First World War, in men working in sewers, and in the women who worked in the fish market of Aberdeen, which at one time was rat-infested. It is rarely fatal, but leads to high fever and jaundice. Penicillin in high dosage or tetracycline may help.

Yaws is also a spirochaetal disease, common in the tropics and particularly in children. It is unpleasant, but not serious, and tends to clear up in a year or so. There are raspberry-like growths on the skin, which disappear with the drugs used in syphilis (although the condition is non-venereal). The Wassermann reaction, positive to syphilis, is also positive in yaws.

Leprosy. Whereas syphilis, relapsing fever, epidemic jaundice, and yaws are caused by spirochaetes, leprosy is caused by a bacillus resembling the bacillus of tuberculosis. Apart from the difficulty of classification, many popular beliefs about the disease are untrue. It is *not* the oldest disease afflicting man; *not* a disease confined to tropical countries; it is *not* very catching; *not* hereditary, *not* incurable; in leprosy the fingers and toes do *not* drop off; it is *not* a divine punishment for wrongdoing.

Leprosy is a serious disease not because of disfiguring light-coloured skin patches and lumps, but because it destroys peripheral nerves. Leprosy may disappear spontaneously, or it may progress until the face is lion-like and the hands and feet wasted and ulcerated. The disease rarely kills, but it is the world's greatest crippler.

Leprosy was once fairly common in colder Western countries, though its extent was exaggerated. The great majority of the millions of people who suffer from leprosy live in tropical countries, but it still exists in Iceland, Japan, Korea and some of the southern states of the United States. Prolonged and intimate contact with an "open" case is said to be the main mode of infection, but only one infected husband in twenty passes leprosy to his wife.

The cheap synthetic drug dapsone is highly effective in leprosy, but problems in delivery to third-world settings has resulted in the emergence of resistant strains, so that much more expensive drugs now have to be used. The WHO has launched an ambitious "multi-drug therapy" programme in an attempt to bring this disease under control. Established deformity (such as claw hand, drop foot, paralysed eyelids) can be mitigated by reconstructive surgery, although lost sensation cannot be restored.

In the past, Christian missions were mainly concerned with the plight of the leprosy sufferer. Now, non-sectarian voluntary agencies, Governments and the World Health Organisation have joined in the fight against the disease. Enough is known to control the disease, but not enough is being done, as only one victim in five is at present getting treatment.

Plague is another disease caused by bacteria, common in Europe at one time, but now largely restricted to Asia. Nevertheless, it caused millions of deaths in Europe during the years 1348–49 and 1665 and was the "Black Death," which, indeed, changed the course of history.

Plague is carried by the bite of the rat flea, but, once people become infected, spread may occur from one to the other by droplet infection—i.e., by coughing and sneezing. After an incubation period of two to ten days, fever develops, rather like severe influenza, and in a day or two the glands in the groin begin to swell, followed perhaps by swelling of the glands elsewhere.

Of this usual glandular type (bubonic plague) half of untreated patients die, but if rapidly treated cure is usual. It is also possible to get disease of the lungs from droplet infection and blood-poisoning from infection of the blood-stream. Both the latter types are almost invariably fatal.

Short courses of antibiotics protect contacts. Vaccination is available but usually not used.

Protozoal Diseases.

Nearly all the diseases caused by protozoa are tropical diseases, although one of the best-known protozoans is the harmless amoeba found in British ponds. Protozoal diseases are caused by these organisms, large in comparison with bacteria, which should really be thought of as one-celled animals. Viruses are neither animals nor plants, are much smaller than the other two groups, and have some distinctive characteristics described elsewhere.

Among the diseases caused by protozoa are sleeping sickness or trypanosomiasis, malaria, and amoebic dysentery (as contrasted with bacillary dysentery), another disease, leishmaniasis—also known by the numerous names of kala-azar, dumdum fever, and, in milder form, Delhi boil, Oriental sore, or Baghdad sore—will also be mentioned briefly. More recently, humans have been affected by cryptosporidosis. This is an intestinal infection usually passed to humans from farm animals (e.g. by infected milk). Symptoms include severe diarrhoea. These infections are few, but important in their influence on man; for, as Dr. Clark-Kennedy has pointed out, until recently was responsible for one-fifth of all human sickness, sleeping sickness not so long ago caused a large part of Central Africa to be uninhabitable, and in some areas of the tropics there are probably more people with, than without, amoebic dysentery.

Malaria. The word, of course, means "bad air." When it was formerly found in Britain it was known as *ague*. Human beings have a natural tendency to suppose that, when two events occur together, then one must be caused by the other. Yet, although malaria and "bad air" may often go together, and influenza and cold, it does not follow that bad air (whatever that may be) causes malaria nor that cold causes influenza. In fact, the Anopheles mosquito carries the amoeba of malaria, and the mosquito prefers climates which some people might describe as "bad," but it is the amoeba, not the air, which causes the disease. Anyhow, the unfortunate mosquito might well use the phrase honoured by many generations of schoolmasters: "It hurts me more than it hurts you!" For the mosquito, too, is sick, and passes on its sickness to the person it bites.

There are several types of plasmodium—which is the scientific name for this amoeba—producing attacks of fever varying in severity and frequency: benign tertian, quartan, and malignant quartan. Entering the body from the mosquito bite, the parasites penetrate the blood cells, multiply there, and finally burst into the blood stream. When this happens the temperature rises, and then they return to the cells to carry out once more the same procedure. Depending on the type, the attacks of fever may be at intervals of two or three days, severe or milder. When someone with malaria is bitten by a mosquito the infection can be transmitted to the next person it meets, but malaria is not infectious from one person to another directly.

Treatment of Malaria. Quinine, of course, is the time-honoured remedy, but many other drugs are now available: mepacrine, primaquine, chloroquine and some sulpha drugs. The drug must be taken long enough for the infection to die out, otherwise relapses can occur even after leaving a malarial country. Trials in 2004 of a ground-breaking new vaccine against malaria were very encouraging. It could mark a milestone in the fight against a disease affecting 500 million people each year (90 per cent in Africa). More than 1 million people die annually from malaria, mainly children under 5 (it is estimated that one child dies every 30 seconds from the disease).

Important as are the drugs used in the treatment of malaria, even more so is the control of the parasite-bearing mosquito. The eggs of mosquitoes hatch in water, and there the young or larval forms can be attacked by pouring oil on the surface of pools so that they are unable to breathe, or by introducing small fish which have a partiality for them. Adult mosquitoes can be killed by insecticides or kept away by repellent creams or nets over beds. Prophylaxis with antimalaria before entering and while living in known malarial zones is important.

Today, many British holidaymakers are now contracting malaria, partly as the result of the emergence of drug-resistant strains of the disease. About 2,000 British travellers a year contract malaria and ten die. Do contact your doctor and take precautions.

Blackwater Fever is a sequel to malaria in tropical Africa and some parts of India. Rather illogically, it is described as "Blackwater," although the urine is red and the skin is yellow but the result is due to breaking down of the red blood cells by some malarial toxin. Possibly too much quinine may help in producing the illness. Treatment is to give plenty of fluids and no quinine or any other anti-malarial drugs in the early stages. The death-rate is about 25 per cent.

Trypanosomiasis or sleeping sickness is essentially an African disease (although also found in tropical America) spread by the tsetse fly. Its cause is the type of protozoan known as a trypanosome, almond-shaped with vibrating membranes at the sides which enable it to move through the bloodstream, rather like a flat fish in the water.

There are three stages of the disease: first, the stage of fever with enlarged glands and a rapid pulse; which may continue off and on for three years; secondly, the stage of trembling hands, legs, and tongue, vacant expression, and slow and stumbling speech; thirdly, and lastly, the stage of low temperature, apathy, wasting of the muscles, and possibly death.

Treatment is with pentamidine, suramin or melarsoprol—which give good results in early cases. Preventive measures in infected areas include the destruction of tsetse flies by insecticide, the cutting down of forests near rivers which are inhabited by tsetse flies, and some authorities have suggested the shooting of big game which may form a "reservoir" of the parasites, whence tsetse flies can carry them to human beings. For similar reasons infected people should not be allowed to move to noninfected areas.

Amoebic Dysentery, also known as *Amoebiasis*, is caused by the *Entamoeba histolytica*, an amoeba whose cysts are found in food and water, or spread by infected fingers or flies. There is mild fever and diarrhoea which contains blood. The disease may become chronic, and can cause abscesses, usually in the liver but sometimes in the lungs. Amoebiasis is treated with chloroquine or nitroimidazoles.

Leishmaniasis, kala-azar, or **dum-dum fever,** is another amoebic disease, probably spread in this instance by the bite of sandflies. It is also known as tropical splenomegaly—enlargement of the spleen in ordinary language—since infection results in enlargement of the spleen and liver, low, irregular fever, and death within a year or so. A milder form, affecting the skin, is known as Delhi boil, Oriental sore, or Baghdad sore, does not lead to kala-azar, and is fairly readily cured. The cure for both conditions is to give injections of antimony compounds which reduce the death-rate from kala-azar from 80 per cent, to 5 per cent.

Diseases Caused by Parasitic Worms.

Many types of worms infest human beings and other animals. They are interesting for such reasons as their size (which may range from the almost invisible to 9 m or more), their life histories, and their serious or trivial consequences on their hosts. We shall mention only a few groups here, and mainly the ones likely to be met with in Europe—the tapeworms, the roundworms, and the threadworms—although some tropical types will be described briefly.

Tapeworms, as we have seen earlier, like many other types of intestinal worm, lead a double life. What usually happens is that the worm breeds in the human intestine, the eggs pass out in the faeces, and are then swallowed by animals eating contaminated material. In the animal the eggs hatch out into larvae—primitive forms which penetrate the muscle, forming cysts—and man is infected in turn by eating its meat. Thus *Taenia solium* gets into the flesh of pigs, which, if imperfectly cooked (measly pork), causes infestation of the intestine in man. It reaches a length of about 3 m. *Taenia saginata*, which reaches a length of about 6 m, is spread in imperfectly cooked beef, and in Baltic countries *Dibothriocephalus latus* gets into the human intestine from caviar or undercooked fish. It reaches the awesome length of 9 m.

Now all the worms we have mentioned so far are found in the human intestine, and the cysts, which are much more dangerous and unpleasant, in the animal's muscles. But in some worms the reverse happens, with the adult in the animal's intestines and the cysts in man. Thus in Australia the dog tapeworm (*Taenia echinococcus*) produces cysts in both sheep and man. This is known as hydatid disease, and may remain unsuspected until cysts in the lungs, liver, or elsewhere become infected or rupture. *Trichinella spiralis* is similar in action, being found in the intestines of pigs and getting into the muscles or other organs of man. The main difference is that this worm migrates from the pig's intestines into its muscles, whence it reaches man in undercooked pork meat or sausages. The muscular cysts cause swellings and sometimes pain. There are changes in the blood, swelling of the face and leg in the early stages, and fever. A minor epidemic occurred in England in 1941. *Taenia echinococcus* and *Trichinella spiralis* are small—not more than 0·5 cm in length—but are more serious in their consequences than the large worms. Treatment is very difficult, and ordinarily all that can be done is to deal with individual cysts when they make themselves apparent.

The large tapeworms, *Taenia solium* and *saginata* and *Dibothriocephalus latus*, produce varying symptoms or none at all. Usually they are not discovered until some segments of the worm are excreted, but there may be mild indigestion, excessive hunger, and occasionally anaemia. However, when the worm is discovered the patient, not unnaturally, is likely to become anxious and uncomfortable at the thought of "having" a tapeworm; these symptoms are caused by the worry rather than the worm.

Treatment is, of course, a matter for a doctor, who now has a number of very effective drugs to choose from. One has to make sure that the head of the worm has been removed, otherwise it will continue to grow.

Roundworms are similar both in appearance and size to ordinary earth-worms and the eggs reach man, not from an animal, but from the contaminated fingers of someone else who handles food. They give rise to no symptoms, and are noticed only when discharged in the faeces or occasionally vomited up. Piperazine is an effective treatment.

Threadworms, as the name suggests, are like small 0·5-1 cm long pieces of white thread. They are very common in children, and live mainly in the caecum—*i.e.*, the part of the large intestine near the appendix. The males, which are the smaller ones, remain there, but the females pass down towards the rectum at night-time and lay their eggs in the area around the anus. Infection is by contaminated hands handling food—especially uncooked food—and water. Threadworms are not serious, and cause few symptoms other than itching around the anus and between the legs, but heavily infected children may show symptoms of anaemia. The nervousness often shown by such children is usually the result of the irritation produced by the worms in the anal region. Infection is not common in adults, and in children tends to disappear at puberty.

Treatment is, in theory, simple; for the worms are easily destroyed by a number of drugs, such as piperazine and other, more modern drugs. Ointment is applied to the itching area, and the child should be prevented from scratching. However, since the eggs may lie about the house for some time, reinfection often happens, especially if there are several small children in the home who may pass the disease from one to another.

The idea that intestinal worms in general are likely to cause loss of weight by absorbing food eaten by the patient is largely mistaken; for although it is true that they do live on this food, the amount taken is certainly not enough to be significant.

Tropical Worms. *Bilharzia* has been mentioned before in connection with its frequency in Egypt, although it is also found in other parts of Africa and the Middle East. There are two main types: one infecting the bladder (*Schistosoma haematobium*), the other the rectum (*Schistosoma mansoni*). *Bilharzia* is more correctly known as *schistosomiasis*.

The parasite's fantastic life-history begins when a man bathes in infected water, and the small swimming forms known as cercariae pierce and enter his skin—or they may enter the body by drinking infected water. From the skin they pass to the portal vein below the liver, remain there six weeks until they become adult and then swim against the blood-stream down to the pelvis, where the female lays eggs which have a sharp spine. The eggs penetrate into the bladder or rectum—depending on the type of fluke—and pass out in the faeces or urine. If they enter water they hatch out into small moving forms which seek out a water-snail, develop further in its body, and leave it in the form of cercariae ready to find a new human victim. The female fluke is slender and round, about 2·5 cm in length, the male, flat and leaf-shaped, is about 2 cm long, and, as we have seen, their grisly courting takes place in the portal vein, whence the impregnated female passes to the bladder (*haematobium*) or rectum (*mansoni*) to lay her eggs.

Infection results in raised temperature and, in the urinary type, blood in the urine; in the intestinal type blood is found in the faeces, and there are symptoms resembling dysentery—*e.g.*, diarrhoea. Treatment in both cases is with niridazole. Needless to say, attempts should be made at prevention by telling people to avoid infected canals (usually easier said than done), and by periodically cutting off the water supply to the canals to kill the snails.

Hookworm Disease, or ankylostomiasis, is found in many parts of the world, especially in miners who work on damp ground. The tiny worm enters the body usually through the feet, passes through the blood-stream to the lungs, eats through into one of the bronchial tubes, climbs the windpipe, and passes down the oesophagus into the stomach to end up in the duodenum. It causes anaemia, can be fairly readily cured, but is occasionally fatal.

Elephantiasis. Some types of parasitic worm are spread by insects. Thus in *Filiarisis* mosquitoes inject by their bites the infantile forms of a tiny worm which enters the lymphatic channels; there the blockade they cause leads to the swelling of the legs and the lower part of the body, known as elephantiasis.

PHYSICAL INJURIES AND FIRST AID.

This section which lists emergencies in alphabetical order is designed for rapid reference. Yet it would be wise to make sure now of knowing very thoroughly the parts dealing with bleeding, burns, resuscitation, shock and unconsciousness, situations which are immediately life threatening.

Nothing can teach first aid as effectively as attending one of the many courses organised by the three main organisations:

St. John Ambulance Association, 1, Grosvenor Crescent, London, SW1.
British Red Cross Society, 9, Grosvenor Crescent, London, SW1.
St. Andrew's Ambulance Association, Milton Street, Glasgow, C4.

Their local addresses are in the telephone directory; enquiry will get details of classes held at various hours of the day.

Purpose of First Aid.

First aid is not treatment proper (which is "Second Aid"). It aims to save life, to prevent further harm or suffering and to keep the victim in the best condition until taken over by a doctor or a nurse.

Under ordinary circumstances attempts to do more can be detrimental. If you limit your help to what is outlined here you cannot go wrong.

General Principles.

There are two priorities:

1. That the patient must breathe.
 (—*see* Choking, Resuscitation, Unconsciousness)
2. That severe bleeding is controlled.
 (—*see* Bleeding)

In any accident scene try to judge quickly which person most needs immediate attention. Treat a victim where he is; do not move him unless the surroundings suggest immediate danger (*e.g.*, fire, fumes, collapsing building).

Handle the patient with gentleness and sympathy yet achieve an atmosphere of reassurance and confidence by firm instructions and methodical actions.

Clear away a crowd (always demoralising to the victim) and use likely bystanders to telephone for an ambulance when necessary. Let your message be clear and written if possible. Let it clearly state the exact locality, the number of patients and the nature of their troubles. Always guard against shock (*q.v.*).

Asthma Attacks.

Breathing becomes very difficult, harsh and wheezing, fighting against air passages narrowed in spasm. Fear aggravates and relaxation relieves spasm. Show calm confidence.

1. Allow fresh air ventilation. Loosen tight clothes.
2. Help the mechanics of breathing by telling the patient
 to sit upright with a straight back but all the rest of the body relaxed;
 to direct breathing movements from the lower part of the chest.
3. Give him medicines he has prescribed for the emergency but avoid overdose.

Bleeding.

Treat mild bleeding as for wounds (*q.v.*).

For severe bleeding aim to let the blood clot by stopping or slowing the flow.

1. Immediately firmly press the edges of the wound together between fingers and thumb or press the palm of the hand hard down on it. (Maintain this at least ten minutes.)
2. Lie the patient down; elevate a bleeding limb (unless you suspect it to be fractured).
3. Slip a thick pad (handkerchief, gauze, wool) under your hand. Replace the hand pressure with a firmly bound bandage (stocking, belt, scarf).
4. If blood still leaks out add another pad and bandage.
5. Protect against shock (*q.v.*).

Nose Bleeding.

1. Have the patient sit up.
2. Get him to pinch between finger and thumb the whole lower half of the nose and maintain this for at least ten minutes. Repeat another ten minutes if necessary.
3. Tell him not to sniff or blow his nose.

Ear Bleeding.

1. Bandage or tape a loosely covering dressing (gauze, handkerchief) over the ear.
2. Lie the patient down towards the injured side.—*Nose or ear bleeding which follows a blow to the head may signify a fractured skull which needs immediate medical attention.*

Tooth Socket Bleeding.

This may follow after a dental extraction. Get the patient to bite hard on to a big pad (gauze, bunched-up handkerchief) placed over the bleeding area. He maintains pressure at least ten minutes sitting with a hand under his chin and the elbow on a table.

Blood Vomited.

This could appear black due to the effect of stomach acids.

1. Lie the patient down, on his side, with his head low.
2. Give him nothing to eat or drink.
3. Get a doctor or ambulance.
4. Guard against shock (*q.v.*).

Blood Coughed Up (*see also* Chest Injury).
Blood from the Back Passage.
Blood in the Urine.

However slight and brief the loss, always seek a doctor's opinion.

Blisters.

Leave them intact and protect them with a simple dressing. But if they are so big as to be in the way and need flattening:—

1. Boil a needle for ten minutes: leave it in the water until needed.
2. Wash the blister area with soap and water.
3. Holding the needle by one end pierce the blister at two opposite points. Press down with clean cloth to squeeze the fluid out.
4. Dress it like a wound (*q.v.*).

Burns (*see also* **Chemical Burns**).

1. Put out flames the quickest way: a douche of water; smothering with cloth (rug, coat, blanket).
2. Remove burnt clothes, but leave on what is adherent to the skin.
3. Cool the burnt part with cold water for at least ten minutes, longer if pain persists. Plunge a limb in a bucket or sink. Cover other parts with a thick cloth soaked in water; renew it if it dries.
4. Lie the patient down; keep a burnt limb elevated; remove possibly constricting things (rings, bracelets) from a burnt region before it swells.
5. Dress the burn as a wound (*q.v.*).
6. Guard against shock (*q.v.*)—in severe burns give to drink half a cupful of tepid water with a pinch of salt and sugar every ten or fifteen minutes.

Car Accidents.

1. Urgently stop severe bleeding (*q.v.*) or give resuscitation (*q.v.*) where this is needed; treat choking (*q.v.*). Unless they are at risk from fire or fumes leave the injured where they are. Look for victims thrown into ditches or over walls and hedges.
2. Minimise risks by forbidding smoking (petrol leak), by switching off the ignition and applying the brakes.
3. Set your own car off the road if possible; at night have its light shining on the scene.
4. Detail bystanders (wearing or carrying white objects at night) to stop approaching traffic on either side.
5. Send a message for help (written down) detailing the exact place, the number injured and the injuries.
6. Give other first aid to those in the cars without trying to move them: attempts to pull them out, especially from a distorted car, can do great harm. Leave to the rescue services.

Chemical Burns.

Rapidly wash away the chemical with copious free-flowing water. Remove any contaminated clothing.

The contaminated eye, closed in painful spasm, may need gently forcing open; let the water flow on it without force and bend the patient towards the affected side so that the washings flow off at once.

Chest Injury.

Where there has been a severe blow or deep wound to the chest, possibly followed by blood being coughed up:

1. Clear the mouth of any obstruction (blood, vomit, dentures).
2. If there is an open wound at once close it with the palm of your hand firmly applied. While you keep it there, improvise a thick pad

(towel, cloth, handkerchief, sock) to replace your hand. Tape or bandage it securely to make an air-tight seal.

3. Loosen tight clothing.

4. Lie the patient down *towards* the injured side. If he has difficulty in breathing have him half propped up with head and shoulders raised.

5. Cover him loosely.

6. Get ambulance urgently.

Choking.

1. With your fingers try to clear any obstruction (food, toy, dentures) from the back of the throat.

2. If this fails tell the patient to relax, to bend well forward; give a hard slap between the shoulder blades. This may loosen the obstruction so that the patient can cough it out. A small child you place head down over your arm or your bent knee. Try up to four separate slaps.

If back slapping fails try to force the matter out by pressure:

1. Patient standing: stand behind him; put both your arms round his waist. Patient lying: turn him on his back; kneel astride him.

2. Place your fist (thumb side first) on his abdomen *between his navel and the lower end of his breast bone*; cover your fist with your other hand.

3. Make firm thrust inwards and upwards. This may propel the obstruction out of his windpipe. Try up to four separate thrusts. If these fail continue alternating four slaps and four thrusts. After each of these be ready to remove immediately any matter propelled into the mouth.

After receiving thrusts the patient must be checked by a doctor lest internal damage has occured. If an obstruction is not cleared and the patient ceases breathing and collapses begin resuscitation (*q.v.*).

Always remember that in the unconscious the tongue may fall back and be an obstruction. *See* Unconsciousness.

Cold Effects. *See* **Exposure and Hypothermia.**

Cramp.

Cramps may follow severe loss of body fluid and minerals—as with severe repeated diarrhoea, vomiting or sweating. Slowly give tepid drinks containing a small pinch of table salt to each cupful or with diluted meat or yeast extracts.

Sudden cramp in a single muscle can be stopped by having the patient strongly stretch the muscle. In the front of the arm: straighten the elbow and swing the arm back. In the front of the thigh bend the knee and swing the leg back. In the back of the thigh: straighten the knee and swing the leg forward. In the calf: bend the foot up at the ankle while straightening the leg.

Diabetes.

Under certain circumstances a diabetic treated with insulin may suddenly collapse through sugar deficiency. Passing through phases of weakness, vagueness, sweating, tremor, uncoordinated actions and slurred speech he may go into a coma.

If he is conscious give him two teaspoonfuls (or lumps) of glucose or sugar in water. Failing this, give anything sweet; jam, honey, chocolate. This should clear him rapidly but repeat the dose after ten minutes.

If he is unconscious send for medical help urgently. Give nothing by mouth and put the patient in the recovery position (*q.v.*).

Ear—object in.

Do not try to poke it out.

A small object (*e.g.*, insect) can sometimes be floated up and out by lying the patient down with the ear uppermost and pouring in a little water or olive oil. But do not try this if the ear drum is possibly damaged or the ear is painful.

Electric Shock.

At once disconnect the current (at the switch or by pulling a plug out). If you cannot do this do not touch the patient but knock him away from his contact with dry non-conducting material; wooden stick, light furniture, folded thick garment.

He may need resuscitation (*q.v.*). He may have sustained a fracture (*q.v.*) or a burn. He may recover, only to collapse later; keep watch and send him to hospital.

Beware of very high voltage currents, as from wires of electric pylons: keep at least 20 feet away and do not try to rescue until the electricity authority has cut the current.

Epileptic Attack.

The patient may suddenly become unconscious, fall and soon begin convulsive jerkings, and sometimes frothing at the mouth.

1. Do not try to stop the jerking, but protect him from banging against furniture. Move the furniture or push cloth in position as buffer.

2. Clear froth from the mouth.

3. Once the convulsions stop put him in the recovery position (*q.v.*)—but beware lest he sustained a fracture (*q.v.*) in falling.

A succession of closely following attacks is dangerous: get medical aid at once.

Exposure.

A hill climber or a worker inadequately dressed against cold weather becomes slow, inefficient, clumsy, drowsy. Eventually he collapses and if not properly treated may die.

1. Put him to rest.

2. If you can, get him into a warm shelter. Otherwise protect him with screens of clothes or blankets and poles.

3. If he is conscious give warm drinks (cocoa, chocolate, tea). On no account give alcohol.

4. Get wet cold clothes off him if possible and put him in warm dry covers (sleeping bag, blankets). A plastic sheet over those helps to retain heat. Include the head, leaving only the face free. Well-prepared walkers will equip themselves with a special survival bag, now widely available.

Gradual rewarming is given when the patient has become cold gradually. When exposure has been sudden, as with falling in extremely cold water, you can warm up the patient fast in a bath at about 40° C. (103° F.).

Eye Injury.

Fix a loosely covering pad over the eye and get medical aid.—Do NOT use drops or ointments.—If the wound is severe and painful keep the patient on his back and cover both eyes (since movement of the good eye entails that of the injured one).

Eye—Object In.

Have the patient seated in a good light and stand behind him. If you can see the object on the white of the eye try to lift it off gently with the rolled-up and moistened twist of a handkerchief. If it does not come easily it may be embedded; leave it alone.

If it is within the coloured part of the eye leave it for a doctor to treat.

If you cannot see it look under the lids. The lower lid you pull down as he looks upwards. The upper lid you must evert as he looks down; lay a matchstick along the "hinge" of the lid; firmly grasp the edge of the lid and roll it up over the matchstick.

Fainting.

Lie the patient down with his legs higher than his head (if this is not possible, get him seated with his head bent low between his knees); loosen any tight clothes: tell him to breathe deeply and slowly. He should soon recover. A drink of water (provided he is conscious) will help. If he has fainted fully treat as for unconsciousness (*q.v.*).

Fractures.

Always suspect a broken bone where a blow or crush near a bone is followed by pain, swelling, deformity, weakened or restricted movement. Not all these features are always present: sometimes relatively slight pain is the only one.

Your task is to prevent movement which could worsen the condition by shifting a broken edge of bone into an important organ, or by making it pierce hitherto unbroken skin (with a risk of infection). No one will blame you for undue caution—but all will hold you responsible if you allow a fractured bone to do more damage by movement which could have been avoided.

When a fracture is suspected:—

1. Warn the patient not to move and bystanders not to try to lift him.
2. At once control any severe bleeding (q.v.). Dress any wound (q.v.) temporarily.
3. Now immobilise the fractured area including the joint at either end. The best splint is the patient's own body; e.g., injured arm secured against chest, injured leg against good leg (move the good leg up to the injured one). Or a thin board or rolled-up newspaper, well buffered with cloths and towels tied round it can be slipped under a fore-arm and wrist. Between the injured part and the splinting surface fill any hollows with firm padding of wool, or bunched-up cloth, socks, handkerchiefs. Tie the whole firmly with bandages (or stocking, thin towels) making the knots over the splint (not the hurt part) and avoiding bandage directly over the level at which you suspect the fracture. Work gently; do not lift or move the injured part.
4. Help to reduce shock (q.v.).

If you expect expert help (doctor, nurse, ambulance) to arrive soon, then omit step 3 above.

The fractured spine. When a blow or fall gives a painful back or neck, the vertebral column may be fractured. Inexpert moving may possibly drive a bone fragment into the spinal cord of nerves, causing paralysis or loss of feeling. It is most important to let the patient lie still until experienced first aiders take over. Keep the patient warm.

Frostbite.

Do not heat the area directly or put it in hot water. Do not rub it.

1. Remove any wet cover (e.g., glove).
2. Remove any tight object (garter, ring, etc.).
3. Cover the area loosely with dry material and let it warm up slowly. Fingers can be tucked under clothes into the opposite armpit. Nose, chin or ear can be covered with a dry hand.

Hanging.

Support the victim by his legs. Get the cord cut and be prepared to receive his weight as he falls. Loosen the cord round the neck. Act fast. Get medical help.

See also **Choking** *and* **Resuscitation.**

Head Injuries.

Blows to the head can cause fracture of the skull and also brain damage.

Fracture of the skull is not always obvious. Skin may swell over the site. Sometimes a fracture of the base of the skull (the body platform within the head at eye and ear level which supports the brain) may show up by bruising round an eye or by blood loss from ear or nose (see **Bleeding**).

Brain Damage may be of two kinds:—

Concussion, a temporary "shaking up" of brain tissue causing immediate "knock-out" unconsciousness. Recovery is in anything from a few seconds to several hours.

Compression of the brain develops from bleeding within the skull, from displacement of a fractured bone or from general swelling of the damaged brain tissues within the hard unyielding skull. The patient gradually (minutes or hours) becomes comatose and perhaps unconscious. This condition is dangerous. *The patient is unconscious*—see unconsciousness.

The patient is dazed: put him in the recovery position (q.v.) and watch him closely until help comes.

The patient recovers after a knock-out (concussion). He may yet develop features of compression as described above. However much he wants to carry on, keep him at rest, under observation and get medical advice.

In all cases remember that head injuries are often accompanied by injuries to other parts of the body.

Heart Attack.

Sudden heart attacks may produce:—

severe gripping pain in the centre of the chest, sometimes spreading to the neck, shoulder or arm; fast weak pulse; breathlessness; pallor and blueness; sweating.

or sudden painless breathlessness with slight cough and very wet bubbly breathing.

In either case send urgently for medical help. Get the patient to rest (in bed if possible). If he is very breathless it will be easier for him to be in a sitting position, against banked-up pillows. Otherwise have him laying down.

Loosen tight clothes. Keep him warmly but loosely covered. Mop any sweat from the face.

Heat Effects.

Heat Exhaustion. Anyone working in an unusually hot atmosphere is helped to remain cool by copious sweating which extracts heat from the body as it evaporates off the skin. But this loss of fluid also carries with it essential minerals from the body. The patient may collapse with his temperature normal or just a little raised; his skin is pale, moist and sunken, his pulse fast and weak. Muscles depleted of minerals go into cramp.

Let him rest in a cool place and give him (slowly) fruit juices or water with half a teaspoonful of salt added to each pint.

Heat Stroke happens in unusually hot and moist areas in rare industrial circumstances and in some tropical zones. Evaporation of sweat cannot take place in an atmosphere already saturated with water vapour. The patient becomes burning hot with a red dry skin and a fast forceful pulse. He may suddenly collapse and go into coma.

He must rest, have his clothes removed and be fanned or sponged down with cold (but not iced) water. The condition is dangerous and needs medical help.

Hypothermia.

Small babies and the elderly are specially susceptible to cold, e.g., overnight in a poorly heated bedroom. They become lethargic, comatose and then unconscious. Extremely cold to touch, even under bedclothes, the skin is white (though in babies it may be deceptively pink). Death may follow.

Cover the patient well including the head, leaving the face free. Put him in the recovery position (q.v.). Warm him GRADUALLY by warming the whole room and by giving slowly warm (not hot) drinks. Do NOT give alcohol. Do NOT use electric blankets or hot-water bottles.

Hyperthermia is the opposite of hypothermia.

Insect Bites.

Cool with water or (better) smooth in antihistamine cream.

If a bee sting has been left in the skin pull it out with fine tweezers: apply these well down near the skin so that they do not squeeze in any venom left at the free top of the sting.

Lightning.

As for electric shock (q.v.) except that the patient can be touched at once as he bears no electric charge. Put a dry dressing over any skin burns.

Nose Bleed. *See* **Bleeding.**

Nose—Object in.

Do not try to probe it. Unless GENTLE nose blowing gets it out consult a doctor.

Poisoning.

Do not try to administer antidotes. Do not give salt solutions.

If the patient is unconscious.

Treat as for unconsciousness (*q.v.*).

If he is conscious.

Give, slowly, soothing drinks to dilute the poison (water, barley water, milk and water).
Put him in the recovery position (*q.v.*) while awaiting the ambulance. He may lose consciousness.

In all cases.

Get the patient urgently to hospital.
Send with him any remaining poison or empty container and a sample of any vomit.
Keep a close watch on him all the time you are with him.

Poisoning by pesticides (weed or insect killers).

The patient must be at complete rest. If his clothes and skin are contaminated with the poison (splashes, spray droplets) remove clothes and wash the skin copiously with water (avoid contaminating yourself). If he is conscious give sweetened drinks.

Poisoning by gases.

Get the victim rapidly out of the contaminated atmosphere, but do not venture within this unless you have a lifeline and respirator, with others to safeguard you.

Recovery Position.

This safeguards the patient's comfort and breathing if he is unconscious, or comatose, or likely to lose consciousness. It consists in having him—
    laying on his side;
    with lower arm and leg stretched out straight behind him;
    upper leg and arm bent forward at right angles at hip, knee, shoulder, elbow;
    face tilted slightly downwards and head bent backwards (NO pillow).

This ensures a clear airway and lets any fluid in the mouth (saliva, blood, vomit) flow out and not choke the patient.
To get him in position:

1. Empty his pockets; remove items like bracelet or wrist watch. Put his belongings away safely. Loosen tight clothing.
2. Kneel alongside him.
3. Straighten his arms alongside his body; tuck the nearer hand below his hip.
4. Put one of your hands under his face to protect it as your other hand pulls him at the hip over towards you, on his side.
5. Adjust the limbs.
6. Cover him with a blanket or coat.

However, do not move the patient if circumstances suggest he received a heavy blow to the backbone. In that case ensure free breathing by keeping his head bent well back (never sideways). Be ready to clear immediately any vomit from his mouth.

Resuscitation.

This is the attempt to restore life to someone who has stopped breathing. NEVER try it unless this really is the case; you will do harm if the patient has collapsed but is still breathing. Do not try it if the problem is that of fighting against choking (*q.v.*).
In cases of drowning do not try to tip the patient up to drain out water; this wastes valuable time.
(It is best to have learnt the technique in organised first aid classes, practising only on a manikin.)

Artificial Respiration.

Act very quickly:—

1. Get the patient on his back.
2. Bend his head fully backwards and keep it thus all the time.

3. With fingers rapidly clear out any obstructing matter from mouth and throat.
4. Hold his mouth open (keep your fingers clear of his lips) and pinch his nose shut.
5. Take a deep breath in: open your mouth wide and seal your lips round his mouth: breathe firmly into his mouth. The air going in should make his chest rise. Do not blow more forcibly than is needed to achieve this.
6. Lift your mouth off. His chest will now sink as air comes out. Meantime you take another breath in.
7. Continue by repeating the breathing processes of steps 5 and 6.

The first four breaths you give quickly. Thereafter time yourself by the rise and the natural fall of the patient's chest.
With small children you need not pinch the nose, but let your mouth seal over both the nose and mouth of the patient. Much gentler blowing is needed, and quite small puffs are right for babies.
Keep on until medical authority takes over.
If patient vomits turn his head to one side and clear out the mouth. Then resume artificial respiration, with the first four breaths quick ones.
Successful artificial respiration should soon improve the patient's colour, and later you may find he begins to breathe for himself, even if only weakly. Watch this closely, for he may cease again.

Heart Compression.

If there is no improvement it may be necessary to add heart compression to artificial respiration. This, however, cannot be safely learnt except from first aid class teaching and demonstration. (See the Introduction to this section.)

Shock.

Failure of the heart and of the circulation of the blood may follow any serious injury (bleeding, wounds, burns, fractures). This can happen in minutes or hours according to the severity of the lesion.
In first aid terms this dangerous physical condition is called Shock. The patient is pale, cold, sweating, faint or comatose, with weak and fast pulse and breathing.
Try to prevent or to minimise the development of shock before it appears by applying the following simple but valuable measures to every badly hurt patient.

1. At once stop severe bleeding (*q.v.*).
2. Treat the patient where he is (unless you both are in an area of danger).
3. Lie him down: keep his head low and his legs raised (but avoid movement where a fracture is suspected).
4. Loosen tight clothing.
5. Keep him warm by covering below and loosely above him—but do not use hot-water bottles.
6. Gently dress any wounds—with the minimum of disturbance.
7. Guard his mental state. Be sympathetic but as optimistically reassuring as possible. Never whisper to others. Never assume that because the patient appears unconscious he cannot hear and understand what is said near him.

Do not give the badly injured patient anything to drink. This could worsen his condition and risk vomiting and choking, especially if he becomes unconscious or needs an anaesthetic. If he is very thirsty let him refresh himself by sucking a moistened handkerchief.

Snake Bite.

The adder is the only dangerous snake in Britain. Its bite can cause collapse and great pain, but only very rarely is it fatal.

1. Lie the patient down.
2. Wipe or wash the bite area. Put on a dry dressing.
3. Cover the area with a thick pad and bandage it in position so that it presses down very firmly.

4. Immobilise the bitten part as if it were a fracture (q.v.).
5. Get the patient rapidly to hospital.
6. Reassure him about his recovery. Give aspirin or paracetamol to minimise pain.

You NEVER cut or suck the bite, or apply chemicals. You NEVER use a tourniquet.

Sprains.

These are stretched and torn ligaments at a joint. Immediately after it happens you can reduce the swelling and pain which will follow by applying a cold compress—a cloth soaked in cold water and then wrung out to be just moist. Keep it in position half an hour, and renew it if it gets dry.

Otherwise support the joint firmly with layers of cotton wool interleaved between turns of crepe bandaging. Beware of making it so tight that it interferes with circulation in the limb.

A severe sprain may be difficult to distinguish from a fracture. If in doubt treat as for the latter.

Strains.

A strain is an overstretching of muscle fibres, and is very like a sprain except that it does not necessarily happen at a joint. Treat it as a sprain.

Strokes.

Some part of the brain has sudden damage of its blood supply. The results are as variable as are the functions of the brain: e.g., poor feeling or power in hand, arm or leg, altered speech, loss of bladder control, paralysis of one side, or unconsciousness.

A temporary stroke-like effect (a "transient ischaemic attack") may be the forerunner of more serious damage. Get the patient to bed, if necessary in the recovery position (q.v.), and keep him under observation until the doctor arrives.

Unconsciousness.

In first aid finding the cause of unconsciousness is less important than protecting the patient's breathing. The unconscious patient lying on his back and with head straight or bent towards the chest is at risk of choking from his lax tongue, flopping against and obstructing his throat. Correct positioning prevents this. Act methodically:—

1. Has the patient stopped breathing? He or she will urgently need resuscitation (q.v.).
2. Is his airway blocked making breathing difficult? Clear any material from his mouth. Bend his head straight back at the neck (but do not twist or turn it), and keep it there (see Choking).
3. Arrest any severe bleeding (q.v.).
4. Dress any wounds (q.v.).
5. Consider the possibilities of fractures (q.v.). If you suspect they might be present do not move him (specially important if he might have injured the backbone); stay by his head to ensure its proper position and to clear out immediately any fluid (saliva, blood, vomit) which threatens to choke.

If he can be moved:—

6. Turn him into the recovery position (q.v.).

Two other important points are that you NEVER try to give anything by mouth to the unconscious or comatose, and that you realise how much you must guard your speech, since these patients may overhear and understand what is spoken near them.

Wounds.

The general treatment is simple, and should avoid the use of antiseptics or ointments.

1. At once control any severe bleeding (q.v.).
2. Sit or lay the patient down.
3. Put a clean temporary dressing on the wound.
4. Wash your hands. Prepare dressings and bandages.
5. Wash *around* the wound (but not the open wound itself) with swabs or clean material moistened with soap and water. Use a fresh swab or material area for each stroke.
6. Cover the wound with a large dry dressing. Over this place a thick soft pad. Bandage firmly.
7. Put the injured part at rest.
8. Take measures against shock (q.v.).

Dressings. Gauze from freshly opened pack. Or improvise from clean handkerchief or small towel, held by corners, allowed to fall open and then refolded so that inside surface comes to outside. A leg or arm can be slipped inside a pillowcase.

Padding. Cotton wool. Or improvise from bunched clean handkerchief, sock.

Bandages can be improvised from stockings, necktie, belt.

Object embedded in wound. Do not try to remove it. Cover it with a clean dressing and over this place a "frame" of padding to surround the side of the object and protect above it. You can now apply further padding and bandages without pressing on the object.

Tetanus (lockjaw) is a risk in wounds contaminated with soil or from animals or thorns. Get medical advice.

St. John Ambulance Brigade.

From its origins in 1887, the organisation now boasts some 62,000 volunteers who deal with over 300,000 casualties each year. These casualties can range from minor upsets such as nose bleeds to victims of heart attacks and broken limbs. The work of the St. John Ambulance is divided into two aspects: the Brigade, which provides volunteers to give first-aid at public meetings etc., and the Association, which is engaged in the task of spreading first-aid education.

THE BLOOD.

Doctors who have made a special study of the blood are known as haematologists. Haematology itself is a complex subject because blood itself is complex and its many functions are not easy to describe and only a brief account is given here.

Blood consists of a fluid, called plasma, in which are suspended red and white blood cells and platelets and in which are dissolved many substances from the simple ones like glucose to the complex like hormones, proteins and fats. Total blood volume amounts to about five litres; the blood donor gives about half a litre at a session and feels no ill effects. Loss of a litre or more induces surgical shock (q.v. **Physical Injuries and First Aid**). Red cells are red because they carry a protein called haemoglobin which is capable of carrying oxygen. There are about five million red cells for each cubic millimetre of blood (that is an average sized drop), a total of 25 million million circulating in the body at any one time. The life of a red cell is about 120 days; new ones are constantly replacing old ones which are "buried" by the spleen.

The haemoglobin from dead cells is recycled; new cells are generated in the marrow of bones, including the breast bone, from which samples of marrow can be taken by a technique known as sternal puncture. Such samples are studied with a microscope to establish diagnoses of various blood disorders. White cells are of five basic types, the names of which need not concern us here. Each type has a specific function—some act as bacterial scavengers, some are concerned with antibodies (*q.v.*) and some with the general defence system of the body which is concerned with the development and maintenance of immunity to various diseases both bacterial and viral. There are also non-cell particles derived from large cells which the marrow produces. These are platelets, which are concerned with blood clotting. They have the capacity to "stick" to any gaps in blood vessels (such as may be caused by injury or, in the minutest of blood vessels, "wear and tear") and initiate blood clotting. All these types of cells can be studied in the test tube after taking a sample from the patient. This is known as venipuncture, a simple and virtually painless procedure, carried out by doctor or nurse or trained "phlebotomist", by inserting a needle on the end of a syringe into a dilated vein in the crook of the arm. Marrow samples can also be taken, as we have said, from the breast bone—but that is a very different procedure, requiring local anaesthetic and much more skill. For the patient it is not a comfortable procedure either.

Plasma, the fluid part of the blood, is more the province of the biochemist than the haematologist. The immunologist is also interested in plasma and all three disciplines tend to overlap to some degree. Plasma can be studied in the same way as whole blood. A venipuncture is carried out, a chemical added to stop clotting and the cells can then be removed in a centrifuge. If blood is allowed to clot in the test tube, the cells are all caught up in the clot and the plasma remains liquid and can be poured off. It is then known as serum. Plasma contains substances which are either dissolved, that is, in solution, or are held "in suspension". By this is meant that the plasma forms an emulsion because fat particles and some proteins are not soluble and can only form suspensions in this way. The protein and fat particles are in suspension in a like manner. The substances both in solution and in suspension are much too numerous to be dealt with here.

The functions of blood are manifold, but essentially blood is a transport medium, concerned with moving gases (oxygen and carbon dioxide), moving food (protein, carbohydrate, fat, minerals and vitamins), eliminating waste products and protecting and repairing the body.

Red Cell Diseases.

These are of two main groups leading to a shortage of red cells (anaemia), or an excess (polycythaemia). Anaemia is much the more common and there are many different kinds. In all of them the shortage of red cells results in a depletion of the capacity of the blood to carry oxygen. This means that the heart must work harder to send more blood than usual to the tissues, and even so the tissues will often go short. The patient will be persistently tired and listless, and if the anaemia is severe the action of the brain and heart will be seriously impeded, even leading to fainting, cardiac pain, and breathlessness on exertion. All these symptoms, however, can be caused by many other conditions. The only way to be sure they are due to anaemia is by a proper examination of the blood, and even this will not lead to the truth if the picture has been spoilt by the patient taking iron tonics and other remedies of his own accord. Therefore do not dose yourself with tonics, in case you really have anaemia. You may make it impossible to arrive at a proper diagnosis later.

Haemorrhagic Anaemia. Anaemia, a shortage of red cells, may be due to a variety of causes, singly or in combination. One very obvious cause is loss of blood or haemorrhage. Following the sudden loss of a half-litre of blood or more, the red-cell-producing bone marrow "factory" will step up its production; but even if it is adequately supplied with all the raw materials such as iron, it may well take many weeks to build up the numbers to normal. A very severe degree of haemorrhagic anaemia is usually treated by blood transfusion. Milder degrees can be treated by

taking extra iron, often over a long period of time.

The supply of iron for making new red-cell pigment is nearly always the bottle-neck which limits production. Haemorrhagic anaemia can commonly occur, however, without a sudden severe haemorrhage. From what has been said about the constant replacement of red cells as they wear out, it must be obvious that even if there is only a slight failure to keep pace with the numbers lost, several months of such a failure can eventually deplete the numbers to the level of very severe anaemia.

This situation is common when small amounts of blood are being continuously or repeatedly lost, and here again it is a shortage of dietary iron which is the usual cause of the failure to replace the lost red cells. Normal menstrual loss in women and girls whose diet is on the border-line of iron deficiency is a common cause of progressive tiredness and lack of energy. Where the menstrual flow is heavier than usual, or where it is frankly excessive in older women due to the various common gynaecological disorders, serious anaemia is surprisingly common. During pregnancy a great deal of iron is lost by the mother to the baby, and this, together with the inevitable blood loss at delivery, often makes for a very tired mother indeed, just at the time when there is an enormous amount of work to be done to manufacture milk and attend to all the extra household tasks of baby care. For these reasons it is almost routinely advisable to build up stocks of iron throughout the pregnancy by remembering to take the pills provided. Men as well as women can lose small amounts of blood continuously in later life from gastro-intestinal conditions such as piles, ulcers, and tropical infestations such as hookworm; and here again the anaemia may be just as severe in the long run as that which inevitably follows a sudden, massive haemorrhage.

One extra word of warning. Do not assume because you are pale that you are anaemic. Pallor is a very poor guide, because it is dependent on so many other things, like the blood vessels in your skin, and its thickness and translucency. Nothing but a blood test (which is so easy for your doctor to do) can really tell you if you are anaemic. And if your anaemia is due to a blood-losing condition, then that too must be treated. So do not be tempted to treat yourself, and never delay seeing your doctor about any unexplained bleeding.

Haemolytic Anaemia occurs when for any reason, there are more blood cells than usual being destroyed in the body. This may be because the cells are abnormally fragile, or because normal cells have been attacked by something to which you are allergic, or rarely because you have become sensitive to your own red cells. Sometimes unborn babies have severe haemolytic anaemia, due to an incompatability of blood group (Rh factor) between the mother and the baby, and the same sort of thing happens if incompatible blood is given by mistake in blood transfusion. Up to a point, in mild haemolytic anaemia, the bone marrow can keep pace with the increased loss of cells, but beyond this point anaemia develops. After incompatible blood transfusions a very dangerous situation results from the effects of the destruction of red cells and the liberation of their products into the blood. One form of jaundice is often produced in haemolytic anaemia, the patient becoming yellow because of the breakdown products of red cells circulating in excess as bile pigments. These latter are normally always present to a small extent due to the normal, comparatively small, rate of destruction of effete red cells.

Aplastic Anaemia is the term given to anaemia due to a virtually total failure of the bone marrow red-cell factory. Sometimes this occurs for no obvious reason. It is sometimes due to a heavy dose of radioactivity or X-rays knocking out the cells of the "factory." It may even be due to cancer cells growing in the bone marrow cavity and not leaving sufficient room for the red marrow cells. It is fortunate that aplastic anaemia is very rare, because it can only be treated by blood transfusions every few weeks for the rest of the patient's life. Very occasionally there have been exceptions to this rule, when the patient's marrow has re-awakened for no apparent reason and suddenly begins to make red cells again. Rapid progress has been made in the treatment of marrow disease with bone marrow grafts.

Pernicious Anaemia. The processes by which red cells are manufactured are complex, and depend, like so many other bodily activities, on the supply of a vitamin containing cobalt, called vitamin B_{12}. This is nearly always present in more than adequate quantities in the diet, but in order for it to be absorbed from the intestine, there must also be a substance called "intrinsic factor" which is normally made by the lining of the stomach. People with pernicious anaemia have suffered a degeneration of the lining of their stomachs, probably because, for some reason, they have become "sensitive" to this part of their own tissue. This kind of civil war within the body is known as an "auto-immune" disease, and is comparable in type with some forms of haemolytic anaemia. In other words they destroy their own stomach lining, fail to produce "intrinsic factor," and as a result fail to absorb vitamin B_{12} into the body. Faced with a failure in the supply of this essential substance, the bone marrow produces too few red cells, and the few that are produced are deformed, much too large, and very fragile. In addition to its role in blood formation, vitamin B_{12} is essential to the normal functioning of the spinal cord, and in long-standing cases of untreated pernicious anaemia, there is often a neurological disability.
Nowadays pernicious anaemia is treated by small occasional injections of the vitamin, whose other name is cyanocobalamin.

Polycythaemia. Too many red cells per cubic millimetre of blood can be found without there being an increase of the total number of red cells in the body. This occurs in dehydration, when there is a loss of plasma without a comparable loss of cells, and is called haemo-concentration. Alternatively, the bone marrow can manufacture more cells than usual as a response to living for long periods at high altitudes. The beneficial result can be that the blood can carry normal amounts of oxygen, even though the supply (in the rarefied air) is reduced.
Finally there is a red cell disease in which the bone marrow factory gets out of control and produces too many cells with no beneficial results. The number in the blood can be double the normal and the blood becomes so thick that the heart has difficulty pumping it round the body. This disease (*polycythaemia rubra vera*) can be treated by repeatedly bleeding the patient to reduce the numbers of cells. It is now treated very successfully with carefully judged amounts of radioactive phosphorus or certain other "antimitotic" chemicals which reduce the rate of multiplication of bone marrow cells.

White Cell Diseases.

Diseases of the white cells are very much less common but are inevitably serious.

Agranulocytosis. In this condition the number of those white cells which are responsible for phagocytosis of bacteria falls precipitously. The result is that one of the main bodily defences against infection fails, and the patient may die from an overwhelming invasion of germs and the accompanying high fever. The usual cause is an abnormal sensitivity to a variety of drugs, often those which are in widespread use and only give trouble in the occasional case. One example among hundreds is the antibiotic chloramphenicol which specifically kills typhoid bacteria and is used for that purpose. It is believed that about one patient in 60,000 becomes sensitive to it and agranulocytosis often fatally follows, though appropriate treatment of infections has greatly reduced the likelihood

of death. The fact that almost any drug *can* do this to some people and yet be quite safe for the majority, is one good reason not to dose yourself unnecessarily with over-the-counter medicines.

Leukaemia comprises a range of diseases which involve the abnormal production of white blood cells. Immature or blast cells are produced at an increased rate and tend to infiltrate various areas of the body, for example, bone marrow, lymph nodes and spleen. They are also found in the peripheral blood and cerebrospinal fluid. In spite of their large numbers these cells, because of their abnormality, are unable to deal effectively with infection and anaemia, sepsis and fever can result. The cause of this type of cancer is open to some speculation but we know there is an increased incidence in those with Down's Syndrome and other chromosomal abnormalities. Viral infections may also be implicated and there is almost certainly an association with ionising radiation.
This latter fact was proved by the increased incidence of leukaemia in those who survived the atomic explosion in Japan at the end of the Second World War. Pregnant women should not be subject to X-Rays as this may cause an increased incidence of leukaemia in their children.
Recent research has suggested that workers exposed to small amounts of radioactive material may suffer abnormal spermatic development so that the tendency to leukaemia may be passed on to their unborn children who may be prone to the disease later in life.
The outcome of the illness largely depends on the specific type. Chronic lymphatic leukaemia for example, which tends to affect older people, may have no clinical signs or symptoms. In fact, it can run a very indolent course, require no treatment and be compatible with a normal lifespan. On the other hand, acute myeloid leukaemia which tends to affect younger adults is a very serious disease with an acute onset and which if not treated can prove to be rapidly fatal.

Chronic Myelogenous Leukaemia (CML) results from a particular "translocation" of cellular DNA. The DNA is swapped to an unusual place and instead of working normally, produces an abnormal protein. A new treatment, Glivec, that blocks the abnormal protein, has demonstrated some dramatic results in patients.

Childhood Leukaemia is the most common form of malignant disease but nevertheless, it is quite rare with an incidence of approximately 25 per 1,000,000 children. Over 85% of all cases involve the type known as acute lymphoblastic leukaemia. With modern treatment, a remission (that is to say, a disease free period) can be induced in over 90% of children and cure rates are very high. Presenting features of acute leukaemia are tiredness, lethargy, abnormal susceptibility to infection, excessive bruising and occasionally bone or joint pain. A blood count usually helps in the diagnosis but this needs to be confirmed by examination of the bone marrow. Treatment involves repeated courses of cytotoxic drugs, sometimes combined with radiotherapy. For those with more resistant forms of the illness, bone marrow transplantation can often provide a cure. Treatment is best performed in specialist centres where the expertise is available to deal with the complicated drug regimes. With modern treatment the outlook for all forms of leukaemia has improved. For children, in particular, the outlook has been dramatically transformed and in a great many cases a cure can be successfully achieved. The address of the Leukaemia Care Society is 14 Kingfisher Court, Venny Bridge, Pinhoe, Exeter, Devon EX4 8JN.

Hodgkin's Disease is a disease in some ways akin to *leukaemia*. Abnormal cells are found in the reticuloedothelial system and proliferate in a disorganised manner, causing enlargement of lymph nodes (glands), spleen and sometimes the liver. Hodgkin's disease, named after a 19th cent. Guy's physician, has been the subject of much research and therapeutic trial. The improvement in outlook for patients with Hodgkin's disease was one of the major success stories of the 1990s. In cases where the disease is caught early, it can be eradicated in over 95 per cent of sufferers (although progress has been less marked with non-Hodgkin's lymphoma).

Haemorrhagic or Bleeding Diseases.

Whenever blood vessels are damaged by injury, there is a remarkable series of mechanisms which automatically come into operation to stem the flow of blood. There is a constriction of all the smaller vessels in the locality. Platelets stick together and release substances which help the vessels to stay constricted as well as others necessary to blood clotting, and yet others which help to bind the clot tightly together. Later, materials appear to prevent too much clotting, and eventually the clot is removed altogether as healing proceeds. There are some very complicated diseases of this blood-conserving mechanism which can lead to abnormal bleeding, sometimes beneath the skin to produce bruising or even smaller leaks; sometimes leading to a greater loss of blood, particularly following a wound. In some kinds of *purpura* (bleeding tendency) the blood vessels are the cause of the trouble, having become fragile and leaky for a number of reasons. This happens in old age (*senile purpura*), in scurvy, or vitamin C deficiency, as an occasional accompaniment to infective diseases, or as an immunological effect on the lining of blood vessels when the patient becomes sensitised to certain substances (*Schönlein-Henoch* or *anaphylactoid purpura*). The latter often follows a streptococcal sore throat, just as rheumatic fever and acute nephritis do; and as well as the purpura there may be joint pains and nephritis. Just as almost any drug or chemical will cause agranulocytosis in some people, so it can also cause anaphylactoid purpura.

Purpura may also be due to a lack of platelets, known as thrombocytopenia (a shortage of thrombocytes or platelets). This can happen if the bone marrow factory is depressed, since this is where platelets too are made. It is therefore a common accompaniment of leukaemia or aplastic anaemia. Or there can be increased destruction of platelets in some diseases of the spleen. Platelets normally last eight to ten days, but their life-span can be shortened in heart failure, and following massive transfusions, or often for no apparent reason ("idiopathic" thrombocytopenia), when removal of the spleen can sometimes help.

Finally, defects of the *clotting mechanism* will lead to a bleeding tendency, and since the mechanism itself is very complex, so is the variety of things which can upset it. The liver provides the blood with many of the substances required for clotting, so it is not surprising that a clotting defect commonly accompanies liver disease. One necessary substance for blood clotting is called "antihaemophilic factor" and is missing from people who have inherited the disease *haemophilia*. These people may die of haemorrhage from quite small cuts or minor surgical procedures.

THE HEART AND BLOOD VESSELS.

The heart consists of about 350g of muscle which makes up the walls of its four chambers. Anatomically the human heart closely resembles the sheeps' hearts to be found in a butcher's shop. Indeed it would be an instructive exercise to dissect one of these in the order described below, since there is no other way of properly appreciating what the chambers, valves, *etc.*, are really like.

There are two quite separate pumps in the heart—one on the owner's right (or on your *left* if you are looking at the front of someone else), and one on his left. The right heart collects spent, deoxygenated, "venous" blood which returns there from the whole of the body, and gives it the comparatively small push required to drive it through the adjacent lungs. The left heart collects the revitalised, oxygenated "arterial" blood as it leaves the lungs, and gives it the enormous push required to build up the arterial blood pressure, so that it can be forced through all the tissues of the body. As may be expected, the right heart chambers have much thinner walls than the left, since their muscle has less work to do. This will help you get your bearings with the sheep's heart. The tip, or apex, is the lowest part. The thick-feeling side is the left, the thin the right; and the great vessels are at the top.

The Right Atrium.

The upper chamber on the right, or right atrium, has two large openings into it through which all the spent blood arrives from the upper and lower great veins (the superior and inferior venae cavae). Cut open the thin wall of the right atrium with scissors between these two holes to lay open the interior of the chamber, noting the "auricle" or "dog's ear" that forms a small cul-de-sac. The whole chamber is sometimes, inaccurately, called the auricle. You should be able to push a finger downwards into the lower chamber—the right ventricle—through a communicating hole guarded by the three thin cusps of the *tricuspid valve*. These will not obstruct your finger, since they are designed to permit blood flow in the same direction.

When the atrium is full of blood, it squeezes its contents through the tricuspid valve into the right ventricle; and when, a split second later, the ventricle is full and contracts, the three cusps come together to prevent the blood from flowing backwards into the atrium again. Instead the spent blood is driven onwards through the *pulmonary valve* (in the upper part of the right ventricle), through the pulmonary artery, to be delivered to the lungs. The pulmonary valve has three very well-defined cusps which prevent blood from coming back into the ventricle as it relaxes to receive more blood from the atrium before the next contraction or beat. It is possible to pass a blade of the scissors from the opened-out right atrium, through the tricuspid valve towards the tip of the heart, and cut along the right border of the heart through the thickness of the ventricular muscle. Then cut upwards again, passing the scissors blade through the pulmonary valve and open up the *pulmonary artery*. If you have done this successfully you will have followed the path taken by the spent blood through the right heart to the lungs. Notice the thick round bands of muscle lining the ventricle, and notice too that you have not entered the left heart, which has no connection with the right except in some congenital malformations (see later). The same dissection can now be made of the left heart. Open up the *left atrium*, noting its "dog's ear" or "auricle," pass the scissors down into the *left ventricle* through the two rather flimsy cusps of the *mitral valve*. Notice how much thicker is the muscle of the left ventricle, and cut upwards through the three well-formed cusps of the *aortic valve* into the main artery of the body—the *aorta*.

The Coronary Arteries.

The aorta as it leaves the left heart is distinguishable from the pulmonary artery as it leaves the right, partly by the extreme toughness of the aortic wall (it has to withstand so much more blood-pressure); and partly by the entrances or orifices of the two small branches given off by the aorta, just beyond the valve cusps, which go to supply the heart muscle itself with blood. These are the *coronary arteries* which are so necessary for the heart's own survival.

Cardiac Output.

The amount of blood pumped in unit time, or the *cardiac output*, can be varied a great deal, according to the needs of the moment. This is accomplished by altering both the heart rate and the stroke volume, the amount expelled per beat. Every minute, the healthy adult man at rest shifts about 5 litres of blood through the heart—an amount equivalent to all the blood he possesses. When exercise is taken, or in response to anxiety or fear, this is stepped up many times, so that the muscles can receive a greatly augmented supply of the materials required for action. The controlling mechanisms which allow these changes to be made automatically are partly organised in the brain by the so-called *cardiac centre*; and partly by local mechanical and chemical stimuli to the heart muscle itself. The cardiac centre is continuously receiving information through nerves about the physical and chemical state of the circulation, and also from the mind; which is partly how certain emotions make the heart beat faster. All the information is integrated, and a cardiac output continuously arranged which is appropriate for current demands.

Cardiac Neurosis.

In ordinary circumstances at rest, most healthy people are not conscious of their heart-beat. However, there are many perfectly healthy people whose hearts slip in an extra beat occasionally. Sometimes their owners are aware of this and become unnecessarily alarmed. Their fear causes palpitations (a pounding of the heart) and the tension mounts. An undue anxiety about the tricks played by a healthy heart sometimes leads people to interpret minor pains in the chest, or even indigestion, as grave symptoms of heart disease, and the consequent anxiety leads to still worse symptoms. If you are one of these worried people, take your worries to your doctor, and let him decide for you whether there is anything wrong. A hundred to one there isn't, and then you will have to find something else to worry about, or better still give up the habit altogether. Many people secretly worry about heart disease and high blood-pressure for years, when very often they are worrying unnecessarily. Even if there is cause for worry, so much can be done for these conditions (as it can for cancer) provided medical advice is taken early in the course of the disease. Remember, too, that the slight feeling of giddiness when you get up suddenly from having been lying down, is often experienced by most normal people; but if you get frightened by it you will begin to breathe more quickly and deeply; and this in itself will make you feel even more faint—and so on.

Heart Failure.

When the cardiac output of blood is too little for the requirements of the body, a state of *circulatory failure* has arisen, and when this is due primarily to the heart itself being at fault, it is more properly called *heart failure*. As will be seen, heart failure is not a disease, but the common result of a large number of different diseases. The signs and symptoms produced are caused by two sorts of process: (*a*) tissues of the body have too little blood flow through them and are therefore undersupplied; (*b*) blood accumulates and stagnates in tissues, causing congestion, since the failing heart cannot move forward the amount of blood presented to it in the great veins. Often the left or right side of the heart fails disproportionately. In *left heart failure* the lungs are congested because they are the territory from which the left heart is failing to move blood. The patient has great difficulty with his breathing, and in advanced cases may not be able to breathe when he lies down, because the lungs become so congested and waterlogged. In *right heart failure* the main veins are congested and the other parts of the body become swollen with excess tissue fluid, mainly in the lower parts such as the legs and ankles. This swelling with fluid is called oedema, and in heart failure is only partly due to the mechanics of the failing heart. It is mainly due to a poorly understood retention of sodium in the body, a situation in which excess water is also retained. Whatever the type of heart failure it is always likely to be a changing condition, since the amount of failure will depend as much on the demands being made as on the state of the heart. For instance, in mild cases at rest when the required cardiac output is small, there may be no signs or symptoms. These may only appear on exertion. Heart failure will be referred to again under the various conditions which cause it.

Treatment of Heart Failure

is quite logical. It is aimed at correcting the imbalance between supply and demand of blood, and at the removal of the accumulated excess fluid. We can therefore (*a*) reduce the body's demand for blood; (*b*) increase the supply or cardiac output; and (*c*) promote the excretion of sodium and fluid. Demand for blood is reduced by rest, both physical and mental, and by reduction of weight, since obesity (being overweight) is an additional demand on the cardiovascular system. The cardiac output can be increased by administering a "tonic" to the heart muscle in the form of *digitalis*, which is a powerful heart stimulant derived from foxglove leaf. Fluid (and hence salt) accumulation can be helped by restricting the intake of salt and by giving drugs which promote its excretion by the kidneys (diuretics). Very occasionally, very large accumulations of fluid in the legs, abdomen, or thorax, are tapped and drained physically, with needles. These remarks are of course very general and must not encourage anyone to treat himself for such a potentially serious condition as heart failure. Even such a simple measure as doing without salt can be practised quite unnecessarily by many people for years, simply as a result of reading a paragraph like the above. If you need to reduce salt intake you should be in your doctor's care, and so please let him decide.

Congenital Heart Disease.

It has been estimated that of all the babies born who survive at least one month, there will be about one in every two hundred with some form of congenital heart disease; that is to say that the heart will have failed to develop properly in embryonic life. In some cases this is associated with a virus disease of the mother (commonly rubella, or German measles) or with certain drugs taken by the mother (*e.g.* thalidomide) at a time, very early in pregnancy, when organs are assuming their adult shape. Parents should see to it that their daughters get German measles vaccine before they grow up; and drugs of all kinds should be avoided where possible during early pregnancy. In most cases of congenital heart disease, however, there is no known cause, and it seems that the manner of formation of the embryonic heart is so delicate that it can be thrown out of gear very easily, perhaps even by chance. Scores of different types of defect occur, singly and in combination.

Any of the valves may be anatomically defective—either failing to close properly (*incompetence*) or being too tight (*stenosis*); the great vessels (pulmonary artery and aorta) may be switched round, or *transposed*, so that they emerge from the wrong ventricle; there may be defects in the wall (*septum*) which separates the atria or the ventricles on each side (*septal defect*, or "hole in the heart"); or there may be a persistence of the vessel which in the foetus normally by-passes the lungs by joining the pulmonary artery to the aorta (*patent ductus arteriosus*). This vessel normally closes at the time of birth when the first breaths are taken, and subsequently disappears, so that the whole output of the heart is then sent round the lungs. Detecting congenital heart disease early is one of the purposes of routine post-natal check-up examinations of the baby. Exact diagnosis requires very complicated techniques, and sometimes the structural defect can be corrected by surgery, with almost miraculous results.

Rheumatic Heart Disease.

Acute rheumatic fever is not to be confused with other forms of rheumatism. Many tissues of the body (particularly the heart) are attacked, as well as the joints, and the trouble is due to a sensitivity which has developed to certain bacteria (*haemolytic streptococci*) which have probably caused a sore throat about three weeks before the onset of the disease. Why acute rheumatism only rarely follows streptococcal sore throat is poorly understood, but this is no consolation to the one per cent or so of the population whose hearts bear its scars. During the acute phase of the illness which usually occurs before the age of fifteen, inflammatory damage occurs to the valves, the heart muscle, and the sac in which the heart lives, the *pericardium*. So there is a *valvulitis* or *endocarditis*, a *myocarditis* and a *pericarditis*. There may be acute heart failure at this stage if the heart is severely affected. The better-known results of rheumatic heart disease, however, are caused in the ensuing years by scarring of the healed valves. The valves are thickened and deformed. They may have lost their elasticity and stretch, so that they do not close properly (*incompetence*); or they may contract and tighten (*stenosis*). In both cases the heart chamber situated next to the affected valve has to work progressively harder, either because it gets no rest in between beats (in *incompetence*); or it has to force the blood through too narrow a hole (in *stenosis*). The end result is some variety of heart failure (*q.v.*).

Mitral Stenosis. The most commonly affected valve is the mitral, usually causing *mitral stenosis*, in which the opening between the left atrium and the left ventricle will sometimes only admit one fingertip instead of three fingers as it should. In time the left atrium becomes much enlarged as it overworks to force blood through this narrow orifice. Later still a back pressure develops in the lungs causing congestion and breathlessness; and even later the right ventricle is strained as it tries to force blood into the already congested lung. This is a classic example of the march of trouble backwards from the site of the damaged valve involving first the chamber "behind" it (the left atrium), then the territory "behind" that (the lungs), then the pulmonary arteries taking blood to the lungs, and finally the right ventricle trying to send blood to the pulmonary artery. This steady march of events is usually very slow, and can commonly take twenty years or longer from the initial attack of acute rheumatism to the severer symptoms of advanced mitral stenosis. Treatment is both medical and surgical. The heart failure is treated medically as already described. These days surgical reopening of the valve is almost commonplace, either by inserting a finger through the left auricle and breaking down the constriction, or by opening up the heart and re-shaping the valve under direct vision. The latter involves the additional problem of by-passing the heart by the use of some sort of external pump and poses additional problems, even though from other points of view it is obviously more convenient.

As always with major surgical procedures much of the problem is in selecting the patients who will benefit from the operation and in whom it is feasible. Quite often there are other valves involved, mainly the aortic or tricuspid or both, and the hydrostatic or "plumbing" problems can be extremely complex. With luck, however, combined with good judgement and good surgery, the lives of incapacitated patients can be transformed by mitral, and other valvular, surgery.

The *aortic valve* is stenosed or narrowed by other degenerative processes besides rheumatism. *Tricuspid stenosis* is nearly always rheumatic in origin.

Coronary Heart Disease. This is the term used whenever the blood supply to the heart muscle (through the coronary arteries) is reduced to such an extent that the heart muscle suffers from a lack of supplies. It has a number of causes, but the only really common one is partial obstruction of the coronary arteries by a condition known as *atheroma* or *atherosclerosis*, and sometimes inaccurately called *arteriosclerosis*. This arterial disease is described later (**Z29**). It takes the form of swellings or lumps on the lining of the artery which, if they become large enough to interfere seriously with the flow of blood, produce a blood starvation or *ischaemia* of the tissue being supplied. Obviously, the smaller the artery, the more easily will a lump of given size impede the flow. Equally obviously the greater the demand for blood, as in exercise, the more blood "starvation" there will be. There are two degrees of

coronary artery disease: one in which the blood flow is reduced to the point where the increased demands of hard work cannot be met, and this results in *angina pectoris* due to *coronary insufficiency*; the other is when the coronary artery becomes completely blocked, preventing the flow of blood altogether, usually by a *thrombus* or clot of blood, and this is *coronary thrombosis*, or heart attack.

Angina Pectoris. Whenever activity is increased in any muscle, the demands for oxygen and nutriments from the blood-stream increase, and as these are used up there is an increased production of waste products known as metabolites. To meet the demands for a greater supply and a more efficient waste-disposal, the blood flow through the exercising muscle must always be increased. If sufficient increase does not occur, not only will there be a shortage of supplies, but there will also be a pile-up of metabolites in the muscle which cannot be carried away. It is mainly because of these latter that pain is caused in ischaemic, or blood-starved muscle, and pain is one of the chief symptoms when heart muscle becomes ischaemic. One important mechanism for increasing blood flow normally to exercising muscle is by automatically dilating the vessels concerned. Diseased vessels, such as coronary arteries when they are affected by atheroma, are not so easily dilated, although certain drugs which are so powerful dilators of arterioles can accomplish a great deal, albeit temporarily. The measures taken to relieve the pain and blood-starvation of angina are two-fold. The patient can reduce the demands of the heart by a few minutes' rest, and a drug (usually nitroglycerin) can be taken to dilate the coronary vessels of supply. Another obvious long-term way to reduce demands is for the overweight patient to eat less, and reduce the load of extra body weight on his circulation. It is very frustrating, to say the least, that such an incapacitating and often lethal condition should be caused by the narrowing or blockage of only 5 or 8 cm of narrow piping about 3·5 mm wide. Coronary bypass operations in which the blocked segment is replaced with a piece of blood vessel taken from another part of the body, are now fairly routine.

Angioplasty is where a small balloon, on a wire, is guided into the narrowed arteries of the heart. The balloon is then inflated, opening up the obstructed vessel and allowing adequate blood to reach the heart beyond the narrowing. The procedure is relatively safe.

Heart Attack (Myocardial Infarction) or Coronary Thrombosis. It should readily be understood from the above description that heart attacks will vary in their severity according to the amount of heart muscle deprived of blood; and this in turn will depend on where in the coronary artery the obstruction occurs. Most usually it is the left ventricular muscle which is cut off from supplies and dies, either in part or in all of its thickness. Since it is the left ventricle which does most of the work of pumping blood to the body, serious heart failure (**Z27**) is to be expected.

If too much muscle is killed, the heart will simply stop, and the patient will suddenly die. It is much more usual, however, for enough muscle to be left for survival, albeit with a greatly reduced cardiac efficiency. A heart attack is usually accompanied by severe pain, similar to the pain of angina but more severe, and unrelieved by rest or by the patient's usual drugs. Very occasionally the event occurs apparently without pain, or with so little that it is ignored. These so-called "silent" coronary attacks can make diagnosis extremely difficult. Since the doctor depends very considerably with heart attacks on an exact, spontaneous description of symptoms for his diagnosis, no description will be given here. There are many over-anxious people who will read these words and could be misled into an unspontaneous description of their own symptoms, and this could make the task of treating them such a problem that they could even be mis-diagnosed as a result. If you have the smallest worry that your chest pain is due to your heart, take your anxiety to your doctor without delay. He will almost certainly be able to reassure you; and if it happens to be your heart after all, you will have taken the first sensible step towards proper treatment. Dangerous as heart attacks are, they are by no means the death warrant that many lay people think, any more than cancer is. The treatment for a true heart attack is urgent and prolonged. Patients must be at complete rest and their pain relieved quickly. The area of heart muscle they have lost must be allowed to heal. Nowadays patients are encouraged to mobilise early, and progressively increase activities over a few days to weeks.

You can help to avoid a heart attack by not smoking, avoiding obesity and living a physically active life. Avoid sudden exercise, however.

Blood Pressure (Hypertension). The blood is under great pressure in the arterial system, since it is this which forces it into all the tissues of the body. It is therefore no more meaningful to say you have "blood pressure" than to say you have a temperature. You would be very badly off without. Blood pressure which is too high (hypertension) can give rise to problems, though not always. It is another of those conditions like angina and cancer, which engender much anxiety among people even when they do not suffer from them. It is not being suggested here that high blood pressure is a trivial condition, but that it is for doctors to worry about rather than patients! If you ever find out your own blood pressure, never try to work out for yourself what the figures mean. It is much too complicated. Finally, it should be mentioned that high blood pressure may occasionally be associated with, or "secondary to," certain kidney diseases (nephritis) including a strange condition known as toxaemia of pregnancy, which lasts only as long as the pregnancy, provided great care is taken. Most high blood pressure is "primary", and without any known association or cause.

Low Blood Pressure. Some people seem normally to have surprisingly low blood pressure all the time. There is nothing whatever wrong with this; indeed it may even be beneficial. At least they are unlikely ever to suffer the effects of high blood pressure. The sudden low blood pressure of circulatory failure or shock (**Z**27) is another matter and must be urgently treated.

Irregularities of the Heart Beat. How quickly or how slowly the heart beats is largely under the control of the cardiac centre in the brain and the level of certain hormones in the blood. The regularity of the beat, however, is controlled by the so-called pace maker in the wall of the right atrium, and by the way impulses from the pacemaker travel through specialised conducting heart cells (the bundle of His and its branches) to the ventricles. When any part of this elaborate mechanism is upset, either by altering the biochemical or electrical conditions of these specialised tissues, or by killing some of them off by deprivation of blood supply in the course of a heart attack, disordered rhythm can result. Increase (tachycardia) or decrease (bradycardia) in rate is nearly always a normal response to exercise, or anxiety. Very occasional irregularity, such as the mis-timing of an occasional beat is also quite normal in some people, although many are alarmed by it. Persistent irregularity, however, is abnormal. Its true nature can usually be elucidated by making an electrical record of the heart beat— an electro cardiogram. The commonest causes are varieties of coronary artery diseases or rheumatic heart disease.

Pericarditis. The heart beats inside a bag or sac. At every beat its outer surface slides against the lining of the sac, lubricated by a small amount of fluid. This is the pericardial sac, the pericardium being strictly the lubricated membrane which lines the sac and which also covers the outer surface of the heart. Sometimes inflammation occurs—pericarditis—and the sliding surfaces become roughened and even separated by a fluid effusion. Very occasionally, so much fluid accumulates that the heart's action is seriously impeded. Pericarditis may be due to infection or to rheumatic fever, and it usually overlies the area of damaged muscle after a heart attack. This illustrates something which people rarely appreciate—that inflammation is not by any means always due to infection by bacteria. The last two varieties of pericarditis are quite free from germs (sterile).

Myocarditis. A term loosely applied to disorders affecting the heart muscle. There are lots of very rare causes. The really common ones are due to acute or chronic rheumatic causes or to coronary artery disease.

Endocarditis or inflammation of the lining of the heart is a term loosely applied to any disorder of the valves or heart lining. All varieties of rheumatic valvular disease (**Z**27) are included. Bacterial endocarditis in its several forms usually involves valves already damaged by rheumatic disease. It is a complication which is still much to be feared, though somewhat less so now that antibiotic drugs are available.

Atheroma or Atherosclerosis. This is the condition referred to above in which lumps arise on the lining of arterial blood-vessels. Although it is therefore a disease of the arteries, its importance lies in the way blood flow is held up, either by the lumps themselves, or by thrombosis ultimately blocking the narrowed portion of the pipework. The effects on the body are therefore those of depriving the tissues of blood.

It is an astonishing fact that in England and America, more people die of the consequences of atheroma than of any other single disease, including all forms of cancer put together. Furthermore, cancer is mainly a disease of old age, whereas many of the effects of atheroma on men occur in early middle age.

Intermittent Claudication. If narrowing of the artery is going to do major harm it is easy to see that it will be of more consequence in those parts of the body where small-bore vessels are supplying tissues whose functions are necessary for life. Exactly such a situation exists in the heart and in the brain. An additional factor is that the arrangement of the blood supply in these tissues is such that any particular area has only one vessel leading to it. This is unusual among the tissues generally, where several alternative, or "collateral" vessels usually supply an area, and where others can take over if one becomes obstructed. We have, therefore, a situation in which perhaps the most important tissues—the heart and the brain—run the greatest risk of deprivation, and this leads to angina and coronary thrombosis on the one hand, and cerebral thrombosis and haemorrhage ("stroke illness") on the other, accounting jointly for about one death in every five. In addition, the effects of atheromatous narrowing are often felt in the legs, where the blood supply to the muscles is inadequate for exercise, leading to intermittent pain comparable with that in the heart in similar circumstances. This is called intermittent claudication, or intermittent closing of the leg arteries. In its most severe forms, it leads to the need for amputation, although in most cases early treatment can avoid this. It is small wonder that there is intensive research into the causes of atheroma.

Raised Cholesterol. A lot of attention has been given to the amounts of certain fats in the circulating blood, particularly cholesterol. This fat is found in larger amounts in the blood of sufferers from atheroma, and is also found in the arterial lumps themselves. Efforts have therefore been made to reduce blood cholesterol by modifications of the diet, but it has been extremely difficult to prove that this has done any good. Many other factors are known to contribute to atheroma, and hence to heart attacks and strokes, some of which can be reduced and others not. Such factors are age, obesity, high blood pressure, and smoking cigarettes.

People who lead an active life seem to have less trouble than others who are less active. Sudden severe exercise, however, is bad if you are not used to it. It is better, and life saving, to take regular, moderate exercise. Women have less atheroma than men, until the menopause when they begin to catch up, so that hormones have something to do with it. Serious starvation, such as occurred in the German occupied territories of Holland and Scandinavia and in the concentration camps conferred one benefit—a freedom from atheroma, but obviously we cannot all starve, and the puzzle remains.

Aortic Disease.

Aortic Disease. The aorta, the main artery of the body, running from the left ventricle down through the chest and abdomen, also suffers from atheroma, but is too wide (about 2·5 cm across) to become obstructed. However, weaknesses occur in the thickness of its wall, sometimes due to syphilis but nowadays much more usually due to atheroma, which results in a ballooning out of a part of the vessel, rather like you sometimes see in an old bicycle inner tube. In days gone by these *aneurysms*, as the dilations are called, reached an enormous size, and would wear away the breastbone and ribs, to appear as large pulsating masses on the chest. Now that advanced syphilis is less common, atheromatous aneurysm, with a predilection for the abdominal aorta, is the one most commonly seen; and these days it is treated by replacement of the diseased portion of vessel. *Dissecting aneurysms* of the aorta are another variety in which the blood, under high pressure, somehow finds its way in between the layers of the aortic wall and then suddenly rips up and down the whole length of the vessel, separating (or dissecting) one layer from another in its path. Sometimes it tracks back towards the heart and suddenly fills the pericardium with blood to stop the heart's action altogether.

Embolism. This term refers to any object travelling in the circulation and becoming impacted when it reaches a vessel too small for it to pass through. It may be a thrombus (**Z30**), a collection of cancer cells, a group of bacteria, a chunk of infected pus from an abscess, a collection of fat droplets or even a bubble of air. If it originates in a vein it travels to the right heart and to the lungs. If it comes from the left heart or an artery, it will impact in any part of the arterial tree. Reasonably enough an arterial embolus will commonly end up in those parts of the body with the richest blood supply, like the brain, the kidneys, the liver or the bone marrow. A thrombotic embolus will cause death of the tissue in the area previously supplied by the blocked vessel, a condition known as *infarction*. Perhaps the commonest source of thrombotic embolism is the lining of the heart chambers where a thrombus has occurred at the site of muscle damaged by a heart attack.

Pulmonary Embolism. Cases of massive *pulmonary (lung) embolism* are usually the result of the thrombosis of the leg veins in people kept immobile following surgery or childbirth. That is why postoperative patients are got out of bed for a while as soon as the first day after the operation. The cells of a cancer embolus usually die; but if they survive, a new cancer deposit begins to grow where the embolus impacts, and this is one of the ways cancer may spread. An infected embolus may infect the vessel wall when it impacts, producing a weakness which may give way. Air embolism, if enough insoluble gas enters the circulation, can kill by making so much froth in the heart chambers as to impede the normal pumping action. If bubbles pass the lungs and enter the brain, all sorts of neurological disorders like scores of tiny strokes arise. The same sort of thing happens all over the body in the "*bends*" or "*caisson*" *disease*, in which nitrogen dissolved in the blood at high pressure, usually in deep-sea diving, bubbles out of solution if decompression is too rapid. Fat embolism sometimes occurs after fractures, due to marrow fat entering damaged veins and being carried away to the lungs.

Thrombosis. This is not quite the same as clotting. It is the mass which arises when platelets adhere to the lining of blood-vessels or heart chambers. Blood clot accumulates among layers of deposited platelets and the thrombus therefore has structure, unlike pure blood clot. Thrombosis usually occurs when the lining of the vessel or chamber is damaged by atheroma or inflammation, or when the circulation becomes very stagnant. One danger is that it will become dislodged and travel as an embolus during the first week or two days of its existence. After this time it is usually firmly incorporated into the vessel walls by cells which migrate into it from the surrounding tissue. The other danger is, of course, that the tissue previously supplied by the blocked vessel will die before a collateral circulation can be established. As previously explained, this is called infarction. All the technical terms in this section are used elsewhere and can be looked up.

Varicose Veins. When veins become swollen they also often become tortuous (wriggly), and particularly on the surface of the leg look very unsightly. They are, however, a sign of a sluggish circulation, and are often due to disease in small valves within the veins which normally prevent the blood from pooling backwards, down towards the feet. They are often a normal maternal accompaniment of pregnancy and disappear after the child is born. If allowed to persist, the sluggish circulation allows the formation of unpleasant ulcers, mainly in elderly people. Treatment is according to severity. In the early stages they are helped by supportive stockings. Later, often as an out-patient, the sufferer may have to have them removed or obliterated by a surgeon.

Raynaud's Disease. This is a strange condition in which the finger tips and in severe cases all the fingers or the whole hand respond in an exaggerated way to cold. The vessels supplying the hand are constricted and the fingers go white as the blood drains from them. Then the capillaries dilate and become distended and filled with blood. But owing to stagnation it is venous and blue, and the fingers are therefore blue. Now we have all experienced this in very cold weather, but sufferers from Raynaud's disease, nearly always women, respond even to very slight cold, like putting their hands into cold water. Even emotional stress will start the process off. In very severe cases the fingers will be so deprived of blood for so long, that sores will develop and fingers can even be lost, but this is very rare, and can be avoided by an operation to cut the nerves which supply the circular muscle of the vessels concerned. In most cases it is sufficient to avoid getting the hands cold.

Frostbite. Strictly speaking, this is literally a freezing of the tissues and usually only occurs at temperatures below −13° C. The patient may feel a pricking feeling at first, and feel an area of firmer, pale skin on the cheeks, nose, ears, fingers, or toes. If these parts are numb with cold, the onset of frostbite may not be felt, and will often only be noticed by others. In countries where extreme cold is prevalent, it is usual for complete strangers to stop each other in the street and point it out when they see it. It is important not to rub the affected part nor to apply direct heat in any form. Rapid warming can be harmful; rewarming by close application of body temperature is good treatment, *e.g.*, fingers can be firmly held in the armpit or a warm hand closely applied to an ear or a nose.

THE RESPIRATORY SYSTEM.

When air is drawn in during the process of breathing, it is brought into very close contact with the blood passing through the lungs. In this way the air we breathe in, which contains 21 per cent oxygen, is confronted with "spent" blood returning from the tissues which contains much less, and oxygen therefore diffuses into the blood from the air. At the same time, the waste gas, carbon dioxide, passes by diffusion in the reverse direction from the blood into the air, because there is much more carbon dioxide in the returning "spent" blood than the tiny amount in the air we breathe. The blood is therefore continually circulating through the lungs and exchanging carbon dioxide for oxygen from the air we breathe in. When we breathe out, we disperse the carbon dioxide into the atmosphere.

When the air enters the nose or mouth, it passes into the windpipe or *trachea*, through the vocal cords in the larynx. The trachea is held open all the time by rings of cartilage and is lined by a mucus-secreting membrane covered by millions of tiny "hairs" or cilia. These continuously waft a sheet of sticky mucus upwards, which traps any dust or other small particles we may have inhaled, until a collection of this material in the pharynx stimulates us to cough and expel the phlegm, usually to be swallowed. At its lower end, the trachea or windpipe divides into two, the right and left main *bronchus*. Each main bronchial tube enters a lung, one on each side, and proceeds to divide repeatedly within the lung until the air is being carried by more and more smaller and ever smaller tubes called *bronchioles*. There are many millions of these on each side, and each one ends in a collection of very small balloon-like structures —the air sacs or *alveoli*. If you were to cut across a lung and examine the cut surface in a good light, you would see that it is a spongy tissue, with many millions of tiny holes, each one just visible to the naked eye. These are the air sacs. In their walls run the blood capillaries, each one of which is a branch of the vessels carrying "spent" blood from the right side of the heart. At this stage, the blood is only separated from the air in the sacs by the walls of the capillaries and of the air sacs themselves. Both structures are extremely thin, making for easy diffusion of the gases between blood and air.

The action of breathing. This is achieved by two muscular mechanisms. One is by the muscles which move the ribs, and the other by the diaphragm, a sheet of muscle which runs across the body, separating the chest cavity from the abdominal cavity. These muscles are all actuated by nerves, just as all other muscles are. Those running to the muscles of breathing are organised by a mechanism in the brain known as the *respiratory centre*. It is this centre—one of the so-called vital centres of the brain—which receives information from many different sources, and translates it into instructions for the breathing mechanism. Thus, when you run for a bus, you will automatically breathe more deeply and more quickly because the respiratory centre has been informed about all the extra carbon dioxide in your blood which has been produced by the exercising leg muscles. Even the conscious instructions involved when you blow a trumpet, inflate a balloon, or during speaking, all pass first to the respiratory centre. It is the death of the cells of this and other vital centres of the brain that is the ultimate cause of death in everyone who dies.

Bronchitis may be acute or chronic. It is an inflammation of the lining mucous membrane of the larger air passages or bronchi, and results in much more secretion than the amount normally produced, mixed with some pus. The acute form is often caused by viruses, with "secondary" infection from bacteria. It may sometimes be caused by irritant gases, like the sulphur dioxide in smog. The chronic, or long-standing form of bronchitis is often associated with *emphysema*, in which the small air sacs of the lung architecture are destroyed or distorted, leaving larger spaces than normal, often surrounded by fibrous scar tissue. Such an arrangement makes the normal gaseous exchange difficult between air and blood. Smoking causes chronic bronchitis and emphysema, as well as lung cancer (see **Z33**). These illnesses can cause even more trouble than lung cancer since, instead of dying in a short time, these patients live for many years in chronic sickness.

Each year in the UK 6000 people die of bronchitis. It certainly is *not* smart to smoke. Patients cough, and produce varying amounts of sputum, or phlegm. They often wheeze like asthmatics. This may go on for many years before the right side of the heart begins to fail. Gradually, during this time, the chest tends to become barrel-shaped. Treatment consists of getting the patient to stop smoking or otherwise contaminating his lungs, preventing infection, particularly during winter months, with germ-killing antibiotics, and breathing exercises.

Smoking. Giving up smoking is a good idea at any stage. Using nicotine replacement gum, patches, or inhalers doubles the chance of successfully quitting. A nicotine-free drug, Zyban, is also available on prescription from your GP. Set a day to stop smoking and reinforce your resolve by telling your family and friends, or getting someone to give up with you. The NHS has a Smoking helpline 0800 169 0 169 on which you can speak to a specialist adviser.

Bronchial Asthma is a condition in which the finer air passages become constricted due to an allergic response. In addition, an increased secretion tends to obstruct them and the patient wheezes. In many cases it can be shown that he is allergic to a particular component of dust, or, less commonly, a foodstuff. This is the same sort of thing as occurs in the upper respiratory passages in hay fever, but the effect is on a different, lower part of the respiratory system. Many other cases are due to respiratory infection of some sort, probably combined with an allergy to the bacteria causing it. A predisposition to asthma is often inherited. Once a patient has become asthmatic, his attacks will be triggered off by such additional things as emotional stress, changes in temperature (particularly sudden cold), irritating fumes or smoke, and physical exertion. These are secondary factors, and although much of the treatment is concerned with them, it is unlikely that any of them is a sole cause of the condition. Treatment is directed at the relief of the breathing difficulty and of the wheezing, as well as the control of the causative factors. Many useful drugs are available to dilate the contracted air passages and reduce the obstructing secretions. Asthma in children often gets better as the patient grows up. Asthma is another condition made much worse by smoking.

A tiny living mite about 0·3 millimetres long exists in large numbers in nearly all mattresses and floor dust. This is the cause of much asthma, and in such cases it is often very helpful to vacuum clean mattresses and floors frequently.

The National Asthma Campaign has found that Britain has more asthma sufferers than any European country (and asthma is now our biggest childhood disease). The statistics are alarming. Over 8 million people have been diagnosed as asthmatic, 5·2 million receive treatment and 1,400 die each year in the UK.

Bronchiectasis. In this condition the bronchial air passages are abnormally and permanently dilated, and the normal structure of the walls destroyed. It is thought to be caused by obstructions of the tubes which lead to dilatation of the parts beyond. Secretions accumulate, and since they cannot easily drain away, they become infected. The infection helps to complete the process of destruction of structures in the bronchial wall. The patient has a chronic cough which often produces large quantities of purulent sputum, and there are often recurrent episodes of pneumonia.

In some cases, where the disease is localised to one part of the lung, it is often a good idea to cut out that portion, and this is particularly true in young people. Vigorous physiotherapy, involving drainage of the lungs by placing the patient in a suitable posture, together with antibiotic drugs for the infection, are other forms of treatment.

Cystic Fibrosis is an inborn disease which affects chiefly the lungs and the digestive system. It is sometimes called *Fibrocystic disease of the Pancreas*, and sometimes "mucoviscidosis".

Today, cystic fibrosis is known to be the commonest genetically determined disorder affecting children in Britain. One child in 2,000 receives one of the abnormal genes from each parent. Such a child therefore has a double dose of the harmful gene, and will have the disease from birth. One person in 25 of the general population carries only one of these abnormal genes, and such an individual will not have the disease, but will be a carrier of the abnormal gene. If such a seemingly normal carrier marries another carrier, there is a one in four chance of each of their children being affected. The children, therefore, who actually develop cystic fibrosis have inherited the disease *equally* from both parents, who are carriers, but are themselves unaffected by the disease.

The disease is inherited recessively and involves a defect in pumping salt across cell membranes, particularly in glands. The prospects for survival into reasonably healthy adult life are steadily improving, but they depend upon early diagnosis and careful management through childhood. In cystic fibrosis most of the damage is caused by the excessive viscidity, or stickiness, of the mucus which is produced in the breathing tubes as a lubricant, and also in the ducts of the pancreatic gland which provides enzymes to help digestion. Being thick and sticky, instead of thin and slimy as in the normal, this mucus tends to block the passages instead of keeping them clear. The pancreatic cells are permanently destroyed. The gland cannot secrete pancreatic enzymes, and the food, especially protein and fat, is not properly absorbed. This deficiency can be compensated fairly well by giving pancreatic extract by mouth with every meal, and by dietary care.

The major clinical problem is in the lungs. The lung passages normally have a thin coating of mucus which is propelled steadily upwards, and is completely renewed in less than one hour. It moves more suddenly on coughing. In cystic fibrosis this upward movement is slowed down and interrupted. There is difficulty in keeping the passages clear, especially when infection with bacteria or viruses greatly increases the amount of mucus. This results in intermittent blocking of the air passages, difficulty in breathing, incomplete use of the lungs, and persistent local pockets of infection. If such infectious processes are not controlled, areas of lung will be destroyed, chronic infection will persist, and multiple lung cavities will develop. These predispose to further infection, interfering with the natural development of the lung—a process not normally complete until halfway through childhood—thus adding to the respiratory problems which the child will face in later life.

Unless a correct diagnosis is made and proper treatment instituted before the first serious lung infection has occurred, the resulting lung damage may well be permanent.

Lung Transplantation can be done, using lungs from a donor who has died, or part of the lungs from each of two living donors. About half of lung transplant recipients are alive five years after this surgery.

Pneumonia. This is an infection of the lung tissue, rather than of the air passages. The lung is the only internal organ which is directly exposed to the air, and since there are germs of all kinds in the air, it is a source of surprise that pneumonia is not a much more common event in all of us. The answer lies, as with all infections, in the fact that it is not simply (or even mainly) bacteria which cause disease, but our own lack of resistance to them. If we allow germs to thrive and multiply by being unhealthy or run down or undernourished, infective disease will occur. If we are fit, the entry of those same harmful germs into the body causes us no inconvenience, unless we are very young, or very old, or unless the invasion of germs is abnormally overwhelming. This helps to explain why pneumonia is so often quoted as a cause of death. In most cases it is merely a terminal event occurring in the elderly sick, whose normal resistance is so far reduced by their illness that they succumb to an invasion which they would normally not notice. There are two main kinds of pneumonia, and in both the air sacs become filled with inflammatory secretions, making the normally porous lung tissue as solid as liver. In *lobar pneumonia*, a whole segment (or lobe) of the lung becomes solid. In *bronchopneumonia*, areas of lung tissue surrounding the smaller bronchioles become consolidated, leaving normal porous lung tissue in between. Bronchopneumonia is the one which occurs in the rather stagnant lungs of people who are already ill or bedridden. Both forms respond to treatment with the appropriate antibiotics, provided any underlying debility does not interfere with the patient's own resistance. In the terminal bronchopneumonia of fatal illness, it is sometimes considered kinder not to treat the additional pneumonia. *Pleurisy* is a natural complication, and before the days of antibiotic drugs *lung abscess* was very much feared. For another form of pneumonia—*viral pneumonia—see* **Z10(2)**.

Pneumoconiosis. This is a term which refers to a large group of different diseases, all of which are caused by breathing in some form of dust over a very long period of time. It is therefore an occupational hazard of certain trades. We have already mentioned the mechanisms of mucus secretion in the air passages which normally trap small particles from the air, and prevent them reaching the lung. However, in some occupations there is so much dust breathed in over the months and years that these normal barriers are defeated. About a quarter of the earth's crust consists of silicon, in quartz, flint, or sand. *Silicosis* occurs in people who have worked for many years in trades like mining, stone crushing, sandblasting, or metal grinding, who are often breathing silicon dust in high concentration. When the particles arrive in the air sacs, they set up an irritant chemical reaction which produces nodules of scar tissue. Silicosis for some reason predisposes to tuberculosis. Emphysema also occurs and there is a general impairment of respiratory function. Coalminer's pneumoconiosis is similar to silicosis but not identical with it. It is more prevalent in some coalfields than others, owing to the different composition of the dust to which these unfortunate men are daily exposed. It is hoped that modern mining methods will help to reduce this dread disease.

Asbestosis. Asbestos is a complex silicate of magnesium, calcium, and iron. *Asbestosis* is caused by inhaling its fine fibres, and often leads to the appearance of a type of lung cancer called mesothelioma. *Berylliosis* is caused by compounds of beryllium, used in the manufacture of fluorescent lamps. *Farmer's lung* is a pneumoconiosis caused by inhaling hay and grain dust, and is similar to *bagassosis* and *byssinosis* caused by sugar cane and cotton dust respectively. The newest pneumoconiosis to be reported is *mushroom worker's lung*, caused by something in the compost in which mushrooms are commercially grown.

Pulmonary Embolism. This catastrophic, yet quite common condition has already been briefly referred to (**Z30(1)**). It is a cause of tragic, sudden death in people who have had operations or have given birth to babies some days previously, or who have been bedridden for any other cause. The first event is that the blood in the veins of the legs becomes stagnant, due to the lack of exercise; and together with the tendency to clot which often follows surgery or childbirth, the whole length of a leg vein may be obstructed for twelve inches or more by an elongated clot of blood. This does little harm to the circulation of the leg, since there are plenty of other veins for returning blood to the heart. The danger is that the clot will become dislodged and be swept upwards towards the heart by the flow of returning blood. When this happens it is carried by way of the right atrium and ventricle into the pulmonary vessels which normally carry spent blood to the lungs. Here, for the first time, it enters vessels which are getting smaller as they divide, and it then impacts in the main pulmonary artery. The patient, who may have been recovering very well, suddenly collapses and not unusually dies there and then. At autopsy a long coiled-up mass of clot is found obstructing the pulmonary vessels. It often can be seen to form a cast of the leg vein and even bears the marks of the small venous valves which are present at its site of origin. With the dramatic advances being made in chest surgery, it is now sometimes possible in selected cases to operate to remove the clot. Thrombolysis, that is using injected drugs to dissolve clots, may also be used rather than pulmonary embolectomy. Three quarters of all cases of pulmonary embolism die within two hours, and therefore the best hope would be to prevent the occurrence altogether. This is not at present possible, but clotting in leg veins can be discouraged by early exercise following surgery and childbirth. Patients often resent having to get up the next day because it is so uncomfortable. Herein, however, lies their best hope of avoiding pulmonary embolism.

Haemoptysis. This means coughing up blood or blood-stained material. It must be distinguished from *haematemesis*, in which the blood is vomited from the stomach. It must always be taken seriously because of the underlying lung disease which may be present. No one who coughs up blood, in however small a quantity, should neglect to inform their doctor so that its source can be determined. Haemoptysis occurs in a variety of lung disease, some of which is not serious but much of which must be treated immediately if it is not to become so. This is a suitable place to repeat our general rule that you should see your doctor without delay if you have any unexplained bleeding from any part of the body, however well you feel. And this includes haemoptysis.

Fat Embolism. Liquid fat sometimes enters the bloodstream following extensive crush injuries to soft tissue and bone. It splits up into millions of small globules which are carried to the lungs, and impact in small blood vessels there, producing obstruction of the lung circulation and consequent difficulties in breathing.

Lung Cancer. This is one of the commonest and at present most incurable forms of cancer which can occur. It is also probably the easiest to prevent. Each year many thousands of people die of lung cancer in Great Britain. Although most are men, the toll among women is rising fast (around 12,000 in 2005, making lung cancer as great a killer as breast cancer). There has been no reasonable doubt for several years now that it is associated with cigarette smoking, and the evidence is overwhelming. However, in spite of this certain knowledge, smoking continues to increase, and every year there are more and more people dying unnecessarily of lung cancer (although it should be stressed not *all* lung cancer originates from smoking).

It seems that nothing the health authorities can do stops people smoking. Intensive campaigns of public advertising of the dangers, and well organised instruction in schools have so far made little impression whatever on the smoking habits even of people who accept the evidence.
In 1997 an EU report blamed *passive smoking* for causing the deaths of 20,000 persons annually across Europe. In Britain alone, around 7·3 million adults and 5 million children are regularly exposed to passive smoking at home.

Lung cancer grows in the wall of a main bronchial air passage. If it grows inwards it can obstruct the airway, choking that part of the lung it is supplying with air. This causes collapse and infection of the lung and may lead to *lung abscess*. The patient will then cough up blood-stained infected and purulent material. Such a case is comparatively lucky, since the disease declares itself early by producing symptoms. In others, the lump may grow outwards into the surrounding lung and produce no symptoms at all in the early stages. Indeed, it may spread to other parts of the body, like brain or bone or liver before causing any trouble to the patient. If this happens he may go to his doctor because of fits, changes of personality, or fracture, only to discover that the origin of the trouble is in the lung.

Cure rates are low, although much can be done to relieve the pain and suffering of the last stages of the illness. Survival rates vary from 16–53% at 5 years, depending on the type and severity of disease. Surgery, by removing the lung, and irradiation of the growth are the standard palliative treatment.

It is not the practice of the Medical Section to alarm the reader unnecessarily, but if only a few are induced to stop giving themselves such a horrible disease, then writing in this way will have been justified. Readers may wish to see the note on **Z31** on giving up smoking and are reminded that every year in Britain *c.* 114,000 smokers die (one fifth of all deaths). Most die of lung cancer.

Secondary Cancer of the Lung. In nearly all forms of cancer, the big problem is that it spreads to other parts of the body. If this were not so it could be eradicated by surgical removal more often than it is. One common way in which it spreads from any part of the body is by entering the bloodstream and being carried as clumps of living cancer cells to distant parts. When these come to rest in smaller blood vessels, they begin to grow and colonise the new environment. Such new colonies are called *secondary deposits* or *metastases*. It so happens that all veins (except portal veins of the liver) lead to the right heart and thence directly to the lungs, and for this reason the lungs are a very common site of *secondary* cancer, which may have begun in the bowel, or breast, or indeed anywhere else in the body.

Other common sites of secondary, blood-borne cancer are the brain, liver, bone marrow, and kidney, since all of them have an abundant blood supply, and there is therefore a high chance of the travelling cells arriving there. Secondary cancer of the lung usually consists of several lumps scattered throughout the lung. Lung cancer itself is usually only one growth. One of the main reasons for the success of early diagnosis is that treatment may be possible before blood-borne and other means of spread have occurred. Unfortunately, in the case of primary cancer of the lung, even early diagnosis is of little avail, but in many other common cancers permanent cure is possible if treatment is begun early enough.

Pleurisy. The chest is lined by one layer of a thin membrane called the *pleura*. The lungs are covered and enclosed by a second, continuous layer of this same membrane. When the lungs move during respiration, the pleura covering the lungs rubs against the pleura lining the chest, lubricated by a very thin layer of pleural fluid separating the two pleura. Whenever the pleural surface becomes inflamed, this is known as *pleurisy*. It is nearly always due to inflammatory disease of the adjoining lung, and is therefore not strictly a disease in its own right. For example, pneumonia, tuberculosis, lung cancer, or a lung infarct will produce a pleurisy if the area of diseased lung adjoins the lung surface. Sometimes the area of inflamed inner pleura will tend to stick to its outer layer or rub painfully against it, producing a sharp pain when the patient breathes.

Sometimes a large effusion of fluid is produced which separates the two layers and collapses the lung by occupying space in the chest which the lung should be occupying. This latter is more usual in tuberculosis or cancer.

The lung can be collapsed by the entry of anything between the normally adjacent layers of pleura, for example by accidental rupture of the lung with emphysema (q.v.). This condition is called *pneumothorax* or "air in the chest." Bleeding into the cavity between the pleura is called *haemothorax.*

THE DIGESTIVE TRACT AND LARGE INTESTINE.

Introduction.

The digestive tract consists of the mouth, pharynx, oesophagus (or gullet), stomach, small intestine, large intestine (or colon), rectum, and anus. The small intestine is very long, and is subdivided into the duodenum, jejunum, and ileum. It ends at the junction of the ileum with the caecum, where there is a small blind side-tube, the appendix. The caecum leads into the colon. The whole tract has two main mechanical functions and two main biochemical ones. Mechanically, food has to be chewed in the mouth and further minced up by muscular squeezing, mainly by the stomach. It has also to be propelled along by an orderly series of squeezing movements known as *peristalsis.* While it is still in the digestive tract, food has to be digested. That is to say, it has to be broken down chemically into suitable materials for absorption into the system, and secondly, it has to be absorbed across the wall of the intestine into the blood stream, itself a highly complex biochemical process. The blood stream it now enters is a special part of the circulation, the "portal" system, which travels directly to the liver without first passing to the heart. In the liver the broken-down foods are processed and issued in their new form into the general, or "systemic" circulation, by which they are finally carried to all the tissues of the body.

Alimentary Canal. As the food passes along the digestive tract (or alimentary canal), it is mixed with various secretions which are either made in the wall of the tract, or by organs outside the wall connected to the main pathway by small tubes. Examples of the latter are bile, manufactured by the liver and sent into the duodenum through the bile ducts; and pancreatic juice, which comes from the pancreas down the pancreatic ducts, also into the duodenum. These secretions are either digestive juices concerned with splitting up the foodstuffs so that they can be absorbed, or they have a lubricant so that the gut contents slide along easily under the influence of peristalsis. Roughly speaking, it may be said that digestive juices give place to lubricant secretions at the junction between the small and large intestine.

The constituents of the diet are dealt with in a later section. The principal classes with whose digestion we are now concerned are carbohydrates, proteins, and fats.

Carbohydrates are sugars and starches. There are many sugars, which may exist alone, in pairs, or with lots of them stuck together. Alone they are such things as glucose or fructose. Common table sugar is a substance called sucrose, formed by sticking one glucose molecule to one fructose molecule. Starch is lots of glucose molecules all stuck together. Digestion of carbohydrates consists of splitting up sugars and starch into single sugars like glucose, since only single sugars can be absorbed into the system. The splitting is done by digestive *enzymes* which are found in the juices secreted into the digestive tract. Sugar-splitters are found in the saliva of the mouth, in the pancreatic juice of the duodenum, and in the duodenum's own juice from its own wall. On the face of it, you might think it would be better to eat glucose which needs no digestion and can be absorbed in this form, than to eat starch which has first to be split; and so a lot of money has been made out of a gullible public by the sale of glucose drinks and powder. In fact digesting starch is no problem whatever, even for the sick, who can obtain their carbohydrate energy just as easily (and much

more cheaply) from potatoes as from expensive glucose. The end result of eating both is the same. The starch-splitting enzyme in saliva is mixed with the food as it is chewed, and it is therefore probably a good idea to chew it well. However, even if the food is bolted it does not seem to matter very much. People without teeth (neither their own nor dentures) seem to digest their carbohydrate quite well, presumably by means of their pancreatic juice at a later stage.

Proteins, which are found in meat, cheese, and eggs, are very large molecules consisting of lots of small ones strung together. Unlike starch, in which all the component glucose molecules are identical, the amino acids of which proteins are composed come in many different types. They all contain nitrogen, and there are about twenty-seven varieties. One protein differs from another in the proportions of the mixture and the order in which they are stuck together. Only single amino acids can be absorbed from the food, and so protein digestion again consists of splitting the material down into its building bricks. There is a strong protein-splitting enzyme in the gastric (or stomach) juice called pepsin, whose job it is to split the long amino-acid chains into shorter chains. Several other protein-splitters in the duodenal and pancreatic juice contrive to break the smaller chains into individual amino acids which are then absorbed and sent to the liver for processing.

Fats mainly consist of glycerol to which are attached three fatty acid molecules for each molecule of glycerol. An enzyme in pancreatic juice splits the fatty acids off the glycerol, but would have some difficulty penetrating the globules of fat without the help of bile. One of the constituents of bile (bile salts) has detergent properties like washing-up powder and breaks the fat globules up into a very fine emulsion so that the enzyme can get at the fat. Some fat particles of this size can even be absorbed as such, without preliminary splitting.

The processes by which all these enzymic secretions are produced are very finely controlled. They are very expensive to make in terms of energy and raw materials, and so it would be very wasteful to produce them all the time, even when there was no food to digest. And so the body has some very well designed automatic arrangements for sampling the foods as they are eaten and passed on, which ensure that exactly the right kind of juice is waiting in every part of the digestive tract for whatever food arrives. As soon as the food is digested the supply of enzymes is automatically switched off, so that there is very little waste of precious materials. It is, of course, beyond the scope of this account to describe the control mechanisms. Suffice it to say that they are operated partly by nerve reflexes which signal the imminent arrival of food, and partly by special hormones produced in various parts of the gut wall. The best secretion is affected even by psychological factors, so that pleasant company and surroundings, attractive appearance of the food, and an eager anticipation of it all make for good digestion and good health. These psychological factors are all capable of proper scientific investigation and proof. The poor health of those who habitually and irregularly bolt unpalatable food is probably due to such factors as these. So is the failure of appetite in the depressed, the anxious adult, or the scolded child.

Nearly all the digestion which has been described occurs in the stomach and upper part of the small intestine (the duodenum, jejunum, and upper ileum). Almost all absorption of the products of digestion occurs in the small intestine which is long and intricately folded to give it a large surface area for this purpose. The colon, or large intestine, is adapted for conserving water, by removing it from the residual waste material. This has then to be eliminated, and being rather dry its passage has to be lubricated by suitable secretions of mucus.

Constipation. For some people it is entirely normal only to pass motions about once or twice a week. For others the normal frequency is once or twice a day. What is abnormal? The answer is that the only thing worth worrying about is pronounced change of bowel habit, particularly in middle-aged and older people. By a change is meant a change from that individual person's normal routine. Such a pronounced change—either in the direction of constipation or diarrhoea—is worth consulting your doctor about if it persists for more than a week or two.

Constipation should be treated first by diet containing plenty of roughage—bran and oatmeal are excellent—plenty of stewed and fresh fruits, and at least 1½ litres of fluid should be taken daily. Failing that take a proprietary product prepared from senna pods. Never to be taken regularly are liquid paraffin, castor oil, preparations of aloes etc.

Oesophagus.

The oesophagus, or gullet, is more than a simple tube for taking the food from the mouth to the stomach. It is normally closed except when swallowing, and the act of swallowing is very complicated. When the material to be swallowed arrives in the back of the throat there is an automatic mechanism which opens the top end of the oesophagus to receive it, and from then onwards everything happens automatically. The next portion of the tube opens and the top closes strongly, so that the food (or drink) is propelled forcibly down the next segment. Then the part below this relaxes and the material is squeezed further downwards and so on until it arrives in the stomach.

This squeezing (or milking) action is similar to the action known as peristalsis which propels contents in other parts of the gut. Thus when you see someone swallowing a glass of beer very quickly in warm weather, it is not going "down the hatch" under the influence of gravity, however much it may look like it. It is perfectly possible to swallow the same, or any other liquid, standing on your head. Getting into that position is the only difficult part. Sometimes this complicated swallowing mechanism gets out of order, leading to difficulties of swallowing, or dysphagia.

Hiatus Hernia. Another disorder known as hiatus hernia occurs at the lower end of the oesophagus as it meets the stomach. At this point the oesophagus has to pass through the diaphragm, the sheet of muscle which separates the chest from the abdomen. The muscular fibres of the diaphragm are normally arranged in a ring around the oesophagus. These help to keep the lower end shut, so that the acid contents of the stomach do not regurgitate upwards, causing inflammation (oesophagitis) or heartburn. A hiatus hernia is when muscle fibres get slack, and the upper end of the stomach can even slide upwards into the chest. People with hiatus hernia get heartburn after meals, and particularly when they bend down or lie down. Except for very severe forms, which need surgical repair, the treatment is to eat less at a time, reduce the acidity with a suitable antacid and reduce weight so that the weight of the abdomen does not press upwards so much.

Cancer of the Oesophagus.

The other disease of the oesophagus, quite unrelated to the above, is cancer of the oesophagus, the cause of which is still unknown in most cases. When cancer occurs in the wall of any tube, it will often encircle the tube and gradually narrow the way through. This is what happens in the oesophagus, leading to difficulty in swallowing, particularly solids. It is a condition usually, of rather elderly men, although it is sometimes associated with a special form of severe anaemia in women.

Treatment is in some way to keep the passage open, either by transplanting a new tube, or more usually, by removing the constricted piece and joining up the remainder.

The Stomach and Duodenum.

By far the commonest diseases of the stomach and duodenum are gastric ulcer and duodenal ulcer. They are actually the same condition in two different sites and are often classed together as peptic ulcer or acid-peptic disease. The ulcers, which are rather like sores on the lining of the stomach or duodenum, may be "acute" or "chronic." Acute ulcers tend to be small and there are often several of them. Chronic ulcers are usually single. They may be small, or they may be several centimetres across. Chronic ulcers smoulder for months and even years, like a sore which will not heal, and a great deal of scar tissue forms in their depths. Thus they may in time erode their way right through the wall of the stomach, destroying all its layers, and begin to eat into surrounding structures like the pancreas or liver. The fact that they do not perforate more frequently is due to all the fibrous scar tissue which is formed during the slow eroding process. Healing of such a destructive ulcer is nevertheless common, and the great problem is how to help the natural healing process to win against the ulcer's tendency to erode.

Treatment of Ulcers.

Ulcers are very commonly associated with the bacterium Helicobacter pylori, which may be the cause of ulcers. Appropriate treatment to eradicate this organism is an important part of ulcer therapy. This extremely common affliction is confined to the human species and has been known since the earliest times. It does not vary very much with diet or with social class. Although occurring at all ages, it usually begins between the ages of twenty and forty, and is most commonly found in men between forty-five and fifty-five. Gastric ulcer is four times, and duodenal ulcer ten times more common in men than in women. It is always due to an inability of the lining to stand up to the normal digestive activity of the stomach contents. These are normally acid and contain a powerful enzyme for digesting proteins. Again it is perhaps more surprising that we all do not digest our own stomachs, rather than that some unfortunate people do digest small areas slowly. In certain abnormal conditions when the stomach stops making acid, ulcers always heal. However, some ulcers occur without excessive secretion of acid and many heal without the acid being neutralised with antacids.

Symptoms of Peptic Ulcers.

All this points to the main trouble being in the response of the lining to acid rather than to the acid itself. Nevertheless, the most effective treatment at present known involves regulating gastric secretion, and particularly its acidity. It is also known that peptic ulcers are more common in people whose occupations involve administrative and professional responsibility, competitive effort and nervous tension, long periods of anxiety or frustration. Presumably the higher nervous system influences these events by the same nerves, which normally help to control secretion.

The main symptom of peptic ulcer is pain, and this usually responds well to proper doses of antacids. Many different varieties are available and a lot of money is made from selling them. When indigestion persists for longer than a few days it is always better to see your doctor so that a proper diagnosis can be made and the best remedies begun. Many other causes exist for similar pains, and you should not try to make the diagnosis yourself. It may be necessary to analyse your gastric secretions in the hospital laboratory. Almost certainly you will have a special X-ray examination, and since the stomach cannot easily be seen on a normal X-ray, they will have to show it up by making you drink a white material containing barium. This will be seen as a silhouette of the stomach and duodenal contents. Searching for an ulcer this way is a highly skilled matter and is performed by doctors specially trained in radiology.

Until recently, no drugs capable of influencing the course of peptic ulcer in any significant manner were available and the physician had to rely on general measures, such as rest, diet and the administration of antacids to relieve pain and discomfort; episodes of acute haemorrhage were not uncommon and required surgical intervention if life were threatened.

Endoscopy. Most ulceration in the stomach and all in the duodenum is due to bacterial infection, *Helicobacter Pylori*. This damages the intestinal wall and makes damage from the stomach's own acid inevitable. Eradication cures the disease, although re-infection may occur. The gastro-enterologist can now pass a *flexible* instrument, the *gastroduodenal endoscope* (the gastroscope is a *rigid* tube), under mild sedation through the patient's gullet and into the stomach and duodenum and view the lesions directly. Once an ulcer is diagnosed, the time has come to stop treating yourself with antacids from the chemist's counter, and to take the ones your doctor decides are best. Smoking should be stopped by ulcer patients because it inhibits healing.

Alcohol tends to increase acid secretion and should be avoided. It is also *extremely important* to avoid taking any form of aspirin, even in quite small amounts, since this can lead to very serious bleeding from the ulcer. The ulcer patient should be warned that hundreds of proprietary preparations contain aspirin and all of them are dangerous for him. Search for the formula in small print on the label before taking any remedy, looking particularly for acetylsalicylic acid—the systematic name for aspirin. Some of the patients with "upset stomach" are, of course, ulcer patients, and some even die of haemorrhage following the ingestion of aspirin.

Complications of Peptic Ulcers.

The main complications of peptic ulcer are bleeding, perforation, and a narrowing of the pylorus, or lower part of the stomach (*pyloric stenosis*). Bleeding is caused by the eroding ulcer eating away at one of the many blood vessels in the stomach or duodenal wall. It leads to the passing of "altered" blood in the stool (*melaena*), or to the vomiting of blood (*haematemesis*). When the initial bleeding occurs, the patient may feel suddenly faint, and a little later will notice the black, tarry colour of his stool. This is sometimes confused with a similiar colour when the patient is taking iron. Peptic ulcer is not the only cause of this very serious haemorrhage, which constitutes a hospital emergency whatever its cause. The treatment, like that of every large haemorrhage, is blood transfusion which must be continued until the bleeding stops, or until the patient is sufficiently fit for surgery, should that be deemed necessary.

Perforation is perhaps the most serious complication of peptic ulcer, leading to the spilling of stomach contents within the abdominal cavity. Treatment is invariably surgical, either the closure of the perforation or the partial removal of the stomach.

Surgical removal of part of the stomach is often the only way to treat a peptic ulcer which has had its chance to heal in other ways. It is tempting for the patient to "have it out and done with," but the time for surgery is a matter of fine judgment. So many ulcers heal by medical means if you give them a chance, and operations are for those which persistently refuse, or which become complicated.

Stomach Cancer. The stomach is a fairly common site for primary cancer. There is no known reason for this, and it is particularly impor-tant to stress that we know of no connection whatever between the peptic ulcers which have just been discussed and cancer. Stomach cancer used to be the commonest cancer of men, but the current rise of lung cancer has pushed it into second place. There are some strange geographical differences in its distribution. For example, it is much commoner in Japan and Scandinavia than in England or the USA. It is difficult to see any reason for this in dietary habits. In Wales it causes three times as many deaths as in South-East England. All this is very puzzling, as is so much of our information about cancer generally. One of the main problems with stomach cancer is that it often causes the patient no inconvenience and thus produces no symptoms of note until the disease is far advanced and it is difficult to do much.

Treatment is by the surgical removal of the growth, and even in the most advanced cases a great deal can often be done to make the patient more comfortable.

The Small Intestine.

The small intestine runs from the stomach to the caecum and comprises the duodenum, jejunum, and ileum in that order. On a more cheerful note it may be remarked that it is very rarely the site of cancer. Its main problems arise in connection with defects in absorption mechanisms, with obstructions, and with a strange inflammatory condition known as *regional enteritis*. Most obstructions are due not to blockages of the tube, but to failures of peristaltic propulsion, the process which is briefly described above under "oesophagus." Such a failure is called *ileus*. When peristalsis stops for any reason, the result is severe dehydration and loss of important chemicals like sodium and chloride from the body. This is because about 9 litres of fluid enter the small intestine each day in the form of digestive juices, and all of this has to be pushed onwards to be reabsorbed into the system at lower levels. If peristalsis fails, this bulk of fluid remains in the small intestine, or is vomited. In both cases it is lost to the body itself, leading to serious dehydration and illness. Treatment is by very careful replacement by transfusion of the fluid and the chemicals lost, and by removal of the trapped fluid within the intestine through a tube threaded down through the mouth.

Regional Enteritis or **Ileitis** is sometimes known as **Crohn's Disease**. It is a very mysterious condition in which the normally supple wall of the small intestine becomes inflamed and gradually replaced by thick fibrous scar tissue, so that it looks and feels like a thick garden hose. Loops of inflamed gut stick together, and channels open between them, and if the disease progresses a mass of adherent, thickened intestine results to which everything in the neighbourhood also adheres. However, for some unknown reason some cases do not progress downhill in this way and get better spontaneously. Surgical treatment is necessary for the majority, however, particularly those with advanced disease leading to complications such as obstruction or perforation. Sometimes an early case can be resolved by cutting out the length of affected gut, although recurrences are unfortunately common.

Appendicitis. This must be one of the best-known surgical diseases of the intestinal tract. The appendix is a narrow, blind-ended side tube attached to the caecum near the end of the small intestine. Appendicitis is when it becomes obstructed, or infected, or both. From its position it is almost predictable that it will get obstructed sooner or later by pieces of faecal matter which pass its entrance and which are normally infected. The surprising thing is that it does not happen more often. Once this has occurred, however, a closed abscess forms, and as the abscess distends the appendix, it first weakens its wall, making it gangrenous, and then bursts into the abdominal cavity causing *peritonitis* (*see later*). It would be useless and misleading to describe the symptoms of acute appendicitis in detail, since it is difficult even for experienced doctors to distinguish them from those of several other conditions. Suffice it to say that any severe, persisting pain in the abdomen, whether continuous or intermittent, whether associated with diarrhoea or not, should lead the sufferer to a doctor for a quick diagnosis. Germ-killing antibiotics are useless against appendicitis, and any laxative is extremely dangerous as it may cause an acutely inflamed appendix to perforate.

The Large Intestine or Colon.

The two main serious diseases of the colon are ulcerative colitis and cancer in its various forms.

Ulcerative Colitis is yet another mysterious disease in which severe ulceration of the lining of the colon gives rise most frequently to diarrhoea with the passage of blood and mucus. In fact it can be like dysentery, and it has often been considered to be due to some form of infection. Unfortunately no particular germ can routinely be found in these cases, and the situation is endlessly confused by the presence in the normal bowel of lots of different germs anyway. Nevertheless the ulcerated lining of the bowel certainly does get infected by the germs normally present, and this makes the disease worse. Therefore germ-killing antibiotics are often helpful in alleviating symptoms and can lead to an earlier settling down of the condition, although not to a cure. It has long been known that certain kinds of psychological upset are often associated, but here again the disease is so unpleasant for the sufferer that he is to be forgiven some despondency as a result of, rather than as a cause of, his troubles. It is also suspected that ulcerative colitis may be an auto-immune disease; that is it may represent rejection by the patient of his own colonic lining in a manner somewhat comparable to the tissue rejection which often follows organ transplantation.

Some of the more alarming complications are perforation through the wall of the ulcerated bowel, and sometimes massive haemorrhage occurs. Treatment is with sulphasalazine or drugs derived from it, together with diet and the occasional use of other drugs to minimise symptoms. Surgery may be required to relieve obstruction, deal with perforation, remove affected parts of the bowel, *etc.*

Cancer of the Colon and Rectum. This is

another very common form of cancer, which can often be completely cured by surgical removal of the growth provided it is caught in the early stages before it has spread. The commonest symptom is a change in bowel habit, either towards constipation or, more often, towards diarrhoea, in the second half of life. There may be rectal bleeding, or the passage of mucus, and there may be abdominal pain. We cannot too often repeat that any such change of bowel habit, or any unexplained bleeding, should lead the patient promptly to his doctor.

Bowel cancer is the second most common cause of cancer death in the UK (after lung cancer). Today there are around 16,000 deaths annually. In 2006 a new initiative offered everyone in the UK over the age of 65 screening for bowel cancer.

Diverticulitis. Some people have small pockets or sacs in the wall of the colon known as diverticula. A minority of these sometimes get inflamed, and this is *diverticulitis*. Occasionally perforation occurs.

Hernia or Rupture. This is a condition in

which abdominal contents, usually a loop of intestine, protrude forwards through the muscular wall of the abdomen. The wall consists of a sheet of muscle fibres running in several directions. They normally become tense when we cough, or strain, or in getting up from a recumbent position. There are places in the groin on each side where there is a way through the muscle for the spermatic cord in the male. In many men a weakness can arise at this point, and if it persists, the way through may enlarge and allow loops of bowel to emerge from behind the muscle sheet to appear as a lump under the skin of the groin. On relaxation the lump can be made to disappear by pushing the contents back the way they came; and they will re-emerge when the patient strains. This is an extremely common complaint in men, and it should be treated by an operation in which the muscle wall is repaired.

Strangulated Hernia is the term used when the muscle tightens around the neck of the protruding loop of bowel, cutting off its blood supply. From then onwards the loop becomes gangrenous and the intestine is obstructed by having a part of itself nipped outside the abdominal wall. The patient is in severe pain, vomits continuously, and quickly is liable to get into such a poor condition that surgical relief is difficult. It is therefore a surgical emergency, and it would have been better to have had the relatively simple repair operation earlier and at leisure. Hernia in the region of the groin is of two types: *inguinal hernia* and *femoral hernia*, the difference between them being technical and of no consequence to the patient. They nearly always occur in men.

Incisional Hernia is when the muscle wall has been weakened at the site of an old abdominal operation and has failed to heal properly.

Umbilical Hernia occurs owing to the natural weakness of the abdominal wall at the navel, and is so common in babies as to be almost normal. When a baby cries and thereby puts a strain on his abdominal wall, a lump often appears in the region of the navel, and this can be very alarming for the parents. They should of course show it to their doctor who will nearly always be able to reassure them. It is self-healing without operation in the majority of cases.

Peritonitis. The cavity of the abdomen in which the intestines and other organs lie is called the peritoneal cavity, and it is lined by a thin membrane called the peritoneum. When this becomes inflamed the condition is a serious one and is called *peritonitis*. Inflammation may be bacterial, as occurs following a burst appendix and the spillage of bacteria and pus in the cavity. It may be a sterile peritonitis as often follows perforation of a peptic ulcer, when the inflammation is caused by the acid contents of the stomach. It is always very dangerous, probably because of the large surface area afforded by the peritoneum for the absorption of inflammatory toxins.

Haemorrhoids are simply varicose veins in the rectal and anal regions. They are very common, and are caused probably in about equal degrees by inherited weakness of the veins, strain such as heavy lifting, and constipation (this is one of the very few conditions in which constipation may do some damage, due to the mechanical pressure of hardened faeces in the rectum on the veins).

Pregnant women may develop haemorrhoids or "*piles,*" as they are commonly called, owing to the pressure of the baby's head in the pelvis.

Haemorrhoids may be external or internal, the former being in the anal region below the sphincter, the latter in the rectum; the two usually go together. There may be no symptoms, but the veins are liable to bleed, to get thrombosed (*i.e.*, a clot forms within) or to become infected. When clotting or infection occurs the piles enlarge and tend to be pushed out through the anus during defaecation, when they form extremely painful external swellings. Treatment in simple cases may be by the use of suppositories—cones of a firm grease containing suitable medicaments which are inserted in the rectum—in other cases the veins may be injected, as with varicose veins of the leg, in order to close them, but when there is much bleeding, thrombosis, infection, or interference with bowel movements they should be removed surgically.

THE LIVER.

The liver is a very large organ and has such a wide variety of known functions (to say nothing of the unknown) that it is also one of the most complicated. Nearly all of its functions are biochemical, and it is often called the laboratory of the body. Medical students, when asked to enumerate the functions of the liver, usually stick at about twenty-five, nearly all of them to do with general metabolism: that is the biochemical processing of substances taking part in structure or as body fuel. For example, the liver makes proteins from the amino-acids absorbed from the gut, and breaks down amino-acids and manufactures a waste product (urea) from them. It stores carbohydrates as glycogen, and conducts many of the processes necessary to turn carbohydrates into energy. It manufactures prothrombin with the help of vitamin K, and this is essential for blood clotting. It makes bile and secretes it into the gall bladder and bile ducts (see later). The three main constituents of bile (cholesterol, bile pigment or bilirubin, and bile acids) all have to be processed, or metabolised, in the liver during the production of bile. Vitamin B_{12} and iron are also stored and dealt with there, and these are involved in preventing various forms of anæmia (q.v.); and in addition to all these things the liver is the place where harmful substances, both from within the body and from outside it, are dealt with and rendered harmless. This last function of "detoxication" is often accomplished by making the offending molecules suitable for rapid excretion by the kidneys, or by altering their chemical shape to make them harmless.

Nearly all of these very different things are done by one single type of cell: the liver cell, and it is one of the remarkable features of the design that this cell can be so versatile. There also have to be some very efficient transport systems in the liver, in addition to the usual blood supply and venous drainage possessed by all other tissues.

The Portal Venous System.

One of these is the "portal venous system." Whenever a substance is absorbed across the gut wall from any part of the intestine into the interior of the body it enters the special draining blood vessels of the portal system, which are arranged throughout the length of the digestive tract. All these veins eventually unite in the main portal vein which enters the liver. Everything absorbed from the gut is therefore taken first to the liver to be processed. After this the products are carried away from the liver in the ordinary veins to the heart, and are distributed to the rest of the body by the arterial system. The liver has arteries of its own by which it receives oxygen and nutriment like any other tissue. The fourth transport system collects the bile as it is formed within the liver and delivers it to the gall bladder and bile ducts, which eventually drain it into the duodenum.

Portal Hypertension means high blood pressure in the portal venous system, and is the usual accompaniment to cirrhosis (see later). When the terminations of the portal veins in the liver are strangled and obstructed by cirrhotic disease, this tends to blow them up, or dilate them with blood. There is a natural escape route for the portal blood where the lower end of the oesophagus or gullet joins the upper end of the stomach. At this place some of the portal veins draining the stomach are connected with the ordinary veins draining the oesophagus so that when pressure rises in the portal system, blood

tends to be diverted into these connecting veins, and they in turn become dilated, or varicose. Trouble begins when these dilated connecting veins, which bulge inwards into the oesophagus, are damaged by food particles passing across them and bleed severely into the stomach. The patient vomits large quantities of blood (haematemesis) or passes tarry altered blood in the stool (melaena). The other main cause of these is the bleeding which occasionally accompanies peptic ulcer (q.v.).

Ascites is a second complication of portal hypertension (and hence of cirrhosis) Large amounts of a lymph-like fluid accumulate in the abdominal cavity. The fluid contains a great deal of precious protein and salt which is lost to the body economy. Ascites also sometimes accompanies cancerous deposits in the abdomen.

Jaundice means being yellow because there is too much yellow bile pigment circulating in the blood, and there are three main possible causes for this. The term "yellow jaundice," like "gastric stomach" is therefore unnecessarily redundant: there is no other kind.
Bile pigment comes from broken-down red blood cells, which normally come to the end of their time after existing for about 120 days. The breakdown products of red cells can always be found in the blood of normal people, but there is normally insufficient colour to show. Abnormal amounts of colour build up quite logically in any of the following three circumstances:

(1) If too many red cells are being destroyed and even the normal liver cannot deal with the amount of bile pigment produced, it piles up in the blood, and haemolytic jaundice is the result. The expression simply means jaundice due to (abnormally large) red-cell destruction.

(2) If the liver cells are themselves sick and unable to cope with the normal amounts of pigment from normal red-cell destruction. Here too the pigment will pile up and cause hepatocellular jaundice, or liver-cell jaundice.

(3) If the bile ducts carrying bile away from the liver are blocked, then bile will pile up behind the blockage and re-enter the blood stream, causing obstructive jaundice. In this case the rate of red-cell breakdown is normal, and the liver cells are normal: at least for a time.

It is enormously important for the treatment of jaundice for the doctor to diagnose its type correctly, since the treatment varies from surgical relief of obstruction to the medical treatment of viral infection or of excess red-cell destruction.
The so-called differential diagnosis of jaundice is often exceptionally difficult, and sometimes requires some very sophisticated laboratory tests and X-rays. At other times it is extremely easy and is obvious from a cursory glance at the urine and the stool. In any case all jaundice is a highly technical matter for the doctor who must be consulted early.

Neonatal Jaundice. There is a special jaundice of newborn babies which resembles haemolytic jaundice and can occasionally have serious consequences for the developing brain (kernicterus) if it is allowed to become too severe. When this is threatened, steps are taken to reduce the level of circulating bile pigment by replacement of the baby's blood or by other means.
The commonest cause of hepatocellular jaundice is infective or viral hepatitis. Obstructive jaundice is usually due either to blockage by gallstones (q.v.) or a lump pressing on the bile ducts from an adjacent cancer. This can often be quite satisfactorily relieved by surgery.

Infective Hepatitis. See **Z10(1).**

Cirrhosis. There are many different kinds of cirrhosis, the commonest of which has already been mentioned under *portal hypertension* above. In all cases, liver cells are slowly poisoned and are killed off over a long period of time. In response to this, the surviving liver cells undergo cell division, trying to make good the numbers lost, and at the same time fibrous scar tissue replaces the damaged tissue throughout the organ. The result is a hard, knobbly liver. The many "knobs" are spherical areas of regenerated new cells, and they are separated by thickened bands of scar tissue. All of this destroys the normal architecture and leads to the portal hypertension and ascites mentioned above. In some countries (*e.g.*, France and the United States) excessive alcohol is the main cause of the original liver damage which starts it all off. In others (*e.g.*, Bantu South Africa) it seems to be nutritional starvation of the liver. In England much less than half the cases are due to alcohol, and many are thought to be due to a previous episode of infective hepatitis (*q.v.*), but this is not certain. Infective hepatitis is quite common but cirrhosis is comparatively rare. So that the great majority of people do not progress from one to the other. One treatment for advanced cirrhosis is to replace the liver by transplantation, but there are still problems to overcome before this can become routine.

Cancer of the Liver. Cancer of the liver is quite common, but it is nearly always cancer which has spread in the blood stream from other parts of the body. The liver is a favourite site for such secondary deposits, since it has a large blood supply and will receive a generous helping of anything being carried. It is also a very "fertile soil" for the cancer seedlings to grow in. Primary cancer of the liver is uncommon, and only occurs in a few cases of pre-existing cirrhosis.

Gallstones. These are "stones" formed by some of the major constituents of bile coming out of solution and forming solid bodies. They are very common, and often cause no trouble at all. When they do, it is usually a colicky intermittent severe pain. This is due to the muscular walls of the bile passages contracting in an effort to expel an obstructing stone into the duodenum. The second common trouble arising from gallstones is obstructive jaundice, described above. It is small consolation to gallstone sufferers that the stones are often very pretty. If they contain calcium they will be visible on an X-ray. Otherwise they are not seen. Stones often occur in conjunction with inflammation of the gall bladder, known as *cholecystitis*. The treatment for gallstones is to remove them surgically together with the gall bladder if they are causing persistent symptoms. Also, a flexible endoscope can be passed into the intestine and a tiny wire basket passed from it into the bile system to remove stones. Twenty years ago, if you had an operation to remove your gall bladder you would have been in hospital for around two weeks. Today, the same operation can be done with keyhole surgery in the morning and you can go home the same day.

The Pancreas is a soft, elongated gland lying behind the stomach; it is *c.* 12·5 cm long and 5 cm wide. Within its tissues lies the duct, which, when it leaves the pancreas, passes into the duodenum near the point of entry of the bile-duct. This duct transmits the juices containing enzymes which aid in the digestion in the small intestine. The pancreas, however, has two main functions: not only does it manufacture these important digestive juices, but in certain specialised areas, known as the islets of Langerhans, it makes insulin, the hormone which makes it possible for the body to utilise sugar.

Diabetes Mellitus (or ordinary diabetes) is a chronic disorder usually caused by a deficient secretion of insulin. The unused sugar accumulates in the blood and acts as a poison, which, in extreme cases, sends the patient into coma and may—indeed, in former times, usually did—result in death. The treatment of diabetes was revolutionised by the discovery of the hormone insulin by Banting and Best in 1921. On the whole, diabetes is more severe in young people than in the elderly, but with correct treatment it is possible for all cases to lead a perfectly normal life except for dietary restrictions and insulin injections. Not to be confused with *Diabetes insipidus* (*q.v.*). The main problem with diabetes mellitus now is that the wrong (albeit slightly) blood sugar levels that are found even with good therapy eventually damage small blood vessels, leading to problems with the eyes, peripheral nerves and kidneys. Diabetes is discussed in greater detail on Z63.

Pancreatitis is a condition where the pancreatic enzymes start digesting the pancreas itself. It may be caused by stones blocking the duct these secretions normally leave the pancreas by, but alcohol is a common cause. It can be a very serious illness.

DIET AND OBESITY.

When considering diet, and the effect it has on our health and well-being, there is more to it than just the things we eat. We must also know about what our body does with the food, and it would be unscientific not to acknowledge the effects of our psychological make-up and our nutritional beliefs on what we eat, what we do with it, and how well (or ill) we feel as a result. We must remember too that, in the Western world, problems of obesity threaten to develop into an epidemic of alarming proportions.

Basic Constituents of Diet.

The basic constituents of any diet are protein, fats, carbohydrates, water, vitamins, minerals, salts, and indigestible roughage (fibre). All are chemicals whose structure and function are reasonably well understood. Even the mystical differences between fine table wines, so beloved of the connoisseur and gourmet, are reasonably well understood in chemical terms. Perhaps that is a pity.

Much nonsense is talked, even by some nutritionists, about minimal daily requirements. In general terms, however, requirements can be described in terms of how many calories there are in the total intake of proteins, fats, and carbohydrates per day, and how these are distributed between the three classes of food. The other substances mentioned above are only required in trace or small amounts except for water; and roughage is only required to aid bowel movement stimulus.

The Process of Digestion.

During the process of digestion (described earlier) all proteins are split into their constituent amino acids; all carbohydrates are split into their constituent simple sugars and most fats are converted into fatty acids and glycerol. At this stage, and not until this stage, all these simpler building bricks derived from the three classes of food are absorbed into the body proper, and taken to the liver and other tissues. Here they are "metabolised." That is to say they are either burned as fuel for the various processes of the body; or they are built up again into proteins, fats, and carbohydrates of the special kinds the body needs. They will either be used to rebuild structures suffering ordinary wear and tear or they will be stored. Many of them will be converted into a different class from the one they came from when they entered the body. For example, excess carbohydrate is converted into fat; or if there is a shortage of carbohydrate, some will be made out of the protein amino-acids which would normally have been used for tissue growth and repair. Thus it is only a generalisation to say that dietary carbohydrates are fuel and proteins are for building bodily structure. The body can convert one into the other, and spoil the calculation.

Diet and Energy.

There is a great deal of confusion in people's minds about *energy*, and that is why the word *fuel* has been used above in connection with carbohydrates. The lay person uses energy as a term meaning something which allows us to leap about, running and jumping and skipping and dancing, and which keeps us from getting tired and run down. Thus, the food industry tells us, we need potatoes or breakfast cereals for these activities or for a hard day's work. This is a deliberate commercial confidence trick, and the scientist is largely to blame. He originally handed out the word energy to an eager food industry and an unsuspecting public, forgetting to explain that he meant it in the strictly scientific sense of fuel for bodily processes. It simply is not true that more potatoes, or more cornflakes will make you more active. Indeed the reverse is the case, and after a certain point they will only be converted into fat and reduce your activity The nutritionist measures energy as calories, which are units of heat, and it is certainly true that you must eat enough of these each day if you wish to remain alive, let alone active.

The Well-Balanced Diet.

All the three main classes of food provide calories, and in an ordinary well-balanced diet about 15% are provided by protein. Carbohydrates produce most of the remainder. Each gram of fat contains about twice the calories of a similar quantity of carbohydrate. We simply eat less fat than carbohydrate, because fat has a "high satiety value." It takes away the appetite for more. Proteins are mostly found in meat, fish, eggs, cheese, and milk. However, there is quite a lot of protein in many predominantly starchy foods like bread, and such grains as wheat, rice, and corn. Carbohydrates are mainly found in bread, potatoes, sugar, pastry, sweets, and so forth. That is one of the words which fortunately seems to be used by both scientists and laymen in much the same sense.

Some substances are absolutely essential to the body if life is to continue, even if they are only needed in trace amounts. These are substances which the body's own factories (like the liver) cannot make for themselves, even if they are provided with the correct ingredients.

Vitamins.

One group of such substances are the *vitamins*. Some of these are found in predominantly fatty foods (milk, butter, cheese and so on) and are known as the fat-soluble vitamins—Vitamins A, D, E and K; the others are water-soluble—the Vitamin B group and Vitamin C. All have now been chemically identified, are manufactured and can be bought over a pharmacist's counter. The myth has grown up that if a little is good for one then a lot more will be better and there are a great many vitamin enthusiasts who consume vast quantities of such manufactured products in the belief that by doing so they will induce extra vitality and energy. Unless your diet is unbalanced in some way (a vegetarian diet may be grossly deficient in Vitamin B₁₂) you will not need extra vitamins.

Fortunately, most people buy food because they like it, not because it does them good; and provided they have normal dietary tastes they will usually get a perfectly adequate selection of the things we have spoken of as necessary for good health. The main danger in England is to have a surfeit and become overweight. In addition there are certain times of life when conscious attention should be paid to what is necessary.

For example babies and nursing mothers have special dietary needs and will hear about them from their Health Visitor or from their Welfare Clinic or Doctor.

Popular Attitudes and Knowledge.

Recent surveys have revealed some interesting facts about people's attitude to food and their knowledge of it. For example, half the people asked knew that meat was a source of protein, a third mentioned eggs and a fifth cheese, fish, and milk. But practically no one knew there was protein in bread. Yet in England about a fifth of our daily protein intake comes from bread, and nearly a third from cereals as a whole. Fish is well known as a source of protein, but did you know that on average we only obtain 4% of our daily protein from fish—less than we get from potatoes (5%)? No one seems to know that potatoes are an important source of vitamin C, although fruit and vegetables are well-known sources. Calcium is recognised in milk, but most people forget its presence in cheese. Most people are very confused about iron. Why does everyone think it is mainly in green vegetables, when these are really such a poor source? For our daily requirement of iron we would each have to eat 1 kg spring greens or peas; or 2 kg. of sprouts! In fact meat provides one of our best sources; one-fifth of our daily needs is contained in bread.

The Problem of Obesity.

Since most of the people who read *Pears* live in Britain let us return finally to our commonest nutritional disease, namely obesity. Call it "being overweight" if you like, but acknowledge that it means being fat. Being fat is not only unattractive and unsightly but it is dangerous to health and carries a high mortality. Ask any life insurance company how they view your chances if you are overweight and you will find they are as worried about it as if you had high blood pressure, or smoke heavily. It is a particularly important cause of heart disease. However, it is very important to know exactly what we mean by fatness. The table below may be of help.

The term *Body Mass Index* is now a common measure of a person's weight relative to their height (above 25 is overweight, above 30 obese).

If you are overweight according to these tables you need to slim, and the question is how? Answer: by will-power. There is no other satisfactory method than to decide to eat less. For the time being eat as much fruit, and green vegetables, as

DESIRABLE WEIGHTS FOR MEN AND WOMEN, AGES 25 AND OVER

Men Height (in shoes 2.5 cm heels)	Weight in kilograms (in indoor clothing)		
	Small frame	Medium frame	Large frame
157	51–54.5	53.5–59	57–64
160	52–56	55–60.5	59–65.5
162	53.5–57	56–62	60–67
165	55–59	58–63	61–69
167	56–60.5	59–65	63–71
170	58–62	61–67	64.5–73
172	60–64	63–69	67–75.5
175	62–66	64.5–71	68.5–77
177	63.5–68	66–72.5	70.5–79
180	65.5–70	68–75	72–81
183	67–72	70–77	74–83.5
185	69–73.5	72–79.5	76–86
188	71–76	73.5–82	78.5–88
190	72.5–77.5	76–84	81–90.5
193	74.5–79.5	78–86	82.5–93

Women Height (in shoes 5 cm heels)	Weight in kilograms (in indoor clothing)		
	Small frame	Medium frame	Large frame
147	42–44.5	43.5–48.5	47–54
150	43–46	44.5–50	48–55.5
152	43.5–47	46–51	49.5–57
155	45–48.5	47–53	51–58
157	46–50	48.5–54	52–59.5
160	48–51	50–55.5	53.5–61
162	49–53	51–57	55–63
165	50.5–54	53–59	57–64.5
167	52–56	54.5–61	59–66
170	53.5–58	56–63	60.5–68
172	55.5–59.5	58–65	62–70
175	57–61	60–67	64–72
177	59–63.5	62–68.5	66–74
180	61–65.5	63.5–70.5	68–76
183	63–67	65.5–72	69.5–78.5

you like, but no sugar, starch, sweets, cakes, pastry, or biscuits, and no eating between meals. And cut down on beer and other alcoholic drinks.

At the same time take more exercise. Walk to work. If you make a real and genuine effort for three months without success, you should ask your doctor for advice. Almost certainly you will have to admit you have not really tried. Good luck!

NUTRITIONAL DISORDERS.

Nutritional Deficiency and Malnutrition.—Until quite recently a consideration of malnutrition would have merely led to an account of how too little food, or a deficiency of certain articles in the diet, produced deficiency diseases at the time of the restriction. For example lack of vitamins of various kinds gives rise to such diseases as rickets, scurvy, beri-beri, and pellagra; and an overall shortage of food to general starvation. These may be considered the immediate or concurrent effects of a poor diet. Modern nutritionists, however, are beginning to be concerned with two more kinds of nutritional disorders; and although the study of both kinds is in its infancy, both will be introduced in this account.

The first deals with the effects of comparatively small amounts of harmful constituents in our diet, introduced either voluntarily or involuntarily, and consumed for a long period of time; and the second with the lasting effects on our adult well-being of nutritional deficiencies in early life even though they have long since been corrected.

When viewed in this light, one or other of these three kinds of nutritional disorder may at this moment be affecting almost every individual in every part of the world, "privileged" or "under-privileged." Let us first define some terms.

Undernutrition, strictly speaking, means a state of affairs in which the quality of the diet is per fectly good. There is the correct balance of the various dietary constituents and all the necessary components are present, but there is simply too little of it. Many hundreds of millions of people throughout the underprivileged world are suffering and dying from this kind of under-nutrition, and the simplicity of the problem must be appreciated: they simply need more food of the kind they are at present getting, and which can often be produced locally

Malnutrition means an imbalance of the various constituents: a relative lack or excess of one or more of them. It usually leads to conditions which are, from the point of view of medical treatment, much more difficult to deal with. And therefore doctors often class them as "more serious."

The diseases of malnutrition range from the widespread protein deficiencies in other parts of the underprivileged world to *obesity* in our own better-off industrial countries, which is usually due to excess carbohydrate. Make no mistake about it: obesity (or being overweight) is a widespread disease of nutritional imbalance, and it kills.

Obesity is the commonest form of malnutrition in (for example) England and America today, and is a consequence of the sophistication of our diet in modern times. Between one-fifth and one-tenth of the population of the United States is more than 20% overweight, and to be 10% or 15% overweight is almost the rule nowadays in people over thirty. There are high authorities in the world of nutritional science who attribute all this overfed malnutrition to the consumption of refined sugar, or sucrose. They say it is not only the amount of refined sugar we put in our tea or on our breakfast cereals, but also the amount in sweet cakes, biscuits, drinks, chocolates and

sweets, and so forth. For some people it adds up to a phenomenal quantity each day. According to this school of thought we are not so much suffering from a surfeit of carbohydrates or starches, but from this single sugar, sucrose. It is interesting to reflect on the recent banning of the artificial sweetener, cyclamate, by many governments. This substance, having been used extensively throughout the world as an apparently harmless non-fattening substitute for sugar, was suddenly banned in America because in very large doses (equivalent to the amount taken in hundreds of cups of coffee per day for a long time) it was found to produce cancer in rats. It has never been shown to do humans any harm, whereas the effects of sugar in producing an overweight population, thereby indirectly kill tens of thousands of British people each year. This is a fascinating example of the difficulties confronting our legislators in making balanced judgments when deciding to ban a foodstuff, a drug, or an artificial fertiliser.

Childhood Malnutrition.

Protein-Calorie Deficiency is much the most widespread form of malnutrition. In very large under-privileged areas of the world, the childhood population receives such an inadequate diet that children live continuously on the brink of nutritional disaster. It only requires a small extra restriction or stress to topple them over into one of the clinical conditions to be described. At this stage they cease to be merely hungry. They become nutritionally ill. Sometimes the force which produces the disaster is a community catastrophe like a famine, an earthquake, or a war. Sometimes it is a family catastrophe like the loss of a lactating mother or a parental delinquency. Parents abandon young children as often in Africa as anywhere else. Sometimes the clinical nutritional disease is unmasked by a common childhood illness like measles, or gastro-enteritis which the well-fed child would have overcome. The starved child reveals his malnutrition instead and frequently dies.

Protein-Caloric Deficiency is a collection of different kinds of childhood malnutrition. Some are due predominantly to deficiency of protein and are collectively called kwashiorkor, a West African word meaning "red-haired boy" (*see below*). Others are mainly due to a severe deficiency of overall foodstuffs and are called *marasmus*. But in any real-life situation the severe *malnutrition* of kwashiorkor exists side-by-side with all gradations between itself and the severe *undernutrition* of marasmus, so that many intermediate forms of "marasmic kwashiorkor" are described. In kwashiorkor the child is typically listless, apathetic, whining, with a reddish discoloration of the hair, a peeling, scaly skin, and with much extra fluid in his tissues causing oedema. He is so listless as not even to be hungry. In marasmus the child is ravenously hungry. He is extremely thin and "starved" looking and is quite a different picture.

There is good reason to believe that even when protein-calorie deficiency is successfully treated, there will always be some lasting restriction of mental function, particularly if the malnutrition occurred as early as the first year of life. This is especially true in situations of appalling poverty in towns, where thousands of babies are not breast-fed because their mothers are at work. Many of them die. Some of them are no heavier than their birth weight at one year of age. Breast feeding in an underprivileged community is an essential insurance for childhood health and survival.

Problems of Additives.

Two new avenues of nutritional inquiry were mentioned at the beginning of this section. The impact of very long continued intake of refined sugar over many years on our bodily health is an example of one of them. Scientists and others are also becoming alarmed at the effects of modern food additives when taken, even in small amounts, over a long period. These additives include colouring matter, decolorising chemicals, taste "enhancers," and so forth, which are present in everyone's diet in a "civilised community." We are as unable to avoid a constant dosage with them as if they had been added to our water supply. It is, however, difficult to strike a balanced attitude. It is one thing to suspect that these additives are harmful and quite another to prove it.

Naturally if any of them are shown to produce harm in animals given reasonable quantities they are invariably withdrawn But in practice it is extremely difficult for animal experiments to mimic the conditions of human intake, especially as the human life span involves eating the substance concerned in small quantities for several decades. Thus it is easy to postulate the harmful effects of monosodium glutamate (a very common taste enhancer) but practically impossible to prove it the question either way. It is not sufficient to condemn "chemicals." All natural foods consist of chemicals, and so do we.

New Views on Nutrition.

The other new topic in nutrition is more soundly based on animal experiment. It has been repeatedly found that if animals do not grow quickly enough at certain early periods of life they not only become small, but they remain smaller than they should be even when they are subsequently given as much as they like to eat. This is true of all animals and birds so far studied. At the moment it is difficult to know whether the same is true of humans and, if so, when is our period of vulnerability. There is some suggestion that the corresponding critical period in humans is during the last part of gestation in the uterus, and the first year or so of postnatal life. This new idea may turn out to be very important for world nutrition. Since there will not be enough food for all the children all the time, it may become important to concentrate our aid to underprivileged countries on certain sections of the population only. It may be a good idea to see that pregnant mothers and small babies are specially fed. In this way we may be able to put off the periods of inevitable malnutrition until a time of life when it is recoverable. Such a plan would also go a long way to safeguarding the development of the brain which also occurs mostly at the same early time of life.

Even in Britain, we need to be aware of this problem. Vitamin deficiency can still occur, however, in elderly people living alone and not having a well-balanced diet. It also occurs for similar reasons in alcoholics, vagrants, etc.

Beri-beri is a group of diseases usually confined to the Far East where a diet of polished rice results in a poor intake of vitamin B_1 (thiamine). In one form there is oedema (q.v.); in another the peripheral nerves are affected leading to tingling and numbness. A similar condition is occasionally seen in alcoholics and diabetics. Treatment is with thiamine, and with other vitamins too, since most sufferers are going short of more than one.

Pellagra is found among maize-eating populations and is due to a deficiency of several vitamins including niacin, another member of the B group of vitamins. There is dermatitis on exposed skin, and soreness of the mouth and tongue, with gastro enteritis.

Scurvy is due to vitamin C deficiency. In children bone growth is affected. At all ages there is bleeding into the skin (bruising), impaired wound healing, mental depression, and anaemia. Most fresh fruit and vegetables contain vitamin C and a diet containing these prevents the disease.

Vitamin A Deficiency is commonly found in children in some underprivileged countries. It causes permanent blindness, with thickening opacity and dryness of the whites of the eyes leading to ulceration of the eye. Beyond a certain stage, therefore, a child's sight cannot be saved. The only real hope is prevention, with an adequate diet.

Rickets, another disease of early childhood, is caused by deficiency of vitamin D. Bones are not properly calcified, and their softness leads to deformities of the legs and many other bones. Vitamin D can either be eaten in the diet or produced under the skin under the influence of sunlight. Therefore rickets commonly occurs when both the diet and the sunlight are inadequate. It was once very common in industrial England, and is still to be seen very occasionally there and in impoverished urban communities in the USA.

THE ENDOCRINE GLANDS.

Glands are structures or organs which manufacture secretions (except for *lymph glands* which are not glands at all and should be called *lymph nodes*). The secretions are of two main kinds. The first are passed down tubes, or ducts, or are secreted directly into the hollow organs, and act locally. Good examples are the salivary glands which make saliva and pass it down ducts into the mouth for digestion of its contents and lubrication. These are *exocrine glands*. The second kind have no ducts, and secrete their product straight into the blood stream. This secretion is called a *hormone* and it is carried to all parts of the body by the blood where it acts at a distance on some remote part. These are the *endocrine glands* or *ductless glands*, and a number of them will be discussed in this section.

The first hormone, or "chemical messenger," was discovered by the British physiologist Starling in 1904, but the effects of removing some of the endocrine glands were known centuries before.

Anterior Pituitary.—Many of the endocrine glands do not act as separate autonomous organs in spite of their great differences. They are organised into a well-disciplined band by a "master-gland" called the anterior pituitary. Somebody once called it the "conductor of the endocrine orchestra" and the phrase is still repeated *ad nauseam* in students' examination papers. The pituitary, consisting of its two parts, anterior and posterior, is not much bigger than a pea and it sits right in the middle of the skull, centrally beneath the brain and joined to the brain by a short stalk. This astonishing tiny nodule of tissue produces at least eight important hormones.

Growth Hormone, which is one of these is necessary for normal growth, and also has an influence on insulin. An excess causes *gigantism* and *acromegaly*, often coinciding with diabetes, and too little results in a form of dwarfism. Three others, known as *gonadotrophic hormones* regulate the cyclical and other activities of the reproductive organs and lactating breast. Another, *thyrotrophic hormone*, regulates thyroid activity.

Adrenocorticotrophic Hormone, or ACTH, as its name implies, looks after the activities of another important endocrine gland, the adrenal cortex. And there are several others.

Hypopituitarism, including *Simmonds' disease* and *Sheehan's disease*, results from destruction of the anterior pituitary. It is extremely rare, and is usually associated with difficult childbirth involving very severe bleeding. There are disturbances of all the functions mentioned above, particularly thyroid and adrenal failure (q.v.) with upset sexual function. Treatment is by replacing the lost hormones.

Hyperpituitarism, including *gigantism* and *acromegaly*, results from over-activity of the anterior pituitary, and is usually due to a tumour or overgrowth of the gland. In acromegaly the growth hormone is produced in excess over a long period of time in an adult. This results in overgrowth of all the organs except the brain, and it is characteristic to find enlarged extremities—feet, hands, and jaw. In gigantism the same has occurred during childhood before the bones have stopped growing and the result is a person who may be 2 m tall or more.

Posterior Pituitary. The posterior part of the gland is really a quite separate gland. The main hormone it produces is concerned with the excretion of urine by the kidney (antidiuretic hormone). Deficiency of the hormone results in *diabetes insipidus*, not to be confused with *diabetes mellitus* or "sugar diabetes." In diabetes insipidus, the patient produces enormous quantities of dilute urine. He consequently has a prodigious thirst and consumes astonishing quantities of fluids. Treatment is by replacing the hormone.

Thyroid. The thyroid gland in the neck secretes an iodine containing hormone called thyroxine. Excess of it causes *hyperthyroidism*, *thyrotoxicosis*, or *Graves' disease*. Lack of it produces *cretinism* in the growing child or *myxoedema* in the adult. Thyroxine is concerned with the metabolic rate of cells throughout the body, or the rate at which they work, as well as with the proper growth of developing tissues, especially the brain. Too much thyroxine as in thyrotoxicosis leads to over-activity, warm sweatiness in an over-excitable patient whose pulse is rapid and who is eating ravenously to try to replace the wasted energy. In spite of his appetite he is very thin, and he often has bulging eyes for a reason not understood. Treatment is by drugs which neutralise the thyroxine or by cutting out some of the gland. A *cretin* is a child usually born with insufficient thyroid. He is destined to grow poorly, and to mental subnormality of a permanent and distressing kind. If the condition is diagnosed soon after birth (and routine testing is now done) treatment with thyroxine can avert most of the trouble. In myxoedema, thyroxine is deficient in an adult. They become slow in all their bodily processes, the hair thins and their flesh is puffy with a dry, wrinkled skin. Treatment is by thyroid replacement.

Goitre means enlargement of the thyroid gland. It may be accompanied by overactivity or underactivity, or with little functional change. One variety (Derbyshire neck) occurs in areas short of iodine in the soil and drinking water.

Adrenal Cortex. The adrenal or suprarenal glands sit, as the name implies, one on top of each kidney. There are two distinct parts: the cortex or outside which secretes steroid hormones, and the *adrenal medulla*, or core, which secretes adrenalin. There are many different steroid hormones in the adrenale cortical secretion, which look after such diverse matters as sodium and potassium balance, sexual function, the reaction of the body to stress, and the regulation of sugar levels.

Addison's Disease results from adrenal cortical insufficiency, and is often due to destruction of the gland by tuberculosis. There is weariness, malaise, pigmentation of skin creases and mucous membranes. They are short of sodium and have excess potassium. Treatment is with cortisone or synthetic steroids to replace the missing hormone, and by extra salt by mouth for the lack of sodium.

Cushing's Disease is due to excessive adrenal cortical function, and sometimes also occurs in patients treated with steroids for other purposes. They have a striking redistribution of fat in the face, neck, and trunk, with stretch marks similar to

those acquired by most women during pregnancy. The facial obesity makes them "moon-faced," and female patients may suffer masculinisation with deepening of the voice and hirsutism.

Testis. The male testes, as well as producing sperm are also endocrine glands producing steroid hormones known as androgens. They are mainly concerned with maintaining secondary sex characteristics. At the time of puberty the controlling secretions from the anterior pituitary begin to appear and androgens are produced. There is a whole range of rare disorders, resulting in everything from precocious puberty to delayed puberty. It should be borne in mind that the normal time of puberty can vary by several years from one boy to another. In passing, it should be noted that any lump or severe pain in a testicle requires urgent medical advice. These may be signs of cancer or twisting of the blood supply, respectively.

Ovary. The human ovary has two functions: to produce ova, or eggs; and to produce two hormones, oestrogen and progesterone. These functions begin at puberty, one of whose features in the female is the onset of menstruation, or menarche. Just as in boys, the timing of normal puberty is very variable, but on the average, girls achieve puberty before boys. As social conditions improve, the age of menarche is getting younger generation by generation. All the secondary sex characteristics are under the control of the ovarian hormones which are released in response to the appropriate anterior pituitary hormones. The changes which occur in the womb and elsewhere in the intervals between menstrual periods and the periods themselves are controlled by a cyclical or rhythmic secretion, first of oestrogen and then of progesterone, by the ovary. This cycle is upset by pregnancy to allow the development of the embryo. It can also be upset by taking certain combinations of the two hormones by mouth. These can prevent the formation of ova, and are a popular form of contraception. In late middle age, the ovaries lose their function, the menstrual cycles cease to occur, and reproductive life is at an end. This is called the *menopause* or "change of life," and is sometimes accompanied for a time by distressing symptoms due to a temporary imbalance between oestrogen and progesterone. Many sexual functions, however, continue well after the menopause into old age.

Parathyroid. Four tiny parathyroid glands are buried behind the thyroid gland and are responsible for regulating the body calcium and phosphate. They are therefore particularly important for the building and maintenance of bones and teeth. Since a proper calcium level in the blood is necessary for muscle (including heart muscle) contraction, and for correct functioning of nerves, disorders of the parathyroids can give rise to muscular spasms as well as loss of bone calcium. The latter can result in fragility and fractures. Overactivity of the glands leads to too much calcium and the formation of stones especially in the kidney.

Pineal. We end this section with a mystery gland. Like the pituitary it is small—about the size of a pea—and sits well back at the base of the brain. It was endowed in ancient times with metaphysical properties all of which remain speculative. In fish and lizards and certain lower vertebrates it is a kind of third eye, and receives light. In higher mammals, like ourselves, it is so far from any source of light that it could scarcely do so. It can be removed without harm. Indeed it normally becomes calcified and inactive about the time of puberty, and its position seen on X-rays of the skull can be a good guide to whether the brain is being pushed to one side by an abnormal mass.

THE URINARY SYSTEM.

Everyone knows what kidneys look like—in fact, the term "kidney-shaped" is used to describe other objects. Within the kidneys the blood-vessels carrying waste materials subdivide and finally end up in little coils or glomeruli through which waste products are filtered into the other system, the system of tubes which, beginning as tiny cups around the glomeruli, become larger and larger until they join the ureter passing out at the foot of the kidney, the hilum, a point at which both the veins and tubes enter and leave. The kidneys, of course, lie one on each side in the loins, so that if one puts one's hands on the hips and then slides them farther back they will cover the area over the left and right kidney The ureters pass down on each side to the bladder, which is the storage tank of the products excreted by the kidneys, and lies in the mid-line down low in the abdomen; it is somewhat pear-shaped, and at its base in men there lies the *prostate gland*—a gland which apparently has few functions but can be a nuisance. Its only known function is that it adds something to the semen from the testes without which the semen would be sterile. Then, from the base of the bladder a single tube, the urethra, passes to the outside. One can, in fact, visualise the urinary system as a capital Y, in which the two upper limbs are the ureters, the place where they meet is the bladder, and the single limb at the foot is the urethra. Clearly, then, there may be diseases of the kidneys, of the ureters, of the bladder, of the prostate gland, or of the urethra.

Urine: Polyuria and Oliguria.

The amount of urine may be increased or diminished. It is *increased* in the following conditions: after drinking excess of fluids; after taking drugs (known as *diuretics*) which are given to increase the flow; in diabetes of both types—mellitus and insipidus; in some types of chronic kidney disease; and finally, in emotional states of excitement. It is *decreased* in the following conditions: acute nephritis; any disease in which fluid is being lost in other ways, such as diarrhoea or sweating in fevers; when the fluid intake is small; and when both ureters are blocked by stones.

Passing a great deal of urine is known as *polyuria*, passing very little is *oliguria*, passing frequent small amounts is simply called *frequency*. Normally, the urine is acid, but in infections of the bladder it may become alkaline owing to decomposition by bacteria. Abnormal substances, or normal substances in abnormal quantities, may occur in the urine and give the doctor an indication of what is wrong. In fact, urine analysis is a very important part of medical diagnosis. Thus urea is a normal component of urine which is increased in fevers, wasting diseases, or diabetes; the amount of urea is to some extent a measure of the degree of tissue breakdown. Uric acid is found in small quantities in normal urine, but the amount is increased in fevers and after an attack of gout (uric acid is important in the causation of gout, but has nothing at all to do with rheumatism in general, so one may disregard the advertisements in the popular press showing unpleasant pictures of joints with sharp crystals of uric acid which are alleged to cause the pain of rheumatic disease).

Oxalates are not ordinarily found in urine, but, since they occur in such foods as rhubarb and strawberries, and some people are unable to deal with them, such individuals may develop problems.

Albumin and Sugar.

Two very important substances which ought not to be in normal urine are albumin and sugar. Albumin is a protein, and its presence in the urine indicates that the filters of the kidney are leaking —they are allowing protein to pass out which ought to remain in the body. Albumin is easily tested for, and its presence may indicate kidney disease or nephritis as it is usually called by doctors. On the other hand, small amounts of albumin occur in fevers and in nervous conditions —*functional albuminuria*. Sugar, too, should not be present, but its presence does not necessarily indicate diabetes; for small amounts may occur in nervous conditions or in some people after taking large quantities of carbohydrate.

Blood in the urine may give it an appearance which varies from bright red to a dark, smoky colour. It is found in many diseases: acute nephritis,

stone, tumours, poisoning by certain drugs, infections such as bilharzia or malaria, papilloma (*i.e.*, non-malignant tumour of the bladder), after injury, in high blood-pressure, scurvy, and blood diseases. Sometimes it occurs for no known reason at all.

Nephritis. It will be remembered that streptococcal infection of the throat may cause in some people disease of the valves in the heart or endocarditis. In such cases, although the germ is found in the throat, it is not found in the heart or anywhere else in the body.

Acute Nephritis occurs in the same circumstances, with the sole difference that it is in the kidneys not the heart which are affected.

The disease appears to be an allergic reaction to the toxins of the Streptococcus. The patient, often a child, has a sore throat (and even this may be absent or fail to be noticed) or sometimes the infection may arise in other sites: after scarlet fever, erysipelas, burns, and disease of the ear. A few days later there is headache, vomiting, pain in the loins, slight rise in temperature, and especially typical is *dropsy* or oedema. This begins in the face, first around the eyelids, and then affects the ankles; later it may become more general and affect the rest of the body. Blood and albumin are found in the urine, and the blood pressure is slightly raised. The outlook is usually good if the kidneys are rested by reducing the amount of protein taken in and also the amounts of salt and water. When this is done, the inflammation soon goes and no permanent harm results. In other cases, however, if treatment is inadequate or the condition severe, the symptoms may go, but the albumin found in the urine persists. This means that permanent damage has been done, and although there may be nothing else to show for many years, *chronic nephritis* develops.

Chronic Nephritis. With this disease, the blood pressure continues to rise, and since the filters of the kidneys no longer work efficiently, urea, the principal waste product of the body to be excreted in the urine, is retained in the blood and only small amounts escape from the system. Hence chronic nephritis sooner or later leads to heart failure or haemorrhage in the brain from the rising blood pressure, or to the form of poisoning known as *uraemia* which results from the retention of urea in the blood. Uraemia may come on suddenly or gradually, but ends in progressive coma, drowsiness, and unconsciousness. There may be convulsions and difficulty in breathing to complicate the picture.

Nephrosis is another type of nephritis which seems to have nothing at all to do with streptococcal infections, and the cause of which is completely unknown. Developing in early adult life, its onset is insidious, and the patient first shows signs of oedema in his white and puffy face and the swelling of his legs. (It should be said here that if you have swelling of the ankles or elsewhere, you would be foolish to jump to conclusions; for such swelling is common in many diseases—in heart disease, in allergic conditions, even hot weather.

When the urine is examined in a case of nephrosis it is found to be full of albumin and, as in chronic nephritis, the blood urea starts to rise. The end results of nephrosis are the same as those of chronic nephritis and depend upon the original damage.

The modern diuretics of the thiazide group help to control the oedema and, provided enough healthy tissue remains, remove both the fluid and the waste-products.

Artificial Kidneys or **Dialysers** as they are known, can now be used in patients' own homes, thus obviating in some cases long journeys to hospital twice a week for treatment. Dialysis is a relatively temporary measure; renal transplants now offer real hope to many sufferers although there are far more suitable recipients than potential donors.

Pyelitis (Pyelonephritis), infection of the pelvis of the kidney, that is to say, of the part where the ureter leaves the kidney. Usually caused by Escherichia coli, which is normally present in the body, or by the Streptococcus. These germs may reach the ureter through the blood-stream or may pass upwards from the bladder. Obstruction anywhere in the urinary tract which causes the urine to stagnate is liable to cause pyelitis. Symptoms come on suddenly, with high fever, pain in the loin (the infection is usually on one side only, and is commoner in women), and pain in the abdomen. When urine is passed there is a burning sensation, and it is passed frequently and in small amounts, On examination, the urine is found to be highly acid and full of Escherichia coli or whatever the causative germ may be. Pyelitis is fairly readily treated by the antibiotics or sulpha drugs. Plenty of fluids should be given and the urine made alkaline.

Cystitis means inflammation of the bladder, either acute or chronic, and its causes are much the same as in the case of pyelitis. There is pain over the lower abdomen, frequency, and sometimes slight fever. The treatment is as for pyelitis.

Urethritis is an inflammation of the urethra, with burning pain on passing water and frequency. The most serious cause (although it can usually be easily dealt with now) is gonorrhoea. But non-specific urethritis is common, especially in the newly wed and in this case various germs or none may bring about pain and frequency; there is often a large neurotic element. Urethritis should be regarded as probably due to gonorrhoea when there is a thick, creamy discharge from the penis or discharge in women following sexual intercourse with an infected person.

Kidney Stones *or* **Renal Calculi** sometimes form, and, as in the case of gall-stones, what causes them is not certain. They may be caused by disorders of metabolism—that is, in the inability of the body to deal with calcium, proteins, uric acid, and other products; or by vitamin deficiency, obstruction in the urinary tract, and urinary infections. But when a stone or stones are formed various events may occur: thus it may remain in the kidney and cause no symptoms; or it may cause repeated attacks of pain, infection, and blood in the urine (haematuria); or it may completely block the passage of urine from the kidney to such a degree that it degenerates and becomes useless; or, lastly, it may pass into the ureter, and when this occurs very severe pain, known as *renal colic*, will occur. A stone passing down the ureter into the bladder may become stuck in the urethra, although this is uncommon, since a stone small enough to get down the ureters is likely to be capable of manoeuvring through the rest of the tract. In fact, about 80–90 per cent. of stones are passed spontaneously.

Stones not passed spontaneously may have to be removed by operation, but whether this is undertaken or not depends on various factors, such as the health of the patient, the amount of trouble caused by the stone, and the health of the other kidney—for it is dangerous to operate on one kidney unless one is sure that the other is functioning efficiently. Lithotripters are also used to fragment stones without needing invasive surgery.

Hydronephrosis. If a stone blocks the passage of urine on one side for any length of time *hydronephrosis* may result, in which the part where the ureter enters the kidney swells with the retained urine. Ultimately much of the kidney may be destroyed by the back-pressure. The same effect may be produced by kinking of the ureter or anything else which causes obstruction. Sometimes children are born with hydronephrosis, and when the dilation is due to kinking of the tube the condition may be intermittent, with attacks of renal colic during which only small amounts of urine are passed; this is followed with relief and the passage of large quantities.

Tumours and Cysts. The kidney may also be the site of tumours and cysts which produce pain in the loins, sometimes a lump over the kidney which can be felt, and blood in the urine. *Cancer of the bladder* is a serious condition in which the bladder may have to be removed, so the urinary flow has then to be directed elsewhere. Either the ureters are brought out on to the skin surface, a procedure known as *cutaneous ureterostomy*, or they are implanted in the large bowel, so that the urine flows out with the faeces. This is described as *uretero-colostomy*.

There may also be benign tumours of the bladder

or *papillomas*, which are soft and bleed easily; a great deal of blood is passed, but there is usually little or no pain. In this, and similar, diseases of the bladder examination of the inside of the organ is carried out by means of a cystoscope, a thin tube which is passed up the urethra with fibre-optic light guides which enable the surgeon to see what is going on. Instruments may also be passed through the tube, and simple papillomas can be cauterised. Similar instruments are used to examine the stomach (gastroscope) and the bronchial tubes (bronchoscope).

When some obstruction in the outlet of the bladder or in the urethra occurs the bladder, of course, fills with urine, which cannot be passed, and very painful dilation occurs. In this case an attempt may be made to pass a catheter, a thin rubber tube, into the bladder to relieve the tension, or if this fails a *suprapubic cystotomy* is performed—an incision is made in the abdomen over the bladder and a tube inserted into it, through which the urine escapes. This is ordinarily a temporary expedient, and later when the patient's health has improved an attempt will be made to remove the cause of obstruction.

The common cause of such obstruction is *enlargement of the prostate gland* at the base of the bladder, which surrounds this area and the beginning of the ureter. About 40 per cent. of men over sixty have some degree of obstruction due to this cause, and about 20 per cent. of these require operation. The gland is about the size of a walnut and, as we have seen, its function is to supply part of the fluid which makes up the semen, the male sex secretion. Enlargement of the prostate may be benign or malignant, and, although nobody knows just why, such benign enlargement tends to occur in most men in later life. There may be no symptoms, but characteristically there is frequency during the day and the need to get up at night to pass water. The flow of urine being impeded by constriction of the urethra, the passage is less forceful than normal, and there is a tendency for dribbling to occur. If the obstruction is severe and not relieved the back-pressure may be transmitted to the ureters and kidneys, resulting finally in kidney failure and uraemia. The prostate, except in cases of very mild enlargement, has to be removed either through the abdomen or through the perineum (the part of the body lying between the sex organs and the anus). Sometimes, in less serious cases, it is possible without an incision to cut away the obstructing part by an electrocautery inserted, as is a cystoscope, through the urethra. Prostatectomy was once a serious operation, all the more so because the patient was usually elderly and not in good condition, but new techniques and the use of antibiotics have greatly improved the outlook.

Cancer of the Prostate is a potentially serious disease, but if diagnosed early and is localised, may be cured by surgery or radiotherapy. If the disease spreads, or has spread at the time of diagnosis, it can often be controlled. *See* **Z62–3.**

THE NERVOUS SYSTEM.

The nervous system consists of the central nervous system and the peripheral nervous system. The brain and spinal cord make up the former. The latter consists of the nerve fibres by which the central nervous system is connected to all parts of the body. Human beings have a more complicated brain than any other animal species, but it is only its complexity which makes it different from the brains of other mammals like rats and pigs and cows. We do not have the largest brains, since whales, for example, have much larger ones. Ours is not even the largest for the size of the body.

Before describing some of the diseases of the nervous system it will be helpful to say a little about how it is made and how it works. Each human brain probably contains about ten thousand million (10,000,000,000) nerve cells and perhaps four or five times this number of supporting "glial" cells. Each nerve cell has many long thin

Z46

branching projections, called dendrites, rather like the branches of a tree, leading to many thousands of "twigs" for each single nerve cell. At the end of each "twig" there is a special structure called a *synapse* by which contact is made with other nerve cells. It is through these connections that very large numbers of nerve cells give information (or send impulses) to each other so that they can be co-ordinated. As well as these dendritic branches, each nerve cell gives off one large trunk called the *axon*, down which initial messages are sent as the result of all the information it receives from its dendrites. Some axons are many feet long. Some end in another synapse, by which the outgoing message is passed to yet another nerve cell. Some axons, those of the peripheral nerves, end directly on organs like muscles or glands, instructing them and making them work.

Transmission of Messages. Messages are passed along dendrites and axons as electrical impulses. These are generated in the nerve cell "body." They are modified according to information received from other nerve cells and propagated down the axon. It is this superficial resemblance to a series of electrical cables which has given rise to comparisons of the brain with a telephone system or a computer, and the comparison is not a bad one. However, the brain generates its own electric power from the fuel brought in its own blood supply; and no spare parts or spare cables are available if the originals should get damaged, except in peripheral nerves. Furthermore the contact of one nerve cell with another through a synapse is not an electrical contact, and neither is the contact between a nerve and the muscle or other organ it is controlling. In both cases the connection is chemical. Thus when an electrical impulse arrives at the end of the nerve fibre, a chemical is released into the gap between it and the next nerve or organ, and it is this chemical which carries the stimulus forward. There is also an arrangement to neutralise the chemical transmitter when the impulse has been transmitted. So the resemblance to a telephone exchange or computer can sometimes be misleading.

Myelin Sheaths.

Many of the nerve axons which transmit electrical impulses are clothed in fatty *myelin sheaths*, a little like the plastic insulation around an electric wire. Here again the resemblance is only partial, since the myelin sheaths are interrupted at regular intervals and these gaps in the insulation play an important role in transmitting the impulse. One of the important functions of the non-nervous *glial* cells of the brain is to manufacture and maintain the myelin sheaths.

The Functions of the Brain.

Many of the functions of the brain are little known, and even the ones we know about are very poorly understood. It is the organ of higher mental function, of the mind and intellect, but much remains to be done on linking the different functions of the brain with the structures found within it. The brain is known to control all bodily functions by means of *motor* and other nerves which carry impulses from the brain outwards to all parts of the body. Sometimes these are under our voluntary control; mostly they are involuntary, reflex or automatic. Reflex actions are the result of impulses passed inwards from the body towards the brain by means of sensory nerves. Information arriving in the brain about the various sensations like heat, pain, touch, position, the need for saliva or gastric juice or even the thought or smell of food, are acted on in the various "centres" in the brain. These send out instructions down the "motor" or "secretary" nerves which instruct the muscles or glands to take appropriate action. Thus a *reflex* has a "sensory ending" which appreciates some sort of sensation. This is converted into an electrical impulse which is sent towards the brain or spinal cord along a sensory or "afferent" nerve. The impulse arrives at a "centre" in the central nervous system which co-ordinates all the relevant

information and issues instructions. These travel as impulses outwards, along "efferent" nerves towards "effector" organs like muscles or glands, and an appropriate action occurs automatically. The pathway from sensory ending to effector organ is called a *reflex arc*. Many reflex activities are partly under voluntary control, although mainly automatic. If you touch something hot you will automatically withdraw your hand. But if it is a hot china cup which has cost you a lot of money, you are capable of overriding the tendency to drop it, at least for a time. Breathing is automatic, but it can also be controlled, again at least for a time.

Clearly the brain is a very delicately organised piece of machinery, and its cells are extremely specialised for their job. Achieving this kind of specialised perfection brings many difficulties, however, and the brain cells have become highly dependent on the proper functioning of the other body systems, especially the blood circulation, the respiratory system, and the systems regulating the detailed nutrient composition of the blood. Failure of these systems, even for a very short time, can damage the nerve cells. Nearly all death is produced this way, by an ultimate interference with nerve cell function.

Vulnerability of the Brain.

We have already mentioned that the brain and spinal cord are unable to repair or replace any components which get damaged. The vulnerability of the brain is even more obvious when it is realised how easily damage and destruction can occur. For example, unless a rich supply of oxygen and glucose is continuously arriving in the blood stream, brain cells will cease to function in a few seconds and will die in a few minutes, and they can never be replaced. This is in marked contrast to other tissues of the body. The leg, for example, may carry on for over half an hour without any blood at all because the muscle and other cells can find other ways of surviving. Thus the brain can be permanently damaged if the blood contains insufficient oxygen (through asphyxia), insufficient glucose, or if the blood supply is blocked or if the blood pressure falls.

All these are likely to happen to any of us at any time, and so there are elaborate mechanisms trying to prevent them occurring. Much of the subject of physiology is concerned with the mechanisms designed to protect the brain, and most of us ultimately die because they eventually fail. One of the clever features of the body design is that all the mechanisms which protect the brain from a supply failure are controlled by the brain itself. Thus the brain has itself been made to control the heart beat and the breathing and the many other systems which are needed for its own survival.

In all that follows it will be seen that the effects of neurological disease on the patient are the direct result of something going wrong with one of the structures or mechanisms we have described.

Diagnostic Techniques in Neurology. The doctor has many ways of testing the nervous system, most of which test its various functions as outlined in the introduction. Thus tests of sensation, muscular movement and reflexes of all kinds as well as the special functions of taste, smell, vision, hearing, speech and intellect play a part. A great deal can be learned about the brain by *arteriography*. In this test a radio-opaque substance is put into the arteries supplying the brain, and an X-ray picture taken immediately afterwards shows up all the blood vessels. *Myelography* is an X-ray of the spinal cord after a radio-opaque substance has been injected into the space between the spinal cord and the bony vertebral canal housing it.

Computerised tomography (CT) scanning and Magnetic Resonance Imaging (MRI) have now made "invasive" diagnostic tests less necessary.

In another development, *radioactive isotopes* can be put into the blood stream and carried into the brain where they can be detected from outside the skull by counters. *Electroencephalography* measures the electrical waves generated by the brain by placing electrodes on the scalp. *Electro-myography* does the same for muscles.

Consciousness and Unconsciousness (Coma). Everyone knows what consciousness is until he tries to define it. Full consciousness is generally taken to imply not only wakefulness but the total complement of human mental faculties. In clinical medicine, however, something less than this is usually meant. For example a demented person, or one whose memory is lost (*amnesia*), or one whose powers of speech are lost (*aphasia*) may still be "conscious." There is really a continuous gradation between full consciousness and coma, passing through drowsiness and even "stupor" in which condition a patient can be aroused from coma but sinks back into it when left alone.

Many different things can cause coma ranging from swelling of the brain, compressing it in its rigid box of bone, to disorders in other body systems resulting in a failure to provide for the brain's needs. Examples of the first are bleeding within the brain or *brain tumours*, both of which occupy space and can only do so by producing compression. In the second category are asphyxia preventing oxygen from reaching the brain, lack of glucose in the blood, circulatory failure in which there is insufficient blood, or insufficient blood pressure. Fainting is a comparatively minor example.

Sleep and Insomnia. Nobody knows what causes sleep, why it is necessary, and how it helps. It is quite different from coma or even stupor, since as much oxygen and glucose is necessary asleep as awake. Insomnia is experienced by everyone at some time, and for some reason is very distressing if it persists. There are three forms: failing to get to sleep, intermittent wakefulness, and awaking early. Nearly all insomniacs sleep more than they think. They should eat light evening meals and avoid stimulants like tea and coffee after mid-day. Elderly people should realise they need less sleep. Being cold or having a full bladder can be a cause. Or simply not being tired. Sedative drugs are a last resort, but they can be useful in "breaking the habit" of wakefulness. Obviously there may be psychological factors such as anxiety and excitement.

Narcolepsy, or a true inability to keep awake is comparatively rare, although it affects 20,000 people in the UK.

Headache. We must distinguish between the very common varieties of comparatively trivial significance and the rare ones due to serious causes. Some headaches are due to continuous tightness in muscles of the scalp, and are often "nervous" or psychological in origin. Others result from nose blockage and congestion, sinus problems, eye strain, toothache, *etc.* Migraine is a special kind and will be described below. Very occasionally indeed headache is due to serious disease like brain tumour. Most headache results from "living it up" or being "run down," or both.

The headache of alcoholic hangover is probably due to dehydration. It can often be avoided by consuming a great quantity of water (a half litre or so, before going to bed), but few people are prepared to do this in the circumstances. Be careful when using aspirin, which is a useful remedy for headache, since it is very dangerous for people with stomach complaints like gastritis or gastric or duodenal ulcer. Occasionally aspirin makes the stomach bleed, and this can be so severe as to kill. Paracetamol is safer.

Migraine. This is a very special variety of "sick headache" and requires special treatment under medical supervision. It has many different forms, but usually there is a definite sequence of events. An attack often starts with some alteration of vision. The patient has shimmering blind spots or other visual disorders. This is followed by a well localised severe headache which may end in nausea or vomiting. The whole thing is caused by a poorly understood disorder of the blood vessels. There are special drugs, which are effective, especially if used when the first signs of an attack appear.

Although there is a direct physical cause for an attack, it is also certain that some of the trouble

is psychological tenseness. People with migraine are often rather anxious, striving and perfectionist people. Also it has been noticed that attacks are much less frequent when the necessary pills are being carried available for use. However, as with all other conditions which are partly "psychological" in origin they are none the less distressing for the patient. It simply means that the treatment is also partly psychological in encouraging him to come to terms with his problems.

Ménière's Disease is one of the conditions in which the organ of balance in the middle ear is affected, giving rise to *vertigo*, a form of giddiness. It usually begins in middle life in the same sort of person who sometimes has migraine. There is buzzing in the ears and some intermittent loss of hearing as well as vertigo. During an attack the patient may be unable to walk because of his loss of balance, and nausea and vomiting are common. Treatment is by special drugs, and occasionally an operation on the ear is necessary.

Epilepsy is a symptom, not a disease, which is common at all ages but especially children. It has been attributed to St. Paul, Julius Caesar and Napoleon. Many varieties of attack occur often in the same patient, the commonest and best known being the *grand mal* or major seizure. In this the patient falls down unconscious and rigid and the jaw is clenched, so that there is danger of the tongue being bitten. This so-called tonic phase is followed, within a minute or so, by a clonic phase in which the limbs contract rhythmically. The attack ends with the patient going limp and gradually recovering consciousness, a process which may take up to an hour. Occasionally the patient has a brief warning, most often an indescribable feeling in the stomach.

There are two common forms of minor seizure, one occurring mainly in children and the other more often in adults. The common minor attacks in children are often called *petit mal* or *absence*, which well describes the instantaneous and brief loss of consciousness often unaccompanied by any change in posture. Recovery is equally instantaneous. On the other hand, in the other forms of epilepsy which arise from various parts of the brain, but especially from the lobe under the temporal region, there is often a warning similar to that which may precede a major seizure. In these cases the patient shows only confusion, no definite loss of posture, but automatic activity such as fumbling with buttons, muttering, and grimacing. After these attacks there may be a period of confusion in which the patient may wander away and even be violent.

Convulsions. Many people have had one or two fits in their lives, maybe at times of physical or psychological stress. "Fever" or "Febrile" convulsions (often called teething fits in the past) are extremely common in young children and are often thought of as something different from epilepsy since the attacks rarely continue in later years. This form of epilepsy and some cases of *petit mal* are the only forms in which hereditary factors are important in the causation, and these are the least serious forms of epilepsy. They are very rarely associated with serious physical or psychological disturbances. Most other forms of epilepsy are due to a scar or other area of brain damage. It is a proportion of these cases which develop the psychological disturbances that are occasionally very serious.

Not every patient who has had one or two fits need necessarily take regular anticonvulsant drugs; that is drugs which damp down the abnormal excessive activity of the brain that leads to the attacks. Many new drugs can now be used effectively. The choice is a matter of skilled medical judgment.

Patients, however, often find it difficult to get work because of the reluctance of employers to take on someone who may be more prone to accidents and whose fits may distress other workers. Obviously there are some jobs which epilepsy sufferers should not do because of the danger involved (from for example, moving machinery), and they should not drive a car. A few cases are so severe that work is almost impossible, but employers have a duty whenever possible to employ these people whose mental health may suffer greatly if they are made to feel outcasts and who ordinarily are as efficient, or even more so, as the next man. It is also hoped that employees will become less prejudiced about epilepsy as the general public become less ignorant about medical matters.

Congenital Malformations.

The proper shape of the brain and spinal cord is achieved quite early in development by about the thirteenth week after conception. During this time very slight changes in the foetal environment can produce disastrous malformations. The drug thalidomide, for example, operated on other body systems while they were passing through this phase of construction. Some viruses can do the same thing. Most malformations are without known cause, but it is certain that something went wrong at this very early stage, and it only needs a very minor interference with the normal process to do the permanent damage. At about this time the bones of the spine are beginning to enclose, or form a roof over the developing spinal cord. Sometimes they fail to complete the process, resulting in *spina bifida*. If the coverings of the cord protrude through the defect, this is a *meningocoele*, and if the cord itself protrudes it is a *meningomyelocoele*. The whole protrusion may be covered with skin, but if it is not, the cord soon becomes infected. The effect on the patient is variable, according to the amount of damage to the nerve fibres in the cord, and there are varying degrees of paralysis and loss of sensation below the area involved and loss of bowel and bladder control. Much help can often be obtained from surgical repair, but many cases remain in a distressing condition always, and the only really useful attack on the problem is research to find the cause and prevent it happening. The same is true of the *malformations of the brain*. In one of these, hydrocephaly, the narrow channel is blocked which transmits the cerebrospinal fluid from the chambers within the brain where it is secreted to the outer coverings to be taken back into the blood stream. Blockage of the channel (or aqueduct) results in distension of the brain by fluid, enlargement of the head, and mental retardation. Sometimes a by-pass valve can be inserted to restore normal fluid circulation with very gratifying results.

Cerebral Palsy

is a physically disabling condition of impaired muscle co-ordination caused before, during or shortly after birth by damage to or maldevelopment in the portion of the brain which controls movement. There are 3 main types: *spasticity*, *athetosis*, and *ataxia* depending on what area of the brain has been affected. Inherited defects do not play a large part in cerebral palsy. The general incidence of the disorder is thought to be 2·5 per 1,000 births. For further information and advice contact: SCOPE, 12 Park Crescent, London W1N 4EQ.

Motor Neurone Disease.

This is a group of related diseases usually occurring in people over 40, in whom the parts of the brain and spinal cord which look after muscular movement degenerate. The group includes *amyotrophic lateral sclerosis*, *progressive muscular atrophy*, *progres-sive bulbar palsy*, and *primary lateral sclerosis*.

The results are paralysis or weakness with wasting of the muscles of the body, including those concerned with arms, legs, breathing, speaking, *etc*. The Motor Neurone Disease Association, 61 Derngate, Northampton, NN1 1UE, provides help and advice. There are around 5,000 sufferers in Britain.

Parkinson's Disease,

formerly known as the shaking palsy, derives its present name from the London physician James Parkinson (1755–1824). It is one of the commonest illnesses to affect the human brain with more than one in 1,000 of the population as a whole (though one in 100 of those above 60 years of age) suffering from it. The average age of onset is about 55 though one in seven contract it before they reach 50. It has three classical features: shaking (or tremor), muscular rigidity and poverty of movement. A stooping, shuffling gait and a mask-like loss of facial expression are common. It is a progressive disease affecting patients in variable degrees of severity and different degrees of progres-

sion. A good deal can now be done to help these patients with drugs and since the condition results from a malfunctioning of brain cells which produce a chemical 'messenger' known as dopamine replacement of this substance by the drug L-Dopa (often accompanied by an additive in a combined preparation) is often the first line of treatment. Occasionally younger patients have benefited from surgical - destruction of small areas of diseased brain.

In rare cases the disease is hereditary, but normally the cause is unknown (although a gene responsible for some cases of Parkinson's has been found).

It is important to remember that many old people have some tremor of the head or hands called *senile tremor* and this is *not* Parkinson's Disease. It is merely one of the features of achieving advanced seniority as a citizen. The Parkinson's Disease Society of 215 Vauxhall Bridge Road, London SW1V 1EJ sponsors medical research and patient welfare.

Chorea.

This is a group of diseases in which there is involuntary muscle movement, weakness, and emotional instability. There will be clumsiness, awkward gait, twitching of limbs, face, hands, trunk, or tongue. They include *acute chorea* or *St. Vitus' dance* occurring in children from 5 to 15, *hereditary* or *Huntington's chorea* occurring in a well-defined genetic pattern and beginning later, between 35 and 50. *Tics* or habit spasms are not part of these diseases but are often of psychological origin. They are usually eye blinking or head shaking.

Stroke Illness or Cerebrovascular Diseases.

Strokes are due to diseases of the brain's blood vessels which either burst or get blocked. The same blood vessel disorders cause heart attacks by blocking the coronary arteries supplying the heart. Strokes and heart attacks together kill more people than any other single cause including cancer. They account for one death in every five. Perhaps less is known of the cause of this disease than is known about cancer, and much more research is needed to find out if it is to be prevented. The cause of the commonest cancer (of the lung) is now known and it can be prevented by stopping smoking. Perhaps the prevention of strokes and heart attacks will mean an equally difficult abstinence from all those foods which make us fat. At least it is known that being overweight leads to death from these causes, just as smoking may lead to death from lung cancer.

Infarction.

If any artery supplying blood to any part of the brain is blocked, the territory supplied will die; and the bodily functions for which that part of the brain is responsible will cease. The process is called *infarction* of the brain, the dead area being an *infarct*. The blockage is usually due to thrombosis of the blood within a vessel, a *thrombus* being a rather complicated clot with a structure of its own. The underlying cause is the arterial disease, *atheroma*, together with stagnation of the circulation. About one blockage in ten is due to a small piece of a much larger thrombus in the heart chambers being flung into the blood stream and impacting in the distant vessel in the brain. This is *cerebral embolism*.

If the area of dead or infarcted brain is not too large the patient will recover from his unconsciousness, but will be left with permanent loss of function (paralysis, *etc*.) related to that part of the brain.

When a blood vessel supplying the brain bursts, this causes *cerebral haemorrhage* or apoplexy. The vessel may be on the surface (*subarachnoid haemorrhage*) or in the depths of the tissue (*intracerebral haemorrhage*). Strokes tend to occur in older people, because the associated arterial disease is a product of age and high blood pressure. Occasionally a subarachnoid haemorrhage occurs in a younger person with an unsuspected malformation of the arteries at the base of the brain known as a *berry aneurysm*. This is a small berry-sized blown-out balloon due to a defect in the wall of the vessel. Berry aneurysms can often be treated surgically. Intracerebral haemorrhage carries a very poor outlook, however, since much brain tissue is often destroyed by the escaping blood, especially the deep tissues responsible for the vital functions. Haemorrhage within the brain cavity can also be caused by injury.

Inflammatory Diseases of the Nervous System.

The membranes covering the brain are called the

meninges. Inflammation of these, nearly always by blood-borne infection or infection following injury, is called *meningitis* (*see* **Z13**(2)). Cerebrospinal or spotted fever was only one variety caused by a germ called "meningococcus."

Almost any other germ may cause meningitis, and when the germ is susceptible to one of the antibiotics it is usually treatable. It will usually be necessary to identify the germ by taking a sample of cerebrospinal fluid from a convenient space around the spinal cord in the lower back. When the disease is caused by the tubercle bacillus (*tuberculous meningitis*) the problem is more difficult because the patient is often not so obviously ill until the later, less treatable stages.

Cerebral Abscess, or abscess of the brain is very serious because it occupies space in the closed box of the skull and compresses the brain, as well as being a destructive process. It may arise due to an infected piece of tissue or pus being carried to the brain in the blood stream from a distant site in the lungs or heart. When the brain or cord tissue is itself inflamed it is called *encephalitis* (brain) or *myelitis* (cord) or *encephalo-myelitis* (both).

Herpes Zoster (Shingles) is a common viral infection of the nervous system which affects sensory nerve roots where they enter the spinal cord. The initial symptoms are of pain in the area supplied by the affected nerves—commonly one side of the trunk, the buttock or the face—followed by the appearance of blisters. Treatment nowadays is usually with a course of the drug Zovirax. Soothing lotions may be applied to the blisters and analgesics given for the pain. The disease is fairly short-lived, but neuralgia may persist for weeks after the blisters have healed.

Shingles is interesting in that it is not a *primary* viral infection, but the result of reactivation of the varicella-zoster virus (so called because it causes *either* chicken pox or shingles) which has lain dormant in nerve root cells, probably since childhood. Primary infection with the virus at whatever age causes chicken pox, not shingles; if an adult who has never had chicken pox or shingles comes into contact with a child with chicken pox or an adult with shingles, he is likely to contract the former but not the latter.

Shingles is infectious from the time the blisters appear until they have crusted over and healed. However, it is not as infectious as chicken pox.

Multiple Sclerosis (MS) is the most important of the *demyelinating diseases* in which the myelin or "fatty" sheaths which insulate nerve fibres appear to disintegrate. This occurs patchily and seemingly randomly throughout the central nervous system (*i.e.* the brain and spinal cord) and results in interference with the passage of impulses through the affected nerves. Changes in sensation, balance or muscular co-ordination occur at varying intervals of time and spaced out over months or years in such a way as to appear unconnected. There is at present no reliable, objective diagnostic test for multiple sclerosis and diagnosis has to be made from the history of such episodic symptoms.

The cause is unknown, but from various pieces of evidence such as the odd distribution of the disease in the world one theory is that multiple sclerosis is the result of a recrudescence of a dormant viral infection which may be picked up during the teenage years. Others hold it to be an auto-immune disease. It is commonly held that once diagnosis of MS is made it means a sentence of years of increasingly severe disablement which will progress relentlessly and inexorably. That may be the case, but in fact such a gloomy picture is very uncommon.

Much research has gone into the natural history of MS and it is clear that there are seven distinct patterns of the disease. These cover a wide range of symptom patterns from that characterised by a sudden onset of symptoms with relatively few relapses after the first year, to that manifested by sudden onset followed by unremitting relapses causing progressively greater degrees of physical impairment which may indeed lead to much distressing disability and relatively early death. But between these two extremes, of which the first is far the commonest form for the disease to take and the latter

relatively infrequent, there lies a whole range of disease patterns and prediction is difficult.

Around 85,000 people in the UK suffer from MS and it is the most common neurological condition affecting young adults.

The Multiple Sclerosis Society exists to sponsor research, to care for patients and to give advice and support to friends and relatives. For more information write to them at their offices at 372, Edgware Road, London, NW2 6ND. The Scottish office is at Ratho Park, 88 Glasgow Road, Ratho Station, Edinburgh, EH28 8PP. The web address is www.mssociety.org.uk.

Brain Tumours. The brain is no exception to the rule that any cell in any tissue of the body can suddenly begin to disobey the body's rules regarding its growth and multiplication. A largely unknown mechanism governs how many cells of a certain type there ought to be and calls a halt to cell multiplication when this number is reached. Every now and then one of them turns a blind eye and goes on dividing, and the result is a tumour, or lump, of anarchic cells which obey no rules. Tumours are commonest in cells which normally go on dividing throughout life, in order to replace those lost by wear and tear. Examples are the cells lining the air passages in the lung, or the alimentary tract in the stomach or large bowel. Fortunately for the brain there is little cell division once it has grown. Nerve cells cannot divide at all in adult life, and the supporting glial cells only do so in response to injury. Primary brain tumours are therefore much less common than those elsewhere. Also many brain tumours like many of those elsewhere, are benign or "innocent" tumours. They are not cancerous, and need only be removed for the patient to be completely cured. The brain, however, is at two major disadvantages compared with other tissues when it comes to tumours. One is that all tumours as they grow take up space, and space in the skull is already fully occupied. Thus even an innocent tumour can compress the brain within its rigid box of bone and become most dangerous until it is removed. The second disadvantage is due to the very large blood supply of the brain. Cancer in other parts of the body spreads partly by sending small pieces of itself to other tissues by way of the blood stream, and those tissues like liver, lung, kidney, and brain which have a big blood supply naturally receive more than their share of other tissues' tumour. These secondary deposits, or *metastases*, cause compression and other trouble in the brain much more frequently than the brain's own primary tumours. Indeed convulsions or other signs of brain disorder may be the first indication that there is a primary tumour in the lung or breast or elsewhere.

Diseases of Peripheral Nerves. Compared with the nerves of the central nervous system (brain and spinal cord), the peripheral nerves are comparatively rarely affected by disease. They have some similarities of structure with central nerve fibres in that their fibres are often covered with myelin sheaths and are arranged in bundles. A special feature, however, is that they are enclosed by connective tissue sheaths and it is probably these which allow a peripheral nerve to grow again, or regenerate, after it has been cut or damaged. Central nerve fibres are unable to do this. After *injury of a peripheral nerve* the part away from the centre is cut off from its parent cell body and it dies. All function, whether motor or sensory, is lost. But in the course of many months the central surviving part grows into the connective tissue sheaths which act like tubes to guide the new nerve to its destination. Provided the cut ends are close enough together and correctly aligned, and provided enough fibres reach their correct destination, good functional recovery is possible.

Neuropathy. A disorder of a peripheral nerve is called a *neuropathy*. There are many kinds. One of the most distressing is *trigeminal neuralgia*, again fortunately rare. The trigeminal or fifth cranial nerve has a motor and sensory territory on the face. In this condition there are paroxysmal episodes of extremely severe pain which may resist all treatment except destruction of the nerve itself with consequent facial paralysis and loss of sensation.

Bell's Palsy is the sudden loss of function of the seventh cranial nerve and there is again paralysis on one side of the face which usually recovers in time. Some bacterial diseases, especially leprosy, invade the nerves themselves. Chronic alcoholism may affect the nerves, as may diabetes, probably by interfering with the nutrition of the nerve cell. So may exposure to arsenic or lead or an unpleasant nerve poison which may contaminate cooking oil known as TOCP, or triorthocresylphosphate.

Muscular Dystrophies. These are a series of diseases of muscle in which there is progressive wasting and weakness of muscle, the causes of which are entirely unknown. They are divided up according to the age of onset and the muscles involved. *Duchenne's muscular dystrophy* occurs in the first decade of life. It affects most of the muscles eventually, including the heart muscle and those concerned with breathing, and so the outlook is not good. Other forms are inherited. The Muscular Dystrophy Group (Nattrass House, 35 Macaulay Rd, London SW4 0QP) gives great assistance to sufferers.

Myasthenia Gravis. This is a strange disorder of the mechanism which transmits instructions from nerve to muscle at the "neuromuscular junction," leading to extreme weakness.

Creutzfeldt-Jakob Disease causes fatal degeneration of the central nervous system. It may be sporadic, genetic or transmitted, and results from the accumulation of abnormally folded proteins in the brain. It is now clear that some cases resulted from eating animals infected with Bovine Spongiform Encephalopathy, BSE or "mad cow disease" (*see* **L69**). These illnesses are caused by mysterious proteins, *prions*, that act in some ways like viruses—making the body produce more of themselves.

MENTAL ILLNESS

Conventionally mental illness is divided into two categories, **psychosis** (madness), and **neurosis** (exaggerated symptoms of commonly experienced states). Psychoses are themselves divided into: *organic*, implying that we can identify a physical cause, and *functional*, where the brain structure appears to be intact but its performance is abnormal. This division is now seen to be very blurred since there are physical diseases and drugs which can lower the threshold for response, or alter a person's perceptions so that he appears to be mad, albeit temporarily. The more research is done, the more organic causes are found for abnormal behaviour, and successful medical intervention.

Organic Psychoses.

The organic psychoses result from actual damage to the brain. This damage can be caused by disease, as in syphilis; by tumours; by dietary deficiencies, as in inadequate vitamin B12 absorption; by poisons such as alcohol and lead; by drugs such as LSD or amphetamine; by problems of blood circulation such as heart failure or atheroma; and by genetic inheritance. The onset of illness can be either an acute confusional state or a chronic reaction known as *dementia*. The acute episode is characterised by an impairment of consciousness which may vary from difficulty in holding on to the point of a story, to actual coma. The chronic reaction, on the other hand, does not affect consciousness but intellect, memory and personality. Characteristically, memory for recent events is lost, while that for remote ones is preserved. About one in ten men and women over the age of 65 is likely to be affected.

Alcohol-Related Problems.

Since it is the most commonly and voluntarily ingested poison, it is worth giving a special mention to alcohol. Alcohol-related disabilities can be classed as social, psychological and physical. Social problems are often noticed first, and include failure to perform an expected role as parent or spouse or at work. Psychological difficulties include increased depression and personality deterioration. *Delirium tremens*, (DTs), is an acute confusional state involving intense fear and restlessness with hallucinations.

Most alcoholics experience blackouts ranging from momentary lapses to memory loss involving several hours. Intellectual impairment can occur and may be permanent, even after alcohol is abandoned. Other physical problems associated with alcoholism include a doubled death rate, liver damage, gastritis, anaemia, increased rates of cancer, and infections such as TB. Sexual incompetence is common. The children of alcoholic mothers are at increased risk of problems.

Schizophrenia.

Functional psychoses broadly fall into two categories: *schizophrenia* and *manic depressive psychosis*. Schizophrenia was a term introduced by Eugene Bleuler in 1911 to describe a group of illnesses in which there was a splitting of the psychic functioning so that the association between two ideas was bizarre, and mood seemed inappropriate to the circumstances. Nowadays schizophrenia is diagnosed on the presence of certain accepted symptoms such as a lack of insight, auditory hallucinations especially of voices discussing the patient in derogatory terms, the idea that radio and TV programmes refer to him directly, unreasonable suspicions, or a flatness of response.

Schizophrenia occurs in all societies, but in less developed countries appears to be more acute yet to offer better prospects for recovery. About one person in a hundred will develop the condition, and there is an increased risk where close relations are affected.

There are many theories of causation though an inheritance factor is clear, but there is argument about what this factor might be, and the extent to which its influence is affected by life events. Theories invoking abnormalities in the substances responsible for the transmission of signals within the brain itself are supported by the fact that some symptoms of schizophrenia can be induced experimentally. But as yet the physical theories are not wholly proven.

The 'double bind' hypothesis of Bateson, that an emotionally disturbed parent, who says one thing to a child but at the same time suggests a deeper, contradictory, message will eventually cause the child to withdraw into a fantasy world, is another explanation.

The personal construct theory of Bannister and Fransella says that we build up constructs and relationships between them in order to understand our world. In this theory if the construct of generous-mean is linked with those of honest–dishonest and gentle–violent, then we expect someone we know to be generous to be also honest and gentle. If these associations are weak or inconsistent, then the world is a chaotic and fearful place. Whatever the role of early experience in the causation of schizophrenia, current stress brings on an attack.

Treatment of schizophrenia. This was revolutionised by the introduction in the 1950s of phenothiazine drugs which not only tranquillise but also have specific anti-psychotic effects. The fact that schizophrenic patients are increasingly returned to their community, able to function, is due in large part to these pharmacological advances, and to the concept of 'milieu therapy' involving group activities, recreation and occupational therapies.

Manic Depression (now known as **Bipolar Disorder** – **BPD**) is characterised by swings of mood between depression and elation without apparent cause, and in this form is called the *bipolar* state. More frequently, the disease is *unipolar*, showing only periods of depression interspersed with periods of normality. The difficulty in defining depression as an illness is firstly to distinguish it from a symptom, and secondly to make a distinction between normal and morbid depression which is depression of greater severity and duration than would be expected in a given population from the apparent cause. This last is a very subjective rating and this makes depression a difficult subject for research. The expectancy that one will suffer a depressive illness in one's lifetime is about one to three per cent, with females more likely than males. Generally it is accepted as a phenomenon of later life, but can occur at any age. In depression the major symptom is of a persisting sad, despairing mood, especially severe on waking up. Agitation or marked slowing down may be present, and hallucinations are not uncommon. Ideas of unworthiness, guilt *etc.* are frequent, loss of appetite, loss of weight, loss of sexual drive and loss of menstruation are also common. Around 1 per cent of the UK population is affected by bipolar disorder.

Causation of Depression. The cause is another area where authorities are in dispute, and theories abound. Seligman points to learned helplessness as a cause. In his experiments animals exposed to repeated stresses beyond their control, exhibited apathy, difficulty in accepting that they could do anything to help themselves, loss of appetite, and reduced sociability. The idea that depression is the result of aggressive feelings which cannot be channelled out and so are turned in on oneself, is a simplified view of what Freud said. Some support is lent to this idea by the fact that depressive illness is less common in time of war. Certain biochemical changes have been found in the brains of depressed patients, and the anti-depressant drugs work in ways to correct these imbalances, but whether these intra-cellular changes are cause or effect, and how this comes about, is still not entirely clear. Treatment is by specific anti-depressant drugs of which there are now many, by psychotherapy of various kinds, and much more rarely now by electro-convulsive therapy (ECT) which can be life-saving in very severe cases.

Mania is a state of elation, hurried speech, and physical overactivity. Irritability is common if the patient is frustrated. Grandiose plans are made and money can be lavishly spent. Gradually as the illness progresses the sufferer becomes confused, angry *etc.* Treatment is usually by lithium.

Neurosis as we now understand it is a concept we owe to Freud, and to him, too, we owe the distinction between the neurotic disorders of *hysteria*, *anxiety* and *obsessionality*, and the disorders of *personality*. Those in the latter category, while having no detectable disease, are treated by psychiatrists as if they had, and this is a decision of society as a whole since the alternative is to refer such people to the legal or social services. Because the category of neurosis is so vague, it is hard to put a figure on how many people may be affected, but researchers in general practice consultations estimate about one in ten women, and half that many men are at risk. The reason for this disparity is not clear, but may be due to factors such as the greater freedom for expression of frustration enjoyed by men in our society than women. The majority of neurotic illnesses clear up, and may do so spontaneously, although obsessional and hypochondriacal symptoms are more persistent.

Anxiety Neurosis as a pathological state is where anxiety is either unrelated to a recognisable threat, or the degree of anxiety is out of proportion to the threat. The mechanism of our response to a threat appears to depend on the level at which the threat is perceived, if at a conscious level, the response is fear, if at an unconscious level, the response is anxiety. Symptoms include weakness, dizziness, sweating and tiredness. The physical symptoms are themselves unpleasant and increase the feelings of being threatened. Treatment may be by reassurance and explanation, by psychotherapy aimed at bringing the threat into conscious appraisal, or by drugs which are now widely, and often inappropriately, prescribed. Phobic anxiety occurs when unreasonable fear is focused on a particular object or situation, and leads to avoidance, Agoraphobia, literally a fear of the market place, claustrophobia, fear of enclosed spaces, and animal phobias are well recognised. Social phobias, such as fear of eating in public or fear of vomiting are often harder for the sufferer to acknowledge. Phobic states are often associated with a traumatic event in the past, and avoidance through fear leads to a form of conditioning which reinforces the fear. Gradually the sufferer extends the range of feared and avoided stimuli. Behavioural therapy offers the chance to reverse this process.
Much is made of the manipulative nature of neurotics, and the idea of secondary gain, where the neurotic is perceived as getting the better of those around him by organising his, and other people's,

lives to fit in with his symptoms. Certainly neurotic people can be very irritating in their demands and social failings, but their conscious experience is of personal suffering, their gains are at an unconscious level, and one cannot but be saddened by the waste their lives represent.

Suicide as a completed act is on the decline, but the rate of attempted suicide is rising. Most attempts are preceded by a warning of intention, often quite explicit.

Mental Illness in Childhood can refer to illness specific to children such as autism (*see below*), to emotional disorders, and to disorders of conduct. Because children are dependent on their families, much interest has centred on relationships within the family and on maternal deprivation as factors in the creation of childhood difficulties. The work of Bowlby highlighted problems consequent on the infant's need for attachment being denied, and he expressed the view that poor early experiences led to failures in later life to develop social relationships. Autism is a state where the child displays abnormalities of language, indifference to people, and ritual behaviour. Autistic children do not grow into schizophrenics, they grow up into autistic adults, and most remain severely handicapped. Phobias and obsessional behaviour are common in children and usually appear and disappear rapidly, especially with prompt intervention. Depressive illness is rare before puberty and where depressive features are seen it is usually in response to environment. Conduct disorders include persistent lying, stealing, disobeying, truanting, fighting or setting fires. The distinction from delinquency is important since the latter implies breaking the law which is quite common in adolescence. There is a high correlation between these behaviours and difficulty in reading, though whether this is because of a shared impairment or the result of educational frustration is not clear. Treatment is by careful assessment of the family situation, and by social and educational intervention. The future is not rosy though, since about half the antisocial boys in one long-term study went on to be antisocial men in later life.

Anorexia Nervosa is usually a disorder of adolescent girls in which food avoidance, weight loss, failure of menstruation and overactivity predominate. Anorexics often display a distorted view of their own bodies, being unable to see how thin they have become. The underlying difficulty may be a need to control something in their life at a time of actual dependence on parents, or an attempt to avoid the challenge of puberty and the demands, particularly of sexuality, that adulthood makes. Treatment is by behaviour modification, supervised weight gain, and psychotherapy.

Bulimia Nervosa is a variant in which meals, often very large meals, are eaten and then vomiting is induced to get rid of them.

Autism is a profound life-long handicap which is now believed to be caused by brain malfunction; often occurring with other disorders, including mental retardation, which affects three times as many boys as girls. The spectrum of the autistic condition encompasses dramatically different degrees of severity, varying from profound handicap through to subtle problems of social understanding in people of apparently normal or even superior intelligence. With the right therapy at an early age, autistic people can become less indifferent to others and can develop social responsiveness at a simple level.
There is no present cure for autism; and it is essential that people with autism are cared for in a special community by dedicated staff.

THE SKIN

The skin in the course of development before birth is particularly closely associated with the nervous system. It is therefore not surprising that so many skin diseases are influenced by emotional states. Other causes of skin disease are infectious, glandular disorders, vitamin deficiencies, and the numerous conditions for which no cause has been discovered, but which presumably are due to metabolic disorders.

Itching (or **Pruritus**) is one of the commonest skin symptoms. It may accompany many different general diseases, for example diabetes and jaundice. It may also be troublesome during the menopause (the change of life in women), in old age, or in nervous conditions. Sedatives and sex hormones sometimes help the itching during the menopause, and there are ointments which may be useful.

Itching in the region of the anus and genital organs is relatively common. It may be caused by worms, by irritating vaginal discharge, or by sugar in the urine, as in diabetes. The alteration in the normal bacteria of the bowel which follows treatment with various antibiotics also often causes anal pruritus and soreness. In many cases however the itching has some psychological cause.

In treatment it is important to avoid ointments and creams which contain a local anaesthetic, because these substances can cause severe allergic reactions if used for longer than a few days, and may thus make the condition much worse. Treatment with a local corticosteroid application is more effective and safer.

Parasites, such as the *scabies* mite or *lice* can cause severe and persistent itching. The scabies mite is very small, and since it burrows under the skin surface, is unlikely to be seen; it is the cause of itching most commonly between the fingers and on the front of the wrists. The itching is worst when the body becomes heated, as in bed. Treatment consists of painting the body from head to foot with benzyl benzoate application, followed the next day by a hot bath. Since scabies is contracted through close personal contact with an infested person it is often desirable for several or all members of a family to be treated at the same time, even though only one of them may be affected.

Lice are also specialists, one type of which affects the scalp, another the body, and a third the genital area. Head lice are destroyed by washing with shampoos containing organophosphorus insecticides such as malathion, body lice by insecticides and genital (pubic) lice by shaving off hair and washing. Obviously, the clothes, especially in the case of body lice, should be disinfested, by using a hot iron particularly over the seams, which lice (for some inexplicable reason) seem to favour. Apart from the discomfort they cause, lice are dangerous as potential carriers of typhus fever.

Baldness, or Alopecia, is a very common and often distressing condition. Baldness is common in men and often hereditary. In the past, men have been sold a large number of ineffective treatments, but there are now some genuine treatments available. These include a lotion applied to scalp, minoxidil, or tablets, finasteride. For most men, no treatment remains the best option.

Even if these medications are successful in halting hair loss, they need to be continued indefinitely for the benefit to continue. Scalp surgery has also been used.

In women the hair often thins out soon after a pregnancy, but a few months later it usually returns to normal. Alopecia is a common side effect of many drugs used in treating cancer, because these drugs affect rapidly-growing cells, including those in hair follicles.

Seborrhoea is a condition in which there is over-activity of the sebaceous glands. The most usual form it takes is *dandruff*. However, it takes other forms, and those who have dandruff may also have rashes on the face, shoulders, and chest. In these areas there is a patchy, greasy, and often itchy, rash which does not clear up until the primary condition in the scalp is dealt with. The scalp should be washed with one of the modern sulphur-containing shampoos at least twice a week, and the affected parts on the face and chest can be dealt with by the use of a sulphur lotion (*not* on any account by greasy ointments). Seborrhoea is not in itself difficult to treat, but since the condition depends on over-secretion of sebum, the skin lubricant, treatment may have to be persisted in during the years of early adulthood, when it is most active.

Erythema Intertrigo is, quite simply, the sort of irritation which occurs usually from excessive sweating under the armpits, between the legs, and under the breasts in women. All that need be done is to wash frequently and to dust the affected areas after washing with powder. This is the condition which, in the tropics, is known as "prickly heat" and elsewhere as a "sweat rash."

Hyperhidrosis or **excessive sweating** is a problem in some people, especially when the sweating is accompanied with body odour. There is little need for anyone in these days to suffer in this way: for the cosmetic firms have produced many highly efficient deodorants which not only control odour but also control the amount of sweating.

Erysipelas is an infection of the skin caused by the haemolytic streptococcus. It begins as a red, raised area anywhere on the body where the germs have been able to enter through a small crack or cut in the skin. The red area advances and spreads over the body until the disease is got under control. Erysipelas is very infectious, and those who look after the patient should wash their hands thoroughly after contact. At one time the disease used to spread as an epidemic throughout the hospital wards, but this is very rare nowadays. Treatment is, of course, a matter for the doctor.

Chilblains used to be common in cold weather, especially in those with poor circulation. Ordinarily they occur in the toes and fingers, but may appear on the nose and ears. The part affected becomes swollen, dusky, and there is pain and itching, sometimes leading to ulceration. Protection of the body, especially the hands and feet, from cold is the best and the only really effective way of preventing chilblains. Warm lined gloves and footwear, and arm stockings or trousers should be worn outdoors. Adequate heating of rooms is essential: a temperature between 18° and 21°C is recommended. Most tablets, medicines, ointment, or creams for chilblains are useless. A skin affection caused by heat is rather grandiosely described as *erythema ab igne*, and used frequently to be seen on the legs of ladies addicted to roasting their legs before the fire. It takes the form of red patches on the front of the legs and can be removed only by avoiding the cause.

Dermatitis means "inflammation of the skin," and therefore the word could be, strictly speaking, applied to any skin disease. In fact the term is used almost interchangeably with the term *eczema*. There are three main types of dermatitis or eczema. The first, *primary irritant dermatitis* results from injury of the skin by some powerful chemical, such as strong alkali or turpentine. The second, *contact dermatitis* is due to sensitisation of the skin to some substance which is normally liable to cause this type of allergic sensitivity; examples are nickel (in jewellery and suspender buckles), epoxy resins, rubber additives, primulas and chrysanthemums, and even ingredients of cosmetics. Contact dermatitis may continue for a long time, even after the patient is no longer in contact with the offending material. The third type is often called *constitutional eczema*. Although the skin is apt to react adversely to various irritants and sensitisers the major part is played by the personality, and there is often a history of eczema, hay fever or asthma in the family. Treatment is more difficult, but local corticosteroids and tar, sedatives and psychological treatment can be of great help. Infantile eczema also belongs in this category, but in most patients it disappears as the child grows up. The National Eczema Society is based at 163 Eversholt Street, London NW1 1BU.

Impetigo is an infectious skin disease caused primarily by the Streptococcus, but later often infected with staphylococci. It usually occurs on the face, and takes the form of blisters filled with pus on a red base; when the blisters burst their place is taken by yellow crusts. Impetigo is very infectious and easily spread by the fingers, dirty towels, or cloths; therefore, one of the first necessities is to prevent infection of others or reinfection of oneself by avoiding scratching and using a different towel each day, which must on no account be used by anyone else. Treatment is simple with an antibacterial ointment, so the main issue is prevention of contamination.

Urticaria or **Nettlerash** is a familiar skin disease in which itching weals appear on the skin, usually for no obvious reason. It is not infectious, and can be caused by nervous stress, certain drugs, allergy to some foods, or even exposure of the skin to cold. In some people it is possible to write on the skin with a fingernail: the "writing" appears in the form of weals. This is known as *dermographism*; it occurs in many normal persons as well as in many patients with urticaria. The antihistamine drugs are the most useful in the treatment of urticaria. Urticarial swelling of the tongue or throat requires urgent medical attention.

Acne, or **"Blackheads,"** is a condition found on the face and shoulders; its appearance is so familiar that no description is necessary. Acne is one of those conditions which is the end result of many factors. There is, first, a greasy skin, the result of glandular upset (which is why the disease usually occurs in adolescence); secondly, there is infection of the skin; and thirdly, there is blockage of the sebaceous ducts, which ordinarily allow the grease from the skin to pass out on to the surface. Since the condition starts with excess secretion of grease, ointments should never be used, and probably the best applications are drying lotions containing some sulphur preparation which inhibits secretion of grease. The face should be frequently washed, and it is possible now to obtain detergent solutions which are both antiseptic and prevent grease formation. In severe cases ultraviolet ray treatment may be necessary. Advances are presently being made in the case of vitamin A in treating acne. Acne is now known to be linked to one's genes.

Rosacea. As has already been implied elsewhere, although the wages of sin may be extremely unpleasant, the wages of extreme virtue may be no less troublesome. Thus *rosacea*, in which the nose and cheeks become red and greasy and the skin coarsened, occurs alike to chronic alcoholics and elderly ladies with no vices other than a preference for strong tea. Both cases are associated with indigestion, since, regrettable as it may seem, strong tea and alcohol are about equally liable to cause the gastritis which may be at the root of this complaint. However, in many patients the chronic flushing is caused in other ways and psychological factors are important.

Lichen Planus is one of the numerous skin diseases which seem to be due to nervous states of tension. It may occur on any part of the body, but is most common on the front of the forearms and legs. The rash takes the form of nodules which are lilac in colour and have a dent on the top; when these disappear a stain is left behind. There is severe itching. Treatment is a matter for a doctor, as it also is in the case of *psoriasis*, a very common disease of largely unknown origin, which is extremely resistant to treatment. It tends to run in families. It takes the form of slightly raised papules, usually on the elbows and knees; typically the papules are covered with dry, silvery-looking scales. Apart from the rash, the patient is usually in perfectly good health and there is no itching. Many drugs have been used in psoriasis, notably chrysarobin, and while it is not difficult to cause the rash (which may occur

anywhere on the body) to disappear in one area or even in all areas for a time it has a strong tendency to return.

Psoriasis. A skin disease which results in patches of inflamed, red skin often covered by silvery scales. It is at present a long-term condition.

Warts, or **Verrucae** are both familiar enough. They are caused by a virus, and are, theoretically at least, contagious. Usually they are found on the hands, but may occur elsewhere. Treatment is best carried out by a doctor, who will use a cautery, a caustic carbon dioxide frozen into "snow." A curious feature of the common wart is that it can sometimes be caused to disappear by suggestion.

Different altogether from the common wart is the *plantar wart*, which occurs on the soles of the feet and often causes a good deal of discomfort. It is best dealt with by a chiropodist or in bad cases by a skin specialist since it is highly infectious.

Ichthyosis is a disorder of skin formation with which some unfortunate people are born. The oil and sweat-producing glands do not function well and the skin is dry and scaly like the skin of a fish. It is, however, possible to help the condition, which does not affect the general health, by frequent alkaline baths to wash off the scales, and the subsequent use of lanolin to replace the lacking oil. Large doses of vitamin A seem to help in some cases, and there have been reports in the medical press of cases being helped by hypnosis; this, however, is very much a matter for speculation.

Skin Cancer. Squamous cell skin cancers occur mostly in old people. They are most common on the face or hands, and usually appear as a nodule which breaks down and produces an ulcer. The glands may later be affected, but such cancers can almost invariably be cured unless a considerable time has elapsed during which they have been neglected. They are much more common in persons over-exposed to the ultraviolet in sunlight, and there is great worry that their frequency will increase as the ozone layer of the atmosphere becomes more depleted. Great care should be taken in direct sunlight, especially when sunbathing. Cases of skin cancer have recently proliferated in the sun-belt states of America and in Australia.

Basal cell skin cancers were also known as "rodent ulcers", because untreated they act by eating into the tissues in the area where it has started. X-ray therapy or operation is necessary, but the outlook is good. *Cysts* on the skin are due to blockage of the sebaceous glands. They may become very large, and are best removed, as they may become infected. They do not turn into cancer, and there is no such thing as "male" and "female" cysts. It does sometimes happen that *moles*, especially of the bluish-black type, may become malignant, forming a cancer called a malignant melanoma. This is a fast growing and extremely dangerous cancer, though cure rates after early treatment are good. Any change in size or shape of any mole must be shown to your doctor immediately.

Skin Grafts.

These are a very complex subject which can be only briefly discussed here. They are used basically for a number of conditions in which large areas of skin have been removed from the body, as in burns or serious accidents. In other cases, as in plastic surgery, grafts may be used to make a new nose, eyelids, and so on. The following are the main types:

Split-thickness Grafts are grafts removed from another part of the body by an instrument known as a dermatome, which cuts sections about 10 by 20 cm. containing part of the deep layers of the skin.

Full-thickness Grafts, on the other hand, are when the whole thickness of the skin is removed from elsewhere and applied to an area which has to bear friction or heavy weights (*e.g.* hand or foot).

Pedicle Grafts, which unfortunately although the most exciting type, are rather difficult to describe. Briefly, if one, for example, wants to make a new nose, one cuts an area of skin and underlying fat about 5 cm wide and 12·5-15 cm long in the abdomen. One end, however, remains attached so that it gets adequate blood supply. The problem is how to get this tissue to the nose, and this is done by a complicated process of leap-frog. First, the free end of the graft is attached to the forearm, whilst its "root" remains in the original site, and when it begins to grow and get its blood supply from the arm, the original "root" is cut. So we now have a "sausage" of tissue attached to the arm. The arm is then lifted to the face and kept firmly in position there until the new free part becomes attached. It is then detached from the arm, modelled to the correct shape, and grows where the nose used to be!

THE JOINTS.

Rheumatism is a word most doctors wish did not exist. This is partly because they do not understand it, but mainly because it is a condition which strictly does not exist: which is small comfort to the many millions of people who are more or less totally incapacitated by it. The truth is it is used for a hotch-potch of very real diseases, in all of which there is pain and stiffness of what is called the musculo-skeletal system, *i.e.*, the muscles and the joints. It may mainly involve the joints, in which case it should be called arthritis; or it may involve other structures near the joints like tendons, muscles and fibrous tissue. Joints may either suffer from inflammation or degeneration or both, and the trouble may be acute or chronic or both; so it is easy to see what a mix-up the subject becomes, especially when we must include the joints of the spine as well as the limbs, feet and hands.

A good deal of arthritis used to be due to various germs, but these types are much less common now that the infections causing them have become rarer or better treated. They used to include gonorrhoea, tuberculosis, septic joints, syphilis, brucellosis, typhoid fever, dysentery and so on. The importance of *rheumatic fever,* which is a reaction to an infection (streptococcal sore throat) rather than being actually caused by the Streptococcus, is not because it involves the joints. This arthritis quickly clears up, but there may also be disease of the heart (*see* **Z27**).

Rheumatoid Arthritis is a completely different condition in which there is non-infective inflammation of connective tissues throughout the body. In the joints, the normally smooth, lubricated synovial membrane lining the joint cavity becomes scarred, leading to distortion, especially of smaller joints like those of the hand. Another characteristic feature is its capacity to vary in severity from time to time, with a strong tendency to unexplainable periods when it gets better or worse. This makes it extremely difficult to know whether any form of treatment is being useful, since any response may have occurred in any case. As in all diseases which behave like this, especially those in which medical men are also baffled, there are almost as many theories and treatments as there are doctors. It has never been satisfactorily shown to be caused by infection, faulty nutrition, "glands," emotions or personality disturbance, nor is it convincingly inherited. The best current theory links it with an increased sensitivity reaction, perhaps to the body's own tissues, known as "autoimmunity." From the patient's point of view there is swelling and deformity of the joints with tenderness on pressure and pain on movement. Treatment involves a lengthy and complicated regime of rest, relief of pain with anti-inflammatory drugs such as aspirin, exercises and the application of heat, with attention to general physical and mental health. At some stage adrenal corticosteroids (cortisone and its derivatives) are often tried, but although these can give great relief they have to be very carefully used to avoid very unpleasant side-effects.

Osteoarthritis is another completely different condition closely related to the normal processes of ageing. Therefore it occurs in older people and tends to be in larger, weight-bearing joints of the spine, hips and knees rather than in the hand; although the end joint of the fingers is commonly affected. Hard wear and tear, especially that caused by overweight, or injury may be the beginning of it. It is *not* due to diet, and dieting has no part in treatment except in those who need to slim. Physiotherapy, including heat, is helpful. It is not such a relentless condition as rheumatoid arthritis and patients should be reassured about this. It is partly inherited.

Osteoporosis is a reduction in bone density without change in the chemical composition of bone, and has many causes including hormone imbalance, poor diet, age and long use of corticosteroid medicines. Hormone replacement therapy after the menopause is partly to prevent osteoporosis. Around 3 million people in the UK suffer from osteoporosis, with a heavy annual toll of hip fractures, wrist fractures *etc.* A new treatment is with bisphosphonate medication.

Fibrositis (now more usually called **Fibromyalgia**) and other vague forms of "rheumatism" are very often manifestations of psychological problems but still very painful.

Backache. A symptom which may be caused by many different diseases—sometimes disease of the vertebrae themselves, sometimes strain of the ligaments, and sometimes inflammation or spasm of the surrounding muscles. "Lumbago" is usually due to inflammation of the muscles in the small of the back. Backache from purely local causes may be treated temporarily by applying heat in the form of a kaolin poultice or a rubber hot-water bottle and taking two aspirin tablets a day. On the other hand, many cases of backache are due to disease elsewhere, so a doctor should be consulted. BackCare is the new name of the National Back Pain Association.

Gout. An excruciatingly painful inflammation of the joints (especially the toe) caused by crystals formed by uric acid. Chronic gout can be avoided by such medication as allopurinol.

EYES AND THROAT.

Eye Diseases. These are very specialised and only very general information can be given here. The most common is inflammation of the conjunctiva causing redness and usually due to infection or some irritant substance or dust. If it persists and leads to hard crusts of yellow pus on waking in the morning, get it seen by a doctor for treatment probably with antibiotics. First-aiders are usually instructed how to remove small particles of grit from under the lids. It is important that these should not scratch the front of the eye—your window on the world—as this may lead to scarring and poor vision. So, above all, do not rub them in. Also, if you are fishing one out of someone else's eye, see it before removing it. Do not have a general sweep round in vague hopes of finding it. If in any doubts, obtain skilled help. Remember the eyes are part of the brain: the only visible part. Perhaps this is why people's eyes are so revealing.

Conditions such as **glaucoma** and **cataract** are beyond the scope of this section.

Sore Throats are a nuisance we all have to put up with from time to time. If they last more than a few days they should be treated professionally. Never prescribe antibiotics for yourself, especially in lozenge form, and only expect your doctor to give them when other measures have failed.

Tonsils and their inflammation may be a problem. It is comparatively rarely that they should be removed. Of course there are many children who benefit so much from having tonsils out that the operation (which has real dangers) is worth doing. But please allow your doctor to decide if it is necessary, and do not pressurise him into recommending it. (The same is true of *circumcision*, for which there are no hygienic, and few medical indications).

DISEASES OF WOMEN.

Internal Sexual Organs. These, as with the urinary system, can best be described as shaped like a capital Y. At the tips of the arms of the Y are the female sex glands, the ovaries: the two arms running downwards are the Fallopian tubes: the point where the arms meet is the womb or uterus: the single leg of the Y is the vagina. These are the *primary sexual organs* of a woman and they undergo regular cyclical changes in response to the control exercised over them by the pituitary gland, situated in the base of the skull. This control is mediated by chemical messengers (hormones) secreted into the circulation. The ovaries also secrete hormones, oestrogen, and progesterone, and a delicate hormonal balance is maintained between the pituitary gland and the ovaries. Each month an egg cell (ovum) matures and is released from the ovary, usually midway between two menstrual periods: the ovum is wafted along the Fallopian tubes by waves of contraction and if fertilised embeds in the lining of the uterus which has been conditioned to nourish it by the ovarian hormones.

If it is not fertilised the ovum escapes from the uterus, altered hormone levels then cause the lining of the uterus to be shed (this is menstruation), usually about 14 days after ovulation. After menstruation a new cycle begins; another ovum matures and a fresh lining grows in the uterus. These cyclical changes recur from puberty to the menopause.

Menstruation does not occur during pregnancy, of which a missed period is often the first sign. However, women do miss periods even though they are not pregnant, and this usually means that some minor and temporary change has occurred in the hormone balance. If three consecutive periods are missed it is wise to consult a doctor.

The Breasts are called *secondary sexual organs* and are also under the influence of the ovarian hormones. Two conditions which need treatment are *mastitis* and *cancer of the breast*, both of which are characterised by lumps within the breast tissue. Mastitis may be uncomfortable but is not dangerous and can be treated medically, whereas cancer is more serious. The distinction between mastitis and cancer can only be made by a doctor and any woman who discovers a lump in her breast must seek medical aid *at once*. Although death rates from breast cancer fell in the 1990s (partly due to use of the drug tamoxifen) it was reported in 2001 that breast cancer has now overtaken lung cancer as the commonest cancer.

Abscesses also occur in the breast, nearly always when the mother is feeding her child. Here again, a lump appears, the breast becomes red and very tender, and the woman may be feverish. Treatment with antibiotics is sometimes successful, especially if the mother consults her doctor quickly, otherwise treatment is by a small operation.

The Ovaries. The two commonest diseases of the ovaries are cysts and disorders arising from hormonal imbalance. The symptoms of ovarian disease are usually abdominal or low back pains, and heavy and painful loss during the periods, which may become irregular. These signs should be taken as a warning to consult a doctor.

The Fallopian Tubes. Infection of the Fallopian tubes is called salpingitis. The membrane lining the tubes is continuous with the lining of the uterus, hence an infection is rarely confined to a circumscribed area in either the tubes or the uterus, and pelvic inflammatory disease is a better name for this condition. Pelvic inflammatory disease often follows an abortion, or childbirth where part of the afterbirth (placenta) has been retained, or can spread from an infection in a nearby organ, for example the appendix. Infection is sometimes conveyed by the blood from another septic source in the body. The gonococcus is another cause of infection. The disease is characterised by pain and tenderness in the lower part of the abdomen, accompanied by fever, general malaise and frequently (but not invariably) a vaginal discharge. The treatment of pelvic inflammatory disease is usually medical and is the same irrespective of the primary site of infection. Before the introduction of antibiotics the disease often became chronic and the Fallopian tubes were frequently blocked by a cicatrising scar, a cause of subsequent sterility.

The Uterus. This is a hollow muscular organ and both its musculature and its lining membrane can be the site of disease. *Fibroids* are non-malignant muscular tumours which develop in many women. The main symptom is a heavy menstrual loss and surgical removal of the uterus (hysterectomy) is often necessary. This can be a major operation, but trans-vaginal hysterectomy, which does not involve opening the abdomen, has made this operation much less daunting. Hysterectomy does not impair sexual pleasure, but no more babies can be conceived. Infection of the lining of the uterus is usually part of a generalised pelvic inflammatory disease (*see* Fallopian tubes).

Cancer of the Uterus and Cervical Smears (Pap Smears). The uterus is pear-shaped and consists of a body and neck. The wide end is uppermost (the body) and the narrow neck (cervix) projects into the top of the vagina. Cancer of the cervix is commonest in middle-aged women who have married young and have had a large family; cancer of the body of the uterus usually occurs after the menopause and is more common in nulliparous women. The symptoms are variable and it is sufficient to emphasise that any woman who has unexpected bleeding, especially after intercourse, whether her periods have stopped or not, *must* see her doctor at once.

The treatment depends on individual circumstances, but is usually by operation. It is now possible to detect cancer of the cervix long before symptoms develop and at a stage when the disease can be eradicated by a relatively small operation. This early detection has been made possible by the development of exfoliative cytology. Cells taken from the cervix (without discomfort to the woman) are examined under a microscope. This test is popularly known as the "cancer test" or "cervical smear." A cervical smear is often taken as part of the routine gynaecological examination by consultants, general practitioners, and family planning doctors, and a nationwide screening programme is now in force. It is a big step forward in preventive medicine and may ultimately solve the problem of cancer of the cervix. Every woman between the ages of 25 and 60 should have the test done at least once every 5 years.

Major advances were announced in 2005 that could lead within 5 years to a vaccine against cervical cancer.

Prolapse means a sagging down of the uterus into the vagina and the cervix may even appear at the outside. It is a result of frequent childbirth and laxness of the ligaments which support the uterus: weakness of the vaginal walls often occurs at the same time. The symptoms of uterine prolapse are low back pain and a heavy dragging feeling in the lower abdomen: these are often overshadowed by the distressingly embarrassing incontinence which results from lax vaginal walls. The stress of only a sneeze, a cough, or a giggle often causes the involuntary escape of urine. The cure is operative and very rewarding.

Dysmenorrhoea or pain with the periods, is very common and most women experience this symptom at some time or another. Very often a girl's first periods are troublesome, but dysmenorrhoea develops after a year or two: this suggests that a psychological element is involved. Dysmenorrhoea is a symptom which has many varying causes, and the sensible thing to do, if pain is troublesome, is to see a doctor.

Amenorrhoea means stopping of the periods in a young woman. It may signify pregnancy or glandular disease or it can be purely psychological and generally occurs in girls with anorexia.

Menopause occurs when the ovaries no longer have any egg cells to release, causing the cessation of the normal menstrual cycle (*see below*). The hormones oestrogen and progesterone are no longer produced, and this change is often accompanied by "hot flushes". Over time women also experience a loss of bone strength (osteoporosis). It was hoped that giving these missing hormones by mouth would improve women's health. However a recent study of 27,000 women showed **"hormone replacement therapy"** caused a small increase in heart attacks, stroke, pulmonary embolus and breast cancers (with one extra such "event" occurring per hundred women treated for five years).

Abortion means the death and expulsion of a foetus before the 24th week of pregnancy. Abortion may happen spontaneously (*i.e.* naturally) or be deliberately induced. If deliberate, it may be legal or illegal (although a woman who aborts herself commits no offence) and the Abortion Act 1967 defines those conditions in which abortion is legal. The two main symptoms of abortion are bleeding and abdominal pain. Any bleeding occurring during pregnancy ought to be reported at once. Pain starts in the back and lower abdomen and is usually spasmodic in character, and like colic it works up to a peak and then temporarily passes off. Any pregnant woman with pain and bleeding should go to bed at once and send for her doctor. When doctors are convinced that a pregnancy should be terminated then an abortion by surgical means may be performed in hospital.

FAMILY PLANNING

In Britain a service of *free* family planning advice and supplies is in operation, that is, *free* to the consumer. The service is available to all men and women.

Sources of the Service.

1. *Area Health Authorities:* provide Family Planning Clinics in local Health Centres and sometimes in other buildings. Some require an appointment but others provide a "walk-in" service at certain specified times.

2. *Family Doctors*

3. *Hospitals:* supply the service mainly for the patients of that hospital referred from other departments and for patients referred by the patients' own doctors (usually for IUCDs).

4. *Private Sector:*
   1. The Family Planning Association still provides clinics in some areas, including some special vasectomy clinics.
   2. Brook Advisory Centres operate in certain places and tend to specialise in advising the young.
   3. The Marie Stopes Clinic is in London (and advertises in the press).
   4. The British Pregnancy Advisory Service provides a pregnancy advisory service in some areas.
   5. Some Family Practitioners undertake vasectomies.
   6. Some hospital consultant surgeons do private vasectomies, female sterilisations and reversals of sterilisation operations.

Anyone wishing to use the service can obtain the address of a clinic or a family doctor from any one of a number of sources.

1. *The Citizens Advice Bureau:* the address is in the telephone directory.
2. *The telephone directory:* Area Health Authority clinics are usually under the heading Health and subheading Clinic for each Health Authority. Private clinics will be under their own names.
3. *Area Health Authorities:* (H.Q. telephone number usually in Directory) Health Centres; Health Visitors; Nurses; Midwives; Family Doctors.*
4. *Family doctors' surgeries.*
5. *School nurses, school teachers, school counsellors.*
6. *Social workers.*

NB If a person goes to a family doctor she may be required to sign a form to the effect that the doctor has undertaken to provide her with contraception for the following 12 months. This is not binding on her and if for any reason she is unable to return to that doctor, or does not wish to, she may still obtain help elsewhere, *e.g.*, at a clinic or from another doctor. The patient has the choice.
   At most, but not all, family planning clinics an appointment system operates.

* The list of Family Doctors issued by the Family Practitioners Committees is available in Public Libraries and Post Offices. Doctors in the list who offer Family Planning Services have "C" or "C+" after their names.

METHODS OF FAMILY PLANNING

"The pill" ("combined oral contraceptive pill").

This consists of two female type hormones, oestrogen (usually pronounced as if the first "o" were another "e", that is eestrogen), and progestogen.

Preparations:

Many different combinations of these two hormones are marketed. Nowadays most formulae contain 30–50 units (micrograms) of oestrogen, whereas twelve years ago most contained 100 units. Even the amount of progestogen has been reduced to the bare minimum which is effective. Most pills have the same amount of hormone throughout the course but some recently produced pills have differing amounts of progestogen during the course, giving the lowest total amount of hormone per month.

Mode of action:

The pill works by stopping the egg cell from being shed from the ovary, and if no egg cell is shed, no fertilisation can take place. They are thus virtually 100% effective as a contraceptive, the tiny proportion of failure which occurs being almost invariably due to human error, *e.g.*, forgetting to take the pill.

The Menstrual Cycle.

Some people may like to have a more detailed description of the way in which the pill affects the normal menstrual cycle.
   The menstrual cycle begins thus: A tiny part of the base of the brain (the *hypothalamus*) sends out a hormone called releasing factor (RF), which stimulates the pituitary gland to release a hormone called follicle stimulating hormone (FSH). This in turn stimulates a group of folicles or egg sacs in the ovary. Each egg sac is a small fluid-filled bubble lined with special cells and containing an immature egg cell. The lining cells are stimulated to produce oestrogen and more and more of this accumulates in the blood stream. Eventually by "negative feedback" the oestrogen causes the pituitary gland to decrease the production of FSH (*i.e.* high level of oestrogen → low level FSH), and by "positive feedback" causes the pituitary gland to produce a sudden surge of another hormone called luteinising hormone, LH (*i.e.*, high level oestrogen → high level of LH). This LH causes the largest egg bubble to burst, releasing the egg cell, which is caught by the fringe at the free end of the uterine tube and wafted down the tube into the uterus,

during which time it can be fertilised. Meanwhile the burst bubble in the ovary turns yellow and is called the "yellow body" (or *corpus luteum*). This produces both oestrogen and another hormone progesterone which are both vital for the continuation and promotion of any pregnancy. If no pregnancy occurs the yellow body collapses after 14 days, the lining of the uterus is shed in menstruation, the level of oestrogen (and progesterone) in the blood drops, and this causes the pituitary gland to step up the output of FSH again.

The combined pill consists of oestrogen and progestogen, similar to those hormones produced by the "yellow body". These act on the pituitary gland as they would in a pregnancy and prevent the release of FSH and LH, so that egg cells are neither prepared nor released. Thus, taking the pill is in some ways like being constantly pregnant, which until the present century was probably the most natural and likely way for a woman in the fertile age group to be.

Method of Taking the Pill.

A woman starts to take the pill initially on the 1st day of a normal period, or on the 5th day of a normal period, depending on the particular pill. If she starts on the first day, she is protected from risk of pregnancy immediately. If she starts on the fifth day she is not protected until she has taken 14 pills. The pill is taken for 21 days followed by a rest interval of 7 days and this pattern is repeated indefinitely. The pills are provided in packets of 21. (There is one pill which is supplied in packs of 22 and a rest interval of only 6 days is required.) During the seven days without the pill the "pill period" comes. This is not a true period, but is simply due to stopping the pill, when such lining of the womb as has been allowed to form, is shed.

Protection from pregnancy is maintained unless:

she is more than 4–12 hours late in taking a pill (depending on the pill dosage)
she misses a pill
she has diarrhoea or vomiting so that the pill is lost before it can be absorbed.

If protection is lost she should continue to take the pills in the ordinary way but use other contraceptives, *e.g.*, the sheath, as well until the end of that packet of pills.

A few pills are put up in packets with 7 inactive tablets as well as 21 active tablets, so that a pill is taken every day. These are useful for people who find the "on-off" regime difficult to remember.

Other Drugs and the Pill.

A few drugs hasten the breakdown of the pill in the body and so make it less effective. Such drugs include some of those used to treat epilepsy and some, but not by any means all, antibiotics, some drugs for treating rheumatism and one or two other drugs more rarely used. Conversely, the pill is suspected of making some other drugs less effective, for example some drugs for treating depression. It is always advisable for a woman to remind any doctor who is prescribing for her that she is taking the pill.

The pill is the commonest method of birth control being used in Britain. 28% of the 11 million women in the fertile age group 15–44 use it. In the under-30 age group, recent estimates are that about 70% are using it. In spite of the fact that the pill affects in some degree, usually slight or moderate, much body chemistry and therefore many body systems, rather as pregnancy does, most people feel no different on the pill.

Pill problems.

Connected with "pill period".

Occasionally slight bleeding happens during the days when pills are being taken, particularly when a woman first starts to take the pill. If it is very slight it is called "spotting", if rather heavier, *i.e.*, necessitating the wearing of some sort of protection, it is referred to as "breakthrough bleeding". If this is in the first month or two of pill-taking it usually settles down spontaneously. If later on, a change of pill may be indicated. It can be due to erratic pill-taking, *i.e.*, being late taking a pill, or forgetting to take a pill, or it can be caused by having to take one of a very few other drugs which have the effect of hastening the breakdown of the pill in the body so that it does not have time to be effective. It is best to consult your doctor if bleeding happens, particularly if it happens when drug treatment is given. To be absolutely safe in those circumstances it is wise to use other contraceptives, *e.g.*, sheaths, as well until the end of that packet of pills.

Other Side Effects.

Occasionally, and usually in the early weeks of pill-taking, other side effects are experienced such as nausea, breast tenderness, headaches or weight gain. If these are troublesome and do not settle the pill may have to be changed or even, rarely, stopped. Some symptoms such as depression, general leg aches, and decreased interest in sex, are more doubtfully attributable to the pill and may have some quite other cause, but all these problems should be discussed with the doctor.

Headaches: Migraine headaches are usually one-sided, often associated with feeling sick or with actual vomiting and sometimes with disturbances of vision. Sometimes these headaches seem to improve when a woman takes the pill, but more often they seem to become more frequent. Sometimes they come only in the pill-free week. Often a change to a pill with a lower dose of oestrogen, or even to a progestogen-only pill, will eliminate such headaches.

It is advisable to stop taking the pill if

(*a*) *migraine occurs for the first time* when the pill is taken or
(*b*) migraine becomes "focal".

By "focal" is meant that other localised symptoms are experienced such as attacks of tingling or weakness on one side of the body, brief episodes of difficulty in speaking or visual disturbances such as transient loss of part of the field of vision. This might be a sign of a brief loss of blood supply to a part of the brain and a warning of the danger of stroke.

Headaches other than migraine: these are of course not uncommon in women who are not taking the pill. They are not uncommon in men. If they should increase when the pill is taken then changing the pill to one with a lower dose of oestrogen, or with a different progestogen (or even to one containing progestogen only) will help.

Blood pressure: In most women the blood pressure rises very slightly on the pill. In a few, it rises to above the normal level. Having a blood pressure higher than normal over a period of time renders a person more liable to diseases of the circulation. Fortunately the blood pressure is easy to monitor regularly.

Blood clotting: Blood clotting is a normal function of the body and is the body's way of sealing a cut or otherwise injured blood vessel. In women who take the pill various factors which influence blood clotting both in the blood itself and in the blood vessel wall, are altered, so that although the blood is slightly more liable to clot, the clot is more liable to be dissolved. The net result is still a slightly increased tendency to blood clotting (thrombosis).

Blood clotting or thrombosis can occur in a vein, or in an artery.

In a vein: It can extremely rarely occur in a normal vein in a person who is not taking the pill. It is only about four times more likely (or four times less unlikely) in a person taking the pill. If it occurs, it is usually in the deep veins of the leg, mainly because blood flow tends to be slowest there. It usually causes relatively little localised damage but very occasionally a piece of the blood clot can break off and be swept in the blood stream through the heart and into the lungs where it can block a blood vessel and even occasionally prove fatal.

NB Moderate varicose veins with no evidence of any past thrombosis are not reasons for not taking the pill.

In an artery (thrombosis) is due to the fact that "hardening of the arteries" (atherosclerosis) affects almost everyone and in the developed world has usually begun by the age of 20. Roughened patches on the artery wall allow blood clots to form on them and occasionally to block them. The pill slightly increases the risk of this happening, again by about 4-5 times. Other factors which more strongly increase the likelihood of this happening are smoking, which at less than 15 cigarettes/day increases the risk by 5 times and at more than 20 cigarettes/day increases the risk by 10 times,

increasing age, particularly the age of 35 years and older,

high blood pressure and

abnormal blood fats. A few people have these from birth, but this is a disorder which runs in families and can be detected by a blood test.

Clotting in an artery of the heart muscle is called coronary thrombosis. Clotting in an artery of the brain, and bleeding from an artery of the brain, which can result from a weak patch in a blood vessel and/or high blood pressure, are known as cerebral thrombosis or a stroke.

In October 1983 the results of one American and one British study of cancer among women using oral contraceptives were published in the medical press. The first of these appeared to suggest that long-term use of certain types of pill by younger women (under 25) may be associated with an increased risk of breast cancer; other previously published studies had shown no such connection. The British study showed that a group of women who had chosen to take a combined oral contraceptive had an increased incidence of cancer of the neck of the womb (cervical cancer) in comparison with a similar group of women who had elected to use intra-uterine contraceptive devices (*e.g.*, the coil). Both studies suggested that the progestogen content of mixed pills could be implicated. All the women in the pill group who had been found to have invasive cervical cancer were treated effectively.

The Committee on Safety of Medicines considered both these studies very carefully and concluded that women should be prescribed pills which had the lowest progestogen content but that there was no need for any woman to make an immediate change. Furthermore, the Committee endorsed the British study authors' recommendation that all long-term users of oral contraceptives should have regular cervical cytology examinations ("smears"). Of course, your family or clinic doctor will have all the Committee of Safety of Medicine's information and any more recent advice on this matter.

Helpful side effects: the pill almost always prevents period pains. It also frequently reduces the unpleasant effects of "premenstrual tension" which some women experience, including feelings of depression, irritability and tenseness.

The Progestogen-only pill.

This pill, as its name implies, contains only one hormone, progestogen. It is sometimes called the mini-pill but as this name is also occasionally used for very low dose combined pills, it will be better to call it the progestogen-only pill, or P-O-P.

Until the past year or two this pill was used mainly by women who were breast feeding as it is 98 per cent effective as a contraceptive, but does not diminish the milk flow. A very small amount of the hormone does get into the milk; it is not known whether this can affect the baby but it is thought that it does not.

Recently the P-O-P is being more widely used, particularly by women over the age of 35, and also by younger women. It is probably the next most effective method of birth control to the combined pill, having a failure rate of rather less than 2 pregnancies among 100 women taking it for a year.

Mode of action: The P-O-P works mainly by making the secretion from the neck of the womb (the cervix) scanty and thick so that the sperms do not get through. The pill does not as a rule stop the egg cell from being shed, so that the periods which come are natural periods, though they may be lighter than usual because the pill does make the lining of the uterus thinner and less suitable for a fertilised egg cell to settle in. It also probably slows down the transporting of the egg cell in the uterine tubes by diminishing the waves of movement in them which normally help to get the egg cell into the uterus.

Side effects: There are two slight risks with the P-O-P. One is the slight risk of unwanted

pregnancy. The other is the risk of the nuisance of irregular bleeding.

The irregular bleeding may take the form of more frequent, usually slight, bleeding or less frequent bleeding. Sometimes the periods cease altogether, or become extremely infrequent. This means that the very small amount of hormone in the pill is having a similar effect on the pituitary gland to that of the combined pill, so that it does not stimulate egg release in the ovaries. Provided it is ascertained that the pill-taker is not pregnant, the contraceptive effect is excellent in these people, and probably be cause the dose of hormone is so small the pituitary gland seems to recover its normal functions very rapidly when this pill is stopped. In general tests have shown that the P-O-P has far less effect on body chemistry than has the combined pill. Blood clotting and blood pressure seem to be little affected.

Method of taking the P-O-P.

The P-O-P is taken continuously and without breaks. Starting on the first day of a period it is taken every day. Because the effect on the secretion from the neck of the womb is greatest for the first six hours after taking it, it is advisable for it to be taken about six or seven o'clock in the evening, so that protection is high at bed time when intercourse is most likely. Because the effect rapidly declines after 24 hours it should be taken at the same time every day and not more than 2 hours late, otherwise the protection is broken. It takes about 2 weeks for the protection to build up initially, and the same after any break in protection due, for example, to being late taking a pill, missing a pill or pills or having a stomach upset.

The Coil or Intra Uterine Contraceptive Device (IUCD).

Coils are devices which are inserted into the uterus and remain there until a pregnancy is desired. All are made of plastic, some have very fine copper wire wound round them to increase their effectiveness. They are all highly effective, having a failure rate of about 2 pregnancies per 100 women using it for a year.

Each device has a thread attached to it which passes through the neck of the womb into the vagina. This can be pulled by the doctor when the coil is to be removed. A woman should never try to remove her coil herself.

The mode of action is not entirely clear, but the coil seems to prevent the fertilised egg cell from embedding in the uterus.

The method is generally considered to be more suitable for women who have had a baby than for those who have not, because in the latter the very slight risk of an infection ensuing is 7 times greater. An infection could occasionally, if untreated, proceed to involve the uterine tubes and, even rarely sealing them. A woman fitted with a coil not infrequently has slightly longer and heavier and occasionally more painful periods than were usual for her. The coil is used by about 5% of the 11 million women in the fertile age group 15–44.

The Cap or Diaphragm.

The cap or diaphragm is a circle of soft rubber with a firm rim which is inserted by the woman into the vagina so that it covers the neck of the womb (the cervix) and so physically prevents sperms from entering it. It is always used with a sperm-killing jelly or cream. There are a few different shapes of cap. Most are flat, but some are variations on a thimble shape and fit closely over the cervix. One of these is also made in plastic and can be used by a person who is allergic to rubber. The suitable cap size has to be estimated and the cap first fitted by a doctor (or nurse).

Method of use:

The cap can be put in anything up to 3 hours before intercourse, or longer if more sperm-killing preparation (spermicide) is inserted. The cap should be left in for 6–8 hours after intercourse, and if this happens again before 6 hours have elapsed, more spermicide is inserted and the cap is left in for a further 6 hours. It is then removed, washed with soft soap and water and stored in its box.

The cap has the advantage of being absolutely harmless to health. It does not affect the periods or the body systems or chemistry in any way.

It is slightly less effective than either pill or coil. The failure rate has been estimated variously as 2–8 per 100 women using it for a year, probably varying with the conscientiousness of the user. It is used by about 3 % of women in the fertile age group.

Method Used by the Man.

The sheath (or condom or "Durex"). The sheath is made of very fine rubber, nowadays almost always including a lubricant and usually including a spermicide. Most have a teat-shaped end to receive the semen.

Method of use: The air should be squeezed out of the teat end before the sheath is put on so that there is room for the semen and the sheath will not burst. The sheath should then be unrolled on to the erect penis before the penis makes any contact with the woman, as there can be a drop of fluid which contains sperms and is quite sufficient to make her pregnant. The man should hold the sheath in place when he withdraws. Unless the sheath contains spermicide the woman should always use a spermicidal pessary or foam in addition.

Advantages: Sheaths are completely harmless and in fact can give some protection against sexually transmitted diseases ("V.D.") They are readily available—*free* (when *prescribed* by the doctor) from all Area Health Authority Family Planning Clinics and on payment from chemists' shops and from slot machines which are found mainly in public houses, hotels, garages and service stations and sometimes in clubs, restaurants and holiday camps.

The failure rate is variously estimated at between 0·4 and 6 per 100 couples using it for a year and can be very low if the method is conscientiously used. The method is second only to the pill in the number of people using it—25 per cent of couples where the woman is in the fertile age-group.

Natural Methods of Birth Control.

Natural methods can have a high effectiveness rate. They are all based on the woman finding out when her egg cell is shed, *i.e.*, her "ovulation time", and avoiding intercourse around that time. Sperms can live in the vagina for up to 5 days and the egg cell lives for up to 24 hours after it is shed.

There are two methods of detecting ovulation time.

The **calendar method** involves the woman in recording her menstrual cycle for *at least 6 months* before it can any way be relied on. The woman must make a note of the first day of bleeding of each cycle. The last day of the cycle is the day before the next onset of bleeding. The calculation of the "safe period" is made by deducting 18 from the shortest cycle and 11 from the longest. For example, with a shortest cycle of 25 days and a longest of 31 the safe period would be *before* day 7 and *after* day 20 (25−18=7; 31−11=20). If only the safe period around day 20 is used the method is considerably more reliable.

The **temperature method** is based on the fact that immediately after ovulation there is a distinct rise in body temperature which persists until the next period starts. The method involves taking the temperature first thing every morning *before* eating, drinking or smoking and plotting it on a chart each day. The safe period begins about four days *after* ovulation (as detected by the rise in temperature) and continues until the next menstrual period begins.

Other home-methods of finding the moment of ovulation continue to be explored, including tests on the mucus from the cervix, which becomes thin, clear and "stringy" at ovulation times; tests on vaginal enzymes; and even urine tests, but no simple test requiring no expertise is yet available.

Coitus Interruptus.

This should be mentioned in this section on "natural methods" because it is probably used at some time by many couples. It means that the man withdraws his penis before climax or ejaculation. This requires great will-power at the height of sexual excitation. Even if withdrawal is achieved, it may be too late. There are enough sperms in the drop of fluid which emerges from the penis in the early stages of sexual stimulation to cause a pregnancy. The method is therefore highly fallible, frustrating and often futile—akin to "shutting the stable door . . ." Although it cannot be recommended, it is a method requiring no expert help or artificial equipment, and is better than nothing. The failure rate is around 17 % .

Sterilisation.

(i) Women: Tubal tie or Tubal ligation.

This means cutting the tubes which carry the egg cells from the ovary to the uterus. Although this is not a major operation it may involve a general anaesthetic and an abdominal operation. It can now sometimes be done through a very small cut under a local anaesthetic with an instrument called a laparoscope, which can shine a light into the abdomen through a quite narrow tube. At operation the uterine tubes are cut and a piece taken out before each end is sealed. In addition the cut end nearest the uterus may also be embedded in the uterine wall to make doubly sure that the two ends do not rejoin. Sometimes the tubes are not cut but gold clips are put on to close the lumens of the tubes.

The operation must be regarded as irreversible as it is extremely rarely possible to reverse it.

(ii) Men: Vasectomy.

Vasectomy means cutting the tubes which carry the sperms into the semen or seminal fluid, which is the fluid produced during intercourse.

The testicles have two functions. One is to produce sperms. The other is to produce the hormone testosterone which gives a man his maleness, for example his deep voice and his beard, and his sex drive. The hormone is carried in the blood stream. The sperms are carried in special tubes called the *vas deferens* which run under the skin of the scrotum. Thus the tubes are easily accessible to the surgeon. At operation the tube on each side is cut and a small piece is removed. This is to leave a gap to prevent the cut ends from re-uniting. The cut ends are sealed and the skin cut closed. The operation takes 15–20 minutes, can be done under general or local anaesthetic, and causes minimal discomfort after wards. The result of the operation is that the sperms formed in the testicle do not get through to the penis. They go on being formed, but are gradually broken down again and reabsorbed by the blood stream. The sperms which are already in the *vas* beyond the cut end will still go into the seminal fluid, and it may be 3 months before they have all been ejected. A sample of fluid is usually checked about 2 months after the operation, and another 2 weeks later. There is no visible change in the fluid, only under the microscope can it be seen that there are no sperms in it. Nor is there any change in a man's virility, potency or sex drive. A man should have the operation only if he is sure he will not wish for further children. Although in some cases it may be possible to reverse the operation and give him back his fertility this can never be certain. He should be prepared to accept that it is irreversible.

DRUG ABUSE AND DRUG DEPENDENCE.

The Problem.

The *abuse* of drugs around the world is at present of large proportions, increasing rapidly and showing no signs of diminishing. It is responsible each year for thousands of deaths by suicide and by accidental overdosage; for an enormous but virtually unmeasurable amount of private suffering; and for the loss to society, in terms of reduced working efficiency, of millions of working hours every year. Around 11 million people in the UK have used illegal drugs and a staggering 500,000 are believed to be drug addicts.

Serious problems are caused by the illegal importation and distribution of drugs such as heroin and cocaine, crack and ecstasy (most prevalent in affluent areas). Other problems arise from the misuse of drugs given by doctors for their effects on the central nervous system—the pain- killers, sleeping pills, "stimulants," and "tranquillisers."

Drugs and Medicines.

To the doctor, any substance is a drug that can be introduced into the body from outside, and that is capable of producing some detectable effect. Most such substances have a beneficial use. They are "medicines," and as such are given by doctors in suitable cases. Others, for example, nicotine (in cigarettes), alcohol (in beer, wine, or spirits), and carbon monoxide (in coal gas), are of doubtful benefit and of certain harm and are used by doctors, if at all, only under certain very special and usually experimental conditions.

Medicines may be classified under four main headings. First, there are those like quinine, or penicillin and other so-called antibiotics, that actually cure diseases by eradicating the organism (bacteria or other parasites) that cause disturbance of normal bodily function. Second, drugs such as insulin or the steroids overcome in the unhealthy the lack of some necessary substance a healthy body manufactures for itself: they must usually continue to be given for life. Third are the drugs which relieve the signs of disease—for example, there are many new drugs that lower the blood pressure or increase the output of urine—without being able to put right the disturbed basic situation which is the cause of the trouble. Fourth are drugs to relieve the patient's symptoms—which make him feel better, less breathless, take away his pain, help him to sleep, and so on—although we seldom know why they are able to do this.

There is no doubt that the genuine advances in beneficial drugs during the last sixty years have been enormous; but the very successes of the penicillins, tetracyclines, antimalarials, hormones, and so on have bred in the public and in the medical profession itself an attitude of uncritical wonder. There have been relatively few drugs in the first and second categories mentioned above; and in the field of mental health, the importance of which is now so rightly emphasised, there are virtually none. Thus, although there are many drugs which act upon the mind, few do this in any fundamental sense; they relieve pain and anxiety, bring sleep and lessening of stress, and may allow the patient to recuperate himself during the relief they provide. But often this deeper change does not occur—sometimes because the doctor has not clearly seen his part in helping to bring it about—and then the symptomatic relief may come to be sought for its own sake.

Dangers of Long-term Use of Drugs acting on the Brain.

1. **Toxic effects.** Drugs which act upon the nervous system, like any others, have characteristic toxic or unwanted effects of their own (incidentally, these may become apparent rapidly; even, on rare occasions, after only a single dose). Such effects may have little or nothing to do with the desired effects for which they are being prescribed and taken. For example, it has only come to be realised quite recently that aspirin is liable to cause bleeding, which is occasionally serious, from the lining of the stomach in a large proportion of people who take aspirin regularly. Some drugs may cause rashes and other allergic reactions in susceptible subjects; and jaundice, fainting, tremors, and motor disorders are known to occur in some patients taking a variety of other drugs.

2. **"Rebound."** The body works in such a way, over a variety of its activities, that it tends to return to a "neutral" position after it has departed from this for any reason. For example, over-eating tends to be followed by a lessening

of appetite, at least for a time; the runner makes up for his air-deficit during the race by breathing more deeply thereafter; and if, at rest, you breathe for a time more rapidly and deeply than you need, this period will be followed by one in which you breathe *less* often than usual until the balance is restored. These illustrations—and there are others—have nothing to do with drugs; but in a similar way, it seems that if a continued pain, or an unpleasant emotional state such as anxiety or depression is changed into its opposite, or removed altogether by the use of a drug, the prior state may return with increased force when the drug is no longer taken. The "rebound" phenomenon, naturally, encourages the patient to take another dose, and so on.

3. **Habit formation.** This alternation of mood-changed-by-drug with the disturbed mood itself leads to the habit of taking the drug. The patient comes to rely upon it and to take it anyway, even before the unpleasant state has returned. At this stage he is said to be "habituated"; he has a psychological need for the drug, and later may become disturbed at the possibility that it will not be available when he needs it. This might not matter so greatly, if it were not that continued use of drugs in this way has physical consequences as well.

4. **Tolerance and habituation.** The body also tends to restore its own balance when drugs are given, too. It "learns" surprisingly quickly how to deal with substances with which it has never before been confronted, so that it eliminates subsequent doses more and more quickly and completely. Thus the effect of each successive dose is smaller and lasts for progressively shorter periods of time. To counter this, the patient tends to increase the dose: and the vicious circle continues. At this point he has become physically dependent upon the drug: and he may suffer physically—sometimes so severely that he dies—if supplies are not continued.

As he increases the dose in this way, so his tolerance of its effects increases, to such an extent that after prolonged use he may be taking doses of a drug that are five or ten times greater than those which will kill somebody not dependent upon them in this way. It sometimes happens that a patient develops a renewed craving at some point after a course of treatment, in which the dose of drug has been reduced without removing the underlying cause of his dependence. He may then obtain and use the dose he habitually took before treatment, not knowing that his body will have lost its tolerance of such doses. That dose is now as high for him as for any other person and so may be lethal. There has been a number of deaths for this reason.

Factors in the Causation of Dependence.

The risk of becoming dependent upon a drug is governed by three main factors; the drug itself, the personality of the individual who takes it, and the circumstances in which it is taken. Most adults have taken alcohol at one time or another, unless it is against their code to do so; yet *relatively* few are dependent upon it (relatively few, but many too many; more than half a million in the United Kingdom alone).

Many of us have had morphine or some other strong analgesic for medical reasons, without becoming dependent upon it (whatever so-called addicts say, it is extremely rare for anyone to become dependent on an opiate because he was introduced to it in a medical setting).

However, if we start to take such a drug "for kicks"—as more and more people, particularly teenagers and young adults are doing—it is extremely probable that we shall become dependent upon it, and sooner rather than later at that.

It is also probable that each one of us would become dependent, were he obliged to take it regularly, for long enough, and in sufficient dosage. Thus, although there are personalities—psychopathic, immature, or unstable—that are more prone than others to become dependent if they are exposed to the drug, there are also drugs that are more likely than others to cause such dependence no matter to whom they are given. The extent of the dependence will vary; with some, it is never physiological but remains psychological (but not the less real or disturbing for that). Also, the rate at which dependence develops may vary; and the picture presented by the dependent subject—the extent to which his normal life is impaired, or to which he becomes dangerous to himself or others—varies as well. In a very much oversimplified way, some of these relationships will now be summarised for certain substances.

Types of Dependence.

Heroin, morphine and cocaine are usually injected. Amphetamines ("Benzedrine") are tablets or capsules, and marijuana ("reefer," hashish) is smoked in cigarettes. Heroin and cocaine are now usually taken together. Combinations of drugs often act differently from their individual constituents and patients dependent upon them are even more difficult to treat.

Psychological dependence is considerable with heroin, morphine, cocaine, and amphetamine, but much less with marijuana.

Physiological dependence is great with heroin and morphine, less with barbiturates, alcohol, and amphetamine in that order, and virtually nil with cocaine and marijuana. Personality plays a greater part in initiating dependence on alcohol, marijuana, and barbiturates than with the others. Heroin, cocaine, and morphine are the cause of more antisocial tendencies in dependent people than alcohol, barbiturates, and amphetamine.

One danger of marijuana is that the search for it will lead the searcher into localities where his risk of exposure to even more dangerous influences is greatly increased. It is thus sometimes argued that if it were legal to consume marijuana, the number of young people who yearly become dependent upon the other more dangerous drugs would in fact decrease. There is as yet no evidence for or against this proposition. The number of drug dependent people in the UK is rising fast for heroin, crack and cocaine.

This number is very large for alcohol, and is increasing in the case of marijuana. Very few people are dependent on morphine, and the number is not growing.

Treatment.

Exhortations, imprisonment, and other moralistic or legalistic approaches are useless. Treatment of any person dependent upon a drug is a matter for a qualified psychotherapist. It is liable to be time-consuming and frustrating for patient and doctor, and it is sometimes unsuccessful. At present, there are too few specialists or centres where treatment can be obtained, although it is to be hoped that this situation will change as the problem is increasingly seen by our society to be of exceptional gravity.

When there is little or no chance of cure, prevention is certainly the best treatment. Drugs should only be taken on the prescription of a doctor; and the patient should remind him from time to time, if this be necessary, that he would like to dispense with his drugs as soon as the doctor thinks it possible.

PART III. SPECIAL TOPICS

SPOTLIGHT ON ALLERGIES

Note Readers of this article may also wish to refer to the section on Asthma (Z31).

Introduction

Allergy is an unwanted response by the immune system to a foreign particle. It is a rapidly growing problem. If the escalating epidemic continues, half of all Europeans may be suffering some form of allergy by 2015. The body may be reacting to a sting, a drug or food. The guilty substance (allergen) may encounter the immune system by swallowing, inhalation, injection or even contact with the skin. One of the most common ten causes of long term disease, allergies range from annoyances to life threatening. Around 20 children a year actually die from food allergies.

The allergic response is from a part of the immune system which arose early in evolution. The immune system consists of white blood cells and proteins in the circulation, recognising any substance which is not part of the human body. It can identify bacteria or cells infected with viruses, produce antibodies which will only attach to them and destroy the invaders flagged up by these antibodies. This is an elegant system which keeps us infection-free with the minimum of damage to healthy body parts.

Other parts of the immune system have a cruder approach. Basic antibodies recognise foreign substances and try to fight them by making the surrounding body part "leaky". This is aimed at diluting the offending poison. Leaky blood vessels allow the intelligent white blood cells to attack the poison more easily. Leakiness is achieved by the simple antibody (immunoglobulin E, or IgE) latching onto a specialised cell (mast cell) which forces it to empty its store of highly active chemicals. Histamine is the most active of these. This is also the start of an allergic response.

Anaphylactic Shock

The most dangerous allergic response is called "anaphylactic shock", shock being the medical term for any severe drop in blood pressure. The victim, perhaps having eaten a peanut or been stung by a wasp, swells up in the face and limbs. The victim then becomes wheezy and finds it increasingly difficult to breath. Low blood pressure leads to inadequate blood flow to the brain and fainting. This dramatic overall response is due to the simple fact of "leakiness". Leaky blood vessels allow water out of the bloodstream and into body tissues, hence swelling. An emptier bloodstream means the heart does not have enough volume to pump and maintain a high enough pressure. Leaky lungs are irritable and constrict, leading to wheeze.

Treatment for Anaphylactic Shock

Treatment for anaphylactic shock needs to be given immediately. Histamine release is the signal which starts the event, and anti-histamine tablets or injections are only of use if given within the first few minutes. The victim *must* go immediately to an Accident & Emergency Department. There, oxygen and drugs to open the lung airways can be given. Fluid can be infused into the blood to restore blood pressure. Steroid tablets or injections will start to calm down the unwanted immune system chemicals. Most importantly, adrenaline, given by a painless injection, will tighten up the leaky blood vessels and reverse the whole process.

Adrenaline Injections

Adrenaline is life-saving and anyone who experiences a bad reaction to food or an insect sting should carry their own injection at all times. Easily-used syringes, for example "epipen" are available. Sufferers' friends and family should be happy with the simple task of rolling up clothes on a swelling-up victim and injecting the ampoule of adrenalin 1cm into a pinched fold of skin over the flank. A trip by ambulance to hospital is then essential, as the patient will need close observation for the next few hours in case of relapse.

Skin Allergies

At the other end of the allergic spectrum, skin allergies occur by smaller amounts of histamine release locally. The skin may be irritated in a self-perpetuating way, as in some forms of eczema, or only when in contact with the allergen (such as reactions to nickel on belt buckles or jewellery). Latex in surgical gloves provokes allergy in 5% of people and is a major problem for the health service. The common and embarrassing problem of anal itchiness is usually caused by a reaction in the sensitive anal puckered skin to soaps or shampoos.

As the immune reaction is local in skin allergy, locally applied steroid creams are the mainstay of treatment. Hydrocortisone, one of the oldest steroid medicines, is safe and effective. Although use every-day for months can lead to permanent skin thinning, short periods of treatment are safe even on the skin of young children. The solution to skin allergy is careful detective work to discover the offending substance.

Medicine Allergies

Penicillin allergy is the most well-known allergic problem with medicines. As with all allergies the response varies, from a mild rash, through wheeziness to full anaphylactic shock. Around 2.5% of the population will show sensitivity to penicillin on skin-testing, but the proportion of these who will suffer a dangerous reaction on receiving the drug will be far smaller. Up to 50 people a year will die from penicillin allergy. Hospital notes are clearly marked if a patient has reacted to penicillin in the past, and the patient will be given a bracelet to wear showing their allergic status. There are many alternative antibiotics which can be safely used instead.

Hay Fever

Hay fever, or allergic rhinitis ("rhinitis" is Greek for swollen nose), is, like asthma, becoming more common. The allergen provoking hay fever is, of course, pollen. Trees, flowers and weeds release their pollens at different times of the year. Sufferers may be allergic to more than one type of pollen, thus experiencing symptoms throughout the year. Otherwise the flowering season of most plants lasts for a minnin only a portion of the summer.

Newer anti-histamine tablets are effective, do not induce drowsiness and last all day. Older tablets were plagued by side-effects, including an interaction with antibiotics or grapefruit juice leading to fatal heart rhythms. These are now off the market. If no relief occurs with anti-histamines, anti-inflammatory nose sprays containing steroids usually control symptoms after a few days' use.

Food Allergies

Food allergies are common and potentially dangerous. Cow's milk, egg, shellfish, peanuts and chocolate are justifiably well-known as potential culprits. A mere 1/40,000th of a peanut kernel can be fatal to a highly allergic individual. Some foods are rich in histamine, the chemical dumped by mast cells which starts the natural allergic response. These include cheeses, wine and tuna. Eating offending examples of these produces an allergic-like reaction, but on other occasions may be eaten with impunity. Food intolerances are not allergies, as seen in milk (lactose) intolerance. This is due to a relative lack of the gut enzyme lactose dehydrogenase, and treatment will be quite different. Treatment of food allergy is the same as for any other allergic reaction.

Allergies in Children

Children are often plagued by allergies as their immune systems are still new to all the chemicals found in the world. Colic is the gut's unhappy response to cow's milk or other foods, and often improves with breast feeding. Mothers can eat foods which baby is allergic to, and pass the trigger chemical in their milk, and thus have to avoid eating the guilty food in future.

Vaccines

The rising rate of childhood allergic diseases—this includes asthma, discussed on Z31(2)—has been suggested to be the fault of vaccines 'irritating' the immune system into oversensitivity. Others suggest that childhood diseases 'strengthen' the immune system. Despite increased immunisation rates for tuberculosis, diphtheria and measles in many countries, studies have not found a matching increase in allergic diseases.

The increase in allergies, with all the nuisance and danger that accompany them, still remains a mystery.

PROBLEMS OF PROSTATE CANCER

Introduction

In 2005 in England and Wales around 27,000 men were diagnosed with this disease and currently 10,000 die from it. Prostate cancer increased by 50 per cent in men under 60 in the years 1980 to 2000. Prostate cancer, after lung and bowel, is the third commonest male cancer. In men, 7% of cancers are of the prostate. By age 80, 80% of men will have early cancer in their prostate glands, although this usually grows slowly and is of no significance. The risks are increased testosterone levels, and the disease runs in families. The prostate gland sits under the bladder and in front of the rectum. It can easily be felt on rectal examination. A normal gland is smooth and has two distinct lobes.

Benign Prostatic Hypertrophy

An important distinction to be made is between prostate cancer and a very common condition called benign prostatic hypertrophy. In two-thirds of men over 70, the prostate gland enlarges under the influence of natural male hormones. Eunuchs do not have this problem. The condition is not a cancer and cannot spread beyond the prostate. However, as the tube which carries urine from the bladder through the penis to the outside world (the urethra) passes close to the prostate gland, enlargement can lead to the urethra becoming obstructed. This is a frequently seen problem leading to urinary retention. Retention of urine is extremely painful and requires a rubber tube to be placed into the bladder through the penis.

Prostate Gland Enlargement

In prostate cancer, islands of cancerous cells arise during the natural turnout of cells in the gland. The speed of their growth is variable. A cancerous prostate gland loses its normal shape and may become very large. Cancer cells may also spread to other parts of the body. Spread to the skeleton can result in the bones breaking even in the absence of an accident.

Medical Examination

A doctor may go about investigating the suspicion of prostate cancer in several ways. Blood tests can measure 'PSA' levels throughout treatment. PSA meaning 'Prostatic Specific Antigen', a chemical signature of an abnormal prostate gland. Unfortunately PSA levels are increased in any other condition affecting the prostate and thus cannot be relied upon to confirm the presence of cancer. Rectal ultrasound, which is not as excruciating as it may sound, can demonstrate gland size and extension clearly. A biopsy can be taken, which involves using a special needle to cut a small section of the gland away for microscopic examination. A radioactive-marker bone scan will reveal presence and location of cancer deposits in the bones. An X-ray of the kidneys using dye may show any obstruction of the kidneys (the path of urine from the kidneys to the outside may be blocked by the cancer).

Current Methods of Treatment

Treatment of advanced prostate cancer relies on the fact that the gland depends on male hormones to give it the necessary signals to continue growing (hence eunuchs, who do not have testes to make testosterone, are rarely affected). A slow release injection can be given which stops male hormone release. This may be a drug called buserelin or gosarelin, the trade name of which is Zoladex. Initially the tumour flares up with treatment, as the injection briefly increases male hormone production. This period needs to be covered with drugs that block the male hormones directly, such as cyproterone acetate. This is a classic example of *hormonal manipulation*. This is an effective technique in most tumours which arise from glandular tissue, such as ovarian cancer or cancer of the breast. A side effect of this treatment is impotence in some men.

A very effective but occasionally unpalatable method of achieving the same result is to remove both testes. This is an easy operation and may halt the disease for one to two years. Surgery is often used for early disease in an attempt at cure. Radiotherapy can also be given to the prostate, as an alternative to surgery, and is the usual treatment for less fit or older men.

Postscript

Trials of a revolutionary non-invasive procedure to dissolve tumours using an advanced ultrasound technique began in Britain in 2004. This new method (Hifu, short for High Intensity Focused Ultrasound) does not involve the debilitating side effects of current treatment, which sometimes involve impotence and incontinence.

FOCUS ON DIABETES

Introduction

The world today (2006) faces a diabetes crisis. Across the globe more than 300 million people are at risk of developing diabetes. The current total of sufferers is 194 million. In the UK alone there are over 2 million diabetics (a surge of 600,000 in the last 8 years). As people live longer, and as obesity continues unchecked, the problem is growing.

Everybody knows someone with diabetes. The term applies to a range of disorders in which the patient's blood sugar (glucose) level is increased. Certain drugs can cause diabetes, but it is usually due to failure of the body's glucose regulation system.

Glucose

Humans need glucose. Whilst fats and proteins can be burnt as fuel in some organs, glucose is the main energy source. Carbohydrate-containing food is broken down and absorbed by the digestive tract and stored in the liver and muscle. The body's signal to mop up glucose and store it away is insulin. Without insulin, glucose levels in the blood rise very high and is simply passed out in urine; the kidneys only being able to keep a small fraction of the glucose passing through them. This is why some diabetics are thin and wasted.

Insulin

Diabetes can come about in two ways. Insulin is not produced in enough quantities, or at all, or the body does not recognise the insulin signal. Insulin is produced from the pancreas, a yellow organ 30cm long that nestles at the back of the abdomen next to the small intestine. Insulin release is prompted by signals sent from the intestine when it senses glucose in the food it contains.

Types of Diabetes

There are two forms of diabetes.

1) Type One, or **Insulin Dependent**. This is the form people have when they are diabetic from childhood.

The body attacks the part of the pancreas where insulin is made, the β-cells of the Islets of Langerhans. This is because of a malfunction of the immune system. Antibodies which should recognise foreign bodies such as bacteria, instead think theses cells are alien and start an immune reaction which destroys them all eventually. People with Type One diabetes need to start on insulin straightaway.

2) Type Two, or **Non-Insulin Dependent**. In this form, the liver, pancreas and all the body's insulin receptors are at fault. The liver fails to make the storage form of glucose (glycogen). The insulin receptors which sit on all cells and look out for insulin are defective. The pancreas does not make enough insulin, and certainly not the extra amounts necessary to stimulate the sluggish, defective receptors. Overweight people need more insulin due to their increased bulk and their pancreases are even more overworked, thus they get diabetes earlier. Whether the intrinsic organ problems lead to obesity is not clear.

Treatment

Diet:

A low carbohydrate diet, which is essentially a good, healthy diet which we all should eat, is the best start to treatment. Starchy foods, sweets and biscuits will harm the diabetes control severely.

Tablets and Injections:

Type Two diabetes can be treated for the first decades with tablets. These tablets make the body more receptive to insulin, and stimulate the tired pancreas to produce more. Tablets such as glibenclamide or gliclazide work this way. The other sort of tablet is the large pill, metformin. This helps the body mop up glucose when insulin is around, but works mainly by stopping the liver producing glucose afresh, which it can by recycling 'burnt' glucose and using muscle protein elements. Metformin helps people lose weight by this block on the liver, forcing their bodies' to burn fat instead.

Type One diabetics, and eventually those with Type Two, must **replace their insulin** directly. Rather than have insulin released directly into their liver and thence the rest of the body from their pancreas, these sufferers must inject themselves with artificial insulin. As insulin is a small, relatively simple molecule, artificial insulin is identical to their own insulin (when they were still able to make it). There is still a role for insulin collected from pigs and cows.

Insulin injection is now often by tiny needles incorporated into 'pens'. These can be injected through clothing and are painless. Although the switch to injected insulin is often feared, it is quickly part of the normal routine. Insulin can either be in a fast form, which stays in the body for a short time, or a slow form, which stays in the body all day. Combinations ensure that there is a low background level of slow insulin, with more 'fast' insulin around at mealtimes.

Medical researchers are now developing a 'patch' that administers insulin through the skin (thus avoiding daily injections). There are hopes it could be available in 5–10 years.

Side Effects of Insulin

Hypo's Hypoglycaemia (Greek for "Low Blood Sugar") is the major side effect of insulin. It does not happen with the tablet treatment of diabetes unless the person has kidney problems. It is the reason why diabetics are so sensitive about going without food. Hypo's comes about because once insulin has been injected, it will tell the body to mop up glucose from the blood regardless of how low the glucose level is. If there is not enough glucose in the blood for the brain to function, the person will pass out, having first got confused, irritable and dizzy. The pulse rate will rise and heart palpitations will be felt. Most diabetics can feel a hypo coming on (an 'aura') and easily avert it by having a sweet drink or a biscuit.

Long-Term Complications

Patients often complain about having to take so

many tablets, or having to inject themselves and having to put up with (possibly dangerous) hypoglycaemic attacks. The reason why aggressive treatment is necessary is because diabetics, untreated, will go blind, have heart attacks, stop urinating and die from kidney failure, have their toes and feet literally fall off, or die of dehydration due to rampant glucose levels.

All these complications deserve a chapter each, but their root cause is high glucose levels causing everything in the body, especially the smaller blood vessels, to get a 'sugar coating'. This stops their proper function. Diabetic eye disease is the commonest cause of blindness in the Western world. It is one of the commonest reasons for people to require kidney dialysis. Diabetic ulcers form on feet and the lower leg, and get infected. Diabetic nerve damage leads to sensation loss. This means sore feet continue to be walked on until joints are destroyed and skin breaks down. Diabetical blood vessel disease leads to loss of blood flow. This is such a problem in the extremities that toes may die. Happily these problems are not seen often nowadays, but diabetics must always realise that they have been burdened with a serious affliction. Thankfully we now have the weapons to fight it.

MEDICAL NEWS AND NOTES

PET Scans

Positron emission tomography (PET) scans are the latest refinement of the technique of injecting a radioactive marker to study disease. New markers have been developed to measure processes such as glucose metabolism. This makes them particularly useful for examining a range of different cancers, and they may show the spread of cancer much earlier than other tests. They can also help accurately target treatments such as radiation therapy. In future, they may give an idea of response to treatments like chemotherapy, long before the results would otherwise be known.

These tests are not only more sensitive and accurate but often also easier on patients.

Health Information on the Internet

The Internet is a powerful tool for finding information, for both patients and doctors. However, much of the material on the Internet may be unreliable or incomplete. If you are looking for health information, a good idea is to start with the Web site of an organisation that you already have confidence in. For example, both the UK and US governments have useful sites—NHS direct (*www.nhsdirect.nhs.uk*) and Medlineplus (*www.medlineplus.gov*).

You may want to visit other sites, such as patient support groups. You should check these sites are not out of date, and it makes sense to verify any information from a range of sources. You should not try to get medical advice over the Internet or attempt self-diagnosis. However the Internet can be very helpful at suggesting questions to discuss with your doctor. Remember that your own doctor knows your medical condition and can tailor any discussion to your personal needs.

Evidence-Based Medicine (EBM)

A surprising amount of medical practice has been based on common sense or opinion rather than scientific studies. "Evidence based medicine" (EBM) is an approach aimed at helping doctors find "the current best available evidence" to manage any particular medical condition. This has been helped by the computer revolution—doctors now have access to databases summarising the scientific evidence.

Often medical experts have prepared reports, after examining all the published research critically and in detail. EBM also makes use of techniques such as "adding together" a number of smaller studies to produce a large study. For example, a review of many studies of bed rest as a treatment for lower back-pain found that it is ineffective and may in fact delay recovery.

Clinical studies are an important way of progressing medical understanding. If you are offered the opportunity to participate in a trial of a new treatment you should consider it carefully. There is some evidence that patients on studies, even if receiving standard treatments, do better. At the same time most of the benefit from taking part will be for future patients in the same situation. Ethics committees will have reviewed the study and ensured patients who participate are not disadvantaged.

One common way of trying to decide which of two possible treatments is better is dividing patients into two groups and treating each differently. To ensure that the only difference is due to the treatment, the group acts as a scientific "control". Such studies are known as *randomised controlled trials*. They are very important in deciding which treatment is better for different medical conditions.

Mouth Cancer (Oral Cancer)

A new awareness programme to highlight the spread of mouth cancer was launched in November 2005. With 4,300 new cases each year in the UK, and around 1,700 deaths annually, cancer of the lips, tongue, cheek and throat has now become more frequent. The mouth should be examined regularly to check for warning signs such as ulcers that do not heal or red and white patches.

Once considered mainly a disease of men over 50, it now affects more younger men (and the number of women with the disease has risen by a third since 1995). Excess alcohol intake, as well as smoking, are being blamed.

PART IV. GLOSSARY

Alternative Medicine. *See* J3.

Alzheimer's Disease, results in slowly advancing dementia affecting all aspects of brain function, leading to personality disintegration. The disease affects one in 20 people over 65 and almost a quarter of those over 85.

Anabolic Steroids. Synthetic hormones which stimulate growth, muscle development and sex drive.

Anaesthetic. Any drug used to abolish pain during an operation.

Ankylosis. Partial or complete fixation of a joint as after some types of arthritis. In other cases deliberately produced by surgery.

Ankylosing Spondylitis (AS). A painful progressive rheumatic disease, mainly but not always of the spine.

Antibiotics, a collective name for any substance derived from micro-organisms or fungi which is capable of destroying infections, *e.g.*, penicillin.

Avian Flu. *See* **Bird Flu** (*below*).

Barium meal. Barium sulphate is opaque to X-rays and before X-ray pictures of the alimentary canal radiologists give a "barium meal" to the patient so that the alimentary canal shows up more clearly. Barium X-rays can reveal diseases of the bowel.

Bird Flu (Avian Flu), typical flu-like symptoms, eye infections, pneumonia and respiratory disease contracted from birds, chickens *etc.* in Asia. There are fears the strain could mutate and transfer between humans.

Blood Groups. Human blood plasma contains factors which clump, or agglutinate, the red cells of some other people's blood. The main blood groups are called A, B, AB, and O. The plasma of group A blood contains an anti-B factor and *vice versa*, so that people of groups A and B cannot accept each other's blood. Group AB contains neither anti-A nor anti-B factor and people with this group can therefore receive transfusions from both but can give to neither. Group O contains both anti-A and anti-B, and can therefore receive blood only from group O but can donate blood to all groups. It is important that transfused cells should not be agglutinated by the factors in the recipient's plasma. Apart from the so-called ABO system, there are several other blood groupings, one of which is mentioned under **Rhesus Factor.**

Cachexia. Extreme wasting due to disease.

Caesarean operation. When the abdomen has to be opened to remove the child.

Carbohydrates. The scientific name for sugars, starches and cellulose, *See* **Z34**(1), **Z39–40**.

Chill. What is ordinarily called a chill is merely an infection by the germs causing cold and influenza. But a chill may be the preliminary to almost any infectious disease

Chlamydia, the most common sexually-transmitted infection in Britain. It can lead to pelvic inflammatory disease and infertility. In the UK, one in eight teenage girls has chlamydia. New nationwide screening is now set to be introduced.

Chronic. A chronic disease is one which is prolonged and relatively mild, as opposed to an acute one which is short and severe.

Claustrophobia. A physical symptom, which causes the individual to be afraid of enclosed spaces. *See under* **Obsessional neurosis, Z51** (1).

Coccyx. The end of the spinal column.

Cortisone. A hormone produced by the adrenal glands. *See* **Z43**(1).

Cryoablation, the freezing of tissue. An increasingly common treatment for corns, warts and also cancer of the kidney, prostate and skin.

Cryosurgery. A pioneering treatment for cancer which destroys tumours by freezing them.

Down's syndrome, a genetic condition caused by the presence of an extra chromosome—47 instead of 46. Those affected have learning disabilities and difficulties in sitting, crawling and walking. Babies born to older mothers have a higher chance of having Down's syndrome.

Dyslexia, a specific learning disability that can affect reading, writing, memory *etc.* It is hereditary and scientists have now discovered the gene responsible for it. New flashing light treatment is having positive results for many sufferers. There are 375,000 children in the UK with dyslexia.

Dyspraxia, a developmental disorder in which the organisation and sequencing of movement is impaired. Boys are four times more likely to be affected than girls. The Dyspraxia Foundation helpline is 01462 454986.

Economy class syndrome is deep vein thrombosis (*see* **Z30**)—a clot in the veins deep in the leg ("deep vein thrombosis") which travels via the bloodstream to the lungs ("pulmonary embolism"). Periods of immobility, such as during long flights, predispose to its development.

Ecstasy ("e" or MDMA) is an illicit drug that stops brain cells from reclaiming a chemical used to signal between cells (*see* **Z46**). This leaves the signal from these cells switched on resulting in an emotional high and a feeling of closeness to others. Users often take it before all night dancing. It occasionally causes an uncontrolled rise in body temperature (hyperthermia) which may be fatal, and may cause depression.

ECT. The abbreviated form of the name for a modern type of treatment for certain psychiatric disorders—electro-convulsive-therapy. *See under* **Psychosis, Z50**(1).

Empyema. A collection of pus in the lung (usually a complication of other diseases)

Endemic. Referring to a disease, means prevalent in a particular area.

Endocarditis. Disease of the valves of the heart, *See* **Z29**(2).

Endometriosis, a condition producing pelvic pain in which the endometrial cells lining the uterus start to flourish elsewhere in the body.

Ganglion. A small cystic swelling, usually on the wrist, dealt with by simple surgical treatment.

Gastritis. Inflammation of the stomach.

Geriatrics. The medical study of old age.

Gingivitis. Inflammation of the gums due to infection and requiring treatment by a dentist.

Haemoglobin. The red pigment in the blood.

Hallucinogen, a drug which acts upon the brain to create sensory illusions or hallucinations with a variety of emotional effects. One of the most widely studied is LSD (*q.v.*) which will produce symptoms very similar to those found in some mental disorders.

Heller's syndrome, a condition similar to autism.

HPV (Human Papilloma Virus), a virus now known to be present in cases of cervical cancer.

Huntington's chorea, a neurological disease which can cause paralysis in middle age.

Hypochondriasis, the unfounded belief that one is suffering from a serious disease.

Hypno-Anaesthesia, the use of medical hypnosis to overcome pain in place of anaesthetic drugs.

IBD. Inflammatory bowel disorder.

IBS. Irritable Bowel Disease. This includes Ulcerative Colitis and Crohn's Disease.

Insulin is a hormone which controls the supply of sugar from the blood to muscles. The breakdown of sugar provides energy. In diabetes there is a lack of insulin, causing a build-up of blood sugar which can be released by the injection of insulin. It is secreted by the islet tissue of the pancreas, from which it was isolated in 1922 by Banting and Best. In 1980 insulin became the first product of genetic engineering techniques to reach clinical trials.

Interferon, identified in 1957 as a defence protein produced in animal cells, is also produced in human immune systems. Its use as a possible anti-cancer agent as well as for other complaints has been limited by extraction problems. Modern production is likely to be by genetic engineering. In 1980 the amino acid sequence was determined for the 150 residues in human interferon.

Legionnaire's Disease, caused by the Legionella bacterium. Very serious outbreaks (as at Stafford hospital in 1985 when 28 people died) can occur. Sometimes the bacterium is found in recirculating and hot-water systems.

LSD (d-lysergic acid diethylamide). An hallucinogenic drug which has provoked much debate. It is active in extremely small quantities and a dose as small as a fifty-millionth part of a gram can cause marked disturbances of the mental function in man. LSD has been used in the study of mental disease because it produces symptoms very similar to mental disorders such as schizophrenia.

Lupus. Disease more prevalent in black people (especially women) which causes the patient's immune system to attack his or her own body tissues. *Lupus: A Guide for Patients* by Graham R V Hughes, £3 including postage is available from Lupus UK, St. James House, Eastern Road, Romford, Essex, RM1 3NH.

ME (Myalgic Encephalomyelitis), chronic fatigue syndrome with symptoms of extreme exhaustion and muscular pain. Now more often called Chronic Fatigue Syndrome (CFS).

MMR, a vaccination which immunises against measles, mumps and rubella (German measles).

MRSA (Methicillin Resistant Staphylococcus Aureus), a bacteria resistant to almost all antibiotics. More than 7,000 annual cases of MRSA are now recorded in England alone and the figure is rising rapidly. Hospital-acquired infections (nearly half drug resistant) total around 100,000 a year.

Narcotic, is a drug that produces stupor; complete insensibility or sleep. In terms of drug addiction, it has been defined as altering the user's perception of himself and of the external world, being taken primarily for that purpose.

Olfactory. To do with the sense of smell.

Opium was known to the ancients, and used by them as a medicine. It is obtained from the poppy (*Papaver somniferum*), the unripe "head" or seed capsule of that flower yielding a juice which when dried becomes the opium of commerce. The poppy is cultivated for the sake of this juice, which yields various alkaloids, such as morphine, narcotine, codeine, *etc.* These days the drug is rarely used medicinally.

Ostectomy. The surgical removal of a bone or part of a bone.

Paediatrics. The study of the diseases of children.

Paget's Disease, a severe bone disease. Symptoms may include curvature of the spine, bowing of the legs *etc.*

Penicillin. An antibiotic drug produced by the mould *Penicillium notatum*, and discovered by Sir Alexander Fleming in 1928. It is one of the most effective chemotherapeutic agents known. The mould produces a number of penicillins, all of which are effective antibiotics.

Pharmacopoeia, an official publication containing information on the recognised drugs used in medicine. Each country has its own pharmacopoeia. The British Pharmacopoeia (BP) is published under the direction of the General Medical Council. The Pharmaceutical Society issues the British Pharmaceutical Codex (BPC); there is also an International Pharmacopoeia (2 vols.), issued by the World Health Organisation.

Placebo, medical treatment that the therapist uses deliberately although he knows it is without any specific effect on the condition being treated. There may be various medical reasons for using placebos, *e.g.*, for the beneficial psychological effect on people who like to feel something is being done for them; for differentiating during clinical trials of a new treatment between those persons given the real thing and those given a placebo or inactive imitation.

Progressive Supranuclear Palsy (PSP), a neuro-degenerative disease which affects the brain stem. It was identified as a separate disease in the 1960s. The cause is not yet known and there is at present no cure.

Prostate Specific Antigen (PSA), the chemical 'signature' of an abnormal prostate gland.

Psoriasis. A skin disease which results in patches of inflamed, red skin often covered by silvery scales. It is at present a long-term condition.

Psychosomatic diseases. Psychosomatic diseases are those physical ailments due to emotional causes. They include such complaints as high blood-pressure, gastric ulcer *etc.*

Pyorrhoea. An infection of the gums which causes the edges of the tooth sockets to bleed easily when the teeth are being brushed.

Quinine, a vegetable alkaloid obtained from the bark of several trees of the *Cinchona* genus. It is colourless and extremely bitter. The drug, sulphate of quinine, is one of the most valuable medicines, forming a powerful tonic. It is anti-periodic, antipyretic and antineuralgic. In cases of malaria it is the most efficacious remedy of natural origin known.

Rhesus Factor. Apart from the ABO blood group system (*see* **Blood Groups**) there is another blood group system (designated the Rh-system or Rhesus system). Everybody is either Rh-positive or Rh-negative. Three positive factors (denoted C, D, E) and three negative factors (denoted c, d, e) are involved. This system of blood factors is inherited separately from the ABO group, so that one may be A Rh+ or A Rh−, *etc.* Both the positive and the negative factors are antigenic, *i.e.*, if introduced into other blood they will stimulate the production of substances which act in some way against the cells introduced.

Rods and Cones are cells in the retina of the eye which convert light into nervous impulses which can be interpreted by the brain.

RSI (Repetitive Strain Injury), an injury most prevalent among computer users and factory workers. It may begin with a minor ache before eventually becoming a persistent pain. Symptoms include pain in the hands, elbow, wrist or shoulder. Around 450,000 British workers now suffer these upper limb problems.

Salpingitis, infection of the Fallopian tubes. *See* **Z55(1)**.

SARS (Severe Acute Respiratory Syndrome), a flu-like virus which spread rapidly from south China and Hong Kong in 2003. The symptoms include fever above 38°C, breathing difficulties, low blood oxygen and a dry cough.

Sciatica, painful affliction radiating along the sciatic nerve, extending from the buttocks down the back of the leg to the foot.

Screening is looking for a disease in the absence of symptoms. It may be extremely effective such as for cervical cancer, which can be detected and treated many years before it would otherwise be found. Screening for prostate cancer is controversial, because some men may have treatment for an illness that might not otherwise harm them.

Sickle-cell disease, a hereditary blood disease characterised by the production of an abnormal type of haemaglobin. This painful disease mainly affects people of African descent (but can be found also in the Middle East and India).

Temperature. The body temperature is regulated by a small area at the base of the brain. Normally it should be about 37°C. *See* **Z9(1)**.

Thalassaemia. A little known but potentially fatal hereditary blood disorder. Around 75% of babies with this disease are born to Asian parents.

Tinnitus. A constant ringing noise in the ears, linked to deafness. The cause is unknown.

Viagra, a drug (in the form of a little blue tablet) which counters impotence in men.

Vitiligo, a common skin condition (affecting 1 in every hundred children and adults) which causes white patches where the skin has lost its pigmentation).

SUBJECT INDEX

Each section has a letter and, where appropriate, the column is given in brackets after the page number,
e.g., T8(1), F25(2). Some of the sections are alphabetically arranged and index themselves. Their contents
are not included here except where it is anticipated some special difficulty may arise. In addition
"The World of Music" has a separate index and glossary. For environmental terms, see Section Y
and historical terms, see Section A. The great majority of biographical entries are in Section B,
Prominent People.

A

Abdication	A40
Abortion	J2
Abortus fever, see Undulant fever, Z13(2)	
Absolute temperature	L3
Abstract Art	N2
Abstract Expressionism	N2
Acid rain	L3, Y26(2)
Acidity See Peptic ulcer, Z35(2)	
Acne	Z53(1)
Acquired Immune Deficiency Syndrome.	Z11(2)
Acromegaly	Z43(1)
Actinomycosis	Z15(1)
Action Painting	N2
Acupuncture	J2
Acute chorea (St. Vitus' dance)	Z48(2)
Acute nephritis	Z44(2)
Addison's disease	Z43(1)
Adlerian Psychology	J2
Adrenal cortex	Z43(1)
Adrenocorticotrophic hormone (ACTH)	Z42(2)
Adventists	J2
Advisory, Conciliation and Arbitration Service (ACAS)	F21(2)
Aesthetic Movement	N2
Aesthetics	N2
Afghanistan, recent events in	C31–2, C51–2
overthrow of Taliban	C51–2
Africa, background to recent events	C36–43
economic stagnation in	F47(1)
Agranulocytosis	Z25(2)
Aid to less-developed countries	F43
AIDS	Z11(2)
economic impact of	F47(2)
Air, composition of	L4
Air glow	L4
Air Pollution	Y25–7
Albigenses	J2–3
Alchemy	J3
Alcohol abuse	Z59–61
Alcohols	L4
Algeria, recent events in	C37
Allergies	Z61–2
Allotropy	L5
Alopecia	Z52(1)
Alpha rays (or particles)	L5, T12(1)
Al-Qaeda	C51–4
Altarpiece	N2
Alternative Medicine	J3
Althorpe (home of Spencers)	A55
Alzheimer's disease	Z65
Amenorrhoea	Z56(1)
America's Cup	S24
American Football	S2
Amino acids	L6, T32(1)
Amnesia	Z47(1)
Amnesty International	L6(2)
Amoebae	Z8(1)
Amoebic dysentery	Z17(2)
Ampère, unit of electric current	L6
Amphetamine	Z61(1)
Amyotrophic lateral sclerosis	Z48(1)
Anabolic steroids	Z65
Anaemias	Z24–5
Anaesthetic	Z65
Analytical Psychology	J3
Anarchism	J3
Anencephaly	Z48(1)
Aneurism	Z30(1)
Angina pectoris	Z28(1)
Angioplasty	Z28(2)
Anglo-Catholicism	J4
Anglo-Irish Agreement	D19(1)
Animal kingdom	T36–41

Animism	J4
Ankylosing Spondylitis	Z65
Ankylosis	Z65
Ankylostomiasis	Z18(2)
Anorexia nervosa	Z51(2)
Antarctic exploration	L7
Anterior pituitary	Z42(2)
Anthrax	Z14(1)
Anthropology	T49–55
(our early ancestors; the hominid lineage; geological dating; Neanderthal Man; Modern Man)	
Anthropomorphism	J4
Anthroposophy	J4
Antibiotics	Z9(1)
Antibodies	Z8(2)
Anti-clericalism	J4
Anti-Globalisation	J4
Antihistamine drugs	Z4 (2), Z5(1)
Antimony	L8
Antisemitism	J4–5
Antiseptics	Z8(2)
Anti-vivisection	J5
Antonine Wall	A55
Anxiety neurosis	Z51(2)
Aortic diseases	Z30(1)
Apartheid	J5
Aphasia	Z47(1)
Aplastic anaemia	Z24(2)
Apocalypse (in Bible)	H5(1)
Apocrypha	H3
Appendicitis	Z36(2)
Aquaculture	L8, Y24
Aquatint	N2
Archbishops of Canterbury (since 1533)	A53
of York (since 1000)	A53
Architecture	N2
Arctic exploration	L8 0
Argentina, recent events in	C46–8
Arianism	J5
Ark of the Covenant	H5
Armed Forces, ranks in	A53
Arminianism	J5
Art Brut	N2
Art (dictionary of terms)	N1–16
Art Deco	N3
Art Nouveau	N3
Arts and Crafts Movement	N3
Arteriography	Z46(2)
Artesian Wells	L9
Arthritis	Z54(1)
Artificial intelligence	V2
Artificial respiration (kiss of life)	Z22(1)
Asbestos (health dangers)	Y26
Asceticism	J5
Ascites	Z38(2)
Ashcan School	N3
Ashes, the	L10
Ashmolean Musuem	L10
Asia, political survey	C27–36
Assassinations	A40
Assassins (Muslim sect)	J5
Association Football	S2–5
Assyria	H5
Asteroids	L10, T3(2)
Asthma	Z31(2)
Astrobiology	L10
Astrology	J5
Astronomers Royal (since 1675)	L10
Astronomical distances	T8
Astronomical unit (earth–sun distance)	L10
Astronomy: outline	T3–8
(planets, stars and galaxies; origin and development of the universe)	
Astrophysics	L10
Atelier	N3

J

K

L

M

X

Y

Z